NIV
Faithlife
STUDY BIBLE

NEW INTERNATIONAL VERSION

NIV
Faithlife
STUDY BIBLE

Intriguing Insights to Inform Your Faith

Feed Your Curiosity

ZONDERVAN®

Biblica provides God's Word to people through translation, publishing and Bible engagement in Africa, Asia Pacific, Europe, Latin America, Middle East, and North America. Through its worldwide reach, Biblica engages people with God's Word so that their lives are transformed through a relationship with Jesus Christ.

Table of Contents

THE OLD TESTAMENT

THE NEW TESTAMENT

Table of Contents:
Visual Content

LARGE TIMELINES

Table of Contents: Articles

Alphabetical List of the Books of the Bible

The books of the New Testament are in *italic*.

Abbreviations

ca.	about, approximately
ch., chs.	chapter, chapters
e.g.	for example
etc.	and so forth
i.e.	that is
lit.	literally, literal
LXX	The Septuagint, the ancient Greek translation of the Old Testament
MT	Masoretic Text
NT	New Testament
OT	Old Testament
p.	page
pp	parallel passage
v., vv.	verse, verses

Editorial Team

GENERAL EDITOR

John D. Barry

ACADEMIC EDITORS

Douglas Mangum, Derek R. Brown,
and Michael S. Heiser

CONTRIBUTING EDITORS

Miles Custis, Elliot Ritzema, and Matthew M. Whitehead

MANAGING EDITORS

Michael R. Grigoni and David Bomar

ASSISTANT EDITORS

Rebecca Brant, Claire Brubaker, Jacob Cerone, Lynnea Fraser,
Rachel Klippenstein, Spencer Jones, Matthew Nerdahl, Britt Rogers,
Abigail Salinger, Abigail Stocker, Jessi Strong, and Elizabeth Vince

MAJOR CONTRIBUTORS

Amy Balogh, Abner Chou, Johnny Cisneros, Seth Ehorn, Israel Loken,
Brian Maiers, Judith Odor, David B. Schreiner, David Seal, Chris Seeman,
E. Tod Twist, William Varner, Lazarus Wentz, and Wendy Widder

Editor's Preface

When you see the Bible in its ancient context, it comes to life as a body of literature that shaped God's people. These are the people who were known first as the sons of Jacob, the people of Israel, and later as the Jewish people, and from them came Jesus and the Christian tradition. This is the true story of the whole world, of every person, and of our deep need for relationship with the God who made the universe. This is the story of how God sought to know us and love us—by sending his Son to die and rise for us, so that we may truly live.

Faithlife Study Bible (FSB) invites you to find your place in this story by understanding the Bible more fully—and to feed your curiosity about God and his work in the world.

VISION

Faithlife Study Bible helps remove the obstacles to understanding the Bible, so people with any level of knowledge and experience can pursue an enriching study of Scripture. We encourage you to read a passage, then read the study notes, and then go back to the passage. Our ultimate goal is to help you engage with God's Word—and with God himself.

Faithlife Study Bible bridges contextual gaps. FSB is your guide to the ancient world of the Old and New Testaments. For each biblical passage, we have curated the most relevant data to illuminate the biblical text, from archaeological findings to manuscript research. Historical, cultural and linguistic details help you understand the background of the Bible so you can interpret its significance. Study notes, media and articles connect the dots from Genesis to Revelation, revealing how the story of God unfolds across different books and eras. FSB also looks at the Bible as a work of literature, explaining how different genres, narrative structures and literary devices shape the text.

The notes provide explanations of the Hebrew, Aramaic and Greek text of the Bible, but they're written for people who don't know those languages. Unlike other study Bibles, FSB was developed on the basis of the original languages of the Bible. Utilizing the technology and data behind Logos Bible Software, we were able to create a study Bible that works with multiple English translations. We call this translation independence. For example, the insights you'll receive from FSB in the New International Version will be just as relevant for a study partner who uses the New King James Version.

Faithlife Study Bible unites scholarship and discipleship. The notes and articles draw from a wide range of academic research to illuminate the Bible, its world and its message. While this certainly is a scholastic effort, it is foremost an endeavor of faith. FSB stands in the Christian tradition summarized by the ancient Apostles' Creed and Nicene Creed. It is committed both to the authority of Scripture and to the challenge of wrestling with its full meaning.

Faithlife Study Bible invites you to be an interpreter. The study notes explain the biblical text while recognizing that God's truth often reflects his mysterious ways and requires guidance from his Spirit. When tradition and scholarship presents diverging views on a passage, FSB explains the interpretive options, so you can reach your own conclusions. Rather than tell you what to think, the notes in FSB help you learn *how* to think about a text and work toward a deeper understanding.

CREATING FAITHLIFE STUDY BIBLE

We began in 2011 with a desire to design a study Bible for the digital age. The following year, we launched the initial project on multiple platforms—mobile, web and desktop (available at FaithlifeBible.com). From the beginning, we were committed to expanding and revising the study Bible in an effort to continually improve it. FSB eventually would involve dozens of contributors and build on the insights of two of our other resources: *Lexham Bible Dictionary* and *DIY Bible Study*. Nearly every note in FSB has been expanded and reshaped by multiple people—those listed as editors or major contributors. As a result of this rich collaboration, FSB's study notes have no single author.

The editors designed FSB to explore questions they had about the text without regard to constraints of space. The digital content often runs much longer than what can fit on the page of a typical study Bible. These lengthy explorations provided an abundance of material for later editors to distill complex discussions into concise notes and articles for the print edition of FSB, which we are pleased to publish in partnership with Zondervan.

OUR HOPE FOR YOU

Understanding a verse or passage in its historical context leads naturally to applying God's Word in our lives. When we see just how amazing the God of history is, we realize how much we want to love and serve that God. We hope and pray that every reader of FSB chooses to trust in the God revealed in the resurrected Savior, Jesus. And if you already know him, we pray that you will be drawn into a closer relationship with him.

Commit to Bible study. Feed your curiosity. Savor. Believe. And be transformed.

With much love for Christ and his work in all of us,

John D. Barry, General Editor
On behalf of the Faithlife Study Bible team
Spring 2016, Bellingham, WA

Preface

The goal of the New International Version (NIV) is to enable English-speaking people from around the world to read and hear God's eternal Word in their own language. Our work as translators is motivated by our conviction that the Bible is God's Word in written form. We believe that the Bible contains the divine answer to the deepest needs of humanity, sheds unique light on our path in a dark world and sets forth the way to our eternal well-being. Out of these deep convictions, we have sought to recreate as far as possible the experience of the original audience—blending transparency to the original text with accessibility for the millions of English speakers around the world. We have prioritized accuracy, clarity and literary quality with the goal of creating a translation suitable for public and private reading, evangelism, teaching, preaching, memorizing and liturgical use. We have also sought to preserve a measure of continuity with the long tradition of translating the Scriptures into English.

The complete NIV Bible was first published in 1978. It was a completely new translation made by over a hundred scholars working directly from the best available Hebrew, Aramaic and Greek texts. The translators came from the United States, Great Britain, Canada, Australia and New Zealand, giving the translation an international scope. They were from many denominations and churches— including Anglican, Assemblies of God, Baptist, Brethren, Christian Reformed, Church of Christ, Evangelical Covenant, Evangelical Free, Lutheran, Mennonite, Methodist, Nazarene, Presbyterian, Wesleyan and others. This breadth of denominational and theological perspective helped to safeguard the translation from sectarian bias. For these reasons, and by the grace of God, the NIV has gained a wide readership in all parts of the English-speaking world.

The work of translating the Bible is never finished. As good as they are, English translations must be regularly updated so that they will continue to communicate accurately the meaning of God's Word. Updates are needed in order to reflect the latest developments in our understanding of the biblical world and its languages and to keep pace with changes in English usage. Recognizing, then, that the NIV would retain its ability to communicate God's Word accurately only if it were regularly updated, the original translators established the Committee on Bible Translation (CBT). The Committee is a self-perpetuating group of biblical scholars charged with keeping abreast of advances in biblical scholarship and changes in English and issuing periodic updates to the NIV. The CBT is an independent, self-governing body and has sole responsibility for the NIV text. The Committee mirrors the original group of translators in its diverse international and denominational makeup and in its unifying commitment to the Bible as God's inspired Word.

In obedience to its mandate, the Committee has issued periodic updates to the NIV. An initial revision was released in 1984. A more thorough revision process was completed in 2005, resulting in the separately published TNIV. The updated NIV you now have in your hands builds on both the original NIV and the TNIV and represents the latest effort of the Committee to articulate God's unchanging Word in the way the original authors might have said it had they been speaking in English to the global English-speaking audience today.

TRANSLATION PHILOSOPHY

The Committee's translating work has been governed by three widely accepted principles about the way people use words and about the way we understand them.

First, the meaning of words is determined by the way that users of the language actually use them at any given time. For the biblical languages, therefore, the Committee utilizes the best and most recent scholarship on the way Hebrew, Aramaic and Greek words were being used in biblical times. At the same time, the Committee carefully studies the state of modern English. Good translation is like good communication: one must know the target audience so that the appropriate choices can be made about which English words to use to represent the original words of Scripture. From its inception, the NIV has had as its target the general English-speaking population all over the world, the "International" in its title reflecting this concern. The aim of the Committee is to put the Scriptures into natural English that will communicate effectively with the broadest possible audience of English speakers.

Modern technology has enhanced the Committee's ability to choose the right English words to convey the meaning of the original text. The field of computational linguistics harnesses the power of computers to provide broadly applicable and current data about the state of the language. Translators can now access huge databases of modern English to better understand the current meaning and usage of key words. The Committee utilized this resource in preparing the 2011 edition of the NIV. An area of especially rapid and significant change in English is the way certain nouns and pronouns are used to refer to human beings. The Committee therefore requested experts in computational linguistics at Collins Dictionaries to pose some key questions about this usage to its database of English—the largest in the world, with over 4.4 billion words, gathered from several English-speaking countries and including both spoken and written English. (The Collins Study, called "The Development and Use of Gender Language in Contemporary English," can be accessed at *http://www.thenivbible.com/about-the-niv/about-the-2011-edition/*.) The study revealed that the most popular words to describe the human race in modern U.S. English were "humanity," "man" and "mankind." The Committee then used this data in the updated NIV, choosing from among these three words (and occasionally others also) depending on the context.

A related issue creates a larger problem for modern translations: the move away from using the third-person masculine singular pronouns—"he/him/his"—to refer to men and women equally. This usage does persist in some forms of English, and this revision therefore occasionally uses these pronouns in a generic sense. But the tendency, recognized in day-to-day usage and confirmed by the Collins study, is away from the generic use of "he," "him" and "his." In recognition of this shift in language and in an effort to translate into the natural English that people are actually using, this revision of the NIV generally uses other constructions when the biblical text is plainly addressed to men and women equally. The reader will encounter especially frequently a "they," "their" or "them" to express a generic singular idea. Thus, for instance, Mark 8:36 reads: "What good is it for someone to gain the whole world, yet forfeit their soul?" This generic use of the "distributive" or "singular" "they/them/their" has been used for many centuries by respected writers of English and has now become established as standard English, spoken and written, all over the world.

A second linguistic principle that feeds into the Committee's translation work is that meaning is found not in individual words, as vital as they are, but in larger clusters: phrases, clauses, sentences, discourses. Translation is not, as many people think, a matter of word substitution: English word *x* in place of Hebrew word *y*. Translators must first determine the meaning of the words of the biblical languages in the context of the passage and then select English words that accurately communicate that meaning to modern listeners and readers. This means that accurate translation will not always reflect the exact structure of the original language. To be sure, there is debate over the degree to which translators should try to preserve the "form" of the original text in English. From the beginning, the NIV has taken a mediating position on this issue. The manual produced when the translation that became the NIV was first being planned states: "If the Greek or Hebrew syntax has a good parallel in modern English, it should be used. But if there is no good parallel, the English syntax appropriate to the meaning of the original is to be chosen." It is fine, in

other words, to carry over the form of the biblical languages into English—but not at the expense of natural expression. The principle that meaning resides in larger clusters of words means that the Committee has not insisted on a "word-for-word" approach to translation. We certainly believe that every word of Scripture is inspired by God and therefore to be carefully studied to determine what God is saying to us. It is for this reason that the Committee labors over every single word of the original texts, working hard to determine how each of those words contributes to what the text is saying. Ultimately, however, it is how these individual words function in combination with other words that determines meaning.

A third linguistic principle guiding the Committee in its translation work is the recognition that words have a spectrum of meaning. It is popular to define a word by using another word, or "gloss," to substitute for it. This substitute word is then sometimes called the "literal" meaning of a word. In fact, however, words have a range of possible meanings. Those meanings will vary depending on the context, and words in one language will usually not occupy the same semantic range as words in another language. The Committee therefore studies each original word of Scripture in its context to identify its meaning in a particular verse and then chooses an appropriate English word (or phrase) to represent it. It is impossible, then, to translate any given Hebrew, Aramaic or Greek word with the same English word all the time. The Committee does try to translate related occurrences of a word in the original languages with the same English word in order to preserve the connection for the English reader. But the Committee generally privileges clear natural meaning over a concern with consistency in rendering particular words.

TEXTUAL BASIS

For the Old Testament the standard Hebrew text, the Masoretic Text as published in the latest edition of *Biblia Hebraica*, has been used throughout. The Masoretic Text tradition contains marginal notations that offer variant readings. These have sometimes been followed instead of the text itself. Because such instances involve variants within the Masoretic tradition, they have not been indicated in the textual notes. In a few cases, words in the basic consonantal text have been divided differently than in the Masoretic Text. Such cases are usually indicated in the textual footnotes. The Dead Sea Scrolls contain biblical texts that represent an earlier stage of the transmission of the Hebrew text. They have been consulted, as have been the Samaritan Pentateuch and the ancient scribal traditions concerning deliberate textual changes. The translators also consulted the more important early versions. Readings from these versions, the Dead Sea Scrolls and the scribal traditions were occasionally followed where the Masoretic Text seemed doubtful and where accepted principles of textual criticism showed that one or more of these textual witnesses appeared to provide the correct reading. In rare cases, the translators have emended the Hebrew text where it appears to have become corrupted at an even earlier stage of its transmission. These departures from the Masoretic Text are also indicated in the textual footnotes. Sometimes the vowel indicators (which are later additions to the basic consonantal text) found in the Masoretic Text did not, in the judgment of the translators, represent the correct vowels for the original text. Accordingly, some words have been read with a different set of vowels. These instances are usually not indicated in the footnotes.

The Greek text used in translating the New Testament has been an eclectic one, based on the latest editions of the Nestle-Aland/United Bible Societies' Greek New Testament. The translators have made their choices among the variant readings in accordance with widely accepted principles of New Testament textual criticism. Footnotes call attention to places where uncertainty remains.

The New Testament authors, writing in Greek, often quote the Old Testament from its ancient Greek version, the Septuagint. This is one reason why some of the Old Testament quotations in the NIV New Testament are not identical to the corresponding passages in the NIV Old Testament. Such quotations in the New Testament are indicated with the footnote "(see Septuagint)."

FOOTNOTES AND FORMATTING

Footnotes in this version are of several kinds, most of which need no explanation. Those giving alternative translations begin with "Or" and generally introduce the alternative with the last word preceding it in the text, except when it is a single-word alternative. When poetry is quoted in a footnote a slash mark indicates a line division.

It should be noted that references to diseases, minerals, flora and fauna, architectural details, clothing, jewelry, musical instruments and other articles cannot always be identified with precision. Also, linear measurements and measures of capacity can only be approximated (see the Table of Weights and Measures). Although *Selah*, used mainly in the Psalms, is probably a musical term, its meaning is uncertain. Since it may interrupt reading and distract the reader, this word has not been kept in the English text, but every occurrence has been signaled by a footnote.

As an aid to the reader, sectional headings have been inserted. They are not to be regarded as part of the biblical text and are not intended for oral reading. It is the Committee's hope that these headings may prove more helpful to the reader than the traditional chapter divisions, which were introduced long after the Bible was written.

Sometimes the chapter and/or verse numbering in English translations of the Old Testament differs from that found in published Hebrew texts. This is particularly the case in the Psalms, where the traditional titles are included in the Hebrew verse numbering. Such differences are indicated in the footnotes at the bottom of the page. In the New Testament, verse numbers that marked off portions of the traditional English text not supported by the best Greek manuscripts now appear in brackets, with a footnote indicating the text that has been omitted (see, for example, Matthew 17:[21]).

Mark 16:9–20 and John 7:53—8:11, although long accorded virtually equal status with the rest of the Gospels in which they stand, have a questionable standing in the textual history of the New Testament, as noted in the bracketed annotations with which they are set off. A different typeface has been chosen for these passages to indicate their uncertain status.

Basic formatting of the text, such as lining the poetry, paragraphing (both prose and poetry), setting up of (administrative-like) lists, indenting letters and lengthy prayers within narratives and the insertion of sectional headings, has been the work of the Committee. However, the choice between single-column and double-column formats has been left to the publishers. Also the issuing of "red-letter" editions is a publisher's choice—one that the Committee does not endorse.

The Committee has again been reminded that every human effort is flawed—including this revision of the NIV. We trust, however, that many will find in it an improved representation of the Word of God, through which they hear his call to faith in our Lord Jesus Christ and to service in his kingdom. We offer this version of the Bible to him in whose name and for whose glory it has been made.

The Committee on Bible Translation

HOW TO STUDY THE BIBLE

As you begin to study the Bible, determine your goals, methods and resources. If you simply want to be a more careful reader of the Bible, perhaps begin by reading a small portion of the text daily with a Bible reading plan. If you want to put serious effort into learning the Bible, you will need to make a greater commitment. Such an approach may involve several hours a week of focused study and the use of resources such as commentaries. If pursuing this level of Bible study, you will benefit from acquiring at least one Bible dictionary and two kinds of commentaries—one-volume Bible commentaries and commentary volumes corresponding to individual books of the Bible are both valuable. Using these as you study the Bible passage by passage will provide you with some of the same help you would get if you were to study the Bible in an academic institution. There are also some basics that apply.

TAKE SERIOUSLY THE IMPORTANCE AND QUALITY OF THE BOOK YOU'RE STUDYING

Although we may wish the Bible were entirely clear, students of literature would never expect that from other important books. When it comes to the Bible, it should be obvious that we have to study the Bible to understand it.

Some writing—a newspaper story, for example—might be understood by almost any mature reader. Other writing—such as a Shakespearean play—might require readers to consult dictionaries, study guides and other aids because of the nature of the language and the subject matter. Yet other writing—a calculus textbook, for example—might require years of prior study as well as patient, focused effort to understand even a single page. The Bible contains literature at all these levels: Some parts any reader can follow, some parts that require help and some that are difficult enough that even seasoned scholars struggle to comprehend them.

This is to be expected. A book claiming to be authored by the One whose thinking and communication can range from the simplest level to far above human understanding should require serious effort from seekers of its truth. It is naïve to think that the Bible differs from other literature in being automatically comprehensible, or that our good intentions and love of God will overcome our need to study in order to appreciate the quality of the ideas he has put into writing for us.

RESPECT THE BIBLE'S GENRES

No serious Bible student can ignore the various genres in the Bible. Ten predominate: narrative, law, wisdom, psalms and prophecy in the Old Testament; and gospel, parable, Acts, letter and apocalypse in the New Testament. To understand and appreciate the Bible's content, each of these genres must be read differently.

Consider two examples: Parables are stories told to willing students, not those who refuse to bother with what seems irrelevant to them (Mt 13:10–17). Thus, they resemble puzzles, containing punch lines that help willing readers see a truth they might have otherwise missed. Western culture is not used to parables, but with reasonable study, the parables of the New Testament reveal a great deal about the nature of God's kingdom.

Similarly, proverbs, part of Old Testament Wisdom literature, frequently present life's choices in a semi-riddle fashion, which require that readers take time to understand them. Those who work out the meaning of a proverb often read it repeatedly and thus learn its content while trying to understand its point.

RESPECT THE FORMAT

The format of the Bible requires appreciating it as an anthology of many books, each of which has its own integrity: Readers of the Bible must start by recognizing the genre of a given book and then reading it as both a unique piece of literature and one that contributes to the overall message of the anthology. The Bible is an integrated and univocal text that benefits the reader at both the individual book level and as a whole.

RESPECT THE HISTORICAL SWEEP AND CONTEXT

In one sense, the Bible is like a world epic: It covers the sweep of history from the very beginning of Creation to the end of history when our universe is radically transformed. Biblical books always deal with something that is part of this very big picture—the story of God's creation, its fall, his ongoing redemption of it and/or the ultimate consummation of all the hopes of God's people for a permanent establishment characterized by God's goodness. Few other books, even other religious scriptures, resemble the scope of the Bible.

RESPECT THE MULTIDISCIPLINARY NATURE OF CAREFUL STUDY

There are several different ways to look at any piece of literature. In the case of the Bible, it pays to look from every angle that might yield a payoff. It is convenient to think of 11 such angles, or steps, in the study process:

1. *Text*—Seeking the original wording to avoid treating a scribal error that accidentally crept into the text as original. (Translations and study notes already depend on this scholastic research.)

2. *Translation*—Studying how to best convey in a modern language the concepts conveyed by the original Hebrew, Aramaic or Greek. (Consulting multiple translations and study notes aids in this process.)

3. *Grammar*—Analyzing the language of the passage under consideration to be sure it is not misunderstood. (Even one-volume commentaries will often explain these issues.)

4. *Lexical content*—Seeking the correct meaning of individual words and phrases found in a passage. (Study notes, commentaries and Bible software aid in this process.)

5. *Form*—Studying the literary category and the characteristics that make any passage special. (Study Bible articles on genre serve this process.)

6. *Structure*—Analyzing the way that the elements of a passage are ordered and how that affects its meaning. (A careful reading of the Biblical text, especially with the aid of commentaries, makes this possible.)

7. *Historical context*—Studying the milieu in which the Bible was revealed, which helps yield the point of its contents. (One-volume commentaries and study notes, like those of the *NIV Faithlife Study Bible*, are designed to reveal this.)

8. *Literary context*—Studying how a passage fits within the book of which it is a part and how that affects its meaning. (Examining how a passage relates to those before and after it, and to the book as a whole, helps with this interpretive step.)

9. *Biblical context*—Analyzing what a passage contributes to the Bible as a whole and what the rest of the Bible contributes to understanding the passage. (Reading through the Bible as a whole, and reading passages that are cross-referenced, help with this.)

10. *Application*—Seeking to conform beliefs and actions to the guidance the Bible imparts. (Act on what the Bible says.)

11. *Secondary literature*—Examining the wisdom and diligent study of others as they have put it into books and articles. (This step should be used throughout study, but it is usually best to do after attempting to draw your own conclusions and is best done in conversation with other believers in Jesus.)

DON'T TRY TO REINVENT THE WHEEL, AND DON'T GO IT ALONE

As you read through the Bible, look up anything you don't fully know or understand. Make use of the many good resources available to help you be a better student of the Bible than you would be on your own.

Bible dictionaries give an overview and a brief analysis of virtually any topic mentioned in the Bible, and they also connect that information to the various books and major doctrines of Scripture. Likewise, Bible commentaries explain Bible passages from an expert angle. Reading with a good study Bible provides additional help. Such resources introduce Bible books and special topics, and provide aids that explain the particular verse or passage under investigation.

TAKE NOTES, LIKE A GOOD READER SHOULD

If you rely entirely on your own memory, you'll eventually lose many valuable insights. But if you develop an external memory—your notes of observations or what you've learned—you will preserve them. Writing down what you have learned also forces you to express your thoughts more cogently and carefully than if you merely relied on memory. Memory fades with time, but written notes provide you with an element of stability and continuity for what you've learned in Bible study.

RESPECT THE DIFFERENCE BETWEEN WORDS AND CONCEPTS

Most people are not aware of the difference between words and concepts, yet respecting these differences is essential to accurately interpreting the Bible. For example, in Luke 10 when Jesus illustrates what it means to "love your neighbor as yourself," he tells the story of the Good Samaritan. This account does not include the words "love," "neighbor" or "self," but the story richly includes the concept of loving neighbor as self and shows how that concept works in an exemplary illustration.

A significant aspect of Bible study is understanding the words used in the text. But even more important is understanding the concepts used—the point, significance or meaning of a passage, verse, statement or word.

PRAY FOR HELP AND STUDY WITH OTHER CHRISTIANS

Ask God for help and guidance in your Bible study. God will empower you with the desire, patience and discernment to recognize the simple truths of the Bible and understand the complicated concepts. In addition, read the Bible in Christian community, as that is a critical component of growing as a Christian.

Douglas Stuart

Broad Timeline of Biblical History

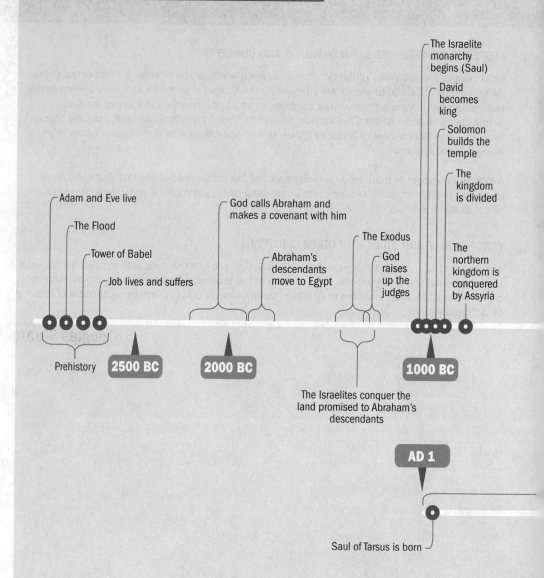

Adam and Eve live

The Flood

Tower of Babel

Job lives and suffers

God calls Abraham and makes a covenant with him

Abraham's descendants move to Egypt

The Exodus

God raises up the judges

The Israelite monarchy begins (Saul)

David becomes king

Solomon builds the temple

The kingdom is divided

The northern kingdom is conquered by Assyria

Prehistory

2500 BC

2000 BC

1000 BC

The Israelites conquer the land promised to Abraham's descendants

AD 1

Saul of Tarsus is born

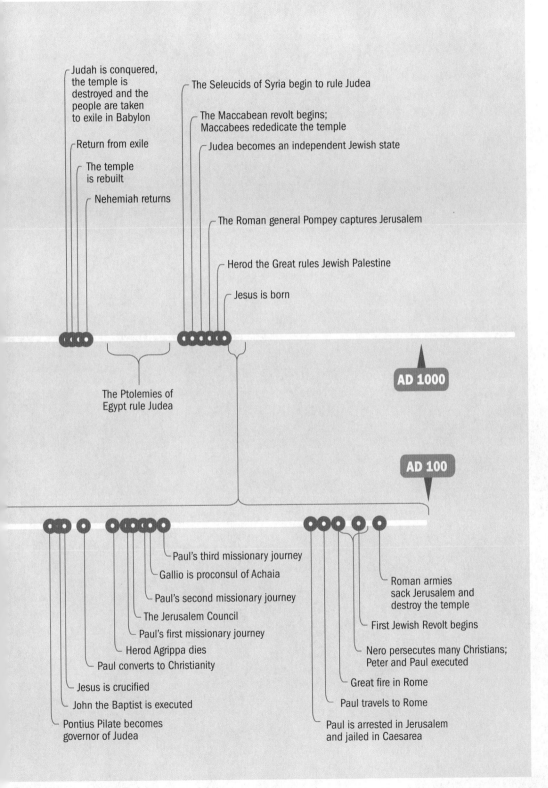

Judah is conquered, the temple is destroyed and the people are taken to exile in Babylon

The Seleucids of Syria begin to rule Judea

The Maccabean revolt begins; Maccabees rededicate the temple

Return from exile

Judea becomes an independent Jewish state

The temple is rebuilt

Nehemiah returns

The Roman general Pompey captures Jerusalem

Herod the Great rules Jewish Palestine

Jesus is born

AD 1000

The Ptolemies of Egypt rule Judea

AD 100

Paul's third missionary journey

Gallio is proconsul of Achaia

Paul's second missionary journey

The Jerusalem Council

Paul's first missionary journey

Herod Agrippa dies

Paul converts to Christianity

Jesus is crucified

John the Baptist is executed

Pontius Pilate becomes governor of Judea

Roman armies sack Jerusalem and destroy the temple

First Jewish Revolt begins

Nero persecutes many Christians; Peter and Paul executed

Great fire in Rome

Paul travels to Rome

Paul is arrested in Jerusalem and jailed in Caesarea

OLD
TESTAMENT

THE FORMATION OF
THE OLD TESTAMENT

The story of the origin of the Old Testament is multi-layered and complex, and no known ancient sources actually tell it. The Protestant, Roman Catholic, Eastern Orthodox, Ethiopian, and Syriac traditions all have slightly different Old Testaments. While they all agree on the books that comprise the Protestant Old Testament, the other groups also include books that Protestants call Apocryphal or Deuterocanonical books. The books agreed upon are the same as those in the Jewish Canon, also known as the Hebrew Bible (or Tanakh), although Christians have them in a different order. Some Jewish religious books that were popular in the time of Jesus and the early church were read as sacred Scripture. They were considered good for teaching by both Jews and Christians, but were later not included in the Old Testament (e.g., 2Pe 2:4–9; Jude 14–15; 2Co 12:1–4). Some of these other books help us piece together the story of the formation of the Christian Bible and provide insight into the context of early Christianity.

Today, the term "Canon" is commonly used to identify those books that comprise the Bible. In antiquity, however, neither the Jews nor the early Christians used the term "Canon" as an official catalog. Jews used the phrase "books that defile the hands" to describe their sacred books, and Christians simply used the term "Scripture" or various formulations such as "as it is written" or "as the Scripture says." Paul initially used the term "Canon" in the New Testament (2Co 10:13,15–16) to speak of the limits of his ministry and the rule (or scope) of the Christian faith (Gal 6:16). "Canon" began to be used by Christians to refer to an official list of authoritative sacred writings in the late fourth century AD.

The basic properties of Scripture, both for ancient Judaism and Christianity, seem to include at least four essential elements: The text is a written document; it is believed to have a divine origin; it communicates the will and truth of God for the believing community; and it provides a source of regulations for the corporate and individual life of the community.

THE BEGINNINGS OF THE IDEA OF SCRIPTURE

Despite the importance of the Law in ancient Israel's identity (e.g., Ex 20), very few authors of the earlier Old Testament Scriptures—such as Judges, 1–2 Samuel, and 1–2 Kings—actually appeal to Scripture directly. While there are references to sacred writings in this period, there are few references to the Law itself (compare 2Ki 22:3–13; 2Ch 34:8–21). At this stage in Israel's history, the Law itself—or the conviction that it is God's Law—may have been largely ignored and thus had little influence in national life. The prophets repeatedly warned the nation to keep the commands of God, but apparently without a positive response.

However, during king Josiah of Judah's reign in the late seventh century BC, his high priest found the "Book of the Law" (probably Deuteronomy; 2Ki 22). After this point, the divinely authoritative status of the sacred writings came to national prominence and several of them were elevated to the status of Scripture, even if they were not yet called "Scripture." When the Jews returned to their homeland under the leadership of Ezra and Nehemiah after captivity in Babylon in the mid-sixth to mid-fifth century BC, many reforms were instituted. Regular reading and interpretation of the laws of Moses (Pentateuch or Torah) began at this time (Ne 8:1–8).

EARLY OLD TESTAMENT COLLECTIONS

Likely between 400–200 BC, some Jews began more widely to recognize the importance and divine origin of many other prophetic Old Testament Scriptures in addition to the Law of Moses. For example, 2 Kings 17:13 references both the Law and some Prophets: "The LORD warned Israel and Judah through all his prophets and seers ... 'in accordance with the entire Law that I commanded your ancestors to obey and that I delivered to you through my servants the prophets.'" Although it is unclear which prophets 2 Kings 17:13 refers to, the verse indicates that some prophets were recognized by around 400 BC (compare 2Ki 17:37, where the admonition to keep the law of God is clear).

The Deuterocanonical book of Sirach (also called Ecclesiasticus) identifies the prophets that were influential among the Jews between 200–180 BC. Sirach contains a reference to many of Israel's heroes, including prophets such as Moses, Nathan, David, Elijah, Elisha, Isaiah, Jeremiah, Ezekiel, Job and Nehemiah (Sirach 49:10). Sirach also includes a reference to the book of the Twelve Minor Prophets and Nehemiah (Sirach 49:6,8,10,13). It is unlikely that Sirach would have known of the heroes he listed without being familiar with the books that tell their stories, suggesting that the books that contain these stories were already accepted as authoritative by his lifetime. Thus, by the late third century or early second century BC, the Israelites recognized many (if not most) of the more familiar Old Testament books as Scripture.

The early first-century BC Deuterocanonical text 2 Maccabees records Judas Maccabeus' actions after the Greek king Antiochus IV Epiphanes' destroyed many Jewish sacred books and committed other heinous acts, stating: "Judas also collected all the books that had been lost on account of the war that had come upon us, and they are in our possession. So if you have need of them, send people to get them for you" (2 Macc 2:14–15 NRSV). It is unclear which sacred books 2 Maccabees refers to, but 1 Maccabees 1:56 suggests the collection involved at least the Law: "The books of the law that they found they tore to pieces and burned with fire" (NRSV). It's unknown, though, whether "books of the law" refers to the Pentateuch (Genesis—Deuteronomy) or to all of the Jewish sacred Scriptures.

It is certain that collections of the Jewish Scriptures were circulating in the land of Israel (Palestine) in the second and first centuries BC; however, it is unknown what writings were included in these collections. All of the books that compose the Hebrew Bible except Esther and Nehemiah were found at Qumran among the Dead Sea Scrolls (dating ca. 250 BC–AD 50). In the Dead Sea Scrolls' document known as *Miqsat Maase Hatorah*, the Jewish sacred writings are described as the "book of Moses, the books of the prophets, and David" (likely a reference to the Psalms). *Miqsat Maase Hatorah* also references the "annals of each generation," which may be a reference to the Historical Books of 1–2 Samuel, 1–2 Kings, and 1–2 Chronicles. Although the specific books of each of these categories are not identified, *Miqsat Maase Hatorah* shows that the Scriptures were grouped into specific, authoritative collections.

At the same time, many other religious books besides those that currently make up the Hebrew Bible were read and circulated among Jews (and later Christians) during the first centuries BC and AD. The Hebrew Bible writings among the Dead Sea Scrolls were found alongside many additional religious texts: Of the more than 900 manuscripts discovered, about 700 were non-Biblical works.

EARLY REFERENCES TO THE OLD TESTAMENT COLLECTIONS AND CANON

The Old Testament—and Jewish literature written between the Old Testament and New Testament—attests to the belief that God has delivered divine messages through prophetic figures (like Moses and Isaiah), as well as through the Psalms. The followers of Jesus inherited this notion of sacred Scripture and the Hebrew Scriptures themselves—although they often read them in Greek. Early Christ followers also inherited the commonly accepted designations for sections of the Scriptures, namely, the Law and the Prophets (e.g., Lk 24:27).

The New Testament generally only includes references to the Law and the Prophets (see Mt 5:17; 7:12; Lk 24:27; Ac 28:23), but in Lk 24:44, Jesus mentions that everything about him in the "Law of Moses, the Prophets and the Psalms" must be fulfilled. The categories may suggest that a third grouping ("psalms") was emerging at that time.

Both Jesus and his followers cited the Jewish Scriptures as an authoritative collection of sacred books (Lk 24:13–35). Those books influenced virtually the entire life and ministry of the community of Jesus' followers. The central teachings of the church were rooted in Scripture (see 1Co 15:3–8), and early Christians regularly incorporated Scripture as they told their story. All of the New Testament authors regularly cite the Jewish Scriptures; in particular, the book of Hebrews includes more Scripture citations than any other New Testament book. The books that are most frequently cited in the New Testament and early church writings are Deuteronomy, Isaiah and the Psalms. Not all of the Old Testament books are cited in the New Testament, and there are allusions to some nonbiblical books (e.g., 1 Enoch in 2Pe 2:4 and Jude 14).

In the late first century AD, the historian Josephus is the first Jewish writer to limit the number of books that make up the Jewish Scriptures. He mentions a limited 22-book collection identified only by category, not specific titles. In *Against Apion*, he writes:

Our books, those which are justly accredited, are but two and twenty, and contain the record of all time. Of these, five are the books of Moses, comprising the laws and the traditional history from the birth of man down to the death of the lawgiver ... The prophets subsequent to Moses wrote the history of the events of their own times in thirteen books. The remaining four books contain hymns to God and precepts for the conduct of human life (*Against Apion* 1.38–40).

While it is not entirely clear which books were included in Josephus' collection, he is likely referring to the books that later comprised the Hebrew Bible, though that is not clear in Josephus' writings.

At about the same time as Josephus, the author of the Jewish apocalyptic work 4 Ezra referred to 24 books to be read by both the worthy and unworthy alike, but 70 others that were reserved for the "wise among your people. For in them is the spring of understanding, the fountain of wisdom, and the river of knowledge" (4 Ezra 14:45–7 NRSV). The 24 books are likely the same as those that Josephus had mentioned, only counted differently by combining books in different ways. The later tripartite Hebrew Bible (Law, Prophets and Writings) appears for the first time in the middle to late second century BC. Those books are also likely the same as those in the Protestant Old Testament, but not in the same order. In the late first century AD we cannot be certain about all of the books that Josephus had in mind, but we can be sure that he wanted the number to be the same as the letters in the Hebrew alphabet (22) by combining the books to equal that number.

THE JEWISH TANAKH AND THE CHRISTIAN OLD TESTAMENT

The Christian Old Testament is divided into four categories: Law (or Pentateuch), History, Poetry (includes Wisdom literature), and Prophets. The Jewish Scriptures are divided into the three categories of Law, Prophets, and Writings.

After the second century AD, it appears that the story of the Christian Old Testament diverges from that of the Jewish Tanakh. This is likely because early Jewish Christians separated from synagogue and temple-based Judaism on two major occasions: when James the brother of Jesus was executed in AD 62, and during the last Jewish revolt against Rome in AD 132–35. In addition, many Jewish Christians welcomed Gentiles into the early church apart from the requirement of their keeping the Law, especially circumcision. Thus, early Christians, when departing from broader Judaism, accepted those Jewish Scriptures that were circulating in Israel in the first centuries BC and AD as authoritative.

THE SCOPE OF THE OLD TESTAMENT

There were no Jewish councils to determine the scope of the Jewish Canon; rather, this process took several centuries. It also took several centuries for Christians to determine the scope of their Old Testament. Several Christian councils in the late fourth century AD affirmed the scope of the Old Testament in use within wider Christianity. The decisions of these councils, and the lists of early church fathers, affirm what is currently the Protestant Old Testament and some of the Deuterocanonical (or Apocryphal) works; they also often list a variety of Deuterocanonical works as valuable for instruction but not canonical. Among the writings of the early church fathers, usage and affirmation (or lack thereof) of the Deuterocanonical books varies. However, the books of the Protestant Old Testament seem to have been affirmed by most Christian churches, though like the Jewish rabbis, some early church fathers questioned the inclusion of Esther, Song of Songs and Ecclesiastes.

Only the Apocryphal or Deuterocanonical works are disputed today. The precise collection and status of these books varies slightly depending on faith tradition. Prior to the Protestant Reformation in the sixteenth century AD, it seems that most Christians accepted most of the books embraced by the Roman Catholic and Eastern Orthodox traditions because they were included in the Greek and Latin Bibles that were most commonly used in the early church. The ancient Christian Bibles Codex Vaticanus, Codex Sinaiticus, and Codex Alexandrinus (dating from the fourth–fifth centuries AD), all include some of these books. The earliest edition of the King James Bible also included the Apocrypha, as did several other Protestant Bibles well into the seventeenth century. Most Protestant Bibles had eliminated the Apocrypha by 1831; those that did include the Apocryphal (or Deuterocanonical) books placed them in an appendix to the Old Testament rather than inside the collection of the other Old Testament books. While all churches have not agreed on the full scope of their Old Testament books, all agree that the books in the Protestant Old Testament should be included.

Lee Martin McDonald

THE PENTATEUCH

The term "Pentateuch" refers to the first five books of the Bible—Genesis, Exodus, Leviticus, Numbers and Deuteronomy. In the Hebrew Bible and Judaism, these books are referred to as the Torah. They are considered sacred and authoritative.

AUTHORSHIP

Jewish and Christian traditions ascribe the Pentateuch to Moses. However, modern scholarship is divided on the authorship and composition history of the Pentateuch. Some have asserted that the Pentateuch was compiled over a period of centuries as multiple authors or communities produced distinct versions of Israel's early history and laws. Julius Wellhausen (1844–1918) articulated the most influential version of this theory, identifying four sources in the Pentateuch that he called J, E, D and P. This model for the origin of the Pentateuch is called the Documentary Hypothesis.

Proponents of the Documentary Hypothesis identify and categorize supposed unique sources within the Pentateuch based on changes in style, vocabulary and content. Over time, according to this view, various editors (called redactors) combined the source documents and added other material to create the Pentateuch as we know it.

However, there is no real consensus about the Documentary Hypothesis in modern scholarship; even among those who hold to the viewpoint, there is great variation in how the theoretical sources are understood, divided, and how many sources there are.

Current opinions on the composition of the Pentateuch vary widely, from affirming traditional Mosaic authorship to complex theories involving multiple sources being woven together over centuries of textual transmission. Nonetheless, J, E, D and P are still often used as convenient labels for identifying different types of content in the Pentateuch, apart from questions of sources or authorship.

CONTENT AND THEMES OF EACH BOOK

The fundamental purpose of the Pentateuch is to define the origin, mission and institutions of Israel as God's elect nation, chosen for his purposes in the world. Utilizing multiple settings, narratives and laws the Pentateuch articulates this viewpoint.

Genesis

In Genesis 12:1–3, Abraham is called by Yahweh to leave his homeland because God has chosen him and will give the land of Canaan to his offspring. This text defines Israel's ultimate mission: All the nations of earth will find blessing through Abraham's offspring.

Genesis 1–11 is a prologue to Abraham's election; it describes a world estranged from God and in need of reconciliation, illustrated by the expulsion from Eden, Cain's murder of Abel, the flood and the Tower of Babel. Genesis 12–50 describes God's special protection and provision for the patriarchs, caring for Abraham even when he was acting dishonorably (Ge 12:10–20) and

using Joseph's brothers' jealousy to secure a place for Israel in Egypt (Ge 50:20). Genesis also continually defines and refines the identity of Israel: The elect people are the offspring of Abraham and not Lot (father of Moab and Ammon), of Isaac and not Ishmael (father of the Ishmaelites), of Jacob and not Esau (father of the Edomites).

Exodus

The history of Israel as a nation (not just a family) begins with Exodus, and Exodus is also in many ways the wellspring of Old Testament theology. Israel is transformed from a mass of migrants and slaves to a unified nation. Their dependence on Yahweh is defined when their liberation is brought about entirely by Yahweh's initiative through the plagues on Egypt (Ex 7–14). Moses emerges as the paradigm for the prophets as he speaks for Yahweh (Ex 9:1–4), does mighty works (Ex 14:21–29), and intercedes when the people sin (Ex 32:11–14). The Sinai (or Mosaic) covenant establishes the bond between Yahweh and Israel (Ex 19:5–6), and the tent of meeting, where Yahweh dwells among his people, demonstrates Israel's privileged status (Ex 25–27). Exodus describes two of Israel's ritual days: Passover (Ex 12:1–32) and the Sabbath (Ex 16:22–30). The Ten Commandments and the statutes of Exodus 21–23 define Israel's duties to Yahweh as well as their civil institutions. Exodus initiates the central sanctuary (Ex 25–27) and the Aaronic priesthood—the descendants of Aaron, Moses' brother (Ex 28–31).

In the golden calf narrative (Ex 32:1–6), Exodus describes the pattern of idolatry that would plague Israel throughout its history and lead to its eventual destruction. Exodus also establishes God's character: He keeps his covenant (Ex 2:24), he is the great victor over evil (as shown at the crossing of the sea in Ex 14), he is holy (Ex 19:10–13), and above all, he is "compassionate and gracious" (Ex 34:6). The theology of Deuteronomy and the prophets is often an expansion of themes in Exodus. Throughout the Old Testament, the exodus, the plagues, the Sinai covenant, the golden calf and other events from the book of Exodus are treated as paradigms.

Leviticus

Leviticus is Israel's guide to holy living—for all the people, not just the priests. Even when Leviticus focuses on rules for the priests (Lev 8–10), the message is that the Aaronic priesthood has been consecrated for the sake of all Israelites. In describing what sacrifices to offer (Lev 1–7), Leviticus tells the people how to worship Yahweh. All of life becomes sacred through the introduction of ritual into matters of food, dress and care for the body (with respect to diet in Lev 11, childbirth in Lev 12, and contagion in Lev 13–14). Holiness, however, is not just a matter of ritual cleanness; Leviticus 18–20 gives extensive teaching on sexual purity, the proper treatment of one's neighbors and idolatrous practices to avoid.

Numbers

Numbers continues the narrative and legal themes begun in Exodus. More information about the nature of the Israelite camp, its relationship to the tent of meeting and the first Passover is given in Numbers 1:1—9:14. Further commands regarding sacrifices, the priests and ritual cleanness appear in Numbers 15–19. The pattern of Israelite disobedience also continues; another incident involving complaints about food and the appearance of quail occurs in Numbers 11:1–35 (compare Ex 16:13), and another incident in Meribah involving thirst takes place in Numbers 20:1–13 (compare Ex 17:1–7). The people again rebel against the directives regarding the invasion of Canaan in Numbers 14:1–45, with catastrophic results—and as with the golden calf, Moses again intercedes for them (Nu 15:13–19; see Ex 32:11–14; 34:6–7). On the other hand, the Balaam episode (Nu 22–24) illustrates the principle from Genesis 12:3 that Yahweh comes to the defense of his people, cursing those who curse Israel.

Deuteronomy
Deuteronomy is both the summation of the Pentateuch and essentially the first book of prophecy. The book is basically Moses' prophetic sermon, and it foretells Israel's disobedience, destruction and eventual restoration (Dt 29:22—30:5). Deuteronomy 1–4 summarizes the story of Israel in the wilderness, and the bulk of Deuteronomy 5–26 restates, expands upon or modifies the laws given in Exodus, Leviticus and Numbers. Deuteronomy 5:1–21, for example, restates the Ten Commandments from Exodus 20:1–17. Deuteronomy is also the restatement of the Sinai Covenant between Yahweh and Israel. The book is similar to suzerain-vassal treaties from the fourteenth century BC. In these treaties, a superior "suzerain" state makes a covenant with a subordinate "vassal" state; this type of relationship is similar to Yahweh's covenant with Israel. Thus Deuteronomy is in some respect similar to these ancient treaties.

THE PENTATEUCH AND THE REST OF SCRIPTURE

Taken as a whole, the Pentateuch is a coherent and unified work. Together these books assert that people are estranged from Yahweh due to sin, but Yahweh chose Israel and gave them a unique identity and mission as his people in order to bring blessing to all the nations of the earth. In the histories and prophecies of the Old Testament, Israel, like the rest of the humanity, demonstrates its sinfulness; but the promise of salvation is sustained as prophets pointed Yahweh's people toward a new and marvelous work that he would do in the future. In the Messiah, Jesus, we see how Yahweh's covenant love finally overcomes human sin and discover that truly "salvation is from the Jews" (Jn 4:22).

Duane Garrett

GENESIS

INTRODUCTION TO GENESIS

Genesis is about beginnings—of the world, of humanity and of Israel. The book focuses on the early stages of God's relationship with humankind, as he sets a plan in motion to redeem the world. God chooses Abraham—known as Abram at the time—and his descendants to participate in this plan. The thrilling stories of Abraham and his family make up the majority of Genesis.

BACKGROUND

The name "Genesis" comes from the Greek word meaning "origins." But there is great debate about the book's origins and the rest of the Pentateuch (the first five books of the Bible). While the text of Genesis does not identify its author, Jewish and Christian traditions ascribe the book to Moses (e.g., Lk 24:44). However, this does not necessarily mean Moses himself wrote the Pentateuch—it may simply be in the tradition of Moses, the first known writing prophet (Ex 20). The Pentateuch may use multiple sources, and multiple people may have added to it and edited it over time—with it reaching its final form in the fifth century BC. Even if Moses had a major hand in shaping this material, certain passages (such as the record of his death in Dt 34:1–12) indicate that it underwent at least some editorial revision.

STRUCTURE

Genesis can be divided into two sections. First, Genesis 1–11 is known as the *primeval history*; this section describes creation and its corruption by sin, with passages about humanity's fall

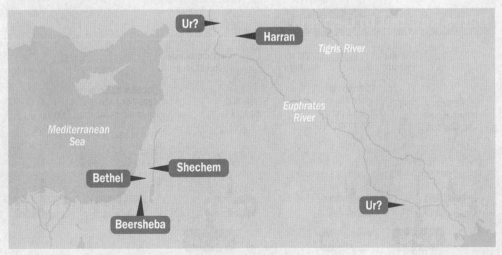

There is disagreement about whether Ur of the Chaldeans is a large city in southern Mesopotamia or a smaller city in northwest Mesopotamia.

(Ge 3), Noah's ark (chs. 6–9) and the tower of Babel (ch. 11). The second section, the *patriarchal narratives* (chs. 12–50), begin with God's promise to Abram—to make him a great nation, bless him and make him a blessing to the world (12:2). As the patriarchal narratives unfold, we discover how Abram and his descendants respond to this promise.

Genesis 1–11 serves as a literary prequel to the rest of the book and to the Pentateuch. Israel's origin is set within the context of the origins of the universe, the earth, humanity and separate people groups and languages. The section concludes with the introduction of Abram (11:27–32), the major character of the patriarchal narratives and the forefather of the Israelites. As a backdrop to the Bible's message, Genesis 1–11 introduces us to God (known as Yahweh)—showing his power in creation and revealing his expectations for humanity.

In Genesis 12–25, God calls Abram to leave his home and move to a new land. God intends to show Abraham a land that he and his descendants will inhabit, the future land of Israel. God also promises that a great nation will descend from Abram and his barren wife, Sarai. As a sign of God and Abram's special relationship—called a "covenant"—God changes the couple's names to Abraham and Sarah (ch. 17). Holding on to a promise but still impatient, the couple decides for Abraham to have a son by Hagar, Sarah's servant; the son is named Ishmael. In spite of this, Sarah eventually gives birth to the son promised by God, Isaac.

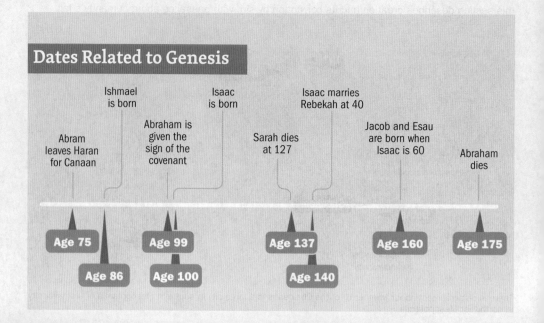

Dates Related to Genesis

Ishmael is born

Isaac is born

Isaac marries Rebekah at 40

Abram leaves Haran for Canaan

Abraham is given the sign of the covenant

Sarah dies at 127

Jacob and Esau are born when Isaac is 60

Abraham dies

Age 75

Age 99

Age 137

Age 160

Age 175

Age 86

Age 100

Age 140

Isaac fathers twins, Esau and Jacob (25:19—36:43). Jacob—whose name God changes to "Israel"—has 12 sons, including Joseph. Through a series of challenging events, Joseph eventually claims a powerful role in Egypt's royal court, and his family joins him in Egypt where, unfortunately, they will one day be enslaved (chs. 37–50; see Exodus).

At every stage of the story, characters take matters into their own hands and often suffer painful consequences, yet God remains faithful to his promises and his people, now known as Israel.

OUTLINE

- Creation, sin and the early history of the nations (1:1—11:32)
- The life of Abraham (12:1—25:18)
- The lives of Isaac and Jacob (25:19—36:43)
- The lives of Joseph and his brothers (37:1—50:26)

THEMES

Adam and Eve's choices compromised our ability to live in God's image; Genesis tells the story of the beginning of God's effort to renew his image in us. In Genesis, the people of Israel are selected to initiate God's grand plan of salvation by being a blessing to the world—a plan that is ultimately fulfilled in Jesus.

The major themes of promise and blessing run throughout the patriarchal narratives, as God's promises are repeated to Abraham, Isaac and Jacob. Their failures send a clear message that God's blessing is not because of any merit or righteousness on their own part; instead, God's blessing reflects his desire to restore humanity to right relationship with him. Genesis is the story of God calling people to turn from the sinful world and obey him.

The Beginning

1 In the beginning God created the heavens and the earth. ²Now the earth was formless and empty, darkness was over the surface of the deep, and the Spirit of God was hovering over the waters.

³And God said, "Let there be light," and there was light. ⁴God saw that the light was good, and he separated the light from the darkness.

⁵God called the light "day," and the darkness he called "night." And there was evening, and there was morning — the first day.

⁶And God said, "Let there be a vault between the waters to separate water from water." ⁷So God made the vault and separated the water under the vault from the water above it. And it was so. ⁸God called the vault "sky." And there was evening, and there was morning — the second day.

1:1 — 2:3 The Bible's opening narrative introduces the Bible's main character — God. The creation account emphasizes God's power as he brings all things into existence through divine decree. God's creative activity occurs over six days in Ge 1:3–31. The account ends with the description of God's rest on the seventh day in 2:1–3. The six-day structure reflects the overall pattern the writer gives to God's work. Creation is organized into three categories: the heavens, the sea and sky, and the earth. God's creative activity forms and then fills each of these categories. The focus of the creation account demonstrates how God brought order and structure to the universe. Throughout the Bible, God's power over creation shows his sovereignty (see Ps 104:1–35 and note; Isa 40:12 and note).

1:1 In the beginning Genesis opens with the Hebrew phrase *bere'shith*, typically translated as "in the beginning." There are two possible interpretations of this phrase: a specific, absolute beginning of all time; or a nonspecific, general beginning of God's work of creation. **God** The Hebrew word used here for "God," *elohim*, is plural. While *elohim* may be used to describe multiple deities, OT authors usually use the term to refer to the singular God of Israel (more than 2,000 instances), such as here. See the infographic "The Days of Creation" on p. 6. **created** The Hebrew word used here is *bara*. Compare Isa 40:26; note on Ge 1:27. **the heavens and the earth** This phrase refers to the entirety of creation. The OT often uses opposing word pairs to refer to a totality.

BARA

The Hebrew word for "create" (*bara*) is used in the OT to refer to divine activity only — Yahweh alone serves as its grammatical subject — implying the writer wanted to emphasize that people cannot create in the way that Yahweh creates and that no other god can claim to be the creator. The verb *bara* also conveys the idea of ordering or determining function, suggesting God's creative activity consists of bringing proper order and function to the cosmos.

1:2 formless and empty The Hebrew terms used here, *tohu* and *bohu,* describe material substance lacking boundary, order and definition. This same word pairing occurs in Jer 4:23, indicating that the meaning of *tohu* and *bohu* is not nonexistence but a nonfunctional, barren state. The Hebrew structure implies that this material existed in a formless and empty state when God began his creative work. This does not mean that God didn't create this material prior to the time period recorded by the Biblical text. Hence, Isa 45:18, which declares that God did not

create the earth empty (*bohu*), does not contradict Ge 1:2, where God orders and fills an initially empty (*bohu*) creation. **darkness** Throughout the Bible darkness represents evil or calamity. Here, darkness refers to the unformed and unfilled conditions of the material of v. 1. **the deep** The Hebrew word used here, *tehom*, refers to the primordial or primeval sea — the cosmic waters of chaos. *Tehom* is similar to the Babylonian words *tamtu* and *Tiamat*. *Tiamat* refers to a chaos deity, and the slaying of a chaos monster is described elsewhere in the OT in the context of creation (Ps 74:12–17). However, a closer parallel can be found in the Ugaritic *thm*, the term for the primeval abyss. Since *thm* is not personified, *tehom* in Ge 1:2 should likewise not be considered a personified god. In both instances, the description credits the God of Israel with subduing the chaotic primordial conditions to bring about an ordered, habitable creation. Although chaos is not eliminated in the OT account, God's action yields order and restraint. The chaos is part of what God deems "very good" in v. 31. It is nevertheless a perpetual danger that will only be finally removed at the end of the age when there is no longer any sea (Rev 21:1). **Spirit of God** Since the Hebrew word used here, *ruach*, can mean "spirit" or "wind," this phrase can be translated "Spirit of God" or "wind from God" (or even "mighty wind"). However, the pairing of *ruach* with God (*elohim*) in Hebrew usually refers to God's Spirit.

1:3 And God said The ordering of creation begins with the spoken word. Only one other ancient Near Eastern creation account, the Egyptian Memphite Theology, includes an example of creation by speech. **Let there be light** God creates light before the creation of the sun (Ge 1:14–18). This reflects an understanding of the world, common in the ancient Near East, that held that the sun does not serve as the source of light. See the infographic "Ancient Hebrew Conception of the Universe" on p. 5.

1:4 good God calls his handiwork good seven times in ch. 1 (vv. 4,10,12,18,21,25,31). The Hebrew word used here, *tov*, has a broad range of meaning but generally describes what is desirable, beautiful or right. In essence, God affirms creation as right and in right relationship with him immediately after he creates it. The material world is good as created by God.

1:5 evening, and there was morning — the first day The expression "evening, and there was morning" specifies the length of a "day" (*yom* in Hebrew). While the author may have meant a 24-hour day, less specific interpretations are possible. The Hebrew word *yom* can refer to a 24-hour cycle, the daylight hours or an unspecified future "someday." The meaning of the word, though, does not settle the debate over whether the passage references a literal six-day creation or symbolic days. In addition, the sun (which marks the change from evening to morning) is not created until the fourth day. Nonliteral interpretations of this phrase fall into two main groups: those that privilege the literary qualities of ch. 1, and those that seek to accommodate scientific conclusions about the

Ancient Hebrew Conception of the Universe

The ancient Israelites divided the world into Heaven, Earth, Sea and the Underworld.

▶ They viewed the sky as a vault resting on foundations—perhaps mountains—with doors and windows that let in the rain. God dwelt above the sky, hidden in cloud and majesty.

▶ The world was viewed as a disk floating on the waters, secured or moored by pillars. The earth was the only known domain—the realm beyond it was considered unknowable.

▶ The Underworld (Sheol) was a watery or dusty prison from which no one returned. Regarded as a physical place beneath the earth, it could be reached only through death.

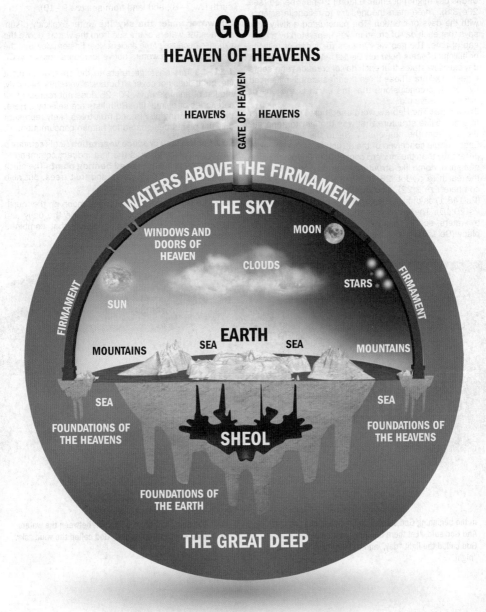

⁹And God said, "Let the water under the sky be gathered to one place, and let dry ground appear." And it was so. ¹⁰God called the dry ground "land," and the gathered waters he called "seas." And God saw that it was good.

¹¹Then God said, "Let the land produce vegetation: seed-bearing plants and trees on the land that bear fruit with seed in it, according to their various kinds." And it was so. ¹²The land produced vegetation: plants bearing seed according to their kinds and trees bearing fruit with seed in it according to their kinds. And God saw that it was good. ¹³And there was evening, and there was morning—the third day.

¹⁴And God said, "Let there be lights in the vault

age of the earth. The first group includes the framework view, in which the days of creation are a literary device that structures the creation account. Also included in this group is the analogical day view, in which each day of creation represents God's work day, but the length of this day might not equal a literal 24-hour period (see 2Pe 3:8). Three main theories try to reconcile science with the days of creation. The punctuated activity view says that each day of creation was separated by a huge gap of time. The gap view argues for a gap of millions or billions of years between Ge 1:1 and 1:2. Finally, the day-age view states that each day of creation represents a geological era. These three theories are all influenced by scientific conclusions that the earth is millions or billions of years old.

1:6 a vault The Hebrew word used here, *raqia'*, refers to a dome-like structure that was thought to separate the sky from the heavens (v. 8). In the ancient Near East, people conceived of the structure of the universe differently than the modern conception. People thought of a solid, dome-like structure encircling and enclosing the earth (e.g., Job 26:10; Pr 8:27–28; Job 37:18; compare Eze 1:22). God dwelled above this expanse (Ps 148:1) as though the earth was his throne (Am 9:6; Ps 29:10). The earth was thought to be surrounded by waters, so the seas were gathered together in one place (Ge 1:9).

1:9–13 The third day of creation involves two more distinct acts of creation. Both are affirmed with the phrase, "And God saw that it was good." The first three days of creation are characterized by three acts of separation: God separates light from darkness (v. 4), heaven from earth (vv. 7–8), and land from sea (vv. 9–10).

1:9 water under the sky The writer explicitly distinguishes the waters of the sea from the waters above the expanse because of the ancient Near Eastern view that the sky held back the waters above (compare note on v. 6).

1:11–13 This passage refers to the creation of plant life, but it does not cover all botanical varieties. Similarly, the list of animals in vv. 20–25 does not represent all categories of animal life. Both lists are selective. Here, the seed-bearing plants and fruit trees likely represent only the plants designated for human consumption.

1:11 Let the land produce vegetation God's command for vegetation to grow is the first indirect command in the creation sequence. **seed-bearing plants** The earth is to produce not only plants and fruit trees, but also plants and fruit trees that bear seeds.

1:14–18 God creates the sun and moon on the fourth day. The sun, moon and stars provide the daily and seasonal cycles required for agriculture that, combined with land and water, sustain life.

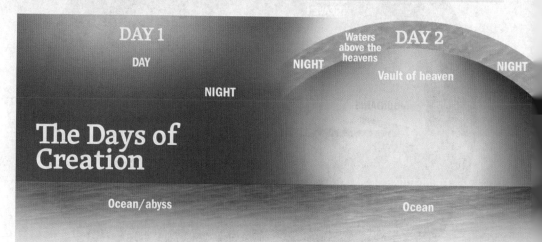

The Days of Creation

DAY 1

DAY

NIGHT

NIGHT

Ocean/abyss

DAY 2

Waters above the heavens

NIGHT

Vault of heaven

NIGHT

Ocean

In the beginning God created the heavens and the earth. And God said, "Let there be light," and there was light. God called the light "day," and the darkness he called "night."

And God said, "Let there be a vault between the waters to separate water from water." God called the vault "sky."

of the sky to separate the day from the night, and let them serve as signs to mark sacred times, and days and years, [15]and let them be lights in the vault of the sky to give light on the earth." And it was so. [16]God made two great lights — the greater light to govern the day and the lesser light to govern the night. He also made the stars. [17]God set them in the vault of the sky to give light on the earth, [18]to govern the day and the night, and to separate light from darkness. And God saw that it was good. [19]And there was evening, and there was morning — the fourth day.

[20]And God said, "Let the water teem with living creatures, and let birds fly above the earth across the vault of the sky." [21]So God created the great creatures of the sea and every living thing with which the water teems and that moves about in it, according to their kinds, and every winged bird according to its kind.

1:14 lights The creation of the lights in the heavens on the fourth day parallels the creation of light in general on the first day. These lights produce another separation — day from night (compare note on vv. 1:9–13). **signs to mark** Celestial phenomena were often understood as divine signs in the ancient Near East (see note on Jer 8:2). **sacred times** The Hebrew word used here, *mo'adim*, could refer to seasons — indicating the natural agricultural cycle — but *mo'adim* also frequently indicates religious festivals or sacred times.

1:16 two great lights This refers to the sun and the moon, but the writer deliberately avoids the words "sun" (*shemesh* in Hebrew) and "moon" (*yareach* in Hebrew) that correspond to the names of West Semitic deities: Shamash and Yarik. Avoiding the Hebrew words for "sun" and "moon" may be part of a larger agenda in the narrative to cast all of the heavenly bodies as natural, created phenomena that are subject to the Creator — not deities in themselves. In this way, Ge 1 offers a subtle critique of prevailing ancient Near Eastern beliefs about the sun, moon and stars.

1:20–25 Creation on the fifth day includes the creatures of the sky and sea. God creates land animals on the sixth day. These creative acts parallel the activity on the second day, when God separates sky and sea, and the third day, when land appears. The description focuses on order and balance in nature. The zoological categories reflect those known to human experience: sea creatures, birds, wild and domesticated animals, and creatures that move along the ground. (The latter description is not restricted to insects as it describes movement, not species.)

1:20 living creatures Here, the Hebrew term *nephesh* refers to animal life.

α Genesis 1:20

NEPHESH
While the Hebrew word *nephesh* (often translated as "soul") can refer to animal life, it can also refer to human life or a person's life force (their soul) along with emotions, intellect, personality and will (see Ge 9:5; 27:4; Ex 23:9; 1Sa 19:11).

1:21 creatures of the sea A translation of the Hebrew word *tannin*, which does not refer to any specific member

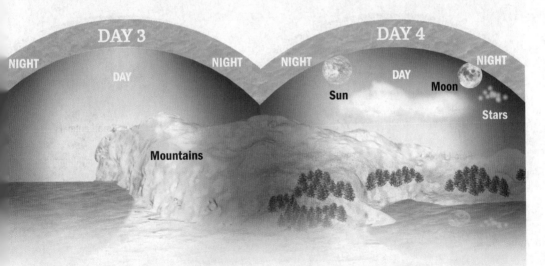

DAY 3
NIGHT
DAY
NIGHT

DAY 4
NIGHT
DAY
NIGHT
Sun
Moon
Stars
Mountains

And God said, "Let the water under the sky be gathered to one place, and let dry ground appear." God called the dry ground "land," and the gathered waters he called "seas." Then God said, "Let the land produce vegetation: seed-bearing plants and trees on the land that bear fruit with seed in it, according to their various kinds."

And God said, "Let there be lights in the vault of the sky to separate the day from the night, and let them serve as signs to mark sacred times, and days and years, and let them be lights in the vault of the sky to give light on the earth." God made two great lights—the greater light to govern the day and the lesser light to govern the night. He also made the stars.

And God saw that it was good. ²²God blessed them and said, "Be fruitful and increase in number and fill the water in the seas, and let the birds increase on the earth." ²³And there was evening, and there was morning—the fifth day.

²⁴And God said, "Let the land produce living creatures according to their kinds: the livestock, the creatures that move along the ground, and the wild animals, each according to its kind." And it was so. ²⁵God made the wild animals according to their kinds, the livestock according to their kinds, and all the creatures that move along the ground according to their kinds. And God saw that it was good.

²⁶Then God said, "Let us make mankind in our image, in our likeness, so that they may rule over the fish in the sea and the birds in the sky, over the livestock and all the wild animals,ᵃ and over all the creatures that move along the ground."

²⁷So God created mankind in his own image,
    in the image of God he created them;
    male and female he created them.

ᵃ 26 Probable reading of the original Hebrew text (see Syriac); Masoretic Text *the earth*

---

of the aquatic kingdom. The term *tannin* occurs in Canaanite mythology for supernatural sea creatures who served the god Yam in his primordial battle with the god Baal. Yam was depicted as Leviathan, a chaotic monster of the primordial deep. Attributing the creation of the *tannin* to the God of Israel served to assert his superiority over the gods of Canaan, especially those symbolizing the watery chaos that existed before God brought order to the world. It was a message of hope that God was the Creator of even the chaos and thus could subdue it.

1:22 Be fruitful and increase in number God created life to be fertile. Here, the capacity for sexual reproduction is cast as a divine blessing.

1:26–31 The creation of man and woman is the climax of God's creative activity. This passage contains several key words and concepts: God's reference to himself in the plural, the concept of the "image of God," the separation of humanity into two genders—male and female—and the divine command for humanity to fill and rule the earth.

1:26 Let us make The occurrence of "us" in this passage has been understood to refer to the plurality of the godhead: the Father, Son and Holy Spirit. This understanding would have been unknown to the authors of the OT. Another possible explanation is the so-called "plural of majesty," but this type of grammatical usage is more common for nouns and adjectives than verbs. A simpler explanation is that "us" reflects an announcement by the single God of Israel to a group in his presence—the heavenly host. Other OT passages support the idea of a heavenly host or divine council (Ps 29:1; see Ps 82:1 and note). This explanation also applies to Ge 11:7. The phrase "our image" then means that the members of the heavenly host also reflect the divine image.

1:27 image of God Being created in the image of God distinguishes people from all other earthly creation. God's image is not described as being possessed in part or given gradually; rather, it is an immediate and inherent part of being human. The image of God likely does not refer to

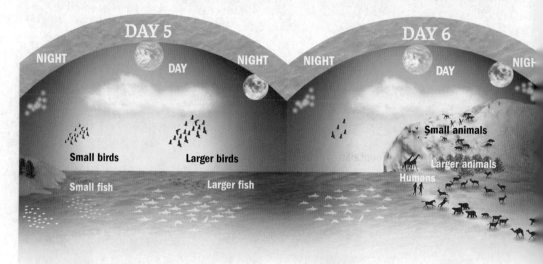

DAY 5 — NIGHT · DAY · NIGHT

Small birds   Larger birds
Small fish   Larger fish

DAY 6 — NIGHT · DAY · NIGH

Small animals
Larger animals
Humans

And God said, "Let the water teem with living creatures, and let birds fly above the earth across the vault of the sky." God blessed them and said, "Be fruitful and increase in number and fill the water in the seas, and let the birds increase on the earth."

And God said, "Let the land produce living creatures according to their kinds: the livestock, the creatures that move along the ground, and the wild animals, each according to its kind." Then God said, "Let us make mankind in our image, in our likeness." God blessed them and said to them, "Be fruitful and increase in number."

²⁸God blessed them and said to them, "Be fruitful and increase in number; fill the earth and subdue it. Rule over the fish in the sea and the birds in the sky and over every living creature that moves on the ground."

²⁹Then God said, "I give you every seed-bearing plant on the face of the whole earth and every tree that has fruit with seed in it. They will be yours for food. ³⁰And to all the beasts of the earth and all the birds in the sky and all the creatures that move along the ground — everything that has the breath of life in it — I give every green plant for food." And it was so.

³¹God saw all that he had made, and it was very good. And there was evening, and there was morning — the sixth day.

2 Thus the heavens and the earth were completed in all their vast array.

²By the seventh day God had finished the work he had been doing; so on the seventh day he rested from all his work. ³Then God blessed the seventh day and made it holy, because on it he rested from all the work of creating that he had done.

Adam and Eve

⁴This is the account of the heavens and the earth when they were created, when the LORD God made the earth and the heavens.

---

any specific ability (intelligence, sentience, emotional capacity, free will, etc.). This would result in an ethical problem, since human beings do not possess these abilities equally. Likewise, connecting the image of God to the internal makeup of a human being—by appealing to the application of the Hebrew words *nephesh* for "soul" or *ruach* for "spirit" for people—does not resolve this issue, as both terms are used to describe members of the animal kingdom. Rather, it refers to our creation as God's image, his unique representatives on earth. People are thus God's agents, functioning as he would if he were embodied. Jesus is the ultimate image of God (Heb 1:3). **male and female** There is no status distinction among bearers of the divine image; they are equal while having distinct capacities and roles in fulfilling the divine mandate to steward the earth. **he created them** The Hebrew verb used here, *bara*, is the same word used in

Ge 1:1. However, the plural declaration "let us make" in v. 26 uses a different verb. The verbs for "make" (*asah*) and "form" (*yatsar*) are also used elsewhere with *bara* to refer to God's work as Creator in chs. 1–2. In ch. 2, yet another verb is used for the fashioning of Adam (*yatsar*). These verbs are synonyms. Compare note on 1:1.

1:28 Be fruitful and increase in number As with the animal kingdom, humanity is created to be fertile. The capacity for sexual reproduction is cast as a divine blessing. **subdue it. Rule over** These terms indicate active power or rule involving physical force or effort (Jer 34:16; Est 7:8; Jos 18:1; Isa 14:2; Eze 29:15). Active rule is not destructive, as creation is meant to sustain people. Humanity is instructed to keep creation under control—to keep the chaotic conditions that God subdued at bay. All must function as God originally ordered it to function (compare Ge 2:15).

1:31 very good The totality of the ordered creation meets the expectations of its Creator.

2:1–3 The seven days of creation end with this description of God's rest. The creation account of Ge 1:1—2:3, where God works for six days and rests on the seventh, provides a theological rationale for the Sabbath observance. The command to observe the Sabbath in Ex 20:8–11 is based directly on the pattern developed in this passage.

2:2 By the seventh day God had finished Some translations render this "on the seventh day," suggesting that God worked on the seventh day in violation of the Sabbath. However, the Hebrew text here can be translated "by the seventh day," resulting in the verb being rendered "had finished," expressing the completion of the act. See the infographic "The Days of Creation" on p. 6.

2:3 God blessed the seventh day The creation week serves as the model for the six-day week and Sabbath rest noted in Ex 20:11 and other Israelite laws.

2:4–25 Leaving behind the cosmic view of creation in Ge 1:1—2:3, the narrative turns to what is happening on earth—specifically, the creation of the first man and the preparation of the Garden of Eden as his home. The narrative presents a more personal view of God interacting with his creation. Rather than presenting two unconnected creation accounts, the narratives of chs. 1 and 2 tell complementary stories, with ch. 2 offering a closer look at the creation of humanity.

2:4 This is the account The formulaic Hebrew phrase used here, *elleh toledoth*, is used throughout Genesis

DAY 7

NIGHT

DAY

NIGHT

Thus the heavens and the earth were completed in all their vast array. By the seventh day God had finished the work he had been doing; so on the seventh day he rested from all his work.

⁵Now no shrub had yet appeared on the earthᵃ and no plant had yet sprung up, for the LORD God had not sent rain on the earth and there was no one to work the ground, ⁶but streamsᵇ came up from the earth and watered the whole surface of the ground. ⁷Then the LORD God formed a manᶜ from the dust of the ground and breathed into his nostrils the breath of life, and the man became a living being.

⁸Now the LORD God had planted a garden in the east, in Eden; and there he put the man he had formed. ⁹The LORD God made all kinds of trees grow out of the ground—trees that were pleasing to the eye and good for food. In the middle of the garden were the tree of life and the tree of the knowledge of good and evil.

¹⁰A river watering the garden flowed from Eden; from there it was separated into four headwaters.

¹¹The name of the first is the Pishon; it winds through the entire land of Havilah, where there is gold. ¹²(The gold of that land is good; aromatic resinᵈ and onyx are also there.) ¹³The name of the second river is the Gihon; it winds through the entire land of Cush.ᵉ ¹⁴The name of the third river is the Tigris; it runs along the east side of Ashur. And the fourth river is the Euphrates.

¹⁵The LORD God took the man and put him in the Garden of Eden to work it and take care of it. ¹⁶And the LORD God commanded the man, "You are free to eat from any tree in the garden; ¹⁷but you must not eat from the tree of the knowledge of good and evil, for when you eat from it you will certainly die."

ᵃ 5 Or *land*; also in verse 6   ᵇ 6 Or *mist*   ᶜ 7 The Hebrew for *man (adam)* sounds like and may be related to the Hebrew for *ground (adamah)*; it is also the name *Adam* (see verse 20).   ᵈ 12 Or *good; pearls*   ᵉ 13 Possibly southeast Mesopotamia

to mark the beginning of major sections (5:1; 6:9; 10:1; 11:10,27; 25:12,19; 36:1,9; 37:2). **LORD God** The first occurrence of the personal divine name Yahweh. Here it is combined with *elohim*, the Hebrew word that identifies God in ch. 1. This combination occurs only 37 times in the OT. Twenty of these instances appear in ch. 2; there is only one more in the rest of the Pentateuch (Ex 9:30). This suggests that Ge 1 and 2 were composed separately and combined with the rest of the book at a later date.
2:5 there was no one to work the ground Verse 5 implies that the earth is barren because there is no one to work the ground, but the man is not assigned this task until he is placed in the Garden of Eden (v. 15). Even so, the garden requires very little work until after the fall (when the people oppose God's will), when the ground is cursed (3:23). Here God sustains plant life in the Garden of Eden without any work on the man's part (see vv. 9–10). The following verse (v. 6) indicates that God uses a "mist" or "streams" (*ed* in Hebrew) to water the ground.
2:7 formed The Hebrew verb used here is *yatsar*, whereas different verbs appear in the declaration and action of 1:26–27 (*asah* and *bara* respectively). See note on 1:27. **man** The Hebrew word used here is *adam*, which is also used in the Bible as the proper name for the first man, Adam (e.g., Ge 3:17; 1Co 15:45). **the breath of life** The Hebrew phrase used here, *nishmath chayyim*, occurs only this one time in the OT. Genesis 6:17 uses the Hebrew phrase *ruach chayyim*, which is regularly translated "breath of life." Genesis 7:22 has a close parallel that combines both: *nishmath ruach chayyim*, which is also often translated "breath of life." The phrases refer broadly to animate life, which was naturally shown by breathing.
2:8 in Eden Eden was distinguished from the entirety of creation and had specific geographical boundaries. The narrative does not say what the rest of the creation was like, only that Eden was the unique dwelling place of God. Thus, it is not certain if all of creation was like Eden—ideal and without death.
2:9 tree of life The wider garden imagery in the ancient Near East helps in understanding the tree of life. The tree of life refers to two concepts: one earthly and the other symbolic of divine life and cosmological wellness. The tree is described as being located in Eden, which is a garden with abundant water and lush vegetation, paradise for those living in agrarian or pastoral settings. In the ancient Near East, garden imagery was used to

describe the abodes of deities, representing luxury and abundance. The divine abode also represented the place where heaven and earth met. The OT often connects trees with divine encounters and sacred geography (21:33; 35:4; Jos 24:26; Jdg 4:5; 6:11,19).
2:10 four headwaters The geographical details positioning Eden in relation to a river that branches into four rivers do not help pinpoint Eden's location. Two of the rivers named here are unknown (the Pishon and Gihon). The references to the Tigris and Euphrates Rivers suggest a connection with Mesopotamia.
2:11 Havilah The precise location of this land is unknown, but it is mentioned again later in Genesis (Ge 10:7,29; 25:18). Genesis 10:7 includes the name in a list of Arabian regions.
2:13 Cush The land of Cush (*kush* in Hebrew) refers to a region of East Africa that likely included southern Egypt and northern Sudan. The Greek Septuagint as well as some modern translations use "Ethiopia" to translate Hebrew *kush*. The Biblical region was probably located further north than modern Ethiopia.
2:14 Tigris The Tigris, the river mentioned here, is the eastern of the two great rivers in Mesopotamia (Da 10:4). **Ashur** The region around the upper Tigris. Later, Assyria would become the center of a major Mesopotamian empire. See note on Isa 10:24. **Euphrates** The western of the two great rivers in Mesopotamia. The ancient city of Babylon was built near the Euphrates. The Euphrates is the largest river in southwest Asia, flowing southeast for nearly 1,800 miles before emptying into the Persian Gulf.

Genesis 2:14

TIGRIS RIVER
The Tigris River begins in the Taurus Mountains of southeastern Turkey and flows southeast for 1,150 miles to the Persian Gulf.

2:15 to work it and take care of it This phrase helps define the language of subduing and ruling in Ge 1:28; people represent God as stewards of his creation—tending to it as he would. People have the power to rule and are told to do so, but are instructed to do so appropriately.
2:17 you must not eat Eating from the tree of the knowledge of good and evil is not what awakened moral

¹⁸The Lord God said, "It is not good for the man to be alone. I will make a helper suitable for him."

¹⁹Now the Lord God had formed out of the ground all the wild animals and all the birds in the sky. He brought them to the man to see what he would name them; and whatever the man called each living creature, that was its name. ²⁰So the man gave names to all the livestock, the birds in the sky and all the wild animals.

But for Adam^a no suitable helper was found. ²¹So the Lord God caused the man to fall into a deep sleep; and while he was sleeping, he took one of the man's ribs^b and then closed up the place with flesh. ²²Then the Lord God made a woman from the rib^c he had taken out of the man, and he brought her to the man.

²³The man said,

"This is now bone of my bones
  and flesh of my flesh;

she shall be called 'woman,'
  for she was taken out of man."

²⁴That is why a man leaves his father and mother and is united to his wife, and they become one flesh.

²⁵Adam and his wife were both naked, and they felt no shame.

The Fall

3 Now the serpent was more crafty than any of the wild animals the Lord God had made. He said to the woman, "Did God really say, 'You must not eat from any tree in the garden'?"

²The woman said to the serpent, "We may eat fruit from the trees in the garden, ³but God did say, 'You must not eat fruit from the tree that is in

^a 20 Or the man   ^b 21 Or took part of the man's side   ^c 22 Or part

---

discernment in humans, since they would need to possess this already to understand God's command. **tree of the knowledge of good and evil** No such tree appears in other ancient Near Eastern texts and traditions. This tree was located within Eden—the dwelling place of God and his heavenly host (see note on 1:26; note on 2:8). This particular tree represents a counterpart to the tree of life, which could bestow immortality (3:22; see note on 2:9). **you will certainly die** This refers to the certainty of death, not to immediate death. Adam and Eve did not immediately die after eating from the tree, but they were cut off from the tree of life and driven from the garden after their disobedience (3:6). Their immortality depended on remaining in God's presence, symbolized by the tree of life and its fruit. Driven out, they would inevitably die, as all mortals do (compare note on 3:22).

2:18 helper The Hebrew term used here, *ezer*, refers broadly to rendering aid. While used to refer to subordinates, the word does not necessarily imply inferiority: God is called Israel's helper (*ezer* in Hebrew; Hos 13:9). *Ezer* does not imply that the woman is inferior to the man, especially since Eve's creation was prompted by a perceived insufficiency in Adam to image God. Through wordplay, the term may also draw attention to Adam's inability to fulfill one of God's primary mandates: procreation (Ge 1:28). The pronunciation of *ezer* resembles *zera'* (often translated as "seed" or "offspring"), which expresses that Eve is an essential part of humanity imaging God as Creator of life. While the naming of Eve by Adam after the fall implies some level of authority on Adam's part (3:20; compare 2:20), the purpose seems to be to bless Eve and properly steward his relationship with her (see note on 2:20). Eve's status remains equal as divine imager (see note on 1:27). Their equivalence (or equality) is indicated by Adam's response to Eve in 2:23—where he refers to her as bone of his bones and flesh of his flesh. In addition, the dominion (stewardship) mandate was issued to both the man and woman at the same time (see 1:28). This shows that Adam's relationship to Eve is not one of dominion; instead, it involves a difference in roles—he blesses creation through his naming of the animals, while she blesses it by continuing the life of humanity (3:20). Eve comes alongside Adam to help him in his mandate to steward creation—Adam leads in the sense that he is already working with creation before she is created.

2:20 gave names to all the livestock In exercising his stewardship over creation, Adam names the animals. In ancient Israelite belief, knowing the name of a thing is what enabled one to do good for the thing named or to pronounce a blessing. In 32:26–29, the divine figure who wrestles with Jacob must know the name of Jacob before he can bless him. Adam also gives Eve her name (3:20), but in the ch. 2 account, Eve is simply called woman, not given a proper name (2:23).

2:21–23 The language used to describe the first man and woman in these verses indicates that they were human and needed all the things necessary to sustain human life. Due to their environment (Eden), Adam and Eve enjoyed perpetual, but contingent, immortality by being able to eat from the tree of life and not sinning against God's command. All of this ended with their fall (ch. 3).

2:21 one of the man's ribs The woman is made from the side (*tsela'* in Hebrew) of the man. Usually used in architectural contexts (Ex 25:12,14; 26:20), this is the only occurrence of the word in reference to human flesh.

2:25 naked In light of the later events, the use of this Hebrew term here, *arom*, involves wordplay—the serpent is described as crafty (*arum* in Hebrew; 3:1). The parallel words indicate a contrast: innocence being transformed into shame.

3:1–24 The idyllic life of the first man and woman in the Garden of Eden is disrupted by the appearance of the serpent. This serpent tempts the woman to break God's command not to eat from the tree of the knowledge of good and evil. Her choice to taste the fruit disturbs the order of creation and damages the relationship between God and his creation, because now part of his creation is out of order (or harmony)—humanity.

3:1 serpent The Hebrew word used here, *nachash*, means "snake" or "serpent." The Hebrew word *satan* does not appear in this passage, but the NT associates the events recorded here with Satan (Rev 12:9; 20:2). The attribution of human characteristics (cleverness and speech) to the *nachash* suggests it is more than an ordinary member of the animal kingdom. Proper nouns of people or cities that include the Hebrew *nachash* indicate that the term may also mean "bronze" or "diviner." Conceptual parallels

the middle of the garden, and you must not touch it, or you will die.'"

⁴"You will not certainly die," the serpent said to the woman. ⁵"For God knows that when you eat from it your eyes will be opened, and you will be like God, knowing good and evil."

⁶When the woman saw that the fruit of the tree was good for food and pleasing to the eye, and also desirable for gaining wisdom, she took some and ate it. She also gave some to her husband, who was with her, and he ate it. ⁷Then the eyes of both of them were opened, and they realized they were naked; so they sewed fig leaves together and made coverings for themselves.

⁸Then the man and his wife heard the sound of the LORD God as he was walking in the garden in the cool of the day, and they hid from the LORD God among the trees of the garden. ⁹But the LORD God called to the man, "Where are you?"

¹⁰He answered, "I heard you in the garden, and I was afraid because I was naked; so I hid."

¹¹And he said, "Who told you that you were naked? Have you eaten from the tree that I commanded you not to eat from?"

¹²The man said, "The woman you put here with me—she gave me some fruit from the tree, and I ate it."

¹³Then the LORD God said to the woman, "What is this you have done?"

The woman said, "The serpent deceived me, and I ate."

¹⁴So the LORD God said to the serpent, "Because you have done this,

"Cursed are you above all livestock
　　and all wild animals!
You will crawl on your belly
　　and you will eat dust
　　all the days of your life.

---

between Ge 3 and ancient Near Eastern material—which also forms the backdrop of passages with similar language (Isa 14; Eze 28)—suggests that the *nachash* in Ge 3 could be understood in two ways. The narrative may refer to a shining divine being—a member of God's heavenly host or council (compare note on 1:26)—in serpentine appearance. In addition, the serpentine imagery may be used to convey the motif of threatening disorder associated with other serpentine figures in the OT (see Ps 74:13–14; 104:26 and note; Job 26:12 and note; Job 41:1 and note). **Did God really say** The serpent's question omits the positive statement made by God in Ge 2:16. The serpent also distorts the earlier statement by presenting God as saying Adam and Eve could not eat from any tree at all. **3:2 We may eat** The woman corrects the serpent's wording, but she does not do so precisely. Instead of echoing 2:16, where God gave the human couple permission to eat from every tree except one, she generalizes the permission, noting simply that they may eat of the trees in the garden. **3:3 you must not touch it** Eve adds to God's original prohibition, which states nothing about touching the fruit from the tree of the knowledge of good and evil. **or you will die** The original threat of 2:17 points to the certainty of death upon disobedience, but it says nothing of an immediate death. The serpent will introduce the idea of an immediate death into the meaning of 2:17 to deceive the woman (see v. 4). **3:5 God** The Hebrew word used here, *elohim*, is plural. Depending on grammar and context, the plural form can be translated as plural or singular—God or gods (divine beings). It is the most common word used in the OT to refer to the singular God of Israel (over 2,000 occurrences). But *elohim* here may be translated as a plural because of v. 22, where *elohim* says (according to a literal rendering of the Hebrew): "they have become as one of us." Like 1:26, the plurality refers to God and those with him in his abode and throne room: the heavenly host or council (compare Dt 32:8–9; Ps 82; note on 82:title–8; 1Ki 22:19–23; note on 22:19). In the ancient Near East, the knowledge of good and evil was believed to be a divine attribute that humans must earn or receive in some fashion. This possibility has seductive power for the woman in the Genesis account and may indicate why God did not reveal this information

earlier. God created the test by issuing the prohibition of Ge 2:16–17, but he did not intend the temptation to be overwhelming. The serpent is the one who makes it seem irresistible. **knowing good and evil** This does not refer only to the ability to choose between right and wrong. If the man and woman did not already possess this ability, the original command would have been meaningless. Rather, knowing good and evil refers to divine wisdom, which corresponds with the idea of becoming like God or the gods (*elohim* in Hebrew). **3:6 husband, who was with her** Since there is no mention of the woman leaving the serpent to find Adam, Adam was most likely present for the entire conversation. **3:7 the eyes of both of them were opened** Both Adam and Eve ate the forbidden fruit (v. 6), so they both experienced the new knowledge of rebellion. **3:8 LORD God as he was walking** This signals that the writer wants the reader to picture God as a human being (an anthropomorphism) present in the Garden of Eden. This is the first theophany in the OT—an appearance of God to human beings in a manner that can be processed by the human senses. See the table "Old Testament Theophanies" on p. 924. **in the cool of the day** Translating this phrase is difficult. The Hebrew term used here, *ruach*, is normally translated "spirit" or "wind" (see note on 1:2), but is often translated here as "cool." This may mean that it is intended to evoke the unmistakable power of God's presence. **3:10 I was afraid** Adam says he is afraid because he is unclothed, but he really fears the shame of appearing naked in God's presence. His awareness of that shame exposes his guilt. Before their disobedience, Adam and Eve had no reason to be ashamed (2:25). **3:11 Who told you that you were naked** God asks not because he lacks information, but to elicit a confession. **3:12 woman you put** Adam tries to pass responsibility to his wife—and perhaps even to God. **3:14 Cursed are you** It is unclear how the serpent (*nachash* in Hebrew) is more cursed than any other animal. This supports the view that the *nachash* is not an ordinary member of the animal kingdom and the serpent imagery evokes other ancient Near Eastern parallels. See note on 3:1. **You will crawl on your belly** The language and context suggest that this condition was new in some way. Since the Hebrew word used for serpent, *nachash*,

15 And I will put enmity
    between you and the woman,
    and between your offspring[a] and hers;
he will crush[b] your head,
    and you will strike his heel."

16 To the woman he said,

"I will make your pains in childbearing very
        severe;
    with painful labor you will give birth to
        children.
Your desire will be for your husband,
    and he will rule over you."

17 To Adam he said, "Because you listened to
your wife and ate fruit from the tree about which
I commanded you, 'You must not eat from it,'

"Cursed is the ground because of you;
    through painful toil you will eat food from it
        all the days of your life.
18 It will produce thorns and thistles for you,
    and you will eat the plants of the field.

19 By the sweat of your brow
    you will eat your food
until you return to the ground,
    since from it you were taken;
for dust you are
    and to dust you will return."

20 Adam[c] named his wife Eve,[d] because she
would become the mother of all the living.
21 The LORD God made garments of skin for Adam
and his wife and clothed them. 22 And the LORD God
said, "The man has now become like one of us, knowing good and evil. He must not be allowed to reach
out his hand and take also from the tree of life and
eat, and live forever." 23 So the LORD God banished
him from the Garden of Eden to work the ground
from which he had been taken. 24 After he drove the
man out, he placed on the east side[e] of the Garden
of Eden cherubim and a flaming sword flashing
back and forth to guard the way to the tree of life.

a 15 Or seed   b 15 Or strike   c 20 Or The man   d 20 Eve
probably means living.   e 24 Or placed in front

and its affiliated imagery are often paired with chaotic
and disorderly forces in opposition to the divine order
in the ancient Near East, there is no need for a literal
zoological explanation. Rather, this passage indicates
that the serpent, God's cosmic enemy, has been made
docile (i.e., he is defeated). **you will eat dust** Ancient
Near Eastern texts, such as the Akkadian work Descent of
Ishtar, depict serpents as inhabitants of the underworld
that feed on dust and clay.
3:15 enmity This word refers to hostility, not fear. The
curse is not aimed at the woman, but at the serpent. Its
language speaks of combat—specifically between the
serpent and its offspring (those that follow its ways),
and the woman and her descendants. The serpent is a
divine enemy of God rather than a member of the animal
kingdom. As such, this text contains a prophecy indicating
that animosity and spiritual war will ensue between the
serpent (nachash in Hebrew) and humanity (compare note
on 3:1). In the NT, the offspring of the devil are equated
with evildoers who oppose God's will and the Messiah,
Jesus (Rev 12:9; Jn 8:44; 1Jn 3:8,12,23). **offspring**
The Hebrew word used here, zera' (which may be literally
rendered "seed"), can refer to one person or many. **he
will crush your head** In the Hebrew text, the singular
pronoun here refers collectively to the offspring (zera' in
Hebrew) of Eve. The NT presents Jesus as the ultimate
human descendant of Eve who defeats Satan or the
devil (Lk 3:38; 10:17–19; Rev 12:9–11; compare Gal
3:16). Paul seems to reference this line when he tells
the Roman Christians that God will give them the power
to crush Satan (Ro 16:20).
3:16 your pains The Hebrew word used here is also
used to describe Adam's punishment: He will work the
ground in pain. The original tasks given to both Adam
and Eve (tending to creation, and being fruitful and
multiplying) now involve great difficulty because they live
outside Eden (Ge 1:28; 3:24). Compare note on 2:18.
Your desire will be for your husband The Hebrew
word used here, teshuqah, occurs elsewhere only twice
(4:7; SS 7:10). In the Song of Songs the term seems to
indicate sexual desire, but that meaning does not work
well in this context. In Ge 4:7 the word connotes desire
to control or desire to conquer (compare note on 4:7).

3:17 Cursed is the ground because of you The context
of the curse shows that serious effort and the overcoming
of obstacles will be necessary to make the earth produce
what human survival requires.
3:19 to dust you will return The consequences of sin
include lifelong toil. This line could be understood as
indicating that only death is the release from that curse
of toil, or that natural death may be another consequence
of sin (compare Ro 5:12). It is unclear whether natural
death existed prior to Adam and Eve's sin—whether in
Eden or elsewhere (see note on Ge 3:22; note on 6:3).
3:20 Adam named his wife Eve Eve's name in Hebrew,
chawwah, is related to the Hebrew verb chayah, which
may be translated "to live." This is wordplay—Eve is
described as the mother of all life.
3:22 The man The Hebrew grammar here can be understood as including Eve. **like one of us** The plural here
refers to more than just the singular God Yahweh—it
speaks of the heavenly host or God's council. See note
on 3:5. **tree of life** See note on 2:9. **live forever** Adam
and Eve had to be driven from the garden. To remain in
God's presence and eat of the tree of life would have
resulted in them becoming immortal, thus thwarting
the penalty for their transgression (2:17). Cut off from
God's presence, immortality was unavailable—they
would eventually die. God's statement here does not
indicate whether Adam and Eve were eating from the tree
of life before their sin and thus it is unclear if they were
immortal (compare 2:16). God could be concerned that
they will start eating from the tree of life or that they be
prevented from continuing to eat from it. However, several
factors seem to hint at their immortality prior to their
sin. The tree of life was probably intended to perpetually
sustain all life in Eden, in order to sustain its ideal state
(2:8–9). In addition, God's original command hints that
Adam and Eve knew what death was but were currently
experiencing an immortal life in God's presence—the
source of life itself (2:16). Adam and Eve also were allowed to eat from any tree but the tree of knowledge of
good and evil (2:17). Compare note on 6:3.
3:24 cherubim The Hebrew term used here is plural.
The noun comes from the Akkadian term karub, which

Cain and Abel

4 Adam[a] made love to his wife Eve, and she became pregnant and gave birth to Cain.[b] She said, "With the help of the LORD I have brought forth[c] a man." [2]Later she gave birth to his brother Abel.

Now Abel kept flocks, and Cain worked the soil. [3]In the course of time Cain brought some of the fruits of the soil as an offering to the LORD. [4]And Abel also brought an offering — fat portions from some of the firstborn of his flock. The LORD looked with favor on Abel and his offering, [5]but on Cain and his offering he did not look with favor. So Cain was very angry, and his face was downcast.

[6]Then the LORD said to Cain, "Why are you angry? Why is your face downcast? [7]If you do what is right, will you not be accepted? But if you do not do what is right, sin is crouching at your door; it desires to have you, but you must rule over it."

[8]Now Cain said to his brother Abel, "Let's go out to the field."[d] While they were in the field, Cain attacked his brother Abel and killed him.

[9]Then the LORD said to Cain, "Where is your brother Abel?"

"I don't know," he replied. "Am I my brother's keeper?"

[10]The LORD said, "What have you done? Listen! Your brother's blood cries out to me from the ground. [11]Now you are under a curse and driven from the ground, which opened its mouth to receive your brother's blood from your hand. [12]When you work the ground, it will no longer yield its crops for you. You will be a restless wanderer on the earth."

[13]Cain said to the LORD, "My punishment is

---

[a] 1 Or *The man*   [b] 1 *Cain* sounds like the Hebrew for *brought forth* or *acquired*.   [c] 1 Or *have acquired*   [d] 8 Samaritan Pentateuch, Septuagint, Vulgate and Syriac; Masoretic Text does not have "Let's go out to the field."

---

refers to a divine throne guardian. These guardians are often depicted in sculptures as sphinx-like — having the body of a lion and the head of a man. They are commonly depicted as guarding the throne of a deity. This fits the context, as the cherubim are placed as guardians of Eden, God's dwelling place (see note on 2:8). **flaming sword flashing back and forth** This phrase occurs only here in the OT. Fire is a very common motif for the presence of Yahweh — as demonstrated by the descriptions of Yahweh on Sinai (Ex 19:18; 24:17; Dt 4:11; 5:4–5) and the fiery throne of Eze 1 (which also includes cherubim; compare Da 7:9).

4:1–26 Genesis 4 introduces the theme of conflict between brothers. This theme will return in the story of Jacob and Esau (25:19–34; 27:1–45) and again with Joseph and his brothers (37:1–35). In each story an older brother is passed over in favor of the younger. The narrative illustrates the deepening effects of sin in the world.

4:1 Cain The meaning of this name is disputed. It likely relates to smithing or metalworking, as in the name Tubal-Cain, forefather of metalworkers (see v. 22). **the LORD** The Hebrew here uses the divine name *yhwh* (Yahweh). See the table "Names of God in the Old Testament" on p. 917.
4:2 Later she gave birth to his brother The text subtly indicates that this story is really about Cain. Instead of stating that Eve bore Abel, the narrator says Eve bore Cain's brother. **Abel** Abel's name in Hebrew, *hevel*, means "breath." Since the chapter does not tie the name to Abel's early death, it may refer generally to brevity of life. Alternatively, the name *hevel* could refer to Abel's occupation, as the related Syriac word *habla* means "herdsman."
4:3 some of the fruits of the soil as an offering The Hebrew word order here may hint that Cain brought whatever was close at hand while Abel brought the best of what he had (v. 4). Cain's offering could also be of poor quality, but there is no direct statement about this in the text.
4:4 firstborn of his flock Abel's offering seems to demonstrate great care and attention to his relationship with Yahweh. He offers exactly what later texts indicate Yahweh requests of his people (Ex 13:12; Nu 18:17). By offering the firstborn and best portions, Abel

makes the greater sacrifice and reflects a righteous attitude (Pr 3:9).
4:5 he did not look with favor Later laws in Leviticus ask for both animal and plant offerings, so it is highly unlikely that Abel's offering was more highly regarded because it was an animal sacrifice (e.g., Lev 2). Rather, Yahweh's favor of Abel's offering may have been related to something about both Cain and Abel as people — such as their intentions. Cain could have been insincere in his devotion to Yahweh, whereas Abel was not (compare Heb 11:4). Compare note on Ge 4:3.
4:7 is crouching The Hebrew verb used here, *ravats*, normally indicates lying down, as in resting (29:2; Isa 11:6); it can also refer to lying in wait like a predator does when waiting for prey (Ge 49:9). The Hebrew word *ravats* is also associated with the Akkadian word *rabitsu*, which in Mesopotamian religion is used in reference to demons that were believed to guard entrances to buildings. Thus, it is possible that sin is being personified here as a demonic force, waiting to pounce on Cain. This fits with the curse of the serpent who God says will strike at the heel of people (3:15). **it desires to have you** The Hebrew word used here, *teshuqah*, also occurs in 3:16 in relation to Eve's desire for her husband. Both here and in the curse of 3:16, the context is negative: The desire represents something to be resisted, as it is connected to sin.
4:8 Cain said to his brother Abel The traditional Hebrew text (the Masoretic Text) does not include what Cain says before he murders Abel. This omission may come from a scribal error in the transmission of the text. Another Hebrew text, the Septuagint (the ancient Greek translation of the OT) and later translations into Syriac preserve a brief statement: "Let's go out to the field."
4:9 I don't know When God confronted Adam and Eve with their sin, they readily confessed (3:11–13). Here, Cain lies to God outright, denying any knowledge of his brother's whereabouts. **my brother's keeper** Cain not only denies knowing anything about Abel's fate but also defiantly objects to the implication that he should be responsible for his brother in any way.
4:11 under a curse and driven from the ground Because Cain spilled Abel's blood on the ground, Yahweh makes Cain's efforts as a farmer futile (compare v. 14).
4:13 punishment The Hebrew word used here, *awon*,

more than I can bear. [14]Today you are driving me from the land, and I will be hidden from your presence; I will be a restless wanderer on the earth, and whoever finds me will kill me."

[15]But the LORD said to him, "Not so[a]; anyone who kills Cain will suffer vengeance seven times over." Then the LORD put a mark on Cain so that no one who found him would kill him. [16]So Cain went out from the LORD's presence and lived in the land of Nod,[b] east of Eden.

[17]Cain made love to his wife, and she became pregnant and gave birth to Enoch. Cain was then building a city, and he named it after his son Enoch. [18]To Enoch was born Irad, and Irad was the father of Mehujael, and Mehujael was the father of Methushael, and Methushael was the father of Lamech.

[19]Lamech married two women, one named Adah and the other Zillah. [20]Adah gave birth to Jabal; he was the father of those who live in tents and raise livestock. [21]His brother's name was Jubal; he was the father of all who play stringed instruments and pipes. [22]Zillah also had a son, Tubal-Cain, who forged all kinds of tools out of[c] bronze and iron. Tubal-Cain's sister was Naamah.

[23]Lamech said to his wives,

"Adah and Zillah, listen to me;
    wives of Lamech, hear my words.
I have killed a man for wounding me,
    a young man for injuring me.
[24]If Cain is avenged seven times,
    then Lamech seventy-seven times."

[25]Adam made love to his wife again, and she gave birth to a son and named him Seth,[d] saying, "God has granted me another child in place of Abel, since Cain killed him." [26]Seth also had a son, and he named him Enosh.

At that time people began to call on[e] the name of the LORD.

[a] 15 Septuagint, Vulgate and Syriac; Hebrew *Very well*
[b] 16 *Nod* means *wandering* (see verses 12 and 14).
[c] 22 Or *who instructed all who work in*   [d] 25 *Seth* probably means *granted*.   [e] 26 Or *to proclaim*

---

is commonly translated as "sin" or "iniquity" (15:16; 2Sa 22:24). It can refer to both the offense and its punishment (1Sa 28:10; see note on Ps 130:3). The idea is that Cain's sin is greater than he can bear. The consequences will overtake him.

4:14 I will be hidden from your presence Part of Cain's anguish is that he fears being cut off from Yahweh. **whoever finds me will kill me** By the time of Abel's murder, there were others living nearby. As with Cain's wife (see Ge 4:17 and note), the narrator has no interest in providing a chronology and description of circumstances that would explain where the people living outside Eden came from. Statements of this nature imply that the Biblical genealogies are selective.

4:15 anyone who kills Cain will suffer vengeance God's intent in punishing Cain is not to cause him harm. **seven times over** This idiomatic phrase indicates severity. **LORD put a mark on Cain** While the precise nature of this mark is unclear, it is visible and it is for Cain's protection. Since the Hebrew preposition here, usually translated "on," may be translated "for," the phrase could be translated: "Yahweh put (or placed) a mark for Cain." This would indicate that Yahweh marked something for Cain's protection, not necessarily him.

4:16 land of Nod This city or region is unknown. It may be symbolic—the Hebrew word *nod* means "wandering" which fits with Yahweh's earlier description of Cain's fate (see vv. 12,14).

4:17 Cain made love to his wife The narrative of ch. 4 does not give a literal chronology of all events that extend from (or are related to) Adam and Eve's life outside Eden. Rather, the narrative shows how Adam and Eve survived, and it traces the beginning of their lineage. The narrative does not say where Cain's wife came from, only that his lineage began through her. Since the narrative is selective and contains no time references concerning how long Adam, Eve and Cain lived after the death of Abel, it is possible (though speculative) that Cain married a woman also birthed by Eve (compare v. 25). Biblical genealogies are typically selective and unconcerned with the precise number of children a couple produced, preferring to follow specific lineages. **building a city** Cain is cast as the originator of urban civilization. There is no indication that God is displeased with Cain or views the building of the city as a rebellion against his punishment (vv. 12,14).

4:18 Irad This name may be associated with Eridu, the first city in Sumerian tradition.

4:19 Lamech married two women Lamech is the first polygamist identified in the Bible.

4:20 Jabal The name Jabal here and Jubal in v. 21 are noticeably similar. Jabal and Jubal may be derived from the Hebrew word *yevul*, meaning "to produce." Jabal, Jubal and Tubal-Cain are all depicted as inventors or founders.

4:22 Tubal-Cain, who forged In addition to being related to Cain's name, this name rhymes with the name Jubal, creating wordplay (see note on v. 20; note on v. 1).

4:23–24 Lamech's poem uses a Hebrew literary technique known as synonymous parallelism—the same concept is stated two different ways in parallel lines. The short poem illustrates Cain's legacy of violence and Lamech's arrogance in thinking his act of killing a man is justified. He addresses the poem to his wives, possibly as a means of intimidating them (compare 3:16 and note).

4:24 seventy-seven Lamech alludes to God's promise regarding the severity of what would happen to any who killed Cain (v. 15). Apparently Lamech sees God's promise as a sign of approval rather than an act of mercy, since he claims for himself even greater vengeance. Either Lamech believes that he, too, will have divine protection, or his arrogant boasting arises from his belief that his own greatness makes divine protection unnecessary.

4:25 named him Seth The Hebrew name *sheth* derives from a verb that means "to put," "to place" or "to set." This subtly relates to the idea that the birth of Seth compensates for the loss of Abel. When not a proper name, the Hebrew noun *sheth* may be translated as "foundation," since a foundation is itself set or put in place (Ps 11:3).

4:26 call on the name of the LORD Up to this point in the narrative, no one has invoked God by his name, *yhwh* (Yahweh).

From Adam to Noah

5 This is the written account of Adam's family line.

When God created mankind, he made them in the likeness of God. ²He created them male and female and blessed them. And he named them "Mankind"ᵃ when they were created.

³When Adam had lived 130 years, he had a son in his own likeness, in his own image; and he named him Seth. ⁴After Seth was born, Adam lived 800 years and had other sons and daughters. ⁵Altogether, Adam lived a total of 930 years, and then he died.

⁶When Seth had lived 105 years, he became the fatherᵇ of Enosh. ⁷After he became the father of Enosh, Seth lived 807 years and had other sons and daughters. ⁸Altogether, Seth lived a total of 912 years, and then he died.

⁹When Enosh had lived 90 years, he became the father of Kenan. ¹⁰After he became the father of Kenan, Enosh lived 815 years and had other sons and daughters. ¹¹Altogether, Enosh lived a total of 905 years, and then he died.

¹²When Kenan had lived 70 years, he became the father of Mahalalel. ¹³After he became the father of Mahalalel, Kenan lived 840 years and had other sons and daughters. ¹⁴Altogether, Kenan lived a total of 910 years, and then he died.

¹⁵When Mahalalel had lived 65 years, he became the father of Jared. ¹⁶After he became the father of Jared, Mahalalel lived 830 years and had other sons and daughters. ¹⁷Altogether, Mahalalel lived a total of 895 years, and then he died.

¹⁸When Jared had lived 162 years, he became the father of Enoch. ¹⁹After he became the father of Enoch, Jared lived 800 years and had other sons and daughters. ²⁰Altogether, Jared lived a total of 962 years, and then he died.

²¹When Enoch had lived 65 years, he became the father of Methuselah. ²²After he became the father of Methuselah, Enoch walked faithfully with God 300 years and had other sons and daughters. ²³Altogether, Enoch lived a total of 365 years. ²⁴Enoch walked faithfully with God; then he was no more, because God took him away.

²⁵When Methuselah had lived 187 years, he became the father of Lamech. ²⁶After he became the father of Lamech, Methuselah lived 782 years and had other sons and daughters. ²⁷Altogether, Methuselah lived a total of 969 years, and then he died.

²⁸When Lamech had lived 182 years, he had a son. ²⁹He named him Noahᶜ and said, "He will comfort us in the labor and painful toil of our hands caused by the ground the LORD has cursed." ³⁰After Noah was born, Lamech lived 595 years and had other sons and daughters. ³¹Altogether, Lamech lived a total of 777 years, and then he died.

³²After Noah was 500 years old, he became the father of Shem, Ham and Japheth.

ᵃ 2 Hebrew *adam*   ᵇ 6 *Father* may mean *ancestor*; also in verses 7-26.   ᶜ 29 *Noah* sounds like the Hebrew for *comfort*.

5:1–32 The genealogy in Ge 5 moves the narrative from one major character (Adam) to the next (Noah). This list of generations traces the descent of Noah one generation at a time, naming one ancestor from each. One of the most striking features of this genealogy is the long lifespans. The notable exception is Enoch (5:22–23), whose time on earth is a comparatively short 365 years. See the people diagram "Adam's Family Tree" on p. 17.

5:1 family line The Hebrew word used here, *toledoth*, is used to mark family histories in Genesis (6:9; 10:1; 11:10,27; 25:12,19; 36:1,9; 37:2). Generally speaking, there are two types of genealogies in the OT, linear and vertical. Linear genealogies focus on one person in each generation—they connect one individual to one specific ancestor in a previous generation. Vertical (segmented) genealogies treat more than one person per generation—they depict relationships within a generation and from one generation to another. **in the likeness of God** See 1:26.

5:3–31 The genealogy of vv. 3–31 is deliberately arranged to conclude with Noah and his sons in preparation for the flood narrative. The generations are described formulaically. Each person is given the same description: When *A* lived *x* years, he fathered *B*. After he fathered *B*, *A* lived *y* years and had other sons and daughters. And all the days of *A* were *x*+*y* years; then he died. The pattern is broken only twice. In vv. 22–23, the unusual case of Enoch requires a break in the formula. The

birth of Noah in v. 29—the climax of the list—also interrupts the pattern, as Noah's father describes his son's special destiny.

5:3 his own likeness, in his own image This phrase echoes God's language about humanity being in his image (see 1:26–27; 5:1).

5:5 930 years It is unclear whether the ages of the individuals in this genealogy are meant to be taken literally or not. The long lifespans are paralleled (and far exceeded) in the Sumerian King List, an ancient Near Eastern document that describes a line of rulers before a great flood.

5:22 Enoch walked faithfully with God This phrase occurs twice, perhaps to demonstrate to readers that Enoch's short life span in this list is not due to negative judgment. The description is also used of Noah (6:9).

5:23 Altogether, Enoch lived a total of 365 years Enoch is the seventh generation from Adam in this genealogy (Jude 14). The number 365 corresponds to the number of days in a solar year, so Enoch became a central figure in later Jewish calendrical mysticism (as seen in the work 1 Enoch).

5:24 he was no more The writer omits the typical formulaic ending referring to the death of the individual (see note on Ge 5:3–31), suggesting that Enoch did not experience a normal death. The NT also asserts that Enoch did not die (Heb 11:5). **took him away** Similar language appears in the description of Elijah's departure from earth in God's fiery chariot (2Ki 2:1,5,9–11).

Wickedness in the World

6 When human beings began to increase in number on the earth and daughters were born to them, ²the sons of God saw that the daughters of humans were beautiful, and they married any of them they chose. ³Then the LORD said, "My Spirit will not contend with*a* humans forever, for they are mortal*b*; their days will be a hundred and twenty years."

⁴The Nephilim were on the earth in those days—and also afterward—when the sons of God went to the daughters of humans and had

a 3 Or *My spirit will not remain in*   *b* 3 Or *corrupt*

6:1–8 This brief narrative bridges the genealogy of Ge 5 and the flood narrative of 6:9–9:29, serving as both a prologue to the flood narrative and a conclusion to the genealogy. As a prologue to the flood narrative, it illustrates the increasing wickedness on earth. As a conclusion to the genealogy, it explains why the long lifespans of ch. 5 have come to an end. Noah serves as the major link between the genealogy and the flood narrative.

6:1 daughters The OT usually refers to the birth of male children when describing a generation. In this case, the reference to daughters deliberately contrasts with the sons of God (see v. 2).

6:2 sons of God This Hebrew phrase, *bene ha'elohim*, and similar phrasings (*bene elohim* and *bene elim*) are used elsewhere in the OT only of heavenly beings (Job 1:6; 2:1; 38:7; Ps 89:6; 82:6; see Dt 32:8 and note). Thus, *bene ha'elohim* could refer to spiritual beings who are members of God's council—the divine council. The Hebrew phrase *bene el-chay* (which may be translated "sons of the living God") is used for the people of Israel in Hos 1:10 and may be an echo of this ancient concept of the divine council (see Hos 1:10 and note). The *bene ha'elohim* could also be human rulers or kings. This idea is based on the OT references to the Davidic king as son of God (Ps 2:7; 2Sa 7:14; 1Ch 17:13). The sons of God could represent the human male line of Seth, while the daughters of men are the descendants of Cain.

6:3 My Spirit The Hebrew word used here, *ruach*, is often used to refer to breath (see Ge 2:7 and note; Job 9:18; 19:17; Ex 15:8; La 4:20). This means that this phrase likely refers to the human life span. **will not contend** The Hebrew word used here, *yadon*, occurs only here in the OT; its origins are unclear. It could mean "remain," "contend" or "be strong." **for they are mortal** The Hebrew grammar here could be understood as an additional thought, rather than the cause of God's decision. God may be asserting that he has the authority to judge humanity since he is God and not flesh. **a hundred and twenty years** It is unclear if this refers to the shortening of the human life span or the amount of time before the flood. If it refers to the span of human life, it would only be a general rule—some individuals after the flood are said to have lived more than 120 years (e.g., Abraham; Ge 25:7).

6:4 Nephilim The Hebrew term used here, *nephilim*, occurs only here and in Nu 13:33, where it is associated with gigantism and people of unusual height. The great height of the Nephilim—who are described as the sons or descendants of Anak in Nu 13:33—discourages the Israelites from conquering the promised land. **afterward** It seems that nephilim were on the earth after the flood (see Nu 13:33). Nonetheless, Noah and his family were the only human

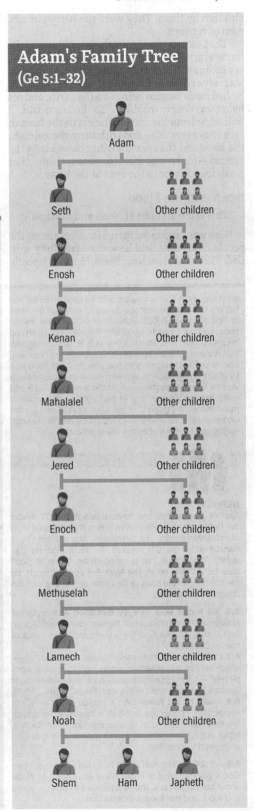

Adam's Family Tree
(Ge 5:1–32)

Adam

Seth — Other children

Enosh — Other children

Kenan — Other children

Mahalalel — Other children

Jered — Other children

Enoch — Other children

Methuselah — Other children

Lamech — Other children

Noah — Other children

Shem   Ham   Japheth

children by them. They were the heroes of old, men of renown.

⁵The LORD saw how great the wickedness of the human race had become on the earth, and that every inclination of the thoughts of the human heart was only evil all the time. ⁶The LORD regretted that he had made human beings on the earth, and his heart was deeply troubled. ⁷So the LORD said, "I will wipe from the face of the earth the human race I have created — and with them the animals, the birds and the creatures that move along the ground — for I regret that I have made them." ⁸But Noah found favor in the eyes of the LORD.

Noah and the Flood

⁹This is the account of Noah and his family.

Noah was a righteous man, blameless among the people of his time, and he walked faithfully with God. ¹⁰Noah had three sons: Shem, Ham and Japheth.

¹¹Now the earth was corrupt in God's sight and was full of violence. ¹²God saw how corrupt the earth had become, for all the people on earth had corrupted their ways. ¹³So God said to Noah, "I am going to put an end to all people, for the earth is filled with violence because of them. I am surely going to destroy both them and the earth. ¹⁴So make yourself an ark of cypressᵃ wood; make rooms in it and coat it with pitch inside and out. ¹⁵This is how you are to build it: The ark is to be three hundred cubits long, fifty cubits wide and thirty cubits high.ᵇ ¹⁶Make a roof for it, leaving below the roof an opening one cubitᶜ high all around.ᵈ Put a door in the side of the ark and make lower, middle and upper decks. ¹⁷I am going to bring floodwaters on

---

ᵃ 14 The meaning of the Hebrew for this word is uncertain.
ᵇ 15 That is, about 450 feet long, 75 feet wide and 45 feet high or about 135 meters long, 23 meters wide and 14 meters high
ᶜ 16 That is, about 18 inches or about 45 centimeters
ᵈ 16 The meaning of the Hebrew for this clause is uncertain.

---

survivors of the flood (compare note on Ge 6:17). Perhaps Noah's family did not escape the cohabitation of the sons of God described in 6:2. Some later extra-Biblical Jewish texts, such as 1 Enoch, agree with this view, but Noah and his generations are called blameless (v. 9), which suggests that none of the members of Noah's family are Nephilim. This would lend credibility to the view that the flood was localized, not global: The Nephilim survived because there was no flood where they were at the time (see 7:19 and note). **heroes** This may refer to the Nephilim—which would make them the offspring of the sons of God and human women (see note on 6:2)—or introduce another ancient mighty group spawned by the sons of God.

Genesis 6:4

NEPHILIM
Ancient Jewish texts and translations of the OT render the Hebrew word *nephilim* with terms that describe men of inordinate height. The Septuagint (the ancient Greek translation of the OT) renders the term *gigantes* ("giants"). The term is not a synonym for "sons of God" (see Ge 6:2 and note); the Nephilim could, though, be the offspring of the sons of God from cohabiting with the daughters of humans.

6:6 his heart was deeply troubled Anthropomorphisms—the attribution of human characteristics to God—suggest that God feels emotions as a result of human behavior.
6:7 I will wipe The Hebrew verb used here, *machah*—which may be translated "to erase" or "to remove completely"—often appears in contexts where something is washed away or erased with water (Nu 5:23; 2Ki 21:13).
6:8 Noah found favor God's choice of Noah is not necessarily connected to Noah's character, although his honorable character is also mentioned in Ge 6:9. Noah finding favor in God's eyes means only that God is inclined to help him.

6:9 — 7:24 The first half of the flood narrative describes God's plan to bring a flood, his instructions to Noah about building an ark, the requirement to bring animals and food, and the flood's destruction.

6:9 account of Noah God chose Noah to survive the great flood along with his wife, his sons, and their wives. See note on Ge 5:1. **blameless** The Hebrew word used here, *tamim*, refers to being free from defect; it is often used in sacrificial contexts to describe an unblemished animal presented to God (Ex 12:5; Lev 1:3,10; 3:1,6). However, this does not mean Noah was sinless (compare Job 1:1 and note). This phrase is similar to the modern descriptions like wholesome, godly or honorable (compare Ge 17:1; Dt 18:13; Ps 15:2). **he walked faithfully with God** The OT describes a pattern of personal, divine encounters that precede a calling for divine service. The pattern begins with Adam, who spoke with God face to face and, along with Eve, received the dominion (stewardship) mandate of Ge 1:26–28. It appears next with Enoch who, as Noah, walked with God (see 5:22 and note).
6:10 Shem Noah's first son is presented as the ancestor of the Semitic people groups, one line of which produces Abraham, Isaac and Jacob (9:26; 11:10–25). **Ham** This name is either derived from a Hebrew word meaning "hot" or "warm" or the Egyptian word *khemet*, meaning "black land"—a name for the land of Egypt that describes the black soil produced by the flooding of the Nile. In the Table of Nations (ch. 10), the descendants of Ham occupy the hot lands of the southern Mediterranean and African regions (10:6–20). The name Ham is also used at times in parallel with Egypt (Ps 78:51; 105:23,27; 106:22). **Japheth** The derivation of this name is uncertain. The Table of Nations (Ge 10) locates Japheth's descendants in Greece and the northern Mediterranean region (10:2–5).

6:11–22 The account of the great flood has many ancient parallels. These stories—especially the Babylonian flood stories like the Epic of Gilgamesh—have detailed similarities and often sharp differences from the Biblical flood story.

6:11–12 As in 6:5, the description conveys totality—a sweeping condition of humanity, not one confined to a small locality.

6:15 ark is to be three hundred cubits long A cubit was roughly 18 inches, so the ark would have been 450 feet by 75 feet by 45 feet. See the infographic "Inside Noah's Ark" on p. 19.
6:17 destroy all life This language could describe a

the earth to destroy all life under the heavens, every creature that has the breath of life in it. Everything on earth will perish. [18]But I will establish my covenant with you, and you will enter the ark — you and your sons and your wife and your sons' wives with you. [19]You are to bring into the ark two of all living creatures, male and female, to keep them alive with you. [20]Two of every kind of bird, of every kind of animal and of every kind

of creature that moves along the ground will come to you to be kept alive. [21]You are to take every kind of food that is to be eaten and store it away as food for you and for them."

[22]Noah did everything just as God commanded him.

7 The LORD then said to Noah, "Go into the ark, you and your whole family, because I have found you righteous in this generation. [2]Take with

global flood or a flood over all the earth in the region. Interpretations over the extent of the flood vary. Because ancient Near Eastern people conceived of the known world as a single land mass surrounded by water, a massive regional flood could have been interpreted as a flood of the entire world. Proponents of a global flood offer explanations that they claim can demonstrate how such an event could have been possible. Supporters of a smaller scale flood point to evidence of local catastrophes

in the ancient world, such as the large flood in the Black Sea region around 5500 BC, when the sea level of the Mediterranean rose suddenly. In that incident, 66,000 square miles of land were flooded over the course of a year. Compare note on 7:19.

6:18 my covenant with you This covenant is given in 8:20 — 9:17.

7:2 seven pairs There is a discrepancy between this figure and the instructions of 6:19 — 20, which speak of

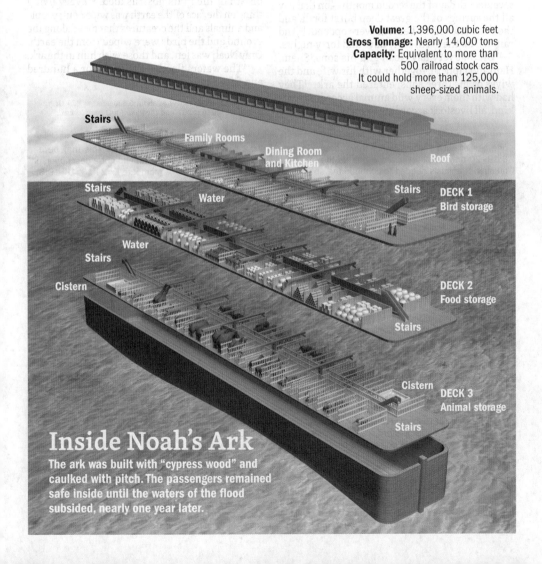

Volume: 1,396,000 cubic feet
Gross Tonnage: Nearly 14,000 tons
Capacity: Equivalent to more than 500 railroad stock cars
It could hold more than 125,000 sheep-sized animals.

Stairs
Family Rooms
Dining Room and Kitchen
Roof

Stairs
Water
Stairs
DECK 1
Bird storage

Water
Stairs
Cistern
DECK 2
Food storage

Stairs
Cistern
DECK 3
Animal storage

Stairs

Inside Noah's Ark

The ark was built with "cypress wood" and caulked with pitch. The passengers remained safe inside until the waters of the flood subsided, nearly one year later.

you seven pairs of every kind of clean animal, a male and its mate, and one pair of every kind of unclean animal, a male and its mate, ³and also seven pairs of every kind of bird, male and female, to keep their various kinds alive throughout the earth. ⁴Seven days from now I will send rain on the earth for forty days and forty nights, and I will wipe from the face of the earth every living creature I have made."

⁵And Noah did all that the LORD commanded him.

⁶Noah was six hundred years old when the floodwaters came on the earth. ⁷And Noah and his sons and his wife and his sons' wives entered the ark to escape the waters of the flood. ⁸Pairs of clean and unclean animals, of birds and of all creatures that move along the ground, ⁹male and female, came to Noah and entered the ark, as God had commanded Noah. ¹⁰And after the seven days the floodwaters came on the earth.

¹¹In the six hundredth year of Noah's life, on the seventeenth day of the second month — on that day all the springs of the great deep burst forth, and the floodgates of the heavens were opened. ¹²And rain fell on the earth forty days and forty nights.

¹³On that very day Noah and his sons, Shem, Ham and Japheth, together with his wife and the wives of his three sons, entered the ark. ¹⁴They had with them every wild animal according to its kind, all livestock according to their kinds, every creature that moves along the ground according to its kind and every bird according to its kind, everything with wings. ¹⁵Pairs of all creatures that have the breath of life in them came to Noah and entered the ark. ¹⁶The animals going in were male and female of every living thing, as God had commanded Noah. Then the LORD shut him in.

¹⁷For forty days the flood kept coming on the earth, and as the waters increased they lifted the ark high above the earth. ¹⁸The waters rose and increased greatly on the earth, and the ark floated on the surface of the water. ¹⁹They rose greatly on the earth, and all the high mountains under the entire heavens were covered. ²⁰The waters rose and covered the mountains to a depth of more than fifteen cubits.ᵃ,ᵇ ²¹Every living thing that moved on land perished — birds, livestock, wild animals, all the creatures that swarm over the earth, and all mankind. ²²Everything on dry land that had the breath of life in its nostrils died. ²³Every living thing on the face of the earth was wiped out; people and animals and the creatures that move along the ground and the birds were wiped from the earth. Only Noah was left, and those with him in the ark.

²⁴The waters flooded the earth for a hundred and fifty days.

ᵃ 20 That is, about 23 feet or about 6.8 meters   ᵇ 20 Or rose more than fifteen cubits, and the mountains were covered

---

one pair of each species rather than seven. Genesis 6:19–20 may speak of a single pair as the minimum number of animals needed to continue the species after the flood, whereas 7:2–3 includes additional clean animals to ensure that proper sacrifice can be made after the flood. **clean animal** The clean and unclean distinction for sacrifice is made explicit only with the law, long after Noah (Ex 20; Lev 11; Dt 14). However, there may have been an earlier awareness of animals that were appropriate and inappropriate for sacrifice. Alternatively, a later editor may have added this detail to remove potential contradictions with the law.

7:4 Seven days from now Presumably the time needed for the animals and humans to board the ark. Seven-day periods are noted elsewhere in the story (Ge 7:10; 8:10,12). See the infographic "Inside Noah's Ark" on p. 19.

7:11 seventeenth day Throughout chs. 6–8, the narrative offers multiple numbers relating to how much time has passed—it is often difficult to tell how these figures relate. This may suggest that Genesis was originally composed of multiple sources. Alternatively, there may be two systems of recording time in the narrative, one that linearly presents the days and what developed during various time spans and the other designating exact dates. **springs of the great deep** This description presumes an ancient Near Eastern cosmology (worldview). This worldview included a domed firmament (or vault) above the visible sky that held back waters that were above the firmament and below the earth. The waters below were called the great deep. It was believed that the waters came to earth (when it rained) through gaps in the firmament—the windows and doors of heaven (compare 1:6 and note). See the infographic "Ancient Hebrew Conception of the Universe" on p. 5.

7:12 forty days and forty nights This may be an idiom for a long period of time and not a description of a precise length of time (compare Ex 24:18; 1Ki 19:8).

7:16 the LORD shut him in Yahweh's role in saving Noah, his family, and the animals comes into full view here. The narrator reminds the audience that the salvation of these few people is an act of divine grace.

7:19 all the high mountains under the entire heavens This description and Ge 7:20–23 may support the idea that this narrative presents a global flood—and perhaps even demand it. In addition, the NT uses the flood account as an analogy for the future judgment of all of humanity (2Pe 3:6–7). On the other hand, extra-Biblical evidence for a global flood is inconclusive. Arguments for both a local and global flood can be supported Biblically (see note on Ge 6:17; note on 7:21).

7:21 Every living thing that moved on land perished In Biblical usage, phrases that appear on the surface to be universal do not always speak of exhaustive, universal participation—particularly with respect to peoples and lands on the other side of the globe from the ancient Near East (e.g., 8:6–7; 41:57; 2Sa 15:23; 1Ch 14:17; 2Ch 9:28). Specifically with regard to the flood, Yahweh himself speaks of destroying all life, yet that is clearly not the case: Noah, his family and the animals with him live (Ge 6:17; 8:21). In addition, if all the water on all the earth had evaporated after the flood, as 8:13–14 seems to imply, everything would have died. Given this literary context, it is possible that the flood, while spoken about in global terms, was limited to a vast area near Noah (compare 6:4 and note; note on 7:19). Nonetheless, this is only an argument based on common literary practice; it is unclear how the narrator actually understood the scope of the flood.

8 But God remembered Noah and all the wild animals and the livestock that were with him in the ark, and he sent a wind over the earth, and the waters receded. ²Now the springs of the deep and the floodgates of the heavens had been closed, and the rain had stopped falling from the sky. ³The water receded steadily from the earth. At the end of the hundred and fifty days the water had gone down, ⁴and on the seventeenth day of the seventh month the ark came to rest on the mountains of Ararat. ⁵The waters continued to recede until the tenth month, and on the first day of the tenth month the tops of the mountains became visible.

⁶After forty days Noah opened a window he had made in the ark ⁷and sent out a raven, and it kept flying back and forth until the water had dried up from the earth. ⁸Then he sent out a dove to see if the water had receded from the surface of the ground. ⁹But the dove could find nowhere to perch because there was water over all the surface of the earth; so it returned to Noah in the ark. He reached out his hand and took the dove and brought it back to himself in the ark. ¹⁰He waited seven more days and again sent out the dove from the ark. ¹¹When the dove returned to him in the evening, there in its beak was a freshly plucked olive leaf! Then Noah knew that the water had receded from the earth. ¹²He waited seven more days and sent the dove out again, but this time it did not return to him.

¹³By the first day of the first month of Noah's six hundred and first year, the water had dried up from the earth. Noah then removed the covering from the ark and saw that the surface of the ground was dry. ¹⁴By the twenty-seventh day of the second month the earth was completely dry.

¹⁵Then God said to Noah, ¹⁶"Come out of the ark, you and your wife and your sons and their wives. ¹⁷Bring out every kind of living creature that is with you — the birds, the animals, and all the creatures that move along the ground — so they can multiply on the earth and be fruitful and increase in number on it."

¹⁸So Noah came out, together with his sons and his wife and his sons' wives. ¹⁹All the animals and all the creatures that move along the ground and all the birds — everything that moves on land — came out of the ark, one kind after another.

²⁰Then Noah built an altar to the Lord and, taking some of all the clean animals and clean birds, he sacrificed burnt offerings on it. ²¹The Lord smelled the pleasing aroma and said in his heart: "Never again will I curse the ground because of humans, even though[a] every inclination of the human heart is evil from childhood. And never again will I destroy all living creatures, as I have done.

²²"As long as the earth endures,
　seedtime and harvest,
　cold and heat,
　summer and winter,
　day and night
　will never cease."

a 21 Or humans, for

8:1–14 After the flood has accomplished its purpose (see 7:22–23), God begins to restore creation. In contrast to God's act of creation in six days, the waters recede and the earth is restored over a period of five months.

8:2 the floodgates of the heavens God is reversing the process from 7:11–12. See note on 7:11. See the infographic "Ancient Hebrew Conception of the Universe" on p. 5.

8:3 hundred and fifty days It is difficult to know how this figure and the one given in 8:4 relate; this is further complicated by difficulties understanding how the calendar in this period of time functioned. See note on 7:11.

8:4 the mountains of Ararat Refers to a mountain range, not necessarily a particular mountain called Ararat. Ararat was the country or region of Urartu. Assyrian records use this place name for a region that corresponds today most closely with Armenia and Turkey.

8:7 sent out a raven No reason for Noah's action is given, but the narrative implies that Noah is checking for signs of land and states this explicitly in v. 8 about his choice to send out a dove.

8:13 six hundred and first year The Hebrew text here does not directly state that this figure is in reference to Noah's life, but that can be inferred from 7:6 and 7:11.

8:14 completely dry The Hebrew verb used here, yavesh, is related to the noun yabbashah (often translated "dry land") used in 1:9–10. The words provide a verbal and thematic link between the two narratives, indicating that the restoration of the world after the flood should be understood as an act of divine re-creation.

8:15–22 This passage describes the process of disembarking from the ark, which concludes with Noah offering a sacrifice to Yahweh. Yahweh accepts the sacrifice and promises never to destroy all life by a flood again (compare note on 7:21).

8:20 altar The first reference to a sacrificial or worship altar in the Bible. See the infographic "Ancient Altars" on p. 127; see the table "Altars in the Old Testament" on p. 249.

8:21 Lord smelled the pleasing aroma This phrase indicates an acceptable offering and appears frequently in the books of Leviticus and Numbers (e.g., Lev 1:9; 2:9; 4:31; Nu 15:3). **curse** The Hebrew term used here, qalal, is different from that of Ge 3:17 (arar), which references the cursing of the ground after the fall. **human heart is evil** An explicit reference to the language of 6:5. God knows that even the flood will not reverse the corruption of the human will and mind.

8:22 As long as the earth endures This wording resolves the tension between the promise of this verse and subsequent descriptions of a final judgment of the world (2Pe 3:12–13). The final apocalypse will produce a new heaven and new earth. God promises to keep his wrath from humanity until the earth—as it is currently known—is no more (or renewed).

God's Covenant With Noah

9 Then God blessed Noah and his sons, saying to them, "Be fruitful and increase in number and fill the earth. ²The fear and dread of you will fall on all the beasts of the earth, and on all the birds in the sky, on every creature that moves along the ground, and on all the fish in the sea; they are given into your hands. ³Everything that lives and moves about will be food for you. Just as I gave you the green plants, I now give you everything.

⁴"But you must not eat meat that has its lifeblood still in it. ⁵And for your lifeblood I will surely demand an accounting. I will demand an accounting from every animal. And from each human being, too, I will demand an accounting for the life of another human being.

⁶ "Whoever sheds human blood,
    by humans shall their blood be shed;
 for in the image of God
    has God made mankind.

⁷As for you, be fruitful and increase in number; multiply on the earth and increase upon it."

⁸Then God said to Noah and to his sons with him: ⁹"I now establish my covenant with you and with your descendants after you ¹⁰and with every living creature that was with you — the birds, the livestock and all the wild animals, all those that came out of the ark with you — every living creature on earth. ¹¹I establish my covenant with you: Never again will all life be destroyed by the waters of a flood; never again will there be a flood to destroy the earth."

¹²And God said, "This is the sign of the covenant I am making between me and you and every living creature with you, a covenant for all generations to come: ¹³I have set my rainbow in the clouds, and it will be the sign of the covenant between me and the earth. ¹⁴Whenever I bring clouds over the earth and the rainbow appears in the clouds, ¹⁵I will remember my covenant between me and you and all living creatures of every kind. Never again will the waters become a flood to destroy all life. ¹⁶Whenever the rainbow appears in the clouds, I will see it and remember the everlasting covenant between

---

9:1–17 God blesses Noah (as a representative of humanity), establishes rules and institutes a covenant. In the process, he gives people permission to kill and eat animals for food, provided they do not consume the blood (Ge 9:3–4). Killing other people, however, is forbidden (vv. 5–6). In the covenant that God institutes, he promises again to humanity and all creation that he won't destroy all life again by a flood (vv. 8–17).

9:1 his sons Shem, Ham and Japheth (see 6:10). See the people diagram "Table of Nations" on p. 26. **fill the earth** A repeat of the mandate to procreate and fill the earth (1:28; 8:17).
9:2 they are given into your hands Emphasizes humanity's authoritative role as stewards of the animal kingdom. Animal flesh is now permitted as food for humanity. This phrase links eating meat with the command to multiply and have dominion, suggesting that the practice of eating meat is not a result of the fall (ch. 3), but an outgrowth of the flood event that is consistent with the original stewardship of humanity (1:28–29; compare 4:4).
9:4 its lifeblood Before animal flesh can be consumed, it must be properly drained of blood. This suggests that the prohibition of consuming blood predates Israel's law (though it is repeated in the law; Lev 17:11,14).
9:5 your lifeblood The ensuing context shows that this phrase means human life, not the blood itself. **I will demand an accounting** Whether human life is taken by an animal or human, there will be a penalty. The wording clearly affirms the sanctity of human life in God's eyes.
9:6 by humans shall their blood be shed Establishes the principle of capital punishment as the consequence for the intentional murder of an innocent human life. This crime results in the forfeiture of one's own life — the offender can no longer be protected by the principle that safeguards innocent human life. This principle is based on people being divine imagers — representations of God on earth (Ge 1:27). Taking an innocent human life was viewed as murdering God in effigy. Later, Mosaic

Law (as primarily seen Exodus, Leviticus, Numbers and Deuteronomy) made capital punishment mandatory for murder, allowing no alternative form of punishment (see Nu 35:31).
9:7 multiply on the earth This command was disobeyed after the flood when the people of the earth migrated to build a city rather than multiply and disperse (Ge 11:1–9).

9:9–13 The covenant Yahweh gives here is established with humanity, with every living creature, and with the earth itself. Genesis 8:22 indicates that God's promise to refrain from destruction (and hence this covenant) will endure indefinitely until that time when God decides to create a new heaven and new earth (compare 2Pe 3:12–13).

9:9 my covenant A covenant is either a contract or — when only one party pledges anything — a promise. The first-person language of this covenant shows that this is a unilateral promise or divine charter. It does not depend on Noah; God's integrity and power serves as its basis. See the table "Covenants in the Old Testament" on p. 469.
9:12 sign of the covenant The sign serves as a reminder of the promise or as a tangible guarantee of God's commitment to keep the promise (compare Ge 17:11; Ex 31:16–17).
9:13 my rainbow The Hebrew word used here, *qesheth*, is most frequently used of an archer's bow. The mention of a cloud indicates it is a rainbow, but the military connotation may still be present. The rainbow may symbolically signify God's war bow — God's wrath via water has ended and he has hung up his bow.
9:16 everlasting covenant The Hebrew phrase used here, *berith-olam*, is often used to describe covenants between God and his people. These everlasting covenants are also frequently linked to special signs. God's covenant with Abraham is also described as a *berith-olam* (Ge 17:7,13,19), with circumcision as the sign. The covenant between God and Israel is similarly called a *berith-olam*, and the sign is Israel's obligation to observe the Sabbath (Ex 31:16).

God and all living creatures of every kind on the earth."

¹⁷So God said to Noah, "This is the sign of the covenant I have established between me and all life on the earth."

The Sons of Noah

¹⁸The sons of Noah who came out of the ark were Shem, Ham and Japheth. (Ham was the father of Canaan.) ¹⁹These were the three sons of Noah, and from them came the people who were scattered over the whole earth.

²⁰Noah, a man of the soil, proceeded*ᵃ* to plant a vineyard. ²¹When he drank some of its wine, he became drunk and lay uncovered inside his tent. ²²Ham, the father of Canaan, saw his father naked and told his two brothers outside. ²³But Shem and Japheth took a garment and laid it across their shoulders; then they walked in backward and covered their father's naked body. Their faces were turned the other way so that they would not see their father naked.

²⁴When Noah awoke from his wine and found out what his youngest son had done to him, ²⁵he said,

"Cursed be Canaan!
    The lowest of slaves
    will he be to his brothers."

²⁶He also said,

"Praise be to the Lord, the God of Shem!
    May Canaan be the slave of Shem.
²⁷May God extend Japheth'sᵇ territory;
    may Japheth live in the tents of Shem,
    and may Canaan be the slave of Japheth."

²⁸After the flood Noah lived 350 years. ²⁹Noah lived a total of 950 years, and then he died.

The Table of Nations

10 This is the account of Shem, Ham and Japheth, Noah's sons, who themselves had sons after the flood.

ᵃ 20 Or *soil, was the first*   ᵇ 27 *Japheth* sounds like the Hebrew for *extend.*

9:18–29 This passage provides a narrative postscript to the flood story, describing how Noah settles into a life of agriculture.

9:18 Ham was the father of Canaan A reminder of the connection between Ham and Canaan; Canaan is cursed by Noah for Ham's actions (Ge 9:22,25). This account also serves to cast the Canaanites in a negative, shameful light. In that sense, the story resembles the account in 19:30–38, which provides a shameful explanation for the paternity of the Ammonites and Moabites.

9:20 a man of the soil The parallel to Adam is evident and signifies continuity with Adam's original blessing and mandated task (see 2:15).

9:21 became drunk The first mention of drunkenness in the Bible. **lay uncovered inside his tent** The ensuing context explains this as nakedness.

9:22–24 Two difficult interpretive issues arise in the incident between Ham and Noah: understanding the nature of Ham's offense and making sense of why Ham's son, Canaan, was cursed instead of Ham (see note on v. 25). The text of 9:22 may be literally rendered as "Ham, the father of Canaan, saw the nakedness of his father." However, this could be an idiom—it may not be about Noah being nude, but an incident that greatly insults Noah. Ham's offense could be explained as voyeurism, castration of Noah, sodomy, or incestuous rape of his mother. The voyeurism view is often defended by what Ham's brothers, Shem and Japheth, do in the wake of the incident—they walk backward into the tent and cover their father's nakedness. This act doesn't explain the offense, though; it simply shows their respect for their father. There is no OT prohibition against seeing one's father naked, so this interpretation would have likely been foreign to the original reader; likewise no such prohibition appears elsewhere in ancient Near Eastern law.

Against the idea that Ham's offense was voyeurism, the Hebrew phrase which may be literally rendered "saw the nakedness" appears elsewhere in the OT referring to illicit sexual contact and intercourse. To "see [*ra'ah* in Hebrew] the nakedness [*erwah* in Hebrew]" of someone is used in the Law (Lev 18; 20) to prohibit certain sexual relations. This idiom suggests that Ham's offense may have been of a sexual nature, perhaps homosexual rape of his father or paternal incest. However, no combination of the relevant Hebrew words—*ra'ah* ("see"), *galah* ("uncover") and *erwah* ("nakedness")—occurs in the OT in reference to homosexuality. The Hebrew phrase for "uncovering the nakedness of [a man]" actually refers to sexual intercourse with a man's wife. For example, in a literal rendering of Lev 18:7, "the nakedness of your father" means "the nakedness of your mother"; in Lev 18:14, a literal rendering of "the nakedness of your father's brother" is clarified as "his wife" and "your aunt" (see Lev 18:8; 20:11,20,21). Although the usual expression in Leviticus is to "uncover [*galah* in Hebrew] the nakedness," both idioms are used in parallel in Lev 20:17. Therefore, Ham's offense may have been maternal incest and the forcible rape of his mother. This explains the curse of Ham's son that follows (see Ge 9:25–27; compare note on 9:25).

9:25 lowest of slaves will he be Noah pronounces a curse on Canaan, not on Ham. Noah does this because Ham likely raped his mother to gain further inheritance (see note on vv. 22–24). Ham's crime of maternal incest would have been an attempt to usurp Noah's position as leader of the family clan. This explains why Ham would announce what he had done to his brothers—he was asserting authority over them (v. 22). The fact that Canaan was cursed suggests that Canaan was the offspring of Ham's sexual intercourse with Noah's wife. The son bore the punishment for the crime of his father. The curse on Canaan forms the backdrop to the later antipathy between Israel and the Canaanites.

9:29 950 years May or may not be intended literally. See 5:5 and note.

10:1–32 This passage is called the Table of Nations because its list explains the origin of most of the peoples of the ancient Near East. The names correspond to Biblical

The Japhethites

10:2-5pp — 1Ch 1:5-7

2 The sons[a] of Japheth:

Gomer, Magog, Madai, Javan, Tubal, Meshek and Tiras.

3 The sons of Gomer:

Ashkenaz, Riphath and Togarmah.

4 The sons of Javan:

Elishah, Tarshish, the Kittites and the Rodanites.[b] **5** (From these the maritime peoples spread out into their territories by their clans within their nations, each with its own language.)

The Hamites

10:6-20pp — 1Ch 1:8-16

6 The sons of Ham:

Cush, Egypt, Put and Canaan.

7 The sons of Cush:

Seba, Havilah, Sabtah, Raamah and Sabteka.

The sons of Raamah:

Sheba and Dedan.

8 Cush was the father[c] of Nimrod, who became a mighty warrior on the earth. **9** He was a mighty hunter before the LORD; that is why it is said, "Like Nimrod, a mighty hunter before the LORD." **10** The first centers of his kingdom were Babylon, Uruk, Akkad and Kalneh, in[d] Shinar.[e] **11** From that land he went to Assyria, where he built Nineveh, Rehoboth Ir,[f] Calah **12** and Resen, which is between Nineveh and Calah — which is the great city.

13 Egypt was the father of

the Ludites, Anamites, Lehabites, Naphtu-

---

[a] *2 Sons* may mean *descendants* or *successors* or *nations*; also in verses 3, 4, 6, 7, 20-23, 29 and 31.   [b] *4* Some manuscripts of the Masoretic Text and Samaritan Pentateuch (see also Septuagint and 1 Chron. 1:7); most manuscripts of the Masoretic Text *Dodanites*   [c] *8 Father* may mean *ancestor* or *predecessor* or *founder*; also in verses 13, 15, 24 and 26.   [d] *10 Or Uruk and Akkad — all of them in*   [e] *10* That is, Babylonia   [f] *11 Or Nineveh with its city squares*

---

names for major people groups, tribes and regions (see 10:31 – 32). The correspondence between the ancestral names and Biblical geography suggests the Table of Nations provides a record of ancient eponymous ancestry (the naming of nations or regions after particular people). The list does not cover all the nations of the earth. Rather, it covers the groups most relevant for Biblical history. The listing is also symbolic, as the number of descendants listed for Shem, Ham and Japheth totals 70. See the people diagram "Table of Nations" on p. 26.

10:1 account The Hebrew word used here, *toledoth*, is used throughout Genesis to refer to genealogical related information. See note on 5:1.

10:2 The sons of Japheth While the descendants of Ham and Shem (10: 6 – 31) would have lived near each other in the ancient Near East, the descendants of Japheth are not all found in regions next to each other. These verses probably reflect an Israelite perspective that all the names therein come from across the Mediterranean Sea. **Gomer** This name refers to the Cimmerians who seem to be the same people group as the Scythians (compare Eze 38:6). **Magog** This term is used in Eze 38:2 and 39:6 to refer to the land of Gog. The region was probably between Armenia and Cappadocia near the Black Sea. See note on Eze 38:1 — 39:24. **Madai** The Hebrew word used here, *madai*, refers in the OT to the land of the Medes (Isa 13:17; 2Ki 17:6). The Medes lived in the northern part of the Iranian plateau, northeast of the Zagros Mountains and southwest of the Caspian Sea. **Tubal, Meshek** These two names often occur together in the OT (e.g., Eze 27:13; 32:26; 38:2; 39:1) and refer to central and eastern Anatolia (Asia Minor, now Turkey and Armenia). **Tiras** This term appears in the work of Jewish historian Josephus in reference to the Thracians (Josephus, *Antiquities* 1.125). The term could also refer to the Pelasgians mentioned among the Sea Peoples in the records of Pharaoh Merenptah.

10:3 Ashkenaz The reference to Ashkenaz in association with Ararat and Minni in Jer 51:27 makes it likely that this refers to the Scythians. Assyrian cuneiform texts also refer to a group called the Ashkuza, who are probably the same people. **Riphath** Called Diphath in the Hebrew text of 1Ch 1:6. The location under either name remains unidentified. **Togarmah** This term seems to refer to Tegarama, north of Harran near Carchemesh.

10:4 Javan This is the generic word for the Hellenic (Greek) peoples used in the OT; it includes the Ionians in western Asia Minor (modern Turkey). **Elishah** This term is mentioned in Eze 27:7 as a source of purple dye. It is possibly to be identified with all or part of Cyprus, which was called "Alashia" in Egyptian, Akkadian and Ugaritic inscriptions. **Tarshish** This could refer to several locations, all of which are westward across the Mediterranean. See Jnh 1:3 and note. **Kittites** Refers to people from Cyprus. **Rodanites** This likely refers to people from Rhodes.

10:5 maritime peoples This suggests that all the peoples from the Mediterranean coastal regions (including Greece and Asia Minor) are descended from Japheth.

10:6 The sons of Ham The line of Ham has four branches: Cush, Mizraim (Egypt), Put and Canaan. All four are probably place names. **Cush** This term refers to the African kingdom of Nubia. See note on Ge 2:13. **Egypt** The Hebrew word used here, *mitsrayim*, is used throughout the OT for Egypt. **Put** The Hebrew term used here occurs six times in the OT and probably refers to Libya (e.g., Jer 46:9; Eze 30:5; 38:4 – 6). **Canaan** Noah cursed Canaan because of Ham's sin (see Ge 9:20 – 27; note on 9:25). Here Canaan is listed last of Ham's sons, indicating either his low standing as a result of Noah's curse or his position as Ham's fourth and youngest son. Like the other names in this section, Canaan also refers to the land and its people. A detailed list is given in 10:15 – 19.

10:7 Seba, Havilah, Sabtah, Raamah and Sabteka The names of the five sons of Cush all refer to areas in or on the outskirts of the region known broadly in later antiquity as Arabia. **Sheba** The location that this term refers to is debatable, but the most plausible location is in the southwest corner of the Arabian Peninsula. **Dedan** This term likely refers to 'Ula in northern Arabia — an important trading center since ancient times near the border of Edom.

hites, ¹⁴Pathrusites, Kasluhites (from whom the Philistines came) and Caphtorites. ¹⁵Canaan was the father of

Sidon his firstborn,ᵃ and of the Hittites, ¹⁶Jebusites, Amorites, Girgashites, ¹⁷Hivites, Arkites, Sinites, ¹⁸Arvadites, Zemarites and Hamathites.

Later the Canaanite clans scattered ¹⁹and the borders of Canaan reached from Sidon toward Gerar as far as Gaza, and then toward Sodom, Gomorrah, Admah and Zeboyim, as far as Lasha.

²⁰These are the sons of Ham by their clans and languages, in their territories and nations.

The Semites
10:21-31pp — Ge 11:10-27; 1Ch 1:17-27

²¹Sons were also born to Shem, whose older brother wasᵇ Japheth; Shem was the ancestor of all the sons of Eber.

ᵃ 15 Or *of the Sidonians, the foremost*   ᵇ 21 Or *Shem, the older brother of*

10:8–11 The digression about Nimrod (vv. 8–12) in this section shifts the focus from Upper Egypt and Arabia to Mesopotamia. This represents the first instance of direct ancestral descent (*A* fathered *B*) in this section; this indicates that the Table of Nations (ch. 10) concerns more than generational descent. See the infographic "The Amarna Letters" on p. 337.

10:8 Nimrod This figure is associated with the founding of the greatest cities of Mesopotamia—Babylon, Uruk, Akkad, Nineveh and Calah.

10:10 Kalneh The location this refers to is unknown. **Shinar** This is another name for Babylonia—encompassing the city states of Sumer and Akkad and extending northward to Assyria. This name does not occur in Mesopotamian material but is found many times in records of the Egyptians and Hittites, as well as the Amarna letters. See the infographic "The Amarna Letters" on p. 337. See note on 11:2.

10:11 Nineveh Located on the east bank of the Tigris River. **Rehoboth Ir** The Hebrew text here could be understood as referring to the open places of the city—an area of Nineveh, rather than a separate city. **Calah** One of the chief cities of Assyria, along with Nineveh and Asshur. The city's association with Nimrod is preserved in the site's medieval and modern name Nimrud. Calah is located on the east bank of the Tigris about 20 miles south of Nineveh.

10:12 Resen This could refer to an unknown town between Nineveh and Calah or be a scribal corruption that was originally a reference to an irrigation system or waterworks. **great city** The Hebrew text here could refer to Calah or Nineveh.

10:13–14 The names in vv. 13–14 are plural in Hebrew, suggesting they refer to people groups despite their presentation as the sons of Egypt. The identification of the people groups in v. 13 is uncertain. These names again connect the line of Ham to Egypt (compare v. 6).

10:13 Ludites This group could be the Lydians from Asia Minor (modern Turkey), but the Hebrew term *lud* used here is also connected elsewhere with North African peoples (Jer 46:9; Eze 30:5). **Lehabites** This could refer to Libyans.

10:14 Pathrusites This refers to people from Upper Egypt (the southern portion), sometimes called Pathros (compare Isa 11:11; Jer 44:1). **Philistines** Elsewhere in the OT, the Philistines are identified as coming from Caphtor (Am 9:7; Dt 2:23; Jer 47:4). Thus, it seems that the editorial comment here should instead come after the reference to Caphtor. Alternatively, this could indicate that the Philistines at one point migrated to Caphtor, similar to how the OT mentions Israel as coming from Egypt (e.g., Nu 22:11; 2Ki 21:15). **Caphtorites** Caphtor may be identified with Crete; it is the place of origin of the Philistines according to other OT texts (see Am 9:7).

10:15 Sidon This term refers to the Sidonians of the famous Phoenician city of Sidon. **Hittites** This reference to the ancestor of the Hittites seems out of place in this verse

because the Hittites are from Asia Minor (modern Turkey), not Egypt, Arabia, Phoenicia or Syria-Palestine, like the other people groups mentioned as the descendants of Canaan. Since the line of Canaan indicates a mixed population of people groups—some of whom migrated into Canaan—this may refer to some of the known Hittite migrations southward.

10:16 Jebusites This term refers to inhabitants of Jebus, which would become Jerusalem after David's conquest of the city (1Ch 11:4–5). Nothing is known of their origin or history. **Amorites** The Hebrew text here probably refers broadly to the Amurru, a nomadic Semitic people group occupying Syria and Canaan in pre-Israelite times. **Girgashites** Little is known about this group. They are regularly mentioned in the lists of Canaanite people groups, but no details are given (Ge 15:21; Dt 7:1; Jos 3:10; 24:11).

Genesis 10:16

AMORITES
The term "Amorite" refers to a West Semitic people, the Amurru, known from Akkadian sources that place them around Babylon about 2000 BC. They migrated westward throughout the Fertile Crescent, including the regions of Phoenicia and Canaan. The term is used in different ways in the OT. In some places, it is used as a generic term for inhabitants of the land of Canaan before the Israelite conquest, like "Canaanites" (e.g., Ge 15:16; Jos 24:15; Jdg 6:10; 1Ki 21:26). In other places it refers more specifically to a people group who lived in the hill country (Dt 1:19–20; Nu 13:29; Jos 11:3) and the Transjordan (Dt 3:8; Jos 12:1–2; Jdg 1:36). In one place, Jos 13:4, it may refer specifically to the kingdom of Amurru in northern Lebanon and western Syria.

10:17 Hivites This Canaanite group is regularly mentioned in the list of pre-Israelite occupants of the promised land (Ex 3:8; Dt 7:1).

10:18 Arvadites, Zemarites and Hamathites These people groups inhabited the region north of Sidon (modern Lebanon).

10:19 Gerar A city of the western Negev region that is in several narratives about the patriarchs. See note on Ge 26:6. **Gaza** One of the five major cities of the Philistines (compare note on 1Sa 4:1). **Sodom, Gomorrah** The inclusion of Sodom and Gomorrah here connects these cities characterized by debauchery to the curse of Canaan by Noah and the sin of Ham (9:22–25). See Ge 13:10.

10:21–31 This list details the line of Shem, outlining Shem's relationship to Japheth (his brother) and Eber (the lead descendant of the list).

10:21 all the sons of Eber The list of the descendants of

Table of Nations
(Ge 10:1–32)

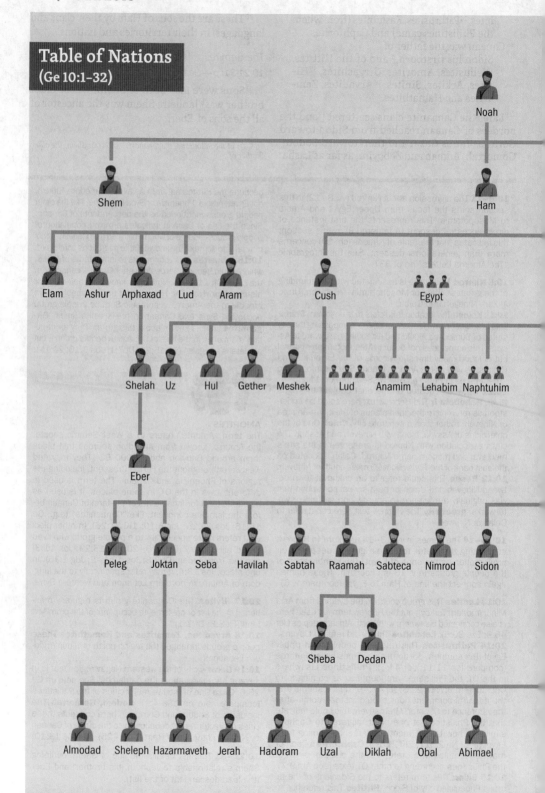

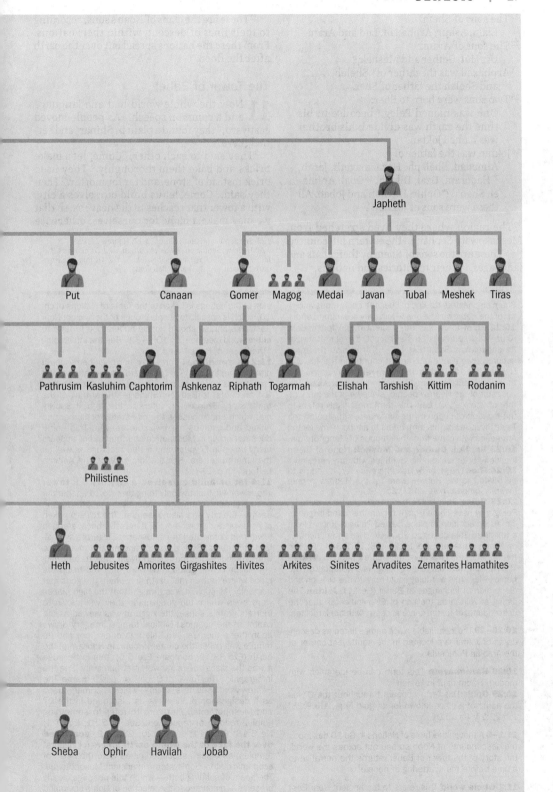

²²The sons of Shem:

Elam, Ashur, Arphaxad, Lud and Aram.
²³The sons of Aram:

Uz, Hul, Gether and Meshek.ᵃ
²⁴Arphaxad was the father ofᵇ Shelah,
and Shelah the father of Eber.
²⁵Two sons were born to Eber:

One was named Peleg,ᶜ because in his
time the earth was divided; his brother
was named Joktan.
²⁶Joktan was the father of

Almodad, Sheleph, Hazarmaveth, Jerah,
²⁷Hadoram, Uzal, Diklah, ²⁸Obal, Abimael, Sheba, ²⁹Ophir, Havilah and Jobab. All
these were sons of Joktan.

³⁰The region where they lived stretched from
Mesha toward Sephar, in the eastern hill country.
³¹These are the sons of Shem by their clans and
languages, in their territories and nations.

³²These are the clans of Noah's sons, according
to their lines of descent, within their nations.
From these the nations spread out over the earth
after the flood.

The Tower of Babel

11 Now the whole world had one language
and a common speech. ²As people moved
eastward,ᵈ they found a plain in Shinarᵉ and settled there.

³They said to each other, "Come, let's make
bricks and bake them thoroughly." They used
brick instead of stone, and tar for mortar. ⁴Then
they said, "Come, let us build ourselves a city,
with a tower that reaches to the heavens, so that
we may make a name for ourselves; otherwise

ᵃ 23 See Septuagint and 1 Chron. 1:17; Hebrew *Mash.*
ᵇ 24 Hebrew; Septuagint *father of Cainan, and Cainan was the
father of* ᶜ 25 *Peleg* means *division.* ᵈ 2 Or *from the east*;
or *in the east* ᵉ 2 That is, Babylonia

Shem emphasizes the line of Eber, the eponymous ancestor of the Hebrews (the one whom they are named after).
10:22 Elam Elam was the ancient name for modern
Khuzestan (southwestern Iran), located east of Babylon.
Its capital was Susa (Est 1:2–5). It is also the most
securely identified easternmost country in the Table of
Nations (Ge 10). **Ashur** This term refers to Assyria and
thus is associated with Mesopotamia. **Arphaxad** The
ancestor of the Hebrew people, since he is the grandfather of Eber (v. 24). **Lud** This term most likely refers to
the location of Ludbu of the Assyrians, situated on the
Tigris River. **Aram** This term refers to a tribal name for the
Arameans who came from the steppes of Mesopotamia.
10:23 Uz, Hul, Gether and Meshek None of these
locations or tribes can be identified with any certainty.
10:24 Eber The Hebrew used here is *ever*. It seems to
be related to the Hebrew word for the Hebrew people
(*ivrim*). Compare note on 10:25.
10:25 Peleg This name can mean "water channel."
Peleg may have come from a region that used irrigation
canals. In addition, a place named Palag is known from
a text from Ebla dating to 2500 BC. He is the ancestor
of Abram (Abraham; Ge 11:18–26; Lk 3:34–35), the
forefather of the Israelites, the Hebrew people. **divided**
The Hebrew word used here, *palag*, is a wordplay on the
name Peleg. This wordplay could refer to the division and
dispersion of languages at Babel (Ge 11). **Joktan** The
listing of Joktan as the son of Eber indicates that the
descendants of Joktan share ancestry with the Israelites.

10:26–29 The identifiable place names listed as descendants of Joktan are located in the southwest corner of
the Arabian Peninsula.

10:26 Hazarmaveth This term can be identified with
modern Hadramaut in Yemen.

10:29 Ophir This term appears throughout the OT as
the name of a place known for its gold (e.g., 1Ki 9:28;
Job 22:24; Ps 45:9).

11:1–9 Although the Table of Nations in Ge 10 describes
the descendants of Noah spread out across the world,
the story of the tower of Babel returns the narrative to
a time before the scattering of people.

11:1 whole world This refers to the ancient Near East
and the Mediterranean world. Since Ge 11 and its disper-

sion of the nations is linked to the Table of Nations of ch.
10, which is specific to people groups of the ancient Near
East, this phrase should not be understood to refer to
entire world (see note on 10:1–32). See the infographic
"The Tower of Babel" on p. 29.
11:2 eastward The Hebrew text here can be rendered
either "from the east" or "eastward." A migration to the
east makes sense: from the Ararat (Urartu) region (see
8:4 and note) to Babylon (Shinar)—the setting of the
tower story. **Shinar** This refers to the land of Babylonia, which encompasses the city states of Sumer and
Akkad and extends northward to Assyria. This name
does not occur in Mesopotamian material but appears
many times in Egyptian and Hittite records, as well as
the Amarna Letters. See the infographic "The Amarna
Letters" on p. 337.
11:4 let us build ourselves a city, with a tower
The tower was not the only thing that would enable the
people to remain together rather than spread over the
earth—the city was also essential. The tower spoken
of here was a ziggurat temple, a massive brick, stepped
tower that dominated the landscape. Ziggurats symbolized mountains. Both ziggurats and natural mountains
were considered in the ancient Near East to be dwelling places of the gods. They were believed to be the
place where heaven met earth and where the gods met
humanity. As such, it was thought that the high places
were sites where the gods made their will known to
mortals. In this sense, the ziggurat was viewed as the
center of the cosmos. Biblical temple imagery draws
upon these themes. Jerusalem (Mount Zion) and its
temple was called the center (*tabbur*, in Hebrew) of the
earth (Eze 38:12; compare Eze 5:5); this is because
it was the place where Yahweh met humanity. See the
infographic "The Tower of Babel" on p. 29. **name** The
Hebrew word used here, *shem*—which is primarily used
as a designation of identity—is also used in the OT
and Mesopotamian literature to refer to something
gaining renown or reputation. See Pr 22:1; Ecc 7:1;
Ne 6:13; Ru 4:11; Jer 32:20; 2Sa 7:9. **scattered
over the face of the whole earth** Towers (or ziggurat
temples) and their associated cities were the heart of
economic distribution systems in ancient Mesopotamia.
The goals of building both—which this passage clearly
presents—amounted to the rejection of God's command
and blessing in Ge 9:7.

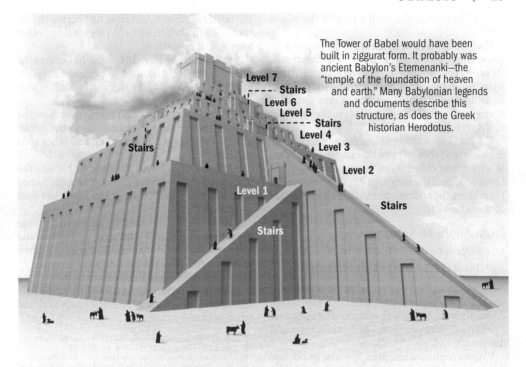

The Tower of Babel would have been built in ziggurat form. It probably was ancient Babylon's Etemenanki—the "temple of the foundation of heaven and earth." Many Babylonian legends and documents describe this structure, as does the Greek historian Herodotus.

Level 7
Stairs
Level 6
Level 5
Stairs
Level 4
Level 3
Level 2
Stairs
Level 1
Stairs
Stairs

The Tower of Babel

Ancients believed that deities dwelt on high places and associated the gods with hills and mountains. Babylon was on low ground—the ziggurat was a substitute mountain. It towered above the dust in the lower air and was an excellent place to observe the stars. From a ziggurat's top, heaven seemed closer.

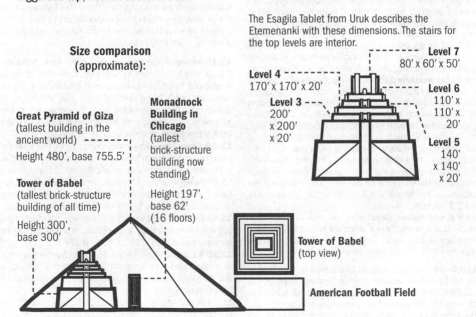

The Esagila Tablet from Uruk describes the Etemenanki with these dimensions. The stairs for the top levels are interior.

Size comparison (approximate):

Great Pyramid of Giza
(tallest building in the ancient world)
Height 480', base 755.5'

Tower of Babel
(tallest brick-structure building of all time)
Height 300', base 300'

Monadnock Building in Chicago
(tallest brick-structure building now standing)
Height 197', base 62' (16 floors)

Level 7
80' x 60' x 50'

Level 4
170' x 170' x 20'

Level 6
110' x 110' x 20'

Level 3
200' x 200' x 20'

Level 5
140' x 140' x 20'

Tower of Babel
(top view)

American Football Field

we will be scattered over the face of the whole earth."

⁵But the LORD came down to see the city and the tower the people were building. ⁶The LORD said, "If as one people speaking the same language they have begun to do this, then nothing they plan to do will be impossible for them. ⁷Come, let us go down and confuse their language so they will not understand each other."

⁸So the LORD scattered them from there over all the earth, and they stopped building the city. ⁹That is why it was called Babel*a* — because there the LORD confused the language of the whole world. From there the LORD scattered them over the face of the whole earth.

From Shem to Abram

11:10-27pp — Ge 10:21-31; 1Ch 1:17-27

¹⁰This is the account of Shem's family line.

Two years after the flood, when Shem was 100 years old, he became the father*b* of Arphaxad. ¹¹And after he became the father of Arphaxad, Shem lived 500 years and had other sons and daughters.

¹²When Arphaxad had lived 35 years, he became the father of Shelah. ¹³And after he became the father of Shelah, Arphaxad lived 403 years and had other sons and daughters.*c*

¹⁴When Shelah had lived 30 years, he became the father of Eber. ¹⁵And after he became the father of Eber, Shelah lived 403 years and had other sons and daughters.

¹⁶When Eber had lived 34 years, he became the father of Peleg. ¹⁷And after he became the father of Peleg, Eber lived 430 years and had other sons and daughters.

¹⁸When Peleg had lived 30 years, he became the father of Reu. ¹⁹And after he became the father of Reu, Peleg lived 209 years and had other sons and daughters.

²⁰When Reu had lived 32 years, he became the father of Serug. ²¹And after he became the father of Serug, Reu lived 207 years and had other sons and daughters.

²²When Serug had lived 30 years, he became the father of Nahor. ²³And after he became the father of Nahor, Serug lived 200 years and had other sons and daughters.

²⁴When Nahor had lived 29 years, he became the father of Terah. ²⁵And after he became the father of Terah, Nahor lived 119 years and had other sons and daughters.

---

a 9 That is, Babylon; *Babel* sounds like the Hebrew for *confused.*
b 10 *Father* may mean *ancestor;* also in verses 11-25.
c 12,13 Hebrew; Septuagint (see also Luke 3:35, 36 and note at Gen. 10:24) *35 years, he became the father of Cainan.* ¹³*And after he became the father of Cainan, Arphaxad lived 430 years and had other sons and daughters, and then he died. When Cainan had lived 130 years, he became the father of Shelah. And after he became the father of Shelah, Cainan lived 330 years and had other sons and daughters*

11:5 LORD came down to see This description follows the pattern seen throughout Genesis of portraying Yahweh as involved in the affairs of humanity. This line is also ironic: While the humans sought to build a tower into the heavens (v. 4), Yahweh must come down to it.

11:7 let us go down As with 1:26, this exhortation is plural. The plural indicates that Yahweh is speaking to the heavenly host or divine council (see 1:26 and note).

11:8 LORD scattered them This dispersal will eventually result in the fulfillment of Yahweh's command after the flood (9:7), but at a terrible price. This event is central to understanding how nations came to worship other gods besides Yahweh who had created them (see chs. 1–2). This is where Yahweh shifts from focusing on all the peoples of the earth to electing Israel (see 12:1–3). In a sense, the Babel event marks Yahweh disowning the nations of the world as his human family in favor of electing Israel, whom he will also use to reclaim the nations as his people (Dt 32:8–9; 4:19–20; compare Isa 2:1–5; Hos 1:8–11).

11:9 it was called Babel Here, Hebrew wordplay connects God's confusion of language with the name for the place. The Hebrew word *balal* ("to confuse") and Hebrew name Babel (*bavel*) sound similar.

11:10–26 This genealogy of Shem differs from that of Ge 10:21–31. It focuses only on firstborn sons and is more detailed than the one in ch. 10. As result, a number of names in this genealogy do not appear in 10:21–31. The genealogy highlights Shem in anticipation of Abram (Abraham) who is Shem's descendant and the patriarch with whom the genealogy culminates. In the genealogy,

Abram is the tenth generation from Shem, just as Noah was the tenth generation from Adam. This indicates that the genealogy is highlighting a specific point: As with the birth of Adam and Noah, the birth of Abram represents a turning point in human history.

11:10 account The Hebrew term used here, *toledoth,* marks family histories in Genesis. See note on 5:1.

Arphaxad This figure is listed as the firstborn of Shem here, but in 10:22 he is listed third. The account here seems to reflect birth order, while the genealogy in ch. 10 seems to change the birth order because it is focused on the geographical distribution of people groups.

11:14 Eber The eponymous ancestor of the Hebrew people (the one whom the people group derives its name from, according to 10:21). See 10:21 and note.

11:16 Peleg The line of Shem described in 10:21–31 follows the line of Joktan, Peleg's brother. The line of Peleg is resumed here, leading to Abram. See note on 10:25.

11:18 Reu This descendant of Shem was not mentioned in the earlier genealogy. In the Bible, this name appears only in genealogies (1Ch 1:25; Lk 3:35).

11:20 Serug Several of Abram's ancestors have names that correspond to cities in Mesopotamia. Serug is the name of a place west of Harran in northwestern Mesopotamia.

11:22 Nahor Abram's grandfather and brother (Ge 11:26) are both named Nahor. A city known as Nahur is located not far from Harran in northwestern Mesopotamia.

11:24 Terah Assyrian sources mention a place name

²⁶After Terah had lived 70 years, he became the father of Abram, Nahor and Haran.

Abram's Family

²⁷This is the account of Terah's family line.

Terah became the father of Abram, Nahor and Haran. And Haran became the father of Lot. ²⁸While his father Terah was still alive, Haran died in Ur of the Chaldeans, in the land of his birth. ²⁹Abram and Nahor both married. The name of Abram's wife was Sarai, and the name of Nahor's wife was Milkah; she was the daughter of Haran, the father of both Milkah and Iskah. ³⁰Now Sarai was childless because she was not able to conceive.

³¹Terah took his son Abram, his grandson Lot son of Haran, and his daughter-in-law Sarai, the wife of his son Abram, and together they set out from Ur of the Chaldeans to go to Canaan. But when they came to Harran, they settled there. ³²Terah lived 205 years, and he died in Harran.

The Call of Abram

12 The Lord had said to Abram, "Go from your country, your people and your father's household to the land I will show you.

² "I will make you into a great nation,
 and I will bless you;
I will make your name great,
 and you will be a blessing.ᵃ
³ I will bless those who bless you,
 and whoever curses you I will curse;
and all peoples on earth
 will be blessed through you."ᵇ

ᵃ 2 Or be seen as blessed   ᵇ 3 Or earth / will use your name in blessings (see 48:20)

---

near Harran that includes the word *turachi*—this likely corresponds to this name (see v. 32).
11:26 Abram The genealogy ends by introducing Abram (Abraham), the next major character in the narrative. **Nahor** Rebekah, who marries Abram's son Isaac, is the granddaughter of this brother of Abram (24:15). **Haran** The name of this brother of Abram and Nahor is not related to the similar sounding (in English) place name in v. 32.

11:27–32 This short section introduces the narratives about Abram (Abraham) and his family. The genealogies in Genesis have so far followed a pattern of ten names between important figures (e.g., Adam to Noah, Noah to Abram). This paragraph includes eight names, possibly foreshadowing the central theme of Abram's story—that the list will become complete again with the birth of Isaac, the child of promise. The ninth and tenth family members are Abram's sons Ishmael and Isaac.

11:27 Lot The origin of his name is unknown.

LOT
Lot was the son of Haran and grandson of Terah (see v. 31). Lot plays an important role at several decisive points in the Abraham narratives. First, Lot accompanies Terah and the rest of the clan from Ur to Harran (v. 31). Later, he accompanies Abram to Canaan (12:5). After they arrive in Canaan, Lot leaves Abram and moves into the Jordan Valley (13:11–12)—a decision that places Abram in the heart of the land that God has promised him. Lot's choice also places him in harm's way, and twice Abram intervenes to save him (14:1–16; 18:22–33). Throughout the Genesis narrative, Lot is characterized by the questionable choices he makes; this stands in contrast to Abram's persistent faith.

11:28 Ur of the Chaldeans Possibly a Sumerian coastal city-state near the Persian Gulf in southern Mesopotamia. Alternatively, another Ur is located in the northwest region of Mesopotamia in proximity to Anatolia (land of the Hittites) and Syria.
11:29 Sarai The name of Abram's wife is changed to Sarah in 17:15. **Milkah and Iskah** These are the daughters of Haran. Only Milkah is significant in the narrative as the grandmother of Rebekah, who becomes the wife of Isaac (22:20,23).
11:30 Sarai was childless Barrenness provides the central drama of the narrative about Sarai (Sarah) and Abram (Abraham).
11:31 Harran A city on the upper Euphrates River in northwestern Mesopotamia. The city is mentioned later in the list of places conquered by Sennacherib, king of Assyria (2Ki 19:12).
11:32 he died in Harran This explains the circumstances of Ge 12:1–6.

12:1–9 The narratives of chs. 12–50 tell the story of Israel's patriarchs: Abram (later called Abraham) and the three generations after him. In 12:1–3, Yahweh calls Abram to leave his home and set out for an unknown land. By following Yahweh's call, Abram demonstrates his trust in Yahweh's promise to bless him and make him a great nation. The patriarchal narratives center on Yahweh promises to Abram in vv. 1–3 for offspring, land and blessing. Genesis 12 marks a shift as Yahweh narrows his focus to Abram and his descendants and begins to work through a specifically chosen people. See the people diagram "Family Tree of the Patriarchs" on p. 52.

12:1 Go from your country Abram is living in Harran in northwestern Mesopotamia. Yahweh's command that Abram go is followed by three details: Abram is to leave his country or land, his birthplace or homeland, and his father's household. The list increases in intimacy and importance. **the land** Referring to the land of Canaan (v. 5). This is the first of three promises to Abram.
12:2 I will make you into a great nation Yahweh's second promise to Abram refers to a miraculous multiplication; Abram and his wife are simply two people and past childbearing age (compare Isa 51:2). It is unclear whether the covenant relationship with Abram begins here or in Ge 15:1–6, but the core promises of the covenant are present here. The covenant in Ge 15:1–6 is one-sided, but when the sign of the covenant (circumcision) is given later in Abram's life, the covenant relationship becomes two-sided—with obligations for Abram (17:1–2; compare Dt 4:23). **your name great** This third promise of Yahweh to Abram is a promise of renown and reputation, but primarily relates to material blessing, as Dt 7:13–14 indicates.

⁴So Abram went, as the LORD had told him; and Lot went with him. Abram was seventy-five years old when he set out from Harran. ⁵He took his wife Sarai, his nephew Lot, all the possessions they had accumulated and the people they had acquired in Harran, and they set out for the land of Canaan, and they arrived there.

⁶Abram traveled through the land as far as the site of the great tree of Moreh at Shechem. At that time the Canaanites were in the land. ⁷The LORD appeared to Abram and said, "To your offspring^a I will give this land." So he built an altar there to the LORD, who had appeared to him.

⁸From there he went on toward the hills east of Bethel and pitched his tent, with Bethel on the west and Ai on the east. There he built an altar to the LORD and called on the name of the LORD.

⁹Then Abram set out and continued toward the Negev.

Abram in Egypt

12:10-20Ref — Ge 20:1-18; 26:1-11

¹⁰Now there was a famine in the land, and Abram went down to Egypt to live there for a while because the famine was severe. ¹¹As he was about to enter Egypt, he said to his wife Sarai, "I know what a beautiful woman you are. ¹²When the Egyptians see you, they will say, 'This is his wife.' Then they will kill me but will let you live. ¹³Say you are my sister, so that I will be treated well for your sake and my life will be spared because of you."

¹⁴When Abram came to Egypt, the Egyptians saw that Sarai was a very beautiful woman. ¹⁵And when Pharaoh's officials saw her, they praised her to Pharaoh, and she was taken into his palace. ¹⁶He treated Abram well for her sake, and Abram ac-

---

^a 7 Or seed

12:4 Lot Lot is Abram's nephew (Ge 11:27). See the people diagram "Lot's Family Tree" on p. 42.

12:5 land of Canaan Refers to the land along the eastern shore of the Mediterranean Sea, all the way north to modern Lebanon and Syria, and inland to the boundary of the Jordan River.

12:6 great tree of Moreh A place of sacred significance since Yahweh appears to Abram here and reveals that he has arrived in the land to which Yahweh originally sent him (Ge 12:7). **Shechem** This later becomes a sacred site commemorating the appearance of Yahweh to Abram, who builds an altar there (v. 7). Other notable events at Shechem include: the rape of Dinah, Jacob's daughter — an act avenged by her brothers Simeon and Levi (ch. 34); the burial of Jacob's household gods (*teraphim* in Hebrew; 35:4); the burial of Joseph's bones (Jos 24:32; compare Ac 7:16); Joshua recording matters in the Book of the Law (Jos 24:26); and Rehoboam's coronation and the splitting of the Israelite kingdom, after which Shechem becomes the first capital of the rival northern kingdom of Israel (1Ki 12). **Canaanites** Refers generically to pre-Israelite inhabitants of the promised land.

12:7 appeared Other passages note Yahweh appearing visibly — even embodied — to Abram (Ge 18). The appearance to Abram marks the continuation of an overarching motif in both testaments — that God or an angelic figure often visibly appears to those chosen to be his representatives and specifically prophets (20:7). **your offspring** The Hebrew word used here, *zera'*, often translated "offspring" or "seed," represents an important element of Yahweh's promise to Abram: The land of Canaan is promised to his descendants. **this land** Yahweh confirms to Abram that he is standing in the promised land. **he built an altar there to the LORD** Abram did not use an existing altar to another deity. See the infographic "Ancient Altars" on p. 127; see the table "Altars in the Old Testament" on p. 249.

12:8 Bethel Bethel means "house of God"; it would become a sacred site for Israelites (see 1Ki 12:26-29).

12:9 the Negev Refers to southern and southeastern Judah around Beersheba.

12:10-20 Abram's trek through southern Canaan (the Negev) results in him journeying to Egypt to avoid a severe famine. Yahweh does not instruct Abram to leave Canaan, but neither does he explicitly demand that he stay. This is different than Yahweh's instructions to Isaac not to leave Canaan during a famine in (Ge 26:2-6).

FAMINES IN GENESIS	
Abram and Sarai Travel to Egypt	Ge 12:10
Isaac and Family Settle in Gerar	Ge 26:1
Joseph's Family Follows Him to Egypt	Ge 41:53 — 42:5

12:11-16 Abram fears that Sarai's beauty will lead the Egyptians to procure her for Pharaoh at any cost. He also believes he will be killed if the Egyptians learn of their marriage, so he has Sarai tell a half-truth about their relationship. Abram's fears are well-founded — the Egyptians kidnap Sarai. While Abram can be faulted for a lack of faith, given the accuracy of his suspicions, the incident can be cast as a dilemma in which Abram was forced to choose between two evils. Yahweh does not chastise Abram for the episode. Abram may have reasoned that at least both he and Sarai would live (though she would be sexually violated) if they deceived the Egyptians. The story can be read as presenting Abram with a choice between human life and human dignity.

12:13 Say you are my sister Denotes a sibling relationship, which was true in a way (see 20:12).

12:15 she was taken into his palace This indicates that Sarai becomes a member of Pharaoh's harem. Unlike the similar story in 20:1-18, this text does not explicitly indicate that Pharaoh does not have sex with Sarai (compare 20:3-4).

12:16 male and female donkeys, male and female servants, and camels Abram profits considerably from his ruse. The Pharaoh's gifts to Abram may have been a type of dowry in exchange for taking Sarai into his harem. The mention of camels is somewhat problematic, as domesticated camels may not have existed in Canaan during the time of the patriarchal stories. Camels are not mentioned in Egyptian texts until centuries after the patriarchal period, during the Persian period. In addition, camels are absent from the Mari texts of Mesopotamia, which provide abundant details about nomadic groups at this time. However, there is some other ambiguous, though suggestive, data that domesticated camels were in Mesopotamia during the patriarchal period.

quired sheep and cattle, male and female donkeys, male and female servants, and camels.

[17]But the LORD inflicted serious diseases on Pharaoh and his household because of Abram's wife Sarai. [18]So Pharaoh summoned Abram. "What have you done to me?" he said. "Why didn't you tell me she was your wife? [19]Why did you say, 'She is my sister,' so that I took her to be my wife? Now then, here is your wife. Take her and go!" [20]Then Pharaoh gave orders about Abram to his men, and they sent him on his way, with his wife and everything he had.

Abram and Lot Separate

13 So Abram went up from Egypt to the Negev, with his wife and everything he had, and Lot went with him. [2]Abram had become very wealthy in livestock and in silver and gold.

[3]From the Negev he went from place to place until he came to Bethel, to the place between Bethel and Ai where his tent had been earlier [4]and where he had first built an altar. There Abram called on the name of the LORD.

[5]Now Lot, who was moving about with Abram, also had flocks and herds and tents. [6]But the land could not support them while they stayed together, for their possessions were so great that they were not able to stay together. [7]And quarreling arose between Abram's herders and Lot's. The Canaanites and Perizzites were also living in the land at that time.

[8]So Abram said to Lot, "Let's not have any quarreling between you and me, or between your herders and mine, for we are close relatives. [9]Is not the whole land before you? Let's part company. If you go to the left, I'll go to the right; if you go to the right, I'll go to the left."

[10]Lot looked around and saw that the whole plain of the Jordan toward Zoar was well watered, like the garden of the LORD, like the land of Egypt. (This was before the LORD destroyed Sodom and Gomorrah.) [11]So Lot chose for himself the whole plain of the Jordan and set out toward the east. The two men parted company: [12]Abram lived in the land of Canaan, while Lot lived among the cities of the plain and pitched his tents near Sodom. [13]Now the people of Sodom were wicked and were sinning greatly against the LORD.

[14]The LORD said to Abram after Lot had parted from him, "Look around from where you are, to the north and south, to the east and west. [15]All the land that you see I will give to you and your offspring[a] forever. [16]I will make your offspring like the dust of the earth, so that if anyone could count the dust, then your offspring could be counted. [17]Go, walk through the length and breadth of the land, for I am giving it to you."

[18]So Abram went to live near the great trees of Mamre at Hebron, where he pitched his tents. There he built an altar to the LORD.

[a] 15 Or *seed*; also in verse 16

12:17 LORD inflicted serious diseases on Pharaoh Instead of chastising Abram, Yahweh punishes Pharaoh. **12:18 Pharaoh summoned Abram** In the similar account in ch. 20, God informs the king of the problem (20:3–7).

13:1–18 Abram and Lot have returned to the Negev after leaving Egypt. Conflict over resources leads Abram to decide that he and Lot should go their separate ways. In the patriarchal narratives, separation is often used as a subtle indicator of rejection (21:14–21; 25:6). Lot's separation from Abram excludes him from the promises intended for Abram's offspring. Lot's exclusion is also evident in his choice of where to settle: the cities of the plain in the Jordan Valley, which are outside the land promised to Abram.

13:3 From the Negev Abram moves from southern and southeastern Judah around Beersheba.
13:7 Canaanites Refers generically to a wide range of people groups. **Perizzites** The Hebrew word used here, *perizzi*, is probably generic, like the Hebrew word for Canaanites. *Perizzi* refers to people who dwell in villages (compare Dt 3:5, where the related Hebrew word *perazi* means "unwalled village"); this distinguishes them from the city dwellers (the Canaanites). Elsewhere, the term *perizzi* occurs with names for distinct ethnic groups. **were also living** Indicates that the area and its resources were already in use by a settled population.
13:10 toward Zoar This apparently refers to the southernmost limit to the plain of Jordan (or the Jordan Valley); it was located on the southeast shore of the Dead Sea.

13:13 wicked and were sinning greatly against the LORD This parenthetical note sets up the episode of Ge 19 and Sodom's destruction by Yahweh. It also serves as a commentary on Lot's character, contrasting it with Abram's.

13:14–17 Yahweh rewards Abram for his decision, which firmly situates him in the promised land of Canaan. Here, Yahweh repeats to Abram the blessings of the covenant relationship (12:1–3).

13:18 great trees of Mamre The place where Yahweh appeared to Abram earlier in the narrative (see 12:6 and note). **Hebron** Also called Kiriath Arba (23:2), this area is where Abraham (Abram) will buy a cave to bury Sarah (Sarai; 23:17).

Genesis 13:18

HEBRON
Hebron was located about 20 miles southwest of Jerusalem. Abram was often in the region of Hebron, and many of the patriarchs and matriarchs were buried there, including Sarah, Abraham, Isaac, Rebekah, Leah and Jacob. David was anointed king at Hebron (2Sa 2:4), and the city was his capital for the first seven and a half years of his reign over Judah (2Sa 5:4–5). See the infographic "Ancient Altars" on p. 127; see the table "Altars in the Old Testament" on p. 249.

Abram Rescues Lot

14 At the time when Amraphel was king of Shinar,[a] Arioch king of Ellasar, Kedorlaomer king of Elam and Tidal king of Goyim, ²these kings went to war against Bera king of Sodom, Birsha king of Gomorrah, Shinab king of Admah, Shemeber king of Zeboyim, and the king of Bela (that is, Zoar). ³All these latter kings joined forces in the Valley of Siddim (that is, the Dead Sea Valley). ⁴For twelve years they had been subject to Kedorlaomer, but in the thirteenth year they rebelled.

⁵In the fourteenth year, Kedorlaomer and the kings allied with him went out and defeated the Rephaites in Ashteroth Karnaim, the Zuzites in Ham, the Emites in Shaveh Kiriathaim ⁶and the Horites in the hill country of Seir, as far as El Paran near the desert. ⁷Then they turned back and went to En Mishpat (that is, Kadesh), and they conquered the whole territory of the Amalekites, as well as the Amorites who were living in Hazezon Tamar.

⁸Then the king of Sodom, the king of Gomor-rah, the king of Admah, the king of Zeboyim and the king of Bela (that is, Zoar) marched out and drew up their battle lines in the Valley of Siddim ⁹against Kedorlaomer king of Elam, Tidal king of Goyim, Amraphel king of Shinar and Arioch king of Ellasar — four kings against five. ¹⁰Now the Valley of Siddim was full of tar pits, and when the kings of Sodom and Gomorrah fled, some of the men fell into them and the rest fled to the hills. ¹¹The four kings seized all the goods of Sodom and Gomorrah and all their food; then they went away. ¹²They also carried off Abram's nephew Lot and his possessions, since he was living in Sodom.

¹³A man who had escaped came and reported this to Abram the Hebrew. Now Abram was living near the great trees of Mamre the Amorite, a brother[b] of Eshkol and Aner, all of whom were allied with Abram. ¹⁴When Abram heard that his relative had been taken captive, he called out the 318 trained men born in his household and went

[a] 1 That is, Babylonia; also in verse 9   [b] 13 Or *a relative*; or *an ally*

14:1–24 This episode recounts a regional war between several Mesopotamian kings. Lot's fateful choice to live near Sodom embroils him in the conflict, and Abram must rescue him from the kings who have conquered Sodom and the surrounding cities. This narrative is the only time Abram is depicted as a warrior, and the themes of promise and blessing — prominent in the other episodes from Abraham's life — are absent here.

14:1 Amraphel was king of Shinar The identity of this person is unknown. **Shinar** Another name for Babylonia (see 11:2). **Arioch** The name Arioch appears in the ancient Near Eastern Mari archives (eighteenth century BC) and the Nuzi tablets (fifteenth century BC). **Ellasar** This may be the Hebrew equivalent of the Akkadian phrase *al ashshur*, which indicates "city of Ashur" (Assyria). **Kedorlaomer** This name does not appear in the known lists of Elamite kings (roughly 40 kings). The first part of the name, however, may correspond to the Akkadian term *kudur* (*kutir* in Elamite), which means "a servant". This element appears in several royal Elamite names. **Elam** The ancient name for modern Khuzestan (southwestern Iran), east of Babylon. **Tidal** This name may be a transcription of the Hittite royal name Tudchaliash. The name is attributed to four Hittite kings, the earliest of whom lived during the seventeenth century BC — chronologically too late to be identified with the king mentioned here. **14:2 Bera king of Sodom, Birsha king of Gomorrah** Neither name is known. However, this may be a wordplay: Bera (*bera'* in Hebrew) and Birsha (*birsha'* in Hebrew) appear to play on the Hebrew words for "evil" (*ra'ah*) and "wicked" (*rasha'*). **14:3 the Dead Sea Valley** The water of the Dead Sea has the highest salt content of any body of water in the world. **14:5 Rephaites in Ashteroth Karnaim** The people groups listed in this verse were clans of giant people — much like the descendants of Anak (see Nu 13:33; Dt 2:10–11; 3:11–13). **14:6 Horites** The inhabitants of the region of Edom before it was taken over by the descendants of Esau

(Ge 36:20–30). The narrator probably intended the Horites to be understood as another Canaanite people group since all the names given in ch. 36 are Semitic. Another possibility, though less likely, is that "Horites" was the Hebrew name for the Hurrians — a non-Semitic people who moved into northwestern Mesopotamia and established the Mitannian Empire in the mid-second millennium BC. There is no evidence that the Hurrians lived in the region of Edom or Seir, though they were occasionally in other parts of Canaan. **Seir** Refers to the mountainous region southeast of the Dead Sea. This name is often used as a synonym for Edom. **El Paran** Generally refers to the desert of the Sinai Peninsula southwest of Palestine (see 21:21; Nu 10:12). **14:7 En Mishpat (that is, Kadesh)** A location in the northern Sinai that later served as a regular campsite for Israel during their wilderness wanderings (Nu 20:1). **the Amalekites** Refers to a nomadic or seminomadic tribe that later occupied parts of Canaan. Genesis portrays them as descendants of Esau, Abraham's grandson (Ge 36:12; compare 1Ch 1:36). **Hazezon Tamar** This location is later equated with En Gedi, a freshwater spring on the west side of the Dead Sea (2Ch 20:2). **14:13 the Hebrew** The Hebrew language word used here, *ivri*, could come from the Hebrew language preposition *ever*, meaning "beyond," resulting in the translation "Abram, the one from beyond (the river Euphrates)." However, this phrase most likely refers to Abram being a descendant of Eber (see Ge 10:21–31; 11:10–26) — whom Genesis seems to present as the forefather of the Hebrew people. **great trees** See note on 12:6. **Mamre the Amorite** Since his own people had been attacked in this war, Mamre had good reason to assist Abram. **14:14 318 trained men** A realistic number for an armed force, but two extra-Biblical examples suggest it may be a symbolic number indicating a large group. In an Egyptian text, Princess Giluchepa of Mitanni arrives with 317 harem attendants. In the Greek work Homer's *Iliad*, 318 men die in a four-day battle. The number 318 is the sum of the 12 prime numbers from 7 to 47, so the number may have symbolic meaning.

in pursuit as far as Dan. [15]During the night Abram divided his men to attack them and he routed them, pursuing them as far as Hobah, north of Damascus. [16]He recovered all the goods and brought back his relative Lot and his possessions, together with the women and the other people.

[17]After Abram returned from defeating Kedorlaomer and the kings allied with him, the king of Sodom came out to meet him in the Valley of Shaveh (that is, the King's Valley).

[18]Then Melchizedek king of Salem brought out bread and wine. He was priest of God Most High, [19]and he blessed Abram, saying,

"Blessed be Abram by God Most High,
    Creator of heaven and earth.
[20] And praise be to God Most High,
    who delivered your enemies into your
        hand."

Then Abram gave him a tenth of everything.

[21]The king of Sodom said to Abram, "Give me the people and keep the goods for yourself."

[22]But Abram said to the king of Sodom, "With raised hand I have sworn an oath to the LORD, God Most High, Creator of heaven and earth, [23]that I will accept nothing belonging to you, not even a thread or the strap of a sandal, so that you will never be able to say, 'I made Abram rich.' [24]I will accept nothing but what my men have eaten and the share that belongs to the men who went with me — to Aner, Eshkol and Mamre. Let them have their share."

The LORD's Covenant With Abram

15 After this, the word of the LORD came to Abram in a vision:

"Do not be afraid, Abram.
    I am your shield,[a]
    your very great reward.[b]"

[2]But Abram said, "Sovereign LORD, what can you give me since I remain childless and the one who will inherit[c] my estate is Eliezer of Damascus?" [3]And Abram said, "You have given me no children; so a servant in my household will be my heir."

[4]Then the word of the LORD came to him: "This man will not be your heir, but a son who is your own flesh and blood will be your heir." [5]He took him outside and said, "Look up at the sky and count the stars — if indeed you can count them." Then he said to him, "So shall your offspring[d] be."

[6]Abram believed the LORD, and he credited it to him as righteousness.

[7]He also said to him, "I am the LORD, who

---

[a] 1 Or *sovereign*   [b] 1 Or *shield; / your reward will be very great*
[c] 2 The meaning of the Hebrew for this phrase is uncertain.
[d] 5 Or *seed*

14:17–24 On the way back from defeating the kings and recovering the captives, Abram is met by the king of Sodom, who is accompanied by Melchizedek, king of Salem (see note on v. 18). Melchizedek, identified as a priest of God Most High, immediately offers a blessing to Abram, giving God the glory for his success. The introduction of Melchizedek provides an opportunity for Abram to demonstrate that his military offensive was not motivated by personal gain. As an answer to Melchizedek's blessing, Abram gives Melchizedek a tenth of the spoil he had recovered (14:16,20), recognizing God's role in his victory. The king of Sodom offers Abram all the plunder taken from Sodom as a reward for his successful venture, but Abram rejects the proposal because it implies dependence on someone or something other than God alone.

14:17 the Valley of Shaveh This site is also mentioned in 2Sa 18:18.

14:18 Melchizedek This name, which is *malki-tsedeq* in Hebrew, likely means "my king is righteous" or "king of righteousness" (compare Heb 7:2). It could also mean "Tsedeq is my king" with Tsedeq referring to a deity's name. Melchizedek is only mentioned once more in the OT, in Ps 110:4, but features prominently in the NT book of Hebrews. **Salem** This location may be, though not certainly, identified with Jerusalem. The name Salem is attested once in parallel with Zion in Ps 76:2, the location of the temple. **priest** Melchizedek was both a king and a priest. Some ancient Near Eastern civilizations combined the two offices, though most separated them. **God Most High** The Hebrew text here uses the phrase *el elyon*; this is the first Biblical occurrence of this phrase.

The word *el* is both the generic word for "god" in Semitic languages and the name of the god El in the Canaanite pantheon (as seen in Ugaritic texts). *Elyon* could refer to the "most high" deity or mean "upper" or "highest." In Ge 14:22, the title is combined in the Hebrew text with the name Yahweh (*yhwh*), so it seems that the narrator identified Yahweh with *el elyon*. See the table "Names of God in the Old Testament" on p. 917.

15:1–8 God speaks again to Abram to reassure him of his promises. Abram's reply to Yahweh demonstrates his frustration at Yahweh's delay in fulfilling what Abram views as the first necessary step in making him a great nation—providing him with a son and heir. Yahweh's answer to Abram addresses his concerns by clarifying that his heir will be his biological son and that his offspring will eventually be as numerous as the stars.

15:1 the word of the LORD came to Abram A phrase common to the prophetic books. Its use here places Abram among the prophets. See 15:4; 20:7. **vision** The Hebrew word used here, *chazon*, usually refers to a revelation received by a prophet.

15:3 a servant in my household will be my heir It was not uncommon in ancient Near Eastern culture for a trusted servant to become heir to a childless couple.

15:5 count the stars The reference to the stars (compare 22:17; 26:4) is similar to how the 12 tribes of Israel will later be described (37:9).

15:6 believed the LORD A clear statement of faith. Paul uses this as an example of salvation by faith (Ro 4:1–8). **as righteousness** Abram's response of faith confirms Yahweh's choice of him for the covenant. An OT parallel to this episode occurs in Ne 9:7–8.

brought you out of Ur of the Chaldeans to give you this land to take possession of it."

⁸But Abram said, "Sovereign LORD, how can I know that I will gain possession of it?"

⁹So the LORD said to him, "Bring me a heifer, a goat and a ram, each three years old, along with a dove and a young pigeon."

¹⁰Abram brought all these to him, cut them in two and arranged the halves opposite each other; the birds, however, he did not cut in half. ¹¹Then birds of prey came down on the carcasses, but Abram drove them away.

¹²As the sun was setting, Abram fell into a deep sleep, and a thick and dreadful darkness came over him. ¹³Then the LORD said to him, "Know for certain that for four hundred years your descendants will be strangers in a country not their own and that they will be enslaved and mistreated there. ¹⁴But I will punish the nation they serve as slaves, and afterward they will come out with great possessions. ¹⁵You, however, will go to your ancestors in peace and be buried at a good old age.

¹⁶In the fourth generation your descendants will come back here, for the sin of the Amorites has not yet reached its full measure."

¹⁷When the sun had set and darkness had fallen, a smoking firepot with a blazing torch appeared and passed between the pieces. ¹⁸On that day the LORD made a covenant with Abram and said, "To your descendants I give this land, from the Wadiᵃ of Egypt to the great river, the Euphrates — ¹⁹the land of the Kenites, Kenizzites, Kadmonites, ²⁰Hittites, Perizzites, Rephaites, ²¹Amorites, Canaanites, Girgashites and Jebusites."

Hagar and Ishmael

16 Now Sarai, Abram's wife, had borne him no children. But she had an Egyptian slave named Hagar; ²so she said to Abram, "The LORD has kept me from having children. Go, sleep with my slave; perhaps I can build a family through her." Abram agreed to what Sarai said. ³So after

ᵃ 18 Or *river*

15:8 how can I know This is not an expression of doubt that would undermine Abram's statement of faith in Ge 15:6. Yahweh now offers Abram land—such transactions in the ancient Near East required a covenant ceremony (compare ch. 23). Abram is asking for this ceremony.

15:9–21 Yahweh's response to Abram is a covenant ceremony that closely follows the pattern of ancient Near Eastern land grant treaties. It is unclear whether the covenant relationship with Abram begins here or in 12:1–3 (see v. 18; note on 12:2). The covenant of 15:9–21 is unilateral (one-sided), but when the sign of the covenant (circumcision) is given later, the covenant relationship becomes two-sided—it includes obligations for Abram (17:1–2,10–14).

15:10 cut them in two The animals are cut in half, and the halves are separated. The most common expression for making a covenant in the OT uses the Hebrew word *karath* (meaning "to cut"). This is because covenants usually involved literally cutting animals. This type of covenant practice was common in the ancient Near East. Ordinarily, those entering into a covenant would walk through the halved carcasses—indicating that they should end up like the animals if they break the agreement (see Jer 34:17–20). The fate of the sacrificial animals is applied onto the participants. In this case, only Yahweh—whose presence is signaled by the firepot and flaming torch—passes through (Ge 15:17).

15:13 four hundred years It is difficult to fit these 400 years into Biblical chronology. There is no information about when this sequence of years begins, and the OT does not state the number of years between Joseph's death and the beginning of the Israelites' enslavement in Egypt. It also appears inconsistent with the mention of the fourth generation in 15:16, and it fails to match the 430-year figure given in Ex 12:40 regarding Israel's time in Egypt. Most likely, the 400 years here is a round number.

15:14 will punish the nation they serve See Ex 7–12; note on Ex 7:3. **they will come out with great possessions** This is fulfilled when the Egyptians send the Hebrew people away with great wealth (Ex 12:33–36).

15:15 to your ancestors in peace This expression for death conveys an optimistic belief about the afterlife. While the OT at times can seem to lack this optimism, the righteous are depicted as hoping that God would remove them from *she'ol*—the Hebrew word for the grave or underworld (e.g., 1Sa 2:6; Pr 15:24; Ps 30:3; 49:15; 73:23–26). See the infographic "Ancient Hebrew Conception of the Universe" on p. 5.

15:16 sin of the Amorites This phrase shows that Yahweh does not later displace those occupying the promised land because of favoritism—he makes a judgment against their abhorrent practices (see Lev 18:24–25; 20:23–24).

15:18 your descendants See note on Ge 12:7. **the Wadi of Egypt** The river (*nahar* in Hebrew) mentioned here is not the Nile, which is referred to with the Hebrew word *ye'or* elsewhere in the OT (41:1; Ex 2:3,5); rather, this river is the Wadi el'Arish.

15:19–21 This passage presents the most complete OT list of the preconquest inhabitants of the promised land. The Kenites, Kenizzites, Kadmonites and Rephaim (Rephaites) appear in no other list like this. This list is also the only one to exclude the Hivites.

15:19 the Kenites This people group seems to be named after Cain (4:1,22). This seminomadic tribe was known for metalworking and are connected to the Midianites and Amalekites (compare Jdg 1:16; 4:11; Nu 24:21–22; 1Sa 15:1–6). **Kenizzites** This group of people are connected to the Edomites—descendants of Esau (Ge 36:4,11,15,42). **Kadmonites** This people group is not mentioned elsewhere in the OT, but may be the same as the Kedemites (a phrase which may be rendered "people of the east") noted in several passages. The Kedemites were seminomadic and ventured as far north as Aram (Syria) and as far south as the Red Sea (Jdg 6:3,33; 7:12; 8:10).

15:20 Perizzites See note on 13:7. **Rephaites** See note on Ge 14:5.

15:21 Amorites See note on 10:16. **Canaanites** A general term for a wide range of people groups. **Girgashites and Jebusites** See note on 10:16.

Abram had been living in Canaan ten years, Sarai his wife took her Egyptian slave Hagar and gave her to her husband to be his wife. [4]He slept with Hagar, and she conceived.

When she knew she was pregnant, she began to despise her mistress. [5]Then Sarai said to Abram, "You are responsible for the wrong I am suffering. I put my slave in your arms, and now that she knows she is pregnant, she despises me. May the LORD judge between you and me."

[6]"Your slave is in your hands," Abram said. "Do with her whatever you think best." Then Sarai mistreated Hagar; so she fled from her.

[7]The angel of the LORD found Hagar near a spring in the desert; it was the spring that is beside the road to Shur. [8]And he said, "Hagar, slave of Sarai, where have you come from, and where are you going?"

"I'm running away from my mistress Sarai," she answered.

[9]Then the angel of the LORD told her, "Go back to your mistress and submit to her." [10]The angel added, "I will increase your descendants so much that they will be too numerous to count."

[11]The angel of the LORD also said to her:

"You are now pregnant
     and you will give birth to a son.
You shall name him Ishmael,[a]
     for the LORD has heard of your misery.

[12]He will be a wild donkey of a man;
     his hand will be against everyone
     and everyone's hand against him,
and he will live in hostility
     toward[b] all his brothers."

[13]She gave this name to the LORD who spoke to her: "You are the God who sees me," for she said, "I have now seen[c] the One who sees me." [14]That is why the well was called Beer Lahai Roi[d]; it is still there, between Kadesh and Bered.

[15]So Hagar bore Abram a son, and Abram gave the name Ishmael to the son she had borne. [16]Abram was eighty-six years old when Hagar bore him Ishmael.

The Covenant of Circumcision

17 When Abram was ninety-nine years old, the LORD appeared to him and said, "I am God Almighty[e]; walk before me faithfully and be blameless. [2]Then I will make my covenant between me and you and will greatly increase your numbers."

[3]Abram fell facedown, and God said to him, [4]"As for me, this is my covenant with you: You will be

---

[a] 11 *Ishmael* means *God hears.*   [b] 12 Or *live to the east / of*
[c] 13 Or *seen the back of*   [d] 14 *Beer Lahai Roi* means *well of the Living One who sees me.*   [e] 1 Hebrew *El-Shaddai*

16:1–16 This narrative shows Abram and Sarai attempting to work around Sarai's barrenness to provide an heir for Abram. Yahweh's reassurance in ch. 15 confirmed for Abram that Yahweh's promise is intended for his biological offspring, but Yahweh did not specify that Sarai would be the mother. Since Sarai has been unable to provide an heir for Abram herself, she offers her servant, Hagar, to Abram as a wife. Hagar conceives, but her success causes strife in light of Sarai's perceived failure. After Sarai makes life difficult for Hagar, the pregnant Hagar leaves the camp, heading back toward her native Egypt. On the way, an angel appears to her and convinces her to return to Sarai.

16:1 Sarai See 11:29 and note. **Hagar** The name may be related to Arabic *hajara*, meaning "to flee"—and thus may parallel her fleeing later in this chapter.
16:2 LORD has kept me from having children In the ancient Near East, barrenness was always considered a female problem due to the belief that the man deposited a seedling child into the woman, where it would grow like a plant. Failure to grow the child was thus viewed as divine judgment against the woman. **I can build a family through her** The procedure of a barren woman providing her husband with a concubine occurred in other ancient Near Eastern cultures, according to both the ancient work Hammurabi's Code and ancient marriage contracts.
16:6 Sarai mistreated Hagar Ancient Near Eastern law codes, like that of Hammurabi, allowed slave owners to harshly punish their slaves for insolence.
16:7 The angel of the LORD Elsewhere, the Hebrew phrase used here, *malak yhwh*, is used in reference to Yahweh made visible or embodied, although it is not clear that the angel is always Yahweh (Ex 23:20–23; Jdg 6). See the table "Angels in the Bible" on p. 2120. **beside the road to Shur** Hagar was journeying toward Egypt, her native country (1Sa 15:7; 27:8).

16:8–10 Hagar is told by the angel to return to Sarai but adds that her son will become a nation. This passage features language similar to the promise to Abram (compare Ge 12:1–3; 15:1–6).

16:11 Ishmael This name in Hebrew, *yishma'el*, means "God hears." See the table "Symbolic Names of People in Hebrew" on p. 1388.
16:14 Beer Lahai Roi This name means "well of the living one who sees me" (see 24:62; 25:11).

17:1–27 Once more, Yahweh appears to Abram to reiterate his covenant promises. To confirm the covenant, Yahweh gives Abram a new name and institutes the practice of circumcision as a sign of the covenant. This event takes place 13 years after the events of ch. 16. Ishmael is now 13 years old (v. 25).

17:1 God Almighty The Hebrew phrase used here, *el shaddai*, which is commonly translated "God Almighty" or "the Almighty God" is translated as such based on English translation tradition; however, this is not based on the original Hebrew but how the Septuagint (the ancient Greek translation of the OT) translates *shaddai* in the book of Job (Job 5:17; 8:5). *Shaddai* is similar to the Hebrew term *shad*, meaning "breast" (Eze 23:3,21,34; SS 4:5; 7:3), but "God of breasts" is not a reasonable translation. The possibly related Akkadian word *shadu* (meaning "mountain")—along with the abundant testimony in the OT associating God with mountains (e.g., Sinai)—suggests that the word means "God of the mountain" or "God of the mountainous wilderness." God is called this name again later in Genesis and in Exodus (Ge 28:3; 35:11; 48:3; Ex 6:3). See the table "Names of God in the Old Testament" on p. 917.
17:2 I will make The Hebrew verb used here, *nathan*,

the father of many nations. ⁵No longer will you be called Abram*a*; your name will be Abraham,*b* for I have made you a father of many nations. ⁶I will make you very fruitful; I will make nations of you, and kings will come from you. ⁷I will establish my covenant as an everlasting covenant between me and you and your descendants after you for the generations to come, to be your God and the God of your descendants after you. ⁸The whole land of Canaan, where you now reside as a foreigner, I will give as an everlasting possession to you and your descendants after you; and I will be their God."

⁹Then God said to Abraham, "As for you, you must keep my covenant, you and your descendants after you for the generations to come. ¹⁰This is my covenant with you and your descendants after you, the covenant you are to keep: Every male among you shall be circumcised. ¹¹You are to undergo circumcision, and it will be the sign of the covenant between me and you. ¹²For the generations to come every male among you who is eight days old must be circumcised, including those born in your household or bought with money from a foreigner — those who are not your offspring. ¹³Whether born in your household or bought with your money, they must be circumcised. My covenant in your flesh is to be an everlasting covenant. ¹⁴Any uncircumcised male, who has not been circumcised in the flesh, will be cut off from his people; he has broken my covenant."

¹⁵God also said to Abraham, "As for Sarai your wife, you are no longer to call her Sarai; her name will be Sarah. ¹⁶I will bless her and will surely give you a son by her. I will bless her so that she will be the mother of nations; kings of peoples will come from her."

¹⁷Abraham fell facedown; he laughed and said to himself, "Will a son be born to a man a hundred years old? Will Sarah bear a child at the age of ninety?" ¹⁸And Abraham said to God, "If only Ishmael might live under your blessing!"

¹⁹Then God said, "Yes, but your wife Sarah will bear you a son, and you will call him Isaac.*c* I will establish my covenant with him as an everlasting covenant for his descendants after him. ²⁰And as

a 5 Abram means *exalted father.*   *b 5* Abraham probably means *father of many.*   *c 19* Isaac means *he laughs.*

can be understood as God establishing or confirming his covenant (see Ge 17:6). The covenant was earlier made in ch. 15 (see 17:4). See the table "Covenants in the Old Testament" on p. 469.

17:5 Abram The name Abram (*avram* in Hebrew) may be related to the names Abiram or Abarama, known from Akkadian texts contemporary with Abraham. The first syllable (*av*) is the Hebrew word for "father." The second syllable (*ram*) likely derives from the Hebrew verb *ram* (meaning "to be raised," or "to be exalted"); this means the name means "exalted father" or "the father is exalted." See the table "Symbolic Names of People in Hebrew" on p. 1388. **Abraham** The new name Abraham (*avraham* in Hebrew) is related to Abraham's role as "father of many nations" or "father of a multitude of nations" — the first part of this phrase, *av hamon*, seems to be a wordplay in Hebrew on Abraham's new name, *avraham*. It is difficult to discern the actual derivation of the Hebrew name *avraham*.

17:6–8 God's promises here reinforce what God had earlier promised to Abram in Ge 12 and Ge 15. Years of Abraham's life separate these repetitions of the promise, but each repetition has the same basic elements: God promises Abraham many descendants and land. See the people diagram "Family Tree of the Patriarchs" on p. 52.

17:10 shall be circumcised Circumcision — the surgical removal of the foreskin of the penis — was required as part of the covenant (see v. 14). Female circumcision is not intended by this statement. Circumcision was not unique to Israel, nor was it invented by the Israelites. The custom is known in Egypt as early as the twenty-third century BC, except that Egyptians slit the foreskin rather than removing it. Ancient Near Eastern art from Syria dating several centuries earlier depicts Syrian warriors as circumcised.

17:12 eight days old While the OT contains examples of adult male circumcision (vv. 23–27; 34:15–24; Jos 5:3–7), the normal practice for Abraham's descendants was infant circumcision.

17:15 Sarai The Hebrew word for "prince" or "ruler" is *sar*; both the name Sarai, and it seems Sarah, are related to this term and mean "princess." **Sarah** Sarah is the only woman renamed by God in the Bible. The context shows Abraham producing "kings" (Ge 17:6,16), and thus her new name, Sarah, may draw attention to Sarah as the matriarch of kings. While the name Sarah could mean "princess" — like Sarai — it could be affiliated with the Hebrew verb *sarah* (commonly translated as "to strive" or "to struggle"); this verb is used when Jacob's name is changed to Israel because he has both striven with God and people (32:28).

17:17 laughed The name Isaac (*yitschaq* in Hebrew) derives from the Hebrew verb used here, *tsachaq*. Abraham's laughter — expressing both joy and surprise — suggests that his original faith expression in 15:6 was not based on a realization that Sarah would be the mother.

17:19 Isaac This name means "he laughs" (see v. 17 and note). See the table "Symbolic Names of People in Hebrew" on p. 1388.

Genesis 17:19

ISAAC
Despite his importance as the child of promise, Isaac plays a relatively minor role in the Genesis narratives. Soon after Abraham dies (ch. 25), Jacob — the next major figure in Genesis — is introduced (ch. 25). After his birth and early years in 21:1–12, Isaac appears as a young man in the story of his binding in ch. 22, where he is a mostly passive character. He is largely absent from the narrative of ch. 24 when Abraham's servant finds Rebekah from among their relatives as Isaac's wife. The remaining narratives involving Isaac alone are nearly identical to incidents from Abraham's life (compare chs. 26; 20–21).

17:20 twelve rulers Equal in number to the 12 tribes

for Ishmael, I have heard you: I will surely bless him; I will make him fruitful and will greatly increase his numbers. He will be the father of twelve rulers, and I will make him into a great nation. ²¹But my covenant I will establish with Isaac, whom Sarah will bear to you by this time next year." ²²When he had finished speaking with Abraham, God went up from him.

²³On that very day Abraham took his son Ishmael and all those born in his household or bought with his money, every male in his household, and circumcised them, as God told him. ²⁴Abraham was ninety-nine years old when he was circumcised, ²⁵and his son Ishmael was thirteen; ²⁶Abraham and his son Ishmael were both circumcised on that very day. ²⁷And every male in Abraham's household, including those born in his household or bought from a foreigner, was circumcised with him.

The Three Visitors

18 The Lord appeared to Abraham near the great trees of Mamre while he was sitting at the entrance to his tent in the heat of the day. ²Abraham looked up and saw three men standing nearby. When he saw them, he hurried from the entrance of his tent to meet them and bowed low to the ground.

³He said, "If I have found favor in your eyes, my lord,ᵃ do not pass your servant by. ⁴Let a little water be brought, and then you may all wash your feet and rest under this tree. ⁵Let me get you something to eat, so you can be refreshed and then go on your way — now that you have come to your servant."

"Very well," they answered, "do as you say."

⁶So Abraham hurried into the tent to Sarah. "Quick," he said, "get three seahsᵇ of the finest flour and knead it and bake some bread."

⁷Then he ran to the herd and selected a choice, tender calf and gave it to a servant, who hurried to prepare it. ⁸He then brought some curds and milk and the calf that had been prepared, and set these before them. While they ate, he stood near them under a tree.

⁹"Where is your wife Sarah?" they asked him.

"There, in the tent," he said.

¹⁰Then one of them said, "I will surely return to you about this time next year, and Sarah your wife will have a son."

Now Sarah was listening at the entrance to the tent, which was behind him. ¹¹Abraham and Sarah were already very old, and Sarah was past the age of childbearing. ¹²So Sarah laughed to herself as she thought, "After I am worn out and my lord is old, will I now have this pleasure?"

¹³Then the Lord said to Abraham, "Why did Sarah laugh and say, 'Will I really have a child, now that I am old?' ¹⁴Is anything too hard for the Lord? I will return to you at the appointed time next year, and Sarah will have a son."

¹⁵Sarah was afraid, so she lied and said, "I did not laugh."

But he said, "Yes, you did laugh."

Abraham Pleads for Sodom

¹⁶When the men got up to leave, they looked down toward Sodom, and Abraham walked along with them to see them on their way. ¹⁷Then the Lord said, "Shall I hide from Abraham what I am about to do? ¹⁸Abraham will surely become a great and powerful nation, and all nations on earth will be blessed through him.ᶜ ¹⁹For I have

---

ᵃ 3 Or *eyes, Lord*   ᵇ 6 That is, probably about 36 pounds or about 16 kilograms   ᶜ 18 Or *will use his name in blessings* (see 48:20)

---

of Israel (also from Abraham), the 12 Ishmaelite princes (or rulers) are listed in 25:12–16.

17:23–27 Abraham obeys the covenant rite of circumcision in complete detail. He, Ishmael and every other male in his household are circumcised.

18:1–15 After God repeats his promise to Abraham (17:15–27), Abraham is visited by three men. These men restate that Sarah will bear a son within a year (v. 10; compare 17:19–21). This time Sarah reacts with laughter, just as Abraham did earlier (v. 12; compare 17:17). Abraham and Sarah's reactions highlight just how surprising and implausible it seems that they will produce a son.

18:1 appeared to Abraham In parallel with earlier events, Yahweh is visibly present with Abraham during this conversation (see 12:7 and note; 15:1 and note; 17:1). **18:2 three men standing** This indicates that these figures were embodied. Genesis 18:1 indicates that one of the men is Yahweh (compare v. 13). **18:3 my lord** It could be that Abraham does not know he is speaking to Yahweh, but this is unlikely. The Hebrew verbs used in this verse are singular, indicating that Abra-

ham addresses only one of the individuals — Yahweh — as *adonay* (meaning "my lord"). The same form of address occurs later in v. 27, when Abraham notes that he has spoken boldly with the Lord (*adonay*). In vv. 4–5, the Hebrew verbs are plural as Abraham includes the other two figures in his invitation.

18:4 rest Abraham fulfills the duties of an ancient Near Eastern host. Besides feeding the men, he ensures that they are rested and refreshed. **18:6 three seahs** This amount would produce more than enough bread for the visitors.

18:16–22 As the three visitors leave, Yahweh considers telling Abraham about his plan to destroy Sodom and Gomorrah. Yahweh then reflects on his promise to Abraham (see v. 18). Here, for the first time, Yahweh mentions an additional reason for choosing Abraham (v. 19). Yahweh ultimately reveals his plan to Abraham (vv. 20–21).

18:19 I have chosen him The Hebrew verb used here, *yada'*, is often used to refer to acknowledging something, knowing something or understanding something — the idea seems to be that Yahweh knows Abraham. Yahweh here also seems to refer to his election of Abraham

chosen him, so that he will direct his children and his household after him to keep the way of the Lord by doing what is right and just, so that the Lord will bring about for Abraham what he has promised him."

²⁰Then the Lord said, "The outcry against Sodom and Gomorrah is so great and their sin so grievous ²¹that I will go down and see if what they have done is as bad as the outcry that has reached me. If not, I will know."

²²The men turned away and went toward Sodom, but Abraham remained standing before the Lord.ᵃ ²³Then Abraham approached him and said: "Will you sweep away the righteous with the wicked? ²⁴What if there are fifty righteous people in the city? Will you really sweep it away and not spareᵇ the place for the sake of the fifty righteous people in it? ²⁵Far be it from you to do such a thing—to kill the righteous with the wicked, treating the righteous and the wicked alike. Far be it from you! Will not the Judge of all the earth do right?"

²⁶The Lord said, "If I find fifty righteous people in the city of Sodom, I will spare the whole place for their sake."

²⁷Then Abraham spoke up again: "Now that I have been so bold as to speak to the Lord, though I am nothing but dust and ashes, ²⁸what if the number of the righteous is five less than fifty? Will you destroy the whole city for lack of five people?"

"If I find forty-five there," he said, "I will not destroy it."

²⁹Once again he spoke to him, "What if only forty are found there?"

He said, "For the sake of forty, I will not do it."

³⁰Then he said, "May the Lord not be angry, but let me speak. What if only thirty can be found there?"

He answered, "I will not do it if I find thirty there."

³¹Abraham said, "Now that I have been so bold as to speak to the Lord, what if only twenty can be found there?"

He said, "For the sake of twenty, I will not destroy it."

³²Then he said, "May the Lord not be angry, but let me speak just once more. What if only ten can be found there?"

He answered, "For the sake of ten, I will not destroy it."

³³When the Lord had finished speaking with Abraham, he left, and Abraham returned home.

Sodom and Gomorrah Destroyed

19 The two angels arrived at Sodom in the evening, and Lot was sitting in the gateway of the city. When he saw them, he got up to meet them and bowed down with his face to the ground. ²"My lords," he said, "please turn aside to your servant's house. You can wash your feet and spend the night and then go on your way early in the morning."

"No," they answered, "we will spend the night in the square."

³But he insisted so strongly that they did go with him and entered his house. He prepared a meal for

---

ᵃ 22 Masoretic Text; an ancient Hebrew scribal tradition *but the Lord remained standing before Abraham*   ᵇ 24 Or *forgive*; also in verse 26

---

and his descendants—the people of Israel—to inherit specific promises and to understand the identity of the true God. **what is right** The Hebrew word used here, *tsedaqah*, refers to what is right or fair (Lev 19:36). It can convey the legal sense of innocence or vindication (Job 6:29; see Ps 4:1 and note). **just** The Hebrew word used here, *mishpat*, can refer to legal decisions that involve both condemning the guilty and acquitting the innocent (1Ki 8:32; see Ps 146:7 and note).

18:20 outcry The Hebrew word used here, *ze'aqah* is used elsewhere to describe oppression and injustice (Ex 3:7; 22:21–23). The crimes of Sodom are more than the general evil of inhospitality and homosexual aggression described in Ge 19.

18:23–33 Abraham intercedes for Sodom and Gomorrah, pleading with Yahweh to spare the cities if fifty righteous people can be found within them, or even ten. The course of this exchange builds dramatic tension—only ten righteous people are needed to save the cities. Until now, Abraham has spoken few words to Yahweh. Here, pleading for the doomed cities, he is far more vocal. Abraham speaks far more here than Yahweh.

18:23 sweep away the righteous with the wicked Abraham shows a concern for righteousness and justice. He argues that by destroying Sodom, God might destroy some righteous people along with the wicked.

18:32 What if only ten can be found It is unclear why

Abraham stops his negotiation at ten. Ultimately there are not even 10 righteous people within the city, and Yahweh destroys it (19:25–26). However, Yahweh remembers Abraham's pleas here and extends his mercy by saving Lot (see 19:29 and note).

19:1–22 After recording Abraham's intercession for Sodom and Gomorrah, the scene shifts to Lot's house in Sodom (see v. 2 and note). When two angels visit Lot, the men of Sodom ask Lot to hand them over so they can violate them (see v. 5 and note). Lot refuses and offers his daughters instead (v. 8). When the men of Sodom refuse this offer, the angels strike them with blindness (vv. 9–11). After the men of Sodom leave, the angels inform Lot of Sodom's impending judgment and warn him to take his family and leave the city (vv. 12–22).

19:1 The two angels Three men had appeared to Abraham. It turned out that one was Yahweh, while the other two were angels (see 18:1 and note; 18:2 and note). The two angels here are the same angels who appeared to Abraham earlier (18:2). See the table "Angels in the Bible" on p. 2120.

19:2 your servant's house Previously, Lot lived in tents outside the wicked city of Sodom (13:12).

19:3 baking bread without yeast A meal that could be prepared on short notice since the bread would not have to rise. See note on Ex 12:8.

them, baking bread without yeast, and they ate. [4]Before they had gone to bed, all the men from every part of the city of Sodom — both young and old — surrounded the house. [5]They called to Lot, "Where are the men who came to you tonight? Bring them out to us so that we can have sex with them."

[6]Lot went outside to meet them and shut the door behind him [7]and said, "No, my friends. Don't do this wicked thing. [8]Look, I have two daughters who have never slept with a man. Let me bring them out to you, and you can do what you like with them. But don't do anything to these men, for they have come under the protection of my roof."

[9]"Get out of our way," they replied. "This fellow came here as a foreigner, and now he wants to play the judge! We'll treat you worse than them." They kept bringing pressure on Lot and moved forward to break down the door.

[10]But the men inside reached out and pulled Lot back into the house and shut the door. [11]Then they struck the men who were at the door of the house, young and old, with blindness so that they could not find the door.

[12]The two men said to Lot, "Do you have anyone else here — sons-in-law, sons or daughters, or anyone else in the city who belongs to you? Get them out of here, [13]because we are going to destroy this place. The outcry to the LORD against its people is so great that he has sent us to destroy it."

[14]So Lot went out and spoke to his sons-in-law, who were pledged to marry[a] his daughters. He said, "Hurry and get out of this place, because the LORD is about to destroy the city!" But his sons-in-law thought he was joking.

[15]With the coming of dawn, the angels urged Lot, saying, "Hurry! Take your wife and your two daughters who are here, or you will be swept away when the city is punished."

[16]When he hesitated, the men grasped his hand and the hands of his wife and of his two daughters and led them safely out of the city, for the LORD was merciful to them. [17]As soon as they had brought them out, one of them said, "Flee for your lives! Don't look back, and don't stop anywhere in the plain! Flee to the mountains or you will be swept away!"

[18]But Lot said to them, "No, my lords,[b] please! [19]Your[c] servant has found favor in your[c] eyes, and you[c] have shown great kindness to me in sparing my life. But I can't flee to the mountains; this disaster will overtake me, and I'll die. [20]Look, here is a town near enough to run to, and it is small. Let me flee to it — it is very small, isn't it? Then my life will be spared."

[21]He said to him, "Very well, I will grant this request too; I will not overthrow the town you speak of. [22]But flee there quickly, because I cannot do anything until you reach it." (That is why the town was called Zoar.[d])

[23]By the time Lot reached Zoar, the sun had risen over the land. [24]Then the LORD rained down burning sulfur on Sodom and Gomorrah — from the LORD out of the heavens. [25]Thus he overthrew those cities and the entire plain, destroying all those living in the cities — and also the vegetation in the land. [26]But Lot's wife looked back, and she became a pillar of salt.

[27]Early the next morning Abraham got up and returned to the place where he had stood before the LORD. [28]He looked down toward Sodom and Gomorrah, toward all the land of the plain, and he saw dense smoke rising from the land, like smoke from a furnace.

[29]So when God destroyed the cities of the plain, he remembered Abraham, and he brought Lot

---

[a] 14 Or were married to   [b] 18 Or No, Lord; or No, my lord
[c] 19 The Hebrew is singular.   [d] 22 Zoar means small.

19:5 we can have sex with them The men of Sodom seek to humiliate Lot's guests by raping them. While the attempted rape is terrible, other OT passages (Lev 18:22,24; 20:13,23) also indicate that homosexuality was regarded as a repugnant Canaanite practice. In addition, Eze 16:49 indicates that Sodom also had a reputation for excess and injustice. Sodom and Gomorrah is regularly used in the OT as an example of general wickedness and lawlessness (e.g., Jer 23:14).

19:8 you can do what you like with them Hospitality toward strangers was generally considered a moral imperative in the ancient Near East. This honor code meant that Lot could not turn the strangers over to the men of Sodom. In a patriarchal culture, daughters would have been viewed in lesser terms than Lot's male guests. However, Mesopotamian law codes parallel to Biblical laws make it clear that violating a betrothed woman—which Lot's daughters were (Ge 19:14)—was a crime punishable by death. According to even ancient Near Eastern customs, then, Lot understood just how evil offering his daughters to the men was, but he may have considered it a lesser evil.

19:9 This fellow came here as a foreigner Lot is an outsider whom the native inhabitants do not consider of equal legal or ethnic status. He cannot appeal to them on the basis of kinship.

19:14 his sons-in-law thought he was joking Lot's sons-in-law cannot take him seriously. Until now, Lot's behavior hasn't reflected a life centered on God's will, so their skepticism comes as no surprise.

19:16 When he hesitated The delay shows either extraordinary stupidity or, more likely, deplorable spiritual character.

19:23–29 After Lot flees from Sodom, Yahweh destroys Sodom and Gomorrah with fire from heaven (see v. 24). Despite the angels' instructions (v. 17), Lot's wife looks back at the destruction and becomes a pillar of salt. Abraham goes to the place where he interceded on behalf of Sodom and sees the destruction (vv. 27–28). The text notes that Yahweh delivered Lot because of Abraham (see v. 29 and note).

19:26 a pillar of salt Lot's wife disobeyed the command of the angels (v. 17). The result of her hesitancy was inclusion in the judgment against Sodom and Gomorrah.

19:29 remembered There were not ten righteous people found in Sodom (see 18:32), but Yahweh extends his mercy beyond what Abraham asked by saving Lot.

out of the catastrophe that overthrew the cities where Lot had lived.

Lot and His Daughters

³⁰Lot and his two daughters left Zoar and settled in the mountains, for he was afraid to stay in Zoar. He and his two daughters lived in a cave. ³¹One day the older daughter said to the younger, "Our father is old, and there is no man around here to give us children — as is the custom all over the earth. ³²Let's get our father to drink wine and then sleep with him and preserve our family line through our father."

³³That night they got their father to drink wine,

and the older daughter went in and slept with him. He was not aware of it when she lay down or when she got up.

³⁴The next day the older daughter said to the younger, "Last night I slept with my father. Let's get him to drink wine again tonight, and you go in and sleep with him so we can preserve our family line through our father." ³⁵So they got their father to drink wine that night also, and the younger daughter went in and slept with him. Again he was not aware of it when she lay down or when she got up.

³⁶So both of Lot's daughters became pregnant by their father. ³⁷The older daughter had a son,

19:30–38 Lot's daughters, worried about their ability to find men to give them offspring, get their father drunk and have sexual relations with him (vv. 32–35). Both women get pregnant and have sons. Their sons produce the Moabites and Ammonites (vv. 37–38); both of these groups are given special protection after the Israelites leave Egypt (Dt 2:9,19). This episode of incest concludes the story of Lot. See the people diagram "Lot's Family Tree" below.

19:32 preserve our family line through our father
While it is possible (Ge 19:31) that the women believed there were no more men left in their region after the cataclysm, the emphasis on Lot's lineage suggests that they believed there were no more relatives left to continue the family line. The absence of a blood heir was akin to being erased from history in an ancient Near Eastern culture. While this does not in any way excuse the incestuous behavior, it helps explain their desperation.

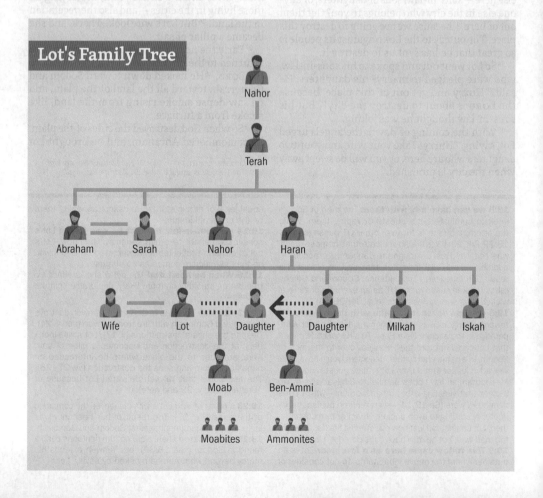

Lot's Family Tree

and she named him Moab[a]; he is the father of the Moabites of today. [38]The younger daughter also had a son, and she named him Ben-Ammi[b]; he is the father of the Ammonites[c] of today.

Abraham and Abimelek

20:1-18Ref — Ge 12:10-20; 26:1-11

20 Now Abraham moved on from there into the region of the Negev and lived between Kadesh and Shur. For a while he stayed in Gerar, [2]and there Abraham said of his wife Sarah, "She is my sister." Then Abimelek king of Gerar sent for Sarah and took her.

[3]But God came to Abimelek in a dream one night and said to him, "You are as good as dead because of the woman you have taken; she is a married woman."

[4]Now Abimelek had not gone near her, so he said, "Lord, will you destroy an innocent nation? [5]Did he not say to me, 'She is my sister,' and didn't she also say, 'He is my brother'? I have done this with a clear conscience and clean hands."

[6]Then God said to him in the dream, "Yes, I know you did this with a clear conscience, and so I have kept you from sinning against me. That is why I did not let you touch her. [7]Now return the man's wife, for he is a prophet, and he will pray for you and you will live. But if you do not return her, you may be sure that you and all who belong to you will die."

[8]Early the next morning Abimelek summoned all his officials, and when he told them all that had happened, they were very much afraid. [9]Then Abimelek called Abraham in and said, "What have you done to us? How have I wronged you that you have brought such great guilt upon me and my kingdom? You have done things to me that should never be done." [10]And Abimelek asked Abraham, "What was your reason for doing this?"

[11]Abraham replied, "I said to myself, 'There is surely no fear of God in this place, and they will kill me because of my wife.' [12]Besides, she really is my sister, the daughter of my father though not of my mother; and she became my wife. [13]And when God had me wander from my father's household, I said to her, 'This is how you can show your love to me: Everywhere we go, say of me, "He is my brother."'"

[14]Then Abimelek brought sheep and cattle and male and female slaves and gave them to Abraham, and he returned Sarah his wife to him. [15]And Abimelek said, "My land is before you; live wherever you like."

[16]To Sarah he said, "I am giving your brother a thousand shekels[d] of silver. This is to cover the offense against you before all who are with you; you are completely vindicated."

[17]Then Abraham prayed to God, and God healed Abimelek, his wife and his female slaves so they could have children again, [18]for the LORD had kept all the women in Abimelek's household from conceiving because of Abraham's wife Sarah.

a 37 Moab sounds like the Hebrew for *from father.* *b 38 Ben-Ammi* means *son of my father's people.* *c 38* Hebrew *Bene-Ammon* *d 16* That is, about 25 pounds or about 12 kilograms

---

19:36–38 The Moabites and Ammonites are both related to Abraham by their incestuous beginnings between Lot (Abraham's nephew) and Lot's daughters.

19:37 Moab The Hebrew word used here sounds like the Hebrew phrase for "from father." **the Moabites** This people group was eventually neighbors of Israel. They lived east of the Dead Sea. See note on Ru 1:1.

19:38 Ben-Ammi The Hebrew word used here means "son of my people." **the Ammonites** This people group lived east of the Jordan River, north of the Moabites. They were eventually neighbors of Israel. See note on 1Ch 19:1.

20:1–18 Abraham repeats the mistake he made in Egypt (Ge 12:10–20). Finding himself in the foreign territory of Gerar, he again claims that Sarah is his sister out of fear of personal harm (vv. 2,11; compare 12:11–12). In both instances God intervenes and protects Abraham. Here, God intervenes by appearing to Abimelek, the foreign king, in a dream (vv. 3–7).

20:1 Negev The narrative about Sodom and Gomorrah places Abraham in Mamre, near Hebron. Now he has migrated to the Negev, the desert area between Canaan and Egypt, southward toward the Sinai Peninsula. **Shur** A defensive wall in the eastern Nile delta. **Gerar** A Canaanite city in the western Negev. See note on 26:6.

20:2 She is my sister Just like when Abraham and Sarah went into Egypt (12:10–20), Abraham fears that his life is in jeopardy. **Abimelek** This is a fairly common personal name in northwest Semitic literature (Ugaritic and Phoenician literature). It means "my father is king," and may be a title.

20:4 Lord In the Hebrew text here it is not the divine name, Yahweh, that is used but *adonay*—the customary address to a divine being (see 18:3 and note).

20:5–7 God affirms Abimelek's innocence and commands him to send Sarah back to Abraham.

20:7 prophet Prophets were essentially spokespersons for and representatives of God. They exhorted people to be loyal and obey his commands lest judgment occur.

20:9 What have you done to us Though forewarned—and despite the fact that he will return Sarah to Abraham without having sexual relations with her (v. 6)—Abimelek is angry with Abraham.

20:11 no fear of God Abraham views Abimelek and his people as lacking any sense of morality that would come from belief in the one true God.

20:12 my sister Sarah is Abraham's half-sister—such marriages seems to have been culturally acceptable at this point in time in the ancient Near East. Despite later prohibitions under the law (see Lev 18), 2Sa 13:13 and Eze 22:11 indicate that close kinship marriages still occurred.

20:18 had kept all the women in Abimelek's household from conceiving This suggests that Sarah was in the king's company long enough for the people in his household to notice the absence of any new pregnancies.

The Birth of Isaac

21 Now the LORD was gracious to Sarah as he had said, and the LORD did for Sarah what he had promised. ²Sarah became pregnant and bore a son to Abraham in his old age, at the very time God had promised him. ³Abraham gave the name Isaac[a] to the son Sarah bore him. ⁴When his son Isaac was eight days old, Abraham circumcised him, as God commanded him. ⁵Abraham was a hundred years old when his son Isaac was born to him.

⁶Sarah said, "God has brought me laughter, and everyone who hears about this will laugh with me." ⁷And she added, "Who would have said to Abraham that Sarah would nurse children? Yet I have borne him a son in his old age."

Hagar and Ishmael Sent Away

⁸The child grew and was weaned, and on the day Isaac was weaned Abraham held a great feast. ⁹But Sarah saw that the son whom Hagar the Egyptian had borne to Abraham was mocking, ¹⁰and she said to Abraham, "Get rid of that slave woman and her son, for that woman's son will never share in the inheritance with my son Isaac."

¹¹The matter distressed Abraham greatly because it concerned his son. ¹²But God said to him, "Do not be so distressed about the boy and your slave woman. Listen to whatever Sarah tells you, because it is through Isaac that your offspring[b] will be reckoned. ¹³I will make the son of the slave into a nation also, because he is your offspring."

¹⁴Early the next morning Abraham took some food and a skin of water and gave them to Hagar.

He set them on her shoulders and then sent her off with the boy. She went on her way and wandered in the Desert of Beersheba.

¹⁵When the water in the skin was gone, she put the boy under one of the bushes. ¹⁶Then she went off and sat down about a bowshot away, for she thought, "I cannot watch the boy die." And as she sat there, she[c] began to sob.

¹⁷God heard the boy crying, and the angel of God called to Hagar from heaven and said to her, "What is the matter, Hagar? Do not be afraid; God has heard the boy crying as he lies there. ¹⁸Lift the boy up and take him by the hand, for I will make him into a great nation."

¹⁹Then God opened her eyes and she saw a well of water. So she went and filled the skin with water and gave the boy a drink.

²⁰God was with the boy as he grew up. He lived in the desert and became an archer. ²¹While he was living in the Desert of Paran, his mother got a wife for him from Egypt.

The Treaty at Beersheba

²²At that time Abimelek and Phicol the commander of his forces said to Abraham, "God is with you in everything you do. ²³Now swear to me here before God that you will not deal falsely with me or my children or my descendants. Show to me and the country where you now reside as a foreigner the same kindness I have shown to you."

²⁴Abraham said, "I swear it."

²⁵Then Abraham complained to Abimelek

---

[a] 3 *Isaac* means *he laughs.*   [b] 12 Or *seed*   [c] 16 Hebrew; Septuagint *the child*

21:1–7 Just as God promised in Ge 17:16–21 and 18:10–14, Sarah conceives and bears a son. Abraham names him Isaac and circumcises him as God instructs (17:10–14).

21:3 Isaac See 17:19 and note.

21:5 a hundred years old Twenty-five years have passed since God promised Abraham that he would make him a great nation (12:2; compare 12:4).

21:6 laughter This is a wordplay on Isaac's name. See 17:17 and note.

21:8–21 After the birth of Isaac, Sarah asks Abraham to banish Hagar and Ishmael, Abraham's son with Hagar (v. 10). Abraham is reluctant, but God tells him that he will also make Ishmael a nation (vv. 11–13; compare 17:20). After Hagar and Ishmael leave, God provides for them and repeats to Hagar his promise to make Ishmael a great nation (vv. 15–21).

21:8 weaned The age that a child was weaned varied within ancient Near Eastern cultures.

21:9 son whom Hagar See 16:1–16 and note; note on 16:1.

21:11 distressed Abraham greatly Abraham is troubled by Sarah's demand that Hagar and Ishmael be driven away, which means he recognized Ishmael as his legal son (16:15; 17:23,25; 25:9,12). Contemporaneous

ancient Near Eastern law codes (such as Hammurabi's Code) presume inheritance rights on behalf of a son accepted by the father. However, the ancient laws of Lipit-Ishtar contain a clause to the effect that if a slave woman and her children are granted freedom by the male owner who fathered those children, the children forfeit their share in his estate. This seems to be Sarah's intent in having Abraham send Hagar and Ishmael away—to forfeit Ishmael's rights.

21:17 angel of God called The interchange of God (who hears in this verse) and the Angel of God (who then speaks) shows a blurring of the distinction between the two—this is because the angel is speaking on behalf of God or is God in a form.

21:22–34 This section continues the narrative about Abraham's relationship with the king of Gerar—Gerar is where Abraham is staying (see 20:1–18 and note). Abraham and the king make a covenant to deal honestly with each other (vv. 23–24). Abraham then confronts the king about his servants seizing a well (vv. 25–26). The two men then make a covenant agreeing that the well belongs to Abraham (vv. 27–32).

21:22 Abimelek See 20:2 and note.

21:24 I swear Promises were frequently formalized in the ancient Near East by oath-taking.

about a well of water that Abimelek's servants had seized. ²⁶But Abimelek said, "I don't know who has done this. You did not tell me, and I heard about it only today."

²⁷So Abraham brought sheep and cattle and gave them to Abimelek, and the two men made a treaty. ²⁸Abraham set apart seven ewe lambs from the flock, ²⁹and Abimelek asked Abraham, "What is the meaning of these seven ewe lambs you have set apart by themselves?"

³⁰He replied, "Accept these seven lambs from my hand as a witness that I dug this well."

³¹So that place was called Beersheba,ᵃ because the two men swore an oath there.

³²After the treaty had been made at Beersheba, Abimelek and Phicol the commander of his forces returned to the land of the Philistines. ³³Abraham planted a tamarisk tree in Beersheba, and there he called on the name of the LORD, the Eternal God. ³⁴And Abraham stayed in the land of the Philistines for a long time.

Abraham Tested

22 Some time later God tested Abraham. He said to him, "Abraham!"

"Here I am," he replied.

²Then God said, "Take your son, your only son, whom you love — Isaac — and go to the region of Moriah. Sacrifice him there as a burnt offering on a mountain I will show you."

³Early the next morning Abraham got up and loaded his donkey. He took with him two of his servants and his son Isaac. When he had cut enough wood for the burnt offering, he set out for the place God had told him about. ⁴On the third day Abraham looked up and saw the place in the distance. ⁵He said to his servants, "Stay here with the donkey while I and the boy go over there. We will worship and then we will come back to you."

⁶Abraham took the wood for the burnt offering and placed it on his son Isaac, and he himself carried the fire and the knife. As the two of them went on together, ⁷Isaac spoke up and said to his father Abraham, "Father?"

"Yes, my son?" Abraham replied.

"The fire and wood are here," Isaac said, "but where is the lamb for the burnt offering?"

⁸Abraham answered, "God himself will provide the lamb for the burnt offering, my son." And the two of them went on together.

⁹When they reached the place God had told him about, Abraham built an altar there and arranged the wood on it. He bound his son Isaac and laid

ᵃ 31 *Beersheba* can mean *well of seven* and *well of the oath.*

21:28 seven ewe lambs These animals may have been sacrifices in a covenant ceremony (compare 15:9–17). However, they may have also been a reciprocation of Abimelek's previous gift to Abraham in 20:14.
21:31 Beersheba This place name means either "well of the oath" or "well of seven." There are seven lambs mentioned in v. 30 and the two men swear an oath there, as this verse indicates. Either meaning involves wordplay (compare 21:24).
21:32 land of the Philistines Abimelek was king of Gerar (20:2). Gerar is here identified as being in the land of the Philistines (*peleset* in Hebrew). In the parallel story about Isaac and Abimelek, Abimelek resides in Gerar and is specifically called king of the Philistines (26:1) — however, Isaac may be encountering Abimelek's son. Genesis does not list the Philistines among the peoples inhabiting the land of Canaan. Archaeologically speaking, evidence of Philistine cities does not appear until centuries after the patriarchs (ca. 1200 BC). References to the Philistines appear in the books of Joshua (Jos 13:2–3) and Judges (e.g., Jdg 3:3,31; 10:6–11; 13:1,5), as well as in texts from the time of the Egyptian Pharaoh Rameses III (twelfth century BC). All these references to Philistines are too late to align with the time of Abraham (ca. 2000 BC). Since Egyptian texts place the *peleset* people group (the Philistines) among the Sea Peoples — marauding people groups from the Aegean — it is possible that the term *peleset* may have been applied generally to peoples settling on the shores of Canaan. This would mean that the Philistines of the Abraham and Isaac stories are not of the same ethnicity as the Philistines of later Israelite history.
21:33 planted a tamarisk tree A practice consistent with earlier commemorations of divine communication. See Ge 12:6.

22:1–19 After waiting 25 years to have a son (see note on 21:5), Abraham faces a test of faith. God instructs him to take Isaac, his only son and the heir to God's promise (17:21), to a mountain and sacrifice him (vv. 1–2). Abraham obeys without question, binding Isaac to the altar (vv. 3–10). God intervenes and provides a ram to offer instead (vv. 11–14). After this resolution, God reiterates his covenant with Abraham (vv. 15–19).
22:1 God tested Abraham God is not in favor of human sacrifice, and he later directly prohibits it (Lev 18:21; Dt 12:31) — Abraham is being tested. The text hints that Isaac will not die (v. 5).
22:2 your only son Since Isaac is not Abraham's only son (he had Ishmael by Hagar earlier; 16:11–16), the Hebrew text here is referring to value, not number. Isaac is Abraham's special son — through him the covenant promises with God will be passed on (17:21). Hebrews 11:17 refers to Isaac with the Greek term *monogenēs*, which is the same word found in Jn 3:16 describing Jesus — above all, this term refers to uniqueness. **Isaac** See Ge 17:17–19. **Moriah** This term occurs only here and in 2Ch 3:1, where it is described as a mountain. Second Chronicles 3:1 notes that Mount Moriah is where Yahweh appeared to David on the threshing floor of Ornan (Araunah) the Jebusite — and in turn, where Solomon built the temple. See the infographic "A Threshing Floor" on p. 497; see the infographic "Ancient Altars" on p. 128.
22:5 I and the boy go over there Abraham tells his servants that not only would he and Isaac go and worship (to sacrifice Isaac, unbeknownst to all but Abraham), but both of them would return. This may mean Abraham was concealing the true purpose of the trip from Isaac. However, the NT book of Hebrews takes this as a statement of Abraham's faith — that God would raise Isaac from the dead (Heb 11:17–19).

him on the altar, on top of the wood. ¹⁰Then he reached out his hand and took the knife to slay his son. ¹¹But the angel of the LORD called out to him from heaven, "Abraham! Abraham!"

"Here I am," he replied.

¹²"Do not lay a hand on the boy," he said. "Do not do anything to him. Now I know that you fear God, because you have not withheld from me your son, your only son."

¹³Abraham looked up and there in a thicket he saw a ram[a] caught by its horns. He went over and took the ram and sacrificed it as a burnt offering instead of his son. ¹⁴So Abraham called that place The LORD Will Provide. And to this day it is said, "On the mountain of the LORD it will be provided."

¹⁵The angel of the LORD called to Abraham from heaven a second time ¹⁶and said, "I swear by myself, declares the LORD, that because you have done this and have not withheld your son, your only son, ¹⁷I will surely bless you and make your descendants as numerous as the stars in the sky and as the sand on the seashore. Your descendants will take possession of the cities of their enemies, ¹⁸and through your offspring[b] all nations on earth will be blessed,[c] because you have obeyed me."

¹⁹Then Abraham returned to his servants, and they set off together for Beersheba. And Abraham stayed in Beersheba.

Nahor's Sons

²⁰Some time later Abraham was told, "Milkah is also a mother; she has borne sons to your brother Nahor: ²¹Uz the firstborn, Buz his brother, Kemuel (the father of Aram), ²²Kesed, Hazo, Pildash, Jidlaph and Bethuel." ²³Bethuel became the father of Rebekah. Milkah bore these eight sons to Abraham's brother Nahor. ²⁴His concubine, whose name was Reumah, also had sons: Tebah, Gaham, Tahash and Maakah.

The Death of Sarah

23 Sarah lived to be a hundred and twenty-seven years old. ²She died at Kiriath Arba (that is, Hebron) in the land of Canaan, and Abraham went to mourn for Sarah and to weep over her.

³Then Abraham rose from beside his dead wife and spoke to the Hittites.[d] He said, ⁴"I am a foreigner and stranger among you. Sell me some property for a burial site here so I can bury my dead."

⁵The Hittites replied to Abraham, ⁶"Sir, listen to us. You are a mighty prince among us. Bury your dead in the choicest of our tombs. None of us will refuse you his tomb for burying your dead."

⁷Then Abraham rose and bowed down before the people of the land, the Hittites. ⁸He said to them, "If you are willing to let me bury my dead, then listen to me and intercede with Ephron son of Zohar on my behalf ⁹so he will sell me the cave of Machpelah, which belongs to him and is at the end of his field. Ask him to sell it to me for the full price as a burial site among you."

¹⁰Ephron the Hittite was sitting among his people and he replied to Abraham in the hearing of all the Hittites who had come to the gate of his city. ¹¹"No, my lord," he said. "Listen to me; I give[e] you the field, and I give[e] you the cave that is in it. I give[e] it to you in the presence of my people. Bury your dead."

---

[a] 13 Many manuscripts of the Masoretic Text, Samaritan Pentateuch, Septuagint and Syriac; most manuscripts of the Masoretic Text *a ram behind him*   [b] 18 Or *seed*   [c] 18 Or *and all nations on earth will use the name of your offspring in blessings* (see 48:20)   [d] 3 Or *the descendants of Heth*; also in verses 5, 7, 10, 16, 18 and 20   [e] 11 Or *sell*

22:11 the angel of the LORD See note on Ge 16:7.
22:12 Now I know The identity between the angel and God is blurred. The angel speaks in the first person as God, but also refers to God in the third person. See the table "Angels in the Bible" on p. 2120.
22:17 the stars in the sky See 15:5 and note.

22:20–24 Chapter 22 concludes with an account of the offspring of Abraham's brother, Nahor, who has not been mentioned since Abraham was introduced (11:29). The genealogy provides a transition to the account of Isaac, as it mentions his future wife, Rebekah (v. 23; compare 24:15–16).

23:1–20 The account of Sarah's death focuses on Abraham's efforts to obtain her burial site. The Hittites (see v. 3 and note) offer their best tombs to Abraham (v. 6). Abraham chooses the cave of Machpelah (v. 9), purchases it and the surrounding area (vv. 10–18), and buries Sarah (vv. 19–20). Later Abraham himself will be buried here, as will many of his descendants.

23:1 Sarah See 11:29; 17:15 and note.
23:2 Kiriath Arba This place—which may be literally rendered "city of Arba"—was later named Hebron (Jdg 1:10). Hebron is also mentioned by name in Ge 13:18. Genesis uses both names here in 23:2 to reflect the updating of the name—a later editor may have added this note for clarity.

23:3 the Hittites There is no archeological evidence supporting a Hittite presence in Canaan (south of Kadesh) at this time. The Hittite Empire never reached as far south as Hebron. This apparent disagreement between the OT and extra-Biblical source material is compounded by the fact that the Hittites in the patriarchal narratives have Semitic names, when Hittite is not a Semitic language (23:8; 26:34; 36:2). However, the term Hittite was used of at least four distinct ethnic groups, and the Hittites of the patriarchal narratives in Genesis can be distinguished from the Hittites of the Hittite Empire: Neo-Assyrian and neo-Babylonian texts use the term "Hatti" for the combined area of Syria-Palestine. See note on 10:15.
23:6 mighty prince This title is likely honorific, having no religious or governing significance for the Hittites.
23:10 all the Hittites who had come to the gate This could describe an assembly of free (non-slave) citizens assembled for a vote.

¹²Again Abraham bowed down before the people of the land ¹³and he said to Ephron in their hearing, "Listen to me, if you will. I will pay the price of the field. Accept it from me so I can bury my dead there."

¹⁴Ephron answered Abraham, ¹⁵"Listen to me, my lord; the land is worth four hundred shekels[a] of silver, but what is that between you and me? Bury your dead."

¹⁶Abraham agreed to Ephron's terms and weighed out for him the price he had named in the hearing of the Hittites: four hundred shekels of silver, according to the weight current among the merchants.

¹⁷So Ephron's field in Machpelah near Mamre — both the field and the cave in it, and all the trees within the borders of the field — was deeded ¹⁸to Abraham as his property in the presence of all the Hittites who had come to the gate of the city. ¹⁹Afterward Abraham buried his wife Sarah in the cave in the field of Machpelah near Mamre (which is at Hebron) in the land of Canaan. ²⁰So the field and the cave in it were deeded to Abraham by the Hittites as a burial site.

Isaac and Rebekah

24 Abraham was now very old, and the LORD had blessed him in every way. ²He said to the senior servant in his household, the one in charge of all that he had, "Put your hand under my thigh. ³I want you to swear by the LORD, the God of heaven and the God of earth, that you will not get a wife for my son from the daughters of the Canaanites, among whom I am living, ⁴but will go to my country and my own relatives and get a wife for my son Isaac."

⁵The servant asked him, "What if the woman is unwilling to come back with me to this land? Shall I then take your son back to the country you came from?"

⁶"Make sure that you do not take my son back there," Abraham said. ⁷"The LORD, the God of heaven, who brought me out of my father's household and my native land and who spoke to me and promised me on oath, saying, 'To your offspring[b] I will give this land' — he will send his angel before you so that you can get a wife for my son from there. ⁸If the woman is unwilling to come back with you, then you will be released from this oath of mine. Only do not take my son back there." ⁹So the servant put his hand under the thigh of his master Abraham and swore an oath to him concerning this matter.

¹⁰Then the servant left, taking with him ten of his master's camels loaded with all kinds of good things from his master. He set out for Aram Naharaim[c] and made his way to the town of Nahor. ¹¹He had the camels kneel down near the well outside the town; it was toward evening, the time the women go out to draw water.

¹²Then he prayed, "LORD, God of my master Abraham, make me successful today, and show

---

[a] 15 That is, about 10 pounds or about 4.6 kilograms
[b] 7 Or seed   [c] 10 That is, Northwest Mesopotamia

23:15 four hundred shekels of silver This may have been a standard price — three texts from Ugarit (ancient Syria) give this amount as the purchase price for a piece of real estate.

23:16 according to the weight current among the merchants The shekel was not a coin at this time, but a unit of weight.

24:1–67 Abraham sends his servant back to his homeland to find a wife for Isaac, warning him not to take Isaac with him (vv. 1–9). The servant encounters Rebekah, the daughter of Abraham's nephew (his great niece; v. 15; compare 22:20–23). After explaining his mission to Rebekah's brother, Laban (vv. 34–49), Laban and Rebekah's father agree that Rebekah should marry Isaac (vv. 50–51). Rebekah agrees and returns with Abraham's servant (vv. 57–67).

24:2 Put your hand under my thigh Swearing oaths typically involved symbolic acts in the ancient Near East. See note on 47:29.

24:3 Canaanites This refers generally to all the inhabitants of Canaan, regardless of individual ethnicity (see 10:19).

24:4 my country and my own relatives In response to this command, the servant does not go to Ur where Abraham is originally from (see note on 11:28). Instead, he goes across the Euphrates (see v. 10) to the country of Nahor, Abraham's brother (see 11:27,29; compare 27:43).

24:5–8 The servant asks what to do if the woman is unwilling — perhaps Isaac should be taken across the river to Ur, where Abraham is originally from. Abraham refuses, letting the servant know that God would lead him to a woman via his angel and that Isaac should not leave the promised land for Abraham's homeland. Abraham nevertheless considers her refusal a possibility, so he informs the servant that his obligation will end once the woman is found and the marriage is offered.

24:6 you do not take my son back there Although the people to whom the servant was sent were Abraham's kin, Abraham did not want the son of Yahweh's covenant promises to leave the promised land.

24:7 send his angel before you Abraham's theology allowed for a refusal on the part of the woman whom God, through his angel, would select.

24:10 Aram Naharaim The Hebrew phrase used here *aram naharayim* does not occur anywhere else in the OT, though it is paralleled by Paddan Aram in 25:20. It is sometimes translated as Mesopotamia because it can be understood as "Aram of the rivers" or "Aram, the land between two rivers" and because the Septuagint (the ancient Greek translation of the OT) translates it as *mesopotamia* (Mesopotamia). **town of Nahor** A city associated with either (or both) Abraham's brother Nahor or Abraham's grandfather who had the same name, Nahor (see 11:24–27).

24:11 the time the women go out to draw water After the normal workday and its requirements have ended, in preparation for the evening meal.

kindness to my master Abraham. [13]See, I am standing beside this spring, and the daughters of the townspeople are coming out to draw water. [14]May it be that when I say to a young woman, 'Please let down your jar that I may have a drink,' and she says, 'Drink, and I'll water your camels too'—let her be the one you have chosen for your servant Isaac. By this I will know that you have shown kindness to my master."

[15]Before he had finished praying, Rebekah came out with her jar on her shoulder. She was the daughter of Bethuel son of Milkah, who was the wife of Abraham's brother Nahor. [16]The woman was very beautiful, a virgin; no man had ever slept with her. She went down to the spring, filled her jar and came up again.

[17]The servant hurried to meet her and said, "Please give me a little water from your jar."

[18]"Drink, my lord," she said, and quickly lowered the jar to her hands and gave him a drink.

[19]After she had given him a drink, she said, "I'll draw water for your camels too, until they have had enough to drink." [20]So she quickly emptied her jar into the trough, ran back to the well to draw more water, and drew enough for all his camels. [21]Without saying a word, the man watched her closely to learn whether or not the LORD had made his journey successful.

[22]When the camels had finished drinking, the man took out a gold nose ring weighing a beka[a] and two gold bracelets weighing ten shekels.[b] [23]Then he asked, "Whose daughter are you? Please tell me, is there room in your father's house for us to spend the night?"

[24]She answered him, "I am the daughter of Bethuel, the son that Milkah bore to Nahor." [25]And she added, "We have plenty of straw and fodder, as well as room for you to spend the night."

[26]Then the man bowed down and worshiped the LORD, [27]saying, "Praise be to the LORD, the God of my master Abraham, who has not abandoned his kindness and faithfulness to my master. As for me, the LORD has led me on the journey to the house of my master's relatives."

[28]The young woman ran and told her mother's household about these things. [29]Now Rebekah had a brother named Laban, and he hurried out to the man at the spring. [30]As soon as he had seen the nose ring, and the bracelets on his sister's arms,

and had heard Rebekah tell what the man said to her, he went out to the man and found him standing by the camels near the spring. [31]"Come, you who are blessed by the LORD," he said. "Why are you standing out here? I have prepared the house and a place for the camels."

[32]So the man went to the house, and the camels were unloaded. Straw and fodder were brought for the camels, and water for him and his men to wash their feet. [33]Then food was set before him, but he said, "I will not eat until I have told you what I have to say."

"Then tell us," Laban said.

[34]So he said, "I am Abraham's servant. [35]The LORD has blessed my master abundantly, and he has become wealthy. He has given him sheep and cattle, silver and gold, male and female servants, and camels and donkeys. [36]My master's wife Sarah has borne him a son in her old age, and he has given him everything he owns. [37]And my master made me swear an oath, and said, 'You must not get a wife for my son from the daughters of the Canaanites, in whose land I live, [38]but go to my father's family and to my own clan, and get a wife for my son.'

[39]"Then I asked my master, 'What if the woman will not come back with me?'

[40]"He replied, 'The LORD, before whom I have walked faithfully, will send his angel with you and make your journey a success, so that you can get a wife for my son from my own clan and from my father's family. [41]You will be released from my oath if, when you go to my clan, they refuse to give her to you—then you will be released from my oath.'

[42]"When I came to the spring today, I said, 'LORD, God of my master Abraham, if you will, please grant success to the journey on which I have come. [43]See, I am standing beside this spring. If a young woman comes out to draw water and I say to her, "Please let me drink a little water from your jar," [44]and if she says to me, "Drink, and I'll draw water for your camels too," let her be the one the LORD has chosen for my master's son.'

[45]"Before I finished praying in my heart, Rebekah came out, with her jar on her shoulder. She went down to the spring and drew water, and I said to her, 'Please give me a drink.'

---

[a] 22 That is, about 1/5 ounce or about 5.7 grams   [b] 22 That is, about 4 ounces or about 115 grams

---

24:15 the daughter of Bethuel son of Milkah Rebekah's genealogy is provided to show that her grandmother was the wife of Nahor (Abraham's brother) and not a concubine (Ge 11:29). Rebekah, as Bethuel's daughter, is Isaac's first cousin once removed.
24:26 worshiped the LORD Rebekah's response is an answer to the prayer of Abraham's servant (v. 24). It reveals that she is related to Abraham and fits the request that Abraham made him swear (vv. 2–4; compare note on 24:15).

24:29–33 Rebekah informs her family about the visitor, Abraham's servant.

24:29 Laban Rebekah's brother and son of Bethuel (see note on v. 50). Laban is Abraham's great nephew and like Rebekah, Isaac's first cousin once removed.

24:34–48 Abraham's servant recounts the story of his journey in precise detail. This type of repetition is common in literature that originated as oral tradition.

⁴⁶"She quickly lowered her jar from her shoulder and said, 'Drink, and I'll water your camels too.' So I drank, and she watered the camels also. ⁴⁷"I asked her, 'Whose daughter are you?'

"She said, 'The daughter of Bethuel son of Nahor, whom Milkah bore to him.'

"Then I put the ring in her nose and the bracelets on her arms, ⁴⁸and I bowed down and worshiped the Lord. I praised the Lord, the God of my master Abraham, who had led me on the right road to get the granddaughter of my master's brother for his son. ⁴⁹Now if you will show kindness and faithfulness to my master, tell me; and if not, tell me, so I may know which way to turn."

⁵⁰Laban and Bethuel answered, "This is from the Lord; we can say nothing to you one way or the other. ⁵¹Here is Rebekah; take her and go, and let her become the wife of your master's son, as the Lord has directed."

⁵²When Abraham's servant heard what they said, he bowed down to the ground before the Lord. ⁵³Then the servant brought out gold and silver jewelry and articles of clothing and gave them to Rebekah; he also gave costly gifts to her brother and to her mother. ⁵⁴Then he and the men who were with him ate and drank and spent the night there.

When they got up the next morning, he said, "Send me on my way to my master."

⁵⁵But her brother and her mother replied, "Let the young woman remain with us ten days or so; then youᵃ may go."

⁵⁶But he said to them, "Do not detain me, now that the Lord has granted success to my journey. Send me on my way so I may go to my master."

⁵⁷Then they said, "Let's call the young woman and ask her about it." ⁵⁸So they called Rebekah and asked her, "Will you go with this man?"

"I will go," she said.

⁵⁹So they sent their sister Rebekah on her way, along with her nurse and Abraham's servant and his men. ⁶⁰And they blessed Rebekah and said to her,

"Our sister, may you increase
    to thousands upon thousands;
may your offspring possess
    the cities of their enemies."

⁶¹Then Rebekah and her attendants got ready and mounted the camels and went back with the man. So the servant took Rebekah and left.

⁶²Now Isaac had come from Beer Lahai Roi, for he was living in the Negev. ⁶³He went out to the field one evening to meditate,ᵇ and as he looked up, he saw camels approaching. ⁶⁴Rebekah also looked up and saw Isaac. She got down from her camel ⁶⁵and asked the servant, "Who is that man in the field coming to meet us?"

"He is my master," the servant answered. So she took her veil and covered herself.

⁶⁶Then the servant told Isaac all he had done. ⁶⁷Isaac brought her into the tent of his mother Sarah, and he married Rebekah. So she became his wife, and he loved her; and Isaac was comforted after his mother's death.

The Death of Abraham

25:1-4pp — 1Ch 1:32-33

25 Abraham had taken another wife, whose name was Keturah. ²She bore him Zimran, Jokshan, Medan, Midian, Ishbak and Shuah.

ᵃ 55 Or *she*   ᵇ 63 The meaning of the Hebrew for this word is uncertain.

24:50 Laban and Bethuel answered In the narrative that follows (and all other OT references to it), Rebekah's father, Bethuel, says and does nothing in negotiations regarding Rebekah. Laban, her brother, handles everything—and his name appears before her father's when the opposite is expected. Laban clearly has guardianship over his sister. When Rebekah goes to tell her family about the man she has met, she informs her mother's household rather than her father's (v. 28).

24:53 costly gifts It is unclear whether these gifts are part of a bride price (called elsewhere in Hebrew *mohar*; see note on Ex 22:16) or are meant to show generosity.

24:55 ten days or so This may be a colloquialism for a long period of time—perhaps longer than a year. Ten days alone would not be a sufficient reason for the servant to protest the imposition.

24:62 Beer Lahai Roi The well where Hagar had a divine encounter (see Ge 16:14 and note).

24:65 my master The man Rebekah asked about is Isaac. Abraham's servant refers to Isaac as his master because Isaac will inherit all of Abraham's wealth, including his servants (compare to 25:5). **took her veil** The story of the Egyptians witnessing Sarah's beauty seems to indicate that Israelite women did not normally veil themselves (12:14). Veiling was, however, part of the marriage ceremony (29:23–25).

25:1–18 The Abraham narrative concludes with two genealogies (see note on 5:1) bracketing the account of his death (vv. 7–11). The first genealogy (vv. 1–6) lists the sons Abraham has with another wife, Keturah. The second genealogy (vv. 12–18) lists the descendants of Ishmael, Abraham's son through Hagar (his wife Sarah's servant). The names in these genealogies, like earlier genealogies in Genesis, seem to correspond to people groups and places. However, of the names in the list, only Midian and Ishbak can be identified with places or people groups with certainty.

25:1 had taken another wife Earlier Abraham's age was once considered an obstacle to having children (Ge 17:17; compare Heb 11:11–12); now he takes another wife and has six more children. Genesis 25:1–6 may be out of chronological sequence. First Chronicles 1:32, which refers to Keturah as a concubine, favors this suggestion. Compare note on 25:12–15.

25:2 Midian The term here refers to the land of Midian, which was in northwest Arabia, east of the Gulf of Aqaba. As a clan (or confederacy of clans), the Midianites were located in a widespread area from Midian to the northern borders of Egypt. Midianite traders purchased Joseph from his brothers (Ge 37:25,28; compare Jdg 8:24)

³Jokshan was the father of Sheba and Dedan; the descendants of Dedan were the Ashurites, the Letushites and the Leummites. ⁴The sons of Midian were Ephah, Epher, Hanok, Abida and Eldaah. All these were descendants of Keturah.

⁵Abraham left everything he owned to Isaac. ⁶But while he was still living, he gave gifts to the sons of his concubines and sent them away from his son Isaac to the land of the east.

⁷Abraham lived a hundred and seventy-five years. ⁸Then Abraham breathed his last and died at a good old age, an old man and full of years; and he was gathered to his people. ⁹His sons Isaac and Ishmael buried him in the cave of Machpelah near Mamre, in the field of Ephron son of Zohar the Hittite, ¹⁰the field Abraham had bought from the Hittites.ᵃ There Abraham was buried with his wife Sarah. ¹¹After Abraham's death, God blessed his son Isaac, who then lived near Beer Lahai Roi.

Ishmael's Sons

25:12-16pp — 1Ch 1:29-31

¹²This is the account of the family line of Abraham's son Ishmael, whom Sarah's slave, Hagar the Egyptian, bore to Abraham.

¹³These are the names of the sons of Ishmael, listed in the order of their birth: Nebaioth the firstborn of Ishmael, Kedar, Adbeel, Mibsam, ¹⁴Mishma, Dumah, Massa, ¹⁵Hadad, Tema, Jetur, Naphish and Kedemah. ¹⁶These were the sons of Ishmael, and these are the names of the twelve tribal rulers according to their settlements and camps. ¹⁷Ishmael lived a hundred and thirty-seven years. He breathed his last and died, and he was gathered to his people. ¹⁸His descendants settled in the area from Havilah to Shur, near the eastern border of Egypt, as you go toward Ashur. And they lived in hostility towardᵇ all the tribes related to them.

Jacob and Esau

¹⁹This is the account of the family line of Abraham's son Isaac.

Abraham became the father of Isaac, ²⁰and Isaac was forty years old when he married Rebekah daughter of Bethuel the Aramean from Paddan Aramᶜ and sister of Laban the Aramean.

²¹Isaac prayed to the LORD on behalf of his wife, because she was childless. The LORD answered his prayer, and his wife Rebekah became pregnant. ²²The babies jostled each other within her, and she said, "Why is this happening to me?" So she went to inquire of the LORD.

ᵃ 10 Or the descendants of Heth   ᵇ 18 Or lived to the east of
ᶜ 20 That is, Northwest Mesopotamia

and sold him to Ishmaelites (Ge 37:28). **Ishbak** The descendants of Ishbak are likely the north Syrian tribe of Iasbuq mentioned in Assyrian sources.

25:3 Ashurites Elsewhere in the OT, this term refers to Assyrians. However, based on chronology (see v. 18, where Assyria is already referred to as a region) as well as ancient Near Eastern sources for the origin of Assyria, it seems that Assyrians are not being referenced here (compare Nu 24:22,24). As is the case with other people terms (e.g., Hittites; see Ge 23:3 and note), another group of people was likely known by this term.

25:6 sent them away from his son Abraham wanted to ensure that the promised line of Isaac through Sarah would be maintained. See note on 21:11.

25:8 gathered to his people This Hebrew phrase is used only in the Pentateuch. It likely refers to death itself, with the presumption of being reunited in the afterlife with family or ancestors.

25:11 Beer Lahai Roi This refers to the well where Hagar had a divine encounter. See 16:14 and note.

25:12–15 Some names in this passage are distinguished by lineage as from Keturah (see vv. 1–4) or Ishmael but such distinctions are not retained in other passages. For example, in Isa 60:6–7, Midian, Ephah and Sheba (from Keturah) are listed beside Kedar and Nebaioth (who are listed as Ishmael's descendants in Ge 25:13). This intermingling in other passages may suggest fluid tribal confederations and allegiances. It also forms a backdrop for later Israelite history, where the people of Abraham through Isaac and Jacob are opposed to those from Abraham by concubines. Keturah, though labeled as a wife of Abraham, is affiliated as a concubine via the connections with Ishmael's line and is actually labeled as a concubine elsewhere (1Ch 1:32). The same problem arises from within the nuclear family of Isaac via the line of Esau — with Jacob's and Esau's lines being enemies.

25:13 Ishmael See note on Ge 16:11.

25:19–26 The birth of Esau and Jacob is a miraculous event. Isaac prays that Rebekah, who is barren, will conceive (see v. 21). Once pregnant, she inquires of God when the children struggle within her. God's answer reveals the future of both sons (v. 23).

25:20 Aramean Genesis seems to connect this term to Aram the son of Kemuel, who was Bethuel's brother thus making Aram Bethuel's nephew (22:20–21). This term refers to western Semitic tribes in the region of what the Hebrew text refers to as *aram naharayim* (see 24:10 and note) and Paddan Aram. According to Dt 26:5, Israelite farmers were to declare that they were descended from a wandering Aramean (Syrian) when they brought their firstfruits offering. **Paddan Aram** Either another name for what the Hebrew text calls *aram naharayim* (see Ge 24:10 and note) or a town in that region (see Hos 12:12). According to Ge 25:11, Isaac and Rebekah were living in Beer Lahai Roi, the place where Hagar encountered the Angel of Yahweh (16:7–14). Rebekah may have been aware of this, as places of divine encounter often became sacred sites for worship and, perhaps, contact with the divine (see 12:6–7; 13:18).

²³The Lord said to her,

"Two nations are in your womb,
    and two peoples from within you will be
        separated;
one people will be stronger than the other,
    and the older will serve the younger."

²⁴When the time came for her to give birth, there were twin boys in her womb. ²⁵The first to come out was red, and his whole body was like a hairy garment; so they named him Esau.ᵃ ²⁶After this, his brother came out, with his hand grasping Esau's heel; so he was named Jacob.ᵇ Isaac was sixty years old when Rebekah gave birth to them.

²⁷The boys grew up, and Esau became a skillful hunter, a man of the open country, while Jacob was content to stay at home among the tents. ²⁸Isaac, who had a taste for wild game, loved Esau, but Rebekah loved Jacob.

²⁹Once when Jacob was cooking some stew, Esau came in from the open country, famished. ³⁰He said to Jacob, "Quick, let me have some of that red stew! I'm famished!" (That is why he was also called Edom.ᶜ)

³¹Jacob replied, "First sell me your birthright."

³²"Look, I am about to die," Esau said. "What good is the birthright to me?"

³³But Jacob said, "Swear to me first." So he swore an oath to him, selling his birthright to Jacob.

³⁴Then Jacob gave Esau some bread and some lentil stew. He ate and drank, and then got up and left.

So Esau despised his birthright.

Isaac and Abimelek

26:1-11Ref — Ge 12:10-20; 20:1-18

26 Now there was a famine in the land — besides the previous famine in Abraham's time — and Isaac went to Abimelek king of the Philistines in Gerar. ²The Lord appeared to Isaac and said, "Do not go down to Egypt; live in the land where I tell you to live. ³Stay in this land for a while, and I will be with you and will bless you. For to you and your descendants I will give all these lands and will confirm the oath I swore to your father Abraham. ⁴I will make your descendants as numerous as the stars in the sky and will give them all these lands, and through your offspringᵈ all nations on earth will be blessed,ᵉ ⁵because Abraham obeyed me and did everything I required

---

ᵃ 25 *Esau* may mean *hairy*.   ᵇ 26 *Jacob* means *he grasps the heel*, a Hebrew idiom for *he deceives*.   ᶜ 30 *Edom* means *red*.   ᵈ 4 Or *seed*   ᵉ 4 Or *and all nations on earth will use the name of your offspring in blessings* (see 48:20)

25:23 older will serve the younger The opposite of the norm for male birth in patriarchal culture.

25:25 red The Hebrew word used here, *admoni*, is used elsewhere only of David (1Sa 16:12; 17:42). It may refer to skin or hair color. *Admoni* and the red food Esau requests from Jacob when giving up his birthright (called in Hebrew *adom*) is connected by wordplay to the Hebrew word *edom* (Edom) — the name of the nation identified with the descendants of Esau (compare Nu 20; 1Sa 14:47; 2Ki 8:22; Ob 11–21). See the people diagram "Esau's Family Tree" on p. 70. **hairy** The Hebrew word used here, *se'ar*, sounds similar to the name Esau and also Seir, the territory of the Edomites (Ge 32:3; 36:8; Dt 2:5).

25:26 hand grasping Esau's heel This seems to be indicative of the prophecy that the older (Esau) would serve the younger (see Hos 12:3). **so he was named Jacob** This is wordplay: In Hebrew, the name Jacob is *ya'aqov*, while the word for "heel" is *aqev*. The name *ya'aqov* is actually derived from the Hebrew word *aqav*, meaning "to protect." *Ya'aqov* is likely an abbreviated version of the name *ya'aqov-el*, meaning "May God protect." Compare Ge 27:36 and note. See the table "Symbolic Names of People in Hebrew" on p. 1388.

25:27–34 The section describes Jacob and Esau's struggle for tribal preeminence. The story (and others that follow) shows Jacob to be a schemer and manipulator as he gains the birthright of the firstborn from Esau. He will later deprive his eldest son (Reuben) of his birthright (49:3–4) and prefer Joseph's younger son over the firstborn in his blessing (48:13). The Mosaic Law will later forbid a father with multiple wives from favoring a younger son merely because he comes from a preferred wife (Dt 21:15–17).

25:30 red The Hebrew word used here, *adom*, echoes the Hebrew word *admoni*, which was employed to describe Esau's appearance at birth (see note on Ge 25:25).

25:31 birthright The right of first inheritance, according to which the firstborn son would receive a double inheritance (Dt 21:17).

25:33 swore In ancient Near Eastern culture, swearing an oath was an irrevocable act.

26:1–5 Abraham had fled to Egypt when he experienced famine (see Ge 12:10–20 and note). Here God appears to Isaac and tells him not to go to Egypt (v. 2). Instead, Isaac should go elsewhere within the land God has promised (v. 3). After giving Isaac this instruction, God repeats the covenant promises he made to Abraham (vv. 4–5). The events of vv. 1–33 may have taken place before the birth of Jacob and Esau (ch. 25), since Isaac's lie about Rebekah not being his wife (v. 7) would likely not have worked otherwise.

26:1 Abimelek This name could be a title and is fairly common, thus this is not necessarily the exact same king Abraham earlier encountered (ch. 20), although it could be. See note on 21:32; compare note on 20:2.

FAMINES IN GENESIS	
Abram and Sarai Travel to Egypt	Ge 12:10
Isaac and Family Settle in Gerar	Ge 26:1
Joseph's Family Follows Him to Egypt	Ge 41:53—42:5

26:2 appeared This could indicate that God appeared in visible form to Isaac, as he did with Abraham at times (ch. 18; see note on 12:7). God coming to Isaac confirms his status as the recipient of the covenant promises given to his father (see 12:1–3; 15). See the table "Old Testament Theophanies" on p. 924.

26:4 stars in the sky See note on 15:5.

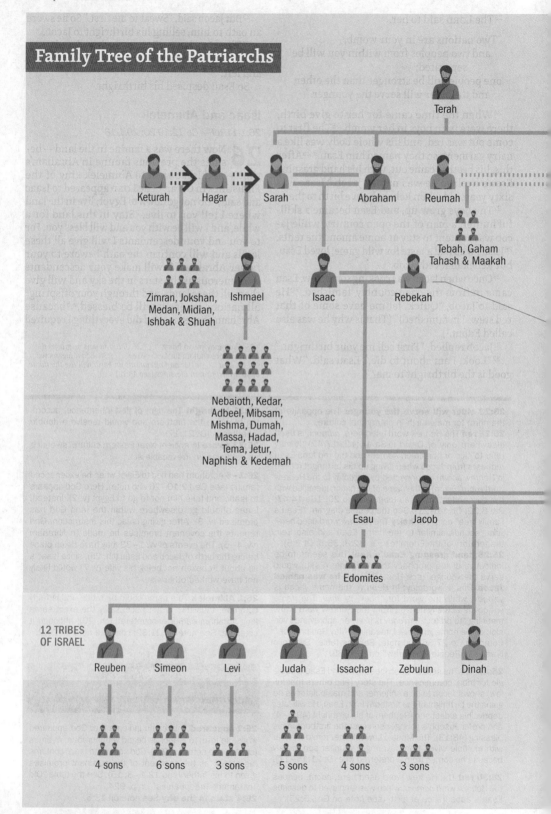

Family Tree of the Patriarchs

Terah

Keturah Hagar Sarah Abraham Reumah

Tebah, Gaham
Tahash & Maakah

Zimran, Jokshan,
Medan, Midian,
Ishbak & Shuah

Ishmael Isaac Rebekah

Nebaioth, Kedar,
Adbeel, Mibsam,
Mishma, Dumah,
Massa, Hadad,
Tema, Jetur,
Naphish & Kedemah

Esau Jacob

Edomites

12 TRIBES
OF ISRAEL

Reuben Simeon Levi Judah Issachar Zebulun Dinah

4 sons 6 sons 3 sons 5 sons 4 sons 3 sons

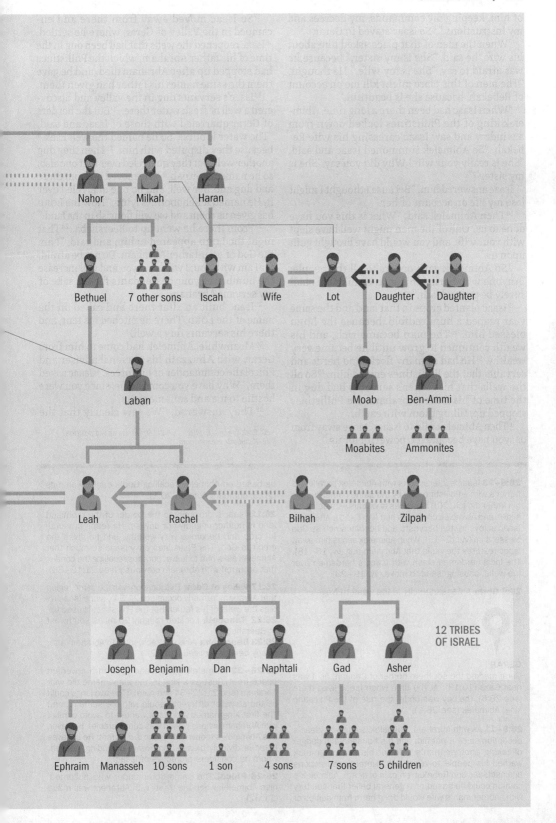

Nahor Milkah Haran

Bethuel 7 other sons Iscah Wife Lot Daughter Daughter

Laban Moab Ben-Ammi

Moabites Ammonites

Leah Rachel Bilhah Zilpah

12 TRIBES
OF ISRAEL

Joseph Benjamin Dan Naphtali Gad Asher

Ephraim Manasseh 10 sons 1 son 4 sons 7 sons 5 children

of him, keeping my commands, my decrees and my instructions." ⁶So Isaac stayed in Gerar.

⁷When the men of that place asked him about his wife, he said, "She is my sister," because he was afraid to say, "She is my wife." He thought, "The men of this place might kill me on account of Rebekah, because she is beautiful."

⁸When Isaac had been there a long time, Abimelek king of the Philistines looked down from a window and saw Isaac caressing his wife Rebekah. ⁹So Abimelek summoned Isaac and said, "She is really your wife! Why did you say, 'She is my sister'?"

Isaac answered him, "Because I thought I might lose my life on account of her."

¹⁰Then Abimelek said, "What is this you have done to us? One of the men might well have slept with your wife, and you would have brought guilt upon us."

¹¹So Abimelek gave orders to all the people: "Anyone who harms this man or his wife shall surely be put to death."

¹²Isaac planted crops in that land and the same year reaped a hundredfold, because the Lord blessed him. ¹³The man became rich, and his wealth continued to grow until he became very wealthy. ¹⁴He had so many flocks and herds and servants that the Philistines envied him. ¹⁵So all the wells that his father's servants had dug in the time of his father Abraham, the Philistines stopped up, filling them with earth.

¹⁶Then Abimelek said to Isaac, "Move away from us; you have become too powerful for us."

¹⁷So Isaac moved away from there and encamped in the Valley of Gerar, where he settled. ¹⁸Isaac reopened the wells that had been dug in the time of his father Abraham, which the Philistines had stopped up after Abraham died, and he gave them the same names his father had given them.

¹⁹Isaac's servants dug in the valley and discovered a well of fresh water there. ²⁰But the herders of Gerar quarreled with those of Isaac and said, "The water is ours!" So he named the well Esek,ᵃ because they disputed with him. ²¹Then they dug another well, but they quarreled over that one also; so he named it Sitnah.ᵇ ²²He moved on from there and dug another well, and no one quarreled over it. He named it Rehoboth,ᶜ saying, "Now the Lord has given us room and we will flourish in the land."

²³From there he went up to Beersheba. ²⁴That night the Lord appeared to him and said, "I am the God of your father Abraham. Do not be afraid, for I am with you; I will bless you and will increase the number of your descendants for the sake of my servant Abraham."

²⁵Isaac built an altar there and called on the name of the Lord. There he pitched his tent, and there his servants dug a well.

²⁶Meanwhile, Abimelek had come to him from Gerar, with Ahuzzath his personal adviser and Phicol the commander of his forces. ²⁷Isaac asked them, "Why have you come to me, since you were hostile to me and sent me away?"

²⁸They answered, "We saw clearly that the

ᵃ 20 Esek means dispute.   ᵇ 21 Sitnah means opposition.
ᶜ 22 Rehoboth means room.

26:6–23 Isaac's interactions with Abimelek parallel his father's with a Philistine king by the same name. Just as his father did (ch. 20), Isaac lies about his wife being his sister, and Abimelek confronts him (vv. 7–11). After this, Isaac enjoys fruitful harvests and becomes rich as God blesses him (vv. 12–15). When Abimelek sends him away, Isaac restores the wells that Abraham dug (vv. 16–18). The local herdsmen clash with Isaac's herdsmen over the wells, causing Isaac to move (vv. 19–23).

26:6 Gerar A Canaanite city in the western Negev.

Genesis 26:6

GERAR
Gerar marked the southern border of Canaan, as it was near Gaza (10:19). At the time when Isaac lived there (see 26:6), the city was under the rule of the Philistine king, Abimelek (see 26:1).

26:9–11 As with Abraham, Abimelek is angry at Isaac's deception since it put him and his household in danger of taking another man's wife for his own. Abimelek warned his people to avoid any ill-intentioned actions against Isaac and Rebekah on pain of death. Abimelek's caution could be based on a general belief that adultery with another man's wife would bring harm from deities or

be based on Abimelek recalling God's earlier warnings (20:3; compare note on 26:1).

26:12 Isaac's proximity to the border of the promised land is neither ungodly nor unwise. He reaps a bountiful crop and becomes very wealthy, and he gives the credit to God. The Philistines envy Isaac so much that Abimelek asks him to leave, perhaps recalling the conflict that occurred with Abraham previously (see 21:19–30).

26:17 Valley of Gerar This location was the same region that Abraham formerly occupied (21:34), since Isaac redigs the wells of his father that the Philistines closed up.
26:22 Rehoboth Located roughly 20 miles southwest of Beersheba.
26:23 Beersheba Where Isaac went with Abraham after nearly being sacrificed (ch. 22).

26:26–33 Abimelek visits Isaac to form a covenant peace treaty, just as a king by the same name did with Abraham (see 21:22–34 and note). (The two kings could be the same or different people with the same name.) The first king named Abimelek wanted to avoid conflict with Abraham (whose wealth was considerable). However, this Abimelek's motive with Isaac is different: He believes Isaac is divinely blessed and fears offending Yahweh, whom he considers protective of Isaac.

26:26 Phicol The same commander who accompanied Abimelek when the treaty with Abraham was made (21:32).

LORD was with you; so we said, 'There ought to be a sworn agreement between us' — between us and you. Let us make a treaty with you ^{29}that you will do us no harm, just as we did not harm you but always treated you well and sent you away peacefully. And now you are blessed by the LORD."

^{30}Isaac then made a feast for them, and they ate and drank. ^{31}Early the next morning the men swore an oath to each other. Then Isaac sent them on their way, and they went away peacefully.

^{32}That day Isaac's servants came and told him about the well they had dug. They said, "We've found water!" ^{33}He called it Shibah,^{a} and to this day the name of the town has been Beersheba.^{b}

Jacob Takes Esau's Blessing

^{34}When Esau was forty years old, he married Judith daughter of Beeri the Hittite, and also Basemath daughter of Elon the Hittite. ^{35}They were a source of grief to Isaac and Rebekah.

27 When Isaac was old and his eyes were so weak that he could no longer see, he called for Esau his older son and said to him, "My son."

"Here I am," he answered.

^{2}Isaac said, "I am now an old man and don't know the day of my death. ^{3}Now then, get your equipment — your quiver and bow — and go out to the open country to hunt some wild game for me. ^{4}Prepare me the kind of tasty food I like and bring it to me to eat, so that I may give you my blessing before I die."

^{5}Now Rebekah was listening as Isaac spoke to his son Esau. When Esau left for the open country to hunt game and bring it back, ^{6}Rebekah said to her son Jacob, "Look, I overheard your father say to your brother Esau, ^{7}'Bring me some game and prepare me some tasty food to eat, so that I may give you my blessing in the presence of the LORD before I die.' ^{8}Now, my son, listen carefully and do what I tell you: ^{9}Go out to the flock and bring me two choice young goats, so I can prepare some tasty food for your father, just the way he likes it. ^{10}Then take it to your father to eat, so that he may give you his blessing before he dies."

^{11}Jacob said to Rebekah his mother, "But my brother Esau is a hairy man while I have smooth skin. ^{12}What if my father touches me? I would appear to be tricking him and would bring down a curse on myself rather than a blessing."

^{13}His mother said to him, "My son, let the curse fall on me. Just do what I say; go and get them for me."

^{14}So he went and got them and brought them to his mother, and she prepared some tasty food, just the way his father liked it. ^{15}Then Rebekah took the best clothes of Esau her older son, which she had in the house, and put them on her younger son Jacob. ^{16}She also covered his hands and the smooth part of his neck with the goatskins. ^{17}Then she handed to her son Jacob the tasty food and the bread she had made.

^{a} 33 Shibah can mean oath or seven. ^{b} 33 Beersheba can mean well of the oath and well of seven.

26:33 Shibah The name of the well (*shiv'ah* in Hebrew) sounds like the Hebrew term for "oath" (*sheva*). *Sheva* was part of the name Beersheba—the place of this covenant and the earlier one between Abimelek and Abraham (26:23; see 21:31 and note). See the table "Covenants in the Old Testament" on p. 469.

26:34 forty years If Esau is 40, Isaac would now be 100 years old (25:20,26). This indication of age provides context for 27:1, where Isaac is aged and blind. **Judith** Nothing else is known of her; she does not appear in the list of Esau's wives (36:2–3). **the Hittite** See note on 23:3. **Basemath** The Hebrew term used here often is used for a spice. It may indicate involvement with the spice trade.

26:35 They were a source of grief Marrying outside the clan (and therefore the divinely chosen lineage) reflects Esau's indifference to the covenant with Yahweh, as did the surrendering of his birthright (25:29–33).

27:1–29 Earlier Jacob manipulated (or entrapped) Esau into selling him his birthright (see 25:27–34 and note). Now Rebekah conspires with Jacob to place him in a position to receive Isaac's blessing in place of Esau. Hearing that Isaac is preparing to bless Esau, Rebekah instructs Jacob to get some goats for her to prepare (vv. 1–10). When Jacob protests that his father will recognize him because Esau is hairy, she gives him Esau's clothes and puts the goat skins on him (vv. 11–17). The ruse works, and Isaac blesses Jacob instead of the firstborn Esau (vv. 18–29).

27:1 Esau At this point, Isaac is likely unaware that

Esau surrendered his birthright to Jacob (25:31–34). The emphasis on the meal here and in the ensuing narrative suggests that it was not incidental to the blessing. It may have been viewed as a ritual element in the father's passing of blessing to the eldest son.

27:4 give you my blessing Esau has already sold his birthright (*bekhorah* in Hebrew) to Jacob (25:29–34). The blessing (*berakhah* in Hebrew) is closely related but is distinct from the birthright. The birthright specifies property and wealth passed from one generation to the other—this has already been given to Jacob by Esau and such an action would be irrevocable by Isaac (25:27–34). The blessing focuses on future wealth and posterity—most profoundly seen in receiving Yahweh's covenant blessings. Compare note on 27:12.

27:6 I overheard your father say See note on 24:34–48.

27:11 hairy man See note on 25:25.

27:12 curse In the ancient Near East, curses were considered powerful if they had divine support—a real threat in this instance since God chose Isaac as his covenant recipient and the one who would pass on the blessings of the covenant to his heirs (26:1–5). This makes Rebekah's promise that she would take any curse upon herself a serious matter (v. 13)—she would be taking on the opposite of the covenant promises (a lack of divine support).

27:15 best clothes This may refer to special clothing worn for festivals and important ceremonies. This would heighten the credulity of Isaac, since he would naturally assume that only Esau would know what was transpiring.

¹⁸He went to his father and said, "My father."

"Yes, my son," he answered. "Who is it?"

¹⁹Jacob said to his father, "I am Esau your first-born. I have done as you told me. Please sit up and eat some of my game, so that you may give me your blessing."

²⁰Isaac asked his son, "How did you find it so quickly, my son?"

"The LORD your God gave me success," he replied.

²¹Then Isaac said to Jacob, "Come near so I can touch you, my son, to know whether you really are my son Esau or not."

²²Jacob went close to his father Isaac, who touched him and said, "The voice is the voice of Jacob, but the hands are the hands of Esau." ²³He did not recognize him, for his hands were hairy like those of his brother Esau; so he proceeded to bless him. ²⁴"Are you really my son Esau?" he asked.

"I am," he replied.

²⁵Then he said, "My son, bring me some of your game to eat, so that I may give you my blessing."

Jacob brought it to him and he ate; and he brought some wine and he drank. ²⁶Then his father Isaac said to him, "Come here, my son, and kiss me."

²⁷So he went to him and kissed him. When Isaac caught the smell of his clothes, he blessed him and said,

"Ah, the smell of my son
　　is like the smell of a field
　　that the LORD has blessed.
²⁸May God give you heaven's dew
　　and earth's richness —
　　an abundance of grain and new wine.
²⁹May nations serve you
　　and peoples bow down to you.
Be lord over your brothers,
　　and may the sons of your mother bow
　　　　down to you.
May those who curse you be cursed
　　and those who bless you be blessed."

³⁰After Isaac finished blessing him, and Jacob had scarcely left his father's presence, his brother Esau came in from hunting. ³¹He too prepared some tasty food and brought it to his father. Then he said to him, "My father, please sit up and eat some of my game, so that you may give me your blessing."

³²His father Isaac asked him, "Who are you?"

"I am your son," he answered, "your firstborn, Esau."

³³Isaac trembled violently and said, "Who was it, then, that hunted game and brought it to me? I ate it just before you came and I blessed him — and indeed he will be blessed!"

³⁴When Esau heard his father's words, he burst out with a loud and bitter cry and said to his father, "Bless me — me too, my father!"

³⁵But he said, "Your brother came deceitfully and took your blessing."

³⁶Esau said, "Isn't he rightly named Jacob^a? This is the second time he has taken advantage of me: He took my birthright, and now he's taken my blessing!" Then he asked, "Haven't you reserved any blessing for me?"

³⁷Isaac answered Esau, "I have made him lord over you and have made all his relatives his servants, and I have sustained him with grain and new wine. So what can I possibly do for you, my son?"

³⁸Esau said to his father, "Do you have only one blessing, my father? Bless me too, my father!" Then Esau wept aloud.

³⁹His father Isaac answered him,

"Your dwelling will be
　　away from the earth's richness,
　　away from the dew of heaven above.
⁴⁰You will live by the sword
　　and you will serve your brother.
But when you grow restless,
　　you will throw his yoke
　　from off your neck."

---

^a 36 Jacob means he grasps the heel, a Hebrew idiom for he takes advantage of or he deceives.

27:20 LORD your God Jacob uses God's covenant name, yhwh (Yahweh), in his lie and refers to Yahweh as his father's God, not yet his own (see 28:21; 32:22–32).

27:23 he proceeded to bless him Though the deception works, the blessing here is simply permission to continue with the meal. The transfer of the actual promise is yet to occur.

27:28 heaven's dew This metaphor speaks of material abundance in crops and, in turn, the ability to sustain large numbers of domesticated livestock. In a region where rainfall was sparse, dew was vital for sustaining life.

27:29 Be lord over your brothers This wording describes the vast scope of the recipient's predominance. Since Isaac was passing on a divinely ordained covenant relationship with Yahweh, this phrase is appropriate. Compare note on 27:4.

27:30–46 Upon returning from hunting, Esau prepares food and brings it to his father only to find that Isaac has already blessed Jacob (vv. 30–33). Upset that his brother stole his blessing, Esau begs his father to bless him also (vv. 34–38; compare 25:34). Isaac gives Esau a blessing, albeit a rather negative one (vv. 39–40). After this, Esau plots to kill his brother, but Rebekah sends Jacob away to her brother, Laban (vv. 41–45).

27:36 has taken advantage Esau uses the Hebrew word 'aqab here, which is a wordplay on Jacob's name in Hebrew, ya-aqov. Ya-aqov means "to protect," and was given to Jacob as a name because of wordplay with a different word (see note on 25:26). Esau suggests that Jacob's name actually has to do with him being a person who supplants or cheats other people. Jacob is a trickster. **birthright, and now he's taken my blessing** See note on 27:4.

⁴¹Esau held a grudge against Jacob because of the blessing his father had given him. He said to himself, "The days of mourning for my father are near; then I will kill my brother Jacob."

⁴²When Rebekah was told what her older son Esau had said, she sent for her younger son Jacob and said to him, "Your brother Esau is planning to avenge himself by killing you. ⁴³Now then, my son, do what I say: Flee at once to my brother Laban in Harran. ⁴⁴Stay with him for a while until your brother's fury subsides. ⁴⁵When your brother is no longer angry with you and forgets what you did to him, I'll send word for you to come back from there. Why should I lose both of you in one day?"

⁴⁶Then Rebekah said to Isaac, "I'm disgusted with living because of these Hittite women. If Jacob takes a wife from among the women of this land, from Hittite women like these, my life will not be worth living."

28 So Isaac called for Jacob and blessed him. Then he commanded him: "Do not marry a Canaanite woman. ²Go at once to Paddan Aram,ᵃ to the house of your mother's father Bethuel. Take a wife for yourself there, from among the daughters of Laban, your mother's brother. ³May God Almightyᵇ bless you and make you fruitful and increase your numbers until you become a community of peoples. ⁴May he give you and your descendants the blessing given to Abraham, so that you may take possession of the land where you now reside as a foreigner, the land God gave to Abraham." ⁵Then Isaac sent Jacob on his way, and he went to Paddan Aram, to Laban son of Bethuel the Aramean, the brother of Rebekah, who was the mother of Jacob and Esau.

⁶Now Esau learned that Isaac had blessed Jacob and had sent him to Paddan Aram to take a wife from there, and that when he blessed him he commanded him, "Do not marry a Canaanite woman," ⁷and that Jacob had obeyed his father and mother and had gone to Paddan Aram. ⁸Esau then realized how displeasing the Canaanite women were to his father Isaac; ⁹so he went to Ishmael and married Mahalath, the sister of Nebaioth and daughter of Ishmael son of Abraham, in addition to the wives he already had.

Jacob's Dream at Bethel

¹⁰Jacob left Beersheba and set out for Harran. ¹¹When he reached a certain place, he stopped for the night because the sun had set. Taking one of the stones there, he put it under his head and lay down to sleep. ¹²He had a dream in which he saw a stairway resting on the earth, with its top reaching to heaven, and the angels of God were ascending and descending on it. ¹³There above itᶜ stood the LORD, and he said: "I am the LORD, the God of your father Abraham and the God of Isaac.

ᵃ 2 That is, Northwest Mesopotamia; also in verses 5, 6 and 7
ᵇ 3 Hebrew El-Shaddai   ᶜ 13 Or There beside him

27:40 by the sword Isaac prophesies that Edom (Esau's descendants; see note on 25:25) is destined to live by pillaging. **you will serve your brother** In the tenth century BC, Esau's descendants, the Edomites, became vassals to Israel under David (2Sa 8:13). **from off your neck** In the ninth century BC, Esau's descendants (Edom) eventually revolted against Jacob's descendants (represented by the southern nation of Judah; 2Ki 8:20–22). The southern kingdom of Judah had several conflicts with Edom thereafter. See the timeline "The Divided Kingdom" on p. 536.

28:1–9 Because of Esau's reaction to Jacob receiving Isaac's blessing, Rebekah warns Jacob to flee to her brother in Harran (Ge 27:41–45). She gives Isaac a reason to send Jacob away: her concern over Esau's Hittite wives (27:46; see 26:35 and note). Isaac sends Jacob away with his blessing to find a wife from Rebekah's family (28:1–5; compare 24:1–9). When Esau sees this, he attempts to gain favor from his parents by taking a wife from the family of Ishmael, Abraham's son through Hagar (vv. 6–9). However, he apparently retained his Hittite wives (26:34).

28:3 a community of peoples Isaac's goodbye echoes the language of the covenant blessings (12:1–3; 15:1–6).

28:5 Genealogical details are listed here to reestablish the intent of the trip: for Jacob to find a wife within the extended family clan.

28:9 Mahalath This wife of Esau is apparently called Basemath in the list of Esau's wives in 36:2–3. Both here and in 36:3 the wife is identified as the daughter of Ishmael and the sister of Nebaioth. Both names may refer to the same woman, but the various passages naming Esau's wives are not identical. In 26:34, for example, Basemath is called the daughter of Elon the Hittite, but in 36:2, Adah is identified as the daughter of Elon the Hittite.

28:10–22 On his way to Harran, Jacob encounters Yahweh in a dream. Yahweh repeats to Jacob the promise he made to Abraham and Isaac (vv. 13–15). Jacob, recognizing Yahweh's presence in the place (vv. 15–17), makes a vow to God (vv. 20–22). His vow is conditional on God's blessing. This vow will prove representative of Jacob's relationship with God (compare 32:22–32).

28:12 He had a dream Dreams and visions are a common mode of divine communication throughout the Bible (see 20:3; 31:11,24; 37:5–10; Mt 1:20; 2:19–22). **stairway** This word, which occurs only here in the OT, derives from either the Hebrew verb salal (meaning "to heap up") or the Akkadian word simmiltu, which is used for a stairway of steps. The description that its top reached to heaven echoes the description of the Tower of Babel, which was a ziggurat (see note on Ge 11:4). See the infographic "The Tower of Babel" on p. 29. **angels of God were ascending** That divine beings used the ladder shows that the staircase marked an entryway to the divine realm (see v. 17). The imagery also suggests that angels regularly visit earth to do God's work. See the table "Angels in the Bible" on p. 2120.

28:13 above it The Hebrew text here can be translated "above it," "beside him" or "beside it." If it is translated

I will give you and your descendants the land on which you are lying. ¹⁴Your descendants will be like the dust of the earth, and you will spread out to the west and to the east, to the north and to the south. All peoples on earth will be blessed through you and your offspring.ᵃ ¹⁵I am with you and will watch over you wherever you go, and I will bring you back to this land. I will not leave you until I have done what I have promised you."

¹⁶When Jacob awoke from his sleep, he thought, "Surely the Lord is in this place, and I was not aware of it." ¹⁷He was afraid and said, "How awesome is this place! This is none other than the house of God; this is the gate of heaven."

¹⁸Early the next morning Jacob took the stone he had placed under his head and set it up as a pillar and poured oil on top of it. ¹⁹He called that place Bethel,ᵇ though the city used to be called Luz.

²⁰Then Jacob made a vow, saying, "If God will be with me and will watch over me on this journey I am taking and will give me food to eat and clothes to wear ²¹so that I return safely to my father's household, then the Lordᶜ will be my God ²²andᵈ this stone that I have set up as a pillar will be God's house, and of all that you give me I will give you a tenth."

Jacob Arrives in Paddan Aram

29 Then Jacob continued on his journey and came to the land of the eastern peoples. ²There he saw a well in the open country, with three flocks of sheep lying near it because the flocks were watered from that well. The stone over the mouth of the well was large. ³When all the flocks were gathered there, the shepherds would roll the stone away from the well's mouth and water the sheep. Then they would return the stone to its place over the mouth of the well.

⁴Jacob asked the shepherds, "My brothers, where are you from?"

"We're from Harran," they replied.

⁵He said to them, "Do you know Laban, Nahor's grandson?"

"Yes, we know him," they answered.

⁶Then Jacob asked them, "Is he well?"

"Yes, he is," they said, "and here comes his daughter Rachel with the sheep."

⁷"Look," he said, "the sun is still high; it is not time for the flocks to be gathered. Water the sheep and take them back to pasture."

⁸"We can't," they replied, "until all the flocks are gathered and the stone has been rolled away from the mouth of the well. Then we will water the sheep."

⁹While he was still talking with them, Rachel came with her father's sheep, for she was a shepherd. ¹⁰When Jacob saw Rachel daughter of his uncle Laban, and Laban's sheep, he went over

---

ᵃ 14 Or will use your name and the name of your offspring in blessings (see 48:20)   ᵇ 19 Bethel means house of God.   ᶜ 20,21 Or Since God . . . father's household, the Lord   ᵈ 21,22 Or household, and the Lord will be my God, ²²then

---

as "beside him" or "beside it" then Yahweh is on the ground standing next to Jacob as he gazed at the cosmic stairway; if translated "above it," then Yahweh is visible at the top of the stairway. See the table "Covenants in the Old Testament" on p. 469.

28:15 I will not leave you Jacob's actions have been factored into a providential plan (25:19–28). Jacob will have to make amends for his sins (32:1–21; 33), but Yahweh will still fulfill his will through Jacob's life.

28:16 Surely the Lord is in this place Unlike Abraham's and Isaac's divine encounters within the land of promise, Jacob's encounter was at a location not yet associated with divine appearances. His astonishment highlights the belief in cosmic geography—that certain places were associated with divine appearances.

28:17 house of God The Hebrew phrase used here, *beth elohim*, is typically used of a temple. Temples were both divine abodes and places where divine activity, as it pertained to humanity, could be witnessed or experienced.

28:18 as a pillar This refers to a sacred standing stone. The OT contains numerous references to their use as religious objects, most often in the context of idolatry. When erected for the worship of false gods—rivals to Yahweh—these stones were to be torn down (e.g., Ex 23:24; Dt 7:5; 16:21–22). Here, Jacob erects one in honor of Yahweh. Other contexts in Israelite religion where they were permissible include memorials for the dead (Ge 35:20), treaties (31:45–54) and other important events (Jos 24:27). **poured oil** The anointing of the pillar with oil likely indicates a holy status.

28:19 Bethel The earlier used Hebrew phrase *beth elohim* is here shortened to *beth el*, meaning "house of God." See note on Ge 28:17. **Luz** Bethel and Luz are distinguished in Jos 16:2. Though the two are identified with each other here and elsewhere (Ge 35:6; Jos 18:13; Jdg 1:23), the term Bethel seems to have been originally applied to a religious area outside the city.

28:20–22 Jacob's vow follows a pattern seen elsewhere in the OT (1Sa 1:11; 2Sa 15:8). His promise to God is a response to divine providence in his own life. All the desired conditions Jacob mentions have already been articulated in God's covenant promises (see Ge 28:15).

29:1–30 Jacob's experience in Harran begins much the same as Abraham's servant's experience (24:1–61). Abraham's servant met Rebekah—Jacob's mother—at a well; Jacob meets Rachel—his future wife—at a well. Both Abraham's servant and Jacob deal with Laban, Rebekah's brother and Rachel's father and thus Jacob's uncle. Whereas Abraham's servant returns quickly with Rebekah, Jacob spends 20 years in Harran (31:41), despite having planned a much shorter stay (27:43–45). Rachel and Leah are Jacob's cousins—it seems that marriage among cousins (called endogamy) was a normal occurrence in the ancient Near East.

29:1 eastern The Hebrew word used here, *qedem*, is often a generic designation for any location to the east of the promised land of Canaan (beyond the border of the Jordan River). It also occurs with respect to territory in other directions outside of Canaan.

29:6 Rachel In Hebrew, the word *rachel* is also the word for an ewe lamb (31:38; 32:14), making this line a conceptual wordplay.

and rolled the stone away from the mouth of the well and watered his uncle's sheep. [11] Then Jacob kissed Rachel and began to weep aloud. [12] He had told Rachel that he was a relative of her father and a son of Rebekah. So she ran and told her father.

[13] As soon as Laban heard the news about Jacob, his sister's son, he hurried to meet him. He embraced him and kissed him and brought him to his home, and there Jacob told him all these things. [14] Then Laban said to him, "You are my own flesh and blood."

Jacob Marries Leah and Rachel

After Jacob had stayed with him for a whole month, [15] Laban said to him, "Just because you are a relative of mine, should you work for me for nothing? Tell me what your wages should be."

[16] Now Laban had two daughters; the name of the older was Leah, and the name of the younger was Rachel. [17] Leah had weak[a] eyes, but Rachel had a lovely figure and was beautiful. [18] Jacob was in love with Rachel and said, "I'll work for you seven years in return for your younger daughter Rachel."

[19] Laban said, "It's better that I give her to you than to some other man. Stay here with me." [20] So Jacob served seven years to get Rachel, but they seemed like only a few days to him because of his love for her.

[21] Then Jacob said to Laban, "Give me my wife. My time is completed, and I want to make love to her."

[22] So Laban brought together all the people of the place and gave a feast. [23] But when evening came, he took his daughter Leah and brought her to Jacob, and Jacob made love to her. [24] And Laban gave his servant Zilpah to his daughter as her attendant.

[25] When morning came, there was Leah! So Jacob said to Laban, "What is this you have done to me? I served you for Rachel, didn't I? Why have you deceived me?"

[26] Laban replied, "It is not our custom here to give the younger daughter in marriage before the older one. [27] Finish this daughter's bridal week; then we will give you the younger one also, in return for another seven years of work."

[28] And Jacob did so. He finished the week with Leah, and then Laban gave him his daughter Rachel to be his wife. [29] Laban gave his servant Bilhah to his daughter Rachel as her attendant. [30] Jacob made love to Rachel also, and his love for Rachel was greater than his love for Leah. And he worked for Laban another seven years.

Jacob's Children

[31] When the LORD saw that Leah was not loved, he enabled her to conceive, but Rachel remained childless. [32] Leah became pregnant and gave birth to a son. She named him Reuben,[b] for she said, "It is because the LORD has seen my misery. Surely my husband will love me now."

[33] She conceived again, and when she gave birth to a son she said, "Because the LORD heard that I am not loved, he gave me this one too." So she named him Simeon.[c]

[34] Again she conceived, and when she gave birth

---

[a] 17 Or *delicate*   [b] 32 *Reuben* sounds like the Hebrew for *he has seen my misery*; the name means *see, a son*.   [c] 33 *Simeon* probably means *one who hears*.

29:11 Jacob kissed Rachel Though Jacob falls in love with Rachel, this is a normal greeting in the ancient Near East.

29:16 Leah The etymology of the Hebrew name *le'ah* is unknown.

29:17 weak eyes It is unclear whether this description is positive or negative. If the Hebrew word used here, *rakh*, is translated "weak" or "dull," it may indicate a lack of brightness in her eyes; lustrous or sparkling eyes were considered a striking sign of beauty (1Sa 16:12; SS 4:1,9). On the other hand, if *rakh* is translated "delicate," "tender" or "lovely," it may indicate that she had one striking feature, while Rachel had many.

29:18 I'll work for Jacob's service is in exchange for the normally expected bride payment price, elsewhere called in Hebrew *mohar* (see note on Ex 22:16). Though the ensuing narrative could hint at Laban expecting the arrangement to involve Jacob's adoption into Laban's household, Jacob had no intention or desire to stay with Laban in Harran. He was a normal day laborer, paying his debt of a bride price (Ge 31:38–42).

29:21 my wife This language is consistent with the ancient Near Eastern cultural view that a betrothed woman had the status of a wife.

29:25 Leah As Jacob had disguised himself to deceive his father (27:1–29), Laban presented the veiled Leah at the wedding instead of Rachel. Ancient Near Eastern evidence indicates that brides were veiled. However, as there is no evidence that Leah was veiled during intercourse that night, Jacob's surprise may be explained by darkness (the wedding occurred in the evening; see v. 23) or severely inebriated, although the text itself does not say this.

29:27 Finish this daughter's bridal week This refers to a seven-day marriage celebration.

29:31—30:24 This extended account of the birth of Jacob's children is framed by references to God opening wombs—first Leah's (29:31) and then Rachel's (30:22). In between, Rachel and Leah compete for their husband's favor by providing offspring for him (29:34; 30:1,15). The 12 sons born to them and their maidservants, Bilhah and Zilpah (11 in this section, plus Benjamin in 35:16–18), eventually become the eponymous (or name-giving) ancestors of the 12 tribes of Israel (49:28).

29:31 remained childless Barrenness was viewed as a divine judgment (see 16:2 and note).

29:32 Reuben This name is a combination of two Hebrew words, meaning "See! A son!" See the table "Symbolic Names of People in Hebrew" on p. 1388.

29:33 Simeon The Hebrew name *Shim'on* derives from the Hebrew for "heard," *shama'*, as Leah indicates.

29:34 Levi The origin of this name is uncertain. It derives from the Hebrew word *lawah*, meaning "to attach."

to a son she said, "Now at last my husband will become attached to me, because I have borne him three sons." So he was named Levi.ᵃ

³⁵She conceived again, and when she gave birth to a son she said, "This time I will praise the LORD." So she named him Judah.ᵇ Then she stopped having children.

30 When Rachel saw that she was not bearing Jacob any children, she became jealous of her sister. So she said to Jacob, "Give me children, or I'll die!"

²Jacob became angry with her and said, "Am I in the place of God, who has kept you from having children?"

³Then she said, "Here is Bilhah, my servant. Sleep with her so that she can bear children for me and I too can build a family through her."

⁴So she gave him her servant Bilhah as a wife. Jacob slept with her, ⁵and she became pregnant and bore him a son. ⁶Then Rachel said, "God has vindicated me; he has listened to my plea and given me a son." Because of this she named him Dan.ᶜ

⁷Rachel's servant Bilhah conceived again and bore Jacob a second son. ⁸Then Rachel said, "I have had a great struggle with my sister, and I have won." So she named him Naphtali.ᵈ

⁹When Leah saw that she had stopped having children, she took her servant Zilpah and gave her to Jacob as a wife. ¹⁰Leah's servant Zilpah bore Jacob a son. ¹¹Then Leah said, "What good fortune!"ᵉ So she named him Gad.ᶠ

¹²Leah's servant Zilpah bore Jacob a second son. ¹³Then Leah said, "How happy I am! The women will call me happy." So she named him Asher.ᵍ

¹⁴During wheat harvest, Reuben went out into the fields and found some mandrake plants, which he brought to his mother Leah. Rachel said to Leah, "Please give me some of your son's mandrakes."

¹⁵But she said to her, "Wasn't it enough that you took away my husband? Will you take my son's mandrakes too?"

"Very well," Rachel said, "he can sleep with you tonight in return for your son's mandrakes."

¹⁶So when Jacob came in from the fields that evening, Leah went out to meet him. "You must sleep with me," she said. "I have hired you with my son's mandrakes." So he slept with her that night.

¹⁷God listened to Leah, and she became pregnant and bore Jacob a fifth son. ¹⁸Then Leah said, "God has rewarded me for giving my servant to my husband." So she named him Issachar.ʰ

¹⁹Leah conceived again and bore Jacob a sixth son. ²⁰Then Leah said, "God has presented me with a precious gift. This time my husband will treat me with honor, because I have borne him six sons." So she named him Zebulun.ⁱ

²¹Some time later she gave birth to a daughter and named her Dinah.

²²Then God remembered Rachel; he listened to her and enabled her to conceive. ²³She became pregnant and gave birth to a son and said, "God has taken away my disgrace." ²⁴She named him Joseph,ʲ and said, "May the LORD add to me another son."

Jacob's Flocks Increase

²⁵After Rachel gave birth to Joseph, Jacob said to Laban, "Send me on my way so I can go back to my own homeland. ²⁶Give me my wives and children,

---

ᵃ 34 *Levi* sounds like and may be derived from the Hebrew for *attached.*   ᵇ 35 *Judah* sounds like and may be derived from the Hebrew for *praise.*   ᶜ 6 *Dan* here means *he has vindicated.*   ᵈ 8 *Naphtali* means *my struggle.*   ᵉ 11 Or "*A troop is coming!*"   ᶠ 11 *Gad* can mean *good fortune* or *a troop.*   ᵍ 13 *Asher* means *happy.*   ʰ 18 *Issachar* sounds like the Hebrew for *reward.*   ⁱ 20 *Zebulun* probably means *honor.*   ʲ 24 *Joseph* means *may he add.*

29:35 Judah As Leah hints, this name derives from the Hebrew word *yadah*, meaning "to praise."

30:2 Am I in the place of God Jacob considers Rachel's plea irrational since he views conception as the province of God. His response to Rachel's barrenness differs sharply from his father's response to Rebekah's barrenness. Both men consider their wives' ability to conceive to be within God's purview, but Isaac petitions God for help, whereas Jacob deflects blame away from himself (compare 25:21).

30:6 Dan As Rachel indicates, this name is derived from the Hebrew word meaning "to judge," "to vindicate" or "to contend." In the Hebrew text, Jacob later makes a similar wordplay as Rachel, but does so when speaking of Dan in unflattering terms (49:16–17). This negative reputation continues in later texts (see Jdg 17:1–18:31; note on Rev 7:4).

30:8 Naphtali Rachel is making a wordplay in naming Naphtali; his name sounds like the Hebrew word *niphtalti* she uses in this verse to refer to her wrestling or struggling with Leah.

30:11 Gad The Hebrew word *gad* can mean "troop," but it is also the word for luck or good fortune, as Leah uses it here. Though there was a god of good fortune in the

ancient Near East (mentioned in Isa 65:11 with "Destiny"), Leah refers here to her good fortune, not the deity.

30:13 Asher *Asher* is also the Hebrew word for happiness—hence Leah's remark in this verse.

30:14 During wheat harvest This corresponds roughly to the month of May. **mandrake plants** Mandrakes (*duda'im* in Hebrew) were believed in the ancient Near East to have magical fertility powers.

30:16 I have hired you The Hebrew verb used here, *sakhar*, is a sound play on the name Issachar (*yissakhar* in Hebrew)—the son who results from the rendezvous between Leah and Jacob (Ge 30:18).

30:18 Issachar See note on 30:16.

30:20 Zebulun The Hebrew name *zevulun* sounds similar to the Hebrew verb *zaval*, meaning "to honor"—hence Leah's remark in this verse.

30:24 Joseph The name Joseph has two possible Hebrew derivations: the Hebrew word *asaph* (meaning "to take away") and the Hebrew word *yasaph* (meaning "to add"). Rachel uses the word *yasaph* in this verse, suggesting that she viewed it as related to that word. However, both possible derivations are pertinent to the story in chs. 37–50. If Joseph's name comes from the Hebrew word *asaph*, it alludes to the loss of Joseph via the treachery

for whom I have served you, and I will be on my way. You know how much work I've done for you." 27But Laban said to him, "If I have found favor in your eyes, please stay. I have learned by divination that the LORD has blessed me because of you." 28He added, "Name your wages, and I will pay them."

29Jacob said to him, "You know how I have worked for you and how your livestock has fared under my care. 30The little you had before I came has increased greatly, and the LORD has blessed you wherever I have been. But now, when may I do something for my own household?"

31"What shall I give you?" he asked.

"Don't give me anything," Jacob replied. "But if you will do this one thing for me, I will go on tending your flocks and watching over them: 32Let me go through all your flocks today and remove from them every speckled or spotted sheep, every dark-colored lamb and every spotted or speckled goat. They will be my wages. 33And my honesty will testify for me in the future, whenever you check on the wages you have paid me. Any goat in my possession that is not speckled or spotted, or any lamb that is not dark-colored, will be considered stolen."

34"Agreed," said Laban. "Let it be as you have said." 35That same day he removed all the male goats that were streaked or spotted, and all the speckled or spotted female goats (all that had white on them) and all the dark-colored lambs, and he placed them in the care of his sons. 36Then he put a three-day journey between himself and

Jacob, while Jacob continued to tend the rest of Laban's flocks.

37Jacob, however, took fresh-cut branches from poplar, almond and plane trees and made white stripes on them by peeling the bark and exposing the white inner wood of the branches. 38Then he placed the peeled branches in all the watering troughs, so that they would be directly in front of the flocks when they came to drink. When the flocks were in heat and came to drink, 39they mated in front of the branches. And they bore young that were streaked or speckled or spotted. 40Jacob set apart the young of the flock by themselves, but made the rest face the streaked and dark-colored animals that belonged to Laban. Thus he made separate flocks for himself and did not put them with Laban's animals. 41Whenever the stronger females were in heat, Jacob would place the branches in the troughs in front of the animals so they would mate near the branches, 42but if the animals were weak, he would not place them there. So the weak animals went to Laban and the strong ones to Jacob. 43In this way the man grew exceedingly prosperous and came to own large flocks, and female and male servants, and camels and donkeys.

Jacob Flees From Laban

31 Jacob heard that Laban's sons were saying, "Jacob has taken everything our father owned and has gained all this wealth from what belonged to our father." 2And Jacob noticed that Laban's attitude toward him was not what it had been.

---

of his brothers. If Joseph's name derives from *yasaph*, it is a reference to his being added to the family through the formerly barren Rachel.

30:27 I have learned by divination Most translations understand the Hebrew verb used here as a reference to divination—discerning the will of a deity based on using an object, omen or method. However in other occurrences in the OT, there is often an explanation of the divination procedure used but one is not offered here (compare 44:15–17; Lev 16:8; Nu 5). **because of you** This seems to be a result of God's promise to Abraham in Ge 12:3 (see 22:18; 26:4). Since God has blessed Jacob, via Abraham and his father Isaac, Jacob's presence blesses others.

30:32–36 In this part of the world, sheep are typically white and goats are dark brown or black. Consequently, the markings Jacob describes on the animals he demands for his wages would lead Laban to presume he was getting the better side of the agreement (v. 34). Jacob is confident he will do well and ultimately becomes successful. Jacob attributes this turn of events not to his own actions, but to God (31:8–9).

30:37–43 For Jacob to succeed in increasing his flock, monochrome sheep and goats must produce offspring with the specified markings. In order to increase his herd, Jacob employs sympathetic magical practices. Sympathetic magic was based on the belief that the user could influence something based on its relationship or resemblance to another thing. Sympathetic magic was employed throughout the ancient Near East. Jacob's actions also reflect the ancient Near Eastern belief that the offspring of an animal was affected by what it saw during the procreation process.

Since Jacob attributes his success to God (31:9–11), he believed he was acting in faith that God would supernaturally increase his flocks. While there is no natural explanation for Jacob's success and God does take credit for Jacob's achievement (31:12), this does not mean that God responded directly to Jacob's techniques—instead, God is simply choosing to look out for Jacob as he promised (see 31:13; compare 28:15).

31:1–55 After manipulating the flocks to increase his wages, Jacob leaves Laban. Jacob originally fled to Laban to escape his brother (see 28:1–9 and note). Now Yahweh tells him to go home (v. 3). Jacob explains to his wives that Laban has cheated him. He recounts a dream in which God appears and reveals that he knows about Laban's wrongs against Jacob (vv. 4–13). Jacob and his wives leave, but Rachel steals the household idols (vv. 14–21). When Laban discovers that Jacob has fled, he pursues him, eventually catching him (vv. 22–25). Rachel hides the stolen idols from her father, and Jacob confronts Laban over the 20 years of mistreatment (vv. 26–42). Jacob and Laban make a covenant not to harm each other, and Laban returns (vv. 43–55).

³Then the LORD said to Jacob, "Go back to the land of your fathers and to your relatives, and I will be with you."

⁴So Jacob sent word to Rachel and Leah to come out to the fields where his flocks were. ⁵He said to them, "I see that your father's attitude toward me is not what it was before, but the God of my father has been with me. ⁶You know that I've worked for your father with all my strength, ⁷yet your father has cheated me by changing my wages ten times. However, God has not allowed him to harm me. ⁸If he said, 'The speckled ones will be your wages,' then all the flocks gave birth to speckled young; and if he said, 'The streaked ones will be your wages,' then all the flocks bore streaked young. ⁹So God has taken away your father's livestock and has given them to me.

¹⁰"In breeding season I once had a dream in which I looked up and saw that the male goats mating with the flock were streaked, speckled or spotted. ¹¹The angel of God said to me in the dream, 'Jacob.' I answered, 'Here I am.' ¹²And he said, 'Look up and see that all the male goats mating with the flock are streaked, speckled or spotted, for I have seen all that Laban has been doing to you. ¹³I am the God of Bethel, where you anointed a pillar and where you made a vow to me. Now leave this land at once and go back to your native land.'"

¹⁴Then Rachel and Leah replied, "Do we still have any share in the inheritance of our father's estate? ¹⁵Does he not regard us as foreigners? Not only has he sold us, but he has used up what was paid for us. ¹⁶Surely all the wealth that God took away from our father belongs to us and our children. So do whatever God has told you."

¹⁷Then Jacob put his children and his wives on camels, ¹⁸and he drove all his livestock ahead of him, along with all the goods he had accumulated in Paddan Aram,ᵃ to go to his father Isaac in the land of Canaan.

¹⁹When Laban had gone to shear his sheep, Rachel stole her father's household gods. ²⁰Moreover, Jacob deceived Laban the Aramean by not telling him he was running away. ²¹So he fled with all he had, crossed the Euphrates River, and headed for the hill country of Gilead.

Laban Pursues Jacob

²²On the third day Laban was told that Jacob had fled. ²³Taking his relatives with him, he pursued Jacob for seven days and caught up with him in the hill country of Gilead. ²⁴Then God came to Laban the Aramean in a dream at night and said to him, "Be careful not to say anything to Jacob, either good or bad."

²⁵Jacob had pitched his tent in the hill country of Gilead when Laban overtook him, and Laban and his relatives camped there too. ²⁶Then Laban said to Jacob, "What have you done? You've deceived me, and you've carried off my daughters like captives in war. ²⁷Why did you run off secretly and deceive me? Why didn't you tell me, so I could send you away with joy and singing to the music of timbrels and harps? ²⁸You didn't even let me kiss my grandchildren and my daughters

ᵃ 18 That is, Northwest Mesopotamia

31:3 Go back to the land of your fathers In view of Laban's negative disposition toward Jacob, this is both a command and a warning.

31:7 by changing my wages ten times This is a rhetorical expression that essentially means time and again.

31:11 angel of God See note on 21:17.

31:12 streaked, speckled or spotted See note on 30:37–43.

31:13 you anointed a pillar and where you made a vow See 28:18–22; note on 28:18.

31:17 on camels See note on 12:16.

31:18 Paddan Aram This could be another name for what the Hebrew text refers to as *aram naharayim* (see note on 24:10) or a town in that region (see Hos 12:12). The identification of Laban with both place names indicates that it is near Harran (see Ge 27:43). See the map "Patriarchal Journeys to and From Haran" on p. 2251.

31:19 household gods The Hebrew text here uses the term *teraphim*. The precise meaning of this Hebrew term is uncertain, but it seems to refer to household gods, idols or figurines that were thought to represent residents of the unseen, spiritual world. The *teraphim* could have been used in household worship, which would have been idolatrous. However, it is also possible that they served another purpose that would not be thought of as idolatry: In 1Sa 19:13–16 the term

teraphim occurs without any suggestion of idolatry. Ancient Near Eastern legal documents from Nuzi, and other ancient Near Eastern parallels, suggest that worshiping and honoring departed spirits of the dead was practiced, and that household gods were part of a person's inheritance. But this does not mean that Laban's *teraphim* were intended for ancestor worship; they may also have been used as tokens to remember the dead—the ancient equivalent of expressing grief or respect for the dead by leaving gifts at grave sites. In Jacob's subsequent demand that his household put away its foreign gods (Ge 35:2), the word used is not *teraphim*. Nevertheless, any image of something or someone could be used in an idolatrous way, so it is understandable that such items would be opposed by Biblical writers elsewhere (see 1Sa 15:23; 2Ki 23:24; Zec 10:2).

31:20 Laban the Aramean See note on Ge 24:29; 25:20 and note.

31:21 hill country of Gilead Harran and Paddan Aram, where Laban is departing from, is located in the bend of the Fertile Crescent, north of Canaan. Gilead would be the first region travelers would encounter in the Transjordan.

31:27 with joy and singing Laban's claims of wanting to wish farewell to Jacob and his daughters with a festive celebration seem disingenuous.

goodbye. You have done a foolish thing. [29]I have the power to harm you; but last night the God of your father said to me, 'Be careful not to say anything to Jacob, either good or bad.' [30]Now you have gone off because you longed to return to your father's household. But why did you steal my gods?"

[31]Jacob answered Laban, "I was afraid, because I thought you would take your daughters away from me by force. [32]But if you find anyone who has your gods, that person shall not live. In the presence of our relatives, see for yourself whether there is anything of yours here with me; and if so, take it." Now Jacob did not know that Rachel had stolen the gods.

[33]So Laban went into Jacob's tent and into Leah's tent and into the tent of the two female servants, but he found nothing. After he came out of Leah's tent, he entered Rachel's tent. [34]Now Rachel had taken the household gods and put them inside her camel's saddle and was sitting on them. Laban searched through everything in the tent but found nothing.

[35]Rachel said to her father, "Don't be angry, my lord, that I cannot stand up in your presence; I'm having my period." So he searched but could not find the household gods.

[36]Jacob was angry and took Laban to task. "What is my crime?" he asked Laban. "How have I wronged you that you hunt me down? [37]Now that you have searched through all my goods, what have you found that belongs to your household? Put it here in front of your relatives and mine, and let them judge between the two of us.

[38]"I have been with you for twenty years now. Your sheep and goats have not miscarried, nor have I eaten rams from your flocks. [39]I did not bring you animals torn by wild beasts; I bore the loss myself. And you demanded payment from me for whatever was stolen by day or night. [40]This was my situation: The heat consumed me in the daytime and the cold at night, and sleep fled from my eyes. [41]It was like this for the twenty years I was in your household. I worked for you fourteen years for your two daughters and six years for your flocks, and you changed my wages ten times. [42]If the God of my father, the God of Abraham and the Fear of Isaac, had not been with me, you would surely have sent me away empty-handed. But God has seen my hardship and the toil of my hands, and last night he rebuked you."

[43]Laban answered Jacob, "The women are my daughters, the children are my children, and the flocks are my flocks. All you see is mine. Yet what can I do today about these daughters of mine, or about the children they have borne? [44]Come now, let's make a covenant, you and I, and let it serve as a witness between us."

[45]So Jacob took a stone and set it up as a pillar. [46]He said to his relatives, "Gather some stones." So they took stones and piled them in a heap, and they ate there by the heap. [47]Laban called it Jegar Sahadutha, and Jacob called it Galeed.[a]

[48]Laban said, "This heap is a witness between you and me today." That is why it was called Galeed. [49]It was also called Mizpah,[b] because he said, "May the LORD keep watch between you and me when we are away from each other. [50]If you mistreat my daughters or if you take any wives besides my daughters, even though no one is with us, remember that God is a witness between you and me."

[51]Laban also said to Jacob, "Here is this heap, and here is this pillar I have set up between you and me. [52]This heap is a witness, and this pillar is a witness, that I will not go past this heap to your side to harm you and that you will not go past this heap and pillar to my side to harm me. [53]May the God of Abraham and the God of Nahor, the God of their father, judge between us."

So Jacob took an oath in the name of the Fear of his father Isaac. [54]He offered a sacrifice there in the hill country and invited his relatives to a meal. After they had eaten, they spent the night there.

[55]Early the next morning Laban kissed his grandchildren and his daughters and blessed them. Then he left and returned home.[c]

[a] 47 The Aramaic *Jegar Sahadutha* and the Hebrew *Galeed* both mean *witness heap.* [b] 49 *Mizpah* means *watchtower.* [c] 55 In Hebrew texts this verse (31:55) is numbered 32:1.

31:35 I'm having my period Rachel claims she cannot get up to show her father proper respect because she is menstruating.
31:42 the Fear of Isaac This is a divine title. It occurs only here and in v. 53. It refers to the one whom Isaac, Jacob's father, revered—Yahweh, the God of Abraham.
31:44 let it serve as a witness Standing pillars and stone memorials often denoted a divine being or supernatural appearance (v. 45,52). In this context, Jacob and Laban commemorate God as witness to their pact of nonaggression (vv. 51–53). See note on 28:18; compare 35:14. See the table "Covenants in the Old Testament" on p. 469.
31:47 Jegar Sahadutha This is an Aramaic term that means "the heap of witness" or "stones of witness," hence Laban's remark in v. 48. **Galeed** Like Laban's naming of the place, Jacob uses a Hebrew term that means "the heap of witness."
31:49 Mizpah The Hebrew term used here, *mispah* is related to the Hebrew verb *taspah* (meaning "to watch"), which Jacob uses here in his description of what he requests Yahweh do.
31:53 the God of Nahor There is no evidence in the stories of Abraham that his brother, Nahor, knew of or followed Yahweh. In addition, the verb often translated as "judge" in this verse is plural in Hebrew, which could indicate that two separate deities are being called on to bear witness by Laban—Yahweh and Nahor's god.

Jacob Prepares to Meet Esau

32 [a] Jacob also went on his way, and the angels of God met him. [2]When Jacob saw them, he said, "This is the camp of God!" So he named that place Mahanaim.[b]

[3]Jacob sent messengers ahead of him to his brother Esau in the land of Seir, the country of Edom. [4]He instructed them: "This is what you are to say to my lord Esau: 'Your servant Jacob says, I have been staying with Laban and have remained there till now. [5]I have cattle and donkeys, sheep and goats, male and female servants. Now I am sending this message to my lord, that I may find favor in your eyes.'"

[6]When the messengers returned to Jacob, they said, "We went to your brother Esau, and now he is coming to meet you, and four hundred men are with him."

[7]In great fear and distress Jacob divided the people who were with him into two groups,[c] and the flocks and herds and camels as well. [8]He thought, "If Esau comes and attacks one group,[d] the group[d] that is left may escape."

[9]Then Jacob prayed, "O God of my father Abraham, God of my father Isaac, LORD, you who said to me, 'Go back to your country and your relatives, and I will make you prosper,' [10]I am unworthy of all the kindness and faithfulness you have shown your servant. I had only my staff when I crossed this Jordan, but now I have become two camps. [11]Save me, I pray, from the hand of my brother Esau, for I am afraid he will come and attack me, and also the mothers with their children. [12]But you have said, 'I will surely make you prosper and will make your descendants like the sand of the sea, which cannot be counted.'"

[13]He spent the night there, and from what he had with him he selected a gift for his brother Esau: [14]two hundred female goats and twenty male goats, two hundred ewes and twenty rams, [15]thirty female camels with their young, forty cows and ten bulls, and twenty female donkeys and ten male donkeys. [16]He put them in the care of his servants, each herd by itself, and said to his servants, "Go ahead of me, and keep some space between the herds."

[17]He instructed the one in the lead: "When my brother Esau meets you and asks, 'Who do you belong to, and where are you going, and who owns all these animals in front of you?' [18]then you are to say, 'They belong to your servant Jacob. They are a gift sent to my lord Esau, and he is coming behind us.'"

[19]He also instructed the second, the third and all the others who followed the herds: "You are to say the same thing to Esau when you meet him. [20]And be sure to say, 'Your servant Jacob is coming behind us.'" For he thought, "I will pacify him with these gifts I am sending on ahead; later, when I see him, perhaps he will receive me." [21]So Jacob's gifts went on ahead of him, but he himself spent the night in the camp.

Jacob Wrestles With God

[22]That night Jacob got up and took his two wives, his two female servants and his eleven sons and crossed the ford of the Jabbok. [23]After he had sent them across the stream, he sent over all his possessions. [24]So Jacob was left alone, and

---

[a] In Hebrew texts 32:1-32 is numbered 32:2-33.   [b] 2 Mahanaim means two camps.   [c] 7 Or camps   [d] 8 Or camp

---

32:1–21 After making a covenant of peace with Laban, Jacob must confront the problem he left to escape: Esau. He sends a message to his brother and learns that Esau is coming with 400 men (32:1–6). Assuming Esau is a threat, Jacob divides his camp so that Esau cannot attack the entire group (vv. 7–8). He prays that God will deliver him and prepares a gift for Esau, hoping to appease him (vv. 13–21).

32:1 angels of God This exact phrase occurs elsewhere only in 28:12—also in connection with Jacob. Spiritual messengers from God, like those Jacob earlier witnessed, now meet him in a tumultuous time. Compare 35:7.
32:2 This is the camp of God This phrase seems to have both military and residential connotations (1Ch 12:22; compare Jdg 18:12). **Mahanaim** The Hebrew word used here, machanayim, is plural and means "two camps." It is unclear why Jacob did not choose to use a singular form when naming this place; Jacob uses a singular form of the same word (machaneh in Hebrew, meaning "camp") in his explanation of the name. The plural form could indicate that Jacob is referencing the meeting of his camp and God's camp (where the angels of God are), or even referencing three different camps: his own, God's and Esau's. Jacob could have seen Esau's

camp by this point or knew it was nearby. The specific site of this location is unknown.
32:3 in the land of Seir, the country of Edom The land of Esau's descendants (see Ge 25:30).
32:5 cattle and donkeys, sheep and goats, male and female servants This listing is probably intended as a hint to Esau that Jacob has wealth to share. This is likely Jacob's way of saying he intends to compensate for Esau's loss of wealth many years ago when he took Esau's birthright (25:31–34; 27:36; compare 32:20).
32:6 four hundred men If other references to this number of men are analogous (1Sa 22:2; 25:13; 30:10,17), 400 appears to have been the normal size of a militia.

32:9–12 Jacob does not pray for Esau's demise, as though Esau were his enemy. Rather, Jacob knows he wronged his brother and is undeserving of God's protection for this reason (Ge 32:10).

32:20 I will pacify The Hebrew word used here, kaphar—which may be literally rendered as "to cover over" (6:14)—is often used in the OT to describe atonement—the covering over of sin (see Lev 4:20 and note; Isa 6:7 and note).

32:22–32 As Jacob anticipates his brother's arrival, God appears as a man (see Ge 32:24 and note) and wrestles

a man wrestled with him till daybreak. 25When the man saw that he could not overpower him, he touched the socket of Jacob's hip so that his hip was wrenched as he wrestled with the man. 26Then the man said, "Let me go, for it is daybreak."

But Jacob replied, "I will not let you go unless you bless me."

27The man asked him, "What is your name?"

"Jacob," he answered.

28Then the man said, "Your name will no longer be Jacob, but Israel,ᵃ because you have struggled with God and with humans and have overcome."

29Jacob said, "Please tell me your name."

But he replied, "Why do you ask my name?" Then he blessed him there.

30So Jacob called the place Peniel,ᵇ saying, "It is because I saw God face to face, and yet my life was spared."

31The sun rose above him as he passed Peniel,ᶜ and he was limping because of his hip. 32Therefore to this day the Israelites do not eat the tendon attached to the socket of the hip, because the socket of Jacob's hip was touched near the tendon.

Jacob Meets Esau

33 Jacob looked up and there was Esau, coming with his four hundred men; so he divided the children among Leah, Rachel and the two female servants. 2He put the female servants and their children in front, Leah and her children next, and Rachel and Joseph in the rear. 3He himself went on ahead and bowed down to the ground seven times as he approached his brother.

4But Esau ran to meet Jacob and embraced him; he threw his arms around his neck and kissed him. And they wept. 5Then Esau looked up and saw the women and children. "Who are these with you?" he asked.

Jacob answered, "They are the children God has graciously given your servant."

6Then the female servants and their children approached and bowed down. 7Next, Leah and her children came and bowed down. Last of all came Joseph and Rachel, and they too bowed down.

8Esau asked, "What's the meaning of all these flocks and herds I met?"

"To find favor in your eyes, my lord," he said.

ᵃ 28 *Israel* probably means *he struggles with God.*   ᵇ 30 *Peniel* means *face of God.*   ᶜ 31 Hebrew *Penuel*, a variant of *Peniel*

---

with Jacob. Jacob refuses to relent until God blesses him (v. 26). After God blesses him, Jacob renames the place to reflect his encounter with God (vv. 29–30). This story explains the origin of the name Israel, as God changes Jacob's name to Israel (see v. 28 and note).

32:22 his eleven sons Jacob's daughter Dinah is not mentioned for literary reasons (30:21). Only the main characters in the narratives that follow are noted—particularly the sons of Jacob, who are the eponymous (or name-giving) ancestors of the 12 tribes of Israel, once Jacob's name is changed (vv. 27–28).

32:24 and a man This man is a divine being in physical, bodily form (vv. 28,30; compare ch. 18). In Hos 12:3–4, the man who visits Jacob is called an angel, but then it is said that Jacob met God at Bethel—this is because the identity of the angel of God (or angel of Yahweh) and Yahweh himself are sometimes blurred. See note on Ge 21:17. **wrestled** The Hebrew word used here, *'avaq*, sounds like Jacob's name (*ya'aqob* in Hebrew). In addition to being wordplay on Jacob's name, there is wordplay here with the place of the scene, the Jabbok (*yabboq* in Hebrew; v. 22). Compare note on 25:26; note on 27:36; note on 32:28.

32:25 he could not overpower him Jacob is quite strong, as he was able to roll away the stone at the well when he arrived in Harran (29:10).

32:26 you bless me Jacob's request for a blessing suggests that he recognizes that his combatant is neither an ordinary man nor out to destroy him. Though not specifically affirmed in the text, there are indications that the man was Yahweh embodied (compare note on 32:24).

32:28 name will no longer be Jacob, but Israel Jacob's name must be changed due to its association with his misdeeds (see note on 25:26; note on 27:36). Here, the reasoning for the name Israel (*yisra'el*, in Hebrew) is the verbal phrase "you have striven with (or struggled with) God." This suggests the name derives from the

Hebrew verb *sarah*, meaning "to struggle," "to strive" or "to fight." The name *yisra'el* itself could mean "God will struggle," "May God struggle" or "God fights," suggesting that the meaning given here is wordplay. See the table "Symbolic Names of People in Hebrew" on p. 1388.

32:29 Why do you ask my name Jacob may make this request because he wishes to honor the one he has wrestled with (compare Jdg 13:17–18), or because of the ancient Near Eastern belief that knowing a spiritual being's name gave a person the ability to evoke the power of that being (compare Ex 20:7; Lk 10:17). Similarly, the man asks Jacob his name before blessing him—indicating that the usage of a name was necessary for a blessing to be given.

32:30 Peniel This name in Hebrew (*penu'el*) means "face of God"—hence the explanation that follows. The place Peniel is mentioned elsewhere in the OT (e.g., Jdg 8:8–9).

32:32 tendon attached Jewish tradition associates this with the sciatic nerve. In refraining from eating this part of an animal, Israelites were reminded of Jacob's name change and God's blessing on Israel. This tradition is only noted here in the OT.

33:1–20 As Esau approaches, Jacob divides his children among their respective mothers and then greets his brother with respect and deference (Ge 33:1–3). Despite Jacob's concerns (see 32:6–8), Esau welcomes Jacob affectionately (vv. 4–7). Esau initially refuses Jacob's gift, but he eventually yields to Jacob's urging (vv. 8–11). Esau then encourages Jacob to return to Edom with him, but Jacob continues to Shechem (vv. 12–20). The chapter ends with Jacob following the pattern of Abraham and Isaac by erecting an altar to God (see v. 20 and note).

33:3 bowed down to the ground seven times The sevenfold prostration was used to express subordination to a superior. See the infographic "The Amarna Letters" on p. 337.

⁹But Esau said, "I already have plenty, my brother. Keep what you have for yourself."

¹⁰"No, please!" said Jacob. "If I have found favor in your eyes, accept this gift from me. For to see your face is like seeing the face of God, now that you have received me favorably. ¹¹Please accept the present that was brought to you, for God has been gracious to me and I have all I need." And because Jacob insisted, Esau accepted it.

¹²Then Esau said, "Let us be on our way; I'll accompany you."

¹³But Jacob said to him, "My lord knows that the children are tender and that I must care for the ewes and cows that are nursing their young. If they are driven hard just one day, all the animals will die. ¹⁴So let my lord go on ahead of his servant, while I move along slowly at the pace of the flocks and herds before me and the pace of the children, until I come to my lord in Seir."

¹⁵Esau said, "Then let me leave some of my men with you."

"But why do that?" Jacob asked. "Just let me find favor in the eyes of my lord."

¹⁶So that day Esau started on his way back to Seir. ¹⁷Jacob, however, went to Sukkoth, where he built a place for himself and made shelters for his livestock. That is why the place is called Sukkoth.ᵃ

¹⁸After Jacob came from Paddan Aram,ᵇ he arrived safely at the city of Shechem in Canaan and camped within sight of the city. ¹⁹For a hundred pieces of silver,ᶜ he bought from the sons of Hamor, the father of Shechem, the plot of ground where he pitched his tent. ²⁰There he set up an altar and called it El Elohe Israel.ᵈ

Dinah and the Shechemites

34 Now Dinah, the daughter Leah had borne to Jacob, went out to visit the women of the land. ²When Shechem son of Hamor the Hivite, the ruler of that area, saw her, he took her and raped her. ³His heart was drawn to Dinah daughter of Jacob; he loved the young woman and spoke tenderly to her. ⁴And Shechem said to his father Hamor, "Get me this girl as my wife."

⁵When Jacob heard that his daughter Dinah had been defiled, his sons were in the fields with his livestock; so he did nothing about it until they came home.

⁶Then Shechem's father Hamor went out to talk

ᵃ 17 Sukkoth means shelters.   ᵇ 18 That is, Northwest Mesopotamia   ᶜ 19 Hebrew hundred kesitahs; a kesitah was a unit of money of unknown weight and value.   ᵈ 20 El Elohe Israel can mean El is the God of Israel or mighty is the God of Israel.

33:9–11 This verbal exchange illustrates the cultural expectations of ancient Near Eastern etiquette with respect to receiving gifts. Whereas Jacob earlier used the Hebrew word *minchah* of his gift to Esau (32:13,18,20,21)—a term associated with offering tribute to a superior—in v. 11 he uses *berakhah* (meaning "blessing"; see note on 27:4). This term, spoken directly to Esau, suggests that Jacob views the gift as reparation for his theft of Esau's blessing years ago.

33:12 I'll accompany you Esau presumed that Jacob traveled to Edomite country in order to visit him. He is unaware of both Jacob's flight from Laban (ch. 31) and Jacob's encounter with God in which he was granted the land of Canaan (28:10–22). As Esau turns south toward Seir, Jacob turns north toward Sukkoth. Jacob's actions betray continuing uncertainty about Esau's feelings toward him.

33:17 to Sukkoth This Hebrew term means "booths" or "shelters," hence the reasoning given for the name in this verse. It is located in the plain north of the Jabbok (32:22) and east of the Jordan River.

33:18 Paddan Aram See 25:20 and note. **Shechem** The city where Abraham built an altar after God appeared to him and promised him the land of Canaan (12:6–7).

33:20 There he set up an altar Jacob's act echoes what Abraham and Isaac had done before him (12:6–8; 26:25). See the infographic "Ancient Altars" on p. 127; see the table "Altars in the Old Testament" on p. 249. **El Elohe Israel** This name means "El (or God), the God of Israel." This name, along with Jacob's own new name of Israel (see note on 32:28), marks the land as belonging to him and his descendants, by mandate of God.

34:1–31 The rape of Dinah in the city of Shechem (33:18–20)—the only daughter mentioned in the account

of Jacob's children (29:31—30:24)—creates conflict between Jacob and his sons and the people of Canaan. Jacob remains mostly passive throughout the passage, allowing his sons to speak for him. After Shechem rapes Dinah, he seeks permission to marry her. Jacob's sons agree on the condition that all the males in the city get circumcised (34:22–24). When the men are recovering, Simeon and Levi return and kill them (vv. 25–29).

34:1 Dinah, the daughter Leah had borne The specific reference to Dinah's mother establishes that Simeon and Levi (v. 25) are her full brothers, not half-brothers. **to visit the women of the land** It would have been unusual in the ancient Near East for young girls (or women) to leave the camp without a chaperone, especially when going to a city in a new land. Dinah's act represents a youthful indiscretion, as it placed her in the company of women not bound to the covenant that Jacob and his family were. However, the narrative does not suggest that Dinah bears responsibility for what happened to her—she is a victim.

34:2 Hivite Nothing is known of the Hivites outside of the Biblical account. They appear in the Table of Nations (10:17) and are often listed among the Canaanite nations (Dt 7:1; Jos 3:10; Jdg 3:3–5). **ruler of that area** Hamor is not described as a king, since this title describes a leadership role over a wide area of land, not just the city. Instead, it seems that Hamor is the leader of the region—perhaps of a tribal confederacy.

34:3 and spoke tenderly to her The perverse Shechem, who has already raped Dinah, now seems to change his approach from forceful and brutal to attempted kindness.

34:5 had been defiled In Hebrew, the term for religious impurity is used here (compare Lev 11:24–44). Its use here suggests that Dinah has been violated in a way that makes her unacceptable to her culture.

with Jacob. [7]Meanwhile, Jacob's sons had come in from the fields as soon as they heard what had happened. They were shocked and furious, because Shechem had done an outrageous thing in[a] Israel by sleeping with Jacob's daughter — a thing that should not be done.

[8]But Hamor said to them, "My son Shechem has his heart set on your daughter. Please give her to him as his wife. [9]Intermarry with us; give us your daughters and take our daughters for yourselves. [10]You can settle among us; the land is open to you. Live in it, trade[b] in it, and acquire property in it."

[11]Then Shechem said to Dinah's father and brothers, "Let me find favor in your eyes, and I will give you whatever you ask. [12]Make the price for the bride and the gift I am to bring as great as you like, and I'll pay whatever you ask me. Only give me the young woman as my wife."

[13]Because their sister Dinah had been defiled, Jacob's sons replied deceitfully as they spoke to Shechem and his father Hamor. [14]They said to them, "We can't do such a thing; we can't give our sister to a man who is not circumcised. That would be a disgrace to us. [15]We will enter into an agreement with you on one condition only: that you become like us by circumcising all your males. [16]Then we will give you our daughters and take your daughters for ourselves. We'll settle among you and become one people with you. [17]But if you will not agree to be circumcised, we'll take our sister and go."

[18]Their proposal seemed good to Hamor and his son Shechem. [19]The young man, who was the most honored of all his father's family, lost no time in doing what they said, because he was delighted with Jacob's daughter. [20]So Hamor and his son Shechem went to the gate of their city to speak to the men of their city. [21]"These men are friendly toward us," they said. "Let them live in our land and trade in it; the land has plenty of room for them. We can marry their daughters and they can marry ours. [22]But the men will agree to live with us as one people only on the condition that our males be circumcised, as they themselves are. [23]Won't their livestock, their property and all their other animals become ours? So let us agree to their terms, and they will settle among us."

[24]All the men who went out of the city gate agreed with Hamor and his son Shechem, and every male in the city was circumcised.

[25]Three days later, while all of them were still in pain, two of Jacob's sons, Simeon and Levi, Dinah's brothers, took their swords and attacked the unsuspecting city, killing every male. [26]They put Hamor and his son Shechem to the sword and took Dinah from Shechem's house and left. [27]The sons of Jacob came upon the dead bodies and looted the city where[c] their sister had been defiled. [28]They seized their flocks and herds and donkeys and everything else of theirs in the city and out in the fields. [29]They carried off all their wealth and all their women and children, taking as plunder everything in the houses.

[30]Then Jacob said to Simeon and Levi, "You have brought trouble on me by making me obnoxious to the Canaanites and Perizzites, the people living in this land. We are few in number, and if they join forces against me and attack me, I and my household will be destroyed."

[31]But they replied, "Should he have treated our sister like a prostitute?"

[a] 7 Or against   [b] 10 Or move about freely; also in verse 21
[c] 27 Or because

34:12 price for the bride The Hebrew term used here, *mohar*, does not refer to purchase money, but compensation for the loss of a daughter whose labor contributed to the tribe — such an action was expected in the ancient Near East in any marriage (see note on Ex 22:16; compare Ge 29:18). It is unclear whether Shechem's offer also included compensation for the loss of an unbetrothed virgin — which would have been expected (compare Dt 22:28–29). Like his father moments earlier, Shechem never actually mentions the crime — there is no apology. Since Dinah was being kept inside the city (Ge 34:17,26), the payment may also have acted as a personal bribe for Jacob to forget the incident and avoid further escalation.

34:15 by circumcising God instructed Abraham to circumcise all males born to him or within his household as a sign of the covenant (see 17:10 and note).

34:18–24 Hamor and Shechem take the terms of the proposal to the citizenry for approval. With the terms agreed to, all the men of the city are circumcised. However, in the conversation with the men of the city Hamor and Shechem are not completely honest. They deliberately omitted the issue that, for many men in the city, would represent an enduring threat to their posterity: the promise of property rights for the outsiders (34:10).

34:23 become ours It is unclear whether Hamor and Shechem plan to take the livestock of Jacob's family. Most likely they are presenting their scheme in the best possible light to convince the men of their city.

34:25 Three days later By waiting until all the males are circumcised, Simeon and Levi ensure that they are all incapacitated.

34:27 came upon the dead bodies The wording distinguishes the rest of Jacob's sons from Simeon and Levi, indicating that only Simeon and Levi did the killing. The other sons came into the city and, seeing the slain men, plundered it (vv. 28–29). Jacob later singles out and pairs Simeon and Levi in his deathbed reprimand, recalling the treachery (49:5–7).

34:30 brought trouble on me After remaining silent throughout the narrative, Jacob finally speaks. His chief concern is not the welfare of his daughter or even his sons' slaughter of innocent people. Instead, Jacob is concerned that their actions may bring trouble against him. **Perizzites** See note on 13:7. **people living in this land** Jacob's comment may reflect that Shechem was a city formed on the basis of tribal confederacy, meaning that the people of the town could have had extended family throughout Canaan.

Jacob Returns to Bethel

35 Then God said to Jacob, "Go up to Bethel and settle there, and build an altar there to God, who appeared to you when you were fleeing from your brother Esau."

²So Jacob said to his household and to all who were with him, "Get rid of the foreign gods you have with you, and purify yourselves and change your clothes. ³Then come, let us go up to Bethel, where I will build an altar to God, who answered me in the day of my distress and who has been with me wherever I have gone." ⁴So they gave Jacob all the foreign gods they had and the rings in their ears, and Jacob buried them under the oak at Shechem. ⁵Then they set out, and the terror of God fell on the towns all around them so that no one pursued them.

⁶Jacob and all the people with him came to Luz (that is, Bethel) in the land of Canaan. ⁷There he built an altar, and he called the place El Bethel,ᵃ because it was there that God revealed himself to him when he was fleeing from his brother.

⁸Now Deborah, Rebekah's nurse, died and was buried under the oak outside Bethel. So it was named Allon Bakuth.ᵇ

⁹After Jacob returned from Paddan Aram,ᶜ God appeared to him again and blessed him. ¹⁰God said to him, "Your name is Jacob,ᵈ but you will no longer be called Jacob; your name will be Israel.ᵉ" So he named him Israel.

¹¹And God said to him, "I am God Almighty;ᶠ be fruitful and increase in number. A nation and a community of nations will come from you, and kings will be among your descendants. ¹²The land I gave to Abraham and Isaac I also give to you, and I will give this land to your descendants after you."

ᵃ 7 *El Bethel* means *God of Bethel.*   ᵇ 8 *Allon Bakuth* means *oak of weeping.*   ᶜ 9 That is, Northwest Mesopotamia; also in verse 26   ᵈ 10 *Jacob* means *he grasps the heel,* a Hebrew idiom for *he deceives.*   ᵉ 10 *Israel* probably means *he struggles with God.*   ᶠ 11 Hebrew *El-Shaddai*

35:1–15 Following the massacre at Shechem (ch. 34), God instructs Jacob to settle at Bethel and build an altar there—this would allow him the opportunity to offer sacrifices. During Jacob's stay in Bethel, God reiterates both his covenant with Abraham (12:1–3) and Jacob's new name (32:28). This encounter recalls God's covenant faithfulness (28:10–22), his divine protection of his people and his plan for Israel's future.

35:1 Bethel See 28:19 and note. **build an altar** When Jacob first encountered God at Bethel (28:10–22), he erected a pillar (*matsevah* in Hebrew) and anointed it (see 28:18–22). Now he is instructed to build an altar at the same location. See the table "Altars in the Old Testament" on p. 249.

35:2 foreign gods The Hebrew phrase used here, *elohe nekhar*, refers to the idols buried by Jacob in v. 4. At his encounter with God at Bethel in 28:10–22, Jacob vowed that if God were to rescue him from exile, then Yahweh shall be his God. However, it seems that those of Jacob's household, and perhaps even him, had been worshipping other gods since then. Although a different Hebrew word is used here than the one used for the figurines (or household gods) that Rachel stole from her father Laban (see 31:19 and note), Jacob could be referring to those figurines. It seems, though, that more than the figurines stolen by Rachel were involved. **purify yourselves and change your clothes** The meaning of these acts is unclear, but the acts likely have to do with meeting God on holy ground (compare Ex 3:5) and may be related to purification needed after the defiling acts of Ge 34. Jacob and his family departed from Shechem (ch. 34), part of the promised land (see 12:1–9). But for Jacob Bethel was one of the most holy places because God had appeared to him there (28:18–22).

35:4 rings The inclusion of the rings suggests they were associated with the foreign gods (perhaps carved with symbols) or used in the worship of foreign gods. God's previous blessings of Jacob—despite the presence of idolatry among his household—represents the fulfillment of Yahweh's promise to Abraham and Isaac (28:13–15). Compare note on 35:2. **oak** Trees often marked sacred sites in Israelite religion. This tree can be identified with the tree of Moreh at Shechem mentioned in Abraham's encounter with Yahweh many years earlier (12:6–7). Burial of the foreign gods and rings at this place, and under this tree, marks a surrender of these items and the people of Jacob's household to the lordship of Yahweh.

35:5 terror of God While it is unclear what this description refers to, it is clear that God makes the safe passage possible. It seems that it was necessary because of the actions of Levi and Simeon at Shechem (see 34:30 and note)—travel was also risky in general in the ancient Near East.

35:6 Luz The earlier name of the city of Bethel, according to 28:19 (see note on 28:19).

35:7 El Bethel This term means the "the God of Bethel." **God** The Hebrew word used here is *ha-elohim*; in the Hebrew text it is accompanied by the definite article ("the"), which at times indicates that Yahweh is the God, set apart from, and superior to, all others (see Dt 4:35). Here, its use indicates the significance of the Bethel event—that the true God, Yahweh, had passed on his promises to Jacob at that time and place (compare note on Ge 35:1–15).

35:8 Allon Bakuth This term means the "oak of weeping."

35:9 God appeared to him again The Hebrew phrase used here could indicate that God appeared again to Jacob during, or upon, his return to Bethel. This would indicate that the narrative of 35:9–13 records a new divine encounter with God that brings together various moments in Jacob's life. If this is the case, the "again" would refer back to an earlier encounter, such as that at Peniel (32:22–32) or Bethel 30 years earlier (28:10–22). Alternatively, the Hebrew phrase may not refer to Jacob having a new encounter with God, but instead indicate that 35:9–13 is a recounting of earlier events with additional details. In 35:7, Jacob's first encounter with God at Bethel (28:10–22) was referenced, suggesting that 35:9–13 could refer to Jacob's second divine encounter at Peniel (32:22–32).

35:10 your name will be Israel See 32:28 and note.

35:11 I am God Almighty See note on 17:1. **kings will be among your descendants** See 49:10; compare 17:6,16.

[13]Then God went up from him at the place where he had talked with him.

[14]Jacob set up a stone pillar at the place where God had talked with him, and he poured out a drink offering on it; he also poured oil on it. [15]Jacob called the place where God had talked with him Bethel.[a]

The Deaths of Rachel and Isaac

35:23-26pp — 1Ch 2:1-2

[16]Then they moved on from Bethel. While they were still some distance from Ephrath, Rachel began to give birth and had great difficulty. [17]And as she was having great difficulty in childbirth, the midwife said to her, "Don't despair, for you have another son." [18]As she breathed her last — for she was dying — she named her son Ben-Oni.[b] But his father named him Benjamin.[c]

[19]So Rachel died and was buried on the way to Ephrath (that is, Bethlehem). [20]Over her tomb Jacob set up a pillar, and to this day that pillar marks Rachel's tomb.

[21]Israel moved on again and pitched his tent beyond Migdal Eder. [22]While Israel was living in that region, Reuben went in and slept with his father's concubine Bilhah, and Israel heard of it.

Jacob had twelve sons:

[23]The sons of Leah:

Reuben the firstborn of Jacob,
Simeon, Levi, Judah, Issachar and Zebulun.

[24]The sons of Rachel:

Joseph and Benjamin.

[25]The sons of Rachel's servant Bilhah:

Dan and Naphtali.

[26]The sons of Leah's servant Zilpah:

Gad and Asher.

These were the sons of Jacob, who were born to him in Paddan Aram.

[27]Jacob came home to his father Isaac in Mamre, near Kiriath Arba (that is, Hebron), where Abraham and Isaac had stayed. [28]Isaac lived a hundred and eighty years. [29]Then he breathed his last and died and was gathered to his people, old and full of years. And his sons Esau and Jacob buried him.

Esau's Descendants

36:10-14pp — 1Ch 1:35-37
36:20-28pp — 1Ch 1:38-42

36 This is the account of the family line of Esau (that is, Edom).

[2]Esau took his wives from the women of Canaan: Adah daughter of Elon the Hittite, and Oholibamah daughter of Anah and granddaughter of Zibeon the Hivite — [3]also Basemath daughter of Ishmael and sister of Nebaioth.

[4]Adah bore Eliphaz to Esau, Basemath bore Reuel, [5]and Oholibamah bore Jeush, Jalam and Korah. These were the sons of Esau, who were born to him in Canaan.

---

[a] 15 *Bethel* means *house of God.*   [b] 18 *Ben-Oni* means *son of my trouble.*   [c] 18 *Benjamin* means *son of my right hand.*

35:14 stone pillar See note on 28:18. **drink offering** This offering involved pouring out liquid, usually wine, in honor of God (compare Ex 29:40–42; Isa 57:6). **oil on it** This marks the pillar as sacred (compare Ge 28:18).

35:16–29 This section describes Jacob's travels south and records the deaths of Rachel and Isaac, as well as an additional tragic incident involving Reuben.

35:16 Ephrath Genesis 35:19 identifies Ephrath with Bethlehem, as do other passages (48:7; 1Sa 17:12; Ru 1:2; 4:11; Mic 5:2). Bethlehem is located in the territory of the tribe of Judah; it is surprising that Rachel is not buried in one of the territories allotted to her sons — Joseph and Benjamin.

35:18 Ben-Oni This Hebrew name can mean either "son of my sorrow," "son of my oath" or "son of my wickedness." Because of the context, "son of my sorrow" is more likely. **his father named him Benjamin** Benjamin (*binyamin* in Hebrew) means "son of the right hand." Since the Hebrew word *yamin* is also used to denote the southern direction (facing east), the name can also mean "son of the south." See the table "Symbolic Names of People in Hebrew" on p. 1388.

35:22 his father's concubine Bilhah Bilhah was Rachel's maidservant. With the matriarch of the family (Rachel) now dead, Reuben's violation of Bilhah ensures she will never replace Rachel as chief wife. Had Bilhah desired this status, her chief rival would have

been Leah — Reuben's mother. Reuben was already the firstborn (Ge 29:32; 35:23), but Jacob's favor of Rachel — and thus her sons — likely concerned him. He may have also been concerned for his mother. Since Reuben was the firstborn, cohabiting with his father's concubine represented a challenge to his aging father's position and authority. Reuben's act is a political move for power, one that recurs elsewhere in the OT for similar reasons (2Sa 3:7–8; 12:7–10; 16:21–22; 1Ki 2:13–25). Jacob commemorates Reuben's failure in his deathbed rebuke, denying Reuben any right to preeminence over his siblings and their families (Ge 49:3–4).

35:27 Kiriath Arba This is an early name for Hebron. See note on 23:2.

36:1–43 There are two genealogies in this passage: vv. 1–8 and vv. 9–43. This passage is the last mention of Esau in Genesis (compare note on 5:1). The remainder of the book (chs. 37–50) focuses on Jacob's descendants.

36:1 Esau See note on 25:25. **Edom** See 25:30 and note.

36:2 Esau took his wives The names of Esau's wives in this account differ from those in 26:34 and 28:9. Despite these variances, all the traditions agree that Esau married foreign wives (see 26:35; 27:46 — 28:9). **women of Canaan** This Hebrew term is used in the Pentateuch to refer to the wide range of peoples living in the region.

Esau's Family Tree
(Ge 36:1-14)

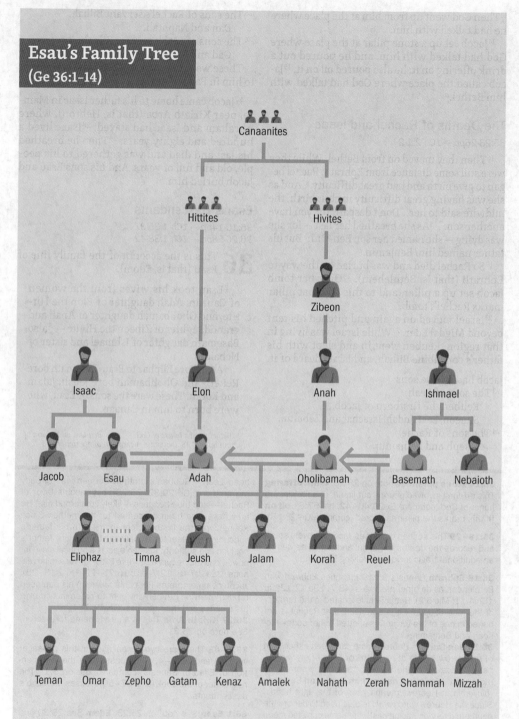

DESCENDANTS OF ESAU

⁶Esau took his wives and sons and daughters and all the members of his household, as well as his livestock and all his other animals and all the goods he had acquired in Canaan, and moved to a land some distance from his brother Jacob. ⁷Their possessions were too great for them to remain together; the land where they were staying could not support them both because of their livestock. ⁸So Esau (that is, Edom) settled in the hill country of Seir.

⁹This is the account of the family line of Esau the father of the Edomites in the hill country of Seir.

¹⁰ These are the names of Esau's sons:
Eliphaz, the son of Esau's wife Adah, and Reuel, the son of Esau's wife Basemath.
¹¹ The sons of Eliphaz:
Teman, Omar, Zepho, Gatam and Kenaz.
¹² Esau's son Eliphaz also had a concubine named Timna, who bore him Amalek. These were grandsons of Esau's wife Adah.
¹³ The sons of Reuel:
Nahath, Zerah, Shammah and Mizzah. These were grandsons of Esau's wife Basemath.
¹⁴ The sons of Esau's wife Oholibamah daughter of Anah and granddaughter of Zibeon, whom she bore to Esau:
Jeush, Jalam and Korah.

¹⁵ These were the chiefs among Esau's descendants:
The sons of Eliphaz the firstborn of Esau:
Chiefs Teman, Omar, Zepho, Kenaz, ¹⁶Korah,ᵃ Gatam and Amalek. These were the chiefs descended from Eliphaz in Edom; they were grandsons of Adah.
¹⁷ The sons of Esau's son Reuel:
Chiefs Nahath, Zerah, Shammah and Mizzah. These were the chiefs descended from Reuel in Edom; they were grandsons of Esau's wife Basemath.
¹⁸ The sons of Esau's wife Oholibamah:
Chiefs Jeush, Jalam and Korah. These were the chiefs descended from Esau's wife Oholibamah daughter of Anah.
¹⁹These were the sons of Esau (that is, Edom), and these were their chiefs.

²⁰These were the sons of Seir the Horite, who were living in the region:
Lotan, Shobal, Zibeon, Anah, ²¹Dishon, Ezer and Dishan. These sons of Seir in Edom were Horite chiefs.
²² The sons of Lotan:
Hori and Homam.ᵇ Timna was Lotan's sister.

ᵃ 16 Masoretic Text; Samaritan Pentateuch (also verse 11 and 1 Chron. 1:36) does not have *Korah*.   ᵇ 22 Hebrew *Hemam*, a variant of *Homam* (see 1 Chron. 1:39)

See note on 13:7. **Hittite** See note on 23:3. **Anah** The Hebrew word used here, *anah*, is a component of known ancient Near Eastern personal names, suggesting that the name may also be that of a god. **Hivite** See note on 34:2. While Esau's wife Oholibamah is identified as a Hivite here, her ancestors (presumably her father and grandfather—Anah and Zibeon), appear in the genealogy of the descendants of Seir the Horite in 36:20–30. The Hivites and Horites are likely both names for the same native Canaanite people. In Hebrew, the names differ by one letter and look very similar.

36:6–8 The migration of Esau and his family clan to Seir at this point in the narrative is chronologically problematic. Earlier Esau was already depicted as living in Seir and then returning to Seir again after his meeting with Jacob (32:3–4; 33:14,16). This means that this chapter likely presents a parenthetical summary and elaboration rather than a chronological account. This would mean that Jacob and Esau living in proximity to one another as adults with large families (36:7–8) occurred at some point between 33:11 and 33:16.

36:8 (that is, Edom) settled in the hill country of Seir This is a name for either part of Edom (e.g., 14:6; Dt 2:1; Jos 12:7) or Edom in its entirety—in both geographical and political terms (e.g., Ge 33:14,16; Nu 24:18; Jos 24:4; Eze 25:8).

36:9–43 This second genealogy of Esau is divided into four sections: Ge 36:9–14; vv. 15–19; vv. 20–30; and vv. 31–43. The first section of this second genealogy (vv. 9–14) repeats the names and relationships of the first one (see vv. 1–4), but it continues the line to the third generation for Adah and Basemath. The sequence

of Esau's wives moves according to the descending number of their children.

36:11 Teman Verse 34 refers to the land of the Temanites, which suggests that Teman was a geographical term for Edom (see Ob 9; Hab 3:3; Eze 25:13).
36:12 Amalek Amalek is in Esau's family line by a concubine, Timna. The OT casts the Amalekites as one of Israel's most bitter foes. The Amalekites are elsewhere not described as part of Edom (see Ex 17:8–15; Nu 24:20), likely because they are descendants of a concubine. This may indicate that they were latecomers to the Edomite tribal confederation. This is supported by Ge 36:22, which describes Timna as the sister of Lotan, an indigenous Horite (v. 20). This suggests that the Edomites who migrated to Seir began to intermarry with the native population.

36:15–19 This portion of Esau's genealogy focuses on Esau's firstborn son, Eliphaz. In this section each individual is described as a "chief" (*alluph* in Hebrew). The term *alluph* is related to the Hebrew word *eleph*, which refers to a clan or subdivision of a tribe.

36:20–30 This portion of the second genealogy traces the lineage of the indigenous Canaanite people—the Horites or Hivites (see 36:2 and note)—who were native to the region taken over by the descendants of Esau (36:8). This list links the family of Esau to the native Horites through his marriage to Oholibamah, daughter of a chief of the Horites (36:25; compare 36:18–19). The placement of this genealogy of the Horites suggests that they were assimilated into the clans of Edom. In this section, Seir is identified as the ancestor of the native clans. The region of Seir was named after him.

²³ The sons of Shobal:

Alvan, Manahath, Ebal, Shepho and Onam.

²⁴ The sons of Zibeon:

Aiah and Anah. This is the Anah who discovered the hot springs[a] in the desert while he was grazing the donkeys of his father Zibeon.

²⁵ The children of Anah:

Dishon and Oholibamah daughter of Anah.

²⁶ The sons of Dishon[b]:

Hemdan, Eshban, Ithran and Keran.

²⁷ The sons of Ezer:

Bilhan, Zaavan and Akan.

²⁸ The sons of Dishan:

Uz and Aran.

²⁹ These were the Horite chiefs:

Lotan, Shobal, Zibeon, Anah, ³⁰Dishon, Ezer and Dishan. These were the Horite chiefs, according to their divisions, in the land of Seir.

The Rulers of Edom

36:31-43pp — 1Ch 1:43-54

³¹These were the kings who reigned in Edom before any Israelite king reigned:

³² Bela son of Beor became king of Edom. His city was named Dinhabah.

³³ When Bela died, Jobab son of Zerah from Bozrah succeeded him as king.

³⁴ When Jobab died, Husham from the land of the Temanites succeeded him as king.

³⁵ When Husham died, Hadad son of Bedad, who defeated Midian in the country of Moab, succeeded him as king. His city was named Avith.

³⁶ When Hadad died, Samlah from Masrekah succeeded him as king.

³⁷ When Samlah died, Shaul from Rehoboth on the river succeeded him as king.

³⁸ When Shaul died, Baal-Hanan son of Akbor succeeded him as king.

³⁹ When Baal-Hanan son of Akbor died, Hadad[c] succeeded him as king. His city was named Pau, and his wife's name was Mehetabel daughter of Matred, the daughter of Me-Zahab.

⁴⁰These were the chiefs descended from Esau, by name, according to their clans and regions:

Timna, Alvah, Jetheth, ⁴¹Oholibamah, Elah, Pinon, ⁴²Kenaz, Teman, Mibzar, ⁴³Magdiel and Iram. These were the chiefs of Edom, according to their settlements in the land they occupied.

This is the family line of Esau, the father of the Edomites.

Joseph's Dreams

37 Jacob lived in the land where his father had stayed, the land of Canaan.

²This is the account of Jacob's family line.

Joseph, a young man of seventeen, was tending the flocks with his brothers, the sons of Bilhah and the sons of Zilpah, his father's wives, and he brought their father a bad report about them.

³Now Israel loved Joseph more than any of his other sons, because he had been born to him in his old age; and he made an ornate[d] robe for him. ⁴When his brothers saw that their father loved him more than any of them, they hated him and could not speak a kind word to him.

⁵Joseph had a dream, and when he told it to his

---

a 24 Vulgate; Syriac *discovered water;* the meaning of the Hebrew for this word is uncertain.   *b 26* Hebrew *Dishan,* a variant of *Dishon*   *c 39* Many manuscripts of the Masoretic Text, Samaritan Pentateuch and Syriac (see also 1 Chron. 1:50); most manuscripts of the Masoretic Text *Hadar*   *d 3* The meaning of the Hebrew for this word is uncertain; also in verses 23 and 32.

36:31–39 This section presents an account of eight kings who ruled in Edom before the Israelite monarchy (v. 31).

36:31 before any Israelite king reigned Since Saul, the first king of the Israelites, came centuries after the era of the patriarchs, this phrase was likely added by an editor to indicate that the prophecy given to Rebekah about Esau's fate had been fulfilled (see 25:23; compare 27:40). According to 1Sa 14:47, Saul fought against the Edomites, and David later dominated Edom (2Sa 8:2,13–14; 1Ki 11:14–17).

36:33 Bozrah The later capital city of Edom; it is sometimes equated with Edom as a whole (Isa 34:6; 63:1; Jer 49:13).

36:40–43 This list of names is not identical to previous ones. Likely arranged by localities, it may reflect Edomite administrative ordering during the time of the last Edomite king (see 1Ch 1:54).

37:1—50:26 The remainder of Genesis presents the story of Joseph and his brothers, as well as the episode of Judah and Tamar (Ge 38) and Jacob's final words (ch. 49). Joseph's story is the longest in the patriarchal narratives. It leads to Israel's descent into Egypt in fulfillment of Yahweh's announcement to Abraham (15:13).

37:1–36 The first part of this chapter (vv. 1–11) gives the reasons for the animosity of Joseph's brothers. The remainder (vv. 12–36) details their response to Jacob's favoritism and what they perceive as Joseph's youthful arrogance.

37:2 Joseph Jacob's eleventh son, the firstborn of his favorite wife, Rachel (30:24–25). See the people diagram "Joseph's, Son of Jacob, Family Tree" on p. 82.

37:3 an ornate robe The meaning of the Hebrew phrase used here, *kethoneth passim,* is uncertain. It also appears in 2Sa 13:18–19, but without any description. While it is clear that Joseph's robe set him apart from his brothers — likely indicating his favored status — it is not clear what set it apart. It could have had long sleeves, been made of expensive material or been a robe of many colors. The idea that the robe had many colors derives from the

brothers, they hated him all the more. [6]He said to them, "Listen to this dream I had: [7]We were binding sheaves of grain out in the field when suddenly my sheaf rose and stood upright, while your sheaves gathered around mine and bowed down to it."

[8]His brothers said to him, "Do you intend to reign over us? Will you actually rule us?" And they hated him all the more because of his dream and what he had said.

[9]Then he had another dream, and he told it to his brothers. "Listen," he said, "I had another dream, and this time the sun and moon and eleven stars were bowing down to me."

[10]When he told his father as well as his brothers, his father rebuked him and said, "What is this dream you had? Will your mother and I and your brothers actually come and bow down to the ground before you?" [11]His brothers were jealous of him, but his father kept the matter in mind.

Joseph Sold by His Brothers

[12]Now his brothers had gone to graze their father's flocks near Shechem, [13]and Israel said to Joseph, "As you know, your brothers are grazing the flocks near Shechem. Come, I am going to send you to them."

"Very well," he replied.

[14]So he said to him, "Go and see if all is well with your brothers and with the flocks, and bring word back to me." Then he sent him off from the Valley of Hebron.

When Joseph arrived at Shechem, [15]a man found him wandering around in the fields and asked him, "What are you looking for?"

[16]He replied, "I'm looking for my brothers. Can you tell me where they are grazing their flocks?"

[17]"They have moved on from here," the man answered. "I heard them say, 'Let's go to Dothan.'"

So Joseph went after his brothers and found them near Dothan. [18]But they saw him in the distance, and before he reached them, they plotted to kill him.

[19]"Here comes that dreamer!" they said to each other. [20]"Come now, let's kill him and throw him into one of these cisterns and say that a ferocious animal devoured him. Then we'll see what comes of his dreams."

[21]When Reuben heard this, he tried to rescue him from their hands. "Let's not take his life," he said. [22]"Don't shed any blood. Throw him into this cistern here in the wilderness, but don't lay a hand on him." Reuben said this to rescue him from them and take him back to his father.

[23]So when Joseph came to his brothers, they stripped him of his robe — the ornate robe he was wearing — [24]and they took him and threw him into the cistern. The cistern was empty; there was no water in it.

[25]As they sat down to eat their meal, they looked up and saw a caravan of Ishmaelites coming from Gilead. Their camels were loaded with spices, balm and myrrh, and they were on their way to take them down to Egypt.

---

way the Septuagint (the ancient Greek translation of the OT) translates *kethoneth passim*. Regardless of its appearance, the robe distinguishes Joseph from his brothers and possibly indicates a position of authority over them.
37:5 Joseph had a dream Dreams were considered a common means of divine communication in the OT and throughout the ancient Near East (Ge 20:3; 28:12; 31:10–11). Particular dreams, like those Joseph has, were also believed to be prophetic. **they hated him all the more** It is difficult to know whether Joseph baits his brothers with a dream that symbolically depicts them as subservient to him, or whether he simply fails to discern their hatred.

37:7 This dream probably refers to Joseph's rise to power in Egypt and his brothers being forced to come to him in order to survive (chs. 42–46).

37:9 the sun and moon and eleven stars This probably refers to Joseph's entire family, as a unit. The sun is a reference to Jacob, while the moon could be Bilhah or Leah—Rachel, Joseph's mother, was already deceased, making Bilhah, Rachel's servant, his stepmother (v. 10) and Leah the chief wife. The 11 stars refers to Joseph's 11 brothers. While Joseph's dream is not literally fulfilled—Jacob is never recorded as bowing down to Joseph—it is in essence when the entire family becomes dependent on Joseph (chs. 42–46).
37:14 Shechem The distance from Hebron to Shechem was about fifty miles, probably at least five days on foot.
37:15 a man The identity of this man is unknown. The overall mystery of the sequence and wording is reminis-

cent of the event when Jacob wrestled a man who turned out to be a divine being (32:24–32; see note on 32:24).
37:17 Dothan Roughly 15 miles north of Shechem.
37:20 these cisterns Referring to human-made containers for storing water.

Genesis 37:20

CISTERN
Ancient Israelites cut cisterns out of solid rock to gather and store water during the rainy season. Many cisterns have been found in Israel, some of which are quite large and deep (over 20 feet).

37:21 Let's not take his life Reuben's motive for intervening is unknown. As the oldest, he may have assumed that he would be held responsible for anything that happened to Joseph. In later years, Reuben still regretted his failure to save Joseph (42:22) and thus takes a different approach when a similar situation later arises involving his youngest brother Benjamin (42:37).
37:25 caravan of Ishmaelites This is a problematic phrase since these Ishmaelites are said to sell Joseph to Potiphar (39:1). Elsewhere, it is Midianite traders who take Joseph from his brothers (v. 28) and sell him to Potiphar (v. 36). This discrepancy could show that two versions of the same story were combined by an editor. It could also be that Joseph changed hands several times, or that the Ishmaelites were the Midianites. Judges 8:24

²⁶Judah said to his brothers, "What will we gain if we kill our brother and cover up his blood? ²⁷Come, let's sell him to the Ishmaelites and not lay our hands on him; after all, he is our brother, our own flesh and blood." His brothers agreed.

²⁸So when the Midianite merchants came by, his brothers pulled Joseph up out of the cistern and sold him for twenty shekels*ᵃ* of silver to the Ishmaelites, who took him to Egypt.

²⁹When Reuben returned to the cistern and saw that Joseph was not there, he tore his clothes. ³⁰He went back to his brothers and said, "The boy isn't there! Where can I turn now?"

³¹Then they got Joseph's robe, slaughtered a goat and dipped the robe in the blood. ³²They took the ornate robe back to their father and said, "We found this. Examine it to see whether it is your son's robe."

³³He recognized it and said, "It is my son's robe! Some ferocious animal has devoured him. Joseph has surely been torn to pieces."

³⁴Then Jacob tore his clothes, put on sackcloth and mourned for his son many days. ³⁵All his sons and daughters came to comfort him, but he refused to be comforted. "No," he said, "I will continue to mourn until I join my son in the grave." So his father wept for him.

³⁶Meanwhile, the Midianites*ᵇ* sold Joseph in Egypt to Potiphar, one of Pharaoh's officials, the captain of the guard.

Judah and Tamar

38 At that time, Judah left his brothers and went down to stay with a man of Adullam named Hirah. ²There Judah met the daughter of a Canaanite man named Shua. He married her and made love to her; ³she became pregnant and gave birth to a son, who was named Er. ⁴She conceived again and gave birth to a son and named him Onan. ⁵She gave birth to still another son and named him Shelah. It was at Kezib that she gave birth to him.

⁶Judah got a wife for Er, his firstborn, and her name was Tamar. ⁷But Er, Judah's firstborn, was wicked in the LORD's sight; so the LORD put him to death.

⁸Then Judah said to Onan, "Sleep with your brother's wife and fulfill your duty to her as a brother-in-law to raise up offspring for your brother." ⁹But Onan knew that the child would not be his; so whenever he slept with his brother's wife, he spilled his semen on the ground to keep from providing offspring for his brother. ¹⁰What he did was wicked in the LORD's sight; so the LORD put him to death also.

¹¹Judah then said to his daughter-in-law Tamar,

ᵃ 28 That is, about 8 ounces or about 230 grams
ᵇ 36 Samaritan Pentateuch, Septuagint, Vulgate and Syriac (see also verse 28); Masoretic Text *Medanites*

---

describes Midianites wearing golden earrings because they were Ishmaelites. It may also be that Ishmaelites was not an ethnic term, but a generic term for nomadic tradesmen. Either way, the narrative is pointing out that Joseph's brothers sold him into slavery to his own kin, but to people outside of the covenant promises of their family—the descendants of both Ishmael and Midian ultimately derive from the line of Abraham (Ge 16:15; 25:1–2). **camels** See note on 12:16.
37:26 Judah The fourth oldest of the 12 sons of Jacob and son of Leah (29:35).
37:29 he tore his clothes A gesture signifying mourning. It seems that Reuben thought Joseph was dead.
37:35 in the grave The Hebrew term used here, *she'ol*, occurs for the first time in the OT here. It refers to the realm of the dead (or the underworld), the grave or death itself. See the infographic "Ancient Hebrew Conception of the Universe" on p. 5.
37:36 Potiphar This same name occurs in the Hebrew text of the Joseph narrative later but as two words: *poti phera'* (41:45,50) in reference to Joseph's father-in-law. While the names probably do not identify the same person, they may share the same derivation. Potiphar means "he whom Ra has given" (*pa-di-pa-ra* in Egyptian). The final element in the name (*ra*) is the name of the sun god whose primary center was at On (Heliopolis). Joseph's father-in-law (Potiphera) is said to have been a priest at this religious center (41:45). However, this Egyptian name form does not occur in Egyptian sources before the nineteenth Dynasty of Egypt (ca. thirteenth century BC) although it reflects an evolution from name forms used in earlier periods, possibly as early as the Middle Kingdom (ca. twentieth to seventeenth century BC). Compare note on 41:14–57.

38:1–30 Judah's earlier suggestion saved Joseph's life (37:26–27), and Joseph in turn saves the nation of Israel (50:20). This narrative interrupts the story of Joseph's tragic betrayal and draws attention to Judah, whose lineage produces King David (see 17:6; 35:11). Every place name in this narrative is located in the later tribal territory of Judah, and several of the characters connect to later biographical details of the life of David. In addition, Jacob selects Judah to lead the family to Egypt (46:28). This narrative shows the moral failures of Judah and the desperate situation in which his inaction put Tamar in. See the people diagram "Judah to David" on p. 618.

38:1 At that time This phrase connects the events of ch. 38 with the events of ch. 37—the selling of Joseph into slavery. **Adullam** A city located in the Judean lowlands.
38:2 Canaanite Marriage with Canaanites was discouraged among the Israelites: Abraham insisted that Isaac not marry a Canaanite (Ge 24:3); Isaac and Rebekah objected to Esau's marriages with foreigners and forbade Jacob to marry outside the clan (27:46—28:1). The law later forbade intermarriage with Canaanites, because of the risk of foreigners leading the Israelites into idolatry (Dt 7:1,3). Compare note on 12:6.
38:5 Kezib A reference to Achzib, a city southwest of Adullam.
38:6 Judah got a wife for Er This describes the customary mode for marriage in a patriarchal culture: the father chooses a bride for his son (see 21:21,24). **Tamar** The only other occurrences of this name in the OT appear with reference to women in David's family (2Sa 13:1; 14:27).
38:7 wicked The Hebrew word used here, *ra'*, is a reverse of the consonants used in Hebrew for Er's name;

"Live as a widow in your father's household until my son Shelah grows up." For he thought, "He may die too, just like his brothers." So Tamar went to live in her father's household.

[12]After a long time Judah's wife, the daughter of Shua, died. When Judah had recovered from his grief, he went up to Timnah, to the men who were shearing his sheep, and his friend Hirah the Adullamite went with him.

[13]When Tamar was told, "Your father-in-law is on his way to Timnah to shear his sheep," [14]she took off her widow's clothes, covered herself with a veil to disguise herself, and then sat down at the entrance to Enaim, which is on the road to Timnah. For she saw that, though Shelah had now grown up, she had not been given to him as his wife.

[15]When Judah saw her, he thought she was a prostitute, for she had covered her face. [16]Not realizing that she was his daughter-in-law, he went over to her by the roadside and said, "Come now, let me sleep with you."

"And what will you give me to sleep with you?" she asked.

[17]"I'll send you a young goat from my flock," he said.

"Will you give me something as a pledge until you send it?" she asked.

[18]He said, "What pledge should I give you?"

"Your seal and its cord, and the staff in your hand," she answered. So he gave them to her and slept with her, and she became pregnant by him. [19]After she left, she took off her veil and put on her widow's clothes again.

[20]Meanwhile Judah sent the young goat by his friend the Adullamite in order to get his pledge back from the woman, but he did not find her. [21]He asked the men who lived there, "Where is the shrine prostitute who was beside the road at Enaim?"

"There hasn't been any shrine prostitute here," they said.

[22]So he went back to Judah and said, "I didn't find her. Besides, the men who lived there said, 'There hasn't been any shrine prostitute here.'"

[23]Then Judah said, "Let her keep what she has, or we will become a laughingstock. After all, I did send her this young goat, but you didn't find her."

[24]About three months later Judah was told, "Your daughter-in-law Tamar is guilty of prostitution, and as a result she is now pregnant."

Judah said, "Bring her out and have her burned to death!"

[25]As she was being brought out, she sent a message to her father-in-law. "I am pregnant by the man who owns these," she said. And she added, "See if you recognize whose seal and cord and staff these are."

[26]Judah recognized them and said, "She is more righteous than I, since I wouldn't give her to my son Shelah." And he did not sleep with her again.

[27]When the time came for her to give birth, there were twin boys in her womb. [28]As she was giving birth, one of them put out his hand; so the midwife took a scarlet thread and tied it on his wrist and said, "This one came out first." [29]But when he drew back his hand, his brother came out, and she said, "So this is how you have broken

---

this creates a wordplay. Er's offense or precisely how he died is unknown.

38:8 fulfill your duty to her as a brother-in-law With the death of Er, his brother, Onan, became responsible for providing children to Onan's wife. This custom is known as levirate marriage and is described in Dt 25. The custom, however, certainly predated Deuteronomy, as suggested by parallel ancient Near Eastern sources (e.g., the laws of Nuzi; Hittite laws). The purpose of the obligation is to ensure that widows were cared for and did not marry outside the clan. In a patriarchal culture, a widow needed sons to provide for her material needs and keep the property of her deceased husband within the family; sons also ensured that the name of the deceased husband would not be forgotten (see Dt 25:5–6).

38:9 the child would not be his This comment reveals the motives for Onan's selfish actions (compare note on Ge 38:8).

38:11 Live as a widow It is unclear whether Judah knew the nature of Er's offense, but he may have known why Yahweh killed Onan. The two deaths seem to discourage him from pursuing another partner for Tamar. This put Tamar in a desperate situation, as her livelihood would have depended on a husband or sons.

38:12 men who were shearing his sheep The springtime shearing of the sheep included feasting and celebration (1Sa 25:11,36; 2Sa 13:23).

38:15 she had covered her face The narrator conveys

that had Judah known the identity of the woman, he would not have had sexual relations with her (Ge 38:16; compare v. 26).

38:18 Your seal Likely a cylinder seal. A cylinder seal is a small, oval-shaped object upon which a personal sign or name was engraved. When rolled over clay, an impression was created. They were often hollowed out in the center, which enabled them to be carried on a cord around the neck. Tens of thousands of cylinder seals are known from archeological excavations.

38:21 shrine prostitute The Hebrew term used here is typically used of a woman in the service of a deity or temple.

38:24 burned to death Since Tamar was waiting for someone to fulfill the obligation of levirate marriage (see note on v. 8), any willful preempting of that obligation on her part was viewed as adultery—a capital offense (see Lev 20:10; Dt 22:22).

38:26 She is more righteous than I Judah knows he is the guilty party and confesses—sparing Tamar's life. She gives birth to twins, one of whom (Perez) appears in the lineage of Jesus (Mt 1:3; Lk 3:33). See the people diagram "Jesus' Family Tree According to Matthew" on p. 1528.

38:29 you have broken out The Hebrew word used here, *perets*, often translated is a pun on the baby's name Perez (*perets*). See the table "Symbolic Names of People in Hebrew" on p. 1388.

out!" And he was named Perez.[a] ³⁰Then his brother, who had the scarlet thread on his wrist, came out. And he was named Zerah.[b]

Joseph and Potiphar's Wife

39 Now Joseph had been taken down to Egypt. Potiphar, an Egyptian who was one of Pharaoh's officials, the captain of the guard, bought him from the Ishmaelites who had taken him there.

²The LORD was with Joseph so that he prospered, and he lived in the house of his Egyptian master. ³When his master saw that the LORD was with him and that the LORD gave him success in everything he did, ⁴Joseph found favor in his eyes and became his attendant. Potiphar put him in charge of his household, and he entrusted to his care everything he owned. ⁵From the time he put him in charge of his household and of all that he owned, the LORD blessed the household of the Egyptian because of Joseph. The blessing of the LORD was on everything Potiphar had, both in the house and in the field. ⁶So Potiphar left everything he had in Joseph's care; with Joseph in charge, he did not concern himself with anything except the food he ate.

Now Joseph was well-built and handsome, ⁷and after a while his master's wife took notice of Joseph and said, "Come to bed with me!"

⁸But he refused. "With me in charge," he told her, "my master does not concern himself with anything in the house; everything he owns he has entrusted to my care. ⁹No one is greater in this house than I am. My master has withheld nothing from me except you, because you are his wife. How then could I do such a wicked thing and sin against God?" ¹⁰And though she spoke to Joseph day after day, he refused to go to bed with her or even be with her.

¹¹One day he went into the house to attend to his duties, and none of the household servants was inside. ¹²She caught him by his cloak and said, "Come to bed with me!" But he left his cloak in her hand and ran out of the house.

¹³When she saw that he had left his cloak in her hand and had run out of the house, ¹⁴she called her household servants. "Look," she said to them, "this Hebrew has been brought to us to make sport of us! He came in here to sleep with me, but I screamed. ¹⁵When he heard me scream for help, he left his cloak beside me and ran out of the house."

¹⁶She kept his cloak beside her until his master came home. ¹⁷Then she told him this story: "That Hebrew slave you brought us came to me to make sport of me. ¹⁸But as soon as I screamed for help, he left his cloak beside me and ran out of the house."

¹⁹When his master heard the story his wife told him, saying, "This is how your slave treated me," he burned with anger. ²⁰Joseph's master took him and put him in prison, the place where the king's prisoners were confined.

---

[a] 29 Perez means breaking out.   [b] 30 Zerah can mean scarlet or brightness.

38:30 Zerah This name means "shining" or "brightness," which is probably an association with the crimson (or scarlet) thread tied to his wrist.

39:1–23 The narrative transitions from the Judah and Tamar episode (ch. 38) back into the account of Joseph. The opening verse repeats information from where the Joseph story left off (compare Ge 37:36; 39:1). This chapter describes how Yahweh protects and blesses Joseph in Potiphar's house and in prison (see note on 39:2), and it hints at Joseph's future in Pharaoh's court.

39:1 Potiphar See note on 37:36.

39:2 LORD was with Joseph This phrase occurs four times in this chapter (vv. 2,3,21,23). The repetition reinforces the providential storyline. **he lived in the house** Joseph was not made to labor in the fields, which suggests that Potiphar discerned abilities that made him more suitable for household management.

39:4 put him in charge of his household The Hebrew phrase used here, al betho—which may be literally rendered "over his house"—and the remainder of the verse indicates that Joseph oversaw everything owned by Potiphar. Slaves in Egypt commonly held occupations of high responsibility in households. For example, the Egyptian document Papyrus Brooklyn (ca. 1800 BC) lists nearly 80 male and female slaves in an Egyptian household by name with their occupations. Many are described as Asiatic, which is an Egyptian term that included Semites like Joseph. However this does not mean that foreigners from Canaan were viewed positively by Egyptians (see note on 46:34; compare 43:32).

39:6 except the food he ate This phrase can be understood literally; the reasoning could be that Joseph is not Egyptian (43:32). It is also possible that this phrase is a euphemism for Potiphar's wife or a figure of speech for Potiphar's private affairs.

39:7 Come to bed with me In addition to the issue of adultery, having sexual relations with the wife or concubine of one's superior was viewed as a usurpation of power (see note on 2Sa 3:7). Sex with Potiphar's wife would constitute an attempt to gain control over his master's property and would likely have led to Joseph's execution.

39:8 he refused Joseph's refusal is immediate and direct. He does not react angrily, knowing his place, but he allows for no flirtatious conversation.

39:10 even be with her This detail probably indicates that Joseph not only refuses to have sex with Potiphar's wife, but also refuses even to be in her presence.

39:16 his master This phrase reveals the loyalties of both the accused and the accuser. Joseph has had Potiphar's best interests in mind for roughly 11 years (see note on Ge 40:1), but Potiphar's wife views her husband as no more than the master of slaves like Joseph.

39:19 he burned with anger The text does not state the object of Potiphar's anger, perhaps suggesting that Potiphar may have been suspicious of his wife.

39:20 prison Joseph's punishment is distinctly Egyptian; incarceration is attested to in Egyptian documents, but does not appear in other ancient Near Eastern law codes.

But while Joseph was there in the prison, [21]the LORD was with him; he showed him kindness and granted him favor in the eyes of the prison warden. [22]So the warden put Joseph in charge of all those held in the prison, and he was made responsible for all that was done there. [23]The warden paid no attention to anything under Joseph's care, because the LORD was with Joseph and gave him success in whatever he did.

The Cupbearer and the Baker

40 Some time later, the cupbearer and the baker of the king of Egypt offended their master, the king of Egypt. [2]Pharaoh was angry with his two officials, the chief cupbearer and the chief baker, [3]and put them in custody in the house of the captain of the guard, in the same prison where Joseph was confined. [4]The captain of the guard assigned them to Joseph, and he attended them.

After they had been in custody for some time, [5]each of the two men — the cupbearer and the baker of the king of Egypt, who were being held in prison — had a dream the same night, and each dream had a meaning of its own.

[6]When Joseph came to them the next morning, he saw that they were dejected. [7]So he asked Pharaoh's officials who were in custody with him in his master's house, "Why do you look so sad today?"

[8]"We both had dreams," they answered, "but there is no one to interpret them."

Then Joseph said to them, "Do not interpretations belong to God? Tell me your dreams."

[9]So the chief cupbearer told Joseph his dream. He said to him, "In my dream I saw a vine in front of me, [10]and on the vine were three branches. As soon as it budded, it blossomed, and its clusters ripened into grapes. [11]Pharaoh's cup was in my hand, and I took the grapes, squeezed them into Pharaoh's cup and put the cup in his hand."

[12]"This is what it means," Joseph said to him. "The three branches are three days. [13]Within three days Pharaoh will lift up your head and restore you to your position, and you will put Pharaoh's cup in his hand, just as you used to do when you were his cupbearer. [14]But when all goes well with you, remember me and show me kindness; mention me to Pharaoh and get me out of this prison. [15]I was forcibly carried off from the land of the Hebrews, and even here I have done nothing to deserve being put in a dungeon."

[16]When the chief baker saw that Joseph had given a favorable interpretation, he said to Joseph, "I too had a dream: On my head were three baskets of bread.[a] [17]In the top basket were all kinds of baked goods for Pharaoh, but the birds were eating them out of the basket on my head."

[18]"This is what it means," Joseph said. "The three baskets are three days. [19]Within three days Pharaoh will lift off your head and impale your body on a pole. And the birds will eat away your flesh."

[20]Now the third day was Pharaoh's birthday, and he gave a feast for all his officials. He lifted up the heads of the chief cupbearer and the chief baker in the presence of his officials: [21]He restored the chief cupbearer to his position, so that he once again put the cup into Pharaoh's hand — [22]but he impaled the chief baker, just as Joseph had said to them in his interpretation.

[23]The chief cupbearer, however, did not remember Joseph; he forgot him.

---

[a] 16 Or *three wicker baskets*

40:1–23 While in prison, Joseph interprets dreams for two of Pharaoh's chief officials. Despite a seemingly bleak outlook for Joseph (see v. 23), his successful interpretations ultimately lead to an encounter with Pharaoh and a promotion (ch. 41). Joseph later interprets his circumstances in Egypt as God sovereignly arranging using particular circumstances to ensure the preservation of his people (see 50:20).

40:1 Some time later While the time frame is not specified here, later chronological references allow for a reconstruction. Two years elapse before Pharaoh has the dream that he calls upon Joseph to interpret (41:1). Joseph is 30 years old when Pharaoh elevates him to high office (41:46), which immediately follows his successful dream interpretation. As a result, Joseph was probably 28 years old when he entered prison. This means he served Potiphar for roughly 11 years (compare 37:2). **cupbearer and the baker of the king of Egypt** These men are the chief officials of their professions in Pharaoh's household (v. 2).

40:2 Pharaoh This word in Egyptian means "great house." In Egyptian records, this term is not used of Egypt's king until the fifteenth century BC and is not paired with the personal name of the king as a title until roughly the tenth century BC. This means that it is probably supplied here by a later writer or editor. **chief cupbearer** A palace official who served Pharaoh's wine and oversaw his drinking needs. Since this position offered regular opportunities to poison the king, the chief cupbearer had to be highly trustworthy.

40:13 lift up your head The Hebrew phrase used here is a common idiom for showing favor or pardoning someone (compare 2Ki 25:27; Jer 52:31).

40:19 will lift off your head Joseph repeats the imagery from v. 13, but with a negative connotation. Unlike the chief cupbearer, the chief baker is not restored or pardoned; he is literally lifted off the ground and impaled (v. 22). **birds will eat away your flesh** This would be especially horrible to an Egyptian. Egyptians at this point in history linked preservation of the body to their wellbeing in the afterlife.

40:22 impaled This could involve execution followed by the public hanging of a body from a large pole, or the execution itself being carried out by impalement.

40:23 chief cupbearer, however, did not remember Joseph's request in v. 14 is forgotten, and he remains in prison. Yet the earlier mention of God's favor with Joseph hints that something good is looming on the horizon, despite the bleak outlook (39:2).

Pharaoh's Dreams

41 When two full years had passed, Pharaoh had a dream: He was standing by the Nile, ²when out of the river there came up seven cows, sleek and fat, and they grazed among the reeds. ³After them, seven other cows, ugly and gaunt, came up out of the Nile and stood beside those on the riverbank. ⁴And the cows that were ugly and gaunt ate up the seven sleek, fat cows. Then Pharaoh woke up.

⁵He fell asleep again and had a second dream: Seven heads of grain, healthy and good, were growing on a single stalk. ⁶After them, seven other heads of grain sprouted—thin and scorched by the east wind. ⁷The thin heads of grain swallowed up the seven healthy, full heads. Then Pharaoh woke up; it had been a dream.

⁸In the morning his mind was troubled, so he sent for all the magicians and wise men of Egypt. Pharaoh told them his dreams, but no one could interpret them for him.

⁹Then the chief cupbearer said to Pharaoh, "Today I am reminded of my shortcomings. ¹⁰Pharaoh was once angry with his servants, and he imprisoned me and the chief baker in the house of the captain of the guard. ¹¹Each of us had a dream the same night, and each dream had a meaning of its own. ¹²Now a young Hebrew was there with us, a servant of the captain of the guard. We told him our dreams, and he interpreted them for us, giving each man the interpretation of his dream. ¹³And things turned out exactly as he interpreted them to us: I was restored to my position, and the other man was impaled."

¹⁴So Pharaoh sent for Joseph, and he was quickly brought from the dungeon. When he had shaved and changed his clothes, he came before Pharaoh.

¹⁵Pharaoh said to Joseph, "I had a dream, and no one can interpret it. But I have heard it said of you that when you hear a dream you can interpret it."

¹⁶"I cannot do it," Joseph replied to Pharaoh, "but God will give Pharaoh the answer he desires."

¹⁷Then Pharaoh said to Joseph, "In my dream I was standing on the bank of the Nile, ¹⁸when out of the river there came up seven cows, fat and sleek, and they grazed among the reeds. ¹⁹After them, seven other cows came up—scrawny and very ugly and lean. I had never seen such ugly cows in all the land of Egypt. ²⁰The lean, ugly cows ate up the seven fat cows that came up first. ²¹But even after they ate them, no one could tell that they had done so; they looked just as ugly as before. Then I woke up.

²²"In my dream I saw seven heads of grain, full and good, growing on a single stalk. ²³After them, seven other heads sprouted—withered and thin and scorched by the east wind. ²⁴The thin heads of grain swallowed up the seven good heads. I told this to the magicians, but none of them could explain it to me."

²⁵Then Joseph said to Pharaoh, "The dreams of Pharaoh are one and the same. God has revealed to Pharaoh what he is about to do. ²⁶The seven good cows are seven years, and the seven good heads of grain are seven years; it is one and the same dream. ²⁷The seven lean, ugly cows that came up afterward are seven years, and so are the seven worthless heads of grain scorched by the east wind: They are seven years of famine.

41:1−36 After being forgotten for two years, Joseph is finally released from prison (compare note on 40:1). The chief cupbearer remembers Joseph's ability to interpret dreams at the most opportune time. Joseph is called upon to interpret Pharaoh's puzzling dreams and subsequently reveals their meaning. The section closes with Joseph awaiting the king's reaction to the interpretation.

41:1 Nile The sustenance of the entire nation depended on the Nile. It flooded every year, providing millions of acres of arable land for the nation's food. Egyptians viewed the pharaoh as the incarnation of a god (Horus) and as the maintainer of the divinely imposed order on earth. Any irregularity in the annual flooding of the Nile was taken as a sign of weakness or illegitimacy with respect to Pharaoh's rule.

41:2−7 Pharaoh's two dreams in this chapter echo Joseph's pair of dreams (37:5−11) and the two dreams of the cupbearer and baker (40:5−19). His first dream features cows, which had a range of symbolic meanings in Egyptian religion. The Egyptian deity Isis, the mother of Horus, was depicted at times as a cow. Since the pharaoh was considered to be Horus incarnate, the cow symbolized the mother of the pharaoh and the pharaoh's own fertility and dynastic line.

41:8 wise men The Hebrew term used here, *chakham*,

occurs often in the OT (see Da 2:12−14; 5:7−8). It refers to people in the king's immediate circle who were either skilled in divination—discerning the will of deities based on using objects, omens or particular methods—or served as advisers.

41:14−57 References to various Egyptian practices in the Joseph story, especially in this passage, may help correlate the narrative with Egyptian history, thereby providing a chronological marker for Joseph, but the proposed correlations are disputed. This debate centers on whether or not elements of the Joseph story correlate with Egypt's Hyksos period (ca. 1700−1570 BC), a time when Semites from Syria-Palestine ruled the eastern delta of Egypt. This debate has effects on the dating of the exodus (see note on Ex 1:1−7; note on Ex 1:8; note on Ex 1:11).

41:14 shaved It is likely that both Joseph's head and beard were shaved. Egyptians were generally clean shaven, though iconography of the Old Kingdom (ca. 2575−2150) indicates that some males had beards or moustaches.

41:17−24 Pharaoh repeats his dreams to Joseph as he did with his magicians and wise men (Ge 41:1−8). Only minor variations between the two accounts appear in the Hebrew text.

²⁸"It is just as I said to Pharaoh: God has shown Pharaoh what he is about to do. ²⁹Seven years of great abundance are coming throughout the land of Egypt, ³⁰but seven years of famine will follow them. Then all the abundance in Egypt will be forgotten, and the famine will ravage the land. ³¹The abundance in the land will not be remembered, because the famine that follows it will be so severe. ³²The reason the dream was given to Pharaoh in two forms is that the matter has been firmly decided by God, and God will do it soon.

³³"And now let Pharaoh look for a discerning and wise man and put him in charge of the land of Egypt. ³⁴Let Pharaoh appoint commissioners over the land to take a fifth of the harvest of Egypt during the seven years of abundance. ³⁵They should collect all the food of these good years that are coming and store up the grain under the authority of Pharaoh, to be kept in the cities for food. ³⁶This food should be held in reserve for the country, to be used during the seven years of famine that will come upon Egypt, so that the country may not be ruined by the famine."

³⁷The plan seemed good to Pharaoh and to all his officials. ³⁸So Pharaoh asked them, "Can we find anyone like this man, one in whom is the spirit of God[a]?"

³⁹Then Pharaoh said to Joseph, "Since God has made all this known to you, there is no one so discerning and wise as you. ⁴⁰You shall be in charge of my palace, and all my people are to submit to your orders. Only with respect to the throne will I be greater than you."

Joseph in Charge of Egypt

⁴¹So Pharaoh said to Joseph, "I hereby put you in charge of the whole land of Egypt." ⁴²Then Pharaoh took his signet ring from his finger and put it on Joseph's finger. He dressed him in robes of fine linen and put a gold chain around his neck. ⁴³He had him ride in a chariot as his second-in-command,[b] and people shouted before him, "Make way[c]!" Thus he put him in charge of the whole land of Egypt.

⁴⁴Then Pharaoh said to Joseph, "I am Pharaoh, but without your word no one will lift hand or foot in all Egypt." ⁴⁵Pharaoh gave Joseph the name Zaphenath-Paneah and gave him Asenath daughter of Potiphera, priest of On,[d] to be his wife. And Joseph went throughout the land of Egypt.

⁴⁶Joseph was thirty years old when he entered the service of Pharaoh king of Egypt. And Joseph went out from Pharaoh's presence and traveled throughout Egypt. ⁴⁷During the seven years of abundance the land produced plentifully. ⁴⁸Joseph collected all the food produced in those seven years of abundance in Egypt and stored it in the

---

[a] 38 Or of the gods   [b] 43 Or in the chariot of his second-in-command; or in his second chariot   [c] 43 Or Bow down
[d] 45 That is, Heliopolis; also in verse 50

41:26–31 Joseph interprets the details of Pharaoh's dreams. God reveals that he will bring seven years of great agricultural abundance to Egypt and afterward seven years of devastating famine. The famine will be so severe that no one will remember the seven years of plenty.

41:37–57 Pharaoh promotes Joseph following the satisfactory interpretation of his dreams (41:26–31). He recognizes that Joseph has been divinely given the interpretation and that if the predicted disaster happens, no one is better positioned to guide Egypt through it. Joseph has already presented Pharaoh with the solution for surviving the seven-year famine.

Pharaoh also elevates Joseph through the ranks of Egyptian society. Pharaoh marries Joseph into a prestigious family. Pharaoh also makes Joseph second in command—which means he appointed Joseph as leader of at least the granaries and palace, and perhaps even as grand vizier of Egypt in general. It is difficult to know what position precisely Joseph obtained since the titles used in this section are Hebrew terms, not words borrowed from Egyptian, although they seem to reflect Egyptian positions. Although the idea of a Semite from Canaan attaining such high status is abnormal, examples of Semitic high officials are known from Egyptian texts. As the years of plenty pass and the famine strikes the land, Joseph will be able to help Egypt, his family and the rest of the world survive.

41:38 spirit of God The Hebrew phrase used here could be a reference to an empowering by Joseph's God, Yahweh, or an Egyptian god. It may also be translated as "the spirit of the gods" and refer to the Egyptian pantheon in general. Since this is spoken by Pharaoh, he likely means that in his perception the Egyptian gods are with Joseph.

41:40 in charge of my palace Compare 39:4 and note. **Only with respect to the throne** It is difficult to identify which office Joseph was appointed to in the Egyptian bureaucracy.

41:42–43 There are many scenes in surviving Egyptian records that depict the bestowal of a reward by a pharaoh or commemorate an appointment to high office (or both). In general, the scenes include the same elements as the Joseph story: bestowal of a seal or insignia of authority, a gold necklace, fine linen garments and an honorific chariot ride (vv. 42–43).

41:42 signet ring This ring signified the Pharaoh's approval, functioning like his signature of approval for a mandate.
41:45 Zaphenath-Paneah Joseph is given an Egyptian name, though the narrative continues to refer to him as Joseph. The precise derivation and meaning of this name is unknown. **Asenath** This name or title likely means "she who belongs to Neith"; Neith is an Egyptian goddess. This name does not appear among extant Egyptian texts. **Potiphera** Likely a variant of the name Potiphar, but probably not the same person as Joseph's former master. See note on 37:36. **On** The central location for Egyptian worship of Ra, the sun god.
41:46 Joseph was thirty years old Roughly 13 years have passed since Joseph was sold into slavery (see 37:2). Compare note on 40:1.

cities. In each city he put the food grown in the fields surrounding it. ⁴⁹Joseph stored up huge quantities of grain, like the sand of the sea; it was so much that he stopped keeping records because it was beyond measure.

⁵⁰Before the years of famine came, two sons were born to Joseph by Asenath daughter of Potiphera, priest of On. ⁵¹Joseph named his firstborn Manasseh*a* and said, "It is because God has made me forget all my trouble and all my father's household." ⁵²The second son he named Ephraim*b* and said, "It is because God has made me fruitful in the land of my suffering."

⁵³The seven years of abundance in Egypt came to an end, ⁵⁴and the seven years of famine began, just as Joseph had said. There was famine in all the other lands, but in the whole land of Egypt there was food. ⁵⁵When all Egypt began to feel the famine, the people cried to Pharaoh for food. Then Pharaoh told all the Egyptians, "Go to Joseph and do what he tells you."

⁵⁶When the famine had spread over the whole country, Joseph opened all the storehouses and sold grain to the Egyptians, for the famine was severe throughout Egypt. ⁵⁷And all the world came to Egypt to buy grain from Joseph, because the famine was severe everywhere.

Joseph's Brothers Go to Egypt

42 When Jacob learned that there was grain in Egypt, he said to his sons, "Why do you just keep looking at each other?" ²He continued, "I have heard that there is grain in Egypt. Go down there and buy some for us, so that we may live and not die."

³Then ten of Joseph's brothers went down to buy grain from Egypt. ⁴But Jacob did not send Benjamin, Joseph's brother, with the others, because he was afraid that harm might come to him. ⁵So Israel's sons were among those who went to buy grain, for there was famine in the land of Canaan also.

⁶Now Joseph was the governor of the land, the person who sold grain to all its people. So when Joseph's brothers arrived, they bowed down to him with their faces to the ground. ⁷As soon as Joseph saw his brothers, he recognized them, but he pretended to be a stranger and spoke harshly to them. "Where do you come from?" he asked.

"From the land of Canaan," they replied, "to buy food."

⁸Although Joseph recognized his brothers, they did not recognize him. ⁹Then he remembered his dreams about them and said to them, "You are spies! You have come to see where our land is unprotected."

¹⁰"No, my lord," they answered. "Your servants have come to buy food. ¹¹We are all the sons of one man. Your servants are honest men, not spies."

¹²"No!" he said to them. "You have come to see where our land is unprotected."

¹³But they replied, "Your servants were twelve brothers, the sons of one man, who lives in the land of Canaan. The youngest is now with our father, and one is no more."

¹⁴Joseph said to them, "It is just as I told you: You are spies! ¹⁵And this is how you will be tested: As surely as Pharaoh lives, you will not leave this

a 51 Manasseh sounds like and may be derived from the Hebrew for *forget.* *b 52 Ephraim* sounds like the Hebrew for *twice fruitful.*

41:51 Manasseh The Hebrew name here, *menashsheh*, roughly means "he who causes to forget," hence Joseph's explanation of the name, in which he uses the similar sounding Hebrew verbal form *nashshani.*

41:52 Ephraim This name is derived from the Hebrew verb, *parah*, meaning "to be fruitful." **made me fruitful** The Hebrew verb form used here, *hiphrani*, is a wordplay on the name Ephraim (*ephrayim* in Hebrew); it describes abundance and prosperity, hence Joseph's explanation of the name. See the people diagram "Joseph's, Son of Jacob, Family Tree" on p. 82.

41:54 seven years of famine References to Nile irregularities and famines—even seven-year famines—have survived in Egyptian records.

FAMINES IN GENESIS	
Abram and Sarai Travel to Egypt	Ge 12:10
Isaac and Family Settle in Gerar	Ge 26:1
Joseph's Family Follows Him to Egypt	Ge 41:53—42:5

42:1–38 Because the famine is widespread throughout the Mediterranean world, starving people from impoverished countries must travel to Egypt to buy food. This sets the stage for Joseph's reunion with his family.

When his brothers arrive to buy grain, they don't recognize Joseph, but Joseph recognizes them. Joseph asks his brothers a series of questions, and he tests them to see whether they have changed over the past twenty or more years. He initially accuses his brothers of spying and has them imprisoned for three days. Since Joseph wants to see Benjamin, he demands that they bring him to Egypt to validate their word. In the meantime, he holds one brother in prison as collateral. When the brothers return home and report what has happened, Jacob refuses to let them take Benjamin, fearing that he will never see the boy again.

42:3 ten of Joseph's brothers There may have been a per capita food distribution rule in Egypt, requiring all ten brothers to make the trip. Compare 29:31–35; 30:1–24.

42:9 dreams This scene is the fulfillment of the dreams that Joseph reported to his family prior to being sold into slavery (37:5–11).

42:13 twelve The brothers must explain this number to Joseph because only ten appear before him.

42:15 As surely as Pharaoh lives Joseph swears on the life of the most powerful authority in the land—the king of Egypt who thought of himself as a god incarnate (compare 1Sa 17:55; 25:26; 2Sa 14:19; 15:21). This

place unless your youngest brother comes here. ¹⁶Send one of your number to get your brother; the rest of you will be kept in prison, so that your words may be tested to see if you are telling the truth. If you are not, then as surely as Pharaoh lives, you are spies!" ¹⁷And he put them all in custody for three days.

¹⁸On the third day, Joseph said to them, "Do this and you will live, for I fear God: ¹⁹If you are honest men, let one of your brothers stay here in prison, while the rest of you go and take grain back for your starving households. ²⁰But you must bring your youngest brother to me, so that your words may be verified and that you may not die." This they proceeded to do.

²¹They said to one another, "Surely we are being punished because of our brother. We saw how distressed he was when he pleaded with us for his life, but we would not listen; that's why this distress has come on us."

²²Reuben replied, "Didn't I tell you not to sin against the boy? But you wouldn't listen! Now we must give an accounting for his blood." ²³They did not realize that Joseph could understand them, since he was using an interpreter.

²⁴He turned away from them and began to weep, but then came back and spoke to them again. He had Simeon taken from them and bound before their eyes.

²⁵Joseph gave orders to fill their bags with grain, to put each man's silver back in his sack, and to give them provisions for their journey. After this was done for them, ²⁶they loaded their grain on their donkeys and left.

²⁷At the place where they stopped for the night one of them opened his sack to get feed for his donkey, and he saw his silver in the mouth of his sack. ²⁸"My silver has been returned," he said to his brothers. "Here it is in my sack."

Their hearts sank and they turned to each other trembling and said, "What is this that God has done to us?"

²⁹When they came to their father Jacob in the land of Canaan, they told him all that had happened to them. They said, ³⁰"The man who is lord over the land spoke harshly to us and treated us as though we were spying on the land. ³¹But we said to him, 'We are honest men; we are not spies. ³²We were twelve brothers, sons of one father. One is no more, and the youngest is now with our father in Canaan.'

³³"Then the man who is lord over the land said to us, 'This is how I will know whether you are honest men: Leave one of your brothers here with me, and take food for your starving households and go. ³⁴But bring your youngest brother to me so I will know that you are not spies but honest men. Then I will give your brother back to you, and you can trade*a* in the land.'"

³⁵As they were emptying their sacks, there in each man's sack was his pouch of silver! When they and their father saw the money pouches, they were frightened. ³⁶Their father Jacob said to them, "You have deprived me of my children. Joseph is no more and Simeon is no more, and now you want to take Benjamin. Everything is against me!"

³⁷Then Reuben said to his father, "You may put both of my sons to death if I do not bring him back to you. Entrust him to my care, and I will bring him back."

³⁸But Jacob said, "My son will not go down there with you; his brother is dead and he is the only one left. If harm comes to him on the journey you are taking, you will bring my gray head down to the grave in sorrow."

The Second Journey to Egypt

43 Now the famine was still severe in the land. ²So when they had eaten all the grain they had brought from Egypt, their father said to them, "Go back and buy us a little more food."

a 34 Or move about freely

---

kind of oath appears in an Egyptian inscription from the twentieth century BC.
42:22 not to sin against the boy This indicates that all ten of Joseph's older brothers are morally at fault for what happened to him. **we must give an accounting for his blood** This could indicate that the brothers never told Reuben what they actually did to Joseph—he seems to think Joseph is dead.
42:24 Simeon The second oldest brother, who was a son of Leah (Ge 29:33), and one of the two brothers who slaughtered the men of Shechem (ch. 34).
42:27 place where they stopped for the night This refers to a temporary encampment, not an inn.

42:29–34 Joseph's ten older brothers recount the misfortunes of their trip to their father Jacob. Perhaps sensing that Jacob does not trust them to take care of Benjamin, they spin the story as positively as they can. They seem to believe that if Jacob will allow Benjamin to accompany them to Egypt, then all tensions will be resolved. Although Jacob is silent during this discussion, the outlook seems favorable until v. 36.

42:37 You may put both of my sons to death Since Reuben had four sons (46:9), the text likely refers to two of his sons.
42:38 to the grave The Hebrew text here uses the word *she'ol* (see note on 37:35).

43:1–34 When the famine grows more severe and food supplies run low, Jacob must send his sons back to Egypt for additional grain. But they refuse to go without Benjamin. Judah—acting as the firstborn in place of Reuben, Simeon and Levi (see note on 49:8)—agrees to take responsibility for Benjamin's safety, and Jacob reluctantly allows Benjamin to travel with him (compare 37:25–28). Once the brothers present Benjamin to Joseph, Simeon is restored to them (compare 42:24). Joseph also prepares a feast and tests them further to see whether they have changed (see 42:11).

Joseph's, Son of Jacob, Family Tree

Abraham = Sarah

Isaac = Rebekah

Potiphera   Esau   Jacob = Rachel

Joseph = Asenath   Benjamin

Manasseh   Ephraim

Asriel   Jair   Makir   Shuthelah   Beker   Tahan   Ezer   Beriah   Sheerah

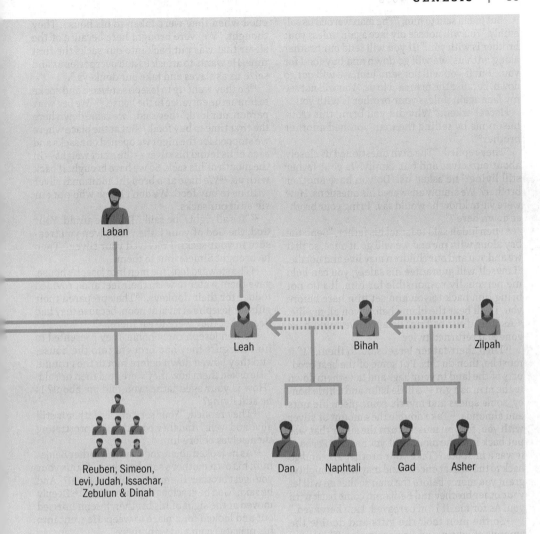

Laban

Leah

Bihah

Zilpah

Reuben, Simeon,
Levi, Judah, Issachar,
Zebulun & Dinah

Dan

Naphtali

Gad

Asher

³But Judah said to him, "The man warned us solemnly, 'You will not see my face again unless your brother is with you.' ⁴If you will send our brother along with us, we will go down and buy food for you. ⁵But if you will not send him, we will not go down, because the man said to us, 'You will not see my face again unless your brother is with you.'"

⁶Israel asked, "Why did you bring this trouble on me by telling the man you had another brother?"

⁷They replied, "The man questioned us closely about ourselves and our family. 'Is your father still living?' he asked us. 'Do you have another brother?' We simply answered his questions. How were we to know he would say, 'Bring your brother down here'?"

⁸Then Judah said to Israel his father, "Send the boy along with me and we will go at once, so that we and you and our children may live and not die. ⁹I myself will guarantee his safety; you can hold me personally responsible for him. If I do not bring him back to you and set him here before you, I will bear the blame before you all my life. ¹⁰As it is, if we had not delayed, we could have gone and returned twice."

¹¹Then their father Israel said to them, "If it must be, then do this: Put some of the best products of the land in your bags and take them down to the man as a gift—a little balm and a little honey, some spices and myrrh, some pistachio nuts and almonds. ¹²Take double the amount of silver with you, for you must return the silver that was put back into the mouths of your sacks. Perhaps it was a mistake. ¹³Take your brother also and go back to the man at once. ¹⁴And may God Almighty[a] grant you mercy before the man so that he will let your other brother and Benjamin come back with you. As for me, if I am bereaved, I am bereaved."

¹⁵So the men took the gifts and double the amount of silver, and Benjamin also. They hurried down to Egypt and presented themselves to Joseph. ¹⁶When Joseph saw Benjamin with them, he said to the steward of his house, "Take these men to my house, slaughter an animal and prepare a meal; they are to eat with me at noon."

¹⁷The man did as Joseph told him and took the men to Joseph's house. ¹⁸Now the men were frightened when they were taken to his house. They thought, "We were brought here because of the silver that was put back into our sacks the first time. He wants to attack us and overpower us and seize us as slaves and take our donkeys."

¹⁹So they went up to Joseph's steward and spoke to him at the entrance to the house. ²⁰"We beg your pardon, our lord," they said, "we came down here the first time to buy food. ²¹But at the place where we stopped for the night we opened our sacks and each of us found his silver—the exact weight—in the mouth of his sack. So we have brought it back with us. ²²We have also brought additional silver with us to buy food. We don't know who put our silver in our sacks."

²³"It's all right," he said. "Don't be afraid. Your God, the God of your father, has given you treasure in your sacks; I received your silver." Then he brought Simeon out to them.

²⁴The steward took the men into Joseph's house, gave them water to wash their feet and provided fodder for their donkeys. ²⁵They prepared their gifts for Joseph's arrival at noon, because they had heard that they were to eat there.

²⁶When Joseph came home, they presented to him the gifts they had brought into the house, and they bowed down before him to the ground. ²⁷He asked them how they were, and then he said, "How is your aged father you told me about? Is he still living?"

²⁸They replied, "Your servant our father is still alive and well." And they bowed down, prostrating themselves before him.

²⁹As he looked about and saw his brother Benjamin, his own mother's son, he asked, "Is this your youngest brother, the one you told me about?" And he said, "God be gracious to you, my son." ³⁰Deeply moved at the sight of his brother, Joseph hurried out and looked for a place to weep. He went into his private room and wept there.

³¹After he had washed his face, he came out and, controlling himself, said, "Serve the food."

³²They served him by himself, the brothers by themselves, and the Egyptians who ate with him by themselves, because Egyptians could not eat with Hebrews, for that is detestable to Egyptians. ³³The

[a] 14 Hebrew *El-Shaddai*

43:7 ourselves and our family This explanation includes details not found in the sons' explanation to Jacob in ch. 42. The former chapter apparently presented a summary.

43:8 boy The Hebrew term used here, *na'ar*, is used to describe Benjamin in 44:22 and 44:30–34. The term can refer to a male from infancy (Ex 2:6) up until young adulthood (Ge 34:19).

43:10 we could have gone and returned twice This is likely hyperbole, but if not, then their brother Simeon has been imprisoned in Egypt for several months (compare 42:24).

43:21 place where we stopped for the night As in 42:27, this refers to a temporary encampment, not an inn.

43:24 to wash their feet In the ancient Near East, people were customarily given water to wash their feet upon being welcomed into someone's home.

43:29 Benjamin Joseph's only full brother. **God be gracious to you, my son** Joseph is probably still using an interpreter (42:23). Up to this point in the narrative, he has not said anything like this to any of the brothers.

43:31 Serve the food Joseph hosts a meal for his brothers; this is an ironic echo of how his brothers had callously sat down to eat and debate his fate after throwing him into a pit (37:25).

men had been seated before him in the order of their ages, from the firstborn to the youngest; and they looked at each other in astonishment. ³⁴When portions were served to them from Joseph's table, Benjamin's portion was five times as much as anyone else's. So they feasted and drank freely with him.

A Silver Cup in a Sack

44 Now Joseph gave these instructions to the steward of his house: "Fill the men's sacks with as much food as they can carry, and put each man's silver in the mouth of his sack. ²Then put my cup, the silver one, in the mouth of the youngest one's sack, along with the silver for his grain." And he did as Joseph said.

³As morning dawned, the men were sent on their way with their donkeys. ⁴They had not gone far from the city when Joseph said to his steward, "Go after those men at once, and when you catch up with them, say to them, 'Why have you repaid good with evil? ⁵Isn't this the cup my master drinks from and also uses for divination? This is a wicked thing you have done.'"

⁶When he caught up with them, he repeated these words to them. ⁷But they said to him, "Why does my lord say such things? Far be it from your servants to do anything like that! ⁸We even brought back to you from the land of Canaan the silver we found inside the mouths of our sacks. So why would we steal silver or gold from your master's house? ⁹If any of your servants is found to have it, he will die; and the rest of us will become my lord's slaves."

¹⁰"Very well, then," he said, "let it be as you say. Whoever is found to have it will become my slave; the rest of you will be free from blame."

¹¹Each of them quickly lowered his sack to the ground and opened it. ¹²Then the steward proceeded to search, beginning with the oldest and ending with the youngest. And the cup was found in Benjamin's sack. ¹³At this, they tore their clothes. Then they all loaded their donkeys and returned to the city.

¹⁴Joseph was still in the house when Judah and his brothers came in, and they threw themselves to the ground before him. ¹⁵Joseph said to them, "What is this you have done? Don't you know that a man like me can find things out by divination?"

¹⁶"What can we say to my lord?" Judah replied. "What can we say? How can we prove our innocence? God has uncovered your servants' guilt. We are now my lord's slaves — we ourselves and the one who was found to have the cup."

¹⁷But Joseph said, "Far be it from me to do such a thing! Only the man who was found to have the cup will become my slave. The rest of you, go back to your father in peace."

¹⁸Then Judah went up to him and said: "Pardon your servant, my lord, let me speak a word to my lord. Do not be angry with your servant, though you are equal to Pharaoh himself. ¹⁹My lord asked

---

43:32 the Egyptians who ate with him by themselves Joseph eats alone because he is a member of the political elite. The other Egyptians eat apart from Joseph's brothers because of a cultural sense of racial superiority. Egyptian art often portrays Semites and other foreigners as inferior. Egyptian artifacts—such as footrests decorated with foreigners—show that foreigners like Semites were viewed as people who could be treaded upon by Egyptians.

44:1–34 Joseph devises one final test to determine his brothers' true character. He hides a divination cup in Benjamin's sack of grain and accuses the brothers of stealing it. Vehemently denying the charge and confident of their innocence, they promise the life of the thief. Much to their chagrin, the silver cup turns up in Benjamin's sack. In response, Judah makes a passionate plea before Joseph and offers his life as a ransom for Benjamin's.

44:2 silver References to silver occur repeatedly in the Joseph story (chs. 37–45). Here, the reference conveys the irony of the situation: Joseph's brothers sold him into slavery for 20 pieces of silver (37:28); now Joseph uses a silver object to test them and drive them into a state of panic.

44:5 uses for divination The narrative never states explicitly that Joseph practiced divination, although Joseph seems to suggest that he did (v. 15). Divination often involved determining the will of a deity by using some sort of object, like the cup referenced in v. 2. If Joseph did practice divination, then he could have practiced it in a way that fit with belief in Yahweh (compare Lev 16:8). Although the usage of a cup in divination is never specifically allowed, the casting of lots is. Joseph also could have practiced Egyptian divination, which was later prohibited, as it meant syncretism and calling upon foreign deities (see Dt 18:9–14). There are some possible indicators that Joseph was an Egyptian diviner: He married the daughter of an Egyptian priest and seems to become fully assimilated as an Egyptian, to the point that his brothers do not even recognize him (Ge 41:42–45; compare note on 42:15).

44:9 he will die Neither OT law nor known Egyptian legal material require the death penalty for property crimes of this nature.

44:13 tore their clothes This was Reuben's response when he thought his brothers had killed Joseph (see Ge 37:29 and note). Jacob exhibited this same response when he learned of Joseph's untimely demise (see 37:34). Now, in light of Benjamin's impending death and their father's certain grief, all the brothers repeat this gesture.

44:15 divination Joseph could be referencing his gift of receiving prophetic dreams and interpreting them or some other form of divination, such as using the cup referenced in 44:2 for divination. See note on 44:5.

44:19–26 In this section Judah recounts the events of 42:10–20 and 43:1–5. By repeating these events and showing Benjamin's importance to his father—particularly in vv. 27–31—Judah provides the basis for his appeal in v. 33. Joseph didn't hear the brothers' conversation with their father in Canaan, so Judah hopes that this background will cause Joseph to consider their father's best interests.

his servants, 'Do you have a father or a brother?' [20]And we answered, 'We have an aged father, and there is a young son born to him in his old age. His brother is dead, and he is the only one of his mother's sons left, and his father loves him.'

[21]"Then you said to your servants, 'Bring him down to me so I can see him for myself.' [22]And we said to my lord, 'The boy cannot leave his father; if he leaves him, his father will die.' [23]But you told your servants, 'Unless your youngest brother comes down with you, you will not see my face again.' [24]When we went back to your servant my father, we told him what my lord had said.

[25]"Then our father said, 'Go back and buy a little more food.' [26]But we said, 'We cannot go down. Only if our youngest brother is with us will we go. We cannot see the man's face unless our youngest brother is with us.'

[27]"Your servant my father said to us, 'You know that my wife bore me two sons. [28]One of them went away from me, and I said, "He has surely been torn to pieces." And I have not seen him since. [29]If you take this one from me too and harm comes to him, you will bring my gray head down to the grave in misery.'

[30]"So now, if the boy is not with us when I go back to your servant my father, and if my father, whose life is closely bound up with the boy's life, [31]sees that the boy isn't there, he will die. Your servants will bring the gray head of our father down to the grave in sorrow. [32]Your servant guaranteed the boy's safety to my father. I said, 'If I do not bring him back to you, I will bear the blame before you, my father, all my life!'

[33]"Now then, please let your servant remain here as my lord's slave in place of the boy, and let the boy return with his brothers. [34]How can I go back to my father if the boy is not with me? No! Do not let me see the misery that would come on my father."

Joseph Makes Himself Known

45 Then Joseph could no longer control himself before all his attendants, and he cried out, "Have everyone leave my presence!" So there was no one with Joseph when he made himself known to his brothers. [2]And he wept so loud-ly that the Egyptians heard him, and Pharaoh's household heard about it.

[3]Joseph said to his brothers, "I am Joseph! Is my father still living?" But his brothers were not able to answer him, because they were terrified at his presence.

[4]Then Joseph said to his brothers, "Come close to me." When they had done so, he said, "I am your brother Joseph, the one you sold into Egypt! [5]And now, do not be distressed and do not be angry with yourselves for selling me here, because it was to save lives that God sent me ahead of you. [6]For two years now there has been famine in the land, and for the next five years there will be no plowing and reaping. [7]But God sent me ahead of you to preserve for you a remnant on earth and to save your lives by a great deliverance.[a]

[8]"So then, it was not you who sent me here, but God. He made me father to Pharaoh, lord of his entire household and ruler of all Egypt. [9]Now hurry back to my father and say to him, 'This is what your son Joseph says: God has made me lord of all Egypt. Come down to me; don't delay. [10]You shall live in the region of Goshen and be near me — you, your children and grandchildren, your flocks and herds, and all you have. [11]I will provide for you there, because five years of famine are still to come. Otherwise you and your household and all who belong to you will become destitute.'

[12]"You can see for yourselves, and so can my brother Benjamin, that it is really I who am speaking to you. [13]Tell my father about all the honor accorded me in Egypt and about everything you have seen. And bring my father down here quickly."

[14]Then he threw his arms around his brother Benjamin and wept, and Benjamin embraced him, weeping. [15]And he kissed all his brothers and wept over them. Afterward his brothers talked with him.

[16]When the news reached Pharaoh's palace that Joseph's brothers had come, Pharaoh and all his officials were pleased. [17]Pharaoh said to Joseph, "Tell your brothers, 'Do this: Load your animals and return to the land of Canaan, [18]and bring your father and your families back to me. I will

---

[a] 7 Or save you as a great band of survivors

44:28 torn to pieces See 37:33.

45:1–28 Joseph can no longer hold back his emotions. Moved by Judah's impassioned plea for Benjamin's release and for the life of his father Jacob, Joseph reveals his identity to his brothers. They are stunned but relieved. Joseph embraces them — particularly Benjamin — and explains that God has used his journey to Egypt for good.

Pharaoh is pleased when he hears of the arrival of Joseph's brothers. He provides the necessary means to transport Joseph's family from Canaan to Egypt. He also gives them the best things Egypt has to offer. Not only will they live comfortably through the famine, they will also have a safe, fertile area in which to increase their wealth and clan. This suggests the value of Joseph to Pharaoh.

45:8 father to Pharaoh In Egyptian literature, titles similar to this one are attributed to Egyptians other than just Pharaoh. It is used for the pharaoh's physical father, tutor and father-in-law. The title could also be used as an honorary title for someone who incurred special favor from the pharaoh, which likely describes Joseph's case.

45:10 Goshen This likely refers to the northeastern region of the Nile delta.

45:18 you can enjoy the fat of the land Refers to the abundance that the land or soil offers — its produce.

give you the best of the land of Egypt and you can enjoy the fat of the land.'

¹⁹"You are also directed to tell them, 'Do this: Take some carts from Egypt for your children and your wives, and get your father and come. ²⁰Never mind about your belongings, because the best of all Egypt will be yours.'"

²¹So the sons of Israel did this. Joseph gave them carts, as Pharaoh had commanded, and he also gave them provisions for their journey. ²²To each of them he gave new clothing, but to Benjamin he gave three hundred shekelsᵃ of silver and five sets of clothes. ²³And this is what he sent to his father: ten donkeys loaded with the best things of Egypt, and ten female donkeys loaded with grain and bread and other provisions for his journey. ²⁴Then he sent his brothers away, and as they were leaving he said to them, "Don't quarrel on the way!"

²⁵So they went up out of Egypt and came to their father Jacob in the land of Canaan. ²⁶They told him, "Joseph is still alive! In fact, he is ruler of all Egypt." Jacob was stunned; he did not believe them. ²⁷But when they told him everything Joseph had said to them, and when he saw the carts Joseph had sent to carry him back, the spirit of their father Jacob revived. ²⁸And Israel said, "I'm convinced! My son Joseph is still alive. I will go and see him before I die."

Jacob Goes to Egypt

46 So Israel set out with all that was his, and when he reached Beersheba, he offered sacrifices to the God of his father Isaac.

²And God spoke to Israel in a vision at night and said, "Jacob! Jacob!"

"Here I am," he replied.

³"I am God, the God of your father," he said. "Do not be afraid to go down to Egypt, for I will make you into a great nation there. ⁴I will go down to Egypt with you, and I will surely bring you back again. And Joseph's own hand will close your eyes."

⁵Then Jacob left Beersheba, and Israel's sons took their father Jacob and their children and their wives in the carts that Pharaoh had sent to transport him. ⁶So Jacob and all his offspring went to Egypt, taking with them their livestock and the possessions they had acquired in Canaan. ⁷Jacob brought with him to Egypt his sons and grandsons and his daughters and granddaughters — all his offspring.

⁸These are the names of the sons of Israel (Jacob and his descendants) who went to Egypt:

Reuben the firstborn of Jacob.
⁹The sons of Reuben:
    Hanok, Pallu, Hezron and Karmi.
¹⁰The sons of Simeon:
    Jemuel, Jamin, Ohad, Jakin, Zohar and Sha-
    ul the son of a Canaanite woman.
¹¹The sons of Levi:
    Gershon, Kohath and Merari.
¹²The sons of Judah:
    Er, Onan, Shelah, Perez and Zerah (but Er
    and Onan had died in the land of Canaan).
The sons of Perez:
    Hezron and Hamul.
¹³The sons of Issachar:
    Tola, Puah,ᵇ Jashubᶜ and Shimron.

ᵃ 22 That is, about 7 1/2 pounds or about 3.5 kilograms
ᵇ 13 Samaritan Pentateuch and Syriac (see also 1 Chron. 7:1); Masoretic Text *Puvah*   ᶜ 13 Samaritan Pentateuch and some Septuagint manuscripts (see also Num. 26:24 and 1 Chron. 7:1); Masoretic Text *Iob*

45:25–28 Although Jacob would have likely asked, there is no indication here or elsewhere that Joseph or his brothers ever discussed with Jacob the story of how Joseph ended up in Egypt. The depiction here is of a father who thinks only of seeing his son, long presumed dead. Once he recovers from the shock of learning that Joseph is not only alive, but at the apex of power in Egypt, Jacob does not hesitate to make the journey.

46:1–27 Jacob gathers the clan and offers sacrifices to God on the way out of Canaan. In a vision, God grants Jacob permission to go to Egypt and promises to make him a great nation there. He also promises to bring Israel back to the land of Canaan—the promised land. This portion of the chapter also catalogues the members of Jacob's family that accompany him to Egypt.

46:1 Israel Jacob, father of Joseph and his brothers (see 32:28). The narrative alternates between his given name at birth, Jacob, and the name Yahweh gave him, Israel. **Beersheba** Jacob's reasons for stopping here are unknown, but this location occurs in other patriarchal narratives (see 21:14,31–33).

46:2 a vision at night This likely refers to a dream, though the normal Hebrew word for dreaming (*chalom*,

which occurs in 20:3; 28:12; 31:11; 37:5–10) is not used here.

46:4 I will go down Though this may seem obvious given God's omnipresence, it is noteworthy in light of the notion of sacred geography—the Israelite notion that the God of Israel allowed foreign nations to be under the jurisdiction of other gods after the Babel event (see 11:1–9; Dt 4:19–20; 32:8–9).

46:8–27 These genealogies—arranged according to the mother of each brother, in the order of Leah, Zilpah, Rachel and Bilhah—contain numerous inconsistencies with other OT genealogies for the sons of Jacob (compare Nu 26; 1Ch 2–8). This could indicate that this genealogy, in parallel with the similar one in Ex 1:1–7, focuses on people—and reaching the symbolic number of 70—while others focus on clans. While 70 nations are listed in Ge 10, here 70 people related to Israel (Jacob) are listed, suggesting that the nation of Israel functions as a new beginning for humanity.

46:9–25 This section lists the names of Jacob's descendants, most of whom accompanied him to Egypt. Joseph and his sons were already there (see 46:19–20). Each list begins with one of Jacob's sons, grouped according to their mothers (compare note on 46:8–27).

[14] The sons of Zebulun:
  Sered, Elon and Jahleel.

[15] These were the sons Leah bore to Jacob in Paddan Aram,[a] besides his daughter Dinah. These sons and daughters of his were thirty-three in all.

[16] The sons of Gad:
  Zephon,[b] Haggi, Shuni, Ezbon, Eri, Arodi and Areli.

[17] The sons of Asher:
  Imnah, Ishvah, Ishvi and Beriah.
  Their sister was Serah.
  The sons of Beriah:
    Heber and Malkiel.

[18] These were the children born to Jacob by Zilpah, whom Laban had given to his daughter Leah — sixteen in all.

[19] The sons of Jacob's wife Rachel:
  Joseph and Benjamin. [20] In Egypt, Manasseh and Ephraim were born to Joseph by Asenath daughter of Potiphera, priest of On.[c]

[21] The sons of Benjamin:
  Bela, Beker, Ashbel, Gera, Naaman, Ehi, Rosh, Muppim, Huppim and Ard.

[22] These were the sons of Rachel who were born to Jacob — fourteen in all.

[23] The son of Dan:
  Hushim.

[24] The sons of Naphtali:
  Jahziel, Guni, Jezer and Shillem.

[25] These were the sons born to Jacob by Bilhah, whom Laban had given to his daughter Rachel — seven in all.

[26] All those who went to Egypt with Jacob — those who were his direct descendants, not counting his sons' wives — numbered sixty-six persons. [27] With the two sons[d] who had been born to Joseph in Egypt, the members of Jacob's family, which went to Egypt, were seventy[e] in all.

[28] Now Jacob sent Judah ahead of him to Joseph to get directions to Goshen. When they arrived in the region of Goshen, [29] Joseph had his chariot made ready and went to Goshen to meet his father Israel. As soon as Joseph appeared before him, he threw his arms around his father[f] and wept for a long time.

[30] Israel said to Joseph, "Now I am ready to die, since I have seen for myself that you are still alive."

[31] Then Joseph said to his brothers and to his father's household, "I will go up and speak to Pharaoh and will say to him, 'My brothers and my father's household, who were living in the land of Canaan, have come to me. [32] The men are shepherds; they tend livestock, and they have brought along their flocks and herds and everything they own.' [33] When Pharaoh calls you in and asks, 'What is your occupation?' [34] you should answer, 'Your servants have tended livestock from our boyhood on, just as our fathers did.' Then you will be allowed to settle in the region of Goshen, for all shepherds are detestable to the Egyptians."

47 Joseph went and told Pharaoh, "My father and brothers, with their flocks and herds and everything they own, have come from the land of Canaan and are now in Goshen." [2] He chose five of his brothers and presented them before Pharaoh.

[3] Pharaoh asked the brothers, "What is your occupation?"

"Your servants are shepherds," they replied to Pharaoh, "just as our fathers were." [4] They also said to him, "We have come to live here for a while, because the famine is severe in Canaan and your servants' flocks have no pasture. So now, please let your servants settle in Goshen."

[5] Pharaoh said to Joseph, "Your father and your brothers have come to you, [6] and the land of Egypt is before you; settle your father and your brothers

---

a 15 That is, Northwest Mesopotamia   *b 16* Samaritan Pentateuch and Septuagint (see also Num. 26:15); Masoretic Text *Ziphion*   *c 20* That is, Heliopolis   *d 27* Hebrew; Septuagint *the nine children*   *e 27* Hebrew (see also Exodus 1:5 and note); Septuagint (see also Acts 7:14) *seventy-five*   *f 29* Hebrew *around him*

46:26 sixty-six The total descendants of Israel (Jacob) given in v. 27 is 70. This can be explained by the figure 66 referring just to those who came to Egypt. Er and Onan did not come to Egypt but died in Canaan before the journey was made (38:1–10). Joseph's two sons, Ephraim and Manasseh, were born in Egypt and could also be subtracted. The figure 66 could also involve adding Dinah and subtracting Joseph.

46:27 seventy This figure may be arrived at by counting the people listed in this genealogy and then adding Joseph, his two sons, and Jacob or Dinah. Compare note on 46:26.

46:28–34 Jacob and Joseph are finally reunited after the nearly two decades since Joseph was sold into slavery. After spending time with his father, Joseph prepares the family for their audience with Pharaoh. He tells them what to say to ensure that they are given Egypt's fertile pastureland to the north.

46:34 detestable to the Egyptians It is unclear why shepherds were held in low social esteem by the Egyptians. The Egyptians may have considered foreign herdsmen competition for resources, which may reflect a general disdain for foreigners from Canaan—called "Asiatics" in Egyptian texts (compare 43:32 and note).

47:1–12 The first part of this chapter focuses on the meeting of Joseph's family's with Pharaoh. Pharaoh meets first with a representative group of Joseph's brothers and gives them the pasturelands of Goshen (vv. 1–6). Then Pharaoh meets Jacob, and Jacob blesses him (vv. 7–10). The section ends by noting the gracious and benevolent way in which Joseph provides for his family (vv. 11–12), which contrasts sharply with the section that follows (vv. 13–31).

47:1 Goshen See note on 45:10.

47:6 in charge of my own livestock The offer to oversee the king's cattle would result in an elevated status for the foreigners, with all the associated legal advantages.

in the best part of the land. Let them live in Goshen. And if you know of any among them with special ability, put them in charge of my own livestock."

⁷Then Joseph brought his father Jacob in and presented him before Pharaoh. After Jacob blessedª Pharaoh, ⁸Pharaoh asked him, "How old are you?"

⁹And Jacob said to Pharaoh, "The years of my pilgrimage are a hundred and thirty. My years have been few and difficult, and they do not equal the years of the pilgrimage of my fathers." ¹⁰Then Jacob blessedᵇ Pharaoh and went out from his presence.

¹¹So Joseph settled his father and his brothers in Egypt and gave them property in the best part of the land, the district of Rameses, as Pharaoh directed. ¹²Joseph also provided his father and his brothers and all his father's household with food, according to the number of their children.

Joseph and the Famine

¹³There was no food, however, in the whole region because the famine was severe; both Egypt and Canaan wasted away because of the famine. ¹⁴Joseph collected all the money that was to be found in Egypt and Canaan in payment for the grain they were buying, and he brought it to Pharaoh's palace. ¹⁵When the money of the people of Egypt and Canaan was gone, all Egypt came to Joseph and said, "Give us food. Why should we die before your eyes? Our money is all gone."

¹⁶"Then bring your livestock," said Joseph. "I will sell you food in exchange for your livestock, since your money is gone." ¹⁷So they brought their livestock to Joseph, and he gave them food in exchange for their horses, their sheep and goats, their cattle and donkeys. And he brought them through that year with food in exchange for all their livestock.

¹⁸When that year was over, they came to him the following year and said, "We cannot hide from our lord the fact that since our money is gone and our livestock belongs to you, there is nothing left for our lord except our bodies and our land. ¹⁹Why should we perish before your eyes — we and our land as well? Buy us and our land in exchange for food, and we with our land will be in bondage to Pharaoh. Give us seed so that we may live and not die, and that the land may not become desolate."

²⁰So Joseph bought all the land in Egypt for Pharaoh. The Egyptians, one and all, sold their fields, because the famine was too severe for them. The land became Pharaoh's, ²¹and Joseph reduced the people to servitude,ᶜ from one end of Egypt to the other. ²²However, he did not buy the land of the priests, because they received a regular allotment from Pharaoh and had food enough from the allotment Pharaoh gave them. That is why they did not sell their land.

²³Joseph said to the people, "Now that I have bought you and your land today for Pharaoh, here is seed for you so you can plant the ground. ²⁴But when the crop comes in, give a fifth of it to Pharaoh. The other four-fifths you may keep as seed for the fields and as food for yourselves and your households and your children."

²⁵"You have saved our lives," they said. "May we find favor in the eyes of our lord; we will be in bondage to Pharaoh."

²⁶So Joseph established it as a law concerning land in Egypt — still in force today — that a fifth of the produce belongs to Pharaoh. It was only the land of the priests that did not become Pharaoh's.

²⁷Now the Israelites settled in Egypt in the region of Goshen. They acquired property there and were fruitful and increased greatly in number.

²⁸Jacob lived in Egypt seventeen years, and the years of his life were a hundred and forty-seven. ²⁹When the time drew near for Israel to die, he called for his son Joseph and said to him, "If I have

ª 7 Or greeted   ᵇ 10 Or said farewell to   ᶜ 21 Samaritan Pentateuch and Septuagint (see also Vulgate); Masoretic Text and he moved the people into the cities

---

47:11 district of Rameses Another name for Goshen. The city of Rameses (Pi-Ramesses) — the capital under Pharaoh Rameses II — was located within this region. That city has been identified as Qantir (which is also called Avaris and Tell ed-Dab'a). The presence of the name Rameses here and elsewhere in the Pentateuch is a focal point in the debate over the chronology of Joseph's time in Egypt and the exodus (see note on Ex 1:11; compare note on Ge 41:14–57).

47:13–31 Joseph initiates and manages a harsh set of reforms, as the severity of the famine requires. The Egyptian people surrender their money, livestock and farmland in exchange for the food necessary for their survival (Ge 47:14–21).

These circumstances ultimately resulted in landowners becoming tenant farmers under the authority of Pharaoh — paying him one-fifth of the produce of the land (vv. 20–26). This was neither serfdom nor slavery, since the people kept 80 percent of the produce. The people express gratitude for the reforms (v. 25) — which were continued after Joseph's death (as indicated by the editorial comment of v. 26) — likely because it gave them a chance to survive, not necessarily because they were pleased with the reforms. A consensus has not been reached on what period in Egypt's history best reflects these reforms.

47:29 put your hand under my thigh The exact Hebrew expression used here only occurs here and in 24:2. The Hebrew word commonly translated as "thigh" (yerekh) is used elsewhere as a euphemism for genitalia — in reference to where children come from (46:26; Ex 1:5; Jdg 8:30). This makes sense, since Ge 24:2 involves the fate of Abraham's child, Isaac. It is unclear precisely what this particular action involved — since there are no ancient Near Eastern parallels — but it seems that one man placed his hand near or on another man's genitalia, perhaps in reference to the sign of the covenant with Yahweh, circumcision (17:1–14).

found favor in your eyes, put your hand under my thigh and promise that you will show me kindness and faithfulness. Do not bury me in Egypt, ³⁰but when I rest with my fathers, carry me out of Egypt and bury me where they are buried."

"I will do as you say," he said.

³¹"Swear to me," he said. Then Joseph swore to him, and Israel worshiped as he leaned on the top of his staff.ᵃ

Manasseh and Ephraim

48 Some time later Joseph was told, "Your father is ill." So he took his two sons Manasseh and Ephraim along with him. ²When Jacob was told, "Your son Joseph has come to you," Israel rallied his strength and sat up on the bed.

³Jacob said to Joseph, "God Almightyᵇ appeared to me at Luz in the land of Canaan, and there he blessed me ⁴and said to me, 'I am going to make you fruitful and increase your numbers. I will make you a community of peoples, and I will give this land as an everlasting possession to your descendants after you.'

⁵"Now then, your two sons born to you in Egypt before I came to you here will be reckoned as mine; Ephraim and Manasseh will be mine, just as Reuben and Simeon are mine. ⁶Any children born to you after them will be yours; in the territory they inherit they will be reckoned under the names of their brothers. ⁷As I was returning from Paddan,ᶜ to my sorrow Rachel died in the land of Canaan while we were still on the way, a little distance from Ephrath. So I buried her there beside the road to Ephrath" (that is, Bethlehem).

⁸When Israel saw the sons of Joseph, he asked, "Who are these?"

⁹"They are the sons God has given me here," Joseph said to his father.

Then Israel said, "Bring them to me so I may bless them."

¹⁰Now Israel's eyes were failing because of old age, and he could hardly see. So Joseph brought his sons close to him, and his father kissed them and embraced them.

¹¹Israel said to Joseph, "I never expected to see your face again, and now God has allowed me to see your children too."

¹²Then Joseph removed them from Israel's knees and bowed down with his face to the ground. ¹³And Joseph took both of them, Ephraim on his right toward Israel's left hand and Manasseh on his left toward Israel's right hand, and brought them close to him. ¹⁴But Israel reached out his right hand and put it on Ephraim's head, though he was the younger, and crossing his arms, he put his left hand on Manasseh's head, even though Manasseh was the firstborn.

¹⁵Then he blessed Joseph and said,

"May the God before whom my fathers
    Abraham and Isaac walked faithfully,
the God who has been my shepherd
    all my life to this day,
¹⁶the Angel who has delivered me from
    all harm
    — may he bless these boys.

ᵃ 31 Or *Israel bowed down at the head of his bed*   ᵇ 3 Hebrew *El-Shaddai*   ᶜ 7 That is, Northwest Mesopotamia

---

47:30 bury me This indicates Jacob's hope that his people would return to the promised land of Canaan (see 15:1–16). **where they are buried** See 25:9; 35:29.
47:31 worshiped The Hebrew text here indicates that Jacob bows; Jacob may be worshiping or expressing thanks—or both.

48:1–22 With his death approaching, Jacob blesses his sons—a process that continues through ch. 49. In this chapter he incorporates Ephraim and Manasseh, Joseph's sons, into the Abrahamic covenant by formally adopting them (12:1–3; 15; 17:1–14). They thereby become entitled to a portion of the promised land and are eventually included in the 12 tribes of Israel. If Manasseh and Ephraim were simply added to the tribes of Israel, their inclusion would make it so that there are more than 12 tribes. However, Manasseh and Ephraim take Joseph's place as a land-inheriting tribe. In addition, Levi is excluded from receiving a proper land inheritance (Jos 13:33; 16–17). This makes it so that the tribes who inherit land equals 12. A total of 12 tribes can also be arrived at by only counting the sons of Jacob (Israel)—with Manasseh and Ephraim being viewed as tribes of Joseph (Josh 16:4). Manasseh is even referred to in later texts as a half-tribe (Jos 1:12; 4:12; 12:6), but this is primarily because half the tribe took an inheritance on the east side of the Jordan River and the other half took territory on the west side (Jos 13:1–14,29–33).

As in other parts of Genesis, this chapter continues the literary motif of the older brother—who would culturally be expected to be the major inheritor and leader of the overall family clan—serving the younger. Despite Joseph's protests, Jacob gives the greater blessing to Ephraim, Joseph's younger son. This is the pattern of Jacob's life, and he continues it here (see Ge 25:23).

48:1 Manasseh and Ephraim See 41:50–52; note on 41:51; note on 41:52.
48:3 God Almighty See note on 17:1. **Luz** See note on 28:19.
48:5 mine Jacob formally adopts his two grandchildren. Intrafamily adoptions are well attested to in the ancient Near East.
48:7 Paddan This refers to Paddan Aram (see 25:20; 28:2,5,6–7). **Rachel** See ch. 29; note on 29:6. **Ephrath** See 35:16–19; note on 35:16.
48:8 Who are these This may be due to Jacob's age—he has poor eyesight (v. 10). However, it is probably an allusion to Isaac's blessing of Jacob, when he took his brother's birthright because in v. 9 Jacob uses the same word Isaac did (compare 27:4 and note). However, the overall wording of the blessing appears to be part of a customary legal procedure (see 27:18).
48:16 the Angel The Hebrew phrase used here, *ha mal'akh*, likely refers to the Angel of God (or Angel of

May they be called by my
name
and the names of my fathers
Abraham and Isaac,
and may they increase greatly
on the earth."

[17]When Joseph saw his father placing his right hand on Ephraim's head he was displeased; so he took hold of his father's hand to move it from Ephraim's head to Manasseh's head. [18]Joseph said to him, "No, my father, this one is the firstborn; put your right hand on his head." [19]But his father refused and said, "I know, my son, I know. He too will become a people, and he too will become great. Nevertheless, his younger brother will be greater than he, and his descendants will become a group of nations." [20]He blessed them that day and said,

"In your[a] name will Israel pronounce this blessing:
'May God make you like Ephraim and Manasseh.'"

So he put Ephraim ahead of Manasseh.
[21]Then Israel said to Joseph, "I am about to die, but God will be with you[b] and take you[b] back to the land of your[b] fathers. [22]And to you I give one more ridge of land[c] than to your brothers, the ridge I took from the Amorites with my sword and my bow."

Jacob Blesses His Sons

49:1-28Ref — Dt 33:1-29

49 Then Jacob called for his sons and said: "Gather around so I can tell you what will happen to you in days to come.

[2]"Assemble and listen, sons of Jacob;
listen to your father Israel.

[3]"Reuben, you are my firstborn,
my might, the first sign of my
strength,
excelling in honor, excelling in power.
[4]Turbulent as the waters, you will no
longer excel,
for you went up onto your father's bed,
onto my couch and defiled it.

[5]"Simeon and Levi are brothers —
their swords[d] are weapons of violence.
[6]Let me not enter their council,
let me not join their assembly,
for they have killed men in their anger
and hamstrung oxen as they pleased.
[7]Cursed be their anger, so fierce,
and their fury, so cruel!
I will scatter them in Jacob
and disperse them in Israel.

[a] 20 The Hebrew is singular.   [b] 21 The Hebrew is plural.
[c] 22 The Hebrew for *ridge of land* is identical with the place name Shechem.   [d] 5 The meaning of the Hebrew for this word is uncertain.

Yahweh), whose identity is often blurred with Yahweh himself (see note on 21:17). This blurring of these identities is fitting with the parallel usage of *ha 'elohim* in Hebrew (which may be literally rendered as "the God") in v. 11 and v. 15. Jacob had divine encounters several times in his life and at several of these times it seems that God appeared to him in bodily form (see 28:13 and note; 32:24 and note) and the Angel of God also appeared to Jacob (see 31:11 and note). **bless** The Hebrew word used here is singular, not plural. The plural form of this word in Hebrew would have distinguished God from the Angel in the blessing. The singular form here blurs their identities.
48:20 Ephraim ahead of Manasseh Ephraim would become the more noteworthy of the two tribes, eventually becoming virtually synonymous with the northern kingdom of Israel (Isa 7:17; Hos 5:12). Compare note on Ge 48:1–22.
48:21 you The Hebrew text here uses a plural form, indicating that Jacob's blessing refers to the whole nation of Israel, not just to Joseph.
48:22 ridge of land The Hebrew word used here, *shekhem*, is identical to the Hebrew name of the location Shechem. Jacob purchased land at Shechem (33:18–19) and Joseph was later buried there (Jos 24:32). **with my sword and my bow** This probably does not refer back to the massacre at Shechem (Ge 34) or Jacob's purchase of land at Shechem (33:19), but to another incident in Jacob's lifetime that is not recorded in Genesis. Jacob did not participate in the massacre at Shechem; instead he condemned it (34:30; 49:5–7).

49:1–27 Commonly referred to as the "Blessing of Jacob," this chapter actually contains a mixture of blessings and curses on his 12 sons who essentially function as the eponymous (or name giving) ancestors of the 12 tribes of Israel (compare note on 48:1–22). Genesis 49 does not follow the birth order of Jacob's children found in chs. 29–30. In chs. 29–30, Zebulun is the tenth son overall (the sixth and last son by Leah). Jacob also blesses Zebulun before Issachar, though Issachar was born before Zebulun (30:17–20); this inversion also occurs in Dt 33:18.
49:1 what will happen to you in days to come Jacob's blessings and curses speak about the distant future of the 12 tribes of Israel. In this way, his words in ch. 49 function prophetically.
49:4 you will no longer excel Jacob demotes Reuben for his immorality. While sexual immorality in certain contexts may not have merited such a demotion — as Judah is not demoted for his actions with Tamar (ch. 38) — Reuben's actions had dishonored his father and were an attempt to usurp his fathers' leadership of the tribe (see note on 35:22).
49:5 their swords are weapons of violence References the murder of the men of Shechem (see ch. 34). The tribe of Simeon quickly lost its importance in Israel's national history. From the exodus (Nu 1:23) to the end of the wilderness wanderings (Nu 26:14), its population decreased from 59,300 to 22,200 people. In addition, rather than obtaining its own region, Simeon's inheritance was allotted within the tribe of Judah's territory (Jos 19:1–9).

8 "Judah,[a] your brothers will praise you;
    your hand will be on the neck of your
        enemies;
    your father's sons will bow down to you.
9 You are a lion's cub, Judah;
    you return from the prey, my son.
Like a lion he crouches and lies down,
    like a lioness — who dares to rouse him?
10 The scepter will not depart from Judah,
    nor the ruler's staff from between his feet,[b]
until he to whom it belongs[c] shall come
    and the obedience of the nations shall be his.
11 He will tether his donkey to a vine,
    his colt to the choicest branch;
he will wash his garments in wine,
    his robes in the blood of grapes.
12 His eyes will be darker than wine,
    his teeth whiter than milk.[d]

13 "Zebulun will live by the seashore
    and become a haven for ships;
    his border will extend toward Sidon.

14 "Issachar is a rawboned[e] donkey
    lying down among the sheep pens.[f]
15 When he sees how good is his resting place
    and how pleasant is his land,
he will bend his shoulder to the burden
    and submit to forced labor.

16 "Dan[g] will provide justice for his people
    as one of the tribes of Israel.
17 Dan will be a snake by the roadside,
    a viper along the path,
that bites the horse's heels
    so that its rider tumbles backward.

18 "I look for your deliverance, Lord.

19 "Gad[h] will be attacked by a band
        of raiders,
    but he will attack them at their heels.

20 "Asher's food will be rich;
    he will provide delicacies fit for a king.

21 "Naphtali is a doe set free
    that bears beautiful fawns.[i]

22 "Joseph is a fruitful vine,
    a fruitful vine near a spring,
    whose branches climb over a wall.[j]

---

[a] 8 *Judah* sounds like and may be derived from the Hebrew for *praise.*   [b] 10 Or *from his descendants*   [c] 10 Or *to whom tribute belongs*; the meaning of the Hebrew for this phrase is uncertain.   [d] 12 Or *will be dull from wine, / his teeth white from milk*   [e] 14 Or *strong*   [f] 14 Or *the campfires*; or *the saddlebags*   [g] 16 *Dan* here means *he provides justice.*   [h] 19 *Gad* sounds like the Hebrew for *attack* and also for *band of raiders.*   [i] 21 Or *free; / he utters beautiful words*   [j] 22 Or *Joseph is a wild colt, / a wild colt near a spring, / a wild donkey on a terraced hill*

49:8 your brothers will praise you Judah takes preeminence since Jacob's first three sons — Reuben, Simeon, and Levi — were dismissed from the blessing normally given to the firstborn. Jacob seems to indicate that this is because Reuben had intercourse with Jacob's concubine (compare note on 49:4) and because Simeon and Levi murdered the men at Shechem, putting the whole family in danger from other people in the region (compare 34:30 and note; note on 49:5). Judah's leadership following the exodus is hinted at elsewhere in the Pentateuch: The tribe of Judah has the largest tribal population in the census (Nu 1:26; 26:22), camps in front of the tent of meeting, and leads the nation in the marching order to the promised land (Nu 2:3,9; 10:14). See the infographic "The Israelite Encampment" on p. 215.

49:9 lion The epithet "lion of Judah" (Rev 5:5) derives from this blessing. Since Mic 5:2 associated Judah with the coming of the ruler of Israel, the lion of Judah became a Messianic motif as well.

49:11 to a vine The animals listed in this verse here would trample any vine to which they were tied. The image suggests that the land of Judah will be so lush and productive that losing vines in this manner will be no cause for concern. **he will wash his garments in wine** This image is intentionally absurd: Only incredibly wealthy people would have so much wine that they could even wash garments in them if they desired. See the infographic "A Winepress in Ancient Israel" on p. 1157.

49:13 the seashore It is difficult to know why Zebulun is connected to the sea here, since none of the territory of Zebulun touched the Mediterranean. (Jos 19:10–16). This could mean that the reference to the sea here is to the Sea of Galilee, which the tribe of Zebulun was near. **Sidon** Zebulun's territory did not border the Phoenician city Sidon. However, here Sidon may refer to the nation of Phoenicia as a whole, as Zebulun's territorial boundaries were adjacent to Phoenicia.

49:14 a rawboned donkey The Hebrew expression used here seems to refer to physical strength. The descriptions that follow in the remainder of this verse and Ge 49:15 likely mean that, despite being known for strength, Issachar would be more content not working.

49:16 will provide justice The Hebrew verb used here, *dayan*, is a wordplay on Dan's name. Compare note on 30:6.

49:17 a snake The Hebrew word used here, *nachash*, is the same term used in ch. 3 for the primeval enemy of Adam and Eve. This means that Jacob is re-characterizing what Dan's name means — he will act as accuser, not one who delivers proper judgment or justice. This is reflected in the later reputation of the tribe of Dan (see note on 30:6).

49:19 Gad will be attacked by a band of raiders With its tribal inheritance located east of the Jordan River, Gad regularly had problems with Ammonites, Moabites, Arameans and an assortment of other semi-nomadic groups.

49:20 Asher's food will be rich The Hebrew expression used here probably refers to a reputation for fine food; however, it could be unflattering. In Jdg 1:32, the tribe of Asher is living among enemy Canaanites, indicating that they could be providing fine food for enemy people groups.

49:21 English translations of this verse vary considerably, since some of the words are homographs (words that are spelled like other words, but have different meanings); this allows for substantially different interpretations of the Hebrew text. While the first part of the verse seems to refer to flourishing, it is unclear whether Jacob's words to Naphtali are ultimately positive or negative.

²³ With bitterness archers attacked him;
    they shot at him with hostility.
²⁴ But his bow remained steady,
    his strong arms stayed[a] limber,
because of the hand of the Mighty One
    of Jacob,
because of the Shepherd, the Rock
    of Israel,
²⁵ because of your father's God, who helps you,
    because of the Almighty,[b] who blesses you
with blessings of the skies above,
    blessings of the deep springs below,
    blessings of the breast and womb.
²⁶ Your father's blessings are greater
    than the blessings of the ancient
      mountains,
    than[c] the bounty of the age-old hills.
Let all these rest on the head of Joseph,
    on the brow of the prince among[d] his
      brothers.
²⁷ "Benjamin is a ravenous wolf;
    in the morning he devours the prey,
    in the evening he divides the plunder."

²⁸ All these are the twelve tribes of Israel, and this is what their father said to them when he blessed them, giving each the blessing appropriate to him.

The Death of Jacob

²⁹ Then he gave them these instructions: "I am about to be gathered to my people. Bury me with my fathers in the cave in the field of Ephron the Hittite, ³⁰ the cave in the field of Machpelah, near Mamre in Canaan, which Abraham bought along with the field as a burial place from Ephron the Hittite. ³¹ There Abraham and his wife Sarah were buried, there Isaac and his wife Rebekah were buried, and there I buried Leah. ³² The field and the cave in it were bought from the Hittites.[e]"

³³ When Jacob had finished giving instructions to his sons, he drew his feet up into the bed, breathed his last and was gathered to his people.

50 Joseph threw himself on his father and wept over him and kissed him. ² Then Joseph directed the physicians in his service to embalm his father Israel. So the physicians embalmed him, ³ taking a full forty days, for that was the time required for embalming. And the Egyptians mourned for him seventy days.

⁴ When the days of mourning had passed, Joseph said to Pharaoh's court, "If I have found favor in your eyes, speak to Pharaoh for me. Tell him, ⁵ 'My father made me swear an oath and said, "I am about to die; bury me in the tomb I dug for myself in the land of Canaan." Now let me go up and bury my father; then I will return.'"

⁶ Pharaoh said, "Go up and bury your father, as he made you swear to do."

⁷ So Joseph went up to bury his father. All Pharaoh's officials accompanied him — the dignitaries of his court and all the dignitaries of Egypt — ⁸ besides all the members of Joseph's household and his brothers and those belonging to his father's household. Only their children and their flocks and herds were left in Goshen. ⁹ Chariots and horsemen[f] also went up with him. It was a very large company.

¹⁰ When they reached the threshing floor of Atad, near the Jordan, they lamented loudly and bitterly; and there Joseph observed a seven-day

---

a 23,24 Or *archers will attack . . . will shoot . . . will remain . . . will stay*   *b 25* Hebrew *Shaddai*   *c 26* Or *of my progenitors, / as great as*   *d 26* Or *of the one separated from*   *e 32* Or *the descendants of Heth*   *f 9* Or *charioteers*

49:22 – 26 The ambiguous and cryptic nature of the Hebrew text of these verses makes interpretation difficult; Jacob could be referring to Joseph positively or negatively, or both.

49:22 Joseph is a fruitful vine The Hebrew phrase used here, *ben porath*, could refer to a "fruitful vine" (or "fruitful bough") or a "wild donkey" (or "wild colt"). Genesis 49:21 uses animal imagery, and vv. 23–24 use military imagery, which may suggest that a translation referring to an animal is more fitting.

49:24 This verse ascribes the success of Jacob to God, using various metaphors and titles for God to do so.

49:24 the Shepherd Shepherd imagery for God and rulers is found throughout the OT (e.g., Nu 27:17; 2Sa 5:2; 1Ki 22:17; Eze 34:23; 37:24).

49:27 Benjamin is a ravenous wolf Given the portrayal of young Benjamin in the Joseph story (Ge 43–45), this description is unexpected. However, it fits later events. For example, in the book of Judges troops from the tribe of Benjamin are described as experts with the sword and sling (Jdg 20:15–25).

49:28 – 33 Following Jacob's blessings and curses, he gives instructions concerning his death and burial. His death causes anxiety for Joseph's brothers—which they express in Ge 50. The end of ch. 49 leaves the reader unsure of how things will turn out.

50:1 – 26 Joseph's brothers view Jacob as a restraining force—Joseph will never hurt his father by punishing his brothers. But when Jacob dies, the brothers fear reprisals for their past actions. Apparently they were unsure of the forgiveness that Joseph had already offered (45:4–15). To ensure their survival, they concoct a story that Joseph ultimately accepts. Their story does not affect the way Joseph treats his brothers; he has already forgiven them. But it does provide Joseph with an opportunity to once again affirm how God has used the situation for good.

50:2 embalm his father Joseph orders his father to be embalmed in the Egyptian manner.
50:3 seventy days Other passages indicate that the normal Hebrew period of mourning was 30 days (see Nu 20:29; Dt 34:8). This means that this period of time likely includes 40 days for embalming.
50:10 the threshing floor of Atad This site is not

period of mourning for his father. [11]When the Canaanites who lived there saw the mourning at the threshing floor of Atad, they said, "The Egyptians are holding a solemn ceremony of mourning." That is why that place near the Jordan is called Abel Mizraim.[a]

[12]So Jacob's sons did as he had commanded them: [13]They carried him to the land of Canaan and buried him in the cave in the field of Machpelah, near Mamre, which Abraham had bought along with the field as a burial place from Ephron the Hittite. [14]After burying his father, Joseph returned to Egypt, together with his brothers and all the others who had gone with him to bury his father.

Joseph Reassures His Brothers

[15]When Joseph's brothers saw that their father was dead, they said, "What if Joseph holds a grudge against us and pays us back for all the wrongs we did to him?" [16]So they sent word to Joseph, saying, "Your father left these instructions before he died: [17]'This is what you are to say to Joseph: I ask you to forgive your brothers the sins and the wrongs they committed in treating you so badly.' Now please forgive the sins of the servants of the God of your father." When their message came to him, Joseph wept.

[18]His brothers then came and threw themselves down before him. "We are your slaves," they said.

[19]But Joseph said to them, "Don't be afraid. Am I in the place of God? [20]You intended to harm me, but God intended it for good to accomplish what is now being done, the saving of many lives. [21]So then, don't be afraid. I will provide for you and your children." And he reassured them and spoke kindly to them.

The Death of Joseph

[22]Joseph stayed in Egypt, along with all his father's family. He lived a hundred and ten years [23]and saw the third generation of Ephraim's children. Also the children of Makir son of Manasseh were placed at birth on Joseph's knees.[b]

[24]Then Joseph said to his brothers, "I am about to die. But God will surely come to your aid and take you up out of this land to the land he promised on oath to Abraham, Isaac and Jacob." [25]And Joseph made the Israelites swear an oath and said, "God will surely come to your aid, and then you must carry my bones up from this place."

[26]So Joseph died at the age of a hundred and ten. And after they embalmed him, he was placed in a coffin in Egypt.

---

[a] 11 Abel Mizraim means mourning of the Egyptians.
[b] 23 That is, were counted as his

---

mentioned elsewhere in the OT and has not been identified with certainty; its significance is unknown. See the infographic "A Threshing Floor" on p. 497.
50:11 Abel Mizraim This alternate name for the threshing floor of Atad means "mourning of Egypt" or "meadow of Egypt."
50:13 field of Machpelah See Ge 49:30; compare 23:9,17–19.

50:20 This climactic statement is the culmination of the Joseph saga.

50:22 a hundred and ten years This may not be Joseph's true age, since 110 years represented the ideal lifespan in Egyptian thought and served as an honorific description.
50:24 out of this land This statement foreshadows the exodus. Compare 15:13–14.
50:25 from this place When the Israelites finally leave Egypt in the exodus under Moses, they fulfill this vow (see Ex 13:19). Compare Jos 24:32.
50:26 he was placed in a coffin The use of a coffin is characteristically Egyptian.

THE OLD TESTAMENT AND THE ANCIENT NEAR EASTERN WORLDVIEW
by Michael S. Heiser

Proper interpretation of the Bible requires an understanding of the original context in which it was written. This is particularly true for the Old Testament. God chose a specific time, place and culture—the ancient Mediterranean and the ancient Near Eastern world of the second and first millennia BC—in which to inspire faithful persons to produce what we read in the Old Testament. Understanding their worldview leads to more faithful understanding on our part, since misinterpretations result from assuming that the Biblical writers thought, believed and acted as we do.

Although this ancient world is unfamiliar to most of us, it would have been even more unfamiliar to students of the Bible living prior to the archeological discoveries of the late 19th and early 20th centuries. The languages of the ancient Sumerians, Babylonians, Egyptians and Canaanites were deciphered within the past 200 years. The intimate relationship between the Old Testament and the literature and ideas of these civilizations became accessible only after such developments in ancient history and archaeology. This opened an extraordinary window for understanding what the Biblical writers meant. These connections are especially significant for our understanding of Genesis 1–2.

WHAT IS COSMOLOGY?

The term "cosmology" refers to the way in which we understand the structure of the universe. The Biblical writers' concept of how the heavens and earth were structured by God represents a particular cosmology. This cosmology involves ideas about where God dwells within the known "universe" and reflects the writer's experience or understanding of the world, not historical or scientific fact. For example, cosmologies include descriptions about places and events humans do not experience until death or unless permitted to do so by an act of God.

OLD TESTAMENT COSMOLOGY

The Israelites believed in a universe structure that was common among the civilizations of the ancient Near East. This structure included three parts: a heavenly realm for the gods, an earthly realm for humans and an underworld for the dead. The vocabulary of the Israelites' cosmology is also similar to that found in the literature of Mesopotamia, Egypt and Canaan.

The three tiers are reflected in the Ten Commandments: "You shall not make for yourself an image in the form of anything in heaven above or on the earth beneath or in the waters below" (Ex 20:4; compare Ps 33:6–8; Pr 8:27–29). This cosmology is also affirmed in Philippians 2:10 and Revelation 5:3.

The Heavens
Genesis 1:6–8 presents a basic understanding of the heavens: "And God said, 'Let there be a vault between the waters to separate water from water.' So God made the vault and separated the water under the vault from the water above it. And it was so. God called the vault 'sky.' And there was evening, and there was morning—the second day." The vaulted dome was believed to be solid and thought to hold back the waters above it, preventing them from falling on the earth.

The vaulted dome, sometimes called the firmament (and sometimes equated with the sky), was seen as connecting to foundations that went deep below the sea. The dome surrounded the earth with its edge meeting at the horizon—the boundary "between light and darkness" (Job 26:10; compare Pr 8:27–28). This explains verses like: "when he established the clouds above and fixed securely the fountains of the deep," (Pr 8:28) and "can you join [God] in spreading out the skies, hard as a mirror of cast bronze?" (Job 37:18).

The vaulted dome was thought to be supported by the tops of mountains because the peaks appeared to touch the sky (e.g., 2Sa 22:8). The heavens had doors and windows through which rain or the waters above could flow upon the earth from their storehouse above the dome (Ge 7:11; 8:2; Ps 78:23; 33:7).

Genesis 1 describes waters above and below the solid firmament, a belief also reflected in Psalm 148:4. God was thought to dwell above the firmament, as described in Job 22:14: "Thick clouds veil him, so he does not see us as he goes about in the vaulted heavens" (compare Am 9:6; Ps 29:10).

The Earth

The earth sat atop the watery deep. The "waters below" refers not only to waters that humans use but also the deeper abyss. Thus, the earth was seen as surrounded by and floating upon the seas (Ge 1:9–10), having arisen out of the water (2Pe 3:5). The earth was thought to be held fast by pillars or sunken foundations (1Sa 2:8; Job 38:4–6; Ps 104:5).

The Underworld

The realm of the dead was believed to be located under the earth. The most frequent Hebrew term for this place was *she'ol*, often transliterated in English Bibles as Sheol or translated as the realm of the dead, or even the grave (Pr 9:18; Ps 6:4–5; 18:4–5). At times, the Hebrew word for "earth" (*'erets*) is also used to describe the underworld, since graves were believed to represent gateways to the underworld. In Job, the realm of the dead is even described in watery terms: "The dead are in deep anguish, those beneath the waters and all that live in them" (Job 26:5). Jonah's description is perhaps the most vivid. Although he is located in the belly of the great fish, Jonah says he is in the underworld: the watery deep at "the roots of the mountains," a "pit" that had "bars" that closed forever (Jnh 2:6).

This worldview shaped the Old Testament and illustrates how the Bible uses the language of its time to explain its perspective and to glorify Yahweh.

EXODUS

INTRODUCTION TO EXODUS

Exodus begins where Genesis leaves off: The descendants of Jacob are living in Egypt and have multiplied into a large community. But Egypt's new king, the pharaoh, regards the Israelites as a threat and forces them into slavery. Exodus tells the story of how God hears the cry of his people, delivers them from Egyptian bondage and leads them to freedom.

BACKGROUND

The title, Exodus, comes from a Greek word that means "going out," which is fitting for the book's subject: the exit of the Hebrew people from Egypt. The text does not name its author, but Jewish and Christian traditions ascribe the book to Moses. However, there is debate about how the first five books of the Bible, known as the Pentateuch, were compiled (see the "Introduction to Genesis").

Assigning the events of Exodus to a specific historical period is difficult because there is little evidence from outside the Bible. The exodus can be dated to sometime during the 15th–13th centuries BC. The story is set mostly in Egypt and the Sinai Peninsula—particularly Mount Sinai. The events surrounding God's call of Moses (Ex 2–4) take place in Midian, just east of Sinai.

STRUCTURE

The book of Exodus divides naturally into two halves (chs. 1–18 and chs. 19–40). The first half tells how God rescues the Israelites from Egypt and leads them to Mount Sinai. God saves the infant Moses and later commissions him to lead the Israelites out of Egypt (chs. 1–4). As God's representative, Moses repeatedly confronts Pharaoh, who refuses to let the Israelites leave despite the devastating plagues sent by God (chs. 5–10). After the 10th plague kills all of the firstborn throughout Egypt, Pharaoh relents; the Israelites leave Egypt and walk across the sea as God holds back the waters (chs. 11–15). In the wilderness, they soon run out of supplies, but God miraculously provides food and water (chs. 16–18).

The second half of Exodus deals with the covenant God makes with the Israelites at Mount Sinai. This section begins with the Israelites camping at the mountain and receiving the Ten Commandments, which are followed by other regulations (chs. 19–24). God also gives Moses detailed plans for the Israelites'

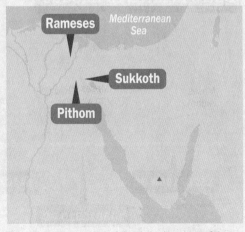

This map depicts some of the major locations of the Exodus narrative.

worship, including instructions for the ark of the covenant, the tabernacle (Israel's portable tent-shrine) and the priesthood (chs. 25–31). While Moses is up on the mountain, the Israelites decide to worship a golden idol shaped like a calf; in the fallout, God teaches the people how important it is to worship him alone (chs. 32–34). The remaining chapters record the Israelites constructing the tabernacle and preparing for worship (chs. 35–40).

OUTLINE

- Deliverance from Egypt (1:1—15:21)
- Journey to Sinai (15:22—18:27)
- The law is given at Sinai (19:1—31:18)
- The Israelites rebel at Sinai (32:1—34:35)
- The tabernacle is completed (35:1—40:38)

THEMES

The core message of Exodus is that God alone can set people free from bondage. The Israelites cannot rescue themselves. Throughout the book, God reveals himself with the repeated statement "I am Yahweh" (e.g., 6:6–8; 20:2; 34:10; this name often appears as "the Lord" in English translations). In doing so, Yahweh affirms that Israel is indeed *his* people.

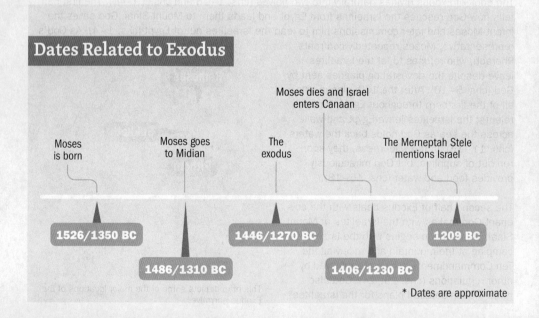

Dates Related to Exodus

Moses dies and Israel enters Canaan

Moses is born	Moses goes to Midian	The exodus		The Merneptah Stele mentions Israel
1526/1350 BC		1446/1270 BC		1209 BC
	1486/1310 BC		1406/1230 BC	

* Dates are approximate

God gives his people guidance about how to live and how to worship. Idolatry is not an option; Yahweh is not like other gods and cannot be worshiped in the same way. By giving the Israelites his law, God teaches them how to live justly. But as Moses indicates, the people need more than God's law; they need his presence to dwell among them (33:15–17; 40:36–38).

Exodus proclaims God's deliverance of Israel. God frees his people and sustains them. He is their great rescuer. This act of deliverance is remembered throughout the Bible as the quintessential example of Yahweh's power to save (Ne 9:9–15; Ps 78; Isa 48:20–21). Just as Yahweh saved them before, he would save them again (Isa 51:9–11; Hos 11:1–11). And, in Christ—the one greater than Moses—we too have a great rescuer (Heb 3:1–6). Jesus came to fulfill the Law of Moses and free us from the bondage of sin (Mt 5:17–20; Gal 5:1). Thanks to Christ's actions on the cross, we also have God's very presence among us, the Holy Spirit (Jn 14:16–17; 16:17).

The message of Exodus is that God has set the captives free and continues to do so. God hears the cries of all who are oppressed, from sin or any worldly or spiritual powers, and he is faithful to answer (Ro 8:31–39; Heb 2).

The Israelites Oppressed

1 These are the names of the sons of Israel who went to Egypt with Jacob, each with his family: [2]Reuben, Simeon, Levi and Judah; [3]Issachar, Zebulun and Benjamin; [4]Dan and Naphtali; Gad and Asher. [5]The descendants of Jacob numbered seventy[a] in all; Joseph was already in Egypt.

[6]Now Joseph and all his brothers and all that generation died, [7]but the Israelites were exceedingly fruitful; they multiplied greatly, increased in numbers and became so numerous that the land was filled with them.

[8]Then a new king, to whom Joseph meant nothing, came to power in Egypt. [9]"Look," he said to his people, "the Israelites have become far too numerous for us. [10]Come, we must deal shrewdly with them or they will become even more numerous and, if war breaks out, will join our enemies, fight against us and leave the country."

[11]So they put slave masters over them to oppress them with forced labor, and they built Pithom and Rameses as store cities for Pharaoh. [12]But the more they were oppressed, the more they multiplied and spread; so the Egyptians came to dread the Israelites [13]and worked them ruthlessly. [14]They made their lives bitter with harsh labor in brick and mortar and with all kinds of work in the fields; in all their harsh labor the Egyptians worked them ruthlessly.

[15]The king of Egypt said to the Hebrew midwives, whose names were Shiphrah and Puah, [16]"When you are helping the Hebrew women during childbirth on the delivery stool, if you see that the baby is a boy, kill him; but if it is a girl, let her live." [17]The midwives, however, feared God and did not do what the king of Egypt had told them to do; they let the boys live. [18]Then the king of Egypt summoned the midwives and asked them, "Why have you done this? Why have you let the boys live?"

[19]The midwives answered Pharaoh, "Hebrew women are not like Egyptian women; they are vigorous and give birth before the midwives arrive."

[20]So God was kind to the midwives and the people increased and became even more numerous. [21]And because the midwives feared God, he gave them families of their own.

[22]Then Pharaoh gave this order to all his people: "Every Hebrew boy that is born you must throw into the Nile, but let every girl live."

---

[a] 5 Masoretic Text (see also Gen. 46:27); Dead Sea Scrolls and Septuagint (see also Acts 7:14 and note at Gen. 46:27) *seventy-five*

1:1–7 The opening verses of the book of Exodus provide the narrative backdrop for the events to follow in Ex 1–19. The descendants of Jacob (or Israel) have been in Egypt for generations. By the time they leave Egypt, they will have spent 430 years there (12:40–41). Since the date of their arrival in Egypt is uncertain, this chronological clue only provides a rough approximation. The exodus most likely occurred sometime in the Late Bronze Age (1550–1200 BC). The two best options for the narrative's historical setting are mid-fifteenth century BC and early thirteenth century BC.

The first half of the book of Exodus describes Israel's oppression in Egypt, Yahweh's calling of Moses as a deliverer for his people, the conflict with Egypt over Israel's freedom, the plagues Yahweh brings on Egypt, Israel's sudden freedom, the miraculous crossing of the sea of reeds (commonly translated as the Red Sea), and their journey to Sinai, the mountain of Yahweh (chs. 1–19). Most of the second half of Exodus is devoted to explaining God's law with an emphasis on the construction of the tabernacle and the ordination of Moses' brother Aaron and his sons as priests (chs. 20–40). The Ten Commandments are enumerated in ch. 20, and the notorious incident with the worship of the golden calf is found in chs. 32–34.

1:1 who went to Egypt This opening verse indicates that the narrative of Exodus is a continuation of the story of Abraham's descendants that began in Ge 12–50. By the end of Genesis, Abraham's grandson Jacob (also known as Israel) has moved his family to Egypt due to famine (Ge 45:5–8). The story of Exodus picks up many years later with the descendants of Israel living under Egyptian rule.

1:8 Joseph meant nothing Because centuries have passed since the time of Joseph (compare note on Ex 1:1), the new pharaoh may not have known of him.

Alternately, he may have known about Joseph, but had no regard for his people or his past service to Egypt.

1:11 oppress them with forced labor The terms here describe harsh oppression. **Pithom and Rameses** These cities, well attested in Egyptian sources, are in the region of Goshen (see note on Ge 47:11). The appearance of the name "Rameses" (also spelled "Raamses") here and in Ex 12:37 provides a clue for dating Joseph's time in Egypt and the exodus. Pharaohs with this name do not appear until the thirteenth century BC. This reference to the city of Rameses could place the exodus event in the thirteenth century BC under Rameses II. The first extrabiblical reference to Israel is found in a stele erected by Ramses II's son, Merneptah, dating to near the end of the thirteenth century BC. However, according to the chronological description of 1Ki 6:1 (which yields a mid-fifteenth century BC exodus), this date is late by two centuries. An earlier date is supported by the possibility that the name Rameses may come from an individual who was not a pharaoh. The mention of Rameses could also represent an updating of the text by a later editor for readers more familiar with the region by its famous city. **as store cities** The Israelites may not have been the actual builders of these cities; Ex 1:14 (compare 5:7–19) shows that they were responsible for producing the building materials. **Pharaoh** The Biblical accounts do not identify any pharaohs by name until a much later period, so the pharaohs involved in the events of Genesis and Exodus are unknown. See note on Ge 40:2.

1:15 Hebrew midwives Despite there being thousands of Hebrew women (see Ex 1:7), the text names only two midwives. They might have been supervisors to other midwives, or they could be representative of the midwives of the time.

1:16 kill him Pharaoh targeted males because they can reproduce with many women—men often had more than one wife in the ancient Near East. Furthermore, since

The Birth of Moses

2 Now a man of the tribe of Levi married a Levite woman, ²and she became pregnant and gave birth to a son. When she saw that he was a fine child, she hid him for three months. ³But when she could hide him no longer, she got a papyrus basket[a] for him and coated it with tar and pitch. Then she placed the child in it and put it among the reeds along the bank of the Nile. ⁴His sister stood at a distance to see what would happen to him.

⁵Then Pharaoh's daughter went down to the Nile to bathe, and her attendants were walking along the riverbank. She saw the basket among the reeds and sent her female slave to get it. ⁶She

---

[a] 3 The Hebrew can also mean *ark*, as in Gen. 6:14.

---

men can serve as soldiers, the Egyptians feared that the Israelites would become a rival military power (v. 9).

2:1–22 This chapter introduces Moses, whom God will call to deliver the Israelites from Egyptian oppression. By showing how he escapes death at birth (vv. 1–10) and again after he commits murder (vv. 11–22), the narrative indicates that he is significant and that God is providentially caring for him.

2:2 fine The Hebrew word used here is the common word for "good" (*tov*). This verse—which combines "she saw" and the word *tov*—parallels God's assessment of

creation in Ge 1:31. This link indicates that a creative act of God is in view—the birth of Moses will lead to the exodus from Egypt and the birth of Israel as a nation. **2:3 papyrus** It was not uncommon to weave the papyrus plant in the manner described to make light, temporary boats. **basket** The Hebrew word used here, *tevah*, is the same term used for Noah's ark (Ge 6:14). **bank of the Nile** Moses' mother now obeys Pharaoh's command of Ex 1:22, but the manner of her compliance actually thwarts Pharaoh's intention. The story of the infant Moses reflects the ancient genre of the Exposed Child. Stories involving the exposure of a child to the elements

The Merneptah Stele

This engraved stone describes the victories of Egyptian Pharaoh Merneptah over Libyan invaders. Various outlying groups of raiders banded together to attack Egypt near the end of the 13th century BC, but Merneptah defeated them.

The stele also seems to mention a victory over Israel, saying, "Israel is a waste, without grain." If so, this indicates that an identifiable Israelite population already existed in the late thirteenth century BC.

opened it and saw the baby. He was crying, and she felt sorry for him. "This is one of the Hebrew babies," she said.

[7]Then his sister asked Pharaoh's daughter, "Shall I go and get one of the Hebrew women to nurse the baby for you?"

[8]"Yes, go," she answered. So the girl went and got the baby's mother. [9]Pharaoh's daughter said to her, "Take this baby and nurse him for me, and I will pay you." So the woman took the baby and nursed him. [10]When the child grew older, she took him to Pharaoh's daughter and he became her son. She named him Moses,[a] saying, "I drew him out of the water."

Moses Flees to Midian

[11]One day, after Moses had grown up, he went out to where his own people were and watched them at their hard labor. He saw an Egyptian beating a Hebrew, one of his own people. [12]Looking this way and that and seeing no one, he killed the Egyptian and hid him in the sand. [13]The next day he went out and saw two Hebrews fighting. He asked the one in the wrong, "Why are you hitting your fellow Hebrew?"

[14]The man said, "Who made you ruler and judge over us? Are you thinking of killing me as you killed the Egyptian?" Then Moses was afraid and thought, "What I did must have become known."

[15]When Pharaoh heard of this, he tried to kill Moses, but Moses fled from Pharaoh and went to live in Midian, where he sat down by a well. [16]Now a priest of Midian had seven daughters, and they came to draw water and fill the troughs to water their father's flock. [17]Some shepherds came along and drove them away, but Moses got up and came to their rescue and watered their flock.

[18]When the girls returned to Reuel their father, he asked them, "Why have you returned so early today?"

[19]They answered, "An Egyptian rescued us from the shepherds. He even drew water for us and watered the flock."

[20]"And where is he?" Reuel asked his daughters. "Why did you leave him? Invite him to have something to eat."

[21]Moses agreed to stay with the man, who gave his daughter Zipporah to Moses in marriage. [22]Zipporah gave birth to a son, and Moses named him Gershom,[b] saying, "I have become a foreigner in a foreign land."

[23]During that long period, the king of Egypt died. The Israelites groaned in their slavery and cried out, and their cry for help because of their slavery went up to God. [24]God heard their groaning and he remembered his covenant with Abraham, with Isaac and with Jacob. [25]So God looked on the Israelites and was concerned about them.

Moses and the Burning Bush

3 Now Moses was tending the flock of Jethro his father-in-law, the priest of Midian, and he led the flock to the far side of the wilderness and

---

[a] 10 *Moses* sounds like the Hebrew for *draw out*.
[b] 22 *Gershom* sounds like the Hebrew for *a foreigner there*.

---

appear in several dozen ancient texts. In most cases, the child is destined for greatness.

2:4 His sister Miriam (see Nu 26:59).

2:6 she felt sorry for him Ironically, Pharaoh's own daughter counteracts his decree.

2:9 will pay God's providence is unmistakable: Moses' mother has gone from desperately complying with Pharaoh's unjust decree to being paid out of his treasury to take care of her own child.

2:10 he became her son Since infant mortality was common in ancient times, formal adoption generally did not occur until a child was weaned—usually around the age of two or three. **Moses** The name "Moses," *mosheh*, is Egyptian in origin. Although the name seems to derive from the Egyptian verb *msy*, translated "to give birth," that verb does not reflect the interpretation given here—"I drew him out of the water." (The Hebrew verb for "draw out" is *mashah*.)

2:11 he went out to where his own people were Though the text does not mention when he learned this, Moses knows he is not Egyptian.

2:12 Looking this way and that In hiding the body in the sand, Moses demonstrates that he knows he has committed a crime (see Ex 2:15).

2:15 he tried to kill Moses While Egypt had the death penalty, ancient sources provide no evidence that it was used in cases of homicide. Pharaoh may have viewed Moses' action as a personal affront to his own authority. **Midian** Known from OT descriptions to have been in northwest Arabia, east of the Gulf of Aqaba.

2:18 Reuel their father Reuel is identified as the priest of Midian (v. 16) and the father of the girls at the well. A different name, Jethro, is used in 3:1, 4:18 and throughout ch. 18. The name Reuel also appears in Nu 10:29. Since Reuel means "friend of God" in Hebrew, it may be an epithet (or nickname) reflecting his priestly office or character.

2:22 Gershom The name Gershom, derived from the Hebrew verb *garash* (meaning "to drive out"), likely had personal significance to Moses given his flight from Egypt and his new circumstances. The verb *garash* appears several times elsewhere in the Hebrew text of the Moses narrative, including the description of Jethro's daughters before they were rescued by Moses (Ex 2:17) and his later confrontations with Pharaoh (6:1; 10:11; 11:1).

2:23 the king of Egypt died Egyptian sources attest to the practice of new pharaohs pardoning criminals. Moses apparently benefited from this policy, since he was not arrested upon his return to Egypt (see 4:19).

2:24 remembered The Hebrew verb used here, *zakhar*, often appears in conjunction with some activity—referring to a memory that prompts a specific course of action.

3:1–22 About 40 years after Moses settles down in Midian (see 7:7; Ac 7:23,30), the angel of Yahweh appears to him in a burning bush and calls him to return to Egypt.

3:1 Jethro See note on Ex 2:18. **Horeb** The name Horeb might be a synonym for Sinai—or, since the word means "desolate" or "dry," it could describe the arid region in

came to Horeb, the mountain of God. ²There the angel of the LORD appeared to him in flames of fire from within a bush. Moses saw that though the bush was on fire it did not burn up. ³So Moses thought, "I will go over and see this strange sight — why the bush does not burn up."

⁴When the LORD saw that he had gone over to look, God called to him from within the bush, "Moses! Moses!"

And Moses said, "Here I am."

⁵"Do not come any closer," God said. "Take off your sandals, for the place where you are standing is holy ground." ⁶Then he said, "I am the God of your father,ᵃ the God of Abraham, the God of Isaac and the God of Jacob." At this, Moses hid his face, because he was afraid to look at God.

⁷The LORD said, "I have indeed seen the misery of my people in Egypt. I have heard them crying out because of their slave drivers, and I am concerned about their suffering. ⁸So I have come down to rescue them from the hand of the Egyptians and to bring them up out of that land into a good and spacious land, a land flowing with milk and honey — the home of the Canaanites, Hittites, Amorites, Perizzites, Hivites and Jebusites. ⁹And now the cry of the Israelites has reached me, and I have seen the way the Egyptians are oppressing them. ¹⁰So now, go. I am sending you to Pharaoh to bring my people the Israelites out of Egypt."

¹¹But Moses said to God, "Who am I that I should go to Pharaoh and bring the Israelites out of Egypt?"

¹²And God said, "I will be with you. And this will be the sign to you that it is I who have sent you: When you have brought the people out of Egypt, youᵇ will worship God on this mountain."

¹³Moses said to God, "Suppose I go to the Israelites and say to them, 'The God of your fathers has sent me to you,' and they ask me, 'What is his name?' Then what shall I tell them?"

¹⁴God said to Moses, "I AM WHO I AM.ᶜ This is what you are to say to the Israelites: 'I AM has sent me to you.'"

¹⁵God also said to Moses, "Say to the Israelites, 'The LORD,ᵈ the God of your fathers — the God of Abraham, the God of Isaac and the God of Jacob — has sent me to you.'

"This is my name forever,
    the name you shall call me
    from generation to generation.

¹⁶"Go, assemble the elders of Israel and say to them, 'The LORD, the God of your fathers — the God of Abraham, Isaac and Jacob — appeared to me and said: I have watched over you and have

ᵃ 6 Masoretic Text; Samaritan Pentateuch (see Acts 7:32) *fathers*   ᵇ 12 The Hebrew is plural.   ᶜ 14 Or *I WILL BE WHAT I WILL BE*   ᵈ 15 The Hebrew for LORD sounds like and may be related to the Hebrew for *I AM* in verse 14.

---

which Mount Sinai was located. **the mountain of God** The location of Mount Sinai is not precisely identified in the OT. Horeb was either located on the east side of the Gulf of Aqaba or the west side of the gulf, just south of Canaan. The traditional site of this mountain (Jebel Musa) is located hundreds of miles south of the Gulf of Aqaba, deep in the Sinai Peninsula. However, it is unlikely that Moses drove the entire flock hundreds of miles to Jebel Musa. Jethro's arrival in ch. 18 also suggests Mount Sinai was closer to Midian than Jebel Musa (compare 18:5–6). The identification of Jebel Musa with Sinai is based on early church tradition, not descriptions like vv. 1–2.

3:2 angel of the LORD Either an embodiment of Yahweh himself or an angelic representative of Yahweh. While the angel of Yahweh is distinguished from Yahweh, the text often blurs or fuses their identities (see Ge 48:15–16; compare Ex 23:20–23; Jdg 2:1–3). Moses' encounter involves the angel of Yahweh and God himself, identified in Hebrew by the names *yahweh* and *elohim* (Ex 3:2–4). See the table "Angels in the Bible" on p. 2120; see the table "Old Testament Theophanies" on p. 924. **fire** Fire is frequently associated with divine presence and divine encounters, both in the OT and other ancient Near Eastern religions (e.g., Ge 15:17; Ex 24:17; Eze 1:27). **3:5 holy ground** The idea of physical ground being sanctified or made holy by divine presence is not unique to Israel; it follows from the ancient Near Eastern belief that a mountain was a divine abode or the location from which God (or the gods) ruled.

3:6 the God of your father Here and at Ex 3:15–16, the references to God encompass the three patriarchs of Gen 12–50 and link their covenant protector, God himself, to all of Israel.

3:8 flowing with milk and honey A common description of Canaan's abundance. **Canaanites, Hittites, Amorites, Perizzites, Hivites and Jebusites** These names appear in other lists of the people who lived in the promised land prior to Israelite occupation. The most comprehensive list — Ge 15:19–21 — includes 10 people groups.

3:12 sign to you It seems odd that God would give a reassuring sign to Moses only after he left Egypt. However, he may be referring to the burning bush, meaning that the encounter at the bush — or the miracle of the bush itself — was the sign given to Moses that God would be with him.

3:13 What is his name It is unlikely that the Israelites do not know the name of the God they worship, or that they were ignorant of the names used by their ancestors for God. Since divine names — and place names associated with divine appearances — often revealed events in the patriarchal stories (e.g., Ge 14:19–20; 16:13–14; 32:30–31), this question is the equivalent of asking what new thing God revealed.

3:14 I AM WHO I AM The revelation of the personal name of God — Israel's Creator (Ex 3:15). In Hebrew, the phrase "I am" is *ehyeh* — a different spelling from *yhwh* ("Yahweh"). The relationship between *ehyeh* and *yhwh* (called the Tetragrammaton) is not entirely clear, but both involve the consonants *y* and *h* in the same order and *yhwh* is used throughout this passage, indicating that both are names for the God of Israel (e.g. Ex 3:4,7,15,16). It seems that the spelling of *yhwh* recalls the revelation here. See the table "Names of God in the Old Testament" on p. 917.

3:16 elders of Israel These are Israel's tribal leaders (e.g., 4:29; 12:21; 18:12; 24:1; Nu 11:16,25).

seen what has been done to you in Egypt. [17]And I have promised to bring you up out of your misery in Egypt into the land of the Canaanites, Hittites, Amorites, Perizzites, Hivites and Jebusites — a land flowing with milk and honey.'

[18]"The elders of Israel will listen to you. Then you and the elders are to go to the king of Egypt and say to him, 'The LORD, the God of the Hebrews, has met with us. Let us take a three-day journey into the wilderness to offer sacrifices to the LORD our God.' [19]But I know that the king of Egypt will not let you go unless a mighty hand compels him. [20]So I will stretch out my hand and strike the Egyptians with all the wonders that I will perform among them. After that, he will let you go.

[21]"And I will make the Egyptians favorably disposed toward this people, so that when you leave you will not go empty-handed. [22]Every woman is to ask her neighbor and any woman living in her house for articles of silver and gold and for clothing, which you will put on your sons and daughters. And so you will plunder the Egyptians."

Signs for Moses

4 Moses answered, "What if they do not believe me or listen to me and say, 'The LORD did not appear to you'?"

[2]Then the LORD said to him, "What is that in your hand?"

"A staff," he replied.

[3]The LORD said, "Throw it on the ground."

Moses threw it on the ground and it became a snake, and he ran from it. [4]Then the LORD said to him, "Reach out your hand and take it by the tail." So Moses reached out and took hold of the snake and it turned back into a staff in his hand. [5]"This," said the LORD, "is so that they may believe that the LORD, the God of their fathers — the God of Abraham, the God of Isaac and the God of Jacob — has appeared to you."

[6]Then the LORD said, "Put your hand inside your cloak." So Moses put his hand into his cloak, and when he took it out, the skin was leprous[a] — it had become as white as snow.

[7]"Now put it back into your cloak," he said. So Moses put his hand back into his cloak, and when he took it out, it was restored, like the rest of his flesh.

[8]Then the LORD said, "If they do not believe you or pay attention to the first sign, they may believe the second. [9]But if they do not believe these two signs or listen to you, take some water from the Nile and pour it on the dry ground. The water you take from the river will become blood on the ground."

[10]Moses said to the LORD, "Pardon your servant, Lord. I have never been eloquent, neither in the past nor since you have spoken to your servant. I am slow of speech and tongue."

[11]The LORD said to him, "Who gave human beings their mouths? Who makes them deaf or mute? Who gives them sight or makes them blind? Is it not I, the LORD? [12]Now go; I will help you speak and will teach you what to say."

[13]But Moses said, "Pardon your servant, Lord. Please send someone else."

[14]Then the LORD's anger burned against Moses and he said, "What about your brother, Aaron the Levite? I know he can speak well. He is already on his way to meet you, and he will be glad to see you. [15]You shall speak to him and put words in his mouth; I will help both of you speak and will teach you what to do. [16]He will speak to the people for you, and it will be as if he were your mouth and as if you were God to him. [17]But take this staff in your hand so you can perform the signs with it."

Moses Returns to Egypt

[18]Then Moses went back to Jethro his father-in-law and said to him, "Let me return to my own people in Egypt to see if any of them are still alive."

Jethro said, "Go, and I wish you well."

[19]Now the LORD had said to Moses in Midian, "Go back to Egypt, for all those who wanted to kill you are dead." [20]So Moses took his wife and

---

[a] 6 The Hebrew word for leprous was used for various diseases affecting the skin.

4:1–17 God responds to Moses' hesitation to obey his call (Ex 4:1; see 3:11,13) by giving him signs to perform before the Israelites and Egyptians: a staff that turns into a snake (vv. 2–5), a hand that becomes leprous (vv. 6–8) and Nile water that turns to blood (v. 9). When Moses continues to balk (vv. 10,13), God gives him his brother Aaron as a spokesman (vv. 14–16).

4:2 staff Moses' staff is nothing out of the ordinary—his power comes from God.

4:3 it became a snake The rod and serpent were two symbols well recognized in Egypt: The rod was a symbol of authority; the snake was the patron deity (goddess) of Lower Egypt (the Delta region).

4:6 leprous The Hebrew word used here, tsara', describes various skin diseases. See note on Lev 14:3.

4:10 never been eloquent Moses might have had a speech impediment—perhaps stuttering—or he may have doubted his fluency in the Egyptian language after living for many years in Midian.

4:14 brother Aaron was three years older than Moses (Ex 7:7). **the Levite** The reason for specifying Aaron's tribe is unclear; both he and Moses were Levites. Rather than be distinguishing Aaron as a Levite, the Hebrew phrasing could emphasize their relationship as fellow Levites.

4:16 God God is not saying that Aaron will worship Moses. Rather, God will either tell Moses what to say and

sons, put them on a donkey and started back to Egypt. And he took the staff of God in his hand.

²¹The LORD said to Moses, "When you return to Egypt, see that you perform before Pharaoh all the wonders I have given you the power to do. But I will harden his heart so that he will not let the people go. ²²Then say to Pharaoh, 'This is what the LORD says: Israel is my firstborn son, ²³and I told you, "Let my son go, so he may worship me." But you refused to let him go; so I will kill your firstborn son.'"

²⁴At a lodging place on the way, the LORD met Moses[a] and was about to kill him. ²⁵But Zipporah took a flint knife, cut off her son's foreskin and touched Moses' feet with it.[b] "Surely you are a

---

[a] 24 Hebrew *him*   [b] 25 The meaning of the Hebrew for this clause is uncertain.

---

then Moses will tell Aaron (v. 15), or Aaron will consider all commands given by Moses as the word of God.

4:20 his wife and sons Until now, only one son has been mentioned: Gershom (2:22). **started back** This seems to contradict 18:2–5, which describes Jethro accompanying Zipporah and her sons from Midian to Sinai to rejoin Moses after the exodus. It could be that the narrative simply leaves out the family's return trip from Egypt to Midian, which presumably occurred sometime before the exodus.

4:21 harden his heart Refers to selfish stubbornness born of arrogance. The hardness of Pharaoh's heart is mentioned repeatedly in Exodus, with references divided between Pharaoh's own disposition (7:13,14,22; 8:15,32; 9:7,34,35; 13:15) and God's role in the hardening (vv. 7:3; 9:12; 10:1,20,27; 11:10; 14:4,8,17).

4:23 your firstborn son Alludes to the tenth plague God will bring against Egypt (11:5).

4:24–26 This bizarre scene presents a number of interpretive issues due to the ambiguity of the narrative. En route to Egypt, Yahweh appears when Moses and his family are camped for the night. The Hebrew text says that Yahweh encountered "him" and intended to kill "him," but it offers no explanation of who exactly Yahweh intended to kill. Moses' name actually does not appear in these verses at all in Hebrew, though many English translations substitute the proper name for one or two of the masculine pronouns. There are two possibilities for the referent of these masculine pronouns: Moses and Moses' oldest son Gershom (2:22). Yahweh attempting to kill Moses seems unlikely in light of the trajectory of chs. 3–4, where Yahweh

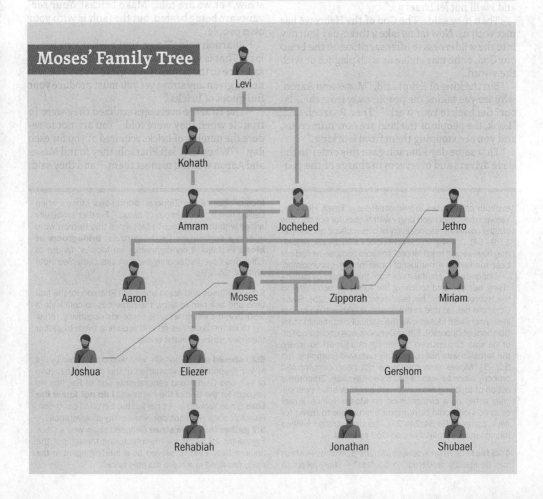

Moses' Family Tree

Levi

Kohath

Amram — Jochebed   Jethro

Aaron   Moses — Zipporah   Miriam

Joshua   Eliezer   Gershom

Rehabiah   Jonathan   Shubael

bridegroom of blood to me," she said. [26]So the Lord let him alone. (At that time she said "bridegroom of blood," referring to circumcision.)

[27]The Lord said to Aaron, "Go into the wilderness to meet Moses." So he met Moses at the mountain of God and kissed him. [28]Then Moses told Aaron everything the Lord had sent him to say, and also about all the signs he had commanded him to perform.

[29]Moses and Aaron brought together all the elders of the Israelites, [30]and Aaron told them everything the Lord had said to Moses. He also performed the signs before the people, [31]and they believed. And when they heard that the Lord was concerned about them and had seen their misery, they bowed down and worshiped.

Bricks Without Straw

5 Afterward Moses and Aaron went to Pharaoh and said, "This is what the Lord, the God of Israel, says: 'Let my people go, so that they may hold a festival to me in the wilderness.'"

[2]Pharaoh said, "Who is the Lord, that I should obey him and let Israel go? I do not know the Lord and I will not let Israel go."

[3]Then they said, "The God of the Hebrews has met with us. Now let us take a three-day journey into the wilderness to offer sacrifices to the Lord our God, or he may strike us with plagues or with the sword."

[4]But the king of Egypt said, "Moses and Aaron, why are you taking the people away from their labor? Get back to your work!" [5]Then Pharaoh said, "Look, the people of the land are now numerous, and you are stopping them from working."

[6]That same day Pharaoh gave this order to the slave drivers and overseers in charge of the people: [7]"You are no longer to supply the people with straw for making bricks; let them go and gather their own straw. [8]But require them to make the same number of bricks as before; don't reduce the quota. They are lazy; that is why they are crying out, 'Let us go and sacrifice to our God.' [9]Make the work harder for the people so that they keep working and pay no attention to lies."

[10]Then the slave drivers and the overseers went out and said to the people, "This is what Pharaoh says: 'I will not give you any more straw. [11]Go and get your own straw wherever you can find it, but your work will not be reduced at all.'" [12]So the people scattered all over Egypt to gather stubble to use for straw. [13]The slave drivers kept pressing them, saying, "Complete the work required of you for each day, just as when you had straw." [14]And Pharaoh's slave drivers beat the Israelite overseers they had appointed, demanding, "Why haven't you met your quota of bricks yesterday or today, as before?"

[15]Then the Israelite overseers went and appealed to Pharaoh: "Why have you treated your servants this way? [16]Your servants are given no straw, yet we are told, 'Make bricks!' Your servants are being beaten, but the fault is with your own people."

[17]Pharaoh said, "Lazy, that's what you are—lazy! That is why you keep saying, 'Let us go and sacrifice to the Lord.' [18]Now get to work. You will not be given any straw, yet you must produce your full quota of bricks."

[19]The Israelite overseers realized they were in trouble when they were told, "You are not to reduce the number of bricks required of you for each day." [20]When they left Pharaoh, they found Moses and Aaron waiting to meet them, [21]and they said,

---

explicitly calls Moses to lead Israel out of Egypt. However, Yahweh may have been angry with Moses for not carrying out the covenant responsibility of circumcising his son (Ge 17:9–14). Drawing on the context of Ex 4:21–23, Yahweh may have sought to kill Moses' firstborn because he had not been marked as a member of Israel through circumcision.

Zipporah delivers the male from this danger by circumcising her son and touching the foreskin, according to the Hebrew text, to "his feet" (see note on v. 25). Since Gershom has no role in the narrative, Yahweh was most likely angry with Moses over the issue of circumcision (not Gershom or Zipporah). Either Gershom was uncircumcised or he was circumcised by the Egyptian method where the foreskin was not completely removed (compare Jos 5:2–5). Moses also may have not been circumcised properly since he was raised as an Egyptian. Zipporah's action of touching the foreskin to him may have symbolically acted as a circumcision on Moses (since a real circumcision would have made him unable to travel for days; compare Ge 34:24–25). The circumcision fulfilled the covenantal obligation, so God relented.

4:25 feet The Hebrew phrase used here, *leraglav*—which may be literally rendered "to his feet"—likely refers to

Moses' feet, since Zipporah addresses Moses when calling him a "bridegroom of blood." Further ambiguity arises with the reference to feet since this Hebrew word is also a euphemism for the genitals. **bridegroom of blood** Perhaps a condemnation on Moses' failure to fulfill this covenantal obligation on his own. See note on Ex 4:24–26.

5:1–23 Moses and Aaron approach Pharaoh for the first time and ask him to allow the Israelites to celebrate a festival in the wilderness. He responds negatively, refusing to let the Israelites go and requiring them to gather their own straw to make bricks.

5:2 I should obey Pharaoh, who was considered by his fellow Egyptians an incarnation of the deity Horus (son of Isis and Osiris) and generational son of Ra, has no respect for the God of the Hebrews. **I do not know the Lord** Since Yahweh is not part of the Egyptian pantheon, Pharaoh does not consider him worthy of reverence.

5:7 gather their own straw Chopped straw was a stock ingredient for mudbrick manufacturing throughout the ancient Near East. It served as a binding agent in the mud, resulting in a more durable brick.

"May the LORD look on you and judge you! You have made us obnoxious to Pharaoh and his officials and have put a sword in their hand to kill us."

God Promises Deliverance

²²Moses returned to the LORD and said, "Why, Lord, why have you brought trouble on this people? Is this why you sent me? ²³Ever since I went to Pharaoh to speak in your name, he has brought trouble on this people, and you have not rescued your people at all."

6 Then the LORD said to Moses, "Now you will see what I will do to Pharaoh: Because of my mighty hand he will let them go; because of my mighty hand he will drive them out of his country."

²God also said to Moses, "I am the LORD. ³I appeared to Abraham, to Isaac and to Jacob as God Almighty,ᵃ but by my name the LORDᵇ I did not make myself fully known to them. ⁴I also established my covenant with them to give them the land of Canaan, where they resided as foreigners. ⁵Moreover, I have heard the groaning of the Israelites, whom the Egyptians are enslaving, and I have remembered my covenant.

⁶"Therefore, say to the Israelites: 'I am the LORD, and I will bring you out from under the yoke of the Egyptians. I will free you from being slaves to them, and I will redeem you with an outstretched arm and with mighty acts of judgment. ⁷I will take you as my own people, and I will be your God. Then you will know that I am the LORD your God, who brought you out from under the yoke of the Egyptians. ⁸And I will bring you to the land I swore with uplifted hand to give to Abraham, to Isaac and to Jacob. I will give it to you as a possession. I am the LORD.'"

⁹Moses reported this to the Israelites, but they did not listen to him because of their discouragement and harsh labor.

¹⁰Then the LORD said to Moses, ¹¹"Go, tell Pharaoh king of Egypt to let the Israelites go out of his country."

¹²But Moses said to the LORD, "If the Israelites will not listen to me, why would Pharaoh listen to me, since I speak with faltering lipsᶜ?"

Family Record of Moses and Aaron

¹³Now the LORD spoke to Moses and Aaron about the Israelites and Pharaoh king of Egypt, and he commanded them to bring the Israelites out of Egypt.

¹⁴These were the heads of their families ᵈ:

The sons of Reuben the firstborn son of Israel were Hanok and Pallu, Hezron and Karmi. These were the clans of Reuben.

¹⁵The sons of Simeon were Jemuel, Jamin, Ohad, Jakin, Zohar and Shaul the son of a Canaanite woman. These were the clans of Simeon.

¹⁶These were the names of the sons of Levi according to their records: Gershon, Kohath and Merari. Levi lived 137 years.

¹⁷The sons of Gershon, by clans, were Libni and Shimei.

¹⁸The sons of Kohath were Amram, Izhar, Hebron and Uzziel. Kohath lived 133 years.

¹⁹The sons of Merari were Mahli and Mushi.

These were the clans of Levi according to their records.

²⁰Amram married his father's sister Jochebed, who bore him Aaron and Moses. Amram lived 137 years.

²¹The sons of Izhar were Korah, Nepheg and Zikri.

ᵃ 3 Hebrew *El-Shaddai*   ᵇ 3 See note at 3:15.   ᶜ 12 Hebrew *I am uncircumcised of lips*; also in verse 30   ᵈ 14 The Hebrew for *families* here and in verse 25 refers to units larger than clans.

6:1–13 In response to Moses' crying out to him in 5:22–23, God reaffirms his plans to rescue the Israelites (vv. 1–8). Moses reports God's message to the people, but they do not believe him (v. 9). God then charges Moses and Aaron to appear again before Pharaoh (vv. 10–13).

6:3 by my name the LORD This appears to indicate that Abraham, Isaac and Jacob did not know the name *yhwh* (Yahweh), the name revealed to Moses at Sinai (3:14–16). If this is true, the many occurrences of the name Yahweh in the Hebrew text before ch. 3 (e.g., Ge 2:5; 4:26) would be considered editorial additions by scribes, indicating for later readers that the same deity is being referred to. Another explanation is that the name Yahweh was actually not new to Moses, but was an existing name that was given new significance (see note on Ex 3:13).

6:6 redeem The Hebrew word used here, *ga'al*, occurs in social and legal contexts with respect to kinship laws and rights. Over time, the term became more abstract

and theological, as it was used to describe God's actions toward Israel, whom he calls his firstborn son (e.g., 4:22).

6:12 speak with faltering lips See note on 4:10.

6:14–30 This genealogy connects the present people with the ancient patriarchs and marks Moses and Aaron transitioning to full dependence on the power of God. The genealogy also anticipates later historical developments. It hints at the elevated status of the tribe of Levi and initiates a merging of the kingly line of Judah and the priestly line of Levi—anticipating elements of Messianic theology. In v. 23, the genealogy refers to Aaron's wife and mentions his father-in-law, Amminadab, and brother-in-law, Nahshon—both of whom belonged to the tribe of Judah (Nu 1:7).

6:20 his father's sister Moses and Aaron were born of a marriage that would later be prohibited under Mosaic Law (marriage to a paternal aunt; see Lev 18:12; 20:19). **Jochebed** Although Moses' mother appears in Ex 2:1–10, she is not named there. **Aaron and Moses** Amram and Jochebed also had a girl, Miriam (Nu 26:59).

²²The sons of Uzziel were Mishael, Elzaphan and Sithri.

²³Aaron married Elisheba, daughter of Amminadab and sister of Nahshon, and she bore him Nadab and Abihu, Eleazar and Ithamar.

²⁴The sons of Korah were Assir, Elkanah and Abiasaph. These were the Korahite clans.

²⁵Eleazar son of Aaron married one of the daughters of Putiel, and she bore him Phinehas.

These were the heads of the Levite families, clan by clan.

²⁶It was this Aaron and Moses to whom the LORD said, "Bring the Israelites out of Egypt by their divisions." ²⁷They were the ones who spoke to Pharaoh king of Egypt about bringing the Israelites out of Egypt — this same Moses and Aaron.

Aaron to Speak for Moses

²⁸Now when the LORD spoke to Moses in Egypt, ²⁹he said to him, "I am the LORD. Tell Pharaoh king of Egypt everything I tell you."

³⁰But Moses said to the LORD, "Since I speak with faltering lips, why would Pharaoh listen to me?"

7 Then the LORD said to Moses, "See, I have made you like God to Pharaoh, and your brother Aaron will be your prophet. ²You are to say everything I command you, and your brother Aaron is to tell Pharaoh to let the Israelites go out of his country.

6:24 sons of Korah Superscriptions of certain psalms refer to the sons of Korah as singers in the temple (e.g., Ps 42; 44; 45; 46).

6:28–30 These verses mark the return to the narrative that was interrupted by the genealogy. Compare Ex 6:12,30.

7:1 like God to Pharaoh In 4:16, God promised that Aaron would consider Moses' words as if they came from the mouth of God himself. The same idea operates here — Moses will act as God to Pharaoh (see v. 2).

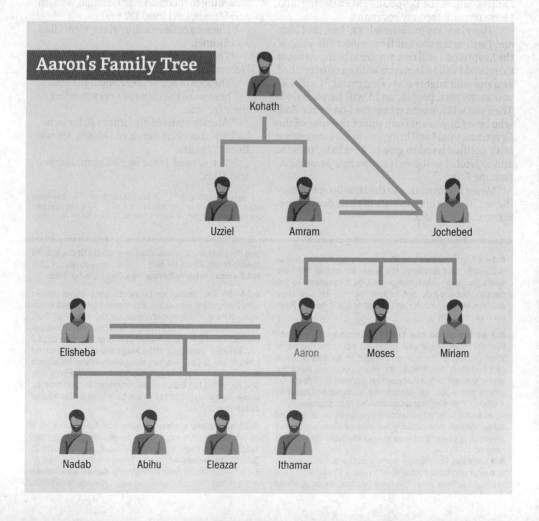

Aaron's Family Tree

Kohath

Uzziel   Amram   Jochebed

Elisheba   Aaron   Moses   Miriam

Nadab   Abihu   Eleazar   Ithamar

³But I will harden Pharaoh's heart, and though I multiply my signs and wonders in Egypt, ⁴he will not listen to you. Then I will lay my hand on Egypt and with mighty acts of judgment I will bring out my divisions, my people the Israelites. ⁵And the Egyptians will know that I am the LORD when I stretch out my hand against Egypt and bring the Israelites out of it."

⁶Moses and Aaron did just as the LORD commanded them. ⁷Moses was eighty years old and Aaron eighty-three when they spoke to Pharaoh.

Aaron's Staff Becomes a Snake

⁸The LORD said to Moses and Aaron, ⁹"When Pharaoh says to you, 'Perform a miracle,' then say to Aaron, 'Take your staff and throw it down before Pharaoh,' and it will become a snake."

¹⁰So Moses and Aaron went to Pharaoh and did just as the LORD commanded. Aaron threw his staff down in front of Pharaoh and his officials, and it became a snake. ¹¹Pharaoh then summoned wise men and sorcerers, and the Egyptian magicians also did the same things by their secret arts: ¹²Each one threw down his staff and it became a snake. But Aaron's staff swallowed up their staffs. ¹³Yet Pharaoh's heart became hard and he would not listen to them, just as the LORD had said.

The Plague of Blood

¹⁴Then the LORD said to Moses, "Pharaoh's heart is unyielding; he refuses to let the people go. ¹⁵Go to Pharaoh in the morning as he goes out to the river. Confront him on the bank of the Nile, and take in your hand the staff that was changed into a snake. ¹⁶Then say to him, 'The LORD, the God of the Hebrews, has sent me to say to you: Let my people go, so that they may worship me in the wilderness. But until now you have not listened. ¹⁷This is what the LORD says: By this you will know that I am the LORD: With the staff that is in my hand I will strike the water of the Nile, and it will be changed into blood. ¹⁸The fish in the Nile will die, and the river will stink; the Egyptians will not be able to drink its water.'"

¹⁹The LORD said to Moses, "Tell Aaron, 'Take your staff and stretch out your hand over the waters of Egypt — over the streams and canals, over the ponds and all the reservoirs — and they will turn to blood.' Blood will be everywhere in Egypt, even in vessels*ᵃ* of wood and stone."

²⁰Moses and Aaron did just as the LORD had commanded. He raised his staff in the presence of Pharaoh and his officials and struck the water of the Nile, and all the water was changed into blood. ²¹The fish in the Nile died, and the river smelled so bad that the Egyptians could not drink its water. Blood was everywhere in Egypt.

²²But the Egyptian magicians did the same things by their secret arts, and Pharaoh's heart became hard; he would not listen to Moses and Aaron, just as the LORD had said. ²³Instead, he turned and went into his palace, and did not take even this to heart. ²⁴And all the Egyptians dug along the Nile to get drinking water, because they could not drink the water of the river.

The Plague of Frogs

²⁵Seven days passed after the LORD struck the Nile.ᵇ ¹Then the LORD said to Moses, "Go to Pharaoh and say to him, 'This is what the

---

ᵃ 19 Or *even on their idols*   *ᵇ* In Hebrew texts 8:1-4 is numbered 7:26-29, and 8:5-32 is numbered 8:1-28.

7:3 will harden Pharaoh's heart See note on 4:21. **signs and wonders** The descriptions here and in v. 4 foreshadow the plagues that God will cast upon Egypt.

7:8–13 This passage recalls the sign God gave to Moses in 4:2–5. However, the Hebrew word used for "snake" here is different from the one used in 4:3. The Hebrew word used here, *tannin*, elsewhere in the OT indicates a great sea serpent (see Ge 1:21 and note). As in Genesis, this passage is intended to communicate the superiority of the Creator God over all created beings, including primordial chaos monsters.

7:11 wise men The Hebrew word used here, *chakham*, is the common Hebrew term for an advisor of royalty, whether skilled in magical arts or not. **sorcerers** Comparative terminology in other Semitic languages indicates the Hebrew term used here may refer to one who concocts potions from plants or herbs. **magicians** The Hebrew word used here, *chartom*, is related to an Egyptian term for a chief lector priest. Lector priests were learned scribes and oracles whose duties included reciting spells and prayers to appeal to the gods for advice. Second Timothy 3:8 identifies the magicians referenced here as Jannes and Jambres. **7:12 swallowed up their staffs** The snake's consumption of the others demonstrates the supremacy of the sign of Moses and Aaron over the deed of the magicians.

7:14–25 This passage narrates the first of ten plagues with which God strikes Egypt. This plague was included in the signs God gave to Moses at the burning bush (see Ex 4:9).

7:17 it will be changed into blood The Hebrew phrasing used here — the verb *haphak* (literally rendered "turn") plus the preposition *l-* (literally rendered "to") — typically describes a complete alteration, often of one thing into its opposite (Dt 23:5; Jer 31:13; Am 5:8). This plague may be understood literally — the water of Egypt changed into blood. See the table "Ten Plagues on Egypt" on p. 110.

7:21 everywhere While some of the plagues did not affect the territory of Goshen where the Israelites live (Ex 8:22; 9:26), no such qualifier is included in this passage. However, the text only records that the Egyptians could not drink the water of the Nile, which may imply that the Israelites were not affected.

8:1–15 Yahweh's second plague against Egypt brings frogs (vv. 1–6). As before, the Egyptian magicians replicate the plague (v. 7). This time, however, Pharaoh pleads with Moses and Aaron to take it away (v. 8). When the plague ends, he hardens his own heart (vv. 9–15; see note on 4:21).

LORD says: Let my people go, so that they may worship me. ²If you refuse to let them go, I will send a plague of frogs on your whole country. ³The Nile will teem with frogs. They will come up into your palace and your bedroom and onto your bed, into the houses of your officials and on your people, and into your ovens and kneading troughs. ⁴The frogs will come up on you and your people and all your officials.'"

⁵Then the LORD said to Moses, "Tell Aaron, 'Stretch out your hand with your staff over the streams and canals and ponds, and make frogs come up on the land of Egypt.'"

⁶So Aaron stretched out his hand over the waters of Egypt, and the frogs came up and covered the land. ⁷But the magicians did the same things by their secret arts; they also made frogs come up on the land of Egypt.

⁸Pharaoh summoned Moses and Aaron and said, "Pray to the LORD to take the frogs away from me and my people, and I will let your people go to offer sacrifices to the LORD."

⁹Moses said to Pharaoh, "I leave to you the honor of setting the time for me to pray for you and your officials and your people that you and your houses may be rid of the frogs, except for those that remain in the Nile."

¹⁰"Tomorrow," Pharaoh said.

Moses replied, "It will be as you say, so that you may know there is no one like the LORD our God. ¹¹The frogs will leave you and your houses, your officials and your people; they will remain only in the Nile."

¹²After Moses and Aaron left Pharaoh, Moses cried out to the LORD about the frogs he had brought on Pharaoh. ¹³And the LORD did what Moses asked. The frogs died in the houses, in the courtyards and in the fields. ¹⁴They were piled into heaps, and the land reeked of them. ¹⁵But when Pharaoh saw that there was relief, he hardened his heart and would not listen to Moses and Aaron, just as the LORD had said.

The Plague of Gnats

¹⁶Then the LORD said to Moses, "Tell Aaron, 'Stretch out your staff and strike the dust of the

---

8:2 frogs The influx of frogs would have been the natural result of a polluted Nile.

8:8 Pray to the LORD Pharaoh has no confidence in the magicians' ability to stop the plague, despite their ability to imitate it. His request suggests that he knows that Yahweh is behind all that has befallen Egypt.

8:10 like the LORD our God While the plagues ultimately succeed at forcing Pharaoh to set the Israelites free,

the supremacy of Yahweh over Egypt's gods (including Pharaoh, considered the incarnation of Horus by his fellow Egyptians) is paramount.

8:15 he hardened his heart See note on 4:21.

8:16–19 In the third plague, small insects overrun Egypt. While the insects may have been gnats, they may also have been lice or mosquitoes (compare note on 8:17).

Ten Plagues on Egypt

PLAGUE*	REFERENCE
1. The Plague of Blood	Ex 7:14-25
2. The Plague of Frogs	Ex 8:1-15
3. The Plague of Gnats	Ex 8:16-19
4. The Plague of Flies	Ex 8:20-32
5. The Plague on Livestock	Ex 9:1-7
6. The Plague of Boils	Ex 9:8-12
7. The Plague of Hail	Ex 9:13-35
8. The Plague of Locusts	Ex 10:1-20
9. The Plague of Darkness	Ex 10:21-29
(Threat of Death of Firstborn)	(Ex 11)
10. Death of Firstborn	Ex 12:29-32

*The terminology "Ten Plagues" does not appear in the Bible. The most detailed rehearsals of the plagues on Egypt are in Psalms 78 and 105. Only six plagues are listed in Psalm 78:42-51, and only eight plagues are listed in 105:28-36.

ground,' and throughout the land of Egypt the dust will become gnats." ¹⁷They did this, and when Aaron stretched out his hand with the staff and struck the dust of the ground, gnats came on people and animals. All the dust throughout the land of Egypt became gnats. ¹⁸But when the magicians tried to produce gnats by their secret arts, they could not.

Since the gnats were on people and animals everywhere, ¹⁹the magicians said to Pharaoh, "This is the finger of God." But Pharaoh's heart was hard and he would not listen, just as the LORD had said.

The Plague of Flies

²⁰Then the LORD said to Moses, "Get up early in the morning and confront Pharaoh as he goes to the river and say to him, 'This is what the LORD says: Let my people go, so that they may worship me. ²¹If you do not let my people go, I will send swarms of flies on you and your officials, on your people and into your houses. The houses of the Egyptians will be full of flies; even the ground will be covered with them.

²²" 'But on that day I will deal differently with the land of Goshen, where my people live; no swarms of flies will be there, so that you will know that I, the LORD, am in this land. ²³I will make a distinction[a] between my people and your people. This sign will occur tomorrow.' "

²⁴And the LORD did this. Dense swarms of flies poured into Pharaoh's palace and into the houses of his officials; throughout Egypt the land was ruined by the flies.

²⁵Then Pharaoh summoned Moses and Aaron and said, "Go, sacrifice to your God here in the land."

²⁶But Moses said, "That would not be right. The sacrifices we offer the LORD our God would be detestable to the Egyptians. And if we offer sacrifices that are detestable in their eyes, will they not stone us? ²⁷We must take a three-day journey into the wilderness to offer sacrifices to the LORD our God, as he commands us."

²⁸Pharaoh said, "I will let you go to offer sacrifices to the LORD your God in the wilderness, but you must not go very far. Now pray for me."

²⁹Moses answered, "As soon as I leave you, I will pray to the LORD, and tomorrow the flies will leave Pharaoh and his officials and his people. Only let Pharaoh be sure that he does not act deceitfully again by not letting the people go to offer sacrifices to the LORD."

³⁰Then Moses left Pharaoh and prayed to the LORD, ³¹and the LORD did what Moses asked. The flies left Pharaoh and his officials and his people; not a fly remained. ³²But this time also Pharaoh hardened his heart and would not let the people go.

The Plague on Livestock

9 Then the LORD said to Moses, "Go to Pharaoh and say to him, 'This is what the LORD, the God of the Hebrews, says: "Let my people go, so that they may worship me." ²If you refuse to let them go and continue to hold them back, ³the hand of the LORD will bring a terrible plague on your livestock in the field — on your horses, donkeys and camels and on your cattle, sheep and goats. ⁴But the LORD will make a distinction between the livestock of Israel and that of Egypt, so that no animal belonging to the Israelites will die.' "

⁵The LORD set a time and said, "Tomorrow the LORD will do this in the land." ⁶And the next day the LORD did it: All the livestock of the Egyptians died, but not one animal belonging to the Israelites died. ⁷Pharaoh investigated and found that not even one of the animals of the Israelites had died. Yet his heart was unyielding and he would not let the people go.

The Plague of Boils

⁸Then the LORD said to Moses and Aaron, "Take handfuls of soot from a furnace and have Moses toss it into the air in the presence of Pharaoh. ⁹It will become fine dust over the whole land of

---

[a] 23 Septuagint and Vulgate; Hebrew *will put a deliverance*

8:17 dust of the ground Neither gnats nor mosquitoes come from the dust of the ground, but lice may have been associated with the ground since they crawl.

8:18 they could not Again, the Egyptian magicians seek to imitate the plague, but this time they do not succeed.

8:20–32 During the fourth plague, the plague of flies, Yahweh calls attention to the different way it will affect Israelites and Egyptians for the first time (vv. 22–24; compare 9:4,26; 10:23).

8:21 flies The Hebrew word used here, *arov*, is ambiguous. Since it literally means mixture, it is often interpreted as a swarm of insects such as flies.

8:26 offer sacrifices that are detestable in their eyes The nature of the Egyptians' revulsion towards the Israelites' sacrifice is unknown.

8:32 hardened his heart See note on 4:21.

9:1–7 The fifth plague affects livestock. This is the first plague to explicitly include death (v. 6), and the second in which a distinction is made between the Israelites and Egyptians (see 8:22–24).

9:3 plague The Hebrew word used here, *dever*, refers to a pestilence or disease. **camels** See note on Ge 12:16.
9:7 his heart was unyielding See note on Ex 4:21.

9:8–12 In the sixth plague, both people and livestock are afflicted with boils. The magicians of Egypt, who had some success in imitating the first two plagues (7:22; 8:7) but could not replicate the third (8:18), are now so far out of their depth that they themselves are afflicted with boils.

9:9 festering boils The description of the boils and the interpretations of the previous plagues suggest the disease is anthrax.

Egypt, and festering boils will break out on people and animals throughout the land."

¹⁰So they took soot from a furnace and stood before Pharaoh. Moses tossed it into the air, and festering boils broke out on people and animals. ¹¹The magicians could not stand before Moses because of the boils that were on them and on all the Egyptians. ¹²But the LORD hardened Pharaoh's heart and he would not listen to Moses and Aaron, just as the LORD had said to Moses.

The Plague of Hail

¹³Then the LORD said to Moses, "Get up early in the morning, confront Pharaoh and say to him, 'This is what the LORD, the God of the Hebrews, says: Let my people go, so that they may worship me, ¹⁴or this time I will send the full force of my plagues against you and against your officials and your people, so you may know that there is no one like me in all the earth. ¹⁵For by now I could have stretched out my hand and struck you and your people with a plague that would have wiped you off the earth. ¹⁶But I have raised you up[a] for this very purpose, that I might show you my power and that my name might be proclaimed in all the earth. ¹⁷You still set yourself against my people and will not let them go. ¹⁸Therefore, at this time tomorrow I will send the worst hailstorm that has ever fallen on Egypt, from the day it was founded till now. ¹⁹Give an order now to bring your livestock and everything you have in the field to a place of shelter, because the hail will fall on every person and animal that has not been brought in and is still out in the field, and they will die.'"

²⁰Those officials of Pharaoh who feared the word of the LORD hurried to bring their slaves and their livestock inside. ²¹But those who ignored the word of the LORD left their slaves and livestock in the field.

²²Then the LORD said to Moses, "Stretch out your hand toward the sky so that hail will fall all over Egypt — on people and animals and on everything growing in the fields of Egypt." ²³When Moses stretched out his staff toward the sky, the LORD sent thunder and hail, and lightning flashed down to the ground. So the LORD rained hail on the land of Egypt; ²⁴hail fell and lightning flashed back and forth. It was the worst storm in all the land of Egypt since it had become a nation. ²⁵Throughout Egypt hail struck everything in the fields — both people and animals; it beat down everything growing in the fields and stripped every tree. ²⁶The only place it did not hail was the land of Goshen, where the Israelites were.

²⁷Then Pharaoh summoned Moses and Aaron. "This time I have sinned," he said to them. "The LORD is in the right, and I and my people are in the wrong. ²⁸Pray to the LORD, for we have had enough thunder and hail. I will let you go; you don't have to stay any longer."

²⁹Moses replied, "When I have gone out of the city, I will spread out my hands in prayer to the LORD. The thunder will stop and there will be no more hail, so you may know that the earth is the LORD's. ³⁰But I know that you and your officials still do not fear the LORD God."

³¹(The flax and barley were destroyed, since the barley had headed and the flax was in bloom. ³²The wheat and spelt, however, were not destroyed, because they ripen later.)

³³Then Moses left Pharaoh and went out of the city. He spread out his hands toward the LORD; the thunder and hail stopped, and the rain no longer poured down on the land. ³⁴When Pharaoh saw that the rain and hail and thunder had stopped, he sinned again: He and his officials hardened their hearts. ³⁵So Pharaoh's heart was hard and he would not let the Israelites go, just as the LORD had said through Moses.

The Plague of Locusts

10 Then the LORD said to Moses, "Go to Pharaoh, for I have hardened his heart and the hearts of his officials so that I may perform these signs of mine among them ²that you may tell your children and grandchildren how I dealt harsh-

---

[a] 16 Or *have spared you*

9:13–35 The description of the seventh plague, hail, is unusually long. It includes Yahweh's explanation to Pharaoh of the rationale behind the plagues (vv. 13–19). This plague includes the death of people for the first time (v. 25).

9:14 against you and against your officials God again makes a distinction between the Egyptians and the Israelites; only the Egyptians will experience this plague (see 8:22; 9:4–6).

9:19 hail will fall on God demonstrates compassion by advising Pharaoh (through Moses) how to avoid loss of life during the impending hailstorm.

9:20 who feared Those who heed Yahweh's warning know that their own gods and Pharaoh cannot protect them—only Yahweh can.

9:22 everything growing in the fields In addition to injuries, hail would also result in severe crop loss.

9:31–32 In addition to listing which of the surviving crops (see vv. 31–32) were left to be consumed by locusts, this parenthetical note also explains why Pharaoh has not yet surrendered. While the destruction of flax—which produced fiber for linen garments—disrupted an important part of Egypt's economy, the survival of wheat and spelt meant that Egypt continued to have a food supply. Pharaoh thus assumed that the nation could endure the hardships already sent.

10:1–20 In the eighth plague, locusts cover the land and eat what the hail in the previous plague had left (v. 12). As with the plague of hail, this plague includes an extended introduction (vv. 1–11).

10:2 your children and grandchildren The plagues are cast as a dramatic example of Yahweh's superiority to

ly with the Egyptians and how I performed my signs among them, and that you may know that I am the LORD."

[3]So Moses and Aaron went to Pharaoh and said to him, "This is what the LORD, the God of the Hebrews, says: 'How long will you refuse to humble yourself before me? Let my people go, so that they may worship me. [4]If you refuse to let them go, I will bring locusts into your country tomorrow. [5]They will cover the face of the ground so that it cannot be seen. They will devour what little you have left after the hail, including every tree that is growing in your fields. [6]They will fill your houses and those of all your officials and all the Egyptians — something neither your parents nor your ancestors have ever seen from the day they settled in this land till now.'" Then Moses turned and left Pharaoh.

[7]Pharaoh's officials said to him, "How long will this man be a snare to us? Let the people go, so that they may worship the LORD their God. Do you not yet realize that Egypt is ruined?"

[8]Then Moses and Aaron were brought back to Pharaoh. "Go, worship the LORD your God," he said. "But tell me who will be going."

[9]Moses answered, "We will go with our young and our old, with our sons and our daughters, and with our flocks and herds, because we are to celebrate a festival to the LORD."

[10]Pharaoh said, "The LORD be with you — if I let you go, along with your women and children! Clearly you are bent on evil.[a] [11]No! Have only the men go and worship the LORD, since that's what you have been asking for." Then Moses and Aaron were driven out of Pharaoh's presence.

[12]And the LORD said to Moses, "Stretch out your hand over Egypt so that locusts swarm over the land and devour everything growing in the fields, everything left by the hail."

[13]So Moses stretched out his staff over Egypt, and the LORD made an east wind blow across the land all that day and all that night. By morning the wind had brought the locusts; [14]they invaded all Egypt and settled down in every area of the country in great numbers. Never before had there been such a plague of locusts, nor will there ever be again. [15]They covered all the ground until it was black. They devoured all that was left after the hail — everything growing in the fields and the fruit on the trees. Nothing green remained on tree or plant in all the land of Egypt.

[16]Pharaoh quickly summoned Moses and Aaron and said, "I have sinned against the LORD your God and against you. [17]Now forgive my sin once more and pray to the LORD your God to take this deadly plague away from me."

[18]Moses then left Pharaoh and prayed to the LORD. [19]And the LORD changed the wind to a very strong west wind, which caught up the locusts and carried them into the Red Sea.[b] Not a locust was left anywhere in Egypt. [20]But the LORD hardened Pharaoh's heart, and he would not let the Israelites go.

The Plague of Darkness

[21]Then the LORD said to Moses, "Stretch out your hand toward the sky so that darkness spreads over Egypt — darkness that can be felt." [22]So Moses stretched out his hand toward the sky, and total darkness covered all Egypt for three days. [23]No one could see anyone else or move about for three days. Yet all the Israelites had light in the places where they lived.

[24]Then Pharaoh summoned Moses and said, "Go, worship the LORD. Even your women and children may go with you; only leave your flocks and herds behind."

[25]But Moses said, "You must allow us to have sacrifices and burnt offerings to present to the LORD our God. [26]Our livestock too must go with us; not a hoof is to be left behind. We have to use

---

[a] 10 Or Be careful, trouble is in store for you!   [b] 19 Or the Sea of Reeds

---

other gods and his bond with Israel. They will serve to instruct the young of each generation, and remind the old of their ancestors' redemption.

10:4 locusts Locust plagues could result in the loss of a population's food supply, making starvation a genuine possibility.

10:6 from the day they settled in this land till now Highlights the supernatural nature of the disaster. This plague would exceed the severity of any similar natural disasters Egypt had ever experienced. Compare v. 14.

10:10 I let you go, along with your women and children Leaving the women and children behind would prevent the permanent loss of this slave labor force.

10:19 very strong west wind A wind from the west would blow the locusts toward the Red Sea (or sea of reeds; see note on 13:18).

10:21–29 Like the third and sixth plagues, the ninth plague begins without warning. This darkening of the sky complements the darkening of the land experienced under the previous plague (v. 15). At the end of it, Pharaoh refuses to grant Moses the opportunity to see him again.

10:21 darkness The severe wind that blew the locusts out of Egypt also could have brought a sandstorm. However, Pharaoh probably would not have been impressed if this were the case; historically, such storms obscured the sun for days. While the Egyptians would have been accustomed to the sky-darkening effect of sandstorms, blotting out the sun nevertheless would convey a frightening spiritual message. Ra, the sun god, was Egypt's supreme deity. The Egyptians took the regular rising of the sun and its traversing of the sky as proof of triumph over death. They would have considered the obstruction of the sun at Moses' command to be an evil omen.

10:23 No one could see anyone else Indicates darkness greater than that caused by a sandstorm.

10:26 Our livestock too must go with us Moses raises his demand by insisting that the Israelites be allowed to take their property.

some of them in worshiping the LORD our God, and until we get there we will not know what we are to use to worship the LORD."

²⁷But the LORD hardened Pharaoh's heart, and he was not willing to let them go. ²⁸Pharaoh said to Moses, "Get out of my sight! Make sure you do not appear before me again! The day you see my face you will die."

²⁹"Just as you say," Moses replied. "I will never appear before you again."

The Plague on the Firstborn

11 Now the LORD had said to Moses, "I will bring one more plague on Pharaoh and on Egypt. After that, he will let you go from here, and when he does, he will drive you out completely. ²Tell the people that men and women alike are to ask their neighbors for articles of silver and gold." ³(The LORD made the Egyptians favorably disposed toward the people, and Moses himself was highly regarded in Egypt by Pharaoh's officials and by the people.)

⁴So Moses said, "This is what the LORD says: 'About midnight I will go throughout Egypt. ⁵Every firstborn son in Egypt will die, from the firstborn son of Pharaoh, who sits on the throne, to the firstborn son of the female slave, who is at her hand mill, and all the firstborn of the cattle as well. ⁶There will be loud wailing throughout Egypt—worse than there has ever been or ever will be again. ⁷But among the Israelites not a dog will bark at any person or animal.' Then you will know that the LORD makes a distinction between Egypt and Israel. ⁸All these officials of yours will come to me, bowing down before me and saying, 'Go, you and all the people who follow you!' After that I will leave." Then Moses, hot with anger, left Pharaoh.

⁹The LORD had said to Moses, "Pharaoh will refuse to listen to you—so that my wonders may be multiplied in Egypt." ¹⁰Moses and Aaron performed all these wonders before Pharaoh, but the LORD hardened Pharaoh's heart, and he would not let the Israelites go out of his country.

The Passover and the Festival of Unleavened Bread

12:14-20pp — Lev 23:4-8; Nu 28:16-25; Dt 16:1-8

12 The LORD said to Moses and Aaron in Egypt, ²"This month is to be for you the first month, the first month of your year. ³Tell the whole community of Israel that on the tenth day of this month each man is to take a lamb*ᵃ* for his family, one for each household. ⁴If any household is too small for a whole lamb, they must share one with their nearest neighbor, having taken into account the number of people there are. You are to determine the amount of lamb needed in accordance with what each person will eat. ⁵The animals you choose must be year-old males without defect, and you may take them from the sheep or the goats. ⁶Take care of them until the fourteenth day of the month, when all the members of the community of Israel must slaughter them at

---

ᵃ 3 The Hebrew word can mean lamb or kid; also in verse 4.

11:1–10 This chapter introduces the tenth and final plague—the death of the firstborn. However, the plague does not take place until 12:29–32. Exodus 11:1–3 reflects a conversation between God and Moses while he is in the presence of Pharaoh (see 10:28–29). Verse 4 continues the conversation between Moses and Pharaoh (see v. 8). See the table "Ten Plagues on Egypt" on p. 110.

11:3 made the Egyptians favorably disposed toward the people This event, which takes place in 12:35–36, is a fulfillment of the promise given in 3:21–22. **highly regarded** Moses was held in fearful awe by the native population who had suffered so much under the plagues.

11:5 Every firstborn son in Egypt will die The Israelites are not exempt from the threat against the firstborn. They must take the precautions instructed by Yahweh (ch. 12), or their firstborn will also die.

11:10 hardened Pharaoh's heart See note on 4:21.

12:1–51 The focus of ch. 12 is the tenth plague where Yahweh brings about the death of all the firstborn of Egypt—the firstborn of both animals and people are struck dead in the night (vv. 29–32). This event finally convinces Pharaoh to release the Israelites, so they leave hurriedly that night (vv. 33–42). The account of the last plague and the departure from Egypt is bracketed by instructions related to observing the Passover (vv. 1–28,43–51). Originally, the Israelites were to place

the blood of a lamb on the doorposts and lintel of their houses to mark them as loyal servants of Yahweh who were to be excluded from the punishment of the plague (vv. 12–13). Yahweh also established that day as a time of annual remembrance, commemorating the events of that night when Yahweh delivered Israel from Egypt (v. 14). Chapter 12 blends instructions about keeping the Passover in the future with instructions relevant for Israel's deliverance from the plague and from Egypt itself.

12:2 the first month The exodus from Egypt is of such profound importance that the Israelite calendar is reoriented to it. The first month of the year will now be the month that Israel left Egypt, and the remaining months are numbered accordingly.

12:3 one for each household Each household has a lamb, and the lambs are killed, prepared and consumed at home (vv. 4–10). The law in Dt 16 turns the slaughter of the Passover lamb into a sacrifice that must be brought to the altar at the central sanctuary, meaning the tabernacle or temple. Deuteronomy also instructs the people to eat the Passover lamb at the central sanctuary, not in their homes (see Dt 16:5–7). The reason for this revision of the law may be that Dt 16 anticipates a different plan for celebrating feasts once Israel had occupied the promised land.

12:5 without defect Using a defective animal for a meal or sacrifice was considered a terrible insult.

twilight. [7]Then they are to take some of the blood and put it on the sides and tops of the doorframes of the houses where they eat the lambs. [8]That same night they are to eat the meat roasted over the fire, along with bitter herbs, and bread made without yeast. [9]Do not eat the meat raw or boiled in water, but roast it over a fire — with the head, legs and internal organs. [10]Do not leave any of it till morning; if some is left till morning, you must burn it. [11]This is how you are to eat it: with your cloak tucked into your belt, your sandals on your feet and your staff in your hand. Eat it in haste; it is the LORD's Passover.

[12]"On that same night I will pass through Egypt and strike down every firstborn of both people and animals, and I will bring judgment on all the gods of Egypt. I am the LORD. [13]The blood will be a sign for you on the houses where you are, and when I see the blood, I will pass over you. No destructive plague will touch you when I strike Egypt.

[14]"This is a day you are to commemorate; for the generations to come you shall celebrate it as a festival to the LORD — a lasting ordinance. [15]For seven days you are to eat bread made without yeast. On the first day remove the yeast from your houses, for whoever eats anything with yeast in it from the first day through the seventh must be cut off from Israel. [16]On the first day hold a sacred assembly, and another one on the seventh day. Do no work at all on these days, except to prepare food for everyone to eat; that is all you may do.

[17]"Celebrate the Festival of Unleavened Bread, because it was on this very day that I brought your divisions out of Egypt. Celebrate this day as a lasting ordinance for the generations to come. [18]In the first month you are to eat bread made without yeast, from the evening of the fourteenth day until the evening of the twenty-first day. [19]For seven days no yeast is to be found in your houses. And anyone, whether foreigner or native-born, who eats anything with yeast in it must be cut

off from the community of Israel. [20]Eat nothing made with yeast. Wherever you live, you must eat unleavened bread."

[21]Then Moses summoned all the elders of Israel and said to them, "Go at once and select the animals for your families and slaughter the Passover lamb. [22]Take a bunch of hyssop, dip it into the blood in the basin and put some of the blood on the top and on both sides of the doorframe. None of you shall go out of the door of your house until morning. [23]When the LORD goes through the land to strike down the Egyptians, he will see the blood on the top and sides of the doorframe and will pass over that doorway, and he will not permit the destroyer to enter your houses and strike you down.

[24]"Obey these instructions as a lasting ordinance for you and your descendants. [25]When you enter the land that the LORD will give you as he promised, observe this ceremony. [26]And when your children ask you, 'What does this ceremony mean to you?' [27]then tell them, 'It is the Passover sacrifice to the LORD, who passed over the houses of the Israelites in Egypt and spared our homes when he struck down the Egyptians.'" Then the people bowed down and worshiped. [28]The Israelites did just what the LORD commanded Moses and Aaron.

[29]At midnight the LORD struck down all the firstborn in Egypt, from the firstborn of Pharaoh, who sat on the throne, to the firstborn of the prisoner, who was in the dungeon, and the firstborn of all the livestock as well. [30]Pharaoh and all his officials and all the Egyptians got up during the night, and there was loud wailing in Egypt, for there was not a house without someone dead.

The Exodus

[31]During the night Pharaoh summoned Moses and Aaron and said, "Up! Leave my people, you and the Israelites! Go, worship the LORD as you

---

12:7 tops of the doorframes The blood of the Passover was a sign that the life of the sacrificed animal was exchanged for the lives of the occupants of the house (vv. 12–13).

12:8 meat roasted over the fire Roasting eliminates the blood entirely; blood was forbidden for consumption (see Lev 3:17; 17:10–14; Dt 15:23). **bread made without yeast** The Hebrew word used here, *matsah*, refers to a type of bread that has no yeast. Since the dough does not rise, it can be baked quickly; it is thus ideal for unexpected guests or eating hastily (see v. 11; Ge 19:3).

12:11 Passover The Hebrew noun used here is *pesach*. The English adjective "paschal" derives from this Hebrew term and is used of both the Passover lamb and Easter (see 1Co 5:7). While only the fourteenth day of the month can technically be called *pesach* (Passover), the term was later applied to the entire week of the observance (Ex 12:15).

12:12 bring judgment on all the gods of Egypt The first reference to the plagues as judgments on Egypt's gods. **12:15 For seven days you are to eat** The narrative moves from the Passover and its use of unleavened bread to the seven-day Festival of Unleavened Bread. Throughout the remainder of the OT and NT, this seven-day feast is considered distinct from — but occurring adjacent to — the Passover. In the very next chapter, the rules for the seven-day feast are again enumerated, with no reference to the Passover (13:6–8). **remove the yeast** The reason for this prohibition of leaven is unknown. During the Passover, the rationale was clearly haste (see note on v. 8), but this cannot be true of a seven-day festival. Leaven may have been viewed as something that had life in itself — because it caused fermentation and the rising of bread — and thus it was not to be burned on the altar (Lev 2:4,11). The prohibition would then be similar to that regarding the consumption of blood (e.g., Lev 3:17; 7:26–27; 17:10–14; Dt 15:23).

have requested. ³²Take your flocks and herds, as you have said, and go. And also bless me."

³³The Egyptians urged the people to hurry and leave the country. "For otherwise," they said, "we will all die!" ³⁴So the people took their dough before the yeast was added, and carried it on their shoulders in kneading troughs wrapped in clothing. ³⁵The Israelites did as Moses instructed and asked the Egyptians for articles of silver and gold and for clothing. ³⁶The LORD had made the Egyptians favorably disposed toward the people, and they gave them what they asked for; so they plundered the Egyptians.

³⁷The Israelites journeyed from Rameses to Sukkoth. There were about six hundred thousand men on foot, besides women and children. ³⁸Many other people went up with them, and also large droves of livestock, both flocks and herds. ³⁹With the dough the Israelites had brought from Egypt, they baked loaves of unleavened bread. The dough was without yeast because they had been driven out of Egypt and did not have time to prepare food for themselves.

⁴⁰Now the length of time the Israelite people lived in Egyptᵃ was 430 years. ⁴¹At the end of the 430 years, to the very day, all the LORD's divisions left Egypt. ⁴²Because the LORD kept vigil that night to bring them out of Egypt, on this night all the Israelites are to keep vigil to honor the LORD for the generations to come.

Passover Restrictions

⁴³The LORD said to Moses and Aaron, "These are the regulations for the Passover meal:

"No foreigner may eat it. ⁴⁴Any slave you have bought may eat it after you have circumcised him,

⁴⁵but a temporary resident or a hired worker may not eat it.

⁴⁶"It must be eaten inside the house; take none of the meat outside the house. Do not break any of the bones. ⁴⁷The whole community of Israel must celebrate it.

⁴⁸"A foreigner residing among you who wants to celebrate the LORD's Passover must have all the males in his household circumcised; then he may take part like one born in the land. No uncircumcised male may eat it. ⁴⁹The same law applies both to the native-born and to the foreigner residing among you."

⁵⁰All the Israelites did just what the LORD had commanded Moses and Aaron. ⁵¹And on that very day the LORD brought the Israelites out of Egypt by their divisions.

Consecration of the Firstborn

13 The LORD said to Moses, ²"Consecrate to me every firstborn male. The first offspring of every womb among the Israelites belongs to me, whether human or animal."

³Then Moses said to the people, "Commemorate this day, the day you came out of Egypt, out of the land of slavery, because the LORD brought you out of it with a mighty hand. Eat nothing containing yeast. ⁴Today, in the month of Aviv, you are leaving. ⁵When the LORD brings you into the land of the Canaanites, Hittites, Amorites, Hivites and Jebusites — the land he swore to your ancestors to give you, a land flowing with milk and honey — you are to observe this ceremony in this

ᵃ 40 Masoretic Text; Samaritan Pentateuch and Septuagint *Egypt and Canaan*

12:34 before the yeast was added Not a reference to the Passover ritual; that had already been performed. Rather, the Egyptians push Israel out of Egypt so quickly that their bread with leaven does not have time to rise.
12:37 six hundred thousand The numbers given here and elsewhere in the story of the exodus and wilderness wanderings are logistically problematic. See note on Nu 1:20–46; note on Nu 1:46.
12:38 Many other people The Hebrew phrase used here, *erev rav*, refers to a mixed group of non-Israelites who joined them in their departure. The incident recorded in Lev 24:10–16 indicates that some Egyptians had joined with the Israelites.

12:43–49 This passage is somewhat redundant, as the Passover rules have already been described (see Ex 12:1–13). However, this section also describes who is ineligible to observe the Passover—likely a necessary clarification in response to foreigners joining Israel (v. 38). No uncircumcised people could participate in the Passover; circumcision is the sign of the covenant between Yahweh and Israel (v. 48; see Ge 17). The necessity of being a member of Israel to partake in the Passover reinforced the connection of the event to Israel's identification as Yahweh's own people.

13:1–16 This passage reiterates some of the requirements for celebrating the Festival of Unleavened Bread and connects the observance to the commemoration of the exodus and the consecration of the firstborn. While this festival and the Passover both celebrate God's deliverance of Israel from Egypt, the description here does not include any of the distinctive features of Passover such as the roasted lamb or the blood on the doorposts. The instructions for Passover in ch. 12, however, also refer to the Festival of Unleavened Bread (12:14–20). Passover was a time to remember how Israel was spared at the tenth plague (12:13). Unleavened bread memorializes the exodus event with a focus on the bread the Israelites had when they left Egypt in a hurry (12:33–34). The regulations in this passage to set apart the firstborn of Israel for Yahweh also connect with the events of ch. 12 since the tenth plague struck down the firstborn of Egypt (12:29–30).

13:2 Consecrate to me every firstborn The firstborn belongs to God by virtue of this decree, not because of any inherent status. Later in Israel's history, the Levites replace the firstborn by way of their priestly role (Nu 3:12; 8:16,18).
13:5 the Canaanites, Hittites, Amorites, Hivites and Jebusites The promised land of Canaan is frequently

month: ⁶For seven days eat bread made without yeast and on the seventh day hold a festival to the Lord. ⁷Eat unleavened bread during those seven days; nothing with yeast in it is to be seen among you, nor shall any yeast be seen anywhere within your borders. ⁸On that day tell your son, 'I do this because of what the Lord did for me when I came out of Egypt.' ⁹This observance will be for you like a sign on your hand and a reminder on your forehead that this law of the Lord is to be on your lips. For the Lord brought you out of Egypt with his mighty hand. ¹⁰You must keep this ordinance at the appointed time year after year.

¹¹"After the Lord brings you into the land of the Canaanites and gives it to you, as he promised on oath to you and your ancestors, ¹²you are to give over to the Lord the first offspring of every womb. All the firstborn males of your livestock belong to the Lord. ¹³Redeem with a lamb every firstborn donkey, but if you do not redeem it, break its neck. Redeem every firstborn among your sons.

¹⁴"In days to come, when your son asks you, 'What does this mean?' say to him, 'With a mighty hand the Lord brought us out of Egypt, out of the land of slavery. ¹⁵When Pharaoh stubbornly refused to let us go, the Lord killed the firstborn of both people and animals in Egypt. This is why I sacrifice to the Lord the first male offspring of every womb and redeem each of my firstborn sons.' ¹⁶And it will be like a sign on your hand and a symbol on your forehead that the Lord brought us out of Egypt with his mighty hand."

Crossing the Sea

¹⁷When Pharaoh let the people go, God did not lead them on the road through the Philistine country, though that was shorter. For God said, "If they face war, they might change their minds and return to Egypt." ¹⁸So God led the people around by the desert road toward the Red Sea.ᵃ The Israelites went up out of Egypt ready for battle.

¹⁹Moses took the bones of Joseph with him because Joseph had made the Israelites swear an oath. He had said, "God will surely come to your aid, and then you must carry my bones up with you from this place."ᵇ

²⁰After leaving Sukkoth they camped at Etham on the edge of the desert. ²¹By day the Lord went ahead of them in a pillar of cloud to guide them on their way and by night in a pillar of fire to give them light, so that they could travel by day or night. ²²Neither the pillar of cloud by day nor the pillar of fire by night left its place in front of the people.

14 Then the Lord said to Moses, ²"Tell the Israelites to turn back and encamp near Pi Hahiroth, between Migdol and the sea. They are to encamp by the sea, directly opposite Baal Zephon. ³Pharaoh will think, 'The Israelites are wandering around the land in confusion, hemmed in by

ᵃ 18 Or *the Sea of Reeds*   ᵇ 19 See Gen. 50:25.

mentioned with lists of three to ten people groups who are to be driven out of the land (see Ge 15:19–21 and note). There are 18 lists like this in Genesis to 2 Kings—including several in Exodus (e.g., Ex 3:8; 23:23; 33:2; 34:11). **13:9 on your forehead** This verse and others led to the Jewish tradition of wearing phylacteries—small, black, leather boxes that contained short passages of Scripture.

13:11–16 While v. 2 detailed the consecration of the firstborn with respect to both people and animals, this section deals with the treatment of the firstborn once Israel moves into the promised land.

The present passage allows for exceptions. The firstborn of unclean animals (e.g., the donkey) are to be redeemed (replaced) by a clean animal for sacrifice (v. 13). In v. 15, the practice of redemption (or replacement) is applied to people: The firstborn of the Israelites are exempted from sacrifice by virtue of their (later) substitution with the tribe of Levi (the Levites were bound to Yahweh's service; see Nu 3:11–13).

13:17–22 This passage transitions back to the narrative of Israel's departure from Egypt with details about the route and method by which God led them into the wilderness.

13:17 on the road through the Philistine country Refers to an ancient road known as "the way of Horus" (later called the Via Maris, meaning the "way of the sea"). This road ran from the northeastern Egyptian delta along the Mediterranean coast toward Canaan. **war** The coastal highway was dotted by Egyptian forts—a threat to the Israelites.

13:18 Red Sea The Hebrew phrase used here, *yam suph*, means "sea of reeds." While it can refer to what is now known as the Red Sea (e.g., 1Ki 9:26), the term is widely used in the Bible. Based on the description in Nu 33, the usage here likely does not refer to the Red Sea, but to another shorter crossing. The Hebrew word *suph* is derived from the Egyptian term for papyrus reeds, which grow abundantly in fresh water. See note on Ex 14:2.

13:19 bones of Joseph When the people leave Egypt, Moses takes the bones of Joseph, fulfilling his deathbed request (Ge 50:25). The Israelites bury the bones when they reach Canaan (Jos 24:32).

13:20 Sukkoth Sukkoth is still in the Egyptian delta. Today, the site is identified as Tell el-Maskhuta.

13:21 a pillar of cloud Besides veiling Yahweh from view and providing direction, the cloud also obscured the entire assembly from view.

14:1–31 This chapter narrates the crossing of the sea of reeds (or Red Sea; see note on Ex 13:18) and serves as a bridge between the exodus from Egypt and Israel's time in the wilderness. Exodus 14:30–31 summarizes Israel's experience of Yahweh's deliverance, his judgment of Egypt, and the people's faith in Yahweh and his servant Moses.

14:2 the sea This is the same body of water the Israelites cross to escape Pharaoh. Identifying the precise location requires knowing exactly where the Israelites were when they turned back to Pi Hahiroth (Nu 33:7–8), and which direction they turned. Neither of these questions can be answered from the text; the location of the crossing is thus unknown. Compare note on 13:18. See the map "Route of the Exodus" on p. 2252.

the desert.' ⁴And I will harden Pharaoh's heart, and he will pursue them. But I will gain glory for myself through Pharaoh and all his army, and the Egyptians will know that I am the LORD." So the Israelites did this.

⁵When the king of Egypt was told that the people had fled, Pharaoh and his officials changed their minds about them and said, "What have we done? We have let the Israelites go and have lost their services!" ⁶So he had his chariot made ready and took his army with him. ⁷He took six hundred of the best chariots, along with all the other chariots of Egypt, with officers over all of them. ⁸The LORD hardened the heart of Pharaoh king of Egypt, so that he pursued the Israelites, who were marching out boldly. ⁹The Egyptians — all Pharaoh's horses and chariots, horsemenᵃ and troops — pursued the Israelites and overtook them as they camped by the sea near Pi Hahiroth, opposite Baal Zephon.

¹⁰As Pharaoh approached, the Israelites looked up, and there were the Egyptians, marching after them. They were terrified and cried out to the LORD. ¹¹They said to Moses, "Was it because there were no graves in Egypt that you brought us to the desert to die? What have you done to us by bringing us out of Egypt? ¹²Didn't we say to you in Egypt, 'Leave us alone; let us serve the Egyptians'? It would have been better for us to serve the Egyptians than to die in the desert!"

¹³Moses answered the people, "Do not be afraid. Stand firm and you will see the deliverance the LORD will bring you today. The Egyptians you see today you will never see again. ¹⁴The LORD will fight for you; you need only to be still."

¹⁵Then the LORD said to Moses, "Why are you crying out to me? Tell the Israelites to move on. ¹⁶Raise your staff and stretch out your hand over the sea to divide the water so that the Israelites can go through the sea on dry ground. ¹⁷I will harden the hearts of the Egyptians so that they will go in after them. And I will gain glory through Phar-

aoh and all his army, through his chariots and his horsemen. ¹⁸The Egyptians will know that I am the LORD when I gain glory through Pharaoh, his chariots and his horsemen."

¹⁹Then the angel of God, who had been traveling in front of Israel's army, withdrew and went behind them. The pillar of cloud also moved from in front and stood behind them, ²⁰coming between the armies of Egypt and Israel. Throughout the night the cloud brought darkness to the one side and light to the other side; so neither went near the other all night long.

²¹Then Moses stretched out his hand over the sea, and all that night the LORD drove the sea back with a strong east wind and turned it into dry land. The waters were divided, ²²and the Israelites went through the sea on dry ground, with a wall of water on their right and on their left.

²³The Egyptians pursued them, and all Pharaoh's horses and chariots and horsemen followed them into the sea. ²⁴During the last watch of the night the LORD looked down from the pillar of fire and cloud at the Egyptian army and threw it into confusion. ²⁵He jammedᵇ the wheels of their chariots so that they had difficulty driving. And the Egyptians said, "Let's get away from the Israelites! The LORD is fighting for them against Egypt."

²⁶Then the LORD said to Moses, "Stretch out your hand over the sea so that the waters may flow back over the Egyptians and their chariots and horsemen." ²⁷Moses stretched out his hand over the sea, and at daybreak the sea went back to its place. The Egyptians were fleeing towardᶜ it, and the LORD swept them into the sea. ²⁸The water flowed back and covered the chariots and horsemen — the entire army of Pharaoh that had followed the Israelites into the sea. Not one of them survived.

²⁹But the Israelites went through the sea on

ᵃ 9 Or *charioteers*; also in verses 17, 18, 23, 26 and 28
ᵇ 25 See Samaritan Pentateuch, Septuagint and Syriac; Masoretic Text *removed*   ᶜ 27 Or *from*

14:4 harden Pharaoh's heart See note on Ex 4:21. Yahweh moves Pharaoh to change his mind and pursue the Israelites, so that he (Yahweh) may show himself triumphant.

14:11 brought us to the desert to die This will not be the last time the people of Israel forget the power of God and blame Moses for their troubles.

14:14 The LORD will fight for you The claim that God will fight on his people's behalf, called the "divine warrior" motif, occurs throughout the Bible (e.g., Dt 28:7; Ne 4:20; Isa 42:13; Zec 14:3).

14:15 Why are you crying out to me Indicates urgency: It is time to act, not to perform a lengthy prayer.

14:16 stretch out your hand Exodus 14:21 suggests that Moses was to stand in front of the water and hold out his staff. **dry ground** The ground could be walked on but still contained enough water that the wheels of the heavy chariots become mired in it (v. 25).

14:19 angel of God In 13:21–22, Yahweh—not the Angel of God—was going in front of Israel in a pillar of cloud or fire. The angel may be (visibly) leading the Israelites with God and now turns to block the Egyptians (v. 20). It is also possible that the angel is in the cloud and is therefore identified with Yahweh himself. See the table "Angels in the Bible" on p. 2120.

14:21 strong east wind God uses a force of nature to divide the sea.

14:24 last watch of the night If the division of the sea took all night, the Israelites crossed it quickly; the Egyptians were already in the sea by morning. **from the pillar** The wording in this passage illustrates how the distinction between Yahweh and this angel is often blurred (compare note on 14:19). Elsewhere in Exodus, this angel is described in the Hebrew text as having Yahweh's name in him and leads Israel to the land (23:20–23; compare Jdg 2:1–3).

dry ground, with a wall of water on their right and on their left. ³⁰That day the LORD saved Israel from the hands of the Egyptians, and Israel saw the Egyptians lying dead on the shore. ³¹And when the Israelites saw the mighty hand of the LORD displayed against the Egyptians, the people feared the LORD and put their trust in him and in Moses his servant.

The Song of Moses and Miriam

15 Then Moses and the Israelites sang this song to the LORD:

"I will sing to the LORD,
  for he is highly exalted.

Both horse and driver
  he has hurled into the sea.
² "The LORD is my strength and my
    defense ᵃ;
  he has become my salvation.
He is my God, and I will praise him,
  my father's God, and I will exalt him.
³ The LORD is a warrior;
    the LORD is his name.
⁴ Pharaoh's chariots and his army
  he has hurled into the sea.
The best of Pharaoh's officers
  are drowned in the Red Sea.ᵇ

ᵃ 2 Or *song*   ᵇ 4 Or *the Sea of Reeds*; also in verse 22

15:1–21 Exodus 15:1–18 is a poem celebrating the victory God won for Israel at the sea (vv. 1–12) and looking forward to their journey toward the promised land (vv. 13–18). Because of its use of the first person, it is often referred to as the "Song of Moses" (see v. 1). It is followed by the shorter "Song of Miriam," sung by Moses and Aaron's sister (vv. 20–21).

15:2 LORD Here the name used for God in the Hebrew text is the abbreviated form of the divine name—*yah*. The shorter form occurs nearly 50 times in the OT, mostly in Psalms (e.g., Ps 68:4; 77:11; 89:8; 150:6).

15:3 a warrior A clear declaration of Yahweh as the divine warrior who fights on behalf of Israel. See Ex 14:14 and note.

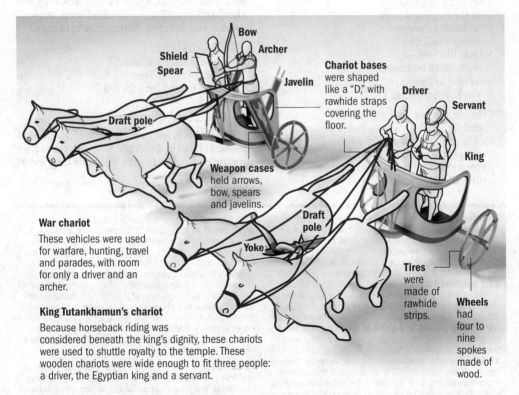

Bow
Shield
Spear
Archer
Javelin
Draft pole

Chariot bases were shaped like a "D," with rawhide straps covering the floor.

Driver
Servant
King

Weapon cases held arrows, bow, spears and javelins.

Draft pole
Yoke

Tires were made of rawhide strips.

Wheels had four to nine spokes made of wood.

War chariot

These vehicles were used for warfare, hunting, travel and parades, with room for only a driver and an archer.

King Tutankhamun's chariot

Because horseback riding was considered beneath the king's dignity, these chariots were used to shuttle royalty to the temple. These wooden chariots were wide enough to fit three people: a driver, the Egyptian king and a servant.

Egyptian Chariots

Two types of chariots used by ancient Egyptians were war and royal chariots. Made mostly of wood and rawhide, these light, horse-drawn chariots could carry two or three people at a time.

⁵ The deep waters have covered them;
    they sank to the depths like a stone.
⁶ Your right hand, LORD,
    was majestic in power.
Your right hand, LORD,
    shattered the enemy.

⁷ "In the greatness of your majesty
    you threw down those who opposed you.
You unleashed your burning anger;
    it consumed them like stubble.
⁸ By the blast of your nostrils
    the waters piled up.
The surging waters stood up like a wall;
    the deep waters congealed in the heart of
        the sea.
⁹ The enemy boasted,
    'I will pursue, I will overtake them.
I will divide the spoils;
    I will gorge myself on them.
I will draw my sword
    and my hand will destroy them.'
¹⁰ But you blew with your breath,
    and the sea covered them.
They sank like lead
    in the mighty waters.
¹¹ Who among the gods
    is like you, LORD?
Who is like you —
    majestic in holiness,
awesome in glory,
    working wonders?

¹² "You stretch out your right hand,
    and the earth swallows your enemies.
¹³ In your unfailing love you will lead
    the people you have redeemed.
In your strength you will guide them
    to your holy dwelling.

¹⁴ The nations will hear and tremble;
    anguish will grip the people of Philistia.
¹⁵ The chiefs of Edom will be terrified,
    the leaders of Moab will be seized with
        trembling,
the people*a* of Canaan will melt away;
¹⁶   terror and dread will fall on them.
By the power of your arm
    they will be as still as a stone —
until your people pass by, LORD,
    until the people you bought*b* pass by.
¹⁷ You will bring them in and plant them
    on the mountain of your inheritance —
the place, LORD, you made for your dwelling,
    the sanctuary, Lord, your hands
        established.

¹⁸ "The LORD reigns
    for ever and ever."

¹⁹ When Pharaoh's horses, chariots and horse-men*c* went into the sea, the LORD brought the waters of the sea back over them, but the Israelites walked through the sea on dry ground. ²⁰ Then Miriam the prophet, Aaron's sister, took a timbrel in her hand, and all the women followed her, with timbrels and dancing. ²¹ Miriam sang to them:

"Sing to the LORD,
    for he is highly exalted.
Both horse and driver
    he has hurled into the sea."

The Waters of Marah and Elim

²² Then Moses led Israel from the Red Sea and they went into the Desert of Shur. For three days they traveled in the desert without finding water.

a 15 Or rulers   b 16 Or created   c 19 Or charioteers

15:5 deep waters The Hebrew word used here, *tehom*, is the same word used in Ge 1:2 for the chaotic primeval deep. The use of this word connects the exodus events to several important themes that begin with Ge 1: God's power over the forces of chaos (see Ge 1:2); the divine power behind creation; and the supremacy of Yahweh over other gods.
15:6 shattered the enemy Possibly another allusion to Yahweh's defeat of the waters of chaos, often personified as a sea dragon violently struck down by God (Ps 74:12–17; Job 26:12–13; Isa 27:1; 51:9; compare note on Ge 1:2).
15:11 Who among the gods is like you This phrase indicates the absolute uniqueness of Yahweh among all other unseen divine beings.
15:12 the earth swallows In ancient Israelite cosmology (their conception of the structure of the cosmos), the primeval deep was thought to be under the earth. In such contexts, earth refers to the underworld—the realm of the dead (compare Jnh 2:1–6). See the infographic "Ancient Hebrew Conception of the Universe" on p. 5.
15:13 unfailing love The Hebrew word used here, *chesed*, denotes loving favor and covenant faithfulness.
your holy dwelling Refers to Mount Sinai in this context.
15:15 Edom The region southeast of the Dead Sea.
Moab Territory east of the Dead Sea and north of Edom.

15:16 bought The Hebrew verb used here, *qanah*, may be rendered as "to acquire" ("purchase" or "buy") or "to create" (compare Ge 14:19,22). Since this poem alludes to the creation imagery of God's victory over chaos, the word here is likely meant in the sense of creation, not acquisition. The exodus event is generally not characterized as an economic transaction either. Yahweh's triumph over Egypt results in the creation of a nation, not its purchase.
15:20 Miriam the prophet Moses' sister has not been named prior to this verse (compare Ex 2:4,7–9). Three other women in the OT are also described as prophets: Deborah (Jdg 4:4), Huldah (2Ki 22:14; 2Ch 34:22) and Noadiah (Ne 6:14).

15:22–27 The account of the bitter water at Marah is the first of several episodes in Exodus and Numbers that detail the harsh nature of the wilderness journey. These accounts illustrate both the difficulties faced by the Israelites and God's care of them. Many of these events show the Israelites' unbelief in spite of their deliverance from Egypt and their experience of God's power over the forces of nature.

15:22 Desert of Shur This location in the northern Sinai peninsula is referred to elsewhere in the OT (Ge

²³When they came to Marah, they could not drink its water because it was bitter. (That is why the place is called Marah.ᵃ) ²⁴So the people grumbled against Moses, saying, "What are we to drink?"

²⁵Then Moses cried out to the LORD, and the LORD showed him a piece of wood. He threw it into the water, and the water became fit to drink.

There the LORD issued a ruling and instruction for them and put them to the test. ²⁶He said, "If you listen carefully to the LORD your God and do what is right in his eyes, if you pay attention to his commands and keep all his decrees, I will not bring on you any of the diseases I brought on the Egyptians, for I am the LORD, who heals you."

²⁷Then they came to Elim, where there were twelve springs and seventy palm trees, and they camped there near the water.

Manna and Quail

16 The whole Israelite community set out from Elim and came to the Desert of Sin, which is between Elim and Sinai, on the fifteenth day of the second month after they had come out of Egypt. ²In the desert the whole community grumbled against Moses and Aaron. ³The Israelites said to them, "If only we had died by the LORD's hand in Egypt! There we sat around pots of meat and ate all the food we wanted, but you have brought us out into this desert to starve this entire assembly to death."

⁴Then the LORD said to Moses, "I will rain down bread from heaven for you. The people are to go out each day and gather enough for that day. In this way I will test them and see whether they will follow my instructions. ⁵On the sixth day they are to prepare what they bring in, and that is to be twice as much as they gather on the other days."

⁶So Moses and Aaron said to all the Israelites,

"In the evening you will know that it was the LORD who brought you out of Egypt, ⁷and in the morning you will see the glory of the LORD, because he has heard your grumbling against him. Who are we, that you should grumble against us?" ⁸Moses also said, "You will know that it was the LORD when he gives you meat to eat in the evening and all the bread you want in the morning, because he has heard your grumbling against him. Who are we? You are not grumbling against us, but against the LORD."

⁹Then Moses told Aaron, "Say to the entire Israelite community, 'Come before the LORD, for he has heard your grumbling.'"

¹⁰While Aaron was speaking to the whole Israelite community, they looked toward the desert, and there was the glory of the LORD appearing in the cloud.

¹¹The LORD said to Moses, ¹²"I have heard the grumbling of the Israelites. Tell them, 'At twilight you will eat meat, and in the morning you will be filled with bread. Then you will know that I am the LORD your God.'"

¹³That evening quail came and covered the camp, and in the morning there was a layer of dew around the camp. ¹⁴When the dew was gone, thin flakes like frost on the ground appeared on the desert floor. ¹⁵When the Israelites saw it, they said to each other, "What is it?" For they did not know what it was.

Moses said to them, "It is the bread the LORD has given you to eat. ¹⁶This is what the LORD has commanded: 'Everyone is to gather as much as they need. Take an omerᵇ for each person you have in your tent.'"

ᵃ 23 *Marah* means *bitter.*   ᵇ 16 That is, possibly about 3 pounds or about 1.4 kilograms; also in verses 18, 32, 33 and 36

25:18; 1Sa 15:7) and is also called the Wilderness of Etham in Nu 33:8.
15:23 Marah The Hebrew word used here, *marah*, means "bitter."
15:25 water became fit to drink The purpose of the piece of wood is not explained.
15:26 diseases This may refer to the plagues, though the OT contains other references to more general diseases suffered in Egypt (e.g., Dt 7:15; 28:60; compare Am 4:10).
15:27 Elim This location was likely situated in the Wadi Gharandel, between the Wilderness of Shur and the Wilderness of Sin.

16:1–36 After the water crisis in Ex 15:22–27 and before another water crisis in 17:1–7, the Israelites now face a food crisis. Yahweh provides for them again, this time with manna and quail. Despite this, however, the Israelites continue to have problems trusting in Yahweh's ability to provide (vv. 20,27).

16:1 Desert of Sin The precise location of the Wilderness of Sin is uncertain, but it likely refers to a central region of the Sinai Peninsula. This wilderness should not be confused with the Wilderness of Zin located southwest of the Dead Sea much closer to Canaan.

16:6 who brought you out The phrasing is virtually identical to that associated with the Passover, which commemorated deliverance at the death of the firstborn of Egypt and the release from captivity (compare 13:9,16).
16:7 glory of the LORD This phrase typically denotes the presence of God (see v. 10).
16:10 glory of the LORD appearing in the cloud Though the cloud is visible, the glory (*kavod* in Hebrew) will also be visible and distinct in appearance from the cloud.
16:12 you will eat meat Refers to the quail that appear in v. 13. **you will be filled with bread** Identifies the manna of v. 15 (compare Ps 78:24; 105:40; Ne 9:15).
16:13 quail Quail migrate in large numbers. Because of long migrations, they often tire and fly very low to the ground, enabling people to catch them in nets or by hand (see Nu 11:31–32).
16:15 What is it The Hebrew phrase used here is *man hu.* The Israelites accordingly name the bread *man* (translated "manna").
16:16 omer In later times, an omer measured approximately a gallon. During the exodus, it likely represented a daily ration. Exodus 16:36 indicates that an omer was one-tenth of an ephah. An ephah was approximately 22 liters.

¹⁷The Israelites did as they were told; some gathered much, some little. ¹⁸And when they measured it by the omer, the one who gathered much did not have too much, and the one who gathered little did not have too little. Everyone had gathered just as much as they needed.

¹⁹Then Moses said to them, "No one is to keep any of it until morning."

²⁰However, some of them paid no attention to Moses; they kept part of it until morning, but it was full of maggots and began to smell. So Moses was angry with them.

²¹Each morning everyone gathered as much as they needed, and when the sun grew hot, it melted away. ²²On the sixth day, they gathered twice as much — two omers* for each person — and the leaders of the community came and reported this to Moses. ²³He said to them, "This is what the LORD commanded: 'Tomorrow is to be a day of sabbath rest, a holy sabbath to the LORD. So bake what you want to bake and boil what you want to boil. Save whatever is left and keep it until morning.'"

²⁴So they saved it until morning, as Moses commanded, and it did not stink or get maggots in it. ²⁵"Eat it today," Moses said, "because today is a sabbath to the LORD. You will not find any of it on the ground today. ²⁶Six days you are to gather it, but on the seventh day, the Sabbath, there will not be any."

²⁷Nevertheless, some of the people went out on the seventh day to gather it, but they found none. ²⁸Then the LORD said to Moses, "How long will you* refuse to keep my commands and my instructions? ²⁹Bear in mind that the LORD has given you the Sabbath; that is why on the sixth day he gives you bread for two days. Everyone is to stay where they are on the seventh day; no one is to go out." ³⁰So the people rested on the seventh day.

³¹The people of Israel called the bread manna.* It was white like coriander seed and tasted like wafers made with honey. ³²Moses said, "This is what the LORD has commanded: 'Take an omer of manna and keep it for the generations to come, so they can see the bread I gave you to eat in the wilderness when I brought you out of Egypt.'"

³³So Moses said to Aaron, "Take a jar and put an omer of manna in it. Then place it before the LORD to be kept for the generations to come."

³⁴As the LORD commanded Moses, Aaron put the manna with the tablets of the covenant law, so that it might be preserved. ³⁵The Israelites ate manna forty years, until they came to a land that was settled; they ate manna until they reached the border of Canaan.

³⁶(An omer is one-tenth of an ephah.)

Water From the Rock

17 The whole Israelite community set out from the Desert of Sin, traveling from place to place as the LORD commanded. They camped at Rephidim, but there was no water for the people to drink. ²So they quarreled with Moses and said, "Give us water to drink."

Moses replied, "Why do you quarrel with me? Why do you put the LORD to the test?"

³But the people were thirsty for water there, and they grumbled against Moses. They said, "Why did you bring us up out of Egypt to make us and our children and livestock die of thirst?"

⁴Then Moses cried out to the LORD, "What am I to do with these people? They are almost ready to stone me."

⁵The LORD answered Moses, "Go out in front of the people. Take with you some of the elders of Israel and take in your hand the staff with which you struck the Nile, and go. ⁶I will stand there before you by the rock at Horeb. Strike the rock, and water will come out of it for the people to

---

ᵃ 22 That is, possibly about 6 pounds or about 2.8 kilograms
ᵇ 28 The Hebrew is plural.   *ᶜ 31 Manna* sounds like the Hebrew for *What is it?* (see verse 15).

16:31 with honey Manna resembles no known modern-day natural phenomenon. The tamarisk bush produces a sweet white secretion that modern Bedouin call manna. Basically a sap, it does not match the description here or in v. 14 as something fine and flake-like on the ground.
16:33 omer of manna God commands that some manna be preserved as a cultural and religious relic. **before the LORD** Here, the manna is to be placed before Yahweh. In v. 34, it is to be placed, as the Hebrew text phrases it, before the testimony (*eduth* in Hebrew). These two statements are not referring to two competing locations. Rather, both phrases come to label the sacred site where Yahweh's earthly presence may be found (compare Lev 1:5). However, the ark and tabernacle had not yet been built (Ex 35–39) nor had Yahweh's presence entered the tabernacle (ch. 40). Compare note on v. 34.
16:34 tablets of the covenant law The Hebrew text here uses the word *eduth*. One of the later labels used for the tabernacle is the *mishkan ha'eduth* (which may be

translated "tabernacle of the testimony" or "tabernacle of the covenant law"; 38:21; Nu 1:50; 10:11). Hebrews 9:4 interprets this verse as saying that the manna was put inside the ark of the covenant. Since the ark was not built at this time, this account likely reports events from a later time after the tabernacle and the ark of the covenant had been built.

17:1–7 In this passage, a location previously called Rephidim is renamed Massah and Meribah after the Israelites complain of a lack of water. Later, this location is known proverbially as the place Israel tested Yahweh (see Dt 6:16; 9:22; 33:8; Ps 95:8).

17:1 Rephidim Exodus 19:2 indicates this as the final stop before the Israelites arrive at Sinai (compare Nu 33:14–15). It is located near Horeb (see Ex 17:6), another term for Mount Sinai (see 3:1 and note).

17:5 Go out in front of the people Instead of reacting with anger, God will show his power.

drink." So Moses did this in the sight of the elders of Israel. [7] And he called the place Massah[a] and Meribah[b] because the Israelites quarreled and because they tested the LORD saying, "Is the LORD among us or not?"

The Amalekites Defeated

[8] The Amalekites came and attacked the Israelites at Rephidim. [9] Moses said to Joshua, "Choose some of our men and go out to fight the Amalekites. Tomorrow I will stand on top of the hill with the staff of God in my hands."

[10] So Joshua fought the Amalekites as Moses had ordered, and Moses, Aaron and Hur went to the top of the hill. [11] As long as Moses held up his hands, the Israelites were winning, but whenever he lowered his hands, the Amalekites were winning. [12] When Moses' hands grew tired, they took a stone and put it under him and he sat on it. Aaron and Hur held his hands up — one on one side, one on the other — so that his hands remained steady till sunset. [13] So Joshua overcame the Amalekite army with the sword.

[14] Then the LORD said to Moses, "Write this on a scroll as something to be remembered and make sure that Joshua hears it, because I will completely blot out the name of Amalek from under heaven."

[15] Moses built an altar and called it The LORD is my Banner. [16] He said, "Because hands were lifted up against[c] the throne of the LORD,[d] the LORD will be at war against the Amalekites from generation to generation."

Jethro Visits Moses

18 Now Jethro, the priest of Midian and father-in-law of Moses, heard of everything God had done for Moses and for his people Israel, and how the LORD had brought Israel out of Egypt.

[2] After Moses had sent away his wife Zipporah, his father-in-law Jethro received her [3] and her two sons. One son was named Gershom,[e] for Moses said, "I have become a foreigner in a foreign land"; [4] and the other was named Eliezer,[f] for he said, "My father's God was my helper; he saved me from the sword of Pharaoh."

[5] Jethro, Moses' father-in-law, together with Moses' sons and wife, came to him in the wilderness, where he was camped near the mountain of God. [6] Jethro had sent word to him, "I, your father-in-law Jethro, am coming to you with your wife and her two sons."

[7] So Moses went out to meet his father-in-law and bowed down and kissed him. They greeted each other and then went into the tent. [8] Moses told his father-in-law about everything the LORD had done to Pharaoh and the Egyptians for Israel's sake and about all the hardships they had met along the way and how the LORD had saved them.

[9] Jethro was delighted to hear about all the good things the LORD had done for Israel in rescuing them from the hand of the Egyptians. [10] He said,

---

[a] 7 Massah means testing.   [b] 7 Meribah means quarreling.
[c] 16 Or to   [d] 16 The meaning of the Hebrew for this clause is uncertain.   [e] 3 Gershom sounds like the Hebrew for a foreigner there.   [f] 4 Eliezer means my God is helper.

17:7 Massah The Hebrew word used here means "testing." **Meribah** The Hebrew word used here means "quarreling." This name and the name Massah derive from the Hebrew verbs used here and in 16:2.

17:8–16 When the Amalekites attack them, the Israelites encounter their first opposition from other people since arriving in the wilderness. The Amalekites apparently interpreted the appearance of the Israelites as a threat to their territory and its resources. Other details of this conflict are found in Dt 25:17–19, which describes a surprise attack by the Amalekites at the back of Israel's wandering assembly.

17:8 Amalekites The Amalekites were descendants of Esau (Edom) (Ge 36:12,16). The territory of the Amalekites was situated in the desert south of Canaan, north of the Israelites' location at this time (Ge 14:7; Nu 13:29).

17:9 Joshua The first reference to Joshua in the OT. He will become Moses' commander-in-chief and lead the Israelites' conquest of Canaan.

17:10 Hur Hur would later be one of the leaders who assisted Aaron in governing the people while Moses was on Mount Sinai (Ex 24:14). He may be the same Hur who was the grandfather of Bezalel—one of the craftsmen who built the tabernacle and its furnishings (see 31:2; 35:30; 38:22; 1Ch 2:20).

17:14 Write this The first mention of writing in the Bible. Although no documents composed in early Hebrew writing before the tenth century BC have survived, the Hebrew alphabet is much older (ca. seventeenth

century BC). **completely blot out the name of Amalek from under heaven** Yahweh commands Moses to write down his promise to destroy the Amalekites; they would suffer the same fate as other people groups targeted in the conquest of Canaan (see Dt 2:34; Jos 2:10; 6:17–21).

18:1–27 In this chapter, the narrative transitions away from the wilderness difficulties of Ex 15:22—17:16 in anticipation of the Israelites receiving the law at Sinai. Here, Moses' father-in-law, Jethro, advises Moses to appoint administrators to ease his burden of leadership.

18:1 Jethro Since Jethro lives in Midian, just east of the Gulf of Aqaba, his visit suggests that Mount Sinai should most likely be located in the eastern region of the Sinai Peninsula. Jebel Musa, the traditional location of Mount Sinai, is much too far south. See note on 2:18; note on 3:1.

18:2 After Moses had sent away his wife Explains 4:20, which says that Moses had left for Egypt with his wife and sons.

18:4 Eliezer This Hebrew name means "my God is help." While 4:20 hinted that Moses had at least two sons, only Gershom has been named until now. See the table "Symbolic Names of People in Hebrew" on p. 1388.

18:10 Praise be to the LORD Though Jethro is a Midianite, not an Israelite, he praises the God of Israel, Yahweh. However, Jethro may have accepted Yahweh as his own God, since his son-in-law was living testimony to Yahweh's amazing triumph in Egypt (see v. 11).

"Praise be to the LORD, who rescued you from the hand of the Egyptians and of Pharaoh, and who rescued the people from the hand of the Egyptians. ¹¹Now I know that the LORD is greater than all other gods, for he did this to those who had treated Israel arrogantly." ¹²Then Jethro, Moses' father-in-law, brought a burnt offering and other sacrifices to God, and Aaron came with all the elders of Israel to eat a meal with Moses' father-in-law in the presence of God.

¹³The next day Moses took his seat to serve as judge for the people, and they stood around him from morning till evening. ¹⁴When his father-in-law saw all that Moses was doing for the people, he said, "What is this you are doing for the people? Why do you alone sit as judge, while all these people stand around you from morning till evening?"

¹⁵Moses answered him, "Because the people come to me to seek God's will. ¹⁶Whenever they have a dispute, it is brought to me, and I decide between the parties and inform them of God's decrees and instructions."

¹⁷Moses' father-in-law replied, "What you are doing is not good. ¹⁸You and these people who come to you will only wear yourselves out. The work is too heavy for you; you cannot handle it alone. ¹⁹Listen now to me and I will give you some advice, and may God be with you. You must be the people's representative before God and bring their disputes to him. ²⁰Teach them his decrees and instructions, and show them the way they are to live and how they are to behave. ²¹But select capable men from all the people — men who fear God, trustworthy men who hate dishonest gain — and appoint them as officials over thousands, hundreds, fifties and tens. ²²Have them serve as judges for the people at all times, but have them bring every difficult case to you; the simple cases they can decide themselves. That will

make your load lighter, because they will share it with you. ²³If you do this and God so commands, you will be able to stand the strain, and all these people will go home satisfied."

²⁴Moses listened to his father-in-law and did everything he said. ²⁵He chose capable men from all Israel and made them leaders of the people, officials over thousands, hundreds, fifties and tens. ²⁶They served as judges for the people at all times. The difficult cases they brought to Moses, but the simple ones they decided themselves.

²⁷Then Moses sent his father-in-law on his way, and Jethro returned to his own country.

At Mount Sinai

19 On the first day of the third month after the Israelites left Egypt — on that very day — they came to the Desert of Sinai. ²After they set out from Rephidim, they entered the Desert of Sinai, and Israel camped there in the desert in front of the mountain.

³Then Moses went up to God, and the LORD called to him from the mountain and said, "This is what you are to say to the descendants of Jacob and what you are to tell the people of Israel: ⁴'You yourselves have seen what I did to Egypt, and how I carried you on eagles' wings and brought you to myself. ⁵Now if you obey me fully and keep my covenant, then out of all nations you will be my treasured possession. Although the whole earth is mine, ⁶you[a] will be for me a kingdom of priests and a holy nation.' These are the words you are to speak to the Israelites."

⁷So Moses went back and summoned the elders of the people and set before them all the words the LORD had commanded him to speak. ⁸The people all responded together, "We will do everything the

---

[a] 5,6 Or possession, for the whole earth is mine. ⁶You

18:16 instructions The Israelites have not yet received the law at Sinai. However, this and other verses indicate that a body of regulations may have begun to take shape before the full revelation of the law (see 15:25–26; 18:20).

18:17 What you are doing is not good Jethro — stunned by the inefficient and burdensome procedure he witnesses — immediately recommends changes. His suggestions lead to the establishment of a judiciary system in Israel.

18:21 as officials over thousands, hundreds The units parallel the later organization and leadership of the Israelite army (e.g., Nu 31:14; 1Sa 22:7–8; 2Sa 18:1; 2Ch 1:2). The Hebrew term used for the leaders, *sar*, is frequently employed in military contexts (e.g., Dt 20:9; 1Sa 14:50; 2Ki 1:9).

19:1–25 Exodus 19 marks the arrival of the Israelites at Sinai. There, they will meet with Yahweh and receive the law and God's instructions for the priesthood, sacrifices, offerings and the tabernacle. Before Israel leaves Sinai, they will have everything needed to function as a nation — except the land itself.

The law informs the Israelites how to approach God and live with their fellow citizens. It was, in effect, a national constitution designed for Israel's theocratic kingdom. In addition to providing Israel's national and spiritual identity, the law was also a covenant treaty between the nation and God. As such, it is arranged in the manner of ancient Near Eastern covenants. See the table "Covenants in the Old Testament" on p. 469.

19:3 mountain Mount Sinai (see v. 11; see note on 3:1).

19:5 treasured possession In ancient Near Eastern covenant-legal literature, the term used here sometimes describes those in covenant with a deity — a context reflected here. **whole earth is mine** Though all the earth and its nations belong to Yahweh, Ge 11:1–9 describes God disinheriting the nations of the world. In the next divine act recorded in the OT, he called Abram and promised him a line of descendants that culminated in the sons of Jacob — the 12 tribes of Israel — who now stand before him at Sinai.

19:6 kingdom of priests The only instance of the Hebrew phrase used here in the OT, although the language of Isa 61:6 is similar. This phrase suggests that the

LORD has said." So Moses brought their answer back to the LORD.

⁹The LORD said to Moses, "I am going to come to you in a dense cloud, so that the people will hear me speaking with you and will always put their trust in you." Then Moses told the LORD what the people had said.

¹⁰And the LORD said to Moses, "Go to the people and consecrate them today and tomorrow. Have them wash their clothes ¹¹and be ready by the third day, because on that day the LORD will come down on Mount Sinai in the sight of all the people. ¹²Put limits for the people around the mountain and tell them, 'Be careful that you do not approach the mountain or touch the foot of it. Whoever touches the mountain is to be put to death. ¹³They are to be stoned or shot with arrows; not a hand is to be laid on them. No person or animal shall be permitted to live.' Only when the ram's horn sounds a long blast may they approach the mountain."

¹⁴After Moses had gone down the mountain to the people, he consecrated them, and they washed their clothes. ¹⁵Then he said to the people, "Prepare yourselves for the third day. Abstain from sexual relations."

¹⁶On the morning of the third day there was thunder and lightning, with a thick cloud over the mountain, and a very loud trumpet blast. Everyone in the camp trembled. ¹⁷Then Moses led the people out of the camp to meet with God, and they stood at the foot of the mountain. ¹⁸Mount Sinai was covered with smoke, because the LORD descended on it in fire. The smoke billowed up from it like smoke from a furnace, and the whole mountain[a] trembled violently. ¹⁹As the sound of the trumpet grew louder and louder, Moses spoke and the voice of God answered him.[b]

²⁰The LORD descended to the top of Mount Sinai and called Moses to the top of the mountain. So Moses went up ²¹and the LORD said to him, "Go down and warn the people so they do not force their way through to see the LORD and many of them perish. ²²Even the priests, who approach the LORD, must consecrate themselves, or the LORD will break out against them."

²³Moses said to the LORD, "The people cannot come up Mount Sinai, because you yourself warned us, 'Put limits around the mountain and set it apart as holy.'"

²⁴The LORD replied, "Go down and bring Aaron up with you. But the priests and the people must not force their way through to come up to the LORD, or he will break out against them."

²⁵So Moses went down to the people and told them.

The Ten Commandments

20:1-17pp — Dt 5:6-21

20 And God spoke all these words:

² "I am the LORD your God, who brought you out of Egypt, out of the land of slavery.

a 18 Most Hebrew manuscripts; a few Hebrew manuscripts and Septuagint and all the people   b 19 Or and God answered him with thunder

---

Israelites (and therefore Israel corporately) were to be Yahweh's representatives to the other disinherited nations of the world (see note on Ex 19:5). This interpretation is supported by NT treatment of this phrase (1Pe 2:9; Rev 1:6) and Ge 12:3. Yahweh chose Israel as his people to ultimately provide a means for all nations to re-enter his family. **holy** This refers to being set apart from that which is common (or profane). It indicates something devoted to God's presence and specific use.

19:9 a dense cloud Cloud, smoke, fire, lightning, thunder and darkness are commonly associated with God's presence (see Ex 14:20; 19:16–18; compare 1Ki 8:12; Ps 77:18; 97:2; Eze 1:4). Divine appearances (theophanies) are common in OT narratives. Exodus 33:20 indicates that humans cannot remain alive if they witness the true, glorious presence of Yahweh. Nevertheless, many OT characters do see God and live. In such encounters, God's presence is veiled or obscured by cloud, darkness, fire, smoke or in the appearance of a man (e.g., Ge 32:30; Ex 24:9–14; Dt 5:24; Jdg 13:22; Isa 6:5). See the table "Old Testament Theophanies" on p. 924.

19:10 consecrate them The steps listed here are designed to make the people holy (see note on Ex 19:6) as preparation for being near God's presence.

19:12 Put limits for the people Mount Sinai is a divine sanctuary or temple. It is thus entirely sacred. God sets limitations for the people—those who are not priests or Moses. As the narrative continues, God allows the priests to be on the mountain. He also allows Moses and Aaron to come even closer. The graded areas of sanctity resemble the later zones of the tabernacle and the temple.

19:13 Only when the ram's horn sounds a long blast The Israelites do not produce the trumpet sound; the sound emanates from the mountain and God's presence (see vv. 16,19; compare Zec 9:14). References to a divine trumpet call in the NT draw from this context (compare Mt 24:31; 1Co 15:52; 1Th 4:16). The NT writers also align the trumpet sound with the voice of the risen Christ or angelic beings (1Th 4:16; Rev 1:10; 4:1).

19:14 washed their clothes By washing themselves of earthly soiling, the Israelites will be reminded that the presence they are coming in contact with is not of the earth.

19:15 Abstain from sexual relations Sexual abstinence in the OT is normally associated with ritual cleanness (Lev 15:18; 1Sa 21:4). Like blood, seminal fluids represented life. Loss of blood (e.g., menstruation; compare Lev 12:2,5) or semen was therefore interpreted as a depletion of life force.

19:22 the priests Since there is no evidence for priests in Israel until after Sinai (see Ex 28–29), this may speak of firstborn males who functioned in service to Yahweh prior to the establishment of the official priesthood (see 13:1–2,13; 24:5; 34:20). After Sinai, they were replaced by Aaron's line (see Nu 3:11–13; 8:16–18). Alternatively, this may be a reference to those who were later consecrated as priests.

20:1–21 While Exodus 20 is known for the Ten Commandments, the Hebrew words for "ten" and "commandment" do not appear in the chapter. The Hebrew phrase *asereth haddevarim*, which may be rendered as "ten words," appears in another passage connected to

3 "You shall have no other gods before[a] me.

4 "You shall not make for yourself an image in the form of anything in heaven above or on the earth beneath or in the waters below. 5 You shall not bow down to them or worship them; for I, the LORD your God, am a jealous God, punishing the children for the sin of the parents to the third and fourth generation of those who hate me, 6 but showing love to a thousand generations of those who love me and keep my commandments.

7 "You shall not misuse the name of the LORD your God, for the LORD will not hold anyone guiltless who misuses his name.

8 "Remember the Sabbath day by keeping it holy. 9 Six days you shall labor and do all your work, 10 but the seventh day is a sabbath to the LORD your God. On it you shall not do any work, neither you, nor your son or daughter, nor your male or female servant, nor your animals, nor any foreigner residing in your towns. 11 For in six days the LORD made the heavens and the earth, the sea, and all that is in them, but he rested on the seventh day. Therefore the LORD blessed the Sabbath day and made it holy.

12 "Honor your father and your mother, so that you may live long in the land the LORD your God is giving you.

13 "You shall not murder.

14 "You shall not commit adultery.

15 "You shall not steal.

---

[a] 3 Or besides

---

the Sinai scene (34:11–28). Those commandments (words) do not exactly match the ten laws in ch. 20 (or the parallel passage in Dt 5). This has generated debate over which commands should be considered the core of the law and how they are to be numbered. The ten laws can be divided into two groups of five. The first five focus on the relationship between a person and God. The second five focus on person-to-person relationships. Since these commands were given to Moses, they are also referred to as the "Law of Moses," a phrase applied elsewhere to the whole of the Pentateuch (a reference to the first five books of the OT—Ge, Ex, Lev, Nu and Dt). These ten laws were written on tablets of stone that were deposited in the ark of the covenant, which was kept in the tabernacle (Ex 24:12; 25:16; Dt 4:13; 1Ki 8:9). This reflects the ancient Near Eastern practice of inscribing treaty stipulations on stone and placing those tablets in a sanctuary.

20:2 I am the LORD your God This statement emphasizes that Yahweh is not to be confused with any other god, and that what follows is to be received as his word alone.
20:3 no other gods before me Forbids any personal loyalty or relationship with any deity besides Yahweh—the core idea behind the modern term "monotheism."
20:4 an image Prohibits the worship of any image created, not the creation of the image. Together, the first two commands describe the sin of idolatry. The core idea behind idolatry was to provide a tangible representative of the deity on earth and to maintain the favor of that deity through caring for its idol. An important element of Israelite religion was that Yahweh was not to be depicted the way other deities were, by means of an idol. See the infographic "Ancient Hebrew Conception of the Universe" on p. 5.
20:5 third and fourth generation Illustrates the concept of corporate responsibility: In addition to the individual being accountable, the community is responsible for the behavior and sin of its members. This passage does not suggest that future innocents will be held morally accountable for the sins of ancestors but refers to the mutual consequences of sins. This concept and its relation to divine grace is illustrated in Ex 34:6–7, where God describes himself as quick to forgive, yet visiting iniquity on the third and fourth generations; i.e., God's forgiveness does not erase consequences.
20:6 love The Hebrew term used here, chesed, is variously translated as "steadfast love," "grace" or "lovingkindness." It denotes loving favor, and is tied to the covenants. The translation "loyal love" may capture the meaning best.
20:7 You shall not misuse the name of the LORD your God Prohibits hypocritical, insincere or frivolous use of God's name.
20:8–11 The Sabbath is not actually instituted in Ex 20:8–11 but was established at creation (see Ge 2:2–3). Further, earlier passages of Exodus contain references to the Sabbath that allude to creation (see Ex 16:23–30; compare 31:13–17). The Sabbath is viewed as a cosmic principle, commemorating Yahweh's rest on the seventh day after his creation of the world in six days (Ge 2:2). The command to stop work on the Sabbath means all of their work for the week is also to be performed in six days rather than seven. Those who observe the Sabbath are not just responsible for resting on the seventh day, but for a diligent work ethic the remaining six days. In this way, the Sabbath is remembered continuously. Everyone was to rest from work on the Sabbath. The Sabbath rest was designed for all levels of society, including servants of both genders, as well as animals. The Sabbath is not a day to be served by others, but of rest and community.
20:8 Sabbath The Hebrew word used here, shabbath, relates to the Hebrew verb shavath (which may be rendered "to rest," or "to cease"). **keeping it holy** The holiness of the Sabbath depends on the people remembering and observing it.
20:12 Honor your father and your mother This acts as a hinge between the two categories of the laws (see note on Ex 20:1–21) since it has elements of both divine and interpersonal relationship. The dual focus demonstrates that faith to God was of central importance for the family.
20:13 murder The Hebrew verb used here, tirtsach, describes the unlawful taking of innocent life.
20:14 adultery The OT regards adultery as sexual intercourse involving a married woman, a man who is not her husband, and mutual consent. The OT definition of adultery reflects the ancient Near Eastern view that wives and daughters were the property of their husbands or fathers.
20:15 steal The Hebrew verb used here, ganav, is ambiguous—the object of the theft is not definable. Just as in modern law, punishments for theft in OT laws have varying degrees of severity.

¹⁶ "You shall not give false testimony against your neighbor.

¹⁷ "You shall not covet your neighbor's house. You shall not covet your neighbor's wife, or his male or female servant, his ox or donkey, or anything that belongs to your neighbor."

¹⁸When the people saw the thunder and lightning and heard the trumpet and saw the mountain in smoke, they trembled with fear. They stayed at a distance ¹⁹and said to Moses, "Speak to us yourself and we will listen. But do not have God speak to us or we will die."

²⁰Moses said to the people, "Do not be afraid. God has come to test you, so that the fear of God will be with you to keep you from sinning."

²¹The people remained at a distance, while Moses approached the thick darkness where God was.

20:16 You shall not give false testimony The wording points to a judicial proceeding intended to determine the truth or falsehood of a criminal accusation.

20:17 covet The Hebrew verb used here, *chamad*, does not condemn the general acquisition of possessions or the desire to collect things. It speaks to obsession or a desire so strong that it compels someone to violate another person's property.

20:18 thunder and lightning Storm imagery is commonly connected with divine appearances in the OT and ancient Near Eastern literature (compare Eze 1:4–14).

Yahweh's presence is accompanied with storm-god imagery similar to how the Canaanite storm-god Baal might be described.

20:20 fear of God will be with you Moses explains that the thunderous scene has a practical function: to move the people to reverence that inspires obedience. Like the storms of the eastern Mediterranean, Yahweh has the power to destroy, but also to give life. By following or not following the law, Israel chooses which side of this power it will experience.

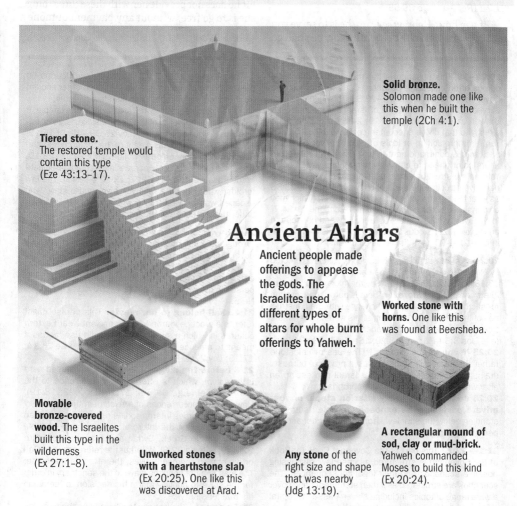

Ancient Altars

Ancient people made offerings to appease the gods. The Israelites used different types of altars for whole burnt offerings to Yahweh.

Solid bronze. Solomon made one like this when he built the temple (2Ch 4:1).

Tiered stone. The restored temple would contain this type (Eze 43:13–17).

Worked stone with horns. One like this was found at Beersheba.

Movable bronze-covered wood. The Israelites built this type in the wilderness (Ex 27:1-8).

Unworked stones with a hearthstone slab (Ex 20:25). One like this was discovered at Arad.

Any stone of the right size and shape that was nearby (Jdg 13:19).

A rectangular mound of sod, clay or mud-brick. Yahweh commanded Moses to build this kind (Ex 20:24).

Idols and Altars

²²Then the LORD said to Moses, "Tell the Israelites this: 'You have seen for yourselves that I have spoken to you from heaven: ²³Do not make any gods to be alongside me; do not make for yourselves gods of silver or gods of gold.

²⁴"'Make an altar of earth for me and sacrifice on it your burnt offerings and fellowship offerings, your sheep and goats and your cattle. Wherever I cause my name to be honored, I will come to you and bless you. ²⁵If you make an altar of stones for me, do not build it with dressed stones, for you will defile it if you use a tool on it. ²⁶And do not go up to my altar on steps, or your private parts may be exposed.'

21 "These are the laws you are to set before them:

Hebrew Servants

21:2-6pp — Dt 15:12-18
21:2-11Ref — Lev 25:39-55

²"If you buy a Hebrew servant, he is to serve you for six years. But in the seventh year, he shall go free, without paying anything. ³If he comes alone, he is to go free alone; but if he has a wife when he comes, she is to go with him. ⁴If his master gives him a wife and she bears him sons or daughters, the woman and her children shall belong to her master, and only the man shall go free.

⁵"But if the servant declares, 'I love my master and my wife and children and do not want to go free,' ⁶then his master must take him before the judges.ᵃ He shall take him to the door or the doorpost and pierce his ear with an awl. Then he will be his servant for life.

⁷"If a man sells his daughter as a servant, she is not to go free as male servants do. ⁸If she does not please the master who has selected her for himself,ᵇ he must let her be redeemed. He has no right to sell her to foreigners, because he has broken faith with her. ⁹If he selects her for his son, he must grant her the rights of a daughter. ¹⁰If he marries another woman, he must not deprive the first one of her food, clothing and marital rights. ¹¹If he does not provide her with these three things, she is to go free, without any payment of money.

ᵃ 6 Or *before God*   ᵇ 8 Or *master so that he does not choose her*

20:22–26 This passage is the transition to the legal corpus often called the Covenant Code (or Book of the Covenant), found in Ex 20:22–23:33. This legal material is bracketed by the narrative of Israel's encounter with Yahweh at Mount Sinai (chs. 19; 24). Verse 22 alludes directly to that divine encounter (compare 19:3–6), and Yahweh's prohibition of idols of gold or silver connects back to the commandment in v. 4. The laws related to altars point ahead to ch. 24, when Moses writes down Yahweh's instructions and builds an altar (24:3–4). The narrative structure presents the laws of 20:22—23:33 as what the Hebrew text calls *sepher habberith* (which may be translated "Book of the Covenant" mentioned in 24:7. In this way, vv. 22–26 act as a literary and conceptual bridge to ch. 21. Exodus 21:1 formally marks the material in chs. 21—23 as a distinct legal corpus.

20:24 altar of earth Describes the kind of altars erected by Noah (Ge 8:20) and the patriarchs (e.g., Ge 12:7,8; 13:18; 22:9; 26:25; 35:1–7). See the infographic "Ancient Altars" on p. 127. **Wherever** There is not yet one location for sacrifice, although that will change with the construction of the tabernacle. However, altars were built after the tabernacle and used in a manner acceptable to Yahweh (e.g., Jos 8:30–31; Jdg 13:20; 1Sa 7:17; 2Sa 24:25).

20:25 if you use a tool on it The use of fieldstone rather than quarried stone serves a practical purpose: drainage. This also ensures that Israel can set up an altar wherever and whenever is appropriate.

20:26 do not go up to my altar on steps, or your private parts may be exposed Prevented someone standing below the altar level from seeing under another person's garments.

21:1—22:17 This part of the Covenant Code (or Book of the Covenant) is structured as case law, discussing possible scenarios and their legal consequences. The scenarios are structured as if-then statements and cover a wide range of topics including slavery, assault, capital crimes and offenses related to property.

The passage in Ex 21:2–11 gives instructions on the treatment of Hebrew slaves. Although other ancient Near Eastern legal codes discuss slavery, Israelite law shows a unique sensitivity toward slaves; for example, it recognizes the humanity of the Hebrew slave. Israelite law refers to a slave as a brother (Lev 25:39–42; Dt 15:12; Jer 34:9,14,17) who has a right to the Sabbath rest and freedom from labor on other holidays (Ex 20:10; 23:12; Dt 5:14; 16:11–12,14). Hebrew slaves could participate in the Passover (Ge 17:13,27; Ex 12:44–45). The law forbids extradition of a fugitive slave, and a slave who escaped was allowed to live where he or she pleased under the protection of the law (Dt 23:15–16).

21:2 buy Hebrews could find themselves in slavery through a variety of circumstances, including extreme poverty or debt. People suffering from terrible poverty could sell themselves into slavery, but it was apparently more common that such a situation fell to a person in overwhelming debt (e.g., 2Ki 4:1; Am 2:6–7; Ne 5:4–5).

21:4 shall belong to her master This phrase might refer to a practice known in other ancient Near Eastern cultures in which a slave's master could use him as a means to produce "house born" slaves (see Ge 14:14; 17:13; Lev 22:11).

21:6 before the judges The Hebrew word used here is *ha'elohim*, which is often used in reference to the God of Israel (e.g., Ge 6:9; 17:18; Ex 2:23; 18:19). However, the occurrences of *ha'elohim* in this legal section are sometimes interpreted as references to human judges—following the interpretations of ancient Bible translations in Greek, Syriac and Aramaic (compare 22:8–9; note on 22:8). Whether the reference is to God or his human representatives, the effect is the same: The master must bring the slave to the sanctuary in order for the slave to publicly affirm his decision to remain in his master's service.

21:7 a servant The Hebrew text here uses the feminine

Personal Injuries

¹²"Anyone who strikes a person with a fatal blow is to be put to death. ¹³However, if it is not done intentionally, but God lets it happen, they are to flee to a place I will designate. ¹⁴But if anyone schemes and kills someone deliberately, that person is to be taken from my altar and put to death.

¹⁵"Anyone who attacks[a] their father or mother is to be put to death.

¹⁶"Anyone who kidnaps someone is to be put to death, whether the victim has been sold or is still in the kidnapper's possession.

¹⁷"Anyone who curses their father or mother is to be put to death.

¹⁸"If people quarrel and one person hits another with a stone or with their fist[b] and the victim does not die but is confined to bed, ¹⁹the one who struck the blow will not be held liable if the other can get up and walk around outside with a staff; however, the guilty party must pay the injured person for any loss of time and see that the victim is completely healed.

²⁰"Anyone who beats their male or female slave with a rod must be punished if the slave dies as a direct result, ²¹but they are not to be punished if the slave recovers after a day or two, since the slave is their property.

²²"If people are fighting and hit a pregnant woman and she gives birth prematurely[c] but there is no serious injury, the offender must be fined whatever the woman's husband demands and the court allows. ²³But if there is serious injury, you are to take life for life, ²⁴eye for eye, tooth for tooth, hand for hand, foot for foot, ²⁵burn for burn, wound for wound, bruise for bruise.

²⁶"An owner who hits a male or female slave in the eye and destroys it must let the slave go free to compensate for the eye. ²⁷And an owner who knocks out the tooth of a male or female slave must let the slave go free to compensate for the tooth.

²⁸"If a bull gores a man or woman to death, the bull is to be stoned to death, and its meat must not be eaten. But the owner of the bull will not be held responsible. ²⁹If, however, the bull has had the habit of goring and the owner has been warned but has not kept it penned up and it kills a man or woman, the bull is to be stoned and its owner also is to be put to death. ³⁰However, if payment is demanded, the owner may redeem his life by the payment of whatever is demanded. ³¹This law also applies if the bull gores a son or daughter. ³²If the bull gores a male or female slave, the owner must pay thirty shekels[d] of silver to the master of the slave, and the bull is to be stoned to death.

³³"If anyone uncovers a pit or digs one and fails to cover it and an ox or a donkey falls into it, ³⁴the

---

a 15 Or *kills*   *b 18* Or *with a tool*   *c 22* Or *she has a miscarriage*   *d 32* That is, about 12 ounces or about 345 grams

---

noun *amah* (which may be rendered "maid") and marks a transition to a different category of slave. In this situation, a man facing devastating debt or poverty could sell his daughter in a transaction that presupposed her marriage to the purchaser.

21:9 for his son, he must grant her the rights of a daughter The girl would receive all the legal protections of a blood daughter—including protection from sexual violation within the household.

21:12 Anyone who strikes a person with a fatal blow Describes premeditated murder (see v. 14; 20:13; compare Lev 24:17,21). **to be put to death** This illustrates the principle of *lex talionis*, the idea that punishment must be meted out in exact equivalence to the crime (e.g., eye for an eye in Ex 21:24).

21:13 they are to flee Foreshadows the establishment of Levitical cities of refuge (see Nu 35; Dt 19). In cases of accidental manslaughter, someone could find refuge in these cities from the victim's family members seeking blood vengeance.

21:15 Anyone who attacks their father or mother The Hebrew verb used here likely implies a severe injury that warrants the death penalty.

21:17 Anyone who curses their father or mother Refers to humiliating someone or treating a person with contempt, a more serious offense than the mere utterance of a word in anger. It is essentially the opposite of the command to honor parents from Ex 20:12.

21:22–25 This passage addresses a potential scenario of injury to a bystander when others are fighting. In the scenario, the injured bystander is a pregnant woman who was hit when two men were fighting. The blow caused the woman to give birth prematurely. The wording of the case leaves a great deal of ambiguity over whether the penalties for causing injury relate to the health of the woman, the survival of the infant, or both.

21:26 compensate for the eye This example and the following one (v. 27) are not strictly cases of *lex talionis* (see note on v. 12). Otherwise, the penalty would be the owner's loss of an eye or tooth rather than release from slavery as compensation for the loss. These verses also reveal that the law for bodily injury was different for slaves than for free citizens; the slave goes free but is not expressly granted the right of retaliation.

21:28–32 This passage presents the rules governing an ox who gores a human. The rules concerning an ox who gores another ox are listed in vv. 35–36. In the case of an ox goring a human, the ox is killed (v. 28); in the case if it goring another ox, it is kept alive and the dead body (presumably the meat) is either shared or traded for the surviving ox (vv. 35–36). The cases are treated separately because the first relates to the bodily injury of a human being while the second relates to property damage.

21:32 thirty shekels of silver A price is set in addition to the death penalty for the ox. The fact that the ox is killed shows that the slave had the same value as a free person. The extra money was to compensate for the loss of the slave's labor, which might have been intended to pay off a debt (compare v. 2).

21:33—22:15 This section is concerned with restitution and property laws. The laws of 21:33–36 focus on proportional compensation for property loss, in this case,

one who opened the pit must pay the owner for the loss and take the dead animal in exchange.

35"If anyone's bull injures someone else's bull and it dies, the two parties are to sell the live one and divide both the money and the dead animal equally. 36However, if it was known that the bull had the habit of goring, yet the owner did not keep it penned up, the owner must pay, animal for animal, and take the dead animal in exchange.

Protection of Property

22ª "Whoever steals an ox or a sheep and slaughters it or sells it must pay back five head of cattle for the ox and four sheep for the sheep.

2"If a thief is caught breaking in at night and is struck a fatal blow, the defender is not guilty of bloodshed; 3but if it happens after sunrise, the defender is guilty of bloodshed.

"Anyone who steals must certainly make restitution, but if they have nothing, they must be sold to pay for their theft. 4If the stolen animal is found alive in their possession — whether ox or donkey or sheep — they must pay back double.

5"If anyone grazes their livestock in a field or vineyard and lets them stray and they graze in someone else's field, the offender must make restitution from the best of their own field or vineyard.

6"If a fire breaks out and spreads into thornbushes so that it burns shocks of grain or standing grain or the whole field, the one who started the fire must make restitution.

7"If anyone gives a neighbor silver or goods for safekeeping and they are stolen from the neighbor's house, the thief, if caught, must pay back double. 8But if the thief is not found, the owner of the house must appear before the judges, and they must^b determine whether the owner of the house has laid hands on the other person's property. 9In all cases of illegal possession of an ox, a donkey, a sheep, a garment, or any other lost property about which somebody says, 'This is mine,' both parties are to bring their cases before the judges.^c The one whom the judges declare^d guilty must pay back double to the other.

10"If anyone gives a donkey, an ox, a sheep or any other animal to their neighbor for safekeeping and it dies or is injured or is taken away while no one is looking, 11the issue between them will be settled by the taking of an oath before the LORD that the neighbor did not lay hands on the other person's property. The owner is to accept this, and no restitution is required. 12But if the animal was stolen from the neighbor, restitution must be made to the owner. 13If it was torn to pieces by a wild animal, the neighbor shall bring in the remains as evidence and shall not be required to pay for the torn animal.

14"If anyone borrows an animal from their neighbor and it is injured or dies while the owner is not present, they must make restitution. 15But

---

^a In Hebrew texts 22:1 is numbered 21:37, and 22:2-31 is numbered 22:1-30.   ^b 8 Or before God, and he will   ^c 9 Or before God   ^d 9 Or whom God declares

---

the loss of an ox or donkey. Since work animals, such as donkeys and oxen, were the means of livelihood and agricultural production for the majority of people, they are the most commonly mentioned possession in this passage. The laws of 22:1–4 address the loss of these animals by theft. Other regulations include protections for agricultural goods (22:5–6) and belongings lent for either safekeeping or use (22:7–15).

22:1–4 These verses address cases of property lost through theft, especially the theft of livestock. The fines required for theft were steep when the thief killed or sold the animal—five oxen to compensate for the theft of one—likely to serve as a deterrent against stealing property for profit. If the stolen animal was recovered alive, the penalty was paying double—presumably meaning the return of the stolen animal plus one more as a fine (compare 22:7,9).

22:3 guilty of bloodshed If the homeowner kills the thief in daylight, he can be held liable for the thief's life. Human life is valued more than property.
22:4 they must pay back double While this could mean the thief had to give two animals in restitution in addition to returning the stolen animal, the parallel in Ge 43:12 suggests the sense is two animals in total.
22:5–15 These laws address property loss due to neglect or unforeseen circumstances (such as theft of borrowed property). Damage to agricultural products required

repayment equivalent to what was lost (Ex 22:5–6). In some cases where the responsibility for property damage or loss was unclear, the parties were to bring their cases before God (or his human representatives) for a determination of guilt (vv. 8–9).

22:8 before the judges The Hebrew text here seems to suggest that in this breach of trust, both parties must submit to God's justice by appearing before him or his representatives (v. 9). Some translations understand the Hebrew word ha'elohim, used here, to refer to judges, but there is no evidence that elohim (literally rendered as "God" or "gods") itself ever means judges or even refers to human agents. At best, the meaning of judges can be inferred in the sense that they would function as earthly representatives of divine justice. See note on 21:6.
22:9 one whom the judges declare guilty In the Hebrew text, the subject of this phrase is elohim (see v. 8 and note). The noun elohim is grammatically plural and the verb used here is also plural. However, the plural is used elsewhere in passages where the subject is clearly the God of Israel (e.g., Ge 20:13; 31:53; 35:7; 2Sa 7:23; Ps 58:11). The idea of God condemning the guilty party recalls other contexts where God's will was determined through casting lots (1Sa 10:16–26; 14:42; Jos 7:14). Since the scenario here is very similar to the one that follows in Ex 22:10–11, God's will may have been determined by an oath taken in the name of Yahweh.

if the owner is with the animal, the borrower will not have to pay. If the animal was hired, the money paid for the hire covers the loss.

Social Responsibility

[16]"If a man seduces a virgin who is not pledged to be married and sleeps with her, he must pay the bride-price, and she shall be his wife. [17]If her father absolutely refuses to give her to him, he must still pay the bride-price for virgins.

[18]"Do not allow a sorceress to live.

[19]"Anyone who has sexual relations with an animal is to be put to death.

[20]"Whoever sacrifices to any god other than the LORD must be destroyed.[a]

[21]"Do not mistreat or oppress a foreigner, for you were foreigners in Egypt.

[22]"Do not take advantage of the widow or the fatherless. [23]If you do and they cry out to me, I will certainly hear their cry. [24]My anger will be aroused, and I will kill you with the sword; your wives will become widows and your children fatherless.

[25]"If you lend money to one of my people among you who is needy, do not treat it like a business deal; charge no interest. [26]If you take your neighbor's cloak as a pledge, return it by sunset, [27]because that cloak is the only covering your neighbor has. What else can they sleep in? When they cry out to me, I will hear, for I am compassionate.

[28]"Do not blaspheme God[b] or curse the ruler of your people.

[29]"Do not hold back offerings from your granaries or your vats.[c]

"You must give me the firstborn of your sons. [30]Do the same with your cattle and your sheep. Let them stay with their mothers for seven days, but give them to me on the eighth day.

[31]"You are to be my holy people. So do not eat the meat of an animal torn by wild beasts; throw it to the dogs.

[a] 20 The Hebrew term refers to the irrevocable giving over of things or persons to the LORD, often by totally destroying them.   [b] 28 Or *Do not revile the judges*   [c] 29 The meaning of the Hebrew for this phrase is uncertain.

22:16–17 This passage designates the penalty for a man who has seduced a virgin who has not been promised in marriage already. The verses follow the case law format that predominates in 21:2–22:15, and they focus on the issue of compensation for loss—the common theme of the laws in 21:28–22:15. Many modern English translations mark a change in topic between 22:15 and 22:16, but the exchange of economic value was a key aspect of marriage in the ancient Near East, so this change in topic is not necessary. The loss of the girl's sexual purity was viewed in the ancient Near East as significantly devaluing her worth as a potential bride. Thus, according to these laws, the man who seduced her must pay her father the bride-price, even if her father refused to give his daughter in marriage. If the girl had been promised in marriage to another, the penalty for the one who violated her was death, regardless of whether the encounter was consensual (Dt 22:23–27).

22:16 he must pay the bride-price Refers to a sum of money paid to the bride's father to cover the loss since he is unable to offer her to other suitors.

22:18 — 23:9 This section of Exodus includes an eclectic assortment of regulations covering forbidden religious practices (Ex 22:18,20), sexual depravity (v. 19), social justice (vv. 21–28), dedication of the firstborn (vv. 29–30), and honest and just treatment of all people (23:1–9). Although it is not clear what binds these particular laws together, they all do, in their own way, work to protect citizens from danger, particularly exploitation.

22:20 any god other than This highlights the polytheistic nature of the historical and religious context out of which Israel emerged. **must be destroyed** The Hebrew verb used here, *charam*, refers to the act of setting someone or something apart as the sacred and exclusive property of a deity. This act frequently entails the destruction of the person or thing devoted to the deity. Destruction ensured the exclusive dedication to Yahweh. See note on Jos 6:17.

22:21–27 These verses describe laws protecting certain social groups—such as foreign-born residents, widows, orphans and the poor—from exploitation. These are the most vulnerable groups in society. The reiteration of how vulnerable social groups should be treated suggests that exploitation was common in the ancient Near East. The laws regarding social justice go beyond avoiding oppression; they demand others to love vulnerable people as God loves them (Lev 19:33–34; Dt 10:18–19) by providing for their basic needs (e.g., Ex 23:12; Lev 19:9–10; Nu 35:15; Dt 26:12–13; compare Pr 22:22–23; 23:10–11).

The OT laws protecting these social groups are aimed at individuals who are able to help, and the punishment that would come for abuse. Citizens should act with compassion as their God acted toward them when redeeming them from bondage (Ex 22:21).

22:24 kill you with the sword Imagery of God killing with the sword usually refers to his use of an invading army (e.g., Jer 5:14–19; 9:16), though sometimes the punishment originates within the community itself (e.g., Ex 32:27–29).

22:25 do not treat it like a business deal This prohibition does not indicate that lending is forbidden; rather it likely forbids oppressive practices like harassment or intimidation associated with attempts to collect the debt (2Ki 4:1). The following verses provide an example of how lending should be done compassionately (Ex 22:26–27). **charge no interest** The law prohibits charging interest to a fellow Israelite who is poor (compare Lev 25:35–38; Dt 23:20–21; 24:10–13). This is gracious in comparison with other ancient Near Eastern law codes in which interest on agricultural goods begins at an average of 25%.

22:28 Both clauses in this verse address treating with contempt someone who should be respected or revered.

22:28 Do not blaspheme God See note on Lev 24:11.

22:29 firstborn The consecration of the firstborn is first commanded just after the tenth plague against Egypt, the death of all their firstborn including livestock (Ex 12:29–32; 13:2,11–16).

Laws of Justice and Mercy

23 "Do not spread false reports. Do not help a guilty person by being a malicious witness.
²"Do not follow the crowd in doing wrong. When you give testimony in a lawsuit, do not pervert justice by siding with the crowd, ³and do not show favoritism to a poor person in a lawsuit.

⁴"If you come across your enemy's ox or donkey wandering off, be sure to return it. ⁵If you see the donkey of someone who hates you fallen down under its load, do not leave it there; be sure you help them with it.

⁶"Do not deny justice to your poor people in their lawsuits. ⁷Have nothing to do with a false charge and do not put an innocent or honest person to death, for I will not acquit the guilty.

⁸"Do not accept a bribe, for a bribe blinds those who see and twists the words of the innocent.

⁹"Do not oppress a foreigner; you yourselves know how it feels to be foreigners, because you were foreigners in Egypt.

Sabbath Laws

¹⁰"For six years you are to sow your fields and harvest the crops, ¹¹but during the seventh year let the land lie unplowed and unused. Then the poor among your people may get food from it, and the wild animals may eat what is left. Do the same with your vineyard and your olive grove.

¹²"Six days do your work, but on the seventh day do not work, so that your ox and your donkey may rest, and so that the slave born in your household and the foreigner living among you may be refreshed.

¹³"Be careful to do everything I have said to you. Do not invoke the names of other gods; do not let them be heard on your lips.

The Three Annual Festivals

¹⁴"Three times a year you are to celebrate a festival to me.

¹⁵"Celebrate the Festival of Unleavened Bread; for seven days eat bread made without yeast, as I commanded you. Do this at the appointed time in the month of Aviv, for in that month you came out of Egypt.

"No one is to appear before me empty-handed.

¹⁶"Celebrate the Festival of Harvest with the firstfruits of the crops you sow in your field.

"Celebrate the Festival of Ingathering at the end of the year, when you gather in your crops from the field.

¹⁷"Three times a year all the men are to appear before the Sovereign LORD.

¹⁸"Do not offer the blood of a sacrifice to me along with anything containing yeast.

"The fat of my festival offerings must not be kept until morning.

23:1–9 In line with previous laws that prohibit exploitative behavior, these rules promote honesty, justice and fairness, particularly in situations where one might be tempted to promote self-interest over justice.

23:1 malicious witness The integrity of ancient legal proceedings depended entirely on the validity of witness testimony. Since a case required at least two witnesses (Dt 19:15), this statement addresses a scenario where a person with ill intent enlists another to aid them in deceiving the court. See note on Ex 20:16.

23:4 your enemy's ox The people of Israel are to act with integrity toward one another, regardless of personal difference or social standing. Even an enemy's belongings are to be treated fairly.

23:8 Do not accept a bribe The OT often portrays bribery as being evil—especially in judicial contexts, which suggests that it might have been a widespread problem (e.g., 1Sa 8:3; Isa 1:23; 33:15; Eze 22:12; Mic 7:3; compare Dt 10:17).

23:9 a foreigner The Hebrew word used here, *ger* (which may be rendered as "resident alien" or "sojourner"), denotes a legal status beyond just being a foreigner. The term *ger* applies to people living somewhere other than the society or community where they were born. They are afforded legal protection since they fall outside the kinship-based social structures of the land where they settled. In some cases, this status is akin to being refugees driven from their homelands due to war or famine (Ru 1:1; 2Sa 4:3). In other cases, people may have left their home country by choice (Ge 21:23,34). See Ex 22:21–27 and note.

23:10–19 The laws in this section relate to sacred time—times that are set apart for sacred purposes. The first two verses prohibit Israelites from working the land during the seventh year or Sabbatical Year (vv. 10–11; compare Lev 25:1–7). Exodus 23:12 then reiterates the importance of observing the Sabbath day (compare 20:8–11; 34:21; 35:2). Verses 14–17 present the agricultural festivals in Israel's sacred calendar (compare 34:18–24). These festivals—which also appear in Dt 16:1–17—are referenced by the Hebrew word *chag*, indicating a pilgrimage. A more complete sacred calendar is found in Lev 23. See the table "Israelite Festivals" on p. 200.

23:13 other gods The issue here is not whether other gods exist, but which god has Israel's loyalty. Promoting the worship of one particular god, without denying the existence of others, is called monolatry. Israel was to be loyal to Yahweh alone, the Creator of all.

23:15 Festival of Unleavened Bread This feast is an annual commemoration of the exodus out of Egypt. See note on Ex 13:1–16.

23:16 Festival of Harvest Also known as the Festival of Weeks (called *shavu'oth* in Hebrew). See note on Lev 23:15–22. **Festival of Ingathering** Refers to the final harvest of crops in autumn. The feast is called ingathering (*asiph* in Hebrew) here and in Ex 34:22, but Dt 16:13 subtly equates gathering (*asaph*) with the Festival of Tabernacles (also called Booths). See note on Lev 23:33–44.

23:17 all the men Since travel in the ancient Near East was difficult and often dangerous, women and children were not required to make these pilgrimages.

[19]"Bring the best of the firstfruits of your soil to the house of the LORD your God.

"Do not cook a young goat in its mother's milk.

God's Angel to Prepare the Way

[20]"See, I am sending an angel ahead of you to guard you along the way and to bring you to the place I have prepared. [21]Pay attention to him and listen to what he says. Do not rebel against him; he will not forgive your rebellion, since my Name is in him. [22]If you listen carefully to what he says and do all that I say, I will be an enemy to your enemies and will oppose those who oppose you. [23]My angel will go ahead of you and bring you into the land of the Amorites, Hittites, Perizzites, Canaanites, Hivites and Jebusites, and I will wipe them out. [24]Do not bow down before their gods or worship them or follow their practices. You must demolish them and break their sacred stones to pieces. [25]Worship the LORD your God, and his blessing will be on your food and water. I will take away sickness from among you, [26]and none will miscarry or be barren in your land. I will give you a full life span.

[27]"I will send my terror ahead of you and throw into confusion every nation you encounter. I will make all your enemies turn their backs and run. [28]I will send the hornet ahead of you to drive the Hivites, Canaanites and Hittites out of your way.

[29]But I will not drive them out in a single year, because the land would become desolate and the wild animals too numerous for you. [30]Little by little I will drive them out before you, until you have increased enough to take possession of the land.

[31]"I will establish your borders from the Red Sea[a] to the Mediterranean Sea,[b] and from the desert to the Euphrates River. I will give into your hands the people who live in the land, and you will drive them out before you. [32]Do not make a covenant with them or with their gods. [33]Do not let them live in your land or they will cause you to sin against me, because the worship of their gods will certainly be a snare to you."

The Covenant Confirmed

24 Then the LORD said to Moses, "Come up to the LORD, you and Aaron, Nadab and Abihu, and seventy of the elders of Israel. You are to worship at a distance, [2]but Moses alone is to approach the LORD; the others must not come near. And the people may not come up with him."

[3]When Moses went and told the people all the LORD's words and laws, they responded with one voice, "Everything the LORD has said we will do." [4]Moses then wrote down everything the LORD had said.

---

[a] 31 Or *the Sea of Reeds* [b] 31 Hebrew *to the Sea of the Philistines*

23:19 best of the firstfruits Relates to the Festival of Harvest (see Ex 23:16) and the dedication of firstfruits to Yahweh (22:29; compare Lev 23:9–14). **Do not cook a young goat in its mother's milk** In Canaanite texts, cooking a goat (kid) in its mother's milk is part of a magic ritual, suggesting that this prohibition relates to pagan practices.

23:20–33 These verses bring an end to this legal section of Ex 21–23 by promising Israel protection and giving them instructions for how to conquer the promised land.

23:20 bring you to the place While here and in 33:2 the angel is specified as leading the Israelites into the promised land, elsewhere God says he himself will lead them (33:14; Dt 4:37). The figure of the Angel of Yahweh is often equated with Yahweh himself (see note on Ex 3:2).

23:23 The groups listed here were some of the native inhabitants of the land at the time of the exodus. See note on Ge 15:19–21.

23:24 break their sacred stones Since worship of other gods is forbidden, the Israelites must destroy the religious objects to other gods. See note on Ge 28:18.

23:26 none will miscarry or be barren Reflects God's promise to make Abraham's descendants like the stars of the sky and sand on the seashore (Ge 12:1–3; 15:1–6).

23:27 I will send my terror ahead of you That is, the Israelites' reputation as conquerors will precede them (compare Ex 15:16; Jos 2:9).

23:30 Little by little The Israelites will gain the promised land through a long, progressive series of campaigns and displacements (see Jos 1–13).

23:31 Red Sea The Hebrew term used here here, *yam suph*, refers in this context (unlike in Ex 13:18) to the

Gulf of Aqaba, the easternmost prong of the Red Sea (compare 1Ki 9:26; see note on Ex 13:18).

23:32 Do not make a covenant Israel was forbidden from forming such agreements, perhaps because they were viewed as serving other gods (Ex 23:33)—a violation of the first commandment (20:3).

24:1–18 Chapter 24 acts as a bridge between the giving of the covenant (chs. 20–23) and the instructions for the tabernacle (chs. 25–31). The passage depicts Israel's acceptance of the terms of the covenant as explained by Moses (v. 3). The scene in vv. 3–8 is the formal, legally binding confirmation of the covenant as a contract between Yahweh and Israel (compare 19:8). This chapter may be divided into four scenes: instructions to Moses (vv. 1–2), sealing of the covenant via sacrifice (vv. 3–8), a divine meal (vv. 9–11) and Moses' second ascent to Mount Sinai (vv. 12–18).

24:1 Nadab and Abihu The older two sons of Aaron who were later killed for offering incense improperly. See note on Lev 10:1. **seventy** Seventy is one of several numbers that is attributed a particular significance in the OT. These 70 elders represent the fullness of what is referred to in the Hebrew text as Yahweh's portion—his people (compare Dt 32:9)—suggesting that Israel was intended to bring the nations and Hebrew people back under Yahweh's dominion as a kingdom of priests (Ex 19:6).

24:2 Moses alone Moses' relationship with Yahweh is marked by an access to the divine presence that is unequalled in all Israel's history.

24:3 we will The people collectively and voluntarily enter into the Sinai covenant with Yahweh (compare 19:8).

24:4 LORD had said Likely refers to the instructions in

He got up early the next morning and built an altar at the foot of the mountain and set up twelve stone pillars representing the twelve tribes of Israel. [5]Then he sent young Israelite men, and they offered burnt offerings and sacrificed young bulls as fellowship offerings to the LORD. [6]Moses took half of the blood and put it in bowls, and the other half he splashed against the altar. [7]Then he took the Book of the Covenant and read it to the people. They responded, "We will do everything the LORD has said; we will obey."

[8]Moses then took the blood, sprinkled it on the people and said, "This is the blood of the covenant that the LORD has made with you in accordance with all these words."

[9]Moses and Aaron, Nadab and Abihu, and the seventy elders of Israel went up [10]and saw the God of Israel. Under his feet was something like a pavement made of lapis lazuli, as bright blue as the sky. [11]But God did not raise his hand against these leaders of the Israelites; they saw God, and they ate and drank.

[12]The LORD said to Moses, "Come up to me on the mountain and stay here, and I will give you the tablets of stone with the law and commandments I have written for their instruction."

[13]Then Moses set out with Joshua his aide, and Moses went up on the mountain of God. [14]He said to the elders, "Wait here for us until we come back to you. Aaron and Hur are with you, and anyone involved in a dispute can go to them."

[15]When Moses went up on the mountain, the cloud covered it, [16]and the glory of the LORD settled on Mount Sinai. For six days the cloud covered the mountain, and on the seventh day the LORD called to Moses from within the cloud. [17]To the Israelites the glory of the LORD looked like a consuming fire on top of the mountain. [18]Then Moses entered the cloud as he went on up the mountain. And he stayed on the mountain forty days and forty nights.

Offerings for the Tabernacle

25:1-7pp — Ex 35:4-9

25 The LORD said to Moses, [2]"Tell the Israelites to bring me an offering. You are to receive the offering for me from everyone whose heart prompts them to give. [3]These are the offerings you are to receive from them: gold, silver and bronze; [4]blue, purple and scarlet yarn and fine linen; goat hair; [5]ram skins dyed red and another type of durable leather[a]; acacia wood; [6]olive oil for the light; spices for the anointing oil and for the fragrant incense; [7]and onyx stones and other gems to be mounted on the ephod and breastpiece.

[8]"Then have them make a sanctuary for me, and

[a] 5 Possibly the hides of large aquatic mammals

---

chs. 20–23. See the infographic "Ancient Altars" on p. 127; see the table "Altars in the Old Testament" on p. 249. **twelve stone pillars** In the patriarchal stories, pillars were erected to commemorate divine encounters (Ge 28:18,22; 31:45; compare Ex 23:24 and note).

24:7 Book of the Covenant Refers to what Moses wrote in v. 4. This phrase is generally considered the Biblical name for the law code in chs. 20–23 (also called the Covenant Code; see note on 20:22–26).

24:8 sprinkled it on the people The blood sprinkled on the altar and upon the people indicated that Yahweh and the people of Israel were bound together in the covenant.

24:10 Under his feet Yahweh is described anthropomorphically—that is, with human features. On the nature of Moses' earthly encounters with Yahweh, see note on 33:20. **a pavement made of lapis lazuli** Similar descriptions of Yahweh's throne room are also found in Eze 1 and Rev 4.

24:12 I have written God writes the commandments on the tablets (compare Ex 31:18; 32:16). Moses also wrote down the commandments of Yahweh (v. 4). Moses will later break these divinely inscribed tablets upon seeing the golden calf (32:15–19) and will write the replacement tablets himself (34:1–4,28–29). These passages link the writing of the laws to both God and Moses.

24:13–15 This is one of the few insights Exodus provides about the leadership hierarchy of Israel during this period. Joshua is Moses' assistant, and in the absence of both of them, Moses' brother Aaron and Hur are in command. Hur is mentioned only twice: here and in the battle against the Amalekites (17:10).

24:16 glory of the LORD Refers to the visible presence of Yahweh. See note on 16:10. **settled on Mount Sinai** The glory of Yahweh appeared to the Israelites as a fiery cloud on the mountain.

24:18 forty days and forty nights The number 40 appears frequently in the OT and is symbolic as a period of separation for the sake of spiritual purification and growth (see 34:28; Dt 9:9–18; 10:10; compare Mt 4).

25:1–9 The next major section of Exodus (Ex 25–31) relays God's instructions to Moses for building the tabernacle, Israel's portable tent shrine, where the presence of God would dwell, beginning with Israel's time in the wilderness and ending with the reign of King Solomon. These instructions are carried out in chs. 35–39, and the tabernacle is assembled and consecrated in ch. 40. This passage in vv. 1–9 serves as the introduction to the instructions, starting with the call for the Israelites to voluntarily bring the materials for the project.

25:3 gold, silver and bronze The value of these metals (listed in descending order) reflects their sanctity: the higher the value, the greater the sanctity.

25:4 blue, purple and scarlet yarn These were among the most costly dyed yarns of the ancient Near East.

25:5 another type of durable leather The Hebrew term used here, *tachash*, refers to some sort of animal skins. The term is almost always used for the protective material covering the tabernacle furnishings in transit. In Eze 16:10, *tachash* is a material that sandals can be made from. Because of the word's similarity to the Arabic word for dolphin (*tukhas*), *tachash* is often understood to mean dolphin, but the evidence for this connection is weak. The Hebrew term may be related to the Akkadian word *tachshia*, which refers to an orange or yellow gemstone.

I will dwell among them. ⁹Make this tabernacle and all its furnishings exactly like the pattern I will show you.

The Ark

25:10-20pp — Ex 37:1-9

¹⁰"Have them make an ark[a] of acacia wood — two and a half cubits long, a cubit and a half wide, and a cubit and a half high.[b] ¹¹Overlay it with pure gold, both inside and out, and make a gold molding around it. ¹²Cast four gold rings for it and fasten them to its four feet, with two rings on one side and two rings on the other. ¹³Then make poles of acacia wood and overlay them with gold. ¹⁴Insert the poles into the rings on the sides of the ark to carry it. ¹⁵The poles are to remain in the rings of this ark; they are not to be removed. ¹⁶Then put in the ark the tablets of the covenant law, which I will give you.

¹⁷"Make an atonement cover of pure gold — two and a half cubits long and a cubit and a half wide. ¹⁸And make two cherubim out of hammered gold at the ends of the cover. ¹⁹Make one cherub on one end and the second cherub on the other; make the cherubim of one piece with the cover, at the two ends. ²⁰The cherubim are to have their wings spread upward, overshadowing the cover with them. The cherubim are to face each other, looking toward the cover. ²¹Place the cover on top of the ark and put in the ark the tablets of the covenant law that I will give you. ²²There, above the cover between the two cherubim that are over the ark of the covenant law, I will meet with you and give you all my commands for the Israelites.

The Table

25:23-29pp — Ex 37:10-16

²³"Make a table of acacia wood — two cubits long, a cubit wide and a cubit and a half high.[c] ²⁴Overlay it with pure gold and make a gold molding around it. ²⁵Also make around it a rim a handbreadth[d] wide and put a gold molding on the rim. ²⁶Make four gold rings for the table and fasten them to the four corners, where the four legs are. ²⁷The rings are to be close to the rim to hold the poles used in carrying the table. ²⁸Make the poles of acacia wood, overlay them with gold and carry the table with them. ²⁹And make its plates and dishes of pure gold, as well as its pitchers and bowls for the pouring out of offerings. ³⁰Put the bread of the Presence on this table to be before me at all times.

---

[a] *10* That is, a chest   [b] *10* That is, about 3 3/4 feet long and 2 1/4 feet wide and high or about 1.1 meters long and 68 centimeters wide and high; similarly in verse 17   [c] *23* That is, about 3 feet long, 1 1/2 feet wide and 2 1/4 feet high or about 90 centimeters long, 45 centimeters wide and 68 centimeters high   [d] *25* That is, about 3 inches or about 7.5 centimeters

---

This stone was used in Mesopotamia for dyeing and tanning the skins of sheep and goats. **acacia wood** A fragrant and waxy wood from the acacia plant.

25:7 ephod and breastpiece The ephod is the priestly robe and the breastpiece is a metal adornment with 12 precious stones, one representing each tribe of Israel.

25:8 sanctuary The Hebrew word used here, *miqdash*, comes from the verb *qadash* (which may be rendered "to be holy" or "make holy") and refers to an enclosed sacred space designated for the presence of Yahweh (compare Ex 33:15).

25:9 this tabernacle The Hebrew term *mishkan* (which may be rendered "dwelling") refers to the Israelites' portable sanctuary used during their journey to the promised land. See note on 26:1. **pattern** The tabernacle was to be an earthly replica of a divine archetype, a cosmic sanctuary where Yahweh dwelled.

25:10–22 The ark of the covenant, as described in vv. 10–22 and elsewhere, is comparable in design to the thrones associated with deities and, sometimes, royalty throughout the ancient Near East (e.g., 1Ki 10:18–20). The defining features are the seat atop the ark itself, and the cherubim that flank either side. The account of the ark's is construction in located in Ex 37:1–9.

25:10 ark The Hebrew word used here, *aron*, refers to a storage chest or box of varying size. The word is commonly used to refer specifically to the ark of the covenant, which symbolized Yahweh's presence among the Israelites. See the infographic "The Ark of the Covenant" on p. 412. **cubits** The measurement from the tip of the fingers to the elbow. A cubit is roughly 18 inches.

25:16 tablets of the covenant law The ark's primary function is to house these tablets.

25:17 atonement cover The lid of the ark, on which the blood of the sacrifice was sprinkled on the Day of Atonement (Lev 16). It is the most holy object mentioned in the OT, because this was the spot from which Yahweh spoke (Ex 25:22).

ATONEMENT COVER (MERCY SEAT)
The Hebrew noun for the lid of the ark, *kapporeth*—literally translated "covering"—is from the verb *kaphar*, meaning "to atone" or "to cover." Similarly *yom kippur* is the Day of Atonement—the one day of the year when the high priest enters the Holy of Holies (Most Holy Place) where the ark is located and sprinkles it with blood for the sins of the people. The *kapporeth* was, in effect, the throne of Yahweh on earth.

25:18 cherubim The spiritual beings called *cherubim* (a plural form in Hebrew) were typically depicted in the ancient Near East with a composite of human, bird and bovine features (compare Eze 1:5–10; 10:1–15).

25:23–30 The plan for the table for bread is similar to that of the ark of the covenant (Ex 25:10–22; 37:1–9) in that it is made of acacia wood, overlain with gold, and carried via four rings and two poles.

25:29 for the pouring out Libations were a common form of divine offering in the ancient Near East, usually consisting of the finest wine available.

25:30 bread of the Presence The table held 12 loaves of bread, symbolizing the 12 tribes of Israel (Lev 24:5–9).

The Lampstand

25:31-39pp — Ex 37:17-24

[31]"Make a lampstand of pure gold. Hammer out its base and shaft, and make its flowerlike cups, buds and blossoms of one piece with them. [32]Six branches are to extend from the sides of the lampstand — three on one side and three on the other. [33]Three cups shaped like almond flowers with buds and blossoms are to be on one branch, three on the next branch, and the same for all six branches extending from the lampstand. [34]And on the lampstand there are to be four cups shaped like almond flowers with buds

---

25:31–40 The golden lampstand (*menorah* in Hebrew) becomes the symbol of the divine presence in early Judaism, because of its association with light and goodness (e.g., Zec 4).

25:31 lampstand The Hebrew word used here, *menorah*, refers to a lampstand with seven branches that was stationed on the tabernacle's southern side (Ex 26:35; 40:24). According to Lev 24:1–4, the lamp was to be kept burning continually.

25:32 Six branches Since the tabernacle was to be the cosmic domain of Yahweh, the *menorah* (see note on 25:31) tree likely symbolized the tree of life from Eden. **25:33 shaped like almond flowers with buds and blossoms** The almond flower symbolized life and its renewal (e.g., Jer 1:11–12; compare Ecc 12:5). The Hebrew term for almond blossoms, *shuqedim*, is related to the verb *shaqad*, which may be rendered "to be watchful." Thus the almond flowers may symbolize Yahweh's watchfulness. In Zechariah's vision of a lampstand, its

---

Altar of burnt offering. Made of acacia wood and covered with bronze, the altar was light enough for the Levites to carry during the wilderness wanderings (Ex 27:1–8).

Bronze Basin. Cast of solid bronze, the basin was used for ceremonial washings (Ex 30:17–21).

Altar of Incense. Placed before the tabernacle curtain, this altar was used regularly to burn incense before Yahweh (Ex 30:1–10).

Table of Showbread. The bread of the Presence lay on it at all times (Ex 25:23–30).

Furnishings of the Tabernacle

The book of Exodus details the construction of the tabernacle and its furnishings. As Yahweh's sanctuary, the tabernacle served as God's dwelling place among the Israelites—the expression of the covenant between Yahweh and his people (Ex 25:8–9).

Golden Lampstand. A symbol of the tree of life, it held seven oil lamps (Ex 25:31–40).

PLACEMENT OF TABERNACLE FURNISHINGS:

Ark of the Covenant
Table of showbread
Bronze Basin
Altar of burnt offering
Court of the Tabernacle
Golden Lampstand
Altar of Incense

Ark of the Covenant. The holiest object of Israelite worship, the ark symbolized God's presence and contained the tablets of the Law (Ex 25:10–22).

and blossoms. [35]One bud shall be under the first pair of branches extending from the lampstand, a second bud under the second pair, and a third bud under the third pair — six branches in all. [36]The buds and branches shall all be of one piece with the lampstand, hammered out of pure gold. [37]"Then make its seven lamps and set them up on it so that they light the space in front of it. [38]Its wick trimmers and trays are to be of pure gold. [39]A talent[a] of pure gold is to be used for the lampstand and all these accessories. [40]See that you make them according to the pattern shown you on the mountain.

The Tabernacle

26:1-37pp — Ex 36:8-38

26 "Make the tabernacle with ten curtains of finely twisted linen and blue, purple and scarlet yarn, with cherubim woven into them by a skilled worker. [2]All the curtains are to be the same size — twenty-eight cubits long and four cubits wide.[b] [3]Join five of the curtains together, and do the same with the other five. [4]Make loops of blue material along the edge of the end curtain in one set, and do the same with the end curtain in the other set. [5]Make fifty loops on one curtain and fifty loops on the end curtain of the other set, with the loops opposite each other. [6]Then make fifty gold clasps and use them to fasten the curtains together so that the tabernacle is a unit.

[7]"Make curtains of goat hair for the tent over the tabernacle — eleven altogether. [8]All eleven curtains are to be the same size — thirty cubits long and four cubits wide.[c] [9]Join five of the curtains together into one set and the other six into another set. Fold the sixth curtain double at the front of the tent. [10]Make fifty loops along the edge of the end curtain in one set and also along the edge of the end curtain in the other set. [11]Then make fifty bronze clasps and put them in the loops to fasten the tent together as a unit. [12]As for the additional length of the tent curtains, the half curtain that is left over is to hang down at the rear of the tabernacle. [13]The tent curtains will be a cubit[d] longer on both sides; what is left will hang over the sides of the tabernacle so as to cover it. [14]Make for the tent a covering of ram skins dyed red, and over that a covering of the other durable leather.[e]

[15]"Make upright frames of acacia wood for the tabernacle. [16]Each frame is to be ten cubits long and a cubit and a half wide,[f] [17]with two projections set parallel to each other. Make all the frames of the tabernacle in this way. [18]Make twenty frames for the south side of the tabernacle [19]and make forty silver bases to go under them — two bases for each frame, one under each projection. [20]For the other side, the north side of the tabernacle, make twenty frames [21]and forty silver bases — two

---

[a] 39 That is, about 75 pounds or about 34 kilograms   [b] 2 That is, about 42 feet long and 6 feet wide or about 13 meters long and 1.8 meters wide   [c] 8 That is, about 45 feet long and 6 feet wide or about 13.5 meters long and 1.8 meters wide   [d] 13 That is, about 18 inches or about 45 centimeters   [e] 14 Possibly the hides of large aquatic mammals (see 25:5)   [f] 16 That is, about 15 feet long and 2 1/4 feet wide or about 4.5 meters long and 68 centimeters wide

---

seven lights represent the eyes of Yahweh (Zec 4:2,10). **buds** The Hebrew word used here, *kaphtor*, is an architectural term (compare Am 9:1; Zep 2:14), describing the top of a column.

25:34 lampstand See note on Ex 25:31.

25:37 seven lamps Since the *menorah* or lampstand has seven lights, it is used in Judaism to commemorate the Sabbath — the day of rest on the seventh day of the week — in line with the fourth commandment (20:8–11).

26:1–37 This passage provides instructions for building the tabernacle itself — Israel's approved house of worship until the temple was built under King Solomon. The tabernacle was dismantled and reassembled whenever the Israelites moved their camp. See the table "Tabernacle Materials and Equipment" on p. 141.

26:1 tabernacle The Hebrew term used here, *mishkan*, refers to the Israelites' portable sanctuary during their journey to the promised land (compare 25:8–9; 35:30 — 36:38). The rectangular structure was 150 feet long, 75 feet wide and 7.5 feet high (27:18). It was surrounded by curtains. Within the tabernacle was another smaller, completely enclosed structure divided into two unequal sections by a heavy veil: the Most Holy Place (also called the Holy of Holies) and the Holy Place. The veil blocked the view into the Holy of Holies, which housed the ark of the covenant (see 25:10–22). Before the veil stood the altar of incense (30:1–10), the seven-branched lamp-

stand (*menorah* in Hebrew; 25:31–40), and the table for the bread of the Presence (25:23–30). Outside the internal structure but still within the enclosure, there was a courtyard area. In this sacred space stood the altar for burnt offerings (30:28; 31:9; 38:1; 40:6–10) and the basin for washing (30:18). See the infographic "The Tabernacle" on p. 138; see the infographic "Furnishings of the Tabernacle" on p. 136.

26:3 Join five of the curtains together They were to be connected to one another at the edge by a series of stitches — a series of loops and clasps, in this case.

26:6 a unit All ten of these curtains were to be attached to one another to form one large curtain. While this would help keep each individual panel in place, it would make the tent very difficult to move due it is sheer size and weight.

26:7 goat hair This hair was collected and spun into a type of wool, which was then woven into these eleven curtains (35:26).

26:15 frames It is unclear how the frames of the tabernacle were held together.

26:17 with two projections This describes a protruding piece of wood that fits into a corresponding groove or slot, carved into whatever object the frame is designed to attach, in this case, another frame.

26:19 forty silver bases Probably both to hold the frames erect and to weigh them down. **silver** The second most precious metal used in the tabernacle construction. See note on 25:3.

under each frame. ²²Make six frames for the far end, that is, the west end of the tabernacle, ²³and make two frames for the corners at the far end. ²⁴At these two corners they must be double from the bottom all the way to the top and fitted into a single ring; both shall be like that. ²⁵So there will be eight frames and sixteen silver bases — two under each frame.

²⁶"Also make crossbars of acacia wood: five for the frames on one side of the tabernacle, ²⁷five for those on the other side, and five for the frames on the west, at the far end of the tabernacle. ²⁸The center crossbar is to extend from end to end at the middle of the frames. ²⁹Overlay the frames with gold and make gold rings to hold the crossbars. Also overlay the crossbars with gold.

³⁰"Set up the tabernacle according to the plan shown you on the mountain.

26:22 far end, that is, the west end of the tabernacle See note on 27:13.

26:30 according to the plan This plan or pattern was shown to Moses earlier (see 25:9).

The Tabernacle

This portable temple was built in the wilderness by the Israelites ca. 1450 BC after they were freed from Egyptian slavery. The tabernacle was the first temple dedicated to God and the first resting place of the ark of the covenant. It served as a place of worship and sacrifices during the Israelites' 40 years in the wilderness.

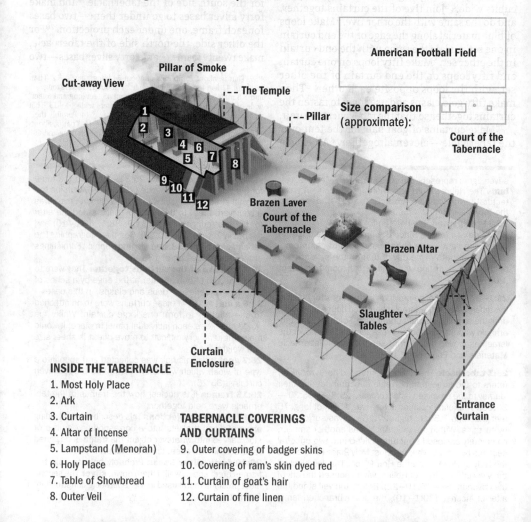

Pillar of Smoke
Cut-away View
The Temple
Pillar

American Football Field

Size comparison
(approximate):

Court of the
Tabernacle

Brazen Laver
Court of the
Tabernacle

Brazen Altar

Slaughter
Tables

Curtain
Enclosure

Entrance
Curtain

INSIDE THE TABERNACLE
1. Most Holy Place
2. Ark
3. Curtain
4. Altar of Incense
5. Lampstand (Menorah)
6. Holy Place
7. Table of Showbread
8. Outer Veil

TABERNACLE COVERINGS AND CURTAINS
9. Outer covering of badger skins
10. Covering of ram's skin dyed red
11. Curtain of goat's hair
12. Curtain of fine linen

31"Make a curtain of blue, purple and scarlet yarn and finely twisted linen, with cherubim woven into it by a skilled worker. 32Hang it with gold hooks on four posts of acacia wood overlaid with gold and standing on four silver bases. 33Hang the curtain from the clasps and place the ark of the covenant law behind the curtain. The curtain will separate the Holy Place from the Most Holy Place. 34Put the atonement cover on the ark of the covenant law in the Most Holy Place. 35Place the table outside the curtain on the north side of the tabernacle and put the lampstand opposite it on the south side.

36"For the entrance to the tent make a curtain of blue, purple and scarlet yarn and finely twisted linen — the work of an embroiderer. 37Make gold hooks for this curtain and five posts of acacia wood overlaid with gold. And cast five bronze bases for them.

The Altar of Burnt Offering

27:1-8pp — Ex 38:1-7

27 "Build an altar of acacia wood, three cubits[a] high; it is to be square, five cubits long and five cubits wide.[b] 2Make a horn at each of the four corners, so that the horns and the altar are of one piece, and overlay the altar with bronze. 3Make all its utensils of bronze — its pots to remove the ashes, and its shovels, sprinkling bowls, meat forks and firepans. 4Make a grating for it, a bronze network, and make a bronze ring at each of the four corners of the network. 5Put it under the ledge of the altar so that it is halfway up the altar. 6Make poles of acacia wood for the altar and overlay them with bronze. 7The poles are to be inserted into the rings so they will be on two sides of the altar when it is carried. 8Make the altar hollow, out of boards. It is to be made just as you were shown on the mountain.

The Courtyard

27:9-19pp — Ex 38:9-20

9"Make a courtyard for the tabernacle. The south side shall be a hundred cubits[c] long and is to have curtains of finely twisted linen, 10with twenty posts and twenty bronze bases and with silver hooks and bands on the posts. 11The north side shall also be a hundred cubits long and is to have curtains, with twenty posts and twenty bronze bases and with silver hooks and bands on the posts.

12"The west end of the courtyard shall be fifty cubits[d] wide and have curtains, with ten posts and ten bases. 13On the east end, toward the sunrise, the courtyard shall also be fifty cubits wide. 14Curtains fifteen cubits[e] long are to be on one

a 1 That is, about 4 1/2 feet or about 1.4 meters   b 1 That is, about 7 1/2 feet or about 2.3 meters long and wide   c 9 That is, about 150 feet or about 45 meters; also in verse 11   d 12 That is, about 75 feet or about 23 meters; also in verse 13   e 14 That is, about 23 feet or about 6.8 meters; also in verse 15

26:31–36 These verses describe the interior layout of the inner tent shrine of the tabernacle. The tabernacle included an outer structure (a curtained fence) and an internal structure, a fully enclosed tent partitioned into two rooms by a thick veil. The inner veil and the screen for the entrance of the tent are made of the same materials as the tabernacle curtains described in v. 1. The pillars for the veil and screen are also made of acacia wood just like the frames for the rest of the tabernacle (v. 15). The innermost section — the Most Holy Place or Holy of Holies — was a 15-foot cube. The larger section was 30 feet long, 15 feet wide, and 15 feet tall.

26:36 a curtain Describes the curtain that hung across the entrance of the tent, closing it off from the courtyard.

27:1–8 This passage lists the instructions for the construction of the bronze altar, which are carried out in 38:1–7. The altar is a hollow wooden box overlaid with bronze, yet it is designed to hold offerings as they burn. The bronze altar described here is the large, main altar for sacrifices that was located in the courtyard of the tabernacle. The altar was situated between the tent sanctuary and the entrance of the tabernacle. See the infographic "Ancient Altars" on p. 127; see the table "Altars in the Old Testament" on p. 249.

27:1 cubits One cubit equals about 1.5 feet.
27:2 a horn Protrusions, mimicking the horns of a bull, at the four corners of the altar. Sacrificial blood was placed on the horns in certain rituals of purification and atonement (e.g., Lev 4:25).

27:9–19 This section describes the courtyard area surrounding the tent sanctuary. The courtyard put distance between the tabernacle's entrance and provided space for the priests and worshipers to prepare the offerings. The sacrificial altar (Ex 30:28; 31:9; 38:1; 40:6–10) and the bronze basin (30:18) were located in this courtyard. The rectangular fence marking the bounds of the courtyard was 150 feet long and 75 feet wide (for a perimeter of 450 feet). Three of the sides were covered by curtains of fine white linen. The east side had a 30-foot opening covered by a screen. The curtains were suspended by ropes from 60 support posts set in bronze bases; the posts were 7.5 feet high and spaced at intervals of 7.5 feet.

27:10 twenty posts The material used for these support posts is not stated explicitly. The same Hebrew words for posts (*ammud* in Hebrew) and bases (*eden* in Hebrew) are used to describe the posts and bases used for the screens separating the sections of the tent sanctuary in ch. 26. Those posts are acacia wood overlaid with gold (see 26:32,37). The support posts for the tabernacle enclosure were likely also acacia wood but with silver bands rather than a full metal overlay. The posts were not pure bronze. The record of what the various precious metals were used for in 38:24–31 only shows the metals used for the bases and capitals of the posts.
27:13 east For some cultures in the ancient Near East, the orientation of a deity's dwelling was very important. The tabernacle and temple were both oriented eastward.

side of the entrance, with three posts and three bases, [15]and curtains fifteen cubits long are to be on the other side, with three posts and three bases.

[16]"For the entrance to the courtyard, provide a curtain twenty cubits[a] long, of blue, purple and scarlet yarn and finely twisted linen — the work of an embroiderer — with four posts and four bases. [17]All the posts around the courtyard are to have silver bands and hooks, and bronze bases. [18]The courtyard shall be a hundred cubits long and fifty cubits wide,[b] with curtains of finely twisted linen five cubits[c] high, and with bronze bases. [19]All the other articles used in the service of the tabernacle, whatever their function, including all the tent pegs for it and those for the courtyard, are to be of bronze.

Oil for the Lampstand

27:20-21pp — Lev 24:1-3

[20]"Command the Israelites to bring you clear oil of pressed olives for the light so that the lamps may be kept burning. [21]In the tent of meeting, outside the curtain that shields the ark of the covenant law, Aaron and his sons are to keep the lamps burning before the LORD from evening till morning. This is to be a lasting ordinance among the Israelites for the generations to come.

The Priestly Garments

28 "Have Aaron your brother brought to you from among the Israelites, along with his sons Nadab and Abihu, Eleazar and Ithamar, so they may serve me as priests. [2]Make sacred garments for your brother Aaron to give him dignity and honor. [3]Tell all the skilled workers to whom I have given wisdom in such matters that they are to make garments for Aaron, for his consecration, so he may serve me as priest. [4]These are the garments they are to make: a breastpiece, an ephod, a robe, a woven tunic, a turban and a sash. They are to make these sacred garments for your brother Aaron and his sons, so they may serve me as priests. [5]Have them use gold, and blue, purple and scarlet yarn, and fine linen.

The Ephod

28:6-14pp — Ex 39:2-7

[6]"Make the ephod of gold, and of blue, purple and scarlet yarn, and of finely twisted linen — the work of skilled hands. [7]It is to have two shoulder pieces attached to two of its corners, so it can be fastened. [8]Its skillfully woven waistband is to be

[a] 16 That is, about 30 feet or about 9 meters   [b] 18 That is, about 150 feet long and 75 feet wide or about 45 meters long and 23 meters wide   [c] 18 That is, about 7 1/2 feet or about 2.3 meters

---

27:16 a curtain A curtain that hung across the main entrance to the tabernacle.

27:20–21 This short section deals with the oil for the lampstand. The lamp was to be kept burning in the tent all night long. Compare note on 25:31.

27:20 clear oil The olive oil was to be clear, free of any particulates.

27:21 tent of meeting In this context, the Hebrew phrase used here, *ohel mo'ed*, refers to the tent shrine within the tabernacle court. In other contexts, the label applies to the entire tabernacle complex (compare Lev 1:1–3). The *ohel mo'ed* referenced in Ex 33:7–11 appears to have been a distinct structure set up outside the camp.

28:1–43 The daily operation of the tabernacle (chs. 25–27) requires the efforts of priests and other staff. In this chapter and the next, Yahweh instructs Moses on the construction of the priestly garments and the consecration of the priests. Aaron and his sons are appointed to the priesthood; the details of their job are given throughout Leviticus. See the table "Functions of Priests" on p. 171.

28:1 Nadab and Abihu Nadab and Abihu were killed by God in response to their improper offering of holy fire (see Lev 10:1 and note). **Eleazar** The eldest surviving son of Aaron who became high priest after Aaron's death (Nu 20:24–29). **Ithamar** Another son of Aaron and a priest who oversaw the tabernacle's construction (Ex 38:21). **priests** Israelite priests were responsible for conducting sacrifices and other religious duties associated with the tabernacle.

28:2 sacred garments The garments were set apart for priestly use only.

28:3 skilled The Hebrew phrase used here, *chakhmei-lev*, means wise of heart. Israelites considered the heart to be the source of intelligence as well as emotions. Hence, to be wise of heart refers to giftedness in intellect and craftsmanship. **consecration** The consecration of the priests, including Aaron, is directed in ch. 29 and carried out in Lev 8–9.

28:4 garments The same materials used for the tabernacle were provided to make the priestly garments. Thus, the priesthood was connected conceptually and materially to the sanctuary. **ephod** A robe or tunic for the upper body to waist level; the most sacred item of clothing worn by the high priest.

Exodus 28:4

EPHOD
An ephod was likely a robe or tunic worn on the upper body above the waist. In certain OT passages, the ephod is presented in a manner resembling the breastpiece, an item worn over the ephod (Ex 28:15). The ephod often is described as though it were an object instead of a garment. Goliath's sword is said to be kept behind the ephod in the sanctuary at Nob (1Sa 21:9). At times, David calls for the ephod to assist him in discerning God's will (1Sa 23:9).

28:5 fine linen The Hebrew term used here, *shesh*, derives from an Egyptian term denoting cloth of very high quality.

28:7 two shoulder pieces attached to two of its corners On each shoulder of the garment was a piece

like it — of one piece with the ephod and made with gold, and with blue, purple and scarlet yarn, and with finely twisted linen.

⁹"Take two onyx stones and engrave on them the names of the sons of Israel ¹⁰in the order of their birth — six names on one stone and the remaining six on the other. ¹¹Engrave the names of the sons of Israel on the two stones the way a gem cutter engraves a seal. Then mount the stones in gold filigree settings ¹²and fasten them on the

holding an onyx stone, on which were written the name of six tribes of Israel (thus twelve in all).
28:9 onyx The Hebrew term used here, *shoham*, refers to a gem of some kind. Possibilities include onyx and lapis lazuli.

28:12 to bear the names on his shoulders The high priest is to bear the people on his shoulders, both literally and metaphorically, by ensuring that the sacrificial duties were carried out properly. **memorial** The names

Tabernacle Materials and Equipment

	PLAN	CONSTRUCTION
Gold	Ex 25:3	Ex 35:5,22
Silver	Ex 25:3	Ex 35:5,24
Bronze	Ex 25:3	Ex 35:5,24
Blue, purple and scarlet yarns	Ex 25:4	Ex 35:6,25
Fine twined linen	Ex 25:4	Ex 35:6,25
Goat's hair	Ex 25:4	Ex 35:6,26
Tanned rams' hides and other hides	Ex 25:5	Ex 35:7,23
Acacia wood	Ex 25:5	Ex 35:7,24
Oil for light and anointing	Ex 25:6	Ex 35:8,28
Spices and incense	Ex 25:6	Ex 35:8,28
Onyx and other stones	Ex 25:7	Ex 35:9,27
Tabernacle*	Ex 26:1–37	Ex 36:8–38
Ark of God	Ex 25:10–22	Ex 37:1–9
Table	Ex 25:23–30	Ex 37:10–16
Lampstand	Ex 25:31–40	Ex 37:17–24
Incense altar	Ex 30:1–10	Ex 37:25–28
Anointing oil	Ex 30:22–33	Ex 37:29
Incense	Ex 30:34–38	Ex 37:29
Bronze altar	Ex 27:1–8	Ex 38:1–7
Bronze basin	Ex 30:17–21	Ex 38:8
Courtyard	Ex 27:9–19	Ex 38:9–20
Ephod	Ex 28:6–14	Ex 39:2–7
Breastpiece	Ex 28:15–30	Ex 39:8–21
Robe	Ex 28:31–35	Ex 39:22–26
Tunic, turban, sash	Ex 28:39	Ex 39:27–29
Gold plating	Ex 28:36–38	Ex 39:30–31

*The tabernacle construction account seems to be organized according to the principle of constructing the most important items first, but hiding them from public view.

shoulder pieces of the ephod as memorial stones for the sons of Israel. Aaron is to bear the names on his shoulders as a memorial before the LORD. [13] Make gold filigree settings [14] and two braided chains of pure gold, like a rope, and attach the chains to the settings.

The Breastpiece

28:15-28pp — Ex 39:8-21

[15] "Fashion a breastpiece for making decisions — the work of skilled hands. Make it like the ephod: of gold, and of blue, purple and scarlet yarn, and of finely twisted linen. [16] It is to be square — a span[a] long and a span wide — and folded double. [17] Then mount four rows of precious stones on it. The first row shall be carnelian, chrysolite and beryl; [18] the second row shall be turquoise, lapis lazuli and emerald; [19] the third row shall be jacinth, agate and amethyst; [20] the fourth row shall be topaz, onyx and jasper.[b] Mount them in gold filigree settings. [21] There are to be twelve stones, one for each of the names of the sons of Israel, each engraved like a seal with the name of one of the twelve tribes.

[22] "For the breastpiece make braided chains of pure gold, like a rope. [23] Make two gold rings for it and fasten them to two corners of the breastpiece. [24] Fasten the two gold chains to the rings at the corners of the breastpiece, [25] and the other ends of the chains to the two settings, attaching them to the shoulder pieces of the ephod at the front. [26] Make two gold rings and attach them to the other two corners of the breastpiece on the inside edge next to the ephod. [27] Make two more gold rings and attach them to the bottom of the shoulder pieces on the front of the ephod, close to the seam just above the waistband of the ephod. [28] The rings of the breastpiece are to be tied to the rings of the ephod with blue cord, connecting it to the waistband, so that the breastpiece will not swing out from the ephod.

[29] "Whenever Aaron enters the Holy Place, he will bear the names of the sons of Israel over his heart on the breastpiece of decision as a continuing memorial before the LORD. [30] Also put the Urim and the Thummim in the breastpiece, so they may be over Aaron's heart whenever he enters the presence of the LORD. Thus Aaron will always bear the means of making decisions for the Israelites over his heart before the LORD.

Other Priestly Garments

28:31-43pp — Ex 39:22-31

[31] "Make the robe of the ephod entirely of blue cloth, [32] with an opening for the head in its center. There shall be a woven edge like a collar[c] around this opening, so that it will not tear. [33] Make pome-

---

[a] 16 That is, about 9 inches or about 23 centimeters
[b] 20 The precise identification of some of these precious stones is uncertain.   [c] 32 The meaning of the Hebrew for this word is uncertain.

---

engraved on this garment served as a constant reminder to both the high priest and to Yahweh that the reason for maintaining the divine favor and presence was the fate of the people to whom Yahweh bound himself.

28:15 a breastpiece Worn over the chest and thus over the ephod. It was approximately nine inches square (Ex 28:16). Twelve gemstones, inscribed with the names of Israel's tribes, were fastened to it in four rows of three (see vv. 17–21 and note on v. 17). The breastpiece also had a pouch containing the Urim and Thummim (see note on v. 30). It is called a *choshen mishpat* in Hebrew (which may be rendered "breastpiece of judgment") because the Urim and Thummim were used to determine God's will.

28:17 precious stones Precise identifications of these gemstones are unknown, but there were active quarries that produced precious stones throughout Egypt and the Sinai Peninsula, long before the exodus. These stones may have been plundered from the Egyptians (12:35–36), or the Israelites had contact with traders who provided such goods. Three of the gems named here appear only in this passage and its parallel in 39:10–13.

28:21 like a seal Refers to a stone engraved with a unique design that may be set into a ring. The seal or signet was used to sign a document by stamping the symbol into the wax seal that secured the document, or, in some instances, the clay envelope that enclosed the document. The comparison of these stones with seals most likely refers to the way in which they were to be engraved.

28:22–28 These verses describe how the gems were attached to the breastpiece: Ropes of pure gold thread were passed through gold rings attached to the top corners of the breastpiece, upon which were rows of filigree mountings. Like the shoulder pieces of the ephod, the breastpiece was connected to the idea of bearing the names of the sons of Israel before Yahweh, for the sake of their remembrance (see v. 12 and note).

28:29 Holy Place Contained the altar of incense, the lampstand, and the table for the bread of the Presence. See note on 26:1. **over his heart** The placement of the names of the tribes over the heart is both literal and symbolic. The literal bearing of the names speaks to the purpose of the priesthood and its significance for the well-being and prosperity of the people of Israel.

28:30 the Urim and the Thummim Two objects that, together, served as a means of discerning God's will when Israel's leaders were unable to do so (see Nu 27:21; 1Sa 28:6; Ezr 2:63; compare Ne 7:65). These items are not mentioned in Ex 39, when the breastpiece is actually constructed. These items could have been lots cast to discern the will of God, a form of divination. However, the Urim and Thummim may have been objects that gave off a supernatural light as a sign to authenticate a message or decision of the high priest. This possibility is based on the apparent relation between the term Urim (*urim* in Hebrew) and the Hebrew word for "light" (*or*).

28:31 robe of the ephod This is the main garment that goes under the ephod, since the ephod only covers above the waist.

28:33 pomegranates This fruit is a symbol of abundance. Pomegranates are listed among the foods available in the promised land (Dt 8:8).

granates of blue, purple and scarlet yarn around the hem of the robe, with gold bells between them. ³⁴The gold bells and the pomegranates are to alternate around the hem of the robe. ³⁵Aaron must wear it when he ministers. The sound of the bells will be heard when he enters the Holy Place before the Lᴏʀᴅ and when he comes out, so that he will not die.

³⁶"Make a plate of pure gold and engrave on it as on a seal: ʜᴏʟʏ ᴛᴏ ᴛʜᴇ Lᴏʀᴅ. ³⁷Fasten a blue cord to it to attach it to the turban; it is to be on the front of the turban. ³⁸It will be on Aaron's forehead, and he will bear the guilt involved in the sacred gifts the Israelites consecrate, whatever their gifts may be. It will be on Aaron's forehead continually so that they will be acceptable to the Lᴏʀᴅ.

³⁹"Weave the tunic of fine linen and make the turban of fine linen. The sash is to be the work of an embroiderer. ⁴⁰Make tunics, sashes and caps for Aaron's sons to give them dignity and honor. ⁴¹After you put these clothes on your brother Aaron and his sons, anoint and ordain them. Consecrate them so they may serve me as priests.

⁴²"Make linen undergarments as a covering for the body, reaching from the waist to the thigh. ⁴³Aaron and his sons must wear them whenever they enter the tent of meeting or approach the altar to minister in the Holy Place, so that they will not incur guilt and die.

"This is to be a lasting ordinance for Aaron and his descendants.

Consecration of the Priests

29:1-37pp — Lev 8:1-36

29 "This is what you are to do to consecrate them, so they may serve me as priests: Take a young bull and two rams without defect. ²And from the finest wheat flour make round loaves without yeast, thick loaves without yeast and with olive oil mixed in, and thin loaves without yeast and brushed with olive oil. ³Put them in a basket and present them along with the bull and the two rams. ⁴Then bring Aaron and his sons to the entrance to the tent of meeting and wash them with water. ⁵Take the garments and dress Aaron with the tunic, the robe of the ephod, the ephod itself and the breastpiece. Fasten the ephod on him by its skillfully woven waistband. ⁶Put the turban on his head and attach the sacred emblem to the turban. ⁷Take the anointing oil and anoint him by pouring it on his head. ⁸Bring his sons and dress them in tunics ⁹and fasten caps on them. Then tie sashes on Aaron and his sons.ᵃ The priesthood is theirs by a lasting ordinance.

"Then you shall ordain Aaron and his sons.

ᵃ 9 Hebrew; Septuagint *on them*

28:35 sound Since only the high priest could go into the Most Holy Place to stand before the ark of the covenant (though only once a year; Lev 16:16–17), the sound of the bells (or lack thereof) would alert Yahweh to his approach and departure. The sound would also allow those outside to know if the priest was alive.

28:36–37 These verses concern the headwear of the high priest.

28:36 a plate Likely a reference to priestly headwear. Elsewhere, the Hebrew word used here, *tsits*, occurs in parallel with the Hebrew word *atarah* (which denotes headwear such as a crown or garland; see Isa 28:1). Additionally, *tsits* occurs in parallel with the Hebrew word *nezer*, which likely refers to an ornamental headband worn by royalty (Ex 39:30; Lev 8:9). **ʜᴏʟʏ ᴛᴏ ᴛʜᴇ Lᴏʀᴅ** This is a literal mark of dedication to Yahweh, setting the high priest apart from all other priests as belonging exclusively to Yahweh.

28:38 bear the guilt Leviticus 22:15–16 indicates that the high priest was accountable for any impropriety in ritual or worship (compare Nu 18:1). **sacred gifts** Items which the people have dedicated to Yahweh, presumably for use by the priests.

28:40–43 These verses are devoted to the clothing worn by the other priests.

28:40 dignity and honor Like the garments of the high priest (Ex 28:2), these garments are also to have a certain aesthetic quality that communicates the status and role of the priest who wears them.

28:41 anoint and ordain them The oil used to anoint priests was forbidden for any other use. Since the tabernacle and the high priest were anointed with the same

oil, the anointing apparently marked the person or thing as set apart for sacred service.

28:42 undergarments The Hebrew phrase used here, *besar erwah*, which is literally rendered "naked flesh," is likely a euphemism. This suggests that the robe under the ephod (28:31) was short enough to risk a sighting of the priest's genitalia. Compare 20:26 and note.

28:43 they will not incur guilt and die The repulsion caused by seeing a priest's genitals is likely connected to the requirement that the priests abstain from sexual contact during their time of service to the sanctuary (compare Lev 22:1–9). Regular priests (that is, not the high priest) did not work in the sanctuary year round, but were on a rotating schedule that allowed them to spend most of the year with their wives and families.

29:1–46 In this chapter, which comes after the description of the priestly garments, Yahweh explains to Moses the ritual procedure for consecrating the priests. This ritual is carried out in Lev 8, after the sacrificial duties of the priests are explained further (Lev 1–7).

29:1 consecrate The Hebrew word used here, *qadash*, refers to being holy or making something holy. The concept of holiness fundamentally indicates separation: Someone or something is set apart for sacred use, as opposed to ordinary use. See note on Ex 19:6. **a young bull and two rams** Only domesticated animals were acceptable sacrifices because the offering was meant to be costly for the worshiper (see 2Sa 24:24).

29:2 without yeast See note on Ex 12:8.

29:4 tent of meeting The tent of meeting is often used synonymously for the entire tabernacle complex which sat in the center of the Israelite camp (see 40:1; Nu 2:2,17).

29:7 anointing oil Anointing oil was used to show that

¹⁰"Bring the bull to the front of the tent of meeting, and Aaron and his sons shall lay their hands on its head. ¹¹Slaughter it in the LORD's presence at the entrance to the tent of meeting. ¹²Take some of the bull's blood and put it on the horns of the altar with your finger, and pour out the rest of it at the base of the altar. ¹³Then take all the fat on the internal organs, the long lobe of the liver, and both kidneys with the fat on them, and burn them on the altar. ¹⁴But burn the bull's flesh and its hide and its intestines outside the camp. It is a sin offering.ᵃ

¹⁵"Take one of the rams, and Aaron and his sons shall lay their hands on its head. ¹⁶Slaughter it and take the blood and splash it against the sides of the altar. ¹⁷Cut the ram into pieces and wash the internal organs and the legs, putting them with the head and the other pieces. ¹⁸Then burn the entire ram on the altar. It is a burnt offering to the LORD, a pleasing aroma, a food offering presented to the LORD.

¹⁹"Take the other ram, and Aaron and his sons shall lay their hands on its head. ²⁰Slaughter it, take some of its blood and put it on the lobes of the right ears of Aaron and his sons, on the thumbs of their right hands, and on the big toes of their right feet. Then splash blood against the sides of the altar. ²¹And take some blood from the altar and some of the anointing oil and sprinkle it on Aaron and his garments and on his sons and their garments. Then he and his sons and their garments will be consecrated.

²²"Take from this ram the fat, the fat tail, the fat on the internal organs, the long lobe of the liver, both kidneys with the fat on them, and the right thigh. (This is the ram for the ordination.) ²³From the basket of bread made without yeast, which is before the LORD, take one round loaf, one thick loaf with olive oil mixed in, and one thin loaf. ²⁴Put all these in the hands of Aaron and his sons and have them wave them before the LORD as a wave offer-

ing. ²⁵Then take them from their hands and burn them on the altar along with the burnt offering for a pleasing aroma to the LORD, a food offering presented to the LORD. ²⁶After you take the breast of the ram for Aaron's ordination, wave it before the LORD as a wave offering, and it will be your share.

²⁷"Consecrate those parts of the ordination ram that belong to Aaron and his sons: the breast that was waved and the thigh that was presented. ²⁸This is always to be the perpetual share from the Israelites for Aaron and his sons. It is the contribution the Israelites are to make to the LORD from their fellowship offerings.

²⁹"Aaron's sacred garments will belong to his descendants so that they can be anointed and ordained in them. ³⁰The son who succeeds him as priest and comes to the tent of meeting to minister in the Holy Place is to wear them seven days.

³¹"Take the ram for the ordination and cook the meat in a sacred place. ³²At the entrance to the tent of meeting, Aaron and his sons are to eat the meat of the ram and the bread that is in the basket. ³³They are to eat these offerings by which atonement was made for their ordination and consecration. But no one else may eat them, because they are sacred. ³⁴And if any of the meat of the ordination ram or any bread is left over till morning, burn it up. It must not be eaten, because it is sacred.

³⁵"Do for Aaron and his sons everything I have commanded you, taking seven days to ordain them. ³⁶Sacrifice a bull each day as a sin offering to make atonement. Purify the altar by making atonement for it, and anoint it to consecrate it. ³⁷For seven days make atonement for the altar and consecrate it. Then the altar will be most holy, and whatever touches it will be holy.

³⁸"This is what you are to offer on the altar regularly each day: two lambs a year old. ³⁹Offer one

ᵃ 14 Or purification offering; also in verse 36

---

an official, such as a priest or king, was chosen by God; the oil was poured on top of the person's head.

29:10 lay their hands A symbolic act acknowledging a connection between the worshiper and the offering.

29:11 at the entrance to the tent of meeting Refers to the open area outside and in front of the tent shrine in the tabernacle. In Ex 27:9, this open area is called in the Hebrew text chatsar hammishkan (which may be rendered as "courtyard of the tabernacle").

29:13 long lobe of the liver Burning this part of the liver might be an act of religious defiance directed against the widespread practice in the ancient Near East of using the liver for divination; the liver was used in rituals to attempt to access supernatural knowledge (Eze 21:21).

29:18 a pleasing aroma The smoke from the burning sacrifice rises up to Yahweh, carrying a smell that satisfies and pleases him. See note on Lev 1:9.

29:20 lobes of the right ears The instruction to place sacrificial blood on someone's ears, thumbs and toes is

found elsewhere only in the context of ritual purification from a skin disease (Lev 14:14–17). The ritual here also likely has purification as its intent.

29:21 will be consecrated The concept of holiness relates to separation—setting apart something for sacred use.

29:30 Holy Place This was the chamber just outside of the Most Holy Place (or Holy of Holies)—which was where the presence of Yahweh dwelled.

29:33 atonement Refers to the purging of ritual impurity. See note on Lev 4:20.

29:37 whatever touches it will be holy Both defilement and holiness are considered contagious. See note on Ex 29:1.

29:38–42 This passage gives instructions about the two burnt offerings that are to be offered by the priests every day. A lamb was sacrificed twice daily (at morning and twilight; vv. 38–39) as a whole burnt offering on the altar. In Hebrew, the offering is called olath tamid, which may be translated "the regular burnt offering" (v. 42).

in the morning and the other at twilight. ⁴⁰With the first lamb offer a tenth of an ephah*a* of the finest flour mixed with a quarter of a hin*b* of oil from pressed olives, and a quarter of a hin of wine as a drink offering. ⁴¹Sacrifice the other lamb at twilight with the same grain offering and its drink offering as in the morning — a pleasing aroma, a food offering presented to the LORD.

⁴²"For the generations to come this burnt offering is to be made regularly at the entrance to the tent of meeting, before the LORD. There I will meet you and speak to you; ⁴³there also I will meet with the Israelites, and the place will be consecrated by my glory.

⁴⁴"So I will consecrate the tent of meeting and the altar and will consecrate Aaron and his sons to serve me as priests. ⁴⁵Then I will dwell among the Israelites and be their God. ⁴⁶They will know that I am the LORD their God, who brought them out of Egypt so that I might dwell among them. I am the LORD their God.

The Altar of Incense

30:1-5pp — Ex 37:25-28

30 "Make an altar of acacia wood for burning incense. ²It is to be square, a cubit long and a cubit wide, and two cubits high*c* — its horns of one piece with it. ³Overlay the top and all the sides and the horns with pure gold, and make a gold molding around it. ⁴Make two gold rings for the altar below the molding — two on each of the opposite sides — to hold the poles used to carry it. ⁵Make the poles of acacia wood and overlay them with gold. ⁶Put the altar in front of the curtain that shields the ark of the covenant law — before the atonement cover that is over the tablets of the covenant law — where I will meet with you.

⁷"Aaron must burn fragrant incense on the altar every morning when he tends the lamps. ⁸He must burn incense again when he lights the lamps at twilight so incense will burn regularly before the LORD for the generations to come. ⁹Do not offer on this altar any other incense or any burnt offering or grain offering, and do not pour a drink offering on it. ¹⁰Once a year Aaron shall make atonement on its horns. This annual atonement must be made with the blood of the atoning sin offering*d* for the generations to come. It is most holy to the LORD."

Atonement Money

¹¹Then the LORD said to Moses, ¹²"When you take a census of the Israelites to count them, each one must pay the LORD a ransom for his life at the time he is counted. Then no plague will come on them when you number them. ¹³Each one who crosses over to those already counted is to give a half shekel,*e* according to the sanctuary shekel, which weighs twenty gerahs. This half shekel is an offering to the LORD. ¹⁴All who cross over, those twenty years old or more, are to give an offering to the LORD. ¹⁵The rich are not to give more than a half shekel and the poor are not to give less when you make the offering to the LORD to atone for your lives. ¹⁶Receive the atonement money from the Israelites and use it for the service of the tent of meeting. It will be a memorial for the Israelites before the LORD, making atonement for your lives."

a 40 That is, probably about 3 1/2 pounds or about 1.6 kilograms   b 40 That is, probably about 1 quart or about 1 liter   c 2 That is, about 1 1/2 feet long and wide and 3 feet high or about 45 centimeters long and wide and 90 centimeters high   d 10 Or purification offering   e 13 That is, about 1/5 ounce or about 5.8 grams; also in verse 15

29:43 will be consecrated Yahweh dwells among the people to set Israel apart from all the peoples of the earth (33:16). **my glory** Refers to the presence of God. See 16:10 and note.

30:1–10 In the first section of ch. 30, Yahweh gives Moses instructions for the altar of incense that will stand before the veil that covers the Most Holy Place (Holy of Holies). This altar is used not for ritual slaughter but for burning incense. The incense altar is similar in design to the main bronze altar (27:1–8). See the infographic "Furnishings of the Tabernacle" on p. 136; see the infographic "Ancient Altars" on p. 127; see the table "Altars in the Old Testament" on p. 249.

30:6 ark of the covenant law The Hebrew phrase used here, *aron ha'eduth*, (often rendered as "ark of the testimony") is one of the common labels for the ark of the covenant (see 40:3; Nu 7:89; Jos 4:16). See note on Ex 25:10. See the infographic "The Ark of the Covenant" on p. 412.

30:7 fragrant incense The ingredients of the incense are listed in v. 34. The recipe uses tree resin, onycha, galbanum and pure frankincense (*nataph, shecheleth, chelbinah* and *levonah* in Hebrew, respectively). People in the ancient Near East burned incense so that the deity would smell the incense and be invited to its location. **30:10 atonement** Refers to purging of ritual impurity. See note on Lev 4:20.

30:11–16 This section prescribes a census of Israelite men (age 20 and older). In order to avoid a plague (30:12), each man must offer one half-shekel to God as a ransom for his life (vv. 12,15–16). The money is designated for the service of the tent of meeting (v. 16). According to 38:25–26, this payment provided silver for the construction of the tabernacle. This is not an annual payment, but a one-time obligation.

30:12 ransom The Hebrew term used here, *kopher*, is related to the verb for making atonement (*kaphar*; see v. 10 and note). This ransom is substituted for a physical consequence, as indicated in 21:30 (compare Nu 35:31–32).

30:13 shekel A unit for weighing metals as currency. **gerahs** Ancient coins found in Israel and marked *gerah* weigh just over half a gram, on average.

30:14 twenty years old The age where a man became eligible for military service (Nu 1:3).

Basin for Washing

[17]Then the LORD said to Moses, [18]"Make a bronze basin, with its bronze stand, for washing. Place it between the tent of meeting and the altar, and put water in it. [19]Aaron and his sons are to wash their hands and feet with water from it. [20]Whenever they enter the tent of meeting, they shall wash with water so that they will not die. Also, when they approach the altar to minister by presenting a food offering to the LORD, [21]they shall wash their hands and feet so that they will not die. This is to be a lasting ordinance for Aaron and his descendants for the generations to come."

Anointing Oil

[22]Then the LORD said to Moses, [23]"Take the following fine spices: 500 shekels[a] of liquid myrrh, half as much (that is, 250 shekels) of fragrant cinnamon, 250 shekels[b] of fragrant calamus, [24]500 shekels of cassia — all according to the sanctuary shekel — and a hin[c] of olive oil. [25]Make these into a sacred anointing oil, a fragrant blend, the work of a perfumer. It will be the sacred anointing oil. [26]Then use it to anoint the tent of meeting, the ark of the covenant law, [27]the table and all its articles, the lampstand and its accessories, the altar of incense, [28]the altar of burnt offering and all its utensils, and the basin with its stand. [29]You shall consecrate them so they will be most holy, and whatever touches them will be holy.

[30]"Anoint Aaron and his sons and consecrate them so they may serve me as priests. [31]Say to the Israelites, 'This is to be my sacred anointing oil for the generations to come. [32]Do not pour it on anyone else's body and do not make any other oil using the same formula. It is sacred, and you are to consider it sacred. [33]Whoever makes perfume like it and puts it on anyone other than a priest must be cut off from their people.'"

Incense

[34]Then the LORD said to Moses, "Take fragrant spices — gum resin, onycha and galbanum — and pure frankincense, all in equal amounts, [35]and make a fragrant blend of incense, the work of a perfumer. It is to be salted and pure and sacred. [36]Grind some of it to powder and place it in front of the ark of the covenant law in the tent of meeting, where I will meet with you. It shall be most holy to you. [37]Do not make any incense with this formula for yourselves; consider it holy to the LORD. [38]Whoever makes incense like it to enjoy its fragrance must be cut off from their people."

Bezalel and Oholiab

31:2-6pp — Ex 35:30-35

31 Then the LORD said to Moses, [2]"See, I have chosen Bezalel son of Uri, the son of Hur, of the tribe of Judah, [3]and I have filled him with the

---

[a] 23 That is, about 12 1/2 pounds or about 5.8 kilograms; also in verse 24   [b] 23 That is, about 6 1/4 pounds or about 2.9 kilograms   [c] 24 That is, probably about 1 gallon or about 3.8 liters

---

30:17–21 The bronze basin (also called the laver) was not mentioned in the earlier instructions for tabernacle furniture in Ex 25–26. While the earlier items were used in the context of worship, the basin is used in preparation for entering the Holy Place (see note on 26:1). In contrast to the other pieces of furniture described, the focus here is on how to use the basin rather than what it looks like. The basin was crafted from bronze mirrors (38:8). The text does not provide dimensions for the basin, or any details about its construction, for that matter. See the infographic "The Tabernacle" on p. 138.

30:20 so that they will not die Here, washing is connected to purity, as any contamination could lead to a dangerous situation when working in the presence of God.

30:22–38 This passage describes the anointing oil and incense first mentioned in 25:6. Spices, perfumes, and incense were generally reserved for use by temples and royalty in the ancient Near East. Their costliness was directly related to the expense of industry required to produce them from raw materials. See the table "Tabernacle Materials and Equipment" on p. 141.

30:25 anointing oil This oil was used to show that an official, such as a priest or king, was chosen by God, by pouring the oil on top of the person's head. Here, the oil is to be used on the tent of meeting, all of its furniture and utensils, and the priests.

30:32 do not make any other oil The uniqueness of the mixture would reinforce the firm distinction between the sacred and the common.

30:33 cut off Likely means shunning or exclusion from the covenant community and its blessings. See note on Nu 15:30.

30:34 gum resin A fragrant tree resin; probably balsam or persimmon. **onycha** The identification of this substance, called *shecheleth* in Hebrew, is uncertain. The Septuagint (the ancient Greek translation of the OT) translates *shecheleth* with the Greek word *onych*, meaning "talon," "claw" or "fingernail." Ancient translations into Aramaic also used a word for claw or fingernail. *Shecheleth* may be understood as the nail-like door (the operculum) of the shell of a sea snail. However, the use of sea snails for sacred incense would be surprising since they are unclean animals (see Lev 11:9–12). Evidence from other ancient Semitic languages suggests that *shecheleth* refers to some type of edible plant — possibly an herb like the garden cress. **galbanum** A plant resin that, when burned, increases the pungency of the ingredients with which it is mixed.

30:35 pure and sacred Purity is a state that enables something or someone to become holy or set apart. A state of ritual purity is necessary for someone or something to enter holy space.

31:1–11 This passage begins with Yahweh telling Moses whom he has chosen to carry out the work of constructing the tabernacle and all its furnishings. The skilled workers mentioned in this passage, Bezalel and Oholiab design the individual pieces, teach others and oversee the labor (see Ex 35:30–36:2). This passage also includes a catalog of all that they are commanded to manufacture.

Spirit of God, with wisdom, with understanding, with knowledge and with all kinds of skills — [4]to make artistic designs for work in gold, silver and bronze, [5]to cut and set stones, to work in wood, and to engage in all kinds of crafts. [6]Moreover, I have appointed Oholiab son of Ahisamak, of the tribe of Dan, to help him. Also I have given ability to all the skilled workers to make everything I have commanded you: [7]the tent of meeting, the ark of the covenant law with the atonement cover on it, and all the other furnishings of the tent — [8]the table and its articles, the pure gold lampstand and all its accessories, the altar of incense, [9]the altar of burnt offering and all its utensils, the basin with its stand — [10]and also the woven garments, both the sacred garments for Aaron the priest and the garments for his sons when they serve as priests, [11]and the anointing oil and fragrant incense for the Holy Place. They are to make them just as I commanded you."

The Sabbath

[12]Then the LORD said to Moses, [13]"Say to the Israelites, 'You must observe my Sabbaths. This will be a sign between me and you for the generations to come, so you may know that I am the LORD, who makes you holy.

[14]"'Observe the Sabbath, because it is holy to you. Anyone who desecrates it is to be put to death; those who do any work on that day must be cut off from their people. [15]For six days work is to be done, but the seventh day is a day of sabbath rest, holy to the LORD. Whoever does any work on the Sabbath day is to be put to death. [16]The Israelites are to observe the Sabbath, celebrating it for the generations to come as a lasting covenant. [17]It will be a sign between me and the Israelites forever, for in six days the LORD made the heavens and the earth, and on the seventh day he rested and was refreshed.'"

[18]When the LORD finished speaking to Moses on Mount Sinai, he gave him the two tablets of the covenant law, the tablets of stone inscribed by the finger of God.

The Golden Calf

32 When the people saw that Moses was so long in coming down from the mountain, they gathered around Aaron and said, "Come, make us gods[a] who will go before us. As for this fellow Moses who brought us up out of Egypt, we don't know what has happened to him."

[2]Aaron answered them, "Take off the gold earrings that your wives, your sons and your

---

[a] 1 Or a god; also in verses 23 and 31

31:3 with the Spirit of God In the OT, specific skills or tasks are often associated with divine enablement.

31:12–18 This passage deals with the observance of the Sabbath. It is actually the seventh literary section describing the tabernacle and its personnel. The patterns of seven—reflecting the creation week—is deliberate: In six units God describes the work, and on the seventh he describes the Sabbath rest (v. 17; compare 16:23; 20:8; 23:12). The tabernacle narrative resumes in ch. 35 with the explanation of the Sabbath laws in abbreviated form (35:1–3).

31:13 Sabbaths The plural here denotes the weekly observance in perpetuity. Its observance is the fourth of the commandments in 20:8–11 (compare 23:12; 31:15–17; 34:21). The principle of the Sabbath is established at creation (see Ge 2:2). **a sign** This connects the Sinai covenant with the Abrahamic covenant, where circumcision is given as a sign (see Ge 12:1–3; 15:1–6; 17:1–14). The Sinai covenant is now at the same level as the Abrahamic; they operate in tandem and are to be honored equally (see Ex 24:3). In connecting the two covenants, obedience to the law becomes linked to inheriting the promises of the Abrahamic covenant.

31:18 two tablets of the covenant law Refers to the commandments of Ex 20 (commonly called the Ten Commandments), which were written on the two tablets (see 24:12–18).

32:1–35 Chapter 32 recounts the episode of the Israelites' apostasy involving the golden calf. Even Aaron, who will become Israel's first high priest, is implicated. After Moses intercedes to save the people from obliteration, God gives them a chance to repent. The tribe of Levi is singled out for its loyalty to Yahweh, and the Levites become the instrument of punishment under the direction of Moses. The narrative continues in chs. 33–34 with Moses and the Israelites dealing with the consequences of the golden calf incident.

32:1 the people saw that Moses was so long This entire episode is in response to the Hebrew people's assumption that something has happened to Moses, and he must be replaced. The people do not ask for Aaron to take Moses' place, but to build a replacement for him by constructing the golden calf. **gods** Israel's sin here is improper and inappropriate worship, but the nature of their offense is open to interpretation. The incident could be understood as an instance of apostasy—Israel worshiping a god other than Yahweh. The Hebrew word used here, *elohim*, is grammatically plural, but the plural form is not only used to refer to multiple gods. For example, *elohim* is frequently used as a name for Yahweh, even in passages that also use *elohim* to refer to other gods (e.g., Ge 31:24–32). The plural can also be used for an individual foreign god (e.g., 1Ki 11:33). This ambiguity allows for either Israel worshiping Yahweh, somehow represented idolatrously by the image, or worshiping another god or gods. *Elohim* is often translated as "gods" in this passage since it occurs with verbs in Hebrew that are plural in form (vv. 1,4,8), but *elohim* occurs elsewhere with plural verbs where a single god is in view (e.g., Ge 20:13; see note on Ex 22:9). It is likely that only one god is in view in this passage since Aaron fashions only one image (v. 4). The case that Israel was worshiping Yahweh improperly is further implied when Aaron associates the golden calf with the god who saved Israel from Egypt (v. 4; compare 1Ki 12:28) and announces that the next day will be a festival for Yahweh (Ex 32:5). With Moses gone, the people may have thought they needed another

daughters are wearing, and bring them to me." ³So all the people took off their earrings and brought them to Aaron. ⁴He took what they handed him and made it into an idol cast in the shape of a calf, fashioning it with a tool. Then they said, "These are your gods,ᵃ Israel, who brought you up out of Egypt."

⁵When Aaron saw this, he built an altar in front of the calf and announced, "Tomorrow there will be a festival to the LORD." ⁶So the next day the people rose early and sacrificed burnt offerings and presented fellowship offerings. Afterward they sat down to eat and drink and got up to indulge in revelry.

⁷Then the LORD said to Moses, "Go down, because your people, whom you brought up out of Egypt, have become corrupt. ⁸They have been quick to turn away from what I commanded them and have made themselves an idol cast in the shape of a calf. They have bowed down to it and sacrificed to it and have said, 'These are your gods, Israel, who brought you up out of Egypt.'

⁹"I have seen these people," the LORD said to Moses, "and they are a stiff-necked people. ¹⁰Now leave me alone so that my anger may burn against them and that I may destroy them. Then I will make you into a great nation."

¹¹But Moses sought the favor of the LORD his God. "LORD," he said, "why should your anger burn against your people, whom you brought out of Egypt with great power and a mighty hand? ¹²Why should the Egyptians say, 'It was with evil intent that he brought them out, to kill them in the mountains and to wipe them off the face of the earth'? Turn from your fierce anger; relent and do not bring disaster on your people. ¹³Remember your servants Abraham, Isaac and Israel, to whom you swore by your own self: 'I will make your descendants as numerous as the stars in the sky and I will give your descendants all this land I promised them, and it will be their inheritance forever.'" ¹⁴Then the LORD relented and did not bring on his people the disaster he had threatened.

¹⁵Moses turned and went down the mountain with the two tablets of the covenant law in his hands. They were inscribed on both sides, front and back. ¹⁶The tablets were the work of God; the writing was the writing of God, engraved on the tablets.

¹⁷When Joshua heard the noise of the people shouting, he said to Moses, "There is the sound of war in the camp."

¹⁸Moses replied:

"It is not the sound of victory,
    it is not the sound of defeat;
    it is the sound of singing that I hear."

¹⁹When Moses approached the camp and saw the calf and the dancing, his anger burned and he threw the tablets out of his hands, breaking them to pieces at the foot of the mountain. ²⁰And he took the calf the people had made and burned it

ᵃ 4 Or *This is your god*; also in verse 8

---

way to hear from Yahweh. While the OT polemic against idolatry often mocks it as worship of a human-made object (see Isa 44:9–20), people in the ancient Near East apparently believed the deity somehow resided in—or associated its presence with—the physical object (compare Ex 40:34–35). After fashioning the idol, the Israelites made sacrifices (v. 8); this was likely to call the deity to localize its presence there so that they could be in communication with it. When the people are chastised in v. 8, they are not explicitly charged with worshiping other gods, but only with fashioning and worshiping an image. This means that they may be in violation of the second commandment, not the first (compare 20:3–6).
32:4 calf The Hebrew word used here, *egel*, refers to a young bull or ox. The bull symbolized strength and fertility in the ancient Near East and was used to depict a range of gods throughout the region. In Ugaritic texts from ancient Syria, the god El is associated with bull imagery. The Semitic term *el* is also used for the God of Israel because it is the generic word for god in Semitic languages—providing a connection between this scene and the god El. Semitic storm gods like Hadad are also sometimes depicted mounted on a bull. The calf image here may have been envisioned as a mount for Yahweh (compare note on 32:1). **tool** The Hebrew word used here, *cheret*, refers to a tool like a chisel or stylus (see Isa 8:1). The calf may have been a wooden object crafted using chisels or carving tools and then overlaid with gold. However, the image is called in Hebrew an *egel massekhah* (which may be literally rendered "cast-

image calf"); *massekhah* typically refers to creating a molten object, which would not necessarily require a tool for carving or engraving. However, *cheret* may also have designated a tool used for shaping a metal object.
32:5 a festival to the LORD Aaron's proclamation has the single deity Yahweh as its focus (see note on Ex 32:1).
32:6 indulge in revelry The Hebrew verb used here, *tsachaq*, commonly refers to laughing, joking or mocking (Ge 17:17; 18:12; 19:14; 21:9). In this context, it may refer to dancing (Ex 32:19). However, usage of *tsachaq* in other contexts suggests that sexual connotations are possible (Ge 26:8; 39:14,17).
32:7 your people This phrase demonstrates God's disgust with the Israelites, and their distance from fellowship with him. Previously, God refers to the Israelites as my people (e.g., Ex 3:7; 5:1; 7:4,16; 9:1,17; 10:3–4).
32:8 what I commanded them Referring to what is commonly called the Ten Commandments and the laws of the covenant (chs. 20–23), particularly the prohibitions against images (20:4–6,23). The people accepted the terms of this covenant in 24:3.
32:12 evil intent Moses appeals to God's good reputation, as well as to the covenant with Abraham (v. 13).
32:14 the LORD relented Repentant intercession elsewhere convinces Yahweh to turn away from punishment completely or lessen its severity (compare 2Sa 24:10–25; Jnh 3:6–10; see note on Ex 32:31–35).
32:19 threw the tablets Breaking tablets on which covenant stipulations were recorded signified that the covenant had been broken by one of its parties.

in the fire; then he ground it to powder, scattered it on the water and made the Israelites drink it.

²¹He said to Aaron, "What did these people do to you, that you led them into such great sin?"

²²"Do not be angry, my lord," Aaron answered. "You know how prone these people are to evil. ²³They said to me, 'Make us gods who will go before us. As for this fellow Moses who brought us up out of Egypt, we don't know what has happened to him.' ²⁴So I told them, 'Whoever has any gold jewelry, take it off.' Then they gave me the gold, and I threw it into the fire, and out came this calf!"

²⁵Moses saw that the people were running wild and that Aaron had let them get out of control and so become a laughingstock to their enemies. ²⁶So he stood at the entrance to the camp and said, "Whoever is for the LORD, come to me." And all the Levites rallied to him.

²⁷Then he said to them, "This is what the LORD, the God of Israel, says: 'Each man strap a sword to his side. Go back and forth through the camp from one end to the other, each killing his brother and friend and neighbor.'" ²⁸The Levites did as Moses commanded, and that day about three thousand of the people died. ²⁹Then Moses said, "You have been set apart to the LORD today, for you were

---

32:24 out came this calf Aaron leaves out his own role in creating the calf (vv. 3–4).

32:26 Levites rallied to him The Levites, the tribe of Moses and Aaron (6:16–20), immediately respond to Moses' ultimatum. The description here establishes that the Levites, who were set apart to Yahweh (chs. 28–29), were still loyal to him.

32:28 did as Moses commanded None of the punishments placed upon the people thus far, from the drinking of tainted water to the massacre of 3,000, are from Yahweh, who relented (v. 14). **three thousand** The fact that this is a round number suggests that it may be symbolic, as both three and 1,000 are significant numbers in the OT.

The Stele of Adad

Adad, chief god of the Babylonian-Assyrian pantheon—and of the Northwest Semitic pantheon as Hadad or Baal—is here pictured on his symbolic animal, the bull. This depiction is from the mid-eighth century BC.

Animals—and bulls, in particular—were often associated with pagan gods. When the Israelites made a golden calf in Exodus 32, they might not have been making an idol of a bull-god (as existed in Egypt as the Apis bull). They could have been making a bull to be associated with Baal, or even with Yahweh under idolatrous forms of worship.

against your own sons and brothers, and he has blessed you this day."

³⁰The next day Moses said to the people, "You have committed a great sin. But now I will go up to the LORD; perhaps I can make atonement for your sin."

³¹So Moses went back to the LORD and said, "Oh, what a great sin these people have committed! They have made themselves gods of gold. ³²But now, please forgive their sin—but if not, then blot me out of the book you have written."

³³The LORD replied to Moses, "Whoever has sinned against me I will blot out of my book. ³⁴Now go, lead the people to the place I spoke of, and my angel will go before you. However, when the time comes for me to punish, I will punish them for their sin."

³⁵And the LORD struck the people with a plague because of what they did with the calf Aaron had made.

33 Then the LORD said to Moses, "Leave this place, you and the people you brought up out of Egypt, and go up to the land I promised on oath to Abraham, Isaac and Jacob, saying, 'I will give it to your descendants.' ²I will send an angel before you and drive out the Canaanites, Amorites, Hittites, Perizzites, Hivites and Jebusites. ³Go up to the land flowing with milk and honey. But I will not go with you, because you are a stiff-necked people and I might destroy you on the way."

⁴When the people heard these distressing words, they began to mourn and no one put on any ornaments. ⁵For the LORD had said to Moses, "Tell the Israelites, 'You are a stiff-necked people. If I were to go with you even for a moment, I might destroy you. Now take off your ornaments and I will decide what to do with you.'" ⁶So the Israelites stripped off their ornaments at Mount Horeb.

The Tent of Meeting

⁷Now Moses used to take a tent and pitch it outside the camp some distance away, calling it the "tent of meeting." Anyone inquiring of the LORD would go to the tent of meeting outside the camp. ⁸And whenever Moses went out to the tent, all the people rose and stood at the entrances to their tents, watching Moses until he entered the tent. ⁹As Moses went into the tent, the pillar of cloud would come down and stay at the entrance, while the LORD spoke with Moses. ¹⁰Whenever the people saw the pillar of cloud standing at the entrance to the tent, they all stood and worshiped, each at the entrance to their tent. ¹¹The LORD would speak to Moses face to face, as one speaks to a friend. Then Moses would return to the camp, but his young aide Joshua son of Nun did not leave the tent.

Moses and the Glory of the LORD

¹²Moses said to the LORD, "You have been telling me, 'Lead these people,' but you have not let

---

32:31–35 Prior to Moses' descent from the mountain, God had relented from his decision to destroy the Israelites (vv. 14–15). Furthermore, the guilty parties were punished with death (vv. 27–28). Even so, Moses tells the people that they sinned greatly in making the calf, and he returns to Yahweh to seek forgiveness on their behalf. God responds that he will punish the people, and he does so with a plague (vv. 34–35).

32:32 book you have written Belief in heavenly books or recountings was common in the ancient Near East. In the NT, this concept appears again as the book of life (e.g., Php 4:3; Rev 20:12,15; 21:27).

33:1–6 In the wake of the golden calf episode, Yahweh decides that he cannot accompany the people to the promised land because it is too dangerous for them—if they anger him again he may wipe them out. Instead, he will send only the angel that he promised in Ex 23:20. The people mourn upon hearing the news.

33:2 an angel In some cases, the angel appears to be Yahweh himself. Here Yahweh makes a clear distinction between his presence and the angel's presence. See note on 23:20. **the Canaanites, Amorites, Hittites, Perizzites, Hivites and Jebusites** These groups were some of the native inhabitants of Canaan at the time. See note on 13:5.

33:3 milk and honey A common phrase used in Exodus, Numbers and Deuteronomy, which refers to the agricultural fertility of the land (e.g., Lev 20:24; Nu 13:27; Dt 6:3; 27:3). This reference to the fertility of the land

appears frequently in connection with lists of the land's pre-Israelite inhabitants (Ex 3:8,17; 13:5).

33:7–11 Here the narrator pauses to give more information about Moses' relationship with Yahweh. This is an important bridge between Yahweh's declaration that he will not go with the people (Ex 33:1–6) and what follows.

33:7 tent of meeting The Hebrew phrase used here, ohel mo'ed, becomes a common label for the tabernacle (see Lev 1:1 and note). Here, however, the tabernacle has not yet been constructed. The ohel mo'ed referenced in Ex 33:7–11 was a distinct structure set up outside the camp. This tent was not associated with the ark of the covenant, an altar or sacrifice. It was a place where Moses met with Yahweh before the tabernacle was constructed. Once the tabernacle was complete, the Hebrew phrase ohel mo'ed (often rendered "tent of meeting") applied either to the internal tented structure within the tabernacle proper or to the tabernacle complex as a whole.

33:9 As Moses went into the tent This emphasizes what was subtle in the previous two verses—that Moses initiates his regular encounters with Yahweh. He does not need to wait for Yahweh's signal or command; Yahweh meets Moses upon Moses' signal.

33:11 would speak to Moses face to face, as one speaks to a friend The wording here uses metaphors for intimacy and accessibility (compare v. 20). In the ancient Near East, it was dishonorable to look a superior in the face. Here, Moses and Yahweh converse as equals even though they are far from it.

me know whom you will send with me. You have said, 'I know you by name and you have found favor with me.' ¹³If you are pleased with me, teach me your ways so I may know you and continue to find favor with you. Remember that this nation is your people."

¹⁴The LORD replied, "My Presence will go with you, and I will give you rest."

¹⁵Then Moses said to him, "If your Presence does not go with us, do not send us up from here. ¹⁶How will anyone know that you are pleased with me and with your people unless you go with us? What else will distinguish me and your people from all the other people on the face of the earth?"

¹⁷And the LORD said to Moses, "I will do the very thing you have asked, because I am pleased with you and I know you by name."

¹⁸Then Moses said, "Now show me your glory."

¹⁹And the LORD said, "I will cause all my goodness to pass in front of you, and I will proclaim my name, the LORD, in your presence. I will have mercy on whom I will have mercy, and I will have compassion on whom I will have compassion. ²⁰But," he said, "you cannot see my face, for no one may see me and live."

²¹Then the LORD said, "There is a place near me where you may stand on a rock. ²²When my glory passes by, I will put you in a cleft in the rock and cover you with my hand until I have passed by. ²³Then I will remove my hand and you will see my back; but my face must not be seen."

The New Stone Tablets

34 The LORD said to Moses, "Chisel out two stone tablets like the first ones, and I will write on them the words that were on the first tablets, which you broke. ²Be ready in the morning, and then come up on Mount Sinai. Present yourself to me there on top of the mountain. ³No one is to come with you or be seen anywhere on the mountain; not even the flocks and herds may graze in front of the mountain."

⁴So Moses chiseled out two stone tablets like the first ones and went up Mount Sinai early in the morning, as the LORD had commanded him; and he carried the two stone tablets in his hands. ⁵Then the LORD came down in the cloud and stood there with him and proclaimed his name, the LORD. ⁶And he passed in front of Moses, proclaiming, "The LORD, the LORD, the compassionate and gracious God, slow to anger, abounding in love and faithfulness, ⁷maintaining love to thousands, and forgiving wickedness, rebellion and sin. Yet he does not leave the guilty unpunished; he punishes

---

33:12–23 The narrator returns to the main narrative. In vv. 1–6, the people learned that Yahweh will not go with them to the promised land and they mourned in response. Here, Moses intercedes on their behalf and convinces Yahweh not only to go with them, but also to reveal more of himself to Moses.

33:12 I know you by name Moses appeals to the personal and intimate nature of his relationship with Yahweh as grounds for the conversation that follows (see vv. 7–11).

33:13 teach me your ways This request should be distinguished from the one in v. 18. Here Moses desires to know Yahweh's decision about leading the people to the promised land (v. 12). Yahweh responds in vv. 14 and 17 that he will accompany them after all.

33:16 me and with your people This is the first time Moses identifies himself with the people since before the golden calf episode (Ex 32).

33:17 I am pleased with you Yahweh signals to Moses that it is indeed their relationship that opens up the possibility of Yahweh residing among the Hebrew people.

33:18 show me your glory Yahweh responds to this request in 33:19–23 and 34:6–7. While Moses wants to know and experience God's essential person, there are limits regarding how much humans can withstand (see v. 20 and note). Yahweh's visible earthly presence is often called his "glory" (*kavod* in Hebrew; see 16:7,10; 24:16–17; 40:34–35).

33:20 you cannot see my face This clarifies that the previous description of Moses as meeting with Yahweh face to face (vv. 11; Nu 12:6–8; Dt 34:10–12) is to be understood metaphorically.

34:1–9 This passage describes the fulfillment of Yahweh's agreement with Moses, to let Moses see a portion—the back side—of Yahweh's glory. This promise was made just prior in Ex 33:17–23. See the table "Old Testament Theophanies" on p. 924.

34:1 like the first Moses broke the first set of tablets, the divinely inscribed ones, upon seeing the golden calf (32:15–19; compare 31:18). **I will write** See note on 24:12.

34:3 not even the flocks and herds The precautions against loss of life due to the danger of God's presence extends even to animals. The issue here is not sin, as in 33:3, but rather the sheer power associated with God's unveiling more of his true form.

34:6 he passed in front In passing, God—whose name Moses already knew (3:14)—calls out his name, Yahweh, along with a list of attributes in accordance with 33:19–23. Yahweh told Moses that he would place him in a cleft in the rock and then shelter him with his own hand so that Moses would not see his presence (*panim* in Hebrew; which may be literally rendered as "face"). Yahweh would then remove his hand once he had passed by Moses so that Moses could see his back (33:23). The Biblical writers use the language of anthropomorphism and embodiment when referring to God as having a face or a hand. **The LORD, the LORD** In Hebrew, the first use of the divine name Yahweh can be the subject of the verb "to proclaim." The result is the rendering, "Yahweh proclaimed, 'Yahweh, the compassionate and gracious God' "—which creates the impression that Yahweh is using the third-person voice to refer to himself. **compassionate and gracious** The attributes listed here emphasize God's benevolent character. These characteristics explain why—despite Israel's apostasy with the golden calf (ch. 32) and the breaking of the covenant (32:19)—God will forgive and renew the covenant in this chapter. **love** The Hebrew term used here,

the children and their children for the sin of the parents to the third and fourth generation."

⁸Moses bowed to the ground at once and worshiped. ⁹"Lord," he said, "if I have found favor in your eyes, then let the Lord go with us. Although this is a stiff-necked people, forgive our wickedness and our sin, and take us as your inheritance."

¹⁰Then the Lord said: "I am making a covenant with you. Before all your people I will do wonders never before done in any nation in all the world. The people you live among will see how awesome is the work that I, the Lord, will do for you. ¹¹Obey what I command you today. I will drive out before you the Amorites, Canaanites, Hittites, Perizzites, Hivites and Jebusites. ¹²Be careful not to make a treaty with those who live in the land where you are going, or they will be a snare among you. ¹³Break down their altars, smash their sacred stones and cut down their Asherah poles.ᵃ ¹⁴Do not worship any other god, for the Lord, whose name is Jealous, is a jealous God.

¹⁵"Be careful not to make a treaty with those who live in the land; for when they prostitute themselves to their gods and sacrifice to them, they will invite you and you will eat their sacrifices. ¹⁶And when you choose some of their daughters as wives for your sons and those daughters prostitute themselves to their gods, they will lead your sons to do the same.

¹⁷"Do not make any idols.

¹⁸"Celebrate the Festival of Unleavened Bread. For seven days eat bread made without yeast, as I commanded you. Do this at the appointed time in the month of Aviv, for in that month you came out of Egypt.

¹⁹"The first offspring of every womb belongs to me, including all the firstborn males of your livestock, whether from herd or flock. ²⁰Redeem the firstborn donkey with a lamb, but if you do not redeem it, break its neck. Redeem all your firstborn sons.

"No one is to appear before me empty-handed.

²¹"Six days you shall labor, but on the seventh day you shall rest; even during the plowing season and harvest you must rest.

²²"Celebrate the Festival of Weeks with the firstfruits of the wheat harvest, and the Festival of Ingathering at the turn of the year.ᵇ ²³Three times a year all your men are to appear before the Sovereign Lord, the God of Israel. ²⁴I will drive out nations before you and enlarge your territory, and no one will covet your land when you go up three times each year to appear before the Lord your God.

²⁵"Do not offer the blood of a sacrifice to me along with anything containing yeast, and do not

ᵃ 13 That is, wooden symbols of the goddess Asherah
ᵇ 22 That is, in the autumn

---

chesed, is directly associated with God's covenant love for Israel and is frequently paired with the Hebrew word *emeth* (which may be rendered as "faithfulness"). See note on 15:13.

34:7 he punishes the children and their children for the sin of the parents At first, the idea of visiting the iniquity of the fathers upon subsequent generations seems counter to the abundance of mercy, grace, love, faithfulness and forgiveness mentioned in vv. 6–7. However, this is not the case. While God does forgive, he does not undo the consequences of sin, and some sins continue to shape people's lives long after the sinner has passed away.

34:10–28 The following passage describes the renewal of the covenant and is crafted with the golden calf incident (ch. 32) in mind. The narrative especially addresses inappropriate worship (vv. 10–17) alongside a rehearsal of Israel's required festivals and rules for worship (vv. 18–26). Some of the obligations are more strict than before. For example, in addition to prohibiting covenants with other people groups, Yahweh now prohibits marrying them (23:23–33; 34:16). Despite some of these contextualized differences, many of the commandments are repeated from chs. 23–24. See the table "Covenants in the Old Testament" on p. 469.

34:13 Break down their altars This command is reiterated in connection with the conquest of the promised land (see 23:23–33; Dt 7:5; 12:3; Jdg 2:2). **smash their sacred stones** See note on Ex 23:24; compare Ex 23:24; Dt 7:5. **Asherah poles** Referring to sacred wooden poles. The Hebrew term used here, *asherim*, derives from the name of the Canaanite goddess Asherah, who

was associated with sexual fertility (Dt 7:5; 16:21; 2Ki 23:7). Archaeologists have recovered Hebrew inscriptions that read "Yahweh and his *asherah*"—which suggests a significant degree of religious syncretism (or blending). Since the OT describes a perversion of Yahweh worship, it is possible that some Israelites wrongly saw Asherah as the wife of Yahweh. See the table "Pagan Deities of the Old Testament" on p. 1287.

34:15 when they prostitute themselves to The Hebrew verb used here and in Ex 34:16 is *zanah*, the term for sexually immoral behavior, especially adultery or prostitution. The word is used frequently in the OT to cast religious infidelity as sexual infidelity (see note on Nu 25:1). **eat their sacrifices** The act of eating a sacrificed animal (a sacrificial meal) was considered participation in the worship of the deity to whom it was offered.

34:18 Festival of Unleavened Bread This festival is associated with Passover and commemorates the exodus from Egypt. See note on Ex 13:1–16.

34:19 first offspring of every womb The consecration of the firstborn is first commanded just after the tenth plague against Egypt, the death of all their firstborn, including livestock (12:29–32; 13:2,12–15).

34:21 during the plowing season and harvest The Sabbath law tested the Israelites' loyalty to Yahweh, as it required them to stop working even during the most critical periods for farming.

34:22 Festival of Weeks Also called the Festival of Harvest or Firstfruits. **Festival of Ingathering** Also known as the Festival of Tabernacles. See 23:16 and note.

34:24 no one will covet your land With the men absent from the fields and homes, an enemy might take advantage by stealing crops, land, property or even a man's

let any of the sacrifice from the Passover Festival remain until morning.

26"Bring the best of the firstfruits of your soil to the house of the LORD your God.

"Do not cook a young goat in its mother's milk."

27Then the LORD said to Moses, "Write down these words, for in accordance with these words I have made a covenant with you and with Israel." 28Moses was there with the LORD forty days and forty nights without eating bread or drinking water. And he wrote on the tablets the words of the covenant — the Ten Commandments.

The Radiant Face of Moses

29When Moses came down from Mount Sinai with the two tablets of the covenant law in his hands, he was not aware that his face was radiant because he had spoken with the LORD. 30When Aaron and all the Israelites saw Moses, his face was radiant, and they were afraid to come near him. 31But Moses called to them; so Aaron and all the leaders of the community came back to him, and he spoke to them. 32Afterward all the Israelites came near him, and he gave them all the commands the LORD had given him on Mount Sinai.

33When Moses finished speaking to them, he put a veil over his face. 34But whenever he entered the LORD's presence to speak with him, he removed the veil until he came out. And when he came out and told the Israelites what he had been commanded, 35they saw that his face was radiant. Then Moses would put the veil back over his face until he went in to speak with the LORD.

Sabbath Regulations

35 Moses assembled the whole Israelite community and said to them, "These are the things the LORD has commanded you to do: 2For six days, work is to be done, but the seventh day shall be your holy day, a day of sabbath rest to the LORD. Whoever does any work on it is to be put to death. 3Do not light a fire in any of your dwellings on the Sabbath day."

Materials for the Tabernacle

35:4-9pp — Ex 25:1-7
35:10-19pp — Ex 39:32-41

4Moses said to the whole Israelite community, "This is what the LORD has commanded: 5From what you have, take an offering for the LORD.

---

wife and children. God promises that if the Israelite men are faithful, he will prevent any such loss.

34:25 This commandment may specifically refer here to the Passover sacrifice (compare 12:1–28; 23:18; 34:18–20). However, a portion from the grain offerings was generally offered along with certain animal sacrifices (see Lev 7:11–18), and all grain offerings placed on the altar were required to be unleavened (see Lev 2:4–11). So this prohibition technically applies to all animal sacrifices since leaven was not permitted on the altar (Lev 2:11).

34:28 Ten Commandments The Hebrew term used here, *asereth haddevarim* (which may be literally rendered as "ten words"), is where the name for the list of laws in Ex 20:1–21 derives from (see note on 20:1–21)—the Ten Commandments. However, the commands given in 34:11–26 do not align exactly with the commandments listed in ch. 20 or Dt 5.

34:29–35 Moses comes down from Mount Sinai, and his face is radiant. This passage uses imagery that is heavily symbolic for its ancient Near Eastern context. A distinctive radiance was associated with divinity, and deities were thought to share this attribute with their chosen earthly representatives, often royalty.

34:29 radiant The Hebrew verb used here, *qaran*, is rare. It likely should be understood as a reference to shining, even though it derives from a word that describes having horns. The interpretation of *qaran* as a verb for shining derives from Hab 3:4 where the poetic parallelism associates the Hebrew word *qarnayim* (which may be literally rendered as "two horns") with bright light. In the NT, the apostle Paul understood this passage as a reference to Moses' face being radiant (2Co 3:7). In the ancient Latin translation, the Vulgate, the Hebrew consonants here in Ex 34:29 were understood as *qeren*

(not *qaran*), resulting in the translation that Moses had horns after he descended from the mountain. This reading has influenced certain artistic depictions of Moses, including a sculpture by Michelangelo.

34:33 veil This veil (*masweh* in Hebrew) acts as a boundary between Moses and the people in perpetuity. The only time he will remove it, unveiling his face, is when he speaks with Yahweh and relays his message to the people.

35:1–29 The description of the construction of the tabernacle begins here with Moses reminding the people of the Sabbath regulations (vv. 1–3). In vv. 4–29, Moses tells the people to bring the materials needed for construction of the tabernacle and its furnishings. The catalog of materials is derived from Yahweh's detailed instructions given to Moses in chs. 25–31. In chs. 35–39, the Israelite craftsmen named in 31:1–11 construct the tabernacle and all of the sacred items detailed earlier.

The account of the work is extremely detailed, narrating the execution of the instructions from chs. 25–30 item by item. The careful mention of every detail, despite the resultant repetition of earlier material, serves to emphasize how the work was completed precisely as instructed. The narrative from 36:8 to 39:32 presents little new information as it painstakingly details the work being carried out according to Yahweh's explicit instructions. The tabernacle itself is constructed in ch. 36. The fabrication of the tabernacle furniture and its utensils follows in chs. 37–38. The priestly garments are made in ch. 39. The account culminates in ch. 40 with the assembly and consecration of the tabernacle. See the table "Tabernacle Materials and Equipment" on p. 141.

35:3 Do not light a fire The Israelites must cook their supply of manna the night before the Sabbath (see 16:23; compare Nu 11:8). Cooking on the Sabbath was forbidden.

Everyone who is willing is to bring to the LORD an offering of gold, silver and bronze; [6]blue, purple and scarlet yarn and fine linen; goat hair; [7]ram skins dyed red and another type of durable leather[a]; acacia wood; [8]olive oil for the light; spices for the anointing oil and for the fragrant incense; [9]and onyx stones and other gems to be mounted on the ephod and breastpiece.

[10]"All who are skilled among you are to come and make everything the LORD has commanded: [11]the tabernacle with its tent and its covering, clasps, frames, crossbars, posts and bases; [12]the ark with its poles and the atonement cover and the curtain that shields it; [13]the table with its poles and all its articles and the bread of the Presence; [14]the lampstand that is for light with its accessories, lamps and oil for the light; [15]the altar of incense with its poles, the anointing oil and the fragrant incense; the curtain for the doorway at the entrance to the tabernacle; [16]the altar of burnt offering with its bronze grating, its poles and all its utensils; the bronze basin with its stand; [17]the curtains of the courtyard with its posts and bases, and the curtain for the entrance to the courtyard; [18]the tent pegs for the tabernacle and for the courtyard, and their ropes; [19]the woven garments worn for ministering in the sanctuary — both the sacred garments for Aaron the priest and the garments for his sons when they serve as priests."

[20]Then the whole Israelite community withdrew from Moses' presence, [21]and everyone who was willing and whose heart moved them came and brought an offering to the LORD for the work on the tent of meeting, for all its service, and for the sacred garments. [22]All who were willing, men and women alike, came and brought gold jewelry of all kinds: brooches, earrings, rings and ornaments. They all presented their gold as a wave offering to the LORD. [23]Everyone who had blue, purple or scarlet yarn or fine linen, or goat hair, ram skins dyed red or the other durable leather

brought them. [24]Those presenting an offering of silver or bronze brought it as an offering to the LORD, and everyone who had acacia wood for any part of the work brought it. [25]Every skilled woman spun with her hands and brought what she had spun — blue, purple or scarlet yarn or fine linen. [26]And all the women who were willing and had the skill spun the goat hair. [27]The leaders brought onyx stones and other gems to be mounted on the ephod and breastpiece. [28]They also brought spices and olive oil for the light and for the anointing oil and for the fragrant incense. [29]All the Israelite men and women who were willing brought to the LORD freewill offerings for all the work the LORD through Moses had commanded them to do.

Bezalel and Oholiab

35:30-35pp — Ex 31:2-6

[30]Then Moses said to the Israelites, "See, the LORD has chosen Bezalel son of Uri, the son of Hur, of the tribe of Judah, [31]and he has filled him with the Spirit of God, with wisdom, with understanding, with knowledge and with all kinds of skills — [32]to make artistic designs for work in gold, silver and bronze, [33]to cut and set stones, to work in wood and to engage in all kinds of artistic crafts. [34]And he has given both him and Oholiab son of Ahisamak, of the tribe of Dan, the ability to teach others. [35]He has filled them with skill to do all kinds of work as engravers, designers, embroiderers in blue, purple and scarlet yarn and fine linen, and weavers — all of them skilled workers and designers. [1]So Bezalel, Oholiab and every skilled person to whom the LORD has given skill and ability to know how to carry out all the work of constructing the sanctuary are to do the work just as the LORD has commanded."

[2]Then Moses summoned Bezalel and Oholiab

36

---

[a] 7 Possibly the hides of large aquatic mammals; also in verse 23

35:5 who is willing The qualification that people give willingly is key to understanding the significance of this building project for the community. The tabernacle was not constructed by forceful means, such as taxation or confiscation. At a later time a tax will be levied for maintenance (Ex 30:11–16).

35:9 ephod and breastpiece See note on 25:7.

35:19 garments Special garments marked the priests, and especially the high priest. Priestly garments were associated with social status.

35:21 whose heart moved them A similar phenomenon happens in Ezra when God stirs the spirit of both King Cyrus and a group of Judeans, in order to rebuild the temple (Ezr 1:1,5). Both instances — the tabernacle construction and the return to the land — are united by the fact that this movement in the spirit results in financial and material support for the erection of the divine dwelling.

35:22 gold jewelry Presumably gold items received or plundered in Egypt (Ex 12:35–36) that were not used for the golden calf (32:2–3).

35:26 spun the goat hair The goats' hair was to be spun into a type of wool, which was then woven into eleven curtains (25:4; 26:7–14).

35:29 freewill offerings An offering given on occasion and out of devotion rather than for an expressed purpose (e.g., guilt, peace, sin; Lev 7:16).

35:30 — 36:38 The account of the building of the tabernacle begins with Moses' call to Bezalel, Oholiab and the other craftsmen (Ex 35:30–35). These men receive the materials in 36:1–7 and construct the tabernacle structure in 36:8–38, following the instructions from ch. 26.

35:34 the ability to teach For these two men, being filled with skill and knowledge came with an innate responsibility to teach others, that more people may take part in the work of fulfilling God's plan as it was revealed to Moses in 25:8–9.

36:1–7 As a prelude to the actual construction of the tabernacle, this passage describes the people's response

and every skilled person to whom the LORD had given ability and who was willing to come and do the work. ³They received from Moses all the offerings the Israelites had brought to carry out the work of constructing the sanctuary. And the people continued to bring freewill offerings morning after morning. ⁴So all the skilled workers who were doing all the work on the sanctuary left what they were doing ⁵and said to Moses, "The people are bringing more than enough for doing the work the LORD commanded to be done."

⁶Then Moses gave an order and they sent this word throughout the camp: "No man or woman is to make anything else as an offering for the sanctuary." And so the people were restrained from bringing more, ⁷because what they already had was more than enough to do all the work.

The Tabernacle

36:8-38pp — Ex 26:1-37

⁸All those who were skilled among the workers made the tabernacle with ten curtains of finely twisted linen and blue, purple and scarlet yarn, with cherubim woven into them by expert hands. ⁹All the curtains were the same size — twenty-eight cubits long and four cubits wide.ᵃ ¹⁰They joined five of the curtains together and did the same with the other five. ¹¹Then they made loops of blue material along the edge of the end curtain in one set, and the same was done with the end curtain in the other set. ¹²They also made fifty loops on one curtain and fifty loops on the end curtain of the other set, with the loops opposite each other. ¹³Then they made fifty gold clasps and used them to fasten the two sets of curtains together so that the tabernacle was a unit.

¹⁴They made curtains of goat hair for the tent over the tabernacle — eleven altogether. ¹⁵All eleven curtains were the same size — thirty cubits long and four cubits wide.ᵇ ¹⁶They joined five of the curtains into one set and the other six into another set. ¹⁷Then they made fifty loops along the edge of the end curtain in one set and also along the edge of the end curtain in the other set.

¹⁸They made fifty bronze clasps to fasten the tent together as a unit. ¹⁹Then they made for the tent a covering of ram skins dyed red, and over that a covering of the other durable leather.ᶜ

²⁰They made upright frames of acacia wood for the tabernacle. ²¹Each frame was ten cubits long and a cubit and a half wide,ᵈ ²²with two projections set parallel to each other. They made all the frames of the tabernacle in this way. ²³They made twenty frames for the south side of the tabernacle ²⁴and made forty silver bases to go under them — two bases for each frame, one under each projection. ²⁵For the other side, the north side of the tabernacle, they made twenty frames ²⁶and forty silver bases — two under each frame. ²⁷They made six frames for the far end, that is, the west end of the tabernacle, ²⁸and two frames were made for the corners of the tabernacle at the far end. ²⁹At these two corners the frames were double from the bottom all the way to the top and fitted into a single ring; both were made alike. ³⁰So there were eight frames and sixteen silver bases — two under each frame.

³¹They also made crossbars of acacia wood: five for the frames on one side of the tabernacle, ³²five for those on the other side, and five for the frames on the west, at the far end of the tabernacle. ³³They made the center crossbar so that it extended from end to end at the middle of the frames. ³⁴They overlaid the frames with gold and made gold rings to hold the crossbars. They also overlaid the crossbars with gold.

³⁵They made the curtain of blue, purple and scarlet yarn and finely twisted linen, with cherubim woven into it by a skilled worker. ³⁶They made four posts of acacia wood for it and overlaid them with gold. They made gold hooks for them and cast their four silver bases. ³⁷For the entrance to the tent they made a curtain of blue, purple

---

ᵃ *9 That is, about 42 feet long and 6 feet wide or about 13 meters long and 1.8 meters wide*   ᵇ *15 That is, about 45 feet long and 6 feet wide or about 14 meters long and 1.8 meters wide*   ᶜ *19 Possibly the hides of large aquatic mammals (see 35:7)*   ᵈ *21 That is, about 15 feet long and 2 1/4 feet wide or about 4.5 meters long and 68 centimeters wide*

---

to Moses' call for contributions for the tabernacle (35:4–29). The skilled workers now arrive, and those who were so inclined bring their contributions. This echoes much of 35:20–29, but with one major difference — here, Moses must command the people to stop bringing contributions because the amount of donated material is more than sufficient, to the point of overwhelming.

36:1 sanctuary Refers to the tabernacle and its furnishings. Compare 25:8.

36:6 people were restrained The Israelite people were so enthusiastic and generous that Moses had to command them to stop giving.

36:8–38 The description of Bezalel's construction of the tabernacle matches the description in ch. 26 precisely.

See note on 35:1–29. See the infographic "The Tabernacle" on p. 138.

36:8 cherubim Refers to supernatural or angelic beings that were regularly depicted in the ancient Near East with a composite of bovine, bird and human attributes (compare Eze 1:5–10; 10:1–15).

36:11 loops These were added to the edge of the curtains in order to hold the clasps that would connect the panels to one another. The row of loops and clasps would then be draped over the tent poles.

36:18 bronze clasps The clasps for holding together the inner curtains of the tent are made of the most precious metal, gold (Ex 36:13). The clasps for these outer curtains are bronze.

36:20 upright frames These wooden frames are the

and scarlet yarn and finely twisted linen — the work of an embroiderer; [38] and they made five posts with hooks for them. They overlaid the tops of the posts and their bands with gold and made their five bases of bronze.

The Ark

37:1-9pp — Ex 25:10-20

37 Bezalel made the ark of acacia wood — two and a half cubits long, a cubit and a half wide, and a cubit and a half high.[a] [2] He overlaid it with pure gold, both inside and out, and made a gold molding around it. [3] He cast four gold rings for it and fastened them to its four feet, with two rings on one side and two rings on the other. [4] Then he made poles of acacia wood and overlaid them with gold. [5] And he inserted the poles into the rings on the sides of the ark to carry it.

[6] He made the atonement cover of pure gold — two and a half cubits long and a cubit and a half wide. [7] Then he made two cherubim out of hammered gold at the ends of the cover. [8] He made one cherub on one end and the second cherub on the other; at the two ends he made them of one piece with the cover. [9] The cherubim had their wings spread upward, overshadowing the cover with them. The cherubim faced each other, looking toward the cover.

The Table

37:10-16pp — Ex 25:23-29

[10] They[b] made the table of acacia wood — two cubits long, a cubit wide and a cubit and a half high.[c] [11] Then they overlaid it with pure gold and made a gold molding around it. [12] They also made around it a rim a handbreadth[d] wide and put a gold molding on the rim. [13] They cast four gold rings for the table and fastened them to the four corners, where the four legs were. [14] The rings were put close to the rim to hold the poles used in carrying the table. [15] The poles for carrying the table were made of acacia wood and were overlaid with gold. [16] And they made from pure gold the articles for the table — its plates and dishes and bowls and its pitchers for the pouring out of drink offerings.

The Lampstand

37:17-24pp — Ex 25:31-39

[17] They made the lampstand of pure gold. They hammered out its base and shaft, and made its flowerlike cups, buds and blossoms of one piece with them. [18] Six branches extended from the sides of the lampstand — three on one side and three on the other. [19] Three cups shaped like almond flowers with buds and blossoms were on one branch, three on the next branch and the same for all six branches extending from the lampstand. [20] And on the lampstand were four cups shaped like almond flowers with buds and blossoms. [21] One bud was under the first pair of branches extending from the lampstand, a second bud under the second pair, and a third bud under the third pair — six branches in all. [22] The buds and the branches were all of one piece with the lampstand, hammered out of pure gold.

[23] They made its seven lamps, as well as its wick trimmers and trays, of pure gold. [24] They made the lampstand and all its accessories from one talent[e] of pure gold.

---

[a] *1* That is, about 3 3/4 feet long and 2 1/4 feet wide and high or about 1.1 meters long and 68 centimeters wide and high; similarly in verse 6   [b] *10* Or *He*; also in verses 11-29   [c] *10* That is, about 3 feet long, 1 1/2 feet wide and 2 1/4 feet high or about 90 centimeters long, 45 centimeters wide and 68 centimeters high   [d] *12* That is, about 3 inches or about 7.5 centimeters   [e] *24* That is, about 75 pounds or about 34 kilograms

---

main structural pieces for the tabernacle. See note on 26:15.

37:1–9 The design for the ark is initially communicated in Ex 25:10–22. In this passage, Bezalel makes the ark exactly as instructed in ch. 25. The ark of the covenant, as described in this passage and elsewhere, is comparable in design to the thrones associated with deities and, sometimes, royalty throughout the ancient Near East (e.g., 1Ki 10:18–20). The defining features are the seat atop the ark itself, and the cherubim that flank either side. The purpose of the design being similar is likely to show that Yahweh is truly and ultimately king of Israel and over all creation — not any person or god. The seat itself also contains no idol, which signals that Yahweh is not worshiped like other gods. See the infographic "The Ark of the Covenant" on p. 412.

37:7 two cherubim Spiritual beings with composite human, bird and bovine features. In the ancient Near East, these beings were guardians of a deity's throne.

37:10–16 The design for this table was given in 25:23–30. See the infographic "Furnishings of the Tabernacle" on p. 136.

37:15 poles for carrying Like the ark of the covenant (25:12–15; 37:1–9), the table is made to be carried with poles, not touched.

37:16 dishes This is one of two places where incense offerings are made within the tabernacle. There is also an altar of incense in the same room of the tabernacle (see vv. 25–29).

37:17–24 The lampstand described in 25:31–40 is now made, probably by Bezalel (v. 1; see 31:2). See note on 25:31.

37:19 shaped like almond flowers See note on 25:33.

37:22 all of one piece Even with modern tools, this would be an incredible feat, especially given the fact that the lampstand and its accessories were to weigh a total of one talent (75 pounds or 34 kilograms; see 25:36,39; 37:24).

The Altar of Incense

37:25-28pp — Ex 30:1-5

[25]They made the altar of incense out of acacia wood. It was square, a cubit long and a cubit wide and two cubits high[a] — its horns of one piece with it. [26]They overlaid the top and all the sides and the horns with pure gold, and made a gold molding around it. [27]They made two gold rings below the molding — two on each of the opposite sides — to hold the poles used to carry it. [28]They made the poles of acacia wood and overlaid them with gold.

[29]They also made the sacred anointing oil and the pure, fragrant incense — the work of a perfumer.

The Altar of Burnt Offering

38:1-7pp — Ex 27:1-8

38 They[b] built the altar of burnt offering of acacia wood, three cubits[c] high; it was square, five cubits long and five cubits wide.[d] [2]They made a horn at each of the four corners, so that the horns and the altar were of one piece, and they overlaid the altar with bronze. [3]They made all its utensils of bronze — its pots, shovels, sprinkling bowls, meat forks and firepans. [4]They made a grating for the altar, a bronze network, to be under its ledge, halfway up the altar. [5]They cast bronze rings to hold the poles for the four corners of the bronze grating. [6]They made the poles of acacia wood and overlaid them with bronze. [7]They inserted the poles into the rings so they would be on the sides of the altar for carrying it. They made it hollow, out of boards.

The Basin for Washing

[8]They made the bronze basin and its bronze stand from the mirrors of the women who served at the entrance to the tent of meeting.

The Courtyard

38:9-20pp — Ex 27:9-19

[9]Next they made the courtyard. The south side was a hundred cubits[e] long and had curtains of finely twisted linen, [10]with twenty posts and twenty bronze bases, and with silver hooks and bands on the posts. [11]The north side was also a hundred cubits long and had twenty posts and twenty bronze bases, with silver hooks and bands on the posts.

[12]The west end was fifty cubits[f] wide and had curtains, with ten posts and ten bases, with silver hooks and bands on the posts. [13]The east end, toward the sunrise, was also fifty cubits wide. [14]Curtains fifteen cubits[g] long were on one side of the entrance, with three posts and three bases, [15]and curtains fifteen cubits long were on the other side of the entrance to the courtyard, with three posts and three bases. [16]All the curtains around the courtyard were of finely twisted linen. [17]The bases for the posts were bronze. The hooks and bands on the posts were silver, and their tops were overlaid with silver; so all the posts of the courtyard had silver bands.

[18]The curtain for the entrance to the courtyard was made of blue, purple and scarlet yarn and finely twisted linen — the work of an embroiderer. It was twenty cubits[h] long and, like the curtains of the courtyard, five cubits[i] high, [19]with four posts

---

[a] 25 That is, about 1 1/2 feet long and wide and 3 feet high or about 45 centimeters long and wide and 90 centimeters high   [b] 1 Or *He*; also in verses 2-9   [c] 1 That is, about 4 1/2 feet or about 1.4 meters   [d] 1 That is, about 7 1/2 feet or about 2.3 meters long and wide   [e] 9 That is, about 150 feet or about 45 meters   [f] 12 That is, about 75 feet or about 23 meters   [g] 14 That is, about 22 feet or about 6.8 meters   [h] 18 That is, about 30 feet or about 9 meters   [i] 18 That is, about 7 1/2 feet or about 2.3 meters

---

37:25–29 This altar of incense was placed before the veil that divided the Holy Place and the Most Holy Place or Holy of Holies (40:26). The smoke from the incense, in addition to the veil, further obscured visibility so that a priest working within the Holy Place would not see the presence of Yahweh behind the veil, in the Most Holy Place. See the table "Tabernacle Materials and Equipment." on p. 141.

37:25 the altar of incense See 30:1–10 and note. **acacia wood** Since this altar had a wooden core, it is likely the incense was not burned directly upon it, but in a bowl that rested between its horns.

38:1–7 The instructions for the bronze altar are given in 27:1–8. In this passage, the altar is constructed in conformity with those instructions. See note on 27:1–8. See the infographic "Ancient Altars" on p. 127; see the table "Altars in the Old Testament" on p. 249.

38:1 acacia wood Since the altar is wood overlaid with bronze, the hollow core was probably filled with earth to give the altar structural stability. This would also allow the bronze altar to conform with the requirement of 20:24. **38:7 hollow, out of boards** The weight of Israel's largest sacrifice, the bull, would be anywhere between 1,100–2,200 pounds (or 500–1,000 kilograms). A hollow altar probably could not have supported this weight; therefore, the animal was butchered as part of the sacrificial process (Lev 1:6).

38:8 bronze basin Instructions for the bronze basin appear in Ex 30:17–21. Little information is given about the design or construction of the piece itself. The text here and in ch. 30 focuses on the function of the basin. **mirrors** Ancient mirrors were not glass, but highly polished discs of copper or bronze, fitted with handles of a variety of costly materials. **women** Nothing is known about this group of women, identified in the Hebrew text in this verse as *tsove'oth*. Similar language is used to describe Levites in the sense that they are qualified to serve as part of the temple workforce (Nu 4:23), so it follows that these women may have worked on behalf of the tabernacle in some capacity.

38:9–20 The plan for the court of the tabernacle is first described in Ex 27:9–19. Now the materials for the courtyard enclosure are constructed. See note on 27:9–19. See the infographic "The Tabernacle" on p. 138; see the table "Tabernacle Materials and Equipment" on p. 141.

and four bronze bases. Their hooks and bands were silver, and their tops were overlaid with silver. 20All the tent pegs of the tabernacle and of the surrounding courtyard were bronze.

The Materials Used

21These are the amounts of the materials used for the tabernacle, the tabernacle of the covenant law, which were recorded at Moses' command by the Levites under the direction of Ithamar son of Aaron, the priest. 22(Bezalel son of Uri, the son of Hur, of the tribe of Judah, made everything the LORD commanded Moses; 23with him was Oholiab son of Ahisamak, of the tribe of Dan—an engraver and designer, and an embroiderer in blue, purple and scarlet yarn and fine linen.) 24The total amount of the gold from the wave offering used for all the work on the sanctuary was 29 talents and 730 shekels,a according to the sanctuary shekel.
25The silver obtained from those of the community who were counted in the census was 100 talentsb and 1,775 shekels,c according to the sanctuary shekel— 26one beka per person, that is, half a shekel,d according to the sanctuary shekel, from everyone who had crossed over to those counted, twenty years old or more, a total of 603,550 men. 27The 100 talents of silver were used to cast the bases for the sanctuary and for the curtain—100 bases from the 100 talents, one talent for each base. 28They used the 1,775 shekels to make the hooks for the posts, to overlay the tops of the posts, and to make their bands.
29The bronze from the wave offering was 70 talents and 2,400 shekels.e 30They used it to make the bases for the entrance to the tent of meeting, the bronze altar with its bronze grating and all its utensils, 31the bases for the surrounding courtyard and those for its entrance and all the tent pegs for the tabernacle and those for the surrounding courtyard.

The Priestly Garments

39 From the blue, purple and scarlet yarn they made woven garments for ministering in the sanctuary. They also made sacred garments for Aaron, as the LORD commanded Moses.

The Ephod

39:2-7pp—Ex 28:6-14

2Theyf made the ephod of gold, and of blue, purple and scarlet yarn, and of finely twisted linen. 3They hammered out thin sheets of gold and cut strands to be worked into the blue, purple and scarlet yarn and fine linen—the work of skilled hands. 4They made shoulder pieces for the ephod, which were attached to two of its corners, so it could be fastened. 5Its skillfully woven waistband was like it—of one piece with the ephod and made with gold, and with blue, purple and scarlet yarn, and with finely twisted linen, as the LORD commanded Moses.
6They mounted the onyx stones in gold filigree

---

a 24 The weight of the gold was a little over a ton or about 1 metric ton.   b 25 That is, about 3 3/4 tons or about 3.4 metric tons; also in verse 27   c 25 That is, about 44 pounds or about 20 kilograms; also in verse 28   d 26 That is, about 1/5 ounce or about 5.7 grams   e 29 The weight of the bronze was about 2 1/2 tons or about 2.4 metric tons.   f 2 Or He; also in verses 7, 8 and 22

38:21–31 These verses present a catalog of all of the materials used for the construction of the tabernacle, Israel's tent shrine. The quantities of gold, silver and bronze used for the project total more than seven tons of precious metals (vv. 24–29). All of the architectural and furniture elements listed here are described in more detail in the previous chapters (25:1—30:38; 35:1–38:19). This closes the account of the tabernacle construction proper (see note on 35:1–29).

38:21 Levites Members of the tribe of Levi. Levites were assigned the duties of erecting, disassembling and transporting the tabernacle during the wilderness journey (Nu 3–4).
38:22 made everything the LORD commanded The work was completed according to the instructions found in Ex 25–30.
38:24 offering This refers to the freewill offering mentioned in 35:29. **talents** A unit of weight used for metals exchanged as currency. One talent was approximately 75 pounds (34 kilograms). **shekels** A unit of weight for weighing metals as currency. One silver shekel weighed approximately 2/5 of an ounce or 11–13 grams.
38:26 beka A unit of weight measuring 1/5 of an ounce or 5.5 grams. **everyone** Official records were often kept in temples and other sacred spaces in the ancient Near East, as many priests often doubled as scribes. **603,550**

The numbers given here and elsewhere in the narratives of the exodus and subsequent wilderness wanderings are logistically problematic. See note on Nu 1:46.
38:30 tent of meeting In this context, this likely refers to the tabernacle. See note on Ex 27:21.

39:1–43 The priestly garments described in ch. 28 are now made, presumably under the supervision of Oholiab, the person chosen by God for his skill in engraving, design, and embroidery (38:23). These garments set the priests and high priest apart as ministers of the tabernacle.

39:1 sanctuary Refers to the first internal chamber of the tabernacle.
39:2 ephod A robe or tunic for the upper body to waist level. See note on 28:4.
39:3 thin sheets of gold Thin sheets of gold used for overlay and other fine work; low quality gold leaf can be found in modern craft stores. These sheets are about as thin as a leaf and fairly small.
39:4 shoulder pieces See 28:7 and note.
39:6 onyx The Hebrew term used here, *shoham*, refers to a gem of some kind. Possibilities include onyx and lapis lazuli. **names of the sons of Israel** Exodus 28:10 specifies that these names are the names of the 12 tribes, and are to be engraved in order of the birth of the sons of Jacob who fathered the tribes (see Ge 29:31—30:24).

settings and engraved them like a seal with the names of the sons of Israel. [7]Then they fastened them on the shoulder pieces of the ephod as memorial stones for the sons of Israel, as the LORD commanded Moses.

The Breastpiece

39:8-21pp — Ex 28:15-28

[8]They fashioned the breastpiece — the work of a skilled craftsman. They made it like the ephod: of gold, and of blue, purple and scarlet yarn, and of finely twisted linen. [9]It was square — a span[a] long and a span wide — and folded double. [10]Then they mounted four rows of precious stones on it. The first row was carnelian, chrysolite and beryl; [11]the second row was turquoise, lapis lazuli and emerald; [12]the third row was jacinth, agate and amethyst; [13]the fourth row was topaz, onyx and jasper.[b] They were mounted in gold filigree settings. [14]There were twelve stones, one for each of the names of the sons of Israel, each engraved like a seal with the name of one of the twelve tribes.

[15]For the breastpiece they made braided chains of pure gold, like a rope. [16]They made two gold filigree settings and two gold rings, and fastened the rings to two of the corners of the breastpiece. [17]They fastened the two gold chains to the rings at the corners of the breastpiece, [18]and the other ends of the chains to the two settings, attaching them to the shoulder pieces of the ephod at the front. [19]They made two gold rings and attached them to the other two corners of the breastpiece on the inside edge next to the ephod. [20]Then they made two more gold rings and attached them to the bottom of the shoulder pieces on the front of the ephod, close to the seam just above the waistband of the ephod. [21]They tied the rings of the breastpiece to the rings of the ephod with blue cord, connecting it to the waistband so that the breastpiece would not swing out from the ephod — as the LORD commanded Moses.

Other Priestly Garments

39:22-31pp — Ex 28:31-43

[22]They made the robe of the ephod entirely of blue cloth — the work of a weaver — [23]with an opening in the center of the robe like the opening of a collar,[c] and a band around this opening, so that it would not tear. [24]They made pomegranates of blue, purple and scarlet yarn and finely twisted linen around the hem of the robe. [25]And they made bells of pure gold and attached them around the hem between the pomegranates. [26]The bells and pomegranates alternated around the hem of the robe to be worn for ministering, as the LORD commanded Moses.

[27]For Aaron and his sons, they made tunics of fine linen — the work of a weaver — [28]and the turban of fine linen, the linen caps and the undergarments of finely twisted linen. [29]The sash was made of finely twisted linen and blue, purple and scarlet yarn — the work of an embroiderer — as the LORD commanded Moses.

[30]They made the plate, the sacred emblem, out of pure gold and engraved on it, like an inscription on a seal: HOLY TO THE LORD. [31]Then they fastened a blue cord to it to attach it to the turban, as the LORD commanded Moses.

Moses Inspects the Tabernacle

39:32-41pp — Ex 35:10-19

[32]So all the work on the tabernacle, the tent of meeting, was completed. The Israelites did everything just as the LORD commanded Moses. [33]Then they brought the tabernacle to Moses: the tent and all its furnishings, its clasps, frames, crossbars, posts and bases; [34]the covering of ram skins dyed red and the covering of another durable leather[d] and the shielding curtain; [35]the ark of the covenant law with its poles and the atonement cover;

---

[a] 9 That is, about 9 inches or about 23 centimeters
[b] 13 The precise identification of some of these precious stones is uncertain.   [c] 23 The meaning of the Hebrew for this word is uncertain.   [d] 34 Possibly the hides of large aquatic mammals

---

39:7 memorial The names engraved on this garment served as a constant reminder of Israel's covenantal relationship with Yahweh.
39:8 breastpiece Worn over the chest and thus over the ephod. See note on Ex 28:15.
39:10 precious stones Precise identifications of these gemstones are unknown. See note on 28:17.
39:22 robe of the ephod The main garment worn under the ephod. See note on 28:31.
39:24 pomegranates Symbolizing abundance (Dt 8:8). The columns in Solomon's temple were decorated with pomegranate figures (1Ki 7:18,20,42; Jer 52:22–23). See note on 28:33.
39:28 undergarments of finely twisted linen These garments served to cover the priests lest they improperly expose themselves in the course of carrying out their duties. See note on Ex 28:42.

39:32–43 This passage summarizes all of the work of the tabernacle, which Moses assembles and consecrates in ch. 40. Similar catalogs are to be found in 25:1–9; 35:4–29; 38:21–31. Each of these items is described in more detail in chs. 25–30; 35–39.

39:32 all the work on the tabernacle All that was commanded in chs. 25–31 and completed in chs. 35–39. See the infographic "The Tabernacle" on p. 138.
39:33 brought the tabernacle to Moses Since Bezalel and Oholiab were chosen by Yahweh and filled with his spirit (31:3; 35:31), Moses did not need to supervise. Here, they present the items to Moses because it is Moses who will assemble the tabernacle (ch. 40). Upon his inspection, Moses sees that the people have done exactly as Yahweh commanded (39:43).

³⁶the table with all its articles and the bread of the Presence; ³⁷the pure gold lampstand with its row of lamps and all its accessories, and the olive oil for the light; ³⁸the gold altar, the anointing oil, the fragrant incense, and the curtain for the entrance to the tent; ³⁹the bronze altar with its bronze grating, its poles and all its utensils; the basin with its stand; ⁴⁰the curtains of the courtyard with its posts and bases, and the curtain for the entrance to the courtyard; the ropes and tent pegs for the courtyard; all the furnishings for the tabernacle, the tent of meeting; ⁴¹and the woven garments worn for ministering in the sanctuary, both the sacred garments for Aaron the priest and the garments for his sons when serving as priests.

⁴²The Israelites had done all the work just as the LORD had commanded Moses. ⁴³Moses inspected the work and saw that they had done it just as the LORD had commanded. So Moses blessed them.

Setting Up the Tabernacle

40 Then the LORD said to Moses: ²"Set up the tabernacle, the tent of meeting, on the first day of the first month. ³Place the ark of the covenant law in it and shield the ark with the curtain. ⁴Bring in the table and set out what belongs on it. Then bring in the lampstand and set up its lamps. ⁵Place the gold altar of incense in front of the ark of the covenant law and put the curtain at the entrance to the tabernacle.

⁶"Place the altar of burnt offering in front of the entrance to the tabernacle, the tent of meeting; ⁷place the basin between the tent of meeting and the altar and put water in it. ⁸Set up the courtyard around it and put the curtain at the entrance to the courtyard.

⁹"Take the anointing oil and anoint the tabernacle and everything in it; consecrate it and all its furnishings, and it will be holy. ¹⁰Then anoint the altar of burnt offering and all its utensils; consecrate the altar, and it will be most holy. ¹¹Anoint the basin and its stand and consecrate them.

¹²"Bring Aaron and his sons to the entrance to the tent of meeting and wash them with water. ¹³Then dress Aaron in the sacred garments, anoint him and consecrate him so he may serve me as priest. ¹⁴Bring his sons and dress them in tunics. ¹⁵Anoint them just as you anointed their father, so they may serve me as priests. Their anointing will be to a priesthood that will continue throughout their generations." ¹⁶Moses did everything just as the LORD commanded him.

¹⁷So the tabernacle was set up on the first day of the first month in the second year. ¹⁸When Moses set up the tabernacle, he put the bases in place, erected the frames, inserted the crossbars and set up the posts. ¹⁹Then he spread the tent over the tabernacle and put the covering over the tent, as the LORD commanded him.

²⁰He took the tablets of the covenant law and placed them in the ark, attached the poles to the ark and put the atonement cover over it. ²¹Then he brought the ark into the tabernacle and hung

---

39:38 gold altar Refers to the small altar stationed in front of the veil leading to the Most Holy Place, where the ark of the covenant was kept. See note on 30:1–10. **anointing oil** The recipe for this oil and the details regarding its use are found in 30:22–33. **fragrant incense** The composition of the incense is detailed in 30:34–38.
39:40 furnishings for the tabernacle For example, the pots and shovels for the bronze altar (27:3–4).
39:41 garments The priestly garments that were described in ch. 28 and fabricated, with a few variations, in vv. 1–31.
39:42 LORD had commanded Moses Confirms the work had been completed according to the instructions given in chs. 25–31.

40:1–38 Moses is the one Yahweh chooses to assemble the tabernacle once its component parts are finished, presented to him, and inspected (39:33,42–43). Since Moses is the only one to whom Yahweh shows the pattern of the tabernacle (25:8–9), Moses is the one who must do the work. He is also tasked with the tabernacle's anointing and consecration (40:9), since the priests are not yet capable of doing so (Lev 8). This chapter is divided into three sections: the first portion records Yahweh's command to Moses (Ex 40:1–15), the second records Moses' completion of the tasks (vv. 16–33) and the closing verses record Yahweh's response (vv. 34–38).
40:2 first day of the first month This marks one year since the people were commanded regarding Passover (see 12:2 and note).

40:8 courtyard around The rectangular fence marking the bounds of the courtyard was 150 feet long and 75 feet wide (for a perimeter of 450 feet).
40:9 consecrate Meaning to set apart for sacred use. Moses is officially designating the tabernacle and all furnishings and utensils for sacred use only.
40:12 wash them with water Bodily hygiene was important in the life of priests throughout the ancient Near East, as the gods did not want to experience the negative aspects of human life. The bronze basin installed in the tabernacle courtyard is designed to meet this need on a regular basis (30:17–21; 38:8). Here, Yahweh is referring to the consecration of the priests as described in ch. 29; Lev 8.

40:16–33 This section records Moses' completion of what Yahweh commands in the previous verses (Ex 40:1–15). Moses assembles the tabernacle, beginning with the Most Holy Place (or Holy of Holies)—the innermost chamber—and works his way outward, ending with the gate of the courtyard walls.

40:17 first day of the first month in the second year At Yahweh's command, the tabernacle is erected one year after the Israelites are warned about the tenth plague (the death of the firstborn) and commanded regarding Passover (12:2; 40:2). The evening after Passover is the evening the people flee from Egypt. Thus, the tabernacle is associated with Israel's freedom from bondage, unto a new life in the presence of Yahweh.

the shielding curtain and shielded the ark of the covenant law, as the LORD commanded him.

²²Moses placed the table in the tent of meeting on the north side of the tabernacle outside the curtain ²³and set out the bread on it before the LORD, as the LORD commanded him.

²⁴He placed the lampstand in the tent of meeting opposite the table on the south side of the tabernacle ²⁵and set up the lamps before the LORD, as the LORD commanded him.

²⁶Moses placed the gold altar in the tent of meeting in front of the curtain ²⁷and burned fragrant incense on it, as the LORD commanded him.

²⁸Then he put up the curtain at the entrance to the tabernacle. ²⁹He set the altar of burnt offering near the entrance to the tabernacle, the tent of meeting, and offered on it burnt offerings and grain offerings, as the LORD commanded him.

³⁰He placed the basin between the tent of meeting and the altar and put water in it for washing, ³¹and Moses and Aaron and his sons used it to wash their hands and feet. ³²They washed whenever they entered the tent of meeting or approached the altar, as the LORD commanded Moses.

³³Then Moses set up the courtyard around the tabernacle and altar and put up the curtain at the entrance to the courtyard. And so Moses finished the work.

The Glory of the LORD

³⁴Then the cloud covered the tent of meeting, and the glory of the LORD filled the tabernacle. ³⁵Moses could not enter the tent of meeting because the cloud had settled on it, and the glory of the LORD filled the tabernacle.

³⁶In all the travels of the Israelites, whenever the cloud lifted from above the tabernacle, they would set out; ³⁷but if the cloud did not lift, they did not set out — until the day it lifted. ³⁸So the cloud of the LORD was over the tabernacle by day, and fire was in the cloud by night, in the sight of all the Israelites during all their travels.

40:34–38 The book of Exodus ends with the presence of Yahweh entering the tabernacle. This brings Israel's relationship with Yahweh to a very different place than where it was when Exodus began. He is no longer far off, hearing his people's cry from a distance (2:23–3:9). He now lives among the people, and his continual presence distinguishes Israel from all the peoples of the earth (33:16). The divine cloud which stood on top of Mount Sinai, which only Moses could enter, now comes to rest on the tabernacle and it is this cloud that will guide the people on their journey into the promised land (vv. 36–38; Nu 10:11–13).

40:34 cloud The presence of Yahweh often appears as a pillar of cloud by day and a pillar of fire by night during Israel's time in the wilderness, but the image of a cloud is used most often (see Ex 13:21–22; 14:19–24; 19:9 and note; 19:16; 24:15–18; 33:9–11; 40:38). The cloud itself is not the presence of Yahweh; Yahweh dwells in the midst of the cloud, while the cloud masks him from view.

40:35 Moses could not enter Moses is able to enter the cloud on other occasions (e.g., 24:18). On this occasion, it was inappropriate for Moses to enter the tabernacle as the rightful owner took possession of his dwelling. The presence of Yahweh filling the entire tabernacle indicated his exclusive ownership.

40:38 in the sight of all the Israelites The cloud and fire have a distinct purpose — to signal to the people that their God is with them continually and to guide them on their journey through the wilderness, toward the promised land.

SHOULD CHRISTIANS FOLLOW OLD TESTAMENT LAW?

by Timothy Keller

Columnists, pundits or journalists often dismiss Christians as inconsistent because "they pick and choose which of the rules in the Bible to obey." The argument proceeds along these lines: "Christians ignore lots of Old Testament texts—about not eating raw meat or pork or shellfish, not executing people for breaking the Sabbath, not wearing garments woven with two kinds of material, and so on. Aren't they just picking and choosing what they want to believe from the Bible?"

The root of the issue is a perceived inconsistency regarding rules mentioned in the Old Testament that are no longer practiced in the New Testament by the people of God. Most Christians don't know how to respond when confronted about this, but the best place to start is often by describing the relationship between the Old Testament and the New Testament.

The Old Testament devotes a good amount of space to describing the various sacrifices that were to be offered in the tabernacle (and later the temple) to atone for sin so that worshipers could approach a holy God. That sacrificial system included a complex set of rules for ceremonial purity and cleanness—you could only approach God in worship if you ate certain foods, wore certain forms of clothing, refrained from touching certain objects, and so on. This code vividly conveyed, over and over, that human beings are spiritually unclean and cannot enter God's presence without purification.

But even in the Old Testament, many passages indicate that the sacrifices and regulations of temple worship point ahead to something beyond them (see 1Sa 15:21–22; Ps 50:12–15; 51:17; Hos 6:6). This "something" was Jesus. Throughout his ministry, Jesus ignored Old Testament regulations regarding purification; he touched lepers and dead bodies, and declared all foods "clean" (Mk 7:19).

The culmination of Jesus' ministry made clear his reason for doing this. When he died on the cross, the veil (curtain) in the temple tore in two, demonstrating that the entire sacrificial system and its ceremonial laws had been done away with (Mt 27:51). It is Jesus, the ultimate sacrifice for sin, not the laws of the Old Testament, that makes us clean now.

The book of Hebrews explains that the Old Testament ceremonial laws were not so much abolished as fulfilled by Christ. Whenever we pray in Jesus' name, we "have confidence to enter the Most Holy Place by the blood of Jesus" (Heb 10:19). As a result, if Christians continued to practice the ceremonial laws, their actions would be deeply inconsistent with the teaching of the Bible as a whole.

The New Testament provides further guidance for reading and understanding the Old Testament. Paul makes clear that the apostles understood the Old Testament moral law to still be binding on us (see Ro 13). In short, the coming of Christ changed how we worship, but not how we live. The moral law outlines God's own character—his integrity, love and faithfulness. Old Testament commandments about loving our neighbor, caring for the poor, being generous with our possessions and being committed to family still apply. The New Testament continues to forbid killing and adultery, and the sexual ethic of the Old Testament is restated throughout the New Testament

(Mt 5:27–30; 1Co 6:9–20; 1Ti 1:8–11). If the New Testament reaffirms an Old Testament commandment, then it continues to have force for us today.

Once you grant the main premise of the Bible—the surpassing significance of Christ and his salvation—then all of the Bible's various parts make sense. Because of Christ, the ceremonial law of the Old Testament is repealed. However, if you reject the idea that Jesus is God's Son and our Savior, then the Bible may contain some insight and wisdom—but most of it would be rejected as foolish or erroneous.

So where does this leave us? There are only two possibilities: If Christ is God, then this way of reading the Bible makes sense and is perfectly consistent with its main premise. If Christ isn't God, then one does not adopt the central proclamation of Christianity, nor can the Bible serve as a guide for much of anything. But the one thing that cannot be said is that Christians are inconsistent to accept the moral statements of the Old Testament while not practicing its ceremonial laws.

One way to respond to the charge of inconsistency may be to ask a counter-question: "Are you asking me to deny the very heart of my Christian beliefs?" If you are asked, "Why do you say that?" you could respond, "If I believe Jesus is the resurrected Son of God, I can't follow all the 'clean laws' of diet and practice, and I can't offer animal sacrifices. All that would be to deny the power of Christ's death on the cross. And so those who really believe in Christ must follow some Old Testament texts and not others."

(This article was adapted from Tim Keller's article, "Old Testament Law and the Change of Inconsistency," originally published in the Redeemer Report.)

LEVITICUS

INTRODUCTION TO LEVITICUS

Leviticus outlines God's covenant expectations. Yahweh and the Hebrew people formally entered into a covenant, a contractual agreement, at Sinai (Ex 24:1–8). As God's chosen people, Israel was expected to live in a way that honored him. While the book of Leviticus elaborates on many laws about rituals and sacrifices, the true focus of the book is holiness—ensuring that the people maintain a community worthy of God's special presence. Holiness means being set apart for a purpose. Maintaining holiness involves having the attitude of respect that God's holiness deserves. In Leviticus, God repeatedly states that his people must be holy because he is holy (e.g., Lev 11:44). Obedience in ritual and ethical matters is essential for the preservation of Israel's holiness. In this way, Leviticus links worship with ethical living.

BACKGROUND

The title, Leviticus, comes from a Greek word that means "having to do with the Levites." The Levites were descendants of Jacob's son Levi and a tribe of Israel (Ge 34; 49:5–7). Moses—the man who led the Hebrew people out of Egypt—was a Levite, as was Moses' brother Aaron. The Levites were responsible for maintaining the tabernacle—the sacred tent where God's presence would dwell among the people.

Leviticus is set during the Israelites' stay at Mount Sinai after the exodus from Egypt (see Ex 19). Most of the book records God explaining his laws to Moses. Many of these laws focus on purity and aim to establish standards for holiness among God's people. Leviticus is the source for what Jesus identifies as the second most important commandment: loving your neighbor as yourself (Lev 19:18; Mt 22:39).

The exact location of Mount Sinai remains uncertain. A variety of locations have been proposed, but the traditional site is Jebel Musa in the southern Sinai Peninsula.

STRUCTURE

Leviticus can be divided into six sections. The first section (Lev 1–7) gives instructions for various sacrifices. The second section (chs. 8–10) narrates the establishment of the priesthood as Aaron and his sons are ordained and God's glory fills the tabernacle, Israel's portable tent-shrine (compare Ex 28–29). In Leviticus 10, two of Aaron's sons are punished for offering worship to God inappropriately. Even the priests need to recognize the importance of obedience in Yahweh's presence. The third section (chs. 11–15) contains regulations about ritual purity and impurity. This section includes the dietary laws about what animals are suitable for food and

what animals must not be eaten (ch. 11). The rules about how to handle skin diseases are also found in this part of Leviticus (chs. 13–14). Jesus acknowledges these laws when he heals a leper, telling the man to visit the priests and follow the proper rituals for purification (Mt 8:1–4).

The fourth section (Lev 16) gives instructions for the annual Day of Atonement, when special sacrifices were offered to cleanse the Israelites of their sins. On this day alone, the high priest could enter the Holy of Holies (Most Holy Place), the inner chamber of the tabernacle. The fifth section (chs. 17–26) is a "holiness code." By following this system of ethics—which reflected God's own holiness—the Israelites confirmed their covenant with God and showed themselves to be his holy people. The sixth section (ch. 27) gives instructions about vows and is patterned more like the earlier chapters of the book (chs. 1–16). It appears to have been placed there to avoid ending the book with the list of curses in Leviticus 26.

OUTLINE

- Laws concerning sacrifices (1:1—7:38)
- The consecration of priests (8:1—10:20)
- Laws concerning purity (11:1—15:33)
- The Day of Atonement (16:1–34)
- Laws concerning holiness (17:1—26:46)
- Laws about vows (27:1–34)

Events in Leviticus

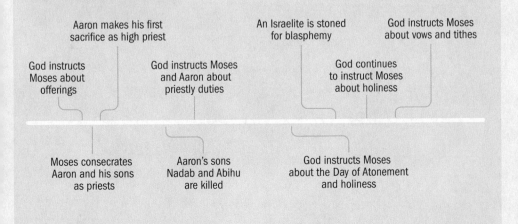

Aaron makes his first sacrifice as high priest

An Israelite is stoned for blasphemy

God instructs Moses about vows and tithes

God instructs Moses about offerings

God instructs Moses and Aaron about priestly duties

God continues to instruct Moses about holiness

Moses consecrates Aaron and his sons as priests

Aaron's sons Nadab and Abihu are killed

God instructs Moses about the Day of Atonement and holiness

THEMES

In Leviticus, holiness is not simply goodness; it refers to being dedicated to God and separated from ordinary things. As a result, much of Leviticus is about setting boundaries—such as the categories of "pure" and "impure." God is holy and separate, yet he invites Israel into relationship. The inner chamber of the tabernacle provides an example of this: Because this sanctuary was God's holy dwelling place, it was dangerous to enter (16:2). However, with an invitation from God, the high priest (representing all of Israel) could enter into God's holy presence and make atonement—signifying that the people are now right before God.

Leviticus contains regulations for Israel for worship and ethics. But it also sets the stage for some of the most important theological developments of the Bible: sacrifice, priesthood and maintaining a right relationship with God himself. Building on the words of the prophets, the New Testament articulates Jesus' death on the cross as an atonement for all of humanity's wrongdoings. This act makes it possible for all believers in Jesus to act as priests ministering to one another—because Jesus himself intercedes today for us as our great high priest in heaven (1Pe 2:5; Heb 4:14–16).

The Burnt Offering

1 The LORD called to Moses and spoke to him from the tent of meeting. He said, 2 "Speak to the Israelites and say to them: 'When anyone among you brings an offering to the LORD, bring as your offering an animal from either the herd or the flock.

3 "'If the offering is a burnt offering from the herd, you are to offer a male without defect. You must present it at the entrance to the tent of meeting so that it will be acceptable to the LORD. 4 You are to lay your hand on the head of the burnt offering, and it will be accepted on your behalf to make atonement for you. 5 You are to slaughter the young bull before the LORD, and then Aaron's sons the priests shall bring the blood and splash it against the sides of the altar at the entrance to the tent of meeting. 6 You are to skin the burnt offering and cut it into pieces. 7 The sons of Aaron the priest are to put fire on the altar and arrange wood on the fire. 8 Then Aaron's sons the priests shall arrange the pieces, including the head and the fat, on the wood that is burning on the altar. 9 You are to wash the internal organs and the legs with water, and the priest is to burn all of it on the altar. It is a burnt offering, a food offering, an aroma pleasing to the LORD.

10 "'If the offering is a burnt offering from the flock, from either the sheep or the goats, you are to

---

1:1–2 The book of Leviticus continues where Exodus left off. Israel is at Mount Sinai and Yahweh's presence has entered the tabernacle (Ex 40:34–38). Leviticus begins with Yahweh instructing Moses on the procedures for sacrifices and offerings that he is to pass on to the people of Israel. The Biblical law given to Israel at Sinai encompasses Ex 20:1—Nu 9:14, including the entire book of Leviticus.

1:1 Moses The intermediary between Yahweh and Israel who receives the law at Sinai (see note on Ex 2:10). **tent of meeting** The Hebrew phrase used here, *ohel mo'ed* (often translated "tent of meeting"), regularly refers to the entire tabernacle complex at the center of the Israelite camp (e.g., Nu 2:2,17). The actual tent of meeting is the tent shrine itself within the tabernacle complex (see Lev 4:4–7). See the infographic "The Tabernacle" on p. 138.

Leviticus 1:1

MOSES
Moses was commissioned by Yahweh to lead his people out of Egypt and bring them to Canaan (see Ge 12:5–7; Ex 1–15), the land that Yahweh had promised to Abraham (see Ge 12:5–7; Ex 1–15). Moses leads Israel for 40 years—until the next generation is on the cusp of entering Canaan (Dt 34:1–8).

1:2 brings an offering to the LORD The Hebrew word used here, *qorban*—often translated "offering" and literally rendered as "gift"—refers generally to anything presented to God when approaching him. **animal** Only domesticated animals were acceptable sacrifices because the offering was meant to be costly for the worshiper (compare 2Sa 24:24).

1:3–17 The first type of sacrifice is called the *olah* in Hebrew—this is often rendered as "burnt offering." The sacrificial animal could be a bull, a ram, a male goat, a turtledove or a pigeon. The procedures for offering the sacrifices are very similar; the only changes regard the birds, since they are smaller animals. Despite the similarity, many of the details are repeated almost verbatim.

The burnt offering (an *olah*) was the most costly type of sacrifice since the entire animal carcass was burned on the altar. A burnt offering was to be offered every morning and evening (Ex 29:38–42).

1:3 burnt offering An offering where the whole sacrificial animal was burned on the altar (Ex 27:1–8). See note on Lev 6:9. See the table "Types of Offerings in the Old Testament" on p. 178. **without defect** The Hebrew adjective used here, *tamim*, refers to something complete and unblemished. See Ex 12:5 and note. **entrance to the tent of meeting** Refers to the open area outside and in front of the tent shrine in the tabernacle. This was the area accessible to laypeople, where they carried out their responsibilities for the sacrificial ritual.

1:4 You are to lay your hand on the head of the burnt offering A symbolic act that acknowledged the relationship between the worshiper and the sacrificial offering. The significance of the symbolism is uncertain. **make atonement** See note on Lev 4:20.

1:5 You are to slaughter the young bull The person bringing the offering slaughtered their own sacrifice. The sacrificial ritual had a clear division of labor between what the worshiper was responsible for and what the priests were responsible for. **before the LORD** The precise location is unspecified, but the entire ritual took place at the entrance of the tent of meeting (v. 3). According to v. 11, the slaughter took place on the north side of the altar. See the table "Functions of Priests" on p. 171. **splash** Sacrificial rituals involved various actions that were to be done with the blood, often sprinkling or pouring the blood on or around the altar (Ex 29:16–20). **altar** Refers to the altar of burnt offering, the large bronze altar in the courtyard of the tabernacle (Ex 27:1–8).

1:6 cut it into pieces The worshiper was generally responsible for skinning the animal and cutting it into pieces that would be placed on the altar.

1:7 fire on the altar and arrange wood The priests were responsible for the altar. Anyone who approached the altar who was not a priest was subject to the death penalty (Nu 18:7).

1:9 You are to wash the internal organs and the legs with water While the priest placed most of the sacrifice on the altar, the worshiper had to wash the animal's hind legs and its entrails, probably to remove the dung (compare Lev 4:11). **food offering** The Hebrew term used here, *isheh*, is commonly associated with the noun *esh*, meaning "fire." This results in the translation of "offering by fire." However, the meaning of *isheh* could be related to cognate terms for "gift" in Arabic (*'atta*) and Ugaritic (*'itt*). Since the translation "offering by fire" is also difficult to support from the general usage of *isheh* in the OT, the word most likely refers to some kind of gift and should probably be understood as referring to a food gift or food offering. **an aroma pleasing** The Hebrew phrase used here, *reach nichoach*, expresses the intended outcome of the sacrifice. The smoke rises up to Yahweh, carrying a smell that satisfies and pleases

offer a male without defect. ¹¹You are to slaughter it at the north side of the altar before the LORD, and Aaron's sons the priests shall splash its blood against the sides of the altar. ¹²You are to cut it into pieces, and the priest shall arrange them, including the head and the fat, on the wood that is burning on the altar. ¹³You are to wash the internal organs and the legs with water, and the priest is to bring all of them and burn them on the altar. It is a burnt offering, a food offering, an aroma pleasing to the LORD.

¹⁴"'If the offering to the LORD is a burnt offering of birds, you are to offer a dove or a young pigeon. ¹⁵The priest shall bring it to the altar, wring off the head and burn it on the altar; its blood shall be drained out on the side of the altar. ¹⁶He is to remove the crop and the feathers[a] and throw them down east of the altar where the ashes are. ¹⁷He shall tear it open by the wings, not dividing it completely, and then the priest shall burn it on the wood that is burning on the altar. It is a burnt offering, a food offering, an aroma pleasing to the LORD.

The Grain Offering

2 "'When anyone brings a grain offering to the LORD, their offering is to be of the finest flour. They are to pour olive oil on it, put incense on it ²and take it to Aaron's sons the priests. The priest shall take a handful of the flour and oil, together with all the incense, and burn this as a memorial[b] portion on the altar, a food offering, an aroma pleasing to the LORD. ³The rest of the grain offering belongs to Aaron and his sons; it is a most holy part of the food offerings presented to the LORD.

⁴"'If you bring a grain offering baked in an oven, it is to consist of the finest flour: either thick loaves made without yeast and with olive oil mixed in or thin loaves made without yeast and brushed with olive oil. ⁵If your grain offering is prepared on a griddle, it is to be made of the finest flour mixed with oil, and without yeast. ⁶Crumble it and pour oil on it; it is a grain offering. ⁷If your grain offering is cooked in a pan, it is to be made of the finest flour and some olive oil. ⁸Bring the grain offering made of these things to the LORD; present it to the priest, who shall take it to the altar. ⁹He shall take out the memorial portion from the grain offering and burn it on the altar as a food offering, an aroma pleasing to the LORD. ¹⁰The rest of the grain offering belongs to Aaron and his sons; it is a most holy part of the food offerings presented to the LORD.

¹¹"'Every grain offering you bring to the LORD must be made without yeast, for you are not to burn any yeast or honey in a food offering pre-

---

[a] 16 Or *crop with its contents*; the meaning of the Hebrew for this word is uncertain.   [b] 2 Or *representative*; also in verses 9 and 16

---

him. The distinction over whether the aroma pleases or appeases Yahweh is significant. Something pleasing Yahweh is much different from something appeasing him. A delight brings enjoyment and pleasure (without reference to wrath). Appeasement refers to allaying his wrath (compare Ge 8:21; Lev 26:31).

1:11 north side of the altar The main difference between the guidelines for the bull and those for a ram or goat is the explicit statement that the flock animal was slaughtered on the north side of the altar.

1:14 birds The last option for an acceptable burnt offering was a bird, specifically a dove or a pigeon.

1:15 wring off the head Due to their small size, birds were not cut in pieces (v. 17).

1:16 where the ashes The crop and contents (or plumage) was not offered on the altar. It was discarded along with the ashes that were removed from the altar every morning (6:8–13).

2:1–16 This passage outlines the procedure for bringing various types of grain offering. The offerings may be either uncooked (vv. 1–3) or cooked (vv. 4–10). For the cooked grain offerings, they could be prepared in a variety of ways, but they all had to be unleavened and mixed with oil. The grain offering was less expensive than an animal sacrifice and so was possibly a poor person's offering.

2:1 anyone The Hebrew word used here, *nephesh*, is commonly translated as "soul," but it can also be used as a generic, neutral term meaning "anyone." **grain offering** The Hebrew phrase used here is *qorban minchah* (v. 1) although this same action is sometimes referred to just with the Hebrew word *minchah* (v. 8). Both terms have a basic sense indicating a gift or offering. *Minchah*

is commonly used as a technical term for the grain offering. The word *qorban* is a common and generic word for all kinds of offerings. While *minchah* could be used in nonreligious contexts, *qorban* is used exclusively for sacrificial offerings. **the finest flour** See note on 6:15. **oil** The grain offerings all included oil (*shemen* in Hebrew)—probably olive oil. **incense** A fragrant resin from a type of tree (the *boswellia*), which is native to the southern Arabian peninsula and northeastern Africa.

2:2 as a memorial portion The Hebrew word used here, *azkarah*, is derived from the Hebrew word *zakhar* (often translated as "to remember"). *Azkarah* always occurs in a religious context, typically designating the representative portion of an offering that is burned on the altar.

2:3 rest While the burnt offering was fully consumed by fire on the altar, only a representative amount of the grain offering was burned up. The rest of the grain offering was for the priests to eat. **most holy part** Grain offerings, purification (sin) offerings and guilt (trespass) offerings are described as most holy (6:17,29; 7:1). This designation meant that the offering could only be eaten by the priests (7:6; 14:13).

2:4–10 The cooked grain offerings could be prepared three different ways—by baking in an oven, by cooking on a griddle and by frying in a pan. In each case, the offering was made of unleavened fine flour (*soleth* in Hebrew) with oil.

2:4 oven The Hebrew word used here, *tannur*, refers to an oven made of mud or clay, which was open on top.
2:9 an aroma pleasing See note on 1:9.

sented to the LORD. ¹²You may bring them to the LORD as an offering of the firstfruits, but they are not to be offered on the altar as a pleasing aroma. ¹³Season all your grain offerings with salt. Do not leave the salt of the covenant of your God out of your grain offerings; add salt to all your offerings.

¹⁴"'If you bring a grain offering of firstfruits to the LORD, offer crushed heads of new grain roasted in the fire. ¹⁵Put oil and incense on it; it is a grain offering. ¹⁶The priest shall burn the memorial portion of the crushed grain and the oil, together with all the incense, as a food offering presented to the LORD.

The Fellowship Offering

3 "'If your offering is a fellowship offering, and you offer an animal from the herd, whether male or female, you are to present before the LORD an animal without defect. ²You are to lay your hand on the head of your offering and slaughter it at the entrance to the tent of meeting. Then Aaron's sons the priests shall splash the blood against the sides of the altar. ³From the fellowship offering you are to bring a food offering to the LORD: the internal organs and all the fat that is connected to them, ⁴both kidneys with the fat on them near the loins, and the long lobe of the liver, which you will remove with the kidneys. ⁵Then Aaron's sons are to burn it on the altar on top of the burnt offering that is lying on the burning wood; it is a food offering, an aroma pleasing to the LORD.

⁶"'If you offer an animal from the flock as a fellowship offering to the LORD, you are to offer a male or female without defect. ⁷If you offer a lamb, you are to present it before the LORD, ⁸lay your hand on its head and slaughter it in front

---

2:11–16 This section provides some miscellaneous rules about the grain offerings (vv. 11–13) and discusses the grain offering of firstfruits (vv. 14–16). The comment that food offerings with leaven or honey could be offered as firstfruits (re'shith in Hebrew, meaning "first things"), but not burned on the altar, likely motivated the further instructions about firstfruits (bikkurim in Hebrew) offerings (see v. 12 and note).

2:11 yeast Leaven (yeast) and honey were probably prohibited because they involved fermentation. The fermentation process may have been connected with death; as such, it could not be associated with the altar, where sacrifices were given to the life-giver—God. Greek and Jewish sources from the ancient world attest to the symbolic connection made between leaven and corruption. The NT and rabbinic literature use leaven as a metaphor for sin and moral decay (e.g., 1Co 5:8; the rabbinic work Babylonian Talmud Berakhot 17a). **honey** This prohibition likely refers to fruit honey (or syrup) since offerings of firstfruits were agricultural produce.

2:12 the firstfruits The Hebrew word used here is re'shith; in Lev 2:14, the Hebrew term used for firstfruits is bikkurim, which refers to first-ripe grain and fruit of the harvest. The first of every living thing—human, animal or plant—belonged to Yahweh and was to be given back to him (compare Dt 18:4).

2:13 The requirement that all grain offerings be salted is repeated three times in this verse. In the Hebrew text, the first statement indicates that all qorban minchah must be salted, using the common term for grain offerings (see note on Lev 2:1). The second refers to the offerings just as minchah. The third statement asserts that salt must be offered on every qorban. The first two references are undoubtedly to the grain offerings. The third is ambiguous (since qorban is a general word for an offering) and could be taken to mean that all sacrificial offerings had to be salted.

2:13 salt of the covenant This phrase could simply underscore that the use of salt was obligatory. However, the references to a covenant of salt in Nu 18:19 and 2Ch 13:5 appear to have a broader meaning. The use of salt as the main preservative in the ancient world could have motivated figurative usage where salt symbolized the preservation of the covenant.

3:1–17 The zevach shelamim (a Hebrew phrase commonly translated as "peace offering" or "fellowship offering") was the main type of sacrifice that provided meat for the people. The priests were given a portion from the peace (or fellowship) offerings—the breast and the right upper thigh (Lev 7:28–34). The fat and the blood were offered to Yahweh. The rest of the meat could be eaten by the worshiper, but it had to be consumed within one or two days (7:15; 19:6–8).

The primary purpose of the peace (fellowship) offering was to provide an acceptable setting for slaughtering sacrificial animals for food (see 17:1–7). See the table "Types of Offerings in the Old Testament" on p. 178.

3:1 fellowship offering The significance of the Hebrew phrase zevach shelamim used here is uncertain, leading to a wide variety of potential translations, such as "peace offering," "well-being offering," "fellowship offering" and "repayment offering." The ambiguity stems from the range of possible meanings associated with shalem—the Hebrew word shelamim derives from—including completion, restoration, compensation, recompense, peace and well-being. **from the herd** As with the burnt offering, the regulations for the peace (fellowship) offerings are repeated for each type of acceptable animal. The order of presentation reflects the relative value of the different animals.

3:2 You are to lay your hand on the head Symbolically associating the offerer with the offering. **against the sides of the altar** The blood ritual for the burnt offering and the peace (fellowship) offering involved the blood being sprinkled all around the alter (in Hebrew, al-hammizbeach saviv). Following Jewish tradition, this is commonly understood to mean the blood was sprinkled against the sides of the altar.

3:3 internal organs and all the fat The fat that is to be offered to Yahweh is listed out explicitly for the peace (fellowship) offerings and the first sin offering (vv. 3–4,9–10,14–15; 4:8–9). The fat portions are primarily the fat around the organs including the entrails, liver and kidneys, not the fat attached to or mixed in the muscle (the consumable flesh) of an animal.

3:4 long lobe of the liver Refers to a finger shaped appendage on the liver known as the caudate lobe.

3:6–17 The procedures for the peace (fellowship) offering are repeated. The only change from vv. 1–5 relates to the type of animal offered.

of the tent of meeting. Then Aaron's sons shall splash its blood against the sides of the altar. [9]From the fellowship offering you are to bring a food offering to the LORD: its fat, the entire fat tail cut off close to the backbone, the internal organs and all the fat that is connected to them, [10]both kidneys with the fat on them near the loins, and the long lobe of the liver, which you will remove with the kidneys. [11]The priest shall burn them on the altar as a food offering presented to the LORD.

[12]"'If your offering is a goat, you are to present it before the LORD, [13]lay your hand on its head and slaughter it in front of the tent of meeting. Then Aaron's sons shall splash its blood against the sides of the altar. [14]From what you offer you are to present this food offering to the LORD: the internal organs and all the fat that is connected to them, [15]both kidneys with the fat on them near the loins, and the long lobe of the liver, which you will remove with the kidneys. [16]The priest shall burn them on the altar as a food offering, a pleasing aroma. All the fat is the LORD's.

[17]"'This is a lasting ordinance for the generations to come, wherever you live: You must not eat any fat or any blood.'"

The Sin Offering

4 The LORD said to Moses, [2]"Say to the Israelites: 'When anyone sins unintentionally and does what is forbidden in any of the LORD's commands—

[3]"'If the anointed priest sins, bringing guilt on the people, he must bring to the LORD a young bull without defect as a sin offering[a] for the sin he has committed. [4]He is to present the bull at the entrance to the tent of meeting before the LORD. He is to lay his hand on its head and slaughter it there before the LORD. [5]Then the anointed priest shall take some of the bull's blood and carry it into the tent of meeting. [6]He is to dip his finger into the blood and sprinkle some of it seven times before the LORD, in front of the curtain of the sanctuary. [7]The priest shall then put some of the blood on the horns of the altar of fragrant incense that is

[a] 3 Or purification offering; here and throughout this chapter

3:6 from the flock May refer to either sheep or goats.
3:9 entire fat tail The type of sheep raised in the southeastern Mediterranean and Arabia are known for their exceptionally broad, fatty tails.
3:11 a food offering The Hebrew phrase used here is lechem isheh, not just isheh as in similar occurrences (1:9; 3:3,9,14; see note on 1:9).
3:16 All the fat is the LORD's The fat and the blood from the sacrifice belonged to Yahweh. This meant that all domestic animals slaughtered for food had to be brought as sacrifices so that the priests could offer their fat on the altar (compare Dt 12:20–24).
3:17 must not eat any fat or any blood The prohibition against eating blood is repeated in Lev 7:26–27.

4:1—5:13 This passage provides a detailed treatment of the chatta'th, a Hebrew word commonly translated as "sin offering" because the Hebrew verb chata means "sin" or "miss the mark." However, the chatta'th is prescribed for situations that do not result from sin, such as the purification needed following childbirth (see ch. 12). Since the verb chata can also be used for purification, describing actions that counter the effects of sin, chatta'th may be more broadly translated as "purification offering." Its purpose was restoring ritual purity to a person (and the sanctuary), as opposed to atoning for a moral offense.

Unlike the discussions of the burnt offerings, grain offerings and peace (fellowship) offerings, which focused on the sacrifice rather than the one bringing the sacrifice, the regulations for purification (or sin) offerings in this section are categorized according to the nature of the offense and the offender. The purification offerings fall into two main categories—ones that purify the sanctuary and the altar and ones that only cleanse the altar. The first type could not be eaten at all (6:30). The second type could be eaten by the priests (see 6:25–29).

4:1 The LORD said to Moses The offerings described in chs. 1–3 were motivated by the willing obedience of the worshiper. The offerings outlined in 4:1—6:8 were required for the atonement of sin.

4:2 When anyone sins unintentionally To sin without intent or inadvertently means the wrong was due to ignorance of the law or negligence that brought about an unintended result, such as accidentally killing someone (Nu 35:11).
4:3 anointed priest Referring to the high priest, the main one who is anointed with oil (see Lev 21:10 and note). This regulation likely addresses violations committed in an official capacity, not the priest's personal sins, since the cure involved cleansing the sacred space of the tabernacle. bringing guilt on the people The sins of the high priest affect the entire congregation because he represents the people before God. See the table "Functions of Priests" on p. 171. sin offering When a person unknowingly sinned, the offense affected the sanctity of the sanctuary. The Hebrew word used here, chatta'th, refers to an offering that cleansed the contamination—in this regard it may be described as a purification (sin) offering (see note on 4:1—5:13).
4:6 sprinkle some of it The blood is the ritual cleanser that purges the impurity. The blood is handled differently in this sacrifice than the burnt offering (1:4–5) or peace (fellowship) offering (3:2). Here it is sprinkled (nazah in Hebrew) in front of the tent shrine, not dashed (zaraq in Hebrew) against the altar. seven times Similar purification rituals also call for sevenfold sprinkling of water, oil or blood. The cleansing rituals for the Day of Atonement also required sprinkling blood on or around the ark of the covenant seven times (16:14). curtain of the sanctuary Refers to the thick curtain separating the two parts of the tent shrine (see note on Ex 26:31–36)—the Holy Place and the Most Holy Place (Holy of Holies). See the infographic "The Tabernacle" on p. 138; see the infographic "Furnishings of the Tabernacle" on p. 136.
4:7 horns Removing the horns from an altar rendered it unusable and defiled (Am 3:14). Placing the blood on the horns served to cleanse the whole altar. altar of fragrant incense The altar inside the tent, directly in front of the veil that separated the Holy Place from the Most Holy Place. See the infographic "The Most Holy

before the LORD in the tent of meeting. The rest of the bull's blood he shall pour out at the base of the altar of burnt offering at the entrance to the tent of meeting. ⁸He shall remove all the fat from the bull of the sin offering — all the fat that is connected to the internal organs, ⁹both kidneys with the fat on them near the loins, and the long lobe of the liver, which he will remove with the kidneys — ¹⁰just as the fat is removed from the oxᵃ sacrificed as a fellowship offering. Then the priest shall burn them on the altar of burnt offering. ¹¹But the hide of the bull and all its flesh, as well as the head and legs, the internal organs and the intestines — ¹²that is, all the rest of the bull — he must take outside the camp to a place ceremonially clean, where the

ᵃ 10 The Hebrew word can refer to either male or female.

Place" on p. 525. **base of the altar of burnt offering** The blood for the purification (sin) offering is used to purify the small incense altar inside the tent shrine and the large sacrificial altar in the courtyard.
4:8 fat from the bull of the sin offering Essentially the same list of fatty portions that should be offered on the altar appears three times in Lev 3 (see 3:3 and note).

4:12 all the rest While the fatty portions are all burned on the altar of burnt offering, the remainder of the bull's carcass — its skin, flesh and other entrails — was taken outside the camp and burned. The rest of the animal could not be eaten because some of the blood had been taken inside the tent of meeting (6:30).

Functions of Priests

TASK	REFERENCE
Supervise and administrate sacrifices and offerings	Lev 1–7
Distinguish between sacred and common	Lev 10:10; 20:24,26
Distinguish between clean and unclean	Lev 10:10; 20:25 (compare Lev 11)
Purify accrued pollution of sin in holy place	Lev 4:1–6:7; 16:1–19
Purify people from impurity	Lev 12:1–8; 15:13–15
Keep gradations of holiness distinct	Nu 3:10
Protect purity of sanctuary	Nu 18:1–7
Interpret skin diseases and bodily discharges	Lev 13:1–46; 14:1–32; 15:1–33
Serve as occasional judges	Dt 17:8–13; 19:16–17; 21:1–5 (see also Nu 5:11–31)
Determine times of rituals	Lev 23:1–44
Assess and collect tithes	Lev 27:1–33; Ex 30:11–16 (compare Nu 18:8–32; Dt 14:22–29; 18:1–8; 26:1–15)
Interpret cultural and religious practices	Lev 18:3,24–28; 20:22–25 (perhaps all of Lev 18–20)
Pronounce divine blessing on people	Nu 6:22–27; Dt 10:8 (compare Lev 9:22)
Teach God's commands	Lev 10:10; Dt 33:10; 2Ch 35:3 (compare Dt 31:9–13; Eze 22:26; Hag 2:11–13)
Give oracles via Urim and Thummim	Nu 27:21; Dt 33:8; Ezr 2:59–63 (compare 1Sa 14:41; 28:6; Ne 7:63–65)
Give speeches before battle	Dt 20:2–4
Sound sacred trumpets	Nu 10:1–10 (compare Nu 31:6)
Supervise the ark of God†	Jos 6:1–14; 1Sa 4:1–4
Give oracles regarding war	Nu 27:18–21; Jdg 18:19–31
Supervise decisions to destroy banned spoils of war	Nu 31:21–31

† The Levites hauled the ark of God, but the priests supervised the process (see Nu 3:31–32; Dt 31:9, 25).

ashes are thrown, and burn it there in a wood fire on the ash heap.

¹³"If the whole Israelite community sins unintentionally and does what is forbidden in any of the LORD's commands, even though the community is unaware of the matter, when they realize their guilt ¹⁴and the sin they committed becomes known, the assembly must bring a young bull as a sin offering and present it before the tent of meeting. ¹⁵The elders of the community are to lay their hands on the bull's head before the LORD, and the bull shall be slaughtered before the LORD. ¹⁶Then the anointed priest is to take some of the bull's blood into the tent of meeting. ¹⁷He shall dip his finger into the blood and sprinkle it before the LORD seven times in front of the curtain. ¹⁸He is to put some of the blood on the horns of the altar that is before the LORD in the tent of meeting. The rest of the blood he shall pour out at the base of the altar of burnt offering at the entrance to the tent of meeting. ¹⁹He shall remove all the fat from it and burn it on the altar, ²⁰and do with this bull just as he did with the bull for the sin offering. In this way the priest will make atonement for the community, and they will be forgiven. ²¹Then he shall take the bull outside the camp and burn it as he burned the first bull. This is the sin offering for the community.

²²"When a leader sins unintentionally and does what is forbidden in any of the commands of the LORD his God, when he realizes his guilt ²³and the sin he has committed becomes known, he must bring as his offering a male goat without defect. ²⁴He is to lay his hand on the goat's head and slaughter it at the place where the burnt offering is slaughtered before the LORD. It is a sin offering. ²⁵Then the priest shall take some of the blood of the sin offering with his finger and put it on the horns of the altar of burnt offering and pour out the rest of the blood at the base of the altar. ²⁶He shall burn all the fat on the altar as he burned the fat of the fellowship offering. In this way the priest will make atonement for the leader's sin, and he will be forgiven.

²⁷"If any member of the community sins unintentionally and does what is forbidden in any

---

4:13–21 This passage addresses unintentional sin for which the entire congregation of Israel is responsible. The ritual procedures for the purification offering for the community's sin are essentially the same as for the unintentional sin of the high priest.

4:13 whole Israelite community Probably refers to the entire nation of Israel—every man, woman and child. This Hebrew phrase is used throughout the Pentateuch (e.g., Ex 17:1; Nu 1:53; 20:1). **sins unintentionally** Possibly, the entire congregation sinned as a result of the high priest making an error. Leviticus 4:1–21 could be addressing a single case where the priest's mistake led to the people inadvertently violating God's commandments.

4:14 a young bull The purification (sin) offering for cleansing the greater impurity caused by a sin of the congregation or the high priest had to be a bull—the most costly sacrificial animal.

4:15 elders of the community The leaders of the community (see Ex 3:16 and note).

4:16–18 The blood ritual described here is identical to that outlined in Lev 4:5–7. The account here was abbreviated slightly as a result.

4:17 in front of the curtain The Hebrew phrasing used here (and in v. 6) could mean either that the blood was sprinkled before the veil (curtain) or directly on the veil (curtain).

4:19 all the fat from it The detailed list of what is meant here can be found in vv. 8–9. Rather than repeat these details for the other purification (sin) offerings, the text simply uses this phrase for the four types discussed in 4:22—5:10.

4:20 make atonement A central purpose of the purification (sin) offering is making atonement or purging uncleanness, which is the focus of the OT sacrificial system. The theological concept of atonement focuses on reconciliation with God, but how that reconciliation happens is debated. Atonement can be understood as appeasing the wrath of God kindled by sin, as making

payment for sin, as removing the guilt incurred through sin or as covering over the guilt.

The Hebrew verb used here for making atonement, *kipper*, can mean: "to cover," "to ransom" or "to wipe away." Interpretations of how atonement works generally use one of these three common meanings of the word as a starting point. Recognizing the result of atonement—the restoration of relationship with God—is more important than discerning whether atonement is based on cleansing, covering over or compensating for sin.

4:22–35 From here through the end of the chapter, the regulations address purification (sin) offerings relevant to sins that do not have the same level of impact on the entire community. The blood ritual described for these offerings differs slightly from the earlier ones (compare vv. 7,18). Only the main altar in the courtyard is involved with blood daubed on the horns and the rest poured out at the base (vv. 25,30,34). Also the priest was permitted to eat the meat of these sin (purification) offerings (6:24–29).

4:23 a male goat The goat was a more common and less costly sacrifice for a sin (purification) offering (*chatta'th* in Hebrew) than the bull.

4:25 the horns of the altar of burnt offering The procedure for this sin (purification) offering is comparable to the other offerings. However, this is a different altar— the previous two sin offerings had the blood placed on the altar of fragrant incense in front of the veil (curtain), inside the tent of meeting (vv. 7,18). See the infographic "Ancient Altars" on p. 127.

4:26 fat of the fellowship offering The parts of the animal offered on the altar are explicitly identified as the same as those offered for the peace (fellowship) offerings (see note on 3:3).

4:27–35 The procedure for the final two sin or purification (*chatta'th* in Hebrew) offerings is essentially the same as that for the leader. The primary difference is that a common person can bring a female goat (vv. 27–31) or sheep (vv. 32–35) instead of a male goat.

of the Lord's commands, when they realize their guilt ²⁸and the sin they have committed becomes known, they must bring as their offering for the sin they committed a female goat without defect. ²⁹They are to lay their hand on the head of the sin offering and slaughter it at the place of the burnt offering. ³⁰Then the priest is to take some of the blood with his finger and put it on the horns of the altar of burnt offering and pour out the rest of the blood at the base of the altar. ³¹They shall remove all the fat, just as the fat is removed from the fellowship offering, and the priest shall burn it on the altar as an aroma pleasing to the Lord. In this way the priest will make atonement for them, and they will be forgiven.

³²"'If someone brings a lamb as their sin offering, they are to bring a female without defect. ³³They are to lay their hand on its head and slaughter it for a sin offering at the place where the burnt offering is slaughtered. ³⁴Then the priest shall take some of the blood of the sin offering with his finger and put it on the horns of the altar of burnt offering and pour out the rest of the blood at the base of the altar. ³⁵They shall remove all the fat, just as the fat is removed from the lamb of the fellowship offering, and the priest shall burn it on the altar on top of the food offerings presented to the Lord. In this way the priest will make atonement for them for the sin they have committed, and they will be forgiven.

5 "'If anyone sins because they do not speak up when they hear a public charge to testify regarding something they have seen or learned about, they will be held responsible.

²"'If anyone becomes aware that they are guilty—if they unwittingly touch anything ceremonially unclean (whether the carcass of an unclean animal, wild or domestic, or of any unclean creature that moves along the ground) and they are unaware that they have become unclean, but then they come to realize their guilt; ³or if they touch human uncleanness (anything that would make them unclean) even though they are unaware of it, but then they learn of it and realize their guilt; ⁴or if anyone thoughtlessly takes an oath to do anything, whether good or evil (in any matter one might carelessly swear about) even though they are unaware of it, but then they learn of it and realize their guilt— ⁵when anyone becomes aware that they are guilty in any of these matters, they must confess in what way they have sinned. ⁶As a penalty for the sin they have committed, they must bring to the Lord a female lamb or goat from the flock as a sin offering[a]; and the priest shall make atonement for them for their sin.

⁷"'Anyone who cannot afford a lamb is to bring two doves or two young pigeons to the Lord as a penalty for their sin—one for a sin offering and the other for a burnt offering. ⁸They are to bring them to the priest, who shall first offer the one for the sin offering. He is to wring its head from its neck, not dividing it completely, ⁹and is to splash some of the blood of the sin offering against the side of the altar; the rest of the blood must be drained out at the base of the altar. It is a sin offering. ¹⁰The priest shall then offer the other as a burnt offering in the prescribed way and make atonement for them for the sin they have committed, and they will be forgiven.

[a] 6 Or purification offering; here and throughout this chapter

---

4:27 community Leviticus 4 has moved in degrees of sanctity—from the high priest, to the Israelite people as a whole, to leaders who were not priests, to other common people (likely non-Israelites)—addressed here.

5:1–6 The procedure for the purification (sin) offering (*chatta'th* in Hebrew) was outlined in ch. 4. This passage provides examples of the kinds of sins that might require such an offering.

5:1 they hear a public charge Refers to someone who has heard a public request for information about an incident or accusation of a violation of the law. **they will be held responsible** Introduces the concept of sin by omission—the failure to do what is right. Sins of omission for an average person fall under the atonement procedure outlined in 4:27–35.

5:2–3 The examples in vv. 2–3 begin the ongoing development of the categories of clean and unclean in Israelite religion. The uncleanness described in v. 2 primarily derives from contact with a dead body (see Nu 19:1–22 and note). The human uncleanness of Lev 5:3 could allude to death or the various bodily functions that caused uncleanness, which are discussed in chs. 12–15.

5:2 they are unaware The unintentional or inadvertent nature of the offense is what allows it to be remedied

via the sin (purification) offering (*chatta'th* in Hebrew). See note on 4:2.

5:4 thoughtlessly takes an oath Refers to a thoughtless promise, perhaps something vowed without full knowledge of its implications.

5:6 As a penalty Just as the Hebrew word *chatta'th* can refer either to an offense or the offering to remedy the offense (see note on 4:1–5:13; note on 4:3), the Hebrew word *asham* used here may refer to the guilt associated with an offense, the penalty for that guilt, or the offering required to atone for the guilt (see note on 5:14—6:7).

5:7–13 The discussion of the sin (purification) offering (*chatta'th* in Hebrew) ends with regulations for people who need to provide such an offering but do not have the economic means to give the prescribed offering of a lamb or goat. The first alternative is offering two birds instead of a sheep or goat (vv. 7–10). The second alternative is bringing a grain offering of fine flour (*soleth* in Hebrew; vv. 11–13; see note on 6:15).

5:7 two doves or two young pigeons The first bird removes the offense and restores the guilty party to ritual purity and fellowship, while the second is offered as an act of worship.

5:8 wring its head The first bird had its neck broken, but the head was not severed, unlike the burnt offering (1:14–15).

¹¹"'If, however, they cannot afford two doves or two young pigeons, they are to bring as an offering for their sin a tenth of an ephah*a* of the finest flour for a sin offering. They must not put olive oil or incense on it, because it is a sin offering. ¹²They are to bring it to the priest, who shall take a handful of it as a memorial*b* portion and burn it on the altar on top of the food offerings presented to the LORD. It is a sin offering. ¹³In this way the priest will make atonement for them for any of these sins they have committed, and they will be forgiven. The rest of the offering will belong to the priest, as in the case of the grain offering.'"

The Guilt Offering

¹⁴The LORD said to Moses: ¹⁵"When anyone is unfaithful to the LORD by sinning unintentionally in regard to any of the LORD's holy things, they are to bring to the LORD as a penalty a ram from the flock, one without defect and of the proper value in silver, according to the sanctuary shekel.*c* It is a guilt offering. ¹⁶They must make restitution for what they have failed to do in regard to the holy things, pay an additional penalty of a fifth of its value and give it all to the priest. The priest will make atonement for them with the ram as a guilt offering, and they will be forgiven.

¹⁷"If anyone sins and does what is forbidden in any of the LORD's commands, even though they do not know it, they are guilty and will be held responsible. ¹⁸They are to bring to the priest as a guilt offering a ram from the flock, one with-out defect and of the proper value. In this way the priest will make atonement for them for the wrong they have committed unintentionally, and they will be forgiven. ¹⁹It is a guilt offering; they have been guilty of*d* wrongdoing against the LORD."

6 *e* The LORD said to Moses: ²"If anyone sins and is unfaithful to the LORD by deceiving a neighbor about something entrusted to them or left in their care or about something stolen, or if they cheat their neighbor, ³or if they find lost property and lie about it, or if they swear falsely about any such sin that people may commit — ⁴when they sin in any of these ways and realize their guilt, they must return what they have stolen or taken by extortion, or what was entrusted to them, or the lost property they found, ⁵or whatever it was they swore falsely about. They must make restitution in full, add a fifth of the value to it and give it all to the owner on the day they present their guilt offering. ⁶And as a penalty they must bring to the priest, that is, to the LORD, their guilt offering, a ram from the flock, one without defect and of the proper value. ⁷In this way the priest will make atonement for them before the LORD, and they will be forgiven for any of the things they did that made them guilty."

---

a 11 That is, probably about 3 1/2 pounds or about 1.6 kilograms   *b* 12 Or representative   *c* 15 That is, about 2/5 ounce or about 12 grams   *d* 19 Or offering; atonement has been made for their   *e* In Hebrew texts 6:1-7 is numbered 5:20-26, and 6:8-30 is numbered 6:1-23.

5:11 finest flour for a sin offering This alternative is unusual since offerings that make atonement for sin and guilt typically require the shedding of blood. The NT notes that virtually everything required blood for purification under the sacrificial system because it was the blood that effected atonement (Heb 9:22; compare Lev 17:11). It seems that in some cases the token amount of the grain offering burned on the altar could substitute for the blood.

5:14—6:7 This passage details the regulations for what the Hebrew text calls the *asham*—guilt, reparation or restitution offering. The Hebrew word *asham* is used in three different senses in the OT. It may refer to the guilt itself that is incurred by wrongdoing, but it also designates either the penalty required to compensate for the offense or the sacrifice that must be offered to atone for the guilt (see 5:6 and note). The distinction between the *asham* and the sin (purification) offering (*chatta'th* in Hebrew) is unclear in 5:15–19. In 5:15–16, the offense related to the *asham* is somehow connected to sacred things; correcting the offense involved offering a ram and paying restitution. However, the scenario in 5:17–19 seems comparable to those in 5:1–6 that relate to offering the *chatta'th*.

The situations requiring the *asham* listed in 6:1–7 appear to involve some level of intent—e.g., fraud, robbery, lying and extortion—which would indicate a different category of offense than the inadvertent sins covered by the *chatta'th*. The offenses in 6:1–7 also all require restitution—restoring the full value of what was taken by theft or fraud and adding a fifth to it. See note on 7:1–7. See the table "Types of Offerings in the Old Testament" on p. 178.

5:15 unfaithful The Hebrew term *ma'al* used here generally refers to disloyalty or infidelity—often disloyalty toward Yahweh or misuse of sacred objects devoted to Yahweh (e.g., Nu 5:6; Jos 7:1). **proper value in silver** The Hebrew phrase used here leaves some ambiguity over whether the offering had to be a ram or just the monetary equivalent of a ram. **guilt offering** The Hebrew word used here, *asham*, is used in two different senses in this verse. It is the penalty or compensation that must be paid as well as the name for the offering itself. The third sense—referring to the guilt (or trespass) itself—occurs in 5:17. In Isa 53:10, the suffering servant's life is made a guilt offering (*asham* in Hebrew)—the suffering servant passages from Isaiah are understood as prophecies about Jesus in the NT (see note on Lk 4:17).

6:1–5 The offenses listed here seem to involve deliberate offenses, not inadvertent errors (see note on Lev 5:14—6:7). The three offenses described in vv. 2–3—deliberate deception in a contractual relationship, outright theft and oppression of a fellow Israelite—all deal with greed.

6:4 realize their guilt The Hebrew verb used here, *asham*, indicates the person is guilty and willing to make amends, thus it is often translated here in a way that reflects people coming to realize their guilt.

The Burnt Offering

[8]The LORD said to Moses: [9]"Give Aaron and his sons this command: 'These are the regulations for the burnt offering: The burnt offering is to remain on the altar hearth throughout the night, till morning, and the fire must be kept burning on the altar. [10]The priest shall then put on his linen clothes, with linen undergarments next to his body, and shall remove the ashes of the burnt offering that the fire has consumed on the altar and place them beside the altar. [11]Then he is to take off these clothes and put on others, and carry the ashes outside the camp to a place that is ceremonially clean. [12]The fire on the altar must be kept burning; it must not go out. Every morning the priest is to add firewood and arrange the burnt offering on the fire and burn the fat of the fellowship offerings on it. [13]The fire must be kept burning on the altar continuously; it must not go out.

The Grain Offering

[14]"These are the regulations for the grain offering: Aaron's sons are to bring it before the LORD, in front of the altar. [15]The priest is to take a handful of the finest flour and some olive oil, together with all the incense on the grain offering, and burn the memorial[a] portion on the altar as an aroma pleasing to the LORD. [16]Aaron and his sons shall eat the rest of it, but it is to be eaten without yeast in the sanctuary area; they are to eat it in the courtyard of the tent of meeting. [17]It must not be baked with yeast; I have given it as their share of the food offerings presented to me. Like the sin offering[b] and the guilt offering, it is most holy. [18]Any male descendant of Aaron may eat it. For all generations to come it is his perpetual share of the food offerings presented to the LORD. Whatever touches them will become holy.[c]'"

[19]The LORD also said to Moses, [20]"This is the offering Aaron and his sons are to bring to the LORD on the day he[d] is anointed: a tenth of an ephah[e] of the finest flour as a regular grain offering, half of it in the morning and half in the evening. [21]It must be prepared with oil on a griddle; bring it well-mixed and present the grain offering broken[f] in pieces as an aroma pleasing to the LORD. [22]The son who is to succeed him as anointed priest shall prepare it. It is the LORD's perpetual share and is to be burned completely. [23]Every grain offering of a priest shall be burned completely; it must not be eaten."

The Sin Offering

[24]The LORD said to Moses, [25]"Say to Aaron and his sons: 'These are the regulations for the sin offering: The sin offering is to be slaughtered before the LORD in the place the burnt offering is slaughtered; it is most holy. [26]The priest who offers it shall eat it; it is to be eaten in the sanctuary area, in the courtyard of the tent of meeting. [27]Whatever touches any of the flesh will become holy, and if any of the blood is spattered on a garment, you must wash it in the sanctuary area. [28]The clay pot the meat is cooked in must be broken; but if it is cooked in a bronze pot, the pot is to be scoured and rinsed with water. [29]Any male in a priest's family may eat it; it is most holy. [30]But any sin offering

---

[a] 15 Or representative   [b] 17 Or purification offering; also in verses 25 and 30   [c] 18 Or Whoever touches them must be holy; similarly in verse 27   [d] 20 Or each   [e] 20 That is, probably about 3 1/2 pounds or about 1.6 kilograms   [f] 21 The meaning of the Hebrew for this word is uncertain.

6:8—7:38 This passage provides additional instructions for the priests regarding how to handle the various sacrifices and offerings. One of the main concerns of the passage is the protocol for distributing and eating portions of the offerings. The major offerings discussed in chs. 1–5 are mentioned again here—sometimes providing new information and sometimes repeating details given earlier. See the table "Types of Offerings in the Old Testament" on p. 178.

6:9 burnt offering Burnt offerings were offered to make atonement and played an important part in public worship (Nu 28–29). Burnt offerings also played a role in the procedures for cleansing various ritual impurities (e.g., Lev 12:6–7; 14:19–20; 15:30). **throughout the night, till morning** The altar was to be kept burning continually with a burnt offering. See note on 1:3–17.
6:14 grain offering Grain offerings were mixed with oil and frankincense and a token amount was burned on the altar.
6:15 finest flour The Hebrew word used here, soleth, probably refers to wheat flour (compare Ex 29:2). Soleth also seems to be high quality flour as opposed to ordinary flour (qemach in Hebrew; compare 1Ki 4:22).
6:16 it is to be eaten without yeast in the sanctuary area The meal had to be eaten in a sacred area—the

courtyard of the tabernacle. See the infographic "The Tabernacle" on p. 138.
6:18 will become holy Not in the sense of moral purity, but in the sense of being set apart.
6:19–23 This passage is specifically about the grain offering that is to be offered when one of Aaron's descendants is anointed as the next high priest (Lev 6:22; compare 21:10). The offerings associated with the ordination of Aaron and his sons included grain offerings and animal sacrifices (Ex 29:1–3).
6:20 he is anointed Aaron and his four sons were anointed when they were ordained as priests (see Lev 8:12,30). According to 21:10, the chief priest was the anointed one, suggesting that anointing was only part of the ordination ceremony for future high priests, not all priests.
6:24–30 Only the purification (sin) offerings described in 4:22–35 could be eaten. The procedure for the offerings in 4:1–21 involved bringing some of the blood inside the tent, giving those sacrifices a higher level of sanctity and making them ineligible for consumption (6:30).
6:28 clay pot The meat of the sacrifice made whatever it was cooked in holy.

whose blood is brought into the tent of meeting to make atonement in the Holy Place must not be eaten; it must be burned up.

The Guilt Offering

7 "'These are the regulations for the guilt offering, which is most holy: ²The guilt offering is to be slaughtered in the place where the burnt offering is slaughtered, and its blood is to be splashed against the sides of the altar. ³All its fat shall be offered: the fat tail and the fat that covers the internal organs, ⁴both kidneys with the fat on them near the loins, and the long lobe of the liver, which is to be removed with the kidneys. ⁵The priest shall burn them on the altar as a food offering presented to the LORD. It is a guilt offering. ⁶Any male in a priest's family may eat it, but it must be eaten in the sanctuary area; it is most holy.

⁷"'The same law applies to both the sin offering[a] and the guilt offering: They belong to the priest who makes atonement with them. ⁸The priest who offers a burnt offering for anyone may keep its hide for himself. ⁹Every grain offering baked in an oven or cooked in a pan or on a griddle belongs to the priest who offers it, ¹⁰and every grain offering, whether mixed with olive oil or dry, belongs equally to all the sons of Aaron.

The Fellowship Offering

¹¹"'These are the regulations for the fellowship offering anyone may present to the LORD:

¹²"'If they offer it as an expression of thankfulness, then along with this thank offering they are to offer thick loaves made without yeast and with olive oil mixed in, thin loaves made without yeast and brushed with oil, and thick loaves of the finest flour well-kneaded and with oil mixed in. ¹³Along with their fellowship offering of thanksgiving they are to present an offering with thick loaves of bread made with yeast. ¹⁴They are to bring one of each kind as an offering, a contribution to the LORD; it belongs to the priest who splashes the blood of the fellowship offering against the altar. ¹⁵The meat of their fellowship offering of thanksgiving must be eaten on the day it is offered; they must leave none of it till morning.

¹⁶"'If, however, their offering is the result of a vow or is a freewill offering, the sacrifice shall be eaten on the day they offer it, but anything left over may be eaten on the next day. ¹⁷Any meat of the sacrifice left over till the third day must be burned up. ¹⁸If any meat of the fellowship offering is eaten on the third day, the one who offered it will not be accepted. It will not be reckoned to their credit, for it has become impure; the person who eats any of it will be held responsible.

¹⁹"'Meat that touches anything ceremonially unclean must not be eaten; it must be burned up. As for other meat, anyone ceremonially clean may eat it. ²⁰But if anyone who is unclean eats any meat of the fellowship offering belonging to the LORD, they must be cut off from their people. ²¹Anyone who touches something unclean— whether human uncleanness or an unclean animal or any unclean creature that moves along the ground[b]—and then eats any of the meat of the fellowship offering belonging to the LORD must be cut off from their people.'"

Eating Fat and Blood Forbidden

²²The LORD said to Moses, ²³"Say to the Israelites: 'Do not eat any of the fat of cattle, sheep or

---

[a] 7 Or purification offering; also in verse 37   [b] 21 A few Hebrew manuscripts, Samaritan Pentateuch, Syriac and Targum (see 5:2); most Hebrew manuscripts any unclean, detestable thing

---

7:1–7 This passage outlines a procedure for handling the guilt offering (asham in Hebrew) that is very similar to the process for handling the peace (fellowship) offering (zevach shelamim in Hebrew; see note on 3:1–17). In the introduction of the asham in 5:14—6:7, no specific procedures were provided, but it was treated as if it was related to the purification (sin) offering (chatta'th in Hebrew; compare 4:27–28 and 5:15)—this connection is made explicit in 7:7.

The guilt (trespass) offering could be considered the same as the purification (sin) offering in that only the priests are entitled to eat it (compare 6:16–18); the ritual procedure is not exactly identical for both.

7:8 hide The hide of an animal offered as a burnt offering became the property of the priest who officiated over the sacrifice.

7:11–36 The longest discussion in this chapter is devoted to the peace (fellowship) offering (zevach shelamim in Hebrew). This passage indicates that this sort of offering was appropriate for a variety of situations and could be given as an expression of thanks (v. 12), in fulfillment of a vow or as an act of worship (v. 16). Only part of the peace offerings belonged to the priests—the breast and right thigh (vv. 31–32). Most of the meat was for the worshiper, but it had to be eaten within the prescribed period of time (vv. 15–18).

7:17 till the third day Those sacrifices that did not have to be eaten on the same day of the sacrifice had to be consumed by the third day—possibly because the meat would spoil.

7:19 anyone ceremonially clean Participation in worship required ritual purity. Maintaining ritual purity is the primary topic of chs. 11–16.

7:20 they must be cut off from their people This phrase indicates a serious punishment and is used frequently to describe the consequences of violating God's law (e.g., Ex 12:15; Lev 23:29; Nu 9:13). The variety of applications of this phrase suggest the punishment could range from loss of social standing to banishment to execution (see Nu 15:30 and note).

7:22–27 This passage reiterates the prohibition from Lev 3:17 against eating fat or blood. This segment provides

goats. [24]The fat of an animal found dead or torn by wild animals may be used for any other purpose, but you must not eat it. [25]Anyone who eats the fat of an animal from which a food offering may be[a] presented to the Lord must be cut off from their people. [26]And wherever you live, you must not eat the blood of any bird or animal. [27]Anyone who eats blood must be cut off from their people.'"

The Priests' Share

[28]The Lord said to Moses, [29]"Say to the Israelites: 'Anyone who brings a fellowship offering to the Lord is to bring part of it as their sacrifice to the Lord. [30]With their own hands they are to present the food offering to the Lord; they are to bring the fat, together with the breast, and wave the breast before the Lord as a wave offering. [31]The priest shall burn the fat on the altar, but the breast belongs to Aaron and his sons. [32]You are to give the right thigh of your fellowship offerings to the priest as a contribution. [33]The son of Aaron who offers the blood and the fat of the fellowship offering shall have the right thigh as his share. [34]From the fellowship offerings of the Israelites, I have taken the breast that is waved and the thigh that is presented and have given them to Aaron the priest and his sons as their perpetual share from the Israelites.'"

[35]This is the portion of the food offerings presented to the Lord that were allotted to Aaron and his sons on the day they were presented to serve the Lord as priests. [36]On the day they were anointed, the Lord commanded that the Israelites give this to them as their perpetual share for the generations to come.

[37]These, then, are the regulations for the burnt offering, the grain offering, the sin offering, the guilt offering, the ordination offering and the fellowship offering, [38]which the Lord gave Moses at Mount Sinai in the Desert of Sinai on the day he commanded the Israelites to bring their offerings to the Lord.

The Ordination of Aaron and His Sons

8:1-36pp — Ex 29:1-37

8 The Lord said to Moses, [2]"Bring Aaron and his sons, their garments, the anointing oil, the bull for the sin offering,[b] the two rams and the basket containing bread made without yeast, [3]and gather the entire assembly at the entrance to the tent of meeting." [4]Moses did as the Lord commanded him, and the assembly gathered at the entrance to the tent of meeting.

[5]Moses said to the assembly, "This is what the Lord has commanded to be done." [6]Then Moses brought Aaron and his sons forward and washed them with water. [7]He put the tunic on Aaron, tied the sash around him, clothed him with the robe and put the ephod on him. He also fastened the ephod with a decorative waistband, which he tied around him. [8]He placed the breastpiece on him and put the Urim and Thummim in the breastpiece. [9]Then he placed the turban on Aaron's head and set the gold plate, the sacred emblem, on the front of it, as the Lord commanded Moses.

[10]Then Moses took the anointing oil and anointed the tabernacle and everything in it, and so consecrated them. [11]He sprinkled some of the oil on

---

[a] 25 Or offering is   [b] 2 Or purification offering; also in verse 14

---

more context for the prohibition—clarifying that no fat at all may be eaten, regardless of whether the fat came from a sacrificial animal. The penalty for violating the prohibition was being cut off from the community, indicating either death or excommunication (compare 20:2–5).

7:26 you must not eat the blood of any bird or animal Prohibits eating meat from which the blood has not been completely drained (compare Lev 3:17; Dt 12:15–16; 1Sa 14:33).

7:30 wave offering The Hebrew word used here, tenuphah, is a priestly, technical term that designates an offering presented to Yahweh but not put on the altar.

7:37–38 These verses are a concluding summary statement to the additional regulations about sacrifices and offerings provided in Lev 6:8–7:36. All of the offerings listed in v. 37 are mentioned by name in 6:8–7:36 with the exception of the ordination (consecration) offering. The reference to ordination may be anticipating the ordination ceremony to follow in chs. 8–9.

7:37 ordination offering This may refer to the priestly grain offering described in 6:19–23.

8:1—9:24 Chapters 8–9 describe the formal beginning of the priesthood and the sacrificial system. The process

for ordaining Aaron and his sons as priests was laid out in Ex 28–29, but the tabernacle had not yet been built at that time. This passage reflects how Moses followed the detailed procedure from Ex 28–29.

8:2 garments, the anointing oil Refers to the priestly garments (Ex 28:2–5) and the anointing oil (Ex 30:23–33) prepared when the tabernacle was constructed (compare Ex 40:13–15). **the bull** The sacrifices for the ordination required a bull as a sin offering and two rams as burnt offerings (Ex 29:1). **bread made without yeast** See Lev 6:19–23 and note.

8:6 washed them with water This cleansing was necessary before they could wear the priestly garments. The washing fulfilled the command of Ex 29:4.

8:7 ephod A priestly garment involved in the practice of seeking God's will through the use of the Urim and Thummim. See note on Ex 28:4; note on 28:30.

8:8 the Urim and Thummim Objects that were likely used in casting lots as a way to discern God's will. See note on Ex 28:30.

8:9 as the Lord commanded Moses This phrase occurs at intervals throughout this passage (Lev 8:1—9:24) and serves to connect the Levitical priesthood (priests from the tribes of Levi) and its system of sacrifices directly with Yahweh's command (e.g., 8:13,29; 9:8–10).

the altar seven times, anointing the altar and all its utensils and the basin with its stand, to consecrate them. [12]He poured some of the anointing oil on Aaron's head and anointed him to consecrate him. [13]Then he brought Aaron's sons forward, put tunics on them, tied sashes around them and fastened caps on them, as the LORD commanded Moses.

[14]He then presented the bull for the sin offering, and Aaron and his sons laid their hands on its head. [15]Moses slaughtered the bull and took some of the blood, and with his finger he put it on all the horns of the altar to purify the altar.

He poured out the rest of the blood at the base of the altar. So he consecrated it to make atonement for it. [16]Moses also took all the fat around the internal organs, the long lobe of the liver, and both kidneys and their fat, and burned it on the altar. [17]But the bull with its hide and its flesh and its intestines he burned up outside the camp, as the LORD commanded Moses.

[18]He then presented the ram for the burnt offering, and Aaron and his sons laid their hands on its head. [19]Then Moses slaughtered the ram and splashed the blood against the sides of the altar. [20]He cut the ram into pieces and burned the head,

---

8:15 horns of the altar See 4:7 and note. **make atonement** The altar, the tabernacle and all the items needed for priestly service had to undergo an initial purification to be acceptable for use in God's service.

Types of Offerings in the Old Testament

OFFERING TYPE*	REFERENCES†	MATERIAL OFFERED	DISTRIBUTION
Whole Burnt	Lev 1:3–17; 6:8–13	Male animal without defect (value varies)	All burned
Grain	Lev 2:1–16; 6:14–23	Grain or cakes	Part burned/remainder to priests
Drink	Nu 15:1–10	Wine	Poured out
Peace/Fellowship	Lev 3:1–17; 7:11–21	Animal without defect (value varies)	Fat burned/remainder shared in meal
Thank	Lev 7:12–15; 22:29	Bread, in addition to the regular peace offering	Fat burned/remainder shared in meal
Vow	Lev 7:16–17; 22:17–20	Animal without defect (value varies)	Fat burned/remainder shared in meal
Freewill	Lev 7:16; 22:18–23	Animal without defect (value varies)	Fat burned/remainder shared in meal
Sin/Purification‡	Lev 4:1–35; 6:24–30	Animals without defect of various value (corresponds to status and wealth of person)	Fat burned/remainder to priests
Guilt/Reparation	Lev 5:14–6:7	Ram	Fat burned/remainder to priests
Ordination	Lev 8:22–30; Ex 29:19–34	Ram	Fat burned/remainder to priests

*This table is structured around the basic framework of Lev 1:1–6:7, with related material added to the appropriate category.

†Lev 1:1–6:7 presents the offerings in overview and Lev 6:8–7:21 reviews the same topics from the perspective of the priests.

‡Note that in Leviticus, the offerings are not presented as they would occur in actual practice. In practice, the offerings would go: (1) Sin/Guilt; (2) Whole Burnt/Grain; (3) Peace.

the pieces and the fat. ²¹He washed the internal organs and the legs with water and burned the whole ram on the altar. It was a burnt offering, a pleasing aroma, a food offering presented to the Lord, as the Lord commanded Moses.

²²He then presented the other ram, the ram for the ordination, and Aaron and his sons laid their hands on its head. ²³Moses slaughtered the ram and took some of its blood and put it on the lobe of Aaron's right ear, on the thumb of his right hand and on the big toe of his right foot. ²⁴Moses also brought Aaron's sons forward and put some of the blood on the lobes of their right ears, on the thumbs of their right hands and on the big toes of their right feet. Then he splashed blood against the sides of the altar. ²⁵After that, he took the fat, the fat tail, all the fat around the internal organs, the long lobe of the liver, both kidneys and their fat and the right thigh. ²⁶And from the basket of bread made without yeast, which was before the Lord, he took one thick loaf, one thick loaf with olive oil mixed in, and one thin loaf, and he put these on the fat portions and on the right thigh. ²⁷He put all these in the hands of Aaron and his sons, and they waved them before the Lord as a wave offering. ²⁸Then Moses took them from their hands and burned them on the altar on top of the burnt offering as an ordination offering, a pleasing aroma, a food offering presented to the Lord. ²⁹Moses also took the breast, which was his share of the ordination ram, and waved it before the Lord as a wave offering, as the Lord commanded Moses.

³⁰Then Moses took some of the anointing oil and some of the blood from the altar and sprinkled them on Aaron and his garments and on his sons and their garments. So he consecrated Aaron and his garments and his sons and their garments.

³¹Moses then said to Aaron and his sons, "Cook the meat at the entrance to the tent of meeting and eat it there with the bread from the basket of ordination offerings, as I was commanded: 'Aaron and his sons are to eat it.' ³²Then burn up the rest of the meat and the bread. ³³Do not leave the entrance to the tent of meeting for seven days, until the days of your ordination are completed, for your ordination will last seven days. ³⁴What has been done today was commanded by the Lord to make atonement for you. ³⁵You must stay at the entrance to the tent of meeting day and night for seven days and do what the Lord requires, so you will not die; for that is what I have been commanded."

³⁶So Aaron and his sons did everything the Lord commanded through Moses.

The Priests Begin Their Ministry

9 On the eighth day Moses summoned Aaron and his sons and the elders of Israel. ²He said to Aaron, "Take a bull calf for your sin offering[a] and a ram for your burnt offering, both without defect, and present them before the Lord. ³Then say to the Israelites: 'Take a male goat for a sin offering, a calf and a lamb—both a year old and without defect—for a burnt offering, ⁴and an ox[b] and a ram for a fellowship offering to sacrifice before the Lord, together with a grain offering mixed with olive oil. For today the Lord will appear to you.'"

[a] 2 Or *purification offering*; here and throughout this chapter
[b] 4 The Hebrew word can refer to either male or female; also in verses 18 and 19.

8:22–29 The procedure for the ordination (consecration) offering outlined in this passage does not fit exactly into one of the categories of sacrifice described in chs. 1–7. The description of the breast and right thigh as a wave offering (*tenuphah* in Hebrew; see note on 7:30) and the allotment of those portions to the priests is part of the ritual for the peace (fellowship) offering (7:28–36). In other respects, the closest parallel is the purification ritual described in 14:10–14.

8:22 ram for the ordination The reference to the ordination (consecration) offering in 7:37 may have been anticipating this sacrifice.
8:23 on the lobe of Aaron's right ear The act of smearing some of the blood on the right ear, right thumb, right toe and on the clothes of Aaron and his sons (vv. 23–24,30) purified them and prepared them for service at the tabernacle.
8:24 splashed blood Parallel to what was done in connection with the Sinai covenant (Ex 24:6–8).
8:35 do what the Lord requires It is unclear whether there was a seven-day waiting period to leave the tabernacle precinct after the ordination rituals were complete or if the rituals described here were repeated over seven days.

9:1–24 Following the seven-day ordination period, Aaron offers the inaugural sacrifices for worship at the tabernacle. Everything offered in this chapter is a representative example (in a way) of the sacrifices and offerings detailed in Lev 1–7. Aaron and his sons follow the prescribed procedures for the purification (sin) offering (ch. 4), the burnt offering (ch. 1), the grain offering (ch. 2), and the peace (fellowship) offering (ch. 3). The continuity between chs. 9 and 10 suggests the events all occurred on the one occasion—the inauguration of the tabernacle that immediately followed the ordination of Aaron and his sons.

9:1 On the eighth day This ceremony marks the culmination of the consecration of the priests, the altar and the tabernacle after the seven days of waiting described in 8:35.
9:2 Take Aaron must offer sacrifices to atone for himself first and then for the community. The distinction between offerings for the priests themselves and those for the community as a whole is also seen in the ceremony for the Day of Atonement (compare 16:3–6).
9:3 a male goat for a sin offering According to 4:22–26, this was the purification (sin) offering (*chatta'th* in Hebrew) sacrifice required for a community leader's

⁵They took the things Moses commanded to the front of the tent of meeting, and the entire assembly came near and stood before the LORD. ⁶Then Moses said, "This is what the LORD has commanded you to do, so that the glory of the LORD may appear to you."

⁷Moses said to Aaron, "Come to the altar and sacrifice your sin offering and your burnt offering and make atonement for yourself and the people; sacrifice the offering that is for the people and make atonement for them, as the LORD has commanded."

⁸So Aaron came to the altar and slaughtered the calf as a sin offering for himself. ⁹His sons brought the blood to him, and he dipped his finger into the blood and put it on the horns of the altar; the rest of the blood he poured out at the base of the altar. ¹⁰On the altar he burned the fat, the kidneys and the long lobe of the liver from the sin offering, as the LORD commanded Moses; ¹¹the flesh and the hide he burned up outside the camp.

¹²Then he slaughtered the burnt offering. His sons handed him the blood, and he splashed it against the sides of the altar. ¹³They handed him the burnt offering piece by piece, including the head, and he burned them on the altar. ¹⁴He washed the internal organs and the legs and burned them on top of the burnt offering on the altar.

¹⁵Aaron then brought the offering that was for the people. He took the goat for the people's sin offering and slaughtered it and offered it for a sin offering as he did with the first one.

¹⁶He brought the burnt offering and offered it in the prescribed way. ¹⁷He also brought the grain offering, took a handful of it and burned it on the altar in addition to the morning's burnt offering.

¹⁸He slaughtered the ox and the ram as the fellowship offering for the people. His sons handed him the blood, and he splashed it against the sides of the altar. ¹⁹But the fat portions of the ox and the ram — the fat tail, the layer of fat, the kidneys and the long lobe of the liver — ²⁰these they laid on the breasts, and then Aaron burned the fat on the altar. ²¹Aaron waved the breasts and the right thigh before the LORD as a wave offering, as Moses commanded.

²²Then Aaron lifted his hands toward the people and blessed them. And having sacrificed the sin offering, the burnt offering and the fellowship offering, he stepped down.

²³Moses and Aaron then went into the tent of meeting. When they came out, they blessed the people; and the glory of the LORD appeared to all the people. ²⁴Fire came out from the presence of the LORD and consumed the burnt offering and the fat portions on the altar. And when all the people saw it, they shouted for joy and fell facedown.

The Death of Nadab and Abihu

10 Aaron's sons Nadab and Abihu took their censers, put fire in them and added incense; and they offered unauthorized fire before the LORD, contrary to his command. ²So fire came out from the presence of the LORD and consumed them, and they died before the LORD. ³Moses then said to Aaron, "This is what the LORD spoke of when he said:

---

inadvertent sin. Here the male goat is apparently brought for the entire community (v. 5). The offering required for a special occasion such as the inauguration of the tabernacle or the Day of Atonement may have differed from the usual offering. If the events of 10:12–20 are connected with this same day of sacrifice, then the offering of a male goat for the community could explain the priests' confusion about whether or not it was to be eaten (10:16–18).

9:8 Aaron came to the altar Aaron presented the sacrifices on the altar as instructed, beginning with the purification (sin) offering for himself.

9:9 brought the blood The handling of the blood for this offering also differs from the instructions in 4:1–12 concerning the purification (sin) offering for the priest. According to 4:5–7, the blood was to be sprinkled before the veil (curtain) in the tent of meeting, smeared on the horns of the altar of incense inside the tent of meeting, and poured out at the base of the altar of burnt offering in the tabernacle courtyard. Here Aaron only smears the blood on the horns of the altar of burnt offering and pours the rest of the blood at the base of the altar. The discrepancy could relate to the requirements of the occasion—the day's offerings were unique as the tabernacle's inaugural sacrifices.

9:15 as he did with the first one The purification (sin) offering for the people was handled just like the one for the priest except that Aaron's was a bull and the people's is a goat.

9:16 in the prescribed way Aaron's actions for the burnt offerings, the grain offering and the peace (fellowship) offerings align with the instructions for those offerings outlined earlier in chs. 1–3.

9:24 Fire came out from the presence of the LORD The visible manifestation of divine presence in 9:23 becomes a visible manifestation of divine power.

10:1–20 The events in ch. 10 continue the narrative of the sacrifices offered on the eighth day after Aaron and his sons were ordained to the priesthood. In the opening scene, Aaron's eldest sons, Nadab and Abihu, are struck dead for violating procedure (vv. 1–3). Following that incident, Yahweh reminds Aaron of the responsibilities inherent in his priestly office (vv. 9–11). The narrative ends with another apparent violation of priestly procedure when the purification (sin) offering is completely burned on the altar instead of eaten by the priests (vv. 16–20).

10:1 Aaron's sons Nadab and Abihu Nadab and Abihu appear to be Aaron's eldest sons (Ex 6:23). **unauthorized fire** The Hebrew phrase for what Nadab and Abihu offered is *esh zarah*. The word *esh* means "fire," and *zarah* is an adjective identifying something as "strange," "foreign" or "illegitimate." English translations generally represent the phrase as "unauthorized fire" or "strange fire." The nature of their offense is not specified, but Ex 30:9 prohibits the offering of *ketoreth zarah* (which may be rendered "illegitimate incense") on the altar of incense. This illegitimate incense was likely incense that was not

"'Among those who approach me
    I will be proved holy;
in the sight of all the people
    I will be honored.'"

Aaron remained silent.

⁴Moses summoned Mishael and Elzaphan, sons of Aaron's uncle Uzziel, and said to them, "Come here; carry your cousins outside the camp, away from the front of the sanctuary." ⁵So they came and carried them, still in their tunics, outside the camp, as Moses ordered.

⁶Then Moses said to Aaron and his sons Eleazar and Ithamar, "Do not let your hair become unkempt*a* and do not tear your clothes, or you will die and the Lord will be angry with the whole community. But your relatives, all the Israelites, may mourn for those the Lord has destroyed by fire. ⁷Do not leave the entrance to the tent of meeting or you will die, because the Lord's anointing oil is on you." So they did as Moses said.

⁸Then the Lord said to Aaron, ⁹"You and your sons are not to drink wine or other fermented drink whenever you go into the tent of meeting, or you will die. This is a lasting ordinance for the generations to come, ¹⁰so that you can distinguish between the holy and the common, between the unclean and the clean, ¹¹and so you can teach the Israelites all the decrees the Lord has given them through Moses."

¹²Moses said to Aaron and his remaining sons, Eleazar and Ithamar, "Take the grain offering left over from the food offerings prepared without yeast and presented to the Lord and eat it beside the altar, for it is most holy. ¹³Eat it in the sanctuary area, because it is your share and your sons' share of the food offerings presented to the Lord; for so I have been commanded. ¹⁴But you and your sons and your daughters may eat the breast that was waved and the thigh that was presented. Eat them in a ceremonially clean place; they have been given to you and your children as your share of the Israelites' fellowship offerings. ¹⁵The thigh that was presented and the breast that was waved must be brought with the fat portions of the food offerings, to be waved before the Lord as a wave offering. This will be the perpetual share for you and your children, as the Lord has commanded."

¹⁶When Moses inquired about the goat of the sin offering*b* and found that it had been burned up, he was angry with Eleazar and Ithamar, Aaron's remaining sons, and asked, ¹⁷"Why didn't you eat the sin offering in the sanctuary area? It is most holy; it was given to you to take away the guilt of the community by making atonement for them before the Lord. ¹⁸Since its blood was not taken into the Holy Place, you should have eaten the goat in the sanctuary area, as I commanded."

¹⁹Aaron replied to Moses, "Today they sacrificed their sin offering and their burnt offering before

---

a 6 Or *Do not uncover your heads*   *b* 16 Or *purification offering*; also in verses 17 and 19

---

prepared according to the instructions in Ex 30:34–38. Alternately, Ex 30:7–8 states that Aaron was to offer the incense in the morning and at twilight, so it could have been that Nadab and Abihu were bringing incense to the altar at an inappropriate time. It seems most likely that it was inappropriate for them, instead of Aaron, to be bringing the incense at all.

10:2 fire came out from the presence of the Lord Parallels Lev 9:24, where fire from God's presence directly consumed the sacrifices on the altar.

10:3 those who approach me Refers to those in close proximity to the divine presence—the priests who had just been consecrated in ch. 9.

10:4 carry your cousins Aaron and his surviving two sons could not touch the bodies because contact with a corpse caused ritual impurity (see Nu 19:1–22 and note).

10:6 Do not let your hair become unkempt The Hebrew phrase used here could refer to exposing the head or to disheveling the hair. The same wording appears in Lev 21:10 where the high priest is forbidden from engaging in outward signs of mourning. Disheveling or pulling out one's hair was an expression of mourning (Jos 7:6; Job 2:12; Ezr 9:3). According to Lev 21:1–3, priests could only become unclean for the dead for the priest's nearest relatives, but even that allowance is forbidden here.

10:7 Lord's anointing oil is on you Aaron and his four sons were anointed when they were ordained as priests (8:12,30; Ex 40:13–15).

10:10 between the holy and the common Refers to the duty of the priests to protect sacred space and sacred objects from being treated as ordinary. See the table "Functions of Priests" on p. 171. **between the**

unclean and the clean The distinction between clean and unclean is the main concern of the regulations outlined in Lev 11–15.

10:12 without yeast and presented to the Lord and eat it beside the altar In vv. 12–15, Moses verbally conveys some of Yahweh's instructions about eating the offerings that had been given in chs. 6–7.

10:14 breast that was waved and the thigh This was the priest's portion from the peace (fellowship) offerings (7:30–38).

10:16 sin offering Refers to the male goat sacrificed as the purification (sin) offering (*chatta'th* in Hebrew) for the community (9:3,15). Any *chatta'th* sacrifice where the blood was not brought inside the tent shrine itself could be eaten by the priests (6:24–30; 10:18). Moses was attempting to confirm that the sacrifice had been handled appropriately. See note on 9:3. **he was angry** Moses is alarmed at this failure to follow proper protocol for the purification (sin) offering. He likely feared that Yahweh would strike down Eleazar and Ithamar for the error, just as he had struck Nadab and Abihu for their violation. Their deaths would have put the future of the priesthood from Aaron's line in jeopardy.

10:17 in the sanctuary area According to 6:26, the purification (sin) offering (*chatta'th* in Hebrew) was to be eaten in the Holy Place (the main room of the tabernacle tent). By eating the offering portions, the priests bear the iniquity of the congregation. The act was part of the atonement process.

10:19 Would the Lord have been pleased Aaron attributes the oversight to the trauma of what happened to Nadab and Abihu.

the LORD, but such things as this have happened to me. Would the LORD have been pleased if I had eaten the sin offering today?" ²⁰When Moses heard this, he was satisfied.

Clean and Unclean Food

11:1-23pp — Dt 14:3-20

11 The LORD said to Moses and Aaron, ²"Say to the Israelites: 'Of all the animals that live on land, these are the ones you may eat: ³You may eat any animal that has a divided hoof and that chews the cud.

⁴"There are some that only chew the cud or only have a divided hoof, but you must not eat them. The camel, though it chews the cud, does not have a divided hoof; it is ceremonially unclean for you. ⁵The hyrax, though it chews the cud, does not have a divided hoof; it is unclean for you. ⁶The rabbit, though it chews the cud, does not have a divided hoof; it is unclean for you. ⁷And the pig, though it has a divided hoof, does not chew the cud; it is unclean for you. ⁸You must not eat their meat or touch their carcasses; they are unclean for you.

⁹"Of all the creatures living in the water of the seas and the streams you may eat any that have fins and scales. ¹⁰But all creatures in the seas or streams that do not have fins and scales — whether among all the swarming things or among all the other living creatures in the water — you are to regard as unclean. ¹¹And since you are to regard them as unclean, you must not eat their meat; you must regard their carcasses as unclean. ¹²Anything living in the water that does not have fins and scales is to be regarded as unclean by you.

¹³"These are the birds you are to regard as unclean and not eat because they are unclean: the eagle,ᵃ the vulture, the black vulture, ¹⁴the red kite, any kind of black kite, ¹⁵any kind of raven, ¹⁶the horned owl, the screech owl, the gull, any kind of hawk, ¹⁷the little owl, the cormorant, the great owl, ¹⁸the white owl, the desert owl, the osprey, ¹⁹the stork, any kind of heron, the hoopoe and the bat.

²⁰"All flying insects that walk on all fours are to be regarded as unclean by you. ²¹There are, however, some flying insects that walk on all fours that you may eat: those that have jointed legs for hopping on the ground. ²²Of these you may eat any kind of locust, katydid, cricket or grasshopper. ²³But all other flying insects that have four legs you are to regard as unclean.

²⁴"You will make yourselves unclean by these; whoever touches their carcasses will be unclean till evening. ²⁵Whoever picks up one of their carcasses must wash their clothes, and they will be unclean till evening. ²⁶Every animal that does not have a divided hoof or that does not chew the cud is unclean for you; whoever touches the carcass of any of them will be unclean. ²⁷Of all the animals that walk on all fours, those that walk on their paws are unclean for you;

ᵃ 13 The precise identification of some of the birds, insects and animals in this chapter is uncertain.

11:1−47 This chapter marks a shift of focus from the rules for the priests about the day-to-day operations of the tabernacle to the obligations for all Israel to maintain holiness (vv. 44−45). The central aspect of holiness was that Israelites were to be set apart for Yahweh and distinct from other peoples (20:22−26). The focus on holiness dominates the rest of the book of Leviticus, but rituals such as washing and offering sacrifice were intimately connected with how the Israelites were to maintain holiness.

Leviticus 11 explains the categories of clean and unclean with reference to animals (vv. 46−47). The focus is avoiding ritual impurity (called uncleanness). These laws were central to a complex system of purity and impurity that affected the sacred space of the sanctuary, the priesthood and the daily life of all Israelites. Avoiding impurity was integral to holiness.

11:3 that has a divided hoof and that chews the cud Clean animals—such as cattle, goats and sheep—have hooves split into two toes. These domesticated animals are also ruminants having a complex digestive system with a stomach of 3 or 4 chambers.

11:4−8 This section identifies some animals that are forbidden because they do not fully meet the criteria of v. 3. To be considered clean, the animals must have both split hooves and chew their cud.

11:7 the pig Swine were widely domesticated in the ancient Near East, so this particular dietary restriction stood out as a mark of identity. Archaeologists have noted that Iron Age sites inhabited by Philistines and Ammonites attest to the popularity of the pig for consumption. By contrast, sites from the central hill country associated with Israel show no evidence of pig domestication or consumption.

11:8 they are unclean for you Israelites were rendered unclean by the prohibited animals only if they ate them or touched a carcass.

11:9−23 The discussion of clean and unclean animals in vv. 3−8 dealt with land animals. The following verses cover animals that live in the water, animals that fly and insects.

11:11 carcasses Death was a key cause of ritual uncleanness, so dead bodies had to be avoided.

11:13 birds The Hebrew word used here, *oph*, may be literally rendered as "flying thing."

11:19 bat Since the Hebrew word *oph* used in v. 13 refers to anything that flies (see note on v. 13), the bat is not out of place in the list even though it is technically classified as a mammal, not a bird.

11:20 flying insects Flying insects are designated by the Hebrew phrase *sherets ha'oph* here, which may be literally rendered as "the swarming things that fly."

11:24−44 Verses 24−28 reiterates the prohibition against touching an animal's carcass and summarizes the content of vv. 3−8. The focus of this section is explaining how impurity can be contracted by touching, as opposed to eating.

whoever touches their carcasses will be unclean till evening. ²⁸Anyone who picks up their carcasses must wash their clothes, and they will be unclean till evening. These animals are unclean for you.

²⁹"'Of the animals that move along the ground, these are unclean for you: the weasel, the rat, any kind of great lizard, ³⁰the gecko, the monitor lizard, the wall lizard, the skink and the chameleon. ³¹Of all those that move along the ground, these are unclean for you. Whoever touches them when they are dead will be unclean till evening. ³²When one of them dies and falls on something, that article, whatever its use, will be unclean, whether it is made of wood, cloth, hide or sackcloth. Put it in water; it will be unclean till evening, and then it will be clean. ³³If one of them falls into a clay pot, everything in it will be unclean, and you must break the pot. ³⁴Any food you are allowed to eat that has come into contact with water from any such pot is unclean, and any liquid that is drunk from such a pot is unclean. ³⁵Anything that one of their carcasses falls on becomes unclean; an oven or cooking pot must be broken up. They are unclean, and you are to regard them as unclean. ³⁶A spring, however, or a cistern for collecting water remains clean, but anyone who touches one of these carcasses is unclean. ³⁷If a carcass falls on any seeds that are to be planted, they remain clean. ³⁸But if water has been put on the seed and a carcass falls on it, it is unclean for you.

³⁹"'If an animal that you are allowed to eat dies, anyone who touches its carcass will be unclean till evening. ⁴⁰Anyone who eats some of its carcass must wash their clothes, and they will be unclean till evening. Anyone who picks up the carcass must wash their clothes, and they will be unclean till evening.

⁴¹"'Every creature that moves along the ground is to be regarded as unclean; it is not to be eaten. ⁴²You are not to eat any creature that moves along the ground, whether it moves on its belly or walks on all fours or on many feet; it is unclean. ⁴³Do not defile yourselves by any of these creatures. Do not make yourselves unclean by means of them or be made unclean by them. ⁴⁴I am the LORD your God; consecrate yourselves and be holy, because I am holy. Do not make yourselves unclean by any creature that moves along the ground. ⁴⁵I am the LORD, who brought you up out of Egypt to be your God; therefore be holy, because I am holy.

⁴⁶"'These are the regulations concerning animals, birds, every living thing that moves about in the water and every creature that moves along the ground. ⁴⁷You must distinguish between the unclean and the clean, between living creatures that may be eaten and those that may not be eaten.'"

Purification After Childbirth

12 The LORD said to Moses, ²"Say to the Israelites: 'A woman who becomes pregnant and gives birth to a son will be ceremonially unclean for seven days, just as she is unclean during her monthly period. ³On the eighth day the boy is to be circumcised. ⁴Then the woman must wait thirty-three days to be purified from her bleeding. She must not touch anything sacred or go to the sanctuary until the days of her purification are over. ⁵If she gives birth to a daughter, for two weeks the woman will be unclean, as during her period. Then she must wait sixty-six days to be purified from her bleeding.

11:32 one of them dies and falls on something The legal discussion distinguishes between things that can be fallen on and things that can be fallen into (v. 33).

11:34 drunk from such a pot Solid food moistened by water becomes unclean when it comes into contact with the carcass. Liquid in a vessel that becomes contaminated is also contaminated.

11:36 A spring, however, or a cistern for collecting water Water from a natural source like a spring or stored in the ground as in a cistern was not contaminated the same way as a ceramic vessel. While the water itself did not become impure, anyone removing a carcass from a spring or a cistern was rendered unclean.

11:44 I am holy The only rationale given for the regulations in this chapter is the requirement to emulate Yahweh's own holiness. In v. 45 this reason is given in a way that could be taken as a blanket statement for the entire discussion of clean and unclean creatures (compare 19:2).

11:46 These are the regulations The final two verses of this chapter provide a concluding summary of the regulations about clean and unclean animals with special reference to whether the animals were acceptable for food.

12:1–8 Chapter 12 addresses the issue of a woman's purification after childbirth. Restoring the woman to a state of ritual purity required waiting a prescribed period of time and then offering a purification sacrifice (*chatta'th* in Hebrew; see note on 4:1—5:13). The nature of the woman's impurity during the waiting period is analogous to menstrual impurity (15:19–24).

12:2 will be ceremonially unclean for seven days Since the woman is ritually unclean, she cannot participate in sacred activities or enter sacred space. **during her monthly period** The birth itself cannot be the cause of uncleanness since the child is considered ritually pure. The impurity ascribed here is likely related to bleeding, since the passage refers to her blood three times (vv. 4,5,7).

12:3 boy is to be circumcised Circumcision symbolized covenant membership in the Israelite community (Ge 17:10–14).

12:4 purified from her bleeding Leviticus 12:4–5 describes a second waiting period for the woman. The Hebrew phrase used here, *bidmei tahorah*—which may be literally rendered as "in blood of cleansing"—is also mentioned in v. 5. This concept blends the beliefs that blood is the source of her impurity (15:19–24) with

6 "'When the days of her purification for a son or daughter are over, she is to bring to the priest at the entrance to the tent of meeting a year-old lamb for a burnt offering and a young pigeon or a dove for a sin offering.ª 7He shall offer them before the LORD to make atonement for her, and then she will be ceremonially clean from her flow of blood.

"'These are the regulations for the woman who gives birth to a boy or a girl. 8But if she cannot afford a lamb, she is to bring two doves or two young pigeons, one for a burnt offering and the other for a sin offering. In this way the priest will make atonement for her, and she will be clean.'"

Regulations About Defiling Skin Diseases

13 The LORD said to Moses and Aaron, 2"When anyone has a swelling or a rash or a shiny spot on their skin that may be a defiling skin disease,ᵇ they must be brought to Aaron the priest or to one of his sonsᶜ who is a priest. 3The priest is to examine the sore on the skin, and if the hair in the sore has turned white and the sore appears to be more than skin deep, it is a defiling skin disease. When the priest examines that person, he shall pronounce them ceremonially unclean. 4If the shiny spot on the skin is white but does not appear to be more

than skin deep and the hair in it has not turned white, the priest is to isolate the affected person for seven days. 5On the seventh day the priest is to examine them, and if he sees that the sore is unchanged and has not spread in the skin, he is to isolate them for another seven days. 6On the seventh day the priest is to examine them again, and if the sore has faded and has not spread in the skin, the priest shall pronounce them clean; it is only a rash. They must wash their clothes, and they will be clean. 7But if the rash does spread in their skin after they have shown themselves to the priest to be pronounced clean, they must appear before the priest again. 8The priest is to examine that person, and if the rash has spread in the skin, he shall pronounce them unclean; it is a defiling skin disease.

9"When anyone has a defiling skin disease, they must be brought to the priest. 10The priest is to examine them, and if there is a white swelling in the skin that has turned the hair white and if there is raw flesh in the swelling, 11it is a chronic skin disease and the priest shall pronounce them unclean. He is not to isolate them, because they are already unclean.

ª 6 Or *purification offering*; also in verse 8   ᵇ 2 The Hebrew word for *defiling skin disease*, traditionally translated "leprosy," was used for various diseases affecting the skin; here and throughout verses 3-46.   ᶜ 2 Or *descendants*

---

the idea that blood is an agent of purification (8:15; 14:5–7; 16:18–19).

12:6 the days of her purification The passage of time brought cleansing so the woman was able to bring offerings to the tabernacle to mark the completion of her purification.

12:7 she will be ceremonially clean from her flow of blood Many types of bodily uncleanness are remedied by waiting a set length of time (e.g., 14:23; 15:1–11). Full purification, however, requires presenting a purification (sin) offering and a burnt offering (compare 15:13–15).

12:8 if she cannot afford a lamb The law made allowance for cheaper alternatives for the burnt offering and the purification (sin) offering for people who did not have the economic means to bring livestock (see 1:14–17; 5:7–10).

13:1–59 In chs. 12–15, the Levitical regulations — regulations for use by the priesthood from the tribe of Levi — concern ritual impurity related to the human body. The main topic of 13:1–14:57 is identified by the Hebrew word *tsara'ath,* commonly translated "leprosy." The Hebrew term did not originally refer to leprosy in the modern sense of the English word, which usually designates a mycobacterial infection called Hansen's disease (an affliction that likely did not exist in the Near East until the Hellenistic period, ca. fourth century BC). The Hebrew word *tsara'ath* is a general term covering a variety of infections that produce visible sores on the skin. From the symptoms described in vv. 1–44, *tsara'ath* likely includes the following skin diseases known to modern medicine: psoriasis, eczema, dermatitis, favus, scabies, vitiligo and perhaps skin cancer. The use of *tsara'ath* for surface infections in textiles and building materials (vv. 47–59; 14:34–53) suggests an even broader range

for the word. When *tsara'ath* applies to a person, a visible skin disease or infection of some kind is meant. When the term applies to inanimate objects, *tsara'ath* probably designates some kind of mold or mildew that can affect cloth and plaster.

Leviticus 13 explains how the priests should go about diagnosing an unclean skin disease. In cases where the unclean nature of the infection is not immediately apparent, the priest would quarantine the person for seven days and inspect the infection again. To be declared clean, the marks would have to not spread and to have visibly healed over the course of 14 days of quarantine. If the condition had worsened on reinspection, then the person was pronounced unclean. The specific criteria used to diagnose the condition vary, but they generally include the color of the skin in the diseased area, the color of the hair in the diseased skin, and the size of the infected area.

13:3 The priest is to examine An inspection by a priest is a required element for all the scenarios of potential unclean skin diseases discussed in chs. 13–14. **unclean** Uncleanness and cleanness refer to a complex system of judging ritual purity and impurity that affected the sacred space of the sanctuary, the priesthood and the everyday life of the Israelites.

13:4 seven days The initial period of quarantine in cases where the nature of the affliction was not immediately apparent was always seven days.

13:9–17 This section addresses a new scenario — the possibility of chronic skin conditions (*tsara'ath* in Hebrew; see note on 13:1–59). The diagnosis of this type of skin disease requires swelling and the presence of raw, open flesh in addition to the whiteness and white hair. If the open flesh heals completely, the person may be pronounced clean.

[12]"If the disease breaks out all over their skin and, so far as the priest can see, it covers all the skin of the affected person from head to foot, [13]the priest is to examine them, and if the disease has covered their whole body, he shall pronounce them clean. Since it has all turned white, they are clean. [14]But whenever raw flesh appears on them, they will be unclean. [15]When the priest sees the raw flesh, he shall pronounce them unclean. The raw flesh is unclean; they have a defiling disease. [16]If the raw flesh changes and turns white, they must go to the priest. [17]The priest is to examine them, and if the sores have turned white, the priest shall pronounce the affected person clean; then they will be clean.

[18]"When someone has a boil on their skin and it heals, [19]and in the place where the boil was, a white swelling or reddish-white spot appears, they must present themselves to the priest. [20]The priest is to examine it, and if it appears to be more than skin deep and the hair in it has turned white, the priest shall pronounce that person unclean. It is a defiling skin disease that has broken out where the boil was. [21]But if, when the priest examines it, there is no white hair in it and it is not more than skin deep and has faded, then the priest is to isolate them for seven days. [22]If it is spreading in the skin, the priest shall pronounce them unclean; it is a defiling disease. [23]But if the spot is unchanged and has not spread, it is only a scar from the boil, and the priest shall pronounce them clean.

[24]"When someone has a burn on their skin and a reddish-white or white spot appears in the raw flesh of the burn, [25]the priest is to examine the spot, and if the hair in it has turned white, and it appears to be more than skin deep, it is a defiling disease that has broken out in the burn. The priest shall pronounce them unclean; it is a defiling skin disease. [26]But if the priest examines it and there is no white hair in the spot and if it is not more than skin deep and has faded, then the priest is to isolate them for seven days. [27]On the seventh day the priest is to examine that person, and if it is spreading in the skin, the priest shall pronounce them unclean; it is a defiling skin disease. [28]If, however, the spot is unchanged and has not spread in the skin but has faded, it is a swelling from the burn, and the priest shall pronounce them clean; it is only a scar from the burn.

[29]"If a man or woman has a sore on their head or chin, [30]the priest is to examine the sore, and if it appears to be more than skin deep and the hair in it is yellow and thin, the priest shall pronounce them unclean; it is a defiling skin disease on the head or chin. [31]But if, when the priest examines the sore, it does not seem to be more than skin deep and there is no black hair in it, then the priest is to isolate the affected person for seven days. [32]On the seventh day the priest is to examine the sore, and if it has not spread and there is no yellow hair in it and it does not appear to be more than skin deep, [33]then the man or woman must shave themselves, except for the affected area, and the priest is to keep them isolated another seven days. [34]On the seventh day the priest is to examine the sore, and if it has not spread in the skin and appears to be no more than skin deep, the priest shall pronounce them clean. They must wash their clothes, and they will be clean. [35]But if the sore does spread in the skin after they are pronounced clean, [36]the priest is to examine them, and if he finds that the sore has spread in the skin, he does not need to look for yellow hair; they are unclean. [37]If, however, the sore is unchanged so far as the priest can see, and if black hair has grown in it, the affected person is healed. They are clean, and the priest shall pronounce them clean.

[38]"When a man or woman has white spots on the skin, [39]the priest is to examine them, and if the spots are dull white, it is a harmless rash that has broken out on the skin; they are clean.

[40]"A man who has lost his hair and is bald is clean. [41]If he has lost his hair from the front of his scalp

---

13:12 from head to foot In a case where the skin condition (tsara'ath in Hebrew) has affected the whole body, the person is considered clean as long as all of the skin is white and no raw flesh appears (vv. 13–14).

13:18–28 This passage addresses skin afflictions that develop following the healing of boils or burns. The diagnostic criteria in these cases are essentially the same as the basic condition described in vv. 1–8.

13:23 a scar If the mark did not spread or worsen, then it was considered to have been a part of the healing process from the original injury—whether burn or boil—and not a new condition (compare v. 28).

13:29–37 The skin irritations in this section relate to the skin of the scalp or face. The most likely condition behind what is described here is favus—a fungal infection, usually affecting the scalp, that produces yellowish, crusted lesions.

13:31 sore The Hebrew phrase used here is nega' hannetheq. The first word refers to an affliction or injury. The meaning of netheq is less clear since the Hebrew word only occurs in this passage and in 14:54. However, the related verb means "tear off," which suggests a scab that might be torn off by scratching. When the crusted lesions of favus tear off, they take the hair as well, so netheq may also refer to the tearing away of hair caused by the disease.

13:38–39 The widespread presence of dull white spots on the skin is not an indicator of impurity unless accompanied by other characteristic symptoms of skin ailments (tsara'ath in Hebrew; vv. 3,10,30). The condition described here could be the disorder known as vitiligo (or leukoderma). Vitiligo is characterized by portions of skin losing pigment.

13:40–44 This section begins by explicitly indicating that hair loss alone is not a cause of uncleanness (vv. 40–41). However, an unclean skin disease may break out on the bald scalp just like any other part of the body (vv. 43–44).

and has a bald forehead, he is clean. ⁴²But if he has a reddish-white sore on his bald head or forehead, it is a defiling disease breaking out on his head or forehead. ⁴³The priest is to examine him, and if the swollen sore on his head or forehead is reddish-white like a defiling skin disease, ⁴⁴the man is diseased and is unclean. The priest shall pronounce him unclean because of the sore on his head.

⁴⁵"Anyone with such a defiling disease must wear torn clothes, let their hair be unkempt,ᵃ cover the lower part of their face and cry out, 'Unclean! Unclean!' ⁴⁶As long as they have the disease they remain unclean. They must live alone; they must live outside the camp.

Regulations About Defiling Molds

⁴⁷"As for any fabric that is spoiled with a defiling mold — any woolen or linen clothing, ⁴⁸any woven or knitted material of linen or wool, any leather or anything made of leather — ⁴⁹if the affected area in the fabric, the leather, the woven or knitted material, or any leather article, is greenish or reddish, it is a defiling mold and must be shown to the priest. ⁵⁰The priest is to examine the affected area and isolate the article for seven days. ⁵¹On the seventh day he is to examine it, and if the mold has spread in the fabric, the woven or knitted material, or the leather, whatever its use, it is a persistent defiling mold; the article is unclean. ⁵²He must burn the fabric, the woven or knitted material of wool or linen, or any leather article that has been spoiled; because the defiling mold is persistent, the article must be burned.

⁵³"But if, when the priest examines it, the mold has not spread in the fabric, the woven or knitted material, or the leather article, ⁵⁴he shall order that the spoiled article be washed. Then he is to isolate it for another seven days. ⁵⁵After the article has been washed, the priest is to examine it again, and if the mold has not changed its appearance, even though it has not spread, it is unclean. Burn it, no matter which side of the fabric has been spoiled. ⁵⁶If, when the priest examines it, the mold has faded after the article has been washed, he is to tear the spoiled part out of the fabric, the leather, or the woven or knitted material. ⁵⁷But if it reappears in the fabric, in the woven or knitted material, or in the leather article, it is a spreading mold; whatever has the mold must be burned. ⁵⁸Any fabric, woven or knitted material, or any leather article that has been washed and is rid of the mold, must be washed again. Then it will be clean."

⁵⁹These are the regulations concerning defiling molds in woolen or linen clothing, woven or knitted material, or any leather article, for pronouncing them clean or unclean.

Cleansing From Defiling Skin Diseases

14 The LORD said to Moses, ²"These are the regulations for any diseased person at the time of their ceremonial cleansing, when they are brought to the priest: ³The priest is to go outside the camp and examine them. If they have been healed of their defiling skin disease,ᵇ ⁴the priest shall order that two live clean birds and some

---

ᵃ 45 Or *clothes, uncover their head*   ᵇ 3 The Hebrew word for *defiling skin disease*, traditionally translated "leprosy," was used for various diseases affecting the skin; also in verses 7, 32, 54 and 57.

13:45–46 These two verses provide general guidelines for following the priest's diagnosis. First, the person must show the outward signs of mourning—wearing torn clothes, having disheveled hair, and covering their mouths or upper lips (compare 10:6; 21:10–11; Eze 24:17,22). Second, they were to call out that they were unclean to warn others to stay away. Third, they had to live outside the camp.

13:46 must live outside the camp People who were ritually impure had to stay outside the camp until they were cleansed because the camp was considered sacred space (Lev 14:1–9; Nu 5:2–4).

13:47–59 This passage discusses *tsara'ath* visible in textiles and leather, which was considered analogous to disease on human skin (see note on Lev 13:1–59). If the problem was still present after a seven-day observation, the item would be burned. If the affected area did not grow larger, it was laundered.

13:49 greenish or reddish The color is likely indicative of some kind of mold or other fungus.

14:1–32 Leviticus 14 details the ritual processes involved for cleansing someone or something contaminated by skin ailments. The first section (vv. 1–32) specifically explains the cleansing ritual for a person.

14:3–8 This passage describes the first phase of the purification process, which takes place outside the camp. If the unclean skin disease was healed, the priest needed two birds, cedar wood, hyssop and red yarn to proceed with the purification ritual (v. 4). The ritual continued with the slaughter of one of the birds (v. 5). The bird's blood was mixed with water; then, the living bird, the cedar wood, hyssop and yarn were dipped in the mixture. The person being cleansed was sprinkled with the mixture seven times and the living bird was released—symbolically carrying away the impurity (v. 7). Once this was done, the person being purified had to wash clothes, shave off all hair, and bathe. Then, the person could reenter the camp but not return home for the first seven days (v. 8).

14:3 skin disease The Hebrew term *tsara'ath* is used here and throughout chs. 13–14 to designate an open-ended category of unclean skin diseases or surface discoloration.
14:4 two live clean birds The birds are not sacrifices. The only explicit requirement for these birds is that they are ritually clean. **cedar wood, scarlet yarn and hyssop** These items are regularly involved in purification rituals (vv. 49; Nu 19:6).

cedar wood, scarlet yarn and hyssop be brought for the person to be cleansed. ⁵Then the priest shall order that one of the birds be killed over fresh water in a clay pot. ⁶He is then to take the live bird and dip it, together with the cedar wood, the scarlet yarn and the hyssop, into the blood of the bird that was killed over the fresh water. ⁷Seven times he shall sprinkle the one to be cleansed of the defiling disease, and then pronounce them clean. After that, he is to release the live bird in the open fields.

⁸"The person to be cleansed must wash their clothes, shave off all their hair and bathe with water; then they will be ceremonially clean. After this they may come into the camp, but they must stay outside their tent for seven days. ⁹On the seventh day they must shave off all their hair; they must shave their head, their beard, their eyebrows and the rest of their hair. They must wash their clothes and bathe themselves with water, and they will be clean.

¹⁰"On the eighth day they must bring two male lambs and one ewe lamb a year old, each without defect, along with three-tenths of an ephah\u1d43 of the finest flour mixed with olive oil for a grain offering, and one log\u1d47 of oil. ¹¹The priest who pronounces them clean shall present both the one to be cleansed and their offerings before the LORD at the entrance to the tent of meeting.

¹²"Then the priest is to take one of the male lambs and offer it as a guilt offering, along with the log of oil; he shall wave them before the LORD as a wave offering. ¹³He is to slaughter the lamb in the sanctuary area where the sin offering\u1d9c and the burnt offering are slaughtered. Like the sin offering, the guilt offering belongs to the priest; it is most holy. ¹⁴The priest is to take some of the blood of the guilt offering and put it on the lobe of the right ear of the one to be cleansed, on the thumb of their right hand and on the big toe of their right foot. ¹⁵The priest shall then take some of the log of oil, pour it in the palm of his own left hand, ¹⁶dip his right forefinger into the oil in his palm, and with his finger sprinkle some of it before the LORD seven times. ¹⁷The priest is to put some of the oil remaining in his palm on the lobe of the right ear of the one to be cleansed, on the thumb of their right hand and on the big toe of their right foot, on top of the blood of the guilt offering. ¹⁸The rest of the oil in his palm the priest shall put on the head of the one to be cleansed and make atonement for them before the LORD.

¹⁹"Then the priest is to sacrifice the sin offering and make atonement for the one to be cleansed from their uncleanness. After that, the priest shall slaughter the burnt offering ²⁰and offer it on the altar, together with the grain offering, and make atonement for them, and they will be clean.

²¹"If, however, they are poor and cannot afford these, they must take one male lamb as a guilt offering to be waved to make atonement for them, together with a tenth of an ephah\u1d48 of the finest flour mixed with olive oil for a grain offering, a log of oil, ²²and two doves or two young pigeons, such as they can afford, one for a sin offering and the other for a burnt offering.

²³"On the eighth day they must bring them for their cleansing to the priest at the entrance to the tent of meeting, before the LORD. ²⁴The priest is to take the lamb for the guilt offering, together with the log of oil, and wave them before the LORD as a wave offering. ²⁵He shall slaughter the lamb for the guilt offering and take some of its blood and put it on the lobe of the right ear of the one to be cleansed, on the thumb of their right hand and on the big toe of their right foot. ²⁶The priest is to pour some of the oil into the palm of his own left hand, ²⁷and with his right forefinger sprinkle some of the oil from his palm seven times before the LORD. ²⁸Some of the oil in his palm he is to put

---

\u1d43 10 That is, probably about 11 pounds or about 5 kilograms   \u1d47 10 That is, about 1/3 quart or about 0.3 liter; also in verses 12, 15, 21 and 24   \u1d9c 13 Or *purification offering*; also in verses 19, 22 and 31   \u1d48 21 That is, probably about 3 1/2 pounds or about 1.6 kilograms

---

14:7 Seven times he shall sprinkle The blood is sprinkled on the person to be cleansed (compare Ex 24:8). The blood of a purification (sin) offering was applied to the altar (Lev 4:30), so the handling of the blood here also indicates this ritual is not a sacrifice. **he is to release the live bird** Since the release of the bird symbolized the impurity being carried away, the bird was probably not a domesticated sacrificial bird like the pigeon or turtledove. Use of domesticated birds would have exposed the community to the possibility that the bird would return and bring back the impurity.

14:9–20 The second phase of the purification ritual took place inside the camp. On the last day of the seven-day waiting period, the person repeated the process of shaving all hair, washing clothes and bathing. On the eighth day, the cleansing was finalized with sacrifices and offerings (compare 12:6–7). The required offerings

for purification included three lambs (two males and a female) and a grain offering (v. 10). The ritual involving the guilt (trespass) offering (*asham* in Hebrew) entails applying the blood to the person being cleansed. This procedure is similar to how Aaron and his sons were originally purified and consecrated for priestly service (see 8:22–29 and note).

14:21–32 Just as with other purification offerings, cheaper alternative offerings are allowed for this purpose as well (e.g., 5:7–13; 12:8). Instead of three lambs and a grain offering, the person may bring one lamb, two birds and a smaller grain offering (vv. 21–22). The process of applying the blood of the guilt (trespass) offering (*asham* in Hebrew) to the person, described in vv. 14–18, is repeated essentially verbatim here (vv. 25–29).

14:21 a tenth of an ephah The grain offering is a third of what was required for the regular ritual (v. 10).

on the same places he put the blood of the guilt offering — on the lobe of the right ear of the one to be cleansed, on the thumb of their right hand and on the big toe of their right foot. ²⁹The rest of the oil in his palm the priest shall put on the head of the one to be cleansed, to make atonement for them before the LORD. ³⁰Then he shall sacrifice the doves or the young pigeons, such as the person can afford, ³¹one as a sin offering and the other as a burnt offering, together with the grain offering. In this way the priest will make atonement before the LORD on behalf of the one to be cleansed."

³²These are the regulations for anyone who has a defiling skin disease and who cannot afford the regular offerings for their cleansing.

Cleansing From Defiling Molds

³³The LORD said to Moses and Aaron, ³⁴"When you enter the land of Canaan, which I am giving you as your possession, and I put a spreading mold in a house in that land, ³⁵the owner of the house must go and tell the priest, 'I have seen something that looks like a defiling mold in my house.' ³⁶The priest is to order the house to be emptied before he goes in to examine the mold, so that nothing in the house will be pronounced unclean. After this the priest is to go in and inspect the house. ³⁷He is to examine the mold on the walls, and if it has greenish or reddish depressions that appear to be deeper than the surface of the wall, ³⁸the priest shall go out the doorway of the house and close it up for seven days. ³⁹On the seventh day the priest shall return to inspect the house. If the mold has spread on the walls, ⁴⁰he is to order that the contaminated stones be torn out and thrown into an unclean place outside the town. ⁴¹He must have all the inside walls of the house scraped and the material that is scraped off dumped into an unclean place outside the town. ⁴²Then they are to take other stones to replace these and take new clay and plaster the house.

⁴³"If the defiling mold reappears in the house after the stones have been torn out and the house scraped and plastered, ⁴⁴the priest is to go and examine it and, if the mold has spread in the house, it is a persistent defiling mold; the house is un-

clean. ⁴⁵It must be torn down — its stones, timbers and all the plaster — and taken out of the town to an unclean place.

⁴⁶"Anyone who goes into the house while it is closed up will be unclean till evening. ⁴⁷Anyone who sleeps or eats in the house must wash their clothes.

⁴⁸"But if the priest comes to examine it and the mold has not spread after the house has been plastered, he shall pronounce the house clean, because the defiling mold is gone. ⁴⁹To purify the house he is to take two birds and some cedar wood, scarlet yarn and hyssop. ⁵⁰He shall kill one of the birds over fresh water in a clay pot. ⁵¹Then he is to take the cedar wood, the hyssop, the scarlet yarn and the live bird, dip them into the blood of the dead bird and the fresh water, and sprinkle the house seven times. ⁵²He shall purify the house with the bird's blood, the fresh water, the live bird, the cedar wood, the hyssop and the scarlet yarn. ⁵³Then he is to release the live bird in the open fields outside the town. In this way he will make atonement for the house, and it will be clean."

⁵⁴These are the regulations for any defiling skin disease, for a sore, ⁵⁵for defiling molds in fabric or in a house, ⁵⁶and for a swelling, a rash or a shiny spot, ⁵⁷to determine when something is clean or unclean.

These are the regulations for defiling skin diseases and defiling molds.

Discharges Causing Uncleanness

15 The LORD said to Moses and Aaron, ²"Speak to the Israelites and say to them: 'When any man has an unusual bodily discharge, such a discharge is unclean. ³Whether it continues flowing from his body or is blocked, it will make him unclean. This is how his discharge will bring about uncleanness:

⁴"'Any bed the man with a discharge lies on will be unclean, and anything he sits on will be unclean. ⁵Anyone who touches his bed must wash their clothes and bathe with water, and they will be unclean till evening. ⁶Whoever sits on anything that the man with a discharge sat on must wash

---

14:33–57 Building materials could become contaminated just as cloth could (see 13:47–59 and note). As with cloth, the problem was likely some sort of mold, identified by greenish or reddish spots in the walls. The process to diagnose whether the contamination caused ritual uncleanness was essentially the same as that for an unclean skin disease (13:1–8): initial inspection, seven-day quarantine and reinspection (vv. 37–39).

14:34 a spreading mold The application of the Hebrew term used here, *tsara'ath*, to plastered walls supports the understanding of it as a general word for surface afflictions, not a term for any one specific skin disease (see note on 13:1–59).

14:54–57 These three verses provide a concluding summary for the entire discussion of unclean skin diseases and surface afflictions — all identified by the Hebrew word *tsara'ath* — found in 13:1—14:53.

15:1–33 This chapter details how bodily discharges from male and female sexual organs caused ritual impurity. The chapter outlines required procedures for restoring purity in the wake of such discharges (male, vv. 1–18; female, vv. 19–30).

15:2 an unusual bodily discharge The Hebrew phrase used here is *zab mibbsaro*. The word *zab* is a general word for any kind of discharge, so it may be used with

their clothes and bathe with water, and they will be unclean till evening.

⁷"'Whoever touches the man who has a discharge must wash their clothes and bathe with water, and they will be unclean till evening.

⁸"'If the man with the discharge spits on anyone who is clean, they must wash their clothes and bathe with water, and they will be unclean till evening.

⁹"'Everything the man sits on when riding will be unclean, ¹⁰and whoever touches any of the things that were under him will be unclean till evening; whoever picks up those things must wash their clothes and bathe with water, and they will be unclean till evening.

¹¹"'Anyone the man with a discharge touches without rinsing his hands with water must wash their clothes and bathe with water, and they will be unclean till evening.

¹²"'A clay pot that the man touches must be broken, and any wooden article is to be rinsed with water.

¹³"'When a man is cleansed from his discharge, he is to count off seven days for his ceremonial cleansing; he must wash his clothes and bathe himself with fresh water, and he will be clean. ¹⁴On the eighth day he must take two doves or two young pigeons and come before the LORD to the entrance to the tent of meeting and give them to the priest. ¹⁵The priest is to sacrifice them, the one for a sin offering*a* and the other for a burnt offer-

ing. In this way he will make atonement before the LORD for the man because of his discharge.

¹⁶"'When a man has an emission of semen, he must bathe his whole body with water, and he will be unclean till evening. ¹⁷Any clothing or leather that has semen on it must be washed with water, and it will be unclean till evening. ¹⁸When a man has sexual relations with a woman and there is an emission of semen, both of them must bathe with water, and they will be unclean till evening.

¹⁹"'When a woman has her regular flow of blood, the impurity of her monthly period will last seven days, and anyone who touches her will be unclean till evening.

²⁰"'Anything she lies on during her period will be unclean, and anything she sits on will be unclean. ²¹Anyone who touches her bed will be unclean; they must wash their clothes and bathe with water, and they will be unclean till evening. ²²Anyone who touches anything she sits on will be unclean; they must wash their clothes and bathe with water, and they will be unclean till evening. ²³Whether it is the bed or anything she was sitting on, when anyone touches it, they will be unclean till evening.

²⁴"'If a man has sexual relations with her and her monthly flow touches him, he will be unclean for seven days; any bed he lies on will be unclean.

²⁵"'When a woman has a discharge of blood for many days at a time other than her monthly

a 15 Or *purification offering*; also in verse 30

---

reference to a discharge associated with illness or one connected with normal bodily processes. The second word—*basar*—is a common word for the body. However, *basar* is also a common euphemism in OT Hebrew for male genitalia (e.g., Eze 16:26; 23:20).

15:3–12 This passage describes how impurity spreads in connection with the man with a discharge. Contact with the man or with things he touched passed on a temporary impurity to others. The instructions to avoid the man's bed or anything that he sits on are later repeated with reference to a woman's menstrual impurity (compare Lev 15:4–6,19–24). The remedy for all cases was the same—washing clothes, bathing and waiting until evening—(probably sunset).

15:11 his hands This rinsing of the hands apparently obstructed the transmission of the sort of temporary impurity described in vv. 5–11.

15:13–15 These verses outline the ritual for final purification after a man's discharge has stopped. The process is somewhat analogous to that for a woman's final purification after childbirth (12:1–8). The cleansing procedure also partly parallels that for a person being cleansed from an unclean skin disease (14:8–9,21–23). The common elements in most purification procedures are a waiting period, bathing, washing clothes and bringing a burnt offering and a purification offering.

15:16–24 This passage addresses uncleanness related to natural bodily functioning, not illness. These types of

impurity were treatable with time, bathing and washing clothes. No sacrificial offerings were required. There are no explicit instructions that the woman should bathe or wash clothes, but it is likely that her impurity was cleansed following the same process as in vv. 16–18. Washing is explicitly noted in many other passages about purification (e.g., 11:25; 15:13; Nu 19:19), suggesting the practice could be assumed from the context.

15:19 anyone who touches her These instructions about impurity spread through contact with the menstruating woman are similar to the detailed comments about how anything a man with a discharge touches becomes unclean (compare Lev 15:3–12 and note).

15:20 Anything she lies on The spread of menstrual impurity appears to be more limited than the impurity from a discharge described in vv. 1–15. Since the impurity is mainly limited to areas where she was lying or sitting, the concern may have been with areas that had direct contact with her menstrual flow.

15:25–30 The final scenario, like the first in vv. 1–15, addresses an abnormal discharge—in this case, a woman who has a discharge of blood that is not related to menstruation. When the discharge stops, she must wait seven days and then bring sacrifices to the priest for final purification. The cleansing procedure described in vv. 28–30 is the same as the one from vv. 14–15. The need for ritual washing in the instructions related to women (vv. 19–30) should be assumed by analogy with the first half of the chapter, which dealt with impurity related to men (vv. 1–18).

period or has a discharge that continues beyond her period, she will be unclean as long as she has the discharge, just as in the days of her period. ²⁶Any bed she lies on while her discharge continues will be unclean, as is her bed during her monthly period, and anything she sits on will be unclean, as during her period. ²⁷Anyone who touches them will be unclean; they must wash their clothes and bathe with water, and they will be unclean till evening.

²⁸"'When she is cleansed from her discharge, she must count off seven days, and after that she will be ceremonially clean. ²⁹On the eighth day she must take two doves or two young pigeons and bring them to the priest at the entrance to the tent of meeting. ³⁰The priest is to sacrifice one for a sin offering and the other for a burnt offering. In this way he will make atonement for her before the LORD for the uncleanness of her discharge.

³¹"'You must keep the Israelites separate from things that make them unclean, so they will not die in their uncleanness for defiling my dwelling place,ᵃ which is among them.'"

³²These are the regulations for a man with a discharge, for anyone made unclean by an emission of semen, ³³for a woman in her monthly period, for a man or a woman with a discharge, and for a man who has sexual relations with a woman who is ceremonially unclean.

The Day of Atonement

16:2-34pp — Lev 23:26-32; Nu 29:7-11

16 The LORD spoke to Moses after the death of the two sons of Aaron who died when they approached the LORD. ²The LORD said to Moses:

"Tell your brother Aaron that he is not to come whenever he chooses into the Most Holy Place behind the curtain in front of the atonement cover on the ark, or else he will die. For I will appear in the cloud over the atonement cover.

³"This is how Aaron is to enter the Most Holy Place: He must first bring a young bull for a sin offeringᵇ and a ram for a burnt offering. ⁴He is to put on the sacred linen tunic, with linen undergarments next to his body; he is to tie the linen sash around him and put on the linen turban. These are sacred garments; so he must bathe himself with water before he puts them on. ⁵From the Israelite community he is to take two male goats for a sin offering and a ram for a burnt offering.

⁶"Aaron is to offer the bull for his own sin offering to make atonement for himself and his household. ⁷Then he is to take the two goats and present them before the LORD at the entrance to the tent of meeting. ⁸He is to cast lots for the two goats — one lot for the LORD and the other for the scapegoat.ᶜ ⁹Aaron shall bring the goat whose lot falls to the LORD and sacrifice it for a sin offering. ¹⁰But the goat chosen by lot as the scapegoat shall be presented alive before the LORD to be used for making atonement by sending it into the wilderness as a scapegoat.

¹¹"Aaron shall bring the bull for his own sin offering to make atonement for himself and his household, and he is to slaughter the bull for his own sin offering. ¹²He is to take a censer full of burning coals from the altar before the LORD and

---

ᵃ 31 Or *my tabernacle*   ᵇ 3 Or *purification offering*; here and throughout this chapter   ᶜ 8 The meaning of the Hebrew for this word is uncertain; also in verses 10 and 26.

15:29 bring them to the priest The passages addressing abnormal discharges (vv. 1–15,25–30) bracket the section on natural discharges (vv. 16–24). Only abnormal discharges required sacrificial offerings for purification.

16:1–34 Chapter 16 describes the rituals for the Day of Atonement, known in Jewish tradition as Yom Kippur. This day—the tenth day of the seventh month—was the one time per year when the high priest was permitted to enter the Holy of Holies (or Most Holy Place) and stand before the ark of the covenant to atone for the sins of the nation (v. 34). The ritual has two basic components: purifying the sanctuary and eliminating the sins that caused the impurity and offended Yahweh.

16:1 who died when they approached the LORD This verse explicitly connects the instructions of ch. 16 with the events of ch. 10, where Aaron's sons Nadab and Abihu died in the tabernacle for violating procedure (see note on 10:1–20). The detailed procedure for the Day of Atonement was needed to prevent a similar tragedy from happening again.

16:2 or else he will die In Biblical passages where Yahweh has appeared to people, they often fear that they will die from having been in the presence of God (e.g., Ge 32:30; Ex 33:20; Jdg 13:21–22).

16:3 sin offering See Lev 4:1—5:13 and note.

16:8 for the LORD The goat designated for Yahweh was the one used to purge the sanctuary (v. 9). **for the scapegoat** The second goat was not sacrificed; it was driven out of the camp after the high priest symbolically transferred the sins of the nation to it. Interpretation of the Hebrew term *aza'zel* used here is debated. The word is usually either translated as scapegoat or treated as the proper name Azazel for a deity or place (such as a cliff). These two possibilities stem from different ways of dividing the Hebrew letters into words. The interpretation of scapegoat derives from dividing the letters into two words: *az* plus *azal*, meaning "the goat that goes away." However, the traditional Hebrew text (the Masoretic Text) preserves these letters as one word, and the sentence is structured in a way that supports reading a proper name here. The name Azazel is known from later Jewish texts, such as 1 Enoch, as the name of a demon associated with the desert (1 Enoch 8:1; 9:6; 10:4–8; 13:1–3). If Azazel, the deity is in view, this is not meant to indicate that the people were offering a sacrifice to this Azazel (Lev 17:7 would prohibit this), but instead that they were sending the goat that carried their sin outside the land deemed holy for Yahweh—into a territory understood to be under Azazel's jurisdiction (see note on 16:22; note on 17:7).

16:10 for making atonement Atonement is typically associated with blood sacrifice—the guilt (trespass)

two handfuls of finely ground fragrant incense and take them behind the curtain. ¹³He is to put the incense on the fire before the LORD, and the smoke of the incense will conceal the atonement cover above the tablets of the covenant law, so that he will not die. ¹⁴He is to take some of the bull's blood and with his finger sprinkle it on the front of the atonement cover; then he shall sprinkle some of it with his finger seven times before the atonement cover.

¹⁵"He shall then slaughter the goat for the sin offering for the people and take its blood behind the curtain and do with it as he did with the bull's blood: He shall sprinkle it on the atonement cover and in front of it. ¹⁶In this way he will make atonement for the Most Holy Place because of the uncleanness and rebellion of the Israelites, whatever their sins have been. He is to do the same for the tent of meeting, which is among them in the midst of their uncleanness. ¹⁷No one is to be in the tent of meeting from the time Aaron goes in to make atonement in the Most Holy Place until he comes out, having made atonement for himself, his household and the whole community of Israel.

¹⁸"Then he shall come out to the altar that is before the LORD and make atonement for it. He shall take some of the bull's blood and some of the goat's blood and put it on all the horns of the altar. ¹⁹He shall sprinkle some of the blood on it with his finger seven times to cleanse it and to consecrate it from the uncleanness of the Israelites.

²⁰"When Aaron has finished making atonement for the Most Holy Place, the tent of meeting and the altar, he shall bring forward the live goat. ²¹He is to lay both hands on the head of the live goat and confess over it all the wickedness and rebellion of the Israelites — all their sins — and put them on the goat's head. He shall send the goat away into the wilderness in the care of someone appointed for the task. ²²The goat will carry on itself all their sins to a remote place; and the man shall release it in the wilderness.

²³"Then Aaron is to go into the tent of meeting and take off the linen garments he put on before he entered the Most Holy Place, and he is to leave them there. ²⁴He shall bathe himself with water in the sanctuary area and put on his regular garments. Then he shall come out and sacrifice the burnt offering for himself and the burnt offering for the people, to make atonement for himself and for the people. ²⁵He shall also burn the fat of the sin offering on the altar.

²⁶"The man who releases the goat as a scapegoat must wash his clothes and bathe himself with water; afterward he may come into the camp. ²⁷The bull and the goat for the sin offerings, whose blood was brought into the Most Holy Place to make atonement, must be taken outside the camp; their hides, flesh and intestines are to be burned up. ²⁸The man who burns them must wash his clothes and bathe himself with water; afterward he may come into the camp.

²⁹"This is to be a lasting ordinance for you: On the tenth day of the seventh month you must deny yourselves[a] and not do any work — whether native-born or a foreigner residing among you — ³⁰because on this day atonement will be made for you, to cleanse you. Then, before the LORD, you will be clean from all your sins. ³¹It is a day of sabbath rest, and you must deny yourselves; it is a lasting ordinance. ³²The priest who is anointed and ordained to succeed his father as high priest is to make atonement. He is to put on the sacred linen garments ³³and make atonement for the Most Holy Place, for the tent of meeting and the altar, and for the priests and all the members of the community.

³⁴"This is to be a lasting ordinance for you: Atonement is to be made once a year for all the sins of the Israelites."

And it was done, as the LORD commanded Moses.

<hr>

a 29 Or must fast; also in verse 31

<hr>

offering (asham in Hebrew) and the purification (sin) offering (chatta'th in Hebrew). No blood is applied to the goat or associated with this part of the ritual (vv. 20–22). See 4:20 and note.

16:12 behind the curtain The Day of Atonement was the only time the priest could go beyond the veil (curtain) that separated the front room of the tent (or later the temple) from the inner room (the Most Holy Place or Holy of Holies).

16:13 conceal the atonement cover The lid of the ark of the covenant was called in Hebrew the kapporeth, which is commonly translated as "atonement cover" or "mercy seat" (see note on Ex 25:17).

16:14 He is to take some of the bull's blood The high priest went behind the veil (curtain) twice — first to sprinkle the blood from the bull used for his own purification (sin) offering and then to sprinkle the blood from the goat that was the people's purification (sin) offering (Lev 16:15). The blood of this goat made the

people ritually clean before Yahweh — but their sins had not yet been removed.

16:20 he shall bring forward the live goat After the blood of the goat for Yahweh was sprinkled inside the tabernacle, the ritual shifts focus to the second goat.

16:22 The goat will carry on itself all their sins The live goat carried away the sins of the congregation. This goat bore the sins of the nation and was subsequently driven out of the camp of Israel — out of holy ground and away from a purified people. Compare Isa 53:10–12.

16:26 man who releases the goat The person who leads the goat into the wilderness becomes ritually impure. This impurity is similar to that caused by contact with a carcass in Lev 11:24–25.

16:29 On the tenth day of the seventh month The date designated for the Day of Atonement is specified here in the Hebrew text as the tenth day of the month Tishri (the seventh month).

Eating Blood Forbidden

17 The Lord said to Moses, [2]"Speak to Aaron and his sons and to all the Israelites and say to them: 'This is what the Lord has commanded: [3]Any Israelite who sacrifices an ox,[a] a lamb or a goat in the camp or outside of it [4]instead of bringing it to the entrance to the tent of meeting to present it as an offering to the Lord in front of the tabernacle of the Lord — that person shall be considered guilty of bloodshed; they have shed blood and must be cut off from their people. [5]This is so the Israelites will bring to the Lord the sacrifices they are now making in the open fields. They must bring them to the priest, that is, to the Lord, at the entrance to the tent of meeting and sacrifice them as fellowship offerings. [6]The priest is to splash the blood against the altar of the Lord at the entrance to the tent of meeting and burn the fat as an aroma pleasing to the Lord. [7]They must no longer offer any of their sacrifices to the goat idols[b] to whom they prostitute themselves. This is to be a lasting ordinance for them and for the generations to come.'

[8]"Say to them: 'Any Israelite or any foreigner residing among them who offers a burnt offering or sacrifice [9]and does not bring it to the entrance to the tent of meeting to sacrifice it to the Lord must be cut off from the people of Israel.

[10]"'I will set my face against any Israelite or any foreigner residing among them who eats blood, and I will cut them off from the people. [11]For the life of a creature is in the blood, and I have given it to you to make atonement for yourselves on the altar; it is the blood that makes atonement for one's life.[c] [12]Therefore I say to the Israelites, "None of you may eat blood, nor may any foreigner residing among you eat blood."

[13]"'Any Israelite or any foreigner residing among you who hunts any animal or bird that may be eaten must drain out the blood and cover it with earth, [14]because the life of every creature is its blood. That is why I have said to the Israelites, "You must not eat the blood of any creature, because the life of every creature is its blood; anyone who eats it must be cut off."

[15]"'Anyone, whether native-born or foreigner, who eats anything found dead or torn by wild animals must wash their clothes and bathe with water, and they will be ceremonially unclean till evening; then they will be clean. [16]But if they do not wash their clothes and bathe themselves, they will be held responsible.'"

Unlawful Sexual Relations

18 The Lord said to Moses, [2]"Speak to the Israelites and say to them: 'I am the Lord your God. [3]You must not do as they do in Egypt, where you used to live, and you must not do as they do in the land of Canaan, where I am bringing you. Do not follow their practices. [4]You must obey my laws and be careful to follow my decrees.

---

[a] 3 The Hebrew word can refer to either male or female.
[b] 7 Or *the demons*   [c] 11 Or *atonement by the life in the blood*

17:1–16 Chapter 17 initiates what is commonly called the Holiness Code (chs. 17–26), where the underlying assumption is that the responsibility of holiness falls on Israel as a nation versus individuals. This idea is expressed clearly in 19:2 where Yahweh commands Israel to be holy because he is holy.

17:3 sacrifices an ox, a lamb or a goat It is unclear whether sacrificial or secular slaughter is in view (i.e., slaughter for any reason besides sacrifice, such as food). It is likely that this requirement is intended to prevent illegitimate sacrifice (compare v. 7).
17:4 instead of bringing it Any animals that were eligible to be sacrifices to Yahweh but were slaughtered outside the tabernacle were to be brought there as sacrificial offerings. Failure to do so brought blood-guilt on the person.
17:5 they are now making in the open fields Before the institution of the tabernacle (see Ex 26), sacrifices were sometimes offered in an open field. **fellowship offerings** Most of the meat of this offering belonged to the one who brought the sacrifice, making this offering the typical one for slaughtering sacrificial animals for food (see note on Lev 3:1–17).
17:7 goat idols Reflects the ancient belief that goat demons (*se'irim* in Hebrew) lived in the wilderness. It is possible that the Israelites were offering sacrifices to divine beings thought to inhabit the desert. The prohibition here aimed to eliminate the practice and bring all sacrifice under the auspices of the priesthood.

17:10–16 This passage provides the process for the proper disposal of an animal's blood before consumption.

17:10 eats blood Refers to eating meat from a slaughtered animal that has not been entirely drained of blood.
17:11 life of a creature is in the blood This statement appears again in v. 14 (compare Ge 9:4; Dt 12:23–24). Since ancient people knew that animals and human beings died from significant blood loss, they identified the essence of life with blood.
17:13 cover it with earth This ensured that the blood was not eaten by the hunter or anyone else. It may have also prevented other animals from consuming the blood.

18:1–18 Leviticus 18 provides the most thorough catalog of laws regulating sexuality in the OT. The initial focus is prohibiting sexual contact with close relatives—condemned as depravity and a violation of the respect commanded by kinship relationships (vv. 6–18). This class of relatives is labeled as *she'er* in Hebrew (v. 6). Only sexual relationships among immediate relatives are forbidden. Marriages to others within the same clan or tribe were common (e.g., Ge 24:1–9; Nu 36:1–13).

18:3 You must not do as they do The sexual standards for Israel are presented as a direct contrast with those of Egypt and Canaan. In this way, the writer references Israel's past and future and reinforces the idea that Israel is to stand apart from its geo-political context. **in the land of Canaan** In the OT, the Canaanites are regularly associated with sexual immorality (Ge 19:5–6; Eze 16:3; compare Dt 20:16–18).

I am the LORD your God. ⁵Keep my decrees and laws, for the person who obeys them will live by them. I am the LORD.

⁶"'No one is to approach any close relative to have sexual relations. I am the LORD.

⁷"'Do not dishonor your father by having sexual relations with your mother. She is your mother; do not have relations with her.

⁸"'Do not have sexual relations with your father's wife; that would dishonor your father.

⁹"'Do not have sexual relations with your sister, either your father's daughter or your mother's daughter, whether she was born in the same home or elsewhere.

¹⁰"'Do not have sexual relations with your son's daughter or your daughter's daughter; that would dishonor you.

¹¹"'Do not have sexual relations with the daughter of your father's wife, born to your father; she is your sister.

¹²"'Do not have sexual relations with your father's sister; she is your father's close relative.

¹³"'Do not have sexual relations with your mother's sister, because she is your mother's close relative.

¹⁴"'Do not dishonor your father's brother by approaching his wife to have sexual relations; she is your aunt.

¹⁵"'Do not have sexual relations with your daughter-in-law. She is your son's wife; do not have relations with her.

¹⁶"'Do not have sexual relations with your brother's wife; that would dishonor your brother.

¹⁷"'Do not have sexual relations with both a woman and her daughter. Do not have sexual relations with either her son's daughter or her daughter's daughter; they are her close relatives. That is wickedness.

¹⁸"'Do not take your wife's sister as a rival wife and have sexual relations with her while your wife is living.

¹⁹"'Do not approach a woman to have sexual relations during the uncleanness of her monthly period.

²⁰"'Do not have sexual relations with your neighbor's wife and defile yourself with her.

²¹"'Do not give any of your children to be sacrificed to Molek, for you must not profane the name of your God. I am the LORD.

²²"'Do not have sexual relations with a man as one does with a woman; that is detestable.

²³"'Do not have sexual relations with an animal and defile yourself with it. A woman must not present herself to an animal to have sexual relations with it; that is a perversion.

²⁴"'Do not defile yourselves in any of these ways, because this is how the nations that I am going to drive out before you became defiled. ²⁵Even the land was defiled; so I punished it for its sin, and the land vomited out its inhabitants. ²⁶But you must keep my decrees and my laws. The native-born and the foreigners residing among you must not do any of these detestable things, ²⁷for all these things were done by the people who lived in the land before you, and the land became defiled. ²⁸And if you defile the land, it will vomit you out as it vomited out the nations that were before you.

²⁹"'Everyone who does any of these detestable things — such persons must be cut off from their people. ³⁰Keep my requirements and do not follow any of the detestable customs that were practiced

---

18:6–18 These laws forbid incestuous relationships and sexual relationships with other close relatives, whether related by blood or marriage.

18:6 close relative The Hebrew idiom here essentially means one's own flesh and blood. However, relatives by marriage are also included in the prohibitions by virtue of their connection with someone who is a flesh and blood relative (see Lev 18:14–16). **sexual relations** A common Hebrew idiom appears here and throughout the chapter; it consists of a form of the Hebrew verb *galah*, meaning "reveal" or "uncover," and the noun *erwah*, meaning "nakedness." The idiom of "uncovering nakedness" is a common euphemism for sexual intercourse (or relations).

18:8 father's wife Refers to a wife other than the individual's mother. In patriarchal, ancient Near Eastern cultures, a man often had more than one wife.

18:9 in the same home or elsewhere Reinforces the prohibition against sexual intercourse with sisters, whether full, half or step.

18:16 brother's wife Forbids sexual relations with a sister-in-law. An exception is made if the brother died without leaving a male heir. In this case, a surviving brother produces an heir for his brother with his brother's widow. This is known as levirate marriage (Dt 25:5–10; compare Ge 38).

18:17 they are her close relatives If a woman is taken as a wife, then sexual relations with her daughters and granddaughters are forbidden.

18:19–30 Besides sexuality within the family, Lev 18 classifies other sexual activities as unclean and abominations (v. 27). The rationale provided for these prohibitions is that they were Canaanite practices that made the land unclean (vv. 24–30).

18:20 your neighbor's wife This prohibition echoes the seventh commandment prohibiting adultery (Ex 20:14; Dt 5:18).

18:21 Molek A Semitic deity worshiped by some Canaanite peoples. Mention of this deity in the OT is often connected with child sacrifice.

18:22 Do not have sexual relations with a man Most major ancient Near Eastern cultures contemporary with OT Israel considered homosexuality—along with other practices like incest or bestiality—to be deviant, but not a capital crime (compare Lev 20:13,15–16,17).

18:28 defile the land By speaking both about the uncleanness of the people and that of the land (polluted by the actions of the people), vv. 27–28 emphasize the

before you came and do not defile yourselves with them. I am the LORD your God.'"

Various Laws

19 The LORD said to Moses, 2"Speak to the entire assembly of Israel and say to them: 'Be holy because I, the LORD your God, am holy.

3"'Each of you must respect your mother and father, and you must observe my Sabbaths. I am the LORD your God.

4"'Do not turn to idols or make metal gods for yourselves. I am the LORD your God.

5"'When you sacrifice a fellowship offering to the LORD, sacrifice it in such a way that it will be accepted on your behalf. 6It shall be eaten on the day you sacrifice it or on the next day; anything left over until the third day must be burned up. 7If any of it is eaten on the third day, it is impure and will not be accepted. 8Whoever eats it will be held responsible because they have desecrated what is holy to the LORD; they must be cut off from their people.

9"'When you reap the harvest of your land, do not reap to the very edges of your field or gather the gleanings of your harvest. 10Do not go over your vineyard a second time or pick up the grapes that have fallen. Leave them for the poor and the foreigner. I am the LORD your God.

11"'Do not steal.

"'Do not lie.

"'Do not deceive one another.

12"'Do not swear falsely by my name and so profane the name of your God. I am the LORD.

13"'Do not defraud or rob your neighbor.

"'Do not hold back the wages of a hired worker overnight.

14"'Do not curse the deaf or put a stumbling block in front of the blind, but fear your God. I am the LORD.

15"'Do not pervert justice; do not show partiality to the poor or favoritism to the great, but judge your neighbor fairly.

16"'Do not go about spreading slander among your people.

"'Do not do anything that endangers your neighbor's life. I am the LORD.

17"'Do not hate a fellow Israelite in your heart. Rebuke your neighbor frankly so you will not share in their guilt.

18"'Do not seek revenge or bear a grudge against anyone among your people, but love your neighbor as yourself. I am the LORD.

19"'Keep my decrees.

"'Do not mate different kinds of animals.

"'Do not plant your field with two kinds of seed.

"'Do not wear clothing woven of two kinds of material.

20"'If a man sleeps with a female slave who is promised to another man but who has not been ransomed or given her freedom, there must be due punishment.ᵃ Yet they are not to be put to

---

ᵃ 20 Or be an inquiry

---

relationship between the cleanness of the land and that of the people inhabiting it.

19:1–37 Leviticus 19 expresses principles that extend from the Ten Commandments (Ex 20:1–17; Dt 5:6–21). This chapter establishes the core morality attached to holiness. Holiness describes something set aside as separate from the common or ordinary.

The passage consists of teaching statements one to three verses long that begin with commands related to either things that must be done or that must be avoided. The statements often end with a formulaic pronouncement grounding the holiness principles in Yahweh's divine authority (e.g., Lev 19:3,4).

19:2 Be holy This command to be holy is rooted in the character of Yahweh.

19:3 must respect your mother and father The command to honor one's parents (Ex 20:12) was critical to Israelite society—such a command was expected in a tribal, patriarchal culture. **you must observe my Sabbaths** According to Ex 20:8–11, keeping the Sabbath meant to rest from work on that day; this became a defining characteristic of the community's ethos.

19:8 Whoever eats it will be held responsible Individuals are expected to adhere to these expectations and will suffer the consequences if they are violated. **they must be cut off from their people** One of the most severe punishments leveled. See note on Lev 7:20.

19:9–18 These verses articulate a communal ethic, defined by mutual provision and respect. The exhortations

offered cover a range of issues, touching on the agricultural, legal and social aspects of life. Jesus' teachings on ethics in the Sermon on the Mount, especially portions of Mt 5:21–48, echo some of the ethical exhortations given in this passage, perhaps explaining and elaborating on the principles here.

19:9 do not reap to the very edges of your field Some of the produce was to be left in the field to provide food for poor people and travelers (compare Ru 2:3–7).

19:12 profane Refers to treating something as though it were not holy. In this context, profaning God's name resulted when oaths were not kept.

19:14 a stumbling block in front of the blind This command and the one immediately preceding it prohibit preying on someone's disability.

19:16 spreading slander This command prohibits financial or commercial fraud, but the Hebrew phrase used here might also be idiomatic for gossiping.

19:18 love your neighbor as yourself Aside from loving God, this is the cardinal point of all the laws and personal holiness. It is the corrective to all the previous negative behaviors. In the NT, Jesus quotes this as the second greatest of all the commandments (Mt 22:39; Mk 12:31).

19:19 different kinds The underlying rationale is imitation of God: These commands seek to avoid violating the separateness that God has woven into creation. What God has separated should not be mixed (compare Lev 20:25).

19:20–22 These verses deal with the violation of a betrothed female slave. It might have been included in this passage on separateness because a slave was

death, because she had not been freed. ²¹The man, however, must bring a ram to the entrance to the tent of meeting for a guilt offering to the LORD. ²²With the ram of the guilt offering the priest is to make atonement for him before the LORD for the sin he has committed, and his sin will be forgiven.

²³"'When you enter the land and plant any kind of fruit tree, regard its fruit as forbidden.^a For three years you are to consider it forbidden^a; it must not be eaten. ²⁴In the fourth year all its fruit will be holy, an offering of praise to the LORD. ²⁵But in the fifth year you may eat its fruit. In this way your harvest will be increased. I am the LORD your God.

²⁶"'Do not eat any meat with the blood still in it.

"'Do not practice divination or seek omens.

²⁷"'Do not cut the hair at the sides of your head or clip off the edges of your beard.

²⁸"'Do not cut your bodies for the dead or put tattoo marks on yourselves. I am the LORD.

²⁹"'Do not degrade your daughter by making her a prostitute, or the land will turn to prostitution and be filled with wickedness.

³⁰"'Observe my Sabbaths and have reverence for my sanctuary. I am the LORD.

³¹"'Do not turn to mediums or seek out spiritists, for you will be defiled by them. I am the LORD your God.

³²"'Stand up in the presence of the aged, show respect for the elderly and revere your God. I am the LORD.

³³"'When a foreigner resides among you in your land, do not mistreat them. ³⁴The foreigner residing among you must be treated as your na-

tive-born. Love them as yourself, for you were foreigners in Egypt. I am the LORD your God.

³⁵"'Do not use dishonest standards when measuring length, weight or quantity. ³⁶Use honest scales and honest weights, an honest ephah^b and an honest hin.^c I am the LORD your God, who brought you out of Egypt.

³⁷"'Keep all my decrees and all my laws and follow them. I am the LORD.'"

Punishments for Sin

20 The LORD said to Moses, ²"Say to the Israelites: 'Any Israelite or any foreigner residing in Israel who sacrifices any of his children to Molek is to be put to death. The members of the community are to stone him. ³I myself will set my face against him and will cut him off from his people; for by sacrificing his children to Molek, he has defiled my sanctuary and profaned my holy name. ⁴If the members of the community close their eyes when that man sacrifices one of his children to Molek and if they fail to put him to death, ⁵I myself will set my face against him and his family and will cut them off from their people together with all who follow him in prostituting themselves to Molek.

⁶"'I will set my face against anyone who turns to mediums and spiritists to prostitute themselves by following them, and I will cut them off from their people.

---

^a 23 Hebrew *uncircumcised*   ^b 36 An ephah was a dry measure having the capacity of about 3/5 of a bushel or about 22 liters.   ^c 36 A hin was a liquid measure having the capacity of about 1 gallon or about 3.8 liters.

---

likely a non-Israelite (see 25:44 and note). Sexual intercourse with a woman who was engaged to be married was considered adultery. Adultery was often punished by the death penalty for one or both people involved, but here the death penalty is not applied—to the female slave or the seducer. Instead, the punishment involved a guilt (trespass) offering (*asham* in Hebrew; see note on 5:14–6:7) and a payment for damages (v. 21). This may be because this law is dealing with an issue involving a non-Israelite and because the female slave—according to ancient Near Eastern customs—was viewed as property (see 25:46 and note).

19:20 there must be due punishment Some sort of recompense or compensation is in view—possibly a bride price. Since the woman was a slave, the price would have been paid to her owner. The money could alternatively have gone to the fiancé in reparation for a broken engagement.

19:23 For three years you are to consider it forbidden Since fruit trees bear little fruit in their early years, the required firstfruits offering was delayed to the fourth year (v. 24), likely the first opportunity for a good harvest. In the fourth year, all the fruit went to Yahweh (v. 24; compare 2:12–14). Israelites could keep the fruit in the fifth year.

19:26 Do not eat any meat with the blood Consuming

blood apparently was associated with idolatrous religious rituals, since the practice is juxtaposed with divination. The prohibition against consuming blood was also given in 3:17 and 7:26–27. **seek omens** Most techniques of soliciting knowledge from the divine world were off limits (see Dt 18:9–14.).

19:28 tattoo marks The Hebrew text here is probably prohibiting bodily disfigurement (see Lev 21:5; Dt 14:1) or practices connected to pagan mourning rites (compare Job 1:20; Isa 22:12).

19:29 by making her a prostitute Since the immediate context concerns the sanctuary (Lev 19:30), this likely refers to devoting her to sacred prostitution (see Ge 38:15).

20:1–27 Leviticus 20 repeats many of the prohibitions of ch. 18, which dealt with forbidden sexual relationships (incest, homosexuality and bestiality). Both chs. 18 and 20 link sexual degeneracy to Canaanite religious practices. However, while the commands of ch. 18 are stated categorically and grouped topically, the laws in ch. 20 describe specific scenarios and apply a penalty to each case.

20:2 Molek A Canaanite deity associated with child sacrifice.

20:3 profaned my holy name The ritualistic sacrifice of one's children is an affront to God's holy name.

7 "'Consecrate yourselves and be holy, because I am the LORD your God. 8 Keep my decrees and follow them. I am the LORD, who makes you holy.

9 "'Anyone who curses their father or mother is to be put to death. Because they have cursed their father or mother, their blood will be on their own head.

10 "'If a man commits adultery with another man's wife — with the wife of his neighbor — both the adulterer and the adulteress are to be put to death.

11 "'If a man has sexual relations with his father's wife, he has dishonored his father. Both the man and the woman are to be put to death; their blood will be on their own heads.

12 "'If a man has sexual relations with his daughter-in-law, both of them are to be put to death. What they have done is a perversion; their blood will be on their own heads.

13 "'If a man has sexual relations with a man as one does with a woman, both of them have done what is detestable. They are to be put to death; their blood will be on their own heads.

14 "'If a man marries both a woman and her mother, it is wicked. Both he and they must be burned in the fire, so that no wickedness will be among you.

15 "'If a man has sexual relations with an animal, he is to be put to death, and you must kill the animal.

16 "'If a woman approaches an animal to have sexual relations with it, kill both the woman and the animal. They are to be put to death; their blood will be on their own heads.

17 "'If a man marries his sister, the daughter of either his father or his mother, and they have sexual relations, it is a disgrace. They are to be publicly removed from their people. He has dishonored his sister and will be held responsible.

18 "'If a man has sexual relations with a woman during her monthly period, he has exposed the source of her flow, and she has also uncovered it. Both of them are to be cut off from their people.

19 "'Do not have sexual relations with the sister of either your mother or your father, for that would dishonor a close relative; both of you would be held responsible.

20 "'If a man has sexual relations with his aunt, he has dishonored his uncle. They will be held responsible; they will die childless.

21 "'If a man marries his brother's wife, it is an act of impurity; he has dishonored his brother. They will be childless.

22 "'Keep all my decrees and laws and follow them, so that the land where I am bringing you to live may not vomit you out. 23 You must not live according to the customs of the nations I am going to drive out before you. Because they did all these things, I abhorred them. 24 But I said to you, "You will possess their land; I will give it to you as an inheritance, a land flowing with milk and honey." I am the LORD your God, who has set you apart from the nations.

25 "'You must therefore make a distinction between clean and unclean animals and between unclean and clean birds. Do not defile yourselves by any animal or bird or anything that moves along the ground — those that I have set apart as unclean for you. 26 You are to be holy to me because I, the LORD, am holy, and I have set you apart from the nations to be my own.

27 "'A man or woman who is a medium or spiritist among you must be put to death. You are to stone them; their blood will be on their own heads.'"

Rules for Priests

21 The LORD said to Moses, "Speak to the priests, the sons of Aaron, and say to them: 'A priest must not make himself ceremonially unclean for any of his people who die, 2 except for a close relative, such as his mother or father, his son or daughter, his brother, 3 or an unmarried sister who is dependent on him since she has no husband — for her he may make himself unclean.

20:11 he has dishonored his father The Hebrew idiom used here, often translated as "uncovering nakedness," is a common euphemism for sexual intercourse. The context here makes it clear that the idiom refers to a son having sex with any of his father's wives.

20:13 sexual relations with a man as one does with a woman One of Leviticus' explicit denouncements of homosexual behavior.

20:17 marries his sister The context indicates that this refers to having sexual relations with a sister.

20:18 during her monthly period Prohibits having sex with a woman who is menstruating (18:19; compare 15:24).

20:20 they will die childless Although the penalty here is not death, having no children would result in the death of the family name and line—which relates to a person being cut off from their people (see note on 7:20).

20:21 marries his brother's wife Levirate marriage is the exception to this case (see note on 18:16).

20:22 may not vomit you out Disobedience is a violation of Israel's covenant with Yahweh; violation results in the loss of Yahweh's blessing of the land.

20:26 You are to be holy to me The exhortation to be holy is rooted in two realities. First Yahweh is holy, and second, he has set his people apart for this purpose.

21:1 — 22:16 Until this point, the book of Leviticus has primarily focused on the holiness of ordinary Israelites. The focus now shifts to the priesthood (chs. 21–22). Even higher standards are expected of the religious leaders.

21:1 must not make himself ceremonially unclean for any of his people who die It was the responsibility of people other than the priest's immediate family to bury the priest's relatives.

⁴He must not make himself unclean for people related to him by marriage,ᵃ and so defile himself.

⁵"'Priests must not shave their heads or shave off the edges of their beards or cut their bodies. ⁶They must be holy to their God and must not profane the name of their God. Because they present the food offerings to the Lord, the food of their God, they are to be holy.

⁷"'They must not marry women defiled by prostitution or divorced from their husbands, because priests are holy to their God. ⁸Regard them as holy, because they offer up the food of your God. Consider them holy, because I the Lord am holy—I who make you holy.

⁹"'If a priest's daughter defiles herself by becoming a prostitute, she disgraces her father; she must be burned in the fire.

¹⁰"'The high priest, the one among his brothers who has had the anointing oil poured on his head and who has been ordained to wear the priestly garments, must not let his hair become unkemptᵇ or tear his clothes. ¹¹He must not enter a place where there is a dead body. He must not make himself unclean, even for his father or mother, ¹²nor leave the sanctuary of his God or desecrate it, because he has been dedicated by the anointing oil of his God. I am the Lord.

¹³"'The woman he marries must be a virgin. ¹⁴He must not marry a widow, a divorced woman, or a woman defiled by prostitution, but only a virgin from his own people, ¹⁵so that he will not defile his offspring among his people. I am the Lord, who makes him holy.'"

¹⁶The Lord said to Moses, ¹⁷"Say to Aaron: 'For the generations to come none of your descendants who has a defect may come near to offer the food of his God. ¹⁸No man who has any defect may come near: no man who is blind or lame, disfigured or deformed; ¹⁹no man with a crippled foot or hand, ²⁰or who is a hunchback or a dwarf, or who has any eye defect, or who has festering or running sores or damaged testicles. ²¹No descendant of Aaron the priest who has any defect is to come near to present the food offerings to the Lord. He has a defect; he must not come near to offer the food of his God. ²²He may eat the most holy food of his God, as well as the holy food; ²³yet because of his defect, he must not go near the curtain or approach the altar, and so desecrate my sanctuary. I am the Lord, who makes them holy.'"

²⁴So Moses told this to Aaron and his sons and to all the Israelites.

22 The Lord said to Moses, ²"Tell Aaron and his sons to treat with respect the sacred offerings the Israelites consecrate to me, so they will not profane my holy name. I am the Lord.

³"Say to them: 'For the generations to come, if any of your descendants is ceremonially unclean and yet comes near the sacred offerings that the Israelites consecrate to the Lord, that person must be cut off from my presence. I am the Lord.

⁴"'If a descendant of Aaron has a defiling skin diseaseᶜ or a bodily discharge, he may not eat the

ᵃ 4 Or *unclean as a leader among his people*   ᵇ 10 Or *not uncover his head*   ᶜ 4 The Hebrew word for *defiling skin disease*, traditionally translated "leprosy," was used for various diseases affecting the skin.

21:2 a close relative This group includes a priest's mother, father, daughter, brother and virgin sister.
21:5 must not shave their heads Shaving the head and cutting the body were mourning customs associated with Canaanite religious practices (see 19:28 and note; Eze 44:20).
21:7 women defiled by prostitution The Hebrew text here seems to refer broadly to a woman who was not sexually pure before marriage.
21:9 disgraces her father Such behavior brings shame to the priestly office.
21:10 high priest, the one among his brothers Refers to the high priest. See note on Lev 6:20. **had the anointing oil poured on his head** This alludes to the high priest's installation ceremony, where special garments were given and oil was used for anointing (Ex 29; Lev 8).
21:11 He must not enter a place where there is a dead body The high priest must follow stricter restrictions than those of vv. 1–3.
21:14 virgin The Hebrew word used here, *bethulah,* is used for a woman who has never been sexually active.
21:15 he will not defile his offspring A marriage to a woman not of the priestly clan and not a virgin would mean that the priest's sons would be ineligible for priestly duty.
21:16–23 The regulations in this section are, like much of the regulations in Leviticus, meant to remind the Israelites that God is set apart (holy) and represents wholeness. These regulations are not meant to make a

statement about the handicapped or prevent them from being a priest (compare note on v. 22). Instead, these regulations are focused on priests who bring offerings into the sanctuary and thus serve as a reminder of the sanctity of God's presence (v. 23). These regulations also ensured that the priests delivering offerings could carry out their duties without a physical issue hindering them.
21:17 a defect Refers to a physical defect, as indicated by the list that follows (v. 18).
21:22 most holy food of his God, as well as the holy food A priest who had a physical defect was not deprived of food from offerings to which priests were entitled. He was merely prohibited from performing priestly duties within sacred space (see v. 17).
21:23 he must not go near the curtain Priests were not allowed to enter sacred space if they had a physical defect.

22:1–16 Priests who were disqualified from their duties due to physical defects nevertheless were allowed to eat priestly food (21:16–24). Verses 1–16 deal with certain circumstances in which this eating was restricted. This was an application of the separation of the clean from the unclean (see note on 11:1–47). The penalty for disobedience was that the priest would be cut off from God's presence (i.e., priestly service; v. 3).
22:3 ceremonially unclean The nature of the disqualifying uncleanness is explained in vv. 4–6. The impure

sacred offerings until he is cleansed. He will also be unclean if he touches something defiled by a corpse or by anyone who has an emission of semen, ⁵or if he touches any crawling thing that makes him unclean, or any person who makes him unclean, whatever the uncleanness may be. ⁶The one who touches any such thing will be unclean till evening. He must not eat any of the sacred offerings unless he has bathed himself with water. ⁷When the sun goes down, he will be clean, and after that he may eat the sacred offerings, for they are his food. ⁸He must not eat anything found dead or torn by wild animals, and so become unclean through it. I am the LORD.

⁹"'The priests are to perform my service in such a way that they do not become guilty and die for treating it with contempt. I am the LORD, who makes them holy.

¹⁰"'No one outside a priest's family may eat the sacred offering, nor may the guest of a priest or his hired worker eat it. ¹¹But if a priest buys a slave with money, or if slaves are born in his household, they may eat his food. ¹²If a priest's daughter marries anyone other than a priest, she may not eat any of the sacred contributions. ¹³But if a priest's daughter becomes a widow or is divorced, yet has no children, and she returns to live in her father's household as in her youth, she may eat her father's food. No unauthorized person, however, may eat it.

¹⁴"'Anyone who eats a sacred offering by mistake must make restitution to the priest for the offering and add a fifth of the value to it. ¹⁵The priests must not desecrate the sacred offerings the Israelites present to the LORD ¹⁶by allowing them to eat the sacred offerings and so bring upon them guilt requiring payment. I am the LORD, who makes them holy.'"

Unacceptable Sacrifices

¹⁷The LORD said to Moses, ¹⁸"Speak to Aaron and his sons and to all the Israelites and say to them: 'If any of you—whether an Israelite or a foreigner residing in Israel—presents a gift for a burnt offering to the LORD, either to fulfill a vow or as a freewill offering, ¹⁹you must present a male without defect from the cattle, sheep or goats in order that it may be accepted on your behalf. ²⁰Do not bring anything with a defect, because it will not be accepted on your behalf. ²¹When anyone brings from the herd or flock a fellowship offering to the LORD to fulfill a special vow or as a freewill offering, it must be without defect or blemish to be acceptable. ²²Do not offer to the LORD the blind, the injured or the maimed, or anything with warts or festering or running sores. Do not place any of these on the altar as a food offering presented to the LORD. ²³You may, however, present as a freewill offering an oxᵃ or a sheep that is deformed or stunted, but it will not be accepted in fulfillment of a vow. ²⁴You must not offer to the LORD an animal whose testicles are bruised, crushed, torn or cut. You must not do this in your own land, ²⁵and you must not accept such animals from the hand of a foreigner and offer them as the food of your God. They will not be accepted on your behalf, because they are deformed and have defects.'"

²⁶The LORD said to Moses, ²⁷"When a calf, a lamb or a goat is born, it is to remain with its mother for seven days. From the eighth day on, it will be acceptable as a food offering presented to the LORD. ²⁸Do not slaughter a cow or a sheep and its young on the same day.

²⁹"When you sacrifice a thank offering to the LORD, sacrifice it in such a way that it will be accepted on your behalf. ³⁰It must be eaten that same day; leave none of it till morning. I am the LORD.

³¹"Keep my commands and follow them. I am the LORD. ³²Do not profane my holy name, for I must be acknowledged as holy by the Israelites. I am the LORD, who made you holy ³³and who brought you out of Egypt to be your God. I am the LORD."

ᵃ 23 The Hebrew word can refer to either male or female.

---

conditions all allude to the various types of uncleanness described in chs. 11–15.

22:7 he will be clean An otherwise-pure priest who touched something (or someone) unclean would be restored to ritual purity if he bathed and waited until nightfall.

they are his food According to 10:13–14, priests are entitled to certain portions of the sacrifices for their own nourishment so long as the proper precautions are taken.

22:9 become guilty and die Disobedience in the area of ritual purity could be punished by death. Ignoring the standards for purity would be met with the stiffest of penalties.

22:12 may not eat any of the sacred contributions A priest's daughter naturally ate from the priest's portion of food. If she later married a priest, her food portion would come from that priest (her husband). If she married outside the priesthood, the privilege expired.

22:14 make restitution to the priest for the offering The person who mistakenly took from the priest's portion of food had to replace the portion plus a fifth of its value.

22:17–25 These verses offer guidelines for acceptable offerings. According to v. 18, the entire nation is in view. Thus, legal stipulations are not merely the responsibility of the priesthood. Verses 22–25 list specific defects that are only generally referenced in vv. 17–21.

22:18 fulfill a vow or as a freewill offering Sacrifices could be brought as an act of worship or in fulfillment of a vow.

22:19 without defect Just as physical defects disqualified priests from duties in the tabernacle (21:17–23), any physical defect disqualified an animal for use as a sacrifice (Dt 17:1; see note on Ex 12:5).

22:26–28 These verses encourage respect for the animal kingdom and restraint in the context of a sacrificial system that demands the death of animals.

22:28 a cow or a sheep and its young May be motivated by compassion for animals.

The Appointed Festivals

23 The LORD said to Moses, [2]"Speak to the Israelites and say to them: 'These are my appointed festivals, the appointed festivals of the LORD, which you are to proclaim as sacred assemblies.

The Sabbath

[3]"There are six days when you may work, but the seventh day is a day of sabbath rest, a day of sacred assembly. You are not to do any work; wherever you live, it is a sabbath to the LORD.

The Passover and the Festival of Unleavened Bread

23:4-8pp — Ex 12:14-20; Nu 28:16-25; Dt 16:1-8

[4]"These are the LORD's appointed festivals, the sacred assemblies you are to proclaim at their appointed times: [5]The LORD's Passover begins at twilight on the fourteenth day of the first month. [6]On the fifteenth day of that month the LORD's Festival of Unleavened Bread begins; for seven days you must eat bread made without yeast. [7]On the first day hold a sacred assembly and do no regular work. [8]For seven days present a food offering to the LORD. And on the seventh day hold a sacred assembly and do no regular work.'"

Offering the Firstfruits

[9]The LORD said to Moses, [10]"Speak to the Israelites and say to them: 'When you enter the land I am going to give you and you reap its harvest, bring to the priest a sheaf of the first grain you harvest. [11]He is to wave the sheaf before the LORD so it will be accepted on your behalf; the priest is to wave it on the day after the Sabbath. [12]On the day you wave the sheaf, you must sacrifice as a burnt offering to the LORD a lamb a year old without defect, [13]together with its grain offering of two-tenths of an ephah[a] of the finest flour mixed with olive oil — a food offering presented to the LORD, a pleasing aroma — and its drink offering of a quarter of a hin[b] of wine. [14]You must not eat any bread, or roasted or new grain, until the very day you bring this offering to your God. This is to be a lasting ordinance for the generations to come, wherever you live.

The Festival of Weeks

23:15-22pp — Nu 28:26-31; Dt 16:9-12

[15]"From the day after the Sabbath, the day you brought the sheaf of the wave offering, count off

---

[a] 13 That is, probably about 7 pounds or about 3.2 kilograms; also in verse 17   [b] 13 That is, about 1 quart or about 1 liter

---

22:31–33 These verses conclude the congregation's responsibility to uphold the sanctity of the sacrificial system by appealing to the character of Yahweh, which is defined by holiness. Yet in Lev 22:33, an appeal is made to the exodus, which also anchors Israel's responsibility in their history.

23:1–44 Chapter 23 lists the holy seasons and celebrations of ancient Israel and their required sacrifices for the entire sacred year. See the table "Israelite Festivals" on p. 200.

23:2 the appointed festivals of the LORD Feasts were tied to astronomical phenomena (e.g., twilight, new moons, seasons) corresponding to the lunar calendar. Therefore, the time of their celebration was considered to have been appointed by God — the Creator of the heavenly bodies (Ge 1:15–16).

23:3 a day of sabbath rest The Sabbath is set on the seventh day of each week, when the Israelites are forbidden from performing work.

23:4–8 This passage and its parallel in Nu 28:16–25 provide further regulations for Passover, which was instituted in Ex 12 (compare Dt 16:1–8). Passover is an annual commemoration of events leading up to the exodus from Egypt (Ex 12–13), when the feast was first established.

23:5 at twilight on the fourteenth day of the first month Establishes the date and time of the Passover sacrifice.

23:6 fifteenth day of that month The Festival of Unleavened Bread begins the day after the Passover sacrifice. During this seven-day feast, only unleavened bread (i.e., bread without yeast) is to be eaten. **LORD's Festival** The Hebrew word used here, *chag* (which may be rendered as "feast" or "festival"), refers to a pilgrimage festival. This word is used to describe the festivals of Unleavened Bread (Lev 23:6), Tabernacles (v. 39) and Weeks (Ex 34:22; Dt 16:16).

23:7 a sacred assembly and do no regular work Given that sacrifices are to be given on the other days of the festival, an absolute statement prohibiting work would not make sense. Rather, work related to a person's occupation is prohibited. Only the special work of Passover may be carried out.

23:8 present a food offering to the LORD The Hebrew term for offering used here is *isheh*, which likely designates some kind of food gift (see note on Lev 1:9).

23:9–14 This passage describes the Festival of Firstfruits, a thank-you to Yahweh for the barley crops he provides Israel, similar to the idea of a tithe. Leviticus 2:11–16 specifies how to prepare the firstfruits offering.

23:10 first grain Giving Yahweh the first yield constitutes an act of trust that the remaining yield will be sufficient for the people's need.

23:11 wave the sheaf Refers to the practice of waving a portion of an offering before Yahweh to symbolize offering it to him. This was called the wave offering (*tenuphah* in Hebrew; see v. 15).

23:13 drink offering Libations were a common form of divine offering in the ancient Near East, usually consisting of the finest wine available (e.g., Ge 35:14; Ex 29:40–41; Nu 15:6–10).

23:14 a lasting ordinance A common refrain in Biblical law, often used to reinforce the timelessness of the command and the importance to continually observe sacred occasions.

23:15–22 The day of the wave offering, which is the defining act of the Festival of Firstfruits (Lev 23:9–14), initiates a period of counting: seven full cycles of seven days (sabbaths or weeks). On the fiftieth day, the second firstfruits offering is performed for the Festival of Weeks, marking the beginning of the grain harvest. This feast was known in later times as Pentecost, deriving its name from the Greek word for fiftieth (compare Ac 2:1 and note).

seven full weeks. ¹⁶Count off fifty days up to the day after the seventh Sabbath, and then present an offering of new grain to the LORD. ¹⁷From wherever you live, bring two loaves made of two-tenths of an ephah of the finest flour, baked with yeast, as a wave offering of firstfruits to the LORD. ¹⁸Present with this bread seven male lambs, each a year old and without defect, one young bull and two rams. They will be a burnt offering to the LORD, together with their grain offerings and drink offerings — a food offering, an aroma pleasing to the LORD. ¹⁹Then sacrifice one male goat for a sin offering[a] and two lambs, each a year old, for a fellowship offering. ²⁰The priest is to wave the two lambs before the LORD as a wave offering, together with the bread of the firstfruits. They are a sacred offering to the LORD for the priest. ²¹On that same day you are to proclaim a sacred assembly and do no regular work. This is to be a lasting ordinance for the generations to come, wherever you live.

²²"'When you reap the harvest of your land, do not reap to the very edges of your field or gather the gleanings of your harvest. Leave them for the poor and for the foreigner residing among you. I am the LORD your God.'"

The Festival of Trumpets
23:23-25pp — Nu 29:1-6

²³The LORD said to Moses, ²⁴"Say to the Israelites: 'On the first day of the seventh month you are to have a day of sabbath rest, a sacred assembly commemorated with trumpet blasts. ²⁵Do no regular work, but present a food offering to the LORD.'"

---

[a] 19 Or purification offering

23:17 baked with yeast The only occasion in Israel's sacred calendar when leavened bread was brought as part of an offering (Lev 2:11; compare 7:13).

23:20 a sacred offering to the LORD for the priest Items that were dedicated to Yahweh were not to be used for any common purpose, but were holy—set apart as belonging to Yahweh.

23:22 This verse is an abridgement of the law in 19:9–10.

23:23–43 This passage describes three celebrations to be held in the seventh month: the Festival of Trumpets; the Day of Atonement (ch. 16); and the Festival of Tabernacles (Booths).

23:24 commemorated with trumpet blasts The shofar horn—made of a ram's horn—was sounded to give advance notice for the Festival of Tabernacles (Booths), the pilgrimage festival that would occur two weeks later.

Israelite Festivals

FESTIVAL	TIME OF CELEBRATION	REFERENCES
Passover	Nisan 14	Ex 12:1–14; 23:15; Lev 23:5; Nu 28:16; Mt 26:17–20
Unleavened Bread*	Nisan 15–21	Ex 12:15–20; 34:18; Lev 23:6–8; Nu 28:17–25
Firstfruits	Nisan 16, Sivan 6	Lev 23:9–14; Nu 28:26
Pentecost (Harvest, Weeks)*	Sivan 6	Ex 23:16; 34:22; Lev 23:15–22; Nu 28:26–31; Dt 16:9–12; Ac 2:1
Trumpets (Rosh Hashanah)	Tishri 1	Lev 23:23–25; Nu 29:1–6
Day of Atonement (Yom Kippur)	Tishri 10	Lev 16:2–34; Lev 23:26–32; Nu 29:7–11; Heb 9:7
Tabernacles (Ingathering, Booths, Sukkot)*	Tishri 15–22	Ex 23:16; 34:22; Lev 23:33–43; Nu 29:12–39; Dt 16:13–17; Ne 8:13–18; Jn 7:2
Dedication (Lights, Hanukkah)†	Chislev 25 (for 8 days)	Jn 10:22
Purim†	Adar 14–15	Est 9:18–32

* The three festivals for which all adult Israelite males had to go to Jerusalem (Ex 23:17; 34:23).

† Festivals that are not prescribed in Leviticus.

The Day of Atonement
23:26-32pp — Lev 16:2-34; Nu 29:7-11

²⁶The Lᴏʀᴅ said to Moses, ²⁷"The tenth day of this seventh month is the Day of Atonement. Hold a sacred assembly and deny yourselves,ᵃ and present a food offering to the Lᴏʀᴅ. ²⁸Do not do any work on that day, because it is the Day of Atonement, when atonement is made for you before the Lᴏʀᴅ your God. ²⁹Those who do not deny themselves on that day must be cut off from their people. ³⁰I will destroy from among their people anyone who does any work on that day. ³¹You shall do no work at all. This is to be a lasting ordinance for the generations to come, wherever you live. ³²It is a day of sabbath rest for you, and you must deny yourselves. From the evening of the ninth day of the month until the following evening you are to observe your sabbath."

The Festival of Tabernacles
23:33-43pp — Nu 29:12-39; Dt 16:13-17

³³The Lᴏʀᴅ said to Moses, ³⁴"Say to the Israelites: 'On the fifteenth day of the seventh month the Lᴏʀᴅ's Festival of Tabernacles begins, and it lasts for seven days. ³⁵The first day is a sacred assembly; do no regular work. ³⁶For seven days present food offerings to the Lᴏʀᴅ, and on the eighth day hold a sacred assembly and present a food offering to the Lᴏʀᴅ. It is the closing special assembly; do no regular work.

³⁷("'These are the Lᴏʀᴅ's appointed festivals, which you are to proclaim as sacred assemblies for bringing food offerings to the Lᴏʀᴅ — the burnt offerings and grain offerings, sacrifices and drink offerings required for each day. ³⁸These offerings are in addition to those for the Lᴏʀᴅ's Sabbaths andᵇ in addition to your gifts and whatever you have vowed and all the freewill offerings you give to the Lᴏʀᴅ.)

³⁹"'So beginning with the fifteenth day of the seventh month, after you have gathered the crops of the land, celebrate the festival to the Lᴏʀᴅ for seven days; the first day is a day of sabbath rest, and the eighth day also is a day of sabbath rest. ⁴⁰On the first day you are to take branches from luxuriant trees — from palms, willows and other leafy trees — and rejoice before the Lᴏʀᴅ your God for seven days. ⁴¹Celebrate this as a festival to the Lᴏʀᴅ for seven days each year. This is to be a lasting ordinance for the generations to come; celebrate it in the seventh month. ⁴²Live in temporary shelters for seven days: All native-born Israelites are to live in such shelters ⁴³so your descendants will know that I had the Israelites live in temporary shelters when I brought them out of Egypt. I am the Lᴏʀᴅ your God.'"

⁴⁴So Moses announced to the Israelites the appointed festivals of the Lᴏʀᴅ.

Olive Oil and Bread Set Before the Lᴏʀᴅ
24:1-3pp — Ex 27:20-21

24 The Lᴏʀᴅ said to Moses, ²"Command the Israelites to bring you clear oil of pressed olives for the light so that the lamps may be kept burning continually. ³Outside the curtain that shields the ark of the covenant law in the tent of meeting, Aaron is to tend the lamps before the Lᴏʀᴅ from evening till morning, continually. This is to be a lasting ordinance for the generations to come. ⁴The lamps on the pure gold lampstand before the Lᴏʀᴅ must be tended continually.

ᵃ *27* Or *and fast*; similarly in verses 29 and 32   ᵇ *38* Or *These festivals are in addition to the Lᴏʀᴅ's Sabbaths, and these offerings are*

23:26–32 The Day of Atonement is the most important occasion on the ancient Israelite calendar and was the holiest day of the year, because the high priest would enter the Holy of Holies (or Most Holy Place) on that day. See 16:1–34 and note.

23:27 deny yourselves Refers to fasting.
23:28 Do not do any work On the Day of Atonement, all work is to cease, not just everyday work.
23:29 Those who do not deny themselves Though rare in Leviticus, the grammatical form of the Hebrew verb used here suggests that the action is self-directed, such as fasting or some other form of self-discipline.
23:32 a day of sabbath rest The Day of Atonement was to be a day of complete rest.

23:33–44 The Festival of Tabernacles (Booths) — *sukkoth* in Hebrew — lasts seven days, with a final celebration on the eighth day. On the first and eighth days, ordinary work is prohibited. During the seven days of the feast, the people make food offerings to God. After the solemnity of the Day of Atonement, the Festival of Tabernacles was intended as a joyous celebration — a reminder that the people were forgiven and chosen by Yahweh.

23:34 Festival of Tabernacles The name for the festival reflects the command (vv. 40–42) that the Israelites take tree branches and fashion them into small huts or booths to stay in during the feast.

23:37–38 These two verses break up the discussion of the Festival of Tabernacles (Booths; vv. 33–36, 39–43) and appear to provide a summary or closing statement for ch. 23 as a whole.

23:43 brought them out of Egypt The historical referent for the Festival of Tabernacles (Booths) is the exodus (Ex 12–15). A perpetual awareness of the exodus event is the expressed purpose of dwelling in tabernacles for these seven days.

24:1–23 Leviticus 24 is a collection of religious laws, with topics ranging from tabernacle procedures (vv. 1–9) to serious crimes like blasphemy (vv. 10–16). The chapter concludes with a clear declaration of the law of commensurate retaliation in vv. 17–23 (known as the principle of an eye for an eye or *lex taliones*; compare Ex 21:23–25; Dt 19:21).

24:3 Outside the curtain The lamp is to be placed

5"Take the finest flour and bake twelve loaves of bread, using two-tenths of an ephah[a] for each loaf. 6Arrange them in two stacks, six in each stack, on the table of pure gold before the LORD. 7By each stack put some pure incense as a memorial[b] portion to represent the bread and to be a food offering presented to the LORD. 8This bread is to be set out before the LORD regularly, Sabbath after Sabbath, on behalf of the Israelites, as a lasting covenant. 9It belongs to Aaron and his sons, who are to eat it in the sanctuary area, because it is a most holy part of their perpetual share of the food offerings presented to the LORD."

A Blasphemer Put to Death

10Now the son of an Israelite mother and an Egyptian father went out among the Israelites, and a fight broke out in the camp between him and an Israelite. 11The son of the Israelite woman blasphemed the Name with a curse; so they brought him to Moses. (His mother's name was Shelomith, the daughter of Dibri the Danite.) 12They put him in custody until the will of the LORD should be made clear to them.

13Then the LORD said to Moses: 14"Take the blasphemer outside the camp. All those who heard him are to lay their hands on his head, and the entire assembly is to stone him. 15Say to the Israelites: 'Anyone who curses their God will be held responsible; 16anyone who blasphemes the name of the LORD is to be put to death. The entire assembly must stone them. Whether foreigner or native-born, when they blaspheme the Name they are to be put to death.

17"'Anyone who takes the life of a human being is to be put to death. 18Anyone who takes the life of someone's animal must make restitution—life for life. 19Anyone who injures their neighbor is to be injured in the same manner: 20fracture for fracture, eye for eye, tooth for tooth. The one who has inflicted the injury must suffer the same injury. 21Whoever kills an animal must make restitution, but whoever kills a human being is to be put to death. 22You are to have the same law for the foreigner and the native-born. I am the LORD your God.'"

23Then Moses spoke to the Israelites, and they took the blasphemer outside the camp and stoned him. The Israelites did as the LORD commanded Moses.

The Sabbath Year

25 The LORD said to Moses at Mount Sinai, 2"Speak to the Israelites and say to them: 'When you enter the land I am going to give you, the land itself must observe a sabbath to the LORD.

---

a 5 That is, probably about 7 pounds or about 3.2 kilograms
b 7 Or representative

---

directly outside the curtain that was to close off the Holy of Holies (or Most Holy Place; Ex 26:31–35).

24:5–9 A similar practice of placing bread before a deity was common in the ancient Near East. The idea was that the gods needed to be served bread and wine for sustenance. The practice outlined here of leaving the bread (Ex 25:30) before Yahweh belongs to this tradition but departs from it significantly since the bread is explicitly designated as food for the priests, not Yahweh (Lev 24:9).

24:6 table of pure gold Refers to the table for the bread of the presence in the Holy Place (compare Ex 25:23–30; 1Ki 7:48; 2Chr 13:11; Heb 9:2).

TABLE OF SHOWBREAD
The table held 12 loaves of bread, probably symbolizing the 12 tribes of Israel. The loaves were displayed in two equal rows. They were not touched during the entire week until the Sabbath, when they were replaced with 12 freshly baked loaves. The old loaves were eaten by the priests in a sacred area (Lev 24:9).

24:7 some pure incense A fragrant resin used as a perfume and as a spice (see note on Lev 2:1).
24:8 Sabbath after Sabbath The command to arrange 12 loaves every Sabbath likely means that fresh loaves were brought on the Sabbath and the loaves from the previous week were consumed. Since regular loaves would have been hardened and spoiled after a week, unleavened bread was probably used for this purpose.

24:10–23 This passage recounts a narrative about a particular incident that demanded a legal decision by Moses. The anecdote emphasizes the severity of blasphemy, but the overall aim of the passage is to make explicit that the same law applies to all—whether an offense is committed by a native Israelite or by a foreigner living among them (e.g., a sojourner or resident alien).

24:10 son of an Israelite mother and an Egyptian father The man guilty of blasphemy is only half Israelite, so his status in the community was ambiguous.
24:11 blasphemed The crime of blasphemy is characterized by slander and contempt toward the sacred. Here the name of God was used in a cursing fashion, reflecting extreme disrespect for Yahweh. Blasphemy was specifically prohibited in Ex 22:28. The penalty was death.
24:14 outside the camp Capital punishment was undertaken outside Israel's normal living space—in part due to the uncleanness of corpses. However, moving the execution scene outside the camp had symbolic impact: It indicated that taking a human life—even if ordered by the law—was a terrible act that should not be associated with sanctified ground.

24:17–22 This segment interrupts the narrative with an explanation of the legal principle of appropriate retaliation (often called *lex talionis*; see note on Lev 24:1–23). The only appropriate restitution for blasphemy is death.

24:22 the same law for the foreigner and the native-born Everyone is under the same law and subject to

³For six years sow your fields, and for six years prune your vineyards and gather their crops. ⁴But in the seventh year the land is to have a year of sabbath rest, a sabbath to the LORD. Do not sow your fields or prune your vineyards. ⁵Do not reap what grows of itself or harvest the grapes of your untended vines. The land is to have a year of rest. ⁶Whatever the land yields during the sabbath year will be food for you — for yourself, your male and female servants, and the hired worker and temporary resident who live among you, ⁷as well as for your livestock and the wild animals in your land. Whatever the land produces may be eaten.

The Year of Jubilee

25:8-38Ref — Dt 15:1-11
25:39-55Ref — Ex 21:2-11; Dt 15:12-18

⁸"'Count off seven sabbath years — seven times seven years — so that the seven sabbath years amount to a period of forty-nine years. ⁹Then have the trumpet sounded everywhere on the tenth day of the seventh month; on the Day of Atonement sound the trumpet throughout your land. ¹⁰Consecrate the fiftieth year and proclaim liberty throughout the land to all its inhabitants. It shall be a jubilee for you; each of you is to return to your family property and to your own clan. ¹¹The fiftieth year shall be a jubilee for you; do not sow and do not reap what grows of itself or harvest the untended vines. ¹²For it is a jubilee

and is to be holy for you; eat only what is taken directly from the fields.

¹³"'In this Year of Jubilee everyone is to return to their own property.

¹⁴"'If you sell land to any of your own people or buy land from them, do not take advantage of each other. ¹⁵You are to buy from your own people on the basis of the number of years since the Jubilee. And they are to sell to you on the basis of the number of years left for harvesting crops. ¹⁶When the years are many, you are to increase the price, and when the years are few, you are to decrease the price, because what is really being sold to you is the number of crops. ¹⁷Do not take advantage of each other, but fear your God. I am the LORD your God.

¹⁸"'Follow my decrees and be careful to obey my laws, and you will live safely in the land. ¹⁹Then the land will yield its fruit, and you will eat your fill and live there in safety. ²⁰You may ask, "What will we eat in the seventh year if we do not plant or harvest our crops?" ²¹I will send you such a blessing in the sixth year that the land will yield enough for three years. ²²While you plant during the eighth year, you will eat from the old crop and will continue to eat from it until the harvest of the ninth year comes in.

²³"'The land must not be sold permanently, because the land is mine and you reside in my land as foreigners and strangers. ²⁴Throughout

---

the same penalty. The law makes no distinction for ethnic origin.

25:1–7 Just as every seventh day was called the Sabbath, every seventh year functioned like a year-long Sabbath called the sabbatical year (or "sabbath year"; see Ex 16:23; 20:8–11). Israelites were not to cultivate crops during the sabbatical year; instead, they were to eat only what grew naturally. After seven sabbatical years, the fiftieth year was called the Jubilee Year, and the same agricultural restrictions were observed (see Lev 25:8–12).

In addition, the Jubilee Year added two provisions that essentially canceled debts throughout Israel. First, any property that had transferred ownership during the previous 49 years was to be returned to the original owner. In addition, Israelites who had sold themselves as indentured laborers were to be released from their debts and freed to return to their families and homes.

25:4 a year of sabbath rest This phrase is repeated at the end of v. 5, functioning as a bracket around specific prohibitions. Thus, the text is clear that the land is not to be farmed in the sabbatical year.

25:6 will be food for you The expectation is that the natural yield of the land will sustain the entire household. This testifies to expectation of Yahweh's provision for his people. **temporary resident** The Hebrew word used here, *toshav*, denotes someone who was temporarily living among the Israelites

25:9 the tenth day of the seventh month The blast on the shofar before the Festival of Tabernacles (Booths) announced the advent of the Jubilee. This day was also the Day of Atonement.

25:10 to return to your family property A family that was not able to pay its debts may have had to sell its property or have the property seized in lieu of payment (vv. 25–28). The practice of Jubilee essentially reversed this transfer of ownership and restored the property to the family.

25:15 the basis of the number of years since the Jubilee A property's value was linked to the number of crop years remaining until the next Jubilee Year—when ownership would be transferred back to the original landholder.

25:19–22 During the sabbatical year, the Israelites could not work the land. Yahweh promises that the sixth year will produce such a bountiful harvest that the Israelites will have enough to eat during the seventh year, the eighth year and into the ninth year, when they are harvesting again.

25:23–28 The land cannot be sold permanently, for it belongs to Yahweh. This passage explains the proper response to a sale or foreclosure: Relatives of the former owner have a duty to keep the property in the clan by redeeming it from the purchaser or creditor (v. 25). However, if no one in the clan had sufficient means to acquire the property, ownership still would transfer back to the original owner when the Jubilee Year came around (v. 28).

25:23 permanently The Hebrew term used here, *tsemithuth*, denotes a final and permanent sale. The concept is known from Akkadian land contracts (which use a related Akkadian term).

the land that you hold as a possession, you must provide for the redemption of the land.

[25]"'If one of your fellow Israelites becomes poor and sells some of their property, their nearest relative is to come and redeem what they have sold. [26]If, however, there is no one to redeem it for them but later on they prosper and acquire sufficient means to redeem it themselves, [27]they are to determine the value for the years since they sold it and refund the balance to the one to whom they sold it; they can then go back to their own property. [28]But if they do not acquire the means to repay, what was sold will remain in the possession of the buyer until the Year of Jubilee. It will be returned in the Jubilee, and they can then go back to their property.

[29]"'Anyone who sells a house in a walled city retains the right of redemption a full year after its sale. During that time the seller may redeem it. [30]If it is not redeemed before a full year has passed, the house in the walled city shall belong permanently to the buyer and the buyer's descendants. It is not to be returned in the Jubilee. [31]But houses in villages without walls around them are to be considered as belonging to the open country. They can be redeemed, and they are to be returned in the Jubilee.

[32]"'The Levites always have the right to redeem their houses in the Levitical towns, which they possess. [33]So the property of the Levites is redeemable — that is, a house sold in any town they hold — and is to be returned in the Jubilee, because the houses in the towns of the Levites are their property among the Israelites. [34]But the pastureland belonging to their towns must not be sold; it is their permanent possession.

[35]"'If any of your fellow Israelites become poor and are unable to support themselves among you, help them as you would a foreigner and stranger, so they can continue to live among you. [36]Do not take interest or any profit from them, but fear your God, so that they may continue to live among you. [37]You must not lend them money at interest or sell them food at a profit. [38]I am the LORD your God, who brought you out of Egypt to give you the land of Canaan and to be your God.

[39]"'If any of your fellow Israelites become poor and sell themselves to you, do not make them work as slaves. [40]They are to be treated as hired workers or temporary residents among you; they are to work for you until the Year of Jubilee. [41]Then they and their children are to be released, and they will go back to their own clans and to the property of their ancestors. [42]Because the Israelites are my servants, whom I brought out of Egypt, they must not be sold as slaves. [43]Do not rule over them ruthlessly, but fear your God.

[44]"'Your male and female slaves are to come from the nations around you; from them you may buy slaves. [45]You may also buy some of the temporary residents living among you and members of their clans born in your country, and they will become your property. [46]You can bequeath them to your children as inherited property and can make them slaves for life, but you must not rule over your fellow Israelites ruthlessly.

[47]"'If a foreigner residing among you becomes rich and any of your fellow Israelites become poor and sell themselves to the foreigner or to a member of the foreigner's clan, [48]they retain the right of redemption after they have sold themselves. One of their relatives may redeem them: [49]An

---

25:25 nearest relative The Hebrew word used here, *go'el*—which is often rendered redeemer—refers to the nearest relative responsible for acquiring the property on behalf of the family.

25:29–31 Rules were different for urban properties (within a walled city; v. 30) than for agricultural lands and villages. When a city property changed hands, clan members had a one-year window to redeem it. After that year, the buyer became the permanent owner and would not have to surrender the property in the Jubilee Year.

25:31 they are to be returned in the Jubilee Houses in unwalled villages are classified as being a part of the fields of the land, which explains why homes in walled cities were not redeemed after a year (compare note on 25:29–31).

25:32 Levites Property within cities allotted to the Levites could be redeemed. However, enclosed areas in the near vicinity of such cities could not be sold (vv. 33–34).

25:33 are their property Because land was not a familial inheritance for the tribe of Levi, homes could be redeemed.

25:35 they can continue to live among you When a family member came on hard times, they were not to be disgraced or shunned. The law also prevented

family members from becoming indentured servants (vv. 39–46).

25:42 brought out of Egypt Yahweh redeemed the people of Israel when they were slaves in Egypt (Ex 12–15). Israelites should not enslave a fellow Israelite because they had no right to each other; they all belonged to Yahweh (compare Ex 22:21,25; 23:9).

25:44 nations around you Israelites were allowed to have non-Israelite slaves. Slavery was common in the ancient Near East, which means this could have been an accommodation for other ancient Near Eastern practices. Accommodation in general seems to have been present in the law; Jesus, for example, notes that divorce was allowed because of the obstinateness of the Israelites (Mt 19:8). Unlike Israel's neighboring cultures, it was prohibited in Israel to mistreat a non-Israelite (Ex 23:9; compare Dt 21:10–14), which would have included foreign slaves, and there are laws meant to protect slaves (Ex 21:20–21,26–27). Compare note on Phm 10; note on 1Pe 2:18; Gal 3:28.

25:46 inherited property The rights of Israelite slaveholders over foreign slaves were akin to the rights of landownership. Slaves could be passed down, inherited and kept within the family. However, this law does not encourage slavery, but instead regulates an already common practice (compare note on 25:44).

uncle or a cousin or any blood relative in their clan may redeem them. Or if they prosper, they may redeem themselves. ⁵⁰They and their buyer are to count the time from the year they sold themselves up to the Year of Jubilee. The price for their release is to be based on the rate paid to a hired worker for that number of years. ⁵¹If many years remain, they must pay for their redemption a larger share of the price paid for them. ⁵²If only a few years remain until the Year of Jubilee, they are to compute that and pay for their redemption accordingly. ⁵³They are to be treated as workers hired from year to year; you must see to it that those to whom they owe service do not rule over them ruthlessly.

⁵⁴"Even if someone is not redeemed in any of these ways, they and their children are to be released in the Year of Jubilee, ⁵⁵for the Israelites belong to me as servants. They are my servants, whom I brought out of Egypt. I am the LORD your God.

Reward for Obedience

26 "'Do not make idols or set up an image or a sacred stone for yourselves, and do not place a carved stone in your land to bow down before it. I am the LORD your God.

²"'Observe my Sabbaths and have reverence for my sanctuary. I am the LORD.

³"'If you follow my decrees and are careful to obey my commands, ⁴I will send you rain in its season, and the ground will yield its crops and the trees their fruit. ⁵Your threshing will continue until grape harvest and the grape harvest will continue until planting, and you will eat all the food you want and live in safety in your land.

⁶"'I will grant peace in the land, and you will lie down and no one will make you afraid. I will remove wild beasts from the land, and the sword will not pass through your country. ⁷You will pursue your enemies, and they will fall by the sword before you. ⁸Five of you will chase a hundred, and a hundred of you will chase ten thousand, and your enemies will fall by the sword before you.

⁹"'I will look on you with favor and make you fruitful and increase your numbers, and I will keep my covenant with you. ¹⁰You will still be eating last year's harvest when you will have to move it out to make room for the new. ¹¹I will put my dwelling place*a* among you, and I will not abhor you. ¹²I will walk among you and be your God, and you will be my people. ¹³I am the LORD your God, who brought you out of Egypt so that you would no longer be slaves to the Egyptians; I broke the bars of your yoke and enabled you to walk with heads held high.

Punishment for Disobedience

¹⁴"'But if you will not listen to me and carry out all these commands, ¹⁵and if you reject my

a 11 Or my tabernacle

25:47–55 In certain circumstances, Israelites may sell themselves to a non-Israelite. In such instances, the redeemer (*go'el* in Hebrew) had responsibilities, but the redemption was to be handled respectfully, with an offer of honest payment.

25:48 may redeem them If an Israelite had to become an indentured servant to a foreigner living in Israel (a resident alien), the Israelite's family members were responsible for redeeming the indentured servant—they had to pay the debt to release their fellow family member. **25:50 count the time** The same computation system described in vv. 15–16. The price was based on the years remaining until the Jubilee Year.

26:1–2 This chapter lists the blessings that would come from obeying Yahweh's commandments and the punishments that would come from breaking them. The first two verses summarize some core requirements of the law—complete loyalty to Yahweh alone, observance of the Sabbath and proper respect for Yahweh's sacred space.

26:1 a sacred stone The OT contains numerous references to the use of these objects in the context of idolatry (e.g., Ex 23:24; Dt 16:22; compare Ge 28:18). **26:2 Observe my Sabbaths** Mentioned in conjunction with a prohibition on idolatry, this exhortation introduces a series of blessings affiliated with the Israelites' covenant with Yahweh (compare note on 26:3–46).

26:3–46 Leviticus 26:3–46 constitutes an epilogue to what is commonly called the Holiness Code (chs.

17–26; see 17:1–16 and note). Yahweh promises the Israelites peace and safety within a prosperous, fertile land if they obey his laws (vv. 3–13). If the Israelites disobey, the opposite will occur (vv. 14–45): Yahweh will send disease, invasion, pestilence, famine, wild animals and natural disasters. As a final punishment, the people will be expelled from the land and scattered among their enemies. The negative consequences of disobedience can be reversed through repentance, atonement and divine mercy. If the people come back to Yahweh, he will remember his covenant with their forefathers. Similar lists of blessings and curses can be found in Dt 27–28 and many ancient Near Eastern treaties.

26:5 in safety The Israelites will live without threat of external hostility, whether by man or beast, or fear of want. The descriptions here mirror and reverse the promised curses for disobedience (Lev 26:14–46). **26:11 I will put my dwelling place among you** Yahweh's presence with the Israelites—in the tent of meeting and tabernacle—will remain if they obey him. **26:12 I will walk among you** Probably means that Yahweh will move about among the Israelites—a reference to his continued presence in the journey to the promised land and—ultimately—the settling of the land (compare 2Sa 7:6–7). **26:13 brought you out of Egypt** Refers to the exodus from Egypt. This event was meant to lead the people into the promised land so that they could live vibrantly and positively. However, their security in the land was contingent upon obedience.

decrees and abhor my laws and fail to carry out all my commands and so violate my covenant, ¹⁶then I will do this to you: I will bring on you sudden terror, wasting diseases and fever that will destroy your sight and sap your strength. You will plant seed in vain, because your enemies will eat it. ¹⁷I will set my face against you so that you will be defeated by your enemies; those who hate you will rule over you, and you will flee even when no one is pursuing you.

¹⁸"If after all this you will not listen to me, I will punish you for your sins seven times over. ¹⁹I will break down your stubborn pride and make the sky above you like iron and the ground beneath you like bronze. ²⁰Your strength will be spent in vain, because your soil will not yield its crops, nor will the trees of your land yield their fruit.

²¹"If you remain hostile toward me and refuse to listen to me, I will multiply your afflictions seven times over, as your sins deserve. ²²I will send wild animals against you, and they will rob you of your children, destroy your cattle and make you so few in number that your roads will be deserted.

²³"If in spite of these things you do not accept my correction but continue to be hostile toward me, ²⁴I myself will be hostile toward you and will afflict you for your sins seven times over. ²⁵And I will bring the sword on you to avenge the breaking of the covenant. When you withdraw into your cities, I will send a plague among you, and you will be given into enemy hands. ²⁶When I cut off your supply of bread, ten women will be able to bake your bread in one oven, and they will dole out the bread by weight. You will eat, but you will not be satisfied.

²⁷"If in spite of this you still do not listen to me but continue to be hostile toward me, ²⁸then in my anger I will be hostile toward you, and I myself will punish you for your sins seven times

over. ²⁹You will eat the flesh of your sons and the flesh of your daughters. ³⁰I will destroy your high places, cut down your incense altars and pile your dead bodies*ᵃ* on the lifeless forms of your idols, and I will abhor you. ³¹I will turn your cities into ruins and lay waste your sanctuaries, and I will take no delight in the pleasing aroma of your offerings. ³²I myself will lay waste the land, so that your enemies who live there will be appalled. ³³I will scatter you among the nations and will draw out my sword and pursue you. Your land will be laid waste, and your cities will lie in ruins. ³⁴Then the land will enjoy its sabbath years all the time that it lies desolate and you are in the country of your enemies; then the land will rest and enjoy its sabbaths. ³⁵All the time that it lies desolate, the land will have the rest it did not have during the sabbaths you lived in it.

³⁶"As for those of you who are left, I will make their hearts so fearful in the lands of their enemies that the sound of a windblown leaf will put them to flight. They will run as though fleeing from the sword, and they will fall, even though no one is pursuing them. ³⁷They will stumble over one another as though fleeing from the sword, even though no one is pursuing them. So you will not be able to stand before your enemies. ³⁸You will perish among the nations; the land of your enemies will devour you. ³⁹Those of you who are left will waste away in the lands of their enemies because of their sins; also because of their ancestors' sins they will waste away.

⁴⁰"But if they will confess their sins and the sins of their ancestors — their unfaithfulness and their hostility toward me, ⁴¹which made me hostile toward them so that I sent them into the land of their enemies — then when their uncircumcised hearts are humbled and they pay for their sin,

ᵃ 30 Or your funeral offerings

26:16 I will do this to you This statement introduces a lengthy list of possible punishments. **wasting diseases and fever** It is unclear what conditions are indicated by these terms (which also appear together in Dt 28:22).
26:17 I will set my face against you Signifying the absence of God's favor or him being in opposition to the people.
26:18 punish you for your sins seven times over Points to repeated, successive punishment (compare Ps 79:12; Pr 24:16) but with the implication that even in the midst of the curses there would be opportunity to repent (Lev 26:21,23,27).
26:19 sky above you like iron and the ground beneath you like bronze Indicates that Yahweh will withhold rain and cause the ground to become hard and dry, unable to yield crops for food.
26:29 You will eat the flesh Compare Dt 28:54–57; La 2:20; 4:10; Eze 5:10; Jer 19:9; 2Ki 6:28–29.
26:30 destroy your high places The high places were places of worship for foreign deities. **dead bodies** A pejorative description of the idol itself—a lifeless, inanimate object (Ps 135:15–17).

26:32 will be appalled This image—of travelers and enemies descending upon the land only to be shocked by its desolation—is a common curse in such listings (e.g., Dt 29:21–24).
26:33 scatter you among the nations A clear reference to the threat of exile (see Eze 6:8; 12:15; 22:15).
26:38 perish among the nations Yahweh threatens that the captive Israelites will die on foreign ground, never to see their homeland again.

26:40–45 The conclusion of this list of punishments and curses (Lev 26:14–45) is structured as a lengthy conditional statement that communicates that a cursed state of affairs is not absolute. There is possibility for salvation. When the people recognize and confess their sins, then Yahweh will remember his covenant and restore them.

26:41 uncircumcised hearts This imagery also occurs elsewhere (Dt 10:16; Jer 9:25; Eze 44:7). Circumcision was a symbol of Yahweh's covenant with his people—he desired for their actions and thoughts to reflect the same kind of obedience.

⁴²I will remember my covenant with Jacob and my covenant with Isaac and my covenant with Abraham, and I will remember the land. ⁴³For the land will be deserted by them and will enjoy its sabbaths while it lies desolate without them. They will pay for their sins because they rejected my laws and abhorred my decrees. ⁴⁴Yet in spite of this, when they are in the land of their enemies, I will not reject them or abhor them so as to destroy them completely, breaking my covenant with them. I am the LORD their God. ⁴⁵But for their sake I will remember the covenant with their ancestors whom I brought out of Egypt in the sight of the nations to be their God. I am the LORD.'"

⁴⁶These are the decrees, the laws and the regulations that the LORD established at Mount Sinai between himself and the Israelites through Moses.

Redeeming What Is the LORD's

27 The LORD said to Moses, ²"Speak to the Israelites and say to them: 'If anyone makes a special vow to dedicate a person to the LORD by giving the equivalent value, ³set the value of a male between the ages of twenty and sixty at fifty shekels[a] of silver, according to the sanctuary shekel[b]; ⁴for a female, set her value at thirty shekels[c]; ⁵for a person between the ages of five and twenty, set the value of a male at twenty shekels[d] and of a female at ten shekels[e]; ⁶for a person between one month and five years, set the value of a male at five shekels[f] of silver and that of a female at three shekels[g] of silver; ⁷for a person sixty years old or more, set the value of a male at fifteen shekels[h] and of a female at ten shekels. ⁸If anyone making the vow is too poor to pay the specified amount, the person being dedicated is to be presented to the priest, who will set the value according to what the one making the vow can afford.

⁹"'If what they vowed is an animal that is acceptable as an offering to the LORD, such an animal given to the LORD becomes holy. ¹⁰They must not exchange it or substitute a good one for a bad one, or a bad one for a good one; if they should substitute one animal for another, both it and the substitute become holy. ¹¹If what they vowed is a ceremonially unclean animal — one that is not acceptable as an offering to the LORD — the animal must be presented to the priest, ¹²who will judge its quality as good or bad. Whatever value the priest then sets, that is what it will be. ¹³If the owner wishes to redeem the animal, a fifth must be added to its value.

¹⁴"'If anyone dedicates their house as something holy to the LORD, the priest will judge its quality as good or bad. Whatever value the priest then sets, so it will remain. ¹⁵If the one who dedicates their

---

[a] *3* That is, about 1 1/4 pounds or about 575 grams; also in verse 16   [b] *3* That is, about 2/5 ounce or about 12 grams; also in verse 25   [c] *4* That is, about 12 ounces or about 345 grams   [d] *5* That is, about 8 ounces or about 230 grams   [e] *5* That is, about 4 ounces or about 115 grams; also in verse 7   [f] *6* That is, about 2 ounces or about 58 grams   [g] *6* That is, about 1 1/4 ounces or about 35 grams   [h] *7* That is, about 6 ounces or about 175 grams

---

26:42 my covenant with Abraham Yahweh will remember his promise to the patriarchs about them having a great number of descendants and a wonderful land (Ge 12:1–3; 15:1–6; 26:4; 28:3). The exact meaning of this phrase is unknown. The promise may mean that the nation of Israel is still the focus of kingdom language and prophecy or it could be applied more broadly to Yahweh remembering the idea behind his covenant and fulfilling its general purposes.

26:44 breaking my covenant with them The discipline described in 26:3–43 was a requirement of the covenant, but Yahweh does not nullify the covenant.

27:1–34 The final chapter of Leviticus focuses on pledges to support the tabernacle's construction. This is possibly a later addition to Leviticus, since ch. 26 already provides a logical ending. Both Deuteronomy and Leviticus avoid ending the book with the list of blessings and curses. The placement of ch. 27 highlights the centerpiece of the Holiness Code (chs. 17–26): the sacredness of the sanctuary—which must be kept absolutely pure as the place where Yahweh interacts with his people.

27:1 The LORD said to Moses This final section of laws in Leviticus follows a common pattern (e.g., 6:1): Yahweh speaks to Moses and explains the laws that Moses should repeat to the Israelites.

27:2–8 Verses 2–8 establish the equivalent value in silver for persons of either gender according to age. This practice of exchanging a set amount of silver for the life of a person is comparable to the custom of redeeming the firstborn (Nu 18:16). This law creates a fixed value and appears to base that value on stereotypical expectations of the time about a person's potential economic contribution. A man in his prime is valued nearly twice as much as a woman of the same age bracket because in a manual labor economy a man was viewed as being able to generate more value.

27:2 makes a special vow to dedicate Describes the practice of rendering a fixed payment in place of lifelong service to the sanctuary. People who were not Levites could pledge themselves or their child to the sanctuary in some role (compare 1Sa 1:11). They also could vow to support the sanctuary with some other resource—in this case, silver (Lev 27:3)—in an amount equivalent to one's life. This practice ensured that the sanctuary received enough financial support to sustain its operations (compare 2Ki 12:5–6).

27:3 fifty shekels of silver A shekel was a unit of weight for weighing metals as currency. In general terms, one silver shekel weighed approximately 11–13 grams, but the weight for other precious metals is not precisely known.

27:9 animal The Israelites could pledge animals to the sanctuary. An animal's value was determined by the priests. If the owner wanted to redeem the animal later, a 20 percent surcharge would be added to the value so that the sanctuary would still profit (v. 13).

27:14 house as something holy Israelites could also pledge houses and land (v. 16) to the sanctuary. The priest was responsible to make a fair valuation of the house or land.

house wishes to redeem it, they must add a fifth to its value, and the house will again become theirs.

16 "'If anyone dedicates to the Lord part of their family land, its value is to be set according to the amount of seed required for it — fifty shekels of silver to a homer[a] of barley seed. 17 If they dedicate a field during the Year of Jubilee, the value that has been set remains. 18 But if they dedicate a field after the Jubilee, the priest will determine the value according to the number of years that remain until the next Year of Jubilee, and its set value will be reduced. 19 If the one who dedicates the field wishes to redeem it, they must add a fifth to its value, and the field will again become theirs. 20 If, however, they do not redeem the field, or if they have sold it to someone else, it can never be redeemed. 21 When the field is released in the Jubilee, it will become holy, like a field devoted to the Lord; it will become priestly property.

22 "'If anyone dedicates to the Lord a field they have bought, which is not part of their family land, 23 the priest will determine its value up to the Year of Jubilee, and the owner must pay its value on that day as something holy to the Lord. 24 In the Year of Jubilee the field will revert to the person from whom it was bought, the one whose land it was. 25 Every value is to be set according to the sanctuary shekel, twenty gerahs to the shekel.

26 "'No one, however, may dedicate the firstborn of an animal, since the firstborn already belongs to the Lord; whether an ox[b] or a sheep, it is the Lord's. 27 If it is one of the unclean animals, it may be bought back at its set value, adding a fifth of the value to it. If it is not redeemed, it is to be sold at its set value.

28 "'But nothing that a person owns and devotes[c] to the Lord — whether a human being or an animal or family land — may be sold or redeemed; everything so devoted is most holy to the Lord.

29 "'No person devoted to destruction[d] may be ransomed; they are to be put to death.

30 "'A tithe of everything from the land, whether grain from the soil or fruit from the trees, belongs to the Lord; it is holy to the Lord. 31 Whoever would redeem any of their tithe must add a fifth of the value to it. 32 Every tithe of the herd and flock — every tenth animal that passes under the shepherd's rod — will be holy to the Lord. 33 No one may pick out the good from the bad or make any substitution. If anyone does make a substitution, both the animal and its substitute become holy and cannot be redeemed.'"

34 These are the commands the Lord gave Moses at Mount Sinai for the Israelites.

---

[a] 16 That is, probably about 300 pounds or about 135 kilograms
[b] 26 The Hebrew word can refer to either male or female.
[c] 28 The Hebrew term refers to the irrevocable giving over of things or persons to the Lord.   [d] 29 The Hebrew term refers to the irrevocable giving over of things or persons to the Lord, often by totally destroying them.

27:16 part of their family land Due to Jubilee laws (ch. 25), rules for pledging land to the sanctuary were more complicated than those for animals or houses. Under the Jubilee principle, land would revert to its original owner in the Jubilee Year (the fiftieth year). **according to the amount of seed required for it** The land being pledged was valued according to the amount of seed required for sowing it annually.

27:17 value that has been set remains Private land in Israel was referred to by the Hebrew term *achuzzah* — which may be rendered "tenured land" or "land holding." The Israelites were essentially Yahweh's tenants, not the outright owners of the land.

27:19 add a fifth to its value As with pledged animals and houses (vv. 9,13–15), land could be redeemed at a 20 percent penalty.

27:21 it will become priestly property If the donor did not redeem the land before the next Jubilee Year, the initial donation was considered permanent.

27:22–23 These verses reflect the rules of 25:25–28. Even if someone had to sell private land (referred to in Hebrew as *achuzzah*; see v. 17 and note), the rights would revert at the next Jubilee Year — which meant that the buyer never became the permanent owner. In the meantime, if the buyer wanted to dedicate the land to the sanctuary, he had to donate its value (in silver) plus the surcharge of 20 percent — since the sanctuary would end up losing the land at the Jubilee Year.

27:26 firstborn already belongs to the Lord The firstborn males of people and animals are dedicated to Yahweh (Ex 13:2).

27:28 nothing that a person owns and devotes to the

Lord The Hebrew word used here, *cherem*, is a technical term used for people and things designated as sacred property — that is, devoted to a deity (compare note on Jos 6:17). In the case of Lev 27:21, certain pieces of property are dedicated exclusively to Yahweh and cannot be redeemed (i.e., no substitute was allowed). In the present verse and v. 29, the term is used with respect to people. The present verse suggests that anything voluntarily dedicated to Yahweh or his service — such as an animal, person, or land — cannot have its status changed.

27:29 devoted to destruction While the same Hebrew term used in 27:28 is used here, *cherem*, here it does not refer to a positive connotation of dedication, but instead to the idea of fulfilling the law (see note on Jos 6:17). This law suggests that a person who has committed an injustice that would result in death (according to the law) must be put to death — they cannot be redeemed from that punishment (compare 24:11 and note).

27:30 A tithe of everything from the land Each year, Israelites donated one-tenth from their crops and vineyards to the sanctuary. The tithe went to support the Levites, who in turn had to tithe to the priests (Nu 18:21–32). Ancient Israelites were obligated to pay three tithes: the general tithe described in Lev 27; a special tithe for the Levites, who were not allotted land (Dt 14:22–27); and a special tithe for the poor, paid every three years (Dt 14:28–29). As with vows, the tithed items could be repurchased based on the value of the object plus 20 percent (Lev 27:31).

27:32 every tenth animal The tithe from livestock was determined by counting every tenth animal that passed under the shepherd's rod (compare Jer 33:13; Eze 20:37).

NUMBERS

INTRODUCTION TO NUMBERS

The book of Numbers is about Israel's 40-year journey through the wilderness toward Canaan, the promised land—a place God had long ago promised to their forefather Abraham (Ge 12:1–3). Numbers begins in the Sinai Desert, shortly after Yahweh gave his law to Moses, the man who led the Israelites out of slavery (see Exodus). Numbers ends with the Israelites on the plains of Moab, across the Jordan River from the promised land. The book contains narratives, laws, poetry and census lists. The various genres create a holistic picture of the Israelites' journey and their developing relationship with God.

BACKGROUND

The title, Numbers, refers to two censuses taken to count the members of Israel's tribes—one at Mount Sinai (Nu 1–4) and one in Moab (ch. 26). The Bible often includes records like these to provide a snapshot of the Hebrew people at significant turning points in their history. This time of wandering likely dates to the 15th or 13th centuries BC.

According to Jewish and Christian traditions, Moses wrote Numbers along with the rest of the Pentateuch (the first five books of the Bible). However, the books of the Pentateuch do not explicitly name Moses as their author and may have been compiled over a long period (see the "Introduction to Genesis"). However, Numbers provides the basis for the traditions crediting Moses as author of the Pentateuch. In Numbers 33:1–2, God commands Moses to record the Israelites' movements during their wanderings between Egypt and the promised land—and the book may have begun as that account. Numbers also mentions additional literary sources (such as the Book of the Wars of Yahweh, in 21:14); references like this suggest that an editor was involved in shaping the book's final form.

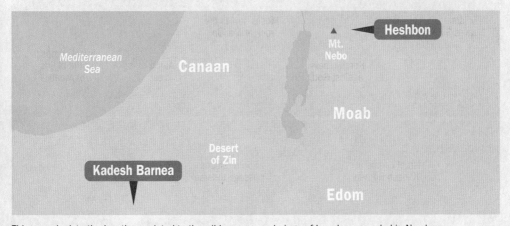

This map depicts the locations related to the wilderness wanderings of Israel as recorded in Numbers.

STRUCTURE

Numbers can be divided into three sections. The first and third sections, which are set 40 years apart, each begin with a census and report the Israelites' preparations for a major move. In the first section (chs. 1–10), the move involves departing from Sinai (10:11–12); in the third section (chs. 26–36), the move involves crossing the Jordan River from Moab into the promised land (an event described in Joshua 3). The intervening section (Nu 11–25) is a collection of stories and laws from the 40-year period between these moves. The book can also be outlined according to the major geographical locations it mentions.

OUTLINE

- Preparing to leave Sinai (1:1—10:10)
- Journey to Kadesh Barnea (10:11—12:16)
- Wilderness wanderings (13:1—20:21)
- Journey to Moab (20:22—22:1)
- On the plains of Moab (22:2—36:13)

THEMES

Numbers focuses on God's provision for the Israelites. In the process, it records detailed laws intended to create a society reflective of Yahweh's holiness and justice. The narrative passages

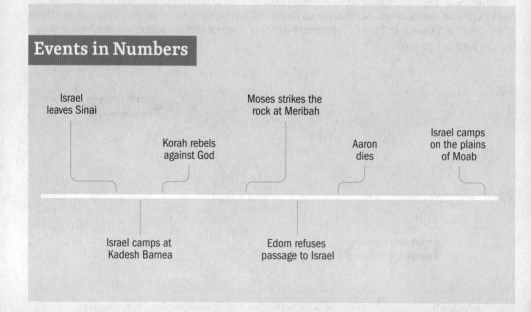

Events in Numbers

Israel leaves Sinai

Korah rebels against God

Israel camps at Kadesh Barnea

Moses strikes the rock at Meribah

Edom refuses passage to Israel

Aaron dies

Israel camps on the plains of Moab

deal mostly with the Israelites' failings, showing what happens when God's people do not live according to his commands. Their mistakes result in calamity and Yahweh's temporary judgment, issued so that he may preserve them from further evil.

Despite Israel's failure, Yahweh honors his promise to Abraham and prepares Israel for entering the promised land. But there is a problem: Terrifying foes inhabit the promised land, and the people see no chance for success against them in war (chs. 13–14). Although the older generation lacks the trust to let Yahweh overcome these foes and dies in the wilderness, the younger generation—plus two faithful men, Caleb and Joshua—have an opportunity to enter the land. This new generation, led by Joshua, is left with a choice: to follow Yahweh or turn away like the previous generation (27:15–23). Although Numbers ends without fully resolving this dilemma, the closing chapters anticipate the people's future in Canaan, the promised land (e.g., ch. 34).

The wilderness journey presents challenges and blessings—all of which invite a faithful response. Numbers shows that trusting God is not merely a mental commitment; it involves action and bold risks. But Numbers emphasizes that a risk taken because of our faith in Yahweh is beautiful. It gives God the opportunity to demonstrate his protection, meet our needs and be present among us. Numbers also shows us that God pursues us, despite our failings. In relationship with Yahweh—facilitated by our great warrior and advocate Jesus—we find all the direction we will ever need (Heb 3–4).

The Census

1 The LORD spoke to Moses in the tent of meeting in the Desert of Sinai on the first day of the second month of the second year after the Israelites came out of Egypt. He said: ²"Take a census of the whole Israelite community by their clans and families, listing every man by name, one by one. ³You and Aaron are to count according to their divisions all the men in Israel who are twenty years old or more and able to serve in the army. ⁴One man from each tribe, each of them the head of his family, is to help you. ⁵These are the names of the men who are to assist you:

from Reuben, Elizur son of Shedeur;
⁶from Simeon, Shelumiel son of Zurishaddai;
⁷from Judah, Nahshon son of Amminadab;
⁸from Issachar, Nethanel son of Zuar;
⁹from Zebulun, Eliab son of Helon;
¹⁰from the sons of Joseph:
from Ephraim, Elishama son of Ammihud;
from Manasseh, Gamaliel son of Pedahzur;
¹¹from Benjamin, Abidan son of Gideoni;
¹²from Dan, Ahiezer son of Ammishaddai;
¹³from Asher, Pagiel son of Okran;
¹⁴from Gad, Eliasaph son of Deuel;
¹⁵from Naphtali, Ahira son of Enan."

¹⁶These were the men appointed from the community, the leaders of their ancestral tribes. They were the heads of the clans of Israel.

¹⁷Moses and Aaron took these men whose names had been specified, ¹⁸and they called the whole community together on the first day of the second month. The people registered their ancestry by their clans and families, and the men twenty years old or more were listed by name, one by one, ¹⁹as the LORD commanded Moses. And so he counted them in the Desert of Sinai:

²⁰From the descendants of Reuben the firstborn son of Israel:
All the men twenty years old or more who were able to serve in the army were listed by name, one by one, according to the records of their clans and families. ²¹The number from the tribe of Reuben was 46,500.

²²From the descendants of Simeon:
All the men twenty years old or more who were able to serve in the army were counted and listed by name, one by one, according to the records of their clans and families. ²³The number from the tribe of Simeon was 59,300.

1:1—10:36 The first 10 chapters of Numbers describe the organization of the camp of Israel during the journey to the promised land. The book continues the narrative begun in the book of Exodus. The Israelites must organize the camp and determine the logistics of the march. They must also make military preparations for the eventual conquest of Canaan. The census recorded in Nu 1–10 took place over 20 days (1:1; 10:11). At the close of this period, the Israelites began their journey—which ended 38 years later (Dt 2:14). These events from Israel's early history date to sometime in the Late Bronze Age (1550–1200 BC).

1:1 tent of meeting Yahweh's voice came from inside the internal tent structure of the tabernacle proper—the Most Holy Place (Holy of Holies) where the ark of the covenant was kept (Ex 25:22; Nu 7:89). The tent was essentially a portable Sinai, where Moses and God conversed in private. See the infographic "The Tabernacle" on p. 138. **Desert of Sinai** Designates an area near Mount Sinai, but not the mountain itself (compare Ex 3:1–2; 19:1–2). All of the communications between Moses and Yahweh in Nu 1–10 occur in the wilderness of Sinai rather than on the mountain bearing the same name.

1:2 Take a census of the whole Israelite community Chapter 1 records a census which was taken to determine the number of fighting men in Israel so that they could organize Israel into a war camp with the tabernacle at the center.

1:3 twenty years old The age of mandatory enlistment in the ancient Israelite army. Compare 2Ch 25:5.

1:4 head The Hebrew term used here, *rosh*, refers to the leader of the household in this instance. In some contexts, it is synonymous with the Hebrew term *nasi* (often translated as "prince" or "chieftain") which is used in Nu 1:16.

1:5–16 The following list includes 24 names—16 of which do not appear elsewhere. One representative from each tribe is chosen by Yahweh to count the men of his own tribe. The list identifies the leaders of the tribes during the days of Moses. The list is arranged according to tribe, but it leaves out the tribe of Levi because the Levites were exempt from military service due to their assignment to the service of the tabernacle sanctuary (vv. 47–53; ch. 18).

1:16 leaders The Hebrew term used here, *nasi*, refers to the recognized leader of the clan (see note on v. 4). Each tribe included multiple clans and their respective leaders (vv. 5–16; 13:1–15; 34:16–29).

1:20–46 This section lists how many men of at least 20 years of age were registered during the census. The listing is given tribe-by-tribe with a summary at the end (vv. 44–46). According to Ex 12:37, about 600,000 men left Egypt, accompanied by additional women and children. The sum total given in this passage yields an army of over 600,000 men. Adding women and children, this number indicates an extremely large population of 2–3 million people for the Israelites, the size of which poses major logistical difficulties (see note on Nu 1:46). The size of the army also poses a major historical difficulty since such a large army was unheard of in the ancient world—even if it was made up of every able-bodied male. The Egyptian army at the time had about 100,000 men total. At the Battle of Kadesh, a major battle of the early thirteenth century BC, the Egyptians fielded an army of about 20,000 against a Hittite force of about 17,000. A few hundred years later, the Assyrians subjugated most of Mesopotamia and the Levant with around 175,000 men. A few hundred years after that, the Persians fielded the largest armies of ancient times with 350,000 to 400,000.

24 From the descendants of Gad:
All the men twenty years old or more who were able to serve in the army were listed by name, according to the records of their clans and families. 25 The number from the tribe of Gad was 45,650.

26 From the descendants of Judah:
All the men twenty years old or more who were able to serve in the army were listed by name, according to the records of their clans and families. 27 The number from the tribe of Judah was 74,600.

28 From the descendants of Issachar:
All the men twenty years old or more who were able to serve in the army were listed by name, according to the records of their clans and families. 29 The number from the tribe of Issachar was 54,400.

30 From the descendants of Zebulun:
All the men twenty years old or more who were able to serve in the army were listed by name, according to the records of their clans and families. 31 The number from the tribe of Zebulun was 57,400.

32 From the sons of Joseph:
From the descendants of Ephraim:
All the men twenty years old or more who were able to serve in the army were listed by name, according to the records of their clans and families. 33 The number from the tribe of Ephraim was 40,500.

34 From the descendants of Manasseh:
All the men twenty years old or more who were able to serve in the army were listed by name, according to the records of their clans and families. 35 The number from the tribe of Manasseh was 32,200.

36 From the descendants of Benjamin:
All the men twenty years old or more who were able to serve in the army were listed by name, according to the records of their clans and families. 37 The number from the tribe of Benjamin was 35,400.

38 From the descendants of Dan:
All the men twenty years old or more who were able to serve in the army were listed by name, according to the records of their clans and families. 39 The number from the tribe of Dan was 62,700.

40 From the descendants of Asher:
All the men twenty years old or more who were able to serve in the army were listed by name, according to the records of their clans and families. 41 The number from the tribe of Asher was 41,500.

42 From the descendants of Naphtali:
All the men twenty years old or more who were able to serve in the army were listed by name, according to the records of their clans and families. 43 The number from the tribe of Naphtali was 53,400.

44 These were the men counted by Moses and Aaron and the twelve leaders of Israel, each one representing his family. 45 All the Israelites twenty years old or more who were able to serve in Israel's army were counted according to their families. 46 The total number was 603,550.

47 The ancestral tribe of the Levites, however, was not counted along with the others. 48 The LORD had said to Moses: 49 "You must not count the tribe of Levi or include them in the census of the other Israelites. 50 Instead, appoint the Levites to be in charge of the tabernacle of the covenant law — over all its furnishings and everything belonging to it.

An Israelite army of 600,000 men, even unarmed and enslaved, had a six-to-one numerical advantage over their captors and would hardly have needed divine intervention to make their escape from Egypt. Similarly, conquering the territory of Canaan would have posed no trouble for such a large force.

The best explanation for the difficulty posed by the total is that the Hebrew words used in this passage — eleph ("thousand") and me'ah ("hundred") — should be understood as terms for military groupings, not as literal numbers (compare 10:4; Ex 18:21; Jos 22:30). Both terms are also used in a way that is analogous to terms for military units like legion, squadron, battalion or platoon (Nu 31:5; 1Sa 8:12; 29:2; 2Sa 18:1; 2Ki 11:4). Therefore, the totals given do not provide any information on the size of the Israelite population.

1:46 603,550 Adding women and children to this number yields a total population of 2–3 million. A population of this size would have taken weeks to pass any single point on the route to the promised land. Furthermore, Yahweh's miraculous provision of food for the Israel-

ites only begins roughly 45 days into their journey (Ex 16:1), meaning about 2 million people had to be fed by other means for that time. If they ate livestock from their flocks and herds for that time, they would have had to leave Egypt with millions of animals. Even after the provision of manna began, a population that size would need to gather over a million gallons of manna per day (see Ex 16:13–21). Either the size of the population is literary hyperbole (exaggeration for effect) or the terms for thousands, hundreds and fifties are not labels for the actual numbers of the groups (see note on Nu 1:20–46).

1:47–54 The tribe of Levi is exempt from military service because the Levites serve in the tabernacle (vv. 50–53; compare ch. 18). Without the integrity of the tabernacle — which enables Yahweh to live among the people — Israel would not succeed in war. In this way, the Levite's guardianship of the tabernacle is a form of military service in that it ensures Yahweh's protection for Israel's soldiers.

They are to carry the tabernacle and all its furnishings; they are to take care of it and encamp around it. ⁵¹Whenever the tabernacle is to move, the Levites are to take it down, and whenever the tabernacle is to be set up, the Levites shall do it. Anyone else who approaches it is to be put to death. ⁵²The Israelites are to set up their tents by divisions, each of them in their own camp under their standard. ⁵³The Levites, however, are to set up their tents around the tabernacle of the covenant law so that my wrath will not fall on the Israelite community. The Levites are to be responsible for the care of the tabernacle of the covenant law."

⁵⁴The Israelites did all this just as the LORD commanded Moses.

The Arrangement of the Tribal Camps

2 The LORD said to Moses and Aaron: ²"The Israelites are to camp around the tent of meeting some distance from it, each of them under their standard and holding the banners of their family."

³On the east, toward the sunrise, the divisions of the camp of Judah are to encamp under their standard. The leader of the people of Judah is Nahshon son of Amminadab. ⁴His division numbers 74,600.

⁵The tribe of Issachar will camp next to them. The leader of the people of Issachar is Nethanel son of Zuar. ⁶His division numbers 54,400.

⁷The tribe of Zebulun will be next. The leader of the people of Zebulun is Eliab son of Helon. ⁸His division numbers 57,400.

⁹All the men assigned to the camp of Judah, according to their divisions, number 186,400. They will set out first.

¹⁰On the south will be the divisions of the camp of Reuben under their standard. The leader of the people of Reuben is Elizur son of Shedeur. ¹¹His division numbers 46,500.

¹²The tribe of Simeon will camp next to them. The leader of the people of Simeon is Shelumiel son of Zurishaddai. ¹³His division numbers 59,300.

¹⁴The tribe of Gad will be next. The leader of the people of Gad is Eliasaph son of Deuel.ᵃ ¹⁵His division numbers 45,650.

¹⁶All the men assigned to the camp of Reuben, according to their divisions, number 151,450. They will set out second.

¹⁷Then the tent of meeting and the camp of the Levites will set out in the middle of the camps. They will set out in the same order as they encamp, each in their own place under their standard.

¹⁸On the west will be the divisions of the camp of Ephraim under their standard. The leader of the people of Ephraim is Elishama son of Ammihud. ¹⁹His division numbers 40,500.

²⁰The tribe of Manasseh will be next to them. The leader of the people of Manasseh is Gamaliel son of Pedahzur. ²¹His division numbers 32,200.

²²The tribe of Benjamin will be next. The leader of the people of Benjamin is Abidan son of Gideoni. ²³His division numbers 35,400.

²⁴All the men assigned to the camp of Ephraim, according to their divisions, number 108,100. They will set out third.

²⁵On the north will be the divisions of the camp of Dan under their standard. The leader of the people of Dan is Ahiezer son of Ammishaddai. ²⁶His division numbers 62,700.

²⁷The tribe of Asher will camp next to them. The leader of the people of Asher is Pagiel son of Okran. ²⁸His division numbers 41,500.

²⁹The tribe of Naphtali will be next. The leader of the people of Naphtali is Ahira son of Enan. ³⁰His division numbers 53,400.

³¹All the men assigned to the camp of Dan number 157,600. They will set out last, under their standards.

³²These are the Israelites, counted according to their families. All the men in the camps, by their divisions, number 603,550. ³³The Levites, however, were not counted along with the other Israelites, as the LORD commanded Moses.

³⁴So the Israelites did everything the LORD commanded Moses; that is the way they encamped under their standards, and that is the way they set out, each of them with their clan and family.

ᵃ 14 Many manuscripts of the Masoretic Text, Samaritan Pentateuch and Vulgate (see also 1:14); most manuscripts of the Masoretic Text *Reuel*

1:53 so that my wrath will not fall The Levites were to camp around the tabernacle as a buffer between the other 11 tribes and the space dedicated to the service of Yahweh.

2:1–34 This chapter describes how the 12 tribes were arranged in the camp with the Levites and the tabernacle at the center.

2:2 around the tent of meeting The order of encampment reflects the birth order of Jacob's sons—the patriarchs of the 12 tribes. See the infographic "The Israelite Encampment" on p. 215.

2:33 Levites, however, were not counted The Levites were exempt from military duty, so they were not included in the census.

Ephraim   Benjamin   Naphtali   Dan

Gershon

Merarites

Tabernacle

Moses,
Aaron,
Priests

Kohathites

The Israelite Encampment

The Book of Numbers describes the layout of the encampment during Israel's 40 years of wilderness wanderings (2:1–34). The tribes encamped around the tabernacle, both in order to stay close to the tent of meeting and to defend it during attack. The four sides were surrounded by four groups, led by Judah, Reuben, Ephraim and Dan. The Levites—specially chosen to be close to God—camped around all sides of the tabernacle.

ARRANGEMENT OF THE CAMPS:

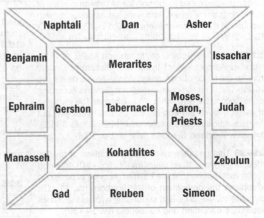

	Naphtali	Dan	Asher
Benjamin		Merarites	Issachar
Ephraim	Gershon	Tabernacle / Moses, Aaron, Priests	Judah
Manasseh		Kohathites	Zebulun
	Gad	Reuben	Simeon

The Levites

3 This is the account of the family of Aaron and Moses at the time the Lord spoke to Moses at Mount Sinai.

²The names of the sons of Aaron were Nadab the firstborn and Abihu, Eleazar and Ithamar. ³Those were the names of Aaron's sons, the anointed priests, who were ordained to serve as priests. ⁴Nadab and Abihu, however, died before the Lord when they made an offering with unauthorized fire before him in the Desert of Sinai. They had no sons, so Eleazar and Ithamar served as priests during the lifetime of their father Aaron.

⁵The Lord said to Moses, ⁶"Bring the tribe of Levi and present them to Aaron the priest to assist him. ⁷They are to perform duties for him and for the whole community at the tent of meeting by doing the work of the tabernacle. ⁸They are to take care of all the furnishings of the tent of meeting, fulfilling the obligations of the Israelites by doing the work of the tabernacle. ⁹Give the Levites to Aaron and his sons; they are the Israelites who are to be given wholly to him.ᵃ ¹⁰Appoint Aaron and his sons to serve as priests; anyone else who approaches the sanctuary is to be put to death."

¹¹The Lord also said to Moses, ¹²"I have taken the Levites from among the Israelites in place of the first male offspring of every Israelite woman. The Levites are mine, ¹³for all the firstborn are mine. When I struck down all the firstborn in Egypt, I set apart for myself every firstborn in Israel, whether human or animal. They are to be mine. I am the Lord."

¹⁴The Lord said to Moses in the Desert of Sinai, ¹⁵"Count the Levites by their families and clans. Count every male a month old or more." ¹⁶So Moses counted them, as he was commanded by the word of the Lord.

¹⁷These were the names of the sons of Levi:
Gershon, Kohath and Merari.
¹⁸These were the names of the Gershonite clans:
Libni and Shimei.
¹⁹The Kohathite clans:
Amram, Izhar, Hebron and Uzziel.
²⁰The Merarite clans:
Mahli and Mushi.
These were the Levite clans, according to their families.

²¹To Gershon belonged the clans of the Libnites and Shimeites; these were the Gershonite clans. ²²The number of all the males a month old or more who were counted was 7,500. ²³The Gershonite clans were to camp on the west, behind the tabernacle. ²⁴The leader of the families of the Gershonites was Eliasaph son of Lael. ²⁵At the tent of meeting the Gershonites were responsible for the care of the tabernacle and tent, its coverings, the curtain at the entrance to the tent of meeting, ²⁶the curtains of the courtyard, the curtain at the entrance to the courtyard surrounding the tabernacle and altar, and the ropes — and everything related to their use.

ᵃ 9 Most manuscripts of the Masoretic Text; some manuscripts of the Masoretic Text, Samaritan Pentateuch and Septuagint (see also 8:16) *to me*

3:1–51 Numbers 3 opens by identifying Aaron's four sons who were ordained as priests (Lev 8–10). Most of the chapter addresses the responsibilities of the Levites, especially as related to taking care of the tabernacle. Each clan of Levites has a particular responsibility and is positioned in a specific location with respect to the tabernacle. The Levites are dedicated to the service of Yahweh in place of all the firstborn of Israel, who were set aside for Yahweh because of the Passover event (Nu 3:11–13,40–51; Ex 13:1–2; see Ex 11–12; 22:29–30; 34:19–20).

3:2 Eleazar The deaths of Nadab and Abihu leave Eleazar as Aaron's eldest living son; therefore, Eleazar inherits the office of high priest upon Aaron's death (Nu 20:22–29). See the people diagram "Levites According to the Second Census" on p. 217. **Ithamar** The youngest of Aaron's four sons who led the Levites in carrying out the responsibilities of the tabernacle (4:28,33; Ex 38:21).

3:4 unauthorized fire See note on Lev 10:1.

3:5–39 This passage describes the duties of the Levites, beginning with an overview (Nu 3:5–10), followed by the explanation that the Levites' service is designed to replace the dedication of the firstborn (vv. 11–13; compare vv. 40–51), and continuing with assignments specific to each clan and household (vv. 14–39).

3:7 They are to perform duties for him and for the whole community One of the Levites' main responsibilities was guarding the priests against defilement from those outside the tabernacle grounds.

3:10 anyone else who approaches God authorized the priests to kill anyone who entered sacred space without authorization.

3:12 in place of the first male offspring of every Israelite woman The substitution of the Levites in place of the firstborn for the service of the tabernacle explains what it meant that the firstborn be dedicated to God (compare Ex 13:1–2; note on Nu 3:1–51).

3:15 a month old The age at which the firstborn became eligible for redemption (see vv. 40–51; compare note on 3:1–51).

3:21–39 The eight clans of Levi—the Libnites and Shimeites descended from Gershon, the Amramites, Izharites, Hebronites and Uzzielites descended from Kohath, and the Mahlites and Mushites descended from Merari—now receive instructions regarding where they will camp when the Israelites are at rest, and what their precise duties will be. See the people diagram "Levites According to the Second Census" on p. 217.

3:25 were responsible for the care The Hebrew term used here, *mishmereth*, refers to trusted service.

3:26 the curtains of the courtyard The Gershonites are entrusted with the outer coverings of the tabernacle courtyard and the material coverings of the tent shrine itself.

Levites According to the Second Census
(Nu 3:14–39)

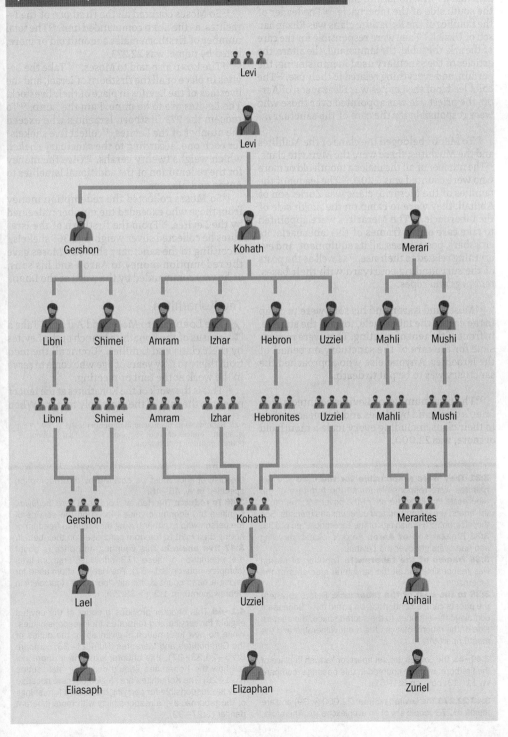

²⁷To Kohath belonged the clans of the Amramites, Izharites, Hebronites and Uzzielites; these were the Kohathite clans. ²⁸The number of all the males a month old or more was 8,600.ᵃ The Kohathites were responsible for the care of the sanctuary. ²⁹The Kohathite clans were to camp on the south side of the tabernacle. ³⁰The leader of the families of the Kohathite clans was Elizaphan son of Uzziel. ³¹They were responsible for the care of the ark, the table, the lampstand, the altars, the articles of the sanctuary used in ministering, the curtain, and everything related to their use. ³²The chief leader of the Levites was Eleazar son of Aaron, the priest. He was appointed over those who were responsible for the care of the sanctuary.

³³To Merari belonged the clans of the Mahlites and the Mushites; these were the Merarite clans. ³⁴The number of all the males a month old or more who were counted was 6,200. ³⁵The leader of the families of the Merarite clans was Zuriel son of Abihail; they were to camp on the north side of the tabernacle. ³⁶The Merarites were appointed to take care of the frames of the tabernacle, its crossbars, posts, bases, all its equipment, and everything related to their use, ³⁷as well as the posts of the surrounding courtyard with their bases, tent pegs and ropes.

³⁸Moses and Aaron and his sons were to camp to the east of the tabernacle, toward the sunrise, in front of the tent of meeting. They were responsible for the care of the sanctuary on behalf of the Israelites. Anyone else who approached the sanctuary was to be put to death.

³⁹The total number of Levites counted at the LORD's command by Moses and Aaron according to their clans, including every male a month old or more, was 22,000.

⁴⁰The LORD said to Moses, "Count all the firstborn Israelite males who are a month old or more and make a list of their names. ⁴¹Take the Levites for me in place of all the firstborn of the Israelites, and the livestock of the Levites in place of all the firstborn of the livestock of the Israelites. I am the LORD."

⁴²So Moses counted all the firstborn of the Israelites, as the LORD commanded him. ⁴³The total number of firstborn males a month old or more, listed by name, was 22,273.

⁴⁴The LORD also said to Moses, ⁴⁵"Take the Levites in place of all the firstborn of Israel, and the livestock of the Levites in place of their livestock. The Levites are to be mine. I am the LORD. ⁴⁶To redeem the 273 firstborn Israelites who exceed the number of the Levites, ⁴⁷collect five shekelsᵇ for each one, according to the sanctuary shekel, which weighs twenty gerahs. ⁴⁸Give the money for the redemption of the additional Israelites to Aaron and his sons."

⁴⁹So Moses collected the redemption money from those who exceeded the number redeemed by the Levites. ⁵⁰From the firstborn of the Israelites he collected silver weighing 1,365 shekels,ᶜ according to the sanctuary shekel. ⁵¹Moses gave the redemption money to Aaron and his sons, as he was commanded by the word of the LORD.

The Kohathites

4 The LORD said to Moses and Aaron: ²"Take a census of the Kohathite branch of the Levites by their clans and families. ³Count all the men from thirty to fifty years of age who come to serve in the work at the tent of meeting.

⁴"This is the work of the Kohathites at the tent of meeting: the care of the most holy things. ⁵When

---

ᵃ 28 Hebrew; some Septuagint manuscripts 8,300   ᵇ 47 That is, about 2 ounces or about 58 grams   ᶜ 50 That is, about 35 pounds or about 16 kilograms

---

3:31 They were responsible for the care The Kohathites were responsible for all the furniture of the tabernacle including the ark of the covenant, the table, the altars, the lampstand and other various utensils. See the infographic "Furnishings of the Tabernacle" on p. 136.

3:32 Eleazar son of Aaron Aaron's eldest surviving son had oversight over the Levites.

3:36 frames of the tabernacle The clan of Merari was responsible for all the structural elements of the tabernacle.

3:38 to the east of the tabernacle Refers to where the priests camped and stood on guard duty. Because it contained the entrance to the sacred space, the eastern side of the tabernacle was the most vulnerable and the most important.

3:40–51 The Levites are set apart for Yahweh in place of the firstborn, who are counted in this passage (compare vv. 11–13; note on 3:1–51).

3:43 22,273 The Levites number 22,000 (v. 39) and are therefore 273 people shy of an even exchange. Therefore,

the discrepancy must be covered by the redemption specified in vv. 46–48.

3:46 To redeem The Hebrew word used here, *peduyim*, signifies the economic value placed on the service of the person who is either buying their right to freedom or having their right to freedom purchased on their behalf.

3:47 five shekels This counting and price is about the redemption of these 273 individual, firstborn lives (compare note on 3:1–51). The Hebrew idiom used for taking a head count is literally "per skull" (*gulgoleth* in Hebrew; compare 1:2; Ex 38:26).

4:1–49 This chapter provides a count of the Levites eligible for service and reiterates their responsibilities. While no new information is given about the duties of the Gershonites and Merarites (Nu 4:21–33; compare 3:25–26,33–37), this chapter explains in more detail how the Kohathites should carry out their duties (vv. 1–20). The Kohathites are singled out here because they are responsible for carrying the sacred furnishings of the tabernacle—a responsibility with more inherent danger (3:27–32).

the camp is to move, Aaron and his sons are to go in and take down the shielding curtain and put it over the ark of the covenant law. [6]Then they are to cover the curtain with a durable leather,[a] spread a cloth of solid blue over that and put the poles in place.

[7]"Over the table of the Presence they are to spread a blue cloth and put on it the plates, dishes and bowls, and the jars for drink offerings; the bread that is continually there is to remain on it. [8]They are to spread a scarlet cloth over them, cover that with the durable leather and put the poles in place.

[9]"They are to take a blue cloth and cover the lampstand that is for light, together with its lamps, its wick trimmers and trays, and all its jars for the olive oil used to supply it. [10]Then they are to wrap it and all its accessories in a covering of the durable leather and put it on a carrying frame.

[11]"Over the gold altar they are to spread a blue cloth and cover that with the durable leather and put the poles in place.

[12]"They are to take all the articles used for ministering in the sanctuary, wrap them in a blue cloth, cover that with the durable leather and put them on a carrying frame.

[13]"They are to remove the ashes from the bronze altar and spread a purple cloth over it. [14]Then they are to place on it all the utensils used for ministering at the altar, including the firepans, meat forks, shovels and sprinkling bowls. Over it they are to spread a covering of the durable leather and put the poles in place.

[15]"After Aaron and his sons have finished covering the holy furnishings and all the holy articles, and when the camp is ready to move, only then are the Kohathites to come and do the carrying. But they must not touch the holy things or they will die. The Kohathites are to carry those things that are in the tent of meeting.

[16]"Eleazar son of Aaron, the priest, is to have charge of the oil for the light, the fragrant incense, the regular grain offering and the anointing oil. He is to be in charge of the entire tabernacle and everything in it, including its holy furnishings and articles."

[17]The LORD said to Moses and Aaron, [18]"See that the Kohathite tribal clans are not destroyed from among the Levites. [19]So that they may live and not die when they come near the most holy things, do this for them: Aaron and his sons are to go into the sanctuary and assign to each man his work and what he is to carry. [20]But the Kohathites must not go in to look at the holy things, even for a moment, or they will die."

The Gershonites

[21]The LORD said to Moses, [22]"Take a census also of the Gershonites by their families and clans. [23]Count all the men from thirty to fifty years of age who come to serve in the work at the tent of meeting.

[a] 6 Possibly the hides of large aquatic mammals; also in verses 8, 10, 11, 12, 14 and 25

4:3 thirty to fifty years of age Twenty-five is the age at which Levites enter their service to Yahweh (8:24), and fifty is the age at which the Levites are required to retire (8:25). Each Levite presumably completed five years of supervised service between the ages of twenty-five and thirty (compare vv. 23,30).

4:5–15 This passage describes the procedures for dismantling and preparing the holy objects for transport.

4:5 Aaron and his sons While the Kohathites carried the objects on their shoulders (v. 15; 7:9), only Aaron and his sons—the priests—were allowed to dismantle and wrap the holy objects. **ark of the covenant law** This is one of the common labels for the ark of the covenant (e.g., Ex 40:3; Nu 7:89; Jos 4:16). See note on Ex 25:10. See the infographic "The Ark of the Covenant" on p. 412.

4:6 a cloth of solid blue The sanctity of the sacred objects may have been indicated by the color and fabric of their covers. All the sacred furnishings must be covered properly by the priests before the Kohathites can touch them (Nu 4:15)

4:10 durable leather The Hebrew term used here, *tachash*, refers to some sort of animal skins (see note on Ex 25:5). The term is almost always used for the protective material covering the tabernacle furnishings in transit.

4:15 they must not touch the holy things This explains why the objects were carried using poles and carrying frames, as well as why it was the duty of the priests to

wrap the items (Nu 4:5) before the Kohathites could carry them.

4:16 Eleazar This eldest living son of Aaron became high priest after his father died.

Numbers 4:16

ELEAZAR
Eleazar oversaw the Kohathites, who transported the sacred objects and ensured that procedures involving these objects were carried out correctly. Eleazar also served as chief of the Levitical guards (Nu 3:32).

4:18–20 God now instructs Moses and Aaron on how to ensure that the Kohathites properly handle the sacred objects, in order to avoid being destroyed by him.

4:20 This verse addresses the possibility that the Kohathites, forbidden from entering the tented structure of the Holy Place and Most Holy Place (Holy of Holies), might encounter that which is holy in an improper manner and, in doing so, bring calamity upon themselves and the people of Israel.

4:21–28 This passage repeats the duties of the Gershonites listed in 3:21–26 and adds the detail that they were responsible for carrying the curtains and coverings used for the walls of the tabernacle court and the tent shrine.

²⁴"This is the service of the Gershonite clans in their carrying and their other work: ²⁵They are to carry the curtains of the tabernacle, that is, the tent of meeting, its covering and its outer covering of durable leather, the curtains for the entrance to the tent of meeting, ²⁶the curtains of the courtyard surrounding the tabernacle and altar, the curtain for the entrance to the courtyard, the ropes and all the equipment used in the service of the tent. The Gershonites are to do all that needs to be done with these things. ²⁷All their service, whether carrying or doing other work, is to be done under the direction of Aaron and his sons. You shall assign to them as their responsibility all they are to carry. ²⁸This is the service of the Gershonite clans at the tent of meeting. Their duties are to be under the direction of Ithamar son of Aaron, the priest.

The Merarites

²⁹"Count the Merarites by their clans and families. ³⁰Count all the men from thirty to fifty years of age who come to serve in the work at the tent of meeting. ³¹As part of all their service at the tent, they are to carry the frames of the tabernacle, its crossbars, posts and bases, ³²as well as the posts of the surrounding courtyard with their bases, tent pegs, ropes, all their equipment and everything related to their use. Assign to each man the specific things he is to carry. ³³This is the service of the Merarite clans as they work at the tent of meeting under the direction of Ithamar son of Aaron, the priest."

The Numbering of the Levite Clans

³⁴Moses, Aaron and the leaders of the community counted the Kohathites by their clans and families. ³⁵All the men from thirty to fifty years of age who came to serve in the work at the tent of meeting, ³⁶counted by clans, were 2,750. ³⁷This was the total of all those in the Kohathite clans who served at the tent of meeting. Moses and Aaron counted them according to the LORD's command through Moses.

³⁸The Gershonites were counted by their clans and families. ³⁹All the men from thirty to fifty years of age who came to serve in the work at the tent of meeting, ⁴⁰counted by their clans and families, were 2,630. ⁴¹This was the total of those in the Gershonite clans who served at the tent of meeting. Moses and Aaron counted them according to the LORD's command.

⁴²The Merarites were counted by their clans and families. ⁴³All the men from thirty to fifty years of age who came to serve in the work at the tent of meeting, ⁴⁴counted by their clans, were 3,200. ⁴⁵This was the total of those in the Merarite clans. Moses and Aaron counted them according to the LORD's command through Moses.

⁴⁶So Moses, Aaron and the leaders of Israel counted all the Levites by their clans and families. ⁴⁷All the men from thirty to fifty years of age who came to do the work of serving and carrying the tent of meeting ⁴⁸numbered 8,580. ⁴⁹At the LORD's command through Moses, each was assigned his work and told what to carry.

Thus they were counted, as the LORD commanded Moses.

The Purity of the Camp

5 The LORD said to Moses, ²"Command the Israelites to send away from the camp anyone who has a defiling skin disease[a] or a discharge of any kind, or who is ceremonially unclean because of a dead body. ³Send away male and female alike;

[a] 2 The Hebrew word for *defiling skin disease*, traditionally translated "leprosy," was used for various diseases affecting the skin.

4:28 Ithamar The youngest of Aaron's four sons, Ithamar, led the Levites in carrying out the responsibilities of the tabernacle (Ex 38:21; Nu 4:33; 7:8). Like Eleazar, who was in charge of the Kohathites (v. 16), Ithamar was responsible for overseeing the Gershonites and the Merarites (see v. 33).

4:29–33 This passage repeats the duties of the Merarites (3:33–37). They were responsible for transporting the structural elements of the tabernacle. All the items listed here are described in the detailed instructions for the construction of the tabernacle (see Ex 26; 27:9–19).

4:31 As part of all their service at the tent, they are to carry The only new information provided about the Merarites' duties is that their responsibility to carry the items in their charge is made explicit.

4:34–49 The passages about the duties of the Levitical clans each started with the command to take a census of each clan (Nu 4:2,21,29). The census of the full clan of Levites was done in ch. 3 (which counted the males

from the age of one-month upward). The count here in ch. 4 was done to determine how many Levites were eligible for service, that is, between the ages of 30 and 50 (see note on v. 3). Of the 22,000 Levite males (3:39), 8,580 were available to bear the items of the tabernacle.

5:1–31 Chapter 5 opens with a concern for eliminating impurity from the Israelite camp before embarking on the journey to the promised land (vv. 1–4). This concern is introduced here as a bridge between the sacred duties of the Levites in protecting the tabernacle and its furnishings (chs. 3–4) and special circumstances among the general population (5:5–6:21).

5:2 a defiling skin disease The Hebrew term used here refers to being afflicted by any of a number of skin diseases (see note on Lev 13:1–59). **a discharge of any kind** Women who have just given birth (Lev 12) or who are menstruating (Lev 15:19–24) are not specifically listed here, indicating that the discharges in view are abnormal.

send them outside the camp so they will not defile their camp, where I dwell among them." ⁴The Israelites did so; they sent them outside the camp. They did just as the LORD had instructed Moses.

Restitution for Wrongs

⁵The LORD said to Moses, ⁶"Say to the Israelites: 'Any man or woman who wrongs another in any way[a] and so is unfaithful to the LORD is guilty ⁷and must confess the sin they have committed. They must make full restitution for the wrong they have done, add a fifth of the value to it and give it all to the person they have wronged. ⁸But if that person has no close relative to whom restitution can be made for the wrong, the restitution belongs to the LORD and must be given to the priest, along with the ram with which atonement is made for the wrongdoer. ⁹All the sacred contributions the Israelites bring to a priest will belong to him. ¹⁰Sacred things belong to their owners, but what they give to the priest will belong to the priest.'"

The Test for an Unfaithful Wife

¹¹Then the LORD said to Moses, ¹²"Speak to the Israelites and say to them: 'If a man's wife goes astray and is unfaithful to him ¹³so that another man has sexual relations with her, and this is hidden from her husband and her impurity is undetected (since there is no witness against her and she has not been caught in the act), ¹⁴and if feelings of jealousy come over her husband and

he suspects his wife and she is impure — or if he is jealous and suspects her even though she is not impure — ¹⁵then he is to take his wife to the priest. He must also take an offering of a tenth of an ephah[b] of barley flour on her behalf. He must not pour olive oil on it or put incense on it, because it is a grain offering for jealousy, a reminder-offering to draw attention to wrongdoing.

¹⁶"The priest shall bring her and have her stand before the LORD. ¹⁷Then he shall take some holy water in a clay jar and put some dust from the tabernacle floor into the water. ¹⁸After the priest has had the woman stand before the LORD, he shall loosen her hair and place in her hands the reminder-offering, the grain offering for jealousy, while he himself holds the bitter water that brings a curse. ¹⁹Then the priest shall put the woman under oath and say to her, "If no other man has had sexual relations with you and you have not gone astray and become impure while married to your husband, may this bitter water that brings a curse not harm you. ²⁰But if you have gone astray while married to your husband and you have made yourself impure by having sexual relations with a man other than your husband" — ²¹here the priest is to put the woman under this curse — "may the LORD cause you to become a curse[c] among your people when he makes your womb miscarry and your abdomen swell. ²²May this water that brings

---

[a] 6 Or *woman who commits any wrong common to mankind*
[b] 15 That is, probably about 3 1/2 pounds or about 1.6 kilograms
[c] 21 That is, may he cause your name to be used in cursing (see Jer. 29:22); or, may others see that you are cursed; similarly in verse 27.

5:5–10 The following section deals with restitution for fraudulent crimes that demonstrate disloyalty to Yahweh and his ideals for Israel's society. The required offerings related to restitution are enumerated in Lev 5 (see note on Lev 5:14—6:7). The legal scenario detailed here involves someone who cheats a fellow Israelite. This chapter provides instructions on what to do if the defrauded person dies before the case is settled, but has no relatives who can accept the restitution on their behalf.

5:7 restitution The Hebrew word used here, *asham*, is also used with respect to guilt offerings (see note on Lev 5:6). To make restitution, the guilty had to make a payment equal to the value of what was stolen plus 20 percent.

5:11–31 This passage describes a trial by ordeal. The ordeal is designed to reveal whether a woman had committed adultery in a case where there was no evidence other than the husband's suspicion (Nu 5:14,29). While OT law forbids adultery (Ex 20:14), the definition of adultery centers around the status of the woman (Lev 20:10). A man was only guilty of adultery for having sex with a woman who was married or engaged (Dt 22:22–27). If a man had sex with an unmarried woman who was still part of her father's household, he was required to marry her if they were discovered (Dt 22:28–29). There is no equivalent test for a woman who suspects her husband of committing adultery.

5:13 her impurity This defilement refers to the status of her womb. Since an adulterous woman's womb is viewed as tainted by the genetic material of a man who is not her husband, the husband's line is in danger; the paternity of future children is now suspect. **no witness against her** The trial by ordeal described here assumes that God serves as a witness.

5:17 tabernacle floor Probably from the floor inside the tent structure (the Holy Place), an area officially consecrated by ritual. See the infographic "The Tabernacle" on p. 138.

5:18 reminder-offering While grain offerings are spoken of elsewhere (see note on Lev 2:1–16), this specific kind of grain offering is mentioned only here.

5:21 a curse The Hebrew phrase here uses two nouns— *alah* (which may be rendered "curse") and *shevu'ah* (which may be rendered "oath")—probably emphasizing the severity of the punishment. The following verses only use *alah* to emphasize the negative aspect since *shevu'ah* does not have negative connotations. The trial by ordeal was a means of divination (such as the Urim and Thummim; see Ex 28:30 and note; Lev 8:8); the Israelites assumed that Yahweh would reveal guilt or innocence through the trial.

5:22 enter your body so that your abdomen swells The curse affects the woman's reproductive system; if she is guilty, she will be unable to bear children.

a curse enter your body so that your abdomen swells or your womb miscarries."

"'Then the woman is to say, "Amen. So be it."

23 "'The priest is to write these curses on a scroll and then wash them off into the bitter water. 24 He shall make the woman drink the bitter water that brings a curse, and this water that brings a curse and causes bitter suffering will enter her. 25 The priest is to take from her hands the grain offering for jealousy, wave it before the Lord and bring it to the altar. 26 The priest is then to take a handful of the grain offering as a memorial[a] offering and burn it on the altar; after that, he is to have the woman drink the water. 27 If she has made herself impure and been unfaithful to her husband, this will be the result: When she is made to drink the water that brings a curse and causes bitter suffering, it will enter her, her abdomen will swell and her womb will miscarry, and she will become a curse. 28 If, however, the woman has not made herself impure, but is clean, she will be cleared of guilt and will be able to have children.

29 "'This, then, is the law of jealousy when a woman goes astray and makes herself impure while married to her husband, 30 or when feelings of jealousy come over a man because he suspects his wife. The priest is to have her stand before the Lord and is to apply this entire law to her. 31 The husband will be innocent of any wrongdoing, but the woman will bear the consequences of her sin.'"

The Nazirite

6 The Lord said to Moses, 2 "Speak to the Israelites and say to them: 'If a man or woman wants to make a special vow, a vow of dedication to the Lord as a Nazirite, 3 they must abstain from wine and other fermented drink and must not drink vinegar made from wine or other fermented drink. They must not drink grape juice or eat grapes or raisins. 4 As long as they remain under their Nazirite vow, they must not eat anything that comes from the grapevine, not even the seeds or skins.

5 "'During the entire period of their Nazirite vow, no razor may be used on their head. They must be holy until the period of their dedication to the Lord is over; they must let their hair grow long.

6 "'Throughout the period of their dedication to the Lord, the Nazirite must not go near a dead body. 7 Even if their own father or mother or brother or sister dies, they must not make themselves ceremonially unclean on account of them, because the symbol of their dedication to God is on their head. 8 Throughout the period of their dedication, they are consecrated to the Lord.

9 "'If someone dies suddenly in the Nazirite's presence, thus defiling the hair that symbolizes their dedication, they must shave their head on the seventh day — the day of their cleansing. 10 Then on the eighth day they must bring two doves or two young pigeons to the priest at the entrance to the tent of meeting. 11 The priest is to offer one as a sin offering[b] and the other as a burnt offering to make atonement for the Nazirite because they sinned by being in the presence of the dead body. That same day they are to consecrate their head again. 12 They must rededicate themselves to the Lord for the same period of dedication and must bring a year-old male lamb as a guilt offering. The previous days do not count, because they became defiled during their period of dedication.

13 "'Now this is the law of the Nazirite when the period of their dedication is over. They are to be brought to the entrance to the tent of meeting. 14 There they are to present their offerings to the Lord: a year-old male lamb without defect for a burnt offering, a year-old ewe lamb without defect for a sin offering, a ram without defect

---

[a] 26 Or representative   [b] 11 Or purification offering; also in verses 14 and 16

5:27 she will become a curse The woman has been rendered barren by God. People in the ancient Near East considered childlessness to be related to divine disfavor (see Ge 20:18; 30:1–3; 1Sa 1:6,11). While severe, the penalty for guilt in this case was not death (Nu 5:22), unlike when a couple was caught in the act of adultery (Lev 20:10; Dt 22:22).

5:31 The husband The Hebrew word used here, *ha'ish*, is a generic word for "man" — so which man is in view is ambiguous. It could possibly refer to the man with whom the woman had relations, although a husband who wrongfully accused his wife is also not held to account.

6:1–21 This passage describes the obligations associated with a Nazirite vow: abstaining from strong drink or any product of the grapevine (Nu 6:3–4), letting the hair grow long (v. 5) and avoiding the ritual impurity caused by contact with a dead body (vv. 6–8). The passage also provides procedures for rectifying defilement caused by

contact with a corpse (vv. 9–12) and gives instructions about how to properly terminate the vow (vv. 13–21).

6:2 Nazirite The Hebrew term used here, *nazir*, means "devoted one." The nature of the vow is described by the related Hebrew verb *nazar* which denotes abstaining. It designates someone who took a vow to live distinctly from the rest of the community. The Nazirite did this by following certain distinctive customs (compare note on 6:1–21).

6:5 no razor may be used on their head The treatment of the hair after the period of the vow ended (vv. 13–21) suggests that uncut hair was central to the Nazirite vow.

6:9 they must shave their head on the seventh day When Nazirites broke their vow through unintentional contact with a corpse, the vow would start again following procedures for purification.

6:10 two doves or two young pigeons These are the least costly animal sacrifices of the sacrificial system.

for a fellowship offering, [15]together with their grain offerings and drink offerings, and a basket of bread made with the finest flour and without yeast — thick loaves with olive oil mixed in, and thin loaves brushed with olive oil.

[16]"The priest is to present all these before the LORD and make the sin offering and the burnt offering. [17]He is to present the basket of unleavened bread and is to sacrifice the ram as a fellowship offering to the LORD, together with its grain offering and drink offering.

[18]"Then at the entrance to the tent of meeting, the Nazirite must shave off the hair that symbolizes their dedication. They are to take the hair and put it in the fire that is under the sacrifice of the fellowship offering.

[19]"After the Nazirite has shaved off the hair that symbolizes their dedication, the priest is to place in their hands a boiled shoulder of the ram, and one thick loaf and one thin loaf from the basket, both made without yeast. [20]The priest shall then wave these before the LORD as a wave offering; they are holy and belong to the priest, together with the breast that was waved and the thigh that was presented. After that, the Nazirite may drink wine.

[21]"This is the law of the Nazirite who vows offerings to the LORD in accordance with their dedication, in addition to whatever else they can afford. They must fulfill the vows they have made, according to the law of the Nazirite.'"

The Priestly Blessing

[22]The LORD said to Moses, [23]"Tell Aaron and his sons, 'This is how you are to bless the Israelites. Say to them:

[24]" '"The LORD bless you
    and keep you;

[25]the LORD make his face shine on you
    and be gracious to you;
[26]the LORD turn his face toward you
    and give you peace.' "

[27]"So they will put my name on the Israelites, and I will bless them."

Offerings at the Dedication of the Tabernacle

7 When Moses finished setting up the tabernacle, he anointed and consecrated it and all its furnishings. He also anointed and consecrated the altar and all its utensils. [2]Then the leaders of Israel, the heads of families who were the tribal leaders in charge of those who were counted, made offerings. [3]They brought as their gifts before the LORD six covered carts and twelve oxen — an ox from each leader and a cart from every two. These they presented before the tabernacle.

[4]The LORD said to Moses, [5]"Accept these from them, that they may be used in the work at the tent of meeting. Give them to the Levites as each man's work requires."

[6]So Moses took the carts and oxen and gave them to the Levites. [7]He gave two carts and four oxen to the Gershonites, as their work required, [8]and he gave four carts and eight oxen to the Merarites, as their work required. They were all under the direction of Ithamar son of Aaron, the priest. [9]But Moses did not give any to the Kohathites, because they were to carry on their shoulders the holy things, for which they were responsible.

[10]When the altar was anointed, the leaders brought their offerings for its dedication and presented them before the altar. [11]For the LORD had said to Moses, "Each day one leader is to bring his offering for the dedication of the altar."

6:20 breast that was waved and the thigh Here, the wave offering (tenuphah in Hebrew) is elevated and offered to God for his special attention and ownership. See note on Lev 7:30.

6:22–27 Yahweh presents Moses with a priestly benediction to pass on to Aaron and his sons, the priests.

6:23 you are to bless the Israelites A priest was responsible for blessing the people in God's name (Dt 10:8; 21:5). See the table "Functions of Priests" on p. 171.

6:25 his face The Hebrew word panim (used here and in Nu 6:26) refers to the physical face. It also may idiomatically refer to someone's presence because seeing a face required being in the person's physical presence (compare Ex 33:20).

6:26 turn his face The Hebrew idiom nasa' panim used here describes looking favorably upon someone (e.g., Ge 19:21; Job 42:8–9). This expression describes how people of superior status implied their acceptance of an inferior when they looked up at them.

7:1–89 Numbers 7 describes the contributions that the 12 tribal chieftains bring to the tabernacle in honor of its consecration: 6 carts and 12 oxen for transporting its structural components (vv. 1–9); silver and gold vessels; and implements filled with flour, oil or incense. Numbers 7–9 describe the final preparations before leaving Sinai for the first time (ch. 10). This includes taking inventory of all items related to the tabernacle as detailed in this chapter.

7:1 the tabernacle The Hebrew term used here, mishkan, is a general word for a tent or dwelling (e.g., 16:24; Isa 32:18). However, the term often refers specifically to Yahweh's dwelling, the tabernacle, which was Israel's portable tent sanctuary used during the journey to the promised land (Nu 16:9; Lev 15:31). The tabernacle was also called in Hebrew the ohel mo'ed (which may be rendered "tent of meeting"; Ex 28:43). See the infographic "The Tabernacle" on p. 138.

7:5 as each man's work requires Refers to the duty of the Levites to dismantle, transport and reassemble the tabernacle and its furnishings.

7:11 Each day one leader Rather than the chiefs bringing everything at once, each brought his tribe's contribution on his own day, meaning the offerings were brought over a 12-day period.

[12]The one who brought his offering on the first day was Nahshon son of Amminadab of the tribe of Judah.

[13]His offering was one silver plate weighing a hundred and thirty shekels[a] and one silver sprinkling bowl weighing seventy shekels,[b] both according to the sanctuary shekel, each filled with the finest flour mixed with olive oil as a grain offering; [14]one gold dish weighing ten shekels,[c] filled with incense; [15]one young bull, one ram and one male lamb a year old for a burnt offering; [16]one male goat for a sin offering[d]; [17]and two oxen, five rams, five male goats and five male lambs a year old to be sacrificed as a fellowship offering. This was the offering of Nahshon son of Amminadab.

[18]On the second day Nethanel son of Zuar, the leader of Issachar, brought his offering.

[19]The offering he brought was one silver plate weighing a hundred and thirty shekels and one silver sprinkling bowl weighing seventy shekels, both according to the sanctuary shekel, each filled with the finest flour mixed with olive oil as a grain offering; [20]one gold dish weighing ten shekels, filled with incense; [21]one young bull, one ram and one male lamb a year old for a burnt offering; [22]one male goat for a sin offering; [23]and two oxen, five rams, five male goats and five male lambs a year old to be sacrificed as a fellowship offering. This was the offering of Nethanel son of Zuar.

[24]On the third day, Eliab son of Helon, the leader of the people of Zebulun, brought his offering.

[25]His offering was one silver plate weighing a hundred and thirty shekels and one silver sprinkling bowl weighing seventy shekels, both according to the sanctuary shekel, each filled with the finest flour mixed with olive oil as a grain offering; [26]one gold dish weighing ten shekels, filled with incense; [27]one young bull, one ram and one male lamb a year old for a burnt offering; [28]one male goat for a sin offering; [29]and two oxen, five rams, five male goats and five male lambs a year old to be sacrificed as a fellowship offering. This was the offering of Eliab son of Helon.

[30]On the fourth day Elizur son of Shedeur, the leader of the people of Reuben, brought his offering.

[31]His offering was one silver plate weighing a hundred and thirty shekels and one silver sprinkling bowl weighing seventy shekels, both according to the sanctuary shekel, each filled with the finest flour mixed with olive oil as a grain offering; [32]one gold dish weighing ten shekels, filled with incense; [33]one

young bull, one ram and one male lamb a year old for a burnt offering; [34]one male goat for a sin offering; [35]and two oxen, five rams, five male goats and five male lambs a year old to be sacrificed as a fellowship offering. This was the offering of Elizur son of Shedeur.

[36]On the fifth day Shelumiel son of Zurishaddai, the leader of the people of Simeon, brought his offering.

[37]His offering was one silver plate weighing a hundred and thirty shekels and one silver sprinkling bowl weighing seventy shekels, both according to the sanctuary shekel, each filled with the finest flour mixed with olive oil as a grain offering; [38]one gold dish weighing ten shekels, filled with incense; [39]one young bull, one ram and one male lamb a year old for a burnt offering; [40]one male goat for a sin offering; [41]and two oxen, five rams, five male goats and five male lambs a year old to be sacrificed as a fellowship offering. This was the offering of Shelumiel son of Zurishaddai.

[42]On the sixth day Eliasaph son of Deuel, the leader of the people of Gad, brought his offering.

[43]His offering was one silver plate weighing a hundred and thirty shekels and one silver sprinkling bowl weighing seventy shekels, both according to the sanctuary shekel, each filled with the finest flour mixed with olive oil as a grain offering; [44]one gold dish weighing ten shekels, filled with incense; [45]one young bull, one ram and one male lamb a year old for a burnt offering; [46]one male goat for a sin offering; [47]and two oxen, five rams, five male goats and five male lambs a year old to be sacrificed as a fellowship offering. This was the offering of Eliasaph son of Deuel.

[48]On the seventh day Elishama son of Ammihud, the leader of the people of Ephraim, brought his offering.

[49]His offering was one silver plate weighing a hundred and thirty shekels and one silver sprinkling bowl weighing seventy shekels, both according to the sanctuary shekel, each filled with the finest flour mixed with olive oil as a grain offering; [50]one gold dish weighing ten shekels, filled with incense; [51]one young bull, one ram and one male lamb a year old for a burnt offering; [52]one male goat for a sin offering; [53]and two oxen, five rams, five male goats and five male lambs a year old to be sacrificed as a fellowship

---

[a] 13 That is, about 3 1/4 pounds or about 1.5 kilograms; also elsewhere in this chapter   [b] 13 That is, about 1 3/4 pounds or about 800 grams; also elsewhere in this chapter   [c] 14 That is, about 4 ounces or about 115 grams; also elsewhere in this chapter   [d] 16 Or purification offering; also elsewhere in this chapter

offering. This was the offering of Elishama son of Ammihud.

⁵⁴On the eighth day Gamaliel son of Pedahzur, the leader of the people of Manasseh, brought his offering.

⁵⁵His offering was one silver plate weighing a hundred and thirty shekels and one silver sprinkling bowl weighing seventy shekels, both according to the sanctuary shekel, each filled with the finest flour mixed with olive oil as a grain offering; ⁵⁶one gold dish weighing ten shekels, filled with incense; ⁵⁷one young bull, one ram and one male lamb a year old for a burnt offering; ⁵⁸one male goat for a sin offering; ⁵⁹and two oxen, five rams, five male goats and five male lambs a year old to be sacrificed as a fellowship offering. This was the offering of Gamaliel son of Pedahzur.

⁶⁰On the ninth day Abidan son of Gideoni, the leader of the people of Benjamin, brought his offering.

⁶¹His offering was one silver plate weighing a hundred and thirty shekels and one silver sprinkling bowl weighing seventy shekels, both according to the sanctuary shekel, each filled with the finest flour mixed with olive oil as a grain offering; ⁶²one gold dish weighing ten shekels, filled with incense; ⁶³one young bull, one ram and one male lamb a year old for a burnt offering; ⁶⁴one male goat for a sin offering; ⁶⁵and two oxen, five rams, five male goats and five male lambs a year old to be sacrificed as a fellowship offering. This was the offering of Abidan son of Gideoni.

⁶⁶On the tenth day Ahiezer son of Ammishaddai, the leader of the people of Dan, brought his offering.

⁶⁷His offering was one silver plate weighing a hundred and thirty shekels and one silver sprinkling bowl weighing seventy shekels, both according to the sanctuary shekel, each filled with the finest flour mixed with olive oil as a grain offering; ⁶⁸one gold dish weighing ten shekels, filled with incense; ⁶⁹one young bull, one ram and one male lamb a year old for a burnt offering; ⁷⁰one male goat for a sin offering; ⁷¹and two oxen, five rams, five male goats and five male lambs a year old to be sacrificed as a fellowship offering. This was the offering of Ahiezer son of Ammishaddai.

⁷²On the eleventh day Pagiel son of Okran, the leader of the people of Asher, brought his offering.

⁷³His offering was one silver plate weighing a hundred and thirty shekels and one silver sprinkling bowl weighing seventy shekels, both according to the sanctuary shekel, each filled with the finest flour mixed with olive oil as a grain offering; ⁷⁴one gold dish weighing ten shekels, filled with incense; ⁷⁵one young bull, one ram and one male lamb a year old for a burnt offering; ⁷⁶one male goat for a sin offering; ⁷⁷and two oxen, five rams, five male goats and five male lambs a year old to be sacrificed as a fellowship offering. This was the offering of Pagiel son of Okran.

⁷⁸On the twelfth day Ahira son of Enan, the leader of the people of Naphtali, brought his offering.

⁷⁹His offering was one silver plate weighing a hundred and thirty shekels and one silver sprinkling bowl weighing seventy shekels, both according to the sanctuary shekel, each filled with the finest flour mixed with olive oil as a grain offering; ⁸⁰one gold dish weighing ten shekels, filled with incense; ⁸¹one young bull, one ram and one male lamb a year old for a burnt offering; ⁸²one male goat for a sin offering; ⁸³and two oxen, five rams, five male goats and five male lambs a year old to be sacrificed as a fellowship offering. This was the offering of Ahira son of Enan.

⁸⁴These were the offerings of the Israelite leaders for the dedication of the altar when it was anointed: twelve silver plates, twelve silver sprinkling bowls and twelve gold dishes. ⁸⁵Each silver plate weighed a hundred and thirty shekels, and each sprinkling bowl seventy shekels. Altogether, the silver dishes weighed two thousand four hundred shekels,ᵃ according to the sanctuary shekel. ⁸⁶The twelve gold dishes filled with incense weighed ten shekels each, according to the sanctuary shekel. Altogether, the gold dishes weighed a hundred and twenty shekels.ᵇ ⁸⁷The total number of animals for the burnt offering came to twelve young bulls, twelve rams and twelve male lambs a year old, together with their grain offering. Twelve male goats were used for the sin offering. ⁸⁸The total number of animals for the sacrifice of the fellowship offering came to twenty-four oxen, sixty rams, sixty male goats and sixty male lambs a year old. These were the offerings for the dedication of the altar after it was anointed.

⁸⁹When Moses entered the tent of meeting to

ᵃ 85 That is, about 60 pounds or about 28 kilograms
ᵇ 86 That is, about 3 pounds or about 1.4 kilograms

7:84–88 What follows is a grand total of all offerings given by the 12 tribes according to Nu 7:12–83.

7:89 the voice speaking to him Refers to the voice of Yahweh, who was seated above the ark. This is one of five verses in the Pentateuch that describe this location as the meeting place of Yahweh and Moses (Ex 25:22; 30:6,36; Nu 17:4). **atonement cover** The lid of the ark of the covenant (see note on Ex 25:17). See the infographic "The Ark of the Covenant" on p. 412.

speak with the LORD, he heard the voice speaking to him from between the two cherubim above the atonement cover on the ark of the covenant law. In this way the LORD spoke to him.

Setting Up the Lamps

8 The LORD said to Moses, 2"Speak to Aaron and say to him, 'When you set up the lamps, see that all seven light up the area in front of the lampstand.'"

3Aaron did so; he set up the lamps so that they faced forward on the lampstand, just as the LORD commanded Moses. 4This is how the lampstand was made: It was made of hammered gold—from its base to its blossoms. The lampstand was made exactly like the pattern the LORD had shown Moses.

The Setting Apart of the Levites

5The LORD said to Moses: 6"Take the Levites from among all the Israelites and make them ceremonially clean. 7To purify them, do this: Sprinkle the water of cleansing on them; then have them shave their whole bodies and wash their clothes. And so they will purify themselves. 8Have them take a young bull with its grain offering of the finest flour mixed with olive oil; then you are to take a second young bull for a sin offering.ᵃ 9Bring the Levites to the front of the tent of meeting and assemble the whole Israelite community. 10You are to bring the Levites before the LORD, and the Israelites are to lay their hands on them. 11Aaron is to present the Levites before the LORD as a wave offering from the Israelites, so that they may be ready to do the work of the LORD.

12"Then the Levites are to lay their hands on the heads of the bulls, using one for a sin offering to the LORD and the other for a burnt offering, to make atonement for the Levites. 13Have the Levites stand in front of Aaron and his sons and then present them as a wave offering to the LORD. 14In this way you are to set the Levites apart from the other Israelites, and the Levites will be mine.

15"After you have purified the Levites and presented them as a wave offering, they are to come to do their work at the tent of meeting. 16They are the Israelites who are to be given wholly to me. I have taken them as my own in place of the firstborn, the first male offspring from every Israelite woman. 17Every firstborn male in Israel, whether human or animal, is mine. When I struck down all the firstborn in Egypt, I set them apart for myself. 18And I have taken the Levites in place of all the firstborn sons in Israel. 19From among all the Israelites, I have given the Levites as gifts to Aaron and his sons to do the work at the tent of meeting on behalf of the Israelites and to make atonement for them so that no plague will strike the Israelites when they go near the sanctuary."

20Moses, Aaron and the whole Israelite community did with the Levites just as the LORD commanded Moses. 21The Levites purified themselves and washed their clothes. Then Aaron presented them as a wave offering before the LORD and made atonement for them to purify them. 22After that, the Levites came to do their work at the tent of meeting under the supervision of Aaron and his sons. They did with the Levites just as the LORD commanded Moses.

23The LORD said to Moses, 24"This applies to the Levites: Men twenty-five years old or more

---

ᵃ 8 Or purification offering; also in verse 12

8:1–4 Numbers 8:1–4 contain instructions for mounting the lamps of the great golden lampstand (the menorah) stationed inside the Holy Place. This passage demonstrates that the Israelites carried out the instructions found in Ex 25:31–40. See the infographic "Furnishings of the Tabernacle" on p. 136.

8:2 Aaron Only the priests conducted activity inside the Holy Place of the tent of meeting once the tabernacle had been constructed (see Nu 3:5–10).

8:4 the pattern the LORD had shown Moses When Yahweh communicated the instructions for the tabernacle and its furnishings to Moses, he showed Moses a pattern or blueprint. See Ex 25:9 and note.

8:5–22 Like the priests (Ex 29; Lev 8), the Levites had to be ritually purified before beginning service. Levites between the ages of 25 and 50 were eligible for service and had to be purified (Nu 8:24–25).

8:6 make them ceremonially clean Although cleansing or purification often involved washing or water, the underlying rationale had little to do with hygiene; rather, washing was an outward gesture that symbolized the purification of the person's being.

8:11 wave offering A wave offering (tenuphah in Hebrew; see note on Lev 7:30) involved elevating the thing offered to God. The use of tenuphah is peculiar in this passage because a group of people are being offered in this way. Normally a wave offering consists of meat (e.g., Ex 29:24–27; Lev 7:30) or grain (e.g., Lev 23:15; Nu 5:25) that is literally lifted up by the priest. This signals that the Levites are consecrated before Yahweh—their lives are devoted to his service. Compare note on 8:14.

8:14 the Levites will be mine The Levites are set apart for the service of Yahweh in place of the firstborn of all Israel (Nu 3:11–13; see note on Nu 3:1–51).

8:17 I set them apart The concept of holiness fundamentally indicates separation: A person or item is set apart for sacred use or duty, as opposed to common, ordinary tasks or purposes.

8:19 no plague When the Israelites did not follow Yahweh's instruction, they risked an outbreak of plague or divine wrath.

8:23–26 This brief section contains instructions about what to do when a Levite reaches 50 years old, the age of retirement.

8:24 twenty-five years old or more See note on 4:3.

shall come to take part in the work at the tent of meeting, ²⁵but at the age of fifty, they must retire from their regular service and work no longer. ²⁶They may assist their brothers in performing their duties at the tent of meeting, but they themselves must not do the work. This, then, is how you are to assign the responsibilities of the Levites."

The Passover

9 The LORD spoke to Moses in the Desert of Sinai in the first month of the second year after they came out of Egypt. He said, ²"Have the Israelites celebrate the Passover at the appointed time. ³Celebrate it at the appointed time, at twilight on the fourteenth day of this month, in accordance with all its rules and regulations."

⁴So Moses told the Israelites to celebrate the Passover, ⁵and they did so in the Desert of Sinai at twilight on the fourteenth day of the first month. The Israelites did everything just as the LORD commanded Moses.

⁶But some of them could not celebrate the Passover on that day because they were ceremonially unclean on account of a dead body. So they came to Moses and Aaron that same day ⁷and said to Moses, "We have become unclean because of a dead body, but why should we be kept from presenting the LORD's offering with the other Israelites at the appointed time?"

⁸Moses answered them, "Wait until I find out what the LORD commands concerning you."

⁹Then the LORD said to Moses, ¹⁰"Tell the Israelites: 'When any of you or your descendants are unclean because of a dead body or are away on a journey, they are still to celebrate the LORD's Passover, ¹¹but they are to do it on the fourteenth day of the second month at twilight. They are to eat the lamb, together with unleavened bread and bitter herbs. ¹²They must not leave any of it till morning or break any of its bones. When they celebrate the Passover, they must follow all the regulations. ¹³But if anyone who is ceremonially clean and not on a journey fails to celebrate the Passover, they must be cut off from their people for not presenting the LORD's offering at the appointed time. They will bear the consequences of their sin.

¹⁴"'A foreigner residing among you is also to celebrate the LORD's Passover in accordance with its rules and regulations. You must have the same regulations for both the foreigner and the native-born.'"

The Cloud Above the Tabernacle

¹⁵On the day the tabernacle, the tent of the covenant law, was set up, the cloud covered it. From evening till morning the cloud above the tabernacle looked like fire. ¹⁶That is how it continued to be; the cloud covered it, and at night it looked like fire. ¹⁷Whenever the cloud lifted from above the tent, the Israelites set out; wherever the cloud settled, the Israelites encamped. ¹⁸At the LORD's command the Israelites set out, and at his command they encamped. As long as the cloud stayed over the tabernacle, they remained in camp. ¹⁹When the cloud remained over the tabernacle a long time, the Israelites obeyed the LORD's order and did not set out. ²⁰Sometimes the cloud was over the tabernacle only a few days; at the LORD's command they would encamp, and then at his command

---

9:1–14 Verses 1–14 concern the observance of the first Passover in the wilderness. It also describes a complaint against Moses by those barred from the Passover because they came into contact with a corpse. Verse 3 indicates that the Passover was to be observed in accordance with Yahweh's instructions. However, while the original rules called for the Israelites to smear blood on their doors and doorposts (Ex 12:7), the Israelites had no such housing while camped at Sinai. Also, since Passover was held annually (not monthly), the extra Passover allowed by Yahweh (Nu 9:1–11) reflects his amending of the Passover due to unique circumstances. See the table "Israelite Festivals" on p. 200.

9:1 the first month of the second year This Passover celebration marks the second year anniversary of the original event (Ex 12–15) and the first time Israel celebrates this holiday in the wilderness.

9:3 rules Regulations for the Passover are found in Ex 12:1–49.

9:6 ceremonially unclean on account of a dead body This was not part of the original stipulations (Ex 12:1–49) because at that point the regulations regarding corpse impurity had not yet been instituted.

9:11 on the fourteenth day of the second month One month after the first celebration (Nu 9:5). **unleavened bread and bitter herbs** The roasted Passover lamb (Ex 12:8) is not mentioned explicitly here, but the prohibition against breaking bones in Nu 9:12 indicates the presence of the lamb along with the unleavened bread and herbs was assumed.

9:13 must be cut off from their people This likely means shunning or exclusion from the covenant community and its blessings. Passover is the only ceremonial observance where those who willfully neglect it are punished in this way (compare Ex 12:19; Lev 7:20 and note).

9:15–23 Numbers 9:15–23 is the first detailed description of how the appearance of Yahweh as a pillar of fire by night and a pillar of cloud by day actually worked to lead the people through the wilderness.

The priestly rules and regulations that began in Lev 1 conclude here. This passage harks back to the end of Exodus and its reference to the pillar of cloud or fire. In doing so, this reference bookends the priestly rules of Exodus and the present section (Lev 1:1–Nu 9:14).

9:15 cloud The cloud that became familiar to the people throughout Exodus as a symbol of Yahweh's presence (e.g., Ex 13:21–22; 19:9; 33:9–10; compare Lev 16:2,13) is now spoken of again, for the first time since Ex 40:34.

they would set out. ²¹Sometimes the cloud stayed only from evening till morning, and when it lifted in the morning, they set out. Whether by day or by night, whenever the cloud lifted, they set out. ²²Whether the cloud stayed over the tabernacle for two days or a month or a year, the Israelites would remain in camp and not set out; but when it lifted, they would set out. ²³At the LORD's command they encamped, and at the LORD's command they set out. They obeyed the LORD's order, in accordance with his command through Moses.

The Silver Trumpets

10 The LORD said to Moses: ²"Make two trumpets of hammered silver, and use them for calling the community together and for having the camps set out. ³When both are sounded, the whole community is to assemble before you at the entrance to the tent of meeting. ⁴If only one is sounded, the leaders—the heads of the clans of Israel—are to assemble before you. ⁵When a trumpet blast is sounded, the tribes camping on the east are to set out. ⁶At the sounding of a second blast, the camps on the south are to set out. The blast will be the signal for setting out. ⁷To gather the assembly, blow the trumpets, but not with the signal for setting out.

⁸"The sons of Aaron, the priests, are to blow the trumpets. This is to be a lasting ordinance for you and the generations to come. ⁹When you go into battle in your own land against an enemy who is oppressing you, sound a blast on the trumpets. Then you will be remembered by the LORD your God and rescued from your enemies. ¹⁰Also at your times of rejoicing—your appointed festivals and New Moon feasts—you are to sound the trumpets over your burnt offerings and fellowship offerings, and they will be a memorial for you before your God. I am the LORD your God."

The Israelites Leave Sinai

¹¹On the twentieth day of the second month of the second year, the cloud lifted from above the tabernacle of the covenant law. ¹²Then the Israelites set out from the Desert of Sinai and traveled from place to place until the cloud came to rest in the Desert of Paran. ¹³They set out, this first time, at the LORD's command through Moses.

¹⁴The divisions of the camp of Judah went first, under their standard. Nahshon son of Amminadab was in command. ¹⁵Nethanel son of Zuar was over the division of the tribe of Issachar, ¹⁶and Eliab son of Helon was over the division of the tribe of Zebulun. ¹⁷Then the tabernacle was taken down, and the Gershonites and Merarites, who carried it, set out.

¹⁸The divisions of the camp of Reuben went next, under their standard. Elizur son of Shedeur was in command. ¹⁹Shelumiel son of Zurishaddai was over the division of the tribe of Simeon, ²⁰and Eliasaph son of Deuel was over the division of the tribe of Gad. ²¹Then the Kohathites set out, carrying the holy things. The tabernacle was to be set up before they arrived.

²²The divisions of the camp of Ephraim went next, under their standard. Elishama son of Ammihud was in command. ²³Gamaliel son of Pedahzur was over the division of the tribe of Manasseh, ²⁴and Abidan son of Gideoni was over the division of the tribe of Benjamin.

²⁵Finally, as the rear guard for all the units, the divisions of the camp of Dan set out under their standard. Ahiezer son of Ammishaddai was in command. ²⁶Pagiel son of Okran was over the division of the tribe of Asher, ²⁷and Ahira son of Enan was over the division of the tribe of Naphtali. ²⁸This was the order of march for the Israelite divisions as they set out.

²⁹Now Moses said to Hobab son of Reuel the Mid-

10:1–10 Numbers 10 is the final chapter before Israel resumes its march to the promised land, after about a year at Mount Sinai. This passage details the creation of the silver trumpets that Moses will sound to signal Israel's departure (compare 9:15–23 and note).

10:3 entrance to the tent of meeting The Hebrew phrase used here, *pethach ohel mo'ed*, refers to the open area in front of the tent shrine in the tabernacle. See the infographic "The Tabernacle" on p. 138.

10:8 sons of Aaron Typically this phrase refers to the priests in general, but since there are only two trumpets, the reference must be to Aaron's two surviving sons—Eleazar and Ithamar (3:2).

10:11–36 The Israelites finally break camp and leave Mount Sinai after camping there for about a year. This passage records their departure. Following Yahweh's leading, the camp moves to the wilderness (or desert) of Paran on the eastern side of the Sinai Peninsula (v. 12). The journey to the wilderness of Paran is the setting for the events in ch. 11 and ch. 12.

10:11 cloud See note on 9:15.

10:12 the cloud came to rest The Israelites set up camp wherever the cloud settled and stayed until it lifted again (9:15–23). **Paran** Paran probably refers to an area of the northeastern Sinai Peninsula, west of Midian, but it may also have been used as a name for the entire northern half of the Sinai Peninsula.

10:17 tabernacle was taken down The Levite clans of the Gershonites and Merarites carried the tabernacle (3:21–26,33–37) ahead of the Kohathites, who transported its furnishings (3:27–32). The order was set so that, by the time the Kohathites arrived at the camp, the other Levites would have the tabernacle set up and ready for the furnishings (10:21).

10:29 Moses' father-in-law There is ambiguity in the Hebrew text here regarding whether Hobab is being identified as Moses' father-in-law (compare Jdg 4:11). However, Ex 2:18 explicitly identifies Moses' father-in-law as Reuel, and Ex 3:1 and Nu 4:18 refer to him as Jethro.

ianite, Moses' father-in-law, "We are setting out for the place about which the LORD said, 'I will give it to you.' Come with us and we will treat you well, for the LORD has promised good things to Israel."

³⁰He answered, "No, I will not go; I am going back to my own land and my own people."

³¹But Moses said, "Please do not leave us. You know where we should camp in the wilderness, and you can be our eyes. ³²If you come with us, we will share with you whatever good things the LORD gives us."

³³So they set out from the mountain of the LORD and traveled for three days. The ark of the covenant of the LORD went before them during those three days to find them a place to rest. ³⁴The cloud of the LORD was over them by day when they set out from the camp.

³⁵Whenever the ark set out, Moses said,

"Rise up, LORD!
  May your enemies be scattered;
  may your foes flee before you."

³⁶Whenever it came to rest, he said,

"Return, LORD,
  to the countless thousands of Israel."

Fire From the LORD

11 Now the people complained about their hardships in the hearing of the LORD, and when he heard them his anger was aroused. Then fire from the LORD burned among them and consumed some of the outskirts of the camp. ²When the people cried out to Moses, he prayed to the LORD and the fire died down. ³So that place was called Taberah,ᵃ because fire from the LORD had burned among them.

Quail From the LORD

⁴The rabble with them began to crave other food, and again the Israelites started wailing and said, "If only we had meat to eat! ⁵We remember the fish we ate in Egypt at no cost — also the cucumbers, melons, leeks, onions and garlic. ⁶But now we have lost our appetite; we never see anything but this manna!"

⁷The manna was like coriander seed and looked like resin. ⁸The people went around gathering it, and then ground it in a hand mill or crushed it in a mortar. They cooked it in a pot or made it into loaves. And it tasted like something made with olive oil. ⁹When the dew settled on the camp at night, the manna also came down.

¹⁰Moses heard the people of every family wailing at the entrance to their tents. The LORD became exceedingly angry, and Moses was troubled. ¹¹He asked the LORD, "Why have you brought this trouble on your servant? What have I done to displease you that you put the burden of all these people on me? ¹²Did I conceive all these people? Did I give them birth? Why do you tell me to carry them in my arms, as a nurse carries an infant, to the land you promised on oath to their ancestors? ¹³Where can I get meat for all these people? They keep wailing to me, 'Give us meat to eat!' ¹⁴I cannot carry all these people by myself; the burden is too heavy for me. ¹⁵If this is how you are going to treat me, please go ahead and kill me — if I have found favor in your eyes — and do not let me face my own ruin."

¹⁶The LORD said to Moses: "Bring me seventy of Israel's elders who are known to you as leaders

ᵃ 3 *Taberah* means *burning*.

10:35–36 These two verses are known as the "Song of the Ark." Ancient Hebrew scribes marked the poem as not part of the original context. The first verse matches Ps 68:1 almost exactly.

10:36 Return, LORD The ark was intimately identified with the presence of Yahweh, since it served as the throne of his presence. See the infographic "The Ark of the Covenant" on p. 412.

11:1–35 As soon as the people set out from the wilderness of Sinai toward the promised land (Nu 10:33), they begin to complain (compare Ex 16), once about their misfortunes in general (Nu 11:1–3), and another time about their craving for meat (vv. 4–15). Yahweh provides the people with meat (vv. 31–32), but those who had craved the meat and complained against Yahweh and Moses are struck by a plague (vv. 33–35).

11:1 people complained about In other instances where Israel complains or grumbles, the issue is either water (Ex 17:3), food (Ex 16:2–8) or the threat of violence (Nu 14:2–3). The reason for their complaint in vv. 1–3 is unknown.

11:4 rabble The Hebrew word used occurs only this one time in the OT, making its meaning uncertain. It

appears to be related to a word for gathering, so it probably designates a smaller group who had gathered together to complain.

11:7–9 These comments about the qualities of the manna address the substance of their complaint, as well as the grounds for Yahweh's and Moses' annoyance.

11:7 like coriander seed Meaning, small, round and off-white in color.

11:9 the manna also came down This highlights that the people do not have to work for the manna, just collect what has been provided for them daily.

11:11 Why have you brought this trouble on your servant Moses sees their complaint as a punishment from Yahweh.

11:16–30 In response to Moses' complaint that he alone must deal with the people, Yahweh commands him to appoint 70 elders who will share the burden. After a portion of the spirit upon Moses is distributed among these 70, they prophesy once, so the people would know their authority came from God.

11:16 seventy Seventy is one of several numbers that is attributed a particular significance in the OT.

and officials among the people. Have them come to the tent of meeting, that they may stand there with you. ¹⁷I will come down and speak with you there, and I will take some of the power of the Spirit that is on you and put it on them. They will share the burden of the people with you so that you will not have to carry it alone.

¹⁸"Tell the people: 'Consecrate yourselves in preparation for tomorrow, when you will eat meat. The LORD heard you when you wailed, "If only we had meat to eat! We were better off in Egypt!" Now the LORD will give you meat, and you will eat it. ¹⁹You will not eat it for just one day, or two days, or five, ten or twenty days, ²⁰but for a whole month—until it comes out of your nostrils and you loathe it—because you have rejected the LORD, who is among you, and have wailed before him, saying, "Why did we ever leave Egypt?"'"

²¹But Moses said, "Here I am among six hundred thousand men on foot, and you say, 'I will give them meat to eat for a whole month!' ²²Would they have enough if flocks and herds were slaughtered for them? Would they have enough if all the fish in the sea were caught for them?"

²³The LORD answered Moses, "Is the LORD's arm too short? Now you will see whether or not what I say will come true for you."

²⁴So Moses went out and told the people what the LORD had said. He brought together seventy of their elders and had them stand around the tent. ²⁵Then the LORD came down in the cloud and spoke with him, and he took some of the power of the Spirit that was on him and put it on the seventy elders. When the Spirit rested on them, they prophesied—but did not do so again.

²⁶However, two men, whose names were Eldad and Medad, had remained in the camp. They were listed among the elders, but did not go out to the tent. Yet the Spirit also rested on them, and they prophesied in the camp. ²⁷A young man ran and told Moses, "Eldad and Medad are prophesying in the camp."

²⁸Joshua son of Nun, who had been Moses' aide since youth, spoke up and said, "Moses, my lord, stop them!"

²⁹But Moses replied, "Are you jealous for my sake? I wish that all the LORD's people were prophets and that the LORD would put his Spirit on them!" ³⁰Then Moses and the elders of Israel returned to the camp.

³¹Now a wind went out from the LORD and drove quail in from the sea. It scattered them up to two cubits*a* deep all around the camp, as far as a day's walk in any direction. ³²All that day and night and all the next day the people went out and gathered quail. No one gathered less than ten homers.*b* Then they spread them out all around the camp. ³³But while the meat was still between their teeth and before it could be consumed, the anger of the LORD burned against the people, and he struck them with a severe plague. ³⁴Therefore the place was named Kibroth Hattaavah,*c* because there they buried the people who had craved other food.

³⁵From Kibroth Hattaavah the people traveled to Hazeroth and stayed there.

Miriam and Aaron Oppose Moses

12 Miriam and Aaron began to talk against Moses because of his Cushite wife, for he had married a Cushite. ²"Has the LORD spoken

a 31 That is, about 3 feet or about 90 centimeters   *b 32* That is, possibly about 1 3/4 tons or about 1.6 metric tons   *c 34* Kibroth Hattaavah means graves of craving.

11:17 some of the power of the Spirit that is on you The Spirit will not be taken from Moses and given to the new elders. Rather, some of the ability or power given by Yahweh to Moses will be given to the new elders.

11:20 Why did we ever leave Egypt The anger Yahweh feels toward Israel is not because of their longing for meat, but because, in their craving, they long for Egypt and thus reject the goodness, provision and power of Yahweh.

11:21 six hundred thousand men on foot See note on 1:46.

11:28 Moses, my lord, stop them Prophetic utterance signified divine empowerment (see v. 25). Joshua, who may have been with Moses at the tent (compare Ex 33:11), is likely concerned that they will threaten Moses' authority. Yet Moses, willing to share authority (Nu 11:14,29), wishes that more would prophesy and have the Spirit upon them (v. 29).

11:31–35 The quail come as promised, but the experience is negative just as Yahweh warned in vv. 18–23 (see Ps 78:29–31; 106:13–15). Their complaint had aroused Yahweh's anger, so those who had craved the meat were struck dead by a plague (Nu 11:33). Compare note on 11:20.

11:31 drove quail in from the sea The migration route

of the quail includes the eastern Mediterranean coast and the Sinai Peninsula.

11:32 homers During the pre-exilic period (pre-586 BC), the capacity of a homer was probably around 100 to 200 liters, roughly 3–6 bushels.

11:33 before it could be consumed The anger of Yahweh is so strong that he punishes them immediately instead of making them loathe the meat after eating it for a whole month (v. 20). Compare note on 11:20.

11:34 the people who had craved Meaning, those who had complained (v. 4); presumably no one else was killed.

11:35 Hazeroth The exact location of Hazeroth is unknown, though it must be somewhere between the wilderness of Sinai and the wilderness of Paran. The events of ch. 12 take place at Hazeroth (12:16).

12:1–16 Chapter 12 focuses on Moses' unique authority. Moses' siblings—Aaron and Miriam—challenge his authority because they also have the gift of prophecy. Moses is shown to be greater than any others who may receive revelation from Yahweh through dreams or visions because he communicates with Yahweh face to face (v. 8).

12:1 his Cushite wife This label may describe Zipporah—Moses' wife—who was from Midian (Ex 2:16–22). It may alternatively indicate that Moses

only through Moses?" they asked. "Hasn't he also spoken through us?" And the LORD heard this.

³(Now Moses was a very humble man, more humble than anyone else on the face of the earth.)

⁴At once the LORD said to Moses, Aaron and Miriam, "Come out to the tent of meeting, all three of you." So the three of them went out. ⁵Then the LORD came down in a pillar of cloud; he stood at the entrance to the tent and summoned Aaron and Miriam. When the two of them stepped forward, ⁶he said, "Listen to my words:

"When there is a prophet among you,
    I, the LORD, reveal myself to them
        in visions,
    I speak to them in dreams.
⁷But this is not true of my servant Moses;
    he is faithful in all my house.
⁸With him I speak face to face,
    clearly and not in riddles;
    he sees the form of the LORD.
Why then were you not afraid
    to speak against my servant Moses?"

⁹The anger of the LORD burned against them, and he left them.

¹⁰When the cloud lifted from above the tent, Miriam's skin was leprous*ᵃ* — it became as white as snow. Aaron turned toward her and saw that she had a defiling skin disease, ¹¹and he said to Moses, "Please, my lord, I ask you not to hold against us the sin we have so foolishly committed. ¹²Do not let her be like a stillborn infant coming from its mother's womb with its flesh half eaten away."

¹³So Moses cried out to the LORD, "Please, God, heal her!"

¹⁴The LORD replied to Moses, "If her father had spit in her face, would she not have been in disgrace for seven days? Confine her outside the camp for seven days; after that she can be brought back." ¹⁵So Miriam was confined outside the camp for seven days, and the people did not move on till she was brought back.

¹⁶After that, the people left Hazeroth and encamped in the Desert of Paran.

Exploring Canaan

13 The LORD said to Moses, ²"Send some men to explore the land of Canaan, which I am giving to the Israelites. From each ancestral tribe send one of its leaders."

³So at the LORD's command Moses sent them out from the Desert of Paran. All of them were leaders of the Israelites. ⁴These are their names:

from the tribe of Reuben, Shammua son
    of Zakkur;
⁵from the tribe of Simeon, Shaphat son of Hori;
⁶from the tribe of Judah, Caleb son of Jephunneh;
⁷from the tribe of Issachar, Igal son of Joseph;
⁸from the tribe of Ephraim, Hoshea son of Nun;
⁹from the tribe of Benjamin, Palti son of Raphu;
¹⁰from the tribe of Zebulun, Gaddiel son of Sodi;
¹¹from the tribe of Manasseh (a tribe of Joseph),
    Gaddi son of Susi;
¹²from the tribe of Dan, Ammiel son of Gemalli;
¹³from the tribe of Asher, Sethur son of Michael;
¹⁴from the tribe of Naphtali, Nahbi son of Vophsi;
¹⁵from the tribe of Gad, Geuel son of Maki.

¹⁶These are the names of the men Moses sent to explore the land. (Moses gave Hoshea son of Nun the name Joshua.)

ᵃ 10 The Hebrew for *leprous* was used for various diseases affecting the skin.

---

had another wife from Cush (usually identified with Ethiopia). However, the term "Cush" is identified with both regions. Ultimately, Aaron and Miriam's objection was based on ethnicity—she was not a native Israelite. This complaint is a pretense, however; the real issue was Moses' authority.

12:2 Hasn't he also spoken through us As Moses' older siblings, Miriam and Aaron may assume they should hold equal authority, failing to recognize God's choice of Moses as his representative.

12:8 face to face, clearly and not in riddles This stands in contrast to the previously mentioned forms of communication that prophets experience—visions and dreams (Nu 12:6)—which are not clear but require interpretation. Moses, on the other hand, converses with Yahweh plainly, without barrier. See the table "Old Testament Theophanies" on p. 924.

12:11 to Moses Aaron's appeal to Moses acknowledges the superiority of Moses' role as intercessor and highlights Aaron's own inability to intercede in this case.

13:1–33 Chapter 13 records the second of the two greatest sins during Israel's journey to the promised land, the first being the golden calf incident in Ex 32.

When the spies (Nu 13:2) return from scoping out the land of Canaan, they express fear of certain occupants (vv. 32–33). The unbelief inspired by this fear dooms Israel to a 38-year period of wandering in the wilderness, just long enough to ensure that the unbelieving generation dies off.

13:2 to explore The spying mission was probably designed to energize the people, not provide intelligence in advance of an invasion. They were to be inspired by the goodness of the land and the living situations of its current occupants (vv. 17–20).

13:3 Paran See note on 10:12.

13:6 Caleb This name is from the Hebrew term *kelev*, meaning "dog." In the ancient Near East, the dog could symbolize an obedient servant.

13:8 Hoshea The name used here is Hoshea, but he is more commonly known as Joshua (see note on Jos 1:1). Hoshea means "he saves," referring to God's saving ability. Moses later renamed him Joshua, which means "Yah is salvation," using a shortened form of God's name, Yahweh (v. 16). Joshua's new name is more specific to Yahweh's name.

¹⁷When Moses sent them to explore Canaan, he said, "Go up through the Negev and on into the hill country. ¹⁸See what the land is like and whether the people who live there are strong or weak, few or many. ¹⁹What kind of land do they live in? Is it good or bad? What kind of towns do they live in? Are they unwalled or fortified? ²⁰How is the soil? Is it fertile or poor? Are there trees in it or not? Do your best to bring back some of the fruit of the land." (It was the season for the first ripe grapes.)

²¹So they went up and explored the land from the Desert of Zin as far as Rehob, toward Lebo Hamath. ²²They went up through the Negev and came to Hebron, where Ahiman, Sheshai and Talmai, the descendants of Anak, lived. (Hebron had been built seven years before Zoan in Egypt.) ²³When they reached the Valley of Eshkol,ᵃ they cut off a branch bearing a single cluster of grapes.

ᵃ 23 *Eshkol* means *cluster*; also in verse 24.

13:17–20 This passage outlines the specific mission of the 12 spies. Their primary objective was to gain information about the productivity of the land and the defensive strength of its inhabitants.

13:17 hill country Refers to the central hill country of Palestine, the mountainous strip of land running from just north of the Negev to the Sea of Galilee on the western side of the Jordan River.

13:20 It was the season for the first ripe grapes The beginning of summer. This underscores the idea that the goal of the expedition is to give the people a preview of the land's bounty and to energize them (in addition to getting them to stop complaining about food; compare Nu 11).

13:21 Desert of Zin Located north of the wilderness of Paran, where the spies initially camped (v. 3). This region is later identified as marking the southern border of the promised land (34:3–4; Jos 15:1). **Rehob** A city in the north of Canaan, which will later be part of the territory of Asher (Jos 19:28). **Lebo Hamath** A city on the Orontes River in the northern part of the Levant. This area is later used to mark the northern extent of the kingdom of Israel (1Ki 8:65; 2Ki 14:25).

13:22 Hebron It was at Hebron that Abraham was first promised the land of Canaan—which makes the Israel-

Spies in Canaan
(Nu 13:1–33)

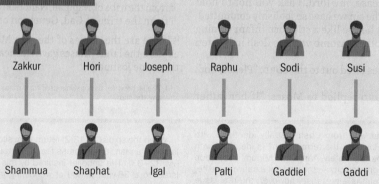

| Zakkur | Hori | Joseph | Raphu | Sodi | Susi |

| Shammua | Shaphat | Igal | Palti | Gaddiel | Gaddi |

GAVE UNFAVORABLE REPORT

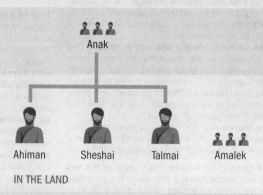

Anak

Ahiman | Sheshai | Talmai | Amalek

IN THE LAND

Two of them carried it on a pole between them, along with some pomegranates and figs. ²⁴That place was called the Valley of Eshkol because of the cluster of grapes the Israelites cut off there. ²⁵At the end of forty days they returned from exploring the land.

Report on the Exploration

²⁶They came back to Moses and Aaron and the whole Israelite community at Kadesh in the Desert of Paran. There they reported to them and to the whole assembly and showed them the fruit of the land. ²⁷They gave Moses this account: "We went into the land to which you sent us, and it does flow with milk and honey! Here is its fruit. ²⁸But the people who live there are powerful, and the cities are fortified and very large. We even saw descendants of Anak there. ²⁹The Amalekites live in the Negev; the Hittites, Jebusites and Amorites live in the hill country; and the Canaanites live near the sea and along the Jordan."

³⁰Then Caleb silenced the people before Moses

ites' apprehension about entering the land all the more shameful (Nu 14:1–4). **descendants of Anak** These people were said to be very large, as they are descended from the Nephilim (v. 33; Ge 6:1–4).

13:25–33 The spies' report is initially balanced. However, as soon as Caleb asserts the inhabitants of the land can be defeated in military engagement, the rest of the spies (except for Joshua) oppose him, arguing that the descendants of Anak, the Anakites, are too strong (see note on 13:32).

13:26 Kadesh This site was on the southern border of the promised land (Nu 34:4). The same location is called by a number of different names: Kadesh Barnea (32:8), En Mishpat (Ge 14:7), Meribah (Nu 20:13), and Meribah Kadesh (27:14).

13:27 flow with milk and honey An image frequently used in the OT for great bounty, as it speaks to both livestock and agricultural produce (e.g., Ex 3:8,17; Nu 14:8).

13:29 Amalekites A nomadic tribe related to Esau (Ge 36:12,16). They may have been the dominant presence in the land at this time (Nu 24:20). **the Canaanites**

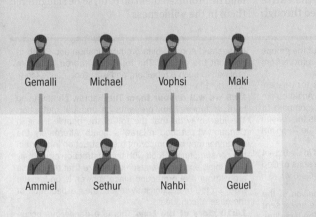

Gemalli Michael Vophsi Maki

Ammiel Sethur Nahbi Geuel

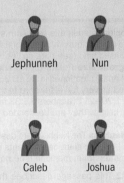

Jephunneh Nun

Caleb Joshua

GAVE FAVORABLE REPORT

Hittites   Jebusites   Amorites   Canaanites   Nephilim

and said, "We should go up and take possession of the land, for we can certainly do it."

³¹But the men who had gone up with him said, "We can't attack those people; they are stronger than we are." ³²And they spread among the Israelites a bad report about the land they had explored. They said, "The land we explored devours those living in it. All the people we saw there are of great size. ³³We saw the Nephilim there (the descendants of Anak come from the Nephilim). We seemed like grasshoppers in our own eyes, and we looked the same to them."

The People Rebel

14 That night all the members of the community raised their voices and wept aloud. ²All the Israelites grumbled against Moses and Aaron, and the whole assembly said to them, "If only we had died in Egypt! Or in this wilderness! ³Why is the LORD bringing us to this land only to let us fall by the sword? Our wives and children will be taken as plunder. Wouldn't it be better for us to go back to Egypt?" ⁴And they said to each other, "We should choose a leader and go back to Egypt."

⁵Then Moses and Aaron fell facedown in front of the whole Israelite assembly gathered there. ⁶Joshua son of Nun and Caleb son of Jephunneh, who were among those who had explored the land, tore their clothes ⁷and said to the entire Israelite assembly, "The land we passed through

and explored is exceedingly good. ⁸If the LORD is pleased with us, he will lead us into that land, a land flowing with milk and honey, and will give it to us. ⁹Only do not rebel against the LORD. And do not be afraid of the people of the land, because we will devour them. Their protection is gone, but the LORD is with us. Do not be afraid of them."

¹⁰But the whole assembly talked about stoning them. Then the glory of the LORD appeared at the tent of meeting to all the Israelites. ¹¹The LORD said to Moses, "How long will these people treat me with contempt? How long will they refuse to believe in me, in spite of all the signs I have performed among them? ¹²I will strike them down with a plague and destroy them, but I will make you into a nation greater and stronger than they."

¹³Moses said to the LORD, "Then the Egyptians will hear about it! By your power you brought these people up from among them. ¹⁴And they will tell the inhabitants of this land about it. They have already heard that you, LORD, are with these people and that you, LORD, have been seen face to face, that your cloud stays over them, and that you go before them in a pillar of cloud by day and a pillar of fire by night. ¹⁵If you put all these people to death, leaving none alive, the nations who have heard this report about you will say, ¹⁶'The LORD was not able to bring these people into the land he promised them on oath, so he slaughtered them in the wilderness.'

The peoples listed in this verse are some of the groups native to Canaan that Yahweh promised to remove from the promised land (see note on Jos 3:10).

13:32 great size Refers to the Anakites (or descendants of Anak) mentioned in Nu 13:33. The Anakites are described as very tall elsewhere in the OT (compare Dt 2:10–11,20–21). Numbers 13:33 provides the reason for their height: They are descended from the Nephilim (see Ge 6:1–4).

13:33 Nephilim The Nephilim are described in Ge 6:1–4 and are likely the giant descendants of the sons of God and daughters of humankind (see note on Ge 6:4).

14:1–12 This passage describes the rebellion of the Israelites following the fearful report of the spies sent to investigate the promised land (Nu 13). The Israelites complain over what they view as a hopeless situation and again yearn to go back to Egypt, imagining life in slavery as better than the certain death that must await them in Canaan (vv. 1–4). Joshua and Caleb urge the people not to rebel against Yahweh, but the mob prepares to stone them when Yahweh appears to punish the rebellious people (vv. 5–12).

14:3 to let us fall by the sword The people believe that facing the inhabitants of the land will mean certain death. They have forgotten that Yahweh has delivered them from death numerous times already, and also that he has promised them victory over these very people (e.g., Ex 33:2; 34:11).

14:5 in front of the whole Israelite assembly gathered there Moses and Aaron do not beseech Yahweh; rather, they beg the people to reconsider their defiance.

Moses and Aaron's plea prompts Joshua and Caleb to confront the people. The four likely feared Yahweh's reaction to such a rebellion, and with good cause (compare Nu 11).

14:9 we will devour them The Hebrew phrase used here, *lachmenu hem*, presents an unusual metaphor. The idea may be that the toil of the people living in Canaan will put food in Israel's mouth. Alternately, the metaphor may be comparing the destruction inherent in the consumption of food with the destruction brought by war. Caleb and Joshua also emphasize that the people are without real protection since Yahweh is on Israel's side, so the metaphor may reflect their expectation of the ease of conquest.

14:10 glory of the LORD This is a dangerous occurrence, as one cannot see the glory of Yahweh and live (compare Ex 33:18–23).

14:12 destroy them The Hebrew verb used here, *yarash*, denotes taking possession of an inheritance. The word can also refer to disinheriting people or driving them out of their land (Dt 2:12; Jdg 1:19; 11:23–24).

14:13–19 Yahweh wants to destroy Israel outright, but as before, Moses pleads with him to relent on the basis of Yahweh's own reputation (compare Ex 32:11–14). Others would hear of the destruction and presume Yahweh lacked the power to bring Israel into the land. Moses' argument is effective: Yahweh spares Israel, but sentences the rebellious generation—everyone over the age of 20—to die in the wilderness (Nu 14:29–32). Of the older generation, only Joshua and Caleb will see and inherit the land.

[17]"Now may the Lord's strength be displayed, just as you have declared: [18]'The LORD is slow to anger, abounding in love and forgiving sin and rebellion. Yet he does not leave the guilty unpunished; he punishes the children for the sin of the parents to the third and fourth generation.' [19]In accordance with your great love, forgive the sin of these people, just as you have pardoned them from the time they left Egypt until now."

[20]The LORD replied, "I have forgiven them, as you asked. [21]Nevertheless, as surely as I live and as surely as the glory of the LORD fills the whole earth, [22]not one of those who saw my glory and the signs I performed in Egypt and in the wilderness but who disobeyed me and tested me ten times — [23]not one of them will ever see the land I promised on oath to their ancestors. No one who has treated me with contempt will ever see it. [24]But because my servant Caleb has a different spirit and follows me wholeheartedly, I will bring him into the land he went to, and his descendants will inherit it. [25]Since the Amalekites and the Canaanites are living in the valleys, turn back tomorrow and set out toward the desert along the route to the Red Sea. [a]"

[26]The LORD said to Moses and Aaron: [27]"How long will this wicked community grumble against me? I have heard the complaints of these grumbling Israelites. [28]So tell them, 'As surely as I live, declares the LORD, I will do to you the very thing I heard you say: [29]In this wilderness your bodies will fall — every one of you twenty years old or more who was counted in the census and who has grumbled against me. [30]Not one of you will enter the land I swore with uplifted hand to make your home, except Caleb son of Jephunneh and Joshua son of Nun. [31]As for your children that you said

would be taken as plunder, I will bring them in to enjoy the land you have rejected. [32]But as for you, your bodies will fall in this wilderness. [33]Your children will be shepherds here for forty years, suffering for your unfaithfulness, until the last of your bodies lies in the wilderness. [34]For forty years — one year for each of the forty days you explored the land — you will suffer for your sins and know what it is like to have me against you.' [35]I, the LORD, have spoken, and I will surely do these things to this whole wicked community, which has banded together against me. They will meet their end in this wilderness; here they will die."

[36]So the men Moses had sent to explore the land, who returned and made the whole community grumble against him by spreading a bad report about it — [37]these men who were responsible for spreading the bad report about the land were struck down and died of a plague before the LORD. [38]Of the men who went to explore the land, only Joshua son of Nun and Caleb son of Jephunneh survived.

[39]When Moses reported this to all the Israelites, they mourned bitterly. [40]Early the next morning they set out for the highest point in the hill country, saying, "Now we are ready to go up to the land the LORD promised. Surely we have sinned!"

[41]But Moses said, "Why are you disobeying the LORD's command? This will not succeed! [42]Do not go up, because the LORD is not with you. You will be defeated by your enemies, [43]for the Amalekites and the Canaanites will face you there. Because you have turned away from the LORD, he will not be with you and you will fall by the sword."

[44]Nevertheless, in their presumption they went

[a] 25 Or *the Sea of Reeds*

14:18 slow to anger Moses reminds Yahweh of how Yahweh has previously described his own character (see Ex 34:6–7). **he punishes the children** The idea that later generations would be punished for the sins of others is qualified in Deuteronomy which implies that Yahweh would punish succeeding generations only if they repeated the sins of their ancestors (Dt 5:9–10; compare Eze 18:4 and note).

14:20–38 In response to the people's rebellion and Moses's plea, Yahweh proclaims that he will not wipe them out, but he will make the people wander for 40 years, until every member of the rebellious generation has passed away (Nu 14:20–35). As for the spies who gave a bad report, Yahweh strikes them with plague (vv. 36–38).

14:20 I have forgiven them, as you asked The people were spared immediate judgment, but they were still punished for their sin.

14:22 ten times This does not necessarily refer to a literal ten times, but is a figure of speech meaning "too many" (compare Ge 31:7).

14:24 follows me wholeheartedly Caleb remained loyal to Yahweh and his promises when he reported that the land was good and that the people should rise up and take it immediately (Nu 13:30).

14:25 along the route to the Red Sea Probably refers to the Gulf of Aqaba (see Ex 10:19; 13:18 and note).

14:29 twenty years old or more who was counted in the census The required age for military service was 20. The individuals in this age group encompass those who refused to enter the land and take it (Nu 1:3).

14:32 your bodies will fall in this wilderness Although not by the sword, as feared, but by old age and the challenges of desert life.

14:33 forty years This length of time allows for the old rebellious generation to pass away, and a new generation to emerge. **your unfaithfulness** Any suffering experienced during this time is attributed to the people's choice in refusing to believe the promises of Yahweh.

14:39–45 The Israelites' response to Yahweh's punishment is a futile effort to overturn the punishment themselves by obeying his original demand to take the land of Canaan. The result is, of course, tragic.

14:41 Why are you disobeying the LORD's command Although this was indeed the original expectation, the time for this generation of Israelites to fight against the people living in the Levant has passed.

14:43 Amalekites and the Canaanites The two dominant people groups in the Levant at the time.

14:44 ark of the LORD's covenant The ark, which served

up toward the highest point in the hill country, though neither Moses nor the ark of the LORD's covenant moved from the camp. ⁴⁵Then the Amalekites and the Canaanites who lived in that hill country came down and attacked them and beat them down all the way to Hormah.

Supplementary Offerings

15 The LORD said to Moses, ²"Speak to the Israelites and say to them: 'After you enter the land I am giving you as a home ³and you present to the LORD food offerings from the herd or the flock, as an aroma pleasing to the LORD — whether burnt offerings or sacrifices, for special vows or freewill offerings or festival offerings — ⁴then the person who brings an offering shall present to the LORD a grain offering of a tenth of an ephahᵃ of the finest flour mixed with a quarter of a hinᵇ of olive oil. ⁵With each lamb for the burnt offering or the sacrifice, prepare a quarter of a hin of wine as a drink offering.

⁶"'With a ram prepare a grain offering of two-tenths of an ephahᶜ of the finest flour mixed with a third of a hinᵈ of olive oil, ⁷and a third of a hin of wine as a drink offering. Offer it as an aroma pleasing to the LORD.

⁸"'When you prepare a young bull as a burnt offering or sacrifice, for a special vow or a fellowship offering to the LORD, ⁹bring with the bull a grain offering of three-tenths of an ephah of the finest flour mixed with half a hinᶠ of olive oil, ¹⁰and also bring half a hin of wine as a

drink offering. This will be a food offering, an aroma pleasing to the LORD. ¹¹Each bull or ram, each lamb or young goat, is to be prepared in this manner. ¹²Do this for each one, for as many as you prepare.

¹³"'Everyone who is native-born must do these things in this way when they present a food offering as an aroma pleasing to the LORD. ¹⁴For the generations to come, whenever a foreigner or anyone else living among you presents a food offering as an aroma pleasing to the LORD, they must do exactly as you do. ¹⁵The community is to have the same rules for you and for the foreigner residing among you; this is a lasting ordinance for the generations to come. You and the foreigner shall be the same before the LORD: ¹⁶The same laws and regulations will apply both to you and to the foreigner residing among you.'"

¹⁷The LORD said to Moses, ¹⁸"Speak to the Israelites and say to them: 'When you enter the land to which I am taking you ¹⁹and you eat the food of the land, present a portion as an offering to the LORD. ²⁰Present a loaf from the first of your ground meal and present it as an offering from the threshing floor. ²¹Throughout the generations to come you are to give this offering to the LORD from the first of your ground meal.

ᵃ 4 That is, probably about 3 1/2 pounds or about 1.6 kilograms
ᵇ 4 That is, about 1 quart or about 1 liter; also in verse 5
ᶜ 6 That is, probably about 7 pounds or about 3.2 kilograms
ᵈ 6 That is, about 1 1/3 quarts or about 1.3 liters; also in verse 7
ᵉ 9 That is, probably about 11 pounds or about 5 kilograms
ᶠ 9 That is, about 2 quarts or about 1.9 liters; also in verse 10

---

as the throne of Yahweh, was supposed to accompany the people in battle to ensure victory (10:35–36).

15:1–41 Chapter 15 presents an eclectic collection of laws. Most of the chapter is concerned with various sacrifices and offerings (vv. 1–31). The chapter closes with the law of the *tsitsith*, the Hebrew word for the tassels worn as a physical reminder of Yahweh's commandments (vv. 37–41; compare Dt 22:12). It is unknown why these laws were placed here, instead of incorporated into other legal collections in Exodus, Leviticus, Numbers or Deuteronomy. Many of the laws are intended for a settled agricultural population living in the land of Canaan (Nu 15:2), whereas Numbers is generally about the people living in the wilderness prior to entering Canaan.

The legal material is interrupted by a brief narrative recounting an incident where a man was found working on the Sabbath (vv. 32–36). The narrative illustrates how law develops in response to situations and how Biblical laws may have needed clarification over time (see note on v. 34).

15:3 you present to the LORD This passage provides a brief survey of sacrifices and specifies the amounts of grain, oil and wine needed for the grain offerings and drink offerings that should accompany the various sacrifices. Most of the offerings are treated in more detail in Lev 1–7. **special vows** Offerings might be brought for a variety of reasons including to give thanks to Yahweh, to fulfill a vow, to commemorate a religious festival or as a freewill offering (see Lev 7:12–18; 22:18–33).

15:7 a drink offering Drink offerings are not covered in the detailed account of the various offerings in Lev 1–7, but they are often mentioned elsewhere in association with various offerings (e.g., Nu 6:15; 28:7; Ex 29:40–41; Lev 23:18). **as an aroma pleasing** See note on Lev 1:9.

15:10 a food offering The Hebrew term used here, *isheh*, most likely designates a gift of food. This Hebrew word has often been interpreted as "offering by fire" based on a sound association with the Hebrew word for fire (*esh*). However, the term is more likely related to another Semitic word for gift (see note on Lev 1:9).

15:13–16 This passage emphasizes that the same laws of sacrifice apply equally to a native-born Israelite (*ezrach* in Hebrew) and to a sojourner (*ger* in Hebrew), a foreigner living among them (compare Nu 15:29). The parallel language between Ex 12:49 and Nu 15:16 is likely intended to evoke a connection between these passages with the implication that circumcision is also necessary for anyone who would offer sacrifice (see Ge 17:9–14).

15:15 You and the foreigner shall be the same This language is used to indicate specific instances where the same law applies to both native-born Israelites and sojourners (e.g., Ex 12:49; see note on Nu 15:13–16).
15:20 from the first of your ground meal The priests received the first of the produce. The amount contributed was likely the first loaf made from the dough (compare Lev 2:14–15).

Offerings for Unintentional Sins

22"'Now if you as a community unintentionally fail to keep any of these commands the LORD gave Moses— 23any of the LORD's commands to you through him, from the day the LORD gave them and continuing through the generations to come— 24and if this is done unintentionally without the community being aware of it, then the whole community is to offer a young bull for a burnt offering as an aroma pleasing to the LORD, along with its prescribed grain offering and drink offering, and a male goat for a sin offering.a 25The priest is to make atonement for the whole Israelite community, and they will be forgiven, for it was not intentional and they have presented to the LORD for their wrong a food offering and a sin offering. 26The whole Israelite community and the foreigners residing among them will be forgiven, because all the people were involved in the unintentional wrong.

27"'But if just one person sins unintentionally, that person must bring a year-old female goat for a sin offering. 28The priest is to make atonement before the LORD for the one who erred by sinning unintentionally, and when atonement has been made, that person will be forgiven. 29One and the same law applies to everyone who sins unintentionally, whether a native-born Israelite or a foreigner residing among you.

30"'But anyone who sins defiantly, whether native-born or foreigner, blasphemes the LORD and must be cut off from the people of Israel. 31Because they have despised the LORD's word and broken his commands, they must surely be cut off; their guilt remains on them.'"

The Sabbath-Breaker Put to Death

32While the Israelites were in the wilderness, a man was found gathering wood on the Sabbath day. 33Those who found him gathering wood brought him to Moses and Aaron and the whole assembly, 34and they kept him in custody, because it was not clear what should be done to him. 35Then the LORD said to Moses, "The man must die. The whole assembly must stone him outside the camp." 36So the assembly took him outside the camp and stoned him to death, as the LORD commanded Moses.

Tassels on Garments

37The LORD said to Moses, 38"Speak to the Israelites and say to them: 'Throughout the generations to come you are to make tassels on the corners of your garments, with a blue cord on each tassel. 39You will have these tassels to look at and so you will remember all the commands of the LORD, that you may obey them and not prostitute yourselves by chasing after the lusts of your own hearts and eyes. 40Then you will remember to obey all my commands and will be consecrated to your God. 41I am the LORD your God, who brought you out of Egypt to be your God. I am the LORD your God.'"

Korah, Dathan and Abiram

16 Korah son of Izhar, the son of Kohath, the son of Levi, and certain Reubenites—Dathan and Abiram, sons of Eliab, and On son of

a 24 Or purification offering; also in verses 25 and 27

15:22–31 Numbers 15:22–31 addresses the offerings needed for atonement for sins related to unintentional violations of God's laws, whether by the community as a whole (vv. 24–26) or by an individual (vv. 27–28), whether native Israelite or sojourner (v. 29). A deliberate sin could not be atoned for by sacrifice, so the guilty person in that circumstance would be cut off from the Israelite people (vv. 30–31; see note on v. 30). The procedures for these purification (sin) offerings are described in more detail in Leviticus 4 (see note on Lev 4:1—5:13).

15:30 who sins defiantly Describes a deliberate and brazen sin. The sin is all the more serious because of the defiant attitude of the sinner which revealed the sinful behavior resulting from willful opposition to God's commands (Nu 15:31). This attitude of rebellion against God was a threat to the entire community (see 16:19–23). cut off The Hebrew term used here, karath, can describe either capital punishment or banishment (see Ex 12:15; 30:33; Lev 7:20–27). Numbers 15:32–36 may illustrate that karath in this context could refer to capital punishment (compare note on v. 34). The seriousness of the sin demanded a serious penalty for the sake of the community (compare Dt 17:12; 19:13).

15:32–36 The story of the man who violated the Sabbath by gathering wood could indicate that everyone was not aware of God's laws. However, the placement of the story immediately after discussion of laws addressing unintentional

sin suggests the passage serves as a case study to illustrate that distinction. The immediately preceding verses indicate that sins committed with intent cannot be remediated (Nu 15:30–31) through the purification offering (or sin offering). The uncertainty in this narrative may reflect a debate over whether the man's sin was intentional. If unintentional, the purification offering applied. If intentional, the penalty of karath applied (see note on v. 30).

15:32 gathering wood on the Sabbath day Work was forbidden on the Sabbath (Ex 20:10; 31:14–15; Lev 23:3). However, OT law does not explicitly define everything that qualifies as work.

15:34 done to him The penalty for violating the Sabbath was death according to Ex 31:14–15. Their uncertainty over how to handle the violation could indicate that this portion of the law had not been fully articulated at this time. There may have been some confusion about whether the man's actions consisted of prohibited work, or Moses may have been waiting for confirmation from Yahweh that the violation had been deliberate and demanded the death penalty.

15:38 you are to make tassels on the corners of your garments The reason or occasion for this rule is unknown. Compare Dt 22:12.

15:39 remember all the commands The tassels served as a physical reminder of the need for the Israelites to remain faithful to God's law.

16:1–50 Numbers 16 describes two rebellions against

Peleth — became insolent[a] ²and rose up against Moses. With them were 250 Israelite men, well-known community leaders who had been appointed members of the council. ³They came as a group to oppose Moses and Aaron and said to them, "You have gone too far! The whole community is holy, every one of them, and the LORD is with them. Why then do you set yourselves above the LORD's assembly?"

⁴When Moses heard this, he fell facedown. ⁵Then he said to Korah and all his followers: "In the morning the LORD will show who belongs to him and who is holy, and he will have that person come near him. The man he chooses he will cause to come near him. ⁶You, Korah, and all your followers are to do this: Take censers ⁷and tomorrow put burning coals and incense in them before the LORD. The man the LORD chooses will be the one who is holy. You Levites have gone too far!"

⁸Moses also said to Korah, "Now listen, you Levites! ⁹Isn't it enough for you that the God of Israel has separated you from the rest of the Israelite community and brought you near himself to do the work at the LORD's tabernacle and to stand before the community and minister to them? ¹⁰He has brought you and all your fellow Levites near himself, but now you are trying to get the priesthood too. ¹¹It is against the LORD that you and all your followers have banded together. Who is Aaron that you should grumble against him?"

¹²Then Moses summoned Dathan and Abiram, the sons of Eliab. But they said, "We will not come! ¹³Isn't it enough that you have brought us up out of a land flowing with milk and honey to kill us in the wilderness? And now you also want to lord it over us! ¹⁴Moreover, you haven't brought us into a land flowing with milk and honey or given us an inheritance of fields and vineyards. Do you want to treat these men like slaves[b]? No, we will not come!"

¹⁵Then Moses became very angry and said to the LORD, "Do not accept their offering. I have not taken so much as a donkey from them, nor have I wronged any of them."

¹⁶Moses said to Korah, "You and all your followers are to appear before the LORD tomorrow — you and they and Aaron. ¹⁷Each man is to take his censer and put incense in it — 250 censers in all — and present it before the LORD. You and Aaron are to present your censers also." ¹⁸So each of them took his censer, put burning coals and incense in it, and stood with Moses and Aaron at the entrance to the tent of meeting. ¹⁹When Korah had gathered all his followers in opposition to them at the entrance to the tent of meeting, the glory of the LORD appeared to the entire assembly. ²⁰The LORD said to Moses and Aaron, ²¹"Separate yourselves from this assembly so I can put an end to them at once."

²²But Moses and Aaron fell facedown and cried out, "O God, the God who gives breath to all living things, will you be angry with the entire assembly when only one man sins?"

---

[a] 1 Or Peleth—took men   [b] 14 Or to deceive these men; Hebrew Will you gouge out the eyes of these men

---

Moses and Aaron: The rebellion of 250 Israelite chieftains at the instigation of Korah, and the uprising of Dathan and Abiram, both of which are woven together in the chapter. Having just been punished to wander the wilderness for 40 years after their faithless refusal to take the promised land (ch. 14), the Israelites may have been susceptible to following other leaders with the hope of improving their lot (compare 14:4).

16:1 Korah son of Izhar, the son of Kohath Korah was the eldest son of Izhar, the second son of Kohath. **Reubenites** Dathan and Abiram were descendants of Reuben, the oldest of Jacob's 12 sons.

16:3 whole community is holy Moses, Aaron and Korah were all of the tribe of Levi, which was set apart for the service of the tabernacle (and later, the temple); Aaron and his sons were set apart even more so as priests, with Aaron as the high priest, and Moses was highest of all. Here, Korah argues that every male Israelite was set apart, not just Moses, Aaron and their inner circle. While this is true to a certain extent (e.g., Ex 19:5–6), a political coup to overthrow God's appointed leadership and priesthood was an affront to Yahweh (Nu 14:8–11).

16:5 followers The Hebrew text here uses a military term for a group of men over a particular number of people. Moses views this act of rebellion as an attempted coup.

16:7 put burning coals and incense in them before the LORD Moses challenges Korah to test his claim that the entire community has an equal right to the priesthood, but in following Moses's command, Korah proves that he and his followers do not know even the basic protocol for how to act before Yahweh.

16:9 to do the work at the LORD's tabernacle Korah was a Kohathite, a clan with the special privilege and responsibility of carrying the holy items of the tabernacle (3:27–32; 4:1–20). Moses accuses him of lusting for influence and power when he should have been thankful for the privilege of his role.

16:12 We will not come Moses apparently hears that Dathan and Abiram have also contested his authority.

16:13 you also want to lord it over us Like Miriam and Aaron in ch. 12, Dathan and Abiram misunderstand Moses' role with respect to the people and Yahweh.

16:14 you want to treat these men like slaves The Hebrew expression used here, which refers to gouging out the eyes, may be an idiom for deceiving people by giving them false hope. The act of gouging out a person's eyes was a punishment for prisoners of war (Jdg 16:21; 2Ki 25:4–7).

16:15 Do not accept their offering This seems to refer to the test involving an incense offering (Nu 16:6–7), though it may include any offering the rebels might offer prior to the morning.

16:17 You and Aaron are to present your censers also Korah was not exempt from the test and neither was Aaron, who would stand against the 250 rebels for the test involving incense (vv. 6–7).

16:19 glory of the LORD Refers to the divine presence.

²³Then the LORD said to Moses, ²⁴"Say to the assembly, 'Move away from the tents of Korah, Dathan and Abiram.'"

²⁵Moses got up and went to Dathan and Abiram, and the elders of Israel followed him. ²⁶He warned the assembly, "Move back from the tents of these wicked men! Do not touch anything belonging to them, or you will be swept away because of all their sins." ²⁷So they moved away from the tents of Korah, Dathan and Abiram. Dathan and Abiram had come out and were standing with their wives, children and little ones at the entrances to their tents.

²⁸Then Moses said, "This is how you will know that the LORD has sent me to do all these things and that it was not my idea: ²⁹If these men die a natural death and suffer the fate of all mankind, then the LORD has not sent me. ³⁰But if the LORD brings about something totally new, and the earth opens its mouth and swallows them, with everything that belongs to them, and they go down alive into the realm of the dead, then you will know that these men have treated the LORD with contempt."

³¹As soon as he finished saying all this, the ground under them split apart ³²and the earth opened its mouth and swallowed them and their households, and all those associated with Korah, together with their possessions. ³³They went down alive into the realm of the dead, with everything they owned; the earth closed over them, and they perished and were gone from the community. ³⁴At their cries, all the Israelites around them fled, shouting, "The earth is going to swallow us too!"

³⁵And fire came out from the LORD and consumed the 250 men who were offering the incense.

³⁶The LORD said to Moses, ³⁷"Tell Eleazar son of Aaron, the priest, to remove the censers from the charred remains and scatter the coals some distance away, for the censers are holy— ³⁸the censers of the men who sinned at the cost of their lives. Hammer the censers into sheets to overlay the altar, for they were presented before the LORD and have become holy. Let them be a sign to the Israelites."

³⁹So Eleazar the priest collected the bronze censers brought by those who had been burned to death, and he had them hammered out to overlay the altar, ⁴⁰as the LORD directed him through Moses. This was to remind the Israelites that no one except a descendant of Aaron should come to burn incense before the LORD, or he would become like Korah and his followers.

⁴¹The next day the whole Israelite community grumbled against Moses and Aaron. "You have killed the LORD's people," they said.

⁴²But when the assembly gathered in opposition to Moses and Aaron and turned toward the tent of meeting, suddenly the cloud covered it and the glory of the LORD appeared. ⁴³Then Moses and Aaron went to the front of the tent of meeting, ⁴⁴and the LORD said to Moses, ⁴⁵"Get away from this assembly so I can put an end to them at once." And they fell facedown.

⁴⁶Then Moses said to Aaron, "Take your censer and put incense in it, along with burning coals from the altar, and hurry to the assembly to make atonement for them. Wrath has come out from the LORD; the plague has started." ⁴⁷So Aaron did as Moses said, and ran into the midst of the assembly. The plague had already started among the people, but Aaron offered the incense and made atonement for them. ⁴⁸He stood between the living and the dead, and the plague stopped. ⁴⁹But 14,700 people died from the plague, in addition to those who had died because of Korah. ⁵⁰Then Aaron returned to Moses at the entrance to the tent of meeting, for the plague had stopped.ᵃ

ᵃ 50 In Hebrew texts 16:36-50 is numbered 17:1-15.

16:24 Move away from the tents Yahweh will not punish the innocent with the guilty; he allows those who will reject the rebels the opportunity to do so.

16:25 elders of Israel Possibly the 70 elders of 11:16. If so, Korah, Dathan and Abiram had no supporters among the other tribes.

16:27 at the entrances to their tents The families of Dathan, Abiram and Korah suffer the consequence of their rebellion, but some of the sons of Korah survive (26:11).

16:32 the earth opened its mouth and swallowed them This imagery reflects the ancient Hebrew belief that the realm of the dead (or Sheol) was located under the earth. See the infographic "Ancient Hebrew Conception of the Universe" on p. 5.

16:37 Eleazar Aaron's eldest remaining son, and therefore second in command among the priests.

16:38 Hammer the censers into sheets to overlay the altar The bronze censers in which the rebels put their incense (vv. 17–18) will be turned into plating for the bronze altar of sacrifice. This was because the incense offering to Yahweh was intended to make censers holy. The men who offered these offerings were not holy or set apart for such a deed, and therefore paid with their lives. See the infographic "Ancient Altars" on p. 127.

16:41 LORD's people The people continue to challenge Moses' authority, suggesting they believed Moses and Aaron were behind the supernatural judgment (vv. 31–35), not Yahweh. They charge Moses and Aaron with murdering their rivals.

16:45 I can put an end to them at once This is Yahweh's greatest threat, one that he brings against Israel only upon the most extreme occasions (e.g., Ex 32:10; Nu 11:1–4; 16:21).

16:48 He stood between the living and the dead The high priest was to avoid all contact with the dead (Lev 21:11). Here Aaron risks contamination to save the living. Aaron succeeds in stopping the plague, but not before many die (Nu 16:49).

16:49 because of Korah That is, the 250 rebels plus the families of Korah, Dathan and Abiram (vv. 28–35).

The Budding of Aaron's Staff

17 [a] The LORD said to Moses, [2]"Speak to the Israelites and get twelve staffs from them, one from the leader of each of their ancestral tribes. Write the name of each man on his staff. [3]On the staff of Levi write Aaron's name, for there must be one staff for the head of each ancestral tribe. [4]Place them in the tent of meeting in front of the ark of the covenant law, where I meet with you. [5]The staff belonging to the man I choose will sprout, and I will rid myself of this constant grumbling against you by the Israelites."

[6]So Moses spoke to the Israelites, and their leaders gave him twelve staffs, one for the leader of each of their ancestral tribes, and Aaron's staff was among them. [7]Moses placed the staffs before the LORD in the tent of the covenant law.

[8]The next day Moses entered the tent and saw that Aaron's staff, which represented the tribe of Levi, had not only sprouted but had budded, blossomed and produced almonds. [9]Then Moses brought out all the staffs from the LORD's presence to all the Israelites. They looked at them, and each of the leaders took his own staff.

[10]The LORD said to Moses, "Put back Aaron's staff in front of the ark of the covenant law, to be kept as a sign to the rebellious. This will put an end to their grumbling against me, so that they will not die." [11]Moses did just as the LORD commanded him.

[12]The Israelites said to Moses, "We will die! We are lost, we are all lost! [13]Anyone who even comes near the tabernacle of the LORD will die. Are we all going to die?"

Duties of Priests and Levites

18 The LORD said to Aaron, "You, your sons and your family are to bear the responsibility for offenses connected with the sanctuary, and you and your sons alone are to bear the responsibility for offenses connected with the priesthood. [2]Bring your fellow Levites from your ancestral tribe to join you and assist you when you and your sons minister before the tent of the covenant law. [3]They are to be responsible to you and are to perform all the duties of the tent, but they must not go near the furnishings of the sanctuary or the altar. Otherwise both they and you will die. [4]They are to join you and be responsible for the care of the tent of meeting — all the work at the tent — and no one else may come near where you are.

[5]"You are to be responsible for the care of the sanctuary and the altar, so that my wrath will not fall on the Israelites again. [6]I myself have selected your fellow Levites from among the Israelites as a gift to you, dedicated to the LORD to do the work at the tent of meeting. [7]But only you and your sons may serve as priests in connection with everything at the altar and inside the curtain. I am giving you the service of the priesthood as a gift. Anyone else who comes near the sanctuary is to be put to death."

Offerings for Priests and Levites

[8]Then the LORD said to Aaron, "I myself have put you in charge of the offerings presented to me; all the holy offerings the Israelites give me I

[a] In Hebrew texts 17:1-13 is numbered 17:16-28.

17:1–13 Following the rebellions and unrest in ch. 16, Yahweh further demonstrates his authority and emphasizes that Aaron and Moses are his designated leaders for the people of Israel. Korah's rebellion in ch. 16 was an attempt to usurp the divinely ordained priesthood; this chapter offers up a test to convince the people that Aaron's authority was greater than that of the tribal chieftains (vv. 1–7).

17:2 staffs The staff was a symbol of leadership (Ge 49:10; Ps 110:2; Eze 19:11).

17:4 ark of the covenant law Refers to the ark of the covenant, sometimes called the ark of the testimony (see note on Nu 4:5). See the infographic "The Ark of the Covenant" on p. 412.

17:5 constant grumbling against you by the Israelites This is intended as a final test to halt the people's complaining against the divinely ordained authority of the priesthood.

17:8 produced almonds Since the almond flower symbolized life and renewal (Jer 1:11–12; Ecc 12:5), the almonds here likely symbolize the renewal of life, which is fitting in light of the tragedy of Nu 16.

17:13 Are we all going to die The people understand the message: Yahweh has chosen the priestly authority, and his choice should not be challenged, lest more people die (v. 10; compare 16:22,45).

18:1–32 This passage provides instructions for Aaron concerning the responsibilities of the priests and the Levites. While his instructions were normally mediated through Moses (e.g., 6:23; 8:2), here Yahweh speaks directly to Aaron (compare Lev 10:8–11). The responsibility for the sanctity of the priesthood falls to Aaron and his descendants. See the table "Functions of Priests" on p. 171.

18:2 Levites from your ancestral tribe The responsibility of the Levites to serve with the priests and guard the sanctuary was outlined in Nu 3:5–10.

18:5 my wrath will not fall on the Israelites again Approaching the sacred space of the tabernacle improperly brought judgment (Lev 10:6; Nu 16:40).

18:7 Anyone else The Hebrew word used here, *zar*, refers to anyone who might approach the sacred area without authorization.

18:8–20 These verses list the 11 priestly portions, which are divided into "most holy" (vv. 9–10) and "holy" (vv. 11–19). The portions include: firstfruits of agricultural produce (compare Lev 2:14), firstborn redeemed male animals not sacrificed (Ex 13:11–16; compare note on Nu 3:1–51), everything categorized as *cherem* (meaning devoted to Yahweh; compare Lev 27:28; see note on Jos 6:17), and the breast and right thigh of the peace offerings

give to you and your sons as your portion, your perpetual share. ⁹You are to have the part of the most holy offerings that is kept from the fire. From all the gifts they bring me as most holy offerings, whether grain or sin[a] or guilt offerings, that part belongs to you and your sons. ¹⁰Eat it as something most holy; every male shall eat it. You must regard it as holy.

¹¹"This also is yours: whatever is set aside from the gifts of all the wave offerings of the Israelites. I give this to you and your sons and daughters as your perpetual share. Everyone in your household who is ceremonially clean may eat it.

¹²"I give you all the finest olive oil and all the finest new wine and grain they give the LORD as the firstfruits of their harvest. ¹³All the land's firstfruits that they bring to the LORD will be yours. Everyone in your household who is ceremonially clean may eat it.

¹⁴"Everything in Israel that is devoted[b] to the LORD is yours. ¹⁵The first offspring of every womb, both human and animal, that is offered to the LORD is yours. But you must redeem every firstborn son and every firstborn male of unclean animals. ¹⁶When they are a month old, you must redeem them at the redemption price set at five shekels[c] of silver, according to the sanctuary shekel, which weighs twenty gerahs.

¹⁷"But you must not redeem the firstborn of a cow, a sheep or a goat; they are holy. Splash their blood against the altar and burn their fat as a food offering, an aroma pleasing to the LORD. ¹⁸Their meat is to be yours, just as the breast of the wave offering and the right thigh are yours. ¹⁹Whatever is set aside from the holy offerings the Israelites present to the LORD I give to you and your sons and daughters as your perpetual share. It is an everlasting covenant of salt before the LORD for both you and your offspring."

²⁰The LORD said to Aaron, "You will have no inheritance in their land, nor will you have any share among them; I am your share and your inheritance among the Israelites.

²¹"I give to the Levites all the tithes in Israel as their inheritance in return for the work they do while serving at the tent of meeting. ²²From now on the Israelites must not go near the tent of meeting, or they will bear the consequences of their sin and will die. ²³It is the Levites who are to do the work at the tent of meeting and bear the responsibility for any offenses they commit against it. This is a lasting ordinance for the generations to come. They will receive no inheritance among the Israelites. ²⁴Instead, I give to the Levites as their inheritance the tithes that the Israelites present as an offering to the LORD. That is why I said concerning them: 'They will have no inheritance among the Israelites.'"

²⁵The LORD said to Moses, ²⁶"Speak to the Levites and say to them: 'When you receive from the Israelites the tithe I give you as your inheritance, you must present a tenth of that tithe as the LORD's offering. ²⁷Your offering will be reckoned to you as grain from the threshing floor or juice from the

---

[a] 9 Or *purification*   [b] 14 The Hebrew term refers to the irrevocable giving over of things or persons to the LORD.   [c] 16 That is, about 2 ounces or about 58 grams

---

(Lev 7:31–34). All gifts to the sanctuary—called in Hebrew the *tenuphah* (often translated "wave offering") and the *terumah* (often translated "contribution")—also belong to the priests.

18:9 from the fire For most sacrifices and offerings, only a representative portion was actually burned on the altar (see note on Lev 2:2). The rest of the offering went to the priests.

18:11 clean Only members of a priestly household who were ritually pure could eat the food received through sacrifices and offerings. If they were unclean, they could transmit their impurity to the offerings and defile them (Lev 22:2–3).

18:12 firstfruits of their harvest The first and best of the oil, wine and grain was to be offered to Yahweh (Pr 3:9). Here the priests are identified as the ultimate recipients of those offerings (compare Dt 18:3–5).

18:14 Everything in Israel that is devoted to the LORD The Hebrew word used here for property devoted to sacred use is *cherem* (see note on Jos 6:17). Most things designated as *cherem* must be completely destroyed. However, at times people and property designated as *cherem* are not destroyed but become property of Yahweh under stewardship of the priests (Lev 27:28; Jos 6:19).

18:15 you must redeem every firstborn son The firstborn of both humankind and animals belonged to Yahweh (Ex 13:2). All human firstborn had to be redeemed (Ex 34:19–20; see note on Nu 3:1–51).

18:16 the redemption price Five silver shekels is the same redemption price given in Nu 3:47. Since the firstborn are redeemed at a month old, the price also lines up with the valuation found in Lev 27:6.

18:19 an everlasting covenant of salt Salt was required for the grain offering and may have been used for all sacrifices (see Lev 2:13 and note; compare Eze 43:24).

18:20 You will have no inheritance in their land The portions and tithes due to the Levites were deemed sufficient, and they had no need of land for agriculture or domestication of animals. However, the Levites were given 48 cities and their surrounding pasturage (Nu 35:1–8).

18:21–32 This passage indicates that the tithe was meant to provide for the Levites, who were a tribal group as well as those who ensured the religious regulations of the Israelites were honored (compare Ne 10:37; 12:44). The compensation for the Levites for their service was the tithe, not the sacrifices which belonged to the priests (Dt 12:6). The distinction here is that not all Levites were priests. In addition to the sacrifices that supported the priesthood, Israel was required to hand over a tenth of all agricultural produce and all livestock to the sanctuary for the Levites (Lev 27:30,32; Dt 14:22).

18:26 a tenth of that tithe The Levites were to give a tenth of the tithe they received from the other tribes to Yahweh.

winepress. ²⁸In this way you also will present an offering to the LORD from all the tithes you receive from the Israelites. From these tithes you must give the LORD's portion to Aaron the priest. ²⁹You must present as the LORD's portion the best and holiest part of everything given to you.'

³⁰"Say to the Levites: 'When you present the best part, it will be reckoned to you as the product of the threshing floor or the winepress. ³¹You and your households may eat the rest of it anywhere, for it is your wages for your work at the tent of meeting. ³²By presenting the best part of it you will not be guilty in this matter; then you will not defile the holy offerings of the Israelites, and you will not die.'"

The Water of Cleansing

19 The LORD said to Moses and Aaron: ²"This is a requirement of the law that the LORD has commanded: Tell the Israelites to bring you a red heifer without defect or blemish and that has never been under a yoke. ³Give it to Eleazar the priest; it is to be taken outside the camp and slaughtered in his presence. ⁴Then Eleazar the priest is to take some of its blood on his finger and sprinkle it seven times toward the front of the tent of meeting. ⁵While he watches, the heifer is to be burned — its hide, flesh, blood and intestines. ⁶The priest is to take some cedar wood, hyssop and scarlet wool and throw them onto the burning heifer. ⁷After that, the priest must wash his clothes and bathe himself with water. He may then come into the camp, but he will be ceremonially unclean till

evening. ⁸The man who burns it must also wash his clothes and bathe with water, and he too will be unclean till evening.

⁹"A man who is clean shall gather up the ashes of the heifer and put them in a ceremonially clean place outside the camp. They are to be kept by the Israelite community for use in the water of cleansing; it is for purification from sin. ¹⁰The man who gathers up the ashes of the heifer must also wash his clothes, and he too will be unclean till evening. This will be a lasting ordinance both for the Israelites and for the foreigners residing among them.

¹¹"Whoever touches a human corpse will be unclean for seven days. ¹²They must purify themselves with the water on the third day and on the seventh day; then they will be clean. But if they do not purify themselves on the third and seventh days, they will not be clean. ¹³If they fail to purify themselves after touching a human corpse, they defile the LORD's tabernacle. They must be cut off from Israel. Because the water of cleansing has not been sprinkled on them, they are unclean; their uncleanness remains on them.

¹⁴"This is the law that applies when a person dies in a tent: Anyone who enters the tent and anyone who is in it will be unclean for seven days, ¹⁵and every open container without a lid fastened on it will be unclean.

¹⁶"Anyone out in the open who touches someone who has been killed with a sword or someone who has died a natural death, or anyone who touches a human bone or a grave, will be unclean for seven days.

18:31 your wages for your work The Levites were also entitled to a portion from the contributions brought to the sanctuary because they risked death in guarding the sanctuary.

19:1–22 Numbers 19:1–10 details the red heifer procedure designed to produce a substance that restores ritual purity to someone contaminated through contact with a corpse. The ritual involves materials and activities similar to other purification rites detailed in Leviticus, especially the sacrifice of the purification (or sin) offering (*chatta'th* in Hebrew; Lev 4) and the cleansing rituals related to skin disease (Lev 14).

The handling of the red heifer has four main components and involves a priest and at least two others. First, the heifer is slaughtered outside the camp. Second, the priest sprinkles some of the blood toward the tent of meeting seven times (compare Lev 4:6). Third, all of the animal is burned up. While it burns, the priest adds cedarwood, hyssop and scarlet yarn to the fire. Finally, the ashes are stored for later use in removing corpse contamination. Numbers 19:11–22 describes certain scenarios related to corpse contamination and explains the proper usage of the ashes to bring about purification.

19:2 red heifer The cow must have reddish hair to be acceptable for the ritual. Since red yarn is also added to the fire, the color may be specified due to its symbolic association with blood. **that has never been under a yoke** Describes a heifer that has never been used for a non-sacred purpose. Compare Dt 21:1–9; 1Sa 6:7.

19:3 Eleazar the priest It is unclear why this duty was not given to Aaron, the high priest, but it was likely related to keeping Aaron from becoming ritually impure. **to be taken outside the camp** The animal is burned up outside the camp, similar to the purification (or sin) offering (Lev 4:12). However, the heifer in this case is also slaughtered outside the camp, not at the sacrificial altar.

19:4 sprinkle it The ritual sprinkling of blood seven times toward the tent of meeting is comparable to the sevenfold sprinkling of blood required for the purification (or sin) offering (Lev 4:6; 16:14).

19:6 cedar wood, hyssop and scarlet wool The same ingredients are used in other purification rituals (e.g., Lev 14:4,51–52).

19:7 unclean The people involved in the ritual are rendered unclean, but their ritual purity is restored after they wash their clothes, bathe and wait until evening (compare Lev 11:25).

19:9 for purification from sin This designation connects the red heifer ritual with the *chatta'th* (the purification or sin offering) and indicates its purpose of providing purification. See note on Lev 4:1—5:13.

19:11 seven days The seven-day length of time is common for purification procedures (e.g., Lev 12:2; 14:9; 15:13).

19:14 anyone who is in it Ancient Israelites conceived of impurity as a physical substance that could be contained (e.g., inside the tent) or spread. They thought it could invade objects (e.g., the vessels in Nu 19:15), or move from one person or object to another (e.g., the grave of the dead in v. 16).

¹⁷"For the unclean person, put some ashes from the burned purification offering into a jar and pour fresh water over them. ¹⁸Then a man who is ceremonially clean is to take some hyssop, dip it in the water and sprinkle the tent and all the furnishings and the people who were there. He must also sprinkle anyone who has touched a human bone or a grave or anyone who has been killed or anyone who has died a natural death. ¹⁹The man who is clean is to sprinkle those who are unclean on the third and seventh days, and on the seventh day he is to purify them. Those who are being cleansed must wash their clothes and bathe with water, and that evening they will be clean. ²⁰But if those who are unclean do not purify themselves, they must be cut off from the community, because they have defiled the sanctuary of the LORD. The water of cleansing has not been sprinkled on them, and they are unclean. ²¹This is a lasting ordinance for them.

"The man who sprinkles the water of cleansing must also wash his clothes, and anyone who touches the water of cleansing will be unclean till evening. ²²Anything that an unclean person touches becomes unclean, and anyone who touches it becomes unclean till evening."

Water From the Rock

20 In the first month the whole Israelite community arrived at the Desert of Zin, and they stayed at Kadesh. There Miriam died and was buried.

²Now there was no water for the community, and the people gathered in opposition to Moses and Aaron. ³They quarreled with Moses and said, "If only we had died when our brothers fell dead before the LORD! ⁴Why did you bring the LORD's community into this wilderness, that we and our livestock should die here? ⁵Why did you bring us up out of Egypt to this terrible place? It has no grain or figs, grapevines or pomegranates. And there is no water to drink!"

⁶Moses and Aaron went from the assembly to the entrance to the tent of meeting and fell facedown, and the glory of the LORD appeared to them. ⁷The LORD said to Moses, ⁸"Take the staff, and you and your brother Aaron gather the assembly together. Speak to that rock before their eyes and it will pour out its water. You will bring water out of the rock for the community so they and their livestock can drink."

⁹So Moses took the staff from the LORD's presence, just as he commanded him. ¹⁰He and Aaron gathered the assembly together in front of the rock and Moses said to them, "Listen, you rebels, must we bring you water out of this rock?" ¹¹Then Moses raised his arm and struck the rock twice with his staff. Water gushed out, and the community and their livestock drank.

¹²But the LORD said to Moses and Aaron, "Because you did not trust in me enough to honor me as holy in the sight of the Israelites, you will not bring this community into the land I give them."

¹³These were the waters of Meribah,ᵃ where the Israelites quarreled with the LORD and where he was proved holy among them.

Edom Denies Israel Passage

¹⁴Moses sent messengers from Kadesh to the king of Edom, saying:

"This is what your brother Israel says: You know about all the hardships that have

ᵃ 13 Meribah means quarreling.

20:1–29 Chapter 20 continues the story of Israel in the wilderness. This chapter mentions the death of Miriam, Moses' and Aaron's sister (v. 1), and then describes Israel's complaints about food and water (vv. 2–7; compare 21:4–9), Moses' sin in striking the rock (vv. 7–13), Edom's opposition to Israel passing through their territory (vv. 14–21) and the death of Aaron (vv. 22–29).

20:1 the first month Based on the travel itinerary given in ch. 33, these events could date to the fortieth and final year of Israel's wandering. **Kadesh** This site was on the southern border of the promised land (34:4). **Miriam** The sister of Moses and Aaron, who was struck with a skin disease when she and Aaron complained against Moses (see ch. 12).

20:2–13 This episode is one of several examples of the Israelites' complaining about resources, only to have Yahweh provide what they need (Ex 15:22—17:7; Nu 11; 14). Here, Moses, in his frustration, offends Yahweh. His punishment is that he and Aaron will not be allowed to enter the promised land.

20:3 our brothers fell dead before the LORD Likely an allusion to the punishment due to the rebellion of Korah, Dathan and Abiram in ch. 16.

20:5 grain or figs, grapevines or pomegranates The same items the spies brought back from the promised land (13:23). The parallel is probably not coincidental, given the complaint in v. 3.

20:8 Take the staff May refer to Aaron's staff that budded (17:8–10) and was kept in the presence of Yahweh (17:10).

20:12 you will not bring this community into the land The exact reason for Moses' punishment is unknown. Essentially, Moses disobeyed Yahweh's instructions: He struck the rock rather than speaking to it (vv. 8,11), and his wording betrayed his personal dissatisfaction with the people.

20:13 Meribah Meribah means "quarreling." The title "waters of quarreling" serves as a reminder of what happened at this place.

20:14–21 The king of Edom, a land on the southeast border of the promised land, refuses to let Israel pass through his territory. Because of this instance, 24:18 says that Edom will be dispossessed; on the other hand, Dt 23:7–8 states that one is not to abhor an Edomite, but to include the third generation into the assembly of Yahweh. This episode is recalled in Jdg 11:17–18.

come on us. [15]Our ancestors went down into Egypt, and we lived there many years. The Egyptians mistreated us and our ancestors, [16]but when we cried out to the Lord, he heard our cry and sent an angel and brought us out of Egypt.

"Now we are here at Kadesh, a town on the edge of your territory. [17]Please let us pass through your country. We will not go through any field or vineyard, or drink water from any well. We will travel along the King's Highway and not turn to the right or to the left until we have passed through your territory."

[18]But Edom answered:

"You may not pass through here; if you try, we will march out and attack you with the sword."

[19]The Israelites replied:

"We will go along the main road, and if we or our livestock drink any of your water, we will pay for it. We only want to pass through on foot — nothing else."

[20]Again they answered:

"You may not pass through."

Then Edom came out against them with a large and powerful army. [21]Since Edom refused to let them go through their territory, Israel turned away from them.

The Death of Aaron

[22]The whole Israelite community set out from Kadesh and came to Mount Hor. [23]At Mount Hor, near the border of Edom, the Lord said to Moses and Aaron, [24]"Aaron will be gathered to his people.

He will not enter the land I give the Israelites, because both of you rebelled against my command at the waters of Meribah. [25]Get Aaron and his son Eleazar and take them up Mount Hor. [26]Remove Aaron's garments and put them on his son Eleazar, for Aaron will be gathered to his people; he will die there."

[27]Moses did as the Lord commanded: They went up Mount Hor in the sight of the whole community. [28]Moses removed Aaron's garments and put them on his son Eleazar. And Aaron died there on top of the mountain. Then Moses and Eleazar came down from the mountain, [29]and when the whole community learned that Aaron had died, all the Israelites mourned for him thirty days.

Arad Destroyed

21 When the Canaanite king of Arad, who lived in the Negev, heard that Israel was coming along the road to Atharim, he attacked the Israelites and captured some of them. [2]Then Israel made this vow to the Lord: "If you will deliver these people into our hands, we will totally destroy[a] their cities." [3]The Lord listened to Israel's plea and gave the Canaanites over to them. They completely destroyed them and their towns; so the place was named Hormah.[b]

The Bronze Snake

[4]They traveled from Mount Hor along the route to the Red Sea,[c] to go around Edom. But the people grew impatient on the way; [5]they spoke against God and against Moses, and said, "Why have you

---

[a] 2 The Hebrew term refers to the irrevocable giving over of things or persons to the Lord, often by totally destroying them; also in verse 3.   [b] 3 Hormah means destruction.   [c] 4 Or the Sea of Reeds

---

20:17 King's Highway The main north-south road through the Transjordan (compare Nu 21:22).

20:18 You may not pass through Edom may be recalling the deception of Jacob (Israel) against his own brother, Esau, Edom's forefather (see Ge 25:19–34; 26:34—27:45).

20:21 turned away from them Edom is not punished for their decision.

20:22–29 This passage reports that Aaron died at Mount Hor (compare Nu 33:38; Dt 32:50), while Dt 10:6 places Aaron's death at Moserah. According to the itinerary of Nu 33:30, Israel reached Moserah (or Moseroth) before Mount Hor. Both accounts may be correct and be due to a geographical overlap between the locations.

20:24 because both of you rebelled This is Aaron's punishment for his part in the waters of Meribah episode. See vv. 2–13.

20:26 put them on his son Eleazar Eleazar is clothed with the special garments of Aaron, the high priest (see Ex 28:1–39), symbolizing the transfer of the office of high priest from father to son.

20:29 thirty days The normal period of mourning was seven days (e.g., Ge 50:10; 1Sa 31:13). This extended period of mourning indicates Aaron's great stature and importance.

21:1–3 Israel now comes into conflict with the Canaanites living in the Negev, namely the king of Arad. The archeological site of Arad, which dates to this period, is important for understanding Canaanite religion as the backdrop of the OT. For example, an altar unearthed at Arad has four horns, similar to the ones described in the OT (e.g., Ex 27:1–8; 30:1–10; Eze 43:15; compare 1Ki 1:50; 2:28).

21:1 Canaanite The generic term for pre-Israelite inhabitants of the promised land.

21:4–9 The Israelites again complain about the lack of food and water, using language similar to their previous complaints (e.g., Ex 15:22—17:7; Nu 11; 14; 20:1–13). This time, God punishes the people with venomous snakes. After Moses prays for the punishment to cease, God instructs him to make a bronze snake, promising to heal all those who look at it.

brought us up out of Egypt to die in the wilderness? There is no bread! There is no water! And we detest this miserable food!"

⁶Then the LORD sent venomous snakes among them; they bit the people and many Israelites died. ⁷The people came to Moses and said, "We sinned when we spoke against the LORD and against you. Pray that the LORD will take the snakes away from us." So Moses prayed for the people.

⁸The LORD said to Moses, "Make a snake and put it up on a pole; anyone who is bitten can look at it and live." ⁹So Moses made a bronze snake and put it up on a pole. Then when anyone was bitten by a snake and looked at the bronze snake, they lived.

The Journey to Moab

¹⁰The Israelites moved on and camped at Oboth. ¹¹Then they set out from Oboth and camped in Iye Abarim, in the wilderness that faces Moab

---

21:6 venomous The Hebrew verb used here, *saraph*, means "burn," but the noun is commonly used for a type of snake (e.g., Dt 8:15). The relationship between the terms likely derives from the burning pain of the venom from a snakebite, although it may also be the ancient Semitic name for a particular species of serpent. **snakes** The Hebrew noun used here, *nachash*, is the common word for "snake." The word sounds similar to *nechosheth*, the word for "bronze," producing the wordplay found in Nu 21:9, *nechash nechosheth* ("bronze serpent"). See the infographic "The Bronze Snake" below.

21:9 looked at the bronze snake, they lived In the ancient Near East, serpents were widely associated with life and healing because they shed their skin. The prescientific observance of this ability led people to assume the serpent had regenerative power.

21:10–20 This passage summarizes Israel's route through the Transjordan. A more detailed description appears in 33:41–49. This section and the next (vv. 21–35) are not in chronological order, since the battle with the Amorites (vv. 21–35) would have likely been before Israel entered the Jordan Valley. As with many OT passages that list numerous locations, many of these sites are unknown.

The Bronze Snake

The Israelites spoke against God and Moses in the desert, and God sent snakes that bit them—and many died. They repented, and Moses prayed for them. Yahweh had Moses make a bronze snake to heal those who looked at it (Nu 21:4-9).

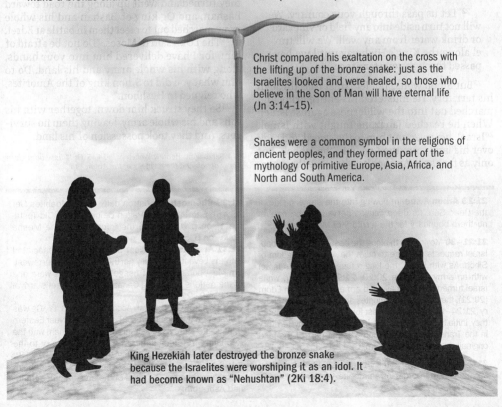

Christ compared his exaltation on the cross with the lifting up of the bronze snake: just as the Israelites looked and were healed, so those who believe in the Son of Man will have eternal life (Jn 3:14-15).

Snakes were a common symbol in the religions of ancient peoples, and they formed part of the mythology of primitive Europe, Asia, Africa, and North and South America.

King Hezekiah later destroyed the bronze snake because the Israelites were worshiping it as an idol. It had become known as "Nehushtan" (2Ki 18:4).

toward the sunrise. ¹²From there they moved on and camped in the Zered Valley. ¹³They set out from there and camped alongside the Arnon, which is in the wilderness extending into Amorite territory. The Arnon is the border of Moab, between Moab and the Amorites. ¹⁴That is why the Book of the Wars of the LORD says:

"... Zahab*ᵃ* in Suphah and the ravines,
 the Arnon ¹⁵and*ᵇ* the slopes of the ravines
that lead to the settlement of Ar
 and lie along the border of Moab."

¹⁶From there they continued on to Beer, the well where the LORD said to Moses, "Gather the people together and I will give them water."

¹⁷Then Israel sang this song:

"Spring up, O well!
 Sing about it,
¹⁸about the well that the princes dug,
 that the nobles of the people sank—
 the nobles with scepters and staffs."

Then they went from the wilderness to Mattanah, ¹⁹from Mattanah to Nahaliel, from Nahaliel to Bamoth, ²⁰and from Bamoth to the valley in Moab where the top of Pisgah overlooks the wasteland.

Defeat of Sihon and Og

²¹Israel sent messengers to say to Sihon king of the Amorites:

²²"Let us pass through your country. We will not turn aside into any field or vineyard, or drink water from any well. We will travel along the King's Highway until we have passed through your territory."

²³But Sihon would not let Israel pass through his territory. He mustered his entire army and marched out into the wilderness against Israel. When he reached Jahaz, he fought with Israel. ²⁴Israel, however, put him to the sword and took over his land from the Arnon to the Jabbok, but only as far as the Ammonites, because their bor-

der was fortified. ²⁵Israel captured all the cities of the Amorites and occupied them, including Heshbon and all its surrounding settlements. ²⁶Heshbon was the city of Sihon king of the Amorites, who had fought against the former king of Moab and had taken from him all his land as far as the Arnon.

²⁷That is why the poets say:

"Come to Heshbon and let it be rebuilt;
 let Sihon's city be restored.

²⁸"Fire went out from Heshbon,
 a blaze from the city of Sihon.
It consumed Ar of Moab,
 the citizens of Arnon's heights.
²⁹Woe to you, Moab!
 You are destroyed, people of Chemosh!
He has given up his sons as fugitives
 and his daughters as captives
 to Sihon king of the Amorites.

³⁰"But we have overthrown them;
 Heshbon's dominion has been destroyed all
 the way to Dibon.
We have demolished them as far as Nophah,
 which extends to Medeba."

³¹So Israel settled in the land of the Amorites. ³²After Moses had sent spies to Jazer, the Israelites captured its surrounding settlements and drove out the Amorites who were there. ³³Then they turned and went up along the road toward Bashan, and Og king of Bashan and his whole army marched out to meet them in battle at Edrei.

³⁴The LORD said to Moses, "Do not be afraid of him, for I have delivered him into your hands, along with his whole army and his land. Do to him what you did to Sihon king of the Amorites, who reigned in Heshbon."

³⁵So they struck him down, together with his sons and his whole army, leaving them no survivors. And they took possession of his land.

ᵃ 14 Septuagint; Hebrew *Waheb*   *ᵇ 14,15* Or *"I have been given from Suphah and the ravines / of the Arnon* ¹⁵*to*

21:13 Arnon A stream flowing into the eastern side of the Dead Sea. Its deep canyon served as the natural northern boundary for the territory of Moab.

21:21–30 Moving north along the eastern edge of Moab, Israel requests passage through the Amorite kingdom of Sihon. As with Edom, the king refuses and meets Israel with an army (compare 20:20; 21:23). However, while Israel turned away and avoided armed conflict with Edom (20:21), they engage the Amorites and conquer their territory (21:24–26). Israel's request for safe passage indicates they initially had no interest in possessing any territory in the Transjordan. This region was not part of the land originally promised to Abraham (Ge 12:1–3; 15:1–6,18).

21:24 Jabbok A river in the Transjordan often described as marking the border of Ammonite territory (Dt 3:16; Jos 12:2).

21:29 Chemosh The patron deity of the Moabites (Jer 48:46). See the table "Pagan Deities of the Old Testament" on p. 1287; see the infographic "The Mesha Stele" on p. 565.

21:31 Amorites An ancient Semitic people associated with the Levant, especially northern Syria and northwestern Mesopotamia. In OT usage, the Amorites were one of the nations occupying Canaan prior to Israel's arrival (Ge 15:19–21).

21:33 Og king of Bashan According to Dt 3:11, Og was a descendant of giants. The OT and ancient Near Eastern Ugaritic literature associate his territory, Bashan, with the Rephaim—referring either to a clan of giants or to the ghosts of dead kings dwelling there (Dt 1:4; 3:1–13).

Edrei A city mentioned in association with the Rephaim on tablets found at the sites of the ancient cities Ugarit and Ashtaroth.

Balak Summons Balaam

22 Then the Israelites traveled to the plains of Moab and camped along the Jordan across from Jericho.

²Now Balak son of Zippor saw all that Israel had done to the Amorites, ³and Moab was terrified because there were so many people. Indeed, Moab was filled with dread because of the Israelites.

⁴The Moabites said to the elders of Midian, "This horde is going to lick up everything around us, as an ox licks up the grass of the field."

So Balak son of Zippor, who was king of Moab at that time, ⁵sent messengers to summon Balaam son of Beor, who was at Pethor, near the Euphrates River, in his native land. Balak said:

"A people has come out of Egypt; they cover the face of the land and have settled next to me. ⁶Now come and put a curse on these people, because they are too powerful for me. Perhaps then I will be able to defeat them and drive them out of the land. For I know that whoever you bless is blessed, and whoever you curse is cursed."

⁷The elders of Moab and Midian left, taking with them the fee for divination. When they came to Balaam, they told him what Balak had said.

⁸"Spend the night here," Balaam said to them, "and I will report back to you with the answer the LORD gives me." So the Moabite officials stayed with him.

⁹God came to Balaam and asked, "Who are these men with you?"

¹⁰Balaam said to God, "Balak son of Zippor, king of Moab, sent me this message: ¹¹'A people that has come out of Egypt covers the face of the land. Now come and put a curse on them for me. Perhaps then I will be able to fight them and drive them away.'"

¹²But God said to Balaam, "Do not go with them. You must not put a curse on those people, because they are blessed."

¹³The next morning Balaam got up and said to Balak's officials, "Go back to your own country, for the LORD has refused to let me go with you."

¹⁴So the Moabite officials returned to Balak and said, "Balaam refused to come with us."

¹⁵Then Balak sent other officials, more numerous and more distinguished than the first. ¹⁶They came to Balaam and said:

"This is what Balak son of Zippor says: Do not let anything keep you from coming to me, ¹⁷because I will reward you handsomely and do whatever you say. Come and put a curse on these people for me."

¹⁸But Balaam answered them, "Even if Balak gave me all the silver and gold in his palace, I could not do anything great or small to go beyond the command of the LORD my God. ¹⁹Now spend the night here so that I can find out what else the LORD will tell me."

²⁰That night God came to Balaam and said, "Since these men have come to summon you, go with them, but do only what I tell you."

Balaam's Donkey

²¹Balaam got up in the morning, saddled his donkey and went with the Moabite officials. ²²But God was very angry when he went, and the angel of the LORD stood in the road to oppose him. Balaam was riding on his donkey, and his two servants were with him. ²³When the donkey saw the angel of the LORD standing in the road with a drawn sword in his hand, it turned off the road into a field. Balaam beat it to get it back on the road.

²⁴Then the angel of the LORD stood in a narrow path through the vineyards, with walls on both

---

22:1–21 Numbers 22–24 contain the story of Balaam, a well-known seer hired by the king of Moab to curse Israel. Chapter 22 includes a miraculous (and possibly satirical) conversation between Balaam and his donkey, and closes with Balaam's arrival in Moab.

22:1 the Jordan across from Jericho The city of Jericho is not in the plains of Moab, but the hill country of Canaan. The Hebrew phrase used here, *yarden yericho* (which may be literally rendered "Jordan of Jericho"), probably refers to a seasonal river on both sides of the Jordan in the vicinity of Jericho.

22:2 Israel had done to the Amorites Refers to the people of the kingdoms of Sihon and Og (see 21:21,25–26,31–35).

22:4 elders of Midian The clans of Midan were somehow allied with the Moabite king, perhaps because many Midianites lived in Moabite territory (Ge 36:35).

22:5 Balaam son of Beor Refers to a seer from Pethor, a place located near a river, although it is not clear from the Biblical text which river is intended.

22:6 put a curse on these people Balak seeks a man who could pronounce a powerful curse on his enemies at will. It was widely believed in the ancient Near East that uttered blessings or curses could literally accomplish blessing or cursing (see Ge 27; 48).

22:12 they are blessed The language of Israel as a blessed people evokes the blessings of the Abrahamic covenant (Ge 12:1–3; 27:33).

22:18 LORD my God Here, Balaam calls Yahweh his God. Balak may have specifically sought out Balaam because he was a follower of Yahweh, believing that Yahweh would listen to one of his own prophets.

22:20 do only what I tell you A directive that Balaam apparently obeys without wavering (Nu 22:35; compare 23:12,26).

22:22 God was very angry when he went It is unknown why God is angry with Balaam for going on a trip which he told him to make (v. 20). Perhaps Balaam's attitude or motivation angered God. The Hebrew wording here echoes other instances where God is angry with people in a rebellious state of mind (compare 12:9). Balaam

sides. ²⁵When the donkey saw the angel of the Lord, it pressed close to the wall, crushing Balaam's foot against it. So he beat the donkey again. ²⁶Then the angel of the Lord moved on ahead and stood in a narrow place where there was no room to turn, either to the right or to the left. ²⁷When the donkey saw the angel of the Lord, it lay down under Balaam, and he was angry and beat it with his staff. ²⁸Then the Lord opened the donkey's mouth, and it said to Balaam, "What have I done to you to make you beat me these three times?"

²⁹Balaam answered the donkey, "You have made a fool of me! If only I had a sword in my hand, I would kill you right now."

³⁰The donkey said to Balaam, "Am I not your own donkey, which you have always ridden, to this day? Have I been in the habit of doing this to you?"

"No," he said.

³¹Then the Lord opened Balaam's eyes, and he saw the angel of the Lord standing in the road with his sword drawn. So he bowed low and fell facedown.

³²The angel of the Lord asked him, "Why have you beaten your donkey these three times? I have come here to oppose you because your path is a reckless one before me.ᵃ ³³The donkey saw me and turned away from me these three times. If it had not turned away, I would certainly have killed you by now, but I would have spared it."

³⁴Balaam said to the angel of the Lord, "I have sinned. I did not realize you were standing in the road to oppose me. Now if you are displeased, I will go back."

³⁵The angel of the Lord said to Balaam, "Go with the men, but speak only what I tell you." So Balaam went with Balak's officials.

³⁶When Balak heard that Balaam was coming, he went out to meet him at the Moabite town on the Arnon border, at the edge of his territory. ³⁷Balak said to Balaam, "Did I not send you an urgent summons? Why didn't you come to me? Am I really not able to reward you?"

³⁸"Well, I have come to you now," Balaam replied. "But I can't say whatever I please. I must speak only what God puts in my mouth."

³⁹Then Balaam went with Balak to Kiriath Huzoth. ⁴⁰Balak sacrificed cattle and sheep, and gave some to Balaam and the officials who were with him. ⁴¹The next morning Balak took Balaam up to Bamoth Baal, and from there he could see the outskirts of the Israelite camp.

Balaam's First Message

23 Balaam said, "Build me seven altars here, and prepare seven bulls and seven rams for me." ²Balak did as Balaam said, and the two of them offered a bull and a ram on each altar.

³Then Balaam said to Balak, "Stay here beside your offering while I go aside. Perhaps the Lord will come to meet with me. Whatever he reveals to me I will tell you." Then he went off to a barren height.

⁴God met with him, and Balaam said, "I have prepared seven altars, and on each altar I have offered a bull and a ram."

⁵The Lord put a word in Balaam's mouth and said, "Go back to Balak and give him this word."

⁶So he went back to him and found him standing beside his offering, with all the Moabite officials. ⁷Then Balaam spoke his message:

"Balak brought me from Aram,
  the king of Moab from the eastern
    mountains.
'Come,' he said, 'curse Jacob for me;
  come, denounce Israel.'

ᵃ 32 The meaning of the Hebrew for this clause is uncertain.

---

may have wanted to curse Israel against God's wishes.
donkey The Hebrew word used here, *athon*, is a common term for a donkey. The point of humor or satire in what follows is that Balaam, a professional seer, cannot see the angel, but his donkey can.
22:31 the Lord opened Balaam's eyes The Hebrew wording used here serves as a deliberate, sarcastic contrast to Balaam's own later claim—that his own eyes are open to God's revelation (24:4,16).
22:32 your path is a reckless one Likely meaning that the purpose of the errand (cursing Israel) was repugnant to God (compare vv. 20,22,34).
22:36 Moabite town The Hebrew name used here, *ir mo'av*, suggests the city is Ar of Moab (21:15,28).
22:38 I must speak only what God puts in my mouth Balaam clearly asserts that he will speak only the words God gives to him.
23:1–30 Chapter 23 contains the first two of Balaam's four oracles and reports his interactions with Balak of Moab. All of his oracles speak of Israel's prosperity and future success. His first oracle in vv. 7–10 expresses his

inability to curse this people because they are blessed by Yahweh. The second oracle in vv. 18–24 similarly acknowledges Yahweh's blessing on Israel and emphasizes that Balaam has no power to take back that blessing. Balak is unhappy that Balaam has not cursed Israel as he had ordered (vv. 11–12,25). After each of the first two oracles, Balak moves Balaam to another location—first Mount Pisgah, then Peor—as Balak hopes for a better outcome (vv. 13–14,27–28).

23:1 seven altars This is the only time that multiple altars are used for one ritual in the OT. The use may reflect a polytheistic perspective with Balaam offering sacrifices and entreating multiple deities at once. See the infographic "Ancient Altars" on p. 127; see the table "Altars in the Old Testament" on p. 249. **seven** Given Balaam's non-Israelite context as a seer, the use of seven here may indicate a broader ancient Near Eastern belief in the mystical quality of the number seven.
23:3 Stay here beside your offering Balak was to stand by his sacrifice while Balaam sought divine revelation in private (see vv. 6,15,17; 24:1).

Altars in the Old Testament

ALTAR*	ALTAR TYPE	MATERIAL	REFERENCE
Noah's altar	open-air	earth	Ge 8:20-22
Abram's altar at Moreh	open-air	earth	Ge 12:6-7 (compare Ge 22:2)
Abram's altar between Bethel and Ai	open-air	earth	Ge 12:8 (compare Ge 13:3-4)
Abram's altar at Mamre/Hebron	open-air	earth	Ge 13:18
Abraham's altar at Moriah	open-air	earth	Ge 22:2,9 (compare Ge 12:6-7)
Isaac's altar at Beersheba	open-air	earth	Ge 26:25
Jacob's altar at Shechem	open-air	earth	Ge 33:20
Jacob's altar at Bethel	open-air	earth	Ge 35:1-7
Moses' altar after the Amalekites	open-air	earth	Ex 17:14-16
Moses' altar at Sinai	open-air	earth	Ex 24:4-8
[Balaam's seven altars]	open-air	earth	Nu 23
Joshua's altar on Ebal	open-air	uncut stone	Jos 8:30-31 (compare Dt 27:4-7)
The eastern tribes' altar of witness	open-air	earth	Jos 22:10-34
Gideon's altar	open-air	stone slab	Jdg 6:17-24
[Altar to Baal built by Gideon's father]	open-air	uncertain	Jdg 6:25-32
Manoah's altar	open-air	stone slab	Jdg 13:19-20
Israelites' altar during crisis with the tribe of Benjamin	open-air	uncertain	Jdg 21:1-7
Samuel's altar at Ramah	open-air	uncertain	1Sa 7:17
Saul's altar	open-air	stone slab	1Sa 14:31-35
David's altar in Jerusalem	open-air	uncertain	2Sa 24:18-25; 1Ch 21:18-27
[Altar of the prophets of Baal]	open-air	uncertain	1Ki 18:22-26
Elijah's altar	open-air	stone	1Ki 18:30-35
[Israelites' altars mentioned by Isaiah]	open-air	brick	Isa 65:3
Altar of the tabernacle	tabernacle‡	acacia wood; bronze	Ex 27:1-8; 40:6-7 (compare 2Ch 1:5)

Altars in the Old Testament (continued)

ALTAR*	ALTAR TYPE	MATERIAL	REFERENCE
Incense altar for tabernacle	tabernacle‡	acacia wood; gold	Ex 30:1–10
Bronze altar for Solomon's temple	temple‡	bronze	2Ch 4:1
Incense altar for Solomon's temple	temple‡	gold	1Ki 6:22; 7:48
Altar at Shiloh	tabernacle‡	unknown	1Sa 2:33
Altar at Gibeon	high place†	unknown	1Ki 3:4; 1Ch 21:29
[Jeroboam's altar at Bethel]	high place†	unknown	1Ki 12:32–33 (compare 2Ki 23:15)
[Ahab's altar to Baal in Samaria]	temple of Baal	unknown	1Ki 16:32
[Ahaz's altar in the temple, and other idolatrous actions]	temple‡	unknown	2Ki 16:10–16; compare 2Ch 28:22–27
[Manasseh's altars to Baal and other deities]	high places†, temple‡	unknown	2Ki 21:1–9; 2Ch 33:1–9 (compare 2Ch 33:10–20)
[Altars destroyed in Asa's reform]	high places†	unknown	2Ch 14:2–5
[Altars to Baal destroyed in Jehoiada's reform]	temple of Baal	unknown	2Ki 11:17–18; 2Ch 23:17
[Illicit altars to Yahweh destroyed by Hezekiah]	high places†, temple‡	unknown	2Ki 18:22; 2Ch 30:14
[Altars to various deities destroyed in Hezekiah's reform]	high places†	unknown	2Ch 31:1
[Altars to various deities destroyed in Josiah's reform]	various	unknown	2Ki 23:1–20; 2Ch 34:1–7
Ezekiel's vision of (bronze) altar	temple‡	uncertain	Eze 43:13–17
Restored altar after Babylonian exile	temple‡	unknown	Ezr 3:2; Ne 10:34
Restored incense altar in the Second Temple	temple‡	unknown	Lk 1:11

*Foreign or illicit altars are in [brackets].

‡The ministry before tabernacle and temple altars was restricted to Aaron and his sons (Nu 18:1–7).

†The various "high places" condemned in Scripture may have had altars at them (compare 2Ki 23:20; 2Ch 34:5).

⁸How can I curse
   those whom God has not cursed?
 How can I denounce
   those whom the LORD has not
      denounced?
⁹From the rocky peaks I see them,
   from the heights I view them.
 I see a people who live apart
   and do not consider themselves one
      of the nations.
¹⁰Who can count the dust of Jacob
   or number even a fourth of Israel?
 Let me die the death of the righteous,
   and may my final end be like theirs!"

¹¹Balak said to Balaam, "What have you done to me? I brought you to curse my enemies, but you have done nothing but bless them!"

¹²He answered, "Must I not speak what the LORD puts in my mouth?"

Balaam's Second Message

¹³Then Balak said to him, "Come with me to another place where you can see them; you will not see them all but only the outskirts of their camp. And from there, curse them for me." ¹⁴So he took him to the field of Zophim on the top of Pisgah, and there he built seven altars and offered a bull and a ram on each altar.

¹⁵Balaam said to Balak, "Stay here beside your offering while I meet with him over there."

¹⁶The LORD met with Balaam and put a word in his mouth and said, "Go back to Balak and give him this word."

¹⁷So he went to him and found him standing beside his offering, with the Moabite officials. Balak asked him, "What did the LORD say?"

¹⁸Then he spoke his message:

"Arise, Balak, and listen;
   hear me, son of Zippor.

¹⁹God is not human, that he should lie,
   not a human being, that he should change
      his mind.
 Does he speak and then not act?
 Does he promise and not fulfill?
²⁰I have received a command to bless;
   he has blessed, and I cannot change it.

²¹"No misfortune is seen in Jacob,
   no misery observed*a* in Israel.
 The LORD their God is with them;
   the shout of the King is among them.
²²God brought them out of Egypt;
   they have the strength of a wild ox.
²³There is no divination against*b* Jacob,
   no evil omens against*b* Israel.
 It will now be said of Jacob
   and of Israel, 'See what God
      has done!'
²⁴The people rise like a lioness;
   they rouse themselves like a lion
 that does not rest till it devours its prey
   and drinks the blood of its victims."

²⁵Then Balak said to Balaam, "Neither curse them at all nor bless them at all!"

²⁶Balaam answered, "Did I not tell you I must do whatever the LORD says?"

Balaam's Third Message

²⁷Then Balak said to Balaam, "Come, let me take you to another place. Perhaps it will please God to let you curse them for me from there." ²⁸And Balak took Balaam to the top of Peor, overlooking the wasteland.

²⁹Balaam said, "Build me seven altars here, and prepare seven bulls and seven rams for me." ³⁰Balak did as Balaam had said, and offered a bull and a ram on each altar.

a 21 Or *He has not looked on Jacob's offenses / or on the wrongs found   *b 23* Or *in*

23:10 count the dust of Jacob Echoes Yahweh's promise to Abram (Abraham) in Ge 13:16. **a fourth** The rare Hebrew word used here, *rova'*, means either a "fourth" or "dust cloud." Most English translations opt for the former (compare 2Ki 6:25), but a reference to dust may better fit the Hebrew parallelism with the preceding poetic line that uses *aphar* (the more common Hebrew word for dust). However, an allusion to just part of the Israelite population also fits the larger context where Balak takes Balaam to sites where he can see different sections of the Israelite camp (Nu 22:41; 23:13).

23:13 another place Balak takes Balaam to another site to see a different section of the Israelite camp (compare 22:41).

23:14 field of Zophim Possibly a location associated with observing the sky for omens. **Pisgah** Likely refers to another mountain of the Abarim range (21:20). **seven altars** Balak reproduces the setup Balaam had ordered

for the first oracle (vv. 1–2), though Balaam does not explicitly ask for it here (compare vv. 29–30).

23:18 Arise, Balak, and listen This oracle is addressed specifically to Balak, the man who hired Balaam to curse Israel.

23:19 that he should change his mind Indicates that God will not change something he has decreed or promised. The message for Balak is that nothing he does will induce God to permit him to curse Israel.

23:25 nor bless them at all Balak reasons that if he cannot get a curse against Israel out of Balaam, neither does he want a blessing.

23:27 to let you curse them for me Balak likely prods Balaam to pronounce a curse and then look for God's approval. This betrays Balak's assumption that certain people had the ability to affect the will of the gods through speech.

23:28 Peor Another mountain in the Abarim range, overlooking Israel's camp (21:11; compare 23:14).

24

Now when Balaam saw that it pleased the LORD to bless Israel, he did not resort to divination as at other times, but turned his face toward the wilderness. [2]When Balaam looked out and saw Israel encamped tribe by tribe, the Spirit of God came on him [3]and he spoke his message:

"The prophecy of Balaam son of Beor,
  the prophecy of one whose eye sees clearly,
[4]the prophecy of one who hears the words
    of God,
  who sees a vision from the Almighty,[a]
  who falls prostrate, and whose eyes are
    opened:

[5]"How beautiful are your tents, Jacob,
  your dwelling places, Israel!

[6]"Like valleys they spread out,
  like gardens beside a river,
like aloes planted by the LORD,
  like cedars beside the waters.
[7]Water will flow from their buckets;
  their seed will have abundant water.

"Their king will be greater than Agag;
  their kingdom will be exalted.

[8]"God brought them out of Egypt;
  they have the strength of a wild ox.
They devour hostile nations
  and break their bones in pieces;
  with their arrows they pierce them.
[9]Like a lion they crouch and lie down,
  like a lioness — who dares to rouse them?

"May those who bless you be blessed
  and those who curse you be cursed!"

[10]Then Balak's anger burned against Balaam. He struck his hands together and said to him, "I summoned you to curse my enemies, but you have blessed them these three times. [11]Now leave at once and go home! I said I would reward you handsomely, but the LORD has kept you from being rewarded."

[12]Balaam answered Balak, "Did I not tell the messengers you sent me, [13]'Even if Balak gave me all the silver and gold in his palace, I could not do anything of my own accord, good or bad, to go beyond the command of the LORD — and I must say only what the LORD says'? [14]Now I am going back to my people, but come, let me warn you of what this people will do to your people in days to come."

Balaam's Fourth Message

[15]Then he spoke his message:

"The prophecy of Balaam son of Beor,
  the prophecy of one whose eye sees clearly,
[16]the prophecy of one who hears the words
    of God,
  who has knowledge from the Most High,
who sees a vision from the Almighty,
  who falls prostrate, and whose eyes are
    opened:

[17]"I see him, but not now;
  I behold him, but not near.
A star will come out of Jacob;
  a scepter will rise out of Israel.
He will crush the foreheads of Moab,
  the skulls[b] of[c] all the people of Sheth.[d]

---

[a] 4 Hebrew *Shaddai*; also in verse 16   [b] 17 Samaritan Pentateuch (see also Jer. 48:45); the meaning of the word in the Masoretic Text is uncertain.   [c] 17 Or possibly *Moab, / batter*   [d] 17 Or *all the noisy boasters*

24:1–14 This passage is the third of Balaam's four oracles. As with the earlier two oracles (ch. 23), Balaam is obligated to speak only what Yahweh authorizes, so he can only speak favorably about Israel (23:26; 24:12–13). By now, Balaam has resigned himself to Yahweh's intent to bless Israel (v. 1), but Balak is again surprised and angered (vv. 10–11).

24:1 he did not resort to divination This is the first time that Balaam's use of divination is mentioned explicitly. He was probably going off alone to seek God through divination before the previous two oracles (23:3,15). Balaam has learned that Yahweh communicates directly, not through typical divination practices like omens (23:23).

24:2 the Spirit of God came on him Instead of receiving messages from Yahweh through omens, a dream (22:9,20), or having Yahweh's words placed directly into his mouth (23:5,16), Balaam speaks prophetically through the power of God's spirit.

24:7 Their king An early reference to an Israelite king. Despite Samuel's later resistance to kingship (1Sa 12), God alludes to the later establishment of a royal line in Israel here and in other passages in the Pentateuch (Ge 17:6,16; 35:11; compare Nu 23:21; Dt 17:14–20).

24:11 has kept you from being rewarded Balak declares that Yahweh has prevented Balaam from being paid and from the honor that comes with his position as a well-known seer.

24:13 I must say only what the LORD says Balaam reminds Balak that he offered no guarantee of cursing, but would say only what Yahweh told him to say.

24:14 what this people will do to your people Balaam's final oracle is a prophecy of Israel's future victory over enemies in the Transjordan including Moab, Edom and Amalek.

24:15–25 Balaam's final oracle predicts the destruction of Moab and other enemies of Israel (compare Nu 23–24). The wording of this oracle often echoes the third oracle. This prophecy may have frightened Balak, the king of Moab, so much that he orchestrated leading Israel to worship other gods so that Yahweh would punish rather than bless them. The account of Israel's idolatry with the Baal of Peor follows this oracle immediately (Nu 25:1–9). Israel was drawn into Baal worship through the influence of Moabite women.

24:17 star Elsewhere in the OT, the Hebrew word used here, *kokhav*, serves as imagery for kingship (Isa 14:12; Eze 32:7). **scepter** The Hebrew word used here, *shevet*, refers to a tool used to punish people for wrongdoing or to oppress them.

[18] Edom will be conquered;
Seir, his enemy, will be conquered,
but Israel will grow strong.
[19] A ruler will come out of Jacob
and destroy the survivors of the city."

Balaam's Fifth Message

[20] Then Balaam saw Amalek and spoke his message:

"Amalek was first among the nations,
but their end will be utter destruction."

Balaam's Sixth Message

[21] Then he saw the Kenites and spoke his message:

"Your dwelling place is secure,
your nest is set in a rock;
[22] yet you Kenites will be destroyed
when Ashur takes you captive."

Balaam's Seventh Message

[23] Then he spoke his message:

"Alas! Who can live when God does this?[a]
[24] Ships will come from the shores of Cyprus;

they will subdue Ashur and Eber,
but they too will come to ruin."

[25] Then Balaam got up and returned home, and Balak went his own way.

Moab Seduces Israel

25 While Israel was staying in Shittim, the men began to indulge in sexual immorality with Moabite women, [2] who invited them to the sacrifices to their gods. The people ate the sacrificial meal and bowed down before these gods. [3] So Israel yoked themselves to the Baal of Peor. And the LORD's anger burned against them.

[4] The LORD said to Moses, "Take all the leaders of these people, kill them and expose them in broad daylight before the LORD, so that the LORD's fierce anger may turn away from Israel."

[5] So Moses said to Israel's judges, "Each of you must put to death those of your people who have yoked themselves to the Baal of Peor."

[6] Then an Israelite man brought into the camp a Midianite woman right before the eyes of Moses

---

[a] 23 Masoretic Text; with a different word division of the Hebrew *The people from the islands will gather from the north.*

24:20 Amalek Probably refers to the Amalekites, a clan of the Edomites (Ge 36:12; 1Ch 1:36) who lived in the Negev desert in the south of Canaan.
24:21 Kenites A tribe of nomadic or semi-nomadic Semitic people living in Canaan and the Sinai Peninsula.

KENITES
A nomadic group associated with Midian, Amalek and Israel through Moses' marriage to Zipporah (see Nu 10:29; Jdg 1:16). The Kenites were the descendants of Moses' father-in-law, who was a Midianite priest (Ex 3:1). At some point, the Kenites merged with the Amalekites, but parted ways after Saul threatened to kill all who lived among the Amalekites (1Sa 15:6–7). In some cases, the Kenites are allies of the Israelites (Jdg 1:16; 4:11).

24:22 when Ashur takes you captive Likely referring to the military conquest of the region by the Assyrians in the eighth century BC.

25:1–18 Although Balaam does not appear in Nu 25, this passage is placed here to connect it to the narrative of chs. 22–24. According to 31:16, Balaam encouraged the Moabites (who were allied with Midian; 22:4,7) to lead Israel into idol worship at Baal Peor. The Israelites may have been guilty of sexual immorality with foreign women, which the OT condemns as invariably leading to worship of their gods (Ex 34:15–16; see note on Nu 25:1).
In response to the idolatry, God sends a pestilence and sentences the leaders to death (25:4–5). When an Israelite man and a Midianite woman begin flaunting their relationship at the entrance to the tabernacle, Phinhas—son of Eleazar the high priest—impales the couple, halting the plague (vv. 6–9). For his zeal, Yahweh rewards Phinehas by granting him and his descendants (the Zadokites) a perpetual place in the priesthood (vv. 10–18).

25:1 Shittim The Hebrew name for this site, *shittim*, comes from the word *shittah*, meaning acacia bush. The site, also called Abel Shittim, was the last stop in Israel's wilderness journey (33:48–49). **to indulge in sexual immorality with** The full extent of Israel's sin is obscured by the use here of the Hebrew word *zanah*. While the term denotes sexual immorality, it is often used metaphorically for apostasy. The worship of gods other than Yahweh is cast as marital infidelity. The warning of Ex 34:15–16 similarly conflates idol worship and sexual immorality. The use of the language of sexual infidelity is often used to infer that Canaanite worship had sexual elements and that Israel is punished here for sexual sin. However, the context of Nu 25:1–5 only supports the inference that Israel was worshiping at a shrine to Baal. For example, the women of Moab were guilty of inviting the people (*ha'am* in Hebrew; v. 1) of Israel to their sacrifices, not just the men. The Hebrew of vv. 1–2 refers to "the people" three times, indicting the nation as a whole for the sin of idolatry rather than accusing the men alone of sexual sin (compare note on v. 8). Other Biblical references to this event also only condemn the idolatry that led to the plague (31:16; Dt 4:3; Jos 22:17; Ps 106:28).
25:2 The people ate A reference to partaking in sacrificial meals dedicated to the regional deities.
25:3 Baal of Peor Baal is a Canaanite and Hebrew word for "lord" as well as the name of a Canaanite god. Peor is the name of the location. Evidence from the OT and Canaanite literature suggests Baal was worshiped in various regional manifestations. See the table "Pagan Deities of the Old Testament" on p. 1287. **burned** Yahweh's anger apparently took the form of a plague (Nu 25:8–9).

25:6–18 The first part of this narrative provided a general account of Israel's apostasy at Peor (vv. 1–5). This passage relates a specific example of an unrepentant Israelite leader (vv. 6–9). See the table "Covenants in the Old Testament" on p. 469.

25:6 they were weeping The Hebrew word used here, *bakhah*, refers to mourning and penitent pleading with

and the whole assembly of Israel while they were weeping at the entrance to the tent of meeting. [7]When Phinehas son of Eleazar, the son of Aaron, the priest, saw this, he left the assembly, took a spear in his hand [8]and followed the Israelite into the tent. He drove the spear into both of them, right through the Israelite man and into the woman's stomach. Then the plague against the Israelites was stopped; [9]but those who died in the plague numbered 24,000.

[10]The LORD said to Moses, [11]"Phinehas son of Eleazar, the son of Aaron, the priest, has turned my anger away from the Israelites. Since he was as zealous for my honor among them as I am, I did not put an end to them in my zeal. [12]Therefore tell him I am making my covenant of peace with him. [13]He and his descendants will have a covenant of a lasting priesthood, because he was zealous for the honor of his God and made atonement for the Israelites."

[14]The name of the Israelite who was killed with the Midianite woman was Zimri son of Salu, the leader of a Simeonite family. [15]And the name of the Midianite woman who was put to death was Kozbi daughter of Zur, a tribal chief of a Midianite family.

[16]The LORD said to Moses, [17]"Treat the Midianites as enemies and kill them. [18]They treated you as enemies when they deceived you in the Peor incident involving their sister Kozbi, the daughter of a Midianite leader, the woman who was killed when the plague came as a result of that incident."

The Second Census

26 After the plague the LORD said to Moses and Eleazar son of Aaron, the priest, [2]"Take a census of the whole Israelite community by families — all those twenty years old or more who are able to serve in the army of Israel." [3]So on the plains of Moab by the Jordan across from Jericho, Moses and Eleazar the priest spoke with them and said, [4]"Take a census of the men twenty years old or more, as the LORD commanded Moses."

These were the Israelites who came out of Egypt:

[5]The descendants of Reuben, the firstborn son of Israel, were:

through Hanok, the Hanokite clan;
through Pallu, the Palluite clan;
[6]through Hezron, the Hezronite clan;
through Karmi, the Karmite clan.

[7]These were the clans of Reuben; those numbered were 43,730.

[8]The son of Pallu was Eliab, [9]and the sons of Eliab were Nemuel, Dathan and Abiram. The same Dathan and Abiram were the community officials who rebelled against Moses and Aaron and were among Korah's followers when they rebelled against the LORD. [10]The earth opened its mouth and swallowed them along with Korah, whose followers died when the fire devoured the 250 men. And they served as a warning sign. [11]The line of Korah, however, did not die out.

Yahweh in the face of hardship. Moses and the people of Israel were weeping due to the outbreak of plague. **at the entrance to the tent of meeting** Refers to the courtyard of the tabernacle (Ex 27:9; see note on Lev 1:3). The offense was not that the man brought a foreigner into the sacred space. Rather, his act was a brash display of impiety in full view of the people entreating Yahweh for mercy (compare note on Nu 25:1; note on 25:1–18; note on 25:8).
25:8 tent The Hebrew word used here, *qubbah*, refers to a domed room or tent. This is the only use of the word in the OT. In later rabbinic literature, *qubbah* is a word for brothel (see the rabbinic work Babylonian Talmud Abodah Zarah 17b). **He drove the spear into both of them, right through** Possibly implying that the couple was engaged in sexual intercourse since Phinehas kills the two with a single thrust of his spear. Their apparent physical position is the primary evidence for inferring a sexual aspect to the incident at Baal Peor, but the summary statement in Nu 25:18 treats this as a matter separate from the idolatry at Peor. **into the woman's stomach** The Hebrew word used here, *qevah*, could refer to either the woman's womb or pubic region, emphasizing that the (likely) sexual relationship was leading to idolatry (see note on 25:1–18). The verse contains wordplay between the Hebrew words *qevah* and *qubbah* (the word for a tent or domed room used earlier in the verse).
25:11 as zealous for my honor among them as I am God interprets Phinehas' act as an act of solidarity with Yahweh, rooted in the proper emotional response for the time to apostasy.

25:13 a covenant of a lasting priesthood It is unclear whether this means that Phinehas' line would succeed Aaron's as high priest, or whether his line (later called the Zadokites; compare Eze 44:15–16) would forever be the exclusive priests who served in the temple (when it was built). The latter is probably correct, since the text refers to the priesthood, not the high priesthood.
25:17 Treat the Midianites as enemies The Israelites do just this in Nu 31. Elsewhere, the Israelites kill the Midianite tribal chiefs, who are called both kings (31:8) and chieftains (Jos 13:21).

26:1–65 As was the case nearly 40 years earlier (Nu 1), Israel conducts a census of all men over 20 years of age able to fight for the promised land. The account of Israel's journeying through the wilderness begins and ends with a census (compare 1:20–43). The first census counted the people by tribe, and the Israelite camp in the wilderness was arranged according to tribe (see ch. 2). This census counts the people by clan, and the tribal allotments described next are organized by clan (vv. 52–65). See note on 1:46.

26:5 descendants of Reuben The four clans of Reuben listed here are identical to those in Ge 46:9; Ex 6:14; and 1Ch 5:3.
26:9 Dathan and Abiram For most tribes, the only information given in this chapter relates to their clans and the size of the tribe. For Reuben, the involvement of Reubenites in the rebellion against Moses in Nu 16 is singled out for comment.

¹²The descendants of Simeon by their clans were:
through Nemuel, the Nemuelite clan;
through Jamin, the Jaminite clan;
through Jakin, the Jakinite clan;
¹³through Zerah, the Zerahite clan;
through Shaul, the Shaulite clan.
¹⁴These were the clans of Simeon; those numbered were 22,200.

¹⁵The descendants of Gad by their clans were:
through Zephon, the Zephonite clan;
through Haggi, the Haggite clan;
through Shuni, the Shunite clan;
¹⁶through Ozni, the Oznite clan;
through Eri, the Erite clan;
¹⁷through Arodi,ᵃ the Arodite clan;
through Areli, the Arelite clan.
¹⁸These were the clans of Gad; those numbered were 40,500.

¹⁹Er and Onan were sons of Judah, but they died in Canaan.
²⁰The descendants of Judah by their clans were:
through Shelah, the Shelanite clan;
through Perez, the Perezite clan;
through Zerah, the Zerahite clan.
²¹The descendants of Perez were:
through Hezron, the Hezronite clan;
through Hamul, the Hamulite clan.
²²These were the clans of Judah; those numbered were 76,500.

²³The descendants of Issachar by their clans were:
through Tola, the Tolaite clan;
through Puah, the Puiteᵇ clan;
²⁴through Jashub, the Jashubite clan;
through Shimron, the Shimronite clan.
²⁵These were the clans of Issachar; those numbered were 64,300.

²⁶The descendants of Zebulun by their clans were:
through Sered, the Seredite clan;
through Elon, the Elonite clan;
through Jahleel, the Jahleelite clan.
²⁷These were the clans of Zebulun; those numbered were 60,500.

²⁸The descendants of Joseph by their clans through Manasseh and Ephraim were:

²⁹The descendants of Manasseh:
through Makir, the Makirite clan (Makir was the father of Gilead);
through Gilead, the Gileadite clan.
³⁰These were the descendants of Gilead:
through Iezer, the Iezerite clan;
through Helek, the Helekite clan;
³¹through Asriel, the Asrielite clan;
through Shechem, the Shechemite clan;
³²through Shemida, the Shemidaite clan;
through Hepher, the Hepherite clan.
³³(Zelophehad son of Hepher had no sons; he had only daughters, whose names were Mahlah, Noah, Hoglah, Milkah and Tirzah.)
³⁴These were the clans of Manasseh; those numbered were 52,700.

³⁵These were the descendants of Ephraim by their clans:
through Shuthelah, the Shuthelahite clan;
through Beker, the Bekerite clan;
through Tahan, the Tahanite clan.
³⁶These were the descendants of Shuthelah:
through Eran, the Eranite clan.
³⁷These were the clans of Ephraim; those numbered were 32,500.

These were the descendants of Joseph by their clans.

³⁸The descendants of Benjamin by their clans were:
through Bela, the Belaite clan;
through Ashbel, the Ashbelite clan;
through Ahiram, the Ahiramite clan;
³⁹through Shupham,ᶜ the Shuphamite clan;
through Hupham, the Huphamite clan.
⁴⁰The descendants of Bela through Ard and Naaman were:
through Ard,ᵈ the Ardite clan;
through Naaman, the Naamite clan.

ᵃ 17 Samaritan Pentateuch and Syriac (see also Gen. 46:16); Masoretic Text *Arod*   ᵇ 23 Samaritan Pentateuch, Septuagint, Vulgate and Syriac (see also 1 Chron. 7:1); Masoretic Text *through Puvah, the Punite*   ᶜ 39 A few manuscripts of the Masoretic Text, Samaritan Pentateuch, Vulgate and Syriac (see also Septuagint); most manuscripts of the Masoretic Text *Shephupham*   ᵈ 40 Samaritan Pentateuch and Vulgate (see also Septuagint); Masoretic Text does not have *through Ard*.

26:12 Simeon by their clans One clan of Simeon found in Ge 46:10 and Ex 6:15 is missing here and in 1Ch 4:24. That clan may have died out by the time this passage was written.

26:20 Perezite The three clans of Judah are Shelah, Perez and Zerah. The line of Perez is highlighted because his second generation sons, Hezron and Hamul, were in the blessing of Jacob (compare Ge 46:12). The kings of Israel would come through this line (Ru 4:18–21; 1Ch 2:4–17), culminating with Jesus of Nazareth (Lk 3:23–33; Mt 1:3–16). See the people diagram "Judah to David" on p. 618.

26:23 descendants of Issachar Issachar's four sons are consistently identified as Tola, Puah, Jashub and Shimron (Ge 46:13; 1Ch 7:1).

26:24 Shimronite clan Both clans are the basis for two place names in the hill country of Ephraim.

26:26 descendants of Zebulun Unlike the other tribes, the Zebulunites are not mentioned in the genealogies outlined in 1Ch 2–8. The reason for this is unknown.

26:28 Manasseh and Ephraim Manasseh and Ephraim are listed by birth order, not the order in which they were blessed (see Ge 48:13–20).

26:33 Zelophehad This reference anticipates the legal case to come in Nu 27:1–11 where Zelophehad's daughters make a case for inheriting their father's land.

26:35 Beker According to Ge 46:21, Beker was a Benjaminite—not an Ephraimite—clan. Ephraim and Benjamin shared a common border, so the clan may have had ties to both tribes.

⁴¹These were the clans of Benjamin; those numbered were 45,600.

⁴²These were the descendants of Dan by their clans:

through Shuham, the Shuhamite clan.

These were the clans of Dan: ⁴³All of them were Shuhamite clans; and those numbered were 64,400.

⁴⁴The descendants of Asher by their clans were:

through Imnah, the Imnite clan;
through Ishvi, the Ishvite clan;
through Beriah, the Beriite clan;
⁴⁵and through the descendants of Beriah:
through Heber, the Heberite clan;
through Malkiel, the Malkielite clan.
⁴⁶(Asher had a daughter named Serah.)
⁴⁷These were the clans of Asher; those numbered were 53,400.

⁴⁸The descendants of Naphtali by their clans were:

through Jahzeel, the Jahzeelite clan;
through Guni, the Gunite clan;
⁴⁹through Jezer, the Jezerite clan;
through Shillem, the Shillemite clan.
⁵⁰These were the clans of Naphtali; those numbered were 45,400.

⁵¹The total number of the men of Israel was 601,730.

⁵²The LORD said to Moses, ⁵³"The land is to be allotted to them as an inheritance based on the number of names. ⁵⁴To a larger group give a larger inheritance, and to a smaller group a smaller one; each is to receive its inheritance according to the number of those listed. ⁵⁵Be sure that the land is distributed by lot. What each group inherits will be according to the names for its ancestral tribe. ⁵⁶Each inheritance is to be distributed by lot among the larger and smaller groups."

⁵⁷These were the Levites who were counted by their clans:

through Gershon, the Gershonite clan;
through Kohath, the Kohathite clan;
through Merari, the Merarite clan.
⁵⁸These also were Levite clans:
the Libnite clan,
the Hebronite clan,
the Mahlite clan,
the Mushite clan,
the Korahite clan.
(Kohath was the forefather of Amram; ⁵⁹the name of Amram's wife was Jochebed, a descendant of Levi, who was born to the Levites[a] in Egypt. To Amram she bore Aaron, Moses and their sister Miriam. ⁶⁰Aaron was the father of Nadab and Abihu, Eleazar and Ithamar. ⁶¹But Nadab and Abihu died when they made an offering before the LORD with unauthorized fire.)

⁶²All the male Levites a month old or more numbered 23,000. They were not counted along with the other Israelites because they received no inheritance among them.

⁶³These are the ones counted by Moses and Eleazar the priest when they counted the Israelites on the plains of Moab by the Jordan across from Jericho. ⁶⁴Not one of them was among those counted by Moses and Aaron the priest when they counted the Israelites in the Desert of Sinai. ⁶⁵For the LORD had told those Israelites they would surely die in the wilderness, and not one of them was left except Caleb son of Jephunneh and Joshua son of Nun.

ᵃ 59 Or Jochebed, a daughter of Levi, who was born to Levi

26:42 descendants of Dan The tribe of Dan is composed of one clan, indicating the tribe was small, despite the large numerical total.
26:44 descendants of Asher Genesis 46:17 and 1Ch 7:30 list four sons for Asher—Imnah, Ishvah, Ishvi and Beriah. However, this verse lists only three clans—Imnites, Ishvites and Beriites. It is possible that Asher had only three sons and that Ishvah and Ishvi are variant spellings of one name.
26:48 The descendants of Naphtali Jacob's son Naphtali was his second son by Bilhah (Ge 30:8). The same four sons of Naphtali are named in Ge 46:24–25 and 1Ch 7:13.
26:51 601,730 See note on Nu 1:46.
26:54 give a larger inheritance The land was allotted according to tribal size but the process also involved drawing lots (vv. 53–56).
26:57 Levites who were counted by their clans The descendants of Levi were in charge of the tabernacle (and later the temple). **Gershonite** The duties assigned to the Gershonites involved care and maintenance of the tent coverings, screens and other cloth materials (3:21–26; 4:24–28). **Kohathite** They were assigned the care of the furnishings of the tabernacle including the altars and the ark of the covenant (3:27–31; 4:34–37; 10:21).
Merarite Their duties involved the structural components of the tabernacle—the frames, pillars, tent pegs and cords (3:33–37; 4:29–33; 10:17).
26:58 Levite clans The five clans listed here are each part of the larger clans of Gershon, Kohath or Merari (3:21,27,33). **Korahite** A clan of the Izharites (see Ex 6:21,24). **Kohath was the forefather of Amram** The genealogy of Levi concludes in Nu 26:58–61 with the priests descended from Kohath through Aaron. See Ex 6:18,20,23.
26:59 their sister Miriam The only women mentioned in this Levitical genealogy appear in this verse—Jochebed and Miriam.
26:61 before the LORD with unauthorized fire The fate of Nadab and Abihu (Nu 3:4; Lev 10:1–2) serves as a warning to future generations of priests.
26:65 they would surely die in the wilderness The first generation of Israelites with Moses in the wilderness all died for their lack of faith except for Caleb and Joshua (Nu 14:28–30).

Zelophehad's Daughters

27:1-11pp — Nu 36:1-12

27 The daughters of Zelophehad son of Hepher, the son of Gilead, the son of Makir, the son of Manasseh, belonged to the clans of Manasseh son of Joseph. The names of the daughters were Mahlah, Noah, Hoglah, Milkah and Tirzah. They came forward ²and stood before Moses, Eleazar the priest, the leaders and the whole assembly at the entrance to the tent of meeting and said, ³"Our father died in the wilderness. He was not among Korah's followers, who banded together against the LORD, but he died for his own sin and left no sons. ⁴Why should our father's name disappear from his clan because he had no son? Give us property among our father's relatives."

⁵So Moses brought their case before the LORD, ⁶and the LORD said to him, ⁷"What Zelophehad's daughters are saying is right. You must certainly give them property as an inheritance among their father's relatives and give their father's inheritance to them.

⁸"Say to the Israelites, 'If a man dies and leaves no son, give his inheritance to his daughter. ⁹If he has no daughter, give his inheritance to his brothers. ¹⁰If he has no brothers, give his inheritance to his father's brothers. ¹¹If his father had no brothers, give his inheritance to the nearest relative in his clan, that he may possess it. This is to have the force of law for the Israelites, as the LORD commanded Moses.'"

Joshua to Succeed Moses

¹²Then the LORD said to Moses, "Go up this mountain in the Abarim Range and see the land I have given the Israelites. ¹³After you have seen it, you too will be gathered to your people, as your brother Aaron was, ¹⁴for when the community rebelled at the waters in the Desert of Zin, both of you disobeyed my command to honor me as holy before their eyes." (These were the waters of Meribah Kadesh, in the Desert of Zin.)

¹⁵Moses said to the LORD, ¹⁶"May the LORD, the God who gives breath to all living things, appoint someone over this community ¹⁷to go out and come in before them, one who will lead them out and bring them in, so the LORD's people will not be like sheep without a shepherd."

¹⁸So the LORD said to Moses, "Take Joshua son of Nun, a man in whom is the spirit of leadership,[a] and lay your hand on him. ¹⁹Have him stand before Eleazar the priest and the entire assembly and commission him in their presence. ²⁰Give him some of your authority so the whole Israelite community will obey him. ²¹He is to stand before Eleazar the priest, who will obtain decisions for him by inquiring of the Urim before the LORD.

---

[a] 18 Or *the Spirit*

27:1-11 Chapter 27 addresses the question of inheritance rights in the case of a clan member who dies with no sons to inherit his property but is survived by daughters. The case presupposes a system where the heirs are generally male but also draws on the principle that land holdings were to remain in the family (see Lev 25:25–34).

In this passage, the daughters of Zelophehad (who died without a male heir) plead their case to Moses; they argue that their father's name will be wiped out unless they inherit his land. Moses brings the question to Yahweh, who informs him that the daughters have the right to inherit. The resolution of their case established a law of succession in inheritance.

27:3 Our father died in the wilderness Their father was part of the first generation of Israelites who were not allowed to enter the promised land due to their rebellion (Nu 14:26–35).

27:4 among our father's relatives The law contains no provisions up to this point for women to inherit a share of their father's property. Hints in the patriarchal narratives, as well as ancient Near Eastern legal codes, do suggest that customs regarding female inheritance rights did exist (e.g., Ge 31:14; compare Naomi's situation in Ruth; see Ru 2:20).

27:7 You must certainly give them property as an inheritance Yahweh sides with Zelophehad's daughters. This passage consequently begins to lay out the rights of Israelite women with respect to property law.

27:8-11 Numbers 27:8–11 provides a sequence of inheritance, in the event that no immediate male heir is

alive: daughter, the deceased man's brothers, and then the nearest living clan relative.

27:11 nearest relative in his clan An example of the nearest kinsman being offered the right of inheritance appears in the legal proceedings of the book of Ruth (Ru 4).

27:12-23 Yahweh commands Moses to ascend the mountains of Abarim to view the promised land before he dies. Moses' death is reported in the final chapter of Deuteronomy (Dt 34). After Nu 27, Yahweh continues to give laws through Moses.

27:14 you disobeyed Moses is reminded of Yahweh's punishment, which he promised after Moses lost his temper against the people (20:12).

27:17 sheep without a shepherd Describes an absence of leadership. Moses is elsewhere described as Israel's shepherd (Isa 63:11; Ps 78:71).

27:18 Joshua Moses' apprentice and military general since the beginning of the Israelite's trek in the wilderness (Ex 17:9; see note on Jos 1:1). **in whom is the spirit** This phrase can be understood as the OT way of describing the working of the Holy Spirit. It may be describing the gift of wisdom (Dt 34:9), special skills (Ex 35:31) or courage (Jos 2:11; 5:1). **lay your hand on him** The transfer of Moses' authority to Joshua was represented by Moses laying his hands on him (Nu 27:23; compare 8:10; Lev 16:21).

27:21 by inquiring of the Urim An abbreviated reference to the Urim and Thummim, a mode of permitted divination by which Israel's high priest determined the will of Yahweh. See Ex 28:30 and note.

At his command he and the entire community of the Israelites will go out, and at his command they will come in."

²²Moses did as the Lᴏʀᴅ commanded him. He took Joshua and had him stand before Eleazar the priest and the whole assembly. ²³Then he laid his hands on him and commissioned him, as the Lᴏʀᴅ instructed through Moses.

Daily Offerings

28 The Lᴏʀᴅ said to Moses, ²"Give this command to the Israelites and say to them: 'Make sure that you present to me at the appointed time my food offerings, as an aroma pleasing to me.' ³Say to them: 'This is the food offering you are to present to the Lᴏʀᴅ: two lambs a year old without defect, as a regular burnt offering each day. ⁴Offer one lamb in the morning and the other at twilight, ⁵together with a grain offering of a tenth of an ephah*ᵃ* of the finest flour mixed with a quarter of a hin*ᵇ* of oil from pressed olives. ⁶This is the regular burnt offering instituted at Mount Sinai as a pleasing aroma, a food offering presented to the Lᴏʀᴅ. ⁷The accompanying drink offering is to be a quarter of a hin of fermented drink with each lamb. Pour out the drink offering to the Lᴏʀᴅ at the sanctuary. ⁸Offer the second lamb at twilight, along with the same kind of grain offering and drink offering that you offer in the morning. This is a food offering, an aroma pleasing to the Lᴏʀᴅ.

Sabbath Offerings

⁹"'On the Sabbath day, make an offering of two lambs a year old without defect, together with its drink offering and a grain offering of two-tenths of an ephah*ᶜ* of the finest flour mixed with olive oil. ¹⁰This is the burnt offering for every Sabbath, in addition to the regular burnt offering and its drink offering.

Monthly Offerings

¹¹"'On the first of every month, present to the Lᴏʀᴅ a burnt offering of two young bulls, one ram and seven male lambs a year old, all without defect. ¹²With each bull there is to be a grain offering of three-tenths of an ephah*ᵈ* of the finest flour mixed with oil; with the ram, a grain offering of two-tenths of an ephah of the finest flour mixed with oil; ¹³and with each lamb, a grain offering of a tenth of an ephah of the finest flour mixed with oil. This is for a burnt offering, a pleasing aroma, a food offering presented to the Lᴏʀᴅ. ¹⁴With each bull there is to be a drink offering of half a hin*ᵉ* of wine; with the ram, a third of a hin*ᶠ*; and with each lamb, a quarter of a hin. This is the monthly burnt offering to be made at each new moon during the year. ¹⁵Besides the regular burnt offering with its drink offering, one male goat is to be presented to the Lᴏʀᴅ as a sin offering.*ᵍ*

The Passover

28:16-25pp — Ex 12:14-20; Lev 23:4-8; Dt 16:1-8

¹⁶"'On the fourteenth day of the first month the Lᴏʀᴅ's Passover is to be held. ¹⁷On the fifteenth day of this month there is to be a festival; for seven days eat bread made without yeast. ¹⁸On the first day hold a sacred assembly and do no regular work. ¹⁹Present to the Lᴏʀᴅ a food offering consisting of a burnt offering of two young bulls, one ram and seven male lambs a year old, all without defect. ²⁰With each bull offer a grain offering of three-tenths of an ephah of the finest

---

ᵃ 5 That is, probably about 3 1/2 pounds or about 1.6 kilograms; also in verses 13, 21 and 29   *ᵇ 5* That is, about 1 quart or about 1 liter; also in verses 7 and 14   *ᶜ 9* That is, probably about 7 pounds or about 3.2 kilograms; also in verses 12, 20 and 28   *ᵈ 12* That is, probably about 11 pounds or about 5 kilograms; also in verses 20 and 28   *ᵉ 14* That is, about 2 quarts or about 1.9 liters   *ᶠ 14* That is, about 1 1/3 quarts or about 1.3 liters   *ᵍ 15* Or *purification offering*; also in verse 22

28:1—29:40 Numbers 28–29 detail the religious calendar the Israelites will follow in the promised land. Leviticus 23 outlines a full calendar. Numbers 28–29 adjusted or supplemented that calendar in several places in order to match later conditions, when Israel actually occupied the land (compare 15:1–12). Verses 1–8 list the daily offerings of the tabernacle, as they are the core of the sacrificial system. The schedule of holidays begins in v. 9. All of the regular offerings are explained in detail in Lev 1–7.

28:2 at the appointed time God considered the sacrifices invalid if they were offered at the wrong times (compare Nu 9:1–14).

28:9–10 The Israelite calendar required offerings beyond the daily offerings described in vv. 1–8. The Sabbath burnt offering described in vv. 9–10 is the same as the daily offering (two lambs), but the Sabbath grain offering is double in size. The comment in v. 10 probably means these two lambs are offered on the Sabbath in addition to the daily offering.

28:9 Sabbath The Sabbath is on the seventh day of each week, when the Israelites are forbidden from performing work. See Ex 20:8–11 and note.

28:11 first of every month Numbers 28:11–15 prescribes a monthly system of offerings that begins anew with each new moon.

28:16–25 This passage and its parallel in Lev 23:4–8 provide further regulations for Passover, the commemoration of Israel's deliverance from bondage in Egypt. See Ex 12:1–51 and note.

28:18 a sacred assembly The Hebrew phrase used here, *miqra qodesh*, refers to a holy event to which people are summoned or invited. **do no regular work** Given that sacrifices are to be given on the other days of the festival, an absolute statement prohibiting work would not make sense. Rather, work related to one's occupation is prohibited. Only the special work of Passover may be carried out.

flour mixed with oil; with the ram, two-tenths; [21]and with each of the seven lambs, one-tenth. [22]Include one male goat as a sin offering to make atonement for you. [23]Offer these in addition to the regular morning burnt offering. [24]In this way present the food offering every day for seven days as an aroma pleasing to the Lord; it is to be offered in addition to the regular burnt offering and its drink offering. [25]On the seventh day hold a sacred assembly and do no regular work.

The Festival of Weeks

28:26-31pp — Lev 23:15-22; Dt 16:9-12

[26]"'On the day of firstfruits, when you present to the Lord an offering of new grain during the Festival of Weeks, hold a sacred assembly and do no regular work. [27]Present a burnt offering of two young bulls, one ram and seven male lambs a year old as an aroma pleasing to the Lord. [28]With each bull there is to be a grain offering of three-tenths of an ephah of the finest flour mixed with oil; with the ram, two-tenths; [29]and with each of the seven lambs, one-tenth. [30]Include one male goat to make atonement for you. [31]Offer these together with their drink offerings, in addition to the regular burnt offering and its grain offering. Be sure the animals are without defect.

The Festival of Trumpets

29:1-6pp — Lev 23:23-25

29 "'On the first day of the seventh month hold a sacred assembly and do no regular work. It is a day for you to sound the trumpets. [2]As an aroma pleasing to the Lord, offer a burnt offering of one young bull, one ram and seven male lambs a year old, all without defect. [3]With the bull offer a grain offering of three-tenths of

an ephah[a] of the finest flour mixed with olive oil; with the ram, two-tenths[b]; [4]and with each of the seven lambs, one-tenth.[c] [5]Include one male goat as a sin offering[d] to make atonement for you. [6]These are in addition to the monthly and daily burnt offerings with their grain offerings and drink offerings as specified. They are food offerings presented to the Lord, a pleasing aroma.

The Day of Atonement

29:7-11pp — Lev 16:2-34; 23:26-32

[7]"'On the tenth day of this seventh month hold a sacred assembly. You must deny yourselves[e] and do no work. [8]Present as an aroma pleasing to the Lord a burnt offering of one young bull, one ram and seven male lambs a year old, all without defect. [9]With the bull offer a grain offering of three-tenths of an ephah of the finest flour mixed with oil; with the ram, two-tenths; [10]and with each of the seven lambs, one-tenth. [11]Include one male goat as a sin offering, in addition to the sin offering for atonement and the regular burnt offering with its grain offering, and their drink offerings.

The Festival of Tabernacles

29:12-39pp — Lev 23:33-43; Dt 16:13-17

[12]"'On the fifteenth day of the seventh month, hold a sacred assembly and do no regular work. Celebrate a festival to the Lord for seven days. [13]Present as an aroma pleasing to the Lord a food offering consisting of a burnt offering of thirteen young bulls, two rams and fourteen male lambs

a 3 That is, probably about 11 pounds or about 5 kilograms; also in verses 9 and 14   b 3 That is, probably about 7 pounds or about 3.2 kilograms; also in verses 9 and 14   c 4 That is, probably about 3 1/2 pounds or about 1.6 kilograms; also in verses 10 and 15   d 5 Or purification offering; also elsewhere in this chapter   e 7 Or must fast

---

28:26–31 The Festival of Weeks commemorates the beginning of the wheat harvest, seven weeks after the barley harvest (Lev 23:9–22).

28:26 firstfruits Giving Yahweh the first yield constitutes an act of trust that the remaining yield will be sufficient for the people's need. See Lev 23:9–22.

29:1–6 Numbers 29 continues the festival calendar, the description of which began in Nu 28. This passage lists the requirements for the Festival of Trumpets, held on the first day of the seventh month. The Festival of Trumpets is also described in Lev 23:23–25. The trumpeting of the shofar horn—made of a ram's horn—was sounded to give advance notice for the Festival of Booths (or Tabernacles), the pilgrimage festival that would occur two weeks later. In later Jewish tradition, this day marks the beginning of the Jewish year, Rosh Hashanah ("the head of the year"). See the table "Israelite Festivals" on p. 200.

29:7–11 The Day of Atonement (or Yom Kippur) was the holiest day of the year on the ancient Israelite calendar. The procedures carried out on this day provided an

annual cleansing or purging of ritual defilement from the tabernacle, especially the Most Holy Place (or Holy of Holies). See Lev 16:1–34 and note.

29:7 You must deny yourselves Traditionally understood to refer to fasting, a practice that is still a defining element of observances for Yom Kippur today.

29:12–38 The Festival of Booths (also known as Tabernacles or *sukkoth*) lasts seven days, with a final celebration on the eighth day. The feast is also discussed in Lev 23:34–43 and Dt 16:13–15. There are three major differences in the descriptions of the festival between Leviticus and Numbers: First, Nu 29:12–38 provides more detail about the large quantities of animal sacrifices required for each of the eight days of the feast, but these offerings are summarized very briefly in Lev 23:36. Second, Lev 23:33–43 emphasizes the celebratory nature of the feast and the purpose of memorializing the period of the wilderness wanderings by dwelling in booths, details that are completely absent from Nu 29:12–38. Finally, Numbers makes no mention of the species of tree involved in the celebration listed in Lev 23:40–43.

a year old, all without defect. ¹⁴With each of the thirteen bulls offer a grain offering of three-tenths of an ephah of the finest flour mixed with oil; with each of the two rams, two-tenths; ¹⁵and with each of the fourteen lambs, one-tenth. ¹⁶Include one male goat as a sin offering, in addition to the regular burnt offering with its grain offering and drink offering.

¹⁷"'On the second day offer twelve young bulls, two rams and fourteen male lambs a year old, all without defect. ¹⁸With the bulls, rams and lambs, offer their grain offerings and drink offerings according to the number specified. ¹⁹Include one male goat as a sin offering, in addition to the regular burnt offering with its grain offering, and their drink offerings.

²⁰"'On the third day offer eleven bulls, two rams and fourteen male lambs a year old, all without defect. ²¹With the bulls, rams and lambs, offer their grain offerings and drink offerings according to the number specified. ²²Include one male goat as a sin offering, in addition to the regular burnt offering with its grain offering and drink offering.

²³"'On the fourth day offer ten bulls, two rams and fourteen male lambs a year old, all without defect. ²⁴With the bulls, rams and lambs, offer their grain offerings and drink offerings according to the number specified. ²⁵Include one male goat as a sin offering, in addition to the regular burnt offering with its grain offering and drink offering.

²⁶"'On the fifth day offer nine bulls, two rams and fourteen male lambs a year old, all without defect. ²⁷With the bulls, rams and lambs, offer their grain offerings and drink offerings according to the number specified. ²⁸Include one male goat as a sin offering, in addition to the regular burnt offering with its grain offering and drink offering.

²⁹"'On the sixth day offer eight bulls, two rams and fourteen male lambs a year old, all without defect. ³⁰With the bulls, rams and lambs, offer their grain offerings and drink offerings according to the number specified. ³¹Include one male goat as a sin offering, in addition to the regular burnt offering with its grain offering and drink offering.

³²"'On the seventh day offer seven bulls, two rams and fourteen male lambs a year old, all without defect. ³³With the bulls, rams and lambs, offer their grain offerings and drink offerings according to the number specified. ³⁴Include one male goat as a sin offering, in addition to the regular burnt offering with its grain offering and drink offering.

³⁵"'On the eighth day hold a closing special assembly and do no regular work. ³⁶Present as an aroma pleasing to the LORD a food offering consisting of a burnt offering of one bull, one ram and seven male lambs a year old, all without defect. ³⁷With the bull, the ram and the lambs, offer their grain offerings and drink offerings according to the number specified. ³⁸Include one male goat as a sin offering, in addition to the regular burnt offering with its grain offering and drink offering.

³⁹"'In addition to what you vow and your freewill offerings, offer these to the LORD at your appointed festivals: your burnt offerings, grain offerings, drink offerings and fellowship offerings.'"

⁴⁰Moses told the Israelites all that the LORD commanded him.ᵃ

Vows

30 ᵇ Moses said to the heads of the tribes of Israel: "This is what the LORD commands: ²When a man makes a vow to the LORD or takes an oath to obligate himself by a pledge, he must not break his word but must do everything he said.

³"When a young woman still living in her father's household makes a vow to the LORD or obligates herself by a pledge ⁴and her father hears about her vow or pledge but says nothing to her, then all her vows and every pledge by which she obligated herself will stand. ⁵But if her father forbids her when he hears about it, none of her vows or the pledges by which she obligated herself will stand; the LORD will release her because her father has forbidden her.

ᵃ 40 In Hebrew texts this verse (29:40) is numbered 30:1.   ᵇ In Hebrew texts 30:1-16 is numbered 30:2-17.

29:18 according to the number specified Possibly referring to the quantities for drink offerings designated in Nu 28:7 or 28:14. This wording is repeated a number of times in this chapter with reference to the drink offerings. However, those designations are related to regular offerings, not offerings for a festival. If those quantities do not apply here, then this phrase refers to some other tradition, likely an oral tradition of the priests that contained this information.

29:39–40 These closing verses echo the introduction to this section on the Israelite calendar in 28:2. They also remind the people that these offerings for specific holidays are in addition to their regular offerings, most of which are detailed in Leviticus 1–7.

30:1–16 Numbers 30 deals with people who elect to make vows to Yahweh. Only one verse is allotted to describe the rules governing a male who makes a vow (v. 2), while the remaining fourteen verses describe the regulations surrounding women who make vows (vv. 3–16). The rules for women are not straightforward because their legal status is defined with respect to fathers or husbands.

30:2 obligate himself by a pledge To swear a vow or oath is no small matter, but is done on one's life, whether male or female (vv. 4,6).

30:3–16 A vow or oath by a woman could be nullified by the man whose authority she was under (usually either her father or husband). If the father or husband made no objection on the day he learned of the vow or oath, then the woman had to fulfill the vow or oath. If he nullified the vow, he had to endure its consequences. Widows and divorced women were exceptions because they were not subject to a male authority.

⁶"If she marries after she makes a vow or after her lips utter a rash promise by which she obligates herself ⁷and her husband hears about it but says nothing to her, then her vows or the pledges by which she obligated herself will stand. ⁸But if her husband forbids her when he hears about it, he nullifies the vow that obligates her or the rash promise by which she obligates herself, and the LORD will release her.

⁹"Any vow or obligation taken by a widow or divorced woman will be binding on her.

¹⁰"If a woman living with her husband makes a vow or obligates herself by a pledge under oath ¹¹and her husband hears about it but says nothing to her and does not forbid her, then all her vows or the pledges by which she obligated herself will stand. ¹²But if her husband nullifies them when he hears about them, then none of the vows or pledges that came from her lips will stand. Her husband has nullified them, and the LORD will release her. ¹³Her husband may confirm or nullify any vow she makes or any sworn pledge to deny herself.ᵃ ¹⁴But if her husband says nothing to her about it from day to day, then he confirms all her vows or the pledges binding on her. He confirms them by saying nothing to her when he hears about them. ¹⁵If, however, he nullifies them some time after he hears about them, then he must bear the consequences of her wrongdoing."

¹⁶These are the regulations the LORD gave Moses concerning relationships between a man and his wife, and between a father and his young daughter still living at home.

Vengeance on the Midianites

31 The LORD said to Moses, ²"Take vengeance on the Midianites for the Israelites. After that, you will be gathered to your people."

³So Moses said to the people, "Arm some of your men to go to war against the Midianites so that they may carry out the LORD's vengeance on them. ⁴Send into battle a thousand men from each of the tribes of Israel." ⁵So twelve thousand men armed for battle, a thousand from each tribe, were supplied from the clans of Israel. ⁶Moses sent them into battle, a thousand from each tribe, along with Phinehas son of Eleazar, the priest, who took with him articles from the sanctuary and the trumpets for signaling.

⁷They fought against Midian, as the LORD commanded Moses, and killed every man. ⁸Among their victims were Evi, Rekem, Zur, Hur and Reba — the five kings of Midian. They also killed Balaam son of Beor with the sword. ⁹The Israelites captured the Midianite women and children and took all the Midianite herds, flocks and goods as plunder. ¹⁰They burned all the towns where the Midianites had settled, as well as all their camps. ¹¹They took all the plunder and spoils, including the people and animals, ¹²and brought the captives, spoils and plunder to Moses and Eleazar the priest and the Israelite assembly at their camp on the plains of Moab, by the Jordan across from Jericho.

¹³Moses, Eleazar the priest and all the leaders of the community went to meet them outside the camp. ¹⁴Moses was angry with the officers of the army — the commanders of thousands and commanders of hundreds — who returned from the battle.

¹⁵"Have you allowed all the women to live?" he asked them. ¹⁶"They were the ones who followed Balaam's advice and enticed the Israelites to be

ᵃ 13 Or to fast

30:6 after she makes a vow This refers to a woman who marries while under a vow approved by her father. The vow here does not refer to her marriage or wedding. **after her lips utter a rash promise** The Hebrew noun used here, *mivta*, occurs only here and in v. 8. It is related to the Hebrew verb *batah* which refers to speaking thoughtlessly (Lev 5:4; Pr 12:18). The sense is that the vow has been made without regard for the consequences or implications.

30:10 a woman living with her husband Meaning that she initiated the vow or oath while they were married.

30:15 he must bear the consequences of her wrongdoing Refers to the responsibility of her vow and the consequences of breaking that vow. In causing his wife to break her vow to Yahweh, it is as if the husband himself has broken it.

31:1–54 This passage continues the story of Israel in the wilderness. The vengeance described in this passage results from the incident of Nu 25, where — presumably on the advice of Balaam — Midianite and Moabite women seduced the Israelites into worshiping Baal at Baal Peor.

31:2 Midianites Old Testament descriptions suggest that Midian was a region in northwest Arabia, east of the Gulf of Aqaba.

31:4 a thousand The Hebrew word used here, *eleph*, could denote a military unit with fewer than 1,000 men, rather than a literal group of 1,000. See note on 1:20–46.

31:6 Phinehas Son of Eleazar the high priest, who showed his zeal for Yahweh in the ordeal at Baal Peor (25:7–11). **articles from the sanctuary** This likely refers to the items used for the service of the tabernacle listed in Ex 37:16: pure gold plates and dishes for incense, and bowls and flagons (pitchers) with which to pour drink offerings.

31:8 Zur The father of the Midianite woman Phinehas slayed (Nu 25:15). This identification provides another link to the incident from ch. 25. **Balaam son of Beor** The seer upon whose advice the Midianites sought to influence Israel (chs. 22–24; 31:16).

31:13 outside the camp The army could not enter the camp because they were ritually impure from contact with human corpses (see 19:11–22; 31:19).

31:15 Have you allowed all the women to live Since the reason for vengeance against the Midianites was the behavior of their women, Moses is appalled at the fact that the soldiers did not kill them, but brought them back to the Israelite encampment.

31:16 enticed the Israelites to be unfaithful to the

unfaithful to the LORD in the Peor incident, so that a plague struck the LORD's people. [17]Now kill all the boys. And kill every woman who has slept with a man, [18]but save for yourselves every girl who has never slept with a man.

[19]"Anyone who has killed someone or touched someone who was killed must stay outside the camp seven days. On the third and seventh days you must purify yourselves and your captives. [20]Purify every garment as well as everything made of leather, goat hair or wood."

[21]Then Eleazar the priest said to the soldiers who had gone into battle, "This is what is required by the law that the LORD gave Moses: [22]Gold, silver, bronze, iron, tin, lead [23]and anything else that can withstand fire must be put through the fire, and then it will be clean. But it must also be purified with the water of cleansing. And whatever cannot withstand fire must be put through that water. [24]On the seventh day wash your clothes and you will be clean. Then you may come into the camp."

Dividing the Spoils

[25]The LORD said to Moses, [26]"You and Eleazar the priest and the family heads of the community are to count all the people and animals that were captured. [27]Divide the spoils equally between the soldiers who took part in the battle and the rest of the community. [28]From the soldiers who fought in the battle, set apart as tribute for the LORD one out of every five hundred, whether people, cattle, donkeys or sheep. [29]Take this tribute from their half share and give it to Eleazar the priest as the LORD's part. [30]From the Israelites' half, select one out of every fifty, whether people, cattle, donkeys, sheep or other animals. Give them to the Levites, who are responsible for the care of the LORD's tabernacle." [31]So Moses and Eleazar the priest did as the LORD commanded Moses.

[32]The plunder remaining from the spoils that the soldiers took was 675,000 sheep, [33]72,000 cattle, [34]61,000 donkeys [35]and 32,000 women who had never slept with a man.

[36]The half share of those who fought in the battle was:

337,500 sheep, [37]of which the tribute for the LORD was 675;
[38]36,000 cattle, of which the tribute for the LORD was 72;
[39]30,500 donkeys, of which the tribute for the LORD was 61;
[40]16,000 people, of whom the tribute for the LORD was 32.

[41]Moses gave the tribute to Eleazar the priest as the LORD's part, as the LORD commanded Moses.

[42]The half belonging to the Israelites, which Moses set apart from that of the fighting men — [43]the community's half — was 337,500 sheep, [44]36,000 cattle, [45]30,500 donkeys [46]and 16,000 people. [47]From the Israelites' half, Moses selected one out of every fifty people and animals, as the LORD commanded him, and gave them to the Levites, who were responsible for the care of the LORD's tabernacle.

[48]Then the officers who were over the units of the army — the commanders of thousands and commanders of hundreds — went to Moses [49]and said to him, "Your servants have counted the soldiers under our command, and not one is missing. [50]So we have brought as an offering to the LORD the gold articles each of us acquired — armlets, bracelets, signet rings, earrings and necklaces — to make atonement for ourselves before the LORD."

[51]Moses and Eleazar the priest accepted from them the gold — all the crafted articles. [52]All the gold from the commanders of thousands and commanders of hundreds that Moses and Eleazar presented as a gift to the LORD weighed 16,750 shekels.[a] [53]Each soldier had taken plunder for himself. [54]Moses and Eleazar the priest accepted the gold from the commanders of thousands and commanders of hundreds and brought it into the tent of meeting as a memorial for the Israelites before the LORD.

The Transjordan Tribes

32 The Reubenites and Gadites, who had very large herds and flocks, saw that the lands of Jazer and Gilead were suitable for livestock.

[a] 52 That is, about 420 pounds or about 190 kilograms

LORD That is, to submit themselves to the Canaanite god Baal at Peor (25:3).
31:17 every woman who has slept with a man In some contexts following a battle, the Israelites were allowed to take women as wives if they were not native Canaanites (Dt 20:14; compare Ge 34:28–29). However, the women described in this passage, who had been involved in the idolatry and apostasy that cost Israelite lives, could not be spared; all the non-virgins were slain.
31:19 purify yourselves Any person contaminated by contact with a corpse (in this case, the army) had to be purified with the ashes of the red heifer on the third and seventh days of the week following the contamination (Nu 19).

31:27 the spoils Yahweh instructs Moses how to divide the spoils of war. One half went to the warriors and the other half was distributed to the rest of the community.
31:29 as the LORD's part One out of every five hundred captives and animals would be used in service of the priesthood whether for work or for sacrifice.
31:50 to make atonement for ourselves before the LORD A ransom paid to Yahweh for his protection over their lives (compare 8:19; Ex 30:11–16; Lev 17:11).
31:53 Each soldier had taken plunder for himself The commanders donated an amount equal to twice that needed as a ransom for the whole army. As a result, each foot soldier who was not an officer kept his own plunder.

²So they came to Moses and Eleazar the priest and to the leaders of the community, and said, ³"Ataroth, Dibon, Jazer, Nimrah, Heshbon, Elealeh, Sebam, Nebo and Beon— ⁴the land the LORD subdued before the people of Israel—are suitable for livestock, and your servants have livestock. ⁵If we have found favor in your eyes," they said, "let this land be given to your servants as our possession. Do not make us cross the Jordan."

⁶Moses said to the Gadites and Reubenites, "Should your fellow Israelites go to war while you sit here? ⁷Why do you discourage the Israelites from crossing over into the land the LORD has given them? ⁸This is what your fathers did when I sent them from Kadesh Barnea to look over the land. ⁹After they went up to the Valley of Eshkol and viewed the land, they discouraged the Israelites from entering the land the LORD had given them. ¹⁰The LORD's anger was aroused that day and he swore this oath: ¹¹'Because they have not followed me wholeheartedly, not one of those who were twenty years old or more when they came up out of Egypt will see the land I promised on oath to Abraham, Isaac and Jacob— ¹²not one except Caleb son of Jephunneh the Kenizzite and Joshua son of Nun, for they followed the LORD wholeheartedly.' ¹³The LORD's anger burned against Israel and he made them wander in the wilderness forty years, until the whole generation of those who had done evil in his sight was gone.

¹⁴"And here you are, a brood of sinners, standing in the place of your fathers and making the LORD even more angry with Israel. ¹⁵If you turn away from following him, he will again leave all this people in the wilderness, and you will be the cause of their destruction."

¹⁶Then they came up to him and said, "We would like to build pens here for our livestock and cities for our women and children. ¹⁷But we will arm ourselves for battle[a] and go ahead of the Israelites until we have brought them to their place. Meanwhile our women and children will live in fortified cities, for protection from the inhabitants of the land. ¹⁸We will not return to our homes until each of the Israelites has received their inheritance. ¹⁹We will not receive any inheritance with them on the other side of the Jordan, because our inheritance has come to us on the east side of the Jordan."

²⁰Then Moses said to them, "If you will do this— if you will arm yourselves before the LORD for battle ²¹and if all of you who are armed cross over the Jordan before the LORD until he has driven his enemies out before him— ²²then when the land is subdued before the LORD, you may return and be free from your obligation to the LORD and to Israel. And this land will be your possession before the LORD.

²³"But if you fail to do this, you will be sinning against the LORD; and you may be sure that your sin will find you out. ²⁴Build cities for your women and children, and pens for your flocks, but do what you have promised."

²⁵The Gadites and Reubenites said to Moses, "We your servants will do as our lord commands. ²⁶Our children and wives, our flocks and herds will remain here in the cities of Gilead. ²⁷But your servants, every man who is armed for battle, will cross over to fight before the LORD, just as our lord says."

²⁸Then Moses gave orders about them to Eleazar the priest and Joshua son of Nun and to the family heads of the Israelite tribes. ²⁹He said to them, "If the Gadites and Reubenites, every man armed for battle, cross over the Jordan with you before the LORD, then when the land is subdued before you, you must give them the land of Gilead as their possession. ³⁰But if they do not cross over with you armed, they must accept their possession with you in Canaan."

³¹The Gadites and Reubenites answered, "Your servants will do what the LORD has said. ³²We will cross over before the LORD into Canaan armed, but the property we inherit will be on this side of the Jordan."

³³Then Moses gave to the Gadites, the Reubenites and the half-tribe of Manasseh son of Joseph

---

[a] 17 Septuagint; Hebrew *will be quick to arm ourselves*

32:1–42 The tribes of Gad and Reuben ask to settle in the Transjordan because the area provides enough space for their large livestock holdings. The request means that they will not receive land in Canaan proper.

32:1 lands of Jazer Numbers 21:32 distinguishes Jazer from the Heshbon region. See Dt 3:12–13; Jos 12:2,5; 13:31.

32:2 Eleazar The allotment of the land involved assigning regions by lot (Nu 26:55–56), and Eleazar, as high priest was responsible for the Urim and Thummim used to determine such a matter (27:21; see note on Ex 28:30).

32:4 the land the LORD subdued The tribes identify the areas they wish to settle by listing nine of the towns conquered in the region (32:3).

32:8 This is what your fathers did Moses suspects that Reuben and Gad, like the ten spies from the previous generation, fear the giant Anakite and Rephaim tribes in Canaan and are making an excuse to remain to the east.

32:12 Caleb Caleb and Joshua were the two spies who gave a favorable report of the land and argued that the people should move ahead in faith.

32:22 be free from your obligation Implies that the soldiers of Gad and Reuben took an oath with respect to their promise.

32:28 Eleazar the priest and Joshua Eleazar, the high priest, and Joshua, Moses' successor and military general, are the leaders who will take the Israelites into the promised land.

32:30 they must accept their possession with you If Gad and Reuben go back on their promise, they would forfeit their preferred land in the Transjordan and live in Canaan instead.

32:33 half-tribe of Manasseh This half-tribe is mentioned as part of the agreement here for the first time. They apparently asked for the same favor. Half of Manasseh settles in the Transjordan while the other half settles in Canaan proper (see Jos 22:7).

the kingdom of Sihon king of the Amorites and the kingdom of Og king of Bashan — the whole land with its cities and the territory around them. [34]The Gadites built up Dibon, Ataroth, Aroer, [35]Atroth Shophan, Jazer, Jogbehah, [36]Beth Nimrah and Beth Haran as fortified cities, and built pens for their flocks. [37]And the Reubenites rebuilt Heshbon, Elealeh and Kiriathaim, [38]as well as Nebo and Baal Meon (these names were changed) and Sibmah. They gave names to the cities they rebuilt.

[39]The descendants of Makir son of Manasseh went to Gilead, captured it and drove out the Amorites who were there. [40]So Moses gave Gilead to the Makirites, the descendants of Manasseh, and they settled there. [41]Jair, a descendant of Manasseh, captured their settlements and called them Havvoth Jair.[a] [42]And Nobah captured Kenath and its surrounding settlements and called it Nobah after himself.

Stages in Israel's Journey

33 Here are the stages in the journey of the Israelites when they came out of Egypt by divisions under the leadership of Moses and Aaron. [2]At the LORD's command Moses recorded the stages in their journey. This is their journey by stages:

[3]The Israelites set out from Rameses on the fifteenth day of the first month, the day after the Passover. They marched out defiantly in full view of all the Egyptians, [4]who were burying all their firstborn, whom the LORD had struck down among them; for the LORD had brought judgment on their gods.

[5]The Israelites left Rameses and camped at Sukkoth.

[6]They left Sukkoth and camped at Etham, on the edge of the desert.

[7]They left Etham, turned back to Pi Hahiroth, to the east of Baal Zephon, and camped near Migdol.

[8]They left Pi Hahiroth[b] and passed through the sea into the desert, and when they had traveled for three days in the Desert of Etham, they camped at Marah.

[9]They left Marah and went to Elim, where there were twelve springs and seventy palm trees, and they camped there.

[10]They left Elim and camped by the Red Sea.[c]

[11]They left the Red Sea and camped in the Desert of Sin.

[12]They left the Desert of Sin and camped at Dophkah.

[13]They left Dophkah and camped at Alush.

[14]They left Alush and camped at Rephidim, where there was no water for the people to drink.

[15]They left Rephidim and camped in the Desert of Sinai.

[16]They left the Desert of Sinai and camped at Kibroth Hattaavah.

[17]They left Kibroth Hattaavah and camped at Hazeroth.

[18]They left Hazeroth and camped at Rithmah.

---

[a] 41 Or *them the settlements of Jair*   [b] 8 Many manuscripts of the Masoretic Text, Samaritan Pentateuch and Vulgate; most manuscripts of the Masoretic Text *left from before Hahiroth*   [c] 10 Or *the Sea of Reeds*; also in verse 11

32:34–38 The following verses list the names of the cities that the Gadites, Reubenites and Manassites rebuilt, then renamed (Nu 32:38). In the ancient Near East, giving something or someone a new name was the equivalent of assigning a new identity.

32:39 Amorites who were there The Amorites were weakened when the Israelites defeated King Sihon in 21:21–30, but they remained in the land. They are never fully removed.

33:1–49 Chapter 33 is the longest and most detailed uninterrupted account of Israel's journey from their exodus from Egypt to their arrival on the border of the promised land. Israel's itinerary is given in 41 stages, starting at the Egyptian city of Rameses and ending at the plains of Moab. The precise route that Israel took through the wilderness is uncertain because some key locations cannot be definitively identified, such as the site of the sea crossing (Ex 14) or the location of Mount Sinai (Ex 19). Since this chapter is a summary of their journey, many of the names and associated events point back to earlier parts of the narrative. Some of the names, however, are unknown outside of this list.

33:2 Moses recorded A few passages mention Moses writing down something specific for current and future generations (e.g., Ex 17:14; 24:4).

33:3 from Rameses Rameses is identified as one of the

two store cities built by the Israelites (Ex 1:11). The city was located in the area of the modern village of Qantir in the northeastern delta of the Nile. See note on Ge 47:11.

33:8 for three days This is the only time the itinerary provides information about how long a stage of the journey lasted. **camped at Marah** As recorded in Ex 15:23. Here, the itinerary focuses on stopping points that have water. The water at this location was not drinkable, hence the name *marah*—meaning "bitter."

33:10 Red Sea It is unclear whether this sea refers to a different location from the sea in Nu 33:8 through which the Israelites passed. See Ex 13:18 and note; 14:2 and note.

33:15 Desert of Sinai Designates an area near Mount Sinai, but the exact location of the mountain itself is unknown (compare Ex 3:1–2; 19:1–2; Nu 1:1). The events of Ex 19–Nu 10 take place in this wilderness.

33:18–34 There is a narrative gap of 38 years in the book of Numbers, from the time the people are told they will not enter the promised land (Nu 14:28–35) until a full 40 years has come to fruition (20:22–28; 33:38–39). Therefore, none of the legs of the journey found in vv. 18–34 appear elsewhere in OT descriptions of Israel's journey. The exact locations of these sites are unknown and most do not appear in written or archeological records. This issue is complicated by the fact that Israel renamed locations as it moved throughout the region (32:38).

¹⁹They left Rithmah and camped at Rimmon Perez.

²⁰They left Rimmon Perez and camped at Libnah.

²¹They left Libnah and camped at Rissah.

²²They left Rissah and camped at Kehelathah.

²³They left Kehelathah and camped at Mount Shepher.

²⁴They left Mount Shepher and camped at Haradah.

²⁵They left Haradah and camped at Makheloth.

²⁶They left Makheloth and camped at Tahath.

²⁷They left Tahath and camped at Terah.

²⁸They left Terah and camped at Mithkah.

²⁹They left Mithkah and camped at Hashmonah.

³⁰They left Hashmonah and camped at Moseroth.

³¹They left Moseroth and camped at Bene Jaakan.

³²They left Bene Jaakan and camped at Hor Haggidgad.

³³They left Hor Haggidgad and camped at Jotbathah.

³⁴They left Jotbathah and camped at Abronah.

³⁵They left Abronah and camped at Ezion Geber.

³⁶They left Ezion Geber and camped at Kadesh, in the Desert of Zin.

³⁷They left Kadesh and camped at Mount Hor, on the border of Edom. ³⁸At the LORD's command Aaron the priest went up Mount Hor, where he died on the first day of the fifth month of the fortieth year after the Israelites came out of Egypt. ³⁹Aaron was a hundred and twenty-three years old when he died on Mount Hor.

⁴⁰The Canaanite king of Arad, who lived in the Negev of Canaan, heard that the Israelites were coming.

⁴¹They left Mount Hor and camped at Zalmonah.

⁴²They left Zalmonah and camped at Punon.

⁴³They left Punon and camped at Oboth.

⁴⁴They left Oboth and camped at Iye Abarim, on the border of Moab.

⁴⁵They left Iye Abarim and camped at Dibon Gad.

⁴⁶They left Dibon Gad and camped at Almon Diblathaim.

⁴⁷They left Almon Diblathaim and camped in the mountains of Abarim, near Nebo.

⁴⁸They left the mountains of Abarim and camped on the plains of Moab by the Jordan across from Jericho. ⁴⁹There on the plains of Moab they camped along the Jordan from Beth Jeshimoth to Abel Shittim.

⁵⁰On the plains of Moab by the Jordan across from Jericho the LORD said to Moses, ⁵¹"Speak to the Israelites and say to them: 'When you cross the Jordan into Canaan, ⁵²drive out all the inhabitants of the land before you. Destroy all their carved images and their cast idols, and demolish all their high places. ⁵³Take possession of the land and settle in it, for I have given you the land to possess. ⁵⁴Distribute the land by lot, according to your clans. To a larger group give a larger inheritance, and to a smaller group a smaller one. Whatever falls to them by lot will be theirs. Distribute it according to your ancestral tribes.

⁵⁵"But if you do not drive out the inhabitants of the land, those you allow to remain will become barbs in your eyes and thorns in your sides. They will give you trouble in the land where you will live. ⁵⁶And then I will do to you what I plan to do to them.'"

Boundaries of Canaan

34 The LORD said to Moses, ²"Command the Israelites and say to them: 'When you enter Canaan, the land that will be allotted to you as an inheritance is to have these boundaries:

³"'Your southern side will include some of the Desert of Zin along the border of Edom. Your

---

33:36 Kadesh Here, Kadesh is near the end of the itinerary, suggesting Israel arrived there near the end of their period of wilderness wandering. See 13:26 and note.
33:49 Abel Shittim It is called Shittim in 25:1.

33:50–56 Yahweh reiterates his previous command to drive out the inhabitants of Canaan when Israel enters the promised land (Ex 23:20–33).

33:52 drive out The Hebrew verb used here, *yarash*, describes taking possession of an inheritance (see Jos 1:11). Several different verbs are used to describe the conquest of the promised land, some of which do not necessarily involve destruction.
33:55 They will give you trouble Yahweh's concern is not only that Israel will have difficulty with the communities living in Canaan, but also that the Israelites will adopt practices that conflict with Yahweh's vision for Israel.

34:1–15 This chapter focuses on the geographical boundaries of the tribal allotments and the promised land. However, certain boundaries given here do not align with the dimensions envisioned in Ge 15:18–21 and Ex 23:31, although the boundaries in Jos 13–22 do appear to conform to Nu 34. The exact location of most of the sites named is uncertain.

34:2 to have these boundaries Canaan was the swath of land between the Mediterranean Sea and Jordan River that now consists of modern Israel, Palestine, Lebanon, and, in some periods, Syria.
34:3 Edom A kingdom and land to the southeast of Canaan, on the eastern side of the Dead Sea.

southern boundary will start in the east from the southern end of the Dead Sea, [4]cross south of Scorpion Pass, continue on to Zin and go south of Kadesh Barnea. Then it will go to Hazar Addar and over to Azmon, [5]where it will turn, join the Wadi of Egypt and end at the Mediterranean Sea.

[6]"'Your western boundary will be the coast of the Mediterranean Sea. This will be your boundary on the west.

[7]"'For your northern boundary, run a line from the Mediterranean Sea to Mount Hor [8]and from Mount Hor to Lebo Hamath. Then the boundary will go to Zedad, [9]continue to Ziphron and end at Hazar Enan. This will be your boundary on the north.

[10]"'For your eastern boundary, run a line from Hazar Enan to Shepham. [11]The boundary will go down from Shepham to Riblah on the east side of Ain and continue along the slopes east of the Sea of Galilee.[a] [12]Then the boundary will go down along the Jordan and end at the Dead Sea.

"'This will be your land, with its boundaries on every side.'"

[13]Moses commanded the Israelites: "Assign this land by lot as an inheritance. The LORD has ordered that it be given to the nine and a half tribes, [14]because the families of the tribe of Reuben, the tribe of Gad and the half-tribe of Manasseh have received their inheritance. [15]These two and a half tribes have received their inheritance east of the Jordan across from Jericho, toward the sunrise."

[16]The LORD said to Moses, [17]"These are the names of the men who are to assign the land for you as an inheritance: Eleazar the priest and Joshua son of Nun. [18]And appoint one leader from each tribe to help assign the land. [19]These are their names:

Caleb son of Jephunneh,
    from the tribe of Judah;
[20]Shemuel son of Ammihud,
    from the tribe of Simeon;
[21]Elidad son of Kislon,
    from the tribe of Benjamin;
[22]Bukki son of Jogli,
    the leader from the tribe of Dan;

[23]Hanniel son of Ephod,
    the leader from the tribe of Manasseh son
    of Joseph;
[24]Kemuel son of Shiphtan,
    the leader from the tribe of Ephraim son
    of Joseph;
[25]Elizaphan son of Parnak,
    the leader from the tribe of Zebulun;
[26]Paltiel son of Azzan,
    the leader from the tribe of Issachar;
[27]Ahihud son of Shelomi,
    the leader from the tribe of Asher;
[28]Pedahel son of Ammihud,
    the leader from the tribe of Naphtali."

[29]These are the men the LORD commanded to assign the inheritance to the Israelites in the land of Canaan.

Towns for the Levites

35 On the plains of Moab by the Jordan across from Jericho, the LORD said to Moses, [2]"Command the Israelites to give the Levites towns to live in from the inheritance the Israelites will possess. And give them pasturelands around the towns. [3]Then they will have towns to live in and pasturelands for the cattle they own and all their other animals.

[4]"The pasturelands around the towns that you give the Levites will extend a thousand cubits[b] from the town wall. [5]Outside the town, measure two thousand cubits[c] on the east side, two thousand on the south side, two thousand on the west and two thousand on the north, with the town in the center. They will have this area as pastureland for the towns.

Cities of Refuge

35:6-34Ref — Dt 4:41-43; 19:1-14; Jos 20:1-9

[6]"Six of the towns you give the Levites will be cities of refuge, to which a person who has

---

[a] 11 Hebrew *Kinnereth*   [b] 4 That is, about 1,500 feet or about 450 meters   [c] 5 That is, about 3,000 feet or about 900 meters

---

34:4 Kadesh Barnea The precise location of this site is uncertain. Possible identifications include Ain Qadesh and Ein el-Qudeirat.

34:5 Wadi of Egypt Refers to the Wadi el-Arish, the ancient, easternmost branch of the Nile, which is no longer in existence, but once served as a natural boundary in north-central Sinai.

34:8 Lebo Hamath An area marking the northern boundary of Canaan; the northern limit to the territory explored by the 12 spies (13:21; compare Jos 13:5).

34:13 nine and a half tribes Refers to the tribes other than those that inherited land in the Transjordan — Reuben, Gad and the other half-tribe Manasseh (Nu 32; compare note on 32:33).

34:16–29 With the exception of Caleb, this is the first reference to the tribal leaders listed here. Joshua and

Eleazar, both of whom were in earlier narratives, are also included in this passage as being involved in the dividing of the promised land. The chieftains listed in 13:3–16 were part of the first generation of Israelites who wandered the wilderness because they refused to believe God would give them the land (ch. 14). Joshua and Caleb were the lone exceptions to such unbelief (14:30,38), and will therefore lead the people into the promised land.

35:1–8 The Levites would not receive a tribal allotment in the promised land (18:23; Lev 25:32–33), but here the other tribes are instructed to set aside specific towns within their territories where the Levites will live. The Levites receive 48 cities along with pasture land around those cities for their livestock. The cities are described in Nu 35:1–8, and the instructions are carried out in Jos 21.

killed someone may flee. In addition, give them forty-two other towns. ⁷In all you must give the Levites forty-eight towns, together with their pasturelands. ⁸The towns you give the Levites from the land the Israelites possess are to be given in proportion to the inheritance of each tribe: Take many towns from a tribe that has many, but few from one that has few."

⁹Then the Lord said to Moses: ¹⁰"Speak to the Israelites and say to them: 'When you cross the Jordan into Canaan, ¹¹select some towns to be your cities of refuge, to which a person who has killed someone accidentally may flee. ¹²They will be places of refuge from the avenger, so that anyone accused of murder may not die before they stand trial before the assembly. ¹³These six towns you give will be your cities of refuge. ¹⁴Give three on this side of the Jordan and three in Canaan as cities of refuge. ¹⁵These six towns will be a place of refuge for Israelites and for foreigners residing among them, so that anyone who has killed another accidentally can flee there.

¹⁶"'If anyone strikes someone a fatal blow with an iron object, that person is a murderer; the murderer is to be put to death. ¹⁷Or if anyone is holding a stone and strikes someone a fatal blow with it, that person is a murderer; the murderer is to be put to death. ¹⁸Or if anyone is holding a wooden object and strikes someone a fatal blow with it, that person is a murderer; the murderer is to be put to death. ¹⁹The avenger of blood shall put the murderer to death; when the avenger comes upon the murderer, the avenger shall put the murderer to death. ²⁰If anyone with malice aforethought shoves another or throws something at them intentionally so that they die ²¹or if out of enmity one person hits another with their fist so that the other dies, that person is to be put to death; that person is a murderer. The avenger of blood shall put the murderer to death when they meet.

²²"'But if without enmity someone suddenly pushes another or throws something at them unintentionally ²³or, without seeing them, drops on them a stone heavy enough to kill them, and they die, then since that other person was not an enemy and no harm was intended, ²⁴the assembly must judge between the accused and the avenger of blood according to these regulations. ²⁵The assembly must protect the one accused of murder from the avenger of blood and send the accused back to the city of refuge to which they fled. The accused must stay there until the death of the high priest, who was anointed with the holy oil.

²⁶"'But if the accused ever goes outside the limits of the city of refuge to which they fled ²⁷and the avenger of blood finds them outside the city, the avenger of blood may kill the accused without being guilty of murder. ²⁸The accused must stay in the city of refuge until the death of the high priest; only after the death of the high priest may they return to their own property.

²⁹"'This is to have the force of law for you throughout the generations to come, wherever you live.

³⁰"'Anyone who kills a person is to be put to death as a murderer only on the testimony of witnesses. But no one is to be put to death on the testimony of only one witness.

³¹"'Do not accept a ransom for the life of a murderer, who deserves to die. They are to be put to death.

³²"'Do not accept a ransom for anyone who has fled to a city of refuge and so allow them to go back and live on their own land before the death of the high priest.

³³"'Do not pollute the land where you are. Bloodshed pollutes the land, and atonement cannot be made for the land on which blood has been shed, except by the blood of the one who shed it.

35:9–34 The six cities of refuge were set up as areas of protection for those who took the life of another person accidentally. Since ancient Near Eastern culture permitted relatives to avenge the blood of their kin, a place of asylum was necessary.

35:12 avenger The Hebrew word used here, *go'el*, refers to the nearest relative to whom fell the obligation to right a wrong on behalf of the family. One of the responsibilities was avenging the death of a family member. In the context of the cities of refuge and blood vengeance, the *go'el* ensures the execution of the offender. See note on Dt 19:6.

35:14 on this side of the Jordan The Transjordan, where the tribes of Gad, Reuben and Manasseh would later settle (Nu 32).

35:16–21 This passage describes an intentional act of violence. Intent is a necessary component of murder, the illegitimate taking of an innocent life. There are six examples of intentional homicide provided in vv. 16–18 and vv. 20–21.

35:22–29 This passage describes cases of accidental homicide and regulations governing the cities of refuge.

35:25 until the death of the high priest When the court determined that the death was unintentional, offenders were returned to the city of refuge, where they stayed until the death of the high priest at the time of the event. As long as they did so, they remained safe from the avenger (*go'el* in Hebrew; see v. 12). In the case of intentional homicide, the blood of the slain person was atoned for by capital punishment: The *go'el* killed the murderer. In the case of an accidental homicide, the blood could not be avenged in this way; instead, atonement was accomplished by the death of the high priest under whose authority the unintentional slayer was sent to a city of refuge.

35:30 on the testimony of only one At least two witnesses were required to establish guilt in a capital case (compare Dt 17:6; 19:15).

35:31 Do not accept a ransom Those who intentionally killed had to be killed through capital punishment; ransom for that person's life was rejected.

³⁴Do not defile the land where you live and where I dwell, for I, the LORD, dwell among the Israelites.'"

Inheritance of Zelophehad's Daughters

36:1-12pp — Nu 27:1-11

36 The family heads of the clan of Gilead son of Makir, the son of Manasseh, who were from the clans of the descendants of Joseph, came and spoke before Moses and the leaders, the heads of the Israelite families. ²They said, "When the LORD commanded my lord to give the land as an inheritance to the Israelites by lot, he ordered you to give the inheritance of our brother Zelophehad to his daughters. ³Now suppose they marry men from other Israelite tribes; then their inheritance will be taken from our ancestral inheritance and added to that of the tribe they marry into. And so part of the inheritance allotted to us will be taken away. ⁴When the Year of Jubilee for the Israelites comes, their inheritance will be added to that of the tribe into which they marry, and their property will be taken from the tribal inheritance of our ancestors."

⁵Then at the LORD's command Moses gave this order to the Israelites: "What the tribe of the descendants of Joseph is saying is right. ⁶This is what the LORD commands for Zelophehad's daughters: They may marry anyone they please as long as they marry within their father's tribal clan. ⁷No inheritance in Israel is to pass from one tribe to another, for every Israelite shall keep the tribal inheritance of their ancestors. ⁸Every daughter who inherits land in any Israelite tribe must marry someone in her father's tribal clan, so that every Israelite will possess the inheritance of their ancestors. ⁹No inheritance may pass from one tribe to another, for each Israelite tribe is to keep the land it inherits."

¹⁰So Zelophehad's daughters did as the LORD commanded Moses. ¹¹Zelophehad's daughters — Mahlah, Tirzah, Hoglah, Milkah and Noah — married their cousins on their father's side. ¹²They married within the clans of the descendants of Manasseh son of Joseph, and their inheritance remained in their father's tribe and clan.

¹³These are the commands and regulations the LORD gave through Moses to the Israelites on the plains of Moab by the Jordan across from Jericho.

36:1-13 In Nu 27, Yahweh determined that Zelophehad's daughters could inherit their father's property because he had no sons (27:1–11). Chapter 36 indicates that this decision raised another legal problem: A daughter may inherit, but if she marries someone from another tribe, the territory would become the possession of that tribe, not the father's tribe (v. 3). To address this potential difficulty for their tribal-oriented land allotment, Moses declares that daughters may inherit, but they must marry within their tribe. Zelophehad's daughters follow this rule by marrying their cousins—the sons of their father's brothers (v. 11). Marrying cousins was a common practice in the ancient Near East.

36:1 son of Makir, the son of Manasseh These are the men who conquered the Amorites in order to settle their land (32:39–40).

36:4 Year of Jubilee Ancestral land that was sold or surrendered due to debt obligation reverts to its original owner in the Year of Jubilee which happened every 50 years (see Lev 25:10).

36:13 plains of Moab This is the final stop of Israel's wilderness wanderings and the setting for the entire book of Deuteronomy, which includes Moses' last words to the people.

DEUTERONOMY

INTRODUCTION TO DEUTERONOMY

Deuteronomy concludes the Pentateuch, the first five books of the Bible, with further instruction from Moses, the man who led the Israelites out of slavery in Egypt and received God's law (see Exodus). In Deuteronomy, Moses reviews teachings and events from the time of the exodus and the people's wilderness wanderings. He exhorts the Israelites to love their God Yahweh and obey his commandments. Deuteronomy ends with the final events of Moses' life, including the official appointment of his successor Joshua—the man who formerly encouraged the Israelites to faithfully conquer the promised land despite terrible foes (Nu 13–14). Deuteronomy records Moses telling the Israelites how to live in the land long ago promised to their forefather Abraham (Ge 12:1–3)—a land they must still conquer.

BACKGROUND

Deuteronomy 31:9 indicates Moses' involvement in writing the law portions of Deuteronomy. For this reason and others, Jewish and Christian traditions ascribe the Pentateuch to Moses, but it may have been completed and edited later (for more information on this debate, see the "Introduction to Genesis").

Deuteronomy's narrative is set on the plains of Moab, just across the Jordan River from the promised land, where the Israelites are camping after their 40 years of wilderness wandering—placing it within the same period as the closing chapters of Numbers.

The title "Deuteronomy" means "second law." The book reiterates the law and the events recorded in Exodus, Leviticus and Numbers. It also establishes a framework for viewing this history: If the Israelites are faithful to God's covenant, they will have peace and receive blessings from Yahweh, but if they turn away, they will experience curses of war, famine and death—all of which are meant to prompt them to stay faithful. This framework is applied to subsequent books that narrate Israel's later history (Joshua, Judges, 1–2 Samuel, 1–2 Kings).

The structure of Deuteronomy resembles ancient Near Eastern treaties between kings and the foreign nations they conquered. In these agreements, both the king and the nation accepted certain obligations; if the nation fulfilled the terms of the treaty, there would be peace. Deuteronomy's similarities with these ancient documents, examples of which date from the fourteenth to the seventh centuries BC, likely indicate that it originated around the same time.

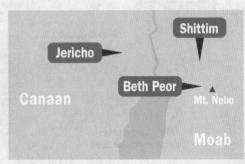

This map depicts the setting of Deuteronomy.

STRUCTURE

Deuteronomy has three major sections followed by an epilogue. Each major section presents a speech by Moses and begins with a special phrase marking it as a distinct unit.

The first speech (Dt 1:1—4:43) is introduced with a phrase stating these are "the words." Moses uses the wilderness journey to teach the Israelites about God. This history shows that Yahweh is faithful to his people and able to overcome their enemies—and that Israel must trust and obey him. If they do not follow Yahweh's ways, they will not be able to live long term in the promised land.

Moses' second speech (4:44—28:68), which is the longest of the three, is introduced with the phrase "this is the law." After Moses repeats a form of the Ten Commandments (5:6–21), he expands on them in the subsequent chapters.

Moses' third speech (29:1—30:20) is introduced with the same phrase that opens the first speech. Moses calls the Israelites to renew their covenant with Yahweh. He warns the Israelites that violating the covenant will lead to death, but he also assures them that repenting and trusting God will lead to life and blessing.

The epilogue (31:1—34:12) deals with the end of Moses' life. Joshua succeeds Moses as leader of the Israelites. Moses sings a farewell song and blesses the people, and his life on this earth ends.

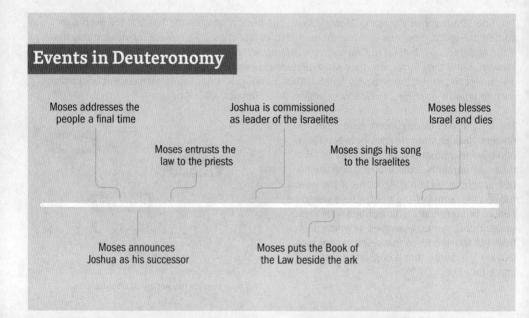

Events in Deuteronomy

Moses addresses the people a final time

Joshua is commissioned as leader of the Israelites

Moses blesses Israel and dies

Moses entrusts the law to the priests

Moses sings his song to the Israelites

Moses announces Joshua as his successor

Moses puts the Book of the Law beside the ark

OUTLINE

- Moses' review of history (1:1—4:43)
- Moses' review of the law (4:44—28:68)
- Moses' review of the covenant (29:1—30:20)
- Moses' final words and death (31:1—34:12)

THEMES

One of the central messages of Deuteronomy is that God loves the Israelites, as seen in his promises to Abraham, Isaac and Jacob. Deuteronomy also indicates that Yahweh showed his love for the Israelites by rescuing them from Egypt and will continue to do so by giving them the promised land. The Israelites should respond to Yahweh's love by believing he can do anything he asks of them—even overcome dreadful foes in the promised land (31:1–6).

Moses commands the people to love Yahweh with all their heart, soul and might—a statement Jesus will later call the greatest commandment (Dt 6:5; Mt 22:36–40). As God's people we are to take courage and boldly embrace whatever he asks us to do, through the power of Christ (Dt 31:6–7; Ac 5). And if we do, we will surely see God at work in our lives, communities and world.

The Command to Leave Horeb

1 These are the words Moses spoke to all Israel in the wilderness east of the Jordan — that is, in the Arabah — opposite Suph, between Paran and Tophel, Laban, Hazeroth and Dizahab. [2] (It takes eleven days to go from Horeb to Kadesh Barnea by the Mount Seir road.)

[3] In the fortieth year, on the first day of the eleventh month, Moses proclaimed to the Israelites all that the LORD had commanded him concerning them. [4] This was after he had defeated Sihon king of the Amorites, who reigned in Heshbon, and at Edrei had defeated Og king of Bashan, who reigned in Ashtaroth.

[5] East of the Jordan in the territory of Moab, Moses began to expound this law, saying:

[6] The LORD our God said to us at Horeb, "You have stayed long enough at this mountain. [7] Break camp and advance into the hill country of the Amorites; go to all the neighboring peoples in the Arabah, in the mountains, in the western foothills, in the Negev and along the coast, to the land of the Canaanites and to Lebanon, as far as the great river, the Euphrates. [8] See, I have given you this land. Go in and take possession of the land the LORD swore he would give to your fathers — to Abraham, Isaac and Jacob — and to their descendants after them."

The Appointment of Leaders

[9] At that time I said to you, "You are too heavy a burden for me to carry alone. [10] The LORD your God has increased your numbers so that today you are as numerous as the stars in the sky. [11] May the LORD, the God of your ancestors, increase you a thousand times and bless you as he has promised! [12] But how can I bear your problems and your burdens and your disputes all by myself? [13] Choose some wise, understanding and respected men from each of your tribes, and I will set them over you."

[14] You answered me, "What you propose to do is good."

[15] So I took the leading men of your tribes, wise and respected men, and appointed them to have authority over you — as commanders of thousands, of hundreds, of fifties and of tens and as tribal officials. [16] And I charged your judges at that time, "Hear the disputes between your people and judge fairly, whether the case is between two Israelites or between an Israelite and a foreigner residing among you. [17] Do not show partiality in judging; hear both small and great alike. Do not be afraid of anyone, for judgment belongs to God. Bring me any case too hard for you, and I will hear it." [18] And at that time I told you everything you were to do.

Spies Sent Out

[19] Then, as the LORD our God commanded us, we set out from Horeb and went toward the hill country of the Amorites through all that vast and dreadful wilderness that you have seen, and so we reached Kadesh Barnea. [20] Then I said to you, "You have reached the hill country of the Amorites, which the LORD our God is giving us. [21] See, the LORD your

---

1:1–8 The introductory passage of Deuteronomy introduces the book and connects it to the events described earlier in Exodus and Numbers, continuing where the book of Numbers left off (Dt 1:1–5; 4:44–49; 29:1; 33:1). This introduction begins by mentioning key geographical markers like Horeb (or Sinai) and Kadesh Barnea. The mention of Horeb serves as a reminder of the covenant established between Yahweh and his people. The reference to Kadesh Barnea (v. 2) is a reminder of how the Israelites failed to trust in Yahweh after he miraculously brought them out of Egypt. Because of their unbelief, Yahweh granted the privilege of inheriting the land to the subsequent generation. Deuteronomy focuses on this new generation that had not been present at Mount Sinai, summarizing Yahweh's commandments before they enter the promised land. The introduction also reminds the Israelites of their victories in the Transjordan over the Amorite kings, Sihon and Og (vv. 4–5; Nu 21). The setting for Moses' address to the nation — which begins in Dt 1:6 — is the plains of Moab, the place where Israel camped after that victory (Nu 22:1).

1:1 words Moses spoke to all Israel Apart from some words of introduction in Dt 1:1–5 and the close of the book (ch. 34), Deuteronomy is presented as Moses' speeches to the Israelites, orally recounting Yahweh's law to the new generation. At various moments, the narrator also speaks. **the Arabah — opposite Suph, between Paran and Tophel** The list in this verse moves from north (the Transjordan) to south, mentioning locations

in the upper Sinai peninsula and the desert region south of the Dead Sea.

1:3 In the fortieth year This note indicates the time of the wilderness wandering was coming to an end (compare Nu 13–14).

1:6 Horeb Another name for Mount Sinai, where Moses received the law from God. The book of Deuteronomy characteristically uses Horeb, not Sinai, as the name of Yahweh's holy mountain. The name Horeb is used a few times in Exodus (see Ex 3:1; 17:6; 33:6), but Sinai is more common in the book (e.g., Ex 24:16; 31:18; 34).

1:8 the LORD swore he would give to your fathers The promises Yahweh made to the patriarchs appear primarily in Genesis (Ge 12:1–3; 15:1–6,18; 17:7–8; 26:3–4; 28:13–14; 50:24).

1:9–18 This passage summarizes the accounts from Ex 18:13–26 and Nu 11:14–17 of how Moses assigned leadership roles to others in the community to alleviate some of his administrative burden. Some of the laws related to serving as a judge are also repeated here (compare Dt 1:17; Ex 23:2–3; Lev 19:18).

1:9 You are too heavy a burden for me to carry alone Alludes to either Ex 18:18 or Nu 11:14.

1:15–16 The title "commander" in these verses refers to leaders of military matters, whereas the title "judge" refers to judicial matters.

1:16 foreigner residing among you The Hebrew word used here, *ger*, designates a legal category of resident alien — someone who is not a native-born citizen but

God has given you the land. Go up and take possession of it as the LORD, the God of your ancestors, told you. Do not be afraid; do not be discouraged."

²²Then all of you came to me and said, "Let us send men ahead to spy out the land for us and bring back a report about the route we are to take and the towns we will come to."

²³The idea seemed good to me; so I selected twelve of you, one man from each tribe. ²⁴They left and went up into the hill country, and came to the Valley of Eshkol and explored it. ²⁵Taking with them some of the fruit of the land, they brought it down to us and reported, "It is a good land that the LORD our God is giving us."

Rebellion Against the LORD

²⁶But you were unwilling to go up; you rebelled against the command of the LORD your God. ²⁷You grumbled in your tents and said, "The LORD hates us; so he brought us out of Egypt to deliver us into the hands of the Amorites to destroy us. ²⁸Where can we go? Our brothers have made our hearts melt in fear. They say, 'The people are stronger and taller than we are; the cities are large, with walls up to the sky. We even saw the Anakites there.'"

²⁹Then I said to you, "Do not be terrified; do not be afraid of them. ³⁰The LORD your God, who is going before you, will fight for you, as he did for you in Egypt, before your very eyes, ³¹and in the wilderness. There you saw how the LORD your God carried you, as a father carries his son, all the way you went until you reached this place."

³²In spite of this, you did not trust in the LORD your God, ³³who went ahead of you on your journey, in fire by night and in a cloud by day, to search out places for you to camp and to show you the way you should go.

³⁴When the LORD heard what you said, he was angry and solemnly swore: ³⁵"No one from this evil generation shall see the good land I swore to give your ancestors, ³⁶except Caleb son of Jephunneh. He will see it, and I will give him and his descendants the land he set his feet on, because he followed the LORD wholeheartedly."

³⁷Because of you the LORD became angry with me also and said, "You shall not enter it, either. ³⁸But your assistant, Joshua son of Nun, will enter it. Encourage him, because he will lead Israel to inherit it. ³⁹And the little ones that you said would be taken captive, your children who do not yet know good from bad — they will enter the land. I will give it to them and they will take possession of it. ⁴⁰But as for you, turn around and set out toward the desert along the route to the Red Sea. ᵃ"

⁴¹Then you replied, "We have sinned against the LORD. We will go up and fight, as the LORD our God commanded us." So every one of you put on his weapons, thinking it easy to go up into the hill country.

⁴²But the LORD said to me, "Tell them, 'Do not go up and fight, because I will not be with you. You will be defeated by your enemies.'"

⁴³So I told you, but you would not listen. You rebelled against the LORD's command and in your arrogance you marched up into the hill country. ⁴⁴The Amorites who lived in those hills came out against you; they chased you like a swarm of bees and beat you down from Seir all the way to Hormah. ⁴⁵You came back and wept before the LORD, but he paid no attention to your weeping and turned a deaf ear to you. ⁴⁶And so you stayed in Kadesh many days — all the time you spent there.

Wanderings in the Wilderness

2 Then we turned back and set out toward the wilderness along the route to the Red Sea,ᵃ as the LORD had directed me. For a long time we made our way around the hill country of Seir.

ᵃ 40,1 Or the Sea of Reeds

---

lives among another people. Old Testament law includes provisions designed to prevent the mistreatment of these people (Ex 23:9; Lev 19:34; 23:22; Nu 15:29).

1:19–46 This passage recounts the Israelites' failure that resulted in the wilderness wandering, a punishment that made the new generation of Israelites a people of the wilderness who would take part in the conquest of the promised land. The events Moses summarizes are recorded in Nu 13–14.

1:21 given you the land Moses' words here directly echo the exhortation to take possession of the land from Dt 1:8.
1:27 the Amorites An ancient Semitic people, who according to OT usage, occupied Canaan prior to the arrival of the Israelites (Ge 15:19–21).
1:28 the Anakites Referring to the descendants of giants whose presence in Canaan inspired Israel's fear (Nu 13:32–33). Israel's fear of the Anakim (or Anakites) was greater than their faith in Yahweh.
1:31 this place Refers to Kadesh Barnea, where Israel was camped while the spies entered Canaan.

1:34 was angry The rebellion of the previous generation provoked Yahweh to anger. Recounting the previous generation's fate functions as a warning for those preparing to enter the promised land.
1:36 Caleb son of Jephunneh Though Caleb, like his fellow spies, saw the strength of the inhabitants of the land, Caleb remained faithful to Yahweh and his promise to deliver the land to the Israelites. He encouraged Israel to enter the land according to Yahweh's command (Nu 13:30; 14:6–8,30). **the land he set his feet on** Refers to Hebron (see Jos 14:6–14).
1:38 Joshua son of Nun Joshua, like Caleb, encouraged the Israelites to follow Yahweh's command and enter the land (Nu 14:6–8,30).
1:40 along the route to the Red Sea This route was well known in the ancient Near East; it began at Kadesh Barnea and extended to the tip of the Red Sea at Elath.

2:1–23 Deuteronomy 2–3 details Israel's departure from Kadesh Barnea, their journey through the Transjordan, and their conquest and settlement of part of the Transjordan. This first part of Moses' speech summarizes

²Then the LORD said to me, ³"You have made your way around this hill country long enough; now turn north. ⁴Give the people these orders: 'You are about to pass through the territory of your relatives the descendants of Esau, who live in Seir. They will be afraid of you, but be very careful. ⁵Do not provoke them to war, for I will not give you any of their land, not even enough to put your foot on. I have given Esau the hill country of Seir as his own. ⁶You are to pay them in silver for the food you eat and the water you drink.'"

⁷The LORD your God has blessed you in all the work of your hands. He has watched over your journey through this vast wilderness. These forty years the LORD your God has been with you, and you have not lacked anything.

⁸So we went on past our relatives the descendants of Esau, who live in Seir. We turned from the Arabah road, which comes up from Elath and Ezion Geber, and traveled along the desert road of Moab.

⁹Then the LORD said to me, "Do not harass the Moabites or provoke them to war, for I will not give you any part of their land. I have given Ar to the descendants of Lot as a possession."

¹⁰(The Emites used to live there—a people strong and numerous, and as tall as the Anakites. ¹¹Like the Anakites, they too were considered Rephaites, but the Moabites called them Emites. ¹²Horites used to live in Seir, but the descendants of Esau drove them out. They destroyed the Horites from before them and settled in their place, just as Israel did in the land the LORD gave them as their possession.)

¹³And the LORD said, "Now get up and cross the Zered Valley." So we crossed the valley.

¹⁴Thirty-eight years passed from the time we left Kadesh Barnea until we crossed the Zered Valley. By then, that entire generation of fighting men had perished from the camp, as the LORD had sworn to them. ¹⁵The LORD's hand was against them until he had completely eliminated them from the camp.

Israel's travels from Kadesh to the border of Amorite territory in the Transjordan (Nu 20:22—21:20). Israel spent most of the period in the wilderness of Zin—forty years—in the vicinity of Kadesh Barnea (Dt 2:14; Nu 20:1,14). See the map "Route of the Exodus" on p. 2252.

2:1 along the route to the Red Sea Here the reference to the Red Sea is likely indicating the Gulf of Elath (see Dt 2:8), the northern prong of the Red Sea.

2:5 I have given Esau the hill country of Seir as his own Seir is a mountain in Edom, and the Edomites are descendants of Esau (Ge 32:3; 36:8; Eze 35:15), which also makes them descendants of Abraham, Esau's grandfather.

2:8 from Elath and Ezion Geber Both locations were situated at the tip of the northern prong of the Red Sea. The precise locations of each have not been determined.

2:10–12 Moses' speech in Dt 2 is interrupted twice—here and in vv. 20–23—for the narrator to provide background information about the ancient inhabitants of southern Canaan and the Transjordan (the region east of the Jordan River and the Dead Sea). Both passages describe the areas as formerly inhabited by giants like those whose presence had frightened the Israelite spies so much that the first generation had given up hope of conquest (Nu 13–14). These other clans of giants are identified by a variety of names in these verses: Emim (Emites), Rephaim (Rephaites), Zamzummim (Zamzummites), and Avvim (Avvites). The explanations of the names in these verses suggest that Rephaim was the general category and that the others were local names for the giant clans (Dt 2:11,20). The narrator's comments in vv. 20–23 indicate that some of Israel's neighbors encountered the giant clans and succeeded in driving them out. In the case of the Ammonites, their ability to prevail over the giants is attributed directly to Yahweh (v. 21). This background information comes in the larger context of Moses' explaining that Israel was not entitled to land that Yahweh allotted to Ammon, Moab and Edom (vv. 5,9,19).

2:10 Emites Refers to one of several giant clans. This term was apparently the Moabite name for the Anakim (also called the Anakites; v. 11). See 1:28 and note.

2:11 Rephaites The Hebrew term used here, *rephaim*, sometimes refers to the spirits of the dead (Isa 26:14), but here the term is associated with the giant clans (see Dt 3:11; compare Jos 12:4; 13:12). In Ge 14:5, both the Rephaim (or Rephaites) and the Emim (or Emites) are mentioned as inhabiting the area east of the Dead Sea during the time of Abraham.

Deuteronomy 2:11

REPHAITES (REPHAIM)
Ancient Near Eastern texts from Phoenicia and Ugarit depict the *rephaim* as divine residents of the underworld. Deuteronomy identifies various clans of giants as *rephaim* (Dt 2:10; 3:11). The *rephaim* are associated with the Anakim (Anakites; see Dt 2:10–11,21) who themselves are affiliated with the Nephilim (Nu 13:33). This creates a connection between the *rephaim* and the ancient giant group the Nephilim, who are likely the descendants of the sons of God and human women (see note on Ge 6:2; note on Ge 6:4). Genesis 14:5 also refers to the *rephaim* as an ancient people group inhabiting Canaan. There are various clans affiliated with the *rephaim* in Deuteronomy. See note on Dt 2:10–12.

2:12 descendants of Esau drove them out In parallel with this passage, Ge 36:20–30 relates a genealogy of Seir the Horite, in-between two lists related to the Edomites. **Horites** See note on Ge 14:6.

2:13–18 This passage marks the transition from the original generation of Israelites who came out of Egypt—those who rebelled in unbelief (Nu 13–14)—to those Israelites who would claim the promised land (compare Dt 1:35). Once they crossed the Wadi Zered—the southern border of Moab—the move toward the conquest of Canaan had begun. However, Israel was not allotted any territory between the Zered and the Arnon (Moab's southern and northern borders). The Israelites do not engage in battle with the Moabites or the Ammonites at this point in their history (vv. 9,19).

[16]Now when the last of these fighting men among the people had died, [17]the LORD said to me, [18]"Today you are to pass by the region of Moab at Ar. [19]When you come to the Ammonites, do not harass them or provoke them to war, for I will not give you possession of any land belonging to the Ammonites. I have given it as a possession to the descendants of Lot."

[20](That too was considered a land of the Rephaites, who used to live there; but the Ammonites called them Zamzummites. [21]They were a people strong and numerous, and as tall as the Anakites. The LORD destroyed them from before the Ammonites, who drove them out and settled in their place. [22]The LORD had done the same for the descendants of Esau, who lived in Seir, when he destroyed the Horites from before them. They drove them out and have lived in their place to this day. [23]And as for the Avvites who lived in villages as far as Gaza, the Caphtorites coming out from Caphtor[a] destroyed them and settled in their place.)

Defeat of Sihon King of Heshbon

[24]"Set out now and cross the Arnon Gorge. See, I have given into your hand Sihon the Amorite, king of Heshbon, and his country. Begin to take possession of it and engage him in battle. [25]This very day I will begin to put the terror and fear of you on all the nations under heaven. They will hear reports of you and will tremble and be in anguish because of you."

[26]From the Desert of Kedemoth I sent messengers to Sihon king of Heshbon offering peace and saying, [27]"Let us pass through your country. We will stay on the main road; we will not turn aside to the right or to the left. [28]Sell us food to eat and water to drink for their price in silver. Only let us pass through on foot— [29]as the descendants of Esau, who live in Seir, and the Moabites, who live in Ar, did for us—until we cross the Jordan into the land the LORD our God is giving us." [30]But Sihon king of Heshbon refused to let us pass through. For the LORD your God had made his spirit stubborn and his heart obstinate in order to give him into your hands, as he has now done.

[31]The LORD said to me, "See, I have begun to deliver Sihon and his country over to you. Now begin to conquer and possess his land."

[32]When Sihon and all his army came out to meet us in battle at Jahaz, [33]the LORD our God delivered him over to us and we struck him down, together with his sons and his whole army. [34]At that time we took all his towns and completely destroyed[b] them—men, women and children. We left no survivors. [35]But the livestock and the plunder from the towns we had captured we carried off for ourselves. [36]From Aroer on the rim of the Arnon Gorge, and from the town in the gorge, even as far as Gilead, not one town was too strong for us. The LORD our God gave us all of them. [37]But in accordance with the command of the LORD our God, you did not encroach on any of the land of the Ammonites, neither the land along the course of the Jabbok nor that around the towns in the hills.

Defeat of Og King of Bashan

3 Next we turned and went up along the road toward Bashan, and Og king of Bashan with his whole army marched out to meet us in battle

[a] 23 That is, Crete   [b] 34 The Hebrew term refers to the irrevocable giving over of things or persons to the LORD, often by totally destroying them.

2:19 as a possession to the descendants of Lot According to Ge 19:30–38, the people of Ammon and Moab descended from Abraham's nephew Lot.
2:20 Zamzummites Another name for the giant clans associated with the region (Dt 2:19–20). See note on 2:10–12.
2:23 Avvites A giant clan associated with the region. This giant clan—who originally inhabited what would later be known as Philistine territory (Jos 13:3)—was expelled prior to the events narrated in Deuteronomy. See note on Dt 2:10–12. **Caphtorites coming out from Caphtor** Refers to the Philistines (Ge 10:14; Jer 47:4; Am 9:7). Caphtor was an island or coastal region of the Aegean—commonly identified as Crete.
2:24–37 Here Moses recounts Israel's defeat of the Amorite king Sihon (see Nu 21:21–32). His territory was in the Transjordan, north of Moab and east of Ammon, extending roughly from the Arnon River to the Jabbok River.
2:24 the Amorite The Amorites were one of the Canaanite people groups who lived in territory that Yahweh had promised to Abraham's descendants (Ge 15:18–21). Yahweh promised to drive them out before Israel (see Jos 3:10).
2:25 the terror and fear of you This is a fear caused not by Israel's military prowess, but by Yahweh himself. See Dt 11:25; 28:10; compare Ex 15:14–16; Jos 2:9–11.
2:30 LORD your God had made his spirit stubborn Exo-

dus 4:21 contains a parallel account involving the Pharaoh of the exodus. Yahweh sometimes hardens the disposition of a rebellious (or evil) person as a means of judgment.
2:34 completely destroyed The Amorites in Sihon's territory were placed under the Hebrew principle of *cherem*—this word designated people or things as sacred property. In some instances, like this one, the designation of *cherem* meant complete destruction (see note on Jos 6:16; note on Jos 6:17). The same approach was taken in Og's domain (see Dt 3:6). The motivation was judgment of wicked nations, likely due to idolatrous practices (see Ge 15:16; Dt 9:4–5). These nations were viewed as completely corrupt and under the jurisdiction of foreign gods (compare note on Dt 4:19).

3:1–22 After defeating Sihon, the king of the Amorites at Heshbon (2:26–37), the Israelites continued north to the Amorite kingdom of Og, ruler of Bashan. Og's territory was north of the Jabbok River and east of the Sea of Galilee. In this passage, Moses recounts the events from Nu 21:33–35 about the defeat of Og (Dt 3:1–3), lists the territories acquired in these victories in the Transjordan (vv. 4–11), and summarizes how the territory was allotted to the tribes of Reuben, Gad and half of Manasseh (vv. 12–22; compare Nu 32).
3:1 Og king of Bashan Og is described as the last of the Rephaim (or Rephaite) giants (see Dt 3:11–13; Jos 12:4),

at Edrei. ²The LORD said to me, "Do not be afraid of him, for I have delivered him into your hands, along with his whole army and his land. Do to him what you did to Sihon king of the Amorites, who reigned in Heshbon."

³So the LORD our God also gave into our hands Og king of Bashan and all his army. We struck them down, leaving no survivors. ⁴At that time we took all his cities. There was not one of the sixty cities that we did not take from them — the whole region of Argob, Og's kingdom in Bashan. ⁵All these cities were fortified with high walls and with gates and bars, and there were also a great many unwalled villages. ⁶We completely destroyed^a them, as we had done with Sihon king of Heshbon, destroying^a every city — men, women and children. ⁷But all the livestock and the plunder from their cities we carried off for ourselves.

⁸So at that time we took from these two kings of the Amorites the territory east of the Jordan, from the Arnon Gorge as far as Mount Hermon. ⁹(Hermon is called Sirion by the Sidonians; the Amorites call it Senir.) ¹⁰We took all the towns on the plateau, and all Gilead, and all Bashan as far as Salekah and Edrei, towns of Og's kingdom in Bashan. ¹¹(Og king of Bashan was the last of the Rephaites. His bed was decorated with iron and was more than nine cubits long and four cubits wide.^b It is still in Rabbah of the Ammonites.)

Division of the Land

¹²Of the land that we took over at that time, I gave the Reubenites and the Gadites the territory north of Aroer by the Arnon Gorge, including half the hill country of Gilead, together with its towns. ¹³The rest of Gilead and also all of Bashan, the kingdom of Og, I gave to the half-tribe of Manasseh. (The whole region of Argob in Bashan used to be known as a land of the Rephaites. ¹⁴Jair, a descendant of Manasseh, took the whole region of Argob as far as the border of the Geshurites and the Maakathites; it

was named after him, so that to this day Bashan is called Havvoth Jair.^c) ¹⁵And I gave Gilead to Makir. ¹⁶But to the Reubenites and the Gadites I gave the territory extending from Gilead down to the Arnon Gorge (the middle of the gorge being the border) and out to the Jabbok River, which is the border of the Ammonites. ¹⁷Its western border was the Jordan in the Arabah, from Kinnereth to the Sea of the Arabah (that is, the Dead Sea), below the slopes of Pisgah.

¹⁸I commanded you at that time: "The LORD your God has given you this land to take possession of it. But all your able-bodied men, armed for battle, must cross over ahead of the other Israelites. ¹⁹However, your wives, your children and your livestock (I know you have much livestock) may stay in the towns I have given you, ²⁰until the LORD gives rest to your fellow Israelites as he has to you, and they too have taken over the land that the LORD your God is giving them across the Jordan. After that, each of you may go back to the possession I have given you."

Moses Forbidden to Cross the Jordan

²¹At that time I commanded Joshua: "You have seen with your own eyes all that the LORD your God has done to these two kings. The LORD will do the same to all the kingdoms over there where you are going. ²²Do not be afraid of them; the LORD your God himself will fight for you."

²³At that time I pleaded with the LORD: ²⁴"Sovereign LORD, you have begun to show to your servant your greatness and your strong hand. For what god is there in heaven or on earth who can do the deeds and mighty works you do? ²⁵Let me go over and see the good land beyond the Jordan — that fine hill country and Lebanon." ²⁶But because of you the LORD was angry with

---

^a 6 The Hebrew term refers to the irrevocable giving over of things or persons to the LORD, often by totally destroying them. ^b 11 That is, about 14 feet long and 6 feet wide or about 4 meters long and 1.8 meters wide   ^c 14 Or *called the settlements of Jair*

---

though the greater region of Bashan is still referred to as the land of the Rephaim (or Rephaites; Dt 3:13).
3:6 completely destroyed See note on 2:34.
3:8 Mount Hermon The southernmost peak of the Antilebanon mountain range.

Deuteronomy 3:8

MOUNT HERMON

Mount Hermon is located northeast of Lake Huleh in the southernmost part of the Antilebanon mountain range, a range that runs southwest—northeast, parallel to the coastal Lebanon range. Mount Hermon represents the northeastern border of Canaan and marks the northernmost extent of the region of Bashan (1Ch 5:23). Like other ancient sources, the term "Hermon" may refer to the entire mountain range in a few Old Testament passages (Jos 12:5; 13:11).

3:10 Gilead The area north and south of the Jabbok River.
3:11 the Rephaites See note on 2:11. **His bed was decorated with iron** Iron was unusual for the time period (Late Bronze Age); this, along with the bed's unusual size, would have accounted for its notoriety. **nine cubits long and four cubits wide** The iron bed was thirteen feet long and six feet wide, presuming a standard cubit of approximately 18 inches. This point is meant to emphasize Og's incredible height—he was a giant. Compare note on 2:11.

3:23–29 Moses closes his historical recap with the account of how he was unable to lead the people into the promised land. Instead, Joshua will lead Israel during the conquest of Canaan. Moses was only allowed to look out and see the land from a distance (Nu 27:12–23). He was forbidden from entering the land because he had disobeyed Yahweh at Meribah (Nu 20:2–13).

3:26 because of you Here and in Dt 1:37 Moses frames the incident at Meribah in a way that blames the Israel-

me and would not listen to me. "That is enough," the LORD said. "Do not speak to me anymore about this matter. ²⁷Go up to the top of Pisgah and look west and north and south and east. Look at the land with your own eyes, since you are not going to cross this Jordan. ²⁸But commission Joshua, and encourage and strengthen him, for he will lead this people across and will cause them to inherit the land that you will see." ²⁹So we stayed in the valley near Beth Peor.

Obedience Commanded

4 Now, Israel, hear the decrees and laws I am about to teach you. Follow them so that you may live and may go in and take possession of the land the LORD, the God of your ancestors, is giving you. ²Do not add to what I command you and do not subtract from it, but keep the commands of the LORD your God that I give you.

³You saw with your own eyes what the LORD did at Baal Peor. The LORD your God destroyed from among you everyone who followed the Baal of Peor, ⁴but all of you who held fast to the LORD your God are still alive today.

⁵See, I have taught you decrees and laws as the LORD my God commanded me, so that you may follow them in the land you are entering to take possession of it. ⁶Observe them carefully, for this will show your wisdom and understanding to the nations, who will hear about all these decrees and say, "Surely this great nation is a wise and understanding people." ⁷What other nation is so great as to have their gods near them the way

the LORD our God is near us whenever we pray to him? ⁸And what other nation is so great as to have such righteous decrees and laws as this body of laws I am setting before you today?

⁹Only be careful, and watch yourselves closely so that you do not forget the things your eyes have seen or let them fade from your heart as long as you live. Teach them to your children and to their children after them. ¹⁰Remember the day you stood before the LORD your God at Horeb, when he said to me, "Assemble the people before me to hear my words so that they may learn to revere me as long as they live in the land and may teach them to their children." ¹¹You came near and stood at the foot of the mountain while it blazed with fire to the very heavens, with black clouds and deep darkness. ¹²Then the LORD spoke to you out of the fire. You heard the sound of words but saw no form; there was only a voice. ¹³He declared to you his covenant, the Ten Commandments, which he commanded you to follow and then wrote them on two stone tablets. ¹⁴And the LORD directed me at that time to teach you the decrees and laws you are to follow in the land that you are crossing the Jordan to possess.

Idolatry Forbidden

¹⁵You saw no form of any kind the day the LORD spoke to you at Horeb out of the fire. Therefore watch yourselves very carefully, ¹⁶so that you do not become corrupt and make for yourselves an idol, an image of any shape, whether formed like a man or a woman, ¹⁷or like any animal on earth or any bird that flies in the air, ¹⁸or like any creature

---

ites for Yahweh's decision to punish him (Nu 20:2–12), but Yahweh will allow no excuse for disobedience of his command. Moses is punished for his own actions, aside from the root cause.

4:1–43 Moses leverages his historical recap and other historical references to call Israel to obey Yahweh. He reminds Israel of Yahweh's judgment brought by their idolatry at Baal Peor (Nu 25) and alludes to their parents' experience of Yahweh's presence at Sinai (Ex 19–24). Now the punishment of wandering is over, and the inheritance of Yahweh's promised land is imminent. This call to obedience stands in stark contrast to the unbelief and rebellion that characterized the Israelites in this same position nearly 40 years earlier (see Dt 2:7,14).

In vv. 1–40, Moses lays out the requirements for a successful conquest. The most important thing that Israel must do is maintain total devotion to Yahweh alone (vv. 15–40). This section concludes with a brief explanation of the cities of refuge (vv. 41–43; see Nu 35; Dt 19).

4:2 This verse could be a prohibition against altering or adding to the laws Yahweh gave through Moses. However, the law is not an exhaustive code that covers every circumstance of life; moreover, regulations are sometimes adapted within the law itself (e.g., the laws for Passover; compare Ex 12; Dt 16).

4:6 great nation This does not refer to numerical size here (compare 7:7) but to the spiritual greatness arising

from Israel's covenant relationship with Yahweh and their ensuing laws (see vv. 7–8).

4:9 the things your eyes have seen This seems to refer to Israel's experiences at Horeb (also called Sinai), which were part of the collective memory of the people (see Ex 19–20; 24; 32; compare note on Dt 4:11). In vv. 9–31 Moses admonishes Israel to reject idolatry based on these experiences.

4:11 stood at the foot of the mountain Although the previous generation—those who were present at Horeb—died in the wilderness, Moses addresses the children of that generation as if they themselves were present. See Ex 19:17.

4:13 Ten Commandments Alluding to the instructions given in Ex 20:1–24. Those commandments are repeated at the beginning of Moses' recitation of the law (Dt 5:6–21).

4:16 an idol Making idols was forbidden in the Ten Commandments (see Ex 20:3–6; Dt 5:8). The backdrop to the prohibition against making idols is the scene at Horeb where the people of Israel saw no visible form of Yahweh (compare note on 4:9). Moses, Aaron, Nadab, Abihu and seventy of Israel's elders, however, did see the God of Israel in a more tangible way (Ex 24:9–12).

4:18 waters below According to ancient Near Eastern cosmology, the earth either floated atop an ocean of water or sat on pillars (or foundations) in the water. See the infographic "Ancient Hebrew Conception of the Universe" on p. 5.

that moves along the ground or any fish in the waters below. ¹⁹And when you look up to the sky and see the sun, the moon and the stars — all the heavenly array — do not be enticed into bowing down to them and worshiping things the LORD your God has apportioned to all the nations under heaven. ²⁰But as for you, the LORD took you and brought you out of the iron-smelting furnace, out of Egypt, to be the people of his inheritance, as you now are.

²¹The LORD was angry with me because of you, and he solemnly swore that I would not cross the Jordan and enter the good land the LORD your God is giving you as your inheritance. ²²I will die in this land; I will not cross the Jordan; but you are about to cross over and take possession of that good land. ²³Be careful not to forget the covenant of the LORD your God that he made with you; do not make for yourselves an idol in the form of anything the LORD your God has forbidden. ²⁴For the LORD your God is a consuming fire, a jealous God.

²⁵After you have had children and grandchildren and have lived in the land a long time — if you then become corrupt and make any kind of idol, doing evil in the eyes of the LORD your God and arousing his anger, ²⁶I call the heavens and the earth as witnesses against you this day that you will quickly perish from the land that you are crossing the Jordan to possess. You will not live there long but will certainly be destroyed. ²⁷The LORD will scatter you among the peoples, and only a few of you will survive among the nations to which the LORD will drive you. ²⁸There you will worship man-made gods of wood and stone, which cannot see or hear or eat or smell. ²⁹But if from there you seek the LORD your God, you will find him if you seek him with all your heart and with all your soul. ³⁰When you are in distress and all these things have happened to you, then in later days you will return to the LORD your God and obey him. ³¹For the LORD your God is a merciful God; he will not abandon or destroy you or forget the covenant with your ancestors, which he confirmed to them by oath.

The LORD Is God

³²Ask now about the former days, long before your time, from the day God created human beings on the earth; ask from one end of the heavens to the other. Has anything so great as this ever happened, or has anything like it ever been heard of? ³³Has any other people heard the voice of God[a]

---

a 33 Or *of a god*

4:19–20 These two verses parallel Dt 32:8–9 and explain that the heavenly host (the celestial forms described here) were considered divine beings who should not be worshiped in place of Yahweh (see 32:8 and note). Belief that the heavenly host represented gods was common in the ancient Near East.

4:19 all the nations under heaven This phrase, combined with the inheritance language in v. 20, suggests that a contrast is being made here between Israel and other nations. Ancient Israelites understood other nations, whom Yahweh had disinherited (Ge 10 — 11; Dt 32:8–9), to be under the leadership of foreign gods, while Israel was under the leadership of Yahweh.

4:20 the iron-smelting furnace, out of Egypt Either a metaphorical reference to the exodus as a refining fire for the fledgling nation (Isa 48:10) or an allusion to the difficulties of slavery in Egypt itself.

4:21 LORD was angry with me See Dt 3:26 and note; compare Nu 20:1–14.

4:23 the covenant of the LORD your God The law given at Sinai — which is also called the Book of the Covenant (Ex 24:7) — constituted the terms of Israel's covenant with Yahweh. It functioned as a sort of legal contract between Yahweh and Israel, providing terms for blessing or judgment. See Ex 24.

4:24 God is a consuming fire The image of God as a fire functions as a warning to Israel against disobedience, specifically idolatry — this is made clear by the statement that God is a jealous God.

4:26 you will quickly perish Here, Moses warns of the severe penalty for the spiritual infidelity of practicing idolatry and worshiping other gods. This type of disobedience will result in death and removal from the promised land (Dt 4:26–28).

4:27 scatter you among the peoples The punishment threatened here, scattering, is the opposite of God's intended blessing of gathering Israel as one nation in the promised land.

4:28 There you will worship This idea does not violate the notion that Yahweh was accessible anywhere (see v. 29), but instead reflects the belief that only the land of Israel was sacred space for the worship of Yahweh in this period of time. Other nations and their lands were rejected as impure — a logical outcome of the worldview described in vv. 19–20 and 32:8–9 (compare Zec 2:8).

4:29 heart In ancient Israelite thought, emotions, thoughts and intentions were associated with the heart (Ge 6:5; Ex 4:21). **soul** In parallel with the heart, the soul represented the center of a person's thoughts and desires (Eze 24:25; Job 23:13; compare note on Dt 6:5). The mention of the heart and the soul here emphasizes that true repentance is a complete change of heart (compare Eze 36:26–32).

4:30 later days This refers to the exile that will inevitably come if Israel fails to stay faithful to Yahweh — the exile will be the punishment Yahweh will issue.

4:31 a merciful God Israel is reminded of God's character (Ex 34:6). **covenant with your ancestors** Yahweh will accept the repentance of his people in faithfulness to the covenant he made with their ancestors (see Ge 15; Ex 24).

4:32–40 Moses follows the dire warning of exile (Dt 4:26–31) with a plea to Israel to maintain fidelity to Yahweh, essentially arguing that history validates Yahweh alone as the true God. No other god has ever accomplished what he did at creation, the exodus, and Mount Sinai; no other god has the power and authority to act in these ways. Compare Dt 4:19–20; compare 32:8–9.

speaking out of fire, as you have, and lived? ³⁴Has any god ever tried to take for himself one nation out of another nation, by testings, by signs and wonders, by war, by a mighty hand and an outstretched arm, or by great and awesome deeds, like all the things the LORD your God did for you in Egypt before your very eyes?

³⁵You were shown these things so that you might know that the LORD is God; besides him there is no other. ³⁶From heaven he made you hear his voice to discipline you. On earth he showed you his great fire, and you heard his words from out of the fire. ³⁷Because he loved your ancestors and chose their descendants after them, he brought you out of Egypt by his Presence and his great strength, ³⁸to drive out before you nations greater and stronger than you and to bring you into their land to give it to you for your inheritance, as it is today.

³⁹Acknowledge and take to heart this day that the LORD is God in heaven above and on the earth below. There is no other. ⁴⁰Keep his decrees and commands, which I am giving you today, so that it may go well with you and your children after you and that you may live long in the land the LORD your God gives you for all time.

Cities of Refuge
4:41-43 Ref — Nu 35:6-34; Dt 19:1-14; Jos 20:1-9

⁴¹Then Moses set aside three cities east of the Jordan, ⁴²to which anyone who had killed a person could flee if they had unintentionally killed a neighbor without malice aforethought. They could flee into one of these cities and save their life. ⁴³The cities were these: Bezer in the wilderness plateau, for the Reubenites; Ramoth in Gilead, for the Gadites; and Golan in Bashan, for the Manassites.

Introduction to the Law

⁴⁴This is the law Moses set before the Israelites. ⁴⁵These are the stipulations, decrees and laws Moses gave them when they came out of Egypt ⁴⁶and were in the valley near Beth Peor east of the Jordan, in the land of Sihon king of the Amorites, who reigned in Heshbon and was defeated by Moses and the Israelites as they came out of Egypt. ⁴⁷They took possession of his land and the land of Og king of Bashan, the two Amorite kings east of the Jordan. ⁴⁸This land extended from Aroer on the rim of the Arnon Gorge to Mount Sirion*a* (that is, Hermon), ⁴⁹and included all the Arabah east of the Jordan, as far as the Dead Sea,*b* below the slopes of Pisgah.

The Ten Commandments
5:6-21pp — Ex 20:1-17

5 Moses summoned all Israel and said:
Hear, Israel, the decrees and laws I declare in your hearing today. Learn them and be sure to follow them. ²The LORD our God made a covenant with us at Horeb. ³It was not with our ancestors*c* that the LORD made this covenant, but with us,

---

a 48 Syriac (see also 3:9); Hebrew *Siyon*   *b 49* Hebrew *the Sea of the Arabah*   *c 3* Or *not only with our parents*

4:32 ask from one end of the heavens to the other The expression means to ask anyone anywhere.
4:33 and lived A direct encounter with God is a life-threatening experience (see Ge 32:30; Ex 3:6; 19:21; 33:20–23; Jdg 13:22).
4:35 besides him there is no other Affirms that Yahweh is utterly unique and no other gods can compare to him.
4:38 nations greater and stronger than you Refers to Israel's victories in the Transjordan over the Amalekites at Rephidim (Ex 17:8–16), the Amorites of king Sihon's region (Nu 21:21–35; Dt 2:26–37), and the kingdom of king Og of Bashan (Dt 3:1–22). Compare Dt 4:44–48.

4:41–43 Moses delineates the location and purpose of the cities of refuge; six cities were chosen, three in the Transjordan (Nu 35:14).

4:42 They could flee into one of these cities The purpose of the city of refuge was providing asylum for someone who had killed a person accidentally. See Nu 35:9–34.

4:44–49 This short section introduces the next major division in Deuteronomy: the main body of legal stipulations connected with Israel's covenant with Yahweh (Dt 4:44—26:19). The legal material is presented in the form of a sermon explaining the laws given at Sinai (also called Horeb; compare note on 1:6) and recorded in the book of Exodus.

4:44 the law Moses recites this law—referring to various passages of moral, legal and religious legislation—in chs. 5–26. The main source for this repetition of Biblical law is the legal material from the book of Exodus, especially the so-called "Covenant Code" in Ex 20–23.

5:1–33 Moses' discourse on God's law begins here with a rehearsal of the Ten Commandments (Dt 5:6–21; compare Ex 20:1–17). One approach to understanding Deuteronomy's law is to view it as an exposition of these Ten Commandments. Moses' teachings in Dt 6–26 can be connected thematically with the legal principles introduced in the Ten Commandments.

The recollection of the appearance of Yahweh at Sinai roots the laws in divine revelation and legitimizes their authority. While many of Israel's laws parallel those of surrounding cultures, Israel's laws were tied to a covenantal relationship with Yahweh. Since most members of the present generation were children when Israel first received the law at Sinai, Moses needed to teach the laws again. Many people either would not have heard or witnessed the divine encounters at Sinai, or they would have been too young to remember it (see v. 5).

5:2 made a covenant with us at Horeb Refers to the giving of the laws at Sinai, another name for the same place (Ex 19–24). Obeying the laws was how Israel held up their end of the contract (or covenant) with Yahweh.
5:3 not with our ancestors Moses impresses upon the people that they too are bound to the covenant made with

with all of us who are alive here today. [4]The Lord spoke to you face to face out of the fire on the mountain. [5](At that time I stood between the Lord and you to declare to you the word of the Lord, because you were afraid of the fire and did not go up the mountain.) And he said:

[6]"I am the Lord your God, who brought you out of Egypt, out of the land of slavery.

[7]"You shall have no other gods before[a] me.

[8]"You shall not make for yourself an image in the form of anything in heaven above or on the earth beneath or in the waters below. [9]You shall not bow down to them or worship them; for I, the Lord your God, am a jealous God, punishing the children for the sin of the parents to the third and fourth generation of those who hate me, [10]but showing love to a thousand generations of those who love me and keep my commandments.

[11]"You shall not misuse the name of the Lord your God, for the Lord will not hold anyone guiltless who misuses his name.

[12]"Observe the Sabbath day by keeping it holy, as the Lord your God has commanded you. [13]Six days you shall labor and do all your work, [14]but the seventh day is a sabbath to the Lord your God. On it you shall not do any work, neither you, nor your son or daughter, nor your male or female servant, nor your ox, your donkey or any of your animals, nor any foreigner residing in your towns, so that your male and female servants may rest, as you do. [15]Remember that you were slaves in Egypt and that the Lord your God brought you out of there with a mighty hand and an outstretched arm. Therefore the Lord your God has commanded you to observe the Sabbath day.

[16]"Honor your father and your mother, as the Lord your God has commanded you, so that you may live long and that it may go well with you in the land the Lord your God is giving you.

[17]"You shall not murder.

[18]"You shall not commit adultery.

[19]"You shall not steal.

[20]"You shall not give false testimony against your neighbor.

[21]"You shall not covet your neighbor's wife. You shall not set your desire on your neighbor's house or land, his male or female servant, his ox or donkey, or anything that belongs to your neighbor."

[22]These are the commandments the Lord proclaimed in a loud voice to your whole assembly there on the mountain from out of the fire, the cloud and the deep darkness; and he added

---

[a] 7 Or besides

---

their ancestors. Though they were not physically present, the enduring nature of the covenant is as applicable to them as is it was to their ancestors.

5:4 face to face The people of Israel may have heard the Ten Commandments from Yahweh directly (see Ex 20:1–17); however, the presence of God was too terrifying, so the people begged Moses to act as an intermediary (see Ex 20:18–21). For this reason, other passages emphasize that Yahweh spoke with Moses face to face (see Dt 34:10; Ex 33:11).

5:6–21 These verses record the Ten Commandments, following the list from Ex 20:1–17 almost precisely. The major divergence is in the rationale given for the Sabbath observance. In Exodus, the command to observe the Sabbath rest is grounded in Yahweh's rest from his work after he finished creating the universe (Ex 20:8–11; Ge 2:1–3). In Deuteronomy, the Sabbath rest is based on Israel's past experience in slavery in Egypt (Dt 5:15).

5:8 waters below The references in this verse to heaven, earth and waters reflect the ancient Hebrew conception of the universe. The commandment prohibits making an idol out of anything found in the universe. The physical world was perceived in Hebrew thought as having these three parts: heaven above, earth itself, and waters under the earth. The land floated on the waters, anchored by pillars (1Sa 2:8). The earth was separated from the heavens by a dome-like vault (Ge 1:6–8).Compare Ex 20:4. See the infographic "Ancient Hebrew Conception of the Universe" on p. 5.

5:9 to the third and fourth generation An expression that describes the normal extent of a long lifespan.

Consequently, rather than referring to a perpetual generational curse, the punishment extends only as long as the descendants of the guilty conceivably lived.

5:11 You shall not misuse the name of the Lord The broader context of this phrase is that of establishing legal testimony. See note on Dt 5:6–21; compare 6:13.

5:16 Honor The Hebrew verb used here, *kaved*, refers to reverence and respect. This verse also assumes that father and mother deserve an equal amount of honor.

5:19 You shall not steal This law likely speaks of personal property rights, but it may involve more.

5:20 You shall not give false testimony The wording here points to a judicial context in which the truth or falsehood of criminal accusations were established. Ancient legal proceedings depended mainly on witness testimony, so this command established the validity of testimony and preserved confidence in the judicial system necessary for a stable society.

5:21 You shall not covet The Hebrew verb used here, *chamad*, speaks of obsession—desire so strong that it compels someone to violate another person's body or property. The command speaks to more than just internal disposition (compare Pr 6:25). Other passages where *chamad* is used indicate this command likely refers to an act of theft (e.g., Ex 34:24; Jos 7:21). Consequently, this command seems to parallel the earlier prohibition against stealing (see Dt 5:19; Ex 20:15). Compare Mt 5:27–30.

5:22–33 In this passage, Moses recounts the scene from Ex 20:18–21 where the people react to having heard the Ten Commandments from Yahweh himself. Moses also describes the scene in more detail, making

nothing more. Then he wrote them on two stone tablets and gave them to me.

²³When you heard the voice out of the darkness, while the mountain was ablaze with fire, all the leaders of your tribes and your elders came to me. ²⁴And you said, "The LORD our God has shown us his glory and his majesty, and we have heard his voice from the fire. Today we have seen that a person can live even if God speaks with them. ²⁵But now, why should we die? This great fire will consume us, and we will die if we hear the voice of the LORD our God any longer. ²⁶For what mortal has ever heard the voice of the living God speaking out of fire, as we have, and survived? ²⁷Go near and listen to all that the LORD our God says. Then tell us whatever the LORD our God tells you. We will listen and obey."

²⁸The LORD heard you when you spoke to me, and the LORD said to me, "I have heard what this people said to you. Everything they said was good. ²⁹Oh, that their hearts would be inclined to fear me and keep all my commands always, so that it might go well with them and their children forever!

³⁰"Go, tell them to return to their tents. ³¹But you stay here with me so that I may give you all the commands, decrees and laws you are to teach them to follow in the land I am giving them to possess."

³²So be careful to do what the LORD your God has commanded you; do not turn aside to the right or to the left. ³³Walk in obedience to all that the LORD your God has commanded you, so that you may live and prosper and prolong your days in the land that you will possess.

Love the LORD Your God

6 These are the commands, decrees and laws the LORD your God directed me to teach you to observe in the land that you are crossing the Jordan to possess, ²so that you, your children and their children after them may fear the LORD your God as long as you live by keeping all his decrees and commands that I give you, and so that you may enjoy long life. ³Hear, Israel, and be careful to obey so that it may go well with you and that you may increase greatly in a land flowing with milk and honey, just as the LORD, the God of your ancestors, promised you.

⁴Hear, O Israel: The LORD our God, the LORD is one.ᵃ ⁵Love the LORD your God with all your heart and with all your soul and with all your strength. ⁶These commandments that I give you today are to be on your hearts. ⁷Impress them on your children. Talk about them when you sit at home and when you walk along the road, when

ᵃ 4 Or *The LORD our God is one LORD*; or *The LORD is our God, the LORD is one*; or *The LORD is our God, the LORD alone*

---

it clear that the people had heard Yahweh's voice (see Dt 5:24; this detail is only implied in Exodus; compare Dt 5:4 and note). After their initial exposure to Yahweh's awesome presence, the people ask Moses to act as the intermediary between them and God. This account of the event includes God's favorable response—he was pleased that Israel was showing an appropriate amount of fear and reverence (vv. 28–29). At that point, the nation was dismissed and Yahweh continued with revealing his commandments directly to Moses (vv. 30–33).

5:31 you stay here with me This episode provides part of the basis for Moses' being considered a prophet. See 18:15–22.

6:1–25 As is the case with Exodus, the Ten Commandments (the Decalogue; ch. 5) enumerated in Deuteronomy are only an entry point to the main thrust of the book: the need for exclusive loyalty to Yahweh. Chapters 6–11 articulate the rationale for that loyalty and set the context for the more detailed laws for Israel given in chs. 12–26. This chapter emphasizes the importance of teaching the laws to future generations and passing on the tradition of complete obedience and loyalty to Yahweh.

6:1 observe in the land Israel's inheritance of the land is once again connected to obedience (Nu 14:23; 32:11. Dt 4:1,5).

6:2 you, your children and their children after them The wording here indicates that Israel's laws had a twofold purpose: They were an expression of reverence for Yahweh and a means of teaching this reverence to the next generation.

6:4 Hear, O Israel The affirmation of loyalty to Yahweh in this verse is traditionally called the "Shema" from this opening call to attention, which in Hebrew is *shema' yisra'el*. The Shema represents the greatest commandment of Judaism and Christianity, as it represents God's expectation that God's people will remain wholly loyal to him. **LORD our God, the LORD is one** The four Hebrew words used here represent the core confession of belief in Yahweh as the one true God. However, the syntactic relationship of these four Hebrew words—*yhwh elohenu yhwh echad*—presents a complicated translation issue. These four words can be understood as a single clause or as two separate clauses. Additional ambiguity over the grammatical function of the final word yields five possible translations for this confession: (1) "Yahweh is our God; Yahweh is one." (2) "Yahweh our God, Yahweh is one." (3) "Yahweh our God is one Yahweh." (4) "Yahweh is our God, Yahweh alone." (5) "Our one God is Yahweh, Yahweh." The problem is that while Hebrew frequently uses nominal sentences (where the verb "to be" is understood), the Shema does not clearly fit the typical patterns for those types of sentences. Every possible reading is open to objection because some aspect violates typical grammatical usage. However, the first two words—*yhwh elohenu*—always mean "Yahweh our God" elsewhere in Deuteronomy where the phrase occurs 24 more times (e.g., 1:6,19,20). This pattern supports favoring option 2—"Yahweh our God, Yahweh is one."

6:5 with all your heart and with all your soul The Hebrew terms *levav* (often translated "heart") and *nephesh* (often translated "soul") do not refer to separate components of the human person. Rather, the terms overlap in meaning, conveying the internal life, dispositions, emotions and intellect.

6:7 Impress them on your children This command presumes that teachers know their content, which in turn presumes concentrated effort and study.

you lie down and when you get up. ⁸Tie them as symbols on your hands and bind them on your foreheads. ⁹Write them on the doorframes of your houses and on your gates.

¹⁰When the LORD your God brings you into the land he swore to your fathers, to Abraham, Isaac and Jacob, to give you — a land with large, flourishing cities you did not build, ¹¹houses filled with all kinds of good things you did not provide, wells you did not dig, and vineyards and olive groves you did not plant — then when you eat and are satisfied, ¹²be careful that you do not forget the LORD, who brought you out of Egypt, out of the land of slavery.

¹³Fear the LORD your God, serve him only and take your oaths in his name. ¹⁴Do not follow other gods, the gods of the peoples around you; ¹⁵for the LORD your God, who is among you, is a jealous God and his anger will burn against you, and he will destroy you from the face of the land. ¹⁶Do not put the LORD your God to the test as you did at Massah. ¹⁷Be sure to keep the commands of the LORD your God and the stipulations and decrees he has given you. ¹⁸Do what is right and good in the LORD's sight, so that it may go well with you and you may go in and take over the good land the LORD promised on oath to your ancestors, ¹⁹thrusting out all your enemies before you, as the LORD said.

²⁰In the future, when your son asks you, "What is the meaning of the stipulations, decrees and laws the LORD our God has commanded you?" ²¹tell him: "We were slaves of Pharaoh in Egypt, but the LORD brought us out of Egypt with a mighty hand. ²²Before our eyes the LORD sent signs and wonders — great and terrible — on Egypt and Pharaoh and his whole household. ²³But he brought us out from there to bring us in and give us the land he promised on oath to our ancestors. ²⁴The LORD commanded us to obey all these decrees and to fear the LORD our God, so that we might always prosper and be kept alive, as is the case today. ²⁵And if we are careful to obey all this law before the LORD our God, as he has commanded us, that will be our righteousness."

Driving Out the Nations

7 When the LORD your God brings you into the land you are entering to possess and drives out before you many nations — the Hittites, Girgashites, Amorites, Canaanites, Perizzites, Hivites and Jebusites, seven nations larger and stronger than you — ²and when the LORD your God has delivered them over to you and you have defeated them, then you must destroy them totally.ᵃ Make no treaty with them, and show them no mercy. ³Do not intermarry with them. Do not give your daughters to their sons or take their daughters

ᵃ 2 The Hebrew term refers to the irrevocable giving over of things or persons to the LORD, often by totally destroying them; also in verse 26.

6:8–9 Not only must the people of Israel memorize and rehearse Yahweh's commands in order to internalize them, they must also wear them on the body (compare Ex 13:9,16) and attach the words to their homes. The Israelites practiced these commands by placing written commandments in leather pouches (*tefillin* or "phylacteries"; compare Mt 23:5) and then literally binding them on their arms and forehead with leather straps. The command to put the laws of Yahweh on doorposts (*mezuzoth* in Hebrew; Dt 6:9) likewise resulted in the Jewish practice of writing passages of Scripture on a small piece of parchment that was rolled and inserted in a case affixed to the doors, lintels and doorposts of private houses. The verses written on those small parchments typically included this passage (vv. 4–9) and 11:13–21.

6:13 take your oaths in his name Swearing by Yahweh's name served as an oath of loyalty (e.g., 10:20; Jos 2:12; Ps 63:11; Isa 45:23; 65:16; Jer 12:16). Compare Mt 5:33–37.

6:14 Do not follow other gods This command is central to the Shema (see Dt 6:4 and note): exclusive loyalty to Yahweh. All other gods are forbidden for the Israelites (see 5:7; 13:6–8; compare 4:19–20; 32:8–9).

6:15 he will destroy you Loyalty to Yahweh is critical not only to Israel's continued occupation of the promised land but to their existence as a people (see Lev 26). Compare Dt 7:16.

6:16 as you did at Massah Moses recalls an earlier incident of the people's rebellion and disloyalty to Yahweh. See Ex 17:1–7.

6:20 stipulations Moses again discusses the duty to teach the next generation, beginning with a person's own children. When children ask about how Israel escaped Egypt (Ex 12–14) and came to dwell in the land, their parents must know how to respond because it is integral to Israel's very identity as a nation governed by Yahweh himself.

7:1–26 This chapter continues the emphasis on the absolute necessity of loyalty to Yahweh and his commands. The first six verses repeat (though not identically) earlier instructions to destroy the indigenous Canaanites and their idols (e.g., Ex 23:24,32–33; 34:12–16; Nu 33:50–56). This passage also forbids intermarriage with the Canaanites on the grounds that it will lead to idolatry (Dt 7:3–4; compare Nu 25:1–3; 1Ki 11:1–11).

7:1 into the land you are entering In Ex 23:20–23, Yahweh told Moses that an angel would bring them to Canaan (which Jdg 2:1–3 validates). The angel is not mentioned here. Instead Yahweh is described as leading the people, an idea consistent with Dt 4:37, where Yahweh said he would bring Israel to the land. Exodus 23 describes the angel as being indwelled by Yahweh's name. This sort of language is part of the name theology of the Hebrew Bible, in which "the name" of Yahweh serves as an expression for Yahweh himself.

7:2 you must destroy them totally The Hebrew concept of *cherem*, which is evoked in the Hebrew text here, meant designating someone or something as sacred property. This designation often involved destruction. See note on Jos 6:16; note on Jos 6:17; compare note on Dt 2:34.

7:3 Do not intermarry with them Intermarriage with the Canaanite populations would lead the Israelites to

for your sons, ⁴for they will turn your children away from following me to serve other gods, and the LORD's anger will burn against you and will quickly destroy you. ⁵This is what you are to do to them: Break down their altars, smash their sacred stones, cut down their Asherah poles[a] and burn their idols in the fire. ⁶For you are a people holy to the LORD your God. The LORD your God has chosen you out of all the peoples on the face of the earth to be his people, his treasured possession.

⁷The LORD did not set his affection on you and choose you because you were more numerous than other peoples, for you were the fewest of all peoples. ⁸But it was because the LORD loved you and kept the oath he swore to your ancestors that he brought you out with a mighty hand and redeemed you from the land of slavery, from the power of Pharaoh king of Egypt. ⁹Know therefore that the LORD your God is God; he is the faithful God, keeping his covenant of love to a thousand generations of those who love him and keep his commandments. ¹⁰But

> those who hate him he will repay to their face
>   by destruction;
> he will not be slow to repay to their face
>   those who hate him.

¹¹Therefore, take care to follow the commands, decrees and laws I give you today.

¹²If you pay attention to these laws and are careful to follow them, then the LORD your God will keep his covenant of love with you, as he swore to your ancestors. ¹³He will love you and bless you and increase your numbers. He will bless the fruit of your womb, the crops of your land — your grain, new wine and olive oil — the calves of your herds and the lambs of your flocks in the land he swore to your ancestors to give you. ¹⁴You will be blessed more than any other people; none of your men or women will be childless, nor will any of your livestock be without young. ¹⁵The LORD will keep you free from every disease. He will not inflict on you the horrible diseases you knew in Egypt, but he will inflict them on all who hate you. ¹⁶You must destroy all the peoples the LORD your God gives over to you. Do not look on them with pity and do not serve their gods, for that will be a snare to you.

¹⁷You may say to yourselves, "These nations are stronger than we are. How can we drive them out?" ¹⁸But do not be afraid of them; remember well what the LORD your God did to Pharaoh and to all Egypt. ¹⁹You saw with your own eyes the great trials, the signs and wonders, the mighty hand and outstretched arm, with which the LORD your God brought you out. The LORD your God will do the same to all the peoples you now fear. ²⁰Moreover, the LORD your God will send the hornet among them until even the survivors who hide from you have perished. ²¹Do not be terrified by them, for the LORD your God, who is among you, is a great and awesome God. ²²The LORD your God will drive out those nations before you, little by little. You will not be allowed to eliminate them all at once, or the wild animals will multiply around you. ²³But the LORD your God will deliver them over to you, throwing them into great confusion until they are destroyed. ²⁴He will give their kings into your hand, and you will wipe out their names from under heaven. No one will be able to stand up against you; you will destroy them. ²⁵The images of their gods you are to burn in the fire. Do not covet the silver and gold on them, and do not take it for yourselves, or you will be ensnared by it, for it is detestable to the LORD your God. ²⁶Do not

---

a 5 That is, wooden symbols of the goddess Asherah; here and elsewhere in Deuteronomy

---

adopt their ways, including their gods — a violation of the first (5:7; Ex 20:3; compare Dt 6:4) and second commandments (5:8–10; Ex 20:4–6). Destruction of those populations would prevent intermarriage with them and idolatry. Compare note on Dt 7:2.

7:5 Break down their altars Israel was to destroy the altars because they were central to the worship of the gods of Canaan through sacrifice. **sacred stones** The Hebrew word used here, *matsevah*, refers to standing stones (whether fashioned by human hands or not) that had religious significance. **Asherah poles** This refers to wooden poles or a tree planted by an altar (see 16:21). The context of some OT passages indicates that the Asherah pole was a symbol for the Canaanite goddess Asherah. At other times, worshipers used the Asherah when there is no mention of the goddess (Jdg 6:25–32). See the table "Pagan Deities of the Old Testament" on p. 1287.

7:6 out of all the peoples Moses links these instructions with those from Ex 19:6; 23:20–33; and 34:10–15, implying that Israel's unique and privileged status requires vehement rejection of other gods and everything associated with devotion to them. **treasured possession** The Hebrew word used here, *segullah*, refers to one's accumulated property. Although Yahweh as creator owns everything, he singles out and cherishes Israel.

7:9 of love The Hebrew term used here, *chesed*, denotes loving favor and is tied to the covenants Yahweh has made with his people (see Ge 15; Ex 24).

7:12 his covenant of love Indicates the link between Yahweh's covenant with the patriarchs (Ge 12:1–3; 15; 17) and loyal obedience to Yahweh as the only God.

7:15 the horrible diseases you knew in Egypt The mention of sickness and disease does not refer to the plagues preceding the exodus (Ex 7–12) but to disease (see Dt 28:27,60).

7:19 LORD your God will do the same Yahweh was successful in bringing his people out of Egypt even though Egypt's population was larger than Israel's. Likewise, Yahweh will destroy Israel's enemies even though they are greater than Israel.

7:25 it is detestable to the LORD your God Moses' words here are not a comprehensive condemnation of wealth; they are directed at idolatrous practices and the idolatry of greed. Compare Jos 7:1,20–21.

7:26 set apart for destruction Meaning to designate the things as sacred property (*cherem* in Hebrew), which often involved complete destruction of the property (see

bring a detestable thing into your house or you, like it, will be set apart for destruction. Regard it as vile and utterly detest it, for it is set apart for destruction.

Do Not Forget the LORD

8 Be careful to follow every command I am giving you today, so that you may live and increase and may enter and possess the land the LORD promised on oath to your ancestors. ²Remember how the LORD your God led you all the way in the wilderness these forty years, to humble and test you in order to know what was in your heart, whether or not you would keep his commands. ³He humbled you, causing you to hunger and then feeding you with manna, which neither you nor your ancestors had known, to teach you that man does not live on bread alone but on every word that comes from the mouth of the LORD. ⁴Your clothes did not wear out and your feet did not swell during these forty years. ⁵Know then in your heart that as a man disciplines his son, so the LORD your God disciplines you.

⁶Observe the commands of the LORD your God, walking in obedience to him and revering him. ⁷For the LORD your God is bringing you into a good land — a land with brooks, streams, and deep springs gushing out into the valleys and hills; ⁸a land with wheat and barley, vines and fig trees, pomegranates, olive oil and honey; ⁹a land where bread will not be scarce and you will lack nothing; a land where the rocks are iron and you can dig copper out of the hills.

¹⁰When you have eaten and are satisfied, praise the LORD your God for the good land he has given you. ¹¹Be careful that you do not forget the LORD your God, failing to observe his commands, his laws and his decrees that I am giving you this day. ¹²Otherwise, when you eat and are satisfied, when you build fine houses and settle down, ¹³and when your herds and flocks grow large and your silver and gold increase and all you have is multiplied, ¹⁴then your heart will become proud and you will forget the LORD your God, who brought you out of Egypt, out of the land of slavery. ¹⁵He led you through the vast and dreadful wilderness, that thirsty and waterless land, with its venomous snakes and scorpions. He brought you water out of hard rock. ¹⁶He gave you manna to eat in the wilderness, something your ancestors had never known, to humble and test you so that in the end it might go well with you. ¹⁷You may say to yourself, "My power and the strength of my hands have produced this wealth for me." ¹⁸But remember the LORD your God, for it is he who gives you the ability to produce wealth, and so confirms his covenant, which he swore to your ancestors, as it is today.

¹⁹If you ever forget the LORD your God and follow other gods and worship and bow down to them, I testify against you today that you will surely be destroyed. ²⁰Like the nations the LORD destroyed before you, so you will be destroyed for not obeying the LORD your God.

Not Because of Israel's Righteousness

9 Hear, Israel: You are now about to cross the Jordan to go in and dispossess nations greater and stronger than you, with large cities that have walls up to the sky. ²The people are strong and tall —

---

note on Dt 7:2). This principle of *cherem* lies behind the entire discussion of driving out the nations of Canaan in ch. 7. The Israelites are engaged in a war against wicked people who have been placed under the judgment of Yahweh (9:4–5); these people will lead the Israelites to idolatry if they are not destroyed. The Israelites will be susceptible to destruction themselves if they adopt the religious practices of the inhabitants of Canaan or take property designated as *cherem* (compare Jos 7:11–15). See note on Jos 6:16; note on Jos 6:17.

8:1–20 Deuteronomy 8 continues the emphasis on exclusive loyalty to Yahweh. The concern in this chapter is that prosperity might weaken Israel's resolve to depend on Yahweh. Israel's history once again provides the backdrop for confronting this potential problem. The Israelites should know by now that their success in the land depends on their God. The prime example in this chapter is Yahweh's provision of manna in the wilderness (see vv. 2,11,14,18–19; compare Ex 16:31–35).

8:1 LORD promised on oath to your ancestors The promises of the Abrahamic covenant (Ge 12:1–3) are once again linked to obedience to the laws of Yahweh (compare Ex 34).

8:3 with manna Yahweh provided for Israel's needs in the wilderness with manna (see Ex 16:15 and note;

16:31–35). **on every word that comes from the mouth of the LORD** Israel's hunger and want in the desert functioned as a testing of their faith and as a lesson. Yahweh gave the Israelites manna to reinforce the knowledge that he would provide (see Dt 8:16). The Israelites are to understand that their prosperity will come from Yahweh's hand and not through their own effort or natural forces. Compare Mt 4:4; Lk 4:4.

8:4 Your clothes did not wear out Israel's prosperity had a divine cause. Under any normal circumstances, clothing would wear out over nearly 40 years of use (the length of time the Israelites were in the wilderness).

8:5 as a man disciplines his son The father-son analogy places discipline in the context of love (compare Pr 3:11–12).

8:15 venomous snakes A reference back to Nu 21:6, where the Israelites encountered poisonous snakes that bit and killed many. **He brought you water out of hard rock** As in Dt 8:3–5, Yahweh's supernatural provision is once again highlighted. Yahweh not only delivered Israel from trials and afflictions, he also provided for their basic needs. See Ex 17:6; Nu 20:11; Ps 78:15.

9:1–12 The address to Israel that begins here continues until Dt 10:22. In this section, Moses' focus shifts to threats to Israel's faith that would be relevant for a

Anakites! You know about them and have heard it said: "Who can stand up against the Anakites?" ³But be assured today that the LORD your God is the one who goes across ahead of you like a devouring fire. He will destroy them; he will subdue them before you. And you will drive them out and annihilate them quickly, as the LORD has promised you.

⁴After the LORD your God has driven them out before you, do not say to yourself, "The LORD has brought me here to take possession of this land because of my righteousness." No, it is on account of the wickedness of these nations that the LORD is going to drive them out before you. ⁵It is not because of your righteousness or your integrity that you are going in to take possession of their land; but on account of the wickedness of these nations, the LORD your God will drive them out before you, to accomplish what he swore to your fathers, to Abraham, Isaac and Jacob. ⁶Understand, then, that it is not because of your righteousness that the LORD your God is giving you this good land to possess, for you are a stiff-necked people.

The Golden Calf

⁷Remember this and never forget how you aroused the anger of the LORD your God in the wilderness. From the day you left Egypt until you arrived here, you have been rebellious against the LORD. ⁸At Horeb you aroused the LORD's wrath so that he was angry enough to destroy you. ⁹When I went up on the mountain to receive the tablets of stone, the tablets of the covenant that the LORD had made with you, I stayed on the mountain forty days and forty nights; I ate no bread and drank no water. ¹⁰The LORD gave me two stone tablets inscribed by the finger of God. On them were all the commandments the LORD proclaimed to you on the mountain out of the fire, on the day of the assembly.

¹¹At the end of the forty days and forty nights, the LORD gave me the two stone tablets, the tablets of the covenant. ¹²Then the LORD told me, "Go down from here at once, because your people whom you brought out of Egypt have become corrupt. They have turned away quickly from what I commanded them and have made an idol for themselves."

¹³And the LORD said to me, "I have seen this people, and they are a stiff-necked people indeed! ¹⁴Let me alone, so that I may destroy them and blot out their name from under heaven. And I will make you into a nation stronger and more numerous than they."

¹⁵So I turned and went down from the mountain while it was ablaze with fire. And the two tablets of the covenant were in my hands. ¹⁶When I looked, I saw that you had sinned against the LORD your God; you had made for yourselves an idol cast in the shape of a calf. You had turned aside quickly from the way that the LORD had commanded you. ¹⁷So I took the two tablets and threw them out of my hands, breaking them to pieces before your eyes.

¹⁸Then once again I fell prostrate before the LORD for forty days and forty nights; I ate no bread and drank no water, because of all the sin you had committed, doing what was evil in the LORD's sight and so arousing his anger. ¹⁹I feared the anger and wrath of the LORD, for he was angry enough with you to destroy you. But again the LORD listened to me. ²⁰And the LORD was angry enough with Aaron to destroy him, but at that time I prayed

---

settled society after the conquest of Canaan. Moses' concern is that Israel will assume that victory resulted from their own strategic skill. While chs. 7–8 stressed that Yahweh would grant success when Israel obeyed, initial successes did not guarantee against future rebellion or forgetfulness of Yahweh. The idolatrous sin of the golden calf (Ex 32) is referenced throughout the chapter.

9:2 Who can stand up against the Anakites An allusion to the giants who were living in Canaan before the conquest. See note on Dt 2:10–12; compare Nu 13:33.
9:3 annihilate them quickly In Dt 7:22, Moses said that Israel's conquest would be gradual. When combined with this verse, the meaning could be that a campaign of conquest will have quick victories but proceed slowly in its totality.
9:4 on account of the wickedness of these nations Moses' comments here recall the warning of 8:11–18. The Israelites should not assume they deserve victory on account of their righteousness and thus take credit for victory. To the contrary, Yahweh will use Israel's armies to remove the Canaanites as judgment for the Canaanites' wickedness. Only by grace will Israel benefit from Yahweh's judgment.
9:7 you aroused the anger of the LORD Alludes to

Israel's idolatrous rebellion at Sinai (Horeb) with the incident of the golden calf (Ex 32). **From the day you left** Israel's complaining began immediately after they departed from Egypt and continued throughout the journey to Sinai (see Ex 14:11; 15:24; 16:2; 17:2). **until you arrived here** Israel is encamped in the plains of Moab near Beth Peor (Dt 3:29). Beth Peor was another site associated with apostasy and rebellion (see Nu 25:1–9).

9:12–21 These verses provide a summary of the events of Ex 32–34 where Israel committed idolatry with a golden calf while Moses was on Sinai (Horeb) receiving the law from Yahweh.

9:12 made an idol for themselves Aaron made the calf from gold ornaments (Ex 32:2,24).
9:14 I may destroy them Yahweh intended to destroy Israel. Moses' intervention prevented that judgment.
9:17 breaking them to pieces Moses' destruction of the two tablets was not simply a reaction of anger, but was an act that symbolically represented a covenant broken by the people's rebellion. See Ex 32:19.
9:20 I prayed for Aaron Because Aaron had made the golden calf (see Ex 32:2–5,21–24). Moses' prayer only partially averted Yahweh's punishment.

for Aaron too. 21Also I took that sinful thing of yours, the calf you had made, and burned it in the fire. Then I crushed it and ground it to powder as fine as dust and threw the dust into a stream that flowed down the mountain.

22You also made the LORD angry at Taberah, at Massah and at Kibroth Hattaavah.

23And when the LORD sent you out from Kadesh Barnea, he said, "Go up and take possession of the land I have given you." But you rebelled against the command of the LORD your God. You did not trust him or obey him. 24You have been rebellious against the LORD ever since I have known you.

25I lay prostrate before the LORD those forty days and forty nights because the LORD had said he would destroy you. 26I prayed to the LORD and said, "Sovereign LORD, do not destroy your people, your own inheritance that you redeemed by your great power and brought out of Egypt with a mighty hand. 27Remember your servants Abraham, Isaac and Jacob. Overlook the stubbornness of this people, their wickedness and their sin. 28Otherwise, the country from which you brought us will say, 'Because the LORD was not able to take them into the land he had promised them, and because he hated them, he brought them out to put them to death in the wilderness.' 29But they are your people, your inheritance that you brought out by your great power and your outstretched arm."

Tablets Like the First Ones

10 At that time the LORD said to me, "Chisel out two stone tablets like the first ones and come up to me on the mountain. Also make a wooden ark.*a* 2I will write on the tablets the words that were on the first tablets, which you broke. Then you are to put them in the ark."

3So I made the ark out of acacia wood and chiseled out two stone tablets like the first ones, and I went up on the mountain with the two tablets in my hands. 4The LORD wrote on these tablets what he had written before, the Ten Commandments he had proclaimed to you on the mountain, out of the fire, on the day of the assembly. And the LORD gave them to me. 5Then I came back down the mountain and put the tablets in the ark I had made, as the LORD commanded me, and they are there now.

6(The Israelites traveled from the wells of Bene Jaakan to Moserah. There Aaron died and was buried, and Eleazar his son succeeded him as priest. 7From there they traveled to Gudgodah and on to Jotbathah, a land with streams of water. 8At that time the LORD set apart the tribe of Levi to carry the ark of the covenant of the LORD, to stand before the LORD to minister and to pronounce blessings in his name, as they still do today. 9That is why the Levites have no share or inheritance among their fellow Israelites; the LORD is their inheritance, as the LORD your God told them.)

10Now I had stayed on the mountain forty days and forty nights, as I did the first time, and the LORD listened to me at this time also. It was not his will to destroy you. 11"Go," the LORD said to me, "and lead the people on their way, so that they may enter and possess the land I swore to their ancestors to give them."

Fear the LORD

12And now, Israel, what does the LORD your God ask of you but to fear the LORD your God, to walk in obedience to him, to love him, to serve the LORD your God with all your heart and with all your soul,

---

a 1 That is, a chest

9:21 that flowed down the mountain Grinding the golden calf to dust and dumping the results into the brook thoroughly dispensed with a ritually impure and repulsive object.
9:22 at Taberah This is where the people complained and fire came down from Yahweh. See Nu 11:1–3. **at Massah** This is where the people complained about lack of water; at Yahweh's command Moses struck a rock and it provided water. See Ex 17:1–7; Dt 6:16. **Kibroth Hattaavah** This is where some of the people complained about not having meat; Yahweh sent quail and a plague. See Nu 11:4–34.

9:27–29 Moses' appeal is to Yahweh's reputation and Yahweh's promises to Israel's patriarchs.

10:1–11 Deuteronomy 10 continues the recollection that Moses had begun in ch. 9, where he recalled receiving Yahweh's laws on tablets of stone and then smashing them at the golden calf incident (see Ex 24:12; 31:18; 32:15–16; compare Dt 4:13; 5:9). The gesture showed that the people broke the covenant with Yahweh as soon as it had been given. By replacing the tablets, Yahweh agreed to restore the covenant. As described in Exodus,

Yahweh reestablished the covenant after the broken tablet incident, but said he would not continue with Israel (see Ex 32:14,34; 33:1–5). Moses, unsatisfied with Yahweh's decision, begged Yahweh to restore his personal relationship with Israel (Ex 33:14–17; 34:1–4,9–28). Deuteronomy 10 recalls Yahweh's decision to once again give his Ten Commandments to Israel.

10:1 Chisel out two stone tablets Although Yahweh inscribes new tablets, he does not make them as in the original instance (Ex 32:16). This suggests a less intimate relationship with Israel. **make a wooden ark** This may not refer to the ark of the covenant. The Hebrew word for "ark" (*aron*) simply denotes a box or chest.
10:6 buried Elsewhere in the narrative about Israel's journey to Canaan (Nu 33:37–39), Aaron's death occurs 40 years after the golden-calf incident. Its mention here prior to entering Canaan may indicate that not seeing the land was a punishment for his role in the golden calf incident. See the map "Route of the Exodus" on p. 2252.
10:9 Levites have no share or inheritance The Levites' portion and inheritance comes through the tithes and offerings given to Yahweh from the Israelites (Nu 18:20–24).

¹³and to observe the LORD's commands and decrees that I am giving you today for your own good?

¹⁴To the LORD your God belong the heavens, even the highest heavens, the earth and everything in it. ¹⁵Yet the LORD set his affection on your ancestors and loved them, and he chose you, their descendants, above all the nations — as it is today. ¹⁶Circumcise your hearts, therefore, and do not be stiff-necked any longer. ¹⁷For the LORD your God is God of gods and Lord of lords, the great God, mighty and awesome, who shows no partiality and accepts no bribes. ¹⁸He defends the cause of the fatherless and the widow, and loves the foreigner residing among you, giving them food and clothing. ¹⁹And you are to love those who are foreigners, for you yourselves were foreigners in Egypt. ²⁰Fear the LORD your God and serve him. Hold fast to him and take your oaths in his name. ²¹He is the one you praise; he is your God, who performed for you those great and awesome wonders you saw with your own eyes. ²²Your ancestors who went down into Egypt were seventy in all, and now the LORD your God has made you as numerous as the stars in the sky.

Love and Obey the LORD

11 Love the LORD your God and keep his requirements, his decrees, his laws and his commands always. ²Remember today that your children were not the ones who saw and experienced the discipline of the LORD your God: his majesty, his mighty hand, his outstretched arm; ³the signs he performed and the things he did in the heart of Egypt, both to Pharaoh king of Egypt and to his whole country; ⁴what he did to the Egyptian army, to its horses and chariots, how he overwhelmed them with the waters of the Red Seaᵃ as they were pursuing you, and how the LORD brought lasting ruin on them. ⁵It was not your children who saw what he did for you in the wilderness until you arrived at this place, ⁶and what he did to Dathan and Abiram, sons of Eliab the Reubenite, when the earth opened its mouth right in the middle of all Israel and swallowed them up with their households, their tents and every living thing that belonged to them. ⁷But it was your own eyes that saw all these great things the LORD has done.

⁸Observe therefore all the commands I am giving you today, so that you may have the strength to go in and take over the land that you are crossing the Jordan to possess, ⁹and so that you may live long in the land the LORD swore to your ancestors to give to them and their descendants, a land flowing with milk and honey. ¹⁰The land you are entering to take over is not like the land of Egypt, from which you have come, where you planted your seed and irrigated it by foot as in a vegetable garden. ¹¹But the land you are crossing the Jordan to take possession of is a land of mountains and valleys that drinks rain from heaven. ¹²It is a land the LORD your God cares for; the eyes of the LORD your God are continually on it from the beginning of the year to its end.

¹³So if you faithfully obey the commands I am giving you today — to love the LORD your God and to serve him with all your heart and with all your soul — ¹⁴then I will send rain on your land in its season, both autumn and spring rains, so that you may gather in your grain, new wine and olive oil. ¹⁵I will provide grass in the fields for your cattle, and you will eat and be satisfied.

¹⁶Be careful, or you will be enticed to turn away

ᵃ 4 Or *the Sea of Reeds*

10:12–22 Yahweh mercifully renewed the covenant and allowed the Israelites to enter into the land rather than destroying them. In light of this, Moses urges the Israelites to obey Yahweh and to adopt a right attitude of the heart rather than blindly obeying Yahweh's commands. To make this point, Moses uses the image of circumcising the heart (see Dt 10:16; compare Lev 26:41; Jer 9:25; Eze 44:7). Circumcision was a sign of Yahweh's covenant with his people (Ge 17); he desired for their actions and thoughts to reflect the same kind of obedience.

10:13 for your own good Yahweh's commandments and statutes were not aimed at restricting Israel's prosperity and joy in the land, but at magnifying it.

10:17 God is God of gods and Lord of lords Israel's attitude should stem from recognizing that Yahweh elected them out of love (Dt 10:15) and that he is superior over all other gods.

10:20 take your oaths in his name Swearing by Yahweh's name served as an expression of loyalty. See note on 6:13.

10:22 as numerous as the stars in the sky The size of the current population is illustrative of Yahweh's faithfulness to his promise. See Ge 15:5 and note; compare Ge 22:17; Ex 32:13.

11:1–32 In Deuteronomy 11, rather than focusing on Yahweh's works of power for Israel, Moses shifts attention to Yahweh's punishment of Egypt, a telling object lesson for the fate of nations that reject Yahweh's will.

11:1 his commands Obedience to Yahweh's commands is the means by which the people will be able to live long in the promised land and how they will demonstrate their love of him and loyalty to him.

11:6 Dathan and Abiram These are Korah's co-conspirators in the rebellion against Moses and Aaron recorded in Nu 16. **households, their tents and every living thing** Reflects the principle of corporate solidarity and punishment that was common in the ancient Near East.

11:13–21 In this passage, Moses explains the implications and conclusions of his sermon — noting that even rainfall in the land of Canaan will depend on Yahweh. Rain, and consequently successful agriculture, will be intertwined with the people's obedience or disobedience to Yahweh. Once again, Moses ties prosperity and life in the land to believing in Yahweh and loyalty to him.

11:16 worship other gods As in Dt 6:12 and 8:11, Moses follows the promise of prosperity with a warning

and worship other gods and bow down to them. [17]Then the LORD's anger will burn against you, and he will shut up the heavens so that it will not rain and the ground will yield no produce, and you will soon perish from the good land the LORD is giving you. [18]Fix these words of mine in your hearts and minds; tie them as symbols on your hands and bind them on your foreheads. [19]Teach them to your children, talking about them when you sit at home and when you walk along the road, when you lie down and when you get up. [20]Write them on the doorframes of your houses and on your gates, [21]so that your days and the days of your children may be many in the land the LORD swore to give your ancestors, as many as the days that the heavens are above the earth.

[22]If you carefully observe all these commands I am giving you to follow — to love the LORD your God, to walk in obedience to him and to hold fast to him — [23]then the LORD will drive out all these nations before you, and you will dispossess nations larger and stronger than you. [24]Every place where you set your foot will be yours: Your territory will extend from the desert to Lebanon, and from the Euphrates River to the Mediterranean Sea. [25]No one will be able to stand against you. The LORD your God, as he promised you, will put the terror and fear of you on the whole land, wherever you go.

[26]See, I am setting before you today a blessing and a curse — [27]the blessing if you obey the commands of the LORD your God that I am giving you today; [28]the curse if you disobey the commands of the LORD your God and turn from the way that I command you today by following other gods, which you have not known. [29]When the LORD your God has brought you into the land you are entering to possess, you are to proclaim on Mount Gerizim the blessings, and on Mount Ebal the curses. [30]As you know, these mountains are across the Jordan, westward, toward the setting sun, near the great trees of Moreh, in the territory of those Canaanites living in the Arabah in the vicinity of Gilgal. [31]You are about to cross the Jordan to enter and take possession of the land the LORD your God is giving you. When you have taken it over and are living there, [32]be sure that you obey all the decrees and laws I am setting before you today.

The One Place of Worship

12 These are the decrees and laws you must be careful to follow in the land that the LORD, the God of your ancestors, has given you to possess — as long as you live in the land. [2]Destroy completely all the places on the high mountains, on the hills and under every spreading tree, where the nations you are dispossessing worship their gods. [3]Break down their altars, smash their sacred stones and burn their Asherah poles in the fire; cut down the idols of their gods and wipe out their names from those places.

[4]You must not worship the LORD your God in their way. [5]But you are to seek the place the LORD

---

regarding the worship of other gods and infidelity to Yahweh.

11:18–20 The list of actions in vv. 18–20 corresponds closely to the list in 6:6–9. See note on 6:8–9.

11:25 the whole land, wherever you go Compare Ge 13:17; Jos 1:3–4; 24:3).

11:26–32 From Dt 5:1 until this point, Moses' speech has served as an introduction to the specific laws he delineates in chs. 12–26. Moses ends this introduction by presenting a choice in v. 26: receive Yahweh's blessing or curse. The promises to Israel's ancestors are available to Moses' audience if they obey. This creates a connection between the Abrahamic and Sinai covenants (Ge 17; Ex 34).

11:29 you are to proclaim Moses anticipates the dramatic covenant ratification ceremony of Dt 27–28 at Shechem. Mount Ebal is north of Shechem and Mount Gerizim is south of Shechem; the two mountains face each other (see 27:4,12–13).

11:30 near the great trees of Moreh This oak marked a sacred site in the patriarchal era (see Ge 12:6).

12:1–28 Deuteronomy 12 begins the main legal code in the book (chs. 12–26). The laws can be divided into three major sections: a collection of laws about worship and religious practices (12:1—16:17); a collection of laws about leadership of the community (16:18—18:22); and a collection of miscellaneous laws (19–26).

This chapter opens the collection of laws about worship by emphasizing that upon entering the promised land

Israel is to worship Yahweh at the one specific place of his choosing (vv. 1–7; compare Jn 4:19–26). Moses forbids the Israelites from setting up altars and worshiping anywhere, as the patriarchs did (Ge 12:7–8; 13:4,18; 22:9; 26:25; 35:1,3,7). Once they complete the conquest, they are to build a central sanctuary in a location that Yahweh will reveal (Dt 12:11). Requiring a single, central place of worship would demand changes in the way the Israelites ordered their life, even to the point of changing the observance of holy days as described in the book of Exodus. This passage of Deuteronomy seems to indicate that the purpose of the centralized sanctuary was to ensure that Israel worshipped Yahweh correctly.

12:2 on the high mountains, on the hills In the ancient Near East, people associated high mountains and hills — remote places that were removed from humans and closer to the sky — as places of worship. They believed these elevated places were sites where divine beings might come down to earth from heaven. In Canaanite mythology, Zaphon was a mountain associated with Baal. Yahweh was associated with Mount Sinai (Horeb). **under every spreading tree** Ancient Canaanites considered trees to be sacred because they symbolized fertility and life. Israelites likewise associated trees with the sacred; trees often marked places of divine encounter (see Ge 12:6–7; compare Jdg 4:4–5).

12:4 in their way The Israelites must not follow the worship practices of other peoples; Yahweh is completely unlike the gods of Canaan (see Dt 12:30–31; compare Ex 23:24).

12:5 the place the LORD your God will choose Deuter-

your God will choose from among all your tribes to put his Name there for his dwelling. To that place you must go; ⁶there bring your burnt offerings and sacrifices, your tithes and special gifts, what you have vowed to give and your freewill offerings, and the firstborn of your herds and flocks. ⁷There, in the presence of the LORD your God, you and your families shall eat and shall rejoice in everything you have put your hand to, because the LORD your God has blessed you.

⁸You are not to do as we do here today, everyone doing as they see fit, ⁹since you have not yet reached the resting place and the inheritance the LORD your God is giving you. ¹⁰But you will cross the Jordan and settle in the land the LORD your God is giving you as an inheritance, and he will give you rest from all your enemies around you so that you will live in safety. ¹¹Then to the place the LORD your God will choose as a dwelling for his Name — there you are to bring everything I command you: your burnt offerings and sacrifices, your tithes and special gifts, and all the choice possessions you have vowed to the LORD. ¹²And there rejoice before the LORD your God — you, your sons and daughters, your male and female servants, and the Levites from your towns who have no allotment or inheritance of their own. ¹³Be careful not to sacrifice your burnt offerings anywhere you please. ¹⁴Offer them only at the place the LORD will choose in one of your tribes, and there observe everything I command you.

¹⁵Nevertheless, you may slaughter your animals in any of your towns and eat as much of the meat as you want, as if it were gazelle or deer, according to the blessing the LORD your God gives you. Both the ceremonially unclean and the clean may eat it. ¹⁶But you must not eat the blood; pour it out on the ground like water. ¹⁷You must not eat in your own towns the tithe of your grain and new wine and olive oil, or the firstborn of your herds and flocks, or whatever you have vowed to give, or your freewill offerings or special gifts. ¹⁸Instead, you are to eat them in the presence of the LORD your God at the place the LORD your God will choose — you, your sons and daughters, your male and female servants, and the Levites from your towns — and you are to rejoice before the LORD your God in everything you put your hand to. ¹⁹Be careful not to neglect the Levites as long as you live in your land.

²⁰When the LORD your God has enlarged your territory as he promised you, and you crave meat and say, "I would like some meat," then you may eat as much of it as you want. ²¹If the place where the LORD your God chooses to put his Name is too far away from you, you may slaughter animals from the herds and flocks the LORD has given you, as I have commanded you, and in your own towns you may eat as much of them as you want. ²²Eat them as you would gazelle or deer. Both the ceremonially unclean and the clean may eat. ²³But be sure you do not eat the blood, because the blood is the life, and you must not eat the life with the meat. ²⁴You must not eat the blood; pour it out on the ground like water. ²⁵Do not eat it, so that it may go well with you and your children after you, because you will be doing what is right in the eyes of the LORD.

²⁶But take your consecrated things and whatever you have vowed to give, and go to the place the LORD will choose. ²⁷Present your burnt offerings on the altar of the LORD your God, both the meat and the blood. The blood of your sacrifices must be poured beside the altar of the LORD your God, but you may eat the meat. ²⁸Be careful to obey all these regulations I am giving you, so that it may always go well with you and your children after you, because you will be doing what is good and right in the eyes of the LORD your God.

²⁹The LORD your God will cut off before you the nations you are about to invade and dispossess. But when you have driven them out and settled in

onomy regularly uses this phrase to refer to the central sanctuary (Dt 12:11,14,18,21,26). From the narrative perspective of Deuteronomy, the location had not yet been determined, but from the later perspective of the historical books, the only legitimate place to worship Yahweh was the Jerusalem temple (see 1Ki 12:25–31; 2Ki 17:9; compare Jn 4:19–26).

12:6 there bring Moses commands that every worship practice associated with the tabernacle be conducted only at this future center of worship (compare Lev 1–5; 27; Nu 18; 28–29). Deuteronomy 12:8–28 explains how the centralization will modify Israelite worship and life. See the infographic "The Tabernacle" on p. 138.

12:7 you and your families shall eat Certain sacrifices involved meals. Once the central sanctuary was in place, people would have to travel to meet these obligations.

12:15 as if it were gazelle or deer Moses may be introducing a modification to earlier legislation. Leviticus 17:1–7 appears to require that all slaughter of animals

for food had to be treated like a sacrifice (see Lev 17:1–7; compare 1Sa 14:31–35). With centralization of worship, it would be impractical to require all people in the land to come to the central sanctuary to slaughter all animals used for food. Here Moses explicitly allows non-sacrificial slaughter, applying the rules for handling the slaughter of wild game to any slaughter that occurs away from the central sanctuary (compare Lev 17:13).

12:16 you must not eat the blood This prohibition against eating blood is consistent throughout OT law (see Lev 3:17; 7:26–27; 17:11–14; compare Ac 15:20).

12:29 — 13:18 Moses' address in this section has a twofold emphasis: Israel is not to worship Yahweh in the manner of Canaanite worship, and Israel must not add to or subtract from Yahweh's commandments (Dt 12:32).

12:29 will cut off The Hebrew verb used here, *karath*, elsewhere expresses the idea of cutting (or making) a covenant with Israel (see note on Ge 15:10). The Canaanite

their land, ³⁰and after they have been destroyed before you, be careful not to be ensnared by inquiring about their gods, saying, "How do these nations serve their gods? We will do the same." ³¹You must not worship the LORD your God in their way, because in worshiping their gods, they do all kinds of detestable things the LORD hates. They even burn their sons and daughters in the fire as sacrifices to their gods.

³²See that you do all I command you; do not add to it or take away from it.ᵃ

Worshiping Other Gods

13ᵇ If a prophet, or one who foretells by dreams, appears among you and announces to you a sign or wonder, ²and if the sign or wonder spoken of takes place, and the prophet says, "Let us follow other gods" (gods you have not known) "and let us worship them," ³you must not listen to the words of that prophet or dreamer. The LORD your God is testing you to find out whether you love him with all your heart and with all your soul. ⁴It is the LORD your God you must follow, and him you must revere. Keep his commands and obey him; serve him and hold fast to him. ⁵That prophet or dreamer must be put to death for inciting rebellion against the LORD your God, who brought you out of Egypt and redeemed you from the land of slavery. That prophet or dreamer tried to turn you from the way the LORD your God commanded you to follow. You must purge the evil from among you.

⁶If your very own brother, or your son or daughter, or the wife you love, or your closest friend secretly entices you, saying, "Let us go and worship other gods" (gods that neither you nor your ancestors have known, ⁷gods of the peoples around you, whether near or far, from one end of the land to the other), ⁸do not yield to them or listen to them. Show them no pity. Do not spare them or shield them. ⁹You must certainly put them to death. Your hand must be the first in putting them to death, and then the hands of all the people. ¹⁰Stone them to death, because they tried to turn you away from the LORD your God, who brought you out of Egypt, out of the land of slavery. ¹¹Then all Israel will hear and be afraid, and no one among you will do such an evil thing again.

¹²If you hear it said about one of the towns the LORD your God is giving you to live in ¹³that troublemakers have arisen among you and have led the people of their town astray, saying, "Let us go and worship other gods" (gods you have not known), ¹⁴then you must inquire, probe and investigate it thoroughly. And if it is true and it has been proved that this detestable thing has been done among you, ¹⁵you must certainly put to the sword all who live in that town. You must destroy it completely,ᶜ both its people and its livestock. ¹⁶You are to gather all the plunder of the town into the middle of the public square and completely burn the town and all its plunder as a whole burnt offering to the LORD your God. That town is to remain a ruin forever, never to be rebuilt, ¹⁷and none of the condemned thingsᶜ are to be found in your hands. Then the LORD will turn from his fierce anger, will show you mercy, and will have compassion on you. He will increase your numbers, as he promised on oath to your ancestors — ¹⁸because you obey the LORD your God by keeping all his commands that I am giving you today and doing what is right in his eyes.

ᵃ 32 In Hebrew texts this verse (12:32) is numbered 13:1.   ᵇ In Hebrew texts 13:1-18 is numbered 13:2-19.   ᶜ 15,17 The Hebrew term refers to the irrevocable giving over of things or persons to the LORD, often by totally destroying them.

---

nations, however, are not brought into a covenant but are cut off from the land—a warning of the fate that will come to Israel if they disregard Yahweh's commandments.
12:31 They even burn their sons and daughters Child sacrifice—a capital crime in Mosaic Law (Lev 18:21; 20:2–5)—illustrates the reprehensible nature of Canaanite religion.

13:1–18 This chapter describes various situations that might result in the people of Israel becoming idolatrous. Here Moses warns against being led astray by false prophets (Dt 13:1–5) or friends and family (vv. 6–11). He also explains how they should proceed if they hear that other Israelites have become idolatrous (vv. 12–18).

13:1 a prophet, or one who foretells by dreams Since prophecy and dreams were associated with divine revelation, Israel must reject any prophet or dreamer whose oracles do not align with Yahweh's commands.
13:2 Let us follow other gods Following other gods would violate the greatest commandment—the central matter pertaining to fidelity to Yahweh (6:4–5)—and would thus endanger Israel's remaining in the land.

13:3 words of that prophet or dreamer Even if the source appears divine, the Israelites must reject the suggestion if the prophet or dreamer suggests violating the commands of Yahweh.
13:8 Do not spare them or shield them People must practice uncompromising fidelity to Yahweh. They must reject and expose even their wives or closest companions if those people promote disloyalty to Yahweh, even though doing so would lead to those people's deaths.
13:9 putting them to death Deuteronomy 17:6–7 requires at least two witnesses to convict a person of the capital crime of worshiping another god. An execution may not occur without a trial to determine guilt.
13:15 You must destroy it completely The Hebrew wording denotes the principle of designating people or things as sacred property (called *cherem* in Hebrew; see note on 7:2). This designation involved judgment from Yahweh and was often associated with idolatry. See note on Jos 6:16; note on 6:17.
13:16 completely burn the town and all its plunder Since the city is devoted to destruction (see note on 13:15), none of its contents can be spared or kept.

Clean and Unclean Food

14:3-20pp — Lev 11:1-23

14 You are the children of the LORD your God. Do not cut yourselves or shave the front of your heads for the dead, [2]for you are a people holy to the LORD your God. Out of all the peoples on the face of the earth, the LORD has chosen you to be his treasured possession.

[3]Do not eat any detestable thing. [4]These are the animals you may eat: the ox, the sheep, the goat, [5]the deer, the gazelle, the roe deer, the wild goat, the ibex, the antelope and the mountain sheep.[a] [6]You may eat any animal that has a divided hoof and that chews the cud. [7]However, of those that chew the cud or that have a divided hoof you may not eat the camel, the rabbit or the hyrax. Although they chew the cud, they do not have a divided hoof; they are ceremonially unclean for you. [8]The pig is also unclean; although it has a divided hoof, it does not chew the cud. You are not to eat their meat or touch their carcasses.

[9]Of all the creatures living in the water, you may eat any that has fins and scales. [10]But anything that does not have fins and scales you may not eat; for you it is unclean.

[11]You may eat any clean bird. [12]But these you may not eat: the eagle, the vulture, the black vulture, [13]the red kite, the black kite, any kind of falcon, [14]any kind of raven, [15]the horned owl, the screech owl, the gull, any kind of hawk, [16]the little owl, the great owl, the white owl, [17]the desert owl, the osprey, the cormorant, [18]the stork, any kind of heron, the hoopoe and the bat.

[19]All flying insects are unclean to you; do not eat them. [20]But any winged creature that is clean you may eat.

[21]Do not eat anything you find already dead. You may give it to the foreigner residing in any of your towns, and they may eat it, or you may sell it to any other foreigner. But you are a people holy to the LORD your God.

Do not cook a young goat in its mother's milk.

Tithes

[22]Be sure to set aside a tenth of all that your fields produce each year. [23]Eat the tithe of your grain, new wine and olive oil, and the firstborn of your herds and flocks in the presence of the LORD your God at the place he will choose as a dwelling for his Name, so that you may learn to revere the LORD your God always. [24]But if that place is too distant and you have been blessed by the LORD your God and cannot carry your tithe (because the place where the LORD will choose to put his

---

[a] 5 The precise identification of some of the birds and animals in this chapter is uncertain.

14:1—15:23 These two chapters present laws related to holiness and ritual purity that closely parallel laws from Exodus and Leviticus (e.g., Ex 21–23; Lev 11–25). For example, the restrictions on mourning customs from Dt 14:1–2 are also found in Leviticus (Lev 19:28; 21:5). The laws about the Sabbath Year in Dt 15:1–18 are paralleled in Lev 25. As in Leviticus, Deuteronomy presents laws about proper worship (Dt 12–13; compare Lev 1–10) before focusing on ritual purity and holiness (Dt 14–15; compare Lev 11–25).

14:1 shave the front of your heads Priests are explicitly commanded to avoid these mourning practices in Lev 21:5. Here the prohibition is extended to the entire people of Israel. The mourning customs of ritual cutting of the skin and shaving of the hair occurred widely in the ancient Near East.

14:2 a people holy to the LORD Israel's status as Yahweh's chosen people requires them to maintain holiness. This holiness was not about morality but about maintaining the separateness of whatever was considered holy. The requirements for ritual purity were designed to maintain the distinction between holy things and everyday things (Lev 10:10–11).

14:3–21 This passage presents the dietary laws for the Israelites, detailing which animals are permitted as food and which are prohibited. The acceptable animals are labeled "clean" while the forbidden animals are labeled "unclean." The categories of clean and unclean relate to the Israelite system of ritual purity. For the most part, the restrictions agree with the list from Lev 11:2–23. Leviticus focuses mainly on identifying what was unclean and only defines the category of clean according to the

criteria in Dt 14:6 (compare Lev 11:3). Deuteronomy provides a list of which animals are considered clean in Dt 14:4–5. See note on Lev 11:1–47.

14:8 The pig See note on Lev 11:7. **You are not to eat their meat or touch their carcasses** Touching the dead body of an unclean animal also caused impurity. Compare Lev 11:26–28.

14:18 the bat See note on Lev 11:19.

14:19 All flying insects are unclean to you Leviticus makes an exception for insects that have jointed legs, so locusts, crickets and grasshoppers are permitted as food (Lev 11:20–23).

14:21 in its mother's milk This prohibition also appears in Exodus, but not in the dietary laws of Leviticus (compare Ex 23:19 and note; Ex 34:26).

14:22–29 This section discusses tithing. The requirement to tithe is also found in Nu 18:20–24, but Numbers designates the tithe for the Levites to provide for their needs since they have no territory of their own (Nu 18:21,24). Here the people are told to bring a tithe to the sanctuary to offer it to Yahweh, but they are instructed to eat the tithe there themselves. The people are still commanded to provide for the Levites since the Levites were given no inheritance (Dt 14:27), but Deuteronomy lacks clear instructions about how to provide for the Levites. Deuteronomy 18:1–8 implies the priests' portions of the food offerings were to be shared with the Levites ministering at the sanctuary, but it is not clear whether this allowance applied to all Levites throughout Israel. Deuteronomy 14:29 puts the Levites in the category of protected classes alongside foreigners, widows and orphans, suggesting they required regular assistance from the community for survival.

Name is so far away), [25] then exchange your tithe for silver, and take the silver with you and go to the place the LORD your God will choose. [26] Use the silver to buy whatever you like: cattle, sheep, wine or other fermented drink, or anything you wish. Then you and your household shall eat there in the presence of the LORD your God and rejoice. [27] And do not neglect the Levites living in your towns, for they have no allotment or inheritance of their own.

[28] At the end of every three years, bring all the tithes of that year's produce and store it in your towns, [29] so that the Levites (who have no allotment or inheritance of their own) and the foreigners, the fatherless and the widows who live in your towns may come and eat and be satisfied, and so that the LORD your God may bless you in all the work of your hands.

The Year for Canceling Debts

15:1-11Ref — Lev 25:8-38

15 At the end of every seven years you must cancel debts. [2] This is how it is to be done: Every creditor shall cancel any loan they have made to a fellow Israelite. They shall not require payment from anyone among their own people, because the LORD's time for canceling debts has been proclaimed. [3] You may require payment from a foreigner, but you must cancel any debt your fellow Israelite owes you. [4] However, there need be no poor people among you, for in the land the LORD your God is giving you to possess as your inheritance, he will richly bless you, [5] if only you fully obey the LORD your God and are careful to follow all these commands I am giving you today. [6] For the LORD your God will bless you as he has promised, and you will lend to many nations but will borrow from none. You will rule over many nations but none will rule over you.

[7] If anyone is poor among your fellow Israelites in any of the towns of the land the LORD your God is giving you, do not be hardhearted or tightfisted toward them. [8] Rather, be openhanded and freely lend them whatever they need. [9] Be careful not to harbor this wicked thought: "The seventh year, the year for canceling debts, is near," so that you do not show ill will toward the needy among your fellow Israelites and give them nothing. They may then appeal to the LORD against you, and you will be found guilty of sin. [10] Give generously to them and do so without a grudging heart; then because of this the LORD your God will bless you in all your work and in everything you put your hand to. [11] There will always be poor people in the land. Therefore I command you to be openhanded toward your fellow Israelites who are poor and needy in your land.

Freeing Servants

15:12-18pp — Ex 21:2-6
15:12-18Ref — Lev 25:38-55

[12] If any of your people — Hebrew men or women — sell themselves to you and serve you six years, in the seventh year you must let them go free. [13] And when you release them, do not send

---

14:25 silver For people who traveled long distances to the central sanctuary (see ch. 12), Moses offers the alternative of making tithes of silver to bring to the sanctuary instead of cattle and crops.

15:1–18 The Sabbath Year (or Sabbatical Year) occurred every seventh year—just as the Sabbath occurred every seventh day (see Ex 20:8–11; 23:10–11). Moreover, every fiftieth year was to be a Year of Jubilee when debts were remitted and property that had been sold reverted to its original owners. The laws for the Sabbath Year and the Year of Jubilee are outlined in Lev 25.

The Sabbath Year and the Jubilee Year were designed for the benefit of the impoverished. Since the poor had limited ability to pay their debts, they often had to work off a debt through indentured servitude. Deuteronomy 15:1–18 is concerned with fair treatment of the impoverished, which included a legal means for them to get out of debt or regain property that economic need had forced them to sell.

This passage addresses a way to deal with the common ancient Near Eastern practice of indentured servitude. It seems that the goal of the Deuteronomy is to prevent the type of poverty that leads to indentured servitude altogether (see 15:4), but with the knowledge that it will likely occur anyway, regulations for dealing with the practice are provided here.

15:2 shall cancel any loan they have made to a fellow Israelite This command is directed at anyone who holds a debt owed by a fellow Israelite. Since the overall concern of the passage is fair treatment of the poor, the debtors are likely impoverished people with no other means to pay the debt. The law may not apply to all types of debt obligations.

15:4 there need be no poor people among you The absence of poverty in the Israelite community is contingent on Israel's complete obedience to Yahweh's law. The conditional nature of this assertion is clear from the rest of vv. 4–6, which alludes to the description of covenantal blessings found in 28:1–14.

15:7 tightfisted toward them The instructions about caring for the impoverished of the community in vv. 7–11 are echoed in Lev 25:35–38. Care for the poor should be motivated by concern for the need of others, not by a desire to make a profit from their misfortune.

15:11 There will always be poor people in the land Moses' statement here (in contrast to Dt 15:4) may reflect his pessimism about the people's obedience (see 31:27–29).

15:12 Hebrew The Hebrew word used here, *ivri*, is the ancient term for Israelites prior to the time of Jacob (Ge 25–50), though it occasionally appears in historical books relating events during the time of Israel's monarchy (1Sa 13:3,7; 14:21). **you must let them go free** It is not just debts that are to be forgiven (Dt 15:2); indentured servants are also to be released in the Sabbath Year (compare Lev 25:39–43). An Israelite, however, could choose to become a permanent member

them away empty-handed. ¹⁴Supply them liberally from your flock, your threshing floor and your winepress. Give to them as the LORD your God has blessed you. ¹⁵Remember that you were slaves in Egypt and the LORD your God redeemed you. That is why I give you this command today.

¹⁶But if your servant says to you, "I do not want to leave you," because he loves you and your family and is well off with you, ¹⁷then take an awl and push it through his earlobe into the door, and he will become your servant for life. Do the same for your female servant.

¹⁸Do not consider it a hardship to set your servant free, because their service to you these six years has been worth twice as much as that of a hired hand. And the LORD your God will bless you in everything you do.

The Firstborn Animals

¹⁹Set apart for the LORD your God every firstborn male of your herds and flocks. Do not put the firstborn of your cows to work, and do not shear the firstborn of your sheep. ²⁰Each year you and your family are to eat them in the presence of the LORD your God at the place he will choose. ²¹If an animal has a defect, is lame or blind, or

has any serious flaw, you must not sacrifice it to the LORD your God. ²²You are to eat it in your own towns. Both the ceremonially unclean and the clean may eat it, as if it were gazelle or deer. ²³But you must not eat the blood; pour it out on the ground like water.

The Passover

16:1-8pp — Ex 12:14-20; Lev 23:4-8; Nu 28:16-25

16 Observe the month of Aviv and celebrate the Passover of the LORD your God, because in the month of Aviv he brought you out of Egypt by night. ²Sacrifice as the Passover to the LORD your God an animal from your flock or herd at the place the LORD will choose as a dwelling for his Name. ³Do not eat it with bread made with yeast, but for seven days eat unleavened bread, the bread of affliction, because you left Egypt in haste — so that all the days of your life you may remember the time of your departure from Egypt. ⁴Let no yeast be found in your possession in all your land for seven days. Do not let any of the meat you sacrifice on the evening of the first day remain until morning.

⁵You must not sacrifice the Passover in any town the LORD your God gives you ⁶except in the place

---

of the household in which he or she served (see Dt 15:16–17; Ex 21:5–6).

15:13 do not send them away empty-handed The person in authority over an indentured servant was obligated to provide material for the released servant to start his new life. Deuteronomy's requirement modifies the law from Exodus where the owner had no obligation to give the released servant anything (compare Ex 21:1–4). Compare note on Dt 15:1–18.

15:17 Do the same for your female servant Unlike the laws of Exodus, Deuteronomy provides the same law for female servants as it does for male servants. In Ex 21:7–11, the rules for freeing female servants differ from those for male servants. In Exodus, a man selling his daughter as a maidservant creates a more permanent arrangement since it is treated as a marriage (compare Ge 30:1–13). Compare note on Dt 15:1–18.

15:19–23 The firstborn of all living things in Israel — human and animal — belong to Yahweh in commemoration of him sparing the firstborn of Israel during the tenth plague on Egypt (Ex 13:1–2; Lev 27:26–28; Nu 3:11–13). The firstborn of people were to be redeemed, but the firstborn of animals were typically sacrificed (Ex 13:12–15; 22:29–30).

15:20 at the place he will choose These animals were to be sacrificed as offerings to Yahweh and eaten at the central sanctuary. See Dt 12:5 and note.

15:21 any serious flaw Any physical defect disqualified an animal for sacrifice to Yahweh. These animals could still be slaughtered and consumed, but they were not brought to the sanctuary. Rather, they could be slaughtered according to the rules for wild game (see 12:15 and note).

15:23 But you must not eat the blood Repeats the prohibition against eating blood from 12:23 (compare Lev 3:17; 7:26–27; 17:11–14).

16:1–17 This passage describes the festivals of Passover, Weeks and Booths (also called Tabernacles). Each of these three festivals commemorates an event from Israel's history. Passover commemorated the exodus event where Israel left Egypt (Ex 12:14). The Festival of Weeks came to be associated with the giving of the law at Sinai (approximately seven weeks into the Israelite's journey; Ex 19:1–3), and the Festival of Tabernacles (Booths) memorialized Israel's period of wandering in the wilderness (Lev 23:42–43).

Israel's sacred calendar is detailed several other times in OT law (Ex 23:10–17; 34:18–24; Lev 23; Nu 28–29). Deuteronomy emphasizes that the seven-day pilgrimage festivals required travel to the central sanctuary. The other accounts in OT law assume the feasts will be celebrated at the tabernacle (Ex 23:14–17) because Israel lived together as one camp prior to the settlement of Canaan. However, Passover was originally celebrated in the home (see Ex 12), and Deuteronomy relocates the celebration to the central sanctuary (Dt 16:5–6). See the table "Israelite Festivals" on p. 200.

16:1 celebrate the Passover The Passover observance served as Israel's annual reminder of Yahweh's deliverance from slavery in Egypt. See note on Ex 12:1–51.

16:2 place the LORD will choose Refers to the central sanctuary (see note on Dt 12:5).

16:3 unleavened bread The Hebrew word used here, matsah, describes bread made without yeast.

16:5–6 These verses note that the Passover must now be celebrated at the central sanctuary. This stipulation is a modification of the procedures established in Ex 12 (see note on Ex 12:3). In Exodus, the Israelites were to eat the meal in their homes (Ex 12:46). Compare note on Dt 16:1–17.

he will choose as a dwelling for his Name. There you must sacrifice the Passover in the evening, when the sun goes down, on the anniversary[a] of your departure from Egypt. [7]Roast it and eat it at the place the LORD your God will choose. Then in the morning return to your tents. [8]For six days eat unleavened bread and on the seventh day hold an assembly to the LORD your God and do no work.

The Festival of Weeks

16:9-12pp — Lev 23:15-22; Nu 28:26-31

[9]Count off seven weeks from the time you begin to put the sickle to the standing grain. [10]Then celebrate the Festival of Weeks to the LORD your God by giving a freewill offering in proportion to the blessings the LORD your God has given you. [11]And rejoice before the LORD your God at the place he will choose as a dwelling for his Name — you, your sons and daughters, your male and female servants, the Levites in your towns, and the foreigners, the fatherless and the widows living among you. [12]Remember that you were slaves in Egypt, and follow carefully these decrees.

The Festival of Tabernacles

16:13-17pp — Lev 23:33-43; Nu 29:12-39

[13]Celebrate the Festival of Tabernacles for seven days after you have gathered the produce of your threshing floor and your winepress. [14]Be joyful at your festival — you, your sons and daughters, your male and female servants, and the Levites, the foreigners, the fatherless and the widows who live in your towns. [15]For seven days celebrate the festival to the LORD your God at the place the LORD will choose. For the LORD your God will bless you in all your harvest and in all the work of your hands, and your joy will be complete.

[16]Three times a year all your men must appear before the LORD your God at the place he will choose: at the Festival of Unleavened Bread, the Festival of Weeks and the Festival of Tabernacles. No one should appear before the LORD empty-handed: [17]Each of you must bring a gift in proportion to the way the LORD your God has blessed you.

Judges

[18]Appoint judges and officials for each of your tribes in every town the LORD your God is giving you, and they shall judge the people fairly. [19]Do not pervert justice or show partiality. Do not accept a bribe, for a bribe blinds the eyes of the wise and twists the words of the innocent. [20]Follow justice and justice alone, so that you may live and possess the land the LORD your God is giving you.

Worshiping Other Gods

[21]Do not set up any wooden Asherah pole beside the altar you build to the LORD your God, [22]and do not erect a sacred stone, for these the LORD your God hates.

---

a 6 Or down, at the time of day

16:7 Roast The Hebrew word used here, *bashal*, appears to be a general term for cooking, but it is often used as a term for boiling. If *bashal* denotes boiling the meat in water, then the instruction here is at odds with Ex 12:9, which explicitly forbids boiling the meat in water. However, while *bashal* is used to refer to cooking by boiling (e.g., Ex 23:19), the term is also often used without any specification about a method of cooking (Ex 29:31). **return to your tents** The sequence of events implied in these instructions is unclear. It appears that the people were to observe Passover at the central sanctuary on the night of the fourteenth and then return home on the morning of the fifteenth to keep the Festival of Unleavened Bread (Dt 16:8).

16:9–12 The Festival of Weeks (known as Pentecost in Greek) was celebrated seven weeks after Passover. This festival was originally a one-day observance celebrating the initial yield from the wheat harvest (Ex 34:22). The holiday is elsewhere called the Festival of Harvest and the day of firstfruits (see Ex 23:16; Nu 28:26), which highlights its celebration of the grain harvest.

16:9 Count off seven weeks The first harvest was ready after seven weeks, a figure confirmed by the Gezer Calendar, a tenth-century-BC inscription.

16:13–17 The Festival of Booths (or Tabernacles) was an autumn festival held in the seventh month (Dt 16:13–15). It was also called the Festival of Ingathering (Ex 23:16; compare Ex 34:22; Lev 23:39), since it commemorated the completion of the harvest. Deuteronomy 16:16–17 is the closing summary statement of 16:1–17; it reiterates that all Israelite males were to appear before Yahweh at his central sanctuary three times per year (vv. 16–17).

16:13 Tabernacles The Hebrew term used here, *sukkoth*, means "huts" or "booths." According to Lev 23:39–43, the people are to construct temporary shelters to live in during the festival as a reminder of life before the settled occupation of the promised land.

16:16 all your men Women are presumably exempted so that they can care for children.

16:18—17:13 Deuteronomy 16:18—17:13 focuses on Israel's judicial system. The text presumes that once settled in the promised land, the Israelites will abolish their earlier system of civil government (1:13–17), which derived from the military nature of the Israelite camp and its march.

16:18 Appoint judges and officials The people must choose their own magistrates to serve their respective communities. No clear distinction is made between the judges and the officials (or officers) mentioned here. See note on 19:12.

16:21—17:7 This passage treats idolatry as a judicial issue, describing how someone found to be worshiping idols should be tried and punished. Compare 13:6–11.

16:21 any wooden Asherah pole Refers to making an idol out of an engraved wooden pole or tree planted by an altar. See note on 7:5.

17 Do not sacrifice to the Lord your God an ox or a sheep that has any defect or flaw in it, for that would be detestable to him.

²If a man or woman living among you in one of the towns the Lord gives you is found doing evil in the eyes of the Lord your God in violation of his covenant, ³and contrary to my command has worshiped other gods, bowing down to them or to the sun or the moon or the stars in the sky, ⁴and this has been brought to your attention, then you must investigate it thoroughly. If it is true and it has been proved that this detestable thing has been done in Israel, ⁵take the man or woman who has done this evil deed to your city gate and stone that person to death. ⁶On the testimony of two or three witnesses a person is to be put to death, but no one is to be put to death on the testimony of only one witness. ⁷The hands of the witnesses must be the first in putting that person to death, and then the hands of all the people. You must purge the evil from among you.

Law Courts

⁸If cases come before your courts that are too difficult for you to judge — whether bloodshed, lawsuits or assaults — take them to the place the Lord your God will choose. ⁹Go to the Levitical priests and to the judge who is in office at that time. Inquire of them and they will give you the verdict. ¹⁰You must act according to the decisions they give you at the place the Lord will choose. Be careful to do everything they instruct you to do. ¹¹Act according to whatever they teach you and the decisions they give you. Do not turn aside from what they tell you, to the right or to the left. ¹²Anyone who shows contempt for the judge or for the priest who stands ministering there to the Lord your God is to be put to death. You must purge the evil from Israel. ¹³All the people will hear and be afraid, and will not be contemptuous again.

The King

¹⁴When you enter the land the Lord your God is giving you and have taken possession of it and settled in it, and you say, "Let us set a king over us like all the nations around us," ¹⁵be sure to appoint over you a king the Lord your God chooses. He must be from among your fellow Israelites. Do not place a foreigner over you, one who is not an Israelite. ¹⁶The king, moreover, must not acquire great numbers of horses for himself or make the people return to Egypt to get more of them, for the Lord has told you, "You are not to go back that way again." ¹⁷He must not take many wives, or his heart will be led astray. He must not accumulate large amounts of silver and gold.

¹⁸When he takes the throne of his kingdom, he is to write for himself on a scroll a copy of this law, taken from that of the Levitical priests. ¹⁹It is to be with him, and he is to read it all the days of his life so that he may learn to revere the Lord his God and follow carefully all the words of this law and these decrees ²⁰and not consider himself better than his fellow Israelites and turn from the law to the right or to the left. Then he and his descendants will reign a long time over his kingdom in Israel.

17:3 sun or the moon People in the ancient Near East considered the sun, moon, stars and other celestial phenomena to be divine beings (see 32:8–9; 1Ki 22:19). The worship of these things violated the first and greatest commandment (see Ex 20:3; Dt 5:7–9; 6:4–5).

17:5 to your city gate A city gate in the ancient Near East usually consisted of a towered entrance and a large open area where people gathered. It functioned similarly to a civic or community center, and the citizens often did business there. Death sentences were likely put into effect outside the city gates (see Lev 24:14; Nu 15:25–36; 1Ki 21:13; compare Dt 22:21).

17:6 two or three witnesses Having multiple witnesses safeguarded against dishonesty or errors in witness testimony. Compare 19:15.

17:8 cases come before your courts These hypothetical examples demonstrate the need for a higher court of appeal for complex legal problems.

17:9 Levitical priests and to the judge The text does not provide specifics about such a court's operations or its members. In addition, no other book in the Pentateuch assigns priests any judicial responsibility. Rather, they assist leaders as needed in determining God's will, especially by using the Urim and Thummim (Ex 28:30; Lev 8:8). In Deuteronomy, priests have some sort of judicial authority, possibly because they were expected to have a knowledge of Yahweh's law (Dt 19:17; 21:5). See the table "Functions of Priests" on p. 171.

17:12 You must purge the evil from Israel A person who disobeys the nation's judicial authority threatens the social order; thus, the law deals with them in the severest terms.

17:14–20 This section describes the role of the king. The laws concerning the king (rather than assigning specific roles and powers) are essentially negative; they forbid the king advocating for a return to Egypt and the acquisition of many horses, multiple wives and great wealth (vv. 16–17). The only positive duty is to learn the law of Yahweh.

17:14 like all the nations around us See 1Sa 8:5,19–20.

17:16 must not acquire great numbers of horses If the king were to form a large cavalry, such an asset would indicate he relies on self-sufficiency instead of Yahweh for the nation's protection (compare Isa 31:1; Hos 14:3; Ps 33:16–17; Pr 21:31).

17:17 many wives Later Israelite history shows that large harems, especially involving foreign wives, led people to tolerate or even embrace the worship of foreign gods. The practice of royal marriages for political alliance was very common in the ancient Near East (see 1Ki 3:1), but for an Israelite such a practice could (and did) lead to idolatry (see 1Ki 11:1–10; 16:31–33).

Offerings for Priests and Levites

18 The Levitical priests — indeed, the whole tribe of Levi — are to have no allotment or inheritance with Israel. They shall live on the food offerings presented to the LORD, for that is their inheritance. [2]They shall have no inheritance among their fellow Israelites; the LORD is their inheritance, as he promised them.

[3]This is the share due the priests from the people who sacrifice a bull or a sheep: the shoulder, the internal organs and the meat from the head. [4]You are to give them the firstfruits of your grain, new wine and olive oil, and the first wool from the shearing of your sheep, [5]for the LORD your God has chosen them and their descendants out of all your tribes to stand and minister in the LORD's name always.

[6]If a Levite moves from one of your towns anywhere in Israel where he is living, and comes in all earnestness to the place the LORD will choose, [7]he may minister in the name of the LORD his God like all his fellow Levites who serve there in the presence of the LORD. [8]He is to share equally in their benefits, even though he has received money from the sale of family possessions.

Occult Practices

[9]When you enter the land the LORD your God is giving you, do not learn to imitate the detestable ways of the nations there. [10]Let no one be found among you who sacrifices their son or daughter in the fire, who practices divination or sorcery, interprets omens, engages in witchcraft, [11]or casts spells, or who is a medium or spiritist or who consults the dead. [12]Anyone who does these things is detestable to the LORD; because of these same detestable practices the LORD your God will

---

18:1–22 This chapter can be divided into three sections of laws related to religious practice: provisions for the support of priests and Levites (Dt 18:1–8); prohibitions against religious practices associated with idolatry (vv. 9–14); and a discussion of the hallmarks of a true prophet (vv. 15–22). All of the laws fall under the general topic of religious leadership, making this chapter the counterpart to ch. 17, which focused on secular leadership. The first section (vv. 1–8) relates to those who officiate at the tabernacle or temple — the priests and Levites. The second (vv. 9–14) and third (vv. 15–22) sections address various types of mediation between the divine realm and the human realm. The forbidden practices mentioned relate primarily to types of forbidden divination that were used to determine the will of divine beings. Israel is to seek Yahweh through priests and prophets, not magic and superstition.

18:1 Levitical priests — indeed, the whole tribe of Levi The priests were members of the tribe of Levi descended from Aaron, Moses' brother (Ex 28:1). The rest of the tribe of Levi — the Levites — served the priests (Nu 3:5–10). The distinction between the duties of a Levite and the duties of a priest is clear in Nu 18:1–7. Deuteronomy blurs the distinction by referring to the priests as "the Levitical priests" (hakkohanim haleviim in Hebrew; see Dt 17:9,18; 24:8). The wording here could be taken as "Levitical priests" in apposition with the entire "tribe of Levi," further blurring the distinction. However, the phrasing could also be taken as clarification that the whole tribe, not just the priests, were not to be given an allotment in the promised land. The reference to the tribe may also imply that the priests' portions from the offerings should be shared either by all the Levites or by the Levites who were serving at the sanctuary with the priests (18:6–8). If sharing of the sacrificial offerings is meant, this passage is modifying the regulations in Lev 7 about who is entitled to consume the priestly portion of a sacrifice.

18:4 the firstfruits of your grain The Israelites were to bring firstfruits as an offering to Yahweh (Ex 23:19; see Lev 2:12 and note). These offerings — which were a portion from the first of the harvested grain, or from the first batch of agricultural products like wine, oil and fleece — were designated for the priests (see Nu 18:12 and note; compare 2Ch 31:5).

18:9–14 Before discussing the legitimate office of prophet (Dt 18:15–22), the narrative focuses on illegitimate sources of divine knowledge (vv. 9–14). This suggests that the office of prophet is more important than that of the king. The prophet, and not the king, is elevated to higher authority, as the true spokesperson for God.

Seeking knowledge from the divine realm (divination) is forbidden due to its association with worship of gods other than Yahweh (see 12:4,30–31; 16:21—17:1). Some Israelites, however, practiced (or otherwise tolerated) divination, sometimes when seeking Yahweh's will (e.g., 1Sa 28:3–19; 2Ki 21:6; Isa 8:19; Jer 27:9).

18:10 who sacrifices their son or daughter in the fire While some passages of the OT clearly refer to child sacrifice (see Dt 12:31), the Hebrew text here is ambiguous. The Hebrew wording describes "one who makes his son or daughter pass through the fire" (ma'avir beno-uvitto ba'esh in Hebrew). The practice prohibited here may be some kind of ritual act of divination, not sacrificing a child by fire. The rest of vv. 10–11 relates explicitly to types of divination. **who practices divination** This expression refers to a variety of practices in which a person attempts to elicit information from a deity or supernatural source by manipulating objects or looking for signs and omens in nature. However, not all forms of divination were prohibited; casting lots was allowed (Lev 16:8; Jos 18:6). **engages in witchcraft** The Hebrew word used here, mekhasheph, is most often translated "sorcerer," but comparative evidence from other Semitic languages suggests the word refers to someone who concocts potions from plants.

18:11 casts spells The Hebrew phrases chover chaver (which is used here) and chover chavarim (see Ps 58:5) refer to someone who casts spells. **who is a medium or spiritist** The first part of the Hebrew phrase used here, sho'el ov, literally means "one who asks of the spirits." The word ov likely refers to nonhuman spirits, not the spirits of human dead. The following term in the second part of the phrase, yidde'oni, probably refers to the spirits of deceased humans. The use of two different words for those who attempt to communicate with spirits suggests two types of spirits that were consulted. **who consults the dead** The Hebrew expression used here refers to someone who practices necromancy — the attempt to contact spirits of the human dead. Compare Lev 19:31; 20:6.

drive out those nations before you. ¹³You must be blameless before the LORD your God.

The Prophet

¹⁴The nations you will dispossess listen to those who practice sorcery or divination. But as for you, the LORD your God has not permitted you to do so. ¹⁵The LORD your God will raise up for you a prophet like me from among you, from your fellow Israelites. You must listen to him. ¹⁶For this is what you asked of the LORD your God at Horeb on the day of the assembly when you said, "Let us not hear the voice of the LORD our God nor see this great fire anymore, or we will die."

¹⁷The LORD said to me: "What they say is good. ¹⁸I will raise up for them a prophet like you from among their fellow Israelites, and I will put my words in his mouth. He will tell them everything I command him. ¹⁹I myself will call to account anyone who does not listen to my words that the prophet speaks in my name. ²⁰But a prophet who presumes to speak in my name anything I have not commanded, or a prophet who speaks in the name of other gods, is to be put to death."

²¹You may say to yourselves, "How can we know when a message has not been spoken by the LORD?" ²²If what a prophet proclaims in the name of the LORD does not take place or come true, that is a message the LORD has not spoken. That prophet has spoken presumptuously, so do not be alarmed.

Cities of Refuge

19:1-14 Ref — Nu 35:6-34; Dt 4:41-43; Jos 20:1-9

19 When the LORD your God has destroyed the nations whose land he is giving you, and when you have driven them out and settled in their towns and houses, ²then set aside for yourselves three cities in the land the LORD your God is giving you to possess. ³Determine the distances involved and divide into three parts the land the LORD your God is giving you as an inheritance, so that a person who kills someone may flee for refuge to one of these cities.

⁴This is the rule concerning anyone who kills a person and flees there for safety — anyone who kills a neighbor unintentionally, without malice aforethought. ⁵For instance, a man may go into the forest with his neighbor to cut wood, and as he swings his ax to fell a tree, the head may fly off and hit his neighbor and kill him. That man may flee to one of these cities and save his life. ⁶Otherwise, the avenger of blood might pursue him in a rage, overtake him if the distance is too great, and kill him even though he is not deserving of death, since he did it to his neighbor without malice aforethought. ⁷This is why I command you to set aside for yourselves three cities.

⁸If the LORD your God enlarges your territory, as he promised on oath to your ancestors, and gives you the whole land he promised them, ⁹because you carefully follow all these laws I command you today — to love the LORD your God and to walk always in obedience to him — then you are to set aside three more cities. ¹⁰Do this so that innocent blood will not be shed in your land, which the LORD your God is giving you as your inheritance, and so that you will not be guilty of bloodshed.

¹¹But if out of hate someone lies in wait, assaults and kills a neighbor, and then flees to one of these cities, ¹²the killer shall be sent for by the town elders,

---

18:15–22 Here Moses describes the role of prophets who speak to the people on behalf of Yahweh—just as he had done. The prophet was to be a mediator of divine revelation, reporting the words of Yahweh to the Israelite people. In the prophetic books, the prophets frequently preface their messages with formulas that identify their words as Yahweh's words, not their own (see Isa 1:10 and note; compare Jer 1:4; Hos 1:1). Prophets who present their own words as if they were Yahweh's words will be subject to divine judgment (see Dt 18:20).

18:15 raise up for you a prophet Yahweh will call a true prophet to speak directly to the Israelites, so they will have no need for the fortune-tellers, sorcerers and diviners used by the Canaanites. **like me** Deuteronomy 34:10, written after Moses' lifetime, indicates that no prophet attained the status of Moses. Consequently, in terms of their ultimate fulfillment, these words later took on a Messianic connotation (compare Jn 1:21,25,45; Ac 3:22; 7:37).

18:22 That prophet has spoken presumptuously The prophet ostensibly reveals the mind of Yahweh, so it is reasonable to have some criterion by which to validate the prophet's identity and role. Accuracy in foretelling the future serves as part of this criterion.

19:1–21 This chapter is a collection of various laws concerning cities of refuge (Dt 19:1–13), property boundaries (v. 14) and judicial witnesses (vv. 15–21). The section on cities of refuge draws on Nu 35. Although the Levites had no allotted tribal land inheritance (Nu 18:23; Lev 25:32–33), 48 cities scattered throughout the promised land were allotted to them. Six of those were designated cities of refuge (Dt 19:2,7–9; Nu 35:6,11–15). Cities of refuge were to function as safe havens for those who accidentally took an innocent human life; an intentional murderer could not resort to a city of refuge.

19:3 Determine the distances involved Each of the cities of refuge was centrally located in the regions described in Dt 34:2.

19:6 avenger The Hebrew word used here, go'el, refers to the nearest relative to whom the obligation fell to right a wrong on behalf of the family. One of the responsibilities was avenging the death of a family member. In the context of the cities of refuge and blood vengeance, the go'el functions as legal executioner when laws about refuge are violated (see note on v. 12). Another duty of the go'el was marrying a brother's widow (a practice known as levirate marriage; see 25:5–10 and note). The go'el was also required to redeem a kinsman from

be brought back from the city, and be handed over to the avenger of blood to die. ¹³Show no pity. You must purge from Israel the guilt of shedding innocent blood, so that it may go well with you.

¹⁴Do not move your neighbor's boundary stone set up by your predecessors in the inheritance you receive in the land the LORD your God is giving you to possess.

Witnesses

¹⁵One witness is not enough to convict anyone accused of any crime or offense they may have committed. A matter must be established by the testimony of two or three witnesses.

¹⁶If a malicious witness takes the stand to accuse someone of a crime, ¹⁷the two people involved in the dispute must stand in the presence of the LORD before the priests and the judges who are in office at the time. ¹⁸The judges must make a thorough investigation, and if the witness proves to be a liar, giving false testimony against a fellow Israelite, ¹⁹then do to the false witness as that witness intended to do to the other party. You must purge the evil from among you. ²⁰The rest of the people will hear of this and be afraid, and never again will such an evil thing be done among you. ²¹Show no pity: life for life, eye for eye, tooth for tooth, hand for hand, foot for foot.

Going to War

20 When you go to war against your enemies and see horses and chariots and an army greater than yours, do not be afraid of them, be-cause the LORD your God, who brought you up out of Egypt, will be with you. ²When you are about to go into battle, the priest shall come forward and address the army. ³He shall say: "Hear, Israel: Today you are going into battle against your enemies. Do not be fainthearted or afraid; do not panic or be terrified by them. ⁴For the LORD your God is the one who goes with you to fight for you against your enemies to give you victory."

⁵The officers shall say to the army: "Has anyone built a new house and not yet begun to live in it? Let him go home, or he may die in battle and someone else may begin to live in it. ⁶Has anyone planted a vineyard and not begun to enjoy it? Let him go home, or he may die in battle and someone else enjoy it. ⁷Has anyone become pledged to a woman and not married her? Let him go home, or he may die in battle and someone else marry her." ⁸Then the officers shall add, "Is anyone afraid or fainthearted? Let him go home so that his fellow soldiers will not become disheartened too." ⁹When the officers have finished speaking to the army, they shall appoint commanders over it.

¹⁰When you march up to attack a city, make its people an offer of peace. ¹¹If they accept and open their gates, all the people in it shall be subject to forced labor and shall work for you. ¹²If they refuse to make peace and they engage you in battle, lay siege to that city. ¹³When the LORD your God delivers it into your hand, put to the sword all the men in it. ¹⁴As for the women, the children, the livestock and everything else in the city, you may take these as plunder for yourselves. And you

---

debt slavery (Lev 25:47–54), or buy back an inherited field lost to debt (Lev 25:25–28,48). Due to the latter two responsibilities, the term *go'el* is often translated as "redeemer."

19:12 the town elders This term generally refers to heads of the families, tribes or towns. It seems that elders are also called judges in Deuteronomy, though the two terms may distinguish two groups (see Dt 16:18; 17:9,12; 19:17–18; 25:2). These leaders act as a judicial body that judges problems of civil and family law.

19:14 your neighbor's boundary stone Landmarks, usually an identifiable stone, indicated property boundaries. Moving them was a serious offense, as it amounted to stealing ancestral land from a neighbor (27:17).

19:15–21 The laws in this section are intended to ensure a correct, proper verdict in legal proceedings and to protect the innocent from wrongful accusation and conviction. The penalty for bearing false witness was severe (vv. 19–21; compare 17:7).

19:15 any crime or offense This clarifies that the requirement was not just for cases involving capital crimes. Compare 17:6.

19:19 do to the false witness as that witness intended This principle—known as *lex talionis* (and summarized by the idea of an "eye for an eye")—requires punishment equivalent to the crime (see Ex 21:24; Lev 24:17–22).

20:1–20 This chapter contains three sections, each focused on some aspect of warfare: preparing an army (Dt 20:1–9); treatment of the vanquished (vv. 10–18); and management of trees in the vicinity of a conquered city (vv. 19–20). Since v. 10 refers to offering terms of peace, and v. 15 indicates that some rules in the chapter pertain to cities outside the promised land of Canaan, these laws are not just limited to the conquest.

20:1 will be with you The Israelite conception of war centered on the idea that Yahweh is the supreme God of all nations and more powerful than their gods (32:8–9). The supreme God fought for Israel, so there was no reason to fear.

20:5–8 This section presents grounds for the deferment of military service, listing important first time personal pleasures that should be conducted before a person risked their life (compare Jer 29:5–6).

20:7 someone else marry her Here, the deferment of going to war is for the sake of the husband; a similar law in Dt 24:5 grants a one-year deferment to a newly married man for the sake of his wife.

20:10 a city Verse 15 makes it clear that the rules of vv. 10–14 apply to cities outside the promised land. Verse 16 transitions to those cities within Canaan.

20:14 plunder for yourselves While the Israelites are to slay the adult males of the cities they attack and defeat, they may take the women, children and livestock

may use the plunder the LORD your God gives you from your enemies. [15]This is how you are to treat all the cities that are at a distance from you and do not belong to the nations nearby.

[16]However, in the cities of the nations the LORD your God is giving you as an inheritance, do not leave alive anything that breathes. [17]Completely destroy[a] them — the Hittites, Amorites, Canaanites, Perizzites, Hivites and Jebusites — as the LORD your God has commanded you. [18]Otherwise, they will teach you to follow all the detestable things they do in worshiping their gods, and you will sin against the LORD your God.

[19]When you lay siege to a city for a long time, fighting against it to capture it, do not destroy its trees by putting an ax to them, because you can eat their fruit. Do not cut them down. Are the trees people, that you should besiege them?[b] [20]However, you may cut down trees that you know are not fruit trees and use them to build siege works until the city at war with you falls.

Atonement for an Unsolved Murder

21 If someone is found slain, lying in a field in the land the LORD your God is giving you to possess, and it is not known who the killer was, [2]your elders and judges shall go out and measure the distance from the body to the neighboring towns. [3]Then the elders of the town nearest the body shall take a heifer that has never been

worked and has never worn a yoke [4]and lead it down to a valley that has not been plowed or planted and where there is a flowing stream. There in the valley they are to break the heifer's neck. [5]The Levitical priests shall step forward, for the LORD your God has chosen them to minister and to pronounce blessings in the name of the LORD and to decide all cases of dispute and assault. [6]Then all the elders of the town nearest the body shall wash their hands over the heifer whose neck was broken in the valley, [7]and they shall declare: "Our hands did not shed this blood, nor did our eyes see it done. [8]Accept this atonement for your people Israel, whom you have redeemed, LORD, and do not hold your people guilty of the blood of an innocent person." Then the bloodshed will be atoned for, [9]and you will have purged from yourselves the guilt of shedding innocent blood, since you have done what is right in the eyes of the LORD.

Marrying a Captive Woman

[10]When you go to war against your enemies and the LORD your God delivers them into your hands and you take captives, [11]if you notice among the captives a beautiful woman and are attracted to her, you may take her as your wife. [12]Bring

[a] 17 The Hebrew term refers to the irrevocable giving over of things or persons to the LORD, often by totally destroying them.
[b] 19 Or down to use in the siege, for the fruit trees are for the benefit of people.

---

captive. Deuteronomy 21:10–14 offers laws governing captive wives.
20:15 do not belong to the nations nearby The preceding laws only pertain to cities outside Canaan. Verse 16 points to the conquest of cities and populations within the promised land.
20:17 Completely destroy The Hebrew wording here invokes the principle of *cherem*, setting a person or thing aside for Yahweh (see 7:2 and note; 7:26). The designation was sometimes associated with idolatry and often involved destruction (compare 20:18 and note). See note on Jos 6:16; note on Jos 6:17.
20:18 do in worshiping their gods The Israelites are to completely destroy certain people groups to prevent them from drawing Israel into worshiping their gods and violating the greatest commandment: absolute loyalty to Yahweh as the lone God of Israel (see Dt 6:4–5; compare 7:23–26).
20:19 do not destroy its trees In order to completely obliterate the enemy's economic viability and, therefore, its ability to recover, armies in the ancient Near East would commonly destroy fields, crops and fruit trees.

21:1–9 As in ch. 19, which dealt with cities of refuge and avenging homicide, the law here in vv. 1–9 seeks to avoid moral culpability for a town when there was a wrongful death but the responsible party is unknown. Since the murderer is unknown, punishment is impossible. In these cases, the law prescribes a complex ritual for purging the land of bloodguilt.

21:3 town nearest the body The leadership in the town nearest the corpse bears the responsibility of purging

the land from bloodguilt. **never been worked and has never worn a yoke** A heifer that had never been used for common purposes would then be fit for sacred purposes.
21:4 not been plowed or planted Like the heifer in v. 3, the valley was not being used for common purposes.
where there is a flowing stream The continuous watering of the valley offset, in part, the bloodguilt resulting from the death of innocent life.
21:8 Accept this atonement Refers to purification or purging of guilt. See note on Lev 4:20.

21:10–23 This section begins the final list of laws in Deuteronomy (Dt 21:10—25:19), a lengthy collection of case law that focuses in large part on the welfare of women and children. The final sections of ch. 21 deal with the treatment of captive wives (vv. 10–14), the rights of the firstborn of a wife who is unloved or disliked (vv. 15–17), an insubordinate son (vv. 18–21) and the disposal of a corpse hung on a tree (vv. 22–23).

21:10–14 Slavery was common in the ancient Near East, and thus laws like these in the OT could represent a response to common practices, not the ideal. The concern of the laws in vv. 10–14 is the protection of female captives of war.

21:11 you notice among the captives a beautiful woman While most women in such circumstances would become servants (see 20:14; Jdg 5:30), some Israelite men would inevitably take them as wives.

21:12 These acts are likely connected to mourning (see v. 13).

her into your home and have her shave her head, trim her nails ¹³and put aside the clothes she was wearing when captured. After she has lived in your house and mourned her father and mother for a full month, then you may go to her and be her husband and she shall be your wife. ¹⁴If you are not pleased with her, let her go wherever she wishes. You must not sell her or treat her as a slave, since you have dishonored her.

The Right of the Firstborn

¹⁵If a man has two wives, and he loves one but not the other, and both bear him sons but the firstborn is the son of the wife he does not love, ¹⁶when he wills his property to his sons, he must not give the rights of the firstborn to the son of the wife he loves in preference to his actual firstborn, the son of the wife he does not love. ¹⁷He must acknowledge the son of his unloved wife as the firstborn by giving him a double share of all he has. That son is the first sign of his father's strength. The right of the firstborn belongs to him.

A Rebellious Son

¹⁸If someone has a stubborn and rebellious son who does not obey his father and mother and will not listen to them when they discipline him, ¹⁹his father and mother shall take hold of him and bring him to the elders at the gate of his town. ²⁰They shall say to the elders, "This son of ours is stubborn and rebellious. He will not obey us. He is a glutton and a drunkard." ²¹Then all the men of his town are to stone him to death. You must purge the evil from among you. All Israel will hear of it and be afraid.

Various Laws

²²If someone guilty of a capital offense is put to death and their body is exposed on a pole, ²³you must not leave the body hanging on the pole overnight. Be sure to bury it that same day, because anyone who is hung on a pole is under God's curse. You must not desecrate the land the LORD your God is giving you as an inheritance.

22 If you see your fellow Israelite's ox or sheep straying, do not ignore it but be sure to take it back to its owner. ²If they do not live near you or if you do not know who owns it, take it home with you and keep it until they come looking for it. Then give it back. ³Do the same if you find their donkey or cloak or anything else they have lost. Do not ignore it.

⁴If you see your fellow Israelite's donkey or ox fallen on the road, do not ignore it. Help the owner get it to its feet.

⁵A woman must not wear men's clothing, nor a man wear women's clothing, for the LORD your God detests anyone who does this.

⁶If you come across a bird's nest beside the road, either in a tree or on the ground, and the mother is sitting on the young or on the eggs, do not take the mother with the young. ⁷You may take the young, but be sure to let the mother go, so that it may go well with you and you may have a long life.

⁸When you build a new house, make a parapet around your roof so that you may not bring the guilt of bloodshed on your house if someone falls from the roof.

⁹Do not plant two kinds of seed in your vineyard; if you do, not only the crops you plant but also the fruit of the vineyard will be defiled.ᵃ

ᵃ 9 Or be forfeited to the sanctuary

21:15–17 These verses outline the rights of the firstborn, an important cultural institution in most ancient Near Eastern cultures. The firstborn son was entitled to a larger portion of his father's property than other sons. Deuteronomy protects that right in the event that a father, seeking either to spite a wife he disliked or to favor another wife (and so her son), would seek to deny firstborn status to a son to whom it belonged.

21:17 That son is the first sign of his father's strength This demonstrates that Israelites considered the basis for firstborn status to be biological, as opposed to preferential.

21:18–21 This section describes the procedure for dealing with a repeatedly rebellious son whose parents consider him beyond reform. If the city elders agree, the son is to be executed. The rationale for such harsh punishment is the need to purge the evil from the community (v. 21)—a refrain repeated regularly in the laws of chs. 12–26 (see 13:5; 17:7,12; 22:21–24). The presence of sin threatened the well-being of the entire community due to the nature of Israel's covenant agreement with Yahweh. Violations of the covenant could lead to consequences that affected everyone (28:15–68).

This potential danger to the community called for serious punishment.

21:22 their body is exposed on a pole Whether they impaled the body or tied it to a pole is unclear. Based on similar Assyrian practices, impalement is more likely. Either way the hanging of the body seems to have occurred after execution. The Egyptians also apparently practiced this on occasion (compare Ge 40:19). The practice of hanging the corpse of someone who had been executed was designed to be a warning to others and a deterrent.

22:1–12 The laws of this section focus mainly on personal property. Deuteronomy 22:1–4 concerns restoring lost animals to their owner. These verses parallel and supplement Ex 23:4–5.

22:5 A woman must not wear men's clothing The rationale for this law is unclear.
22:6 mother with the young See Lev 22:28 and note.
22:8 someone falls from the roof Israelite and Canaanite houses had flat roofs used for storage or socializing.
22:9 Do not plant two kinds of seed This law resembles Lev 19:19. Forbidding such mixtures may have been to observe boundaries established in creation, but the

¹⁰Do not plow with an ox and a donkey yoked together.

¹¹Do not wear clothes of wool and linen woven together.

¹²Make tassels on the four corners of the cloak you wear.

Marriage Violations

¹³If a man takes a wife and, after sleeping with her, dislikes her ¹⁴and slanders her and gives her a bad name, saying, "I married this woman, but when I approached her, I did not find proof of her virginity," ¹⁵then the young woman's father and mother shall bring to the town elders at the gate proof that she was a virgin. ¹⁶Her father will say to the elders, "I gave my daughter in marriage to this man, but he dislikes her. ¹⁷Now he has slandered her and said, 'I did not find your daughter to be a virgin.' But here is the proof of my daughter's virginity." Then her parents shall display the cloth before the elders of the town, ¹⁸and the elders shall take the man and punish him. ¹⁹They shall fine him a hundred shekels*ᵃ* of silver and give them to the young woman's father, because this man has given an Israelite virgin a bad name. She shall continue to be his wife; he must not divorce her as long as he lives.

²⁰If, however, the charge is true and no proof of the young woman's virginity can be found, ²¹she shall be brought to the door of her father's house and there the men of her town shall stone her to death. She has done an outrageous thing in Israel by being promiscuous while still in her father's house. You must purge the evil from among you.

²²If a man is found sleeping with another man's wife, both the man who slept with her and the woman must die. You must purge the evil from Israel.

²³If a man happens to meet in a town a virgin pledged to be married and he sleeps with her, ²⁴you shall take both of them to the gate of that town and stone them to death—the young woman because she was in a town and did not scream for help, and the man because he violated another man's wife. You must purge the evil from among you.

²⁵But if out in the country a man happens to meet a young woman pledged to be married and rapes her, only the man who has done this shall die. ²⁶Do nothing to the woman; she has committed no sin deserving death. This case is like that of someone who attacks and murders a neighbor, ²⁷for the man found the young woman out in the country, and though the betrothed woman screamed, there was no one to rescue her.

²⁸If a man happens to meet a virgin who is not pledged to be married and rapes her and they are discovered, ²⁹he shall pay her father fifty shekels*ᵇ* of silver. He must marry the young woman, for he has violated her. He can never divorce her as long as he lives.

³⁰A man is not to marry his father's wife; he must not dishonor his father's bed.*ᶜ*

ᵃ 19 That is, about 2 1/2 pounds or about 1.2 kilograms   *ᵇ 29* That is, about 1 1/4 pounds or about 575 grams   *ᶜ 30* In Hebrew texts this verse (22:30) is numbered 23:1.

---

practice here is not hybridization. The original purpose, possibly cultural or practical, is no longer known.

22:10 an ox and a donkey yoked together Since these two animals are unequal in strength, working them as a team may fatigue or harm one or both of the partners.

22:11 clothes of wool and linen woven together The law does not prohibit the combining of the two materials, but rather wearing apparel made from a combination of the two. The rationale behind the law is unknown.

22:12 Make tassels A more detailed version of this requirement appears in Nu 15:37–41.

22:13–30 This section of laws focuses on sexual immorality. Compare Lev 18.

22:13 after sleeping with her The Hebrew verb used here, *bo'*, is a common euphemism for sexual intercourse (e.g., Ge 16:4; 38:9; 2Sa 12:24).

22:14 proof of her virginity This likely refers to suspicion of sexual activity prior to marriage based on the initial act of marital intercourse not resulting in bleeding (see Dt 22:17).

22:15 proof that she was a virgin The evidence is a cloth with the woman's blood on it (v. 17). A newly married young woman was expected to retain the bedclothes from the wedding night and present it to her mother for keeping.

22:21 door of her father's house Sexual relations produced children who would inherit ancestral lands and family property—the very means of survival in a tribal agrarian culture. This meant that illicit sexual relationships potentially threatened all the lives entangled in the results; for this reason, the authorities dealt with the matter severely.

22:22 both the man who slept with her and the woman must die See note on Ex 20:14.

22:23 a virgin pledged to be married Refers to a young woman engaged to be married. In ancient Near Eastern culture, betrothal created a legal relationship akin to marriage, which is why violating the betrothal was viewed as adultery.

22:24 because she was in a town and did not scream for help Those judging the case took the lack of a cry for help—which likely would have been heard in a small town—as indicating consent.

22:25 only the man who has done this If the deed occurred in open country, where few people would have been present to hear a cry for help, the law presumes the woman is guiltless.

22:29 He must marry the young woman Exodus 22:16–17 adds that the violated woman's father must let the guilty man marry his daughter.

22:30 dishonor his father's bed The law here could refer to a case where a son marries one of his father's wives who was not his own mother, likely after his father's death. Compare 27:20; Lev 18:8.

Exclusion From the Assembly

23 [a] No one who has been emasculated by crushing or cutting may enter the assembly of the LORD.

[2] No one born of a forbidden marriage[b] nor any of their descendants may enter the assembly of the LORD, not even in the tenth generation.

[3] No Ammonite or Moabite or any of their descendants may enter the assembly of the LORD, not even in the tenth generation. [4] For they did not come to meet you with bread and water on your way when you came out of Egypt, and they hired Balaam son of Beor from Pethor in Aram Naharaim[c] to pronounce a curse on you. [5] However, the LORD your God would not listen to Balaam but turned the curse into a blessing for you, because the LORD your God loves you. [6] Do not seek a treaty of friendship with them as long as you live.

[7] Do not despise an Edomite, for the Edomites are related to you. Do not despise an Egyptian, because you resided as foreigners in their country. [8] The third generation of children born to them may enter the assembly of the LORD.

Uncleanness in the Camp

[9] When you are encamped against your enemies, keep away from everything impure. [10] If one of your men is unclean because of a nocturnal emission, he is to go outside the camp and stay there. [11] But as evening approaches he is to wash himself, and at sunset he may return to the camp. [12] Designate a place outside the camp where you can go to relieve yourself. [13] As part of your equipment have something to dig with, and when you relieve yourself, dig a hole and cover up your excrement. [14] For the LORD your God moves about in your camp to protect you and to deliver your enemies to you. Your camp must be holy, so that he will not see among you anything indecent and turn away from you.

Miscellaneous Laws

[15] If a slave has taken refuge with you, do not hand them over to their master. [16] Let them live among you wherever they like and in whatever town they choose. Do not oppress them.

[17] No Israelite man or woman is to become a shrine prostitute. [18] You must not bring the earnings of a female prostitute or of a male prostitute[d] into the house of the LORD your God to pay any vow, because the LORD your God detests them both.

[19] Do not charge a fellow Israelite interest, whether on money or food or anything else that may earn interest. [20] You may charge a foreigner interest, but not a fellow Israelite, so that the LORD

---

[a] In Hebrew texts 23:1-25 is numbered 23:2-26.   [b] 2 Or one of illegitimate birth   [c] 4 That is, Northwest Mesopotamia   [d] 18 Hebrew of a dog

---

23:1–8 This passage restricts three classes of people (with one exception) from the *qehal yhwh* (often translated as "assembly of Yahweh"). This "assembly" does not directly refer to the tabernacle precinct (see Ex 25–27) or tent of meeting (see Ex 27:21). It may refer to the collective Israelite community (see Ex 16:3; Lev 16:17; Nu 19:20; Dt 31:30) or, more narrowly, an assembly of adult males (Jdg 21:5,8; 1Ki 12:3). However, certain aspects of these laws are similar to OT ritual purity laws dealing with access to sacred space.

23:2 one born of a forbidden marriage The meaning of the Hebrew term used here, *mamzer*, is unclear, but ancient Judaism has traditionally defined the word with reference to children born of illegitimate relationships. The illegitimacy could derive from the marriage of an Israelite to a non-Israelite or from birth out of wedlock.

23:3 Ammonite or Moabite Both of these people groups were related to the Israelites through Lot, Abraham's nephew (Ge 19:36–38). Despite their kinship, they opposed Israel on their journey to Canaan.

23:4 Pethor in Aram Naharaim Pethor was a city in northern Syria.

23:7 you resided as foreigners in their country The hostility of the Ammonites and Moabites is viewed as a worse offense, probably because these two people groups were kin to Israel (see note on Dt 23:3).

23:9–14 Deuteronomy 23:9—26:19 presents the remainder of Deuteronomy's law code—mostly a collection of miscellaneous rules covering a range of disparate subjects. Deuteronomy 23:9–14 provides regulations for

maintaining the ritual purity of an Israelite army camp. Since the Israelite army assumed Yahweh's presence was among them, the laws governing its purity are strict and resemble ritual purity regulations for occupying sacred space.

23:14 moves about in your camp Though the language here describing Yahweh is anthropomorphic, it likely does not refer to God visibly moving about the camp but rather traveling with the Israelite camp as they go to war (see 20:4).

23:17 shrine prostitute The Hebrew terms used here—*qadesh* and *qedeshah*, often translated "shrine prostitute" or "cult prostitute"—are related to the Hebrew word for holiness. The basic meaning seems to be "holy person," referring to some sort of individual set apart for religious service. In the OT, these terms typically point to those officiating at Canaanite shrines (1Ki 15:12; 22:46; 2Ki 23:7), so this prohibition may relate to Israelites serving as officials of Canaanite gods. However, in Ge 38, *qedeshah* is used as a synonym for *zonah* (the common Hebrew word for "prostitute"; compare Ge 38:15,21–22). Since the context of Ge 38 is clearly sexual, it is possible that the official duties of the *qadesh* or *qedeshah* involved prostitution. See Dt 23:18 and note.

23:18 earnings of a female prostitute The use of income gained through an illicit, condemned practice was viewed as an abomination. This verse uses the usual Hebrew word for a female prostitute—*zonah*. Earnings from prostitution may be in view, or the law may simply forbid giving to Yahweh from wages acquired in serving as an official for other gods (see v. 17 and note).

your God may bless you in everything you put your hand to in the land you are entering to possess.

²¹If you make a vow to the LORD your God, do not be slow to pay it, for the LORD your God will certainly demand it of you and you will be guilty of sin. ²²But if you refrain from making a vow, you will not be guilty. ²³Whatever your lips utter you must be sure to do, because you made your vow freely to the LORD your God with your own mouth.

²⁴If you enter your neighbor's vineyard, you may eat all the grapes you want, but do not put any in your basket. ²⁵If you enter your neighbor's grainfield, you may pick kernels with your hands, but you must not put a sickle to their standing grain.

24 If a man marries a woman who becomes displeasing to him because he finds something indecent about her, and he writes her a certificate of divorce, gives it to her and sends her from his house, ²and if after she leaves his house she becomes the wife of another man, ³and her second husband dislikes her and writes her a certificate of divorce, gives it to her and sends her from his house, or if he dies, ⁴then her first husband, who divorced her, is not allowed to marry her again after she has been defiled. That would be detestable in the eyes of the LORD. Do not bring sin upon the land the LORD your God is giving you as an inheritance.

⁵If a man has recently married, he must not be sent to war or have any other duty laid on him. For one year he is to be free to stay at home and bring happiness to the wife he has married.

⁶Do not take a pair of millstones — not even the upper one — as security for a debt, because that would be taking a person's livelihood as security.

⁷If someone is caught kidnapping a fellow Israelite and treating or selling them as a slave, the kidnapper must die. You must purge the evil from among you.

⁸In cases of defiling skin diseases,ᵃ be very careful to do exactly as the Levitical priests instruct you. You must follow carefully what I have commanded them. ⁹Remember what the LORD your God did to Miriam along the way after you came out of Egypt.

¹⁰When you make a loan of any kind to your neighbor, do not go into their house to get what is offered to you as a pledge. ¹¹Stay outside and let the neighbor to whom you are making the loan bring the pledge out to you. ¹²If the neighbor is poor, do not go to sleep with their pledge in your possession. ¹³Return their cloak by sunset so that your neighbor may sleep in it. Then they will thank you, and it will be regarded as a righteous act in the sight of the LORD your God.

¹⁴Do not take advantage of a hired worker who is poor and needy, whether that worker is a fellow Israelite or a foreigner residing in one of your towns. ¹⁵Pay them their wages each day before sunset, because they are poor and are counting on it. Otherwise they may cry to the LORD against you, and you will be guilty of sin.

¹⁶Parents are not to be put to death for their children, nor children put to death for their parents; each will die for their own sin.

ᵃ 8 The Hebrew word for *defiling skin diseases*, traditionally translated "leprosy," was used for various diseases affecting the skin.

23:21 do not be slow to pay it The subject of vv. 21–23 is making vows. A vow was a conditional promise (i.e., if X happens, then I will do Y). Whereas Nu 30:2 warns Israelites about breaking a vow, the command here warns against procrastinating in acting upon a vow.

23:22 refrain from making a vow It is better to not vow at all than to vow and be unable to act upon it. The ethic here is similar to Jesus' teaching on avoiding vows and oaths (see Mt 5:33–37).

24:1–4 This passage continues a larger section of miscellaneous laws begun in Dt 23:10. These verses address the subject of divorce, but rather than provide general guidelines for the practice, they discuss the hypothetical scenario of whether a man can remarry a woman he divorced if she has been married to someone else in the interim. There is no clear indication in this passage of what qualifies as grounds for divorce, but the husband is permitted to issue his wife a certificate of divorce. Compare Mt 5:31–32; 19:1–12.

24:1 he finds something indecent about her The Hebrew word used here, *erwah*, literally means "nakedness." The idiom used here and in 23:14—*erwath davar* (which may be literally rendered "naked thing")—appears to refer to anything indecent or unseemly. **he writes her a certificate of divorce** Possibly a written document, though this could also refer to an oral decree or public gesture by the husband.

24:5—25:4 The miscellaneous laws in this passage cover a wide variety of subjects, but many of the laws relate generally to maintaining ideals of justice and fairness.

24:6 Do not take a pair of millstones This law forbids creditors from taking this important implement for grinding grain for food as collateral. Similarly, the laws in vv. 10–13 and v. 17 restrict oppressive lending practices.

24:8 cases of defiling skin diseases The Hebrew word used here, *tsara'ath*, is a general term for a range of skin diseases. See note on Lev 14:3.

24:9 did to Miriam When Miriam was struck with a skin disease, Yahweh refused to instantly heal her, even though Moses pleaded with Yahweh to do so. Instead, she was required to remain secluded outside the camp for seven days, after which she was permitted to re-enter the camp (Nu 12:10–15).

24:13 Return their cloak by sunset A lender was forbidden from taking a cloth or cloak used for warmth as a pledge except for in daylight hours, when the debtor would not need it for warmth.

24:16 for their own sin This verse emphasizes individual accountability for sin. Other passages allude to corporate responsibility such as Dt 5:9 and Ex 20:5. Corporate responsibility for sin does not mean succeeding generations are punished for the sins of earlier generations. But, the consequences of the sins of earlier generations may effect later generations. See note on Ex 20:5.

[17]Do not deprive the foreigner or the fatherless of justice, or take the cloak of the widow as a pledge. [18]Remember that you were slaves in Egypt and the Lord your God redeemed you from there. That is why I command you to do this.

[19]When you are harvesting in your field and you overlook a sheaf, do not go back to get it. Leave it for the foreigner, the fatherless and the widow, so that the Lord your God may bless you in all the work of your hands. [20]When you beat the olives from your trees, do not go over the branches a second time. Leave what remains for the foreigner, the fatherless and the widow. [21]When you harvest the grapes in your vineyard, do not go over the vines again. Leave what remains for the foreigner, the fatherless and the widow. [22]Remember that you were slaves in Egypt. That is why I command you to do this.

25 When people have a dispute, they are to take it to court and the judges will decide the case, acquitting the innocent and condemning the guilty. [2]If the guilty person deserves to be beaten, the judge shall make them lie down and have them flogged in his presence with the number of lashes the crime deserves, [3]but the judge must not impose more than forty lashes. If the guilty party is flogged more than that, your fellow Israelite will be degraded in your eyes.

[4]Do not muzzle an ox while it is treading out the grain.

[5]If brothers are living together and one of them dies without a son, his widow must not marry outside the family. Her husband's brother shall take her and marry her and fulfill the duty of a brother-in-law to her. [6]The first son she bears shall carry on the name of the dead brother so that his name will not be blotted out from Israel.

[7]However, if a man does not want to marry his brother's wife, she shall go to the elders at the town gate and say, "My husband's brother refuses to carry on his brother's name in Israel. He will not fulfill the duty of a brother-in-law to me." [8]Then the elders of his town shall summon him and talk to him. If he persists in saying, "I do not want to marry her," [9]his brother's widow shall go up to him in the presence of the elders, take off one of his sandals, spit in his face and say, "This is what is done to the man who will not build up his brother's family line." [10]That man's line shall be known in Israel as The Family of the Unsandaled.

[11]If two men are fighting and the wife of one of them comes to rescue her husband from his assailant, and she reaches out and seizes him by his private parts, [12]you shall cut off her hand. Show her no pity.

[13]Do not have two differing weights in your bag — one heavy, one light. [14]Do not have two differing measures in your house — one large, one small. [15]You must have accurate and honest weights and measures, so that you may live long in the land the Lord your God is giving you. [16]For the Lord your God detests anyone who does these things, anyone who deals dishonestly.

[17]Remember what the Amalekites did to you along the way when you came out of Egypt. [18]When you were weary and worn out, they met

---

24:17 foreigner or the fatherless The law protected certain groups who would have been especially vulnerable in ancient Near Eastern society—foreigners, orphans and widows.

24:19–22 Israel is called upon to care for the impoverished in the land by rejecting the scrupulous practice of harvesting every sheaf, olive or grape of their crop. Instead, land owners were to make one pass through their fields and leave the remainder as a provision for the poor in the land (see Ru 2; compare Lev 19:9–10; 23:22).

25:3 must not impose more than forty lashes Punishment in excess of 40 lashes might result in incredibly degrading circumstances—such as a person losing control of their bowels; they could even die from such a punishment.

25:4 while it is treading out the grain It was normal for animals threshing grain—pulling a threshing sledge over the stalks—to eat some of the crop.

25:5–10 This passage describes the obligations and purposes of a practice called levirate marriage. Genesis 38 and other ancient Near Eastern parallels make clear that the custom predated Mosaic Law. The law had several purposes: to retain property within the family, to provide a widow with sons to provide for her material needs, and to ensure that the name of the deceased would not be forgotten (see Dt 25:5–6). Examples of the levirate procedure in the OT include Ge 38 and Ru 4.

25:9 take off one of his sandals While the Biblical text provides no explanation for this gesture, it is well known from other literatures in the eastern Mediterranean. Both this act and the spitting that follows—both performed by the woman—humiliate the kinsman who refused the marital obligation (Dt 25:9–10).

25:11–16 This passage contains another list of miscellaneous laws. These laws also relate to the general theme of fairness and justice, continuing the section from 24:4—25:4.

25:12 you shall cut off her hand In the ancient Near East, a person's name (memory) was understood to be erased without heirs. Thus, the act of grabbing the genitals functioned like a death sentence since the man might then be unable to have children. In ancient Israelite thought, his name would then cease to exist.

25:13–16 The laws of vv. 13–16 concern righteous practices for using weights and measures. A lack thereof was the equivalent of defrauding someone.

25:17–19 These verses offer a historical retrospective, looking back on how the Amalekites mistreated Israel. For their past behavior toward Israel, this passage commands the Israelites to eventually destroy the Amalekites completely. Compare note on Jos 6:16; note on Jos 6:17.

25:17 what the Amalekites did to you The Amalekites lived in the Negev, the desert area south of Israel. Moses

you on your journey and attacked all who were lagging behind; they had no fear of God. ¹⁹When the LORD your God gives you rest from all the enemies around you in the land he is giving you to possess as an inheritance, you shall blot out the name of Amalek from under heaven. Do not forget!

Firstfruits and Tithes

26 When you have entered the land the LORD your God is giving you as an inheritance and have taken possession of it and settled in it, ²take some of the firstfruits of all that you produce from the soil of the land the LORD your God is giving you and put them in a basket. Then go to the place the LORD your God will choose as a dwelling for his Name ³and say to the priest in office at the time, "I declare today to the LORD your God that I have come to the land the LORD swore to our ancestors to give us." ⁴The priest shall take the basket from your hands and set it down in front of the altar of the LORD your God. ⁵Then you shall declare before the LORD your God: "My father was a wandering Aramean, and he went down into Egypt with a few people and lived there and became a great nation, powerful and numerous. ⁶But the Egyptians mistreated us and made us suffer, subjecting us to harsh labor. ⁷Then we cried out to the LORD, the God of our ancestors, and the LORD heard our voice and saw our misery, toil and oppression. ⁸So the LORD brought us out of Egypt with a mighty hand and an outstretched arm, with great terror and with signs and wonders. ⁹He brought us to this place and gave us this land, a land flowing with milk and honey; ¹⁰and now I bring the firstfruits of the soil that you, LORD, have given me." Place the basket before the LORD your God and bow down before him. ¹¹Then you and the Levites and the foreigners residing among you shall rejoice in all the good things the LORD your God has given to you and your household.

¹²When you have finished setting aside a tenth of all your produce in the third year, the year of the tithe, you shall give it to the Levite, the foreigner, the fatherless and the widow, so that they may eat in your towns and be satisfied. ¹³Then say to the LORD your God: "I have removed from my house the sacred portion and have given it to the Levite, the foreigner, the fatherless and the widow, according to all you commanded. I have not turned aside from your commands nor have I forgotten any of them. ¹⁴I have not eaten any of the sacred portion while I was in mourning, nor have I removed any of it while I was unclean, nor have I offered any of it to the dead. I have obeyed the LORD my God; I have done everything you commanded me. ¹⁵Look down from heaven, your holy dwelling place, and bless your people Israel and the land you have given us as you promised on oath to our ancestors, a land flowing with milk and honey."

Follow the LORD's Commands

¹⁶The LORD your God commands you this day to follow these decrees and laws; carefully observe them with all your heart and with all your soul. ¹⁷You have declared this day that the LORD is your God and that you will walk in obedience to him, that you will keep his decrees, commands and laws—that you will listen to him. ¹⁸And the LORD has declared this day that you are his people, his treasured possession as he promised, and that you are to keep all his commands. ¹⁹He has declared that he will set you in praise, fame and honor high above all the nations he has made and that you will be a people holy to the LORD your God, as he promised.

The Altar on Mount Ebal

27 Moses and the elders of Israel commanded the people: "Keep all these commands that I give you today. ²When you have crossed the Jordan

26:13 **I have removed from my house the sacred portion** This tithe supports those in Israel particularly at risk of poverty or destitution.

26:14 **while I was in mourning** The mourning context created the possible circumstance that the farmer might be ritually impure due to contact with a dead body. See Nu 19; Hos 9:4. **nor have I offered any of it to the dead** The ancient Israelites believed the dead became part of the underworld (called *she'ol* in Hebrew). Such offerings maintained some connection with deceased loved ones.

27:1–26 This chapter describes the covenant ceremony the Israelites must perform upon entering the land of Canaan. The Israelites must erect an altar on Mount Ebal, offer sacrifices, inscribe the words of the covenant between Yahweh and Israel on stone pillars, and then proclaim the blessings and curses that will come with obedience or disobedience. Joshua follows these instructions when they enter the land (see Jos 8:30–35).

and Israel encountered and defeated them in battle on their way to Sinai (Ex 17:8–16).

26:1–19 This section describes a liturgical procedure for Israelite farmers to follow when they bring their annual firstfruits offering to the central sanctuary (see Dt 12) and when bringing a tithe for the poor every three years. These laws supplement, but do not replace, other Mosaic laws pertaining to these offerings (see Ex 23:19; Nu 18:12–13; Dt 12:6; 14:28–29).

26:5 **My father was a wandering Aramean** This is primarily a reference to Jacob (see Ge 46:1–7; Nu 20:15–16), though it could also apply to his ancestors—Abraham and Isaac—and even his own children (see note on Ge 24:10). The phrase Aramean refers to someone from Paddan Aram in northwest Mesopotamia (Ge 24:4,10; 25:20).

26:9 **a land flowing with milk and honey** A Hebrew idiom for fertility and prosperity.

into the land the Lord your God is giving you, set up some large stones and coat them with plaster. ³Write on them all the words of this law when you have crossed over to enter the land the Lord your God is giving you, a land flowing with milk and honey, just as the Lord, the God of your ancestors, promised you. ⁴And when you have crossed the Jordan, set up these stones on Mount Ebal, as I command you today, and coat them with plaster. ⁵Build there an altar to the Lord your God, an altar of stones. Do not use any iron tool on them. ⁶Build the altar of the Lord your God with fieldstones and offer burnt offerings on it to the Lord your God. ⁷Sacrifice fellowship offerings there, eating them and rejoicing in the presence of the Lord your God. ⁸And you shall write very clearly all the words of this law on these stones you have set up."

Curses From Mount Ebal

⁹Then Moses and the Levitical priests said to all Israel, "Be silent, Israel, and listen! You have now become the people of the Lord your God. ¹⁰Obey the Lord your God and follow his commands and decrees that I give you today."

¹¹On the same day Moses commanded the people:

¹²When you have crossed the Jordan, these tribes shall stand on Mount Gerizim to bless the people: Simeon, Levi, Judah, Issachar, Joseph and Benjamin. ¹³And these tribes shall stand on Mount Ebal to pronounce curses: Reuben, Gad, Asher, Zebulun, Dan and Naphtali.

¹⁴The Levites shall recite to all the people of Israel in a loud voice:

¹⁵"Cursed is anyone who makes an idol—a thing detestable to the Lord, the work of skilled hands—and sets it up in secret."

Then all the people shall say, "Amen!"

¹⁶"Cursed is anyone who dishonors their father or mother."

Then all the people shall say, "Amen!"

¹⁷"Cursed is anyone who moves their neighbor's boundary stone."

Then all the people shall say, "Amen!"

¹⁸"Cursed is anyone who leads the blind astray on the road."

Then all the people shall say, "Amen!"

¹⁹"Cursed is anyone who withholds justice from the foreigner, the fatherless or the widow."

Then all the people shall say, "Amen!"

²⁰"Cursed is anyone who sleeps with his father's wife, for he dishonors his father's bed."

Then all the people shall say, "Amen!"

²¹"Cursed is anyone who has sexual relations with any animal."

Then all the people shall say, "Amen!"

²²"Cursed is anyone who sleeps with his sister, the daughter of his father or the daughter of his mother."

Then all the people shall say, "Amen!"

²³"Cursed is anyone who sleeps with his mother-in-law."

Then all the people shall say, "Amen!"

²⁴"Cursed is anyone who kills their neighbor secretly."

Then all the people shall say, "Amen!"

²⁵"Cursed is anyone who accepts a bribe to kill an innocent person."

Then all the people shall say, "Amen!"

²⁶"Cursed is anyone who does not uphold the words of this law by carrying them out."

Then all the people shall say, "Amen!"

While Dt 27:9–14 describes this ceremony along with its blessings and curses, vv. 15–26 delineate separate curses for the Levites to pronounce on anyone guilty of sins done in secret. The blessings and curses related to covenant loyalty are listed in more detail in ch. 28.

27:2 you have crossed the Jordan into the land According to v. 4, the Israelites are to enact the covenant terms on Mount Ebal, located approximately 30 miles from where Israel will actually cross into Canaan. **some large stones and coat them with plaster** The practice of plastering walls and pillars for the purpose of writing or painting was common in Egypt. Covering stone with plaster created a smooth writing surface that was easy to either engrave or write on with ink.

27:4 on Mount Ebal Located north of Shechem, a city of significance in the earlier patriarchal era. Shechem was Abram's first recorded stopping point in his own journey into Canaan (Ge 12:6).

27:5 an altar of stones Inscribing the covenant on standing stones is not typical of OT covenant ceremonies. The Israelites are not to establish other places of sacrifice in the land apart from the central sanctuary (see Dt 12); since this is a one-time event specifically commanded, it does not violate that law. **Do not use any iron tool on them** The Israelites are to make the altar out of natural stones, not hewn stones (see Ex 20:24–25).

27:12 stand on Mount Gerizim to bless the people In the procedure for the covenant ratification ceremony, six of the twelve tribes stand on the mountain to pronounce the blessings, while the other six stand opposite on Mount Ebal to declare the curses (see v. 13).

27:20–24 The next four curses focus on sexual sins. The Mosaic Law prohibits and condemns all of these sins elsewhere (see Ex 22:19; Lev 18:6–23; 20:10–21).

Blessings for Obedience

28 If you fully obey the LORD your God and carefully follow all his commands I give you today, the LORD your God will set you high above all the nations on earth. ²All these blessings will come on you and accompany you if you obey the LORD your God:

³You will be blessed in the city and blessed in the country.

⁴The fruit of your womb will be blessed, and the crops of your land and the young of your livestock—the calves of your herds and the lambs of your flocks.

⁵Your basket and your kneading trough will be blessed.

⁶You will be blessed when you come in and blessed when you go out.

⁷The LORD will grant that the enemies who rise up against you will be defeated before you. They will come at you from one direction but flee from you in seven.

⁸The LORD will send a blessing on your barns and on everything you put your hand to. The LORD your God will bless you in the land he is giving you.

⁹The LORD will establish you as his holy people, as he promised you on oath, if you keep the commands of the LORD your God and walk in obedience to him. ¹⁰Then all the peoples on earth will see that you are called by the name of the LORD, and they will fear you. ¹¹The LORD will grant you abundant prosperity—in the fruit of your womb, the young of your livestock and the crops of your ground—in the land he swore to your ancestors to give you.

¹²The LORD will open the heavens, the storehouse of his bounty, to send rain on your land in season and to bless all the work of your hands. You will lend to many nations but will borrow from none. ¹³The LORD will make you the head, not the tail. If you pay attention to the commands of the LORD your God that I give you this day and carefully follow them, you will always be at the top, never at the bottom. ¹⁴Do not turn aside from any of the commands I give you today, to the right or to the left, following other gods and serving them.

Curses for Disobedience

¹⁵However, if you do not obey the LORD your God and do not carefully follow all his commands and decrees I am giving you today, all these curses will come on you and overtake you:

¹⁶You will be cursed in the city and cursed in the country.

¹⁷Your basket and your kneading trough will be cursed.

¹⁸The fruit of your womb will be cursed, and the crops of your land, and the calves of your herds and the lambs of your flocks.

¹⁹You will be cursed when you come in and cursed when you go out.

²⁰The LORD will send on you curses, confusion and rebuke in everything you put your hand to, until you are destroyed and come to sudden ruin because of the evil you have done in forsaking him.[a] ²¹The LORD will plague you with diseases until he has destroyed you from the land you are entering to possess. ²²The LORD will strike you with wasting disease, with fever and inflammation, with scorching heat and drought, with blight and mildew, which will plague you until you perish. ²³The sky over your head will be bronze, the

---

[a] 20 Hebrew *me*

28:1–14 This chapter offers a detailed description of the ways Israel will either be blessed for obedience, or cursed for disobedience, according to the terms of their covenant with Yahweh. The chapter naturally divides into two parts: the blessings (Dt 28:1–14) and the curses (vv. 15–68). The chapter distinguishes blessings (vv. 3–6) from positive circumstances that extend from those blessings (vv. 7–13).

28:6 when you go out This Hebrew idiom might describe a person's regular movements during the day (e.g., 2Ki 11:8; Jer 37:4), travel to and from a location (e.g., Jos 6:1; 1Ki 15:17; Zec 8:10) or the marching forth and returning of armies (e.g., Dt 28:7; Nu 27:17,21; 1Sa 18:13,16; 29:6).

28:7 flee from you in seven This is idiomatic for being scattered in defeat and retreat.

28:8 bless you in the land he is giving you This presents the link between blessing, obedience and the promised land (see Dt 4:26–28,40; 5:30–33; 6:16–19; 7:12; 8:1).

28:9 his holy people The Israelites were chosen so that they might become a holy nation. See 7:6 and note.

28:14 following other gods and serving them The greatest commandment—to worship only Yahweh—is the central idea of obedience (e.g., 6:4–5; 8:19; 13:2–3).

28:15–68 The curses for disobedience in this section resemble those of Lev 26. In both instances, the link between obedience to the law and possession of the land of Canaan is made explicit (compare Dt 4:26–28,40; 5:30–33; 6:16–19; 7:12; 8:1). A curse generally describes the mirror-opposite of a particular blessing: Yahweh, through nature, will punish Israel with drought, disease and famine and will cause Israel to suffer defeat before the nation's enemies. Many of the curses reverse the language of the respective blessings.

28:20 until you are destroyed Although the later-disobedient nation was sent into exile, a remnant of Israelites were preserved and brought back. This suggests that either this curse is hyperbole, or due to Yahweh's mercy, was not fully enacted. Compare 30:1–20 and note. **come to sudden ruin** This refers to the threats that follow, which fall into three categories: pestilence (vv. 21–22), drought and its aftereffects (vv. 23–24), and war (vv. 25–26).

ground beneath you iron. ²⁴The LORD will turn the rain of your country into dust and powder; it will come down from the skies until you are destroyed.

²⁵The LORD will cause you to be defeated before your enemies. You will come at them from one direction but flee from them in seven, and you will become a thing of horror to all the kingdoms on earth. ²⁶Your carcasses will be food for all the birds and the wild animals, and there will be no one to frighten them away. ²⁷The LORD will afflict you with the boils of Egypt and with tumors, festering sores and the itch, from which you cannot be cured. ²⁸The LORD will afflict you with madness, blindness and confusion of mind. ²⁹At midday you will grope about like a blind person in the dark. You will be unsuccessful in everything you do; day after day you will be oppressed and robbed, with no one to rescue you.

³⁰You will be pledged to be married to a woman, but another will take her and rape her. You will build a house, but you will not live in it. You will plant a vineyard, but you will not even begin to enjoy its fruit. ³¹Your ox will be slaughtered before your eyes, but you will eat none of it. Your donkey will be forcibly taken from you and will not be returned. Your sheep will be given to your enemies, and no one will rescue them. ³²Your sons and daughters will be given to another nation, and you will wear out your eyes watching for them day after day, powerless to lift a hand. ³³A people that you do not know will eat what your land and labor produce, and you will have nothing but cruel oppression all your days. ³⁴The sights you see will drive you mad. ³⁵The LORD will afflict your knees and legs with painful boils that cannot be cured, spreading from the soles of your feet to the top of your head.

³⁶The LORD will drive you and the king you set over you to a nation unknown to you or your ancestors. There you will worship other gods, gods of wood and stone. ³⁷You will become a thing of horror, a byword and an object of ridicule among all the peoples where the LORD will drive you.

³⁸You will sow much seed in the field but you will harvest little, because locusts will devour it. ³⁹You will plant vineyards and cultivate them but you will not drink the wine or gather the grapes, because worms will eat them. ⁴⁰You will have olive trees throughout your country but you will not use the oil, because the olives will drop off. ⁴¹You will have sons and daughters but you will not keep them, because they will go into captivity. ⁴²Swarms of locusts will take over all your trees and the crops of your land.

⁴³The foreigners who reside among you will rise above you higher and higher, but you will sink lower and lower. ⁴⁴They will lend to you, but you will not lend to them. They will be the head, but you will be the tail.

⁴⁵All these curses will come on you. They will pursue you and overtake you until you are destroyed, because you did not obey the LORD your God and observe the commands and decrees he gave you. ⁴⁶They will be a sign and a wonder to you and your descendants forever. ⁴⁷Because you did not serve the LORD your God joyfully and gladly in the time of prosperity, ⁴⁸therefore in hunger and thirst, in nakedness and dire poverty, you will serve the enemies the LORD sends against you. He will put an iron yoke on your neck until he has destroyed you.

⁴⁹The LORD will bring a nation against you from far away, from the ends of the earth, like an eagle swooping down, a nation whose language you will not understand, ⁵⁰a fierce-looking nation without respect for the old or pity for the young. ⁵¹They will devour the young of your livestock and the crops of your land until you are destroyed. They will leave you no grain, new wine or olive oil, nor any calves of your herds or lambs of your flocks until you are ruined. ⁵²They will lay siege to all the cities throughout your land until the high fortified walls in which you trust fall down. They will besiege all the cities throughout the land the LORD your God is giving you.

⁵³Because of the suffering your enemy will inflict on you during the siege, you will eat the fruit

---

28:25 flee from them in seven This is a precise reversal of v. 7. See note on v. 7.

28:26 food for all the birds Israel's unburied dead will be food for scavengers. This fate would be especially horrific in light of 21:23, which forbids prolonged exposure of a corpse because it is an affront to God and may imply rejection in the afterlife.

28:27 with the boils of Egypt A possible reference to one of the plagues at the time of the exodus (Ex 9:1–12; compare Dt 7:15).

28:29 you will be oppressed and robbed Israel suffered all these things at the hands of their enemy captors, Assyria in 722 BC and Babylon from 605–586 BC. See the timeline "Dates Related to Isaiah and 2 Kings" on p. 1116.

28:30 take her and rape her The Hebrew verb used here, *shagal*, denotes rape, not normal sexual relations (compare Isa 13:16; Zec 14:2).

28:43 will rise above you higher and higher This curse reverses the blessing of Dt 28:12–13, where agricultural abundance would overflow to other nations.

28:46 sign and a wonder Both of the Hebrew terms used here, *oth* and *mopheth*, are used to describe the ten plagues Yahweh sent on Egypt (see 4:34; 6:22; 34:11). This evokes the idea that a role reversal will take place between Egypt and Israel—Israel will endure what Yahweh brought upon Egypt. See 28:68.

28:48 destroyed you See note on 28:20.

28:53–57 Verses 53–57 describe famine conditions that will be so severe that even the wealthy must resort to cannibalism, even to the point of eating a woman's afterbirth (v. 57). Such episodes are later reported in Samaria and Jerusalem, the capitals of the separate kingdoms of Israel and Judah (see 2Ki 6:28–29; Isa 9:19–20; La 2:20; 4:10).

of the womb, the flesh of the sons and daughters the LORD your God has given you. ⁵⁴Even the most gentle and sensitive man among you will have no compassion on his own brother or the wife he loves or his surviving children, ⁵⁵and he will not give to one of them any of the flesh of his children that he is eating. It will be all he has left because of the suffering your enemy will inflict on you during the siege of all your cities. ⁵⁶The most gentle and sensitive woman among you — so sensitive and gentle that she would not venture to touch the ground with the sole of her foot — will begrudge the husband she loves and her own son or daughter ⁵⁷the afterbirth from her womb and the children she bears. For in her dire need she intends to eat them secretly because of the suffering your enemy will inflict on you during the siege of your cities.

⁵⁸If you do not carefully follow all the words of this law, which are written in this book, and do not revere this glorious and awesome name — the LORD your God — ⁵⁹the LORD will send fearful plagues on you and your descendants, harsh and prolonged disasters, and severe and lingering illnesses. ⁶⁰He will bring on you all the diseases of Egypt that you dreaded, and they will cling to you. ⁶¹The LORD will also bring on you every kind of sickness and disaster not recorded in this Book of the Law, until you are destroyed. ⁶²You who were as numerous as the stars in the sky will be left but few in number, because you did not obey the LORD your God. ⁶³Just as it pleased the LORD to make you prosper and increase in number, so it will please him to ruin and destroy you. You will be uprooted from the land you are entering to possess.

⁶⁴Then the LORD will scatter you among all nations, from one end of the earth to the other. There you will worship other gods — gods of wood and stone, which neither you nor your ancestors have known. ⁶⁵Among those nations you will find no repose, no resting place for the sole of your foot. There the LORD will give you an anxious mind, eyes weary with longing, and a despairing heart. ⁶⁶You will live in constant suspense, filled with dread both night and day, never sure of your life. ⁶⁷In the morning you will say, "If only it were evening!" and in the evening, "If only it were morning!" — because of the terror that will fill your hearts and the sights that your eyes will see. ⁶⁸The LORD will send you back in ships to Egypt on a journey I said you should never make again. There you will offer yourselves for sale to your enemies as male and female slaves, but no one will buy you.

Renewal of the Covenant

29ᵃ These are the terms of the covenant the LORD commanded Moses to make with the Israelites in Moab, in addition to the covenant he had made with them at Horeb.

²Moses summoned all the Israelites and said to them:

Your eyes have seen all that the LORD did in Egypt to Pharaoh, to all his officials and to all his land. ³With your own eyes you saw those great trials, those signs and great wonders. ⁴But to this day the LORD has not given you a mind that understands or eyes that see or ears that hear. ⁵Yet the LORD says, "During the forty years that I led you through the wilderness, your clothes did not wear out, nor did the sandals on your feet. ⁶You ate no bread and drank no wine or other fermented drink. I did this so that you might know that I am the LORD your God."

⁷When you reached this place, Sihon king of Heshbon and Og king of Bashan came out to fight against us, but we defeated them. ⁸We took their land and gave it as an inheritance to the Reubenites, the Gadites and the half-tribe of Manasseh.

⁹Carefully follow the terms of this covenant, so

ᵃ In Hebrew texts 29:1 is numbered 28:69, and 29:2-29 is numbered 29:1-28.

28:63 This verse summarizes the principle of dramatic reversal that is so prominent in the chapter's enumerated blessings and curses.

28:68 you should never make again This is the ironic and tragic climax of Israel's cursing—the nation will end up back in the nation of its original bondage (Ex 1).

29:1–29 Moses has finished explaining to Israel the particulars of Yahweh's law in Dt 4:44—28:68; throughout chs. 29–30, he continues to urge them to truly obey Yahweh. In ch. 29, he recounts Israel's history with Yahweh (vv. 1–8) and warns the people that their consenting to the covenant binds them and all subsequent generations (vv. 9–14).

29:1 in addition to the covenant The wording here treats the covenant represented by Deuteronomy as somewhat distinct from the covenant Yahweh made with Israel at Horeb (or Sinai; Ex 20–24). However, the distinction is primarily the audience of each covenant. Deuteronomy articulates Yahweh's laws to the second generation—the children of those who had stood at Sinai (Horeb), whereas former laws, as represented by Exodus and Numbers, were addressed to the former generation. All the laws Yahweh gave through Moses are the terms of the covenant, so the covenants are essentially identical.

29:4 a mind that understands Moses here suggests that up until now, Yahweh himself had not actually enabled Israel to discern the true importance of these deeds with respect to their own relationship to him. Deuteronomy 29:6–7, however, confirms that now Israel does understand. The text here may employ hyperbole. Alternatively, it may reflect Moses' own resignation to the people's hopeless stubbornness; only now that the unbelieving generation has died off (Nu 14:29; 32:11) will the people understand.

that you may prosper in everything you do. ¹⁰All of you are standing today in the presence of the LORD your God — your leaders and chief men, your elders and officials, and all the other men of Israel, ¹¹together with your children and your wives, and the foreigners living in your camps who chop your wood and carry your water. ¹²You are standing here in order to enter into a covenant with the LORD your God, a covenant the LORD is making with you this day and sealing with an oath, ¹³to confirm you this day as his people, that he may be your God as he promised you and as he swore to your fathers, Abraham, Isaac and Jacob. ¹⁴I am making this covenant, with its oath, not only with you ¹⁵who are standing here with us today in the presence of the LORD our God but also with those who are not here today.

¹⁶You yourselves know how we lived in Egypt and how we passed through the countries on the way here. ¹⁷You saw among them their detestable images and idols of wood and stone, of silver and gold. ¹⁸Make sure there is no man or woman, clan or tribe among you today whose heart turns away from the LORD our God to go and worship the gods of those nations; make sure there is no root among you that produces such bitter poison.

¹⁹When such a person hears the words of this oath and they invoke a blessing on themselves, thinking, "I will be safe, even though I persist in going my own way," they will bring disaster on the watered land as well as the dry. ²⁰The LORD will never be willing to forgive them; his wrath and zeal will burn against them. All the curses written in this book will fall on them, and the LORD will blot out their names from under heaven. ²¹The LORD will single them out from all the tribes of Israel for disaster, according to all the curses of the covenant written in this Book of the Law.

²²Your children who follow you in later generations and foreigners who come from distant lands will see the calamities that have fallen on the land and the diseases with which the LORD has afflicted it. ²³The whole land will be a burning waste of salt and sulfur — nothing planted, nothing sprouting, no vegetation growing on it. It will be like the destruction of Sodom and Gomorrah, Admah and Zeboyim, which the LORD overthrew in fierce anger. ²⁴All the nations will ask: "Why has the LORD done this to this land? Why this fierce, burning anger?"

²⁵And the answer will be: "It is because this people abandoned the covenant of the LORD, the God of their ancestors, the covenant he made with them when he brought them out of Egypt. ²⁶They went off and worshiped other gods and bowed down to them, gods they did not know, gods he had not given them. ²⁷Therefore the LORD's anger burned against this land, so that he brought on it all the curses written in this book. ²⁸In furious anger and in great wrath the LORD uprooted them from their land and thrust them into another land, as it is now."

²⁹The secret things belong to the LORD our God, but the things revealed belong to us and to our children forever, that we may follow all the words of this law.

Prosperity After Turning to the LORD

30 When all these blessings and curses I have set before you come on you and you take them to heart wherever the LORD your God disperses you among the nations, ²and when you and your children return to the LORD your God and obey him with all your heart and with all your soul according to everything I command you today, ³then the LORD your God will restore your fortunes[a] and have compassion on you and gather you again from all the nations where he scattered you. ⁴Even if you have been banished to the most distant land under

---

[a] 3 Or will bring you back from captivity

29:14 not only with you The people's agreement to Yahweh's covenant with them would be binding on succeeding generations.

29:26 he had not given them This verse foreshadows the worldview description of Dt 32:8–9 (compare 4:19–20). Israel is Yahweh's possession, but he has allowed other nations to be governed by different supernatural beings.

29:27 LORD's anger burned against this land The wording in vv. 25–28 views Israel's apostasy as a past event, possibly indicating the passage was an editorial comment written much later in Israel's history, after the fall of the northern kingdom of Israel in 722 BC. Second Kings 17:7–20 also explains that the northern kingdom's fall was caused by their apostasy. The theological perspective of Dt 29:25–28 runs through the historical books that make up the Deuteronomistic History (Joshua—2 Kings). Israel's failure to keep their covenant with Yahweh brought about the divine judgment promised in the terms of the covenant itself.

29:28 as it is now This phrase indicates that this verse, and possibly also vv. 25–27, may have been added after Moses' lifetime (see note on 29:27).

30:1–20 While chs. 28–29 emphasized the judgment Israel would experience for violating their covenant with Yahweh, this chapter offers the hope of possible restoration following the judgment. If Israel turned back to Yahweh, then he would restore his people (Lev 26:40–45). Even if the covenant was broken and Israel experienced judgment, Yahweh would still be faithful to his agreement if they repented. Moses emphasizes the choice Israel has between obedience and disobedience, life and death, blessings and curses.

30:2 with all your heart Undivided loyalty to Yahweh is the necessary condition for Israel to return from a future exile (Dt 30:3–5).

30:3 where he scattered you If Israel returns to Yahweh after their disobedience, he will one day return them from exile.

the heavens, from there the LORD your God will gather you and bring you back. ⁵He will bring you to the land that belonged to your ancestors, and you will take possession of it. He will make you more prosperous and numerous than your ancestors. ⁶The LORD your God will circumcise your hearts and the hearts of your descendants, so that you may love him with all your heart and with all your soul, and live. ⁷The LORD your God will put all these curses on your enemies who hate and persecute you. ⁸You will again obey the LORD and follow all his commands I am giving you today. ⁹Then the LORD your God will make you most prosperous in all the work of your hands and in the fruit of your womb, the young of your livestock and the crops of your land. The LORD will again delight in you and make you prosperous, just as he delighted in your ancestors, ¹⁰if you obey the LORD your God and keep his commands and decrees that are written in this Book of the Law and turn to the LORD your God with all your heart and with all your soul.

The Offer of Life or Death

¹¹Now what I am commanding you today is not too difficult for you or beyond your reach. ¹²It is not up in heaven, so that you have to ask, "Who will ascend into heaven to get it and proclaim it to us so we may obey it?" ¹³Nor is it beyond the sea, so that you have to ask, "Who will cross the sea to get it and proclaim it to us so we may obey it?" ¹⁴No, the word is very near you; it is in your mouth and in your heart so you may obey it.

¹⁵See, I set before you today life and prosperity, death and destruction. ¹⁶For I command you today to love the LORD your God, to walk in obedience to him, and to keep his commands, decrees and laws; then you will live and increase, and the LORD your God will bless you in the land you are entering to possess. ¹⁷But if your heart turns away and you are not obedient, and if you are drawn away to bow down to other gods and worship them, ¹⁸I declare to you this day that you will certainly be destroyed. You

will not live long in the land you are crossing the Jordan to enter and possess.

¹⁹This day I call the heavens and the earth as witnesses against you that I have set before you life and death, blessings and curses. Now choose life, so that you and your children may live ²⁰and that you may love the LORD your God, listen to his voice, and hold fast to him. For the LORD is your life, and he will give you many years in the land he swore to give to your fathers, Abraham, Isaac and Jacob.

Joshua to Succeed Moses

31 Then Moses went out and spoke these words to all Israel: ²"I am now a hundred and twenty years old and I am no longer able to lead you. The LORD has said to me, 'You shall not cross the Jordan.' ³The LORD your God himself will cross over ahead of you. He will destroy these nations before you, and you will take possession of their land. Joshua also will cross over ahead of you, as the LORD said. ⁴And the LORD will do to them what he did to Sihon and Og, the kings of the Amorites, whom he destroyed along with their land. ⁵The LORD will deliver them to you, and you must do to them all that I have commanded you. ⁶Be strong and courageous. Do not be afraid or terrified because of them, for the LORD your God goes with you; he will never leave you nor forsake you."

⁷Then Moses summoned Joshua and said to him in the presence of all Israel, "Be strong and courageous, for you must go with this people into the land that the LORD swore to their ancestors to give them, and you must divide it among them as their inheritance. ⁸The LORD himself goes before you and will be with you; he will never leave you nor forsake you. Do not be afraid; do not be discouraged."

Public Reading of the Law

⁹So Moses wrote down this law and gave it to the Levitical priests, who carried the ark of the

---

30:6 circumcise your hearts Earlier, this idiom negatively described Israel's stubbornness (see 10:16; note on 10:12–22). Here, it indicates the removal of the impediment of stubbornness so that Israel can turn toward Yahweh.

30:11–20 The choice facing the Israelites is clear: They can choose life and prosperity or death and exile. There is no middle ground.

30:16 to keep his commands According to 4:13 and 5:2–22, the content of the Horeb (Sinai) covenant was the Decalogue—the Ten Commandments—which Moses reiterated in ch. 5. Yahweh gave the later laws to Moses in private, and Moses then revealed them to Israel in his lengthy address in 4:44—28:68.
30:20 hold fast to him Moses links the promises Yahweh gave to the patriarchs and their descendants (Israel) to obedience to the Sinai covenant (29:1).

31:1–8 Moses appoints his apprentice Joshua son of Nun as his successor to lead the people of Israel (compare Nu 27:12–23).

31:2 You shall not cross the Jordan Yahweh will not allow Moses to enter the promised land due to his earlier sin (see Nu 20:12; compare Dt 1:37; 3:27; 4:21–22).
31:3 God himself will cross over Moses reminds Israel that Yahweh's presence is indispensable for a successful conquest of the promised land.

31:9–13 Moses instructs the priests to read Yahweh's law to all Israel once every seven years when all the people are gathered to celebrate the Festival of Booths (also called the Festival of Tabernacles; compare Ne 8:1–3,13–18).

31:9 who carried the ark of the covenant of the LORD This refers to the Kohathites (see Nu 4:1–15).

covenant of the LORD, and to all the elders of Israel. [10]Then Moses commanded them: "At the end of every seven years, in the year for canceling debts, during the Festival of Tabernacles, [11]when all Israel comes to appear before the LORD your God at the place he will choose, you shall read this law before them in their hearing. [12]Assemble the people — men, women and children, and the foreigners residing in your towns — so they can listen and learn to fear the LORD your God and follow carefully all the words of this law. [13]Their children, who do not know this law, must hear it and learn to fear the LORD your God as long as you live in the land you are crossing the Jordan to possess."

Israel's Rebellion Predicted

[14]The LORD said to Moses, "Now the day of your death is near. Call Joshua and present yourselves at the tent of meeting, where I will commission him." So Moses and Joshua came and presented themselves at the tent of meeting.

[15]Then the LORD appeared at the tent in a pillar of cloud, and the cloud stood over the entrance to the tent. [16]And the LORD said to Moses: "You are going to rest with your ancestors, and these people will soon prostitute themselves to the foreign gods of the land they are entering. They will forsake me and break the covenant I made with them. [17]And in that day I will become angry with them and forsake them; I will hide my face from them, and they will be destroyed. Many disasters and calamities will come on them, and in that day they will ask, 'Have not these disasters come on us because our God is not with us?' [18]And I will certainly hide my face in that day because of all their wickedness in turning to other gods.

[19]"Now write down this song and teach it to the Israelites and have them sing it, so that it may be a witness for me against them. [20]When I have brought them into the land flowing with milk and honey, the land I promised on oath to their ancestors, and when they eat their fill and thrive, they will turn to other gods and worship them, rejecting me and breaking my covenant. [21]And when many disasters and calamities come on them, this song will testify against them, because it will not be forgotten by their descendants. I know what they are disposed to do, even before I bring them into the land I promised them on oath." [22]So Moses wrote down this song that day and taught it to the Israelites.

[23]The LORD gave this command to Joshua son of Nun: "Be strong and courageous, for you will bring the Israelites into the land I promised them on oath, and I myself will be with you."

[24]After Moses finished writing in a book the words of this law from beginning to end, [25]he gave this command to the Levites who carried the ark of the covenant of the LORD: [26]"Take this Book of the Law and place it beside the ark of the covenant of the LORD your God. There it will remain as a witness against you. [27]For I know how rebellious and stiff-necked you are. If you have been rebellious against the LORD while I am still alive and with you, how much more will you rebel after I die! [28]Assemble before me all the elders of your tribes and all your officials, so that I can speak these words in their hearing and call the heavens and the earth to testify against them. [29]For I know that after my death you are sure to become utterly corrupt and to turn from the way I have commanded you. In days to come, disaster will fall on you because you will do evil in the sight of the LORD and arouse his anger by what your hands have made."

The Song of Moses

[30]And Moses recited the words of this song from beginning to end in the hearing of the whole assembly of Israel:

32 Listen, you heavens, and I will speak;
  hear, you earth, the words of my mouth.
[2]Let my teaching fall like rain
   and my words descend like dew,
  like showers on new grass,
   like abundant rain on tender plants.

31:10 At the end of every seven years This refers to the Sabbatical Year (Lev 25:1–7). See Dt 15:1–18 and note. **Festival of Tabernacles** An autumn harvest festival held in the seventh month. See 16:13–15.
31:11 at the place he will choose The central sanctuary (see 12:5 and note).

31:14–23 Here Yahweh commissions Moses' apprentice Joshua directly, affirming Moses' choice of successor (vv. 1–8). Yahweh's words of encouragement to Joshua echo those of Moses (vv. 6,23). Yahweh also warns Moses that soon after Moses' death, Israel will begin to turn away and worship other gods (vv. 16–21). In doing so, they will break their covenant with Yahweh and bring judgment on themselves. Moses is to write a song to be passed down as a reminder to Israel to remain faithful to Yahweh (vv. 19,22). The song is probably the poem of ch. 32.

31:16 break the covenant Yahweh knows that the Israelites will indeed fail to uphold their agreement. When they break their contract with Yahweh, they will become subject to the penalties outlined in 28:15–68.
31:18 in turning to other gods Holding to the covenant means nothing less than exclusive loyalty and devotion to Yahweh as Israel's only God.

31:24–30 Moses had commanded the priests to read the law to the people once every seven years (vv. 9–13). Now he formally finishes writing the law and turns it over to the priests to deposit in the ark of the covenant. Moses then warns Israel against turning away from Yahweh and recites them his song—the Song of Moses from ch. 32 (v. 30; compare v. 22).

31:30 the words of this song This verse introduces the Song of Moses which follows in ch. 32.

³I will proclaim the name of the LORD.
Oh, praise the greatness of our God!
⁴He is the Rock, his works are perfect,
and all his ways are just.
A faithful God who does no wrong,
upright and just is he.

⁵They are corrupt and not his children;
to their shame they are a warped and
crooked generation.
⁶Is this the way you repay the LORD,
you foolish and unwise people?
Is he not your Father, your Creator,ᵃ
who made you and formed you?

⁷Remember the days of old;
consider the generations long past.
Ask your father and he will tell you,
your elders, and they will explain to you.
⁸When the Most High gave the nations their
inheritance,
when he divided all mankind,
he set up boundaries for the peoples
according to the number of the sons
of Israel.ᵇ
⁹For the LORD's portion is his people,
Jacob his allotted inheritance.

¹⁰In a desert land he found him,
in a barren and howling waste.

He shielded him and cared for him;
he guarded him as the apple of his eye,
¹¹like an eagle that stirs up its nest
and hovers over its young,
that spreads its wings to catch them
and carries them aloft.
¹²The LORD alone led him;
no foreign god was with him.

¹³He made him ride on the heights of the land
and fed him with the fruit of the fields.
He nourished him with honey from the rock,
and with oil from the flinty crag,
¹⁴with curds and milk from herd and flock
and with fattened lambs and goats,
with choice rams of Bashan
and the finest kernels of wheat.
You drank the foaming blood of the grape.

¹⁵Jeshurunᶜ grew fat and kicked;
filled with food, they became heavy and
sleek.
They abandoned the God who made them
and rejected the Rock their Savior.
¹⁶They made him jealous with their foreign gods
and angered him with their detestable idols.

ᵃ 6 Or *Father, who bought you*   ᵇ 8 Masoretic Text; Dead Sea
Scrolls (see also Septuagint) *sons of God*   ᶜ 15 *Jeshurun* means
the upright one, that is, Israel.

32:1–43 This passage presents the Song of Moses, a poetic overview of how the nations of the world known to the ancient Israelites came to serve other gods—even though descended from Noah and his sons—and how Israel became Yahweh's own chosen people. Israel's origin and God's selection of them as his people tragically form the backdrop to their anticipated betrayal of Yahweh. Each verse of the Song of Moses consists of two poetic lines that exhibit some type of parallelism that is characteristic of Hebrew poetry.

32:3 I will proclaim the name of the LORD This means to extol Yahweh's attributes and nature, specifically in connection with the deeds he has done (see Ex 33:19; 34:5).

32:4–6 Deuteronomy 32:4–6 proclaims Yahweh's attributes and simultaneously highlights Israel's wretched unfaithfulness.

32:5 They are corrupt The Hebrew term used here, *shicheth*, in this case describes Israel's treachery with the golden calf in 9:12.

32:8 When the Most High gave the nations their inheritance The fragmentation of humankind after the flood into nations occurred at the Tower of Babel incident (Ge 11:1–9; compare Ge 10). Deuteronomy 32:8–9 (compare 4:19–20) notes that Yahweh then chose Israel for himself as a nation. The nations would have no direct relationship with Yahweh, but instead were allowed to worship and follow other gods. Other passages envision the future reversal of this situation with the nations coming to Jerusalem to worship Yahweh (e.g., Isa 2:2–4; compare Ro 1:16–17; 3:29; 9). **number of the sons of Israel** While many translations read "sons of Israel" in v. 8 (following the traditional

Hebrew text's reading of *benei yisrael*), "sons of God" (*benei elohim* in Hebrew) is the more probable original Hebrew reading based on manuscript evidence from the Dead Sea Scrolls (ca. 250 BC–AD 50). The Septuagint, the ancient Greek translation of the OT, also attests to reading "God," not "Israel" for this verse. These "sons of God" seem to have been spiritual beings who were part of Yahweh's divine council prior to their downfall (see Ge 6:2 and note). Verses 8–9, along with its parallel in 4:19–20, provide a connection between other nations and the gods they worship and the nations' opposition to Yahweh and his people, Israel. The nations are under the dominion of other divine beings because Yahweh allowed for them to be so, while Yahweh chose Israel as his own (Ge 12:1–3).

32:9 Jacob his allotted inheritance Israel is Yahweh's chosen people. Jacob is another name for Israel, because Jacob was renamed Israel (see Ge 32:28).

32:12 no foreign god was with him Israel's apostasy and spiritual infidelity were heinous because they did not owe any other deity their loyalty; Yahweh alone cared for the Israelites (see Dt 32:39), who had experienced his protection through 40 years of wandering (e.g., Dt 8:2–4).

32:14 Bashan A mountainous area in the northern Transjordan known for its favorable pastureland.

32:15 Jeshurun grew fat The name Jeshurun (*yeshurun* in Hebrew) derives from the Hebrew word *yashar*, meaning "upright." This word is used of God in v. 4. With deliberate irony, the writer uses *yashar*, which is normally used of God, as a pun on Israel, whose Hebrew pronunciation (*yisra'el*) sounds similar to *yashar*. The irony is that Israel was hardly upright—they kicked like a stubborn animal after growing fat on God's blessings.

¹⁷ They sacrificed to false gods, which are not
God —
gods they had not known,
gods that recently appeared,
gods your ancestors did not fear.
¹⁸ You deserted the Rock, who fathered you;
you forgot the God who gave you birth.

¹⁹ The Lord saw this and rejected them
because he was angered by his sons and
daughters.
²⁰ "I will hide my face from them," he said,
"and see what their end will be;
for they are a perverse generation,
children who are unfaithful.
²¹ They made me jealous by what is no god
and angered me with their worthless idols.
I will make them envious by those who are
not a people;
I will make them angry by a nation that
has no understanding.
²² For a fire will be kindled by my wrath,
one that burns down to the realm of
the dead below.
It will devour the earth and its harvests
and set afire the foundations
of the mountains.

²³ "I will heap calamities on them
and spend my arrows against them.
²⁴ I will send wasting famine against them,
consuming pestilence and deadly plague;
I will send against them the fangs of wild
beasts,
the venom of vipers that glide in the dust.
²⁵ In the street the sword will make them
childless;
in their homes terror will reign.
The young men and young women will perish,
the infants and those with gray hair.

²⁶ I said I would scatter them
and erase their name from human
memory,
²⁷ but I dreaded the taunt of the enemy,
lest the adversary misunderstand
and say, 'Our hand has triumphed;
the Lord has not done all this.'"

²⁸ They are a nation without sense,
there is no discernment in them.
²⁹ If only they were wise and would understand
this
and discern what their end will be!
³⁰ How could one man chase a thousand,
or two put ten thousand to flight,
unless their Rock had sold them,
unless the Lord had given them up?
³¹ For their rock is not like our Rock,
as even our enemies concede.
³² Their vine comes from the vine of Sodom
and from the fields of Gomorrah.
Their grapes are filled with poison,
and their clusters with bitterness.
³³ Their wine is the venom of serpents,
the deadly poison of cobras.

³⁴ "Have I not kept this in reserve
and sealed it in my vaults?
³⁵ It is mine to avenge; I will repay.
In due time their foot will slip;
their day of disaster is near
and their doom rushes upon them."

³⁶ The Lord will vindicate his people
and relent concerning his servants
when he sees their strength is gone
and no one is left, slave or free.^a
³⁷ He will say: "Now where are their gods,
the rock they took refuge in,

^a 36 Or and they are without a ruler or leader

32:17 to false gods The Hebrew word used here, *shedim*, occurs rarely in the OT; it is only found elsewhere in Ps 106:37. The word is most likely related to the Akkadian name for protective spirits, known as *shadu*—beings with far less power than Yahweh. This verse and Ps 106:37 may be describing Israel as worshiping lesser spiritual beings instead of worshiping God (compare Lev 17:7). **which are not God** The Hebrew term used here, *eloah*, is singular. It is a common poetic reference to God. The sacrifices were illegitimate since the Israelites did not offer them to the true God of Israel but to inferior spiritual entities. **gods they had not known** The Hebrew term used here, *elohim*, refers in this instance to the *shedim* referenced earlier in this verse. The text here casts these gods as real, albeit inferior, spiritual entities that Israel should have avoided. Israel's worship of spiritual beings other than Yahweh is the focus of the segment of the poem in Dt 32:15–21.
32:19 rejected Yahweh rejected Israel because of unfaithfulness. They broke the covenant and brought judgment on themselves. During the wilderness journey, Israel had provoked Yahweh's anger such that he sought to

destroy them completely (Ex 32:9–10; Nu 14:11–12). The only thing preventing God from totally annihilating Israel was that the nations—and their gods—would see and rejoice (see Dt 9:14; 32:26–31).
32:22 realm of the dead The Hebrew term used here, *she'ol*, is the name for the underworld—the realm of the dead—which people in the ancient Near East considered to be a dark abyss under the earth. See the infographic "Ancient Hebrew Conception of the Universe" on p. 5.

32:23–27 The descriptions of vv. 23–27 appear among the curses Yahweh said would come upon Israel for disloyalty to him and his covenant with them. See the curses in 28:15–68.

32:28 They are a nation without sense It is not completely clear which nation is the subject here—Israel or the nation of fools (v. 21). This likely refers to the nation of fools (those without understanding); if that is the case, Yahweh is explaining that the nation is delusional in thinking that they deserve credit for conquering Israel, when Israel is his people and he could easily protect them (see vv. 8–9). Compare 32:43 and note.

[38] the gods who ate the fat of their sacrifices
   and drank the wine of their drink
      offerings?
Let them rise up to help you!
   Let them give you shelter!

[39] "See now that I myself am he!
   There is no god besides me.
I put to death and I bring to life,
   I have wounded and I will heal,
   and no one can deliver out of my hand.
[40] I lift my hand to heaven and solemnly swear:
   As surely as I live forever,
[41] when I sharpen my flashing sword
   and my hand grasps it in judgment,
I will take vengeance on my adversaries
   and repay those who hate me.
[42] I will make my arrows drunk with blood,
   while my sword devours flesh:
the blood of the slain and the captives,
   the heads of the enemy leaders."

[43] Rejoice, you nations, with his people,[a,b]
   for he will avenge the blood of his servants;
he will take vengeance on his enemies
   and make atonement for his land and
      people.

[44] Moses came with Joshua[c] son of Nun and
spoke all the words of this song in the hearing of
the people. [45] When Moses finished reciting all
these words to all Israel, [46] he said to them, "Take
to heart all the words I have solemnly declared
to you this day, so that you may command your
children to obey carefully all the words of this law.
[47] They are not just idle words for you — they are
your life. By them you will live long in the land
you are crossing the Jordan to possess."

Moses to Die on Mount Nebo

[48] On that same day the LORD told Moses, [49] "Go
up into the Abarim Range to Mount Nebo in Moab,
across from Jericho, and view Canaan, the land I
am giving the Israelites as their own possession.
[50] There on the mountain that you have climbed
you will die and be gathered to your people, just
as your brother Aaron died on Mount Hor and
was gathered to his people. [51] This is because both
of you broke faith with me in the presence of the
Israelites at the waters of Meribah Kadesh in the
Desert of Zin and because you did not uphold my
holiness among the Israelites. [52] Therefore, you
will see the land only from a distance; you will not
enter the land I am giving to the people of Israel."

Moses Blesses the Tribes

33:1-29 Ref — Ge 49:1-28

33 This is the blessing that Moses the man of
God pronounced on the Israelites before
his death. [2] He said:

"The LORD came from Sinai
   and dawned over them from Seir;
   he shone forth from Mount Paran.
He came with[d] myriads of holy ones
   from the south, from his mountain
      slopes.[e]
[3] Surely it is you who love the people;
   all the holy ones are in your hand.
At your feet they all bow down,
   and from you receive instruction,
[4] the law that Moses gave us,
   the possession of the assembly of Jacob.
[5] He was king over Jeshurun[f]
   when the leaders of the people
      assembled,
   along with the tribes of Israel.

---

[a] 43 Or *Make his people rejoice, you nations*   [b] 43 Masoretic
Text; Dead Sea Scrolls (see also Septuagint) *people, / and let all
the angels worship him, /*   [c] 44 Hebrew *Hoshea,* a variant of
Joshua   [d] 2 Or *from*   [e] 2 The meaning of the Hebrew for
this phrase is uncertain.   [f] 5 *Jeshurun* means *the upright one,*
that is, Israel; also in verse 26.

32:39 There is no god besides me The other inferior
gods (v. 17) are incomparable to Yahweh (see 4:35,39;
compare Ps 82).

32:41 I sharpen my flashing sword This phrase alludes
to flashes of lightning. Yahweh ultimately reigns over the
forces of nature and will use them in judgment.

32:43 he will take vengeance on his enemies Yahweh's use of a wicked nation in judgment on Israel does
not at all prevent him from punishing that nation's own
wickedness. Compare Hab 1–2.

32:48–52 Yahweh reminds Moses that he cannot enter
the promised land. He instructs Moses to go view the
land from Mount Nebo before he dies. He also informs
him that he will die on the mountain.

32:49 Mount Nebo In the Abarim mountain range.
32:50 be gathered to your people A euphemistic
expression for death, carrying with it the hope of being
reunited with family or ancestors in the afterlife. See
Ge 25:8 and note.

33:1–29 This chapter presents Moses' last words to
Israel. While Exodus and Deuteronomy consistently cast
Moses as stern, mouthing Yahweh's rebuke to his people,
this chapter reveals another side of Moses. Instead of
continuing to berate his audience, Moses bids farewell
on a high note, wishing for Israel's blessing.

33:2 he shone forth from Mount Paran Deuteronomy
33:2–4 describes Yahweh's journey with the camp of
Israel from Sinai to Canaan. Despite difficulties in the
passage, it basically agrees with similar passages that
describe Yahweh's presence localized south of Canaan,
somewhere in the upper Sinai peninsula, such as Seir
Edom, Teman, Mount Paran (e.g., Jdg 5:4–5; Hab
3:3–15; Ps 68:8–9,15–18; Zec 9:14). See the map
"Route of the Exodus" on p. 2252. **myriads of holy ones**
The Hebrew phrase used here, *rivvoth qodesh*, seems to
refer to the heavenly host but it could also mean "myriads
of Kodesh" or "myriads of Kadesh"—describing the large
Israelite camp. It might also be a place name.
33:5 Jeshurun A name for Israel. See note on Dt 32:15.

6 "Let Reuben live and not die,
  nor[a] his people be few."

7 And this he said about Judah:

"Hear, Lord, the cry of Judah;
  bring him to his people.
With his own hands he defends his cause.
  Oh, be his help against his foes!"

8 About Levi he said:

"Your Thummim and Urim belong
  to your faithful servant.
You tested him at Massah;
  you contended with him at the waters
    of Meribah.
9 He said of his father and mother,
  'I have no regard for them.'
He did not recognize his brothers
  or acknowledge his own children,
but he watched over your word
  and guarded your covenant.
10 He teaches your precepts to Jacob
  and your law to Israel.
He offers incense before you
  and whole burnt offerings on your altar.
11 Bless all his skills, Lord,
  and be pleased with the work of his hands.
Strike down those who rise against him,
  his foes till they rise no more."

12 About Benjamin he said:

"Let the beloved of the Lord rest secure in him,
  for he shields him all day long,
and the one the Lord loves rests between
    his shoulders."

13 About Joseph he said:

"May the Lord bless his land
  with the precious dew from heaven above
    and with the deep waters that lie below;
14 with the best the sun brings forth
    and the finest the moon can yield;
15 with the choicest gifts of the ancient
      mountains
    and the fruitfulness of the everlasting hills;

16 with the best gifts of the earth and its fullness
    and the favor of him who dwelt in the
      burning bush.
Let all these rest on the head of Joseph,
    on the brow of the prince among[b] his
      brothers.
17 In majesty he is like a firstborn bull;
    his horns are the horns of a wild ox.
With them he will gore the nations,
    even those at the ends of the earth.
Such are the ten thousands of Ephraim;
    such are the thousands of Manasseh."

18 About Zebulun he said:

"Rejoice, Zebulun, in your going out,
    and you, Issachar, in your tents.
19 They will summon peoples to the
      mountain
    and there offer the sacrifices of the
      righteous;
they will feast on the abundance of the seas,
    on the treasures hidden in the sand."

20 About Gad he said:

"Blessed is he who enlarges Gad's domain!
    Gad lives there like a lion,
    tearing at arm or head.
21 He chose the best land for himself;
    the leader's portion was kept for him.
When the heads of the people assembled,
    he carried out the Lord's righteous will,
    and his judgments concerning Israel."

22 About Dan he said:

"Dan is a lion's cub,
    springing out of Bashan."

23 About Naphtali he said:

"Naphtali is abounding with the favor
      of the Lord
    and is full of his blessing;
he will inherit southward to the lake."

---

[a] 6 Or but let   [b] 16 Or of the one separated from

33:6–25 In this passage, Moses provides a blessing for each tribe of Israel. The patriarch Jacob similarly blessed his twelve sons when he was on his deathbed (Ge 49), although some of Jacob's words were negative. Some of the blessings express sentiments that echo Jacob's blessings for his sons, such as the blessing for Judah (compare Dt 33:7 and Ge 49:8).

33:8 The juxtaposition of Massah and Meribah (see Ex 17:7) with the Levites' privileged possession of the Thummim and Urim could indicate that they were awarded to the priesthood for some loyalty performed at those two locations.

33:8 Your Thummim and Urim Objects the priests used for discerning God's will; they may have been used similarly to the casting of lots (see Nu 27:21; 1Sa 28:6; Ezr 2:63).

33:13 Joseph Ephraim and Manasseh (Joseph's sons) are here subsumed under the tribe of Joseph.

33:16 the prince among his brothers This description seems to allude to the tribe of Ephraim's primacy in the northern kingdom after the split of the monarchy (see 1Ch 5:1–2).

33:17 the horns of a wild ox A familiar metaphor for power and strength (see Nu 23:22).

33:20 Blessed is he who enlarges Gad's domain This probably refers to population. The tribes of Gad and Reuben both take territory in the Transjordan (Nu 32).

33:22 Dan is a lion's cub Imagery related to a warrior's skill (see Ge 49:9).

33:23 he will inherit southward to the lake Naphtali's territory (later known as upper Galilee) is quite fertile. The lake referenced here is Lake Tiberias, also known as the Sea of Galilee.

24 About Asher he said:

"Most blessed of sons is Asher;
 let him be favored by his brothers,
 and let him bathe his feet in oil.
25 The bolts of your gates will be iron and
  bronze,
 and your strength will equal your days.

26 "There is no one like the God of Jeshurun,
 who rides across the heavens to help you
 and on the clouds in his majesty.
27 The eternal God is your refuge,
 and underneath are the everlasting
  arms.
He will drive out your enemies before you,
 saying, 'Destroy them!'
28 So Israel will live in safety;
 Jacob will dwell[a] secure
in a land of grain and new wine,
 where the heavens drop dew.
29 Blessed are you, Israel!
 Who is like you,
 a people saved by the LORD?
He is your shield and helper
 and your glorious sword.
Your enemies will cower before you,
 and you will tread on their heights."

The Death of Moses

34 Then Moses climbed Mount Nebo from the plains of Moab to the top of Pisgah, across from Jericho. There the LORD showed him the whole land — from Gilead to Dan, 2 all of Naphtali, the territory of Ephraim and Manasseh, all the land of Judah as far as the Mediterranean Sea, 3 the Negev and the whole region from the Valley of Jericho, the City of Palms, as far as Zoar. 4 Then the LORD said to him, "This is the land I promised on oath to Abraham, Isaac and Jacob when I said, 'I will give it to your descendants.' I have let you see it with your eyes, but you will not cross over into it."

5 And Moses the servant of the LORD died there in Moab, as the LORD had said. 6 He buried him[b] in Moab, in the valley opposite Beth Peor, but to this day no one knows where his grave is. 7 Moses was a hundred and twenty years old when he died, yet his eyes were not weak nor his strength gone. 8 The Israelites grieved for Moses in the plains of Moab thirty days, until the time of weeping and mourning was over.

9 Now Joshua son of Nun was filled with the spirit[c] of wisdom because Moses had laid his hands on him. So the Israelites listened to him and did what the LORD had commanded Moses. 10 Since then, no prophet has risen in Israel like Moses, whom the LORD knew face to face, 11 who did all those signs and wonders the LORD sent him to do in Egypt — to Pharaoh and to all his officials and to his whole land. 12 For no one has ever shown the mighty power or performed the awesome deeds that Moses did in the sight of all Israel.

---

a 28 Septuagint; Hebrew *Jacob's spring is*   *b* 6 Or *He was buried*   *c* 9 Or *Spirit*

33:26 who rides across the heavens to help you The motif of the "rider on the clouds" or "he who comes on the clouds," referring to Yahweh, occurs several times in the OT (e.g., Ps 68:4; 104:3; Isa 19:1). It was a common epithet outside the Bible for the Canaanite god Baal. By implication, Yahweh — not Baal — brings rain and fertility to the land.

34:1–12 After wishing his countrymen farewell in Dt 33, Moses dies on Mount Nebo — but not before seeing the promised land of Canaan from a distance.

34:1 from Gilead to Dan Part of the Transjordan territory Israel took from the Amorite kings, Sihon and Og (see Nu 21; Dt 2–3).

34:2 land of Judah as far as the Mediterranean Sea Moses' view pans counterclockwise from his original vantage point to the Mediterranean Sea.

34:3 the Negev The region south of the region of Canaan. **as far as Zoar** Located south of the Dead Sea. Moses' panoramic view has now come full circle.

34:4 you will not cross over into it Moses is once again reminded that God will not permit him to enter into the promised land on account of his former sin. See 32:48–52.

34:6 He buried him in Moab, in the valley This location is near Israel's encampment (see 3:29), so the Israelites would have known the general location of Moses' burial place, though not the exact site of his grave. **no one knows where his grave is** The note that Yahweh buried Moses would serve to deter anyone from trying to discover Moses' tomb and turning it into a shrine.

34:9 filled with the spirit of wisdom Joshua has a divine gifting for leading Israel. **Moses had laid his hands on him** Laying on of hands symbolized the transfer of authority from Moses to Joshua.

34:10 like Moses Throughout the rest of the OT, no prophetic figure rivals Moses' direct communication with Yahweh or his displays of divine power.

THE HISTORICAL BOOKS

Twelve books in the Protestant canon of the Old Testament are commonly called the Historical Books: Joshua, Judges, Ruth, 1–2 Samuel, 1–2 Kings, 1–2 Chronicles, Ezra—Nehemiah and Esther. This term does not imply that the other books in the Bible (or portions thereof) should not also be considered historical, but describes these 12 books in their largely narrative character as they tell the story of God's dealings with his people over many centuries. They cover Israel's entry into the land of Canaan as a nation (Joshua); the chaotic period of apostasy in the time of the judges (Judges and Ruth); the establishment of the Davidic monarchy (1–2 Samuel and 1 Chronicles); the history of Israel's life under its kings (1–2 Kings and 2 Chronicles) and Israel's exile in another land and what happened afterward (Esther and Ezra—Nehemiah).

These books were not written to tell history for history's sake but to show how God works through history. Their immediate audience would have been any of God's people in their respective eras, but the preservation of these books centuries beyond shows that their messages endure for all generations.

AUTHORSHIP

All 12 of the Historical Books are anonymous. None makes any claim of authorship, and nowhere else in the Bible is there any such claim for these books. A good case can be made for the independent authorship of each, with 1–2 Samuel, 1–2 Kings, 1–2 Chronicles, and Ezra—Nehemiah each considered as one book.

CONTEXT AND BACKGROUND

The historical background to these books spans close to 1,000 years, beginning with Israel's entry into the land of Canaan around 1400 BC–1200 BC (depending on an early or late dating of the exodus). This was a time of great turmoil in Canaan and elsewhere, and the chaos of the time of the judges should not be surprising against such a backdrop.

With the rise of David and the establishment of a monarchy in Israel around 1000 BC, life in the land stabilized. The large empires (Egypt, Assyria, Babylon) were relatively quiet at this time, which allowed Israel to be established as a regional power under David and Solomon.

However, Solomon's sins prompted God to partition the land, resulting in a divided kingdom (ca. 930 BC). The kingdoms of Israel (in the north) and Judah (in the south) maintained an uneasy co-existence for about 200 years, until the fall of Israel to the Assyrians in 722 BC. Judah continued as an independent kingdom until the fall of Jerusalem to the Babylonians in 586 BC.

When the Persians under Cyrus conquered Babylon in 539 BC, the Jews were allowed to return to Jerusalem and rebuild the temple and the city's walls. The final events of the Historical Books took place in 433 BC, when Nehemiah returned to Jerusalem from Babylon (Ne 13).

BASIC THEOLOGICAL THEMES

Joshua

The book of Joshua describes God giving the promised land of Canaan to his people Israel as an inheritance. The book looks back at the many promises God made to Abraham and his descendants. It also looks ahead as the first account of Israel living in the promised land.

Judges

Judges exposes a deepening apostasy throughout Israel that spirals into spiritual, societal and political chaos. The book looks ahead to the establishment of a legitimate, God-honoring monarchy, rooted in the ideal king of Deuteronomy 17.

Ruth

This book shows God's providence in the life of one family in David's line. The genealogy at the end of the account connects David with the promises that God gave to Judah centuries earlier and points the way to the establishment of a legitimate monarchy under David.

1–2 Samuel

This book tells the story of Israel's transition from chaotic life under the judges, where "everyone did as they saw fit" (Jdg 17:6; 21:25), to life under God's chosen king, David. David was "a man after [God's] own heart" (1Sa 13:14), to whom God promised an everlasting throne and lineage (2Sa 7:16).

1–2 Kings

Kings begins with the story of the slow unraveling of the monarchy in David's last days and especially under his son Solomon. Israel divides into two kingdoms, Israel and Judah, until the fall of Israel in 722 BC and the fall of Judah in 586 BC. The tragic ends to these kingdoms are rooted in the continuing unfaithfulness of their kings and people. Yet a few godly kings lead their people back to the Lord, and God's promises to David endure even under perilous circumstances.

1–2 Chronicles

This book parallels 1–2 Samuel and 1–2 Kings, focusing particularly on David and his descendants (the kings of Judah) while ignoring the history of the northern kingdom of Israel. They emphasize godliness, proper worship in the temple, the reward of the righteous and the punishment of the unrighteous. It ends on the uplifting note that Cyrus had released the Jews from captivity.

Ezra — Nehemiah

The story of postexilic Judah is told in these closely related books, beginning with the first return of an Israelite remnant from exile in 538 BC. The account narrates the rebuilding of the temple, followed by the ministries of Ezra and Nehemiah about a century later. These two men were instrumental in renewing a discouraged people, encouraging loyalty to God's covenant, rebuilding the walls of Jerusalem and undertaking other reforms.

Esther

In this book God's unseen hand is seen at work in the lives of Jews in exile, showing his favor

through the leadership of Esther and Mordecai. The book does not mention God by name, however, suggesting that his people sometimes need to discern his presence through indirect hints and glimpses.

RELATIONSHIP TO THE LARGER BIBLICAL NARRATIVE AND THEMES

Throughout the Historical Books, three major Old Testament covenants—the Abrahamic, the Mosaic and the Davidic—point ahead to the new covenant. The Historical Books build on the first two covenants and introduce readers to the third.

The Abrahamic Covenant

God promised Abraham that he and his descendants would be a blessing to all peoples of the earth (Ge 12:1–3). This is demonstrated in the stories of Rahab, Ruth, Naaman and others; all were foreigners who embraced Israel's God and became Israelites—not by virtue of bloodlines, but by their faith (Jos 2:1–21; Ru 1:6–18; 2Ki 5:1–15). Furthermore, the foundations for the Davidic covenant appear in the promises about kings coming from Abraham's line (Ge 17:6,16; 35:11; 49:10).

The Mosaic Covenant

The covenant that God made through Moses—the terms of which are laid out in the Law given at Mount Sinai—was to guide Israel in how to live under the umbrella of the Abrahamic covenant. Abraham himself lived in a way that could later be recognized as keeping the Law (Ge 26:5). The Mosaic Law was the foundation for true, godly leadership, and Israel's kings were to be rooted in it (Jos 1:7–9; Dt 17:18–20).

The Davidic Covenant

In fulfillment of the promises to the patriarchs, God established a kingdom for his people under a godly king, David. The Davidic covenant was God's promise to David that his descendants would rule in Israel forever (2Sa 7:16). There was an important spiritual dimension of this kingdom as well (compare 1Ch 13:8; 28:5; 29:23; 2Ch 9:8). The kingdom of Israel was not only a geo-political entity, it was God's kingdom—responsibility for which was vested in the line of David.

Specific themes found throughout the rest of the Bible—such as obedience, the consequences of sin, true worship, faithfulness, proper behavior, godly leadership and prayer—also find expression in the Historical Books. These books present in narrative form the great truths of the Bible and richly reward careful study.

David M. Howard, Jr.

JOSHUA

INTRODUCTION TO JOSHUA

Joshua is about bravery, rooted in faith in Yahweh. The book of Joshua takes place just after the death of Moses, Israel's longtime leader. It begins with God commissioning Moses' successor, Joshua, to lead the Israelites across the Jordan River to take possession of the land that had long ago been promised to their forefather Abraham (Jos 1:1–5; compare Ge 17:8). In the narrative, the Israelites engage in a military campaign against the nations that already live in the promised land, Canaan. Eventually, through God's intervention, they settle the land and allot territories to their 12 tribes (Jos 14:1–5).

The narrative does not merely recount the events of the conquest of Canaan; it also interprets these events theologically. At the end of the book, Joshua charges Israel to choose Yahweh as their God, and the Israelites symbolically renew their covenant with Yahweh.

BACKGROUND

Joshua and the subsequent OT books (Judges, 1–2 Samuel and 1–2 Kings) relate Israel's history using the framework set out in Deuteronomy: When the Israelites are faithful to their covenant with Yahweh, things go well for them and they receive God's blessing. But when they violate the covenant, they experience war and suffering.

The historical period for Israel's conquests described in Joshua is uncertain, but there are two common options—either around 1400 BC or around 1220 BC. Both dates fall within the period of ancient Near Eastern history known as the Late Bronze Age (1550–1200 BC). This was a time of upheaval and regional conflict in Canaan.

STRUCTURE

Joshua can be divided into three sections. The first section (Jos 1–12) describes the conquest of Canaan, including the battle of Jericho and the observance of the first Passover in the promised land.

The second section (chs. 13–21) outlines the allotment of land to the 12 tribes of Israel. The Levites receive no tribal territory, but rather settle in cities throughout the other tribes' lands where they can serve as spiritual leaders (ch. 21).

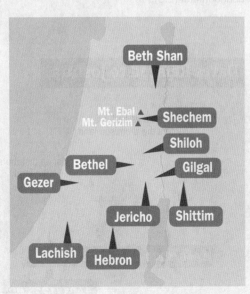

This map depicts some of the major locations mentioned in Joshua, which primarily focuses on the Israelites' campaign to take the promised land.

The third section deals with the Israelites' covenant with Yahweh (chs. 22–24). The tribes that settle east of the Jordan build a commemorative altar, which raises concerns that they are violating regulations about the proper place of worship (ch. 22). The now-elderly Joshua assembles the Israelites at the city of Shechem and leads them in reaffirming their commitment to serve Yahweh alone (chs. 23–24).

OUTLINE

- God commissions Joshua (1:1–18)
- Israel conquers the land (2:1—12:24)
- Joshua distributes the land (13:1—21:45)
- Joshua's farewell address (22:1—24:33)

THEMES

The book of Joshua emphasizes the importance of faith, in both times of war and peace. Joshua's faith in Yahweh allows him to act courageously as he takes over for Moses and leads Israel into the promised land. He acts in obedience, even when God's strategy does not seem to make sense—such as marching around Jericho and blowing trumpets until the city's walls collapse (ch. 6). Joshua's faith is an act of obedience grounded in Yahweh's promise to never fail him or abandon him (1:5).

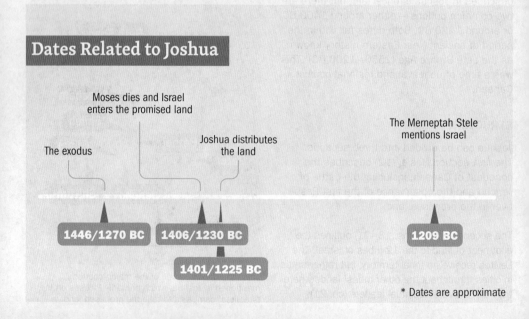

Dates Related to Joshua

Moses dies and Israel
enters the promised land

The Merneptah Stele
mentions Israel

Joshua distributes
the land

The exodus

1446/1270 BC   1406/1230 BC   1209 BC

1401/1225 BC

* Dates are approximate

The prostitute Rahab also acts faithfully by risking her life and the lives of her family to hide the spies Joshua sent into Jericho. She has seen the powerful acts of Yahweh and acknowledges that he is the God of heaven and earth (2:8–11). In addition, the tribes that settle east of the Jordan—Reuben, Gad and the half-tribe of Manasseh—act in faith by returning to their territories and building their own altar as a symbol that they are also part of Yahweh's covenant people, united with the tribes west of the Jordan (22:21–30). Joshua gathers all the tribes at Shechem, where they renew their pledge of faithfulness to Yahweh (24:1–28).

Behind the physical warfare of Joshua is a spiritual battle. Yahweh issues war on nations ruled by evil powers (Lev 18:24–30; Nu 22; Dt 9:4–6; 12:31; 32:8–9,43; 1Sa 5; compare Eph 6:12); Yahweh aims to show that he is the God of order and justice who will rightfully lay claim to the world that is his. Yahweh uses the land of Israel as a starting point to reclaim the world.

Although the book of Joshua tells about the Israelites' battles, the main focus is on Yahweh's faithfulness to his people—as he protects them in battle, gives them the land he had promised and restores peace among them. The people of Israel were responsible for choosing to follow God and wholeheartedly obey his covenant (Jos 1:7; 23:6), just as we are responsible to follow and obey him today. If we do, we too will know God's faithfulness.

Yahweh continues to fight against sin and evil (Eph 6:12). As followers of Jesus, God calls us to take up his armor and join him in this spiritual battle for the betterment of our broken world (Eph 6:1–10).

Joshua Installed as Leader

1 After the death of Moses the servant of the LORD, the LORD said to Joshua son of Nun, Moses' aide: ²"Moses my servant is dead. Now then, you and all these people, get ready to cross the Jordan River into the land I am about to give to them—to the Israelites. ³I will give you every place where you set your foot, as I promised Moses. ⁴Your territory will extend from the desert to Lebanon, and from the great river, the Euphrates—all the Hittite country—to the Mediterranean Sea in the west. ⁵No one will be able to stand against you all the days of your life. As I was with Moses, so I will be with you; I will never leave you nor forsake you. ⁶Be strong and courageous, because you will lead these people to inherit the land I swore to their ancestors to give them.

⁷"Be strong and very courageous. Be careful to obey all the law my servant Moses gave you; do not turn from it to the right or to the left, that you may be successful wherever you go. ⁸Keep this Book of the Law always on your lips; meditate on it day and night, so that you may be careful to do everything written in it. Then you will be prosperous and successful. ⁹Have I not commanded you? Be strong and courageous. Do not be afraid; do not be discouraged, for the LORD your God will be with you wherever you go."

¹⁰So Joshua ordered the officers of the people: ¹¹"Go through the camp and tell the people, 'Get your provisions ready. Three days from now you will cross the Jordan here to go in and take possession of the land the LORD your God is giving you for your own.'"

¹²But to the Reubenites, the Gadites and the half-tribe of Manasseh, Joshua said, ¹³"Remember the command that Moses the servant of the LORD gave you after he said, 'The LORD your God will give you rest by giving you this land.' ¹⁴Your wives, your children and your livestock may stay in the land that Moses gave you east of the Jordan, but all your fighting men, ready for battle, must cross over ahead of your fellow Israelites. You are to help them ¹⁵until the LORD gives them rest, as he has done for you, and until they too have taken possession of the land the LORD your God is giving them. After that, you may go back and occupy your own land, which Moses the servant of the LORD gave you east of the Jordan toward the sunrise."

¹⁶Then they answered Joshua, "Whatever you have commanded us we will do, and wherever you

---

1:1–18 Joshua 1:1—5:15 describes the Israelites' preparations, under Joshua's leadership, for taking possession of the land. In the first chapter, Yahweh charges Joshua to keep his law diligently (vv. 1–9). Joshua then assumes command (vv. 10–18).

The conquest of Canaan described in the book of Joshua is set sometime in the Late Bronze Age (ca. 1550–1200 BC). The Israelites under Joshua invade Canaan from the eastern side of the Jordan River from their encampment in the plains of Moab (see Nu 33:48–50). The preparation and the invasion itself is mainly recounted in Jos 1–12. The allotment of the land to the various tribes of Israel is the main focus of the second half of the book (chs. 13–24). See the timeline "Broad Timeline of Biblical History" on p. xxvi.

1:1 death of Moses The man under whom God delivered the Israelites from Egypt (Ex 7–14) and gave Israel the law (Ex 20; 24; compare Dt 34:1–5). See diagram "Moses' Family Tree" on p. 105. **Joshua** Moses' trusted second-in-command. Joshua is first mentioned in the OT when Moses appoints him to command the Israelite army in the battle against the Amalekites (Ex 17:8–13).

JOSHUA
Joshua is first mentioned in the OT when Moses appoints him to command the Israelite army in the battle against the Amalekites (see Ex 17:8–13). Joshua is regularly identified as Moses' servant in the sense of an executive officer or aide-de-camp (Ex 24:13; 33:11; Nu 11:28). Moses formally identifies Joshua as his successor to lead the Israelites in Nu 27:18–20.

1:2 cross the Jordan River The Jordan River was the eastern boundary to the promised land (except for the Transjordan regions noted in Nu 32). **I am about to give to them** Yahweh promised Abraham that his descendants would possess the land of Canaan (see Ge 12:1–7; compare Nu 14:23; 32:11; Dt 4:1–5).

1:4 the desert A general term for the desert regions either south of Canaan or west of the Jordan River. **Hittite country** The Hittite Empire was centered in Asia Minor (modern-day Turkey) but controlled territory north of Lebanon (and north/northwest of the Euphrates). However, some OT references to Hittites are most likely referring to a group of native Canaanites, descendants of Heth, son of Canaan (1Ch 1:13), and not to the Hittite Empire (see Ge 23:10; 27:46). The Canaanite Hittites are most likely meant here (compare Dt 7:1; Eze 16:3). See note on Jos 3:10.

1:7 do not turn from it to the right or to the left This formulaic expression occurs many times in Deuteronomy, indicating that Yahweh is referring to the laws of that book (see Dt 2:27; 5:32; 17:11,20; 28:14).

1:8 this Book of the Law Likely refers to the laws of Deuteronomy. **meditate on it day and night** Yahweh commands Joshua specifically, not the nation.

1:9 Have I not commanded you Joshua should be certain that it is Yahweh speaking to him. Having accompanied Moses in earlier divine encounters, he had heard him before (see Ex 24:13; 33:11; Dt 31:14).

1:12 Reubenites, the Gadites and the half-tribe of Manesseh Reuben, Gad and the half-tribe of Manasseh had earlier requested to settle in the Transjordan, which was outside Canaan.

1:14 ready for battle, must cross over ahead of your fellow Israelites In Nu 32:28–32, Moses charged Reuben, Gad and the half-tribe of Manasseh with helping the other tribes win their land before permanently settling in the Transjordan.

send us we will go. ¹⁷Just as we fully obeyed Moses, so we will obey you. Only may the LORD your God be with you as he was with Moses. ¹⁸Whoever rebels against your word and does not obey it, whatever you may command them, will be put to death. Only be strong and courageous!"

Rahab and the Spies

2 Then Joshua son of Nun secretly sent two spies from Shittim. "Go, look over the land," he said, "especially Jericho." So they went and entered the house of a prostitute named Rahab and stayed there.

²The king of Jericho was told, "Look, some of the Israelites have come here tonight to spy out the land." ³So the king of Jericho sent this message to Rahab: "Bring out the men who came to you and entered your house, because they have come to spy out the whole land."

⁴But the woman had taken the two men and hidden them. She said, "Yes, the men came to me, but I did not know where they had come from. ⁵At dusk, when it was time to close the city gate, they left. I don't know which way they went. Go after them quickly. You may catch up with them." ⁶(But she had taken them up to the roof and hidden them under the stalks of flax she had laid out on the roof.) ⁷So the men set out in pursuit of the spies on the road that leads to the fords of the Jordan, and as soon as the pursuers had gone out, the gate was shut.

⁸Before the spies lay down for the night, she went up on the roof ⁹and said to them, "I know that the LORD has given you this land and that a great fear of you has fallen on us, so that all who live in this country are melting in fear because of you. ¹⁰We have heard how the LORD dried up the water of the Red Sea[a] for you when you came out of Egypt, and what you did to Sihon and Og, the two kings of the Amorites east of the Jordan, whom you completely destroyed.[b] ¹¹When we heard of it, our hearts melted in fear and everyone's courage failed because of you, for the LORD your God is God in heaven above and on the earth below.

¹²"Now then, please swear to me by the LORD that you will show kindness to my family, because I have

---

[a] 10 Or *the Sea of Reeds*   [b] 10 The Hebrew term refers to the irrevocable giving over of things or persons to the LORD, often by totally destroying them.

1:17 so we will obey you The men of the tribes in the Transjordan honor their promise to Moses by pledging their allegiance to Joshua, his successor.

2:1–24 In this chapter, Joshua sends spies to Jericho where Rahab, motivated by faith in Yahweh, protects them.

2:1 Shittim The precise location of Shittim, which means "acacia trees," is unknown (see Nu 25:1 and note; Nu 33:49 and note). **entered the house of a prostitute** The narrative avoids terminology that would suggest any sexual contact took place. Going to a prostitute's house was a logical choice for gathering intelligence, as men who visited the prostitute would likely have included soldiers who might inadvertently provide them with useful information. The Jewish historian Josephus, writing much later, describes Rahab as an innkeeper, not a prostitute (*Antiquities* 5.6–30), suggesting that her house may have also served as an inn.

2:5 I don't know Rahab lies and provides the king's men with misinformation to put them off the track of the Israelite spies (see Jos 2:9). The events that follow (6:17–25) demonstrate that Rahab believes in the God of Israel. New Testament references to Rahab also indicate that her faith was genuine: Rahab is included in the list of faithful people in Hebrews (Heb 11:31). James presents her along with Abraham as an example of faith (Jas 2:25). Scripture affirms the need for truth telling; however, Rahab's incident demonstrates that this needs to be contextualized to allow for situations like hers. God himself uses deception to judge evil or preserve life (e.g., 1Sa 16:1–13), and Jesus commands his followers to withhold information about himself and his works (e.g., Lk 5:14; 8:56; 9:21).

2:6 roof While this may refer to a bare roof, it likely refers to the second story of the house. See the infographic "Ancient Israelite House" on p. 1205.

2:9 the LORD has given you this land Rahab confesses belief in Yahweh as the supremely powerful God. The statement is noteworthy, since the Canaanites worshiped multiple deities (see Ex 23:24,32–33; 34:15; Dt 11:16,28; 12:2–3,30–31). See Jos 2:11. **a great fear of you has fallen on us** This fear was prophesied at the crossing of the sea (Ex 15:16). At the end of the Sinai law code, God promised to send the fear of himself on the Canaanites (Ex 23:27).

2:10 Sihon and Og Kings who led the Amorites in the Transjordan. Og was a Rephaite giant related to the Anakite, the group of giant people before whom Israel cowered, resulting in the punishment of the 40 years of wilderness wandering (Nu 13–14). See Nu 21; Dt 2–3. **whom you completely destroyed** The Hebrew term used here, *cherem*, refers to the destruction of life—human and otherwise—as an act of devotion to a deity (here, Yahweh of Israel; see note on Ex 22:20). Joshua and his armies were responsible for devoting the inhabitants of Canaan to destruction (Dt 7:2; 20:17). However, the verb is only found only in select passages, suggesting that the *cherem* was targeted, not indiscriminate (Jos 6:17–18,21; 8:26; 10:1,28,35,37,39–40; 11:11–12,20–21). Other verbs not associated with the destruction of life are also used to describe the task of conquest: *garash* ("to drive out": 24:12,18); *yarash* ("to dispossess, drive out": 3:10; 12:1; 13:6; 17:12,13; 23:5,9).

2:11 in heaven above and on the earth below Rahab confesses the absolute and unique sovereignty of Yahweh. The only other uses of this phrase in the OT also appear in the context of God's exclusive claim to sovereignty (Ex 20:4; Dt 4:39; 5:8). Rahab is an example of a non-Israelite (Gentile) who comes to faith in Yahweh. She is included in the genealogy of Jesus in Mt 1 along with three other women who were also Gentiles (Tamar, Ruth and Bathsheba).

2:12 Give me a sure sign The Hebrew phrase used here, *oth emeth*, literally means "sign of truth." The spies comply (see Jos 2:12–14,16–21).

shown kindness to you. Give me a sure sign ¹³that you will spare the lives of my father and mother, my brothers and sisters, and all who belong to them—and that you will save us from death."

¹⁴"Our lives for your lives!" the men assured her. "If you don't tell what we are doing, we will treat you kindly and faithfully when the LORD gives us the land."

¹⁵So she let them down by a rope through the window, for the house she lived in was part of the city wall. ¹⁶She said to them, "Go to the hills so the pursuers will not find you. Hide yourselves there three days until they return, and then go on your way."

¹⁷Now the men had said to her, "This oath you made us swear will not be binding on us ¹⁸unless, when we enter the land, you have tied this scarlet cord in the window through which you let us down, and unless you have brought your father and mother, your brothers and all your family into your house. ¹⁹If any of them go outside your house into the street, their blood will be on their own heads; we will not be responsible. As for those who are in the house with you, their blood will be on our head if a hand is laid on them. ²⁰But if you tell what we are doing, we will be released from the oath you made us swear."

²¹"Agreed," she replied. "Let it be as you say."

So she sent them away, and they departed. And she tied the scarlet cord in the window.

²²When they left, they went into the hills and stayed there three days, until the pursuers had searched all along the road and returned without finding them. ²³Then the two men started back. They went down out of the hills, forded the river and came to Joshua son of Nun and told him everything that had happened to them. ²⁴They said to Joshua, "The LORD has surely given the whole land into our hands; all the people are melting in fear because of us."

Crossing the Jordan

3 Early in the morning Joshua and all the Israelites set out from Shittim and went to the Jordan, where they camped before crossing over. ²After three days the officers went throughout the camp, ³giving orders to the people: "When you see the ark of the covenant of the LORD your God, and the Levitical priests carrying it, you are to move out from your positions and follow it. ⁴Then you will know which way to go, since you have never been this way before. But keep a distance of about two thousand cubits[a] between you and the ark; do not go near it."

⁵Joshua told the people, "Consecrate yourselves, for tomorrow the LORD will do amazing things among you."

⁶Joshua said to the priests, "Take up the ark of the covenant and pass on ahead of the people." So they took it up and went ahead of them.

⁷And the LORD said to Joshua, "Today I will begin to exalt you in the eyes of all Israel, so they may know that I am with you as I was with Moses. ⁸Tell the priests who carry the ark of the covenant: 'When you reach the edge of the Jordan's waters, go and stand in the river.'"

⁹Joshua said to the Israelites, "Come here and listen to the words of the LORD your God. ¹⁰This is how you will know that the living God is among you and that he will certainly drive out before you the Canaanites, Hittites, Hivites, Perizzites, Girgashites, Amorites and Jebusites. ¹¹See, the ark of the covenant of the Lord of all the earth will go into the Jordan ahead of you. ¹²Now then, choose twelve men from the tribes of Israel, one from each tribe. ¹³And as soon as the priests who carry the ark of the LORD—the Lord of all the earth—set foot in the Jordan, its waters flowing downstream will be cut off and stand up in a heap."

[a] 4 That is, about 3,000 feet or about 900 meters

2:14 Our lives for your lives The spies take a blood oath, pledging their lives against hers and her family's.
2:15 house she lived in was part of the city wall It is unclear how Rahab speaks to the men after lowering them out her window.
2:18 this scarlet cord in the window The cord is not a condition of the oath (see v. 12) but a practical means to identify Rahab's house. If she forgets the cord, they would be guiltless if she died, since they would have difficulty identifying her location.

3:1–17 Chapters 3–4 describe Israel's entrance into the promised land. The description emphasizes the solemn observance and commemoration of the event and draws parallels to the momentous passage through the Red Sea (Ex 14; Jos 3).

3:3 ark of the covenant In Joshua, the ark is the visible token of Yahweh's presence among the Israelites in their quest to take the promised land. See the infographic "The Ark of the Covenant" on p. 412. **Levitical priests** Other books of the Pentateuch assign the task

of carrying the ark to the Kohathites, who were Levites but not priests (see Nu 4:15). See the table "Functions of Priests" on p. 171.
3:4 do not go near it This enabled the Israelites to see the ark from a distance since they needed to follow it.
3:7 to exalt you God exalts Joshua to make it clear to Israel that he is with him.
3:10 the living God The Hebrew phrase used here occurs only three other times in the OT (Ps 42:2; 84:2; Hos 1:10) and speaks to the direct presence of an active God.
Canaanites, Hittites, Hivites, Perizzites, Girgashites, Amorites and Jebusites The list of nations echoes the list God gave to the patriarchs, confirming that he is acting to fulfill the ancient promises (see Ge 15:19–21; Ex 3:8,17; 23:23; 33:2; 34:11; Dt 7:1; 20:17). The OT contains nearly 24 lists like this one, including five in Joshua (Jos 3:10; 9:1; 11:3; 12:8; 24:11).
3:13 stand up in a heap When the priests step into the water, the river will stop flowing. The description of the water heaping up parallels the description of events at the Red Sea (see Ex 14:21–22; compare Ps 78:13).

¹⁴So when the people broke camp to cross the Jordan, the priests carrying the ark of the covenant went ahead of them. ¹⁵Now the Jordan is at flood stage all during harvest. Yet as soon as the priests who carried the ark reached the Jordan and their feet touched the water's edge, ¹⁶the water from upstream stopped flowing. It piled up in a heap a great distance away, at a town called Adam in the vicinity of Zarethan, while the water flowing down to the Sea of the Arabah (that is, the Dead Sea) was completely cut off. So the people crossed over opposite Jericho. ¹⁷The priests who carried the ark of the covenant of the LORD stopped in the middle of the Jordan and stood on dry ground, while all Israel passed by until the whole nation had completed the crossing on dry ground.

4 When the whole nation had finished crossing the Jordan, the LORD said to Joshua, ²"Choose twelve men from among the people, one from each tribe, ³and tell them to take up twelve stones from the middle of the Jordan, from right where the priests are standing, and carry them over with you and put them down at the place where you stay tonight."

⁴So Joshua called together the twelve men he had appointed from the Israelites, one from each tribe, ⁵and said to them, "Go over before the ark of the LORD your God into the middle of the Jordan. Each of you is to take up a stone on his shoulder, according to the number of the tribes of the Israelites, ⁶to serve as a sign among you. In the future, when your children ask you, 'What do these stones mean?' ⁷tell them that the flow of the Jordan was cut off before the ark of the covenant of the LORD. When it crossed the Jordan, the waters of the Jordan were cut off. These stones are to be a memorial to the people of Israel forever."

⁸So the Israelites did as Joshua commanded them. They took twelve stones from the middle of the Jordan, according to the number of the tribes of the Israelites, as the LORD had told Joshua; and they carried them over with them to their camp, where they put them down. ⁹Joshua set up the twelve stones that had been[a] in the middle of the Jordan at the spot where the priests who carried the ark of the covenant had stood. And they are there to this day.

¹⁰Now the priests who carried the ark remained standing in the middle of the Jordan until everything the LORD had commanded Joshua was done by the people, just as Moses had directed Joshua. The people hurried over, ¹¹and as soon as all of them had crossed, the ark of the LORD and the priests came to the other side while the people watched. ¹²The men of Reuben, Gad and the half-tribe of Manasseh crossed over, ready for battle, in front of the Israelites, as Moses had directed them. ¹³About forty thousand armed for battle crossed over before the LORD to the plains of Jericho for war.

¹⁴That day the LORD exalted Joshua in the sight of all Israel; and they stood in awe of him all the days of his life, just as they had stood in awe of Moses.

¹⁵Then the LORD said to Joshua, ¹⁶"Command the priests carrying the ark of the covenant law to come up out of the Jordan."

¹⁷So Joshua commanded the priests, "Come up out of the Jordan."

¹⁸And the priests came up out of the river carrying the ark of the covenant of the LORD. No sooner had they set their feet on the dry ground than the waters of the Jordan returned to their place and ran at flood stage as before.

¹⁹On the tenth day of the first month the people went up from the Jordan and camped at Gilgal on

---

[a] 9 Or Joshua also set up twelve stones

3:15 all during harvest At harvest time, the river would be in its annual flood stage. Based on modern analogy, it was probably roughly 100 feet wide and 5–10 feet deep.
3:16 Adam Located in the Jordan Valley. The wording suggests that the waters of the Jordan were stopped up at this location, not that it was the place where the priests entered the Jordan. **Sea of the Arabah** This body of water is known as the Salt Sea and as the Dead Sea.

4:1–24 Joshua 4 continues to describe Israel's entrance into Canaan (see note on 3:1–17), focusing on the commemoration of this event. The Israelites erect a permanent memorial for the succeeding generations to remember the spectacular stoppage of the Jordan River (see 3:5).

4:3 right where the priests are standing The Israelites were to erect the monument using stones from the dry, solid ground, which God produced by stopping the water.
4:5 into the middle of the Jordan The Israelites were not to take the memorial stones from the shores of the Jordan, but from the middle, highlighting the fact that they crossed over on dry ground.

4:6 a sign The Hebrew term used here, *oth*, can mean pledge or omen, or refer to a display of miraculous power. Here, it refers to a memorial object which will remind the present generation and future generations of this event.
4:9 where the priests who carried the ark of the covenant had stood This verse seems to indicate that the Israelites erected a second memorial of 12 stones in the middle of the Jordan, which would be covered over by water; the first memorial would be a visible sign, while the second would mark where the priests had stood, perhaps becoming visible at times when the Jordan was low. More likely, however, v. 9 is a parenthetical thought, and there would be only one memorial. **to this day** Indicates that the book of Joshua was written sometime after the events it describes (e.g., 5:9; 7:26; 9:27).
4:12 The men of Reuben, Gad and the half-tribe of Manasseh See note on 1:12.
4:14 as they had stood in awe of Moses See 1:5.
4:16 covenant law Refers to the tablets containing the Ten Commandments that were stored within the ark (see Ex 31:18; 32:15).
4:19 tenth day of the first month Coincides with the day that the Israelites were to select the Passover lamb

the eastern border of Jericho. ²⁰And Joshua set up at Gilgal the twelve stones they had taken out of the Jordan. ²¹He said to the Israelites, "In the future when your descendants ask their parents, 'What do these stones mean?' ²²tell them, 'Israel crossed the Jordan on dry ground.' ²³For the LORD your God dried up the Jordan before you until you had crossed over. The LORD your God did to the Jordan what he had done to the Red Sea^a when he dried it up before us until we had crossed over. ²⁴He did this so that all the peoples of the earth might know that the hand of the LORD is powerful and so that you might always fear the LORD your God."

⁵ Now when all the Amorite kings west of the Jordan and all the Canaanite kings along the coast heard how the LORD had dried up the Jordan before the Israelites until they^b had crossed over, their hearts melted in fear and they no longer had the courage to face the Israelites.

Circumcision and Passover at Gilgal

²At that time the LORD said to Joshua, "Make flint knives and circumcise the Israelites again." ³So Joshua made flint knives and circumcised the Israelites at Gibeath Haaraloth.^c

⁴Now this is why he did so: All those who came out of Egypt—all the men of military age—died in the wilderness on the way after leaving Egypt. ⁵All the people that came out had been circumcised, but all the people born in the wilderness during the journey from Egypt had not. ⁶The Israelites had moved about in the wilderness forty years until all the men who were of military age when they left Egypt had died, since they had not obeyed the LORD. For the LORD had sworn to them that they would not see the land he had solemnly promised their ancestors to give us, a land flowing with milk and honey. ⁷So he raised up their sons in their place, and these were the ones Joshua circumcised. They were still uncircumcised because they had not been circumcised on the way. ⁸And after the whole nation had been circumcised, they remained where they were in camp until they were healed.

⁹Then the LORD said to Joshua, "Today I have rolled away the reproach of Egypt from you." So the place has been called Gilgal^d to this day.

¹⁰On the evening of the fourteenth day of the month, while camped at Gilgal on the plains of Jericho, the Israelites celebrated the Passover. ¹¹The day after the Passover, that very day, they ate some of the produce of the land: unleavened bread and roasted grain. ¹²The manna stopped the day after^e they ate this food from the land; there was no longer any manna for the Israelites, but that year they ate the produce of Canaan.

^a 23 Or the Sea of Reeds   ^b 1 Another textual tradition we
^c 3 Gibeath Haaraloth means the hill of foreskins.   ^d 9 Gilgal sounds like the Hebrew for roll.   ^e 12 Or the day

---

(Ex 12:3) and therefore anticipates Jos 5:10, where the Israelites will keep the Passover on the fourteenth day of the same month (Ex 12:6,18). See the table "Israelite Festivals" on p. 200. **Gilgal** The first of several important religious sites for the Israelites at this time of conquest (also Shiloh, Jos 18:1; and Shechem, 24:1; compare 8:30).

GILGAL
The Israelites celebrated Passover at Gilgal and circumcised all their males there in accord with the Abrahamic covenant—a practice which they had not performed during the wilderness wanderings (see Jos 5:5,7). Later, the Israelites built an altar and sanctuary to God at Gilgal (4:19–20) before the central sanctuary was built (see Dt 12). Gilgal would remain a holy site into the days of the judges and the monarchy (1Sa 7:16; 10:8; 11:14–15). During the period of the divided kingdom, the site became associated with false worship (Hos 9:15; 12:11; Am 4:4; 5:5).

4:23 your God did to the Jordan what he had done to the Red Sea Identifies the parallel between this crossing and the crossing of the Red Sea (Ex 14:21).
4:24 the hand of the LORD is powerful The people will be intimidated in the manner described by Rahab (see Jos 2:10–11; 5:1).

5:1–15 This chapter describes the Israelites' initial actions after crossing the Jordan into Canaan, including circumcising all males (vv. 1–9) and observing the Passover (vv. 10–12). Joshua also encounters the divine commander of Yahweh's hosts (vv. 13–15).

5:1 Canaanite kings The Amorites and Canaanites were two of the native populations mentioned in 3:10. They were perhaps the largest, since they appear to represent all the nations here. **their hearts melted** They were overcome with fear.
5:2 At that time The first thing Joshua does after entering Canaan and erecting the memorial of stones (see ch. 4) is circumcise the males of Israel. **circumcise the Israelites again** See vv. 4–5,8.
5:4 this is why he did so Circumcision was a sign of membership in the covenant community. See Ge 17:10 and note.
5:6 they would not see the land See Nu 14:29; 26:64–65; Dt 2:14–16. **he had solemnly promised their ancestors** See Ge 12:1–3; 15:1–6,18; 28:13; 35:12; 48:21.
5:9 the reproach of Egypt May indicate that the Israelite males in the initial generation who had escaped Egypt were circumcised by the Egyptian method (compare Jos 5:2, which indicates some Israelites were circumcised a second time). The Israelite method removed the foreskin completely, while the Egyptian method merely slit it. See note on Ge 17:10. **Gilgal** This name sounds like the Hebrew word galal, which means "roll away" (see note on Jos 4:9). **to this day** See note on 4:9.
5:11 Passover The Passover commemorated God's deliverance of Israel from slavery in Egypt (see Ex 12:1–28). The Israelites celebrated the Passover at least once in the wilderness (Nu 9:1–5).
5:12 manna The bread Yahweh provided to the Israelites during their time in the wilderness (Ex 16:31–35).

The Fall of Jericho

¹³Now when Joshua was near Jericho, he looked up and saw a man standing in front of him with a drawn sword in his hand. Joshua went up to him and asked, "Are you for us or for our enemies?"

¹⁴"Neither," he replied, "but as commander of the army of the LORD I have now come." Then Joshua fell facedown to the ground in reverence, and asked him, "What message does my Lord^a have for his servant?"

¹⁵The commander of the LORD's army replied, "Take off your sandals, for the place where you are standing is holy." And Joshua did so.

6 Now the gates of Jericho were securely barred because of the Israelites. No one went out and no one came in.

²Then the LORD said to Joshua, "See, I have delivered Jericho into your hands, along with its king and its fighting men. ³March around the city once with all the armed men. Do this for six days. ⁴Have seven priests carry trumpets of rams' horns in front of the ark. On the seventh day, march around the city seven times, with the priests blowing the trumpets. ⁵When you hear them sound a long blast on the trumpets, have the whole army give a loud shout; then the wall of the city will collapse and the army will go up, everyone straight in."

⁶So Joshua son of Nun called the priests and said to them, "Take up the ark of the covenant of the LORD and have seven priests carry trumpets in front of it." ⁷And he ordered the army, "Advance! March around the city, with an armed guard going ahead of the ark of the LORD."

⁸When Joshua had spoken to the people, the seven priests carrying the seven trumpets before the LORD went forward, blowing their trumpets, and the ark of the LORD's covenant followed them. ⁹The armed guard marched ahead of the priests who blew the trumpets, and the rear guard followed the ark. All this time the trumpets were sounding. ¹⁰But Joshua had commanded the army, "Do not give a war cry, do not raise your voices, do not say a word until the day I tell you to shout. Then shout!" ¹¹So he had the ark of the LORD carried around the city, circling it once. Then the army returned to camp and spent the night there. ¹²Joshua got up early the next morning and the

^{a} 14 Or lord

5:13 Jericho A major Canaanite city just west of the Jordan. **a man standing** This "man" is not human (compare Ge 18; 32:22–32; Ex 15:3). **with a drawn sword in his hand** This phrase occurs only two other times in the OT (Nu 22:22–23; 1Ch 21:16). In these instances, the sword-bearer is the Angel of Yahweh (compare Jos 5:15).

Joshua 5:13

JERICHO
Located on the fertile plain just northwest of the Dead Sea. The site is well-positioned for agriculture and has been settled since pre-historic times. The city eventually became part of Benjamin's allotment (Jos 18:12,21). Due to its central role in the Biblical narrative of the conquest (see ch. 6), it has been a focal point for archeological excavation.

5:14 commander of the army of the LORD Refers to Yahweh himself as the divine warrior (Ex 15:3). See Jos 5:15. **Joshua fell facedown to the ground** Joshua falls prostrate as soon as he hears the voice of the being before him. Joshua has heard the voice of God—who is appearing as the Angel (Ex 23:20–23) at other times as well (Ex 24:13; 33:11; Jos 1:1; 3:7).

5:15 the place where you are standing is holy This is similar to what happens at the burning bush event when Moses encounters Yahweh (Ex 3:1–6).

6:1–27 Jericho falls to Joshua and the Israelites after the city's walls fall down, leaving the city vulnerable. Joshua precisely followed Yahweh's instructions for approaching the city, despite their unconventional nature. Yahweh commanded Joshua to march Israel's army around the city once a day for six days (Jos 6:3). On the seventh day, they were to circle the city seven times—then the walls would fall down (v. 5). The fall of Jericho has become one of the most contested subjects for those studying the history and archaeology of the Biblical world. The debate centers on how to interpret the archeological record from Jericho and how to relate that archeological data to the Biblical story. Part of the problem stems from the lack of certainty over the date of the exodus from Egypt.

Proponents of an exodus around 1446 BC look for evidence of Joshua's conquest around 1400 BC. Middle Bronze Age Jericho was an impressively fortified city, so its fallen walls are sometimes attributed to Joshua. However, the Middle Bronze Age ends around 1550 BC, so the destruction of Middle Bronze Age Jericho would appear to be too early to attribute to Joshua. It is possible that while the Middle Bronze generally ended around 1550 that some Middle Bronze fortified cities stood into the Late Bronze Age (1550–1200 BC). The Jericho of the Late Bronze Age was in decline and unfortified.

Proponents of a later exodus in the mid-thirteenth century BC look for evidence of Joshua's attack around 1200 BC, but the city of Jericho continued to be small and unfortified through the Late Bronze and early Iron Ages. The debate is far from settled and conclusions about archeological data should be considered more tentative than decisive. See the infographic "Ancient Jericho" on p. 330.

6:3 Do this for six days The Israelites' behavior is essentially a spiritual exercise—a ritual act of obedience to Yahweh.

6:4 seven times The number seven is used symbolically in Scripture to denote completeness or totality (for example, the Sabbath week).

6:5 wall of the city will collapse The text does not specify that every wall in every place would fall. Archaeological excavation indicates that the walls fell flat in various places (see 6:15–21).

6:8 before the LORD Before the ark, which symbolized God's presence (see Ex 25:10 and note).

priests took up the ark of the Lord. ¹³The seven priests carrying the seven trumpets went forward, marching before the ark of the Lord and blowing the trumpets. The armed men went ahead of them and the rear guard followed the ark of the Lord, while the trumpets kept sounding. ¹⁴So on the second day they marched around the city once and returned to the camp. They did this for six days.

¹⁵On the seventh day, they got up at daybreak and marched around the city seven times in the same manner, except that on that day they circled the city seven times. ¹⁶The seventh time around, when the priests sounded the trumpet blast, Joshua commanded the army, "Shout! For the Lord has given you the city! ¹⁷The city and all that is in it are to be devoted*ᵃ* to the Lord. Only Rahab the prostitute and all who are with her in her house

ᵃ 17 The Hebrew term refers to the irrevocable giving over of things or persons to the Lord, often by totally destroying them; also in verses 18 and 21.

6:16 the Lord has given you the city The Biblical account is clear that Israel's invasion of Canaan was authorized by Yahweh (compare Jos 10:29–30; 11:6) and that Yahweh would be assisting them to ensure success (see Ex 23:27–28). While the idea of divinely sanctioned warfare involving the wholesale destruction of towns and cities appears troublesome, the Biblical justification for this approach is rooted in the idea that all of these nations have rejected Yahweh and are under the authority of divine beings—so-called "sons of god" who rule unjustly (compare Dt 32:8; Ps 82:1–2,6–7). Israel

is under the authority of Yahweh alone (Dt 4:19–20). Over and against these other divine beings, Yahweh is laying claim to what is rightfully his (Dt 32:9). This is a war against the people and the nations that worship other gods (compare Nu 13:32–33). When Yahweh promises the land to Abraham and his descendants, he says the people will return to the land after the sin of the Amorites has reached its pinnacle (Ge 15:16–21)—showing that they were given nearly 500 years to change their ways. Later when Yahweh gives Moses instructions related to the future conquest of Canaan, the command to destroy

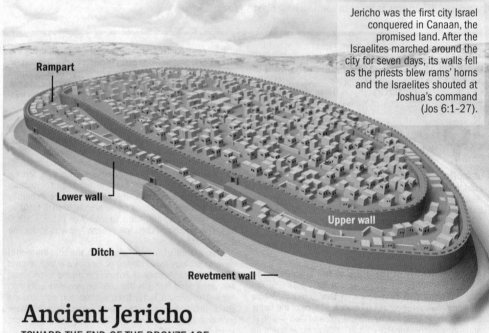

Jericho was the first city Israel conquered in Canaan, the promised land. After the Israelites marched around the city for seven days, its walls fell as the priests blew rams' horns and the Israelites shouted at Joshua's command (Jos 6:1–27).

Rampart

Lower wall

Upper wall

Ditch

Revetment wall

Ancient Jericho
TOWARD THE END OF THE BRONZE AGE

Archaeological excavations reveal that Jericho was violently destroyed sometime toward the end of the Bronze Age. The walls seem to have been thrown down by sudden force, as if by an earthquake. Charred wood shows that what was left of the city was burned. Excavators have also found food supplies buried in the destroyed city, which shows it was not captured by siege.

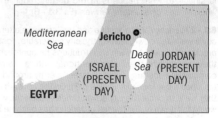

Mediterranean Sea

Jericho

Dead JORDAN
ISRAEL Sea (PRESENT
(PRESENT DAY)
DAY)

EGYPT

shall be spared, because she hid the spies we sent. [18]But keep away from the devoted things, so that you will not bring about your own destruction by taking any of them. Otherwise you will make the camp of Israel liable to destruction and bring trouble on it. [19]All the silver and gold and the articles of bronze and iron are sacred to the LORD and must go into his treasury."

[20]When the trumpets sounded, the army shouted, and at the sound of the trumpet, when the men gave a loud shout, the wall collapsed; so everyone charged straight in, and they took the city. [21]They devoted the city to the LORD and destroyed with the sword every living thing in it — men and women, young and old, cattle, sheep and donkeys.

[22]Joshua said to the two men who had spied out the land, "Go into the prostitute's house and bring her out and all who belong to her, in accordance with your oath to her." [23]So the young men who had done the spying went in and brought out Rahab, her father and mother, her brothers and sisters and all who belonged to her. They brought out her entire family and put them in a place outside the camp of Israel.

[24]Then they burned the whole city and everything in it, but they put the silver and gold and the articles of bronze and iron into the treasury of the LORD's house. [25]But Joshua spared Rahab the prostitute, with her family and all who belonged to her, because she hid the men Joshua had sent as spies to Jericho — and she lives among the Israelites to this day.

[26]At that time Joshua pronounced this solemn oath: "Cursed before the LORD is the one who undertakes to rebuild this city, Jericho:

"At the cost of his firstborn son
   he will lay its foundations;
at the cost of his youngest
   he will set up its gates."

[27]So the LORD was with Joshua, and his fame spread throughout the land.

Achan's Sin

7 But the Israelites were unfaithful in regard to the devoted things[a]; Achan son of Karmi, the son of Zimri,[b] the son of Zerah, of the tribe of Judah, took some of them. So the LORD's anger burned against Israel.

---

[a] 1 The Hebrew term refers to the irrevocable giving over of things or persons to the LORD, often by totally destroying them; also in verses 11, 12, 13 and 15.   [b] 1 See Septuagint and 1 Chron. 2:6; Hebrew Zabdi; also in verses 17 and 18.

---

the native Canaanite peoples is closely linked with the potential that Israel will be led into idolatry by any survivors (Ex 23:23–33; compare Dt 7:1–6; 20:18; 32:15–17).

6:17 to be devoted to the LORD The act is described using the Hebrew noun *cherem* which indicates things being set apart as sacred property. (There is no good English equivalent for this concept, so translations usually discuss things being put "under the ban" or "devoted to destruction" to represent the idea.) No one was allowed to profit personally from the attack (Jos 7:1). The spoils of war belonged to God, so their destruction ensured no one else acquired them. However, some of the valuables were not destroyed but placed in Yahweh's treasury (v. 19). Compare note on 2:10.

Joshua 6:17

CHEREM
The Hebrew verb *charam* (used in Jos 6:18) always designates a special action of setting something or someone apart permanently as the property of God. The noun *cherem* sometimes indicates something or someone that has been set apart for service or use in the sanctuary (Lev 27:28; Mic 4:13). These items were devoted to sacred use and not necessarily destroyed (Jos 6:19). The priests took possession of these items as the ones in charge of Yahweh's sanctuary (Nu 18:14; Eze 44:29).

However, the act of placing entire cities or populations under *cherem* often entailed the complete annihilation of a place and its people. The word is used when God instructs Moses to devote to destruction certain cities and populations in the land of Canaan (Nu 21:2–3; Dt 7:2; 9:5; 13:15; 20:17). Joshua was charged with carrying out these instructions as well, and he did so

(Jos 6:18–21; 8:26; 10:28–40; 11:11–21). The practice of *cherem* was not unique to ancient Israel. In the Mesha Stele, King Mesha of Moab describes how he captured Israelite cities and killed all the people because he had designated them as *cherem* for the Moabite god Chemosh. However, Yahweh is not like other gods. Yahweh demands rules of engagement—including that this action can only happen by his command (Dt 20)—and goes so far as to provide provisions for female captives (Dt 21:10–14; compare Ex 23:9).

6:19 sacred to the LORD Indicates that they are set apart to Yahweh for his ownership and use. This command relates to the *cherem* (see note on v. 17).

6:22 the prostitute's house Refers to Rahab; see 2:1 and note.

6:26 at the cost of his youngest Similar to Moses' directions in Dt 13:12–16 that cities tolerating the worship of other gods besides Yahweh should be destroyed.

7:1–26 Joshua 7–8 details Israel's wars against the city of Ai. Chapter 7 focuses on Israel's defeat at Ai, because Achan violated the principle of *cherem* (see note on 6:17). Several contrastive parallels are apparent between ch. 7 and ch. 2. Chapter 7 describes a disobedient Israelite who costs Israel a military victory. Chapter 2 recounted the faith of Rahab, a Canaanite, whose protection of the spies assisted in the defeat of Jericho. Rahab and Achan are contrasting characters—a faithful outsider contrasted with a foolish insider.

7:1 the Israelites were unfaithful The Hebrew word used here, *ma'al*, elsewhere describes adultery (Nu 5:12–13; see note on 1Ch 5:25). Achan's violation exceeded theft—it was akin to spiritual adultery against Yahweh for breaking the *cherem* principle. **in regard to the devoted things** Refers to breaking the rules of *cherem*; see note on Jos 6:17.

²Now Joshua sent men from Jericho to Ai, which is near Beth Aven to the east of Bethel, and told them, "Go up and spy out the region." So the men went up and spied out Ai.

³When they returned to Joshua, they said, "Not all the army will have to go up against Ai. Send two or three thousand men to take it and do not weary the whole army, for only a few people live there." ⁴So about three thousand went up; but they were routed by the men of Ai, ⁵who killed about thirty-six of them. They chased the Israelites from the city gate as far as the stone quarries and struck them down on the slopes. At this the hearts of the people melted in fear and became like water.

⁶Then Joshua tore his clothes and fell facedown to the ground before the ark of the LORD, remaining there till evening. The elders of Israel did the same, and sprinkled dust on their heads. ⁷And Joshua said, "Alas, Sovereign LORD, why did you ever bring this people across the Jordan to deliver us into the hands of the Amorites to destroy us? If only we had been content to stay on the other side of the Jordan! ⁸Pardon your servant, Lord. What can I say, now that Israel has been routed by its enemies? ⁹The Canaanites and the other people of the country will hear about this and they will surround us and wipe out our name from the earth. What then will you do for your own great name?"

¹⁰The LORD said to Joshua, "Stand up! What are you doing down on your face? ¹¹Israel has sinned; they have violated my covenant, which I commanded them to keep. They have taken some of the devoted things; they have stolen, they have lied, they have put them with their own possessions. ¹²That is why the Israelites cannot stand against their enemies; they turn their backs and run because they have been made liable to destruction. I will not be with you anymore unless you destroy whatever among you is devoted to destruction.

¹³"Go, consecrate the people. Tell them, 'Consecrate yourselves in preparation for tomorrow; for this is what the LORD, the God of Israel, says: There are devoted things among you, Israel. You cannot stand against your enemies until you remove them.

¹⁴"'In the morning, present yourselves tribe by tribe. The tribe the LORD chooses shall come forward clan by clan; the clan the LORD chooses shall come forward family by family; and the family the LORD chooses shall come forward man by man. ¹⁵Whoever is caught with the devoted things shall be destroyed by fire, along with all that belongs to him. He has violated the covenant of the LORD and has done an outrageous thing in Israel!'"

¹⁶Early the next morning Joshua had Israel come forward by tribes, and Judah was chosen. ¹⁷The clans of Judah came forward, and the Zerahites were chosen. He had the clan of the Zerahites come forward by families, and Zimri was chosen. ¹⁸Joshua had his family come forward man by man, and Achan son of Karmi, the son of Zimri, the son of Zerah, of the tribe of Judah, was chosen.

¹⁹Then Joshua said to Achan, "My son, give glory to the LORD, the God of Israel, and honor him. Tell me what you have done; do not hide it from me."

²⁰Achan replied, "It is true! I have sinned against the LORD, the God of Israel. This is what I have done: ²¹When I saw in the plunder a beautiful robe from Babylonia,ᵃ two hundred shekelsᵇ of silver and a bar of gold weighing fifty shekels,ᶜ I coveted them and took them. They are hidden in the ground inside my tent, with the silver underneath."

ᵃ 21 Hebrew *Shinar*   ᵇ 21 That is, about 5 pounds or about 2.3 kilograms   ᶜ 21 That is, about 1 1/4 pounds or about 575 grams

---

7:2 Joshua sent men The narrative contains no indication that Joshua consulted God before this decision. While this omission may suggest a reason for the defeat at Ai, the text nevertheless explicitly attributes the defeat to Achan's sin (see vv. 10–12). **Ai** The site of Biblical Ai is commonly identified with et-Tell, a large (27 acres) site southeast of Bethel. The nearby site of Khirbet el-Maqatir is the most plausible alternative location for Biblical Ai.

7:4–5 These two verses describe the Israelites' short engagement with Ai where 36 Israelites die. While the number is small, Israel had suffered no casualties against Jericho. For this reason, the Israelites lose heart, believing this defeat should not have happened.

7:6 The elders of Israel The heads of the families and also of political units to which they belong (e.g., town or tribe).

7:7 hands of the Amorites to destroy us Associated with the ancient indigenous Canaanite giant clans (see Nu 32:33,39; Dt 1:4; 2:24; 3:2,8–9). This was one of the people-group terms regularly used to describe the nations in Canaan (see Jos 3:10; 9:1).

7:9 What then will you do for your own great name Joshua appeals to the reputation of God—his ability to bring Israel into the land as he promised.

7:11 Israel has sinned This reflects the idea of corporate responsibility, a notion prevalent in ancient Near Eastern cultures and the OT. **they have violated my covenant** Since the principle of *cherem* had been articulated in Moses' sermons in Deuteronomy (Dt 7:2; 20:17)—the reiteration of the Sinai covenant—this was a covenantal violation. See note on Jos 6:16; note on 6:17.

7:12 they have been made liable to destruction The wording is ominous: Either Israel obeys God's command about *cherem*, or it will itself become the object of *cherem*.

7:20 I have sinned against the LORD, the God of Israel Achan confesses immediately, knowing that God has exposed him through the lot.

7:21 in the plunder On other occasions, Israelite warriors were allowed to take plunder from the conquered (e.g., Nu 31:11–12). However, when the enemy is placed under *cherem*, everything belongs to God (see note on Jos 6:17).

²²So Joshua sent messengers, and they ran to the tent, and there it was, hidden in his tent, with the silver underneath. ²³They took the things from the tent, brought them to Joshua and all the Israelites and spread them out before the LORD.

²⁴Then Joshua, together with all Israel, took Achan son of Zerah, the silver, the robe, the gold bar, his sons and daughters, his cattle, donkeys and sheep, his tent and all that he had, to the Valley of Achor. ²⁵Joshua said, "Why have you brought this trouble on us? The LORD will bring trouble on you today."

Then all Israel stoned him, and after they had stoned the rest, they burned them. ²⁶Over Achan they heaped up a large pile of rocks, which remains to this day. Then the LORD turned from his fierce anger. Therefore that place has been called the Valley of Achorᵃ ever since.

Ai Destroyed

8 Then the LORD said to Joshua, "Do not be afraid; do not be discouraged. Take the whole army with you, and go up and attack Ai. For I have delivered into your hands the king of Ai, his people, his city and his land. ²You shall do to Ai and its king as you did to Jericho and its king, except that you may carry off their plunder and livestock for yourselves. Set an ambush behind the city."

³So Joshua and the whole army moved out to attack Ai. He chose thirty thousand of his best fighting men and sent them out at night ⁴with these orders: "Listen carefully. You are to set an ambush behind the city. Don't go very far from it. All of you be on the alert. ⁵I and all those with me will advance on the city, and when the men come out against us, as they did before, we will flee from them. ⁶They will pursue us until we have lured them away from the city, for they will say, 'They are running away from us as they did before.' So when we flee from them, ⁷you are to rise up from ambush and take the city. The LORD your God will give it into your hand. ⁸When you have taken the city, set it on fire. Do what the LORD has commanded. See to it; you have my orders."

⁹Then Joshua sent them off, and they went to the place of ambush and lay in wait between Bethel and Ai, to the west of Ai — but Joshua spent that night with the people.

¹⁰Early the next morning Joshua mustered his army, and he and the leaders of Israel marched before them to Ai. ¹¹The entire force that was with him marched up and approached the city and arrived in front of it. They set up camp north of Ai, with the valley between them and the city. ¹²Joshua had taken about five thousand men and set them in ambush between Bethel and Ai, to the west of the city. ¹³So the soldiers took up their positions — with the main camp to the north of the city and the ambush to the west of it. That night Joshua went into the valley.

¹⁴When the king of Ai saw this, he and all the men of the city hurried out early in the morning to meet Israel in battle at a certain place overlooking the Arabah. But he did not know that an ambush had been set against him behind the city. ¹⁵Joshua and all Israel let themselves be driven back before them, and they fled toward the wilderness. ¹⁶All the men of Ai were called to pursue them, and they pursued Joshua and were lured away from the city. ¹⁷Not a man remained in Ai or Bethel who did not go after Israel. They left the city open and went in pursuit of Israel.

¹⁸Then the LORD said to Joshua, "Hold out

ᵃ 26 *Achor* means *trouble*.

7:23 spread them out before the Lord Suggests that the entire scene — the choosing by lots, the confession and now the resolution — took place before the entry to the sanctuary, God's abode.

7:24 his sons and daughters Points to the principle of corporate responsibility. The unfortunate death of Achan's family ensured that his name was blotted out of Israel. In effect, Achan and his family were given to God in place of the stolen objects that violated the *cherem* (see note on Jos 6:17). **his cattle, donkeys and sheep** The inclusion of livestock, which cannot bear moral responsibility, indicates that Achan's household was punished because of corporate responsibility, not due to their participation. **to the Valley of Achor** The exact location of this valley is unknown. The name "Achor" is a play on words, as it comes from the Hebrew verb *akhar*, which means "to bring disaster."

7:26 to this day See note on 4:9.

8:1–29 Chapter 8 continues to recount Israel's battles with Ai (see note on 7:1–26) and describes Israel's victory over Ai following the execution of Achan. This chapter presents one of the most detailed accounts of military strategy in the OT.

8:1 I have delivered into your hands God, who had ensured the Israelites' previous defeat, declares they will now succeed.

8:2 as you did to Jericho See ch. 6.

8:4–8 God at times uses deception to judge his enemies. God is not violating his own commandment not to bear false witness, as that command has judicial proceedings in mind.

8:9–23 These verses describe the strategic maneuvers of Joshua's army. It is unknown, however, whether they convey a coherent chronology. The account may simply relay key stages of the episode (compare Ex 16; Jos 2; Jdg 20).

8:12 to the west of the city The men of Ai do not see this secondary force.

8:14 When the king of Ai saw this He saw the force to his north, who were positioned so that they would be seen. **overlooking the Arabah** The valley in which Jericho is situated. The king of Ai could look down into this valley and see Israel's army — exactly what Joshua intended.

toward Ai the javelin that is in your hand, for into your hand I will deliver the city." So Joshua held out toward the city the javelin that was in his hand. [19]As soon as he did this, the men in the ambush rose quickly from their position and rushed forward. They entered the city and captured it and quickly set it on fire.

[20]The men of Ai looked back and saw the smoke of the city rising up into the sky, but they had no chance to escape in any direction; the Israelites who had been fleeing toward the wilderness had turned back against their pursuers. [21]For when Joshua and all Israel saw that the ambush had taken the city and that smoke was going up from it, they turned around and attacked the men of Ai. [22]Those in the ambush also came out of the city against them, so that they were caught in the middle, with Israelites on both sides. Israel cut them down, leaving them neither survivors nor fugitives. [23]But they took the king of Ai alive and brought him to Joshua.

[24]When Israel had finished killing all the men of Ai in the fields and in the wilderness where they had chased them, and when every one of them had been put to the sword, all the Israelites returned to Ai and killed those who were in it. [25]Twelve thousand men and women fell that day — all the people of Ai. [26]For Joshua did not draw back the hand that held out his javelin until he had destroyed[a] all who lived in Ai. [27]But Israel did carry off for themselves the livestock and plunder of this city, as the LORD had instructed Joshua.

[28]So Joshua burned Ai[b] and made it a permanent heap of ruins, a desolate place to this day. [29]He impaled the body of the king of Ai on a pole and left it there until evening. At sunset, Joshua ordered them to take the body from the pole and throw it down at the entrance of the city gate. And they raised a large pile of rocks over it, which remains to this day.

The Covenant Renewed at Mount Ebal

[30]Then Joshua built on Mount Ebal an altar to the LORD, the God of Israel, [31]as Moses the servant of the LORD had commanded the Israelites. He built it according to what is written in the Book of the Law of Moses — an altar of uncut stones, on which no iron tool had been used. On it they offered to the LORD burnt offerings and sacrificed fellowship offerings. [32]There, in the presence of the Israelites, Joshua wrote on stones a copy of the law of Moses. [33]All the Israelites, with their elders, officials and judges, were standing on both sides of the ark of the covenant of the LORD, facing the Levitical priests who carried it. Both the foreigners living among them and the native-born were there. Half of the people stood in front of Mount Gerizim and half of them in front of Mount Ebal, as Moses the servant of the LORD had formerly commanded when he gave instructions to bless the people of Israel.

[34]Afterward, Joshua read all the words of the law — the blessings and the curses — just as it is written in the Book of the Law. [35]There was not a word of all that Moses had commanded that Joshua did not read to the whole assembly of Israel, including the women and children, and the foreigners who lived among them.

---

[a] 26 The Hebrew term refers to the irrevocable giving over of things or persons to the LORD, often by totally destroying them.
[b] 28 Ai means the ruin.

8:21 attacked the men of Ai Joshua and his men were part of the first assault group that had faked defeat and fled.
8:22 Those in the ambush also came out of the city The soldiers of Ai were now trapped.
8:26 he had destroyed all who lived in Ai See note on Jos 6:17.
8:29 a large pile of rocks The pile of stones at the entrance to Ai stood as a memorial to Israel's victory. The purpose is the same as that of the memorial stones erected in the Jordan (see 4:9 and note) and of the stones piled atop Achan and his household (7:26).

8:30–35 This section may be out of place in the traditional Masoretic Text of the Hebrew Bible. Some Dead Sea Scroll manuscripts, reflecting a Hebrew text 1000 years closer to the time of writing than the Masoretic Text, have this content just before 5:2 (see note on 5:2). The first thing Israel was to do upon entering the land was to renew the covenant at Mount Ebal (8:30) and Mount Gerizim (v. 33). The placement of these verses before 5:2, as in the Dead Sea Scrolls, casts Joshua as immediately obeying that command.

8:30 Mount Ebal The scene here at Mount Ebal — located north of Shechem in the central hill country of Israel — reflects the ceremony of covenant renewal that Moses commanded in Dt 27:1–13. The construction of the altar, the sacrifices of burnt offerings and peace offerings, the copying of the Law of Moses, and the arrangement of the tribes opposite each other on Mount Ebal and Mount Gerizim aligns directly with Moses' instructions in Dt 27 (compare Dt 11:29).

8:31 an altar of uncut stones The command to make such an altar is found in Dt 27:5–7.
8:32 wrote on stones Joshua was following the command from Dt 27:8 to write the law on the stones.
8:33 Mount Gerizim This peak is just south of Mount Ebal. The bases of the two mountains are only about 500 yards apart. The association of Gerizim with blessing and Ebal with cursing arises from geography. Israel reckons direction according to the physical orientation of a person standing with back to the Mediterranean and facing east. From that position, the left hand was north and the right hand was south. The right hand had positive connotations of wisdom, favor and blessing (Ps 16:11), while the left hand had negative connotations of foolishness, disfavor and cursing (Ecc 10:2). See Dt 27:11–13.
8:34 it is written in the Book of the Law Likely refers to the content of Deuteronomy, Moses' reiteration of the law before his death.

The Gibeonite Deception

9 Now when all the kings west of the Jordan heard about these things — the kings in the hill country, in the western foothills, and along the entire coast of the Mediterranean Sea as far as Lebanon (the kings of the Hittites, Amorites, Canaanites, Perizzites, Hivites and Jebusites) — ²they came together to wage war against Joshua and Israel.

³However, when the people of Gibeon heard what Joshua had done to Jericho and Ai, ⁴they resorted to a ruse: They went as a delegation whose donkeys were loaded ͣ with worn-out sacks and old wineskins, cracked and mended. ⁵They put worn and patched sandals on their feet and wore old clothes. All the bread of their food supply was dry and moldy. ⁶Then they went to Joshua in the camp at Gilgal and said to him and the Israelites, "We have come from a distant country; make a treaty with us."

⁷The Israelites said to the Hivites, "But perhaps you live near us, so how can we make a treaty with you?"

⁸"We are your servants," they said to Joshua.

But Joshua asked, "Who are you and where do you come from?"

⁹They answered: "Your servants have come from a very distant country because of the fame of the LORD your God. For we have heard reports of him: all that he did in Egypt, ¹⁰and all that he did to the two kings of the Amorites east of the Jordan — Sihon king of Heshbon, and Og king of Bashan, who reigned in Ashtaroth. ¹¹And our elders and all those living in our country said

to us, 'Take provisions for your journey; go and meet them and say to them, "We are your servants; make a treaty with us."' ¹²This bread of ours was warm when we packed it at home on the day we left to come to you. But now see how dry and moldy it is. ¹³And these wineskins that we filled were new, but see how cracked they are. And our clothes and sandals are worn out by the very long journey."

¹⁴The Israelites sampled their provisions but did not inquire of the LORD. ¹⁵Then Joshua made a treaty of peace with them to let them live, and the leaders of the assembly ratified it by oath.

¹⁶Three days after they made the treaty with the Gibeonites, the Israelites heard that they were neighbors, living near them. ¹⁷So the Israelites set out and on the third day came to their cities: Gibeon, Kephirah, Beeroth and Kiriath Jearim. ¹⁸But the Israelites did not attack them, because the leaders of the assembly had sworn an oath to them by the LORD, the God of Israel.

The whole assembly grumbled against the leaders, ¹⁹but all the leaders answered, "We have given them our oath by the LORD, the God of Israel, and we cannot touch them now. ²⁰This is what we will do to them: We will let them live, so that God's wrath will not fall on us for breaking the oath we swore to them." ²¹They continued, "Let them live, but let them be woodcutters and water carriers in the service of the whole assembly." So the leaders' promise to them was kept.

ͣ 4 Most Hebrew manuscripts; some Hebrew manuscripts, Vulgate and Syriac (see also Septuagint) *They prepared provisions and loaded their donkeys*

9:1–27 Joshua 9 continues the conquest narrative. Up to this point, the Israelites had attacked and taken individual cities. Now, they encounter coalitions of cities and people groups: Six kings come against the Israelites (vv. 1–2). The Gibeonites choose not to fight in this coalition, instead opting to trick Joshua into a treaty (vv. 3–15). The latter part of the chapter deals with the consequences of having made a treaty with the Gibeonites (vv. 16–27). Though enacted by deception, the treaty was binding upon Israel, forcing Joshua to come to Gibeon's aid in ch. 10. During the period of the monarchy, the Israelites — including David — were still honoring this treaty (see 2Sa 21:1–8).

9:3–15 The Gibeonites concoct a scheme to dupe Israel into a treaty. They take great care to appear as though they have traveled a long distance in order to convince the Israelites that they were not native Canaanites, who were to be destroyed (see Dt 20:17; compare note on Jos 6:17). See the table "Covenants in the Old Testament" on p. 469.

9:3 Gibeon Located about five miles away from Ai (presuming Ai is et-Tell; see Jos 7:2 and note). Gibeon would eventually be folded into Benjamin (18:25–28) and be named a Levitical city (21:17; compare Lev 25:32–33).

9:6 make a treaty with us God had not prohibited the Israelites from entering into a covenant with people outside of Canaan, just the peoples of Canaan whose

territory Israel was moving into (see Ex 34:11–12; Dt 20:10–18). The Gibeonites apparently knew about this prohibition (Jos 2:9–11; 9:9–10).

9:9 that he did in Egypt Joshua 2:9–11 indicates that Canaanites had heard about Yahweh's miraculous defeat of the Egyptians.

9:10 Sihon king of Heshbon See Nu 21; Dt 2–3.

9:14 did not inquire of the LORD The key element of the narrative and the ultimate reason that Israel was deceived is that they failed to seek Yahweh's guidance on the matter. Numbers 27:21 indicates that Joshua's leadership role involved inquiring of Yahweh through the priest's use of the Urim (a method of casting lots). Since the men were soliciting a treaty, it would have made good sense for Joshua to inquire of Yahweh.

9:17 Gibeon, Kephirah, Beeroth and Kiriath Jearim Like the Philistines and their five-city confederation (Jos 13:3; Jdg 3:3; 1Sa 6:16–18), the Gibeonite cities were formally allied. All of the cities fall into Benjamin's tribal allotment (Jos 18:25–26,28) and are located within 10 miles of Jerusalem.

9:18 grumbled against the leaders The people were likely uneasy that this violation of the *cherem* command (see note on 6:17; compare Dt 20:17) would result in retaliation from Yahweh, or perhaps withdrawal of his help.

9:21 woodcutters and water carriers The Israelites spared the Gibeonites because of the treaty but made them slaves.

²²Then Joshua summoned the Gibeonites and said, "Why did you deceive us by saying, 'We live a long way from you,' while actually you live near us? ²³You are now under a curse: You will never be released from service as woodcutters and water carriers for the house of my God."

²⁴They answered Joshua, "Your servants were clearly told how the Lord your God had commanded his servant Moses to give you the whole land and to wipe out all its inhabitants from before you. So we feared for our lives because of you, and that is why we did this. ²⁵We are now in your hands. Do to us whatever seems good and right to you."

²⁶So Joshua saved them from the Israelites, and they did not kill them. ²⁷That day he made the Gibeonites woodcutters and water carriers for the assembly, to provide for the needs of the altar of the Lord at the place the Lord would choose. And that is what they are to this day.

The Sun Stands Still

10 Now Adoni-Zedek king of Jerusalem heard that Joshua had taken Ai and totally destroyed^a it, doing to Ai and its king as he had done to Jericho and its king, and that the people of Gibeon had made a treaty of peace with Israel and had become their allies. ²He and his people were very much alarmed at this, because Gibeon was an important city, like one of the royal cities; it was larger than Ai, and all its men were good fighters. ³So Adoni-Zedek king of Jerusalem appealed to Hoham king of Hebron, Piram king of Jarmuth, Japhia king of Lachish and Debir king of Eglon. ⁴"Come up and help me attack Gibeon,"

he said, "because it has made peace with Joshua and the Israelites."

⁵Then the five kings of the Amorites — the kings of Jerusalem, Hebron, Jarmuth, Lachish and Eglon — joined forces. They moved up with all their troops and took up positions against Gibeon and attacked it.

⁶The Gibeonites then sent word to Joshua in the camp at Gilgal: "Do not abandon your servants. Come up to us quickly and save us! Help us, because all the Amorite kings from the hill country have joined forces against us."

⁷So Joshua marched up from Gilgal with his entire army, including all the best fighting men. ⁸The Lord said to Joshua, "Do not be afraid of them; I have given them into your hand. Not one of them will be able to withstand you."

⁹After an all-night march from Gilgal, Joshua took them by surprise. ¹⁰The Lord threw them into confusion before Israel, so Joshua and the Israelites defeated them completely at Gibeon. Israel pursued them along the road going up to Beth Horon and cut them down all the way to Azekah and Makkedah. ¹¹As they fled before Israel on the road down from Beth Horon to Azekah, the Lord hurled large hailstones down on them, and more of them died from the hail than were killed by the swords of the Israelites.

¹²On the day the Lord gave the Amorites over to Israel, Joshua said to the Lord in the presence of Israel:

a 1 The Hebrew term refers to the irrevocable giving over of things or persons to the Lord, often by totally destroying them; also in verses 28, 35, 37, 39 and 40.

9:26 they did not kill them Indicates again that Israelites in the camp wanted to kill the Gibeonites, despite the treaty (compare Jos 9:21).
9:27 for the assembly, to provide for the needs of the altar The Gibeonite labor force would also cut the timber needed for the sacrificial altar and draw water for ritual washing. **at the place the Lord would choose** Refers to the central sanctuary, which would become the focus of Israelite worship after the conquest (see Dt 12:5).

10:1–15 Joshua 10 describes the southern campaign of the conquest of Canaan. Victories at Jericho and Ai gave the Israelites a foothold in the center of the land, effectively dividing it and preventing the southern and northern cities from taking a united front. The chapter also includes an incident in which Israel is bound to defend Gibeon because of their treaty (see ch. 9). When five Canaanite kings join forces and attack, Israel fights the coalition on their behalf and defeats the enemies. This battle is the occasion for Joshua's famous prayer that the sun stand still. Most of the personal and place names in this chapter are known from external sources, such as the Amarna Letters and the Annals of Thutmose III. See the infographic "The Amarna Letters" on p. 337.

10:1 Adoni-Zedek Means "My Lord is Righteous," with "righteous" translating the Hebrew word *tsedeq* (compare

Ge 14:18). *Tsedeq* was a Canaanite deity known in Jerusalem. **totally destroyed it** See note on Jos 6:17.

10:3 The cities of this five-king coalition are situated southwest of Jerusalem. This suggests the current coalition is different from the one in 9:1–2, where the kings are said to be from various locations in Canaan.

10:3 Hebron Hebron was formerly called Kiriath-Arba, which was the city of the Anakite giant clan in Nu 13:22,32–33 (the population that caused Israel to doubt God, leading to the 40 years of wilderness wandering; compare Jos 14:13–15). Hebron was eventually given to Caleb, since he was one of the two spies who did not doubt God's promise. It was also one of the Levitical cities (20:7).
10:5 five kings of the Amorites The term "Amorites" was occasionally used with reference to giant clans (see v. 3; Dt 1:4; 2:22–24; 3:10–13; 4:47; 31:4). The Israelite southern campaign is heading directly into the territory of the enemies they feared 40 years earlier.
10:7 entire army The Israelites honor the treaty with Gibeon, despite having been tricked into joining it (see Jos 9).
10:9 After an all-night march from Gilgal Gilgal was approximately 21 miles from Gibeon.
10:10 threw them into confusion The Hebrew verb used here, *hamam*, frequently occurs in descriptions where God helps Israel in battle — especially when God uses meteorological phenomena (see Ex 14:24; Ps 77:16–18;

"Sun, stand still over Gibeon,
and you, moon, over the Valley of Aijalon."
¹³ So the sun stood still,
and the moon stopped,
till the nation avenged itself on*a* its
enemies,

as it is written in the Book of Jashar.
The sun stopped in the middle of the sky and delayed going down about a full day. ¹⁴ There has never been a day like it before or since, a day when

the LORD listened to a human being. Surely the LORD was fighting for Israel!

¹⁵ Then Joshua returned with all Israel to the camp at Gilgal.

Five Amorite Kings Killed

¹⁶ Now the five kings had fled and hidden in the cave at Makkedah. ¹⁷ When Joshua was told that the five kings had been found hiding in the cave

a 13 Or nation triumphed over

Jdg 4:15; 5:20–21; 1Sa 7:10; 2Sa 22:15; Ps 18:14; 144:6; compare Jos 10:11).

10:12 Sun, stand still over Gibeon The sun's location over Gibeon in the east suggests this event occurs in the morning.

10:13 the moon stopped The account suggests that the sun and moon stopped at the same time on opposite horizons. Several theories try to explain this event. One option holds that the sun and moon stayed visible until the end of the battle. Another possibility is that Joshua requests continued light for fighting. A third suggestion is that Joshua was praying for a solar eclipse—an event

universally viewed as an omen. Joshua would have prayed for this sign to frighten the enemy. A fourth option is that Joshua asked for a celestial omen from God to either encourage his own army or demoralize the enemy. **the Book of Jashar** Nothing else is known of this book. It apparently was a chronicle of epic and nationalistic poems (see 2Sa 1:19–27; 1Ki 8:12–13 may have also come from this book).

10:14 There has never been a day like it before or since The exceptional nature is due to the specificity of the prayer and immediacy of the response.

The Amarna Letters

This collection of cuneiform tablets is named after the place they were discovered—modern Amarna, the ancient Egyptian city of Akhetaten. Written in the late 14th century BC, these letters record correspondence between Egypt (under Pharaohs Akhenaten and Tutankhamun) and its vassal states. They provide information about trade and government of the time.

The Amarna letters and the biblical text describe the land of Canaan similarly. Both indicate that Canaan had several territories, various kings, and chariots that served as the means of military control.

The Amarna letters describe the city of Shechem as a dangerous place full of political intrigue; the book of Judges does the same at a later date. The Amarna letters also show that the kingdoms of Canaan were under military pressure from nomadic tribes.

The Amarna letters are a collection of 388 tablets, with the largest measuring about 8 in. by 4 in.

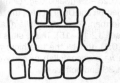

at Makkedah, 18he said, "Roll large rocks up to the mouth of the cave, and post some men there to guard it. 19But don't stop; pursue your enemies! Attack them from the rear and don't let them reach their cities, for the LORD your God has given them into your hand."

20So Joshua and the Israelites defeated them completely, but a few survivors managed to reach their fortified cities. 21The whole army then returned safely to Joshua in the camp at Makkedah, and no one uttered a word against the Israelites.

22Joshua said, "Open the mouth of the cave and bring those five kings out to me." 23So they brought the five kings out of the cave—the kings of Jerusalem, Hebron, Jarmuth, Lachish and Eglon. 24When they had brought these kings to Joshua, he summoned all the men of Israel and said to the army commanders who had come with him, "Come here and put your feet on the necks of these kings." So they came forward and placed their feet on their necks.

25Joshua said to them, "Do not be afraid; do not be discouraged. Be strong and courageous. This is what the LORD will do to all the enemies you are going to fight." 26Then Joshua put the kings to death and exposed their bodies on five poles, and they were left hanging on the poles until evening.

27At sunset Joshua gave the order and they took them down from the poles and threw them into the cave where they had been hiding. At the mouth of the cave they placed large rocks, which are there to this day.

Southern Cities Conquered

28That day Joshua took Makkedah. He put the city and its king to the sword and totally destroyed everyone in it. He left no survivors. And he did to the king of Makkedah as he had done to the king of Jericho.

29Then Joshua and all Israel with him moved on from Makkedah to Libnah and attacked it. 30The LORD also gave that city and its king into Israel's hand. The city and everyone in it Joshua put to the sword. He left no survivors there. And he did to its king as he had done to the king of Jericho.

31Then Joshua and all Israel with him moved on from Libnah to Lachish; he took up positions against it and attacked it. 32The LORD gave Lachish into Israel's hands, and Joshua took it on the second day. The city and everyone in it he put to the sword, just as he had done to Libnah. 33Meanwhile, Horam king of Gezer had come up to help Lachish, but Joshua defeated him and his army—until no survivors were left.

34Then Joshua and all Israel with him moved on from Lachish to Eglon; they took up positions against it and attacked it. 35They captured it that same day and put it to the sword and totally destroyed everyone in it, just as they had done to Lachish.

36Then Joshua and all Israel with him went up from Eglon to Hebron and attacked it. 37They took the city and put it to the sword, together with its king, its villages and everyone in it. They left no survivors. Just as at Eglon, they totally destroyed it and everyone in it.

38Then Joshua and all Israel with him turned around and attacked Debir. 39They took the city, its king and its villages, and put them to the sword. Everyone in it they totally destroyed. They left no survivors. They did to Debir and its king as they had done to Libnah and its king and to Hebron.

40So Joshua subdued the whole region, including the hill country, the Negev, the western foothills

---

10:20 managed to reach their fortified cities This battle was in defense of the Gibeonites; it was not part of the *cherem* (see note on Ex 22:20; note on Jos 2:10).
10:21 whole army Apparently refers to the Gibeonites. Given the victory, no one from Gibeon should complain about Israel's loyalty to the treaty (see v. 6).
10:24 put your feet on the necks A gesture of contempt for a defeated foe.
10:25 Do not be afraid Joshua uses the victory as an object lesson. The cities of these kings were home to the Canaanites they feared most—the giant clans (see vv. 3–5).
10:27 they took them down from the poles See 8:29; compare Dt 21:22.

10:28–43 Joshua now moves to secure southern Canaan. The Israelites conquer seven more cities in Jos 10:28–39 (Makkedah, Libnah, Lachish, Gezer, Eglon, Hebron and Debir). Later, the text adds four cities (Geder, Hormah, Arad and Adullam) as having been conquered (see 12:13–15). These sites are under the *cherem* (see 10:1), though the text hints that the Israelites did not always accomplish or carry out the *cherem* fully (see v. 33 and note).

10:28 totally destroyed everyone This engagement was independent of the Gibeonite defense, so the principle of *cherem* is once again operative. See note on 6:16; note on 6:17.
10:30 He left no survivors there According to the *cherem* principle (see note on 6:17).
10:31 he took up positions against it The Hebrew phrase used here is not *cherem* (see v. 1), but v. 32 indicates that the Israelites had followed the principle of *cherem* (6:16–17).
10:32 and everyone in it The king of Lachish had already been killed—he was one of the five kings in collaboration against Israel (see vv. 23–27).
10:33 until no survivors were left The language of *cherem* (see note on 6:16; note on 6:17; compare 10:35). The Israelites killed only the king of Gezer and his army, not the entire population of Gezer. This is consistent with comments in 16:10 and Jdg 1:29 that Gezer's population was not entirely destroyed.
10:36 Hebron The king of Hebron had already been killed, as he was one of the five kings in collaboration against Gibeon (see Jos 10:23–27).
10:38 Debir Refers to the city of Debir, not the king of Eglon (whose name is Debir; v. 3).

and the mountain slopes, together with all their kings. He left no survivors. He totally destroyed all who breathed, just as the LORD, the God of Israel, had commanded. ⁴¹Joshua subdued them from Kadesh Barnea to Gaza and from the whole region of Goshen to Gibeon. ⁴²All these kings and their lands Joshua conquered in one campaign, because the LORD, the God of Israel, fought for Israel.

⁴³Then Joshua returned with all Israel to the camp at Gilgal.

Northern Kings Defeated

11 When Jabin king of Hazor heard of this, he sent word to Jobab king of Madon, to the kings of Shimron and Akshaph, ²and to the northern kings who were in the mountains, in the Arabah south of Kinnereth, in the western foothills and in Naphoth Dor on the west; ³to the Canaanites in the east and west; to the Amorites, Hittites, Perizzites and Jebusites in the hill country; and to the Hivites below Hermon in the region of Mizpah. ⁴They came out with all their troops and a large number of horses and chariots — a huge army, as numerous as the sand on the seashore. ⁵All these kings joined forces and made camp together at the Waters of Merom to fight against Israel.

⁶The LORD said to Joshua, "Do not be afraid of them, because by this time tomorrow I will hand all of them, slain, over to Israel. You are to hamstring their horses and burn their chariots."

⁷So Joshua and his whole army came against them suddenly at the Waters of Merom and attacked them, ⁸and the LORD gave them into the hand of Israel. They defeated them and pursued them all the way to Greater Sidon, to Misrephoth Maim, and to the Valley of Mizpah on the east, until no survivors were left. ⁹Joshua did to them as the LORD had directed: He hamstrung their horses and burned their chariots.

¹⁰At that time Joshua turned back and captured Hazor and put its king to the sword. (Hazor had been the head of all these kingdoms.) ¹¹Everyone in it they put to the sword. They totally destroyedᵃ them, not sparing anyone that breathed, and he burned Hazor itself.

¹²Joshua took all these royal cities and their kings and put them to the sword. He totally destroyed them, as Moses the servant of the LORD had commanded. ¹³Yet Israel did not burn any of the cities built on their mounds — except Hazor, which Joshua burned. ¹⁴The Israelites carried off for themselves all the plunder and livestock of these cities, but all the people they put to the sword until they completely destroyed them, not sparing anyone that breathed. ¹⁵As the LORD commanded his servant Moses, so Moses commanded Joshua, and Joshua did it; he left nothing undone of all that the LORD commanded Moses.

¹⁶So Joshua took this entire land: the hill country, all the Negev, the whole region of Goshen, the

---

ᵃ *11* The Hebrew term refers to the irrevocable giving over of things or persons to the LORD, often by totally destroying them; also in verses 12, 20 and 21.

10:40 the Negev Often refers to the territory at the southern border of Canaan (the northern Sinai), but can also refer to a desert area. **LORD, the God of Israel, had commanded** Other passages in Joshua and Judges indicate that the complete destruction of some of these people groups was not completed until sometime later (compare note on Jos 6:17). For example, Hebron (15:13–14; Jdg 1:9–10,20) and Debir (Jos 15:15–17; Jdg 1:11–13) are mentioned later in the book as still needing subjugation. Joshua 10:28–40 seems to present a complete annihilation of the Canaanite population throughout the region, but later passages suggest this conquest was not that exhaustive and complete (see 11:22; 13:2–6; 14:12; 15:63; 16:10; 17:12–13; 18:2–3; 19:47; 23:4–5,7,12–13; Jdg 1). The language of this passage is meant to indicate that Joshua made every effort to be obedient to God's earlier mandate (see note on Jos 6:16).
10:41 Goshen Not the Goshen located in the Nile Delta in Egypt (see Ge 45:10).

11:1–23 Joshua 11:1–15 chronicles the subjugation of northern Canaan. The chapter closes (Jos 11:16–23) with a summary of Israel's successes, effectively bringing the description of the conquest of Canaan to a close. Chapter 11 describes a military coalition formed against Israel. The leader of the coalition is Jabin, king of Hazor.

11:1 Jabin This chapter is sometimes connected with the story of Deborah and Barak, which also refers to Jabin (Jdg 4). However, the Biblical narrative presents them as two distinct events. Jabin may have been a hereditary title borne by successive kings of Hazor (compare "Abimelek," Ge 20–21,26). **Jobab king of Madon** Possibly identified with Qarn Hattin, west of Tiberias.
11:2 northern kings who were in the mountains Having mentioned some specific kings and cities, the writer now refers more generally to several regions to the north, south and west who take a "last stand" against Israel.
11:3 the Canaanites The peoples named here frequently appear in lists of enemies targeted for destruction in the conquest (see note on Jos 3:10; compare Ex 3:8; Dt 7:1).
11:8 LORD gave them into the hand Unlike Jos 10, this chapter does not describe the battle in detail.
11:11 They totally destroyed them According to the *cherem* principle. See note on 6:17.
11:12 Moses the servant of the LORD had commanded See Dt 20:16–17.
11:13 did not burn any of the cities built on their mounds May indicate that the Israelites only needed to utterly destroy Hazor to ensure no resistance in the future. It may also point to retaliation, since Hazor had led the opposition alliance.
11:14 all the plunder and livestock of these cities The text apparently makes some distinction between certain items allowed for plunder and what was considered *cherem* (see note on Jos 6:17; compare 8:2).

11:16–17 This passage notes the regions Israel conquered (compare 10:40–41) and indicates the northern and southern boundaries of their territory.

11:16 whole region of Goshen Not the Goshen in Egypt. Possibly the region between the hill country of Judah and the Negev.

western foothills, the Arabah and the mountains of Israel with their foothills, 17from Mount Halak, which rises toward Seir, to Baal Gad in the Valley of Lebanon below Mount Hermon. He captured all their kings and put them to death. 18Joshua waged war against all these kings for a long time. 19Except for the Hivites living in Gibeon, not one city made a treaty of peace with the Israelites, who took them all in battle. 20For it was the LORD himself who hardened their hearts to wage war against Israel, so that he might destroy them totally, exterminating them without mercy, as the LORD had commanded Moses.

21At that time Joshua went and destroyed the Anakites from the hill country: from Hebron, Debir and Anab, from all the hill country of Judah, and from all the hill country of Israel. Joshua totally destroyed them and their towns. 22No Anakites were left in Israelite territory; only in Gaza, Gath and Ashdod did any survive.

23So Joshua took the entire land, just as the LORD had directed Moses, and he gave it as an inheritance to Israel according to their tribal divisions. Then the land had rest from war.

List of Defeated Kings

12 These are the kings of the land whom the Israelites had defeated and whose territory they took over east of the Jordan, from the Arnon Gorge to Mount Hermon, including all the eastern side of the Arabah:

2Sihon king of the Amorites, who reigned in Heshbon.

He ruled from Aroer on the rim of the Arnon Gorge — from the middle of the gorge — to the Jabbok River, which is the border of the Ammonites. This included half of Gilead. 3He also ruled over the eastern Arabah from the Sea of Galilee*a* to the Sea of the Arabah (that is, the Dead Sea), to Beth Jeshimoth, and then southward below the slopes of Pisgah.

4And the territory of Og king of Bashan, one of the last of the Rephaites, who reigned in Ashtaroth and Edrei.

5He ruled over Mount Hermon, Salekah, all of Bashan to the border of the people of Geshur and Maakah, and half of Gilead to the border of Sihon king of Heshbon.

6Moses, the servant of the LORD, and the Israelites conquered them. And Moses the servant of the LORD gave their land to the Reubenites, the Gadites and the half-tribe of Manasseh to be their possession.

7Here is a list of the kings of the land that Joshua and the Israelites conquered on the west side of the Jordan, from Baal Gad in the Valley of Lebanon to Mount Halak, which rises toward Seir. Joshua gave their lands as an inheritance to the tribes of Israel according to their tribal divisions. 8The lands included the hill country, the western foothills, the Arabah, the mountain slopes, the wilderness and the Negev. These were the lands of the Hittites, Amorites, Canaanites,

a 3 Hebrew Kinnereth

11:18 Joshua waged war against all these kings for a long time See note on 10:40.
11:21 destroyed the Anakites This verse may summarize the demise of the Anakite giant clan in connection with the southern campaign of ch. 10, or it describes a separate campaign. Elsewhere, the OT connects the eradication of giant clans with a homeland for God's own people (Dt 2:8–12). While the giant clans in Canaan were interspersed with other people groups, their presence is apparent in many of the sites and regions specifically included in the destruction narrative. This probably relates theologically to Nu 13–14, where the presence of the Anakite lead the people to doubt God. **Joshua totally destroyed them** See note on Jos 6:17.
11:22 Gaza, Gath and Ashdod Philistine cities (see 13:3). This side comment is noteworthy in regard to the later accounts of Philistine giants (also associated with the Rephaites; see 13:12).
11:23 their tribal divisions See chs. 14–19; Nu 26:52–56.

12:1–6 Joshua 12 serves as a summary of the first 11 chapters of the book. The chapter reiterates the territories the Israelites conquered, noting which ones Moses defeated (in the Transjordan; vv. 1–6) and which ones Joshua defeated (vv. 7–24). The account includes the Transjordanian territories for sake of completeness; Israel is now in possession of its inheritance.

12:2–3 These verses repeat the information of Dt 2–3 with respect to the regions taken before crossing into Canaan proper (compare Dt 2:36–37; Jos 3:16–17).
12:4 Og king of Bashan See Nu 21:33–35; Dt 3:1–11 (compare Nu 32:33). **the Rephaites** A term associated with the giant clans. See Dt 2:10–11; 3:11–13. **who reigned in Ashtaroth and Edrei** Og's territory was in Bashan (see Nu 21:33; Dt 1:4; 3:1,10). The half-tribe of Manasseh inherited these two cities. Ashtaroth became one of the Levitical cities (see Jos 21:27; compare Lev 25:32–33).
12:5 Bashan Also associated with giant clans, the Rephaites (Dt 1:4; 3:10–11).
12:6 Reubenites See Nu 32:1–42 and note.

12:7–24 This passage lists the territory conquered (Jos 12:7–8), the native Canaanite peoples targeted in the conquest (v. 8; compare Dt 7:1; 20:17; Jos 3:10), and the various kings subjugated by the Israelites (vv. 9–24). The list of kings mainly includes those listed in the campaigns of chs. 10–11 as well as the kings of Jericho and Ai from chs. 6–8. Some names from vv. 13–16 are associated with the southern campaign of ch. 10, but they are not explicitly mentioned in ch. 10. Several names in vv. 17–22 relate to the northern campaign of ch. 11, but they are not explicitly mentioned in ch. 11.

12:7 according to their tribal divisions Describes the northern and southern limits of the conquered territory.

Perizzites, Hivites and Jebusites. These were the kings:

9	the king of Jericho	one
	the king of Ai (near Bethel)	one
10	the king of Jerusalem	one
	the king of Hebron	one
11	the king of Jarmuth	one
	the king of Lachish	one
12	the king of Eglon	one
	the king of Gezer	one
13	the king of Debir	one
	the king of Geder	one
14	the king of Hormah	one
	the king of Arad	one
15	the king of Libnah	one
	the king of Adullam	one
16	the king of Makkedah	one
	the king of Bethel	one
17	the king of Tappuah	one
	the king of Hepher	one
18	the king of Aphek	one
	the king of Lasharon	one
19	the king of Madon	one
	the king of Hazor	one
20	the king of Shimron Meron	one
	the king of Akshaph	one
21	the king of Taanach	one
	the king of Megiddo	one
22	the king of Kedesh	one
	the king of Jokneam in Carmel	one
23	the king of Dor (in Naphoth Dor)	one
	the king of Goyim in Gilgal	one
24	the king of Tirzah	one

thirty-one kings in all.

Land Still to Be Taken

13 When Joshua had grown old, the LORD said to him, "You are now very old, and there are still very large areas of land to be taken over.

2 "This is the land that remains: all the regions of the Philistines and Geshurites, 3 from the Shihor River on the east of Egypt to the territory of Ekron on the north, all of it counted as Canaanite though held by the five Philistine rulers in Gaza, Ashdod, Ashkelon, Gath and Ekron; the territory of the Avvites 4 on the south; all the land of the Canaanites, from Arah of the Sidonians as far as Aphek and the border of the Amorites; 5 the area of Byblos; and all Lebanon to the east, from Baal Gad below Mount Hermon to Lebo Hamath.

6 "As for all the inhabitants of the mountain regions from Lebanon to Misrephoth Maim, that is, all the Sidonians, I myself will drive them out before the Israelites. Be sure to allocate this land to Israel for an inheritance, as I have instructed you, 7 and divide it as an inheritance among the nine tribes and half of the tribe of Manasseh."

12:14 king of Arad See Nu 21:1; 33:40.

12:15 king of Adullam Mentioned only here.

12:18 king of Aphek This is a different Aphek from others mentioned elsewhere (see Jos 13:4; 19:30; 1Ki 20:26,30; 2Ki 13:17).

12:21 king of Taanach Megiddo and Taanach became part of the territory of Manasseh (Jos 17:11; 21:25; compare Lev 25:32–33).

12:22 king of Kedesh Likely refers to the Kedesh between Megiddo and Taanach, not the one associated with the sanctuary city in the remote north of the territory allotted to the tribe of Naphtali (Jos 19:37). **king of Jokneam in Carmel** Located on Zebulun's border with Manasseh (19:11).

12:23 king of Goyim in Gilgal The identity of the king and region indicated here is uncertain. The Hebrew word used here, *goiim*, means "nations" and is otherwise unknown as a place name. However, it must be a place name to meet the mathematical total of 31 kings given in v. 24.

12:24 king of Tirzah Will become the initial capital city of the northern kingdom of Israel when Jeroboam takes the kingship of the ten northern tribes (1Ki 14–16).

13:1–33 This chapter begins the second half of Joshua. The first half focused on the conquest of Canaan; the second half (Jos 13–24) features lists and catalogues rather than battles. The focus is on the allotment of the land to the Israelite tribes (chs. 13–21). Chapter 13 addresses the allotments in the Transjordan and reiterates that the Levites receive no inheritance (vv. 14,33; compare Nu 18:20–32). The lands west of the Jordan are distributed in Jos 14–19, reflecting the order in which the lands were conquered. Caleb's inheritance is listed first (14:1–15), a position of honor in view of his faithfulness. Judah and Joseph (Ephraim and Manasseh) are described in order in chs. 15–17. The lists conclude in chs. 20–21 with the cities of refuge (ch. 20) and the Levitical cities (ch. 21).

13:3 Shihor River The location of this river (the Sihor or Shihor) is unknown. In Isa 23:3 and Jer 2:18, Shihor refers to the Nile. Here, it is to the east of Egypt, suggesting it may be a branch of the Nile in the delta region. **five Philistine rulers** The first mention of the Philistines in Joshua. According to Egyptian texts, the Philistines were part of a group of seafaring cultures from the Aegean known as the Sea Peoples. They settled in Canaan in roughly 1200 BC.

13:4 from Arah This site is unknown, but if it was under the control of Sidon, it was likely in north of Israel. **Aphek** Probably to be identified with Afqa, which is in the north, east of Byblos in Lebanon. This location is more likely than the Philistine Aphek in the Sharon (see Jos 12:18). **the Amorites** Exercised control of territory in the northern part of the land (Nu 21; Dt 2–3).

13:5 Baal Gad below Mount Hermon to Lebo Hamath Baal Gad and Lebo Hamath (also called "the entrance to Hamath") probably marked the southern and northern points of the same valley.

13:6 Sidonians Refers to Phoenicians from the city of Sidon. **I myself will drive them out** God's promise that he will drive out the remaining opposition is intended as encouragement in view of the fact that Joshua is quite old and will not live much longer (Jos 13:1). Joshua must now apportion the land among the tribes (vv. 6–7) before he dies.

13:7 nine tribes and half of the tribe of Manasseh The other two tribes (Reuben and Gad) and the other half

Division of the Land East of the Jordan

[8]The other half of Manasseh,[a] the Reubenites and the Gadites had received the inheritance that Moses had given them east of the Jordan, as he, the servant of the LORD, had assigned it to them.

[9]It extended from Aroer on the rim of the Arnon Gorge, and from the town in the middle of the gorge, and included the whole plateau of Medeba as far as Dibon, [10]and all the towns of Sihon king of the Amorites, who ruled in Heshbon, out to the border of the Ammonites. [11]It also included Gilead, the territory of the people of Geshur and Maakah, all of Mount Hermon and all Bashan as far as Salekah — [12]that is, the whole kingdom of Og in Bashan, who had reigned in Ashtaroth and Edrei. (He was the last of the Rephaites.) Moses had defeated them and taken over their land. [13]But the Israelites did not drive out the people of Geshur and Maakah, so they continue to live among the Israelites to this day.

[14]But to the tribe of Levi he gave no inheritance, since the food offerings presented to the LORD, the God of Israel, are their inheritance, as he promised them.

[15]This is what Moses had given to the tribe of Reuben, according to its clans:

[16]The territory from Aroer on the rim of the Arnon Gorge, and from the town in the middle of the gorge, and the whole plateau past Medeba [17]to Heshbon and all its towns on the plateau, including Dibon, Bamoth Baal, Beth Baal Meon, [18]Jahaz, Kedemoth, Mephaath, [19]Kiriathaim, Sibmah, Zereth Shahar on the hill in the valley, [20]Beth Peor, the slopes of Pisgah, and Beth Jeshimoth — [21]all the towns on the plateau and the entire realm of Sihon king of the Amorites, who ruled at Heshbon. Moses had defeated him and the Midianite chiefs, Evi, Rekem, Zur, Hur and Reba — princes allied with Sihon — who lived in that country. [22]In addition to those slain in battle, the Israelites had put to the sword Balaam son of Beor, who practiced divination. [23]The boundary of the Reubenites was the bank of the Jordan. These towns and their villages were the inheritance of the Reubenites, according to their clans.

[24]This is what Moses had given to the tribe of Gad, according to its clans:

[25]The territory of Jazer, all the towns of Gilead and half the Ammonite country as far as Aroer, near Rabbah; [26]and from Heshbon to Ramath Mizpah and Betonim, and from Mahanaim to the territory of Debir; [27]and in the valley, Beth Haram, Beth Nimrah, Sukkoth and Zaphon with the rest of the realm of Sihon king of Heshbon (the east side of the Jordan, the territory up to the end of the Sea of Galilee[b]). [28]These towns and their villages were the inheritance of the Gadites, according to their clans.

[29]This is what Moses had given to the half-tribe of Manasseh, that is, to half the family of the descendants of Manasseh, according to its clans:

[a] 8 Hebrew *With it* (that is, with the other half of Manasseh)
[b] 27 Hebrew *Kinnereth*

---

of Manasseh had their inheritance in the Transjordan (see vv. 8–33; compare Nu 32).

13:8–33 After listing the general extent of the territory Israel controlled in the Transjordan (Jos 13:8–14), this passage specifies the territory assigned to Reuben, Gad and the half-tribe of Manasseh. Their allotments are given from south to north beginning with Reuben, then Gad and then Manasseh (vv. 15–33). The territory formerly controlled by Sihon from Heshbon is apparently split between Reuben and Gad (vv. 21,27), but the border between their territories is not clearly indicated. However, the extent of Israel's control of the Transjordan region is unclear. Prophetic oracles denouncing Moab indicate cities from this area are prominent Moabite cities (e.g, Isa 15:1–9; Jer 48:1–2,21–25). Jeremiah indicates that Ammon eventually drove Gad out of its territory (Jer 49:1–2). Jephthah's conflict with the Ammonites in Jdg 11 also indicates control of this region was contested. The ninth-century BC Moabite inscription known as the Mesha Stele also reveals that Moab fought with Israel over control of the cities north of the Arnon.

13:9 from Aroer A city in the Transjordan on the Arnon River. **whole plateau of Medeba** This plateau runs from the Arnon northward to the city of Heshbon. Dibon is modern Dhiban, which later became the capital of Moab (Isa 15:2; Jer 48:18,22).

13:12 Rephaites The Hebrew term here, *rephaim*, is used in the OT for giant clans and the spirits of those fallen warriors in Sheol (Isa 14:9).

13:13 to this day Illustrates that the conquest was not actually fully accomplished when the book of Joshua was written, years after Joshua's own time.

13:14 to the tribe of Levi The Levites were responsible for the service and maintenance of the tabernacle. Though they were given several cities in the land (see Jos 21; compare Dt 10:8–9), they were supported by offerings (compare Dt 18:1–5).

13:17 Heshbon This city is identified in the description of territory allotted to Reuben and in the description of territory given to Gad (Jos 13:26). Heshbon is elsewhere described as a Levitical city in the territory of Gad, not Reuben (see 21:38–39). The location was apparently on the border of the two tribal allotments, showing that overlap in territorial perception was possible. The city was northeast of Mount Nebo near Reuben's northern border and Gad's southern border. **all its towns on the plateau** A list of cities that the Reubenites rebuilt is found in Nu 32:37–38.

13:23 the Jordan A natural boundary separating the Transjordan from Canaan (Nu 32).

13:25 near Rabbah The principal city of the Ammonites, located just over 20 miles east of the Jordan.

30The territory extending from Mahanaim and including all of Bashan, the entire realm of Og king of Bashan—all the settlements of Jair in Bashan, sixty towns, 31half of Gilead, and Ashtaroth and Edrei (the royal cities of Og in Bashan). This was for the descendants of Makir son of Manasseh—for half of the sons of Makir, according to their clans.

32This is the inheritance Moses had given when he was in the plains of Moab across the Jordan east of Jericho. 33But to the tribe of Levi, Moses had given no inheritance; the LORD, the God of Israel, is their inheritance, as he promised them.

Division of the Land West of the Jordan

14 Now these are the areas the Israelites received as an inheritance in the land of Canaan, which Eleazar the priest, Joshua son of Nun and the heads of the tribal clans of Israel allotted to them. 2Their inheritances were assigned by lot to the nine and a half tribes, as the LORD had commanded through Moses. 3Moses had granted the two and a half tribes their inheritance east of the Jordan but had not granted the Levites an inheritance among the rest, 4for Joseph's descendants had become two tribes—Manasseh and Ephraim. The Levites received no share of the land but only towns to live in, with pasturelands for their flocks and herds. 5So the Israelites divided the land, just as the LORD had commanded Moses.

Allotment for Caleb

6Now the people of Judah approached Joshua at Gilgal, and Caleb son of Jephunneh the Kenizzite said to him, "You know what the LORD said to Moses the man of God at Kadesh Barnea about you and me. 7I was forty years old when Moses the servant of the LORD sent me from Kadesh Barnea to explore the land. And I brought him back a report according to my convictions, 8but my fellow Israelites who went up with me made the hearts of the people melt in fear. I, however, followed the LORD my God wholeheartedly. 9So on that day Moses swore to me, 'The land on which your feet have walked will be your inheritance and that of your children forever, because you have followed the LORD my God wholeheartedly.'[a]

10"Now then, just as the LORD promised, he has kept me alive for forty-five years since the time he said this to Moses, while Israel moved about in the wilderness. So here I am today, eighty-five years old! 11I am still as strong today as the day Moses sent me out; I'm just as vigorous to go out to battle now as I was then. 12Now give me this hill country that the LORD promised me that day. You yourself heard then that the Anakites were there and their cities were large and fortified, but, the LORD helping me, I will drive them out just as he said."

13Then Joshua blessed Caleb son of Jephunneh and gave him Hebron as his inheritance. 14So Hebron has belonged to Caleb son of Jephunneh the Kenizzite ever since, because he followed the LORD, the God of Israel, wholeheartedly. 15(Hebron used to be called Kiriath Arba after Arba, who was the greatest man among the Anakites.)

Then the land had rest from war.

Allotment for Judah

15:15-19pp — Jdg 1:11-15

15 The allotment for the tribe of Judah, according to its clans, extended down to the territory of Edom, to the Desert of Zin in the extreme south.

a 9 Deut. 1:36

13:30 Mahanaim The allotment in this verse borders Gad, since Mahanaim is also placed in Gad's territory (see Jos 13:26). There is no definite northern boundary point given, but the reference to Mount Hermon in v. 11 likely indicates the northern extent of the territory. Manasseh's allotment includes all of Bashan, formerly the Amorite kingdom of Og (Nu 32; Dt 3).

13:31 the descendants of Makir son of Manasseh The tribe is sometimes associated with Makir, a son of Manasseh and grandson of Joseph (Ge 50:23).

14:1–5 Joshua 14–19 describes the tribal allotments west of the Jordan: Canaan proper. This chapter discusses Caleb's inheritance.

14:1 Joshua son of Nun See note on 1:1.

14:2 by lot The Israelites cast lots to determine the inheritance to show the people that God himself was behind the allotment decisions (see 18:6,8,10; compare Pr 16:33). Casting lots was a common form of divination used to discern the will of gods or spirits. Other cultures were known to throw small stones or clay markers. Elsewhere in Joshua and the Bible, lots are described as being "cast" (Jos 18:6,8), so this parallel may be appropriate.

14:4 Joseph's descendants had become two tribes There were actually 13 tribes because Joseph's was split into two; however, the Levites did not receive land, so the text still refers to 12 tribes.

14:6 Gilgal The Israelite headquarters for the conquest (4:20; 5:9–10). Since Caleb, the focus of the rest of the chapter, comes from Judah, the discussion of the allotment of Judah's inheritance begins with this verse.

14:8 I, however, followed the LORD my God wholeheartedly Caleb and Joshua were the only two spies to express confidence that God would deliver Canaan to the Israelites (Nu 13:25–33).

14:12 give me this hill country Caleb asks for the hill and country of Judah, vowing to drive out the remaining Anakite (Jos 14:6–12).

14:15 Arba The father of Anak (15:13). **Anakites** One of Canaan's giant clans, which Caleb had encountered while a spy (Dt 2:10–11,20–21; 3:10–13; compare Nu 13:25–33).

15:1–63 Discussion of Judah's inheritance began in 14:6. Judah emerged as the most important tribe, having received a special blessing from his father, Jacob, many

²Their southern boundary started from the bay at the southern end of the Dead Sea, ³crossed south of Scorpion Pass, continued on to Zin and went over to the south of Kadesh Barnea. Then it ran past Hezron up to Addar and curved around to Karka. ⁴It then passed along to Azmon and joined the Wadi of Egypt, ending at the Mediterranean Sea. This is their*a* southern boundary.

⁵The eastern boundary is the Dead Sea as far as the mouth of the Jordan.

The northern boundary started from the bay of the sea at the mouth of the Jordan, ⁶went up to Beth Hoglah and continued north of Beth Arabah to the Stone of Bohan son of Reuben. ⁷The boundary then went up to Debir from the Valley of Achor and turned north to Gilgal, which faces the Pass of Adummim south of the gorge. It continued along to the waters of En Shemesh and came out at En Rogel. ⁸Then it ran up the Valley of Ben Hinnom along the southern slope of the Jebusite city (that is, Jerusalem). From there it climbed to the top of the hill west of the Hinnom Valley at the northern end of the Valley of Rephaim. ⁹From the hilltop the boundary headed toward the spring of the waters of Nephtoah, came out at the towns of Mount Ephron and went down toward Baalah (that is, Kiriath Jearim). ¹⁰Then it curved westward from Baalah to Mount Seir, ran along the northern slope of Mount Jearim (that is, Kesalon), continued down to Beth Shemesh and crossed to Timnah. ¹¹It went to the northern slope of Ekron, turned toward Shikkeron, passed along to Mount Baalah and reached Jabneel. The boundary ended at the sea.

¹²The western boundary is the coastline of the Mediterranean Sea.

These are the boundaries around the people of Judah by their clans.

¹³In accordance with the LORD's command to him, Joshua gave to Caleb son of Jephunneh a portion in Judah — Kiriath Arba, that is, Hebron. (Arba was the forefather of Anak.) ¹⁴From Hebron Caleb drove out the three Anakites — Sheshai, Ahiman and Talmai, the sons of Anak. ¹⁵From there he marched against the people living in Debir (formerly called Kiriath Sepher). ¹⁶And Caleb said, "I will give my daughter Aksah in marriage to the man who attacks and captures Kiriath Sepher." ¹⁷Othniel son of Kenaz, Caleb's brother, took it; so Caleb gave his daughter Aksah to him in marriage.

¹⁸One day when she came to Othniel, she urged him*b* to ask her father for a field. When she got off her donkey, Caleb asked her, "What can I do for you?"

¹⁹She replied, "Do me a special favor. Since you have given me land in the Negev, give me also springs of water." So Caleb gave her the upper and lower springs.

²⁰This is the inheritance of the tribe of Judah, according to its clans:

²¹The southernmost towns of the tribe of Judah in the Negev toward the boundary of Edom were:

a 4 Septuagint; Hebrew *your*   *b 18* Hebrew and some Septuagint manuscripts; other Septuagint manuscripts (see also note at Judges 1:14) *Othniel, he urged her*

---

years prior while the nation of Israel was still in Egypt (Ge 49:8–12). This blessing associated Judah with rulership (see Ge 49:10). Judah's inheritance (Jos 15:1–12) is geographically the largest of the tribes in Canaan proper.

15:3 continued on to Zin Judah's inheritance extended southward to the border of Edom.

15:4 Wadi of Egypt Refers to the Wadi el-Arish, not the Nile. This wadi flows from the northern Sinai Peninsula into the Mediterranean Sea.

15:6 to the Stone of Bohan The identification of this site is uncertain. "Bohan" may derive from the Hebrew word for "thumb" (*bohen*), suggesting the name may derive from the shape of a rock formation.

15:8 the Valley of Ben Hinnom The Hebrew text sometimes refers to this valley as *gei ben hinnom* ("Valley of the Son of Hinnom") and other times just as *gei hinnom* ("Valley of Hinnom"). The latter rendering became "Gehenna" in Greek (Mt 23:33). The valley encircles the Old City of Jerusalem on the south and west. See note on Jer 7:31.

15:10 Mount Seir Not the Mount Seir in Edom, since the other geographical locations mentioned in this verse are in the western region of Judah. This is the only reference to a Mount Seir in the western hills of Judah, but one of the Amarna letters (number EA 288) may refer to a Seir near Jerusalem.

15:14 Sheshai, Ahiman and Talmai These three Anakites—who are part of a clan of giant people—were alive 40 years earlier when Caleb spied out the land (compare note on 14:15).

15:15–19 These verses describe sites in the hill country south of Hebron.

15:15 people living in Debir Caleb gets credit for attacking Debir; however, v. 17 indicates that Debir was captured by Othniel, Caleb's kinsman. In 10:36–39, the capture of Debir is credited to Joshua. These varying accounts likely describe separate engagements since the narrator stated that the conquest took a long time (see 13:1–6). Since Othniel and Caleb were related, it is also possible that Othniel's conquest within the inheritance given to Caleb accounts for the wording here.

15:17 gave his daughter Aksah to him in marriage Othniel was Caleb's nephew and a member of the Kenizzite clan.

15:20–63 These verses delineate the territory of Judah by listing 60 cities belonging to Judah according to geographical region. The list closes with the note that Jerusalem, the city of the Jebusites, remained under Canaanite control (v. 63).

Kabzeel, Eder, Jagur, ²²Kinah, Dimonah, Adadah, ²³Kedesh, Hazor, Ithnan, ²⁴Ziph, Telem, Bealoth, ²⁵Hazor Hadattah, Kerioth Hezron (that is, Hazor), ²⁶Amam, Shema, Moladah, ²⁷Hazar Gaddah, Heshmon, Beth Pelet, ²⁸Hazar Shual, Beersheba, Biziothiah, ²⁹Baalah, Iyim, Ezem, ³⁰Eltolad, Kesil, Hormah, ³¹Ziklag, Madmannah, Sansannah, ³²Lebaoth, Shilhim, Ain and Rimmon — a total of twenty-nine towns and their villages.

³³In the western foothills:

Eshtaol, Zorah, Ashnah, ³⁴Zanoah, En Gannim, Tappuah, Enam, ³⁵Jarmuth, Adullam, Sokoh, Azekah, ³⁶Shaaraim, Adithaim and Gederah (or Gederothaim)*a* — fourteen towns and their villages.

³⁷Zenan, Hadashah, Migdal Gad, ³⁸Dilean, Mizpah, Joktheel, ³⁹Lachish, Bozkath, Eglon, ⁴⁰Kabbon, Lahmas, Kitlish, ⁴¹Gederoth, Beth Dagon, Naamah and Makkedah — sixteen towns and their villages.

⁴²Libnah, Ether, Ashan, ⁴³Iphtah, Ashnah, Nezib, ⁴⁴Keilah, Akzib and Mareshah — nine towns and their villages.

⁴⁵Ekron, with its surrounding settlements and villages; ⁴⁶west of Ekron, all that were in the vicinity of Ashdod, together with their villages; ⁴⁷Ashdod, its surrounding settlements and villages; and Gaza, its settlements and villages, as far as the Wadi of Egypt and the coastline of the Mediterranean Sea.

⁴⁸In the hill country:

Shamir, Jattir, Sokoh, ⁴⁹Dannah, Kiriath Sannah (that is, Debir), ⁵⁰Anab, Eshtemoh, Anim, ⁵¹Goshen, Holon and Giloh — eleven towns and their villages.

⁵²Arab, Dumah, Eshan, ⁵³Janim, Beth Tappuah, Aphekah, ⁵⁴Humtah, Kiriath Arba (that is, Hebron) and Zior — nine towns and their villages.

⁵⁵Maon, Carmel, Ziph, Juttah, ⁵⁶Jezreel, Jokdeam, Zanoah, ⁵⁷Kain, Gibeah and Timnah — ten towns and their villages.

⁵⁸Halhul, Beth Zur, Gedor, ⁵⁹Maarath, Beth Anoth and Eltekon — six towns and their villages.*b*

⁶⁰Kiriath Baal (that is, Kiriath Jearim) and Rabbah — two towns and their villages.

⁶¹In the wilderness:

Beth Arabah, Middin, Sekakah, ⁶²Nibshan, the City of Salt and En Gedi — six towns and their villages.

⁶³Judah could not dislodge the Jebusites, who were living in Jerusalem; to this day the Jebusites live there with the people of Judah.

Allotment for Ephraim and Manasseh

16 The allotment for Joseph began at the Jordan, east of the springs of Jericho, and went up from there through the desert into the hill country of Bethel. ²It went on from Bethel (that is, Luz),*c* crossed over to the territory of the Arkites in Ataroth, ³descended westward to the territory of the Japhletites as far as the region of Lower Beth Horon and on to Gezer, ending at the Mediterranean Sea. ⁴So Manasseh and Ephraim, the descendants of Joseph, received their inheritance.

⁵This was the territory of Ephraim, according to its clans:

The boundary of their inheritance went from Ataroth Addar in the east to Upper Beth Horon ⁶and continued to the Mediterranean Sea. From Mikmethath on the north it curved eastward to Taanath Shiloh, passing by it

---

a 36 Or *Gederah and Gederothaim*　　*b* 59 The Septuagint adds another district of eleven towns, including Tekoa and Ephrathah (Bethlehem).　　*c* 2 Septuagint; Hebrew *Bethel to Luz*

15:63 the Jebusites Jebus, the city of the Jebusites, is identified with Jerusalem (see 18:28; Jdg 19:10 – 11). Judges supports this comment about Israel's failure to drive out the Jebusites (Jdg 1:21), but the failure is attributed to the tribe of Benjamin. According to Jos 18:28, Jebus was part of the territory allotted to Benjamin. However, Jdg 1:8 states that the men of Judah successfully captured the city. Jerusalem straddles the boundary of Benjamin and Judah, so that would explain how it could be identified with both tribes (see Jos 15:8; 18:16,28). David is also credited with conquering Jerusalem (2Sa 5:6 – 10). The varying reports about the conquest and allotment of Jebus may indicate that efforts on the part of the Judahites were only temporarily successful, while Benjamin suffered a complete failure.

16:1 — 17:18 Joshua 16 – 17 outlines the inheritance for the tribes of Joseph: Ephraim and Manasseh. The land allotted to these tribes was situated west of the Jordan. The Manasseh allotment was for half the tribe, as the other half received an allotment in the Transjordan

(see 13:29 – 31). The present chapter summarizes Ephraim and Manasseh's mutual southern boundary (16:1 – 4) and designates Ephraim's land (16:5 – 10). The same sort of description for Manasseh comes in the next chapter (17:1 – 13). The author seems to consider the two tribes of Joseph to be one, as they receive one allotment by the casting of one lot (16:1). The tribes complain about this process (17:14 – 18), demonstrating that they considered themselves separate entities.

16:1 The allotment The inheritances of the tribes were determined by casting lots (see 14:2). **Joseph** The descendants of Joseph through his two sons born in Egypt, Manasseh and Ephraim (see Ge 41:50 – 52).

16:2 Ataroth Not the Ataroth on Ephraim's northern boundary (Jos 16:7); that Ataroth was part of Benjamin (v. 5; 18:13).

16:3 Gezer According to v. 10, Gezer was not fully conquered at this time. Gezer only came under Israelite control when an unnamed Egyptian pharaoh gave it to Solomon as a marriage dowry for his daughter (1Ki 9:16).

to Janoah on the east. ⁷Then it went down from Janoah to Ataroth and Naarah, touched Jericho and came out at the Jordan. ⁸From Tappuah the border went west to the Kanah Ravine and ended at the Mediterranean Sea. This was the inheritance of the tribe of the Ephraimites, according to its clans. ⁹It also included all the towns and their villages that were set aside for the Ephraimites within the inheritance of the Manassites.

¹⁰They did not dislodge the Canaanites living in Gezer; to this day the Canaanites live among the people of Ephraim but are required to do forced labor.

17 This was the allotment for the tribe of Manasseh as Joseph's firstborn, that is, for Makir, Manasseh's firstborn. Makir was the ancestor of the Gileadites, who had received Gilead and Bashan because the Makirites were great soldiers. ²So this allotment was for the rest of the people of Manasseh — the clans of Abiezer, Helek, Asriel, Shechem, Hepher and Shemida. These are the other male descendants of Manasseh son of Joseph by their clans.

³Now Zelophehad son of Hepher, the son of Gilead, the son of Makir, the son of Manasseh, had no sons but only daughters, whose names were Mahlah, Noah, Hoglah, Milkah and Tirzah. ⁴They went to Eleazar the priest, Joshua son of Nun, and the leaders and said, "The LORD commanded Moses to give us an inheritance among our relatives." So Joshua gave them an inheritance along with the brothers of their father, according to LORD's command. ⁵Manasseh's share consisted of ten tracts of land besides Gilead and Bashan east of the Jordan, ⁶because the daughters of the tribe of Manasseh received an inheritance among the

sons. The land of Gilead belonged to the rest of the descendants of Manasseh.

⁷The territory of Manasseh extended from Asher to Mikmethath east of Shechem. The boundary ran southward from there to include the people living at En Tappuah. ⁸(Manasseh had the land of Tappuah, but Tappuah itself, on the boundary of Manasseh, belonged to the Ephraimites.) ⁹Then the boundary continued south to the Kanah Ravine. There were towns belonging to Ephraim lying among the towns of Manasseh, but the boundary of Manasseh was the northern side of the ravine and ended at the Mediterranean Sea. ¹⁰On the south the land belonged to Ephraim, on the north to Manasseh. The territory of Manasseh reached the Mediterranean Sea and bordered Asher on the north and Issachar on the east.

¹¹Within Issachar and Asher, Manasseh also had Beth Shan, Ibleam and the people of Dor, Endor, Taanach and Megiddo, together with their surrounding settlements (the third in the list is Naphoth[a]).

¹²Yet the Manassites were not able to occupy these towns, for the Canaanites were determined to live in that region. ¹³However, when the Israelites grew stronger, they subjected the Canaanites to forced labor but did not drive them out completely.

¹⁴The people of Joseph said to Joshua, "Why have you given us only one allotment and one portion for an inheritance? We are a numerous people, and the LORD has blessed us abundantly." ¹⁵"If you are so numerous," Joshua answered, "and if the hill country of Ephraim is too small

[a] 11 That is, Naphoth Dor

16:6–7 Most of the sites listed in Jos 16:6–7 are unknown. Taanath Shiloh and Naarah are mentioned only in these two verses.

16:10 required to do forced labor Israelites were allowed to enslave inhabitants of cities outside the promised land, but they were supposed to completely destroy those living in the land (Dt 20:10–16).

17:1 for the tribe of Manasseh Chapter 16 dealt with the allotment of Ephraim. Manasseh follows here, an order probably reflecting the position of the blessing in Ge 48. **Gilead and Bashan** Located in the Transjordan. Makir's descendants had already inherited land in the Transjordan (see Jos 13:29–31). He is noted here as inheritor of the portion in Canaan, since he was Manasseh's only son (Ge 50:23; Nu 26:29).

17:2 Abiezer The hometown of Gideon (Jdg 6:11,24,34); identified as Iezer in Nu 26:30.

17:3 had no sons but only daughters See note on Nu 27:1–11.

17:4 They went to Eleazar the priest, Joshua son of Nun The daughters approached Eleazar and Joshua because the matter had earlier been decided while Moses was in leadership (see Nu 27:1–11).

17:7–11 Manasseh's inheritance is given in what is essentially a list of boundary markers, though there are geographical gaps in it.

17:7 Shechem One of the cities of refuge (Jos 20:7) and a Levitical city (see 21:21). It would be the site of covenant renewal before Joshua dies (ch. 24).

17:11 Issachar and Asher Some towns designated to Manasseh were inside the boundaries of Issachar and Asher—likely reflecting a degree of fluidity in the borders of their territories.

17:12 the Canaanites were determined to live in that region Another example of a tribe failing to drive out the Canaanites (see 15:63; 16:10).

17:14 Why have you given us only one allotment The people of Joseph considered themselves two tribes, not one. See note on 16:1–17:18.

17:15–18 Joshua responds to the complaint by challenging Joseph's descendants to clear the forested land of the Perizzites and Rephaites. They complain that they are at a military disadvantage: The enemy has iron chariots (v. 16). Joshua is confident that they will drive out the Canaanites anyway (vv. 17–18).

for you, go up into the forest and clear land for yourselves there in the land of the Perizzites and Rephaites."

[16]The people of Joseph replied, "The hill country is not enough for us, and all the Canaanites who live in the plain have chariots fitted with iron, both those in Beth Shan and its settlements and those in the Valley of Jezreel."

[17]But Joshua said to the tribes of Joseph — to Ephraim and Manasseh — "You are numerous and very powerful. You will have not only one allotment [18]but the forested hill country as well. Clear it, and its farthest limits will be yours; though the Canaanites have chariots fitted with iron and though they are strong, you can drive them out."

Division of the Rest of the Land

18 The whole assembly of the Israelites gathered at Shiloh and set up the tent of meeting there. The country was brought under their control, [2]but there were still seven Israelite tribes who had not yet received their inheritance.

[3]So Joshua said to the Israelites: "How long will you wait before you begin to take possession of the land that the Lord, the God of your ancestors, has given you? [4]Appoint three men from each tribe. I will send them out to make a survey of the land and to write a description of it, according to the inheritance of each. Then they will return to me. [5]You are to divide the land into seven parts. Judah is to remain in its territory on the south and the tribes of Joseph in their territory on the north. [6]After you have written descriptions of the seven parts of the land, bring them here to me and I will cast lots for you in the presence of the Lord our God. [7]The Levites, however, do not get a portion among you, because the priestly service of the Lord is their inheritance. And Gad, Reuben and the half-tribe of Manasseh have already received their inheritance on the east side of the Jordan. Moses the servant of the Lord gave it to them."

[8]As the men started on their way to map out the land, Joshua instructed them, "Go and make a survey of the land and write a description of it. Then return to me, and I will cast lots for you here at Shiloh in the presence of the Lord." [9]So the men left and went through the land. They wrote its description on a scroll, town by town, in seven parts, and returned to Joshua in the camp at Shiloh. [10]Joshua then cast lots for them in Shiloh in the presence of the Lord, and there he distributed the land to the Israelites according to their tribal divisions.

Allotment for Benjamin

[11]The first lot came up for the tribe of Benjamin according to its clans. Their allotted territory lay between the tribes of Judah and Joseph:

[12]On the north side their boundary began at the Jordan, passed the northern slope of Jericho and headed west into the hill country, coming out at the wilderness of Beth Aven. [13]From there it crossed to the south slope of Luz (that is, Bethel) and went down to Ataroth Addar on the hill south of Lower Beth Horon.

[14]From the hill facing Beth Horon on the south the boundary turned south along the western side and came out at Kiriath Baal (that is, Kiriath Jearim), a town of the people of Judah. This was the western side.

[15]The southern side began at the outskirts of Kiriath Jearim on the west, and the boundary came out at the spring of the waters of Nephtoah. [16]The boundary went down to the foot of the hill facing the Valley of Ben Hinnom, north of the Valley of Rephaim. It continued down the Hinnom Valley along the southern slope of the Jebusite city and so to En Rogel. [17]It then curved north, went to En Shemesh, continued to Geliloth, which faces the Pass of Adummim, and ran down to the Stone of Bohan son of Reuben. [18]It continued to the northern slope of Beth Arabah[a] and on down into the Arabah. [19]It then went to the northern slope of Beth Hoglah and came out at the northern bay of the Dead Sea, at the mouth of the Jordan in the south. This was the southern boundary.

[20]The Jordan formed the boundary on the eastern side.

These were the boundaries that marked out the inheritance of the clans of Benjamin on all sides.

[21]The tribe of Benjamin, according to its clans, had the following towns:

a 18 Septuagint; Hebrew *slope facing the Arabah*

18:1–10 Chapters 18–19 describe the allotments of the tribes other than Judah, Ephraim and Manasseh, while also summarizing those earlier inheritances. Chapter 18 recounts the Israelites' meeting at Shiloh to divide the rest of the land. Once that task was completed, lots were cast to decide the distribution.

18:1 gathered at Shiloh Indicates that the Israelites' camp moved from Gilgal (e.g., 5:9; 9:6; 10:6) to Shiloh.
18:5 You are to divide the land into seven parts For the remaining tribes.

18:7 priestly service of the Lord is their inheritance The Levites do not receive an allotment of territory (see note on 13:14). Compare Nu 18:20–24; Dt 10:9.
18:14 Kiriath Baal (that is, Kiriath Jearim) This location is also identified among Judah's cities (Jos 15:60) and boundary markers (15:9).
18:17 Geliloth The sequence of locations around Jerusalem follows 15:6–8 except that Geliloth appears instead of Gilgal. "Geliloth" in Hebrew literally means "districts" (compare 13:2; Joel 3:4). The two terms are related, so the reference may be the same.

Jericho, Beth Hoglah, Emek Keziz, 22Beth Arabah, Zemaraim, Bethel, 23Avvim, Parah, Ophrah, 24Kephar Ammoni, Ophni and Geba—twelve towns and their villages.

25Gibeon, Ramah, Beeroth, 26Mizpah, Kephirah, Mozah, 27Rekem, Irpeel, Taralah, 28Zelah, Haeleph, the Jebusite city (that is, Jerusalem), Gibeah and Kiriath—fourteen towns and their villages.

This was the inheritance of Benjamin for its clans.

Allotment for Simeon

19:2-10pp — 1Ch 4:28-33

19 The second lot came out for the tribe of Simeon according to its clans. Their inheritance lay within the territory of Judah. 2It included:

Beersheba (or Sheba),*a* Moladah, 3Hazar Shual, Balah, Ezem, 4Eltolad, Bethul, Hormah, 5Ziklag, Beth Markaboth, Hazar Susah, 6Beth Lebaoth and Sharuhen—thirteen towns and their villages;

7Ain, Rimmon, Ether and Ashan—four towns and their villages— 8and all the villages around these towns as far as Baalath Beer (Ramah in the Negev).

This was the inheritance of the tribe of the Simeonites, according to its clans. 9The inheritance of the Simeonites was taken from the share of Judah, because Judah's portion was more than they needed. So the Simeonites received their inheritance within the territory of Judah.

Allotment for Zebulun

10The third lot came up for Zebulun according to its clans:

The boundary of their inheritance went as far as Sarid. 11Going west it ran to Maralah, touched Dabbesheth, and extended to the ravine near Jokneam. 12It turned east from Sarid toward the sunrise to the territory of Kisloth Tabor and went on to Daberath and up to Japhia. 13Then it continued eastward to Gath Hepher and Eth Kazin; it came out at Rimmon and turned toward Neah. 14There the boundary went around on the north to Hannathon and ended at the Valley of Iphtah El. 15Included were Kattath, Nahalal, Shimron, Idalah and Bethlehem. There were twelve towns and their villages.

16These towns and their villages were the inheritance of Zebulun, according to its clans.

Allotment for Issachar

17The fourth lot came out for Issachar according to its clans. 18Their territory included:

Jezreel, Kesulloth, Shunem, 19Hapharaim, Shion, Anaharath, 20Rabbith, Kishion, Ebez, 21Remeth, En Gannim, En Haddah and Beth Pazzez. 22The boundary touched Tabor, Shahazumah and Beth Shemesh, and ended at the Jordan. There were sixteen towns and their villages.

23These towns and their villages were the inheritance of the tribe of Issachar, according to its clans.

Allotment for Asher

24The fifth lot came out for the tribe of Asher according to its clans. 25Their territory included:

Helkath, Hali, Beten, Akshaph, 26Allammelek, Amad and Mishal. On the west the boundary touched Carmel and Shihor Libnath. 27It then turned east toward Beth Dagon, touched Zebulun and the Valley of Iphtah El, and went north to Beth Emek and Neiel, passing Kabul on the left. 28It went to

a 2 Or Beersheba, Sheba; 1 Chron. 4:28 does not have Sheba.

18:28 the Jebusite city See note on Jos 15:63.

19:1–9 In ch. 19, Simeon, Zebulun, Issachar, Asher, Naphtali and Dan receive their territorial allotments. The last three verses of the chapter include a special inheritance for Joshua as well. See note on 18:1–10.

19:1 territory of Judah Simeon was not given its own distinct inheritance. Instead, its allotment fell within Judah's territory. According to v. 9, Judah's land exceeded the needs of its population. In 15:21–42, ten cities previously allotted to Judah are given to Simeon. Jacob's prophetic curse on Simeon in Ge 49:5–7 is likely another reason Simeon lacked its own independent allotment. While Jacob also cursed Levi in the same passage, Levi redeemed itself via loyalty to Yahweh at the golden calf incident (Ex 32).

19:10–16 Zebulun is the first of the remaining small tribes to receive its inheritance. This section is essentially a standard boundary and city list. However, the information given is inconsistent. Joshua 19:15 specifies that Zebulun received twelve cities. However, only five cities are named in v. 15. Some of the names may have been omitted by scribal error in the process of copying the Biblical text.

19:13 Rimmon Likely refers to Rummaneh, located roughly ten miles northeast of Nazareth.

19:17–23 Issachar was a small tribe whose inheritance was in the region later known as Galilee. Verse 22 states that Issachar had 16 cities; however, Tabor generally refers to a mountain, not a town, leaving the list at 15 cities. Arriving at 16 cities for this list then requires either dividing Shahazumah into two place names or adding Beeroth (included in the Greek Septuagint version of this list). The existence of a village named Tabor is still possible, especially since Tabor is listed as a Levitical city in 1Ch 6:77 (though taken from the territory of Zebulun, not Issachar).

19:18 Kesulloth Probably the same as the Kisloth Tabor mentioned in Jos 19:12.

19:24–31 Unlike the preceding descriptions, Asher's inheritance is not given as a city list. Instead, small clusters of cities appear.

19:28 Greater Sidon A Phoenician city. The two major Phoenician cities of Tyre and Sidon are mentioned here

Abdon,ᵃ Rehob, Hammon and Kanah, as far as Greater Sidon. ²⁹The boundary then turned back toward Ramah and went to the fortified city of Tyre, turned toward Hosah and came out at the Mediterranean Sea in the region of Akzib, ³⁰Ummah, Aphek and Rehob. There were twenty-two towns and their villages. ³¹These towns and their villages were the inheritance of the tribe of Asher, according to its clans.

Allotment for Naphtali

³²The sixth lot came out for Naphtali according to its clans:

³³Their boundary went from Heleph and the large tree in Zaanannim, passing Adami Nekeb and Jabneel to Lakkum and ending at the Jordan. ³⁴The boundary ran west through Aznoth Tabor and came out at Hukkok. It touched Zebulun on the south, Asher on the west and the Jordanᵇ on the east. ³⁵The fortified towns were Ziddim, Zer, Hammath, Rakkath, Kinnereth, ³⁶Adamah, Ramah, Hazor, ³⁷Kedesh, Edrei, En Hazor, ³⁸Iron, Migdal El, Horem, Beth Anath and Beth Shemesh. There were nineteen towns and their villages. ³⁹These towns and their villages were the inheritance of the tribe of Naphtali, according to its clans.

Allotment for Dan

⁴⁰The seventh lot came out for the tribe of Dan according to its clans. ⁴¹The territory of their inheritance included:

Zorah, Eshtaol, Ir Shemesh, ⁴²Shaalabbin, Aijalon, Ithlah, ⁴³Elon, Timnah, Ekron, ⁴⁴Eltekeh, Gibbethon, Baalath, ⁴⁵Jehud, Bene Berak, Gath Rimmon, ⁴⁶Me Jarkon and Rakkon, with the area facing Joppa.

⁴⁷(When the territory of the Danites was lost to them, they went up and attacked Leshem, took it, put it to the sword and occupied it. They settled in Leshem and named it Dan after their ancestor.) ⁴⁸These towns and their villages were the inheritance of the tribe of Dan, according to its clans.

Allotment for Joshua

⁴⁹When they had finished dividing the land into its allotted portions, the Israelites gave Joshua son of Nun an inheritance among them, ⁵⁰as the LORD had commanded. They gave him the town he asked for—Timnath Serahᶜ in the hill country of Ephraim. And he built up the town and settled there.

⁵¹These are the territories that Eleazar the priest, Joshua son of Nun and the heads of the tribal clans of Israel assigned by lot at Shiloh in the presence of the LORD at the entrance to the tent of meeting. And so they finished dividing the land.

Cities of Refuge

20:1-9Ref — Nu 35:9-34; Dt 4:41-43; 19:1-14

20 Then the LORD said to Joshua: ²"Tell the Israelites to designate the cities of refuge, as I instructed you through Moses, ³so that anyone who kills a person accidentally and unintentionally may flee there and find protection from the avenger of blood. ⁴When they flee to one of these cities, they are to stand in the entrance of the city gate and state their case before the elders of that city. Then the elders are to admit the fugitive into their city and provide a place to live among them. ⁵If the avenger of blood comes

ᵃ 28 Some Hebrew manuscripts (see also 21:30); most Hebrew manuscripts Ebron   ᵇ 34 Septuagint; Hebrew west, and Judah, the Jordan,   ᶜ 50 Also known as Timnath Heres (see Judges 2:9)

---

to indicate that Asher's allotment extended to the border with Phoenicia.

19:32–39 Several cities enumerated in Naphtali's allotment (vv. 35–38) have names identical to cities elsewhere. For example, Ramah (v. 36) is a town in the allotment of Asher (v. 29); Edrei (v. 37) is also a town in the Transjordan, a city of Og (13:12); and Kedesh (v. 37) appears in the allotment of Judah (15:23).

19:33 large tree in Zaanannim Likely a sacred tree of the type known from the patriarchal narratives (e.g., Ge 12:6; 13:18) and the story of Deborah (Jdg 4:11).

19:40–48 Dan is the last tribe to receive its inheritance. Dan was unable to conquer its allotted territory described here and eventually migrated north to an entirely different region (Jdg 1:34; 18:1). The description includes note of this migration (Jos 19:47), indicating either that the verse is a later editorial note or that the book was written after this occurred. Dan was unique among the tribes of Israel in that it forsook the inheritance Yahweh gave them (compare 14:2 and note).

19:47 Leshem Judges indicates that the name of the city

Dan conquered and renamed was Laish, not Leshem, a name that appears only here (see Jdg 18:7,14,27,29). The use of Leshem here is likely a spelling error in Hebrew. Both Septuagint (ancient Greek translation) versions seem to confirm that Laish is in view here.

19:49 gave Joshua son of Nun Compare Caleb's special inheritance in Jos 14:6–15. Following God's command, the people give Joshua the city of Timnath Serah as an inheritance within the territory of Ephraim, his own tribe (vv. 49–50).

20:1—21:45 This chapter and the next describe, respectively, the six Israelite cities of refuge and the 48 Levitical cities. A city of refuge was a Levitical city designated as a place of asylum for anyone who took the life of another person by accident (Nu 35:6). Anyone guilty of unintentional homicide could flee to one of these cities for protection from relatives of the deceased seeking blood revenge (see Nu 35:9–29).

20:2 cities of refuge See Nu 35:9–34 and note.
20:4 city gate City gates functioned similarly to a civic or community center; citizens often conducted business there (see Ru 4:11; 1Ki 21:13).

in pursuit, the elders must not surrender the fugitive, because the fugitive killed their neighbor unintentionally and without malice aforethought. ⁶They are to stay in that city until they have stood trial before the assembly and until the death of the high priest who is serving at that time. Then they may go back to their own home in the town from which they fled."

⁷So they set apart Kedesh in Galilee in the hill country of Naphtali, Shechem in the hill country of Ephraim, and Kiriath Arba (that is, Hebron) in the hill country of Judah. ⁸East of the Jordan (on the other side from Jericho) they designated Bezer in the wilderness on the plateau in the tribe of Reuben, Ramoth in Gilead in the tribe of Gad, and Golan in Bashan in the tribe of Manasseh. ⁹Any of the Israelites or any foreigner residing among them who killed someone accidentally could flee to these designated cities and not be killed by the avenger of blood prior to standing trial before the assembly.

Towns for the Levites

21:4-39pp — 1Ch 6:54-80

21 Now the family heads of the Levites approached Eleazar the priest, Joshua son of Nun, and the heads of the other tribal families of Israel ²at Shiloh in Canaan and said to them, "The LORD commanded through Moses that you give us towns to live in, with pasturelands for our livestock." ³So, as the LORD had commanded, the Israelites gave the Levites the following towns and pasturelands out of their own inheritance:

⁴The first lot came out for the Kohathites, according to their clans. The Levites who were descendants of Aaron the priest were allotted thirteen towns from the tribes of Judah, Simeon and Benjamin. ⁵The rest of Kohath's descendants were allotted ten towns from the clans of the tribes of Ephraim, Dan and half of Manasseh.

⁶The descendants of Gershon were allotted thirteen towns from the clans of the tribes of Issachar, Asher, Naphtali and the half-tribe of Manasseh in Bashan.

⁷The descendants of Merari, according to their clans, received twelve towns from the tribes of Reuben, Gad and Zebulun.

⁸So the Israelites allotted to the Levites these towns and their pasturelands, as the LORD had commanded through Moses.

⁹From the tribes of Judah and Simeon they allotted the following towns by name ¹⁰(these towns were assigned to the descendants of Aaron who were from the Kohathite clans of the Levites, because the first lot fell to them):

¹¹They gave them Kiriath Arba (that is, Hebron), with its surrounding pastureland, in the hill country of Judah. (Arba was the forefather of Anak.) ¹²But the fields and villages around the city they had given to Caleb son of Jephunneh as his possession.

¹³So to the descendants of Aaron the priest they gave Hebron (a city of refuge for one accused of murder), Libnah, ¹⁴Jattir, Eshtemoa, ¹⁵Holon, Debir, ¹⁶Ain, Juttah and Beth Shemesh, together with their pasturelands — nine towns from these two tribes.

¹⁷And from the tribe of Benjamin they gave them Gibeon, Geba, ¹⁸Anathoth and Almon,

---

20:7-8 These two verses list the six cities of refuge. There were three to the west of the Jordan (Jos 20:7) and three to the east (v. 8).

20:7 Kedesh A city in Naphtali's territory in Galilee (see 12:22; 19:37). **Shechem** A city in Ephraim on the western border of Manasseh and Ephraim, in the central region of the land (see 17:2,7). **Kiriath Arba (that is, Hebron)** Located in the south (see 11:21; 14:13-15; 15:13-14).

20:8 Bezer Located in Reuben's territory, east of the Dead Sea. **in Bashan** Located east of the Sea of Kinnereth (Galilee), in Manasseh.

21:1-45 In ch. 21, the Israelites designate 48 cities from the territories of the other tribes to be Levitical cities (see Nu 35:1-8; note on Jos 20:1-21:45). Since Levi had no land allotment in Canaan (see 13:14 and note; compare 13:33; 14:3; 18:7), these cities were provided where the Levites could live and raise their livestock. The cities were apportioned by lot to the Levitical clans descended from Levi's three sons: Kohath, Gershon and Merari (Ge 46:11). The Kohathites were further subdivided into priestly and non-priestly lines according to descent from Aaron (see Jos 21:4-8). The chapter closes in vv. 43-45 with a summary statement that concludes the account of the allotment of Canaan begun in ch. 13.

21:1 Eleazar the priest See note on Nu 4:16.
21:2 through Moses See Nu 35:1-8.
21:4 descendants of Aaron Since Aaron's descendants made up the priesthood (Ex 28-29; Nu 18), their Levitical cities were in the south near Jerusalem.
21:5 Kohath's descendants Levites responsible for transporting the ark and other tabernacle furniture during the wilderness journey (see Nu 3:1,17-20; 4:15-20; 7:9; Ex 6:16-19).
21:6 descendants of Gershon Levites responsible for transporting the tabernacle's textiles, screens and coverings during the wilderness journey (Nu 3:25-26; 4:24-26).
21:7 descendants of Merari Levites who guarded the tabernacle and transported its poles and various fixtures during the journey in the wilderness (Nu 1:47-53; 3:33-37; 4:29-33).

21:9-19 This passage lists the cities allotted to the priestly branch of the Kohathites, that is, the ones descended from Aaron.

21:13 Hebron See Jos 14:6-15; note on 10:3; note on 20:7.
21:16 nine towns from these two tribes The 12 tribes (see note on 13:14) averaged four Levitical cities each. Here, however, Judah and Simeon break the pattern

together with their pasturelands — four towns.

19 The total number of towns for the priests, the descendants of Aaron, came to thirteen, together with their pasturelands.

20 The rest of the Kohathite clans of the Levites were allotted towns from the tribe of Ephraim:

21 In the hill country of Ephraim they were given Shechem (a city of refuge for one accused of murder) and Gezer, 22 Kibzaim and Beth Horon, together with their pasturelands — four towns.

23 Also from the tribe of Dan they received Eltekeh, Gibbethon, 24 Aijalon and Gath Rimmon, together with their pasturelands — four towns.

25 From half the tribe of Manasseh they received Taanach and Gath Rimmon, together with their pasturelands — two towns.

26 All these ten towns and their pasturelands were given to the rest of the Kohathite clans.

27 The Levite clans of the Gershonites were given:
from the half-tribe of Manasseh,
Golan in Bashan (a city of refuge for one accused of murder) and Be Eshterah, together with their pasturelands — two towns;
28 from the tribe of Issachar,
Kishion, Daberath, 29 Jarmuth and En Gannim, together with their pasturelands — four towns;
30 from the tribe of Asher,
Mishal, Abdon, 31 Helkath and Rehob, together with their pasturelands — four towns;
32 from the tribe of Naphtali,
Kedesh in Galilee (a city of refuge for one accused of murder), Hammoth Dor and Kartan, together with their pasturelands — three towns.

33 The total number of towns of the Gershonite clans came to thirteen, together with their pasturelands.

34 The Merarite clans (the rest of the Levites) were given:
from the tribe of Zebulun,
Jokneam, Kartah, 35 Dimnah and Nahalal, together with their pasturelands — four towns;
36 from the tribe of Reuben,
Bezer, Jahaz, 37 Kedemoth and Mephaath, together with their pasturelands — four towns;
38 from the tribe of Gad,
Ramoth in Gilead (a city of refuge for one accused of murder), Mahanaim, 39 Heshbon and Jazer, together with their pasturelands — four towns in all.

40 The total number of towns allotted to the Merarite clans, who were the rest of the Levites, came to twelve.

41 The towns of the Levites in the territory held by the Israelites were forty-eight in all, together with their pasturelands. 42 Each of these towns had pasturelands surrounding it; this was true for all these towns.

43 So the LORD gave Israel all the land he had sworn to give their ancestors, and they took possession of it and settled there. 44 The LORD gave them rest on every side, just as he had sworn to their ancestors. Not one of their enemies withstood them; the LORD gave all their enemies into their hands. 45 Not one of all the LORD's good promises to Israel failed; every one was fulfilled.

Eastern Tribes Return Home

22 Then Joshua summoned the Reubenites, the Gadites and the half-tribe of Manasseh 2 and said to them, "You have done all that Moses the servant of the LORD commanded, and you have obeyed me in everything I commanded. 3 For

---

and combine for nine. This was to make up for Naphtali, where three cities were selected (v. 32).

21:20–26 This passage lists the cities given to the Kohathites who were not of the priestly line of Aaron.

21:21 Gezer See note on 16:3.

21:23 from the tribe of Dan As with Gezer, it was not until the era of David and Solomon that this area came under Israelite control.

21:43–45 These verses conclude the account of the allotment of territory to the tribes. The passage affirms that God has fulfilled his promises by bringing his people into their land (Dt 6:10) and by giving them rest from war (Dt 12:9–10). However, while this text presents the conquest as complete and successful, other texts indicate that Israel was unable to subdue certain cities and peoples (Jos 13:13; 15:63; 16:10; 17:12–13; Jdg 1:21). The opening of the book of Judges also suggests the conquest was still going on after the death of Joshua (Jdg 1:1). The confident statements of Jos 21:43–45 could then be

understood as reflecting an ideal not immediately and fully realized by Israel. Alternately, the conquest could be viewed as a success because the nations of Canaan no longer presented any strong, united opposition as described in chs. 6–12, even though isolated areas of opposition remained.

21:43 the land he had sworn to give See Ge 12:1–3; 15:1–6,18; 28:13; 35:12; 48:21.

22:1–34 In ch. 22, the tribes whose allotment was in the Transjordan return to their territory (vv. 1–9), because the land west of the Jordan was reasonably secured. The Transjordanian tribes erect an altar on the shared border with Canaan (v. 10). The Israelites living in Canaan perceive this as a secessionist gesture and a provocation for war. The Israelites in Canaan send representatives to the tribes in the Transjordan to voice their concern (vv. 11–20). The initiative is successful after they are assured by their countrymen to the west that the altar is not for a separate religious system (vv. 21–34).

a long time now — to this very day — you have not deserted your fellow Israelites but have carried out the mission the LORD your God gave you. [4]Now that the LORD your God has given them rest as he promised, return to your homes in the land that Moses the servant of the LORD gave you on the other side of the Jordan. [5]But be very careful to keep the commandment and the law that Moses the servant of the LORD gave you: to love the LORD your God, to walk in obedience to him, to keep his commands, to hold fast to him and to serve him with all your heart and with all your soul."

[6]Then Joshua blessed them and sent them away, and they went to their homes. [7](To the half-tribe of Manasseh Moses had given land in Bashan, and to the other half of the tribe Joshua gave land on the west side of the Jordan along with their fellow Israelites.) When Joshua sent them home, he blessed them, [8]saying, "Return to your homes with your great wealth — with large herds of livestock, with silver, gold, bronze and iron, and a great quantity of clothing — and divide the plunder from your enemies with your fellow Israelites."

[9]So the Reubenites, the Gadites and the half-tribe of Manasseh left the Israelites at Shiloh in Canaan to return to Gilead, their own land, which they had acquired in accordance with the command of the LORD through Moses.

[10]When they came to Geliloth near the Jordan in the land of Canaan, the Reubenites, the Gadites and the half-tribe of Manasseh built an imposing altar there by the Jordan. [11]And when the Israelites heard that they had built the altar on the border of Canaan at Geliloth near the Jordan on the Israelite side, [12]the whole assembly of Israel gathered at Shiloh to go to war against them.

[13]So the Israelites sent Phinehas son of Eleazar, the priest, to the land of Gilead — to Reuben, Gad and the half-tribe of Manasseh. [14]With him they sent ten of the chief men, one from each of the tribes of Israel, each the head of a family division among the Israelite clans.

[15]When they went to Gilead — to Reuben, Gad and the half-tribe of Manasseh — they said to them: [16]"The whole assembly of the LORD says: 'How could you break faith with the God of Israel like this? How could you turn away from the LORD and build yourselves an altar in rebellion against him now? [17]Was not the sin of Peor enough for us? Up to this very day we have not cleansed ourselves from that sin, even though a plague fell on the community of the LORD! [18]And are you now turning away from the LORD?

"'If you rebel against the LORD today, tomorrow he will be angry with the whole community of Israel. [19]If the land you possess is defiled, come over to the LORD's land, where the LORD's tabernacle stands, and share the land with us. But do not rebel against the LORD or against us by building an altar for yourselves, other than the altar of the LORD our God. [20]When Achan son of Zerah was unfaithful in regard to the devoted things,[a] did not wrath come on the whole community of Israel? He was not the only one who died for his sin.'"

[21]Then Reuben, Gad and the half-tribe of Manasseh replied to the heads of the clans of Israel: [22]"The Mighty One, God, the LORD! The Mighty One, God, the LORD! He knows! And let Israel know! If this has been in rebellion or disobedience to the LORD, do not spare us this day. [23]If we have built our own altar to turn away from the LORD and to offer burnt offerings and grain offerings, or to sacrifice fellowship offerings on it, may the LORD himself call us to account.

[24]"No! We did it for fear that some day your descendants might say to ours, 'What do you have to do with the LORD, the God of Israel? [25]The LORD

---

[a] 20 The Hebrew term refers to the irrevocable giving over of things or persons to the LORD, often by totally destroying them.

22:3 you have not deserted your fellow Israelites The Transjordanian tribes had fulfilled the promise they had made to Moses to fight for their fellows in Canaan proper when the time came (see Nu 32:28–32).

22:5 the law that Moses the servant of the LORD gave you The reference to Moses' earlier instructions likely refers to Deuteronomy, which is presented as a sermon Moses delivered to Israel on the plains of Moab (Jos 22:4; Dt 1:1–5). Joshua's words also closely echo statements of Moses from Deuteronomy (Dt 4:29; 6:5–6; 10:12–13; 11:13).

22:8 with your fellow Israelites Refers to those tribe members who had stayed in the Transjordan while their kinsmen had gone into Canaan to fight for their fellow tribes.

22:10 built an imposing altar there by the Jordan If this region is Gilgal, they may have built an altar at or near the already existing altar there (see Jos 4:19–20; 5:9–10). See the infographic "Ancient Altars" on p. 127; see the table "Altars in the Old Testament" on p. 249.

22:12 gathered at Shiloh to go to war against them The tribes in Canaan reacted to the new altar by gathering for war (see vv. 16–20). They interpreted the construction of the altar as a sign that the tribes in Transjordan were abandoning Yahweh (v. 16).

22:18 with the whole community of Israel The congregation feared that any violation of the worship of Yahweh meant punishment for the nation (as at Baal of Peor; Nu 25:3).

22:19 building an altar for yourselves To prevent conflict, the tribes in Canaan proper urge their brothers to move into Canaan rather than violate the true worship of Yahweh.

22:21–29 The tribes in the Transjordan defend themselves against the charge of religious apostasy. They had never intended for the altar to be an alternative worship site—not even for Yahweh; rather, it was to commemorate for posterity (Jos 22:26–27) that they were members of one nation with the tribes on the other side of the Jordan.

has made the Jordan a boundary between us and you — you Reubenites and Gadites! You have no share in the LORD.' So your descendants might cause ours to stop fearing the LORD.

²⁶"That is why we said, 'Let us get ready and build an altar — but not for burnt offerings or sacrifices.' ²⁷On the contrary, it is to be a witness between us and you and the generations that follow, that we will worship the LORD at his sanctuary with our burnt offerings, sacrifices and fellowship offerings. Then in the future your descendants will not be able to say to ours, 'You have no share in the LORD.'

²⁸"And we said, 'If they ever say this to us, or to our descendants, we will answer: Look at the replica of the LORD's altar, which our ancestors built, not for burnt offerings and sacrifices, but as a witness between us and you.'

²⁹"Far be it from us to rebel against the LORD and turn away from him today by building an altar for burnt offerings, grain offerings and sacrifices, other than the altar of the LORD our God that stands before his tabernacle."

³⁰When Phinehas the priest and the leaders of the community — the heads of the clans of the Israelites — heard what Reuben, Gad and Manasseh had to say, they were pleased. ³¹And Phinehas son of Eleazar, the priest, said to Reuben, Gad and Manasseh, "Today we know that the LORD is with us, because you have not been unfaithful to the LORD in this matter. Now you have rescued the Israelites from the LORD's hand."

³²Then Phinehas son of Eleazar, the priest, and the leaders returned to Canaan from their meeting with the Reubenites and Gadites in Gilead and reported to the Israelites. ³³They were glad to hear the report and praised God. And they talked no more about going to war against them to devastate the country where the Reubenites and the Gadites lived.

³⁴And the Reubenites and the Gadites gave the altar this name: A Witness Between Us — that the LORD is God.

Joshua's Farewell to the Leaders

23 After a long time had passed and the LORD had given Israel rest from all their enemies around them, Joshua, by then a very old man, ²summoned all Israel — their elders, leaders, judges and officials — and said to them: "I am very old. ³You yourselves have seen everything the LORD your God has done to all these nations for your sake; it was the LORD your God who fought for you. ⁴Remember how I have allotted as an inheritance for your tribes all the land of the nations that remain — the nations I conquered — between the Jordan and the Mediterranean Sea in the west. ⁵The LORD your God himself will push them out for your sake. He will drive them out before you, and you will take possession of their land, as the LORD your God promised you.

⁶"Be very strong; be careful to obey all that is written in the Book of the Law of Moses, without turning aside to the right or to the left. ⁷Do not associate with these nations that remain among you; do not invoke the names of their gods or swear by them. You must not serve them or bow down to them. ⁸But you are to hold fast to the LORD your God, as you have until now.

⁹"The LORD has driven out before you great and powerful nations; to this day no one has been able to withstand you. ¹⁰One of you routs a thousand, because the LORD your God fights for you, just as he promised. ¹¹So be very careful to love the LORD your God.

¹²"But if you turn away and ally yourselves with the survivors of these nations that remain among you and if you intermarry with them and associate with them, ¹³then you may be sure that the LORD your God will no longer drive out these nations

---

22:25 your descendants The Transjordanian tribes feared that the next generation of Israelites in Canaan would think the tribes in the Transjordan were foreigners and exclude them from worship of Yahweh.

22:28 as a witness between us and you The altar at the border would be a visual reminder that the tribes on the two sides were one people.

23:1–16 Chapter 23 includes Joshua's farewell address, which resembles the final addresses given by other important figures in Israelite history (e.g., Jacob in Ge 48–49; Joseph in Ge 50:22–26; and Moses, recorded throughout the book of Deuteronomy). Joshua reminds his people of all that God has done for them, especially with respect to the conquest (Jos 23:2–11). He calls the nation to remain faithful to Yahweh and reject all other gods (vv. 12–16).

23:1 the LORD had given Israel rest See note on 21:43–45.

23:4 nations that remain Despite the note in v. 1 that the land "had rest," this verse acknowledges that the

Israelites have not completely expelled the indigenous inhabitants of Canaan.

23:5 will push them out for your sake Reflects the theme that God was the power behind the conquest (see 13:6; 23:13; compare Ex 23:30; 33:2; 34:11; Dt 11:23).

as the LORD your God promised you This promise occurs multiple times in the book of Genesis (Ge 12:1–3; 15:1–6,18; 28:13; 35:12; compare Ge 48:21).

23:7 Do not associate with these nations The forbidden mixing refers primarily to idolatry — avoiding contamination from the worship of foreign gods by non-Israelite peoples.

23:12 intermarry with them The prohibition against intermarrying with the surrounding Canaanite nations was stated explicitly in Dt 7:1–6. The rationale behind forbidding intermarriage was directly related to the temptation towards idolatry (see note on Ezr 9:1—10:44; compare 1Ki 11:1–8).

23:13 until you perish from this good land Reflects the severe curses listed in Moses' farewell sermon (Dt 28:15–68).

before you. Instead, they will become snares and traps for you, whips on your backs and thorns in your eyes, until you perish from this good land, which the Lord your God has given you.

¹⁴"Now I am about to go the way of all the earth. You know with all your heart and soul that not one of all the good promises the Lord your God gave you has failed. Every promise has been fulfilled; not one has failed. ¹⁵But just as all the good things the Lord your God has promised you have come to you, so he will bring on you all the evil things he has threatened, until the Lord your God has destroyed you from this good land he has given you. ¹⁶If you violate the covenant of the Lord your God, which he commanded you, and go and serve other gods and bow down to them, the Lord's anger will burn against you, and you will quickly perish from the good land he has given you."

The Covenant Renewed at Shechem

24 Then Joshua assembled all the tribes of Israel at Shechem. He summoned the elders, leaders, judges and officials of Israel, and they presented themselves before God.

²Joshua said to all the people, "This is what the Lord, the God of Israel, says: 'Long ago your ancestors, including Terah the father of Abraham and Nahor, lived beyond the Euphrates River and worshiped other gods. ³But I took your father Abraham from the land beyond the Euphrates and led him throughout Canaan and gave him many descendants. I gave him Isaac, ⁴and to Isaac I gave Jacob and Esau. I assigned the hill country of Seir to Esau, but Jacob and his family went down to Egypt.

⁵"'Then I sent Moses and Aaron, and I afflicted the Egyptians by what I did there, and I brought you out. ⁶When I brought your people out of Egypt, you came to the sea, and the Egyptians pursued them with chariots and horsemen[a] as far as the Red Sea.[b] ⁷But they cried to the Lord for help, and he put darkness between you and the Egyptians; he brought the sea over them and covered them. You saw with your own eyes what I did to the Egyptians. Then you lived in the wilderness for a long time.

⁸"'I brought you to the land of the Amorites who lived east of the Jordan. They fought against you, but I gave them into your hands. I destroyed them from before you, and you took possession of their land. ⁹When Balak son of Zippor, the king of Moab, prepared to fight against Israel, he sent for Balaam son of Beor to put a curse on you. ¹⁰But I would not listen to Balaam, so he blessed you again and again, and I delivered you out of his hand.

¹¹"'Then you crossed the Jordan and came to Jericho. The citizens of Jericho fought against you, as did also the Amorites, Perizzites, Canaanites, Hittites, Girgashites, Hivites and Jebusites, but I gave them into your hands. ¹²I sent the hornet ahead of you, which drove them out before you — also the two Amorite kings. You did not do it with your own sword and bow. ¹³So I gave you a land on which you did not toil and cities you did not build; and you live in them and eat from vineyards and olive groves that you did not plant.'

¹⁴"Now fear the Lord and serve him with all faithfulness. Throw away the gods your ancestors worshiped beyond the Euphrates River and in Egypt, and serve the Lord. ¹⁵But if serving the Lord seems undesirable to you, then choose for yourselves this day whom you will serve, whether the gods your ancestors served beyond the Eu-

---

[a] 6 Or charioteers   [b] 6 Or the Sea of Reeds

23:15 destroyed you from this good land The context for these curses is the potential transgression of the covenant mentioned in Jos 23:16.

24:1–28 Joshua addresses the people, citing key events from their past. Following his address, the Israelites perform a ceremony at Shechem to renew their covenant with Yahweh—committing themselves to worship him only and follow his laws. See the table "Covenants in the Old Testament" on p. 469.

24:1 Shechem Joshua probably chose Shechem because of its ancient significance. In Ge 33:18–20, Jacob purchased a parcel of ground from the native Shechemites and built an altar to Yahweh there.

24:3 I took your father Abraham See Ge 12:1–7. **I gave him Isaac** See Ge 21:1–3.

24:4 to Isaac I gave Jacob and Esau See Ge 25:19–26. **I assigned the hill country of Seir to Esau** See Ge 36:8 (compare Dt 2:5). **Jacob and his family went down to Egypt** See Ge 46:1–6.

24:5 I sent Moses and Aaron See Ex 4:13–17. **I afflicted the Egyptians** See Ex 7–12.

24:6 you came to the sea See Ex 14:1–4.

24:7 between you and the Egyptians See Ex 14:5–28. **you lived in the wilderness for a long time** See Jos 5:6 (compare Nu 14:33–34; Dt 2:7).

24:8 to the land of the Amorites A reference to Sihon and Og (see Nu 21:21–35; Dt 2–3).

24:9 for Balaam son of Beor See Nu 22–24.

24:11 The removal of the people groups mentioned here is listed as a sign in the beginning of Joshua that God is with his people (Jos 3:10).

24:11 citizens of Jericho See chs. 2; 6. **I gave them into your hands** See chs. 6–12.

24:14 Now fear the Lord In light of their miraculous history (vv. 1–13), the Israelites must decide whether to recommit themselves to following Yahweh. **Throw away the gods** A reference to their remote ancestor Terah (v. 2) and any gods they had adopted while being in Egypt.

24:15 gods your ancestors served Shechem was the place at which Jacob had earlier buried the gods that his wives and concubines had brought from Haran (Ge 35:2–4). **Amorites** Here "Amorites" refers generally to the Canaanites.

phrates, or the gods of the Amorites, in whose land you are living. But as for me and my household, we will serve the LORD."

¹⁶Then the people answered, "Far be it from us to forsake the LORD to serve other gods! ¹⁷It was the LORD our God himself who brought us and our parents up out of Egypt, from that land of slavery, and performed those great signs before our eyes. He protected us on our entire journey and among all the nations through which we traveled. ¹⁸And the LORD drove out before us all the nations, including the Amorites, who lived in the land. We too will serve the LORD, because he is our God."

¹⁹Joshua said to the people, "You are not able to serve the LORD. He is a holy God; he is a jealous God. He will not forgive your rebellion and your sins. ²⁰If you forsake the LORD and serve foreign gods, he will turn and bring disaster on you and make an end of you, after he has been good to you."

²¹But the people said to Joshua, "No! We will serve the LORD."

²²Then Joshua said, "You are witnesses against yourselves that you have chosen to serve the LORD."

"Yes, we are witnesses," they replied.

²³"Now then," said Joshua, "throw away the foreign gods that are among you and yield your hearts to the LORD, the God of Israel."

²⁴And the people said to Joshua, "We will serve the LORD our God and obey him."

²⁵On that day Joshua made a covenant for the people, and there at Shechem he reaffirmed for them decrees and laws. ²⁶And Joshua recorded these things in the Book of the Law of God. Then he took a large stone and set it up there under the oak near the holy place of the LORD.

²⁷"See!" he said to all the people. "This stone will be a witness against us. It has heard all the words the LORD has said to us. It will be a witness against you if you are untrue to your God."

²⁸Then Joshua dismissed the people, each to their own inheritance.

Buried in the Promised Land

24:29-31pp — Jdg 2:6-9

²⁹After these things, Joshua son of Nun, the servant of the LORD, died at the age of a hundred and ten. ³⁰And they buried him in the land of his inheritance, at Timnath Serah*ᵃ* in the hill country of Ephraim, north of Mount Gaash.

³¹Israel served the LORD throughout the lifetime of Joshua and of the elders who outlived him and who had experienced everything the LORD had done for Israel.

³²And Joseph's bones, which the Israelites had brought up from Egypt, were buried at Shechem in the tract of land that Jacob bought for a hundred pieces of silver*ᵇ* from the sons of Hamor, the father of Shechem. This became the inheritance of Joseph's descendants.

³³And Eleazar son of Aaron died and was buried at Gibeah, which had been allotted to his son Phinehas in the hill country of Ephraim.

ᵃ 30 Also known as *Timnath Heres* (see Judges 2:9)
ᵇ 32 Hebrew *hundred kesitahs*; a kesitah was a unit of money of unknown weight and value.

24:16 Far be it from us Initiates the people's agreement to the covenant terms of remaining faithful to Yahweh.

24:17 from that land of slavery Israel should remain committed to Yahweh because he delivered them from slavery in Egypt.

24:19 he is a jealous God This description is often used in connection with absolute loyalty to Yahweh; see Ex 20:5; 34:14; Dt 4:24; 5:9; 6:15. **He will not forgive your rebellion** Indicates judgment for disloyalty according to the covenant Moses outlined in his farewell sermon (Jos 23:12–15; Dt 28:15–68).

24:26 in the Book of the Law of God The words of the ceremony were added to the body of laws already written, those in the book of Deuteronomy (Dt 31:9,19,22), which the priests kept with the ark (Dt 31:9,25–26). **he took a large stone** A stela or pillar on which the covenant would be written—a common practice in the ancient Near Eastern world.

24:29 at the age of a hundred and ten This same number is given for Joseph's lifespan (Ge 50:26), whose bones are referenced in Jos 24:32.

24:32 Joseph's bones Joseph believed that God would help his people and that someday his bones would be brought with God's people out of Egypt (Ge 50:25); Moses ensured this action was carried out (Ex 13:19). **that Jacob bought for a hundred pieces of silver from the sons of Hamor** Since Joseph was a son of Jacob, this refers to the family burial plot (see Ge 33:19).

24:33 Eleazar son of Aaron died The high priest instrumental in the tribal allotments (see Jos 14:1) also died. Phinehas is mentioned for the sake of continuity; the high priest's office was to be filled by the oldest son of the previous high priest.

JUDGES

INTRODUCTION TO JUDGES

The book of Judges is a startling narrative about the pain of a life without God and about the wonder of God's intervention. The stories in Judges begin shortly after the death of Joshua, who led the Israelites into the promised land (Jos 24:29–33; Jdg 1:1). The people no longer have a leader like Moses or Joshua, and they neglect their relationship with Yahweh. The result is a recurring cycle of sin, punishment, repentance and rescue by a "judge"—a leader sent by God.

BACKGROUND

The events in Judges take place shortly after the conquest of the promised land but before the selection of Saul as Israel's first king—roughly 1210–1051 BC. The book's narrative centers on military leaders, whom the narrative calls judges; this relates them to the leaders Moses appointed to arbitrate disputes among the Israelites, but only the judge Deborah clearly serves that role (Ex 18:21,26; compare Jdg 4:4–5). Most of the judges are warriors leading the tribes of Israel against nearby enemies, including Moabites, Canaanites, Ammonites and Philistines.

The period of the judges is marked by violence and moral decline; the end of the book attributes this to an absence of centralized leadership resulting in a lack of accountability and unity (e.g., 17:6; 21:25). Judges opens by referring back to the book of Joshua (1:1). In this way, it functions to bring clarity to the end of Joshua: Although the Israelites had settled in Canaan (Jos 24:28), enemies still abounded (Jdg 1:27–36). In line with the viewpoint of Deuteronomy, foreign oppression

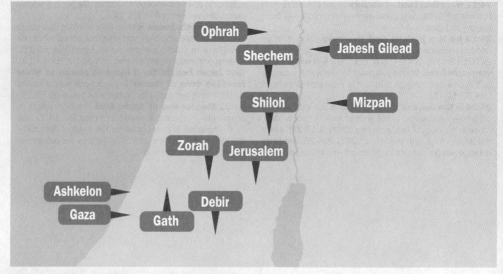

This map depicts some of the major locations mentioned in Judges.

is directly related to the sinfulness of the people (Jdg 17:6). But whenever the people repent, a judge arises to save them.

STRUCTURE

Judges opens with a description of political and religious turmoil in Israel (Jdg 1–2). After this comes a sequence of hero stories about the judges, Israel's leaders. Major judges include Ehud (3:12–30), Deborah (chs. 4–5), Gideon (chs. 6–8), Abimelek (ch. 9), Jephthah (chs. 10–11) and Samson (chs. 13–16). The same pattern occurs in each story: Israel falls into sin; God allows a foreign nation to oppress Israel as punishment; Israel repents; God sends a judge to deliver Israel from foreign oppression. The last five chapters of Judges emphasize the social and moral decline within Israel rather than conflict with outside enemies.

OUTLINE

- Incomplete occupation of the land (1:1—3:6)
- Judges deliver Israel (3:7—16:31)
- Israel's depravity under the judges (17:1—21:25)

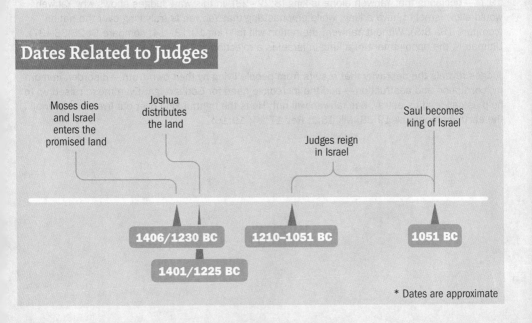

Dates Related to Judges

Moses dies and Israel enters the promised land

Joshua distributes the land

Judges reign in Israel

Saul becomes king of Israel

1406/1230 BC   **1210–1051 BC**   **1051 BC**

1401/1225 BC

* Dates are approximate

THEMES

The Israelites' failures during the period of the judges undo many of Joshua's accomplishments. By failing to finish the conquest Joshua started, they lose much of the land he led them in occupying (ch. 1); and they break the covenant (contract) they had renewed under his leadership (ch. 2). In addition, most of their heroes do not rise to Joshua's standard of leadership (chs. 3–16). At the end of the book, these failures remain unresolved.

But kingship is not necessarily the answer. Judges shows the problem of kingship: Gideon does not allow himself to be made king because that role belongs to God alone (8:23). Yet, his son Abimelek's name means "my father is king," and Abimelek kills his 70 brothers in an attempt to claim the kingship for himself (9:5). This foray into kingship ends in disaster and profoundly demonstrates the evils of monarchy.

On the other hand, the final section of Judges (chs. 17–21) includes stories about Israel's disarray, showing the need for centralized leadership. Without a godly governance, Israel's tragic cycle—idolatry, punishment, pleas for mercy, God's appointment of a judge and the return to idolatry—would undoubtedly continue. There is a contrast here: Joshua's leadership exemplified faithfulness, but the lack of leadership in Judges results in everyone doing what is right in their own eyes (e.g., 17:6; 21:25).

Judges simultaneously endorses and critiques the need for a king in Israel (compare 18:1; 19:1)—declaring that Yahweh alone is king (8:22–23). In this way, Judges shows why Yahweh would allow Israel to have a king, while emphasizing that Yahweh is truly king over the nation (compare 1Sa 8:5). Without Yahweh, the nation will fail (Jdg 10:13–14; compare Dt 28:36–37). Ultimately, the appointment of a king in Israel is a rejection of their true king (1Sa 8).

Judges reveals the depravity that results from people living by their own truth—disorder, immorality, corruption and destruction—and the incredible need for God's reign. Even those raised up to help us can lead us astray, but Yahweh will not. He is the rightful king over our lives and over all the earth (compare Lk 19:38; Mk 15:2; Rev 17:14; 19:16).

Israel Fights the Remaining Canaanites

1:11-15pp — Jos 15:15-19

1 After the death of Joshua, the Israelites asked the LORD, "Who of us is to go up first to fight against the Canaanites?"

²The LORD answered, "Judah shall go up; I have given the land into their hands."

³The men of Judah then said to the Simeonites their fellow Israelites, "Come up with us into the territory allotted to us, to fight against the Canaanites. We in turn will go with you into yours." So the Simeonites went with them.

⁴When Judah attacked, the LORD gave the Canaanites and Perizzites into their hands, and they struck down ten thousand men at Bezek. ⁵It was there that they found Adoni-Bezek and fought against him, putting to rout the Canaanites and Perizzites. ⁶Adoni-Bezek fled, but they chased him and caught him, and cut off his thumbs and big toes.

⁷Then Adoni-Bezek said, "Seventy kings with their thumbs and big toes cut off have picked up scraps under my table. Now God has paid me back for what I did to them." They brought him to Jerusalem, and he died there.

⁸The men of Judah attacked Jerusalem also and took it. They put the city to the sword and set it on fire.

⁹After that, Judah went down to fight against the Canaanites living in the hill country, the Negev and the western foothills. ¹⁰They advanced against the Canaanites living in Hebron (formerly called Kiriath Arba) and defeated Sheshai, Ahiman and Talmai. ¹¹From there they advanced against the people living in Debir (formerly called Kiriath Sepher).

¹²And Caleb said, "I will give my daughter Aksah in marriage to the man who attacks and captures Kiriath Sepher." ¹³Othniel son of Kenaz, Caleb's younger brother, took it; so Caleb gave his daughter Aksah to him in marriage.

¹⁴One day when she came to Othniel, she urged him[a] to ask her father for a field. When she got off her donkey, Caleb asked her, "What can I do for you?"

¹⁵She replied, "Do me a special favor. Since you have given me land in the Negev, give me also springs of water." So Caleb gave her the upper and lower springs.

¹⁶The descendants of Moses' father-in-law, the Kenite, went up from the City of Palms[b] with the

---

[a] 14 Hebrew; Septuagint and Vulgate *Othniel, he urged her*
[b] 16 That is, Jericho

1:1–36 The events in the book of Judges take place roughly 1210–1051 BC and center on key military leaders; it is unclear whether the narrative is organized chronologically or thematically. The opening chapter summarizes the conquests described in Joshua but presents a different outlook on the conquest. The writer of Judges acknowledges a partial failure in displacing the Canaanites (see Jdg 1:19–33). The account in ch. 1 likely presents a more realistic view of Israel's ongoing struggle to take control of the region while statements like those of Jos 21:43–45 may reflect an ideal that the tribes are still attempting to accomplish (see note on Jos 21:43–45). The book of Joshua also indicates that the conquest was incomplete (Jos 13:1,13; 15:63; 16:10; 17:13). Joshua 23:1–5 and 23:13 assert both that the task of taking Canaan was largely accomplished and that God would expel the remaining Canaanites—provided the Israelites heed Joshua's farewell admonition. See the timeline "Broad Timeline of Biblical History" on p. xxvi.

1:1 Who of us is to go up first Joshua's death has left a vacuum of leadership. The people nevertheless assume the necessity of finishing the conquest as directed by Joshua in his farewell address (Jos 23:4–5).

1:2 Judah shall go up Judah is cast as the leading tribe in the same language as God's promise to Joshua ("I have given the land into their hands"; compare Jos 24:8,11).

1:4 the Canaanites and Perizzites See note on Jos 3:10; compare Ex 3:8; Dt 7:1; 20:17; Jos 9:1. See the map "Tribal Distribution of Palestine" on p. 2253.

1:6 cut off his thumbs and big toes Maiming the king in this way ensured that he would never again be able to take up arms in battle or effectively fight as a foot soldier.

1:8 set it on fire There are differing Biblical reports of the conquest of Jerusalem. In Jdg 1:5–8, Judah defeats Adoni Bezek and then moves immediately toward Jerusalem (which is occupied by the Jebusites; v. 21; Jos 15:8) and destroys it. According to Jos 15:63, Judah was unable to drive the Jebusites out of the city, and it appears to have remained in Canaanite hands until King David conquered it 2Sa 5:6–9. Furthermore, Jerusalem was part of Benjamin's allotted territory (Jos 18:16,28). While Judah is depicted conquering Jerusalem here, Benjamin is said to have failed to conquer the city later in this chapter (Jdg 1:21). It is likely that the different reports reflect various attempts to conquer the city over the years. Judah's victory here was only temporary.

1:10 formerly called Kiriath Arba Verses 5–10 parallel Jos 15:13–14, where Caleb defeats the three Anakites named here. **Sheshai, Ahiman and Talmai** Descendants of Anak, head of the Anakites giant clan that had often troubled the Israelites (see Nu 13:29–33; compare Jos 15:13–14; Dt 2:10–11,20–21).

1:13 Othniel son of Kenaz Othniel is the first judge in the book of Judges (Jdg 3:9). **Caleb's younger brother** Likely meant in the sense of a brother in arms or a distant relative. Othniel and Caleb are likely distantly related, since the name Kenaz is affiliated with them both (Jos 14:14). Caleb is specifically identified as a son of Jephunneh or Hezron, not Kenaz, and Othniel is never listed as a son of Jephunneh or Hezron (Nu 32:12; 1Ch 2:9,18; compare 1Ch 4:13; Jos 15:17). **took it** See Jdg 1:10–12; compare Jos 15:13–14. **gave his daughter** In Biblical times, fathers often gave their daughters in the manner described here. Aksah would likely have been honored to be awarded to a war hero such as Othniel, though she was not pleased with the land gifted to Othniel by her father (see note on v. 15).

1:15 the upper and lower springs Aksah apparently feels her father's gift of land, which lacks a water supply, is inadequate and undesirable.

people of Judah to live among the inhabitants of the Desert of Judah in the Negev near Arad.

¹⁷Then the men of Judah went with the Simeonites their fellow Israelites and attacked the Canaanites living in Zephath, and they totally destroyed*a* the city. Therefore it was called Hormah.*b* ¹⁸Judah also took*c* Gaza, Ashkelon and Ekron — each city with its territory.

¹⁹The Lord was with the men of Judah. They took possession of the hill country, but they were unable to drive the people from the plains, because they had chariots fitted with iron. ²⁰As Moses had promised, Hebron was given to Caleb, who drove from it the three sons of Anak. ²¹The Benjamites, however, did not drive out the Jebusites, who were living in Jerusalem; to this day the Jebusites live there with the Benjamites.

²²Now the tribes of Joseph attacked Bethel, and the Lord was with them. ²³When they sent men to spy out Bethel (formerly called Luz), ²⁴the spies saw a man coming out of the city and they said to him, "Show us how to get into the city and we will see that you are treated well." ²⁵So he showed them, and they put the city to the sword but spared the man and his whole family. ²⁶He then went to the land of the Hittites, where he built a city and called it Luz, which is its name to this day.

²⁷But Manasseh did not drive out the people of Beth Shan or Taanach or Dor or Ibleam or Megiddo and their surrounding settlements, for the Canaanites were determined to live in that land. ²⁸When Israel became strong, they pressed the Canaanites into forced labor but never drove them out completely. ²⁹Nor did Ephraim drive out the Canaanites living in Gezer, but the Canaanites continued to live

there among them. ³⁰Neither did Zebulun drive out the Canaanites living in Kitron or Nahalol, so these Canaanites lived among them, but Zebulun did subject them to forced labor. ³¹Nor did Asher drive out those living in Akko or Sidon or Ahlab or Akzib or Helbah or Aphek or Rehob. ³²The Asherites lived among the Canaanite inhabitants of the land because they did not drive them out. ³³Neither did Naphtali drive out those living in Beth Shemesh or Beth Anath; but the Naphtalites too lived among the Canaanite inhabitants of the land, and those living in Beth Shemesh and Beth Anath became forced laborers for them. ³⁴The Amorites confined the Danites to the hill country, not allowing them to come down into the plain. ³⁵And the Amorites were determined also to hold out in Mount Heres, Aijalon and Shaalbim, but when the power of the tribes of Joseph increased, they too were pressed into forced labor. ³⁶The boundary of the Amorites was from Scorpion Pass to Sela and beyond.

The Angel of the Lord at Bokim

2 The angel of the Lord went up from Gilgal to Bokim and said, "I brought you up out of Egypt and led you into the land I swore to give to your ancestors. I said, 'I will never break my covenant with you, ²and you shall not make a covenant with the people of this land, but you shall break down their altars.' Yet you have disobeyed me. Why have you done this? ³And I have also said,

---

a 17 The Hebrew term refers to the irrevocable giving over of things or persons to the Lord, often by totally destroying them. *b* 17 *Hormah* means *destruction.*   *c* 18 Hebrew; Septuagint *Judah did not take*

1:17 it was called Hormah This verse recalls an earlier incident recorded in Nu 21:1–3, where Arad (Jdg 1:16) was destroyed and the place was renamed "Hormah" (*chormah*); it obtained this name because it was put under the principle called (in Hebrew) *cherem* (see note on Jos 6:17).

1:19 they had chariots fitted with iron The cities conquered in Jdg 1:18 are on the low-lying plain, where the Canaanite chariots forced the Israelites into the hills. The Israelites, however, may have taken only the areas immediately surrounding these cities, in the hill country, where chariots were basically useless.

1:21 to this day the Jebusites live there See v. 8 and note; compare Jos 15:63 and note.

1:25 they put the city to the sword This success does not appear in Joshua. Bethel and Ai were allies, with Bethel apparently donating a military force to Ai's defense (Jos 8:17). The two were also close geographically (Jos 8:9,12).

1:26 the land of the Hittites The Hittite Empire was in Anatolia (now Turkey), but the designated land of the Hittites also referred to Syria, which was under Hittite control (see Jos 1:4 and note).

1:27–36 Judges 1:27–36 catalogs unconquered territory, foreshadowing that Israel has broken the covenant with Yahweh (see 2:1–3; compare Jos 24). See the map "Tribal Distribution of Palestine" on p. 2253.

1:28 Israel became strong Manasseh's failure (Jdg 1:27) is attributed to the nation. **into forced labor** Forced labor was acceptable only for inhabitants of cities outside the promised land (Dt 20:10–16).

1:29 the Canaanites living in Gezer See Jos 16:10.

1:34 come down into the plain The Danites' failure to take possession of their original inheritance anticipates their later migration (Jdg 18; Jos 19:47–48).

1:35 the Amorites Remnants of the giant clans were associated with an Amorite population (Dt 3:1–11; Am 2:9).

2:1–5 The Angel of Yahweh—a figure closely associated with earthly appearances of Yahweh himself—rebukes Israel for failing to fully drive out the Canaanites as commanded. Since they have not upheld their covenant responsibilities, Yahweh is no longer going to work to drive out the peoples, just as Moses and Joshua had warned (Nu 33:55; Jos 23:13).

2:1 the angel of the Lord See Ex 3:2 and note. See the table "Angels in the Bible" on p. 2120. **from Gilgal** As Joshua's headquarters, Gilgal may have had a symbolic status as the center of Yahweh's activity—so the angel comes from there to judge Israel (Jos 9:6; 10:6–9,15,43; 14:6).

2:3 I will not drive them out before you God's promise to complete the conquest by expelling the nations (Jos 13:6; 23:5) was contingent on Israel's faithfulness to his laws, particularly regarding the worship of Yahweh only (Jdg 2:21; compare Jos 23:15).

'I will not drive them out before you; they will become traps for you, and their gods will become snares to you.'"

⁴When the angel of the Lᴏʀᴅ had spoken these things to all the Israelites, the people wept aloud, ⁵and they called that place Bokim.ᵃ There they offered sacrifices to the Lᴏʀᴅ.

Disobedience and Defeat

2:6-9pp — Jos 24:29-31

⁶After Joshua had dismissed the Israelites, they went to take possession of the land, each to their own inheritance. ⁷The people served the Lᴏʀᴅ throughout the lifetime of Joshua and of the elders who outlived him and who had seen all the great things the Lᴏʀᴅ had done for Israel.

⁸Joshua son of Nun, the servant of the Lᴏʀᴅ, died at the age of a hundred and ten. ⁹And they buried him in the land of his inheritance, at Timnath Heresᵇ in the hill country of Ephraim, north of Mount Gaash.

¹⁰After that whole generation had been gathered to their ancestors, another generation grew up who knew neither the Lᴏʀᴅ nor what he had done for Israel. ¹¹Then the Israelites did evil in the eyes of the Lᴏʀᴅ and served the Baals. ¹²They forsook the Lᴏʀᴅ, the God of their ancestors, who had brought them out of Egypt. They followed and worshiped various gods of the peoples around them. They aroused the Lᴏʀᴅ's anger ¹³because they forsook him and served Baal and the Ashtoreths. ¹⁴In his anger against Israel the Lᴏʀᴅ gave them into the hands of raiders who plundered them. He sold them into the hands of their enemies all around, whom they were no longer able to resist. ¹⁵Whenever Israel went out to fight, the hand of the Lᴏʀᴅ was against them to defeat them, just as he had sworn to them. They were in great distress.

¹⁶Then the Lᴏʀᴅ raised up judges,ᶜ who saved them out of the hands of these raiders. ¹⁷Yet they would not listen to their judges but prostituted themselves to other gods and worshiped them. They quickly turned from the ways of their ancestors, who had been obedient to the Lᴏʀᴅ's commands. ¹⁸Whenever the Lᴏʀᴅ raised up a judge for them, he was with the judge and saved them out of the hands of their enemies as long as the judge lived; for the Lᴏʀᴅ relented because of their groaning under those who oppressed and afflicted them. ¹⁹But when the judge died, the people returned to ways even more corrupt than those of their ancestors, following other gods and serving and worshiping them. They refused to give up their evil practices and stubborn ways.

²⁰Therefore the Lᴏʀᴅ was very angry with Israel and said, "Because this nation has violated the covenant I ordained for their ancestors and has not listened to me, ²¹I will no longer drive out before them any of the nations Joshua left when he died. ²²I will use them to test Israel and see whether they will keep the way of the Lᴏʀᴅ and walk in it as their ancestors did." ²³The Lᴏʀᴅ had allowed those nations to remain; he did not drive them out at once by giving them into the hands of Joshua.

3 These are the nations the Lᴏʀᴅ left to test all those Israelites who had not experienced any of the wars in Canaan ²(he did this only to

---

ᵃ *5 Bokim* means *weepers.*   ᵇ *9* Also known as *Timnath Serah* (see Joshua 19:50 and 24:30)   ᶜ *16* Or *leaders;* similarly in verses 17-19

2:6–10 The book of Joshua ends with Joshua's death. Here, his death is reported to transition to the leadership of the judges in Israel.

2:7 the elders Israel served God under Joshua's leadership and under the leadership of those who had lived to see Yahweh's work on their behalf in bringing them into the land (Jos 24:31).

2:9 they buried him See note on Jdg 2:6–10; Jos 24:29–30.

2:10 that whole generation Not the generation of Joshua directly since only Joshua and Caleb survived to enter Canaan out of the first generation of Israelites who had escaped Egypt (Nu 14:26–35). The generation referred to here is likely the next generation who had undertaken the conquest (Nu 14:31).

2:11–15 Judges 2:11 marks a transition from Israel's failure in the more distant past (following the death of Joshua) to the fallout of that failure in the more recent past. Verses 11–19 describe a cycle that repeats itself over the next several centuries of Israelite history: spiritual apostasy; judgment and suffering; calling out to Yahweh for forgiveness and deliverance; and the appearance of a leader (or judge) to deliver Israel from oppression.

2:11 did evil The Israelites disobeyed God's covenant, to which they had sworn allegiance (Jos 24:16–18,24).

2:13 served Baal and the Ashtoreths Indicates that Israel began worshiping Canaanite gods, likely with multiple idols at multiple worship sites. Baal was the Canaanite storm god. Astarte was a Canaanite goddess. See the table "Pagan Deities of the Old Testament" on p. 1287.

2:16 judges The Hebrew word used here and throughout the book, *shophetim*, does not necessarily designate arbiters of law. The judges are mainly military leaders. Only Deborah is described as sitting in judgment of the people's legal cases (4:4–5; compare Moses' role in Ex 18:13–16).

2:22–23 Judges 2:22–23 provides a theological explanation for Israel's failure. If the conquest had been incomplete, it was because God had chosen not to immediately annihilate the nations to test his people. Israel, however, quickly failed the test.

2:22 to test Israel The people are tested in whether they will stay true to the Law Yahweh had provided, despite foreign influence, and whether they would depend upon Yahweh for their salvation. The people are also supposed to remove the remaining people groups from the promised land (compare note on Jos 6:16).

3:2 to teach warfare This skill would help secure

teach warfare to the descendants of the Israelites who had not had previous battle experience): ³the five rulers of the Philistines, all the Canaanites, the Sidonians, and the Hivites living in the Lebanon mountains from Mount Baal Hermon to Lebo Hamath. ⁴They were left to test the Israelites to see whether they would obey the LORD's commands, which he had given their ancestors through Moses.

⁵The Israelites lived among the Canaanites, Hittites, Amorites, Perizzites, Hivites and Jebusites. ⁶They took their daughters in marriage and gave their own daughters to their sons, and served their gods.

Othniel

⁷The Israelites did evil in the eyes of the LORD; they forgot the LORD their God and served the Baals and the Asherahs. ⁸The anger of the LORD burned against Israel so that he sold them into the hands of Cushan-Rishathaim king of Aram Naharaim,ᵃ to whom the Israelites were subject for eight years. ⁹But when they cried out to the LORD, he raised up for them a deliverer, Othniel son of Kenaz, Caleb's younger brother, who saved them. ¹⁰The Spirit of the LORD came on him, so that he became Israel's judgeᵇ and went to war. The LORD gave Cushan-Rishathaim king of Aram into

the hands of Othniel, who overpowered him. ¹¹So the land had peace for forty years, until Othniel son of Kenaz died.

Ehud

¹²Again the Israelites did evil in the eyes of the LORD, and because they did this evil the LORD gave Eglon king of Moab power over Israel. ¹³Getting the Ammonites and Amalekites to join him, Eglon came and attacked Israel, and they took possession of the City of Palms.ᶜ ¹⁴The Israelites were subject to Eglon king of Moab for eighteen years.

¹⁵Again the Israelites cried out to the LORD, and he gave them a deliverer — Ehud, a left-handed man, the son of Gera the Benjamite. The Israelites sent him with tribute to Eglon king of Moab. ¹⁶Now Ehud had made a double-edged sword about a cubitᵈ long, which he strapped to his right thigh under his clothing. ¹⁷He presented the tribute to Eglon king of Moab, who was a very fat man. ¹⁸After Ehud had presented the tribute, he sent on their way those who had carried it. ¹⁹But on reaching the stone images near Gilgal he himself went back to Eglon and said, "Your Majesty, I have a secret message for you."

ᵃ 8 That is, Northwest Mesopotamia   ᵇ 10 Or leader
ᶜ 13 That is, Jericho   ᵈ 16 That is, about 18 inches or about 45 centimeters

---

Israel's nationhood, though military power was never a substitute for trust in Yahweh (see Dt 17:16).
3:3 five rulers of the Philistines The leaders of the five Philistine cities along the coast (see Jos 13:3 and note).
the Hivites The Gibeonites, the people who deceived Joshua and the rest of Israel into making a treaty with them, were Hivites (Jos 9).
3:4 left to test the Israelites See note on 2:22.
3:5 the Canaanites, Hittites, Amorites, Perizzites, Hivites and Jebusites The six nations listed here were the native peoples that the Israelites were to completely destroy (Ex 3:8; 23:23; Dt 7:1–2). Israel was not to live among them as described here.
3:6 served their gods Intermarriage with the neighboring nations was specifically forbidden to prevent this kind of behavior (see note on Jos 23:12; compare Ex 34:16; Dt 7:3).
3:7–11 This narrative begins the cycle of apostasy, judgment, repentance and deliverance that will repeat throughout the book (see note on Jdg 2:11–15). This cycle, summarized in 2:11–23, provides the template for the story of every judge: Israel turns from God, God allows them to be oppressed, Israel calls out to God for help, God raises up a deliverer, Israel is delivered, the judge dies and Israel turns from God again. See the table "Judges and Their Rule" on p. 364.
3:7 Baals See note on 2:13. **the Asherahs** Refers to idols or objects devoted to the goddess Asherah. See Ex 34:13 and note.
3:8 Cushan-Rishathaim king of Aram Naharaim This king probably comes from a region east of the Euphrates. He is not otherwise known from records of Syria or Mesopotamia.

3:9 a deliverer The Hebrew term used here (moshia'), often translated as "deliverer," is not the word for "judge" (shophet). The related Hebrew verb yasha' appears in Jdg 2:16 describing what the judges did.
3:10 The Spirit of the LORD came on him In the OT, the Spirit comes upon people to enable them to perform divinely appointed tasks.
3:12–30 The cycle of the book of Judges continues: The previous judge dies and the people turn away again (see note on vv. 7–11). God then raises up Ehud to deliver the people from Moab. See the table "Judges and Their Rule" on p. 364.
3:12 Eglon king of Moab The list in vv. 3–6 does not mention the Moabites as one of the enemy peoples that should have been expelled from Canaan. Moab's territory was in the Transjordan, and Israel had problems with them during their journey to Canaan (see Nu 22–25). Eglon appears to have led a coalition that included the Ammonites and Amalekites.
3:13 they took possession of the City of Palms Perhaps a reference to Jericho (Dt 34:3).
3:15 left-handed man The name "Benjamin" means "son of the right hand" in Hebrew. The narrative ironically notes Ehud was left-handed, but this detail is crucial to the success of his plan to deliver Israel from Moab. **the son of Gera the Benjamite** The fact that a Benjamite acts as savior is significant since deliverance at the hands of a Benjamite dramatically reverses the portrayal of Benjamin and Judah (compare Jdg 1:8,21; compare chs. 19–21).
3:16 about a cubit long A cubit was the length of a man's arm from elbow to fingertips, roughly 18 inches on average. **strapped to his right thigh under his clothing**

The king said to his attendants, "Leave us!" And they all left.

²⁰Ehud then approached him while he was sitting alone in the upper room of his palace*ᵃ* and said, "I have a message from God for you." As the king rose from his seat, ²¹Ehud reached with his left hand, drew the sword from his right thigh and plunged it into the king's belly. ²²Even the handle sank in after the blade, and his bowels discharged. Ehud did not pull the sword out, and the fat closed in over it. ²³Then Ehud went out to the porch*ᵇ*; he shut the doors of the upper room behind him and locked them.

²⁴After he had gone, the servants came and found the doors of the upper room locked. They said, "He must be relieving himself in the inner room of the palace." ²⁵They waited to the point of embarrassment, but when he did not open the doors of the room, they took a key and unlocked them. There they saw their lord fallen to the floor, dead.

²⁶While they waited, Ehud got away. He passed by the stone images and escaped to Seirah. ²⁷When he arrived there, he blew a trumpet in the hill country of Ephraim, and the Israelites went down with him from the hills, with him leading them.

²⁸"Follow me," he ordered, "for the LORD has given Moab, your enemy, into your hands." So they followed him down and took possession of the fords of the Jordan that led to Moab; they al-lowed no one to cross over. ²⁹At that time they struck down about ten thousand Moabites, all vigorous and strong; not one escaped. ³⁰That day Moab was made subject to Israel, and the land had peace for eighty years.

Shamgar

³¹After Ehud came Shamgar son of Anath, who struck down six hundred Philistines with an ox-goad. He too saved Israel.

Deborah

4 Again the Israelites did evil in the eyes of the LORD, now that Ehud was dead. ²So the LORD sold them into the hands of Jabin king of Canaan, who reigned in Hazor. Sisera, the commander of his army, was based in Harosheth Haggoyim. ³Because he had nine hundred chariots fitted with iron and had cruelly oppressed the Israelites for twenty years, they cried to the LORD for help.

⁴Now Deborah, a prophet, the wife of Lappidoth, was leading*ᶜ* Israel at that time. ⁵She held court under the Palm of Deborah between Ramah and Bethel in the hill country of Ephraim, and the Israelites went up to her to have their disputes

ᵃ 20 The meaning of the Hebrew for this word is uncertain; also in verse 24.   *ᵇ 23* The meaning of the Hebrew for this word is uncertain.   *ᶜ 4* Traditionally *judging*

Since most warriors were right-handed, they wore such weapons on their left thigh, reaching across their bodies to draw them. Ehud would have appeared unarmed. **3:19 on reaching the stone images near Gilgal** Possibly boundary stones fashioned into idol images or with idolatrous images carved on them.

3:22 the blade The writer makes the scene more memorable in this verse by playing on the similar sounds of the Hebrew words for blade (*lahav*), fat (*helev*) and sword (*herev*).

3:24 relieving himself A common Biblical euphemism (see 1Sa 24:3). The king's private chamber would have had its own bathroom, hence the reluctance of Eglon's servants to interrupt him (Jdg 3:25).

3:28 Moab, your enemy, into your hands Ehud's daring assassination of Eglon catalyzes an Israelite rebellion against their Moabite oppressors. **the fords of the Jordan** Occupying this strategic location prevented both the Moabites' escape and Moabite assistance from the other side. See the map "Tribal Distribution of Palestine" on p. 2253.

3:31 Shamgar son of Anath Anat (or Anath) was the Canaanite goddess of war. This may mean that Shamgar was at one time a follower of Anat but now worshipped Yahweh. Since Anat was a warrior goddess, the label "son of Anath," could simply mean "warrior." Shamgar is the first of the so-called minor judges—judges whom the Biblical account gives little information (compare note on 10:1–5). **an oxgoad** The Hebrew word used here, *malmad*, refers to a wooden pointer, at times tipped with metal, that was used to control livestock; it could easily have been wielded as a javelin or spear.

4:1–24 Chapters 4 and 5 present parallel accounts of the same event: the victory of Deborah and Barak over the Canaanites.

4:2 Jabin king of Canaan, who reigned in Hazor Joshua also defeated a king named Jabin from Hazor in Jos 11:1–11. Jabin was likely a dynastic name used at Hazor, a practice known elsewhere in the ancient Near East (e.g., the multiple pharaohs of the nineteenth and twentieth Dynasties named Ramesses; the name Abimelek for two different kings in Ge 20; 26). **Sisera** The spelling of this proper name may indicate someone not of native Canaanite ancestry.

4:3 chariots fitted with iron See Jdg 1:19 and note.

4:4 Deborah, a prophet A prophet was, broadly speaking, someone who spoke for God. Other women prophets include Miriam (Ex 15:20) and Huldah (2Ki 22:14). Receiving revelation from God is not the normal role of a judge in the book of Judges. Most of the judges are only described as warriors leading the tribes of Israel into battle against their enemies. No other judge, except for Samuel (also called a prophet), dispenses revelation from God. Consequently, Deborah's role may be different than the other judges. The description of her leadership in Jdg 4:5 reflects a role more like the judges appointed by Moses in Ex 18:13–26. Moses links this function as judge to divine revelation when he says the people come to him to inquire of God (Ex 18:15) and he tells them God's instructions (Ex 18:16). The precise date of Deborah's efforts is unknown; the overall timeframe of the judges is roughly 1210–1051 BC.

4:5 under the Palm of Deborah The association between trees and divine encounters is well known in the patriarchal narratives (Ge 12:6; 13:18; 18:1; Jos 24:26).

decided. ⁶She sent for Barak son of Abinoam from Kedesh in Naphtali and said to him, "The Lord, the God of Israel, commands you: 'Go, take with you ten thousand men of Naphtali and Zebulun and lead them up to Mount Tabor. ⁷I will lead Sisera, the commander of Jabin's army, with his chariots and his troops to the Kishon River and give him into your hands.'"

⁸Barak said to her, "If you go with me, I will go; but if you don't go with me, I won't go."

⁹"Certainly I will go with you," said Deborah. "But because of the course you are taking, the honor will not be yours, for the Lord will deliver Sisera into the hands of a woman." So Deborah went with Barak to Kedesh. ¹⁰There Barak summoned Zebulun and Naphtali, and ten thousand men went up under his command. Deborah also went up with him.

¹¹Now Heber the Kenite had left the other Kenites, the descendants of Hobab, Moses'

4:6 Mount Tabor At 1,300 feet high, Mount Tabor was an unmistakable meeting place. The mountain marked the boundary between Naphtali and Zebulun.

4:8 I won't go Barak's hesitancy is not necessarily a mark of cowardice, but it may reflect a lack of faith. He feels Deborah's presence would ensure Yahweh's presence.

4:9 into the hands of a woman This verse seems to indicate that Deborah is referring to herself, but the climax of the story demonstrates otherwise (Jdg 4:18–21).

4:10 Deborah also went up with him The Israelites recognized Deborah as Yahweh's oracle, and her presence with Barak would have given confidence to the troops and certified Barak's leadership as deliverer.

4:11 Heber the Kenite This sets up the narrative of the downfall of Sisera, since it is Heber's wife, Jael, who will

---

Judges and Their Rule

JUDGE	OPPRESSOR	YEARS OF OPPRESSION/REST*	REFERENCE
Othniel	Cushan-Rishathaim, king of Mesopotamia (also called Aram Naharaim)	8 years oppression/40 years rest	Jdg 3:7 – 11
Ehud	Eglon, king of Moab	18 years oppression/80 years rest	Jdg 3:12 – 30
Shamgar	Philistines	–	Jdg 3:31
Deborah	Jabin, king of Canaan	20 years oppression/40 years rest	Jdg 4:1 – 5:31
Gideon	Midianites	7 years oppression/ 40 years rest	Jdg 6:1 – 8:28
Tola	Abimelek	3 years oppression/23 years rest	Jdg 10:1 – 2
Jair	–	22 years rest	Jdg 10:3 – 5
Jephthah	Philistines, Ammonites	18 years oppression/6 years rest	Jdg 10:7 – 12:7
Ibzan	–	7 years rest	Jdg 12:8 – 10
Elon	–	10 years rest	Jdg 12:11 – 12
Abdon	–	8 years rest	Jdg 12:13 – 15
Samson	Philistines	40 years oppression/20 years rest	Jdg 13:1 – 16:31
Eli	–	40 years rest	1Sa 4:18
Samuel	–	–	1Sa 7:15 – 17

*"Years rest" includes the entire amount of time that a judge served, though the phrase "and the land rested" only occurs with Othniel, Ehud, Deborah and Gideon.

brother-in-law,^{a} and pitched his tent by the great tree in Zaanannim near Kedesh.

^{12}When they told Sisera that Barak son of Abinoam had gone up to Mount Tabor, ^{13}Sisera summoned from Harosheth Haggoyim to the Kishon River all his men and his nine hundred chariots fitted with iron.

^{14}Then Deborah said to Barak, "Go! This is the day the LORD has given Sisera into your hands. Has not the LORD gone ahead of you?" So Barak went down Mount Tabor, with ten thousand men following him. ^{15}At Barak's advance, the LORD routed Sisera and all his chariots and army by the sword, and Sisera got down from his chariot and fled on foot.

^{16}Barak pursued the chariots and army as far as Harosheth Haggoyim, and all Sisera's troops fell by the sword; not a man was left. ^{17}Sisera, meanwhile, fled on foot to the tent of Jael, the wife of Heber the Kenite, because there was an alliance between Jabin king of Hazor and the family of Heber the Kenite.

^{18}Jael went out to meet Sisera and said to him, "Come, my lord, come right in. Don't be afraid." So he entered her tent, and she covered him with a blanket.

^{19}"I'm thirsty," he said. "Please give me some water." She opened a skin of milk, gave him a drink, and covered him up.

^{20}"Stand in the doorway of the tent," he told her. "If someone comes by and asks you, 'Is anyone in there?' say 'No.'"

^{21}But Jael, Heber's wife, picked up a tent peg and a hammer and went quietly to him while he lay fast asleep, exhausted. She drove the peg through his temple into the ground, and he died.

^{22}Just then Barak came by in pursuit of Sisera, and Jael went out to meet him. "Come," she said, "I will show you the man you're looking for." So he went in with her, and there lay Sisera with the tent peg through his temple — dead.

^{23}On that day God subdued Jabin king of Canaan before the Israelites. ^{24}And the hand of the Israelites pressed harder and harder against Jabin king of Canaan until they destroyed him.

The Song of Deborah

5 On that day Deborah and Barak son of Abinoam sang this song:

^{2} "When the princes in Israel take the lead,
　when the people willingly offer
　　themselves —
　praise the LORD!

^{3} "Hear this, you kings! Listen, you rulers!
　I, even I, will sing to^b the LORD;
　I will praise the LORD, the God of Israel,
　　in song.

^{4} "When you, LORD, went out from Seir,
　when you marched from the land of Edom,
　the earth shook, the heavens poured,
　　the clouds poured down water.
^{5} The mountains quaked before the LORD, the
　　One of Sinai,
　before the LORD, the God of Israel.

^{6} "In the days of Shamgar son of Anath,
　in the days of Jael, the highways were
　　abandoned;
　travelers took to winding paths.

^{a} 11 Or *father-in-law*　^{b} 3 Or *of*

---

kill Sisera (5:24–26). **Hobab, Moses' brother-in-law** The Hebrew text here uses the term "father-in-law of Moses" to describe Hobab, however, the same Hebrew word could be slightly modified to read "brother-in-law." This is more fitting, since according to Nu 10:29, Hobab is the son of Reuel, the father-in-law of Moses, making him Moses' brother-in-law (compare Nu 10:29 and note). Moses' father-in-law is called both by the names Jethro and Reuel (Ex 3:1; 2:18; 4:18).

4:15 fled on foot The chariots proved useless along the banks of the Kishon (Jdg 4:12; compare 5:19–21).
4:17 Jael Heber's wife, Jael, is instrumental in the rest of the story. **there was an alliance between** This formal alliance with the Kenites affiliated with Heber and Jabin, the king of Hazor, explains why Sisera expected protection.
4:21 while he lay fast asleep The milk and warmth of the rug (along with Sisera's undoubted exhaustion) have the desired effect, making him a prone target. This act fulfills Deborah's words that a woman would get the glory for Sisera's defeat (v. 9).
4:22 lay Sisera Jael transgressed several cultural norms — inviting a man into her tent and rendering hospitality as a pretext for murder — and violated an agreement of peace. But Jabin (king of Hazor) would fall from

power, so the Kenites would not need to fear retaliation for killing the general of Jabin's army (4:2).

5:1–31 This chapter, often called the Song of Deborah, is a poetic account of the events described in ch. 4.

5:2 the princes in Israel take the lead The Hebrew phrasing here, which refers to long hair, can be understood as idiomatic for leadership (compare Dt 32:42). The idiom alludes to the practice of leaving hair uncut to fulfill a vow (Nu 6:5,18).

5:4–5 These verses describe a theophany — or appearance of God — associated with the people's journey to Canaan: It alludes to the pillar of fire and cloud and the Angel of Yahweh (Ex 23:20–23).

5:4 from the land of Edom Seir and Edom are south of Canaan, reflecting the Israelite tradition that Yahweh had journeyed with Israel from the south via the Transjordan (Nu 33:37; Dt 2; compare Dt 33:1–2; Hab 3:3).

5:6–8 These verses describe the socially deplorable conditions of life under the oppression of Jabin, the king of Hazor whom Deborah and Barak overthrew.

5:6 travelers took to winding paths Because the land was unsafe for travel.

[7] Villagers in Israel would not fight;
  they held back until I, Deborah, arose,
  until I arose, a mother in Israel.
[8] God chose new leaders
  when war came to the city gates,
  but not a shield or spear was seen
  among forty thousand in Israel.
[9] My heart is with Israel's princes,
  with the willing volunteers among
    the people.
  Praise the LORD!

[10] "You who ride on white donkeys,
  sitting on your saddle blankets,
  and you who walk along the road,
  consider [11] the voice of the singers[a]
    at the watering places.
  They recite the victories of the LORD,
  the victories of his villagers in Israel.

  "Then the people of the LORD
    went down to the city gates.
[12] 'Wake up, wake up, Deborah!
  Wake up, wake up, break out in song!
  Arise, Barak!
  Take captive your captives, son
    of Abinoam.'

[13] "The remnant of the nobles came down;
  the people of the LORD came down to me
    against the mighty.
[14] Some came from Ephraim, whose roots were
    in Amalek;
  Benjamin was with the people who
    followed you.
  From Makir captains came down,
  from Zebulun those who bear
    a commander's[a] staff.
[15] The princes of Issachar were with Deborah;
  yes, Issachar was with Barak,
  sent under his command into the valley.

  In the districts of Reuben
    there was much searching of heart.
[16] Why did you stay among the sheep pens[b]
  to hear the whistling for the flocks?
  In the districts of Reuben
    there was much searching of heart.
[17] Gilead stayed beyond the Jordan.
  And Dan, why did he linger by the ships?
  Asher remained on the coast
    and stayed in his coves.
[18] The people of Zebulun risked their very lives;
  so did Naphtali on the terraced fields.

[19] "Kings came, they fought,
  the kings of Canaan fought.
  At Taanach, by the waters of Megiddo,
    they took no plunder of silver.
[20] From the heavens the stars fought,
  from their courses they fought against
    Sisera.
[21] The river Kishon swept them away,
  the age-old river, the river Kishon.
  March on, my soul; be strong!
[22] Then thundered the horses' hooves—
  galloping, galloping go his mighty steeds.
[23] 'Curse Meroz,' said the angel of the LORD.
  'Curse its people bitterly,
  because they did not come to help the LORD,
  to help the LORD against the mighty.'

[24] "Most blessed of women be Jael,
  the wife of Heber the Kenite,
  most blessed of tent-dwelling women.
[25] He asked for water, and she gave him milk;
  in a bowl fit for nobles she brought him
    curdled milk.
[26] Her hand reached for the tent peg,
  her right hand for the workman's hammer.

[a] 11,14 The meaning of the Hebrew for this word is uncertain.
[b] 16 Or the campfires; or the saddlebags

5:8 among forty thousand in Israel A fighting force of 40,000 fighting men is far smaller than the numbers recorded at the outset of Israel's conquest of Canaan (see Nu 1:46 and note).

5:11 the city gates A city gate in the ancient Near East consisted of a towered entrance and a large open area where people gathered.

5:13–18 This passage discusses how the tribes of Israel responded to the summons for battle. According to Jdg 4:6–10, Barak's force of 10,000 warriors came from the tribes of Zebulun and Naphtali who are praised in v. 18. This passage implies that the tribes of Benjamin, Ephraim, Manasseh and Issachar joined them while Reuben, Gad, Dan and Asher did not. The tribes of Judah and Simeon are not mentioned.

5:14 Benjamin was with the people who followed you Ephraim and Benjamin are probably mentioned first because of their association with Deborah (see 4:5).

5:17 Gilead stayed beyond the Jordan Likely an allusion to the tribe of Gad since most of the region of Gilead

in the Transjordan belonged to Gad (Jos 13:24–25). The eastern half of the tribe of Manasseh also lived in Gilead (Jos 13:31). The references to Reuben (Jdg 5:16) and Gilead together likely sum up the responses of all three tribes in the Transjordan. **why did he linger by the ships** The tribe of Dan was allotted territory along the coast far southwest of where this battle occurred. The tribe's coastal territory was just northwest of Judah, but Dan had not been able to possess its inheritance (1:34).

5:19 Kings came The plural here suggests that King Jabin of Hazor was part of a confederacy, a pattern evident earlier during the conquest where Canaanite kings formed coalitions to oppose Israel (Jos 11:1–5).

5:21 The river Kishon swept them away The flood swept away the enemy chariots. Any remaining chariots would naturally have been stuck in the mud and rendered useless.

5:24 of tent-dwelling women Refers to the Kenites, who were seminomadic.

5:25 she brought him curdled milk See Jdg 4:19.

She struck Sisera, she crushed his head,
she shattered and pierced his temple.
²⁷ At her feet he sank,
he fell; there he lay.
At her feet he sank, he fell;
where he sank, there he fell — dead.

²⁸ "Through the window peered Sisera's
mother;
behind the lattice she cried out,
'Why is his chariot so long in coming?
Why is the clatter of his chariots delayed?'
²⁹ The wisest of her ladies answer her;
indeed, she keeps saying to herself,
³⁰ 'Are they not finding and dividing the spoils:
a woman or two for each man,
colorful garments as plunder for Sisera,
colorful garments embroidered,
highly embroidered garments for my neck —
all this as plunder?'

³¹ "So may all your enemies perish, LORD!
But may all who love you be like the sun
when it rises in its strength."

Then the land had peace forty years.

Gideon

6 The Israelites did evil in the eyes of the LORD,
and for seven years he gave them into the
hands of the Midianites. ²Because the power of
Midian was so oppressive, the Israelites prepared
shelters for themselves in mountain clefts, caves
and strongholds. ³Whenever the Israelites planted
their crops, the Midianites, Amalekites and other eastern peoples invaded the country. ⁴They
camped on the land and ruined the crops all the
way to Gaza and did not spare a living thing for
Israel, neither sheep nor cattle nor donkeys. ⁵They
came up with their livestock and their tents like
swarms of locusts. It was impossible to count them
or their camels; they invaded the land to ravage it.
⁶Midian so impoverished the Israelites that they
cried out to the LORD for help.

⁷When the Israelites cried out to the LORD because of Midian, ⁸he sent them a prophet, who
said, "This is what the LORD, the God of Israel,
says: I brought you up out of Egypt, out of the
land of slavery. ⁹I rescued you from the hand of
the Egyptians. And I delivered you from the hand
of all your oppressors; I drove them out before you
and gave you their land. ¹⁰I said to you, 'I am the
LORD your God; do not worship the gods of the
Amorites, in whose land you live.' But you have
not listened to me."

¹¹The angel of the LORD came and sat down under the oak in Ophrah that belonged to Joash the
Abiezrite, where his son Gideon was threshing
wheat in a winepress to keep it from the Midianites. ¹²When the angel of the LORD appeared to
Gideon, he said, "The LORD is with you, mighty
warrior."

¹³"Pardon me, my lord," Gideon replied, "but if
the LORD is with us, why has all this happened to us?
Where are all his wonders that our ancestors told
us about when they said, 'Did not the LORD bring us

5:28 Through the window peered The poet imagines
the reaction of Sisera's mother to his death.
5:30 Are they not finding and dividing the spoils In
the poet's extended conjecture, the maidens of v. 29
suggest that Sisera has not returned yet because he
and his soldiers are dividing the spoils of their presumed
conquest of the Israelites — expensive fabrics and more
women for their beds.
5:31 So may all your enemies perish Deborah rejoices
over the fall of the wicked in language reminiscent of Nu
10:35, where the Israelites take the ark of the covenant
into battle. **the land had peace forty years** Israel
did not suffer under foreign oppression for 40 years. A
statement that the land had peace for a time is typical
in the cyclical narrative of Judges. The judge delivers the
people and all is well for a time (see note on Jdg 3:7–11).

6:1—8:35 The story of Gideon, recorded in 6:1—8:35,
is the first of several extended narratives focused on
the career of a single leader. The narratives recounting the lives of the judges vary greatly in length. Some
are terse references of a few verses (3:31; 10:1–5;
12:8–15); others are relatively brief self-contained tales
(3:7–11,12–30; 4:1–24) while others are more extensive. Gideon is the first major judge with an extended
multi-scene story. While Gideon's death is reported in
8:32–35, his story leads directly into ch. 9 — the tale
of how Gideon's son Abimelek attempts to set himself
up as a king. The other two judges featured in extended
narratives are Jephthah (10:6—12:7) and Samson

(chs. 13–16). The precise date for individual judges
is unknown, but the overall timeframe of the judges is
roughly 1210–1051 BC. See the table "Judges and
Their Rule" on p. 364.

6:1 The Israelites did evil The wording used here
situates the narrative at the beginning of the repetitive
cycle that reverberates throughout the book (see note
on 2:11–15; note on 3:7–11).
6:8 he sent them a prophet In the standard narrative
template, God raises up a judge as deliverer at this point
(compare 3:15).
6:11 The angel of the LORD This label is often inter-
changed with the name Yahweh or other names for
Yahweh (see Ge 16:7 and note; Ex 3:2 and note). Often
this figure is Yahweh in human appearance (see note
on Ge 48:16; see note on Ex 23:20). In this scene,
the figure that appears to Gideon may be identified
as both the Angel of Yahweh (vv. 11–12,22) and as
Yahweh himself (vv. 14,16,23). **Ophrah** Gideon's hometown (8:27,32; 9:5). The overall geographic setting of
Gideon's activity suggests Ophrah was located east
of Megiddo in the Jezreel Valley. A different Ophrah is
part of the territory of Benjamin (Jos 18:23). **threshing
wheat in a winepress** The oppressive conditions of
the time (see Jdg 6:2–6) are driving the Israelites to
be secretive about food production and use unusual
methods; a winepress would not be the normal place
for processing wheat. See the infographic "A Winepress
in Ancient Israel" on p. 1157.

up out of Egypt?' But now the LORD has abandoned us and given us into the hand of Midian."

¹⁴The LORD turned to him and said, "Go in the strength you have and save Israel out of Midian's hand. Am I not sending you?"

¹⁵"Pardon me, my lord," Gideon replied, "but how can I save Israel? My clan is the weakest in Manasseh, and I am the least in my family."

¹⁶The LORD answered, "I will be with you, and you will strike down all the Midianites, leaving none alive."

¹⁷Gideon replied, "If now I have found favor in your eyes, give me a sign that it is really you talking to me. ¹⁸Please do not go away until I come back and bring my offering and set it before you."

And the LORD said, "I will wait until you return."

¹⁹Gideon went inside, prepared a young goat, and from an ephah[a] of flour he made bread without yeast. Putting the meat in a basket and its broth in a pot, he brought them out and offered them to him under the oak.

²⁰The angel of God said to him, "Take the meat and the unleavened bread, place them on this rock, and pour out the broth." And Gideon did so. ²¹Then the angel of the LORD touched the meat and the unleavened bread with the tip of the staff that was in his hand. Fire flared from the rock, consuming the meat and the bread. And the angel of the LORD disappeared. ²²When Gideon realized that it was the angel of the LORD, he exclaimed, "Alas, Sovereign LORD! I have seen the angel of the LORD face to face!"

²³But the LORD said to him, "Peace! Do not be afraid. You are not going to die."

²⁴So Gideon built an altar to the LORD there and called it The LORD Is Peace. To this day it stands in Ophrah of the Abiezrites.

²⁵That same night the LORD said to him, "Take the second bull from your father's herd, the one seven years old.[b] Tear down your father's altar to Baal and cut down the Asherah pole[c] beside it. ²⁶Then build a proper kind of[d] altar to the LORD your God on the top of this height. Using the wood of the Asherah pole that you cut down, offer the second[e] bull as a burnt offering."

²⁷So Gideon took ten of his servants and did as the LORD told him. But because he was afraid of his family and the townspeople, he did it at night rather than in the daytime.

²⁸In the morning when the people of the town got up, there was Baal's altar, demolished, with the Asherah pole beside it cut down and the second bull sacrificed on the newly built altar!

²⁹They asked each other, "Who did this?"

When they carefully investigated, they were told, "Gideon son of Joash did it."

³⁰The people of the town demanded of Joash, "Bring out your son. He must die, because he has broken down Baal's altar and cut down the Asherah pole beside it."

³¹But Joash replied to the hostile crowd around him, "Are you going to plead Baal's cause? Are you trying to save him? Whoever fights for him shall be put to death by morning! If Baal really is a god, he can defend himself when someone breaks down his altar." ³²So because Gideon broke down

---

[a] 19 That is, probably about 36 pounds or about 16 kilograms
[b] 25 Or *Take a full-grown, mature bull from your father's herd*
[c] 25 That is, a wooden symbol of the goddess Asherah; also in verses 26, 28 and 30   [d] 26 Or *build with layers of stone an*
[e] 26 Or *full-grown*; also in verse 28

6:14 The LORD turned to him The text uses the divine name, Yahweh, meaning either that the text identifies the Angel of Yahweh (vv. 11–12) as Yahweh or that Yahweh now joins the discussion. The narrative may suggest the presence of two supernatural figures in vv. 21–23.

6:15 lord The traditional Hebrew text uses *adonai* ("Lord," but not the divine name, Yahweh) here. The usage of *adonai* implies that Gideon recognizes that there is something unusual about the person with whom he is talking. However, Gideon expresses surprise in v. 22 when he realizes the figure was the Angel of Yahweh.

6:16 The LORD answered Again the text reports Yahweh, not the Angel of Yahweh, speaking to Gideon (see v. 14 and note). Deliberate ambiguity in the text makes it unclear whether one or two individuals are talking to Gideon.

6:17 give me a sign Gideon may believe he is speaking to a prophet who here gives him the words of Yahweh, not Yahweh himself. This interpretation makes sense of Gideon's surprise in v. 22 at having been in the presence of the Angel of Yahweh.

6:21 And the angel of the LORD disappeared The Angel of Yahweh departs at this point, but Gideon is not left alone (see v. 23 and note).

6:22 I have seen the angel of the LORD face to face Gideon fears he will die, as ancient Israelites believed that face-to-face divine encounters could be lethal (see Ex 24:9–11; 33:20; Dt 34:1).

6:23 the LORD said to him Yahweh is still in the scene even though the angel has left. This could indicate that only the voice of Yahweh speaks to Gideon now or that Yahweh is still present after the Angel of Yahweh has left, with them both speaking to Gideon earlier as two separate figures (see Jdg 6:11 and note; note on 6:14). Considering that the text does not indicate that just a voice speaks to Gideon, it seems that Yahweh and the Angel of Yahweh appeared to Gideon as two separate figures and that their identities are intentionally blurred.

6:25 cut down the Asherah pole Gideon's own family is involved in worship of the Canaanite gods Baal and Asherah. Gideon must destroy the religious center on his father's land (compare Dt 7:5; 12:3). Worship of Asherah involved trees or wood poles which would supply the wood for Gideon to burn a sacrifice to Yahweh (Jdg 6:26). See the table "Pagan Deities of the Old Testament" on p. 1287.

6:31 he can defend himself Joash refuses to slay his son, arguing that if a deity like Baal had any real power, he ought to be able to defeat his own enemies.

6:32 Jerub-Baal Gideon's new name would always conjure the idea his father expresses: "Baal will deal with you!" (presuming Baal has any power). Every day Gideon lived would be an indictment on Baal's power. See the table "Symbolic Names of People in Hebrew" on p. 1388.

Baal's altar, they gave him the name Jerub-Baal[a] that day, saying, "Let Baal contend with him."

33Now all the Midianites, Amalekites and other eastern peoples joined forces and crossed over the Jordan and camped in the Valley of Jezreel. 34Then the Spirit of the LORD came on Gideon, and he blew a trumpet, summoning the Abiezrites to follow him. 35He sent messengers throughout Manasseh, calling them to arms, and also into Asher, Zebulun and Naphtali, so that they too went up to meet them.

36Gideon said to God, "If you will save Israel by my hand as you have promised — 37look, I will place a wool fleece on the threshing floor. If there is dew only on the fleece and all the ground is dry, then I will know that you will save Israel by my hand, as you said." 38And that is what happened. Gideon rose early the next day; he squeezed the fleece and wrung out the dew — a bowlful of water.

39Then Gideon said to God, "Do not be angry with me. Let me make just one more request. Allow me one more test with the fleece, but this time make the fleece dry and let the ground be covered with dew." 40That night God did so. Only the fleece was dry; all the ground was covered with dew.

Gideon Defeats the Midianites

7 Early in the morning, Jerub-Baal (that is, Gideon) and all his men camped at the spring of Harod. The camp of Midian was north of them in the valley near the hill of Moreh. 2The LORD said to Gideon, "You have too many men. I cannot deliver Midian into their hands, or Israel would boast against me, 'My own strength has saved me.' 3Now announce to the army, 'Anyone who trembles with fear may turn back and leave Mount Gilead.'" So twenty-two thousand men left, while ten thousand remained.

4But the LORD said to Gideon, "There are still too many men. Take them down to the water, and I will thin them out for you there. If I say, 'This one shall go with you,' he shall go; but if I say, 'This one shall not go with you,' he shall not go."

5So Gideon took the men down to the water. There the LORD told him, "Separate those who lap the water with their tongues as a dog laps from those who kneel down to drink." 6Three hundred of them drank from cupped hands, lapping like dogs. All the rest got down on their knees to drink.

7The LORD said to Gideon, "With the three hundred men that lapped I will save you and give the Midianites into your hands. Let all the others go home." 8So Gideon sent the rest of the Israelites home but kept the three hundred, who took over the provisions and trumpets of the others.

Now the camp of Midian lay below him in the valley. 9During that night the LORD said to Gideon, "Get up, go down against the camp, because I am going to give it into your hands. 10If you are afraid to attack, go down to the camp with your servant Purah 11and listen to what they are saying. Afterward, you will be encouraged to attack the camp." So he and Purah his servant went down to the outposts of the camp. 12The Midianites, the Amalekites and all the other eastern peoples had settled in the valley, thick as locusts. Their camels could no more be counted than the sand on the seashore.

13Gideon arrived just as a man was telling a friend his dream. "I had a dream," he was saying. "A round loaf of barley bread came tumbling into the Midianite camp. It struck the tent with such force that the tent overturned and collapsed."

14His friend responded, "This can be nothing other than the sword of Gideon son of Joash, the Israelite. God has given the Midianites and the whole camp into his hands."

15When Gideon heard the dream and its interpretation, he bowed down and worshiped. He

---

a 32 Jerub-Baal probably means let Baal contend.

6:34 summoning the Abiezrites to follow him That Gideon's own clan (vv. 11,24) follows him shows that they have had a change of heart about Baal and now follow Gideon in his fight for Yahweh.

6:35 into Asher, Zebulun and Naphtali Manasseh's northern neighbors. See the map "Tribal Distribution of Palestine" on p. 2253.

6:36–40 Gideon seems to lack confidence in Yahweh's protection. Nevertheless, Yahweh does not condemn Gideon's uncertainty here; rather, he patiently acts to encourage his faith by granting the signs for which Gideon asks.

7:1–18 Gideon and his army take up positions at a spring called Harod, likely located at the foot of Mount Gilboa. Gideon's army begins at 32,000 men, but God reduces it to 300 through a series of divine tests, reinforcing that the glory for victory belongs to Yahweh and not the army.

7:3 Mount Gilead The Hebrew text here reads Mount Gil-

ead (hargl'd), but this may have arisen from a misspelling of Mount Gilboa (harglb'), which looks similar in Hebrew. The placement of the encounter in the Jezreel Valley suggests the location is Mount Gilboa. Alternately, the reference to Gilead could be another name for the spring where Gideon camped, at the base of the mountain.

7:5 Separate those who lap the water While the narrative provides no specific rationale for the meaning of this test, the manner of drinking seems to indicate alertness. Those deemed fit to go to war with Gideon scooped up the water, then lapped (or sipped) the water out of their hands; this would allow for them to still see their surroundings.

7:8 who took over the provisions They were likely carrying the jars, the trumpets and a weapon (probably a sword or spear; see 7:16).

7:13 a man was telling a friend his dream God was the source of the dream that Gideon and Purah overhear, making it clear why God suggested Gideon eavesdrop in the first place (see v. 11).

returned to the camp of Israel and called out, "Get up! The LORD has given the Midianite camp into your hands." ¹⁶Dividing the three hundred men into three companies, he placed trumpets and empty jars in the hands of all of them, with torches inside.

¹⁷"Watch me," he told them. "Follow my lead. When I get to the edge of the camp, do exactly as I do. ¹⁸When I and all who are with me blow our trumpets, then from all around the camp blow yours and shout, 'For the LORD and for Gideon.'"

¹⁹Gideon and the hundred men with him reached the edge of the camp at the beginning of the middle watch, just after they had changed the guard. They blew their trumpets and broke the jars that were in their hands. ²⁰The three companies blew the trumpets and smashed the jars. Grasping the torches in their left hands and holding in their right hands the trumpets they were to blow, they shouted, "A sword for the LORD and for Gideon!" ²¹While each man held his position around the camp, all the Midianites ran, crying out as they fled.

²²When the three hundred trumpets sounded, the LORD caused the men throughout the camp to turn on each other with their swords. The army fled to Beth Shittah toward Zererah as far as the border of Abel Meholah near Tabbath. ²³Israelites from Naphtali, Asher and all Manasseh were called out, and they pursued the Midianites. ²⁴Gideon sent messengers throughout the hill country of Ephraim, saying, "Come down against the Midianites and seize the waters of the Jordan ahead of them as far as Beth Barah."

So all the men of Ephraim were called out and they seized the waters of the Jordan as far as Beth Barah. ²⁵They also captured two of the Midianite leaders, Oreb and Zeeb. They killed Oreb at the rock of Oreb, and Zeeb at the winepress of Zeeb. They pursued the Midianites and brought the heads of Oreb and Zeeb to Gideon, who was by the Jordan.

Zebah and Zalmunna

8 Now the Ephraimites asked Gideon, "Why have you treated us like this? Why didn't you call us when you went to fight Midian?" And they challenged him vigorously.

²But he answered them, "What have I accomplished compared to you? Aren't the gleanings of Ephraim's grapes better than the full grape harvest of Abiezer? ³God gave Oreb and Zeeb, the Midianite leaders, into your hands. What was I able to do compared to you?" At this, their resentment against him subsided.

⁴Gideon and his three hundred men, exhausted yet keeping up the pursuit, came to the Jordan and crossed it. ⁵He said to the men of Sukkoth, "Give my troops some bread; they are worn out, and I am still pursuing Zebah and Zalmunna, the kings of Midian."

⁶But the officials of Sukkoth said, "Do you already have the hands of Zebah and Zalmunna in your possession? Why should we give bread to your troops?"

⁷Then Gideon replied, "Just for that, when the LORD has given Zebah and Zalmunna into my hand, I will tear your flesh with desert thorns and briers."

⁸From there he went up to Peniel[a] and made

---

a 8 Hebrew *Penuel*, a variant of *Peniel*; also in verses 9 and 17

7:16 with torches inside The jars prevent anyone from seeing the torches in the night while Gideon's men move; they also prevent the torches from blowing out in the wind. The jars, after functioning as a camouflage, then function as a means of noise to startle and confuse the Midianites.

7:18 For the LORD and for Gideon The order of Gideon's words demonstrate that he recognizes that the battle is Yahweh's, Israel's true leader (compare note on Jos 6:16).

7:19 reached the edge of the camp Gideon and his small fighting force are stationed at various points around the enemy's perimeter. The ensuing noise and sudden appearance of flames once the jars are broken misleads the Midianites into assuming that they are surrounded and outnumbered.

7:22 to turn on each other with their swords Thinking that a large military force is besieging them under cover of darkness, the Midianites accidentally kill many of their own men in the frenzy.

7:24 as far as Beth Barah Gideon sends messengers to the tribe of Ephraim, whose geographical position would allow them to cut off the Midianites' retreat to their home territory. **seized the waters of the Jordan** An instruction to form a blockade (or fight) near the Jordan River.

8:1–21 The men of Ephraim had answered Gideon's call to cut off the fleeing Midianites, but Gideon now learns that they are incensed at not being included in the original call for battle against the Midianites (Jdg 8:1). Gideon is able to resolve the situation with Ephraim (vv. 1–3) and continue the pursuit of Midian. Lacking food for his men, Gideon requests supplies from Sukkoth and then Peniel. Both cities rudely refuse and Gideon promises retaliation once he returns from defeating Midan (vv. 4–9). Following Gideon's decisive attack and victory over the Midianite rulers Zebah and Zalmunna (vv. 10–12), he returns to Peniel and Sukkoth, punishing the cities as he had promised (vv. 13–17). The last scene of the conflict with Midian depicts Gideon's execution of the kings Zebah and Zalmunna (vv. 18–21).

8:3 What was I able to do Gideon's gracious answer to Ephraim turns away their anger; they have captured and killed two princes of Midian, whereas he has currently captured and killed no one.

8:6 should we give bread to your troops Sukkoth refuses to choose sides until Gideon and his band have completely defeated the Midianites.

8:7 I will tear your flesh Gideon promises to retaliate against what he rightly views as their betrayal of fellow Israelites.

the same request of them, but they answered as the men of Sukkoth had. ⁹So he said to the men of Peniel, "When I return in triumph, I will tear down this tower."

¹⁰Now Zebah and Zalmunna were in Karkor with a force of about fifteen thousand men, all that were left of the armies of the eastern peoples; a hundred and twenty thousand swordsmen had fallen. ¹¹Gideon went up by the route of the nomads east of Nobah and Jogbehah and attacked the unsuspecting army. ¹²Zebah and Zalmunna, the two kings of Midian, fled, but he pursued them and captured them, routing their entire army.

¹³Gideon son of Joash then returned from the battle by the Pass of Heres. ¹⁴He caught a young man of Sukkoth and questioned him, and the young man wrote down for him the names of the seventy-seven officials of Sukkoth, the elders of the town. ¹⁵Then Gideon came and said to the men of Sukkoth, "Here are Zebah and Zalmunna, about whom you taunted me by saying, 'Do you already have the hands of Zebah and Zalmunna in your possession? Why should we give bread to your exhausted men?'" ¹⁶He took the elders of the town and taught the men of Sukkoth a lesson by punishing them with desert thorns and briers. ¹⁷He also pulled down the tower of Peniel and killed the men of the town.

¹⁸Then he asked Zebah and Zalmunna, "What kind of men did you kill at Tabor?"

"Men like you," they answered, "each one with the bearing of a prince."

¹⁹Gideon replied, "Those were my brothers, the sons of my own mother. As surely as the LORD lives, if you had spared their lives, I would not kill you." ²⁰Turning to Jether, his oldest son, he said,

"Kill them!" But Jether did not draw his sword, because he was only a boy and was afraid.

²¹Zebah and Zalmunna said, "Come, do it yourself. 'As is the man, so is his strength.'" So Gideon stepped forward and killed them, and took the ornaments off their camels' necks.

Gideon's Ephod

²²The Israelites said to Gideon, "Rule over us — you, your son and your grandson — because you have saved us from the hand of Midian."

²³But Gideon told them, "I will not rule over you, nor will my son rule over you. The LORD will rule over you." ²⁴And he said, "I do have one request, that each of you give me an earring from your share of the plunder." (It was the custom of the Ishmaelites to wear gold earrings.)

²⁵They answered, "We'll be glad to give them." So they spread out a garment, and each of them threw a ring from his plunder onto it. ²⁶The weight of the gold rings he asked for came to seventeen hundred shekels,ᵃ not counting the ornaments, the pendants and the purple garments worn by the kings of Midian or the chains that were on their camels' necks. ²⁷Gideon made the gold into an ephod, which he placed in Ophrah, his town. All Israel prostituted themselves by worshiping it there, and it became a snare to Gideon and his family.

Gideon's Death

²⁸Thus Midian was subdued before the Israelites and did not raise its head again. During Gideon's lifetime, the land had peace forty years. ²⁹Jerub-Baal son of Joash went back home to live. ³⁰He had seventy sons of his own, for he

ᵃ *26* That is, about 43 pounds or about 20 kilograms

8:9 I will tear down this tower Gideon vows retaliation against Peniel (see v. 17) similar to that against Sukkoth.
8:18 What kind of men did you kill at Tabor In addition to ravaging the land and forcing the Israelites into caves and the hill country (6:4–5), the Midianites have apparently murdered people in the local population, some of whom were related to Gideon. As the Law's instructions on blood vengeance indicate (Nu 35), the cultural norm dictated capital punishment by next of kin.

8:22–28 Fresh from his victory over Midian, Gideon is offered the kingship of Israel. He refuses, emphasizing Israel's allegiance to Yahweh, but he then uses about 40 pounds (or 18 kilograms) of gold to make an ephod as a symbol of his authority.
8:22 Rule over us A request for Gideon to become their king and begin dynastic rule in Israel.
8:23 The LORD will rule over you Here, Gideon insists that Yahweh should be the sole king in Israel. Despite his refusal, Gideon seems to have ruled as a de facto king (compare Jdg 9:2).
8:26 ornaments, the pendants While Gideon may be seeking payment for his military service by asking for gold,

the use of it to make an ephod suggests that Gideon is setting himself up as the highest authority in the land.
8:27 Gideon made the gold into an ephod An ephod was a type of sacred object used in divination — to discern the will of God (1Sa 23:6–12). **All Israel prostituted themselves by worshiping it there** The same language is used to describe idolatry in Jdg 8:33 (compare 2:17).

8:29–35 This passage reports the death of Gideon (v. 32) and indicates that Israel's return to apostasy followed his death (vv. 33–35). The role of judge is not inherited, so most of the stories make no reference to the judge's descendants. That Gideon's rule approximated that of a king is suggested by the reference to his many wives and many sons — a common practice of kings (vv. 29–31). In 9:2, his son Abimelek implies that Gideon's 70 sons are ruling in his place, but the statement in 9:28 suggests Israel felt no particular loyalty to Gideon's descendants. See the people diagram "Gideon's Family Tree" on p. 372.

8:30 he had many wives Gideon multiplies his harem, effectively creating a regional dynastic household.

had many wives. ³¹His concubine, who lived in Shechem, also bore him a son, whom he named Abimelek. ³²Gideon son of Joash died at a good old age and was buried in the tomb of his father Joash in Ophrah of the Abiezrites.

Gideon's Family Tree
(Jdg 3:20—9:5)

Joash

Gideon

70 other sons | Jether | Abimelek | Jotham

³³No sooner had Gideon died than the Israelites again prostituted themselves to the Baals. They set up Baal-Berith as their god ³⁴and did not remember the Lᴏʀᴅ their God, who had rescued them from the hands of all their enemies on every side. ³⁵They also failed to show any loyalty to the family of Jerub-Baal (that is, Gideon) in spite of all the good things he had done for them.

Abimelek

9 Abimelek son of Jerub-Baal went to his mother's brothers in Shechem and said to them and to all his mother's clan, ²"Ask all the citizens of Shechem, 'Which is better for you: to have all seventy of Jerub-Baal's sons rule over you, or just one man?' Remember, I am your flesh and blood."
³When the brothers repeated all this to the citizens of Shechem, they were inclined to follow Abimelek, for they said, "He is related to us." ⁴They gave him seventy shekels* of silver from the temple of Baal-Berith, and Abimelek used it to hire reckless scoundrels, who became his followers. ⁵He went to his father's home in Ophrah and on one stone murdered his seventy brothers, the sons of Jerub-Baal. But Jotham, the youngest son of Jerub-Baal, escaped by hiding. ⁶Then all the citizens of Shechem and Beth Millo gathered beside the great tree at the pillar in Shechem to crown Abimelek king.
⁷When Jotham was told about this, he climbed up on the top of Mount Gerizim and shouted to them, "Listen to me, citizens of Shechem, so that God may listen to you. ⁸One day the trees went out to anoint a king for themselves. They said to the olive tree, 'Be our king.'

a 4 That is, about 1 3/4 pounds or about 800 grams

8:31 whom he named Abimelek Though Gideon refused Israel's request that he rule them as a king, he gave a son a name that means "my father is king" (compare v. 23 and note).
8:33 the Baals The Hebrew text here is plural, indicating multiple Baals; this is likely a reference to multiple idols and worship sites (compare note on 2:11). Baal can mean "lord" or refer directly to the Canaanite storm god. **set up Baal-Berith as their god** This god's name means "Baal (or lord) of the covenant." In Jdg 9:46, there is a reference to the god El-Berith, meaning "El (or god) of the covenant." The connection between these two references suggests that the Israelites had made a covenant with Baal and El (or with one god whom they referenced with both titles)—their covenant was supposed to be with Yahweh. El was the creator god and chief deity of the Canaanite pantheon, who fathered Baal.

9:1–21 This chapter details the attempt of Abimelek, one of Gideon's sons, to take his father's place of authority. Abimelek's choice indicates that Gideon (also called Jerub-Baal), despite refusing kingship (8:22–23), lived and governed in the manner of a king. The events of this narrative suggest the existence of an influential

native Canaanite populace within Israel at Shechem—a city with a long history dating back to the patriarchal period. In ch. 9 the Shechemites are described as the men of Hamor (v. 28), alluding to the Canaanite leader of the city from Ge 34. This designation suggests that the city is either back under Canaanite control or home to a considerable Canaanite population.

9:4 Baal-Berith See note on Jdg 8:33.
9:5 to his father's home in Ophrah Gideon's hometown (see note on 6:11). **on one stone** May refer to a stone altar; if the stone is an altar, Abimelek may have murdered his brothers as human sacrifices to Baal.
9:6 to crown Abimelek king While all Israel had offered Gideon the kingship (8:22–23), it was only the leaders of Shechem and Beth Millo who declared Abimelek to be their king.
9:7–15 Jotham, the only other remaining son of Gideon, shouts to the people of Shechem. He uses a parable to draw attention to the Shechemites' foolish behavior. In the parable, the people's standards for a king diminish with each new object they request be their leader. The first object seems to be Abimelek's father, Gideon (also called Jerub-Baal). The last object is a reference to Abimelek.

⁹"But the olive tree answered, 'Should I give up my oil, by which both gods and humans are honored, to hold sway over the trees?'

¹⁰"Next, the trees said to the fig tree, 'Come and be our king.'

¹¹"But the fig tree replied, 'Should I give up my fruit, so good and sweet, to hold sway over the trees?'

¹²"Then the trees said to the vine, 'Come and be our king.'

¹³"But the vine answered, 'Should I give up my wine, which cheers both gods and humans, to hold sway over the trees?'

¹⁴"Finally all the trees said to the thornbush, 'Come and be our king.'

¹⁵"The thornbush said to the trees, 'If you really want to anoint me king over you, come and take refuge in my shade; but if not, then let fire come out of the thornbush and consume the cedars of Lebanon!'

¹⁶"Have you acted honorably and in good faith by making Abimelek king? Have you been fair to Jerub-Baal and his family? Have you treated him as he deserves? ¹⁷Remember that my father fought for you and risked his life to rescue you from the hand of Midian. ¹⁸But today you have revolted against my father's family. You have murdered his seventy sons on a single stone and have made Abimelek, the son of his female slave, king over the citizens of Shechem because he is related to you. ¹⁹So have you acted honorably and in good faith toward Jerub-Baal and his family today? If you have, may Abimelek be your joy, and may you be his, too! ²⁰But if you have not, let fire come out from Abimelek and consume you, the citizens of Shechem and Beth Millo, and let fire come out from you, the citizens of Shechem and Beth Millo, and consume Abimelek!"

²¹Then Jotham fled, escaping to Beer, and he lived there because he was afraid of his brother Abimelek.

²²After Abimelek had governed Israel three years, ²³God stirred up animosity between Abimelek and the citizens of Shechem so that they acted treacherously against Abimelek. ²⁴God did this in order that the crime against Jerub-Baal's sev-enty sons, the shedding of their blood, might be avenged on their brother Abimelek and on the citizens of Shechem, who had helped him murder his brothers. ²⁵In opposition to him these citizens of Shechem set men on the hilltops to ambush and rob everyone who passed by, and this was reported to Abimelek.

²⁶Now Gaal son of Ebed moved with his clan into Shechem, and its citizens put their confidence in him. ²⁷After they had gone out into the fields and gathered the grapes and trodden them, they held a festival in the temple of their god. While they were eating and drinking, they cursed Abimelek. ²⁸Then Gaal son of Ebed said, "Who is Abimelek, and why should we Shechemites be subject to him? Isn't he Jerub-Baal's son, and isn't Zebul his deputy? Serve the family of Hamor, Shechem's father! Why should we serve Abimelek? ²⁹If only this people were under my command! Then I would get rid of him. I would say to Abimelek, 'Call out your whole army!'"ᵃ

³⁰When Zebul the governor of the city heard what Gaal son of Ebed said, he was very angry. ³¹Under cover he sent messengers to Abimelek, saying, "Gaal son of Ebed and his clan have come to Shechem and are stirring up the city against you. ³²Now then, during the night you and your men should come and lie in wait in the fields. ³³In the morning at sunrise, advance against the city. When Gaal and his men come out against you, seize the opportunity to attack them."

³⁴So Abimelek and all his troops set out by night and took up concealed positions near Shechem in four companies. ³⁵Now Gaal son of Ebed had gone out and was standing at the entrance of the city gate just as Abimelek and his troops came out from their hiding place.

³⁶When Gaal saw them, he said to Zebul, "Look, people are coming down from the tops of the mountains!"

Zebul replied, "You mistake the shadows of the mountains for men."

³⁷But Gaal spoke up again: "Look, people are coming down from the central hill,ᵇ and a

ᵃ 29 Septuagint; Hebrew him." Then he said to Abimelek, "Call out your whole army!"   ᵇ 37 The Hebrew for this phrase means the navel of the earth.

9:15 consume the cedars of Lebanon Brambles were used for fire. Abimelek is not only worthless—he will also produce destruction.

9:22–57 The narrative moves ahead three years to a time when Shechem and the surrounding region is no longer satisfied with Abimelek's leadership. This passage recounts the rising opposition to Abimelek and his ultimate fall from power.

9:22 had governed Israel Abimelek's control seems to have been localized to the general vicinity of Shechem since the other towns mentioned in this account are within 15 miles of Shechem. Abimelek's original power base may have largely derived from the Canaanite popu-lation of Shechem (see note on vv. 1–21; compare v. 28 and note).

9:23 God stirred up animosity God causes a rift between Abimelek and the leaders of the city—the same people who had supported his bloody coup against his brothers (see vv. 1–6).

9:26 citizens put their confidence in him A new character, Gaal, emerges as a rival who may deliver them from Abimelek.

9:28 Zebul Zebul is the leader of Shechem, where Gaal also lives. Zebul rules under the authority of Abimelek; Abimelek lives in Arumah (v. 41). **family of Hamor, Shechem's father** Gaal argues that only native Shechemites should rule Shechem.

company is coming from the direction of the diviners' tree."

³⁸Then Zebul said to him, "Where is your big talk now, you who said, 'Who is Abimelek that we should be subject to him?' Aren't these the men you ridiculed? Go out and fight them!"

³⁹So Gaal led out*ᵃ* the citizens of Shechem and fought Abimelek. ⁴⁰Abimelek chased him all the way to the entrance of the gate, and many were killed as they fled. ⁴¹Then Abimelek stayed in Arumah, and Zebul drove Gaal and his clan out of Shechem.

⁴²The next day the people of Shechem went out to the fields, and this was reported to Abimelek. ⁴³So he took his men, divided them into three companies and set an ambush in the fields. When he saw the people coming out of the city, he rose to attack them. ⁴⁴Abimelek and the companies with him rushed forward to a position at the entrance of the city gate. Then two companies attacked those in the fields and struck them down. ⁴⁵All that day Abimelek pressed his attack against the city until he had captured it and killed its people. Then he destroyed the city and scattered salt over it.

⁴⁶On hearing this, the citizens in the tower of Shechem went into the stronghold of the temple of El-Berith. ⁴⁷When Abimelek heard that they had assembled there, ⁴⁸he and all his men went up Mount Zalmon. He took an ax and cut off some branches, which he lifted to his shoulders. He ordered the men with him, "Quick! Do what you have seen me do!" ⁴⁹So all the men cut branches and followed Abimelek. They piled them against the stronghold and set it on fire with the people still inside. So all the people in the tower of Shechem, about a thousand men and women, also died.

⁵⁰Next Abimelek went to Thebez and besieged it and captured it. ⁵¹Inside the city, however, was a strong tower, to which all the men and women—all the people of the city—had fled. They had locked themselves in and climbed up on the tower roof. ⁵²Abimelek went to the tower and attacked it. But as he approached the entrance to the tower to set it on fire, ⁵³a woman dropped an upper millstone on his head and cracked his skull. ⁵⁴Hurriedly he called to his armor-bearer, "Draw your sword and kill me, so that they can't say, 'A woman killed him.'" So his servant ran him through, and he died. ⁵⁵When the Israelites saw that Abimelek was dead, they went home.

⁵⁶Thus God repaid the wickedness that Abimelek had done to his father by murdering his seventy brothers. ⁵⁷God also made the people of Shechem pay for all their wickedness. The curse of Jotham son of Jerub-Baal came on them.

Tola

10 After the time of Abimelek, a man of Issachar named Tola son of Puah, the son of Dodo, rose to save Israel. He lived in Shamir, in the hill country of Ephraim. ²He led*ᵇ* Israel twenty-three years; then he died, and was buried in Shamir.

Jair

³He was followed by Jair of Gilead, who led Israel twenty-two years. ⁴He had thirty sons, who rode thirty donkeys. They controlled thirty towns in Gilead, which to this day are called Havvoth Jair.*ᶜ* ⁵When Jair died, he was buried in Kamon.

ᵃ 39 Or Gaal went out in the sight of   ᵇ 2 Traditionally judged; also in verse 3   ᶜ 4 Or called the settlements of Jair

---

9:41 Arumah Abimelek's capital city, located about five miles southeast of Shechem.

9:42 the people of Shechem went out to the fields Forces are apparently still camped outside the city; the leaders of Shechem still want Abimelek removed (see vv. 22–25), despite Gaal's failure.

9:45 scattered salt Sowing with salt renders land infertile; Abimelek ensures no crops will grow in or around the city in the future, keeping it uninhabitable.

9:46 El-Berith See note on 8:33.

9:49 about a thousand men and women Just as Jotham's parable foreshadowed, fire goes out from Abimelek—the bramble (kindling)—destroying Shechem's leaders who supported Abimelek's murderous coup (see v. 20).

9:50 Thebez Likely the town of Tubas about 13 miles northeast of Shechem. It seems that Abimelek, having suppressed the rebellion at Shechem, now decides to expand his area of governance by force.

9:52 to set it on fire Abimelek plans to burn the tower just as he did at Shechem (vv. 48–49).

9:53 cracked his skull An unnamed woman drops a grinding stone out a window in the tower and fractures Abimelek's skull. Abimelek's proximity to the tower made this possible.

9:55 the Israelites The narrative here identifies Abim-

elek's soldiers (or at least part of his army) as Israelite, though the extent of his reign in Israel seems to have been limited (see note on v. 22). Nonetheless, Abimelek could have been influential among the Israelites and thus able to gather Israelites from beyond his jurisdiction.

10:1–5 This passage briefly acknowledges the careers of two judges—Tola and Jair. There are passing references to six minor judges throughout the book, bringing the total number of judges to twelve.

10:1 Tola son of Puah One of the so-called minor judges—judges about whom the Biblical text gives little information. Nothing is known of Tola's career apart from what is included here. See the table "Judges and Their Rule" on p. 364. **Shamir, in the hill country of Ephraim** The location of Shamir is uncertain, but the hill country of Ephraim includes the general vicinity of Shechem, where Abimelek caused so much chaos (ch. 9).

10:3 He was followed by Jair The description here is the extent of what is known about this judge. **Gilead** A hilly territory and border territory occupied by the tribes of Manasseh, Gad and Reuben (Nu 32). This suggests Jair and his sons came to the aid of multiple tribes. There was also a clan called Gilead, to which Jair may have belonged (Nu 26:28–33).

10:4 to this day are called Havvoth Jair Jair's time

Jephthah

⁶Again the Israelites did evil in the eyes of the LORD. They served the Baals and the Ashtoreths, and the gods of Aram, the gods of Sidon, the gods of Moab, the gods of the Ammonites and the gods of the Philistines. And because the Israelites forsook the LORD and no longer served him, ⁷he became angry with them. He sold them into the hands of the Philistines and the Ammonites, ⁸who that year shattered and crushed them. For eighteen years they oppressed all the Israelites on the east side of the Jordan in Gilead, the land of the Amorites. ⁹The Ammonites also crossed the Jordan to fight against Judah, Benjamin and Ephraim; Israel was in great distress. ¹⁰Then the Israelites cried out to the LORD, "We have sinned against you, forsaking our God and serving the Baals."

¹¹The LORD replied, "When the Egyptians, the Amorites, the Ammonites, the Philistines, ¹²the Sidonians, the Amalekites and the Maonitesᵃ oppressed you and you cried to me for help, did I not save you from their hands? ¹³But you have forsaken me and served other gods, so I will no longer save you. ¹⁴Go and cry out to the gods you have chosen. Let them save you when you are in trouble!"

¹⁵But the Israelites said to the LORD, "We have sinned. Do with us whatever you think best, but please rescue us now." ¹⁶Then they got rid of the foreign gods among them and served the LORD. And he could bear Israel's misery no longer.

¹⁷When the Ammonites were called to arms and camped in Gilead, the Israelites assembled and camped at Mizpah. ¹⁸The leaders of the people of Gilead said to each other, "Whoever will take the lead in attacking the Ammonites will be head over all who live in Gilead."

11 Jephthah the Gileadite was a mighty warrior. His father was Gilead; his mother was a prostitute. ²Gilead's wife also bore him sons, and when they were grown up, they drove Jephthah away. "You are not going to get any inheritance in our family," they said, "because you are the son of another woman." ³So Jephthah fled from his brothers and settled in the land of Tob, where a gang of scoundrels gathered around him and followed him.

⁴Some time later, when the Ammonites were fighting against Israel, ⁵the elders of Gilead went to get Jephthah from the land of Tob. ⁶"Come," they said, "be our commander, so we can fight the Ammonites."

⁷Jephthah said to them, "Didn't you hate me and drive me from my father's house? Why do you come to me now, when you're in trouble?"

⁸The elders of Gilead said to him, "Nevertheless, we are turning to you now; come with us to fight the Ammonites, and you will be head over all of us who live in Gilead."

⁹Jephthah answered, "Suppose you take me back to fight the Ammonites and the LORD gives them to me — will I really be your head?"

¹⁰The elders of Gilead replied, "The LORD is our witness; we will certainly do as you say." ¹¹So Jephthah went with the elders of Gilead, and the people

ᵃ 12 Hebrew; some Septuagint manuscripts *Midianites*

---

as judge is connected in some way to the conquest of Havvoth Jair ("the tent villages of Jair") described in Nu 32:39–42 and Dt 3:14.

10:6–18 This narrative introduces the Jephthah cycle, which extends to Jdg 12:7. This cycle does not follow the typical pattern of the judges repeated throughout the book: apostasy, judgment and suffering, calling out to Yahweh and deliverance (see note on 2:11–15).

While it begins with a cry to Yahweh for relief, the narrative does not mention Yahweh raising up a judge to deliver his people. This omission suggests that Jephthah's rise is initiated by people rather than God (see 11:5–11). However, there is a reference to the Spirit empowering Jephthah, which gives him some divine legitimacy (11:29); yet Jephthah's foolish vow overshadows this positive aspect (11:30–40). Jephthah's narrative also contains elements that parallel the preceding stories of Gideon and Abimelek.

10:7 Philistines and the Ammonites The Philistines occupied the coastal region of Canaan (Jos 13:3; 15:45–46), whereas Ammon was in the Transjordan. Jephthah, from Gilead, is in proximity to the Ammonite oppression (see note on Jdg 10:3). After the Jephthah cycle ends in ch. 12, the narrative switches to the judge who takes on the Philistine oppressors: Samson. See the table "Judges and Their Rule" on p. 364.

10:16 Then they got rid of the foreign gods Israel had

acknowledged that worshiping idols was sinful (v. 10), but they apparently had not fully demonstrated their sincerity and repentance, as they do here. **could bear Israel's misery no longer** Meaning Yahweh is now willing to deliver the Israelites since they fully turned from their idolatry (v. 13).

10:17 Ammonites A people group from the Transjordan who the Israelites were instructed to leave alone (Dt 2:19–21,37); nonetheless, Israel ended up acquiring some land belonging to the Ammonites (Jos 13:24–25).

11:1–28 With battle against the Ammonites imminent in Gilead, the elders of Gilead seek out Jephthah—an outcast and outlaw—to lead their army (Jdg 11:1–11). Jephthah's negotiations with the Ammonite king reveal that the conflict is a territorial dispute—they assert the Israelites took their land (vv. 12–13). Jephthah's reply rehearses the story of Israel's exodus from Egypt and their journey through the wilderness to the Transjordan, emphasizing how Israel took the territory from the Amorites, not the Ammonites (vv. 14–28).

11:3 a gang of scoundrels gathered around him Jephthah becomes leader over a gang of outlaws. In the Hebrew text, the same description is used for Abimelek's hired thugs (9:4).

11:11 before the LORD in Mizpah That Jephthah insists on a formal covenant ceremony invoking Yahweh shows his faith but does not necessarily mean that he viewed

made him head and commander over them. And he repeated all his words before the LORD in Mizpah.

¹²Then Jephthah sent messengers to the Ammonite king with the question: "What do you have against me that you have attacked my country?"

¹³The king of the Ammonites answered Jephthah's messengers, "When Israel came up out of Egypt, they took away my land from the Arnon to the Jabbok, all the way to the Jordan. Now give it back peaceably."

¹⁴Jephthah sent back messengers to the Ammonite king, ¹⁵saying:

"This is what Jephthah says: Israel did not take the land of Moab or the land of the Ammonites. ¹⁶But when they came up out of Egypt, Israel went through the wilderness to the Red Sea[a] and on to Kadesh. ¹⁷Then Israel sent messengers to the king of Edom, saying, 'Give us permission to go through your country,' but the king of Edom would not listen. They sent also to the king of Moab, and he refused. So Israel stayed at Kadesh.

¹⁸"Next they traveled through the wilderness, skirted the lands of Edom and Moab, passed along the eastern side of the country of Moab, and camped on the other side of the Arnon. They did not enter the territory of Moab, for the Arnon was its border.

¹⁹"Then Israel sent messengers to Sihon king of the Amorites, who ruled in Heshbon, and said to him, 'Let us pass through your country to our own place.' ²⁰Sihon, however, did not trust Israel[b] to pass through his territory. He mustered all his troops and encamped at Jahaz and fought with Israel.

²¹"Then the LORD, the God of Israel, gave Sihon and his whole army into Israel's hands, and they defeated them. Israel took over all the land of the Amorites who lived in that country, ²²capturing all of it from the Arnon to the Jabbok and from the desert to the Jordan.

²³"Now since the LORD, the God of Israel, has driven the Amorites out before his people Israel, what right have you to take it over? ²⁴Will you not take what your god Chemosh gives you? Likewise, whatever the LORD our God has given us, we will possess. ²⁵Are you any better than Balak son of Zippor, king of Moab? Did he ever quarrel with Israel or fight with them? ²⁶For three hundred years Israel occupied Heshbon, Aroer, the surrounding settlements and all the towns along the Arnon. Why didn't you retake them during that time? ²⁷I have not wronged you, but you are doing me wrong by waging war against me. Let the LORD, the Judge, decide the dispute this day between the Israelites and the Ammonites."

²⁸The king of Ammon, however, paid no attention to the message Jephthah sent him.

²⁹Then the Spirit of the LORD came on Jephthah. He crossed Gilead and Manasseh, passed through

---

a 16 Or *the Sea of Reeds*   *b* 20 Or *however, would not make an agreement for Israel*

Yahweh as his only god. Mizpah may have been home to a sanctuary of Yahweh (see Ge 31:48–49).

11:13 from the Arnon to the Jabbok, all the way to the Jordan Ammon's contention with Israel amounts to a territorial dispute. The Ammonite king charges Israel with stealing their land, and he intends to invade Gilead to reclaim it. According to the Biblical account, the region of Gilead was not Ammonite territory when Israel conquered the Transjordan. Israel had obtained the territory in the days of Moses via the conquest of the Amorite king, Sihon (Nu 21:21–34; Dt 2:24–32). Nonetheless, the mention of the region as belonging to the Ammonites in Jos 13:24–25 suggests that at one point it did belong to the Ammonites.

11:16 through the wilderness to the Red Sea See Ex 12–14. **on to Kadesh** See Nu 13:26.

11:17 Give us permission to go through your country See Nu 20:14–21.

11:18 eastern side of the country of Moab See Nu 21:11.

11:19 Israel sent messengers According to the Biblical account, the Arnon was the boundary between Moab and the Amorites, not the Ammonites (Nu 21:13). **Let us pass** See Nu 21:21–26; Dt 2:26–37.

11:24 what your god Chemosh gives you Chemosh was the god of Moab, as both the OT and the Mesha (Moabite) Stele make evident. The Ammonites' god was Molek (or Milcom; see 1Ki 11:5 and note; 11:33). It is possible that Jephthah indicates the wrong deity, either in error or by deliberate insult. See the table "Pagan Deities of the Old Testament" on p. 1287. **LORD our God has given us** Jephthah argues that each army or nation should be content with the land their respective god has given.

11:26 For three hundred years This phrase may be a reference to a long period of time, rather than a literal 300 years. However, if it is a reference to a literal 300 years then it introduces difficulty for those who argue that the exodus took place ca. 1260 BC (the late exodus date). A late exodus allows for less than 200 years between the exodus and the kingship under Saul (ca. 1051 BC) (compare note on Ex 1:11). **along the Arnon** The dominance of the nation of Ammon in the Transjordan (Jdg 10:8–9) suggests the possibility that Ammon had already conquered Moab and controlled the area south of the Arnon (the territory of Chemosh; compare note on v. 24). Now they were attempting to subdue the territory north of the Arnon.

11:29–40 Negotiations failed, so Jephthah advanced to meet the Ammonites in battle (Jdg 11:29–32). While on the way, Jephthah vowed to offer a burnt offering to Yahweh on his return if God would grant him a victory. Oddly, he vowed to sacrifice whoever or whatever came out of his house first to greet him when he returned home. This foolish vow has tragic consequences.

11:29 the Spirit of the LORD Indicating that Jephthah was divinely empowered to carry out his task to defend Israel from the Ammonites (3:10; 6:34).

Mizpah of Gilead, and from there he advanced against the Ammonites. ³⁰And Jephthah made a vow to the LORD: "If you give the Ammonites into my hands, ³¹whatever comes out of the door of my house to meet me when I return in triumph from the Ammonites will be the LORD's, and I will sacrifice it as a burnt offering."

³²Then Jephthah went over to fight the Ammonites, and the LORD gave them into his hands. ³³He devastated twenty towns from Aroer to the vicinity of Minnith, as far as Abel Keramim. Thus Israel subdued Ammon.

³⁴When Jephthah returned to his home in Mizpah, who should come out to meet him but his daughter, dancing to the sound of timbrels! She was an only child. Except for her he had neither son nor daughter. ³⁵When he saw her, he tore his clothes and cried, "Oh no, my daughter! You have brought me down and I am devastated. I have made a vow to the LORD that I cannot break."

³⁶"My father," she replied, "you have given your word to the LORD. Do to me just as you promised, now that the LORD has avenged you of your enemies, the Ammonites. ³⁷But grant me this one request," she said. "Give me two months to roam the hills and weep with my friends, because I will never marry."

³⁸"You may go," he said. And he let her go for two months. She and her friends went into the hills and wept because she would never marry. ³⁹After the two months, she returned to her father, and he did to her as he had vowed. And she was a virgin.

From this comes the Israelite tradition ⁴⁰that each year the young women of Israel go out for four days to commemorate the daughter of Jephthah the Gileadite.

Jephthah and Ephraim

12 The Ephraimite forces were called out, and they crossed over to Zaphon. They said to Jephthah, "Why did you go to fight the Ammonites without calling us to go with you? We're going to burn down your house over your head."

²Jephthah answered, "I and my people were engaged in a great struggle with the Ammonites, and although I called, you didn't save me out of their hands. ³When I saw that you wouldn't help, I took my life in my hands and crossed over to fight the Ammonites, and the LORD gave me the victory over them. Now why have you come up today to fight me?"

⁴Jephthah then called together the men of Gilead and fought against Ephraim. The Gileadites struck them down because the Ephraimites had said, "You Gileadites are renegades from Ephraim and Manasseh." ⁵The Gileadites captured the fords of the Jordan leading to Ephraim, and whenever a survivor of Ephraim said, "Let me cross over," the men of Gilead asked him, "Are you an Ephraimite?" If he replied, "No," ⁶they said, "All right, say 'Shibboleth.'" If he said, "Sibboleth," because he could not pronounce the word correctly, they seized him and killed him at the fords of the Jordan. Forty-two thousand Ephraimites were killed at that time.

⁷Jephthah led*ᵃ* Israel six years. Then Jephthah the Gileadite died and was buried in a town in Gilead.

Ibzan, Elon and Abdon

⁸After him, Ibzan of Bethlehem led Israel. ⁹He had thirty sons and thirty daughters. He gave his

---

ᵃ 7 Traditionally *judged*; also in verses 8-14

11:31 whatever comes out The wording used here in Hebrew is ambiguous and could be understood as "whoever" or "whatever."

11:34 who should come out to meet him but his daughter Jephthah's daughter is the first to emerge from the house when Jephthah returns, causing him great anguish—but he does not relent on the vow (vv. 35,39). Breaking a vow was a serious matter because it could anger God and bring misfortune (Dt 23:21–23; Ecc 5:5–6). Jephthah wrongfully assumes that a human life is less important than keeping his vow. Jephthah's vow is foolish and unnecessary and shows his failure to trust God. Jephthah incorrectly believes that Yahweh needs to be coaxed or bartered with to deliver the people of Gilead. All this points to Jephthah treating Yahweh like a foreign god (compare Jdg 11:24).

11:37 weep with my friends Jephthah's daughter does not fight the vow but asks instead for time to mourn the fact that she will never marry. It is possible that instead of sacrificing his daughter to Yahweh, Jephthah may have simply forbid her from marrying. Jephthah could have understood his daughter's perpetual virginity—perhaps linked to some spiritual service to Yahweh—as fulfilling his vow.

11:39 as he had vowed The language of weeping and lament in vv. 37–40 leaves the impression that Jepthah's daughter may have died as a human sacrifice—a capital crime according to Mosaic Law (Lev 18:21; 20:2–5)—but

she is also said to be weeping over her virginity (see note on Jdg 11:37).

12:1–7 This passage records a conflict between Jephthah and the Ephraimites after Jephthah's victory over the Ammonites (see 11:32–34).

12:2 you didn't save me out of their hands Jephthah claims that he did request help from the Ephraimites, but was denied. Chapter 11 records no such request, but Jephthah may have sent messengers as Gideon had (6:35; 7:24).

12:4 Jephthah then called together the men of Gilead The situation degenerates quickly. Jephthah reassembles his army, which has just returned home.

12:6 say 'Shibboleth' The Gileadites use differences of dialect as a test of identity. The Ephraimites were unable to properly articulate the *sh* of *shibboleth*. The Ephraimites likely could not even hear the distinction between *shibboleth* and *sibboleth*.

12:8–15 The three judges in this section—Ibzan, Elon and Abdon—are among the so-called minor judges—judges about whom the Biblical account gives little information. Mention of six minor judges brings the total number covered in the book to twelve (3:31; 10:1–5). It is unlikely, however, that these twelve were the only such figures during the period of the judges. The writer probably

daughters away in marriage to those outside his clan, and for his sons he brought in thirty young women as wives from outside his clan. Ibzan led Israel seven years. ¹⁰Then Ibzan died and was buried in Bethlehem.

¹¹After him, Elon the Zebulunite led Israel ten years. ¹²Then Elon died and was buried in Aijalon in the land of Zebulun.

¹³After him, Abdon son of Hillel, from Pirathon, led Israel. ¹⁴He had forty sons and thirty grandsons, who rode on seventy donkeys. He led Israel eight years. ¹⁵Then Abdon son of Hillel died and was buried at Pirathon in Ephraim, in the hill country of the Amalekites.

The Birth of Samson

13 Again the Israelites did evil in the eyes of the LORD, so the LORD delivered them into the hands of the Philistines for forty years.

²A certain man of Zorah, named Manoah, from the clan of the Danites, had a wife who was childless, unable to give birth. ³The angel of the LORD appeared to her and said, "You are barren and childless, but you are going to become pregnant and give birth to a son. ⁴Now see to it that you drink no wine or other fermented drink and that you do not eat anything unclean. ⁵You will become pregnant and have a son whose head is never to be touched by a razor because the boy is to be a Nazirite, dedicated to God from the womb. He will take the lead in delivering Israel from the hands of the Philistines."

⁶Then the woman went to her husband and told him, "A man of God came to me. He looked like an angel of God, very awesome. I didn't ask him where he came from, and he didn't tell me his name. ⁷But he said to me, 'You will become pregnant and have a son. Now then, drink no wine or other fermented drink and do not eat anything unclean, because the boy will be a Nazirite of God from the womb until the day of his death.'"

⁸Then Manoah prayed to the LORD: "Pardon your servant, Lord. I beg you to let the man of God you sent to us come again to teach us how to bring up the boy who is to be born."

⁹God heard Manoah, and the angel of God came again to the woman while she was out in the field; but her husband Manoah was not with her. ¹⁰The woman hurried to tell her husband, "He's here! The man who appeared to me the other day!"

¹¹Manoah got up and followed his wife. When he came to the man, he said, "Are you the man who talked to my wife?"

---

selected representative stories that well illustrated the conflict and chaos of the period. See the table "Judges and Their Rule" on p. 364.

12:10 buried in Bethlehem Ibzan was either from the Bethlehem in Zebulun (Jos 19:15) or the one in Judah (Jdg 17:7; 19:1). It is uncertain which is in view here, but the other references to Bethlehem of Judah in the book of Judges explicitly mention that the location is in Judah (17:7; 19:1; compare Ru 1:1). However, Jdg 12:11 suggests an association with Zebulun.

12:15 the Amalekites The reference to Amalekites suggests they had once lived in the region. The Amalekites were one of the Canaanite peoples occupying the land before Israel (Nu 13:29; 14:43–45; Dt 25:17–19).

13:1–25 The story of Samson—the last of the judges to be featured in the book—begins in Jdg 13:1 and continues to 16:31. The story seems to be set in the period of Philistine oppression alluded to in 10:7.

Samson is the only judge with a birth narrative signaling his auspicious arrival. In vv. 1–25, the Angel of Yahweh appears to his barren mother to announce that she would have a son and that he was to be set apart as a lifelong Nazirite (see Nu 6). While the precise date for Samson is unknown, the overall timeframe of the judges is roughly 1210–1051 BC, leading up to the time of the narrative of Samuel the judge—depicted in 1 Samuel. See the table "Judges and Their Rule" on p. 364.

13:1 the Philistines The Philistines settled on the coast of Canaan around 1200 BC. Their territory centered around five cities in the coastal region west of Judah (Ashkelon, Ashdod, Ekron, Gaza and Gath; Jos 13:3). They had already pressed into Israelite territory, but the judge Shamgar drove them back (Jdg 3:31).

13:2 Zorah One of the towns allotted to the tribe of Dan (Jos 15:33; 19:41). This area was part of the Shephelah—the foothills west of the hill country of Judah. The Shephelah was a border region between Israel and the coastal plain controlled by the Philistines.

a wife who was childless People in the ancient Near East often considered barrenness a divine curse. The motif of barrenness is often used in connection with stories of the divinely enabled birth of an important figure to a formerly barren woman. Conception and birth after a long period of barrenness is often presented in the Bible as a divine blessing for the woman and an answer to prayer (Ge 25:21; 1Sa 1:9–11,20).

13:3 angel of the LORD appeared The OT elsewhere identifies this angel with Yahweh (see Jdg 6:11 and note).

13:4 anything unclean These restrictions are stipulations of the Nazirite vow, under which the child will be born.

13:5 the boy is to be a Nazirite Numbers 6:1–21 describes the rules related to this vow in detail.

13:6 A man of God The Angel of Yahweh appeared to Samson's mother as a man (see note on Jdg 13:3). The phrase "man of God" raises the possibility that Manoah's wife assumed the figure was a prophet (compare Dt 33:1; 1Sa 2:27; 9:6). **he didn't tell me his name** Angels in the OT typically do not provide their name (see Jdg 13:17–18; Ge 32:29). This may reflect the ancient Near Eastern belief that knowing the name of a divine being gave one power over the entity.

13:7 the boy will be a Nazirite The Nazirite vow (Nu 6:1–21) can be either a temporary or a lifelong commitment. Samson and Samuel appear to have been lifelong Nazirites (compare 1Sa 1:11).

13:11 he came to the man Once again, the angel is cast as human in appearance. **"I am," he said** The angel's answer in Hebrew is simply the pronoun *ani* ("I") with the verb implied; this response is consistent with the angel's subsequent refusal to reveal his name (Jdg 13:17–18).

"I am," he said.

¹²So Manoah asked him, "When your words are fulfilled, what is to be the rule that governs the boy's life and work?"

¹³The angel of the Lord answered, "Your wife must do all that I have told her. ¹⁴She must not eat anything that comes from the grapevine, nor drink any wine or other fermented drink nor eat anything unclean. She must do everything I have commanded her."

¹⁵Manoah said to the angel of the Lord, "We would like you to stay until we prepare a young goat for you."

¹⁶The angel of the Lord replied, "Even though you detain me, I will not eat any of your food. But if you prepare a burnt offering, offer it to the Lord." (Manoah did not realize that it was the angel of the Lord.)

¹⁷Then Manoah inquired of the angel of the Lord, "What is your name, so that we may honor you when your word comes true?"

¹⁸He replied, "Why do you ask my name? It is beyond understanding.ᵃ" ¹⁹Then Manoah took a young goat, together with the grain offering, and sacrificed it on a rock to the Lord. And the Lord did an amazing thing while Manoah and his wife watched: ²⁰As the flame blazed up from the altar toward heaven, the angel of the Lord ascended in the flame. Seeing this, Manoah and his wife fell with their faces to the ground. ²¹When the angel of the Lord did not show himself again to Manoah and his wife, Manoah realized that it was the angel of the Lord.

²²"We are doomed to die!" he said to his wife. "We have seen God!"

²³But his wife answered, "If the Lord had meant to kill us, he would not have accepted a burnt offering and grain offering from our hands, nor shown us all these things or now told us this."

²⁴The woman gave birth to a boy and named him Samson. He grew and the Lord blessed him, ²⁵and the Spirit of the Lord began to stir him while he was in Mahaneh Dan, between Zorah and Eshtaol.

Samson's Marriage

14 Samson went down to Timnah and saw there a young Philistine woman. ²When he returned, he said to his father and mother, "I have seen a Philistine woman in Timnah; now get her for me as my wife."

³His father and mother replied, "Isn't there an acceptable woman among your relatives or among all our people? Must you go to the uncircumcised Philistines to get a wife?"

But Samson said to his father, "Get her for me. She's the right one for me." ⁴(His parents did not know that this was from the Lord, who was seeking an occasion to confront the Philistines; for at that time they were ruling over Israel.)

⁵Samson went down to Timnah together with his father and mother. As they approached the vineyards of Timnah, suddenly a young lion came roaring toward him. ⁶The Spirit of the Lord came powerfully upon him so that he tore the lion apart

ᵃ 18 Or is wonderful

13:13 must do The Nazirite status is critical to the child's mission, which becomes clear later when the Nazirite status explains the mystery behind God's enablement of Samson's extraordinary strength.

13:18 It is beyond understanding The Hebrew word used here, *peli,* elsewhere describes miraculous signs from God (see Ex 15:11; Ps 78:12; compare Ps 77:12,14; Isa 25:1).

13:19 did an amazing thing Manoah offers sacrifices to Yahweh in acknowledgement of Yahweh's power to perform wonders. The Hebrew term used here is a verbal form of the word *peli* used in v. 18.

13:22 We have seen God People in the ancient Near East considered an encounter with a divine being potentially fatal (see Ex 24:9–11; 33:20).

13:24 named him Samson A name meaning "little sun." The name may metaphorically suggest that the child would be a ray of light in an otherwise dark time. However, it may be connected to sun worship. Beth Shemesh (meaning "house of the sun") was close to Zorah (where Samson's family lived; Jdg 13:2). Sun worship was common in Canaan. For followers of Yahweh, Samson's name would have spoken of the power of the sun—and the God behind that power.

13:25 the Spirit of the Lord Yahweh's power enabled the success of many judges (see 6:34; 9:23; 11:29). **in Mahaneh Dan** This name means "camp of Dan" (see 18:12); the precise location is unknown.

14:1–20 Samson, now a grown man, asks his parents to arrange for him to marry a Philistine girl he saw in the nearby town of Timnah. This passage records Samson's feat of slaying a lion with his bare hands and the riddle he devised after seeing bees had made a hive in the lion's carcass. The narrative then turns to Samson's wedding celebration.

14:1 Samson went down to Timnah Near Zorah, Samson's hometown. **a young Philistine woman** The presence of Philistine women in Timnah most likely indicates the Philistines occupied the city.

14:2 get her for me as my wife Motivated by lust, Samson desires a Philistine woman. Marriages in ancient Near Eastern culture were generally handled like business transactions (compare Ge 29:15–20).

14:3 an acceptable woman among your relatives Samson's parents are unhappy with the idea of Samson marrying a non-Israelite woman since it could lead to idolatry (see Ex 34:16; Dt 7:1–6; 17:17).

14:4 time they were ruling over Israel God will use Samson's lust to initiate judgment on the Philistines for oppressing Israel.

14:5 to Timnah together with his father and mother So that they could negotiate the marriage transaction (see note on Jdg 14:2).

14:6 The Spirit of the Lord came powerfully upon him This statement usually indicates Yahweh's empowering

with his bare hands as he might have torn a young goat. But he told neither his father nor his mother what he had done. ⁷Then he went down and talked with the woman, and he liked her.

⁸Some time later, when he went back to marry her, he turned aside to look at the lion's carcass, and in it he saw a swarm of bees and some honey. ⁹He scooped out the honey with his hands and ate as he went along. When he rejoined his parents, he gave them some, and they too ate it. But he did not tell them that he had taken the honey from the lion's carcass.

¹⁰Now his father went down to see the woman. And there Samson held a feast, as was customary for young men. ¹¹When the people saw him, they chose thirty men to be his companions.

¹²"Let me tell you a riddle," Samson said to them. "If you can give me the answer within the seven days of the feast, I will give you thirty linen garments and thirty sets of clothes. ¹³If you can't tell me the answer, you must give me thirty linen garments and thirty sets of clothes."

"Tell us your riddle," they said. "Let's hear it." ¹⁴He replied,

"Out of the eater, something to eat;
     out of the strong, something sweet."

For three days they could not give the answer.

¹⁵On the fourthᵃ day, they said to Samson's wife, "Coax your husband into explaining the riddle for us, or we will burn you and your father's house-

hold to death. Did you invite us here to steal our property?"

¹⁶Then Samson's wife threw herself on him, sobbing, "You hate me! You don't really love me. You've given my people a riddle, but you haven't told me the answer."

"I haven't even explained it to my father or mother," he replied, "so why should I explain it to you?" ¹⁷She cried the whole seven days of the feast. So on the seventh day he finally told her, because she continued to press him. She in turn explained the riddle to her people.

¹⁸Before sunset on the seventh day the men of the town said to him,

"What is sweeter than honey?
     What is stronger than a lion?"

Samson said to them,

"If you had not plowed with my heifer,
     you would not have solved my riddle."

¹⁹Then the Spirit of the LORD came powerfully upon him. He went down to Ashkelon, struck down thirty of their men, stripped them of everything and gave their clothes to those who had explained the riddle. Burning with anger, he returned to his father's home. ²⁰And Samson's wife was given to one of his companions who had attended him at the feast.

ᵃ 15 Some Septuagint manuscripts and Syriac; Hebrew *seventh*

---

of a judge to accomplish deliverance (see 3:10; 6:34). In Samson's case, the Spirit comes when he performs exceptional feats of physical strength (compare vv. 19; 15:14). **But he told neither his father nor his mother** The reason for Samson's secrecy is unstated and unknown. Samson may have thought he had violated his lifelong Nazirite vow by touching a dead carcass (see Nu 6:6).

14:9 He scooped out the honey with his hands Since it is not a product of the vine (Nu 6:3–4), honey is not listed as a food prohibited for Nazirites. Since Samson continues to receive Yahweh's empowering until his hair is cut, none of his prior actions (including touching the lion's carcass here) appear to be violations of his lifelong Nazirite vow (see Jdg 16:17–19).

14:10 his father went down to see the woman To complete the transaction and prepare the wedding celebration (see note on v. 2). **as was customary for young men** Samson is responsible for the wedding feast, but it will take place in the bride's home, something not customary in an Israelite ceremony.

14:11 they chose thirty men to be his companions These are not Samson's friends; rather, the people at the wedding in Timnah bring these men once Samson arrives. They may be invited guests of the woman's family.

14:12 Let me tell you a riddle Samson entertains the gathering with a challenging riddle. He has no reason to suspect anyone will solve it since he alone knows about the incident with the lion (see v. 9,16). **within the seven days of the feast** By the end of the marriage feast. **thirty linen garments and thirty sets of clothes** The prize is costly and desirable, though the cost would be distributed

for the thirty men. Even the cost of one change of clothes each apparently represented a significant expense based on the men's protest in v. 15. Most people in ancient Near Eastern cultures would have owned few garments.

14:14 out of the strong, something sweet Samson here refers to the lion and the honey within it (vv. 8–9).

14:18 the men of the town The description here and in v. 17 clarifies that the 30 men are all Philistines from Timnah. **you had not plowed with my heifer** An idiom meaning "had you not intimidated my wife."

14:19 Spirit of the LORD came powerfully upon him Although Samson is acting out of rage, Yahweh empowers Samson with strength because the Philistines have been oppressing the Israelites (see v. 4). **struck down thirty of their men** Samson travels 20 miles to the Philistine city of Ashkelon (Jos 13:3) and murders 30 random Philistine men. **stripped them of everything and gave their clothes** Samson takes each man's belongings and presents them to fulfill his obligation. The Hebrew phrasing used here involves rhyme and wordplay and leaves ambiguity about what Samson gave the men. The translation "clothes" or "garments" is often supplied here because of Samson's wager in Jdg 14:12–13, but different terminology is used in vv. 12–13. Samson may have given the men the battle gear or equipment of those he killed, as 2Sa 2:21 uses the same Hebrew word in reference to weaponry. Samson's inclusion of weaponry would send the men a clear message: They would be wise not to trifle with someone who could kill 30 armed Philistines single-handedly.

14:20 And Samson's wife was given to one of his companions Samson, having gone home in a rage, does

Samson's Vengeance on the Philistines

15 Later on, at the time of wheat harvest, Samson took a young goat and went to visit his wife. He said, "I'm going to my wife's room." But her father would not let him go in.

2"I was so sure you hated her," he said, "that I gave her to your companion. Isn't her younger sister more attractive? Take her instead."

3Samson said to them, "This time I have a right to get even with the Philistines; I will really harm them." 4So he went out and caught three hundred foxes and tied them tail to tail in pairs. He then fastened a torch to every pair of tails, 5lit the torches and let the foxes loose in the standing grain of the Philistines. He burned up the shocks and standing grain, together with the vineyards and olive groves.

6When the Philistines asked, "Who did this?" they were told, "Samson, the Timnite's son-in-law, because his wife was given to his companion."

So the Philistines went up and burned her and her father to death. 7Samson said to them, "Since you've acted like this, I swear that I won't stop until I get my revenge on you." 8He attacked them viciously and slaughtered many of them. Then he went down and stayed in a cave in the rock of Etam.

9The Philistines went up and camped in Judah, spreading out near Lehi. 10The people of Judah asked, "Why have you come to fight us?"

"We have come to take Samson prisoner," they answered, "to do to him as he did to us."

11Then three thousand men from Judah went down to the cave in the rock of Etam and said to Samson, "Don't you realize that the Philistines are rulers over us? What have you done to us?"

He answered, "I merely did to them what they did to me."

12They said to him, "We've come to tie you up and hand you over to the Philistines."

Samson said, "Swear to me that you won't kill me yourselves."

13"Agreed," they answered. "We will only tie you up and hand you over to them. We will not kill you." So they bound him with two new ropes and led him up from the rock. 14As he approached Lehi, the Philistines came toward him shouting. The Spirit of the LORD came powerfully upon him. The ropes on his arms became like charred flax, and the bindings dropped from his hands. 15Finding a fresh jawbone of a donkey, he grabbed it and struck down a thousand men.

16Then Samson said,

> "With a donkey's jawbone
>   I have made donkeys of them.*a*
> With a donkey's jawbone
>   I have killed a thousand men."

17When he finished speaking, he threw away the jawbone; and the place was called Ramath Lehi.*b*

18Because he was very thirsty, he cried out to the LORD, "You have given your servant this great victory. Must I now die of thirst and fall into the hands of the uncircumcised?" 19Then God opened up the hollow place in Lehi, and water came out of it. When Samson drank, his strength returned and

---

a 16 Or *made a heap or two*; the Hebrew for *donkey* sounds like the Hebrew for *heap*.   *b* 17 *Ramath Lehi* means *jawbone hill*.

---

not actually consummate his marriage. Instead, his wife is given to one of the Philistine men present.

15:1–20 In Jdg 14 God used the occasion of Samson's desire for a Philistine woman to bring judgment on the Philistines (14:4,10–20). The antagonism begun in that chapter sets the stage for Samson's exploits recorded here.

15:1 I'm going to my wife's room Samson never consummated the marriage. Nevertheless, he assumes the woman is his wife, unaware that her father has given her to another man after his departure (14:20).

15:2 Take her instead To avoid offense or perhaps out of fear, the man offers Samson the sister of the woman he presumed was his wife. Samson, however, is not satisfied by the offer.

15:4 caught three hundred foxes Probably a number intended to indicate a large amount, not an exact figure, since foxes are not abundant in the region.

15:6 burned her and her father to death The Philistine populace exacts revenge on Samson's intended bride and her father for their role in Samson's treachery.

15:8 He attacked them viciously and slaughtered The Hebrew phrase used here, *shoq al-yarekh*, literally rendered "he struck them thigh upon loin," is an idiomatic expression. It most likely indicates that Samson inflicted a thorough, violent beating. It is possible that the Hebrew

text here is suggesting that Samson killed men at this moment, but it is not entirely clear. **the rock of Etam** The precise location of this rock is unknown; the ensuing context requires that it be in Judah's territory (v. 9).

15:11 three thousand men from Judah went down The men of Judah conduct their own search for the fugitive Samson to surrender him to their Philistine overlords (14:4). **Don't you realize** The men of Judah face a serious threat. If the Philistines retaliate, they could ravage Judah. The only way to appease them is to present them with Samson.

15:13 led him up from the rock Samson complies to ensure that the Philistines do not attack Judah.

15:14 Spirit of the LORD came powerfully upon him See 14:6 and note.

15:15 struck The Hebrew word used here, *nakhah*, likely means "kill" in this instance (e.g., Ex 2:12), though it may refer to other wounds that rendered the men unable to fight back.

15:16 I have made donkeys of them The Hebrew phrase here seems to be a pun. The Hebrew text could be understood as Samson stating that he has made his Philistine enemies into "many heaps" or that he has made them seem like donkeys by simply using the jawbone of a donkey.

15:18 he cried out to the LORD The first mention of Samson praying.

he revived. So the spring was called En Hakkore,[a] and it is still there in Lehi.

[20] Samson led[b] Israel for twenty years in the days of the Philistines.

Samson and Delilah

16 One day Samson went to Gaza, where he saw a prostitute. He went in to spend the night with her. [2] The people of Gaza were told, "Samson is here!" So they surrounded the place and lay in wait for him all night at the city gate. They made no move during the night, saying, "At dawn we'll kill him."

[3] But Samson lay there only until the middle of the night. Then he got up and took hold of the doors of the city gate, together with the two posts, and tore them loose, bar and all. He lifted them to his shoulders and carried them to the top of the hill that faces Hebron.

[4] Some time later, he fell in love with a woman in the Valley of Sorek whose name was Delilah. [5] The rulers of the Philistines went to her and said, "See if you can lure him into showing you the secret of his great strength and how we can overpower him so we may tie him up and subdue him. Each one of us will give you eleven hundred shekels[c] of silver."

[6] So Delilah said to Samson, "Tell me the secret of your great strength and how you can be tied up and subdued."

[7] Samson answered her, "If anyone ties me with seven fresh bowstrings that have not been dried, I'll become as weak as any other man."

[8] Then the rulers of the Philistines brought her seven fresh bowstrings that had not been dried, and she tied him with them. [9] With men hidden in the room, she called to him, "Samson, the Philistines are upon you!" But he snapped the bowstrings as easily as a piece of string snaps when it comes close to a flame. So the secret of his strength was not discovered.

[10] Then Delilah said to Samson, "You have made a fool of me; you lied to me. Come now, tell me how you can be tied."

[11] He said, "If anyone ties me securely with new ropes that have never been used, I'll become as weak as any other man."

[12] So Delilah took new ropes and tied him with them. Then, with men hidden in the room, she called to him, "Samson, the Philistines are upon you!" But he snapped the ropes off his arms as if they were threads.

---

[a] 19 *En Hakkore* means *caller's spring.*   [b] 20 Traditionally *judged*   [c] 5 That is, about 28 pounds or about 13 kilograms

---

16:1–22 In this passage, Samson's lust continues to draw him into conflict with the Philistines. First, he visits a prostitute in the Philistine city of Gaza (Jdg 16:1–3) and then begins his relationship with Delilah (vv. 4–22). The notice in 15:20 that Samson judged Israel for 20 years suggests that the episode with Delilah occurred at the end of this time. However, the timing of the incident in vv. 1–3 is not given. It may have been soon after the events of 15:14–19 or closer to the following events with Delilah in vv. 4–22.

16:1 Gaza One of the five Philistine cities on the coast of Canaan (Jos 13:3). Gaza was the furthest south of the Philistine cities. See the map "Tribal Distribution of Palestine" on p. 2253.

16:2 The people of Gaza The men of Gaza, aware of what Samson had done to their Philistine kinsmen (Jdg 14–15), want him dead. Since Gaza is a major Philistine stronghold deep in Philistine territory, it would be surprising if this incident follows soon after the events of 15:14–19. Samson's conflict with the Philistines was likely ongoing throughout his twenty-year time as judge. The episodes recounted in the book of Judges are selective and meant to be representative of each judge's character and accomplishments.

16:3 and took hold of the doors Samson's other great feats of strength happen when he is empowered by Yahweh (see 14:6 and note; compare 14:19; 15:14). Here there is no mention of God's Spirit coming upon him; he simply picks up the gate. However, the narrative in vv. 1–22 consistently assumes Samson's strength comes from God, even though it does not explicitly state that God empowers him each time (vv. 9,12,14). Once Samson's hair has been cut, he loses his strength and the narrative explains that Yahweh had left him (v. 20). **carried them to the top of the hill** In another feat of supernatural strength, Samson carries the doors and

doorposts of the city gate to the top of a hill nearly 40 miles away. The city of Hebron is about 40 miles east of Gaza.

16:4 the Valley of Sorek This valley, only named here, likely refers to the fertile valley that marked the border between the territories of Judah and Dan (Jos 15:9–10; 19:40–46). The valley was Samson's home region where Zorah, Eshtaol, Timnah and Ekron were located. The cities of Beth Shemesh and Lehi in the territory of Judah are in the southern part of this valley (see Jdg 15:9–19). The region is also the borderland between Philistine territory and Israelite territory (1Sa 6:9–20; 2Ch 28:18).

16:5 eleven hundred shekels of silver The amount is substantial—5,500 silver pieces in all, assuming one lord for each of the five cities of the Philistines.

16:6 how you can be tied up Delilah asks the question openly. Samson fails to suspect her of treachery. His lust for Delilah may have clouded his judgment, or he is arrogantly sure of his ability to overcome any foe. Since he continues to play along as she asks the secret of his strength and tests his answer, he is likely overconfident; this is evident in his assumption in v. 20 that he will break free again.

16:8 and she tied him with them Delilah tests all of Samson's answers, but the story is unclear whether she tries each method immediately after he gives the answer or some time later. In testing the bowstrings, she first has to notify the Philistines who provide the bowstrings and wait in ambush.

16:12 men hidden Delilah had Philistines waiting to overpower Samson when she tests the bowstrings (v. 9) and when she tests the new ropes. It is possible these incidents happened at the same time. The men lying in ambush are not mentioned in vv. 13–14, and the Philistines have to be summoned again in v. 18 because some days have passed (v. 16).

[13] Delilah then said to Samson, "All this time you have been making a fool of me and lying to me. Tell me how you can be tied."

He replied, "If you weave the seven braids of my head into the fabric on the loom and tighten it with the pin, I'll become as weak as any other man." So while he was sleeping, Delilah took the seven braids of his head, wove them into the fabric [14] and[a] tightened it with the pin.

Again she called to him, "Samson, the Philistines are upon you!" He awoke from his sleep and pulled up the pin and the loom, with the fabric.

[15] Then she said to him, "How can you say, 'I love you,' when you won't confide in me? This is the third time you have made a fool of me and haven't told me the secret of your great strength." [16] With such nagging she prodded him day after day until he was sick to death of it.

[17] So he told her everything. "No razor has ever been used on my head," he said, "because I have been a Nazirite dedicated to God from my mother's womb. If my head were shaved, my strength would leave me, and I would become as weak as any other man."

[18] When Delilah saw that he had told her everything, she sent word to the rulers of the Philistines, "Come back once more; he has told me everything." So the rulers of the Philistines returned with the silver in their hands. [19] After putting him to sleep on her lap, she called for someone to shave off the seven braids of his hair, and so began to subdue him.[b] And his strength left him.

[20] Then she called, "Samson, the Philistines are upon you!"

He awoke from his sleep and thought, "I'll go out as before and shake myself free." But he did not know that the LORD had left him.

[21] Then the Philistines seized him, gouged out his eyes and took him down to Gaza. Binding him with bronze shackles, they set him to grinding grain in the prison. [22] But the hair on his head began to grow again after it had been shaved.

The Death of Samson

[23] Now the rulers of the Philistines assembled to offer a great sacrifice to Dagon their god and to celebrate, saying, "Our god has delivered Samson, our enemy, into our hands."

[24] When the people saw him, they praised their god, saying,

"Our god has delivered our enemy
    into our hands,
the one who laid waste our land
    and multiplied our slain."

[25] While they were in high spirits, they shouted, "Bring out Samson to entertain us." So they called Samson out of the prison, and he performed for them.

When they stood him among the pillars, [26] Samson said to the servant who held his hand, "Put me where I can feel the pillars that support the temple, so that I may lean against them." [27] Now the temple was crowded with men and women; all the rulers of the Philistines were there, and on the roof were about three thousand men and women watching Samson perform. [28] Then Samson prayed to the LORD, "Sovereign LORD, remember me. Please, God, strengthen me just once more, and let me with one blow get revenge on the Philistines for my two eyes." [29] Then Samson reached toward the two central pillars on which the temple stood. Bracing himself against them, his right hand on the one and his left hand on the other, [30] Samson said, "Let me die with the

---

[a] 13,14 Some Septuagint manuscripts; Hebrew replied, "I can if you weave the seven braids of my head into the fabric on the loom." [14] So she   [b] 19 Hebrew; some Septuagint manuscripts and he began to weaken

---

16:17 God Samson uses the generic Hebrew word *elohim* instead of the divine name Yahweh, which Samson never utters until his death. This word choice highlights Samson's spiritual detachment from Yahweh, who has guarded and empowered him through his life but whom he now betrays by revealing the secret.

16:18 When Delilah saw Something may have changed in Samson's manner that causes Delilah to know he is telling the truth.

16:19 putting him to sleep on her lap This may indicate that Delilah drugged Samson in some way to put him to sleep. **began to subdue him** Delilah is probably trying to awaken Samson from some sort of drug-induced stupor and, seeing him begin to stir, calls out as before.

16:21 they set him to grinding grain in the prison The Philistines easily capture the now-powerless Samson. After blinding him, they imprison him at Gaza, enslaving him and giving him what was considered a woman's work: probably grinding corn with a hand mill.

16:23–31 The Samson narrative ends with this account of Samson's final act of great strength where he is empowered by Yahweh one last time to bring destruction on the Philistines, Israel's oppressive foe.

16:23 to Dagon their god The Philistine god Dagon was most likely a corn or vegetation god. The noun *dagan* was a common Semitic word for "grain." A temple to Dagon is known from Ugarit (ca. fourteenth century BC). Dagon was worshiped in Canaan during the reign of Saul (1Sa 31:10; compare 1Ch 10:10).

16:24 they praised their god Samson's betrayal of Yahweh gives the Philistines occasion to praise their lesser, foreign deity Dagon.

16:25 they stood him among the pillars Assuming this temple's structure is similar to that of several pagan temples discovered in the wider region, this temple would have been covered by a roof supported by a series of pillars.

16:28 Then Samson prayed to the LORD Samson calls to God with the divine name, Yahweh. Samson has apparently regained his faith, or he is at least repentant (see Jdg 16:17).

16:30 down came the temple on the rulers Though it is unclear which two pillars the Philistines place Samson

Philistines!" Then he pushed with all his might, and down came the temple on the rulers and all the people in it. Thus he killed many more when he died than while he lived.

³¹Then his brothers and his father's whole family went down to get him. They brought him back and buried him between Zorah and Eshtaol in the tomb of Manoah his father. He had led*a* Israel twenty years.

Micah's Idols

17 Now a man named Micah from the hill country of Ephraim ²said to his mother, "The eleven hundred shekels*b* of silver that were taken from you and about which I heard you utter a curse — I have that silver with me; I took it."

Then his mother said, "The LORD bless you, my son!"

³When he returned the eleven hundred shekels of silver to his mother, she said, "I solemnly consecrate my silver to the LORD for my son to make an image overlaid with silver. I will give it back to you."

⁴So after he returned the silver to his mother, she took two hundred shekels*c* of silver and gave them to a silversmith, who used them to make the idol. And it was put in Micah's house.

⁵Now this man Micah had a shrine, and he made an ephod and some household gods and installed one of his sons as his priest. ⁶In those days Israel had no king; everyone did as they saw fit.

⁷A young Levite from Bethlehem in Judah, who had been living within the clan of Judah, ⁸left that town in search of some other place to stay. On his way*d* he came to Micah's house in the hill country of Ephraim.

⁹Micah asked him, "Where are you from?"

"I'm a Levite from Bethlehem in Judah," he said, "and I'm looking for a place to stay."

¹⁰Then Micah said to him, "Live with me and be my father and priest, and I'll give you ten shekels*e* of silver a year, your clothes and your food." ¹¹So the Levite agreed to live with him, and the young man became like one of his sons to him. ¹²Then Micah installed the Levite, and the young man became his priest and lived in his house. ¹³And Micah said, "Now I know that the LORD will be good to me, since this Levite has become my priest."

The Danites Settle in Laish

18 In those days Israel had no king.

And in those days the tribe of the Danites was seeking a place of their own where they might settle, because they had not yet come into an inheritance among the tribes of Israel. ²So the Danites sent five of their leading men from Zorah and Eshtaol to spy out the land and explore it. These

---

a 31 Traditionally *judged*   *b 2* That is, about 28 pounds or about 13 kilograms   *c 4* That is, about 5 pounds or about 2.3 kilograms   *d 8* Or *To carry on his profession*   *e 10* That is, about 4 ounces or about 115 grams

---

between (v. 26), it likely did not matter. The upper terrace or roof area of the structure, compromised by the collapse of two of its pillars, topples under the weight of the numerous spectators (v. 27).
16:31 He had led Israel twenty years See 15:20.

17:1 — 18:31 The final five chapters of Judges (chs. 17–21) do not offer an account of any additional judges; rather, they provide a glimpse into life during the period. These chapters recount two stories. The first is focused on the idolatry of an Ephraimite named Micah and his encounter with the tribe of Dan (chs. 17–18). The second story relates an incident that instigates war between the tribe of Benjamin and the other tribes (chs. 19–21). While Israel's experience of oppression earlier in the book was attributed to their persistent idolatry (2:11–19), the stories in chs. 17–21 emphasize the near anarchy that existed in Israel before there was a king.

17:2 eleven hundred shekels of silver that were taken Micah confesses to stealing silver from his mother. **LORD bless you, my son** Micah's mother uses the divine name, Yahweh. She is therefore probably a worshiper of Yahweh, though likely not one who worships Yahweh exclusively.
17:3 I solemnly consecrate my silver to the LORD Micah's mother apparently sees no problem with dedicating 200 pieces of the silver to make an idol for Yahweh, a clear violation of Ex 20:4–5 and Dt 5:8–9.
17:5 an ephod See Jdg 8:27 and note. **household gods** Likely figurines of ancestors or other objects connected with ancestors. **sons as his priest** Since Micah appoints his own son as priest, he may have seen himself in the role of a high priest. Micah may be attempting to worship Yahweh but was woefully ignorant of the Law of Moses.

Micah may also have been motivated by making a living through operating a worship and sacrificial center.
17:6 everyone did as they saw fit In chs. 17–21, the familiar refrain of the narrative that the Israelites did evil before Yahweh or did what was right in their own eyes (see 2:11) leads to a new expression that highlights the near anarchy that persisted without a king in Israel (18:1; 19:1; 21:25). Religious apostasy is now connected to a lack of central governance.
17:9 I'm a Levite from Bethlehem in Judah The Levite's name is Jonathan (18:30).
17:10 my father and priest A spiritual leader. Micah may wish to add a priest to increase business or add a greater level of credibility to his shrine. Alternatively, Micah's deference to the Levite as a source of spiritual authority may suggest that his actions in vv. 2–6, though severely misguided, were well-intentioned. **ten shekels of silver a year** Normally priests were supported materially from the sacrifices brought to the tabernacle, so Micah's offer of a small stipend is not suspect.
17:11 agreed to live with him The Levite should know that Yahweh should be worshiped only at the tabernacle, the central sanctuary (Dt 12).
17:12 installed This term can refer to appointment to a priestly office (e.g., Ex 29:29), but here, it may also refer to Micah paying the Levite.

18:1–31 Judges 17 introduced Micah, an Israelite from Ephraim who worshiped Yahweh using an idol and his own household shrine. After meeting a Levite from Judah, Micah invites the Levite to be his personal priest. In this chapter, the migrating Danites encounter the Levite.

18:1 Israel had no king See note on 17:6. **they had**

men represented all the Danites. They told them, "Go, explore the land."

So they entered the hill country of Ephraim and came to the house of Micah, where they spent the night. ³When they were near Micah's house, they recognized the voice of the young Levite; so they turned in there and asked him, "Who brought you here? What are you doing in this place? Why are you here?"

⁴He told them what Micah had done for him, and said, "He has hired me and I am his priest."

⁵Then they said to him, "Please inquire of God to learn whether our journey will be successful."

⁶The priest answered them, "Go in peace. Your journey has the LORD's approval."

⁷So the five men left and came to Laish, where they saw that the people were living in safety, like the Sidonians, at peace and secure. And since their land lacked nothing, they were prosperous.ᵃ Also, they lived a long way from the Sidonians and had no relationship with anyone else.ᵇ

⁸When they returned to Zorah and Eshtaol, their fellow Danites asked them, "How did you find things?"

⁹They answered, "Come on, let's attack them! We have seen the land, and it is very good. Aren't you going to do something? Don't hesitate to go there and take it over. ¹⁰When you get there, you will find an unsuspecting people and a spacious land that God has put into your hands, a land that lacks nothing whatever."

¹¹Then six hundred men of the Danites, armed for battle, set out from Zorah and Eshtaol. ¹²On their way they set up camp near Kiriath Jearim in Judah. This is why the place west of Kiriath Jearim is called Mahaneh Danᶜ to this day. ¹³From there they went on to the hill country of Ephraim and came to Micah's house.

¹⁴Then the five men who had spied out the land of Laish said to their fellow Danites, "Do you know that one of these houses has an ephod, some household gods and an image overlaid with silver? Now you know what to do." ¹⁵So they turned in there and went to the house of the young Levite at Micah's place and greeted him. ¹⁶The six hundred Danites, armed for battle, stood at the entrance of the gate. ¹⁷The five men who had spied out the land went inside and took the idol, the ephod and the household gods while the priest and the six hundred armed men stood at the entrance of the gate.

¹⁸When the five men went into Micah's house and took the idol, the ephod and the household gods, the priest said to them, "What are you doing?"

¹⁹They answered him, "Be quiet! Don't say a word. Come with us, and be our father and priest. Isn't it better that you serve a tribe and clan in Israel as priest rather than just one man's household?" ²⁰The priest was very pleased. He took the ephod, the household gods and the idol and went along with the people. ²¹Putting their little children, their livestock and their possessions in front of them, they turned away and left.

²²When they had gone some distance from

ᵃ 7 The meaning of the Hebrew for this clause is uncertain.
ᵇ 7 Hebrew; some Septuagint manuscripts *with the Arameans*
ᶜ 12 *Mahaneh Dan* means *Dan's camp.*

---

not yet come into an inheritance among the tribes of Israel The wording here does not mean that Dan had not received an inheritance, only that Dan had not secured their inheritance. While Jos 19:40–48 describes the inheritance of Dan, Jos 19:47 notes that they had lost this inheritance. Judges 1:34 indicates that the Danites were unable to defeat the Amorites. The story of Samson also indicates the Philistines had a strong presence in the region in the city of Timnah (14:1). Consequently, the tribe of Dan decided to leave the territory it was allotted and migrate north.

18:2 from Zorah and Eshtaol Zorah and Eshtaol were towns in the Shephelah—the lowlands west of the hill country of Judah—allotted to the tribe of Dan (Jos 15:33). The region bordered the coastal plain controlled by the Philistines.

18:3 near Micah's house The Danite scouts probably come to Micah's house because it has a reputation as a religious sanctuary (see Jdg 17:5 and note).

18:6 has the LORD's approval The priest, who has already proven himself to be breaking Yahweh's regulations, proclaims that Yahweh will bless the Danites' abandonment of their divinely given inheritance (Jos 19:40). Although the Danites are successful, as the priest proclaims, this does not mean that the priest spoke truthfully—the Danites' success in the battle is predictable (Jdg 18:7).

18:7 came to Laish Laish was at the foot of Mount Hermon in the northern region of Israel's land (also called Leshem; compare Jos 19:47). The city was the northernmost extent of Israel (see note on Jdg 20:1). **like the Sidonians** The Sidonians were Phoenicians from Sidon. Their city was on the Mediterranean coast northwest of Laish. The comparison with the Sidonians could mean that the people of Laish were also Phoenicians or that Sidon considered the area part of their territory.

18:10 God has put into your hands The Danites presume God endorses their plan to violently invade Laish, perhaps because of God's original conquest command (e.g., Dt 11:23; Jos 3:10; compare note on Jos 6:16), but more likely because of the priest's proclamation (see Jdg 18:6 and note).

18:11 six hundred men of the Danites Since Laish was unguarded, a large army would be unnecessary.

18:12 is called Mahaneh Dan The first stop on the migratory journey is near Kiriath Jearim, a city of Judah on the border with Dan. Mahaneh Dan means "camp of Dan."

18:14–20 The Danites return to Micah's home, where earlier the Levite had told them that Yahweh would bless their migration efforts (v. 6). Upon seeing that the desired site would be easy to capture and thus that the Levite's words appeared to be true, they believed he had access to God. The Levite apparently stands outside speaking to the armed Danites after they inquire of his welfare (v. 15).

18:22 near Micah were called together Seeing that the Danites have raided their cult sanctuary, someone

Micah's house, the men who lived near Micah were called together and overtook the Danites. ²³As they shouted after them, the Danites turned and said to Micah, "What's the matter with you that you called out your men to fight?"

²⁴He replied, "You took the gods I made, and my priest, and went away. What else do I have? How can you ask, 'What's the matter with you?'"

²⁵The Danites answered, "Don't argue with us, or some of the men may get angry and attack you, and you and your family will lose your lives." ²⁶So the Danites went their way, and Micah, seeing that they were too strong for him, turned around and went back home.

²⁷Then they took what Micah had made, and his priest, and went on to Laish, against a people at peace and secure. They attacked them with the sword and burned down their city. ²⁸There was no one to rescue them because they lived a long way from Sidon and had no relationship with anyone else. The city was in a valley near Beth Rehob.

The Danites rebuilt the city and settled there. ²⁹They named it Dan after their ancestor Dan, who was born to Israel — though the city used to be called Laish. ³⁰There the Danites set up for themselves the idol, and Jonathan son of Gershom, the son of Moses,ᵃ and his sons were priests for the tribe of Dan until the time of the captivity of the land. ³¹They continued to use the idol Micah had made, all the time the house of God was in Shiloh.

A Levite and His Concubine

19 In those days Israel had no king.
Now a Levite who lived in a remote area in the hill country of Ephraim took a concubine from Bethlehem in Judah. ²But she was unfaithful to him. She left him and went back to her parents' home in Bethlehem, Judah. After she had

been there four months, ³her husband went to her to persuade her to return. He had with him his servant and two donkeys. She took him into her parents' home, and when her father saw him, he gladly welcomed him. ⁴His father-in-law, the woman's father, prevailed on him to stay; so he remained with him three days, eating and drinking, and sleeping there.

⁵On the fourth day they got up early and he prepared to leave, but the woman's father said to his son-in-law, "Refresh yourself with something to eat; then you can go." ⁶So the two of them sat down to eat and drink together. Afterward the woman's father said, "Please stay tonight and enjoy yourself." ⁷And when the man got up to go, his father-in-law persuaded him, so he stayed there that night. ⁸On the morning of the fifth day, when he rose to go, the woman's father said, "Refresh yourself. Wait till afternoon!" So the two of them ate together.

⁹Then when the man, with his concubine and his servant, got up to leave, his father-in-law, the woman's father, said, "Now look, it's almost evening. Spend the night here; the day is nearly over. Stay and enjoy yourself. Early tomorrow morning you can get up and be on your way home." ¹⁰But, unwilling to stay another night, the man left and went toward Jebus (that is, Jerusalem), with his two saddled donkeys and his concubine.

¹¹When they were near Jebus and the day was almost gone, the servant said to his master, "Come, let's stop at this city of the Jebusites and spend the night."

¹²His master replied, "No. We won't go into any city whose people are not Israelites. We will go on to Gibeah." ¹³He added, "Come, let's try to reach

---

ᵃ 30 Many Hebrew manuscripts, some Septuagint manuscripts and Vulgate; many other Hebrew manuscripts and some other Septuagint manuscripts *Manasseh*

(likely Micah himself; see v. 23) calls the men near Micah's household to arms.
18:28 near Beth Rehob If this is the Rehob of Nu 13:21, it is the northernmost city that the original 12 spies observed on their journey from Sinai many years earlier.
18:30 Jonathan son of Gershom Here, the narrative reveals that the Levite's name is Jonathan, son of Gershom, son of Moses (or Manasseh). The traditional Hebrew text reads "Manasseh," but the only known Gershom in the OT before the time of Ezra is the son of Moses (Ex 2:22; compare Ezr 8:2). The Septuagint, the ancient Greek translation of the OT, reads "Moses" here. The names are similar in Hebrew.

19:1—21:25 The closing narrative of the book of Judges is the most graphic in its depiction of the lawlessness that existed during the time before the monarchy.

19:1 days Israel had no king See note on Jdg 17:6.
a concubine A woman who was a sexual partner and part of the man's household but with a social status below that of a wife. **from Bethlehem in Judah** The contrast between Ephraim and Judah is evident in the narrative's identification of the home territories of the

Levite and the concubine. The woman is from Bethlehem, the hometown of David.
19:2 unfaithful The Hebrew verb used here, *zanah*, is a common word for describing sexual immorality (Ge 38:24; Jos 6:22). However, the Septuagint, the ancient Greek translation of the OT, says that the woman became angry with the Levite, reading a homonym for *zanah* that means to become angry or hate.
19:4 he remained with him three days Such hospitality was common in ancient Near Eastern culture; inhospitality was a cause for shame (compare Jdg 19:17–23).
19:10 that is, Jerusalem Jebus was an ancient name for Jerusalem (or a settlement very close to it) prior to David's capture of the city. The Jebusites were among the native peoples of Canaan (Ge 10:16). Other passages apparently equate Jebus with Jerusalem (Jos 15:8; 18:28; compare 2Sa 5:6–9; 24:18–25).
19:12 We will go on to Gibeah The Levite either favors staying in a town inhabited by fellow Israelites, perhaps because he thinks it will be safer, or is motivated by ethnic bigotry against the foreign Jebusites (see note on Jdg 19:10).
19:13 Gibeah or Ramah and spend the night Gibeah

Gibeah or Ramah and spend the night in one of those places." ¹⁴So they went on, and the sun set as they neared Gibeah in Benjamin. ¹⁵There they stopped to spend the night. They went and sat in the city square, but no one took them in for the night.

¹⁶That evening an old man from the hill country of Ephraim, who was living in Gibeah (the inhabitants of the place were Benjamites), came in from his work in the fields. ¹⁷When he looked and saw the traveler in the city square, the old man asked, "Where are you going? Where did you come from?"

¹⁸He answered, "We are on our way from Bethlehem in Judah to a remote area in the hill country of Ephraim where I live. I have been to Bethlehem in Judah and now I am going to the house of the LORD.ª No one has taken me in for the night. ¹⁹We have both straw and fodder for our donkeys and bread and wine for ourselves your servants—me, the woman and the young man with us. We don't need anything."

²⁰"You are welcome at my house," the old man said. "Let me supply whatever you need. Only don't spend the night in the square." ²¹So he took him into his house and fed his donkeys. After they had washed their feet, they had something to eat and drink.

²²While they were enjoying themselves, some of the wicked men of the city surrounded the house. Pounding on the door, they shouted to the old man who owned the house, "Bring out the man who came to your house so we can have sex with him."

²³The owner of the house went outside and said to them, "No, my friends, don't be so vile. Since this man is my guest, don't do this outrageous thing. ²⁴Look, here is my virgin daughter, and his concubine. I will bring them out to you now, and you can use them and do to them whatever you wish. But as for this man, don't do such an outrageous thing."

²⁵But the men would not listen to him. So the man took his concubine and sent her outside to them, and they raped her and abused her throughout the night, and at dawn they let her go. ²⁶At daybreak the woman went back to the house where her master was staying, fell down at the door and lay there until daylight.

²⁷When her master got up in the morning and opened the door of the house and stepped out to continue on his way, there lay his concubine, fallen in the doorway of the house, with her hands on the threshold. ²⁸He said to her, "Get up; let's go." But there was no answer. Then the man put her on his donkey and set out for home.

²⁹When he reached home, he took a knife and cut up his concubine, limb by limb, into twelve parts and sent them into all the areas of Israel. ³⁰Everyone who saw it was saying to one another, "Such a thing has never been seen or done, not since the day the Israelites came up out of Egypt. Just imagine! We must do something! So speak up!"

The Israelites Punish the Benjamites

20 Then all Israel from Dan to Beersheba and from the land of Gilead came together as one and assembled before the LORD in Mizpah. ²The leaders of all the people of the tribes of Israel

ª 18 Hebrew, Vulgate, Syriac and Targum; Septuagint *going home*

(not to be confused with Gibeon) was about four miles beyond Jebus, and Ramah was near Gibeah. Both cities were within Benjamite territory (19:14,16).
19:18 house of the LORD It is unclear why the Levite would reference visiting Shiloh (or Bethel), where it seems the ark of the covenant was kept (18:31; 20:18). This may be why the Septuagint, the ancient Greek translation of the OT, reads "my house" instead (compare 19:29).

19:22–30 The account draws on the episode of Sodom in Ge 19. The two stories contain the same number of words and share common vocabulary. This story shows that Gibeah of Benjamin had become like Sodom.

19:24 don't do such an outrageous thing The cultural expectations related to hospitality demanded the Levite's protection and safety. The rest of the tribes were appalled by the Benjamites' savagery toward the concubine (Jdg 19:28–30; ch. 20).

19:25 abused her throughout the night This horrific act casts both the tribes of Ephraim and Benjamin in a dishonorable light. The victim—the concubine—is from Judah, while the men who offer the innocent women are from Ephraim; the men who perpetuate the crime are from Benjamin (v. 1,14,16,22,24).

19:28 Then the man put her on his donkey It is unclear whether the concubine is already dead. In view of 19:29, she is dead by the time the Levite returns to Bethlehem.

19:29 into all the areas of Israel It seems that the Levite does this hideous act to prove the truthfulness of his story and prompt others to action (20:4–7).

19:30 Just imagine! We must do something Suggests that the Levite sent a message with the pieces of the corpse. This explains how the tribes knew where to meet in ch. 20.

20:1–48 War with Benjamin erupts in response to the heinous crime that the inhabitants of Gibeah committed in ch. 19. The account of chs. 19–21 emphasizes the moral degradation of Israelite society that occurred when there was no centralized civil authority in Israel. In this way, the narrative promotes the idea of kingship, but the negative portrayal of the tribe of Benjamin indicates disapproval of the kingship of Saul, who was also a Benjamite (see 1Sa 9:21). Further, the negative characterization of Ephraim in Jdg 19 suggests a subtle critique of the northern kingdom of Israel in contrast with Judah, the southern kingdom (compare note on 19:1). These emphases indicate the narrative reflects a perspective favoring Davidic kingship (from Judah), written after the division of Israel into the northern and southern kingdoms.

20:1 from Dan to Beersheba An idiomatic phrase for the northern and southern extent of the promised land. See the map "Tribal Distribution of Palestine"

took their places in the assembly of God's people, four hundred thousand men armed with swords. ³(The Benjamites heard that the Israelites had gone up to Mizpah.) Then the Israelites said, "Tell us how this awful thing happened."

⁴So the Levite, the husband of the murdered woman, said, "I and my concubine came to Gibeah in Benjamin to spend the night. ⁵During the night the men of Gibeah came after me and surrounded the house, intending to kill me. They raped my concubine, and she died. ⁶I took my concubine, cut her into pieces and sent one piece to each region of Israel's inheritance, because they committed this lewd and outrageous act in Israel. ⁷Now, all you Israelites, speak up and tell me what you have decided to do."

⁸All the men rose up together as one, saying, "None of us will go home. No, not one of us will return to his house. ⁹But now this is what we'll do to Gibeah: We'll go up against it in the order decided by casting lots. ¹⁰We'll take ten men out of every hundred from all the tribes of Israel, and a hundred from a thousand, and a thousand from ten thousand, to get provisions for the army. Then, when the army arrives at Gibeah*a* in Benjamin, it can give them what they deserve for this outrageous act done in Israel." ¹¹So all the Israelites got together and united as one against the city.

¹²The tribes of Israel sent messengers throughout the tribe of Benjamin, saying, "What about this awful crime that was committed among you? ¹³Now turn those wicked men of Gibeah over to us so that we may put them to death and purge the evil from Israel."

But the Benjamites would not listen to their fellow Israelites. ¹⁴From their towns they came together at Gibeah to fight against the Israelites. ¹⁵At once the Benjamites mobilized twenty-six thousand swordsmen from their towns, in ad-

dition to seven hundred able young men from those living in Gibeah. ¹⁶Among all these soldiers there were seven hundred select troops who were left-handed, each of whom could sling a stone at a hair and not miss.

¹⁷Israel, apart from Benjamin, mustered four hundred thousand swordsmen, all of them fit for battle.

¹⁸The Israelites went up to Bethel*b* and inquired of God. They said, "Who of us is to go up first to fight against the Benjamites?"

The Lord replied, "Judah shall go first."

¹⁹The next morning the Israelites got up and pitched camp near Gibeah. ²⁰The Israelites went out to fight the Benjamites and took up battle positions against them at Gibeah. ²¹The Benjamites came out of Gibeah and cut down twenty-two thousand Israelites on the battlefield that day. ²²But the Israelites encouraged one another and again took up their positions where they had stationed themselves the first day. ²³The Israelites went up and wept before the Lord until evening, and they inquired of the Lord. They said, "Shall we go up again to fight against the Benjamites, our fellow Israelites?"

The Lord answered, "Go up against them."

²⁴Then the Israelites drew near to Benjamin the second day. ²⁵This time, when the Benjamites came out from Gibeah to oppose them, they cut down another eighteen thousand Israelites, all of them armed with swords.

²⁶Then all the Israelites, the whole army, went up to Bethel, and there they sat weeping before the Lord. They fasted that day until evening and presented burnt offerings and fellowship offerings to the Lord. ²⁷And the Israelites inquired of the Lord. (In those days the ark of the covenant

a 10 One Hebrew manuscript; most Hebrew manuscripts *Geba,* a variant of *Gibeah*   *b 18* Or *to the house of God*; also in verse 26

on p. 2253. **before the Lord** The phrase used here likely indicates the presence of some sort of sanctuary. **Mizpah** This location is a little less than three miles from Gibeah. Samuel also summoned Israel to gather at Mizpah when he proclaimed Saul as the first king of Israel (1Sa 10:17–27).

20:4–7 The Levite summarizes the events from Jdg 19:14–30. Presumably he had sent a message with the body parts of his dead concubine (19:28–30), but now the group wants an explanation of what happened that warranted summoning everyone to Mizpah.

20:9 by casting lots The people cast lots as a means of determining Yahweh's will; this and v. 27 implies that Yahweh supports the punishment of the city of Gibeah.

20:13 so that we may put them to death The coalition first asks for local authorities from Benjamin to turn over those guilty of the offense.

20:15 twenty-six thousand swordsmen The army of Benjamin is dramatically smaller (see vv. 2,17).

20:16 who were left-handed Being left-handed gave

this group of Benjamites an usual advantage in war—their striking and throwing hands were the opposite of what would be expected (compare note on 3:15; note on 3:16). This helps explain the Benjamites' ability to defeat the Israelites twice, even though the Israelite force is drastically larger (vv. 17,21,25).

20:18 went up to Bethel The tribes inquire of Yahweh about the decision to go to battle against Benjamin.

20:21 cut down twenty-two thousand Israelites on the battlefield that day Despite being vastly outnumbered, the Benjamites win the first two encounters—killing 40,000 (see v. 25).

20:23 and they inquired of the Lord The people ask God for help against Gibeah. They are second-guessing the decision to go up; they expected a victory since Yahweh endorsed the attack. The failure reinforces that the victory will not be by their superior numbers but by God's help (compare v. 28).

20:27 inquired of the Lord After the second defeat, they return to confirm that their attack is indeed supported by Yahweh (compare v. 23).

of God was there, [28]with Phinehas son of Eleazar, the son of Aaron, ministering before it.) They asked, "Shall we go up again to fight against the Benjamites, our fellow Israelites, or not?"

The LORD responded, "Go, for tomorrow I will give them into your hands."

[29]Then Israel set an ambush around Gibeah. [30]They went up against the Benjamites on the third day and took up positions against Gibeah as they had done before. [31]The Benjamites came out to meet them and were drawn away from the city. They began to inflict casualties on the Israelites as before, so that about thirty men fell in the open field and on the roads — the one leading to Bethel and the other to Gibeah. [32]While the Benjamites were saying, "We are defeating them as before," the Israelites were saying, "Let's retreat and draw them away from the city to the roads."

[33]All the men of Israel moved from their places and took up positions at Baal Tamar, and the Israelite ambush charged out of its place on the west[a] of Gibeah.[b] [34]Then ten thousand of Israel's able young men made a frontal attack on Gibeah. The fighting was so heavy that the Benjamites did not realize how near disaster was. [35]The LORD defeated Benjamin before Israel, and on that day the Israelites struck down 25,100 Benjamites, all armed with swords. [36]Then the Benjamites saw that they were beaten.

Now the men of Israel had given way before Benjamin, because they relied on the ambush they had set near Gibeah. [37]Those who had been in ambush made a sudden dash into Gibeah, spread out and put the whole city to the sword. [38]The Israelites had arranged with the ambush that they should send up a great cloud of smoke from the city, [39]and then the Israelites would counterattack.

The Benjamites had begun to inflict casualties on the Israelites (about thirty), and they said, "We are defeating them as in the first battle."

[40]But when the column of smoke began to rise from the city, the Benjamites turned and saw the whole city going up in smoke. [41]Then the Israelites counterattacked, and the Benjamites were terrified, because they realized that disaster had come on them. [42]So they fled before the Israelites in the direction of the wilderness, but they could not escape the battle. And the Israelites who came out of the towns cut them down there. [43]They surrounded the Benjamites, chased them and easily[c] overran them in the vicinity of Gibeah on the east. [44]Eighteen thousand Benjamites fell, all of them valiant fighters. [45]As they turned and fled toward the wilderness to the rock of Rimmon, the Israelites cut down five thousand men along the roads. They kept pressing after the Benjamites as far as Gidom and struck down two thousand more.

[46]On that day twenty-five thousand Benjamite swordsmen fell, all of them valiant fighters. [47]But six hundred of them turned and fled into the wilderness to the rock of Rimmon, where they stayed four months. [48]The men of Israel went back to Benjamin and put all the towns to the sword, including the animals and everything else they found. All the towns they came across they set on fire.

Wives for the Benjamites

21 The men of Israel had taken an oath at Mizpah: "Not one of us will give his daughter in marriage to a Benjamite."

[2]The people went to Bethel,[d] where they sat before God until evening, raising their voices and weeping bitterly. [3]"LORD, God of Israel," they cried, "why has this happened to Israel? Why should one tribe be missing from Israel today?"

---

[a] 33 Some Septuagint manuscripts and Vulgate; the meaning of the Hebrew for this word is uncertain.   [b] 33 Hebrew *Geba*, a variant of *Gibeah*   [c] 43 The meaning of the Hebrew for this word is uncertain.   [d] 2 Or *to the house of God*

20:28 I will give them into your hands The first time God explicitly promises victory.

20:29–48 Israel's ultimate victory over Gibeah, recounted in 20:29–48, echoes Joshua's victory over Ai (compare Jos 8:1–29).

20:35 that day the Israelites struck down 25,100 Benjamites This is a near total annihilation. Less than 1,000 adult males now remain in Benjamin. Compare Jdg 20:15.

20:44 Eighteen thousand Benjamites fell Verses 44–45 breaks down the 25,100 of v. 35 into the approximation of 18,000 here, then the 5,000 and 2,000 of v. 45.

20:46 twenty-five thousand Benjamite swordsmen A discrepancy exists between this number and the 25,100 of v. 35. The number here may be an approximation.

20:47 they stayed 600 Benjamites succeed in hiding out at a natural rock fortification.

20:48 All the towns they came across Other cities

in Benjamin are now subject to destruction since the Benjamites refused to surrender the guilty people of Gibeah (see vv. 12–13). This seems to indicate that the Israelites viewed this as an act of divine warfare because Yahweh had endorsed their original plans to battle against the city of Gibeah (v. 28; see note on Jos 6:16; note on Jos 6:17). However, Yahweh does not endorse their destruction of these additional cities or the actions that follow—and the Israelites seem to regret this action (Jdg 21:6; compare note on 21:10).

21:1–25 This chapter follows in the wake of the slaughter of Benjamin at the hands of the other 11 tribes of Israel (ch. 20) in response to Gibeah's crime (ch. 19). Now the tribe of Benjamin's survival is at stake.

21:1 at Mizpah This vow was not reported in ch. 20.
21:3 Why should one tribe be missing from Israel Given that some Benjamites remain, the language here does not mean the Benjamites are entirely gone but rather dangerously close to being gone.

⁴Early the next day the people built an altar and presented burnt offerings and fellowship offerings.

⁵Then the Israelites asked, "Who from all the tribes of Israel has failed to assemble before the LORD?" For they had taken a solemn oath that anyone who failed to assemble before the LORD at Mizpah was to be put to death.

⁶Now the Israelites grieved for the tribe of Benjamin, their fellow Israelites. "Today one tribe is cut off from Israel," they said. ⁷"How can we provide wives for those who are left, since we have taken an oath by the LORD not to give them any of our daughters in marriage?" ⁸Then they asked, "Which one of the tribes of Israel failed to assemble before the LORD at Mizpah?" They discovered that no one from Jabesh Gilead had come to the camp for the assembly. ⁹For when they counted the people, they found that none of the people of Jabesh Gilead were there.

¹⁰So the assembly sent twelve thousand fighting men with instructions to go to Jabesh Gilead and put to the sword those living there, including the women and children. ¹¹"This is what you are to do," they said. "Kill every male and every woman who is not a virgin." ¹²They found among the people living in Jabesh Gilead four hundred young women who had never slept with a man, and they took them to the camp at Shiloh in Canaan.

¹³Then the whole assembly sent an offer of peace to the Benjamites at the rock of Rimmon. ¹⁴So the Benjamites returned at that time and were given the women of Jabesh Gilead who had been spared. But there were not enough for all of them.

¹⁵The people grieved for Benjamin, because the LORD had made a gap in the tribes of Israel. ¹⁶And the elders of the assembly said, "With the women of Benjamin destroyed, how shall we provide wives for the men who are left? ¹⁷The Benjamite survivors must have heirs," they said, "so that a tribe of Israel will not be wiped out. ¹⁸We can't give them our daughters as wives, since we Israelites have taken this oath: 'Cursed be anyone who gives a wife to a Benjamite.' ¹⁹But look, there is the annual festival of the LORD in Shiloh, which lies north of Bethel, east of the road that goes from Bethel to Shechem, and south of Lebonah."

²⁰So they instructed the Benjamites, saying, "Go and hide in the vineyards ²¹and watch. When the young women of Shiloh come out to join in the dancing, rush from the vineyards and each of you seize one of them to be your wife. Then return to the land of Benjamin. ²²When their fathers or brothers complain to us, we will say to them, 'Do us the favor of helping them, because we did not get wives for them during the war. You will not be guilty of breaking your oath because you did not give your daughters to them.'"

²³So that is what the Benjamites did. While the young women were dancing, each man caught one and carried her off to be his wife. Then they returned to their inheritance and rebuilt the towns and settled in them.

²⁴At that time the Israelites left that place and went home to their tribes and clans, each to his own inheritance.

²⁵In those days Israel had no king; everyone did as they saw fit.

21:5 solemn oath In v. 5, the Israelites interrupt their mourning for Benjamin to confront another issue. Apparently, when the Levite of the incident described in ch. 19 sent the pieces of his dead concubine throughout Israel, the enraged Israelites threatened any city that failed to respond to the call for justice with death.

21:9 from Jabesh Gilead Since Jabesh Gilead had failed to participate in bringing justice on Benjamin, the Israelite men decide that the city must now be punished. They seemed to have viewed this decision as falling within a provision of divine war (see note on 20:48). The Israelite men probably decided to spare a group of virgins because Moses had previously made a similar decision (Nu 31:17–18). This is how they end up providing women for the remaining Benjamite men, so that the Benjamite tribe may continue to exist.

21:10 the women and children While the people assemble at Bethel (v. 2) and lament before God for Benjamin, they never consult Yahweh for a solution. This, and the overall absurdity of the decisions of the Israelite men, suggests that although the Israelite men thought they were following Yahweh's principles, they weren't.

21:11 what you are to do The tribes of Israel impose the principle of *cherem* on Jabesh Gilead, sparing only virgin girls (see note on Jos 6:17).

21:14 there were not enough for all of them Since the Israelites were able to take only 400 virgins from Jabesh Gilead, and there are 600 Benjamite men (Jdg 20:47), the Israelites must find 200 more virgins.

21:19 annual festival of the LORD in Shiloh Many people would be attending this annual feast, providing an occasion for 200 more virgins to be kidnapped for the men of Benjamin.

21:22 You will not be guilty of breaking your oath The leaders of Israel admit their complicity in the kidnappings. They contrive an excuse for the fathers whose daughters have been kidnapped that exempts them from the earlier vow (see note on 21:5). Apparently the instructions to the men of Benjamin were given without the men from Shiloh knowing.

21:25 everyone did as they saw fit See note on 17:6.

RUTH

INTRODUCTION TO RUTH

Ruth is a story about self-sacrificial love against all odds. The title character is a Moabite woman who marries into an Israelite family but becomes an impoverished widow. Ruth refuses to abandon her mother-in-law, Naomi—also a widow. Together, they travel from Moab to Bethlehem, where Ruth works to provide for them both. Ruth then marries Boaz, a relative of Naomi's husband, and gives Naomi a grandchild—redeeming them from poverty and restoring Naomi's joy.

BACKGROUND

The book of Ruth is mainly set in the town of Bethlehem of Judah—the hometown of David and birthplace of Jesus (Mt 2:1–6; Jn 7:42). The narrative opens explaining how famine in Judah drove Naomi's husband, Elimelek, to move his family to Moab. The story is set during the period of the judges (roughly 1210–1051 BC) and serves as a bridge between this lawless era—when every-one did what was right in their own eyes (Jdg 17:6; 21:25)—and the era of Israel's monarchy.

Like many stories in the OT, Ruth presents an unexpected reversal of the common expectations of the time. In the patriarchal culture of ancient Israel, a childless widow like Ruth would have been limited to the lowest levels of society. Her status as a foreigner from Israel's sometime-enemy Moab (Jdg 3:12–21) would have reduced her social status even further. However, through her faithfulness to Naomi and her marriage to Boaz, she moves from the margins to mainline society.

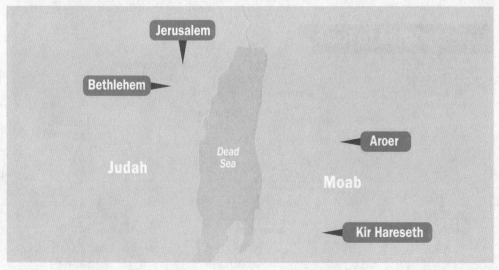

This map depicts Moab in relation to Israel. Bethlehem is the only town mentioned by name in the book; other towns are provided for context.

The marriage of Ruth and Boaz depicts an ancient Near Eastern custom called "levirate marriage" (described in Dt 25:5–10). After a man died, a relative (often his brother) was expected to marry the deceased man's widow; the Hebrew text calls this as acting as a *go'el*, which may be broadly defined as a redeemer. This custom preserved the deceased man's lineage and his family's inheritance. It also provided support for the widow—redeeming her from an otherwise desperate existence without a family and income.

STRUCTURE

Ruth may be divided into four acts bookended by a prologue and an epilogue, with the story moving thematically from death to life. The prologue (Ru 1:1–5) sets the stage with an Israelite family migrating to Moab during a famine. The father and his sons die, leaving his wife, Naomi, and the sons' Moabite wives, Ruth and Orpah. In the first major section (1:6–22), Naomi and Ruth journey to Israel. Rather than remaining in Moab and marrying a husband from her own people, Ruth insists on committing herself to Naomi and Naomi's God—the God of Israel, Yahweh (1:15–18).

In the second section (2:1–23), Ruth gathers food for herself and Naomi by gleaning barley in the field of Boaz, a relative of Naomi. The third section (3:1–18) describes Ruth following Naomi's advice and sleeping on the threshing floor at Boaz's feet. Ruth asks Boaz to redeem her by marrying her, and he agrees. In the fourth major section (4:1–12), Boaz successfully negotiates with a closer relative, who has the first right to act as Ruth's redeemer (*go'el* in Hebrew). In

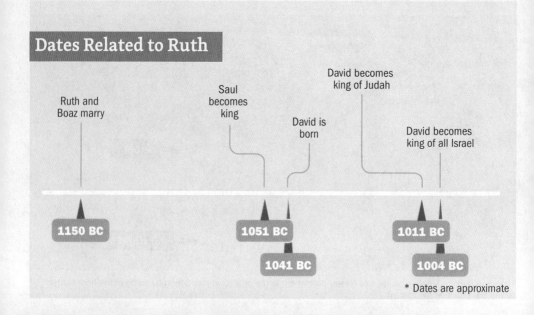

Dates Related to Ruth

Ruth and Boaz marry

Saul becomes king

David becomes king of Judah

David is born

David becomes king of all Israel

1150 BC

1051 BC

1041 BC

1011 BC

1004 BC

* Dates are approximate

the epilogue (4:13–22), Boaz marries Ruth, and she gives birth to a son, Obed, who becomes the grandfather of King David.

OUTLINE

- Prologue: The family line ends (1:1–5)
- Ruth joins Naomi (1:6–22)
- Ruth meets Boaz (2:1–23)
- Ruth sleeps at Boaz's feet (3:1–18)
- Boaz redeems Ruth (4:1–12)
- Epilogue: The family line continues (4:13–22)

THEMES

Redemption is at the center of Ruth. At the beginning of the book, Naomi believes that Yahweh has turned against her (1:13,20–21). Despite this, Ruth demonstrates her love by staying with Naomi instead of returning to her own family. These two marginalized women travel together to Israel in hope of a better life. Through Ruth's kindness and self-sacrifice, God works to renew Naomi's faith and redeem Ruth from the bleak existence of widowhood in the ancient world.

The book emphasizes the vital role women play in God's plan for humanity. By the standards of Israelite society, Ruth and Naomi would be powerless and inconsequential. But God's plan turns societal expectations upside down, and the women become central figures in the story of God's people.

Underlying this story of redemption is Yahweh himself, who is with his people even in foreign lands—unlike Moab's gods. The story shows that Yahweh desires to incorporate outsiders into his people, even into the lineage of Israel's great king, David, and its ultimate king, Jesus (Mt 1:5–6; compare Gal 3:28–29). Ruth demonstrates that Yahweh can use any of us to further his work in the world and that he will go anywhere for any of us.

Naomi Loses Her Husband and Sons

1 In the days when the judges ruled,[a] there was a famine in the land. So a man from Bethlehem in Judah, together with his wife and two sons, went to live for a while in the country of Moab. ²The man's name was Elimelek, his wife's name was Naomi, and the names of his two sons were Mahlon and Kilion. They were Ephrathites from Bethlehem, Judah. And they went to Moab and lived there.

³Now Elimelek, Naomi's husband, died, and she was left with her two sons. ⁴They married Moabite women, one named Orpah and the other Ruth. After they had lived there about ten years, ⁵both Mahlon and Kilion also died, and Naomi was left without her two sons and her husband.

Naomi and Ruth Return to Bethlehem

⁶When Naomi heard in Moab that the Lord had come to the aid of his people by providing food for them, she and her daughters-in-law prepared to return home from there. ⁷With her two daughters-in-law she left the place where she had been living and set out on the road that would take them back to the land of Judah.

⁸Then Naomi said to her two daughters-in-law, "Go back, each of you, to your mother's home. May the Lord show you kindness, as you have shown kindness to your dead husbands and to me. ⁹May the Lord grant that each of you will find rest in the home of another husband."

Then she kissed them goodbye and they wept aloud ¹⁰and said to her, "We will go back with you to your people."

¹¹But Naomi said, "Return home, my daughters. Why would you come with me? Am I going to have any more sons, who could become your husbands? ¹²Return home, my daughters; I am too old to have another husband. Even if I thought there was still hope for me — even if I had a husband tonight and then gave birth to sons — ¹³would you wait until they grew up? Would you remain unmarried for them? No, my daughters. It is more bitter for me than for you, because the Lord's hand has turned against me!"

¹⁴At this they wept aloud again. Then Orpah kissed her mother-in-law goodbye, but Ruth clung to her.

¹⁵"Look," said Naomi, "your sister-in-law is going back to her people and her gods. Go back with her."

¹⁶But Ruth replied, "Don't urge me to leave you or to turn back from you. Where you go I will go, and where you stay I will stay. Your people will

[a] 1 Traditionally *judged*

1:1–5 The story of Ruth occurs during the time of the judges, which began with Joshua's death (Jdg 1:1) and ended with Saul's coronation as king (1Sa 10; roughly 1210–1051 BC).

The opening verses of the book of Ruth provide the exposition for the story, giving the background necessary for understanding the events about to unfold. A family from Bethlehem of the tribe of Judah moves to the neighboring country of Moab to escape famine. The plot is set in motion by the circumstances described here in Ru 1:1–5: A man and his two sons die, leaving three women widowed and destitute.

1:1 when the judges ruled The judges were local leaders raised up by Yahweh to deliver the tribes of Israel from their enemies. The time of the judges was sometimes unstable and chaotic (Jdg 21:25), but the rule of a strong and capable judge could bring peace to a region for decades (Jdg 8:28). The lack of unrest or political instability in the book of Ruth suggests the events are set during one of those periods of peace. **famine in the land** Famines were common in the ancient world. The exact circumstances of this famine are unknown. God is sometimes depicted in the OT as using famine as a means of punishment (Lev 26:18–20; Dt 28:23–24; Isa 3:1). See the infographic "The Amarna Letters" on p. 337. **Bethlehem** It is ironic that a famine has afflicted Bethlehem, which means "house of bread." This city in the territory of Judah was the home of the family of David (1Sa 17:12) and eventually came to be known as the city of David (Lk 2:4). **Moab** Judah's closest neighbor to the east. Moab and Israel were often in conflict. Their history of mutual animosity adds depth to Ruth's proclamation of loyalty to Naomi (Ru 1:16).

Ruth 1:1

MOAB
The region east of the Jordan River and the Dead Sea. According to Genesis, the people of Moab descended from Abraham's nephew Lot (Ge 19:30–38). In the time of the exodus, Balak, the king of Moab, unsuccessfully hired Balaam to curse the Israelites (Nu 22:1—24:25). During the period of the judges, Moab asserted control over Israel at times (Jdg 3:12–30). Israel and Moab occasionally fought during the reigns of Saul and David, and Israel was usually the victor (1Sa 14:47; 2Sa 8:2). See the infographic "The Mesha Stele" on p. 565.

1:2 Naomi The name Naomi is derived from a Hebrew word meaning "pleasant." See note on v. 20.

1:4 Moabite women Israelites were commanded not to intermarry with the surrounding Canaanite nations (Dt 7:1–4), but intermarriage with the Moabites was not explicitly forbidden. During the wilderness wanderings, some Israelites slept with Moabite women who encouraged the men to worship their gods, specifically Baal of Peor (Nu 25:1–5). Intermarriage was viewed as potentially leading to idolatry (compare 1Ki 11:1–8). However, intermarriage with Moabite women here resulted in a Moabite—Ruth—worshiping Israel's God (Ru 1:16–17).

ten years Both Orpah and Ruth may have been barren (see 4:13), as ten years would have been enough time for the couples to conceive.

1:5 without her two sons and her husband Naomi's situation is truly dire because a widow with no heirs would

be my people and your God my God. ¹⁷Where you die I will die, and there I will be buried. May the LORD deal with me, be it ever so severely, if even death separates you and me." ¹⁸When Naomi realized that Ruth was determined to go with her, she stopped urging her.

¹⁹So the two women went on until they came to Bethlehem. When they arrived in Bethlehem, the whole town was stirred because of them, and the women exclaimed, "Can this be Naomi?"

²⁰"Don't call me Naomi,ᵃ" she told them. "Call me Mara,ᵇ because the Almightyᶜ has made my life very bitter. ²¹I went away full, but the LORD has brought me back empty. Why call me Naomi? The LORD has afflictedᵈ me; the Almighty has brought misfortune upon me."

²²So Naomi returned from Moab accompanied by Ruth the Moabite, her daughter-in-law, arriving in Bethlehem as the barley harvest was beginning.

Ruth Meets Boaz in the Grain Field

2 Now Naomi had a relative on her husband's side, a man of standing from the clan of Elimelek, whose name was Boaz.

²And Ruth the Moabite said to Naomi, "Let me go to the fields and pick up the leftover grain behind anyone in whose eyes I find favor."

Naomi said to her, "Go ahead, my daughter."

ᵃ 20 *Naomi* means *pleasant.*   ᵇ 20 *Mara* means *bitter.*
ᶜ 20 Hebrew *Shaddai*; also in verse 21   ᵈ 21 Or *has testified against*

---

be unable to support herself. Without any additional protection, a widow could be exploited or oppressed (Job 22:8–9; Isa 10:1–2).

1:6 LORD had come to the aid of his people God is viewed as the one who provides for his people (Dt 10:18; 28:8; Ps 104:14; 136:25; Eze 16:19).

1:8 Go back, each of you Naomi encourages her daughters-in-law to go back to their families. They were probably young enough that they could remarry (Ru 1:9). **kindness** The Hebrew term used here, *chesed*, speaks to God's covenantal love, faithfulness, mercy, favor and kindness (Ex 34:6–7; Dt 7:9; 1Sa 20:14; Ps 118:29; Isa 54:10).

1:11 my daughters Naomi refers to them as her "daughters" rather than her "daughters-in-law," suggesting their relationship was very intimate. **Am I going to have any more sons** Naomi is past the age of childbearing and cannot produce an heir for Orpah or Ruth to marry. Naomi argues that it would be better for them to return home where they will have a chance to remarry. The practice of levirate marriage, where a surviving brother would marry his widowed sister-in-law, provides the background for Naomi's words in Ru 1:11–13 (see Dt 25:5–10; compare Ge 38). An extension of the practice to the nearest male relatives factors into later events in which Naomi and Ruth seek help from Boaz as a redeemer (Ru 2:20; 3:9; 4:1–12; compare Lev 25:25).

1:13 LORD's hand has turned After experiencing famine, the death of her husband, and the death of both her sons, Naomi is convinced that Yahweh is against her.

1:15 to her people and her gods Nationality in the ancient Near East was closely tied to religion. For Orpah and Ruth, going back to their people included returning to the deities of that land. Conversely, for Ruth, the choice to follow Naomi is also the choice to worship Yahweh (Ru 1:16).

1:16 your God my God Ruth's devotion to Naomi's God is striking considering Naomi has just ascribed her difficulties to God's hand being against her (see note on v. 13).

1:17 LORD Ruth uses the divine name Yahweh, illustrating that she is indeed viewing Naomi's God as her God.

1:18 determined to go with her Ruth was determined to stay with Naomi. The word *mith'ammetseth* ("determined") here comes from the word *amats*, denoting strength, firmness, and persistence.

1:19 they came to Bethlehem They returned to Naomi's hometown after she was away for at least a decade. See note on v. 1.

1:20 Mara The name Mara means "bitter." Given her circumstances, Naomi thinks "bitter" is a more fitting

name than "pleasant" (see note on v. 2). However, she is never referred to as Mara because—despite her claim—Yahweh did not deal bitterly with her (see 4:14–15).

1:21 Almighty has brought misfortune upon me Naomi attributed the loss of her husband and sons to God. Like Job, Naomi felt God had become her enemy (Job 16:9; 19:11). However, just as with Job, Naomi's tragedy was part of a larger series of events that would result in God's blessing (Ru 4:14–15).

1:22 Ruth the Moabite Ruth's non-Israelite ethnicity is emphasized throughout the book (2:2,6,21; 4:5,10). Foreigners were generally excluded from worship (e.g., Ex 12:43; Eze 44:9) and often viewed as enemies (Isa 1:7). Against this backdrop, the story of a Moabite widow receiving Yahweh's favor and being included in the lineage of David (Ru 4:17–22) is remarkable. **barley harvest was beginning** Naomi left Bethlehem with her husband and sons because of famine. Now, she returns with Ruth at the time of harvest, when food would be plentiful. The barley harvest began in late April and was followed by the wheat harvest (2:23).

2:1–23 In ch. 2, Ruth works to provide food for herself and her mother-in-law by gleaning grain behind the workers who were harvesting barley. Biblical law designated the gleanings to provide for the poor including orphans and widows (see Dt 24:19–21; compare Lev 19:9–10; 23:22). Ruth chooses to work in a field that happens to be owned by Boaz, a close relative of Naomi's husband, Elimelek. Boaz takes notice of Ruth and shows exceptional kindness toward her, advising her to work only in his fields. He shows concern for her safety and quietly advises his workers to make sure Ruth is able to gather a significant amount of grain.

2:1 on her husband's side, a man of standing The Hebrew phrase used here, *gibbor chayil*, likely identifies Boaz as a wealthy landowner, a member of the upper class. **Elimelek** Since Boaz is from the same family as Elimelek (Naomi's late husband), he can act as a redeemer (*go'el*) for Ruth and Naomi due to the provisions of levirate law. See note on Ru 1:11.

2:2 Let me go to the fields and pick up Ruth takes the initiative to gather food for herself and Naomi. Harvesters were supposed to allow the poor to pick up the grain that fell during the harvesting process. **I find favor** While Biblical law required landowners to allow this, Ruth seems to have asked permission before gleaning (v. 7)—suggesting the poor may not always have been allowed to glean.

³So she went out, entered a field and began to glean behind the harvesters. As it turned out, she was working in a field belonging to Boaz, who was from the clan of Elimelek.

⁴Just then Boaz arrived from Bethlehem and greeted the harvesters, "The Lᴏʀᴅ be with you!"

"The Lᴏʀᴅ bless you!" they answered.

⁵Boaz asked the overseer of his harvesters, "Who does that young woman belong to?"

⁶The overseer replied, "She is the Moabite who came back from Moab with Naomi. ⁷She said, 'Please let me glean and gather among the sheaves behind the harvesters.' She came into the field and has remained here from morning till now, except for a short rest in the shelter."

⁸So Boaz said to Ruth, "My daughter, listen to me. Don't go and glean in another field and don't go away from here. Stay here with the women who work for me. ⁹Watch the field where the men are harvesting, and follow along after the women. I have told the men not to lay a hand on you. And whenever you are thirsty, go and get a drink from the water jars the men have filled."

¹⁰At this, she bowed down with her face to the ground. She asked him, "Why have I found such favor in your eyes that you notice me—a foreigner?"

¹¹Boaz replied, "I've been told all about what you have done for your mother-in-law since the death of your husband—how you left your father and mother and your homeland and came to live with a people you did not know before. ¹²May the Lᴏʀᴅ repay you for what you have done. May you be richly rewarded by the Lᴏʀᴅ, the God of Israel, under whose wings you have come to take refuge."

¹³"May I continue to find favor in your eyes, my lord," she said. "You have put me at ease by speaking kindly to your servant—though I do not have the standing of one of your servants."

¹⁴At mealtime Boaz said to her, "Come over here. Have some bread and dip it in the wine vinegar."

When she sat down with the harvesters, he offered her some roasted grain. She ate all she wanted and had some left over. ¹⁵As she got up to glean, Boaz gave orders to his men, "Let her gather among the sheaves and don't reprimand her. ¹⁶Even pull out some stalks for her from the bundles and leave them for her to pick up, and don't rebuke her."

¹⁷So Ruth gleaned in the field until evening. Then she threshed the barley she had gathered, and it amounted to about an ephah.ᵃ ¹⁸She carried it back to town, and her mother-in-law saw how much she had gathered. Ruth also brought

---

ᵃ 17 That is, probably about 30 pounds or about 13 kilograms

2:3 As it turned out While Ruth's coming to Boaz's field seems coincidental, Naomi later recognizes that God is at work (v. 20).

2:5 Who does that young woman belong to Boaz's question may be driven by curiosity about the new woman working in his field; it may also indicate an attraction to Ruth.

2:6 She is the Moabite Boaz's servant identifies Ruth first by her Moabite ethnicity (see note on 1:22). He also indicates that Ruth is the woman who accompanied Naomi back from Moab.

2:7 Please let me glean Ruth shows courtesy by asking permission to do something that should have been her legal right (see note on v. 2).

2:8–13 Not only does Boaz give Ruth permission to glean, he instructs her to stay in his field and work with his female servants. He also provides protection from any harassment she may have faced and allows her to drink from the water drawn by his workers. Boaz's kindness exceeds normal expectations. When Ruth expresses surprise at his excessive attention, Boaz explains he was impressed by her exceptional loyalty and kindness toward Naomi (vv. 10–12).

2:8 My daughter Boaz's use of this address likely reflects an age difference between him and Ruth (3:10). He may have been closer in age to Naomi's deceased husband, Elimelek.

2:9 not to lay a hand on you Boaz instructed his workers not to bother Ruth. The Hebrew verb used here can denote causing bodily harm (Ge 26:11,29), but it can also be a sexual euphemism (Ge 20:6; Pr 6:29).

2:10 Why have I found such favor Ruth recognizes the great privilege Boaz has awarded to her.

2:12 May the Lᴏʀᴅ repay you Ironically, Boaz himself can fulfill this wish. See note on Ru 3:9. **under whose wings** Boaz recognizes that Ruth has not only expressed loyalty to Naomi, but to Yahweh, the God of Israel (1:16). In this context, the Hebrew word *kenaphaim* is usually translated as "wings."

KENAPHAIM

The Hebrew word *kenaphaim* ("wings") commonly appears in the OT as an image of finding shelter or refuge under God's wings. This image—especially prevalent in the Psalms (Ps 17:8; 36:7; 57:1; 61:4; 63:7; 91:4)—compares the tender way God loves and cares for his people with the way birds protect and care for their young (Dt 32:11). Those who seek refuge under God's wings find satisfaction (Ps 36:7–8; 63:5–8) and protection from danger (Ps 57:1; 91:3–6).

2:13 speaking kindly to your servant The Hebrew phrase used here describes speaking comfort or encouragement (Ge 50:21; Isa 40:2) and can also be used to show attraction between a man and a woman (Ge 34:3; Jdg 19:3; Hos 2:14). While the first meaning is probably intended here, the second meaning anticipates the later events of the story.

2:14 Come over here. Have some bread In addition to allowing Ruth to work with his female servants, Boaz also provides a meal for her. She is invited to eat with the workers, where Boaz himself serves her—a type of respect reserved for special guests.

2:15 Let her gather Boaz further extends his kindness to Ruth by telling his workers to let her glean among the

out and gave her what she had left over after she had eaten enough.

[19] Her mother-in-law asked her, "Where did you glean today? Where did you work? Blessed be the man who took notice of you!"

Then Ruth told her mother-in-law about the one at whose place she had been working. "The name of the man I worked with today is Boaz," she said.

[20] "The LORD bless him!" Naomi said to her daughter-in-law. "He has not stopped showing his kindness to the living and the dead." She added, "That man is our close relative; he is one of our guardian-redeemers. [a]"

[21] Then Ruth the Moabite said, "He even said to me, 'Stay with my workers until they finish harvesting all my grain.'"

[22] Naomi said to Ruth her daughter-in-law, "It will be good for you, my daughter, to go with the women who work for him, because in someone else's field you might be harmed."

[23] So Ruth stayed close to the women of Boaz to glean until the barley and wheat harvests were finished. And she lived with her mother-in-law.

Ruth and Boaz at the Threshing Floor

3 One day Ruth's mother-in-law Naomi said to her, "My daughter, I must find a home [b] for you, where you will be well provided for. [2] Now Boaz, with whose women you have worked, is a relative of ours. Tonight he will be winnowing barley on the threshing floor. [3] Wash, put on perfume, and get dressed in your best clothes. Then go down to the threshing floor, but don't let him know you are there until he has finished eating and drinking. [4] When he lies down, note the place where he is lying. Then go and uncover his feet and lie down. He will tell you what to do."

[a] 20 The Hebrew word for *guardian-redeemer* is a legal term for one who has the obligation to redeem a relative in serious difficulty (see Lev. 25:25-55).   [b] 1 Hebrew *find rest* (see 1:9)

---

sheaves (or stocks of grain). Normally, a person in Ruth's position would be allowed to gather only what workers missed or left behind (Lev 19:9–10; Dt 24:19–22).

2:17 ephah An ephah of barley would have weighed approximately 30 pounds—enough for Ruth and Naomi to live on for several weeks.

2:19 Blessed be the man who took notice The amount of grain Ruth returns with shows Naomi that she received special treatment.

2:20 He has not stopped showing his kindness Naomi reverses her former claim that Yahweh dealt bitterly with her (Ru 1:13,20–21). She now recognizes that God has not removed his kindness (*chesed*; see 1:8 and note). **the living and the dead** In blessing Naomi and Ruth, God also blesses Naomi's deceased husband and sons (4:5; compare Dt 25:6). **our guardian-redeemers** Boaz was a close enough relative to Naomi and Ruth to be a redeemer (*go'el*). If Boaz exercised his responsibility as a redeemer by marrying Ruth, he would provide an heir for Naomi (see Ru 4:5). The responsibilities of a redeemer or *go'el* according to the law included buying back family land that had been sold (Lev 25:25), buying a family member who had sold himself into slavery (Lev 25:47–49), or marrying the childless widow of a family member (Dt 25:5–10).

2:23 barley and wheat harvests were finished A period close to two months: late April—early June. Ruth continued to work to provide for herself and Naomi.

3:1–18 The plot reaches its climax in the events of Ru 3. Naomi sees a chance to restore their economic standing by marrying Ruth to Boaz (vv. 1–2). She instructs Ruth to wash, dress nicely and approach Boaz privately at the threshing floor after the harvest celebration had ended. Ruth is to lie down by Boaz and "uncover his feet" (vv. 3–4). The possible sexual subtext of this scene is widely debated and hinges somewhat on the significance of this act of uncovering his feet (since "feet" may be a sexual euphemism). The scene has certainly been crafted to appear *as though* Naomi is sending Ruth off to seduce Boaz. The reader is left in suspense by the ambiguity over what is about to happen and what Naomi may be expecting to happen.

Naomi's plan for Ruth to meet Boaz in the dark outside of town seems out of character based on her earlier concern for Ruth's welfare (1:9–13; 3:1). Perhaps Naomi trusts Boaz to act with integrity toward Ruth and expects Ruth to use the privacy of the threshing floor and the cover of night to request redemption. However, Ruth would be quite vulnerable, alone at night lying in the hay with a powerful man. The tension of this scene arises from the way Boaz and Ruth have been characterized as people of integrity. If Boaz does not take advantage of Ruth in this vulnerable state, then he truly is a worthy man. Reading ch. 3 as a moonlight roll in the hay goes against the narrative's characterization of Boaz, Ruth and Naomi. The scene certainly builds with sexual tension, but Boaz's words in vv. 10–13 suggest that he was concerned for Ruth's reputation and that nothing happened between them that night.

3:1 I must find a home for you Since Ruth stayed with her, Naomi seeks a way to provide her with the safety and security of marriage.

3:2 winnowing The process of separating grain from plant stalks. Grain was crushed and then tossed into the air for the wind to blow away the chaff. **the threshing floor** An open area outside of town where the process of winnowing grain took place. Threshing floors were located outside of a village (1Ki 22:10), making them vulnerable to thieves (1Sa 23:1). Because of this, farmers sometimes guarded their threshing floors by sleeping on them (Ru 3:7). See the infographic "A Threshing Floor" on p. 497.

3:3 Wash, put on perfume Ruth's actions could be viewed as preparation for marriage or a sexual encounter (2Sa 11:2; 1Ki 22:38; Eze 16:9; 23:40). Ruth may have been washing and anointing her body in connection with removing her widow's garments to mark the potential end of her widowhood (Ge 38:14).

3:4 uncover his feet The nature and significance of this action is unclear. If uncovering Boaz's feet was meant literally, the purpose may have been to wake him by making his feet cold. The Hebrew word *regel* ("foot") is clearly used as a euphemism for the pubic area a few times in the OT (e.g., Ex 4:25; Isa 7:20). However, many cases are ambiguous, and a euphemistic reading is possible but uncertain. The meaning in this passage is further complicated by the form of *regel* used in this

⁵"I will do whatever you say," Ruth answered. ⁶So she went down to the threshing floor and did everything her mother-in-law told her to do.

⁷When Boaz had finished eating and drinking and was in good spirits, he went over to lie down at the far end of the grain pile. Ruth approached quietly, uncovered his feet and lay down. ⁸In the middle of the night something startled the man; he turned—and there was a woman lying at his feet!

⁹"Who are you?" he asked.

"I am your servant Ruth," she said. "Spread the corner of your garment over me, since you are a guardian-redeemer*a* of our family."

¹⁰"The LORD bless you, my daughter," he replied. "This kindness is greater than that which you showed earlier: You have not run after the younger men, whether rich or poor. ¹¹And now, my daughter, don't be afraid. I will do for you all you ask. All the people of my town know that you are a woman of noble character. ¹²Although it is true that I am a guardian-redeemer of our family, there is another who is more closely related than I. ¹³Stay here for the night, and in the morning if he wants to do his duty as your guardian-redeemer, good; let him redeem you. But if he is not willing, as surely as the LORD lives I will do it. Lie here until morning."

¹⁴So she lay at his feet until morning, but got up before anyone could be recognized; and he said, "No one must know that a woman came to the threshing floor."

---

a 9 The Hebrew word for *guardian-redeemer* is a legal term for one who has the obligation to redeem a relative in serious difficulty (see Lev. 25:25-55); also in verses 12 and 13.

---

passage—*margeloth*—which likely means "place of the feet." See note on Ru 3:7. **lie down** The Hebrew word used here, *shakav* ("to lie down"), is used eight times in vv. 4–14; this term is often used as a euphemism for sexual intercourse (Ge 30:15–16; 2Sa 11:4; 13:14). However, since Boaz and Ruth are presented as virtuous and blessed by Yahweh (Ru 2:11–12,20; 3:10–11; 4:11–12), such sexual activity outside marriage would be out of character for them.

3:7 was in good spirits The Hebrew phrase used here, *wayyitab libbo*, does not necessarily indicate drunkenness (Jdg 18:20). When it does indicate drunkenness, that fact is made more explicit (1Sa 25:36; 2Sa 13:28). While Boaz's feasting likely included alcoholic drinks, it should not be assumed that he was drunk. **uncovered his feet** The interpretation of Ruth's action is uncertain (compare note on 3:4). The Hebrew term used for "feet" throughout this chapter is *margeloth*, not the usual *regel* ("foot") or *raglaim* ("feet"). Hebrew nouns using a pattern beginning with the letter *mem* ("m") often refer to an abstract place. This pattern suggests that *margeloth* means "place of the feet" in the same way that *mera'ashoth* indicates the "place of the head" when someone is lying down asleep (1Sa 19:13; 26:7; 1Ki 19:6). This interpretation of *margeloth* also makes the best sense of its use in Ru 3:14 where Ruth is said to have spent the entire night lying at Boaz's feet.

3:9 Spread the corner of your garment over The Hebrew term used here, *kanaph* ("wing"), refers to both a literal wing and the corner of a garment. There is a play on words here; this term is also found in 2:12, where Boaz notes that Ruth has taken refuge under the wings of Yahweh and prays that Yahweh would bless her (see note on 2:12). Here, Boaz is able to fulfill that appeal as Ruth looks for shelter under his "wings." Placing the edge of a garment over a woman symbolized taking her in marriage (Eze 16:8).

3:10 LORD bless you Boaz responds favorably to Ruth's request. His instructions to her in Ru 3:10–13 indicate his willingness to help her. There is no indication that anything sexual occurred between them. See note on vv. 1–18. **kindness is greater than that which you showed earlier** Earlier Boaz was impressed by Ruth's willingness to leave her home out of loyalty to Naomi (2:11). Now he admires her decision to seek a redeemer to provide an heir for Naomi. **You have not run after the younger men** Ruth could have pursued remarriage with other, younger men. Instead, she looked for a marriage that would benefit Naomi and the family of her late husband (see note on 4:5; note on 4:6).

3:11 a woman of noble character The Hebrew phrase used here, *esheth chayil,* is also used in Pr 31:10 to introduce the section on the ideal wife (Pr 31:10–31). Ruth is known throughout the town as a hardworking and capable woman. The sequence of Biblical books in the Hebrew Bible is different than most English Bibles. In one ordering of the Hebrew Bible, Ruth comes directly after Proverbs. This would form a close association between the description of the ideal wife at the end of Proverbs and the character of Ruth.

3:12 who is more closely related than I The closer relative would have the first right to act as the redeemer according to levirate law. See note on Ru 1:11.

3:13 Stay here for the night The Hebrew term used here means "to spend the night" (Ge 28:11; 2Sa 12:16). He likely has her remain because it was safer than sending her home in the middle of the night. **if he is not willing** This closer relative would have the first right of redemption. The responsibility of redemption would go first to the deceased person's brother, then uncle, then cousin, then another "close relative" (Lev 25:48–49). **as surely as the LORD lives** Signifies a binding oath (1Ki 1:29–30; 22:14; Jer 5:2; 12:16). Making an oath on God's name was the strongest form of swearing. Failing to fulfill the oath would make the swearer a blasphemer.

3:14 she lay See note on Ru 3:4. **No one must know** It is unclear who Boaz is addressing with this instruction. In vv. 10–13 and v. 15 he is clearly talking to Ruth. Here he could be telling Ruth to depart before anyone (even his workers) knows that a woman visited him at the threshing floor that night. However, he refers to Ruth as "the woman" (*ha-ishah*) and uses passive voice in the command, saying that no one can know *the* woman was there. This wording suggests he could be addressing his workers, commanding them to keep Ruth's presence a secret. **a woman came to the threshing floor** Ruth stayed at the threshing floor with Boaz for the entire night. Boaz does not want Ruth to be viewed as a prostitute visiting a man at the threshing floor (Hos 9:1). He knows her presence could be easily misconstrued and wants to avoid gossip and speculation. However, Boaz's statement could also be taken as a wish to keep her presence secret to cover up for their sexual relationship. The virtue ascribed to Ruth and Boaz, as well as Naomi's intentions (see note on Ru 3:4), make the latter interpretation unlikely.

[15]He also said, "Bring me the shawl you are wearing and hold it out." When she did so, he poured into it six measures of barley and placed the bundle on her. Then he[a] went back to town.

[16]When Ruth came to her mother-in-law, Naomi asked, "How did it go, my daughter?"

Then she told her everything Boaz had done for her [17]and added, "He gave me these six measures of barley, saying, 'Don't go back to your mother-in-law empty-handed.'"

[18]Then Naomi said, "Wait, my daughter, until you find out what happens. For the man will not rest until the matter is settled today."

Boaz Marries Ruth

4 Meanwhile Boaz went up to the town gate and sat down there just as the guardian-redeemer[b] he had mentioned came along. Boaz said, "Come over here, my friend, and sit down." So he went over and sat down.

[2]Boaz took ten of the elders of the town and said, "Sit here," and they did so. [3]Then he said to the guardian-redeemer, "Naomi, who has come back from Moab, is selling the piece of land that belonged to our relative Elimelek. [4]I thought I should bring the matter to your attention and suggest that you buy it in the presence of these seated here and in the presence of the elders of my people. If you will redeem it, do so. But if you[c] will not, tell me, so I will know. For no one has the right to do it except you, and I am next in line."

"I will redeem it," he said.

[5]Then Boaz said, "On the day you buy the land from Naomi, you also acquire Ruth the Moabite, the[d] dead man's widow, in order to maintain the name of the dead with his property."

[6]At this, the guardian-redeemer said, "Then I cannot redeem it because I might endanger my own estate. You redeem it yourself. I cannot do it."

[7](Now in earlier times in Israel, for the redemption and transfer of property to become final, one party took off his sandal and gave it to the other. This was the method of legalizing transactions in Israel.)

[8]So the guardian-redeemer said to Boaz, "Buy it yourself." And he removed his sandal.

[9]Then Boaz announced to the elders and all the people, "Today you are witnesses that I have bought from Naomi all the property of Elimelek, Kilion and Mahlon. [10]I have also acquired Ruth the Moabite, Mahlon's widow, as my wife, in order to maintain the name of the dead with his property, so that his name will not disappear from among his family or from his hometown. Today you are witnesses!"

[11]Then the elders and all the people at the gate said, "We are witnesses. May the LORD make the

---

a 15 Most Hebrew manuscripts; many Hebrew manuscripts, Vulgate and Syriac *she*   *b 1* The Hebrew word for *guardian-redeemer* is a legal term for one who has the obligation to redeem a relative in serious difficulty (see Lev. 25:25-55); also in verses 3, 6, 8 and 14.   *c 4* Many Hebrew manuscripts, Septuagint, Vulgate and Syriac; most Hebrew manuscripts *he*   *d 5* Vulgate and Syriac; Hebrew (see also Septuagint) *Naomi and from Ruth the Moabite, you acquire the*

3:15 six measures of barley Boaz's generosity is again evident (see note on 2:8–13).

3:18 the man will not rest Boaz is possibly in a rush because he loves Ruth and wants to act quickly to marry her. However, he made an oath to Yahweh in v. 13 and probably does not want to waste time fulfilling his oath. **matter is settled today** Boaz had sworn an oath to redeem Ruth if the closer redeemer would not. Naomi trusts that Boaz—a man of integrity—will act quickly to fulfill this oath.

4:1–12 Boaz follows through on his promise to redeem Ruth, negotiating with the other relative for the right of redemption. The scene takes place at the city gate with ten of the elders serving as witnesses to the transaction. What transpires at the city gate between Boaz and the elders resembles the legal procedure described in Dt 25:7–9.

4:1 gate The social hub of a city. People passed through the gate on their way to fields or threshing floors. The gate was a marketplace (2Ki 7:1), a place of assembly where prophets would speak (1Ki 22:10), and the location where city elders (Dt 21:19; 22:15) or kings (2Sa 15:2) made legal rulings.

4:2 elders of the town By presenting the situation before the city elders, Boaz acts in accordance with the procedures for the levirate law outlined in Dt 25:5–10.

4:3 piece of land Initially, Boaz does not mention Ruth—he simply focuses on the land. A redeemer was responsible for buying land to keep it in the family (Lev 25:25).

4:4 I will redeem it The man initially agrees to redeem

the land without knowing about Ruth. He probably recognizes this as an opportunity to make a good investment. See note on Ru 4:6.

4:5 you also acquire Ruth Boaz now inserts the condition: The redeemer would not only redeem the land, he would also marry Ruth. **maintain the name of the dead** The redeemer was responsible for producing an heir to continue the line of the deceased (Dt 25:6).

4:6 I might endanger my own estate Redeeming Ruth and producing an heir for the line of Elimelek would damage his own children's inheritance. Redeeming the land by itself would have been a good investment because the land would be inherited by the redeemer's own children. But redeeming Ruth with the land would result in its being left to Ruth's offspring (for the line of Elimelek). Any resources spent on redeeming the land and raising the offspring would damage his own children's inheritance since it would benefit the line of Elimelek. See note on Ge 38:8.

4:7 in earlier times Apparently, this custom was unfamiliar to the original audience and required an explanation. **took off his sandal** The actions described here differ slightly from those described in Dt 25:8–10, where the widow removes the sandal. Here the exchange of the sandal merely indicates the man's decision to pass his right of redemption to Boaz. In Dt 25, the person who refuses his duty as redeemer is disgraced, but that sentiment is absent here.

4:10 Mahlon's widow This is the first mention of which of Naomi's sons Ruth married.

Ruth's Family Tree

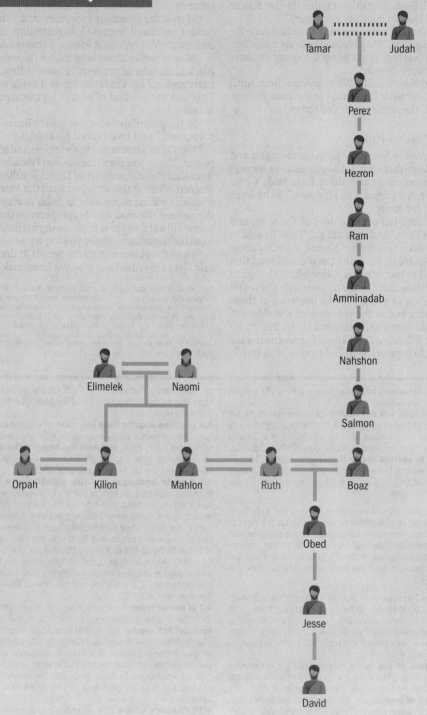

Tamar .... Judah

Perez

Hezron

Ram

Amminadab

Nahshon

Salmon

Elimelek — Naomi

Orpah — Kilion   Mahlon — Ruth — Boaz

Obed

Jesse

David

woman who is coming into your home like Rachel and Leah, who together built up the family of Israel. May you have standing in Ephrathah and be famous in Bethlehem. [12]Through the offspring the LORD gives you by this young woman, may your family be like that of Perez, whom Tamar bore to Judah."

Naomi Gains a Son

[13]So Boaz took Ruth and she became his wife. When he made love to her, the LORD enabled her to conceive, and she gave birth to a son. [14]The women said to Naomi: "Praise be to the LORD, who this day has not left you without a guardian-redeemer. May he become famous throughout Israel! [15]He will renew your life and sustain you in your old age. For your daughter-in-law, who loves you and who is better to you than seven sons, has given him birth."

[16]Then Naomi took the child in her arms and cared for him. [17]The women living there said, "Naomi has a son!" And they named him Obed. He was the father of Jesse, the father of David.

The Genealogy of David

4:18-22pp — 1Ch 2:5-15; Mt 1:3-6; Lk 3:31-33

[18]This, then, is the family line of Perez:

Perez was the father of Hezron,
[19]Hezron the father of Ram,
Ram the father of Amminadab,
[20]Amminadab the father of Nahshon,
Nahshon the father of Salmon,[a]
[21]Salmon the father of Boaz,
Boaz the father of Obed,
[22]Obed the father of Jesse,
and Jesse the father of David.

[a] 20 A few Hebrew manuscripts, some Septuagint manuscripts and Vulgate (see also verse 21 and Septuagint of 1 Chron. 2:11); most Hebrew manuscripts *Salma*

4:12 Perez An ancestor of Boaz (Ru 4:18–22), Perez was born to Judah through circumstances related to the practice of levirate marriage (Ge 38).

4:13 LORD enabled her to conceive Ruth may have been barren, as she was Mahlon's wife for ten years without producing any offspring. Conception and birth after a long period of barrenness is considered a sign of God's blessing on the woman. Both the OT and NT contain examples of formerly barren women becoming pregnant through God's intervention including Sarah (Ge 11:30; 21:1–7), Rebekah (Ge 25:21), Rachel (Ge 29:31; 30:22–23), Hannah (1Sa 1:1–20), and Elizabeth, the mother of John the Baptist (Lk 1:7–25).

4:14 LORD, who this day has not left you without In Ru 1:19–21, Naomi complained that Yahweh dealt bitterly with her. Here, the women point out that Yahweh has been with her the whole time and has now provided a redeemer.

4:15 better to you than seven sons A strong statement about the value of Ruth. Sons were more valuable because the inheritance and family name was passed

through the male heir (see note on v. 6). The number seven is symbolic of completeness.

4:17 Naomi has a son Although the child was born to Boaz and Ruth, it would continue the lineage of Naomi and her deceased husband and son. See note on v. 5; note on v. 6. **the father of Jesse, the father of David** The story ends by revealing the son born to Ruth and Boaz was the grandfather of King David.

4:18 family line The book closes with a short genealogy covering Perez to David. This genealogy is repeated in 1Ch 2:4–15 and Mt 1:3–6. See note on Ge 5:1.

4:21 Salmon the father of Boaz Boaz's mother was Rahab, the prostitute who hid Israelite spies (Jos 2:1–21) and was delivered when Jericho was destroyed (Jos 6). See Mt 1:5.

4:22 Jesse the father of David The genealogical information in these final verses of the book reveals the importance of the story. Obed was King David's grandfather. Obed's birth does not simply offer a satisfying resolution to the story of Naomi and Ruth. The redemption of Ruth ultimately leads to the birth of King David. See the people diagram "Ruth's Family Tree" on p. 400.

RUTH, NAOMI AND GOD'S LOVE OF THE MARGINALIZED
by Carolyn Custis James

C ontrary to popular belief, the book of Ruth is not really a love story—at least, not as it's usually presented as a love story between Boaz and Ruth. It is a story of God's love for all people, and it shows that God is with us through our sufferings, even when we feel abandoned. The book of Ruth is a story of tragedy, hope and the transforming power of God's love in the lives of Ruth, Naomi and Boaz.

The story of Ruth is cast against the backdrop of an ancient patriarchal culture, where a woman's identity and security depended on her relationships with men, especially her father and/or husband. Her value as a wife and contributor to society was measured by counting her sons. By these cultural standards, it is puzzling that a Gentile like Ruth the Moabitess (today a Jordanian)—a non-Israelite outsider who is widowed, childless and barren for most of the story—became a luminary of biblical history. Yet she is unquestionably one of the most significant women in the Bible. She and her mother-in-law Naomi represent God's love for the outsider and the marginalized.

RUTH'S STORY WITHIN THE BIBLICAL STORY

Ruth's story forms a historical and theological bridge from the era of the judges (Ru 1:1)—when the people of Israel did evil in Yahweh's sight (Jdg 2:10–19)—to Israel's monarchy. In contrast to Israel's unfaithfulness to Yahweh, Ruth embodies the courageous, self-giving, sacrificial way that God's image-bearers are supposed to live. The book's genealogy (Ru 4:18–22) establishes the historic significance of her actions. This surprising ending reveals that the family line she battles to save is the royal line of King David (Ru 4:18–22). Matthew expands Ruth's significance by naming her in Jesus' genealogy (Mt 1:5) as an ancestor of the Messiah.

OUTSIDERS AND OLD TESTAMENT LAW

Ruth enters the story on the arm of her husband, Mahlon (Ru 1:3–4; 4:10). Her mother-in-law, Naomi, has suffered a series of calamities, including the untimely deaths of her husband, Elimelek, and her sons, Mahlon and Kilion. Naomi's sons' marriages to pagan Moabite girls may have compounded Naomi's grief, as no believing Israelite would rejoice over such a union (Ru 1:1–5). Suffering engulfed Ruth as well, with 10 long years of barrenness followed by the death of her husband. Widows without sons would drop to the bottom of the social ladder, defenseless against abuse and exploitation. Thus Naomi is not a marginal figure whose plight sets the stage for a romance between Ruth and Boaz; there is something far deeper and more powerful taking place in this story than a romance.

Naomi's plight reminds one of the trials of Job. Like Job her sufferings raise painful questions about God's love for her. The entire narrative centers on the important Hebrew word *chesed* (loyal love). This is no ordinary love; it is a stubborn, costly, sacrificial, voluntary love. It is the love God has for his people—the bedrock of their faith. Naomi's losses convince her that she has lost God's *chesed*. Indeed, she (like Job) is persuaded that God has turned against her (Ru 1:13,20–21; compare Job 13:20–28). The crux of the story is that God has not turned against Naomi. She awakens to this reality as God speaks *chesed* to her through the selfless, loving actions of Ruth.

Three Mosaic laws inform Ruth's actions, and she creatively presses them to the breaking point. Gleaning laws required landowners to permit the poor to scavenge for leftover grain (Lev 19:9–10; Dt 24:19–22). If a man died without a male heir, the levirate law compelled the man's biological brother to marry his widow. A son born to this union carried on the dead man's line and inherited his portion of the family estate (Dt 25:5–9). The kinsman-redeemer law placed responsibility on a man's nearest relative to buy back his land if he fell on hard times (Lev 25:25). Ruth will challenge all three laws, taking the law from the letter to the spirit.

The letter of the law permits Ruth to glean, but the spirit of the law is to feed the poor. Instead of settling for picking up leftover scraps of grain as the law permits, Ruth presses Boaz for permission to glean where his hired female harvesters are bundling freshly cut grain (Ru 2:7). Remarkably, Boaz puts his full weight behind Ruth's mission, and she hauls home a staggering 29 pounds of winnowed barley (Ru 2:17–18)—more than a half-month's pay for a male harvester, according to ancient Babylonian records. This marks a turning point for Naomi, who realizes she has not lost God's love after all (Ru 2:20).

THE MARGINALIZED AND THE LOVE OF GOD

God's *chesed* for Naomi is manifested through the counter cultural actions of her Moabite daughter-in-law. The tide begins to turn for Naomi when, despite the harsh realities and vulnerabilities ahead in Bethlehem, Ruth stubbornly clings to Naomi and embraces Naomi's God. From the shelter of Yahweh's wing, Ruth draws courage, strength and wisdom. At enormous risk to herself, she assumes responsibility for Naomi and for the family.

When Naomi feels most forsaken on the road to Bethlehem, she is held in a human embrace, hearing fierce words of love spoken by her daughter-in-law (Ru 1:16–17). When Ruth goes to glean, she and Boaz meet, not as prospective lovers, but in a powerful Blessed Alliance embodying God's love for Naomi.[1]

At the threshing floor, barren Ruth takes *chesed* to new heights by volunteering to bear a son to rescue Naomi's family. She calls Boaz to fulfill the spirit of the levirate law by marrying her and fathering a child. Boaz is neither Elimelek's blood brother nor his nearest relative. But where *chesed* is at work, none of that matters. Buying Elimelek's land is a losing investment if Ruth bears a son (Ru 4:6), yet despite financial risks, Boaz joins Ruth in rescuing Elimelek's family, and he redeems Elimelek's land. In a final act of *chesed*, Ruth gives her son to Naomi.

---

1 Carolyn Custis James, *Lost Women of the Bible: Finding Strength and Significance through Their Stories* (Grand Rapids: Zondervan, 2005), 37.

1 SAMUEL

INTRODUCTION TO 1 SAMUEL

First Samuel shows Israel's transition from a group of tribes to a centralized monarchy. The book begins with the birth of the last judge, Samuel, who also is a prophet (1Sa 3:20; 7:15–17). During Samuel's leadership, the Israelites clamor for a king. Samuel cautions against this. Yahweh— in anguish over Israel's decision to reject him as their rightful king—grants the request (ch. 8). Samuel then anoints Saul as king (chs. 9–10). After Saul goes against Yahweh's ways, Yahweh rejects Saul and chooses David, who is then a youth (chs. 15–16). The remainder of the book depicts the difficulties between Saul and David. First Samuel illustrates the tension between God's ideal will and people's choices.

BACKGROUND

First Samuel is set in the eleventh century BC, a period marked by regional conflicts such as those between the Philistines and the Israelites (e.g., ch. 17). Egypt no longer had much influence in Canaan—which Israel inhabited—so local city-states and tribal confederations vied for dominance. This atmosphere lies behind 1 Samuel.

The Hebrew Bible presents 1–2 Samuel as a single book called Samuel. (The Septuagint, an ancient Greek translation, split the book into two.) The collective work of 1–2 Samuel—along with Deuteronomy, Joshua, Judges and 1–2 Kings—presents the history of Israel in light of the covenant (contractual) blessings and curses set forth in Deuteronomy. These writings, including 1–2 Samuel, probably reached their final form in the sixth or fifth century BC through the work of Jewish scribes who compiled and edited earlier sources.

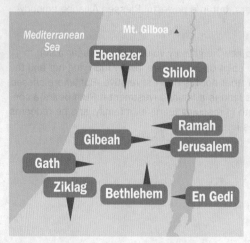

This map depicts some of the major locations related to 1 Samuel.

Much of 1–2 Samuel centers around Deuteronomy's framework: When Israel and its king follow Yahweh, they experience his blessings, but when Yahweh's commands are opposed, hardship ensues. Saul is measured this way, and David is chosen because of his love for Yahweh (13:14; 15:10–11,22–25; 16:7).

STRUCTURE

The narrative of 1–2 Samuel includes three cycles of leadership stories. First Samuel presents the cycles about Samuel and Saul and introduces David, while 2 Samuel contains the cycle about David's reign.

The Samuel cycle (chs. 1–7) starts with the miraculous birth of Samuel and continues

through his time as prophet and last ruling judge of Israel. Samuel's time as prophet continues into Saul's reign as king. This introduces a new structure for Israel's leadership: a king with a consulting prophet, with both reporting to Yahweh. The king is a regent under Yahweh and is supposed to obey Yahweh's prophet.

The Saul cycle (1Sa 8–31) can be divided into two parts. The first part (chs. 8–15) covers Israel's request for a king, the selection of Saul and the beginning of Saul's reign. Toward the end of this section, Saul disobeys Yahweh; as a consequence, his descendants will not inherit the kingship. In the second part of the cycle (chs. 16–31), Samuel anoints young David as king, and conflict develops between David and Saul. The text portrays Saul negatively and David positively. First Samuel ends with Saul's death, which sets the stage for the David cycle in 2 Samuel.

OUTLINE

- God calls Samuel as judge (1:1—7:17)
- God calls Saul as king (8:1—12:25)
- God rejects Saul as king (13:1—15:35)
- God calls David as king (16:1—31:13)

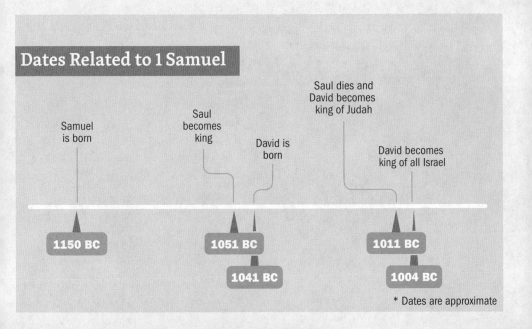

Dates Related to 1 Samuel

Samuel is born — 1150 BC

Saul becomes king — 1051 BC

David is born — 1041 BC

Saul dies and David becomes king of Judah — 1011 BC

David becomes king of all Israel — 1004 BC

* Dates are approximate

THEMES

The various relationships portrayed in 1 Samuel exemplify the startling differences between Yahweh's followers and those who ignore him. Following Yahweh means recognizing his place as ultimate king. The narrative of 1–2 Samuel shows that the power of Israel's king comes only from Yahweh. Even after Saul takes the throne, he can only rule successfully as long as he respects Yahweh's authority. But Saul lets fear take control and loses his way (15:24), even though Yahweh appointed him (15:35). The only thing certain is Yahweh—and the uncertainty of people leads even Yahweh to feel remorse (15:10–11).

Unlike Saul, young David seems to fear only Yahweh, and Yahweh is with him (18:12). The choice of David from among his older, stronger brothers shows Yahweh's love of those who love him. Yahweh looks at the heart and is not swayed by outward appearances (1Sa 16:7). During all of David's struggles against Saul, including his time as an outlaw, he respects both Yahweh and Saul, Yahweh's king (e.g., ch. 24).

First Samuel also brings to the forefront the concept of a messiah—an anointed leader chosen by God to lead his people. Saul fails in this role, while David, for a time, epitomizes the role. David defeats the Amalekites, and Philistine hostilities decline under his leadership. David's reliance on Yahweh brings favor to Israel. And through David's line the true and ultimate messiah, Jesus, brings salvation to the world.

The Birth of Samuel

1 There was a certain man from Ramathaim, a Zuphite[a] from the hill country of Ephraim, whose name was Elkanah son of Jeroham, the son of Elihu, the son of Tohu, the son of Zuph, an Ephraimite. [2] He had two wives; one was called Hannah and the other Peninnah. Peninnah had children, but Hannah had none.

[3] Year after year this man went up from his town to worship and sacrifice to the LORD Almighty at Shiloh, where Hophni and Phinehas, the two sons of Eli, were priests of the LORD. [4] Whenever the day came for Elkanah to sacrifice, he would give portions of the meat to his wife Peninnah and to all her sons and daughters. [5] But to Hannah he gave a double portion because he loved her, and the LORD had closed her womb. [6] Because the LORD had closed Hannah's womb, her rival kept provoking her in order to irritate her. [7] This went on year after year. Whenever Hannah went up to the house of the LORD, her rival provoked her till she wept and would not eat. [8] Her husband Elkanah would say to her, "Hannah, why are you weeping? Why don't you eat? Why are you downhearted? Don't I mean more to you than ten sons?"

[9] Once when they had finished eating and drinking in Shiloh, Hannah stood up. Now Eli the priest was sitting on his chair by the doorpost of the LORD's house. [10] In her deep anguish Hannah prayed to the LORD, weeping bitterly. [11] And she made a vow, saying, "LORD Almighty, if you will only look on your servant's misery and remember me, and not forget your servant but give her a son, then I will give him to the LORD for all the days of his life, and no razor will ever be used on his head."

[12] As she kept on praying to the LORD, Eli observed her mouth. [13] Hannah was praying in her heart, and her lips were moving but her voice was not heard. Eli thought she was drunk [14] and said to her, "How long are you going to stay drunk? Put away your wine."

[15] "Not so, my lord," Hannah replied, "I am a woman who is deeply troubled. I have not been drinking wine or beer; I was pouring out my soul to the LORD. [16] Do not take your servant for a

---

a 1 See Septuagint and 1 Chron. 6:26-27,33-35; or *from Ramathaim Zuphim.*

1:1–20 The narrative of 1 Samuel begins in the eleventh century BC, where the book of Judges left off. First Samuel focuses on the tumultuous relationship of Saul and David, Israel's first two kings; the narrative of 1 Samuel ends with Saul's death (ca. 1011 BC).

The opening section tells the birth story of Samuel, Israel's last judge—a figure empowered by Yahweh to temporarily protect and lead God's people. Hannah, who is barren, prays to Yahweh for a son. God grants her request; in gratitude, she dedicates Samuel to a lifetime of service to God.

1:1 Ramathaim, a Zuphite Shortened to Ramah in 1Sa 1:19. Several areas named Ramah existed during this time; the narrative later indicates that Samuel lived in Ramah (7:17; 25:1). **Ephraimite** Likely describes Elkanah's geographic designation. Genealogically, he was a Levite (1Ch 6:33–34). Joshua 24:33 describes Levites as living in the hill country of Ephraim. Since Samuel later becomes a priest, he must have been a Levite. First Chronicles places him within the family line of Kohath the Levite (1Ch 6:22–28,33–38).

1:2 He had two wives Polygamy recalls the patriarchs of Genesis, particularly Abraham and Jacob (see Ge 16:3; 29:21–28; 30:4,9). It is possible that Hannah was Elkanah's first wife, and he married Peninnah because Hannah did not bear children. **Hannah had none** The narrative portrays Hannah in the same manner as the matriarchs of Genesis—Sarah, Rebekah and Rachel (Ge 21:1–5; 25:21; 29:31—30:2). The text indicates that her conception of a child will be an act of God, and that her child will do great things for God and his people.

1:3 Shiloh Where the tabernacle was. See Jos 18:1.

1:4 he would give portions of the meat to his wife Peninnah Elkanah gave Peninnah food portions based on the number of children she had.

1:5 double portion These annual pilgrimages and their accompanying feasts would have been a source of great shame for Hannah. Peninnah would receive larger portions of food because she had given birth to many children. Elkanah probably didn't intend to cause her shame; however, this single or select portion would have perpetually reminded Hannah of her barrenness.

1:8 Don't I mean more to you In the ancient Near East, husbands were essential for a woman's survival, but children brought them honor. Without children, Hannah would have felt only shame. **ten sons** This could be hyperbole to connote an abundant blessing from God. This number also recalls the ten sons that Jacob's other wives bore to him while Rachel was barren (see Ge 29:31—30:21).

1:9 Hannah stood up Hannah is portrayed as the paragon of faith among the women of the Hebrew Bible. No other woman in the OT goes to the house of Yahweh (except Peninnah, by inference).

1:11 made a vow The only woman recorded in the OT as having made and kept a vow to God. **LORD Almighty** Hannah calls God by the Hebrew title *yhwh tseva'oth*, which identifies him as a commander of armies—those of Israel, as well as heavenly armies. **no razor will ever be used on his head** Indicates that Hannah will set her son aside to become a Nazirite (see Nu 6:5). According to the law, Elkanah could have voided Hannah's vow (see Nu 30:6–15). It is a testimony to his piety that he does not.

1:13 Eli thought she was drunk She was praying intensely and inaudibly.

1:15 I was pouring out my soul to the LORD In contrast to some of the matriarchs in Genesis, Hannah took her problems directly to God in prayer (compare Ge 16:1–3; 30:1–21).

1:16 a wicked woman The Hebrew term used here, *bath beliyya'al*, refers to a woman guilty of heinous and indiscreet acts against the law. People referred to by the term *beliyya'al* are often characterized as wicked, worthless and treacherous. In 1–2 Samuel, the text uses masculine versions of this term to describe men such as Hophni, Phinehas, King Saul's opponents, inciters in David's militia, Nabal and Sheba (see 1Sa 2:12 and note; 10:27; 25:17; 30:22).

wicked woman; I have been praying here out of my great anguish and grief."

¹⁷Eli answered, "Go in peace, and may the God of Israel grant you what you have asked of him."

¹⁸She said, "May your servant find favor in your eyes." Then she went her way and ate something, and her face was no longer downcast.

¹⁹Early the next morning they arose and worshiped before the LORD and then went back to their home at Ramah. Elkanah made love to his wife Hannah, and the LORD remembered her. ²⁰So in the course of time Hannah became pregnant and gave birth to a son. She named him Samuel,ᵃ saying, "Because I asked the LORD for him."

Hannah Dedicates Samuel

²¹When her husband Elkanah went up with all his family to offer the annual sacrifice to the LORD and to fulfill his vow, ²²Hannah did not go. She said to her husband, "After the boy is weaned, I will take him and present him before the LORD, and he will live there always."ᵇ

²³"Do what seems best to you," her husband Elkanah told her. "Stay here until you have weaned him; only may the LORD make good hisᶜ word." So the woman stayed at home and nursed her son until she had weaned him.

²⁴After he was weaned, she took the boy with her, young as he was, along with a three-year-old bull,ᵈ an ephahᵉ of flour and a skin of wine, and brought him to the house of the LORD at Shiloh. ²⁵When the bull had been sacrificed, they brought the boy to Eli, ²⁶and she said to him, "Pardon me, my lord. As surely as you live, I am the woman who stood here beside you praying to the LORD. ²⁷I prayed for this child, and the LORD has granted me what I asked of him. ²⁸So now I give him to the LORD. For his whole life he will be given over to the LORD." And he worshiped the LORD there.

Hannah's Prayer

2 Then Hannah prayed and said:

"My heart rejoices in the LORD;
  in the LORD my hornᶠ is lifted high.
My mouth boasts over my enemies,
  for I delight in your deliverance.

² "There is no one holy like the LORD;
  there is no one besides you;
  there is no Rock like our God.

³ "Do not keep talking so proudly
  or let your mouth speak such arrogance,
for the LORD is a God who knows,
  and by him deeds are weighed.

⁴ "The bows of the warriors are broken,
  but those who stumbled are armed
    with strength.
⁵ Those who were full hire themselves out
    for food,
  but those who were hungry are hungry
    no more.
She who was barren has borne seven
  children,
  but she who has had many sons pines
    away.

⁶ "The LORD brings death and makes alive;
  he brings down to the grave and raises up.
⁷ The LORD sends poverty and wealth;
  he humbles and he exalts.
⁸ He raises the poor from the dust
  and lifts the needy from the ash heap;

ᵃ 20 *Samuel* sounds like the Hebrew for *heard by God.*
ᵇ 22 Masoretic Text; Dead Sea Scrolls *always. I have dedicated him as a Nazirite—all the days of his life."*   ᶜ 23 Masoretic Text; Dead Sea Scrolls, Septuagint and Syriac *your*   ᵈ 24 Dead Sea Scrolls, Septuagint and Syriac; Masoretic Text *with three bulls*
ᵉ 24 That is, probably about 36 pounds or about 16 kilograms
ᶠ 1 *Horn* here symbolizes strength; also in verse 10.

1:19 Ramah A shorter name for Ramathaim-zophim (see note on v. 1). **LORD remembered her** Indicates that Yahweh now turns his attention to her; he had not forgotten her (see Ge 8:1; 30:22; Ex 2:24). Through Hannah, God initiates a new phase in his plan for Israel (compare Ge 8:1; Ex 2:24).
1:20 Samuel Means "his name is God" or "name of God"—an emphasis on God's role in Samuel's life. Hannah's explanation of the name is a wordplay based on a similar-sounding Hebrew phrase meaning "heard from God."

SAMUEL
The son of Elkanah and Hannah, Samuel served as a priest, prophet and judge in 1 Samuel. He was God's instrument in Israel's transition from the period of the judges to the monarchy, and he functioned as God's

kingmaker. Samuel anointed both Saul (1Sa 10:1) and David (16:13). He served God faithfully during Saul's reign but died before David took the throne.

1:21–28 Keeping her vow, Hannah dedicates Samuel to God. After he is weaned, she presents him to Eli, the priest at Shiloh, to serve in the house of God.

1:24 a three-year-old bull A lavish gift according to the standards of the Pentateuch.

2:1–11 Hannah praises God for his great provision and answer to prayer.

2:1 My heart rejoices in the LORD This poem may have served as a model for Mary's song (Lk 1:46–55). They share many similarities in content, and the circumstances under which they were composed are also similar. **horn** A symbol of power and strength. **your deliverance** Refers to God's gift of a son.
2:5 borne seven children Symbolizes a large family. Hannah eventually had six children (1Sa 2:21).

he seats them with princes
  and has them inherit a throne of honor.

"For the foundations of the earth are
    the Lord's;
  on them he has set the world.
⁹ He will guard the feet of his faithful servants,
  but the wicked will be silenced in the place
    of darkness.

"It is not by strength that one prevails;
¹⁰ those who oppose the Lord will be
      broken.
  The Most High will thunder from heaven;
    the Lord will judge the ends of the earth.

"He will give strength to his king
  and exalt the horn of his anointed."

¹¹Then Elkanah went home to Ramah, but the boy ministered before the Lord under Eli the priest.

Eli's Wicked Sons

¹²Eli's sons were scoundrels; they had no regard for the Lord. ¹³Now it was the practice of the priests that, whenever any of the people offered a sacrifice, the priest's servant would come with a three-pronged fork in his hand while the meat was being boiled ¹⁴and would plunge the fork into the pan or kettle or caldron or pot. Whatever the fork brought up the priest would take for himself. This is how they treated all the Israelites who came to Shiloh. ¹⁵But even before the fat was burned, the priest's servant would come and say to the person who was sacrificing, "Give the priest some meat to roast; he won't accept boiled meat from you, but only raw."

¹⁶If the person said to him, "Let the fat be burned first, and then take whatever you want," the servant would answer, "No, hand it over now; if you don't, I'll take it by force."

¹⁷This sin of the young men was very great in the Lord's sight, for they* were treating the Lord's offering with contempt.

¹⁸But Samuel was ministering before the Lord — a boy wearing a linen ephod. ¹⁹Each year his mother made him a little robe and took it to him when she went up with her husband to offer the annual sacrifice. ²⁰Eli would bless Elkanah and his wife, saying, "May the Lord give you children by this woman to take the place of the one she prayed for and gave toᵇ the Lord." Then they would go home. ²¹And the Lord was gracious to Hannah; she gave birth to three sons and two daughters. Meanwhile, the boy Samuel grew up in the presence of the Lord.

²²Now Eli, who was very old, heard about everything his sons were doing to all Israel and how they slept with the women who served at the entrance to the tent of meeting. ²³So he said to them, "Why do you do such things? I hear from all the people about these wicked deeds of yours. ²⁴No, my sons; the report I hear spreading among the Lord's people is not good. ²⁵If one person sins against another, Godᶜ may mediate for the offender; but if anyone sins against the Lord, who will intercede for them?" His sons, however, did

---

a 17 Dead Sea Scrolls and Septuagint; Masoretic Text *people*
b 20 Dead Sea Scrolls; Masoretic Text *and asked from*
c 25 Or *the judges*

2:10 He will give strength to his king Possibly a prophetic anticipation of the monarchy. **his anointed** The Hebrew word used here, *mashiach*, often translated as messiah, refers to a king in this instance; Israelites anointed their kings with oil (see 10:1; 16:13; Ps 2:2 and note). Over time, this same Hebrew term would come to refer to a coming anointed one of God — called the Christ in Greek (see note on Mk 1:1).
2:11 Eli the priest The narrative shifts from focusing on Elkanah, who was a good father, to Eli, who was a poor father (indicated by his worthless sons in 1Sa 2:12).
2:12–21 Eli's sons (1:3) are reintroduced. Their sinfulness and contempt for Yahweh (v. 17) is contrasted with Samuel's faithful service (v. 18).
2:12 Eli's sons The narrative first mentions these sons in 1:3 without indicating their true character. **scoundrels** The Hebrew text here calls Eli's sons *benei beliyya'al*, which is literally rendered as "sons of Belial." A similar term is used in the NT to refer to the antithesis of Christ (see note on 1:16; note on 2Co 6:15). **they had no regard for the Lord** Contrasts Samuel's behavior. Even though young Samuel did not yet know God (see 1Sa 3:7), the narrative hints that he is righteous. He is worthy to take over the priesthood once God destroys Eli's line.
2:14 priest would take for himself Priests were allowed to take specific parts of sacrifices for themselves (see

Lev 7:28–34; 10:12–15; Nu 18:17–19). Here, Eli's sons take more than what is allotted to them by the Law.
2:15 before the fat was burned A grossly sacrilegious act; they also served themselves before serving God. See Lev 3:3–5; 7:22–25,31.
2:16 I'll take it by force Eli's sons use violence to carry out their lawlessness.
2:17 with contempt They had no regard for the sacred office or its function (compare Jdg 17:6; 19:1).
2:18 Samuel was ministering before the Lord Unlike Hophni and Phinehas, who were stealing and being gluttonous with Yahweh's portion.
2:21 in the presence of the Lord The Hebrew phrase used here also appears in Exodus to describe Moses' experience (Ex 34:28).
2:22–26 Eli rebukes his sons for their sinful behavior and tries to reason with them. The word of judgment delivered by the man of God (1Sa 2:27,29) implies that Eli was apathetic toward his sons' offenses and even might have participated in some of them.
2:22 slept with the women who served The sons either rape the women or treat them as temple prostitutes.
2:25 who will intercede Eli presents an argument to his wayward sons, but he does nothing to stop their sinful activities. Eli had the authority to remove his sons and legitimize the worship, but he did not. His ineffectual

not listen to their father's rebuke, for it was the LORD's will to put them to death.

²⁶And the boy Samuel continued to grow in stature and in favor with the LORD and with people.

Prophecy Against the House of Eli

²⁷Now a man of God came to Eli and said to him, "This is what the LORD says: 'Did I not clearly reveal myself to your ancestor's family when they were in Egypt under Pharaoh? ²⁸I chose your ancestor out of all the tribes of Israel to be my priest, to go up to my altar, to burn incense, and to wear an ephod in my presence. I also gave your ancestor's family all the food offerings presented by the Israelites. ²⁹Why do youᵃ scorn my sacrifice and offering that I prescribed for my dwelling? Why do you honor your sons more than me by fattening yourselves on the choice parts of every offering made by my people Israel?'

³⁰"Therefore the LORD, the God of Israel, declares: 'I promised that members of your family would minister before me forever.' But now the LORD declares: 'Far be it from me! Those who honor me I will honor, but those who despise me will be disdained. ³¹The time is coming when I will cut short your strength and the strength of your priestly house, so that no one in it will reach old age, ³²and you will see distress in my dwelling. Although good will be done to Israel, no one in your family line will ever reach old age. ³³Every

one of you that I do not cut off from serving at my altar I will spare only to destroy your sight and sap your strength, and all your descendants will die in the prime of life.

³⁴"'And what happens to your two sons, Hophni and Phinehas, will be a sign to you—they will both die on the same day. ³⁵I will raise up for myself a faithful priest, who will do according to what is in my heart and mind. I will firmly establish his priestly house, and they will minister before my anointed one always. ³⁶Then everyone left in your family line will come and bow down before him for a piece of silver and a loaf of bread and plead, "Appoint me to some priestly office so I can have food to eat."'"

The LORD Calls Samuel

3 The boy Samuel ministered before the LORD under Eli. In those days the word of the LORD was rare; there were not many visions.

²One night Eli, whose eyes were becoming so weak that he could barely see, was lying down in his usual place. ³The lamp of God had not yet gone out, and Samuel was lying down in the house of the LORD, where the ark of God was. ⁴Then the LORD called Samuel.

Samuel answered, "Here I am." ⁵And he ran to Eli and said, "Here I am; you called me."

But Eli said, "I did not call; go back and lie down." So he went and lay down.

ᵃ 29 The Hebrew is plural.

---

attempt at rebuke is a further mark against him as a father and priest. See 3:13 and note.
2:26 grow in stature and in favor The narrative again contrasts Samuel with Eli's sons. See vv. 17–18.

2:27–36 God sends a prophet to pronounce judgment on the house of Eli. As result of Eli's apathy and Hophni and Phinehas's heinous sins, God chooses to remove the line of Eli from the priesthood.

2:27 a man of God An unnamed prophet. **your ancestor's** Refers to Levi, ancestor of the priestly tribe.
2:31 I will cut short your strength The Hebrew text used here refers to cutting off Eli's arm, which was a common symbol of strength. **so that no one in it will reach old age** Indicates that the members of Eli's house will die young.
2:33 all your descendants will die This prophecy comes to fulfillment in Abiathar (22:18–23; 1Ki 2:26–27). **will die** Eli's sons are killed in 1Sa 4:11; other descendants are killed in 22:18–19.
2:35 I will raise up for myself a faithful priest This could be speaking of Samuel as the fulfillment of that promise, but Samuel's sons did not continue in his faithful ways. Alternatively, the narrative might be referring to Zadok, the high priest in the time of David. He first appears in 2Sa 8:17. **I will firmly establish his priestly house** God's judgment against Eli and his house allows God to reestablish the priestly line of Aaron's son Eleazar. In Nu 25:10–13, God had promised Eleazar the priesthood. This promise eventually is fulfilled in Zadok (1Ki 2:35). **before my anointed one** Refers to the king (see note on 1Sa 2:10).

3:1–21 After he pronounces destruction on the house of Eli, God calls Samuel as a prophet.

3:1 the word of the LORD was rare During the period of the judges, the nation is characterized by flagrant sin. The lack of communication from God indicates his displeasure. **there were not many visions** In this chapter, the word of Yahweh is actually an appearance of Yahweh (v. 10). This visual encounter of Yahweh himself is an important backdrop for the NT teaching of John that Jesus was the Word (Jn 1:1–14).
3:2 whose eyes were becoming so weak Eli's physical malady reflects his spiritual dullness and lack of perception. In 1Sa 1:13–14, he mistook Hannah's posture of prayer as drunkenness, and in 2:22–26 he weakly rebuked his sons.
3:3 lamp of God had not yet gone out Indicating that it was nearly dawn (see Ex 27:20–21). The narrative might be subtly referring to Samuel as well: Despite the darkness that characterized Shiloh at this time, a glimmer of hope is found in Samuel. **the house of the LORD** The Hebrew term used here, hekhal, refers to the tabernacle. It also might indicate the large main room of the tabernacle, separated by a veil from the Holy of Holies (Most Holy Place). The setting highlights Samuel's proximity to God: In this moment, he is the closest Israelite to Yahweh. See the infographic "The Tabernacle" on p. 138. **ark of God** Refers to the ark of the covenant, a chest that represented God's presence among his people (Ex 25:10–22; see note on Ex 25:10). See the infographic "The Ark of the Covenant" on p. 412.
3:4 Here I am Echoes the obedient responses of the

⁶Again the LORD called, "Samuel!" And Samuel got up and went to Eli and said, "Here I am; you called me."

"My son," Eli said, "I did not call; go back and lie down."

⁷Now Samuel did not yet know the LORD: The word of the LORD had not yet been revealed to him.

⁸A third time the LORD called, "Samuel!" And Samuel got up and went to Eli and said, "Here I am; you called me."

Then Eli realized that the LORD was calling the boy. ⁹So Eli told Samuel, "Go and lie down, and if he calls you, say, 'Speak, LORD, for your servant is listening.'" So Samuel went and lay down in his place.

¹⁰The LORD came and stood there, calling as at the other times, "Samuel! Samuel!"

Then Samuel said, "Speak, for your servant is listening."

¹¹And the LORD said to Samuel: "See, I am about to do something in Israel that will make the ears of everyone who hears about it tingle. ¹²At that time I will carry out against Eli everything I spoke against his family—from beginning to end. ¹³For I told him that I would judge his family forever because of the sin he knew about; his sons blasphemed God,ᵃ and he failed to restrain them. ¹⁴Therefore I swore to the house of Eli, 'The guilt of Eli's house will never be atoned for by sacrifice or offering.'"

¹⁵Samuel lay down until morning and then opened the doors of the house of the LORD. He was afraid to tell Eli the vision, ¹⁶but Eli called him and said, "Samuel, my son."

Samuel answered, "Here I am."

¹⁷"What was it he said to you?" Eli asked. "Do not hide it from me. May God deal with you, be it ever so severely, if you hide from me anything he told you." ¹⁸So Samuel told him everything, hiding nothing from him. Then Eli said, "He is the LORD; let him do what is good in his eyes."

¹⁹The LORD was with Samuel as he grew up, and he let none of Samuel's words fall to the ground. ²⁰And all Israel from Dan to Beersheba recognized that Samuel was attested as a prophet of the LORD. ²¹The LORD continued to appear at Shiloh, and there he revealed himself to Samuel through his word.

4 And Samuel's word came to all Israel.

The Philistines Capture the Ark

Now the Israelites went out to fight against the Philistines. The Israelites camped at Ebenezer, and the Philistines at Aphek. ²The Philistines deployed their forces to meet Israel, and as the battle spread, Israel was defeated by the Philistines, who killed about four thousand of them on the battlefield. ³When the soldiers returned to camp, the elders of Israel asked, "Why did the LORD bring defeat on us

---

ᵃ *13* An ancient Hebrew scribal tradition (see also Septuagint); Masoretic Text *sons made themselves contemptible*

---

patriarchs and Moses (Ge 22:1,11; 31:11; 46:2; Ex 3:4; compare Isa 6:8).

3:5 ran to Eli Indicates that Samuel was readily available to serve and quick to obey.

3:7 Samuel did not yet know the LORD This verse explains how Samuel could initially fail to recognize Yahweh's voice: He was not yet a prophet. Although Samuel knew of Yahweh and served him daily, he had not yet been called to his prophetic office.

3:8 Eli realized that the LORD was calling The only time Eli is perceptive; it takes three times for him to discern God's call.

3:10 LORD came and stood there Language about God standing is sometimes used to describe the closeness of his presence (Ge 28:13; Ex 34:5). **Samuel! Samuel!** Echoes God's calls to Abraham and Moses (Ge 22:11; Ex 3:4). **Speak, for your servant is listening** Samuel's response varies slightly from Eli's instructions (1Sa 3:9), omitting the divine name.

3:11 ears of everyone who hears An expression describing the reception of terrible news (compare 2Ki 21:12; Jer 19:3).

3:12 everything I spoke against his family See 1Sa 2:30–36.

3:13 he failed to restrain them Eli's rebuke in 2:22–25 was only halfhearted. Though he had the authority and responsibility to act against them, he did not (see note on 2:25).

3:14 The guilt of Eli's house will never be atoned for Eli and his sons had committed high-handed, flagrant sin (2:12–17,31; compare Nu 15:30–31).

3:17 May God deal with you A characteristic oath formula that calls for divine action against a person for failing or refusing to obey (see Ru 1:17; 1 Sa 14:44; 20:13; 25:22; 2 Sa 3:9,35; 19:13). Samuel is forced to speak due to the oath.

3:18 let him do what is good in his eyes Eli acquiesces and accepts God's punishment.

3:19 he let none of Samuel's words fall to the ground This expression conveys the hallmark of a true prophet: His prophecies come to pass (see Dt 18:21–22).

3:20 Dan to Beersheba An expression that indicates all of Israel, from its northernmost city to its southernmost city.

4:1—7:2 The next three chapters interrupt the narrative about Samuel, who will reemerge in 1Sa 7 as Israel's new leader. Chapter 4 reports the fulfillment of God's judgment against the house of Eli. Chapters 5–6 focus on the ark of the covenant, which has been captured by the Philistines.

4:1–11 The Israelites' fight against the Philistines is not going well. They call for the ark to be brought to the battlefield, and Hophni and Phinehas come along with it. They are killed in the ensuing slaughter, and the ark is captured.

4:1 Samuel's word came to all Israel Ties this chapter thematically with ch. 3. Samuel is absent from the next three chapters, emblematic of Israel as a people without a prophet in the time of the judges. **Philistines** The Israelites' archenemies during this time.

today before the Philistines? Let us bring the ark of the LORD's covenant from Shiloh, so that he may go with us and save us from the hand of our enemies."

⁴So the people sent men to Shiloh, and they brought back the ark of the covenant of the LORD Almighty, who is enthroned between the cherubim. And Eli's two sons, Hophni and Phinehas, were there with the ark of the covenant of God.

⁵When the ark of the LORD's covenant came into the camp, all Israel raised such a great shout

PHILISTINES

The Philistines likely were among the Sea Peoples who appear to have migrated from various parts of the Mediterranean to the coastlands of Palestine (see Nu 24:24; Jer 47:4; Am 9:7). They seem to have arrived around the same time as the Israelites (ca. 1200 BC). They were fierce in battle, defeating the Hittite, Ugaritic and Amurru kingdoms, as well as the Egyptians and Israelites. By the time of the Samuel narratives, the Philistines have already claimed a few coastal cities, and they are trying to push eastward to conquer Israelite territory.

4:2 The Philistines deployed their forces to meet Israel The first confrontation between the Israelites and the Philistines in 1–2 Samuel. With the exception of a few brief periods of peace, these two groups continuously engage in warfare. **four thousand** This staggering loss is only the beginning of Israel's defeat.

4:3 ark of the LORD's covenant The Israelites treat the ark as a good luck charm rather than giving it the respect it deserves. See note on Ex 25:10; see the infographic "The Ark of the Covenant" below.

4:4 who is enthroned between the cherubim Refers to the cherubim on the ark (see Ex 25:17–22). The Israelites apparently believed that having the ark close by would make it more likely that God would help them. **Eli's two sons, Hophni and Phinehas** Their introduction in a battle scene recalls the prophecy concerning their death (1Sa 2:33–34) and signals disaster.

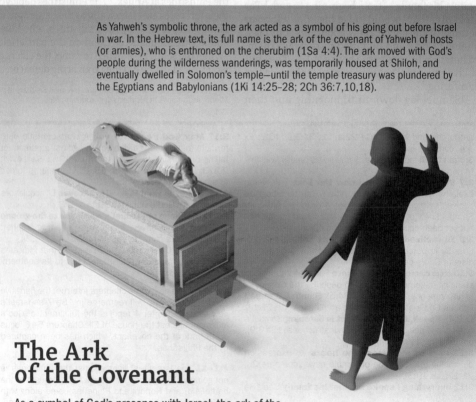

As Yahweh's symbolic throne, the ark acted as a symbol of his going out before Israel in war. In the Hebrew text, its full name is the ark of the covenant of Yahweh of hosts (or armies), who is enthroned on the cherubim (1Sa 4:4). The ark moved with God's people during the wilderness wanderings, was temporarily housed at Shiloh, and eventually dwelled in Solomon's temple—until the temple treasury was plundered by the Egyptians and Babylonians (1Ki 14:25-28; 2Ch 36:7,10,18).

The Ark of the Covenant

As a symbol of God's presence with Israel, the ark of the covenant was the center of Yahweh worship and was brought into the temple each year at Passover (Ps 24:7-9). It housed the covenant tablets; a gold jar of manna and Aaron's staff that had budded were either set before the ark or in it (1Ki 8:9; Heb 9:4).

that the ground shook. 6Hearing the uproar, the Philistines asked, "What's all this shouting in the Hebrew camp?"

When they learned that the ark of the LORD had come into the camp, 7the Philistines were afraid. "A god has*a* come into the camp," they said. "Oh no! Nothing like this has happened before. 8We're doomed! Who will deliver us from the hand of these mighty gods? They are the gods who struck the Egyptians with all kinds of plagues in the wilderness. 9Be strong, Philistines! Be men, or you will be subject to the Hebrews, as they have been to you. Be men, and fight!"

10So the Philistines fought, and the Israelites were defeated and every man fled to his tent. The slaughter was very great; Israel lost thirty thousand foot soldiers. 11The ark of God was captured, and Eli's two sons, Hophni and Phinehas, died.

Death of Eli

12That same day a Benjamite ran from the battle line and went to Shiloh with his clothes torn and dust on his head. 13When he arrived, there was Eli sitting on his chair by the side of the road, watching, because his heart feared for the ark of God. When the man entered the town and told what had happened, the whole town sent up a cry.

14Eli heard the outcry and asked, "What is the meaning of this uproar?"

The man hurried over to Eli, 15who was ninety-eight years old and whose eyes had failed so that he could not see. 16He told Eli, "I have just come from the battle line; I fled from it this very day."

Eli asked, "What happened, my son?"

17The man who brought the news replied, "Israel fled before the Philistines, and the army has suffered heavy losses. Also your two sons, Hophni and Phinehas, are dead, and the ark of God has been captured."

18When he mentioned the ark of God, Eli fell backward off his chair by the side of the gate. His neck was broken and he died, for he was an old man, and he was heavy. He had led*b* Israel forty years.

19His daughter-in-law, the wife of Phinehas, was pregnant and near the time of delivery. When she heard the news that the ark of God had been captured and that her father-in-law and her husband were dead, she went into labor and gave birth, but was overcome by her labor pains. 20As she was dying, the women attending her said, "Don't despair; you have given birth to a son." But she did not respond or pay any attention.

21She named the boy Ichabod,*c* saying, "The Glory has departed from Israel" — because of the capture of the ark of God and the deaths of her father-in-law and her husband. 22She said, "The Glory has departed from Israel, for the ark of God has been captured."

The Ark in Ashdod and Ekron

5 After the Philistines had captured the ark of God, they took it from Ebenezer to Ashdod. 2Then they carried the ark into Dagon's temple and

a 7 Or "Gods have (see Septuagint)   *b* 18 Traditionally judged
c 21 Ichabod means no glory.

4:5 the ground shook Indicates that the sound of their rejoicing could be felt in the ground.
4:7 A god has come into the camp The Hebrew word used here, elohim, can refer to Yahweh, a particular unnamed god, or multiple pagan deities (gods). The Philistines probably are thinking of multiple gods (elohim); it seems unlikely that they would have properly identified Israel's God or viewed him as the supreme deity.
4:8 the gods who struck the Egyptians Although the Philistines likely believe that multiple gods rescued the Israelite people from Egypt, they still show an awareness that the Israelites' rescue was a divine act. The Philistines fear the same sort of reprisals the Egyptians experienced. **in the wilderness** Misidentifies the setting for the plagues. This mistake, along with the likely reference to polytheism, could be indented to show the Philistines' ignorance.
4:10 thirty thousand foot soldiers In their second skirmish, the Philistines obliterate the Israelite forces.
4:11 Hophni and Phinehas, died Fulfills the details of the prophecy in 2:33–34.
4:12–22 Upon hearing about the ark's capture, Eli falls over and dies.
4:12 Shiloh The final mention of this place in 1–2 Samuel (with the exception of a reference to Eli in 14:3). See note on 14:3. **clothes torn and dust on his head** Signs of mourning.
4:13 his heart feared for the ark of God Eli is concerned for the ark, not his sons. See v. 18.

4:17 Israel fled before the Philistines The report comes to Eli in four parts, each more tragic than the one that precedes it: Israel has fled, many troops have died, his sons have been killed, and the ark of God has been captured.
4:18 fell backward off his chair The narrative artfully portrays the fall of Eli's line by speaking of Eli's literal tumble. See the table "Judges and Their Rule" on p. 364. **heavy** A play on words. The Hebrew term used here, kaved, can describe being important, oppressive or weighty. Eli seems to have been all three. He was important; he and his sons dealt oppressively with the people (2:12–17); and he apparently was overweight from eating sacrificial meat (2:29).
4:19 the ark of God had been captured The narrative lists the capture of the ark first, perhaps hinting that this was the greatest tragedy of the day. The structure of this verse suggests this may have been the most significant loss to Phinehas' wife as well (compare 2:22; 4:21,22).

5:1–12 The Philistines return home from battle victorious, having captured the ark of the God of Israel. However, when they bring the ark into their temple, it desecrates their god, Dagon. When they send it throughout the Philistine cities, God afflicts the people with tumors and causes great suffering—the outcome of their irreverence.
5:1 Ebenezer The site of the Israelite camp (4:1). **Ashdod** One of the five major cities of the Philistines.
5:2 Dagon A god of the Philistines. Due to their victory in

set it beside Dagon. ³When the people of Ashdod rose early the next day, there was Dagon, fallen on his face on the ground before the ark of the LORD! They took Dagon and put him back in his place. ⁴But the following morning when they rose, there was Dagon, fallen on his face on the ground before the ark of the LORD! His head and hands had been broken off and were lying on the threshold; only his body remained. ⁵That is why to this day neither the priests of Dagon nor any others who enter Dagon's temple at Ashdod step on the threshold.

⁶The LORD's hand was heavy on the people of Ashdod and its vicinity; he brought devastation on them and afflicted them with tumors.ᵃ ⁷When the people of Ashdod saw what was happening, they said, "The ark of the god of Israel must not stay here with us, because his hand is heavy on us and on Dagon our god." ⁸So they called together all the rulers of the Philistines and asked them, "What shall we do with the ark of the god of Israel?"

They answered, "Have the ark of the god of Israel moved to Gath." So they moved the ark of the God of Israel.

⁹But after they had moved it, the LORD's hand was against that city, throwing it into a great panic. He afflicted the people of the city, both young and old, with an outbreak of tumors.ᵇ ¹⁰So they sent the ark of God to Ekron.

As the ark of God was entering Ekron, the people of Ekron cried out, "They have brought the ark of the god of Israel around to us to kill us and our people." ¹¹So they called together all the rulers of the Philistines and said, "Send the ark of the god of Israel away; let it go back to its own place, or itᶜ will kill us and our people." For death had filled the city with panic; God's hand was very heavy on it. ¹²Those who did not die were afflicted with tumors, and the outcry of the city went up to heaven.

The Ark Returned to Israel

6 When the ark of the LORD had been in Philistine territory seven months, ²the Philistines called for the priests and the diviners and said, "What shall we do with the ark of the LORD? Tell us how we should send it back to its place."

³They answered, "If you return the ark of the

ᵃ 6 Hebrew; Septuagint and Vulgate *tumors. And rats appeared in their land, and there was death and destruction throughout the city*   ᵇ 9 Or *with tumors in the groin* (see Septuagint)   ᶜ 11 Or *he*

---

battle, the Philistines believe that Israel's God must be subservient to their god (see Jer 43:12 and note). See the table "Pagan Deities of the Old Testament" on p. 1287.
5:3 fallen on his face on the ground A posture of worship and subservience. The Philistine god, who they thought prevailed in battle, pays homage to the God of Israel. **put him back in his place** Demonstrates Dagon's true lack of power; he cannot even stand up on his own. This phrase serves as a subtle critique of idolatry. Ancients believed their pagan gods accompanied them on the battlefield and gave them victory. The Philistines believed their god, Dagon, had triumphed over Yahweh. In reality, Dagon needed the help of his priests to simply stand up—a humorous contrast to the image of a warring deity. Compare Isa 44:9–20; Jer 10:5.
5:4 following morning when they rose This occurs on two successive days, showing it was not an accident.
5:5 step on the threshold This seems to indicate that people no longer entered this temple of Dagon. However, the text could also be alluding to some ritual that involved stepping over the threshold of the door rather than on it—showing a sign of respect upon entering the temple. This decision reflects the ancient Near Eastern worldview that geographical regions were under the dominion of various gods (see Dt 32:8 and note). In the minds of the Philistines, the temple of Dagon was now under Yahweh's jurisdiction, since he had conquered Dagon. The Philistines are testifying to the superiority of Yahweh over Dagon.
5:6 with tumors Many translations read "tumors" or "hemorrhoids" here based on a suggestion in the margin of the traditional Hebrew Bible—which literally refers to mounds or bulges. But the main Hebrew text refers to "swellings." In an attempt to alleviate this plague, the Philistines later send five gold rodents and five other gold objects back to Israel with the ark of the covenant (1Sa 6:4–5). The reference to rodents suggests the Philistines' crops were being ravished and that they may have been

experiencing the bubonic plague; in line with this, the ancient Greek translation of the OT (the Septuagint) adds a reference to rodents here in 5:6. However, in 6:4, the same Hebrew word used here in 5:6 refers to the shape of the second set of gold objects, making the reading of "tumors" or "hemorrhoids" odd. Archaeological discoveries at the Philistine city of Ashkelon revealed bronze vessels in the form of male phalluses, which means that the Philistines in 6:4 likely created phallic objects. This suggests that the bodily infirmity of the Philistines was some sort of genital affliction. This combined with their crops being destroyed would have been a mockery of their entire religion—Dagon was a god affiliated with grain and the harvest, and Philistine religion in general focused on fertility.
5:8 rulers of the Philistines The leaders of the five major Philistine cities: Ashdod, Gath, Ekron, Ashkelon and Gaza.
5:10 people of Ekron cried out This was apparently not part of the plan formulated in v. 8; the ark is unwelcome in Ekron.
5:11 let it go back to its own place They recognize that Yahweh's power is directed against them. The God of Israel does not need an army to fight for him—he can handle the Philistines himself. Consequently, they wisely advise that it be returned to its proper place before it kills all of them.
5:12 went up to heaven This does not imply that they are praying specifically to Yahweh.

6:1—7:2 After God has inflicted the Philistines with some sort of swelling and assaulted their god, they decide to send the ark back to Israel, along with a guilt offering to Yahweh.

6:3 guilt offering The Philistines' own religion may have required a guilt offering to appease an offended deity. On Israel's regulations for guilt offerings, see Lev 5:14—6:7 and note.

god of Israel, do not send it back to him without a gift; by all means send a guilt offering to him. Then you will be healed, and you will know why his hand has not been lifted from you."

⁴The Philistines asked, "What guilt offering should we send to him?"

They replied, "Five gold tumors and five gold rats, according to the number of the Philistine rulers, because the same plague has struck both you and your rulers. ⁵Make models of the tumors and of the rats that are destroying the country, and give glory to Israel's god. Perhaps he will lift his hand from you and your gods and your land. ⁶Why do you harden your hearts as the Egyptians and Pharaoh did? When Israel's god dealt harshly with them, did they not send the Israelites out so they could go on their way?

⁷"Now then, get a new cart ready, with two cows that have calved and have never been yoked. Hitch the cows to the cart, but take their calves away and pen them up. ⁸Take the ark of the LORD and put it on the cart, and in a chest beside it put the gold objects you are sending back to him as a guilt offering. Send it on its way, ⁹but keep watching it. If it goes up to its own territory, toward Beth Shemesh, then the LORD has brought this great disaster on us. But if it does not, then we will know that it was not his hand that struck us but that it happened to us by chance."

¹⁰So they did this. They took two such cows and hitched them to the cart and penned up their calves. ¹¹They placed the ark of the LORD on the cart and along with it the chest containing the gold rats and the models of the tumors. ¹²Then the cows went straight up toward Beth Shemesh, keeping on the road and lowing all the way; they did not turn to the right or to the left. The rulers of the Philistines followed them as far as the border of Beth Shemesh.

¹³Now the people of Beth Shemesh were harvesting their wheat in the valley, and when they looked up and saw the ark, they rejoiced at the sight. ¹⁴The cart came to the field of Joshua of Beth Shemesh, and there it stopped beside a large rock. The people chopped up the wood of the cart and sacrificed the cows as a burnt offering to the LORD. ¹⁵The Levites took down the ark of the LORD, together with the chest containing the gold objects, and placed them on the large rock. On that day the people of Beth Shemesh offered burnt offerings and made sacrifices to the LORD. ¹⁶The five rulers of the Philistines saw all this and then returned that same day to Ekron.

¹⁷These are the gold tumors the Philistines sent as a guilt offering to the LORD — one each for Ashdod, Gaza, Ashkelon, Gath and Ekron. ¹⁸And the number of the gold rats was according to the number of Philistine towns belonging to the five rulers — the fortified towns with their country villages. The large rock on which the Levites set the ark of the LORD is a witness to this day in the field of Joshua of Beth Shemesh.

¹⁹But God struck down some of the inhabitants of Beth Shemesh, putting seventy[a] of them to death because they looked into the ark of the LORD. The people mourned because of the heavy blow the LORD had dealt them. ²⁰And the people of Beth Shemesh asked, "Who can stand in the presence of the LORD, this holy God? To whom will the ark go up from here?"

²¹Then they sent messengers to the people of

─────

a 19 A few Hebrew manuscripts; most Hebrew manuscripts and Septuagint *50,070*

─────

6:4 Five gold tumors and five gold rats The diviners call for offerings of gold representing each Philistine ruler and city (see 1Sa 6:17–18). The Philistines apparently believed that these golden likenesses had magical properties. Sending them away was a rite by which they hoped to rid themselves of their suffering. See note on 5:6.

6:6 harden your hearts See note on Ex 4:21. **did they not send the Israelites out** Refers to the exodus (Ex 12:31–33).

6:7 new cart This goes against the procedures given by Yahweh, which required the ark to be carried on poles (Ex 25:13–14). **that have calved and have never been yoked** Refers to untrained cows that were not accustomed to being used for transportation or farming. **take their calves away and pen them up** If the cows pulling the cart resist their maternal instincts and deliver the ark to Israel, then Yahweh's involvement is confirmed.

6:9 then the LORD has brought this great disaster on us In addition to gaining healing, the Philistines also send the ark away (1Sa 6:3) to determine whether their suffering came from Israel's God. If the cows ignore the cries of their calves and successfully transport the ark, the Philistines' misery was certainly an act of vengeance from Israel's God.

6:12 cows went straight Confirms that Yahweh had afflicted the Philistines.

6:13 Beth Shemesh A city of the Levites, who were tasked with taking care of the ark (Nu 3:31; Dt 10:8; Jos 21:16). Their behavior when it comes to them, however, shows that they were not as aware of how to handle the ark as they should have been.

6:14 beside a large rock The stone could be used for an altar. **as a burnt offering to the LORD** A violation of the law, which stipulated male animals for the burnt offering (Lev 1:3).

6:19 seventy Most English translations put the number killed at 70, following the cue of a small number of Hebrew manuscripts. This emendation goes against both the traditional Hebrew text and the Septuagint (the ancient Greek translation of the OT), which awkwardly indicate a much higher number (literally "70 men, 50,000 men"). The population of the small town of Beth Shemesh would have been considerably under 50,000. **they looked into the ark** A violation of the law, which calls for the ark to be shielded from view (Nu 4:5–6).

6:20 To whom will the ark go The people of Beth Shemesh wish to be rid of the ark, just like the Philistines.

6:21 Kiriath Jearim A nearby city located northeast of Beth Shemesh.

Kiriath Jearim, saying, "The Philistines have returned the ark of the LORD. Come down and take

7 it up to your town." ¹So the men of Kiriath Jearim came and took up the ark of the LORD. They brought it to Abinadab's house on the hill and consecrated Eleazar his son to guard the ark of the LORD. ²The ark remained at Kiriath Jearim a long time — twenty years in all.

Samuel Subdues the Philistines at Mizpah

Then all the people of Israel turned back to the LORD. ³So Samuel said to all the Israelites, "If you are returning to the LORD with all your hearts, then rid yourselves of the foreign gods and the Ashtoreths and commit yourselves to the LORD and serve him only, and he will deliver you out of the hand of the Philistines." ⁴So the Israelites put away their Baals and Ashtoreths, and served the LORD only.

⁵Then Samuel said, "Assemble all Israel at Mizpah, and I will intercede with the LORD for you." ⁶When they had assembled at Mizpah, they drew water and poured it out before the LORD. On that day they fasted and there they confessed, "We have sinned against the LORD." Now Samuel was serving as leader*a* of Israel at Mizpah.

⁷When the Philistines heard that Israel had assembled at Mizpah, the rulers of the Philistines came up to attack them. When the Israelites heard of it, they were afraid because of the Philistines. ⁸They said to Samuel, "Do not stop crying out to the LORD our God for us, that he may rescue us from the hand of the Philistines." ⁹Then Samuel took a suckling lamb and sacrificed it as a whole burnt offering to the LORD. He cried out to the LORD on Israel's behalf, and the LORD answered him.

¹⁰While Samuel was sacrificing the burnt offering, the Philistines drew near to engage Israel in battle. But that day the LORD thundered with loud thunder against the Philistines and threw them into such a panic that they were routed before the Israelites. ¹¹The men of Israel rushed out of Mizpah and pursued the Philistines, slaughtering them along the way to a point below Beth Kar.

¹²Then Samuel took a stone and set it up between Mizpah and Shen. He named it Ebenezer,*b* saying, "Thus far the LORD has helped us."

¹³So the Philistines were subdued and they stopped invading Israel's territory. Throughout Samuel's lifetime, the hand of the LORD was against the Philistines. ¹⁴The towns from Ekron to Gath that the Philistines had captured from Israel were restored to Israel, and Israel delivered the neighboring territory from the hands of the Philistines. And there was peace between Israel and the Amorites.

¹⁵Samuel continued as Israel's leader all the days of his life. ¹⁶From year to year he went on a circuit from Bethel to Gilgal to Mizpah, judging Israel in all those places. ¹⁷But he always went

---

a 6 Traditionally *judge*; also in verse 15   *b* 12 *Ebenezer* means *stone of help.*

7:1 They brought it to Abinadab's house The Israelites do not return the ark to Shiloh, suggesting that the city had been destroyed (see note on 1Sa 14:3). **Eleazar** His name (common among priests during this period) and the fact that he was not killed in his caretaking duties suggest that Eleazar was a Levite.

7:2 turned back to the LORD The exact meaning of the Hebrew phrase used here is uncertain; the Israelites may have repented or returned to God while lamenting for their sin (compare v. 3).

7:3–17 The narrative reintroduces Samuel, signaling a positive change for Israel. This passage establishes the background for Samuel's career as a prophet, priest and judge.

7:3 then rid yourselves of the foreign gods The period of the judges was characterized by spiritual defection and idolatry (e.g., Jdg 2:12–13; 3:7; 8:33–34; 10:6–13). **Ashtoreths** Refers to idols of the Canaanite fertility goddess Ashtoreth (also known as Astarte). Some Israelites may have worshiped her along with Yahweh as his wife or consort. If so, Samuel is attempting to correct this practice. See the table "Pagan Deities of the Old Testament" on p. 1287.

7:4 Baals Refers to idols of the Canaanite storm god Baal, the masculine counterpart to Ashtoreth.

7:6 poured it out before the LORD This pouring out could indicate that, along with fasting, the people would not drink water until Samuel had finished interceding on their behalf (compare Jnh 3:7; 2Sa 23:16). Alternatively, this action may be emblematic of a purification ritual to cleanse the land of pagan worship. Ultimately, Samuel is acting as judge and calling the people to repentance.

7:7 rulers of the Philistines came up Following the two defeats in 1Sa 4:1–11, Israel probably was subservient to the Philistines (see 13:19–20). The Philistines likely imposed harsh restrictions on clan and tribal meetings, which could be used to incite revolt. When they hear that Israel is gathering, they send a military dispatch to enforce their regulation and protect their interests.

7:9 whole burnt offering A sacrifice that is entirely burned up before God (Ex 29:18; Lev 8:21; Dt 13:16). **the LORD answered him** Signals a shift in God's interaction with Israel (compare 1Sa 3:1 and note).

7:10 thundered with loud thunder This language recalls imagery from Hannah's song (2:10). God demonstrates that he, not Baal, is in charge of the weather. See the table "Miracles of the Prophets" on p. 1366.

7:12 Ebenezer Meaning "stone of the warrior" or "stone of the helper." This name in 4:1 may refer to a different place.

7:14 Amorites A generic term for people who inhabited the land prior to Israel's arrival (see Ge 10:16 and note). Rather than continue to fight the emerging power, they sought terms of peace.

7:16 he went on a circuit Samuel traveled from place to place as a judge. See the table "Judges and Their Rule" on p. 364.

7:17 he built an altar there to the LORD Indicates that Samuel probably moved the religious headquarters to

back to Ramah, where his home was, and there he also held court for Israel. And he built an altar there to the Lord.

Israel Asks for a King

8 When Samuel grew old, he appointed his sons as Israel's leaders.[a] [2]The name of his firstborn was Joel and the name of his second was Abijah, and they served at Beersheba. [3]But his sons did not follow his ways. They turned aside after dishonest gain and accepted bribes and perverted justice.

[4]So all the elders of Israel gathered together and came to Samuel at Ramah. [5]They said to him, "You are old, and your sons do not follow your ways; now appoint a king to lead[b] us, such as all the other nations have."

[6]But when they said, "Give us a king to lead us," this displeased Samuel; so he prayed to the Lord. [7]And the Lord told him: "Listen to all that the people are saying to you; it is not you they have rejected, but they have rejected me as their king. [8]As they have done from the day I brought them up out of Egypt until this day, forsaking me and serving other gods, so they are doing to you. [9]Now listen to them; but warn them solemnly and let them know what the king who will reign over them will claim as his rights."

[10]Samuel told all the words of the Lord to the people who were asking him for a king. [11]He said, "This is what the king who will reign over you will claim as his rights: He will take your sons and make them serve with his chariots and horses, and they will run in front of his chariots. [12]Some he will assign to be commanders of thousands and commanders of fifties, and others to plow his ground and reap his harvest, and still others to make weapons of war and equipment for his chariots. [13]He will take your daughters to be perfumers and cooks and bakers. [14]He will take the best of your fields and vineyards and olive groves and give them to his attendants. [15]He will take a tenth of your grain and of your vintage and give it to his officials and attendants. [16]Your male and female servants and the best of your cattle[c] and donkeys he will take for his own use. [17]He will take a tenth of your flocks, and you yourselves will become his slaves. [18]When that day comes, you will cry out for relief from the king you have chosen, but the Lord will not answer you in that day."

[19]But the people refused to listen to Samuel. "No!" they said. "We want a king over us. [20]Then we will be like all the other nations, with a king to lead us and to go out before us and fight our battles."

---

[a] 1 Traditionally *judges*   [b] 5 Traditionally *judge*; also in verses 6 and 20   [c] 16 Septuagint; Hebrew *young men*

Ramah. This is further evidence that Shiloh had been destroyed (see note on 4:12). See the table "Altars in the Old Testament" on p. 249.

8:1–9 This chapter marks the beginning of Israel's transition to a monarchy. Because Samuel's sons were not righteous like their father, Israel's tribal leaders request that Samuel appoint a king. Their request, however, ultimately amounts to a rejection of God's rule over the nation. Nevertheless, God permits Samuel to grant their request.

8:1 he appointed his sons as Israel's leaders Samuel makes his sons judges like himself (see 7:6,15), but being a judge was not an office that could be inherited (compare Jdg 8:22–23). It is therefore unsurprising that this move was not successful.

8:2 Beersheba The southern extremity of Israel's territory, outside Samuel's regular circuit (1Sa 7:16).

8:3 did not follow Samuel's sons are like Eli's; they fail to practice righteousness or keep the law (compare 2:12 and note). **accepted bribes and perverted justice** Against the command of Dt 16:19.

8:4 elders of Israel Probably refers to the leaders of the family clans and tribes (see Dt 31:28).

8:5 such as all the other nations God had intended for Israel to be distinct from the other nations (Lev 20:26).

8:6 he prayed to the Lord Prayer is always Samuel's first response.

8:7 they have rejected me as their king God was Israel's king; Samuel and other judges were his administrators (Nu 23:21; Jdg 8:22–23).

8:10–18 Samuel heeds God's counsel and warns the people about the burdens of a monarchy.

8:11 the king who will reign over you The people demand a king like all the other nations — and he will behave like all other kings, relying on taxation and conscription to maintain his rule. **take your sons and make them serve** Describes forced military service.

8:12 to plow his ground In addition to serving in the military, some Israelites will have to work and keep the king's land.

8:14 give them to his attendants He will appropriate the best of the people's land and give it to those who serve him.

8:17 you yourselves will become his slaves This is the climax of Samuel's message. Israelites will no longer be free; they will be forced to work in support of the king and his kingdom.

8:18 you will cry out Recalls the motif from Judges, where the people cry out to God for deliverance from their oppressors (Jdg 3:9,15; 6:6). This time it is not a foreign oppressor but their own king. **the Lord will not answer you** A result of their willful rejection of his rule.

8:19–22 The people reject Samuel's warning and demand a king. They do not care about the consequences of replacing God's rule with a human monarch. They are willing to accept taxation and conscription for the sake of being like all the other nations.

8:20 fight our battles In addition to their apprehension about Samuel's sons as leaders (1Sa 8:5), the Israelites also want a king who will lead them in battle. Previously, it was God who led the Israelites in battle (e.g., Dt 1:30; 20:1–4). Now, despite God's great victory over the Philistines in 1Sa 7, they reject God as commander of their armies.

²¹When Samuel heard all that the people said, he repeated it before the LORD. ²²The LORD answered, "Listen to them and give them a king."

Then Samuel said to the Israelites, "Everyone go back to your own town."

Samuel Anoints Saul

9 There was a Benjamite, a man of standing, whose name was Kish son of Abiel, the son of Zeror, the son of Bekorath, the son of Aphiah of Benjamin. ²Kish had a son named Saul, as handsome a young man as could be found anywhere in Israel, and he was a head taller than anyone else.

³Now the donkeys belonging to Saul's father Kish were lost, and Kish said to his son Saul, "Take one of the servants with you and go and look for the donkeys." ⁴So he passed through the hill country of Ephraim and through the area around Shalisha, but they did not find them. They went on into the district of Shaalim, but the donkeys were not there. Then he passed through the territory of Benjamin, but they did not find them.

⁵When they reached the district of Zuph, Saul said to the servant who was with him, "Come, let's go back, or my father will stop thinking about the donkeys and start worrying about us."

⁶But the servant replied, "Look, in this town there is a man of God; he is highly respected, and everything he says comes true. Let's go there now. Perhaps he will tell us what way to take."

⁷Saul said to his servant, "If we go, what can we give the man? The food in our sacks is gone. We have no gift to take to the man of God. What do we have?"

⁸The servant answered him again. "Look," he said, "I have a quarter of a shekelᵃ of silver. I will give it to the man of God so that he will tell us what way to take." ⁹(Formerly in Israel, if someone went to inquire of God, they would say, "Come, let us go to the seer," because the prophet of today used to be called a seer.)

¹⁰"Good," Saul said to his servant. "Come, let's go." So they set out for the town where the man of God was.

¹¹As they were going up the hill to the town, they met some young women coming out to draw water, and they asked them, "Is the seer here?"

¹²"He is," they answered. "He's ahead of you. Hurry now; he has just come to our town today, for the people have a sacrifice at the high place. ¹³As soon as you enter the town, you will find him before he goes up to the high place to eat. The people will not begin eating until he comes, because he must bless the sacrifice; afterward, those who are invited will eat. Go up now; you should find him about this time."

¹⁴They went up to the town, and as they were entering it, there was Samuel, coming toward them on his way up to the high place.

¹⁵Now the day before Saul came, the LORD had revealed this to Samuel: ¹⁶"About this time tomorrow I will send you a man from the land of Benjamin. Anoint him ruler over my people Israel; he will de-

---

ᵃ 8 That is, about 1/10 ounce or about 3 grams

9:1–27 This section introduces Israel's first human king. Saul's reign is presented with a sense of foreboding, with hints of his ineptness and spiritual ignorance. The nation of Israel gets exactly what it asked for (see 8:5,10–20).

9:1 There was a Benjamite Similar to 1:1, where the narrative introduced Samuel's father with a four-generation genealogy and tribal designation. Samuel and Saul are contrasted throughout the story. Samuel is presented as a capable and righteous leader, whereas Saul is cast as incompetent and, eventually, wicked. In addition to being introduced with the genealogies of their fathers, both men came from the same general region in Israel. Both also led the Israelite forces in battle against the Philistines and built altars to God. See people diagram "King Saul's Family Tree" on p. 428.

9:2 handsome Calling attention to Saul's attractive appearance here may be intended to underscore the fact that appearances can be deceiving (see 16:7; 2Sa 14:25). **a head taller than anyone else** Saul is one of the only Israelites singled out for his tall stature. This description identifies him as being like the kings of other nations. Other people or groups described as being tall in the Hebrew Bible generally are enemies of Israel: the Nephilim (Nu 13:33); the Emites and Anakites (Dt 2:10); Goliath (1Sa 17:4); the four descendants of the giants from Gath, including the giant with six fingers and six toes (2Sa 21:15–22); an Egyptian (1Ch 11:23); the Cushites (Isa 18:1–2); the Sabeans (Isa 45:14); and the Amorites (Am 2:9). David's older brother Eliab,

whom God rejected as king, also is distinguished by his height (1Sa 16:7).

9:3 donkeys belonging to Saul's father Kish were lost The literary motif of a bad shepherd is used for Saul throughout 1 Samuel. Not only is he inept at leading animals, but he also is incompetent when leading people. Rather than being a godly ruler, Saul reflects the leaders of other nations and does not follow God's law. In contrast, the narrative upholds David as the ultimate shepherd (see 2Sa 5:2). In the Bible, leaders are often described with the shepherd motif (e.g., 1Ch 11:2; Ps 78:70–71; Isa 44:28). The patriarchs of Genesis (Abraham, Isaac and Jacob), Moses, Saul and David are all described in this way. The motif also is used in Psalms and in the Prophets, including Isaiah, Jeremiah, Ezekiel, Micah, Nahum and Zechariah. Jesus employs this imagery in the Gospel of John (Jn 10:11–18), and NT authors refer to him in similar terms (e.g., Heb 13:20; 1Pe 2:25; 5:4).

9:4 but they did not find them Saul's inability to locate a herd of large animals displays his incompetence as a shepherd.

9:6 the servant replied Throughout this episode, the servant—not Saul—is shown to have wise instincts.

9:8 I have a quarter of a shekel of silver Unlike Saul, the servant is prepared.

9:11 young women coming out to draw water The narrative's use of the woman at the well motif links this event to significant events in the lives of the patriarchs and Moses (e.g., Ge 24:13–27; 29:9–12; Ex 2:15–22).

9:12 he has just come Samuel apparently was traveling on his circuit. See 1Sa 7:16.

liver them from the hand of the Philistines. I have looked on my people, for their cry has reached me."

[17] When Samuel caught sight of Saul, the LORD said to him, "This is the man I spoke to you about; he will govern my people."

[18] Saul approached Samuel in the gateway and asked, "Would you please tell me where the seer's house is?"

[19] "I am the seer," Samuel replied. "Go up ahead of me to the high place, for today you are to eat with me, and in the morning I will send you on your way and will tell you all that is in your heart. [20] As for the donkeys you lost three days ago, do not worry about them; they have been found. And to whom is all the desire of Israel turned, if not to you and your whole family line?"

[21] Saul answered, "But am I not a Benjamite, from the smallest tribe of Israel, and is not my clan the least of all the clans of the tribe of Benjamin? Why do you say such a thing to me?"

[22] Then Samuel brought Saul and his servant into the hall and seated them at the head of those who were invited — about thirty in number. [23] Samuel said to the cook, "Bring the piece of meat I gave you, the one I told you to lay aside."

[24] So the cook took up the thigh with what was on it and set it in front of Saul. Samuel said, "Here is what has been kept for you. Eat, because it was set aside for you for this occasion from the time I said, 'I have invited guests.'" And Saul dined with Samuel that day.

[25] After they came down from the high place to the town, Samuel talked with Saul on the roof of his house. [26] They rose about daybreak, and Samuel called to Saul on the roof, "Get ready, and I will send you on your way." When Saul got ready, he and Samuel went outside together. [27] As they were going down to the edge of the town, Samuel said to Saul, "Tell the servant to go on ahead of us" — and the servant did so — "but you stay here for a while, so that I may give you a message from God."

10 Then Samuel took a flask of olive oil and poured it on Saul's head and kissed him, saying, "Has not the LORD anointed you ruler over his inheritance?[a] [2] When you leave me today, you will meet two men near Rachel's tomb, at Zelzah on the border of Benjamin. They will say to you, 'The donkeys you set out to look for have been found. And now your father has stopped thinking about them and is worried about you. He is asking, "What shall I do about my son?"'

[3] "Then you will go on from there until you reach the great tree of Tabor. Three men going up to worship God at Bethel will meet you there. One will be carrying three young goats, another three loaves of bread, and another a skin of wine. [4] They will greet you and offer you two loaves of bread, which you will accept from them.

[5] "After that you will go to Gibeah of God, where there is a Philistine outpost. As you approach the town, you will meet a procession of prophets coming down from the high place with lyres, timbrels, pipes and harps being played before them, and they will be prophesying. [6] The Spirit of the LORD will come powerfully upon you, and you will prophesy with them; and you will be changed into a different person. [7] Once these signs are fulfilled, do whatever your hand finds to do, for God is with you.

[8] "Go down ahead of me to Gilgal. I will surely

---

[a] 1 Hebrew; Septuagint and Vulgate *over his people Israel? You will reign over the LORD's people and save them from the power of their enemies round about. And this will be a sign to you that the LORD has anointed you ruler over his inheritance:*

9:18 Saul approached Samuel Saul doesn't recognize Samuel, highlighting his spiritual blindness.

9:21 am I not a Benjamite Saul expresses surprise because, during this period, the Benjamites would have been the least among Israel's tribes in both size and esteem. In Judges, the tribe of Benjamin was nearly eradicated after the men from Saul's hometown, Gibeah, committed one of the most heinous acts since Israel left Egypt (Jdg 19:22–26; 20:35,48).

9:24 the thigh The choice part of the animal reserved for priests from the wave offering (Ex 29:27; Lev 7:32–34).

9:25 on the roof The most desirable sleeping location, due to the breeze.

9:27 As they were going down to the edge of the town Samuel is presented as a gracious host throughout this episode: He invited Saul and his servant to dinner, gave them the best part of the evening sacrifice, provided them with the best location for sleeping, and accompanied them to the edge of town.

10:1–16 This section records Saul's trip home. Before leaving the prophet's house, Saul is anointed king over Israel. As a testimony to his prophetic word, Samuel tells Saul what he will encounter on his journey back to Gibeah. God's word is confirmed, and Saul is set to take over the kingdom.

10:2 Rachel's tomb See Ge 35:20. **donkeys you set out to look for have been found** This first sign will authenticate Samuel's words in 1Sa 9:20.

10:3 Three men going up to worship God at Bethel The items these men carry are for offerings.

10:4 offer you two loaves of bread This second sign confirms Samuel's act of anointing Saul. The men had intended for these loaves to be used by an anointed person—a priest. In accepting the loaves, Saul essentially accepts his kingly anointing (compare note on 2:10).

10:5 a procession of prophets Samuel himself is seen at the head of such a group in 19:20. **with lyres, timbrels, pipes and harps** Music sometimes accompanied prophetic ministry (e.g., 2Ki 3:15).

10:6 Spirit of the LORD will come powerfully This third sign will confirm that God has selected Saul and empowered him to fight against the Philistines (1Sa 9:16).

10:8 Gilgal One of the cities on Samuel's circuit (7:16). Saul would later be crowned king there (11:15). **you must wait seven days** Even though 13:7–8 refers to Samuel asking Saul to wait seven days at Gilgal, that probably does not refer to this event. Since the intervening chapters seem to narrate a long period of time, they were likely several years apart.

come down to you to sacrifice burnt offerings and fellowship offerings, but you must wait seven days until I come to you and tell you what you are to do."

Saul Made King

⁹As Saul turned to leave Samuel, God changed Saul's heart, and all these signs were fulfilled that day. ¹⁰When he and his servant arrived at Gibeah, a procession of prophets met him; the Spirit of God came powerfully upon him, and he joined in their prophesying. ¹¹When all those who had formerly known him saw him prophesying with the prophets, they asked each other, "What is this that has happened to the son of Kish? Is Saul also among the prophets?"

¹²A man who lived there answered, "And who is their father?" So it became a saying: "Is Saul also among the prophets?" ¹³After Saul stopped prophesying, he went to the high place.

¹⁴Now Saul's uncle asked him and his servant, "Where have you been?"

"Looking for the donkeys," he said. "But when we saw they were not to be found, we went to Samuel."

¹⁵Saul's uncle said, "Tell me what Samuel said to you."

¹⁶Saul replied, "He assured us that the donkeys had been found." But he did not tell his uncle what Samuel had said about the kingship.

¹⁷Samuel summoned the people of Israel to the LORD at Mizpah ¹⁸and said to them, "This is what the LORD, the God of Israel, says: 'I brought Israel up out of Egypt, and I delivered you from the power of Egypt and all the kingdoms that oppressed you.' ¹⁹But you have now rejected your God, who saves you out of all your disasters and calamities. And you have said, 'No, appoint a king over us.' So now present yourselves before the LORD by your tribes and clans."

²⁰When Samuel had all Israel come forward by tribes, the tribe of Benjamin was taken by lot. ²¹Then he brought forward the tribe of Benjamin, clan by clan, and Matri's clan was taken. Finally Saul son of Kish was taken. But when they looked for him, he was not to be found. ²²So they inquired further of the LORD, "Has the man come here yet?"

And the LORD said, "Yes, he has hidden himself among the supplies."

²³They ran and brought him out, and as he stood among the people he was a head taller than any of the others. ²⁴Samuel said to all the people, "Do you see the man the LORD has chosen? There is no one like him among all the people."

Then the people shouted, "Long live the king!"

²⁵Samuel explained to the people the rights and duties of kingship. He wrote them down on a scroll and deposited it before the LORD. Then Samuel dismissed the people to go to their own homes.

²⁶Saul also went to his home in Gibeah, accompanied by valiant men whose hearts God had touched. ²⁷But some scoundrels said, "How can this fellow save us?" They despised him and brought him no gifts. But Saul kept silent.

Saul Rescues the City of Jabesh

11 Nahash[a] the Ammonite went up and besieged Jabesh Gilead. And all the men of Jabesh said to him, "Make a treaty with us, and we will be subject to you."

---

[a] 1 Masoretic Text; Dead Sea Scrolls *gifts. Now Nahash king of the Ammonites oppressed the Gadites and Reubenites severely. He gouged out all their right eyes and struck terror and dread in Israel. Not a man remained among the Israelites beyond the Jordan whose right eye was not gouged out by Nahash king of the Ammonites, except that seven thousand men fled from the Ammonites and entered Jabesh Gilead. About a month later,* ¹Nahash

---

10:9 God changed Saul's heart This new heart will be conditioned to do his work (compare ch. 11), but this change in Saul is not permanent (16:14). **all these signs were fulfilled** Confirms Samuel's prophetic office, as well as Saul's selection as king.

10:10 Gibeah The Hebrew word used here can refer generically to a hill, or it can be a proper noun referring to Gibeah, Saul's hometown (see v. 5).

10:11 Is Saul also among the prophets A derisive statement by those in his hometown (compare Mt 13:54–57). This emphasizes the incongruity between his current behavior and his previous behavior.

10:16 the donkeys had been found This deceptively incomplete answer hints at Saul's true character. The rest of his story portrays him as dishonest, reluctant and fearful.

10:17–27 Samuel recalls the people he dismissed in 1Sa 8:22. The search for Israel's king is over, and Samuel is ready to reveal God's selection. Saul shows his true self by timidly hiding among the baggage rather than boldly seizing his throne. With the exception of the events in ch. 11, Saul will be characterized by fear, reluctance, incompetence and impetuousness.

10:17 Mizpah The same gathering place where the Israelites confessed their sin in 7:5–6. In Judges, Mizpah is where the chiefs decided to eradicate the tribe of Benjamin—Saul's tribe (Jdg 20:1–11).

10:19 rejected your God See 1Sa 8:7 and note.

10:20 was taken Casting lots were sometimes used to discern God's will (see Jos 14:2 and note; compare Ac 1:26).

10:22 hidden himself among the supplies While this might seem modest at first, Saul has already been anointed as king and received signs confirming that anointing. Saul should have been confident in God by this point, but he is characterized throughout the narrative as a fearful and insecure man. Saul always fears the wrong things—his calling as king, the Philistine hordes (13:7; 28:5), his own army (15:24), Goliath (17:11,24), David (18:12,15,29), a coup (22:7–8) and Samuel's prophecy about his death and defeat (28:20,21). In contrast, David is said to fear only two things: Achish, king of Gath, in a situation that stemmed from David's own foolishness (21:12); and God (2Sa 6:9).

10:27 some scoundrels The Hebrew term used here also occurs in 2:12 (see note on 2:12; compare note on 1:16). **brought him no gifts** They do not acknowledge

²But Nahash the Ammonite replied, "I will make a treaty with you only on the condition that I gouge out the right eye of every one of you and so bring disgrace on all Israel."

³The elders of Jabesh said to him, "Give us seven days so we can send messengers throughout Israel; if no one comes to rescue us, we will surrender to you."

⁴When the messengers came to Gibeah of Saul and reported these terms to the people, they all wept aloud. ⁵Just then Saul was returning from the fields, behind his oxen, and he asked, "What is wrong with everyone? Why are they weeping?" Then they repeated to him what the men of Jabesh had said.

⁶When Saul heard their words, the Spirit of God came powerfully upon him, and he burned with anger. ⁷He took a pair of oxen, cut them into pieces, and sent the pieces by messengers throughout Israel, proclaiming, "This is what will be done to the oxen of anyone who does not follow Saul and Samuel." Then the terror of the LORD fell on the people, and they came out together as one. ⁸When Saul mustered them at Bezek, the men of Israel numbered three hundred thousand and those of Judah thirty thousand.

⁹They told the messengers who had come, "Say to the men of Jabesh Gilead, 'By the time the sun is hot tomorrow, you will be rescued.'" When the messengers went and reported this to the men of Jabesh, they were elated. ¹⁰They said to the Ammonites, "Tomorrow we will surrender to you, and you can do to us whatever you like."

¹¹The next day Saul separated his men into three divisions; during the last watch of the night they broke into the camp of the Ammonites and slaughtered them until the heat of the day. Those who survived were scattered, so that no two of them were left together.

---

his kingship. **Saul kept silent** Rather than having them killed, Saul acts diplomatically.

11:1–11 This chapter records the one glorious moment in Saul's career. After being threatened by an Ammonite tyrant, Saul musters Israel's troops and skillfully defeats the enemy. However, after this remarkable beginning to his kingship, Saul goes on to ignominy and disgrace.

In the traditional version of the Hebrew Bible called the Masoretic Text—which many Bible translations follow—the narrative jumps from 10:27 to 11:1, which results in an awkward transition. For this reason, some translations follow the Dead Sea Scrolls' version of 1 Samuel here. Between 10:27 and 11:1, the Dead Sea Scrolls' version adds that Nahash, the Ammonite king, had been oppressing the Gadites and Reubenites and had previously gouged out all their right eyes (making them basically incapable of fighting). The addition also notes that 7,000 men had managed to escape the Ammonites and were in Jabesh Gilead—the place of the conflict in 11:1. The Dead Sea Scrolls' addition is likely original to 1 Samuel, because both the addition and 11:1 begin the same—a scribe's eye could easily have unintentionally skipped lines. The addition also explains 11:2, which seems like an odd response otherwise.

11:1 Nahash The Hebrew term used here, *nachash* (often transliterated in English as Nahash), means "snake" or "serpent." **Ammonite** Ammon is east of the Jordan River, northeast of the Dead Sea. A fragment of this section of 1 Samuel, found among the Dead Sea Scrolls, provides the background to ch. 11. This previously lost paragraph has been restored in several Bible translations. **Jabesh Gilead** Located in the area of the half-tribe of Manasseh, just north of Gadite territory. When Moses apportioned the land to Israel, the Reubenites, Gadites and the half-tribe of Manasseh settled east of the Jordan River. The Reubenites settled in the region of Moab to the south, east of the Dead Sea; the half-tribe of Manasseh settled in Ammon to the north (southeast of the Sea of Galilee); and the Gadites settled in the region between Reuben and Manasseh (Nu 34:13–15). Nahash felt entitled to these territories, which formerly belonged to his ancestors

(compare Jdg 11:13). The Gadites and Reubenites had fled to Jabesh Gilead after Nahash's most recent attack, and he was pursuing them. Because the inhabitants of Jabesh Gilead harbored the fleeing Israelites, they were Nahash's enemies as well. **Make a treaty** The Hebrew phrase used here refers to cutting a covenant. In antiquity, covenant making often was accompanied by a formal ceremony involving a sacrifice. Participants would cut animals into pieces and then pass between them. This signified what would befall the person who violated the terms of the agreement—they would be cut into pieces (see Ge 15:7–21).

11:2 gouge out the right eye of every one of you Nahash's tactic disgraced his opponents and would make any retaliation by them virtually impossible. Although Nahash's enemies could not properly wield a weapon in battle, they could still do slow, agricultural work, allowing for Nahash to still retrieve tribute from them.

11:3 if no one comes to rescue us Nahash will allow them to gain more support because, if he wins, he will gain greater return in battle. The more people who show up to fight, the greater the king's spoils will be. He may have presumed that he could defeat any Israelite coalition; alternatively, he may have doubted that the elders of Jabesh would find much support based on historical precedence (see Jdg 11:4–11).

11:6 Spirit of God As was the case with Samson, the Spirit here empowers Saul in his battle against the enemies of God's people (Jdg 14:6,19; 15:14; compare 1Sa 10:10; 19:23).

11:7 cut them into pieces Compare Jdg 19:29, where the cut-up pieces of a concubine murdered in Gibeah are sent through Israel as a message.

11:9 you will be rescued Only here does Saul display the type of faith and fortitude that characterizes his successor, David.

11:10 They said The men of Jabesh suggest to Nahash that they will surrender, prompting the Ammonites to let down their guard.

11:11 three divisions Indicates the Israelites will conduct a three-sided attack. **no two of them were left together** Signifies total defeat. See the table "Battles of Saul and David" on p. 433.

Saul Confirmed as King

¹²The people then said to Samuel, "Who was it that asked, 'Shall Saul reign over us?' Turn these men over to us so that we may put them to death."

¹³But Saul said, "No one will be put to death today, for this day the Lᴏʀᴅ has rescued Israel."

¹⁴Then Samuel said to the people, "Come, let us go to Gilgal and there renew the kingship." ¹⁵So all the people went to Gilgal and made Saul king in the presence of the Lᴏʀᴅ. There they sacrificed fellowship offerings before the Lᴏʀᴅ, and Saul and all the Israelites held a great celebration.

Samuel's Farewell Speech

12 Samuel said to all Israel, "I have listened to everything you said to me and have set a king over you. ²Now you have a king as your leader. As for me, I am old and gray, and my sons are here with you. I have been your leader from my youth until this day. ³Here I stand. Testify against me in the presence of the Lᴏʀᴅ and his anointed. Whose ox have I taken? Whose donkey have I taken? Whom have I cheated? Whom have I oppressed? From whose hand have I accepted a bribe to make me shut my eyes? If I have done any of these things, I will make it right."

⁴"You have not cheated or oppressed us," they replied. "You have not taken anything from anyone's hand."

⁵Samuel said to them, "The Lᴏʀᴅ is witness against you, and also his anointed is witness this day, that you have not found anything in my hand."

"He is witness," they said.

⁶Then Samuel said to the people, "It is the Lᴏʀᴅ who appointed Moses and Aaron and brought your ancestors up out of Egypt. ⁷Now then, stand here, because I am going to confront you with evidence before the Lᴏʀᴅ as to all the righteous acts performed by the Lᴏʀᴅ for you and your ancestors.

⁸"After Jacob entered Egypt, they cried to the Lᴏʀᴅ for help, and the Lᴏʀᴅ sent Moses and Aaron, who brought your ancestors out of Egypt and settled them in this place.

⁹"But they forgot the Lᴏʀᴅ their God; so he sold them into the hand of Sisera, the commander of the army of Hazor, and into the hands of the Philistines and the king of Moab, who fought against them. ¹⁰They cried out to the Lᴏʀᴅ and said, 'We have sinned; we have forsaken the Lᴏʀᴅ and served the Baals and the Ashtoreths. But now deliver us from the hands of our enemies, and we will serve you.' ¹¹Then the Lᴏʀᴅ sent Jerub-Baal,ᵃ Barak,ᵇ Jephthah and Samuel,ᶜ and he delivered you from the hands of your enemies all around you, so that you lived in safety.

¹²"But when you saw that Nahash king of the Ammonites was moving against you, you said to me, 'No, we want a king to rule over us' — even though the Lᴏʀᴅ your God was your king. ¹³Now here is the king you have chosen, the one you asked for; see, the Lᴏʀᴅ has set a king over you. ¹⁴If you fear the Lᴏʀᴅ and serve and obey him and do not rebel against his commands, and if both

---

ᵃ 11 Also called *Gideon*   ᵇ 11 Some Septuagint manuscripts and Syriac; Hebrew *Bedan*   ᶜ 11 Hebrew; some Septuagint manuscripts and Syriac *Samson*

11:12–15 After proving himself able in battle, Saul is heralded by all as Israel's new king (see 1Sa 8:20). To show their goodwill and support, the leaders decide to renew their commitment to Saul. They wish to kill everyone who previously opposed his kingship, but he does not allow it.

11:12 Shall Saul reign over us See 10:25–27.
11:13 No one will be put to death Saul diplomatically defuses the situation. He will not repeat this technique in subsequent episodes.
11:14 the kingship Refers to their commitment to serve King Saul.

12:1–25 Samuel defends his ministry to the people of Israel, once again calling them to repentance. He leads the nation in renewing its commitment to God, and at the close of this chapter Saul and Israel are poised to reap God's covenant blessings. However, the warning in v. 25 hints at what awaits Israel and its new king.

12:2 Now you have a king as your leader Samuel is transitioning out of his role as Israel's leader.
12:3 Testify against me in the presence of the Lᴏʀᴅ Samuel speaks rhetorically here. His ministry was characterized by integrity; none of the charges he mentions could be applied to him. This verse contrasts Samuel with his warning about a king (compare 8:10–18). **his anointed** Refers to King Saul (10:1; see note on 2:10).

12:4 You have not cheated or oppressed us The people affirm the prophet's character.

12:6–17 In this speech, Samuel reviews the history that brought them to the monarchy (vv. 6–12), urges the people to obey Yahweh in this new situation (vv. 13–15) and performs a sign to validate his words (vv. 16–17). This passage recalls Moses' covenant renewal and farewell in Dt 29–30.

12:8 Egypt See Ex 12:31–37,51.
12:9 Sisera See Jdg 4:1–2. **the Philistines** See Jdg 13:1. **the king of Moab** See Jdg 3:12.
12:10 the Baals and the Ashtoreths Refers to idols of Canaanite deities (Jdg 10:6–10; 1Sa 7:3–4).
12:11 Jerub-Baal See Jdg 6:32. **Barak** Although the Hebrew word used here is *bedan*, most English translations follow the Septuagint (the ancient Greek translation of the OT) and read "Barak" (Jdg 4:6), because Bedan is not referenced in the book of Judges, but Barak is mentioned in Jdg 4:6. **Jephthah** See Jdg 11. **Samuel** Samuel may mention himself as the last in the line of the judges. Alternatively, the Septuagint reads "Samson" here (Jdg 13–16).
12:12 Nahash See 1Sa 11. **we want a king to rule over us** Refers to the people's demand for an earthly king to fight their battles (8:19–20).
12:14 If you fear the Lᴏʀᴅ Compare the covenant blessings for faithfulness in Dt 28:1–14.

you and the king who reigns over you follow the Lord your God — good! ¹⁵But if you do not obey the Lord, and if you rebel against his commands, his hand will be against you, as it was against your ancestors.

¹⁶"Now then, stand still and see this great thing the Lord is about to do before your eyes! ¹⁷Is it not wheat harvest now? I will call on the Lord to send thunder and rain. And you will realize what an evil thing you did in the eyes of the Lord when you asked for a king."

¹⁸Then Samuel called on the Lord, and that same day the Lord sent thunder and rain. So all the people stood in awe of the Lord and of Samuel.

¹⁹The people all said to Samuel, "Pray to the Lord your God for your servants so that we will not die, for we have added to all our other sins the evil of asking for a king."

²⁰"Do not be afraid," Samuel replied. "You have done all this evil; yet do not turn away from the Lord, but serve the Lord with all your heart. ²¹Do not turn away after useless idols. They can do you no good, nor can they rescue you, because they are useless. ²²For the sake of his great name the Lord will not reject his people, because the Lord was pleased to make you his own. ²³As for me, far be it from me that I should sin against the Lord by failing to pray for you. And I will teach you the way that is good and right. ²⁴But be sure to fear the Lord and serve him faithfully with all your heart; consider what great things he has done for you. ²⁵Yet if you persist in doing evil, both you and your king will perish."

Samuel Rebukes Saul

13 Saul was thirty[a] years old when he became king, and he reigned over Israel forty-[b] two years.

²Saul chose three thousand men from Israel; two thousand were with him at Mikmash and in the hill country of Bethel, and a thousand were with Jonathan at Gibeah in Benjamin. The rest of the men he sent back to their homes.

³Jonathan attacked the Philistine outpost at Geba, and the Philistines heard about it. Then Saul had the trumpet blown throughout the land and said, "Let the Hebrews hear!" ⁴So all Israel heard the news: "Saul has attacked the Philistine outpost, and now Israel has become obnoxious to the Philistines." And the people were summoned to join Saul at Gilgal.

⁵The Philistines assembled to fight Israel, with three thousand[c] chariots, six thousand charioteers, and soldiers as numerous as the sand on the seashore. They went up and camped at Mikmash, east of Beth Aven. ⁶When the Israelites saw that their situation was critical and that their army was hard pressed, they hid in caves and thickets, among the rocks, and in pits and cisterns. ⁷Some Hebrews even crossed the Jordan to the land of Gad and Gilead.

Saul remained at Gilgal, and all the troops with him were quaking with fear. ⁸He waited seven

a 1 A few late manuscripts of the Septuagint; Hebrew does not have *thirty*.   b 1 Probable reading of the original Hebrew text (see Acts 13:21); Masoretic Text does not have *forty-*.   c 5 Some Septuagint manuscripts and Syriac; Hebrew *thirty thousand*

12:15 if you do not obey Compare the covenant curses for disobedience in Dt 28:15–68.

12:17 to send thunder and rain A sign of God's displeasure over their insistence on an earthly king. Such a storm during the dry season would have been unusual — and, due to flash flooding, potentially deadly (as the people's response in 1Sa 12:19 indicates).

12:22 will not reject his people Even with an earthly king ruling in his place, God will honor the covenant he made with his people.

12:23 failing to pray for you Part of Samuel's role as prophet and priest was to pray for the nation.

12:25 will perish The fate of Israel and its king hinges on being faithful to Yahweh.

13:1–14:52 Although Saul began his career well (ch. 11), two actions soon demonstrate his inability to lead God's people: First, he disobeys Samuel's instructions and the law (ch. 13); second, he interrupts an effort to seek God's counsel and relies instead on his own oath (ch. 14). Since Israel depended on revelation from God for its very livelihood, Saul's decision to act on his own is hazardous for the nation. God vows to remove the kingdom from Saul and give it to someone more obedient.

13:1–7 Despite an initial victory over the Philistines (v. 3), Saul's leadership does not inspire confidence among the people.

13:1 Saul was thirty years old The details of Saul's age

and the length of his reign have been lost, or deliberately omitted, from the Hebrew text. Acts 13:21 indicates that he ruled for 40 years. The Jewish historian Josephus says he reigned 20 years (*Antiquities* 10.143), but elsewhere he also seems to suggest 40 (*Antiquities* 6.378).

13:2 Jonathan Saul's son. Jonathan was loyal to his father until the end of his life (1Sa 31:2). However, he also recognized that David's anointing in the place of Saul was legitimate (23:15–18). He and David were close friends (see 18:1–5); Jonathan helped David escape from Saul several times. The narrative often praises Jonathan for his valor, piety and loyalty (e.g., 14:44; 19:1–2; 20:12–13).

13:3 Geba Possibly refers to Gibeah. Jonathan was stationed at Gibeah (v. 2) and a Philistine garrison has already been mentioned there (10:5). However, the OT also speaks of a city named Geba in the territory of Benjamin (Jos 21:17); the two are probably separate places. **Let the Hebrews hear** Saul proclaims their victory over the Philistines. He might have anticipated that the Philistines would respond with their military; this proclamation would allow him to muster a larger army for battle.

13:6 they hid They seek to avoid what they perceive as certain death at the hands of the Philistines. Their fear later becomes a taunt among the Philistine troops (14:11).

13:7 land of Gad and Gilead East of the Jordan River. See note on 11:1. **quaking with fear** Reflecting the disposition of their leader (compare 10:22 and note).

days, the time set by Samuel; but Samuel did not come to Gilgal, and Saul's men began to scatter. ⁹So he said, "Bring me the burnt offering and the fellowship offerings." And Saul offered up the burnt offering. ¹⁰Just as he finished making the offering, Samuel arrived, and Saul went out to greet him.

¹¹"What have you done?" asked Samuel.

Saul replied, "When I saw that the men were scattering, and that you did not come at the set time, and that the Philistines were assembling at Mikmash, ¹²I thought, 'Now the Philistines will come down against me at Gilgal, and I have not sought the LORD's favor.' So I felt compelled to offer the burnt offering."

¹³"You have done a foolish thing," Samuel said. "You have not kept the command the LORD your God gave you; if you had, he would have established your kingdom over Israel for all time. ¹⁴But now your kingdom will not endure; the LORD has sought out a man after his own heart and appointed him ruler of his people, because you have not kept the LORD's command."

¹⁵Then Samuel left Gilgal[a] and went up to Gibeah in Benjamin, and Saul counted the men who were with him. They numbered about six hundred.

Israel Without Weapons

¹⁶Saul and his son Jonathan and the men with them were staying in Gibeah[b] in Benjamin, while the Philistines camped at Mikmash. ¹⁷Raiding parties went out from the Philistine camp in three detachments. One turned toward Ophrah in the vicinity of Shual, ¹⁸another toward Beth Horon, and the third toward the borderland overlooking the Valley of Zeboyim facing the wilderness.

¹⁹Not a blacksmith could be found in the whole land of Israel, because the Philistines had said, "Otherwise the Hebrews will make swords or spears!" ²⁰So all Israel went down to the Philistines to have their plow points, mattocks, axes and sickles[c] sharpened. ²¹The price was two-thirds of a shekel[d] for sharpening plow points and mattocks, and a third of a shekel[e] for sharpening forks and axes and for repointing goads.

²²So on the day of the battle not a soldier with Saul and Jonathan had a sword or spear in his hand; only Saul and his son Jonathan had them.

Jonathan Attacks the Philistines

²³Now a detachment of Philistines had gone out to the pass at Mikmash. **14** ¹One day Jonathan son of Saul said to his young armorbearer, "Come, let's go over to the Philistine outpost on the other side." But he did not tell his father.

²Saul was staying on the outskirts of Gibeah under a pomegranate tree in Migron. With him were about six hundred men, ³among whom was

a 15 Hebrew; Septuagint *Gilgal and went his way; the rest of the people went after Saul to meet the army, and they went out of Gilgal*   *b 16* Two Hebrew manuscripts; most Hebrew manuscripts *Geba,* a variant of *Gibeah*   *c 20* Septuagint; Hebrew *plow points*   *d 21* That is, about 1/4 ounce or about 8 grams   *e 21* That is, about 1/8 ounce or about 4 grams

---

13:8–23 Saul's desperation leads him to disobey Samuel's instructions, as well as the law regarding sacrifices. This passage serves to justify David's dynasty: God rejects Saul because of his disobedience and anoints David in his place.

13:8 seven days Samuel instructed Saul to wait at Gilgal seven days in 10:8, but the attempt to link that event with this verse results in several inconsistencies. In terms of location, Samuel comes to Gilgal in 11:14–15 after the defeat of the Ammonites; however, he must have left again, because he is not in Gilgal in 13:8. In terms of chronology, the mustering of Israelite forces in 11:7–8 and the subsequent battle with Nahash probably would have taken longer than seven days. Furthermore, although Saul was called a young man in 9:2, he now has an adult son. Although they likely referred to different events, the inclusion of 13:8 as a link to 10:8 serves to highlight the theme of Saul's disobedience in the narrative. **men began to scatter** The people were losing confidence in Saul. They observed their king's apprehension and fear, and they fled.

13:9 Bring me the burnt offering Such offerings were made before fighting to atone for the sins of the troops. In addition to disobeying Samuel's instructions, Saul is not qualified to make this offering. He ignores the law and places himself above God's priest, showing that he is unfit to lead God's people.

13:11 the men Rather than take responsibility for his actions, Saul blames three other people or groups: the people, Samuel and the Philistines. Saul associates himself with the sin only by stating that he offered the sacrifice under duress (v. 12).

13:14 your kingdom will not endure Saul's punishment for acting like a king from other nations (8:5,20) and disobeying God's commands. **a man after his own heart** This description likely is included to contrast the disobedient Saul with a king who follows Yahweh.

13:19 Not a blacksmith could be found The Philistines were restricting the Israelites' access to weapons.

13:21 The price The rates given here are extraordinarily high. In this way, the Philistines could exact additional money from the Israelites, thereby impoverishing them further.

13:22 only Saul and his son Jonathan had them The Philistines' control was so effective that only the Israelite king and one of his generals had metal weapons.

14:1–23 Chapter 14 records a bold act of valor. Jonathan and his armor bearer sneak into a Philistine military outpost and slaughter the troops. This act shifts the momentum in the ongoing conflict.

14:1 he did not tell his father Indicates that this is a covert operation. Saul, who is characterized by fear and doubt, probably would have vetoed a surprise attack.

14:2 pomegranate tree The Hebrew word used here, *rimmon* which means pomegranate, could be a place name (e.g., Jos 19:7; Nu 33:19) or an obscure reference to a pomegranate tree. Judges 20:45–47 refers to the rock of Rimmon—located near Saul's hometown of Gibeah—where 600 men take shelter. This suggests that this is a reference to a cave or outcropping used for military purposes.

Ahijah, who was wearing an ephod. He was a son of Ichabod's brother Ahitub son of Phinehas, the son of Eli, the LORD's priest in Shiloh. No one was aware that Jonathan had left.

⁴On each side of the pass that Jonathan intended to cross to reach the Philistine outpost was a cliff; one was called Bozez and the other Seneh. ⁵One cliff stood to the north toward Mikmash, the other to the south toward Geba.

⁶Jonathan said to his young armor-bearer, "Come, let's go over to the outpost of those uncircumcised men. Perhaps the LORD will act in our behalf. Nothing can hinder the LORD from saving, whether by many or by few."

⁷"Do all that you have in mind," his armor-bearer said. "Go ahead; I am with you heart and soul."

⁸Jonathan said, "Come on, then; we will cross over toward them and let them see us. ⁹If they say to us, 'Wait there until we come to you,' we will stay where we are and not go up to them. ¹⁰But if they say, 'Come up to us,' we will climb up, because that will be our sign that the LORD has given them into our hands."

¹¹So both of them showed themselves to the Philistine outpost. "Look!" said the Philistines. "The Hebrews are crawling out of the holes they were hiding in." ¹²The men of the outpost shouted to Jonathan and his armor-bearer, "Come up to us and we'll teach you a lesson."

So Jonathan said to his armor-bearer, "Climb up after me; the LORD has given them into the hand of Israel."

¹³Jonathan climbed up, using his hands and feet, with his armor-bearer right behind him. The Philistines fell before Jonathan, and his armor-bearer followed and killed behind him. ¹⁴In that first attack Jonathan and his armor-bearer killed some twenty men in an area of about half an acre.

Israel Routs the Philistines

¹⁵Then panic struck the whole army — those in the camp and field, and those in the outposts and raiding parties — and the ground shook. It was a panic sent by God.ᵃ

¹⁶Saul's lookouts at Gibeah in Benjamin saw the army melting away in all directions. ¹⁷Then Saul said to the men who were with him, "Muster the forces and see who has left us." When they did, it was Jonathan and his armor-bearer who were not there.

¹⁸Saul said to Ahijah, "Bring the ark of God." (At that time it was with the Israelites.)ᵇ ¹⁹While Saul was talking to the priest, the tumult in the Philistine camp increased more and more. So Saul said to the priest, "Withdraw your hand."

²⁰Then Saul and all his men assembled and went to the battle. They found the Philistines in total confusion, striking each other with their swords. ²¹Those Hebrews who had previously been with the Philistines and had gone up with them to their camp went over to the Israelites who were with Saul and Jonathan. ²²When all the Israelites who had hidden in the hill country of Ephraim

---

ᵃ 15 Or *a terrible panic*   ᵇ 18 Hebrew; Septuagint *"Bring the ephod." (At that time he wore the ephod before the Israelites.)*

14:3 who was wearing an ephod See note on v. 18. **Ichabod's** See 1Sa 4:19–22.

SHILOH
Shiloh was likely destroyed by the Philistines contemporary to the battles described in 1Sa 4. Other passages in the OT allude to Shiloh's destruction (e.g., Jer 7:12–14; 26:6,9). Psalm 78:58–61 states that God abandoned Shiloh because of Israel's idolatry. It also refers to the capture of the ark (1Sa 4:11). After the ark is returned, it is kept in the house of Abinadab in Kiriath Jearim — not Shiloh — for roughly 20 years (7:1–2). Samuel operated out of Ramah rather than Shiloh, also suggesting that Shiloh was destroyed, perhaps as part of God's judgment (see 7:17). However, Shiloh may have later been partly reconstructed, since it is mentioned as the home of Ahijah during Jeroboam's reign (ca. 930–909 BC; 1Ki 14:2,4).

14:6 those uncircumcised men This derogatory term highlights that the Philistines were excluded from God's covenant with Israel. **Nothing can hinder the LORD from saving** In contrast to his father, Jonathan provides a model of great faith.
14:10 LORD has given them into our hands If the

Philistines call them up to the garrison, Jonathan will take it as a sign of Yahweh's support.
14:11 Hebrews are crawling out of the holes A taunt reflecting the Israelites' tendency to hide in fear (13:6).
14:12 into the hand of Israel Jonathan does not claim the victory for himself; he notes that it will benefit the nation.
14:13 fell before Jonathan Jonathan probably attacked the garrison and wounded them, and his armor bearer stabbed them to ensure that they died. Alternatively, Jonathan may have killed the soldiers coming at him head on, while his armor bearer killed those who attacked from behind.
14:14 twenty men A sure sign of God's blessing: Two Israelites killed about 20 Philistines (compare 9:16).
14:18 Bring the ark of God The Septuagint, an ancient Greek translation of the OT, has the word "ephod" in place of "ark"; this probably represents the original wording. The high priest wore the ephod (v. 3; Ex 28:4). Mentions of the ephod in 1 Samuel likely indicate the presence of the Urim and Thummim, which were used to discern God's will (1Sa 23:6,9–12; 30:7–8; see Ex 28:30 and note).
14:19 Withdraw your hand Saul tells the priest to stop inquiring of God with regard to the battle. By interrupting the effort to seek God's counsel, Saul reveals that he is not fit to lead God's people.
14:21 went over to the Israelites Previously, some Israelites had joined with the Philistines. Now, they turn and fight against them. Compare 1Sa 29:1–7.

heard that the Philistines were on the run, they joined the battle in hot pursuit. ²³So on that day the LORD saved Israel, and the battle moved on beyond Beth Aven.

Jonathan Eats Honey

²⁴Now the Israelites were in distress that day, because Saul had bound the people under an oath, saying, "Cursed be anyone who eats food before evening comes, before I have avenged myself on my enemies!" So none of the troops tasted food.

²⁵The entire army entered the woods, and there was honey on the ground. ²⁶When they went into the woods, they saw the honey oozing out; yet no one put his hand to his mouth, because they feared the oath. ²⁷But Jonathan had not heard that his father had bound the people with the oath, so he reached out the end of the staff that was in his hand and dipped it into the honeycomb. He raised his hand to his mouth, and his eyes brightened.*^a* ²⁸Then one of the soldiers told him, "Your father bound the army under a strict oath, saying, 'Cursed be anyone who eats food today!' That is why the men are faint."

²⁹Jonathan said, "My father has made trouble for the country. See how my eyes brightened when I tasted a little of this honey. ³⁰How much better it would have been if the men had eaten today some of the plunder they took from their enemies. Would not the slaughter of the Philistines have been even greater?"

³¹That day, after the Israelites had struck down the Philistines from Mikmash to Aijalon, they were exhausted. ³²They pounced on the plunder and, taking sheep, cattle and calves, they butchered them on the ground and ate them, together with the blood. ³³Then someone said to Saul, "Look, the men are sinning against the LORD by eating meat that has blood in it."

"You have broken faith," he said. "Roll a large stone over here at once." ³⁴Then he said, "Go out among the men and tell them, 'Each of you bring me your cattle and sheep, and slaughter them here and eat them. Do not sin against the LORD by eating meat with blood still in it.'"

So everyone brought his ox that night and slaughtered it there. ³⁵Then Saul built an altar to the LORD; it was the first time he had done this.

³⁶Saul said, "Let us go down and pursue the Philistines by night and plunder them till dawn, and let us not leave one of them alive."

"Do whatever seems best to you," they replied. But the priest said, "Let us inquire of God here."

³⁷So Saul asked God, "Shall I go down and pursue the Philistines? Will you give them into Israel's hand?" But God did not answer him that day. ³⁸Saul therefore said, "Come here, all you who are leaders of the army, and let us find out what sin has been committed today. ³⁹As surely as the LORD who rescues Israel lives, even if the guilt lies with my son Jonathan, he must die." But not one of them said a word.

⁴⁰Saul then said to all the Israelites, "You stand over there; I and Jonathan my son will stand over here."

"Do what seems best to you," they replied.

⁴¹Then Saul prayed to the LORD, the God of Israel, "Why have you not answered your servant today? If the fault is in me or my son Jonathan, respond with Urim, but if the men of Israel are at fault,*^b* respond with Thummim." Jonathan and Saul were taken by lot, and the men were cleared. ⁴²Saul said, "Cast the lot between me and Jonathan my son." And Jonathan was taken.

⁴³Then Saul said to Jonathan, "Tell me what you have done."

So Jonathan told him, "I tasted a little honey with the end of my staff. And now I must die!"

⁴⁴Saul said, "May God deal with me, be it ever so severely, if you do not die, Jonathan."

⁴⁵But the men said to Saul, "Should Jonathan

---

^a 27 Or *his strength was renewed*; similarly in verse 29
^b 41 Septuagint; Hebrew does not have *"Why . . . at fault."*

14:24–46 After interrupting the process of seeking God's counsel (v. 19), Saul compounds the trouble he is in by making a rash vow. He forbids the Israelites to eat, even though they probably could achieve better results if they were allowed food (vv. 29–30). When Jonathan—ignorant of his father's vow—eats honey, Saul attempts to kill him. The episode confirms further that Saul does not follow Yahweh (12:14) and is unfit to lead God's people.

14:24 Cursed be anyone who eats food Saul's vow effectively debilitates his own forces. The extreme physical exertion of battle requires that the soldiers eat to stay energized. **I have avenged myself on my enemies** Saul sees the Philistine war as a personal vendetta rather than a holy war.

14:29 made trouble for Possibly an allusion to the Achan incident in Jos 7:17–26. Joshua uses the same Hebrew term to describe the sin of Achan (Jos 7:25), who sinned in a time of war and was punished with death.

14:32 ate them, together with the blood This was a violation of the law (Ge 9:4; Lev 7:26–27; Dt 12:23–24). Israelites were to elevate the animals they killed so that the blood would drain out.

14:33 large stone Used to elevate the animals and drain the blood.

14:37 Saul asked God By means of the ephod. See note on 1Sa 14:18.

14:38 let us find out Saul demands to know whose sin has caused God to remain silent.

14:39 even if the guilt lies with my son Jonathan Another rash vow (compare v. 24). Saul will kill the sinner even if it turns out to be his son.

14:43 now I must die Jonathan recognizes that Saul's oath was made before God. In his piety, he agrees to suffer the consequences of his actions.

14:45 he did this today with God's The people save Jonathan by crediting him with carrying out God's will, leading to victory for Israel.

die — he who has brought about this great deliverance in Israel? Never! As surely as the LORD lives, not a hair of his head will fall to the ground, for he did this today with God's help." So the men rescued Jonathan, and he was not put to death.

⁴⁶Then Saul stopped pursuing the Philistines, and they withdrew to their own land.

⁴⁷After Saul had assumed rule over Israel, he fought against their enemies on every side: Moab, the Ammonites, Edom, the kings[a] of Zobah, and the Philistines. Wherever he turned, he inflicted punishment on them.[b] ⁴⁸He fought valiantly and defeated the Amalekites, delivering Israel from the hands of those who had plundered them.

Saul's Family

⁴⁹Saul's sons were Jonathan, Ishvi and Malki-Shua. The name of his older daughter was Merab, and that of the younger was Michal. ⁵⁰His wife's name was Ahinoam daughter of Ahimaaz. The name of the commander of Saul's army was Abner son of Ner, and Ner was Saul's uncle. ⁵¹Saul's father Kish and Abner's father Ner were sons of Abiel.

⁵²All the days of Saul there was bitter war with the Philistines, and whenever Saul saw a mighty or brave man, he took him into his service.

The LORD Rejects Saul as King

15 Samuel said to Saul, "I am the one the LORD sent to anoint you king over his people Israel; so listen now to the message from the LORD. ²This is what the LORD Almighty says: 'I will punish the Amalekites for what they did to Israel when they waylaid them as they came up from Egypt. ³Now go, attack the Amalekites and totally destroy[c] all that belongs to them. Do not spare them; put to death men and women, children and infants, cattle and sheep, camels and donkeys.'"

⁴So Saul summoned the men and mustered them at Telaim — two hundred thousand foot soldiers and ten thousand from Judah. ⁵Saul went to the city of Amalek and set an ambush in the ravine. ⁶Then he said to the Kenites, "Go away, leave the Amalekites so that I do not destroy you along with them; for you showed kindness to all the Israelites when they came up out of Egypt." So the Kenites moved away from the Amalekites.

⁷Then Saul attacked the Amalekites all the way from Havilah to Shur, near the eastern border of Egypt. ⁸He took Agag king of the Amalekites alive, and all his people he totally destroyed with the

---

a 47 Masoretic Text; Dead Sea Scrolls and Septuagint *king*
b 47 Hebrew; Septuagint *he was victorious*   *c 3* The Hebrew term refers to the irrevocable giving over of things or persons to the LORD, often by totally destroying them; also in verses 8, 9, 15, 18, 20 and 21.

14:47–52 These verses provide a summary of Saul's military career as king (vv. 47–48,52) and a brief genealogy (vv. 49–51).

14:47 he inflicted punishment Reflects Saul's divinely appointed mission (9:16; 10:1).

14:49 Ishvi This son of Saul is mentioned only here. It is possible that he is the same person as the later Ish-Bosheth (who is also called Esh-Baal). See 2Sa 2:8 and note.

14:50 Abner The only official named here is Abner, perhaps because he will play a significant role in the later narrative.

ABNER
Abner is presented in 1 Samuel as King Saul's cousin. He commanded Saul's forces until the king died, then made his son, Ish-Bosheth (also known as Esh-Baal; see 1Chr 8:33), king in his place (see 2Sa 2:8–9). However, Ish-Bosheth accused Abner of having sex with Rizpah, one of the king's concubines — an act that amounted to usurping the throne (see 2Sa 3:7 and note; 16:22 and note). As a result, Abner aligns himself with David and — as one who controls the army — transfers the kingdom to David (see 3:9–10). David welcomed him in peace, but Abner was later killed without the king's knowledge by David's military commander Joab, who wrongfully avenged the death of his brother, Asahel (see 2Sa 2:18–23; 3:26–30).

14:52 he took him into his service Recalls Samuel's warning about an earthly king (1Sa 8:11–12).

15:1–35 After another episode of disobedience in which he fails to destroy the Amalekites (vv. 1–9), Saul has a final confrontation with Samuel (vv. 10–35). In the next chapter, the narrative will move on to focus on Saul's replacement.

15:2 LORD Almighty This title identifies God as the leader of armies, both of Israel and of heaven. **as they came up from Egypt** For Amalek's opposition to Israel, see Ex 17:8–16.

15:3 Amalekites It seems that this was supposed to be the fulfillment of the prophecy against the Amalekites, which called for their total destruction (see Nu 24:20; Dt 25:17–19). In performing this action, the Israelites were to execute God's judgment on them (see Lev 27:28 and note; note on Jos 6:16; note on Jos 6:17).

15:6 the Kenites The Kenites were the people of Moses' father-in-law (Jdg 1:16; Nu 24:21). Jael, who killed one of Israel's enemies during the time of the judges, was another Kenite who had showed kindness to Israel (see Jdg 4:17,21).

15:8 totally destroyed This verse notes that at least one Amalekite — Agag — was left alive, until Samuel kills him (1Sa 15:33). However, the presence of Amalekites in 27:8 and 30:1–20 (400 are noted in 30:17) indicates that Saul had likely left alive far more than just Agag. Esther 3:1 also describes Haman, the enemy of the Jews, as an Agagite — this derogatory title could indicate that Haman is somehow related to the Amalekites and perhaps owes his existence to Agag himself. Haman's Jewish opponent, Mordecai, is connected with the family of Saul (Est 2:5), making

sword. ⁹But Saul and the army spared Agag and the best of the sheep and cattle, the fat calvesᵃ and lambs — everything that was good. These they were unwilling to destroy completely, but everything that was despised and weak they totally destroyed.

¹⁰Then the word of the LORD came to Samuel:

¹¹"I regret that I have made Saul king, because he has turned away from me and has not carried out my instructions." Samuel was angry, and he cried out to the LORD all that night.

¹²Early in the morning Samuel got up and went

ᵃ 9 Or *the grown bulls*; the meaning of the Hebrew for this phrase is uncertain.

the book of Esther a kind of rematch between Saul and Amalek. Compare note on Est 3:1.
15:9 spared Agag By letting Agag live, Saul does not fully obey the divine decree of 1Sa 15:3. His selective obedience to God's commands emphasizes that he needs to be replaced as king.

15:11 I regret that I have made Saul king See v. 29 and note. **he has turned away from me** Contrasts the description of a man after God's own heart (see 13:14 and note). This could be the narrator's way of indicating that Saul acted like a king of other nations when he should have been acting as Yahweh's servant (see 8:5,20).

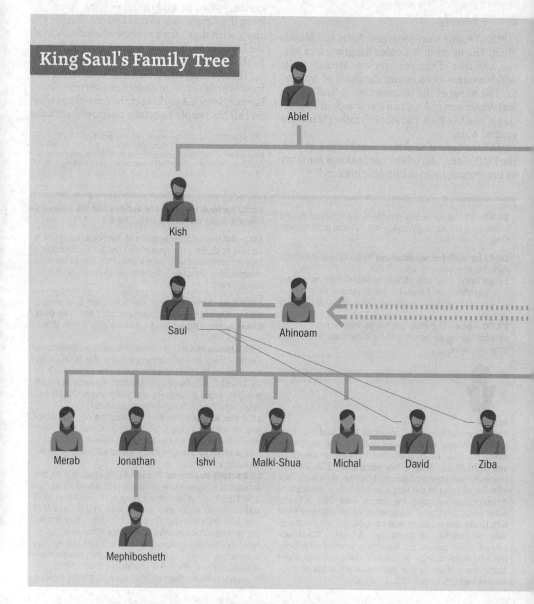

King Saul's Family Tree

Abiel

Kish

Saul — Ahinoam

Merab   Jonathan   Ishvi   Malki-Shua   Michal   David   Ziba

Mephibosheth

to meet Saul, but he was told, "Saul has gone to Carmel. There he has set up a monument in his own honor and has turned and gone on down to Gilgal."

¹³When Samuel reached him, Saul said, "The Lord bless you! I have carried out the Lord's instructions."

¹⁴But Samuel said, "What then is this bleating of sheep in my ears? What is this lowing of cattle that I hear?"

¹⁵Saul answered, "The soldiers brought them from the Amalekites; they spared the best of the sheep and cattle to sacrifice to the Lord your God, but we totally destroyed the rest."

15:12 Carmel Refers to a Judahite town, not Mount Carmel (Jos 15:55; 1Sa 25:2). **a monument in his own honor** Saul honors himself for having carried out God's command, indicating how self-deceived he was (see 2Sa 18:18).
15:13 I have carried out the Lord's instructions Saul

was so deluded by this point that he appears to have actually thought God would be happy with his halfhearted obedience.
15:14 this bleating of sheep in my ears God had commanded the slaughter of all Amalekite livestock (1Sa 15:3).
15:15 they spared Sensing Samuel's displeasure,

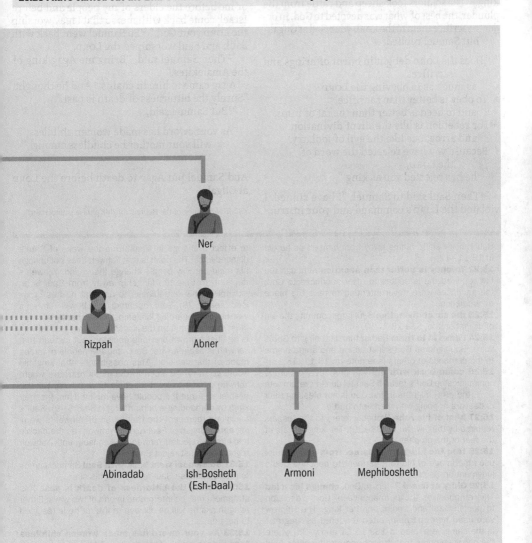

Ner

Rizpah   Abner

Abinadab   Ish-Bosheth   Armoni   Mephibosheth
(Esh-Baal)

¹⁶"Enough!" Samuel said to Saul. "Let me tell you what the LORD said to me last night."

"Tell me," Saul replied.

¹⁷Samuel said, "Although you were once small in your own eyes, did you not become the head of the tribes of Israel? The LORD anointed you king over Israel. ¹⁸And he sent you on a mission, saying, 'Go and completely destroy those wicked people, the Amalekites; wage war against them until you have wiped them out.' ¹⁹Why did you not obey the LORD? Why did you pounce on the plunder and do evil in the eyes of the LORD?"

²⁰"But I did obey the LORD," Saul said. "I went on the mission the LORD assigned me. I completely destroyed the Amalekites and brought back Agag their king. ²¹The soldiers took sheep and cattle from the plunder, the best of what was devoted to God, in order to sacrifice them to the LORD your God at Gilgal."

²²But Samuel replied:

"Does the LORD delight in burnt offerings and
        sacrifices
    as much as in obeying the LORD?
To obey is better than sacrifice,
    and to heed is better than the fat of rams.
²³For rebellion is like the sin of divination,
    and arrogance like the evil of idolatry.
Because you have rejected the word of
        the LORD,
    he has rejected you as king."

²⁴Then Saul said to Samuel, "I have sinned. I violated the LORD's command and your instruc-tions. I was afraid of the men and so I gave in to them. ²⁵Now I beg you, forgive my sin and come back with me, so that I may worship the LORD."

²⁶But Samuel said to him, "I will not go back with you. You have rejected the word of the LORD, and the LORD has rejected you as king over Israel!"

²⁷As Samuel turned to leave, Saul caught hold of the hem of his robe, and it tore. ²⁸Samuel said to him, "The LORD has torn the kingdom of Israel from you today and has given it to one of your neighbors — to one better than you. ²⁹He who is the Glory of Israel does not lie or change his mind; for he is not a human being, that he should change his mind."

³⁰Saul replied, "I have sinned. But please honor me before the elders of my people and before Israel; come back with me, so that I may worship the LORD your God." ³¹So Samuel went back with Saul, and Saul worshiped the LORD.

³²Then Samuel said, "Bring me Agag king of the Amalekites."

Agag came to him in chains.ᵃ And he thought, "Surely the bitterness of death is past."

³³But Samuel said,

"As your sword has made women childless,
    so will your mother be childless among
        women."

And Samuel put Agag to death before the LORD at Gilgal.

ᵃ 32 The meaning of the Hebrew for this phrase is uncertain.

Saul quickly shifts blame away from himself as he did in 13:11–12.

15:22 To obey is better than sacrifice Although the law required the Israelites to offer sacrifices to God, the sacrifices were never intended to take the place of obedience.

15:23 the sin of divination Saul later commits the sin of divination too. See 28:7–19.

15:24 I gave in to them Rather than listening to God's voice, Saul ignores God's instruction and shifts blame to the demands of others (see note on 13:11; 15:15).

15:25 come back with me The prophet's presence communicated God's favor. If Samuel doesn't return with Saul, the army might fear that God is not blessing their endeavors or going with them into battle.

15:27 hem of his robe Probably refers to the tassels required by the law (Nu 15:38–39). The king grovels at the feet of the prophet.

15:28 torn the kingdom of Israel from you Samuel uses the image of his torn garment to describe God's judgment on Saul.

15:29 Glory of Israel Refers to God. **change his mind** This emphasizes the permanence of God's decision to punish Saul and anoint another king. The Hebrew verb used here, *nacham*, often rendered as "regret," is the same verb used in 1Sa 15:11 and v. 35, where the narrative notes that Yahweh regretted making Saul king. Since Saul has disobeyed the stipulations of God's promise to make him king — which specified certain expectations from Saul (12:14–15) — the language of regret in 15:11 and v. 35 reflects Yahweh's decision to effect a change in kingship in the wake of Saul's disobedience. The point is that Yahweh does not change his mind the way people change their mind. Yahweh's decision to take the kingship away from Saul is an example of his faithfulness to do what he has promised (see Dt 28). Saul repeatedly disobeyed Yahweh's instructions regarding kingship. Consequently, Yahweh must remove him from the kingship. It is not that Yahweh is against his own previous decision, but instead that Yahweh is against what Saul, and the people of Israel, made of that decision. This possibility — that kingship would go awry — is seen in the initial narrative where Yahweh agrees to let the people have a king; Yahweh even states that the people have rejected him (as their king) by demanding a human king (1Sa 8:6–9). Saul's decisions represent the realization of Yahweh's warning about kingship. Saul rejects Yahweh, as the people had already rejected Yahweh, and consequently Yahweh regrettably must reject Saul.

15:31 So Samuel went back with Saul Samuel agrees to return because Saul recognized his sin.

15:32 Surely the bitterness of death is past This statement may be interpreted in one of two ways: Either Agag thinks he will be allowed to live, or he is resigned to his fate.

15:33 As your sword has made women childless Agag and the Amalekites were in no way innocent victims of God's command for total destruction (see 15:18; note on v. 3). **Samuel put Agag to death** Samuel fulfills God's command to destroy the Amalekites completely (v. 3).

³⁴Then Samuel left for Ramah, but Saul went up to his home in Gibeah of Saul. ³⁵Until the day Samuel died, he did not go to see Saul again, though Samuel mourned for him. And the Lord regretted that he had made Saul king over Israel.

Samuel Anoints David

16 The Lord said to Samuel, "How long will you mourn for Saul, since I have rejected him as king over Israel? Fill your horn with oil and be on your way; I am sending you to Jesse of Bethlehem. I have chosen one of his sons to be king."

²But Samuel said, "How can I go? If Saul hears about it, he will kill me."

The Lord said, "Take a heifer with you and say, 'I have come to sacrifice to the Lord.' ³Invite Jesse to the sacrifice, and I will show you what to do. You are to anoint for me the one I indicate."

⁴Samuel did what the Lord said. When he arrived at Bethlehem, the elders of the town trembled when they met him. They asked, "Do you come in peace?"

⁵Samuel replied, "Yes, in peace; I have come to sacrifice to the Lord. Consecrate yourselves and come to the sacrifice with me." Then he consecrated Jesse and his sons and invited them to the sacrifice.

⁶When they arrived, Samuel saw Eliab and thought, "Surely the Lord's anointed stands here before the Lord."

⁷But the Lord said to Samuel, "Do not consider his appearance or his height, for I have rejected him. The Lord does not look at the things people look at. People look at the outward appearance, but the Lord looks at the heart."

⁸Then Jesse called Abinadab and had him pass in front of Samuel. But Samuel said, "The Lord has not chosen this one either." ⁹Jesse then had Shammah pass by, but Samuel said, "Nor has the Lord chosen this one." ¹⁰Jesse had seven of his sons pass before Samuel, but Samuel said to him, "The Lord has not chosen these." ¹¹So he asked Jesse, "Are these all the sons you have?"

"There is still the youngest," Jesse answered. "He is tending the sheep."

Samuel said, "Send for him; we will not sit down until he arrives."

¹²So he sent for him and had him brought in. He was glowing with health and had a fine appearance and handsome features.

15:35 the Lord regretted See note on v. 29.

16:1–13 After recording God's second and final rejection of Saul (ch. 15), the narrative focuses on Saul's replacement. God instructs Samuel to travel to Bethlehem, where he will find Israel's next king. Once there, Samuel anoints David, the protagonist for the remainder of the collective work of 1–2 Samuel. See the people diagram "Judah to David" on p. 618.

16:1 horn with oil See 2:10 and note. **Jesse** The son of Obed and grandson of Boaz and Ruth (see Ru 4:17; 1Ch 2:12–15).

JESSE
Jesse belongs to the tribe of Judah and appears in 1 Samuel as a civic leader in the town of Bethlehem (see 1Sa 16:1,4–5). He is best known for being the father of King David, who was the youngest of his eight sons (see 16:10–11). Jesse appears in 1Sa 16 and 17 as an obedient servant to the king, sending his son to serve Saul as well as deliver supplies to his army. The legacy of his name continued throughout Israel's history due to its connection with Davidic Messianic hopes. This is especially the case in Isa 11:1,10; Ps 72; Ac 13:22; Ro 15:12; compare the book of Sirach (45:25).

16:2 If Saul hears Samuel fears that Saul, being jealous for his kingdom, will kill him and the newly anointed king. **Take a heifer** God understands Samuel's fear, so he gives Samuel a means to deceive those who might do evil against the prophet.

16:4 trembled Their fear may result from the unexpected visit from God's prophet. Deuteronomy 21:1–9 demands that in instances of unsolved murder, the elders and judges of the town were to have a Levite sacrifice a heifer to atone for the sin. Since Samuel, a judge and a Levite, arrived in Bethlehem with a heifer, the elders may be assuming the worst. Or they may assume that he visits them at Saul's bidding.

16:6 the Lord's anointed Like Saul, Eliab was impressive in appearance and stature (see 1Sa 9:2 and note).

16:7 the heart God emphasizes that superficial and non-spiritual considerations are not to be critical criteria for the choice of God's leaders.

16:8 The Lord has not chosen this one either The narrative does not record exactly how God communicated with Samuel. The prophet may have used the Urim and Thummim. Alternatively, God may have communicated internally or in a voice that only the prophet could hear.

16:10 seven of his sons Jesse is also recorded as having eight sons (including David) in 17:12. First Chronicles 2:13–15 records that Jesse has seven sons total, not seven plus David. The seven sons there may have referred to only the sons of prominence—those who had other sons to carry on the family name. Alternatively, the narrative in 1 Samuel may be arranging the material for thematic reasons. As the seventh son, David would have held a place of honor and blessing. But as the eighth son, he would have been seen as one among many; David has a humble and insignificant standing within the family.

16:11 youngest The Hebrew word used here, *qatan*, can mean "young" or "small." Since Saul and Eliab are singled out for their height, the narrative is likely establishing a deliberate contrast between their stature and David's. **He is tending the sheep** The narrative calls David a shepherd in the introduction. Leaders are often described as shepherds in the Bible (see 1Sa 9:3 and note). The shepherd motif also occurs in ancient Near Eastern literature.

Then the LORD said, "Rise and anoint him; this is the one."

¹³So Samuel took the horn of oil and anointed him in the presence of his brothers, and from that day on the Spirit of the LORD came powerfully upon David. Samuel then went to Ramah.

David in Saul's Service

¹⁴Now the Spirit of the LORD had departed from Saul, and an evil[a] spirit from the LORD tormented him.

¹⁵Saul's attendants said to him, "See, an evil spirit from God is tormenting you. ¹⁶Let our lord command his servants here to search for someone who can play the lyre. He will play when the evil spirit from God comes on you, and you will feel better."

¹⁷So Saul said to his attendants, "Find someone who plays well and bring him to me."

¹⁸One of the servants answered, "I have seen a son of Jesse of Bethlehem who knows how to play the lyre. He is a brave man and a warrior. He speaks well and is a fine-looking man. And the LORD is with him."

¹⁹Then Saul sent messengers to Jesse and said, "Send me your son David, who is with the sheep." ²⁰So Jesse took a donkey loaded with bread, a skin of wine and a young goat and sent them with his son David to Saul.

²¹David came to Saul and entered his service. Saul liked him very much, and David became one of his armor-bearers. ²²Then Saul sent word to Jesse, saying, "Allow David to remain in my service, for I am pleased with him."

²³Whenever the spirit from God came on Saul, David would take up his lyre and play. Then relief would come to Saul; he would feel better, and the evil spirit would leave him.

David and Goliath

17 Now the Philistines gathered their forces for war and assembled at Sokoh in Judah. They pitched camp at Ephes Dammim, between Sokoh and Azekah. ²Saul and the Israelites assembled and camped in the Valley of Elah and drew up their battle line to meet the Philistines. ³The

---

a 14 Or *and a harmful*; similarly in verses 15, 16 and 23

16:13 Spirit of the LORD Compare the Spirit coming upon Saul to empower him to act as king in 10:6,9–10; 11:6. Also, contrast with v. 14, where the Spirit departs from Saul. **David** Jesse's youngest son.

1 Samuel 16:13

DAVID
David shepherded his father's flocks until his conscription into Saul's service (see 1Sa 16:11,19,21–22; 17:15,20; 1Ch 2:13–16). There, he achieved widespread fame through his military successes and garnered the love of the people (see 1Sa 18:7,13–16,30). Chosen by God and anointed by Samuel, David assumed the throne at age 30, following Saul's death, and reigned for 40 years (see 1Sa 13:14; 15:28; 16:13; 2Sa 2:4; 5:3–5). Though beset with personal difficulties, his reign is characterized by military success and economic prosperity. He defeated his enemies, expanded his territory, secured his borders and increased Israel's national revenue. His achievements paved the way for Solomon's prosperous and peaceful reign.

16:14–23 As Samuel had predicted in 8:11–12, Saul took David into his military service. Initially conscripted for his musical capabilities, the young David would prove to be far more valuable (see v. 21 and note; see especially ch. 17).

16:14 Spirit of the LORD had departed A deliberate contrast to David in the preceding verse. God's Spirit departing from Saul means that he is no longer divinely empowered to act as God's anointed king over his people and fight his enemies. Saul has rejected the guidance of the Spirit throughout his reign, and now the Spirit leaves him for good (see 18:12; 28:15). **an evil spirit from**

the LORD Saul has made himself God's enemy and is treated as such from now on (see 18:10; 19:9). The exact nature of this spirit is unknown. The Hebrew word used here, *ruach*, may describe some form of mental anguish or a general sense of calamity. Nevertheless, a literal spiritual being sent from Yahweh is also possible (compare Ex 12:23). Yahweh sometimes uses physical force—and, at times, spiritual beings implementing that force—to end the reign of a wicked ruler or cause them to give in to his will (compare Jdg 9:23; 2Ki 19:32–37). This is for the greater good of his people and is one way that he brings justice.

16:16 lyre Refers to an instrument with six to eight strings, used in celebrations, worship and prophecy (1Sa 10:5). **you will feel better** Ancients believed that music warded off evil spirits.

16:18 a brave man The Hebrew phrase used here, *gibbor chayil*, denotes a mighty warrior (e.g., Jdg 11:1) or a person of significant social stature (Ru 2:1; 1Sa 9:1). Here, this characteristic functions in a list that cumulatively establishes David's character and abilities.

16:19 with the sheep The narrative again hints at future kingship (see v. 11 and note).

16:21 liked him very much A feeling that would soon depart. The king attempts to kill David approximately 16 times (see 18:11,17,25; 19:1,10,11,15,20–21,22; 23:8,15; 24:2; 26:2). **one of his armor-bearers** Armor-bearers were close attendants and advisors (see Jdg 9:54; 1Sa 14:1; 31:4–6).

17:1–58 In this chapter, David proves his valor and demonstrates that he is fit to be Israel's next king. The Philistine giant, Goliath, taunted the armies of Israel daily. When David came to deliver food to his brothers, he heard the haughty giant and was grievously offended. He charged Goliath with only a shepherd's implements and struck him down. As a demonstration against the Philistines, David decapitated the giant and took his armor. This was Israel's first victory at the hands of David.

Philistines occupied one hill and the Israelites another, with the valley between them.

⁴A champion named Goliath, who was from Gath, came out of the Philistine camp. His height was six cubits and a span.^a ⁵He had a bronze hel-

met on his head and wore a coat of scale armor of bronze weighing five thousand shekels^b; ⁶on his legs he wore bronze greaves, and a bronze

^a 4 That is, about 9 feet 9 inches or about 3 meters   ^b 5 That is, about 125 pounds or about 58 kilograms

17:2 Valley of Elah This valley was in the Shephelah, the western foothills of Israel. It ran between Philistine territory in the west and Judah in the east. The Philistines were on the north side of the valley, and the Israelites on the south.

17:4 champion Commanders of opposing armies in the ancient Near East would occasionally avoid engaging all their forces; instead, each would select his best fighter to engage in a death match with the best fighter from the other army. The winner determined the outcome of the battle (see v. 9). Goliath was this type of fighter. **six cubits and a span** The Hebrew Bible, the Septuagint (the ancient Greek translation of the OT), and the Dead Sea Scrolls vary with regard to Goliath's height. The Hebrew Bible states that he was six cubits and a span—roughly nine and a half feet tall (or perhaps a few inches more).

This would make him about half a foot taller than the world's tallest man in medical history (8 feet, 11 inches). The latter two sources, however, describe him as four cubits and a span—roughly six and a half feet tall. It is possible that the number "six" in the Hebrew text ("six cubits and a span") could have been inadvertently introduced when the scribe's eye saw "six" a few lines below in v. 7. The point of the passage, however, is not to ascertain Goliath's exact height but to note his size and skill compared to David. The young, inexperienced David is victorious over the Philistine champion because Yahweh assisted him (see vv. 37,46–47). Although Goliath appears invincible, God's declaration in 16:7 indicates that height is insignificant.

17:5 a bronze helmet This article, and the others, contrast the simply clothed Israelites.

Battles of Saul and David

COMBATANTS	LOCATION	WINNER	REFERENCES
Saul vs. Ammonites	Jabesh Gilead	Saul	1Sa 11:11
Saul vs. Philistines	Mikmash	Saul	1Sa 13:2-23
Saul vs. Amalekites	Havilah to Shur	Saul	1Sa 15:7-9
David vs. Goliath	Valley of Elah	David	1Sa 17:40-51
David vs. Philistines	—	David	1Sa 18:30; 23:1-5
David vs. Amalekites	—	David	1Sa 30:16-20
Saul vs. Philistines	Mount Gilboa	Philistines	1Sa 31:1-7; 1Ch 10:1-7
David (Joab) vs. Ish-Bosheth (Abner)	Gibeon	David	2Sa 2:12-29
David vs. Philistines	Valley of Rephaim	David	2Sa 5:17-21; 1Ch 14:8-12
David vs. Philistines	Gibeon to Gezer	David	2Sa 5:22-25; 1Ch 14:13-17
David vs. Moabites	—	David	2Sa 8:2; 1Ch 18:2
David vs. Hadadezer and Arameans	—	David	2Sa 8:3-8; 1Ch 18:3-8
David vs. Edomites	Valley of Salt	David	2Sa 8:13-14; 1Ch 18:12-13
David (Joab) vs. Ammonites	Medeba	David	2Sa 10:9-14; 1Ch 19:7-15
David vs. Arameans	Helam	David	2Sa 10:15-19; 1Ch 19:16-19
David (Joab) vs. Ammonites	Rabbah	David	2Sa 11:1; 2Sa 12:26-31; 1Ch 20:1-3
David (Joab) vs. Absalom	forest of Ephraim	David	2Sa 18:6-17
David vs. Philistines	—	David	2Sa 21:15-17
David vs. Philistines	Gob/Gezer	David	2Sa 21:18-19; 1Ch 20:4-5
David vs. Philistines	Gath	David	2Sa 21:20-22; 1Ch 20:6-8

javelin was slung on his back. [7]His spear shaft was like a weaver's rod, and its iron point weighed six hundred shekels.[a] His shield bearer went ahead of him.

[8]Goliath stood and shouted to the ranks of Israel, "Why do you come out and line up for battle? Am I not a Philistine, and are you not the servants of Saul? Choose a man and have him come down to me. [9]If he is able to fight and kill me, we will become your subjects; but if I overcome him and kill him, you will become our subjects and serve us." [10]Then the Philistine said, "This day I defy the armies of Israel! Give me a man and let us fight each other." [11]On hearing the Philistine's words, Saul and all the Israelites were dismayed and terrified.

[12]Now David was the son of an Ephrathite named Jesse, who was from Bethlehem in Judah. Jesse had eight sons, and in Saul's time he was very old. [13]Jesse's three oldest sons had followed Saul to the war: The firstborn was Eliab; the second, Abinadab; and the third, Shammah. [14]David was the youngest. The three oldest followed Saul, [15]but David went back and forth from Saul to tend his father's sheep at Bethlehem.

[16]For forty days the Philistine came forward every morning and evening and took his stand.

[17]Now Jesse said to his son David, "Take this ephah[b] of roasted grain and these ten loaves of bread for your brothers and hurry to their camp. [18]Take along these ten cheeses to the commander of their unit. See how your brothers are and bring back some assurance[c] from them. [19]They are with Saul and all the men of Israel in the Valley of Elah, fighting against the Philistines."

[20]Early in the morning David left the flock in the care of a shepherd, loaded up and set out, as Jesse had directed. He reached the camp as the army was going out to its battle positions, shouting the war cry. [21]Israel and the Philistines were drawing up their lines facing each other. [22]David left his things with the keeper of supplies, ran to the battle lines and asked his brothers how they were. [23]As he was talking with them, Goliath, the Philistine champion from Gath, stepped out from his lines and shouted his usual defiance, and David heard it. [24]Whenever the Israelites saw the man, they all fled from him in great fear.

[25]Now the Israelites had been saying, "Do you see how this man keeps coming out? He comes out to defy Israel. The king will give great wealth to the man who kills him. He will also give him his daughter in marriage and will exempt his family from taxes in Israel."

[26]David asked the men standing near him, "What will be done for the man who kills this Philistine and removes this disgrace from Israel? Who is this uncircumcised Philistine that he should defy the armies of the living God?"

[27]They repeated to him what they had been saying and told him, "This is what will be done for the man who kills him."

[28]When Eliab, David's oldest brother, heard him speaking with the men, he burned with anger at him and asked, "Why have you come down here? And with whom did you leave those few sheep in the wilderness? I know how conceited you are and how wicked your heart is; you came down only to watch the battle."

[29]"Now what have I done?" said David. "Can't I even speak?" [30]He then turned away to someone else and brought up the same matter, and the men answered him as before. [31]What David said was overheard and reported to Saul, and Saul sent for him.

[32]David said to Saul, "Let no one lose heart on account of this Philistine; your servant will go and fight him."

[33]Saul replied, "You are not able to go out against this Philistine and fight him; you are only a young man, and he has been a warrior from his youth."

[34]But David said to Saul, "Your servant has been keeping his father's sheep. When a lion or a bear came and carried off a sheep from the flock, [35]I went after it, struck it and rescued the sheep from its mouth. When it turned on me, I seized it by its

---

[a] 7 That is, about 15 pounds or about 6.9 kilograms [b] 17 That is, probably about 36 pounds or about 16 kilograms [c] 18 Or some token; or some pledge of spoils

---

17:9 If he is able Goliath's explanation of representative warfare may indicate that Israel is ignorant of or inexperienced with the custom. See note on v. 4.

17:10 This day I defy the armies of Israel Goliath's boast is the reason for David's anger in v. 26.

17:11 terrified The most common adjective used of Saul (see 10:22 and note).

17:13 Jesse's three oldest sons Eliab, Abinidab and Shammah (16:6,8,9). According to Nu 1:3, only men older than 20 years are permitted to go to war, which may explain why only three of David's brothers are in the camp.

17:17 hurry to their camp Due to the lengthy standoff in 1Sa 17:16, the army was running low on rations. Families of the troops help provide for the army.

17:18 bring back some assurance from them Proof that they were alive and well.

17:25 king will give great wealth to the man who kills him This man would receive three benefits: riches, Saul's daughter in marriage, and his extended family would be free from taxation.

17:26 armies of the living God David perceives that Goliath is not just insulting Israel, but Israel's God.

17:28 he burned with anger Eliab may have been bitter at being passed over for the kingship, or perhaps David's courage clashed with his fear.

17:31 What David said was overheard Regardless of David's intentions, the word of his discussions with the members of the army eventually got back to the king, who in turn summoned him.

hair, struck it and killed it. [36]Your servant has killed both the lion and the bear; this uncircumcised Philistine will be like one of them, because he has defied the armies of the living God. [37]The LORD who rescued me from the paw of the lion and the paw of the bear will rescue me from the hand of this Philistine."

Saul said to David, "Go, and the LORD be with you."

[38]Then Saul dressed David in his own tunic. He put a coat of armor on him and a bronze helmet on his head. [39]David fastened on his sword over the tunic and tried walking around, because he was not used to them.

"I cannot go in these," he said to Saul, "because I am not used to them." So he took them off. [40]Then he took his staff in his hand, chose five smooth stones from the stream, put them in the pouch of his shepherd's bag and, with his sling in his hand, approached the Philistine.

[41]Meanwhile, the Philistine, with his shield bearer in front of him, kept coming closer to David. [42]He looked David over and saw that he was little more than a boy, glowing with health and handsome, and he despised him. [43]He said to David, "Am I a dog, that you come at me with sticks?" And the Philistine cursed David by his gods. [44]"Come here," he said, "and I'll give your flesh to the birds and the wild animals!"

[45]David said to the Philistine, "You come against me with sword and spear and javelin, but I come against you in the name of the LORD Almighty, the God of the armies of Israel, whom you have defied. [46]This day the LORD will deliver you into my hands, and I'll strike you down and cut off your head. This very day I will give the carcasses of the Philistine army to the birds and the wild animals, and the whole world will know that there is a God in Israel. [47]All those gathered here will know that it is not by sword or spear that the LORD saves; for the battle is the LORD's, and he will give all of you into our hands."

[48]As the Philistine moved closer to attack him, David ran quickly toward the battle line to meet him. [49]Reaching into his bag and taking out a stone, he slung it and struck the Philistine on the forehead. The stone sank into his forehead, and he fell facedown on the ground.

[50]So David triumphed over the Philistine with a sling and a stone; without a sword in his hand he struck down the Philistine and killed him.

[51]David ran and stood over him. He took hold of the Philistine's sword and drew it from the sheath. After he killed him, he cut off his head with the sword.

When the Philistines saw that their hero was dead, they turned and ran. [52]Then the men of Israel and Judah surged forward with a shout and pursued the Philistines to the entrance of Gath[a] and to the gates of Ekron. Their dead were strewn along the Shaaraim road to Gath and Ekron. [53]When the Israelites returned from chasing the Philistines, they plundered their camp.

[54]David took the Philistine's head and brought it to Jerusalem; he put the Philistine's weapons in his own tent.

---

a 52 Some Septuagint manuscripts; Hebrew *of a valley*

17:36 this uncircumcised Philistine A pejorative phrase that is made worse by the equation of him with the beasts of the field.

17:37 LORD be with you Ironically, it is a shepherd boy, and not the king, who represents Israel on the battlefield and shows faith in Yahweh. Saul's resignation to allow David to fight is another indictment of his fear.

17:38 a coat of armor In terms of battlefield strategy, Saul assumes that heavy infantry should be met with heavy infantry.

17:39 he took them off He stripped down to his standard attire, likely just a tunic and belt. He decides to meet heavy infantry with light artillery (his sling and stones), which is substantially more mobile and can give one the advantage in certain battlefield contexts.

17:42 he despised him The text recounts that Goliath's disdain is rooted in David's youth and appearance. Goliath is also offended by David's approach to battle (v. 43). The narrative deliberately contrasts Goliath's stature with David's, further highlighting David's spiritual qualification and divine anointing (with the Spirit) as Israel's next king.

17:45 David said These verses begin David's battlefield declaration, which communicates the theological payoff for the episode. The victory will serve as a proclamation of the Lord's salvation for his people.

17:46 the whole world will know This match was so improbable that the people could only see David's victory as divinely enabled.

17:47 gathered here will know David's victory would also reassure the Israelites that God was fighting for them. **not by sword or spear that the LORD saves** Weapons did not determine the final outcome of the battle. This was encouraging to the Israelites, who had fewer weapons than the Philistines (see 13:19–22; note on 13:19).

17:48 David ran quickly In contrast to Saul and his fleeing army (see v. 24), David runs toward the Philistine giant.

17:49 he slung it David's use of a sling and a stone allow him to fight from a distance, something Goliath's arsenal did not permit (see note on v. 39). **into his forehead** David hits Goliath beneath the front of his helmet (see v. 5), demonstrating his accuracy.

17:51 cut off his head Earlier, God decapitated the Philistine's god on whom they relied in battle (see 5:4). Now, David decapitates their champion.

17:52 the entrance of Gath and to the gates of Ekron Roughly ten miles away.

17:54 Jerusalem Jerusalem did not yet belong to Israel; it was in Jebusite hands (see 2Sa 5:6–7). Since the narratives were composed and edited after the events they describe, events that occurred later were sometimes placed in the text as if they had already happened. Alternatively, this may have been a move designed to intimidate Israel's enemies in that city: It would serve as a warning of what was to befall Jerusalem's inhabitants

⁵⁵As Saul watched David going out to meet the Philistine, he said to Abner, commander of the army, "Abner, whose son is that young man?"

Abner replied, "As surely as you live, Your Majesty, I don't know."

⁵⁶The king said, "Find out whose son this young man is."

⁵⁷As soon as David returned from killing the Philistine, Abner took him and brought him before Saul, with David still holding the Philistine's head.

⁵⁸"Whose son are you, young man?" Saul asked him.

David said, "I am the son of your servant Jesse of Bethlehem."

Saul's Growing Fear of David

18 After David had finished talking with Saul, Jonathan became one in spirit with David, and he loved him as himself. ²From that day Saul kept David with him and did not let him return home to his family. ³And Jonathan made a covenant with David because he loved him as himself. ⁴Jonathan took off the robe he was wearing and gave it to David, along with his tunic, and even his sword, his bow and his belt.

⁵Whatever mission Saul sent him on, David was so successful that Saul gave him a high rank in the army. This pleased all the troops, and Saul's officers as well.

⁶When the men were returning home after David had killed the Philistine, the women came out from all the towns of Israel to meet King Saul with singing and dancing, with joyful songs and with timbrels and lyres. ⁷As they danced, they sang:

"Saul has slain his thousands,
   and David his tens of thousands."

⁸Saul was very angry; this refrain displeased him greatly. "They have credited David with tens of thousands," he thought, "but me with only thousands. What more can he get but the kingdom?" ⁹And from that time on Saul kept a close eye on David.

¹⁰The next day an evil[a] spirit from God came forcefully on Saul. He was prophesying in his house, while David was playing the lyre, as he usually did. Saul had a spear in his hand ¹¹and he hurled it, saying to himself, "I'll pin David to the wall." But David eluded him twice.

¹²Saul was afraid of David, because the LORD was with David but had departed from Saul. ¹³So he sent David away from him and gave him command over a thousand men, and David led the troops in their campaigns. ¹⁴In everything he did

---

[a] 10 Or *a harmful*

---

when the Israelite army came to attack. **the Philistine's weapons** David would later dedicate these items to God, as was called for by Yahweh in this type of warfare (see 1Sa 21:9; note on Jos 6:17).

17:55 whose son is that It is unclear why Saul asks this question, since 1Sa 16 indicates they knew each other (compare 17:15). This story may have occurred sometime before 16:21. Alternatively, it may be that David's bravery on this occasion causes Saul to take a more active interest in him than he had before.

18:1–5 Saul's son Jonathan quickly befriends David. Jonathan was loyal to David until his death, and David honored his commitments to Jonathan even after his friend had died. Their friendship is an example of loyalty in the midst of fierce opposition.

18:1 as himself Demonstrates that the men were like-minded in their observance of God's Law and zeal for Israel.

18:2 did not let him return David was forcibly conscripted into service.

18:3 covenant with David The establishment of a covenant demonstrates the commitment between David and Jonathan. Also, a covenantal context provides the lens for understanding the love between Jonathan and David. See the table "Covenants in the Old Testament" on p. 469.

18:4 robe May describe a royal robe, or something indicative of his status as the king's son. Monarchs in antiquity were often identified by their clothing (see Mt 6:29). His gift of royal clothing and weaponry may symbolize an attempt to transfer the kingdom to David.

18:5 Whatever mission Saul sent him on, David was so successful David's success becomes a contributing factor to Saul's jealousy and thus heightens the contrast between David's rise and Saul's demise.

18:6–16 This section returns to the narrative framework of 1Sa 17. Upon returning home from successfully routing the Philistine forces, Saul hears women singing David's praises. He immediately becomes jealous and suspicious. The narrative presents Saul's first two attempts to kill David.

18:6 to meet King Saul Celebrating the homecoming of the victorious king was a common custom (compare Mt 21:10 and note).

18:7 David his tens of thousands This chorus celebrates David in the face of Saul. In antiquity, kings, not soldiers, received credit for battle.

18:8 Saul was very angry Saul's anger comes directly from the celebration of David.

18:9 from that time on Saul kept a close eye on David For the rest of his life, Saul will view David with suspicion or outright hostility.

18:10 an evil spirit from God See 1Sa 16:14 and note. **spear in his hand** The narrative often portrays Saul as being close to his spear (see 19:9; 22:6). The king's spear seems to be used as a symbol of Saul's madness and paranoia.

18:11 David eluded him twice David apparently shows great loyalty. Even after Saul had thrown the first spear, David continued to play his lyre to ease Saul's madness.

18:12 afraid of David See v. 29; 10:22 and note. Saul's anger toward David is accompanied by fear, which stems from his awareness that God was with David but not with him.

18:13 gave him command Saul may hope to bring about David's death in the natural course of battle. However, because God was with David and not with Saul, this plan backfires (see vv. 14,16).

18:14 he had great success David's success in battle resulted in great gains for Israel. David also gained re-

he had great success, because the LORD was with him. [15]When Saul saw how successful he was, he was afraid of him. [16]But all Israel and Judah loved David, because he led them in their campaigns.

[17]Saul said to David, "Here is my older daughter Merab. I will give her to you in marriage; only serve me bravely and fight the battles of the LORD." For Saul said to himself, "I will not raise a hand against him. Let the Philistines do that!"

[18]But David said to Saul, "Who am I, and what is my family or my clan in Israel, that I should become the king's son-in-law?" [19]So[a] when the time came for Merab, Saul's daughter, to be given to David, she was given in marriage to Adriel of Meholah.

[20]Now Saul's daughter Michal was in love with David, and when they told Saul about it, he was pleased. [21]"I will give her to him," he thought, "so that she may be a snare to him and so that the hand of the Philistines may be against him." So Saul said to David, "Now you have a second opportunity to become my son-in-law."

[22]Then Saul ordered his attendants: "Speak to David privately and say, 'Look, the king likes you, and his attendants all love you; now become his son-in-law.'"

[23]They repeated these words to David. But David said, "Do you think it is a small matter to become the king's son-in-law? I'm only a poor man and little known."

[24]When Saul's servants told him what David had said, [25]Saul replied, "Say to David, 'The king wants no other price for the bride than a hundred Philistine foreskins, to take revenge on his ene-

mies.'" Saul's plan was to have David fall by the hands of the Philistines.

[26]When the attendants told David these things, he was pleased to become the king's son-in-law. So before the allotted time elapsed, [27]David took his men with him and went out and killed two hundred Philistines and brought back their foreskins. They counted out the full number to the king so that David might become the king's son-in-law. Then Saul gave him his daughter Michal in marriage.

[28]When Saul realized that the LORD was with David and that his daughter Michal loved David, [29]Saul became still more afraid of him, and he remained his enemy the rest of his days.

[30]The Philistine commanders continued to go out to battle, and as often as they did, David met with more success than the rest of Saul's officers, and his name became well known.

Saul Tries to Kill David

19 Saul told his son Jonathan and all the attendants to kill David. But Jonathan had taken a great liking to David [2]and warned him, "My father Saul is looking for a chance to kill you. Be on your guard tomorrow morning; go into hiding and stay there. [3]I will go out and stand with my father in the field where you are. I'll speak to him about you and will tell you what I find out."

[4]Jonathan spoke well of David to Saul his father and said to him, "Let not the king do wrong to his servant David; he has not wronged you, and what he

[a] 19 Or However,

---

spect among Israel's military leadership, the devotion of the army and the love of the people.

18:16 all Israel and Judah Even early in his career, David was a charismatic leader who united the country through his military achievements.

18:17–30 This section records Saul's further attempts to kill David. Twice Saul encourages David to marry one of his daughters; he hopes that, through these marriages, he might rid himself of the increasingly popular hero. David initially refuses, stating that he is poor and cannot afford the dowry. However, when Saul indicates that the bride price is dead Philistines, David accepts the challenge and marries Saul's youngest daughter, Michal.

18:17 Let the Philistines do that Saul attempts to lure David into a more dangerous military role by offering him his daughter, Merab, in marriage.

18:19 in marriage to Adriel of Meholah Unlike v. 25, no further negotiations occur between Saul and David; the king gives Merab to another man.

18:21 a snare to him Saul may view Michal as a snare because she practices idolatry (see 19:13) or because Saul uses her to lure David into a more dangerous position (see v. 17 and note).

18:25 a hundred Philistine foreskins Israelites removed the foreskin in the ritual act of circumcision (see Ge 17:10–14). This identified them as participants in God's covenant. Those who were uncircumcised, and therefore outside the covenant, were an object of the

Israelites' derision (e.g., 1Sa 14:6; 17:26; 31:4). **David fall** Saul's fourth attempt to kill David (see 16:21 and note).

18:27 killed two hundred Philistines David provides double the bride price (v. 25).

18:29 Saul became still more afraid See v. 12; 10:22 and note.

19:1–24 In this chapter, Saul attempts to kill David eight times. He initially tries to persuade Jonathan to murder David, but Jonathan refuses and asserts his friend's innocence (vv. 1–5). In response, Saul vows not to harm David. However, he goes back on his word a short time later (vv. 9–10). David flees to Samuel at Ramah and goes into hiding.

19:1 kill David Saul's fifth attempt to kill David. **had taken a great liking to David** Saul likely asserted that Jonathan would lose the throne if David continued to live (see 20:31). Though he would benefit from David's death, Jonathan could not be swayed to turn on his friend. See 18:1–5 and note.

19:2 warned him Jonathan remains loyal to his friend David but betrays his father's trust.

19:3 in the field Their first of two clandestine meetings in a field (see 20:11–42).

19:4 he has not wronged you Jonathan asserts that there was no need for retaliation; David had done nothing wrong. **benefited you** David defeated Saul's enemies on several occasions.

has done has benefited you greatly. [5]He took his life in his hands when he killed the Philistine. The LORD won a great victory for all Israel, and you saw it and were glad. Why then would you do wrong to an innocent man like David by killing him for no reason?"

[6]Saul listened to Jonathan and took this oath: "As surely as the LORD lives, David will not be put to death."

[7]So Jonathan called David and told him the whole conversation. He brought him to Saul, and David was with Saul as before.

[8]Once more war broke out, and David went out and fought the Philistines. He struck them with such force that they fled before him.

[9]But an evil[a] spirit from the LORD came on Saul as he was sitting in his house with his spear in his hand. While David was playing the lyre, [10]Saul tried to pin him to the wall with his spear, but David eluded him as Saul drove the spear into the wall. That night David made good his escape.

[11]Saul sent men to David's house to watch it and to kill him in the morning. But Michal, David's wife, warned him, "If you don't run for your life tonight, tomorrow you'll be killed." [12]So Michal let David down through a window, and he fled and escaped. [13]Then Michal took an idol and laid it on the bed, covering it with a garment and putting some goats' hair at the head.

[14]When Saul sent the men to capture David, Michal said, "He is ill."

[15]Then Saul sent the men back to see David and told them, "Bring him up to me in his bed so that I may kill him." [16]But when the men entered, there was the idol in the bed, and at the head was some goats' hair.

[17]Saul said to Michal, "Why did you deceive me like this and send my enemy away so that he escaped?"

Michal told him, "He said to me, 'Let me get away. Why should I kill you?'"

[18]When David had fled and made his escape, he went to Samuel at Ramah and told him all that Saul had done to him. Then he and Samuel went to Naioth and stayed there. [19]Word came to Saul: "David is in Naioth at Ramah"; [20]so he sent men to capture him. But when they saw a group of prophets prophesying, with Samuel standing there as their leader, the Spirit of God came on Saul's men, and they also prophesied. [21]Saul was told about it, and he sent more men, and they prophesied too. Saul sent men a third time, and they also prophesied. [22]Finally, he himself left for Ramah and went to the great cistern at Seku. And he asked, "Where are Samuel and David?"

"Over in Naioth at Ramah," they said.

[23]So Saul went to Naioth at Ramah. But the Spirit of God came even on him, and he walked along prophesying until he came to Naioth. [24]He stripped off his garments, and he too prophesied in Samuel's presence. He lay naked all that day and all that night. This is why people say, "Is Saul also among the prophets?"

David and Jonathan

20 Then David fled from Naioth at Ramah and went to Jonathan and asked, "What have I done? What is my crime? How have I wronged your father, that he is trying to kill me?"

---

[a] 9 Or But a harmful

19:6 As surely as the LORD lives Saul's subsequent actions reveal his complete spiritual deterioration. After invoking God's name in an oath—thereby making him a witness—Saul breaks his oath.
19:7 with Saul as before Suggests that despite fulfilling his military function, David continued to play the lyre for Saul in his court as well (see v. 9).
19:9 an evil spirit from the LORD See 16:14 and note. **with his spear** A subtle indication that Saul is suffering mentally. Though he is in the safest place in his territory, he is armed (see 18:10 and note). The similarity of this event to 18:10–11 indicates that Saul has not changed.
19:10 but David eluded him Saul's sixth attempt to kill David (see 16:21 and note).
19:11 Michal, David's wife, warned him Like Jonathan, Michal betrays her father's confidence for the sake of saving David, whom she loves (see v. 2 and note). **tomorrow** Michal's knowledge of the timing of Saul's attack indicates she may have been aware of the plot.
19:13 idol Saul may have considered Michal a snare to David because of her idolatry (see 1Sa 18:21 and note). Apparently, these idols could be life-sized or nearly so, since the guards mistook it for David.
19:15 I may kill him Saul's eighth attempt to kill David (see 16:21 and note).
19:17 Why should I kill you Michal lies to her father to cover up her deceit.

19:18 he and Samuel went By portraying them together, the narrative implies that God and his prophet are loyal to David. **Naioth** The name of this place means "tents"; perhaps it was a camp or compound where the prophets lived.
19:20 he sent men Saul attempts to kill David for the ninth time. **they also prophesied** God confounds David's enemies and causes them to prophesy.
19:21 he sent more men Saul's tenth attempt to kill David. **sent men a third time** Saul's eleventh effort to kill David.
19:22 he himself left Saul takes matters into his own hands. This marks his twelfth attempt to kill David (see 16:21 and note).
19:24 stripped off his garments Saul removes his regal robes when encountering God, confirming the judgment of 15:23,28. This involuntary prophesying seems designed to humiliate Saul and show that, despite the trappings of power, he is helpless before God. **in Samuel's presence** In the Hebrew text, this scene stands in tension with 15:35, which notes that Samuel did not see Saul again until the day of his death (or for the rest of his life). This suggests that 15:35 is out of chronological sequence; the comment at 15:35 is likely intended to note Samuel's disdain for Saul following the events of ch. 15. **among the prophets** The second time this proverb is referenced (see 10:11 and note).

²"Never!" Jonathan replied. "You are not going to die! Look, my father doesn't do anything, great or small, without letting me know. Why would he hide this from me? It isn't so!"

³But David took an oath and said, "Your father knows very well that I have found favor in your eyes, and he has said to himself, 'Jonathan must not know this or he will be grieved.' Yet as surely as the LORD lives and as you live, there is only a step between me and death."

⁴Jonathan said to David, "Whatever you want me to do, I'll do for you."

⁵So David said, "Look, tomorrow is the New Moon feast, and I am supposed to dine with the king; but let me go and hide in the field until the evening of the day after tomorrow. ⁶If your father misses me at all, tell him, 'David earnestly asked my permission to hurry to Bethlehem, his hometown, because an annual sacrifice is being made there for his whole clan.' ⁷If he says, 'Very well,' then your servant is safe. But if he loses his temper, you can be sure that he is determined to harm me. ⁸As for you, show kindness to your servant, for you have brought him into a covenant with you before the LORD. If I am guilty, then kill me yourself! Why hand me over to your father?"

⁹"Never!" Jonathan said. "If I had the least inkling that my father was determined to harm you, wouldn't I tell you?"

¹⁰David asked, "Who will tell me if your father answers you harshly?"

¹¹"Come," Jonathan said, "let's go out into the field." So they went there together.

¹²Then Jonathan said to David, "I swear by the LORD, the God of Israel, that I will surely sound out my father by this time the day after tomorrow! If he is favorably disposed toward you, will I not send you word and let you know? ¹³But if my father intends to harm you, may the LORD deal with Jonathan, be it ever so severely, if I do not let you know and send you away in peace. May the LORD be with you as he has been with my father. ¹⁴But show me unfailing kindness like the LORD's kindness as long as I live, so that I may not be killed, ¹⁵and do not ever cut off your kindness from my family—not even when the LORD has cut off every one of David's enemies from the face of the earth."

¹⁶So Jonathan made a covenant with the house of David, saying, "May the LORD call David's enemies to account." ¹⁷And Jonathan had David reaffirm his oath out of love for him, because he loved him as he loved himself.

¹⁸Then Jonathan said to David, "Tomorrow is the New Moon feast. You will be missed, because your seat will be empty. ¹⁹The day after tomorrow, toward evening, go to the place where you hid when this trouble began, and wait by the stone Ezel. ²⁰I will shoot three arrows to the side of it, as though I were shooting at a target. ²¹Then I will send a boy and say, 'Go, find the arrows.' If I say to him, 'Look, the arrows are on this side of you; bring them here,' then come, because, as surely as the LORD lives, you are safe; there is no danger. ²²But if I say to the boy, 'Look, the arrows are beyond you,' then you must go, because the LORD has sent you away. ²³And about the matter you and I discussed—remember, the LORD is witness between you and me forever."

²⁴So David hid in the field, and when the New Moon feast came, the king sat down to eat. ²⁵He sat in his customary place by the wall, opposite Jonathan,^a and Abner sat next to Saul, but David's place was empty. ²⁶Saul said nothing that day, for he

---

^a 25 Septuagint; Hebrew *wall. Jonathan arose*

20:1–42 In this chapter, David approaches Jonathan and asks why Saul wants him killed (v. 1). Jonathan asserts that Saul means him no harm. They devise a plan to test the king, which confirms David's suspicions (vv. 3–34). Remaining faithful to his covenant (see 18:1–4), Jonathan warns David, who has gone into hiding, that Saul will try to kill him (vv. 35–40). The men make vows of friendship to one another, and Jonathan sends David away in peace (vv. 41–42).

20:2 Never Jonathan moves to assure David that Saul will not succeed.

20:3 as surely as the LORD lives David's oaths function to emphasize the gravity of the situation as perceived by David.

20:5 tomorrow is the New Moon feast David decides to exploit customary religious practices (see Nu 10:10; 28:11–15).

20:6 to Bethlehem, his hometown David asks Jonathan to lie for him. This is the first character flaw in David that the narrator mentions; he has otherwise been blameless to this point.

20:8 kill me yourself In keeping with their covenant (see 1Sa 18:1–4), David asks Jonathan to kill him if he

knows of any guilt that would merit Saul's wrath. Apparently, neither party considered the proposed lie to be wrong, since it protected an innocent life.

20:11 into the field See 19:3 and note.

20:13 as he has been Jonathan uses the past tense to note God's favorable dealings with Saul. This may also hint at Jonathan's understanding of David's future kingship.

20:14 as long as I live Jonathan realizes that he is endangering his own life by helping David.

20:15 do not ever cut off David honors this covenant even after Jonathan's death. Rather than killing every descendant of Saul, he elevates Jonathan's son Mephibosheth to a position of honor (see 2Sa 9). David also exercises restraint by not killing Mephibosheth after a perceived attempted coup (see 2Sa 16:3; 19:24–30).

20:16 David's enemies Refers to Jonathan's own father—Saul.

20:17 he loved him On the dynamics of Jonathan's love for David, see 1Sa 18:1 and note.

20:25 customary place by the wall Likely located at the head of the table. This would also prevent anyone from approaching the king from behind.

20:26 to make him ceremonially unclean Saul's initial

thought, "Something must have happened to David to make him ceremonially unclean — surely he is unclean." ²⁷But the next day, the second day of the month, David's place was empty again. Then Saul said to his son Jonathan, "Why hasn't the son of Jesse come to the meal, either yesterday or today?"

²⁸Jonathan answered, "David earnestly asked me for permission to go to Bethlehem. ²⁹He said, 'Let me go, because our family is observing a sacrifice in the town and my brother has ordered me to be there. If I have found favor in your eyes, let me get away to see my brothers.' That is why he has not come to the king's table."

³⁰Saul's anger flared up at Jonathan and he said to him, "You son of a perverse and rebellious woman! Don't I know that you have sided with the son of Jesse to your own shame and to the shame of the mother who bore you? ³¹As long as the son of Jesse lives on this earth, neither you nor your kingdom will be established. Now send someone to bring him to me, for he must die!"

³²"Why should he be put to death? What has he done?" Jonathan asked his father. ³³But Saul hurled his spear at him to kill him. Then Jonathan knew that his father intended to kill David.

³⁴Jonathan got up from the table in fierce anger; on that second day of the feast he did not eat, because he was grieved at his father's shameful treatment of David.

³⁵In the morning Jonathan went out to the field for his meeting with David. He had a small boy with him, ³⁶and he said to the boy, "Run and find the arrows I shoot." As the boy ran, he shot an arrow beyond him. ³⁷When the boy came to the place where Jonathan's arrow had fallen, Jonathan called out after him, "Isn't the arrow beyond you?" ³⁸Then he shouted, "Hurry! Go quickly! Don't stop!" The boy picked up the arrow and returned to his master. ³⁹(The boy knew nothing about all this; only Jonathan and David knew.) ⁴⁰Then Jonathan gave his weapons to the boy and said, "Go, carry them back to town."

⁴¹After the boy had gone, David got up from the south side of the stone and bowed down before Jonathan three times, with his face to the ground. Then they kissed each other and wept together — but David wept the most.

⁴²Jonathan said to David, "Go in peace, for we have sworn friendship with each other in the name of the LORD, saying, 'The LORD is witness between you and me, and between your descendants and my descendants forever.'" Then David left, and Jonathan went back to the town.ᵃ

David at Nob

21 ᵇ David went to Nob, to Ahimelek the priest. Ahimelek trembled when he met him, and asked, "Why are you alone? Why is no one with you?"

²David answered Ahimelek the priest, "The king sent me on a mission and said to me, 'No one is to know anything about the mission I am sending you on.' As for my men, I have told them to meet me at a certain place. ³Now then, what do you have on hand? Give me five loaves of bread, or whatever you can find."

⁴But the priest answered David, "I don't have any ordinary bread on hand; however, there is

---

ᵃ 42 In Hebrew texts this sentence (20:42b) is numbered 21:1.
ᵇ In Hebrew texts 21:1-15 is numbered 21:2-16.

---

assessment gives the benefit of the doubt to David. He assumes that David will not violate the Law by attending a festal celebration while ceremonially unclean (see Lev 7:20–21).

20:27 son of Jesse Saul refuses to call David by his name; going forward he uses this moniker to identify David as his enemy (e.g., 1Sa 20:30–31; 22:7–9,13).
20:29 my brother has ordered me Jonathan takes liberties in his response to Saul (compare with v. 6). Apparently David's oldest brother, Eliab, has taken over family leadership responsibilities from their father.
20:30 perverse and rebellious woman In his angry outburst, Saul shames Jonathan's mother, Ahinoam (see 14:50).
20:31 neither you nor your kingdom Saul makes one final appeal to Jonathan's personal security. However, this statement is yet another indictment of Saul's disconnect and paranoia. The kingship has already been taken from him, and it is not his to pass on.
20:33 Saul hurled his spear at him In his delusion and rage, Saul attempts to murder his own son, the crown prince.
20:38 he shouted This is an additional message for David: He needed to leave town quickly.
20:41 they kissed each other A customary ancient Near Eastern sign of familial love, goodwill and friendship used in greetings, farewells and blessings (e.g., Ge

29:13; 31:28; 33:4; Ex 4:27; Ru 1:9; 1Sa 10:1; 2Sa 14:33; Ac 20:37).

21:1–9 In flight from Saul, David stops at Nob to gather supplies. This proves to be a fateful event for the priests there.

21:1 Nob A priestly compound between Gibeah and Jerusalem, similar to the camp of the prophets in Naioth (see 1Sa 19:18 and note). It seems to have become the center of priestly activity in Israel after the destruction of Shiloh (see 4:12 and note). **Ahimelek the priest** The great-grandson of Eli. **trembled** Ahimelek senses that something is out of the ordinary. He surmises that David is a fugitive, and he fears reprisals from Saul for assisting him.
21:2 king sent me David's second lie leads to the slaughter of many innocent people (see 20:6 and note; v. 7; 22:18–22). **my men** David's mention of others traveling with him aims to further convince Ahimelek.
21:3 five loaves of bread David continues the ruse to secure more food and supplies.
21:4 some consecrated bread Refers to the bread of the Presence (see v. 6; Ex 25:30). **kept themselves from women** Indicates the men have not had sexual relations with women, a stipulation often attached to holy war and worship ceremonies (e.g., Ex 19:15). The men needed to be ceremonially clean to eat the holy bread.

some consecrated bread here — provided the men have kept themselves from women."

⁵David replied, "Indeed women have been kept from us, as usual whenever*ᵃ* I set out. The men's bodies are holy even on missions that are not holy. How much more so today!" ⁶So the priest gave him the consecrated bread, since there was no bread there except the bread of the Presence that had been removed from before the LORD and replaced by hot bread on the day it was taken away.

⁷Now one of Saul's servants was there that day, detained before the LORD; he was Doeg the Edomite, Saul's chief shepherd.

⁸David asked Ahimelek, "Don't you have a spear or a sword here? I haven't brought my sword or any other weapon, because the king's mission was urgent."

⁹The priest replied, "The sword of Goliath the Philistine, whom you killed in the Valley of Elah, is here; it is wrapped in a cloth behind the ephod. If you want it, take it; there is no sword here but that one."

David said, "There is none like it; give it to me."

David at Gath

¹⁰That day David fled from Saul and went to Achish king of Gath. ¹¹But the servants of Achish said to him, "Isn't this David, the king of the land? Isn't he the one they sing about in their dances:

" 'Saul has slain his thousands,
  and David his tens of thousands'?"

¹²David took these words to heart and was very much afraid of Achish king of Gath. ¹³So he pretended to be insane in their presence; and while he was in their hands he acted like a madman, making marks on the doors of the gate and letting saliva run down his beard.

¹⁴Achish said to his servants, "Look at the man! He is insane! Why bring him to me? ¹⁵Am I so short of madmen that you have to bring this fellow here to carry on like this in front of me? Must this man come into my house?"

David at Adullam and Mizpah

22 David left Gath and escaped to the cave of Adullam. When his brothers and his father's household heard about it, they went down to him there. ²All those who were in distress or in debt or discontented gathered around him, and he became their commander. About four hundred men were with him.

³From there David went to Mizpah in Moab and said to the king of Moab, "Would you let my

ᵃ 5 Or from us in the past few days since

21:5 men's bodies The Hebrew word used here, *keli*, is a euphemism for sexual organs. The men have not defiled themselves by having sex at a time when abstinence was required.

21:6 bread of the Presence Only priests were allowed to eat the bread of the Presence (Lev 24:9). Jesus later uses this incident to argue that meeting people's needs is more important than focusing on rituals, since the rituals are meant to serve people (see Mt 12:3–4 and parallels).

21:7 detained before the LORD The exact nature of Doeg's detainment is uncertain. He may have been fulfilling a vow, or it may have been related to sin. **Edomite** The descendants of Esau were some of Israel's most hated enemies. Saul had waged war against them (1Sa 14:47); Doeg may have been a prisoner of war. **Saul's chief shepherd** Refers to the royal shepherd. See 9:3 and note. David, the good shepherd, left his sheep in the care of another shepherd when he delivered food to his brothers (see 17:20). Saul entrusts his sheep to a foreigner—one of Israel's most reviled enemies.

21:8 urgent David has to leave quickly and is therefore ill-equipped. However, he still covers up the nature of his hasty retreat.

21:9 sword of Goliath David apparently dedicated the weapon to God in a manner similar to the events of 17:54. **behind the ephod** May describe an idol rather than a priestly garment (compare Jdg 8:27). This would indicate that spiritual corruption in the days of Saul—as in the days of Eli—continued to be widespread. **There is none like it** The sword was unique—perhaps in size, tensile strength, appearance or composition.

21:10–15 Since he has nowhere else to turn, David flees to Philistia. He could have returned home to his enemy, Saul, but instead he decides to take his chances among his other enemies. David only barely escapes.

21:10 Achish king of Gath David flees to his archenemy, Achish, wearing the sword of Achish's dead champion, Goliath, whom David killed.

21:11 David, the king The Philistines probably recognize David as Israel's king because of his military success against them. **David his tens of thousands** See 1Sa 18:7 and note.

21:12 words to heart After hearing these words, David realizes the implications. When this happens, he has to feign madness before the Philistines can take revenge on him. **was very much afraid** See 10:22 and note.

21:13 letting saliva run down his beard Defilement of the beard—particularly with saliva—was a mark of shame and dishonor (see Dt 25:9; Job 17:6; 30:10); no sane Israelite man would do this intentionally.

21:15 Am I so short of madmen This sarcasm is likely meant to be humorous.

22:1–5 After fleeing Gath, David escapes to the cave of Adullam. He then reunites with his family and acquires an army of outcasts and malcontents. Together, they journey to Moab, where David leaves his family in the care of the king. After receiving a warning from the prophet Gad, David enters Judah and hides in the forest.

22:1 Adullam About halfway between Gath and Bethlehem (Ge 38:1; Jos 12:15; Ne 11:30). **his brothers** They probably join their warrior relative because they are also in danger from Saul.

22:2 All those who were in distress Those oppressed or unhappy with Saul's regime. As a result, he amasses a standing army that supports him as king.

father and mother come and stay with you until I learn what God will do for me?" [4]So he left them with the king of Moab, and they stayed with him as long as David was in the stronghold.

[5]But the prophet Gad said to David, "Do not stay in the stronghold. Go into the land of Judah." So David left and went to the forest of Hereth.

Saul Kills the Priests of Nob

[6]Now Saul heard that David and his men had been discovered. And Saul was seated, spear in hand, under the tamarisk tree on the hill at Gibeah, with all his officials standing at his side. [7]He said to them, "Listen, men of Benjamin! Will the son of Jesse give all of you fields and vineyards? Will he make all of you commanders of thousands and commanders of hundreds? [8]Is that why you have all conspired against me? No one tells me when my son makes a covenant with the son of Jesse. None of you is concerned about me or tells me that my son has incited my servant to lie in wait for me, as he does today."

[9]But Doeg the Edomite, who was standing with Saul's officials, said, "I saw the son of Jesse come to Ahimelek son of Ahitub at Nob. [10]Ahimelek inquired of the LORD for him; he also gave him provisions and the sword of Goliath the Philistine." [11]Then the king sent for the priest Ahimelek son of Ahitub and all the men of his family, who were the priests at Nob, and they all came to the king. [12]Saul said, "Listen now, son of Ahitub."

"Yes, my lord," he answered.

[13]Saul said to him, "Why have you conspired against me, you and the son of Jesse, giving him bread and a sword and inquiring of God for him, so that he has rebelled against me and lies in wait for me, as he does today?"

[14]Ahimelek answered the king, "Who of all your servants is as loyal as David, the king's son-in-law, captain of your bodyguard and highly respected in your household? [15]Was that day the first time I inquired of God for him? Of course not! Let not the king accuse your servant or any of his father's family, for your servant knows nothing at all about this whole affair."

[16]But the king said, "You will surely die, Ahimelek, you and your whole family."

[17]Then the king ordered the guards at his side: "Turn and kill the priests of the LORD, because they too have sided with David. They knew he was fleeing, yet they did not tell me."

But the king's officials were unwilling to raise a hand to strike the priests of the LORD.

[18]The king then ordered Doeg, "You turn and strike down the priests." So Doeg the Edomite turned and struck them down. That day he killed eighty-five men who wore the linen ephod. [19]He also put to the sword Nob, the town of the priests, with its men and women, its children and infants, and its cattle, donkeys and sheep.

[20]But one son of Ahimelek son of Ahitub, named Abiathar, escaped and fled to join David. [21]He told David that Saul had killed the priests of the LORD. [22]Then David said to Abiathar, "That day, when Doeg the Edomite was there, I knew he would be sure to tell Saul. I am responsible for the death of your whole family. [23]Stay with me; don't be afraid.

22:4 Moab Located beyond the Jordan, east of the Dead Sea. This area is out of Saul's jurisdiction. Israel and Moab were bitter enemies (see 1Sa 14:47), yet David leaves his family with the king of Moab. Since David is an enemy of Saul, he was an ally to Moab. Additionally, David had Moabite roots; his great-grandmother, Ruth, was from Moab (see Ru 1:4; 4:13,17–18).

22:5 Do not stay If he remained in the stronghold, he would violate the Law by promoting the welfare of the Edomites (see Dt 23:3–6). **forest of Hereth** A hideout for fugitives.

22:6–23 Saul acts sacrilegiously by massacring the priests from Nob because Ahimelek had helped David.

22:6 spear in hand See 1Sa 18:10 and note.
22:7 men of Benjamin Saul appeals to tribal affiliation in an attempt to muster loyalty. **son of Jesse** See 20:27 and note.
22:9 Doeg the Edomite See 21:7 and note. **son of Jesse** In an effort to gain favor with the king, Doeg reports what he perceives as a potential conspiracy against the throne.
22:10 inquired of the LORD Doeg portrays Ahimelek as loyal to David.
22:11 Nob See 21:1 and note.
22:12 son of Ahitub Saul addresses his enemies in this manner (see 20:27 and note).
22:13 rebelled against me Saul accuses Ahimelek of aiding and abetting a rival to the throne. There is

little concern from Saul whether his conclusions are well founded, which attests to his increasing paranoia.
22:14 as loyal as David Ahimelek begins his defense by pointing out the incontrovertible reality that David has been faithful to Saul and his throne.
22:15 the first time I inquired Ahimelek admits to performing his duties as a priest, which included making inquiries for the king and his people. **knows nothing** Ahimelek eventually pleads ignorance.
22:17 kill the priests of the LORD Saul orders the deaths of a group of Levites—God's chosen tribe to fulfill the priestly functions. By doing so, he is virtually indistinguishable from the kings of other nations (compare also 28:3–25). **the king's officials were unwilling** Unlike their king, these servants still fear God.
22:18 strike down the priests Because he is an Edomite, Doeg has no regard for the priests of Israel's God. **eighty-five men** The priests apparently did not resist or fight back. This also fulfills the prophecy against Eli's house in 2:27–36.
22:19 to the sword Ironically, this verse describes the very act Saul failed to accomplish against the Amalekites in ch. 15, and for which he lost the kingdom. However, rather than an anointed Israelite king obliterating a pagan nation, a pagan mercenary obliterates God's anointed priests.
22:20 Abiathar, escaped This begins the fulfillment of 2:33; see 1Ki 2:26.
22:22 I am responsible for the death David admits culpability for this tragedy, which testifies to his maturity and difference from Saul.

The man who wants to kill you is trying to kill me too. You will be safe with me."

David Saves Keilah

23 When David was told, "Look, the Philistines are fighting against Keilah and are looting the threshing floors," ²he inquired of the LORD, saying, "Shall I go and attack these Philistines?"

The LORD answered him, "Go, attack the Philistines and save Keilah."

³But David's men said to him, "Here in Judah we are afraid. How much more, then, if we go to Keilah against the Philistine forces!"

⁴Once again David inquired of the LORD, and the LORD answered him, "Go down to Keilah, for I am going to give the Philistines into your hand." ⁵So David and his men went to Keilah, fought the Philistines and carried off their livestock. He inflicted heavy losses on the Philistines and saved the people of Keilah. ⁶(Now Abiathar son of Ahimelek had brought the ephod down with him when he fled to David at Keilah.)

Saul Pursues David

⁷Saul was told that David had gone to Keilah, and he said, "God has delivered him into my hands, for David has imprisoned himself by entering a town with gates and bars." ⁸And Saul called up all his forces for battle, to go down to Keilah to besiege David and his men.

⁹When David learned that Saul was plotting against him, he said to Abiathar the priest, "Bring the ephod." ¹⁰David said, "LORD, God of Israel, your servant has heard definitely that Saul plans to come to Keilah and destroy the town on account of me. ¹¹Will the citizens of Keilah surrender me to him? Will Saul come down, as your servant has heard? LORD, God of Israel, tell your servant."

And the LORD said, "He will."

¹²Again David asked, "Will the citizens of Keilah surrender me and my men to Saul?"

And the LORD said, "They will."

¹³So David and his men, about six hundred in number, left Keilah and kept moving from place to place. When Saul was told that David had escaped from Keilah, he did not go there.

¹⁴David stayed in the wilderness strongholds and in the hills of the Desert of Ziph. Day after day Saul searched for him, but God did not give David into his hands.

¹⁵While David was at Horesh in the Desert of Ziph, he learned that[a] Saul had come out to take his life. ¹⁶And Saul's son Jonathan went to David at Horesh and helped him find strength in God. ¹⁷"Don't be afraid," he said. "My father Saul will not lay a hand on you. You will be king over Israel, and I will be second to you. Even my father Saul knows this." ¹⁸The two of them made a covenant before the LORD. Then Jonathan went home, but David remained at Horesh.

¹⁹The Ziphites went up to Saul at Gibeah and said, "Is not David hiding among us in the

---

a 15 Or *he was afraid because*

23:1–14 Faced with an opportunity to kill more Philistines, David rescues the city of Keilah. However, learning of Saul's pursuit, he flees from Keilah, thereby diverting Saul's wrath on his troops as well as the city.

23:1 Keilah A city in the territory of the Philistines. **looting the threshing floors** Threshing floors were areas outside the city where people would separate the seeds or kernels of harvested grain from the rest of the stalk. See the infographic "A Threshing Floor" on p. 497. **23:2 he inquired** Based on 1Sa 23:6, Abiathar had fled to David with the ephod, which was used to inquire of Yahweh (see 14:18 and note). If Abiathar was not yet with David at this point, the inquiry may have been done through Gad the prophet (see 22:5). **The LORD answered** Unlike Saul (see 14:37), David receives a response from God.
23:3 we are afraid If they fear the forces of a deranged leader, they certainly would not want to challenge the army of a competent king.
23:4 David inquired of the LORD To instill confidence in his men, David receives confirmation from God that their mission will be successful.
23:7 God has delivered him into my hands A testimony to Saul's delusion. After he has repeatedly disobeyed divine decree and massacred God's priests, he still thinks that God is with him (see 16:14; 22:17–18).
23:8 besiege David Saul's thirteenth attempt to kill David (see 16:21 and note).
23:9 Bring the ephod Like Samuel, and unlike Saul,

David always seeks divine counsel in his decision making; in this case, he seeks it through the ephod.
23:12 They will The inhabitants of Keilah likely know of Saul's action against the city of Nob and fear similar reprisals (see 22:19). To avoid being destroyed by the king, they are willing to hand over David and his men.
23:13 six hundred David's forces had gained an additional 200 men since 22:2.
23:14 strongholds Refers to natural shelters and hiding places in the wilderness, such as caves and outcroppings of rocks. **Desert of Ziph** Located west of the Dead Sea and south of Gibeah and other cities under Saul's control.

23:15–29 Saul continues to pursue David, but he is diverted when the Philistines raid Israelite territory. The narrative describes David's situation as desperate, hinting that his deliverance is due to divine intervention.

23:15 take his life The fourteenth time Saul tries to kill David (see 16:21 and note).
23:16 Jonathan went to David The last recorded meeting between David and Jonathan.
23:17 You will be king Jonathan recognizes that David is God's anointed choice for the kingship of Israel.
23:18 made a covenant The third covenant David and Jonathan make (see 18:3; 20:16).
23:19 The Ziphites went up to Saul The king's destruction of Nob has far-reaching effects (see 22:13,19). The cities within his jurisdiction fear reprisals for harboring David, and they disclose the fugitive's whereabouts. The Keilahites would have done the same thing (see v. 12 and note).

strongholds at Horesh, on the hill of Hakilah, south of Jeshimon? ²⁰Now, Your Majesty, come down whenever it pleases you to do so, and we will be responsible for giving him into your hands."

²¹Saul replied, "The Lord bless you for your concern for me. ²²Go and get more information. Find out where David usually goes and who has seen him there. They tell me he is very crafty. ²³Find out about all the hiding places he uses and come back to me with definite information. Then I will go with you; if he is in the area, I will track him down among all the clans of Judah."

²⁴So they set out and went to Ziph ahead of Saul. Now David and his men were in the Desert of Maon, in the Arabah south of Jeshimon. ²⁵Saul and his men began the search, and when David was told about it, he went down to the rock and stayed in the Desert of Maon. When Saul heard this, he went into the Desert of Maon in pursuit of David.

²⁶Saul was going along one side of the mountain, and David and his men were on the other side, hurrying to get away from Saul. As Saul and his forces were closing in on David and his men to capture them, ²⁷a messenger came to Saul, saying, "Come quickly! The Philistines are raiding the land." ²⁸Then Saul broke off his pursuit of David and went to meet the Philistines. That is why they call this place Sela Hammahlekoth.ᵃ ²⁹And David went up from there and lived in the strongholds of En Gedi.ᵇ

David Spares Saul's Life

24ᶜ After Saul returned from pursuing the Philistines, he was told, "David is in the Desert of En Gedi." ²So Saul took three thousand able young men from all Israel and set out to look for David and his men near the Crags of the Wild Goats.

³He came to the sheep pens along the way; a cave was there, and Saul went in to relieve himself. David and his men were far back in the cave. ⁴The men said, "This is the day the Lord spoke of when he saidᵈ to you, 'I will give your enemy into your hands for you to deal with as you wish.'" Then David crept up unnoticed and cut off a corner of Saul's robe.

⁵Afterward, David was conscience-stricken for having cut off a corner of his robe. ⁶He said to his men, "The Lord forbid that I should do such a thing to my master, the Lord's anointed, or lay my hand on him; for he is the anointed of the Lord." ⁷With these words David sharply rebuked his men and did not allow them to attack Saul. And Saul left the cave and went his way.

⁸Then David went out of the cave and called out to Saul, "My lord the king!" When Saul looked behind him, David bowed down and prostrated himself with his face to the ground. ⁹He said to Saul, "Why do you listen when men say, 'David is bent on harming you'? ¹⁰This day you have seen with your own eyes how the Lord delivered you into my hands in the cave. Some urged me to kill you, but I spared you; I said, 'I will not lay my hand on my lord, because he is the Lord's anointed.' ¹¹See, my father, look at this piece of your robe in my hand! I cut off the corner of your robe but did not kill you. See that there is nothing in my hand to indicate that I am guilty of wrongdoing or rebellion. I have not wronged you, but you are hunting me down to take my life. ¹²May the Lord judge between you and me. And may the Lord avenge the wrongs you have done to me, but my hand will not touch you. ¹³As the old saying goes, 'From evildoers come evil deeds,' so my hand will not touch you.

ᵃ 28 *Sela Hammahlekoth* means *rock of parting.*   ᵇ 29 In Hebrew texts this verse (23:29) is numbered 24:1.   ᶜ In Hebrew texts 24:1-22 is numbered 24:2-23.   ᵈ 4 Or *"Today the Lord is saying*

23:21 The Lord bless you Ironically, Saul pronounces Yahweh's blessing on them for betraying his anointed.

23:26 away from Saul David refused to kill Saul, God's anointed, because he hadn't directed him to do so (see 24:6; 26:11). If God wanted David to be king, he would have removed Saul from the throne.

23:27 a messenger came to Saul The timing suggests divine providence.

23:29 strongholds of En Gedi See v. 14 and note.

24:1–22 Saul resumes his pursuit of David. Though David has an opportunity to kill Saul, he refuses. David then reveals himself to Saul and calls attention to the fact that he didn't act against the king—evidence of his faithfulness and lack of ill will. Saul acknowledges his sin in pursuing David.

24:2 set out to look for David The fifteenth time Saul seeks to kill David (see 16:21 and note).

24:4 give your enemy into your hands This prophecy, perhaps invented by his men, is not recorded in the Bible. **cut off a corner of Saul's robe** Proves that David is close enough to kill Saul. Saul's regnal robe

would have identified him as the king of Israel. David's act may symbolically represent his usurpation of the kingdom. Furthermore, he brings Saul's robe into a state of nonconformity with legal standards (see Nu 15:37–41; Dt 22:12). Therefore, his act may be seen as an invalidation of Saul's kingship.

24:6 Lord's anointed In spite of Saul's behavior toward him, David still respects him as God's anointed. Only God can remove his anointed person (see note on 1Sa 23:26). This will work in David's favor once he assumes the throne.

24:8 My lord the king David uses this phrase, his most exalted address for the king, when he has a chance to kill Saul (compare 26:19). **bowed down and prostrated himself with his face to the ground** David shows proper respect and deference.

24:11 See, my father In contrast to Saul's epithet for David, "son of Jesse" (see 20:27 and note; 20:29 and note), David refers to Saul in a loving and respectful manner.

24:12 Lord judge between you and me David introduces a series of proclamations designed to pronounce his innocence.

24:13 From evildoers David may be saying that if he

¹⁴"Against whom has the king of Israel come out? Who are you pursuing? A dead dog? A flea? ¹⁵May the LORD be our judge and decide between us. May he consider my cause and uphold it; may he vindicate me by delivering me from your hand."

¹⁶When David finished saying this, Saul asked, "Is that your voice, David my son?" And he wept aloud. ¹⁷"You are more righteous than I," he said. "You have treated me well, but I have treated you badly. ¹⁸You have just now told me about the good you did to me; the LORD delivered me into your hands, but you did not kill me. ¹⁹When a man finds his enemy, does he let him get away unharmed? May the LORD reward you well for the way you treated me today. ²⁰I know that you will surely be king and that the kingdom of Israel will be established in your hands. ²¹Now swear to me by the LORD that you will not kill off my descendants or wipe out my name from my father's family."

²²So David gave his oath to Saul. Then Saul returned home, but David and his men went up to the stronghold.

David, Nabal and Abigail

25 Now Samuel died, and all Israel assembled and mourned for him; and they buried him at his home in Ramah. Then David moved down into the Desert of Paran.[a]

²A certain man in Maon, who had property there at Carmel, was very wealthy. He had a thousand goats and three thousand sheep, which he was shearing in Carmel. ³His name was Nabal and his wife's name was Abigail. She was an intelligent and beautiful woman, but her husband was surly and mean in his dealings — he was a Calebite.

⁴While David was in the wilderness, he heard that Nabal was shearing sheep. ⁵So he sent ten young men and said to them, "Go up to Nabal at Carmel and greet him in my name. ⁶Say to him: 'Long life to you! Good health to you and your household! And good health to all that is yours!

⁷"'Now I hear that it is sheep-shearing time. When your shepherds were with us, we did not mistreat them, and the whole time they were at Carmel nothing of theirs was missing. ⁸Ask your own servants and they will tell you. Therefore be favorable toward my men, since we come at a festive time. Please give your servants and your son David whatever you can find for them.'"

⁹When David's men arrived, they gave Nabal this message in David's name. Then they waited.

¹⁰Nabal answered David's servants, "Who is this David? Who is this son of Jesse? Many servants are breaking away from their masters these days. ¹¹Why should I take my bread and water, and the meat I have slaughtered for my shearers, and give it to men coming from who knows where?"

¹²David's men turned around and went back. When they arrived, they reported every word. ¹³David said to his men, "Each of you strap on your sword!" So they did, and David strapped his on as well. About four hundred men went up with David, while two hundred stayed with the supplies.

¹⁴One of the servants told Abigail, Nabal's wife, "David sent messengers from the wilderness to

---

[a] 1 Hebrew and some Septuagint manuscripts; other Septuagint manuscripts *Maon*

---

was really as wicked as Saul thought, he would have killed Saul. Jesus uses a similar maxim in the NT (Mt 12:35; compare Da 12:10; Mt 7:16–20).

24:16 my son Rather than referring to him as "the son of Jesse," he once again claims David as his own son (see 1Sa 24:11 and note).

24:20 you will surely be king This is Saul's first public admission of David's future succession.

24:21 you will not kill off my descendants Saul knew that kings secured their rule by killing other possible claimants to the throne, and he asks David to not act in the usual way. This also resembles the second covenant David made with Jonathan (see 20:15).

24:22 David gave his oath This anticipates his future benevolence toward Mephibosheth (see 20:15 and note).

25:1 Now Samuel died Samuel dies just after Saul has come to terms with God's judgment on him (announced by Samuel in 13:14) and David's becoming king.

25:2–44 On a festal day, David sends some of his servants to collect a gift of food from a local landowner. David and his men had protected the wealthy man's shepherds and flocks while they were pasturing the sheep in the wilderness. In return, David seeks some remuneration for his services. When the wealthy man refuses David's request, David and 400 men set out to destroy his estate. However, the man's wife intercedes, provides them with food and pleads for mercy. David

obliges and blesses the woman. God then judges the wealthy man, and David takes his widow to be his wife.

25:2 at Carmel Refers to a Judahite town, not Mount Carmel (Jos 15:55; 1Sa 15:12). **which he was shearing** Preparation for the upcoming festival.

25:3 Nabal Means "fool." **he was a Calebite** Most translations render the Hebrew phrase used here as "he was a Calebite.", but some translate "he was as his heart." There is a difference between what is written in the Hebrew and how it has traditionally been read. "As his heart" is what is written, and "Calebite" is how it is traditionally read. The name "Calebite" may indicate that Nabal is a descendant of Caleb, one of the faithful spies (Nu 13–14) whose inheritance was in the area of Hebron, where this story takes place (Jos 14:13–14; 15:13). Also, since the Hebrew name Caleb (*kalev*) sounds similar to the Hebrew word for "dog" (*kelev*), this may be a play on words that indicates both Nabal's ancestry and his churlish character—dogs were viewed negatively in ancient Israel.

25:7 we did not mistreat them Indicates that they treated the shepherds well (see 1Sa 25:15–16).

25:10 Who is this David Nabal implies that David is insignificant. He also uses Saul's adversarial nickname for David, "son of Jesse" (see 20:27 and note). **breaking away** Nabal equates David with a runaway slave.

give our master his greetings, but he hurled insults at them. [15]Yet these men were very good to us. They did not mistreat us, and the whole time we were out in the fields near them nothing was missing. [16]Night and day they were a wall around us the whole time we were herding our sheep near them. [17]Now think it over and see what you can do, because disaster is hanging over our master and his whole household. He is such a wicked man that no one can talk to him."

[18]Abigail acted quickly. She took two hundred loaves of bread, two skins of wine, five dressed sheep, five seahs[a] of roasted grain, a hundred cakes of raisins and two hundred cakes of pressed figs, and loaded them on donkeys. [19]Then she told her servants, "Go on ahead; I'll follow you." But she did not tell her husband Nabal.

[20]As she came riding her donkey into a mountain ravine, there were David and his men descending toward her, and she met them. [21]David had just said, "It's been useless — all my watching over this fellow's property in the wilderness so that nothing of his was missing. He has paid me back evil for good. [22]May God deal with David,[b] be it ever so severely, if by morning I leave alive one male of all who belong to him!"

[23]When Abigail saw David, she quickly got off her donkey and bowed down before David with her face to the ground. [24]She fell at his feet and said: "Pardon your servant, my lord, and let me speak to you; hear what your servant has to say. [25]Please pay no attention, my lord, to that wicked man Nabal. He is just like his name — his name means Fool, and folly goes with him. And as for me, your servant, I did not see the men my lord sent. [26]And now, my lord, as surely as the LORD your God lives and as you live, since the LORD has kept you from bloodshed and from avenging yourself with your own hands, may your enemies and all who are intent on harming my lord be like Nabal. [27]And let this gift, which your servant has brought to my lord, be given to the men who follow you.

[28]"Please forgive your servant's presumption. The LORD your God will certainly make a lasting dynasty for my lord, because you fight the LORD's battles, and no wrongdoing will be found in you as long as you live. [29]Even though someone is pursuing you to take your life, the life of my lord will be bound securely in the bundle of the living by the LORD your God, but the lives of your enemies he will hurl away as from the pocket of a sling. [30]When the LORD has fulfilled for my lord every good thing he promised concerning him and has appointed him ruler over Israel, [31]my lord will not have on his conscience the staggering burden of needless bloodshed or of having avenged himself. And when the LORD your God has brought my lord success, remember your servant."

[32]David said to Abigail, "Praise be to the LORD, the God of Israel, who has sent you today to meet me. [33]May you be blessed for your good judgment and for keeping me from bloodshed this day and from avenging myself with my own hands. [34]Otherwise, as surely as the LORD, the God of Israel, lives, who has kept me from harming you, if you had not come quickly to meet me, not one male belonging to Nabal would have been left alive by daybreak."

[35]Then David accepted from her hand what she had brought him and said, "Go home in peace. I have heard your words and granted your request."

[36]When Abigail went to Nabal, he was in the house holding a banquet like that of a king. He was in high spirits and very drunk. So she told him nothing at all until daybreak. [37]Then in the

---

[a] 18 That is, probably about 60 pounds or about 27 kilograms
[b] 22 Some Septuagint manuscripts; Hebrew with David's enemies

---

25:16 herding our sheep In addition to being a good shepherd himself, David was a protector of shepherds. See 9:3 and note.

25:21 evil for good Nabal's actions reflect Saul's (see 24:17). In response to David's protection, Nabal demeaned David (see v. 10).

25:22 alive one male The Hebrew euphemism used here refers to someone who urinates against a wall. It is a term of contempt used in the Hebrew text of the OT to refer to the killing of complete annihilation of groups of men (e.g., 1Ki 16:11; 21:21; 2Ki 9:8).

25:23 with her face to the ground See 1Sa 24:8 and note.

25:24 Pardon your servant She assumes responsibility for her husband's actions, perhaps assuming that David will not exact revenge on a woman.

25:26 kept you from bloodshed If David had carried out his revenge on Nabal, countless innocent people would have died, and David would have been guilty (had bloodguilt) before God (see Ex 23:7).

25:28 a lasting dynasty May reveal her confidence in David's future kingship.

25:29 pocket of a sling Alludes to David's victory over Goliath (see 1Sa 17:49).

25:31 needless bloodshed Such a flagrant transgression may have undermined his qualification for kingship. See v. 26 and note. **the LORD your God has brought my lord success** Abigail anticipates that David will do the right thing and be rewarded, so she requests that he remember her. **remember your servant** Perhaps a proposal for marriage, if the previous clause refers to Nabal.

25:32 sent you today David sees Abigail's interception as divine intervention that keeps him from incurring bloodguilt (see v. 33).

25:33 May you be blessed for your good judgment See v. 3, where Abigail is noted for her discretion. Here, David admits his fault in attempting to take vengeance on Nabal.

25:34 one male See v. 22 and note.

25:37 his heart failed him The exact illness that befalls Nabal is unclear; it may have been a coma, stroke or heart attack. **became like a stone** Nabal does not die at this time (v. 38).

morning, when Nabal was sober, his wife told him all these things, and his heart failed him and he became like a stone. [38]About ten days later, the LORD struck Nabal and he died.

[39]When David heard that Nabal was dead, he said, "Praise be to the LORD, who has upheld my cause against Nabal for treating me with contempt. He has kept his servant from doing wrong and has brought Nabal's wrongdoing down on his own head."

Then David sent word to Abigail, asking her to become his wife. [40]His servants went to Carmel and said to Abigail, "David has sent us to you to take you to become his wife."

[41]She bowed down with her face to the ground and said, "I am your servant and am ready to serve you and wash the feet of my lord's servants." [42]Abigail quickly got on a donkey and, attended by her five female servants, went with David's messengers and became his wife. [43]David had also married Ahinoam of Jezreel, and they both were his wives. [44]But Saul had given his daughter Michal, David's wife, to Paltiel[a] son of Laish, who was from Gallim.

David Again Spares Saul's Life

26 The Ziphites went to Saul at Gibeah and said, "Is not David hiding on the hill of Hakilah, which faces Jeshimon?"

[2]So Saul went down to the Desert of Ziph, with his three thousand select Israelite troops, to search there for David. [3]Saul made his camp beside the road on the hill of Hakilah facing Jeshimon, but David stayed in the wilderness. When he saw that Saul had followed him there, [4]he sent out scouts and learned that Saul had definitely arrived.

[5]Then David set out and went to the place where Saul had camped. He saw where Saul and Abner son of Ner, the commander of the army, had lain

down. Saul was lying inside the camp, with the army encamped around him.

[6]David then asked Ahimelek the Hittite and Abishai son of Zeruiah, Joab's brother, "Who will go down into the camp with me to Saul?"

"I'll go with you," said Abishai.

[7]So David and Abishai went to the army by night, and there was Saul, lying asleep inside the camp with his spear stuck in the ground near his head. Abner and the soldiers were lying around him.

[8]Abishai said to David, "Today God has delivered your enemy into your hands. Now let me pin him to the ground with one thrust of the spear; I won't strike him twice."

[9]But David said to Abishai, "Don't destroy him! Who can lay a hand on the LORD's anointed and be guiltless? [10]As surely as the LORD lives," he said, "the LORD himself will strike him, or his time will come and he will die, or he will go into battle and perish. [11]But the LORD forbid that I should lay a hand on the LORD's anointed. Now get the spear and water jug that are near his head, and let's go."

[12]So David took the spear and water jug near Saul's head, and they left. No one saw or knew about it, nor did anyone wake up. They were all sleeping, because the LORD had put them into a deep sleep.

[13]Then David crossed over to the other side and stood on top of the hill some distance away; there was a wide space between them. [14]He called out to the army and to Abner son of Ner, "Aren't you going to answer me, Abner?"

Abner replied, "Who are you who calls to the king?"

[15]David said, "You're a man, aren't you? And who is like you in Israel? Why didn't you guard your lord the king? Someone came to destroy your

---

a 44 Hebrew Palti, a variant of Paltiel

25:38 the LORD struck Nabal David interprets this act as divine judgment for Nabal's insult against God's anointed.
25:43 Ahinoam of Jezreel This Ahinoam—the mother of David's oldest son, Amnon (2Sa 3:2)—is different from Saul's wife in 1Sa 14:50.
25:44 to Paltiel After threatening the princess (1Sa 19:17), Saul gave Michal to another man. David apparently did not consent to the divorce (2Sa 3:13–16).
26:1–25 This account shares several similarities with 1Sa 23:19—24:22. The narrative likely includes this retelling to emphasize David's piety. Despite having two opportunities to kill his pursuer, David refuses to kill God's anointed. The main difference between these chapters is that here, David ventures into Saul's camp rather than encountering him in a cave.
26:1 Ziphites went to Saul The Ziphites had given away David's position once before; see 23:19.
26:2 search there for David This is the sixteenth time Saul tries to kill David (see 16:21 and note).
26:3 David stayed in the wilderness During Saul's

ongoing pursuit of him, David and his men took refuge in the wilderness regions of Judah. See 23:29; 24:1.
26:5 Saul was lying inside the camp This location provided Saul with the most protection while he slept.
26:7 spear stuck in the ground Compare 18:10 and note.
26:8 with one thrust of the spear David could kill Saul with the same weapon that Saul repeatedly used to try to kill him.
26:9 lay a hand on the LORD's anointed See 24:6 and note.
26:10 he will go into battle David insists that God will be the orchestrator of Saul's death. This statement foreshadows 31:1–6.
26:12 LORD had put them into a deep sleep God allows David to succeed, further testimony that he is with him (see 16:13).
26:13 other side David stands in the opposite direction of his forces so that, if Saul attacks, David's men will not be initially overrun; they could pursue from behind.
wide space between them Gives David time to retreat if necessary.
26:15 your lord the king See 24:8 and note.

lord the king. ¹⁶What you have done is not good. As surely as the LORD lives, you and your men must die, because you did not guard your master, the LORD's anointed. Look around you. Where are the king's spear and water jug that were near his head?"

¹⁷Saul recognized David's voice and said, "Is that your voice, David my son?"

David replied, "Yes it is, my lord the king." ¹⁸And he added, "Why is my lord pursuing his servant? What have I done, and what wrong am I guilty of? ¹⁹Now let my lord the king listen to his servant's words. If the LORD has incited you against me, then may he accept an offering. If, however, people have done it, may they be cursed before the LORD! They have driven me today from my share in the LORD's inheritance and have said, 'Go, serve other gods.' ²⁰Now do not let my blood fall to the ground far from the presence of the LORD. The king of Israel has come out to look for a flea — as one hunts a partridge in the mountains."

²¹Then Saul said, "I have sinned. Come back, David my son. Because you considered my life precious today, I will not try to harm you again. Surely I have acted like a fool and have been terribly wrong."

²²"Here is the king's spear," David answered. "Let one of your young men come over and get it. ²³The LORD rewards everyone for their righteousness and faithfulness. The LORD delivered you into my hands today, but I would not lay a hand on the LORD's anointed. ²⁴As surely as I valued your life today, so may the LORD value my life and deliver me from all trouble."

²⁵Then Saul said to David, "May you be blessed, David my son; you will do great things and surely triumph."

So David went on his way, and Saul returned home.

David Among the Philistines

27 But David thought to himself, "One of these days I will be destroyed by the hand of Saul. The best thing I can do is to escape to the land of the Philistines. Then Saul will give up searching for me anywhere in Israel, and I will slip out of his hand."

²So David and the six hundred men with him left and went over to Achish son of Maok king of Gath. ³David and his men settled in Gath with Achish. Each man had his family with him, and David had his two wives: Ahinoam of Jezreel and Abigail of Carmel, the widow of Nabal. ⁴When Saul was told that David had fled to Gath, he no longer searched for him.

⁵Then David said to Achish, "If I have found favor in your eyes, let a place be assigned to me in one of the country towns, that I may live there. Why should your servant live in the royal city with you?"

⁶So on that day Achish gave him Ziklag, and it has belonged to the kings of Judah ever since. ⁷David lived in Philistine territory a year and four months.

⁸Now David and his men went up and raided the Geshurites, the Girzites and the Amalekites. (From ancient times these peoples had lived in the land extending to Shur and Egypt.) ⁹Whenever David attacked an area, he did not leave a man or woman alive, but took sheep and cattle, donkeys and camels, and clothes. Then he returned to Achish.

¹⁰When Achish asked, "Where did you go raiding today?" David would say, "Against the Negev of Judah" or "Against the Negev of Jerahmeel" or "Against the Negev of the Kenites." ¹¹He did not leave a man or woman alive to be brought to Gath, for he thought, "They might inform on us and say, 'This is what David did.'" And such was his

---

26:17 David my son See 24:16 and note.

27:1–12 David again flees to the king of the Philistines for asylum (see 21:10–15). However, unlike his previous venture, he arrives in Gath with a standing army. Achish gives David and his company a city to live in, and they make raids on the surrounding cities and villages. Achish is unaware of David's actions, thinking he has become a true enemy of Israel.

27:1 Saul will give up By going to the Philistines, Saul would cease to pursue him.

27:2 six hundred men The first time David went to Gath, he was either alone or accompanied by a few soldiers (apparently no more than five people; see 21:3). Now, he is accompanied by his army and has little reason to fear Achish or the forces in Gath (see 21:12; 22:1).

27:3 the widow of Nabal Refers to Abigail; the author of 1–2 Samuel frequently refers to her in this manner (e.g., 30:5; 2Sa 2:2; 3:3).

27:4 he no longer searched for him David's plan to rid himself of Saul's pursuit is successful.

27:5 country towns A location on the fringe of Philistine territory allows David to accomplish his goals without Achish knowing (1Sa 27:8–9,11).

27:6 Ziklag Located north of Beersheba (see 3:20 and note), close to the southernmost border of Israel.

27:7 a year and four months During this 16-month respite from Saul's attacks, David must wait for God to carry out his purposes with regard to the rejected king.

27:8 the Geshurites, the Girzites and the Amalekites Israel should have exterminated these ancient enemies during their conquest of the promised land (see Dt 20:16–17). David is thus fulfilling the Law and does not incur bloodguilt for their deaths (compare 1Sa 25:26 and note). With regard to the Amalekites, David's actions against them accomplish what Saul did not (see ch. 15).

27:9 he did not leave a man or woman alive Prevents anyone from reporting back to Achish (v. 11).

27:10 Against the Negev David lies, claiming that he has been raiding the southern desert territories of Judah or specific Judahite clans. Achish, who appears thoroughly enamored with David throughout the remainder of the narrative, believes his lie (v. 12).

practice as long as he lived in Philistine territory. ¹²Achish trusted David and said to himself, "He has become so obnoxious to his people, the Israelites, that he will be my servant for life."

28 In those days the Philistines gathered their forces to fight against Israel. Achish said to David, "You must understand that you and your men will accompany me in the army."

²David said, "Then you will see for yourself what your servant can do."

Achish replied, "Very well, I will make you my bodyguard for life."

Saul and the Medium at Endor

³Now Samuel was dead, and all Israel had mourned for him and buried him in his own town of Ramah. Saul had expelled the mediums and spiritists from the land.

⁴The Philistines assembled and came and set up camp at Shunem, while Saul gathered all Israel and set up camp at Gilboa. ⁵When Saul saw the Philistine army, he was afraid; terror filled his heart. ⁶He inquired of the Lord, but the Lord did not answer him by dreams or Urim or prophets. ⁷Saul then said to his attendants, "Find me a woman who is a medium, so I may go and inquire of her."

"There is one in Endor," they said.

⁸So Saul disguised himself, putting on other clothes, and at night he and two men went to the woman. "Consult a spirit for me," he said, "and bring up for me the one I name."

⁹But the woman said to him, "Surely you know what Saul has done. He has cut off the mediums and spiritists from the land. Why have you set a trap for my life to bring about my death?"

¹⁰Saul swore to her by the Lord, "As surely as the Lord lives, you will not be punished for this."

¹¹Then the woman asked, "Whom shall I bring up for you?"

"Bring up Samuel," he said.

¹²When the woman saw Samuel, she cried out at the top of her voice and said to Saul, "Why have you deceived me? You are Saul!"

¹³The king said to her, "Don't be afraid. What do you see?"

The woman said, "I see a ghostly figure[a] coming up out of the earth."

¹⁴"What does he look like?" he asked.

"An old man wearing a robe is coming up," she said.

Then Saul knew it was Samuel, and he bowed

---

a 13 Or see spirits; or see gods

28:1–2 In these verses, Achish falsely assumes that since David has been raiding the Israelites, he will fight against them in battle. David agrees to do so before the narrative is interrupted in 29:3, making readers wait to see how David will escape this predicament.

28:2 you will see David is intentionally ambiguous. Achish correctly perceives that David is referring to his skill in obliterating his enemies. However, he incorrectly perceives the identity of David's true enemies. As in 23:26; 24:6; 26:9; and 27:8–12, David will not strike God's anointed or kill his people. David probably would have followed Achish into battle and then turned on the Philistines as the fight ensued. **make you my bodyguard** The Hebrew phrase used here, which is literally rendered as "keeper of my head," may allude to the Goliath incident (compare 17:51–54, where David "kept" Goliath's severed head).

28:3–25 Yahweh had stopped communicating with Saul because of Saul's sin (16:14). Under threat of Philistine invasion, Saul now seeks divine counsel before battle — an ironic act, since Saul rarely inquired of God earlier in the narrative. With no prophet or word from God, Saul violates the Law and consults a medium. In the encounter with the medium, the prophet Samuel appears. Apparently, God allowed this to happen so that he could pronounce a death sentence on Saul and his sons. This is the final demonstration of Saul's true character — he is a king like those of all the other nations (compare 8:20). This episode further justifies Saul's rejection from the kingship and David's accession to power.

28:3 Samuel was dead The mentioning of the dead prophet sets up the narrative that follows and prepares the reader for Samuel's reappearance. See 25:1. **mediums and spiritists** Those who allegedly communicate

with the spirits of the dead. Saul may have acted at Samuel's urging, which would make the encounter in vv. 12–19 more ironic. The Law demands that mediums and necromancers, as well as Israelites who seek their services, are to be killed (see Lev 19:31; 20:6,27; Dt 18:10–12). Saul does not follow the Law completely; he had cast the mediums out of the land but hadn't put them to death.

28:4 Shunem This site was in the Jezreel Valley in the north of Israel, and was part of the tribal allotment of Issachar (Jos 19:17–18). See 2Ki 4:8 and note. **Gilboa** Mount Gilboa was on the south side of the Jezreel Valley, about ten miles away from Shunem.

28:5 he was afraid See 1Sa 10:22 and note.

28:6 Lord did not answer him Saul had earlier attempted to inquire of Yahweh; compare 14:37. **Urim** See note on 14:18.

28:7 in Endor The servants apparently knew exactly where to find the nearest medium.

28:8 on other clothes Refers to garments other than his regnal robes (see 24:4 and note).

28:10 by the Lord Ironically, the king invokes God's covenant name to assure the medium that she will not be punished for breaking God's covenant.

28:11 Bring up Samuel Samuel was apparently famous enough that his title, lineage or hometown did not need to be mentioned.

28:12 she cried out The medium seems surprised to see Samuel. This is perhaps an indication that God brought about his appearance, not the medium.

28:13 I see a ghostly figure The Hebrew word used here is *elohim*, which is often translated as "God" or "gods." Samuel looks like a divine being.

28:14 face to the ground Saul assumes a position that communicates his complete submission.

down and prostrated himself with his face to the ground.

¹⁵Samuel said to Saul, "Why have you disturbed me by bringing me up?"

"I am in great distress," Saul said. "The Philistines are fighting against me, and God has departed from me. He no longer answers me, either by prophets or by dreams. So I have called on you to tell me what to do."

¹⁶Samuel said, "Why do you consult me, now that the LORD has departed from you and become your enemy? ¹⁷The LORD has done what he predicted through me. The LORD has torn the kingdom out of your hands and given it to one of your neighbors — to David. ¹⁸Because you did not obey the LORD or carry out his fierce wrath against the Amalekites, the LORD has done this to you today. ¹⁹The LORD will deliver both Israel and you into the hands of the Philistines, and tomorrow you and your sons will be with me. The LORD will also give the army of Israel into the hands of the Philistines."

²⁰Immediately Saul fell full length on the ground, filled with fear because of Samuel's words. His strength was gone, for he had eaten nothing all that day and all that night.

²¹When the woman came to Saul and saw that he was greatly shaken, she said, "Look, your servant has obeyed you. I took my life in my hands and did what you told me to do. ²²Now please listen to your servant and let me give you some food so you may eat and have the strength to go on your way."

²³He refused and said, "I will not eat."

But his men joined the woman in urging him, and he listened to them. He got up from the ground and sat on the couch.

²⁴The woman had a fattened calf at the house, which she butchered at once. She took some flour, kneaded it and baked bread without yeast. ²⁵Then she set it before Saul and his men, and they ate. That same night they got up and left.

Achish Sends David Back to Ziklag

29 The Philistines gathered all their forces at Aphek, and Israel camped by the spring in Jezreel. ²As the Philistine rulers marched with their units of hundreds and thousands, David and his men were marching at the rear with Achish. ³The commanders of the Philistines asked, "What about these Hebrews?"

Achish replied, "Is this not David, who was an officer of Saul king of Israel? He has already been with me for over a year, and from the day he left Saul until now, I have found no fault in him."

⁴But the Philistine commanders were angry with Achish and said, "Send the man back, that he may return to the place you assigned him. He must not go with us into battle, or he will turn against us during the fighting. How better could he regain his master's favor than by taking the heads of our own men? ⁵Isn't this the David they sang about in their dances:

"'Saul has slain his thousands,
and David his tens of thousands'?"

⁶So Achish called David and said to him, "As surely as the LORD lives, you have been reliable, and I would be pleased to have you serve with me in the army. From the day you came to me until today, I have found no fault in you, but the rulers don't approve of you. ⁷Now turn back and

---

28:16 departed from you This may refer to the Spirit of Yahweh being withdrawn (see 16:14 and note). It could also refer to Saul's perpetual failures and hardships.

28:17 given it to one of your neighbors Compare 13:14; 15:28 and note.

28:18 carry out his fierce wrath Saul's inability to carry out God's judgment on the Amalekites had lasting repercussions. See 15:1–3.

28:19 you and your sons Recalls the fate of Eli and his sons (3:13–14; 4:11,18). **with me** This phrase probably refers to their death or their presence in Sheol, the place of the dead (see Ge 37:35 and note).

28:20 filled with fear See 1Sa 10:22 and note. **eaten nothing** Saul has apparently fasted for his encounter with Samuel as a display of piety. Ironically, he abstains from food to demonstrate his fervent religious reflection in preparation for heinously violating the Law, continuing the theme of selective obedience in his life.

29:1–11 The Philistines are mounting another attack on the Israelite forces. When the Philistines learn that their king, Achish, has taken David with him into battle (see 28:2), they demand that Achish send David back to Ziklag. The king obliges, giving David an alibi for any accusations that he aided the Philistine attack.

29:1 Aphek Resumes the story from 28:2. This is the second time in 1 Samuel the Philistines have gathered their forces at Aphek (4:1).

29:2 Philistine rulers See 5:8 and note. **at the rear** The perfect position for a surprise attack. In the midst of the battle, David and his 600 troops could attack the king from behind while Saul engaged them at the front battle line.

29:3 these Hebrews The Philistines typically referred to the Israelites as Hebrews (4:6,9; 13:3,19; 14:11). **no fault in him** Like Eli and Saul, Achish is not a good judge of character.

29:4 the place you assigned him Refers to Ziklag (1Sa 27:6). **he will turn** Understandably, they were cautious that David would turn on them and fight for Israel. The last time Israelites were in the Philistine ranks, they did switch sides during the battle (14:21). **heads of our own men** Perhaps an allusion to David's taking of Goliath's head in 17:51–54 (compare 28:2 and note). As with the Philistine giant, David would give the heads of these Philistines to King Saul, winning back his favor.

29:6 As surely as the LORD lives Israel's greatest enemy uses the covenant name of Israel's God, Yahweh. Either David persuaded Achish to become a follower of Yahweh, or Achish is making a vow in the name of David's God out of courtesy to David. **you have been reliable** An ironic statement in light of 27:8–12. David had thoroughly deceived Achish.

go in peace; do nothing to displease the Philistine rulers."

[8] "But what have I done?" asked David. "What have you found against your servant from the day I came to you until now? Why can't I go and fight against the enemies of my lord the king?"

[9] Achish answered, "I know that you have been as pleasing in my eyes as an angel of God; nevertheless, the Philistine commanders have said, 'He must not go up with us into battle.' [10] Now get up early, along with your master's servants who have come with you, and leave in the morning as soon as it is light."

[11] So David and his men got up early in the morning to go back to the land of the Philistines, and the Philistines went up to Jezreel.

David Destroys the Amalekites

30 David and his men reached Ziklag on the third day. Now the Amalekites had raided the Negev and Ziklag. They had attacked Ziklag and burned it, [2] and had taken captive the women and everyone else in it, both young and old. They killed none of them, but carried them off as they went on their way.

[3] When David and his men reached Ziklag, they found it destroyed by fire and their wives and sons and daughters taken captive. [4] So David and his men wept aloud until they had no strength left to weep. [5] David's two wives had been captured — Ahinoam of Jezreel and Abigail, the widow of Nabal of Carmel. [6] David was greatly distressed because the men were talking of stoning him;

each one was bitter in spirit because of his sons and daughters. But David found strength in the LORD his God.

[7] Then David said to Abiathar the priest, the son of Ahimelek, "Bring me the ephod." Abiathar brought it to him, [8] and David inquired of the LORD, "Shall I pursue this raiding party? Will I overtake them?"

"Pursue them," he answered. "You will certainly overtake them and succeed in the rescue."

[9] David and the six hundred men with him came to the Besor Valley, where some stayed behind. [10] Two hundred of them were too exhausted to cross the valley, but David and the other four hundred continued the pursuit.

[11] They found an Egyptian in a field and brought him to David. They gave him water to drink and food to eat — [12] part of a cake of pressed figs and two cakes of raisins. He ate and was revived, for he had not eaten any food or drunk any water for three days and three nights.

[13] David asked him, "Who do you belong to? Where do you come from?"

He said, "I am an Egyptian, the slave of an Amalekite. My master abandoned me when I became ill three days ago. [14] We raided the Negev of the Kerethites, some territory belonging to Judah and the Negev of Caleb. And we burned Ziklag."

[15] David asked him, "Can you lead me down to this raiding party?"

He answered, "Swear to me before God that you will not kill me or hand me over to my master, and I will take you down to them."

29:8 my lord the king David uses this title of Saul elsewhere in 1 Samuel (24:8; 26:17). It is possible that he was being intentionally ambiguous, and that Saul was the king he had in mind here. He wants to fight against Saul's enemies: the Philistines.

29:11 David and his men got up early in the morning to go back This plot point distances David from the scene of Saul's death.

30:1–15 While the Philistine forces were away, Amalekite raiders pillaged Ziklag. On their return (see 29:9–11), David and his men find their city burned and their families gone (30:1–3). God confirms that David should pursue the raiders.

30:1 on the third day Following Achish's dismissing David from Aphek (29:9–11). Aphek was located approximately 50 miles north of Ziklag. **Amalekites had raided** They may have acted in retaliation (compare 27:8). On the continued presence of the Amalekites, see note on 15:8. **Ziklag** See 27:6 and note.

30:2 They killed none of them They simply took them as spoils of war.

30:5 widow of Nabal See 27:3 and note.

30:6 talking of stoning him They perceived that David's plan to beguile the Philistines caused their loss. **the LORD his God** Here, Yahweh is called David's God. In contrast, Saul refers to Yahweh as Samuel's God (compare 15:15, 21, 30). This is the book's final comparison between righteous David and wicked Saul. Saul disregarded the Law

while David obeyed it. Saul inquired of a dead prophet while David inquired of Yahweh himself. Saul consulted a medium while David consulted a priest. Saul received a message of death and destruction while David receives a message of life and victory.

30:7 ephod David uses the ephod to inquire of Yahweh and receives his confirmation to pursue his enemies and rescue his men's families. See 14:18 and note.

30:8 You will certainly overtake them and succeed in the rescue This assurance strengthens David to lead his men even though they are doubting him.

30:10 too exhausted They have been traveling continuously for several days. Many of them are likely traveling on foot and carrying equipment.

30:13 My master abandoned me Being too sick, the raiders left him behind.

30:14 We raided He was part of the marauding horde that sacked Ziklag as well as much of southern Israel. **Kerethites** The identity of this ethnic group is unknown, though they appear to have been closely related to the Philistines and may have been one of the Sea Peoples (see note on 4:1; Eze 25:16; Zep 2:5). When David became king, Kerethites became part of his personal guard (2Sa 8:18; 15:18; 1Ki 1:38,44).

30:15 before God The Hebrew word used here, *elohim*, is plural and can refer to the God, Yahweh or the gods. Since this Egyptian is likely not a follower of Yahweh, and probably does not know of David's God Yahweh, the Egyptian is probably making an oath before the gods.

[16]He led David down, and there they were, scattered over the countryside, eating, drinking and reveling because of the great amount of plunder they had taken from the land of the Philistines and from Judah. [17]David fought them from dusk until the evening of the next day, and none of them got away, except four hundred young men who rode off on camels and fled. [18]David recovered everything the Amalekites had taken, including his two wives. [19]Nothing was missing: young or old, boy or girl, plunder or anything else they had taken. David brought everything back. [20]He took all the flocks and herds, and his men drove them ahead of the other livestock, saying, "This is David's plunder."

[21]Then David came to the two hundred men who had been too exhausted to follow him and who were left behind at the Besor Valley. They came out to meet David and the men with him. As David and his men approached, he asked them how they were. [22]But all the evil men and troublemakers among David's followers said, "Because they did not go out with us, we will not share with them the plunder we recovered. However, each man may take his wife and children and go."

[23]David replied, "No, my brothers, you must not do that with what the LORD has given us. He has protected us and delivered into our hands the raiding party that came against us. [24]Who will listen to what you say? The share of the man who stayed with the supplies is to be the same as that of him who went down to the battle. All will share alike." [25]David made this a statute and ordinance for Israel from that day to this.

[26]When David reached Ziklag, he sent some of the plunder to the elders of Judah, who were his friends, saying, "Here is a gift for you from the plunder of the LORD's enemies."

[27]David sent it to those who were in Bethel, Ramoth Negev and Jattir; [28]to those in Aroer, Siphmoth, Eshtemoa [29]and Rakal; to those in the towns of the Jerahmeelites and the Kenites; [30]to those in Hormah, Bor Ashan, Athak [31]and Hebron; and to those in all the other places where he and his men had roamed.

Saul Takes His Life
31:1-13pp — 2Sa 1:4-12; 1Ch 10:1-12

31 Now the Philistines fought against Israel; the Israelites fled before them, and many fell dead on Mount Gilboa. [2]The Philistines were in hot pursuit of Saul and his sons, and they killed his sons Jonathan, Abinadab and Malki-Shua. [3]The fighting grew fierce around Saul, and when the archers overtook him, they wounded him critically.

[4]Saul said to his armor-bearer, "Draw your sword and run me through, or these uncircumcised fellows will come and run me through and abuse me."

But his armor-bearer was terrified and would not do it; so Saul took his own sword and fell on it. [5]When the armor-bearer saw that Saul was dead, he too fell on his sword and died with him. [6]So Saul and his three sons and his armor-bearer and all his men died together that same day.

[7]When the Israelites along the valley and those across the Jordan saw that the Israelite army had fled and that Saul and his sons had died, they abandoned their towns and fled. And the Philistines came and occupied them.

[8]The next day, when the Philistines came to

30:16–31 The abandoned Egyptian takes David and his forces to the Amalekite raiders. In fulfillment of God's word in 1Sa 30:8, David and his men defeat their enemies, rescue their families, and recover all of their stolen property.

30:17 except four hundred young men Apparently, the enemy force is much larger than David's; the narrative does not indicate that 400 escapees is a large number. David's success despite the disparity in army size shows the divine nature of his mission. See the table "Battles of Saul and David" on p. 433.

30:18 David recovered everything the Amalekites had taken By recovering the families, David restores the confidence of his men in his ability to lead and deliver.

30:20 This is David's plunder He later gives this these spoils as gifts to those who supported him during his wanderings (see vv. 26–31).

30:22 evil men and troublemakers among David's followers The Hebrew phrase used here is derogatory and similar to the phrase used at 2:22, signaling that some of David's company deserved their derided reputations.

30:24 All will share alike David accords those who protect the baggage with equal honor and spoils.

30:26 his friends Refers to those who were kind to him and provided for him while he fled from Saul (see v. 31).

30:31 roamed Since they consumed the resources of the land wherever they roamed, David pays back the landowners for their support.

31:1–13 In fulfillment of Samuel's prophecy (see 28:19), Saul and his sons engage the Philistines in battle and are killed. The era of Saul draws to a close with their defeat at the hands of Israel's archenemy. In the wake of Saul's death, the narrative sets the stage for David's monarchy and Israel's finest hour.

31:4 these uncircumcised A pejorative title that Israel used to refer to the Philistines. Compare 14:6 and note; 17:26,36. **abuse me** In the ancient Near East, enemies often tortured captured royalty or high-ranking military officials as a display of superiority.

31:5 he too fell on his sword Perhaps he also feared being tortured and saw escape as unattainable.

31:6 Saul and his three sons and his armor-bearer and all his men died Fulfills 28:19. For a parallel account, see 1Ch 10:1–6.

31:8 they found Saul Armies usually promptly removed their slain dignitaries from the battlefield, but here, no one was left to take care of the bodies.

strip the dead, they found Saul and his three sons fallen on Mount Gilboa. ⁹They cut off his head and stripped off his armor, and they sent messengers throughout the land of the Philistines to proclaim the news in the temple of their idols and among their people. ¹⁰They put his armor in the temple of the Ashtoreths and fastened his body to the wall of Beth Shan.

¹¹When the people of Jabesh Gilead heard what the Philistines had done to Saul, ¹²all their valiant men marched through the night to Beth Shan. They took down the bodies of Saul and his sons from the wall of Beth Shan and went to Jabesh, where they burned them. ¹³Then they took their bones and buried them under a tamarisk tree at Jabesh, and they fasted seven days.

31:9 cut off his head According to 1Ch 10:10, the Philistines fastened Saul's head to the temple of Dagon. Ironically, they replaced the head of their decapitated god with that of the king whose God decapitated Dagon (see 1Sa 5:4).

31:10 in the temple of the Ashtoreths Spoils of war were often deposited in the victor's temple, as in 5:2. The Philistines do to Saul what David had done to Goliath (21:9).

31:11 people of Jabesh Gilead Saul delivered these inhabitants in his only crowning achievement as king (see 11:1–11). As a Benjamite, he may have been linked genealogically with them (compare Jdg 21:10–14).

31:12 where they burned them This is not a normal Israelite custom. They may have done this to prevent further shame or desecration to the corpses.

2 SAMUEL

INTRODUCTION TO 2 SAMUEL

Second Samuel continues where 1 Samuel left off. Although David is a significant figure in 1 Samuel, that book focuses on Israel's last judge, Samuel, and Israel's first king, Saul. In 2 Samuel, the attention is on David and his relationships with Yahweh and with other people. God establishes a covenant with David, promising that his throne will be established forever (2Sa 7). Even when David commits horrendous sins, the covenant stands. Throughout 2 Samuel, as all others fail, Yahweh's faithfulness is profoundly seen, as are the painful effects of sin on sinners, those around them and those whom they lead.

BACKGROUND

Samuel himself does not appear in 2 Samuel; the book is named after him because 1–2 Samuel are a single book in the Hebrew Bible. As such, 1–2 Samuel may be outlined and understood as one narrative reflecting the same perspective (see the "Introduction to 1 Samuel").

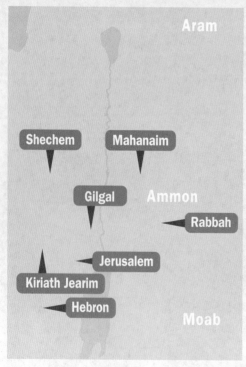

This map depicts some of the major locations related to 2 Samuel.

The events recorded in 2 Samuel date to the late eleventh and early tenth centuries BC. During this period, life in Israel and neighboring regions became less rural and more urban. A stronger Israelite monarchy under David likely brought some regional stability, though not until later in his reign.

STRUCTURE

First Samuel contains two cycles of stories about Samuel and Saul. Second Samuel presents a third cycle about David, beginning with his rise to kingship after Saul's death. This third cycle, which takes up the entirety of 2 Samuel, can be divided into three sections.

In the first section (chs. 1–10), things go well with David. He establishes his rule, first over the tribe of Judah (chs. 1–4) and then over all of Israel (chs. 5–10). He brings the ark of the covenant to Jerusalem (ch. 6). Yahweh then establishes his everlasting covenant with David (ch. 7). David shows kindness to Saul's grandson Mephibosheth, and his army defeats various enemies (chs. 9–10).

In the second section (chs. 11–20), David falls into sin, and things go drastically wrong. The problems start when David, who is home while his men are at war, commits adultery with Bathsheba. He then has her husband killed in battle so he can marry her (ch. 11). When the Prophet Nathan confronts David, he repents, but the effects of his sins are already at work (ch. 12). First, Bathsheba and David's son dies (12:15–25). After this, violence overtakes David's household (chs. 13–14). One son, Absalom, begins a revolt that drives David into hiding and ends with Absalom's death (chs. 15–19). The section concludes by recounting the rebellion of Sheba (ch. 20).

The third section (chs. 21–24) deals with the later part of David's reign. It includes a song by David praising God for rescuing him (ch. 22) and a poem identified as David's last words (23:1–7). In the final chapter, David conducts an unauthorized census, and Yahweh punishes Israel for this by sending a plague that kills 70,000 Israelites (ch. 24). David's death and final decisions as king are recorded in 1Ki 1:1—2:12; he hands his kingdom over to Bathsheba and his second son, Solomon.

OUTLINE

- David reigns over Judah (2Sa 1:1—4:12)
- David reigns over the united Israel (5:1—10:19)
- David's sins and their consequences (11:1—20:26)
- The conclusion of David's reign (21:1—24:25)

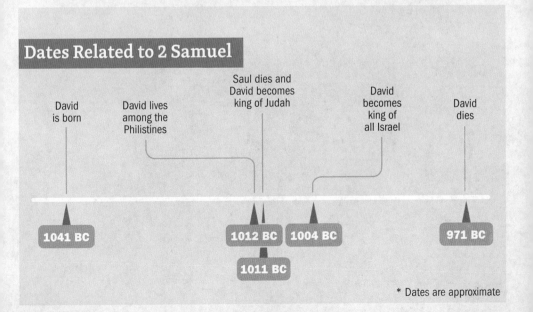

Dates Related to 2 Samuel

| David is born | David lives among the Philistines | Saul dies and David becomes king of Judah | David becomes king of all Israel | David dies |

| 1041 BC | | 1012 BC | 1004 BC | 971 BC |

1011 BC

* Dates are approximate

THEMES

The fast-paced and often heartbreaking narrative of 2 Samuel shows how a person's connection to Yahweh affects their ability to lead, as does each decision they make. After David becomes king over the united Israel, he has the ark of the covenant—which signified Yahweh's presence—brought to Jerusalem, and the city becomes the central site for Israel's worship (6:1–19). David intends to build a "house" (temple) for Yahweh, but Yahweh has other plans (ch. 7). He tells David not to build him a house (temple), but that he will build a house (royal dynasty) for David instead.

In his sin, David squanders this beautiful relationship. But Yahweh still shows unfailing love for David. At the end of the book, David seeks to restore his relationship with Yahweh by building an altar in Jerusalem at a threshing floor—the place where Yahweh stops the plague that is destroying Israel (24:16–25). It is David's son, Solomon, who later builds Yahweh's house, the temple, at this site (2Ch 3:1)—fulfilling one part of Yahweh's promise to David (2Sa 7:12–13).

The eternal nature of Yahweh's promise to David is fulfilled in the birth of Jesus, who is from David's line (Mt 1:1). Second Samuel shows that while people may sin and ruin their lives in the process, Yahweh is loyal—offering eternal relationship with him via Jesus.

David Hears of Saul's Death

1:4-12pp — 1Sa 31:1-13; 1Ch 10:1-12

1 After the death of Saul, David returned from striking down the Amalekites and stayed in Ziklag two days. ²On the third day a man arrived from Saul's camp with his clothes torn and dust on his head. When he came to David, he fell to the ground to pay him honor.

³"Where have you come from?" David asked him.

He answered, "I have escaped from the Israelite camp."

⁴"What happened?" David asked. "Tell me."

"The men fled from the battle," he replied. "Many of them fell and died. And Saul and his son Jonathan are dead."

⁵Then David said to the young man who brought him the report, "How do you know that Saul and his son Jonathan are dead?"

⁶"I happened to be on Mount Gilboa," the young man said, "and there was Saul, leaning on his spear, with the chariots and their drivers in hot pursuit. ⁷When he turned around and saw me, he called out to me, and I said, 'What can I do?'

⁸"He asked me, 'Who are you?'

"'An Amalekite,' I answered.

⁹"Then he said to me, 'Stand here by me and kill me! I'm in the throes of death, but I'm still alive.'

¹⁰"So I stood beside him and killed him, because I knew that after he had fallen he could not survive. And I took the crown that was on his head and the band on his arm and have brought them here to my lord."

¹¹Then David and all the men with him took hold of their clothes and tore them. ¹²They mourned and wept and fasted till evening for Saul and his son Jonathan, and for the army of the LORD and for the nation of Israel, because they had fallen by the sword.

¹³David said to the young man who brought him the report, "Where are you from?"

"I am the son of a foreigner, an Amalekite," he answered.

¹⁴David asked him, "Why weren't you afraid to lift your hand to destroy the LORD's anointed?"

¹⁵Then David called one of his men and said, "Go, strike him down!" So he struck him down, and he died. ¹⁶For David had said to him, "Your blood be on your own head. Your own mouth testified against you when you said, 'I killed the LORD's anointed.'"

1:1–16 Second Samuel continues the narrative begun in 1 Samuel—the two books were originally one work in antiquity as a 200 BC manuscript from the Dead Sea Scrolls shows. Following his successful mission against the Amalekite raiders (1Sa 30:17–20), David returns to rebuild Ziklag. Three days later, a young man arrives with a report from the war between the Israelites and Philistines (1Sa 31). David learns of Saul's death, ca. 1011 BC, and kills the man claiming to be responsible for ending Saul's life.

1:1 death of Saul See 1Sa 31:4–5,8–13. **striking down the Amalekites** See 1Sa 30:17–20. **Ziklag** See 1Sa 30:1–6,26.

1:2 clothes torn and dust on his head Traditional signs of mourning. **to David** The narrative may provide details on David's distance from the battle in order to avoid any implication that David had a part in Saul's death. See note on 1Sa 29:11. **to pay him honor** See 1Sa 24:8 and note.

1:4 What happened David's inquiry suggests that he anticipates a negative report. Given the words that follow, David is concerned about the lives of Saul and Jonathan.

1:5 How do you know Word of mouth will not suffice; he desires eyewitness details as further confirmation.

1:6 I happened to be The young man's story conflicts with 1Sa 31 at several points, including whether the young man killed Saul or Saul killed himself (1Sa 31:4). The young man may be attempting to deliver what he believes will be good news to David for the sake of gaining a reward. **Mount Gilboa** Though it appears that much of the battle took place there (1Sa 31:1), the young man's claim may be false.

1:8 An Amalekite Ironically, in this account Saul orders an Amalekite to kill him. Earlier, he disobeyed Yahweh by failing to kill the Amalekite king (see 1Sa 15).

1:9 kill me First Samuel 31:4 indicates that Saul asked his armor-bearer to kill him. Saul's armor-bearer also killed himself after seeing that Saul was dead (1Sa 31:5).

1:10 crown The crown and the armband were symbols of kingship. If the Amalekite was lying in his account of Saul's death, he may have taken these off Saul's body after he was dead. **brought them here** The young man expects a reward; he does not anticipate David's reaction or the fact that he would consider this to be bad news.

1:11 tore them A sign of mourning and extreme anguish.

1:12 fasted In addition to being an act of religious devotion, fasting can also serve as a sign of mourning (compare Ne 1:4; Mt 9:15).

1:13 son of a foreigner Indicates he is a resident alien, a Gentile who was incorporated into the Israelite community (Lev 19:33–34). As a resident alien, he is under the same obligation as the rest of the members of the covenant community to honor Yahweh's anointed. As an Amalekite, he is a sworn enemy of Israel (see 1Sa 15).

1:14 destroy the LORD's anointed See note on 1Sa 23:26; 24:6 and note.

1:15 and he died David's soldier kills the young man for killing Yahweh's anointed. David may have been attempting to establish a precedent with regard to the treatment of Yahweh's anointed, as well as making it clear that he had no hand in Saul's death. This aligns with David's overall viewpoint on Saul—that he respects Saul's position as Yahweh's anointed but not Saul himself (1Sa 24:6; 26:8–9). However, David had previously indicated that he desired to fight against the Israelites himself and had even referred to a Philistine as lord and king (1Sa 29:8).

1:16 on your own head The young man is guilty and must accept his punishment. He, not David, is responsible for his own death.

David's Lament for Saul and Jonathan

¹⁷David took up this lament concerning Saul and his son Jonathan, ¹⁸and he ordered that the people of Judah be taught this lament of the bow (it is written in the Book of Jashar):

¹⁹"A gazelle*ᵃ* lies slain on your heights, Israel.
How the mighty have fallen!

²⁰"Tell it not in Gath,
proclaim it not in the streets of Ashkelon,
lest the daughters of the Philistines be glad,
lest the daughters of the uncircumcised
rejoice.

²¹"Mountains of Gilboa,
may you have neither dew nor rain,
may no showers fall on your terraced
fields.ᵇ
For there the shield of the mighty was
despised,
the shield of Saul — no longer rubbed
with oil.

²²"From the blood of the slain,
from the flesh of the mighty,
the bow of Jonathan did not turn back,
the sword of Saul did not return
unsatisfied.

²³Saul and Jonathan —
in life they were loved and admired,
and in death they were not parted.
They were swifter than eagles,
they were stronger than lions.

²⁴"Daughters of Israel,
weep for Saul,
who clothed you in scarlet and finery,
who adorned your garments with
ornaments of gold.

²⁵"How the mighty have fallen in battle!
Jonathan lies slain on your heights.

²⁶I grieve for you, Jonathan my brother;
you were very dear to me.
Your love for me was wonderful,
more wonderful than that
of women.

²⁷"How the mighty have fallen!
The weapons of war have perished!"

David Anointed King Over Judah

2 In the course of time, David inquired of the LORD. "Shall I go up to one of the towns of Judah?" he asked.

The LORD said, "Go up."

David asked, "Where shall I go?"

"To Hebron," the LORD answered.

²So David went up there with his two wives, Ahinoam of Jezreel and Abigail, the widow of Nabal of Carmel. ³David also took the men who were with him, each with his family, and they settled in Hebron and its towns. ⁴Then the men of Judah came to Hebron, and there they anointed David king over the tribe of Judah.

When David was told that it was the men from Jabesh Gilead who had buried Saul, ⁵he sent messengers to them to say to them, "The LORD bless you for showing this kindness to Saul your master by burying him. ⁶May the LORD now show you kindness and faithfulness, and I too will show you the same favor because you have done this. ⁷Now then, be strong and brave, for Saul your master is dead, and the people of Judah have anointed me king over them."

ᵃ *19 Gazelle* here symbolizes a human dignitary.   ᵇ *21 Or / nor fields that yield grain for offerings*

1:17–27 Rather than celebrating the death of his enemy, David composes a lamentation for Saul. David also mourns the loss of his dearest friend, Jonathan, his ally and confidant during these turbulent years. He remembers both men for their valor and strength in battle, identifying them as mighty men who accomplished great things for the nation of Israel.

1:18 Book of Jashar A lost book, most likely a collection of Israelite poetry (compare Jos 10:13).

1:19 gazelle Refers to Saul and Jonathan. **How the mighty have fallen** The narrative repeats this refrain three times for emphasis (2Sa 1:25,27).

1:20 Tell it not in Gath Gath and Ashkelon were two of the main cities of the Philistines (see note on 1Sa 5:8). David cannot bear to think of Philistines celebrating Saul's death. **the uncircumcised** See 1Sa 14:6 and note.

1:21 Mountains of Gilboa The location where Saul and Jonathan were slain (1Sa 31:1).

1:24 clothed you in scarlet and finery Saul's reign appears to have been a time of economic success and prosperity for Israel.

1:26 Your love for me See note on 2Sa 1:17–27; 1Sa 18:1 and note.

2:1–7 Following the death of Saul, David asks Yahweh if he should go into the territory of Judah to begin consolidating his kingdom. Yahweh advises him to do so, and the people of Judah anoint David as their king.

2:1 inquired of the LORD David probably seeks Yahweh's counsel through Abiathar's ephod (see 1Sa 14:18 and note; 23:9–12; 30:7–8). **Shall I go up** David asks Yahweh whether he should begin his tenure as king. **Hebron** Hebron was a city of refuge in the territory of Judah (Jos 21:13) and part of the inheritance of Caleb (Jos 14:14; 15:13; Jdg 1:20). In the time of the patriarchs, it was called Kiriath Arba (see Ge 23:2 and note).

2:2 Ahinoam of Jezreel See 1Sa 25:43 and note. **widow of Nabal** See 1Sa 27:3 and note.

2:3 men who were with him All the disenfranchised men who gravitated toward David. See 1Sa 22:2; 23:13.

2:4 anointed David king This anointing serves as a public confirmation of his kingship to the people of Judah. Compare 1Sa 16:13. **men from Jabesh Gilead** See 1Sa 31:11–13.

2:7 be strong In a wise political move, David pronounces a blessing on Saul's most ardent followers in hopes of gaining their support.

War Between the Houses of David and Saul

3:2-5pp — 1Ch 3:1-4

[8] Meanwhile, Abner son of Ner, the commander of Saul's army, had taken Ish-Bosheth son of Saul and brought him over to Mahanaim. [9] He made him king over Gilead, Ashuri and Jezreel, and also over Ephraim, Benjamin and all Israel.

[10] Ish-Bosheth son of Saul was forty years old when he became king over Israel, and he reigned two years. The tribe of Judah, however, remained loyal to David. [11] The length of time David was king in Hebron over Judah was seven years and six months.

[12] Abner son of Ner, together with the men of Ish-Bosheth son of Saul, left Mahanaim and went to Gibeon. [13] Joab son of Zeruiah and David's men went out and met them at the pool of Gibeon. One group sat down on one side of the pool and one group on the other side.

[14] Then Abner said to Joab, "Let's have some of the young men get up and fight hand to hand in front of us."

"All right, let them do it," Joab said.

[15] So they stood up and were counted off — twelve men for Benjamin and Ish-Bosheth son of Saul, and twelve for David. [16] Then each man grabbed his opponent by the head and thrust his dagger into his opponent's side, and they fell down together. So that place in Gibeon was called Helkath Hazzurim.[a]

[17] The battle that day was very fierce, and Abner and the Israelites were defeated by David's men.

[18] The three sons of Zeruiah were there: Joab, Abishai and Asahel. Now Asahel was as fleet-footed as a wild gazelle. [19] He chased Abner, turning neither to the right nor to the left as he pursued him. [20] Abner looked behind him and asked, "Is that you, Asahel?"

"It is," he answered.

[21] Then Abner said to him, "Turn aside to the right or to the left; take on one of the young men and strip him of his weapons." But Asahel would not stop chasing him.

---

[a] 16 *Helkath Hazzurim* means *field of daggers* or *field of hostilities.*

2:8–11 Abner, Saul's cousin and the commander of his army (1Sa 14:50–51), initially rejects David's claim to kingship and installs Saul's son, Ish-Bosheth as king of Israel.

2:8 Abner son of Ner Saul's cousin. Abner's father Ner was Saul's uncle, the brother of Saul's father Kish (see 1Sa 10:14; 14:50). See the people diagram "King Saul's Family Tree" on p. 428. **Ish-Bosheth** One of Saul's remaining sons — three of Saul's sons were killed by the Philistines at the battle of Mount Gilboa (1Sa 31:1–2; compare 2Sa 21:5–9). It appears that Ish-Bosheth was now the rightful heir to the throne, according to progeny based kingship. Abner is attempting to keep Saul's dynasty intact. Ish-Bosheth is called Esh-Baal in 1 Chronicles (see 1Ch 8:33 and note; 9:39) and also may be the same person as the Ishvi mentioned in 1Sa 14:49. **Mahanaim** Located in the region east of the Jordan River where support for Saul's dynasty appeared to be strongest.

2:10 he reigned two years Compare 1Sa 13:1 and note.

2:11 seven years and six months Ish-Bosheth's two-year reign is included in this summary statement. David appears to have been the only ruler in Israel for a period of five years and six months; this period took place prior to his moving the capital city to Jerusalem (see 2Sa 5:5–10).

2:12–32 The remainder of this chapter recounts a period of bitter war between the houses of Saul and David. Ultimately, the rivals call a temporary truce, and peace is restored in Israel.

2:12 Gibeon Located in Benjamite territory, among those loyal to Saul's dynasty (compare Jos 21:17; 1Sa 9:1–2). See the table "Battles of Saul and David" on p. 433.

2:13 Joab A son of Zeruiah, David's sister (1Ch 2:13–16). He was the head of David's army (2Sa 20:23; 1Ch 27:34).

2 Samuel 2:13

JOAB

Joab and his two brothers — Abishai and Asahel — were crucial to David's consolidation efforts. With Joab at the helm, they established David's military power and killed his enemies as David brought the kingdom under his control. Despite his familial connection with the king, Joab fell into disrepute after wrongly avenging the death of his youngest brother, Asahel (see 2Sa 3:22–39). Later, he killed David's rebellious son, Absalom, against David's command (see 18:14); he also killed David's nephew, Amasa (see 17:25 and note; 19:13; 20:10). On his deathbed, David ordered his son, Solomon, to assassinate Joab (see 1Ki 2:5–6,28–35).

2:14 fight hand to hand in front of us They apparently call the young men to compete in representative combat, similar to the Goliath incident (see 1Sa 17:4 and note).

2:16 they fell down together Simultaneous mortal wounds. All 24 men die in the contest. **Helkath Hazzurim** The Hebrew phrase used here means "Field of the Sword Edges" or "Field of Blades." The place name commemorates this unusual and tragic event.

2:18 Joab, Abishai and Asahel David's nephews (sons of his sister Zeruiah) and brothers of Joab (1Ch 2:13–16).

2:19 turning neither to the right nor to the left Asahel pursues Abner with singular focus.

2:21 take on one of the young men Abner encourages Asahel to fight someone else, apparently convinced that he is better prepared to win against another man. Asahel may have been able to run quickly because he lacked armor and weaponry, whereas Abner appears to have been heavily armed. Abner encourages Asahel to arm himself with equipment taken from a defeated combatant, perhaps attempting to level the playing field.

²²Again Abner warned Asahel, "Stop chasing me! Why should I strike you down? How could I look your brother Joab in the face?"

²³But Asahel refused to give up the pursuit; so Abner thrust the butt of his spear into Asahel's stomach, and the spear came out through his back. He fell there and died on the spot. And every man stopped when he came to the place where Asahel had fallen and died.

²⁴But Joab and Abishai pursued Abner, and as the sun was setting, they came to the hill of Ammah, near Giah on the way to the wasteland of Gibeon. ²⁵Then the men of Benjamin rallied behind Abner. They formed themselves into a group and took their stand on top of a hill.

²⁶Abner called out to Joab, "Must the sword devour forever? Don't you realize that this will end in bitterness? How long before you order your men to stop pursuing their fellow Israelites?"

²⁷Joab answered, "As surely as God lives, if you had not spoken, the men would have continued pursuing them until morning."

²⁸So Joab blew the trumpet, and all the troops came to a halt; they no longer pursued Israel, nor did they fight anymore.

²⁹All that night Abner and his men marched through the Arabah. They crossed the Jordan, continued through the morning hours*a* and came to Mahanaim.

³⁰Then Joab stopped pursuing Abner and assembled the whole army. Besides Asahel, nineteen of David's men were found missing. ³¹But David's men had killed three hundred and sixty Benja-

mites who were with Abner. ³²They took Asahel and buried him in his father's tomb at Bethlehem. Then Joab and his men marched all night and arrived at Hebron by daybreak.

3 The war between the house of Saul and the house of David lasted a long time. David grew stronger and stronger, while the house of Saul grew weaker and weaker.

²Sons were born to David in Hebron:

His firstborn was Amnon the son of Ahinoam of Jezreel;

³his second, Kileab the son of Abigail the widow of Nabal of Carmel;

the third, Absalom the son of Maakah daughter of Talmai king of Geshur;

⁴the fourth, Adonijah the son of Haggith;

the fifth, Shephatiah the son of Abital;

⁵and the sixth, Ithream the son of David's wife Eglah.

These were born to David in Hebron.

Abner Goes Over to David

⁶During the war between the house of Saul and the house of David, Abner had been strengthening his own position in the house of Saul. ⁷Now Saul had had a concubine named Rizpah daughter of Aiah. And Ish-Bosheth said to Abner, "Why did you sleep with my father's concubine?"

⁸Abner was very angry because of what Ish-Bosheth said. So he answered, "Am I a dog's head—on Judah's side? This very day I am loyal to the

a 29 See Septuagint; the meaning of the Hebrew for this phrase is uncertain.

2:22 could I look your brother Joab in the face Abner does not want to be responsible for killing the brother of his rival general, Joab. He probably understands that reprisals will follow.

2:23 butt of his spear Asahel is behind Abner, about to overtake him. Abner probably means to keep Asahel at a distance, not to kill him, since he uses the blunted end of the spear rather than the blade. **the spear came out through his back** Attesting to the violence of the wound. This does not appear to be Abner's original intention (2Sa 2:22). **stopped** The people are probably shocked at the death of their leader and surprised at the manner in which he dies.

2:24 Joab and Abishai They pursue him in order to exact revenge for their brother's death; this is exactly what Abner was trying to avoid (see v. 22 and note).

2:28 they no longer pursued Israel Abner and Joab agree to call a temporary end to their civil war.

2:31 three hundred and sixty Benjamites who were with Abner Abner lost 18 times more men than David did.

3:1–25 Ish-Bosheth accuses Abner—who is Saul's cousin and loyal to Saul's dynasty—of having sex with one of Saul's concubines. Outraged, Abner abandons his loyalty to Saul's son and offers to help David consolidate all of Israel under his authority. The two agree, and David honors Abner's efforts with a feast. This is a critical moment for David, since Abner was also Saul's army commander.

3:1 David grew stronger The writer implies that Yahweh is with David and against Saul's house.

3:2 Sons were born to David in Hebron For the parallel account, see 1Ch 3:1–4.

3:6 Abner had been strengthening Indicates that Abner, Saul's cousin (see 2Sa 2:8 and note) is growing in political authority and military power.

3:7 a concubine This refers to a secondary wife who had a lower status than a regular wife. The patriarchs Abraham (Ge 25:6) and Jacob (Ge 30:1–13) had concubines, and the practice continued into Israel's early monarchy (e.g., 2Sa 5:13; 1Ki 11:3). **Ish-Bosheth** Saul's son who succeeded Saul as king of Israel. See 2Sa 2:8 and note. **did you sleep with** The Hebrew word used here is a common verb for coming in or going in, which can be a euphemism for sex. Sleeping with the wife or concubine of a past king was a public signal of an attempt to usurp the throne (e.g., 16:21–22). Ish-Bosheth is accusing Abner of an attempted coup.

3:8 Abner was very angry The narrative never reveals whether Ish-Bosheth's accusation is true. However, Abner is so offended that he immediately switches loyalties; the man whom he helped to inherit Saul's throne (2:8–9) now accuses him of subversion. **a dog's head** First and Second Samuel contain frequent comparisons to dogs that are meant to be degrading (e.g., 1Sa 17:43; 24:14; 2Sa 9:8; 16:9).

house of your father Saul and to his family and friends. I haven't handed you over to David. Yet now you accuse me of an offense involving this woman! [9]May God deal with Abner, be it ever so severely, if I do not do for David what the LORD promised him on oath [10]and transfer the kingdom from the house of Saul and establish David's throne over Israel and Judah from Dan to Beersheba." [11]Ish-Bosheth did not dare to say another word to Abner, because he was afraid of him.

[12]Then Abner sent messengers on his behalf to say to David, "Whose land is it? Make an agreement with me, and I will help you bring all Israel over to you."

[13]"Good," said David. "I will make an agreement with you. But I demand one thing of you: Do not come into my presence unless you bring Michal daughter of Saul when you come to see me." [14]Then David sent messengers to Ish-Bosheth son of Saul, demanding, "Give me my wife Michal, whom I betrothed to myself for the price of a hundred Philistine foreskins."

[15]So Ish-Bosheth gave orders and had her taken away from her husband Paltiel son of Laish. [16]Her husband, however, went with her, weeping behind her all the way to Bahurim. Then Abner said to him, "Go back home!" So he went back.

[17]Abner conferred with the elders of Israel and said, "For some time you have wanted to make David your king. [18]Now do it! For the LORD promised David, 'By my servant David I will rescue my people Israel from the hand of the Philistines and from the hand of all their enemies.'"

[19]Abner also spoke to the Benjamites in person. Then he went to Hebron to tell David everything that Israel and the whole tribe of Benjamin wanted to do. [20]When Abner, who had twenty men with him, came to David at Hebron, David prepared a feast for him and his men. [21]Then Abner said to David, "Let me go at once and assemble all Israel for my lord the king, so that they may make a covenant with you, and that you may rule over all that your heart desires." So David sent Abner away, and he went in peace.

Joab Murders Abner

[22]Just then David's men and Joab returned from a raid and brought with them a great deal of plunder. But Abner was no longer with David in Hebron, because David had sent him away, and he had gone in peace. [23]When Joab and all the soldiers with him arrived, he was told that Abner son of Ner had come to the king and that the king had sent him away and that he had gone in peace.

[24]So Joab went to the king and said, "What have you done? Look, Abner came to you. Why did you let him go? Now he is gone! [25]You know Abner son of Ner; he came to deceive you and observe your movements and find out everything you are doing."

[26]Joab then left David and sent messengers after Abner, and they brought him back from the cistern at Sirah. But David did not know it. [27]Now when Abner returned to Hebron, Joab took him aside into an inner chamber, as if to speak with him privately. And there, to avenge the blood of his brother Asahel, Joab stabbed him in the stomach, and he died.

[28]Later, when David heard about this, he said, "I and my kingdom are forever innocent before the LORD concerning the blood of Abner son of

---

3:9 May God deal with Abner Compare 1Sa 3:17 and note. **what the LORD promised him on oath** Offended, Abner pronounces his allegiance to David.

3:10 transfer the kingdom from the house of Saul Military commanders held great power, as they held the army's loyalty. **from Dan to Beersheba** See 1Sa 3:20 and note.

3:11 he was afraid of him Reminiscent of his father, Saul (see 1Sa 10:22 and note).

3:13 Michal daughter of Saul Refers to David's first wife, who loved David and had previously saved his life (1Sa 18:20; 19:12–17). Saul had ultimately given Michal to another man (1Sa 25:44).

3:14 Ish-Bosheth son of Saul It is unclear why Ish-Bosheth is involved in this process, especially since Abner is working for David. It is possible that only a king could make such a demand, or perhaps he was involved through his status as Michal's brother. **a hundred Philistine foreskins** Since David and Michal had not been divorced and the bride price (or its equivalent) had not been returned to him, they were still married (see 1Sa 18:25).

3:17 you have wanted to make David your king The ease with which the rest of the kingdom is transferred to David suggests that some leaders likely preferred David as king.

3:21 he went in peace Though Abner had killed David's nephew, Asahel (see 2Sa 2:18 and note; 2:23), David and Abner are now on friendly terms.

3:22 Joab David's nephew and the brother of Asahel, whom Abner had killed. See 2:18–23; note on 2:18.

3:25 came to deceive you Joab suspects the worst of his rival general, but Abner's intentions are pure. Joab is likely trying to turn David against Abner.

3:26–30 Without David's knowledge, Joab pursues and kills Abner. The narrative indicates that David is innocent in the matter.

3:27 stabbed him Joab kills Abner in the same way that Abner killed his brother, Asahel—by stabbing him in the stomach (see 2:23 and note). According to the Law, Joab was not supposed to kill Abner to avenge his brother. Asahel's death was not premeditated, and Abner is in a designated city of refuge (Jos 21:13; compare Nu 35:9–28). However, Joab—functioning illegitimately as the "avenger of blood"—ignores the sanctity of Hebron as a city of refuge and slays Abner there. David harshly condemns Joab for disregarding the Law and unjustifiably murdering Abner.

3:28 I and my kingdom are forever innocent Indicates that David had no knowledge of the plan to kill Abner and hadn't sanctioned the murder.

Ner. ²⁹May his blood fall on the head of Joab and on his whole family! May Joab's family never be without someone who has a running sore or leprosyᵃ or who leans on a crutch or who falls by the sword or who lacks food."

³⁰(Joab and his brother Abishai murdered Abner because he had killed their brother Asahel in the battle at Gibeon.)

³¹Then David said to Joab and all the people with him, "Tear your clothes and put on sackcloth and walk in mourning in front of Abner." King David himself walked behind the bier. ³²They buried Abner in Hebron, and the king wept aloud at Abner's tomb. All the people wept also.

³³The king sang this lament for Abner:

"Should Abner have died as the lawless die?
³⁴   Your hands were not bound,
        your feet were not fettered.
You fell as one falls before the wicked."

And all the people wept over him again. ³⁵Then they all came and urged David to eat something while it was still day; but David took an oath, saying, "May God deal with me, be it ever so severely, if I taste bread or anything else before the sun sets!"

³⁶All the people took note and were pleased; indeed, everything the king did pleased them. ³⁷So on that day all the people there and all Israel knew that the king had no part in the murder of Abner son of Ner.

³⁸Then the king said to his men, "Do you not realize that a commander and a great man has fallen in Israel this day? ³⁹And today, though I am the anointed king, I am weak, and these sons of Zeruiah are too strong for me. May the LORD repay the evildoer according to his evil deeds!"

Ish-Bosheth Murdered

4 When Ish-Bosheth son of Saul heard that Abner had died in Hebron, he lost courage, and all Israel became alarmed. ²Now Saul's son had two men who were leaders of raiding bands. One was named Baanah and the other Rekab; they were sons of Rimmon the Beerothite from the tribe of Benjamin — Beeroth is considered part of Benjamin, ³because the people of Beeroth fled to Gittaim and have resided there as foreigners to this day.

⁴(Jonathan son of Saul had a son who was lame in both feet. He was five years old when the news about Saul and Jonathan came from Jezreel. His nurse picked him up and fled, but as she hurried to leave, he fell and became disabled. His name was Mephibosheth.)

⁵Now Rekab and Baanah, the sons of Rimmon

ᵃ 29 The Hebrew for *leprosy* was used for various diseases affecting the skin.

3:29 May his blood fall on the head of Joab David pronounces a rather broad curse on Joab. However, he leaves it to his son, Solomon, to kill him (see 1Ki 2:5–6,28–35). David may restrain himself because Joab's mother is his sister, or because as commander of the army Joab is simply too useful to kill. **a running sore or leprosy** Refers to those who are ceremonially unclean. The constituent parts of the curse have a similar function to the curses that befall the enemies of Yahweh in Dt 28:15–68. **a crutch** This Hebrew word could refer to a crutch or staff, in which case this curse would refer to physical disability. However it could also refer to a distaff or spindle. If that is the case, this is a reference to the work of spinning, which in the ancient Near East was associated with women (compare Pr 31:19). The curse then would reference the men of Joab's household becoming like women. **falls by the sword** Describes the way in which Joab killed Abner. **who lacks food** Refers to starvation.

3:30 his brother Abishai Although 2Sa 3:26–27 doesn't explicitly mention Abishai, he apparently conspired with Joab and was likely present at the city gate with him (see v. 27).

3:31–39 In an effort to clear his name, David mourns Abner and commands others to do the same, but he does not punish Joab for his crime.

3:31 Tear your clothes and put on sackcloth Traditional signs of mourning (compare 1:2,11). **walk in mourning in front of Abner** David scorns Joab, commanding him and his coconspirators to mourn Abner. This is the second of three instances where David mourns publicly (1:11–27; 19:1–8).

3:35 May God deal with me See note on 1Sa 3:17.

I taste bread Fasting was a sign of mourning (compare 2Sa 1:12 and note).

3:37 the king had no part Describes the primary motivation behind David's actions. A better course of action, according to the Law, would have been to exact justice for the murder (Nu 35:16–21) — an action David leaves to his heir (see 2Sa 3:29 and note).

3:39 too strong for me David compares his restraint to the unbridled vengeance of the brothers.

4:1–12 Chapter 4 records the death of Ish-Bosheth. As with the deaths of Saul, Saul's sons, and Abner, the narrative clearly specifies that David is innocent. Two of Ish-Bosheth's captains kill him and bring his head to David. As with the young man in 1:14–16, these men receive a different reward than they were anticipating.

4:1 he lost courage Without Abner, Ish-Bosheth knows that it is only a matter of time before his kingdom is overrun. **all Israel became alarmed** The nation also knows that Ish-Bosheth's reign can no longer be sustained.

4:2 tribe of Benjamin The territory of Benjamin is loyal to Saul's dynasty, which explains why they continue to support Ish-Bosheth rather than David (see 2:8 and note, 2:9).

4:3 people of Beeroth fled to Gittaim This event is not recorded in Scripture. Since Beeroth was one of the cities of the Gibeonites (Jos 9:17), the residents of Beeroth may have fled to Gittaim when Saul put the Gibeonites to death (see 2Sa 21:1).

4:4 became disabled Even after the death of Ish-Bosheth narrated in this chapter, a descendant of Saul still exists. His youth and physical disability are likely mentioned to explain why he was not a threat to take the throne. His lameness will later save his life (19:24–30).

the Beerothite, set out for the house of Ish-Bosheth, and they arrived there in the heat of the day while he was taking his noonday rest. ⁶They went into the inner part of the house as if to get some wheat, and they stabbed him in the stomach. Then Rekab and his brother Baanah slipped away.

⁷They had gone into the house while he was lying on the bed in his bedroom. After they stabbed and killed him, they cut off his head. Taking it with them, they traveled all night by way of the Arabah. ⁸They brought the head of Ish-Bosheth to David at Hebron and said to the king, "Here is the head of Ish-Bosheth son of Saul, your enemy, who tried to kill you. This day the LORD has avenged my lord the king against Saul and his offspring."

⁹David answered Rekab and his brother Baanah, the sons of Rimmon the Beerothite, "As surely as the LORD lives, who has delivered me out of every trouble, ¹⁰when someone told me, 'Saul is dead,' and thought he was bringing good news, I seized him and put him to death in Ziklag. That was the reward I gave him for his news! ¹¹How much more — when wicked men have killed an innocent man in his own house and on his own bed — should I not now demand his blood from your hand and rid the earth of you!"

¹²So David gave an order to his men, and they killed them. They cut off their hands and feet and hung the bodies by the pool in Hebron. But they took the head of Ish-Bosheth and buried it in Abner's tomb at Hebron.

David Becomes King Over Israel

5:1-3pp — 1Ch 11:1-3

5 All the tribes of Israel came to David at Hebron and said, "We are your own flesh and blood. ²In the past, while Saul was king over us, you were the one who led Israel on their military campaigns. And the LORD said to you, 'You will shepherd my people Israel, and you will become their ruler.'"

³When all the elders of Israel had come to King David at Hebron, the king made a covenant with them at Hebron before the LORD, and they anointed David king over Israel.

⁴David was thirty years old when he became king, and he reigned forty years. ⁵In Hebron he reigned over Judah seven years and six months, and in Jerusalem he reigned over all Israel and Judah thirty-three years.

David Conquers Jerusalem

5:6-10pp — 1Ch 11:4-9
5:11-16pp — 1Ch 3:5-9; 14:1-7

⁶The king and his men marched to Jerusalem to attack the Jebusites, who lived there. The Jebusites said to David, "You will not get in here; even the blind and the lame can ward you off." They

---

His name was Mephibosheth In the Hebrew text of 1 Chronicles, this character is called Merib-Baal (1Ch 8:34; 9:40). The Baal part of Merib-Baal likely refers to the Canaanite storm god, Baal. This means that the name Mephibosheth could have been an alternate name used to avoid mentioning Baal (see note on 1Ch 8:34).
4:6 they stabbed him Sensing a coming change in the monarchy, Rekab and Baanah seize the opportunity to eliminate David's rival king. They kill him in the same manner as Abner was killed (2Sa 3:27). Ish-Bosheth's head is later buried in Abner's tomb (v. 12).
4:7 they cut off his head For other examples of beheading in 1 and 2 Samuel, see 1Sa 5:4; 17:51 and note; 1Sa 31:9 and note; 2Sa 20:21–22. **way of the Arabah** They travel through valley lands to avoid detection.
4:8 brought the head The last time someone brought a head before a king was in 1Sa 17:57, when David brought the head of Goliath to Saul. David was rewarded by being given a position in the king's court, made part of the royal family, and freed from taxation along with his family (1Sa 17:25). Rekab and Baanah probably expect a similar reward. **LORD has avenged** Rekab and Baanah wrongly attribute their murder to Yahweh. To show the error of their action, David also cites God's covenant name, Yahweh, in his rebuttal (2Sa 4:9).
4:11 wicked men Refers to Rekab and Baanah. **should I not now demand his blood** David declares that they have committed murder against an innocent man and deserve to die (see Ge 9:6; Ex 21:12; Lev 24:17; Nu 35:31).
4:12 hung the bodies Symbolizes that they are accursed (see Dt 21:22–23).

5:1–16 Following Ish-Bosheth's death (2Sa 4), all of the tribes of Israel submit to David as king. His first act as king of the newly united confederation is to move the capital to Jerusalem. He accomplishes this by ridding the city of the Jebusites and transferring his administration there. Yahweh blesses David's efforts, establishes his royal residence and multiplies his offspring.

5:1 tribes of Israel Refers to the northern tribes previously under the control of Ish-Bosheth, son of Saul (see 2:8–10). Yet they pronounce to David that they are his kin, demonstrating the bonds between tribes.
5:2 who led Israel Referring to David's leadership in battle (compare 1Sa 18:5,13,16; 19:8). **shepherd** See 1Sa 9:3 and note.
5:3 covenant See note on 1Sa 11:1. **anointed David king** David is anointed for a third time (see 1Sa 16:13; 2Sa 2:4).
5:4 he reigned forty years David reigns over Judah ca. 1011–1004 BC; ca. 1004–971 BC, David reigned over all of Israel, including Judah. See the timeline "The United Kingdom" on p. 464.
5:5 seven years and six months See 2:11 and note.
5:6 marched to Jerusalem From this central location, David could unite the northern and southern tribes. See 1Sa 17:54 and note. **Jebusites** The Canaanite inhabitants of Jerusalem. **blind and the lame** The inhabitants of Jerusalem think that their city is impenetrable. They are so confident that no one can enter that they declare that their weakest citizens are all that is necessary to keep David out.

thought, "David cannot get in here." ⁷Nevertheless, David captured the fortress of Zion — which is the City of David.

⁸On that day David had said, "Anyone who conquers the Jebusites will have to use the water shaft to reach those 'lame and blind' who are David's enemies.ᵃ" That is why they say, "The 'blind and lame' will not enter the palace."

⁹David then took up residence in the fortress and called it the City of David. He built up the area around it, from the terracesᵇ inward. ¹⁰And he became more and more powerful, because the LORD God Almighty was with him.

¹¹Now Hiram king of Tyre sent envoys to David, along with cedar logs and carpenters and stonemasons, and they built a palace for David. ¹²Then David knew that the LORD had established him as king over Israel and had exalted his kingdom for the sake of his people Israel.

¹³After he left Hebron, David took more concubines and wives in Jerusalem, and more sons and daughters were born to him. ¹⁴These are the names of the children born to him there: Shammua, Shobab, Nathan, Solomon, ¹⁵Ibhar,

ᵃ 8 Or are hated by David   ᵇ 9 Or the Millo

JEBUSITES
Ancient inhabitants of Jerusalem and its environs. They were sworn enemies of Israel and were among the people groups that God instructed the Israelites to obliterate (see Ex 34:11; Dt 7:1–2; 20:17). However, the Israelites were unable to drive the Jebusites out of the land (see Jos 15:63; Jdg 1:21).

5:7 City of David David renames the crown jewel of Israel after himself—a move that is not unparalleled in the OT (compare Nu 32:41–42; 2Sa 12:28).

5:8 water shaft Possibly a reference to the subterranean waterway now known as Warren's Shaft. **those 'lame and blind'** While this idea is difficult, it is possible to understand David's statements not as an order to attack all lame (crippled) or blind people, but as orders to attack all Jebusites. The Jebusites had inadvertently characterized their whole city by its weakest members (see v. 6 and note). Now that David has conquered their city, he refers to all of its inhabitants by their initial taunt, turning it into a mocking epithet. **palace** The Hebrew text here, which simply refers to a "house," may be a reference to the royal residence or to Israel's place of worship (see Lev 21:17–23).

5:10 LORD God Almighty The Hebrew title used here, *yhwh elohe tseva'oth,* which may be literally rendered as "Yahweh, God of hosts," identifies the God of Israel,

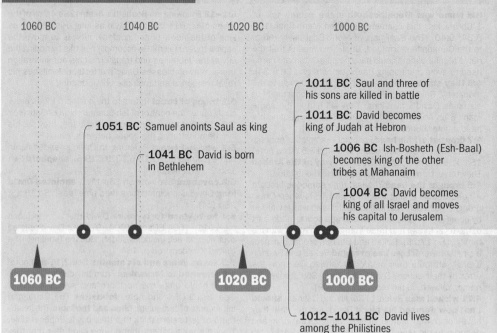

The United Kingdom

1060 BC   1040 BC   1020 BC   1000 BC

1051 BC Samuel anoints Saul as king

1041 BC David is born in Bethlehem

1011 BC Saul and three of his sons are killed in battle

1011 BC David becomes king of Judah at Hebron

1006 BC Ish-Bosheth (Esh-Baal) becomes king of the other tribes at Mahanaim

1004 BC David becomes king of all Israel and moves his capital to Jerusalem

1060 BC   1020 BC   1000 BC

1012–1011 BC David lives among the Philistines

All dates are approximate

Elishua, Nepheg, Japhia, ¹⁶Elishama, Eliada and Eliphelet.

David Defeats the Philistines

5:17-25pp — 1Ch 14:8-17

¹⁷When the Philistines heard that David had been anointed king over Israel, they went up in full force to search for him, but David heard about it and went down to the stronghold. ¹⁸Now the Philistines had come and spread out in the Valley of Rephaim; ¹⁹so David inquired of the Lord, "Shall I go and attack the Philistines? Will you deliver them into my hands?"

The Lord answered him, "Go, for I will surely deliver the Philistines into your hands."

²⁰So David went to Baal Perazim, and there he defeated them. He said, "As waters break out, the Lord has broken out against my enemies before me." So that place was called Baal Perazim.ᵃ ²¹The Philistines abandoned their idols there, and David and his men carried them off.

²²Once more the Philistines came up and spread out in the Valley of Rephaim; ²³so David inquired of the Lord, and he answered, "Do not go straight up, but circle around behind them and attack them in front of the poplar trees. ²⁴As soon as you hear the sound of marching in the tops of the poplar trees, move quickly, because that will mean the Lord has gone out in front of you to strike the

ᵃ 20 *Baal Perazim* means *the lord who breaks out.*

Yahweh, as a commander of armies—those of Israel and heaven.
5:13 wives in Jerusalem Though David breaks Yahweh's command from Dt 17:17, Yahweh still blesses David with more offspring. David may have entered into these marriages to establish treaties and alliances with foreign powers. As part of the ratification process, kings in antiquity often married the daughters of those with whom they made treaties. This practice was intended to prevent rebellion or war between the two parties because a king would not normally attack his extended family. See the people diagram "King David's Family Tree" on p. 620.

5:17–25 The text provides an example of Yahweh, the God of armies, fighting for Israel (see note on 5:10).

5:17 they went up The Philistines intend to make war with him. They likely feel betrayed because he formerly lived among them and feigned friendship (1Sa 27:1—28:2; 29:1–10). See the table "Battles of Saul and David" on p. 433.
5:19 inquired of the Lord As he did when making previous important decisions, David inquires of Yahweh. See 1Sa 23:2,4; 30:8; 2Sa 2:1; note on 1Ch 14:10.
5:20 Baal Perazim Means "The Lord of Bursting Forth."
5:24 the sound of marching Indicates the presence

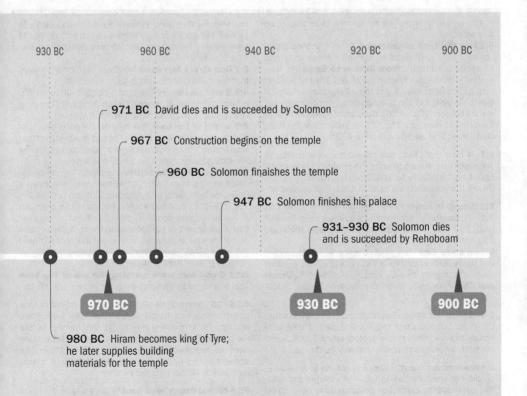

Philistine army." [25] So David did as the LORD commanded him, and he struck down the Philistines all the way from Gibeon[a] to Gezer.

The Ark Brought to Jerusalem

6:1-11pp — 1Ch 13:1-14
6:12-19pp — 1Ch 15:25 – 16:3

6 David again brought together all the able young men of Israel — thirty thousand. [2] He and all his men went to Baalah[b] in Judah to bring up from there the ark of God, which is called by the Name,[c] the name of the LORD Almighty, who is enthroned between the cherubim on the ark. [3] They set the ark of God on a new cart and brought it from the house of Abinadab, which was on the hill. Uzzah and Ahio, sons of Abinadab, were guiding the new cart [4] with the ark of God on it,[d] and Ahio was walking in front of it. [5] David and all Israel were celebrating with all their might before the LORD, with castanets,[e] harps, lyres, timbrels, sistrums and cymbals.

[6] When they came to the threshing floor of Nakon, Uzzah reached out and took hold of the ark of God, because the oxen stumbled. [7] The LORD's anger burned against Uzzah because of his irreverent act; therefore God struck him down, and he died there beside the ark of God.

[8] Then David was angry because the LORD's wrath had broken out against Uzzah, and to this day that place is called Perez Uzzah.[f]

[9] David was afraid of the LORD that day and said, "How can the ark of the LORD ever come to me?" [10] He was not willing to take the ark of the LORD to be with him in the City of David. Instead, he took it to the house of Obed-Edom the Gittite. [11] The ark of the LORD remained in the house of Obed-Edom the Gittite for three months, and the LORD blessed him and his entire household.

[12] Now King David was told, "The LORD has blessed the household of Obed-Edom and everything he has, because of the ark of God." So David went to bring up the ark of God from the house of Obed-Edom to the City of David with rejoicing. [13] When those who were carrying the ark of the LORD had taken six steps, he sacrificed a bull and a fattened calf. [14] Wearing a linen ephod, David was dancing before the LORD with all his might, [15] while he and all Israel were bringing up the ark of the LORD with shouts and the sound of trumpets.

[16] As the ark of the LORD was entering the City of David, Michal daughter of Saul watched from a window. And when she saw King David leaping

---

[a] 25 Septuagint (see also 1 Chron. 14:16); Hebrew *Geba*
[b] 2 That is, Kiriath Jearim (see 1 Chron. 13:6)   [c] 2 Hebrew; Septuagint and Vulgate do not have *the Name*.   [d] 3,4 Dead Sea Scrolls and some Septuagint manuscripts; Masoretic Text *cart* [4] *and they brought it with the ark of God from the house of Abinadab, which was on the hill*   [e] 5 Masoretic Text; Dead Sea Scrolls and Septuagint (see also 1 Chron. 13:8) *songs*   [f] 8 *Perez Uzzah* means *outbreak against Uzzah*.

---

of the heavenly army, led by Yahweh (see 2Sa 5:10 and note).

5:25 as the LORD commanded David's actions again contrast Saul's, who defied Yahweh's commands and usurped his authority. **from Gibeon to Gezer** An overwhelming defeat spanning over 20 miles. The Hebrew text here names Geba (resulting in some translations changing this to Gibeon), but the parallel account in 1 Chronicles names Gibeon (1Ch 14:16). Geba and Gibeon were both towns in this area (see 1Sa 13:3 and note). See the table "Battles of Saul and David" on p. 433.

6:1–4 Now that David has moved the royal capital to Jerusalem, he wishes to bring the symbol of Israel's religious heritage there as well. David and his army escort the ark from its temporary location amid great celebration.

6:2 Baalah in Judah Kiriath Jearim (see Jos 15:9; 1Sa 7:1–2). **Name** The ark denoted the presence of Yahweh (e.g., 2Sa 7:13; 1Ki 9:3; 11:36; 14:21). **cherubim** See 1Sa 4:4 and note; Ex 25:17–22.

6:3 on a new cart They violate the law, which demanded that the Israelites carry the ark using poles. Their violation results in tragedy. See Ex 25:13–14; 2Sa 6:7. **Uzzah and Ahio** Probably Levites (compare with Eleazar in 1Sa 7:1 and note).

6:5–15 Tragedy strikes David's joyous celebration when Uzzah foolishly touches the ark and dies. Those who handle the ark break proper protocol (see 2Sa 6:3 and note); this results in Uzzah's untimely death.

6:6 reached out Though Uzzah's intentions seem pure — he did not want the ark to fall — he violated the Law: The ark was to be carried on poles and was never to be

touched. Furthermore, Yahweh did not need people to protect the ark for him, a lesson the Israelites should have learned the last time the ark was transported (see 1Sa 5:1–5; 6:19–21).

6:7 God struck him down Numbers 4:15 clearly states that the penalty for touching the ark is death.

6:8 David was angry The joyous celebration turns into a time of mourning. **Perez Uzzah** Meaning "Bursting Out Against Uzzah." Compare 1Ch 13:11.

6:9 afraid of the LORD This may be intended as a contrast between David and Saul. The text never states that Saul feared Yahweh; Saul is regularly depicted as fearing the wrong things (see 1Sa 10:22 and note).

6:10 Obed-Edom the Gittite Obed-Edom's name indicates he was from Gath. Obed-Edom may have been a Philistine from Gath who returned with David (1Sa 27; 29; 2Sa 15:18). Alternatively, he may have been an Israelite who was born in Gath — 1Sa 5:8 may suggest that a contingent of Israelites lived there. A third option is that he was an Israelite from a city that incorporated the word "Gath" (which means "winepress"), such as Gath Hepher or Gath Rimmon.

6:13 those who were carrying the ark of the LORD They now correctly transport the ark (compare 1Ch 15:15).

6:16–23 The narrative of the ark's resettlement in Jerusalem ends with a marital spat. Michal, Saul's daughter, accuses David of acting in an undignified manner before the people. David rebukes her by stating that his actions were before Yahweh, who chose him over her father. The account closes by noting the perpetual state of shame ascribed to Michal until her death.

6:16 Michal daughter of Saul In this episode, Michal is

and dancing before the LORD, she despised him in her heart.

[17]They brought the ark of the LORD and set it in its place inside the tent that David had pitched for it, and David sacrificed burnt offerings and fellowship offerings before the LORD. [18]After he had finished sacrificing the burnt offerings and fellowship offerings, he blessed the people in the name of the LORD Almighty. [19]Then he gave a loaf of bread, a cake of dates and a cake of raisins to each person in the whole crowd of Israelites, both men and women. And all the people went to their homes.

[20]When David returned home to bless his household, Michal daughter of Saul came out to meet him and said, "How the king of Israel has distinguished himself today, going around half-naked in full view of the slave girls of his servants as any vulgar fellow would!"

[21]David said to Michal, "It was before the LORD, who chose me rather than your father or anyone from his house when he appointed me ruler over the LORD's people Israel — I will celebrate before the LORD. [22]I will become even more undignified than this, and I will be humiliated in my own eyes. But by these slave girls you spoke of, I will be held in honor."

[23]And Michal daughter of Saul had no children to the day of her death.

God's Promise to David

7:1-17pp — 1Ch 17:1-15

7 After the king was settled in his palace and the LORD had given him rest from all his enemies around him, [2]he said to Nathan the prophet, "Here I am, living in a house of cedar, while the ark of God remains in a tent."

[3]Nathan replied to the king, "Whatever you have in mind, go ahead and do it, for the LORD is with you."

[4]But that night the word of the LORD came to Nathan, saying:

[5]"Go and tell my servant David, 'This is what the LORD says: Are you the one to build me a house to dwell in? [6]I have not dwelt in a house from the day I brought the Israelites up out of Egypt to this day. I have been moving from place to place with a tent as my dwelling. [7]Wherever I have moved with all the Israelites, did I ever say to any of their rulers whom I commanded to shepherd my people Israel, "Why have you not built me a house of cedar?"'

[8]"Now then, tell my servant David, 'This is what the LORD Almighty says: I took you from the pasture, from tending the flock, and

---

primarily identified as Saul's daughter (see 2Sa 6:20,23), not as David's wife. Compare note on 3:13.

6:20 going around half-naked David was wearing a linen ephod (v. 14; 1Ch 15:27), so it may be that Michal's contempt toward David causes her to exaggerate his state of undress. **any vulgar fellow** Michal insinuates that David is not honorable enough to occupy the throne of Israel.

6:21 before the LORD David's focus is solely upon Yahweh; he has no concern with what the audience thought.

6:22 I will become even more undignified David asserts that he will continue to act as he sees fit, regardless of Michal's opinions.

6:23 had no children Women in the ancient Near East felt shame when they could not conceive. David and Michal may have ceased having sexual relations from this point forward, but that is not clear. The point is that her childlessness, however it came about, is associated with her contempt for David.

7:1–17 This chapter records the Davidic covenant, where Yahweh promises to give David an enduring dynasty, throne and kingdom (see 2Sa 7:16). Yahweh makes ten promises concerning David, his offspring and Israel — each one demarcated in the Hebrew text by an "I will" statement. Ethan the Ezrahite, a Jewish sage who lived in the time of Solomon, celebrates this covenant in Ps 89 (compare 1Ki 4:31).

7:1 rest David's kingdom was solidified and there were no significant or imminent threats.

7:2 Nathan A court prophet during the reign of David. **in a tent** David, who is Yahweh's servant, dwells in a royal palace while Yahweh himself (whose presence was focused on earth via the ark of the covenant) dwells in a tent. David seeks to more properly accommodate Yahweh.

2 Samuel 7:2

NATHAN
Nathan is introduced in 2Sa 7:2 as a prophet who is instrumental in David's reign. God uses him to confront the king, uphold righteousness and to make his word known. Nathan is portrayed as a faithful prophet and does not take part in attempts to usurp Davidic or Solomonic rule. He surfaces in three primary accounts: the Davidic covenant (2Sa 7); the rebuke of David for his sin with Bathsheba (2Sa 12); and Solomon's coronation (1Ki 1). In each instance he proves faithful to Yahweh's standards and will.

7:3 Whatever you have in mind, go ahead and do it Nathan initially agrees that something must be done. Yahweh will later give clarification to the prophet on the matter (see 2Sa 7:4–17).

7:5 build me a house Yahweh begins to realign David's presuppositions about what it means to be a king under his reign.

7:6 with a tent Although Shiloh was a centralized place of worship during the period of the judges and the place of worship there had been called a temple (1Sa 1:9) or house of Yahweh (1Sa 3:15), it was not a permanent residence (e.g., Jos 18:1; 1Sa 2:22; Ps 78:60). It also seems that Shiloh had previously been ransacked, leaving the place to meet Yahweh as a tent in Jerusalem (2Sa 6:17).

7:7 did I ever say Signifies a rhetorical question, anticipating a negative answer. **commanded to shepherd my people Israel** Compare note on 1Sa 9:3.

7:8 I took you from the pasture See 1Sa 16:11; 17:15,20,34.

appointed you ruler over my people Israel. [9]I have been with you wherever you have gone, and I have cut off all your enemies from before you. Now I will make your name great, like the names of the greatest men on earth. [10]And I will provide a place for my people Israel and will plant them so that they can have a home of their own and no longer be disturbed. Wicked people will not oppress them anymore, as they did at the beginning [11]and have done ever since the time I appointed leaders[a] over my people Israel. I will also give you rest from all your enemies.

"'The LORD declares to you that the LORD himself will establish a house for you: [12]When your days are over and you rest with your ancestors, I will raise up your offspring to succeed you, your own flesh and blood, and I will establish his kingdom. [13]He is the one who will build a house for my Name, and I will establish the throne of his kingdom forever. [14]I will be his father, and he will be my son. When he does wrong, I will punish him with a rod wielded by men, with floggings inflicted by human hands. [15]But my love will never be taken away from him, as I took it away from Saul, whom I removed from before you. [16]Your house and your kingdom will endure forever before me[b]; your throne will be established forever.'"

[17]Nathan reported to David all the words of this entire revelation.

David's Prayer

7:18-29pp — 1Ch 17:16-27

[18]Then King David went in and sat before the LORD, and he said:

"Who am I, Sovereign LORD, and what is my family, that you have brought me this far? [19]And as if this were not enough in your sight, Sovereign LORD, you have also spoken about the future of the house of your servant — and this decree, Sovereign LORD, is for a mere human![c]

[20]"What more can David say to you? For you know your servant, Sovereign LORD. [21]For the sake of your word and according to your will, you have done this great thing and made it known to your servant.

---

[a] 11 Traditionally *judges*   [b] 16 Some Hebrew manuscripts and Septuagint; most Hebrew manuscripts *you*   [c] 19 Or *for the human race*

7:9-15 The Hebrew text of this section contains ten "I will" statements by Yahweh (2Sa 7:10,11,12,14,15). Each one highlights a promise Yahweh makes to David, his offspring or Israel. The promise in v. 13 is a reiteration of the second promise in v. 12. See the table "Covenants in the Old Testament" on p. 469.

7:9 I will make your name great Yahweh first promises to make David's immediate reputation and his enduring legacy great.

7:10 a place The Hebrew word used here, *maqom*, could refer to the temple—the house that David wants to build for Yahweh. Alternatively, it may refer to the land over which David is now reigning, thus reflecting an earlier promise Yahweh made to Abraham (see Ge 15:7; 17:8). **will plant them** Yahweh's third promise is related to the second; not only will he designate a place for his people, he will also ensure that they are firmly established there.

7:11 rest Yahweh promises David security and peace (compare 2Sa 7:1 and note). **will establish a house for you** David desires to build Yahweh a house, but Yahweh tells David instead that David's house (his dynasty) shall be established. This blessing had already begun in 3:2–5 and 5:13–16.

7:12 raise up your offspring Yahweh's sixth promise refers to Solomon, as evidenced by the following promise, which refers to the descendant's kingdom (see 1Ki 1:29–30). In addition, 2Sa 7:13 states that this person will build a house for Yahweh's name, a feat Solomon accomplishes in 1Ki 5–6. **establish his kingdom** Yahweh guarantees that David's son (Solomon) will rule in his place.

7:13 build a house for my Name Refers to the temple (see 1Ki 5–6). According to 1Ki 5:3, David could not build the temple until he had achieved rest from his enemies; 1Ki 5:3 and 2Sa 7:11 suggest that the rest David was already experiencing, mentioned in 2Sa 7:1,

was temporary. **establish the throne** A reiteration of Yahweh's seventh promise (see 2Sa 7:12 and note). Here, Yahweh adds that the Davidic throne will endure into perpetuity. Compare note on 7:16.

7:14 father Yahweh promises to adopt David's offspring; this reflects the common ancient Near Eastern custom of the king being adopted by his god. In the near term, this refers to Solomon. In the long term, however, it refers to the Messiah; Hebrews 1:5 cites this passage (along with Ps 2:7) and applies the promise to Jesus. Paul also applies this passage collectively to God's adoption of believers in 2Co 6:18.

7:15 love will never be taken away Yahweh's tenth and final promise is comforting—he promises that his love for David's offspring will endure (compare Ps 89:33–35).

7:16 The three promises in this verse—the permanence of David's dynasty, kingdom and throne—summarize Yahweh's ten promises in 2Sa 7:9–15. They are mentioned three times in Ps 89:4,29,36. Central to the NT is the understanding of Jesus as the culmination and ultimate fulfillment of the Davidic covenant. All four Gospels recognize Jesus as the Son of David (especially Luke; see Lk 1:32,69). The "kingdom of God" (or "kingdom of heaven") language of the Gospel accounts also affirm the other aspects of 2Sa 7:16, identifying Jesus' kingdom as inaugurated on earth but not yet fully realized—with its full realization happening in Jesus' return. Paul likewise testifies to Jesus' Davidic heritage, particularly in Ro 1:3 and 2Ti 2:8. In addition, Revelation acknowledges Jesus' ancestry (see Rev 5:5; 22:16). By identifying Jesus as a descendant of David, the NT authors affirm their conviction that Jesus is Yahweh's ultimate anointed ruler (Messiah or Christ) from the Davidic line.

7:18–29 David expresses a sense of awe at Yahweh's gracious promises and conveys his deepest gratitude. Compare 1Ch 17:16–27.

Covenants in the Old Testament

PARTY ONE	PARTY TWO	DESCRIPTION	REFERENCE
Yahweh	Noah, his descendants, all living creatures	Yahweh will never again destroy the earth with a flood. He will establish covenants with Noah's descendants.	Ge 6:18; 9:9-17
Yahweh	Abram	Yahweh promises the land between the river of Egypt and the Euphrates to Abraham and his descendants	Ge 15:18; see also Ge 12:1-8; 22:15-18; Ex 2:24, etc.
Yahweh	Abram/Abraham	Abram receives the name Abraham; he will be a father of many nations; Yahweh will maintain covenants with Abraham's descendants; the institution of circumcision; the promise of a child by Sarah	Ge 17:1-21; see also Ge 12:1-8; 22:15-18; Ex 2:24, etc.
Yahweh	Abraham (Isaac)	Technically not a covenant between Yahweh and Isaac; Yahweh informs Isaac of the continuing relevance of the Abrahamic covenant	Ge 26:2-5,24
Yahweh	Abraham (Jacob)	Yahweh affirms the Abrahamic covenant; Yahweh promises Jacob the land, many descendants, that he and his descendants will be a blessing, and continued protection	Ge 28:12-22
Yahweh	Moses and the people of Israel	Yahweh and Israel will enjoy a unique relationship; Moses receives the Torah, including the Decalogue	Ex 19:1-24:8; 34:10
Yahweh	Aaron and his descendants	Yahweh provides instructions for Aaron and his descendants, who are a hereditary line of priests	Ex 28:1-30:37; compare Ne 13:29; Mal 2:8
Yahweh	Phinehas	Yahweh grants Phinehas a "covenant of peace," promising a hereditary line of priests	Nu 25:10-13
Yahweh	David	Yahweh promises David an eternal royal line and that his son will build the temple	2Sa 7:12-16; compare Ps 89:3,28,34,39; 132:12; Isa 55:3; Jer 33:20-25
Israelites (under Joshua)	Gibeonites	The inhabitants of Gibeon trick Israel into making a peace-covenant	Jos 9:3-15
Joshua	the tribes of Israel	The Israelite tribes renew their commitment to the Mosaic covenant	Jos 24:25
Jehoiada the priest	the captains of the Carites	Jehoiada conscripts the Carites to guard the young Joash	2Ki 11:4
David	elders of Israel	David is made king of Israel	1Ch 11:3

22"How great you are, Sovereign LORD! There is no one like you, and there is no God but you, as we have heard with our own ears. 23And who is like your people Israel — the one nation on earth that God went out to redeem as a people for himself, and to make a name for himself, and to perform great and awesome wonders by driving out nations and their gods from before your people, whom you redeemed from Egypt?a 24You have established your people Israel as your very own forever, and you, LORD, have become their God.

25"And now, LORD God, keep forever the promise you have made concerning your servant and his house. Do as you promised, 26so that your name will be great forever. Then people will say, 'The LORD Almighty is God over Israel!' And the house of your servant David will be established in your sight. 27"LORD Almighty, God of Israel, you have

revealed this to your servant, saying, 'I will build a house for you.' So your servant has found courage to pray this prayer to you. 28Sovereign LORD, you are God! Your covenant is trustworthy, and you have promised these good things to your servant. 29Now be pleased to bless the house of your servant, that it may continue forever in your sight; for you, Sovereign LORD, have spoken, and with your blessing the house of your servant will be blessed forever."

David's Victories

8:1-14pp — 1Ch 18:1-13

8 In the course of time, David defeated the Philistines and subdued them, and he took Metheg Ammah from the control of the Philistines.

a 23 See Septuagint and 1 Chron. 17:21; Hebrew *wonders for your land and before your people, whom you redeemed from Egypt, from the nations and their gods*.

Covenants in the Old Testament (continued)

PARTY ONE	PARTY TWO	DESCRIPTION	REFERENCE
Joash	the Levites and leaders of Israel, under the direction of Jehoiada	Joash is confirmed king	2Ch 23:3; compare 2Ki 11:4
Zedekiah	the inhabitants of Jerusalem	Agreement that no Judean shall hold another Judean as a slave	Jer 34:8 – 10
Solomon	Hiram, King of Tyre	The two make a peace-covenant	1Ki 5:12
King Asa of Judah	King Ben-Hadad of Aram	The two make an alliance against King Baasha of Israel	1Ki 15:19; 2Ch 16:3
King Ahab of Israel	King Ben-Hadad of Aram	The two make a peace-covenant	1Ki 20:34
The king of Babylon	"member of the royal family"	Judah will be permitted to stand if it humbles itself to Babylon	Eze 17:12 – 14
Abram	Mamre, Eshkol, Aner	Unspecified; for some form of mutual benefit	Ge 14:13
Abraham	Abimelek, Phicol	For honest dealings	Ge 21:27,32
Isaac	Abimelek, Phicol, Ahuzzath	For peaceful relations	Ge 26:28 – 33
Jacob	Laban	For well-treatment of Laban's daughters	Ge 31:44 – 53
Jonathan	David	Jonathan and David maintain a sacred covenant of love/friendship	1Sa 18:3; 20:8; 23:18
David	Abner	David agrees to make a covenant, provided that Abner bring him his wife-by-right, Michal	2Sa 3:12 – 13
A husband	A wife	Marriage is treated as a sacred covenant	Pr 2:17; Mal 2:14

²David also defeated the Moabites. He made them lie down on the ground and measured them off with a length of cord. Every two lengths of them were put to death, and the third length was allowed to live. So the Moabites became subject to David and brought him tribute.

³Moreover, David defeated Hadadezer son of Rehob, king of Zobah, when he went to restore his monument at*ᵃ* the Euphrates River. ⁴David captured a thousand of his chariots, seven thousand charioteersᵇ and twenty thousand foot soldiers. He hamstrung all but a hundred of the chariot horses.

⁵When the Arameans of Damascus came to help Hadadezer king of Zobah, David struck down twenty-two thousand of them. ⁶He put garrisons in the Aramean kingdom of Damascus, and the Arameans became subject to him and brought tribute. The LORD gave David victory wherever he went.

⁷David took the gold shields that belonged to the officers of Hadadezer and brought them to Jerusalem. ⁸From Tebahᶜ and Berothai, towns that belonged to Hadadezer, King David took a great quantity of bronze.

⁹When Touᵈ king of Hamath heard that David had defeated the entire army of Hadadezer, ¹⁰he sent his son Joramᵉ to King David to greet him and congratulate him on his victory in battle over Hadadezer, who had been at war with Tou. Joram brought with him articles of silver, of gold and of bronze.

¹¹King David dedicated these articles to the LORD, as he had done with the silver and gold from all the nations he had subdued: ¹²Edomᶠ and Moab, the Ammonites and the Philistines, and Amalek. He also dedicated the plunder taken from Hadadezer son of Rehob, king of Zobah.

¹³And David became famous after he returned from striking down eighteen thousand Edomitesᵍ in the Valley of Salt.

¹⁴He put garrisons throughout Edom, and all the Edomites became subject to David. The LORD gave David victory wherever he went.

David's Officials

8:15-18pp — 1Ch 18:14-17

¹⁵David reigned over all Israel, doing what was just and right for all his people. ¹⁶Joab son of Zeruiah was over the army; Jehoshaphat son of Ahilud was recorder; ¹⁷Zadok son of Ahitub and Ahimelek

---

ᵃ 3 Or *his control along*   ᵇ 4 Septuagint (see also Dead Sea Scrolls and 1 Chron. 18:4); Masoretic Text *captured seventeen hundred of his charioteers*   ᶜ 8 See some Septuagint manuscripts (see also 1 Chron. 18:8); Hebrew *Betah*.   ᵈ 9 Hebrew *Toi*, a variant of *Tou*; also in verse 10   ᵉ 10 A variant of *Hadoram*   ᶠ 12 Some Hebrew manuscripts, Septuagint and Syriac (see also 1 Chron. 18:11); most Hebrew manuscripts *Aram*   ᵍ 13 A few Hebrew manuscripts, Septuagint and Syriac (see also 1 Chron. 18:12); most Hebrew manuscripts *Aram* (that is, Arameans)

8:1–14 This section summarizes the wars that occurred during David's reign. The list is not necessarily all-inclusive (other campaigns are listed later), nor in chronological order. It seems to narrate David's victories over enemies in the west (Philistines), the east (Moabites), the north (Aram) and the south (Edom). The overall intent is to show that Yahweh gives David success (2Sa 8:6,14), and the victories he achieves secure his borders in all directions.

8:1 David defeated the Philistines This brief description represents the cessation of the Philistine threat for a portion of David's reign. See 7:1 and note.

8:2 Moabites David attacks the Moabites even though they had formerly shown kindness to him and were his distant relatives (1Sa 22:4; compare 1Ch 18:2). See the table "Battles of Saul and David" on p. 433. **with a length of cord** The line was long enough to cover three men, and two out of the three were put to death. He left some alive in order to collect tribute from them, but he killed enough so that they no longer posed a military threat to his eastern border. **tribute** Refers to taxes levied against a conquered people.

8:3 Zobah A northern enemy in the region of Syria, north of Damascus and south of Hamath. Saul had earlier fought against Zobah (1Sa 14:47). **monument** The Hebrew word used here, *yad*, may refer to a monument, or more generally to power or control. In the Hebrew text it is unclear whether David or Hadadezer is performing this action. If it was David, he may have erected a monument on his northern border (compare 1Sa 15:12; 2Sa 18:18). This would have alerted travelers that they were about to enter into his kingdom.

8:4 He hamstrung all but a hundred of the chariot horses By doing so, David ensures they cannot be used against him in battle.

8:6 garrisons in the Aramean kingdom Intended to police the region and prevent rebellion.

8:9 Hamath Like Zobah, Hamath was located in the region of Syria.

8:10 greet him and congratulate him on his victory in battle A politically beneficial move; Tou (or Toi) makes peace with David and offers gifts commemorating David's military victories.

8:11 dedicated these articles to the LORD David also dedicates the gold shields of Hadadezer's servants to Yahweh.

8:13 became famous The Hebrew text here speaks of making a name for oneself, which in the ancient Near East can refer to the establishment of a monument. See 2Sa 7:9 and note; note on v. 3.

8:14 garrisons throughout Edom See v. 6 and note.

8:15–18 This chapter closes by listing David's cabinet (compare 20:23–26).

8:15 doing what was just and right The hallmark of a noble ruler.

8:16 Joab David's nephew (see 2:13 and note).

8:17 Zadok See note on 1Sa 2:35; Eze 40:46 and note. **Ahimelek son of Abiathar** This may be a scribal error. Ahimelek is the priest of Nob who gives David holy bread and a sword (1Sa 21:6,8–9)—prompting Saul to order the slaughter of all the priests of Nob (1Sa 22:18). The lone survivor is Ahimelek's son Abiathar (1Sa 22:20), who becomes David's priest (1Sa 30:7). Two later lists of David's officials have Abiathar instead of Ahimelek (2Sa 20:25;

son of Abiathar were priests; Seraiah was secretary; [18]Benaiah son of Jehoiada was over the Kerethites and Pelethites; and David's sons were priests.[a]

David and Mephibosheth

9 David asked, "Is there anyone still left of the house of Saul to whom I can show kindness for Jonathan's sake?"

[2]Now there was a servant of Saul's household named Ziba. They summoned him to appear before David, and the king said to him, "Are you Ziba?"

"At your service," he replied.

[3]The king asked, "Is there no one still alive from the house of Saul to whom I can show God's kindness?"

Ziba answered the king, "There is still a son of Jonathan; he is lame in both feet."

[4]"Where is he?" the king asked.

Ziba answered, "He is at the house of Makir son of Ammiel in Lo Debar."

[5]So King David had him brought from Lo Debar, from the house of Makir son of Ammiel.

[6]When Mephibosheth son of Jonathan, the son of Saul, came to David, he bowed down to pay him honor.

David said, "Mephibosheth!"

"At your service," he replied.

[7]"Don't be afraid," David said to him, "for I will surely show you kindness for the sake of your father Jonathan. I will restore to you all the land that belonged to your grandfather Saul, and you will always eat at my table."

[8]Mephibosheth bowed down and said, "What is your servant, that you should notice a dead dog like me?"

[9]Then the king summoned Ziba, Saul's steward, and said to him, "I have given your master's grandson everything that belonged to Saul and his family. [10]You and your sons and your servants are to farm the land for him and bring in the crops, so that your master's grandson may be provided for. And Mephibosheth, grandson of your master, will always eat at my table." (Now Ziba had fifteen sons and twenty servants.)

[11]Then Ziba said to the king, "Your servant will do whatever my lord the king commands his servant to do." So Mephibosheth ate at David's[b] table like one of the king's sons.

[12]Mephibosheth had a young son named Mika, and all the members of Ziba's household were servants of Mephibosheth. [13]And Mephibosheth lived in Jerusalem, because he always ate at the king's table; he was lame in both feet.

David Defeats the Ammonites

10:1-19pp — 1Ch 19:1-19

10 In the course of time, the king of the Ammonites died, and his son Hanun succeeded him as king. [2]David thought, "I will show kindness to Hanun son of Nahash, just as his father showed kindness to me." So David sent a delegation to

---

[a] 18 Or *were chief officials* (see Septuagint and Targum; see also 1 Chron. 18:17)   [b] 11 Septuagint; Hebrew *my*

1Ki 4:4). On the other hand, it may be that Abiathar named his son Ahimelek after his father, and that is the Ahimelek mentioned here (see 1Ch 18:16; 24:3,6,31).

8:18 Kerethites and Pelethites Foreign mercenary troops comprising the royal bodyguard (2Sa 23:22–23).

David's sons were priests Even though David was not from the tribe of Levi, his sons are named with the typical Hebrew word for a priest, *kohen*. For this reason, some translations use "ministers" here to indicate that they were not Levitical priests but served as royal advisors or administrators (compare 1Ch 18:17).

9:1–13 Recalling his covenant with Jonathan, David seeks to find a survivor from the house of Saul upon whom he may bestow kindness. Jonathan's crippled son, Mephibosheth, is still alive, so David gives him Saul's property and a seat at his own table.

9:1 anyone still left of the house of Saul David seeks to show kindness to Saul's descendants, as Jonathan had asked him to do (see 1Sa 20:15 and note). He had also promised Saul he would not wipe out his family (1Sa 24:21–22). See the people diagram "King Saul's Family Tree" on p. 428.

9:3 he is lame in both feet As a crippled person (see 2Sa 4:4), Mephibosheth posed no threat to David's throne. He was unable to go to war, and he would have been unfit to bear anointed status (compare Lev 21:17 and note). Consequently, David could safely allow him to live (compare 2Sa 21:1–14).

9:4 Lo Debar This was a town on the east side of the Jor-

dan near Mahanaim (see 2:8; 17:27–29). Mephibosheth may be staying here rather than Saul's hometown of Gibeah (which was only three miles from Jerusalem) because of his tenuous position as Saul's descendant.

9:6 At your service Mephibosheth understands the power structures and his language publicly acknowledges this.

9:7 Don't be afraid As a relative of Saul, he likely thinks that he will be executed. Descendants of deposed kings and other rival claimants to the throne were often put to death. **eat at my table** By bestowing this great honor on Mephibosheth, David can also keep track of the activities of the descendant of Saul.

9:8 dead dog See 3:8 and note.

9:10 Ziba Ziba was probably the manager of Saul's estate. From this point on, he is the manager of Mephibosheth's estate. Based on his later behavior, he may have resented this change in circumstances (see 16:1–4; 19:24–30).

9:13 he was lame in both feet This fact is relevant later in the narrative. See 19:24–30.

10:1–19 Chapter 10 opens with the death of Nahash, king of the Ammonites. David sends envoys to Nahash's son, Hanun, out of respect and insists that he honor their previous arrangement. After receiving foolish advice from his fellow Ammonites (see 10:3 and note), Hanun rebels and enlists the Arameans (Syrians) to assist him (10:6). Since Yahweh is with David wherever he goes (8:6,14), David defeats the rebellious vassals and regains control of their regions. A parallel account occurs in 1Ch 19.

express his sympathy to Hanun concerning his father.

When David's men came to the land of the Ammonites, [3] the Ammonite commanders said to Hanun their lord, "Do you think David is honoring your father by sending envoys to you to express sympathy? Hasn't David sent them to you only to explore the city and spy it out and overthrow it?" [4] So Hanun seized David's envoys, shaved off half of each man's beard, cut off their garments at the buttocks, and sent them away.

[5] When David was told about this, he sent messengers to meet the men, for they were greatly humiliated. The king said, "Stay at Jericho till your beards have grown, and then come back."

[6] When the Ammonites realized that they had become obnoxious to David, they hired twenty thousand Aramean foot soldiers from Beth Rehob and Zobah, as well as the king of Maakah with a thousand men, and also twelve thousand men from Tob.

[7] On hearing this, David sent Joab out with the entire army of fighting men. [8] The Ammonites came out and drew up in battle formation at the entrance of their city gate, while the Arameans of Zobah and Rehob and the men of Tob and Maakah were by themselves in the open country.

[9] Joab saw that there were battle lines in front of him and behind him; so he selected some of the best troops in Israel and deployed them against the Arameans. [10] He put the rest of the men under the command of Abishai his brother and deployed them against the Ammonites. [11] Joab said, "If the Arameans are too strong for me, then you are to come to my rescue; but if the Ammonites are too strong for you, then I will come to rescue you. [12] Be strong, and let us fight bravely for our people

and the cities of our God. The LORD will do what is good in his sight."

[13] Then Joab and the troops with him advanced to fight the Arameans, and they fled before him. [14] When the Ammonites realized that the Arameans were fleeing, they fled before Abishai and went inside the city. So Joab returned from fighting the Ammonites and came to Jerusalem.

[15] After the Arameans saw that they had been routed by Israel, they regrouped. [16] Hadadezer had Arameans brought from beyond the Euphrates River; they went to Helam, with Shobak the commander of Hadadezer's army leading them.

[17] When David was told of this, he gathered all Israel, crossed the Jordan and went to Helam. The Arameans formed their battle lines to meet David and fought against him. [18] But they fled before Israel, and David killed seven hundred of their charioteers and forty thousand of their foot soldiers.[a] He also struck down Shobak the commander of their army, and he died there. [19] When all the kings who were vassals of Hadadezer saw that they had been routed by Israel, they made peace with the Israelites and became subject to them.

So the Arameans were afraid to help the Ammonites anymore.

David and Bathsheba

11 In the spring, at the time when kings go off to war, David sent Joab out with the king's men and the whole Israelite army. They destroyed the Ammonites and besieged Rabbah. But David remained in Jerusalem.

a 18 Some Septuagint manuscripts (see also 1 Chron. 19:18); Hebrew *horsemen*

10:1 Ammonites The Ammonites lived on the eastern border of David's territory.

10:2 Nahash See 1Sa 11:1–11. **his father showed kindness** Nahash had probably showed loyalty by making a treaty with David.

10:3 Hanun Hanun listens to the suspicions of his advisors, similar to how Rehoboam, another naïve young ruler, will later listen to bad advice (1Ki 12:6–11).

10:4 half of each man's beard Hanun defaces their symbol of masculinity (see note on 1Sa 21:13). **cut off their garments** Symbolizes castration. See note on 1Ch 19:4.

10:5 they were greatly humiliated Hanun brings great dishonor on David's servants by desecrating their bodies and garments and exposing their genitals. **Stay at Jericho** David orders them to stay because they no longer conform to the standards of the Law in appearance or attire (see Lev 19:27; Nu 15:38–39).

10:6 Aramean foot soldiers from Beth Rehob The Ammonites hire mercenaries from four Aramean (Syrian) kingdoms to the east and northeast of Israel. These mercenaries naturally would jump at any opportunity to attack David.

10:7 Joab David's nephew and the commander of his army. See 2Sa 2:13 and note.

10:8 at the entrance of their city gate A siege battle was established. Compare 1Ch 19:9. **in the open country** Another battle front was established in an open field.

10:10 Abishai his brother See 2Sa 2:18 and note.

10:12 let us fight bravely In the Hebrew text, this pronouncement recalls Jos 1:6,7,9.

10:15 they regrouped They prepare for a counterattack.

10:16 Hadadezer See 2Sa 8:3–12.

10:17 Helam Located northeast of Ammon, where the Aramean (Syrian) forces are positioned (see v. 16).

10:19 vassals of Hadadezer Likely refers to smaller city-states in the northern regions of Syria and just beyond the Euphrates River. See the table "Battles of Saul and David" on p. 433. **Arameans were afraid** Their most recent alliance with the Ammonites resulted in the deaths of roughly 41,000 Arameans (Syrians; see 10:6,18) and brought about their subjugation to David.

11:1–27 This passage narrates David's committing adultery with Bathsheba and having her husband, Uriah, killed to cover up his sin. This narrative (11:1—12:25) is bracketed in 2 Samuel by Israel's defeat of the Ammonites (ch. 10; 12:26–31). The parallel account of the Ammonite defeat in 1 Chronicles (1Ch 19:1—20:3) omits this episode.

²One evening David got up from his bed and walked around on the roof of the palace. From the roof he saw a woman bathing. The woman was very beautiful, ³and David sent someone to find out about her. The man said, "She is Bathsheba, the daughter of Eliam and the wife of Uriah the Hittite." ⁴Then David sent messengers to get her. She came to him, and he slept with her. (Now she was purifying herself from her monthly uncleanness.) Then she went back home. ⁵The woman conceived and sent word to David, saying, "I am pregnant."

⁶So David sent this word to Joab: "Send me Uriah the Hittite." And Joab sent him to David. ⁷When Uriah came to him, David asked him how Joab was, how the soldiers were and how the war was going. ⁸Then David said to Uriah, "Go down to your house and wash your feet." So Uriah left the palace, and a gift from the king was sent after him. ⁹But Uriah slept at the entrance to the palace with all his master's servants and did not go down to his house.

¹⁰David was told, "Uriah did not go home." So he asked Uriah, "Haven't you just come from a military campaign? Why didn't you go home?"

¹¹Uriah said to David, "The ark and Israel and Judah are staying in tents,ᵃ and my commander Joab and my lord's men are camped in the open country. How could I go to my house to eat and drink and make love to my wife? As surely as you live, I will not do such a thing!"

¹²Then David said to him, "Stay here one more day, and tomorrow I will send you back." So Uriah remained in Jerusalem that day and the next. ¹³At David's invitation, he ate and drank with him, and David made him drunk. But in the evening Uriah went out to sleep on his mat among his master's servants; he did not go home.

¹⁴In the morning David wrote a letter to Joab and sent it with Uriah. ¹⁵In it he wrote, "Put Uriah out in front where the fighting is fiercest. Then withdraw from him so he will be struck down and die."

¹⁶So while Joab had the city under siege, he put Uriah at a place where he knew the strongest defenders were. ¹⁷When the men of the city came out and fought against Joab, some of the men in David's army fell; moreover, Uriah the Hittite died.

¹⁸Joab sent David a full account of the battle. ¹⁹He instructed the messenger: "When you have finished giving the king this account of the battle, ²⁰the king's anger may flare up, and he may ask you, 'Why did you get so close to the city to fight? Didn't you know they would shoot arrows from the wall? ²¹Who killed Abimelek son of Jerub-Beshethᵇ? Didn't a woman drop an upper millstone on him from the wall, so that he died in Thebez? Why did you get so close to the wall?' If he asks you this, then say to him, 'Moreover, your servant Uriah the Hittite is dead.'"

²²The messenger set out, and when he arrived he told David everything Joab had sent him to say.

ᵃ 11 Or staying at Sukkoth   ᵇ 21 Also known as Jerub-Baal (that is, Gideon)

11:1 In the spring, at the time when kings go off to war People in the ancient Near East primarily fought battles in the spring rather than in the winter. Fighting in the colder months could endanger the soldiers and required more resources. **kings go off** Rather than going out himself, David sends Joab out against the Ammonites. This may be a subtle indication that something is amiss. **Joab** David's nephew and the commander of his army. See 2Sa 2:13 and note. **They destroyed the Ammonites** The Ammonites had rebelled in ch. 10. See the table "Battles of Saul and David" on p. 433.

11:2 a woman bathing She may be bathing to be cleansed from the impurity of her menstrual cycle, as prescribed by the law of the time (see Lev 15:19–30).

11:3 to find out about her If Bathsheba had not been married, David probably would have added her to his harem, which is a prerogative of the king. **Eliam** Possibly the son of Ahithophel, who was David's advisor (2Sa 23:34; 15:12–17:23). **Uriah the Hittite** One of David's 30 mighty men (23:39). The designation "the Hittite" might indicate that he was a resident alien.

11:4 he slept with her The Hebrew phrase used here is a euphemism for sexual intercourse. **her monthly uncleanness** The Hebrew text here may refer to the Law's regulations concerning impurity created by having illicit sexual intercourse (Lev 18:20; Nu 5:19–21) or to the regulations concerning a woman's menstruation period (Lev 15:25–30).

11:6 Send me Uriah David immediately begins to conceal his immorality.

11:8 wash your feet The Hebrew phrase used here is a euphemism for sexual intercourse. Feet were sometimes referenced euphemistically to refer to male genitalia (e.g., Ex 4:25; Isa 7:20).

11:9 with all his master's servants Uriah slept where the men serving David slept. This may be a reference to David's 30 mighty men (2Sa 23:24–39). **did not go down** Uriah may sense that he is being tested. In an effort to prove his faithfulness to David's standards for warfare—which seem to have applied to holy war in general—he does not have sexual intercourse with his wife and instead guards the king (compare 1Sa 21:4–5; Ex 19:15).

11:11 and make love to my wife Uriah refuses to participate in privileges that his superiors and peers cannot enjoy. **I will not do such a thing** Uriah considers the action disrespectful in light of what Yahweh and his fellow warriors were forced to endure. This contrasts Uriah's character with David's.

11:13 he did not go home David probably intended for Uriah to have intercourse with Bathsheba to cover up Bathsheba's pregnancy; David's ruse is prevented when Uriah once again does not go home. David is forced to come up with another plan.

11:14 sent it with Uriah Uriah unknowingly carries his own death warrant.

11:15 withdraw from him Uriah would be unprotected by his fellow soldiers and left completely exposed.

11:17 moreover, Uriah the Hittite died Joab carries out David's plan by intentionally getting his soldiers too close to the city wall, where they could easily be bombarded (see vv. 20–21); this results in more than Uriah's death.

11:21 Who killed Abimelek See Jdg 9:52–53; note on 9:53. **Uriah the Hittite is dead** Uriah's death would appease the king's anger against Joab. David's main objective was achieved.

²³The messenger said to David, "The men overpowered us and came out against us in the open, but we drove them back to the entrance of the city gate. ²⁴Then the archers shot arrows at your servants from the wall, and some of the king's men died. Moreover, your servant Uriah the Hittite is dead."

²⁵David told the messenger, "Say this to Joab: 'Don't let this upset you; the sword devours one as well as another. Press the attack against the city and destroy it.' Say this to encourage Joab."

²⁶When Uriah's wife heard that her husband was dead, she mourned for him. ²⁷After the time of mourning was over, David had her brought to his house, and she became his wife and bore him a son. But the thing David had done displeased the LORD.

Nathan Rebukes David

11:1; 12:29-31pp — 1Ch 20:1-3

12 The LORD sent Nathan to David. When he came to him, he said, "There were two men in a certain town, one rich and the other poor. ²The rich man had a very large number of sheep and cattle, ³but the poor man had nothing except one little ewe lamb he had bought. He raised it, and it grew up with him and his children. It shared his food, drank from his cup and even slept in his arms. It was like a daughter to him.

⁴"Now a traveler came to the rich man, but the rich man refrained from taking one of his own sheep or cattle to prepare a meal for the traveler who had come to him. Instead, he took the ewe lamb that belonged to the poor man and prepared it for the one who had come to him."

⁵David burned with anger against the man and said to Nathan, "As surely as the LORD lives, the man who did this must die! ⁶He must pay for that lamb four times over, because he did such a thing and had no pity."

⁷Then Nathan said to David, "You are the man! This is what the LORD, the God of Israel, says: 'I anointed you king over Israel, and I delivered you from the hand of Saul. ⁸I gave your master's house to you, and your master's wives into your arms. I gave you all Israel and Judah. And if all this had been too little, I would have given you even more. ⁹Why did you despise the word of the LORD by doing what is evil in his eyes? You struck down Uriah the Hittite with the sword and took his wife to be your own. You killed him with the sword of the Ammonites. ¹⁰Now, therefore, the sword will never depart from your house, because you despised me and took the wife of Uriah the Hittite to be your own.'

¹¹"This is what the LORD says: 'Out of your own household I am going to bring calamity on you. Before your very eyes I will take your wives and give them to one who is close to you, and he will sleep with your wives in broad daylight. ¹²You did it in secret, but I will do this thing in broad daylight before all Israel.'"

¹³Then David said to Nathan, "I have sinned against the LORD."

Nathan replied, "The LORD has taken away your sin. You are not going to die. ¹⁴But because by doing this you have shown utter contempt for*ᵃ* the LORD, the son born to you will die."

ᵃ 14 An ancient Hebrew scribal tradition; Masoretic Text for the enemies of

---

11:25 the sword devours Perhaps an ancient proverb indicating that sometimes even the best soldiers die in battle. David feigns ignorance of any wrongdoing. He encourages Joab to continue with his mission of overthrowing Rabbah.
11:27 she became his wife Similar to his marriage to the widow Abigail (1Sa 25:39–42). **displeased the LORD** The first time this is said of David. By closing this section with this statement, the narrative leaves readers wondering what will happen.

12:1–15 In this section, Yahweh pronounces judgment upon David for his murder and adultery. He sends the prophet Nathan to deliver his message, and Nathan delivers it in the form of a parable. The consequences for David's actions will plague him for the rest of his life.
12:1 Nathan A court prophet during the reign of David. **There were two men in a certain town** Nathan tells David a parable, but he acts as though he is presenting him with a legal dispute. This presentation is effective as it causes David to pronounce judgment upon himself (see 2 Sa 12:5–6).
12:4 he took The point of the parable: Nathan describes how the greedy, lustful King David stole Bathsheba from Uriah.
12:5 the man who did this must die The king unwittingly pronounces his own death sentence (see Ex 20:14; Lev 20:10).

12:6 He must pay for that lamb four times over Aligns with the requirements of the Law (see Ex 22:1). David was well acquainted with the Law, but he failed to apply it to himself in his affair with Bathsheba.
12:8 your master's wives David inherited Saul's harem, symbolizing that he had seized the throne (compare 2Sa 3:7 and note; 16:22).
12:9 You struck down Uriah the Hittite Even though the Ammonites killed Uriah, David was as responsible for Uriah's death as he would have been if he had done the deed himself.
12:10 sword will never depart Refers to internal strife among the royal family. The remainder of the book recounts this judgment, especially chs. 13 and 15. The mention of the sword recalls David's tool of murder in the preceding verse.
12:11 I will take See v. 8 and note. **he will sleep** This second judgment happens via Absalom in 16:22.
12:12 broad daylight This will occur in plain sight of all Israel.
12:13 I have sinned against the LORD David acknowledges his wrongdoing (see Ps 51). **You are not going to die** Death was the usual penalty for adultery (Lev 20:10).
12:14 the son born to you will die According to the Law, the consequence for David's sin was death. However, rather than requiring the life of the king (which would destroy the nation; see 11:1 and note; 21:17), his child dies. This third judgment seems to be an example of

¹⁵After Nathan had gone home, the LORD struck the child that Uriah's wife had borne to David, and he became ill. ¹⁶David pleaded with God for the child. He fasted and spent the nights lying in sackcloth*a* on the ground. ¹⁷The elders of his household stood beside him to get him up from the ground, but he refused, and he would not eat any food with them.

¹⁸On the seventh day the child died. David's attendants were afraid to tell him that the child was dead, for they thought, "While the child was still living, he wouldn't listen to us when we spoke to him. How can we now tell him the child is dead? He may do something desperate."

¹⁹David noticed that his attendants were whispering among themselves, and he realized the child was dead. "Is the child dead?" he asked.

"Yes," they replied, "he is dead."

²⁰Then David got up from the ground. After he had washed, put on lotions and changed his clothes, he went into the house of the LORD and worshiped. Then he went to his own house, and at his request they served him food, and he ate.

²¹His attendants asked him, "Why are you acting this way? While the child was alive, you fasted and wept, but now that the child is dead, you get up and eat!"

²²He answered, "While the child was still alive, I fasted and wept. I thought, 'Who knows? The LORD may be gracious to me and let the child live.' ²³But now that he is dead, why should I go on fasting? Can I bring him back again? I will go to him, but he will not return to me."

²⁴Then David comforted his wife Bathsheba, and he went to her and made love to her. She gave birth to a son, and they named him Solomon. The LORD loved him; ²⁵and because the LORD loved him, he sent word through Nathan the prophet to name him Jedidiah.*b*

²⁶Meanwhile Joab fought against Rabbah of the Ammonites and captured the royal citadel. ²⁷Joab then sent messengers to David, saying, "I have fought against Rabbah and taken its water supply. ²⁸Now muster the rest of the troops and besiege the city and capture it. Otherwise I will take the city, and it will be named after me." ²⁹So David mustered the entire army and went to Rabbah, and attacked and captured it. ³⁰David took the crown from their king's*c* head, and it was placed on his own head. It weighed a talent*d* of gold, and it was set with precious stones. David

---

a 16 Dead Sea Scrolls and Septuagint; Masoretic Text does not have *in sackcloth*.   *b* 25 *Jedidiah* means *loved by the LORD.*
c 30 Or *from Milkom's* (that is, Molek's)   *d* 30 That is, about 75 pounds or about 34 kilograms

---

intergenerational punishment (Ex 20:5; 34:7; Dt 5:9) and may align with the curse the Law prescribed for a woman found to be adulterous—that she would be barren (Nu 5:22), although Bathsheba is not barren forever (see 2Sa 12:24–25).

12:15 Uriah's wife Like the widow of Nabal (Abigail), the text frequently describes Bathsheba as belonging to someone else (compare 1Sa 27:3 and note). She is called David's wife in 2Sa 12:24, indicating that legitimacy has been granted to their marriage after judgment on David's sin is carried out.

12:16–23 The third judgment Yahweh notes will come against David happens first (see v. 14 and note).

12:16 spent the nights lying in sackcloth on the ground A shameful act meant to communicate the depth of his sorrow and repentance.

12:18 He may do something desperate David's servants fear that the king will harm himself because it was his sin that caused the child to die.

12:20 house of the LORD Refers to the tabernacle. **worshiped** David's response is astonishing and pious—though it was Yahweh who had demanded the life of the child (v. 14), David still worships him.

12:21 Why are you acting this way David's servants consider his response to the situation to be incongruous. His actions before the child's death resemble the mourning ritual following a death. His actions after the child's death suggest that the period of mourning is over, when it should have just begun.

12:22 I fasted and wept David grieved over his sin and the punishment against his child. He demonstrated his remorse and repentance to Yahweh in the hope that he might spare the child.

12:23 I will go to him Reflects David's conviction that he will be reunited with his departed child after his own

death. This reality appears to comfort David (v. 20). He is therefore able to console his wife in v. 24.

12:24–25 Yahweh allows Bathsheba to conceive again after her first child dies. He blesses David and Bathsheba with a son, Solomon, who will later succeed David as king.

12:24 they named him Solomon Even in judgment, Yahweh is merciful. He gives David and Bathsheba another son who will be as great as his father. **The LORD loved him** Solomon is the only person in the OT of whom it is said, "Yahweh loved him."

12:25 Jedidiah To commemorate his love for Solomon, Yahweh instructs David to give him the name Jedidiah ("beloved of Yahweh"). This name for Solomon is not mentioned anywhere else. It is possible that Jedidiah was his given name, and Solomon was his throne name. It was not unusual in the ancient Near East for kings to reign under a different name than their given name.

12:26–31 The narrative now resumes the Ammonite battle from ch. 11 (see note on 11:1–27). Joab takes the water supply, which will inevitably lead to the Ammonites' defeat. He summons David to finish the job so that the king will receive the glory for the victory.

12:26 Joab David's nephew and the commander of his army. See 2Sa 2:13 and note. **Rabbah of the Ammonites** See Eze 21:20 and note; 2Sa 11:25.

12:27 its water supply If Joab had taken their water supply, the inhabitants of the city could only survive for a short time.

12:28 besiege the city By following Joab's instructions, the king will receive the honor of a military victory rather than his general. **it will be named after me** Compare 5:7 and note.

12:30 king's The Hebrew text may refer to the king of the Ammonites, whose name is not mentioned here.

took a great quantity of plunder from the city ³¹and brought out the people who were there, consigning them to labor with saws and with iron picks and axes, and he made them work at brickmaking.ᵃ David did this to all the Ammonite towns. Then he and his entire army returned to Jerusalem.

Amnon and Tamar

13 In the course of time, Amnon son of David fell in love with Tamar, the beautiful sister of Absalom son of David.

²Amnon became so obsessed with his sister Tamar that he made himself ill. She was a virgin, and it seemed impossible for him to do anything to her.

³Now Amnon had an adviser named Jonadab son of Shimeah, David's brother. Jonadab was a very shrewd man. ⁴He asked Amnon, "Why do you, the king's son, look so haggard morning after morning? Won't you tell me?"

Amnon said to him, "I'm in love with Tamar, my brother Absalom's sister."

⁵"Go to bed and pretend to be ill," Jonadab said. "When your father comes to see you, say to him, 'I would like my sister Tamar to come and give me something to eat. Let her prepare the food in my sight so I may watch her and then eat it from her hand.'"

⁶So Amnon lay down and pretended to be ill. When the king came to see him, Amnon said to him, "I would like my sister Tamar to come and make some special bread in my sight, so I may eat from her hand."

⁷David sent word to Tamar at the palace: "Go to the house of your brother Amnon and prepare some food for him." ⁸So Tamar went to the house of her brother Amnon, who was lying down. She took some dough, kneaded it, made the bread in his sight and baked it. ⁹Then she took the pan and served him the bread, but he refused to eat.

"Send everyone out of here," Amnon said. So everyone left him. ¹⁰Then Amnon said to Tamar, "Bring the food here into my bedroom so I may eat from your hand." And Tamar took the bread she had prepared and brought it to her brother Amnon in his bedroom. ¹¹But when she took it to him to eat, he grabbed her and said, "Come to bed with me, my sister."

¹²"No, my brother!" she said to him. "Don't force me! Such a thing should not be done in Israel! Don't do this wicked thing. ¹³What about me? Where could I get rid of my disgrace? And what about you? You would be like one of the wicked

---

ᵃ *31* The meaning of the Hebrew for this clause is uncertain.

Alternatively, the Hebrew word used here, *malkum*, could refer to Molek (Milcom), the primary Ammonite deity (see 1Ki 11:5,33; Jer 49:1 and note). This may have been a statue or idol of Molek upon which a crown was set.

12:31 consigning them to labor David enslaves the inhabitants of Ammon because of their rebellion (see 2Sa 10:1–19 and note).

13:1–33 This account reflects the continuation of the judgment Yahweh pronounced against David and his house in 12:10. David is guilty of adultery and murder (see ch. 11). Here, his daughter is raped (13:6–14) and his firstborn son is murdered. In David's sin, he has created an environment where his family both victimizes other people and become victims themselves.

13:1 Amnon son of David Amnon was Tamar's half-brother through their father David; Amnon's mother was Ahinoam of Jezreel (3:2). Amnon was the crown prince—the one who would inherit the throne, according to the rules of kingship based on order of birth. **beautiful sister** Tamar was Absalom's full sister (v. 4); they had the same mother, Maakah (3:2–3). **Absalom** David's third eldest son, beloved by David and renowned for his good looks (14:25).

2 Samuel 13:1

ABSALOM
The son of David and Maakah, daughter of king Talmai of Geshur, Absalom is David's third born (see 2Sa 3:3; 1Ch 3:2). At some unspecified point, David's second son, Kileab (called Daniel in 1Ch 3:1), may have died. Therefore, after Absalom murdered Amnon (David's firstborn) for raping his sister, Tamar, he was next in

line to assume the throne (see 2Sa 13). However, he fled from David and lived with his grandfather, Talmai, in Geshur for three years (see 2Sa 13:37–38). Joab brought him back from hiding, and he was reconciled with King David after two years. A short time later he led a coup against David's throne, which appeared to succeed (see 2Sa 15–17), but Absalom was ultimately killed in battle due to the strategic advice of Hushai the Arkite (see 2Sa 17:5–14; 18:1–18).

13:2 seemed impossible Amnon may have been hindered due to their familial relation or her status as the king's daughter.

13:3 Shimeah, David's brother Shimeah was the third son of David's father, Jesse, making Jonadab Amnon's cousin (1Ch 2:13). **shrewd** The Hebrew word used here, while sometimes translated "wise," has negative connotations in this instance.

13:5 Go to bed Jonadab instructs Amnon to feign illness to attract the attention of the king (see 2Sa 13:3 and note). When the king visits, Amnon is to request that Tamar come and prepare food for him. While she is there, he will have the chance to rape her.

13:6 special bread This food may have been infused with healing herbs or other remedies. The Hebrew word for it, *levivah*, is related to the Hebrew word for the heart, suggesting that these were heart-shaped or intended to benefit the heart.

13:7 to the house of your brother Amnon Members of the royal family may have had private residences, or perhaps this was only the prerogative of the crown prince. The privacy provides the perfect setting for Amnon to carry out his plot.

13:9 everyone Refers to his household stewards (v. 17).

13:12 Such a thing Refers to rape, incest or both (Ge 34:7; Lev 18:9).

13:13 my disgrace Tamar would be forever shamed

fools in Israel. Please speak to the king; he will not keep me from being married to you." [14]But he refused to listen to her, and since he was stronger than she, he raped her.

[15]Then Amnon hated her with intense hatred. In fact, he hated her more than he had loved her. Amnon said to her, "Get up and get out!"

[16]"No!" she said to him. "Sending me away would be a greater wrong than what you have already done to me."

But he refused to listen to her. [17]He called his personal servant and said, "Get this woman out of my sight and bolt the door after her." [18]So his servant put her out and bolted the door after her. She was wearing an ornate[a] robe, for this was the kind of garment the virgin daughters of the king wore. [19]Tamar put ashes on her head and tore the ornate robe she was wearing. She put her hands on her head and went away, weeping aloud as she went.

[20]Her brother Absalom said to her, "Has that Amnon, your brother, been with you? Be quiet for now, my sister; he is your brother. Don't take this thing to heart." And Tamar lived in her brother Absalom's house, a desolate woman.

[21]When King David heard all this, he was furious. [22]And Absalom never said a word to Amnon, either good or bad; he hated Amnon because he had disgraced his sister Tamar.

Absalom Kills Amnon

[23]Two years later, when Absalom's sheepshearers were at Baal Hazor near the border of Ephraim, he invited all the king's sons to come there. [24]Absalom went to the king and said, "Your ser-vant has had shearers come. Will the king and his attendants please join me?"

[25]"No, my son," the king replied. "All of us should not go; we would only be a burden to you." Although Absalom urged him, he still refused to go but gave him his blessing.

[26]Then Absalom said, "If not, please let my brother Amnon come with us."

The king asked him, "Why should he go with you?" [27]But Absalom urged him, so he sent with him Amnon and the rest of the king's sons.

[28]Absalom ordered his men, "Listen! When Amnon is in high spirits from drinking wine and I say to you, 'Strike Amnon down,' then kill him. Don't be afraid. Haven't I given you this order? Be strong and brave." [29]So Absalom's men did to Amnon what Absalom had ordered. Then all the king's sons got up, mounted their mules and fled.

[30]While they were on their way, the report came to David: "Absalom has struck down all the king's sons; not one of them is left." [31]The king stood up, tore his clothes and lay down on the ground; and all his attendants stood by with their clothes torn.

[32]But Jonadab son of Shimeah, David's brother, said, "My lord should not think that they killed all the princes; only Amnon is dead. This has been Absalom's express intention ever since the day Amnon raped his sister Tamar. [33]My lord the king should not be concerned about the report that all the king's sons are dead. Only Amnon is dead."

[34]Meanwhile, Absalom had fled.

Now the man standing watch looked up and

[a] 18 The meaning of the Hebrew for this word is uncertain; also in verse 19.

and stigmatized by this act (compare Lev 21:14). **he will not keep me** It is not likely that their marriage would be allowed because it would be considered incest (Lev 20:17; Dt 27:22). She may be desperate for any way out of this situation and is saying whatever she needs to in order to convince Amnon to let her leave.

13:16 Sending me away The Law required Amnon to marry her (see Ex 22:16–17 and note; Dt 22:28–29; note on 22:29).

13:18 an ornate robe See Ge 37:3 and note.

13:19 tore the ornate robe Symbolizes her grief over Amnon's sin against her.

13:20 a desolate woman A shameful designation indicating that she was single and without children.

13:21 he was furious In addition to Amnon's reprehensible act, he also betrayed his father, David (see 2Sa 13:6–7).

13:23 sheepshearers They were preparing for an upcoming festival (compare 1Sa 25:2).

13:24 the king Absalom's later rebellion may indicate that he intended to kill David, in addition to Amnon, for failing to punish Amnon.

13:25 he still refused to go David may have sensed that it would be a bad idea for the king and all of his sons to be in the same place at the same time. A surprise attack from an enemy would eliminate the Israelite monarchy.

13:26 let my brother Amnon come Because the king refuses to attend, Absalom requests the presence of the crown prince. Absalom's revenge on Amnon served the dual purpose of killing his sister's attacker as well as eliminating the only brother ahead of him in the line of succession. Absalom was technically third in line, but their second brother appears to have already died (see Kileab/Daniel in 2Sa 3:3; 1Ch 3:1–2). If David had attended and been killed, Absalom would have become king (see note on 2Sa 13:24). **Why should he go** David may sense Absalom's evil intentions. However, he may have assumed that Amnon would be safe—as the crown prince, he likely had a detachment of bodyguards accompanying him.

13:28 is in high spirits from drinking wine Absalom instructs his servants to kill Amnon when he is drunk.

13:29 mounted their mules The mode of kingly transportation in ancient Israel (see 18:9; 1Ki 1:33,44).

13:31 lay down on the ground See 2Sa 12:16 and note.

13:32 Jonadab See v. 3 and note. **This has been Absalom's express intention** It is unclear why Jonadab didn't disclose this information sooner—especially since he was Amnon's friend (v. 3). David does not punish him for withholding this information.

13:34–39 Fearing reprisals from the king, Absalom flees David's kingdom, waiting until a more opportune time to seize the throne.

saw many people on the road west of him, coming down the side of the hill. The watchman went and told the king, "I see men in the direction of Horonaim, on the side of the hill."[a]

[35]Jonadab said to the king, "See, the king's sons have come; it has happened just as your servant said."

[36]As he finished speaking, the king's sons came in, wailing loudly. The king, too, and all his attendants wept very bitterly.

[37]Absalom fled and went to Talmai son of Ammihud, the king of Geshur. But King David mourned many days for his son.

[38]After Absalom fled and went to Geshur, he stayed there three years. [39]And King David longed to go to Absalom, for he was consoled concerning Amnon's death.

Absalom Returns to Jerusalem

14 Joab son of Zeruiah knew that the king's heart longed for Absalom. [2]So Joab sent someone to Tekoa and had a wise woman brought from there. He said to her, "Pretend you are in mourning. Dress in mourning clothes, and don't use any cosmetic lotions. Act like a woman who has spent many days grieving for the dead. [3]Then go to the king and speak these words to him." And Joab put the words in her mouth.

[4]When the woman from Tekoa went[b] to the king, she fell with her face to the ground to pay him honor, and she said, "Help me, Your Majesty!"

[5]The king asked her, "What is troubling you?"

She said, "I am a widow; my husband is dead. [6]I your servant had two sons. They got into a fight with each other in the field, and no one was there to separate them. One struck the other and killed him. [7]Now the whole clan has risen up against your servant; they say, 'Hand over the one who struck his brother down, so that we may put him to death for the life of his brother whom he killed; then we will get rid of the heir as well.' They would put out the only burning coal I have left, leaving my husband neither name nor descendant on the face of the earth."

[8]The king said to the woman, "Go home, and I will issue an order in your behalf."

[9]But the woman from Tekoa said to him, "Let my lord the king pardon me and my family, and let the king and his throne be without guilt."

[10]The king replied, "If anyone says anything to you, bring them to me, and they will not bother you again."

[11]She said, "Then let the king invoke the LORD his God to prevent the avenger of blood from adding to the destruction, so that my son will not be destroyed."

"As surely as the LORD lives," he said, "not one hair of your son's head will fall to the ground."

[12]Then the woman said, "Let your servant speak a word to my lord the king."

"Speak," he replied.

[13]The woman said, "Why then have you devised a thing like this against the people of God? When the king says this, does he not convict himself, for the king has not brought back his banished son? [14]Like water spilled on the ground, which cannot

---

[a] 34 Septuagint; Hebrew does not have this sentence.
[b] 4 Many Hebrew manuscripts, Septuagint, Vulgate and Syriac; most Hebrew manuscripts *spoke*

13:35 it has happened just as your servant said When everyone else around him is mourning for Amnon, the crafty Jonadab—who was Amnon's friend (see v. 3 and note)—takes this opportunity to point out that he was right.
13:37 Talmai Absalom's maternal grandfather (see 3:3). His family connection probably secured political refuge. **Geshur** Located east of the Jordan River.
13:39 King David longed to go to Absalom David probably desires to be reunited with his son (14:1).

14:1–33 Joab devises a plan to bring Absalom back to Jerusalem. Absalom is banished to his royal residence for two years—no doubt under strict observation—before finally being welcomed back into the king's presence.
14:1 Joab David's nephew and the commander of his army. See 2Sa 2:13 and note. **king's heart longed for** The meaning of this phrase is ambiguous; it only means that Absalom was on his mind.
14:2 Tekoa Located south of Jerusalem, between Hebron and Bethlehem, David's hometown. Tekoa was later the hometown of the prophet Amos (Am 1:1).
14:4 she fell with her face to the ground She exhibits proper protocol to the monarch (compare 1Sa 24:8 and note; 2Sa 9:6,8; and 1Ki 1:16,23).
14:5 I am a widow Joab has formulated a story specifically designed to grab David's attention. The king was

specially charged with taking care of widows (e.g., Ex 22:22–24; Dt 24:17–21). Her case is especially poignant since the death of both her sons—one by murder and the other by death penalty—would mean that her family line would be destroyed.
14:6 One struck the other Recalls Absalom's murder of Amnon. These sons of David were half-brothers (see note on 2Sa 13:1).
14:7 Hand over the one who struck his brother down In accordance with the Law, the brother should be put to death (Lev 24:17; Nu 35:16–21). The woman is asking David to overrule this decision and exercise mercy.
14:9 Let my lord the king pardon me The woman indicates that the family may hold her responsible for this leniency in the face of the Law's demands.
14:11 avenger of blood See 2Sa 3:27 and note. **As surely as the LORD lives** David takes an oath to protect the murderer in this woman's story; he unwittingly agrees to protect Absalom, whose situation is the same. **not one hair of your son's head will fall to the ground** David unwittingly foreshadows Absalom's fate (see v. 26; 18:9).
14:13 king Like Nathan with his parable of the sheep in 12:1–6, the woman brings this fictional case before David so that he might pronounce judgment on himself (see 12:1 and note).
14:14 a banished person does not remain banished The woman appeals to God's actions in order to prompt the king to respond accordingly in the case of Absalom.

be recovered, so we must die. But that is not what God desires; rather, he devises ways so that a banished person does not remain banished from him.

[15] "And now I have come to say this to my lord the king because the people have made me afraid. Your servant thought, 'I will speak to the king; perhaps he will grant his servant's request. [16] Perhaps the king will agree to deliver his servant from the hand of the man who is trying to cut off both me and my son from God's inheritance.'

[17] "And now your servant says, 'May the word of my lord the king secure my inheritance, for my lord the king is like an angel of God in discerning good and evil. May the LORD your God be with you.'"

[18] Then the king said to the woman, "Don't keep from me the answer to what I am going to ask you."

"Let my lord the king speak," the woman said.

[19] The king asked, "Isn't the hand of Joab with you in all this?"

The woman answered, "As surely as you live, my lord the king, no one can turn to the right or to the left from anything my lord the king says. Yes, it was your servant Joab who instructed me to do this and who put all these words into the mouth of your servant. [20] Your servant Joab did this to change the present situation. My lord has wisdom like that of an angel of God — he knows everything that happens in the land."

[21] The king said to Joab, "Very well, I will do it. Go, bring back the young man Absalom."

[22] Joab fell with his face to the ground to pay him honor, and he blessed the king. Joab said, "Today your servant knows that he has found favor in your eyes, my lord the king, because the king has granted his servant's request."

[23] Then Joab went to Geshur and brought Absalom back to Jerusalem. [24] But the king said, "He must go to his own house; he must not see my face." So Absalom went to his own house and did not see the face of the king.

[25] In all Israel there was not a man so highly praised for his handsome appearance as Absalom. From the top of his head to the sole of his foot there was no blemish in him. [26] Whenever he cut the hair of his head — he used to cut his hair once a year because it became too heavy for him — he would weigh it, and its weight was two hundred shekels[a] by the royal standard.

[27] Three sons and a daughter were born to Absalom. His daughter's name was Tamar, and she became a beautiful woman.

[28] Absalom lived two years in Jerusalem without seeing the king's face. [29] Then Absalom sent for Joab in order to send him to the king, but Joab refused to come to him. So he sent a second time, but he refused to come. [30] Then he said to his servants, "Look, Joab's field is next to mine, and he has barley there. Go and set it on fire." So Absalom's servants set the field on fire.

[31] Then Joab did go to Absalom's house, and he said to him, "Why have your servants set my field on fire?"

[32] Absalom said to Joab, "Look, I sent word to you and said, 'Come here so I can send you to the king to ask, "Why have I come from Geshur? It would be better for me if I were still there!"' Now then, I want to see the king's face, and if I am guilty of anything, let him put me to death."

[33] So Joab went to the king and told him this. Then the king summoned Absalom, and he came in and bowed down with his face to the ground before the king. And the king kissed Absalom.

Absalom's Conspiracy

15 In the course of time, Absalom provided himself with a chariot and horses and with fifty men to run ahead of him. [2] He would get up early and stand by the side of the road leading to the city gate. Whenever anyone came with a com-

---

[a] 26 That is, about 5 pounds or about 2.3 kilograms

14:17 like an angel of God Compare 1Sa 29:9; 2Sa 19:27.

14:24 his own house Compare 13:7 and note. **he must not see my face** David allows Absalom to come back, but he will not give him an audience.

14:25 handsome The description of Absalom in vv. 25–26 indicates that appearances can be deceiving (see 1Sa 9:2 and note), and also foreshadows his manner of death (2Sa 18:9).

14:26 hair of his head See v. 11 and note.

14:27 Three sons These sons may have died young (see 18:18 and note). **Tamar** Absalom's daughter is named for his disgraced sister (see 13:7–22).

14:29 in order to send him to the king Absalom sends Joab because he cannot approach the king himself.

14:30 set the field on fire Absalom sets Joab's field on fire to gain his attention. His actions demonstrate his violent nature and foreshadow his deceitful conduct in subsequent chapters.

14:33 bowed down with his face to the ground Compare v. 4; 1Sa 24:8 and note. This submission is short-lived, as Absalom still intends to take over the kingdom (see 2Sa 15–18). **king kissed Absalom** Signals their reconciliation.

15:1–12 Absalom's subservience to David is short-lived (see 14:33). Soon after the king welcomes him back, Absalom begins to incite rebellion among the people and turn their hearts from following David.

15:1 with a chariot and horses and with fifty men Suggests that Absalom is laying claim to his father's throne (compare 1Sa 8:11; 1Ki 1:5) — a treasonous act since David is still alive.

15:2 He would get up early By doing so, he can intercept people who are bringing legal disputes to the king. **stand by the side of the road leading to the city gate** The location where the Israelites conducted business and other legal matters.

plaint to be placed before the king for a decision, Absalom would call out to him, "What town are you from?" He would answer, "Your servant is from one of the tribes of Israel." ³Then Absalom would say to him, "Look, your claims are valid and proper, but there is no representative of the king to hear you." ⁴And Absalom would add, "If only I were appointed judge in the land! Then everyone who has a complaint or case could come to me and I would see that they receive justice."

⁵Also, whenever anyone approached him to bow down before him, Absalom would reach out his hand, take hold of him and kiss him. ⁶Absalom behaved in this way toward all the Israelites who came to the king asking for justice, and so he stole the hearts of the people of Israel.

⁷At the end of four*ᵃ* years, Absalom said to the king, "Let me go to Hebron and fulfill a vow I made to the LORD. ⁸While your servant was living at Geshur in Aram, I made this vow: 'If the LORD takes me back to Jerusalem, I will worship the LORD in Hebron.*ᵇ*'"

⁹The king said to him, "Go in peace." So he went to Hebron.

¹⁰Then Absalom sent secret messengers throughout the tribes of Israel to say, "As soon as you hear the sound of the trumpets, then say, 'Absalom is king in Hebron.'" ¹¹Two hundred men from Jerusalem had accompanied Absalom.

They had been invited as guests and went quite innocently, knowing nothing about the matter. ¹²While Absalom was offering sacrifices, he also sent for Ahithophel the Gilonite, David's counselor, to come from Giloh, his hometown. And so the conspiracy gained strength, and Absalom's following kept on increasing.

David Flees

¹³A messenger came and told David, "The hearts of the people of Israel are with Absalom."

¹⁴Then David said to all his officials who were with him in Jerusalem, "Come! We must flee, or none of us will escape from Absalom. We must leave immediately, or he will move quickly to overtake us and bring ruin on us and put the city to the sword."

¹⁵The king's officials answered him, "Your servants are ready to do whatever our lord the king chooses."

¹⁶The king set out, with his entire household following him; but he left ten concubines to take care of the palace. ¹⁷So the king set out, with all the people following him, and they halted at the edge of the city. ¹⁸All his men marched past him,

ᵃ 7 Some Septuagint manuscripts, Syriac and Josephus; Hebrew *forty* *ᵇ 8* Some Septuagint manuscripts; Hebrew does not have *in Hebron.*

15:3 there is no representative of the king to hear you Absalom notes flaws in David's administration in order to foster discontent against David among the people.
15:4 I would see that they receive justice This was the prerogative of the king; Absalom is subtly indicating that he could be a better king than David is.
15:5 to bow down before him People paid homage to kings, not heirs.
15:6 stole the hearts of the people of Israel The Hebrew word used here, *ganav*, can refer to deceiving as well as to stealing (see Ge 31:20,26). Both senses of the word work here: Absalom steals the people's affections away from David by deception.
15:7 At the end of four years While the Hebrew text here literally reads "forty years," this may be a scribal error. Some other ancient versions say "four years." If the correct reference is four years, then these events take place two years after the events of 2Sa 14. **Let me go to Hebron and fulfill a vow** Absalom's pious request hides his ulterior motives.
15:8 Geshur See 13:37–38; 14:23.
15:9 he went to Hebron Recalls 2:1,3. This oath is merely a façade to enable Absalom to safely travel to the former royal capital (see 5:1–10). David had made his initial claim to the throne in Hebron and gained the support of one of the most important cities in Judah. Absalom patterns his rise to power on his father's. He may also be attempting to gain support from Hebron's inhabitants, who may feel the sting of diminished importance now that Jerusalem is the capital.
15:11 Two hundred men from Jerusalem Probably men of prominence whom Absalom could manipulate into supporting his revolt. Absalom invites them to partake in the meal that will follow his sacrifices.

15:12 Ahithophel the Gilonite, David's counselor His presence with Absalom lends credence to the prince's claim to the throne (see v. 31). It is unclear whether Ahithophel is aware of Absalom's rebellion, but his presence would indicate to the onlookers that he supports Absalom.

15:13–37 Rather than quelling the rebellion and killing his son, David leaves the royal city. While exiting, he makes arrangements to remain informed about Absalom's plans. This section recalls the period when David fled from Saul and patiently waited on Yahweh to give him the throne.

15:14 none of us will escape from Absalom David feels that his only option is to flee, suggesting Absalom enlisted the support of the military as well. If this is the case, the scope of the conspiracy is larger than the narrative suggests (see v. 12). **to the sword** David is convinced that if he remains in Jerusalem, Absalom will make war on the capital city. In order to protect his subjects, he flees and allows Absalom to peacefully occupy the city.

15:16 his entire household Includes rival claimants to the throne, whom Absalom would likely have killed. **to take care of the palace** Indicates that concubines also served the practical function of looking after the household and tending to daily administrative tasks (see 3:7 and note). This act foreshadows the events of 16:20–22 and recalls the judgment of 12:11–12.

15:17 at the edge of the city Probably located close to the city's main gate.

15:18 the Kerethites and Pelethites See 8:18 and note. **who had accompanied him from Gath** See 1Sa 27; 29.

along with all the Kerethites and Pelethites; and all the six hundred Gittites who had accompanied him from Gath marched before the king.

¹⁹The king said to Ittai the Gittite, "Why should you come along with us? Go back and stay with King Absalom. You are a foreigner, an exile from your homeland. ²⁰You came only yesterday. And today shall I make you wander about with us, when I do not know where I am going? Go back, and take your people with you. May the LORD show you kindness and faithfulness."ᵃ

²¹But Ittai replied to the king, "As surely as the LORD lives, and as my lord the king lives, wherever my lord the king may be, whether it means life or death, there will your servant be."

²²David said to Ittai, "Go ahead, march on." So Ittai the Gittite marched on with all his men and the families that were with him.

²³The whole countryside wept aloud as all the people passed by. The king also crossed the Kidron Valley, and all the people moved on toward the wilderness.

²⁴Zadok was there, too, and all the Levites who were with him were carrying the ark of the covenant of God. They set down the ark of God, and Abiathar offered sacrifices until all the people had finished leaving the city.

²⁵Then the king said to Zadok, "Take the ark of God back into the city. If I find favor in the LORD's eyes, he will bring me back and let me see it and his dwelling place again. ²⁶But if he says, 'I am not pleased with you,' then I am ready; let him do to me whatever seems good to him."

²⁷The king also said to Zadok the priest, "Do you understand? Go back to the city with my blessing. Take your son Ahimaaz with you, and also Abiathar's son Jonathan. You and Abiathar return with your two sons. ²⁸I will wait at the fords in the wilderness until word comes from you to inform me." ²⁹So Zadok and Abiathar took the ark of God back to Jerusalem and stayed there.

³⁰But David continued up the Mount of Olives, weeping as he went; his head was covered and he was barefoot. All the people with him covered their heads too and were weeping as they went up. ³¹Now David had been told, "Ahithophel is among the conspirators with Absalom." So David prayed, "LORD, turn Ahithophel's counsel into foolishness."

³²When David arrived at the summit, where people used to worship God, Hushai the Arkite was there to meet him, his robe torn and dust on his head. ³³David said to him, "If you go with me, you will be a burden to me. ³⁴But if you return to the city and say to Absalom, 'Your Majesty, I will be your servant; I was your father's servant in the past, but now I will be your servant,' then you can help me by frustrating Ahithophel's advice. ³⁵Won't the priests Zadok and Abiathar be there with you? Tell them anything you hear in the king's palace. ³⁶Their two sons, Ahimaaz son of Zadok and Jonathan son of Abiathar, are there with them. Send them to me with anything you hear."

³⁷So Hushai, David's confidant, arrived at Jerusalem as Absalom was entering the city.

David and Ziba

16 When David had gone a short distance beyond the summit, there was Ziba, the steward of Mephibosheth, waiting to meet him. He had a string of donkeys saddled and loaded with two hundred loaves of bread, a hundred cakes of raisins, a hundred cakes of figs and a skin of wine.

²The king asked Ziba, "Why have you brought these?"

Ziba answered, "The donkeys are for the king's household to ride on, the bread and fruit are for the men to eat, and the wine is to refresh those who become exhausted in the wilderness."

ᵃ 20 Septuagint; Hebrew *May kindness and faithfulness be with you*

15:19 Ittai the Gittite The commander of the Gittite mercenaries from 2Sa 15:18.

15:20 You came only yesterday A figure of speech meaning "recently."

15:21 whether it means life or death The Philistines were usually archenemies of Israel, but this Philistine is more loyal than the members of David's own household.

15:23 the Kidron Valley Located east of Jerusalem, between the city and the Mount of Olives. **the wilderness** Recalls David's flight from Saul in 1Sa 21–26.

15:24 Abiathar See 2Sa 8:17 and note.

15:25 Take the ark of God back The ark would have slowed David's escape because it had to be handled in a specific, careful manner (see ch. 6).

15:28 to inform me The priests serve as David's informants, something Absalom would not have expected (see v. 35). They will pass information along to their sons, who will be in contact with David (see 17:17).

15:30 his head was covered and he was barefoot Signs of mourning.

15:31 Ahithophel is among the conspirators with Absalom See 2Sa 15:12 and note. **turn Ahithophel's counsel into foolishness** Yahweh answers this prayer in 17:14,23.

15:32 Hushai the Arkite In answer to David's prayer, another advisor who will frustrate Ahithophel's advice to Absalom (see 17:5–14) appears immediately. The Arkites were a clan who lived in the territory of Benjamin, near Bethel (Jos 16:2).

16:1–4 Ziba, Mephibosheth's servant, brings David gifts of transportation and sustenance. In addition, he accuses Mephibosheth of rebelling against David, which is surprising because David showed great kindness to Mephibosheth (see 2Sa 9). In response to Ziba's kindness, David bequeaths him all that he formerly gave to Mephibosheth (see 9:7). Later, Mephibosheth will give a different version of events (19:24–30).

16:2 men Refers to soldiers (e.g., 1:15; 2:14); these were military rations.

³The king then asked, "Where is your master's grandson?"

Ziba said to him, "He is staying in Jerusalem, because he thinks, 'Today the Israelites will restore to me my grandfather's kingdom.'"

⁴Then the king said to Ziba, "All that belonged to Mephibosheth is now yours."

"I humbly bow," Ziba said. "May I find favor in your eyes, my lord the king."

Shimei Curses David

⁵As King David approached Bahurim, a man from the same clan as Saul's family came out from there. His name was Shimei son of Gera, and he cursed as he came out. ⁶He pelted David and all the king's officials with stones, though all the troops and the special guard were on David's right and left. ⁷As he cursed, Shimei said, "Get out, get out, you murderer, you scoundrel! ⁸The LORD has repaid you for all the blood you shed in the household of Saul, in whose place you have reigned. The LORD has given the kingdom into the hands of your son Absalom. You have come to ruin because you are a murderer!"

⁹Then Abishai son of Zeruiah said to the king, "Why should this dead dog curse my lord the king? Let me go over and cut off his head."

¹⁰But the king said, "What does this have to do with you, you sons of Zeruiah? If he is cursing because the LORD said to him, 'Curse David,' who can ask, 'Why do you do this?'"

¹¹David then said to Abishai and all his officials, "My son, my own flesh and blood, is trying to kill me. How much more, then, this Benjamite! Leave him alone; let him curse, for the LORD has told him to. ¹²It may be that the LORD will look upon my misery and restore to me his covenant blessing instead of his curse today."

¹³So David and his men continued along the road while Shimei was going along the hillside opposite him, cursing as he went and throwing stones at him and showering him with dirt. ¹⁴The king and all the people with him arrived at their destination exhausted. And there he refreshed himself.

The Advice of Ahithophel and Hushai

¹⁵Meanwhile, Absalom and all the men of Israel came to Jerusalem, and Ahithophel was with him. ¹⁶Then Hushai the Arkite, David's confidant, went to Absalom and said to him, "Long live the king! Long live the king!"

¹⁷Absalom said to Hushai, "So this is the love you show your friend? If he's your friend, why didn't you go with him?"

¹⁸Hushai said to Absalom, "No, the one chosen by the LORD, by these people, and by all the men of Israel — his I will be, and I will remain with him. ¹⁹Furthermore, whom should I serve? Should I not serve the son? Just as I served your father, so I will serve you."

²⁰Absalom said to Ahithophel, "Give us your advice. What should we do?"

²¹Ahithophel answered, "Sleep with your father's concubines whom he left to take care of the palace. Then all Israel will hear that you have made yourself obnoxious to your father, and the hands of everyone with you will be more resolute." ²²So they pitched a tent for Absalom on the

---

16:3 Israelites will restore to me A lie, if Mephibosheth's later account is to be believed (see 19:24–30).

16:4 All that belonged to Mephibosheth The king rewards Ziba for his loyalty, but apparently he does not punish Mephibosheth. He may be honoring his covenant with Jonathan (see 1Sa 20:15 and note) or showing pity.

16:5–14 As David travels toward the wilderness, Shimei, one of Saul's relatives, hurls stones and shouts curses at him. David's nephew Abishai asks to decapitate Shimei, but David will not allow him, figuring that he is an instrument of Yahweh or, if not, that Yahweh will punish him. The king and his entourage continue in shame until they reach the Jordan River.

16:6 He pelted David and all the king's officials with stones A physical attack against the king or royal family was punishable by death (see 2Sa 16:9). In light of David's edict against harming Yahweh's anointed (see 1:15 and note), it is surprising that Shimei goes unpunished.

16:7 you murderer Shimei calls David a murderer, possibly suggesting that the events of 21:1–14 preceded this encounter. Alternatively, he may hold David responsible for the deaths of Ish-Bosheth (4:5–8), Abner (3:22–30) or possibly even Saul himself. **you scoundrel** See 1Sa 2:12 and note.

16:9 Abishai son of Zeruiah David's nephew. See 2Sa 2:18 and note. **dead dog** See 3:8 and note.

16:10 sons of Zeruiah Occasionally used in a derogatory manner to indicate their violence (see 2Sa 3:39; 19:22).

16:11 LORD has told him David allows Shimei to curse him because he presumes that Yahweh may have told Shimei to do so.

16:15–23 Absalom makes a royal procession through the city and assumes his father's throne. Hushai greets him there and cunningly convinces Absalom that he is loyal to him. Absalom then has sex with his father's concubines as a testimony to everyone that he is making a claim to David's throne.

16:15 Ahithophel was with him David's former counselor, now definitely loyal to Absalom. See 15:12 and note.

16:16 Hushai Sent by David to act as a false counselor to Absalom. See 15:32–37. **Long live the king** Hushai is intentionally ambiguous. He could be pronouncing blessings upon David, not Absalom.

16:18 the one chosen by Another ambiguous reference to David (compare v. 16).

16:21 Sleep with your father's concubines Ahithophel instructs Absalom to have sex with the concubines, thereby signifying his occupation of his father's throne (see 3:7 and note). **whom he left** See 15:16 and note.

16:22 he slept with his father's concubines Fulfills Nathan's prophecy in 12:11–12. Following this act, all three of Yahweh's judgments against David for his murder of Uriah and adultery with Bathsheba have come to pass

roof, and he slept with his father's concubines in the sight of all Israel.

²³Now in those days the advice Ahithophel gave was like that of one who inquires of God. That was how both David and Absalom regarded all of Ahithophel's advice.

17 Ahithophel said to Absalom, "I would[a] choose twelve thousand men and set out tonight in pursuit of David. ²I would attack him while he is weary and weak. I would strike him with terror, and then all the people with him will flee. I would strike down only the king ³and bring all the people back to you. The death of the man you seek will mean the return of all; all the people will be unharmed." ⁴This plan seemed good to Absalom and to all the elders of Israel.

⁵But Absalom said, "Summon also Hushai the Arkite, so we can hear what he has to say as well." ⁶When Hushai came to him, Absalom said, "Ahithophel has given this advice. Should we do what he says? If not, give us your opinion."

⁷Hushai replied to Absalom, "The advice Ahithophel has given is not good this time. ⁸You know your father and his men; they are fighters, and as fierce as a wild bear robbed of her cubs. Besides, your father is an experienced fighter; he will not spend the night with the troops. ⁹Even now, he is hidden in a cave or some other place. If he should attack your troops first,[b] whoever hears about it will say, 'There has been a slaughter among the troops who follow Absalom.' ¹⁰Then even the bravest soldier, whose heart is like the heart of a lion, will melt with fear, for all Israel knows that your father is a fighter and that those with him are brave.

¹¹"So I advise you: Let all Israel, from Dan to Beersheba — as numerous as the sand on the seashore — be gathered to you, with you yourself leading them into battle. ¹²Then we will attack him wherever he may be found, and we will fall on him as dew settles on the ground. Neither he nor any of his men will be left alive. ¹³If he withdraws into a city, then all Israel will bring ropes to that city, and we will drag it down to the valley until not so much as a pebble is left."

¹⁴Absalom and all the men of Israel said, "The advice of Hushai the Arkite is better than that

---

a 1 Or Let me   *b* 9 Or When some of the men fall at the first attack

---

(see 12:10–14). The child of their unlawful union died (12:14,19); feuding among the royal family was initiated and persisted (12:10; 13:14,28–29); and now David's son attempts to usurp the throne (12:11–12). Taking a king's concubines was a common way in the ancient Near East of indicating a claim to the throne.
16:23 one who inquires of God Indicates that Ahithophel's advice was held in the highest esteem.

17:1–29 In response to David's prayer in 15:31, Yahweh raises up Hushai the Arkite to defeat the counsel of Ahithophel. Yahweh also ensures that the needs of David and his entourage are met while in the wilderness.

17:1 I would choose twelve thousand men An overwhelming force that is much larger than David's. David is accompanied by his band of disenfranchised warriors (1Sa 22:2; 23:13), the Gittite mercenaries (2Sa 15:18), governmental officials (15:14–17) and the members of his household (15:16). This group probably totals about 2,000 people. **tonight in pursuit of David** Communicates the urgency of Ahithophel's counsel. Because Absalom needs to gain total control of the throne, Ahithophel suggests an immediate surprise attack on David and his forces at night.
17:2 people with him will flee Ahithophel claims that David's companions will flee when they see the response of their ruler; this reaction is typical of Saul (see 1Sa 10:22 and note), not David — a point that Hushai highlights in 2Sa 17:8. **I would strike down only the king** Ahithophel assumes that David's forces will not fight back, which is unlikely given their reputation as warriors (e.g., 23:8–23). This aspect of the plan would only be possible if they had all fled.
17:3 bring all the people back If only the king is killed (v. 2), then all his followers will be forced to surrender to Absalom. The language here reflects the earlier note that Absalom stole the heart of the people (15:6,12–13).
17:4 This plan seemed good Ahithophel's plan is tactically brilliant; nevertheless, Yahweh preserves David.
17:5 Hushai Sent by David to act as a false counselor to Absalom. See 15:32–37; note on 15:32.

17:7 not good Contrasts the reaction to Ahithophel's previous advice (see 16:23 and note).
17:8 as fierce As opposed to being weary and discouraged (v. 2). Although Ahithophel's assessment of David and his men reflects their true state (see 15:30; 16:14), Hushai paints a different picture based on David's reputation as a warrior. **he will not spend the night** David, expecting an attack, would hide himself so he could not be easily found by Absalom's soldiers.
17:9 If he should attack your troops This statement contrasts the notion that all of David's men will flee and leave him vulnerable to attack (compare vv. 2–3).
17:10 will melt with fear If David kills some of Ahithophel's forces, the military mystique surrounding King David would cause Ahithophel's 12,000 troops to flee.
17:11 Let all Israel, from Dan to Beersheba After undermining Ahithophel's strategy (vv. 7–10), Hushai proposes a new plan that contradicts Ahithophel's. He advises that Absalom should summon all of Israel's warriors to battle, not merely 12,000 men (compare v. 1). This would take some time, but would almost guarantee David's defeat. In reality, Hushai is buying time for David to rest and regroup. Leading the army into battle was usually the prerogative of the king (compare 11:1 and note). In this instance, Absalom's presence on the battlefield would function as a claim to the throne much like the events of 16:21–22.
17:12 we will attack him Since David will be hard to find (vv. 8–9), Absalom should take the time to assemble a massive force and scour the land until he is found. **Neither he nor any of his men will be left alive** Hushai contends that all of David's forces should be eliminated, not just David (vv. 2–3).
17:13 we will drag it down to the valley With all of Israel's forces gathered for battle, Absalom will be able to besiege any city to which David might flee. This would not be possible with merely 12,000 troops (see v. 1) because individual cities would likely have their own defenses in addition to David's skilled mercenaries.
17:14 The advice of Hushai the Arkite is better

of Ahithophel." For the LORD had determined to frustrate the good advice of Ahithophel in order to bring disaster on Absalom.

[15]Hushai told Zadok and Abiathar, the priests, "Ahithophel has advised Absalom and the elders of Israel to do such and such, but I have advised them to do so and so. [16]Now send a message at once and tell David, 'Do not spend the night at the fords in the wilderness; cross over without fail, or the king and all the people with him will be swallowed up.'"

[17]Jonathan and Ahimaaz were staying at En Rogel. A female servant was to go and inform them, and they were to go and tell King David, for they could not risk being seen entering the city. [18]But a young man saw them and told Absalom. So the two of them left at once and went to the house of a man in Bahurim. He had a well in his courtyard, and they climbed down into it. [19]His wife took a covering and spread it out over the opening of the well and scattered grain over it. No one knew anything about it.

[20]When Absalom's men came to the woman at the house, they asked, "Where are Ahimaaz and Jonathan?"

The woman answered them, "They crossed over the brook."[a] The men searched but found no one, so they returned to Jerusalem.

[21]After they had gone, the two climbed out of the well and went to inform King David. They said to him, "Set out and cross the river at once; Ahithophel has advised such and such against you." [22]So David and all the people with him set out and crossed the Jordan. By daybreak, no one was left who had not crossed the Jordan.

[23]When Ahithophel saw that his advice had not been followed, he saddled his donkey and set out for his house in his hometown. He put his house in order and then hanged himself. So he died and was buried in his father's tomb.

Absalom's Death

[24]David went to Mahanaim, and Absalom crossed the Jordan with all the men of Israel. [25]Absalom had appointed Amasa over the army in place of Joab. Amasa was the son of Jether,[b] an Ishmaelite[c] who had married Abigail,[d] the daughter of Nahash and sister of Zeruiah the mother of Joab. [26]The Israelites and Absalom camped in the land of Gilead.

[27]When David came to Mahanaim, Shobi son of Nahash from Rabbah of the Ammonites, and Makir son of Ammiel from Lo Debar, and Barzillai the Gileadite from Rogelim [28]brought bedding and bowls and articles of pottery. They also brought wheat and barley, flour and roasted grain, beans and lentils,[e] [29]honey and curds, sheep, and cheese from cows' milk for David and his people to eat. For they said, "The people have become exhausted and hungry and thirsty in the wilderness."

18 David mustered the men who were with him and appointed over them commanders of thousands and commanders of hundreds. [2]David sent out his troops, a third under the command

---

[a] 20 Or "They passed by the sheep pen toward the water." [b] 25 Hebrew *Ithra*, a variant of *Jether* [c] 25 Some Septuagint manuscripts (see also 1 Chron. 2:17); Hebrew and other Septuagint manuscripts *Israelite* [d] 25 Hebrew *Abigal*, a variant of *Abigail* [e] 28 Most Septuagint manuscripts and Syriac; Hebrew *lentils, and roasted grain*

This is not necessarily true, but it reflects the attitude of Absalom and his court. Ahithophel's suggestion of a surprise attack by night with six times the forces against David's weary troops would have been better for Absalom. However, Yahweh ordained that the king and his advisors would listen to Hushai, not Ahithophel. **LORD had determined** In answer to David's prayer in 15:31. **17:15 told Zadok and Abiathar, the priests** Loyal to David. See 15:35. **17:16 Do not spend the night** They prepare for the possibility that Absalom will change his mind and follow Ahithophel's advice. **17:17 Jonathan and Ahimaaz** The sons of Abiathar and Zadok. They were loyal to David. See 15:27,36. **En Rogel** A water source approximately a quarter mile from Jerusalem. **female servant was to go and inform them** Jonathan and Ahimaaz use the everyday task of obtaining water as a cover to relay information to David. **17:18 in Bahurim** Located roughly one mile south of Jerusalem. **17:23 then hanged himself** Ahithophel may sense that Absalom will die if he follows Hushai's advice. If Absalom died and David returned, Ahithophel would be killed for treason. In addition, the shame associated with his public scorn may have been too much for him to endure. **17:24 David went to Mahanaim** See 2:8 and note. **17:25 Amasa** David's nephew and the son of David's sister Abigail (1Ch 2:16–17). Absalom appointed him

over the army because Joab was with David (2Sa 18:2). **Abigal, the daughter of Nahash** This may be a copying error in which the scribe saw "Nahash" in v. 27 and wrote that instead of "Jesse." Abigail is presented as the daughter of Jesse in 1 Chronicles (see 1Ch 2:13–17). **Joab** David's nephew and the commander of his army. See 2Sa 2:13 and note. **17:26 land of Gilead** A region very loyal to Saul's dynasty (see 2:8 and note; 2:9). The Gileadites may harbor feelings of bitterness against David, despite affirming him as king in 2:4–7, since they are letting his enemies camp in their territory. **17:27 Shobi son of Nahash** Perhaps the brother of Hanun, who may have been killed due to his rebellion (10:2; 12:26–31). Shobi appears more favorably disposed to David than Hanun. **Makir son of Ammiel from Lo Debar** See 9:4.

18:1–18 Before Absalom can seize full control of Israel and Judah, he must kill his father, David. David strategically moves the battle to a site that suits the strengths of his army. The result is an overwhelming victory by David's forces and the death of his rebellious son, Absalom.

18:1 mustered the men who were with him Seems to imply that David has had time to regroup while at Mahanaim and enlist the support of additional forces. See 17:1 and note. **18:2 Joab** David's nephew and the commander of his

of Joab, a third under Joab's brother Abishai son of Zeruiah, and a third under Ittai the Gittite. The king told the troops, "I myself will surely march out with you."

³But the men said, "You must not go out; if we are forced to flee, they won't care about us. Even if half of us die, they won't care; but you are worth ten thousand of us.ᵃ It would be better now for you to give us support from the city."

⁴The king answered, "I will do whatever seems best to you."

So the king stood beside the gate while all his men marched out in units of hundreds and of thousands. ⁵The king commanded Joab, Abishai and Ittai, "Be gentle with the young man Absalom for my sake." And all the troops heard the king giving orders concerning Absalom to each of the commanders.

⁶David's army marched out of the city to fight Israel, and the battle took place in the forest of Ephraim. ⁷There Israel's troops were routed by David's men, and the casualties that day were great — twenty thousand men. ⁸The battle spread out over the whole countryside, and the forest swallowed up more men that day than the sword.

⁹Now Absalom happened to meet David's men. He was riding his mule, and as the mule went under the thick branches of a large oak, Absalom's hair got caught in the tree. He was left hanging in midair, while the mule he was riding kept on going. ¹⁰When one of the men saw what had happened,

he told Joab, "I just saw Absalom hanging in an oak tree."

¹¹Joab said to the man who had told him this, "What! You saw him? Why didn't you strike him to the ground right there? Then I would have had to give you ten shekelsᵇ of silver and a warrior's belt."

¹²But the man replied, "Even if a thousand shekelsᶜ were weighed out into my hands, I would not lay a hand on the king's son. In our hearing the king commanded you and Abishai and Ittai, 'Protect the young man Absalom for my sake.ᵈ' ¹³And if I had put my life in jeopardyᵉ — and nothing is hidden from the king — you would have kept your distance from me."

¹⁴Joab said, "I'm not going to wait like this for you." So he took three javelins in his hand and plunged them into Absalom's heart while Absalom was still alive in the oak tree. ¹⁵And ten of Joab's armor-bearers surrounded Absalom, struck him and killed him.

¹⁶Then Joab sounded the trumpet, and the troops stopped pursuing Israel, for Joab halted them. ¹⁷They took Absalom, threw him into a big pit in the forest and piled up a large heap of rocks over him. Meanwhile, all the Israelites fled to their homes.

ᵃ 3 Two Hebrew manuscripts, some Septuagint manuscripts and Vulgate; most Hebrew manuscripts care; for now there are ten thousand like us   ᵇ 11 That is, about 4 ounces or about 115 grams   ᶜ 12 That is, about 25 pounds or about 12 kilograms   ᵈ 12 A few Hebrew manuscripts, Septuagint, Vulgate and Syriac; most Hebrew manuscripts may be translated Absalom, whoever you may be.   ᵉ 13 Or Otherwise, if I had acted treacherously toward him

---

army. See 2:13 and note. **Ittai the Gittite** The commander of a band of mercenaries from Gath. He maintained loyalty to David (see 15:18–22). **I myself will surely march out** David may wish to accompany his troops to ensure that Absalom is not killed if captured (see 18:5).
18:3 You must not go out David's death is Absalom's primary objective in this confrontation (see 17:2–3). In order to protect him, David's men urge him to remain in Mahanaim while they fight (compare 11:1).
18:4 the king stood beside the gate Although he does not accompany the army to battle, David exercises his role as commander in chief and hails them as they set out.
18:5 Be gentle David attempts to absolve himself of any involvement in Absalom's death. Similar events occur in regard to the deaths of Saul, Jonathan, Abner, Ish-Bosheth and Amnon (see 1Sa 29:11 and note; note on 2Sa 3:31–39; note on 4:1–12; 13:21 and note). **all the troops heard** David's order, coupled with his mourning in ch. 19, creates a conflict of interest for his army (see 19:2–3).
18:6 forest of Ephraim This rugged terrain provides a strategic advantage for David and his men because they are accustomed to hiding in the dense environment provided by forests (e.g., 1Sa 22:5). This forest was apparently located east of the Jordan River (compare Jos 17:14–18). See the table "Battles of Saul and David" on p. 433.
18:8 whole countryside Refers to the country of Ammon (2Sa 17:24,27). **the forest swallowed up** Absalom's army is not used to fighting in the forest, which is better suited for David's smaller force.
18:9 hair got caught He is caught by his hair, a masterful

literary connection to David's statement in 14:11. This image recalls Dt 21:23, which declares Yahweh's curse on criminals hung from trees. The act of affixing lawbreakers to trees (or other elevated objects) was originally intended to deter further rebellion against the state and Yahweh's covenant. In this instance, Absalom's twofold violation of the Law (see Dt 27:16,20) warranted such a display, even if unintentional. **the mule he was riding kept on going** Absalom loses his kingly transportation, symbolizing his loss of Israel's throne (see 2Sa 13:29 and note).
18:11 ten shekels of silver and a warrior's belt Joab's reward for the person who kills Absalom shows that he intends to defy the king's order (see v. 5).
18:12 I would not lay a hand The unnamed soldier appears more righteous than his commander, Joab.
18:14 I'm not going to wait Surprisingly, Joab does nothing to the soldier for his insolence. Instead, he proceeds immediately to Absalom's location, intent on killing him. **plunged them into Absalom's heart** Joab may have thrown javelins to dislodge Absalom from the tree's branches in addition to killing him. Though Absalom apparently survived the initial blows (see v. 15), the wounds were probably fatal.
18:15 ten of Joab's armor-bearers Multiple participants means that no individual was culpable for Absalom's death. **and killed him** Perhaps intended to remove direct bloodguilt from Joab, who speared Absalom three times.
18:16 Joab sounded the trumpet Signals the end of the battle.
18:17 a large heap of rocks Recalls the Achan incident (see Jos 7:26).

[18]During his lifetime Absalom had taken a pillar and erected it in the King's Valley as a monument to himself, for he thought, "I have no son to carry on the memory of my name." He named the pillar after himself, and it is called Absalom's Monument to this day.

David Mourns

[19]Now Ahimaaz son of Zadok said, "Let me run and take the news to the king that the LORD has vindicated him by delivering him from the hand of his enemies."

[20]"You are not the one to take the news today," Joab told him. "You may take the news another time, but you must not do so today, because the king's son is dead."

[21]Then Joab said to a Cushite, "Go, tell the king what you have seen." The Cushite bowed down before Joab and ran off.

[22]Ahimaaz son of Zadok again said to Joab, "Come what may, please let me run behind the Cushite."

But Joab replied, "My son, why do you want to go? You don't have any news that will bring you a reward."

[23]He said, "Come what may, I want to run."

So Joab said, "Run!" Then Ahimaaz ran by way of the plain[a] and outran the Cushite.

[24]While David was sitting between the inner and outer gates, the watchman went up to the roof of the gateway by the wall. As he looked out, he saw a man running alone. [25]The watchman called out to the king and reported it.

The king said, "If he is alone, he must have good news." And the runner came closer and closer.

[26]Then the watchman saw another runner, and he called down to the gatekeeper, "Look, another man running alone!"

The king said, "He must be bringing good news, too."

[27]The watchman said, "It seems to me that the first one runs like Ahimaaz son of Zadok."

"He's a good man," the king said. "He comes with good news."

[28]Then Ahimaaz called out to the king, "All is well!" He bowed down before the king with his face to the ground and said, "Praise be to the LORD your God! He has delivered up those who lifted their hands against my lord the king."

[29]The king asked, "Is the young man Absalom safe?"

Ahimaaz answered, "I saw great confusion just as Joab was about to send the king's servant and me, your servant, but I don't know what it was."

[30]The king said, "Stand aside and wait here." So he stepped aside and stood there.

[31]Then the Cushite arrived and said, "My lord the king, hear the good news! The LORD has vindicated you today by delivering you from the hand of all who rose up against you."

[32]The king asked the Cushite, "Is the young man Absalom safe?"

The Cushite replied, "May the enemies of my lord the king and all who rise up to harm you be like that young man."

[33]The king was shaken. He went up to the room over the gateway and wept. As he went, he said: "O my son Absalom! My son, my son Absalom! If only I had died instead of you — O Absalom, my son, my son!"[b]

19[c] Joab was told, "The king is weeping and mourning for Absalom." [2]And for the whole army the victory that day was turned into

---

[a] 23 That is, the plain of the Jordan   [b] 33 In Hebrew texts this verse (18:33) is numbered 19:1.   [c] In Hebrew texts 19:1-43 is numbered 19:2-44.

18:18 in the King's Valley Possibly identical to the Valley of Shaveh (Ge 14:17). The precise location is unknown. **I have no son** Second Samuel 14:27 states that Absalom had three sons. They apparently died, leaving Absalom with no legitimate heir; alternatively, he may have erected the monument before they were born.

18:19-33 In this section, David learns of his victory over Absalom's forces, and of his son's death.

18:19 Let me run and take the news Ahimaaz, mentioned earlier as one of David's spies (17:17), wants to report the news of their victory over Absalom's forces to David.

18:20 the king's son is dead Joab knows that David will not be happy to receive the news of Absalom's death. He may fear that the king will kill one of his prized runners (news bearers).

18:21 Cushite A foreigner. Traditionally identified as a person from Ethiopia.

18:22 let me run behind the Cushite Perhaps knowing that the Cushite (a foreigner) would be unfamiliar with the territory and the fastest route, Ahimaaz asks permission to run after him. His motive appears to be

that if he outran the Cushite, Ahimaaz could choose to offer only partial news. By reporting victory and omitting the news of Absalom's death, Ahimaaz could remain in the king's good graces.

18:25 he must have good news The fact that he is alone distinguishes him as a runner, a royal or military messenger.

18:29 I don't know Ahimaaz feigns ignorance (compare v. 22 and note). He leaves the task of reporting the bad news to the Cushite.

18:32 like that young man The Cushite assumes that Absalom's death will be good news to the king.

19:1-8 Casting formality and protocol aside, Joab sharply criticizes David for mourning his dead son. The king's actions present a conflict of interest for his army and communicate contempt for them. Joab urges David to be wise so that he will not lose control of his kingdom.

19:1 Joab David's nephew and the commander of his army. See 2:13 and note. **weeping and mourning** See 3:31 and note.

19:2 turned into mourning Rather than expressing gratitude by celebrating their extraordinary victory, the

mourning, because on that day the troops heard it said, "The king is grieving for his son." ³The men stole into the city that day as men steal in who are ashamed when they flee from battle. ⁴The king covered his face and cried aloud, "O my son Absalom! O Absalom, my son, my son!"

⁵Then Joab went into the house to the king and said, "Today you have humiliated all your men, who have just saved your life and the lives of your sons and daughters and the lives of your wives and concubines. ⁶You love those who hate you and hate those who love you. You have made it clear today that the commanders and their men mean nothing to you. I see that you would be pleased if Absalom were alive today and all of us were dead. ⁷Now go out and encourage your men. I swear by the LORD that if you don't go out, not a man will be left with you by nightfall. This will be worse for you than all the calamities that have come on you from your youth till now."

⁸So the king got up and took his seat in the gateway. When the men were told, "The king is sitting in the gateway," they all came before him.

Meanwhile, the Israelites had fled to their homes.

David Returns to Jerusalem

⁹Throughout the tribes of Israel, all the people were arguing among themselves, saying, "The king delivered us from the hand of our enemies; he is the one who rescued us from the hand of the Philistines. But now he has fled the country to escape from Absalom; ¹⁰and Absalom, whom we anointed to rule over us, has died in battle. So why do you say nothing about bringing the king back?"

¹¹King David sent this message to Zadok and Abiathar, the priests: "Ask the elders of Judah, 'Why should you be the last to bring the king back to his palace, since what is being said throughout Israel has reached the king at his quarters? ¹²You are my relatives, my own flesh and blood. So why should you be the last to bring back the king?' ¹³And say to Amasa, 'Are you not my own flesh and blood? May God deal with me, be it ever so severely, if you are not the commander of my army for life in place of Joab.'"

¹⁴He won over the hearts of the men of Judah so that they were all of one mind. They sent word to the king, "Return, you and all your men." ¹⁵Then the king returned and went as far as the Jordan.

Now the men of Judah had come to Gilgal to go out and meet the king and bring him across the Jordan. ¹⁶Shimei son of Gera, the Benjamite from Bahurim, hurried down with the men of Judah to meet King David. ¹⁷With him were a thousand Benjamites, along with Ziba, the steward of Saul's household, and his fifteen sons and twenty servants. They rushed to the Jordan, where the king was. ¹⁸They crossed at the ford to take the king's household over and to do whatever he wished.

When Shimei son of Gera crossed the Jordan, he fell prostrate before the king ¹⁹and said to him,

---

king mourns his dead rival and offends his troops. Absalom betrayed his father (see 13:24 and note, 13:27), killed the crown prince (13:28–29), treasonously claimed his father's throne while David was still alive (15:1), undermined his father's authority (15:2–6), conspired against the king (15:10–12), usurped the throne (15:13; 16:15), had sex with his father's concubines (16:20–22) and attempted to kill David in battle (17:24–26; 18:6). Despite all of this, David mourns his death.

19:3 who are ashamed when they flee David's mourning stifles the joy of victory and shames his troops.

19:6 those who hate you Refers to Absalom, his disloyal and rebellious son. **those who love you** Refers to his army and those who faithfully support him.

19:7 not a man will be left Joab assures David that such persistent disrespect for his troops will lead them to abandon him.

19:8 took his seat in the gateway David listens to Joab and positions himself in the sight of all his soldiers (compare 18:4). His presence among them communicates that he supports their efforts. **Israelites had fled** Refers to those who fought with Absalom against David (see 18:7).

19:9–15 Following Joab's rebuke and David's subsequent commendation of the army, the king returns home to Jerusalem to reclaim his throne.

19:9 all the people were arguing After returning home from their defeat in battle, the Israelites dispute among themselves about what they should do next. They conclude that their only option is to welcome home the king (v. 10), which leads to the conflict in vv. 41–43.

19:11 to Zadok and Abiathar They had remained loyal to David. See 15:27–28. **Ask the elders of Judah** David has already been informed of the northern tribes' recommitment to his kingship. As he attempts to reconsolidate his kingdom, he exploits the rivalry between north and south to urge the people of Judah to recommit themselves as well.

19:12 You are my relatives David, a Judahite, urges his kinsmen to bring him back into his capital city.

19:13 my own flesh and blood Amasa was David's nephew (see 17:25 and note), but so was Joab (see 2:13 and note). However, by giving him Joab's military post at this time, David places Amasa in a position to sway Judahite leadership and unite the army. **in place of Joab** Joab's disobedience concerning Absalom (see 18:5) leads to him being replaced. His replacement, Amasa, had been Absalom's army commander (see 17:25).

19:15 Gilgal The place of kingship renewal (see 1Sa 11:14–15).

19:16–43 As David returns, those who opposed him when Absalom took over (or at least appeared to have opposed him, e.g., Mephibosheth) attempt to make restitution. David appears to pardon them, but never forgives them for rebellion (see 1Ki 2).

19:16 Shimei A relative of Saul who had cursed David. See 2Sa 16:5–14 and note.

19:17 a thousand Benjamites Shimei may be attempting to show his influence to David in hopes that the king will let him live. **Ziba, the steward** The servant of Saul's grandson Mephibosheth. See 9:10 and note; 16:1–4

"May my lord not hold me guilty. Do not remember how your servant did wrong on the day my lord the king left Jerusalem. May the king put it out of his mind. ²⁰For I your servant know that I have sinned, but today I have come here as the first from the tribes of Joseph to come down and meet my lord the king."

²¹Then Abishai son of Zeruiah said, "Shouldn't Shimei be put to death for this? He cursed the LORD's anointed."

²²David replied, "What does this have to do with you, you sons of Zeruiah? What right do you have to interfere? Should anyone be put to death in Israel today? Don't I know that today I am king over Israel?" ²³So the king said to Shimei, "You shall not die." And the king promised him on oath.

²⁴Mephibosheth, Saul's grandson, also went down to meet the king. He had not taken care of his feet or trimmed his mustache or washed his clothes from the day the king left until the day he returned safely. ²⁵When he came from Jerusalem to meet the king, the king asked him, "Why didn't you go with me, Mephibosheth?"

²⁶He said, "My lord the king, since I your servant am lame, I said, 'I will have my donkey saddled and will ride on it, so I can go with the king.' But Ziba my servant betrayed me. ²⁷And he has slandered your servant to my lord the king. My lord the king is like an angel of God; so do whatever you wish. ²⁸All my grandfather's descendants deserved nothing but death from my lord the king, but you gave your servant a place among those who eat at your table. So what right do I have to make any more appeals to the king?"

²⁹The king said to him, "Why say more? I order you and Ziba to divide the land."

³⁰Mephibosheth said to the king, "Let him take everything, now that my lord the king has returned home safely."

³¹Barzillai the Gileadite also came down from Rogelim to cross the Jordan with the king and to send him on his way from there. ³²Now Barzillai was very old, eighty years of age. He had provided for the king during his stay in Mahanaim, for he was a very wealthy man. ³³The king said to Barzillai, "Cross over with me and stay with me in Jerusalem, and I will provide for you."

³⁴But Barzillai answered the king, "How many more years will I live, that I should go up to Jerusalem with the king? ³⁵I am now eighty years old. Can I tell the difference between what is enjoyable and what is not? Can your servant taste what he eats and drinks? Can I still hear the voices of male and female singers? Why should your servant be an added burden to my lord the king? ³⁶Your servant will cross over the Jordan with the king for a short distance, but why should the king reward me in this way? ³⁷Let your servant return, that I may die in my own town near the tomb of my father and mother. But here is your servant Kimham. Let him cross over with my lord the king. Do for him whatever you wish."

³⁸The king said, "Kimham shall cross over with me, and I will do for him whatever you wish. And anything you desire from me I will do for you."

³⁹So all the people crossed the Jordan, and then the king crossed over. The king kissed Barzillai and bid him farewell, and Barzillai returned to his home.

⁴⁰When the king crossed over to Gilgal, Kimham crossed with him. All the troops of Judah and half the troops of Israel had taken the king over.

⁴¹Soon all the men of Israel were coming to the king and saying to him, "Why did our brothers, the men of Judah, steal the king away and bring

---

and note. **They rushed** The absence of Mephibosheth, Ziba's master (who shows up in vv. 24–30), suggests that Ziba was attempting to cover his earlier lies about Mephibosheth (16:1–4).

19:20 the tribes of Joseph Represents the northern tribes (see v. 17 and note).

19:21 Abishai David's nephew (see 2Sa 2:18 and note). **cursed the LORD's anointed** Assumes that David had established a precedent for the treatment of Yahweh's anointed (see 1:15 and note).

19:22 sons of Zeruiah See 16:10 and note.

19:23 You shall not die David allows Shimei to live until 1Ki 2:8–9 when, with his dying words, David orders his son Solomon to kill him.

19:24 had not taken care of his feet Mephibosheth's signs of mourning for David's exile demonstrate that, in contrast to Ziba's statement in 2Sa 16:3, he had not rebelled against the king.

19:26 your servant am lame Mephibosheth explains that he could not saddle a donkey and make the journey himself because of his physical condition (see 4:4 and note). Apparently, Mephibosheth ordered Ziba to saddle a donkey for him, but Ziba—sensing an opportunity to gain favor with the king—disobeyed and went to David

himself. Mephibosheth's other servants were Ziba's sons (see 9:10) and probably disinclined to help their master.

19:27 like an angel of God Refers to his ability to make clear judgments (14:17; 1Sa 29:9).

19:28 deserved nothing but death Incoming kings would normally kill the offspring of their predecessor in order to avoid rival claimants to the throne. **eat at your table** See 2Sa 9:7 and note.

19:29 divide the land David honors his promise to Ziba (16:4) but does not fully disinherit Mephibosheth since he was clearly tricked.

19:30 Let him take everything Mephibosheth only cares about the king's safe return, not his familial land.

19:32 had provided for the king David remembers Barzillai's kindness in his final instructions to Solomon (see 17:27–29; 1Ki 2:7).

19:37 here is your servant Kimham Barzillai states that at his age, he prefers to stay in his own city. He sends another man, presumably his son, in his place.

19:41 did our brothers, the men of Judah, steal the king away The men of Israel perceive that the men of Judah are attempting to sneak David back, possibly to win favor with the reinstated king over against the men of Israel.

him and his household across the Jordan, together with all his men?"

⁴²All the men of Judah answered the men of Israel, "We did this because the king is closely related to us. Why are you angry about it? Have we eaten any of the king's provisions? Have we taken anything for ourselves?"

⁴³Then the men of Israel answered the men of Judah, "We have ten shares in the king; so we have a greater claim on David than you have. Why then do you treat us with contempt? Weren't we the first to speak of bringing back our king?"

But the men of Judah pressed their claims even more forcefully than the men of Israel.

Sheba Rebels Against David

20 Now a troublemaker named Sheba son of Bikri, a Benjamite, happened to be there. He sounded the trumpet and shouted,

"We have no share in David,
no part in Jesse's son!
Every man to his tent, Israel!"

²So all the men of Israel deserted David to follow Sheba son of Bikri. But the men of Judah stayed by their king all the way from the Jordan to Jerusalem.

³When David returned to his palace in Jerusalem, he took the ten concubines he had left to take care of the palace and put them in a house under guard. He provided for them but had no sexual relations with them. They were kept in confinement till the day of their death, living as widows.

⁴Then the king said to Amasa, "Summon the men of Judah to come to me within three days, and be here yourself." ⁵But when Amasa went to summon Judah, he took longer than the time the king had set for him.

⁶David said to Abishai, "Now Sheba son of Bikri will do us more harm than Absalom did. Take your master's men and pursue him, or he will find fortified cities and escape from us."[a] ⁷So Joab's men and the Kerethites and Pelethites and all the mighty warriors went out under the command of Abishai. They marched out from Jerusalem to pursue Sheba son of Bikri.

⁸While they were at the great rock in Gibeon, Amasa came to meet them. Joab was wearing his military tunic, and strapped over it at his waist was a belt with a dagger in its sheath. As he stepped forward, it dropped out of its sheath.

⁹Joab said to Amasa, "How are you, my brother?" Then Joab took Amasa by the beard with his right hand to kiss him. ¹⁰Amasa was not on his guard against the dagger in Joab's hand, and Joab plunged it into his belly, and his intestines spilled out on the ground. Without being stabbed again, Amasa died. Then Joab and his brother Abishai pursued Sheba son of Bikri.

¹¹One of Joab's men stood beside Amasa and said, "Whoever favors Joab, and whoever is for David, let him follow Joab!" ¹²Amasa lay wallowing in his blood in the middle of the road, and the man saw that all the troops came to a halt there. When he realized that everyone who came up to Amasa stopped, he dragged him from the road into a field

---

a 6 Or *and do us serious injury*

19:42 eaten any of the king's provisions The Judahites state that, despite familial connections, they have not abused their privileged position.

19:43 ten shares A reference to the other ten tribes. In contrast to the Judahites, who are only one tribe, the Israelites represent the bulk of the nation. **bringing back our king** See 2Sa 19:9 and note.

20:1–26 Following the heated exchange in 19:41–43, Sheba leads the Israelites in a rebellion against David. The rebellion is finally quelled by a wise woman who presents Joab with Sheba's severed head.

20:1 a troublemaker See 1Sa 1:16 and note. **a Benjamite** He was a member of Saul's tribe. **He sounded the trumpet** Announces a military maneuver (2Sa 18:16; 20:22). **We have no share** Disgruntled about David's perceived preferential treatment of Judah, Sheba claims that the northern tribes have no place in David's regime. **Every man to his tent** Signals military withdrawal from David.

20:3 ten concubines he had left See 15:16 and note. **had no sexual relations with them** Absalom had defiled these concubines (16:20–22).

20:4 Amasa David's nephew and now the commander of David's army in place of Joab. See 19:13 and note. **Summon the men of Judah to come to me** David intends to reunify the Judahites by pursuing the Israelite rebels. **three days** David wants to suppress the rebellion quickly in order to prevent it from gaining momentum.

20:6 Abishai Joab's brother and David's nephew. Abishai was a commander in David's army (19:21). **your master's men** A reference to David's disenfranchised warriors (v. 7; 1Sa 22:2; 23:13) and the Gittite mercenaries (2Sa 15:18). **pursue him** Amasa delays, so David seeks another course of action (compare v. 4 and note).

20:7 Joab's men Although he is no longer the supreme commander of David's forces, Joab still commands some warriors. **the Kerethites and Pelethites** See 8:18 and note; 15:18.

20:8 Joab The mention of Joab following Amasa's reintroduction signals that something wicked is about to happen. **it dropped out** Joab likely planned this mishap so that he could inconspicuously place a sword in his hand. Soldiers normally carried their swords in their right hands (see note on Jdg 3:16). Joab could inconspicuously pick up his sword or dagger with his left hand while leaving his right hand free to greet Amasa (2Sa 20:9). Joab appears to stab Amasa with his left hand (v. 10), an unexpected action.

20:10 was not on his guard against the dagger See v. 8 and note. **Joab plunged it into his belly** Recalls Joab's executions of Abner (3:26–30) and Absalom (18:14). **Joab and his brother Abishai pursued Sheba** Since Amasa is dead, Joab apparently reclaims his former role (see v. 23 and note).

20:12 all the troops came to a halt Compare 2:23 and note. **threw a garment over him** The man hides the body so that the men will not be distracted but will focus on pursuing Sheba.

and threw a garment over him. [13]After Amasa had been removed from the road, everyone went on with Joab to pursue Sheba son of Bikri.

[14]Sheba passed through all the tribes of Israel to Abel Beth Maakah and through the entire region of the Bikrites,[a] who gathered together and followed him. [15]All the troops with Joab came and besieged Sheba in Abel Beth Maakah. They built a siege ramp up to the city, and it stood against the outer fortifications. While they were battering the wall to bring it down, [16]a wise woman called from the city, "Listen! Listen! Tell Joab to come here so I can speak to him." [17]He went toward her, and she asked, "Are you Joab?"

"I am," he answered.

She said, "Listen to what your servant has to say."

"I'm listening," he said.

[18]She continued, "Long ago they used to say, 'Get your answer at Abel,' and that settled it. [19]We are the peaceful and faithful in Israel. You are trying to destroy a city that is a mother in Israel. Why do you want to swallow up the LORD's inheritance?"

[20]"Far be it from me!" Joab replied, "Far be it from me to swallow up or destroy! [21]That is not the case. A man named Sheba son of Bikri, from the hill country of Ephraim, has lifted up his hand against the king, against David. Hand over this one man, and I'll withdraw from the city."

The woman said to Joab, "His head will be thrown to you from the wall."

[22]Then the woman went to all the people with her wise advice, and they cut off the head of Sheba son of Bikri and threw it to Joab. So he sounded the trumpet, and his men dispersed from the city, each returning to his home. And Joab went back to the king in Jerusalem.

David's Officials

[23]Joab was over Israel's entire army; Benaiah son of Jehoiada was over the Kerethites and Pelethites; [24]Adoniram[b] was in charge of forced labor; Jehoshaphat son of Ahilud was recorder; [25]Sheva was secretary; Zadok and Abiathar were priests; [26]and Ira the Jairite[c] was David's priest.

The Gibeonites Avenged

21 During the reign of David, there was a famine for three successive years; so David sought the face of the LORD. The LORD said, "It is on account of Saul and his blood-stained house; it is because he put the Gibeonites to death."

[2]The king summoned the Gibeonites and spoke to them. (Now the Gibeonites were not a part of Israel but were survivors of the Amorites; the Israelites had sworn to spare them, but Saul in his zeal for Israel and Judah had tried to annihilate them.) [3]David asked the Gibeonites, "What shall I do for you? How shall I make atonement so that you will bless the LORD's inheritance?"

[4]The Gibeonites answered him, "We have no right to demand silver or gold from Saul or his family, nor do we have the right to put anyone in Israel to death."

"What do you want me to do for you?" David asked.

[5]They answered the king, "As for the man who destroyed us and plotted against us so that we have been decimated and have no place anywhere

---

[a] 14 See Septuagint and Vulgate; Hebrew *Berites*.   [b] 24 Some Septuagint manuscripts (see also 1 Kings 4:6 and 5:14); Hebrew *Adoram*   [c] 26 Hebrew; some Septuagint manuscripts and Syriac (see also 23:38) *Ithrite*

20:14 passed through all the tribes of Israel Sheba attempts to rally support. **to Abel Beth Maakah** Located in the northernmost part of the land. **Bikrites** While the Hebrew text here refers to "Berites," they are mentioned only here in the Bible. This may be a scribal error; the Hebrew text probably should have read "Bichrites" (also rendered as "Bikrites"), Sheba's family or clan (see v. 1). If this is the case, Sheba's rallying efforts were unsuccessful—only his family enters the city with him. **20:15 They built a siege ramp** Compare Eze 4:2 and note. **20:18 Get your answer at Abel** May refer to inquiring of God or attempting to determine God's will in a matter such as a legal dispute. The woman argues that her city has an honorable reputation and does not deserve to be treated this way. **20:21 Hand over this one man** Joab's singular objective is to kill Sheba. His death will end the confrontation. **20:22 they cut off the head of Sheba** The people of Abel would rather give up Sheba than see their city destroyed. **he sounded the trumpet** See 2Sa 20:1 and note. **20:23–26** This list (vv. 23–26) is similar to that of 8:16–18. Joab, Benaiah, Zadok and Jehoshaphat have the same roles. Abiathar replaces Ahimelek as priest (see note on 8:17); Sheva replaces Seraiah as secretary; Ira the Jairite replaces David's sons as a priest (see note on 8:18); and Adoram is added as the supervisor of forced labor (see 1Ki 12:18).

20:23 Joab was over Israel's entire army Joab may have reassumed his role after murdering Amasa.

21:1–14 At some point in his reign, Saul attempted to exterminate the Gibeonites, with whom the Israelites had a covenant (see Jos 9). In the time of David (perhaps early in his career; see 2Sa 21:6 and note), the people experience a famine related to Saul's sin. David learns the cause of the famine and asks the Gibeonites how he can make restitution. They ask for seven descendants of Saul to be killed, and David grants their request.

21:1 David sought the face of the LORD David may intend to plead for deliverance (see v. 14) or seek Yahweh to determine the cause of the famine. Deuteronomy 28:22–24 indicates that famine could be a sign of divine disfavor. **put the Gibeonites to death** This act is not recorded in the OT (see note on 2Sa 4:3). **21:2 Amorites** Residents of Canaan prior to Israel's arrival (see note on Ge 10:16). **21:4 to put anyone in Israel to death** The Gibeonites recognize that they are subservient to the nation of Israel and make no request at David's first offering. **21:5 the man who destroyed us** Refers to Saul (2Sa 21:1–2).

in Israel, [6]let seven of his male descendants be given to us to be killed and their bodies exposed before the LORD at Gibeah of Saul — the LORD's chosen one."

So the king said, "I will give them to you."

[7]The king spared Mephibosheth son of Jonathan, the son of Saul, because of the oath before the LORD between David and Jonathan son of Saul. [8]But the king took Armoni and Mephibosheth, the two sons of Aiah's daughter Rizpah, whom she had borne to Saul, together with the five sons of Saul's daughter Merab,[a] whom she had borne to Adriel son of Barzillai the Meholathite. [9]He handed them over to the Gibeonites, who killed them and exposed their bodies on a hill before the LORD. All seven of them fell together; they were put to death during the first days of the harvest, just as the barley harvest was beginning.

[10]Rizpah daughter of Aiah took sackcloth and spread it out for herself on a rock. From the beginning of the harvest till the rain poured down from the heavens on the bodies, she did not let the birds touch them by day or the wild animals by night. [11]When David was told what Aiah's daughter Rizpah, Saul's concubine, had done, [12]he went and took the bones of Saul and his son Jonathan from the citizens of Jabesh Gilead. (They had stolen their bodies from the public square at Beth Shan, where the Philistines had hung them after they struck Saul down on Gilboa.) [13]David brought the bones of Saul and his son Jonathan from there, and the bones of those who had been killed and exposed were gathered up.

[14]They buried the bones of Saul and his son Jonathan in the tomb of Saul's father Kish, at Zela in Benjamin, and did everything the king commanded. After that, God answered prayer in behalf of the land.

Wars Against the Philistines
21:15-22pp — 1Ch 20:4-8

[15]Once again there was a battle between the Philistines and Israel. David went down with his men to fight against the Philistines, and he became exhausted. [16]And Ishbi-Benob, one of the descendants of Rapha, whose bronze spearhead weighed three hundred shekels[b] and who was armed with a new sword, said he would kill David. [17]But Abishai son of Zeruiah came to David's rescue; he struck the Philistine down and killed him. Then David's men swore to him, saying, "Never again will you go out with us to battle, so that the lamp of Israel will not be extinguished."

[18]In the course of time, there was another battle

---

[a] 8 Two Hebrew manuscripts, some Septuagint manuscripts and Syriac (see also 1 Samuel 18:19); most Hebrew and Septuagint manuscripts *Michal* [b] 16 That is, about 7 1/2 pounds or about 3.5 kilograms

---

21:6 seven of his male descendants The Gibeonites use Israel's own Law against its first king, Saul. The Law demands that murderers are to be killed. Leviticus 24 makes no distinction between Israelites and foreigners but places both under the same law of retaliation (see Lev 24:17–22). Since Saul is no longer living, the Gibeonites ask that seven of his descendants be killed. The number seven had symbolic value, so this action allows for the Gibeonites to symbolically carry out the one-to-one retaliation against their attackers. **I will give them to you** This act eliminates rival claimants to David's throne, which makes it easy for David to agree to it. This event may have occurred early in David's reign, sometime before 9:1.

21:7 king spared Mephibosheth Refers to Saul's grandson, the son of Jonathan (see ch. 9) — not to Mephibosheth, son of Saul (v. 8). **because of the oath before the LORD** See 1Sa 20:15 and note.

21:8 Aiah's daughter Rizpah Saul's concubine (2Sa 3:7). **Merab** The traditional Hebrew text references Michal here — Saul's youngest daughter and David's first wife (1Sa 14:49; 18:27) — however other Hebrew manuscripts refer to Merab, Saul's oldest daughter. Merab seems to be correct, since Michal did not have children (2Sa 6:23) and Merab is elsewhere recorded as marrying Adriel the Meholathite (1Sa 18:19). See the people diagram "King Saul's Family Tree" on p. 428.

21:9 before the LORD Although this execution is done in a way that implies Yahweh's endorsement, Yahweh himself never endorses this action. David and the Gibeonites draw their own conclusions about what Yahweh desires. It is not until the bodies are taken down and buried that God answers David's prayer to remove the famine from

the land — this seems to imply that God is displeased with this action and that God's only wish was that David would reconcile with the Gibeonites (2Sa 21:14). **barley harvest** April–May. This foreshadows the end of the famine (21:14).

21:12 citizens of Jabesh Gilead See 1Sa 31:11–13.

21:13 the bones of Saul To honor Rizpah's motherly vigilance (2Sa 21:10), David exhumes the bones of Jonathan and Saul and gives them a proper burial in the tomb of Saul's father, Kish. He likewise ensures that the seven slain descendants of Saul receive a proper burial.

21:15–22 The Philistines now reappear after a lengthy absence from the narrative (see 2Sa 8:1 and note). In this section, four of David's great champions defeat four of the Philistines' great champions.

21:15 Once again there was a battle See 8:1 and note. See the table "Battles of Saul and David" on p. 433. **he became exhausted** David may have been aged by this point in his career; alternatively, he may have grown weary because he was the primary focus of the Philistine attack once they knew he was on the battlefield. This event may have occurred early in David's career; he tends to defer battlefield leadership to others from ch. 11 onward (see 11:1 and note). This event could have established a precedent that David did not usually accompany his troops into battle (compare 12:29).

21:16 descendants of Rapha See 1Ch 20:4 and note.

21:17 Abishai son of Zeruiah He is accorded special honor among David's mighty men in 2Sa 23:18–19. **Never again will you go out** Compare 11:1 and note; v. 15 and note.

21:18 Sibbekai the Hushathite This is one of David's

with the Philistines, at Gob. At that time Sibbekai the Hushathite killed Saph, one of the descendants of Rapha.

¹⁹In another battle with the Philistines at Gob, Elhanan son of Jair[a] the Bethlehemite killed the brother of[b] Goliath the Gittite, who had a spear with a shaft like a weaver's rod.

²⁰In still another battle, which took place at Gath, there was a huge man with six fingers on each hand and six toes on each foot — twenty-four in all. He also was descended from Rapha. ²¹When he taunted Israel, Jonathan son of Shimeah, David's brother, killed him.

²²These four were descendants of Rapha in Gath, and they fell at the hands of David and his men.

David's Song of Praise

22:1-51pp — Ps 18:1-50

22 David sang to the LORD the words of this song when the LORD delivered him from the hand of all his enemies and from the hand of Saul. ²He said:

"The LORD is my rock, my fortress and my
    deliverer;
³   my God is my rock, in whom I take refuge,
    my shield[c] and the horn[d] of my salvation.
He is my stronghold, my refuge and my
        savior —
    from violent people you save me.

⁴ "I called to the LORD, who is worthy of praise,
    and have been saved from my enemies.
⁵ The waves of death swirled about me;
    the torrents of destruction
        overwhelmed me.
⁶ The cords of the grave coiled around me;
    the snares of death confronted me.

⁷ "In my distress I called to the LORD;
    I called out to my God.
From his temple he heard my voice;
    my cry came to his ears.
⁸ The earth trembled and quaked,
    the foundations of the heavens[e] shook;
    they trembled because he was angry.
⁹ Smoke rose from his nostrils;
    consuming fire came from his mouth,
    burning coals blazed out of it.

¹⁰ He parted the heavens and came down;
    dark clouds were under his feet.
¹¹ He mounted the cherubim and flew;
    he soared[f] on the wings of the wind.
¹² He made darkness his canopy around him —
    the dark[g] rain clouds of the sky.
¹³ Out of the brightness of his presence
    bolts of lightning blazed forth.
¹⁴ The LORD thundered from heaven;
    the voice of the Most High resounded.
¹⁵ He shot his arrows and scattered the enemy,
    with great bolts of lightning he routed
        them.
¹⁶ The valleys of the sea were exposed
    and the foundations of the earth laid bare
at the rebuke of the LORD,
    at the blast of breath from his nostrils.

¹⁷ "He reached down from on high and took
        hold of me;
    he drew me out of deep waters.
¹⁸ He rescued me from my powerful enemy,
    from my foes, who were too strong for me.
¹⁹ They confronted me in the day of my
        disaster,
    but the LORD was my support.
²⁰ He brought me out into a spacious place;
    he rescued me because he delighted
        in me.

²¹ "The LORD has dealt with me according to my
        righteousness;
    according to the cleanness of my hands he
        has rewarded me.
²² For I have kept the ways of the LORD;
    I am not guilty of turning from my God.
²³ All his laws are before me;
    I have not turned away from his decrees.
²⁴ I have been blameless before him
    and have kept myself from sin.
²⁵ The LORD has rewarded me according to my
        righteousness,
    according to my cleanness[h] in his sight.

---

a 19 See 1 Chron. 20:5; Hebrew *Jaare-Oregim.*   *b 19* See 1 Chron. 20:5; Hebrew does not have *the brother of.*   *c 3* Or *sovereign*   *d 3* Horn here symbolizes strength.   *e 8* Hebrew; Vulgate and Syriac (see also Psalm 18:7) *mountains*   *f 11* Many Hebrew manuscripts (see also Psalm 18:10); most Hebrew manuscripts *appeared*   *g 12* Septuagint (see also Psalm 18:11); Hebrew *massed*   *h 25* Hebrew; Septuagint and Vulgate (see also Psalm 18:24) *to the cleanness of my hands*

---

mighty men on the chronicler's list (see 1Ch 11:29; 20:4; 27:11).

21:19 killed the brother of Goliath the Gittite According to 1Sa 17, David killed Goliath of Gath (the Gittite). The Hebrew text here claims a man named Elhanan killed Goliath, but this is a scribal mistake that was introduced at some point in the book's transmission history. First Chronicles 20:5 clarifies by stating that Elhanan killed Lahmi, the brother of Goliath.

21:21 Jonathan son of Shimeah Jonathan was David's nephew. His father Shimei (also known as Shimea or Shimeah, not to be confused with the Shimei of 2Sa 16:5–14), was the third son of David's father, Jesse (see 1Ch 2:13).

22:1–51 This psalm is inserted after David's final defeat of the Philistines (see 2Sa 21:15–22). It is nearly identical to Ps 18 and expresses David's gratitude to Yahweh for his salvation, deliverance and covenant faithfulness. Its position here is especially meaningful because David appears — at least from the human perspective — to be susceptible to defeat in 21:15–16.

26 "To the faithful you show yourself faithful,
  to the blameless you show yourself
    blameless,
27 to the pure you show yourself pure,
  but to the devious you show yourself
    shrewd.
28 You save the humble,
  but your eyes are on the haughty to bring
    them low.
29 You, LORD, are my lamp;
  the LORD turns my darkness into light.
30 With your help I can advance against a troop *a*;
  with my God I can scale a wall.

31 "As for God, his way is perfect:
  The LORD's word is flawless;
  he shields all who take refuge in him.
32 For who is God besides the LORD?
  And who is the Rock except our God?
33 It is God who arms me with strength *b*
  and keeps my way secure.
34 He makes my feet like the feet of a deer;
  he causes me to stand on the heights.
35 He trains my hands for battle;
  my arms can bend a bow of bronze.
36 You make your saving help my shield;
  your help has made *c* me great.
37 You provide a broad path for my feet,
  so that my ankles do not give way.

38 "I pursued my enemies and crushed them;
  I did not turn back till they were destroyed.
39 I crushed them completely, and they could
    not rise;
  they fell beneath my feet.
40 You armed me with strength for battle;
  you humbled my adversaries before me.
41 You made my enemies turn their backs
    in flight,
  and I destroyed my foes.
42 They cried for help, but there was no one
    to save them—
  to the LORD, but he did not answer.
43 I beat them as fine as the dust of the earth;
  I pounded and trampled them like mud in
    the streets.

44 "You have delivered me from the attacks
    of the peoples;
  you have preserved me as the head
    of nations.
  People I did not know now serve me,
45   foreigners cower before me;
  as soon as they hear of me, they
    obey me.
46 They all lose heart;
  they come trembling *d* from their
    strongholds.

47 "The LORD lives! Praise be to my Rock!
  Exalted be my God, the Rock, my Savior!
48 He is the God who avenges me,
  who puts the nations under me,
49   who sets me free from my enemies.
  You exalted me above my foes;
  from a violent man you rescued me.
50 Therefore I will praise you, LORD, among
    the nations;
  I will sing the praises of your name.

51 "He gives his king great victories;
  he shows unfailing kindness to his
    anointed,
  to David and his descendants forever."

David's Last Words

23 These are the last words of David:

"The inspired utterance of David son of Jesse,
  the utterance of the man exalted by the
    Most High,
the man anointed by the God of Jacob,
  the hero of Israel's songs:

2 "The Spirit of the LORD spoke through me;
  his word was on my tongue.
3 The God of Israel spoke,
  the Rock of Israel said to me:

---

a 30 Or *can run through a barricade*   *b* 33 Dead Sea Scrolls,
some Septuagint manuscripts, Vulgate and Syriac (see also Psalm
18:32); Masoretic Text *who is my strong refuge*   *c* 36 Dead Sea
Scrolls; Masoretic Text *shield; / you stoop down to make*
d 46 Some Septuagint manuscripts and Vulgate (see also Psalm
18:45); Masoretic Text *they arm themselves*

23:1–7 This section describes the righteous king, his
reign and the fate of his enemies. Such a king was to
be a channel of blessing and an administrator of justice.

23:1 last words of David The Biblical writers sometimes
memorialize great men by including poetic discourses
near the end of their lives (compare Jacob in Ge 49;
and Moses in Dt 32–33). **inspired utterance** The
Hebrew word used here occurs frequently in prophetic
literature; it indicates that this is David's last prophetic
oracle, not his final words. David speaks throughout
the remainder of the narrative and in 1Ki 1–2. **son of
Jesse** The text ascribes honor to David's lineage with
this title, which Saul had formerly used as a derisive
epithet (1Sa 20:27,30). By identifying David as a son of

Jesse, the text distinguishes him as a Judahite, to whom
the monarchy rightly belonged (see Ge 49:10). See the
people diagram "Judah to David" on p. 618. **the man
anointed** Recalls 2Sa 22:51 (see 1Sa 2:10 and note;
Ps 2:2 and note). **God of Jacob** This connection with
Jacob adds monumental significance to David's career;
Jacob founded a nation, and David founded its dynasty.
23:2 The Spirit of the LORD spoke through me Highlights David's prophetic role.
23:3 When one rules over people in righteousness
This and the following verse describe the ideal king and
the effect that his righteousness has on his kingdom. An
upright king is a channel of blessing; he brings hope and
prosperity to his subjects. **when he rules in the fear of
God** Contrasts David with Saul (see 1Sa 10:22 and note).

'When one rules over people in
 righteousness,
 when he rules in the fear of God,
[4] he is like the light of morning at sunrise
 on a cloudless morning,
 like the brightness after rain
 that brings grass from the earth.'

[5] "If my house were not right with God,
 surely he would not have made with me
  an everlasting covenant,
 arranged and secured in every part;
 surely he would not bring to fruition my
  salvation
 and grant me my every desire.
[6] But evil men are all to be cast aside like thorns,
 which are not gathered with the hand.
[7] Whoever touches thorns
 uses a tool of iron or the shaft of a spear;
 they are burned up where they lie."

David's Mighty Warriors

23:8-39pp — 1Ch 11:10-41

[8] These are the names of David's mighty warriors:
Josheb-Basshebeth,[a] a Tahkemonite,[b] was chief
of the Three; he raised his spear against eight
hundred men, whom he killed[c] in one encounter.
[9] Next to him was Eleazar son of Dodai the Ahohite. As one of the three mighty warriors, he was
with David when they taunted the Philistines
gathered at Pas Dammim[d] for battle. Then the Israelites retreated, [10] but Eleazar stood his ground
and struck down the Philistines till his hand grew
tired and froze to the sword. The LORD brought
about a great victory that day. The troops returned
to Eleazar, but only to strip the dead.
[11] Next to him was Shammah son of Agee the
Hararite. When the Philistines banded together
at a place where there was a field full of lentils, Israel's troops fled from them. [12] But Shammah took
his stand in the middle of the field. He defended
it and struck the Philistines down, and the LORD
brought about a great victory.

[13] During harvest time, three of the thirty chief
warriors came down to David at the cave of Adullam, while a band of Philistines was encamped in
the Valley of Rephaim. [14] At that time David was
in the stronghold, and the Philistine garrison was
at Bethlehem. [15] David longed for water and said,
"Oh, that someone would get me a drink of water
from the well near the gate of Bethlehem!" [16] So the
three mighty warriors broke through the Philistine lines, drew water from the well near the gate
of Bethlehem and carried it back to David. But he
refused to drink it; instead, he poured it out before
the LORD. [17] "Far be it from me, LORD, to do this!"
he said. "Is it not the blood of men who went at the
risk of their lives?" And David would not drink it.

Such were the exploits of the three mighty
warriors.

[18] Abishai the brother of Joab son of Zeruiah was
chief of the Three.[e] He raised his spear against three
hundred men, whom he killed, and so he became as
famous as the Three. [19] Was he not held in greater
honor than the Three? He became their commander, even though he was not included among them.

[20] Benaiah son of Jehoiada, a valiant fighter
from Kabzeel, performed great exploits. He struck
down Moab's two mightiest warriors. He also went
down into a pit on a snowy day and killed a lion.
[21] And he struck down a huge Egyptian. Although
the Egyptian had a spear in his hand, Benaiah
went against him with a club. He snatched the
spear from the Egyptian's hand and killed him
with his own spear. [22] Such were the exploits of
Benaiah son of Jehoiada; he too was as famous
as the three mighty warriors. [23] He was held in
greater honor than any of the Thirty, but he was
not included among the Three. And David put him
in charge of his bodyguard.

[a] *8* Hebrew; some Septuagint manuscripts suggest *Ish-Bosheth*,
that is, *Esh-Baal* (see also 1 Chron. 11:11 *Jashobeam*).
[b] *8* Probably a variant of *Hakmonite* (see 1 Chron. 11:11)
[c] *8* Some Septuagint manuscripts (see also 1 Chron. 11:11);
Hebrew and other Septuagint manuscripts *Three; it was Adino the
Eznite who killed eight hundred men*   [d] *9* See 1 Chron. 11:13;
Hebrew *gathered there.*   [e] *18* Most Hebrew manuscripts (see
also 1 Chron. 11:20); two Hebrew manuscripts and Syriac *Thirty*

23:5 an everlasting covenant See 2Sa 7:1–17.
23:6 evil men See 1Sa 1:16 and note. **cast aside like
thorns** David compares the evildoers in his empire to
thorns in a field that are killed and burned.

23:8–39 The following list details the exploits of David's
finest warriors. They are divided into two groups: the
three and the thirty (although the thirty contains more
than thirty men; see 23:39). This list is essentially the
same as 1Ch 11:10–47, but the Chronicler alters the
accounts slightly and expands the register of names.
In addition, he places this catalog at the beginning of
David's reign, indicating that these warriors and their
feats helped David to consolidate his kingdom (see 1Ch
11:10; note on 11:10–47).

23:8 eight hundred First Chronicles reduces this number
to 300 men (see 1Ch 11:11).

23:9 Eleazar First Chronicles conflates the stories of
Eleazar and Shammah, attributing both accounts to
Eleazar (see 1Ch 11:12–14).
23:11 Shammah Omitted from the Chronicler's account
(see 2Sa 23:9 and note).
23:12 took his stand Although this story is attributed to
Eleazar, the Chronicler states that David stood and fought
with him while the rest of the army fled (see 1Ch 11:14).
23:13 During harvest time Indicates that the weather
was dry and hot; this sets up David's request for water
in 2Sa 23:15. **the thirty** May refer to the three (2Sa
23:8–12; compare 1Ch 11:18) or to three anonymous
warriors.
23:16 he poured it out before the LORD Probably as a
libation (or drink) offering to Yahweh (compare Nu 28:7),
which translated into a great honor for the three soldiers
who brought David the water.

²⁴Among the Thirty were:
  Asahel the brother of Joab,
  Elhanan son of Dodo from Bethlehem,
²⁵Shammah the Harodite,
  Elika the Harodite,
²⁶Helez the Paltite,
  Ira son of Ikkesh from Tekoa,
²⁷Abiezer from Anathoth,
  Sibbekai*a* the Hushathite,
²⁸Zalmon the Ahohite,
  Maharai the Netophathite,
²⁹Heled*b* son of Baanah the Netophathite,
  Ithai son of Ribai from Gibeah in Benjamin,
³⁰Benaiah the Pirathonite,
  Hiddai*c* from the ravines of Gaash,
³¹Abi-Albon the Arbathite,
  Azmaveth the Barhumite,
³²Eliahba the Shaalbonite,
  the sons of Jashen,
  Jonathan ³³son of*d* Shammah the Hararite,
  Ahiam son of Sharar*e* the Hararite,
³⁴Eliphelet son of Ahasbai the Maakathite,
  Eliam son of Ahithophel the Gilonite,
³⁵Hezro the Carmelite,
  Paarai the Arbite,
³⁶Igal son of Nathan from Zobah,
  the son of Hagri,*f*
³⁷Zelek the Ammonite,
  Naharai the Beerothite, the armor-bearer
  of Joab son of Zeruiah,
³⁸Ira the Ithrite,
  Gareb the Ithrite
³⁹and Uriah the Hittite.
There were thirty-seven in all.

David Enrolls the Fighting Men

24:1-17pp — 1Ch 21:1-17

24 Again the anger of the LORD burned against Israel, and he incited David against them, saying, "Go and take a census of Israel and Judah."

²So the king said to Joab and the army commanders*g* with him, "Go throughout the tribes of Israel from Dan to Beersheba and enroll the fighting men, so that I may know how many there are."

³But Joab replied to the king, "May the LORD your God multiply the troops a hundred times over, and may the eyes of my lord the king see it. But why does my lord the king want to do such a thing?"

⁴The king's word, however, overruled Joab and the army commanders; so they left the presence of the king to enroll the fighting men of Israel.

⁵After crossing the Jordan, they camped near Aroer, south of the town in the gorge, and then went through Gad and on to Jazer. ⁶They went to Gilead and the region of Tahtim Hodshi, and on to Dan Jaan and around toward Sidon. ⁷Then they went toward the fortress of Tyre and all the towns of the Hivites and Canaanites. Finally, they went on to Beersheba in the Negev of Judah.

⁸After they had gone through the entire land, they came back to Jerusalem at the end of nine months and twenty days.

⁹Joab reported the number of the fighting men to the king: In Israel there were eight hundred thousand able-bodied men who could handle a sword, and in Judah five hundred thousand.

¹⁰David was conscience-stricken after he had counted the fighting men, and he said to the LORD, "I have sinned greatly in what I have done. Now, LORD, I beg you, take away the guilt of your servant. I have done a very foolish thing."

¹¹Before David got up the next morning, the word of the LORD had come to Gad the prophet,

a 27 Some Septuagint manuscripts (see also 21:18; 1 Chron. 11:29); Hebrew *Mebunnai*   *b* 29 Some Hebrew manuscripts and Vulgate (see also 1 Chron. 11:30); most Hebrew manuscripts *Heleb*   *c* 30 Hebrew; some Septuagint manuscripts (see also 1 Chron. 11:32) *Hurai*   *d* 33 Some Septuagint manuscripts (see also 1 Chron. 11:34); Hebrew does not have *son of.*   *e* 33 Hebrew; some Septuagint manuscripts (see also 1 Chron. 11:35) *Sakar*   *f* 36 Some Septuagint manuscripts (see also 1 Chron. 11:38); Hebrew *Haggadi*   *g* 2 Septuagint (see also verse 4 and 1 Chron. 21:2); Hebrew *Joab the army commander*

23:25 Elika the Harodite Not listed in 1Ch 11.
23:34 Eliam son of Ahithophel the Gilonite Not listed in 1Ch 11.
23:39 thirty-seven in all It is unclear how the narrator calculated this total. The text lists 35 men, not 37 (three in 2Sa 23:8–12 [probably the same three as vv. 13–17]; two in vv. 18–23; and 30 in vv. 24–39). He may include Joab and someone like Amasa (see 19:13).

24:1–25 The collective narrative of 1–2 Samuel concludes with an account of David commissioning a census and incurring the judgment of Yahweh. However, David's repentance, Yahweh's forgiveness and the purchase of Araunah's threshing floor provide an element of hope. David's acquisition of the threshing floor anticipates the events that follow in 1Ki 5–6. Solomon, David's son, will build Yahweh's temple on the same site his father procured. The parallel account occurs in 1Ch 21, which differs slightly.

24:1 he incited David Here, Yahweh incites David to number the people, whereas the parallel account in 1Ch 21 has an accuser or adversary (called *satan* in Hebrew) inciting David's census. One way to account for this difference is to say that Yahweh allowed the adversary (or accuser) to incite David. See 1Ch 21:1 and note.

24:10 sinned It is unclear why David's census is considered sinful, especially since Yahweh prompts it (2Sa 24:1). It may have been that Yahweh was testing David and David failed. This would also explain why the Chronicler ascribes the initial prompting of David to a figure called *satan* in the Hebrew text (see note on 2Sa 24:1); this parallels the depiction of the *satan* figure in Job (see note on Job 1:6). The Law allowed for censuses (Ex 30:11–16), and Yahweh even commanded them at various times (Nu 1:2; 26:2). However, the Israelites were to carry them out according to Yahweh's stipulations. David's fault may have been in how he carried out the census, such as excusing the half-shekel requirement

David's seer: [12]"Go and tell David, 'This is what the LORD says: I am giving you three options. Choose one of them for me to carry out against you.'"

[13]So Gad went to David and said to him, "Shall there come on you three[a] years of famine in your land? Or three months of fleeing from your enemies while they pursue you? Or three days of plague in your land? Now then, think it over and decide how I should answer the one who sent me."

[14]David said to Gad, "I am in deep distress. Let us fall into the hands of the LORD, for his mercy is great; but do not let me fall into human hands."

[15]So the LORD sent a plague on Israel from that morning until the end of the time designated, and seventy thousand of the people from Dan to Beersheba died. [16]When the angel stretched out his hand to destroy Jerusalem, the LORD relented concerning the disaster and said to the angel who was afflicting the people, "Enough! Withdraw your hand." The angel of the LORD was then at the threshing floor of Araunah the Jebusite.

[17]When David saw the angel who was striking down the people, he said to the LORD, "I have sinned; I, the shepherd,[b] have done wrong. These are but sheep. What have they done? Let your hand fall on me and my family."

David Builds an Altar
24:18-25pp — 1Ch 21:18-26

[18]On that day Gad went to David and said to him, "Go up and build an altar to the LORD on the threshing floor of Araunah the Jebusite." [19]So David went up, as the LORD had commanded through Gad. [20]When Araunah looked and saw the king and his officials coming toward him, he went out

---

[a] 13 Septuagint (see also 1 Chron. 21:12); Hebrew *seven*
[b] 17 Dead Sea Scrolls and Septuagint; Masoretic Text does not have *the shepherd*.

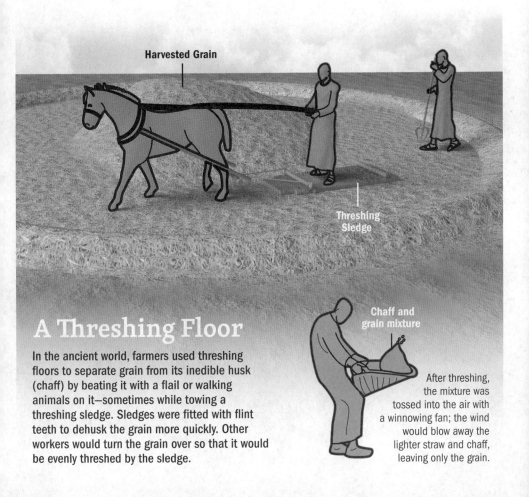

Harvested Grain

Threshing Sledge

Chaff and grain mixture

A Threshing Floor

In the ancient world, farmers used threshing floors to separate grain from its inedible husk (chaff) by beating it with a flail or walking animals on it—sometimes while towing a threshing sledge. Sledges were fitted with flint teeth to dehusk the grain more quickly. Other workers would turn the grain over so that it would be evenly threshed by the sledge.

After threshing, the mixture was tossed into the air with a winnowing fan; the wind would blow away the lighter straw and chaff, leaving only the grain.

and bowed down before the king with his face to the ground.

²¹Araunah said, "Why has my lord the king come to his servant?"

"To buy your threshing floor," David answered, "so I can build an altar to the LORD, that the plague on the people may be stopped."

²²Araunah said to David, "Let my lord the king take whatever he wishes and offer it up. Here are oxen for the burnt offering, and here are threshing sledges and ox yokes for the wood. ²³Your Majesty, Araunah*ᵃ* gives all this to the king." Araunah also said to him, "May the LORD your God accept you."

²⁴But the king replied to Araunah, "No, I insist on paying you for it. I will not sacrifice to the LORD my God burnt offerings that cost me nothing."

So David bought the threshing floor and the oxen and paid fifty shekelsᵇ of silver for them. ²⁵David built an altar to the LORD there and sacrificed burnt offerings and fellowship offerings. Then the LORD answered his prayer in behalf of the land, and the plague on Israel was stopped.

ᵃ 23 Some Hebrew manuscripts and Septuagint; most Hebrew manuscripts *King Araunah*   ᵇ 24 That is, about 1 1/4 pounds or about 575 grams

---

(Ex 30:13), or in his motivation for the census, such as undertaking it to number the military-age males out of pride in his great army rather than dependence on Yahweh (2Sa 24:4,9).

24:25 sacrificed burnt offerings The sacrifice for atonement in this place looks forward to the eventual construction of the temple (see 1Ch 22:1).

THE COVENANTS OF GOD
by Daniel I. Block

The notion of covenant applies to the creation and governance of relationships as varied as marriage, adoption, employment, political alliances and worship. Such covenantal relationships belong no less to the contemporary world than to the ancient world of the Bible. In broadest terms, covenants are agreements between parties either of equal status (e.g., Jacob and Laban, Ge 31:43–55) or of unequal status (e.g., the king of the Assyrian Empire and the king of Judah, 2Ki 16:7). In the ancient world the latter were often called suzerainty treaties. For example, in the fourteenth century BC, such a treaty would involve a superior "suzerain" power making an agreement with a less powerful "vassal" state; the suzerain was always in a position to set the terms. Theologically, the most important covenants in Scripture involve agreements between unequal parties, specifically God himself entering into covenant with his creatures. This meant that God initiated his covenants, chose the covenant partners, announced the terms, identified the signs of the covenant (e.g., a rainbow, Ge 9:12–17; circumcision, Ge 17:9–14), and determined the consequences of his partners' actions (blessings for fidelity; curses for rebellion). Those with whom God entered into covenant had only to accept the terms offered (and enjoy the benefits) or reject them (and suffer the consequences).

The biblical covenants may be grouped under three broad types (from most comprehensive to most specific): God's covenant with all of creation; God's covenant with Israel through Abraham and Moses; and God's royal covenants with Noah (as a second Adam) and King David and his heirs. The NT describes how they all come together and are fulfilled in Jesus Christ.

GOD'S COVENANT WITH ALL OF CREATION

Among all living creatures, God created human beings to bear his image—that is, to serve as his representatives and deputies in governing the world (Ge 1:26–28; Ps 8). Genesis 2 portrays Adam as a king in a royal garden, ruling under God's guidance and authority (Ge 2:16–17) and caring for the world and the garden on God's behalf (Ge 1:26–28; 2:15). The two special trees in the garden—the tree of life and the tree of the knowledge of good and evil—symbolize the blessings and curses that would become a regular feature of ancient treaties: The tree of life represented blessings for faithfulness, and the tree of the knowledge of good and evil represented curses for rebellion.

Because of the sin of the human beings God placed in charge of the world—which resulted in the disintegration of the relationship between the Creator and creation—the blessing of being fruitful and multiplying (Ge 1:20–30) was replaced by the curse of death that eventually led to the great flood (Ge 6–8). Even so, humanity's calling as vassal of God and caretaker of the earth remained. After the flood, through Noah, God graciously established a covenant with creation (Ge 6:18; 8:20—9:17). Later prophets occasionally allude to this covenant (Isa 54:9–10; Jer 31:35–37), treating it as the foundation for the final recreation of the cosmos, when sin and its effects will be removed and righteousness will reign (Isa 65:17; 66:22).

In the New Testament, John 3:16 portrays the cosmic context of Jesus' incarnation using covenant language: "God demonstrated his covenant commitment (love) to the world by giving his one and only son that all who believe in him might not perish but have eternal life" (author's transla-

tion). Paul anticipated the ultimate liberation of all creation in fulfillment of the cosmic covenant (Ro 8:20–22), while Peter's vision of the cosmos' future involved the transformation and recreation of the present order so that righteousness may finally dwell in the new heavens and earth (2Pe 3:10–13). Revelation envisions this renewed creation as a holy city, where the covenant relationship involving God, the earth, and all its inhabitants live in covenant peace (Rev 21:1–4).

GOD'S COVENANT WITH ISRAEL THROUGH ABRAHAM AND MOSES

As the answer for a world under the curse, God chose Abraham and his descendants to be parties to a new covenant that would serve as a microcosm of the creation covenant and be the means by which ultimate blessing could replace the curse. Within this new covenant, God promised Abraham that he and his offspring would enjoy God's personal presence and protection (Ge 12:3; 17:7; 26:24; 28:13–15). God also promised innumerable descendants, who would become a great nation (Ge 12:2; 13:16; 15:5), and that kings would be among them (Ge 17:6,16; 35:11). The land of Canaan would be their homeland (Ge 13:15,17; 15:7–21). Indeed, Abraham's offspring would be God's agents of blessing to the entire world (Ge 12:2; 18:18; 22:18). In response, Abraham and his descendants were called to trust God (Ge 15:6) and demonstrate this trust through a blameless life (Ge 17:1), obedience to God's commands (Ge 12:1,4; 22:1), and conformity to his will (Ge 26:6). God instituted circumcision as the sign of this covenant (Ge 17:9–14,22–27).

The patriarchs experienced the anticipated benefits of God's covenant with Abraham only in part, but God promised to confirm it with their descendants (Ge 17:7). At Sinai, God made the people of Israel his own and committed himself to be their God (Ex 20:2; Lev 26:12). He commissioned them for the mission that he first announced to Abraham: blessing the world (Ex 19:4–6). He also reiterated his commitment to give them the land of Canaan (Ex 6:4–8; 23:20–33; Lev 14:34; 25:38) and revealed in detail how Israel's response to their salvation from Egyptian slavery and the privilege of enjoying this covenant relationship should look. He gave them the seventh-day Sabbath as the sign of the enduring quality of the covenant (Ex 31:16–17; Lev 24:8) and bound himself to them irrevocably through a ritual involving the sprinkling of blood on the altar (Ex 24:6). Meanwhile, the Israelites promised to listen to God's voice and keep his covenant (Ex 19:8; 24:3,7); they bound themselves to the covenant by having Moses sprinkle the blood on them as well (Ex 24:8).

After they had celebrated the ratification of the covenant with a feast on Sinai (Ex 24:9–11), God gave Moses two copies of the covenant on tablets of stone (Ex 24:12; 31:18) to be stored in the ark of the covenant (Ex 40:20; Dt 10:5). God's further revelation was interrupted by the Israelites' worship of the golden calf, which caused Moses to smash the tablets as a symbolic gesture of the broken covenant. Still, in response to Moses' prayer, God took Israel back and provided new tablets; he again expressed his personal commitment to Israel, as well as their obligations to him. The record of God's revelation ends with covenant blessings and curses (Lev 26:1–39) and a reminder of the covenant's irrevocability: If God should ever impose curses on Israel, this would not be the final word; ultimately, he would remember his covenant and restore his relationship with Israel (Lev 26:40–46; Dt 4:25–31; 30:1–10).

Yet the generation that ratified the covenant at Sinai died in the desert because of their unfaithfulness. For this reason Moses presided over a covenant renewal ceremony on the plains of Moab

as his last official act, a ceremony reflected in Deuteronomy. In his farewell addresses to the nation in this book, Moses focused on the theme of God's covenant and the life of covenant righteousness the Israelites were called to live after entering the promised land.

From the perspective of the covenant, the history of Israel in the promised land was a history of failure—not the failure of God's covenant but of the people to honor it. The people forgot their gracious redeemer and worshiped other gods. God eventually had enough of their rebellion, and, in precise fulfillment of the covenant curses, he sent the Assyrians to destroy the northern kingdom of Israel in 722 BC (2Ki 17); the southern kingdom of Judah followed, falling to the Babylonians in 586 BC. However, even these events did not signal the end of the covenant. Rather, as Daniel 9:1–19 recognizes, this judgment represented the application of the terms of the covenant to a disobedient people (Da 9:7–14).

The terms of the covenant included God's promise that Israel's history would not end in judgment (Lev 26:40–45; Dt 30); God would remember his covenant, gather the people again and restore their relationship to the land. The prophets refer to this new relationship as a "covenant of peace" (Isa 54:9–10; Eze 34:25; 37:26), an "everlasting covenant" (Isa 55:3; 61:8; Jer 32:40; Eze 16:60), and a "new covenant" (Jer 31:31). This covenant stands in continuity with the covenant that God first made with Abraham (Ge 17:7,13,19; 1Ch 16:15–18; compare Ps 105:8–11) and then confirmed with Israel at Sinai (Ex 24:8). When God establishes the new/eternal/peace covenant, a transformed Israel will finally realize the ideals of the covenant made centuries earlier and anticipated by Moses (Dt 30).

Jeremiah offers further insight into the nature of the new covenant (Jer 30:1—33:26), focusing on the future of his own people, Israel. (Outsiders enter the picture only as agents of God's judgment, as in Jer 32:26–35, or as the objects of Yahweh's judgment, as in Jer 30:8–11.) Jeremiah's vision of the restored covenant pictures among God's people the internalization of the Torah (Jer 31:33); renewal of the covenant relationship, expressed in the formula, "I will be their God, and they will be my people" (Jer 31:33); knowledge of God; and forgiveness of sin (Jer 31:34). The only significantly new element is represented in the word "all": "They will all know me, from the least of them to the greatest" (Jer 31:34). Here God anticipates a day when the boundaries of spiritual Israel will finally match the boundaries of physical Israel. This covenant represents the fulfillment of the original Israelite covenant first made with Abraham, then ratified with his descendants at Sinai, and later confirmed with a new generation on the plains of Moab.

The NT presents the coming of Jesus as the climax of Israel's history (Mt 1) and Jesus as the embodiment of Israel, the true offspring of Abraham (Gal 3:15–16). Through his sacrificial death on the cross (Lk 22:20; 1Co 11:25; Heb 8:8–13), Jesus effects the new covenant, reconciling humanity to God (Col 1:20) and liberating us from sin (Ro 8:18–25); he makes us new creations so that we may be true images of God (2Co 5:17).

Paul speaks of the church as God's dwelling place (1Co 3:16) and applies Israel's covenant formula also to Christians: "I will live with them and walk among them, and I will be their God, and they will be my people" (2Co 6:16; compare Ge 17:7; Ex 6:7; Dt 26:17; Jer 30:22; Eze 36:28).

The book of Acts traces the worldwide spread of the covenant community; each new advance was accompanied by a fresh outpouring of the Spirit of God. The process began with Jews from all over the world who believed in Jesus (Ac 2:4,33,38) and then was extended to Samaritans (Ac 8:14–17), Gentile converts (see Ac 10:44–48; compare Ac 11:16), and finally to anyone in the world (see Ac 19:6). However, this universal extension of the covenant did not mean God was no longer interested in his covenant people, Israel. Through coming to Jesus, they return from exile. In Romans 9–11 Paul anticipates the ultimate realization of the goal of the original covenant: All Israel will be saved (Ro 11:25–32; compare Dt 30; Jer 31:31–37).

GOD'S ROYAL COVENANT

In the original creation order, God had ordained Adam (and all humanity) with the status and responsibility of governing the world on his behalf. Through a covenant, God renewed this role with Noah as a second Adam after the flood (Ge 9:1–7). Just as the covenant involving God, Israel and the land of Canaan was a microcosm of the covenant involving God, all living creatures and the whole cosmos, so God's covenant with David established in Israel a microcosm of the role humanity was to play in creation. David bore the title son of God (2Sa 7:14; Ps 2:7; 89:26–27), and God promised that he and his sons would have a never-ending title to the throne of Israel (2Sa 7:13). David acknowledged the significance of his reign for Israel (2Sa 7:23–27), but he also recognized its universal import: "This is a revelation concerning humanity!" (2Sa 7:19; author's translation). The cosmic implications of David's kingship are celebrated by psalmists (Ps 2; 72; 110) and prophets (Isa 11:1–9; Mic 5:2–5).

While Jesus is God, the creator of heaven and earth, and the Father's only Son (Jn 1:1–2,18; Col 1:16–20), he is also the last Adam (1Co 15:45), whose ancestry is traced back to the original Adam (Lk 3:38). As the new Adam, Jesus is the fountainhead of a new spiritual race (Ro 5:14–19; 1Co 15:45), and as the perfect image of God (Ro 8:28–29; Col 1:15; Heb 1:2–4), he reconciles the world to God, exercising authority over the whole cosmos (Mt 28:18–19) and accomplishing all things perfectly (Col 1:18–20). However, the New Testament tends to focus specifically on Jesus' role as true heir to the royal covenant with David. His title, "Christ," is a royal title. He is the Messiah, the son of David (Mt 1:1; 21:9; Mk 10:47; Lk 18:39; Ro 1:3; 2Ti 2:8; Rev 5:5; 22:16) and Son of God (Mt 3:17; 17:5). But this royal role is also reflected in epithets like "the Lion of the tribe of Judah" (Rev 5:5) and "the son/root of Jesse" (Lk 3:32; Ac 13:22; Ro 15:12). And in his death he fulfilled the role of the suffering (royal) servant of Isaiah 53.

Ultimately, the reality and effectiveness of all God's covenants—whether cosmic, Israelite or royal—are grounded in the person and work of Christ. As universal Lord, he is the source and end of all things (Col 1:16–17). He is the redeemer of his people—ethnic and spiritual Israel (Ro 10:13). He is both the Son of God and son of David, whose sacrificial work guarantees the fulfillment of all covenant promises to the praise and the glory of God.

1 KINGS

INTRODUCTION TO 1 KINGS

First Kings testifies to Yahweh's presence among Israel, but also shows just how far a nation can fall when Yahweh is ignored. First Kings begins at the end of David's reign, as his sons Adonijah and Solomon compete for the throne. Solomon is selected, and he builds a temple for Yahweh. But after Solomon, the once-prosperous nation splits into two kingdoms. Most of the kings on both sides fail to follow Yahweh and allow idolatry to flourish. Meanwhile, prophets, most notably Elijah, boldly call unfaithful kings to account.

BACKGROUND

The books of 1–2 Kings originally formed a single work, which was probably divided because its length required two scrolls. The division between 1–2 Kings is not based on a natural break in the text; it splits the story of Elijah between the two books.

The whole work of 1–2 Kings deals with the period from 971 BC (the transition from David to Solomon) to 586 BC (the Babylonian exile). First Kings covers about 120 years of that span, starting just before Solomon's accession and ending shortly after Ahab's reign over the northern kingdom (853 BC).

STRUCTURE

The combined work of 1–2 Kings can be divided into three parts. The first section (1Ki 1–11) opens with an aging David and a political coup by his son Adonijah. Following the advice of the

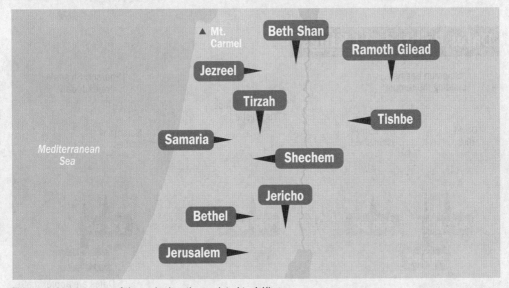

This map depicts some of the major locations related to 1 Kings.

Prophet Nathan, David is able to repair his kingdom by appointing another son, Solomon, to the throne (chs. 1–2). Shortly thereafter, Yahweh comes to Solomon and asks him what he desires; Solomon requests wisdom, which Yahweh grants him (chs. 3–4). Solomon then builds Yahweh's temple (compare 2Sa 7)—representing Yahweh's visible presence on earth—and then continues his building projects with his own palace (1Ki 5–7). However, Solomon ends up worshiping the gods of his foreign wives (11:1–8). Yahweh consequently declares that Solomon's son will lose control over most of his kingdom (11:9–13). The section ends with Solomon's death.

In the second section (1Ki 12—2 Kgs 17), we see Yahweh's declaration against Solomon played out. A civil war divides the nation into a southern kingdom, known as Judah, and a northern kingdom, called Israel. The northern kingdom of Israel is comprised of 10 of the 12 tribes of God's people, with the tribe of Benjamin joining Judah in the south (1Ki 12:21). Solomon's descendants reign over Judah, but Israel is ruled by kings not from the Davidic line. Most kings on both sides are unfaithful to Yahweh. Throughout this section, the prophet Elijah is a major figure (1Ki 17—2 Kgs 2:12). Although 1 Kings ends in the middle of Elijah's ministry, this section of the narrative continues through 2Ki 17, which describes the fall of the northern kingdom of Israel. The third section (2Ki 18–25) deals with the southern kingdom of Judah until it, too, is conquered.

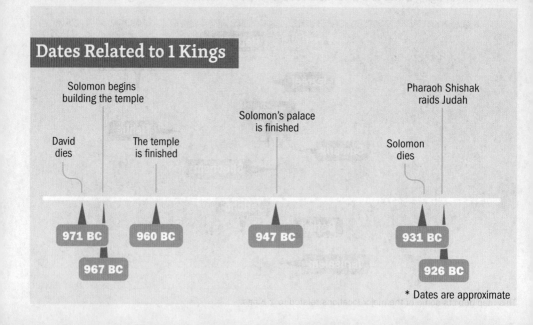

Dates Related to 1 Kings

Solomon begins building the temple		Pharaoh Shishak raids Judah
David dies	The temple is finished	Solomon's palace is finished	Solomon dies
971 BC	960 BC	947 BC	931 BC
967 BC			926 BC

* Dates are approximate

OUTLINE

- Solomon comes to the throne (1:1—2:46)
- Solomon's reign (3:1—11:43)
- Israel is divided after Solomon's death (12:1—22:53)

THEMES

In 1 Kings, priests lead God's people astray when they should have been interceding on their behalf; and kings, who are expected to be godly examples, are selfish and idolatrous. After Solomon's death, almost all rulers of the northern kingdom do evil by continuing the idolatrous shrines established by the first northern king, Jeroboam. (The one exception is Jehu, who receives a mixed evaluation; see 2Ki 10:28–31.) Most leaders of the southern kingdom also receive negative or mixed evaluations, but two—Hezekiah and Josiah—are regarded positively.

First Kings profoundly illustrates just how faith in national identity or leadership can lead to failure. Meanwhile, a faithful relationship with Yahweh is reflected in the life of Elijah, who predicts droughts, resurrects the son of a widow, and calls down fire upon the prophets of the god Baal (1Ki 17–18). Elijah and a few others bravely show strength in the midst of religious persecution (e.g., 18:1–16). We see that these courageous few have the most powerful ally of all, Yahweh, who provides whatever they need (17:2–6) and speaks truth in a still small voice (19:9–18).

First Kings leads us to reflect on what kind of people we will turn out to be. We can choose to stand nearly alone like Elijah, proclaiming righteousness in an unjust time, or we can choose to follow after failed leaders—or worse, become like them. The choice to follow Yahweh—or not—is ours to make.

Adonijah Sets Himself Up as King

1 When King David was very old, he could not keep warm even when they put covers over him. ²So his attendants said to him, "Let us look for a young virgin to serve the king and take care of him. She can lie beside him so that our lord the king may keep warm."

³Then they searched throughout Israel for a beautiful young woman and found Abishag, a Shunammite, and brought her to the king. ⁴The woman was very beautiful; she took care of the king and waited on him, but the king had no sexual relations with her.

⁵Now Adonijah, whose mother was Haggith, put himself forward and said, "I will be king." So he got chariots and horses*a* ready, with fifty men to run ahead of him. ⁶(His father had never rebuked him by asking, "Why do you behave as you do?" He was also very handsome and was born next after Absalom.)

⁷Adonijah conferred with Joab son of Zeruiah and with Abiathar the priest, and they gave him their support. ⁸But Zadok the priest, Benaiah son of Jehoiada, Nathan the prophet, Shimei and Rei and David's special guard did not join Adonijah.

a 5 Or *charioteers*

1:1–4 Building on the narrative of 2 Samuel, 1 Kings opens with an account of the final days of King David's reign (971 BC) and the transfer of the united kingdom of Israel from David to Solomon. In contrast to other ancient Near Eastern accounts of kings' lives, 1 Kings emphasizes David's frailty and humanity—a theme that continues until his death (1Ki 1:1–4,15; 2:1–2,10). The political drama that unfolds in these opening chapters sets the stage for the remaining years of Israel's Monarchic Period, characterized by turmoil from the inside out—ultimately leading to the division of the nation into Israel in the north and Judah in the south.

First Kings narrates about 120 years of Israel's history until shortly after the reign of King Ahab over the northern kingdom of Israel (853 BC). Chapters 1–2 concludes the traditions regarding the Davidic court in 2Sa 9–20. Together these chapters comprise a single narrative about the establishment of David's line. The narrative presents the stories of David and Bathsheba (2Sa 10–12), Absalom's revolt (2Sa 13–19), and Solomon's rise to the throne (1Ki 1–2). The legitimacy of David's reign (e.g., 2Sa 12:30–31; 18:31; 19:8–15), as well as Solomon's (2Sa 12:24–25; 1Ki 1:6,11–14), appears as a central theme throughout this account, likely reflecting the concerns of the period when 1–2 Samuel and 1–2 Kings were compiled. See the people diagram "King David's Family Tree" on p. 620.

1:1 A number of years seem to have elapsed between the events recorded in 2 Samuel and 2 Kings 1. See the timeline "The United Kingdom" on p. 464.

1:1 King David The youngest son of Jesse, David, was a shepherd boy from Bethlehem in Judah when Samuel anointed him king in place of Saul (1Sa 16). **very old** The Hebrew phrase used here, *zaqen ba bayyamim*, occurs only three times elsewhere in the OT: Ge 24:1 in reference to Abraham; Jos 13:1 and 23:1 in reference to Joshua. Its usage here identifies David with two of Israel's greatest figures.

DAVID
King David was a skilled warrior (1Sa 17; 2Sa 8) and a man after God's own heart (1Sa 13:13–14). He reigned for 40 years (1011–971 BC): seven years in Hebron and 33 years in Jerusalem.

1:2 young virgin The Hebrew phrase used here involves two terms: *bethulah*, which refers to a virgin, and *na'arah*, which refers to a young girl or female attendant.

1:3 Israel David expanded the borders of Israel in all directions by battling the Philistines (2Sa 5; 8:1), Amalekites (1Sa 30), Edomites, Moabites (2Sa 8), Ammonites and Arameans (Syrians) (2Sa 10). **Abishag, a Shunammite** Abishag was from the northern town of Shunem (modern-day Solem), located in the Jezreel Valley near Mount Gilboa (1Sa 28:4) and Megiddo. The wealthy woman who provided food and shelter for Elisha and whose son Elisha resurrected also was from Shunem (2Ki 4:8–37). The female lover in Song of Songs may have been from Shunem, as well (see SS 6:13 and note).

1:4 but the king had no sexual relations with her The Hebrew text insists that David did not "know" Abishag (using a Hebrew euphemism for sexual intercourse) because his eldest living son, Adonijah, later asks to marry her after David's death (1Ki 2:13–25); Lev 18 prohibits men from having sexual relations with their father's wife and relatives (see note on Lev 18:1–30). In the ancient Near East, new kings commonly adopted their predecessor's harem. When Adonijah asks Bathsheba if he may take Abishag as a wife, Solomon becomes outraged and has Adonijah killed (1Ki 2:13–25). While Solomon's reason for doing so does not appear in the text, his actions suggest that Adonijah's request represented a serious threat to the throne. If Solomon's outrage was related to the practice of adopting the king's harem, then Abishag's virginity must be explained by her being part of the harem while still maintaining her virginity—similar to how Esther's status is described prior to her first visitation with the king (Est 2:3,8,14).

1:5–10 Like Absalom, his rebellious brother, Adonijah amasses chariots, horses and footmen (2Sa 15:1; 1Ki 1:5). As David's eldest surviving son, Adonijah represents the most likely candidate for the throne, because David's son Absalom has already died (2Sa 18:14–15). However, high-ranking officials did not agree on whether he should be king.

1:5 Adonijah Means "Yahweh is my lord" or "Yahweh is my master." **I will be king** Parallels with Absalom's rebellion suggest that Adonijah was planning a military coup (compare 2Sa 13–18). Alternatively, the declaration might not have represented a threat, since Adonijah was David's eldest surviving son. In the ancient Near East, the eldest son took his father's throne upon his death. **he got chariots and horses ready** In order to go on royal procession throughout the city. This amounted to a formal declaration of his kingship (1Ki 1:11).

1:6 Absalom See 2Sa 3:3; 13–18.

1:7 Joab David's nephew and the commander of his

⁹Adonijah then sacrificed sheep, cattle and fattened calves at the Stone of Zoheleth near En Rogel. He invited all his brothers, the king's sons, and all the royal officials of Judah, ¹⁰but he did not invite Nathan the prophet or Benaiah or the special guard or his brother Solomon.

¹¹Then Nathan asked Bathsheba, Solomon's mother, "Have you not heard that Adonijah, the son of Haggith, has become king, and our lord David knows nothing about it? ¹²Now then, let me advise you how you can save your own life and the life of your son Solomon. ¹³Go in to King David and say to him, 'My lord the king, did you not swear to me your servant: "Surely Solomon your son shall be king after me, and he will sit on my throne"? Why then has Adonijah become king?'

---

army (2Sa 8:16; 20:23). **Abiathar** One of David's high priests and a life-long supporter (1Sa 22:20; 2Sa 20:25).

1:8 Zadok David's other high priest (2Sa 8:17; 20:25). The high priesthood eventually would belong solely to Zadok's descendants. Zadok and Abiathar were co-high priests under David. When Adonijah took over David's throne, Abiathar supported him (v. 7), while Zadok supported Solomon (v. 8). Once Solomon takes Adonijah's place, he expels Abiathar (2:26–27) and makes Zadok the sole high priest (2:35). **Benaiah** The commander of David's bodyguard (see note on 1:38; compare 2Sa 20:23; 23:20–23). **Nathan** The prophet who advised David and delivered the Davidic Covenant (2Sa 7). **Shimei and Rei** Their identities are unknown, but the former may be associated with the Shimei of 2Sa 16:5–14. **David's special guard** A group of warriors who supported David during the period before his kingship. Their names and exploits appear in 2Sa 21:15–22; 23:8–39 and 1Ch 11:10–47.

1:9 En Rogel A spring close to Jerusalem, on the border between the tribal lands of Benjamin and Judah (Jos 15:7; 18:16).

1:11–27 In their conversation with David, Nathan and Bathsheba appeal to an oath not included in the books of Samuel or 1–2 Kings. Nathan advises Bathsheba to speak to David to preserve her life and the life of her son, Solomon—presumably because Adonijah would kill them once he became king, to avoid a threat to the throne (1Ki 1:12). Solomon does not play an active role in this plot until after he assumes the throne (v. 46).

Verse 11 presents the first mention of Bathsheba and Solomon since Solomon's birth.

Second Samuel 12:24–25 records that Yahweh loved Solomon and sent a message by Nathan. This message earns Solomon the name Jedidah ("beloved of Yahweh"), leading Bathsheba and Nathan to believe that Solomon has a special status among David's sons. Despite the fact that David's eldest living son, Adonijah, represents the most likely heir to the throne, this status sets Solomon apart according to 1Ki 1–2.

1:11 Bathsheba The widow of Uriah the Hittite (2Sa 11). **our lord David knows nothing about it** Although David still has the authority to make important decisions, his condition has deteriorated such that he is no longer informed about the happenings in his own kingdom.

BATHSHEBA
David watched Bathsheba while she bathed (2Sa 11:2) and had sex with her while her husband, Uriah, was at battle (2Sa 11:3–5). At first, David tried to hide the affair; when that plan failed, he had Uriah killed (2Sa 11:6–25). After a period of mourning, Bathsheba became David's wife and gave birth to their child (2Sa 11:26–27). The child died (2Sa 12:15–23), but the couple conceived again and Bathsheba gave birth to Solomon (2Sa 12:24–25).

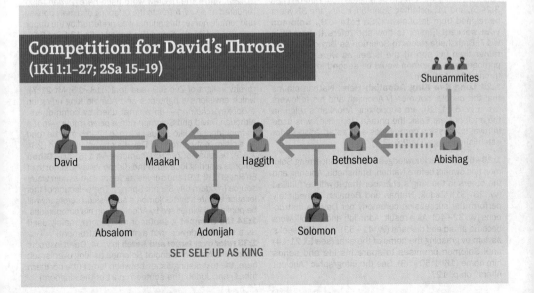

Competition for David's Throne
(1Ki 1:1–27; 2Sa 15–19)

Shunammites

David — Maakah — Haggith — Bethsheba — Abishag

Absalom — Adonijah — Solomon

SET SELF UP AS KING

¹⁴While you are still there talking to the king, I will come in and add my word to what you have said."

¹⁵So Bathsheba went to see the aged king in his room, where Abishag the Shunammite was attending him. ¹⁶Bathsheba bowed down, prostrating herself before the king.

"What is it you want?" the king asked.

¹⁷She said to him, "My lord, you yourself swore to me your servant by the LORD your God: 'Solomon your son shall be king after me, and he will sit on my throne.' ¹⁸But now Adonijah has become king, and you, my lord the king, do not know about it. ¹⁹He has sacrificed great numbers of cattle, fattened calves, and sheep, and has invited all the king's sons, Abiathar the priest and Joab the commander of the army, but he has not invited Solomon your servant. ²⁰My lord the king, the eyes of all Israel are on you, to learn from you who will sit on the throne of my lord the king after him. ²¹Otherwise, as soon as my lord the king is laid to rest with his ancestors, I and my son Solomon will be treated as criminals."

²²While she was still speaking with the king, Nathan the prophet arrived. ²³And the king was told, "Nathan the prophet is here." So he went before the king and bowed with his face to the ground.

²⁴Nathan said, "Have you, my lord the king, declared that Adonijah shall be king after you, and that he will sit on your throne? ²⁵Today he has gone down and sacrificed great numbers of cattle, fattened calves, and sheep. He has invited all the king's sons, the commanders of the army and Abiathar the priest. Right now they are eating and drinking with him and saying, 'Long live King Adonijah!' ²⁶But me your servant, and Zadok the priest, and Benaiah son of Jehoiada, and your servant Solomon he did not invite. ²⁷Is this something my lord the king has done without letting his servants know who should sit on the throne of my lord the king after him?"

David Makes Solomon King

1:28-53pp — 1Ch 29:21-25

²⁸Then King David said, "Call in Bathsheba." So she came into the king's presence and stood before him.

²⁹The king then took an oath: "As surely as the LORD lives, who has delivered me out of every trouble, ³⁰I will surely carry out this very day what I swore to you by the LORD, the God of Israel: Solomon your son shall be king after me, and he will sit on my throne in my place."

³¹Then Bathsheba bowed down with her face to the ground, prostrating herself before the king, and said, "May my lord King David live forever!"

³²King David said, "Call in Zadok the priest, Nathan the prophet and Benaiah son of Jehoiada." When they came before the king, ³³he said to them: "Take your lord's servants with you and have Solomon my son mount my own mule and take him down to Gihon. ³⁴There have Zadok the priest and Nathan the prophet anoint him king over Israel. Blow the trumpet and shout, 'Long live King Solomon!' ³⁵Then you are to go up with

---

1:15 Abishag Her presence makes her a witness to the following conversation.

1:17 your servant Bathsheba appeals to David as his servant or handmaid, rather than as his wife (compare 2Sa 11:27).

1:19 the king's sons David had 17 sons: 6, including Adonijah, during the 7 years he reigned from Hebron (2Sa 3:2–5), and 11, including Solomon, during the 33 years he reigned from Jerusalem (2Sa 5:14–16). **Solomon your servant** Similar to how she refers to herself in v. 17, Bathsheba refers to Solomon as David's servant rather than his son. If the Israelites were practicing primogeniture, Solomon would be second in line to the throne after Adonijah.

1:25 Long live King Adonijah Here, Nathan claims that the people, not merely Adonijah and his followers (as in vv. 5,11,18), are supporting Adonijah's reign. In the ancient Near East, the phrase "long live" was used in royal succession ceremonies and as an address for established kings (Da 2:4; 3:9).

1:28–53 David acknowledges his oath concerning Solomon and swears before Nathan, Bathsheba, Abishag and the others in the king's chamber that it will be fulfilled (vv. 28–31). Zadok, Nathan and Benaiah immediately perform the succession ceremony per David's instructions (vv. 32–40). As a result, Adonijah and his followers become afraid and disband (vv. 41–53). Adonijah seeks asylum by grasping the horns of the altar (see Ex 21:14) until Solomon promises to spare his life and sends him home (1Ki 1:50–53). See the infographic "Ancient Altars" on p. 127.

1:31 May my lord King David live forever While Bathsheba responds properly with this exclamation, it is ironic given the context of David's quickly approaching death.

1:33 your lord's servants Later specified as the Kerethites and Pelethites (v. 38 and note; see 2Sa 8:18 and note), who are under the command of Benaiah (2Sa 20:23). **mule** The Hebrew word used here, *pirdah* (also rendered as *pered*) refers to the offspring of a male donkey and female horse; this animal was preferred by the upper classes and royalty during this period (2Sa 13:29; 18:9). David's and Solomon's use of a mule may be connected to Dt 17:16, which prohibits Israel's kings from amassing horses. When Jesus enters the city of Jerusalem on a donkey, the crowd interprets Jesus' action as a claim to royalty in light of Zec 9:9 (see Jn 12:13–15; Mt 21:7), which envisions a righteous and humble king riding on a donkey (*chamor*)—an animal used by commoners. Although David and Solomon ride a *pered* (mule)—not a *chamor* (donkey) like Jesus—Jn 12:12–15 may be read as a claim to the throne of David's eternal kingdom (2Sa 7:13), because of Zec 9:9 (compare Mt 1:6–16). **Gihon** Gihon is a spring located in the Kidron Valley just north of En Rogel (1Ki 1:9) and serves as Jerusalem's main water source (modern-day Siloam Spring). The selection of this location ensures that Solomon's succession ceremony will be public and witnessed by Adonijah and his companions.

1:34 the trumpet A shofar or ram's horn, mainly used as a signaling device, not a musical instrument.

1:35 ruler over Israel and Judah In v. 34, David instructs Zadok and Nathan to anoint Solomon as king over Israel; here, the text distinguishes between Israel (the northern tribes) and Judah (the southern part of the kingdom).

him, and he is to come and sit on my throne and reign in my place. I have appointed him ruler over Israel and Judah."

36Benaiah son of Jehoiada answered the king, "Amen! May the LORD, the God of my lord the king, so declare it. 37As the LORD was with my lord the king, so may he be with Solomon to make his throne even greater than the throne of my lord King David!"

38So Zadok the priest, Nathan the prophet, Benaiah son of Jehoiada, the Kerethites and the Pelethites went down and had Solomon mount King David's mule, and they escorted him to Gihon. 39Zadok the priest took the horn of oil from the sacred tent and anointed Solomon. Then they sounded the trumpet and all the people shouted, "Long live King Solomon!" 40And all the people went up after him, playing pipes and rejoicing greatly, so that the ground shook with the sound.

41Adonijah and all the guests who were with him heard it as they were finishing their feast. On hearing the sound of the trumpet, Joab asked, "What's the meaning of all the noise in the city?"

42Even as he was speaking, Jonathan son of Abiathar the priest arrived. Adonijah said, "Come in. A worthy man like you must be bringing good news."

43"Not at all!" Jonathan answered. "Our lord King David has made Solomon king. 44The king has sent with him Zadok the priest, Nathan the prophet, Benaiah son of Jehoiada, the Kerethites and the Pelethites, and they have put him on the king's mule, 45and Zadok the priest and Nathan the prophet have anointed him king at Gihon. From there they have gone up cheering, and the city resounds with it. That's the noise you hear. 46Moreover, Solomon has taken his seat on the royal throne. 47Also, the royal officials have come to congratulate our lord King David, saying, 'May your God make Solomon's name more famous than yours and his throne greater than yours!' And the king bowed in worship on his bed 48and said, 'Praise be to the LORD, the God of Israel, who has allowed my eyes to see a successor on my throne today.'"

49At this, all Adonijah's guests rose in alarm and dispersed. 50But Adonijah, in fear of Solomon, went and took hold of the horns of the altar. 51Then Solomon was told, "Adonijah is afraid of King Solomon and is clinging to the horns of the altar. He says, 'Let King Solomon swear to me today that he will not put his servant to death with the sword.'"

52Solomon replied, "If he shows himself to be worthy, not a hair of his head will fall to the ground; but if evil is found in him, he will die." 53Then King Solomon sent men, and they brought him down from the altar. And Adonijah came and bowed down to King Solomon, and Solomon said, "Go to your home."

David's Charge to Solomon

2:10-12pp — 1Ch 29:26-28

2 When the time drew near for David to die, he gave a charge to Solomon his son.

2"I am about to go the way of all the earth," he said. "So be strong, act like a man, 3and observe

---

1:38 Kerethites and the Pelethites Refers to part of David's personal mercenary forces (2Sa 20:23) under the command of Benaiah (see 2Sa 8:18 and note; 1Ch 18:17). They also supported David when he fled from Absalom (2Sa 15:18) and when Sheba rebelled (2Sa 20:7). They do not appear in the Biblical record after David's death and may have been disbanded. Originally from the Aegean (likely the island of Crete), the Kerethites (*kerethi*) settled along the southern coast of Israel (1Sa 30:14). Their relationship to the Philistines is unclear, but the OT mentions them together (Eze 25:16; Zep 2:5). The Pelethites are mentioned only alongside the Kerethites in the OT. The origin of the Pelethites (*pelethi*) is unclear, but they might have been Philistines (*pelishti*).

1:39 horn of oil Zadok must have taken the oil to Gihon in anticipation of Solomon's anointing. Such oil would have been made by a perfumer and mixed with costly spices (Ex 30:23–33). **the sacred tent** Likely refers to the tent of Yahweh (1Ki 2:28) that was pitched in the City of David to house the ark of the covenant (2Sa 6). See note on Ex 27:21. **anointed Solomon** Echoes the consecrations of both Saul (1Sa 10:1) and David (1Sa 16:1–13; Ps 89:20).

1:42 Jonathan son of Abiathar Jonathan also was the messenger who brought word of Absalom's rebellion (2Sa 15:27–28,36; 17:17–21).

1:47 May your God make Solomon's name more famous than yours Refers to fame and reputation achieved through brave deeds (2Sa 7:23; 23:18,22).

the king bowed in worship on his bed Indicates that, despite being bedridden, David still showed gratitude.

1:48 allowed my eyes to see a successor on my throne David recalls the covenant that Yahweh made with him in 2Sa 7:12 (compare 1Ki 3:6). This covenant is particularly important in the Gospels of Matthew and Luke, which trace Jesus' genealogy through David's line (Mt 1:6–16; Lk 3:23–32).

1:50 took hold of the horns of the altar Someone who inadvertently committed certain crimes could seek asylum by grabbing the horns of the altar (Ex 21:14). See note on Ex 27:2.

1:53 Go to your home Solomon deals with Adonijah in the same way that David dealt with his rebellious son, Absalom (2Sa 14:24). Adonijah is pardoned, so long as he keeps out of official business.

2:1–9 David's final instructions to Solomon signal a transfer of power and set the stage for the establishment of Solomon's throne (1Ki 2:13–46). Verses 3–4 echo Deuteronomy (e.g., Dt 4:29,40; 6:5; 10:12; 17:14–20) and refers to the Davidic covenant (2Sa 7). Most of David's instructions command Solomon to punish his personal enemies (1Ki 2:5–9). In the ancient Near East, it was common to eliminate individuals who represented a potential threat to the newly established king, particularly if the king acceded to the throne in an unusual fashion.

2:2 I am about to go the way of all the earth A

what the LORD your God requires: Walk in obedience to him, and keep his decrees and commands, his laws and regulations, as written in the Law of Moses. Do this so that you may prosper in all you do and wherever you go ⁴and that the LORD may keep his promise to me: 'If your descendants watch how they live, and if they walk faithfully before me with all their heart and soul, you will never fail to have a successor on the throne of Israel.'

⁵"Now you yourself know what Joab son of Zeruiah did to me — what he did to the two commanders of Israel's armies, Abner son of Ner and Amasa son of Jether. He killed them, shedding their blood in peacetime as if in battle, and with that blood he stained the belt around his waist and the sandals on his feet. ⁶Deal with him according to your wisdom, but do not let his gray head go down to the grave in peace.

⁷"But show kindness to the sons of Barzillai of Gilead and let them be among those who eat at your table. They stood by me when I fled from your brother Absalom.

⁸"And remember, you have with you Shimei son of Gera, the Benjamite from Bahurim, who called down bitter curses on me the day I went to Mahanaim. When he came down to meet me at the Jordan, I swore to him by the LORD: 'I will not put you to death by the sword.' ⁹But now, do not consider him innocent. You are a man of wisdom; you will know what to do to him. Bring his gray head down to the grave in blood."

¹⁰Then David rested with his ancestors and was buried in the City of David. ¹¹He had reigned forty years over Israel — seven years in Hebron and thirty-three in Jerusalem. ¹²So Solomon sat on the throne of his father David, and his rule was firmly established.

Solomon's Throne Established

¹³Now Adonijah, the son of Haggith, went to Bathsheba, Solomon's mother. Bathsheba asked him, "Do you come peacefully?"

He answered, "Yes, peacefully." ¹⁴Then he added, "I have something to say to you."

"You may say it," she replied.

¹⁵"As you know," he said, "the kingdom was mine. All Israel looked to me as their king. But things changed, and the kingdom has gone to my brother; for it has come to him from the LORD. ¹⁶Now I have one request to make of you. Do not refuse me."

---

euphemism for death; also found in Joshua's farewell address (Jos 23:14). **act like a man** The Philistines used this same phrase to encourage themselves in fighting the Israelites (1Sa 4:9). It serves as an informal call to be strong and courageous.

2:3 Law of Moses The Historical Books (Joshua — Nehemiah) attribute the "Book of the Law" mentioned in Deuteronomy and the laws therein to Moses himself (Dt 28:61; 29:21; 30:10; 31:26). The title "Law of Moses" is the most consistently used title for this collection of laws (see Jos 8:31–32; 2Ki 23:25; 2Ch 23:18; 30:16; Ezr 3:2; 7:6; compare Da 9:11–13; Mal 4:4).

2:4 your descendants The Hebrew terminology used here can refer to David's 17 sons or to all of his descendants. In this context, the broader meaning is probably intended. **watch** God's promise to David through Nathan did not include stipulations (2Sa 7:11–16). However, 1 Kings makes several references to the conditional nature of the covenant (1Ki 8:25; 9:5–7). **soul** Typically translated as "soul," the Hebrew word used here, *nephesh*, refers to a person's inner being or emotional self. Rather than sharply distinguish between soul and body, the OT understands *nephesh* and the body as an integrated whole.

2:5 Abner Saul's commander and the companion of Saul's son, Ishbaal. Joab had Abner killed in revenge for the slaying of his brother (2Sa 2:18–23; 3:27). **Amasa** One of David's nephews (1Ch 2:17). He supported Absalom (2Sa 17:25) but later was appointed as one of David's army commanders (2Sa 19:13–14). Joab killed Amasa — his personal rival — during the rebellion of Sheba (2Sa 20:9–10). **in peacetime** Abner and Amasa were at peace with David when Joab killed them, making Joab accountable for both murders (see Ge 9:6; Ex 21:12; Lev 24:17; Nu 35:31).

2:6 to the grave By using the noun *she'ol*, the Hebrew text here refers to the abode of the dead. See the info-

graphic "Ancient Hebrew Conception of the Universe" on p. 5.

1 Kings 2:6

SHEOL
The grave (sheol) is described as a dark (Job 17:16; La 3:6), dusty (Ps 7:5; Job 17:16; 21:26) and silent (Ps 31:17–18; 94:17; 115:17; Isa 47:5) place to which a person descends after death (Nu 16:30; Job 7:9; Isa 57:9). This description resembles Mesopotamian conceptions of the underworld. Sheol is said to have gates (Job 38:17; Isa 38:10) and is spoken of as the place of no return (Job 7:9). However, Yahweh is capable of bringing a person out of Sheol (1Sa 2:6; Am 9:2). The ancient Greek translation, the Septuagint, normally translates the Hebrew word *sheol* into Greek as *hades* (compare note on 1Pe 3:19).

2:7 Barzillai A wealthy, elderly man who was hospitable to David during his stay in Gilead and refused compensation (2Sa 17:27–29).

2:8 Shimei A man who publicly cursed David for killing members of Saul's family (2Sa 16:5–13). David later swore that he would not kill Shimei; he likely made this promise because Shimei approached him with 1,000 men from the tribe of Benjamin (2Sa 19:16–23). Solomon would not have been bound to this oath (see 2Sa 19:23 and note). See the map "Tribal Distribution of Palestine" on p. 2253.

2:10 rested with his ancestors An idiom meaning "died peacefully." It also can have a literal meaning, denoting burial in a family plot (e.g., Ge 47:29–30). **buried in the City of David** Royal tombs just outside Jerusalem were used by the Davidic dynasty until the

"You may make it," she said.

[17]So he continued, "Please ask King Solomon — he will not refuse you — to give me Abishag the Shunammite as my wife."

[18]"Very well," Bathsheba replied, "I will speak to the king for you."

[19]When Bathsheba went to King Solomon to speak to him for Adonijah, the king stood up to meet her, bowed down to her and sat down on his throne. He had a throne brought for the king's mother, and she sat down at his right hand.

[20]"I have one small request to make of you," she said. "Do not refuse me."

The king replied, "Make it, my mother; I will not refuse you."

[21]So she said, "Let Abishag the Shunammite be given in marriage to your brother Adonijah."

[22]King Solomon answered his mother, "Why do you request Abishag the Shunammite for Adonijah? You might as well request the kingdom for him — after all, he is my older brother — yes, for him and for Abiathar the priest and Joab son of Zeruiah!"

[23]Then King Solomon swore by the LORD: "May God deal with me, be it ever so severely, if Adonijah does not pay with his life for this request! [24]And now, as surely as the LORD lives — he who has established me securely on the throne of my father David and has founded a dynasty for me as he promised — Adonijah shall be put to death today!" [25]So King Solomon gave orders to Benaiah son of Jehoiada, and he struck down Adonijah and he died.

[26]To Abiathar the priest the king said, "Go back to your fields in Anathoth. You deserve to die, but I will not put you to death now, because you carried the ark of the Sovereign LORD before my father David and shared all my father's hardships." [27]So Solomon removed Abiathar from the priesthood of the LORD, fulfilling the word the LORD had spoken at Shiloh about the house of Eli.

[28]When the news reached Joab, who had conspired with Adonijah though not with Absalom, he fled to the tent of the LORD and took hold of the horns of the altar. [29]King Solomon was told that Joab had fled to the tent of the LORD and was beside the altar. Then Solomon ordered Benaiah son of Jehoiada, "Go, strike him down!"

[30]So Benaiah entered the tent of the LORD and said to Joab, "The king says, 'Come out!'"

---

reign of Manasseh (2Ki 21:18). **City of David** David had renamed the stronghold of Jerusalem the "City of David" after displacing the Jebusites (2Sa 5:6–10).

2:11 Hebron David's first capital city, when he ruled only Judah. After he became king over all Israel, he made Jerusalem the capital (2Sa 5:5).

2:12 his rule was firmly established The Hebrew phrase used here is repeated in 1Ki 2:46 after David's instructions have been carried out, forming a literary structure called an inclusio (or envelope structure).

2:13–46 Solomon begins his reign by killing Adonijah (vv. 13–25), expelling Abiathar the priest (vv. 26–27) and carrying out David's final instructions regarding Joab (vv. 28–35) and Shimei (vv. 36–46). In eliminating the competition and avenging his father, Solomon establishes his throne and asserts his competency as king. The power dynamics of this passage demonstrate the cutthroat nature of ancient Israelite politics. Solomon accedes to the throne in a manner that even the narrator—who favors Solomon—acknowledges as controversial (vv. 15,22). Solomon continues by expelling or killing anyone who poses a threat to his reign in the name of Yahweh (vv. 23,27,32–33,42–43).

However, David's instructions to Solomon concerning Joab and Shimei do not include mention of Yahweh, but require Solomon to act according to his own wisdom (vv. 6,9). This suggests that the theological statements in vv. 13–46 serve to legitimize Solomon's actions and reign.

2:13 Do you come peacefully Implies that the tension between Solomon and Adonijah has not been resolved.

2:17 to give me Abishag the Shunammite as my wife Adonijah's motive is suspect and probably represents a move to usurp Solomon's throne. See note on 1:4.

2:19 bowed down to her King Solomon shows respect to Bathsheba, suggesting she has attained an elevated status. **king's mother** The Hebrew phrase used here, em hammelekh, indicates that the primary context of this scene involves Bathsheba and Solomon's mother-son relationship. If her political status were primary, the official term "queen mother" would probably be used (gevirah; 15:13). **at his right hand** The seat at the king's right hand is the highest seat of honor (e.g., Ps 110:1). The resurrected Jesus is often described as seated at the right hand of God (e.g., Mt 22:44; Mk 12:36; Lk 22:69; Ac 2:33; Ro 8:34; Heb 8:1; 1Pe 3:22).

2:22 Why do you request Solomon interprets Adonijah's request as a threat—a rival claim to the kingship. This reaction suggests that Abishag was a concubine in David's harem (see 1:4 and note).

2:24 as surely as the LORD lives This phrase signals that a formal oath will follow. **as he promised** Yahweh does not explicitly promise to establish Solomon's house. This passage represents the view that Solomon embodies God's fulfillment of the promise to David, despite the ambiguity of the promise itself (2Sa 7:11–16).

2:26 Anathoth A Levitical city in the territory of Benjamin (Jos 21:18), about three miles northeast of Jerusalem. **You deserve to die** Presumably for aligning himself with Adonijah. **you carried the ark of the Sovereign LORD** Abiathar and Zadok, both high priests, carried the ark of the covenant to Jerusalem at David's command (2Sa 15:24–29). **shared all my father's hardships** Abiathar had joined David after escaping from Nob (1Sa 22:20–23) and remained faithful until David's death.

2:27 fulfilling the word the LORD Abiathar was the last descendant of Eli, whose priestly line fell out of favor with God. A man of God had prophesied that Eli's house would lose power and eventually vanish (1Sa 2:31). Here, this prophecy is fulfilled, signaling the rise of the line of Zadok. See the people diagram "Competition for David's Throne" on p. 507.

2:28 the horns of the altar See note on 1Ki 1:50.

2:29 strike him down Earlier, Solomon had granted Adonijah sanctuary (1:50–53). His decision to not spare Joab implies that Solomon considered him a greater threat.

But he answered, "No, I will die here." Benaiah reported to the king, "This is how Joab answered me."

³¹Then the king commanded Benaiah, "Do as he says. Strike him down and bury him, and so clear me and my whole family of the guilt of the innocent blood that Joab shed. ³²The LORD will repay him for the blood he shed, because without my father David knowing it he attacked two men and killed them with the sword. Both of them — Abner son of Ner, commander of Israel's army,

and Amasa son of Jether, commander of Judah's army — were better men and more upright than he. ³³May the guilt of their blood rest on the head of Joab and his descendants forever. But on David and his descendants, his house and his throne, may there be the LORD's peace forever."

³⁴So Benaiah son of Jehoiada went up and struck down Joab and killed him, and he was buried at his home out in the country. ³⁵The king put Benaiah son of Jehoiada over the army in Joab's position and replaced Abiathar with Zadok the priest.

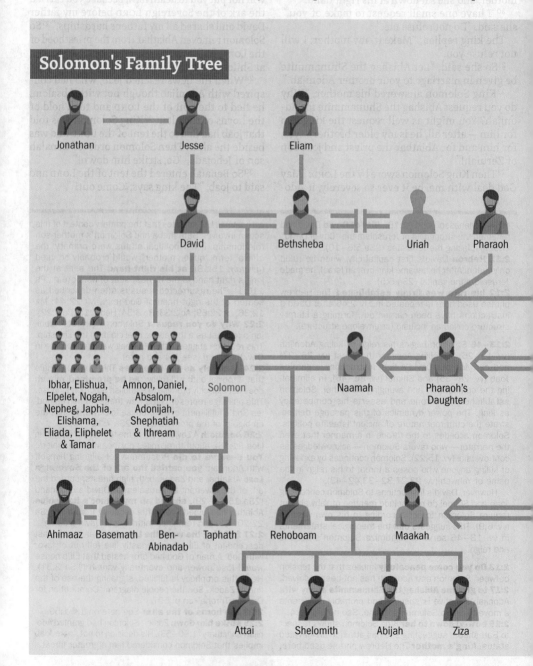

Solomon's Family Tree

Jonathan | Jesse | Eliam

David | Bethsheba | Uriah | Pharaoh

Ibhar, Elishua, Elpelet, Nogah, Nepheg, Japhia, Elishama, Eliada, Eliphelet & Tamar | Amnon, Daniel, Absalom, Adonijah, Shephatiah & Ithream | Solomon | Naamah | Pharaoh's Daughter

Ahimaaz | Basemath | Ben-Abinadab | Taphath | Rehoboam | Maakah

Attai | Shelomith | Abijah | Ziza

[36]Then the king sent for Shimei and said to him, "Build yourself a house in Jerusalem and live there, but do not go anywhere else. [37]The day you leave and cross the Kidron Valley, you can be sure you will die; your blood will be on your own head."

2:34 at his home House burials were common throughout Canaan, but they appear to have been reserved for important leaders in ancient Israel, including Samuel (1Sa 25:1). Despite being executed, Joab is granted an honorable burial.
2:35 over the army Benaiah previously worked alongside Joab as the commander of mercenary forces. Benaiah's

status resulted in him taking Joab's position upon Joab's death. **replaced Abiathar with Zadok the priest** Zadok and Abiathar were co-high priests before Abiathar was expelled (2Sa 8:17; compare note on 1Ki 2:27).
2:37 Kidron Valley To get to his home in Bahurim (v. 8), Shimei would have to cross the Wadi Kidron, Jerusalem's

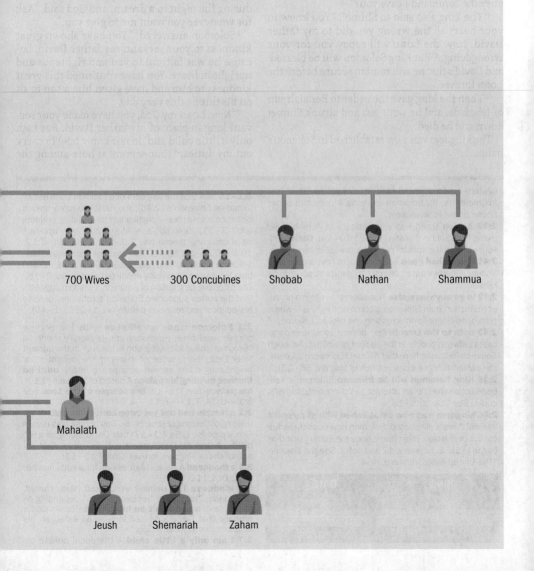

700 Wives   300 Concubines   Shobab   Nathan   Shammua

Mahalath

Jeush   Shemariah   Zaham

³⁸Shimei answered the king, "What you say is good. Your servant will do as my lord the king has said." And Shimei stayed in Jerusalem for a long time.

³⁹But three years later, two of Shimei's slaves ran off to Achish son of Maakah, king of Gath, and Shimei was told, "Your slaves are in Gath." ⁴⁰At this, he saddled his donkey and went to Achish at Gath in search of his slaves. So Shimei went away and brought the slaves back from Gath.

⁴¹When Solomon was told that Shimei had gone from Jerusalem to Gath and had returned, ⁴²the king summoned Shimei and said to him, "Did I not make you swear by the LORD and warn you, 'On the day you leave to go anywhere else, you can be sure you will die'? At that time you said to me, 'What you say is good. I will obey.' ⁴³Why then did you not keep your oath to the LORD and obey the command I gave you?"

⁴⁴The king also said to Shimei, "You know in your heart all the wrong you did to my father David. Now the LORD will repay you for your wrongdoing. ⁴⁵But King Solomon will be blessed, and David's throne will remain secure before the LORD forever."

⁴⁶Then the king gave the order to Benaiah son of Jehoiada, and he went out and struck Shimei down and he died.

The kingdom was now established in Solomon's hands.

Solomon Asks for Wisdom
3:4-15pp — 2Ch 1:2-13

3 Solomon made an alliance with Pharaoh king of Egypt and married his daughter. He brought her to the City of David until he finished building his palace and the temple of the LORD, and the wall around Jerusalem. ²The people, however, were still sacrificing at the high places, because a temple had not yet been built for the Name of the LORD. ³Solomon showed his love for the LORD by walking according to the instructions given him by his father David, except that he offered sacrifices and burned incense on the high places.

⁴The king went to Gibeon to offer sacrifices, for that was the most important high place, and Solomon offered a thousand burnt offerings on that altar. ⁵At Gibeon the LORD appeared to Solomon during the night in a dream, and God said, "Ask for whatever you want me to give you."

⁶Solomon answered, "You have shown great kindness to your servant, my father David, because he was faithful to you and righteous and upright in heart. You have continued this great kindness to him and have given him a son to sit on his throne this very day.

⁷"Now, LORD my God, you have made your servant king in place of my father David. But I am only a little child and do not know how to carry out my duties. ⁸Your servant is here among the

eastern border. Instead of killing Shimei as David had instructed (v. 9), Solomon essentially puts him under house arrest in Jerusalem.
2:39 Achish David was a mercenary to Achish while hiding from Saul in Philistia (1Sa 21:10–14). **Gath** A Philistine city on the coastal plain, southwest of Jerusalem.
2:41 Shimei had gone Solomon might have interpreted Shimei's journey as an attempt to gather support for a rebellion.
2:42 to go anywhere else This seems to reflect a broader restriction than Solomon's command in v. 37, which prohibited Shimei from crossing the brook of Kidron.
2:43 oath to the LORD Deities served as witnesses to oaths between people in the ancient Near East. Although Solomon indicates here that Shimei had sworn an oath, the earlier dialogue does not reflect this (vv. 36–38).
2:45 King Solomon will be blessed Solomon's self-benediction may be an attempt to counteract Shimei's curse. See 2Sa 16:5–13.
2:46 kingdom was now established With all potential internal threats eliminated, Solomon now possesses full control over Israel. This phrase ends the literary unit that began in 1Ki 2:12 (see v. 12 and note). See the timeline "The United Kingdom" on p. 464.

KING	DATE
Saul	1051–1011 BC
David	1011–971 BC
Solomon	971–931 BC

3:1–15 Now that the kingdom of Israel has been established as Solomon's (2:46), the narrative turns toward Solomon's activities—particularly his building projects (chs. 3–11). Solomon's wisdom (2:6) also appears as a recurring theme (vv. 3:3–28; 4:29–34; 5:12; 10:1–10,23–25; 11:41). This passage briefly introduces Solomon's political and religious activities (vv. 1–2) and then focuses on his divinely appointed wisdom (vv. 3–15). The extensive description of Solomon's wisdom suggests that the author supported Solomon's activities, despite his political and religious pitfalls (vv. 1–2; 11:1–40).

3:1 Solomon made an alliance with The Hebrew phrase used here, *yithchatten eth*, is literally rendered "Solomon made himself a son-in-law to." In the ancient Near East, the practice of marrying the daughters of neighboring rulers served as a peace treaty. **until he finished building his palace** A period of 20 years (9:10). **his palace** See 7:1–12. **the temple of the LORD** See 5:1—6:38; 7:13—8:11.
3:2 a temple had not yet been built Foreshadows the building of the temple (chs. 5–8). This phrase also recalls God's promise (2Sa 7:1–17) that David's offspring will build a house for God's name and, in return, God will establish his kingdom forever (2Sa 7:12–16).
3:4 a thousand A general expression for a large number (e.g., Dt 1:11).
3:6 kindness The Hebrew word used here, *chesed*, also means "loyalty" or "reciprocal love," depending on the context. **a son to sit on his throne** Recalls God's promise that David's descendant would establish his kingdom forever (2Sa 7:13).
3:7 I am only a little child A rhetorical phrase ex-

people you have chosen, a great people, too numerous to count or number. ⁹So give your servant a discerning heart to govern your people and to distinguish between right and wrong. For who is able to govern this great people of yours?"

¹⁰The Lord was pleased that Solomon had asked for this. ¹¹So God said to him, "Since you have asked for this and not for long life or wealth for yourself, nor have asked for the death of your enemies but for discernment in administering justice, ¹²I will do what you have asked. I will give you a wise and discerning heart, so that there will never have been anyone like you, nor will there ever be. ¹³Moreover, I will give you what you have not asked for — both wealth and honor — so that in your lifetime you will have no equal among kings. ¹⁴And if you walk in obedience to me and keep my decrees and commands as David your father did, I will give you a long life." ¹⁵Then Solomon awoke — and he realized it had been a dream.

He returned to Jerusalem, stood before the ark of the Lord's covenant and sacrificed burnt offerings and fellowship offerings. Then he gave a feast for all his court.

A Wise Ruling

¹⁶Now two prostitutes came to the king and stood before him. ¹⁷One of them said, "Pardon me, my lord. This woman and I live in the same house, and I had a baby while she was there with me. ¹⁸The third day after my child was born, this woman also had a baby. We were alone; there was no one in the house but the two of us.

¹⁹"During the night this woman's son died because she lay on him. ²⁰So she got up in the middle of the night and took my son from my side while I your servant was asleep. She put him by her breast and put her dead son by my breast. ²¹The next morning, I got up to nurse my son — and he was dead! But when I looked at him closely in the morning light, I saw that it wasn't the son I had borne."

²²The other woman said, "No! The living one is my son; the dead one is yours."

But the first one insisted, "No! The dead one is yours; the living one is mine." And so they argued before the king.

²³The king said, "This one says, 'My son is alive and your son is dead,' while that one says, 'No! Your son is dead and mine is alive.'"

²⁴Then the king said, "Bring me a sword." So they brought a sword for the king. ²⁵He then gave an order: "Cut the living child in two and give half to one and half to the other."

²⁶The woman whose son was alive was deeply moved out of love for her son and said to the king, "Please, my lord, give her the living baby! Don't kill him!"

But the other said, "Neither I nor you shall have him. Cut him in two!"

²⁷Then the king gave his ruling: "Give the living baby to the first woman. Do not kill him; she is his mother."

²⁸When all Israel heard the verdict the king had given, they held the king in awe, because they

---

pressing inexperience and humility (compare Jer 1:6). Solomon is an adult; he had already fathered Rehoboam, his eldest son, by this time (1Ki 11:42–43; 14:21). **do not know how to carry out my duties** Indicates the king's willingness to accept instruction in matters of public duty—especially war (Nu 27:17,21; Dt 31:2; Jos 14:11; 1Sa 18:16).

3:9 a discerning heart The Hebrew phrase used here, *lev shomea'*, literally means "hearing heart"; *lev* means "inner person," "mind," "will" or "heart," while *shomea'* means "hearing" or sometimes "observant." The heart was considered the organ of comprehension in ancient Near Eastern physiology. The Akkadian word *uznu* (meaning "ear") served as a figure of speech or idiom that referred to wisdom. In Egyptian, wisdom and understanding was achieved through a "hearing heart." The OT reflects the belief that wisdom was attained through hearing (e.g., Dt 4:1–2; 6:4; 2Sa 15:3; 1Ki 4:34; Ps 81:8; Isa 21:10; 44:1). **great** The Hebrew word used here, *kaved*, literally means "heavy"; here, it means "numerous" (compare Ex 12:38).

3:11 the death of your enemies The only item God does not grant in 1Ki 3:12–14, presumably because Solomon has no more enemies after the events of 2:13–46—until God raises adversaries at the end of his reign (11:9–40).

3:15 He returned to Jerusalem This is in contrast to the great high place at Gibeon (vv. 3–5) where Solomon had the dream and offered sacrifices. Solomon's newfound wisdom affected his decision regarding where to wor-

ship. Second Chronicles 1:5 adds that Solomon offered these sacrifices on the bronze altar that Bezalel built in the desert (Ex 36:1–2) and David installed before the ark of the covenant (2Sa 6:16–17). See the infographic "Solomon's Bronze Altar" on p. 667; see the infographic "Ancient Altars" on p. 127. **ark of the Lord's covenant** David brought the ark of the covenant to Jerusalem and housed it in a tent (2Sa 6).

3:16–28 This example demonstrates Solomon's wisdom and the fulfillment of God's promise (see 1Ki 3:1–15). The story's composition features dialogue, a defining characteristic of oral stories. As such, it was likely part of a collection of oral literature about Solomon from which the author of 1–2 Kings drew when compiling sources. The story of Solomon's wise decision resembles other ancient Near Eastern stories about the wisdom of rulers.

3:16 two prostitutes The only mention of their profession; otherwise, they are referred to as "the (other) woman." Despite their low social standing, the women are allowed to appear in court; the text even describes one positively (v. 26).

3:18 The third day An indefinite measure of time common in storytelling (e.g., Ge 22:4; 31:22; Jos 9:17; 1Sa 30:1; 2Sa 1:2; Est 5:1).

3:28 he had wisdom from God The Hebrew phrase used here does not occur elsewhere in the OT. Divine wisdom is more than knowledge, which Solomon possessed in abundance (1Ki 4:29–34). It also includes the ability to

saw that he had wisdom from God to administer justice.

Solomon's Officials and Governors

4 So King Solomon ruled over all Israel. ²And these were his chief officials:

Azariah son of Zadok — the priest;
³Elihoreph and Ahijah, sons of Shisha — secretaries;
Jehoshaphat son of Ahilud — recorder;
⁴Benaiah son of Jehoiada — commander in chief;
Zadok and Abiathar — priests;
⁵Azariah son of Nathan — in charge of the district governors;
Zabud son of Nathan — a priest and adviser to the king;
⁶Ahishar — palace administrator;
Adoniram son of Abda — in charge of forced labor.

⁷Solomon had twelve district governors over all Israel, who supplied provisions for the king and the royal household. Each one had to provide supplies for one month in the year. ⁸These are their names:

Ben-Hur — in the hill country of Ephraim;
⁹Ben-Deker — in Makaz, Shaalbim, Beth Shemesh and Elon Bethhanan;

¹⁰Ben-Hesed — in Arubboth (Sokoh and all the land of Hepher were his);
¹¹Ben-Abinadab — in Naphoth Dor (he was married to Taphath daughter of Solomon);
¹²Baana son of Ahilud — in Taanach and Megiddo, and in all of Beth Shan next to Zarethan below Jezreel, from Beth Shan to Abel Meholah across to Jokmeam;
¹³Ben-Geber — in Ramoth Gilead (the settlements of Jair son of Manasseh in Gilead were his, as well as the region of Argob in Bashan and its sixty large walled cities with bronze gate bars);
¹⁴Ahinadab son of Iddo — in Mahanaim;
¹⁵Ahimaaz — in Naphtali (he had married Basemath daughter of Solomon);
¹⁶Baana son of Hushai — in Asher and in Aloth;
¹⁷Jehoshaphat son of Paruah — in Issachar;
¹⁸Shimei son of Ela — in Benjamin;
¹⁹Geber son of Uri — in Gilead (the country of Sihon king of the Amorites and the country of Og king of Bashan). He was the only governor over the district.

Solomon's Daily Provisions

²⁰The people of Judah and Israel were as numerous as the sand on the seashore; they ate, they drank and they were happy. ²¹And Solomon ruled over all the kingdoms from the Euphrates River to the land of the Philistines, as far as the border of

---

render difficult judgments. Moses sought this quality in his own judgments and in the judges he appointed (Ex 18:13–26; Dt 1:13–18; 16:19).

4:1–19 These administrative lists provide insight into the life of Israel: how Israel governed itself, which political parties were favored, who occupied positions of authority, and which cities were considered important. Several of the cities mentioned in 1Ki 4:1–19 represent major archeological sites today, such as Megiddo, Taanach and Beth Shan. These sites provide information about Israel during the period of the monarchy (ca. eleventh to sixth centuries BC).

4:3 secretaries Refers to scribes. **recorder** The Hebrew word used here means "to remember" and literally means "one who reminds." It most likely refers to someone in charge of keeping public records.
4:4 Benaiah Commander of Solomon's army (2:28–35). **Zadok and Abiathar** See note on 1:7; 1:8 and note.
4:5 Nathan See note on 1:8.
4:6 palace administrator Possibly the highest office next to the king (Ge 39:4,5; 41:40–45; Isa 22:15–24). **Adoniram** His title first appears during David's reign (2Sa 20:24).
4:7 twelve district governors The division of Israel into 12 prefects, or districts, as described in vv. 7–19 does not coincide with the boundaries of the tribal divisions (Jos 13–21). The new divisions assume that each district represents its own economic unit capable of meeting Solomon's demands (see 1Ki 4:22–23). See the map "Tribal Distribution of Palestine" on p. 2253.

4:8 the hill country of Ephraim This district does not include all of the land allotted to the tribe of Ephraim. The tribal allotment reached to the coast (Jos 16:3,6,8).
4:9 Makaz This city is not mentioned elsewhere. **Shaalbim** May refer to the city Shaalabbin, which belonged to the tribe of Dan (Jos 19:42). **Beth Shemesh** May refer to Ir Shemesh ("City of Shemesh [the Sun]"), which was allotted to the tribe of Dan (Jos 19:41), or Beth Shemesh, which was allotted to Judah (Jos 15:10). **Elon Bethhanan** Elon is a city allotted to Dan (Jos 19:42), but the Hebrew designation beth-chanan is otherwise unattested.
4:10 Sokoh Allotted to the tribe of Judah (Jos 15:35). **land of Hepher** Joshua and the Israelites conquered the king of Hepher (Jos 12:7,17).
4:12 Zarethan A city on the eastern bank of the Jordan where the bronze vessels for the temple were cast (1Ki 7:46).
4:13 Bashan and its sixty large walled cities Moses and the Israelites defeated these cities (Dt 3:3–7).
4:14 Mahanaim A city on the border of Gad and Manasseh (Jos 13:30) that served a strategic function in 2 Sam (2Sa 2:8,12,29; 17:24,27; 19:32).
4:15 Naphtali A tribal allotment in upper Galilee that includes the city of Hazor (Jos 19:32–34; 1Ki 9:15).
4:16 Asher A tribe in western Galilee (Jos 19:24–30). **in Aloth** This location is unknown.
4:17 Issachar A tribal allotment in lower Galilee (Jos 19:18–22).
4:19 Sihon king of the Amorites and the country of Og king of Bashan Moses and the Israelites defeated these leaders (Nu 21:21–35; Dt 2:24–3:11).

Egypt. These countries brought tribute and were Solomon's subjects all his life.

²²Solomon's daily provisions were thirty cors[a] of the finest flour and sixty cors[b] of meal, ²³ten head of stall-fed cattle, twenty of pasture-fed cattle and a hundred sheep and goats, as well as deer, gazelles, roebucks and choice fowl. ²⁴For he ruled over all the kingdoms west of the Euphrates River, from Tiphsah to Gaza, and had peace on all sides. ²⁵During Solomon's lifetime Judah and Israel, from Dan to Beersheba, lived in safety, everyone under their own vine and under their own fig tree.

²⁶Solomon had four[c] thousand stalls for chariot horses, and twelve thousand horses.[d]

²⁷The district governors, each in his month, supplied provisions for King Solomon and all who came to the king's table. They saw to it that nothing was lacking. ²⁸They also brought to the proper place their quotas of barley and straw for the chariot horses and the other horses.

Solomon's Wisdom

²⁹God gave Solomon wisdom and very great insight, and a breadth of understanding as measureless as the sand on the seashore. ³⁰Solomon's wisdom was greater than the wisdom of all the people of the East, and greater than all the wisdom of Egypt. ³¹He was wiser than anyone else, including Ethan the Ezrahite — wiser than Heman, Kalkol and Darda, the sons of Mahol. And his fame spread to all the surrounding nations. ³²He spoke three thousand proverbs and his songs numbered a thousand and five. ³³He spoke about plant life, from the cedar of Lebanon to the hyssop that grows out of walls. He also spoke about animals and birds, reptiles and fish. ³⁴From all nations people came to listen to Solomon's wisdom, sent by all the kings of the world, who had heard of his wisdom.[e]

Preparations for Building the Temple
5:1-16pp — 2Ch 2:1-18

5[f] When Hiram king of Tyre heard that Solomon had been anointed king to succeed his father David, he sent his envoys to Solomon, because he had always been on friendly terms with David. ²Solomon sent back this message to Hiram:

³"You know that because of the wars waged against my father David from all sides, he could

[a] 22 That is, probably about 5 1/2 tons or about 5 metric tons
[b] 22 That is, probably about 11 tons or about 10 metric tons
[c] 26 Some Septuagint manuscripts (see also 2 Chron. 9:25); Hebrew *forty*   [d] 26 Or *charioteers*   [e] 34 In Hebrew texts 4:21-34 is numbered 5:1-14.   [f] In Hebrew texts 5:1-18 is numbered 5:15-32.

4:20–34 Solomon's wealth and wisdom are linked throughout the narrative of his reign. The account of Solomon's wealth and Israel's prosperity during his reign (1Ki 4:20–28) is preceded by examples of his wisdom in daily affairs (3:16–28) and national governance (4:1–19). The way Solomon divided Israel ensured that the wealth of the palace was maintained, albeit through taxation (vv. 7,22–23). All of these passages are placed between two lengthy descriptions of Solomon's wisdom (3:3–15; 4:29–34). Proverbs 3:16 also links wealth and wisdom.

4:20 Judah and Israel In contrast to "all Israel" (3:28; 4:1,7), the northern kingdom of Israel and southern kingdom of Judah are distinguished here. **the sand on the seashore** Recalls the blessing God placed upon Abraham in Ge 22:17 compare Hos 1:10). First Kings portrays Solomon as the fulfillment of God's covenant with David (2Sa 7:8–16; 1Ki 2:4; 3:6; 8:23–26), as well as the king who sees the fulfillment of God's promise to Abraham—that his descendants would be as numerous as the sand on the seashore.

4:21 tribute Hebrew word used here, *minchah*, describes a required payment brought from a lesser power to its governing power (compare 2Ki 17:3; Jdg 3:15,17; 2Sa 8:2,6).

4:25 During Solomon's lifetime 40 years (1Ki 11:42). **everyone under their own vine** A proverbial image of security and peace (compare 2Ki 18:31; Zec 3:10; Mic 4:4).

4:26 four thousand stalls for chariot horses The Hebrew text here says 40,000; the parallel account in 2Ch 9:25 puts the number of stalls at 4,000. Both figures seem to represent a violation of the law (see Dt 17:16 and note). These numbers reflect a royal literary genre that exaggerates the number of goods, captives, and dead enemies amassed by a king for the sake of showing divine blessing. They probably should not be taken literally.

4:27 district governors Refers to the 12 prefects (see 4:7–19; note on v. 7) under Azariah (v. 5) who took turns providing for the king's table.

4:30 all the people of the East Refers to all of the regions Solomon had contact with. Wise teachings were recorded throughout the ancient Near East, often in the name of a ruler. Wise sayings of the OT often reflect other ancient Near Eastern wisdom texts (such as the parallel between Pr 22:17—23:11 and the Instruction of Amenemope). Wise men were part of the royal court and often served as the king's advisers (e.g., Ge 41:8; Da 2:12). The book of Proverbs includes sayings from two such wise men: Agur (Pr 30:1) and King Lemuel (Pr 31:1).

4:32 three thousand proverbs Indicates a great number, not necessarily 3,000 exactly. This verse connects Solomon's wisdom to the book of Proverbs (Pr 1:1; 10:1; 25:1). **his songs** This connects Solomon to Song of Songs (SS 1:1) and Ps 72; 127. **a thousand and five** Conveys the idea of "many, and then some."

4:33 animals and birds, reptiles and fish The ability to learn through observing the natural world, particularly the animal world, was a large component of what it meant to be wise in the ancient Near East. Both the book of Proverbs and Job reflect this (Job 12:7–8; 38–41).

5:1–18 Chapter 5 shifts away from Solomon's wisdom and focuses on his political and building activities. In this passage, Solomon obtains the basic materials for the construction of the temple. This text details the trade agreement between Solomon and Hiram, king of Tyre, who supplied wood in exchange for wheat and oil (vv. 1–12).

5:1 Hiram The king of Tyre who supplied David and

not build a temple for the Name of the Lord his God until the Lord put his enemies under his feet. [4] But now the Lord my God has given me rest on every side, and there is no adversary or disaster. [5] I intend, therefore, to build a temple for the Name of the Lord my God, as the Lord told my father David, when he said, 'Your son whom I will put on the throne in your place will build the temple for my Name.'

[6] "So give orders that cedars of Lebanon be cut for me. My men will work with yours, and I will pay you for your men whatever wages you set. You know that we have no one so skilled in felling timber as the Sidonians."

[7] When Hiram heard Solomon's message, he was greatly pleased and said, "Praise be to the Lord today, for he has given David a wise son to rule over this great nation."

[8] So Hiram sent word to Solomon:

"I have received the message you sent me and will do all you want in providing the cedar and juniper logs. [9] My men will haul them down from Lebanon to the Mediterranean Sea, and I will float them as rafts by sea to the place you specify. There I will separate them and you can take them away. And you are to grant my wish by providing food for my royal household."

[10] In this way Hiram kept Solomon supplied with all the cedar and juniper logs he wanted, [11] and Solomon gave Hiram twenty thousand cors[a] of wheat as food for his household, in addition to twenty thousand baths[b,c] of pressed olive oil. Solomon continued to do this for Hiram year after year. [12] The Lord gave Solomon wisdom, just as he had promised him. There were peaceful relations between Hiram and Solomon, and the two of them made a treaty.

[13] King Solomon conscripted laborers from all Israel—thirty thousand men. [14] He sent them off to Lebanon in shifts of ten thousand a month, so that they spent one month in Lebanon and two months at home. Adoniram was in charge of the forced labor. [15] Solomon had seventy thousand carriers and eighty thousand stonecutters in the

---

[a] 11 That is, probably about 3,600 tons or about 3,250 metric tons
[b] 11 Septuagint (see also 2 Chron. 2:10); Hebrew *twenty cors*
[c] 11 That is, about 120,000 gallons or about 440,000 liters

---

Solomon with cedar, carpenters, tradesmen and sailors for various building projects (2Sa 5:11; 1Ki 5:1–12,18; 7:13,40,45; 9:11–14,27; 10:11–22; 1Ch 14:1; 2Ch 2:3,11–12; 4:11; 8:2,18; 9:10,21). **he had always been on friendly terms with David** Describes a treaty relationship and not a personal one. See 2Sa 5:11; 1Ch 14:1.

5:3 that because of the wars waged against my father David from all sides Verses 3–6 suggests that David did not build the temple because he was still at war; however, 2Sa 7:1 states that David wanted to build the temple because Yahweh had finally given him rest from his enemies. In 2 Samuel, God objects to David building the temple because he had never requested a temple (2Sa 7:1–7). First Kings considers ongoing warfare the reason for God's objection because the last of David's enemies were not killed until Solomon's reign (1Ki 2:13–46). By the time of 1–2 Chronicles, the reason is generalized as David shedding so much blood (1Ch 22:8).

5:5 Your son Solomon sees himself as the fulfillment of God's covenant with David (2Sa 7:13) who will bring about a new era. Newly established kings in the ancient Near East often began their reign by constructing a temple and palace (1Ki 5–7). This marked a period of change and ensured that both the god(s) and the king were properly enthroned.

5:6 cedars of Lebanon Cedar wood from Lebanon was famed from as early as the third millennium BC until 300 BC. **You know** Hiram demonstrates that he does know this when he counters Solomon's offer in v. 9. Solomon may have hoped to gain knowledge about how the Sidonians cut their timber by sending his own laborers to help Hiram's crew. Hiram suspects this and takes advantage of the situation (v. 9). **Sidonians** Another name for the Phoenicians. The port of Sidon was used to transport lumber throughout the Mediterranean.

5:7 Praise be to the Lord today Hiram's use of the personal name Yahweh does not mean that he followed Yahweh. Those making a formal agreement in the ancient Near East often included the names of their respective deities.

5:8 cedar The Hebrew word used here, *erez*, refers to the Cedrus libani, a tree which can reach a height of 100 feet (30 meters). Ancients praised cedar for its beauty and fragrance; the Biblical authors refer to cedar as the envy of all trees (Eze 31:3–7; compare 2Ki 14:9; 19:23; Isa 2:13; 10:34; Hos 14:5–6; SS 4:11). People throughout the ancient Near East demanded cedar from Lebanon for the construction of buildings and ships because of its durability. **cedar and juniper logs** The Hebrew word used here, *berosh*, refers to the *Juniperus excels*, a species of fir.

5:9 you are to grant my wish Hiram offers to have his own people cut and transport the lumber to the port Solomon chooses, after which Solomon's workers will take over. In return, Hiram demands provisions for the royal house instead of the wage initially proposed by Solomon (5:6). He may be trying to maintain Lebanon's monopoly on cedar production, since no one else knew how to cut timber like the Sidonians (v. 6).

5:11 pressed olive oil Describes the process by which fine olive oil was obtained. **year after year** Solomon also gave Hiram 20 towns in Galilee once the temple and palace were complete (9:11–14).

5:12 as he had promised him See the table "Covenants in the Old Testament" on p. 469. **peaceful relations** The use of the Hebrew word *shalom* here suggests that this treaty was more than an exchange of timber for food. Other verses provide more detail about the relationship between Hiram and Solomon (vv. 18; 9:26–28; 10:11,22).

5:13 conscripted laborers from all Israel This might indicate that Solomon conscripted 30,000 of his own people. However, 9:15–22 claims that Solomon did not enslave Israelites but drafted laborers from the Amorites, Hittites, Perizzites, Hivites and Jebusites who remained in the land.

5:14 He sent them off to Lebanon Solomon's actions contradict the terms of the agreement (vv. 6–10).

5:15 carriers The Hebrew word used here, *sabbal*, refers to some kind of state service in Israel; a similar

hills, [16]as well as thirty-three hundred[a] foremen who supervised the project and directed the workers. [17]At the king's command they removed from the quarry large blocks of high-grade stone to provide a foundation of dressed stone for the temple. [18]The craftsmen of Solomon and Hiram and workers from Byblos cut and prepared the timber and stone for the building of the temple.

Solomon Builds the Temple

6:1-29pp — 2Ch 3:1-14

6 In the four hundred and eightieth[b] year after the Israelites came out of Egypt, in the fourth year of Solomon's reign over Israel, in the month of Ziv, the second month, he began to build the temple of the LORD.

[2]The temple that King Solomon built for the LORD was sixty cubits long, twenty wide and thirty high.[c] [3]The portico at the front of the main hall of the temple extended the width of the temple, that is twenty cubits,[d] and projected ten cubits[e] from the front of the temple. [4]He made narrow windows high up in the temple walls. [5]Against the walls of the main hall and inner sanctuary he built a structure around the building, in which there were side rooms. [6]The lowest floor was five cubits[f] wide, the middle floor six cubits[g] and the third floor seven.[h] He made offset ledges around the outside of the temple so that nothing would be inserted into the temple walls.

[7]In building the temple, only blocks dressed at the quarry were used, and no hammer, chisel or

---

[a] 16 Hebrew; some Septuagint manuscripts (see also 2 Chron. 2:2,18) *thirty-six hundred*   [b] 1 Hebrew; Septuagint *four hundred and fortieth*   [c] 2 That is, about 90 feet long, 30 feet wide and 45 feet high or about 27 meters long, 9 meters wide and 14 meters high   [d] 3 That is, about 30 feet or about 9 meters; also in verses 16 and 20   [e] 3 That is, about 15 feet or about 4.5 meters; also in verses 23-26   [f] 6 That is, about 7 1/2 feet or about 2.3 meters; also in verses 10 and 24   [g] 6 That is, about 9 feet or about 2.7 meters   [h] 6 That is, about 11 feet or about 3.2 meters

---

Hebrew term, *sevel*, is used in 11:28 (compare 12:1–4). **hills** Located in northern Israel, which contains stone to quarry—particularly limestone.
5:17 high-grade stone to provide a foundation This description matches 7:10–11. **dressed stone** Laborers dressed or cut stones at the quarry, then transported them to the building site so that tools did not sound in the house during its construction (6:7). **for the temple** Refers to the house or temple of Yahweh (vv. 3–5; 6:1–38; 7:13–51).
5:18 workers from Byblos Refers to skilled workers from the Phoenician port city of Gebal (also called Byblos; compare Jos 13:5; Eze 27:9).

6:1–38 The description of Solomon's temple is divided into two parts: vv. 2–10 describes the exterior of the temple, while vv. 14–38 describes the interior. The account is divided by a word from Yahweh regarding his promise to David, and Solomon's duty to obey his commands (vv. 11–13).
The building of this temple marked a new era and required divine sanction (2Sa 7:13; 1Ki 5:3–5; 6:12–13), preparation (5:6–18), execution (chs. 6–7), dedication of the building (ch. 8) and blessing for the builder and his offspring (9:1–5). All of these elements appear in the account of Solomon's temple. While this description contains much detail, it doesn't provide enough to reproduce the structure with certainty. The author's knowledge of the inner sanctuary—which the high priest only entered once a year—and priestly quarters suggests that he was either a high priest who officiated after the dedication (ch. 8), or that he saw the inner sanctuary before Yahweh took up residence within it (8:11).
However, since the author does not include the ritual function or symbolism of what he describes, the suggestion that he was a priest may not be tenable. The author's knowledge of the temple's floor plan, including specific dimensions and building materials, suggests he was involved in the temple's construction—possibly one of the 3,300 supervisors Solomon appointed to oversee the work (5:16). See the infographic "Solomon's Temple" on p. 520.

6:1 four hundred and eightieth year This number is based on the calculation of 12 generations of 40 years.

The ancient Greek translation of the OT, the Septuagint, reads 440 years, perhaps counting only 11 generations of priests from Aaron to Zadok (1Ch 6:1–12). See the timeline "Broad Timeline of Biblical History" on p. xxvi. **fourth year of Solomon's reign over Israel** The narrative may have been taken from a royal archive (1Ki 14:29) or the book of the acts (or annals) of Solomon (11:41). **month of Ziv** The second month in the Phoenician calendar (April—May); one of several Phoenician month names to appear in this narrative (see vv. 37–38; 8:2). The concentration of Phoenician month names in chs. 6–8 and their absence in the rest of the OT suggest that this building report comes from a document that was contemporary to the temple building. Phoenicians cut and transported the lumber for the temple and were also involved in its building (5:6,18; see note on 5:6). The Phoenicians were influential in Israel throughout the period of the judges and the Monarchic Period (ca. thirteenth to sixth centuries BC). Their influence is most clearly seen in archeological sites along the Mediterranean coast (e.g., Naphath-Dor; see 4:11). See the table "Israelite Calendar" on p. 763. **temple of the LORD** The Hebrew phrase used here, *beth yhwh*, a frequent title for the temple, reflects the ancient Near Eastern belief that deities resided in houses built for their names. It is unclear whether the ancients believed their gods literally dwelt in temples or whether they thought of idols and other physical representations as depictions of the deity.
6:2 sixty cubits long A cubit is approximately 18 inches long. The temple was 90 feet long, 30 feet wide and 45 feet high.
6:3 portico The Hebrew word used here, *ulam*, describes a porch or entrance hall. **main hall of the temple** The Hebrew phrase used here is *hekhal habbayith*. The word *hekhal* refers to the sanctuary, whereas *habbayith* refers to the house. This is the main hall between the *ulam* (vestibule) and the *devir* (inner chamber or Most Holy Place, also called the Holy of Holies).
6:5 inner sanctuary This is the inner chamber of the temple where Yahweh resided. Only the high priest could enter it and only once a year—on the Day of Atonement. See note on Lev 16:1–34. **a structure around the building** May describe a stepped platform on which to build the side chambers (v. 6).

any other iron tool was heard at the temple site while it was being built.

⁸The entrance to the lowest[a] floor was on the south side of the temple; a stairway led up to the middle level and from there to the third. ⁹So he built the temple and completed it, roofing it with beams and cedar planks. ¹⁰And he built the side rooms all along the temple. The height of each was five cubits, and they were attached to the temple by beams of cedar.

¹¹The word of the Lord came to Solomon: ¹²"As for this temple you are building, if you follow my decrees, observe my laws and keep all my commands and obey them, I will fulfill through you the promise I gave to David your father. ¹³And I will live among the Israelites and will not abandon my people Israel."

¹⁴So Solomon built the temple and completed it. ¹⁵He lined its interior walls with cedar boards,

---

a 8 Septuagint; Hebrew *middle*

6:8 stairway The Hebrew word used here, *lul*, may describe a winding staircase. It may be related to the term *lula'ot*, the loops that held up the fabric of the tabernacle (Ex 26:4).
6:12 promise I gave to David your father Echoes the Davidic covenant (2Sa 7:8–16). First Kings 6:12 understands the covenant as conditional, but the record of the covenant does not include any stipulations (2Sa 7:8–16). The condition of Solomon's faithfulness reappears in God's response to the temple dedication (1Ki 9:4–5).

Solomon's Temple

The First Temple, erected by King Solomon, was built to replace the tabernacle and house the ark of the covenant. The Temple was completed in 960 BC after seven years of labor, but it was destroyed by the Babylonians in 586 BC.

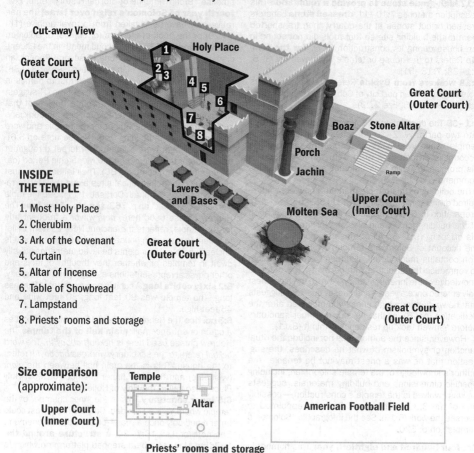

Cut-away View

Great Court (Outer Court)

Holy Place

Great Court (Outer Court)

Boaz   **Stone Altar**

Porch

Jachin   Ramp

INSIDE THE TEMPLE

Lavers and Bases

Great Court (Outer Court)

Molten Sea

Upper Court (Inner Court)

1. Most Holy Place
2. Cherubim
3. Ark of the Covenant
4. Curtain
5. Altar of Incense
6. Table of Showbread
7. Lampstand
8. Priests' rooms and storage

Great Court (Outer Court)

Size comparison (approximate):

Upper Court (Inner Court)

Temple   Altar

American Football Field

Priests' rooms and storage

paneling them from the floor of the temple to the ceiling, and covered the floor of the temple with planks of juniper. ¹⁶He partitioned off twenty cubits at the rear of the temple with cedar boards from floor to ceiling to form within the temple an inner sanctuary, the Most Holy Place. ¹⁷The main hall in front of this room was forty cubits[a] long. ¹⁸The inside of the temple was cedar, carved with gourds and open flowers. Everything was cedar; no stone was to be seen.

¹⁹He prepared the inner sanctuary within the temple to set the ark of the covenant of the LORD there. ²⁰The inner sanctuary was twenty cubits long, twenty wide and twenty high. He overlaid the inside with pure gold, and he also overlaid the altar of cedar. ²¹Solomon covered the inside of the temple with pure gold, and he extended gold chains across the front of the inner sanctuary, which was overlaid with gold. ²²So he overlaid the whole interior with gold. He also overlaid with gold the altar that belonged to the inner sanctuary.

²³For the inner sanctuary he made a pair of cherubim out of olive wood, each ten cubits high. ²⁴One wing of the first cherub was five cubits long, and the other wing five cubits — ten cubits from wing tip to wing tip. ²⁵The second cherub also measured ten cubits, for the two cherubim were identical in size and shape. ²⁶The height of each cherub was ten cubits. ²⁷He placed the cherubim inside the innermost room of the temple, with their wings spread out. The wing of one cherub touched one wall, while the wing of the other touched the other wall, and their wings touched each other in the middle of the room. ²⁸He overlaid the cherubim with gold. ²⁹On the walls all around the temple, in both the inner and outer rooms, he carved cherubim, palm trees and open flowers. ³⁰He also covered the floors of both the inner and outer rooms of the temple with gold.

³¹For the entrance to the inner sanctuary he made doors out of olive wood that were one fifth of the width of the sanctuary. ³²And on the two olive-wood doors he carved cherubim, palm trees and open flowers, and overlaid the cherubim and palm trees with hammered gold. ³³In the same way, for the entrance to the main hall he made doorframes out of olive wood that were one fourth of the width of the hall. ³⁴He also made two doors out of juniper wood, each having two leaves that turned in sockets. ³⁵He carved cherubim, palm trees and open flowers on them and overlaid them with gold hammered evenly over the carvings.

³⁶And he built the inner courtyard of three courses of dressed stone and one course of trimmed cedar beams.

³⁷The foundation of the temple of the LORD was laid in the fourth year, in the month of Ziv. ³⁸In the eleventh year in the month of Bul, the eighth month, the temple was finished in all its details according to its specifications. He had spent seven years building it.

Solomon Builds His Palace

7 It took Solomon thirteen years, however, to complete the construction of his palace. ²He built the Palace of the Forest of Lebanon a hundred cubits long, fifty wide and thirty high,[b]

---

[a] 17 That is, about 60 feet or about 18 meters [b] 2 That is, about 150 feet long, 75 feet wide and 45 feet high or about 45 meters long, 23 meters wide and 14 meters high

---

6:16 Most Holy Place The Hebrew phrase used here, *qodesh haqqodashim*, also appears in priestly descriptions of the area reserved for the ark of the covenant in the tabernacle (see Ex 26:33–34; Nu 4:4,19).

6:19 to set the ark of the covenant of the LORD there Describes the purpose of the inner sanctuary (see v. 5 and note; 8:6). Before the temple was built, the ark was housed in the tabernacle's inner sanctuary. For a description of the ark, see Ex 25:10–22. See the infographic "The Most Holy Place" on p. 525; see the infographic "The Ark of the Covenant" on p. 412.

6:20 he also overlaid the altar of cedar A wooden altar overlaid with gold would have only been suitable for incense offerings (see Ex 30:1–10; 1Ch 28:18). See the infographic "Ancient Altars" on p. 127; see the table "Altars in the Old Testament" on p. 249.

6:23 a pair of cherubim Mythical hybrid creatures attached to the lid of the ark of the covenant (Eze 10:3; Ex 25:18–20; Ge 3:24; 1Sa 4:4). According to some OT traditions, Yahweh is enthroned between these two cherubim (2Sa 6:2; 2Ki 19:15; 1Ch 13:6; Ps 99:1; Isa 37:16). Images of cherubim and other hybrid creatures are found guarding entrances to palaces and temples throughout the ancient Near East. **olive wood** Olive wood is naturally oily and does not need to be treated, unlike most wood. As such, it was appropriate for the inner sanctuary, since only the high priest could enter the Most Holy Place (Holy of Holies) once a year. Native to Israel, the olive wood was not imported from Hiram and the Sidonians (1Ki 5:6–10). However, olive trees are small and slow growing, and a high number would have been necessary to build these cherubim. For this reason, the term here is sometimes taken as referring to a different species, such as pine.

6:27 innermost room of the temple Refers to the inner sanctuary, which measures 20 cubits in each direction (vv. 19–20). Together, the 2 cherubim take up a space 20 cubits wide, 10 cubits deep, and 10 cubits high. The cherubim of the inner sanctuary overshadow or protect the ark of the covenant, where God is enthroned (Ex 25:20; 37:9; 1Ki 8:7; 2Ch 5:8; compare 2Sa 6:2; 2Ki 19:15; 1Ch 13:6; Ps 80:1; Isa 37:16). **their wings** In Ezekiel, cherubim are depicted as having four wings (Eze 10:21).

6:29 cherubim, palm trees and open flowers Common images used in sacred spaces in the ancient Near East.

6:38 month of Bul The eighth month in the Phoenician calendar (Sept—Oct). **seven years** Since seven is an ideal number, the additional six months are rounded off (vv. 1,37–38).

7:1–12 After finishing the temple (6:38; 7:1; 9:10), Solomon turns his attention to the palace compound. This compound includes the House of the Forest of Lebanon, Hall of Pillars, Hall of the Throne, Hall of Judgment, his

with four rows of cedar columns supporting trimmed cedar beams. [3] It was roofed with cedar above the beams that rested on the columns — forty-five beams, fifteen to a row. [4] Its windows were placed high in sets of three, facing each other. [5] All the doorways had rectangular frames; they were in the front part in sets of three, facing each other.[a]

[6] He made a colonnade fifty cubits long and thirty wide.[b] In front of it was a portico, and in front of that were pillars and an overhanging roof.

[7] He built the throne hall, the Hall of Justice, where he was to judge, and he covered it with cedar from floor to ceiling.[c] [8] And the palace in which he was to live, set farther back, was similar in design. Solomon also made a palace like this hall for Pharaoh's daughter, whom he had married.

[9] All these structures, from the outside to the great courtyard and from foundation to eaves, were made of blocks of high-grade stone cut to size and smoothed on their inner and outer faces. [10] The foundations were laid with large stones of good quality, some measuring ten cubits[d] and some eight.[e] [11] Above were high-grade stones, cut to size, and cedar beams. [12] The great courtyard was surrounded by a wall of three courses of dressed stone and one course of trimmed cedar beams, as was the inner courtyard of the temple of the Lord with its portico.

The Temple's Furnishings

7:23-26pp — 2Ch 4:2-5
7:38-51pp — 2Ch 4:6,10 - 5:1

[13] King Solomon sent to Tyre and brought Huram,[f] [14] whose mother was a widow from the tribe of Naphtali and whose father was from Tyre and a skilled craftsman in bronze. Huram was filled with wisdom, with understanding and with knowledge to do all kinds of bronze work. He came to King Solomon and did all the work assigned to him.

[15] He cast two bronze pillars, each eighteen cubits high and twelve cubits in circumference.[g] [16] He also made two capitals of cast bronze to set on the tops of the pillars; each capital was five cubits[h] high. [17] A network of interwoven chains adorned the capitals on top of the pillars, seven for each capital. [18] He made pomegranates in two rows[i] encircling each network to decorate the capitals

[a] 5 The meaning of the Hebrew for this verse is uncertain. [b] 6 That is, about 75 feet long and 45 feet wide or about 23 meters long and 14 meters wide   [c] 7 Vulgate and Syriac; Hebrew *floor*   [d] 10 That is, about 15 feet or about 4.5 meters; also in verse 23   [e] 10 That is, about 12 feet or about 3.6 meters [f] 13 Hebrew *Hiram*, a variant of *Huram*; also in verses 40 and 45 [g] 15 That is, about 27 feet high and 18 feet in circumference or about 8.1 meters high and 5.4 meters in circumference [h] 16 That is, about 7 1/2 feet or about 2.3 meters; also in verse 23   [i] 18 Two Hebrew manuscripts and Septuagint; most Hebrew manuscripts *made the pillars, and there were two rows*

own house and a house for Pharaoh's daughter (3:1; 7:8) — all made of large, costly stone and cedar. These buildings are described briefly in comparison to the temple (ch. 6) and its furnishings (7:13–51). Since the description of the palace complex is little more than a list of the various building sections, and no archeological remains have been found, it is difficult to reconstruct even a basic floor plan.

However, the House of the Forest of Lebanon is approximately twice the size of the temple and contains rows of pillars (6:2; 7:2–3). This suggests that Solomon's palace compound may have been similar to the Syrian construction model know as *bit hilani*; this was a common housing model in the north during this period (tenth — eighth century BC) and included numerous halls and courtyards surrounded by smaller rooms and a pillared porch (e.g., Tell Tainat, Zincirli). Similar architecture can also be found at Megiddo (9:15). See the infographic "Solomon's Temple" on p. 520.

7:1 his palace Refers to the palace compound, including Solomon's personal residence (v. 8).
7:2 Palace of the Forest of Lebanon The name was probably inspired by the building's use of cedar. This building was used, in part, as an armory (10:17; Isa 22:8), but its size suggests that it had multiple uses. Compare 1Ki 5:6 and note; 5:8 and note.
7:6 fifty cubits long A cubit is about 18 inches. Fifty cubits is thus about 75 feet. **overhanging** The exact meaning of the Hebrew word used here, *av*, is unclear; it also appears in Eze 41:25, where it likewise describes something wooden.
7:8 similar in design It is unclear what building or hall Solomon's residence is being compared to. **for**

Pharaoh's daughter Identifies her privileged position among Solomon's wives.
7:10 with large stones of good quality This verse may provide more details about the stones described in v. 9; alternatively, it may describe a different course of stone.
7:12 portico The Hebrew word used here, *ulam*, describes a porch or entrance hall. It is unclear whether the author is referring to the house of Yahweh (the temple) or Solomon's residence.

7:13–51 Descriptions of Huram's bronze work are arranged according to size — from large items like pillars to small items like utensils (vv. 13–40). A summary of Huram's work and a few details about his method follow (vv. 41–47). The most precious utensils used in the temple are attributed to Solomon (vv. 48–50), although the text refers to Huram (or Hiram) as possessing wisdom and skill in bronze work (v. 14). The temple was considered complete once the vessels consecrated by David were transported into the temple treasury (v. 51).

7:14 filled with wisdom, with understanding and with knowledge Bezalel, whom Yahweh filled with the Spirit of God to carry out the work of the tabernacle, also possessed these qualities (Ex 31:2–6; 35:30–31).
bronze The Hebrew word used here, *nechosheth*, means "copper ore," but it typically referred to the bronze alloy used throughout the ancient Near East by the second millennium BC. **did all the work assigned to him** He may work under Solomon's supervision.
7:15 eighteen cubits A cubit is about 18 inches. 18 cubits is about 27 feet.
7:18 pomegranates In the ancient Near East, pomegranates were a symbol of abundance.

on top of the pillars.^a He did the same for each capital. ¹⁹The capitals on top of the pillars in the portico were in the shape of lilies, four cubits^b high. ²⁰On the capitals of both pillars, above the bowl-shaped part next to the network, were the two hundred pomegranates in rows all around. ²¹He erected the pillars at the portico of the temple. The pillar to the south he named Jakin^c and the one to the north Boaz.^d ²²The capitals on top were in the shape of lilies. And so the work on the pillars was completed.

²³He made the Sea of cast metal, circular in shape, measuring ten cubits from rim to rim and five cubits high. It took a line of thirty cubits^e to measure around it. ²⁴Below the rim, gourds encircled it — ten to a cubit. The gourds were cast in two rows in one piece with the Sea.

²⁵The Sea stood on twelve bulls, three facing north, three facing west, three facing south and three facing east. The Sea rested on top of them, and their hindquarters were toward the center. ²⁶It was a handbreadth^f in thickness, and its rim was like the rim of a cup, like a lily blossom. It held two thousand baths.^g

²⁷He also made ten movable stands of bronze; each was four cubits long, four wide and three high.^h ²⁸This is how the stands were made: They had side panels attached to uprights. ²⁹On the panels between the uprights were lions, bulls and cherubim — and on the uprights as well. Above and below the lions and bulls were wreaths of hammered work. ³⁰Each stand had four bronze wheels with bronze axles, and each had a basin resting on four supports, cast with wreaths on each side. ³¹On the inside of the stand there was an opening that had a circular frame one cubitⁱ deep. This opening was round, and with its basework it measured a cubit and a half.^j Around its opening there was engraving. The panels of the stands were square, not round. ³²The four wheels were under the panels, and the axles of the wheels were attached to the stand. The diameter of each wheel was a cubit and a half. ³³The wheels were made like chariot wheels; the axles, rims, spokes and hubs were all of cast metal.

³⁴Each stand had four handles, one on each corner, projecting from the stand. ³⁵At the top of the stand there was a circular band half a cubit^k deep. The supports and panels were attached to the top of the stand. ³⁶He engraved cherubim, lions and palm trees on the surfaces of the supports and on the panels, in every available space, with wreaths all around. ³⁷This is the way he made the ten stands. They were all cast in the same molds and were identical in size and shape.

³⁸He then made ten bronze basins, each holding forty baths^l and measuring four cubits across, one basin to go on each of the ten stands. ³⁹He placed five of the stands on the south side of the temple and five on the north. He placed the Sea on the south side, at the southeast corner of the temple. ⁴⁰He also made the pots^m and shovels and sprinkling bowls.

So Huram finished all the work he had undertaken for King Solomon in the temple of the LORD:

⁴¹the two pillars;
the two bowl-shaped capitals on top of the pillars;
the two sets of network decorating the two bowl-shaped capitals on top of the pillars;
⁴²the four hundred pomegranates for the two sets of network (two rows of pomegranates for each network decorating the bowl-shaped capitals on top of the pillars);
⁴³the ten stands with their ten basins;
⁴⁴the Sea and the twelve bulls under it;
⁴⁵the pots, shovels and sprinkling bowls.

^a 18 Many Hebrew manuscripts and Syriac; most Hebrew manuscripts *pomegranates*   ^b 19 That is, about 6 feet or about 1.8 meters; also in verse 38   ^c 21 *Jakin* probably means *he establishes.*   ^d 21 *Boaz* probably means *in him is strength.*   ^e 23 That is, about 45 feet or about 14 meters   ^f 26 That is, about 3 inches or about 7.5 centimeters   ^g 26 That is, about 12,000 gallons or about 44,000 liters; the Septuagint does not have this sentence.   ^h 27 That is, about 6 feet long and wide and about 4 1/2 feet high or about 1.8 meters long and wide and 1.4 meters high   ⁱ 31 That is, about 18 inches or about 45 centimeters   ^j 31 That is, about 2 1/4 feet or about 68 centimeters; also in verse 32   ^k 35 That is, about 9 inches or about 23 centimeters   ^l 38 That is, about 240 gallons or about 880 liters   ^m 40 Many Hebrew manuscripts, Septuagint, Syriac and Vulgate (see also verse 45 and 2 Chron. 4:11); many other Hebrew manuscripts *basins*

7:21 Jakin The Hebrew word used here, *yakhin*, means "he will establish." The names of these two pillars likely represent catchwords of sentences that were inscribed on the pillars. Mesopotamian doors and gates often bore names asking the gods for protection and blessing. **Boaz** The Hebrew word used here, *boaz*, means "in strength."

7:23 ten cubits from rim to rim This makes the diameter of the Sea 15 feet wide and the height 7.5 feet tall. The function of the Sea is uncertain.

7:24 two rows in one piece The Sea and the decorations surrounding it were a single piece of bronze.

7:25 bulls Used as work animals throughout the ancient world, oxen (or bulls) symbolized strength. Ahaz later eliminated the cast oxen and had the Sea set on stone (2Ki 16:17).

7:26 handbreadth Refers to the width of four fingers

(roughly 3 inches). **two thousand baths** A bath is about 22 liters, meaning the Sea could hold 44,000 liters (12,000 gallons). The parallel account in 1–2 Chronicles puts the volume of the Sea even higher — 3,000 baths (2Ch 4:5).

7:27 ten movable stands of bronze Each stand was paired with one of ten basins (1Ki 7:38–39).

7:37 were identical in size and shape The Hebrew words used here, *middah* (meaning "measure") and *qetsev* (meaning "form"), also are used to describe the two identical cherubim (6:25).

7:38 forty baths A bath is approximately 22 liters, meaning each basin holds about 880 liters.

7:40 the pots and shovels and sprinkling bowls Listed as utensils in the tabernacle (Ex 27:3; 38:3). The pots and shovels are used to remove ashes from the altar. The

All these objects that Huram made for King Solomon for the temple of the LORD were of burnished bronze. ⁴⁶The king had them cast in clay molds in the plain of the Jordan between Sukkoth and Zarethan. ⁴⁷Solomon left all these things unweighed, because there were so many; the weight of the bronze was not determined.

⁴⁸Solomon also made all the furnishings that were in the LORD's temple:

the golden altar;
the golden table on which was the bread of the Presence;
⁴⁹the lampstands of pure gold (five on the right and five on the left, in front of the inner sanctuary);
the gold floral work and lamps and tongs;
⁵⁰the pure gold basins, wick trimmers, sprinkling bowls, dishes and censers;
and the gold sockets for the doors of the innermost room, the Most Holy Place, and also for the doors of the main hall of the temple.

⁵¹When all the work King Solomon had done for the temple of the LORD was finished, he brought in the things his father David had dedicated — the silver and gold and the furnishings — and he placed them in the treasuries of the LORD's temple.

The Ark Brought to the Temple

8:1-21pp — 2Ch 5:2 – 6:11

8 Then King Solomon summoned into his presence at Jerusalem the elders of Israel, all the heads of the tribes and the chiefs of the Israelite families, to bring up the ark of the LORD's covenant from Zion, the City of David. ²All the Israelites came together to King Solomon at the time of the festival in the month of Ethanim, the seventh month.

³When all the elders of Israel had arrived, the priests took up the ark, ⁴and they brought up the ark of the LORD and the tent of meeting and all the sacred furnishings in it. The priests and Levites carried them up, ⁵and King Solomon and the entire

---

basins are used to collect sacrificial blood for splashing against the altar (Ex 24:6). The basins also might have been used for libation rituals (Am 6:6; Zec 9:15).

7:45 burnished bronze Another detail about the utensils mentioned in v. 40. The Hebrew word used here, *marat*, refers to making bald, bare, or smooth (Eze 29:18; Ezr 9:3; Ne 13:25; compare Isa 18:2). This description likely refers to smoothing away imperfection or polishing (Eze 21:11).

7:46 plain The Hebrew word used here, *kikkar* (meaning "district," or "circle"), can refer to either side of the Jordan. Succoth and Zarethan are on the east bank.

7:48 Solomon also made all the furnishings Solomon commissioned all of these objects, but probably did not craft them himself. **golden altar** May have been used to burn incense (see 1Ki 6:20). **golden table on which was the bread of the Presence** The dimensions and construction of this table may be similar to the golden table built for the same function in the tabernacle (Ex 25:23–28). **bread of the Presence** Leviticus 24:5–9 describes the ritual involving the bread of the Presence. David acquires this bread at Nob (1Sa 21:2–7).

7:49 lampstands of pure gold The ten lampstands described here contrast the single lampstand used to light the tabernacle (Ex 25:31–37). **floral work** The tabernacle lampstand also displays a floral motif (Ex 25:31,33; Nu 8:4). **lamps** Refers to oil lamps. Archaeological remains show that lamps of varying styles and sizes were used at this time. **tongs** A tool associated with lamps, possibly used for adjusting the wick.

7:50 the pure gold basins The Hebrew word used here, *saph*, refers to a container to hold liquid, such as blood (Ex 12:22). **dishes** The Hebrew word used here, *kaph*, often refers to the palm of the hand. Here, it likely describes spoon-shaped utensils used for incense (Ex 25:29; 37:16; Nu 4:7; 7:14). **censers** Associated with the incense altar (Lev 16:12), not the sacrificial altar (Ex 27:1–3) or lampstands (Ex 25:38). **sockets** The Hebrew word used here, *poth*, can refer to hinges, an entrance or keys to the door.

7:51 This final summary statement concludes the narrative of the temple building and the construction of the temple furnishings. The Hebrew word *kalah* (meaning "to complete") is used to mark the completion of various stages of the project (1Ki 6:9,14,38; 7:1,40). It echoes God's completion of the phases of creation (Ge 1:1—2:4). Similarly, this summary statement uses the Hebrew word *shalem* (meaning "to complete" or "to be whole"), most likely as a play on words with Solomon's name in Hebrew, *shelomoh*. See the infographic "The Days of Creation" on p. 6; see the timeline "The United Kingdom" on p. 464.

7:51 his father David Refers to the spoil and tribute David collected from his enemies and vassals, which he then dedicated to Yahweh (2Sa 8:9–12).

EVENT	DATE
Solomon becomes king	971 BC
Solomon begins construction on the temple	967 BC
Solomon finishes the temple	960 BC

8:1–11 The installation of the ark of the covenant in the Most Holy Place (Holy of Holies) marks the end of the temple's construction (chs. 6–7) and signifies the presence of God. According to some OT traditions, including vv. 1–11, Yahweh sits enthroned on top of the ark and may be transported from place to place (1Sa 4:4; 2Sa 6:2; 2Ki 19:15; 1Ch 13:6; Ps 99:1; Isa 37:16). The ark was previously housed in the City of David, in the tent David pitched for it (2Sa 6; 1Ki 8:1). A detailed description of the ark appears in Ex 25:10–22. See the infographic "The Ark of the Covenant" on p. 412.

8:2 Israelites The Hebrew phrase used here, *ish yisra'el*, specifies a group of men — possibly the army. **festival** Refers to Succoth or the Festival of Tabernacles (or Booths) (Lev 23:33–43; Nu 29:12–40; Dt 16:13–15). See the table "Israelite Festivals" on p. 200. **Ethanim** The seventh month in the Phoenician calendar (Aug—Sept), one of several Phoenician month names to appear in this narrative (see 1Ki 6:1 and note).

8:3 priests Traditional custodians of the ark of the covenant (Dt 31:9; 2Sa 15:24).

assembly of Israel that had gathered about him were before the ark, sacrificing so many sheep and cattle that they could not be recorded or counted.

⁶The priests then brought the ark of the LORD's covenant to its place in the inner sanctuary of the temple, the Most Holy Place, and put it beneath the wings of the cherubim. ⁷The cherubim spread their wings over the place of the ark and overshad-owed the ark and its carrying poles. ⁸These poles were so long that their ends could be seen from the Holy Place in front of the inner sanctuary, but not from outside the Holy Place; and they are still there today. ⁹There was nothing in the ark except the two stone tablets that Moses had placed in it at Horeb, where the LORD made a covenant with the Israelites after they came out of Egypt.

8:4 tent of meeting Refers to the Holy Place associated with Moses and the desert wandering period of the Israelite people (Ex 26; 36:8–38). The tent of meeting is rarely mentioned in the books of Joshua—1–2 Kings (Jos 18:1; 19:51; 1Sa 2:22). See the infographic "The Tabernacle" on p. 138. **sacred furnishings** Refers to the vessels associated with the tent of meeting (Ex 25–30; 35–40).

8:6 inner sanctuary See 1Ki 6:5 and note; 6:19 and note; 6:27 and note. **temple** Refers to the house of Yahweh (chs. 6–7). **Most Holy Place** The Hebrew phrase used here, *qodesh haqqodashim*, also appears in priestly

descriptions of the area reserved for the ark of the covenant in the tabernacle (see Ex 26:33–34; Nu 4:4,19). **wings of the cherubim** See 1Ki 6:23–28; note on 6:23. **8:8 ends** The poles' length is unspecified (Ex 25:13–15), but the inner sanctuary measures 20 cubits (30 feet) in each direction (1Ki 6:20). **Holy Place** The Hebrew word used here, *qodesh*, refers to the outer sanctuary leading up to the inner sanctuary, or Most Holy Place (Holy of Holies).

8:9 except the two stone tablets By the time of the NT, traditions about what was in the ark of the covenant had grown to include a golden urn holding the manna,

---

The Most Holy Place

The Most Holy Place (Holy of Holies) was the innermost chamber of Solomon's temple; it contained only two gold-inlaid cherubim and the ark of the covenant (1Ki 8:6). The high priest was permitted to enter The Most Holy Place only once a year to bring an offering of blood. This was the Day of Atonement, now known as Yom Kippur.

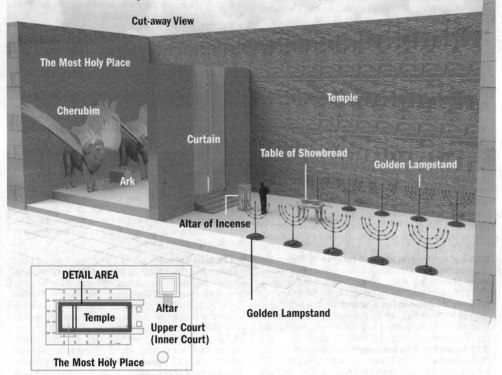

Cut-away View

The Most Holy Place

Cherubim

Temple

Curtain

Table of Showbread

Golden Lampstand

Ark

Altar of Incense

Golden Lampstand

DETAIL AREA

Temple

Altar

Upper Court
(Inner Court)

The Most Holy Place

[10]When the priests withdrew from the Holy Place, the cloud filled the temple of the LORD. [11]And the priests could not perform their service because of the cloud, for the glory of the LORD filled his temple.

[12]Then Solomon said, "The LORD has said that he would dwell in a dark cloud; [13]I have indeed built a magnificent temple for you, a place for you to dwell forever."

[14]While the whole assembly of Israel was standing there, the king turned around and blessed them. [15]Then he said:

"Praise be to the LORD, the God of Israel, who with his own hand has fulfilled what he promised with his own mouth to my father David. For he said, [16]'Since the day I brought my people Israel out of Egypt, I have not chosen a city in any tribe of Israel to have a temple built so that my Name might be there, but I have chosen David to rule my people Israel.'

[17]"My father David had it in his heart to build a temple for the Name of the LORD, the God of Israel. [18]But the LORD said to my father David, 'You did well to have it in your heart to build a temple for my Name. [19]Nevertheless, you are not the one to build the temple, but your son, your own flesh and blood—he is the one who will build the temple for my Name.'

[20]"The LORD has kept the promise he made: I have succeeded David my father and now I sit on the throne of Israel, just as the LORD promised, and I have built the temple for the Name of the LORD, the God of Israel. [21]I have provided a place there for the ark, in which is the covenant of the LORD that he made with our ancestors when he brought them out of Egypt."

Solomon's Prayer of Dedication

8:22-53pp — 2Ch 6:12-40

[22]Then Solomon stood before the altar of the LORD in front of the whole assembly of Israel, spread out his hands toward heaven [23]and said:

"LORD, the God of Israel, there is no God like you in heaven above or on earth below— you who keep your covenant of love with

---

and Aaron's staff that budded, in addition to the stone tablets (see Heb 9:4). See Ex 24:7–8,12; 25:21; 40:20; Dt 10:2–5.

8:10 cloud The common description of God's appearance throughout the wilderness wanderings of the Israelite people (see Ex 16:10; 33:9). At times, fire is included in this description (e.g., Ex 24:17).

8:11 could not perform their service because of the cloud Similarly, Moses could not enter the Most Holy Place (Holy of Holies) of the tabernacle when the cloud filled the tent (Ex 40:34–35). The presence of the cloud signifies that Yahweh now resides in the temple (see Ex 40:34).

8:12–21 Solomon's blessing recalls the covenant God made to David concerning the temple and his descendants (2Sa 7:1–17). Solomon portrays his reign and his accomplishments as the fulfillment of God's promises to David.

8:12 dark cloud The Hebrew word used here, *araphel*, describes a thick darkness that masks God's glory (v. 11) and permits approach (compare Ex 20:21; Dt 4:11; 5:22; Job 22:13). The word *araphel* is often paired with *anan* (meaning "cloud"), where God resides (1Ki 8:10–11; Dt 4:11; 5:22; Ps 97:2). Such imagery is intended to convey God's power and numinous qualities (2Sa 22:10; Ps 18:11; 97:2).

8:13 a place for you to dwell forever This reference to an earthly abode stands in tension with other verses in this chapter that insist that God lives in the heavens (1Ki 8:39,43,49; compare Ex 15:17; Isa 66:1).

8:16 I have not chosen a city Here, the building is delayed because God had yet to choose a city. According to 2Sa 7:6–7, the building is delayed because God had not yet commanded Israel to build a temple.

8:17 David had it in his heart The word *levav* means "inner-person," "mind," "will" or "heart." People in the ancient Near East associated the heart with comprehension, not emotion.

8:20 sit on the throne of Israel See 2Sa 7:12–13. **I have built the temple** See 1Ki 6–7.

8:22–53 After blessing Yahweh before the assembly (vv. 12–21), Solomon turns toward the altar and recites a lengthy prayer. He begins by reiterating that he is the fulfillment of God's promise to David (vv. 23–26; 2Sa 7:13–17), hinting that his throne will be established forever (2Sa 7:16). He then focuses on many of the same themes as the book of Deuteronomy, including the consequences of disobedience and the desire for justice (1Ki 8:31–53). The theological and practical content of the prayer suggests that the author has two audiences in mind: Yahweh and whoever hears or reads the prayer.

Verses 22–53 acknowledge that the temple has great social and religious significance as Israel's central shrine, but evidences a struggle with the idea that God can be contained in a space measuring 20 cubits (30 feet) in all directions. As a result, two related ideas run throughout Solomon's dedication prayer: that God dwells in heaven while his name resides in the temple (vv. 27,29,39,43,49), and that the temple serves as a building for people to pray toward so that God hears their prayers from the heavens (vv. 29,33,35,38,42,44). While sacrifices are offered at the temple (vv. 62–64), Solomon's prayer emphasizes the role of the temple in the daily life of the people.

8:22 stood before A posture of prayer (compare Jer 18:20; Ps 106:30; Ne 9:2). **altar of the LORD** The only altar mentioned in the building narrative is the incense altar in the Most Holy Place, also called the Holy of Holies (1Ki 6:20,22). The sacrificial altar is not mentioned in the account of the temple building or the lists of furnishings (chs. 6–7), but it appears later (vv. 31,64; 9:25; 2Ki 16:10–16; 2Ch 4:1). See the infographic "Solomon's Bronze Altar" on p. 667; see the infographic "Ancient Altars" on p. 127. **spread out his hands** A posture expressing need or help during prayer or supplication (see Ex 9:29; Ps 88:9; Isa 1:15; 65:2; La 1:17; 2:19; 3:41).

your servants who continue wholeheartedly in your way. ²⁴You have kept your promise to your servant David my father; with your mouth you have promised and with your hand you have fulfilled it — as it is today.

²⁵"Now LORD, the God of Israel, keep for your servant David my father the promises you made to him when you said, 'You shall never fail to have a successor to sit before me on the throne of Israel, if only your descendants are careful in all they do to walk before me faithfully as you have done.' ²⁶And now, God of Israel, let your word that you promised your servant David my father come true.

²⁷"But will God really dwell on earth? The heavens, even the highest heaven, cannot contain you. How much less this temple I have built! ²⁸Yet give attention to your servant's prayer and his plea for mercy, LORD my God. Hear the cry and the prayer that your servant is praying in your presence this day. ²⁹May your eyes be open toward this temple night and day, this place of which you said, 'My Name shall be there,' so that you will hear the prayer your servant prays toward this place. ³⁰Hear the supplication of your servant and of your people Israel when they pray toward this place. Hear from heaven, your dwelling place, and when you hear, forgive.

³¹"When anyone wrongs their neighbor and is required to take an oath and they come and swear the oath before your altar in this temple, ³²then hear from heaven and act. Judge between your servants, condemning the guilty by bringing down on their heads what they have done, and vindicating the in-nocent by treating them in accordance with their innocence.

³³"When your people Israel have been defeated by an enemy because they have sinned against you, and when they turn back to you and give praise to your name, praying and making supplication to you in this temple, ³⁴then hear from heaven and forgive the sin of your people Israel and bring them back to the land you gave to their ancestors.

³⁵"When the heavens are shut up and there is no rain because your people have sinned against you, and when they pray toward this place and give praise to your name and turn from their sin because you have afflicted them, ³⁶then hear from heaven and forgive the sin of your servants, your people Israel. Teach them the right way to live, and send rain on the land you gave your people for an inheritance.

³⁷"When famine or plague comes to the land, or blight or mildew, locusts or grasshoppers, or when an enemy besieges them in any of their cities, whatever disaster or disease may come, ³⁸and when a prayer or plea is made by anyone among your people Israel — being aware of the afflictions of their own hearts, and spreading out their hands toward this temple — ³⁹then hear from heaven, your dwelling place. Forgive and act; deal with everyone according to all they do, since you know their hearts (for you alone know every human heart), ⁴⁰so that they will fear you all the time they live in the land you gave our ancestors.

⁴¹"As for the foreigner who does not belong to your people Israel but has come from a

---

8:23 covenant Solomon may have a specific covenant in mind, or he may be speaking of God's covenants in general. The mention of a promise to David in 1Ki 8:24 suggests that he has the Davidic Covenant in mind (2Sa 7:1–17). **love** The Hebrew word used here, *chesed*, also means "loyalty" or "reciprocal love," depending on the context. **who continue wholeheartedly in your way** The Hebrew phrase used here, *halakh liphne*, means "to serve" and always appears in reference to kings serving God (see also 1Ki 8:25; 9:4; 2Ki 20:3).
8:24 your promise Refers to God's promise that David's son will reign and build the temple (2Sa 7:12–13). The promise that his dynasty will be eternal was yet to be fulfilled (2Sa 7:13–16).
8:25 if only your descendants are careful See note on 2:4.
8:28 cry The Hebrew word used here, *rinnah*, indicates a strong raising of the voice that can be either a cry of fright (22:36) or a cry of joy (Isa 35:10; Ps 105:43; 126:2).
8:29 toward this temple This suggests that God actually resides not in the temple, but in the heavens (1Ki 8:27,39,43,49; compare Ex 15:17; Isa 66:1). Solomon makes multiple references to praying toward the temple (1Ki 8:33,35,38,42,44). He also mentions praying toward Jerusalem (v. 44) and the land of Israel (v. 48).
8:32 by bringing down on their heads what they have
done A common idiom throughout the OT expressing just punishment (Jdg 9:57; 1Ki 2:44; Eze 9:10; 22:31).
8:33 because they have sinned against you In the OT, God threatens to turn Israel over to its enemies as punishment for abandoning his ways (e.g., Dt 28:25). This reflects a common ancient Near Eastern belief that the god of a nation protected his people so long as he was satisfied with them.
8:35 there is no rain because your people have sinned Indicates that Israel's behavior determines the weather and fertility of the land (Dt 11:13–17; 28:24; compare 1Ki 17:1–7; 18:41–46).
8:37 blight or mildew A pair of contrasting calamities (see Dt 28:22; Am 4:9; Hag 2:17). The first Hebrew word used here, *shiddaphon* (meaning "blight" or "blasting"), refers to scorching caused by the east wind (Ge 41:6; 2Ki 19:26). The second word, *yeraqon* (meaning "greenness" or "yellowness"), refers to mildew caused by too much rain. **locusts or grasshoppers** The Hebrew words used here, *arbeh* (meaning "locust"), and *hasil* (meaning "grasshopper," "caterpillar" or "locust"), are commonly associated with the destruction of agriculture as divine punishment (see Ex 10:13–15; Joel 1).
8:41 foreigner The Hebrew word used here, *nokhri*, describes a foreigner who dwells abroad but visits Israel, not the "resident alien" (*ger*) who lives in the land.

distant land because of your name — [42]for they will hear of your great name and your mighty hand and your outstretched arm — when they come and pray toward this temple, [43]then hear from heaven, your dwelling place. Do whatever the foreigner asks of you, so that all the peoples of the earth may know your name and fear you, as do your own people Israel, and may know that this house I have built bears your Name.

[44]"When your people go to war against their enemies, wherever you send them, and when they pray to the LORD toward the city you have chosen and the temple I have built for your Name, [45]then hear from heaven their prayer and their plea, and uphold their cause.

[46]"When they sin against you — for there is no one who does not sin — and you become angry with them and give them over to their enemies, who take them captive to their own lands, far away or near; [47]and if they have a change of heart in the land where they are held captive, and repent and plead with you in the land of their captors and say, 'We have sinned, we have done wrong, we have acted wickedly'; [48]and if they turn back to you with all their heart and soul in the land of their enemies who took them captive, and pray to you toward the land you gave their ancestors, toward the city you have chosen and the temple I have built for your Name; [49]then from heaven, your dwelling place, hear their prayer and their plea, and uphold their cause. [50]And forgive your people, who have sinned against you; forgive all the offenses they have committed against you, and cause their captors to show them mercy; [51]for they are your people and your inheritance, whom you brought out of Egypt, out of that iron-smelting furnace.

[52]"May your eyes be open to your servant's plea and to the plea of your people Israel, and may you listen to them whenever they cry out to you. [53]For you singled them out from all the nations of the world to be your own inheritance, just as you declared through your servant Moses when you, Sovereign LORD, brought our ancestors out of Egypt."

[54]When Solomon had finished all these prayers and supplications to the LORD, he rose from before the altar of the LORD, where he had been kneeling with his hands spread out toward heaven. [55]He stood and blessed the whole assembly of Israel in a loud voice, saying:

[56]"Praise be to the LORD, who has given rest to his people Israel just as he promised. Not one word has failed of all the good promises he gave through his servant Moses. [57]May the LORD our God be with us as he was with our ancestors; may he never leave us nor forsake us. [58]May he turn our hearts to him, to walk in obedience to him and keep the commands, decrees and laws he gave our ancestors. [59]And may these words of mine, which I have prayed before the LORD, be near to the LORD our God day and night, that he may uphold the cause of his servant and the cause of his people Israel according to each day's need, [60]so that all the peoples of the earth may know that the LORD is God and that there is no other. [61]And may your hearts be fully committed to the LORD our God, to live by his decrees and obey his commands, as at this time."

The Dedication of the Temple

8:62-66pp — 2Ch 7:1-10

[62]Then the king and all Israel with him offered sacrifices before the LORD. [63]Solomon offered a sacrifice of fellowship offerings to the LORD: twenty-two thousand cattle and a hundred and twenty thousand sheep and goats. So the king and all the Israelites dedicated the temple of the LORD.

8:42 your mighty hand and your outstretched arm Images of Yahweh's might (see Ex 6:1; 32:11; Dt 4:34; 5:15; 7:19; 11:2; 26:8; Jer 21:5).

8:43 bears your Name In the ancient Near East, proclaiming one's name over a person, place or thing indicated ownership (Dt 28:10; 2Sa 6:2; 12:27–28; Isa 4:1; Am 9:12).

8:44 wherever you send them In the ancient Near East, deities had to commission or approve battles (see Nu 27:21; Dt 2:24).

8:46 there is no one who does not sin This idea also appears in OT Wisdom literature and the NT (Pr 20:9; Ecc 7:20; Ro 3:9; 1Jn 1:8–10). **take them captive to their own lands** Conquering armies in the ancient Near East commonly displaced the conquered by systematically sending them to other lands (compare 2Ki 17:24).

8:51 your people and your inheritance The idea that Israel is God's inheritance is often tied to the exodus from Egypt (see Ex 19:4–5; Dt 9:26–29; 32:9). See the table "Parallelism in Hebrew Poetry" on p. 1008. **iron-smelting furnace** A metaphor for harsh living conditions (Dt 4:20; Jer 11:4).

8:53 just as you declared through your servant Moses See Ex 19:4–5; Lev 20:24.

8:54–61 After praying before the altar (1Ki 8:22–53), Solomon turns to bless the people of Israel (vv. 54–61). Like the preceding prayer, Solomon's benediction has many of the same themes and phrases as the book of Deuteronomy. Solomon emphasizes faithfulness to God's statutes, rules and commands.

8:56 who has given rest to his people Israel The period of rest began once Israel completed its conquest of Canaan (Dt 12:9–11; Jos 21:43–45). For the author of 1–2 Kings, this period comes during the reign of Solomon (1Ki 4:24).

8:61 fully committed to Describes being wholehearted (compare 11:4; 15:3,14; 2Ki 20:3).

⁶⁴On that same day the king consecrated the middle part of the courtyard in front of the temple of the LORD, and there he offered burnt offerings, grain offerings and the fat of the fellowship offerings, because the bronze altar that stood before the LORD was too small to hold the burnt offerings, the grain offerings and the fat of the fellowship offerings.

⁶⁵So Solomon observed the festival at that time, and all Israel with him — a vast assembly, people from Lebo Hamath to the Wadi of Egypt. They celebrated it before the LORD our God for seven days and seven days more, fourteen days in all. ⁶⁶On the following day he sent the people away. They blessed the king and then went home, joyful and glad in heart for all the good things the LORD had done for his servant David and his people Israel.

The LORD Appears to Solomon

9:1-9pp — 2Ch 7:11-22

9 When Solomon had finished building the temple of the LORD and the royal palace, and had achieved all he had desired to do, ²the LORD ap-peared to him a second time, as he had appeared to him at Gibeon. ³The LORD said to him:

"I have heard the prayer and plea you have made before me; I have consecrated this temple, which you have built, by putting my Name there forever. My eyes and my heart will always be there.

⁴"As for you, if you walk before me faithfully with integrity of heart and uprightness, as David your father did, and do all I command and observe my decrees and laws, ⁵I will establish your royal throne over Israel forever, as I promised David your father when I said, 'You shall never fail to have a successor on the throne of Israel.'

⁶"But if you[a] or your descendants turn away from me and do not observe the commands and decrees I have given you[a] and go off to serve other gods and worship them, ⁷then I will cut off Israel from the land I have given them and will reject this temple I have consecrated for my Name. Israel will then

---

[a] 6 The Hebrew is plural.

8:62–66 At first glance, the description of Solomon's inaugural sacrifices (1Ki 8:62–66) may appear to be an elaboration on the sacrifices offered in v. 5. However, the sacrifices in v. 5 are part of the ark of the covenant's procession into the Most Holy Place (Holy of Holies), while the latter sacrifices mark the end of the temple dedication. Kings in the ancient Near East were often said to have performed priestly duties, but it is unlikely that royalty would single-handedly perform mass sacrifices, even if they had priestly training. Furthermore, no priestly duties are required of Israel's kings (Dt 17:14–20).

8:63 twenty-two thousand cattle and a hundred and twenty thousand sheep and goats These numbers are likely exaggerated (see 1Ki 4:26 and note). Royal literature in antiquity frequently exaggerated numbers associated with wartime and religious events. This was an acceptable custom and functioned to show both divine blessing on the king as well as the king's excessive devotion to his god (or to Yahweh in the case of Israel). The fact that this is a literary convention makes it unlikely that these numbers are literal. Such extensive slaughtering (142,000 animals) likely would have had a devastating impact on the national economy. **dedicated the temple of the LORD** Describes sealing the ceremony with sacrificial offerings.

8:64 burnt offerings See Lev 1:3 and note. **grain offerings** See Lev 2:1 and note. **fellowship offerings** See Lev 3:1 and note.

8:65 festival Refers to Succoth or the Festival of Tabernacles (or Booths) (Lev 23:33–43; Nu 29:12–40; Dt 16:13–15).

8:66 On the following day Deuteronomy's version of the Festival of Tabernacles (or Booths) does not include special practices for the eighth day (Dt 16:13,15). Other descriptions of the festival include gathering and presenting food on this day (Lev 23:36; Nu 29:35); the book of Chronicles does not fully address the matter (2Ch 7:9–10). **joyful and glad in heart** The Hebrew phrase used here, *tov lev*, refers to lightheartedness that comes with drinking

(Ru 3:7; Est 1:10; 5:9; Ecc 9:7), partying (Pr 15:15) and a sense of accomplishment (Jdg 16:25; 18:20). **David** This reference brings the narrative of Solomon's dedication back to Yahweh's promise to David (1Ki 8:15–26).

9:1–9 God responds to the completion of Solomon's building projects (chs. 6–8) by appearing to him a second time, presumably in a dream (3:5; 9:2; 11:9). God affirms he has heard Solomon's prayer (8:22–53; 9:3), reiterates the Davidic covenant and its conditions (vv. 4–5), and warns Israel of the risk of disobedience using vocabulary reminiscent of the book of Deuteronomy (1Ki 9:4–9). The covenant faithfulness of the king and his people determines the fate of both the throne and the nation.

9:1 the royal palace Refers to the House of the Forest of Lebanon, Hall of Pillars, Hall of the Throne, Hall of Judgment, Solomon's own house and a house for Pharaoh's daughter, Solomon's wife (7:1–12). This complex took 13 years to build (7:1). **had achieved all he had desired to do** Possibly refers to the projects in vv. 15–28.

9:3 I have consecrated this temple Usually, humans serve as the subject of the Hebrew verb used here — meaning they are consecrated by God (e.g., 2Sa 8:11). Here, God endows the temple with holiness, receives Solomon's gifts and resides in the temple (1Ki 8:10–11). **by putting my Name there forever** Continues the tension between the concept of an earthly abode and the insistence that God does not live on earth, but in the heavens (8:13,27,29,39,43–44,49; compare Ex 15:17; Isa 66:1).

9:4 with integrity of heart and uprightness Used to describe David (Ps 78:72; compare Job 1:1,8). **as David your father did** David's obedience to Yahweh serves as the standard that all Israelite kings should emulate.

9:6 turn away The Hebrew text of vv. 6–9 switches from singular to plural. This may refer to Solomon's descendants or Israel itself. The author may have switched from singular to plural to accommodate for the fact that, while Solomon does not keep God's commands and worships other gods (see 11:1–13), God does not destroy Israel

become a byword and an object of ridicule among all peoples. [8]This temple will become a heap of rubble. All[a] who pass by will be appalled and will scoff and say, 'Why has the LORD done such a thing to this land and to this temple?' [9]People will answer, 'Because they have forsaken the LORD their God, who brought their ancestors out of Egypt, and have embraced other gods, worshiping and serving them — that is why the LORD brought all this disaster on them.'"

Solomon's Other Activities

9:10-28pp — 2Ch 8:1-18

[10]At the end of twenty years, during which Solomon built these two buildings — the temple of the LORD and the royal palace — [11]King Solomon gave twenty towns in Galilee to Hiram king of Tyre, because Hiram had supplied him with all the cedar and juniper and gold he wanted. [12]But when Hiram went from Tyre to see the towns that Solomon had given him, he was not pleased with them. [13]"What kind of towns are these you have given me, my brother?" he asked. And he called them the Land of Kabul,[b] a name they have to this day. [14]Now Hiram had sent to the king 120 talents[c] of gold.

[15]Here is the account of the forced labor King Solomon conscripted to build the LORD's temple, his own palace, the terraces,[d] the wall of Jerusalem, and Hazor, Megiddo and Gezer. [16](Pharaoh king of Egypt had attacked and captured Gezer.

He had set it on fire. He killed its Canaanite inhabitants and then gave it as a wedding gift to his daughter, Solomon's wife. [17]And Solomon rebuilt Gezer.) He built up Lower Beth Horon, [18]Baalath, and Tadmor[e] in the desert, within his land, [19]as well as all his store cities and the towns for his chariots and for his horses[f] — whatever he desired to build in Jerusalem, in Lebanon and throughout all the territory he ruled.

[20]There were still people left from the Amorites, Hittites, Perizzites, Hivites and Jebusites (these peoples were not Israelites). [21]Solomon conscripted the descendants of all these peoples remaining in the land — whom the Israelites could not exterminate[g] — to serve as slave labor, as it is to this day. [22]But Solomon did not make slaves of any of the Israelites; they were his fighting men, his government officials, his officers, his captains, and the commanders of his chariots and charioteers. [23]They were also the chief officials in charge of Solomon's projects — 550 officials supervising those who did the work.

[24]After Pharaoh's daughter had come up from the City of David to the palace Solomon had built for her, he constructed the terraces.

[25]Three times a year Solomon sacrificed burnt

---

a 8 See some Septuagint manuscripts, Old Latin, Syriac, Arabic and Targum; Hebrew And though this temple is now imposing, all   b 13 Kabul sounds like the Hebrew for good-for-nothing. c 14 That is, about 4 1/2 tons or about 4 metric tons   d 15 Or the Millo; also in verse 24   e 18 The Hebrew may also be read Tamar.   f 19 Or charioteers   g 21 The Hebrew term refers to the irrevocable giving over of things or persons to the LORD, often by totally destroying them.

---

and the temple as he vows to here (vv. 6–9). **serve other gods** Describes apostasy, the reason for the fall of both the northern and southern kingdoms (2Ki 17:7–23; 21:10–18).

9:7 will reject In contrast, Ezekiel envisions God leaving the temple (Eze 10).

9:8 All who pass by will be appalled and will scoff The prophets frequently use this proverbial image (Jer 18:16; 19:8; 49:17; 50:13; La 2:15; Eze 27:36; Zep 2:15).

9:10–28 This passage contains a list of Solomon's lesser-known projects and actions. It records a disagreement between Solomon and Hiram (1Ki 9:11–13) and gives an account of Solomon's forced labor at odds with 5:13 (vv. 20–22; compare 12:4). This passage sets the stage for the coming conflict (ch. 11).

9:11 twenty towns in Galilee In addition to the yearly provisions listed in 5:11. **Hiram king of Tyre** See note on 5:1. **cedar** See 5:6 and note; 5:8 and note. **juniper** See note on 5:8.

9:13 Kabul The meaning of the word used here, *kavul*, is uncertain. The same name is applied to a border town of the tribe of Asher (Jos 19:27).

9:14 120 talents of gold May describe a tribute payment (Jdg 3:15,17; 2Sa 8:2,6; 2Ki 17:3). The Queen of Sheba brings the same amount (1Ki 10:10). See note on 4:21.

9:15 terraces The meaning of the Hebrew word used here is unclear. The consensus among archaeologists is that it refers to a terraced earthwork that was part of a large retaining wall in Jerusalem. **Hazor, Megiddo**

and Gezer These cities represent important sites in the archeological debate over the history of Israel during the Monarchic Period and the usefulness of the OT for reconstructing history.

9:16 Canaanite inhabitants Though Gezer was located near the Philistine cities of Ekron, Gath and Ashkelon, it remained a Canaanite city. **his daughter, Solomon's wife** Solomon married Pharaoh's daughter early in his reign (3:1). The construction of a house built for her attests to her elevated status among Solomon's 700 wives (7:8; 11:3). See note on 3:1.

9:19 store cities The Hebrew phrase used here, *are hammiskenoth*, refers to the type of city that the Hebrew slaves were forced to build in Egypt (Ex 1:11). First Kings 5:13 states that Solomon conscripted 30,000 people for these projects (compare 12:4). **for his horses** The large stables at Megiddo suggest that it may have served as one of Solomon's cavalry cities.

9:20 There were still people left Lists the people groups residing in the land before the Israelites arrived. Lists like this one vary from five to ten groups (see Ge 15:19–21; Ex 23:23; Dt 7:1).

9:21 descendants of all these peoples remaining in the land Deuteronomy 7:1–5 and 20:16–18 specify that these cities were to be destroyed completely.

9:22 Solomon did not make slaves Although this seems to emphasize that Solomon conscripted only non-Israelites, the language of 5:13 leaves more room for interpretation.

9:25 Three times A possible reference to three pilgrim-

offerings and fellowship offerings on the altar he had built for the LORD, burning incense before the LORD along with them, and so fulfilled the temple obligations.

²⁶King Solomon also built ships at Ezion Geber, which is near Elath in Edom, on the shore of the Red Sea.ᵃ ²⁷And Hiram sent his men — sailors who knew the sea — to serve in the fleet with Solomon's men. ²⁸They sailed to Ophir and brought back 420 talentsᵇ of gold, which they delivered to King Solomon.

The Queen of Sheba Visits Solomon

10:1-13pp — 2Ch 9:1-12

10 When the queen of Sheba heard about the fame of Solomon and his relationship to the LORD, she came to test Solomon with hard questions. ²Arriving at Jerusalem with a very great caravan — with camels carrying spices, large quantities of gold, and precious stones — she came to Solomon and talked with him about all that she had on her mind. ³Solomon answered all her questions; nothing was too hard for the king to explain to her. ⁴When the queen of Sheba saw all the wisdom of Solomon and the palace he had built, ⁵the food on his table, the seating of his officials, the attending servants in their robes, his cupbearers, and the burnt offerings he made atᶜ the temple of the LORD, she was overwhelmed.

⁶She said to the king, "The report I heard in my own country about your achievements and your wisdom is true. ⁷But I did not believe these things until I came and saw with my own eyes. Indeed, not even half was told me; in wisdom and wealth you have far exceeded the report I heard. ⁸How happy your people must be! How happy your officials, who continually stand before you and hear your wisdom! ⁹Praise be to the LORD your God, who has delighted in you and placed you on the throne of Israel. Because of the LORD's eternal love for Israel, he has made you king to maintain justice and righteousness."

¹⁰And she gave the king 120 talentsᵈ of gold, large quantities of spices, and precious stones. Never again were so many spices brought in as those the queen of Sheba gave to King Solomon.

¹¹(Hiram's ships brought gold from Ophir; and from there they brought great cargoes of almugwoodᵉ and precious stones. ¹²The king used the almugwood to make supportsᶠ for the temple of the LORD and for the royal palace, and to make harps and lyres for the musicians. So much almugwood has never been imported or seen since that day.)

¹³King Solomon gave the queen of Sheba all she desired and asked for, besides what he had given her out of his royal bounty. Then she left and returned with her retinue to her own country.

ᵃ 26 Or *the Sea of Reeds*   ᵇ 28 That is, about 16 tons or about 14 metric tons   ᶜ 5 Or *the ascent by which he went up to*   ᵈ 10 That is, about 4 1/2 tons or about 4 metric tons   ᵉ 11 Probably a variant of *algumwood*; also in verse 12   ᶠ 12 The meaning of the Hebrew for this word is uncertain.

---

age festivals, when the Israelites went to Jerusalem (Ex 23:14–17; Dt 16:1–17). **the altar** See note on 8:22.
9:27 his men Hiram's servants were Sidonians—men from the city of Sidon. Sidonians cut and transported the lumber for the temple; they were also involved in building the temple (5:6,18). Historically, the Sidonians are better known as Phoenicians—a people known for seafaring and trade. See note on 6:1.
9:28 Ophir A region known for very fine gold (Job 28:16; Isa 13:12). Its exact location is unknown, but it is thought to have been on the southern Arabian Peninsula on the Red Sea. **420 talents of gold** An exaggerated number; 120 talents of gold probably represents a more appropriate tribute (1Ki 9:14; 10:10). Compare note on 8:63.

10:1–13 The Queen of Sheba's visit highlights the secular and intellectual influence of King Solomon. While the narrative emphasizes Solomon's wisdom and its relationship to his material possessions, it does not provide details about the exchange between Solomon and the queen.
10:1 Sheba Possibly located in the southwestern part of the Arabian Peninsula. Sheba was associated with gold and spices (Isa 60:6; Jer 6:20; Eze 27:22). **hard questions** The Hebrew word used here, *chidah*, can describe a riddle (Jdg 14:12–20) or a teaching from elders (Pr 1:6; Ps 78:2).
10:2 her mind The Hebrew term used here, *levav*, comes from the Hebrew word *lev*, which means "inner person," "mind," "will" or "heart."

10:4 wisdom of Solomon Solomon's wisdom includes knowledge of nature (1Ki 4:33) and the ability to speak proverbs, compose songs (4:32), reorganize a nation (4:1–28) and judge difficult cases (3:16–28).
10:5 cupbearers Perhaps refers to waiters (2Ch 9:4). **burnt offerings he made** Solomon offered burnt sacrifices three times per year (1Ki 9:25). On burnt offerings, see note on Lev 1:3.
10:10 120 talents of gold Likely a tribute payment (see 1Ki 4:21 and note). Hiram presents Solomon with the same amount (9:14).
10:11 Hiram's ships See note on 5:1. **almugwood** This is the only occurrence in the OT of the Hebrew word used here, *almuggim*. The exact identification of this species of wood is uncertain, but it is to be understood as a luxury item.
10:12 to make supports The Hebrew term *mis'ad*—which occurs only here in the OT—comes from the word *sa'ad*, meaning "to support." The exact meaning of this architectural term is uncertain. **musicians** Singers provided entertainment in the royal court (2Sa 19:35; 2Ch 35:25) and also took part in ritual services (Eze 40:44).
10:13 all she desired and asked for May indicate that this was a diplomatic mission and the two negotiated an agreement. **out of his royal bounty** The Hebrew phrase used here, *keyad hammelekh shelomoh*, refers to the king's generosity (see also Est 1:7; 2:18). Solomon apparently gave the Queen of Sheba gifts in return (compare 1Ki 10:2).

Solomon's Splendor

10:14-29pp — 2Ch 1:14-17; 9:13-28

[14]The weight of the gold that Solomon received yearly was 666 talents,[a] [15]not including the revenues from merchants and traders and from all the Arabian kings and the governors of the territories.

[16]King Solomon made two hundred large shields of hammered gold; six hundred shekels[b] of gold went into each shield. [17]He also made three hundred small shields of hammered gold, with three minas[c] of gold in each shield. The king put them in the Palace of the Forest of Lebanon.

[18]Then the king made a great throne covered with ivory and overlaid with fine gold. [19]The throne had six steps, and its back had a rounded top. On both sides of the seat were armrests, with a lion standing beside each of them. [20]Twelve lions stood on the six steps, one at either end of each step. Nothing like it had ever been made for any other kingdom. [21]All King Solomon's goblets were gold, and all the household articles in the Palace of the Forest of Lebanon were pure gold. Nothing was made of silver, because silver was considered of little value in Solomon's days. [22]The king had a fleet of trading ships[d] at sea along with the ships of Hiram. Once every three years it returned, carrying gold, silver and ivory, and apes and baboons.

[23]King Solomon was greater in riches and wisdom than all the other kings of the earth. [24]The whole world sought audience with Solomon to hear the wisdom God had put in his heart. [25]Year after year, everyone who came brought a gift — articles of silver and gold, robes, weapons and spices, and horses and mules.

[26]Solomon accumulated chariots and horses; he had fourteen hundred chariots and twelve thousand horses,[e] which he kept in the chariot cities and also with him in Jerusalem. [27]The king made silver as common in Jerusalem as stones, and cedar as plentiful as sycamore-fig trees in the foothills. [28]Solomon's horses were imported from Egypt and from Kue[f] — the royal merchants purchased them from Kue at the current price. [29]They imported a chariot from Egypt for six hundred shekels of

---

[a] 14 That is, about 25 tons or about 23 metric tons   [b] 16 That is, about 15 pounds or about 6.9 kilograms; also in verse 29   [c] 17 That is, about 3 3/4 pounds or about 1.7 kilograms; or perhaps reference is to double minas, that is, about 7 1/2 pounds or about 3.5 kilograms.   [d] 22 Hebrew *of ships of Tarshish*   [e] 26 Or *charioteers*   [f] 28 Probably *Cilicia*

10:14–29 This catalog of Solomon's possessions may be read as either evidence of a "golden age" brought about by Solomon's wisdom or a critique of amassing wealth. This passage appears between the Queen of Sheba's visit with Solomon, whose wisdom leaves her overwhelmed (v. 5), and the account of Solomon's foreign wives, who lead him astray (11:9).

10:14 yearly The Hebrew terminology here is vague; it might be referring to the gold that Solomon received in one certain year, rather than an annual amount. **666 talents** Perhaps an approximate summary of the stated amount of gold from Hiram (120 talents; 9:14), Ophir (420 talents; 9:28), and Sheba (120 talents; v. 10). A talent was about 75 pounds (34 kilograms). These 666 talents are equal to almost 50,000 pounds (22,600 kilograms).
10:15 governors of the territories Administrators from the 12 provinces of Israel were responsible for providing a month's worth of royal provisions (4:1–28).
10:16 two hundred large shields of hammered gold The Hebrew word used here, *tsinnah*, describes a body-length shield, possibly with three sides (Ps 5:12). An attendant carried this same type of shield for Goliath (1Sa 17:7). Despite their size, gold is a relatively soft metal and thus these shields would not hold up in battle. **six hundred shekels of gold** A shekel is about 0.4 ounces (11 grams). Each shield weighed 15 pounds (6.6 kilograms).
10:17 three hundred small shields The Hebrew word used here, *magen*, refers to small, hand-held shields. **three minas** A mina is about 1.25 pounds (0.6 kilograms). Each shield weighed 3.75 pounds (1.8 kilograms). **in the Palace of the Forest of Lebanon** See note on 7:2.
10:18 a great throne covered with ivory Likely a wood throne with ivory inlays. Costly furniture in the ancient Near East often had carved ivory plates inlaid in the woodwork.

10:19 a rounded top The traditional Hebrew text refers to the round top of the throne; round-topped chairs and bovine imagery were common throughout the ancient Near East. However, the ancient Greek translation, the Septuagint, suggests the top of the throne had a carving of a calf or bull's head. It may be that the Greek text is more original, since the calf imagery would have been seen as related to idolatry and thus the Hebrew text may have later been altered (Ex 32; compare 1Ki 12:25–33). **a lion standing beside each** Symbols of strength and power throughout the ancient Near East (Eze 19:1–9; Na 2:12–13). In the OT, lion imagery is associated with Judah, King David's tribe (Ge 49:9).
10:20 Nothing like it had ever been made It is unclear in what way Solomon's throne was unique, since archeological discoveries reveal similar thrones.
10:22 three years Indicates a very long journey, not necessarily the exact length of the voyage.
10:23 in riches and wisdom Concerning amassing riches, see Dt 17:14–20 and note.
10:25 a gift The Hebrew word used here, *minchah*, describes a required payment brought from a lesser power to its governing power (2Ki 17:3; Judg 3:15,17; 2Sa 8:2,6).
10:26 twelve thousand horses Coincides with the 12,000 horses listed in 1Ki 4:26. **chariot cities** Perhaps includes some of the cities listed in 9:15–18. The large stables at Megiddo suggest that it may have served as one of Solomon's cavalry cities.
10:27 cedar See 5:6 and note; 5:8 and note. **sycamore-fig trees** The Hebrew word used here, *shiqmah*, refers to the *ficus sycomorus*, a tree which was common in the low hills of Israel and suitable for roofing. **foothills** Refers to the low hills in Judah between the coastal plain and Jerusalem.
10:28 Kue A kingdom in southeast Asia Minor (modern-day Turkey).
10:29 They imported a chariot The Hebrew phrase

silver, and a horse for a hundred and fifty.[a] They also exported them to all the kings of the Hittites and of the Arameans.

Solomon's Wives

11 King Solomon, however, loved many foreign women besides Pharaoh's daughter — Moabites, Ammonites, Edomites, Sidonians and Hittites. [2] They were from nations about which the LORD had told the Israelites, "You must not intermarry with them, because they will surely turn your hearts after their gods." Nevertheless, Solomon held fast to them in love. [3] He had seven hundred wives of royal birth and three hundred concubines, and his wives led him astray. [4] As Solomon grew old, his wives turned his heart after other gods, and his heart was not fully devoted to the LORD his God, as the heart of David his father had been. [5] He followed Ashtoreth the goddess of the Sidonians, and Molek the detestable god of the Ammonites. [6] So Solomon did evil in the eyes of the LORD; he did not follow the LORD completely, as David his father had done.

[7] On a hill east of Jerusalem, Solomon built a high place for Chemosh the detestable god of Moab, and for Molek the detestable god of the Ammonites.

[8] He did the same for all his foreign wives, who burned incense and offered sacrifices to their gods.

[9] The LORD became angry with Solomon because his heart had turned away from the LORD, the God of Israel, who had appeared to him twice. [10] Although he had forbidden Solomon to follow other gods, Solomon did not keep the LORD's command. [11] So the LORD said to Solomon, "Since this is your attitude and you have not kept my covenant and my decrees, which I commanded you, I will most certainly tear the kingdom away from you and give it to one of your subordinates. [12] Nevertheless, for the sake of David your father, I will not do it during your lifetime. I will tear it out of the hand of your son. [13] Yet I will not tear the whole kingdom from him, but will give him one tribe for the sake of David my servant and for the sake of Jerusalem, which I have chosen."

Solomon's Adversaries

[14] Then the LORD raised up against Solomon an adversary, Hadad the Edomite, from the royal line of Edom. [15] Earlier when David was fighting with

[a] 29 That is, about 3 3/4 pounds or about 1.7 kilograms

---

used here, literally "would go up and out," implies that chariots were purchased with the intent to resell. Solomon amasses wealth through both trade and tribute. **six hundred shekels of silver** A shekel is about 0.4 ounces (11 grams). A chariot cost about 15 pounds (6.6 kilograms) of silver. **Hittites** See Ge 10:15 and note.

HITTITES
The Hittite empire, based in Asia Minor (modern-day Turkey), was a major power in the ancient Near East during the seventeenth–twelfth centuries BC (prior to Israel's monarchy). Groups of Hittites migrated south, eventually settling in the hill country of Canaan near Hebron (Ge 23:19–20; Nu 13:29). Notable Hittites in the Bible include Ephron, from whom Abraham purchased a burial site (Ge 23) and Uriah, one of David's mighty men (2Sa 23:39). Esau married two Hittites (Ge 26:34), and Solomon had Hittite women in his harem (1Ki 11:1).

11:1–8 Solomon's worship of other gods becomes the theological rationale for the division of the kingdom after his death (1Ki 9–13; 12:16–24). Solomon's love of foreign women and his marriage alliances with other nations represent the cause of his unfaithfulness to Yahweh. See note on 3:1.

11:1 Pharaoh's daughter The last of five references to this marriage (3:1; 7:8; 9:16,24). Solomon built a house for Pharaoh's daughter, indicating her privileged status among Solomon's wives (7:8; 9:24).

11:2 You must not intermarry with them The law forbade Israelites from taking foreign wives because such a relationship could lead to the worship of other gods (Dt 7:1–5). See note on Ezr 9:1—10:44.

11:3 seven hundred wives of royal birth and three hundred concubines See Dt 17:17 and note.

11:4 his heart See note on 1Ki 8:17. **David his father** See 1:1 and note; 9:4 and note.

11:5 Ashtoreth Canaanite fertility goddess (also known as Astarte). **Molek** The patron god of the Ammonites, Milcom, also may have been known by the name Molek (v. 7; see note on Jer 49:1).

11:7 hill east of Jerusalem Likely refers to the Mount of Olives (see note on 2Ki 23:13). **Chemosh** Patron deity of the Moabites. See note on Nu 21:29.

11:9–43 In response to Solomon's unfaithfulness, God raises three adversaries against him: Hadad from the east (1Ki 11:14–22), Rezon from the north (vv. 23–25) and Jeroboam from one of Israel's own tribes (vv. 26–40). Through these adversaries, God destabilizes the peace that Solomon established both within Israel and at her borders (4:24–25) and leads to the division of the kingdom.

11:9 who had appeared to him twice God appeared to Solomon at Gibeon (3:1–15) and after the temple dedication (9:1–9).

11:11 covenant The Hebrew word used here, berith, appears throughout 1–2 Kings (e.g., 19:10,14; 2Ki 17:15,35; 18:12; 23:2–3,21) in reference to covenants between God and humanity. It also can refer to political treaties (e.g., 1Ki 5:12; 15:19; 20:34). **your subordinates** A reference to Jeroboam, who is described as a servant of Solomon (v. 26).

11:12 for the sake of David your father Perhaps in reference to the Davidic covenant, which promised that God would not remove his steadfast love from David's reigning son (2Sa 7:15).

11:13 one tribe Later specified as Judah, the tribe of David (1Ki 12:20).

11:15 when David was fighting with Edom Refers to 2Sa 8:1–16 (compare Dt 20:13; 1Ch 18:12).

Edom, Joab the commander of the army, who had gone up to bury the dead, had struck down all the men in Edom. [16]Joab and all the Israelites stayed there for six months, until they had destroyed all the men in Edom. [17]But Hadad, still only a boy, fled to Egypt with some Edomite officials who had served his father. [18]They set out from Midian and went to Paran. Then taking people from Paran with them, they went to Egypt, to Pharaoh king of Egypt, who gave Hadad a house and land and provided him with food.

[19]Pharaoh was so pleased with Hadad that he gave him a sister of his own wife, Queen Tahpenes, in marriage. [20]The sister of Tahpenes bore him a son named Genubath, whom Tahpenes brought up in the royal palace. There Genubath lived with Pharaoh's own children.

[21]While he was in Egypt, Hadad heard that David rested with his ancestors and that Joab the commander of the army was also dead. Then Hadad said to Pharaoh, "Let me go, that I may return to my own country."

[22]"What have you lacked here that you want to go back to your own country?" Pharaoh asked.

"Nothing," Hadad replied, "but do let me go!"

[23]And God raised up against Solomon another adversary, Rezon son of Eliada, who had fled from his master, Hadadezer king of Zobah. [24]When David destroyed Zobah's army, Rezon gathered a band of men around him and became their leader; they went to Damascus, where they settled and took control. [25]Rezon was Israel's adversary as long as Solomon lived, adding to the trouble caused by Hadad. So Rezon ruled in Aram and was hostile toward Israel.

Jeroboam Rebels Against Solomon

[26]Also, Jeroboam son of Nebat rebelled against the king. He was one of Solomon's officials, an Ephraimite from Zeredah, and his mother was a widow named Zeruah.

[27]Here is the account of how he rebelled against the king: Solomon had built the terraces[a] and had filled in the gap in the wall of the city of David his father. [28]Now Jeroboam was a man of standing, and when Solomon saw how well the young man did his work, he put him in charge of the whole labor force of the tribes of Joseph.

[29]About that time Jeroboam was going out of Jerusalem, and Ahijah the prophet of Shiloh met him on the way, wearing a new cloak. The two of them were alone out in the country, [30]and Ahijah took hold of the new cloak he was wearing and tore it into twelve pieces. [31]Then he said to Jeroboam, "Take ten pieces for yourself, for this is what the LORD, the God of Israel, says: 'See, I am going to tear the kingdom out of Solomon's hand and give you ten tribes. [32]But for the sake of my servant David and the city of Jerusalem, which I have chosen out of all the tribes of Israel, he will have one tribe. [33]I will do this because they have[b] forsaken me and worshiped Ashtoreth the goddess of the Sidonians, Chemosh the god of the Moabites, and Molek the god of the Ammonites, and have not walked in obedience to me, nor done what is right in my eyes, nor kept my decrees and laws as David, Solomon's father, did.

[34]"'But I will not take the whole kingdom out of Solomon's hand; I have made him ruler all the days of his life for the sake of David my servant, whom I chose and who obeyed my commands and decrees. [35]I will take the kingdom from his son's hands and give you ten tribes. [36]I will give one tribe to his son so that David my servant may always have a lamp before me in Jerusalem, the city where I chose to put my Name. [37]However, as for you, I will take you, and you will rule over all that your heart desires; you will be king over Israel. [38]If you do whatever I command you and walk in obedience to me and do what is right in my eyes by obeying my decrees and commands, as David my servant did, I will be with you. I will

---

[a] 27 Or *the Millo*   [b] 33 Hebrew; Septuagint, Vulgate and Syriac *because he has*

11:18 Paran The exact location of this place in the wilderness is unknown (see Ge 21:21; Nu 12:16; 13:26; Dt 33:2; 1Sa 25:1; Hab 3:3). **taking people from Paran with them** Describes guides familiar with the territory.

11:19 Tahpenes Likely a transliteration of the Egyptian phrase *t-h-p-nsw*, meaning "wife of the king."

11:20 There Genubath Genubath was half Egyptian and, like Moses, was weaned in Pharaoh's household.

11:21 rested with his ancestors See 1Ki 2:10 and note. **Joab the commander of the army was also dead** Solomon had ordered Joab's execution (2:28–35). **my own country** Refers to Edom.

11:24 Damascus See 2Sa 8:5.

11:25 Rezon was Israel's adversary as long as Solomon lived Contrasts 1Ki 4:24–25, which claims that Solomon's reign was a time of peace, both inside the land and at Israel's borders.

11:26 Jeroboam Means "may the kin increase." **Zeredah** Possibly synonymous with Zarethan (4:12), a city on the eastern bank of the Jordan where the bronze vessels for the temple were cast (7:46).

11:27 terraces See note on 9:15.

11:30 twelve pieces One for each of Israel's tribes.

11:33 they have forsaken me The traditional Hebrew text here reads "they have forsaken me," which is an ambiguous reference; Greek, Syriac and Latin manuscripts read "he has forsaken," referring to Solomon (vv. 1–8).

11:35 ten tribes Refers to the northern ten tribes of Israel.

11:36 a lamp The Hebrew word used here, *nir*, describes a sign of life and hope (1Sa 3:3; 2Sa 21:17). **where I chose to put my Name** Yahweh chose to put his name inside the temple (1Ki 9:3).

11:37 your heart The Hebrew word used here is *nephesh*, which is often translated as "soul." See note on 2:4.

build you a dynasty as enduring as the one I built for David and will give Israel to you. ³⁹I will humble David's descendants because of this, but not forever.'"

⁴⁰Solomon tried to kill Jeroboam, but Jeroboam fled to Egypt, to Shishak the king, and stayed there until Solomon's death.

Solomon's Death

11:41-43pp — 2Ch 9:29-31

⁴¹As for the other events of Solomon's reign — all he did and the wisdom he displayed — are they not written in the book of the annals of Solomon? ⁴²Solomon reigned in Jerusalem over all Israel forty years. ⁴³Then he rested with his ancestors and was buried in the city of David his father. And Rehoboam his son succeeded him as king.

Israel Rebels Against Rehoboam

12:1-24pp — 2Ch 10:1 – 11:4

12 Rehoboam went to Shechem, for all Israel had gone there to make him king. ²When Jeroboam son of Nebat heard this (he was still in Egypt, where he had fled from King Solomon), he returned from*ᵃ* Egypt. ³So they sent for Jeroboam, and he and the whole assembly of Israel went to Rehoboam and said to him: ⁴"Your father put a heavy yoke on us, but now lighten the harsh labor and the heavy yoke he put on us, and we will serve you."

⁵Rehoboam answered, "Go away for three days and then come back to me." So the people went away.

⁶Then King Rehoboam consulted the elders who had served his father Solomon during his lifetime. "How would you advise me to answer these people?" he asked.

⁷They replied, "If today you will be a servant to these people and serve them and give them a favorable answer, they will always be your servants."

⁸But Rehoboam rejected the advice the elders gave him and consulted the young men who had grown up with him and were serving him. ⁹He asked them, "What is your advice? How should we answer these people who say to me, 'Lighten the yoke your father put on us'?"

ᵃ 2 Or he remained in

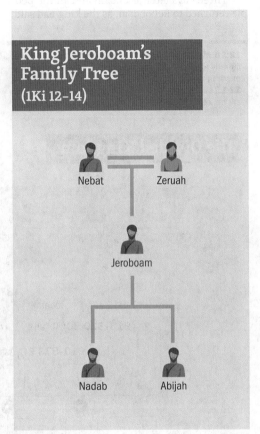

King Jeroboam's Family Tree (1Ki 12–14)

Nebat — Zeruah

Jeroboam

Nadab   Abijah

11:41 the book of the annals of Solomon The author of 1–2 Kings may have drawn from this source, which is no longer extant.
11:42 forty years David also reigned 40 years (2:11). The number 40 signified completeness or success.
11:43 he rested with his ancestors See note on 2:10.

12:1–15 Following the death of Solomon, Rehoboam becomes king of Israel. Ancient Near Eastern monarchies typically practiced primogeniture succession, the right of the eldest son to succeed to the throne. While this served as an easy way of determining the next king, it did not ensure that the position was given to the best candidate, as was the case with Rehoboam. The contrast between Solomon's wise judgment (3:16–28) and Rehoboam's folly (vv. 1–15) further emphasizes Rehoboam's shortcomings.

12:1 Shechem Located 40 miles north of Jerusalem. It is unclear why the Israelites held Rehoboam's coronation at Shechem instead of Jerusalem, the capital.

12:4 put a heavy yoke on us Likely refers to heavy taxation (4:22–28) and perhaps forced labor (5:13–18).
12:5 three days A common literary phrase indicating a short period of time (see Ge 22:4; 34:25; 1Ki 3:18; 2Ki 20:5; Est 5:1).
12:6 the elders The identity of this group is unknown; the Hebrew term used here, *zaqen*, can denote either "old man" or "elder," and likely includes some of the officials listed in 1Ki 4:1–19.
12:7 give them a favorable answer The phrase used here is composed of two Hebrew words: *davar* (meaning "word," "matter" or "thing") and *tov* (meaning "good" or "well"). The phrase means more than a favorable verbal response (Pr 12:25; Zec 1:13); it also means improving conditions by showing grace—in this case, by lightening the peoples' burden.
12:8 young men Generationally identifiable with Rehoboam and lacking the wisdom of their predecessors.

¹⁰The young men who had grown up with him replied, "These people have said to you, 'Your father put a heavy yoke on us, but make our yoke lighter.' Now tell them, 'My little finger is thicker than my father's waist. ¹¹My father laid on you a heavy yoke; I will make it even heavier. My father scourged you with whips; I will scourge you with scorpions.'"

¹²Three days later Jeroboam and all the people returned to Rehoboam, as the king had said,

"Come back to me in three days." ¹³The king answered the people harshly. Rejecting the advice given him by the elders, ¹⁴he followed the advice of the young men and said, "My father made your yoke heavy; I will make it even heavier. My father scourged you with whips; I will scourge you with scorpions." ¹⁵So the king did not listen to the people, for this turn of events was from the LORD, to fulfill the word the LORD had spoken to Jeroboam son of Nebat through Ahijah the Shilonite.

12:10 My little finger The Hebrew term used here, literally rendered as "my little [thing]," may be a euphemism for the penis.
12:11 scorpions While the Hebrew word used here usually denotes the animal, it also can refer to a barbed whip.

12:15 this turn of events was from the LORD This brings the events in line with the prophecy of Ahijah (1Ki 11:29–39) and validates the division of the kingdom.

The Divided Kingdom

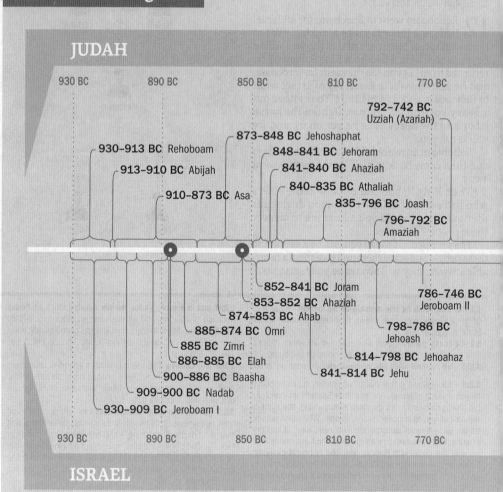

JUDAH

930 BC   890 BC   850 BC   810 BC   770 BC

792–742 BC Uzziah (Azariah)
873–848 BC Jehoshaphat
930–913 BC Rehoboam
848–841 BC Jehoram
913–910 BC Abijah
841–840 BC Ahaziah
840–835 BC Athaliah
910–873 BC Asa
835–796 BC Joash
796–792 BC Amaziah

852–841 BC Joram
786–746 BC Jeroboam II
853–852 BC Ahaziah
874–853 BC Ahab
885–874 BC Omri
798–786 BC Jehoash
885 BC Zimri
886–885 BC Elah
814–798 BC Jehoahaz
900–886 BC Baasha
841–814 BC Jehu
909–900 BC Nadab
930–909 BC Jeroboam I

930 BC   890 BC   850 BC   810 BC   770 BC

ISRAEL

All dates are approximate

¹⁶When all Israel saw that the king refused to listen to them, they answered the king:

"What share do we have in David,
what part in Jesse's son?
To your tents, Israel!
Look after your own house, David!"

So the Israelites went home. ¹⁷But as for the Israelites who were living in the towns of Judah, Rehoboam still ruled over them.

¹⁸King Rehoboam sent out Adoniram,ᵃ who was in charge of forced labor, but all Israel stoned him to death. King Rehoboam, however, managed to get into his chariot and escape to Jerusalem.

ᵃ 18 Some Septuagint manuscripts and Syriac (see also 4:6 and 5:14); Hebrew *Adoram*

12:16–24 From this point on, the kingdom is divided into two nations: Israel and Judah. Israel consists of the northern ten tribes, while Judah includes the two southernmost tribes—Judah and Benjamin. It is unclear why Benjamin paired with Judah, particularly since Saul (1Sa 9:1–2) and Sheba the rebel (2Sa 20) were Benjamites. Although war did not accompany the division of the kingdom, skirmishes between the two powers continued for a number of years (1Ki 14:30).

12:16 To your tents, Israel! Look after your own house, David The statements here reflect the northern tribes' decision to cut ties with Judah, the tribe of David and Rehoboam (v. 20).

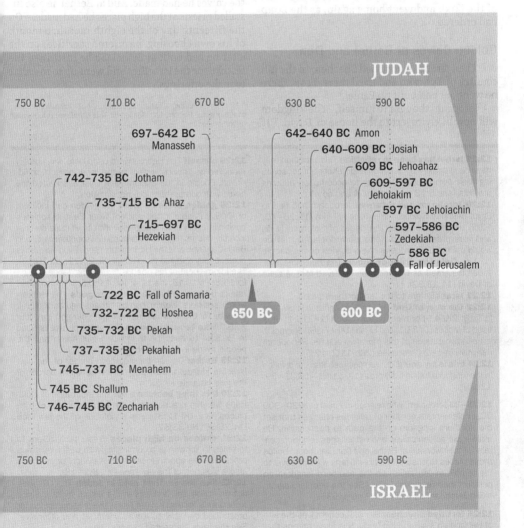

JUDAH

750 BC 710 BC 670 BC 630 BC 590 BC

697–642 BC Manasseh
642–640 BC Amon
640–609 BC Josiah
742–735 BC Jotham
609 BC Jehoahaz
735–715 BC Ahaz
609–597 BC Jehoiakim
597 BC Jehoiachin
715–697 BC Hezekiah
597–586 BC Zedekiah
586 BC Fall of Jerusalem

722 BC Fall of Samaria
650 BC   600 BC
732–722 BC Hoshea
735–732 BC Pekah
737–735 BC Pekahiah
745–737 BC Menahem
745 BC Shallum
746–745 BC Zechariah

750 BC 710 BC 670 BC 630 BC 590 BC

ISRAEL

¹⁹So Israel has been in rebellion against the house of David to this day.

²⁰When all the Israelites heard that Jeroboam had returned, they sent and called him to the assembly and made him king over all Israel. Only the tribe of Judah remained loyal to the house of David.

²¹When Rehoboam arrived in Jerusalem, he mustered all Judah and the tribe of Benjamin — a hundred and eighty thousand able young men — to go to war against Israel and to regain the kingdom for Rehoboam son of Solomon.

²²But this word of God came to Shemaiah the man of God: ²³"Say to Rehoboam son of Solomon king of Judah, to all Judah and Benjamin, and to the rest of the people, ²⁴'This is what the LORD says: Do not go up to fight against your brothers, the Israelites. Go home, every one of you, for this is my doing.'" So they obeyed the word of the LORD and went home again, as the LORD had ordered.

Golden Calves at Bethel and Dan

²⁵Then Jeroboam fortified Shechem in the hill country of Ephraim and lived there. From there he went out and built up Peniel.ᵃ

²⁶Jeroboam thought to himself, "The kingdom will now likely revert to the house of David. ²⁷If these people go up to offer sacrifices at the temple of the LORD in Jerusalem, they will again give their allegiance to their lord, Rehoboam king of Judah. They will kill me and return to King Rehoboam."

²⁸After seeking advice, the king made two golden calves. He said to the people, "It is too much for you to go up to Jerusalem. Here are your gods, Israel, who brought you up out of Egypt." ²⁹One he set up in Bethel, and the other in Dan. ³⁰And this thing became a sin; the people came to worship the one at Bethel and went as far as Dan to worship the other.ᵇ

³¹Jeroboam built shrines on high places and appointed priests from all sorts of people, even though they were not Levites. ³²He instituted a festival on the fifteenth day of the eighth month, like the festival held in Judah, and offered sacrifices on the altar. This he did in Bethel, sacrificing to the calves he had made. And at Bethel he also installed priests at the high places he had made. ³³On the fifteenth day of the eighth month, a month of his own choosing, he offered sacrifices on the altar he had built at Bethel. So he instituted the festival for the Israelites and went up to the altar to make offerings.

ᵃ 25 Hebrew *Penuel*, a variant of *Peniel*   ᵇ 30 Probable reading of the original Hebrew text; Masoretic Text *people went to the one as far as Dan*

12:19 Israel has been in rebellion This rebellion may have been caused by Solomon and Rehoboam conscripting their own people for labor to accomplish building projects (see 5:13 and note; v. 4 and note).

12:20 Jeroboam had returned Jeroboam had fled to Egypt because Solomon sought to kill him (11:26–40; 12:2). He returned after the death of Solomon (v. 2) and was present when Rehoboam declared that he would maintain his father's heavy burden on the people (v. 12). **Only the tribe of Judah** The first time that Judah is named as the one tribe reserved for the sake of David (11:13,32).

12:21 Israel Refers to the ten northern tribes.

12:22 the man of God This title designates a prophet (17:18; 2Ki 4:9) or messenger of God (1Ki 13:1). It is used of Moses (Dt 33:1) and Elijah (1Ki 17:18). Shemaiah is unknown outside of this narrative and the Rehoboam narrative in 1–2 Chronicles (2Ch 11:2; 12:5).

12:24 this is my doing Yahweh declares that the division in the kingdom fulfills his words (1Ki 11:11–13,31–39; 12:15).

12:25–33 Jeroboam, who reigned in Israel ca. 930–909 BC, implements a number of religious changes that set the northern kingdom on the path to destruction. He makes two golden calves and establishes religious centers for their worship at Bethel and Dan. Jeroboam builds these places to ensure that his citizens will not travel to the temple in Jerusalem (in the southern kingdom) to perform their religious duties. See the people diagram "King Jeroboam's Family Tree" on p. 535.

12:25 fortified Shechem Since Shechem was the site of Rehoboam's coronation (v. 1), this likely means that Jeroboam either rebuilt or fortified the city.

12:26 himself The Hebrew word used here, *lev*, literally rendered as "heart," refers to the inner person, mind, or will. People in the ancient Near East associated the heart with comprehension, not emotion.

12:28 golden calves Echoes the golden calf incident of Ex 32. People in the ancient Near East associated bovine imagery and iconography with chief male deities, including Horus (Egypt), Gugalanna (Mesopotamia), El and Baal (Canaan), and the Hittite storm god. Even Yahweh is occasionally referred to as a bull (Nu 23:22; Isa 10:13). The idiom "heat of his nostrils," meaning "anger" (e.g., Ex 15:8; Ps 18:15; Isa 11:4; Job 4:9; 15:30), also might reflect this ancient metaphor. **your gods** The Hebrew word used here, *elohim*, can be either singular or plural, allowing for the alternate renderings "your god" or "your gods." **who brought you up** The same phrase is used in Ex 32:4 to describe the golden calf Aaron and the people made in Moses' absence.

12:29 Bethel City on the southern border of the new Israelite kingdom. **Dan** City on the northern border of the new Israelite kingdom.

12:30 this thing became a sin The institution of idolatrous worship practices and the establishment of high places (see 1Ki 12:31) was a violation of the law (see Lev 26:30; Nu 33:52).

12:31 shrines on high places Presumably refers to temples to Yahweh or a comingling with pagan religious practices. The appointment of non-Levitical priests was also a violation of the law (see Dt 18:1–18).

12:32 like the festival held in Judah The OT does not prescribe any festivals in the eighth month. Since Jeroboam's festival did not follow the religious calendar prescribed by Yahweh, it was unofficial and offensive. See the table "Israelite Festivals" on p. 200.

The Man of God From Judah

13 By the word of the LORD a man of God came from Judah to Bethel, as Jeroboam was standing by the altar to make an offering. ²By the word of the LORD he cried out against the altar: "Altar, altar! This is what the LORD says: 'A son named Josiah will be born to the house of David. On you he will sacrifice the priests of the high places who make offerings here, and human bones will be burned on you.'" ³That same day the man of God gave a sign: "This is the sign the LORD has declared: The altar will be split apart and the ashes on it will be poured out."

⁴When King Jeroboam heard what the man of God cried out against the altar at Bethel, he stretched out his hand from the altar and said, "Seize him!" But the hand he stretched out toward the man shriveled up, so that he could not pull it back. ⁵Also, the altar was split apart and its ashes poured out according to the sign given by the man of God by the word of the LORD.

⁶Then the king said to the man of God, "Intercede with the LORD your God and pray for me that my hand may be restored." So the man of God interceded with the LORD, and the king's hand was restored and became as it was before.

⁷The king said to the man of God, "Come home with me for a meal, and I will give you a gift."

⁸But the man of God answered the king, "Even if you were to give me half your possessions, I would not go with you, nor would I eat bread or drink water here. ⁹For I was commanded by the word of the LORD: 'You must not eat bread or drink water or return by the way you came.'" ¹⁰So he took another road and did not return by the way he had come to Bethel.

¹¹Now there was a certain old prophet living in Bethel, whose sons came and told him all that the man of God had done there that day. They also told their father what he had said to the king. ¹²Their father asked them, "Which way did he go?" And his sons showed him which road the man of God from Judah had taken. ¹³So he said to his sons, "Saddle the donkey for me." And when they had saddled the donkey for him, he mounted it ¹⁴and rode after the man of God. He found him sitting under an oak tree and asked, "Are you the man of God who came from Judah?"

"I am," he replied.

¹⁵So the prophet said to him, "Come home with me and eat."

¹⁶The man of God said, "I cannot turn back and go with you, nor can I eat bread or drink water with you in this place. ¹⁷I have been told by the word of the LORD: 'You must not eat bread or drink water there or return by the way you came.'"

¹⁸The old prophet answered, "I too am a prophet, as you are. And an angel said to me by the word of the LORD: 'Bring him back with you to your house so that he may eat bread and drink water.'" (But he was lying to him.) ¹⁹So the man of God returned with him and ate and drank in his house.

²⁰While they were sitting at the table, the word of the LORD came to the old prophet who had brought him back. ²¹He cried out to the man of God who had come from Judah, "This is what the LORD says: 'You have defied the word of the LORD and have not kept the command the LORD your

---

13:1–10 This chapter details a man of God's confrontation with Jeroboam, and it can be split into two acts: 1Ki 13:1–10 and vv. 11–34. The chapter shows how different characters respond to the word of Yahweh and the consequences of their disobedience.

13:1 the word of the LORD This phrase appears repeatedly in ch. 13 and serves as the central theme of the passage. **to make an offering** Priests were typically responsible for making offerings.

13:2 Josiah Judah's last righteous king and reformer (2Ki 22–23). Josiah reigned ca. 640–609 BC. See the people diagram "Josiah's Family Tree" on p. 704. **human bones will be burned on you** Describes an act of disrespect to the dead and the ultimate defilement of the altar. Josiah fulfills this word of Yahweh in 2Ki 23:20.

13:3 the sign The Hebrew word used here, *mopheth* (often rendered as "portent" or "omen"), describes a miraculous sign that validates the divine word (Ex 7:9; Dt 13:2). It is often paired with the word *oth* (meaning "sign") when describing Yahweh's acts in Egypt (see Dt 4:34; 7:19). **the ashes on it will be poured out** The law instructs priests to pour out ashes of legitimate sacrifices in a "clean place" (Lev 1:16).

13:6 Intercede with the LORD The man of God did not bring this punishment upon Jeroboam, yet Jeroboam begs him to intercede.

13:7 Come home May refer to Shechem (1Ki 12:25) or a second home in Bethel, where this scene takes place (v. 1). **I will give you a gift** Those who called upon prophets customarily offered gifts (1Sa 9:7–8; 1Ki 14:3). **13:8 Even if you were to give me half your possessions** The prophet uses this idiom to declare that nothing can entice him to disobey God's word.

13:9 or return by the way you came These peculiar restrictions suggest that Yahweh has completely rejected Bethel.

13:11–34 This second half of the chapter describes the prophet's disobedience. See note on vv. 1–10.

13:11 a certain old prophet The distinction between the two main characters—the "prophet" and the "man of God"—is maintained throughout most of the narrative.

13:13 the donkey The Hebrew word used here, *chamor*, describes the common donkey, which was used for transport (e.g., Ex 4:20; 1Sa 25:42; Zec 9:9) and as a beast of burden (e.g., Ge 22:3; 1Sa 16:20). In contrast, the upper class and royalty during this period preferred the hybrid mule (the *pered*; e.g., 2Sa 13:29; 18:9). Compare 1Ki 1:33 and note.

13:16 this place Refers to Bethel.

13:18 he was lying to him The lie refers to the prophet's message, not his statement about being a prophet. He later receives the word of Yahweh (v. 20).

God gave you. ²²You came back and ate bread and drank water in the place where he told you not to eat or drink. Therefore your body will not be buried in the tomb of your ancestors.'"

²³When the man of God had finished eating and drinking, the prophet who had brought him back saddled his donkey for him. ²⁴As he went on his way, a lion met him on the road and killed him, and his body was left lying on the road, with both the donkey and the lion standing beside it. ²⁵Some people who passed by saw the body lying there, with the lion standing beside the body, and they went and reported it in the city where the old prophet lived.

²⁶When the prophet who had brought him back from his journey heard of it, he said, "It is the man of God who defied the word of the LORD. The LORD has given him over to the lion, which has mauled him and killed him, as the word of the LORD had warned him."

²⁷The prophet said to his sons, "Saddle the donkey for me," and they did so. ²⁸Then he went out and found the body lying on the road, with the donkey and the lion standing beside it. The lion had neither eaten the body nor mauled the donkey. ²⁹So the prophet picked up the body of the man of God, laid it on the donkey, and brought it back to his own city to mourn for him and bury him. ³⁰Then he laid the body in his own tomb, and they mourned over him and said, "Alas, my brother!"

³¹After burying him, he said to his sons, "When I die, bury me in the grave where the man of God is buried; lay my bones beside his bones. ³²For the message he declared by the word of the LORD against the altar in Bethel and against all the shrines on the high places in the towns of Samaria will certainly come true."

³³Even after this, Jeroboam did not change his evil ways, but once more appointed priests for the high places from all sorts of people. Anyone who wanted to become a priest he consecrated for the high places. ³⁴This was the sin of the house of Jeroboam that led to its downfall and to its destruction from the face of the earth.

Ahijah's Prophecy Against Jeroboam

14 At that time Abijah son of Jeroboam became ill, ²and Jeroboam said to his wife, "Go, disguise yourself, so you won't be recognized as the wife of Jeroboam. Then go to Shiloh. Ahijah the prophet is there — the one who told me I would be king over this people. ³Take ten loaves of bread with you, some cakes and a jar of honey, and go to him. He will tell you what will happen to the boy." ⁴So Jeroboam's wife did what he said and went to Ahijah's house in Shiloh.

Now Ahijah could not see; his sight was gone because of his age. ⁵But the LORD had told Ahijah, "Jeroboam's wife is coming to ask you about her son, for he is ill, and you are to give her such and such an answer. When she arrives, she will pretend to be someone else."

13:22 body will not be buried in the tomb of your ancestors Burial in a family plot was the custom at this time (compare Ge 47:30; 50:25). The man of God's body is further disgraced when it is left lying on the roadside (1Ki 13:24–25).

13:24 a lion met him A lion killing a man of God from Judah is ironic, since in the Bible, lion imagery is associated with Judah, the tribe of King David (Ge 49:9; Rev 5:5). The motif of a devouring lion as a means of divine punishment also is associated with Bethel (e.g., 2Ki 17:25–28). **his body** The Hebrew word *nevelah* is a degrading term referring to a carcass. It describes an unwanted body, human or animal (see Jos 8:29; 2Ki 9:37; Jer 26:23; 36:30). **and the lion standing beside** Suggests that this attack was divinely appointed.

13:26 word of the LORD This is the ninth occurrence of this phrase in ch. 13 and communicates both the origin and significance of the message (see vv. 1,2,5,9,17,18,20,21). This enigmatic story demonstrates the viewpoint of the book of Deuteronomy: Listen to the voice of God and live; listen to the voice of people and die. The first aspect of this principle is demonstrated most clearly in v. 9 when, in obedience to the word of Yahweh, the man of God refuses to associate with the king. However, vv. 18–19 demonstrates the second aspect of this principle as the man of God listens to the voice of the prophet and subsequently incurs God's wrath (vv. 20–22). This event acts as a type of foreshadowing for the rest of the narrative—which is also narrated through the viewpoint of Deuteronomy.

13:30 Alas, my brother A formulaic funerary lament (Jer 22:18; 34:5).

13:32 the message he declared See 1Ki 13:2–3, which are fulfilled in the events of 2Ki 23:15–20. **shrines on the high places** Refers to temples that were likely on hills. **Samaria** This place-name can refer to the city of Samaria or to the territory of the northern kingdom. King Omri of Israel founded the city of Samaria (see 1Ki 16:24 and note). After the Assyrian conquest and resettlement of the land (722 BC), the kingdom of Israel was renamed the province of Samaria (2Ki 17:24). Since the city of Samaria—and the province—did not exist during the events of 1Ki 13, the reference here suggests that the text was edited later. See the timeline "The Divided Kingdom" on p. 536.

13:34 This was the sin Refers to the destruction of the altar and the withering of Jeroboam's hand (vv. 4–5).

14:1–18 In 11:29–39, the prophet Ahijah told Jeroboam that if he walked in the ways of Yahweh, Yahweh would make him a dynasty (11:38). Since Jeroboam did not do so, Ahijah brings this prophecy against him. Ahijah's initial prophecy both legitimizes and condemns Jeroboam's reign (v. 11). God's promise to Jeroboam through Ahijah (11:36–39) parallels the conditional version of his covenant with David. See note on 2:4.

14:1 Abijah Means "my father is Yahweh." He is referred to both by the Hebrew word *na'ar* (meaning "boy" or "adolescent"; vv. 3,17) and *yeled* (meaning "child"; v. 12).

14:3 Take ten loaves of bread with you Those seeking advice or prayers on their behalf (intercession) from a prophet often brought the prophet a gift (1Sa 9:7; 2Ki 5:15; 8:8).

[6]So when Ahijah heard the sound of her footsteps at the door, he said, "Come in, wife of Jeroboam. Why this pretense? I have been sent to you with bad news. [7]Go, tell Jeroboam that this is what the LORD, the God of Israel, says: 'I raised you up from among the people and appointed you ruler over my people Israel. [8]I tore the kingdom away from the house of David and gave it to you, but you have not been like my servant David, who kept my commands and followed me with all his heart, doing only what was right in my eyes. [9]You have done more evil than all who lived before you. You have made for yourself other gods, idols made of metal; you have aroused my anger and turned your back on me.

[10]"'Because of this, I am going to bring disaster on the house of Jeroboam. I will cut off from Jeroboam every last male in Israel—slave or free.[a] I will burn up the house of Jeroboam as one burns dung, until it is all gone. [11]Dogs will eat those belonging to Jeroboam who die in the city, and the birds will feed on those who die in the country. The LORD has spoken!'

[12]"As for you, go back home. When you set foot in your city, the boy will die. [13]All Israel will mourn for him and bury him. He is the only one belonging to Jeroboam who will be buried, because he is the only one in the house of Jeroboam in whom the LORD, the God of Israel, has found anything good.

[14]"The LORD will raise up for himself a king over Israel who will cut off the family of Jeroboam. Even now this is beginning to happen.[b] [15]And the LORD will strike Israel, so that it will be like a reed swaying in the water. He will uproot Israel from this good land that he gave to their ancestors and scatter them beyond the Euphrates River, because they aroused the LORD's anger by making Asherah poles.[c] [16]And he will give Israel up because of the sins Jeroboam has committed and has caused Israel to commit."

[17]Then Jeroboam's wife got up and left and went to Tirzah. As soon as she stepped over the threshold of the house, the boy died. [18]They buried him, and all Israel mourned for him, as the LORD had said through his servant the prophet Ahijah.

[19]The other events of Jeroboam's reign, his wars and how he ruled, are written in the book of the annals of the kings of Israel. [20]He reigned for twenty-two years and then rested with his ancestors. And Nadab his son succeeded him as king.

Rehoboam King of Judah

14:21,25-31pp — 2Ch 12:9-16

[21]Rehoboam son of Solomon was king in Judah. He was forty-one years old when he became king, and he reigned seventeen years in Jerusalem, the city the LORD had chosen out of all the tribes of Israel in which to put his Name. His mother's name was Naamah; she was an Ammonite.

[a] 10 Or Israel—every ruler or leader   [b] 14 The meaning of the Hebrew for this sentence is uncertain.   [c] 15 That is, wooden symbols of the goddess Asherah; here and elsewhere in 1 Kings

14:7 I raised you up from among the people Refers to Ahijah's earlier prophecy concerning Jeroboam (1Ki 11:29–39).

14:9 other gods, idols made of metal The Hebrew word used here denotes "molten" or "metal images" and refers to Jeroboam's golden calves (12:28–29).

14:10 dung Used as fuel in the ancient Near East.

14:11 birds will feed on Yahweh promises the same punishment to those who break a covenant with him (Dt 28:26), suggesting that Jeroboam violated the terms of his appointment (1Ki 11:38). **LORD has spoken** Marks the closing of a divine word.

14:13 who will be buried Instead of being eaten by dogs or birds (v. 11).

14:14 a king over Israel Refers to Baasha, who assassinates Jeroboam's son, Nadab (15:27–30).

14:15 Israel The focus of the prophecy shifts from the actions of Jeroboam to the sinful ways of the whole nation. **scatter them beyond the Euphrates River** This is fulfilled when the Assyrians take control of the northern kingdom of Israel and scatter the people among Assyria's provinces in 722 BC (2Ki 17:6,24). See the timeline "The Divided Kingdom" on p. 536. **Asherah poles** Sacred poles connected to the worship of the Canaanite goddess Asherah; they are also sometimes affiliated with altars of the Canaanite god Baal (Jdg 6:25).

14:16 sins Refers to Jeroboam's installation of the golden calves and establishment of high places.

14:17 Tirzah The capital of the northern kingdom, Israel, from the time of Jeroboam (see 1Ki 15:21,33; 16:6–17) to Omri, who moved the capital to Samaria (16:23–24).

14:19-20 Jeroboam's death—like the death of most of Israel's and Judah's kings—is recounted with a fairly standardized formula.

14:19 annals of the kings of Israel The author of 1–2 Kings may have drawn from this source, which apparently is different from the Biblical book of Chronicles (given that the Chronicler refers to it, as well; see note on 1Ch 9:1). The mention of this separate volume suggests that the Biblical book of Kings was not intended to be merely a record of events; such information could be found elsewhere.

14:20 rested with his ancestors See note on 1Ki 2:10.

14:21-31 The story now returns to Rehoboam—Solomon's son and successor, and the first king to reign over the southern kingdom of Judah. First Kings 11:43—12:24 attributed the division of the kingdom to Rehoboam's foolish arrogance. In contrast, this account is subdued and lacks detail. The narrative of Rehoboam's early career (11:43—12:24) and the account of his reign presented here (vv. 21–31) likely were drawn from different sources (v. 29).

NORTHERN KING	DATE	SOUTHERN KING	DATE
Jeroboam	930–909 BC	Rehoboam	930–913 BC
Nadab	909–900 BC	Abijah	913–910 BC
Baasha	900–886 BC	Asa	910–873 BC

14:21 in which to put his Name Yahweh put his name in the temple in Jerusalem (9:3). **His mother's name**

[22]Judah did evil in the eyes of the Lord. By the sins they committed they stirred up his jealous anger more than those who were before them had done. [23]They also set up for themselves high places, sacred stones and Asherah poles on every high hill and under every spreading tree. [24]There were even male shrine prostitutes in the land; the people engaged in all the detestable practices of the nations the Lord had driven out before the Israelites.

[25]In the fifth year of King Rehoboam, Shishak king of Egypt attacked Jerusalem. [26]He carried off the treasures of the temple of the Lord and the treasures of the royal palace. He took everything, including all the gold shields Solomon had made. [27]So King Rehoboam made bronze shields to replace them and assigned these to the commanders of the guard on duty at the entrance to the royal palace. [28]Whenever the king went to the Lord's temple, the guards bore the shields, and afterward they returned them to the guardroom.

[29]As for the other events of Rehoboam's reign, and all he did, are they not written in the book of the annals of the kings of Judah? [30]There was continual warfare between Rehoboam and Jeroboam. [31]And Rehoboam rested with his ancestors and was buried with them in the City of David. His mother's name was Naamah; she was an Ammonite. And Abijah[a] his son succeeded him as king.

Abijah King of Judah

15:1-2,6-8pp — 2Ch 13:1-2,22 - 14:1

15 In the eighteenth year of the reign of Jeroboam son of Nebat, Abijah[b] became king of Judah, [2]and he reigned in Jerusalem three years. His mother's name was Maakah daughter of Abishalom.[c]

[3]He committed all the sins his father had done before him; his heart was not fully devoted to the Lord his God, as the heart of David his forefather had been. [4]Nevertheless, for David's sake the Lord his God gave him a lamp in Jerusalem by raising up a son to succeed him and by making Jerusalem strong. [5]For David had done what was right in the eyes of the Lord and had not failed to keep any of the Lord's commands all the days of his life — except in the case of Uriah the Hittite.

[6]There was war between Abijah[d] and Jeroboam throughout Abijah's lifetime. [7]As for the other events of Abijah's reign, and all he did, are they not written in the book of the annals of the kings of Judah? There was war between Abijah and Jeroboam. [8]And Abijah rested with his ancestors and was buried in the City of David. And Asa his son succeeded him as king.

Asa King of Judah

15:9-22pp — 2Ch 14:2-3; 15:16 - 16:6
15:23-24pp — 2Ch 16:11 - 17:1

[9]In the twentieth year of Jeroboam king of Israel, Asa became king of Judah, [10]and he reigned in Jerusalem forty-one years. His grandmother's name was Maakah daughter of Abishalom.

a 31 Some Hebrew manuscripts and Septuagint (see also 2 Chron. 12:16); most Hebrew manuscripts *Abijam*   *b 1* Some Hebrew manuscripts and Septuagint (see also 2 Chron. 12:16); most Hebrew manuscripts *Abijam*; also in verses 7 and 8   *c 2* A variant of *Absalom*; also in verse 10   *d 6* Some Hebrew manuscripts and Syriac *Abijam* (that is, Abijah); most Hebrew manuscripts *Rehoboam*

---

was Naamah; she was an Ammonite The narrative of 1–2 Kings notes only the mothers of those kings descended from David; thus this is a mark of prestige, even if Rehoboam bears the social stigma of his mother being a foreign wife (Dt 7:1–5; 1Ki 11:1–8).

14:24 male shrine prostitutes The Hebrew word used here denotes a sacred, consecrated person (e.g., 15:12; 22:46; 2Ki 23:7). The connection between these people and prostitution can only be inferred. Two verses in Deuteronomy have led to the association of sacred persons with prostitutes. Deuteronomy 23:17 prohibits any of the daughters or sons of Israel from becoming "shrine prostitutes." The following verse prohibits Israelites from bringing the wages of a prostitute into the house (Dt 23:18).

14:25 fifth year Dated events are rare in 1–2 Kings.
Shishak First king of the twenty-second Dynasty of Egypt (reigned ca. 931–910 BC). Shishak had harbored Jeroboam after Solomon sought to kill him (1Ki 11:40).

14:26 gold shields Solomon kept these shields in the House of the Forest of Lebanon See 10:16–17.

14:27 Rehoboam made bronze shields to replace them Signifies that the splendor of Solomon's reign was gone. **to the commanders** Rehoboam gave the shields to those who would use them, rather than keeping them in a storehouse (10:17). This also might suggest that Rehoboam needed to keep his bodyguards fully armed

at all times, a sign that the peace of Solomon's reign was gone as well.

15:1 reign of Jeroboam King over the northern kingdom, Israel. See note on 12:25–33.

15:2 Maakah daughter of Abishalom Maakah is identified as both the mother of Abijah and the mother of Asa (v. 10), Abijah's son (v. 8). The nature of their relationship is unclear since the Hebrew word for "mother" also can mean "grandmother." In v. 13, Maakah seems to have had the role of queen mother, a role she still may have had as grandmother to the reigning king.

15:3 all the sins his father had done The narrative does not mention Abijah's specific sins. He apparently allowed the abominations instituted by Rehoboam, his father, to continue (14:22–24).

15:4 lamp The Hebrew word used here, *nir* (meaning "lamp"), describes a sign of life and hope (1Sa 3:3; 2Sa 21:17).

15:5 except in the case of Uriah the Hittite The only misdeed (2Sa 11) mentioned in this praise of David (compare 1Ki 3:6; 9:4; 11:38).

15:6 Abijah Several manuscripts read "Rehoboam" here, while others read "Abijah" (see 14:30; 15:7).

15:9 Asa became king of Judah Asa reigned from approximately 910–873 BC. Six different northern kings ruled during Asa's reign in the south. The author of 1–2 Chronicles gives more details about his reign. See

[11]Asa did what was right in the eyes of the LORD, as his father David had done. [12]He expelled the male shrine prostitutes from the land and got rid of all the idols his ancestors had made. [13]He even deposed his grandmother Maakah from her position as queen mother, because she had made a repulsive image for the worship of Asherah. Asa cut it down and burned it in the Kidron Valley. [14]Although he did not remove the high places, Asa's heart was fully committed to the LORD all his life. [15]He brought into the temple of the LORD the silver and gold and the articles that he and his father had dedicated.

[16]There was war between Asa and Baasha king of Israel throughout their reigns. [17]Baasha king of Israel went up against Judah and fortified Ramah to prevent anyone from leaving or entering the territory of Asa king of Judah.

[18]Asa then took all the silver and gold that was left in the treasuries of the LORD's temple and of his own palace. He entrusted it to his officials and sent them to Ben-Hadad son of Tabrimmon, the son of Hezion, the king of Aram, who was ruling in Damascus. [19]"Let there be a treaty between me and you," he said, "as there was between my father and your father. See, I am sending you a gift of silver and gold. Now break your treaty with Baasha king of Israel so he will withdraw from me."

[20]Ben-Hadad agreed with King Asa and sent the commanders of his forces against the towns of Israel. He conquered Ijon, Dan, Abel Beth Maakah and all Kinnereth in addition to Naphtali. [21]When Baasha heard this, he stopped building Ramah and withdrew to Tirzah. [22]Then King Asa issued an order to all Judah — no one was exempt — and they carried away from Ramah the stones and timber Baasha had been using there. With them King Asa built up Geba in Benjamin, and also Mizpah.

[23]As for all the other events of Asa's reign, all his achievements, all he did and the cities he built, are they not written in the book of the annals of the kings of Judah? In his old age, however, his feet became diseased. [24]Then Asa rested with his ancestors and was buried with them in the city of his father David. And Jehoshaphat his son succeeded him as king.

Nadab King of Israel

[25]Nadab son of Jeroboam became king of Israel in the second year of Asa king of Judah, and he reigned over Israel two years. [26]He did evil in the eyes of the LORD, following the ways of his father and committing the same sin his father had caused Israel to commit.

[27]Baasha son of Ahijah from the tribe of Issachar plotted against him, and he struck him down at Gibbethon, a Philistine town, while Nadab and all Israel were besieging it. [28]Baasha killed Nadab in the third year of Asa king of Judah and succeeded him as king.

2Ch 14:1 — 16:14 and note. See the timeline "The Divided Kingdom" on p. 536.

NORTHERN KING	DATE
Nadab	909–900 BC
Baasha	900–886 BC
Elah	886–885 BC
Zimri	885 BC
Omri	885–874 BC
Ahab	874–853 BC

KING OF ARAM/SYRIA	DATE	SOUTHERN KING	DATE
Tabrimmon	930–885 BC	Rehoboam	930–913 BC
Ben-Hadad I	885–860 BC	Abijah	913–910 BC
Ben-Hadad II (Hadadezer)	860–843 BC	Asa	910–873 BC

15:13 from her position as queen mother The Hebrew word used here, *gevirah* (meaning "queen mother"), is an official title. The exact function of this office is unclear. **Asherah** A Canaanite goddess. **Kidron Valley** Runs along Jerusalem's eastern border. The Kidron Valley became a common disposal site for idols (e.g., 2Ki 23:6,12; 2Ch 15:16).
15:14 high places Refers to a site for pagan worship.
15:16 Baasha king of Israel See 15:27 — 16:7.
15:17 Ramah A city located five miles north of Jerusalem; originally allotted to the tribe of Benjamin (Jos 18:25).
15:18 the silver and gold that was left Refers to the treasures that still remained following the raid of Shishak, king of Egypt (1Ki 14:25–26). These gifts had been dedicated to Yahweh by Asa's ancestors and stored in the temple. **Ben-Hadad son of Tabrimmon** Asa asks for military aid from the king of Aram (also called "Syria"), Israel's northern neighbor.

15:19 he will withdraw from me Asa's immediate reaction was to request aid rather than confront Baasha. This suggests that the kingdom of Judah was politically and militarily weaker than the kingdom of Israel at this time. Aram (Syria) also served as a strategic ally for Judah against Israel due to Israel's geographic position (with Judah to the south and Syria to the north).

15:20 The cities in this verse cover the entire Upper Galilee region, down to the Sea of Galilee. These towns are listed from north to south.

15:22 Geba in Benjamin, and also Mizpah Those who controlled these two locations also controlled the north — south mountain road that leads to and from Jerusalem. As a result, Asa turned the tables on Baasha's blockade.
15:23 In his old age, however, his feet became diseased Implies that this disease led to his death.
15:24 Jehoshaphat his son succeeded him as king See 22:41–50; see the people diagram "King Jehoshaphat's Family Tree" on p. 681.
15:25 Nadab The only descendent of Jeroboam to rule over Israel. He reigned ca. 909–900 BC.
15:26 committing the same sin his father had caused

²⁹As soon as he began to reign, he killed Jeroboam's whole family. He did not leave Jeroboam anyone that breathed, but destroyed them all, according to the word of the LORD given through his servant Ahijah the Shilonite. ³⁰This happened because of the sins Jeroboam had committed and had caused Israel to commit, and because he aroused the anger of the LORD, the God of Israel.

³¹As for the other events of Nadab's reign, and all he did, are they not written in the book of the annals of the kings of Israel? ³²There was war between Asa and Baasha king of Israel throughout their reigns.

Baasha King of Israel

³³In the third year of Asa king of Judah, Baasha son of Ahijah became king of all Israel in Tirzah, and he reigned twenty-four years. ³⁴He did evil in the eyes of the LORD, following the ways of Jeroboam and committing the same sin Jeroboam had caused Israel to commit.

16 Then the word of the LORD came to Jehu son of Hanani concerning Baasha: ²"I lifted you up from the dust and appointed you ruler over my people Israel, but you followed the ways of Jeroboam and caused my people Israel to sin and to arouse my anger by their sins. ³So I am about to wipe out Baasha and his house, and I will make your house like that of Jeroboam son of Nebat. ⁴Dogs will eat those belonging to Baasha who die in the city, and birds will feed on those who die in the country."

⁵As for the other events of Baasha's reign, what he did and his achievements, are they not written in the book of the annals of the kings of Israel? ⁶Baasha rested with his ancestors and was buried in Tirzah. And Elah his son succeeded him as king.

⁷Moreover, the word of the LORD came through the prophet Jehu son of Hanani to Baasha and his house, because of all the evil he had done in the eyes of the LORD, arousing his anger by the things he did, becoming like the house of Jeroboam—and also because he destroyed it.

Elah King of Israel

⁸In the twenty-sixth year of Asa king of Judah, Elah son of Baasha became king of Israel, and he reigned in Tirzah two years.

⁹Zimri, one of his officials, who had command of half his chariots, plotted against him. Elah was in Tirzah at the time, getting drunk in the home of Arza, the palace administrator at Tirzah. ¹⁰Zimri came in, struck him down and killed him in the twenty-seventh year of Asa king of Judah. Then he succeeded him as king.

¹¹As soon as he began to reign and was seated on the throne, he killed off Baasha's whole family. He did not spare a single male, whether relative or friend. ¹²So Zimri destroyed the whole family of Baasha, in accordance with the word of the LORD spoken against Baasha through the prophet Jehu— ¹³because of all the sins Baasha and his son Elah had committed and had caused Israel to commit, so that they aroused the anger of the LORD, the God of Israel, by their worthless idols.

¹⁴As for the other events of Elah's reign, and all he did, are they not written in the book of the annals of the kings of Israel?

Israel to commit As with Abijah (see v. 3), the narrative does not mention Nadab's specific sins.

15:27 Issachar One of the 12 tribes of Israel. **Gibbethon** A Levitical city in the territory of the tribe of Dan (Jos 19:44; 21:23). It is located just a few miles west of Gezer, meaning that the Philistines had pushed their way inland by this time (compare 1Ki 16:15).

15:29 he killed Jeroboam's whole family Baasha thoroughly eliminated political competition (compare 16:12; 2Ki 10:1–11). **according to the word of the LORD** See the prophecy of Ahijah in 1Ki 14:7–16.

15:30 he aroused the anger of the LORD Yahweh is provoked because Israel worshiped other gods (Ex 20:5).

15:34 the ways of Jeroboam Refers to Jeroboam's installation of the golden calves and establishment of high places for worship (see 1Ki 12:28–30; note on 12:28).

16:1 Jehu son of Hanani This is the only episode about Jehu in 1–2 Kings. In contrast, 1–2 Chronicles incorporates other traditions concerning him (2Ch 16:7; 19:2–3; 20:34).

16:2–4 These verses refer to a prophecy that is otherwise unknown. This suggests that a prophet or prophecy may have supported Baasha's rise to the throne, similar to Ahijah's support of Jeroboam (1Ki 11:29–39).

16:2 the ways of Jeroboam Indicates that practices initiated by Jeroboam—primarily the worship of golden calves and other idols—continued under Baasha (see 1Ki 12:28–30; note on 12:28).

16:3 like that of Jeroboam This prophecy against Baasha resembles Ahijah's prophecy against Jeroboam (14:10–11).

16:4 birds will feed on These terms were likely the same as those presented in Jeroboam's prophecy (see 14:11 and note).

16:5 annals of the kings of Israel See note on 14:19.

16:6 rested with his ancestors See note on 2:10.

16:8 twenty-sixth year of Asa See note on 15:9.

16:9 Zimri This name later becomes an insult, indicating someone who murders his or her master (2Ki 9:31). **Tirzah** Capital of the northern kingdom of Israel at this time.

16:11 Baasha's whole family Like Baasha, Zimri eliminates political competition (Jdg 9:1–6; 1Ki 15:29; 2Ki 10:1–11).

16:13 their worthless idols The Hebrew word used here, *hevel*, means "meaningless," "vapor," "breath" or "vanity" (compare vv. 26; Ecc 1:2). *Hevel* does not directly relate to idols, but it often appears in reference to them (see Jer 10:15; 16:19; 51:18). Israel's "following after *hevel*" is the official reason for the fall of the northern kingdom (2Ki 17:15).

Zimri King of Israel

¹⁵In the twenty-seventh year of Asa king of Judah, Zimri reigned in Tirzah seven days. The army was encamped near Gibbethon, a Philistine town. ¹⁶When the Israelites in the camp heard that Zimri had plotted against the king and murdered him, they proclaimed Omri, the commander of the army, king over Israel that very day there in the camp. ¹⁷Then Omri and all the Israelites with him withdrew from Gibbethon and laid siege to Tirzah. ¹⁸When Zimri saw that the city was taken, he went into the citadel of the royal palace and set the palace on fire around him. So he died, ¹⁹because of the sins he had committed, doing evil in the eyes of the LORD and following the ways of Jeroboam and committing the same sin Jeroboam had caused Israel to commit.

²⁰As for the other events of Zimri's reign, and the rebellion he carried out, are they not written in the book of the annals of the kings of Israel?

Omri King of Israel

²¹Then the people of Israel were split into two factions; half supported Tibni son of Ginath for king, and the other half supported Omri. ²²But Omri's followers proved stronger than those of Tibni son of Ginath. So Tibni died and Omri became king.

²³In the thirty-first year of Asa king of Judah, Omri became king of Israel, and he reigned twelve years, six of them in Tirzah. ²⁴He bought the hill of Samaria from Shemer for two talents*a* of silver and built a city on the hill, calling it Samaria, after Shemer, the name of the former owner of the hill.

²⁵But Omri did evil in the eyes of the LORD and sinned more than all those before him. ²⁶He followed completely the ways of Jeroboam son of Nebat, committing the same sin Jeroboam had caused Israel to commit, so that they aroused the anger of the LORD, the God of Israel, by their worthless idols.

²⁷As for the other events of Omri's reign, what he did and the things he achieved, are they not written in the book of the annals of the kings of Israel? ²⁸Omri rested with his ancestors and was buried in Samaria. And Ahab his son succeeded him as king.

Ahab Becomes King of Israel

²⁹In the thirty-eighth year of Asa king of Judah, Ahab son of Omri became king of Israel, and he reigned in Samaria over Israel twenty-two years. ³⁰Ahab son of Omri did more evil in the eyes of the LORD than any of those before him. ³¹He not only considered it trivial to commit the sins of Jeroboam son of Nebat, but he also married Jezebel daughter of Ethbaal king of the Sidonians,

a 24 That is, about 150 pounds or about 68 kilograms

16:15 Gibbethon See note on 1Ki 15:27.

16:19 he had committed The account of Zimri's brief seven-day reign in 885 BC records the backlash of his coup. It is difficult to know what sins he committed within this week.

16:21–28 Omri is one of few individuals from the Bible whose name has been preserved in another source. An inscription on the Mesha Stele (a pillar or obelisk that dates to about 830 BC) mentions the Israelite kings Omri and Ahab by name (see note on 2Ki 3:1–27). The archeological site associated with Samaria, Omri's capital, attests to the grandeur and prosperity of the Omride dynasty. See the infographic "The Mesha Stele" on p. 565.

OMRIDE DYNASTY	885–841 BC
Omri	885–874 BC
Ahab	874–853 BC
Ahaziah	853–852 BC
Joram/Jehoram	852–841 BC

16:21 Tibni Nothing more is known about this individual.
16:23 he reigned twelve years, six of them in Tirzah Omri captured Tirzah from Zimri (1Ki 16:18).
16:24 Samaria This region of the central highlands of Israel was deep in the heart of Israelite territory. The hill where Omri built this new capital city for the northern kingdom offered a commanding view of the surrounding area.

1 Kings 16:24

SAMARIA
Samaria, the capital city of the northern kingdom of Israel, was strategically located at the intersection of major highways and sat atop a hill 300 feet over the surrounding valleys. The site was about 25 miles east of the Mediterranean and about 40 miles north of Jerusalem. The Assyrians destroyed the city in 722 BC.

The city of Samaria was rebuilt after the Assyrian destruction and served as the administrative center for the province of Samaria under Assyrian, Babylonian and Persian rule. Samaria was an important regional center into Roman times. The Hasmonean ruler John Hyrcanus destroyed the city in 108 BC, but Herod the Great rebuilt it around 30 BC and renamed it Sebaste.

16:26 the ways of Jeroboam The idolatry initiated by Jeroboam apparently continued during Omri's reign (see 1Ki 12:28–30).

16:29–34 These six verses set the backdrop for the story of Elijah (1Ki 17—2 Ki 2) and introduce King Ahab, whose story continues in chs. 18; 20–22. See the people diagram "King Ahab's Family Tree" on p. 546.

16:31 He not only considered it trivial Ahab goes beyond Jeroboam's sins (involving the golden calves and the high places; 1Ki 12:28–33) and draws Israel into

and began to serve Baal and worship him. ³²He set up an altar for Baal in the temple of Baal that he built in Samaria. ³³Ahab also made an Asherah pole and did more to arouse the anger of the LORD, the God of Israel, than did all the kings of Israel before him.

King Ahab's Family Tree

Omri

Ethbaal

Ahab

Jezebel

Athaliah   Joram   Ahaziah

³⁴In Ahab's time, Hiel of Bethel rebuilt Jericho. He laid its foundations at the cost of his firstborn son Abiram, and he set up its gates at the cost of his youngest son Segub, in accordance with the word of the LORD spoken by Joshua son of Nun.

Elijah Announces a Great Drought

17 Now Elijah the Tishbite, from Tishbe[a] in Gilead, said to Ahab, "As the LORD, the God of Israel, lives, whom I serve, there will be neither dew nor rain in the next few years except at my word."

Elijah Fed by Ravens

²Then the word of the LORD came to Elijah: ³"Leave here, turn eastward and hide in the Kerith Ravine, east of the Jordan. ⁴You will drink from the brook, and I have directed the ravens to supply you with food there."

⁵So he did what the LORD had told him. He went to the Kerith Ravine, east of the Jordan, and stayed there. ⁶The ravens brought him bread and meat in the morning and bread and meat in the evening, and he drank from the brook.

Elijah and the Widow at Zarephath

⁷Some time later the brook dried up because there had been no rain in the land. ⁸Then the word of the LORD came to him: ⁹"Go at once to Zarephath in the region of Sidon and stay there. I have directed a widow there to supply you with food." ¹⁰So he went to Zarephath. When he came to the town gate, a widow was there gathering sticks. He called to her and asked, "Would you bring me a little water in a jar so I may have a drink?" ¹¹As

---

[a] 1 Or *Tishbite, of the settlers*

---

a political and religious relationship with the Sidonians, who worshiped Baal, the Canaanite storm god. **Sidonians** Refers to the people of Sidon, a major Canaanite and Phoenician city-state on the Mediterranean coast.
16:33 an Asherah pole Typically refers to a sacred pole used to worship the Canaanite goddess Asherah, but worship of the Canaanite god Baal and Asherah were often affiliated (Jdg 6:25–30).
16:34 laid its foundations Laying the foundation and setting up the gates mark the beginning and end of the construction process. **spoken by Joshua** After the fall of Jericho, Joshua set a curse against any who would rebuild the city (Jos 6:26). This may explain the deaths of Hiel's firstborn and youngest sons, who may or may not have been involved in the actual construction of Jericho. See the infographic "Ancient Jericho" on p. 330.

17:1–7 The catalog of the kings of Israel and Judah (1Ki 15–16) is interrupted by a series of stories (1Ki 17 — 2Ki 2) about the prophet Elijah and his conflicts with Ahab, king of Israel (16:29–34). The story about Elijah and the drought continues through ch. 18.

17:1 As the LORD, the God of Israel, lives A statement indicating that a formal oath will follow. **there will be neither dew nor rain** A form of divine punishment. Israel's behavior determines the weather and fertility of the land (Dt 11:13–17; compare 1Ki 8:35; 18:41–46).

FAMINE	REFERENCE
Three-Year Famine in the Time of David	2Sa 21:1
Famine in the Northern Kingdom in the Time of Elijah and Ahab	1Ki 17:1; 18:1–2
Famine in the Time of Elisha	2Ki 4:38

17:3 Kerith Ravine An unidentified riverbed.
17:4 You will drink from the brook Indicates a miracle; riverbeds in Israel dried up for most of the year.

17:8–16 The drought mentioned in vv. 1–7 sets the stage for this scene. The story of the widow of Zarephath demonstrates God's care for both his prophet, Elijah, and the poor woman's household.

she was going to get it, he called, "And bring me, please, a piece of bread."

12"As surely as the LORD your God lives," she replied, "I don't have any bread — only a handful of flour in a jar and a little olive oil in a jug. I am gathering a few sticks to take home and make a meal for myself and my son, that we may eat it — and die."

13Elijah said to her, "Don't be afraid. Go home and do as you have said. But first make a small loaf of bread for me from what you have and bring it to me, and then make something for yourself and your son. 14For this is what the LORD, the God of Israel, says: 'The jar of flour will not be used up and the jug of oil will not run dry until the day the LORD sends rain on the land.'"

15She went away and did as Elijah had told her. So there was food every day for Elijah and for the woman and her family. 16For the jar of flour was not used up and the jug of oil did not run dry, in keeping with the word of the LORD spoken by Elijah.

17Some time later the son of the woman who owned the house became ill. He grew worse and worse, and finally stopped breathing. 18She said to Elijah, "What do you have against me, man of God? Did you come to remind me of my sin and kill my son?"

19"Give me your son," Elijah replied. He took him from her arms, carried him to the upper room where he was staying, and laid him on his bed. 20Then he cried out to the LORD, "LORD my God, have you brought tragedy even on this widow I am staying with, by causing her son to die?" 21Then he stretched himself out on the boy three times and cried out to the LORD, "LORD my God, let this boy's life return to him!"

22The LORD heard Elijah's cry, and the boy's life returned to him, and he lived. 23Elijah picked up the child and carried him down from the room into the house. He gave him to his mother and said, "Look, your son is alive!"

24Then the woman said to Elijah, "Now I know that you are a man of God and that the word of the LORD from your mouth is the truth."

Elijah and Obadiah

18 After a long time, in the third year, the word of the LORD came to Elijah: "Go and present yourself to Ahab, and I will send rain on the land." 2So Elijah went to present himself to Ahab.

Now the famine was severe in Samaria, 3and Ahab had summoned Obadiah, his palace administrator. (Obadiah was a devout believer in the LORD. 4While Jezebel was killing off the LORD's prophets, Obadiah had taken a hundred prophets and hidden them in two caves, fifty in each, and had supplied them with food and water.) 5Ahab had said to Obadiah, "Go through the land to all the springs and valleys. Maybe we can find some grass to keep the horses and mules alive so we will not have to kill any of our animals." 6So they divided the land they were to cover, Ahab going in one direction and Obadiah in another.

17:9 Zarephath A Phoenician city on the Mediterranean coast.

17:10 a widow She was presumably newly widowed, since she could be recognized by her mourning garment (compare Ge 38:14).

17:14 until the day the LORD sends rain Three years later (1Ki 18:1), after the drought and the accompanying famine.

17:15 There was food every day for Elijah and for the woman and her family Apparently Elijah lived with the widow and her son for at least a period of time (v. 19).

17:17–24 Elijah's reviving of the widow's son demonstrates the effectiveness of his petition and his ability to mediate divine power. It sets the stage for the more dramatic, large-scale events that follow (18:20–46). See the table "Miracles of the Prophets" on p. 1366.

17:17 finally stopped breathing The Hebrew word used here, *neshamah*, describes the force that animates all living creatures (Ge 2:7; Dt 20:16; Jos 11:11,14). Its loss marks the end of life (Job 34:14–15).

17:18 man of God This title designates a prophet or messenger of God. It also is used in reference to Moses (Dt 33:1).

17:21 three times A common number in rituals. **life** The Hebrew word used here, *nephesh*, is typically translated "soul," but can also refer to "breath," "life" or "inner being." See note on 1Ki 2:4.

17:22 he lived The Hebrew word *chayah* simply means "to live," but is sometimes translated as "he revived."

The child is never referred to using the Hebrew word *mwtmwt*, meaning "dead."

17:24 Now I know that The revival of the widow's son elicits an affirmation of Elijah's prophetic office, a response not present with the miracle of the flour and oil (v. 16).

18:1–19 The account of Ahab's reign is intertwined with the account of Elijah's prophetic activities. The story of Elijah confronting Ahab sets the stage for a contest between Yahweh and Baal, the Canaanite storm god. Israel's worship of Baal is attributed to king Ahab and his wife, Jezebel, who instituted Baal worship on a national level (16:31–32). See the table "Pagan Deities of the Old Testament" on p. 1287.

18:1 Ahab See 16:29–34; see the people diagram "King Ahab's Family Tree" on p. 546.

18:2 Samaria The capital city established under Ahab's father, Omri (see note on 16:24).

18:3 Obadiah The Obadiah who prophesied against Edom, whose oracles appear in the book of Obadiah, is likely a different person. **his palace administrator** Refers to the royal residence in Samaria. It is unclear what responsibilities Obadiah's position entailed; it was likely the highest attainable office in the ancient Near East, making Obadiah second only to King Ahab (Ge 39:4–5; 41:40–45; 1Ki 4:6; 2Ki 15:5; Isa 22:15–24).

18:4 caves The Hebrew word here suggests a specific cave or set of caves. Since the following scene occurs on Mount Carmel (1Ki 18:19–40), tradition holds that

⁷As Obadiah was walking along, Elijah met him. Obadiah recognized him, bowed down to the ground, and said, "Is it really you, my lord Elijah?"

⁸"Yes," he replied. "Go tell your master, 'Elijah is here.'"

⁹"What have I done wrong," asked Obadiah, "that you are handing your servant over to Ahab to be put to death? ¹⁰As surely as the LORD your God lives, there is not a nation or kingdom where my master has not sent someone to look for you. And whenever a nation or kingdom claimed you were not there, he made them swear they could not find you. ¹¹But now you tell me to go to my master and say, 'Elijah is here.' ¹²I don't know where the Spirit of the LORD may carry you when I leave you. If I go and tell Ahab and he doesn't find you, he will kill me. Yet I your servant have worshiped the LORD since my youth. ¹³Haven't you heard, my lord, what I did while Jezebel was killing the prophets of the LORD? I hid a hundred of the LORD's prophets in two caves, fifty in each, and supplied them with food and water. ¹⁴And now you tell me to go to my master and say, 'Elijah is here.' He will kill me!"

¹⁵Elijah said, "As the LORD Almighty lives, whom I serve, I will surely present myself to Ahab today."

Elijah on Mount Carmel

¹⁶So Obadiah went to meet Ahab and told him, and Ahab went to meet Elijah. ¹⁷When he saw Elijah, he said to him, "Is that you, you troubler of Israel?"

¹⁸"I have not made trouble for Israel," Elijah replied. "But you and your father's family have. You have abandoned the LORD's commands and have followed the Baals. ¹⁹Now summon the people from all over Israel to meet me on Mount Carmel. And bring the four hundred and fifty prophets of Baal and the four hundred prophets of Asherah, who eat at Jezebel's table."

²⁰So Ahab sent word throughout all Israel and assembled the prophets on Mount Carmel. ²¹Elijah went before the people and said, "How long will you waver between two opinions? If the LORD is God, follow him; but if Baal is God, follow him."

But the people said nothing.

²²Then Elijah said to them, "I am the only one of the LORD's prophets left, but Baal has four hundred and fifty prophets. ²³Get two bulls for us. Let Baal's prophets choose one for themselves, and let them cut it into pieces and put it on the wood but not set fire to it. I will prepare the other bull and put it on the wood but not set fire to it. ²⁴Then you call on the name of your god, and I will call on the name of the LORD. The god who answers by fire — he is God."

Then all the people said, "What you say is good."

²⁵Elijah said to the prophets of Baal, "Choose one of the bulls and prepare it first, since there are so many of you. Call on the name of your god, but do not light the fire." ²⁶So they took the bull given them and prepared it.

Then they called on the name of Baal from morning till noon. "Baal, answer us!" they shouted. But there was no response; no one answered. And they danced around the altar they had made.

---

the cave(s) of the prophets were in the Carmel mountain range.

18:7 recognized him Elijah was recognizable because he wore a hairy garment with a leather belt (2Ki 1:8).
my lord Elijah Referring to Elijah as "lord" or "master" suggests that Obadiah willingly subjected himself to the prophet, despite being Elijah's superior.
18:9 to be put to death Obadiah expresses this fear three times (vv. 9,12,14).
18:10 As surely as the LORD your God lives A formula indicating that a formal oath will follow. **he made them swear** Since Elijah's words threatened Ahab's regime, the king could call upon his allies to search for Elijah and extradite him.
18:12 Spirit of the LORD The Hebrew word used here, *ruach*, means "breath," "wind" or "spirit," which fits with the idea of Yahweh's Spirit carrying someone from one location (or activity) to another — it can move them and be in them.
18:15 LORD Almighty A common title for God used by the prophets. The Hebrew word term used here, *yhwh tseva'ot* (literally rendered as "Yahweh of armies"), portrays Yahweh as the commander of either Israel's army or the heavenly hosts.
18:17 you troubler The Hebrew word used here, *okheri*, denotes the idea of causing a disturbance or stirring up trouble.
18:18 Baals Refers to various renderings of the Canaanite storm god, Baal. See the table "Pagan Deities of the Old Testament" on p. 1287.

DEITY	COUNTRY
Asherah	Canaan
Baal	Canaan
Chemosh	Moab
Molek	Ammon

18:19 Mount Carmel A mountain range that extends to the Mediterranean coast near the modern city of Haifa. This particular mountain is symbolic of fertility and grandeur (compare Isa 35:2; Jer 50:19).

18:20–40 First Kings 18:20–40 records the contest between Elijah and the prophets of Baal. The miraculous burning of the sacrifice to Yahweh serves a double purpose: It turns Israel's heart back to him and results in the deaths of 450 prophets of Baal.

18:21 opinions The Hebrew word used here, *sa'ip*, typically refers to the boughs of a tree (Isa 17:6; Eze 31:6,8) or clefts in a rock (Isa 2:21; 57:5), but it also can refer to divided thoughts (Job 4:13; 20:2). The usage here creates the image of a bird hopping between branches or rock clefts.
18:22 only one of the LORD's prophets left An exaggeration, since 100 of Yahweh's prophets have already been mentioned (1Ki 18:4,13), and other prophets of Yahweh are mentioned later (20:13; 22:1–28).
18:24 you call on the name of your god Assumes that all the people of Israel worship Baal.

²⁷At noon Elijah began to taunt them. "Shout louder!" he said. "Surely he is a god! Perhaps he is deep in thought, or busy, or traveling. Maybe he is sleeping and must be awakened." ²⁸So they shouted louder and slashed themselves with swords and spears, as was their custom, until their blood flowed. ²⁹Midday passed, and they continued their frantic prophesying until the time for the evening sacrifice. But there was no response, no one answered, no one paid attention.

³⁰Then Elijah said to all the people, "Come here to me." They came to him, and he repaired the altar of the LORD, which had been torn down. ³¹Elijah took twelve stones, one for each of the tribes descended from Jacob, to whom the word of the LORD had come, saying, "Your name shall be Israel." ³²With the stones he built an altar in the name of the LORD, and he dug a trench around it large enough to hold two seahs^a of seed. ³³He arranged the wood, cut the bull into pieces and laid it on the wood. Then he said to them, "Fill four large jars with water and pour it on the offering and on the wood."

³⁴"Do it again," he said, and they did it again.

"Do it a third time," he ordered, and they did it the third time. ³⁵The water ran down around the altar and even filled the trench.

³⁶At the time of sacrifice, the prophet Elijah stepped forward and prayed: "LORD, the God of Abraham, Isaac and Israel, let it be known today that you are God in Israel and that I am your servant and have done all these things at your command. ³⁷Answer me, LORD, answer me, so these people will know that you, LORD, are God, and that you are turning their hearts back again."

³⁸Then the fire of the LORD fell and burned up the sacrifice, the wood, the stones and the soil, and also licked up the water in the trench.

³⁹When all the people saw this, they fell prostrate and cried, "The LORD — he is God! The LORD — he is God!"

⁴⁰Then Elijah commanded them, "Seize the prophets of Baal. Don't let anyone get away!" They seized them, and Elijah had them brought down to the Kishon Valley and slaughtered there.

⁴¹And Elijah said to Ahab, "Go, eat and drink, for there is the sound of a heavy rain." ⁴²So Ahab went off to eat and drink, but Elijah climbed to the top of Carmel, bent down to the ground and put his face between his knees.

⁴³"Go and look toward the sea," he told his servant. And he went up and looked.

"There is nothing there," he said.

Seven times Elijah said, "Go back."

⁴⁴The seventh time the servant reported, "A cloud as small as a man's hand is rising from the sea."

So Elijah said, "Go and tell Ahab, 'Hitch up your chariot and go down before the rain stops you.'"

⁴⁵Meanwhile, the sky grew black with clouds, the wind rose, a heavy rain started falling and Ahab rode off to Jezreel. ⁴⁶The power of the LORD came on Elijah and, tucking his cloak into his belt, he ran ahead of Ahab all the way to Jezreel.

Elijah Flees to Horeb

19 Now Ahab told Jezebel everything Elijah had done and how he had killed all the prophets with the sword. ²So Jezebel sent a messenger to Elijah to say, "May the gods deal with me, be it ever so severely, if by this time tomorrow I do not make your life like that of one of them."

³Elijah was afraid^b and ran for his life. When he came to Beersheba in Judah, he left his servant

---

^a 32 That is, probably about 24 pounds or about 11 kilograms
^b 3 Or Elijah saw

18:26 they danced around the altar Possibly refers to a ritual dance. See the table "Altars in the Old Testament" on p. 249.

18:28 slashed themselves A sign of mourning and distress that was outlawed for the Israelites (Dt 14:1; Lev 19:28; 21:5).

18:30 repaired the altar of the LORD The people of Israel apparently had disassembled the altars of Yahweh throughout the land (1Ki 19:10).

18:31 Elijah took twelve stones Marks the participation of the "original" Israel—the 12 tribes that were divided into the kingdoms of Israel and Judah.

18:38 fire of the LORD Fire often symbolizes Yahweh's presence (Ex 3:2; 19:18; Lev 9:24; 2Ch 7:3), divine approval (Jdg 6:21; 1Ch 21:26; 2Ch 7:1) and divine judgment (Nu 11:1; 16:35).

18:40 Kishon Valley The Wadi Kishon gathers the runoff from the many springs and streams in the Jezreel Valley and directs the waters west, past Mount Carmel and into the Mediterranean Sea.

18:41–46 After three years of drought (1Ki 18:1), Elijah intercedes and rain returns to the land.

18:43 Go They may ascend to a different peak; Elijah and his servant are already on top of Mount Carmel (v. 42).

18:46 The power of the LORD A phrase used to indicate an extreme sensory experience (see Eze 1:3). **he ran ahead of Ahab** Elijah miraculously outruns Ahab's chariot.

19:1–8 The account of Elijah's flight from Jezebel contains many allusions to traditions about Moses: 40 days and nights in the wilderness (Ex 24:18; 1Ki 19:8), the lack of bread and water (Ex 34:28; 1Ki 19:8), and waiting in a cave in anticipation of a theophany, or divine appearance (Ex 33:22; 1Ki 19:8). See the table "Old Testament Theophanies" on p. 924.

19:2 May the gods deal Similar oaths are used throughout 1–2 Kings (e.g., 1Ki 2:23; 20:10; 2Ki 6:31).

19:3 afraid Hebrew manuscripts use a word that denotes "he saw," but Greek, Syriac and Latin manuscripts read "he was afraid." **to Beersheba** Elijah presumably flees from Mount Carmel (1Ki 18:42). He runs a distance of approximately 125 miles (200 km)—plus a day's journey (v. 4)—in less than 24 hours (v. 2; see 18:46

there, [4]while he himself went a day's journey into the wilderness. He came to a broom bush, sat down under it and prayed that he might die. "I have had enough, LORD," he said. "Take my life; I am no better than my ancestors." [5]Then he lay down under the bush and fell asleep.

All at once an angel touched him and said, "Get up and eat." [6]He looked around, and there by his head was some bread baked over hot coals, and a jar of water. He ate and drank and then lay down again.

[7]The angel of the LORD came back a second time and touched him and said, "Get up and eat, for the journey is too much for you." [8]So he got up and ate and drank. Strengthened by that food, he traveled forty days and forty nights until he reached Horeb, the mountain of God. [9]There he went into a cave and spent the night.

The LORD Appears to Elijah

And the word of the LORD came to him: "What are you doing here, Elijah?"

[10]He replied, "I have been very zealous for the LORD God Almighty. The Israelites have rejected your covenant, torn down your altars, and put your prophets to death with the sword. I am the only one left, and now they are trying to kill me too."

[11]The LORD said, "Go out and stand on the mountain in the presence of the LORD, for the LORD is about to pass by."

Then a great and powerful wind tore the mountains apart and shattered the rocks before the LORD, but the LORD was not in the wind. After the wind there was an earthquake, but the LORD was not in the earthquake. [12]After the earthquake came a fire, but the LORD was not in the fire. And after the fire came a gentle whisper. [13]When Elijah heard it, he pulled his cloak over his face and went out and stood at the mouth of the cave.

Then a voice said to him, "What are you doing here, Elijah?"

[14]He replied, "I have been very zealous for the LORD God Almighty. The Israelites have rejected your covenant, torn down your altars, and put your prophets to death with the sword. I am the only one left, and now they are trying to kill me too."

[15]The LORD said to him, "Go back the way you came, and go to the Desert of Damascus. When you get there, anoint Hazael king over Aram. [16]Also, anoint Jehu son of Nimshi king over Israel, and anoint Elisha son of Shaphat from Abel Meholah to succeed you as prophet. [17]Jehu will put to death any who escape the sword of Hazael, and Elisha will put to death any who escape the sword of Jehu. [18]Yet I reserve seven thousand in Israel — all whose knees have not bowed down to Baal and whose mouths have not kissed him."

The Call of Elisha

[19]So Elijah went from there and found Elisha son of Shaphat. He was plowing with twelve yoke of oxen, and he himself was driving the twelfth pair. Elijah went up to him and threw his cloak around him. [20]Elisha then left his oxen and ran after Elijah. "Let me kiss my father and mother goodbye," he said, "and then I will come with you."

"Go back," Elijah replied. "What have I done to you?"

[21]So Elisha left him and went back. He took his

---

and note). **in Judah** Indicates that Elijah is now outside of Ahab's jurisdiction.

19:4 broom bush A desert shrub common to the southernmost region of Judah (the Negev) and Sinai that could be eaten in times of need (Job 30:4) or burned as fuel (Ps 120:4).

19:6 some bread baked The same type of cake that Elijah had commanded the widow to make (1Ki 17:13).

19:9–18 Like the preceding narrative, the account of Elijah's experience on Mount Horeb contains literary allusions to traditions about Moses. God passes by both Moses and Elijah (Ex 33:22; 1Ki 19:11), who cover their faces when he appears (Ex 3:6; 1Ki 19:13). Also, both men experience fire and thunder as part of God's presence (Ex 3:2; 19:18; 1Ki 19:11–12). However, Elijah is not a new Moses (the giver of the law), but a prophet.

19:10 The Israelites have rejected your covenant In contrast, 18:39 claims that the people of Israel acknowledged Yahweh after the contest with the prophets of Baal (18:22–38). The contrasting traditions may indicate that the Horeb story and the Carmel story (18:20–40) originally come from independent sources. Alternatively, the prophet might be exaggerating—the Israelite king has rejected Yahweh. **torn down your altars** The altar at Carmel had been destroyed (18:30). **put your prophets to death with the sword** Jezebel persecuted Yahweh's prophets (18:4). **I am the only one left** In contrast,

18:4 and 18:13 state that Obadiah saved 100 of God's prophets, which means that Elijah is exaggerating.

19:12 fire Wind, earthquakes and fire are often associated with a divine appearance or theophany (see Ex 19:16–18; 20:18; Jdg 5:4–5; Ps 18:7–9; Hab 3:4–7). Here, they precede Yahweh like a messenger (Ps 104:4).

19:13 he pulled his cloak over his face Elijah's reaction to hide from the divine presence is natural (Jdg 6:22; 13:20–22), since Yahweh declared that viewing his face would result in death (Ex 33:20–23).

19:15 Hazael Hazael does not appear in 1–2 Kings until he approaches Elisha on behalf of Ben-Hadad, king of Aram (Syria), whom he succeeds (2Ki 8:8,15).

19:16 Jehu One of Elisha's servants—not Elijah—anoints Jehu (2Ki 9:1–6). **anoint Elisha son of Shaphat from Abel Meholah to succeed you as prophet** Elijah anoints Elisha symbolically by casting his cloak upon him (1Ki 19:19).

19:19 with twelve yoke of oxen A large team that symbolizes wealth, representing what Elisha would have to give up to follow Elijah. **threw his cloak around him** Elijah is the first prophet to be identified by his garment (2Ki 1:8; compare Zec 13:4; Mt 3:4; Mk 1:6). Elijah's cloak does not belong to Elisha until after Elijah is taken to heaven (2Ki 2:14). Elijah's cloak may have functioned like a priest's ephod or even have been one (see Ex 28:4 and note).

19:21 slaughtered them The Hebrew word used here can refer to both slaughtering for a sacrifice and cooking (Dt

yoke of oxen and slaughtered them. He burned the plowing equipment to cook the meat and gave it to the people, and they ate. Then he set out to follow Elijah and became his servant.

Ben-Hadad Attacks Samaria

20 Now Ben-Hadad king of Aram mustered his entire army. Accompanied by thirty-two kings with their horses and chariots, he went up and besieged Samaria and attacked it. ²He sent messengers into the city to Ahab king of Israel, saying, "This is what Ben-Hadad says: ³'Your silver and gold are mine, and the best of your wives and children are mine.'"

⁴The king of Israel answered, "Just as you say, my lord the king. I and all I have are yours."

⁵The messengers came again and said, "This is what Ben-Hadad says: 'I sent to demand your silver and gold, your wives and your children. ⁶But about this time tomorrow I am going to send my officials to search your palace and the houses of your officials. They will seize everything you value and carry it away.'"

⁷The king of Israel summoned all the elders of the land and said to them, "See how this man is looking for trouble! When he sent for my wives and my children, my silver and my gold, I did not refuse him."

⁸The elders and the people all answered, "Don't listen to him or agree to his demands."

⁹So he replied to Ben-Hadad's messengers, "Tell my lord the king, 'Your servant will do all you demanded the first time, but this demand I cannot meet.'" They left and took the answer back to Ben-Hadad.

¹⁰Then Ben-Hadad sent another message to Ahab: "May the gods deal with me, be it ever so severely, if enough dust remains in Samaria to give each of my men a handful."

¹¹The king of Israel answered, "Tell him: 'One who puts on his armor should not boast like one who takes it off.'"

¹²Ben-Hadad heard this message while he and the kings were drinking in their tents,ᵃ and he ordered his men: "Prepare to attack." So they prepared to attack the city.

Ahab Defeats Ben-Hadad

¹³Meanwhile a prophet came to Ahab king of Israel and announced, "This is what the LORD says: 'Do you see this vast army? I will give it into your hand today, and then you will know that I am the LORD.'"

¹⁴"But who will do this?" asked Ahab.

The prophet replied, "This is what the LORD says: 'The junior officers under the provincial commanders will do it.'"

"And who will start the battle?" he asked.

The prophet answered, "You will."

¹⁵So Ahab summoned the 232 junior officers under the provincial commanders. Then he assembled the rest of the Israelites, 7,000 in all. ¹⁶They set out at noon while Ben-Hadad and the 32 kings allied with him were in their tents getting drunk. ¹⁷The junior officers under the provincial commanders went out first.

Now Ben-Hadad had dispatched scouts, who reported, "Men are advancing from Samaria."

¹⁸He said, "If they have come out for peace, take

ᵃ 12 Or *in Sukkoth*; also in verse 16

12:15; 1Sa 28:24; 2Ch 18:2). It is unclear whether Elisha made a sacrifice or simply killed and cooked the oxen. **became his servant** Joshua also assisted Moses before succeeding him (Ex 33:11; Nu 11:28; Jos 1:1). The Hebrew word used here, *shereth*, (implying "to minster,") also is used of priests (1Ki 8:11) and royal servants (1:4; 10:5).

20:1–12 The conflict between Aram (Syria) and Israel began when King Asa of Judah allied with King Ben-Hadad of Aram in order to fight King Baasha of Israel (15:18–20). The Syrian forces emerged victorious, and Israel became subservient. In this passage, Ben-Hadad reignites the conflict.

20:1 Ben-Hadad See 15:18–20, where King Asa of Judah asks Ben-Hadad for military aid against Israel. **Aram** This kingdom was located north of Israel, with its capital at Damascus. The Hebrew text here calls the nation "Aram," but it later became known as Syria (not to be confused with Assyria, the imperial power). **thirty-two kings** Although OT and ancient Near Eastern sources attest to such alliances (see Ge 14), no other sources confirm such a large number of allied kings. Ben-Hadad's leadership over them (1Ki 20:12,24) suggests they were likely tribal chieftains rather than kings. **Samaria** The capital of Israel since the time of Omri (16:24 and note).

20:7 elders of the land Refers to heads of prominent families throughout Israel responsible for managing day-to-day operations and executing justice (21:8,11; 2Ki 10:1). **this man** The Hebrew word used here, *zeh*, simply means "this"; "man" is supplied in translation. Referring to Ben-Hadad as "this" instead of "he" or "him" both dehumanizes him and conveys the narrator's disgust (compare 1Ki 22:27).

20:9 all you demanded the first time Refers to silver, gold, wives and children (v. 3). **this demand I cannot meet** Refers to allowing Ben-Hadad's servants to take whatever is valuable to Ahab (v. 6), which could mean the destruction or usurpation of the royal city.

20:11 One who puts on his armor should not boast A proverbial saying reminding Ben-Hadad that victory cannot be assured until the battle is over.

20:12 their tents The Hebrew word used here, *sukkoth*, could refer to tents, or it could indicate that Ben-Hadad was in Sukkoth, a town in the central Jordan Valley (7:46).

20:13–25 Despite the disparity between Aram's massive army and the small force of Israel, Ahab defeats Ben-Hadad with the help of an unnamed prophet.

20:15 7,000 While likely a symbolic number (see 19:18), 7,000 is a small force in comparison to the forces Ben-Hadad mustered (vv. 1,29–30; compare v. 27).

them alive; if they have come out for war, take them alive."

¹⁹The junior officers under the provincial commanders marched out of the city with the army behind them ²⁰and each one struck down his opponent. At that, the Arameans fled, with the Israelites in pursuit. But Ben-Hadad king of Aram escaped on horseback with some of his horsemen. ²¹The king of Israel advanced and overpowered the horses and chariots and inflicted heavy losses on the Arameans.

²²Afterward, the prophet came to the king of Israel and said, "Strengthen your position and see what must be done, because next spring the king of Aram will attack you again."

²³Meanwhile, the officials of the king of Aram advised him, "Their gods are gods of the hills. That is why they were too strong for us. But if we fight them on the plains, surely we will be stronger than they. ²⁴Do this: Remove all the kings from their commands and replace them with other officers. ²⁵You must also raise an army like the one you lost — horse for horse and chariot for chariot — so we can fight Israel on the plains. Then surely we will be stronger than they." He agreed with them and acted accordingly.

²⁶The next spring Ben-Hadad mustered the Arameans and went up to Aphek to fight against Israel. ²⁷When the Israelites were also mustered and given provisions, they marched out to meet them. The Israelites camped opposite them like two small flocks of goats, while the Arameans covered the countryside.

²⁸The man of God came up and told the king of Israel, "This is what the LORD says: 'Because the Arameans think the LORD is a god of the hills and not a god of the valleys, I will deliver this vast army into your hands, and you will know that I am the LORD.'"

²⁹For seven days they camped opposite each other, and on the seventh day the battle was joined. The Israelites inflicted a hundred thousand casualties on the Aramean foot soldiers in one day. ³⁰The rest of them escaped to the city of Aphek, where the wall collapsed on twenty-seven thousand of them. And Ben-Hadad fled to the city and hid in an inner room.

³¹His officials said to him, "Look, we have heard that the kings of Israel are merciful. Let us go to the king of Israel with sackcloth around our waists and ropes around our heads. Perhaps he will spare your life."

³²Wearing sackcloth around their waists and ropes around their heads, they went to the king of Israel and said, "Your servant Ben-Hadad says: 'Please let me live.'"

The king answered, "Is he still alive? He is my brother."

³³The men took this as a good sign and were quick to pick up his word. "Yes, your brother Ben-Hadad!" they said.

"Go and get him," the king said. When Ben-Hadad came out, Ahab had him come up into his chariot.

³⁴"I will return the cities my father took from your father," Ben-Hadad offered. "You may set up your own market areas in Damascus, as my father did in Samaria."

Ahab said, "On the basis of a treaty I will set you free." So he made a treaty with him, and let him go.

A Prophet Condemns Ahab

³⁵By the word of the LORD one of the company of the prophets said to his companion, "Strike me with your weapon," but he refused.

20:22 Strengthen The Hebrew word used here, *chazaq*, conveys the sense of "do your best" (Nu 13:20), "strengthening" (2Sa 3:6), or "be strong" (1Sa 4:9; 2Sa 10:12). **next spring the king of Aram will attack you again** Refers to the time of year when kings typically engaged in warfare (see 2Sa 11:1 and note), because the weather was good and provisions were plentiful.

20:23 if we fight them on the plains, surely we will be stronger than they Foot soldiers were no match for Ben-Hadad's chariots and horses on flat ground (1Ki 20:1), whereas the Israelites had an advantage on hills and rough terrain.

20:24 replace them with other officers All of the forces were to be brought under Ben-Hadad's authority.

20:26–34 After determining that Ahab's first victory was a fluke (vv. 21–25), Ben-Hadad fights Israel using a different tactic. However, Israel wins again, and the Arameans (Syrians) who survive the battle flee to the city of Aphek. Ben-Hadad hides in an inner chamber, where he is found and taken captive. Instead of killing his enemy, Ahab goes against God's will and makes a covenant with Ben-Hadad (vv. 32–34,42).

20:26 Aphek Several places are called Aphek in the OT.

This one is likely located across the Jordan River from Israel, three miles east of the Sea of Galilee.

20:28 man of God This title identifies a prophet or messenger of God. Here, it might refer to the same prophet mentioned in vv. 13,22.

20:31 ropes around our heads Refers to a practice connected to leading war captives away, as depicted in many ancient Near Eastern reliefs.

20:32 He is my brother A diplomatic phrase used between parties of equal status (e.g., Jdg 9:3). At the beginning of the account, Ahab was subservient to Ben-Hadad (1Ki 20:4); now, Ahab is in control.

20:33 took this as a good sign The Hebrew word used here, *nachash*, implies the practice of divination. **had him come up** A mutual, public recognition of one another's status.

20:34 your father Refers to Omri (16:21–28). However, the text does not mention Omri losing cities to an enemy. **Ahab said, "On the basis of a treaty I will set you free"** The Hebrew text leaves unclear whether these words are spoken by Ben-Hadad or Ahab. However, since Ahab is the victor, it makes sense that he has final say in the terms of their agreement. See the table "Covenants in the Old Testament" on p. 469.

³⁶So the prophet said, "Because you have not obeyed the LORD, as soon as you leave me a lion will kill you." And after the man went away, a lion found him and killed him.

³⁷The prophet found another man and said, "Strike me, please." So the man struck him and wounded him. ³⁸Then the prophet went and stood by the road waiting for the king. He disguised himself with his headband down over his eyes. ³⁹As the king passed by, the prophet called out to him, "Your servant went into the thick of the battle, and someone came to me with a captive and said, 'Guard this man. If he is missing, it will be your life for his life, or you must pay a talent^a of silver.' ⁴⁰While your servant was busy here and there, the man disappeared."

"That is your sentence," the king of Israel said. "You have pronounced it yourself."

⁴¹Then the prophet quickly removed the headband from his eyes, and the king of Israel recognized him as one of the prophets. ⁴²He said to the king, "This is what the LORD says: 'You have set free a man I had determined should die.^b Therefore it is your life for his life, your people for his people.'" ⁴³Sullen and angry, the king of Israel went to his palace in Samaria.

Naboth's Vineyard

21 Some time later there was an incident involving a vineyard belonging to Naboth the Jezreelite. The vineyard was in Jezreel, close to the palace of Ahab king of Samaria. ²Ahab said to Naboth, "Let me have your vineyard to use for a vegetable garden, since it is close to my palace. In exchange I will give you a better vineyard or, if you prefer, I will pay you whatever it is worth."

³But Naboth replied, "The LORD forbid that I should give you the inheritance of my ancestors."

⁴So Ahab went home, sullen and angry because Naboth the Jezreelite had said, "I will not give you the inheritance of my ancestors." He lay on his bed sulking and refused to eat.

⁵His wife Jezebel came in and asked him, "Why are you so sullen? Why won't you eat?"

⁶He answered her, "Because I said to Naboth the Jezreelite, 'Sell me your vineyard; or if you prefer, I will give you another vineyard in its place.' But he said, 'I will not give you my vineyard.'"

⁷Jezebel his wife said, "Is this how you act as king over Israel? Get up and eat! Cheer up. I'll get you the vineyard of Naboth the Jezreelite."

⁸So she wrote letters in Ahab's name, placed his seal on them, and sent them to the elders and nobles who lived in Naboth's city with him. ⁹In those letters she wrote:

"Proclaim a day of fasting and seat Naboth in a prominent place among the people. ¹⁰But seat two scoundrels opposite him and have them bring charges that he has cursed both God and the king. Then take him out and stone him to death."

¹¹So the elders and nobles who lived in Naboth's city did as Jezebel directed in the letters she had

---

^a 39 That is, about 75 pounds or about 34 kilograms
^b 42 The Hebrew term refers to the irrevocable giving over of things or persons to the LORD, often by totally destroying them.

20:35 company of the prophets The first mention of prophetic groups in the 1–2 Kings (compare 2Ki 2:3).
20:36 a lion found him and killed him Yahweh punished the man of God from Judah in this same way for not obeying his word (1Ki 13:24).
20:39 a talent of silver An extremely large sum (see note on 10:15).
20:40 You have pronounced it yourself The Hebrew word used here, *charats,* (implying "to maim" "to cut" or "to sharpen"; Lev 22:22), here means to decide a case (compare Isa 10:23; 28:22; Da 9:26). The prophet designed this parable to trap the king into making a judgment against himself, just as Nathan did with David over the matter of Uriah (2Sa 12:1–12).
20:41 king of Israel recognized him Since Ahab had several interactions with prophets (1Ki 17:1; 18:17–19,41–46; 20:13–28), he may have known this particular prophet from a previous encounter.
20:43 Sullen and angry The Hebrew expression used here is also used to describe Ahab's anger at Naboth for refusing to sell his vineyard (see 21:1–4).

21:1–16 This chapter records Ahab's acquisition of Naboth's vineyard, focusing on personal rights and the abuse of royal power. Jezebel's deception and mistreatment of Naboth show her disregard for all who follow Yahweh, not just his prophets (18:4,13; 19:1–2).

21:1 Jezreel This Israelite city is in a fertile valley with the same name; it is about 25 miles (40 kilometers) north of Samaria, Israel's capital. Starting with Ahab, Jezreel was the location of the Israelite king's winter residence.
21:3 LORD forbid that I should give Literally "it is a profanation for me from Yahweh." The use of the Hebrew word connoting "profanation" suggests that the sale would desecrate the land and should be avoided (Jos 22:29; 1Sa 12:23; 26:11; 2Sa 23:17). Naboth's viewpoint is rooted in Biblical law, which specifies that the land of Israel belongs to Yahweh; the Israelites temporarily "borrow" the land allotted to them by Yahweh. For this reason, they cannot sell the land in perpetuity or outside of the family. Property also reverts back to its owner in the Year of Jubilee (Lev 25:23–28; Nu 36:7).
21:5 Jezebel Daughter of Ethbaal, king of the Sidonians. Jezebel attacked Yahweh's prophets (1Ki 18:4,13; 19:1–2) and supported the prophets of Baal (18:19).
21:8 placed his seal Jezebel implicates Ahab, although the narrative does not mention his direct involvement until v. 16. See the infographic "Royal Seals of Judah" on p. 593.
21:9 fasting A sign of sorrow and grief in hope that God will grant mercy and forgiveness (1Sa 7:5–6; 2Sa 12:22; Isa 58:3).
21:10 two scoundrels Refers to false witnesses. The law demanded two witnesses for a conviction (Dt 17:6; 19:15; Nu 35:30).
21:11 Naboth's city This could refer to the city of Jezreel or another city in the Jezreel Valley (see note on 1Ki 21:1).

written to them. ¹²They proclaimed a fast and seated Naboth in a prominent place among the people. ¹³Then two scoundrels came and sat opposite him and brought charges against Naboth before the people, saying, "Naboth has cursed both God and the king." So they took him outside the city and stoned him to death. ¹⁴Then they sent word to Jezebel: "Naboth has been stoned to death."

¹⁵As soon as Jezebel heard that Naboth had been stoned to death, she said to Ahab, "Get up and take possession of the vineyard of Naboth the Jezreelite that he refused to sell you. He is no longer alive, but dead." ¹⁶When Ahab heard that Naboth was dead, he got up and went down to take possession of Naboth's vineyard.

¹⁷Then the word of the LORD came to Elijah the Tishbite: ¹⁸"Go down to meet Ahab king of Israel, who rules in Samaria. He is now in Naboth's vineyard, where he has gone to take possession of it. ¹⁹Say to him, 'This is what the LORD says: Have you not murdered a man and seized his property?' Then say to him, 'This is what the LORD says: In the place where dogs licked up Naboth's blood, dogs will lick up your blood—yes, yours!'"

²⁰Ahab said to Elijah, "So you have found me, my enemy!"

"I have found you," he answered, "because you have sold yourself to do evil in the eyes of the LORD. ²¹He says, 'I am going to bring disaster on you. I will wipe out your descendants and cut off from Ahab every last male in Israel—slave or free.ᵃ ²²I will make your house like that of Jeroboam son of Nebat and that of Baasha son of Ahijah, because you have aroused my anger and have caused Israel to sin.'

²³"And also concerning Jezebel the LORD says: 'Dogs will devour Jezebel by the wall ofᵇ Jezreel.'

²⁴"Dogs will eat those belonging to Ahab who die in the city, and the birds will feed on those who die in the country."

²⁵(There was never anyone like Ahab, who sold himself to do evil in the eyes of the LORD, urged on by Jezebel his wife. ²⁶He behaved in the vilest manner by going after idols, like the Amorites the LORD drove out before Israel.)

²⁷When Ahab heard these words, he tore his clothes, put on sackcloth and fasted. He lay in sackcloth and went around meekly.

²⁸Then the word of the LORD came to Elijah the Tishbite: ²⁹"Have you noticed how Ahab has humbled himself before me? Because he has humbled himself, I will not bring this disaster in his day, but I will bring it on his house in the days of his son."

Micaiah Prophesies Against Ahab

22:1-28pp — 2Ch 18:1-27

22 For three years there was no war between Aram and Israel. ²But in the third year Jehoshaphat king of Judah went down to see the king of Israel. ³The king of Israel had said to his officials, "Don't you know that Ramoth Gilead belongs to us and yet we are doing nothing to retake it from the king of Aram?"

⁴So he asked Jehoshaphat, "Will you go with me to fight against Ramoth Gilead?"

Jehoshaphat replied to the king of Israel, "I am

ᵃ 21 Or Israel—every ruler or leader   ᵇ 23 Most Hebrew manuscripts; a few Hebrew manuscripts, Vulgate and Syriac (see also 2 Kings 9:26) the plot of ground at

---

21:13 they took him outside the city In doing so, they avoid being contaminated by the corpse (Lev 24:14,23; Nu 15:35–36).

21:14 they sent word to Jezebel The letter was signed and sealed with Ahab's name (1Ki 21:8). Somehow, the elders knew who penned the letter.

21:16 to take possession King Ahab's right to the land is debatable. The only time property is automatically transferred to a king in the OT is when the owner has left the country (2Ki 8:4–6). Naboth's conviction as a criminal may have given Ahab the right to confiscate the vineyard.

21:17–24 Elijah curses Ahab with language that resembles the prophetic curses brought against kings Jeroboam and Baasha of Israel, who also provoked Yahweh (1Ki 14:9; 16:2; 21:22).

21:19 dogs will lick up your blood The statement from Yahweh describes an "eye for an eye" punishment—their corpses will be left like Naboth's (v. 13; compare Ex 21:24; 1Sa 15:33; 2Sa 12:9–11)—and echoes the prophecies against earlier kings of Israel, Jeroboam (1Ki 14:10–11) and Baasha (16:3–4).

21:23 Dogs will devour Jezebel A punishment similar to the prophecies against Jeroboam (14:10–11), Baasha (16:3–4) and Ahab (21:19–24). But unlike the prophecies against the kings, Elijah does not imply that Jezebel will be dead when the dogs eat her.

21:24 those belonging to Ahab who die The judgment against Jezebel is expanded to include all of Ahab's family.

21:25 urged on by Jezebel his wife Deuteronomy 13:6–11 commands that if anyone entices a person to serve other gods, he or she shall be killed by stoning at the hand of that person.

21:29 in the days of his son The punishment Elijah prophesies in 1Ki 21:19–24 is delayed one generation; it takes place with the assassination of Ahab's son, Joram (2Ki 9). Earlier, Solomon's punishment was delayed a generation for the sake of David (1Ki 11:11–13).

22:1–12 After Ahab, king of Israel, and Jehoshaphat, king of Judah, agree to recapture Ramoth Gilead from the Arameans (the Syrians), they inquire of Yahweh through 400 prophets of the royal court. The prophets ensure the kings that Ramoth Gilead will be given to Ahab. The kings summon the prophet Micaiah for a second opinion.

22:1 no war between Aram and Israel This peace probably resulted from the treaty between Ahab and Ben-Hadad (20:32–34), after Israel defeated Aram (Syria) twice.

22:2 Jehoshaphat Son and successor of Asa (15:24). Jehoshaphat's reign is briefly recorded after the death of Ahab (vv. 41–50).

22:3 Ramoth Gilead belongs to us It is unclear when Ramoth Gilead came under Aramean (Syrian) control.

as you are, my people as your people, my horses as your horses." [5]But Jehoshaphat also said to the king of Israel, "First seek the counsel of the LORD."

[6]So the king of Israel brought together the prophets—about four hundred men—and asked them, "Shall I go to war against Ramoth Gilead, or shall I refrain?"

"Go," they answered, "for the Lord will give it into the king's hand."

[7]But Jehoshaphat asked, "Is there no longer a prophet of the LORD here whom we can inquire of?"

[8]The king of Israel answered Jehoshaphat, "There is still one prophet through whom we can inquire of the LORD, but I hate him because he never prophesies anything good about me, but always bad. He is Micaiah son of Imlah."

"The king should not say such a thing," Jehoshaphat replied.

[9]So the king of Israel called one of his officials and said, "Bring Micaiah son of Imlah at once."

[10]Dressed in their royal robes, the king of Israel and Jehoshaphat king of Judah were sitting on their thrones at the threshing floor by the entrance of the gate of Samaria, with all the prophets prophesying before them. [11]Now Zedekiah son of Kenaanah had made iron horns and he declared, "This is what the LORD says: 'With these you will gore the Arameans until they are destroyed.'"

[12]All the other prophets were prophesying the same thing. "Attack Ramoth Gilead and be victorious," they said, "for the LORD will give it into the king's hand."

[13]The messenger who had gone to summon Micaiah said to him, "Look, the other prophets without exception are predicting success for the king. Let your word agree with theirs, and speak favorably."

[14]But Micaiah said, "As surely as the LORD lives, I can tell him only what the LORD tells me."

[15]When he arrived, the king asked him, "Micaiah, shall we go to war against Ramoth Gilead, or not?"

"Attack and be victorious," he answered, "for the LORD will give it into the king's hand."

[16]The king said to him, "How many times must I make you swear to tell me nothing but the truth in the name of the LORD?"

[17]Then Micaiah answered, "I saw all Israel scattered on the hills like sheep without a shepherd, and the LORD said, 'These people have no master. Let each one go home in peace.'"

[18]The king of Israel said to Jehoshaphat, "Didn't I tell you that he never prophesies anything good about me, but only bad?"

[19]Micaiah continued, "Therefore hear the word of the LORD: I saw the LORD sitting on his throne with all the multitudes of heaven standing around him on his right and on his left. [20]And the LORD said, 'Who will entice Ahab into attacking Ramoth Gilead and going to his death there?'

"One suggested this, and another that. [21]Finally, a spirit came forward, stood before the LORD and said, 'I will entice him.'

[22]"'By what means?' the LORD asked.

"'I will go out and be a deceiving spirit in the mouths of all his prophets,' he said.

"'You will succeed in enticing him,' said the LORD. 'Go and do it.'

[23]"So now the LORD has put a deceiving spirit in the mouths of all these prophets of yours. The LORD has decreed disaster for you."

[24]Then Zedekiah son of Kenaanah went up and

First Kings 4:13 names it as one of Solomon's provinces; according to Ahab's agreement with Ben-Hadad (20:32–34), Aram was to return to Israel all Aramean cities formerly under Israel's control.

22:6 Lord While multiple Hebrew manuscripts and the Aramaic translations (or Targums) have God's personal name, Yahweh, here, most manuscripts read *adonay*, meaning "lord"—a generic term that can be applied to any master, whether human or divine. The use of *adonay* suggests that the word from the 400 prophets is not from Yahweh.

22:7 a prophet of the LORD Ahab's 400 prophets did not satisfy Jehoshaphat, who calls specifically for a prophet of Yahweh.

22:10 threshing floor Winnowing was a seasonal activity, so the threshing floor would have been empty the rest of the year. See the infographic "A Threshing Floor" on p. 497.

22:11 With these you will gore the Arameans Ancient Near Eastern literature from as early as 3400 BC, including the OT, portrays kings and gods as bulls pushing down their enemies with their horns (e.g., the Hittite "Crossing of the Taurus"; compare Nu 23:22–24; Dt 33:17; Ps 22:12; 92:10).

22:16 How many times Since Micaiah was known for giving King Ahab only bad news (v. 8), his favorable response causes Ahab to suspect that he is lying or being sarcastic.

22:17 sheep without a shepherd Comparing kings and leaders to shepherds is a common motif in ancient Near Eastern literature, including the OT (e.g., Nu 27:17; 2Sa 5:2; 7:7; Jer 23:1–4; Eze 34:1–6; Zec 13:7). Here, the leaderless flock will be Israel's army.

22:19 the multitudes of heaven Here, this phrase refers to members of the heavenly court (Ps 82; Job 1–2) who are allowed to decide how to carry out Yahweh's divine decree that Ahab must die (1Ki 22:21–23). Elsewhere, the same terminology is broadly used to refer to celestial bodies, which other nations worshiped; Israel was forbidden from this type of worship (e.g., Dt 4:19; 17:3; 2Ki 17:16; 21:3; Jer 8:2; 19:13).

22:21 a spirit Refers to a specific spirit. The actions of this spirit resemble those of the adversary who comes forward to test Job (Job 1–2; see note on Job 1:6); however, that term is not used to describe the spirit in this passage.

22:22 a deceiving spirit The Hebrew here indicates that this is a spirit of deception.

22:24 Zedekiah son of Kenaanah One of the 400 prophets who foretold victory for Ahab (1Ki 22:11). **slapped Micaiah in the face** A gesture meant to humiliate. **Which way did the spirit from the LORD go when**

slapped Micaiah in the face. "Which way did the spirit from[a] the Lord go when he went from me to speak to you?" he asked.

²⁵Micaiah replied, "You will find out on the day you go to hide in an inner room."

²⁶The king of Israel then ordered, "Take Micaiah and send him back to Amon the ruler of the city and to Joash the king's son ²⁷and say, 'This is what the king says: Put this fellow in prison and give him nothing but bread and water until I return safely.'"

²⁸Micaiah declared, "If you ever return safely, the Lord has not spoken through me." Then he added, "Mark my words, all you people!"

Ahab Killed at Ramoth Gilead

22:29-36pp — 2Ch 18:28-34

²⁹So the king of Israel and Jehoshaphat king of Judah went up to Ramoth Gilead. ³⁰The king of Israel said to Jehoshaphat, "I will enter the battle in disguise, but you wear your royal robes." So the king of Israel disguised himself and went into battle.

³¹Now the king of Aram had ordered his thirty-two chariot commanders, "Do not fight with anyone, small or great, except the king of Israel." ³²When the chariot commanders saw Jehoshaphat, they thought, "Surely this is the king of Israel." So they turned to attack him, but when Jehoshaphat cried out, ³³the chariot commanders saw that he was not the king of Israel and stopped pursuing him.

³⁴But someone drew his bow at random and hit the king of Israel between the sections of his armor. The king told his chariot driver, "Wheel around and get me out of the fighting. I've been wounded." ³⁵All day long the battle raged, and the king was propped up in his chariot facing the Arameans. The blood from his wound ran onto the floor of the chariot, and that evening he died. ³⁶As the sun was setting, a cry spread through the army: "Every man to his town. Every man to his land!"

³⁷So the king died and was brought to Samaria, and they buried him there. ³⁸They washed the chariot at a pool in Samaria (where the prostitutes bathed),[b] and the dogs licked up his blood, as the word of the Lord had declared.

³⁹As for the other events of Ahab's reign, including all he did, the palace he built and adorned with ivory, and the cities he fortified, are they not written in the book of the annals of the kings of Israel? ⁴⁰Ahab rested with his ancestors. And Ahaziah his son succeeded him as king.

Jehoshaphat King of Judah

22:41-50pp — 2Ch 20:31 – 21:1

⁴¹Jehoshaphat son of Asa became king of Judah in the fourth year of Ahab king of Israel. ⁴²Jehoshaphat was thirty-five years old when he became king, and he reigned in Jerusalem twenty-five years. His mother's name was Azubah daughter of Shilhi.

---

a 24 Or *Spirit of*   *b* 38 Or *Samaria and cleaned the weapons*

---

he went from me to speak to you Zedekiah does not recognize that he speaks with a spirit of deception and therefore accuses Micaiah of doing so.

22:25 in an inner room Similarly, Ben-Hadad hid in an inner chamber in the city of Aphek during his second battle against Ahab (20:30).

22:27 this fellow See note on 20:7.

22:28 the Lord has not spoken through me The proof of a valid prophet is whether his prophecy comes true (Dt 18:21–22).

22:30 you wear your royal robes This would make Jehoshaphat the prime target for the enemy.

22:32 Surely this is the king of Israel Jehoshaphat's true identity is confirmed upon closer inspection (1Ki 20:33). **Jehoshaphat cried out** The content of this cry is unknown. 1–2 Chronicles adds that Jehoshaphat called upon Yahweh, who helped him (2Ch 18:31).

22:34 drew his bow at random The archer disobeys Ben-Hadad's command to fight only against the king of Israel (1Ki 22:31). **Wheel around** This gesture both turns the chariot and signals a change in direction to the forces (see 2Ki 9:23).

22:35 the king was propped up in his chariot Contrary to his wish to be carried away from battle, the king is made to stand.

22:36 Every man to his land Fulfills the rest of Micaiah's prophecy (1Ki 22:17).

22:38 the prostitutes Elijah does not mention prostitutes in his prophecy concerning Ahab's death (21:19–24). The

Targums (ancient Aramaic translations) and ancient Syriac translations interpret the Hebrew word used here, *zonah* (meaning "harlot" or "prostitute"), as *zena* (meaning "armor"), resulting in the translation "the armor was washed." This spelling correction to the Hebrew text makes sense of this otherwise enigmatic line. **the dogs licked up his blood** A parallel to Elijah's prophecy (21:19).

22:39 palace he built and adorned with ivory See note on 10:18. The ivory inlays were probably set into the paneling. Archeologists have excavated more than 500 ivory fragments, carved in Phoenician style, in a burnt building at Samaria. While the date of this stratum is debated, it may date to the ninth-century and the Omride kings—especially Ahab. **cities he fortified** Many archeological sites in northern Israel that were once ascribed to the building activities of Solomon (9:10–22)—such as Hazor, Megiddo and Gezer (9:15)—have been redated to the ninth-century and the Omride kings, especially Ahab. **annals of the kings of Israel** See note on 14:19.

22:40 rested with his ancestors See note on 2:10.

22:41–50 The author first introduced Jehoshaphat in 15:24, as the son and successor of Asa, king of Judah. Although the narrator has already recounted Jehoshaphat's involvement with Ahab and Israel's war against Syria (vv. 1–33), this is the first time the narrator formally describes Jehoshaphat's reign.

22:42 he reigned in Jerusalem twenty-five years Jehoshaphat reigned from about 873–848 BC. See 2Ch

[43]In everything he followed the ways of his father Asa and did not stray from them; he did what was right in the eyes of the LORD. The high places, however, were not removed, and the people continued to offer sacrifices and burn incense there.[a] [44]Jehoshaphat was also at peace with the king of Israel.

[45]As for the other events of Jehoshaphat's reign, the things he achieved and his military exploits, are they not written in the book of the annals of the kings of Judah? [46]He rid the land of the rest of the male shrine prostitutes who remained there even after the reign of his father Asa. [47]There was then no king in Edom; a provincial governor ruled.

[48]Now Jehoshaphat built a fleet of trading ships[b] to go to Ophir for gold, but they never set sail — they were wrecked at Ezion Geber. [49]At that time Ahaziah son of Ahab said to Jehoshaphat, "Let my men sail with yours," but Jehoshaphat refused.

[50]Then Jehoshaphat rested with his ancestors and was buried with them in the city of David his father. And Jehoram his son succeeded him as king.

Ahaziah King of Israel

[51]Ahaziah son of Ahab became king of Israel in Samaria in the seventeenth year of Jehoshaphat king of Judah, and he reigned over Israel two years. [52]He did evil in the eyes of the LORD, because he followed the ways of his father and mother and of Jeroboam son of Nebat, who caused Israel to sin. [53]He served and worshiped Baal and aroused the anger of the LORD, the God of Israel, just as his father had done.

[a] 43 In Hebrew texts this sentence (22:43b) is numbered 22:44, and 22:44-53 is numbered 22:45-54.   [b] 48 Hebrew *of ships of Tarshish*

17:1—21:1. See the timeline "The Divided Kingdom" on p. 536.

NORTHERN KING	DATE	SOUTHERN KING	DATE
Ahab	874–853 BC	Jehoshaphat	873–848 BC
Ahaziah	853–852 BC		
Jehoram/Joram	852–841 BC	Jehoram	848–841 BC

22:43 The high places, however, were not removed Jehoshaphat's father, Asa, also allowed the high places to remain, yet he was found faithful—suggesting that in the viewpoint of 1 Kings, they were not used for idolatrous worship during his time (1Ki 15:14).

22:44 also at peace with the king of Israel The Hebrew word used here, *shalem*, conveys the sense of surrender (Dt 20:12; Jos 10:1; 11:19). Israel and Judah wage war from the time the monarchy splits (see 1Ki 14:30; 15:16,32) until Jehoram's marriage to Ahab's daughter (2Ki 8:18).

22:46 male shrine prostitutes See note on 1Ki 14:24.

22:47 There was then no king in Edom The last king of Edom mentioned was Hadad, who rebelled against Solomon (11:14–22).

22:48 trading ships to go to Ophir Second Chronicles 20:35–37 fills in a few details about this ill-fated attempt to resume the maritime activities of Solomon (1Ki 9:26–28; 10:11,22). The Hebrew text refers to these ships as of Tarshish type; Tarshish was a distant trading port (see note on Jnh 1:3). Ophir, also mentioned here, was possibly in Arabia and was known for fine gold (see note on Job 28:16).

22:52 mother Probably refers to Jezebel. **of Jeroboam** Apparently, the idolatrous practices begun by Jeroboam (1Ki 12:25–33) remained in place during Ahaziah's reign.

22:53 Baal The Canaanite storm god.

2 KINGS

INTRODUCTION TO 2 KINGS

Second Kings is about truth versus falsehood, played out on an international scale. The book opens with the prophet Elijah being taken to heaven in a chariot of fire and Elisha succeeding him (2Ki 2; compare 1Ki 19:19–21). The stories of these prophets are intertwined with accounts of the kings of Israel and Judah. Both kingdoms are heading toward disaster. In the northern kingdom of Israel, the kings persistently support idolatry. The southern kingdom of Judah fares only slightly better. Two kings—Hezekiah and Josiah—try to turn the people from idolatry (2Ki 18:3–6; 23:1–25), but their reforms are short lived (21:2–9; 23:32,37).

BACKGROUND

The books of 1–2 Kings—along with Joshua, Judges and 1–2 Samuel—interpret Israel's history in light of the book of Deuteronomy, showing how God's people are blessed when they follow their covenant (contract) with Yahweh and how they are cursed when they break it. In 2 Kings, this is seen in a recurring formula that evaluates each king on the basis of whether he does good or evil in the eyes of Yahweh. Evil is characterized by idolatry, improper worship and rejecting Yahweh for other gods (e.g., 13:2; 21:1–9). Doing good means taking action against idolatry, following Yahweh's law and supporting proper worship (e.g., 10:28–30; 18:3–6; 23:21–25).

Second Kings begins in 852 BC and marks the period of Israel's history when people and events mentioned in the Bible can be confirmed by other sources. For example, Moab's rebellion against

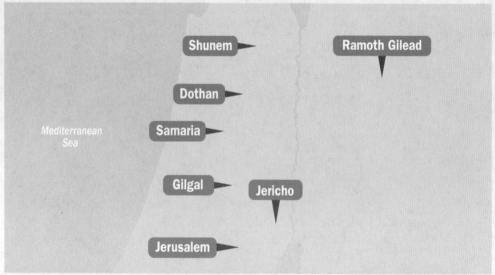

This map depicts some of the major locations related to 2 Kings.

Israel (ch. 3) is known from a Moabite inscription; an Assyrian obelisk depicts the Israelite king Jehu (chs. 9–10) paying tribute; and a Hebrew inscription confirms Hezekiah's work on Jerusalem's water system (20:20).

For most of 2 Kings, the historical backdrop is the imminent threat posed by the powerful Assyrian Empire. Second Kings depicts how Israel and Judah are subjected to Assyrian rule. During this period, those who opposed Assyria were brutally subdued, while others paid tribute to avoid the same fate. By the late seventh century BC, Assyrian power had waned, and Babylon took over as the imperial power in the region. This shift in the balance contextualizes Judah's final years (chs. 23–25).

Nearly all the kings of Israel and Judah place their own agendas above Yahweh's, leading the people into idolatry (e.g., 17:7–23; 21:10–15). Their actions catch up with them, and Yahweh uses foreign powers to bring judgment upon them. Assyria conquers the northern kingdom of Israel and deports its citizens (ch. 17). The southern kingdom of Judah is conquered by the Babylonians and its people, too, are exiled (chs. 24–25).

STRUCTURE

Second Kings begins partway through the second section (1Ki 12—2 Kgs 17) of the combined work of 1–2 Kings, which originally were a single literary unit (see the "Introduction to 1 Kings"). After Elijah's ministry is handed off to his apprentice Elisha (in 852 BC), the remainder of the

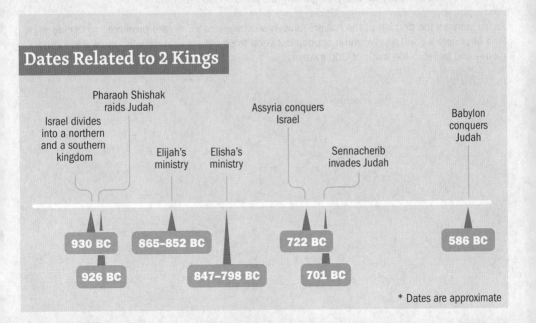

Dates Related to 2 Kings

Israel divides into a northern and a southern kingdom — 930 BC / 926 BC

Pharaoh Shishak raids Judah

Elijah's ministry — 865–852 BC

Elisha's ministry — 847–798 BC

Assyria conquers Israel — 722 BC

Sennacherib invades Judah — 701 BC

Babylon conquers Judah — 586 BC

* Dates are approximate

narrative focuses on the miraculous deeds of Elisha—including resurrection, feeding people during a famine and a healing. This is interspersed with narratives about the kings of Israel and Judah. After Elisha's death, there is brief coverage of the kings of Israel and Judah until 722 BC, when the Assyrians conquer Israel. The third section (2Ki 18–25) focuses on the southern kingdom of Judah until, in 586 BC, the Babylonians destroy Jerusalem and destroy Yahweh's temple.

Throughout 2 Kings, each king's reign is described using a literary motif known as the regnal formula: King A died; King B took his place and ruled for so many years; King B did evil (or good) in the eyes of Yahweh; King B died; and King C took his place (e.g., 21:18–26). Some reigns are covered briefly, with little more than the regnal formula, while others are described with detailed narratives.

OUTLINE

- From the end of Elijah's ministry to the fall of Israel (1:1—17:41)
- From Hezekiah's reign to the fall of Judah (18:1—25:30)

THEMES

Second Kings cuts through the complications of politics and warfare to bring clarity via Yahweh's perspective. There is evil, there is good, and there are those like Elisha who discern between the two. In the midst of it all, we see how gloomy life without God really is.

As we witness the demise of the nation Yahweh originally chose, we are prompted to decide what kind of people we will be. We must choose between false beliefs—in nations, gods and ideologies—and belief in the truth of God's ways.

The LORD's Judgment on Ahaziah

1 After Ahab's death, Moab rebelled against Israel. ²Now Ahaziah had fallen through the lattice of his upper room in Samaria and injured himself. So he sent messengers, saying to them, "Go and consult Baal-Zebub, the god of Ekron, to see if I will recover from this injury."

³But the angel of the LORD said to Elijah the Tishbite, "Go up and meet the messengers of the king of Samaria and ask them, 'Is it because there is no God in Israel that you are going off to consult Baal-Zebub, the god of Ekron?' ⁴Therefore this is what the LORD says: 'You will not leave the bed you are lying on. You will certainly die!'" So Elijah went.

⁵When the messengers returned to the king, he asked them, "Why have you come back?"

⁶"A man came to meet us," they replied. "And he said to us, 'Go back to the king who sent you and tell him, "This is what the LORD says: Is it because there is no God in Israel that you are sending messengers to consult Baal-Zebub, the god of Ekron? Therefore you will not leave the bed you are lying on. You will certainly die!"'"

⁷The king asked them, "What kind of man was it who came to meet you and told you this?"

⁸They replied, "He had a garment of hair[a] and had a leather belt around his waist."

The king said, "That was Elijah the Tishbite."

⁹Then he sent to Elijah a captain with his company of fifty men. The captain went up to Elijah, who was sitting on the top of a hill, and said to him, "Man of God, the king says, 'Come down!'"

¹⁰Elijah answered the captain, "If I am a man of God, may fire come down from heaven and consume you and your fifty men!" Then fire fell from heaven and consumed the captain and his men.

¹¹At this the king sent to Elijah another captain with his fifty men. The captain said to him, "Man of God, this is what the king says, 'Come down at once!'"

¹²"If I am a man of God," Elijah replied, "may fire come down from heaven and consume you and your fifty men!" Then the fire of God fell from heaven and consumed him and his fifty men.

¹³So the king sent a third captain with his fifty men. This third captain went up and fell on his knees before Elijah. "Man of God," he begged, "please have respect for my life and the lives of these fifty men, your servants! ¹⁴See, fire has

---

a 8 Or *He was a hairy man*

1:1–18 The narrative of 1–2 Kings was originally one work that was divided in antiquity, likely because its length required two scrolls. Second Kings begins shortly after King Ahab's death (853 BC). Ahab's son, Ahaziah, is now reigning over the northern kingdom of Israel. (In 930 BC, the kingdom was divided into Israel in the north and Judah in the south.)

Second Kings continues the contrast between apostasy of the Israelite kings and Elijah's zeal for Yahweh (1Ki 17–2Ki 2). Here, the story of Elijah denouncing King Ahaziah uses repetition as a literary device. The tension mounts each time Ahaziah sends a military unit to Elijah, until the pattern of destruction by fire finally ends (2Ki 1:15).

1:1 Moab rebelled against Israel Despite its appearance in the opening verse, the story of Moab's rebellion is put on hold until ch. 3. Apparently, Ahab had either defeated or made an alliance with Moab. See note on 3:4. **rebelled** The Hebrew term used here, *pasha'*, means "to transgress," and is frequently used in legal and religious contexts. In political contexts, *pasha'* refers to the rebellion of a vassal king against his overlord (e.g., 1Ki 12:19; compare 2Ki 3:5).

1:2 Ahaziah First Kings 22:51–53 introduces Ahaziah as one of the kings of Israel who did evil in the sight of Yahweh. He reigned over Israel briefly ca. 853 BC. **Baal-Zebub, the god of Ekron** The name Baal-Zebub literally means "lord of flies." Ekron was one of five major Philistine cities on the border of ancient Israel (Jos 13:3). See the table "Pagan Deities of the Old Testament" on p. 1287.

1:3 the angel of the LORD The Angel of Yahweh often appears with messages to individuals such as Moses (Ex 3:2), Balaam (Nu 22:22–23) or Hagar (Ge 16:7–13). At times, the Angel of Yahweh seems to be a form of Yahweh himself (Jdg 2:1–5). Other times, however, the

Angel appears to be distinct from Yahweh (Ex 23:20–23). The Angel also appears as a mighty warrior defeating Israel's enemies (2Ki 19:35; compare Ps 34:7 and note).

the king of Samaria Refers to Ahaziah. Samaria was the capital city of Israel from the reign of Omri until its destruction at the hands of the Assyrian Empire (1Ki 16:24; 2Ki 17:6).

1:8 He had a garment of hair The Hebrew text here reads literally as "owner of hair." The idea is that Elijah's garment was distinctive. The narrative mentions Elijah's garment several times elsewhere (1Ki 19:13,19; 2Ki 2:8,13,14; compare Zec 13:4). John the Baptist, who is frequently associated with Elijah, wears a hairy garment (see Mt 3:4 and note; Mk 1:6 and note; compare Mt 11:14; Mk 9:13; Lk 1:17).

1:9 a captain with his company of fifty men A military unit comprising 50 men and their officer (1Sa 8:12; Isa 3:3). **Man of God** This title designates a true prophet or messenger of God in the book of Kings (1Ki 12:22; 13:21; 17:18; 2Ki 4:9). It also is used of Moses (Dt 33:1).

1:10 fire come down from heaven Fire in the OT is associated with the divine presence (see note on 2Ki 1:12). In 1Ki 18, divine fire provides the sign of the true God in Elijah's contest with the prophets of Baal (1Ki 18:24,38).

1:11 Come down at once The second officer commands Elijah more forcefully than the first.

1:12 the fire of God The Hebrew phrase used here, *esh-elohim*, may be understood as "fire of God" or indicate the power of the fire, as a translation "mighty fire" or "awesome fire" would imply.

1:13 respect for my life and the lives of these fifty men The third captain changes his approach to Elijah. Instead of coming with orders from the king, he comes humbly and asks Elijah to spare his life. He recognizes that the authority and power behind Elijah is greater than that of Ahaziah.

fallen from heaven and consumed the first two captains and all their men. But now have respect for my life!"

15The angel of the LORD said to Elijah, "Go down with him; do not be afraid of him." So Elijah got up and went down with him to the king.

16He told the king, "This is what the LORD says: Is it because there is no God in Israel for you to consult that you have sent messengers to consult Baal-Zebub, the god of Ekron? Because you have done this, you will never leave the bed you are lying on. You will certainly die!" 17So he died, according to the word of the LORD that Elijah had spoken.

Because Ahaziah had no son, Joram[a] succeeded him as king in the second year of Jehoram son of Jehoshaphat king of Judah. 18As for all the other events of Ahaziah's reign, and what he did, are they not written in the book of the annals of the kings of Israel?

Elijah Taken Up to Heaven

2 When the LORD was about to take Elijah up to heaven in a whirlwind, Elijah and Elisha were on their way from Gilgal. 2Elijah said to Elisha, "Stay here; the LORD has sent me to Bethel."

But Elisha said, "As surely as the LORD lives and as you live, I will not leave you." So they went down to Bethel.

3The company of the prophets at Bethel came out to Elisha and asked, "Do you know that the LORD is going to take your master from you today?"

"Yes, I know," Elisha replied, "so be quiet."

4Then Elijah said to him, "Stay here, Elisha; the LORD has sent me to Jericho."

And he replied, "As surely as the LORD lives and as you live, I will not leave you." So they went to Jericho.

5The company of the prophets at Jericho went up to Elisha and asked him, "Do you know that the LORD is going to take your master from you today?"

"Yes, I know," he replied, "so be quiet."

6Then Elijah said to him, "Stay here; the LORD has sent me to the Jordan."

And he replied, "As surely as the LORD lives and as you live, I will not leave you." So the two of them walked on.

7Fifty men from the company of the prophets went and stood at a distance, facing the place where Elijah and Elisha had stopped at the Jordan. 8Elijah took his cloak, rolled it up and struck the

[a] 17 Hebrew Jehoram, a variant of Joram

1:17 The Hebrew text of this verse can be confusing, as it lists both a king of Israel and a king of Judah who went by the same name yehoram (Jehoram). An alternate rendering of this name is yoram (Joram; 2Ki 8:16). To remove the ambiguity between the king of Judah and the king of Israel, some translations always refer to the king of Israel as Joram and the king of Judah as Jehoram.

1:17 Joram succeeded him as king This king reigned over Israel ca. 852–841 BC; he was Ahaziah of Israel's younger brother and Ahab's son (2Ki 3:1). In the ancient Near East, the eldest son usually took the throne upon his father's death. In the absence of a son, a brother could ascend to the throne. **the second year of Jehoram son of Jehoshaphat king of Judah** It is difficult to determine a precise chronology of the two kings named Jehoram (one in Israel, one in Judah). The information given in 1:17; 3:1; and 8:16 appears to conflict. It is possible that the reference to the second year of Jehoram, king of Judah (1:17), involves a period of coregency with his father, Jehoshaphat (who reigned ca. 873–848 BC); in that case, 8:16 would indicate the beginning of his sole reign in Judah, which would have lasted from approximately 848–841 BC. See the timeline "The Divided Kingdom" on p. 536.

NORTHERN KING	DATE	SOUTHERN KING	DATE
Ahab	874–853 BC	Jehoshaphat	873–848 BC
Ahaziah	853–852 BC		
Jehoram/Joram	852–841 BC	Jehoram	848–841 BC

1:18 annals of the kings of Israel The author of 1–2 Kings may have drawn from this source, which apparently is different from the Biblical books of 1–2 Chron-

icles (given that the Chronicler refers to it, as well; see note on 1Ch 9:1). The mention of this separate volume suggests that the Biblical book of Kings was not intended to be merely a record of events; such information could be found elsewhere.

2:1–14 The narrative shifts to Elijah's mysterious ascent into heaven on God's fiery chariot, which marks the end of the prophet's career (compare Ge 5:24). This narrative marks the beginning of Elisha's career as the head of the prophets of Yahweh (2 Ki 2:15–16; compare 1Ki 19:19–21).

2:1 a whirlwind The Hebrew word used here, se'arah, is associated with both the appearance of God (a theophany) and divine judgment—here it is a testament of God's presence (Job 38:1; 40:6; Jer 23:19; Zec 9:14). **Elijah and Elisha** Elisha was a young farmer living with his parents when he was called to be Elijah's successor (1Ki 19:19–21).

2:2 As surely as the LORD lives This signifies the swearing of an oath.

2:3 The company of the prophets A guild or brotherhood of prophets mentioned in 1Ki 20:35 but more common in the Elisha stories (2Ki 4:1; 5:22; 6:1). Such guilds were stationed in cities throughout the land of Israel, including Bethel and Jericho (vv. 5,15). **from you** This phrase expresses Elijah and Elisha's relationship in terms of master and servant—Elisha's apprenticeship is about to end.

2:8 The water divided Elisha's repetition of this action demonstrates his ability to take Elijah's place (see v. 14). This account parallels Joshua's parting of the Jordan, which likewise demonstrated God's presence with Joshua shortly after he succeeded Moses (Jos 3:7–8,15–17; Ex 14). See the table "Miracles of the Prophets" on p. 1366.

water with it. The water divided to the right and to the left, and the two of them crossed over on dry ground.

⁹When they had crossed, Elijah said to Elisha, "Tell me, what can I do for you before I am taken from you?"

"Let me inherit a double portion of your spirit," Elisha replied.

¹⁰"You have asked a difficult thing," Elijah said, "yet if you see me when I am taken from you, it will be yours — otherwise, it will not."

¹¹As they were walking along and talking together, suddenly a chariot of fire and horses of fire appeared and separated the two of them, and Elijah went up to heaven in a whirlwind. ¹²Elisha saw this and cried out, "My father! My father! The chariots and horsemen of Israel!" And Elisha saw him no more. Then he took hold of his garment and tore it in two.

¹³Elisha then picked up Elijah's cloak that had fallen from him and went back and stood on the bank of the Jordan. ¹⁴He took the cloak that had fallen from Elijah and struck the water with it. "Where now is the LORD, the God of Elijah?" he asked. When he struck the water, it divided to the right and to the left, and he crossed over.

¹⁵The company of the prophets from Jericho, who were watching, said, "The spirit of Elijah is resting on Elisha." And they went to meet him and bowed to the ground before him. ¹⁶"Look," they said, "we your servants have fifty able men. Let them go and look for your master. Perhaps the Spirit of the LORD has picked him up and set him down on some mountain or in some valley."

"No," Elisha replied, "do not send them."

¹⁷But they persisted until he was too embarrassed to refuse. So he said, "Send them." And they sent fifty men, who searched for three days but did not find him. ¹⁸When they returned to Elisha, who was staying in Jericho, he said to them, "Didn't I tell you not to go?"

Healing of the Water

¹⁹The people of the city said to Elisha, "Look, our lord, this town is well situated, as you can see, but the water is bad and the land is unproductive."

²⁰"Bring me a new bowl," he said, "and put salt in it." So they brought it to him.

²¹Then he went out to the spring and threw the salt into it, saying, "This is what the LORD says: 'I have healed this water. Never again will it cause death or make the land unproductive.'" ²²And the water has remained pure to this day, according to the word Elisha had spoken.

Elisha Is Jeered

²³From there Elisha went up to Bethel. As he was walking along the road, some boys came out of the town and jeered at him. "Get out of here, baldy!" they said. "Get out of here, baldy!" ²⁴He turned around, looked at them and called down a curse on them in the name of the LORD. Then two bears came out of the woods and mauled forty-two

---

2:9 a double portion The Hebrew phrase used here, *pi shenayim* (literally rendered "according to two shares"), echoes the legal terminology of Dt 21:17, according to which the firstborn was to receive a double share (*pi shenayim*) of the inheritance. Elisha desires for his spiritual inheritance to be like that of a firstborn son — double in share in comparison to Elijah's other spiritual children, such as other prophets (compare Jn 14:12–14). **of your spirit** As with Moses, the spirit of Elijah is transferrable to others (Nu 11:16–17,24–26). The office of head prophet is transferred from Elijah to Elisha — just as the office of commander of Israel is transferred from Moses to Joshua. This includes the transferring of the Spirit of Yahweh, which was at work in Elijah, to Elisha. Yahweh was the one who originally made this decision (1Ki 19:16).

2:11 a chariot of fire and horses of fire Fire in the OT is associated with God's presence (compare 2Ki 1:10,12).

2:12 My father In the OT, groups sometimes applied the Hebrew word used here, *av*, denoting "father," to their leaders (1Sa 10:12; 2Ki 6:21; 13:14). Elisha's use of *av* may suggest Elijah was head of the prophets of Yahweh, or it may simply reflect Elisha's close relationship with Elijah (compare 1Ki 20:34; 2Ki 2:3; 4:1; 5:22; 6:1). **tore it in two** A gesture of grief.

2:14 the cloak that had fallen from Elijah This seems to be the same cloak Elijah draped on Elisha in 1Ki 19:19 to signify his prophetic calling.

2:15–25 Elisha's actions in this string of narratives demonstrate that he has the spirit of Elijah (2Ki 2:15).

While Elisha's healing of the waters of Jericho (vv. 19–22) attests to the power of the prophetic word to bring life, his cursing of the youths at Bethel (vv. 23–25) attests to the power of the prophetic word to bring death.

2:15 The spirit of Elijah is resting on Elisha See note on v. 9.

2:16 fifty able men This phrase typically appears in reference to military forces. Here, it may simply indicate that they are able to traverse long distances quickly or refer to their prophetic abilities. **the Spirit of the LORD** This phrase can also be translated "Yahweh's wind," since the Hebrew word for spirit, *ruach*, also denotes wind (compare 1Ki 19:11; Jn 3:5–8).

2:21 I have healed this water Draws a parallel between Elisha and Moses, who made bitter water sweet by throwing a log into the waters of Marah (Ex 15:23–25).

2:22 to this day A formula regularly used in etiologies — stories concerned with origins (e.g., 2Ki 8:22; 10:27; 16:6; 17:34).

2:23 Bethel This city was the site of one of Jeroboam's golden calves and his altar that was torn apart (1Ki 12:29; 13) and a location Elisha had visited earlier with Elijah (2Ki 2:2–3). **some boys** There is no indication in the Hebrew text of the age of the boys; they may have been adolescents. **jeered at him** Since Elisha acts so harshly and is at a location where idolatrous worship took place (at least at one point), it's likely that he was condemned for his presence as a prophet. **Get out of here** The Hebrew text here uses the word *alah*, which (ironically) is the same word used for Elijah's ascent to

of the boys. ²⁵And he went on to Mount Carmel and from there returned to Samaria.

Moab Revolts

3 Joramª son of Ahab became king of Israel in Samaria in the eighteenth year of Jehoshaphat king of Judah, and he reigned twelve years. ²He did evil in the eyes of the LORD, but not as his father and mother had done. He got rid of the sacred stone of Baal that his father had made. ³Nevertheless he clung to the sins of Jeroboam son of Nebat, which he had caused Israel to commit; he did not turn away from them.

⁴Now Mesha king of Moab raised sheep, and he had to pay the king of Israel a tribute of a hundred thousand lambs and the wool of a hundred thousand rams. ⁵But after Ahab died, the king of Moab rebelled against the king of Israel. ⁶So at that time King Joram set out from Samaria and mobilized all Israel. ⁷He also sent this message to Jehoshaphat king of Judah: "The king of Moab has rebelled against me. Will you go with me to fight against Moab?"

"I will go with you," he replied. "I am as you are, my people as your people, my horses as your horses."

⁸"By what route shall we attack?" he asked.

"Through the Desert of Edom," he answered.

⁹So the king of Israel set out with the king of Judah and the king of Edom. After a roundabout march of seven days, the army had no more water for themselves or for the animals with them.

ª 1 Hebrew *Jehoram*, a variant of *Joram*; also in verse 6

---

heaven (v. 1). **baldy** Elisha's baldness was most likely natural and not associated with his prophetic office. Uncut hair was the accepted norm among ascetics (those who abstained from pleasure or comfort) as reflected in the Nazirite laws (Nu 6:5; Jdg 13:5); moreover, the law prohibited cutting hair for ritual purposes (Lev 19:27; 21:5; Dt 14:1). The text's repetition of the same phrase suggests incessant mocking of Elisha's appearance and spiritual status.

2:24 two bears The image of a female bear robbed of her cubs is used several times in the OT to describe an angry or destructive force (2Sa 17:8; Pr 17:12; Hos 13:8).

2:25 Mount Carmel A peak within the mountain range that extends to the Mediterranean coast at the modern city of Haifa. Mount Carmel was the site of Elijah's confrontation with Ahab and contest with the prophets of Baal (1Ki 18). **Samaria** See note on 2Ki 1:3.

3:1–27 The narrative briefly begun in 1:1 continues here. While the Biblical account of Moab's rebellion against Israel focuses on the role of Elisha the prophet, another account appears on the Mesha Stele (also known as the Moabite Stone). This stone, an inscribed pillar or obelisk, dates to about 830 BC and commemorates the achievements of King Mesha of Moab—especially his defeat of Israel.

The inscription mentions the Israelite kings Omri and Ahab by name, making it one of the earliest references to Israel outside the Bible. It also names Yahweh, stating that Mesha "took from there the vessels of Yahweh and dragged them before Chemosh" (lines 17–18). (Chemosh is a Moabite god.) See the infographic "The Mesha Stele" on p. 565.

3:1 Joram son of Ahab The final king in the Omride dynasty (see note on 1Ki 16:21–28); he succeeded his brother, King Ahaziah of Israel, since Ahaziah did not have a son (2Ki 1:17). He is not the same person as the king of Judah, who in the Hebrew text shares the same name, *yehoram* (Jehoram; compare note on 1:17). **in Samaria** Capital city of the northern kingdom of Israel. **Jehoshaphat king of Judah** An ally of King Ahab of Israel (1Ki 22); Jehoshaphat attempted to revive the sea trade established under Solomon (1Ki 22:48–49).

OMRIDE DYNASTY	885–841 BC
Omri	885–874 BC
Ahab	874–853 BC
Ahaziah	853–852 BC
Joram/Jehoram	852–841 BC

3:2 but not as his father and mother had done Refers to King Ahab and Jezebel, who instituted the worship of the Canaanite storm god Baal and Canaanite fertility goddess Asherah and persecuted the prophets of Yahweh (see 1Ki 16:31–33; 18:4).

3:3 the sins of Jeroboam Refers to the installation of the golden calves and the establishment of high places and their accompanying temples, where people worshiped other gods along with Yahweh (1Ki 11:26–33; 13:33–34). Jeroboam reigned over the northern kingdom of Israel, after the nation split into Israel and Judah (ca. 930–909 BC).

3:4 Mesha king of Moab Mesha's name and ancestry appear in the opening line of the Mesha Stele, an inscription that describes Mesha's interactions with King Ahab of Israel. See note on 2Ki 3:1–27.

2 Kings 3:4

MOABITES
The Moabites were descendants of Moab (son of Lot and his older daughter; Ge 19:30–38) and lived east of the Jordan River and the Dead Sea. Moab was an enemy of Israel throughout its history. It periodically controlled parts of Israel during the period of the judges (Jdg 3:12–30) and opposed Israel during the reigns of Saul (1Sa 14:47) and David (2Sa 8:2). Solomon made a marriage alliance with the Moabites that resulted in him creating a high place for their god, Chemosh (1Ki 11:1–8). In addition to King Mesha, notable Moabites in the OT include: Balak, the king who hired Balaam to curse the Israelites (Nu 22–24); Eglon, the king who was assassinated by Ehud (Jdg 3:15–30); and Ruth, the widow of Mahlon and wife of Boaz (Ru 4:10,13).

3:5 Moab rebelled against the king of Israel See 1:1 and note.

3:8 Through the Desert of Edom The invasion route (through the wilderness of Edom) is critical to the storyline. Due to the circuitous nature of their chosen approach to Moab, the invading armies soon found themselves in desert terrain without water (v. 9). Edom, located southeast of Israel and Judah, was the territory settled by the descendants of the Esau (Ge 25:25; 36:1,8).

3:9 the king of Edom This verse probably is referring to Edom's governor or deputy, because 1Ki 22:47 says there was no king in Edom during the reign of Jehoshaphat.

[10]"What!" exclaimed the king of Israel. "Has the LORD called us three kings together only to deliver us into the hands of Moab?"

[11]But Jehoshaphat asked, "Is there no prophet of the LORD here, through whom we may inquire of the LORD?"

An officer of the king of Israel answered, "Elisha son of Shaphat is here. He used to pour water on the hands of Elijah. [a]"

[12]Jehoshaphat said, "The word of the LORD is with him." So the king of Israel and Jehoshaphat and the king of Edom went down to him.

[13]Elisha said to the king of Israel, "Why do you want to involve me? Go to the prophets of your father and the prophets of your mother."

"No," the king of Israel answered, "because it was the LORD who called us three kings together to deliver us into the hands of Moab."

[14]Elisha said, "As surely as the LORD Almighty lives, whom I serve, if I did not have respect for the presence of Jehoshaphat king of Judah, I would not pay any attention to you. [15]But now bring me a harpist."

---

[a] 11 That is, he was Elijah's personal servant.

3:11 Is there no prophet of the LORD here Jehoshaphat made a similar request when aligning with Ahab against the Syrians because he was not satisfied with Ahab's prophets of Baal and Asherah (1Ki 22:5–8). **we may inquire of the LORD** Compare 1Ki 22:5. **pour water on the hands of Elijah** An image of servitude.

3:13 prophets of your father Refers to the prophets of Ahab and Jezebel, who served the deities Baal and Asherah (see 1Ki 18:19).
3:14 As surely as the LORD Almighty lives This kind of phrase signals the start of an oath. This particular oath refers to Yahweh as the leader of hosts or armies

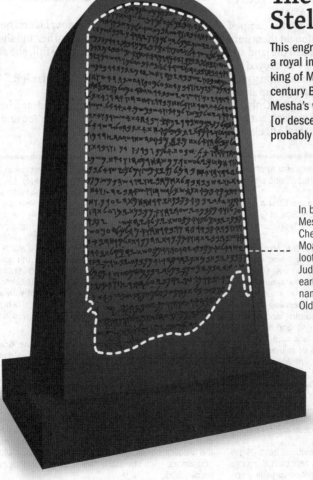

The Mesha Stele

This engraved stone contains a royal inscription by Mesha, king of Moab during the ninth century BC. It celebrates Mesha's victory over the "son [or descendant] of Omri," probably Joram (Jehoram).

In boasting of his victories, Mesha gives glory to Chemosh—the chief god of the Moabites—and describes his looting of the temple vessels of Judah. The stele contains the earliest known reference to the name "Yahweh" outside of the Old Testament.

The stele supports the biblical account of events during Joram's reign of Israel. Second Kings 3:21-27 describes the king of Moab offering his son as a sacrifice, after which great wrath came upon Israel. On the stele, Mesha credits his god, Chemosh, as conquering his enemies.

While the harpist was playing, the hand of the Lord came on Elisha ¹⁶and he said, "This is what the Lord says: I will fill this valley with pools of water. ¹⁷For this is what the Lord says: You will see neither wind nor rain, yet this valley will be filled with water, and you, your cattle and your other animals will drink. ¹⁸This is an easy thing in the eyes of the Lord; he will also deliver Moab into your hands. ¹⁹You will overthrow every fortified city and every major town. You will cut down every good tree, stop up all the springs, and ruin every good field with stones."

²⁰The next morning, about the time for offering the sacrifice, there it was—water flowing from the direction of Edom! And the land was filled with water.

²¹Now all the Moabites had heard that the kings had come to fight against them; so every man, young and old, who could bear arms was called up and stationed on the border. ²²When they got up early in the morning, the sun was shining on the water. To the Moabites across the way, the water looked red—like blood. ²³"That's blood!" they said. "Those kings must have fought and slaughtered each other. Now to the plunder, Moab!"

²⁴But when the Moabites came to the camp of Israel, the Israelites rose up and fought them until they fled. And the Israelites invaded the land and slaughtered the Moabites. ²⁵They destroyed the towns, and each man threw a stone on every good field until it was covered. They stopped up all the springs and cut down every good tree. Only Kir Hareseth was left with its stones in place, but men armed with slings surrounded it and attacked it.

²⁶When the king of Moab saw that the battle had gone against him, he took with him seven hundred swordsmen to break through to the king of Edom, but they failed. ²⁷Then he took his firstborn son, who was to succeed him as king, and offered him as a sacrifice on the city wall. The fury against Israel was great; they withdrew and returned to their own land.

The Widow's Olive Oil

4 The wife of a man from the company of the prophets cried out to Elisha, "Your servant my husband is dead, and you know that he revered the Lord. But now his creditor is coming to take my two boys as his slaves."

²Elisha replied to her, "How can I help you? Tell me, what do you have in your house?"

"Your servant has nothing there at all," she said, "except a small jar of olive oil."

³Elisha said, "Go around and ask all your neighbors for empty jars. Don't ask for just a few. ⁴Then go inside and shut the door behind you and your sons. Pour oil into all the jars, and as each is filled, put it to one side."

⁵She left him and shut the door behind her and her sons. They brought the jars to her and she kept pouring. ⁶When all the jars were full, she said to her son, "Bring me another one."

But he replied, "There is not a jar left." Then the oil stopped flowing.

⁷She went and told the man of God, and he said, "Go, sell the oil and pay your debts. You and your sons can live on what is left."

(1Sa 17:45). **whom I serve** This expression often appears in both kingly court scenes (1Ki 1:2) and prophetic contexts (1Ki 17:1; 18:15; 2Ki 5:16).
3:15 the hand of the Lord came on Elisha In 1Sa 10:5, the band of prophets that meets Saul at Gibeah of God (Gibeath-elohim, "the hill of God") also uses music to elicit prophetic oracles.
3:19 cut down every good tree The Mosaic Law prohibits the felling of fruit-producing trees during a siege. Armies may, however, cut down trees that are not good for food to create siege works against a city (Dt 20:19–20).
3:20 the time for offering the sacrifice The Law required the Israelites to offer morning and evening sacrifices every day (see Ex 29:38–42 and note).
3:23 That's blood Flowing blood is a common motif in ancient Near Eastern accounts of military victory. Upon arriving at the place of battle, the Moabites were fooled by the standing water, which was completely out of place and appeared red as blood against the ground with the sun's reflection (2Ki 3:21–22). They assumed it was blood and that the invading armies (often enemies themselves) had erupted in battle against each other. When they approached to strip the dead and take spoil, they were ambushed (v. 24).
3:27 offered him as a sacrifice Leviticus 20:1–5 prohibits sacrificing children to Molek. Jephthah the judge may have offered his child as a sacrifice to fulfill a vow

(Jdg 11:30–31; Lev 27:29). **fury** The Hebrew term used here describes anger toward wrongdoers (Nu 18:5; Dt 29:27; Jos 9:20; 22:20), but it is uncertain whose wrath the text refers to here. It may be the perceived anger of Chemosh, Moab's patron god, leading to the Israelites' defeat. However, this account does not portray a defeat of Yahweh by Chemosh; instead it depicts a defeat of God's people after they lost faith in Yahweh's ability. The OT portrays the Israelites as believing that the gods of other nations were real. Those gods were originally assigned to the nations by Yahweh (Dt 32:8–9). Given this worldview, which presumes the superiority of Yahweh, it seems that the Israelites were frightened by the human sacrifice, believed that the Moabites' god was angry, and retreated.

4:1–7 The narrative transitions away from the kings of Israel and Judah and refocuses on Elisha. Elisha's ability to perform miracles thematically links the four stories in 2Ki 4. He aids a widow in need (vv. 1–7), rewards kindness and revives a child (vv. 8–37), neutralizes poison (vv. 38–41) and feeds the hungry (vv. 42–44).

4:1 the company of the prophets See 2:3 and note.
4:7 man of God Refers to Elisha. See 1:9 and note.
can live on what is left This miracle not only meets the widow's needs, but leaves her and her sons with an abundance. See the table "Miracles of the Prophets" on p. 1366.

The Shunammite's Son Restored to Life

8One day Elisha went to Shunem. And a well-to-do woman was there, who urged him to stay for a meal. So whenever he came by, he stopped there to eat. 9She said to her husband, "I know that this man who often comes our way is a holy man of God. 10Let's make a small room on the roof and put in it a bed and a table, a chair and a lamp for him. Then he can stay there whenever he comes to us."

11One day when Elisha came, he went up to his room and lay down there. 12He said to his servant Gehazi, "Call the Shunammite." So he called her, and she stood before him. 13Elisha said to him, "Tell her, 'You have gone to all this trouble for us. Now what can be done for you? Can we speak on your behalf to the king or the commander of the army?'"

She replied, "I have a home among my own people."

14"What can be done for her?" Elisha asked.

Gehazi said, "She has no son, and her husband is old."

15Then Elisha said, "Call her." So he called her, and she stood in the doorway. 16"About this time next year," Elisha said, "you will hold a son in your arms."

"No, my lord!" she objected. "Please, man of God, don't mislead your servant!"

17But the woman became pregnant, and the next year about that same time she gave birth to a son, just as Elisha had told her.

18The child grew, and one day he went out to his father, who was with the reapers. 19He said to his father, "My head! My head!"

His father told a servant, "Carry him to his mother." 20After the servant had lifted him up and carried him to his mother, the boy sat on her lap until noon, and then he died. 21She went up and laid him on the bed of the man of God, then shut the door and went out.

22She called her husband and said, "Please send me one of the servants and a donkey so I can go to the man of God quickly and return."

23"Why go to him today?" he asked. "It's not the New Moon or the Sabbath."

"That's all right," she said.

24She saddled the donkey and said to her servant, "Lead on; don't slow down for me unless I tell you." 25So she set out and came to the man of God at Mount Carmel.

When he saw her in the distance, the man of God said to his servant Gehazi, "Look! There's the Shunammite! 26Run to meet her and ask her, 'Are you all right? Is your husband all right? Is your child all right?'"

"Everything is all right," she said.

27When she reached the man of God at the mountain, she took hold of his feet. Gehazi came over to push her away, but the man of God said, "Leave her alone! She is in bitter distress, but the LORD has hidden it from me and has not told me why."

28"Did I ask you for a son, my lord?" she said. "Didn't I tell you, 'Don't raise my hopes'?"

29Elisha said to Gehazi, "Tuck your cloak into your belt, take my staff in your hand and run. Don't greet anyone you meet, and if anyone greets you, do not answer. Lay my staff on the boy's face."

30But the child's mother said, "As surely as the LORD lives and as you live, I will not leave you." So he got up and followed her.

31Gehazi went on ahead and laid the staff on the boy's face, but there was no sound or response. So Gehazi went back to meet Elisha and told him, "The boy has not awakened."

32When Elisha reached the house, there was the boy lying dead on his couch. 33He went in, shut the door on the two of them and prayed to the LORD. 34Then he got on the bed and lay on the boy, mouth to mouth, eyes to eyes, hands to hands. As he stretched himself out on him, the boy's body grew warm. 35Elisha turned away and walked back and forth in the room and then got on the bed and stretched out on him once

---

4:8 Shunem A northern town located in the Jezreel Valley near Mount Gilboa and Megiddo (1Sa 28:4). King David's female attendant, Abishag, is from Shunem (1Ki 1:3,15), and the female lover from Song of Songs may have also been from this town (see SS 6:13 and note). **well-to-do** The Hebrew term here denotes greatness and describes an esteemed person of high status (2Ki 5:1; 10:6,11; Jnh 3:7; Na 3:10).

4:13 Can we speak on your behalf Elisha's offer suggests that he holds a position of influence among high government officials. **I have a home among my own people** The woman politely declines Elisha's offer, indicating that her family and clan can provide for her needs.

4:16 About this time next year The Hebrew idiom used here, which literally reads, "as a time of life" (Ge 18:10,14), seems to be specifically connected to the theme of promised births.

4:23 not the New Moon Israelites marked the new moon by sacrifice, by sounding a ram's horn and by feasting with family (Nu 28:11–15; 1Sa 20:5,26–29). The husband's question suggests the new moon was also a time for visiting prophets.

4:25 Mount Carmel Where Elijah's contest with the prophets of Baal took place (1Ki 18).

4:27 she took hold of his feet An action that accompanies praise or supplication (Mt 28:9). **the LORD has hidden it from me** Elisha is taken aback because prophets in similar circumstances in Israel's history had been forewarned (e.g., 1Sa 9:15; 1Ki 14:5).

4:29 Tuck your cloak into your belt See note on 2Ki 9:1.

4:30 As surely as the LORD lives See 2:2 and note.

4:31 response The Hebrew terminology here denotes a response to spoken word. This suggests that Gehazi also gave an oral command to the woman's son (compare 5:11; Mk 5:41).

4:35 The boy sneezed seven times Indicating that his breath had returned. The number seven is symbolic of completeness (compare Ru 4:15; Job 1:2).

more. The boy sneezed seven times and opened his eyes.

³⁶Elisha summoned Gehazi and said, "Call the Shunammite." And he did. When she came, he said, "Take your son." ³⁷She came in, fell at his feet and bowed to the ground. Then she took her son and went out.

Death in the Pot

³⁸Elisha returned to Gilgal and there was a famine in that region. While the company of the prophets was meeting with him, he said to his servant, "Put on the large pot and cook some stew for these prophets."

³⁹One of them went out into the fields to gather herbs and found a wild vine and picked as many of its gourds as his garment could hold. When he returned, he cut them up into the pot of stew, though no one knew what they were. ⁴⁰The stew was poured out for the men, but as they began to eat it, they cried out, "Man of God, there is death in the pot!" And they could not eat it.

⁴¹Elisha said, "Get some flour." He put it into the pot and said, "Serve it to the people to eat." And there was nothing harmful in the pot.

Feeding of a Hundred

⁴²A man came from Baal Shalishah, bringing the man of God twenty loaves of barley bread baked from the first ripe grain, along with some heads of new grain. "Give it to the people to eat," Elisha said.

⁴³"How can I set this before a hundred men?" his servant asked.

But Elisha answered, "Give it to the people to eat. For this is what the LORD says: 'They will eat and have some left over.'" ⁴⁴Then he set it before them, and they ate and had some left over, according to the word of the LORD.

Naaman Healed of Leprosy

5 Now Naaman was commander of the army of the king of Aram. He was a great man in the sight of his master and highly regarded, because through him the LORD had given victory to Aram. He was a valiant soldier, but he had leprosy.ᵃ

²Now bands of raiders from Aram had gone out and had taken captive a young girl from Israel, and she served Naaman's wife. ³She said to her mistress, "If only my master would see the prophet who is in Samaria! He would cure him of his leprosy."

⁴Naaman went to his master and told him what the girl from Israel had said. ⁵"By all means, go," the king of Aram replied. "I will send a letter to the king of Israel." So Naaman left, taking with him ten talentsᵇ of silver, six thousand shekelsᶜ of gold and ten sets of clothing. ⁶The letter that he took to the king of Israel read: "With this letter I am sending my servant Naaman to you so that you may cure him of his leprosy."

⁷As soon as the king of Israel read the letter, he tore his robes and said, "Am I God? Can I kill and bring back to life? Why does this fellow send someone to me to be cured of his leprosy? See how he is trying to pick a quarrel with me!"

⁸When Elisha the man of God heard that the king of Israel had torn his robes, he sent him this message: "Why have you torn your robes? Have the man come to me and he will know that there is a prophet in Israel." ⁹So Naaman went with his horses and chariots and stopped at the door of Elisha's house. ¹⁰Elisha sent a messenger to say to him, "Go, wash yourself seven times in the Jordan, and your flesh will be restored and you will be cleansed."

¹¹But Naaman went away angry and said, "I

ᵃ 1 The Hebrew for *leprosy* was used for various diseases affecting the skin; also in verses 3, 6, 7, 11 and 27.   ᵇ 5 That is, about 750 pounds or about 340 kilograms   ᶜ 5 That is, about 150 pounds or about 69 kilograms

---

4:36 he said, "Take your son." Elisha's command echoes the promise that the Shunammite woman would bear and embrace a son (2Ki 4:16).
4:38 the company of the prophets See note on 2:3.
4:39 gourds Possibly *Citrullus colocynthis*, a small yellow melon known to be fatal.
4:40 Man of God See note on 1:9.
4:44 and had some left over Jesus' feeding of the large crowds recalls Elisha's feeding the prophets here (Mt 14:13–21; 15:32–38; Mk 8:1–10).

5:1–14 The narrative transitions to offer the backstory for another event involving Elisha. The healing of Naaman, commander of the Aramean (Syrian) army, highlights God's care for even Israel's enemy and the contrast between faith and disbelief. Both the king of Aram (Syria) and the Israelite child—who is a spoil of war—believe in Elisha's abilities. Naaman and the king of Israel, ironically, do not believe healing is possible. The account of Naaman's healing (2Ki 5:1–14) is followed by a description of his newfound commitment to the God of Israel (vv. 15–19). See the table "Miracles of the Prophets" on p. 1366.

5:1 the king of Aram Most likely Ben-Hadad (see 6:24 and note). **he had leprosy** The Hebrew term here refers to a wide variety of human skin diseases (see Lev 13:1–59 and note).
5:3 Samaria Capital of the northern kingdom of Israel. **cure** The Hebrew word used here, literally rendered as "he will gather," refers to the readmission of the suspected leper into society after having been quarantined (2Ki 5:6; Nu 12:14–15).
5:7 he tore his robes A gesture of grief. **Can I kill and bring back to life** Echoes Yahweh's description of himself in the Song of Moses (Dt 32:39). **he is trying to pick a quarrel with me** The king of Israel, presumably Joram/Jehoram (2Ki 3:1; see note on 1:17), assumes that the king of Aram (Syria) has commanded an impossible task, so that failure to comply would provide a pretense for a raid.
5:8 Elisha the man of God Compare note on 1:9.
5:10 seven times Compare note on 4:35.
5:11 cure me of my leprosy Naaman expects Elisha to perform a ritual like other healers.

thought that he would surely come out to me and stand and call on the name of the LORD his God, wave his hand over the spot and cure me of my leprosy. ¹²Are not Abana and Pharpar, the rivers of Damascus, better than all the waters of Israel? Couldn't I wash in them and be cleansed?" So he turned and went off in a rage.

¹³Naaman's servants went to him and said, "My father, if the prophet had told you to do some great thing, would you not have done it? How much more, then, when he tells you, 'Wash and be cleansed'!" ¹⁴So he went down and dipped himself in the Jordan seven times, as the man of God had told him, and his flesh was restored and became clean like that of a young boy.

¹⁵Then Naaman and all his attendants went back to the man of God. He stood before him and said, "Now I know that there is no God in all the world except in Israel. So please accept a gift from your servant."

¹⁶The prophet answered, "As surely as the LORD lives, whom I serve, I will not accept a thing." And even though Naaman urged him, he refused.

¹⁷"If you will not," said Naaman, "please let me, your servant, be given as much earth as a pair of mules can carry, for your servant will never again make burnt offerings and sacrifices to any other god but the LORD. ¹⁸But may the LORD forgive your servant for this one thing: When my master enters the temple of Rimmon to bow down and he is leaning on my arm and I have to bow there also — when I bow down in the temple of Rimmon, may the LORD forgive your servant for this."

¹⁹"Go in peace," Elisha said.

After Naaman had traveled some distance, ²⁰Gehazi, the servant of Elisha the man of God, said to himself, "My master was too easy on Naaman, this Aramean, by not accepting from him what he brought. As surely as the LORD lives, I will run after him and get something from him."

²¹So Gehazi hurried after Naaman. When Naaman saw him running toward him, he got down from the chariot to meet him. "Is everything all right?" he asked.

²²"Everything is all right," Gehazi answered. "My master sent me to say, 'Two young men from the company of the prophets have just come to me from the hill country of Ephraim. Please give them a talent[a] of silver and two sets of clothing.'"

²³"By all means, take two talents," said Naaman. He urged Gehazi to accept them, and then tied up the two talents of silver in two bags, with two sets of clothing. He gave them to two of his servants, and they carried them ahead of Gehazi. ²⁴When Gehazi came to the hill, he took the things from the servants and put them away in the house. He sent the men away and they left.

²⁵When he went in and stood before his master, Elisha asked him, "Where have you been, Gehazi?"

"Your servant didn't go anywhere," Gehazi answered.

²⁶But Elisha said to him, "Was not my spirit with you when the man got down from his chariot to meet you? Is this the time to take money or to accept clothes — or olive groves and vineyards, or flocks and herds, or male and female slaves? ²⁷Naaman's leprosy will cling to you and to your descendants forever." Then Gehazi went from Elisha's presence and his skin was leprous — it had become as white as snow.

An Axhead Floats

6 The company of the prophets said to Elisha, "Look, the place where we meet with you is too small for us. ²Let us go to the Jordan, where

a 22 That is, about 75 pounds or about 34 kilograms

5:13 My father In the OT, the Hebrew term for father sometimes applies to a leader (1Sa 10:12; 2Ki 2:12; 6:21; 13:14). In ancient Near Eastern diplomacy, familial language was often used to express the relationship between greater and lesser powers. It seems that the servants' use of "father" likely conveys Naaman's superiority. It also might reflect the closeness of their relationship to Naaman and their genuine concern for his well-being.

5:15–27 The story of Gehazi's greed and punishment forms the second part of the account of Naaman's healing (vv. 1–14). Naaman's faithfulness and Elisha's modesty stand in direct contrast to the king of Israel's disbelief and Gehazi's greed and deception (see vv. 1–14,8,15,20–23). Furthermore, the role reversal in the opening and closing verses of this narrative (vv. 1,27) — the respected foreign general trusts Elisha and is healed, while Elisha's close attendant acts deceitfully and is inflicted with the same disease — suggests that ch. 5 is a single narrative rather than two separate episodes.

5:16 As surely as the LORD lives See note on 2:2.
5:17 as much earth as a pair of mules can carry Naaman wants holy ground (the dirt) with him so that he can have Yahweh with him while outside Israel. The request reflects a belief that Israel's territory belonged

to Yahweh, while other nations were under the dominion of other, lesser gods (Dt 32:8–9). Naaman now believes in Yahweh and vows to never sacrifice to another god, but his official duties (v. 18) require that he accompany his elderly king into the temple of Rimmon.

5:22 the company of the prophets See note on 2:3.
5:23 take two talents A considerable amount of silver, although only one-fifth of the silver that Naaman brought with him (5:5).
5:24 the hill The Hebrew word here is a topographic term that describes the elevated part of a city, usually the center.
5:26 my spirit The Hebrew term used here can mean "inner person," "mind," "will" or "heart." In the ancient Near East, the heart was associated with comprehension, not emotion.
5:27 his skin was leprous — it had become as white as snow The same imagery occurs when God turns Moses' hand leprous as a sign (Ex 4:6) and when Miriam opposes Moses in the wilderness (Nu 12:10). See note on 2Ki 5:1.

6:1–7 The narrative of Aram and Syria is briefly interrupted by a story of a floating axhead. Like the stories in chs. 4–5, this narrative centers on Elisha's prophetic

each of us can get a pole; and let us build a place there for us to meet."

And he said, "Go."

³Then one of them said, "Won't you please come with your servants?"

"I will," Elisha replied. ⁴And he went with them. They went to the Jordan and began to cut down trees. ⁵As one of them was cutting down a tree, the iron axhead fell into the water. "Oh no, my lord!" he cried out. "It was borrowed!"

⁶The man of God asked, "Where did it fall?" When he showed him the place, Elisha cut a stick and threw it there, and made the iron float. ⁷"Lift it out," he said. Then the man reached out his hand and took it.

Elisha Traps Blinded Arameans

⁸Now the king of Aram was at war with Israel. After conferring with his officers, he said, "I will set up my camp in such and such a place."

⁹The man of God sent word to the king of Israel: "Beware of passing that place, because the Arameans are going down there." ¹⁰So the king of Israel checked on the place indicated by the man of God. Time and again Elisha warned the king, so that he was on his guard in such places.

¹¹This enraged the king of Aram. He summoned his officers and demanded of them, "Tell me! Which of us is on the side of the king of Israel?"

¹²"None of us, my lord the king," said one of his officers, "but Elisha, the prophet who is in Israel, tells the king of Israel the very words you speak in your bedroom."

¹³"Go, find out where he is," the king ordered, "so I can send men and capture him." The report came back: "He is in Dothan." ¹⁴Then he sent horses and chariots and a strong force there. They went by night and surrounded the city.

¹⁵When the servant of the man of God got up and went out early the next morning, an army with horses and chariots had surrounded the city. "Oh no, my lord! What shall we do?" the servant asked.

¹⁶"Don't be afraid," the prophet answered. "Those who are with us are more than those who are with them."

¹⁷And Elisha prayed, "Open his eyes, Lord, so that he may see." Then the Lord opened the servant's eyes, and he looked and saw the hills full of horses and chariots of fire all around Elisha.

¹⁸As the enemy came down toward him, Elisha prayed to the Lord, "Strike this army with blindness." So he struck them with blindness, as Elisha had asked.

¹⁹Elisha told them, "This is not the road and this is not the city. Follow me, and I will lead you to the man you are looking for." And he led them to Samaria.

²⁰After they entered the city, Elisha said, "Lord, open the eyes of these men so they can see." Then the Lord opened their eyes and they looked, and there they were, inside Samaria.

²¹When the king of Israel saw them, he asked Elisha, "Shall I kill them, my father? Shall I kill them?"

²²"Do not kill them," he answered. "Would you kill those you have captured with your own sword or bow? Set food and water before them so that they may eat and drink and then go back to their master." ²³So he prepared a great feast for them, and after they had finished eating and drinking, he sent them away, and they returned to their

---

ability to work miracles. See the table "Miracles of the Prophets" on p. 1366.

6:1 The company of the prophets See note on 2:3.
6:6 The man of God Refers to Elisha. Compare note on 1:9.

6:8–23 This story transitions back to the narratives about Aram (Syria) and Israel. Elisha's ability to stop raids on Israel highlights his power. He knows what others plan behind closed doors (vv. 10–12) and sees supernatural beings that are invisible to other people (v. 17). Elisha's word, moreover, affects the vision of both his servant and his enemies (6:17–18,20). This story gives very little specific historical data; it names neither the king of Israel nor the king of Aram, which makes it difficult to place within Israel's history.

6:8 such and such a place The Hebrew phrase used here refers to both unnamed places (1Sa 21:2) and people (Ru 4:1). The author withholds this information either because he does not have it or because he wants to emphasize something other than historical data.

6:13 in Dothan Dothan was situated near the mountain road that ran through the Jezreel Valley.

6:16 Don't be afraid This Hebrew phrase functions as the opening to prophecies of salvation throughout the OT (e.g., Ge 15:1; Isa 41:10; La 3:57).

6:17 the hills The Hebrew word used here, *har*, can be translated as "mountain" or "hill." It most likely indicates the high point inside the city from which Elisha and the servant can see the opposing army (2Ki 6:15). **horses and chariots of fire** Fire is often association with the divine presence. Chariots and horses of fire appeared when Elijah was taken into heaven (2:11).

6:18 came down toward him The city of Dothan was built on high ground, so the army is coming down in a metaphorical, hostile sense (compare 1Sa 17:8).

6:19 lead you to the man you are looking for Although the Syrian troops are commissioned to capture Elisha, he leads them instead to the king of Israel (compare 2Ki 6:13–14). **Samaria** Capital city of Israel (the northern kingdom); located roughly 12 miles south of Dothan.

6:21 father In the OT, the Hebrew word used here, *av*, is sometimes applied to a leader (see 2:12 and note). By using it here, the king shows respect toward Elisha.

6:23 great feast This seems to stand in tension with his command to give the captives bread; he didn't say to have a feast. **stopped raiding Israel's territory** This story could have occurred chronologically after Israel's later military conflicts with Aram (Syria; see note

master. So the bands from Aram stopped raiding Israel's territory.

Famine in Besieged Samaria

²⁴Some time later, Ben-Hadad king of Aram mobilized his entire army and marched up and laid siege to Samaria. ²⁵There was a great famine in the city; the siege lasted so long that a donkey's head sold for eighty shekels*ᵃ* of silver, and a quarter of a cab*ᵇ* of seed pods*ᶜ* for five shekels.*ᵈ*

²⁶As the king of Israel was passing by on the wall, a woman cried to him, "Help me, my lord the king!"

²⁷The king replied, "If the LORD does not help you, where can I get help for you? From the threshing floor? From the winepress?" ²⁸Then he asked her, "What's the matter?"

She answered, "This woman said to me, 'Give up your son so we may eat him today, and tomorrow we'll eat my son.' ²⁹So we cooked my son and ate him. The next day I said to her, 'Give up your son so we may eat him,' but she had hidden him."

³⁰When the king heard the woman's words, he tore his robes. As he went along the wall, the people looked, and they saw that, under his robes, he had sackcloth on his body. ³¹He said, "May God deal with me, be it ever so severely, if the head of Elisha son of Shaphat remains on his shoulders today!"

³²Now Elisha was sitting in his house, and the elders were sitting with him. The king sent a messenger ahead, but before he arrived, Elisha said to the elders, "Don't you see how this murderer is sending someone to cut off my head? Look, when the messenger comes, shut the door and hold it shut against him. Is not the sound of his master's footsteps behind him?" ³³While he was still talking to them, the messenger came down to him.

The king said, "This disaster is from the LORD. Why should I wait for the LORD any longer?"

7 Elisha replied, "Hear the word of the LORD. This is what the LORD says: About this time tomorrow, a seah*ᵉ* of the finest flour will sell for a shekel*ᶠ* and two seahs*ᵍ* of barley for a shekel at the gate of Samaria."

²The officer on whose arm the king was leaning said to the man of God, "Look, even if the LORD should open the floodgates of the heavens, could this happen?"

"You will see it with your own eyes," answered Elisha, "but you will not eat any of it!"

The Siege Lifted

³Now there were four men with leprosy*ʰ* at the entrance of the city gate. They said to each other, "Why stay here until we die? ⁴If we say, 'We'll go

---

ᵃ 25 That is, about 2 pounds or about 920 grams   *ᵇ 25* That is, probably about 1/4 pound or about 100 grams   *ᶜ 25* Or *of doves' dung*   *ᵈ 25* That is, about 2 ounces or about 58 grams   *ᵉ 1* That is, probably about 12 pounds or about 5.5 kilograms of flour; also in verses 16 and 18   *ᶠ 1* That is, about 2/5 ounce or about 12 grams; also in verses 16 and 18   *ᵍ 1* That is, probably about 20 pounds or about 9 kilograms of barley; also in verses 16 and 18   *ʰ 3* The Hebrew for *leprosy* was used for various diseases affecting the skin; also in verse 8.

---

on 6:8–23) or this line could refer to a short period of peace between Israel and Aram.

6:24–33 Aram's siege of Samaria, part of a series of military conflicts between the two nations, leads to severe famine during which the citizens of Samaria resort to horrifying measures, including cannibalism (see 1Ki 20; 2Ki 6–8). As a last resort, the king of Israel sends for Elisha (vv. 31–33). The account of this siege sets the stage for the following narrative (ch. 7). Ancient sieges of cities involved complete blockades and the slow building of ramps so that soldiers could eventually go over city walls.

6:24 Ben-Hadad king of Aram Ben-Hadad, meaning "son of [the god] Hadad," was the name of more than one king. This section appears to reference the same person who was King Ahab of Israel's enemy (1Ki 20) and the same person the narrative of 2Ki 8:7–15 is about.

6:25 lasted so long that a donkey's head sold for eighty shekels The extreme survival measures taken by the residents of Samaria—paying exorbitant prices for things usually discarded—attest to the effectiveness of the siege.

6:26 cried The Hebrew word used here is a legal term of appeal to a chief arbiter (compare 2Sa 14:4–5; 2Ki 8:3).

6:29 she had hidden him The woman's horrific story is characteristic of texts describing cities under siege in Biblical and other ancient Near Eastern literature (compare Dt 28:52–57; La 2:20; 4:10; Eze 5:10).

6:31 the head of Elisha The king blames Elisha for the siege.

6:32 the elders were sitting with him The Hebrew phrase used here implies that the city elders, like the prophets mentioned earlier, are learning from Elisha (2Ki 4:38; 6:1) or acting as his disciples (Eze 8:1; 14:1; 20:1).

6:33 Why should I wait for the LORD Expresses a lack of hope for Yahweh's deliverance (compare Ps 42:11; 43:5; 130:5; La 3:21,24).

7:1 two seahs of barley for a shekel This contrasts with the outrageous cost of undesirable food sources mentioned in 2Ki 6:25. **at the gate of Samaria** City gates in the ancient Near East were located next to an open plaza where citizens conducted business transactions and handled legal matters (e.g., Ge 23:10; 34:20; Dt 21:19; 25:7; Ru 4:2,11; see note on Job 29:7).

7:2 floodgates of the heavens Refers to rainfall (Ge 7:11; 8:2). The objection here is that, even if God brought rain today, grain could not be sold for such prices tomorrow.

7:3–20 The preceding narrative (2Ki 6:24—7:2) concludes with an account of the Aramean (Syrian) army abandoning its siege of Samaria. Four lepers inadvertently fulfill Elisha's prophecy that grain will be plentiful within 24 hours (vv. 1–2).

7:3 leprosy The Hebrew term used here, *tsara'*, refers to an array of skin diseases (see note on Lev 13:1–59).

7:4 We'll go into the city Lepers, according to Mosaic Law, were forbidden to enter cities (Lev 13:46; Nu 12:14–16).

into the city' — the famine is there, and we will die. And if we stay here, we will die. So let's go over to the camp of the Arameans and surrender. If they spare us, we live; if they kill us, then we die."

⁵At dusk they got up and went to the camp of the Arameans. When they reached the edge of the camp, no one was there, ⁶for the Lord had caused the Arameans to hear the sound of chariots and horses and a great army, so that they said to one another, "Look, the king of Israel has hired the Hittite and Egyptian kings to attack us!" ⁷So they got up and fled in the dusk and abandoned their tents and their horses and donkeys. They left the camp as it was and ran for their lives.

⁸The men who had leprosy reached the edge of the camp, entered one of the tents and ate and drank. Then they took silver, gold and clothes, and went off and hid them. They returned and entered another tent and took some things from it and hid them also.

⁹Then they said to each other, "What we're doing is not right. This is a day of good news and we are keeping it to ourselves. If we wait until daylight, punishment will overtake us. Let's go at once and report this to the royal palace."

¹⁰So they went and called out to the city gatekeepers and told them, "We went into the Aramean camp and no one was there — not a sound of anyone — only tethered horses and donkeys, and the tents left just as they were." ¹¹The gatekeepers shouted the news, and it was reported within the palace.

¹²The king got up in the night and said to his officers, "I will tell you what the Arameans have done to us. They know we are starving; so they have left the camp to hide in the countryside, thinking, 'They will surely come out, and then we will take them alive and get into the city.'"

¹³One of his officers answered, "Have some men take five of the horses that are left in the city. Their plight will be like that of all the Israelites left here — yes, they will only be like all these Israelites who are doomed. So let us send them to find out what happened."

¹⁴So they selected two chariots with their horses, and the king sent them after the Aramean army. He commanded the drivers, "Go and find out what has happened." ¹⁵They followed them as far as the Jordan, and they found the whole road strewn with the clothing and equipment the Arameans had thrown away in their headlong flight. So the messengers returned and reported to the king. ¹⁶Then the people went out and plundered the camp of the Arameans. So a seah of the finest flour sold for a shekel, and two seahs of barley sold for a shekel, as the Lord had said.

¹⁷Now the king had put the officer on whose arm he leaned in charge of the gate, and the people trampled him in the gateway, and he died, just as the man of God had foretold when the king came down to his house. ¹⁸It happened as the man of God had said to the king: "About this time tomorrow, a seah of the finest flour will sell for a shekel and two seahs of barley for a shekel at the gate of Samaria."

¹⁹The officer had said to the man of God, "Look, even if the Lord should open the floodgates of the heavens, could this happen?" The man of God had replied, "You will see it with your own eyes, but you will not eat any of it!" ²⁰And that is exactly what happened to him, for the people trampled him in the gateway, and he died.

The Shunammite's Land Restored

8 Now Elisha had said to the woman whose son he had restored to life, "Go away with your family and stay for a while wherever you can, because the Lord has decreed a famine in the land that will last seven years." ²The woman proceeded to do as the man of God said. She and her family went away and stayed in the land of the Philistines seven years.

7:6 Hittite and Egyptian This phrase suggests that the Arameans (Syrians) felt surrounded, since the Hittites lived to the north and the Egyptians lived to the south. In earlier centuries, the Hittite Empire and Egypt had clashed in the land that later became Israel and Aram. By the time of Elisha, the Hittites controlled only a few city-states in the north of Aram.

7:12 hide The king was worried about an ambush (compare Jos 8:3–28).

7:13 who are doomed This suggests that the siege against Samaria, Israel's capital city, had far-reaching effects on the rest of the nation.

7:14 sent them after the Aramean army Sending spies or scouts was a common practice in ancient warfare (e.g., Nu 13; Jos 2; 1Sa 26:4).

7:17 just as the man of God had foretold In 2Ki 7:17–20, the author reiterates and explains the fulfillment of Elisha's prophecy, which was originally said in 7:1–2.

7:20 that is exactly what happened to him The narrative does not suggest that Yahweh dictated this fate for the captain of the guard, but instead that Elisha knew it would occur. However, this could be viewed as divine retribution because the captain had doubted Elisha's word about Yahweh's provision (compare note on 6:33).

8:1–6 The narrative of ch. 8 continues the story of the Shunammite woman from earlier. Elisha had prophesied that she would have a son; later, Elisha would raise him from the dead (4:8–37). Both the woman's landholdings and her ability to appeal directly to the king attest to her position as a wealthy woman (4:8).

8:1 stay for a while wherever you can People often migrated in times of famine to escape hunger (see Ge 12:10; 26:1; Ru 1:1).

8:2 the land of the Philistines Philistia was on the southern part of Israel's Mediterranean coast. The woman's sojourn into Philistine territory suggests that the famine was not widespread.

³At the end of the seven years she came back from the land of the Philistines and went to appeal to the king for her house and land. ⁴The king was talking to Gehazi, the servant of the man of God, and had said, "Tell me about all the great things Elisha has done." ⁵Just as Gehazi was telling the king how Elisha had restored the dead to life, the woman whose son Elisha had brought back to life came to appeal to the king for her house and land.

Gehazi said, "This is the woman, my lord the king, and this is her son whom Elisha restored to life." ⁶The king asked the woman about it, and she told him.

Then he assigned an official to her case and said to him, "Give back everything that belonged to her, including all the income from her land from the day she left the country until now."

Hazael Murders Ben-Hadad

⁷Elisha went to Damascus, and Ben-Hadad king of Aram was ill. When the king was told, "The man of God has come all the way up here," ⁸he said to Hazael, "Take a gift with you and go to meet the man of God. Consult the LORD through him; ask him, 'Will I recover from this illness?'"

⁹Hazael went to meet Elisha, taking with him as a gift forty camel-loads of all the finest wares of Damascus. He went in and stood before him, and said, "Your son Ben-Hadad king of Aram has sent me to ask, 'Will I recover from this illness?'"

¹⁰Elisha answered, "Go and say to him, 'You will certainly recover.' Nevertheless,ᵃ the LORD has revealed to me that he will in fact die." ¹¹He stared at him with a fixed gaze until Hazael was embarrassed. Then the man of God began to weep.

¹²"Why is my lord weeping?" asked Hazael.

"Because I know the harm you will do to the Israelites," he answered. "You will set fire to their fortified places, kill their young men with the sword, dash their little children to the ground, and rip open their pregnant women."

¹³Hazael said, "How could your servant, a mere dog, accomplish such a feat?"

"The LORD has shown me that you will become king of Aram," answered Elisha.

¹⁴Then Hazael left Elisha and returned to his master. When Ben-Hadad asked, "What did Elisha say to you?" Hazael replied, "He told me that you would certainly recover." ¹⁵But the next day he took a thick cloth, soaked it in water and spread it over the king's face, so that he died. Then Hazael succeeded him as king.

Jehoram King of Judah

8:16-24pp — 2Ch 21:5-10,20

¹⁶In the fifth year of Joram son of Ahab king of Israel, when Jehoshaphat was king of Judah, Jehoram son of Jehoshaphat began his reign as king of Judah. ¹⁷He was thirty-two years old when he became king, and he reigned in Jerusalem eight

---

ᵃ 10 The Hebrew may also be read Go and say, 'You will certainly not recover,' for.

8:3 appeal to the king for her house and land The Shunammite's direct appeal to the king and the absence of a third party in the narrative suggest that the royal government had seized the property. See note on 2Ki 6:26.
8:4 Gehazi Elisha's servant, whom he struck with leprosy in 5:27. **the man of God** Refers to Elisha. Compare note on 1:9.
8:5 This is the woman The woman's case is settled favorably because Gehazi happened to be telling the king how Elisha restored her son to life at the moment she comes to appeal.

8:7-15 The narrative refocuses on Aram (Syria). Hazael's reign in Aram (Syria) surfaces in Assyrian inscriptions dating to the period of his rule (843–796 BC); they refer to him as Hazael of Damascus, "son of a nobody," who suffers a humiliating defeat at the hands of the Assyrians because he fights without the support of his allies. The Biblical story of Hazael's rise to power describes his atrocities against Israel.

8:7 Damascus The capital city of Aram (Syria). **Ben-Hadad king of Aram** See note on 6:24.
8:8 Take a gift with you Taking a gift to a prophet when seeking advice or intercession was common practice (e.g., 1Sa 9:7; 1Ki 14:3).
8:9 forty camel-loads An amount worthy of royalty and likely intended to overwhelm the accommodations wherever the prophet was lodging. **Your son** Through

his messenger (Hazael), Ben-Hadad addresses Elisha as a son would address his father, showing great respect for the prophet.

8:10 Here, Elisha prophesies to Hazael that Ben-Hadad will recover but still die. The narrative of 2 Kings seems to imply that Ben-Hadad would have recovered and Elisha's prophecy would have been fulfilled if Hazael had not murdered him so soon (see 8:15 and note).

8:12 You will set fire to their fortified places Elisha's poetic description of Hazael's later attack is similar to that found in the book of Amos (Am 1:3–4,13).
8:13 your servant, a mere dog Dogs were despised and viewed as scavengers in the ancient Near East (Ex 22:31). This implies that Hazael views himself as lowly (1Sa 17:43; 24:14). See the infographic "The Lachish Letters" on p. 1228. **such a feat** The Hebrew term used here conveys the sense of "exceptional" or "extraordinary" (see Dt 4:32; 1Sa 12:16).
8:15 he died It seems that Hazael murders Ben-Hadad by suffocating him (compare note on 8:10).

8:16-24 The narrative transitions from the nation of Aram (Syria) and focuses on Jehoram, king of Judah. Although both a king of Israel and Judah went by the same Hebrew name, yehoram (Jehoram), which is also rendered as yoram (Joram), they are two different kings (compare note on 2Ki 1:17).
8:16 son of Jehoshaphat The chronological information

years. [18]He followed the ways of the kings of Israel, as the house of Ahab had done, for he married a daughter of Ahab. He did evil in the eyes of the LORD. [19]Nevertheless, for the sake of his servant David, the LORD was not willing to destroy Judah. He had promised to maintain a lamp for David and his descendants forever.

[20]In the time of Jehoram, Edom rebelled against Judah and set up its own king. [21]So Jehoram[a] went to Zair with all his chariots. The Edomites surrounded him and his chariot commanders, but he rose up and broke through by night; his army, however, fled back home. [22]To this day Edom has been in rebellion against Judah. Libnah revolted at the same time.

[23]As for the other events of Jehoram's reign, and all he did, are they not written in the book of the annals of the kings of Judah? [24]Jehoram rested with his ancestors and was buried with them in the City of David. And Ahaziah his son succeeded him as king.

Ahaziah King of Judah

8:25-29pp — 2Ch 22:1-6

[25]In the twelfth year of Joram son of Ahab king of Israel, Ahaziah son of Jehoram king of Judah began to reign. [26]Ahaziah was twenty-two years old when he became king, and he reigned in Jerusalem one year. His mother's name was Athaliah, a granddaughter of Omri king of Israel. [27]He followed the ways of the house of Ahab and did evil in the eyes of the LORD, as the house of Ahab had done, for he was related by marriage to Ahab's family.

[28]Ahaziah went with Joram son of Ahab to war against Hazael king of Aram at Ramoth Gilead. The Arameans wounded Joram; [29]so King Joram returned to Jezreel to recover from the wounds the Arameans had inflicted on him at Ramoth[b] in his battle with Hazael king of Aram.

Then Ahaziah son of Jehoram king of Judah

---

[a] 21 Hebrew *Joram*, a variant of *Jehoram*; also in verses 23 and 24   [b] 29 Hebrew *Ramah*, a variant of *Ramoth*

---

given here seems to conflict with earlier statements, suggesting a period of coregency might be involved. See note on 2Ki 1:17.

SOUTHERN KING	DATE
Asa	910–873 BC
Jehoshaphat	873–848 BC
Jehoram	848–841 BC

8:18 as the house of Ahab had done Just as David was the standard for uprightness (see 1Ki 9:4 and note), Ahab serves as the standard for evil behavior (2Ki 21:3). Ahab, who is described as committing the sins of Jeroboam, maintained worship of the golden calves and use of high places and their accompanying temples, where the people worshiped other gods along with Yahweh (see 1Ki 11:26–33; 13:33–34). Ahab also took a foreign wife and instituted Baal worship (see 1Ki 16:31). **he married a daughter of Ahab** Portrays Jehoram, king of Judah, as another ruler who does evil under the influence of a foreign wife (along with Solomon in 1Ki 11:1–10 and Ahab in 1Ki 16:31). Jehoram's marriage to Ahab's daughter might have been orchestrated by his father, Jehoshaphat (see 2Ch 18:1 and note). This wife is later named as Athaliah (2Ki 8:26; 11:1) who may have been the daughter of Ahab and Jezebel — both Ahab and Jezebel engaged in idolatrous worship of foreign deities. **8:19 He had promised to maintain a lamp** Refers to Yahweh's promise to Solomon to preserve one tribe for his son to rule (1Ki 11:11–13). Here and elsewhere in 1–2 Kings and 1–2 Chronicles, references to this promise use the Hebrew word *nir*, which denotes a lamp and can signify life and hope (1Ki 11:36; 15:4; 2Ch 21:7; compare 2Sa 21:17). **8:20 set up its own king** Edom had been without a king for an undetermined amount of time. It had been suppressed by Judah, who had set up a deputy to rule there (1Ki 22:47). **8:21–24** The Hebrew text of this passage can be confusing, as it uses the variant rendering *yoram* (Joram) in reference to *yehoram* (Jehoram), king of Judah. Starting in v. 25, the narrative shifts its focus to a king of Israel who also goes by the name *yoram* (Joram). Compare note on 1:17.

8:22 Libnah A Levitical city in the hill country of Judah (Jos 21:13). See the infographic "Sennacherib's Prism" on p. 597. **8:23 annals of the kings of Judah** See note on 2Ki 1:18. **8:24 rested with his ancestors** This idiom means to die peacefully. Sometimes it refers specifically to burial in a family plot (e.g., Ge 47:29–30). **8:25–29** The narrative continues by describing the reign of another king of Judah, Ahaziah; the narrative uses the reign of Joram, king of Israel, as a reference point for the chronology, and then proceeds to describe an alliance between the two kings. **8:25 Joram** Although the two kings are sometimes called by the same name, this king of Israel is distinct from the king of Judah, Jehoram, also mentioned in this verse. See note on 8:21–24. **Ahaziah** This king of Judah, who reigned ca. 841–840 BC, shares the same name as an earlier king of Israel (who reigned ca. 853–852 BC; 1Ki 22:51 — 2Ki 1:18). **8:26 Athaliah** The daughter of Ahab whom Jehoram, king of Judah, married (see 8:18 and note). The Hebrew text here and in 2Ch 22:2 literally refers to Athaliah as the daughter of Omri, but this seems to be a reference to her being Omri's descendent (his granddaughter). Athaliah is described in 2Ch 22:3 as the counselor to Ahaziah in acting wickedly. **Omri king of Israel** See 1Ki 16:21–28. **8:27 as the house of Ahab** See 2Ki 8:18 and note. **related by marriage to Ahab's family** This seems to be a reference to the marriage of Ahaziah's parents, Jehoram and Athaliah, not a reference to Ahaziah marrying someone related to Ahab (compare note on 8:18). King Ahaziah of Judah was negatively influenced by his relatives, who were from Ahab of Israel's family. **8:28 Joram son of Ahab** The king of Israel, who is related to Ahaziah. Ahab is both Joram's father and the father of Athaliah, Ahaziah's mother (compare note on 8:18). **Hazael king of Aram** See vv. 7–15. **Ramoth Gilead** A city on the border of Israel and Syria where Ahab, king of Israel, met his downfall during a clash with the Syrian army (1Ki 22). **8:29 Jehoram** Although sometimes called by the same name in the Hebrew text, this king of Judah and the king of Israel, Joram, are two distinct people. Compare note

went down to Jezreel to see Joram son of Ahab, because he had been wounded.

Jehu Anointed King of Israel

9 The prophet Elisha summoned a man from the company of the prophets and said to him, "Tuck your cloak into your belt, take this flask of olive oil with you and go to Ramoth Gilead. ²When you get there, look for Jehu son of Jehoshaphat, the son of Nimshi. Go to him, get him away from his companions and take him into an inner room. ³Then take the flask and pour the oil on his head and declare, 'This is what the LORD says: I anoint you king over Israel.' Then open the door and run; don't delay!"

⁴So the young prophet went to Ramoth Gilead. ⁵When he arrived, he found the army officers sitting together. "I have a message for you, commander," he said.

"For which of us?" asked Jehu.

"For you, commander," he replied.

⁶Jehu got up and went into the house. Then the prophet poured the oil on Jehu's head and declared, "This is what the LORD, the God of Israel, says: 'I anoint you king over the LORD's people Israel. ⁷You are to destroy the house of Ahab your master, and I will avenge the blood of my servants

the prophets and the blood of all the LORD's servants shed by Jezebel. ⁸The whole house of Ahab will perish. I will cut off from Ahab every last male in Israel — slave or free.ᵃ ⁹I will make the house of Ahab like the house of Jeroboam son of Nebat and like the house of Baasha son of Ahijah. ¹⁰As for Jezebel, dogs will devour her on the plot of ground at Jezreel, and no one will bury her.'" Then he opened the door and ran.

¹¹When Jehu went out to his fellow officers, one of them asked him, "Is everything all right? Why did this maniac come to you?"

"You know the man and the sort of things he says," Jehu replied.

¹²"That's not true!" they said. "Tell us."

Jehu said, "Here is what he told me: 'This is what the LORD says: I anoint you king over Israel.'"

¹³They quickly took their cloaks and spread them under him on the bare steps. Then they blew the trumpet and shouted, "Jehu is king!"

Jehu Kills Joram and Ahaziah
9:21-29pp — 2Ch 22:7-9

¹⁴So Jehu son of Jehoshaphat, the son of Nimshi, conspired against Joram. (Now Joram and all

---

ᵃ 8 Or *Israel — every ruler or leader*

---

on 8:25. Jezreel Israelite city in a fertile valley with the same name. Starting with Ahab, Jezreel was the location of the Israelite king's winter residence (1Ki 21:1).

9:1-13 Here, the narrative transitions from focusing on the kingdom of Judah to a narrative primarily about the kingdom of Israel. This is the longest sustained narrative of 2 Kings (2Ki 9:1—10:27) and begins when a prophet anoints Jehu king of Israel. Jehu reigned ca. 841–814 BC after killing all of Ahab's descendants. Since a prophet of Yahweh makes Jehu king, and instructs him to annihilate the house of Ahab (Omri's son), his overthrow of the Omride dynasty is legitimized (2Ki 9:7-10).

OMRIDE DYNASTY	885–841 BC
Omri	885–874 BC
Ahab	874–853 BC
Ahaziah	853–852 BC
Joram/Jehoram	852–841 BC

9:1 the company of the prophets See 2:3 and note. **Tuck your cloak into your belt** The long garments common in the ancient Near East were not suitable for running. The instruction to tie them up indicates that the message is to be delivered with urgent speed. **to Ramoth Gilead** Location of the war between Aram (Syria) and the kings of Israel and Judah (8:28).
9:2 Jehu son of Jehoshaphat, the son of Nimshi It seems that Jehu commanded Israel's army at Ramoth Gilead. It is unusual for an introduction such as this to include the grandfather's name, which might be provided to avoid implying that Jehu's father was Jehoshaphat, king of Judah. Jehu is the son of a different Jehoshaphat who is otherwise unknown.

9:3 I anoint you king over Israel In the ancient Near East, priests usually anointed royalty (e.g., 1Ki 1:39). In the OT, this duty also can fall to a prophet (e.g., 1Sa 10:1; 16:1). The OT mentions anointing only upon the founding of a new dynasty or to attest the legitimacy of the new king. Yahweh had earlier asked Elijah to anoint Jehu (1Ki 19:16), which suggests that Elijah passed this task to Elisha, who then passed it to another unnamed prophet.
9:7 the blood of all the LORD's servants shed by Jezebel Jezebel, wife of King Ahab of Israel, had killed many prophets of Yahweh (1Ki 18:13). She also tried to kill the prophet Elijah (1Ki 19:1-3) and succeeded in arranging Naboth's death (1Ki 21).

9:8-10 The language in 2Ki 9:8 and v. 10 reflects earlier curses against the Israelite kings Jeroboam and Baasha (1Ki 14:10-11; 16:4). Elijah had cursed Ahab and Jezebel in a similar fashion (1Ki 21:21-24). Ahab's death is recorded in 1Ki 22:34-38; the curse against Jezebel is fulfilled in 2Ki 9:30-37.

9:10 the plot of ground at Jezreel See note on v. 21. **no one will bury her** People in the ancient Near East considered it a curse to be left unburied (1Ki 14:11; 16:4; Jer 22:19).
9:11 maniac The Hebrew word used here refers to uncontrollable behavior (1Sa 21:15; 2Ki 9:20; Jer 29:26; Hos 9:7).
9:13 took their cloaks and spread them In Matthew's Gospel, the description of Jesus' triumphal entry into Jerusalem is similar to this scene (Mt 21:8). **they blew the trumpet and shouted** The words and actions in this verse constitute a regular part of enthronement ceremonies.

Israel had been defending Ramoth Gilead against Hazael king of Aram, [15]but King Joram[a] had returned to Jezreel to recover from the wounds the Arameans had inflicted on him in the battle with Hazael king of Aram.) Jehu said, "If you desire to make me king, don't let anyone slip out of the city to go and tell the news in Jezreel." [16]Then he got into his chariot and rode to Jezreel, because Joram was resting there and Ahaziah king of Judah had gone down to see him.

[17]When the lookout standing on the tower in Jezreel saw Jehu's troops approaching, he called out, "I see some troops coming."

"Get a horseman," Joram ordered. "Send him to meet them and ask, 'Do you come in peace?'"

[18]The horseman rode off to meet Jehu and said, "This is what the king says: 'Do you come in peace?'"

"What do you have to do with peace?" Jehu replied. "Fall in behind me."

The lookout reported, "The messenger has reached them, but he isn't coming back."

[19]So the king sent out a second horseman. When he came to them he said, "This is what the king says: 'Do you come in peace?'"

Jehu replied, "What do you have to do with peace? Fall in behind me."

[20]The lookout reported, "He has reached them, but he isn't coming back either. The driving is like that of Jehu son of Nimshi — he drives like a maniac."

[21]"Hitch up my chariot," Joram ordered. And when it was hitched up, Joram king of Israel and Ahaziah king of Judah rode out, each in his own chariot, to meet Jehu. They met him at the plot of ground that had belonged to Naboth the Jezreelite. [22]When Joram saw Jehu he asked, "Have you come in peace, Jehu?"

"How can there be peace," Jehu replied, "as long as all the idolatry and witchcraft of your mother Jezebel abound?"

[23]Joram turned about and fled, calling out to Ahaziah, "Treachery, Ahaziah!"

[24]Then Jehu drew his bow and shot Joram between the shoulders. The arrow pierced his heart and he slumped down in his chariot. [25]Jehu said to Bidkar, his chariot officer, "Pick him up and throw him on the field that belonged to Naboth the Jezreelite. Remember how you and I were riding together in chariots behind Ahab his father when the LORD spoke this prophecy against him: [26]'Yesterday I saw the blood of Naboth and the blood of his sons, declares the LORD, and I will surely make you pay for it on this plot of ground, declares the LORD.'[b] Now then, pick him up and throw him on that plot, in accordance with the word of the LORD."

[27]When Ahaziah king of Judah saw what had happened, he fled up the road to Beth Haggan.[c] Jehu chased him, shouting, "Kill him too!" They wounded him in his chariot on the way up to Gur near Ibleam, but he escaped to Megiddo and died there. [28]His servants took him by chariot to Jerusalem and buried him with his ancestors in his tomb in the City of David. [29](In the eleventh year of Joram son of Ahab, Ahaziah had become king of Judah.)

[a] 15 Hebrew *Jehoram*, a variant of *Joram*; also in verses 17 and 21-24   [b] 26 See 1 Kings 21:19.   [c] 27 Or *fled by way of the garden house*

9:14–29 To establish his throne, Jehu must eliminate the competition. Fortunately for Jehu, the kings of Israel and Judah happen to be in the same place (compare 8:28–29). Jehu kills Joram, king of Israel, and then orders his archers to shoot Ahaziah, king of Judah.

9:14 Joram The king of Israel (see note on 2Ki 1:17).
9:15 Jezreel See note on v. 21. **Jehu said** Jehu apparently is speaking to the men who proclaimed him king in v. 13. **the city** Refers to Ramoth Gilead.
9:16 to see him Ahaziah and Joram are related and allies against Aram (Syria) at this time (see note on 8:28).

9:18–20 Jehu convinces two horseback riders from Jezreel, who report to King Joram of Israel, to not return to Joram. He is likely able to do so because of his position as commander; the messengers either do not expect treachery or respect (or fear) Jehu enough not to oppose him.

9:21 the plot of ground that had belonged to Naboth the Jezreelite By setting this scene at Naboth's property in Jezreel, the narrative foreshadows the fates of Joram (king of Israel) and Jezebel (vv. 24–26,30–37). Jezebel had arranged Naboth's death, which allowed Ahab to seize his property; this was the initial reason for the curse against them and their house (1Ki 21; 2Ki 9:7–10).
9:22 idolatry The Hebrew word used here, *zenunim*, is a derogatory term that refers to following wantonly or whoring — a common metaphor for unfaithfulness to Yahweh (Ex 34:16; Lev 17:7; Jdg 2:17; Jer 3; Eze 16).
witchcraft Biblical law forbids sorcery; both Saul and Josiah outlaw it (Lev 19:31; 20:6; 1Sa 28:3; 2Ki 23:24).
9:26 in accordance with the word of the LORD Elijah's curse against Ahab (1Ki 21:19), fulfilled only partially in 1Ki 22:38, is now fulfilled entirely with the death of King Joram of Israel, Ahab's last reigning descendant.
9:27 to Beth Haggan This place-name means "garden house"; its location is uncertain. **Megiddo** City in the Jezreel Valley.
9:28 took him by chariot to Jerusalem Ahaziah receives a king's burial even though he is said to have done evil in the eyes of Yahweh (2Ki 8:27). The parallel account in 1–2 Chronicles explains that this honor is because of his grandfather, Jehoshaphat, who sought Yahweh with his whole heart (2Ch 22:9).
9:29 the eleventh year of Joram 841 BC. This comment by the narrator functions as a closing statement, referencing the beginning of Ahaziah's reign, which has actually now ended. According to 2 Kings 8:25, Ahaziah, king of Judah, began to reign in the twelfth year of Joram, king of Israel. The discrepancy likely reflects different methods of counting a king's first year. One method begins counting the years only after the first year of his reign.

Jezebel Killed

³⁰Then Jehu went to Jezreel. When Jezebel heard about it, she put on eye makeup, arranged her hair and looked out of a window. ³¹As Jehu entered the gate, she asked, "Have you come in peace, you Zimri, you murderer of your master?"*a*

³²He looked up at the window and called out, "Who is on my side? Who?" Two or three eunuchs looked down at him. ³³"Throw her down!" Jehu said. So they threw her down, and some of her blood spattered the wall and the horses as they trampled her underfoot.

³⁴Jehu went in and ate and drank. "Take care of that cursed woman," he said, "and bury her, for she was a king's daughter." ³⁵But when they went out to bury her, they found nothing except her skull, her feet and her hands. ³⁶They went back and told Jehu, who said, "This is the word of the Lᴏʀᴅ that he spoke through his servant Elijah the Tishbite: On the plot of ground at Jezreel dogs will devour Jezebel's flesh.*b* ³⁷Jezebel's body will be like dung on the ground in the plot at Jezreel, so that no one will be able to say, 'This is Jezebel.'"

Ahab's Family Killed

10 Now there were in Samaria seventy sons of the house of Ahab. So Jehu wrote letters and sent them to Samaria: to the officials of Jezreel,*c* to the elders and to the guardians of Ahab's children. He said, ²"You have your master's sons with you and you have chariots and horses, a fortified city and weapons. Now as soon as this letter reaches you, ³choose the best and most worthy of your master's sons and set him on his father's throne. Then fight for your master's house."

⁴But they were terrified and said, "If two kings could not resist him, how can we?"

⁵So the palace administrator, the city governor, the elders and the guardians sent this message to Jehu: "We are your servants and we will do anything you say. We will not appoint anyone as king; you do whatever you think best."

⁶Then Jehu wrote them a second letter, saying, "If you are on my side and will obey me, take the heads of your master's sons and come to me in Jezreel by this time tomorrow."

Now the royal princes, seventy of them, were with the leading men of the city, who were rearing them. ⁷When the letter arrived, these men took the princes and slaughtered all seventy of them. They put their heads in baskets and sent them to Jehu in Jezreel. ⁸When the messenger arrived, he told Jehu, "They have brought the heads of the princes."

Then Jehu ordered, "Put them in two piles at the entrance of the city gate until morning."

⁹The next morning Jehu went out. He stood before all the people and said, "You are innocent. It

---

a 31 Or *"Was there peace for Zimri, who murdered his master?"*
b 36 See 1 Kings 21:23.   *c 1* Hebrew; some Septuagint manuscripts and Vulgate *of the city*

9:30–37 Jezebel's execution—at the hands of her own servants—marks the fulfillment of Elijah's curse against her (1Ki 21:23).

9:30 Jezreel Location of the Israelite king's winter residence and Naboth's vineyard (see note on v. 21).
9:31 Zimri Refers to the servant of Elah, king of Israel. Zimri killed Elah and ruled in his place for seven days before dying in a conflict with Omri (1Ki 16:8–20).
9:32 Two or three eunuchs Refers to servants of Jezebel.
9:34 bury her Jehu's command opposes the word of the prophet who anointed him king (2Ki 9:10).
9:36 dogs will devour Jezebel's flesh Elijah first proclaimed this curse against Jezebel for arranging the death of Naboth (1Ki 21:23). Similar curses against Jeroboam, Baasha and Ahab refer to dogs desecrating corpses (i.e., the victims were already dead; 1Ki 14:11; 16:4; 21:19,24). However, the curse against Jezebel is worded differently, indicating that dogs will eat Jezebel (1Ki 21:23). Jehu's description of Jezebel's death seems to confirm this distinction (compare 2Ki 9:33–35).
9:37 Jezebel's body will be like dung Jehu's words here are the first mention of this portion of the curse against Jezebel. Dung in an open field is a common simile for an unburied corpse (see Jer 8:2; 9:22; 25:33; Ps 83:10).

10:1–17 Chapter 10 continues the narrative of Jehu's overthrow of the house of Ahab (2Ki 9:1—10:27). In vv. 1–17, all who have a rightful claim to the throne— along with government officials, priests and family friends—are slaughtered.

10:1 seventy sons Likely a symbolic number that refers to all of Ahab's remaining descendants. **Samaria** Capital of the northern kingdom of Israel.
10:4 two kings Refers to Joram of Israel and Ahaziah of Judah, whom Jehu assassinated (9:14–28).
10:6 the heads of your master's sons The Hebrew phrase used here seems to be intentionally ambiguous. Jehu's request could be construed as asking for the leaders to bring the guardians of Ahab's sons (mentioned in vv. 1,6) and come to Jezreel. However, his request could also be construed as asking them to murder Ahab's descendants. Jehu clearly expected them to take the latter sense (v. 8), but the ambiguity allows him to distance himself from the act itself (v. 9). **Jezreel** The place where Jehu had just killed King Joram, King Ahaziah and Jezebel (9:21–33; see note on 9:21); located about 25 miles (40 kilometers) from Samaria.
10:7 and slaughtered all seventy of them The city leaders interpret Jehu's letter as a command to decapitate Ahab's descendants.
10:8 entrance of the city gate until morning In the ancient Near East, displaying an enemy's body or body parts in plain view was a common way to intimidate citizens into cooperating.
10:9 who killed all these Although Jehu's lack of astonishment in v. 8 suggests that he anticipated the decapitations, his remark here to all the people again leaves room for ambiguity (see note on v. 6).

was I who conspired against my master and killed him, but who killed all these? ¹⁰Know, then, that not a word the LORD has spoken against the house of Ahab will fail. The LORD has done what he announced through his servant Elijah." ¹¹So Jehu killed everyone in Jezreel who remained of the house of Ahab, as well as all his chief men, his close friends and his priests, leaving him no survivor.

¹²Jehu then set out and went toward Samaria. At Beth Eked of the Shepherds, ¹³he met some relatives of Ahaziah king of Judah and asked, "Who are you?"

They said, "We are relatives of Ahaziah, and we have come down to greet the families of the king and of the queen mother."

¹⁴"Take them alive!" he ordered. So they took them alive and slaughtered them by the well of Beth Eked — forty-two of them. He left no survivor.

¹⁵After he left there, he came upon Jehonadab son of Rekab, who was on his way to meet him. Jehu greeted him and said, "Are you in accord with me, as I am with you?"

"I am," Jehonadab answered.

"If so," said Jehu, "give me your hand." So he did, and Jehu helped him up into the chariot. ¹⁶Jehu said, "Come with me and see my zeal for the LORD." Then he had him ride along in his chariot.

¹⁷When Jehu came to Samaria, he killed all who were left there of Ahab's family; he destroyed them, according to the word of the LORD spoken to Elijah.

Servants of Baal Killed

¹⁸Then Jehu brought all the people together and said to them, "Ahab served Baal a little; Jehu will serve him much. ¹⁹Now summon all the prophets of Baal, all his servants and all his priests. See that no one is missing, because I am going to hold a great sacrifice for Baal. Anyone who fails to come will no longer live." But Jehu was acting deceptively in order to destroy the servants of Baal.

²⁰Jehu said, "Call an assembly in honor of Baal." So they proclaimed it. ²¹Then he sent word throughout Israel, and all the servants of Baal came; not one stayed away. They crowded into the temple of Baal until it was full from one end to the other. ²²And Jehu said to the keeper of the wardrobe, "Bring robes for all the servants of Baal." So he brought out robes for them.

²³Then Jehu and Jehonadab son of Rekab went into the temple of Baal. Jehu said to the servants of Baal, "Look around and see that no one who serves the LORD is here with you — only servants of Baal." ²⁴So they went in to make sacrifices and burnt offerings. Now Jehu had posted eighty men outside with this warning: "If one of you lets any of the men I am placing in your hands escape, it will be your life for his life."

²⁵As soon as Jehu had finished making the burnt offering, he ordered the guards and officers: "Go in and kill them; let no one escape." So they cut them down with the sword. The guards and officers threw the bodies out and then entered the inner shrine of the temple of Baal. ²⁶They brought the sacred stone out of the temple of Baal and burned it. ²⁷They demolished the sacred stone of Baal and tore down the temple of Baal, and people have used it for a latrine to this day.

²⁸So Jehu destroyed Baal worship in Israel. ²⁹However, he did not turn away from the sins of Jeroboam son of Nebat, which he had caused Israel to commit — the worship of the golden calves at Bethel and Dan.

³⁰The LORD said to Jehu, "Because you have done well in accomplishing what is right in my eyes and have done to the house of Ahab all I had in mind to do, your descendants will sit on the throne of Israel to the fourth generation." ³¹Yet Jehu was not careful to keep the law of the LORD, the God of Israel, with all his heart. He did not turn away from the sins of Jeroboam, which he had caused Israel to commit.

³²In those days the LORD began to reduce the

10:10 through his servant Elijah The prophet Elijah had cursed the house of Ahab (1Ki 21:17–24; 2Ki 9:7–10).
10:13 the queen mother The Hebrew word used here, *gevirah*, meaning "queen mother," is a formal title, but the function of this office is unclear.
10:15 Jehonadab son of Rekab The book of Jeremiah identifies the Rekabites as an ascetic group that denied themselves any form of comfort or pleasure. They rejected the agricultural lifestyle of the Canaanites and faithfully kept the teachings of Jehonadab, their leader (Jer 35). Given Jehu's mission to wipe out the prophets of the Canaanite god Baal (2Ki 10:18–27), Jehu's partnership with Jehonadab makes sense.

10:18–27 After killing off the entire house of Ahab, Jehu destroys all traces of Baal worship in Samaria, which King Ahab and Jezebel promoted (1Ki 16:31–33). In the ancient Near East, kings who took the throne in an unusual manner often initiated reform as a way to break with the previous regime.

10:18 Baal The Canaanite storm god.
10:23 no one who serves the LORD Jehu wants to ensure that no servant of Yahweh is accidentally killed along with the worshipers of Baal.
10:25 threw the bodies out The Hebrew term used here refers to leaving a corpse unburied (1Ki 13:25; Isa 14:19).
10:29 at Bethel and Dan Jeroboam erected these idols to rival the temple of Yahweh in Jerusalem (see 1Ki 12:25–33 and note; 1Ki 12:28 and note).
10:30 all I had in mind Jehu had done what God desired by killing every male descended from Ahab (1Ki 21:21; compare note on Jos 6:16). This is because their regime was fraught with evil (see note on 2Ki 8:18).
10:31 sins of Jeroboam A reference to the synchronistic and idolatrous worship of Jeroboam's reign. See note on 3:3.
10:32 Hazael Refers to the king of Aram (Syria). Ahaziah, king of Judah, and Joram, king of Israel, had joined forces against Hazael (8:28–29) shortly before Jehu

size of Israel. Hazael overpowered the Israelites throughout their territory [33]east of the Jordan in all the land of Gilead (the region of Gad, Reuben and Manasseh), from Aroer by the Arnon Gorge through Gilead to Bashan.

[34]As for the other events of Jehu's reign, all he did, and all his achievements, are they not written in the book of the annals of the kings of Israel?

[35]Jehu rested with his ancestors and was buried in Samaria. And Jehoahaz his son succeeded him as king. [36]The time that Jehu reigned over Israel in Samaria was twenty-eight years.

Athaliah and Joash

11:1-21pp — 2Ch 22:10 – 23:21

11 When Athaliah the mother of Ahaziah saw that her son was dead, she proceeded to destroy the whole royal family. [2]But Jehosheba, the daughter of King Jehoram[a] and sister of Ahaziah, took Joash son of Ahaziah and stole him away from among the royal princes, who were about to be murdered. She put him and his nurse in a

---

[a] 2 Hebrew *Joram*, a variant of *Jehoram*

---

assassinated them (9:21–28). Elisha had prophesied that Hazael would do evil against Israel (8:12). See the infographic "The Tel Dan Stele" on p. 1080.
10:34 book of the annals of the kings of Israel See note on 1:18.
10:35 rested with his ancestors See note on 8:24.

11:1–3 The narrative shifts back in time to address events in the kingdom of Judah which took place shortly after the narrative of 9:1–29. Athaliah, the daughter of King Ahab of Israel, married Jehoram, king of Judah (who reigned ca. 848–41). She bore Ahaziah (king of Judah, who reigned ca. 841–840 BC). After Jehu kills

The Black Obelisk of Shalmaneser III

This black limestone obelisk depicts five kings conquered by Shalmaneser III, king of Assyria from 858–824 BC. Each side of the obelisk portrays the five kings in postures of submission to Shalmaneser, either in prostration to him or bringing tribute. The second is Jehu of the house of Omri, king of Israel. This account is found only here; it is not recorded in the Bible.

This obelisk does align with the biblical account of Jehu's later reign (2Ki 10:32–36) and provides the earliest known depiction of an Israelite. It also supplies evidence for the style of clothing worn in royal Israelite households. It depicts Jehu in a short-sleeved, fringed robe with a belt and slouched conical hat. Since he likely would not have been dressed in his finest robes when appearing as a captive, these represent simpler, everyday garments.

bedroom to hide him from Athaliah; so he was not killed. ³He remained hidden with his nurse at the temple of the LORD for six years while Athaliah ruled the land.

⁴In the seventh year Jehoiada sent for the commanders of units of a hundred, the Carites and the guards and had them brought to him at the temple of the LORD. He made a covenant with them and put them under oath at the temple of the LORD. Then he showed them the king's son. ⁵He commanded them, saying, "This is what you are to do: You who are in the three companies that are going on duty on the Sabbath — a third of you guarding the royal palace, ⁶a third at the Sur Gate, and a third at the gate behind the guard, who take turns guarding the temple — ⁷and you who are in the other two companies that normally go off Sabbath duty are all to guard the temple for the king. ⁸Station yourselves around the king, each of you with weapon in hand. Anyone who approaches your ranksᵃ is to be put to death. Stay close to the king wherever he goes."

⁹The commanders of units of a hundred did just as Jehoiada the priest ordered. Each one took his men — those who were going on duty on the Sabbath and those who were going off duty — and came to Jehoiada the priest. ¹⁰Then he gave the commanders the spears and shields that had belonged to King David and that were in the temple of the LORD. ¹¹The guards, each with weapon in hand, stationed themselves around the king — near the altar and the temple, from the south side to the north side of the temple.

¹²Jehoiada brought out the king's son and put the crown on him; he presented him with a copy of the covenant and proclaimed him king. They anointed him, and the people clapped their hands and shouted, "Long live the king!"

¹³When Athaliah heard the noise made by the guards and the people, she went to the people at the temple of the LORD. ¹⁴She looked and there was the king, standing by the pillar, as the custom was. The officers and the trumpeters were beside the king, and all the people of the land were rejoicing and blowing trumpets. Then Athaliah tore her robes and called out, "Treason! Treason!"

¹⁵Jehoiada the priest ordered the commanders of units of a hundred, who were in charge of the troops: "Bring her out between the ranksᵇ and put to the sword anyone who follows her." For the priest had said, "She must not be put to death in the temple of the LORD." ¹⁶So they seized her as she reached the place where the horses enter the palace grounds, and there she was put to death.

ᵃ 8 Or approaches the precincts   ᵇ 15 Or out from the precincts

---

King Ahaziah, Athaliah takes his place and becomes queen of Judah. She is a descendant of Ahab, king of Israel, and thus not part of the Davidic line. In contrast to the description of Jehoram's reign in 8:16–24, the author of 2 Kings gives very little information about her rule, which lasted ca. 840–835 BC. This is most likely because Athaliah was a usurper and an illegitimate ruler. See note on 8:26.

11:1 royal family The Hebrew phrase here, often translated as "royal family," literally means "royal seed." It can indicate any member of the royal family who would be in line for the throne. Athaliah, the daughter of King Ahab, tries to eliminate the Davidic royal line. Jehu, king of Israel, had already killed many of the relatives of Ahaziah (Athaliah's son) when he was wiping out Ahab's descendants (10:12–14).

11:2 Jehosheba Jehosheba is the wife of Jehoiada, who is a priest—possibly even a high priest (2Ch 22:11; compare 2Ch 24:6–7). As the sister of Ahaziah (the king of Judah who was assassinated by Jehu), Jehosheba is the aunt of Joash, the rightful king of Judah. The text does not indicate if Athaliah is also Jehosheba's mother, but Athaliah is Ahaziah's mother (2Ki 11:1). (Jehoram could have had multiple wives or concubines.) **Jehoram** The Hebrew text here reads *yoram* (Joram), but this is certainly a reference to the king of Judah, Jehoram (*yehoram*; 2Ch 22:11). *Yoram* is an alternate rendering of *yehoram*. **stole him away from among the royal princes** The Hebrew word here denoting theft appears elsewhere to describe kidnapping (Ex 21:16; Dt 24:7).

11:3 at the temple of the LORD The temple of Yahweh in Jerusalem, which is described in 1Ki 6–7.

11:4–20 In this section, Jehoiada the priest and his wife, Jehosheba, intervene in Judah's politics to reinstate the Davidic dynasty and renew the covenant between Yahweh and his people.

11:4 the Carites Part of the royal guard. The Hebrew word used here, *kari* ("Carites"), appears alongside *pelethi* ("Pelethites") in 2Sa 20:23. This suggests that these guards might be better known as the Kerethites, a group of mercenaries employed by David who served under the command of Benaiah (2Sa 8:18; 20:23; 1Ch 18:17). The Pelethites and Kerethites appear together whenever a challenge to the throne emerged, but the groups remain distinct from the regular army. For instance, they support David when he flees from Absalom, when Sheba rebels, and at Solomon's coronation (see 2Sa 15:18; 20:7; 1Ki 1:38,44).

11:9 those who were going off duty Jehoiada divides the captains based on Sabbath duties. These duties and divisions are not explained and probably were well known. It appears that, during the week, the temple was guarded by one division (which rotated throughout the week). During the Sabbath, when the temple would be busier, two divisions would guard the temple. Jehoiada instructs all divisions to be active to ensure that Joash is inaugurated as king of Judah without incident.

11:10 shields that had belonged to King David Jehoiada's use of these weapons symbolizes the return of the Davidic dynasty and legitimizes Joash's succession.

11:12 presented him with a copy of the covenant This might be a reference to Jehoiada obeying Dt 17:18–20, which commands that the king receive, copy and meditate on the Torah once he is seated on the throne.

11:14 the pillar Perhaps one of the two pillars outside the temple (1Ki 7:15–22). **the people of the land**

[17]Jehoiada then made a covenant between the LORD and the king and people that they would be the LORD's people. He also made a covenant between the king and the people. [18]All the people of the land went to the temple of Baal and tore it down. They smashed the altars and idols to pieces and killed Mattan the priest of Baal in front of the altars.

Then Jehoiada the priest posted guards at the temple of the LORD. [19]He took with him the commanders of hundreds, the Carites, the guards and all the people of the land, and together they brought the king down from the temple of the LORD and went into the palace, entering by way of the gate of the guards. The king then took his place on the royal throne. [20]All the people of the land rejoiced, and the city was calm, because Athaliah had been slain with the sword at the palace.

[21]Joash[a] was seven years old when he began to reign.[b]

Joash Repairs the Temple

12:1-21pp — 2Ch 24:1-14,23-27

12 [c] In the seventh year of Jehu, Joash[d] became king, and he reigned in Jerusalem forty years. His mother's name was Zibiah; she was from Beersheba. [2]Joash did what was right in the eyes of the LORD all the years Jehoiada the priest instructed him. [3]The high places, however, were not removed; the people continued to offer sacrifices and burn incense there.

[4]Joash said to the priests, "Collect all the money that is brought as sacred offerings to the temple of the LORD — the money collected in the census, the money received from personal vows and the money brought voluntarily to the temple. [5]Let every priest receive the money from one of the treasurers, then use it to repair whatever damage is found in the temple."

[6]But by the twenty-third year of King Joash the priests still had not repaired the temple. [7]Therefore King Joash summoned Jehoiada the priest and the other priests and asked them, "Why aren't you repairing the damage done to the temple? Take no more money from your treasurers, but hand it over for repairing the temple." [8]The priests agreed that they would not collect any more money from the people and that they would not repair the temple themselves.

[9]Jehoiada the priest took a chest and bored a hole in its lid. He placed it beside the altar, on the right side as one enters the temple of the LORD. The priests who guarded the entrance put into the chest all the money that was brought to the temple of the LORD. [10]Whenever they saw that there was a large amount of money in the chest, the royal secretary and the high priest came, counted the money that had been brought into the temple of the LORD and put it into bags. [11]When the amount had been determined, they gave the money to the men appointed to supervise the work on the temple. With it they paid those who worked on the temple of the LORD — the carpenters and builders,

---

[a] *21* Hebrew *Jehoash*, a variant of *Joash*   [b] *21* In Hebrew texts this verse (11:21) is numbered 12:1.   [c] In Hebrew texts 12:1-21 is numbered 12:2-22.   [d] *1* Hebrew *Jehoash*, a variant of *Joash*; also in verses 2, 4, 6, 7 and 18

The Hebrew term used here seems to refer to a distinct social group that was active during crises involving the Davidic royal line (2Ki 15:5; 21:24). **tore her robes** A gesture of grief.
11:17 they would be the LORD's people A shorthand expression for the terms of Israel's covenant with God (Dt 4:20; 7:6; compare Jer 7:23; 11:4).
11:18 the temple of Baal The previously mentioned temple of Baal (the Canaanite storm god) — which presumably was in Israel — was already destroyed by King Jehu (2Ki 10:27–28). This suggests that some other temple of Baal had been erected during Queen Athaliah's reign in Judah and it seems this temple was in Jerusalem.

11:21 — 12:18 The Hebrew text of this passage calls the king of Judah *yeho'ash* (Jehoash), which is an alternate spelling of *yo'ash* (Joash); *yeho'ash* (Jehoash) is also the name of an Israelite king (see note on 13:9–13). In 12:19, the Hebrew text refers to this same king of Judah as *yo'ash* (Joash). To avoid confusion, some translations always refer to this king of Judah as Joash and the king of Israel as Jehoash.

12:1 seventh year Joash reigned over Judah ca. 835–796 BC. See the timeline "The Divided Kingdom" on p. 536. **Jehu** The king of Israel at the time, whose succession and reign is narrated in 9:1—10:36. **Joash** See note on 2Ki 11:21—12:18.

NORTHERN KING	DATE	SOUTHERN KING	DATE
Jehu	841–814 BC	Joash	835–796 BC
Jehoahaz	814–798 BC		
Jehoash	798–786 BC	Amaziah	796–792 BC

12:3 high places Unsanctioned places of worship.

12:4–18 By the time of the coronation of Joash (also called Jehoash), the temple of Yahweh that was built and furnished under Solomon (1Ki 6–8) had fallen into disrepair. Moreover, the priests' unwillingness to apply the designated money to temple repairs suggests that this was a period of complacency among Israel's religious leaders.

12:4 the money that is brought as sacred offerings Refers to money from taxes and donations. **money received from personal vows** Most likely refers to the census tax (Ex 30:14).
12:6 twenty-third year of King Joash Approximately 812 BC. This is one of the few instances in the collective work of 1–2 Kings that specifies a date during a king's reign (e.g., 1Ki 14:25), which suggests that the narrative draws from either a royal or priestly chronicle.
12:7 Why aren't you repairing the damage done to the temple The passage implies not only neglect and

12the masons and stonecutters. They purchased timber and blocks of dressed stone for the repair of the temple of the Lord, and met all the other expenses of restoring the temple.

13The money brought into the temple was not spent for making silver basins, wick trimmers, sprinkling bowls, trumpets or any other articles of gold or silver for the temple of the Lord; 14it was paid to the workers, who used it to repair the temple. 15They did not require an accounting from those to whom they gave the money to pay the workers, because they acted with complete honesty. 16The money from the guilt offerings and sin offerings*a* was not brought into the temple of the Lord; it belonged to the priests.

17About this time Hazael king of Aram went up and attacked Gath and captured it. Then he turned to attack Jerusalem. 18But Joash king of Judah took all the sacred objects dedicated by his predecessors — Jehoshaphat, Jehoram and Ahaziah, the kings of Judah — and the gifts he himself had dedicated and all the gold found in the treasuries of the temple of the Lord and of the royal palace, and he sent them to Hazael king of Aram, who then withdrew from Jerusalem.

19As for the other events of the reign of Joash, and all he did, are they not written in the book of the annals of the kings of Judah? 20His officials conspired against him and assassinated him at Beth Millo, on the road down to Silla. 21The officials who murdered him were Jozabad son of Shimeath and Jehozabad son of Shomer. He died and was buried with his ancestors in the City of David. And Amaziah his son succeeded him as king.

Jehoahaz King of Israel

13 In the twenty-third year of Joash son of Ahaziah king of Judah, Jehoahaz son of Jehu became king of Israel in Samaria, and he reigned seventeen years. 2He did evil in the eyes of the Lord by following the sins of Jeroboam son of Nebat, which he had caused Israel to commit, and he did not turn away from them. 3So the Lord's anger burned against Israel, and for a long time he kept them under the power of Hazael king of Aram and Ben-Hadad his son.

4Then Jehoahaz sought the Lord's favor, and the Lord listened to him, for he saw how severely the king of Aram was oppressing Israel. 5The Lord provided a deliverer for Israel, and they escaped from the power of Aram. So the Israelites lived in their own homes as they had before. 6But they did not turn away from the sins of the house of Jeroboam, which he had caused Israel to commit; they continued in them. Also, the Asherah pole*b* remained standing in Samaria.

7Nothing had been left of the army of Jehoahaz except fifty horsemen, ten chariots and ten thousand foot soldiers, for the king of Aram had destroyed the rest and made them like the dust at threshing time.

8As for the other events of the reign of Jehoa-

---

a 16 Or *purification offerings*   *b* 6 That is, a wooden symbol of the goddess Asherah; here and elsewhere in 2 Kings

---

apathy on the part of the priests, but also dishonesty. For years, it seems, they have taken the money without making the repairs.
12:13 silver basins, wick trimmers, sprinkling bowls, trumpets The vessels mentioned here also appear in the list of Solomon's temple furnishings (1Ki 7:50), as well as in the list of items carried off as booty by King Nebuchadnezzar of Babylon (2Ki 25:14–15).
12:17 Hazael This king, who had usurped the throne of Aram (Syria; 8:7–15), had already successfully conquered parts of Israel (10:32–33; see note on 10:32).
12:18 all the sacred objects Royal dedications symbolized piety and could be used to pay off attackers if the situation necessitated it (see 1Ki 7:51; 15:15,18; 2Ki 18:15).
12:19 the other events of the reign The account in 2 Chronicles explains that Joash became unfaithful after the death of Jehoiada (2Ch 24:17–19). He killed Jehoiada's son, Zechariah, before being assassinated by his own servants (2Ch 24:20–27). **Joash** Here, the Hebrew text begins referring to this king of Judah as *yo'ash* (Joash), an alternate spelling of *yeho'ash* (Jehoash; see note on 2Ki 11:21–12:18). This spelling continues for the remainder of this narrative, which ceases at 13:1; 13:10–13 then refers to him again by the same name. Confusingly, at 13:9, a different king, a king of Israel, is also referred to by the Hebrew text as *yo'ash*. See note on 13:9–13.
annals of the kings of Judah See note on 1:18.

13:1 The narrative now moves back in time, to give an account of the Israelite king, Jehoahaz, Jehu's son (10:35).

13:1 twenty-third year of Joash Around 814 BC. Jehoahaz reigned over Israel until ca. 798 BC.
13:2 sins of Jeroboam Refers to syncretistic and idolatrous worship. See note on 3:3.
13:3 Hazael king of Aram Elisha had prophesied that Hazael would do evil against Israel (see 8:7–15 and note) and he had already successfully done so (10:32–33; see note on 10:32). See the infographic "The Tel Dan Stele" on p. 1080. **Ben-Hadad** This was the name of the king Hazael usurped; Hazael and his son, who adopts this name, were not related by blood to the former Ben-Hadad. Compare note on 6:24.
13:5 Lord provided a deliverer for Israel The Hebrew word used here, *moshia'*, often rendered as "savior," can denote a "deliverer" or "helper." This seems to refer to Jehoahaz, though a divine figure helping Israel is also a possibility (compare 13:23; 14:27). This help seems to be a temporary reprieve from warfare, because 13:22 states that Israel was at war with Aram (Syria) all the days of Jehoahaz.
13:6 the Asherah pole A sacred pole associated with the cult of the Canaanite goddess Asherah. King Ahab was responsible for erecting the Asherah in Samaria (1Ki 16:33).
13:7 like the dust at threshing time A common image for vanquishing an enemy (see Isa 28:27; 41:15; Am 1:3). Threshing involved crushing grain to separate the edible kernels from the husks.
13:8 annals of the kings of Israel See note on 2Ki 1:18.

haz, all he did and his achievements, are they not written in the book of the annals of the kings of Israel? [9]Jehoahaz rested with his ancestors and was buried in Samaria. And Jehoash[a] his son succeeded him as king.

Jehoash King of Israel

[10]In the thirty-seventh year of Joash king of Judah, Jehoash son of Jehoahaz became king of Israel in Samaria, and he reigned sixteen years. [11]He did evil in the eyes of the LORD and did not turn away from any of the sins of Jeroboam son of Nebat, which he had caused Israel to commit; he continued in them.

[12]As for the other events of the reign of Jehoash, all he did and his achievements, including his war against Amaziah king of Judah, are they not written in the book of the annals of the kings of Israel? [13]Jehoash rested with his ancestors, and Jeroboam succeeded him on the throne. Jehoash was buried in Samaria with the kings of Israel.

[14]Now Elisha had been suffering from the illness from which he died. Jehoash king of Israel went down to see him and wept over him. "My father! My father!" he cried. "The chariots and horsemen of Israel!"

[15]Elisha said, "Get a bow and some arrows," and he did so. [16]"Take the bow in your hands," he said to the king of Israel. When he had taken it, Elisha put his hands on the king's hands.

[17]"Open the east window," he said, and he opened it. "Shoot!" Elisha said, and he shot. "The LORD's arrow of victory, the arrow of victory over Aram!" Elisha declared. "You will completely destroy the Arameans at Aphek."

[18]Then he said, "Take the arrows," and the king took them. Elisha told him, "Strike the ground." He struck it three times and stopped. [19]The man of God was angry with him and said, "You should have struck the ground five or six times; then you would have defeated Aram and completely destroyed it. But now you will defeat it only three times."

[20]Elisha died and was buried.

Now Moabite raiders used to enter the country every spring. [21]Once while some Israelites were burying a man, suddenly they saw a band of raiders; so they threw the man's body into Elisha's tomb. When the body touched Elisha's bones, the man came to life and stood up on his feet.

[22]Hazael king of Aram oppressed Israel throughout the reign of Jehoahaz. [23]But the LORD was gracious to them and had compassion and showed concern for them because of his covenant with Abraham, Isaac and Jacob. To this day he has been unwilling to destroy them or banish them from his presence.

[24]Hazael king of Aram died, and Ben-Hadad his son succeeded him as king. [25]Then Jehoash

[a] 9 Hebrew *Joash*, a variant of *Jehoash*; also in verses 12-14 and 25

13:9–13 The narrative continues focusing on the nation of Israel by detailing the reign of another king of Israel. This brief passage can be confusing because both Judah and Israel had kings named Joash (*yo'ash*), which also can be rendered "Jehoash" (*yeho'ash*)—*yeho'ash* is an alternate spelling of *yo'ash*. In v. 9, the Hebrew text uses the spelling *yo'ash* (Joash) to refer to the king of Israel (who is the son of Jehoahaz). But in v. 10, to distinguish the two kings, the Hebrew text switches to the spelling *yeho'ash* (Jehoash) for the king of Israel and uses the spelling *yo'ash* (Joash) for the king of Judah (who is the son of Ahaziah). Starting in 13:12, however, the Hebrew text reverts to the spelling of v. 9 for the king of Israel, calling him *yo'ash* (Joash) until 13:25. Some English translations resolve this confusion by always calling the king of Israel Jehoash and always referring to the king of Judah as Joash.

13:9 rested with his ancestors See note on 8:24.

13:10 The narrative here mentions the death of Jehoash (also called Joash), king of Israel, but the narrative about him actually continues until 14:17.

13:10 thirty-seventh year of Joash king of Judah Around 798 BC.

13:11 sins of Jeroboam See note on v. 2.

13:14–25 The prophetic service of Elisha (who was introduced in 1Ki 19:19–21) lasts nearly half a century. He continues to prophesy while terminally ill, and his bones retain divine power even after his death.

13:14 The chariots and horsemen of Israel This is the same cry Elisha uttered when God transported his master, Elijah, to heaven (2Ki 2:12).

13:15 Get a bow and some arrows Elisha uses a sign-act to prophesy about Israel's victory. Prophets often used sign-acts to serve as practical examples of how God's word would be accomplished.

13:17 Aphek The OT mentions several places named Aphek. This one is likely in the Transjordan region, three miles east of the Sea of Galilee. In 1 Kings, Ben-Hadad (not to be confused with the Ben-Hadad in 2Ki 8:7–15) and his troops clash with the Israelites and then flee to Aphek, where they suffer defeat (see 1Ki 20:1–34).

13:18 three times The number three appears often in OT rituals (e.g., 1Ki 17:21). Joash apparently assumes that Elisha meant for him to follow this convention.

13:19 The man of God Refers to Elisha. Compare note on 2Ki 1:9.

13:20 Moabite The Israelites constantly had to repel these neighbors to the east (compare 1:1 and note; 3:5).

every spring The season for war in the ancient Near East (2Sa 11:1; 1Ki 20:22,26).

13:23 covenant with Abraham, Isaac and Jacob The collective work of 1–2 Kings mentions Israel's patriarchs only one other time—when Elijah prays to Yahweh during his contest with the prophets of Baal (1Ki 18:36). The author of 1–2 Kings cites Yahweh's faithfulness to his covenant as the reason for his mercy on Israel. It is a reference to God's promise to make Abraham a great nation and multiply his offspring (Ge 12:1–3; 13:14–17; 15:5–21). God reiterates this promise to both Isaac (Ge 26:2–5) and Jacob (Ge 28:13–15). In addition, Moses appealed to the covenant when God

son of Jehoahaz recaptured from Ben-Hadad son of Hazael the towns he had taken in battle from his father Jehoahaz. Three times Jehoash defeated him, and so he recovered the Israelite towns.

Amaziah King of Judah

14:1-7pp — 2Ch 25:1-4,11-12
14:8-22pp — 2Ch 25:17 - 26:2

14 In the second year of Jehoash[a] son of Jehoahaz king of Israel, Amaziah son of Joash king of Judah began to reign. ²He was twenty-five years old when he became king, and he reigned in Jerusalem twenty-nine years. His mother's name was Jehoaddan; she was from Jerusalem. ³He did what was right in the eyes of the LORD, but not as his father David had done. In everything he followed the example of his father Joash. ⁴The high places, however, were not removed; the people continued to offer sacrifices and burn incense there.

⁵After the kingdom was firmly in his grasp, he executed the officials who had murdered his father the king. ⁶Yet he did not put the children of the assassins to death, in accordance with what is written in the Book of the Law of Moses where the LORD commanded: "Parents are not to be put to death for their children, nor children put to death for their parents; each will die for their own sin."[b]

⁷He was the one who defeated ten thousand Edomites in the Valley of Salt and captured Sela in battle, calling it Joktheel, the name it has to this day.

⁸Then Amaziah sent messengers to Jehoash son of Jehoahaz, the son of Jehu, king of Israel, with the challenge: "Come, let us face each other in battle."

⁹But Jehoash king of Israel replied to Amaziah king of Judah: "A thistle in Lebanon sent a message to a cedar in Lebanon, 'Give your daughter to my son in marriage.' Then a wild beast in Lebanon came along and trampled the thistle underfoot.

---

[a] 1 Hebrew *Joash*, a variant of *Jehoash*; also in verses 13, 23 and 27
[b] 6 Deut. 24:16

---

was preparing to punish the Israelites after the golden calf incident (Ex 32:13).

13:25 Jehoash The Hebrew text here refers to this Israelite king again as *yeho'ash* (Jehoash), which is an alternate spelling of *yo'ash* (Joash), which he is otherwise called by in the narrative of 13:12—14:7 (compare note on 13:9–13). **Three times** A fulfillment of Elisha's prophecy (13:19). **he recovered the Israelite towns** The cities Jehoahaz lost must have been west of the Jordan, since Hazael had already taken the territories to the east in the days of Jehu (2Ki 10:32–33; 12:18). Joash's victories at Aphek stopped Aram's (Syria's) expansion and paved the way for Jeroboam II to reclaim the land (14:23,25).

14:1 The narrative here shifts its focus back to the kingdom of Judah. Like 13:9–13, this verse can be confusing, because the Hebrew text here calls a king of Judah and a king of Israel by the same name, *yo'ash* (Joash). Amaziah king of Judah's father is not the same person as the king of Israel who goes by the same name (who is the son of Jehoahaz); Amaziah's father is the son of Ahaziah. See note on 13:9–13.

NORTHERN KING	DATE	SOUTHERN KING	DATE
Jehoash	798–786 BC	Joash	835–796 BC
Jeroboam II	786–746 BC	Amaziah	796–792 BC
Zechariah	746–746 BC	Uzziah (Azariah)	792–742 BC

14:1 second year of Jehoash Amaziah reigned in Judah alone from about 796–792 BC. He shared the throne with his son, Uzziah, for the final 25 years of his reign (see note on 2Ch 26:3). See the timeline "The Divided Kingdom" on p. 536.

14:3 not as his father David had done David was the standard for good, kingly behavior because of his desire to live a worshipful, Yahweh honoring life (1Ki 3:6; 9:4; 11:4). **In everything he followed the example of his father Joash** Although Joash, king of Judah, is described as doing right in the eyes of Yahweh, the text also notes that he failed to take down the high places where people made unsanctioned offerings (2Ki 12:2–3).

14:5 who had murdered his father the king See 12:20–21.

14:6 Book of the Law of Moses See note on 1Ki 2:3. **for their own sin** See Dt 24:16 and note. In the ancient Near East, the practice of killing a person's entire household in revenge was common, particularly if a royal throne was at stake (Jdg 9:3–6; compare 2Ki 10; note on 9:1–13).

14:7 the one who defeated ten thousand Edomites This battle is covered in greater detail in 2Ch 25:5–12. **the Valley of Salt** The site of earlier battles with the Edomites in the time of David (2Sa 8:13; Ps 60:title). **Sela** The precise location of Sela is uncertain, but the book of Judges locates it on the border of Amorite territory (Jdg 1:36).

14:8 Jehoash To distinguish the king of Israel from Amaziah's father who shared the same name, the Hebrew text here refers to the king of Israel as *yeho'ash* (Jehoash). The last time he was mentioned, he was referred to in the Hebrew text as *yo'ash* (14:1). *Yeho'ash* (Jehoash) is an alternate spelling of *yo'ash* (Joash). The king of Israel is referred to as *yeho'ash* (Jehoash) until 14:23. **let us face each other in battle** From the wording of the Hebrew text, it is unclear whether Amaziah's invitation is meant to be a threat, but Jehoash's response seems to indicate that he understood it as one (2Ki 14:9–10). The account in 2 Chronicles indicates a cause for tension between Amaziah and the northern kingdom. Amaziah had hired mercenaries from Israel to help him battle against Edom (2Ch 25:6). However, after a prophet instructed him to fight without Israel's help, he discharged them (2Ch 25:7–10). The discharged northern troops then raided some towns of Judah, killing 3,000 people (2Ch 25:13).

14:9 Amaziah's statement in 2Ki 14:8 appears to be calling Jehoash to meet in battle (compare 23:29). To answer, Jehoash uses a nature parable. In the parable, Jehoash is the cedar; Amaziah is the thistle (or thornbush). The thistle was a thorny plant that grew wild on unattended properties (Job 31:40; Isa 34:13; Hos 9:6). The symbolism is meant to warn Amaziah against arrogance. Despite his recent victory, Amaziah (king of Judah) should not presume to set himself on the same

¹⁰You have indeed defeated Edom and now you are arrogant. Glory in your victory, but stay at home! Why ask for trouble and cause your own downfall and that of Judah also?"

¹¹Amaziah, however, would not listen, so Jehoash king of Israel attacked. He and Amaziah king of Judah faced each other at Beth Shemesh in Judah. ¹²Judah was routed by Israel, and every man fled to his home. ¹³Jehoash king of Israel captured Amaziah king of Judah, the son of Joash, the son of Ahaziah, at Beth Shemesh. Then Jehoash went to Jerusalem and broke down the wall of Jerusalem from the Ephraim Gate to the Corner Gate — a section about four hundred cubits long.ᵃ ¹⁴He took all the gold and silver and all the articles found in the temple of the LORD and in the treasuries of the royal palace. He also took hostages and returned to Samaria.

¹⁵As for the other events of the reign of Jehoash, what he did and his achievements, including his war against Amaziah king of Judah, are they not written in the book of the annals of the kings of Israel? ¹⁶Jehoash rested with his ancestors and was buried in Samaria with the kings of Israel. And Jeroboam his son succeeded him as king.

¹⁷Amaziah son of Joash king of Judah lived for fifteen years after the death of Jehoash son of Jehoahaz king of Israel. ¹⁸As for the other events of Amaziah's reign, are they not written in the book of the annals of the kings of Judah?

¹⁹They conspired against him in Jerusalem, and he fled to Lachish, but they sent men after him to Lachish and killed him there. ²⁰He was brought back by horse and was buried in Jerusalem with his ancestors, in the City of David.

²¹Then all the people of Judah took Azariah,ᵇ who was sixteen years old, and made him king in place of his father Amaziah. ²²He was the one who rebuilt Elath and restored it to Judah after Amaziah rested with his ancestors.

Jeroboam II King of Israel

²³In the fifteenth year of Amaziah son of Joash king of Judah, Jeroboam son of Jehoash king of Israel became king in Samaria, and he reigned forty-one years. ²⁴He did evil in the eyes of the LORD and did not turn away from any of the sins of Jeroboam son of Nebat, which he had caused Israel to commit. ²⁵He was the one who restored the boundaries of Israel from Lebo Hamath to the Dead Sea,ᶜ in accordance with the word of the LORD, the God of Israel, spoken through his servant Jonah son of Amittai, the prophet from Gath Hepher.

²⁶The LORD had seen how bitterly everyone in Israel, whether slave or free, was suffering;ᵈ there was no one to help them. ²⁷And since the

---

ᵃ 13 That is, about 600 feet or about 180 meters   ᵇ 21 Also called Uzziah   ᶜ 25 Hebrew *the Sea of the Arabah*   ᵈ 26 Or *Israel was suffering. They were without a ruler or leader, and*

---

level as Jehoash, king of Israel. The thistle's request for a wife might imply that Amaziah asked for an Israelite princess as a wife, or it could simply serve to illustrate a presumptuous request.

Both the request for a wife and the challenge to a battle would indicate a presumption of equal status on the part of Amaziah. Jehoash's response warns against such a presumption; he even mentions the possible trampling of the thistle by a wild beast, which is probably symbolic of any nation who could destroy Judah.

14:11 would not listen This seems to imply that Amaziah, king of Judah, continued to threaten Jehoash, king of Israel, and perhaps even brought armed forces against Israel. **Beth Shemesh in Judah** This clarification is given because there were several places called Beth Shemesh (Jos 19:22,38; Jdg 1:33; 1Ki 4:9).
14:13 son of Joash The Hebrew text here refers to Amaziah's father using the alternate spelling of his name *yeho'ash* (Jehoash). Compare note on 13:9–13. **the Ephraim Gate to the Corner Gate** The Ephraim Gate is on the north side of Jerusalem; the Corner Gate is most likely on the western side of Jerusalem.
14:14 Samaria The capital of the northern kingdom of Israel. See note on 2Ki 1:3.
14:15 annals of the kings of Israel See note on 1:18.
14:16–17 Here, the Hebrew text clearly distinguishes between the king of Judah and the king of Israel who shared the same name, by spelling the king of Israel's name *yeho'ash* (Jehoash) and the king of Judah's name *yo'ash* (Joash). See note on 14:8; compare note on 13:9–13.

14:16 rested with his ancestors See note on 8:24.

14:19 They conspired The text does not note who murdered Amaziah, but presumably it was people from within his own government. **Lachish** A city in the Judean hill country (Jos 15:39). See the infographic "The Lachish Letters" on p. 1228.
14:21 Azariah The narrative about this king of Judah, who is also called Uzziah (2Ch 26:1) continues at 2Ki 15:1.
14:22 Elath A site on the northern coast of the Gulf of Aqaba; associated with Ezion Geber, one of Solomon's sea ports (1Ki 9:26). Rebuilding Elath would have required defeating the Edomites.
14:23 The narrative about Azariah, king of Judah, is interrupted, as the narrator focuses on events that chronologically took place earlier. The narrator tells the story of Jeroboam II, king of Israel, who reigned ca. 786–746 BC. The Hebrew text here can be confusing, since both a king of Israel and a king of Judah are referred to as *yo'ash* (Joash). However, they are two distinct people. For this reason, some translations refer to the king of Israel as Jehoash, which is based on an alternate spelling. Compare note on 13:9–13.

14:24 sins of Jeroboam Refers to the idolatrous and syncretistic worship of the much earlier king of Israel, Jeroboam I (who reigned ca. 930–909 BC). See note on 3:3.
14:25 Dead Sea The Hebrew text refers here to the Arabah, the arid valley that runs from the Sea of Galilee to the Gulf of Aqaba and includes the Dead Sea. **Jonah son of Amittai, the prophet** See Jnh 1:1 and note. Apart from the book of Jonah, this is the only OT reference to the prophet Jonah.
14:27 blot out the name of Israel This Hebrew phrase occurs only here and in Dt 9:14; 29:20. It denotes

King Jeroboam II's Family Tree

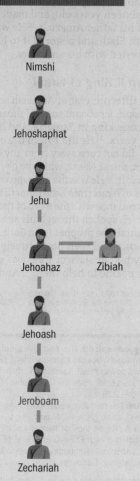

Nimshi

Jehoshaphat

Jehu

Jehoahaz = Zibiah

Jehoash

Jeroboam

Zechariah

LORD had not said he would blot out the name of Israel from under heaven, he saved them by the hand of Jeroboam son of Jehoash.

²⁸As for the other events of Jeroboam's reign, all he did, and his military achievements, including how he recovered for Israel both Damascus and Hamath, which had belonged to Judah, are they not written in the book of the annals of the kings of Israel? ²⁹Jeroboam rested with his ancestors, the kings of Israel. And Zechariah his son succeeded him as king.

Azariah King of Judah

15:1-7pp — 2Ch 26:3-4,21-23

15 In the twenty-seventh year of Jeroboam king of Israel, Azariah[a] son of Amaziah king of Judah began to reign. ²He was sixteen years old when he became king, and he reigned in Jerusalem fifty-two years. His mother's name was Jekoliah; she was from Jerusalem. ³He did what was right in the eyes of the LORD, just as his father Amaziah had done. ⁴The high places, however, were not removed; the people continued to offer sacrifices and burn incense there.

⁵The LORD afflicted the king with leprosy[b] until the day he died, and he lived in a separate house.[c] Jotham the king's son had charge of the palace and governed the people of the land.

⁶As for the other events of Azariah's reign, and all he did, are they not written in the book of the annals of the kings of Judah? ⁷Azariah rested with his ancestors and was buried near them in the City of David. And Jotham his son succeeded him as king.

Zechariah King of Israel

⁸In the thirty-eighth year of Azariah king of Judah, Zechariah son of Jeroboam became king of Israel in Samaria, and he reigned six months.

---

[a] 1 Also called *Uzziah*; also in verses 6, 7, 8, 17, 23 and 27
[b] 5 The Hebrew for *leprosy* was used for various diseases affecting the skin.   [c] 5 Or *in a house where he was relieved of responsibilities*

"blotting out" or "erasing" and calls to mind the image of washing a scroll in order to reuse it. This particular reference could refer to Yahweh's promise to Jehu in 2Ki 10:30, since the point of the narrative seems to be that Yahweh is getting tired of Israel's sin. **Jehoash** The Hebrew text here, when referring to this king of Israel, uses the alternate spelling of *yeho'ash* (Jehoash), which is *yo'ash* (Joash). See note on 13:9–13.

14:28 Damascus and Hamath This would have required a defeat of the nation of Aram (Syria), as Damascus was their capital and Hamath was in their territory at this time (compare 8:7). **annals of the kings of Israel** See note on 1:18.

15:1 The narrative once again shifts chronologically back in time; the focus shifts from the nation of Israel to the nation of Judah, picking up the narrative begun in 14:21–22.

15:1 Azariah Also called Uzziah, king of Judah (v. 13; Isa 1:1; 6:1; Hos 1:1). He reigned ca. 792–742 BC.

15:3 his father Amaziah had done Although both kings do what is right in the eyes of Yahweh, they fail to take down the high places where people make unsanctioned offerings (2Ki 14:3–4; compare 12:2–3).

15:5 leprosy The Hebrew word used here, *tsara'*, can refer to various skin diseases (see note on Lev 13:1–59). The account in 2Ch 26:16–21 explains how Azariah became afflicted. **he lived in a separate house** In accordance with ritual laws concerning skin disease (Lev 13:46). Since Azariah had to be isolated, his son, Jotham, governed the land during the final years of Azariah's reign.

15:6 annals of the kings See note on 2Ki 1:18.

15:8–31 This section chronologically ventures back in time to describe a period of unrest for Israel, as several kings—with the exception of Menahem (vv. 17–22)—are murdered by someone who takes over the throne. Their reigns are generally short, with six kings ruling within

[9]He did evil in the eyes of the LORD, as his predecessors had done. He did not turn away from the sins of Jeroboam son of Nebat, which he had caused Israel to commit.

[10]Shallum son of Jabesh conspired against Zechariah. He attacked him in front of the people,[a] assassinated him and succeeded him as king. [11]The other events of Zechariah's reign are written in the book of the annals of the kings of Israel. [12]So the word of the LORD spoken to Jehu was fulfilled: "Your descendants will sit on the throne of Israel to the fourth generation."[b]

Shallum King of Israel

[13]Shallum son of Jabesh became king in the thirty-ninth year of Uzziah king of Judah, and he reigned in Samaria one month. [14]Then Menahem son of Gadi went from Tirzah up to Samaria. He attacked Shallum son of Jabesh in Samaria, assassinated him and succeeded him as king. [15]The other events of Shallum's reign, and the conspiracy he led, are written in the book of the annals of the kings of Israel.

[16]At that time Menahem, starting out from Tirzah, attacked Tiphsah and everyone in the city and its vicinity, because they refused to open their gates. He sacked Tiphsah and ripped open all the pregnant women.

Menahem King of Israel

[17]In the thirty-ninth year of Azariah king of Judah, Menahem son of Gadi became king of Israel, and he reigned in Samaria ten years. [18]He did evil in the eyes of the LORD. During his entire reign he did not turn away from the sins of Jeroboam son of Nebat, which he had caused Israel to commit. [19]Then Pul[c] king of Assyria invaded the land, and Menahem gave him a thousand talents[d] of silver to gain his support and strengthen his own hold on the kingdom. [20]Menahem exacted this money from Israel. Every wealthy person had to contribute fifty shekels[e] of silver to be given to the king of Assyria. So the king of Assyria withdrew and stayed in the land no longer.

[21]As for the other events of Menahem's reign, and all he did, are they not written in the book of the annals of the kings of Israel? [22]Menahem rested with his ancestors. And Pekahiah his son succeeded him as king.

Pekahiah King of Israel

[23]In the fiftieth year of Azariah king of Judah, Pekahiah son of Menahem became king of Israel in Samaria, and he reigned two years. [24]Pekahiah did evil in the eyes of the LORD. He did not turn away from the sins of Jeroboam son of Nebat, which he had caused Israel to commit. [25]One of his chief officers, Pekah son of Remaliah, conspired against him. Taking fifty men of Gilead with him, he assassinated Pekahiah, along with Argob and Arieh, in the citadel of the royal palace at Samaria. So Pekah killed Pekahiah and succeeded him as king.

[26]The other events of Pekahiah's reign, and all he did, are written in the book of the annals of the kings of Israel.

Pekah King of Israel

[27]In the fifty-second year of Azariah king of Judah, Pekah son of Remaliah became king of Israel in Samaria, and he reigned twenty years.

[a] 10 Hebrew; some Septuagint manuscripts *in Ibleam*   [b] 12 2 Kings 10:30   [c] 19 Also called *Tiglath-Pileser*   [d] 19 That is, about 38 tons or about 34 metric tons   [e] 20 That is, about 1 1/4 pounds or about 575 grams

---

about 25 years. The passage highlights the kings' wickedness and emphasizes the growing Assyrian threat. It concludes with the first Assyrian deportation of Israelites, which occurred around 734 BC (see v. 29 and note). See the timeline "The Divided Kingdom" on p. 536.

15:9 sins of Jeroboam Refers to idolatrous and syncretistic worship. See note on 3:3.

15:12 the word of the LORD Yahweh made this promise to King Jehu of Israel because he eliminated the house of Ahab, king of Israel, and Baal worship (10:30).

15:13 Uzziah king of Judah An alternate name for Azariah, king of Judah (see note on 15:1). **Samaria** Capital of the northern kingdom of Israel. See 1:3 and note.

15:14 Tirzah The previous capital of Israel, from the time of Jeroboam (1Ki 14:17) until Omri moved the capital to Samaria (1Ki 16:23–24).

15:19 Pul king of Assyria Refers to Tiglath-Pileser III (see 2Ki 15:29 and note). This is the first mention in 2 Kings of the Assyrian Empire, which conquers Israel (ch. 17). **a thousand talents of silver** This sum is comparable to amounts that other countries paid Tiglath-Pileser III. This tribute was paid ca. 738 BC.

15:22 rested with his ancestors An idiom meaning to die peacefully. Of the five reigns covered in vv. 8–31, Menahem is the only king who is not murdered.

15:25 fifty men This detail—that 50 men were able to seize the fortified palace in Samaria—indicates the weakness of Israel at this point. **Gilead** Gilead was a region east of the Jordan River inhabited by the tribes of Reuben, Gad and Manasseh. It is possible that Pekah ruled over Gilead before overthrowing Pekahiah (see v. 27 and note).

15:27 he reigned twenty years The chronology of the northern kings does not allow for a 20-year reign for Pekah. The northern kingdom went into Assyrian captivity in 722 BC, nine years into the reign of Pekah's successor, Hoshea (17:6). If Pekah actually reigned over Israel for 20 years, that would mean he began his reign before 750 BC, which does not align with the dates described for the other kings of Israel. There are several possibilities that might account for this discrepancy. One is that the report of a 20-year reign is a textual error. This is unlikely, however, since the author later uses Pekah's seventeenth year as a marker for Ahaz's ascension to the throne in Judah (16:1). A second and more likely option is that Pekah established himself as a ruler over some part of Israel several years before becoming king

²⁸He did evil in the eyes of the LORD. He did not turn away from the sins of Jeroboam son of Nebat, which he had caused Israel to commit.

²⁹In the time of Pekah king of Israel, Tiglath-Pileser king of Assyria came and took Ijon, Abel Beth Maakah, Janoah, Kedesh and Hazor. He took Gilead and Galilee, including all the land of Naphtali, and deported the people to Assyria. ³⁰Then Hoshea son of Elah conspired against Pekah son of Remaliah. He attacked and assassinated him, and then succeeded him as king in the twentieth year of Jotham son of Uzziah.

³¹As for the other events of Pekah's reign, and all he did, are they not written in the book of the annals of the kings of Israel?

Jotham King of Judah

15:33-38pp — 2Ch 27:1-4,7-9

³²In the second year of Pekah son of Remaliah king of Israel, Jotham son of Uzziah king of Judah began to reign. ³³He was twenty-five years old when he became king, and he reigned in Jerusalem sixteen years. His mother's name was Jerusha daughter of Zadok. ³⁴He did what was right in the eyes of the LORD, just as his father Uzziah had done. ³⁵The high places, however, were not removed; the people continued to offer sacrifices and burn incense there. Jotham rebuilt the Upper Gate of the temple of the LORD.

³⁶As for the other events of Jotham's reign, and what he did, are they not written in the book of the annals of the kings of Judah? ³⁷(In those days the LORD began to send Rezin king of Aram and Pekah son of Remaliah against Judah.) ³⁸Jotham rested with his ancestors and was buried with them in the City of David, the city of his father. And Ahaz his son succeeded him as king.

Ahaz King of Judah

16:1-20pp — 2Ch 28:1-27

16 In the seventeenth year of Pekah son of Remaliah, Ahaz son of Jotham king of Judah began to reign. ²Ahaz was twenty years old when he became king, and he reigned in Jerusalem sixteen years. Unlike David his father, he did not do what was right in the eyes of the LORD his God. ³He followed the ways of the kings of Israel and even sacrificed his son in the fire, engaging in the detestable practices of the nations the LORD had driven out before the Israelites. ⁴He offered sacrifices and burned incense at the high places, on the hilltops and under every spreading tree.

⁵Then Rezin king of Aram and Pekah son of Remaliah king of Israel marched up to fight

---

over the entire northern kingdom. He probably ruled in Gilead east of the Jordan, which would account for the men of Gilead joining him in overthrowing Pekahiah (see v. 25). See the timeline "The Divided Kingdom" on p. 536.
15:29 deported the people to Assyria This is the first Assyrian deportation of Israel's people (ca. 734 BC; compare 16:9; 17:6). This deportation seems to have been brought on by King Ahaz of Judah's deal with Assyria, recorded in 16:5–18. King Menahem of Israel (ca. 745–737 BC) had already paid tribute to Tiglath-Pileser III of Assyria (15:19–20). But it seems Ahaz's greater tribute (ca. 734 BC) prompted Tiglath-Pileser III to turn on Israel, who was Ahaz's enemy (see note on 16:1–20). See the timeline "Dates Related to Isaiah and 2 Kings" on p. 1116.

DATE	EVENT
745 BC	Tiglath-Pileser III becomes king
738 BC	Menahem becomes vassal of Tiglath-Pileser
734 BC	Tiglath-Pileser defeats Pekah
727 BC	Shalmaneser V becomes king

15:32 The narrative shifts chronologically back in time, refocusing on the southern kingdom of Judah—this picks up the narrative begun in 15:7.
15:32 Jotham son of Uzziah Because of Uzziah's leprosy (v. 5), Jotham probably reigned in conjunction with his father for a time. Jotham likely may have reigned ca. 742–735 BC.
15:34 what was right in the eyes of the LORD The account of Jotham in 2 Chronicles describes his victory over the Ammonites, who paid him an annual tribute. His military success is attributed to his obedience (2Ch 27:5–6).

15:35 high places Unsanctioned worship locations.
Upper Gate of the temple of the LORD Also known as the Benjamin Gate (see Jer 20:2 and note). In addition to building the upper gate, Jotham rebuilt a portion of the wall (2Ch 27:3).
15:36 annals of the kings of Judah See note on 2Ki 1:18.

16:1–20 During the reign of Judah's King Ahaz (ca. 735–715 BC), the kingdoms of Israel, Aram (Syria) and Edom ally against him. (This alliance occurred in ca. 734 BC prior to the first deportation of Israel recorded in 15:29.) In response, Ahaz buys protection from Tiglath-Pileser III of Assyria by giving him all the temple treasures and precious metals, as well as the frames of the bronze stands and the 12 oxen that hold up the sea of cast metal (vv. 5–9,17; 1Ki 7:23–37). Assyrian records from the period corroborate this account, listing Ahaz of Judah among the kings who pay tribute to the throne. See the timeline "The Divided Kingdom" on p. 536.

16:2 David his father Because of his desire to worship Yahweh, David was the standard for upright kingly behavior (1Ki 3:6; 9:4; 11:4).
16:3 even sacrificed his son in the fire The OT forbids child sacrifice (Lev 20:1–5; Dt 18:9–14; Eze 16:21; 20:31), but Israel's neighbors practiced it (2Ki 3:27). The kingdom of Israel and King Manasseh of Judah also were guilty of this evil (17:17; 21:6).
16:4 high places, on the hilltops and under every spreading tree A standard phrase describing the location of Canaanite religious sites, which often were associated with fertility (Dt 12:2–3; Jer 2:20; Eze 6:13).
16:5 Rezin king of Aram The last of this kingdom's rulers before it was conquered by Assyria. Rezin was executed by Tiglath-Pileser III in 732 BC.

against Jerusalem and besieged Ahaz, but they could not overpower him. ⁶At that time, Rezin king of Aram recovered Elath for Aram by driving out the people of Judah. Edomites then moved into Elath and have lived there to this day.

⁷Ahaz sent messengers to say to Tiglath-Pileser king of Assyria, "I am your servant and vassal. Come up and save me out of the hand of the king of Aram and of the king of Israel, who are attacking me." ⁸And Ahaz took the silver and gold found in the temple of the LORD and in the treasuries of the royal palace and sent it as a gift to the king of Assyria. ⁹The king of Assyria complied by attacking Damascus and capturing it. He deported its inhabitants to Kir and put Rezin to death.

¹⁰Then King Ahaz went to Damascus to meet Tiglath-Pileser king of Assyria. He saw an altar in Damascus and sent to Uriah the priest a sketch of the altar, with detailed plans for its construction. ¹¹So Uriah the priest built an altar in accordance with all the plans that King Ahaz had sent from Damascus and finished it before King Ahaz returned. ¹²When the king came back from Damascus and saw the altar, he approached it and presented offerings*a* on it. ¹³He offered up his burnt offering and grain offering, poured out his drink offering, and splashed the blood of his fellowship offerings against the altar. ¹⁴As for the bronze altar that stood before the LORD, he brought it from the front of the temple — from between the new altar and the temple of the LORD — and put it on the north side of the new altar.

¹⁵King Ahaz then gave these orders to Uriah the priest: "On the large new altar, offer the morning burnt offering and the evening grain offering, the king's burnt offering and his grain offering, and the burnt offering of all the people of the land, and their grain offering and their drink offering. Splash against this altar the blood of all the burnt offerings and sacrifices. But I will use the bronze altar for seeking guidance." ¹⁶And Uriah the priest did just as King Ahaz had ordered.

¹⁷King Ahaz cut off the side panels and removed the basins from the movable stands. He removed the Sea from the bronze bulls that supported it and set it on a stone base. ¹⁸He took away the Sabbath canopy*b* that had been built at the temple and removed the royal entryway outside the temple of the LORD, in deference to the king of Assyria.

¹⁹As for the other events of the reign of Ahaz, and what he did, are they not written in the book of the annals of the kings of Judah? ²⁰Ahaz rested with his ancestors and was buried with them in the City of David. And Hezekiah his son succeeded him as king.

Hoshea Last King of Israel

17:3-7pp — 2Ki 18:9-12

17 In the twelfth year of Ahaz king of Judah, Hoshea son of Elah became king of Israel in Samaria, and he reigned nine years. ²He did evil

---

a 12 Or *and went up*   *b 18* Or *the dais of his throne* (see Septuagint)

KING OF SYRIA	DATE	SOUTHERN KING	DATE
Rezin	740–732 BC	Jotham	742–735 BC
		Ahaz	735–715 BC

16:6 Elath See 2Ki 14:22 and note.

16:7 your servant Ahaz makes Judah a vassal of the Assyrian Empire.

16:8 a gift The Hebrew word here connotes a bribe and this decision involves Judah willingly being subjected to a foreign power and its gods (compare Dt 5:6–7). Mosaic Law forbade the offering of bribes, and other OT passages highly criticize the practice (e.g., Ex 23:8; Dt 16:19; Pr 17:23). According to Assyrian accounts, Ahaz also pays tribute to Tiglath-Pileser III, which could be a reference to his gift (or bribe); Ahaz likely also had to pay regular tribute. See the timeline "Dates Related to Isaiah and 2 Kings" on p. 1116.

DATE	EVENT
745 BC	Tiglath-Pileser III becomes king
734 BC	Tiglath-Pileser defeats Pekah
727 BC	Shalmaneser V becomes king
725–722 BC	Assyrians besiege Samaria. The Israelites are defeated and sent into exile.

16:9 Kir Likely refers to a region of Mesopotamia; the precise location is unknown. Amos 9:7 indicates that Kir is where the Arameans (Syrians) originated.

16:10 Uriah the priest A supporter of the prophet Isaiah (Isa 8:2), which suggests he is faithful to Yahweh (at least later on).

16:13 He offered up his burnt offering Kings often inaugurated new altars by performing sacrifices (e.g., 2Sa 6:17–18; 1Ki 8:63; 12:32). See the table "Altars in the Old Testament" on p. 249.

16:14 bronze altar Likely a reference to the altar established during Solomon's era (1Ki 8:64).

16:17 cut off the side panels Ahaz dismantled certain bronze features of Solomon's temple — possibly in order to give the metal to Tiglath-Pileser III (2Ki 16:8). For details regarding the stands, see 1Ki 7:27–37; for details on the sea and oxen, see 1Ki 7:23–26.

16:18 in deference to the King of Assyria The Hebrew phrase used here may indicate that Ahaz had been ordered by Tiglath-Pileser III to make these changes to the temple, in order to obtain the goods necessary for his tribute payment to Assyria. It could also be a reference to Ahaz setting aside this portion of the temple so it would be out of sight of anyone from Assyria.

16:19 annals of the kings of Judah See note on 2Ki 1:18.

17:1 The narrative once again shifts back in time, to detail the reign of the final king of Israel, Hoshea (who reigned ca. 732–722 BC). The Assyrian king who opposes Hoshea, Shalmaneser V (who began reigning ca. 727 BC), was the son of Tiglath-Pilesar III, who had earlier made the nation of Israel a vassal to the Assyrian Empire.

Hezekiah's Family Tree

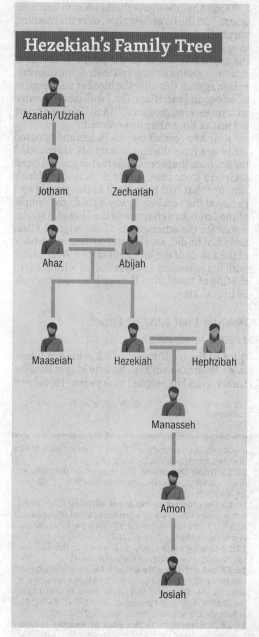

Azariah/Uzziah

Jotham — Zechariah

Ahaz — Abijah

Maaseiah — Hezekiah — Hephzibah

Manasseh

Amon

Josiah

in the eyes of the LORD, but not like the kings of Israel who preceded him.

³Shalmaneser king of Assyria came up to attack Hoshea, who had been Shalmaneser's vassal and had paid him tribute. ⁴But the king of Assyria discovered that Hoshea was a traitor, for he had sent envoys to So[a] king of Egypt, and he no longer paid tribute to the king of Assyria, as he had done year by year. Therefore Shalmaneser seized him and put him in prison. ⁵The king of Assyria invaded the entire land, marched against Samaria and laid siege to it for three years. ⁶In the ninth year of Hoshea, the king of Assyria captured Samaria and deported the Israelites to Assyria. He settled them in Halah, in Gozan on the Habor River and in the towns of the Medes.

Israel Exiled Because of Sin

⁷All this took place because the Israelites had sinned against the LORD their God, who had brought them up out of Egypt from under the power of Pharaoh king of Egypt. They worshiped other gods ⁸and followed the practices of the nations the LORD had driven out before them, as well as the practices that the kings of Israel had introduced. ⁹The Israelites secretly did things against the LORD their God that were not right. From watchtower to fortified city they built themselves high places in all their towns. ¹⁰They set up sacred stones and Asherah poles on every high hill and under every spreading tree. ¹¹At every high place they burned incense, as the nations whom the LORD had driven out before them had done. They did wicked things that aroused the LORD's anger. ¹²They worshiped idols, though the LORD had said, "You shall not do this."[b] ¹³The LORD warned Israel and Judah through all his prophets and seers: "Turn from your evil ways. Observe my commands and decrees, in accordance with the entire Law that I commanded your ancestors to obey and that I delivered to you through my servants the prophets."

¹⁴But they would not listen and were as stiff-necked as their ancestors, who did not trust in the LORD their God. ¹⁵They rejected his decrees

a 4 So is probably an abbreviation for Osorkon.
b 12 Exodus 20:4,5

17:3 Hoshea, who had been Shalmaneser's vassal It is unclear whether Hoshea submitted willingly to Assyria, as Ahaz, king of Judah, had done (16:7–9).
17:4 discovered that Hoshea was a traitor The actions described in this verse suggest that Hoshea was trying to mount a revolt against Assyria and was seeking help from Egypt. **So king of Egypt** Outside of this verse, there is no evidence for an Egyptian king named So. **year by year** Vassal nations typically paid annual tribute to their ruling powers. During the peak of Solomon's rule, Israel received an abundance of tribute from lesser nations (1Ki 10:25).

17:6 The siege of Samaria and the deportation of the Israelites in 722 BC marks the end of the northern kingdom of Israel. The actual deportation was probably conducted by King Sargon II of Assyria (compare Isa 20:1). Assyria later resettles the land with captives from other nations (2Ki 17:24). Unlike the southern kingdom of Judah, the northern kingdom of Israel will never be restored, and there is no account of deportees returning to the land.

17:6 Samaria Capital of the northern kingdom of Israel. See 1:3 and note. **deported the Israelites to Assyria** The second deportation of Israel's people recorded in

and the covenant he had made with their ancestors and the statutes he had warned them to keep. They followed worthless idols and themselves became worthless. They imitated the nations around them although the Lord had ordered them, "Do not do as they do."

¹⁶They forsook all the commands of the Lord their God and made for themselves two idols cast in the shape of calves, and an Asherah pole. They bowed down to all the starry hosts, and they worshiped Baal. ¹⁷They sacrificed their sons and daughters in the fire. They practiced divination and sought omens and sold themselves to do evil in the eyes of the Lord, arousing his anger.

¹⁸So the Lord was very angry with Israel and removed them from his presence. Only the tribe of Judah was left, ¹⁹and even Judah did not keep the commands of the Lord their God. They followed the practices Israel had introduced. ²⁰Therefore the Lord rejected all the people of Israel; he afflicted them and gave them into the hands of plunderers, until he thrust them from his presence.

²¹When he tore Israel away from the house of David, they made Jeroboam son of Nebat their king. Jeroboam enticed Israel away from following the Lord and caused them to commit a great sin. ²²The Israelites persisted in all the sins of Jeroboam and did not turn away from them ²³until the Lord removed them from his presence, as he had warned through all his servants the prophets. So the people of Israel were taken from their homeland into exile in Assyria, and they are still there.

Samaria Resettled

²⁴The king of Assyria brought people from Babylon, Kuthah, Avva, Hamath and Sepharvaim and settled them in the towns of Samaria to replace the Israelites. They took over Samaria and lived in its towns. ²⁵When they first lived there, they did not worship the Lord; so he sent lions among them and they killed some of the people. ²⁶It was reported to the king of Assyria: "The people you deported and resettled in the towns of Samaria do not know what

---

1–2 Kings (compare 2Ki 15:29). See the timeline "Dates Related to Isaiah and 2 Kings" on p. 1116.

17:7–23 This passage gives extensive commentary on the sins of the northern kingdom of Israel, describing how Israel allowed other nations to influence them and how Israel adopted the despicable practices of these nations. In turn, Israel passed along these same practices to the kingdom of Judah (v. 19). Ultimately, Yahweh expelled the Israelites from the promised land and handed them over to their enemies (see vv. 18,20).

17:7 They worshiped other gods The primary cause of the Israelites' expulsion is their worship of other gods, which violates the command to follow Yahweh (Ex 20:3–6; Dt 5:6–10; 6:4–15).

17:8 followed the practices of the nations The law forbids Israel from adopting the practices of the previous inhabitants of the promised land (Lev 18:3; Dt 7:1–6; 18:9).

17:9 high places in all their towns In violation of the law, the Israelites had established their own worship sites and incorporated foreign altars, idols and practices into their worship of Yahweh. They disobeyed the command to worship Yahweh at the place of his choosing, namely the Jerusalem temple. See Dt 12:2–7.

17:10 sacred stones A pillar or set apart stone; the context of this instance implies that these were in honor of foreign gods or some sort of idols that were intended, albeit wrongfully, to honor Yahweh. **Asherah poles** Refers to sacred poles that were affiliated with the worship of the Canaanite fertility goddess Asherah. **under every spreading tree** Refers to pagan worship. Canaanites considered trees to be sacred because they symbolized fertility and life.

17:12 idols The Hebrew word used here, *gillulim*, may be literally rendered as "dung." It is often used as a disparaging term for idols (see Eze 14:3 and note; 18:6).

17:13 seers Refers to a divine messenger (or visionary).

17:15 rejected The Hebrew word used here, *ma'as*, often refers to violating God's commands (Lev 26:15; Eze 5:6; 20:13). It also is used when the Israelites reject God's rule and ask for a human king (1Sa 10:19).

17:16 idols cast in the shape of calves Refers to the idols built by Jeroboam (see 1Ki 12:25–33 and note). **all the starry hosts** Refers to the sun, moon, stars and planets (2Ki 23:5). Astral worship was forbidden by the law (e.g., Dt 4:19). **Baal** The Canaanite storm god. King Ahab had promoted Baal worship in Israel after he married Jezebel (1Ki 16:31–32).

17:17 sacrificed their sons and daughters in the fire The OT forbids child sacrifice (Dt 18:10). Compare note on 2Ki 16:3. **practiced divination** Prohibited in Lev 20:6 and Dt 18:10–14.

17:18 Only the tribe of Judah was left Although the northern kingdom falls to Assyria, the kingdom of Judah continues to exist until it is conquered by Babylon in 586 BC (2Ki 25:1–21).

17:20 he thrust them from his presence In 1Ki 9:6–9, Yahweh warned that he would expel Israel from the promised land if Solomon or his descendants rejected Yahweh for other gods. Compare Lev 26:27–33; Dt 28:58–63.

17:21 he tore Israel away from the house of David Refers to the division of the kingdom, which occurred because Solomon rejected Yahweh (1Ki 11:9–13).

17:22 all the sins of Jeroboam and did not turn away Jeroboam instituted syncretistic and idolatrous worship (see note on 2Ki 3:3).

17:23 through all his servants the prophets A reference to the prophets Elijah, Elisha and others.

17:24–41 In the ancient Near East, it was common for a conquering nation to uproot people from their homeland and resettle them in various regions, resulting in diverse populations with little likelihood of developing a centralized power base. The people who were forced to settle in the land that formerly belonged to Israel naturally brought their own religious practices with them—the same types of practices that caused Yahweh to reject Israel in the first place.

17:24 the towns of Samaria From this point forward, Samaria refers primarily to the entire region of what used to be the northern kingdom of Israel. The people living in this region eventually became known as Samaritans.

17:25 he sent lions among them A devouring lion was

the god of that country requires. He has sent lions among them, which are killing them off, because the people do not know what he requires."

[27]Then the king of Assyria gave this order: "Have one of the priests you took captive from Samaria go back to live there and teach the people what the god of the land requires." [28]So one of the priests who had been exiled from Samaria came to live in Bethel and taught them how to worship the LORD.

[29]Nevertheless, each national group made its own gods in the several towns where they settled, and set them up in the shrines the people of Samaria had made at the high places. [30]The people from Babylon made Sukkoth Benoth, those from Kuthah made Nergal, and those from Hamath made Ashima; [31]the Avvites made Nibhaz and Tartak, and the Sepharvites burned their children in the fire as sacrifices to Adrammelek and Anammelek, the gods of Sepharvaim. [32]They worshiped the LORD, but they also appointed all sorts of their own people to officiate for them as priests in the shrines at the high places. [33]They worshiped the LORD, but they also served their own gods in accordance with the customs of the nations from which they had been brought.

[34]To this day they persist in their former practices. They neither worship the LORD nor adhere to the decrees and regulations, the laws and commands that the LORD gave the descendants of Jacob, whom he named Israel. [35]When the LORD made a covenant with the Israelites, he commanded them: "Do not worship any other gods or bow down to them, serve them or sacrifice to them. [36]But the LORD, who brought you up out of Egypt with mighty power and outstretched arm, is the one you must worship. To him you shall bow down and to him offer sacrifices. [37]You must always be careful to keep the decrees and regulations, the laws and commands he wrote for you. Do not worship other gods. [38]Do not forget the covenant I have made with you, and do not worship other gods. [39]Rather, worship the LORD your God; it is he who will deliver you from the hand of all your enemies."

[40]They would not listen, however, but persisted in their former practices. [41]Even while these people were worshiping the LORD, they were serving their idols. To this day their children and grandchildren continue to do as their ancestors did.

Hezekiah King of Judah

18:2-4pp — 2Ch 29:1-2; 31:1
18:5-7pp — 2Ch 31:20-21
18:9-12pp — 2Ki 17:3-7

18 In the third year of Hoshea son of Elah king of Israel, Hezekiah son of Ahaz king of Judah began to reign. [2]He was twenty-five years

---

a common motif for divine punishment (1Ki 13:24; 20:36; Am 3:8; Na 2:12–13). Lion imagery also is associated with the tribe of Judah (Ge 49:9; Rev 5:5).

17:27 one of the priests you took captive A priest originally from the kingdom of Israel; however, this priest likely would have been synchronistic and idolatrous since these practices were prevalent in Israel before the Israelites' exile.

17:28 Bethel Where Jeroboam had set up one of his golden calves (1Ki 12:28–29). **worship the LORD** The king of Assyria, believing that Yahweh is angry, decides that he must ensure the people of Israel worship Yahweh, so that he may be appeased. In the OT, various lands are described as being aligned with particular gods (Dt 32:8–9). It appears the king of Assyria views the land of Israel (Samaria) as aligned with Yahweh and thus decides Yahweh must be appeased for the people to be safe.

17:30–31 The identities of most of these places and deities are uncertain. The city of Kuthah (or Cuth) in central Babylon was holy to Nergal, the god of plague and lord of the underworld. The city of Hamath was about 120 miles north of Damascus. See the table "Pagan Deities of the Old Testament" on p. 1281.

17:33 but they also served their own gods Like the Israelites, the new residents of Samaria fuse worship of Yahweh with foreign practices.

17:34–40 This passage contains a summary of Yahweh's covenant with Israel and explains that while the people newly settled in the region were taught about Yahweh, they were not observing the terms of his covenant with Israel which demanded sole worship of Yahweh (Ex 20:1–5). The wording in this passage is a pastiche of phrases from the Pentateuch (compare Ex 6:6; 20:5; Dt 4:23,34; 5:32; 6:13).

17:37 he wrote for you Alluding to when Moses wrote down God's law (Ex 34:27–28).

17:40 The narrative about Israel (Samaria) closes with a tragic comment about synchronistic worship, indicating that it became the norm for everyone in Israel, across generations.

18:1–8 The narrative shifts back in time to focus on the nation of Judah; Judah is the focus for the remainder of 2 Kings. This passage relates how Hezekiah enacted religious reform in Judah around the time the nation of Israel fell to Assyria. Hezekiah's trust in Yahweh enables him to rebel against Assyria and regain the Philistine territory. Other accounts of Hezekiah's reign appear in 2Ch 29–32 and Isa 36–39. See the timeline "The Divided Kingdom" on p. 536.

18:1 Hezekiah son of Ahaz King of Judah from ca. 715–697 BC; praised for his devotion to Yahweh. See the people diagram "Hezekiah's Family Tree" on p. 590.

2 Kings 18:1

HEZEKIAH
Hezekiah, who reigned ca. 715–697 BC, demonstrated his loyalty to Yahweh by restoring the temple and reestablishing the sacrificial system. He reorganized the priests and meticulously outlined their responsibilities. He also tore down the high places and altars dedicated to pagan idolatry and even destroyed the bronze serpent that Moses had fashioned in the Sinai desert (2Ki 18:4).

old when he became king, and he reigned in Jerusalem twenty-nine years. His mother's name was Abijah[a] daughter of Zechariah. [3]He did what was right in the eyes of the LORD, just as his father David had done. [4]He removed the high places, smashed the sacred stones and cut down the Asherah poles. He broke into pieces the bronze snake Moses had made, for up to that time the Israelites had been burning incense to it. (It was called Nehushtan.[b])

[a] 2 Hebrew *Abi*, a variant of *Abijah* [b] 4 *Nehushtan* sounds like the Hebrew for both *bronze* and *snake*.

Around 722 BC, the Assyrians conquered Israel and exiled the inhabitants of the northern kingdom. The southern kingdom survived, but it remained a vassal state of Assyria and continued to pay tribute to the Assyrian king. The situation changed dramatically around 705 BC when Hezekiah severed Judah's ties with Assyria (2Ki 18:7). The Assyrian king, Sennacherib, invaded Judah in 701 BC, destroying dozens of cities (2Ki 18:13). He blockaded Jerusalem and taunted Hezekiah for trusting in Yahweh. Hezekiah cried out to God, who saved Jerusalem by sending the Angel of Yahweh to destroy the Assyrian army (2Ki 19:14–37.

18:3 just as his father David had done David was the standard for good, kingly behavior because he chose to worship Yahweh and Yahweh alone. Hezekiah and Josiah provide the only fully positive comparisons with David (2Ki 22:2).
18:4 Asherah poles A wooden pole or tree planted by an altar associated with the cult of the Canaanite goddess Asherah. See note on Dt 7:5. **Nehushtan** The

Royal Seals of Judah

Ancient kings sealed important correspondence with a lump of wet clay, stamping the clay with a seal. These seals were often engraved in semi-precious stones such as brown carnelian. The seals of the kings of Judah featured handles similar to this one.

HANDLE
The center of the handle is a winged sun-disk—a pagan image. This handle was no more than an inch tall, and the seals were about the size of dimes.

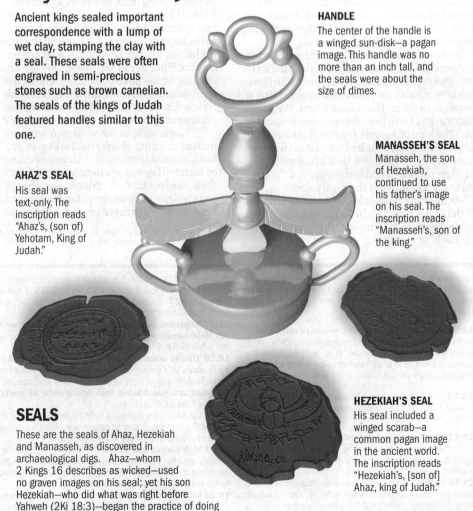

AHAZ'S SEAL
His seal was text-only. The inscription reads "Ahaz's, (son of) Yehotam, King of Judah."

MANASSEH'S SEAL
Manasseh, the son of Hezekiah, continued to use his father's image on his seal. The inscription reads "Manasseh's, son of the king."

HEZEKIAH'S SEAL
His seal included a winged scarab—a common pagan image in the ancient world. The inscription reads "Hezekiah's, [son of] Ahaz, king of Judah."

SEALS
These are the seals of Ahaz, Hezekiah and Manasseh, as discovered in archaeological digs. Ahaz—whom 2 Kings 16 describes as wicked—used no graven images on his seal; yet his son Hezekiah—who did what was right before Yahweh (2Ki 18:3)—began the practice of doing so. Manasseh, his wicked son, did so as well.

⁵Hezekiah trusted in the Lᴏʀᴅ, the God of Israel. There was no one like him among all the kings of Judah, either before him or after him. ⁶He held fast to the Lᴏʀᴅ and did not stop following him; he kept the commands the Lᴏʀᴅ had given Moses. ⁷And the Lᴏʀᴅ was with him; he was successful in whatever he undertook. He rebelled against the king of Assyria and did not serve him. ⁸From watchtower to fortified city, he defeated the Philistines, as far as Gaza and its territory.

⁹In King Hezekiah's fourth year, which was the seventh year of Hoshea son of Elah king of Israel, Shalmaneser king of Assyria marched against Samaria and laid siege to it. ¹⁰At the end of three years the Assyrians took it. So Samaria was captured in Hezekiah's sixth year, which was the ninth year of Hoshea king of Israel. ¹¹The king of Assyria deported Israel to Assyria and settled them in Halah, in Gozan on the Habor River and in towns of the Medes. ¹²This happened because they had not obeyed the Lᴏʀᴅ their God, but had violated his covenant — all that Moses the servant of the Lᴏʀᴅ commanded. They neither listened to the commands nor carried them out.

¹³In the fourteenth year of King Hezekiah's reign, Sennacherib king of Assyria attacked all the fortified cities of Judah and captured them. ¹⁴So Hezekiah king of Judah sent this message to the king of Assyria at Lachish: "I have done wrong. Withdraw from me, and I will pay whatever you demand of me." The king of Assyria exacted from Hezekiah king of Judah three hundred talents*ᵃ* of silver and thirty talents*ᵇ* of gold. ¹⁵So Hezekiah gave him all the silver that was found in the temple of the Lᴏʀᴅ and in the treasuries of the royal palace.

¹⁶At this time Hezekiah king of Judah stripped off the gold with which he had covered the doors and doorposts of the temple of the Lᴏʀᴅ, and gave it to the king of Assyria.

Sennacherib Threatens Jerusalem

18:13,17-37pp — Isa 36:1-22
18:17-35pp — 2Ch 32:9-19

¹⁷The king of Assyria sent his supreme commander, his chief officer and his field commander with a large army, from Lachish to King Hezekiah at Jerusalem. They came up to Jerusalem and stopped at the aqueduct of the Upper Pool, on the road to the Washerman's Field. ¹⁸They called for the king; and Eliakim son of Hilkiah the palace administrator, Shebna the secretary, and Joah son of Asaph the recorder went out to them.

¹⁹The field commander said to them, "Tell Hezekiah:

"'This is what the great king, the king of Assyria, says: On what are you basing this confidence of yours? ²⁰You say you have the counsel and the might for war — but you speak only empty words. On whom are you depending, that you rebel against me? ²¹Look, I know you are depending on Egypt, that splintered reed of a staff, which pierces the hand of anyone who leans on it! Such is Pharaoh king of Egypt to all who depend on him. ²²But if you say to me, "We are depending on the Lᴏʀᴅ our God" — isn't he the one whose high places and altars Hezekiah removed, saying to Judah and Jerusalem, "You must worship before this altar in Jerusalem"?

²³"'Come now, make a bargain with my master, the king of Assyria: I will give you two thousand horses — if you can put riders on them! ²⁴How can you repulse one officer of the least of my master's officials, even though you are depending on Egypt for chariots and horsemen*ᶜ*? ²⁵Furthermore, have I come to

ᵃ 14 That is, about 11 tons or about 10 metric tons   ᵇ 14 That is, about 1 ton or about 1 metric ton   ᶜ 24 Or *charioteers*

Hebrew word used here, *nechushtan*, suggests both the material *nechosheth* ("bronze") and the shape *nachash* ("serpent"). See Nu 21:9. See the infographic "The Bronze Snake" on p. 245.

18:9–12 This recap of the same events (and reasoning) described in 2Ki 17 juxtaposes Hezekiah's righteous reign with the happenings in Israel. This demonstrates the absolute need for a reign like Hezekiah's and why other kings of Judah should follow in his practices.

18:13–37 The account of Sennacherib's campaign against Judah (701 BC) begins here and continues through ch. 19. Parallel accounts occur in 2Ch 32 and Isa 36–37.

18:13 Sennacherib king of Assyria Reigned ca. 705–681 BC. See the timeline "Dates Related to Isaiah and 2 Kings" on p. 1116; see the infographic "Sennacherib's Prism" on p. 597.

18:14 Lachish Apparently Sennacherib's armies were encamped there. One of Judah's fortified cities, strategic for guarding the route from the Mediterranean coast to Jerusalem. The siege of Lachish is depicted in reliefs

discovered at Sennacherib's palace in Nineveh. See the infographic "The Lachish Letters" on p. 1228. **I have done wrong** Presumably means that Hezekiah did not submit to Sennacherib's rule.

18:17 supreme commander, his chief officer and his field commander The Hebrew text here supplies the titles of top Assyrian officials. Compare Isa 36:2.

18:19 This is what the great king, the king of Assyria, says This speech matches Isa 36:4–20 verbatim; most likely there was an official record of the speech. **On what are you basing this confidence of yours** Compare Isa 36:5 and note.

18:21 Egypt The kingdoms in Syria-Palestine commonly sought Egyptian support to resist the Mesopotamian empires during the eighth to sixth centuries BC.

18:22 high places and altars The Assyrian messenger wrongly assumes that Hezekiah has angered Yahweh by removing these sites of idolatry. It is highly likely that some people in Judah also held this perspective.

18:25 Lᴏʀᴅ himself told me Assyrian royal inscriptions often describe gods of other nations as leaving their own people to support the Assyrians. Second Kings attests

attack and destroy this place without word from the LORD? The LORD himself told me to march against this country and destroy it.'"

²⁶Then Eliakim son of Hilkiah, and Shebna and Joah said to the field commander, "Please speak to your servants in Aramaic, since we understand it. Don't speak to us in Hebrew in the hearing of the people on the wall."

²⁷But the commander replied, "Was it only to your master and you that my master sent me to say these things, and not to the people sitting on the wall — who, like you, will have to eat their own excrement and drink their own urine?"

²⁸Then the commander stood and called out in Hebrew, "Hear the word of the great king, the king of Assyria! ²⁹This is what the king says: Do not let Hezekiah deceive you. He cannot deliver you from my hand. ³⁰Do not let Hezekiah persuade you to trust in the LORD when he says, 'The LORD will surely deliver us; this city will not be given into the hand of the king of Assyria.'

³¹"Do not listen to Hezekiah. This is what the king of Assyria says: Make peace with me and come out to me. Then each of you will eat fruit from your own vine and fig tree and drink water from your own cistern, ³²until I come and take you to a land like your own — a land of grain and new wine, a land of bread and vineyards, a land of olive trees and honey. Choose life and not death!

"Do not listen to Hezekiah, for he is misleading you when he says, 'The LORD will deliver us.' ³³Has the god of any nation ever delivered his land from the hand of the king of Assyria? ³⁴Where are the gods of Hamath and Arpad? Where are the gods of Sepharvaim, Hena and Ivvah? Have they rescued Samaria from my hand? ³⁵Who of all the gods of these countries has been able to save his land from me? How then can the LORD deliver Jerusalem from my hand?"

³⁶But the people remained silent and said nothing in reply, because the king had commanded, "Do not answer him."

³⁷Then Eliakim son of Hilkiah the palace administrator, Shebna the secretary, and Joah son of Asaph the recorder went to Hezekiah, with their clothes torn, and told him what the field commander had said.

Jerusalem's Deliverance Foretold

19:1-13pp — Isa 37:1-13

19 When King Hezekiah heard this, he tore his clothes and put on sackcloth and went into the temple of the LORD. ²He sent Eliakim the palace administrator, Shebna the secretary and the leading priests, all wearing sackcloth, to the prophet Isaiah son of Amoz. ³They told him, "This is what Hezekiah says: This day is a day of distress and rebuke and disgrace, as when children come to the moment of birth and there is no strength to deliver them. ⁴It may be that the LORD your God will hear all the words of the field commander, whom his master, the king of Assyria, has sent to ridicule the living God, and that he will rebuke him for the words the LORD your God has heard. Therefore pray for the remnant that still survives."

⁵When King Hezekiah's officials came to Isaiah, ⁶Isaiah said to them, "Tell your master, 'This is what the LORD says: Do not be afraid of what you have heard — those words with which the underlings of the king of Assyria have blasphemed me. ⁷Listen! When he hears a certain report, I will make him want to return to his own country, and there I will have him cut down with the sword.'"

⁸When the field commander heard that the king of Assyria had left Lachish, he withdrew and found the king fighting against Libnah.

⁹Now Sennacherib received a report that Tirhakah, the king of Cush,ᵃ was marching out to fight against him. So he again sent messengers to Hezekiah with this word: ¹⁰"Say to Hezekiah king of Judah: Do not let the god you depend on deceive you when he says, 'Jerusalem will not be given into the hands of the king of Assyria.' ¹¹Surely you have heard what the kings of Assyria have done to all the countries, destroying them completely. And will you be delivered? ¹²Did the gods of the nations that were destroyed by my predecessors deliver them — the gods of Gozan,

---

ᵃ 9 That is, the upper Nile region

---

elsewhere to the idea that Yahweh communicated with non-Israelite leaders (see 2Ki 8:7–15).

18:26 speak to your servants in Aramaic Aramaic was the official language west of the Euphrates at this time. Although Hezekiah's leading officials apparently spoke Aramaic, most of the people of Judah spoke only Hebrew.

18:31 Then each of you will eat A proverbial image of security and peace (see 1Ki 4:25; Zec 3:10; Mic 4:4).

18:34 Hamath and Arpad The official implies that Yahweh is unable or unwilling to defend Jerusalem—just like the gods of these cities (conquered by Assyria).

18:37 with their clothes torn A gesture of grief.

19:1–37 Isaiah 37 contains a parallel account of this chapter.

19:1 put on sackcloth A mourning rite.

19:2 Isaiah The same prophet affiliated with the book of Isaiah. See note on Isa 1:1.

19:4 to ridicule the living God Hezekiah's words express an appeal not for rescue, but for the defense of Yahweh's honor. This perspective is echoed in Isaiah's response (2Ki 19:6,28). **the remnant that still survives** Jerusalem was the only fortified city of Judah that had not yet been conquered (18:13).

19:7 he hears a certain report Perhaps a report of a rebellion or a foreign army. Compare Isa 37:7 and note.

19:8 Libnah A city in the Judean hill country.

19:9 Tirhakah, the king of Cush Suggests that Egypt might have been supporting Judah (see note on Isa 37:9).

Harran, Rezeph and the people of Eden who were in Tel Assar? [13]Where is the king of Hamath or the king of Arpad? Where are the kings of Lair, Sepharvaim, Hena and Ivvah?"

Hezekiah's Prayer

19:14-19pp — Isa 37:14-20

[14]Hezekiah received the letter from the messengers and read it. Then he went up to the temple of the LORD and spread it out before the LORD. [15]And Hezekiah prayed to the LORD: "LORD, the God of Israel, enthroned between the cherubim, you alone are God over all the kingdoms of the earth. You have made heaven and earth. [16]Give ear, LORD, and hear; open your eyes, LORD, and see; listen to the words Sennacherib has sent to ridicule the living God.

[17]"It is true, LORD, that the Assyrian kings have laid waste these nations and their lands. [18]They have thrown their gods into the fire and destroyed them, for they were not gods but only wood and stone, fashioned by human hands. [19]Now, LORD our God, deliver us from his hand, so that all the kingdoms of the earth may know that you alone, LORD, are God."

Isaiah Prophesies Sennacherib's Fall

19:20-37pp — Isa 37:21-38
19:35-37pp — 2Ch 32:20-21

[20]Then Isaiah son of Amoz sent a message to Hezekiah: "This is what the LORD, the God of Israel, says: I have heard your prayer concerning Sennacherib king of Assyria. [21]This is the word that the LORD has spoken against him:

"'Virgin Daughter Zion
    despises you and mocks you.
Daughter Jerusalem
    tosses her head as you flee.
[22]Who is it you have ridiculed and blasphemed?
    Against whom have you raised your voice
and lifted your eyes in pride?
    Against the Holy One of Israel!
[23]By your messengers
    you have ridiculed the Lord.

And you have said,
    "With my many chariots
I have ascended the heights of the
        mountains,
    the utmost heights of Lebanon.
I have cut down its tallest cedars,
    the choicest of its junipers.
I have reached its remotest parts,
    the finest of its forests.
[24]I have dug wells in foreign lands
    and drunk the water there.
With the soles of my feet
    I have dried up all the streams of Egypt."

[25]"'Have you not heard?
    Long ago I ordained it.
In days of old I planned it;
    now I have brought it to pass,
that you have turned fortified cities
    into piles of stone.
[26]Their people, drained of power,
    are dismayed and put to shame.
They are like plants in the field,
    like tender green shoots,
like grass sprouting on the roof,
    scorched before it grows up.

[27]"'But I know where you are
    and when you come and go
    and how you rage against me.
[28]Because you rage against me
    and because your insolence has reached
        my ears,
I will put my hook in your nose
    and my bit in your mouth,
and I will make you return
    by the way you came.'

[29]"This will be the sign for you, Hezekiah:

"This year you will eat what grows by itself,
    and the second year what springs from
        that.
But in the third year sow and reap,
    plant vineyards and eat their fruit.
[30]Once more a remnant of the kingdom
        of Judah
    will take root below and bear fruit above.

19:13 the king of Hamath or the king of Arpad See 2Ki 18:34 and note.

19:14–19 Hezekiah's prayer contains thematic parallels to Solomon's prayer in 1Ki 8:22–53.

19:15 cherubim Spiritual beings commonly depicted as guardians (see Ge 3:24 and note). Their mention here refers to the ark of the covenant (Ex 25:17–22). See the infographic "The Ark of the Covenant" on p. 412.

19:19 kingdoms of the earth may know The desire for the nations to know Yahweh also surfaces in Solomon's prayer (1Ki 8:43) and is a theme in Isaiah (e.g., Isa 2:2–4; 49).

19:21 tosses her head as you flee A gesture of mocking (as here) or sorrow and sympathy (compare Ps 22:7; 109:25; La 2:15).

19:22 the Holy One of Israel A title for God frequently used in Isaiah (Isa 5:24; 17:7; 43:3; 49:7; 55:5).

19:27 you come Refers to watchfulness, whether for protection (Ps 121:8) or for surveillance (2Sa 3:25).

19:28 my bit in your mouth Alludes to preparing an ox for labor. This dehumanizing imagery symbolizes taking a person captive.

19:29 But in the third year sow and reap According to Isaiah's prophecy, it will take several years for Judah to recover from Sennacherib's invasion (2Ki 18:13).

³¹ For out of Jerusalem will come a
　　remnant,
　　and out of Mount Zion a band of
　　　　survivors.

"The zeal of the LORD Almighty will accomplish
this.

³² "Therefore this is what the LORD says concerning the king of Assyria:

"'He will not enter this city
　　or shoot an arrow here.
He will not come before it with shield
　　or build a siege ramp against it.

³³ By the way that he came he will return;
　　he will not enter this city,
　　　　　　declares the LORD.
³⁴ I will defend this city and save it,
　　for my sake and for the sake of David my
　　　　servant.'"

³⁵ That night the angel of the LORD went out
and put to death a hundred and eighty-five thousand in the Assyrian camp. When the people got
up the next morning — there were all the dead
bodies! ³⁶ So Sennacherib king of Assyria broke
camp and withdrew. He returned to Nineveh and
stayed there.

19:32 build a siege ramp The Assyrian account of
Sennacherib's campaign confirms that he did not employ
siege tactics against Jerusalem, as he did elsewhere in
Judah. Images of siege works appear on a relief from
Lachish (see 18:14 and note). See note on Eze 4:2. See
the infographic "Sennacherib's Prism" below.
19:34 for my sake Refers to God acting to protect his

reputation. **for the sake of David my servant** Refers
to Yahweh's statement to Solomon in 1Ki 11:11–13:
Yahweh had promised to continue the Davidic dynasty,
which meant the survival of the tribe of Judah (2Sa 7:16).
19:35 angel of the LORD See note on 2Ki 1:3.
19:36 broke camp and withdrew Sennacherib's record
of this campaign states that he left Hezekiah cooped

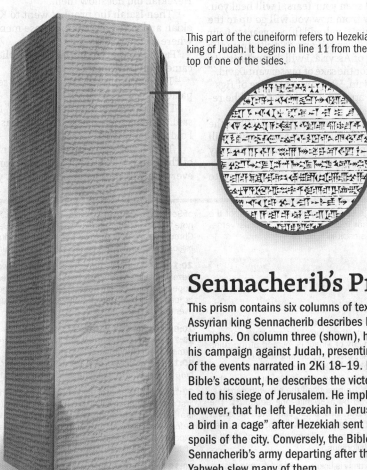

This part of the cuneiform refers to Hezekiah,
king of Judah. It begins in line 11 from the
top of one of the sides.

Sennacherib's Prism

This prism contains six columns of text in which
Assyrian king Sennacherib describes his
triumphs. On column three (shown), he recounts
his campaign against Judah, presenting a version
of the events narrated in 2Ki 18–19. Like the
Bible's account, he describes the victories that
led to his siege of Jerusalem. He implies,
however, that he left Hezekiah in Jerusalem "like
a bird in a cage" after Hezekiah sent him the
spoils of the city. Conversely, the Bible describes
Sennacherib's army departing after the Angel of
Yahweh slew many of them.

37One day, while he was worshiping in the temple of his god Nisrok, his sons Adrammelek and Sharezer killed him with the sword, and they escaped to the land of Ararat. And Esarhaddon his son succeeded him as king.

Hezekiah's Illness

20:1-11pp — 2Ch 32:24-26; Isa 38:1-8

20 In those days Hezekiah became ill and was at the point of death. The prophet Isaiah son of Amoz went to him and said, "This is what the LORD says: Put your house in order, because you are going to die; you will not recover."

2Hezekiah turned his face to the wall and prayed to the LORD, 3"Remember, LORD, how I have walked before you faithfully and with wholehearted devotion and have done what is good in your eyes." And Hezekiah wept bitterly.

4Before Isaiah had left the middle court, the word of the LORD came to him: 5"Go back and tell Hezekiah, the ruler of my people, 'This is what the LORD, the God of your father David, says: I have heard your prayer and seen your tears; I will heal you. On the third day from now you will go up to the temple of the LORD. 6I will add fifteen years to your life. And I will deliver you and this city from the hand of the king of Assyria. I will defend this city for my sake and for the sake of my servant David.'"

7Then Isaiah said, "Prepare a poultice of figs." They did so and applied it to the boil, and he recovered.

8Hezekiah had asked Isaiah, "What will be the sign that the LORD will heal me and that I will go up to the temple of the LORD on the third day from now?"

9Isaiah answered, "This is the LORD's sign to you that the LORD will do what he has promised: Shall the shadow go forward ten steps, or shall it go back ten steps?"

10"It is a simple matter for the shadow to go forward ten steps," said Hezekiah. "Rather, have it go back ten steps."

11Then the prophet Isaiah called on the LORD, and the LORD made the shadow go back the ten steps it had gone down on the stairway of Ahaz.

Envoys From Babylon

20:12-19pp — Isa 39:1-8
20:20-21pp — 2Ch 32:32-33

12At that time Marduk-Baladan son of Baladan king of Babylon sent Hezekiah letters and a gift, because he had heard of Hezekiah's illness. 13Hezekiah received the envoys and showed them all that was in his storehouses — the silver, the gold, the spices and the fine olive oil — his armory and everything found among his treasures. There was nothing in his palace or in all his kingdom that Hezekiah did not show them.

14Then Isaiah the prophet went to King Hezekiah and asked, "What did those men say, and where did they come from?"

"From a distant land," Hezekiah replied. "They came from Babylon."

15The prophet asked, "What did they see in your palace?"

"They saw everything in my palace," Hezekiah said. "There is nothing among my treasures that I did not show them."

16Then Isaiah said to Hezekiah, "Hear the word of the LORD: 17The time will surely come when everything in your palace, and all that your pre-

---

up "like a bird in a cage." It makes no mention of the catastrophic defeat indicated by the previous verse. **Nineveh** Assyria's capital.

NINEVEH
The city of Nineveh was located on the east bank of the Tigris River in northeastern Mesopotamia (modern Iraq). The modern city of Mosul is located at the ruins of Nineveh. The Assyrian king Sennacherib (705–681 BC) tripled the size of Nineveh and made it the Assyrian capital. He constructed a magnificent palace that covered five acres. He beautified the city with gardens, which were watered by a 30-mile-long aqueduct. The population of Nineveh has been estimated at about 200,000 during the reign of Sennacherib. Nineveh was destroyed in 612 BC by a military alliance of Medes, Scythians and Babylonians.

19:37 Nisrok This deity is unknown. See the table "Pagan Deities of the Old Testament" on p. 1287. **killed him with the sword** Other ancient sources corroborate this report

of Sennacherib's death, which occurred ca. 681 BC. See note on Isa 37:38. See the infographic "The Babylonian Chronicles" on p. 605. **the land of Ararat** Mountainous region north of Assyria, in modern-day Armenia.

20:1–11 The author provides a brief narrative of King Hezekiah's illness and recovery; a more detailed version appears in Isa 38. Second Kings 20:6 suggests that at least part of Hezekiah's illness occurred during the events of ch. 19.

20:6 my sake See 2Ki 19:34 and note.
20:7 a poultice of figs Ancient Near Eastern texts often attribute healing properties to figs.
20:11 the stairway of Ahaz The Hebrew terminology here could refer to a staircase or perhaps a sundial.

20:12–21 The arrival of the Babylonian envoys marks the first mention of Babylon in the book of 2 Kings (compare Isa 39:1–8). Although several generations will pass before the Babylonian Empire conquers Assyria and expands its borders, this passage foreshadows the fall of Judah to the Babylonians in 586 BC (chs. 24–25).

20:12 Marduk-Baladan son of Baladan Reigned from 722–710 BC and again for nine months in 704–703 BC. See note on Isa 39:1.

decessors have stored up until this day, will be carried off to Babylon. Nothing will be left, says the LORD. ¹⁸And some of your descendants, your own flesh and blood who will be born to you, will be taken away, and they will become eunuchs in the palace of the king of Babylon."

¹⁹"The word of the LORD you have spoken is good," Hezekiah replied. For he thought, "Will there not be peace and security in my lifetime?"

²⁰As for the other events of Hezekiah's reign, all his achievements and how he made the pool and the tunnel by which he brought water into the city,

---

20:17 time will surely come A common phrase in prophetic oracles; Jeremiah uses it more than Isaiah (e.g., Jer 7:32; 9:25; 16:14; 19:6). **will be carried off to Babylon** Isaiah's prophecy is fulfilled in 2Ki 24:10—25:21.

20:18 eunuchs Refers to government officials in the ancient Near East. By the Persian period, an official who was a eunuch was often a male who had been castrated (see note on Est 1:10).

20:19 Will there not be peace and security in my lifetime Although Isaiah's prophecy envisions Judah being stripped of its wealth, Hezekiah is satisfied that it will not happen during his lifetime.

20:20 the pool and the tunnel Archaeologists have discovered several ancient water-delivery systems connecting the Gihon Spring, just east of Jerusalem, to the Pool of Siloam, inside the city. Hezekiah is associated with two of these systems—the Siloam Channel (2Ch 32:30) and Hezekiah's Tunnel—although his role in each project remains debated (compare 2Ki 18:17; Isa 7:3). Preparations for war included ensuring access to water in the event of a siege, often in the form of digging a tunnel from inside the fortification wall to a water source outside the city. See the infographic "Inscription From Hezekiah's Tunnel" below. **annals of the kings of Judah** See note on 2Ki 1:18.

Inscription From Hezekiah's Tunnel

Hezekiah, king of Judah, fortified Jerusalem at the end of the 8th century BC, just before the invasion of Sennacherib. As part of his building project, Hezekiah brought water into the city of Jerusalem through a tunnel carved from over half a kilometer of bedrock (2Ki 20:20). A six percent gradient was designed into the excavation to allow water to flow from the Gihon spring into the Pool of Siloam (compare Jn 9:7).

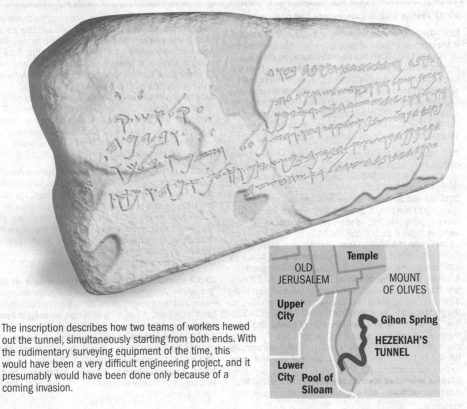

The inscription describes how two teams of workers hewed out the tunnel, simultaneously starting from both ends. With the rudimentary surveying equipment of the time, this would have been a very difficult engineering project, and it presumably would have been done only because of a coming invasion.

Temple

OLD JERUSALEM

MOUNT OF OLIVES

Upper City

Gihon Spring

HEZEKIAH'S TUNNEL

Lower City   Pool of Siloam

are they not written in the book of the annals of the kings of Judah? ²¹Hezekiah rested with his ancestors. And Manasseh his son succeeded him as king.

Manasseh King of Judah

21:1-10pp — 2Ch 33:1-10
21:17-18pp — 2Ch 33:18-20

21 Manasseh was twelve years old when he became king, and he reigned in Jerusalem fifty-five years. His mother's name was Hephzibah. ²He did evil in the eyes of the LORD, following the detestable practices of the nations the LORD had driven out before the Israelites. ³He rebuilt the high places his father Hezekiah had destroyed; he also erected altars to Baal and made an Asherah pole, as Ahab king of Israel had done. He bowed down to all the starry hosts and worshiped them. ⁴He built altars in the temple of the LORD, of which the LORD had said, "In Jerusalem I will put my Name." ⁵In the two courts of the temple of the LORD, he built altars to all the starry hosts. ⁶He sacrificed his own son in the fire, practiced divination, sought omens, and consulted mediums and spiritists. He did much evil in the eyes of the LORD, arousing his anger.

⁷He took the carved Asherah pole he had made and put it in the temple, of which the LORD had said to David and to his son Solomon, "In this temple and in Jerusalem, which I have chosen out of all the tribes of Israel, I will put my Name forever. ⁸I will not again make the feet of the Israelites wander from the land I gave their ancestors, if only they will be careful to do everything I commanded them and will keep the whole Law that my servant Moses gave them." ⁹But the people did not listen. Manasseh led them astray, so that they did more evil than the nations the LORD had destroyed before the Israelites.

¹⁰The LORD said through his servants the prophets: ¹¹"Manasseh king of Judah has committed these detestable sins. He has done more evil than the Amorites who preceded him and has led Judah into sin with his idols. ¹²Therefore this is what the LORD, the God of Israel, says: I am going to bring such disaster on Jerusalem and Judah that the ears of everyone who hears of it will tingle. ¹³I will stretch out over Jerusalem the measuring line used against Samaria and the plumb line used against the house of Ahab. I will wipe out Jerusalem as one wipes a dish, wiping it and turning it upside down. ¹⁴I will forsake the remnant of my inheritance and give them into the hands of enemies. They will be looted and plundered by all their enemies; ¹⁵they have done evil in my eyes and have aroused my anger from the day their ancestors came out of Egypt until this day."

¹⁶Moreover, Manasseh also shed so much innocent blood that he filled Jerusalem from end to

---

20:21 rested with his ancestors See note on 8:24.

21:1–18 According to the author of 1–2 Kings, Manasseh is the epitome of evil. Not only does he undo the reforms of his father, Hezekiah, but he also violates more religious precepts than any king before him—even more than the Canaanites and Amorites (21:9,11). Many of Manasseh's sins mirror those that caused the downfall of the northern kingdom of Israel (17:7–18), so it is no surprise that he is blamed for the fall of Judah. See note on Jer 15:4. See the timeline "The Divided Kingdom" on p. 536; see the infographic "Royal Seals of Judah" on p. 593.

21:1 Manasseh The longest-reigning king in either Judah or Israel (55 years: 697–642 BC). He also is described as one of the most wicked kings to rule either nation. See note on 2Ch 33:1.

21:2 He did evil The author lays similar accusations upon King Ahaz of Judah (2Ki 16:3) and the kingdom of Israel generally (17:8). **detestable practices of the nations** Described in Dt 18:9–14.

21:3 rebuilt the high places Manasseh undoes Hezekiah's reforms (2Ki 18:4–7). **an Asherah pole** A sacred pole associated with the cult of the Canaanite goddess Asherah. **Ahab king of Israel** The author of 1–2 Kings considers Ahab the most sinful king of the northern kingdom of Israel, primarily because he instituted worship of the god Baal and the goddess Asherah (1Ki 16:30–33). See 2Ki 8:18 and note. **all the starry hosts** The sun, moon, stars and planets (23:5). The book of 2 Kings first mentions this kind of idolatry, called astral worship, in the list of Israel's sins (17:16). Biblical law expressly forbids such worship (Dt 4:19).

21:6 He sacrificed his own son in the fire See 2Ki 16:3 and note. **mediums and spiritists** Forbidden in Lev 20:6

and Dt 18:9–14. People who interacted with the spirit world were expelled from the land by Saul (1Sa 28:3,9).

21:7 I will put my Name The author reiterates God's covenant with David and Solomon (see 2Sa 7:13 and note) to show that Manasseh's actions had violated it. By placing an idol in the temple, Manasseh defiled the place where God had chosen to put his name.

21:8 they will be careful to do Yahweh's promise is contingent on obedience to the law (see Dt 28; 1Ki 9:3–9).

21:9 LORD had destroyed Refers to the prior inhabitants of the promised land (e.g., Canaanites, Amorites) who were driven out because of their idolatry (which Israel and Judah later adopted; Dt 18:9–14; 2Ki 17:8; 21:2).

21:12–15 The judgment and exile of Judah are described here as a direct result of Manasseh's sins, which violated God's covenant (see note on v. 7). In 2 Kings, Manasseh and his sins are presented as the main reason for the Babylonian exile. Second Chronicles, however, gives Manasseh's story a different ending, as the wicked king repents, removes the idols and restores proper worship of Yahweh. This account highlights the Chronicler's message of repentance and restoration (see note on 2Ch 33:13).

21:13 plumb line used against the house of Ahab Yahweh will apply the same standard of judgment to Jerusalem and Manasseh that he applied to Samaria (Israel's capital city) and Ahab, king of Israel. **turning it upside down** To ensure that any leftover scraps are removed.

21:14 the remnant of my inheritance Refers to the last of God's people remaining in the promised land and particularly the tribe of Judah (2Ki 17:18).

21:16 innocent blood In prophetic addresses, shedding innocent blood refers to oppressing the poor (Jer 7:6; 22:3; Eze 22:7).

end — besides the sin that he had caused Judah to commit, so that they did evil in the eyes of the LORD.

[17] As for the other events of Manasseh's reign, and all he did, including the sin he committed, are they not written in the book of the annals of the kings of Judah? [18] Manasseh rested with his ancestors and was buried in his palace garden, the garden of Uzza. And Amon his son succeeded him as king.

Amon King of Judah

21:19-24pp — 2Ch 33:21-25

[19] Amon was twenty-two years old when he became king, and he reigned in Jerusalem two years. His mother's name was Meshullemeth daughter of Haruz; she was from Jotbah. [20] He did evil in the eyes of the LORD, as his father Manasseh had done. [21] He followed completely the ways of his father, worshiping the idols his father had worshiped, and bowing down to them. [22] He forsook the LORD, the God of his ancestors, and did not walk in obedience to him.

[23] Amon's officials conspired against him and assassinated the king in his palace. [24] Then the people of the land killed all who had plotted against King Amon, and they made Josiah his son king in his place.

[25] As for the other events of Amon's reign, and what he did, are they not written in the book of the annals of the kings of Judah? [26] He was buried in his tomb in the garden of Uzza. And Josiah his son succeeded him as king.

The Book of the Law Found

22:1-20pp — 2Ch 34:1-2,8-28

22 Josiah was eight years old when he became king, and he reigned in Jerusalem thirty-one years. His mother's name was Jedidah daughter of Adaiah; she was from Bozkath. [2] He did what was right in the eyes of the LORD and followed completely the ways of his father David, not turning aside to the right or to the left.

[3] In the eighteenth year of his reign, King Josiah sent the secretary, Shaphan son of Azaliah, the son of Meshullam, to the temple of the LORD. He said: [4] "Go up to Hilkiah the high priest and have him get ready the money that has been brought into the temple of the LORD, which the doorkeepers have collected from the people. [5] Have them entrust it to the men appointed to supervise the work on the temple. And have these men pay the workers who repair the temple of the LORD — [6] the carpenters, the builders and the masons. Also have them purchase timber and dressed stone to repair the temple. [7] But they need not account for the money entrusted to them, because they are honest in their dealings."

[8] Hilkiah the high priest said to Shaphan the secretary, "I have found the Book of the Law in the temple of the LORD." He gave it to Shaphan, who read it. [9] Then Shaphan the secretary went to the king and reported to him: "Your officials have paid out the money that was in the temple of the LORD and have entrusted it to the workers and supervisors at the temple." [10] Then Shaphan the secretary informed the king, "Hilkiah the priest has given me a book." And Shaphan read from it in the presence of the king.

[11] When the king heard the words of the Book of the Law, he tore his robes. [12] He gave these orders to Hilkiah the priest, Ahikam son of Shaphan, Akbor son of Micaiah, Shaphan the secretary and Asaiah the king's attendant: [13] "Go and inquire of the LORD for me and for the people and for all Judah about what is written in this book that has been found. Great is the LORD's anger that burns against us because those who have gone before us have not obeyed

---

21:18 palace garden, the garden of Uzza Manasseh is the first king to be buried here; previous kings of Judah (ending with Hezekiah) were buried in the City of David. This garden might have belonged to King Uzziah the leper (also called Azariah; ch. 15) or perhaps to the Uzzah who was killed for touching the ark of the covenant (2Sa 6:3–8).

21:19–26 The reign of Amon (ca. 642–640 BC) is overshadowed by the sins of his father, Manasseh (2Ki 21:1–18), and the reforms of his son, Josiah (chs. 22–23). Amon's evil suggests that Manasseh's sins took hold in Judah. See the timeline "The Divided Kingdom" on p. 536.

21:24 the people of the land The Hebrew phrase used here, *am ha'arets*, may describe a distinct upper-class social group — a sort of aristocracy — that is active during crises involving David's royal line (compare 11:12–20).

21:25 annals of the kings of Judah See note on 1:18.

21:26 the garden of Uzza See note on 21:18.

22:1–7 This marks the beginning of the narrative of Josiah's reign; he is the last righteous king of Judah, who reigned ca. 640–609 BC. A parallel account of his reign begins in 2Ch 34. The report of Josiah rebuilding

the temple (2Ki 22:3–7) has many similarities to the account of Jehoash's repairs in 12:4–16.

22:3 eighteenth year of his reign Approximately 622 BC.

22:4 Hilkiah the high priest According to later genealogical lists, Hilkiah's father was Meshullam of the family of Zadok, the high priest who supported both David and Solomon (1Ch 9:10–11; Ezr 7:1; Ne 11:11).
doorkeepers Refers to priests who were stationed at the temple gates to collect funds for repairs to the temple.

22:8–20 The text does not provide the circumstances of Hilkiah's discovery; most likely, the Book of the Law turned up during the temple's renovation (2Ki 22:3–7). Although it is unclear what this book contained, Josiah's actions and certain phrases (in 2 Kings and 2 Chronicles) suggest that Hilkiah found some form of Deuteronomy (compare 2Ch 34:19).

22:11 he tore his robes A gesture of grief, presumably because of the curses found in the Book of the Law (2Ki 22:13).

22:13 inquire of the LORD for me In times of distress, people often inquired of prophets to discern Yahweh's will (e.g., 1Ki 14:1–18; Jer 21:1–7).

the words of this book; they have not acted in accordance with all that is written there concerning us."

[14]Hilkiah the priest, Ahikam, Akbor, Shaphan and Asaiah went to speak to the prophet Huldah, who was the wife of Shallum son of Tikvah, the son of Harhas, keeper of the wardrobe. She lived in Jerusalem, in the New Quarter.

[15]She said to them, "This is what the LORD, the God of Israel, says: Tell the man who sent you to me, [16]'This is what the LORD says: I am going to bring disaster on this place and its people, according to everything written in the book the king of Judah has read. [17]Because they have forsaken me and burned incense to other gods and aroused my anger by all the idols their hands have made,[a] my anger will burn against this place and will not be quenched.' [18]Tell the king of Judah, who sent you to inquire of the LORD, 'This is what the LORD, the God of Israel, says concerning the words you heard: [19]Because your heart was responsive and you humbled yourself before the LORD when you heard what I have spoken against this place and its people — that they would become a curse[b] and be laid waste — and because you tore your robes and wept in my presence, I also have heard you, declares the LORD. [20]Therefore I will gather you to your ancestors, and you will be buried in peace. Your eyes will not see all the disaster I am going to bring on this place.'"

So they took her answer back to the king.

Josiah Renews the Covenant

23:1-3pp — 2Ch 34:29-32
23:4-20Ref — 2Ch 34:3-7,33
23:21-23pp — 2Ch 35:1,18-19
23:28-30pp — 2Ch 35:20 – 36:1

23 Then the king called together all the elders of Judah and Jerusalem. [2]He went up to the temple of the LORD with the people of Judah,

the inhabitants of Jerusalem, the priests and the prophets — all the people from the least to the greatest. He read in their hearing all the words of the Book of the Covenant, which had been found in the temple of the LORD. [3]The king stood by the pillar and renewed the covenant in the presence of the LORD — to follow the LORD and keep his commands, statutes and decrees with all his heart and all his soul, thus confirming the words of the covenant written in this book. Then all the people pledged themselves to the covenant.

[4]The king ordered Hilkiah the high priest, the priests next in rank and the doorkeepers to remove from the temple of the LORD all the articles made for Baal and Asherah and all the starry hosts. He burned them outside Jerusalem in the fields of the Kidron Valley and took the ashes to Bethel. [5]He did away with the idolatrous priests appointed by the kings of Judah to burn incense on the high places of the towns of Judah and on those around Jerusalem — those who burned incense to Baal, to the sun and moon, to the constellations and to all the starry hosts. [6]He took the Asherah pole from the temple of the LORD to the Kidron Valley outside Jerusalem and burned it there. He ground it to powder and scattered the dust over the graves of the common people. [7]He also tore down the quarters of the male shrine prostitutes that were in the temple of the LORD, the quarters where women did weaving for Asherah.

[8]Josiah brought all the priests from the towns of Judah and desecrated the high places, from Geba to Beersheba, where the priests had burned incense. He broke down the gateway at the entrance of the Gate of Joshua, the city governor, which was on

---

[a] 17 Or by everything they have done   [b] 19 That is, their names would be used in cursing (see Jer. 29:22); or, others would see that they are cursed.

22:14 the prophet Huldah Huldah is the only female prophet in the books of 1–2 Samuel, 1–2 Kings and 1–2 Chronicles. Given that the king's advisors consulted Huldah on matters of state, she might have been an official court prophet. Earlier in Israel's history, Deborah was a prophet (Jdg 4:4).
22:16 disaster on this place Huldah's message echoes the statement of judgment delivered because of Manasseh's sins (compare 2Ki 21:12–15 and note).
22:20 I will gather you to your ancestors Josiah is the only king to whom the author applies this archaic expression. Otherwise, the phrase appears in the Bible only in reference to the patriarchs, Aaron and Moses (Ge 25:8,17; 35:29; Nu 20:24; Dt 32:50).

23:1–20 Josiah's reign occurred during the decline of the Assyrian Empire. As Assyria's influence waned, a power vacuum formed in the province of Samaria (formerly the kingdom of Israel), allowing Judah to expand its northern border and extend Josiah's religious reforms into this region (2Ki 23:8,19). Josiah instituted worship of Yahweh as prescribed in Deuteronomy — which supports the view that the Book of the Law found by Hilkiah was a version of Deuteronomy (22:8–20). See the timeline "The Divided Kingdom" on p. 536.

23:1 the elders of Judah and Jerusalem Heads of prominent families who were responsible for day-to-day operations and executing justice (e.g., 1Ki 8:1; 20:7).
23:2 from the least to the greatest A common way of referring to the entire population (e.g., 1Sa 30:2; Jer 31:34).
23:3 the pillar Perhaps one of the two pillars outside the temple (1Ki 7:15–22). **covenant** A legally binding agreement between two or more parties. **his commands, statutes and decrees** Three different terms for the law (compare note on Ps 19:7–9).
23:4 for Baal and Asherah Refers to Canaanite deities (2Ki 17:16; 21:3–5).
23:6 the Kidron Valley Runs along Jerusalem's eastern border; a common disposal site for idols (e.g., v. 12; 1Ki 15:13; 2Ch 15:16).
23:7 male shrine prostitutes The Hebrew word used here, qedeshim, literally refers to "sacred, consecrated people" and is often understood to refer to male prostitutes set apart for pagan worship (also in 1Ki 14:24; 15:12). The notion that such people played a sexual role is inferred from Dt 23:17–18, which prohibits the daughters or sons of Israel from becoming a qedesh or

the left of the city gate. ⁹Although the priests of the high places did not serve at the altar of the LORD in Jerusalem, they ate unleavened bread with their fellow priests.

¹⁰He desecrated Topheth, which was in the Valley of Ben Hinnom, so no one could use it to sacrifice their son or daughter in the fire to Molek. ¹¹He removed from the entrance to the temple of the LORD the horses that the kings of Judah had dedicated to the sun. They were in the courtᵃ near the room of an official named Nathan-Melek. Josiah then burned the chariots dedicated to the sun.

¹²He pulled down the altars the kings of Judah had erected on the roof near the upper room of Ahaz, and the altars Manasseh had built in the two courts of the temple of the LORD. He removed them from there, smashed them to pieces and threw the rubble into the Kidron Valley. ¹³The king also desecrated the high places that were east of Jerusalem on the south of the Hill of Corruption — the ones Solomon king of Israel had built for Ashtoreth the vile goddess of the Sidonians, for Chemosh the vile god of Moab, and for Molek the detestable god of the people of Ammon. ¹⁴Josiah smashed the sacred stones and cut down the Asherah poles and covered the sites with human bones.

¹⁵Even the altar at Bethel, the high place made by Jeroboam son of Nebat, who had caused Israel to sin — even that altar and high place he demolished. He burned the high place and ground it to powder, and burned the Asherah pole also. ¹⁶Then Josiah looked around, and when he saw the tombs that were there on the hillside, he had the bones removed from them and burned on the altar to defile it, in accordance with the word of the LORD proclaimed by the man of God who foretold these things.

¹⁷The king asked, "What is that tombstone I see?"

The people of the city said, "It marks the tomb of the man of God who came from Judah and pronounced against the altar of Bethel the very things you have done to it."

¹⁸"Leave it alone," he said. "Don't let anyone disturb his bones." So they spared his bones and those of the prophet who had come from Samaria.

¹⁹Just as he had done at Bethel, Josiah removed all the shrines at the high places that the kings of Israel had built in the towns of Samaria and that had aroused the LORD's anger. ²⁰Josiah slaughtered all the priests of those high places on the altars and burned human bones on them. Then he went back to Jerusalem.

²¹The king gave this order to all the people: "Celebrate the Passover to the LORD your God, as it is written in this Book of the Covenant." ²²Neither in the days of the judges who led Israel nor in the days of the kings of Israel and the kings of Judah had any such Passover been observed. ²³But in the eighteenth year of King Josiah, this Passover was celebrated to the LORD in Jerusalem.

²⁴Furthermore, Josiah got rid of the mediums and spiritists, the household gods, the idols and all the other detestable things seen in Judah and Jerusalem. This he did to fulfill the requirements of the law written in the book that Hilkiah the priest had discovered in the temple of the LORD. ²⁵Neither before nor after Josiah was there a king like him who turned to the LORD as he did — with

---

ᵃ 11 The meaning of the Hebrew for this word is uncertain.

---

qadesh ("sacred person") and then prohibits bringing the wages of a zonah ("whore") into Yahweh's house.
23:8 from Geba to Beersheba Suggests that Josiah's reforms reached into the Assyrian province of Samaria (formerly the kingdom of Israel). The similar phrase "from Dan to Beersheba" is used to indicate all of Israel (see 1Sa 3:20 and note; note on Jer 4:15).
23:10 Topheth A cultic site just outside Jerusalem where worshipers sacrificed children to the god Molek. See 2Ki 16:3 and note; note on Jer 7:31.
23:11 dedicated to the sun In the ancient Near East, many cultures associated horses with the Mesopotamian sun god, Shamash, who was said to ride a horse-drawn chariot on feast days. This reference suggests that similar ideas had gained popularity in Judah.
23:13 the Hill of Corruption Refers to the Mount of Olives, where Solomon had built shrines to pagan gods for his foreign wives (1Ki 11:7). The Hebrew text contains a play on words, as the Hebrew name har hammishchah, meaning "Mount of Ointment" (the Mount of Olives) is very similar to the Hebrew for Mount (or Hill) of Corruption, har hammashchith.
23:15 the altar at Bethel Established after Israel had divided, so that people in the northern kingdom of Israel did not have to travel to Jerusalem (in the southern kingdom) to worship. See 1Ki 12:25–33 and note.

23:16 in accordance with the word of the LORD Refers to 1Ki 13:1–3, where a man of God comes from Judah to Bethel and prophesies that Josiah will defile (ruin) the altar.
23:18 the prophet who had come from Samaria This prophet was buried in the same grave as the man of God from Judah (1Ki 13:31).
23:21–27 The parallel account of the Passover celebration in 2Ch 35 is significantly longer and more detailed.
23:21 Passover A celebration commemorating Yahweh's deliverance of Israel from slavery and their departure from Egypt (Ex 12:1–30; Dt 16:1–8).
23:23 in Jerusalem Josiah had eliminated all the shrines that competed with the Jerusalem temple.
23:24 the household gods The Hebrew word used here, teraphim, refers to household deities common throughout Israel's history, since the time of the patriarchs (Ge 31:19; Jdg 17:5; 1Sa 19:13). The exact nature and function of these deities is unclear. **the book that Hilkiah the priest had discovered** See 2Ki 22:8–20.
23:25 Neither before nor after Josiah was there a king like him The author of 1–2 Kings considered Josiah to be more devoted to Yahweh than even David, who was the standard for worshipful behavior (1Ki 3:6; 9:4; 11:4). **with all his heart** Alludes to Israel's central commandment in Dt 6:5.

all his heart and with all his soul and with all his strength, in accordance with all the Law of Moses.

²⁶Nevertheless, the LORD did not turn away from the heat of his fierce anger, which burned against Judah because of all that Manasseh had done to arouse his anger. ²⁷So the LORD said, "I will remove Judah also from my presence as I removed Israel, and I will reject Jerusalem, the city I chose, and this temple, about which I said, 'My Name shall be there.'^a"

²⁸As for the other events of Josiah's reign, and all he did, are they not written in the book of the annals of the kings of Judah?

²⁹While Josiah was king, Pharaoh Necho king of Egypt went up to the Euphrates River to help the king of Assyria. King Josiah marched out to meet him in battle, but Necho faced him and killed him at Megiddo. ³⁰Josiah's servants brought his body in a chariot from Megiddo to Jerusalem and buried him in his own tomb. And the people of the land took Jehoahaz son of Josiah and anointed him and made him king in place of his father.

Jehoahaz King of Judah
23:31-34pp — 2Ch 36:2-4

³¹Jehoahaz was twenty-three years old when he became king, and he reigned in Jerusalem three months. His mother's name was Hamutal daughter of Jeremiah; she was from Libnah. ³²He did evil in the eyes of the LORD, just as his predecessors had done. ³³Pharaoh Necho put him in chains at Riblah in the land of Hamath so that he might not reign in Jerusalem, and he imposed on Judah a levy of a hundred talents^b of silver and a talent^c of gold. ³⁴Pharaoh Necho made Eliakim son of Josiah king in place of his father Josiah and changed Eliakim's name to Jehoiakim. But he took Jehoahaz and carried him off to Egypt, and there he died. ³⁵Jehoiakim paid Pharaoh Necho the silver and gold he demanded. In order to do so, he taxed the land and exacted the silver and gold from the people of the land according to their assessments.

Jehoiakim King of Judah
23:36-24:6pp — 2Ch 36:5-8

³⁶Jehoiakim was twenty-five years old when he became king, and he reigned in Jerusalem eleven years. His mother's name was Zebidah daughter of Pedaiah; she was from Rumah. ³⁷And he did evil in the eyes of the LORD, just as his predecessors had done.

24 During Jehoiakim's reign, Nebuchadnezzar king of Babylon invaded the land, and Jehoiakim became his vassal for three years. But then he turned against Nebuchadnezzar and rebelled.

^a 27 1 Kings 8:29   ^b 33 That is, about 3 3/4 tons or about 3.4 metric tons   ^c 33 That is, about 75 pounds or about 34 kilograms

---

23:26 Manasseh had done to arouse his anger See 2Ki 21.

23:27 from my presence The repeated use of this phrase, earlier used in reference to the northern kingdom of Israel, foreshadows a similar fate for Judah. God already had exiled the kingdom of Israel (17:20,23), expelling it from the land and scattering its inhabitants as he promised he would do if Israel did not obey him (e.g., 1Ki 9:6–9).

23:28–30 The politics of Judah's last few kings center on their shifting allegiances between Egypt (allied with a collapsing Assyria) and Babylon. The narrative does not say why Josiah goes up to meet with Egypt and Assyria, nor why Necho kills him on sight. Necho may have believed he could gain power from killing Josiah (which he does; 2Ki 23:29) or he may have thought Judah was allied with Babylon (compare 20:12–13). Second Chronicles offers a longer account of Josiah's untimely death (2Ch 35:20–27).

DATE	EVENT
609–595 BC	Reign of Pharaoh Necho II
609 BC	Necho defeats and kills King Josiah of Judah at Megiddo
605 BC	Babylon defeats Egypt and Assyria
597 BC	Babylon captures Jerusalem

23:28 annals of the kings of Judah See note on 2Ki 1:18.

23:29 Pharaoh Necho See note on Jer 46:2. Necho and his forces are responding to Assyria's request for aid against Babylon. **Megiddo** A city in the fertile plain of the Jezreel Valley; its origins date to 7000 BC. The death of Josiah—regarded as Israel's most righteous king (2Ki 23:25)—at Megiddo led to the idea that the end-times battle between good and evil would occur there. The Hebrew phrase used here, *har megiddo* ("Mount Megiddo"), is the basis for the place-name "Armageddon" (Rev 16:16).

23:30 Jehoahaz This king who reigned only three months, ca. 609 BC, is distinct from the Israelite king with the same name who reigned much earlier (ca. 814–798 BC). **anointed him** The anointing of kings occurs only three times in 1–2 Kings. In the case of Solomon (1Ki 1:45) and Jehoash (Joash) (2Ki 11:12; see note on 1:17), it is clear that their successions take place under irregular circumstances. The same is likely true of Jehoahaz.

23:33 Riblah An Assyrian administrative and military center in the Lebanon Valley.

23:34 made Eliakim son of Josiah king Necho replaces Jehoahaz with his brother, Jehoiakim; he probably does so to ensure that Judah stays unstable (see Jer 22:10 and note). **changed Eliakim's name to Jehoiakim** Eliakim means "God will establish," and Jehoiakim means "Yahweh will establish." Babylonian kings often changed the names of conquered people to give them a new identity; apparently Pharaoh Necho also used this practice (2Ki 24:17; Da 4:8).

23:35 paid Pharaoh Necho The nation of Judah is now a vassal state to Egypt and owes them regular tribute.

22:36–37 Although these verses offer what seem to be closing statements about Jehoiakim's reign, the narrative about his reign continues through 2Ki 23:7.

²The LORD sent Babylonian,ª Aramean, Moabite and Ammonite raiders against him to destroy Judah, in accordance with the word of the LORD proclaimed by his servants the prophets. ³Surely these things happened to Judah according to the LORD's command, in order to remove them from his presence because of the sins of Manasseh and

all he had done, ⁴including the shedding of innocent blood. For he had filled Jerusalem with innocent blood, and the LORD was not willing to forgive.

⁵As for the other events of Jehoiakim's reign, and all he did, are they not written in the book

ª 2 Or *Chaldean*

24:1–7 The conflict between Judah and Babylon that leads to the nation's downfall begins during the reign of Jehoiakim (ca. 609–597 BC). Jehoiakim accepts being a vassal of Babylon, presumably to avoid the destruction of Jerusalem, but then later rebels against Nebuchadnezzar II, king of Babylon. In response to his rebellion, King Nebuchadnezzar of Babylon deploys troops from the surrounding nations in order to destroy Judah. However, the text directly attributes these actions to Yahweh. Yahweh uses the actions of the Babylonian Empire to issue judgment on Judah for the nation's sins. See the timeline "The Divided Kingdom" on p. 536.

24:1 Nebuchadnezzar See note on Jer 21:2. This is the second scene in 2 Kings involving Babylon. In the first, Hezekiah took Babylonian envoys on a tour of the royal treasure houses, and Isaiah prophesied that they would return and carry everything off (2Ki 20:12–21).

24:2 Babylonian The Hebrew text uses "Babylonians" and "Chaldeans" interchangeably. **in accordance with the word of the LORD** Includes the word that Isaiah spoke to Hezekiah (20:16–18), the word of unnamed prophets concerning Manasseh's sins (21:10–15) and the word of Huldah to Josiah (22:15–20).

24:3 according to the LORD's command The author makes it clear that Nebuchadnezzar and Babylon are fulfilling Yahweh's word. Earlier, the sins of Manasseh were given as the reason for Judah's defeat and the exile (see 21:12–15 and note).

24:4 the shedding of innocent blood See note on 21:16.

The Babylonian Chronicles

The Babylonian Chronicles are a series of clay tablets inscribed with Babylonian history. They were written at different times, beginning around the sixth century BC. They narrate events beginning in the eighth century BC and cover nearly 500 years of history. Some describe events of biblical history—including Jehoiakim's refusal to pay tribute (2Ki 24:1), Nebuchadnezzar's siege of Jerusalem (2Ki 24:10–11) and Jehoiachin's capture (2Ki 24:12).

One of these—the Nabonidus Chronicle—describes the reign and downfall of the last king before Cyrus: Nabonidus. This tablet also mentions that Nabonidus had a regent, his son Bēl-šarra-uṣur—the Belshazzar of the book of Daniel. The banquet described in Daniel presumably took place during Belshazzar's regency, when Nabonidus was away from Babylon (Da 5:1–4).

of the annals of the kings of Judah? ⁶Jehoiakim rested with his ancestors. And Jehoiachin his son succeeded him as king.

⁷The king of Egypt did not march out from his own country again, because the king of Babylon had taken all his territory, from the Wadi of Egypt to the Euphrates River.

Jehoiachin King of Judah

24:8-17pp — 2Ch 36:9-10

⁸Jehoiachin was eighteen years old when he became king, and he reigned in Jerusalem three months. His mother's name was Nehushta daughter of Elnathan; she was from Jerusalem. ⁹He did evil in the eyes of the LORD, just as his father had done.

¹⁰At that time the officers of Nebuchadnezzar king of Babylon advanced on Jerusalem and laid siege to it, ¹¹and Nebuchadnezzar himself came up to the city while his officers were besieging it. ¹²Jehoiachin king of Judah, his mother, his attendants, his nobles and his officials all surrendered to him.

In the eighth year of the reign of the king of Babylon, he took Jehoiachin prisoner. ¹³As the LORD had declared, Nebuchadnezzar removed the treasures from the temple of the LORD and from the royal palace, and cut up the gold articles that Solomon king of Israel had made for the temple of the LORD. ¹⁴He carried all Jerusalem

---

24:6 The Hebrew text of this verse can be confusing, as it mentions both *yehoyaqim* (Jehoiakim), king of Judah, and his son *yehoyakhin* (Jehoiachin), who takes his place.

24:6 rested with his ancestors See note on 8:24.

24:10–17 The conflict between Judah and Babylon reaches Jerusalem during the reign of Jehoiachin (see vv. 10–12). Nebuchadnezzar, king of Babylon, proceeds

---

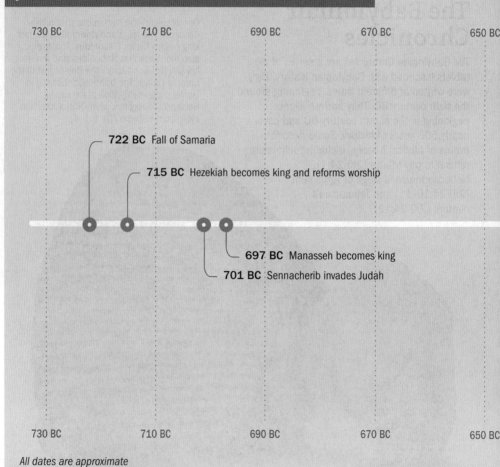

Judah From the Fall of Samaria to the Exile

730 BC   710 BC   690 BC   670 BC   650 BC

722 BC Fall of Samaria

715 BC Hezekiah becomes king and reforms worship

697 BC Manasseh becomes king

701 BC Sennacherib invades Judah

730 BC   710 BC   690 BC   670 BC   650 BC

All dates are approximate

into exile: all the officers and fighting men, and all the skilled workers and artisans — a total of ten thousand. Only the poorest people of the land were left.

[15]Nebuchadnezzar took Jehoiachin captive to Babylon. He also took from Jerusalem to Babylon the king's mother, his wives, his officials and the prominent people of the land. [16]The king of Babylon also deported to Babylon the entire force of seven thousand fighting men, strong and fit for war, and a thousand skilled workers and artisans. [17]He made Mattaniah, Jehoiachin's uncle, king in his place and changed his name to Zedekiah.

Zedekiah King of Judah

24:18-20pp — 2Ch 36:11-16; Jer 52:1-3

[18]Zedekiah was twenty-one years old when he became king, and he reigned in Jerusalem eleven

---

to take captive all the people of Jerusalem (ca. 597 BC), except the poor (v. 14); he then loots the temple and treasuries (compare note on v. 1).

24:12 In the eighth year of the reign Dating an event by the regnal year of a foreign ruler is unusual.

24:13 As the Lord had declared Refers to Isaiah's prophecy in 20:17. **cut up** Nebuchadnezzar's actions suggest that Judah refused to pay tribute. Earlier in 2 Kings, Ahaz and Hezekiah had used bronze, silver and

gold from the temple to fund Judah's tribute (16:17–18; 18:15–16).

24:14 He carried all Jerusalem into exile The first of two Babylonian exiles of Judah's people (25:11 describes the second). The prophet Ezekiel is exiled with this first group (see note on Eze 1:2).

24:17 Zedekiah Babylonian kings often changed the names of conquered people (2Ki 23:34). On Zedekiah, Jehoiachin's uncle, see note on Jer 21:1.

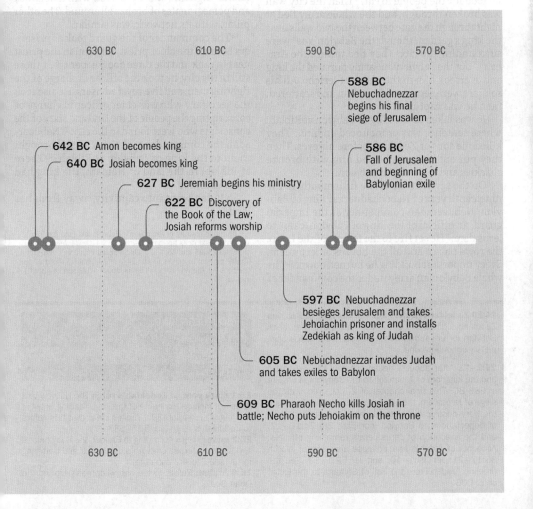

630 BC   610 BC   590 BC   570 BC

588 BC Nebuchadnezzar begins his final siege of Jerusalem

642 BC Amon becomes king

640 BC Josiah becomes king

627 BC Jeremiah begins his ministry

586 BC Fall of Jerusalem and beginning of Babylonian exile

622 BC Discovery of the Book of the Law; Josiah reforms worship

597 BC Nebuchadnezzar besieges Jerusalem and takes Jehoiachin prisoner and installs Zedekiah as king of Judah

605 BC Nebuchadnezzar invades Judah and takes exiles to Babylon

609 BC Pharaoh Necho kills Josiah in battle; Necho puts Jehoiakim on the throne

630 BC   610 BC   590 BC   570 BC

years. His mother's name was Hamutal daughter of Jeremiah; she was from Libnah. [19]He did evil in the eyes of the LORD, just as Jehoiakim had done. [20]It was because of the LORD's anger that all this happened to Jerusalem and Judah, and in the end he thrust them from his presence.

The Fall of Jerusalem

25:1-12pp — Jer 39:1-10
25:1-21pp — 2Ch 36:17-20; Jer 52:4-27
25:22-26pp — Jer 40:7-9; 41:1-3,16-18

Now Zedekiah rebelled against the king of Babylon.

25 So in the ninth year of Zedekiah's reign, on the tenth day of the tenth month, Nebuchadnezzar king of Babylon marched against Jerusalem with his whole army. He encamped outside the city and built siege works all around it. [2]The city was kept under siege until the eleventh year of King Zedekiah.

[3]By the ninth day of the fourth[a] month the famine in the city had become so severe that there was no food for the people to eat. [4]Then the city wall was broken through, and the whole army fled at night through the gate between the two walls near the king's garden, though the Babylonians[b] were surrounding the city. They fled toward the Arabah,[c] [5]but the Babylonian[d] army pursued the king and overtook him in the plains of Jericho. All his soldiers were separated from him and scattered, [6]and he was captured.

He was taken to the king of Babylon at Riblah, where sentence was pronounced on him. [7]They killed the sons of Zedekiah before his eyes. Then they put out his eyes, bound him with bronze shackles and took him to Babylon.

[8]On the seventh day of the fifth month, in the nineteenth year of Nebuchadnezzar king of Babylon, Nebuzaradan commander of the imperial guard, an official of the king of Babylon, came to Jerusalem. [9]He set fire to the temple of the LORD, the royal palace and all the houses of Jerusalem. Every important building he burned down. [10]The whole Babylonian army under the commander of the imperial guard broke down the walls around Jerusalem. [11]Nebuzaradan the commander of the guard carried into exile the people who remained in the city, along with the rest of the populace and those who had deserted to the king of Babylon. [12]But the commander left behind some of the poorest people of the land to work the vineyards and fields.

[13]The Babylonians broke up the bronze pillars, the movable stands and the bronze Sea that were at the temple of the LORD and they carried the bronze to Babylon. [14]They also took away the pots, shovels, wick trimmers, dishes and all the bronze articles used in the temple service. [15]The commander of the imperial guard took away the censers and sprinkling bowls — all that were made of pure gold or silver.

[16]The bronze from the two pillars, the Sea and the movable stands, which Solomon had made for the temple of the LORD, was more than could be weighed. [17]Each pillar was eighteen cubits[e] high. The bronze capital on top of one pillar was three cubits[f] high and was decorated with a network and pomegranates of bronze all around. The other pillar, with its network, was similar.

[18]The commander of the guard took as prisoners Seraiah the chief priest, Zephaniah the priest next in rank and the three doorkeepers. [19]Of those still in the city, he took the officer in charge of the fighting men, and five royal advisers. He also took the secretary who was chief officer in charge of conscripting the people of the land and sixty of the conscripts who were found in the city. [20]Nebuzaradan the commander took them all and brought them to the king of Babylon at Riblah. [21]There at Riblah, in the land of Hamath, the king had them executed.

So Judah went into captivity, away from her land.

---

[a] *3* Probable reading of the original Hebrew text (see Jer. 52:6); Masoretic Text does not have *fourth.*   [b] *4* Or *Chaldeans*; also in verses 13, 25 and 26   [c] *4* Or *the Jordan Valley*   [d] *5* Or *Chaldean*; also in verses 10 and 24   [e] *17* That is, about 27 feet or about 8.1 meters   [f] *17* That is, about 4 1/2 feet or about 1.4 meters

---

24:20 Zedekiah rebelled against the king of Babylon Zedekiah's decision here is the final move that leads Babylon to turn Judah from a vassal state into a completely conquered one.

25:1–21 After about a decade of conflict, Jerusalem and the kingdom of Judah fell to the Babylonian Empire in 586 BC. This final chapter of 2 Kings recounts the siege of Jerusalem, the blinding and binding of Zedekiah, the fiery destruction of the temple, the second wave of deportations to Babylon (compare 2Ki 24:10–17) and the execution of Jerusalem's remaining officials. Accounts of Judah's final collapse also appear in 2Ch 36:17–21; Jer 39:1–10; and Jer 52:1–30. See the timeline "Judah From the Fall of Samaria to the Exile" on p. 606.

SOUTHERN KING	DATE
Jehoiakim	609–597 BC
Jehoiachin	597 BC
Zedekiah	597–586 BC

25:1 ninth year of Zedekiah's reign The Hebrew text does not include the name of the king, reading only "of his reign." Jeremiah 39:1 makes clear that this refers to Zedekiah's reign (ca. 597–586 BC).
25:2 under siege According to Ezekiel, the Babylonians laid siege to Jerusalem with siege works and battering rams (see Eze 4:2 and note).
25:4 Arabah Refers to the arid wilderness around the Dead Sea.

²²Nebuchadnezzar king of Babylon appointed Gedaliah son of Ahikam, the son of Shaphan, to be over the people he had left behind in Judah. ²³When all the army officers and their men heard that the king of Babylon had appointed Gedaliah as governor, they came to Gedaliah at Mizpah — Ishmael son of Nethaniah, Johanan son of Kareah, Seraiah son of Tanhumeth the Netophathite, Jaazaniah the son of the Maakathite, and their men. ²⁴Gedaliah took an oath to reassure them and their men. "Do not be afraid of the Babylonian officials," he said. "Settle down in the land and serve the king of Babylon, and it will go well with you."

²⁵In the seventh month, however, Ishmael son of Nethaniah, the son of Elishama, who was of royal blood, came with ten men and assassinated Gedaliah and also the men of Judah and the Babylonians who were with him at Mizpah. ²⁶At this, all the people from the least to the greatest, together with the army officers, fled to Egypt for fear of the Babylonians.

Jehoiachin Released

25:27-30pp — Jer 52:31-34

²⁷In the thirty-seventh year of the exile of Jehoiachin king of Judah, in the year Awel-Marduk became king of Babylon, he released Jehoiachin king of Judah from prison. He did this on the twenty-seventh day of the twelfth month. ²⁸He spoke kindly to him and gave him a seat of honor higher than those of the other kings who were with him in Babylon. ²⁹So Jehoiachin put aside his prison clothes and for the rest of his life ate regularly at the king's table. ³⁰Day by day the king gave Jehoiachin a regular allowance as long as he lived.

25:6 Riblah See note on 2Ki 23:33.
25:8 the fifth month See 24:12 and note.
25:11 the commander of the guard carried into exile Refers to the second wave of deportations in 586 BC (the first was reported in 24:14–16).
25:12 work the vineyards and fields Fieldworkers were left to supply agricultural goods for the empire.
25:14 all the bronze articles Nebuchadnezzar had taken the vessels of gold to Babylon with the first wave of captives (24:13).

25:22–26 This passage reports that some Jews fled to Egypt in the aftermath of Judah's collapse. The book of Jeremiah includes a lengthy account of these events (Jer 41–46).

25:22 Gedaliah See note on Jer 39:14.
25:23 Mizpah With the destruction of Jerusalem, Judah's administrative center shifts roughly seven miles north to the city of Mizpah.
25:25 the men of Judah and the Babylonians Ishmael and his men attack those who are assisting Gedaliah and thereby supporting the Babylonian Empire, regardless of nationality.

25:27–30 Jehoiachin's release from prison concludes the narrative of 1–2 Kings with a sense of hope that David's royal line will continue and that the kingdom will one day be restored. This hope corresponds with God's covenant with David (2Sa 7:13). Thus, the narrative of 1–2 Kings ends where it began—with the expectation that David's descendants will reign over Israel forever (1Ki 2:4; compare Mt 1:1).

25:27 Awel-Marduk Nebuchadnezzar's successor.
25:28 kings who were with him in Babylon Refers to deposed kings of other nations that Babylon had destroyed.

THE SIGNIFICANCE OF NAMES IN THE BIBLE

by Mark D. Futato

Although it's not always obvious to English speakers, Hebrew names all mean something. Some names are simple nouns like Jonah (*yonah*)—which means "dove"—while others are more complex. Some are compound nouns with implied verbs, as in Elijah (*eli*, "my God" + *yahu*, a short form of "Yahweh"), which means "My God is Yahweh." Others are compound nouns without implied verbs: Absalom (*av*, "father" + *shalom*, "peace") means "father of peace." Still others combine nouns and verbs, as in Nethanel (*nethan*, "has given" + *el*, "God"), which means "God has given." Gaining familiarity with the construction and meaning of Biblical names enriches Bible study.

The Biblical text often explains the significance of names. However, the linguistic meaning of a Biblical name isn't always directly related to its theological significance. In the case of Samuel, the theological significance is related to a play on the name's sound rather than its actual meaning: 1 Samuel says, "She named him Samuel, saying, 'Because I asked the LORD for him'" (1Sa 1:20). The name Samuel does not mean "I requested him from Yahweh"; in Hebrew, *shemu'el* means "name of God." However, it sounds like the Hebrew for "heard by God"—and since her prayer was heard by God, Hannah named her son Samuel.

However, names' meanings often play significant roles in the narratives that feature them. The names in the early chapters of Genesis, for instance, reflect the theological significance of the story. *Adam* means "humanity"—and Adam was the representative of the human race (see Ro 5:12–18). Adam gave to the woman the name Eve (*chawwah*), which means "living," because Eve was the mother of all of the living (Ge 3:20). Cain (*qayin*) sounds like the word for "I have acquired" (*qanithi*), as Eve said she acquired a male child with the help of the Lord (Ge 4:1). Abel (*hevel*) means "vanity"—his life being lived in vain since Cain killed him in his prime. Seth (*sheth*) means "give," because God gave Eve a son in place of the one she lost (Ge 4:25).

The story of Ruth also demonstrates a clear relationship between the meanings of characters' names and the theological significance of the narrative. Elimelek (*eli*, "my God" + *melekh*, "king") means "my God is King," but Elimelek contradicted the meaning of his name, when—rather than trusting his God—he left the land of promise for a foreign land in a time of famine. Naomi's name (*na'omi*) means "pleasantness," but she changed her name to Mara (*mara*), which means "bitterness." The change in name aptly describes the change in her circumstances; she says, "'Don't call me Naomi,' she told them. 'Call me Mara, because the Almighty has made my life very bitter. I went away full, but the LORD has brought me back empty.'" (Ru 1:20–21). Mahlon (*machlon*) and Kilion (*kilyon*), the two sons, mean "sickness" and "annihilation," and both died young. Ruth (*ruth*) sounds like the word for "friendship"—and Ruth is the epitome of covenant friendship in the narrative. Boaz (*bo'az*) sounds like the words for "in him is strength," and he proves to be a man of strong character. Conversely, the first guardian-redeemer, who exhibits a lack of character by refusing to fulfill his covenant responsibilities, has no name in the story. The child born at the end of the story is named Obed (*oved*), which means "servant," because he was to serve Naomi in her old age (Ru 4:15).

The most significant person in the Bible is Jesus. His name stems from Joshua (*yeho*, a short form of "Yahweh" + *shua'*, "salvation"), which means "Yahweh is salvation." This is why the angel said, "She will give birth to a son, and you are to give him the name Jesus, because he will save his people from their sins" (Mt 1:21). Matthew goes on to tell us that Jesus' birth fulfilled Isaiah 7:14: "The virgin will conceive and give birth to a son, and they will call him Immanuel" (Mt 1:23). Emmanuel (*immanu*, "with us" + *el*, "God") means "God is with us."

1 CHRONICLES

INTRODUCTION TO 1 CHRONICLES

History always has the advantage of hindsight. The narrative of 1–2 Chronicles is based on history, but leverages it for something greater: theological lessons. These books tell the story of Israel and Judah, starting with Adam and ending with the return of the Jewish exiles from Babylon (538 BC). The account begins with a collection of genealogies (1Ch 1–9) then shifts to King David (in the remainder of 1 Chronicles) and his descendants (in 2 Chronicles).

BACKGROUND

The books of 1–2 Chronicles were originally a single literary work; they probably were divided because, in antiquity, its length required two scrolls. About half of the content of 1–2 Chronicles is based on 1–2 Samuel and 1–2 Kings, while the genealogies of 1 Chronicles 1–9 rely on the Pentateuch (the first five books of the Bible) and the book of Joshua. Chronicles reworks its sources to emphasize the importance of the temple, priests, King David and later faithful kings of David's line. Chronicles also mentions now-lost texts that probably provided some of the material not found in Samuel and Kings (e.g., 1Ch 29:29–30; 2Ch 12:15).

Chronicles pairs nicely with Ezra and Nehemiah, as they pick up where Chronicles leaves off (538 BC)—completing the story of God's people all the way up to the rebuilding of the temple and Jerusalem, and the accompanying religious reforms (432 BC). This and other factors suggest 1–2 Chronicles was written in the fifth century BC.

The narrative of 1–2 Chronicles is a response to the needs of a formerly exiled Jewish people. In 586 BC the Babylonians conquered the southern kingdom of Judah and deported its people to Babylon (2Ki 25:1–30). In 539 BC the Persians conquered Babylon and by 538 BC, the Jewish exiles had permission to return to Jerusalem and rebuild the temple. In this new context, history must be understood—if the Jewish people understood how to live, from positive examples, then they could establish their lives based on what Yahweh intended.

STRUCTURE

The narrative of 1–2 Chronicles can be divided into three major sections. The first

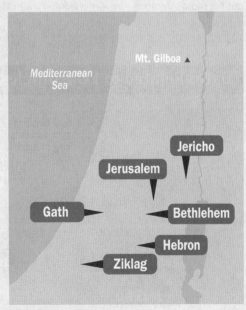

This map depicts some of the major locations related to 1 Chronicles.

section (1Ch 1–9) includes genealogies and information about people and groups listed in the genealogies. The second section (which straddles both books: 1Ch 10—2Ch 9) addresses the united monarchy under David and Solomon. The text says little about King Saul; it simply reports his death in 1 Chronicles 10 to set the stage for David's reign—the focus throughout the rest of 1 Chronicles. Starting with 1 Chronicles 22, the book focuses on David's preparations for the Jerusalem temple: His instructions to his son Solomon for building it; his organization of priests and musicians; and his directions about temple worship and sacrifices. First Chronicles ends with David's death, but the narrative of the united monarchy continues in 2 Chronicles, opening with the start of Solomon's reign and concluding with his death at the end of 2 Chronicles 9. The third major section of Chronicles (2Ch 10–36) focuses on the kings of Judah, the southern kingdom, during the divided monarchy.

OUTLINE

- Genealogy from Adam to Saul (1:1—9:44)
- David's reign (10:1—29:30)

THEMES

The Chronicler portrays David as a model king who followed Yahweh. This account of David leaves out his most infamous sins—his adultery with Bathsheba and his plot to kill her husband, Uriah

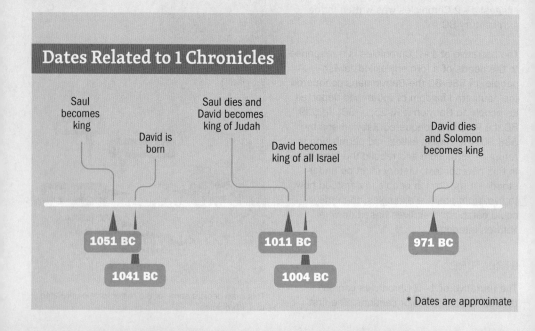

Dates Related to 1 Chronicles

Saul becomes king

David is born

Saul dies and David becomes king of Judah

David becomes king of all Israel

David dies and Solomon becomes king

1051 BC

1041 BC

1011 BC

1004 BC

971 BC

* Dates are approximate

(2Sa 11)—and focuses on the ways in which he was faithful. David embraces God's ways, establishes Jerusalem as a center for worship and leads the people in praise (e.g., 1Ch 16). Yahweh then makes his covenant with David, promising to bless his household forever, and gives David victory over his enemies.

Even the strange and troubling story of David's misguided census (1Ch 21) points to his heart for God. When David recognizes his sin, he repents and relies on God's mercy (21:8,13,17). The episode ends with David building an altar and offering sacrifices to Yahweh—and vowing that the site will become the house of Yahweh (21:18; 22:1).

When 1 Chronicles is contextualized as a work for a Jewish community recovering from military defeat and exiled to a foreign land, it becomes apparent that its portrayal of David's partnership with Yahweh is a message of encouragement, meant to call people to worship and obedience with their full heart. It also is a message of hope, assuring God's people of his blessings and his covenant promises. First Chronicles challenges us to truly seek Yahweh (16:11; 22:19), to set our minds on his purposes and rejoice in his presence. As we see David not exactly as he was, but more as he should have been, we are given the model of a worshipful life.

Historical Records From Adam to Abraham

To Noah's Sons

1 Adam, Seth, Enosh, [2]Kenan, Mahalalel, Jared, [3]Enoch, Methuselah, Lamech, Noah.

[4] The sons of Noah:[a]
Shem, Ham and Japheth.

The Japhethites

1:5-7pp — Ge 10:2-5

[5] The sons[b] of Japheth:
Gomer, Magog, Madai, Javan, Tubal, Meshek and Tiras.
[6] The sons of Gomer:
Ashkenaz, Riphath[c] and Togarmah.
[7] The sons of Javan:
Elishah, Tarshish, the Kittites and the Rodanites.

The Hamites

1:8-16pp — Ge 10:6-20

[8] The sons of Ham:
Cush, Egypt, Put and Canaan.
[9] The sons of Cush:
Seba, Havilah, Sabta, Raamah and Sabteka.
The sons of Raamah:
Sheba and Dedan.
[10] Cush was the father[d] of
Nimrod, who became a mighty warrior on earth.
[11] Egypt was the father of
the Ludites, Anamites, Lehabites, Naphtuhites, [12]Pathrusites, Kasluhites (from whom the Philistines came) and Caphtorites.

[13] Canaan was the father of
Sidon his firstborn,[e] and of the Hittites, [14]Jebusites, Amorites, Girgashites, [15]Hivites, Arkites, Sinites, [16]Arvadites, Zemarites and Hamathites.

The Semites

1:17-23pp — Ge 10:21-31; 11:10-27

[17] The sons of Shem:
Elam, Ashur, Arphaxad, Lud and Aram.
The sons of Aram:[f]
Uz, Hul, Gether and Meshek.
[18] Arphaxad was the father of Shelah,
and Shelah the father of Eber.
[19] Two sons were born to Eber:
One was named Peleg,[g] because in his time the earth was divided; his brother was named Joktan.
[20] Joktan was the father of
Almodad, Sheleph, Hazarmaveth, Jerah, [21]Hadoram, Uzal, Diklah, [22]Obal,[h] Abimael, Sheba, [23]Ophir, Havilah and Jobab. All these were sons of Joktan.

[24] Shem, Arphaxad,[i] Shelah,
[25] Eber, Peleg, Reu,
[26] Serug, Nahor, Terah
[27] and Abram (that is, Abraham).

---

[a] 4 Septuagint; Hebrew does not have this line.   [b] 5 *Sons* may mean *descendants* or *successors* or *nations*; also in verses 6-9, 17 and 23.   [c] 6 Many Hebrew manuscripts and Vulgate (see also Septuagint and Gen. 10:3); most Hebrew manuscripts *Diphath*   [d] 10 *Father* may mean *ancestor* or *predecessor* or *founder*; also in verses 11, 13, 18 and 20.   [e] 13 Or *of the Sidonians, the foremost*   [f] 17 One Hebrew manuscript and some Septuagint manuscripts (see also Gen. 10:23); most Hebrew manuscripts do not have this line.   [g] 19 *Peleg* means *division*.   [h] 22 Some Hebrew manuscripts and Syriac (see also Gen. 10:28); most Hebrew manuscripts *Ebal*   [i] 24 Hebrew; some Septuagint manuscripts *Arphaxad, Cainan* (see also note at Gen. 11:10)

1:1—9:44 The books of 1 and 2 Chronicles retell the history of Israel for the restored Jewish community living around Jerusalem in the fifth century BC. The book's original purpose was to remind the people of the nation's past greatness to encourage their efforts to rebuild a community devoted to Yahweh.

First Chronicles begins that history with a lengthy genealogy that starts with Adam, spans virtually all of the tribes of Israel, and ends by repeating the genealogy of Saul, Israel's first king. The Chronicler summarizes the genealogy of the nations (1Ch 1:1–54), tracing Israel's ancestry back to creation and highlighting God's special purpose for Israel in the world. This emphasis on Israel as God's chosen people would be of special significance to a nation that had been in exile.

In the ancient world, lineage or pedigree was closely connected to prestige, status and identity. Genealogies may serve to assert the legitimacy of certain social, political or religious hierarchies. For example, priests who returned from exile could not serve unless they could prove their priestly lineage (Ezr 2:62). The genealogies of 1Ch 1–9 should be viewed through this evident concern for pedigree in Second Temple Judah.

1:1 Adam The Chronicler uses the format of a genealogy starting with Adam to review the story of the OT from Genesis to the postexilic period of Ezra and Nehemiah. The people listed in 1:1–4 are mentioned in more detail in the genealogy of Ge 5.

1:4 Noah The man God saved from the flood, along with his sons and their families. See Ge 6–9.

1:5–23 This list is based closely on the Table of Nations in Ge 10. The Table of Nations divides up the known world according to its descent from the sons of Noah. See note on Ge 10:1–32.

1:19 in his time the earth was divided The name "Peleg" comes from the Hebrew word *palag*, meaning "to divide."

1:24–27 This list of the descendants of Shem includes the names, but not the details, from the genealogy in Ge 11:10–26 (see note on Ge 11:10–26).

1:27 Abram (that is, Abraham) "Abram" means "exalted father" while "Abraham" means "father of many." God changed his name from "Abram" to "Abraham" after making a covenant with him (see Ge 17:5 and note). See the people diagram "Family Tree of the Patriarchs" on p. 52.

The Family of Abraham

28 The sons of Abraham:

Isaac and Ishmael.

Descendants of Hagar

1:29-31pp — Ge 25:12-16

29 These were their descendants:

Nebaioth the firstborn of Ishmael, Kedar, Adbeel, Mibsam, **30** Mishma, Dumah, Massa, Hadad, Tema, **31** Jetur, Naphish and Kedemah. These were the sons of Ishmael.

Descendants of Keturah

1:32-33pp — Ge 25:1-4

32 The sons born to Keturah, Abraham's concubine:

Zimran, Jokshan, Medan, Midian, Ishbak and Shuah.

The sons of Jokshan:

Sheba and Dedan.

33 The sons of Midian:

Ephah, Epher, Hanok, Abida and Eldaah.

All these were descendants of Keturah.

Descendants of Sarah

1:35-37pp — Ge 36:10-14

34 Abraham was the father of Isaac.

The sons of Isaac:

Esau and Israel.

Esau's Sons

35 The sons of Esau:

Eliphaz, Reuel, Jeush, Jalam and Korah.

36 The sons of Eliphaz:

Teman, Omar, Zepho,*a* Gatam and Kenaz; by Timna: Amalek.*b*

37 The sons of Reuel:

Nahath, Zerah, Shammah and Mizzah.

The People of Seir in Edom

1:38-42pp — Ge 36:20-28

38 The sons of Seir:

Lotan, Shobal, Zibeon, Anah, Dishon, Ezer and Dishan.

39 The sons of Lotan:

Hori and Homam. Timna was Lotan's sister.

40 The sons of Shobal:

Alvan,*c* Manahath, Ebal, Shepho and Onam.

The sons of Zibeon:

Aiah and Anah.

41 The son of Anah:

Dishon.

The sons of Dishon:

Hemdan,*d* Eshban, Ithran and Keran.

42 The sons of Ezer:

Bilhan, Zaavan and Akan.*e*

The sons of Dishan*f*:

Uz and Aran.

The Rulers of Edom

1:43-54pp — Ge 36:31-43

43 These were the kings who reigned in Edom before any Israelite king reigned:

Bela son of Beor, whose city was named Dinhabah.

44 When Bela died, Jobab son of Zerah from Bozrah succeeded him as king.

45 When Jobab died, Husham from the land of the Temanites succeeded him as king.

---

a 36 Many Hebrew manuscripts, some Septuagint manuscripts and Syriac (see also Gen. 36:11); most Hebrew manuscripts *Zephi*   *b 36* Some Septuagint manuscripts (see also Gen. 36:12); Hebrew *Gatam, Kenaz, Timna and Amalek*   *c 40* Many Hebrew manuscripts and some Septuagint manuscripts (see also Gen. 36:23); most Hebrew manuscripts *Alian*   *d 41* Many Hebrew manuscripts and some Septuagint manuscripts (see also Gen. 36:26); most Hebrew manuscripts *Hamran*   *e 42* Many Hebrew and Septuagint manuscripts (see also Gen. 36:27); most Hebrew manuscripts *Zaavan, Jaakan*   *f 42* See Gen. 36:28; Hebrew *Dishon,* a variant of *Dishan*

1:28–42 While the Genesis narrative emphasizes the sons who inherited God's promise to Abraham, Isaac and Jacob, this list includes the descendants of the sons who did not receive the promise—Ishmael and Esau, as well as Abraham's sons by Keturah. The genealogies for these branches of Abraham's family are found in Ge 25; 36.

1:29 Ishmael Abraham's son by Hagar, Sarah's servant. Since Sarah had not borne any children, she offered her servant to Abraham as an alternate means for him to gain a son and heir (Ge 16:1–4). After Isaac was born, Sarah insisted that Hagar and Ishmael be sent away (Ge 21:10).

1:32 Keturah Abraham's third wife or concubine (Ge 25:1). She is not mentioned until after Sarah has died (Ge 23:1–2; 24:67), giving the impression that Abraham took her as a wife after Sarah's death. Her six sons represent Arab tribes associated with the incense trade in the Arabian desert (Ge 25:1–6).

1:33 Midian Ancestor of the Midianites and the name

of a region in the northwest Arabian peninsula, east of the Gulf of Aqaba and north of the Red Sea.

1:34 Isaac The son God promised to Abraham and Sarah (Ge 17:16; 18:9–15). Isaac also was Abraham's primary heir (Ge 24:36; compare Ge 25:6). This verse refers to Jacob as "Israel"—the name he was given by God (Ge 32:27–28).

1:35 Esau Isaac's oldest son (Ge 25:25); also called "Edom" (Ge 36:8). He is the ancestor of the Edomites. Esau's younger brother Jacob acquires his blessing and birthright.

1:38 Seir The region where Esau settled (Ge 32:3) and where the Edomites lived (Dt 2:4). The Horites lived in the area before the Edomites (Ge 14:6; Dt 2:12,22). The names given here in 1Ch 1:38–42 and in Ge 36:20–30 are not descendants of Esau but of Seir the Horite (Ge 36:20–21). Often Seir and Edom are used synonymously for the same general territory (e.g., Nu 24:18).

1:43–54 This passage about the ancient kings of Edom is virtually identical to Ge 36:31–43. The list of kings also follows the similar genealogy of Esau in Ge 36:9–30. See note on Ge 36:31–39.

⁴⁶When Husham died, Hadad son of Bedad, who defeated Midian in the country of Moab, succeeded him as king. His city was named Avith.

⁴⁷When Hadad died, Samlah from Masrekah succeeded him as king.

⁴⁸When Samlah died, Shaul from Rehoboth on the river*a* succeeded him as king.

⁴⁹When Shaul died, Baal-Hanan son of Akbor succeeded him as king.

⁵⁰When Baal-Hanan died, Hadad succeeded him as king. His city was named Pau,*b* and his wife's name was Mehetabel daughter of Matred, the daughter of Me-Zahab. ⁵¹Hadad also died.

The chiefs of Edom were:
Timna, Alvah, Jetheth, ⁵²Oholibamah, Elah, Pinon, ⁵³Kenaz, Teman, Mibzar, ⁵⁴Magdiel and Iram. These were the chiefs of Edom.

Israel's Sons

2:1-2pp — Ge 35:23-26

2 These were the sons of Israel:
Reuben, Simeon, Levi, Judah, Issachar, Zebulun, ²Dan, Joseph, Benjamin, Naphtali, Gad and Asher.

Judah

2:5-15pp — Ru 4:18-22; Mt 1:3-6

To Hezron's Sons

³The sons of Judah:
Er, Onan and Shelah. These three were born to him by a Canaanite woman, the daughter of Shua. Er, Judah's firstborn,

was wicked in the LORD's sight; so the LORD put him to death. ⁴Judah's daughter-in-law Tamar bore Perez and Zerah to Judah. He had five sons in all.

⁵The sons of Perez:
Hezron and Hamul.

⁶The sons of Zerah:
Zimri, Ethan, Heman, Kalkol and Darda*c* — five in all.

⁷The son of Karmi:
Achar,*d* who brought trouble on Israel by violating the ban on taking devoted things.*e*

⁸The son of Ethan:
Azariah.

⁹The sons born to Hezron were:
Jerahmeel, Ram and Caleb.*f*

From Ram Son of Hezron

¹⁰Ram was the father of
Amminadab, and Amminadab the father of Nahshon, the leader of the people of Judah. ¹¹Nahshon was the father of Salmon,*g* Salmon the father of Boaz, ¹²Boaz the father of Obed and Obed the father of Jesse.

¹³Jesse was the father of
Eliab his firstborn; the second son was Abinadab, the third Shimea, ¹⁴the fourth Nethanel, the fifth Raddai, ¹⁵the sixth

---

a 48 Possibly the Euphrates   *b 50* Many Hebrew manuscripts, some Septuagint manuscripts, Vulgate and Syriac (see also Gen. 36:39); most Hebrew manuscripts *Pai*   *c 6* Many Hebrew manuscripts, some Septuagint manuscripts and Syriac (see also 1 Kings 4:31); most Hebrew manuscripts *Dara*   *d 7 Achar* means *trouble*; *Achar* is called *Achan* in Joshua.   *e 7* The Hebrew term refers to the irrevocable giving over of things or persons to the LORD, often by totally destroying them.   *f 9* Hebrew *Kelubai*, a variant of *Caleb*   *g 11* Septuagint (see also Ruth 4:21); Hebrew *Salma*

2:1 the sons of Israel The previous section (1Ch 1:28–53) mainly listed descendants of Abraham who were not the heirs of God's promise. The rest of the genealogies (1Ch 2:1—9:44) focus on the descendants of Israel (Jacob) by tribe. (Israel is first identified as Isaac's son in 1:34.)

2:3—4:23 This lengthy summary of the genealogy of Judah draws on genealogies from Ge 46:12–13; Nu 26:19–22; Ru 4:18–22; 2Sa 3:2–5; 5:13–16, as well as the history of the kings. The Chronicler gives more detail and attention to the genealogy of Judah than any other tribe; Naphtali, for example, gets only one verse (1Ch 7:13). This is because David and the Davidic royal family descend from the line of Judah (see 3:1–24 and note).

The genealogy of Judah reflects many connections with other tribes such as Reuben and Manasseh and mentions various groups and families who are otherwise little known. Since one purpose of the genealogies is to connect people to a major group, some of these families may have been on the margins of Israelite society. The Chronicler presents their ancestral connection to the tribe to affirm they are legitimately part of Judah (e.g., the Jerahmeelites in 2:25–41). See people diagram "Judah to David" on p. 618.

2:3 The sons of Judah Compare Ge 46:12–13; Nu 26:19–22. **so the LORD put him to death** The account

in Genesis does not explain what Er did to incur divine wrath (Ge 38:7).

2:4 daughter-in-law Tamar See Ge 38:1–30 and note.

2:7 Achar, who brought trouble on Israel Achan sinned by taking devoted things from Jericho. His sin caused Israel to be defeated at Ai. See Jos 7:1–26 and note.

2:9 Hezron The list of the descendants of Perez through Hezron takes up the rest of the chapter (1Ch 2:9–55). The line of descent through Hezron's son Ram is significant as the pedigree for King David (vv. 10–17). Compare Ru 4:18–22. The genealogical information for Jerahmeel and Caleb (also called Chelubai) comes primarily from this passage.

2:10 Nahshon The chief of the tribe of Judah during the period of wandering in the wilderness (Nu 1:7; 2:3; 7:12; 10:14).

2:12 Boaz the father of Obed Boaz fathered Obed with Ruth, the daughter-in-law of Naomi. See Ru 4:13–17.

2:15 seventh David David was Jesse's youngest son. The rise of a younger son to prominence over his older brothers is a recurring theme in the OT. The theme is used to show that divine calling trumps traditional leadership customs. David alludes to this himself when he says that Yahweh chose him to be king out of all his father's sons and has chosen Solomon as king out of all of his sons (1Ch 28:4–5).

Ozem and the seventh David. ¹⁶Their sisters were Zeruiah and Abigail. Zeruiah's three sons were Abishai, Joab and Asahel. ¹⁷Abigail was the mother of Amasa, whose father was Jether the Ishmaelite.

Caleb Son of Hezron

¹⁸ Caleb son of Hezron had children by his wife Azubah (and by Jerioth). These were her sons: Jesher, Shobab and Ardon. ¹⁹When Azubah died, Caleb married Ephrath, who bore him Hur. ²⁰Hur was the father of Uri, and Uri the father of Bezalel.

²¹Later, Hezron, when he was sixty years old, married the daughter of Makir the father of Gilead. He made love to her, and she bore him Segub. ²²Segub was the father of Jair, who controlled twenty-three towns in Gilead. ²³(But Geshur and Aram captured Havvoth Jair,ᵃ as well as Kenath with its surrounding settlements—sixty towns.) All these were descendants of Makir the father of Gilead.

²⁴ After Hezron died in Caleb Ephrathah, Abijah the wife of Hezron bore him Ashhur the fatherᵇ of Tekoa.

Jerahmeel Son of Hezron

²⁵ The sons of Jerahmeel the firstborn of Hezron: Ram his firstborn, Bunah, Oren, Ozem andᶜ Ahijah. ²⁶Jerahmeel had another wife, whose name was Atarah; she was the mother of Onam.

²⁷The sons of Ram the firstborn of Jerahmeel: Maaz, Jamin and Eker.

²⁸The sons of Onam: Shammai and Jada. The sons of Shammai: Nadab and Abishur.

²⁹ Abishur's wife was named Abihail, who bore him Ahban and Molid.

³⁰The sons of Nadab: Seled and Appaim. Seled died without children.

³¹The son of Appaim: Ishi, who was the father of Sheshan. Sheshan was the father of Ahlai.

³²The sons of Jada, Shammai's brother: Jether and Jonathan. Jether died without children.

³³The sons of Jonathan: Peleth and Zaza. These were the descendants of Jerahmeel.

³⁴Sheshan had no sons—only daughters. He had an Egyptian servant named Jarha. ³⁵Sheshan gave his daughter in marriage to his servant Jarha, and she bore him Attai.

³⁶ Attai was the father of Nathan, Nathan the father of Zabad, ³⁷Zabad the father of Ephlal, Ephlal the father of Obed, ³⁸Obed the father of Jehu, Jehu the father of Azariah, ³⁹Azariah the father of Helez, Helez the father of Eleasah, ⁴⁰Eleasah the father of Sismai, Sismai the father of Shallum, ⁴¹Shallum the father of Jekamiah, and Jekamiah the father of Elishama.

The Clans of Caleb

⁴²The sons of Caleb the brother of Jerahmeel: Mesha his firstborn, who was the father of Ziph, and his son Mareshah,ᵈ who was the father of Hebron.

⁴³The sons of Hebron: Korah, Tappuah, Rekem and Shema. ⁴⁴Shema was the father of Raham, and Raham the father of Jorkeam. Rekem was the father of Shammai. ⁴⁵The son of Shammai was Maon, and Maon was the father of Beth Zur.

⁴⁶Caleb's concubine Ephah was the mother of Haran, Moza and Gazez. Haran was the father of Gazez.

⁴⁷The sons of Jahdai: Regem, Jotham, Geshan, Pelet, Ephah and Shaaph.

⁴⁸Caleb's concubine Maakah was the mother of Sheber and Tirhanah. ⁴⁹She also gave birth to Shaaph the father of Madmannah and to Sheva the father of Makbenah and Gibea. Caleb's daughter was Aksah. ⁵⁰These were the descendants of Caleb.

The sons of Hur the firstborn of Ephrathah: Shobal the father of Kiriath Jearim, ⁵¹Salma the father of Bethlehem, and Hareph the father of Beth Gader.

⁵²The descendants of Shobal the father of Kiriath Jearim were: Haroeh, half the Manahathites, ⁵³and the clans of Kiriath Jearim: the Ithrites,

---

ᵃ 23 Or captured the settlements of Jair   ᵇ 24 Father may mean civic leader or military leader; also in verses 42, 45, 49-52 and possibly elsewhere.   ᶜ 25 Or Oren and Ozem, by
ᵈ 42 The meaning of the Hebrew for this phrase is uncertain.

2:16 Zeruiah's three sons David's nephews—Joab, Abishai and Asahel—were trusted members of his army (2Sa 2:18; 18:2; 21:17). Joab was commander of David's army (2Sa 8:16; 1Ch 11:6). **2:18 Caleb** Also called Chelubai (v. 9). Not the Caleb who spied out Canaan and participated in the conquest (Nu 13:30; Jos 14:6–15).

2:20 Bezalel The craftsman chosen by Yahweh to build the ark and the tabernacle (Ex 31:1–5). **2:34 Sheshan had no sons** A puzzling statement since 1Ch 2:31 identifies Ahlai as the son of Sheshan. It is possible that sons referred to in the Hebrew text of v. 31 is meant in the sense of "descendants of" and that Ahlai is the unnamed daughter mentioned in v. 35.

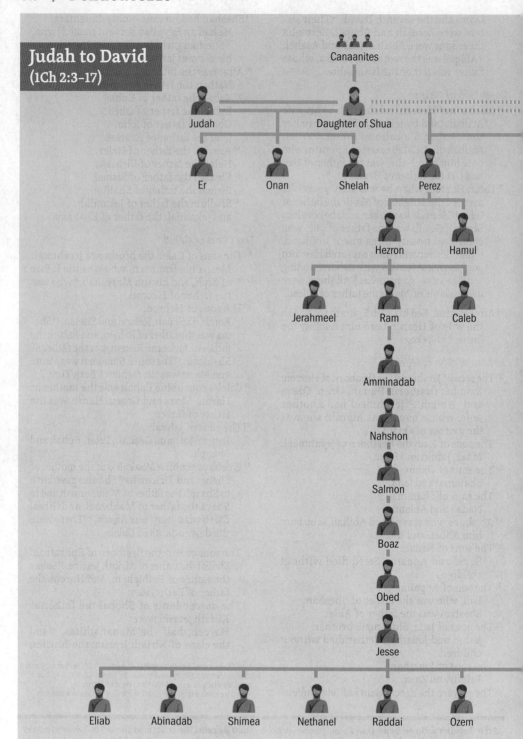

Judah to David
(1Ch 2:3–17)

Canaanites

Judah — Daughter of Shua

Er

Onan

Shelah

Perez

Hezron

Hamul

Jerahmeel

Ram

Caleb

Amminadab

Nahshon

Salmon

Boaz

Obed

Jesse

Eliab

Abinadab

Shimea

Nethanel

Raddai

Ozem

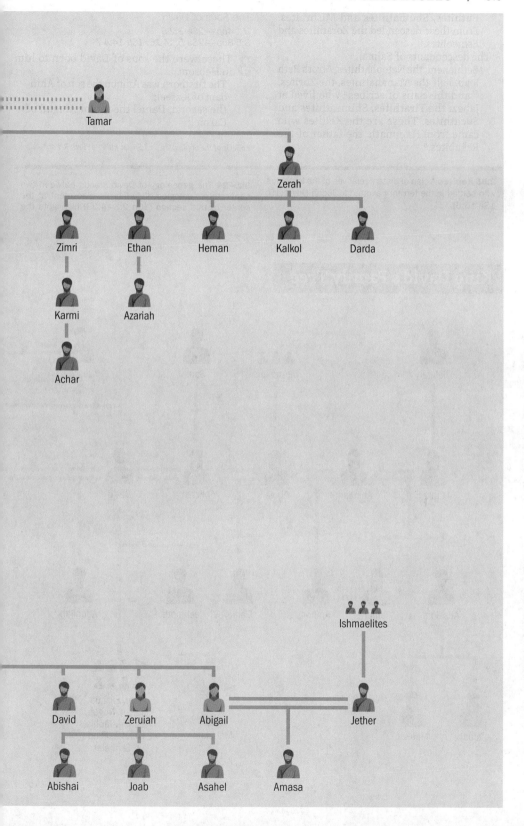

Puthites, Shumathites and Mishraites. From these descended the Zorathites and Eshtaolites.

⁵⁴The descendants of Salma:

Bethlehem, the Netophathites, Atroth Beth Joab, half the Manahathites, the Zorites, ⁵⁵and the clans of scribesᵃ who lived at Jabez: the Tirathites, Shimeathites and Sucathites. These are the Kenites who came from Hammath, the father of the Rekabites.ᵇ

The Sons of David
3:1-4pp — 2Sa 3:2-5
3:5-8pp — 2Sa 5:14-16; 1Ch 14:4-7

3 These were the sons of David born to him in Hebron:

The firstborn was Amnon the son of Ahinoam of Jezreel;

the second, Daniel the son of Abigail of Carmel;

ᵃ 55 Or *of the Sopherites*   ᵇ 55 Or *father of Beth Rekab*

2:55 Kenites A clan of distant relatives of the Israelites who settled in the territory allotted to Judah (Jdg 1:16; 1Sa 15:6).

3:1–24 The genealogy of David stands between two separate genealogies of Judah. Its placement at the center of this section (1Ch 2:3–4:23) highlights the

---

King David's Family Tree

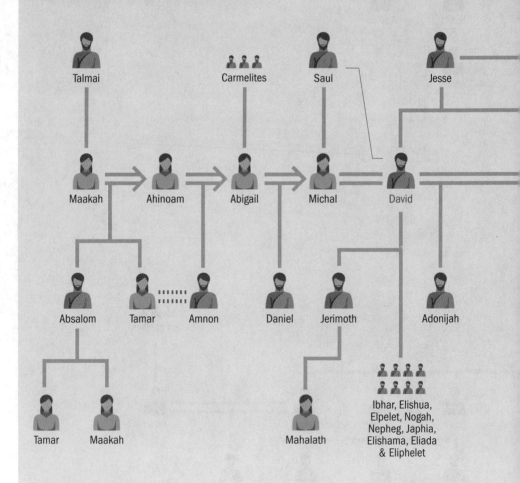

Talmai

Carmelites

Saul

Jesse

Maakah — Ahinoam — Abigail — Michal — David

Absalom   Tamar   Amnon   Daniel   Jerimoth   Adonijah

Tamar   Maakah

Mahalath

Ibhar, Elishua, Elpelet, Nogah, Nepheg, Japhia, Elishama, Eliada & Eliphelet

²the third, Absalom the son of Maakah daughter of Talmai king of Geshur; the fourth, Adonijah the son of Haggith; ³the fifth, Shephatiah the son of Abital; and the sixth, Ithream, by his wife Eglah. ⁴These six were born to David in Hebron, where he reigned seven years and six months.

David reigned in Jerusalem thirty-three years, ⁵and these were the children born to him there: Shammua,ᵃ Shobab, Nathan and Solomon. These four were by Bathshebaᵇ daughter of Ammiel. ⁶There were also Ibhar,

ᵃ 5 Hebrew *Shimea*, a variant of *Shammua*   ᵇ 5 One Hebrew manuscript and Vulgate (see also Septuagint and 2 Samuel 11:3); most Hebrew manuscripts *Bathshua*

Chronicler's emphasis on the Davidic monarchy. Here, the Chronicler lists all the sons of David (vv. 1–9) followed by each of the Davidic kings (vv. 10–16). He finishes the genealogy with the generations from the exilic and postexilic eras (vv. 17–24). See the people diagram "King David's Family Tree" on p. 620.

3:1 born to him in Hebron David had moved to Hebron after Saul's death (2Sa 2:1–2). He reigned there as king over Judah for seven years (2Sa 2:11; 5:5).
3:5 the children born to him there After David was anointed king over all Israel (2Sa 5:1–3), he conquered Jerusalem and made it his capital (2Sa 5:6–10).

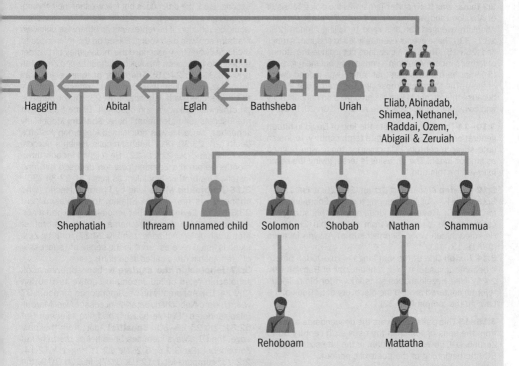

Elishua,[a] Eliphelet, [7]Nogah, Nepheg, Japhia, [8]Elishama, Eliada and Eliphelet — nine in all. [9]All these were the sons of David, besides his sons by his concubines. And Tamar was their sister.

The Kings of Judah

[10] Solomon's son was Rehoboam,
Abijah his son,
Asa his son,
Jehoshaphat his son,
[11]Jehoram[b] his son,
Ahaziah his son,
Joash his son,
[12]Amaziah his son,
Azariah his son,
Jotham his son,
[13]Ahaz his son,
Hezekiah his son,
Manasseh his son,
[14]Amon his son,
Josiah his son.
[15]The sons of Josiah:
Johanan the firstborn,
Jehoiakim the second son,
Zedekiah the third,
Shallum the fourth.

[16]The successors of Jehoiakim:
Jehoiachin[c] his son,
and Zedekiah.

The Royal Line After the Exile

[17]The descendants of Jehoiachin the captive:
Shealtiel his son, [18]Malkiram, Pedaiah, Shenazzar, Jekamiah, Hoshama and Nedabiah.
[19]The sons of Pedaiah:
Zerubbabel and Shimei.
The sons of Zerubbabel:
Meshullam and Hananiah.
Shelomith was their sister.
[20]There were also five others:
Hashubah, Ohel, Berekiah, Hasadiah and Jushab-Hesed.
[21]The descendants of Hananiah:
Pelatiah and Jeshaiah, and the sons of Rephaiah, of Arnan, of Obadiah and of Shekaniah.
[22]The descendants of Shekaniah:
Shemaiah and his sons:
Hattush, Igal, Bariah, Neariah and Shaphat — six in all.

[a] 6 Two Hebrew manuscripts (see also 2 Samuel 5:15 and 1 Chron. 14:5); most Hebrew manuscripts *Elishama*
[b] 11 Hebrew *Joram*, a variant of *Jehoram*   [c] 16 Hebrew *Jeconiah*, a variant of *Jehoiachin*; also in verse 17

3:9 Tamar was their sister Tamar was the biological sister of Absalom and was raped by her half-brother, Amnon. Absalom avenged Tamar's rape by killing Amnon (2Sa 13:1–33). These events eventually led to Absalom's rebellion (2Sa 15). The Chronicler does not include the stories of Tamar's rape or Absalom's conspiracy, but the reference to Tamar here shows that that author was indeed aware of them. The Chronicler most likely omitted these stories because they do not fit with his emphasis on national unity and covenant faithfulness (see note on 1Ch 20:1–3).

3:10–14 The Chronicler lists the line of David in fifteen generations from Solomon (late tenth century) to Josiah (late seventh century BC), covering those who reigned as king of Judah. The phrasing is terse, giving the name followed by "his son."

3:12 Azariah Also called Uzziah (2Ch 26:1; Isa 1:1).
3:13 Ahaz King of Judah during the Syro-Ephraimite War (ca. 735 BC). **Hezekiah** A king known for his attempt to get the people to turn away from idol-worship (2Ki 18:4). He ruled Judah when Sennacherib of Assyria invaded (2Ki 18:13–16).
3:14 Josiah One of the last kings to rule Judah before it became a vassal of Nebuchadnezzar of Babylon (2Ki 24:1). Like Hezekiah, Josiah is known for his religious reforms centered around the discovery of a "Book of the Law" in the temple (2Ki 22).

3:15–19 This passage covers the descendants of David from the sons of Josiah in the early sixth century BC to Zerubbabel, governor of Judah, in the late sixth century BC (the beginning of the postexilic period).

3:15 sons of Josiah During this period, three different sons and one grandson of Josiah reigned over Judah—two for only very brief periods of about three months. Although Josiah's sons here are identified by number (firstborn,

second, etc.), the order does not follow either their chronological age or the sequence of their reigns. The exception would be Johanan, if he represents an otherwise unknown firstborn son who died young. Based on the references to their ages when they ascended the throne, their birth order appears to have been Jehoiakim, Jehoahaz and Zedekiah (2Ki 23:31,36; 24:18). The order of their reigns was Jehoahaz, Jehoiakim, then Zedekiah. **Johanan** Possibly to be identified with Jehoahaz (2Ki 23:30), or perhaps an otherwise unknown son of Josiah. Some Septuagint manuscripts read "Jehoahaz" here. **Shallum** Most likely Jehoahaz, since he was proclaimed king upon Josiah's death (2Ki 23:30–31); Jeremiah calls Josiah's successor "Shallum" (Jer 22:11–12). He reigned for only three months before the Egyptian pharaoh deposed him and installed his brother Jehoiakim as king (2Ki 23:34–36).
3:16 Jehoiakim Made king by Pharaoh Necho, who changed his name from Eliakim to Jehoiakim (2Ki 23:34–36). **Zedekiah** Either Jehoiakim also had a son named Zedekiah (the same name given to his brother Mattaniah by Nebuchadnezzar; 2Ki 24:17), or King Zedekiah is listed here as "son" in the sense of "successor of" Jehoiachin (also called Jeconiah).
3:17 Jehoiachin the captive Nebuchadnezzar took Jehoiachin (also called Jeconiah) captive to Babylon (2Ki 24:15). Apparently he was imprisoned for about 37 years before Nebuchadnezzar's successor Awel-Marduk (also rendered "Evil-Merodach") had him released (Jer 52:31; 2Ki 25:27–30). **Shealtiel** Apart from this passage, the OT always identifies Shealtiel as the father of Zerubbabel (Ezr 3:2,8; 5:2; Ne 12:1; Hag 1:1,12,14; 2:2,23; compare Mt 1:12; Lk 3:27). In 1Ch 3:19, the Septuagint has Shealtiel, not Pedaiah, listed as the father of Zerubbabel and Shimei.
3:19 Zerubbabel A central figure in the period following the exile. He was appointed governor of Judah by the

²³ The sons of Neariah:

Elioenai, Hizkiah and Azrikam — three in all.

²⁴ The sons of Elioenai:

Hodaviah, Eliashib, Pelaiah, Akkub, Johanan, Delaiah and Anani — seven in all.

Other Clans of Judah

4 The descendants of Judah:

Perez, Hezron, Karmi, Hur and Shobal.

² Reaiah son of Shobal was the father of Jahath, and Jahath the father of Ahumai and Lahad. These were the clans of the Zorathites.

³ These were the sons[a] of Etam:

Jezreel, Ishma and Idbash. Their sister was named Hazzelelponi. ⁴ Penuel was the father of Gedor, and Ezer the father of Hushah.

These were the descendants of Hur, the firstborn of Ephrathah and father[b] of Bethlehem.

⁵ Ashhur the father of Tekoa had two wives, Helah and Naarah.

⁶ Naarah bore him Ahuzzam, Hepher, Temeni and Haahashtari. These were the descendants of Naarah.

⁷ The sons of Helah:

Zereth, Zohar, Ethnan, ⁸ and Koz, who was the father of Anub and Hazzobebah and of the clans of Aharhel son of Harum.

⁹ Jabez was more honorable than his brothers. His mother had named him Jabez,[c] saying, "I gave birth to him in pain." ¹⁰ Jabez cried out to the God of Israel, "Oh, that you would bless me and enlarge my territory! Let your hand be with me, and keep me from harm so that I will be free from pain." And God granted his request.

¹¹ Kelub, Shuhah's brother, was the father of Mehir, who was the father of Eshton. ¹² Eshton was the father of Beth Rapha, Paseah and Tehinnah the father of Ir Nahash.[d] These were the men of Rekah.

¹³ The sons of Kenaz:

Othniel and Seraiah.

The sons of Othniel:

Hathath and Meonothai.[e] ¹⁴ Meonothai was the father of Ophrah.

Seraiah was the father of Joab,

the father of Ge Harashim.[f] It was called this because its people were skilled workers.

¹⁵ The sons of Caleb son of Jephunneh:

Iru, Elah and Naam.

The son of Elah:

Kenaz.

¹⁶ The sons of Jehallelel:

Ziph, Ziphah, Tiria and Asarel.

¹⁷ The sons of Ezrah:

Jether, Mered, Epher and Jalon. One of Mered's wives gave birth to Miriam, Shammai

---

[a] 3 Some Septuagint manuscripts (see also Vulgate); Hebrew *father*   [b] 4 *Father* may mean *civic leader* or *military leader*; also in verses 12, 14, 17, 18 and possibly elsewhere.   [c] 9 *Jabez* sounds like the Hebrew for *pain*.   [d] 12 Or *of the city of Nahash*   [e] 13 Some Septuagint manuscripts and Vulgate; Hebrew does not have *and Meonothai*.   [f] 14 *Ge Harashim* means *valley of skilled workers*.

Persians and oversaw the work to rebuild the temple in Jerusalem (ca. 516 BC). See Ezr 3:2 and note.

4:1–23 After the detailed treatment of the line of David (1Ch 3:1–24), the genealogy of the tribe of Judah picks up again more or less where it left off at the end of 1 Chr 2. Most of vv. 2–20 consists of distinct, brief lineages without clear connections to the line of Judah as a whole. For the final few verses (vv. 21–23), the genealogy turns to Shelah, son of Judah (Ge 38:5,11,14).

4:1 The descendants of Judah The five listed here are descendants of Judah, but only Perez was directly his son. They represent five successive generations from Judah (see note on 1Ch 2:3–4:23). See the people diagram "Judah's Family Tree" on p. 624.

4:2 Reaiah Called "Haroeh" in 2:52, but that is likely a misspelling of Reaiah.

4:4 Gedor Genealogies often include place-names, and the phrase "father of" also can be construed as "founder of." Gedor is part of the territory allotted to Judah (Jos 15:58).

4:9 Jabez This short anecdote about Jabez in 1Ch 4:9–10 is a narrative aside, stylistically distinct from the surrounding context. **more honorable** The Hebrew word used here, *kaved*, denotes weightiness—both literal as the weight of a physical object and metaphorical as honor, glory or wealth. Most translations follow the latter sense and indicate Jabez was more honorable than his brothers. However, understanding *kaved* in the physical sense would indicate that Jabez was heavier than his brothers. This reading makes better sense of his mother's statement that she bore him in pain. **I gave birth to him in pain** Jabez' name in Hebrew, *yabets*, is a wordplay on the Hebrew word *atsab*, meaning "pain." The last part of Jabez' prayer in v. 10 is a request to be free from pain (*atsab*).

4:10 And God granted his request Jabez's prayer for a larger border serves as a reminder to the postexilic community that God answers prayers and is able to bring blessing instead of pain. The prayer of Jabez is only one of several examples in 1–2 Chronicles where God answers the prayers of those who call on him (5:20–22; 2Ch 20:6–12; 32:24). Prayer is a prominent theme throughout 1–2 Chronicles, so there is no particular justification for overemphasizing God's response to Jabez. Other anecdotes in 1Ch 1–9 reflect the belief that God punishes disobedience but rewards those who trust him (e.g., 5:20–26).

4:13 Kenaz Brother of Caleb son of Jephunneh (Jos 15:17). **Othniel** The nephew of Caleb son of Jephunneh who earned the right to marry Caleb's daughter Aksah (Jdg 1:13).

4:15 Caleb son of Jephunneh One of the 12 spies to enter Canaan (Nu 13:6) and the only member of his generation besides Joshua son of Nun to take part in the conquest (Jos 14:6–15).

Judah's Family Tree

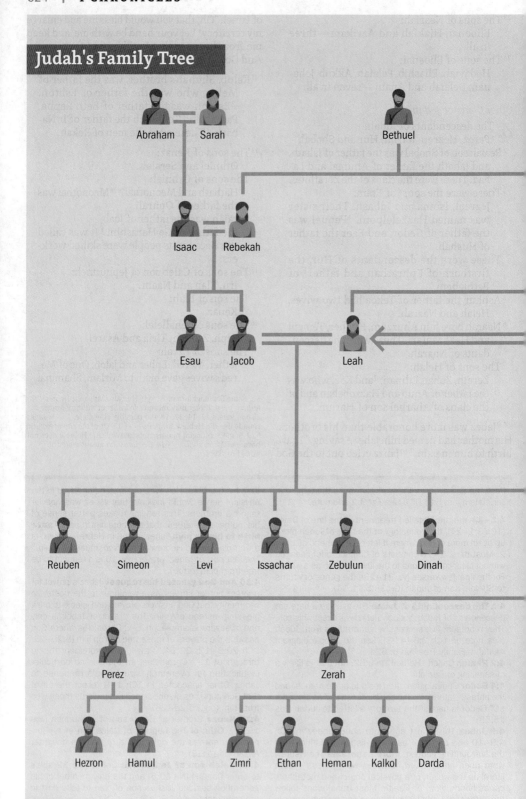

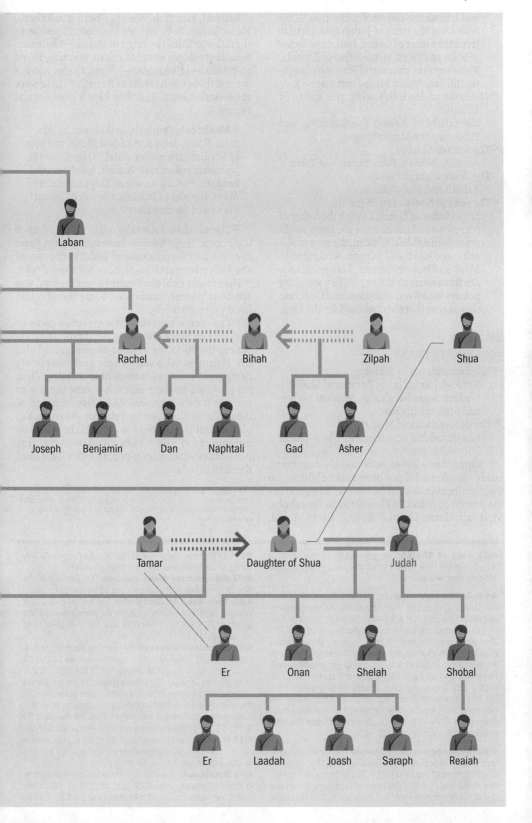

and Ishbah the father of Eshtemoa. [18](His wife from the tribe of Judah gave birth to Jered the father of Gedor, Heber the father of Soko, and Jekuthiel the father of Zanoah.) These were the children of Pharaoh's daughter Bithiah, whom Mered had married.

[19]The sons of Hodiah's wife, the sister of Naham:
the father of Keilah the Garmite, and Eshtemoa the Maakathite.

[20]The sons of Shimon:
Amnon, Rinnah, Ben-Hanan and Tilon.
The descendants of Ishi:
Zoheth and Ben-Zoheth.

[21]The sons of Shelah son of Judah:
Er the father of Lekah, Laadah the father of Mareshah and the clans of the linen workers at Beth Ashbea, [22]Jokim, the men of Kozeba, and Joash and Saraph, who ruled in Moab and Jashubi Lehem. (These records are from ancient times.) [23]They were the potters who lived at Netaim and Gederah; they stayed there and worked for the king.

Simeon

4:28-33pp — Jos 19:2-10

[24]The descendants of Simeon:
Nemuel, Jamin, Jarib, Zerah and Shaul;
[25]Shallum was Shaul's son, Mibsam his son and Mishma his son.

[26]The descendants of Mishma:
Hammuel his son, Zakkur his son and Shimei his son.

[27]Shimei had sixteen sons and six daughters, but his brothers did not have many children; so their entire clan did not become as numerous as the people of Judah. [28]They lived in Beersheba, Moladah, Hazar Shual, [29]Bilhah, Ezem, Tolad, [30]Bethuel, Hormah, Ziklag, [31]Beth Markaboth, Hazar Susim, Beth Biri and Shaaraim. These were their towns until the reign of David. [32]Their surrounding villages were Etam, Ain, Rimmon, Token and Ashan — five towns — [33]and all the villages around these towns as far as Baalath.[a] These were their settlements. And they kept a genealogical record.

[34]Meshobab, Jamlech, Joshah son of Amaziah, [35]Joel, Jehu son of Joshibiah, the son of Seraiah, the son of Asiel, [36]also Elioenai, Jaakobah, Jeshohaiah, Asaiah, Adiel, Jesimiel, Benaiah, [37]and Ziza son of Shiphi, the son of Allon, the son of Jedaiah, the son of Shimri, the son of Shemaiah.

[38]The men listed above by name were leaders of their clans. Their families increased greatly, [39]and they went to the outskirts of Gedor to the east of the valley in search of pasture for their flocks. [40]They found rich, good pasture, and the land was spacious, peaceful and quiet. Some Hamites had lived there formerly.

[41]The men whose names were listed came in the days of Hezekiah king of Judah. They attacked the Hamites in their dwellings and also the Meunites who were there and completely destroyed[b] them, as is evident to this day. Then they settled in their place, because there was pasture for their flocks. [42]And five hundred of these Simeonites, led by Pelatiah, Neariah, Rephaiah and Uzziel, the sons of Ishi, invaded the hill country of Seir. [43]They killed the remaining Amalekites who had escaped, and they have lived there to this day.

---

[a] 33 Some Septuagint manuscripts (see also Joshua 19:8); Hebrew *Baal*   [b] 41 The Hebrew term refers to the irrevocable giving over of things or persons to the LORD, often by totally destroying them.

4:21 sons of Shelah The genealogy of the tribe of Judah ends with a brief list of the descendants from Judah's son Shelah.

4:24–43 After providing a lengthy and detailed account of the genealogy of Judah, the Chronicler gives shorter genealogies of Simeon (1Ch 4:24–43), Reuben (5:1–10), Gad (5:11–22) and the half-tribe of Manasseh (5:23–26). This genealogy for the tribe of Simeon also includes explicit information about their settlements. Whereas the genealogy of Judah only alluded to geographic areas, the cities and villages of Simeon are named as such (4:28–33). The geographic details closely parallel the list of settlements from Jos 19:2–8. After listing the names of the men who were heads of the Simeonite clans (1Ch 4:34–38), the Chronicler tells how the tribe expanded its territory (vv. 39–43).

4:24 The descendants of Simeon The tribe of Simeon was closely associated with Judah during the conquest and allotment of the land (Jdg 1:3; Jos 19:1). In the census at the beginning of the book of Numbers, they were one of the larger tribes (Nu 1:23). By the end of Numbers, they had become the smallest (Nu 26:14). Eventually they came to be absorbed into the tribe of Judah.

4:27 did not have many children The decline in the size of the tribe is attributed here to its low birth rate.

4:28 They lived in Beersheba The list of cities and villages here essentially repeats the description of the territory allotted to Simeon in Jos 19:1–9 (see note on Jos 19:1).

4:33 genealogical record The Hebrew term for genealogical record — *hithyaches* — appears only in postexilic texts, mainly in 1–2 Chronicles (1Ch 5:7; 7:5; 9:22; 2Ch 12:15; Ezr 8:1). This likely indicates an increased interest in pedigree after the exile. This reference to the genealogical record of the Simeonites is likely the introduction to the list of names that follows in 1Ch 4:34–37, since the previous material was geographical.

4:38 leaders The Hebrew word used here, *nasi* (which means "prince"), often designates those who are leaders of clans or tribes (Nu 36:1; Jos 22:14).

4:41 Meunites An unknown people group mentioned only in postexilic texts (2Ch 26:7; Ezr 2:50; Ne 7:52). They may have been residents of Maon (Jdg 10:12) or even

Reuben

5 The sons of Reuben the firstborn of Israel (he was the firstborn, but when he defiled his father's marriage bed, his rights as firstborn were given to the sons of Joseph son of Israel; so he could not be listed in the genealogical record in accordance with his birthright, ²and though Judah was the strongest of his brothers and a ruler came from him, the rights of the firstborn belonged to Joseph) — ³the sons of Reuben the firstborn of Israel:

Hanok, Pallu, Hezron and Karmi.
⁴The descendants of Joel:
Shemaiah his son, Gog his son,
Shimei his son, ⁵Micah his son,
Reaiah his son, Baal his son,
⁶and Beerah his son, whom Tiglath-Pileser*a* king of Assyria took into exile. Beerah was a leader of the Reubenites.
⁷Their relatives by clans, listed according to their genealogical records:
Jeiel the chief, Zechariah, ⁸and Bela son of Azaz, the son of Shema, the son of Joel.
They settled in the area from Aroer to Nebo and Baal Meon. ⁹To the east they occupied the land up to the edge of the desert that extends to the Euphrates River, because their livestock had increased in Gilead.

¹⁰During Saul's reign they waged war against the Hagrites, who were defeated at their hands; they occupied the dwellings of the Hagrites throughout the entire region east of Gilead.

Gad

¹¹The Gadites lived next to them in Bashan, as far as Salekah:
¹²Joel was the chief, Shapham the second, then Janai and Shaphat, in Bashan.
¹³Their relatives, by families, were:
Michael, Meshullam, Sheba, Jorai, Jakan, Zia and Eber — seven in all.
¹⁴These were the sons of Abihail son of Huri, the son of Jaroah, the son of Gilead, the son of Michael, the son of Jeshishai, the son of Jahdo, the son of Buz.
¹⁵Ahi son of Abdiel, the son of Guni, was head of their family.
¹⁶The Gadites lived in Gilead, in Bashan and its outlying villages, and on all the pasturelands of Sharon as far as they extended.
¹⁷All these were entered in the genealogical records during the reigns of Jotham king of Judah and Jeroboam king of Israel.

a 6 Hebrew *Tilgath-Pilneser*, a variant of *Tiglath-Pileser*; also in verse 26

Minaeans. The varied ways of spelling this name suggests the possibility of multiple groups with similar names.

5:1–10 The genealogies of Reuben given here and in Nu 26:5–11 emphasize two of the most unfavorable events associated with the tribe of Reuben. In Nu 26, the text singles out their involvement in Korah's rebellion against Moses from Nu 16. In this passage, the most notorious mistake from Reuben's past is highlighted. Reuben's sin against Jacob by sexually violating his concubine Bilhah was effectively a rebellion against Jacob's headship of the family (Ge 35:22 and note).

5:1 he defiled his father's marriage bed Because Reuben slept with his father's concubine, he was not given the preeminence typically due the firstborn son. See Ge 35:22 and note; compare Ge 49:4 and note. **Joseph** The comments in 1Ch 5:1–2 explain that while Reuben was technically "firstborn of Israel," his actions disqualified him from the benefits of his firstborn status. The birthright was given to Joseph, the favorite son of Jacob (Ge 48:15–22).

5:2 Judah Jacob's three eldest sons all made themselves unworthy to receive the birthright and blessing of the firstborn (Ge 34–35). The Chronicler acknowledges that Judah was next in line, but the birthright still went to Joseph (second youngest of twelve sons). Nevertheless, Judah was blessed in significant ways and attained greater status, power and prestige than most of the other tribes.

5:3 the sons of Reuben the firstborn of Israel The four men identified here are consistently listed as the sons of Reuben and the founders of the Reubenite clans (Ge 46:9; Ex 6:14; Nu 26:5–6).

5:4 descendants of Joel This genealogy of Joel is

not directly connected with the previous verse, so it is unknown how many generations came between Reuben and Joel. The names listed here are unattested outside this passage.

5:6 took into exile According to 2Ki 15:29, Tiglath-Pileser III conquered territory in Israel when he invaded the region during the Syro-Ephraimite War. He deported people from those regions and took them into exile in Assyria (compare 1Ch 5:26). It is likely that those deported would be prominent people like Beerah, chief of the Reubenites. Deporting leaders was an effective way to control a rebellious region by removing the leadership (compare 2Ki 24:14).

5:7 Their relatives Refers to other relatives of Beerah. Bela, mentioned in 1Ch 5:8–9, also is a descendant of Joel through his son Shema (or Shemaiah; v. 4).

5:10 war against the Hagrites The Hagrites appear to have been a seminomadic group in the Transjordan region. Outside of 1 Chronicles, they are mentioned only in Ps 83:6. According to 1Ch 5:18–22, the tribes of Gad and Manasseh also were involved in this conflict.

5:11–26 Along with the tribe of Reuben, the tribe of Gad and the half-tribe of Manasseh resided in the Transjordan (east of the Jordan River), occupying the fertile regions of Gilead and Bashan. These genealogical lists for Gad (vv. 11–22) and eastern Manasseh (vv. 23–24) indicate that the three tribes were allies in success (vv. 18–22) and failure (vv. 25–26).

5:11 Gadites The tribe of Gad lived north of the tribe of Reuben. **Salekah** This town marks the eastern edge of the Transjordan and the approximate border between Bashan and Gilead (Dt 3:10; Jos 12:5).

¹⁸The Reubenites, the Gadites and the half-tribe of Manasseh had 44,760 men ready for military service — able-bodied men who could handle shield and sword, who could use a bow, and who were trained for battle. ¹⁹They waged war against the Hagrites, Jetur, Naphish and Nodab. ²⁰They were helped in fighting them, and God delivered the Hagrites and all their allies into their hands, because they cried out to him during the battle. He answered their prayers, because they trusted in him. ²¹They seized the livestock of the Hagrites — fifty thousand camels, two hundred fifty thousand sheep and two thousand donkeys. They also took one hundred thousand people captive, ²²and many others fell slain, because the battle was God's. And they occupied the land until the exile.

The Half-Tribe of Manasseh

²³The people of the half-tribe of Manasseh were numerous; they settled in the land from Bashan to Baal Hermon, that is, to Senir (Mount Hermon). ²⁴These were the heads of their families: Epher, Ishi, Eliel, Azriel, Jeremiah, Hodaviah and Jahdiel. They were brave warriors, famous men, and heads of their families. ²⁵But they were unfaithful to the God of their ancestors and prostituted themselves to the gods of the peoples of the land, whom God had destroyed before them. ²⁶So the God of Israel stirred up the spirit of Pul king of Assyria (that is, Tiglath-Pileser king of Assyria), who took the Reubenites, the Gadites and the half-tribe of Manasseh into exile. He took them to Halah, Habor, Hara and the river of Gozan, where they are to this day.

Levi

6 ᵃ The sons of Levi:
  Gershon, Kohath and Merari.
²The sons of Kohath:
  Amram, Izhar, Hebron and Uzziel.
³The children of Amram:
  Aaron, Moses and Miriam.
 The sons of Aaron:
  Nadab, Abihu, Eleazar and Ithamar.
    ⁴Eleazar was the father of Phinehas,
    Phinehas the father of Abishua,
    ⁵Abishua the father of Bukki,
    Bukki the father of Uzzi,
    ⁶Uzzi the father of Zerahiah,
    Zerahiah the father of Meraioth,
    ⁷Meraioth the father of Amariah,
    Amariah the father of Ahitub,
    ⁸Ahitub the father of Zadok,

ᵃ In Hebrew texts 6:1-15 is numbered 5:27-41, and 6:16-81 is numbered 6:1-66.

5:18 Reubenites, the Gadites and the half-tribe of Manasseh The tribes of the Transjordan are often mentioned together (e.g., Dt 3:12–16; 29:7–8; Jos 13:8–31; 1Ch 12:37). They are unified by their inheritance of territory east of the Jordan River, separate from the other tribes.
5:19 Jetur, Naphish Descendants of Ishmael according to 1:30–31 (compare Ge 25:15).
5:20 because they cried out to him As with the prayer of Jabez (1Ch 4:10 and note), the Chronicler emphasizes that God answers prayers.
5:23 half-tribe of Manasseh The half-tribe of Manasseh lived in the Bashan region of the Transjordan, north of the territory of Gad. See Nu 32:33 and note.
5:24 brave warriors The Hebrew phrase used here, *gibbor chayil*, denotes men of strength or men of ability. It often refers to warriors (28:1; see 26:6 and note).
5:25 they were unfaithful to the God of their ancestors The Chronicler attributes this first phase of the Assyrian exile to the tribes' breach of faith, using the Hebrew word *ma'al*.

MA'AL
The Hebrew word used here, *ma'al*, indicates a violation of covenant trust (e.g., Lev 5:15). It is used to describe adultery in terms of a woman being unfaithful to her husband (Nu 5:12,27). More often, however, it is used to describe idolatry or unfaithfulness to Yahweh (e.g., Dt 32:51; Jos 7:1). The word is used throughout Chronicles (e.g., 1Ch 2:7; 2Ch 12:2; 26:16–18) and is listed as the reason for the exile (1Ch 5:25; 2Ch 36:14–21).

6:1–81 In his genealogy of the Levites, the Chronicler adapts genealogies in Exodus and Numbers, as well as material in Joshua about the allotment of the land. The placement, as well as the detail given to the genealogy of the Levites, highlights the importance of the priestly function and temple worship. The Chronicler often focuses on the role of the Levites in the events of Israel's history. See note on 1:1—9:44.
6:1 The sons of Levi The families of the Levites are introduced in Ex 6:16–25, which lists the generations from Levi to Aaron's grandson Phinehas. The major Levitical clans are descended from Gershon, Kohath and Merari (see note on Nu 26:57).
6:2 Kohath The list here in 1Ch 6:1–15 covers the line of Kohath. Since Kohath was the ancestor of Aaron and Moses, the members of the Kohathite clan who were descended from Aaron were priests. This genealogy follows the line of Aaron down to the time of the exile. This list probably does not identify all the high priests; rather, it demonstrates continuity from a line of priests in postexilic Judah back to priests who were serving before the temple's destruction in 586 BC (compare Ne 7:63–64). **Izhar** Father of Korah and uncle to Aaron, Moses and Miriam.
6:3 Aaron, Moses and Miriam Prominent leaders of Israel during the exodus (Ex 6:26–27; 15:20). **Nadab, Abihu, Eleazar and Ithamar** The four sons of Aaron have prominent roles in the narrative of Lev 10. The eldest two sons — Nadab and Abihu — die for not following appropriate procedures in offering incense before Yahweh (Lev 10:1).
6:4 Eleazar Became high priest after the death of Aaron (see Nu 20:26–28).
6:8 Zadok Served as high priest under David and Solomon (2Sa 8:17; 1Ki 2:35). See note on Eze 40:46.

Zadok the father of Ahimaaz,
⁹Ahimaaz the father of Azariah,
Azariah the father of Johanan,
¹⁰Johanan the father of Azariah (it was he who served as priest in the temple Solomon built in Jerusalem),
¹¹Azariah the father of Amariah,
Amariah the father of Ahitub,
¹²Ahitub the father of Zadok,
Zadok the father of Shallum,
¹³Shallum the father of Hilkiah,
Hilkiah the father of Azariah,
¹⁴Azariah the father of Seraiah,
and Seraiah the father of Jozadak.ᵃ
¹⁵Jozadak was deported when the LORD sent Judah and Jerusalem into exile by the hand of Nebuchadnezzar.

¹⁶The sons of Levi:
Gershon,ᵇ Kohath and Merari.
¹⁷These are the names of the sons of Gershon:
Libni and Shimei.
¹⁸The sons of Kohath:
Amram, Izhar, Hebron and Uzziel.
¹⁹The sons of Merari:
Mahli and Mushi.
These are the clans of the Levites listed according to their fathers:
²⁰Of Gershon:
Libni his son, Jahath his son,
Zimmah his son, ²¹Joah his son,
Iddo his son, Zerah his son
and Jeatherai his son.
²²The descendants of Kohath:
Amminadab his son, Korah his son,
Assir his son, ²³Elkanah his son,
Ebiasaph his son, Assir his son,
²⁴Tahath his son, Uriel his son,
Uzziah his son and Shaul his son.
²⁵The descendants of Elkanah:
Amasai, Ahimoth,

²⁶Elkanah his son,ᶜ Zophai his son,
Nahath his son, ²⁷Eliab his son,
Jeroham his son, Elkanah his son
and Samuel his son.ᵈ
²⁸The sons of Samuel:
Joelᵉ the firstborn
and Abijah the second son.
²⁹The descendants of Merari:
Mahli, Libni his son,
Shimei his son, Uzzah his son,
³⁰Shimea his son, Haggiah his son
and Asaiah his son.

The Temple Musicians
6:54-80pp — Jos 21:4-39

³¹These are the men David put in charge of the music in the house of the LORD after the ark came to rest there. ³²They ministered with music before the tabernacle, the tent of meeting, until Solomon built the temple of the LORD in Jerusalem. They performed their duties according to the regulations laid down for them.

³³Here are the men who served, together with their sons:

From the Kohathites:
Heman, the musician,
the son of Joel, the son of Samuel,
³⁴the son of Elkanah, the son of Jeroham,
the son of Eliel, the son of Toah,
³⁵the son of Zuph, the son of Elkanah,
the son of Mahath, the son of Amasai,
³⁶the son of Elkanah, the son of Joel,
the son of Azariah, the son of Zephaniah,

ᵃ 14 Hebrew *Jehozadak*, a variant of *Jozadak*; also in verse 15   ᵇ 16 Hebrew *Gershom*, a variant of *Gershon*; also in verses 17, 20, 43, 62 and 71   ᶜ 26 Some Hebrew manuscripts, Septuagint and Syriac; most Hebrew manuscripts *Ahimoth ²⁶and Elkanah. The sons of Elkanah:*   ᵈ 27 Some Septuagint manuscripts (see also 1 Samuel 1:19,20 and 1 Chron. 6:33,34); Hebrew does not have *and Samuel his son.*   ᵉ 28 Some Septuagint manuscripts and Syriac (see also 1 Samuel 8:2 and 1 Chron. 6:33); Hebrew does not have *Joel.*

6:10 Azariah Perhaps the son of Zadok who was a priest during Solomon's reign (1Ki 4:2).

6:13 Azariah Possibly the priest who opposed King Uzziah's attempt to burn incense in the temple (2Ch 26:16–18).

6:15 Jozadak The conclusion of this priestly genealogy with Jehozadak (also rendered as "Jozadak") offers a clue as to the list's purpose. The high priest of the Jewish community re-established after the exile was Joshua son of Jehozadak (see Ezr 3:2; Hag 1:1; Zec 6:11).

6:16 The sons of Levi The previous section focused on descendants of Kohath through Amram (see note on 1Ch 6:2). This list includes the descendants from Gershon and Merari, as well as descendants of Kohath through his son Izhar (called "Amminadab" in v. 22). **Gershon** Throughout the remainder of this chapter (vv. 16–80), the name of Gershon, son of Levi, is spelled "Gershom" in the traditional Hebrew text. Elsewhere in 1 Chronicles and the rest of the OT, the name is consistently spelled "Gershon" (Ge 46:11; Ex 6:16; Nu 3:17; 1Ch 6:1; 23:6–7).

6:22 Amminadab Elsewhere the father of Korah and son of Kohath is known as "Izhar" (see vv. 37–38; compare Ex 6:18,21; Nu 3:19; 16:1). See note on 1Ch 6:2.

6:27 Elkanah his son Apart from minor differences that are likely the result of spelling variations, the genealogies of Elkanah given here and in vv. 34–35 agree substantially with the lineage of Elkanah given in 1Sa 1:1. Some Septuagint manuscripts add "and Samuel his son" to the end of this verse (compare 1Ch 6:33–35).

6:28 The sons of Samuel The sons of Samuel were unjust judges. Their failure as leaders was instrumental in the people asking that Samuel appoint a king. See 1Sa 8:1–9.

6:31 the men David put in charge After moving the ark to Jerusalem, David appointed certain Levites to minister before the ark. Later, he organized some Levites to serve as temple musicians (see 1Ch 25:1–31 and note). The following list (vv. 31–47) provides the genealogies for the Levites in charge of music.

37 the son of Tahath, the son of Assir,
    the son of Ebiasaph, the son of Korah,
38 the son of Izhar, the son of Kohath,
    the son of Levi, the son of Israel;
39 and Heman's associate Asaph, who served at
    his right hand:
    Asaph son of Berekiah, the son of Shimea,
40 the son of Michael, the son of Baaseiah,ᵃ
    the son of Malkijah, 41 the son of Ethni,
    the son of Zerah, the son of Adaiah,
42 the son of Ethan, the son of Zimmah,
    the son of Shimei, 43 the son of Jahath,
    the son of Gershon, the son of Levi;
44 and from their associates, the Merarites, at
    his left hand:
    Ethan son of Kishi, the son of Abdi,
    the son of Malluk, 45 the son of Hashabiah,
    the son of Amaziah, the son of Hilkiah,
46 the son of Amzi, the son of Bani,
    the son of Shemer, 47 the son of Mahli,
    the son of Mushi, the son of Merari,
    the son of Levi.

48 Their fellow Levites were assigned to all
the other duties of the tabernacle, the house
of God. 49 But Aaron and his descendants were
the ones who presented offerings on the altar
of burnt offering and on the altar of incense in
connection with all that was done in the Most
Holy Place, making atonement for Israel, in accordance with all that Moses the servant of God
had commanded.

50 These were the descendants of Aaron:
    Eleazar his son, Phinehas his son,
    Abishua his son, 51 Bukki his son,
    Uzzi his son, Zerahiah his son,
52 Meraioth his son, Amariah his son,
    Ahitub his son, 53 Zadok his son
    and Ahimaaz his son.

54 These were the locations of their settlements
allotted as their territory (they were assigned to
the descendants of Aaron who were from the Kohathite clan, because the first lot was for them):
55 They were given Hebron in Judah with
its surrounding pasturelands. 56 But the fields
and villages around the city were given to
Caleb son of Jephunneh.

57 So the descendants of Aaron were given
Hebron (a city of refuge), and Libnah,ᵇ Jattir,
Eshtemoa, 58 Hilen, Debir, 59 Ashan, Juttahᶜ
and Beth Shemesh, together with their pasturelands. 60 And from the tribe of Benjamin
they were given Gibeon,ᵈ Geba, Alemeth and
Anathoth, together with their pasturelands.

The total number of towns distributed
among the Kohathite clans came to thirteen.
61 The rest of Kohath's descendants were allotted ten towns from the clans of half the tribe of
Manasseh.

62 The descendants of Gershon, clan by clan,
were allotted thirteen towns from the tribes of
Issachar, Asher and Naphtali, and from the part
of the tribe of Manasseh that is in Bashan.

63 The descendants of Merari, clan by clan, were
allotted twelve towns from the tribes of Reuben,
Gad and Zebulun.

64 So the Israelites gave the Levites these towns
and their pasturelands. 65 From the tribes of Judah,
Simeon and Benjamin they allotted the previously
named towns.

66 Some of the Kohathite clans were given as
their territory towns from the tribe of Ephraim.
67 In the hill country of Ephraim they were
given Shechem (a city of refuge), and Gezer,ᵉ
68 Jokmeam, Beth Horon, 69 Aijalon and Gath
Rimmon, together with their pasturelands.
70 And from half the tribe of Manasseh the
Israelites gave Aner and Bileam, together
with their pasturelands, to the rest of the
Kohathite clans.

71 The Gershonites received the following:
    From the clan of the half-tribe of Manasseh
        they received Golan in Bashan and also Ash-
        taroth, together with their pasturelands;
72 from the tribe of Issachar
    they received Kedesh, Daberath, 73 Ra-
    moth and Anem, together with their
    pasturelands;

ᵃ 40 Most Hebrew manuscripts; some Hebrew manuscripts, one
Septuagint manuscript and Syriac *Maaseiah*   ᵇ 57 See Joshua
21:13; Hebrew *given the cities of refuge: Hebron, Libnah.*
ᶜ 59 Syriac (see also Septuagint and Joshua 21:16); Hebrew does
not have *Juttah.*   ᵈ 60 See Joshua 21:17; Hebrew does not have
Gibeon.   ᵉ 67 See Joshua 21:21; Hebrew *given the cities of
refuge: Shechem, Gezer.*

6:39 Asaph Associated with many Psalms. See note
on Ps 73:title.
6:48 assigned to all the other duties Besides serving as musicians, the Levites had a variety of other
responsibilities, such as assisting with sacrifices and
offerings and seeing to the maintenance of the temple
facility (see 1Ch 23:24–32).
6:49 But Aaron and his descendants The writer di-
gresses from genealogical lists in order to emphasize
the division of labor in the temple. Only the priests, descendants of Aaron, were allowed to present sacrifices
on the altar.

6:54–81 This list of cities allotted to the priests and
Levites is substantially similar to the description of the
allotment in Jos 21:1–40 (see note on Jos 21:1–45).

6:61 ten towns Based on 1Ch 6:66–70 and the parallel in Jos 21:5, it appears that this verse has lost the
references to the tribes of Ephraim and Dan. Comparison
between the list in Joshua and other textual witnesses
for this passage suggest a fair number of copying errors
throughout. For example, the details from Jos 21:23
appear to have dropped out completely between 1Ch
6:68 and 6:69.

[74] from the tribe of Asher
> they received Mashal, Abdon, [75] Hukok and Rehob, together with their pasturelands;

[76] and from the tribe of Naphtali
> they received Kedesh in Galilee, Hammon and Kiriathaim, together with their pasturelands.

[77] The Merarites (the rest of the Levites) received the following:
> From the tribe of Zebulun
> they received Jokneam, Kartah,[a] Rimmono and Tabor, together with their pasturelands;

[78] from the tribe of Reuben across the Jordan east of Jericho
> they received Bezer in the wilderness, Jahzah, [79] Kedemoth and Mephaath, together with their pasturelands;

[80] and from the tribe of Gad
> they received Ramoth in Gilead, Mahanaim, [81] Heshbon and Jazer, together with their pasturelands.

Issachar

7 The sons of Issachar:
> Tola, Puah, Jashub and Shimron — four in all.

[2] The sons of Tola:
> Uzzi, Rephaiah, Jeriel, Jahmai, Ibsam and Samuel — heads of their families. During the reign of David, the descendants of Tola listed as fighting men in their genealogy numbered 22,600.

[3] The son of Uzzi:
> Izrahiah.

The sons of Izrahiah:
> Michael, Obadiah, Joel and Ishiah. All five of them were chiefs. [4] According to their family genealogy, they had 36,000 men ready for battle, for they had many wives and children.

[5] The relatives who were fighting men belonging to all the clans of Issachar, as listed in their genealogy, were 87,000 in all.

Benjamin

[6] Three sons of Benjamin:
> Bela, Beker and Jediael.

[7] The sons of Bela:
> Ezbon, Uzzi, Uzziel, Jerimoth and Iri, heads of families — five in all. Their genealogical record listed 22,034 fighting men.

[8] The sons of Beker:
> Zemirah, Joash, Eliezer, Elioenai, Omri, Jeremoth, Abijah, Anathoth and Alemeth. All these were the sons of Beker. [9] Their genealogical record listed the heads of families and 20,200 fighting men.

[10] The son of Jediael:
> Bilhan.

The sons of Bilhan:
> Jeush, Benjamin, Ehud, Kenaanah, Zethan, Tarshish and Ahishahar. [11] All these sons of Jediael were heads of families. There were 17,200 fighting men ready to go out to war.

[12] The Shuppites and Huppites were the descendants of Ir, and the Hushites[b] the descendants of Aher.

---

a 77 See Septuagint and Joshua 21:34; Hebrew does not have *Jokneam, Kartah.* *b 12* Or *Ir. The sons of Dan: Hushim,* (see Gen. 46:23); Hebrew does not have *The sons of Dan.*

7:1–5 This passage provides a brief genealogy of the descendants of Issachar. The priorities of the Chronicler can be deduced from the lengthy treatment of the tribes of Judah (chs. 2–4) and Levi (ch. 6) compared to the other tribes (chs. 5,7). Six tribes, mainly representing the northern kingdom of Israel, are covered in the 40 verses of ch. 7. The Chronicler is concerned primarily with establishing the ethnic boundaries of the postexilic community of Judah—especially identifying those who belong to the tribes of Judah, Benjamin and Levi.

7:1 Issachar Ninth son of Jacob; his mother was Leah (Ge 30:17–18). Issachar's four sons are consistently identified as Tola, Puah, Jashub and Shimron (Ge 46:13; Nu 26:23–24).

7:2 Tola This brief genealogy covers only the descendants of Issachar's oldest son, Tola. The other clans are referenced only indirectly, through the total given in 1Ch 7:5.

7:6–12 The genealogy of Benjamin is continued in 8:1–40, where it primarily follows the line of Bela. The last verse in the segment appears to have been corrupted in copying over time. Initially, it might have contained the missing genealogy for the tribe of Dan (see note on v. 12).

7:6 Three While this verse lists only three sons of Benjamin, 1Ch 8:1 indicates that he had five sons. In Ge

46:21, ten names are given as sons of Benjamin. Based on comparison with 1Ch 8:1–5, the lists of the sons of Benjamin in Ge 46:21 and the clans in Nu 26:38–39 also must include grandsons. **sons of Benjamin** Jacob's twelfth and youngest son, Benjamin, was his second son by Rachel, who died in childbirth (Ge 35:16–19). Benjamin's sons Bela and Beker are listed in Ge 46:21, but Jediael is not.

7:12 Shuppites and Huppites These names appear to be variations on descendants of Benjamin listed in Ge 46:21 and Nu 26:39. The inclusion of the names here outside the syntax of the main genealogy of Benjamin in 1Ch 7:6–11 suggests that the names possibly were inserted so as not to omit the names of two clans of Benjamin. **descendants of Ir** The name "Ir" is otherwise unknown, but the word also is a Hebrew noun for "city." The absence of a genealogy for Dan in this passage supports the possibility that "Ir" is a corruption of "Dan." The likelihood that this verse contained a genealogy of Dan is strengthened by the parallel sequence of Benjamin, Dan and Naphtali in the genealogies of Ge 46:21–24 and Nu 26:38–50. Further, the following reference to the Hushites (Hushim) is best explained as a reference to the son of Dan from Ge 46:23. The genealogy of Naphtali in 1Ch 7:13 concludes by mentioning the descendants of Bilhah—a reference to Dan and Naphtali

Naphtali

[13] The sons of Naphtali:
Jahziel, Guni, Jezer and Shillem[a] — the descendants of Bilhah.

Manasseh

[14] The descendants of Manasseh:
Asriel was his descendant through his Aramean concubine. She gave birth to Makir the father of Gilead. [15] Makir took a wife from among the Huppites and Shuppites. His sister's name was Maakah.

Another descendant was named Zelophehad, who had only daughters.

[16] Makir's wife Maakah gave birth to a son and named him Peresh. His brother was named Sheresh, and his sons were Ulam and Rakem.

[17] The son of Ulam:
Bedan.

These were the sons of Gilead son of Makir, the son of Manasseh. [18] His sister Hammoleketh gave birth to Ishhod, Abiezer and Mahlah.

[19] The sons of Shemida were:
Ahian, Shechem, Likhi and Aniam.

Ephraim

[20] The descendants of Ephraim:
Shuthelah, Bered his son,

Tahath his son, Eleadah his son, Tahath his son, [21] Zabad his son and Shuthelah his son.

Ezer and Elead were killed by the native-born men of Gath, when they went down to seize their livestock. [22] Their father Ephraim mourned for them many days, and his relatives came to comfort him. [23] Then he made love to his wife again, and she became pregnant and gave birth to a son. He named him Beriah,[b] because there had been misfortune in his family. [24] His daughter was Sheerah, who built Lower and Upper Beth Horon as well as Uzzen Sheerah.

[25] Rephah was his son, Resheph his son,[c] Telah his son, Tahan his son, [26] Ladan his son, Ammihud his son, Elishama his son, [27] Nun his son and Joshua his son.

[28] Their lands and settlements included Bethel and its surrounding villages, Naaran to the east, Gezer and its villages to the west, and Shechem and its villages all the way to Ayyah and its villages. [29] Along the borders of Manasseh were Beth Shan, Taanach, Megiddo and Dor, together with their villages. The descendants of Joseph son of Israel lived in these towns.

[a] 13 Some Hebrew and Septuagint manuscripts (see also Gen. 46:24 and Num. 26:49); most Hebrew manuscripts *Shallum* [b] 23 *Beriah* sounds like the Hebrew for *misfortune.* [c] 25 Some Septuagint manuscripts; Hebrew does not have *his son.*

(Ge 30:4–8). **the Hushites** Identified as the only son of Dan in Ge 46:23 and the only clan of Danites according to Nu 26:42–43. The spelling difference between the name "Hushim" (compare Ge 46:23) and "Shuham" in Nu 26:42 reflects a transposition of the first two Hebrew letters. **descendants of Aher** As with "Ir," the Hebrew word used here, *acher,* is a common noun, not a proper name. *Acher* means "another," so the full phrase used here, *benei acher,* technically means "sons of another." The plural "sons" also is unusual since only one name is given. Both of these difficulties are explained by connecting Hushim with the tribe of Dan. The phrase *benei acher* contains two of the letters most easily misread in the handwriting of ancient Hebrew manuscripts. When those two letters are changed to the alternatives, the phrase becomes *beno echad* ("his one son"). This reading aligns this verse with Ge 46:23, which lists Hushim as Dan's only son. Alternately, Aher could be equated with Aharah from 1Ch 8:1 or Ahiram from Nu 26:38 to keep Hushim associated with the tribe of Benjamin.
7:13 The sons of Naphtali Jacob's son Naphtali was his second son by Bilhah (Ge 30:8). The same four sons of Naphtali are named in Ge 46:24–25 and Nu 26:48–49.
7:14–19 The tribe of Manasseh was mentioned briefly in 1Ch 5:23–24. Some of the people listed in this passage also are known from Jos 17:1–3.
7:14 The descendants of Manasseh Joseph's oldest son was Manasseh (Ge 41:50–51). Jacob's blessing in Ge 48 placed Manasseh and Ephraim at the same level as their uncles, as founders of tribes of Israel. Manasseh's

son Makir and grandson Gilead are mentioned in Nu 26:29 and Jos 17:1.
7:15 who had only daughters The fact that Zelophehad had only daughters and not sons was the basis for the legal question of whether daughters could inherit. See note on Nu 27:1–11; compare Jos 17:3–4.
7:20–29 The clans of Ephraim are noted in Nu 26:35–37. Some of the names here likely refer to the same men as those listed in Nu 26:35. This genealogy contains a short narrative recounting how two of Ephraim's sons died in a conflict with the men of Gath (1Ch 7:21–23). The tribe of Ephraim had been the dominant tribe of the northern kingdom, and the name "Ephraim" commonly is used to refer to all ten tribes of the northern kingdom of Israel (Isa 7:2–5; Hos 6:4).
7:20 The descendants of Ephraim Joseph's younger son (Ge 41:50–52). Shuthelah is known from Nu 26:35. The names of the sons Bered and Tahath might be alternatives or misspellings for Beker and Tahan from Nu 26:35.
7:23 there had been misfortune in his family The Hebrew word here for disaster, *bera'ah,* is very similar to the Hebrew spelling of "Beriah" (*beri'ah*).
7:24 Lower and Upper Beth Horon Upper and Lower Beth Horon represent the southern border of Ephraim. Solomon fortifies these cities during his reign (2Ch 8:5).
7:27 Joshua his son The successor to Moses who led the Israelites' conquest of Canaan. See note on Jos 1:1.
7:28 Their lands The territory indicated in 1Ch 7:28–29 is substantially the same as the allotment given to Ephraim in Jos 16:1–9 (compare Jos 17:11).

Asher

30 The sons of Asher:
Imnah, Ishvah, Ishvi and Beriah. Their sister was Serah.
31 The sons of Beriah:
Heber and Malkiel, who was the father of Birzaith.
32 Heber was the father of Japhlet, Shomer and Hotham and of their sister Shua.
33 The sons of Japhlet:
Pasak, Bimhal and Ashvath.
These were Japhlet's sons.
34 The sons of Shomer:
Ahi, Rohgah,[a] Hubbah and Aram.
35 The sons of his brother Helem:
Zophah, Imna, Shelesh and Amal.
36 The sons of Zophah:
Suah, Harnepher, Shual, Beri, Imrah, 37 Bezer, Hod, Shamma, Shilshah, Ithran[b] and Beera.
38 The sons of Jether:
Jephunneh, Pispah and Ara.
39 The sons of Ulla:
Arah, Hanniel and Rizia.
40 All these were descendants of Asher — heads of families, choice men, brave warriors and outstanding leaders. The number of men ready for battle, as listed in their genealogy, was 26,000.

The Genealogy of Saul the Benjamite
8:28-38pp — 1Ch 9:34-44

8 Benjamin was the father of Bela his firstborn, Ashbel the second son, Aharah the third, 2 Nohah the fourth and Rapha the fifth.
3 The sons of Bela were:
Addar, Gera, Abihud,[c] 4 Abishua, Naaman, Ahoah, 5 Gera, Shephuphan and Huram.

6 These were the descendants of Ehud, who were heads of families of those living in Geba and were deported to Manahath:
7 Naaman, Ahijah, and Gera, who deported them and who was the father of Uzza and Ahihud.
8 Sons were born to Shaharaim in Moab after he had divorced his wives Hushim and Baara. 9 By his wife Hodesh he had Jobab, Zibia, Mesha, Malkam, 10 Jeuz, Sakia and Mirmah. These were his sons, heads of families. 11 By Hushim he had Abitub and Elpaal.
12 The sons of Elpaal:
Eber, Misham, Shemed (who built Ono and Lod with its surrounding villages), 13 and Beriah and Shema, who were heads of families of those living in Aijalon and who drove out the inhabitants of Gath.
14 Ahio, Shashak, Jeremoth, 15 Zebadiah, Arad, Eder, 16 Michael, Ishpah and Joha were the sons of Beriah.
17 Zebadiah, Meshullam, Hizki, Heber, 18 Ishmerai, Izliah and Jobab were the sons of Elpaal.
19 Jakim, Zikri, Zabdi, 20 Elienai, Zillethai, Eliel, 21 Adaiah, Beraiah and Shimrath were the sons of Shimei.
22 Ishpan, Eber, Eliel, 23 Abdon, Zikri, Hanan, 24 Hananiah, Elam, Anthothijah, 25 Iphdeiah and Penuel were the sons of Shashak.
26 Shamsherai, Shehariah, Athaliah, 27 Jaareshiah, Elijah and Zikri were the sons of Jeroham.
28 All these were heads of families, chiefs as listed in their genealogy, and they lived in Jerusalem.

a 34 Or of his brother Shomer: Rohgah   b 37 Possibly a variant of Jether   c 3 Or Gera the father of Ehud

---

7:30-40 Asher's descendants listed in 1Ch 7:30-31 are consistent with the genealogical information from Ge 46:17 and Nu 26:44-45. Asher and his older brother Gad were Jacob's sons by Zilpah, Leah's maid (Ge 30:10-13). A similar genealogy for Gad is not provided in 1Ch 1-9. In the genealogy of Ge 46, Gad's descendants are listed immediately before Asher's (Ge 46:16-17). However, the tribe of Gad later became associated more closely with the tribes of Reuben and eastern Manasseh, after settling with them in the Transjordan region (Nu 34:14; Jos 18:7; 20:8; 22:9-34). This affiliation likely explains why Gad appears in 1Ch 1-9 only in connection with the tribes of the Transjordan in 5:11-18. See note on 5:11-26.

7:30 The sons of Asher Jacob's eighth son, Asher, was his second son by Zilpah. This verse and Ge 46:17 list four sons for Asher—Imnah, Ishvah, Ishvi and Beriah. However, the identification of the clans of Asher in Nu 26:44 lists only three clans—Imnites, Ishvites and Beriites. The extremely similar spelling of "Ishvah" and "Ishvi" raises the possibility that Asher had only three sons (and that a copying error produced the repetition in Ge 46:17).

8:1-40 The genealogy of Israel with an expanded genealogy of Benjamin (1Ch 7:6-12). The return to Benjamin might reflect the Chronicler's concern for the tribes of the southern kingdom (Judah and Benjamin). It also provides the background for the main historical narrative in ch. 10, which begins with the death of Saul, a Benjamite and Israel's first king. The final section (vv. 29-40) gives the genealogy of Saul's family, and much of the same material is essentially repeated in 9:35-44, as the Chronicler shifts from the genealogy to historical narrative (10:1-14).

8:1 Benjamin See note on 7:6. **Bela his firstborn** Aside from listing the names of other sons in v. 1, the genealogy follows only the line of Bela, Benjamin's oldest son.

8:6 Ehud A judge who delivered Israel by killing Eglon, the king of Moab (Jdg 3:12-30). He is identified as a son of Gera in Jdg 3:15 (compare 1Ch 8:5). The circumstances surrounding the exile of his sons are unclear as this is the only reference to the incident.

29 Jeiel[a] the father[b] of Gibeon lived in Gibeon. His wife's name was Maakah, 30 and his firstborn son was Abdon, followed by Zur, Kish, Baal, Ner,[c] Nadab, 31 Gedor, Ahio, Zeker 32 and Mikloth, who was the father of Shimeah. They too lived near their relatives in Jerusalem.

33 Ner was the father of Kish, Kish the father of Saul, and Saul the father of Jonathan, Malki-Shua, Abinadab and Esh-Baal.[d]

34 The son of Jonathan:

Merib-Baal,[e] who was the father of Micah.

35 The sons of Micah:

Pithon, Melek, Tarea and Ahaz.

36 Ahaz was the father of Jehoaddah, Jehoaddah was the father of Alemeth, Azmaveth and Zimri, and Zimri was the father of Moza. 37 Moza was the father of Binea; Raphah was his son, Eleasah his son and Azel his son.

38 Azel had six sons, and these were their names:

Azrikam, Bokeru, Ishmael, Sheariah, Obadiah and Hanan. All these were the sons of Azel.

39 The sons of his brother Eshek:

Ulam his firstborn, Jeush the second son and Eliphelet the third. 40 The sons of Ulam were brave warriors who could handle the bow. They had many sons and grandsons — 150 in all.

All these were the descendants of Benjamin.

9 All Israel was listed in the genealogies recorded in the book of the kings of Israel and Judah. They were taken captive to Babylon because of their unfaithfulness.

The People in Jerusalem

9:1-17pp — Ne 11:3-19

2 Now the first to resettle on their own property in their own towns were some Israelites, priests, Levites and temple servants.

3 Those from Judah, from Benjamin, and from Ephraim and Manasseh who lived in Jerusalem were:

4 Uthai son of Ammihud, the son of Omri, the son of Imri, the son of Bani, a descendant of Perez son of Judah.

5 Of the Shelanites[f]:

Asaiah the firstborn and his sons.

6 Of the Zerahites:

Jeuel.

The people from Judah numbered 690.

7 Of the Benjamites:

Sallu son of Meshullam, the son of Hodaviah, the son of Hassenuah;

8 Ibneiah son of Jeroham; Elah son of Uzzi, the son of Mikri; and Meshullam son of Shephatiah, the son of Reuel, the son of Ibnijah.

9 The people from Benjamin, as listed in their genealogy, numbered 956. All these men were heads of their families.

10 Of the priests:

Jedaiah; Jehoiarib; Jakin;

11 Azariah son of Hilkiah, the son of Meshullam, the son of Zadok, the son of Meraioth,

---

[a] 29 Some Septuagint manuscripts (see also 9:35); Hebrew does not have Jeiel.   [b] 29 Father may mean civic leader or military leader.   [c] 30 Some Septuagint manuscripts (see also 9:36); Hebrew does not have Ner.   [d] 33 Also known as Ish-Bosheth   [e] 34 Also known as Mephibosheth   [f] 5 See Num. 26:20; Hebrew Shilonites.

8:29–40 The remainder of the Benjamite genealogy focuses on the line of Saul, Israel's first king. The people listed in vv. 33–34 are some of the ones involved in the events of the early monarchy under Saul and David — including Saul himself, his sons Jonathan (1Sa 13–14) and Esh-Baal (Ish-Bosheth, 2Sa 2:8), and his grandson Merib-Baal (Mephibosheth; 2Sa 4:4).

8:33 Ner was the father of Kish According to 1 Samuel, Abiel was father of both Kish and Ner, making Ner the uncle of Saul (see 1Sa 9:1; 1Sa 14:50–51). It is unclear why Ner would be listed here and in 1Ch 9:39 as father of Kish and grandfather of Saul. **Esh-Baal** Known in 2 Samuel as Ish-Bosheth (compare 2Sa 2:8 and note). The Hebrew word used here, eshbaal, means "man of Baal." The writer of 2 Samuel may have wanted to avoid giving prominence to the name of the Canaanite god Baal and changed it to "Ish-Bosheth," meaning "man of shame." For Biblical names containing the element baal, it was not unusual for some Biblical writers to substitute bosheth for baal (compare Jdg 6:32; 2Sa 11:21).

9:1–34 In this passage, the Chronicler shifts from a mostly pre-exilic genealogy to a catalog of the returned exiles, but the list is almost completely devoted to information about returning priests and Levites (1Ch 9:10–34),

aside from the brief mention of some members of other tribes (vv. 3–9).

9:1 book of the kings The Chronicler refers to this source several times (e.g., 2Ch 27:7; 35:27). The exact nature of the source is unknown, but it most likely is not the same work as the Biblical 1–2 Kings, which includes no such genealogies. Also, 1–2 Chronicles refers to this source in contexts for which 1–2 Kings gives no further information (compare 2Ch 27:1–9; 2Ki 15:32–38).

9:3 who lived in Jerusalem Similar material appears in Ne 11:4–9. Despite the reference to Ephraim and Manasseh here, the list of names in 1Ch 9:4–9 and the comparable list in Ne 11:4–9 appear to refer only to returnees from Judah and Benjamin.

9:5 Shelanites Possibly a surviving clan from Ephraim, since Shiloh was a city of Ephraim located northeast of Bethel (Judg 21:19). However, the parallel reference to a Shilonite in Ne 11:5 connects to the tribe of Judah.

9:10–34 This list of religious workers closely aligns with the material from Ne 11:10–19. Both lists cover the same offices in the same order, identifying those who served as priests (1Ch 9:10–13; Ne 11:10–14), Levites (1Ch 9:14–16; Ne 11:15–18) and gatekeepers (1Ch 9:17–27; Ne 11:19).

the son of Ahitub, the official in charge of the house of God;

[12] Adaiah son of Jeroham, the son of Pashhur, the son of Malkijah; and Maasai son of Adiel, the son of Jahzerah, the son of Meshullam, the son of Meshillemith, the son of Immer.

[13] The priests, who were heads of families, numbered 1,760. They were able men, responsible for ministering in the house of God.

[14] Of the Levites:

Shemaiah son of Hasshub, the son of Azrikam, the son of Hashabiah, a Merarite; [15] Bakbakkar, Heresh, Galal and Mattaniah son of Mika, the son of Zikri, the son of Asaph; [16] Obadiah son of Shemaiah, the son of Galal, the son of Jeduthun; and Berekiah son of Asa, the son of Elkanah, who lived in the villages of the Netophathites.

[17] The gatekeepers:

Shallum, Akkub, Talmon, Ahiman and their fellow Levites, Shallum their chief [18] being stationed at the King's Gate on the east, up to the present time. These were the gatekeepers belonging to the camp of the Levites. [19] Shallum son of Kore, the son of Ebiasaph, the son of Korah, and his fellow gatekeepers from his family (the Korahites) were responsible for guarding the thresholds of the tent just as their ancestors had been responsible for guarding the entrance to the dwelling of the LORD. [20] In earlier times Phinehas son of Eleazar was the official in charge of the gatekeepers, and the LORD was with him. [21] Zechariah son of Meshelemiah was the gatekeeper at the entrance to the tent of meeting.

[22] Altogether, those chosen to be gatekeepers at the thresholds numbered 212. They were registered by genealogy in their villages. The gatekeepers had been assigned to their positions of trust by David and Samuel the seer. [23] They and their descendants were in charge of guarding the gates of the house of the LORD — the house called the tent of meeting. [24] The gatekeepers were on the four sides: east, west, north and south. [25] Their fellow Levites in their villages had to come from time to time and share their duties for seven-day periods. [26] But the four principal gatekeepers, who were Levites, were entrusted with the responsibility for the rooms and treasuries in the house of God. [27] They would spend the night stationed around the house of God, because they had to guard it; and they had charge of the key for opening it each morning.

[28] Some of them were in charge of the articles used in the temple service; they counted them when they were brought in and when they were taken out. [29] Others were assigned to take care of the furnishings and all the other articles of the sanctuary, as well as the special flour and wine, and the olive oil, incense and spices. [30] But some of the priests took care of mixing the spices. [31] A Levite named Mattithiah, the firstborn son of Shallum the Korahite, was entrusted with the responsibility for baking the offering bread. [32] Some of the Kohathites, their fellow Levites, were in charge of preparing for every Sabbath the bread set out on the table.

[33] Those who were musicians, heads of Levite families, stayed in the rooms of the temple and were exempt from other duties because they were responsible for the work day and night.

[34] All these were heads of Levite families, chiefs as listed in their genealogy, and they lived in Jerusalem.

The Genealogy of Saul

9:34-44pp — 1Ch 8:28-38

[35] Jeiel the father[a] of Gibeon lived in Gibeon.

His wife's name was Maakah, [36] and his firstborn son was Abdon, followed by Zur, Kish, Baal, Ner, Nadab, [37] Gedor, Ahio, Zechariah and Mikloth. [38] Mikloth was the father of Shimeam. They too lived near their relatives in Jerusalem.

[39] Ner was the father of Kish, Kish the father of Saul, and Saul the father of Jonathan, Malki-Shua, Abinadab and Esh-Baal.[b]

[40] The son of Jonathan:

Merib-Baal,[c] who was the father of Micah.

[41] The sons of Micah:

Pithon, Melek, Tahrea and Ahaz.[d]

a 35 Father may mean *civic leader* or *military leader.* *b 39* Also known as *Ish-Bosheth* *c 40* Also known as *Mephibosheth* *d 41* Vulgate and Syriac (see also Septuagint and 8:35); Hebrew does not have *and Ahaz.*

9:22 David and Samuel the seer The authorization for these Levitical families to serve as the official temple guards or gatekeepers goes all the way back to the time of King David and Samuel the prophet. Samuel's early duties at the tabernacle might have involved serving as a guard to protect the sanctuary from defilement (1Sa 3:1–3).

9:35–44 The Chronicler concludes his lengthy genealogical section (1Ch 1:1—9:44) by repeating information from the genealogy of Saul given in 8:29–33. After the digression about returned exiles in vv. 1–34, the repeated material returns the reader to the chronological context of the main historical narrative beginning in ch. 10. See note on 8:1–40.

9:39 Saul As Israel's first king, Saul reigned from about 1051 to 1011 BC. Saul was anointed by Samuel. Initially described as Yahweh's choice (1Sa 10:24), he was rejected as king after performing an unlawful sacrifice (1Sa 13:8–14). Samuel then anointed David as king. Saul spent much of his later life trying to destroy David in order to preserve his own reign (1Sa 18–31).

[42] Ahaz was the father of Jadah, Jadah[a] was the father of Alemeth, Azmaveth and Zimri, and Zimri was the father of Moza. [43] Moza was the father of Binea; Rephaiah was his son, Eleasah his son and Azel his son.

[44] Azel had six sons, and these were their names:

Azrikam, Bokeru, Ishmael, Sheariah, Obadiah and Hanan. These were the sons of Azel.

Saul Takes His Life

10:1-12pp — 1Sa 31:1-13; 2Sa 1:4-12

10 Now the Philistines fought against Israel; the Israelites fled before them, and many fell dead on Mount Gilboa. [2] The Philistines were in hot pursuit of Saul and his sons, and they killed his sons Jonathan, Abinadab and Malki-Shua. [3] The fighting grew fierce around Saul, and when the archers overtook him, they wounded him.

[4] Saul said to his armor-bearer, "Draw your sword and run me through, or these uncircumcised fellows will come and abuse me."

But his armor-bearer was terrified and would not do it; so Saul took his own sword and fell on it. [5] When the armor-bearer saw that Saul was dead, he too fell on his sword and died. [6] So Saul and his three sons died, and all his house died together.

[7] When all the Israelites in the valley saw that the army had fled and that Saul and his sons had died, they abandoned their towns and fled. And the Philistines came and occupied them.

[8] The next day, when the Philistines came to strip the dead, they found Saul and his sons fallen on Mount Gilboa. [9] They stripped him and took his head and his armor, and sent messengers throughout the land of the Philistines to proclaim the news among their idols and their people. [10] They put his armor in the temple of their gods and hung up his head in the temple of Dagon.

[11] When all the inhabitants of Jabesh Gilead heard what the Philistines had done to Saul, [12] all their valiant men went and took the bodies of Saul and his sons and brought them to Jabesh. Then they buried their bones under the great tree in Jabesh, and they fasted seven days.

[13] Saul died because he was unfaithful to the LORD; he did not keep the word of the LORD and even consulted a medium for guidance, [14] and did not inquire of the LORD. So the LORD put him to death and turned the kingdom over to David son of Jesse.

David Becomes King Over Israel

11:1-3pp — 2Sa 5:1-3

11 All Israel came together to David at Hebron and said, "We are your own flesh and blood. [2] In the past, even while Saul was king, you were the one who led Israel on their military campaigns. And the LORD your God said to you, 'You will shepherd my people Israel, and you will become their ruler.'"

[3] When all the elders of Israel had come to King David at Hebron, he made a covenant with them at Hebron before the LORD, and they anointed David king over Israel, as the LORD had promised through Samuel.

David Conquers Jerusalem

11:4-9pp — 2Sa 5:6-10

[4] David and all the Israelites marched to Jerusalem (that is, Jebus). The Jebusites who lived

---

[a] 42 Some Hebrew manuscripts and Septuagint (see also 8:36); most Hebrew manuscripts *Jarah, Jarah*

10:1–14 The historical narrative of 1–2 Chronicles begins with the story of Saul's death (see 1Sa 31). The Chronicler does not devote any attention to Saul's reign or to David's rise to prominence (topics covered by 1Sa 9–30). Instead, 1–2 Chronicles focuses entirely on the Davidic monarchy. This chapter mostly follows the narrative of Samuel, ending with an assessment of Saul's death (see 1Ch 10:13–14).

10:1 the Philistines Israel's main enemies during this period (1Sa 4:1–2). **Mount Gilboa** Located roughly 25 miles (40 kilometers) southwest of the Sea of Galilee.
10:2 Jonathan, Abinadab and Malki-Shua The Samuel account reveals that Saul's son, Jonathan, had a very close friendship with David (1Sa 13:2; 18:1–5).
10:4 abuse me See note on 1Sa 31:4. **terrified** The armor-bearer did not want to be responsible for the death of God's anointed king.
10:5 fell on his sword He probably feared being captured and tortured, just as Saul did.
10:6 all his house died Not all of Saul's sons were killed in battle. Saul's son Esh-Baal (or Ish-Bosheth; see

note on 1Ch 8:33) reigned for a time in northern Israel (2Sa 2:8—4:12). Saul's lineage also continued through Jonathan's son, Merib-Baal (or Mephibosheth; see note on 1Ch 8:34; 2Sa 9:1–13).
10:10 temple of Dagon The main Philistine deity.
10:11 Jabesh Gilead A town Saul had saved from the Ammonites (1Sa 11:1–11; 31:11–13).
10:13 he was unfaithful See note on 1Ch 5:25.

11:1–9 The Chronicler moves directly from Saul's death to David's anointing as king over all of Israel and his capture of Jerusalem (compare 2Sa 5:1–10). 1–2 Chronicles skips the period when David ruled over Judah and Ish-Bosheth (Esh-Baal) reigned in Israel (2Sa 2:1—4:12). This is most likely because the Chronicler wanted to emphasize national unity for his audience of returned exiles (2Ch 15:9–15; 30:1–12).

11:2 shepherd The Bible often uses shepherd imagery to describe leaders. See note on 1Sa 9:3.
11:4 Jebusites Listed among the prior inhabitants of the promised land (Ge 15:21). See 2Sa 5:6 and note.

there ⁵said to David, "You will not get in here." Nevertheless, David captured the fortress of Zion—which is the City of David.

⁶David had said, "Whoever leads the attack on the Jebusites will become commander-in-chief." Joab son of Zeruiah went up first, and so he received the command.

⁷David then took up residence in the fortress, and so it was called the City of David. ⁸He built up the city around it, from the terraces^a to the surrounding wall, while Joab restored the rest of the city. ⁹And David became more and more powerful, because the LORD Almighty was with him.

David's Mighty Warriors

11:10-41pp — 2Sa 23:8-39

¹⁰These were the chiefs of David's mighty warriors—they, together with all Israel, gave his kingship strong support to extend it over the whole land, as the LORD had promised— ¹¹this is the list of David's mighty warriors:

Jashobeam,^b a Hakmonite, was chief of the officers^c; he raised his spear against three hundred men, whom he killed in one encounter.

¹²Next to him was Eleazar son of Dodai the Ahohite, one of the three mighty warriors. ¹³He was with David at Pas Dammim when the Philistines gathered there for battle. At a place where there was a field full of barley, the troops fled from the Philistines. ¹⁴But they took their stand in the middle of the field. They defended it and struck the Philistines down, and the LORD brought about a great victory.

¹⁵Three of the thirty chiefs came down to David to the rock at the cave of Adullam, while a band of Philistines was encamped in the Valley of Rephaim. ¹⁶At that time David was in the stronghold, and the Philistine garrison was at Bethlehem. ¹⁷David longed for water and said, "Oh, that someone would get me a drink of water from the well near the gate of Bethlehem!" ¹⁸So the Three broke through the Philistine lines, drew water from the well near the gate of Bethlehem and carried it back to David. But he refused to drink it; instead, he poured it out to the LORD. ¹⁹"God forbid that I should do this!" he said. "Should I drink the blood of these men who went at the risk of their lives?"

Because they risked their lives to bring it back, David would not drink it.

Such were the exploits of the three mighty warriors.

²⁰Abishai the brother of Joab was chief of the Three. He raised his spear against three hundred men, whom he killed, and so he became as famous as the Three. ²¹He was doubly honored above the Three and became their commander, even though he was not included among them.

²²Benaiah son of Jehoiada, a valiant fighter from Kabzeel, performed great exploits. He struck down Moab's two mightiest warriors. He also went down into a pit on a snowy day and killed a lion. ²³And he struck down an Egyptian who was five cubits^d tall. Although the Egyptian had a spear like a weaver's rod in his hand, Benaiah went against him with a club. He snatched the spear from the Egyptian's hand and killed him with his own spear. ²⁴Such were the exploits of Benaiah son of Jehoiada; he too was as famous as the three mighty warriors. ²⁵He was held in greater honor than any of the Thirty, but he was not included among the Three. And David put him in charge of his bodyguard.

²⁶The mighty warriors were:
Asahel the brother of Joab,
Elhanan son of Dodo from Bethlehem,
²⁷Shammoth the Harorite,
Helez the Pelonite,
²⁸Ira son of Ikkesh from Tekoa,
Abiezer from Anathoth,
²⁹Sibbekai the Hushathite,
Ilai the Ahohite,
³⁰Maharai the Netophathite,
Heled son of Baanah the Netophathite,
³¹Ithai son of Ribai from Gibeah in Benjamin,
Benaiah the Pirathonite,
³²Hurai from the ravines of Gaash,
Abiel the Arbathite,
³³Azmaveth the Baharumite,
Eliahba the Shaalbonite,
³⁴the sons of Hashem the Gizonite,
Jonathan son of Shagee the Hararite,

---

^a 8 Or *the Millo*   ^b 11 Possibly a variant of *Jashob-Baal*
^c 11 Or *Thirty*; some Septuagint manuscripts *Three* (see also 2 Samuel 23:8)   ^d 23 That is, about 7 feet 6 inches or about 2.3 meters

---

11:7 City of David David gives Jerusalem this name (2Sa 5:6–10).

11:8 terraces Refers to a platform constructed to provide a suitable building surface.

11:9 LORD Almighty This title portrays Yahweh as the commander of armies—either Israel's forces or the heavenly hosts.

11:10–47 This list of David's mighty men corresponds to a similar report in 2Sa 23:8–39, with some spelling variations and additions (1Ch 11:42–47). The placement of the list at the beginning of David's reign—rather than

the end, as in 2 Samuel—serves to validate David's kingship (see v. 10).

11:15 cave of Adullam Where David hid from Saul (1Sa 22:1–2).

11:23 five cubits The Hebrew cubit was around 1.5 feet (five cubits = 7 feet, 6 inches).

11:26 Asahel In 2Sa, Asahel dies before David is anointed (2Sa 2:23).

11:29 Sibbekai the Hushathite Kills one of the Philistine giants (1Ch 20:4).

³⁵ Ahiam son of Sakar the Hararite,
Eliphal son of Ur,
³⁶ Hepher the Mekerathite,
Ahijah the Pelonite,
³⁷ Hezro the Carmelite,
Naarai son of Ezbai,
³⁸ Joel the brother of Nathan,
Mibhar son of Hagri,
³⁹ Zelek the Ammonite,
Naharai the Berothite, the armor-bearer
of Joab son of Zeruiah,
⁴⁰ Ira the Ithrite,
Gareb the Ithrite,
⁴¹ Uriah the Hittite,
Zabad son of Ahlai,
⁴² Adina son of Shiza the Reubenite, who was
chief of the Reubenites, and the thirty with
him,
⁴³ Hanan son of Maakah,
Joshaphat the Mithnite,
⁴⁴ Uzzia the Ashterathite,
Shama and Jeiel the sons of Hotham the
Aroerite,
⁴⁵ Jediael son of Shimri,
his brother Joha the Tizite,
⁴⁶ Eliel the Mahavite,
Jeribai and Joshaviah the sons of Elnaam,
Ithmah the Moabite,
⁴⁷ Eliel, Obed and Jaasiel the Mezobaite.

Warriors Join David

12 These were the men who came to David at Ziklag, while he was banished from the presence of Saul son of Kish (they were among the warriors who helped him in battle; ² they were armed with bows and were able to shoot arrows or to sling stones right-handed or left-handed; they were relatives of Saul from the tribe of Benjamin):

³ Ahiezer their chief and Joash the sons of Shemaah the Gibeathite; Jeziel and Pelet the sons of Azmaveth; Berakah, Jehu the Anathothite, ⁴ and Ishmaiah the Gibeonite, a mighty warrior among the Thirty, who was a leader of the Thirty; Jeremiah, Jahaziel, Johanan, Jozabad the Gederathite,^a ⁵ Eluzai,

Jerimoth, Bealiah, Shemariah and Shephati-ah the Haruphite; ⁶ Elkanah, Ishiah, Azarel, Joezer and Jashobeam the Korahites; ⁷ and Joelah and Zebadiah the sons of Jeroham from Gedor.

⁸ Some Gadites defected to David at his stronghold in the wilderness. They were brave warriors, ready for battle and able to handle the shield and spear. Their faces were the faces of lions, and they were as swift as gazelles in the mountains.

⁹ Ezer was the chief,
Obadiah the second in command, Eliab the
third,
¹⁰ Mishmannah the fourth, Jeremiah the fifth,
¹¹ Attai the sixth, Eliel the seventh,
¹² Johanan the eighth, Elzabad the ninth,
¹³ Jeremiah the tenth and Makbannai the eleventh.

¹⁴ These Gadites were army commanders; the least was a match for a hundred, and the greatest for a thousand. ¹⁵ It was they who crossed the Jordan in the first month when it was overflowing all its banks, and they put to flight everyone living in the valleys, to the east and to the west.

¹⁶ Other Benjamites and some men from Judah also came to David in his stronghold. ¹⁷ David went out to meet them and said to them, "If you have come to me in peace to help me, I am ready for you to join me. But if you have come to betray me to my enemies when my hands are free from violence, may the God of our ancestors see it and judge you." ¹⁸ Then the Spirit came on Amasai, chief of the Thirty, and he said:

"We are yours, David!
We are with you, son of Jesse!
Success, success to you,
and success to those who help you,
for your God will help you."

So David received them and made them leaders of his raiding bands.

¹⁹ Some of the tribe of Manasseh defected to David when he went with the Philistines to fight against Saul. (He and his men did not help the

^a 4 In Hebrew texts the second half of this verse (*Jeremiah . . . Gederathite*) is numbered 12:5, and 12:5-40 is numbered 12:6-41.

11:41 Uriah the Hittite Husband of Bathsheba. In 2Sa 11, David has an affair with Bathsheba and arranges for Uriah to be killed in battle. Uriah marks the end of 2 Samuel's list of mighty men (2Sa 23:39). The Chronicler probably used a separate source to compose the rest of his list.

12:1–40 The Chronicler identifies men from each tribe who support David's kingship. Some came to David's aid at Ziklag when Saul was pursuing him (1Ch 12:1–22); others came when David was stationed in Hebron after Saul's death (vv. 23–40). The emphasis is on the Israelites' common desire to help David and establish him as king (vv. 18,21–22,38).

12:1 Ziklag Town near Israel's southwestern border. It was given to David by the Philistine king Achish when David was fleeing from Saul (1Sa 27:5–7). He lived there more than a year, until Saul's death (2Sa 1:1—2:4).

12:18 Spirit came on In the OT, this phrase is used to describe people who are enabled to perform divinely appointed tasks. It is similar to descriptions of Yahweh's Spirit coming upon people (e.g., Jdg 3:10). In Samuel, the Spirit confirms Saul's anointing as king (1Sa 10:6,10). When David is anointed, the Spirit of Yahweh comes upon him and departs from Saul (1Sa 16:13–14).

12:19 their rulers sent him away Parallels account in 1Sa 29:1–11.

Philistines because, after consultation, their rulers sent him away. They said, "It will cost us our heads if he deserts to his master Saul.") [20]When David went to Ziklag, these were the men of Manasseh who defected to him: Adnah, Jozabad, Jediael, Michael, Jozabad, Elihu and Zillethai, leaders of units of a thousand in Manasseh. [21]They helped David against raiding bands, for all of them were brave warriors, and they were commanders in his army. [22]Day after day men came to help David, until he had a great army, like the army of God.[a]

Others Join David at Hebron

[23]These are the numbers of the men armed for battle who came to David at Hebron to turn Saul's kingdom over to him, as the LORD had said:
[24]from Judah, carrying shield and spear — 6,800 armed for battle;
[25]from Simeon, warriors ready for battle — 7,100;
[26]from Levi — 4,600, [27]including Jehoiada, leader of the family of Aaron, with 3,700 men, [28]and Zadok, a brave young warrior, with 22 officers from his family;
[29]from Benjamin, Saul's tribe — 3,000, most of whom had remained loyal to Saul's house until then;
[30]from Ephraim, brave warriors, famous in their own clans — 20,800;
[31]from half the tribe of Manasseh, designated by name to come and make David king — 18,000;
[32]from Issachar, men who understood the times and knew what Israel should do — 200 chiefs, with all their relatives under their command;
[33]from Zebulun, experienced soldiers prepared for battle with every type of weapon, to help David with undivided loyalty — 50,000;
[34]from Naphtali — 1,000 officers, together with 37,000 men carrying shields and spears;
[35]from Dan, ready for battle — 28,600;

[36]from Asher, experienced soldiers prepared for battle — 40,000;
[37]and from east of the Jordan, from Reuben, Gad and the half-tribe of Manasseh, armed with every type of weapon — 120,000.
[38]All these were fighting men who volunteered to serve in the ranks. They came to Hebron fully determined to make David king over all Israel. All the rest of the Israelites were also of one mind to make David king. [39]The men spent three days there with David, eating and drinking, for their families had supplied provisions for them. [40]Also, their neighbors from as far away as Issachar, Zebulun and Naphtali came bringing food on donkeys, camels, mules and oxen. There were plentiful supplies of flour, fig cakes, raisin cakes, wine, olive oil, cattle and sheep, for there was joy in Israel.

Bringing Back the Ark

13:1-14pp — 2Sa 6:1-11

13 David conferred with each of his officers, the commanders of thousands and commanders of hundreds. [2]He then said to the whole assembly of Israel, "If it seems good to you and if it is the will of the LORD our God, let us send word far and wide to the rest of our people throughout the territories of Israel, and also to the priests and Levites who are with them in their towns and pasturelands, to come and join us. [3]Let us bring the ark of our God back to us, for we did not inquire of[b] it[c] during the reign of Saul." [4]The whole assembly agreed to do this, because it seemed right to all the people.

[5]So David assembled all Israel, from the Shihor River in Egypt to Lebo Hamath, to bring the ark of God from Kiriath Jearim. [6]David and all Israel went to Baalah of Judah (Kiriath Jearim) to bring up from there the ark of God the LORD, who is enthroned between the cherubim — the ark that is called by the Name.

[7]They moved the ark of God from Abinadab's

---

[a] 22 Or *a great and mighty army*   [b] 3 Or *we neglected*
[c] 3 Or *him*

---

house on a new cart, with Uzzah and Ahio guiding it. ⁸David and all the Israelites were celebrating with all their might before God, with songs and with harps, lyres, timbrels, cymbals and trumpets.

⁹When they came to the threshing floor of Kidon, Uzzah reached out his hand to steady the ark, because the oxen stumbled. ¹⁰The LORD's anger burned against Uzzah, and he struck him down because he had put his hand on the ark. So he died there before God.

¹¹Then David was angry because the LORD's wrath had broken out against Uzzah, and to this day that place is called Perez Uzzah.ᵃ

¹²David was afraid of God that day and asked, "How can I ever bring the ark of God to me?" ¹³He did not take the ark to be with him in the City of David. Instead, he took it to the house of Obed-Edom the Gittite. ¹⁴The ark of God remained with the family of Obed-Edom in his house for three months, and the LORD blessed his household and everything he had.

David's House and Family

14:1-7pp — 2Sa 5:11-16; 1Ch 3:5-8

14 Now Hiram king of Tyre sent messengers to David, along with cedar logs, stonemasons and carpenters to build a palace for him. ²And David knew that the LORD had established him as king over Israel and that his kingdom had been highly exalted for the sake of his people Israel.

³In Jerusalem David took more wives and became the father of more sons and daughters. ⁴These are the names of the children born to him there: Shammua, Shobab, Nathan, Solomon, ⁵Ibhar, Elishua, Elpelet, ⁶Nogah, Nepheg, Japhia, ⁷Elishama, Beeliadaᵇ and Eliphelet.

David Defeats the Philistines

14:8-17pp — 2Sa 5:17-25

⁸When the Philistines heard that David had been anointed king over all Israel, they went up in full force to search for him, but David heard about it and went out to meet them. ⁹Now the Philistines had come and raided the Valley of Rephaim; ¹⁰so David inquired of God: "Shall I go and attack the Philistines? Will you deliver them into my hands?"

The LORD answered him, "Go, I will deliver them into your hands."

¹¹So David and his men went up to Baal Perazim, and there he defeated them. He said, "As waters break out, God has broken out against my enemies by my hand." So that place was called Baal Perazim.ᶜ ¹²The Philistines had abandoned their gods there, and David gave orders to burn them in the fire.

¹³Once more the Philistines raided the valley; ¹⁴so David inquired of God again, and God answered him, "Do not go directly after them, but circle around them and attack them in front of the poplar trees. ¹⁵As soon as you hear the sound of marching in the tops of the poplar trees, move out to battle, because that will mean God has gone out in front of you to strike the Philistine army." ¹⁶So David did as God commanded him, and they struck down the Philistine army, all the way from Gibeon to Gezer.

¹⁷So David's fame spread throughout every land, and the LORD made all the nations fear him.

The Ark Brought to Jerusalem

15:25 - 16:3pp — 2Sa 6:12-19

15 After David had constructed buildings for himself in the City of David, he prepared a place for the ark of God and pitched a tent for it. ²Then David said, "No one but the Levites may carry the ark of God, because the LORD chose them to carry the ark of the LORD and to minister before him forever."

³David assembled all Israel in Jerusalem to bring up the ark of the LORD to the place he had prepared for it. ⁴He called together the descendants of Aaron and the Levites:

ᵃ 11 *Perez Uzzah* means *outbreak against Uzzah.*   ᵇ 7 A variant of *Eliada*   ᶜ 11 *Baal Perazim* means *the lord who breaks out.*

13:8–14 This section is nearly identical to the account in 2Sa 6:5–15.

13:10 struck him down Yahweh had warned that touching the ark would lead to death (Nu 4:15; compare 2Sa 6:7 and note).

13:11 Perez The Hebrew word used here, *perets*, means "to breach" or "to break out."

13:13 Obed-Edom the Gittite Possibly an Israelite who was born in the Philistine city of Gath. See note on 2Sa 6:10.

14:1–17 The Chronicler uses material from 2Sa 5:11–25 to interrupt the story of the ark being brought to Jerusalem (2Sa 6). By rearranging the narrative, the Chronicler emphasizes that God blessed David even without the presence of the ark. This chapter describes David's blessings in terms of friendship and provisions from a foreign nation (1Ch 14:1–2), a fruitful lineage (vv. 3–7) and victory in

battle (vv. 8–17). This provides further contrast between David and Saul, who was defeated in battle (10:1–13).

14:1 Hiram king of Tyre Assisted David and Solomon in their building projects (e.g., 1Ki 5:1–12).

14:8 the Philistines See note on 1Sa 4:1. See the table "Battles of Saul and David" on p. 433.

14:10 inquired of God David's inquiring of God portrays him in contrast to Saul, who inquired of a medium (1Ch 10:13).

14:11 Baal Perazim Means "Lord of bursting forth."

14:12 gave orders to burn The Chronicler portrays David as being faithful to the command to destroy foreign gods (Dt 7:5).

14:16 from Gibeon to Gezer A span of about 20 miles.

14:17 David's fame The Hebrew phrase used here, *shem-dawid*, refers to "the name of David"; it evokes the ancient Near Eastern idea that someone's reputation (and ability) is represented by their name. The writers of

[5] From the descendants of Kohath,
Uriel the leader and 120 relatives;
[6] from the descendants of Merari,
Asaiah the leader and 220 relatives;
[7] from the descendants of Gershon,[a]
Joel the leader and 130 relatives;
[8] from the descendants of Elizaphan,
Shemaiah the leader and 200 relatives;
[9] from the descendants of Hebron,
Eliel the leader and 80 relatives;
[10] from the descendants of Uzziel,
Amminadab the leader and 112 relatives.

[11] Then David summoned Zadok and Abiathar the priests, and Uriel, Asaiah, Joel, Shemaiah, Eliel and Amminadab the Levites. [12] He said to them, "You are the heads of the Levitical families; you and your fellow Levites are to consecrate yourselves and bring up the ark of the LORD, the God of Israel, to the place I have prepared for it. [13] It was because you, the Levites, did not bring it up the first time that the LORD our God broke out in anger against us. We did not inquire of him about how to do it in the prescribed way." [14] So the priests and Levites consecrated themselves in order to bring up the ark of the LORD, the God of Israel. [15] And the Levites carried the ark of God with the poles on their shoulders, as Moses had commanded in accordance with the word of the LORD.

[16] David told the leaders of the Levites to appoint their fellow Levites as musicians to make a joyful sound with musical instruments: lyres, harps and cymbals.

[17] So the Levites appointed Heman son of Joel; from his relatives, Asaph son of Berekiah; and from their relatives the Merarites, Ethan son of Kushaiah; [18] and with them their relatives next in rank: Zechariah,[b] Jaaziel, Shemiramoth, Jehiel, Unni, Eliab, Benaiah, Maaseiah, Mattithiah, Eliphelehu, Mikneiah, Obed-Edom and Jeiel,[c] the gatekeepers.

[19] The musicians Heman, Asaph and Ethan were to sound the bronze cymbals; [20] Zechariah, Jaaziel,[d] Shemiramoth, Jehiel, Unni, Eliab, Maaseiah and Benaiah were to play the lyres according to *alamoth,*[e] [21] and Mattithiah, Eliphelehu, Mikneiah, Obed-Edom, Jeiel and Azaziah were to play the harps, directing according to *sheminith.*[e] [22] Kenaniah the head Levite was in charge of the singing; that was his responsibility because he was skillful at it.

[23] Berekiah and Elkanah were to be doorkeepers for the ark. [24] Shebaniah, Joshaphat, Nethanel, Amasai, Zechariah, Benaiah and Eliezer the priests were to blow trumpets before the ark of God. Obed-Edom and Jehiah were also to be doorkeepers for the ark.

[25] So David and the elders of Israel and the commanders of units of a thousand went to bring up the ark of the covenant of the LORD from the house of Obed-Edom, with rejoicing. [26] Because God had helped the Levites who were carrying the ark of the covenant of the LORD, seven bulls and seven rams were sacrificed. [27] Now David was clothed in a robe of fine linen, as were all the Levites who were carrying the ark, and as were the musicians, and Kenaniah, who was in charge of the singing of the choirs. David also wore a linen ephod. [28] So all Israel brought up the ark of the covenant of the LORD with shouts, with the sounding of rams' horns and trumpets, and of cymbals, and the playing of lyres and harps.

[29] As the ark of the covenant of the LORD was entering the City of David, Michal daughter of Saul watched from a window. And when she saw King David dancing and celebrating, she despised him in her heart.

---

[a] 7 Hebrew *Gershom,* a variant of *Gershon*   [b] 18 Three Hebrew manuscripts and most Septuagint manuscripts (see also verse 20 and 16:5); most Hebrew manuscripts *Zechariah son and* or *Zechariah, Ben and*   [c] 18 Hebrew; Septuagint (see also verse 21) *Jeiel and Azaziah*   [d] 20 See verse 18; Hebrew *Aziel,* a variant of *Jaaziel.*   [e] 20,21 Probably a musical term

---

Psalms often appeal to God's name when seeking his help (Ps 25:11; 31:3).

15:1–29 The ark's journey to Jerusalem, which began in 1Ch 13:1–14, is completed here. The Chronicler's account differs from 2Sa 6:12–16. It describes David's preparations (1Ch 15:1) and the care he took to ensure that the ark was carried properly (vv. 2–15). The Chronicler also shows David's concern for the celebration that accompanied the ark (vv. 16–24).

15:1 City of David A name for Jerusalem (11:4–5).
15:3 all Israel The Chronicler emphasizes the participation of the entire nation.

15:5–7 Kohath, Merari and Gershon were sons of Levi (Nu 3:17).

15:8–10 Uzziel and Hebron were sons of Kohath (Nu 3:19); Elizaphan was a son of Uzziel (Nu 3:30).

15:12 to consecrate yourselves The Hebrew word used for this practice, *hitheqaddeshu,* refers to making oneself holy (see note on Lev 6:18). It involved a separation from any uncleanness, according to the law.
15:13 broke out See 1Ch 13:11.
15:20 alamoth Meaning uncertain; probably a musical term.
15:21 sheminith See Ps 6:title and note.
15:24 trumpets See Nu 10:1–10.
15:26 seven bulls and seven rams The number seven symbolizes completeness.
15:27 linen ephod See Ex 28:4 and note.
15:28 all Israel The Chronicler again emphasizes the unity of Israel (see note on 1Ch 15:3; compare Ps 24; 68).
15:29 Michal The portrayal of Michal's response is shorter here than in Samuel (2Sa 6:16,20–23). It further highlights the contrast between the houses of David and Saul (1Ch 13:3; 14:10 and note), as Saul's daughter is the only one in Israel not celebrating the ark's return.

Ministering Before the Ark

16:8-22pp — Ps 105:1-15
16:23-33pp — Ps 96:1-13
16:34-36pp — Ps 106:1,47-48

16 They brought the ark of God and set it inside the tent that David had pitched for it, and they presented burnt offerings and fellowship offerings before God. ²After David had finished sacrificing the burnt offerings and fellowship offerings, he blessed the people in the name of the LORD. ³Then he gave a loaf of bread, a cake of dates and a cake of raisins to each Israelite man and woman.

⁴He appointed some of the Levites to minister before the ark of the LORD, to extol,ᵃ thank, and praise the LORD, the God of Israel: ⁵Asaph was the chief, and next to him in rank were Zechariah, then Jaaziel,ᵇ Shemiramoth, Jehiel, Mattithiah, Eliab, Benaiah, Obed-Edom and Jeiel. They were to play the lyres and harps, Asaph was to sound the cymbals, ⁶and Benaiah and Jahaziel the priests were to blow the trumpets regularly before the ark of the covenant of God.

⁷That day David first appointed Asaph and his associates to give praise to the LORD in this manner:

⁸ Give praise to the LORD, proclaim his name;
    make known among the nations what he
       has done.
⁹ Sing to him, sing praise to him;
    tell of all his wonderful acts.
¹⁰ Glory in his holy name;
    let the hearts of those who seek the LORD
       rejoice.
¹¹ Look to the LORD and his strength;
    seek his face always.

¹² Remember the wonders he has done,
    his miracles, and the judgments he
       pronounced,
¹³ you his servants, the descendants of Israel,
    his chosen ones, the children of Jacob.

¹⁴ He is the LORD our God;
    his judgments are in all the earth.

¹⁵ He remembersᶜ his covenant forever,
    the promise he made, for a thousand
       generations,
¹⁶ the covenant he made with Abraham,
    the oath he swore to Isaac.
¹⁷ He confirmed it to Jacob as a decree,
    to Israel as an everlasting covenant:
¹⁸ "To you I will give the land of Canaan
    as the portion you will inherit."

¹⁹ When they were but few in number,
    few indeed, and strangers in it,
²⁰ theyᵈ wandered from nation to nation,
    from one kingdom to another.
²¹ He allowed no one to oppress them;
    for their sake he rebuked kings:
²² "Do not touch my anointed ones;
    do my prophets no harm."

²³ Sing to the LORD, all the earth;
    proclaim his salvation day after day.
²⁴ Declare his glory among the nations,
    his marvelous deeds among all peoples.

²⁵ For great is the LORD and most worthy
       of praise;
    he is to be feared above all gods.
²⁶ For all the gods of the nations are idols,
    but the LORD made the heavens.
²⁷ Splendor and majesty are before him;
    strength and joy are in his dwelling place.

²⁸ Ascribe to the LORD, all you families
       of nations,
    ascribe to the LORD glory and strength.

ᵃ *4* Or *petition*; or *invoke*   ᵇ *5* See 15:18,20; Hebrew *Jeiel*, possibly another name for *Jaaziel.*   ᶜ *15* Some Septuagint manuscripts (see also Psalm 105:8); Hebrew *Remember*   ᵈ *18-20* One Hebrew manuscript, Septuagint and Vulgate (see also Psalm 105:12); most Hebrew manuscripts *inherit, /* ¹⁹*though you are but few in number, / few indeed, and strangers in it." /* ²⁰*They*

16:1-43 In the first section (1Ch 16:1-3), the Chronicler closely follows Samuel's account of the ark being brought to Jerusalem (2Sa 6:17-19). However, he then adds to it significantly. The Chronicler's additions focus on worship, as the ark—the symbol of God's presence—has returned to prominence. First, he notes David's appointment of Levites to serve the worship at Jerusalem (1Ch 16:4-7). Then he gives a lengthy thanksgiving psalm (vv. 8-36 and note). Finally, he lists the priests and Levites appointed for worship in both Jerusalem (vv. 37-38) and Gibeon (vv. 39-42).

16:1 inside the tent See note on Ps 15:1.
16:2 the burnt offerings See Ex 29:38-42 and note. **fellowship offerings** See Lev 3:1 and note.
16:5 Asaph Associated with several psalms. See Ps 73:title and note.

16:8-36 This thanksgiving psalm is a combination of other psalms. The first half (1Ch 16:8-22) comes from Ps 105:1-15; most of the second half (1Ch 16:23-33) is taken from Ps 96, while the final two verses (1Ch 16:35-36) reflect Ps 106:1,47-48.

16:11 Look to the LORD This is a theme throughout 1-2 Chronicles. See note on 2Ch 11:16.
16:13 children of Jacob See note on Ps 105:6.
16:16 he made with Abraham A reference to God's promise to make Abraham a great nation (Ge 12:1-3; 13:14-17; 15:5-21).
16:17 everlasting covenant This terminology is first used to describe God's covenant with humanity after the flood (Ge 9:16). God uses it in reference to his covenant with Abraham in Ge 17:7.
16:22 my anointed ones See note on Ps 105:15.
16:23 salvation The Hebrew word used here, *yeshu'ah,* can refer to help or deliverance. In Psalms, it often refers to God's help in defeating enemies (Ps 33:16-17).
16:26 idols See note on Ps 96:5.

²⁹ Ascribe to the Lᴏʀᴅ the glory due his name;
bring an offering and come before him.
Worship the Lᴏʀᴅ in the splendor of his^a
holiness.
³⁰ Tremble before him, all the earth!
The world is firmly established; it cannot
be moved.

³¹ Let the heavens rejoice, let the earth be glad;
let them say among the nations, "The Lᴏʀᴅ
reigns!"
³² Let the sea resound, and all that is in it;
let the fields be jubilant, and everything
in them!
³³ Let the trees of the forest sing,
let them sing for joy before the Lᴏʀᴅ,
for he comes to judge the earth.

³⁴ Give thanks to the Lᴏʀᴅ, for he is good;
his love endures forever.
³⁵ Cry out, "Save us, God our Savior;
gather us and deliver us from the nations,
that we may give thanks to your holy name,
and glory in your praise."
³⁶ Praise be to the Lᴏʀᴅ, the God of Israel,
from everlasting to everlasting.

Then all the people said "Amen" and "Praise the Lᴏʀᴅ."

³⁷ David left Asaph and his associates before the ark of the covenant of the Lᴏʀᴅ to minister there regularly, according to each day's requirements. ³⁸ He also left Obed-Edom and his sixty-eight associates to minister with them. Obed-Edom son of Jeduthun, and also Hosah, were gatekeepers. ³⁹ David left Zadok the priest and his fellow priests before the tabernacle of the Lᴏʀᴅ at the high place in Gibeon ⁴⁰ to present burnt offerings to the Lᴏʀᴅ on the altar of burnt offering regularly, morning and evening, in accordance with everything written in the Law of the Lᴏʀᴅ, which he had given Israel. ⁴¹ With them were Heman and Jeduthun and the rest of those chosen and designated by name to give thanks to the Lᴏʀᴅ, "for his love endures forever." ⁴² Heman and Je-

duthun were responsible for the sounding of the trumpets and cymbals and for the playing of the other instruments for sacred song. The sons of Jeduthun were stationed at the gate.

⁴³ Then all the people left, each for their own home, and David returned home to bless his family.

God's Promise to David

17:1-15pp — 2Sa 7:1-17

17 After David was settled in his palace, he said to Nathan the prophet, "Here I am, living in a house of cedar, while the ark of the covenant of the Lᴏʀᴅ is under a tent."

² Nathan replied to David, "Whatever you have in mind, do it, for God is with you."

³ But that night the word of God came to Nathan, saying:

⁴ "Go and tell my servant David, 'This is what the Lᴏʀᴅ says: You are not the one to build me a house to dwell in. ⁵ I have not dwelt in a house from the day I brought Israel up out of Egypt to this day. I have moved from one tent site to another, from one dwelling place to another. ⁶ Wherever I have moved with all the Israelites, did I ever say to any of their leaders^b whom I commanded to shepherd my people, "Why have you not built me a house of cedar?"'

⁷ "Now then, tell my servant David, 'This is what the Lᴏʀᴅ Almighty says: I took you from the pasture, from tending the flock, and appointed you ruler over my people Israel. ⁸ I have been with you wherever you have gone, and I have cut off all your enemies from before you. Now I will make your name like the names of the greatest men on earth. ⁹ And I will provide a place for my people Israel and will plant them so that they can have a home of their own and no longer be disturbed. Wicked people will

---

^a 29 Or Lᴏʀᴅ *with the splendor of*   ^b 6 Traditionally *judges*; also in verse 10

16:34 his love endures forever This refrain acts as a repeated chorus in some psalms (Ps 118:1–4; 136:1–26).
16:35 nations The Chronicler inserts this verse from Ps 106, a psalm that reflects on Israel's history from the perspective of the exile. This verse would remind the Chronicler's audience of returned exiles how God faithfully delivered them and returned them to the covenant land (1Ch 16:18).

16:37–43 The Chronicler concludes the story of the ark's placement in Jerusalem by listing the specific Levites who were charged with ministering before the ark.

16:39 before the tabernacle See Ex 26:1 and note.
Gibeon City in Benjamin, just north of Jerusalem.
16:40 altar of burnt offering See Ex 27:1–8 and note.
16:41 Heman Grandson of the prophet Samuel (1Ch

6:33). **Jeduthun** Associated with three of psalms (see Ps 39:title; 62:title; 77:title).

17:1–15 This description of the Davidic covenant follows Samuel's account closely (2Sa 7:1–17). In it, God denies David's request to build a house for the ark. Instead, God promises to build a "house" for David: From David's line would come a king whose throne would be established forever (compare Mk 12:35–37; Mt 21:9–11). This promise would be especially relevant to the Chronicler's audience of returned exiles.

17:1 to Nathan the prophet See 2Sa 7:2 and note.
17:7 Lᴏʀᴅ Almighty The Hebrew phrase used here, *yhwh tseva'oth*, has military connotations; it refers to Yahweh as the leader of armies. **tending the flock** David had been a shepherd. See 1Sa 16:11; 17:34.

not oppress them anymore, as they did at the beginning [10]and have done ever since the time I appointed leaders over my people Israel. I will also subdue all your enemies.

"'I declare to you that the LORD will build a house for you: [11]When your days are over and you go to be with your ancestors, I will raise up your offspring to succeed you, one of your own sons, and I will establish his kingdom. [12]He is the one who will build a house for me, and I will establish his throne forever. [13]I will be his father, and he will be my son. I will never take my love away from him, as I took it away from your predecessor. [14]I will set him over my house and my kingdom forever; his throne will be established forever.'"

[15]Nathan reported to David all the words of this entire revelation.

David's Prayer

17:16-27pp — 2Sa 7:18-29

[16]Then King David went in and sat before the LORD, and he said:

"Who am I, LORD God, and what is my family, that you have brought me this far? [17]And as if this were not enough in your sight, my God, you have spoken about the future of the house of your servant. You, LORD God, have looked on me as though I were the most exalted of men.

[18]"What more can David say to you for honoring your servant? For you know your servant, [19]LORD. For the sake of your servant and according to your will, you have done this great thing and made known all these great promises.

[20]"There is no one like you, LORD, and there is no God but you, as we have heard with our own ears. [21]And who is like your people Israel — the one nation on earth whose God went out to redeem a people for himself, and to make a name for yourself, and to perform great and awesome wonders by driving out nations from before your people, whom you redeemed from Egypt? [22]You made your people Israel your very own forever, and you, LORD, have become their God.

[23]"And now, LORD, let the promise you have made concerning your servant and his house be established forever. Do as you promised, [24]so that it will be established and that your name will be great forever. Then people will say, 'The LORD Almighty, the God over Israel, is Israel's God!' And the house of your servant David will be established before you.

[25]"You, my God, have revealed to your servant that you will build a house for him. So your servant has found courage to pray to you. [26]You, LORD, are God! You have promised these good things to your servant. [27]Now you have been pleased to bless the house of your servant, that it may continue forever in your sight; for you, LORD, have blessed it, and it will be blessed forever."

David's Victories

18:1-13pp — 2Sa 8:1-14

18 In the course of time, David defeated the Philistines and subdued them, and he took Gath and its surrounding villages from the control of the Philistines.

[2]David also defeated the Moabites, and they became subject to him and brought him tribute.

17:10 will build a house for you Refers to a royal dynasty.

17:12 build a house Refers to the Jerusalem temple, which Solomon builds (2Ch 2–7). The temple as the center of worship is a central aspect of 1–2 Chronicles. The final eight chapters of 1 Chronicles (1Ch 22:2—29:30) give a detailed account of David's preparations for the temple. The beginning of 2 Chronicles shows Solomon's preparation and building of the temple and its furnishings. The Chronicler also gives detailed accounts of the repairs made to the temple during the reforms of Joash (2Ch 24:1–14) and Hezekiah (2Ch 29:3–36).

17:13 from your predecessor Refers to Saul, who was rejected as king (1Ch 10:13–14; 1Sa 15:10–11,26–29).

17:14 my kingdom In the Chronicler's view, David's dynasty is closely associated with the kingdom of God (e.g., 1Ch 28:5; 29:23; 2Ch 13:8). This connection is unique to 1–2 Chronicles. In the OT, references to God's kingdom appear in Ps 45:6; 103:19; 145:11–13; Da 4:3. In the NT, Jesus is portrayed as ushering in God's kingdom (Mk 1:15 and note; Ac 1:3 and note).

17:16–27 David responds in prayer, humbly thanking God for his promised blessing. This account is mostly unchanged from 2Sa 7:18–29.

17:20 There is no one like you David upholds the incomparable greatness of Yahweh. Solomon echoes this phrase at the temple's dedication (2Ch 6:14). Frequent declarations are made regarding the incomparable nature of God in the OT. These statements often come in songs of praise. The Song of Moses points out God's unique status and power when compared to other gods (Ex 15:11). In Hannah's prayer, after giving birth to Samuel, she declares that there is none holy like Yahweh (1Sa 2:2). The psalmist often rhetorically asks who is like God (Ps 35:10; 71:19; 113:5). The prophets frequently point out the incomparable greatness of Yahweh as they condemn the worship of idols (Isa 40:18–19; Jer 10:6).

17:21 redeem The Hebrew word used here, *padah*, means to buy something back.

17:22 your very own forever David echoes the covenant formula of Lev 26:12.

18:1–17 This account, taken from 2Sa 8:1–18, attributes David's military success to God's blessing (1Ch 18:6,13). David's victories in this section give him security in all directions. The Philistines (v. 1) were to the west; Moab (v. 2) was to the east; Zobah-Hamath and Syria (also called Aram) were to the north (vv. 3–8), and the Edomites (vv. 12–13) were to the south.

³Moreover, David defeated Hadadezer king of Zobah, in the vicinity of Hamath, when he went to set up his monument at^a the Euphrates River. ⁴David captured a thousand of his chariots, seven thousand charioteers and twenty thousand foot soldiers. He hamstrung all but a hundred of the chariot horses.

⁵When the Arameans of Damascus came to help Hadadezer king of Zobah, David struck down twenty-two thousand of them. ⁶He put garrisons in the Aramean kingdom of Damascus, and the Arameans became subject to him and brought him tribute. The LORD gave David victory wherever he went.

⁷David took the gold shields carried by the officers of Hadadezer and brought them to Jerusalem. ⁸From Tebah^b and Kun, towns that belonged to Hadadezer, David took a great quantity of bronze, which Solomon used to make the bronze Sea, the pillars and various bronze articles.

⁹When Tou king of Hamath heard that David had defeated the entire army of Hadadezer king of Zobah, ¹⁰he sent his son Hadoram to King David to greet him and congratulate him on his victory in battle over Hadadezer, who had been at war with Tou. Hadoram brought all kinds of articles of gold, of silver and of bronze.

¹¹King David dedicated these articles to the LORD, as he had done with the silver and gold he had taken from all these nations: Edom and Moab, the Ammonites and the Philistines, and Amalek.

¹²Abishai son of Zeruiah struck down eighteen thousand Edomites in the Valley of Salt. ¹³He put garrisons in Edom, and all the Edomites became subject to David. The LORD gave David victory wherever he went.

David's Officials

18:14-17pp — 2Sa 8:15-18

¹⁴David reigned over all Israel, doing what was just and right for all his people. ¹⁵Joab son of Zeruiah was over the army; Jehoshaphat son of Ahilud was recorder; ¹⁶Zadok son of Ahitub and Ahimelek^c son of Abiathar were priests; Shavsha was secretary; ¹⁷Benaiah son of Jehoiada was over the Kerethites and Pelethites; and David's sons were chief officials at the king's side.

David Defeats the Ammonites

19:1-19pp — 2Sa 10:1-19

19 In the course of time, Nahash king of the Ammonites died, and his son succeeded him as king. ²David thought, "I will show kindness to Hanun son of Nahash, because his father showed kindness to me." So David sent a delegation to express his sympathy to Hanun concerning his father.

When David's envoys came to Hanun in the land of the Ammonites to express sympathy to him, ³the Ammonite commanders said to Hanun, "Do you think David is honoring your father

---

^a 3 Or *to restore his control over*   ^b 8 Hebrew *Tibhath,* a variant of *Tebah*   ^c 16 Some Hebrew manuscripts, Vulgate and Syriac (see also 2 Samuel 8:17); most Hebrew manuscripts *Abimelek*

18:1 the Philistines See note on 1Sa 4:1. **Gath** A Philistine city.

18:2 Moabites See note on 2Sa 8:2. See the table "Battles of Saul and David" on p. 433. **tribute** A payment made by a defeated people in exchange for peace.

18:3 set up his monument See 2Sa 8:3 and note.

18:4 He hamstrung all This would prevent them from being used in battle again.

18:6 garrisons By leaving soldiers in the region, David aimed to prevent rebellion.

18:9 Tou king of Hamath Tou is an alternate form of Toi (2Sa 8:9). Hamath was located about 120 miles north of Damascus on the Orontes River.

18:12 Abishai The account in Samuel says that David, not Abishai, struck down the 18,000 Edomites (2Sa 8:13).

18:15 Joab See note on 2Sa 2:13.

18:16 Zadok son of Ahitub and Ahimelek son of Abiathar This verse and 1Ch 24:6 appear to follow 2Sa 8:17 in identifying David's co-high priests as Zadok and Ahimelek. However, this detail conflicts with references throughout 1–2 Samuel and 1–2 Kings that identify David's priests as Zadok and Abiathar. See note on 2Sa 8:17.

18:17 Kerethites and Pelethites See note on 1Ki 1:38.

19:1–19 This chapter describes another military victory; the parallel account appears in 2Sa 10:1–19. 1–2 Chronicles skips the story of David's kindness to

Saul's grandson, Mephibosheth (2Sa 9:1–13), having stated earlier that Saul's entire house had died (see 1Ch 10:6 and note).

19:1 Nahash king of the Ammonites See note on 1Sa 11:1. The Ammonites were distant relatives of the Israelites (Ge 19:38) and had a history of conflict with them.

AMMONITES
The Ammonites were descendants of Ben-Ammi (Lot's son with his younger daughter; Ge 19:30–38) and lived on the eastern side of the Jordan River. Their territory essentially was surrounded by the Jabbok River and its tributaries. The earliest report of hostilities between Ammon and Israel comes in Jdg 3:12–14, where the Ammonites join the coalition formed by Eglon, king of Moab. Jephthah later defeats an unnamed king of Ammon (Jdg 11). Solomon wrongfully built a sanctuary for Molek, the chief god of the Ammonites, on the Mount of Olives (1Ki 11:7). Child sacrifice was a significant part of the Ammonite religion (Lev 18:21; 20:2–5; 2Ki 23:10; Jer 32:35).

by sending envoys to you to express sympathy? Haven't his envoys come to you only to explore and spy out the country and overthrow it?" ⁴So Hanun seized David's envoys, shaved them, cut off their garments at the buttocks, and sent them away.

⁵When someone came and told David about the men, he sent messengers to meet them, for they were greatly humiliated. The king said, "Stay at Jericho till your beards have grown, and then come back."

⁶When the Ammonites realized that they had become obnoxious to David, Hanun and the Ammonites sent a thousand talents*ᵃ* of silver to hire chariots and charioteers from Aram Naharaim,*ᵇ* Aram Maakah and Zobah. ⁷They hired thirty-two thousand chariots and charioteers, as well as the king of Maakah with his troops, who came and camped near Medeba, while the Ammonites were mustered from their towns and moved out for battle.

⁸On hearing this, David sent Joab out with the entire army of fighting men. ⁹The Ammonites came out and drew up in battle formation at the entrance to their city, while the kings who had come were by themselves in the open country.

¹⁰Joab saw that there were battle lines in front of him and behind him; so he selected some of the best troops in Israel and deployed them against the Arameans. ¹¹He put the rest of the men under the command of Abishai his brother, and they were deployed against the Ammonites. ¹²Joab said, "If the Arameans are too strong for me, then you are to rescue me; but if the Ammonites are too strong for you, then I will rescue you. ¹³Be strong, and let us fight bravely for our people and the cities of our God. The Lᴏʀᴅ will do what is good in his sight."

¹⁴Then Joab and the troops with him advanced to fight the Arameans, and they fled before him. ¹⁵When the Ammonites realized that the Arameans were fleeing, they too fled before his brother Abishai and went inside the city. So Joab went back to Jerusalem.

¹⁶After the Arameans saw that they had been routed by Israel, they sent messengers and had Arameans brought from beyond the Euphrates River, with Shophak the commander of Hadadezer's army leading them.

¹⁷When David was told of this, he gathered all Israel and crossed the Jordan; he advanced against them and formed his battle lines opposite them. David formed his lines to meet the Arameans in battle, and they fought against him. ¹⁸But they fled before Israel, and David killed seven thousand of their charioteers and forty thousand of their foot soldiers. He also killed Shophak the commander of their army.

¹⁹When the vassals of Hadadezer saw that they had been routed by Israel, they made peace with David and became subject to him.

So the Arameans were not willing to help the Ammonites anymore.

The Capture of Rabbah

20:1-3pp — 2Sa 11:1; 12:29-31

20 In the spring, at the time when kings go off to war, Joab led out the armed forces. He laid waste the land of the Ammonites and went to Rabbah and besieged it, but David remained in Jerusalem. Joab attacked Rabbah and left it in ruins. ²David took the crown from the head of their king*ᶜ* — its weight was found to be a talent*ᵈ* of gold, and it was set with precious stones — and it was placed on David's head. He took a great quantity of plunder from the city ³and brought out the people who were there, consigning them to labor with saws and with iron picks and axes. David did this to all the Ammonite towns. Then David and his entire army returned to Jerusalem.

ᵃ 6 That is, about 38 tons or about 34 metric tons   *ᵇ* 6 That is, Northwest Mesopotamia   *ᶜ* 2 Or *of Milkom,* that is, Molek
ᵈ 2 That is, about 75 pounds or about 34 kilograms

19:4 shaved them The Samuel account states that he shaved half their beards — a way of humiliating one's enemies (2Sa 10:4). **cut off their garments at the buttocks** Leaving them naked from the hips down. This type of shaming was used for prisoners of war (Isa 20:4).
19:5 Stay at Jericho See 2Sa 10:5 and note.
19:6 a thousand talents of silver A talent was about 75 pounds (34 kilograms). **Aram Naharaim, Aram Maakah and Zobah** These mercenary fighters, from north of Israel, also were David's vassals (1Ch 18:3–8).
19:7 camped near Medeba Located east of the Dead Sea, about 20 miles south of Ammon's capital.
19:8 fighting men See 11:10–47.
19:9 at the entrance to their city Most likely the Ammonite capital of Rabbah, located about 24 miles east of the Jordan River at modern-day Amman, Jordan.
19:16 Hadadezer's army David had already defeated Hadadezer once (18:3–8). See the table "Battles of Saul and David" on p. 433.

19:19 the vassals of Hadadezer Probably small city-states.

20:1–3 In the Samuel account, the battles against Ammon are broken up by the story of David's sin with Bathsheba (2Sa 11–12), which 1–2 Chronicles omits. That episode in David's life would have been well-known to the Chronicler and his audience; however, this book focuses on themes of faithfulness to Yahweh, national unity and proper temple worship (see note on 1Ch 1:1 — 9:44).

20:1 the time when kings go off to war Military campaigns typically were waged during the spring, because the weather was good and provisions were plentiful. **David remained in Jerusalem** An allusion to David's affair with Bathsheba, which occurred while his army was besieging Rabbah (2Sa 11:2—12:23).
20:2 David took the crown When Joab was close to taking Rabbah, he sent for David to join the battle (2Sa

War With the Philistines

20:4-8pp — 2Sa 21:15-22

⁴In the course of time, war broke out with the Philistines, at Gezer. At that time Sibbekai the Hushathite killed Sippai, one of the descendants of the Rephaites, and the Philistines were subjugated.

⁵In another battle with the Philistines, Elhanan son of Jair killed Lahmi the brother of Goliath the Gittite, who had a spear with a shaft like a weaver's rod.

⁶In still another battle, which took place at Gath, there was a huge man with six fingers on each hand and six toes on each foot — twenty-four in all. He also was descended from Rapha. ⁷When he taunted Israel, Jonathan son of Shimea, David's brother, killed him.

⁸These were descendants of Rapha in Gath, and they fell at the hands of David and his men.

David Counts the Fighting Men

21:1-26pp — 2Sa 24:1-25

21 Satan rose up against Israel and incited David to take a census of Israel. ²So David said to Joab and the commanders of the troops, "Go and count the Israelites from Beersheba to Dan. Then report back to me so that I may know how many there are."

³But Joab replied, "May the LORD multiply his troops a hundred times over. My lord the king, are they not all my lord's subjects? Why does my lord want to do this? Why should he bring guilt on Israel?"

⁴The king's word, however, overruled Joab; so Joab left and went throughout Israel and then came back to Jerusalem. ⁵Joab reported the number of the fighting men to David: In all Israel there were one million one hundred thousand men who could handle a sword, including four hundred and seventy thousand in Judah.

⁶But Joab did not include Levi and Benjamin in the numbering, because the king's command was repulsive to him. ⁷This command was also evil in the sight of God; so he punished Israel.

⁸Then David said to God, "I have sinned greatly by doing this. Now, I beg you, take away the guilt of your servant. I have done a very foolish thing."

⁹The LORD said to Gad, David's seer, ¹⁰"Go and tell David, 'This is what the LORD says: I am giving you three options. Choose one of them for me to carry out against you.'"

¹¹So Gad went to David and said to him, "This is what the LORD says: 'Take your choice: ¹²three years of famine, three months of being swept away*a* before your enemies, with their swords overtaking you, or three days of the sword of the LORD — days of plague in the land, with the angel of the LORD ravaging every part of Israel.' Now then, decide how I should answer the one who sent me."

¹³David said to Gad, "I am in deep distress. Let me fall into the hands of the LORD, for his mercy is very great; but do not let me fall into human hands."

¹⁴So the LORD sent a plague on Israel, and seventy thousand men of Israel fell dead. ¹⁵And God sent an angel to destroy Jerusalem. But as the angel

---

a 12 Hebrew; Septuagint and Vulgate (see also 2 Samuel 24:13) *of fleeing*

12:27 – 29). See the table "Battles of Saul and David" on p. 433. **a talent of gold** About 75 pounds (34 kilograms).

20:4 – 8 Compare 2Sa 21:18 – 22. The Chronicler skips the events of 2Sa 13:1 — 21:17.

20:4 with the Philistines See note on 1Sa 4:1. **descendants of the Rephaites** The Hebrew text describes Sippai as belonging to the Rephaim, a term sometimes translated as "giants" (see note on Dt 3:11).

21:1 — 22:1 The Chronicler presents the account of David's census and God's punishment with several notable differences from the account in 2Sa 24:1 – 25 (see note on 2Sa 24:1; note on 24:10). The most significant variation is that the episode in 1 – 2 Chronicles leads to David's purchase of the temple site (1Ch 21:28 — 22:1).

21:1 Satan rose up against Israel The Hebrew word used here, *satan*, means "accuser" or "adversary." In this instance, the term could refer to an anonymous human adversary (e.g., Nu 22:22,32; 1Sa 29:4; Ps 109:6). Alternatively, it could function as a proper noun and refer to the accuser of the divine court — identified in later tradition as the devil, the enemy of God (e.g., Job 1 – 2; Zec 3:1 – 2). The account in Samuel says that Yahweh's anger is what incites David to take a census (2Sa 24:1).

21:2 from Beersheba to Dan Refers to all of Israel, from south to north.

21:3 guilt It is not clear why the census would incur guilt, or why Joab would be repulsed by the command (1Ch 21:6). See note on v. 7.

21:5 men who could handle a sword This suggests David took the census to assess his military strength.

21:6 did not include Levi and Benjamin Joab excludes the tribe of Levi because it was exempt from military service (Nu 1:47 – 50). His reason for excluding Benjamin is less certain. It might have been because the tabernacle was located in Benjamin, at Gibeon (1Ch 21:29).

21:7 evil in the sight of God The reason for Yahweh's objection to the census is not clear. It is possible that David's apparent motivation — to evaluate his military strength (v. 5) — was the issue. Another possibility is that the census was conducted in a way that violated the law. According to Ex 30:11 – 16, a census should include a half shekel "ransom" for each person; perhaps David ignored this stipulation.

21:9 Gad Advised David when he was fleeing from Saul (1Sa 22:5).

21:13 mercy The Hebrew term used here, *rachamim*, refers to God's deeply felt compassion. It often occurs in passages that refer to God's forgiveness or redemption (Ps 51:1; 103:4; Isa 54:7).

21:15 threshing floor See note on Ru 3:2. See the infographic "A Threshing Floor" on p. 497. **Araunah the Jebusite** The Hebrew name "Ornan" reflects a different

was doing so, the Lord saw it and relented concerning the disaster and said to the angel who was destroying the people, "Enough! Withdraw your hand." The angel of the Lord was then standing at the threshing floor of Araunah[a] the Jebusite.

¹⁶David looked up and saw the angel of the Lord standing between heaven and earth, with a drawn sword in his hand extended over Jerusalem. Then David and the elders, clothed in sackcloth, fell facedown.

¹⁷David said to God, "Was it not I who ordered the fighting men to be counted? I, the shepherd,[b] have sinned and done wrong. These are but sheep. What have they done? Lord my God, let your hand fall on me and my family, but do not let this plague remain on your people."

David Builds an Altar

¹⁸Then the angel of the Lord ordered Gad to tell David to go up and build an altar to the Lord on the threshing floor of Araunah the Jebusite. ¹⁹So David went up in obedience to the word that Gad had spoken in the name of the Lord.

²⁰While Araunah was threshing wheat, he turned and saw the angel; his four sons who were with him hid themselves. ²¹Then David approached, and when Araunah looked and saw him, he left the threshing floor and bowed down before David with his face to the ground.

²²David said to him, "Let me have the site of your threshing floor so I can build an altar to the Lord, that the plague on the people may be stopped. Sell it to me at the full price."

²³Araunah said to David, "Take it! Let my lord the king do whatever pleases him. Look, I will give the oxen for the burnt offerings, the threshing sledges for the wood, and the wheat for the grain offering. I will give all this."

²⁴But King David replied to Araunah, "No, I insist on paying the full price. I will not take for the Lord what is yours, or sacrifice a burnt offering that costs me nothing."

²⁵So David paid Araunah six hundred shekels[c] of gold for the site. ²⁶David built an altar to the Lord there and sacrificed burnt offerings and fellowship offerings. He called on the Lord, and the Lord answered him with fire from heaven on the altar of burnt offering.

²⁷Then the Lord spoke to the angel, and he put his sword back into its sheath. ²⁸At that time, when David saw that the Lord had answered him on the threshing floor of Araunah the Jebusite, he offered sacrifices there. ²⁹The tabernacle of the Lord, which Moses had made in the wilderness, and the altar of burnt offering were at that time on the high place at Gibeon. ³⁰But David could not go before it to inquire of God, because he was afraid of the sword of the angel of the Lord.

22 Then David said, "The house of the Lord God is to be here, and also the altar of burnt offering for Israel."

Preparations for the Temple

²So David gave orders to assemble the foreigners residing in Israel, and from among them he appointed stonecutters to prepare dressed stone for building the house of God. ³He provided a large amount of iron to make nails for the doors of the gateways and for the fittings, and more bronze than could be weighed. ⁴He also provided more cedar logs than could be counted, for the Sidonians and Tyrians had brought large numbers of them to David.

⁵David said, "My son Solomon is young and inexperienced, and the house to be built for the Lord should be of great magnificence and fame and splendor in the sight of all the nations. Therefore I will make preparations for it." So David made extensive preparations before his death.

⁶Then he called for his son Solomon and charged him to build a house for the Lord, the God of Isra-

---

a 15 Hebrew *Ornan*, a variant of *Araunah*; also in verses 18-28
b 17 Probable reading of the original Hebrew text (see 2 Samuel 24:17 and note); Masoretic Text does not have *the shepherd*.
c 25 That is, about 15 pounds or about 6.9 kilograms

---

spelling of "Araunah," which appears in the Hebrew text of 2Sa 24. The Jebusites were Jerusalem's previous inhabitants, whom David had defeated (1Ch 11:4–9).
21:16 angel of the Lord See note on Ps 34:7. See the table "Angels in the Bible" on p. 2120. **clothed in sackcloth** A sign of mourning (see note on Job 16:15).
21:17 These are but sheep Refers to the people of Israel. See note on 1Sa 9:3.
21:26 fire from heaven Fire often symbolizes Yahweh's presence (Ex 3:2; 19:18; Lev 9:24; 2Ch 7:3) or divine approval (Jdg 6:21; 2Ch 7:1) or divine judgment (Nu 11:1; 16:35). Here, it likely indicates Yahweh's approval of David's sacrifice.
22:1 house of the Lord God The story of David's census segues into his preparations for the temple (1Ch 22:2–29:31). Because God answered his prayers and sacrifices at Araunah's (Ornan) threshing floor, David chooses this site for the future temple (2Ch 3:1).

22:2–5 First Chronicles 22–29 describe David's preparations for the temple. This material is unique to 1–2 Chronicles, and the degree of detail shows the Chronicler's emphasis on establishing temple worship.
22:2 foreigners The Hebrew term used here, *ger*, typically refers to a non-Israelite who is living peaceably in Israel (Lev 19:34). Here it seems to refer to foreign forced-laborers (2Sa 20:24).
22:4 Sidonians and Tyrians See 1Ki 5:6 and note.
22:5 fame and splendor The temple needed to be great because it was the earthly representation of God's heavenly dwelling, representing his sovereignty.
22:6–19 In this speech to Solomon, David charges him with building the temple. He explains why he did not build the temple himself (1Ch 22:7–10) and encourages Solomon to remain faithful to the law (vv. 11–13). He

el. [7]David said to Solomon: "My son, I had it in my heart to build a house for the Name of the LORD my God. [8]But this word of the LORD came to me: 'You have shed much blood and have fought many wars. You are not to build a house for my Name, because you have shed much blood on the earth in my sight. [9]But you will have a son who will be a man of peace and rest, and I will give him rest from all his enemies on every side. His name will be Solomon,[a] and I will grant Israel peace and quiet during his reign. [10]He is the one who will build a house for my Name. He will be my son, and I will be his father. And I will establish the throne of his kingdom over Israel forever.'

[11]"Now, my son, the LORD be with you, and may you have success and build the house of the LORD your God, as he said you would. [12]May the LORD give you discretion and understanding when he puts you in command over Israel, so that you may keep the law of the LORD your God. [13]Then you will have success if you are careful to observe the decrees and laws that the LORD gave Moses for Israel. Be strong and courageous. Do not be afraid or discouraged.

[14]"I have taken great pains to provide for the temple of the LORD a hundred thousand talents[b] of gold, a million talents[c] of silver, quantities of bronze and iron too great to be weighed, and wood and stone. And you may add to them. [15]You have many workers: stonecutters, masons and carpenters, as well as those skilled in every kind of work [16]in gold and silver, bronze and iron — craftsmen beyond number. Now begin the work, and the LORD be with you."

[17]Then David ordered all the leaders of Israel to help his son Solomon. [18]He said to them, "Is not the LORD your God with you? And has he not granted you rest on every side? For he has given the inhabitants of the land into my hands, and the land is subject to the LORD and to his people. [19]Now devote your heart and soul to seeking the LORD your God. Begin to build the sanctuary of the LORD God, so that you may bring the ark of the covenant of the LORD and the sacred articles belonging to God into the temple that will be built for the Name of the LORD."

The Levites

23 When David was old and full of years, he made his son Solomon king over Israel. [2]He also gathered together all the leaders of Israel, as well as the priests and Levites. [3]The Levites thirty years old or more were counted, and the total number of men was thirty-eight thousand. [4]David said, "Of these, twenty-four thousand are to be in charge of the work of the temple of the LORD and six thousand are to be officials and judges. [5]Four thousand are to be gatekeepers and four thousand are to praise the LORD with the musical instruments I have provided for that purpose."

[6]David separated the Levites into divisions corresponding to the sons of Levi: Gershon, Kohath and Merari.

Gershonites

[7]Belonging to the Gershonites:
  Ladan and Shimei.
[8]The sons of Ladan:
  Jehiel the first, Zetham and Joel — three in all.
[9]The sons of Shimei:
  Shelomoth, Haziel and Haran — three in all.
  These were the heads of the families of Ladan.

---

[a] 9 *Solomon* sounds like and may be derived from the Hebrew for *peace.*   [b] 14 That is, about 3,750 tons or about 3,400 metric tons
[c] 14 That is, about 37,500 tons or about 34,000 metric tons

---

notes the preparations he has made (vv. 14–16) and charges all of Israel's leaders to help Solomon and seek God (vv. 17–19).

22:6 Solomon David's son by Bathsheba (2Sa 12:24). See note on 2Ch 1:1.
22:8 shed much blood David explains that God objected to David building the temple because David was a man of war. See note on 1Ki 5:3.
22:9 peace and quiet The Hebrew word for peace, *shalom,* is very similar to Solomon's name in Hebrew, *shelomoh.*
22:10 build a house Yahweh's statement here envisions the fulfillment of his promise to establish David's kingdom. See 1Ch 17:1–15.
22:13 Be strong and courageous David's charge to Solomon shares many similarities with God's commission of Joshua. Both men are encouraged to be strong and courageous, and both are told to not be afraid or dismayed (Jos 1:6,9). Like Joshua, Solomon is encouraged to keep the law and is promised success if he is faithful (1Ch 22:12; Jos 1:7–8).

22:14 a hundred thousand talents of gold An exceptionally large amount. Solomon's annual tribute as king was only 666 talents of gold (2Ch 9:13).

23:1—26:32 The Chronicler describes David's preparations in great detail. Not only does he provide the materials for constructing the temple (1Ch 22:2–5), but he also prepares the personnel to minister in the temple. He organizes the Levites (23:1–32), the priests (24:1–30), the musicians (25:1–31), the gatekeepers (26:1–19), and the treasurers and other officials (26:20–32). By highlighting David's planning, the Chronicler shows the importance of the temple, not just as a building, but as a place to worship Yahweh.

23:1 he made his son Solomon king See 29:22 and note.
23:3 thirty years old The law stipulated 30 as the age for service (Nu 4:3,23,30).
23:6 the sons of Levi The major Levitical clans are descended from three brothers: Gershon, Kohath and Merari (see note on Nu 26:57).

10 And the sons of Shimei:

Jahath, Ziza,[a] Jeush and Beriah.

These were the sons of Shimei—four in all.

11 Jahath was the first and Ziza the second, but Jeush and Beriah did not have many sons; so they were counted as one family with one assignment.

Kohathites

12 The sons of Kohath:

Amram, Izhar, Hebron and Uzziel—four in all.

13 The sons of Amram:

Aaron and Moses.

Aaron was set apart, he and his descendants forever, to consecrate the most holy things, to offer sacrifices before the LORD, to minister before him and to pronounce blessings in his name forever. 14 The sons of Moses the man of God were counted as part of the tribe of Levi.

15 The sons of Moses:

Gershom and Eliezer.

16 The descendants of Gershom:

Shubael was the first.

17 The descendants of Eliezer:

Rehabiah was the first.

Eliezer had no other sons, but the sons of Rehabiah were very numerous.

18 The sons of Izhar:

Shelomith was the first.

19 The sons of Hebron:

Jeriah the first, Amariah the second, Jahaziel the third and Jekameam the fourth.

20 The sons of Uzziel:

Micah the first and Ishiah the second.

Merarites

21 The sons of Merari:

Mahli and Mushi.

The sons of Mahli:

Eleazar and Kish.

22 Eleazar died without having sons: he had only daughters. Their cousins, the sons of Kish, married them.

23 The sons of Mushi:

Mahli, Eder and Jerimoth—three in all.

24 These were the descendants of Levi by their families—the heads of families as they were registered under their names and counted individually, that is, the workers twenty years old or more who served in the temple of the LORD. 25 For David had said, "Since the LORD, the God of Israel, has granted rest to his people and has come to dwell in Jerusalem forever, 26 the Levites no longer need to carry the tabernacle or any of the articles used in its service." 27 According to the last instructions of David, the Levites were counted from those twenty years old or more.

28 The duty of the Levites was to help Aaron's descendants in the service of the temple of the LORD: to be in charge of the courtyards, the side rooms, the purification of all sacred things and the performance of other duties at the house of God. 29 They were in charge of the bread set out on the table, the special flour for the grain offerings, the thin loaves made without yeast, the baking and the mixing, and all measurements of quantity and size. 30 They were also to stand every morning to thank and praise the LORD. They were to do the same in the evening 31 and whenever burnt offerings were presented to the LORD on the Sabbaths, at the New Moon feasts and at the appointed festivals. They were to serve before the LORD regularly in the proper number and in the way prescribed for them.

32 And so the Levites carried out their responsibilities for the tent of meeting, for the Holy Place and, under their relatives the descendants of Aaron, for the service of the temple of the LORD.

The Divisions of Priests

24 These were the divisions of the descendants of Aaron:

The sons of Aaron were Nadab, Abihu, Eleazar and Ithamar. 2 But Nadab and Abihu died before their father did, and they had no sons; so Eleazar and Ithamar served as the priests. 3 With the help of Zadok a descendant of Eleazar and Ahimelek a descendant of Ithamar, David separated them into divisions for their appointed order of ministering. 4 A larger number of leaders were found among Eleazar's descendants than among Ithamar's, and they were divided accordingly: sixteen heads of fami-

---

[a] 10 One Hebrew manuscript, Septuagint and Vulgate (see also verse 11); most Hebrew manuscripts *Zina*

23:24 twenty years old Earlier, David had numbered the Levites 30 years and older (1Ch 23:3). The OT gives different ages for Levitical service; see Nu 8:24 and note.
23:26 to carry the tabernacle The Levites were responsible for transporting the structural components and furnishings of the tabernacle, including the ark of the covenant (Nu 4).
23:29 bread set out on the table See Ex 25:30 and note. **grain offerings** See Lev 2:1 and note.
23:30 to thank and praise Probably associated with the daily sacrifices (Ex 29:35–42).
23:31 Sabbaths, at the New Moon feasts See note

on Isa 1:13; note on Isa 1:14. See the table "Israelite Festivals" on p. 200.
23:32 carried out their responsibilities See Nu 3:7 and note.

24:1–31 The Chronicler continues describing David's preparations for temple worship (see note on 1Ch 23:1—26:32). Here, David organizes the priests, who were responsible for religious duties associated with the temple (Ex 28:1–43 and note). He organizes them into 24 divisions.

24:2 Nadab and Abihu See Lev 10:1 and note.

lies from Eleazar's descendants and eight heads of families from Ithamar's descendants. [5]They divided them impartially by casting lots, for there were officials of the sanctuary and officials of God among the descendants of both Eleazar and Ithamar.

[6]The scribe Shemaiah son of Nethanel, a Levite, recorded their names in the presence of the king and of the officials: Zadok the priest, Ahimelek son of Abiathar and the heads of families of the priests and of the Levites — one family being taken from Eleazar and then one from Ithamar.

[7]The first lot fell to Jehoiarib,
the second to Jedaiah,
[8]the third to Harim,
the fourth to Seorim,
[9]the fifth to Malkijah,
the sixth to Mijamin,
[10]the seventh to Hakkoz,
the eighth to Abijah,
[11]the ninth to Jeshua,
the tenth to Shekaniah,
[12]the eleventh to Eliashib,
the twelfth to Jakim,
[13]the thirteenth to Huppah,
the fourteenth to Jeshebeab,
[14]the fifteenth to Bilgah,
the sixteenth to Immer,
[15]the seventeenth to Hezir,
the eighteenth to Happizzez,
[16]the nineteenth to Pethahiah,
the twentieth to Jehezkel,
[17]the twenty-first to Jakin,
the twenty-second to Gamul,
[18]the twenty-third to Delaiah
and the twenty-fourth to Maaziah.

[19]This was their appointed order of ministering when they entered the temple of the LORD, according to the regulations prescribed for them by their ancestor Aaron, as the LORD, the God of Israel, had commanded him.

The Rest of the Levites

[20]As for the rest of the descendants of Levi:
from the sons of Amram: Shubael;
from the sons of Shubael: Jehdeiah.

[21]As for Rehabiah, from his sons:
Ishiah was the first.
[22]From the Izharites: Shelomoth;
from the sons of Shelomoth: Jahath.
[23]The sons of Hebron: Jeriah the first,[a] Amariah the second, Jahaziel the third and Jekameam the fourth.
[24]The son of Uzziel: Micah;
from the sons of Micah: Shamir.
[25]The brother of Micah: Ishiah;
from the sons of Ishiah: Zechariah.
[26]The sons of Merari: Mahli and Mushi.
The son of Jaaziah: Beno.
[27]The sons of Merari:
from Jaaziah: Beno, Shoham, Zakkur and Ibri.
[28]From Mahli: Eleazar, who had no sons.
[29]From Kish: the son of Kish:
Jerahmeel.
[30]And the sons of Mushi: Mahli, Eder and Jerimoth.

These were the Levites, according to their families. [31]They also cast lots, just as their relatives the descendants of Aaron did, in the presence of King David and of Zadok, Ahimelek, and the heads of families of the priests and of the Levites. The families of the oldest brother were treated the same as those of the youngest.

The Musicians

25 David, together with the commanders of the army, set apart some of the sons of Asaph, Heman and Jeduthun for the ministry of prophesying, accompanied by harps, lyres and cymbals. Here is the list of the men who performed this service:

[2]From the sons of Asaph:
Zakkur, Joseph, Nethaniah and Asarelah. The sons of Asaph were under the supervision of Asaph, who prophesied under the king's supervision.

---

[a] 23 Two Hebrew manuscripts and some Septuagint manuscripts (see also 23:19); most Hebrew manuscripts *The sons of Jeriah:*

24:5 They divided them impartially by casting lots Casting lots was a common way of determining God's will. Here, it would ensure that David did not give any families preferential treatment. See note on Ne 11:1.
24:6 Zadok the priest, Ahimelek son of Abiathar This verse and 1Ch 18:16 appear to follow 2Sa 8:17 in identifying David's co-high priests as Zadok and Ahimelek. However, this detail conflicts with references throughout 1–2 Samuel and 1–2 Kings that identify David's priests as Zadok and Abiathar. See note on 2Sa 8:17.
24:19 by their ancestor Aaron The Chronicler indicates that, although David is organizing the priests, he is not determining their duties, which were prescribed by God's commands to Aaron (e.g., Ex 29–30; Lev 1–7).

25:1–31 David now organizes the temple musicians into 24 divisions, just as he did the priests (1Ch 24). While David organized the Levites and priests so they could fulfill their duties as spelled out in the law (23:28–31; 24:19), there were no instructions in the law regarding musicians. According to 2Ch 29:25, God commanded David about the musicians through the prophets Gad and Nathan.

25:1 Asaph Leading musician for the ark's procession into Jerusalem (1Ch 16:5). See note on Ps 73:title.
Heman Grandson of the prophet Samuel (1Ch 6:33).
Jeduthun Associated with three of psalms (Ps 39:title; 62:title; 77:title).

3 As for Jeduthun, from his sons:

Gedaliah, Zeri, Jeshaiah, Shimei,[a] Hashabiah and Mattithiah, six in all, under the supervision of their father Jeduthun, who prophesied, using the harp in thanking and praising the LORD.

4 As for Heman, from his sons:

Bukkiah, Mattaniah, Uzziel, Shubael and Jerimoth; Hananiah, Hanani, Eliathah, Giddalti and Romamti-Ezer; Joshbekashah, Mallothi, Hothir and Mahazioth. 5 (All these were sons of Heman the king's seer. They were given him through the promises of God to exalt him. God gave Heman fourteen sons and three daughters.)

6 All these men were under the supervision of their father for the music of the temple of the LORD, with cymbals, lyres and harps, for the ministry at the house of God.

Asaph, Jeduthun and Heman were under the supervision of the king. 7 Along with their relatives — all of them trained and skilled in music for the LORD — they numbered 288. 8 Young and old alike, teacher as well as student, cast lots for their duties.

9 The first lot, which was for Asaph,
fell to Joseph,
his sons and relatives[b]   12[c]
the second to Gedaliah,
him and his relatives and sons   12
10 the third to Zakkur,
his sons and relatives   12
11 the fourth to Izri,[d]
his sons and relatives   12
12 the fifth to Nethaniah,
his sons and relatives   12
13 the sixth to Bukkiah,
his sons and relatives   12
14 the seventh to Jesarelah,[e]
his sons and relatives   12
15 the eighth to Jeshaiah,
his sons and relatives   12
16 the ninth to Mattaniah,
his sons and relatives   12
17 the tenth to Shimei,
his sons and relatives   12
18 the eleventh to Azarel,[f]
his sons and relatives   12
19 the twelfth to Hashabiah,
his sons and relatives   12
20 the thirteenth to Shubael,
his sons and relatives   12
21 the fourteenth to Mattithiah,
his sons and relatives   12

22 the fifteenth to Jerimoth,
his sons and relatives   12
23 the sixteenth to Hananiah,
his sons and relatives   12
24 the seventeenth to Joshbekashah,
his sons and relatives   12
25 the eighteenth to Hanani,
his sons and relatives   12
26 the nineteenth to Mallothi,
his sons and relatives   12
27 the twentieth to Eliathah,
his sons and relatives   12
28 the twenty-first to Hothir,
his sons and relatives   12
29 the twenty-second to Giddalti,
his sons and relatives   12
30 the twenty-third to Mahazioth,
his sons and relatives   12
31 the twenty-fourth to Romamti-Ezer,
his sons and relatives   12.

The Gatekeepers

26 The divisions of the gatekeepers:

From the Korahites: Meshelemiah son of Kore, one of the sons of Asaph.

2 Meshelemiah had sons:
Zechariah the firstborn,
Jediael the second,
Zebadiah the third,
Jathniel the fourth,
3 Elam the fifth,
Jehohanan the sixth
and Eliehoenai the seventh.
4 Obed-Edom also had sons:
Shemaiah the firstborn,
Jehozabad the second,
Joah the third,
Sakar the fourth,
Nethanel the fifth,
5 Ammiel the sixth,
Issachar the seventh
and Peullethai the eighth.
(For God had blessed Obed-Edom.)

6 Obed-Edom's son Shemaiah also had sons, who were leaders in their father's family because they were very capable men. 7 The sons of Shemaiah: Othni, Rephael, Obed and Elzabad; his relatives Elihu and Sem-

---

a 3 One Hebrew manuscript and some Septuagint manuscripts (see also verse 17); most Hebrew manuscripts do not have *Shimei.*   *b 9* See Septuagint; Hebrew does not have *his sons and relatives.*   *c 9* See the total in verse 7; Hebrew does not have *twelve.*   *d 11* A variant of *Zeri*   *e 14* A variant of *Asarelah*   *f 18* A variant of *Uzziel*

25:5 seer The Hebrew word used here, *chozeh*, is essentially equivalent to the title of prophet (2Sa 24:11).
25:7 they numbered 288 Divided into 24 groups of 12 (1Ch 25:9–31).
25:8 cast lots See note on 24:5.

26:1–19 Continuing with his preparations for the temple, David now divides the gatekeepers and assigns them to specific gates.

26:1 gatekeepers Responsible for guarding the temple

akiah were also able men. [8]All these were descendants of Obed-Edom; they and their sons and their relatives were capable men with the strength to do the work — descendants of Obed-Edom, 62 in all.

[9]Meshelemiah had sons and relatives, who were able men — 18 in all.

[10]Hosah the Merarite had sons: Shimri the first (although he was not the firstborn, his father had appointed him the first), [11]Hilkiah the second, Tabaliah the third and Zechariah the fourth. The sons and relatives of Hosah were 13 in all.

[12]These divisions of the gatekeepers, through their leaders, had duties for ministering in the temple of the Lord, just as their relatives had. [13]Lots were cast for each gate, according to their families, young and old alike.

[14]The lot for the East Gate fell to Shelemiah.[a] Then lots were cast for his son Zechariah, a wise counselor, and the lot for the North Gate fell to him. [15]The lot for the South Gate fell to Obed-Edom, and the lot for the storehouse fell to his sons. [16]The lots for the West Gate and the Shalleketh Gate on the upper road fell to Shuppim and Hosah.

Guard was alongside of guard: [17]There were six Levites a day on the east, four a day on the north, four a day on the south and two at a time at the storehouse. [18]As for the court[b] to the west, there were four at the road and two at the court[b] itself.

[19]These were the divisions of the gatekeepers who were descendants of Korah and Merari.

The Treasurers and Other Officials

[20]Their fellow Levites were[c] in charge of the treasuries of the house of God and the treasuries for the dedicated things.

[21]The descendants of Ladan, who were Gershonites through Ladan and who were heads of families belonging to Ladan the Gershonite, were Jehieli, [22]the sons of Jehieli, Zetham and his brother Joel. They were in charge of the treasuries of the temple of the Lord.

[23]From the Amramites, the Izharites, the Hebronites and the Uzzielites:

[24]Shubael, a descendant of Gershom son of Moses, was the official in charge of the treasuries. [25]His relatives through Eliezer: Rehabiah his son, Jeshaiah his son, Joram his son, Zikri his son and Shelomith his son. [26]Shelomith and his relatives were in charge of all the treasuries for the things dedicated by King David, by the heads of families who were the commanders of thousands and commanders of hundreds, and by the other army commanders. [27]Some of the plunder taken in battle they dedicated for the repair of the temple of the Lord. [28]And everything dedicated by Samuel the seer and by Saul son of Kish, Abner son of Ner and Joab son of Zeruiah, and all the other dedicated things were in the care of Shelomith and his relatives.

[29]From the Izharites: Kenaniah and his sons were assigned duties away from the temple, as officials and judges over Israel.

[30]From the Hebronites: Hashabiah and his relatives — seventeen hundred able men — were responsible in Israel west of the Jordan for all the work of the Lord and for the king's service. [31]As for the Hebronites, Jeriah was their chief according to the genealogical records of their families. In the fortieth year of David's reign a search was made in the records, and capable men among the Hebronites were found at Jazer in Gilead. [32]Jeriah had twenty-seven hundred relatives, who were able men and heads of families, and King David put them in charge of the Reubenites, the Gadites and the half-tribe of Manasseh for every matter pertaining to God and for the affairs of the king.

---

[a] 14 A variant of *Meshelemiah* [b] 18 The meaning of the Hebrew for this word is uncertain. [c] 20 Septuagint; Hebrew *As for the Levites, Ahijah was*

---

and preventing unlawful entry (2Ch 23:19; see Nu 3:10 and note). They also collected money (2Ki 12:9–10) and the freewill offering (2Ch 31:14), assisted with some religious duties and participated in purification rites (Ne 12:44).

26:6 capable men The Hebrew phrase used here, *gibbor chayil*, can refer to capability (1Ki 11:28), wealth (2Ki 15:20), bravery (Jdg 6:12) or character (Ru 2:1).

26:14 lot for the East Gate The east gate was known as the "King's Gate" (1Ch 9:18). There were more gatekeepers posted there than at the other gates (vv. 17–18).

26:20–32 The section on temple personnel concludes with a list of treasurers (vv. 20–28) and positions of service outside the temple (vv. 29–32).

26:22 treasuries of the temple of the Lord Probably refers to treasuries at the gatehouses (9:26; 26:15).

26:26 treasuries for the things dedicated Most likely refers to the spoils of war that were dedicated to God (18:11; compare note on Jos 6:17).

26:28 Samuel the seer Prophet and leader of Israel before Saul. See note on 1Sa 1:20. **Saul** Israel's first king (1Ch 10:1–14). **Abner** Saul's cousin and commander of his army (1Sa 14:50). **Joab** Commander of David's army (1Ch 11:6).

26:29 assigned duties away from the temple These officials had both religious and administrative responsibilities.

26:30 in Israel west of the Jordan Refers to all the tribes except those listed in v. 32.

26:32 the Reubenites, the Gadites and the half-tribe of Manasseh These tribes lived east of the Jordan River.

Temple Treasurers and Other Officials
(1Ch 26:20–32)

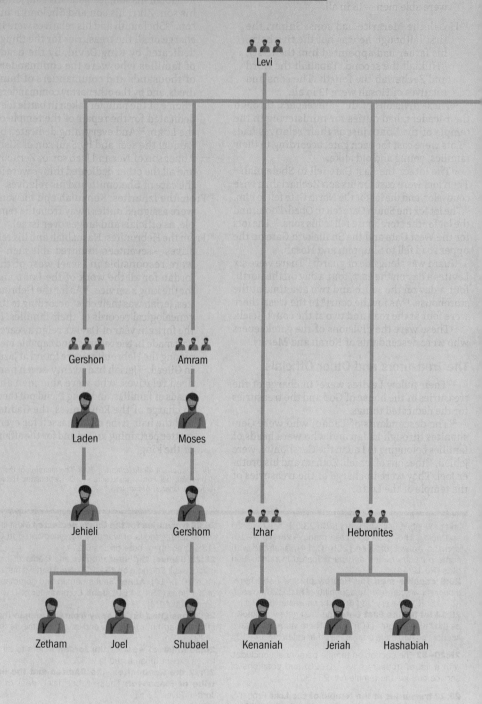

Levi

Gershon

Amram

Laden

Moses

Jehieli

Gershom

Izhar

Hebronites

Zetham

Joel

Shubael

Kenaniah

Jeriah

Hashabiah

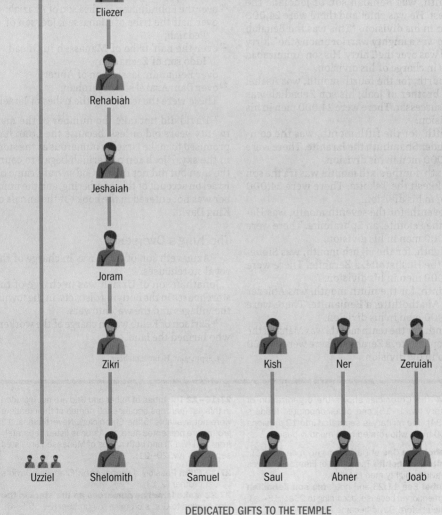

DEDICATED GIFTS TO THE TEMPLE

Army Divisions

27 This is the list of the Israelites — heads of families, commanders of thousands and commanders of hundreds, and their officers, who served the king in all that concerned the army divisions that were on duty month by month throughout the year. Each division consisted of 24,000 men.

² In charge of the first division, for the first month, was Jashobeam son of Zabdiel. There were 24,000 men in his division. ³ He was a descendant of Perez and chief of all the army officers for the first month.
⁴ In charge of the division for the second month was Dodai the Ahohite; Mikloth was the leader of his division. There were 24,000 men in his division.
⁵ The third army commander, for the third month, was Benaiah son of Jehoiada the priest. He was chief and there were 24,000 men in his division. ⁶ This was the Benaiah who was a mighty warrior among the Thirty and was over the Thirty. His son Ammizabad was in charge of his division.
⁷ The fourth, for the fourth month, was Asahel the brother of Joab; his son Zebadiah was his successor. There were 24,000 men in his division.
⁸ The fifth, for the fifth month, was the commander Shamhuth the Izrahite. There were 24,000 men in his division.
⁹ The sixth, for the sixth month, was Ira the son of Ikkesh the Tekoite. There were 24,000 men in his division.
¹⁰ The seventh, for the seventh month, was Helez the Pelonite, an Ephraimite. There were 24,000 men in his division.
¹¹ The eighth, for the eighth month, was Sibbekai the Hushathite, a Zerahite. There were 24,000 men in his division.
¹² The ninth, for the ninth month, was Abiezer the Anathothite, a Benjamite. There were 24,000 men in his division.
¹³ The tenth, for the tenth month, was Maharai the Netophathite, a Zerahite. There were 24,000 men in his division.

¹⁴ The eleventh, for the eleventh month, was Benaiah the Pirathonite, an Ephraimite. There were 24,000 men in his division.
¹⁵ The twelfth, for the twelfth month, was Heldai the Netophathite, from the family of Othniel. There were 24,000 men in his division.

Leaders of the Tribes

¹⁶ The leaders of the tribes of Israel:

over the Reubenites: Eliezer son of Zikri;
over the Simeonites: Shephatiah son of Maakah;
¹⁷ over Levi: Hashabiah son of Kemuel;
over Aaron: Zadok;
¹⁸ over Judah: Elihu, a brother of David;
over Issachar: Omri son of Michael;
¹⁹ over Zebulun: Ishmaiah son of Obadiah;
over Naphtali: Jerimoth son of Azriel;
²⁰ over the Ephraimites: Hoshea son of Azaziah;
over half the tribe of Manasseh: Joel son of Pedaiah;
²¹ over the half-tribe of Manasseh in Gilead: Iddo son of Zechariah;
over Benjamin: Jaasiel son of Abner;
²² over Dan: Azarel son of Jeroham.
These were the leaders of the tribes of Israel.

²³ David did not take the number of the men twenty years old or less, because the LORD had promised to make Israel as numerous as the stars in the sky. ²⁴ Joab son of Zeruiah began to count the men but did not finish. God's wrath came on Israel on account of this numbering, and the number was not entered in the book[a] of the annals of King David.

The King's Overseers

²⁵ Azmaveth son of Adiel was in charge of the royal storehouses.
Jonathan son of Uzziah was in charge of the storehouses in the outlying districts, in the towns, the villages and the watchtowers.
²⁶ Ezri son of Kelub was in charge of the workers who farmed the land.

---

[a] 24 Septuagint; Hebrew *number*

27:1–34 The Chronicler shows the organization of the military (vv. 1–15) and other appointed leaders (vv. 16–34). The military is separated into 12 divisions of 24,000 men, who rotated on a monthly basis.

27:2 Jashobeam One of David's mighty men (11:11).
27:4 Dodai the Ahohite The father of Eleazar, who was one of David's mighty men (11:12).
27:7 Asahel See 11:26 and note. **his son Zebadiah** Probably mentioned because, according to 2Sa 2:18–23, Asahel died before David became king.

27:8–15 The division leaders identified here are listed among David's mighty men in 1Ch 11:27–31.

27:16–22 The tribes of Asher and Gad are not included in this list (perhaps because the names of their leaders were not available to the Chronicler). Nevertheless, 12 groups are presented here, as Aaron is listed separately from Levi (v. 17) and both halves of Manasseh are listed separately (vv. 20–21).

27:18 Elihu Possibly a scribal error; Eliab was David's oldest brother (2:13).
27:23 make Israel as numerous as the stars in the sky Alludes to God's promise to Abraham (Ge 15:5–6).
27:24 began to count A reference to the census David ordered (1Ch 21:1–2). **did not finish** See 21:6 and note. **wrath came on Israel** See note on 21:7. **book of the**

[27] Shimei the Ramathite was in charge of the vineyards.

Zabdi the Shiphmite was in charge of the produce of the vineyards for the wine vats.

[28] Baal-Hanan the Gederite was in charge of the olive and sycamore-fig trees in the western foothills.

Joash was in charge of the supplies of olive oil.

[29] Shitrai the Sharonite was in charge of the herds grazing in Sharon.

Shaphat son of Adlai was in charge of the herds in the valleys.

[30] Obil the Ishmaelite was in charge of the camels.

Jehdeiah the Meronothite was in charge of the donkeys.

[31] Jaziz the Hagrite was in charge of the flocks.

All these were the officials in charge of King David's property.

[32] Jonathan, David's uncle, was a counselor, a man of insight and a scribe. Jehiel son of Hakmoni took care of the king's sons.

[33] Ahithophel was the king's counselor.

Hushai the Arkite was the king's confidant.

[34] Ahithophel was succeeded by Jehoiada son of Benaiah and by Abiathar.

Joab was the commander of the royal army.

David's Plans for the Temple

28 David summoned all the officials of Israel to assemble at Jerusalem: the officers over the tribes, the commanders of the divisions in the service of the king, the commanders of thousands and commanders of hundreds, and the officials in charge of all the property and livestock belonging to the king and his sons, together with the palace officials, the warriors and all the brave fighting men.

[2] King David rose to his feet and said: "Listen to me, my fellow Israelites, my people. I had it in my heart to build a house as a place of rest for the ark of the covenant of the LORD, for the footstool of our God, and I made plans to build it. [3] But God said to me, 'You are not to build a house for my Name, because you are a warrior and have shed blood.'

[4] "Yet the LORD, the God of Israel, chose me from my whole family to be king over Israel forever. He chose Judah as leader, and from the tribe of Judah he chose my family, and from my father's sons he was pleased to make me king over all Israel. [5] Of all my sons — and the LORD has given me many — he has chosen my son Solomon to sit on the throne of the kingdom of the LORD over Israel. [6] He said to me: 'Solomon your son is the one who will build my house and my courts, for I have chosen him to be my son, and I will be his father. [7] I will establish his kingdom forever if he is unswerving in carrying out my commands and laws, as is being done at this time.'

[8] "So now I charge you in the sight of all Israel and of the assembly of the LORD, and in the hearing of our God: Be careful to follow all the commands of the LORD your God, that you may possess this good land and pass it on as an inheritance to your descendants forever.

[9] "And you, my son Solomon, acknowledge the God of your father, and serve him with wholehearted devotion and with a willing mind, for the LORD searches every heart and understands every desire and every thought. If you seek him, he will be found by you; but if you forsake him, he will reject you forever. [10] Consider now, for the LORD has chosen you to build a house as the sanctuary. Be strong and do the work."

[11] Then David gave his son Solomon the plans for the portico of the temple, its buildings, its storerooms, its upper parts, its inner rooms and the place of atonement. [12] He gave him the plans of all that the Spirit had put in his mind for the courts of the temple of the LORD and all the surrounding rooms, for the treasuries of the temple

---

annals of King David Probably refers to an official royal record of the events of David's reign.
27:28 western foothills Refers to the low hills in Judah between the coastal plain and Jerusalem. This was a fertile area known for its vineyards, grain and olive groves.
27:29 Sharon A fertile plane on the Mediterranean coast.
27:33 Ahithophel A key figure in Absalom's rebellion (2Sa 15:12). He killed himself after Absalom did not follow his counsel (2Sa 17:23). **Hushai the Arkite** Hushai pretended to be loyal to Absalom in order to counter the counsel of Ahithophel (2Sa 15:32–37). He gave Absalom bad advice, which eventually caused his defeat (2Sa 17:1–16).
27:34 Abiathar Served as a priest with Zadok (2Sa 15:29,35). **Joab** See note on 2Sa 2:13.

28:1–21 David addresses all the leaders of Israel, presenting Solomon as God's choice to succeed him and build the temple (1Ch 28:2–7). He then addresses Solomon directly and instructs him to faithfully seek

God (vv. 9–10). David also hands off the plans for the temple (vv. 11–19) and gives Solomon a final commission (vv. 20–21).

28:3 have shed blood See 22:8.
28:4 chose me David emphasizes God's initiative and support for his kingship.
28:6 his father See note on 2Sa 7:14.
28:7 establish his kingdom The Chronicler closely associates the Davidic dynasty with God's kingdom. See 1Ch 17:14 and note.
28:8 possess this good land David's language is reminiscent of Moses' charges to Israel before they entered the land (see Dt 30:16 and note).
28:9 acknowledge The Hebrew verb used here, *yada'*, implies recognizing God's power and sovereignty. **wholehearted devotion** The Hebrew phrase used here, *levav shalem*, is common in 1–2 Chronicles and often refers to national unity (1Ch 12:38; 29:9).

of God and for the treasuries for the dedicated things. [13]He gave him instructions for the divisions of the priests and Levites, and for all the work of serving in the temple of the LORD, as well as for all the articles to be used in its service. [14]He designated the weight of gold for all the gold articles to be used in various kinds of service, and the weight of silver for all the silver articles to be used in various kinds of service: [15]the weight of gold for the gold lampstands and their lamps, with the weight for each lampstand and its lamps; and the weight of silver for each silver lampstand and its lamps, according to the use of each lampstand; [16]the weight of gold for each table for consecrated bread; the weight of silver for the silver tables; [17]the weight of pure gold for the forks, sprinkling bowls and pitchers; the weight of gold for each gold dish; the weight of silver for each silver dish; [18]and the weight of the refined gold for the altar of incense. He also gave him the plan for the chariot, that is, the cherubim of gold that spread their wings and overshadow the ark of the covenant of the LORD.

[19]"All this," David said, "I have in writing as a result of the LORD's hand on me, and he enabled me to understand all the details of the plan."

[20]David also said to Solomon his son, "Be strong and courageous, and do the work. Do not be afraid or discouraged, for the LORD God, my God, is with you. He will not fail you or forsake you until all the work for the service of the temple of the LORD is finished. [21]The divisions of the priests and Levites are ready for all the work on the temple of God, and every willing person skilled in any craft will help you in all the work. The officials and all the people will obey your every command."

Gifts for Building the Temple

29 Then King David said to the whole assembly: "My son Solomon, the one whom God has chosen, is young and inexperienced. The task is great, because this palatial structure is not for man but for the LORD God. [2]With all my resources I have provided for the temple of my God — gold for the gold work, silver for the silver, bronze for the bronze, iron for the iron and wood for the wood, as well as onyx for the settings, turquoise,[a] stones of various colors, and all kinds of fine stone and marble — all of these in large quantities. [3]Besides, in my devotion to the temple of my God I now give my personal treasures of gold and silver for the temple of my God, over and above everything I have provided for this holy temple: [4]three thousand talents[b] of gold (gold of Ophir) and seven thousand talents[c] of refined silver, for the overlaying of the walls of the buildings, [5]for the gold work and the silver work, and for all the work to be done by the craftsmen. Now, who is willing to consecrate themselves to the LORD today?"

[6]Then the leaders of families, the officers of the tribes of Israel, the commanders of thousands and commanders of hundreds, and the officials in charge of the king's work gave willingly. [7]They gave toward the work on the temple of God five thousand talents[d] and ten thousand darics[e] of gold, ten thousand talents[f] of silver, eighteen thousand talents[g] of bronze and a hundred thousand talents[h] of iron. [8]Anyone who had precious stones gave them to the treasury of the temple of the LORD in the custody of Jehiel the Gershonite. [9]The people rejoiced at the willing response of their leaders, for they had given freely and wholeheartedly to the LORD. David the king also rejoiced greatly.

David's Prayer

[10]David praised the LORD in the presence of the whole assembly, saying,

"Praise be to you, LORD,
   the God of our father Israel,
   from everlasting to everlasting.
[11]Yours, LORD, is the greatness and the power
   and the glory and the majesty and the
      splendor,
   for everything in heaven and earth is yours.
Yours, LORD, is the kingdom;
   you are exalted as head over all.
[12]Wealth and honor come from you;
   you are the ruler of all things.
In your hands are strength and power
   to exalt and give strength to all.

---

[a] 2 The meaning of the Hebrew for this word is uncertain.
[b] 4 That is, about 110 tons or about 100 metric tons   [c] 4 That is, about 260 tons or about 235 metric tons   [d] 7 That is, about 190 tons or about 170 metric tons   [e] 7 That is, about 185 pounds or about 84 kilograms   [f] 7 That is, about 380 tons or about 340 metric tons   [g] 7 That is, about 675 tons or about 610 metric tons [h] 7 That is, about 3,800 tons or about 3,400 metric tons

---

28:20 Be strong and courageous See 22:13 and note.
28:21 your every command Earlier, David had charged the leaders to support Solomon (22:17–19).

29:1–9 David completes his preparations by taking an offering for the temple.

29:4 three thousand talents of gold See note on 22:14. **Ophir** A region (likely in Arabia) known for fine gold (Job 28:16; Isa 13:12).
29:9 wholeheartedly Refers to a unified purpose. See note on 1Ch 28:9.

29:10–19 David's final action in 1–2 Chronicles is a public prayer of thanksgiving to God.

29:11 head While the Hebrew word used here, *rosh*, literally means "head," it often is used to mean "first" (Pr 8:26) or "chief" (Dt 1:13; 33:5). Here, it indicates that God is exalted as the ultimate ruler of all creation.
29:12 Wealth and honor come from you David attributes his success and wealth to God's blessing.

[13] Now, our God, we give you thanks,
and praise your glorious name.

[14] "But who am I, and who are my people, that we should be able to give as generously as this? Everything comes from you, and we have given you only what comes from your hand. [15] We are foreigners and strangers in your sight, as were all our ancestors. Our days on earth are like a shadow, without hope. [16] LORD our God, all this abundance that we have provided for building you a temple for your Holy Name comes from your hand, and all of it belongs to you. [17] I know, my God, that you test the heart and are pleased with integrity. All these things I have given willingly and with honest intent. And now I have seen with joy how willingly your people who are here have given to you. [18] LORD, the God of our fathers Abraham, Isaac and Israel, keep these desires and thoughts in the hearts of your people forever, and keep their hearts loyal to you. [19] And give my son Solomon the wholehearted devotion to keep your commands, statutes and decrees and to do everything to build the palatial structure for which I have provided."

[20] Then David said to the whole assembly, "Praise the LORD your God." So they all praised the LORD, the God of their fathers; they bowed down, prostrating themselves before the LORD and the king.

Solomon Acknowledged as King

29:21-25pp — 1Ki 1:28-53

[21] The next day they made sacrifices to the LORD and presented burnt offerings to him: a thousand bulls, a thousand rams and a thousand male lambs, together with their drink offerings, and other sacrifices in abundance for all Israel. [22] They ate and drank with great joy in the presence of the LORD that day.

Then they acknowledged Solomon son of David as king a second time, anointing him before the LORD to be ruler and Zadok to be priest. [23] So Solomon sat on the throne of the LORD as king in place of his father David. He prospered and all Israel obeyed him. [24] All the officers and warriors, as well as all of King David's sons, pledged their submission to King Solomon.

[25] The LORD highly exalted Solomon in the sight of all Israel and bestowed on him royal splendor such as no king over Israel ever had before.

The Death of David

29:26-28pp — 1Ki 2:10-12

[26] David son of Jesse was king over all Israel. [27] He ruled over Israel forty years — seven in Hebron and thirty-three in Jerusalem. [28] He died at a good old age, having enjoyed long life, wealth and honor. His son Solomon succeeded him as king.

[29] As for the events of King David's reign, from beginning to end, they are written in the records of Samuel the seer, the records of Nathan the prophet and the records of Gad the seer, [30] together with the details of his reign and power, and the circumstances that surrounded him and Israel and the kingdoms of all the other lands.

29:14 who are my people Compared to the greatness and sovereignty of God, David recognizes their humble position.

29:15 foreigners and strangers in your sight See Lev 25:23, where Yahweh describes the Israelites as travelers on his land.

29:20–25 The Chronicler describes the anointing of Solomon as a great celebration. It lasts two days, and the people offer sacrifices and feast.

29:21 burnt offerings See Ex 29:38–42 and note.
29:22 anointing him before the LORD to be ruler This description of Solomon's anointing leaves out some of the conflict described in 1Ki 1:5–53. Presumably, the Chronicler did not include this information because it was not relevant to his emphasis on national unity. **Zadok to be priest** See note on 1Ki 1:8.
29:27 forty years Approximately 1011–971 BC.

29:29 The Chronicler seems to be referencing three different sources associated with the spiritual figures of Samuel, Nathan and Gad (1Sa 1; 2Sa 7; 24:11–14)— presumably these were works about, or by, each of these prophetic figures. It could also be that that this is a broad reference to a collective work involving information pertaining to the ministries of prophetic figures (compare note on 2Ch 33:19).

2 CHRONICLES

INTRODUCTION TO 2 CHRONICLES

Second Chronicles shows the power and importance of God's presence. The narrative of 1–2 Chronicles views Israel's story through the lens of God's covenant (contract) with David. David desired to build a temple for Yahweh; Yahweh responded by telling David that from his line would come one whose throne would be established forever (1Ch 17). By showing Judah's history in relation to the house of David and the house of Yahweh—the temple—the book emphasizes the importance of proper worship and invites God's people to fully commit to following God's ways.

BACKGROUND

Second Chronicles begins shortly after David's death (971 BC) as Solomon ascends the throne and establishes Yahweh's temple—a concrete sign of God's presence among his people (2Ch 1–7). The narrative highlights the glory of these years by omitting Solomon's idolatry and lustfulness (compare 1Ki 11:1–13). The focus on the positive elements of the glory years of Israel is intended to encourage Jewish people living in the fifth century BC to honor God and be worshipful (see "Introduction to 1 Chronicles").

After Solomon's death (931 BC), the nation of Israel was divided into two kingdoms—one in the north that kept the name "Israel," and one in the south called "Judah" (using the name of the tribal territory that included Jerusalem). Because the emphasis is on David's descendants,

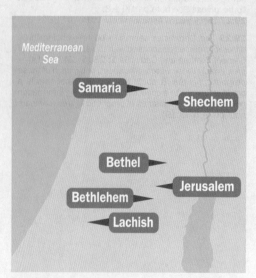

This map depicts some of the major locations related to 2 Chronicles.

2 Chronicles says little about the kings of Israel (who are not in his lineage) and focuses on the Davidic kings of Judah. The book traces the history of Judah for more than 300 years, until Nebuchadnezzar's army destroyed Jerusalem and the temple and deported its people to Babylon (586 BC). Nonetheless, the book concludes on a hopeful note, reporting the royal decree—from a Persian king, who had conquered Babylon—allowing the exiles to return to Judah (538 BC). This decree connects 2 Chronicles with the book of Ezra (compare 2Ch 36:22–23 to Ezr 1:1–3).

STRUCTURE

Second Chronicles starts partway through the second section (1Ch 10—2Ch 9) of 1–2 Chronicles, which originally were a single literary unit (see "Introduction to 1 Chronicles"). The remainder of 2 Chronicles

(2Ch 10–36) focuses on the southern kingdom of Judah. Chapters 10–12 are about Solomon's son Rehoboam, whose oppressive rule prompted the northern tribes of Israel to break off into their own kingdom. Chapters 13–36 recount the reigns of 18 more kings in David's line, describing their power struggles, military conflicts and their faithfulness—or unfaithfulness—to Yahweh. Chapter 36 summarizes the fall of Judah and the people's exile to Babylon and then jumps forward in time to the return from exile.

OUTLINE

- Solomon's reign (1:1—9:31)
- Kings of Judah (10:1—36:23)

THEMES

Second Chronicles' narrative generally depicts kings as either doing right in Yahweh's eyes or doing evil. This recurring theme is reflected in how each king and generation relates to Yahweh. For example, King Rehoboam does evil by refusing to seek Yahweh (2Ch 12:14). King Uzziah disregards proper worship by entering the temple and offering incense himself instead of having a priest do so; as punishment, he is stricken with leprosy (26:15–20). King Asa repairs the altar at the temple and abolishes idolatry throughout Judah (15:8–15), but later relies on political alliances more than Yahweh—his failure leads to war (16:7–9). King Manasseh places idols in

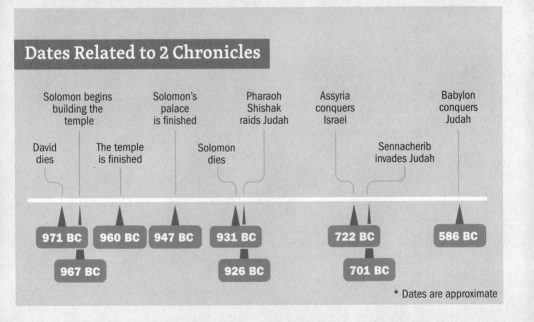

Dates Related to 2 Chronicles

Solomon begins building the temple	Solomon's palace is finished	Pharaoh Shishak raids Judah	Assyria conquers Israel		Babylon conquers Judah
David dies	The temple is finished		Solomon dies	Sennacherib invades Judah	
971 BC	**960 BC**	**947 BC**	**931 BC**	**722 BC**	**586 BC**
	967 BC		**926 BC**	**701 BC**	

* Dates are approximate

the temple and even sacrifices his own sons, but later prayerfully repents and is able to gain back God's favor (33:12–16; compare 2Ki 21:1–18).

Overall, the Chronicler depicts kings as either walking in the ways of David or opposing what David stood for (e.g., 2Ch 23:3,18; 28:1; compare 33:7). The narrative of 1–2 Chronicles overlooks David's mistakes and emphasizes his worshipful attitude—in doing so, David becomes the model of a worshipful king. King Hezekiah is described as being like David because he restores proper worship at the temple and organizes a Passover celebration for the people of Judah and Israel (chs. 29–31). God blesses Judah during his reign, saving them from the Assyrians (ch. 32). King Josiah also removes idols from the land and temple, instructs the people in the ways of Yahweh's law and celebrates Passover (chs. 34–35).

Second Chronicles demonstrates how Yahweh is good to those in relationship with him but against those who oppose him—this presents a healthy understanding of what relationship with him entails. Second Chronicles shows us that when we humble ourselves, seek God and repent of our sins, he is faithful to listen, forgive and heal (7:14). Today, by the power of the one who rules from David's throne (Lk 1:32)—Jesus—we can eternally live in God's presence (Jn 3:16–17).

Solomon Asks for Wisdom

1:2-13pp — 1Ki 3:4-15
1:14-17pp — 1Ki 10:26-29; 2Ch 9:25-28

1 Solomon son of David established himself firmly over his kingdom, for the LORD his God was with him and made him exceedingly great.

²Then Solomon spoke to all Israel — to the commanders of thousands and commanders of hundreds, to the judges and to all the leaders in Israel, the heads of families — ³and Solomon and the whole assembly went to the high place at Gibeon, for God's tent of meeting was there, which Moses the LORD's servant had made in the wilderness. ⁴Now David had brought up the ark of God from Kiriath Jearim to the place he had prepared for it, because he had pitched a tent for it in Jerusalem. ⁵But the bronze altar that Bezalel son of Uri, the son of Hur, had made was in Gibeon in front of the tabernacle of the LORD; so Solomon and the assembly inquired of him there. ⁶Solomon went up to the bronze altar before the LORD in the tent of meeting and offered a thousand burnt offerings on it.

⁷That night God appeared to Solomon and said to him, "Ask for whatever you want me to give you."

⁸Solomon answered God, "You have shown great kindness to David my father and have made me king in his place. ⁹Now, LORD God, let your promise to my father David be confirmed, for you have made me king over a people who are as numerous as the dust of the earth. ¹⁰Give me wisdom and knowledge, that I may lead this people, for who is able to govern this great people of yours?"

¹¹God said to Solomon, "Since this is your heart's desire and you have not asked for wealth, possessions or honor, nor for the death of your enemies, and since you have not asked for a long life but for wisdom and knowledge to govern my people over whom I have made you king, ¹²therefore wisdom and knowledge will be given you. And I will also give you wealth, possessions and honor, such as no king who was before you ever had and none after you will have."

¹³Then Solomon went to Jerusalem from the high place at Gibeon, from before the tent of meeting. And he reigned over Israel.

¹⁴Solomon accumulated chariots and horses; he had fourteen hundred chariots and twelve

---

1:1-13 First Chronicles ends with David's death; 2 Chronicles begins with the continuation of the united monarchy under David's son, Solomon (971 BC). The narrative of 1-2 Chronicles seems to be one work that was divided in antiquity because its length required two scrolls. Collectively, 1-2 Chronicles retells Israel's history for the Jewish community living around Jerusalem in the fifth century BC. The book reminds the Jewish people of how great the nation once was, encouraging them to be completely committed to Yahweh.

In its omission of the details of Solomon's conflict with Adonijah, the opening narrative of 2 Chronicles illustrates how this retelling works; the Chronicler omits certain details to highlight the themes of national unity, proper temple worship and faithfulness. (see 1Ki 1:5—2:25; note on 1Ch 29:22).

1:1 Solomon son of David Solomon was the third and final king of a united Israel. He reigned from about 971–931 BC.

SOLOMON
Solomon's name, *shlomo*, is related to the word *shalom*, meaning "peace." During his reign, Israel experienced an unparalleled period of peace and prosperity. He built the temple as well as other buildings. He also established positive relationships with other nations, which enabled him to import goods used for the temple's construction. Solomon was renowned for his wisdom. His reputation spread far enough that the queen of Sheba visited him to test him (1Ki 10:1–5). Solomon made marriage alliances with many foreign nations. These foreign wives eventually led him into idolatry (1Ki 11:1–8). His worship of foreign deities resulted in God's punishment and the division of Israel into two nations (1Ki 11:9–13).

1:2 Solomon spoke to all Israel The Chronicler emphasizes the unity of Israel as Solomon begins his reign. Throughout 1-2 Chronicles, the narrative portrays all Israel assembled together, often for worship.
1:3 God's tent of meeting See Ex 26:1 and note.
1:4 David had brought up the ark of God The story of David bringing the ark to Jerusalem is found in 1Ch 13; 15 and 16.
1:5 bronze altar See Ex 27:1–8.
1:8 kindness The Hebrew word used here, *chesed*, refers to God's unfailing love. It is related to God's mercy, as God is said to forgive because of his *chesed* (e.g., Ne 9:17). The praise of God's *chesed* as something that endures forever, like in 2Ch 5:13, emphasizes the unceasing nature of God's commitment to fulfilling his promises (see note on Ps 136:1). **king in his place** See 1Ch 28:5–7.
1:9 your promise to my father David A reference to the promise God made to David to establish his kingdom forever. See 1Ch 17:1–15 and note. **a people who are as numerous as the dust** A reference to God's promise to Abraham (Ge 13:16).
1:10 Give me wisdom and knowledge In the account in 1 Kings, Solomon asks for an understanding mind (literally rendered from Hebrew as "heart of hearing"; see note on 1Ki 3:9). In 1 Kings this relates to his ability to discern between good and evil. Both accounts emphasize that Solomon desired wisdom to help him judge the people.
1:14-17 This material is taken from 1Ki 10:26–29. The account in 1 Kings follows Solomon's request for wisdom with a story showing his wisdom (1Ki 3:16–28). The Chronicler follows it with this account of Solomon's wealth, to emphasize that God fulfilled his promise to give Solomon riches, possessions and honor (2Ch 1:12).

1:14 chariot cities See 1Ki 10:26 and note.

thousand horses,ᵃ which he kept in the chariot cities and also with him in Jerusalem. ¹⁵The king made silver and gold as common in Jerusalem as stones, and cedar as plentiful as sycamore-fig trees in the foothills. ¹⁶Solomon's horses were imported from Egypt and from Kueᵇ — the royal merchants purchased them from Kue at the current price. ¹⁷They imported a chariot from Egypt for six hundred shekelsᶜ of silver, and a horse for a hundred and fifty.ᵈ They also exported them to all the kings of the Hittites and of the Arameans.

Preparations for Building the Temple

2:1-18pp — 1Ki 5:1-16

2ᵉ Solomon gave orders to build a temple for the Name of the LORD and a royal palace for himself. ²He conscripted 70,000 men as carriers and 80,000 as stonecutters in the hills and 3,600 as foremen over them.

³Solomon sent this message to Hiramᶠ king of Tyre:

"Send me cedar logs as you did for my father David when you sent him cedar to build a palace to live in. ⁴Now I am about to build a temple for the Name of the LORD my God and to dedicate it to him for burning fragrant incense before him, for setting out the consecrated bread regularly, and for making burnt offerings every morning and evening and on the Sabbaths, at the New Moons and at the appointed festivals of the LORD our God. This is a lasting ordinance for Israel.

⁵"The temple I am going to build will be great, because our God is greater than all other gods. ⁶But who is able to build a temple for him, since the heavens, even the highest heavens, cannot contain him? Who then am I to build a temple for him, except as a place to burn sacrifices before him?

⁷"Send me, therefore, a man skilled to work in gold and silver, bronze and iron, and in purple, crimson and blue yarn, and experienced in the art of engraving, to work in Judah and Jerusalem with my skilled workers, whom my father David provided.

⁸"Send me also cedar, juniper and algumᵍ logs from Lebanon, for I know that your servants are skilled in cutting timber there. My servants will work with yours ⁹to provide me with plenty of lumber, because the temple I build must be large and magnificent. ¹⁰I will give your servants, the woodsmen who cut the timber, twenty thousand corsʰ of ground wheat, twenty thousand corsⁱ of barley, twenty thousand bathsʲ of wine and twenty thousand baths of olive oil."

¹¹Hiram king of Tyre replied by letter to Solomon:

"Because the LORD loves his people, he has made you their king."

¹²And Hiram added:

"Praise be to the LORD, the God of Israel, who made heaven and earth! He has given King David a wise son, endowed with intel-

---

ᵃ *14* Or *charioteers*   ᵇ *16* Probably Cilicia   ᶜ *17* That is, about 15 pounds or about 6.9 kilograms   ᵈ *17* That is, about 3 3/4 pounds or about 1.7 kilograms   ᵉ In Hebrew texts 2:1 is numbered 1:18, and 2:2-18 is numbered 2:1-17.   ᶠ *3* Hebrew *Huram,* a variant of *Hiram*; also in verses 11 and 12   ᵍ *8* Probably a variant of *almug*   ʰ *10* That is, probably about 3,600 tons or about 3,200 metric tons of wheat   ⁱ *10* That is, probably about 3,000 tons or about 2,700 metric tons of barley   ʲ *10* That is, about 120,000 gallons or about 440,000 liters

---

1:15 foothills The low hills in Judah between the coastal plain and Jerusalem.

1:16 from Egypt and from Kue Importing horses, especially from Egypt, was forbidden in the law. See Dt 17:16 and note. Kue was a kingdom in southeast Asia Minor (modern-day Turkey).

2:1–18 The Chronicler continues his emphasis on worship by moving to Solomon's greatest achievement: the building of the temple. He leaves out material found in 1Ki 3:16—4:34, focusing instead on the fulfillment of God's promise to David that David's son would build him a house and God would establish his kingdom (see 1Ch 22:10 and note).

2:2 He conscripted The account in 1 Kings notes that he drafted laborers. Most likely these were foreigners (2Ch 2:17–18; 1Ki 9:20–23), although the language of 1Ki 5:13 leaves more room for interpretation.

2:3 Hiram king of Tyre Hiram had showed kindness to David by sending him materials and workers to build a house shortly after David became king (1Ch 14:1–2). Hiram's gift gave legitimacy to David's newly established monarchy (see 1Ch 14:2).

2:4 dedicate it to him In 1 Kings, the account of Solomon's message to Hiram focuses on God's word to David

that Solomon would build the temple (1Ki 5:3–6). Here, the Chronicler emphasizes the worship of Yahweh and the greatness of Yahweh. **setting out the consecrated bread regularly** See Ex 25:30 and note. **burnt offerings every morning and evening** See note on Ezr 3:3. **on the Sabbaths** See note on Ex 20:8–11. **New Moons and at the appointed festivals** See note on Isa 1:13.

2:5 our God is greater than all other gods Solomon echoes David's concern that the temple be magnificent because it represents God's superiority and sovereignty (compare 1Ch 22:5).

2:6 cannot contain him Solomon recognizes that, while the temple would represent God's presence, it could not contain God's greatness. See Ps 11:4 and note.

2:8 logs from Lebanon An area famous for its cedar trees. By sending his servants to work alongside Hiram's crew, Solomon might have been seeking insights into timber-cutting.

2:10 twenty thousand cors Totaling about 4,400 cubic meters. **ground wheat** Wheat that had already been winnowed.

2:12 who made heaven and earth Hiram's response in 2 Chronicles is longer than in the parallel account (1Ki 5:7). Not only does he bless Yahweh, but he also acknowledges Yahweh as Creator.

ligence and discernment, who will build a temple for the LORD and a palace for himself. 13"I am sending you Huram-Abi, a man of great skill, 14whose mother was from Dan and whose father was from Tyre. He is trained to work in gold and silver, bronze and iron, stone and wood, and with purple and blue and crimson yarn and fine linen. He is experienced in all kinds of engraving and can execute any design given to him. He will work with your skilled workers and with those of my lord, David your father.

15"Now let my lord send his servants the wheat and barley and the olive oil and wine he promised, 16and we will cut all the logs from Lebanon that you need and will float them as rafts by sea down to Joppa. You can then take them up to Jerusalem."

17Solomon took a census of all the foreigners residing in Israel, after the census his father David had taken; and they were found to be 153,600. 18He assigned 70,000 of them to be carriers and 80,000 to be stonecutters in the hills, with 3,600 foremen over them to keep the people working.

Solomon Builds the Temple

3:1-14pp — 1Ki 6:1-29

3 Then Solomon began to build the temple of the LORD in Jerusalem on Mount Moriah, where the LORD had appeared to his father David. It was on the threshing floor of Araunah[a] the Jebusite, the place provided by David. 2He began building on the second day of the second month in the fourth year of his reign.

3The foundation Solomon laid for building the temple of God was sixty cubits long and twenty cubits wide[b] (using the cubit of the old standard). 4The portico at the front of the temple was twenty cubits[c] long across the width of the building and twenty[d] cubits high.

He overlaid the inside with pure gold. 5He paneled the main hall with juniper and covered it with fine gold and decorated it with palm tree and chain designs. 6He adorned the temple with precious stones. And the gold he used was gold of Parvaim. 7He overlaid the ceiling beams, doorframes, walls and doors of the temple with gold, and he carved cherubim on the walls.

8He built the Most Holy Place, its length corresponding to the width of the temple — twenty cubits long and twenty cubits wide. He overlaid the inside with six hundred talents[e] of fine gold. 9The gold nails weighed fifty shekels.[f] He also overlaid the upper parts with gold.

10For the Most Holy Place he made a pair of

---

a 1 Hebrew *Ornan,* a variant of *Araunah*   *b 3* That is, about 90 feet long and 30 feet wide or about 27 meters long and 9 meters wide   *c 4* That is, about 30 feet or about 9 meters; also in verses 8, 11 and 13   *d 4* Some Septuagint and Syriac manuscripts; Hebrew *and a hundred and twenty*   *e 8* That is, about 23 tons or about 21 metric tons   *f 9* That is, about 1 1/4 pounds or about 575 grams

---

2:13 Huram-Abi This craftsman is identified as "Huram" in 1Ki 7:13 (not to be confused with Hiram, the king of Tyre). **skill** The Hebrew word used here, *chakham,* also can refer to wisdom.

2:14 He is trained to work Huram-Abi is seen as a craftsman like Bezalel, who led the work on the tabernacle (Ex 31:1–11). Compare 1Ki 7:14.

2:17 foreigners The Hebrew word used here, *ger,* typically refers to a non-Israelite who is living peaceably in Israel (Lev 19:34). Here, it probably describes forced laborers.

3:1–17 This chapter, which parallels 1Ki 6, describes the temple as Solomon builds it. After indicating the location and time of construction (2Ch 3:1–2), the Chronicler gives the temple's exterior measurements (v. 3). He then provides measurements for the porch (v. 4), the main sanctuary (vv. 5–7), and the Most Holy Place (Holy of Holies; vv. 8–13). In addition, he describes the curtain (v. 14) and the front pillars (vv. 15–17). The version here is shorter than the account in 1–2 Kings. This is surprising given the Chronicler's detailed account of the preparations made for the temple (see 1Ch 23:1 — 26:32 and note). However, the main focus is not the temple itself, but the proper worship of Yahweh that occurs at the temple. The building is important only because it represents God's sovereignty and authority (2Ch 2:5; 1Ch 22:5).

3:1 the temple of the LORD See 1Ki 6:1 and note. **Mount Moriah** In Genesis, Moriah is the place where Abraham went to sacrifice Isaac. It is unclear whether the two locations are the same. See Ge 22:2 and note. **threshing floor of Araunah the Jebusite** David had

chosen this location for the temple after God responded to his sacrifices there. See 1Ch 21:26 — 22:1. **Araunah the Jebusite** The Hebrew name "Ornan" reflects a different spelling of "Araunah." See note on 1Ch 21:15.

3:2 the fourth year of his reign Around 967 BC. The account in 1–2 Kings gives a more detailed date (see 1Ki 6:1).

3:3 foundation Solomon laid A cubit is approximately 18 inches in length. The total dimensions would have been about 90 feet long and 30 feet wide. See the infographic "Solomon's Temple" on p. 520.

3:4 portico Refers to a porch or entrance hall.

3:6 Parvaim This location is not mentioned elsewhere in the OT. It most likely refers to a place in Arabia.

3:7 cherubim The Hebrew word *cherubim* is a plural noun, derived from an Akkadian term referring to a being that guards a divine throne. These figures sometimes have the body of a lion and the head of a man; in other contexts, they could be a composite of human, bird and bovine features. In Genesis, God places cherubim at the garden of Eden (Ge 3:24); in Exodus, he instructs Moses to craft golden cherubim for the ark of the covenant (Ex 25:18–20) and to weave their image into the tabernacle curtains (Ex 26:1,31). The prophet Ezekiel sees a vision involving cherubim (Eze 10).

3:8 the Most Holy Place The inner part of the temple where the ark — and Yahweh — would reside (2Ch 5:7). Only the high priest could enter this area, and only on the Day of Atonement. See note on Lev 16:1–34.

3:10 a pair of sculptured cherubim See note on 2Ch 3:7, where images of cherubim were carved on the walls. Here, the cherubim seem to be free-standing statues.

sculptured cherubim and overlaid them with gold. [11]The total wingspan of the cherubim was twenty cubits. One wing of the first cherub was five cubits[a] long and touched the temple wall, while its other wing, also five cubits long, touched the wing of the other cherub. [12]Similarly one wing of the second cherub was five cubits long and touched the other temple wall, and its other wing, also five cubits long, touched the wing of the first cherub. [13]The wings of these cherubim extended twenty cubits. They stood on their feet, facing the main hall.[b]

[14]He made the curtain of blue, purple and crimson yarn and fine linen, with cherubim worked into it.

[15]For the front of the temple he made two pillars, which together were thirty-five cubits[c] long, each with a capital five cubits high. [16]He made interwoven chains[d] and put them on top of the pillars. He also made a hundred pomegranates and attached them to the chains. [17]He erected the pillars in the front of the temple, one to the south and one to the north. The one to the south he named Jakin[e] and the one to the north Boaz.[f]

The Temple's Furnishings

4:2-6,10 – 5:1pp — 1Ki 7:23-26,38-51

4 He made a bronze altar twenty cubits long, twenty cubits wide and ten cubits high.[g] [2]He made the Sea of cast metal, circular in shape, measuring ten cubits from rim to rim and five cubits[h] high. It took a line of thirty cubits[i] to measure around it. [3]Below the rim, figures of bulls encircled it — ten to a cubit.[j] The bulls were cast in two rows in one piece with the Sea.

[4]The Sea stood on twelve bulls, three facing north, three facing west, three facing south and three facing east. The Sea rested on top of them,

and their hindquarters were toward the center. [5]It was a handbreadth[k] in thickness, and its rim was like the rim of a cup, like a lily blossom. It held three thousand baths.[l]

[6]He then made ten basins for washing and placed five on the south side and five on the north. In them the things to be used for the burnt offerings were rinsed, but the Sea was to be used by the priests for washing.

[7]He made ten gold lampstands according to the specifications for them and placed them in the temple, five on the south side and five on the north.

[8]He made ten tables and placed them in the temple, five on the south side and five on the north. He also made a hundred gold sprinkling bowls.

[9]He made the courtyard of the priests, and the large court and the doors for the court, and overlaid the doors with bronze. [10]He placed the Sea on the south side, at the southeast corner.

[11]And Huram also made the pots and shovels and sprinkling bowls.

So Huram finished the work he had undertaken for King Solomon in the temple of God:

[12]the two pillars;
the two bowl-shaped capitals on top of the pillars;
the two sets of network decorating the two bowl-shaped capitals on top of the pillars;

---

[a] 11 That is, about 7 1/2 feet or about 2.3 meters; also in verse 15   [b] 13 Or facing inward   [c] 15 That is, about 53 feet or about 16 meters   [d] 16 Or possibly made chains in the inner sanctuary; the meaning of the Hebrew for this phrase is uncertain.   [e] 17 Jakin probably means he establishes.   [f] 17 Boaz probably means in him is strength.   [g] 1 That is, about 30 feet long and wide and 15 feet high or about 9 meters long and wide and 4.5 meters high   [h] 2 That is, about 7 1/2 feet or about 2.3 meters   [i] 2 That is, about 45 feet or about 14 meters   [j] 3 That is, about 18 inches or about 45 centimeters   [k] 5 That is, about 3 inches or about 7.5 centimeters   [l] 5 That is, about 18,000 gallons or about 66,000 liters

---

3:14 He made the curtain The account in 1 – 2 Kings does not mention this curtain (or "veil"). God instructed Moses to hang a similar curtain in the tabernacle (Ex 26:31 – 33). Three of the Gospels mention a curtain in Herod's temple being torn in two as Jesus died (Mt 27:51; Mk 15:38; Lk 23:45). This likely symbolizes unrestricted access to God (see note on Mt 27:51).

3:16 pomegranates A symbol of abundance in the ancient Near East.

3:17 Jakin This Hebrew word means "he will establish." See note on 1Ki 7:21. **Boaz** This Hebrew word means "in strength."

4:1 — 5:1 Second Chronicles does not include a description of Solomon's palace (compare 1Ki 7:1 – 12). Instead, it shifts directly to describing the temple's furnishings. As with the report of the temple itself (2Ch 3:1 – 17), 2 Chronicles provides fewer details than 1 Kings (compare 1Ki 7:13 – 51).

4:1 He made a bronze altar Compare Eze 43:13 – 27 and note. See the infographic "Solomon's Bronze Altar" on p. 667; see the infographic "Ancient Altars" on p. 127.

4:2 ten cubits from rim to rim About 15 feet in diameter (a cubit is roughly 1.5 feet).

4:3 cast in two rows in one piece Indicates that the Sea and its decorations were made from a single piece of bronze.

4:4 stood on twelve bulls See 1Ki 7:25 and note. See the infographic "Solomon's Temple" on p. 520.

4:5 handbreadth Refers to the width of a person's four fingers held together, approximately three inches. **It held three thousand baths** Approximately 17,500 gallons. The volume given here differs from that in 1Ki 7:26 (2,000 baths).

4:6 He then made ten basins According to the account in 1 Kings, each of these held 40 baths, or approximately 230 gallons (1Ki 7:38 – 39).

4:7 ten gold lampstands In connection with the tabernacle, Yahweh gave Moses instructions for a single lampstand (see Ex 25:31 and note).

4:8 He made ten tables Most likely for the showbread (2Ch 4:19; 1Ch 28:16).

4:11 the pots and shovels and sprinkling bowls Utensils used for sacrifices. See 1Ki 7:40 and note; Ex 27:3.

¹³ the four hundred pomegranates for the two sets of network (two rows of pomegranates for each network, decorating the bowl-shaped capitals on top of the pillars);

¹⁴ the stands with their basins;

¹⁵ the Sea and the twelve bulls under it;

¹⁶ the pots, shovels, meat forks and all related articles.

All the objects that Huram-Abi made for King Solomon for the temple of the LORD were of polished bronze. ¹⁷ The king had them cast in clay molds in the plain of the Jordan between Sukkoth and Zarethan.ᵃ ¹⁸ All these things that Solomon made amounted to so much that the weight of the bronze could not be calculated.

¹⁹ Solomon also made all the furnishings that were in God's temple:

the golden altar;

the tables on which was the bread of the Presence;

²⁰ the lampstands of pure gold with their lamps, to burn in front of the inner sanctuary as prescribed;

²¹ the gold floral work and lamps and tongs (they were solid gold);

²² the pure gold wick trimmers, sprinkling bowls, dishes and censers; and the gold doors of the temple: the inner doors to the Most Holy Place and the doors of the main hall.

5 When all the work Solomon had done for the temple of the LORD was finished, he brought in the things his father David had dedicated — the silver and gold and all the furnishings — and he placed them in the treasuries of God's temple.

ᵃ 17 Hebrew *Zeredatha*, a variant of *Zarethan*

4:16 Huram-Abi The craftsman from Tyre (introduced in 2Ch 2:13–14).

4:17 Sukkoth and Zarethan Cities along the eastern bank of the Jordan River.

4:19 the golden altar Modeled after the altar of incense in the tabernacle (Ex 30:1–10). See the infographic "Furnishings of the Tabernacle" on p. 136. **bread of the Presence** See Lev 24:5–9; note on Lev 24:6.

4:22 dishes Probably refers to a spoon-shaped utensil used for incense (Ex 25:29). **the gold doors of the temple** The Hebrew phrase used here, *phethach habbayith*, may be literally rendered as "the opening of the house." The account in 1 Kings uses the word *pothoth*, which can indicate door hinges (1Ki 7:50).

5:1 was finished Solomon completed the temple approximately 960 BC. See 1Ki 7:51 and note. See the timeline "The United Kingdom" on p. 464. **the things**

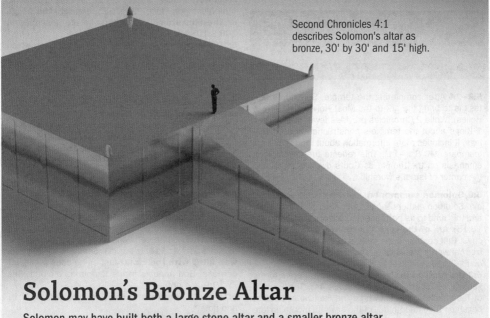

Second Chronicles 4:1 describes Solomon's altar as bronze, 30' by 30' and 15' high.

Solomon's Bronze Altar

Solomon may have built both a large stone altar and a smaller bronze altar. Ahaz moved Solomon's bronze altar—a considerable feat given its weight and dimensions (2Ki 16:14). Asa also "repaired" this altar—implying that it was made of materials that could fall into disrepair (2Ch 15:8).

The Ark Brought to the Temple

5:2 – 6:11pp — 1Ki 8:1-21

²Then Solomon summoned to Jerusalem the elders of Israel, all the heads of the tribes and the chiefs of the Israelite families, to bring up the ark of the LORD's covenant from Zion, the City of David. ³And all the Israelites came together to the king at the time of the festival in the seventh month.

⁴When all the elders of Israel had arrived, the Levites took up the ark, ⁵and they brought up the ark and the tent of meeting and all the sacred furnishings in it. The Levitical priests carried them up; ⁶and King Solomon and the entire assembly of Israel that had gathered about him were before the ark, sacrificing so many sheep and cattle that they could not be recorded or counted.

⁷The priests then brought the ark of the LORD's covenant to its place in the inner sanctuary of the temple, the Most Holy Place, and put it beneath the wings of the cherubim. ⁸The cherubim spread their wings over the place of the ark and covered the ark and its carrying poles. ⁹These poles were so long that their ends, extending from the ark, could be seen from in front of the inner sanctuary, but not from outside the Holy Place; and they are still there today. ¹⁰There was nothing in the ark except the two tablets that Moses had placed in it at Horeb, where the LORD made a covenant with the Israelites after they came out of Egypt.

¹¹The priests then withdrew from the Holy Place. All the priests who were there had consecrated themselves, regardless of their divisions. ¹²All the Levites who were musicians — Asaph, Heman, Jeduthun and their sons and relatives — stood on the east side of the altar, dressed in fine linen and playing cymbals, harps and lyres. They were accompanied by 120 priests sounding trumpets. ¹³The trumpeters and musicians joined in unison to give praise and thanks to the LORD. Accompanied by trumpets, cymbals and other instruments, the singers raised their voices in praise to the LORD and sang:

"He is good;
    his love endures forever."

Then the temple of the LORD was filled with the cloud, ¹⁴and the priests could not perform their service because of the cloud, for the glory of the LORD filled the temple of God.

6 Then Solomon said, "The LORD has said that he would dwell in a dark cloud; ²I have built a magnificent temple for you, a place for you to dwell forever."

³While the whole assembly of Israel was stand-

---

his father David had dedicated Refers to the spoils of war collected by David (1Ch 18:7–11).

EVENT	DATE
Solomon becomes king	971 BC
Solomon begins construction on the temple	967 BC
Solomon finishes the temple	960 BC

5:2–14 After completing the temple, Solomon's first task is to bring the ark to the Most Holy Place (Holy of Holies). While 2 Chronicles provides fewer details than 1 Kings about the temple's construction and furnishings, it includes more information about moving the ark (compare 1Ki 8:1–11). This reflects the Chronicler's emphasis on the temple as God's dwelling place and the center of Israel's worship.

5:2 Solomon summoned Just as his father, David, did, Solomon gathers the leaders of Israel to move the ark, this time to its permanent residence (compare 1Ch 13;15). **ark of the LORD's covenant** A wooden box or chest that contained the tablets of the law and symbolized Yahweh's presence among the Israelites. See note on Ex 25:10.

5:3 the festival in the seventh month Refers to the Festival of Tabernacles (Lev 23:33–44). The Festival of Tabernacles, also known as the Festival of Booths, began on the fifteenth day of the seventh month (in late September or October). It was a seven-day celebration of the autumn harvest. The Israelites lived in temporary shelters (booths) during the feast to remind themselves of the wilderness wanderings (Lev 23:42). All males were required to assemble in the presence of God (Dt 16:16). See the table "Israelite Festivals" on p. 200.

5:7 the inner sanctuary See 1Ki 6:5 and note. **the Most Holy Place** Compare Lev 16. See the infographic "The Most Holy Place" on p. 525. **beneath the wings of the cherubim** These cherubim are described in 2Ch 3:10–13.

5:10 the two tablets Refers to the tablets on which the Ten Commandments were inscribed (Ex 34:1–5; Dt 10:1–5). Later tradition indicates that the ark also contained Aaron's staff and a jar of manna (compare Heb 9:4).

5:11 consecrated themselves See note on Ex 29:1. **regardless of their divisions** The Chronicler emphasizes the priests' commitment to unity and worship.

5:12 All the Levites who were musicians See 1Ch 25:1–31 and note. **Asaph, Heman, Jeduthun** These same men led the worship when David moved the ark to Jerusalem (1Ch 16:37,42). David later appointed them as the temple musicians (1Ch 25:1).

5:13 He is good; his love endures forever This refrain is part of the thanksgiving psalm sung when David brought the ark to Jerusalem (1Ch 16:8–36 and note). The quotation here most likely reflects Ps 106:1, but the phrase is common throughout Psalms (e.g., Ps 107:1; 118:1; 136:1). See note on 2Ch 1:8. **was filled with the cloud** Just as he does in the wilderness, God appears in the temple as a cloud. See Ex 19:9 and note.

5:14 could not perform their service See 1Ki 8:11 and note.

6:1–11 The Chronicler's account of Solomon's blessing closely follows 1Ki 8:12–21.

6:1 dark cloud Refers to God's appearance at Mount Sinai (compare Ex 19:9).

ing there, the king turned around and blessed them. ⁴Then he said:

"Praise be to the LORD, the God of Israel, who with his hands has fulfilled what he promised with his mouth to my father David. For he said, ⁵'Since the day I brought my people out of Egypt, I have not chosen a city in any tribe of Israel to have a temple built so that my Name might be there, nor have I chosen anyone to be ruler over my people Israel. ⁶But now I have chosen Jerusalem for my Name to be there, and I have chosen David to rule my people Israel.'

⁷"My father David had it in his heart to build a temple for the Name of the LORD, the God of Israel. ⁸But the LORD said to my father David, 'You did well to have it in your heart to build a temple for my Name. ⁹Nevertheless, you are not the one to build the temple, but your son, your own flesh and blood — he is the one who will build the temple for my Name.'

¹⁰"The LORD has kept the promise he made. I have succeeded David my father and now I sit on the throne of Israel, just as the LORD promised, and I have built the temple for the Name of the LORD, the God of Israel. ¹¹There I have placed the ark, in which is the covenant of the LORD that he made with the people of Israel."

Solomon's Prayer of Dedication

6:12-40pp — 1Ki 8:22-53
6:41-42pp — Ps 132:8-10

¹²Then Solomon stood before the altar of the LORD in front of the whole assembly of Israel and spread out his hands. ¹³Now he had made a bronze platform, five cubits long, five cubits wide and three cubits high,ᵃ and had placed it in the center of the outer court. He stood on the platform and then knelt down before the whole assembly of Israel and spread out his hands toward heaven. ¹⁴He said:

"LORD, the God of Israel, there is no God like you in heaven or on earth — you who keep your covenant of love with your servants who continue wholeheartedly in your way. ¹⁵You have kept your promise to your servant David my father; with your mouth you have promised and with your hand you have fulfilled it — as it is today.

¹⁶"Now, LORD, the God of Israel, keep for your servant David my father the promises you made to him when you said, 'You shall never fail to have a successor to sit before me on the throne of Israel, if only your descendants are careful in all they do to walk before me according to my law, as you have done.' ¹⁷And now, LORD, the God of Israel, let your word that you promised your servant David come true.

¹⁸"But will God really dwell on earth with humans? The heavens, even the highest heavens, cannot contain you. How much less this temple I have built! ¹⁹Yet, LORD my God, give attention to your servant's prayer and his plea for mercy. Hear the cry and the prayer that your servant is praying in your presence. ²⁰May your eyes be open toward this temple day and night, this place of which you said you would put your Name there. May you hear the prayer your servant prays toward this place. ²¹Hear the supplications of your servant and of your people Israel when they pray toward this place. Hear from heaven, your dwelling place; and when you hear, forgive.

²²"When anyone wrongs their neighbor and is required to take an oath and they come and swear the oath before your altar in this

ᵃ 13 That is, about 7 1/2 feet long and wide and 4 1/2 feet high or about 2.3 meters long and wide and 1.4 meters high

---

6:4 what he promised with his mouth A reference to God's covenant with David (1Ch 17:1–15).

6:6 I have chosen Jerusalem Second Chronicles 6:5–6 expands on the statement in 1Ki 8:16. The Chronicler regarded the building of the temple as a fulfillment of God's promise to establish David's dynasty (1Ch 22:10). Moreover, both the temple and David's dynasty are associated with the kingdom of God (1Ch 17:14 and note).

6:12–42 Solomon's prayer here parallels 1Ki 8:22–53.

6:13 a bronze platform This verse does not appear in 1 Kings, which describes Solomon standing before the altar of Yahweh (1Ki 8:22). Nothing is known of this platform, which might have been used only for this occasion (compare Ne 8:4). **then knelt down** A position of humility. Solomon, king of Israel, publicly shows proper respect for God.

6:14 love The Hebrew word used here, *chesed*, indicates God's faithful love (compare Ex 34:6). See note on 2Ch 1:8.

6:16 your descendants The Hebrew terminology can refer to David's 17 sons or to all of his descendants. In this context, the broader meaning is probably intended. **walk before me according to my law** The parallel phrase in 1Ki 8:25 refers to walking before God, with no explicit mention of the law.

6:20 toward this temple See 1Ki 8:29 and note.

6:21 Hear from heaven, your dwelling place As Solomon indicates in 2Ch 6:18, the temple was only a symbol of God's dwelling place—an earthly representation of God's heavenly temple (compare Ps 11:4 and note). By praying toward the temple, the people were directing their prayers toward the symbol of God's presence. However, Solomon acknowledges that God would answer from heaven.

temple, ²³then hear from heaven and act. Judge between your servants, condemning the guilty and bringing down on their heads what they have done, and vindicating the innocent by treating them in accordance with their innocence.

²⁴"When your people Israel have been defeated by an enemy because they have sinned against you and when they turn back and give praise to your name, praying and making supplication before you in this temple, ²⁵then hear from heaven and forgive the sin of your people Israel and bring them back to the land you gave to them and their ancestors.

²⁶"When the heavens are shut up and there is no rain because your people have sinned against you, and when they pray toward this place and give praise to your name and turn from their sin because you have afflicted them, ²⁷then hear from heaven and forgive the sin of your servants, your people Israel. Teach them the right way to live, and send rain on the land you gave your people for an inheritance.

²⁸"When famine or plague comes to the land, or blight or mildew, locusts or grasshoppers, or when enemies besiege them in any of their cities, whatever disaster or disease may come, ²⁹and when a prayer or plea is made by anyone among your people Israel — being aware of their afflictions and pains, and spreading out their hands toward this temple — ³⁰then hear from heaven, your dwelling place. Forgive, and deal with everyone according to all they do, since you know their hearts (for you alone know the human heart), ³¹so that they will fear you and walk in obedience to you all the time they live in the land you gave our ancestors.

³²"As for the foreigner who does not belong to your people Israel but has come from a distant land because of your great name and your mighty hand and your outstretched arm — when they come and pray toward this temple, ³³then hear from heaven, your dwelling place. Do whatever the foreigner asks of you, so that all the peoples of the earth may know your name and fear you, as do your own people Israel, and may know that this house I have built bears your Name.

³⁴"When your people go to war against their enemies, wherever you send them, and when they pray to you toward this city you have chosen and the temple I have built for your Name, ³⁵then hear from heaven their prayer and their plea, and uphold their cause.

³⁶"When they sin against you — for there is no one who does not sin — and you become angry with them and give them over to the enemy, who takes them captive to a land far away or near; ³⁷and if they have a change of heart in the land where they are held captive, and repent and plead with you in the land of their captivity and say, 'We have sinned, we have done wrong and acted wickedly'; ³⁸and if they turn back to you with all their heart and soul in the land of their captivity where they were taken, and pray toward the land you gave their ancestors, toward the city you have chosen and toward the temple I have built for your Name; ³⁹then from heaven, your dwelling place, hear their prayer and their pleas, and uphold their cause. And forgive your people, who have sinned against you.

⁴⁰"Now, my God, may your eyes be open and your ears attentive to the prayers offered in this place.

⁴¹"Now arise, LORD God, and come to your
    resting place,
you and the ark of your might.
May your priests, LORD God, be clothed
    with salvation,
    may your faithful people rejoice in
      your goodness.
⁴²LORD God, do not reject your anointed one.
    Remember the great love promised to
      David your servant."

The Dedication of the Temple

7:1-10pp — 1Ki 8:62-66

7 When Solomon finished praying, fire came down from heaven and consumed the burnt offering and the sacrifices, and the glory of the LORD filled the temple. ²The priests could not

---

6:24 they have sinned against you See 1Ki 8:33 and note.

6:26 there is no rain One of the consequences of breaking the law (Dt 11:16–17).

6:28 locusts or grasshoppers Insects commonly associated with the destruction of agriculture (see note on 1Ki 8:37).

6:32 foreigner The Hebrew word used here, *nokhri*, indicates someone who lives outside Israel and visits.

6:36 there is no one who does not sin See note on 1Ki 8:46.

6:37 in the land of their captivity This section of Solomon's prayer undoubtedly held special significance for the Chronicler's audience of returned exiles.

6:40–42 At this point, the two versions of the prayer diverge. The Chronicler concludes by having Solomon recite Ps 132:8–10 (2Ch 6:41–42). In 1 Kings, the prayer has a longer ending that invokes Moses and the exodus (1Ki 8:50–53). It also describes Solomon rising to his feet, blessing the assembly and calling the people to remain faithful to Yahweh (1Ki 8:54–61).

enter the temple of the Lord because the glory of the Lord filled it. ³When all the Israelites saw the fire coming down and the glory of the Lord above the temple, they knelt on the pavement with their faces to the ground, and they worshiped and gave thanks to the Lord, saying,

"He is good;
his love endures forever."

⁴Then the king and all the people offered sacrifices before the Lord. ⁵And King Solomon offered a sacrifice of twenty-two thousand head of cattle and a hundred and twenty thousand sheep and goats. So the king and all the people dedicated the temple of God. ⁶The priests took their positions, as did the Levites with the Lord's musical instruments, which King David had made for praising the Lord and which were used when he gave thanks, saying, "His love endures forever." Opposite the Levites, the priests blew their trumpets, and all the Israelites were standing.

⁷Solomon consecrated the middle part of the courtyard in front of the temple of the Lord, and there he offered burnt offerings and the fat of the fellowship offerings, because the bronze altar he had made could not hold the burnt offerings, the grain offerings and the fat portions.

⁸So Solomon observed the festival at that time for seven days, and all Israel with him—a vast assembly, people from Lebo Hamath to the Wadi of Egypt. ⁹On the eighth day they held an assembly, for they had celebrated the dedication of the altar for seven days and the festival for seven days more. ¹⁰On the twenty-third day of the seventh month he sent the people to their homes, joyful and glad in heart for the good things the Lord had done for David and Solomon and for his people Israel.

The Lord Appears to Solomon
7:11-22pp — 1Ki 9:1-9

¹¹When Solomon had finished the temple of the Lord and the royal palace, and had succeeded in carrying out all he had in mind to do in the temple of the Lord and in his own palace, ¹²the Lord appeared to him at night and said:

"I have heard your prayer and have chosen this place for myself as a temple for sacrifices.

¹³"When I shut up the heavens so that there is no rain, or command locusts to devour the land or send a plague among my people, ¹⁴if my people, who are called by my name, will humble themselves and pray and seek my face and turn from their wicked ways, then I will hear from heaven, and I will forgive their sin and will heal their land. ¹⁵Now my eyes will be open and my ears attentive to the prayers offered in this place. ¹⁶I have chosen and consecrated this temple so that my Name may be there forever. My eyes and my heart will always be there.

¹⁷"As for you, if you walk before me faithfully as David your father did, and do all I command, and observe my decrees and laws, ¹⁸I will establish your royal throne, as I covenanted with David your father when I said, 'You shall never fail to have a successor to rule over Israel.'

¹⁹"But if you[a] turn away and forsake the decrees and commands I have given you[a]

---

[a] 19 The Hebrew is plural.

7:1–3 God responds to Solomon's prayer of dedication (2Ch 6:12–42) by filling the temple with his glory. His presence is signaled by fire coming down and consuming the sacrifices (compare 1Ki 18:38 and note). There is no indication that sacrifices have been made for the fire to consume, which suggests that 2Ch 7:1–3 either acts as a type of preface (or summary) for the rest of the chapter or that the priests had already prepared the sacrifices. A similar event occurs in 1Ch 21:26 and Lev 9:23–24. Theophanies (appearances of God to people) often are accompanied by smoke, fire or storms. God appeared to Moses from a burning bush (Ex 3:2). When God appeared on Mount Sinai, he descended with fire and smoke (Ex 19:16–20). The Psalms also associate God's appearance with smoke, fire and storms (see Ps 18:7–19 and note). See the table "Old Testament Theophanies" on p. 924.

7:2 glory of the Lord See note on Ex 16:10.
7:3 his love endures forever This is the same refrain that the Levitical singers sang earlier (2Ch 5:13). It is found throughout Psalms (Ps 106:1; 107:1; 118:1; 136:1).

7:4–10 This section describes the sacrifices offered by Solomon. It largely follows 1Ki 8:62–66, with the Chronicler inserting two verses that call attention to worship practices (2Ch 7:6) and ceremonial rites (v. 9).

7:8 observed the festival at that time for seven days Refers to the Festival of Tabernacles (see note on 5:3).

7:11–22 Yahweh appears to Solomon and reaffirms the covenant; the parallel passage appears in 1Ki 9:1–9. The Chronicler adds to the 1 Kings material at 2Ch 7:13–15: Yahweh affirms that, if the people will show humility and repentance, he will respond with forgiveness and healing.

7:14 heal their land God's response in 2 Chronicles is somewhat different from 1 Kings. While 1 Kings focuses on the faithfulness only of Solomon (1Ki 9:4–5), the additional material in 2 Chronicles expresses the need for God's people to be faithful. This call to return to Yahweh, along with his promise of restoration, would have been especially significant for the Chronicler's audience of returned exiles.

7:19 you turn away The "you" here is plural. God might be addressing Solomon and his descendants or perhaps Solomon and all the people of Israel. **to serve other gods** The northern and southern kingdoms eventually are exiled; in both cases, the text of 2 Kings identifies idolatry as the cause (2Ki 17:7–23; 21:10–18).

and go off to serve other gods and worship them, [20]then I will uproot Israel from my land, which I have given them, and will reject this temple I have consecrated for my Name. I will make it a byword and an object of ridicule among all peoples. [21]This temple will become a heap of rubble. All[a] who pass by will be appalled and say, 'Why has the LORD done such a thing to this land and to this temple?' [22]People will answer, 'Because they have forsaken the LORD, the God of their ancestors, who brought them out of Egypt, and have embraced other gods, worshiping and serving them — that is why he brought all this disaster on them.'"

Solomon's Other Activities

8:1-18pp — 1Ki 9:10-28

8 At the end of twenty years, during which Solomon built the temple of the LORD and his own palace, [2]Solomon rebuilt the villages that Hiram[b] had given him, and settled Israelites in them. [3]Solomon then went to Hamath Zobah and captured it. [4]He also built up Tadmor in the desert and all the store cities he had built in Hamath. [5]He rebuilt Upper Beth Horon and Lower Beth Horon as fortified cities, with walls and with gates and bars, [6]as well as Baalath and all his store cities, and all the cities for his chariots and for his horses[c] — whatever he desired to build in Jerusalem, in Lebanon and throughout all the territory he ruled. [7]There were still people left from the Hittites, Amorites, Perizzites, Hivites and Jebusites (these people were not Israelites). [8]Solomon conscripted the descendants of all these people remaining in the land — whom the Israelites had not destroyed — to serve as slave labor, as it is to this day. [9]But Solomon did not make slaves of the Israelites for his work; they were his fighting men, commanders of his captains, and commanders of his chariots and charioteers. [10]They were also King Solomon's chief officials — two hundred and fifty officials supervising the men.

[11]Solomon brought Pharaoh's daughter up from the City of David to the palace he had built for her, for he said, "My wife must not live in the palace of David king of Israel, because the places the ark of the LORD has entered are holy."

[12]On the altar of the LORD that he had built in front of the portico, Solomon sacrificed burnt offerings to the LORD, [13]according to the daily requirement for offerings commanded by Moses for the Sabbaths, the New Moons and the three annual festivals — the Festival of Unleavened Bread, the Festival of Weeks and the Festival of Tabernacles. [14]In keeping with the ordinance of his father David, he appointed the divisions of the priests for their duties, and the Levites to lead the praise and to assist the priests according to each day's requirement. He also appointed the gatekeepers by divisions for the various gates, because this was what David the man of God had ordered. [15]They did not deviate from the king's commands to the priests or to the Levites in any matter, including that of the treasuries.

[16]All Solomon's work was carried out, from the day the foundation of the temple of the LORD was laid until its completion. So the temple of the LORD was finished.

[17]Then Solomon went to Ezion Geber and Elath on the coast of Edom. [18]And Hiram sent him ships

---

[a] 21 See some Septuagint manuscripts, Old Latin, Syriac, Arabic and Targum; Hebrew *And though this temple is now so imposing, all*   [b] 2 Hebrew *Huram*, a variant of *Hiram*; also in verse 18   [c] 6 Or *charioteers*

7:20 a byword and an object of ridicule Refers to a taunt or mocking saying (compare Isa 14:4 and note; Jer 24:9).

8:1–18 For the most part, this chapter runs parallel to 1Ki 9:10–28, offering an account of Solomon's achievements after building the temple.

8:2 Hiram The king of Tyre (see note on 2Ch 2:3).

8:3–6 This description of Solomon's military conquests and subsequent building projects is not found in the 1 Kings account.

8:4 Tadmor in the desert Tadmor, along with Hamath Zobah, represents the northern extent of Solomon's kingdom.

8:5 Upper Beth Horon Upper and Lower Beth-Horon were located near Jerusalem, most likely on trade routes.

8:6 Baalath A town in the tribe of Dan (Jos 19:44). **store cities** See 1Ki 9:19 and note.

8:8 whom the Israelites had not destroyed Before the Israelites had entered the promised land, God had instructed them to completely destroy these nations (Dt 7:1–6).

8:11 Pharaoh's daughter Soon after becoming king, Solomon had married Pharaoh's daughter to make an alliance with Egypt. This event is not narrated in 2 Chronicles; see 1Ki 3:1 and note. **the places the ark of the LORD has entered are holy** Unlike 1Ki 9:24, the Chronicler's report explains why Solomon built a house for Pharaoh's daughter. Most likely, she was a foreigner who retained her pagan religion (see 1Ki 11:4–8).

8:13 commanded by Moses In this addition to the 1 Kings account, the Chronicler emphasizes Solomon's faithfulness in worship. Here, he shows Solomon's adherence to the commands of Moses. **for the Sabbaths** See Nu 28:9–10 and note. **the New Moons** Refers to the required monthly sacrifices (Nu 28:11–15). **the three annual festivals** For details about these feasts, see Lev 23:9–22,33–44.

8:14 the ordinance of his father David Solomon follows David's plan for organizing the temple personnel (see 1Ch 23:1–26:32).

8:16 All Solomon's work was carried out This completes the building of the temple that began in 2Ch 2:1. Including David's preparations, most of 1Ch 22:2—2Ch 8:16 is devoted to the temple — a reflection of the Chronicler's emphasis on proper worship.

commanded by his own men, sailors who knew the sea. These, with Solomon's men, sailed to Ophir and brought back four hundred and fifty talents[a] of gold, which they delivered to King Solomon.

The Queen of Sheba Visits Solomon

9:1-12pp — 1Ki 10:1-13

9 When the queen of Sheba heard of Solomon's fame, she came to Jerusalem to test him with hard questions. Arriving with a very great caravan — with camels carrying spices, large quantities of gold, and precious stones — she came to Solomon and talked with him about all she had on her mind. [2]Solomon answered all her questions; nothing was too hard for him to explain to her. [3]When the queen of Sheba saw the wisdom of Solomon, as well as the palace he had built, [4]the food on his table, the seating of his officials, the attending servants in their robes, the cupbearers in their robes and the burnt offerings he made at[b] the temple of the LORD, she was overwhelmed.

[5]She said to the king, "The report I heard in my own country about your achievements and your wisdom is true. [6]But I did not believe what they said until I came and saw with my own eyes. Indeed, not even half the greatness of your wisdom was told me; you have far exceeded the report I heard. [7]How happy your people must be! How happy your officials, who continually stand before you and hear your wisdom! [8]Praise be to the LORD your God, who has delighted in you and placed you on his throne as king to rule for the LORD your God. Because of the love of your God for Israel and his desire to uphold them forever, he has made you king over them, to maintain justice and righteousness."

[9]Then she gave the king 120 talents[c] of gold, large quantities of spices, and precious stones. There had never been such spices as those the queen of Sheba gave to King Solomon.

[10](The servants of Hiram and the servants of Solomon brought gold from Ophir; they also brought algumwood[d] and precious stones. [11]The king used the algumwood to make steps for the temple of the LORD and for the royal palace, and to make harps and lyres for the musicians. Nothing like them had ever been seen in Judah.)

[12]King Solomon gave the queen of Sheba all she desired and asked for; he gave her more than she had brought to him. Then she left and returned with her retinue to her own country.

Solomon's Splendor

9:13-28pp — 1Ki 10:14-29; 2Ch 1:14-17

[13]The weight of the gold that Solomon received yearly was 666 talents,[e] [14]not including the revenues brought in by merchants and traders. Also all the kings of Arabia and the governors of the territories brought gold and silver to Solomon.

[15]King Solomon made two hundred large shields of hammered gold; six hundred shekels[f] of hammered gold went into each shield. [16]He also made three hundred small shields of hammered gold, with three hundred shekels[g] of gold in each shield. The king put them in the Palace of the Forest of Lebanon.

[17]Then the king made a great throne covered with ivory and overlaid with pure gold. [18]The throne had six steps, and a footstool of gold was attached to it. On both sides of the seat were armrests, with a lion standing beside each of them. [19]Twelve lions stood on the six steps, one at either end of each step. Nothing like it had ever been made for any other kingdom. [20]All King Solomon's goblets were gold, and all the household articles

---

[a] *18* That is, about 17 tons or about 15 metric tons   [b] *4* Or *and the ascent by which he went up to*   [c] *9* That is, about 4 1/2 tons or about 4 metric tons   [d] *10* Probably a variant of *almugwood*   [e] *13* That is, about 25 tons or about 23 metric tons   [f] *15* That is, about 15 pounds or about 6.9 kilograms   [g] *16* That is, about 7 1/2 pounds or about 3.5 kilograms

---

8:18 Ophir A region possibly located in Arabia and known for fine gold (Job 28:16; Isa 13:12).

9:1–12 This account of Solomon's visit from the Queen of Sheba runs parallel to 1Ki 10:1–13.

9:1 Sheba May refer to an Arabian kingdom. See 1Ki 10:1 and note. **hard questions** The Hebrew word used here, *chidah*, can describe a riddle or a teaching from elders (compare Jdg 14:12–20; Pr 1:6; Ps 78:2). **9:4 she was overwhelmed** The Queen of Sheba is left breathless at the extravagance of Solomon's wisdom and wealth.

9:8 placed you on his throne The account in 1 Kings refers to the throne of Israel rather than the throne of God (1Ki 10:9). In 1–2 Chronicles, the reign of the Davidic king is closely related to God's kingdom. See note on 1Ch 17:14.

9:10 algumwood and precious stones The servants of Hiram and Solomon return (see 2Ch 8:18). The kind

of wood they bring is unknown, but it apparently was a luxury item.

9:13–28 This description of Solomon's wealth—also found in 1Ki 10:14–29—emphasizes God fulfilling his promise to grant Solomon riches, possessions and honor (2Ch 1:11–12). The passage repeats some material found in ch. 1 (see 1:14–17 and note).

9:14 the governors of the territories Leaders of Israel's tribes (1Ch 27:16–22).

9:15 two hundred large shields Refers to body-length shields. See 1Ki 10:16 and note.

9:16 three hundred small shields Refers to smaller, handheld shields. **Palace of the Forest of Lebanon** See 1Ki 7:1–12.

9:17 a great throne covered with ivory Most likely wood with inlaid ivory. Such costly items were condemned by the prophet Amos (Am 6:4 and note).

9:18 a lion Lions were associated with the tribe of Judah and the royal line of David (see Ge 49:9 and note).

in the Palace of the Forest of Lebanon were pure gold. Nothing was made of silver, because silver was considered of little value in Solomon's day. [21]The king had a fleet of trading ships[a] manned by Hiram's[b] servants. Once every three years it returned, carrying gold, silver and ivory, and apes and baboons.

[22]King Solomon was greater in riches and wisdom than all the other kings of the earth. [23]All the kings of the earth sought audience with Solomon to hear the wisdom God had put in his heart. [24]Year after year, everyone who came brought a gift—articles of silver and gold, and robes, weapons and spices, and horses and mules.

[25]Solomon had four thousand stalls for horses and chariots, and twelve thousand horses,[c] which he kept in the chariot cities and also with him in Jerusalem. [26]He ruled over all the kings from the Euphrates River to the land of the Philistines, as far as the border of Egypt. [27]The king made silver as common in Jerusalem as stones, and cedar as plentiful as sycamore-fig trees in the foothills. [28]Solomon's horses were imported from Egypt and from all other countries.

Solomon's Death

9:29-31pp — 1Ki 11:41-43

[29]As for the other events of Solomon's reign, from beginning to end, are they not written in the records of Nathan the prophet, in the prophecy of Ahijah the Shilonite and in the visions of Iddo the seer concerning Jeroboam son of Nebat? [30]Solomon reigned in Jerusalem over all Israel forty years. [31]Then he rested with his ancestors and was buried in the city of David his father. And Rehoboam his son succeeded him as king.

Israel Rebels Against Rehoboam

10:1–11:4pp — 1Ki 12:1-24

10 Rehoboam went to Shechem, for all Israel had gone there to make him king. [2]When Jeroboam son of Nebat heard this (he was in Egypt, where he had fled from King Solomon), he returned from Egypt. [3]So they sent for Jeroboam, and he and all Israel went to Rehoboam and said to him: [4]"Your father put a heavy yoke on us, but now lighten the harsh labor and the heavy yoke he put on us, and we will serve you."

[5]Rehoboam answered, "Come back to me in three days." So the people went away.

[6]Then King Rehoboam consulted the elders who had served his father Solomon during his lifetime. "How would you advise me to answer these people?" he asked.

[7]They replied, "If you will be kind to these people and please them and give them a favorable answer, they will always be your servants."

[8]But Rehoboam rejected the advice the elders

---

[a] 21 Hebrew *of ships that could go to Tarshish*   [b] 21 Hebrew *Huram*, a variant of *Hiram*   [c] 25 Or *charioteers*

9:21 a fleet of trading ships The Hebrew text here references Tarshish, a distant port (see note on Jnh 1:3). **apes and baboons** The translation of the Hebrew words used here, *qophim* and *thukkiyyim*, is uncertain. They represent exotic animals, most likely different species of monkeys.

9:22–26 Expanding on 1Ki 10:23–25, the Chronicler emphasizes Solomon's place of prominence among the kings of the earth.

9:24 everyone who came brought a gift Most likely a tribute. See note on 1Ki 4:21.

9:26 from the Euphrates River The boundaries given here correspond with God's promise to Abraham. See Ge 15:7–8.

9:27 foothills A region of low hills between Jerusalem and the coastal plain.

9:28 Solomon's horses were imported Importing horses, especially from Egypt, was forbidden in the law. See Dt 17:16 and note.

9:29 The Chronicler references three other sources—one associated with Nathan the prophet (2Sa 7), another with Ahijah the Shilonite (1Ki 11:29–39), and a third associated with Iddo, a figure known only from 2 Chronicles (compare note on 2Ch 13:22). These seem to have been works about, or by, these prophetic figures.

9:29 the other events of Solomon's reign, from beginning to end A common epitaph for deceased kings (compare 1Ki 11:41; 14:19). Second Chronicles does not refer to Solomon's foreign wives, his idolatry or God's condemnation of his behavior (1Ki 11:1–40).

Although this information would have been familiar to the Chronicler and his audience, it does not fit with the book's theological emphasis on restoring national unity and proper temple worship. **visions of Iddo the seer** See note on 2Ch 13:22.

9:30 forty years An idealized number, indicating a successful reign. David also reigned for 40 years (1Ch 29:27).

9:31 he rested with his ancestors An idiom meaning "died peacefully." It also can have a literal meaning, denoting burial in a family plot (e.g., Ge 47:29–30).

10:1–19 The Chronicler's account of the division of the kingdom under Rehoboam largely follows the account in 1Ki 12:1–15. However, the Chronicler ignores any details of the northern kingdom (Israel) that do not relate to the southern kingdom (Judah), in part because his audience is composed of returned exiles from Judah. Also, the Chronicler emphasizes national unity and the importance of David's royal line (see note on 1Ch 1:1—9:44), both of which were rejected by the northern tribes (2Ch 10:16,19).

10:1 Shechem Located 40 miles north of Jerusalem. It is unclear why the Israelites held Rehoboam's coronation at Shechem instead of Jerusalem, the capital.

10:2 where he had fled from King Solomon The Chronicler does not include the story of Jeroboam's rebellion against Solomon (see 1Ki 11:26–40).

10:4 Your father put a heavy yoke on us Refers to Solomon's heavy taxation and forced labor.

10:7 give them a favorable answer The advice offered by the old men included lightening the people's burden.

gave him and consulted the young men who had grown up with him and were serving him. ⁹He asked them, "What is your advice? How should we answer these people who say to me, 'Lighten the yoke your father put on us'?"

¹⁰The young men who had grown up with him replied, "The people have said to you, 'Your father put a heavy yoke on us, but make our yoke lighter.' Now tell them, 'My little finger is thicker than my father's waist. ¹¹My father laid on you a heavy yoke; I will make it even heavier. My father scourged you with whips; I will scourge you with scorpions.'"

¹²Three days later Jeroboam and all the people returned to Rehoboam, as the king had said, "Come back to me in three days." ¹³The king answered them harshly. Rejecting the advice of the elders, ¹⁴he followed the advice of the young men and said, "My father made your yoke heavy; I will make it even heavier. My father scourged you with whips; I will scourge you with scorpions." ¹⁵So the king did not listen to the people, for this turn of events was from God, to fulfill the word the LORD had spoken to Jeroboam son of Nebat through Ahijah the Shilonite.

¹⁶When all Israel saw that the king refused to listen to them, they answered the king:

"What share do we have in David,
    what part in Jesse's son?
To your tents, Israel!
    Look after your own house, David!"

So all the Israelites went home. ¹⁷But as for the Israelites who were living in the towns of Judah, Rehoboam still ruled over them.

¹⁸King Rehoboam sent out Adoniram,ᵃ who was in charge of forced labor, but the Israelites stoned him to death. King Rehoboam, however, managed to get into his chariot and escape to Jerusalem. ¹⁹So Israel has been in rebellion against the house of David to this day.

11 When Rehoboam arrived in Jerusalem, he mustered Judah and Benjamin — a hundred and eighty thousand able young men — to go to war against Israel and to regain the kingdom for Rehoboam.

²But this word of the LORD came to Shemaiah the man of God: ³"Say to Rehoboam son of Solomon king of Judah and to all Israel in Judah and Benjamin, ⁴'This is what the LORD says: Do not go up to fight against your fellow Israelites. Go home, every one of you, for this is my doing.'" So they obeyed the words of the LORD and turned back from marching against Jeroboam.

Rehoboam Fortifies Judah

⁵Rehoboam lived in Jerusalem and built up towns for defense in Judah: ⁶Bethlehem, Etam, Tekoa, ⁷Beth Zur, Soko, Adullam, ⁸Gath, Mareshah, Ziph, ⁹Adoraim, Lachish, Azekah, ¹⁰Zorah, Aijalon and Hebron. These were fortified cities in Judah and Benjamin. ¹¹He strengthened their defenses and put commanders in them, with supplies of food, olive oil and wine. ¹²He put shields and spears in all the cities, and made them very strong. So Judah and Benjamin were his.

¹³The priests and Levites from all their districts throughout Israel sided with him. ¹⁴The Levites even abandoned their pasturelands and property and came to Judah and Jerusalem, because Jeroboam and his sons had rejected them as priests of the LORD ¹⁵when he appointed his own priests for the high places and for the goat and calf idols he had made. ¹⁶Those from every tribe of Israel who set their hearts on seeking the LORD, the God of Israel, followed the Levites to Jerusalem to offer sacrifices to the LORD, the God of their ancestors. ¹⁷They strengthened the kingdom of Judah and supported Rehoboam son of Solomon three

---

ᵃ 18 Hebrew *Hadoram*, a variant of *Adoniram*

10:10 My little finger The Hebrew phrase here is most likely a euphemism for the penis (see note on 1Ki 12:10).

10:11 I will scourge you with scorpions The Hebrew word here denoting "scorpions" may refer to barbed whips.

10:15 to fulfill the word the LORD While the Chronicler does not include an account of this prophecy, he nevertheless attributes the division of the kingdom to God's word (see 1Ki 11:29–39).

10:16 So all the Israelites went home This marks the division into two kingdoms—the northern kingdom of Israel (10 tribes), and the southern kingdom of Judah (the tribes of Judah and Benjamin). See note on 1Ki 12:16–24.

10:18 Adoniram In the Hebrew text, this figure is called both "Hadoram" and "Adoniram" (1Ki 4:6; 5:13–14). Considering his position over the forced labor, he was a foolish choice to mediate reconciliation.

10:19 So Israel has been in rebellion See 1Ki 12:19 and note.

11:1–23 While the beginning of the Rehoboam account follows 1 Kings (compare 2Ch 11:1–4; 1Ki 12:21–24), the Chronicler adds details about Rehoboam's fortifications (2Ch 11:5–12) and genealogy (vv. 18–23). The Chronicler also emphasizes that Jerusalem remained the center of proper worship. He explains that Jeroboam banished the priests and Levites, and that those who wanted to seek Yahweh came to Jerusalem (vv. 13–17).

11:2 Shemaiah See 1Ki 12:22 and note.

11:5–10 Rehoboam built up fortifications in cities spanning the southern, eastern and western borders around Jerusalem. He does not build up defenses on the northern border.

11:13 The priests and Levites This account of the priests and Levites leaving the northern kingdom strengthens the Chronicler's emphasis on temple worship and the Davidic monarchy (see note on 2Ch 6:6).

11:15 for the high places While the Chronicler mostly

years, following the ways of David and Solomon during this time.

Rehoboam's Family

[18]Rehoboam married Mahalath, who was the daughter of David's son Jerimoth and of Abihail, the daughter of Jesse's son Eliab. [19]She bore him sons: Jeush, Shemariah and Zaham. [20]Then he married Maakah daughter of Absalom, who bore him Abijah, Attai, Ziza and Shelomith. [21]Rehoboam loved Maakah daughter of Absalom more than any of his other wives and concubines. In all, he had eighteen wives and sixty concubines, twenty-eight sons and sixty daughters.

[22]Rehoboam appointed Abijah son of Maakah as crown prince among his brothers, in order to make him king. [23]He acted wisely, dispersing some of his sons throughout the districts of Judah and Benjamin, and to all the fortified cities. He gave them abundant provisions and took many wives for them.

Shishak Attacks Jerusalem

12:9-16pp — 1Ki 14:21,25-31

12 After Rehoboam's position as king was established and he had become strong, he and all Israel[a] with him abandoned the law of the LORD. [2]Because they had been unfaithful to the LORD, Shishak king of Egypt attacked Jerusalem in the fifth year of King Rehoboam. [3]With twelve hundred chariots and sixty thousand horsemen and the innumerable troops of Libyans, Sukkites and Cushites[b] that came with him from Egypt, [4]he captured the fortified cities of Judah and came as far as Jerusalem.

[5]Then the prophet Shemaiah came to Rehoboam and to the leaders of Judah who had assembled in Jerusalem for fear of Shishak, and he said to them, "This is what the LORD says, 'You have abandoned me; therefore, I now abandon you to Shishak.'"

[6]The leaders of Israel and the king humbled themselves and said, "The LORD is just."

[7]When the LORD saw that they humbled themselves, this word of the LORD came to Shemaiah: "Since they have humbled themselves, I will not destroy them but will soon give them deliverance. My wrath will not be poured out on Jerusalem through Shishak. [8]They will, however, become subject to him, so that they may learn the difference between serving me and serving the kings of other lands."

[9]When Shishak king of Egypt attacked Jerusalem, he carried off the treasures of the temple of the LORD and the treasures of the royal palace. He took everything, including the gold shields Solomon had made. [10]So King Rehoboam made bronze shields to replace them and assigned these to the commanders of the guard on duty at the entrance to the royal palace. [11]Whenever the king went to the LORD's temple, the guards went with him, bearing the shields, and afterward they returned them to the guardroom.

[12]Because Rehoboam humbled himself, the LORD's anger turned from him, and he was not totally destroyed. Indeed, there was some good in Judah.

[13]King Rehoboam established himself firmly in Jerusalem and continued as king. He was forty-one years old when he became king, and he reigned seventeen years in Jerusalem, the city the LORD had chosen out of all the tribes of Israel in which to put his Name. His mother's name was Naamah; she was an Ammonite. [14]He did evil because he had not set his heart on seeking the LORD.

---

[a] 1 That is, Judah, as frequently in 2 Chronicles   [b] 3 That is, people from the upper Nile region

---

ignores the account of Jeroboam, he alludes to Jeroboam's idolatry in this passage. See 1Ki 12:25–33 and note. **for the goat** Sacrificing to "goat idols" or "goat demons" is specifically prohibited in the law. See Lev 17:7 and note. **calf idols** See 1Ki 12:28 and note. Reminiscent of the golden calf that Aaron made while Moses was on Mount Sinai (Ex 32).

11:16 on seeking the LORD, the God o f Israel People from all the tribes who were seeking Yahweh came to Jerusalem to worship. As he does throughout, the Chronicler emphasizes seeking God as evidence of faithfulness. Saul's death is attributed partially to his failure to seek God (1Ch 10:14). David, in contrast, sought God when he brought the ark to Jerusalem. When making preparations for the temple, David encouraged Israel's leaders to seek God (1Ch 22:17–19). He also encouraged Solomon to faithfully seek God (1Ch 28:9).

11:23 dispersing some of his sons Placing his sons in positions of power throughout the kingdom would help guard against rebellion.

12:1–16 The Chronicler's report of Shishak's attack on Jerusalem differs from the account in 1Ki 14:21–28. It includes details about Rehoboam humbling himself and God relenting from destroying Jerusalem (2Ch 12:5–8). It also largely downplays Rehoboam's sin (see note on v. 1).

12:1 he and all Israel with him abandoned the law of the LORD The account in 1 Kings gives more details, indicating that Rehoboam made high places for idol worship and allowed cult prostitution (1Ki 14:22–24).

12:2 Shishak First king of the twenty-second Dynasty of Egypt (reigned ca. 931–910 BC). Shishak had harbored Jeroboam after Solomon sought to kill him (1Ki 11:40).

12:6 The LORD is just Recognizing their sin, Rehoboam and the leaders of Israel humble themselves and acknowledge that God is just in punishing them.

12:7 I will not destroy them In relenting from punishing Rehoboam, God fulfills the promise he made to Solomon (2Ch 7:12–18). This message of God's mercy after repentance would have resonated with the Chronicler's audience of returned exiles.

12:8 they may learn the difference between serving me God allows Rehoboam to suffer some consequences for abandoning the law (see Dt 28:47–50).

12:9 He took everything Since Shishak did not take Jerusalem, it is likely that Rehoboam bought him off with a large, one-time tribute payment.

12:14 on seeking the LORD The importance of seeking God is a recurring theme in 1–2 Chronicles; see note on 2Ch 11:16.

¹⁵As for the events of Rehoboam's reign, from beginning to end, are they not written in the records of Shemaiah the prophet and of Iddo the seer that deal with genealogies? There was continual warfare between Rehoboam and Jeroboam. ¹⁶Rehoboam rested with his ancestors and was buried in the City of David. And Abijah his son succeeded him as king.

Abijah King of Judah

13:1-2,22 – 14:1pp — 1Ki 15:1-2,6-8

13 In the eighteenth year of the reign of Jeroboam, Abijah became king of Judah, ²and he reigned in Jerusalem three years. His mother's name was Maakah,ᵃ a daughterᵇ of Uriel of Gibeah.

There was war between Abijah and Jeroboam. ³Abijah went into battle with an army of four hundred thousand able fighting men, and Jeroboam drew up a battle line against him with eight hundred thousand able troops.

⁴Abijah stood on Mount Zemaraim, in the hill country of Ephraim, and said, "Jeroboam and all Israel, listen to me! ⁵Don't you know that the LORD, the God of Israel, has given the kingship of Israel to David and his descendants forever by a covenant of salt? ⁶Yet Jeroboam son of Nebat, an official of Solomon son of David, rebelled against his master. ⁷Some worthless scoundrels gathered around him and opposed Rehoboam son of Solomon when he was young and indecisive and not strong enough to resist them.

⁸"And now you plan to resist the kingdom of the LORD, which is in the hands of David's descendants. You are indeed a vast army and have with you the golden calves that Jeroboam made to be your gods. ⁹But didn't you drive out the priests of the LORD, the sons of Aaron, and the Levites, and make priests of your own as the peoples of other lands do? Whoever comes to consecrate himself with a young bull and seven rams may become a priest of what are not gods.

¹⁰"As for us, the LORD is our God, and we have not forsaken him. The priests who serve the LORD are sons of Aaron, and the Levites assist them. ¹¹Every morning and evening they present burnt offerings and fragrant incense to the LORD. They set out the bread on the ceremonially clean table and light the lamps on the gold lampstand every evening. We are observing the requirements of the LORD our God. But you have forsaken him. ¹²God is with us; he is our leader. His priests with their trumpets will sound the battle cry against you. People of Israel, do not fight against the LORD, the God of your ancestors, for you will not succeed."

¹³Now Jeroboam had sent troops around to the rear, so that while he was in front of Judah the ambush was behind them. ¹⁴Judah turned and saw that they were being attacked at both front and rear. Then they cried out to the LORD. The priests blew their trumpets ¹⁵and the men of Judah raised the battle cry. At the sound of their battle cry, God routed Jeroboam and all Israel before Abijah and Judah. ¹⁶The Israelites fled before Judah, and God delivered them into their hands. ¹⁷Abijah and his troops inflicted heavy losses on them, so that there were five hundred thousand casualties among Israel's able men. ¹⁸The Israelites were subdued on that occasion, and the people of Judah were victorious because they relied on the LORD, the God of their ancestors.

¹⁹Abijah pursued Jeroboam and took from him the towns of Bethel, Jeshanah and Ephron, with their surrounding villages. ²⁰Jeroboam did not regain power during the time of Abijah. And the LORD struck him down and he died.

ᵃ 2 Most Septuagint manuscripts and Syriac (see also 11:20 and 1 Kings 15:2); Hebrew *Micaiah*   ᵇ 2 Or *granddaughter*

12:15 records of Shemaiah the prophet This source was apparently information recorded by or about Shemaiah the prophet (11:2; 12:5–7). **Iddo the seer** See note on 13:22.
12:16 rested with his ancestors See note on 9:31.
13:1–22 Abijah's reign and his battle with Jeroboam receive more coverage in 2 Chronicles than in 1 Kings (1Ki 15:1–8). Here, Abijah is portrayed in a positive light as he rebukes Jeroboam for his idolatry (2Ch 13:8–9) and expresses faithfulness to God (vv. 10–12). God rewards Abijah by giving him victory over Jeroboam (vv. 15–18).
13:1 In the eighteenth year of the reign of Jeroboam According to 1Ki 14:20, Jeroboam reigned over the northern kingdom for 22 years (ca. 930–909 BC). See the timeline "The Divided Kingdom" on p. 536.

NORTHERN KING	DATE	SOUTHERN KING	DATE
Jeroboam	930–909 BC	Rehoboam	930–913 BC
Nadab	909–900 BC	Abijah	913–910 BC
Baasha	900–886 BC	Asa	910–873 BC

13:2 Maakah The Hebrew text here identifies Abijah's mother as Micaiah, a variant form of Maakah (which appears in 2Ch 11:20).
13:3 four hundred thousand able fighting men These numbers may be symbolic or exaggerated. The point is that Jeroboam's army outnumbered Abijah's army two to one.
13:5 by a covenant of salt Salt was used in certain sacrifices. See Nu 18:19 and note.
13:8 the kingdom of the LORD The Chronicler associates David's royal line with the kingdom of God (1Ch 17:14). By rejecting the Davidic monarchy—God's chosen king—Jeroboam had rejected God's kingdom. **golden calves** Refers to idols built by Jeroboam. See 1Ki 12:25–33 and note.
13:9 didn't you drive out the priests See 2Ch 11:13 and note.
13:11 the bread on the ceremonially clean table See Lev 24:5–6. **gold lampstand** See 2Ch 4:7 and note.
13:17 there were five hundred thousand casualties among Israel's able men See note on v. 3.
13:20 and he died According to 1 Kings, Jeroboam died

²¹But Abijah grew in strength. He married fourteen wives and had twenty-two sons and sixteen daughters.

²²The other events of Abijah's reign, what he did and what he said, are written in the annotations of the prophet Iddo.

14 *ᵃ* And Abijah rested with his ancestors and was buried in the City of David. Asa his son succeeded him as king, and in his days the country was at peace for ten years.

Asa King of Judah

14:2-3pp — 1Ki 15:11-12

²Asa did what was good and right in the eyes of the LORD his God. ³He removed the foreign altars and the high places, smashed the sacred stones and cut down the Asherah poles.*ᵇ* ⁴He commanded Judah to seek the LORD, the God of their ancestors, and to obey his laws and commands. ⁵He removed the high places and incense altars in every town in Judah, and the kingdom was at peace under him. ⁶He built up the fortified cities of Judah, since the land was at peace. No one was at war with him during those years, for the LORD gave him rest.

⁷"Let us build up these towns," he said to Judah, "and put walls around them, with towers, gates and bars. The land is still ours, because we have sought the LORD our God; we sought him and he has given us rest on every side." So they built and prospered.

⁸Asa had an army of three hundred thousand men from Judah, equipped with large shields and with spears, and two hundred and eighty thousand from Benjamin, armed with small shields and with bows. All these were brave fighting men.

⁹Zerah the Cushite marched out against them with an army of thousands upon thousands and three hundred chariots, and came as far as Mareshah. ¹⁰Asa went out to meet him, and they took up battle positions in the Valley of Zephathah near Mareshah.

¹¹Then Asa called to the LORD his God and said, "LORD, there is no one like you to help the powerless against the mighty. Help us, LORD our God, for we rely on you, and in your name we have come against this vast army. LORD, you are our God; do not let mere mortals prevail against you."

¹²The LORD struck down the Cushites before Asa and Judah. The Cushites fled, ¹³and Asa and his army pursued them as far as Gerar. Such a great number of Cushites fell that they could not recover; they were crushed before the LORD and his forces. The men of Judah carried off a large amount of plunder. ¹⁴They destroyed all the villages around Gerar, for the terror of the LORD had fallen on them. They looted all these villages, since there was much plunder there. ¹⁵They also attacked the camps of the herders and carried off droves of sheep and goats and camels. Then they returned to Jerusalem.

Asa's Reform

15:16-19pp — 1Ki 15:13-16

15 The Spirit of God came on Azariah son of Oded. ²He went out to meet Asa and said to him, "Listen to me, Asa and all Judah and Ben-

---

ᵃ In Hebrew texts 14:1 is numbered 13:23, and 14:2-15 is numbered 14:1-14. *ᵇ* 3 That is, wooden symbols of the goddess Asherah; here and elsewhere in 2 Chronicles

---

during the reign of Abijah's successor, Asa (1Ki 15:25). Most likely the Chronicler does not intend this note to be chronological. Instead, he is contrasting the success of Abijah with the eventual demise of Jeroboam.

13:22 The other events A common epitaph for deceased kings (compare 1Ki 11:41; 14:19). **written in the annotations of the prophet Iddo** Iddo is earlier identified as a visionary (or seer); nothing else is known about him. He is mentioned only in the context of the Chronicler's source materials (2Ch 9:29; 12:15).

14:1—16:14 As with Abijah, 2 Chronicles devotes more attention to Asa than does the parallel account in 1 Kings (compare 1Ki 15:9–24). The main themes of Asa's reign are reliance on God and seeking God (see note on 2Ch 14:4).

14:1 Asa his son succeeded him as king Asa reigned in the southern kingdom of Judah from about 910–873 BC. His reign spanned the reign of six different northern kings. See the timeline "The Divided Kingdom" on p. 536.

NORTHERN KING	DATE	NORTHERN KING	DATE
Nadab	909–900 BC	Zimri	885 BC
Baasha	900–886 BC	Omri	885–874 BC
Elah	886–885 BC	Ahab	874–853 BC

14:3 removed the foreign altars and the high places Built during Rehoboam's reign (see note on 12:1). See the table "Altars in the Old Testament" on p. 249. **Asherah poles** Typically refers to sacred poles or trees used to worship the Canaanite goddess Asherah (Dt 16:21), who is associated with sexual fertility and sacred prostitution (2Ki 23:7; see note on Ex 34:13). Asherah often is mentioned alongside Baal (Jdg 3:7; 1Ki 18:19).

14:4 to seek the LORD The theme of seeking God, present throughout 1–2 Chronicles, is especially prevalent in the account of Asa (see note on 2Ch 11:16).

14:9 Zerah the Cushite The identity of Zerah is unknown. **with an army of thousands upon thousands** Literally "a thousand thousands." This phrase indicates a large army rather than a specific number.

14:10 Mareshah A fortified city (11:8) south of Jerusalem.

14:13 Gerar A town in the Negev, the arid region of southern Judah.

15:1–19 The Chronicler continues to give Asa's reign an expanded treatment (see note on 14:1—16:14). While the account in 1 Kings covers some of Asa's reforms (1Ki 15:13–15), only 2 Chronicles includes the prophecy of Azariah (2Ch 15:1–8) and Asa's response (vv. 9–15).

15:1 The Spirit of God came The coming of the "Spirit of God" or "Spirit of Yahweh" is an indication of prophetic

jamin. The LORD is with you when you are with him. If you seek him, he will be found by you, but if you forsake him, he will forsake you. ³For a long time Israel was without the true God, without a priest to teach and without the law. ⁴But in their distress they turned to the LORD, the God of Israel, and sought him, and he was found by them. ⁵In those days it was not safe to travel about, for all the inhabitants of the lands were in great turmoil. ⁶One nation was being crushed by another and one city by another, because God was troubling them with every kind of distress. ⁷But as for you, be strong and do not give up, for your work will be rewarded."

⁸When Asa heard these words and the prophecy of Azariah son of ᵃ Oded the prophet, he took courage. He removed the detestable idols from the whole land of Judah and Benjamin and from the towns he had captured in the hills of Ephraim. He repaired the altar of the LORD that was in front of the portico of the LORD's temple.

⁹Then he assembled all Judah and Benjamin and the people from Ephraim, Manasseh and Simeon who had settled among them, for large numbers had come over to him from Israel when they saw that the LORD his God was with him.

¹⁰They assembled at Jerusalem in the third month of the fifteenth year of Asa's reign. ¹¹At that time they sacrificed to the LORD seven hundred head of cattle and seven thousand sheep and goats from the plunder they had brought back. ¹²They entered into a covenant to seek the LORD, the God of their ancestors, with all their heart and soul. ¹³All who would not seek the LORD, the God of Israel, were to be put to death, whether small or great, man or woman. ¹⁴They took an oath to the LORD with loud acclamation, with shouting and with trumpets and horns. ¹⁵All Judah rejoiced

about the oath because they had sworn it wholeheartedly. They sought God eagerly, and he was found by them. So the LORD gave them rest on every side.

¹⁶King Asa also deposed his grandmother Maakah from her position as queen mother, because she had made a repulsive image for the worship of Asherah. Asa cut it down, broke it up and burned it in the Kidron Valley. ¹⁷Although he did not remove the high places from Israel, Asa's heart was fully committed to the LORD all his life. ¹⁸He brought into the temple of God the silver and gold and the articles that he and his father had dedicated.

¹⁹There was no more war until the thirty-fifth year of Asa's reign.

Asa's Last Years
16:1-6pp — 1Ki 15:17-22
16:11-17:1pp — 1Ki 15:23-24

16 In the thirty-sixth year of Asa's reign Baasha king of Israel went up against Judah and fortified Ramah to prevent anyone from leaving or entering the territory of Asa king of Judah.

²Asa then took the silver and gold out of the treasuries of the LORD's temple and of his own palace and sent it to Ben-Hadad king of Aram, who was ruling in Damascus. ³"Let there be a treaty between me and you," he said, "as there was between my father and your father. See, I am sending you silver and gold. Now break your treaty with Baasha king of Israel so he will withdraw from me."

⁴Ben-Hadad agreed with King Asa and sent the commanders of his forces against the towns

ᵃ 8 Vulgate and Syriac (see also Septuagint and verse 1); Hebrew does not have *Azariah son of*.

---

inspiration or divine authority. The Chronicler uses the term several times, always to indicate a prophetic oracle (20:14; 24:20). **15:8 He removed the detestable idols** Either Asa's earlier removal of the foreign altars was incomplete, or the Chronicler's presentation is not chronological (compare 14:3). **towns he had captured in the hills of Ephraim** This suggests that Asa had clashed with the northern tribes prior to the conflict over Ramah (16:1–6). **He repaired the altar of the LORD** There is no report of prior damage to this altar (built by Solomon; 4:1). The omission is not surprising, since the Chronicler is not presenting an exhaustive history. See the infographic "Solomon's Bronze Altar" on p. 667. **15:13 to be put to death** While this may seem harsh, it aligns with the law's punishment for idolatry (Dt 13:6–11; 17:2–7). **15:16 queen mother** The Hebrew word used here, *gevirah*, designates an official position in the royal court. **for the worship of Asherah** The Canaanite fertility goddess. See note on 2Ch 14:3. See the table "Pagan Deities of the Old Testament" on p. 1287. **the Kidron Valley** Located on the eastern side of Jerusalem, the

Kidron Valley became a common place to dispose of idols (e.g., 29:16; 1Ki 15:13; 2Ki 23:6,12). **15:18 the articles** Refers to spoils of war dedicated to God.

16:1–14 Both 1 Kings and 2 Chronicles describe Asa's conflict with Baasha and his covenant with Ben-Hadad (1Ki 15:16–22; 2Ch 16:1–6). However, 2 Chronicles includes a rebuke from Hanani that is not mentioned in 1 Kings (16:7–10). By including this material, the Chronicler warns his audience of returned exiles to rely on God rather than neighboring nations.

16:1 Baasha king of Israel The Chronicler gives very few details about the northern kings. Baasha ruled ca. 900–886 BC, having become king after killing Nadab, Jeroboam's successor (see 1Ki 15:25–16:7). **Ramah** A city about five miles north of Jerusalem in the tribal territory of Benjamin. A military presence in Ramah would pose an imminent threat against Judah. **16:2 out of the treasuries** The same spoils of war that he had dedicated to God (see 2Ch 15:18). **Aram** Kingdom located north of Israel (the northern kingdom)—and thus a strategic ally for Judah (the southern kingdom).

of Israel. They conquered Ijon, Dan, Abel Maim[a] and all the store cities of Naphtali. ⁵When Baasha heard this, he stopped building Ramah and abandoned his work. ⁶Then King Asa brought all the men of Judah, and they carried away from Ramah the stones and timber Baasha had been using. With them he built up Geba and Mizpah.

⁷At that time Hanani the seer came to Asa king of Judah and said to him: "Because you relied on the king of Aram and not on the Lord your God, the army of the king of Aram has escaped from your hand. ⁸Were not the Cushites[b] and Libyans a mighty army with great numbers of chariots and horsemen[c]? Yet when you relied on the Lord, he delivered them into your hand. ⁹For the eyes of the Lord range throughout the earth to strengthen those whose hearts are fully committed to him. You have done a foolish thing, and from now on you will be at war."

¹⁰Asa was angry with the seer because of this; he was so enraged that he put him in prison. At the same time Asa brutally oppressed some of the people.

¹¹The events of Asa's reign, from beginning to end, are written in the book of the kings of Judah and Israel. ¹²In the thirty-ninth year of his reign Asa was afflicted with a disease in his feet. Though his disease was severe, even in his illness he did not seek help from the Lord, but only from the physicians. ¹³Then in the forty-first year of his reign Asa died and rested with his ancestors. ¹⁴They buried him in the tomb that he had cut out for himself in the City of David. They laid him on a bier covered with spices and various blended perfumes, and they made a huge fire in his honor.

Jehoshaphat King of Judah

17 Jehoshaphat his son succeeded him as king and strengthened himself against Israel. ²He stationed troops in all the fortified cities of Judah and put garrisons in Judah and in the towns of Ephraim that his father Asa had captured.

³The Lord was with Jehoshaphat because he followed the ways of his father David before him. He did not consult the Baals ⁴but sought the God of his father and followed his commands rather than the practices of Israel. ⁵The Lord established the kingdom under his control; and all Judah brought gifts to Jehoshaphat, so that he had great wealth and honor. ⁶His heart was devoted to the ways of the Lord; furthermore, he removed the high places and the Asherah poles from Judah.

⁷In the third year of his reign he sent his officials Ben-Hail, Obadiah, Zechariah, Nethanel and Micaiah to teach in the towns of Judah. ⁸With them were certain Levites—Shemaiah, Nethaniah, Zebadiah, Asahel, Shemiramoth, Jehonathan, Adonijah, Tobijah and Tob-Adonijah—and the priests Elishama and Jehoram. ⁹They taught throughout Judah, taking with them the Book of

---

[a] 4 Also known as *Abel Beth Maakah*   [b] 8 That is, people from the upper Nile region   [c] 8 Or *charioteers*

Although the Hebrew text refers to this nation as "Aram," it is sometimes called by its later name, "Syria."

KING OF ARAM/ SYRIA	DATE	KING OF JUDAH	DATE
Tabrimmon	930–885 BC	Rehoboam	930–913 BC
Ben-Hadad I	885–860 BC	Abijah	913–910 BC
Ben-Hadad II (Hadadezer)	860–843 BC	Asa	910–873 BC

16:6 Geba and Mizpah Strategic cities north of Jerusalem. See 1Ki 15:22 and note.
16:7 Hanani the seer Mentioned only here in the Bible.
16:8 mighty army See 2Ch 14:9 and note.
16:9 from now on you will be at war Earlier, Asa was given peace when he sought God (14:6–7; 15:19).
16:11 book of the kings of Judah and Israel The Chronicler refers to this source several times (e.g., 27:7; 35:27). The exact nature of the source is unknown, but it most likely is not the same work as the Biblical 1–2 Kings. Second Chronicles refers to this source in contexts for which 1–2 Kings gives no further information. Compare 27:1–9; 2Ki 15:32–38.
16:13 rested with his ancestors See note on 2Ch 9:31.
16:14 spices and various blended perfumes A sign of honor (compare Jer 34:5). Even though Asa's story ends with several failings, the honor he received in death corresponds with the positive assessment of him in 2Ch 14:2.

17:1—21:1 Jehoshaphat receives extensive coverage in 2 Chronicles. He is portrayed in a mostly positive light (17:3–4; 22:9), but he also is criticized for his alliances with the northern kings Ahab and Ahaziah (19:2; 20:37). The Chronicler focuses on Jehoshaphat's reforms, which include sending officials throughout the cities of Judah to teach the people (17:7–9) and appointing judges to administer justice throughout Judah (19:5–11). By including the criticism of Jehoshaphat's alliances, the Chronicler emphasizes reliance on God.

17:1 succeeded him as king Jehoshaphat reigned for 25 years (20:31; 1Ki 22:42). See the timeline "The Divided Kingdom" on p. 536.

NORTHERN KING	DATE	SOUTHERN KING	DATE
Ahab	874–853 BC	Jehoshaphat	873–848 BC
Ahaziah	853–852 BC		
Jehoram/Joram	852–841 BC	Jehoram	848–841 BC

17:3 the Baals Refers to idols of Baal, the Canaanite storm deity.
17:6 the high places and the Asherah poles See note on 2Ch 14:3.
17:7 In the third year of his reign This could indicate that Jehoshaphat ruled jointly for three years with his father, Asa, while Asa was diseased (16:12). If this is the case, then this would be the first year of his independent reign. **to teach in the towns of Judah** By focusing on

King Jehoshaphat's Family Tree

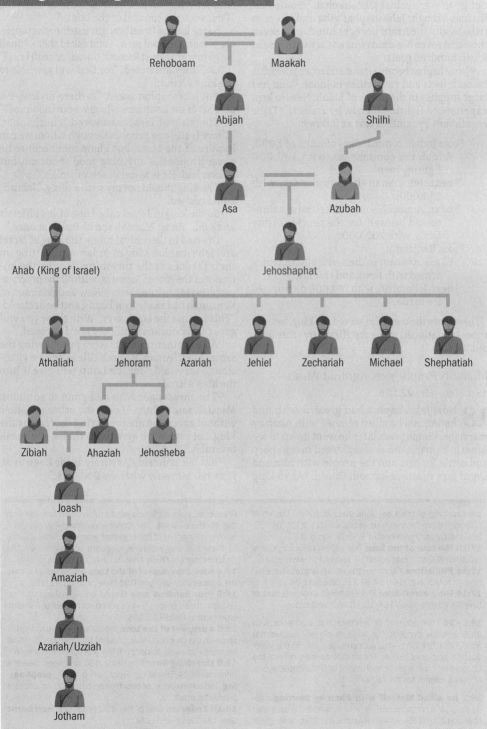

the Law of the LORD; they went around to all the towns of Judah and taught the people.

¹⁰The fear of the LORD fell on all the kingdoms of the lands surrounding Judah, so that they did not go to war against Jehoshaphat. ¹¹Some Philistines brought Jehoshaphat gifts and silver as tribute, and the Arabs brought him flocks: seven thousand seven hundred rams and seven thousand seven hundred goats.

¹²Jehoshaphat became more and more powerful; he built forts and store cities in Judah ¹³and had large supplies in the towns of Judah. He also kept experienced fighting men in Jerusalem. ¹⁴Their enrollment by families was as follows:

From Judah, commanders of units of 1,000:
Adnah the commander, with 300,000 fighting men;
¹⁵next, Jehohanan the commander, with 280,000;
¹⁶next, Amasiah son of Zikri, who volunteered himself for the service of the LORD, with 200,000.
¹⁷From Benjamin:
Eliada, a valiant soldier, with 200,000 men armed with bows and shields;
¹⁸next, Jehozabad, with 180,000 men armed for battle.

¹⁹These were the men who served the king, besides those he stationed in the fortified cities throughout Judah.

Micaiah Prophesies Against Ahab

18:1-27pp — 1Ki 22:1-28

18 Now Jehoshaphat had great wealth and honor, and he allied himself with Ahab by marriage. ²Some years later he went down to see Ahab in Samaria. Ahab slaughtered many sheep and cattle for him and the people with him and urged him to attack Ramoth Gilead. ³Ahab king of Israel asked Jehoshaphat king of Judah, "Will you go with me against Ramoth Gilead?"

Jehoshaphat replied, "I am as you are, and my people as your people; we will join you in the war." ⁴But Jehoshaphat also said to the king of Israel, "First seek the counsel of the LORD."

⁵So the king of Israel brought together the prophets — four hundred men — and asked them, "Shall we go to war against Ramoth Gilead, or shall I not?"

"Go," they answered, "for God will give it into the king's hand."

⁶But Jehoshaphat asked, "Is there no longer a prophet of the LORD here whom we can inquire of?"

⁷The king of Israel answered Jehoshaphat, "There is still one prophet through whom we can inquire of the LORD, but I hate him because he never prophesies anything good about me, but always bad. He is Micaiah son of Imlah."

"The king should not say such a thing," Jehoshaphat replied.

⁸So the king of Israel called one of his officials and said, "Bring Micaiah son of Imlah at once."

⁹Dressed in their royal robes, the king of Israel and Jehoshaphat king of Judah were sitting on their thrones at the threshing floor by the entrance of the gate of Samaria, with all the prophets prophesying before them. ¹⁰Now Zedekiah son of Kenaanah had made iron horns, and he declared, "This is what the LORD says: 'With these you will gore the Arameans until they are destroyed.'"

¹¹All the other prophets were prophesying the same thing. "Attack Ramoth Gilead and be victorious," they said, "for the LORD will give it into the king's hand."

¹²The messenger who had gone to summon Micaiah said to him, "Look, the other prophets without exception are predicting success for the king. Let your word agree with theirs, and speak favorably."

¹³But Micaiah said, "As surely as the LORD lives, I can tell him only what my God says."

---

the teaching of the Law, Jehoshaphat fulfills the ideal responsibilities for royalty as established in Dt 17:18–20. See the table "Functions of Priests" on p. 171.
17:10 The fear of the LORD The surrounding kingdoms recognized God's protection of Judah and were afraid.
17:11 Philistines Often portrayed as aggressive enemies of Israel (e.g., 1Ch 14:8–17). See note on 1Sa 4:1.
17:14 Their enrollment The list here is reminiscent of David's mighty men (1Ch 11:10–47 and note).

18:1–34 This account of Jehoshaphat's alliance with Ahab and the prophecy of Micaiah closely follows the account in 1Ki 22:1–40, with changes only in the introduction and conclusion. Those differences reflect the Chronicler's focus on Jehoshaphat and the implications of these events for his reign.

18:1 he allied himself with Ahab by marriage Jehoshaphat's firstborn son, Jehoram, married a daughter of Ahab (2Ch 21:6). As with Baasha, the Chronicler gives no introduction to Ahab (for Baasha, see 16:1 and note).

Presumably his audience would have been familiar with the northern kings. The Chronicler mostly ignores the northern kingdom of Israel except when it relates directly to events in the southern kingdom of Judah. See the people diagram "King Ahab's Family Tree" on p. 546.
18:4 seek the counsel of the LORD Jehoshaphat shows his concern for seeking God (see note on 11:16).
18:5 four hundred men Based on Jehoshaphat's response, these probably were prophets of Baal or Asherah (compare v. 6; 1Ki 18:19).
18:6 a prophet of the LORD Jehoshaphat was not satisfied with the prophets Ahab brought out. He specifies that he wants to seek guidance from a prophet of Yahweh.
18:9 threshing floor See 1Ki 22:10 and note. See the infographic "A Threshing Floor" on p. 497. **prophesying** Indicates an ecstatic frenzy common in ancient prophetic practice.
18:10 Zedekiah One of the 400 prophets. **iron horns** See 1Ki 22:11 and note.
18:13 As surely as the LORD lives Signifies an oath.

¹⁴When he arrived, the king asked him, "Micaiah, shall we go to war against Ramoth Gilead, or shall I not?"

"Attack and be victorious," he answered, "for they will be given into your hand."

¹⁵The king said to him, "How many times must I make you swear to tell me nothing but the truth in the name of the LORD?"

¹⁶Then Micaiah answered, "I saw all Israel scattered on the hills like sheep without a shepherd, and the LORD said, 'These people have no master. Let each one go home in peace.'"

¹⁷The king of Israel said to Jehoshaphat, "Didn't I tell you that he never prophesies anything good about me, but only bad?"

¹⁸Micaiah continued, "Therefore hear the word of the LORD: I saw the LORD sitting on his throne with all the multitudes of heaven standing on his right and on his left. ¹⁹And the LORD said, 'Who will entice Ahab king of Israel into attacking Ramoth Gilead and going to his death there?'

"One suggested this, and another that. ²⁰Finally, a spirit came forward, stood before the LORD and said, 'I will entice him.'

"'By what means?' the LORD asked.

²¹"'I will go and be a deceiving spirit in the mouths of all his prophets,' he said.

"'You will succeed in enticing him,' said the LORD. 'Go and do it.'

²²"So now the LORD has put a deceiving spirit in the mouths of these prophets of yours. The LORD has decreed disaster for you."

²³Then Zedekiah son of Kenaanah went up and slapped Micaiah in the face. "Which way did the spirit from[a] the LORD go when he went from me to speak to you?" he asked.

²⁴Micaiah replied, "You will find out on the day you go to hide in an inner room."

²⁵The king of Israel then ordered, "Take Micaiah and send him back to Amon the ruler of the city and to Joash the king's son, ²⁶and say, 'This is what the king says: Put this fellow in prison and give him nothing but bread and water until I return safely.'"

²⁷Micaiah declared, "If you ever return safely, the LORD has not spoken through me." Then he added, "Mark my words, all you people!"

Ahab Killed at Ramoth Gilead

18:28-34pp — 1Ki 22:29-36

²⁸So the king of Israel and Jehoshaphat king of Judah went up to Ramoth Gilead. ²⁹The king of Israel said to Jehoshaphat, "I will enter the battle in disguise, but you wear your royal robes." So the king of Israel disguised himself and went into battle.

³⁰Now the king of Aram had ordered his chariot commanders, "Do not fight with anyone, small or great, except the king of Israel." ³¹When the chariot commanders saw Jehoshaphat, they thought, "This is the king of Israel." So they turned to attack him, but Jehoshaphat cried out, and the LORD helped him. God drew them away from him, ³²for when the chariot commanders saw that he was not the king of Israel, they stopped pursuing him.

³³But someone drew his bow at random and hit the king of Israel between the breastplate and the scale armor. The king told the chariot driver, "Wheel around and get me out of the fighting. I've been wounded." ³⁴All day long the battle raged, and the king of Israel propped himself up in his chariot facing the Arameans until evening. Then at sunset he died.

19 When Jehoshaphat king of Judah returned safely to his palace in Jerusalem, ²Jehu the seer, the son of Hanani, went out to meet him and said to the king, "Should you help the wicked and love[b] those who hate the LORD? Because of this, the wrath of the LORD is on you. ³There is, however, some good in you, for you have rid the land of the Asherah poles and have set your heart on seeking God."

Jehoshaphat Appoints Judges

⁴Jehoshaphat lived in Jerusalem, and he went out again among the people from Beersheba to the

---

a 23 Or Spirit of   b 2 Or and make alliances with

18:15 nothing but the truth Ahab is skeptical, due to his past experience with unfavorable prophecies from Micaiah (2Ch 18:7).
18:18 all the multitudes of heaven Refers to heavenly beings who were part of God's divine council (see Ps 82:1 and note).
18:23 slapped Micaiah in the face A gesture meant for humiliation and rebuke. Zedekiah reacts harshly to the claim that he had spoken with a spirit of deception.
18:24 to hide in an inner room Refers to hiding from an invasion or battle (as Ben-Hadad did in Aphek; 1Ki 20:30).
18:26 until I return safely Signals that Ahab has chosen to believe his 400 prophets.
18:29 disguised himself Likely as a precaution, to guard against the possibility that he might be killed as Micaiah foretold (see 2Ch 18:19).

18:31 and the LORD helped him This line is not in the 1 Kings account (compare 1Ki 22:32). The Chronicler emphasizes that God rescued Jehoshaphat in response to his cries.
18:34 propped himself up in his chariot See 1Ki 22:35 and note. **at sunset he died** The account in 1 Kings gives further details surrounding the death of Ahab and the dishonor he faced (1Ki 22:37–38).

19:1–11 As with his predecessor, Asa, Jehoshaphat is rebuked for making a foreign alliance (see 2Ch 16:1–14 and note).

19:2 Jehu the seer, the son of Hanani Jehu rebukes Jehoshaphat for allying with Israel in its battle against Syria.
19:3 have set your heart on seeking God Despite being rebuked, Jehoshaphat is upheld for his faithfulness. See note on 11:16.

hill country of Ephraim and turned them back to the LORD, the God of their ancestors. ⁵He appointed judges in the land, in each of the fortified cities of Judah. ⁶He told them, "Consider carefully what you do, because you are not judging for mere mortals but for the LORD, who is with you whenever you give a verdict. ⁷Now let the fear of the LORD be on you. Judge carefully, for with the LORD our God there is no injustice or partiality or bribery."

⁸In Jerusalem also, Jehoshaphat appointed some of the Levites, priests and heads of Israelite families to administer the law of the LORD and to settle disputes. And they lived in Jerusalem. ⁹He gave them these orders: "You must serve faithfully and wholeheartedly in the fear of the LORD. ¹⁰In every case that comes before you from your people who live in the cities — whether bloodshed or other concerns of the law, commands, decrees or regulations — you are to warn them not to sin against the LORD; otherwise his wrath will come on you and your people. Do this, and you will not sin.

¹¹"Amariah the chief priest will be over you in any matter concerning the LORD, and Zebadiah son of Ishmael, the leader of the tribe of Judah, will be over you in any matter concerning the king, and the Levites will serve as officials before you. Act with courage, and may the LORD be with those who do well."

Jehoshaphat Defeats Moab and Ammon

20 After this, the Moabites and Ammonites with some of the Meunites[a] came to wage war against Jehoshaphat.

²Some people came and told Jehoshaphat, "A vast army is coming against you from Edom,[b] from the other side of the Dead Sea. It is already in Hazezon Tamar" (that is, En Gedi). ³Alarmed, Jehoshaphat resolved to inquire of the LORD, and he proclaimed a fast for all Judah. ⁴The people of Judah came together to seek help from the LORD; indeed, they came from every town in Judah to seek him.

⁵Then Jehoshaphat stood up in the assembly of Judah and Jerusalem at the temple of the LORD in the front of the new courtyard ⁶and said:

"LORD, the God of our ancestors, are you not the God who is in heaven? You rule over all the kingdoms of the nations. Power and might are in your hand, and no one can withstand you. ⁷Our God, did you not drive out the inhabitants of this land before your people Israel and give it forever to the descendants of Abraham your friend? ⁸They have lived in it and have built in it a sanctuary for your Name, saying, ⁹'If calamity comes upon us, whether the sword of judgment, or plague or famine, we will stand in your presence before this temple that bears your Name and will cry out to you in our distress, and you will hear us and save us.'

¹⁰"But now here are men from Ammon, Moab and Mount Seir, whose territory you would not allow Israel to invade when they came from Egypt; so they turned away from them and did not destroy them. ¹¹See how they are repaying us by coming to drive us out of the possession you gave us as an inheritance. ¹²Our God, will you not judge them? For we have no power to face this vast army that is attacking us. We do not know what to do, but our eyes are on you."

¹³All the men of Judah, with their wives and children and little ones, stood there before the LORD.

---

a 1 Some Septuagint manuscripts; Hebrew *Ammonites*
b 2 One Hebrew manuscript; most Hebrew manuscripts, Septuagint and Vulgate *Aram*

19:4 from Beersheba to the hill country of Ephraim Indicates the entire area of the southern kingdom of Judah.

19:10 Jehoshaphat uses four different Hebrew terms for kinds of laws.

19:10 law The Hebrew word used here, *torah*, functions as a summary for all of God's instructions in Deuteronomy (see note on Ps 119:1). **commands** The Hebrew term *mitswah* refers to a specific commandment that should be observed (see note on Ps 119:6). **decrees** The Hebrew word *chuqqim* refers to written laws or boundaries (see note on Ps 119:5). **regulations** The Hebrew term *mishpat* refers to a ruling or decision (see note on Ps 119:7).

20:1–34 The Chronicler concludes the story of Jehoshaphat with a lengthy account of a battle between Judah and several enemy nations. The story highlights Jehoshaphat's reliance on God (2Ch 20:6–12,18–21) and God's protection of his people (vv. 15–17,22–25).

20:1 Moabites and Ammonites Enemies on Judah's eastern border. See note on Ru 1:1. **Meunites** Most likely refers to residents of Maan in Edom.

20:2 Edom One Hebrew manuscript refers to Edom, the area to the southeast of Judah, while others refer to Aram, a country to the north of Israel. The difference in Hebrew is only one letter. See note on Ps 108:9.

20:3 resolved to inquire of the LORD As he did earlier, Jehoshaphat shows his faithfulness (compare 2Ch 17:4; 18:4). See note on 11:16. **and he proclaimed a fast** Fasting often accompanied a time of anxiety as a way of showing humility or repentance.

20:6 LORD, the God of our ancestors Jehoshaphat's prayer is very much in line with corporate lament psalms expressing grief or sadness. Compare Ps 44.

20:7 drive out the inhabitants Jehoshaphat refers to God's past acts of deliverance.

20:9 calamity comes upon us Jehoshaphat summarizes Solomon's prayer at the temple's dedication (2Ch 6:12–42).

20:12 our eyes are on you A statement showing Jehoshaphat's reliance on God.

¹⁴Then the Spirit of the LORD came on Jahaziel son of Zechariah, the son of Benaiah, the son of Jeiel, the son of Mattaniah, a Levite and descendant of Asaph, as he stood in the assembly.

¹⁵He said: "Listen, King Jehoshaphat and all who live in Judah and Jerusalem! This is what the LORD says to you: 'Do not be afraid or discouraged because of this vast army. For the battle is not yours, but God's. ¹⁶Tomorrow march down against them. They will be climbing up by the Pass of Ziz, and you will find them at the end of the gorge in the Desert of Jeruel. ¹⁷You will not have to fight this battle. Take up your positions; stand firm and see the deliverance the LORD will give you, Judah and Jerusalem. Do not be afraid; do not be discouraged. Go out to face them tomorrow, and the LORD will be with you.'"

¹⁸Jehoshaphat bowed down with his face to the ground, and all the people of Judah and Jerusalem fell down in worship before the LORD. ¹⁹Then some Levites from the Kohathites and Korahites stood up and praised the LORD, the God of Israel, with a very loud voice.

²⁰Early in the morning they left for the Desert of Tekoa. As they set out, Jehoshaphat stood and said, "Listen to me, Judah and people of Jerusalem! Have faith in the LORD your God and you will be upheld; have faith in his prophets and you will be successful." ²¹After consulting the people, Jehoshaphat appointed men to sing to the LORD and to praise him for the splendor of his[a] holiness as they went out at the head of the army, saying:

"Give thanks to the LORD,
    for his love endures forever."

²²As they began to sing and praise, the LORD set ambushes against the men of Ammon and Moab and Mount Seir who were invading Judah, and they were defeated. ²³The Ammonites and Moabites rose up against the men from Mount Seir to destroy and annihilate them. After they finished slaughtering the men from Seir, they helped to destroy one another.

²⁴When the men of Judah came to the place that overlooks the desert and looked toward the vast army, they saw only dead bodies lying on the ground; no one had escaped. ²⁵So Jehoshaphat and his men went to carry off their plunder, and they found among them a great amount of equipment and clothing[b] and also articles of value — more than they could take away. There was so much plunder that it took three days to collect it. ²⁶On the fourth day they assembled in the Valley of Berakah, where they praised the LORD. This is why it is called the Valley of Berakah[c] to this day.

²⁷Then, led by Jehoshaphat, all the men of Judah and Jerusalem returned joyfully to Jerusalem, for the LORD had given them cause to rejoice over their enemies. ²⁸They entered Jerusalem and went to the temple of the LORD with harps and lyres and trumpets.

²⁹The fear of God came on all the surrounding kingdoms when they heard how the LORD had fought against the enemies of Israel. ³⁰And the kingdom of Jehoshaphat was at peace, for his God had given him rest on every side.

The End of Jehoshaphat's Reign

20:31 – 21:1pp — 1Ki 22:41-50

³¹So Jehoshaphat reigned over Judah. He was thirty-five years old when he became king of Judah, and he reigned in Jerusalem twenty-five years. His mother's name was Azubah daughter of Shilhi. ³²He followed the ways of his father Asa and did not stray from them; he did what was right in the eyes of the LORD. ³³The high places, however, were not removed, and the people still had not set their hearts on the God of their ancestors.

³⁴The other events of Jehoshaphat's reign, from beginning to end, are written in the annals of Jehu son of Hanani, which are recorded in the book of the kings of Israel.

³⁵Later, Jehoshaphat king of Judah made an alliance with Ahaziah king of Israel, whose ways

---

a 21 Or *him with the splendor of*   *b 25* Some Hebrew manuscripts and Vulgate; most Hebrew manuscripts *corpses*   *c 26 Berakah* means *praise.*

20:14 Then the Spirit of the LORD came on Jahaziel Signifying Jahaziel's validity as a prophet. **Levite and descendant of Asaph** One of the families in charge of the temple music (see 1Ch 25:1–29).

20:19 from the Kohathites and Korahites Prominent Levitical families appointed by David to serve at the temple (1Ch 23:6; 26:1).

20:21 his love endures forever See note on 2Ch 5:13.

20:22 LORD set ambushes God responds to the people's praise by causing the enemy nations to destroy each other. **Mount Seir** Refers to Edom.

20:25 equipment and clothing and also articles of value In addition to delivering Judah from the enemy, God supplies provisions and wealth.

20:26 the Valley of Berakah Meaning "valley of blessing."

20:29 The fear of God Just as they had at the begin-ning of Jehoshaphat's reign, the surrounding nations recognized God's protection of Judah (17:10).

20:31 he reigned in Jerusalem twenty-five years Roughly 873 to 848 BC.

20:33 high places Sites for worshiping foreign deities.

20:34 The other events A common epitaph for deceased kings (compare 1Ki 11:41; 14:19). **annals of Jehu** The chronicles of Jehu the son of Hanani seem to have been a section or smaller work included within the larger work called the Book of the Kings of Israel. For a similar situation, compare the vision of Isaiah (2Ch 32:32 and note). **book of the kings of Israel** See note on 16:11.

20:35 made an alliance with Ahaziah king of Israel The story of Jehoshaphat ends with him repeating an earlier mistake. Just as his alliance with Ahab resulted in defeat, his alliance with Ahaziah is not fruitful (18:28–34; 20:37).

were wicked. ³⁶He agreed with him to construct a fleet of trading ships.ᵃ After these were built at Ezion Geber, ³⁷Eliezer son of Dodavahu of Mareshah prophesied against Jehoshaphat, saying, "Because you have made an alliance with Ahaziah, the LORD will destroy what you have made." The ships were wrecked and were not able to set sail to trade.ᵇ

21 Then Jehoshaphat rested with his ancestors and was buried with them in the City of David. And Jehoram his son succeeded him as king. ²Jehoram's brothers, the sons of Jehoshaphat, were Azariah, Jehiel, Zechariah, Azariahu, Michael and Shephatiah. All these were sons of Jehoshaphat king of Israel.ᶜ ³Their father had given them many gifts of silver and gold and articles of value, as well as fortified cities in Judah, but he had given the kingdom to Jehoram because he was his firstborn son.

Jehoram King of Judah

21:5-10,20pp — 2Ki 8:16-24

⁴When Jehoram established himself firmly over his father's kingdom, he put all his brothers to the sword along with some of the officials of Israel. ⁵Jehoram was thirty-two years old when he became king, and he reigned in Jerusalem eight years. ⁶He followed the ways of the kings of Israel, as the house of Ahab had done, for he married a daughter of Ahab. He did evil in the eyes of the LORD. ⁷Nevertheless, because of the covenant the LORD had made with David, the LORD was not willing to destroy the house of David. He had promised to maintain a lamp for him and his descendants forever.

⁸In the time of Jehoram, Edom rebelled against Judah and set up its own king. ⁹So Jehoram went there with his officers and all his chariots. The Edomites surrounded him and his chariot commanders, but he rose up and broke through by night. ¹⁰To this day Edom has been in rebellion against Judah.

Libnah revolted at the same time, because Je-

horam had forsaken the LORD, the God of his ancestors. ¹¹He had also built high places on the hills of Judah and had caused the people of Jerusalem to prostitute themselves and had led Judah astray.

¹²Jehoram received a letter from Elijah the prophet, which said:

"This is what the LORD, the God of your father David, says: 'You have not followed the ways of your father Jehoshaphat or of Asa king of Judah. ¹³But you have followed the ways of the kings of Israel, and you have led Judah and the people of Jerusalem to prostitute themselves, just as the house of Ahab did. You have also murdered your own brothers, members of your own family, men who were better than you. ¹⁴So now the LORD is about to strike your people, your sons, your wives and everything that is yours, with a heavy blow. ¹⁵You yourself will be very ill with a lingering disease of the bowels, until the disease causes your bowels to come out.'"

¹⁶The LORD aroused against Jehoram the hostility of the Philistines and of the Arabs who lived near the Cushites. ¹⁷They attacked Judah, invaded it and carried off all the goods found in the king's palace, together with his sons and wives. Not a son was left to him except Ahaziah,ᵈ the youngest.

¹⁸After all this, the LORD afflicted Jehoram with an incurable disease of the bowels. ¹⁹In the course of time, at the end of the second year, his bowels came out because of the disease, and he died in great pain. His people made no funeral fire in his honor, as they had for his predecessors.

²⁰Jehoram was thirty-two years old when he became king, and he reigned in Jerusalem eight years. He passed away, to no one's regret, and was buried in the City of David, but not in the tombs of the kings.

ᵃ 36 Hebrew *of ships that could go to Tarshish*   ᵇ 37 Hebrew *sail for Tarshish*   ᶜ 2 That is, Judah, as frequently in 2 Chronicles   ᵈ 17 Hebrew *Jehoahaz*, a variant of *Ahaziah*

21:1—22:12. Following Jehoshaphat's reign, Judah is led by a series of wicked rulers, including the queen Athaliah (2Ch 22:10–12). These rulers are characterized as following the example of the northern king Ahab (21:6; 22:3). See 2Ki 8:16–24.

21:1 rested with his ancestors See note on 9:31.
21:4 he put all his brothers to the sword Jehoram kills his brothers to ensure he will have no rivals to the throne.
21:6 the ways of the kings of Israel As opposed to Jehoshaphat, who walked in the ways of David (17:3). **he married a daughter of Ahab** Jehoram married one of Ahab's daughters as part of the alliance Jehoshaphat made with Ahab (18:1 and note).
21:7 maintain a lamp See 2Ki 8:19 and note.

21:10 Libnah revolted A Levitical city in the Judean hill country (Jos 21:13).
21:11 had caused the people of Jerusalem to prostitute themselves Idolatry in the OT is often compared to adultery (compare Hos 1:2–11).
21:12 from Elijah the prophet Because the prophecies of Elijah primarily concern the kings of Israel, he is not a major character in 2 Chronicles—which focuses on the kings of Judah.
21:17 and carried off A fulfillment of Elijah's prophecy (2Ch 21:14). The invaders capture Jehoram's family except for his son Ahaziah (also identified as "Jehoahaz"), who succeeds him. Although it is not mentioned here, the enemy forces apparently leave behind Ahaziah's mother, Athaliah, who rules as queen after Ahaziah (ca. 840–835 BC; 22:10).

Ahaziah King of Judah

22:1-6pp — 2Ki 8:25-29
22:7-9pp — 2Ki 9:21-29

22 The people of Jerusalem made Ahaziah, Jehoram's youngest son, king in his place, since the raiders, who came with the Arabs into the camp, had killed all the older sons. So Ahaziah son of Jehoram king of Judah began to reign.

²Ahaziah was twenty-two*ª* years old when he became king, and he reigned in Jerusalem one year. His mother's name was Athaliah, a granddaughter of Omri.

³He too followed the ways of the house of Ahab, for his mother encouraged him to act wickedly. ⁴He did evil in the eyes of the LORD, as the house of Ahab had done, for after his father's death they became his advisers, to his undoing. ⁵He also followed their counsel when he went with Joram*ᵇ* son of Ahab king of Israel to wage war against Hazael king of Aram at Ramoth Gilead. The Arameans wounded Joram; ⁶so he returned to Jezreel to recover from the wounds they had inflicted on him at Ramoth*ᶜ* in his battle with Hazael king of Aram.

Then Ahaziah*ᵈ* son of Jehoram king of Judah went down to Jezreel to see Joram son of Ahab because he had been wounded.

⁷Through Ahaziah's visit to Joram, God brought about Ahaziah's downfall. When Ahaziah arrived, he went out with Joram to meet Jehu son of Nimshi, whom the LORD had anointed to destroy the house of Ahab. ⁸While Jehu was executing judgment on the house of Ahab, he found the officials of Judah and the sons of Ahaziah's relatives, who had been attending Ahaziah, and he killed them. ⁹He then went in search of Ahaziah, and his men captured him while he was hiding in Samaria. He was brought to Jehu and put to death. They buried him, for they said, "He was a son of Jehoshaphat, who sought the LORD with all his heart." So there was no one in the house of Ahaziah powerful enough to retain the kingdom.

Athaliah and Joash

22:10 - 23:21pp — 2Ki 11:1-21

¹⁰When Athaliah the mother of Ahaziah saw that her son was dead, she proceeded to destroy the whole royal family of the house of Judah. ¹¹But Jehosheba,*ᵉ* the daughter of King Jehoram, took Joash son of Ahaziah and stole him away from among the royal princes who were about to be murdered and put him and his nurse in a bedroom. Because Jehosheba,*ᵉ* the daughter of King Jehoram and wife of the priest Jehoiada, was Ahaziah's sister, she hid the child from Athaliah so she could not kill him. ¹²He remained hidden with them at the temple of God for six years while Athaliah ruled the land.

23 In the seventh year Jehoiada showed his strength. He made a covenant with the commanders of units of a hundred: Azariah son of Jeroham, Ishmael son of Jehohanan, Azariah son of Obed, Maaseiah son of Adaiah, and Elishaphat son of Zikri. ²They went throughout Judah and gathered the Levites and the heads of Israelite families from all the towns. When they came to

---

ª 2 Some Septuagint manuscripts and Syriac (see also 2 Kings 8:26); Hebrew forty-two   ᵇ 5 Hebrew Jehoram, a variant of Joram; also in verses 6 and 7   ᶜ 6 Hebrew Ramah, a variant of Ramoth   ᵈ 6 Some Hebrew manuscripts, Septuagint, Vulgate and Syriac (see also 2 Kings 8:29); most Hebrew manuscripts Azariah   ᵉ 11 Hebrew Jehoshabeath, a variant of Jehosheba

---

22:1–10 The Hebrew text of this section can be confusing, as it lists both a king of Israel and a king of Judah who went by the same name *yehoram* (Jehoram). An alternate rendering of this name is *yoram* (Joram; 2Ki 8:16). To remove the ambiguity between the king of Judah and the king of Israel, some translations always refer to the king of Israel as Joram and the king of Judah as Jehoram.

22:2 a granddaughter of Omri Refers to the northern king Omri, the father of Ahab.

22:3 the ways of the house of Ahab The Chronicler regards Ahab's deeds as the standard for evil behavior.

22:5 at Ramoth Gilead A city on the border of Israel and Syria.

22:6 Jezreel Location of the Israelite king's winter residence (1Ki 21:1).

22:7 God brought about The Chronicler emphasizes God's involvement in the events of 2Ch 22:7–9, which are described more fully in 2Ki 9:1–28. Jehu, the commander of Israel's army, is anointed to be king and to destroy the house of Ahab—leading to the deaths of both King Joram of Israel and King Ahaziah of Judah. Because the Chronicler focuses on Judah, he emphasizes that God had ordained Ahaziah's downfall, leaving out most of the story about Jehu and Joram. See the infographic "The Black Obelisk of Shalmaneser III" on p. 579.

22:9 powerful enough to retain the kingdom Jehu had killed not only Ahaziah, king of Judah, but also several of his relatives (2Ch 22:8). Ahaziah's remaining son apparently was an infant (v. 11).

22:10 destroy the whole royal family Because Ahaziah had no heir suitable to rule, Athaliah seeks to eliminate the rest of David's royal line and seize the throne for herself (vv. 8–9,12).

22:11 Jehosheba, the daughter of King Jehoram She is the daughter of King Jehoram and sister of King Ahaziah, both of whom are now dead. **stole him away** When Athaliah, the queen mother, executes the royal family, Jehoshabeath (Jehosheba) heroically protects David's lineage by hiding Joash—King Ahaziah's infant son.

22:12 He remained hidden with them at the temple of God Joash and his nurse take refuge in the temple.

23:1–21 The Chronicler largely follows 2 Kings for this account of Joash's enthronement and Athaliah's execution, with some additions (compare 2Ki 11:4–20).

23:1 Jehoiada The priest who hid Joash in the temple (2Ch 22:11–12).

23:2 and gathered the Levites The Chronicler emphasizes the role that the Levites and other temple officials played in Joash's enthronement. He also shows that representatives came from all the cities of Judah. By

Jerusalem, [3] the whole assembly made a covenant with the king at the temple of God.

Jehoiada said to them, "The king's son shall reign, as the LORD promised concerning the descendants of David. [4] Now this is what you are to do: A third of you priests and Levites who are going on duty on the Sabbath are to keep watch at the doors, [5] a third of you at the royal palace and a third at the Foundation Gate, and all the others are to be in the courtyards of the temple of the LORD. [6] No one is to enter the temple of the LORD except the priests and Levites on duty; they may enter because they are consecrated, but all the others are to observe the LORD's command not to enter.[a] [7] The Levites are to station themselves around the king, each with weapon in hand. Anyone who enters the temple is to be put to death. Stay close to the king wherever he goes."

[8] The Levites and all the men of Judah did just as Jehoiada the priest ordered. Each one took his men — those who were going on duty on the Sabbath and those who were going off duty — for Jehoiada the priest had not released any of the divisions. [9] Then he gave the commanders of units of a hundred the spears and the large and small shields that had belonged to King David and that were in the temple of God. [10] He stationed all the men, each with his weapon in his hand, around the king — near the altar and the temple, from the south side to the north side of the temple.

[11] Jehoiada and his sons brought out the king's son and put the crown on him; they presented him with a copy of the covenant and proclaimed him king. They anointed him and shouted, "Long live the king!"

[12] When Athaliah heard the noise of the people running and cheering the king, she went to them at the temple of the LORD. [13] She looked, and there was the king, standing by his pillar at the entrance. The officers and the trumpeters were beside the king, and all the people of the land were rejoicing and blowing trumpets, and musicians with their instruments were leading the praises. Then Athaliah tore her robes and shouted, "Treason! Treason!"

[14] Jehoiada the priest sent out the commanders of units of a hundred, who were in charge of the troops, and said to them: "Bring her out between the ranks[b] and put to the sword anyone who follows her." For the priest had said, "Do not put her to death at the temple of the LORD." [15] So they seized her as she reached the entrance of the Horse Gate on the palace grounds, and there they put her to death.

[16] Jehoiada then made a covenant that he, the people and the king[c] would be the LORD's people. [17] All the people went to the temple of Baal and tore it down. They smashed the altars and idols and killed Mattan the priest of Baal in front of the altars.

[18] Then Jehoiada placed the oversight of the temple of the LORD in the hands of the Levitical priests, to whom David had made assignments in the temple, to present the burnt offerings of the LORD as written in the Law of Moses, with rejoicing and singing, as David had ordered. [19] He also stationed gatekeepers at the gates of the LORD's temple so that no one who was in any way unclean might enter.

[20] He took with him the commanders of hundreds, the nobles, the rulers of the people and all the people of the land and brought the king down from the temple of the LORD. They went into the palace through the Upper Gate and seated the king on the royal throne. [21] All the people of the land rejoiced, and the city was calm, because Athaliah had been slain with the sword.

Joash Repairs the Temple

24:1-14pp — 2Ki 12:1-16
24:23-27pp — 2Ki 12:17-21

24 Joash was seven years old when he became king, and he reigned in Jerusalem forty years. His mother's name was Zibiah; she was from Beersheba. [2] Joash did what was right in the eyes of the LORD all the years of Jehoiada

---

[a] 6 Or *are to stand guard where the LORD has assigned them*
[b] 14 Or *out from the precincts*   [c] 16 Or *covenant between the LORD and the people and the king that they* (see 2 Kings 11:17)

---

including these details, the Chronicler highlights his concern for proper temple worship as well as the unity of the people.

23:3 concerning the descendants of David Jehoiada reveals to the assembly that Joash had survived Athaliah's massacre six years earlier (22:10–12). In his speech, he emphasizes God's promise to establish David's kingdom forever (1Ch 17:1–15). By installing Joash as king, Judah is acting in accordance with God's word. See the table "Covenants in the Old Testament" on p. 469.

23:7 The Levites are to station themselves around the king The instruction for the Levites to guard the king with weapons drawn may reflect an extension of their responsibility to guard Yahweh's sanctuary (e.g.

Nu 1:53; 31:30). Here, they defend not only Yahweh's temple, but also his covenant with David.

23:9 that had belonged to King David The use of these weapons symbolizes the return of David's dynasty.

23:11 a copy of the covenant See 2Ki 11:12 and note.

23:13 Treason Athaliah's cry is rather ironic, given that she had executed the rest of the royal family (2Ch 22:10).

23:15 the entrance of the Horse Gate See note on Ne 3:28.

23:16 would be the LORD's people Refers to the terms of Israel's covenant with Yahweh.

23:17 temple of Baal The Bible does not mention a temple of Baal (the Canaanite storm god) in Jerusalem.

23:18 as written in the Law of Moses Jehoiada reestablishes proper temple worship.

the priest. ³Jehoiada chose two wives for him, and he had sons and daughters.

⁴Some time later Joash decided to restore the temple of the LORD. ⁵He called together the priests and Levites and said to them, "Go to the towns of Judah and collect the money due annually from all Israel, to repair the temple of your God. Do it now." But the Levites did not act at once.

⁶Therefore the king summoned Jehoiada the chief priest and said to him, "Why haven't you required the Levites to bring in from Judah and Jerusalem the tax imposed by Moses the servant of the LORD and by the assembly of Israel for the tent of the covenant law?"

⁷Now the sons of that wicked woman Athaliah had broken into the temple of God and had used even its sacred objects for the Baals.

⁸At the king's command, a chest was made and placed outside, at the gate of the temple of the LORD. ⁹A proclamation was then issued in Judah and Jerusalem that they should bring to the LORD the tax that Moses the servant of God had required of Israel in the wilderness. ¹⁰All the officials and all the people brought their contributions gladly, dropping them into the chest until it was full. ¹¹Whenever the chest was brought in by the Levites to the king's officials and they saw that there was a large amount of money, the royal secretary and the officer of the chief priest would come and empty the chest and carry it back to its place. They did this regularly and collected a great amount of money. ¹²The king and Jehoiada gave it to those who carried out the work required for the temple of the LORD. They hired masons and carpenters to restore the LORD's temple, and also workers in iron and bronze to repair the temple.

¹³The men in charge of the work were diligent, and the repairs progressed under them. They rebuilt the temple of God according to its original design and reinforced it. ¹⁴When they had finished, they brought the rest of the money to the king and Jehoiada, and with it were made articles for the LORD's temple: articles for the service and for the burnt offerings, and also dishes and other objects of gold and silver. As long as Jehoiada lived, burnt offerings were presented continually in the temple of the LORD.

¹⁵Now Jehoiada was old and full of years, and he died at the age of a hundred and thirty. ¹⁶He was buried with the kings in the City of David, because of the good he had done in Israel for God and his temple.

The Wickedness of Joash

¹⁷After the death of Jehoiada, the officials of Judah came and paid homage to the king, and he listened to them. ¹⁸They abandoned the temple of the LORD, the God of their ancestors, and worshiped Asherah poles and idols. Because of their guilt, God's anger came on Judah and Jerusalem. ¹⁹Although the LORD sent prophets to the people to bring them back to him, and though they testified against them, they would not listen.

²⁰Then the Spirit of God came on Zechariah son of Jehoiada the priest. He stood before the people and said, "This is what God says: 'Why do you disobey the LORD's commands? You will not prosper. Because you have forsaken the LORD, he has forsaken you.'"

²¹But they plotted against him, and by order of the king they stoned him to death in the courtyard of the LORD's temple. ²²King Joash did not remember the kindness Zechariah's father Jehoiada had shown him but killed his son, who said as he lay dying, "May the LORD see this and call you to account."

²³At the turn of the year,ᵃ the army of Aram marched against Joash; it invaded Judah and

---

ᵃ 23 Probably in the spring

24:1–27 There are considerable differences between this account and that in 2 Kings. The Chronicler adds that it was necessary to restore the temple because Athaliah's sons had used many of the temple utensils for Baal worship (2Ch 24:7). He emphasizes that people gave with joy (v. 10) and includes details about Jehoiada's death (vv. 15–16) and Joash's subsequent apostasy (vv. 18–22).

24:1 Joash was seven years old Joash reigned in Judah from about 835 to 796 BC. See the timeline "The Divided Kingdom" on p. 536.

NORTHERN KING	DATE	SOUTHERN KING	DATE
Jehu	841–814 BC	Joash	835–796 BC
Jehoahaz	814–798 BC		
Jehoash	798–786 BC	Amaziah	796–792 BC

24:2 all the years of Jehoiada the priest The Chroni-

cler clarifies that Joash's faithfulness lasted only while Jehoiada was alive (vv. 17–18).

24:3 Jehoiada chose two wives for him Since most of the house of David had been destroyed by Jehu and Athaliah, Jehoiada needed to ensure that Joash would have descendants to continue David's royal line (see 22:8–10).

24:6 the tax imposed by Moses Most likely refers to the census tax (Ex 30:12–14).

24:14 burnt offerings were presented See note on Ezr 3:3.

24:16 with the kings Jehoiada the priest is given a king's burial, but Joash the king is not (2Ch 24:25).

24:20 he has forsaken you A fulfillment of David's warning to Solomon (1Ch 28:9), as well as Azariah's prophecy to Asa (2Ch 15:2).

24:21 the courtyard of the LORD's temple Zechariah, Jehoiada's son, is killed inside the temple. Earlier, Jehoiada had been careful to keep the temple pure, ordering Athaliah to be executed outside the temple (23:14).

Jerusalem and killed all the leaders of the people. They sent all the plunder to their king in Damascus. [24]Although the Aramean army had come with only a few men, the LORD delivered into their hands a much larger army. Because Judah had forsaken the LORD, the God of their ancestors, judgment was executed on Joash. [25]When the Arameans withdrew, they left Joash severely wounded. His officials conspired against him for murdering the son of Jehoiada the priest, and they killed him in his bed. So he died and was buried in the City of David, but not in the tombs of the kings.

[26]Those who conspired against him were Zabad,[a] son of Shimeath an Ammonite woman, and Jehozabad, son of Shimrith[b] a Moabite woman. [27]The account of his sons, the many prophecies about him, and the record of the restoration of the temple of God are written in the annotations on the book of the kings. And Amaziah his son succeeded him as king.

Amaziah King of Judah

25:1-4pp — 2Ki 14:1-6
25:11-12pp — 2Ki 14:7
25:17-28pp — 2Ki 14:8-20

25 Amaziah was twenty-five years old when he became king, and he reigned in Jerusalem twenty-nine years. His mother's name was Jehoaddan; she was from Jerusalem. [2]He did what was right in the eyes of the LORD, but not wholeheartedly. [3]After the kingdom was firmly in his control, he executed the officials who had murdered his father the king. [4]Yet he did not put their children to death, but acted in accordance with what is written in the Law, in the Book of Moses, where the LORD commanded: "Parents shall not be put to death for their children, nor

children be put to death for their parents; each will die for their own sin."[c]

[5]Amaziah called the people of Judah together and assigned them according to their families to commanders of thousands and commanders of hundreds for all Judah and Benjamin. He then mustered those twenty years old or more and found that there were three hundred thousand men fit for military service, able to handle the spear and shield. [6]He also hired a hundred thousand fighting men from Israel for a hundred talents[d] of silver.

[7]But a man of God came to him and said, "Your Majesty, these troops from Israel must not march with you, for the LORD is not with Israel — not with any of the people of Ephraim. [8]Even if you go and fight courageously in battle, God will overthrow you before the enemy, for God has the power to help or to overthrow."

[9]Amaziah asked the man of God, "But what about the hundred talents I paid for these Israelite troops?"

The man of God replied, "The LORD can give you much more than that."

[10]So Amaziah dismissed the troops who had come to him from Ephraim and sent them home. They were furious with Judah and left for home in a great rage.

[11]Amaziah then marshaled his strength and led his army to the Valley of Salt, where he killed ten thousand men of Seir. [12]The army of Judah also captured ten thousand men alive, took them to the top of a cliff and threw them down so that all were dashed to pieces.

[13]Meanwhile the troops that Amaziah had sent back and had not allowed to take part in the war

---

[a] 26 A variant of Jozabad   *[b] 26 A variant of* Shomer
[c] 4 Deut. 24:16   *[d] 6* That is, about 3 3/4 tons or about 3.4 metric tons; also in verse 9

24:24 LORD delivered into their hands A reversal of the normal situation in 1–2 Chronicles. Several kings of Judah achieve victory over large armies by relying on God (13:3–20; 14:9–15). Here, the Syrians defeat the larger army of Judah because of Judah's faithlessness.
24:25 they killed him in his bed A fulfillment of Zechariah's request that God avenge his death (v. 22).
24:27 book of the kings See note on 16:11.

25:1–28 The Chronicler follows the account of Amaziah's reign in 2Ki 14:1–20, with some additions. Most notably, the Chronicler includes several prophecies not present in 2 Kings. In the first, Amaziah responds positively and is rewarded with victory (2Ch 25:7–12). After this, however, Amaziah worships foreign gods (v. 14). God sends a prophet to rebuke him, but Amaziah rejects the prophet (vv. 15–16) and is defeated as punishment for his idolatry (vv. 17–22).

25:2 not wholeheartedly Just like his father, Joash, Amaziah was faithful only for a time (compare 24:2).
25:3 who had murdered his father the king See 24:20–26.

25:4 each will die for their own sin Quoted from Dt 24:16.

25:5–10 The Chronicler includes more details than the 2 Kings account of Amaziah's battle with the Edomites (2Ki 14:7). This story highlights the Chronicler's theme of relying on God rather than foreign alliances.

25:5 three hundred thousand men fit for military service Amaziah's army is much smaller than the ones amassed by Asa (2Ch 14:8) and Jehoshaphat (17:14–18). This probably accounts for his decision to hire soldiers from Israel.
25:6 for a hundred talents of silver A talent was about 75 pounds (34 kilograms).
25:7 a man of God A common term for a prophet (1Sa 2:27; 1Ki 13:1; 17:24). **LORD is not with Israel** During the reign of Amaziah, Israel worshiped foreign gods.
25:11 Valley of Salt The location of this battleground is uncertain. **Seir** The hill country of Edom, southeast of Judah.
25:13 carried off great quantities of plunder Angry that they were sent home and denied the opportunity to

raided towns belonging to Judah from Samaria to Beth Horon. They killed three thousand people and carried off great quantities of plunder.

[14]When Amaziah returned from slaughtering the Edomites, he brought back the gods of the people of Seir. He set them up as his own gods, bowed down to them and burned sacrifices to them. [15]The anger of the LORD burned against Amaziah, and he sent a prophet to him, who said, "Why do you consult this people's gods, which could not save their own people from your hand?"

[16]While he was still speaking, the king said to him, "Have we appointed you an adviser to the king? Stop! Why be struck down?"

So the prophet stopped but said, "I know that God has determined to destroy you, because you have done this and have not listened to my counsel."

[17]After Amaziah king of Judah consulted his advisers, he sent this challenge to Jehoash[a] son of Jehoahaz, the son of Jehu, king of Israel: "Come, let us face each other in battle."

[18]But Jehoash king of Israel replied to Amaziah king of Judah: "A thistle in Lebanon sent a message to a cedar in Lebanon, 'Give your daughter to my son in marriage.' Then a wild beast in Lebanon came along and trampled the thistle underfoot. [19]You say to yourself that you have defeated Edom, and now you are arrogant and proud. But stay at home! Why ask for trouble and cause your own downfall and that of Judah also?"

[20]Amaziah, however, would not listen, for God so worked that he might deliver them into the hands of Jehoash, because they sought the gods of Edom. [21]So Jehoash king of Israel attacked. He and Amaziah king of Judah faced each other at Beth Shemesh in Judah. [22]Judah was routed by Israel, and every man fled to his home. [23]Jehoash king of Israel captured Amaziah king of Judah, the son of Joash, the son of Ahaziah,[b] at Beth Shemesh. Then Jehoash brought him to Jerusalem and broke down the wall of Jerusalem from the Ephraim Gate to the Corner Gate—a section about four hundred cubits[c] long. [24]He took all the gold and silver and all the articles found in the temple of God that had been in the care of Obed-Edom, together with the palace treasures and the hostages, and returned to Samaria.

[25]Amaziah son of Joash king of Judah lived for fifteen years after the death of Jehoash son of Jehoahaz king of Israel. [26]As for the other events of Amaziah's reign, from beginning to end, are they not written in the book of the kings of Judah and Israel? [27]From the time that Amaziah turned away from following the LORD, they conspired against him in Jerusalem and he fled to Lachish, but they sent men after him to Lachish and killed him there. [28]He was brought back by horse and was buried with his ancestors in the City of Judah.[d]

Uzziah King of Judah

26:1-4pp — 2Ki 14:21-22; 15:1-3
26:21-23pp — 2Ki 15:5-7

26 Then all the people of Judah took Uzziah,[e] who was sixteen years old, and made him king in place of his father Amaziah. [2]He was the one who rebuilt Elath and restored it to Judah after Amaziah rested with his ancestors.

---

[a] 17 Hebrew *Joash*, a variant of *Jehoash*; also in verses 18, 21, 23 and 25   [b] 23 Hebrew *Jehoahaz*, a variant of *Ahaziah*
[c] 23 That is, about 600 feet or about 180 meters   [d] 28 Most Hebrew manuscripts; some Hebrew manuscripts, Septuagint, Vulgate and Syriac (see also 2 Kings 14:20) *David*   [e] 1 Also called *Azariah*

---

gather war spoils, the hired soldiers from Israel decide to plunder Judah (see 2Ch 25:10).
25:17 Jehoash The Hebrew text here reads *yo'ash* (Joash), which is a variant spelling of *yeho'ash* (Jehoash) used in 2Ki 14:8 (see note on 2Ki 13:9–13). **let us face each other** It is unclear whether Amaziah's message to Joash (Jehoash) is meant to be friendly. It is possible he was looking to join in a marriage alliance like Jehoshaphat did with Ahab (2Ch 18:1). He also could have been looking to face Joash in battle as a response to the actions of the Israelite soldier's raids (v. 13). However Amaziah meant his message, Joash interprets it as a sign of arrogance.
25:18 thistle See note on 2Ki 14:9.
25:23 four hundred cubits Joash (Jehoash) damages about 600 feet of Jerusalem's city wall.
25:24 in the care of Obed-Edom Refers to the family that David appointed as gatekeepers.
25:26 the other events A common epitaph for deceased kings (compare 1Ki 11:41; 14:19).
25:27 and he fled to Lachish One of Judah's fortified cities (2Ch 11:5–10 and note).

26:1–23 Uzziah (Azariah) receives far more coverage in 2 Chronicles than in 2 Kings (compare 2Ki 14:21–22; 15:1–7). His story shares similarities with those of Joash (2Ch 23:1—24:27) and Amaziah (25:1–28). All three kings were faithful at the beginning of their reigns but eventually fell away. Their stories would have been a reminder to the Chronicler's audience of returned exiles to remain faithful.

26:1 Uzziah Also known as Azariah (2Ki 15:1).

UZZIAH
Uzziah was an early eighth-century BC king of Judah. His name means "Yahweh is (my) strength." Uzziah enjoyed a long reign, and the kingdom of Judah experienced its greatest prosperity since Solomon. Uzziah improved the defenses of Judah and expanded its territory through a series of military successes. According to 2 Kings and 2 Chronicles, Yahweh struck Uzziah with leprosy—likely because he did not remove false worship sites (2Ki 15:4). The disease forced Uzziah to hand over control of the kingdom to his son, Jotham, while he spent the remainder of his life in isolation.

³Uzziah was sixteen years old when he became king, and he reigned in Jerusalem fifty-two years. His mother's name was Jekoliah; she was from Jerusalem. ⁴He did what was right in the eyes of the LORD, just as his father Amaziah had done. ⁵He sought God during the days of Zechariah, who instructed him in the fear*a* of God. As long as he sought the LORD, God gave him success.

⁶He went to war against the Philistines and broke down the walls of Gath, Jabneh and Ashdod. He then rebuilt towns near Ashdod and elsewhere among the Philistines. ⁷God helped him against the Philistines and against the Arabs who lived in Gur Baal and against the Meunites. ⁸The Ammonites brought tribute to Uzziah, and his fame spread as far as the border of Egypt, because he had become very powerful.

⁹Uzziah built towers in Jerusalem at the Corner Gate, at the Valley Gate and at the angle of the wall, and he fortified them. ¹⁰He also built towers in the wilderness and dug many cisterns, because he had much livestock in the foothills and in the plain. He had people working his fields and vineyards in the hills and in the fertile lands, for he loved the soil.

¹¹Uzziah had a well-trained army, ready to go out by divisions according to their numbers as mustered by Jeiel the secretary and Maaseiah the officer under the direction of Hananiah, one of the royal officials. ¹²The total number of family leaders over the fighting men was 2,600. ¹³Under their command was an army of 307,500 men trained for war, a powerful force to support the king against his enemies. ¹⁴Uzziah provided shields, spears, helmets, coats of armor, bows and slingstones for the entire army. ¹⁵In Jerusalem he made devices invented for use on the towers and on the corner defenses so that soldiers could shoot arrows and hurl large stones from the walls. His fame spread far and wide, for he was greatly helped until he became powerful.

¹⁶But after Uzziah became powerful, his pride led to his downfall. He was unfaithful to the LORD his God, and entered the temple of the LORD to burn incense on the altar of incense. ¹⁷Azariah the priest with eighty other courageous priests of the LORD followed him in. ¹⁸They confronted King Uzziah and said, "It is not right for you, Uzziah, to burn incense to the LORD. That is for the priests, the descendants of Aaron, who have been consecrated to burn incense. Leave the sanctuary, for you have been unfaithful; and you will not be honored by the LORD God."

¹⁹Uzziah, who had a censer in his hand ready to burn incense, became angry. While he was raging at the priests in their presence before the incense altar in the LORD's temple, leprosy*b* broke out on his forehead. ²⁰When Azariah the chief priest and all the other priests looked at him, they saw that he had leprosy on his forehead, so they hurried him out. Indeed, he himself was eager to leave, because the LORD had afflicted him.

²¹King Uzziah had leprosy until the day he died. He lived in a separate house*c* — leprous, and banned from the temple of the LORD. Jotham his son had charge of the palace and governed the people of the land.

²²The other events of Uzziah's reign, from beginning to end, are recorded by the prophet Isaiah son of Amoz. ²³Uzziah rested with his ancestors

a 5 Many Hebrew manuscripts, Septuagint and Syriac; other Hebrew manuscripts *vision*   *b 19* The Hebrew for *leprosy* was used for various diseases affecting the skin; also in verses 20, 21 and 23.   *c 21* Or *in a house where he was relieved of responsibilities*

26:2 He was the one who rebuilt Elath A site on the Gulf of Aqaba (see note on 2Ki 14:22). **rested with his ancestors** See note on 2Ch 9:31.
26:3 he reigned in Jerusalem fifty-two years From approximately 792–742 BC. Uzziah's reign most likely included periods of coregency. He apparently ruled when his father, Amaziah, fled to Lachish (25:27–28; 26:1). Uzziah's son, Jotham, served as coregent after Uzziah contracted leprosy (26:21). See the timeline "The Divided Kingdom" on p. 536.

NORTHERN KING	DATE	SOUTHERN KING	DATE
Jehoash	798–786 BC	Amaziah	796–792 BC
Jeroboam II	786–746 BC	Uzziah (Azariah)	792–742 BC
Zechariah	746–746 BC	Jotham	742–735 BC

26:5 He sought God See note on 11:16. **during the days of Zechariah** Nothing is known about this Zechariah, who apparently acted as an advisor to Uzziah just as Jehoiada did for Joash (24:2). **God gave him success** The theme of faithfulness leading to prosperity is seen throughout 1–2 Chronicles (e.g., 13:18; 14:11–12; 20:20).

26:6 Philistines See note on 1Sa 4:1. **Gath** A Philistine city. **Jabneh** A town on Judah's northern border; also called "Jabneel" (Jos 15:11). **Ashdod** A major Philistine city.
26:7 Meunites Probably residents of Maan in Edom.
26:8 Ammonites Judah's neighbors (and often enemies) to the east, across the Jordan River.
26:9 at the Corner Gate Uzziah probably repairs the damage to the wall caused by Jehoash, king of Israel (2Ch 25:23).
26:10 foothills The low hills west of central Judah.
26:15 so that soldiers could shoot arrows and hurl large stones The exact nature of these inventions is uncertain. There is no evidence of devices like catapults existing in the ancient Near East until around 400 BC.
26:16 altar of incense Because he is not a priest, Uzziah is not qualified to burn incense in the temple (Nu 16:40). Saul was rejected as king for a similar offense (1Sa 13:9).
26:19 leprosy The Hebrew word used here, *tsara'ath*, can indicate a variety of skin diseases (see note on Lev 13:1–59). People afflicted with such skin diseases were considered unclean and were forced to live in isolation (Lev 13:46; 2Ki 7:3).
26:20 so they hurried him out To avoid defiling the temple.
26:22 recorded by the prophet Isaiah son of Amoz

and was buried near them in a cemetery that belonged to the kings, for people said, "He had leprosy." And Jotham his son succeeded him as king.

Jotham King of Judah

27:1-4,7-9pp — 2Ki 15:33-38

27 Jotham was twenty-five years old when he became king, and he reigned in Jerusalem sixteen years. His mother's name was Jerusha daughter of Zadok. ²He did what was right in the eyes of the LORD, just as his father Uzziah had done, but unlike him he did not enter the temple of the LORD. The people, however, continued their corrupt practices. ³Jotham rebuilt the Upper Gate of the temple of the LORD and did extensive work on the wall at the hill of Ophel. ⁴He built towns in the hill country of Judah and forts and towers in the wooded areas.

⁵Jotham waged war against the king of the Ammonites and conquered them. That year the Ammonites paid him a hundred talents*ᵃ* of silver, ten thousand cors*ᵇ* of wheat and ten thousand cors*ᶜ* of barley. The Ammonites brought him the same amount also in the second and third years.

⁶Jotham grew powerful because he walked steadfastly before the LORD his God.

⁷The other events in Jotham's reign, including all his wars and the other things he did, are written in the book of the kings of Israel and Judah. ⁸He was twenty-five years old when he became king, and he reigned in Jerusalem sixteen years. ⁹Jotham rested with his ancestors and was buried in the City of David. And Ahaz his son succeeded him as king.

Ahaz King of Judah

28:1-27pp — 2Ki 16:1-20

28 Ahaz was twenty years old when he became king, and he reigned in Jerusalem sixteen years. Unlike David his father, he did not do what was right in the eyes of the LORD. ²He followed the ways of the kings of Israel and also made idols for worshiping the Baals. ³He burned sacrifices in the Valley of Ben Hinnom and sacrificed his children in the fire, engaging in the detestable practices of the nations the LORD had driven out before the Israelites. ⁴He offered sacrifices and burned incense at the high places, on the hilltops and under every spreading tree.

⁵Therefore the LORD his God delivered him into the hands of the king of Aram. The Arameans defeated him and took many of his people as prisoners and brought them to Damascus.

He was also given into the hands of the king of Israel, who inflicted heavy casualties on him. ⁶In one day Pekah son of Remaliah killed a hundred and twenty thousand soldiers in Judah — because Judah had forsaken the LORD, the God of their ancestors. ⁷Zikri, an Ephraimite warrior, killed Maaseiah the king's son, Azrikam the officer in charge of the palace, and Elkanah, second to the king. ⁸The men of Israel took captive from their fellow Israelites who were from Judah two hundred thousand wives, sons and daughters. They

---

ᵃ 5 That is, about 3 3/4 tons or about 3.4 metric tons   *ᵇ 5* That is, probably about 1,800 tons or about 1,600 metric tons of wheat   *ᶜ 5* That is, probably about 1,500 tons or about 1,350 metric tons of barley

---

This does not refer to the canonical book of Isaiah. While Isaiah might have been active during Uzziah's reign, his full ministry did not begin until the year of Uzziah's death (see Isa 1:1; 6:1 and note).

27:1 and he reigned in Jerusalem sixteen years Jotham probably reigned in conjunction with his father, Uzziah, for a time (see note on 2Ch 26:3). Jotham made repairs to the temple and found military success (vv. 3–5), but the Chronicler does not devote much attention to his reign. This may be attributed to his coregency with his father, Uzziah. The author of 2 Kings also says little about Jotham (2Ki 15:32–38).

27:2 corrupt practices While Jotham's reign is characterized as positive, he failed to remove the high places used to worship idols (2Ki 15:35).

27:3 Upper Gate Also known as the Benjamin Gate. See Jer 20:2 and note. **the wall at the hill of Ophel** Most likely on the southeastern side of Jerusalem, between the temple and the Kidron Valley.

27:5 a hundred talents of silver A talent is about 75 pounds (34 kilograms). **ten thousand cors of wheat** A cor is about 220 liters.

27:6 Jotham grew powerful Jotham becomes strong just as his father, Uzziah, did (2Ch 26:15–16). Jotham's success, however, does not lead to pride.

27:7 book of the kings of Israel and Judah See note on 16:11.

28:1–27 The Chronicler's account of Ahaz follows 2Ki 16:1—17:5.

28:2 the ways of the kings of Israel Ahaz followed after the pattern of the wicked northern kings. Ironically, the northern kingdom of Israel repents during Ahaz's reign (2Ch 28:9–15).

28:3 in the Valley of Ben Hinnom See note on Jer 7:31. **and sacrificed his children** See 2Ki 16:3 and note.

28:4 on the hilltops A standard reference to the location of Canaanite religious sites. **under every spreading tree** See note on Jer 2:20.

28:5 king of Aram Elsewhere identified as Rezin (2Ki 16:5). Rezin was the last king of Aram (Syria) before it was conquered by Assyria.

KING OF SYRIA	DATE	SOUTHERN KING	DATE
Ben-Hadad III	796–792 BC	Uzziah (Azariah)	792–742 BC
Rezin	740–732 BC	Jotham	742–735 BC
		Ahaz	735–715 BC

28:6 Pekah The king in Israel when the Assyrians first began deporting people from the northern kingdom (2Ki 15:29).

28:8 wives, sons and daughters By referring to relatives, the Chronicler emphasizes the close relationship between the northern and southern kingdoms, Israel and

also took a great deal of plunder, which they carried back to Samaria.

⁹But a prophet of the LORD named Oded was there, and he went out to meet the army when it returned to Samaria. He said to them, "Because the LORD, the God of your ancestors, was angry with Judah, he gave them into your hand. But you have slaughtered them in a rage that reaches to heaven. ¹⁰And now you intend to make the men and women of Judah and Jerusalem your slaves. But aren't you also guilty of sins against the LORD your God? ¹¹Now listen to me! Send back your fellow Israelites you have taken as prisoners, for the LORD's fierce anger rests on you."

¹²Then some of the leaders in Ephraim—Azariah son of Jehohanan, Berekiah son of Meshillemoth, Jehizkiah son of Shallum, and Amasa son of Hadlai—confronted those who were arriving from the war. ¹³"You must not bring those prisoners here," they said, "or we will be guilty before the LORD. Do you intend to add to our sin and guilt? For our guilt is already great, and his fierce anger rests on Israel."

¹⁴So the soldiers gave up the prisoners and plunder in the presence of the officials and all the assembly. ¹⁵The men designated by name took the prisoners, and from the plunder they clothed all who were naked. They provided them with clothes and sandals, food and drink, and healing balm. All those who were weak they put on donkeys. So they took them back to their fellow Israelites at Jericho, the City of Palms, and returned to Samaria.

¹⁶At that time King Ahaz sent to the kings[a] of Assyria for help. ¹⁷The Edomites had again come and attacked Judah and carried away prisoners, ¹⁸while the Philistines had raided towns in the foothills and in the Negev of Judah. They captured and occupied Beth Shemesh, Aijalon and Gederoth, as well as Soko, Timnah and Gimzo, with their surrounding villages. ¹⁹The LORD had

humbled Judah because of Ahaz king of Israel,[b] for he had promoted wickedness in Judah and had been most unfaithful to the LORD. ²⁰Tiglath-Pileser[c] king of Assyria came to him, but he gave him trouble instead of help. ²¹Ahaz took some of the things from the temple of the LORD and from the royal palace and from the officials and presented them to the king of Assyria, but that did not help him.

²²In his time of trouble King Ahaz became even more unfaithful to the LORD. ²³He offered sacrifices to the gods of Damascus, who had defeated him; for he thought, "Since the gods of the kings of Aram have helped them, I will sacrifice to them so they will help me." But they were his downfall and the downfall of all Israel.

²⁴Ahaz gathered together the furnishings from the temple of God and cut them in pieces. He shut the doors of the LORD's temple and set up altars at every street corner in Jerusalem. ²⁵In every town in Judah he built high places to burn sacrifices to other gods and aroused the anger of the LORD, the God of his ancestors.

²⁶The other events of his reign and all his ways, from beginning to end, are written in the book of the kings of Judah and Israel. ²⁷Ahaz rested with his ancestors and was buried in the city of Jerusalem, but he was not placed in the tombs of the kings of Israel. And Hezekiah his son succeeded him as king.

Hezekiah Purifies the Temple

29:1-2pp — 2Ki 18:2-3

29 Hezekiah was twenty-five years old when he became king, and he reigned in Jerusalem twenty-nine years. His mother's name was

---

[a] *16* Most Hebrew manuscripts; one Hebrew manuscript, Septuagint and Vulgate (see also 2 Kings 16:7) *king*   [b] *19* That is, Judah, as frequently in 2 Chronicles   [c] *20* Hebrew *Tilgath-Pilneser,* a variant of *Tiglath-Pileser*

Judah. **Samaria** This city became the capital of the northern kingdom after King Omri purchased it (1Ki 16:24).

28:9 you have slaughtered them in a rage Although God gave Judah into the Israelites' hand, they exceeded what God allowed.

28:10 aren't you also guilty of sins As the leaders of Ephraim acknowledge, Israel's guilt was already great (2Ch 28:13).

28:16 to the kings of Assyria Faced with challenges from both the Edomites and the Philistines, Ahaz turns to Assyria instead of turning to God. The importance of relying on God instead of foreign alliances is a theme throughout 2 Chronicles.

28:19 had been most unfaithful The Hebrew word used here, *ma'al*, occurs throughout 1–2 Chronicles to describe a breach of faith (see note on 1Ch 5:25). The form used here, *ma'ol ma'al*, is meant to emphasize the extent of Ahaz's faithlessness.

28:20 he gave him trouble The Assyrians did help Judah by eliminating some of its enemies and bringing a temporary peace (2Ki 16:9). However, this came at a

cost to Judah both financially and spiritually (2 Ch 28:21; 2Ki 16:10–16).

28:21 but that did not help him The Chronicler highlights the ineffective help from other nations, contrasting it with the powerful help that comes from God (e.g., 2Ch 14:11; 16:12; 18:31; 20:4; 25:8; 26:7).

28:24 cut them in pieces The parallel statement in 2Ki 16:17 describes Ahaz separating bronze stands from their frames. These stands, commissioned by Solomon, are described in detail in 1Ki 7:27–37.

28:27 rested with his ancestors See note on 2Ch 9:31.

29:1—32:33 The collective work of 1–2 Chronicles devotes more time to the reign of Hezekiah than any other king except David and Solomon. While 2Ki 18–20 covers Hezekiah's conflict with Assyria, the account in 1–2 Chronicles focuses on his religious reforms. This fits with the Chronicler's emphasis on proper temple worship (see note on 1Ch 1:1—9:44).

29:1 Hezekiah King of Judah ca. 715–697 BC. Praised as one of the best rulers of Judah due to his devotion to

Abijah daughter of Zechariah. [2]He did what was right in the eyes of the LORD, just as his father David had done.

[3]In the first month of the first year of his reign, he opened the doors of the temple of the LORD and repaired them. [4]He brought in the priests and the Levites, assembled them in the square on the east side [5]and said: "Listen to me, Levites! Consecrate yourselves now and consecrate the temple of the LORD, the God of your ancestors. Remove all defilement from the sanctuary. [6]Our parents were unfaithful; they did evil in the eyes of the LORD our God and forsook him. They turned their faces away from the LORD's dwelling place and turned their backs on him. [7]They also shut the doors of the portico and put out the lamps. They did not burn incense or present any burnt offerings at the sanctuary to the God of Israel. [8]Therefore, the anger of the LORD has fallen on Judah and Jerusalem; he has made them an object of dread and horror and scorn, as you can see with your own eyes. [9]This is why our fathers have fallen by the sword and why our sons and daughters and our wives are in captivity. [10]Now I intend to make a covenant with the LORD, the God of Israel, so that his fierce anger will turn away from us. [11]My sons, do not be negligent now, for the LORD has chosen you to stand before him and serve him, to minister before him and to burn incense."

[12]Then these Levites set to work:

from the Kohathites,
 Mahath son of Amasai and Joel son of
 Azariah;
from the Merarites,
 Kish son of Abdi and Azariah son of
 Jehallelel;
from the Gershonites,
 Joah son of Zimmah and Eden son of Joah;
[13]from the descendants of Elizaphan,
 Shimri and Jeiel;
from the descendants of Asaph,
 Zechariah and Mattaniah;
[14]from the descendants of Heman,
 Jehiel and Shimei;
from the descendants of Jeduthun,
 Shemaiah and Uzziel.

[15]When they had assembled their fellow Levites and consecrated themselves, they went in to purify the temple of the LORD, as the king had ordered, following the word of the LORD. [16]The priests went into the sanctuary of the LORD to purify it. They brought out to the courtyard of the LORD's temple everything unclean that they found in the temple of the LORD. The Levites took it and carried it out to the Kidron Valley. [17]They began the consecration on the first day of the first month, and by the eighth day of the month they reached the portico of the LORD. For eight more days they consecrated the temple of the LORD itself, finishing on the sixteenth day of the first month.

[18]Then they went in to King Hezekiah and reported: "We have purified the entire temple of the LORD, the altar of burnt offering with all its utensils, and the table for setting out the consecrated bread, with all its articles. [19]We have prepared and consecrated all the articles that King Ahaz removed in his unfaithfulness while he was king. They are now in front of the LORD's altar."

[20]Early the next morning King Hezekiah gathered the city officials together and went up to the temple of the LORD. [21]They brought seven bulls, seven rams, seven male lambs and seven male goats as a sin offering[a] for the kingdom, for the sanctuary and for Judah. The king commanded the priests, the descendants of Aaron, to offer these on the altar of the LORD. [22]So they slaughtered the bulls, and the priests took the blood and splashed it against the altar; next they slaughtered the rams and splashed their blood against the altar; then they slaughtered the lambs and splashed their blood against the altar. [23]The goats for the sin

---

[a] 21 Or *purification offering*; also in verses 23 and 24

Yahweh. See the timeline "The Divided Kingdom" on p. 536; see the infographic "Sennacherib's Prism" on p. 597.
29:5 Remove all defilement from the sanctuary Hezekiah's father, Ahaz, apparently had used the temple and its materials for his idolatry.
29:8 Therefore, the anger of the LORD has fallen Yahweh's wrath on Judah during Ahaz's time caused defeat by Israel (2Ch 28:11) and led Judah to become a vassal of Assyria (28:16–21).
29:9 are in captivity See 28:8.
29:10 Now I intend A similar Hebrew phrase is used to describe David's intention to build the temple (1Ch 22:7).

29:12–14 The Chronicler lists Levites according to the divisions established by David, with two representatives from each family. The first three families were part of David's divisions of Levites (1Ch 23:6–23); the final three were part of David's divisions of temple musicians (1Ch 25:1–7); the middle family—the descendants of Elizaphan—is mentioned in 1Chr 15:8.

29:13 Asaph Associated with many Psalms. See Ps 73:title and note.
29:14 Heman Associated with Ps 88. **Jeduthun** Associated with Ps 39; 62; 77.
29:15 following the word of the LORD The cleansing of the temple and the return to proper worship is linked with the reestablishment of a covenant between God and the Davidic king (2Ch 29:10).
29:16 to the Kidron Valley Located on the east side of Jerusalem; often used to dispose of idols (e.g., 15:16; 1Ki 15:13; 2Ki 23:6,12).
29:19 all the articles that King Ahaz removed See 2Ch 28:24.
29:20 gathered the city officials together Just as David and Solomon had done when the ark of the covenant was moved (see 1:2 and note; 5:2 and note).
29:21 as a sin offering Intended to restore the sanctity of the temple, which had been contaminated by the people's sins. Compare Lev 4:3 and note.

offering were brought before the king and the assembly, and they laid their hands on them. ²⁴The priests then slaughtered the goats and presented their blood on the altar for a sin offering to atone for all Israel, because the king had ordered the burnt offering and the sin offering for all Israel.

²⁵He stationed the Levites in the temple of the LORD with cymbals, harps and lyres in the way prescribed by David and Gad the king's seer and Nathan the prophet; this was commanded by the LORD through his prophets. ²⁶So the Levites stood ready with David's instruments, and the priests with their trumpets.

²⁷Hezekiah gave the order to sacrifice the burnt offering on the altar. As the offering began, singing to the LORD began also, accompanied by trumpets and the instruments of David king of Israel. ²⁸The whole assembly bowed in worship, while the musicians played and the trumpets sounded. All this continued until the sacrifice of the burnt offering was completed.

²⁹When the offerings were finished, the king and everyone present with him knelt down and worshiped. ³⁰King Hezekiah and his officials ordered the Levites to praise the LORD with the words of David and of Asaph the seer. So they sang praises with gladness and bowed down and worshiped.

³¹Then Hezekiah said, "You have now dedicated yourselves to the LORD. Come and bring sacrifices and thank offerings to the temple of the LORD." So the assembly brought sacrifices and thank offerings, and all whose hearts were willing brought burnt offerings.

³²The number of burnt offerings the assembly brought was seventy bulls, a hundred rams and two hundred male lambs — all of them for burnt offerings to the LORD. ³³The animals consecrated as sacrifices amounted to six hundred bulls and three thousand sheep and goats. ³⁴The priests, however, were too few to skin all the burnt offerings; so their relatives the Levites helped them until the task was finished and until other priests had been consecrated, for the Levites had been more conscientious in consecrating themselves than the priests had been. ³⁵There were burnt offerings in abundance, together with the fat of the fellowship offerings and the drink offerings that accompanied the burnt offerings.

So the service of the temple of the LORD was re-established. ³⁶Hezekiah and all the people rejoiced at what God had brought about for his people, because it was done so quickly.

Hezekiah Celebrates the Passover

30 Hezekiah sent word to all Israel and Judah and also wrote letters to Ephraim and Manasseh, inviting them to come to the temple of the LORD in Jerusalem and celebrate the Passover to the LORD, the God of Israel. ²The king and his officials and the whole assembly in Jerusalem decided to celebrate the Passover in the second month. ³They had not been able to celebrate it at the regular time because not enough priests had consecrated themselves and the people had not assembled in Jerusalem. ⁴The plan seemed right both to the king and to the whole assembly. ⁵They decided to send a proclamation throughout Israel, from Beersheba to Dan, calling the people to come to Jerusalem and celebrate the Passover to the LORD, the God of Israel. It had not been celebrated in large numbers according to what was written.

⁶At the king's command, couriers went throughout Israel and Judah with letters from the king and from his officials, which read:

"People of Israel, return to the LORD, the God of Abraham, Isaac and Israel, that he may

---

29:24 to atone Signifies forgiveness of sins. See Lev 4:20 and note. **all Israel** This probably includes the northern kingdom, as well as Judah.
29:25 Gad Prophet who advised David (1Sa 22:5; 2Sa 24:11–19: 1Ch 21:9–19). **Nathan** See 2Sa 7:2 and note.
29:30 the words of David and of Asaph A reference to the psalms, many of which name David and Asaph in the title.
29:34 conscientious The Hebrew phrase used here, *yishrath levav,* may be literally rendered as "upright in heart"; it also is used by Solomon to describe David (1Ki 3:6).
30:1–27 In this account of Hezekiah's Passover celebration, the Chronicler focuses on the themes of return and redemption. In the wake of Assyria's victory over the northern kingdom of Israel, Hezekiah invites the remaining Israelites—those who were not dead or deported—to join the people of Judah in celebrating Passover at the temple (2Ch 30:5). Hezekiah calls the Israelites to return to the God of their fathers (v. 6). If they do, God will be

compassionate and merciful (v. 9). Those who respond to Hezekiah's message are pardoned, even though they are not ritually clean (v. 18). Throughout the passage, the Chronicler also highlights the joy associated with worship (vv. 21,23,26).

30:1 Ephraim and Manasseh These tribes represent the northern kingdom as a whole. See note on Hos 4:17. **celebrate the Passover** Passover regulations are recorded in Ex 12:3–20 and Dt 16:1–8.
30:3 They had not been able to celebrate it at the regular time Because the temple was still being consecrated, Hezekiah delayed the Passover celebration from the first month to the second (see 2Ch 29:17). There was precedent for this in the law (Nu 9:10–11; see note on Nu 9:1–14).
30:5 from Beersheba to Dan A figurative way of referring to all of Israel, including the southern and northern extents.
30:6 return to the LORD Hezekiah reminds the remaining Israelites of God's promise at the temple's original dedication: If the people humble themselves and return

return to you who are left, who have escaped from the hand of the kings of Assyria. [7]Do not be like your parents and your fellow Israelites, who were unfaithful to the LORD, the God of their ancestors, so that he made them an object of horror, as you see. [8]Do not be stiff-necked, as your ancestors were; submit to the LORD. Come to his sanctuary, which he has consecrated forever. Serve the LORD your God, so that his fierce anger will turn away from you. [9]If you return to the LORD, then your fellow Israelites and your children will be shown compassion by their captors and will return to this land, for the LORD your God is gracious and compassionate. He will not turn his face from you if you return to him."

[10]The couriers went from town to town in Ephraim and Manasseh, as far as Zebulun, but people scorned and ridiculed them. [11]Nevertheless, some from Asher, Manasseh and Zebulun humbled themselves and went to Jerusalem. [12]Also in Judah the hand of God was on the people to give them unity of mind to carry out what the king and his officials had ordered, following the word of the LORD.

[13]A very large crowd of people assembled in Jerusalem to celebrate the Festival of Unleavened Bread in the second month. [14]They removed the altars in Jerusalem and cleared away the incense altars and threw them into the Kidron Valley.

[15]They slaughtered the Passover lamb on the fourteenth day of the second month. The priests and the Levites were ashamed and consecrated themselves and brought burnt offerings to the temple of the LORD. [16]Then they took up their regular positions as prescribed in the Law of Moses the man of God. The priests splashed against the altar the blood handed to them by the Levites. [17]Since many in the crowd had not consecrated themselves, the Levites had to kill the Passover lambs for all those who were not ceremonially clean and could not consecrate their lambs[a] to the LORD. [18]Although most of the many people who came from Ephraim, Manasseh, Issachar and Zebulun had not purified themselves, yet they ate the Passover, contrary to what was written. But Hezekiah prayed for them, saying, "May the LORD, who is good, pardon everyone [19]who sets their heart on seeking God — the LORD, the God of their ancestors — even if they are not clean according to the rules of the sanctuary." [20]And the LORD heard Hezekiah and healed the people.

[21]The Israelites who were present in Jerusalem celebrated the Festival of Unleavened Bread for seven days with great rejoicing, while the Levites and priests praised the LORD every day with resounding instruments dedicated to the LORD.[b]

[22]Hezekiah spoke encouragingly to all the Levites, who showed good understanding of the service of the LORD. For the seven days they ate their assigned portion and offered fellowship offerings and praised[c] the LORD, the God of their ancestors.

[23]The whole assembly then agreed to celebrate the festival seven more days; so for another seven days they celebrated joyfully. [24]Hezekiah king of Judah provided a thousand bulls and seven thousand sheep and goats for the assembly, and the officials provided them with a thousand bulls and ten thousand sheep and goats. A great number of priests consecrated themselves. [25]The entire assembly of Judah rejoiced, along with the priests and Levites and all who had assembled from Israel, including the foreigners who had come from Israel and also those who resided in Judah. [26]There was great joy in Jerusalem, for since the days of Solomon son of David king of Israel there had been nothing like this in Jerusalem. [27]The priests and the Levites stood to bless the people, and God heard them, for their prayer reached heaven, his holy dwelling place.

31 When all this had ended, the Israelites who were there went out to the towns of Judah, smashed the sacred stones and cut down the Asherah poles. They destroyed the high places and the altars throughout Judah and Benjamin and in Ephraim and Manasseh. After they had

---

[a] 17 Or *consecrate themselves*   [b] 21 Or *priests sang to the LORD every day, accompanied by the LORD's instruments of praise*   [c] 22 Or *and confessed their sins to*

---

to Yahweh, then he will forgive them and heal their land (see 2Ch 7:14 and note).

30:7 he made them an object of horror A fulfillment of God's promise at the temple's original dedication (see 7:19–22).

30:11 some from Asher, Manasseh and Zebulun Only three of the ten tribes responded positively to Hezekiah's invitation.

30:13 Festival of Unleavened Bread See note on Lev 23:6.

30:14 the Kidron Valley See note on 2Ch 29:16.

30:18 from Ephraim, Manasseh, Issachar and Zebulun While only three tribes responded positively to Hezekiah's invitation (v. 11), it appears that individuals from other tribes (e.g., Ephraim and Issachar) also came.

30:20 and healed the people The Hebrew word used here, *rapha*, can refer to a physical healing (Lev 13:18). It also carries the sense of "to make whole" or "to restore." This represents a fulfillment of Yahweh's promise at the temple's dedication (see 2Ch 7:14 and note).

30:23 seven more days This celebration lasts twice as long as the one at the temple's original dedication.

30:26 nothing like this in Jerusalem After Solomon's reign, the kingdom was divided into Israel in the north and Judah in the south. No celebration since had included both kingdoms.

30:27 reached heaven, his holy dwelling place See note on 6:21.

31:1 Israelites who were there went out Like other faithful kings, Hezekiah removed all the high places and Asherim (see 14:3 and note). However, this case is unique in that all the people participated in the destruction of

destroyed all of them, the Israelites returned to their own towns and to their own property.

Contributions for Worship

31:20-21pp — 2Ki 18:5-7

²Hezekiah assigned the priests and Levites to divisions — each of them according to their duties as priests or Levites — to offer burnt offerings and fellowship offerings, to minister, to give thanks and to sing praises at the gates of the Lord's dwelling. ³The king contributed from his own possessions for the morning and evening burnt offerings and for the burnt offerings on the Sabbaths, at the New Moons and at the appointed festivals as written in the Law of the Lord. ⁴He ordered the people living in Jerusalem to give the portion due the priests and Levites so they could devote themselves to the Law of the Lord. ⁵As soon as the order went out, the Israelites generously gave the firstfruits of their grain, new wine, olive oil and honey and all that the fields produced. They brought a great amount, a tithe of everything. ⁶The people of Israel and Judah who lived in the towns of Judah also brought a tithe of their herds and flocks and a tithe of the holy things dedicated to the Lord their God, and they piled them in heaps. ⁷They began doing this in the third month and finished in the seventh month. ⁸When Hezekiah and his officials came and saw the heaps, they praised the Lord and blessed his people Israel.

⁹Hezekiah asked the priests and Levites about the heaps; ¹⁰and Azariah the chief priest, from the family of Zadok, answered, "Since the people began to bring their contributions to the temple of the Lord, we have had enough to eat and plenty to spare, because the Lord has blessed his people, and this great amount is left over."

¹¹Hezekiah gave orders to prepare storerooms in the temple of the Lord, and this was done. ¹²Then they faithfully brought in the contributions, tithes and dedicated gifts. Konaniah, a Levite, was the overseer in charge of these things, and his brother Shimei was next in rank. ¹³Jehiel, Azaziah, Nahath, Asahel, Jerimoth, Jozabad, Eliel,

Ismakiah, Mahath and Benaiah were assistants of Konaniah and Shimei his brother. All these served by appointment of King Hezekiah and Azariah the official in charge of the temple of God.

¹⁴Kore son of Imnah the Levite, keeper of the East Gate, was in charge of the freewill offerings given to God, distributing the contributions made to the Lord and also the consecrated gifts. ¹⁵Eden, Miniamin, Jeshua, Shemaiah, Amariah and Shekaniah assisted him faithfully in the towns of the priests, distributing to their fellow priests according to their divisions, old and young alike.

¹⁶In addition, they distributed to the males three years old or more whose names were in the genealogical records — all who would enter the temple of the Lord to perform the daily duties of their various tasks, according to their responsibilities and their divisions. ¹⁷And they distributed to the priests enrolled by their families in the genealogical records and likewise to the Levites twenty years old or more, according to their responsibilities and their divisions. ¹⁸They included all the little ones, the wives, and the sons and daughters of the whole community listed in these genealogical records. For they were faithful in consecrating themselves.

¹⁹As for the priests, the descendants of Aaron, who lived on the farmlands around their towns or in any other towns, men were designated by name to distribute portions to every male among them and to all who were recorded in the genealogies of the Levites.

²⁰This is what Hezekiah did throughout Judah, doing what was good and right and faithful before the Lord his God. ²¹In everything that he undertook in the service of God's temple and in obedience to the law and the commands, he sought his God and worked wholeheartedly. And so he prospered.

Sennacherib Threatens Jerusalem

32:9-19pp — 2Ki 18:17-35; Isa 36:2-20
32:20-21pp — 2Ki 19:35-37; Isa 37:36-38

32 After all that Hezekiah had so faithfully done, Sennacherib king of Assyria came and invaded Judah. He laid siege to the fortified

---

the pagan altars. **Ephraim and Manasseh** See note on 30:1. For the first time, the destruction of the high places includes the tribes of the northern kingdom.

31:2-21 Hezekiah's reforms conclude with his organization of the priests and Levites, following the example of David (see note on 1Ch 23:1—26:32).

31:3 from his own possessions Hezekiah follows David's example by giving his own wealth to support the temple work (see 1Ch 29:2-5). **morning and evening burnt offerings** See note on Ex 29:38-42. **New Moons** See note on Isa 1:13.

31:4 portion due the priests Hezekiah restores support for the priests and Levites. See Nu 18:8-20 and note.

31:10 Lord has blessed his people The Chronicler

draws a specific connection between the faithfulness of the people and the blessing of God.

31:14 keeper of the East Gate A position of responsibility. In David's original division, the east gate had the most gatekeepers (see 1Ch 26:14 and note).

31:20 what was good and right and faithful Just as in 2 Kings, Hezekiah is portrayed as an example of faithfulness (e.g., 2Ki 18:5-7).

31:21 he sought his God See note on 2Ch 11:16. **And so he prospered** The Chronicler again shows that those who seek God are blessed and prosperous (13:18; 14:7; 20:20; 26:5).

32:1-23 Sennacherib's invasion of Judah also is recorded in 2Ki 18:13—19:37 and Isa 36:1—37:38. The Chronicler provides fewer details than those accounts.

cities, thinking to conquer them for himself. ²When Hezekiah saw that Sennacherib had come and that he intended to wage war against Jerusalem, ³he consulted with his officials and military staff about blocking off the water from the springs outside the city, and they helped him. ⁴They gathered a large group of people who blocked all the springs and the stream that flowed through the land. "Why should the kings*a* of Assyria come and find plenty of water?" they said. ⁵Then he worked hard repairing all the broken sections of the wall and building towers on it. He built another wall outside that one and reinforced the terraces*b* of the City of David. He also made large numbers of weapons and shields.

⁶He appointed military officers over the people and assembled them before him in the square at the city gate and encouraged them with these words: ⁷"Be strong and courageous. Do not be afraid or discouraged because of the king of Assyria and the vast army with him, for there is a greater power with us than with him. ⁸With him is only the arm of flesh, but with us is the LORD our God to help us and to fight our battles." And the people gained confidence from what Hezekiah the king of Judah said.

⁹Later, when Sennacherib king of Assyria and all his forces were laying siege to Lachish, he sent his officers to Jerusalem with this message for Hezekiah king of Judah and for all the people of Judah who were there:

¹⁰"This is what Sennacherib king of Assyria says: On what are you basing your confidence, that you remain in Jerusalem under siege? ¹¹When Hezekiah says, 'The LORD our God will save us from the hand of the king of Assyria,' he is misleading you, to let you die of hunger and thirst. ¹²Did not Hezekiah himself remove this god's high places and altars, saying to Judah and Jerusalem, 'You must worship before one altar and burn sacrifices on it'?

¹³"Do you not know what I and my predecessors have done to all the peoples of the other lands? Were the gods of those nations ever able to deliver their land from my hand? ¹⁴Who of all the gods of these nations that my predecessors destroyed has been able to save his people from me? How then can your god deliver you from my hand? ¹⁵Now do not let Hezekiah deceive you and mislead you like this. Do not believe him, for no god of any nation or kingdom has been able to deliver his people from my hand or the hand of my predecessors. How much less will your god deliver you from my hand!"

¹⁶Sennacherib's officers spoke further against the LORD God and against his servant Hezekiah. ¹⁷The king also wrote letters ridiculing the LORD, the God of Israel, and saying this against him: "Just as the gods of the peoples of the other lands did not rescue their people from my hand, so the god of Hezekiah will not rescue his people from my hand." ¹⁸Then they called out in Hebrew to

a 4 Hebrew; Septuagint and Syriac *king*   *b* 5 Or *the Millo*

32:1 After all that Hezekiah had so faithfully done The Chronicler emphasizes the connection between Hezekiah's faithful restoration of temple worship and God's protection of Judah from Sennacherib's attack. Second Kings and Isaiah set these events in the fourteenth year of Hezekiah's reign. See Isa 36:1 and note.
Sennacherib king of Assyria Sennacherib ruled Assyria around 705–681 BC. See the timeline "Dates Related to Isaiah and 2 Kings" on p. 1116; see the infographic "Sennacherib's Prism" on p. 597.

DATE	EVENT
725–722 BC	Assyrians besiege Samaria. The Israelites are defeated and sent into exile.
705 BC	Sennacherib becomes king.
701 BC	Sennacherib invades Judah.
681 BC	Sennacherib is assassinated by two of his sons.

32:2 that he intended to wage war against Jerusalem The Chronicler does not include details of Hezekiah's attempt to buy peace from Assyria (2Ki 18:14–16).
32:3–6 Hezekiah takes several measures to protect Jerusalem. He cuts off the water supply outside the city, in order to hinder the Assyrians. He also repairs the wall and constructs fortifications. Finally, he builds more weapons and organizes the army.

32:7 Be strong and courageous Hezekiah's speech echoes Yahweh's encouragement to Joshua (Jos 1:6–9), as well as David's charge to Solomon (1Ch 22:13).
32:8 to help us and to fight our battles Hezekiah focuses not on his own preparations, but on Yahweh's help. He contrasts the human power of the Assyrian army with the divine power on Judah's side.

32:9–19 Sennacherib's speech in 2 Chronicles combines several separate speeches (see 2Ki 18:19–25,28–35; 19:9–13). A parallel account of this episode appears in Isa 36.

32:9 Lachish A fortified city about 25 miles southwest of Jerusalem.
32:11 to let you die of hunger and thirst The language in 2 Kings is more graphic, as the Assyrian commander warns that the people will have to eat their own dung and drink their own urine (2Ki 18:27). Blockades such as this often led to desperate measures, as the enemy cut off a city's food and water supply (compare 2Ki 6:24–29).
32:12 high places and altars Sennacherib wrongly assumes that the high places were devoted to Yahweh, and that their removal would turn him against Hezekiah (2Ch 31:1).
32:13 the gods of those nations Sennacherib equates Yahweh with the deities of nations that he already had defeated. See 2Ki 18:34; Isa 36:19.
32:18 in Hebrew Rather than in Aramaic, the common

the people of Jerusalem who were on the wall, to terrify them and make them afraid in order to capture the city. ¹⁹They spoke about the God of Jerusalem as they did about the gods of the other peoples of the world — the work of human hands.

²⁰King Hezekiah and the prophet Isaiah son of Amoz cried out in prayer to heaven about this. ²¹And the LORD sent an angel, who annihilated all the fighting men and the commanders and officers in the camp of the Assyrian king. So he withdrew to his own land in disgrace. And when he went into the temple of his god, some of his sons, his own flesh and blood, cut him down with the sword.

²²So the LORD saved Hezekiah and the people of Jerusalem from the hand of Sennacherib king of Assyria and from the hand of all others. He took care of them[a] on every side. ²³Many brought offerings to Jerusalem for the LORD and valuable gifts for Hezekiah king of Judah. From then on he was highly regarded by all the nations.

Hezekiah's Pride, Success and Death

32:24-33pp — 2Ki 20:1-21; Isa 37:21-38; 38:1-8

²⁴In those days Hezekiah became ill and was at the point of death. He prayed to the LORD, who answered him and gave him a miraculous sign. ²⁵But Hezekiah's heart was proud and he did not respond to the kindness shown him; therefore the LORD's wrath was on him and on Judah and Jerusalem. ²⁶Then Hezekiah repented of the pride of his heart, as did the people of Jerusalem; therefore the LORD's wrath did not come on them during the days of Hezekiah.

²⁷Hezekiah had very great wealth and honor, and he made treasuries for his silver and gold and for his precious stones, spices, shields and all kinds of valuables. ²⁸He also made buildings to store the harvest of grain, new wine and olive oil; and he made stalls for various kinds of cattle, and pens for the flocks. ²⁹He built villages and acquired great numbers of flocks and herds, for God had given him very great riches.

³⁰It was Hezekiah who blocked the upper outlet of the Gihon spring and channeled the water down to the west side of the City of David. He succeeded in everything he undertook. ³¹But when envoys were sent by the rulers of Babylon to ask him about the miraculous sign that had occurred in the land, God left him to test him and to know everything that was in his heart.

³²The other events of Hezekiah's reign and his acts of devotion are written in the vision of the prophet Isaiah son of Amoz in the book of the kings of Judah and Israel. ³³Hezekiah rested with his ancestors and was buried on the hill where the tombs of David's descendants are. All Judah and the people of Jerusalem honored him when he died. And Manasseh his son succeeded him as king.

Manasseh King of Judah

33:1-10pp — 2Ki 21:1-10
33:18-20pp — 2Ki 21:17-18

33 Manasseh was twelve years old when he became king, and he reigned in Jerusalem fifty-five years. ²He did evil in the eyes of the LORD, following the detestable practices of the nations

---

a 22 Hebrew; Septuagint and Vulgate *He gave them rest*

---

international language during this period. See note on Isa 36:11.

32:20–23 The Chronicler gives a very short account of God's protection of Jerusalem. Unlike the parallel accounts in 2Ki 19 and Isa 37, the 2 Chronicles passage does not provide the prayers of Hezekiah and Isaiah, focusing instead on God's response. The defeat of the Assyrian forces demonstrates God's involvement in the course of human events. Victories in 1–2 Chronicles are typically attributed to God (1Ch 18:13; 2Ch 13:16), and peace is seen as coming from God (14:6; 15:15; 20:30). Several times, God's hand is seen directing the course of specific battles (18:31; 20:22). Only here, though, does God take such dramatic and visible control of events.

32:21 LORD sent an angel Elsewhere described as the "angel of Yahweh" (2Ki 19:35; Isa 37:36). See note on Ps 34:7. **who annihilated all the fighting men** See Isa 37:36. **So he withdrew to his own land in disgrace** Sennacherib describes his siege of Jerusalem in his official annals, stating that he trapped Hezekiah "like a bird in a cage." However, he does not include any information about his defeat. See the infographic "Sennacherib's Prism" on p. 597.
32:24 Hezekiah became ill See Isa 38:1–22 and note.
32:26 during the days of Hezekiah See Isa 39:8 and note.
32:27 very great wealth and honor A sign of God's blessing and Hezekiah's faithfulness. Similar statements are made regarding David (1Ch 29:28), Solomon (2Ch 1:14–17 and note; 9:22) and Jehoshaphat (17:5; 18:1).
32:30 the Gihon spring See 2Ki 20:20 and note. See the infographic "Inscription From Hezekiah's Tunnel" on p. 599.
32:32 vision of the prophet Isaiah Appears to refer to a section or smaller work included in the larger work called the Book of the Kings of Israel and Judah. For a similar situation, compare the chronicles of Jehu (2Ch 20:34 and note). The vision of Isaiah mentioned here may be the same as the work attributed to Isaiah in 26:22. **book of the kings of Judah and Israel** See note on 16:11.
32:33 rested with his ancestors See note on 9:31.

33:1–20 Second Chronicles and 2 Kings both focus on Manasseh's wickedness, portraying him as the worst of Judah's kings (vv. 2–9; compare 2Ki 21:1–18). However, 2 Kings does not record Manasseh's imprisonment and subsequent repentance (2Ch 33:10–13), which are central to the Chronicler's account. This emphasis shows God fulfilling his promise to restore those who humble themselves (see 7:14) — a lesson that would resonate with the Chronicler's audience of returned exiles.

33:1 Manasseh The longest-reigning king of either Israel or Judah — as well as one of the most wicked. Manasseh, the son of Hezekiah (through Hephzibah) and the grandfather of Josiah, reigned ca. 697–642 BC.

the Lord had driven out before the Israelites. ³He rebuilt the high places his father Hezekiah had demolished; he also erected altars to the Baals and made Asherah poles. He bowed down to all the starry hosts and worshiped them. ⁴He built altars in the temple of the Lord, of which the Lord had said, "My Name will remain in Jerusalem forever." ⁵In both courts of the temple of the Lord, he built altars to all the starry hosts. ⁶He sacrificed his children in the fire in the Valley of Ben Hinnom, practiced divination and witchcraft, sought omens, and consulted mediums and spiritists. He did much evil in the eyes of the Lord, arousing his anger.

⁷He took the image he had made and put it in God's temple, of which God had said to David and to his son Solomon, "In this temple and in Jerusalem, which I have chosen out of all the tribes of Israel, I will put my Name forever. ⁸I will not again make the feet of the Israelites leave the land I assigned to your ancestors, if only they will be careful to do everything I commanded them concerning all the laws, decrees and regulations given through Moses." ⁹But Manasseh led Judah and the people of Jerusalem astray, so that they did more evil than the nations the Lord had destroyed before the Israelites.

¹⁰The Lord spoke to Manasseh and his people, but they paid no attention. ¹¹So the Lord brought against them the army commanders of the king of Assyria, who took Manasseh prisoner, put a hook in his nose, bound him with bronze shackles and took him to Babylon. ¹²In his distress he sought the favor of the Lord his God and humbled him-

self greatly before the God of his ancestors. ¹³And when he prayed to him, the Lord was moved by his entreaty and listened to his plea; so he brought him back to Jerusalem and to his kingdom. Then Manasseh knew that the Lord is God.

¹⁴Afterward he rebuilt the outer wall of the City of David, west of the Gihon spring in the valley, as far as the entrance of the Fish Gate and encircling the hill of Ophel; he also made it much higher. He stationed military commanders in all the fortified cities in Judah.

¹⁵He got rid of the foreign gods and removed the image from the temple of the Lord, as well as all the altars he had built on the temple hill and in Jerusalem; and he threw them out of the city. ¹⁶Then he restored the altar of the Lord and sacrificed fellowship offerings and thank offerings on it, and told Judah to serve the Lord, the God of Israel. ¹⁷The people, however, continued to sacrifice at the high places, but only to the Lord their God.

¹⁸The other events of Manasseh's reign, including his prayer to his God and the words the seers spoke to him in the name of the Lord, the God of Israel, are written in the annals of the kings of Israel.ᵃ ¹⁹His prayer and how God was moved by his entreaty, as well as all his sins and unfaithfulness, and the sites where he built high places and set up Asherah poles and idols before he humbled himself — all these are written in the records of the seers.ᵇ ²⁰Manasseh rested with his ancestors

ᵃ 18 That is, Judah, as frequently in 2 Chronicles
ᵇ 19 One Hebrew manuscript and Septuagint; most Hebrew manuscripts *of Hozai*

MANASSEH

Manasseh's reputation for wickedness was based on his devotion to Canaanite idols. He rebuilt the high places that his father, Hezekiah, had torn down. He also constructed altars for Baal and made Asherah poles. The king sacrificed his own son to a god and practiced witchcraft and divination. The Chronicler records that Manasseh's wickedness led to his deportation to Babylon by the king of Assyria (1Ch 33:10–11). The Chronicler also records that while in Babylon, Manasseh repented, humbled himself before Yahweh and prayed for mercy (33:12–13). Yahweh responded favorably to Manasseh's prayer and returned him to power in Jerusalem. Manasseh removed the foreign idols and destroyed their altars. He restored the temple, offered sacrifices to Yahweh and commanded the people to worship Yahweh.

33:2 He did evil The Chronicler also makes this judgment of Jehoram (21:6) and Ahaziah (22:4). **detestable practices of the nations** Manasseh's sins (especially in v. 6) closely follow the list of abominable practices in Deuteronomy. See Dt 18:9–14 and note.
33:3 He rebuilt the high places Manasseh reverses the reforms made by Hezekiah (2Ch 31:1). **made Asherah**

poles See note on 14:3. **He bowed down to all the starry hosts** Refers to worshiping celestial objects. See note on Jer 8:2.
33:6 He sacrificed his children in the fire Manasseh follows the example of his grandfather, Ahaz (compare 2Ch 28:3; see note on 2Ki 16:3). **in the Valley of Ben Hinnom** See note on Jer 7:31.
33:7 In this temple The Chronicler contrasts Manasseh's violations of the covenant with this reiteration of it. By placing an idol in the temple, Manasseh defiled the place where God had chosen to put his name.
33:9 the nations the Lord had destroyed Refers to the prior inhabitants of the promised land, who were driven out because of their idolatry.
33:10 but they paid no attention Indicates that Manasseh had opportunity to repent.
33:13 Then Manasseh knew that the Lord is God The story of Manasseh's repentance and restoration undoubtedly would have resonated with the Chronicler's audience of returned exiles. Just like Manasseh, they had been taken captive to Babylon and then restored to the land of promise.
33:15 removed the image Manasseh reverses his earlier practices (2Ch 33:4–5).
33:18 his prayer to his God This epitaph focuses on Manasseh's prayer of repentance rather than his evil (compare 2Ki 21:17). **annals of the kings of Israel** See note on 2Ch 16:11.
33:19 records of the seers This is the only reference to the Chronicles of the Seers (or "of Hozai")—the specific

and was buried in his palace. And Amon his son succeeded him as king.

Amon King of Judah

33:21-25pp — 2Ki 21:19-24

²¹Amon was twenty-two years old when he became king, and he reigned in Jerusalem two years. ²²He did evil in the eyes of the LORD, as his father Manasseh had done. Amon worshiped and offered sacrifices to all the idols Manasseh had made. ²³But unlike his father Manasseh, he did not humble himself before the LORD; Amon increased his guilt.

²⁴Amon's officials conspired against him and assassinated him in his palace. ²⁵Then the people of the land killed all who had plotted against King Amon, and they made Josiah his son king in his place.

Josiah's Reforms

34:1-2pp — 2Ki 22:1-2
34:3-7Ref — 2Ki 23:4-20
34:8-13pp — 2Ki 22:3-7

34 Josiah was eight years old when he became king, and he reigned in Jerusalem thirty-one years. ²He did what was right in the eyes of the LORD and followed the ways of his father David, not turning aside to the right or to the left.

³In the eighth year of his reign, while he was still young, he began to seek the God of his father David. In his twelfth year he began to purge Judah and Jerusalem of high places, Asherah poles and idols. ⁴Under his direction the altars of the Baals were torn down; he cut to pieces the incense altars that were above them, and smashed the Ashe-

rah poles and the idols. These he broke to pieces and scattered over the graves of those who had sacrificed to them. ⁵He burned the bones of the priests on their altars, and so he purged Judah and Jerusalem. ⁶In the towns of Manasseh, Ephraim and Simeon, as far as Naphtali, and in the ruins around them, ⁷he tore down the altars and the Asherah poles and crushed the idols to powder and cut to pieces all the incense altars throughout Israel. Then he went back to Jerusalem.

⁸In the eighteenth year of Josiah's reign, to purify the land and the temple, he sent Shaphan son of Azaliah and Maaseiah the ruler of the city, with Joah son of Joahaz, the recorder, to repair the temple of the LORD his God.

⁹They went to Hilkiah the high priest and gave him the money that had been brought into the temple of God, which the Levites who were the gatekeepers had collected from the people of Manasseh, Ephraim and the entire remnant of Israel and from all the people of Judah and Benjamin and the inhabitants of Jerusalem. ¹⁰Then they entrusted it to the men appointed to supervise the work on the LORD's temple. These men paid the workers who repaired and restored the temple. ¹¹They also gave money to the carpenters and builders to purchase dressed stone, and timber for joists and beams for the buildings that the kings of Judah had allowed to fall into ruin.

¹²The workers labored faithfully. Over them to direct them were Jahath and Obadiah, Levites descended from Merari, and Zechariah and Meshullam, descended from Kohath. The Levites — all who were skilled in playing musical instruments — ¹³had charge of the laborers and supervised all the workers from job to job.

---

seer or seers referenced seem to be among those who spoke to Manasseh (v. 18), although this could be a reference to a larger collection of information from, or about, seers of Israel and Judah (compare 1Ch 29:29).

33:21–25 The reign of Amon (ca. 642–640 BC) is given very little treatment in 2 Chronicles and 2 Kings (see 2Ki 21:19–26 and note). He is wicked like his father, Manasseh, but he does not humble himself (2Ch 33:23). He is killed by his servants, just as Joash was (24:25), although neither 2 Chronicles nor 2 Kings provides details of the conspiracy.

33:25 the people of the land See note on 2Ki 11:14.

34:1 — 35:27 Josiah, Judah's last good king, was similar to several of his predecessors. He re-established proper temple worship and celebrated the Passover, much like Hezekiah (2Ch 29:1 — 32:33). He came to the throne at a young age, just like Joash (24:1). And just as Joash had done (24:4–14), Josiah restored the temple and destroyed idols (34:3–7). The most significant event in Josiah's reign is the discovery of the Book of the Law (vv. 8–21), which led him to renew the covenant (vv. 29–33) and celebrate Passover (35:1–19). A parallel account of Josiah appears in 2Ki 22–23.

34:2 not turning aside The Chronicler emphasizes Josiah's faithfulness. Even the best kings—like Asa (2Ch 16:10–12), Joash (24:18), Uzziah (26:16) and Hezekiah (32:25)—turned aside at some point. Josiah, however, remained faithful.

34:4 Asherah poles See note on 14:3.

34:5 burned the bones of the priests Second Kings 23:20 explains that Josiah sacrificed these priests on their altars. Burning their bones accords with the earlier prophecy about Josiah (see 1Ki 13:2).

34:6 as far as Naphtali The geographical references here indicate that Josiah extended his reforms to the territories of the northern tribes, just as Hezekiah did (see 2Ch 30:1–27 and note).

34:9 gatekeepers Refers to Levites who collected funds for repairs to the temple—the same approach employed during Joash's repairs (24:5–6).

34:12–13 Josiah appoints Levites from the families of Merari and Kohath to supervise the temple's repairs. The musicians mentioned here were most likely from the families of Asaph, Heman and Jeduthun. All of these families were part of David's divisions of temple personnel (1Ch 23:6–23; 25:1–8), and they played leading roles in Hezekiah's reforms (2Ch 29:12–14 and note).

Some of the Levites were secretaries, scribes and gatekeepers.

The Book of the Law Found

34:14-28pp — 2Ki 22:8-20
34:29-32pp — 2Ki 23:1-3

¹⁴While they were bringing out the money that had been taken into the temple of the LORD, Hilkiah the priest found the Book of the Law of the LORD that had been given through Moses. ¹⁵Hilkiah said to Shaphan the secretary, "I have found the Book of the Law in the temple of the LORD." He gave it to Shaphan.

¹⁶Then Shaphan took the book to the king and reported to him: "Your officials are doing everything that has been committed to them. ¹⁷They have paid out the money that was in the temple of the LORD and have entrusted it to the supervisors and workers." ¹⁸Then Shaphan the secretary informed the king, "Hilkiah the priest has given me a book." And Shaphan read from it in the presence of the king.

¹⁹When the king heard the words of the Law, he tore his robes. ²⁰He gave these orders to Hilkiah, Ahikam son of Shaphan, Abdon son of Micah,[a] Shaphan the secretary and Asaiah the king's attendant: ²¹"Go and inquire of the LORD for me and for the remnant in Israel and Judah about what is written in this book that has been found. Great is the LORD's anger that is poured out on us because those who have gone before us have not kept the word of the LORD; they have not acted in accordance with all that is written in this book."

²²Hilkiah and those the king had sent with him[b] went to speak to the prophet Huldah, who was the wife of Shallum son of Tokhath,[c] the son of Hasrah,[d] keeper of the wardrobe. She lived in Jerusalem, in the New Quarter.

²³She said to them, "This is what the LORD, the God of Israel, says: Tell the man who sent you to me, ²⁴'This is what the LORD says: I am going to bring disaster on this place and its people — all the curses written in the book that has been read in the presence of the king of Judah. ²⁵Because they have forsaken me and burned incense to other gods and aroused my anger by all that their hands have made,[e] my anger will be poured out on this place and will not be quenched.' ²⁶Tell the king of Judah, who sent you to inquire of the LORD, 'This is what the LORD, the God of Israel, says concerning the words you heard: ²⁷Because your heart was responsive and you humbled yourself before God when you heard what he spoke against this place and its people, and because you humbled yourself before me and tore your robes and wept in my presence, I have heard you, declares the LORD. ²⁸Now I will gather you to your ancestors, and you will be buried in peace. Your eyes will not see all the disaster I am going to bring on this place and on those who live here.'"

So they took her answer back to the king.

²⁹Then the king called together all the elders of Judah and Jerusalem. ³⁰He went up to the temple of the LORD with the people of Judah, the inhabitants of Jerusalem, the priests and the Levites — all the people from the least to the greatest. He read in their hearing all the words of the Book of the Covenant, which had been found in the temple of the LORD. ³¹The king stood by his pillar and renewed the covenant in the presence of the LORD — to follow the LORD and keep his commands, statutes and decrees with all his heart and all his soul, and to obey the words of the covenant written in this book.

³²Then he had everyone in Jerusalem and Benjamin pledge themselves to it; the people of

---

a 20 Also called *Akbor son of Micaiah*   *b 22* One Hebrew manuscript, Vulgate and Syriac; most Hebrew manuscripts do not have *had sent with him.*   *c 22* Also called *Tikvah*   *d 22* Also called *Harhas*   *e 25* Or *by everything they have done*

34:14–21 The Book of the Law that Hilkiah found was probably some form of Deuteronomy, an identification based on several factors. First, Josiah's reaction would be a natural response to some of the sections of curses in Deuteronomy (e.g, Dt 27:9–26; 28:15–68). The words of Huldah (2Ch 34:24–25) also are consistent with these curses. In addition, Josiah's observation of the Passover (35:1–19) is consistent with the Passover stipulations in Dt 16:1–8.

34:19 he tore his robes A typical gesture of mourning. Josiah's reaction amounts to a display of repentance, showing that he recognizes Judah's recent sin. Ezra reacts the same way when he hears about the people intermarrying in his call for repentance (Ezr 9:3). The prophet Joel includes mourning rituals in his call for repentance (Joel 1:13).
34:21 inquire of the LORD In times of distress, people often inquired of prophets to discern Yahweh's will (e.g., 1Ki 14:1–18; Jer 21:1–7).
34:22 prophet Huldah See 2Ki 22:14 and note.
34:27 you humbled yourself before God Reminiscent

of God's promise at the temple's dedication (see 2Ch 7:14). Humbling oneself is an important theme throughout 1–2 Chronicles. Rehoboam humbled himself, preventing the complete destruction of Jerusalem (12:12). Hezekiah humbled himself and delayed the judgment of God (32:26). Manasseh humbled himself and was able to return from captivity in Babylon (33:12–13).
34:28 I will gather you to your ancestors See 2Ki 22:20 and note.
34:29–33 Josiah responds to Huldah's message of God's judgment by gathering all the people to renew the covenant. He reads aloud the Book of the Law, just as Ezra does later with the postexilic community (Ne 8:1–8).
34:29 all the elders of Judah and Jerusalem Refers to the heads of the leading families — those responsible for administering justice and managing the affairs of the community.
34:31 his commands, statutes and decrees Three different terms for the law (see note on Ps 19:7–9; note on 2Ch 19:10).

Josiah's Family Tree

Manasseh   Meshullemeth

Amon

Josiah

Jehoiakim

Jehoiachin

Zedekiah   Shealtiel   Malkiram   Pedaiah   Shenazzar

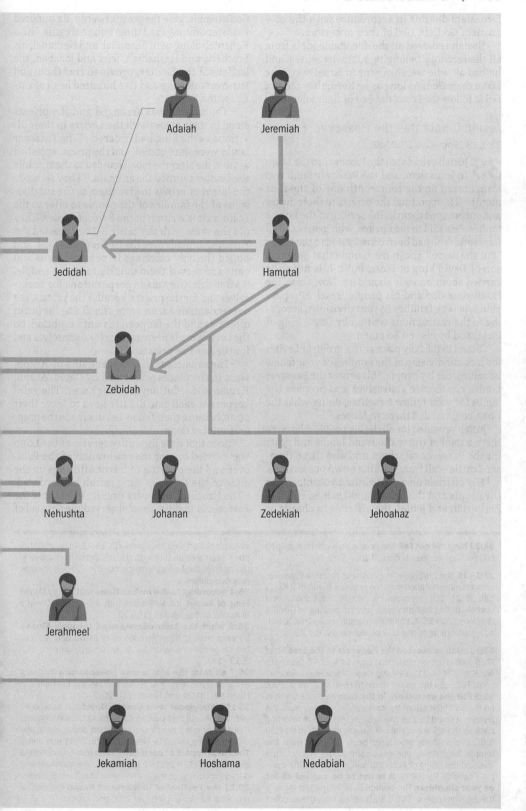

Jerusalem did this in accordance with the covenant of God, the God of their ancestors.

[33]Josiah removed all the detestable idols from all the territory belonging to the Israelites, and he had all who were present in Israel serve the LORD their God. As long as he lived, they did not fail to follow the LORD, the God of their ancestors.

Josiah Celebrates the Passover

35:1,18-19pp — 2Ki 23:21-23

35 Josiah celebrated the Passover to the LORD in Jerusalem, and the Passover lamb was slaughtered on the fourteenth day of the first month. [2]He appointed the priests to their duties and encouraged them in the service of the LORD's temple. [3]He said to the Levites, who instructed all Israel and who had been consecrated to the LORD: "Put the sacred ark in the temple that Solomon son of David king of Israel built. It is not to be carried about on your shoulders. Now serve the LORD your God and his people Israel. [4]Prepare yourselves by families in your divisions, according to the instructions written by David king of Israel and by his son Solomon.

[5]"Stand in the holy place with a group of Levites for each subdivision of the families of your fellow Israelites, the lay people. [6]Slaughter the Passover lambs, consecrate yourselves and prepare the lambs for your fellow Israelites, doing what the LORD commanded through Moses."

[7]Josiah provided for all the lay people who were there a total of thirty thousand lambs and goats for the Passover offerings, and also three thousand cattle — all from the king's own possessions. [8]His officials also contributed voluntarily to the people and the priests and Levites. Hilkiah, Zechariah and Jehiel, the officials in charge of

God's temple, gave the priests twenty-six hundred Passover offerings and three hundred cattle. [9]Also Konaniah along with Shemaiah and Nethanel, his brothers, and Hashabiah, Jeiel and Jozabad, the leaders of the Levites, provided five thousand Passover offerings and five hundred head of cattle for the Levites.

[10]The service was arranged and the priests stood in their places with the Levites in their divisions as the king had ordered. [11]The Passover lambs were slaughtered, and the priests splashed against the altar the blood handed to them, while the Levites skinned the animals. [12]They set aside the burnt offerings to give them to the subdivisions of the families of the people to offer to the LORD, as it is written in the Book of Moses. They did the same with the cattle. [13]They roasted the Passover animals over the fire as prescribed, and boiled the holy offerings in pots, caldrons and pans and served them quickly to all the people. [14]After this, they made preparations for themselves and for the priests, because the priests, the descendants of Aaron, were sacrificing the burnt offerings and the fat portions until nightfall. So the Levites made preparations for themselves and for the Aaronic priests.

[15]The musicians, the descendants of Asaph, were in the places prescribed by David, Asaph, Heman and Jeduthun the king's seer. The gatekeepers at each gate did not need to leave their posts, because their fellow Levites made the preparations for them.

[16]So at that time the entire service of the LORD was carried out for the celebration of the Passover and the offering of burnt offerings on the altar of the LORD, as King Josiah had ordered. [17]The Israelites who were present celebrated the Passover at that time and observed the Festival of

---

34:33 they did not fail The people as a whole remained faithful, just as Josiah did (34:2).

35:1–19 The Chronicler's account of Josiah's Passover is much more detailed than the account found in 2 Kings (2Ki 23:21–23). It focuses on the role of the priests and Levites, noting that they were used according to David's divisions (2Ch 35:4,15). It also emphasizes that Josiah acted according to the Law of Moses (vv. 6,12).

35:1 Josiah celebrated the Passover to the LORD Most likely following the regulations from Dt 16:1–8 (see note on 2Ch 34:14–21). See the table "Israelite Calendar" on p. 763; see the table "Israelite Festivals" on p. 200.
35:3 Put the sacred ark in the temple Since there is no record of the ark of the covenant's removal from the temple, it could be that the Hebrew text here is referring back to the ark's original placement in the temple (1Ki 8:6). The ark may also have been removed from the temple for military purposes, since Josiah's reforms involved the killing of heretical priests (2Ki 23:20; compare note on Ps 24:7). **It is not to be carried about on your shoulders** The Levites were instructed to carry the ark with poles; 1Ch 15:15 notes that these poles

were placed on their shoulders (Ex 25:13–15). Josiah's point seems to be that with the ark deposited safely in the temple, the Levites may devote themselves to other religious duties.
35:4 according to the instructions written by David king of Israel Josiah insists that they follow David's divisions of the Levites (1Ch 23).
35:6 what the LORD commanded through Moses By emphasizing the instructions of David and Moses, the Chronicler likens Josiah to Solomon (compare 2Ch 8:13–14).
35:7 all from the king's own possessions By giving of his own possessions, Josiah follows the examples of Hezekiah (31:3) and David (1Ch 29:2–5).
35:15 in the places prescribed by David Just as he does with the priests and Levites (2Ch 35:4), Josiah ensures that the temple singers are organized according to the divisions established by David (1Ch 25:1–31 and note). **The gatekeepers at each gate** David also organized the gatekeepers (1Ch 26:1–19 and note). The gatekeepers' duties included guarding the temple and collecting money.
35:17 the Festival of Unleavened Bread Begins the day after Passover (see Lev 23:6 and note).

Unleavened Bread for seven days. [18] The Passover had not been observed like this in Israel since the days of the prophet Samuel; and none of the kings of Israel had ever celebrated such a Passover as did Josiah, with the priests, the Levites and all Judah and Israel who were there with the people of Jerusalem. [19] This Passover was celebrated in the eighteenth year of Josiah's reign.

The Death of Josiah

35:20–36:1pp — 2Ki 23:28-30

[20] After all this, when Josiah had set the temple in order, Necho king of Egypt went up to fight at Carchemish on the Euphrates, and Josiah marched out to meet him in battle. [21] But Necho sent messengers to him, saying, "What quarrel is there, king of Judah, between you and me? It is not you I am attacking at this time, but the house with which I am at war. God has told me to hurry; so stop opposing God, who is with me, or he will destroy you."

[22] Josiah, however, would not turn away from him, but disguised himself to engage him in battle. He would not listen to what Necho had said at God's command but went to fight him on the plain of Megiddo.

[23] Archers shot King Josiah, and he told his officers, "Take me away; I am badly wounded." [24] So they took him out of his chariot, put him in his other chariot and brought him to Jerusalem, where he died. He was buried in the tombs of his ancestors, and all Judah and Jerusalem mourned for him.

[25] Jeremiah composed laments for Josiah, and to this day all the male and female singers commemorate Josiah in the laments. These became a tradition in Israel and are written in the Laments.

[26] The other events of Josiah's reign and his acts of devotion in accordance with what is written in the Law of the LORD — [27] all the events, from beginning to end, are written in the book of the kings of Israel and Judah.

36

[1] And the people of the land took Jehoahaz son of Josiah and made him king in Jerusalem in place of his father.

Jehoahaz King of Judah

36:2-4pp — 2Ki 23:31-34

[2] Jehoahaz[a] was twenty-three years old when he became king, and he reigned in Jerusalem three months. [3] The king of Egypt dethroned him in Jerusalem and imposed on Judah a levy of a hundred talents[b] of silver and a talent[c] of gold. [4] The king of Egypt made Eliakim, a brother of Jehoahaz, king over Judah and Jerusalem and

---

[a] 2 Hebrew *Joahaz*, a variant of *Jehoahaz*; also in verse 4 [b] 3 That is, about 3 3/4 tons or about 3.4 metric tons [c] 3 That is, about 75 pounds or about 34 kilograms

---

35:18 Passover had not been observed like this Perhaps because Hezekiah's Passover was observed later than prescribed (2Ch 30:2–3), the Chronicler apparently upholds Josiah's as superior (see note on 2Ch 30:3). **since the days of the prophet Samuel** The parallel statement in 2 Kings refers to the days of the judges (2Ki 23:22). Most likely, the Chronicler's reference to Samuel (Israel's last judge) is intended to indicate the entire period of the judges.

35:20–27 This account of Josiah's death expands on the shorter version in 2Ki 23:28–30.
35:20 Necho king of Egypt Reigned ca. 609–595 BC. See note on Jer 46:2. In addition to killing Josiah, Pharaoh Necho also deposed Josiah's son and successor, Jehoahaz (2Ch 36:3–4). **Carchemish on the Euphrates** Egypt eventually was defeated by Babylon at Carchemish (see note on Jer 2:15).
35:21 It is not you I am attacking at this time Necho was joining forces with Assyria to quell the rising Babylonian kingdom.
35:22 disguised himself to engage him in battle Josiah's actions mirror the wicked northern king, Ahab, who also was killed in battle after disguising himself (2Ch 18:29–34). It is ironic that one of Judah's best kings suffers the same fate as Israel's worst king. **Megiddo** See 2Ki 23:29 and note.
35:24 where he died Since Josiah was killed in battle, his death is not described in terms of resting with his ancestors, which indicates a peaceful death (see 1Ki 2:10 and note).
35:25 Jeremiah composed laments for Josiah The book of Lamentations is traditionally attributed to Jeremiah (see note on La 1:1–5:22); however, it includes no laments about Josiah. Jeremiah most likely uttered a lament similar to David's lament for Saul and Jonathan (2Sa 1:17–27 and note).
35:26 his acts of devotion As with Hezekiah (2Ch 32:32), the epitaph for Josiah focuses on his faithfulness.
35:27 book of the kings of Israel and Judah See note on 16:11.

36:1–16 The Chronicler presents Judah's final four kings in quick succession, leaving out many of the details found in 2 Kings (2Ki 23:31—25:30). The focus in 2 Chronicles is less on the reigns of these kings and more on the sequence of events that led to the exile of all of Judah (2Ch 36:20–21). See the timeline "Judah From the Fall of Samaria to the Exile" on p. 606.

SOUTHERN KING	DATE
Jehoahaz	609 BC
Jehoiakim	609–597 BC
Jehoiachin	597 BC
Zedekiah	597–586 BC

36:1 Jehoahaz son of Josiah Also known as Shallum (see 1Ch 3:15 and note).
36:2 he reigned in Jerusalem three months Although the Chronicler does not assess Jehoahaz's brief reign (ca. 609 BC), 2Ki 23:32 states that he was an evil king.
36:3 The king of Egypt Refers to Pharaoh Necho. **a hundred talents** A talent was about 75 pounds (34 kilograms).
36:4 Necho took Eliakim's brother Jehoahaz It is unclear why Necho deposed Jehoahaz and installed

changed Eliakim's name to Jehoiakim. But Necho took Eliakim's brother Jehoahaz and carried him off to Egypt.

Jehoiakim King of Judah

36:5-8pp — 2Ki 23:36–24:6

[5]Jehoiakim was twenty-five years old when he became king, and he reigned in Jerusalem eleven years. He did evil in the eyes of the LORD his God. [6]Nebuchadnezzar king of Babylon attacked him and bound him with bronze shackles to take him to Babylon. [7]Nebuchadnezzar also took to Babylon articles from the temple of the LORD and put them in his temple[a] there.

[8]The other events of Jehoiakim's reign, the detestable things he did and all that was found against him, are written in the book of the kings of Israel and Judah. And Jehoiachin his son succeeded him as king.

Jehoiachin King of Judah

36:9-10pp — 2Ki 24:8-17

[9]Jehoiachin was eighteen[b] years old when he became king, and he reigned in Jerusalem three months and ten days. He did evil in the eyes of the LORD. [10]In the spring, King Nebuchadnezzar sent for him and brought him to Babylon, together with articles of value from the temple of the LORD, and he made Jehoiachin's uncle,[c] Zedekiah, king over Judah and Jerusalem.

Zedekiah King of Judah

36:11-16pp — 2Ki 24:18-20; Jer 52:1-3

[11]Zedekiah was twenty-one years old when he became king, and he reigned in Jerusalem eleven years. [12]He did evil in the eyes of the LORD his God and did not humble himself before Jeremiah the prophet, who spoke the word of the LORD. [13]He also rebelled against King Nebuchadnezzar, who had made him take an oath in God's name. He became stiff-necked and hardened his heart and would not turn to the LORD, the God of Israel. [14]Furthermore, all the leaders of the priests and the people became more and more unfaithful, following all the detestable practices of the nations and defiling the temple of the LORD, which he had consecrated in Jerusalem.

The Fall of Jerusalem

36:17-20pp — 2Ki 25:1-21; Jer 52:4-27
36:22-23pp — Ezr 1:1-3

[15]The LORD, the God of their ancestors, sent word to them through his messengers again and again, because he had pity on his people and on his dwelling place. [16]But they mocked God's messengers, despised his words and scoffed at his prophets until the wrath of the LORD was aroused against his people and there was no remedy. [17]He brought up against them the king of the Babylonians,[d] who killed their young men with the sword in the sanctuary, and did not spare young men or young women, the elderly or the infirm. God gave them all into the hands of Nebuchadnezzar. [18]He carried to Babylon all the articles from the temple of God, both large and small, and the treasures of the LORD's temple and the treasures of the king and his officials. [19]They set fire to God's temple and broke down the wall of Jerusalem; they burned all the palaces and destroyed everything of value there.

[20]He carried into exile to Babylon the remnant, who escaped from the sword, and they became

---

a 7 Or *palace*   *b 9* One Hebrew manuscript, some Septuagint manuscripts and Syriac (see also 2 Kings 24:8); most Hebrew manuscripts *eight*   *c 10* Hebrew *brother,* that is, relative (see 2 Kings 24:17)   *d 17* Or *Chaldeans*

Jehoiakim as king. Most likely, Jehoiakim was a stronger supporter of Egypt's efforts against Babylon (see note on Jer 22:10).

36:6 Nebuchadnezzar The second king of the Chaldean dynasty, who reigned ca. 605–562 BC. His father, Nabopolassar, had rebelled against Assyrian rule, defeating Assyria about six years before Nebuchadnezzar's reign. See note on Jer 21:2. Judah's exile into Babylon did not happen all at once. It begins here as Nebuchadnezzar deports Jehoiakim along with the temple vessels. (The ancient tablets known as the Babylonian Chronicles describe Jehoiakim's refusal to pay tribute; compare 2Ki 24:1.) Jehoiachin then becomes king, but Nebuchadnezzar soon deports him, as well—along with much of the population of Judah (2Ki 24:10–17; see Da 1:1 and note). Another wave of deportations occurs when Nebuchadnezzar besieges Jerusalem during the reign of Zedekiah (ca. 597–586 BC; see 2Ki 25:1–21). The book of Jeremiah describes one additional deportation (Jer 52:28–30 and note). See the infographic "The Babylonian Chronicles" on p. 605.

36:10 brought him to Babylon The account in 2 Kings describes Nebuchadnezzar's siege and plunder of Jerusalem in greater detail (2Ki 24:10–17 and note).

36:12 did not humble himself Unlike many of his predecessors—including Rehoboam (2Ch 12:12), Hezekiah (32:26), Manasseh (33:12–13) and Josiah (34:27)—Zedekiah does not humble himself. See note on 34:27.

36:14 became more and more unfaithful The Hebrew term used here, *ma'al*, indicates a violation of covenant trust. First Chronicles 5:25 cites unfaithfulness to Yahweh as the reason for the northern kingdom's exile.

36:15 sent word to them through his messengers again and again The Chronicler makes it clear that people of Judah had plenty of opportunities to humble themselves and repent.

36:17–21 After roughly ten years of hostilities, Judah's conflict with Babylon comes to a fiery conclusion. More extensive accounts of Jerusalem's fall are provided in 2Ki 25:1–21 and Jer 39:1–10; 52:1–30.

36:17 He brought up against them The Chronicler emphasizes God's role in Judah's collapse and exile (compare 2Ki 25:1).

servants to him and his successors until the kingdom of Persia came to power. ²¹The land enjoyed its sabbath rests; all the time of its desolation it rested, until the seventy years were completed in fulfillment of the word of the LORD spoken by Jeremiah.

²²In the first year of Cyrus king of Persia, in order to fulfill the word of the LORD spoken by Jeremiah, the LORD moved the heart of Cyrus king of Persia to make a proclamation throughout his realm and also to put it in writing:

²³"This is what Cyrus king of Persia says:

"'The LORD, the God of heaven, has given me all the kingdoms of the earth and he has appointed me to build a temple for him at Jerusalem in Judah. Any of his people among you may go up, and may the LORD their God be with them.'"

36:21 until the seventy years were completed See Jer 25:11 and note. **spoken by Jeremiah** Jeremiah had warned repeatedly about the coming Babylonian exile (see Jer 37:1–10 and note; 38:14–28 and note).

36:22–23 The Chronicler ends his account the same way that the book of Ezra begins—with Cyrus' decree that the Jewish exiles should return to Judah and build the temple (Ezr 1:1–4).

36:22 In the first year of Cyrus Refers to the first year after Cyrus II (the Great) conquered Babylon (539 BC). See note on Ezr 1:1. **the LORD moved** As he does throughout 2 Chronicles (2Ch 10:15; 22:7; 25:20; 36:17), the Chronicler emphasizes God's involvement in human events.

EVENT	DATE
Cyrus becomes king of Persia	559 BC
Cyrus conquers Babylon	539 BC
Cyrus allows Jews to return to Jerusalem	538 BC

36:23 to build a temple for him at Jerusalem The collective work of 1–2 Chronicles ends with Cyrus's proclamation authorizing the rebuilding of the temple. This conclusion is appropriate, considering the Chronicler's emphasis on establishing proper temple worship. A large section of 1 Chronicles revolves around David's preparation for the temple (see 1Ch 23:1—26:32 and note). The Chronicler also focuses on Solomon's building of the temple (2Ch 2–7) and emphasizes the efforts of several kings to cleanse the temple and restore worship there (24:4–14; 29:3–36; 34:8–13). **may go up** The Hebrew term for "go up" is used throughout the OT to designate a trip to Jerusalem (e.g., 2Sa 19:34; 1Ki 12:27; Zec 14:17). Since Jerusalem is situated at the top of a mountain, travelers literally climb up to the city.

EZRA

INTRODUCTION TO EZRA

The book of Ezra shows Yahweh's faithfulness and emphasizes the loyalty he rightfully deserves. The narrative begins with the fulfillment of Jeremiah's prophecy: After 70 years of exile in Babylon, the Jewish people would return to their homeland (Jer 25:11–12; 29:10–14; Ezr 1:1). Upon their return, the people began rebuilding the Jerusalem temple—the symbol of God's presence among them. The book of Ezra depicts the difficulties of rebuilding a community based on faithfulness to Yahweh.

BACKGROUND

Approximately 50 years before the narrative of Ezra begins (in 586 BC), the Babylonians conquered Jerusalem, destroyed the temple and took the residents of Judah into exile. By the time the book of Ezra opens in 538 BC, the balance of world power had shifted from the Babylonians to the Persians. A year after conquering Babylon, Cyrus, the king of Persia, issued a decree that any Jews who wished to return to Judah and rebuild the temple would not only be allowed to do so, but would receive government support (Ezr 1:2–4).

Judah's territory was now only a small area centered around Jerusalem. Instead of being self-governed, Judah was ruled as a province of the Persian Empire. The events in Ezra primarily take place in this location, with a few references to Persian concerns related to other locations.

The Jewish exiles did not leave Babylon all at once; the return to Judah happened in waves. Ezra led the third main group in 458 BC (80 years after King Cyrus' decree). The book of Ezra probably was written a few decades later, around 445–430 BC. The text was originally part of a single work that also included Nehemiah.

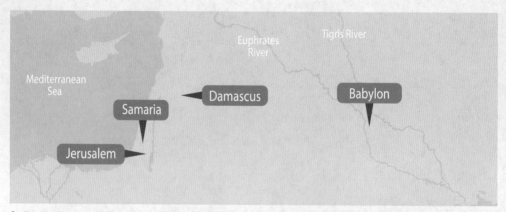

God's people returned from exile in Babylon to Jerusalem and the surrounding region.

STRUCTURE

Ezra may be divided into two sections. The first section (chs. 1–6) records events that happened before Ezra's time. It opens with King Cyrus' proclamation permitting the Jewish exiles to return to Judah (1:1–4; 538 BC). The first two waves were led by Judah's first two governors under Persian rule: Sheshbazzar and Zerubbabel (1:5–11; 2:1–70). Zerubbabel and Joshua (also called Jeshua) the high priest unite to lead the temple rebuilding project. The returned Jewish exiles soon find themselves in conflict with other people living in the area and ultimately at odds with the government, and the work to rebuild the temple comes to a halt (chs. 3–5). With encouragement from the prophets Haggai and Zechariah (Hag 1:4,9; Zec 1:16; 4:9), temple construction resumes around 520 BC (Ezr 6). In 516 BC, the temple, the symbol of God's presence among his people, is rededicated—signifying the completion of the 70 years Jeremiah had proclaimed (Jer 29:10,12).

Ezra 7–10 concentrates on a later period, starting in 458 BC. A command by the Persian king Artaxerxes (who reigned about 60 years after Cyrus) sends a scribe and chief priest named Ezra to Judah as an authority in the law of God (Ezr 7:6,25–28). When he arrives, he appoints and trains judges and magistrates for the leadership of Judah. Ezra's attention first goes to the issue of intermarriage between men from Judah and foreign women from the local people living in the land (9:1–2). God's people had disobeyed his command to live separately as a holy nation, and the intermarriages had likely led to synchronism of Yahweh worship with that of foreign gods (compare 1Ki 11:1–8; Ne 13:26). Under Ezra's leadership, the people repent, and the men give up their foreign wives.

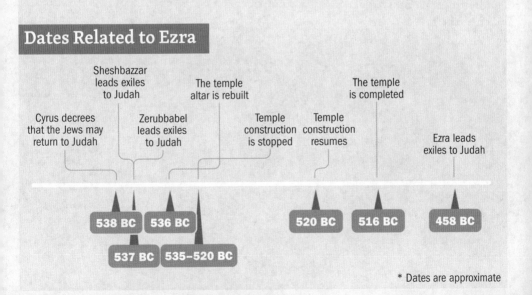

Dates Related to Ezra

Cyrus decrees that the Jews may return to Judah — 538 BC

Sheshbazzar leads exiles to Judah — 537 BC

Zerubbabel leads exiles to Judah — 536 BC

The temple altar is rebuilt — 535–520 BC

Temple construction is stopped — 520 BC

Temple construction resumes — 516 BC

The temple is completed

Ezra leads exiles to Judah — 458 BC

* Dates are approximate

OUTLINE

- Return from exile and rebuilding of the temple (1:1—6:22)
- Ezra's return and reforms (7:1—10:44)

THEMES

The book of Ezra is about the importance of staying faithful, and God's strength to fulfill his promises. Against all odds, God worked in the heart of King Cyrus to allow the exiles to return. Despite this powerful sign of God's favor, the temple was neglected for years because God's people feared local opposition. It took the people receiving a message from two of God's prophets to restart the project (Haggai and Zechariah; see Ezr 5:1). During Ezra's time, the community again showed unfaithfulness in disobeying Yahweh's commands about marriage (chs. 9–10). Returning to live in the promised land was not enough; the people needed to abide by God's law. They needed to be faithful to the one who had redeemed them from exile.

Being people of God comes with blessings and responsibilities. Although we experience his transforming power and grace, we also confront daily choices about the depth of our commitment. Trusting God is often about both seizing the opportunities to do his work and acting faithfully even when those around us do not.

Cyrus Helps the Exiles to Return

1:1-3pp — 2Ch 36:22-23

1 In the first year of Cyrus king of Persia, in order to fulfill the word of the LORD spoken by Jeremiah, the LORD moved the heart of Cyrus king of Persia to make a proclamation throughout his realm and also to put it in writing:

² "This is what Cyrus king of Persia says:

" 'The LORD, the God of heaven, has given me all the kingdoms of the earth and he has appointed me to build a temple for him at Jerusalem in Judah. ³ Any of his people among you may go up to Jerusalem in Judah and build the temple of the LORD, the God of Israel, the God who is in Jerusalem, and may their God be with them. ⁴ And in any locality where survivors may now be living, the people are to provide them with silver and gold, with goods and livestock, and with freewill offerings for the temple of God in Jerusalem.' "

⁵ Then the family heads of Judah and Benjamin, and the priests and Levites — everyone whose heart God had moved — prepared to go up and build the house of the LORD in Jerusalem. ⁶ All their neighbors assisted them with articles of silver and gold, with goods and livestock, and with valuable gifts, in addition to all the freewill offerings.

⁷ Moreover, King Cyrus brought out the articles belonging to the temple of the LORD, which Nebuchadnezzar had carried away from Jerusalem and

---

1:1–11 The book of Ezra begins with Cyrus' proclamation allowing the Israelites to return to Jerusalem and rebuild the temple (compare 2Ch 36:22–23). The book recounts the efforts of the returned exiles to re-establish a Judean community centered on Jerusalem. Ezra 1–6 focuses primarily on the first groups to return and rebuild the temple (ca. 538–516 BC). Chapters 7–10 focus on the community nearly 60 years later when Ezra, the scribe and priest, arrives with another group of exiles returning from Babylon (ca. 458 BC). Ezra is authorized by the king of Persia to teach God's law to the people. The account continues in the book of Nehemiah where Ezra is still serving the people as priest and teacher (Ne 7:73—8:12; ca. 444–433 BC). Together, the books of Ezra and Nehemiah provide an account of the restoration community for over a century after Cyrus' proclamation in 538 BC.

1:1 first year of Cyrus 539 BC, the year in which Cyrus conquered Babylon and became king over all of Mesopotamia. Cyrus founded the Persian Empire. See the timeline "Dates Related to Ezra, Nehemiah and Esther" on p. 716. **spoken by Jeremiah** Likely refers to Jer 25:11–12 and Jer 29:10, where the prophet predicted 70 years of captivity for the Jews. See note on Jer 25:11. **moved the heart** Via God's influence, Cyrus willingly allowed the Jews to return to Jerusalem. Likewise, God gave individual Jews a desire to return to the land (Ezr 1:5).

CYRUS
Cyrus II (the Great) was the son of Cambyses I, a Persian, and Mandane, the daughter of Astyages, king of the Medes. Cyrus became king of the Persians in 559 BC. Originally a vassal of Astyages, Cyrus led a successful revolt against the Medes in 550 BC and continued to build and solidify his empire until his death in 530 BC. His son Cambyses II inherited the throne after his death.

EVENT	DATE
Cyrus becomes king of Persia	559 BC
Cyrus conquers Babylon	539 BC
Cyrus allows Jews to return to Jerusalem	538 BC

1:2 God of heaven Rarely used prior to the exile, this title for God became popular among the Jews during and after the exile (see 5:11,12; Ne 1:4,5; Da 2:18,19). **given me all the kingdoms of the earth** A similar decree appears on the Cyrus Cylinder. See the infographic "The Cyrus Cylinder" on p. 714. **a temple** The original temple in Jerusalem, built by Solomon, was burned by the armies of Nebuchadnezzar when they destroyed Jerusalem in 586 BC (2Ki 25:9; 2Ch 36:19).

1:3 Any of his people While the Assyrians and Babylonians regularly exiled vanquished nations and transplanted foreigners to conquered territories, the Persians allowed captive nations to return to their homelands. **go up to Jerusalem** The Hebrew term for "go up" is used throughout the OT to designate a trip to Jerusalem (e.g., 2Sa 19:34; 1Ki 12:27; 2Ki 12:17; Zec 14:17). Many Jews chose not to return to Jerusalem, showing that Cyrus' decree was probably optional. However, from God's perspective, returning to the land was obligatory. Both Isaiah and Jeremiah implore the nation to return following the exile (e.g., Isa 48:20; Jer 31:16–21). See the infographic "Jerusalem" on p. 1607. **God of Israel** Demonstrates the Persians' tolerance of other religions.

1:5 Judah and Benjamin The primary tribes taken to Babylon when Nebuchadnezzar destroyed Jerusalem. While only these tribes are mentioned, they are not the only ones who were exiled. Even before the northern kingdom fell to Assyria, many priests and Levites were living in Judah, the southern kingdom, having been expelled from the northern kingdom by Jeroboam (see 2Ch 11:14). Many families from the other tribes likewise lived in the southern kingdom (see 2Ch 11:16–17). The descendants of these men would have been taken to Babylon along with the tribes of Judah and Benjamin. First Chronicles 9:3 indicates that representatives of the tribes of Ephraim and Manasseh lived in Jerusalem after the exile. **the priests and Levites** Those who return are divided into three social groups: laity, priests and Levites. This threefold designation is repeatedly used in Ezra to denote the entire population (see Ezr 2:1–58; 3:8,12; 6:16; 7:7,13; 8:15,29; 9:1; 10:5,18–43).

1:7 articles belonging to the temple of the LORD Nebuchadnezzar took the vessels to Babylon during his campaigns against Judah (605–586 BC). The return of the temple vessels vindicated Yahweh and showed his power over the patron gods of Babylon. It also fulfilled the prophecy of Isa 52:11, where the prophet predicted their return.

had placed in the temple of his god.[a] [8]Cyrus king of Persia had them brought by Mithredath the treasurer, who counted them out to Sheshbazzar the prince of Judah.

[9]This was the inventory:

gold dishes	30
silver dishes	1,000
silver pans[b]	29

[10]gold bowls	30
matching silver bowls	410
other articles	1,000

[11]In all, there were 5,400 articles of gold and of silver. Sheshbazzar brought all these along with

---

[a] 7 Or gods   [b] 9 The meaning of the Hebrew for this word is uncertain.

1:8 Mithredath the treasurer Probably the senior Persian financial officer in Babylon. **Sheshbazzar** The Babylonian name Sheshbazzar means "may Shamash protect the son." Shamash was the Babylonian sun god. Sheshbazzar's exact identity is unknown. The epithet "prince of Judah" indicates that Sheshbazzar was a member of the royal family. Sheshbazzar is sometimes identified with the Shenazzar of 1Ch 3:18. It is also possible that Sheshbazzar was simply an unknown foreign official, which explains his foreign name and his being given credit for the project (Ezr 5:14–16). The Persians may have considered Sheshbazzar the official leader of the return, while the Jews recognized Zerubbabel as the unofficial leader; the Persians may have been hesitant to appoint someone of the royal line to be governor.

1:11 5,400 articles of gold and of silver The total number of the temple vessels identified in vv. 9–10 is 2,499. The reason for this discrepancy is unknown. It is possible that vv. 9–10 lists only the largest, most important articles, whereas v. 11 records the total number of all vessels, including the less significant ones. It is also possible that the articles enumerated in vv. 9–10 were those taken by Nebuchadnezzar and returned by Cyrus, whereas the total in v. 11 includes the articles donated by the neighbors of the Jews (compare vv. 4,6). It is also possible that the list is incomplete or corrupted. **Babylon** Babylon was one of the oldest cities of civilization. See note on Mic 4:10. **to Jerusalem** Even in the midst of their march into exile, God promised the Jews that he would bring them back to the land that had been promised to them and here he does so (Jer 31:15–17).

The Cyrus Cylinder

This ancient clay cylinder dates from the sixth century BC and contains a declaration from Cyrus the Great. The first section describes Cyrus' greatness and mercy—common themes in such declarations. The second section, composed of Cyrus' own words, describes how he returned captive peoples and their gods to their native lands. It also records his hope that all the returned gods will intercede before Bel and Nabu (the chief Babylonian gods) on his behalf. The description of Cyrus' mercy and efforts to return captives supports the biblical account of Israel's restoration from exile (see Ezr 1).

the exiles when they came up from Babylon to Jerusalem.

The List of the Exiles Who Returned

2:1-70pp — Ne 7:6-73

2 Now these are the people of the province who came up from the captivity of the exiles, whom Nebuchadnezzar king of Babylon had taken captive to Babylon (they returned to Jerusalem and Judah, each to their own town, ²in company with Zerubbabel, Joshua, Nehemiah, Seraiah, Reelaiah, Mordecai, Bilshan, Mispar, Bigvai, Rehum and Baanah):

The list of the men of the people of Israel:

³ the descendants of Parosh	2,172
⁴ of Shephatiah	372
⁵ of Arah	775
⁶ of Pahath-Moab (through the line of Jeshua and Joab)	2,812
⁷ of Elam	1,254
⁸ of Zattu	945
⁹ of Zakkai	760
¹⁰ of Bani	642
¹¹ of Bebai	623
¹² of Azgad	1,222
¹³ of Adonikam	666
¹⁴ of Bigvai	2,056
¹⁵ of Adin	454
¹⁶ of Ater (through Hezekiah)	98
¹⁷ of Bezai	323
¹⁸ of Jorah	112
¹⁹ of Hashum	223
²⁰ of Gibbar	95
²¹ the men of Bethlehem	123
²² of Netophah	56
²³ of Anathoth	128
²⁴ of Azmaveth	42
²⁵ of Kiriath Jearim,ᵃ Kephirah and Beeroth	743
²⁶ of Ramah and Geba	621
²⁷ of Mikmash	122
²⁸ of Bethel and Ai	223
²⁹ of Nebo	52
³⁰ of Magbish	156
³¹ of the other Elam	1,254
³² of Harim	320
³³ of Lod, Hadid and Ono	725
³⁴ of Jericho	345
³⁵ of Senaah	3,630

³⁶ The priests:

the descendants of Jedaiah (through the family of Jeshua)	973
³⁷ of Immer	1,052
³⁸ of Pashhur	1,247
³⁹ of Harim	1,017

⁴⁰ The Levites:

the descendants of Jeshua and Kadmiel (of the line of Hodaviah)	74

⁴¹ The musicians:

the descendants of Asaph	128

⁴² The gatekeepers of the temple:

the descendants of Shallum, Ater, Talmon, Akkub, Hatita and Shobai	139

⁴³ The temple servants:

the descendants of
Ziha, Hasupha, Tabbaoth,
⁴⁴ Keros, Siaha, Padon,
⁴⁵ Lebanah, Hagabah, Akkub,
⁴⁶ Hagab, Shalmai, Hanan,
⁴⁷ Giddel, Gahar, Reaiah,
⁴⁸ Rezin, Nekoda, Gazzam,
⁴⁹ Uzza, Paseah, Besai,
⁵⁰ Asnah, Meunim, Nephusim,
⁵¹ Bakbuk, Hakupha, Harhur,

ᵃ 25 See Septuagint (see also Neh. 7:29); Hebrew *Kiriath Arim.*

2:1–70 This chapter lists the Jews who returned to Jerusalem from Babylon. For the book's original audience, this passage presents the great heroes of the past — those who had taken the first step toward rebuilding the nation of Israel. The list is organized according to laity (Ezr 2:2–35), priests (vv. 36–39) and Levites, including singers, gatekeepers, temple servants and Solomon's servants (vv. 40–58). This threefold designation may allude to 1:5, where the social distinctions appear in the same order. The list concludes with a record of those who could not prove their ancestry (vv. 59–63). A nearly identical list is found in Ne 7.

2:2 in company Eleven names are recorded here. Nehemiah includes another — Nahamani (Ne 7:7). **Zerubbabel, Joshua** Leaders in Ezr 1–6. Zerubbabel and Jeshua (or Joshua) are routinely mentioned together (see 3:2,8; 4:3; 5:2). With the exception of 3:2, Zerubbabel is always mentioned first. Zerubbabel served as the governor of Judah, while Jeshua served as the high priest. Together they represent the political and religious leadership of the nation. Both work together to return to the land (2:2), lay the foundation of the temple (3:8–10), respond to the enemies of Judah (4:1–3) and resume the rebuilding of the temple (5:2). The prophet Zechariah uses their partnership to describe the coming "Branch" (Zec 6:11–12) — which Jer 23:5 indicates will come from the line of David and will reign as king. Zechariah uses Jeshua to illustrate that this "Branch" will also build the temple of Yahweh and be a priest on his throne (Zec 6:12–13). The "Branch" is a prophetic reference to Jesus Christ, who unites the offices of King and Priest (compare Ps 110; Heb 7). **Mordecai** This is not the Mordecai mentioned in Esther; he was in the Persian capital of Susa some 50 years after the return from exile.

⁵²Bazluth, Mehida, Harsha,
⁵³Barkos, Sisera, Temah,
⁵⁴Neziah and Hatipha

⁵⁵The descendants of the servants of Solomon:

the descendants of
    Sotai, Hassophereth, Peruda,
⁵⁶Jaala, Darkon, Giddel,
⁵⁷Shephatiah, Hattil,
    Pokereth-Hazzebaim and Ami

⁵⁸The temple servants and the descendants
of the servants of Solomon   392

⁵⁹The following came up from the towns
of Tel Melah, Tel Harsha, Kerub, Addon and
Immer, but they could not show that their
families were descended from Israel:

⁶⁰The descendants of
    Delaiah, Tobiah and Nekoda   652

⁶¹And from among the priests:

The descendants of
    Hobaiah, Hakkoz and Barzillai (a
    man who had married a daughter of
    Barzillai the Gileadite and was called
    by that name).
⁶²These searched for their family records,
but they could not find them and so were
excluded from the priesthood as unclean.
⁶³The governor ordered them not to eat any of

2:62 they could not find them Some of the individuals who returned could not prove their ancestry. This proof would likely have consisted of a genealogy tracing one's heritage to one of the sons of Israel; the Jews routinely kept genealogies to prove their Jewish ancestry (see 1Ch 5:17; Ne 7:5). Genealogies were also used to exclude those with foreign blood. A pure line was of great importance to the Jews (see Ezr 9–10; Ne 13:23–28). Although the individuals named here could not prove their ancestry, they were still allowed to return with the rest of the exiles.

2:63 governor A Persian title, perhaps similar in meaning to "excellency." The governor alluded to here is probably Sheshbazzar or Zerubbabel. **Urim and Thummim** Two

---

Dates Related to Ezra, Nehemiah and Esther

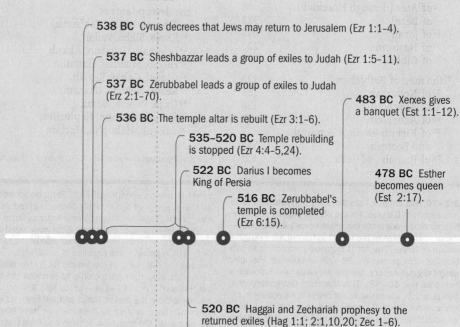

525 BC

538 BC Cyrus decrees that Jews may return to Jerusalem (Ezr 1:1-4).

537 BC Sheshbazzar leads a group of exiles to Judah (Ezr 1:5-11).

537 BC Zerubbabel leads a group of exiles to Judah (Erz 2:1-70).

536 BC The temple altar is rebuilt (Ezr 3:1-6).

535–520 BC Temple rebuilding is stopped (Ezr 4:4-5,24).

522 BC Darius I becomes King of Persia

516 BC Zerubbabel's temple is completed (Ezr 6:15).

483 BC Xerxes gives a banquet (Est 1:1-12).

478 BC Esther becomes queen (Est 2:17).

520 BC Haggai and Zechariah prophesy to the returned exiles (Hag 1:1; 2:1,10,20; Zec 1-6).

520 BC Temple building resumes (Erz 5:1-2; Hag 1:14-15).

525 BC

All dates are approximate

the most sacred food until there was a priest ministering with the Urim and Thummim.

[64]The whole company numbered 42,360, [65]besides their 7,337 male and female slaves; and they also had 200 male and female singers. [66]They had 736 horses, 245 mules, [67]435 camels and 6,720 donkeys.

[68]When they arrived at the house of the LORD in Jerusalem, some of the heads of the families gave freewill offerings toward the rebuilding of the house of God on its site. [69]According to their ability they gave to the treasury for this work 61,000 darics[a] of gold, 5,000 minas[b] of silver and 100 priestly garments.

[70]The priests, the Levites, the musicians, the gatekeepers and the temple servants settled in their own towns, along with some of the other

[a] 69 That is, about 1,100 pounds or about 500 kilograms
[b] 69 That is, about 3 tons or about 2.8 metric tons

---

small objects used to discern the will of God. The Urim and Thummim were placed in the breastpiece of the high priest (see note on Ex 28:30; Lev 8:8). The exact use and form of the Urim and Thummim are unknown. **2:64 42,360** The sum of the various groups mentioned in this chapter is only 29,818, which is 12,542 less than the number given in this verse. It is possible that women and children were not included in the initial numbers but were included in the final tally. It is also possible that not all families are listed in the individual tabulations. If there were only 12,542 women and children among the returned exiles, this seems quite low compared to the number of men. The difficulties of the journey and

the uncertainty of what awaited them in Judah may have caused many women and children to remain in Babylon. Also, many single young men likely returned since it would have been easier for them to leave Babylon on short notice. The discrepancy may also be explained by a scribal error. However, Ne 7:66 has the same number, making this option unlikely. **2:65 male and female slaves** The servants were likely regarded as property rather than as part of the congregation. The majority of these servants were probably foreigners. The servants composed about one-seventh of the total number of returnees, suggesting the Jews had prospered in Babylon.

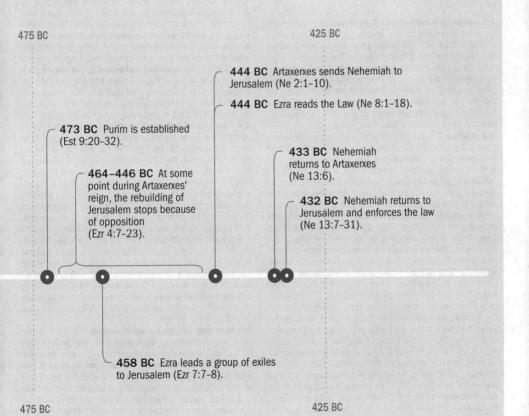

475 BC

425 BC

444 BC Artaxerxes sends Nehemiah to Jerusalem (Ne 2:1–10).

444 BC Ezra reads the Law (Ne 8:1–18).

473 BC Purim is established (Est 9:20–32).

433 BC Nehemiah returns to Artaxerxes (Ne 13:6).

464–446 BC At some point during Artaxerxes' reign, the rebuilding of Jerusalem stops because of opposition (Ezr 4:7–23).

432 BC Nehemiah returns to Jerusalem and enforces the law (Ne 13:7–31).

458 BC Ezra leads a group of exiles to Jerusalem (Ezr 7:7–8).

475 BC

425 BC

people, and the rest of the Israelites settled in their towns.

Rebuilding the Altar

3 When the seventh month came and the Israelites had settled in their towns, the people assembled together as one in Jerusalem. ²Then Joshua son of Jozadak and his fellow priests and Zerubbabel son of Shealtiel and his associates began to build the altar of the God of Israel to sacrifice burnt offerings on it, in accordance with what is written in the Law of Moses the man of God. ³Despite their fear of the peoples around them, they built the altar on its foundation and sacrificed burnt offerings on it to the LORD, both the morning and evening sacrifices. ⁴Then in accordance with what is written, they celebrated the Festival of Tabernacles with the required number of burnt offerings prescribed for each day. ⁵After that, they presented the regular burnt offerings, the New Moon sacrifices and the sacrifices for all the appointed sacred festivals of the LORD, as well as those brought as freewill offerings to the LORD. ⁶On the first day of the seventh month they began to offer burnt offerings to the LORD, though the foundation of the LORD's temple had not yet been laid.

Rebuilding the Temple

⁷Then they gave money to the masons and carpenters, and gave food and drink and olive oil to the people of Sidon and Tyre, so that they would

---

3:1–7 The returned Jewish exiles begin by building an altar to Yahweh. This was the first step in establishing proper worship of Yahweh in the land—for which the sacrificial system was of paramount importance. The building of an altar was also a way of thanking Yahweh for restoring them to the land. Abraham built an altar to Yahweh immediately after entering the land for the first time (Ge 12:7). Joshua likewise built an altar to Yahweh after entering the land following the exodus (Jos 8:30–31).

3:1 seventh month Tishri (late September and early October) according to the Jewish calendar. The year is probably 538 BC. The exiles probably traveled during the spring, leaving Babylon early in the month of Iyyar (also called Ziv; late April and early May) and arriving in Jerusalem in the month of Tammuz (late June and early July). In doing so, they avoided the winter, early spring (which included rains and the flood season) and summer—the most difficult times of the year for traveling. See the table "Israelite Calendar" on p. 763.

3:2 Joshua The name "Jeshua" (or "Joshua"), which means "Yahweh is salvation," is the OT equivalent of the name Jesus. Jeshua was the son of Jozadak and of the priestly family of Jedaiah, one of the 24 priestly families organized by David (compare 1Ch 24:7). He was also the grandson of Seraiah, the high priest during the destruction of Jerusalem (compare 1Ch 6:14; 2Ki 25:18). Jeshua was the first high priest of the Jewish community that returned from exile. This is the only passage in the Bible where Jeshua precedes Zerubbabel (see note on Ezr 2:2). Here, Jeshua is probably mentioned first because this section narrates the reinstitution of worship, which was the responsibility of the priests. **Zerubbabel** Means "the seed of Babel" or "born in Babel." Zerubbabel served as the governor of Judah. Since Sheshbazzar is not mentioned here, he may have died by this time. Or, he may have returned to Babylon after leading the returnees back to Judah. Zerubbabel was the grandson of Jeconiah (Jehoiachin), one of the last kings of Judah (1Ch 3:17–19). While Ezr 3:2 and several other accounts identify Zerubbabel's father as Shealtiel, 1Ch 3:19 lists Pedaiah, a brother of Shealtiel, as Zerubbabel's father (see note on 1Ch 3:17). One possible explanation for this difference is that if Shealtiel died without an heir, Pedaiah could have followed levirate law and married his widow, producing an heir for his brother (see Dt 25:5–10). The child would take Shealtiel's family name

while Pedaiah would have been his biological father. See the timeline "Dates Related to Ezra, Nehemiah and Esther" on p. 716; see the infographic "Ancient Altars" on p. 127; see the table "Altars in the Old Testament" on p. 249. **man of God** A commonly used title to denote a prophet of Yahweh (1Sa 2:27; 9:6; 1Ki 13:1). Here it likely refers to Dt 33:1, where the phrase is applied to Moses (Jos 14:6).

3:3 Despite their fear of the peoples around them In order to build the new altar, the people had to destroy the previous one used by the Jews, Samaritans and foreigners who lived near Jerusalem during the exile (Jer 41:5). The destruction of the altar surely infuriated these groups, which may account for the rift between those who returned from Babylon and those who remained in the land (Ezr 4:1–5). **morning and evening sacrifices** Each day, morning and evening, the burnt offering consisted of a lamb prepared with flour, oil and wine (Ex 29:38–42; Nu 28:2–8). These sacrifices were previously restored by Joash (2Ch 24:14) and Hezekiah (2Ch 29:7,27–29).

3:4 Festival of Tabernacles One of the three pilgrimage festivals where every Jewish male was expected to be in Jerusalem (Dt 16:16). The Festival of Booths (or Tabernacles) was an autumn harvest festival celebrated from the fifteenth to the twenty-first day of the seventh month (Tishri) (see note on Lev 23:33–44). This passage does not mention the Day of Atonement, which is celebrated the week before the Festival of Booths. Nehemiah 8 likewise contains no mention of the Day of Atonement. This may be due to the emphasis in both passages on the community's attitude of celebration. The Day of Atonement was a solemn observance and does not fit with the flow of the narrative. See the infographic "The Ark of the Covenant" on p. 412; see the table "Israelite Festivals" on p. 200; see the table "Israelite Calendar" on p. 763.

3:5 freewill offerings A voluntary sacrifice that could be offered whenever an individual felt led to do so (Lev 22:18–23; Nu 29:39).

3:6 first day of the seventh month The date of the Festival of Trumpets, or Rosh Hashanah. Assuming a year of 538 BC, the date was September 17. **the foundation of the LORD's temple had not yet been laid** The next major section of the book deals with the rebuilding of the temple. Even though the altar had been rebuilt and the sacrificial system reinstituted, the work was not complete. God wanted the entire temple rebuilt (Hag 1).

3:7 money The Jews prepare to build the temple's foundation by hiring masons and carpenters, whose skills

bring cedar logs by sea from Lebanon to Joppa, as authorized by Cyrus king of Persia.

⁸In the second month of the second year after their arrival at the house of God in Jerusalem, Zerubbabel son of Shealtiel, Joshua son of Jozadak and the rest of the people (the priests and the Levites and all who had returned from the captivity to Jerusalem) began the work. They appointed Levites twenty years old and older to supervise the building of the house of the Lᴏʀᴅ. ⁹Joshua and his sons and brothers and Kadmiel and his sons (descendants of Hodaviah*ᵃ*) and the sons of Henadad and their sons and brothers — all Levites — joined together in supervising those working on the house of God.

¹⁰When the builders laid the foundation of the temple of the Lᴏʀᴅ, the priests in their vestments and with trumpets, and the Levites (the sons of Asaph) with cymbals, took their places to praise the Lᴏʀᴅ, as prescribed by David king of Israel. ¹¹With praise and thanksgiving they sang to the Lᴏʀᴅ:

"He is good;
  his love toward Israel endures forever."

And all the people gave a great shout of praise to the Lᴏʀᴅ, because the foundation of the house of the Lᴏʀᴅ was laid. ¹²But many of the older priests and Levites and family heads, who had seen the former temple, wept aloud when they saw the foundation of this temple being laid, while many others shouted for joy. ¹³No one could distinguish the sound of the shouts of joy from the sound of weeping, because the people made so much noise. And the sound was heard far away.

Opposition to the Rebuilding

4 When the enemies of Judah and Benjamin heard that the exiles were building a temple for the Lᴏʀᴅ, the God of Israel, ²they came to Zerubbabel and to the heads of the families and said, "Let us help you build because, like you, we seek your God and have been sacrificing to him since the time of Esarhaddon king of Assyria, who brought us here." ³But Zerubbabel, Joshua and the rest of the heads of the families of Israel answered, "You have no part with us in building a temple to our God. We alone will build it for the Lᴏʀᴅ, the God of Israel, as King Cyrus, the king of Persia, commanded us." ⁴Then the peoples around them set out to discourage the people of Judah and make them afraid to go on building.*ᵇ* ⁵They bribed officials to work

ᵃ 9 Hebrew *Yehudah,* a variant of *Hodaviah*   *ᵇ* 4 Or *and troubled them as they built*

---

were essential to the project. These skilled laborers were hired with money likely taken from the treasury referred to in Ezr 2:69. **gave food and drink and olive oil** Following the example of Solomon, the people contracted the Phoenicians to bring timber from Lebanon to the port city of Joppa (compare 2Ch 2:16). The Phoenicians were paid with food, drink and oil — just as they had been during the time of Solomon. **people of Sidon** Sidon was a city located on the shores of the Mediterranean Sea, about 20 miles north of Tyre and about 95 miles north of Joppa. **Tyre** Tyre was a city located on the shores of the Mediterranean Sea, about 20 miles south of Sidon. **cedar logs** Cedars from Lebanon — greatly prized throughout the ancient Near East — appear throughout the OT as a symbol of worldly strength, surpassed only by Yahweh's power (see Ps 29:5; Isa 2:13; Am 2:9; Zec 11:2). They were also used to build the Jewish temple at Elephantine in Egypt (see note on Isa 49:12).
3:8 the second year The rebuilding of the foundation occurs about seven months after the events of Ezr 3:4–6. **twenty years old and older** Levites now took on responsibility at the age of 20 (1Ch 23:24; 2Ch 31:17). Originally, one had to be 25 (Nu 8:24) — and those who carried the tabernacle were required to be at least 30 (Nu 4:3,23,30).
3:10 foundation of the temple The returned exiles may have simply repaired the foundation of Solomon's temple rather than building a new one from scratch. Second Kings 25:9 indicates only that the temple was burned, which makes it possible that the original foundation remained intact.
3:11 love toward Israel endures forever This celebration echoes 2Ch 5:13. This refrain is used throughout the Psalms (Ps 100:5; 106:1; 107:1; 118:1; 136:1).
3:12 older priests and Levites and family heads, who had seen The first temple was destroyed in 586

BC. The date is now ca. 537 BC, meaning that these men are well over 50 years old. The scene described here is echoed in Hag 2:3. This is also the reality behind Zechariah's piercing question in Zec 4:10.

4:1–5 The following passage builds on the previous chapter by detailing the response of neighboring people to the efforts of the Jews. By this time, the neighbors had lived in Judah for decades, many likely born in the land. Now, the returned exiles — whom they regard as "foreigners" — are taking their land and influence away.

4:1 enemies In their first appearance in the narrative, the neighbors of the Jews are identified as adversaries. As a result, their request in Ezr 4:2 represents a veiled attempt to hinder the work of the Jewish people rather than a sincere request to join the project.
4:2 Esarhaddon Originally another Assyrian king, Sargon, had brought in colonists from a number of Mesopotamian towns when Samaria fell in 722 BC (2Ki 17:24). Additional colonists were later brought in during the reigns of Esarhaddon (681–669 BC) and Ashurbanipal (669–627 BC). While colonization of Israel is unattested in extra-Biblical literature, it is known that Esarhaddon settled easterners in Sidon after a successful campaign in Syria and Palestine. The foreign policy of the Assyrians involved exiling vanquished nations and transplanting foreigners into conquered territories. This was done in hopes of preventing rebellions throughout their vast empire; the mixture of different cultures, languages and religions made a unified rebellion nearly impossible. See the timeline "Dates Related to Isaiah and 2 Kings" on p. 1116.
4:3 You have no part with us Passages like Isa 56:6–8 indicate that foreigners were allowed to worship in the temple. However, Isaiah presents standards the foreigners must meet in order to do so (Isa 56:6) — standards they likely did not meet since they are identified as

against them and frustrate their plans during the entire reign of Cyrus king of Persia and down to the reign of Darius king of Persia.

Later Opposition Under Xerxes and Artaxerxes

⁶At the beginning of the reign of Xerxes,ᵃ they lodged an accusation against the people of Judah and Jerusalem.

⁷And in the days of Artaxerxes king of Persia, Bishlam, Mithredath, Tabeel and the rest of his associates wrote a letter to Artaxerxes. The letter was written in Aramaic script and in the Aramaic language.ᵇ,ᶜ

⁸Rehum the commanding officer and Shimshai the secretary wrote a letter against Jerusalem to Artaxerxes the king as follows:

⁹Rehum the commanding officer and Shimshai the secretary, together with the rest of their associates — the judges, officials and administrators over the people from Persia, Uruk and Babylon, the Elamites of Susa, ¹⁰and the other people whom the great and honorable Ashurbanipal deported and settled in the city of Samaria and elsewhere in Trans-Euphrates.

ᵃ 6 Hebrew *Ahasuerus*   ᵇ 7 Or *written in Aramaic and translated*   ᶜ 7 The text of 4:8–6:18 is in Aramaic.

---

enemies. king of Persia, commanded Cyrus' original decree granted only those who returned from exile the right to rebuild the temple.

4:4 make them afraid to go on building There was little the Jews could do to protect themselves: The supply lines from Tyre and Sidon were long and unguarded. The small group of Jewish people in Jerusalem were surrounded on all sides by enemies; they were completely vulnerable.

4:5 officials The Hebrew word used here is the same word used of the Persian king's advisers in Ezr 7:28 and 8:25. The foreigners may have bribed the Persian authorities to frustrate the rebuilding project. **Darius king of Persia** Darius ruled from 522–486 BC.

Ezra 4:5

DARIUS
Darius the Great assumed the Persian throne in 522 BC. Darius' father was Hystaspes, the governor of Parthia. Darius served as an officer alongside Cambyses, the son of Cyrus (see note on Ezr 1:1). Since Darius was not an obvious heir, revolts erupted throughout the Persian Empire in the early years of his reign, yet he eventually succeeded in solidifying his hold on the throne. Darius proved to be an extraordinary administrator and implemented far-reaching reforms. Chief among these was the standardization of coinage, weights and measures, which helped facilitate trade and commerce throughout the empire. In addition, he erected a magnificent palace in Susa, referred to as the "citadel of Susa" in Ne 1:1. Darius was followed on the throne by his son Xerxes (Ahasuerus) (see Ezr 4:6 and note).

4:6–23 The following passage is a parenthesis in the narrative. Ezra—in an attempt to illustrate some of the measures used by the enemies of the Jews—references events that took place between 50 and 80 years *after* the events of vv. 1–5. However, the account only indicates a change in time period by referring to different kings. Knowledge of these kings and the dates of their reigns is essential for making sense of this account. The kings mentioned in this passage are Ahasuerus, better known as Xerxes (v. 6; 486–465 BC), and his successor Artaxerxes (vv. 7,8,11; 464–424 BC). See the infographic "The Bowls of Darius and Artaxerxes" on p. 724.

4:6 Xerxes The Persian king Ahasuerus is better known by his Greek name, Xerxes. Xerxes became king in December 486 BC and reigned over the Persian Empire until

465 BC. Xerxes is a central figure in the book of Esther. **accusation** The accusations contained in this letter were probably the same ones mentioned in vv. 13–16. Evidently, nothing happened as a result of this attempt. **4:7 Artaxerxes** Artaxerxes reigned over the Persian Empire from 464–424 BC. Ezra led a return to Israel in the seventh year of Artaxerxes, and Nehemiah served as the king's cupbearer. See note on Ne 2:1. **Aramaic** Ezra 4:8—6:18 was written in Aramaic, as was 7:12–26. Aramaic is a Northwest Semitic language related to Hebrew and Phoenician. It became the common language (or *lingua franca*) of the ancient Near East because of the abundance of Aramaean merchants in the region. Eventually, Aramaic became the official language of the Persian Empire. Daniel 2:4—7:28 is the only other significant section of the OT written in Aramaic.

4:8 Rehum The primary author of the letter. **a letter** A different letter than the one mentioned in Ezr 4:7. While the letter is not dated, it was likely written prior to the time of Nehemiah (444 BC), since he successfully completed the rebuilding of the walls of Jerusalem. It is probably best dated between 458–444 BC, assuming v. 12 refers to the return of Ezra and his party in 458 BC. **4:9 Uruk** The city of Erech (or Uruk) was one of the cities founded by Nimrod in southern Mesopotamia (Ge 10:10). It is identified with modern Warka, located on the western bank of the Euphrates. The city was known for its celebrated shrine to the goddess Ishtar. **Susa** The capital of Elam and later one of the capitals of the Persian Empire.

Ezra 4:9

SUSA
The city of Susa is located in the southwestern portion of modern Iran, about 150 miles north of the Persian Gulf. Its ideal winter climate made it a favorite retreat for the Persian kings. The region was brutally oppressive during the summer months, with incredibly high temperatures. The ancient writer Strabo notes that snakes and lizards crossing the street at noon in the summer heat were roasted to death (*Geography* 15.3.10). Nehemiah served as the king's cupbearer in Susa (Ne 1), and Daniel pictured himself there in his vision of the ram and male goat (Da 8).

4:10 Ashurbanipal The Assyrian king Ashurbanipal (reigned 668–627 BC) is here referred to as "Osnappar" in Aramaic. His father was Esarhaddon, the Assyrian king

11(This is a copy of the letter they sent him.)

To King Artaxerxes,

From your servants in Trans-Euphrates:

12The king should know that the people who came up to us from you have gone to Jerusalem and are rebuilding that rebellious and wicked city. They are restoring the walls and repairing the foundations. 13Furthermore, the king should know that if this city is built and its walls are restored, no more taxes, tribute or duty will be paid, and eventually the royal revenues will suffer.a 14Now since we are under obligation to the palace and it is not proper for us to see the king dishonored, we are sending this message to inform the king, 15so that a search may be made in the archives of your predecessors. In these records you will find that this city is a rebellious city, troublesome to kings and provinces, a place with a long history of sedition. That is why this city was destroyed. 16We inform the king that if this city is built and its walls are restored, you will be left with nothing in Trans-Euphrates.

17The king sent this reply:

To Rehum the commanding officer, Shimshai the secretary and the rest of their associates living in Samaria and elsewhere in Trans-Euphrates:

Greetings.

18The letter you sent us has been read and translated in my presence. 19I issued an order and a search was made, and it was found that this city has a long history of revolt against kings and has been a place of rebellion and sedition. 20Jerusalem has had powerful kings ruling over the whole of Trans-Euphrates, and taxes, tribute and duty were paid to them. 21Now issue an order to these men to stop work, so that this city will not be rebuilt until I so order. 22Be careful not to neglect this matter. Why let this threat grow, to the detriment of the royal interests?

23As soon as the copy of the letter of King Artaxerxes was read to Rehum and Shimshai the secretary and their associates, they went immediately to the Jews in Jerusalem and compelled them by force to stop.

24Thus the work on the house of God in Jerusalem came to a standstill until the second year of the reign of Darius king of Persia.

a 13 The meaning of the Aramaic for this clause is uncertain.

---

referred to in Ezr 4:2. Ashurbanipal invaded the territory that included Erech (Uruk), evidently exiling some of the inhabitants to the region of Samaria. **in Trans-Euphrates** This phrase (used throughout Ezra as well as in Ne 2:7,9; 3:7) is the name of a Persian province, indicating the region west and south of the Euphrates River. This province stretched from the Euphrates to the border of Egypt, encompassing the whole of the Levant (which includes Syria, Lebanon and Israel). Babylon was the administrative center of this province until the later reign of Darius.
4:12 people who came up to us from you A reference to the return of Ezra and his party in 458 BC. The term "Jews" became the common name of the people of Israel after the exiles to Assyria and Babylon (Ne 1:2; Est 2:5; Da 3:8). **restoring the walls** The walls had lain in ruins since Nebuchadnezzar's destruction of the city in 586 BC, and their rebuilding became a priority during the days of Ezra and Nehemiah.
4:15 archives Probably alluding to the official records of the earlier ancient Near Eastern empires of Assyria and Babylon who had conquered Israel and Judah. The former capitals of those empires were now cities under Persian control. **rebellious city** The southern kingdom of Judah rebelled against the Assyrians in the days of Hezekiah (2Ki 18:7). They also rebelled against the Babylonian king Nebuchadnezzar in the days of Jehoiakim (597 BC; 2Ki 24:1) and Zedekiah (588 BC; 2Ki 24:20).
4:17–21 This section contains the reply of Artaxerxes to the letter of Ezr 4:11–16. Artaxerxes takes seriously the exaggerated rhetoric of his officials concerning what is happening in Jerusalem.

4:17 Samaria The Persian administrative center in the region. The city of Samaria was built by King Omri of Israel, who made it his capital. He named the city after Shemer, the previous owner of the hill on which it was built (1Ki 16:23–24). Samaria was destroyed by the Assyrians in 722 BC, and was subsequently rebuilt by the Samaritans. See note on 1Ki 16:24.
4:20 powerful kings Possibly refers to the Israelite kings David and Solomon, and maybe Uzziah and Hezekiah. **ruling over the whole** May exaggerate the threat posed by the inhabitants of Jerusalem. Even during the reigns of David and Solomon, the Israelites did not govern such a vast territory.
4:23 compelled them by force to stop While the Jews are forced to quit working to rebuild Jerusalem, the walls of the city will eventually be completed by Nehemiah. Ironically, they would be completed by a decree of the same king who ordered the work to stop. The opposition described in Ezr 4:7–23 dates to the reign of Artaxerxes (464–424 BC). See note on vv. 6–23.
4:24 Thus Here the text resumes the narrative from v. 5 concerning the opposition Zerubbabel faced which resulted in about a 15-year pause in the work to rebuild the temple. This verse introduces the narrative of chs. 5–6. **came to a standstill** The Jewish people in Jerusalem stopped working on the temple in 535 BC. They did not work on the temple for the rest of the reign of Cyrus (until 530 BC) and the entire reigns of Cambyses (530–522 BC) and Pseudo-Smerdis (522 BC). **second year of the reign of Darius** The second year of Darius' reign would be 520 BC (see note on v. 5). The mention of Darius in this verse has been a source of confusion

Tattenai's Letter to Darius

5 Now Haggai the prophet and Zechariah the prophet, a descendant of Iddo, prophesied to the Jews in Judah and Jerusalem in the name of the God of Israel, who was over them. ²Then Zerubbabel son of Shealtiel and Joshua son of Jozadak set to work to rebuild the house of God in Jerusalem. And the prophets of God were with them, supporting them.

³At that time Tattenai, governor of Trans-Euphrates, and Shethar-Bozenai and their associates went to them and asked, "Who authorized you to rebuild this temple and to finish it?" ⁴They[a] also asked, "What are the names of those who are constructing this building?" ⁵But the eye of their God was watching over the elders of the Jews, and they were not stopped until a report could go to Darius and his written reply be received.

⁶This is a copy of the letter that Tattenai, governor of Trans-Euphrates, and Shethar-Bozenai and their associates, the officials of Trans-Euphrates, sent to King Darius. ⁷The report they sent him read as follows:

To King Darius:

Cordial greetings.

⁸The king should know that we went to the district of Judah, to the temple of the great God. The people are building it with large stones and placing the timbers in the walls. The work is being carried on with diligence and is making rapid progress under their direction.

⁹We questioned the elders and asked them, "Who authorized you to rebuild this temple and to finish it?" ¹⁰We also asked them their names, so that we could write down the names of their leaders for your information.

¹¹This is the answer they gave us:

---

a 4 See Septuagint; Aramaic *We.*

---

since it follows the reference to Artaxerxes' letter in v. 23. By mistakenly assuming the kings in this chapter are listed in chronological sequence, one might conclude the Darius named here is Darius II whose second year was 422 BC (a time frame much too late for the setting of Ezra and Nehemiah). Rather, the reference points back to Darius I from v. 5 and marks a return to the earlier time and setting of the community of returnees under Zerubbabel and Jeshua (Joshua). Darius I was on the throne when the Jews completed the rebuilding of the temple (522–486 BC). He was the predecessor of (Xerxes) Ahasuerus, mentioned in v. 6.

5:1–5 This passage narrates the restarting of the temple building project in the second year of the reign of Darius I. This was the perfect time to restart the project, as the early years of Darius' reign were filled with political turmoil. See the timeline "Dates Related to Ezra, Nehemiah and Esther" on p. 716.

5:1 Haggai The prophet's message motivating the people to resume work on the temple is recorded in Hag 1:1–11. Haggai appears to have been well known; he is routinely identified as "the prophet," but no information is ever given about his ancestry (e.g., Ezr 6:14; Hag 1:1,3,12). See the timeline "Approximate Dates of Old Testament Prophets" on p. 1070; see the table "Israelite Calendar" on p. 763. **Zechariah** Zechariah was a Levite, probably born in Babylon (Ne 12:1,16). He was the son of Berekiah and the grandson of Iddo (Zec 1:1). Ezra identifies the prophet simply as "the son of Iddo," to indicate he was a member of the priestly family of which Iddo was the head (Ne 12:16).

5:3 went to them Their chief concern was whether the Jews' actions involved subversion. The Persian Empire had been teeming with revolts since the death of Cyrus, and the political situation became worse when Darius took the throne. See note on Ezr 4:5. Their concern may have also been based on the Jewish expectations of their coming Messiah, who was to rescue his people from bondage and build an empire from which he would rule the earth (e.g., Isa 9:6–7; 11:1–16; Jer 23:5–6; Da 2:44; 7:13–14; Mic 5:2–4). Zechariah himself fuels the speculation concerning the coming Messiah with his prophecies concerning the "Branch." According to

Zechariah, this Branch will build the temple of Yahweh and then rule on his throne (Zec 6:12–13). Jeremiah had written earlier that the Branch would reign as king (Jer 23:5). Naturally, these prophecies would not have pleased the Persian king currently ruling over Israel, especially since both Zechariah and Haggai singled out Zerubbabel as specially chosen by God (Hag 2:23; Zec 4:6–9). See the infographic "The Bowls of Darius and Artaxerxes" on p. 724. **Who authorized you** The Jews could not produce the credentials necessary to prove their right to rebuild the temple. The governor needed to investigate their claim.

5:5 the eye of their God A similar phrase occurs elsewhere in the Bible: Dt 11:12 uses it to describe Yahweh's concern for the land of Israel, and it appears in Job 36:7 to describe Yahweh's providential care for the righteous (compare Ps 34:15; Ps 33:18).

5:6–17 Although the exact date of this letter is not mentioned, various passages aid in narrowing the possibilities. It could not have been written prior to August or September, 520 BC (the month of Elul), when the Jews resumed the building of the temple after Haggai delivered his rebuke to them for halting the project (Hag 1:15). It must have been written prior to February or March 516 BC (the month of Adar), when the temple was completed (Ezr 6:15). Considering the length of time needed for all the events to occur, the letter was probably not written later than 517 BC. Therefore, any date between August or September 520 BC and the end of 517 BC is possible. A date near the end of 520 BC is most likely. The form of this letter and its response are similar to those of ch. 4.

5:8 great The Aramaic term used here can mean "chief" or "head" as well as "great." Since this reference is made by an unbeliever, a translation such as "chief god" or "head god" is most appropriate. **placing the timbers in the walls** The technique of laying timber between layers of stone or brick was common in the ancient Near East. It was probably used as a means of strengthening buildings against earthquakes as well as to help bond the building. See note on 6:4.

5:10 their names Tattenai was probably withholding the names until he heard from the king concerning the validity of the claims.

"We are the servants of the God of heaven and earth, and we are rebuilding the temple that was built many years ago, one that a great king of Israel built and finished. [12]But because our ancestors angered the God of heaven, he gave them into the hands of Nebuchadnezzar the Chaldean, king of Babylon, who destroyed this temple and deported the people to Babylon.

[13]"However, in the first year of Cyrus king of Babylon, King Cyrus issued a decree to rebuild this house of God. [14]He even removed from the temple[a] of Babylon the gold and silver articles of the house of God, which Nebuchadnezzar had taken from the temple in Jerusalem and brought to the temple[a] in Babylon. Then King Cyrus gave them to a man named Sheshbazzar, whom he had appointed governor, [15]and he told him, 'Take these articles and go and deposit them in the temple in Jerusalem. And rebuild the house of God on its site.'

[16]"So this Sheshbazzar came and laid the foundations of the house of God in Jerusalem. From that day to the present it has been under construction but is not yet finished."

[17]Now if it pleases the king, let a search be made in the royal archives of Babylon to see if King Cyrus did in fact issue a decree to rebuild this house of God in Jerusalem. Then let the king send us his decision in this matter.

The Decree of Darius

6 King Darius then issued an order, and they searched in the archives stored in the treasury at Babylon. [2]A scroll was found in the citadel of Ecbatana in the province of Media, and this was written on it:

Memorandum:

[3]In the first year of King Cyrus, the king issued a decree concerning the temple of God in Jerusalem:

Let the temple be rebuilt as a place to present sacrifices, and let its foundations be laid. It is to be sixty cubits[b] high and sixty cubits wide, [4]with three courses of large stones and one of timbers. The costs are to be paid by the royal treasury. [5]Also, the gold and silver articles of the house of God, which Nebuchadnezzar took from the temple in Jerusalem and brought to Babylon, are to be returned to their places in the temple in Jerusalem; they are to be deposited in the house of God.

---

[a] 14 Or *palace*   [b] 3 That is, about 90 feet or about 27 meters

---

5:11 God of heaven and earth A popular title for God after the exile. See note on 1:2.
5:12 our ancestors angered the God The Jews were well aware of the reason for their exile. They acknowledged that their ancestors provoked Yahweh by worshiping other gods (Eze 23; Hos 2:1–13). As a result, Yahweh punished them by scattering them among the nations (Lev 26:33; Dt 28:64) and allowing their temple to be destroyed (2Ch 7:20–22).
5:13 Cyrus king of Babylon Although unusual, this title is not without precedent: Cyrus refers to himself as the king of Babylon in the Cyrus Cylinder. The title is used here to emphasize Cyrus' power over Nebuchadnezzar, king of Babylon (Ezr 5:12). See note on 1:1. See the infographic "The Cyrus Cylinder" on p. 714.
5:14 Sheshbazzar See note on Ezr 1:8. **he had appointed governor** This term for "governor" may refer to the governor of a province or administrative district (v. 3; Ne 12:26) or to a royal commissioner.
6:1 Babylon Since the community of returned exiles originated in Babylon, Darius assumed the decree was made there. Darius likely knew that Cyrus stayed in Babylon following his conquest of the city.
6:2 Ecbatana A summer capital of the Persian kings, called Hagmatana in Persian, Ecbatana in Greek and Achmetha in Aramaic. The city was situated in a mountainous region with a temperate climate. The Greek historian Xenophon reports that Cyrus lived in Babylon for seven months during the winter season, in Susa during the spring for three months and two months in Ecbatana during the height of summer (see Xenophon, *Cyropaedia* 8.6.22; compare *Anabasis* 3.5.15). Ecbatana (modern Hamadan) was located in the province of Media and was the capital of the Medes until they fell under the control

of Cyrus in 550 BC. **Memorandum** The Aramaic term used here, *dikhron*, is related to a Hebrew word for "memorial" (*zikkaron*) that can designate a commemorative symbol including a text (Ex 17:14; 28:12; 30:16). The same Aramaic term was used in a document granting permission to the Jews at Elephantine to build a temple there. This title was usually placed on records of lists and inventories.

6:3–5 The decree of Cyrus recorded here is similar to that of the first chapter but has some notable differences. The differences may indicate the information came from two different sources. The edict of Ezr 1:2–4 may have been a portion of the decree that heralds would proclaim in each city as they journeyed throughout the empire—a shortened form of the official decree suitable for posting. The decree of vv. 3–5 could have been taken from the official records of the Persian king, which would contain the full text of the original, thus detailing all of the particulars.

6:3 cubits The measurement from the tip of the fingers to the elbow. While a standard cubit is roughly 18 inches, a "royal" or "great" cubit was 20.4 inches. These dimensions called for the rebuilt temple to be twice as high and three times as wide as Solomon's temple (1Ki 6:2). This would make the new temple six times larger than Solomon's. Cyrus wanted the glory of this temple to surpass that of Solomon's. Evidently, the Jews did not take advantage of this opportunity (Ezr 3:12–13; Hag 2:3).
6:4 one of timbers The mention of timber reveals that this temple was built with the same techniques employed by Solomon. This verse even prescribes the same ratio of stone to timber (three to one) as Solomon (1Ki 6:36).

⁶Now then, Tattenai, governor of Trans-Euphrates, and Shethar-Bozenai and you other officials of that province, stay away from there. ⁷Do not interfere with the work on this temple of God. Let the governor of the Jews and the Jewish elders rebuild this house of God on its site.

⁸Moreover, I hereby decree what you are to do for these elders of the Jews in the construction of this house of God:

Their expenses are to be fully paid out of the royal treasury, from the revenues of Trans-Eu-phrates, so that the work will not stop. ⁹Whatever is needed — young bulls, rams, male lambs for burnt offerings to the God of heaven, and wheat, salt, wine and olive oil, as requested by the priests in Jerusalem — must be given them daily without fail, ¹⁰so that they may offer sacrifices pleasing to the God of heaven and pray for the well-being of the king and his sons.

¹¹Furthermore, I decree that if anyone defies this edict, a beam is to be pulled from their house and they are to be impaled on it. And for this crime their house is to be made

---

6:6 stay away from there This command directs the Persian officials of the province to not interfere with the project. The governor of the province certainly would have been allowed access for inspections and other such situations.

6:7 governor of the Jews Tattenai is the governor of the entire Persian province of Trans-Euphrates (called in Aramaic *avar-naharah* or "Beyond the River"). This province extended from the Euphrates River in the north to Egypt in the south. Zerubbabel is only the governor of the Jews. Darius viewed Zerubbabel as subordinate to Tattenai.

6:9 young bulls, rams, male lambs The most valuable and important sacrifices in the religious worship of the Jews (Nu 7:87–88; 1Ch 29:21; compare Lev 1).

6:10 pray for the well-being of the king The Cyrus Cylinder records a similar decree: "May all the gods whom I have placed within their sanctuaries address a daily prayer in my favor before Bel and Nabu, that my days may be long." According to Greek historian Herodotus, it was customary among the Persians to utter a prayer for the king whenever a sacrifice was offered (Herodotus, *Histories* 1.132). See the infographic "The Cyrus Cylinder" on p. 714.

6:11 they are to be impaled on it The punishment involves the violator either being nailed to a beam from his house and hanged on it or being impaled by the beam.

The Bowls of Darius and Artaxerxes

Darius "the Great" ruled the Persian Empire from 522–486 BC. Artaxerxes I ruled from 464–424 BC. Ezra–Nehemiah often mentions both, as Darius authorized the rebuilding of the house of God (Ezr 6:5).

DARIUS
The inscription on the rim reads "Darius the great king" in Old Persian, Babylonian and Elamite—the three official languages of the Persian Empire.

ARTAXERXES
The inscription on the rim reads "Artaxerxes the Great King, King of Kings, King of Nations, son of Xerxes the King, of Xerxes son of Darius the King. In whose palace this silver dish was made." The letter which he wrote to Ezra had a similar beginning, "Artaxerxes, king of kings …" (Ezr 7:12).

a pile of rubble. [12]May God, who has caused his Name to dwell there, overthrow any king or people who lifts a hand to change this decree or to destroy this temple in Jerusalem.

I Darius have decreed it. Let it be carried out with diligence.

Completion and Dedication of the Temple

[13]Then, because of the decree King Darius had sent, Tattenai, governor of Trans-Euphrates, and Shethar-Bozenai and their associates carried it out with diligence. [14]So the elders of the Jews continued to build and prosper under the preaching of Haggai the prophet and Zechariah, a descendant of Iddo. They finished building the temple according to the command of the God of Israel and the decrees of Cyrus, Darius and Artaxerxes, kings of Persia. [15]The temple was completed on the third day of the month Adar, in the sixth year of the reign of King Darius.

[16]Then the people of Israel — the priests, the Levites and the rest of the exiles — celebrated the dedication of the house of God with joy. [17]For the dedication of this house of God they offered a hundred bulls, two hundred rams, four hundred male lambs and, as a sin offering[a] for all Israel, twelve male goats, one for each of the tribes of Israel. [18]And they installed the priests in their divisions and the Levites in their groups for the service of God at Jerusalem, according to what is written in the Book of Moses.

The Passover

[19]On the fourteenth day of the first month, the exiles celebrated the Passover. [20]The priests and Levites had purified themselves and were all ceremonially clean. The Levites slaughtered the Passover lamb for all the exiles, for their relatives the priests and for themselves. [21]So the Israelites who had returned from the exile ate it, together with all who had separated themselves from the unclean practices of their Gentile neighbors in order to seek the LORD, the God of Israel. [22]For seven days they celebrated with joy the Festival of Unleavened Bread, because the LORD had filled them with joy by changing the attitude of the king of Assyria so that he assisted them in the work on the house of God, the God of Israel.

Ezra Comes to Jerusalem

7 After these things, during the reign of Artaxerxes king of Persia, Ezra son of Seraiah, the son of Azariah, the son of Hilkiah, [2]the son of Shallum, the son of Zadok, the son of Ahitub,

[a] 17 Or purification offering

The wording is vague, literally stating "being raised up, let him be struck upon it." It is unclear whether the raising up of the victim or of the beam is in view.
6:12 diligence The Aramaic term used here, *osparna*, has the sense of "completely" or "thoroughly."

6:13–18 This passage narrates the completion and dedication of the temple, the climax of the first half of the book of Ezra.

6:13 with diligence The Aramaic term used here is also used to describe the building efforts of the Jewish people (5:8), the urgency of the king's decree (v. 12) and the actions of Tattenai and his colleagues in carrying out that decree.

6:15 the month Adar February or March 516 BC — about four years after the Jewish people restarted the project and approximately 20 years after they laid the foundation. The temple was rebuilt 70 years after its destruction. Solomon's temple stood for almost 400 years (959–586 BC). This temple would stand for almost 600 years (until its destruction by the Romans in AD 70). See the timeline "Dates Related to Ezra, Nehemiah and Esther" on p. 716; see the table "Israelite Calendar" on p. 763.

EVENT	DATE
Cyrus allows Jews to return to Jerusalem	538 BC
Temple altar is rebuilt	536 BC
Temple building is stopped	535–520 BC
Temple is completed	516 BC

6:16 dedication This term eventually becomes the name of an annual festival commemorating the rededication of

the temple after its defilement at the hands of Antiochus Epiphanes. See Jn 10:22 and note.
6:17 a hundred bulls, two hundred rams, four hundred male lambs While this was a significant sacrifice for the impoverished returned Jewish exiles, it pales in comparison to the 22,000 oxen and 120,000 sheep offered in dedication to Solomon's temple (1Ki 8:63).
for all Israel Lev 4:22–24 prescribed the offering of a male goat as a sin offering. Each tribe of Israel was represented in this offering.

6:19–22 Here, the language of the narrative reverts back to Hebrew (see note on Ezr 4:7).

6:19 first month This date can be calculated to March or April 516 BC. **Passover** On Passover, each household sacrificed a one-year-old unblemished lamb at twilight (Ex 12:6). The lamb was then eaten with unleavened bread and bitter herbs (Nu 9:11). The Passover holiday commemorated Yahweh's redemption of the nation of Israel from bondage in Egypt.
6:21 their Gentile neighbors Possibly a reference to Gentile converts who returned to Israel from Babylon with the Jews. It may also refer to Jews who remained in the land throughout the exile, but now separated themselves from foreigners, recommitting themselves to worship of Yahweh alone.
6:22 Festival of Unleavened Bread This celebration began on the day following Passover and lasted seven days (Lev 23:6–8). During this week, the Jews were forbidden from eating leavened bread (Dt 16:3). The first and seventh days were to be days of rest (Ex 12:16). **king of Assyria** The kings have now been identified as the "king of Persia" (Ezr 1:1,2,8; 3:7; 4:3,5,7,24; 6:14), the "king of Babylon" (5:13) and the "king of Assyria."

³the son of Amariah, the son of Azariah, the son of Meraioth, ⁴the son of Zerahiah, the son of Uzzi, the son of Bukki, ⁵the son of Abishua, the son of Phinehas, the son of Eleazar, the son of Aaron the chief priest— ⁶this Ezra came up from Babylon. He was a teacher well versed in the Law of Moses, which the LORD, the God of Israel, had given. The king had granted him everything he asked, for the hand of the LORD his God was on him. ⁷Some of the Israelites, including priests, Levites, musicians, gatekeepers and temple servants, also came up to Jerusalem in the seventh year of King Artaxerxes.

⁸Ezra arrived in Jerusalem in the fifth month of the seventh year of the king. ⁹He had begun his journey from Babylon on the first day of the first month, and he arrived in Jerusalem on the first day of the fifth month, for the gracious hand of his God was on him. ¹⁰For Ezra had devoted himself to the study and observance of the Law of the LORD, and to teaching its decrees and laws in Israel.

King Artaxerxes' Letter to Ezra

¹¹This is a copy of the letter King Artaxerxes had given to Ezra the priest, a teacher of the Law, a man learned in matters concerning the commands and decrees of the LORD for Israel:

¹²Artaxerxes, king of kings,

To Ezra the priest, teacher of the Law of the God of heaven:

Greetings.

¹³Now I decree that any of the Israelites in my kingdom, including priests and Levites, who volunteer to go to Jerusalem with you, may go. ¹⁴You are sent by the king and his seven advisers to inquire about Judah and Jerusalem with regard to the Law of your God, which is in your hand. ¹⁵Moreover, you are to take with you the silver and gold that the king and his advisers have freely given to the God of Israel, whose dwelling is in Jerusalem, ¹⁶together with all the silver and gold you may obtain from the province of Babylon, as well as the freewill offerings of the people and priests for the temple of their God in Jerusalem. ¹⁷With this money be sure to buy bulls, rams and male lambs, together with their grain offerings and drink offerings, and sacrifice them on the altar of the temple of your God in Jerusalem.

¹⁸You and your fellow Israelites may then do whatever seems best with the rest of the silver and gold, in accordance with the will of your God. ¹⁹Deliver to the God of Jerusalem all the articles entrusted to you for worship in the temple of your God. ²⁰And anything else needed for the temple of your God that you are responsible to supply, you may provide from the royal treasury.

²¹Now I, King Artaxerxes, decree that all

The title is probably used here to denote the reversal of the foreign policy of the Assyrians.

7:1—10:44 The remainder of the book contains an account of the ministry of Ezra, the scribe and priest. Ezra's mission is twofold: to lead a second major return to Jerusalem and to implement observance of the Torah, God's law, among the Jewish people. The events of these chapters take place during the reign of Artaxerxes, 58 years after the events of chs. 1–6.

7:1 Artaxerxes king of Persia Refers to Artaxerxes I, the third son of Xerxes (or Ahasuerus) and Amestris who reigned from 464–424 BC. See the infographic "The Bowls of Darius and Artaxerxes" on p. 724. **Ezra** The text supplies an extensive genealogy for Ezra (vv. 1–5) designed to emphasize his descent from Aaron, the first high priest of Israel. Despite its length, Ezra's genealogy skips the generations from Seraiah (2Ki 25:18) to Ezra and omits six generations from the Levitical genealogy in 1Ch 6:1–15. The omission of names in Biblical genealogies is common. The phrase "son of" can simply mean "descendant of."

7:6 a teacher The Hebrew term used here refers to a Persian office. It also refers to the professional class of scholars who had the ability to read and write. **everything he asked** He likely requested the items that were granted to him in Artaxerxes' letter (Ezr 7:12–26). This may be why the king's letter demonstrates such extensive knowledge of Jewish practices. **hand of the LORD** This phrase is used extensively throughout Ezra (Ezr 7:6,9,28; 8:18,22,31). It is also found in Ne 2:8,18.

7:7 musicians, gatekeepers and temple servants

The guilds listed in this verse are commonly associated with the Levites (e.g., 2:70; 7:24). **seventh year of King Artaxerxes** The year was 458 BC. Artaxerxes reigned from 464–424 BC. See note on Ne 2:1.

7:8 The trip from Babylon to Jerusalem took four months and covered roughly 900 miles. A direct route would have covered around 500 miles, but this was avoided because of the Arabian Desert. Ezra's group would have followed the Euphrates River north, then journeyed west across the plains to Damascus, and finally south through Samaria to Jerusalem.

7:12 king of kings A popular title in the Persian courts designed to describe the Persian king's sovereign rule over many peoples.

7:13 any of the Israelites in my kingdom, including priests and Levites Ezra separates the laity from the clergy (see Ezr 1:5 and note).

7:14 seven advisers It was customary in the ancient Near East for rulers to have a group of royal advisers. The Persian king's council was made up of seven princes (compare Est 1:14; Xenophon, *Anabasis*, 1.6.4–5) who were permitted to enter the king's presence uninvited and unannounced. **Law of your God** Likely refers to the entire Pentateuch. **which is in your hand** A reference to Ezra's mastering and becoming proficient in the interpretation of the Law.

7:17 bulls, rams and male lambs Goats were also probably included (Ezr 6:17).

7:19 the articles entrusted to you Not the vessels that had been taken from Solomon's temple—those had already been returned by Cyrus.

the treasurers of Trans-Euphrates are to provide with diligence whatever Ezra the priest, the teacher of the Law of the God of heaven, may ask of you — [22]up to a hundred talents[a] of silver, a hundred cors[b] of wheat, a hundred baths[c] of wine, a hundred baths[c] of olive oil, and salt without limit. [23]Whatever the God of heaven has prescribed, let it be done with diligence for the temple of the God of heaven. Why should his wrath fall on the realm of the king and of his sons? [24]You are also to know that you have no authority to impose taxes, tribute or duty on any of the priests, Levites, musicians, gatekeepers, temple servants or other workers at this house of God.

[25]And you, Ezra, in accordance with the wisdom of your God, which you possess, appoint magistrates and judges to administer justice to all the people of Trans-Euphrates — all who know the laws of your God. And you are to teach any who do not know them. [26]Whoever does not obey the law of your God and the law of the king must surely be punished by death, banishment, confiscation of property, or imprisonment.[d]

[27]Praise be to the LORD, the God of our ancestors, who has put it into the king's heart to bring honor to the house of the LORD in Jerusalem in this way [28]and who has extended his good favor to me before the king and his advisers and all the king's powerful officials. Because the hand of the LORD my God was on me, I took courage and gathered leaders from Israel to go up with me.

List of the Family Heads Returning With Ezra

8 These are the family heads and those registered with them who came up with me from Babylon during the reign of King Artaxerxes:

[2]of the descendants of Phinehas, Gershom;
of the descendants of Ithamar, Daniel;
of the descendants of David, Hattush [3]of the descendants of Shekaniah;

of the descendants of Parosh, Zechariah, and with him were registered 150 men;
[4]of the descendants of Pahath-Moab, Eliehoenai son of Zerahiah, and with him 200 men;
[5]of the descendants of Zattu,[e] Shekaniah son of Jahaziel, and with him 300 men;
[6]of the descendants of Adin, Ebed son of Jonathan, and with him 50 men;
[7]of the descendants of Elam, Jeshaiah son of Athaliah, and with him 70 men;
[8]of the descendants of Shephatiah, Zebadiah son of Michael, and with him 80 men;
[9]of the descendants of Joab, Obadiah son of Jehiel, and with him 218 men;

[a] 22 That is, about 3 3/4 tons or about 3.4 metric tons
[b] 22 That is, probably about 18 tons or about 16 metric tons
[c] 22 That is, about 600 gallons or about 2,200 liters
[d] 26 The text of 7:12-26 is in Aramaic.   [e] 5 Some Septuagint manuscripts (also 1 Esdras 8:32); Hebrew does not have Zattu.

7:22 a hundred talents of silver A Babylonian talent weighed approximately 75 pounds (around 34 kg). One hundred talents of silver would have weighed almost four tons. **wine** Wine is commonly mentioned as an offering in the OT (e.g., Ex 29:40; Lev 23:13; Nu 15:5,7,10). **a hundred baths** About 607 gallons. A cor was equal to 10 baths (Eze 45:14).
7:25 Trans-Euphrates Refers to the Jews who live in the province of Trans-Euphrates. See note on Ezr 4:10.
7:26 law of the king Probably refers to the specific decree of vv. 12–26, not the laws of the Persians.
7:27 bring honor The Hebrew term used here is also used by Isaiah to refer to the future work of Yahweh to glorify his sanctuary (Isa 60:7,13). Ezra may deliberately use this word to signify an initial fulfillment of Isaiah's prophecy.
7:28 to me While the use of the first person is common in Hebrew prophetic literature (Jeremiah, Ezekiel, Habakkuk), it is unusual in OT historical narrative. Nehemiah is the only historical book written primarily in the first person.
8:1–20 Like the list of returnees who accompanied Zerubbabel in Ezr 2, this passage specifies who was part of the group that returned from Babylon with Ezra. Since exiles are still returning decades after Cyrus gave permission for them to return, it is clear that some Jews initially decided to stay in Babylon. From God's perspective, the return to the land seems to have been obligatory — both Isaiah and Jeremiah call on the nation to return following the exile (e.g., Isa 48:20; Jer 31:16–21). However,

respected Biblical characters such as Ezra, Nehemiah, Mordecai and Esther remained in exile. Thus, remaining in exile was not always viewed negatively.
As an expert in the Scriptures (Ezr 7:6,10), Ezra would have recognized that Yahweh wanted the Jews to return to Israel. But both Ezra and Nehemiah may have been prevented from returning because they held official positions in the king's court. Both seem to require the express permission of the Persian king to return. The majority of the Jews were likely unable to return for financial reasons. Those who remained in Babylon had probably exhausted their resources by assisting those who initially returned (see 1:4,6). Over time, those who remained built up their resources in order to return with Ezra.

8:2 Phinehas The only son of Aaron's third son, Eleazar (Ex 6:23–25). This was also the genealogical line of which Ezra was a member (Ezr 7:5). **Ithamar** Aaron's fourth son (Ex 6:23). Eleazar and Ithamar were the only sons of Aaron who had children. **Hattush** The great-great-grandson of Zerubbabel (1Ch 3:17–22).
8:3–14 Ezra 8:3–14 identifies 12 families. A common number in Scripture, 12 may have been used by Ezra to correspond to the 12 tribes of Israel. Each of the families mentioned here appears in the list of 2:3–15, with the exceptions of Shecaniah and Shelomith. In 2:6, Joab is included as part of the Pahath-Moab family, but here he is independent. None of the names from 2:16–20 appear here.

[10] of the descendants of Bani,[a] Shelomith son of Josiphiah, and with him 160 men;

[11] of the descendants of Bebai, Zechariah son of Bebai, and with him 28 men;

[12] of the descendants of Azgad, Johanan son of Hakkatan, and with him 110 men;

[13] of the descendants of Adonikam, the last ones, whose names were Eliphelet, Jeuel and Shemaiah, and with them 60 men;

[14] of the descendants of Bigvai, Uthai and Zakkur, and with them 70 men.

The Return to Jerusalem

[15] I assembled them at the canal that flows toward Ahava, and we camped there three days. When I checked among the people and the priests, I found no Levites there. [16] So I summoned Eliezer, Ariel, Shemaiah, Elnathan, Jarib, Elnathan, Nathan, Zechariah and Meshullam, who were leaders, and Joiarib and Elnathan, who were men of learning, [17] and I ordered them to go to Iddo, the leader in Kasiphia. I told them what to say to Iddo and his fellow Levites, the temple servants in Kasiphia, so that they might bring attendants to us for the house of our God. [18] Because the gracious hand of our God was on us, they brought us Sherebiah, a capable man, from the descendants of Mahli son of Levi, the son of Israel, and Sherebiah's sons and brothers, 18 in all; [19] and Hashabiah, together with Jeshaiah from the descendants of Merari, and his brothers and nephews, 20 in all. [20] They also brought 220 of the temple servants — a body that David and the officials had established to assist the Levites. All were registered by name.

[21] There, by the Ahava Canal, I proclaimed a fast, so that we might humble ourselves before our God and ask him for a safe journey for us and our children, with all our possessions. [22] I was ashamed to ask the king for soldiers and horsemen to protect us from enemies on the road, because we had told the king, "The gracious hand of our God is on everyone who looks to him, but his great anger is against all who forsake him." [23] So we fasted and petitioned our God about this, and he answered our prayer.

[24] Then I set apart twelve of the leading priests, namely, Sherebiah, Hashabiah and ten of their brothers, [25] and I weighed out to them the offering of silver and gold and the articles that the king, his advisers, his officials and all Israel present there had donated for the house of our God. [26] I weighed out to them 650 talents[b] of silver, silver articles weighing 100 talents,[c] 100 talents[c] of gold, [27] 20 bowls of gold valued at 1,000 darics,[d] and two fine articles of polished bronze, as precious as gold.

[28] I said to them, "You as well as these articles are consecrated to the LORD. The silver and gold are a freewill offering to the LORD, the God of your ancestors. [29] Guard them carefully until you weigh them out in the chambers of the house of the LORD in Jerusalem before the leading priests and the Levites and the family heads of Israel." [30] Then the priests and Levites received the silver and gold and sacred articles that had been weighed out to be taken to the house of our God in Jerusalem.

---

[a] 10 Some Septuagint manuscripts (also 1 Esdras 8:36); Hebrew does not have *Bani*.   [b] 26 That is, about 24 tons or about 22 metric tons   [c] 26 That is, about 3 3/4 tons or about 3.4 metric tons   [d] 27 That is, about 19 pounds or about 8.4 kilograms

---

8:13 last ones The Hebrew phrase used here indicates that these men constitute the rest of that family that had remained in Babylon. No other members of the family of Adonikam remained in Babylon after the return of Ezra.
8:15 the canal that flows toward Ahava One irrigation canal of the many that ran from the Euphrates to the Tigris, which flowed at a slightly lower elevation. Ahava and Kasiphia (mentioned in v. 17) are probably in the general vicinity of Babylon. **no Levites** Sheshbazzar also had difficulty finding Levites who were willing to return to Jerusalem (2:40–42). It is possible that a relatively low number of Levites were originally taken into captivity. Many may have been among the poorest people of the land (2Ki 24:14).
8:16 who were men of learning This expression is best understood as "diplomats" in light of the nature of their role.
8:17 leader Probably indicates that Iddo served as the head priest at the sanctuary located in Kasiphia. **Kasiphia** Possibly the location of a Jewish sanctuary. Support for this suggestion is found in the repeated use of the Hebrew term *hammaqom* ("the place") in the OT to designate locations (e.g., Ge 13:3; Nu 11:3; Jer 27:22). The Hebrew term here is occasionally used with the meaning of "sanctuary" (e.g., Dt 12:5; Jer 7:3,6,7).
8:18 a capable man Perhaps a reference to his abilities in the law.

8:21–30 This passage recounts the preparations Ezra made at Ahava, praying for a safe journey and assigning priests to guard the gold, silver and other precious objects bound for the temple in Jerusalem.

8:21 There, by the Ahava Canal, I proclaimed a fast Fasting commonly accompanies a time of great anxiety. Fasting is common throughout the OT: David fasts while pleading for the life of his child (2Sa 12:16); the inhabitants of Nineveh fast upon hearing news of imminent judgment (Jnh 3:5); Nehemiah fasts upon hearing the bad news concerning the state of Jerusalem (Ne 1:4); and King Darius fasts while Daniel is in the lions' den (Da 6:18).
8:23 petitioned our God The combination of fasting with prayer is common in Scripture (Ne 1:4; Da 9:3; Lk 2:37; 5:33; Ac 13:3; 14:23).
8:24 twelve of the leading priests Ezra selects 12 priests. In the Pentateuch, the priests and Levites were given the responsibility of caring for the furnishings of the tabernacle (Nu 3–4). In this passage, these groups are essentially given the same responsibility—with coins and vessels replacing furniture.
8:27 1,000 darics A thick gold coin that was named after the Persian king Darius. One side of the coin had a picture of the king with his crown while holding a bow and arrow (or javelin or dagger?).

³¹On the twelfth day of the first month we set out from the Ahava Canal to go to Jerusalem. The hand of our God was on us, and he protected us from enemies and bandits along the way. ³²So we arrived in Jerusalem, where we rested three days.

³³On the fourth day, in the house of our God, we weighed out the silver and gold and the sacred articles into the hands of Meremoth son of Uriah, the priest. Eleazar son of Phinehas was with him, and so were the Levites Jozabad son of Jeshua and Noadiah son of Binnui. ³⁴Everything was accounted for by number and weight, and the entire weight was recorded at that time.

³⁵Then the exiles who had returned from captivity sacrificed burnt offerings to the God of Israel: twelve bulls for all Israel, ninety-six rams, seventy-seven male lambs and, as a sin offering,ᵃ twelve male goats. All this was a burnt offering to the Lord. ³⁶They also delivered the king's or-

ders to the royal satraps and to the governors of Trans-Euphrates, who then gave assistance to the people and to the house of God.

Ezra's Prayer About Intermarriage

9 After these things had been done, the leaders came to me and said, "The people of Israel, including the priests and the Levites, have not kept themselves separate from the neighboring peoples with their detestable practices, like those of the Canaanites, Hittites, Perizzites, Jebusites, Ammonites, Moabites, Egyptians and Amorites. ²They have taken some of their daughters as wives for themselves and their sons, and have mingled the holy race with the peoples around them. And the leaders and officials have led the way in this unfaithfulness."

ᵃ 35 Or *purification offering*

8:28 consecrated Set apart for a divine purpose.

8:31–36 After announcing their departure from Ahava in Ezr 8:31, the narrative immediately reports their arrival at Jerusalem in v. 32. According to 7:8–9, the journey took about four months. After a few days rest, the group turned over the silver and gold to the temple and offered sacrifices to Yahweh, probably in thanks for a safe journey.

8:31 twelfth day of the first month April 20, 458 BC, two days before Passover. See the table "Israelite Calendar" on p. 763; see the table "Israelite Festivals" on p. 200.

8:32 we arrived in Jerusalem The company arrived on August 4, 458 BC (7:9).

8:33 Meremoth Meremoth was of the line of Hakkoz, which had been unable to prove its ancestry (see 2:61–63; Ne 3:4,21). Evidently, the family had been accepted when evaluated by the priest with Urim and Thummim.

8:36 satraps and to the governors Ezra presents his authorization to the local Persian officials (see Ezr 7:21–24). A satrap was typically a chief governor who ruled a satrapy that might be made up of smaller provinces and administrative districts, each overseen by a governor who reported to the satrap. Darius I divided the empire into 20 satrapies according to the Greek historian Herodotus (*Histories* 3.89). Syria-Palestine was part of the fifth satrapy, following Darius' divisions (*Histories* 3.89). The plural reference to satraps here is unusual since a satrapy like Trans-Euphrates would have had a single satrap but multiple governors. The term is likely used generically for Persian officials. **the people** Probably refers to the new group of returnees being added to the Jewish presence in the land. Those who had returned previously were in need of additional numbers since they were surrounded by enemies (Ezr 4:1).

9:1–10:44 The main topic addressed in the rest of the book of Ezra is the issue of intermarriage. The community of returned exiles has intermarried with the local population. Deuteronomy 7:1–6 prohibited intermarriage with the seven nations who lived in Canaan prior to the conquest. These seven are identified as Hittites, Girgashites, Amorites, Canaanites, Perizzites, Hivites and Jebusites (Dt 7:1). The list of groups the Jews intermarried with in Ezr 9:1 includes five of those seven—Hittites, Amorites, Canaanites, Perizzites and Jebusites—and adds three

more—Ammonites, Moabites and Egyptians. The OT never explicitly prohibits intermarriage with those last three groups, though Dt 23:3–6 could imply disapproval of marriage with Ammonites and Moabites. However, the book of Ruth depicts intermarriage with Moabites positively and notes that a Moabite woman was the great-grandmother of King David (Ru 4:21–22). The book of Genesis also has Joseph married to an Egyptian woman (Ge 41:45). The underlying issue does not appear to be opposition to intermarriage per se. Rather, intermarriage was viewed as a gateway to idolatry (Dt 7:3–6; compare Nu 25:1–5; 1Ki 16:31–33). King Solomon had many foreign wives who eventually led him to worship their gods (1Ki 11:1–8).

The addition of Ammonites, Moabites and Egyptians here likely resulted from interpreting Dt 7:1–6 in light of 1Ki 11:1–2 which explicitly indicates Solomon married Egyptian, Moabite and Ammonite women (among others) and then goes on to paraphrase the prohibition from Dt 7:3–4. The problem behind Ezr 9–10 (and Ne 13) is religious, not ethnic. Ruth was a Moabite, but she made Yahweh her God (Ru 1:16). The scenario described to Ezra in Ezr 9:1–2 is worded precisely to evoke the memory of what had happened to earlier generations. Moses had warned them that intermarriage would result in idolatry and that idolatry would bring judgment from Yahweh (Dt 7:4). Israel and Judah had not heeded that warning (1Ki 11), and eventually Yahweh brought judgment, expelling them from their land (2Ki 24–25). The possibility that history could be repeating itself explains Ezra's strong reaction.

9:1 these things Refers to delivering the king's edicts to his officials (see Ezr 8:36). Several months have passed since the company arrived in Jerusalem; it is now the ninth month (see 10:9). See the timeline "Dates Related to Ezra, Nehemiah and Esther" on p. 716. **the neighboring peoples** A representative list, reminiscent of several similar lists in the Pentateuch (compare Ge 15:19–21; Ex 23:23; 33:2; Dt 7:1–6; 20:17). The Ammonites and Moabites may have been added to this list based on Dt 23:3–6 (see note on Ezr 9:1—10:44).

9:2 some of their daughters The issue at stake is religious, not ethnic. Jewish men had married foreign women and made the mistake of adopting their wives' gods (Mal 2:10–16). This opposed God's desire to be

³When I heard this, I tore my tunic and cloak, pulled hair from my head and beard and sat down appalled. ⁴Then everyone who trembled at the words of the God of Israel gathered around me because of this unfaithfulness of the exiles. And I sat there appalled until the evening sacrifice.

⁵Then, at the evening sacrifice, I rose from my self-abasement, with my tunic and cloak torn, and fell on my knees with my hands spread out to the Lord my God ⁶and prayed:

"I am too ashamed and disgraced, my God, to lift up my face to you, because our sins are higher than our heads and our guilt has reached to the heavens. ⁷From the days of our ancestors until now, our guilt has been great. Because of our sins, we and our kings and our priests have been subjected to the sword and captivity, to pillage and humiliation at the hand of foreign kings, as it is today.

⁸"But now, for a brief moment, the Lord our God has been gracious in leaving us a remnant and giving us a firm place[a] in his sanctuary, and so our God gives light to our eyes and a little relief in our bondage. ⁹Though we are slaves, our God has not forsaken us in our bondage. He has shown us kindness in the sight of the kings of Persia: He has granted us new life to rebuild the house of our God and repair its ruins, and he has given us a wall of protection in Judah and Jerusalem.

¹⁰"But now, our God, what can we say after this? For we have forsaken the commands ¹¹you gave through your servants the prophets when you said: 'The land you are entering to possess is a land polluted by the corruption of its peoples. By their detestable practices they have filled it with their impurity from one end to the other. ¹²Therefore, do not give your daughters in marriage to their sons or take their daughters for your sons. Do not seek a treaty of friendship with them at any time, that you may be strong and eat the good things of the land and leave it to your children as an everlasting inheritance.'

¹³"What has happened to us is a result of our evil deeds and our great guilt, and yet, our God, you have punished us less than our sins deserved and have given us a remnant like this. ¹⁴Shall we then break your commands again and intermarry with the peoples who commit such detestable practices? Would you not be angry enough with us to destroy us, leaving us no remnant or survivor? ¹⁵Lord, the God of Israel, you are righteous! We are left this day as a remnant. Here we are before you in our guilt, though because of it not one of us can stand in your presence."

The People's Confession of Sin

10 While Ezra was praying and confessing, weeping and throwing himself down before the house of God, a large crowd of Israelites — men, women and children — gathered around him. They too wept bitterly. ²Then Shekaniah son of Jehiel, one of the descendants of Elam, said to Ezra, "We have been unfaithful to our God by marrying foreign women from the peoples around us. But in spite of this, there is still hope for Israel. ³Now let us make a covenant before our God to send away all these women and their children, in accordance with the counsel of my lord and of those who fear the commands of our God. Let it be done according to the Law. ⁴Rise up; this matter is in your hands. We will support you, so take courage and do it."

⁵So Ezra rose up and put the leading priests and

---

[a] 8 Or *a foothold*

worshiped exclusively and threatened the survival of the nation. **mingled** The use here of the Hebrew verb *arav* ("mix") may be alluding to Ps 106:34–36, which describes how mixing with the nations led Israel into idolatry. **the holy race** The Hebrew phrase used here, *zera' haqqodesh* ("the holy seed"), echoes the sentiment of Dt 7:6 (*am qodesh*; "holy people") that identifies Israel as a people set apart for Yahweh. The phrase is also likely an allusion to Isa 6:13 where the *zera' qodesh* ("holy seed") refers to the remnant of Jewish people restored to the land after judgment.

9:3 I tore my tunic and cloak A common mourning ritual in the ancient Near East (see Ge 37:29,34; 44:13; Nu 14:6; Jos 7:6; Jdg 11:35). Ezra tears both his undergarment and outer garment.

9:4 everyone who trembled Refers to those among the Jewish community who were attempting to live according to God's law. **evening sacrifice** Offered at twilight (Ex 29:41).

9:5 with my hands spread out Describes a common position for prayer (compare Da 6:10; 1Ki 18:42; Ps 88:9; Isa 1:15; perhaps La 1:17). Solomon assumed this same position when he offered his prayer of dedication for the temple (1Ki 8:54; 2Ch 6:13).

9:8 a brief moment Refers to the 80 years from Cyrus' decree to the present time (538–458 BC). **remnant** The Hebrew term for "remnant" means "survivor" (compare Ge 45:7; Isa 4:2; Eze 14:22). Ezra uses the term four times in his prayer to refer to the community of those who returned from exile (Ezr 9:8,13,14,15; compare Ne 1:2).

9:15 stand The Hebrew term used here is a legal term meaning "to be acquitted" (Ps 1:5; 130:3). None are regarded as guiltless before Yahweh.

10:2 Elam The family of Elam returned to Jerusalem from Babylon with Zerubbabel and Jeshua (or Joshua; see Ezr 2:2,7). Elam is also mentioned in 8:7 and 10:26, indicating it was likely one of the most significant families in the postexilic community. **been unfaithful** The Hebrew term used here is a technical term for violating an oath. It is often used in the context of a covenant. See note on 1Ch 5:25.

10:3 send away all these women and their children

Levites and all Israel under oath to do what had been suggested. And they took the oath. ⁶Then Ezra withdrew from before the house of God and went to the room of Jehohanan son of Eliashib. While he was there, he ate no food and drank no water, because he continued to mourn over the unfaithfulness of the exiles.

⁷A proclamation was then issued throughout Judah and Jerusalem for all the exiles to assemble in Jerusalem. ⁸Anyone who failed to appear within three days would forfeit all his property, in accordance with the decision of the officials and elders, and would himself be expelled from the assembly of the exiles.

⁹Within the three days, all the men of Judah and Benjamin had gathered in Jerusalem. And on the twentieth day of the ninth month, all the people were sitting in the square before the house of God, greatly distressed by the occasion and because of the rain. ¹⁰Then Ezra the priest stood up and said to them, "You have been unfaithful; you have married foreign women, adding to Israel's guilt. ¹¹Now honor*a* the LORD, the God of your ancestors, and do his will. Separate yourselves from the peoples around you and from your foreign wives."

¹²The whole assembly responded with a loud voice: "You are right! We must do as you say. ¹³But there are many people here and it is the rainy season; so we cannot stand outside. Besides, this matter cannot be taken care of in a day or two, because we have sinned greatly in this thing. ¹⁴Let our officials act for the whole assembly. Then let everyone in our towns who has married a foreign woman come at a set time, along with the elders and judges of each town, until the fierce anger of our God in this matter is turned away from us." ¹⁵Only Jonathan son of Asahel and Jahzeiah son of Tikvah, supported by Meshullam and Shabbethai the Levite, opposed this.

¹⁶So the exiles did as was proposed. Ezra the priest selected men who were family heads, one from each family division, and all of them designated by name. On the first day of the tenth month they sat down to investigate the cases, ¹⁷and by the first day of the first month they finished dealing with all the men who had married foreign women.

Those Guilty of Intermarriage

¹⁸Among the descendants of the priests, the following had married foreign women:

From the descendants of Joshua son of Jozadak, and his brothers: Maaseiah, Eliezer, Jarib and Gedaliah. ¹⁹(They all gave their hands in pledge to put away their wives, and for their guilt they each presented a ram from the flock as a guilt offering.)
²⁰From the descendants of Immer:
Hanani and Zebadiah.
²¹From the descendants of Harim:
Maaseiah, Elijah, Shemaiah, Jehiel and Uzziah.

a 11 Or *Now make confession to*

In the ancient Near East, mothers received custody of the children when they divorced (see Ge 21:14). The Jewish men were thus divorcing both their foreign wives and the offspring created by their union. **according to the Law** Refers to Dt 24:1–4, which provides procedures for divorce if a husband finds some indecency in his wife (Dt 24:1). Foreign wives were leading their Jewish husbands to worship their gods, hence the need for divorce. See note on Ezr 9:1—10:44.
10:6 room One of the many rooms of the temple complex (8:29). A building of storerooms and accommodations for those who worked in the temple was located adjacent to the temple. **drank no water** At this point, Ezra has performed all the typical acts of mourning: torn his garments, pulled out his hair and beard, sat down, fallen on his knees, stretched out his hands, prayed, made confession, wept, prostrated himself, taken an oath and fasted (see 9:3,5; 10:1,5,6).
10:8 within three days Judah was a relatively small territory at this time. Jerusalem could easily be reached within three days from anywhere in the territory. **would forfeit** The Hebrew word used here (*charam* or the related noun *cherem*) often had religious implications, referring to the destruction of people and things who would threaten Israel's distinctiveness as a nation committed to Yahweh (Dt 7:2). However, the word was also used for things that were devoted to sacred use (Lev 27:21,28–29; Eze 44:29; Mic 4:13). Here the property of anyone who did not comply with Ezra's ruling about intermarriage would become the official property of the temple (see the historical work of Josephus, *Antiquities* 11.148). Since the penalty of *charam*

was also leveled on people of Israel who engaged in idolatry (Ex 22:20; Dt 13:12–18), the use of the term here may be intended to evoke that aspect as well. The narratives of the conquest of Canaan use the word to denote the complete destruction of Israel's enemies; both the people and their possessions were destroyed (see Dt 2:34; 3:6; Jos 6:21; 8:26; 10:28; 11:20; compare 1Sa 15:3,18).
10:9 ninth month Chislev (late November and early December) of 458 BC. See the table "Israelite Calendar" on p. 763; see the timeline "Dates Related to Ezra, Nehemiah and Esther" on p. 716. **square before the house of God** Probably the only place in the city large enough to hold this gathering. A large portion of the city likely still lay in ruins (see Ne 1:3).
10:15 opposed this These four individuals are probably not against the decision to divorce; they simply wished to resolve the matter as quickly as possible.
10:16 first day of the tenth month December 29, 458 BC.
10:17 first day of the first month March 27, 457 BC.
10:18–44 Assuming that the list is complete, a total of 113 Jews had married foreign women. Most of the names listed are theophoric, meaning they include a component representing the name of Yahweh. Nine of the 33 families from Ezr 2:3–35 are represented here. Two new families are added: a second Bani family (10:34) and that of Binnui (v. 38). The roster includes 17 priests and 10 Levites, composing almost one-fourth of the total.
10:18 Joshua son of Jozadak The family of the high priest is mentioned first.

22 From the descendants of Pashhur:
Elioenai, Maaseiah, Ishmael, Nethanel, Jozabad and Elasah.

23 Among the Levites:

Jozabad, Shimei, Kelaiah (that is, Kelita), Pethahiah, Judah and Eliezer.

24 From the musicians:
Eliashib.
From the gatekeepers:
Shallum, Telem and Uri.

25 And among the other Israelites:

From the descendants of Parosh:
Ramiah, Izziah, Malkijah, Mijamin, Eleazar, Malkijah and Benaiah.

26 From the descendants of Elam:
Mattaniah, Zechariah, Jehiel, Abdi, Jeremoth and Elijah.

27 From the descendants of Zattu:
Elioenai, Eliashib, Mattaniah, Jeremoth, Zabad and Aziza.

28 From the descendants of Bebai:
Jehohanan, Hananiah, Zabbai and Athlai.

29 From the descendants of Bani:
Meshullam, Malluk, Adaiah, Jashub, Sheal and Jeremoth.

30 From the descendants of Pahath-Moab:
Adna, Kelal, Benaiah, Maaseiah, Mattaniah, Bezalel, Binnui and Manasseh.

31 From the descendants of Harim:
Eliezer, Ishijah, Malkijah, Shemaiah, Shimeon, 32 Benjamin, Malluk and Shemariah.

33 From the descendants of Hashum:
Mattenai, Mattattah, Zabad, Eliphelet, Jeremai, Manasseh and Shimei.

34 From the descendants of Bani:
Maadai, Amram, Uel, 35 Benaiah, Bedeiah, Keluhi, 36 Vaniah, Meremoth, Eliashib, 37 Mattaniah, Mattenai and Jaasu.

38 From the descendants of Binnui:[a]
Shimei, 39 Shelemiah, Nathan, Adaiah, 40 Maknadebai, Shashai, Sharai, 41 Azarel, Shelemiah, Shemariah, 42 Shallum, Amariah and Joseph.

43 From the descendants of Nebo:
Jeiel, Mattithiah, Zabad, Zebina, Jaddai, Joel and Benaiah.

44 All these had married foreign women, and some of them had children by these wives.[b]

a 37,38 See Septuagint (also 1 Esdras 9:34); Hebrew *Jaasu* 38*and Bani and Binnui.*   b 44 Or *and they sent them away with their children*

10:44 foreign women The foreign wives likely returned to the homes of their fathers, where they would then either remarry or live as widows (compare Ru 1:8–9). See note on Ezr 9:2.

NEHEMIAH

INTRODUCTION TO NEHEMIAH

The book of Nehemiah is about strength under pressure—having the fortitude to follow Yahweh, no matter what. In 445 BC the king of Persia sent Nehemiah, his Jewish cupbearer, to oversee the rebuilding of the wall of Jerusalem. Nehemiah was accompanied by Jewish exiles—descendants of the captives who were taken to Babylon in 586 BC. When they arrived in Judah, the people already living there opposed the changes they wanted to make. But despite opposition, Nehemiah and his supporters finished the wall.

BACKGROUND

Nehemiah starts where Ezra left off, in 444 BC. Ezra has led a third group of exiles back to Jerusalem and now Nehemiah leads a fourth. This continuity is evident in that Ezra and Nehemiah were treated as a single book in antiquity.

The events of Nehemiah occur between 444 and 432 BC during King Artaxerxes' reign over the Persian Empire (which included Judah). While the text of Nehemiah portrays Artaxerxes positively in his dealings with the Jews, historical sources present a broader picture: He killed his opponents—including his older brother Darius, who was the true heir to the throne. He also put down two significant rebellions (in 460 and 448 BC). Nehemiah's return to Jerusalem took place shortly after the second rebellion. Nehemiah was likely Artaxerxes' choice for governor of Judah because the ruler wanted a loyal subject overseeing the area, which was strategically located between Babylon (modern-day Iraq) and unstable Egypt.

The narrative is set in two cities: Susa and Jerusalem. Susa (sometimes translated "Shushan") was the empire's winter capital and was located on the Karkheh River, roughly 150 miles north of the Persian Gulf. Nehemiah was the royal cupbearer in the palace at Susa (Ne 1:11). Once he became governor of Judah, he lived in Jerusalem, which is the setting for Ne 2:11—13:31.

During Nehemiah's tenure as governor, Judah was less than 900 square miles, small enough that it could be ruled from a single fortification. The non-Jewish people living in Judah strongly opposed the rebuilding of Jerusalem's wall: The building of the wall would effectively allow the Jews to secure the city as a central fortress—and, thus, to once again

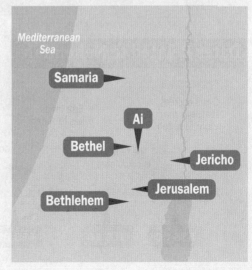

This map depicts many of the major locations related to Nehemiah. Susa, where the book begins, is east of Babylon (see the map for the book of Esther).

dominate the region. On the other hand, if the wall was *not* restored, the Jews would essentially be unable to resist an enemy's attack.

Sanballat the Samaritan, Tobiah the Ammonite and Geshem the Arab—the governors of their respective regions—led the foreigners. They ruled over the nations surrounding Judah on three sides: Samaria in the north, Ammon in the east and Arabia in the south.

STRUCTURE

The book begins with a distressing report that the wall of Jerusalem was in ruins, followed by the announcement of Nehemiah's mission (1:1—2:8). Nehemiah then travels to Jerusalem to rebuild the wall (2:9—7:73). Like the work to restore the temple in Ezr 3–6, the fortification of the wall incites opposition, but the project is finished eventually (Ne 3–4; 6:15—7:4). Along the way, Nehemiah enacts an initial reform to deal with conflicts and injustice among the people, leading by example (5:1–19). He also foils a conspiracy his enemies had concocted against him (6:1–14).

After the wall is restored, Nehemiah focuses on restoring the Jewish people. Ezra the priest reads God's law, and the people respond by confessing their sin (chs. 8–9) and drafting a covenant (a contract) outlining the basic rules of the community (10:28–39). After the wall of Jerusalem is dedicated, the people worship at the temple (12:27–47). A series of further reforms follows (13:4–31).

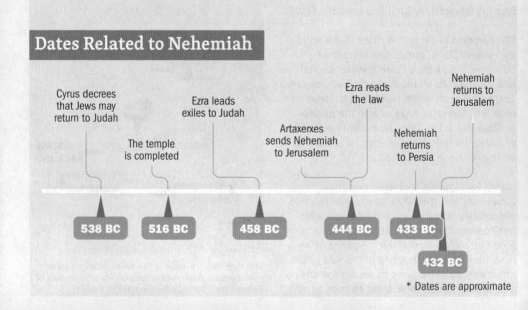

Dates Related to Nehemiah

Cyrus decrees that Jews may return to Judah

The temple is completed

Ezra leads exiles to Judah

Artaxerxes sends Nehemiah to Jerusalem

Ezra reads the law

Nehemiah returns to Persia

Nehemiah returns to Jerusalem

538 BC   516 BC   458 BC   444 BC   433 BC   432 BC

* Dates are approximate

OUTLINE

- The wall is rebuilt (1:1—7:73)
- The covenant is renewed (8:1—10:39)
- Society is reformed (11:1—13:31)

THEMES

Originally a single work, the books of Ezra and Nehemiah were intended to encourage the Jewish community to remain obedient to God's covenant in the face of hardship. Decades after the Babylonian exile had ended, the people were struggling to restore Jerusalem, where insecurity abounded and so did ungodly values.

In the face of this adversity, Nehemiah faithfully perseveres. For Nehemiah, loyalty to God and his people looks like leaving his position as the king's cupbearer—a trusted and esteemed role. Nehemiah then acts upon the plans God places on his heart, acting with integrity and calling others to do the same (2:12; 7:5).

Nehemiah continually calls the Jews' attention to their identity, as people in relationship with Yahweh. Being God's people comes with responsibilities, challenges and sacrifices. In each new generation, God's work continues, and his people, who today are those who have chosen Jesus, carry it forward. We are called to make the world a more just and God-honoring place.

Nehemiah's Prayer

1 The words of Nehemiah son of Hakaliah:

In the month of Kislev in the twentieth year, while I was in the citadel of Susa, ²Hanani, one of my brothers, came from Judah with some other men, and I questioned them about the Jewish remnant that had survived the exile, and also about Jerusalem.

³They said to me, "Those who survived the exile and are back in the province are in great trouble and disgrace. The wall of Jerusalem is broken down, and its gates have been burned with fire."

⁴When I heard these things, I sat down and wept. For some days I mourned and fasted and prayed before the God of heaven. ⁵Then I said:

"Lord, the God of heaven, the great and awesome God, who keeps his covenant of love with those who love him and keep his commandments, ⁶let your ear be attentive and your eyes open to hear the prayer your servant is praying before you day and night for your servants, the people of Israel. I confess the sins we Israelites, including myself and my father's family, have committed against you. ⁷We have acted very wickedly toward you. We have not obeyed the commands, decrees and laws you gave your servant Moses.

⁸"Remember the instruction you gave your servant Moses, saying, 'If you are unfaithful, I will scatter you among the nations, ⁹but if you return to me and obey my commands, then even if your exiled people are at the farthest horizon, I will gather them from there and bring them to the place I have chosen as a dwelling for my Name.'

¹⁰"They are your servants and your people, whom you redeemed by your great strength and your mighty hand. ¹¹Lord, let your ear be attentive to the prayer of this your servant and to the prayer of your servants who delight in revering your name. Give your servant success today by granting him favor in the presence of this man."

I was cupbearer to the king.

1:1–3 In the Hebrew Bible, the books of Nehemiah and Ezra are combined into one book. Both books describe the challenges faced by the postexilic community in Jerusalem. Nehemiah focuses on rebuilding the walls of Jerusalem. The book opens in 445 BC, with Nehemiah who is a Jew, serving in the court of the Persian king Artaxerxes. See note on Ezr 1:1–11.

1:1 Nehemiah Means "Yahweh comforts"; the name comes from the same root word as the name Nahum, meaning "comfort." Nehemiah's father's name is mentioned to distinguish him from other individuals named Nehemiah (Ezr 2:2; Ne 3:16; 7:7). **month of Kislev** Corresponds to November or December. Hanani likely planned his trip to Judah with the intention of returning to Susa before the onset of winter. See the table "Israelite Calendar" on p. 763. **twentieth year** The twentieth year of the reign of Artaxerxes was 445 BC. See note on 2:1. See the timeline "Dates Related to Ezra, Nehemiah and Esther" on p. 716. **Susa** See note on Ezr 4:9.

1:2 Hanani A shortened form of Hananiah, which means "Yahweh has been gracious." Hanani is mentioned again in Ne 7:2. **one of my brothers** While the Hebrew term used here could refer broadly to a kinsman, Hanani may be a biological brother of Nehemiah. **had survived the exile** Refers to those Jews who returned to Jerusalem following the Babylonian exile, which ended ca. 538 BC.

1:3 the province Refers to the province of the Trans-Euphrates (or "Beyond the River"), of which Judah was a part. See note on Ezr 4:10. **wall of Jerusalem is broken down** More than 90 years had passed since Cyrus' decree allowing Jews to return to Jerusalem in 538 BC. A number of factors probably led to the failure of the returned exiles to rebuild the city during this time, including fear of enemies (Ezr 4:1–4; Ne 4–6) and the denial of permission earlier in Artaxerxes' reign (see Ezr 4:7–23). In addition, they may have had misplaced priorities, as happened earlier in the case of rebuilding the temple (Hag 1). If the Jews were reluctant to rebuild the temple, they may also have been reluctant to rebuild the city.

1:4–11 This is the first of 12 prayers recorded in the book. The prayer is in the form of an inclusio, which occurs when similar or identical phrases, motifs or episodes begin and end a literary unit. The words of Nehemiah's prayer are an allusion to Dt 30:1–4. At times, Nehemiah paraphrases the text; at other times he directly quotes it.

1:4 I sat A customary posture during mourning and fasting (Ezr 9:3; Job 2:8,13). **mourned** Nehemiah's mourning likely went on for four months—until the events of Ne 2. **1:5 great and awesome** These words were originally used to describe Yahweh in Dt 7:21. Nehemiah also uses them in Ne 4:14 and 9:32. **his covenant of love** Linking covenant with *chesed*—the Hebrew word for Yahweh's covenant love—suggests that Yahweh would honor the covenant he made with his people because of his loyal love. **those who love him and keep his commandments** A reference to Ex 20:6 and Dt 5:10. Daniel uses this same phraseology to begin his prayer concerning the 70 years of captivity predicted by Jeremiah (Da 9:4).

1:6 servant The Hebrew word used here appears eight times in this prayer to refer to Nehemiah himself, Moses or the people of Israel in general. **day and night** Nehemiah uttered this prayer on a regular basis for the four months between the report of Hanani and the cupbearer's opportunity to make his request of the king.

1:7 the commands, decrees and laws Nehemiah uses three different Hebrew terms synonymously to refer to God's law. The variation and repetition is similar to that of psalms praising the Law like Psalm 19 or Psalm 119 (compare Ps 19:7–9).

1:9 the place Refers to the city of Jerusalem (Dt 12:5,11; 1Ki 11:13).

1:10 your mighty hand Alludes to Ex 32:11 and other passages (see Dt 7:8; 9:26) where the same phrases are used in reference to Yahweh's redemption of the nation from Egypt.

1:11 this man Refers to the Persian king, Artaxerxes. As the king's cupbearer, Nehemiah would ordinarily use a title of honor and respect for his king. Nehemiah may use

Artaxerxes Sends Nehemiah to Jerusalem

2 In the month of Nisan in the twentieth year of King Artaxerxes, when wine was brought for him, I took the wine and gave it to the king. I had not been sad in his presence before, ²so the king asked me, "Why does your face look so sad when you are not ill? This can be nothing but sadness of heart."

I was very much afraid, ³but I said to the king, "May the king live forever! Why should my face not look sad when the city where my ancestors are buried lies in ruins, and its gates have been destroyed by fire?"

⁴The king said to me, "What is it you want?"

Then I prayed to the God of heaven, ⁵and I answered the king, "If it pleases the king and if your servant has found favor in his sight, let him send me to the city in Judah where my ancestors are buried so that I can rebuild it."

⁶Then the king, with the queen sitting beside him, asked me, "How long will your journey take, and when will you get back?" It pleased the king to send me; so I set a time.

⁷I also said to him, "If it pleases the king, may I have letters to the governors of Trans-Euphrates, so that they will provide me safe-conduct until I arrive in Judah? ⁸And may I have a letter to Asaph, keeper of the royal park, so he will give me timber to make beams for the gates of the citadel by the temple and for the city wall and for the residence I will occupy?" And because the gracious hand of my God was on me, the king granted my requests. ⁹So I went to the governors of Trans-Euphrates

---

this phrase to emphasize that the powerful Persian king was a mere man in comparison to Nehemiah's God. See the infographic "The Bowls of Darius and Artaxerxes" on p. 724. **cupbearer to the king** An important occupation in the ancient Near East (see note on Ge 40:1). Nehemiah's occupation as cupbearer demonstrates that he was already a person of impeccable character with excellent administrative skill. The cupbearer often served as a personal confidant to the king, and therefore possessed great influence.

2:1 month of Nisan March or April of 444 BC, four months after the events of chapter one. Nisan was the first month of the year in the Jewish calendar. Nehemiah may have waited four months to make his request of Artaxerxes because the king had been absent. This would also explain why the king had not noticed the change in Nehemiah's countenance (compare Ne 2:2) prior to this time. **King Artaxerxes** The ruler of the Persian Empire from 464–424 BC.

KING ARTAXERXES
Artaxerxes I, third son of Xerxes and Amestris, ruler of the Persian Empire from 464–424 BC. Plutarch notes that Artaxerxes was the "most remarkable" of all the kings of Persia for a "gentle and noble spirit" (*Artaxerxes* 1.1). There were two other Persian kings identified by this name: Artaxerxes II (404–358 BC), and Artaxerxes III (359–338 BC).

EVENT	DATE
Cyrus allows Jews to return to Jerusalem	538 BC
Temple is completed	516 BC
Ezra leads a group of exiles to Jerusalem	458 BC
Nehemiah goes to Jerusalem	444 BC

2:2 Why does your face look so sad Nehemiah's activities of the past few months—mourning, fasting and praying—began to affect him physically. Compare note on 2:1. **very much afraid** Nehemiah may have feared the loss of his livelihood, since court etiquette required those in the king's presence to have a cheerful countenance. It is also possible that Nehemiah was nervous because he knew that if his request were refused he might not get another opportunity.

2:3 where my ancestors are buried Ancestral tombs were universally respected throughout the ancient Near East, especially among the nobility and royalty. Nehemiah is presenting his case in a way that Artaxerxes can sympathize with.

2:6 so I set a time The specific time is not given here, but it is later mentioned that Nehemiah returned to Susa after 12 years in Jerusalem (5:14; 13:6).

2:7 Trans-Euphrates Refers to the name of a Persian province. See note on Ezr 4:10.

2:8 the royal park The location of this park or forest is unclear. Since Asaph is a Hebrew name, it may refer to a forest within Israel such as Solomon's Garden at Etham, about six miles south of Jerusalem. It may also refer to a forest in Lebanon, a region famed for its magnificent cedar trees (see note on Isa 14:8). However, the relative cost of importing the cedars from Lebanon—especially for the task of building city walls—makes this alternative unlikely. **city wall** While most of the city wall was likely made of stone and brick, wood was needed for placement and support. **gracious hand of my God** Reminiscent of similar phraseology used throughout the book of Ezra (Ezr 7:6,9,28; 8:18,22,31). **granted my requests** Artaxerxes may have allowed the return to ensure that Judah remained loyal to the Persians. The land of Judah presented a natural buffer against the many rebellions in the western portion of the empire, assuming it stayed loyal to the Persians. With someone as trusted as Nehemiah as the governor of the territory, the king could feel relatively secure that Judah would not join the occasional uprisings. Regardless of the Persian king's reasoning, Nehemiah attributes his success to God.

2:9 I went to the governors The amount of time between the events of Ne 2:8 and 2:9 was long enough for Nehemiah to gather supplies and make the long journey from Susa to Jerusalem. Nehemiah probably arrived in Jerusalem in the late summer of 444 BC. Nehemiah's journey likely would have taken him from Susa to Babylon, then north up the Euphrates River, west to Damascus, and finally south to Samaria and Jerusalem. **army officers and cavalry** A military escort ensured Nehemiah a safe journey to his homeland and gave him an aura of imperial authority when he got there.

and gave them the king's letters. The king had also sent army officers and cavalry with me.

[10]When Sanballat the Horonite and Tobiah the Ammonite official heard about this, they were very much disturbed that someone had come to promote the welfare of the Israelites.

Nehemiah Inspects Jerusalem's Walls

[11]I went to Jerusalem, and after staying there three days [12]I set out during the night with a few others. I had not told anyone what my God had put in my heart to do for Jerusalem. There were no mounts with me except the one I was riding on. [13]By night I went out through the Valley Gate toward the Jackal[a] Well and the Dung Gate, examining the walls of Jerusalem, which had been broken down, and its gates, which had been destroyed by fire. [14]Then I moved on toward the Fountain Gate and the King's Pool, but there was not enough room for my mount to get through; [15]so I went up the valley by night, examining the wall. Finally, I turned back and reentered through the Valley Gate. [16]The officials did not know where I had gone or what I was doing, because as yet I had said nothing to the Jews or the priests or nobles or officials or any others who would be doing the work.

[17]Then I said to them, "You see the trouble we are in: Jerusalem lies in ruins, and its gates have been burned with fire. Come, let us rebuild the wall of Jerusalem, and we will no longer be in disgrace." [18]I also told them about the gracious hand of my God on me and what the king had said to me.

They replied, "Let us start rebuilding." So they began this good work.

[19]But when Sanballat the Horonite, Tobiah the Ammonite official and Geshem the Arab heard about it, they mocked and ridiculed us. "What is this you are doing?" they asked. "Are you rebelling against the king?"

[20]I answered them by saying, "The God of heaven will give us success. We his servants will start rebuilding, but as for you, you have no share in Jerusalem or any claim or historic right to it."

Builders of the Wall

3 Eliashib the high priest and his fellow priests went to work and rebuilt the Sheep Gate. They dedicated it and set its doors in place, building as far as the Tower of the Hundred, which they dedicated, and as far as the Tower of Hananel. [2]The

---

[a] 13 Or *Serpent* or *Fig*

2:10 Sanballat the Horonite In extra-Biblical sources Sanballat is identified as the governor of Samaria. He is associated with Samaria in 4:1–2, but his title is never given in Nehemiah. **Tobiah the Ammonite** Possibly the Persian governor of Ammon. The Ammonites were descendants of Ben-Ammi, son of Abraham's nephew Lot. They settled in territory east of the Jordan River. See note on 1Ch 19:1. Tobiah was married to the daughter of Shecaniah (Ne 6:18). His son, Jehohanan, was married to the daughter of Meshullam, who helped rebuild the walls of Jerusalem (3:4). The Tobiad family exercised considerable influence and authority over the region of Ammon for several generations during the Hellenistic period (beginning ca. late fourth century BC). The Tobiah named here may have been an ancestor of that family. **to promote the welfare of the Israelites** Nehemiah's governorship effectively took away any authority these opponents had over the region of Judah. Nehemiah's efforts would also strengthen the Jews. The opposition group evidently regarded this strengthening as a military threat. **2:11 three days** Nehemiah was probably resting after his long journey. Ezra's caravan also rested for three days following its journey to Jerusalem (Ezr 8:32). **2:12 a few others** Probably refers to residents of Jerusalem who knew their way around the city. They may also have been guards responsible for Nehemiah's safety. **2:13 Valley Gate** Probably located near the southwest corner of the city. From here, Nehemiah seems to have proceeded in a counterclockwise direction, but did not go all the way around the city. **Jackal Well** The Hebrew word used here can mean "dragon," "serpent" or "jackal." The spring is probably a source of water in the Tyropoeon Valley, now dried up. **Dung Gate** From the Valley Gate to the Dung Gate was a distance of about 1,500 feet (Ne 3:13). This was the southernmost gate, leading to the Hinnom Valley. It is probably to be identified as the Potsherd Gate mentioned in Jer 19:2. **had been broken**

down The gates and walls of Jerusalem were destroyed by Nebuchadnezzar in 586 BC (2Ki 25:8–12). **2:14 Fountain Gate** Probably led to the En Rogel spring in the southeastern corner of Jerusalem. **King's Pool** Possibly the Pool of Siloam. The Pool of Siloam was fed by an aqueduct created during the reign of Hezekiah that brought water from the Gihon spring. See the infographic "Inscription From Hezekiah's Tunnel" on p. 599. **there was not enough room** The homes on this side of the city were terraced down into the valley. When the wall was destroyed, all the homes collapsed and fell on top of one another, creating a considerable amount of debris. **2:15 the valley** The Kidron Valley, east of the city. **I turned back** Nehemiah's tour of inspection was limited to the southern part of the city wall. **2:16 nobles** This may refer to landowners. Since the Hebrew word used here can be translated "citizens," it is possible that they were simply residents of Jerusalem. However, the common residents of the city seem to be included by the general term "Jews." **2:19 Geshem the Arab** "Arab" is a reference to Geshem's ancestry, as well as to his control of the Arab regions east and south of Judah. If this is the same Geshem mentioned in extra-Biblical inscriptions, he ruled a league of Arabian tribes that took control of northern Arabia, Moab, Edom and the Negev. **heard** The enemies of the Jews were well informed, possibly by traitors within Jerusalem. **they mocked** Together, the three groups mentioned represent the contempt of the nations surrounding Jerusalem and the territory of Judah on all three sides—Samaria to the north, Ammon to the east and Arabia to the south (the Mediterranean Sea borders Judah to the west). **rebelling against the king** The leaders of the opposition group themselves were guilty of what they were accusing Nehemiah of. They were aware that Nehemiah was acting with the king's authority (Ne 2:9). **2:20 share in Jerusalem or any claim or historic right**

men of Jericho built the adjoining section, and Zakkur son of Imri built next to them.

³The Fish Gate was rebuilt by the sons of Hassenaah. They laid its beams and put its doors and bolts and bars in place. ⁴Meremoth son of Uriah, the son of Hakkoz, repaired the next section. Next to him Meshullam son of Berekiah, the son of Meshezabel, made repairs, and next to him Zadok son of Baana also made repairs. ⁵The next section was repaired by the men of Tekoa, but their nobles would not put their shoulders to the work under their supervisors.ᵃ

⁶The Jeshanahᵇ Gate was repaired by Joiada son of Paseah and Meshullam son of Besodeiah. They laid its beams and put its doors with their bolts and bars in place. ⁷Next to them, repairs were made by men from Gibeon and Mizpah — Melatiah of Gibeon and Jadon of Meronoth — places under the authority of the governor of Trans-Euphrates. ⁸Uzziel son of Harhaiah, one of the goldsmiths, repaired the next section; and Hananiah, one of the perfume-makers, made repairs next to that. They restored Jerusalem as far as the Broad Wall. ⁹Repha-

iah son of Hur, ruler of a half-district of Jerusalem, repaired the next section. ¹⁰Adjoining this, Jedaiah son of Harumaph made repairs opposite his house, and Hattush son of Hashabneiah made repairs next to him. ¹¹Malkijah son of Harim and Hasshub son of Pahath-Moab repaired another section and the Tower of the Ovens. ¹²Shallum son of Hallohesh, ruler of a half-district of Jerusalem, repaired the next section with the help of his daughters.

¹³The Valley Gate was repaired by Hanun and the residents of Zanoah. They rebuilt it and put its doors with their bolts and bars in place. They also repaired a thousand cubitsᶜ of the wall as far as the Dung Gate.

¹⁴The Dung Gate was repaired by Malkijah son of Rekab, ruler of the district of Beth Hakkerem. He rebuilt it and put its doors with their bolts and bars in place.

¹⁵The Fountain Gate was repaired by Shallum son of Kol-Hozeh, ruler of the district of Mizpah.

ᵃ 5 Or *their Lord* or *the governor*   ᵇ 6 Or *Old*   ᶜ 13 That is, about 1,500 feet or about 450 meters

---

to it Nehemiah is claiming that the opponents of the Jews have no civic, legal or religious rights in Jerusalem.

3:1–32 This section describes the rebuilding of the Jerusalem wall, which begins at the northeast corner and moves around the city in a counterclockwise direction: the north wall (vv. 1–5); west wall (vv. 6–13); south wall (vv. 14–15); east wall (vv. 16–31); and the eastern stretch of the north wall (v. 32). In some places, the wall needed to be built from the ground up; in other places, repairs needed to be made to the existing wall.

The description centers on the ten gates of the city: the Sheep Gate (vv. 1,32); the Fish Gate (v. 3); the Jeshanah (or Old) Gate (v. 6); the Valley Gate (v. 13); the Dung Gate (v. 14); the Fountain Gate (v. 15); the Water Gate (v. 26); the Horse Gate (v. 28); the East Gate (v. 29); and the Inspection (or Muster) Gate (v. 31). Since the gates were the most vulnerable sections of ancient walls, these were the most important segments of the project.

3:1 Eliashib The grandson of Jeshua (also called Joshua), the high priest during the time of Zerubbabel's rebuilding projects (Ezr 3:2). **Sheep Gate** Located at the northeastern corner of the wall, near the Pool of Bethesda (Jn 5:2). The gate probably took its name from the sheep that were brought through it to be offered on the altar at the nearby temple. The Sheep Gate may have been the same as the Benjamin Gate (Jer 20:2; 37:13). **Tower of the Hundred** The headquarters for the commander of a company of 100 men. The towers mentioned throughout this chapter were specially fortified areas where city inhabitants could make their strongest defense. Archers and slingers stationed in towers could shower attacking enemies with projectiles in relative safety. Since the effectiveness of archers and slingers depended upon their range, these towers were placed strategically throughout the city's walls. **Tower of Hananel** Located at the northernmost part of the wall (Zec 14:10).

3:2 next to them The first part of this chapter (Ne 3:1–15) is joined together by frequent occurrences of the phrases "next to him" or "next to them."

3:3 Fish Gate Near the northwest corner of the city, possibly close to a fish market.

3:4 Meremoth One of the leaders of the priests (Ezr 8:33). He is mentioned later as repairing a second section of the wall (Ne 3:21). **Meshullam** The father-in-law of Jehohanan, the son of Tobiah (6:17–18).

3:5 by the men of Tekoa The city of Tekoa was located about 12 miles south of Jerusalem in an open plain in the Judean wilderness. It was the home of the prophet Amos (Am 1:1). **nobles would not put their shoulders to the work** The only time in this passage where individuals are identified as refusing to participate in the rebuilding project. The leaders of the city may have anticipated the opposition to the rebuilding project, and they did not want to join ranks with Nehemiah, thereby giving opponents a reason to attack their city. The men of Tekoa seem to have compensated for the faults of their nobles by repairing two sections of the wall (Ne 3:27). **supervisors** The Hebrew word used here is plural and can be understood as referring to God (in which case the translation would be "Lord") or to human masters (in which case the translation would be "masters" or "supervisors").

3:6 Jeshanah Gate The name of this gate can be translated "Old" or transliterated as "Jeshanah." If it is the latter, then it likely refers to a town of that name near Bethel (2Ch 13:19).

3:7 places under the authority of the governor The meaning of this phrase is unclear, because the Hebrew word *kisse* used here could refer to a seat (a physical site of authority) or to authority. It likely refers to Mizpah as the official residence of the provincial governor when he visited Judah (for Mizpah as an administrative center, see 2Ki 25:23; Jer 40:5–12).

3:8 Broad Wall Located between the Ephraim Gate and the Tower of the Ovens (Ne 12:38–39).

3:9 ruler of a half-district Jerusalem was divided into two districts, each governed by an official.

3:10 opposite his house Nehemiah assigned workers to repair areas near where they lived or worked.

3:15 Pool of Siloam Probably the same as the King's

He rebuilt it, roofing it over and putting its doors and bolts and bars in place. He also repaired the wall of the Pool of Siloam,ᵃ by the King's Garden, as far as the steps going down from the City of David. ¹⁶Beyond him, Nehemiah son of Azbuk, ruler of a half-district of Beth Zur, made repairs up to a point opposite the tombsᵇ of David, as far as the artificial pool and the House of the Heroes.

¹⁷Next to him, the repairs were made by the Levites under Rehum son of Bani. Beside him, Hashabiah, ruler of half the district of Keilah, carried out repairs for his district. ¹⁸Next to him, the repairs were made by their fellow Levites under Binnuiᶜ son of Henadad, ruler of the other half-district of Keilah. ¹⁹Next to him, Ezer son of Jeshua, ruler of Mizpah, repaired another section, from a point facing the ascent to the armory as far as the angle of the wall. ²⁰Next to him, Baruch son of Zabbai zealously repaired another section, from the angle to the entrance of the house of Eliashib the high priest. ²¹Next to him, Meremoth son of Uriah, the son of Hakkoz, repaired another section, from the entrance of Eliashib's house to the end of it. ²²The repairs next to him were made by the priests from the surrounding region. ²³Beyond them, Benjamin and Hasshub made repairs in front of their house; and next to them, Azariah son of Maaseiah, the son of Ananiah, made repairs beside his house. ²⁴Next to him, Binnui son of Henadad repaired another section, from Azariah's house to the angle and the corner, ²⁵and Palal son of Uzai worked opposite the angle and the tower projecting from the upper palace near the court of the guard. Next to him, Pedaiah son of Parosh ²⁶and the temple servants living on the hill of Ophel made repairs up to a point opposite

the Water Gate toward the east and the projecting tower. ²⁷Next to them, the men of Tekoa repaired another section, from the great projecting tower to the wall of Ophel.

²⁸Above the Horse Gate, the priests made repairs, each in front of his own house. ²⁹Next to them, Zadok son of Immer made repairs opposite his house. Next to him, Shemaiah son of Shekaniah, the guard at the East Gate, made repairs. ³⁰Next to him, Hananiah son of Shelemiah, and Hanun, the sixth son of Zalaph, repaired another section. Next to them, Meshullam son of Berekiah made repairs opposite his living quarters. ³¹Next to him, Malkijah, one of the goldsmiths, made repairs as far as the house of the temple servants and the merchants, opposite the Inspection Gate, and as far as the room above the corner; ³²and between the room above the corner and the Sheep Gate the goldsmiths and merchants made repairs.

Opposition to the Rebuilding

4ᵈ When Sanballat heard that we were rebuilding the wall, he became angry and was greatly incensed. He ridiculed the Jews, ²and in the presence of his associates and the army of Samaria, he said, "What are those feeble Jews doing? Will they restore their wall? Will they offer sacrifices? Will they finish in a day? Can they bring the stones back to life from those heaps of rubble — burned as they are?"

ᵃ 15 Hebrew *Shelah*, a variant of *Shiloah*, that is, Siloam
ᵇ 16 Hebrew; Septuagint, some Vulgate manuscripts and Syriac *tomb*   ᶜ 18 Two Hebrew manuscripts and Syriac (see also Septuagint and verse 24); most Hebrew manuscripts *Bavvai*
ᵈ In Hebrew texts 4:1-6 is numbered 3:33-38, and 4:7-23 is numbered 4:1-17.

Pool (see note on 2:14). **King's Garden** Probably located near the southeastern corner of the wall.
3:16 Beyond him The sections in the remainder of the chapter are joined by the Hebrew term *acharai*, meaning "after him." See note on v. 2. **House of the Heroes** This may have been a military barracks; the name associates it with David's mighty men (2Sa 23:8–39).
3:18 under Binnui son of Henadad Most Hebrew manuscripts read "Bavvai" here, but it most likely refers to the Binnui of Ne 3:24 and 10:9. The name Bavvai is unknown in Hebrew. Verse 24 also states that Binnui repaired another section, implying that he had previously completed a different one — likely the section mentioned here.
3:25 court of the guard The site where King Zedekiah imprisoned the prophet Jeremiah for prophesying that Jerusalem would fall to the Babylonians and that he would be taken captive by Nebuchadnezzar (Jer 32:2).
3:26 Ophel The beginning of the hill on which the temple was located (see 2Ch 27:3; 33:14). **Water Gate** Located near the Gihon spring, the main water source for Jerusalem.
3:27 wall of Ophel An internal wall running from east to west that divided the City of David in the south from the Temple Mount in the north (2Ch 27:3).
3:28 Horse Gate The easternmost part of the city (Jer

31:40) overlooking the Kidron Valley. This gate may have been an entrance for cavalry into the palace courtyard.
3:29 East Gate Probably a gate of the temple court, not a gate of the city wall.
3:30 his living quarters Possibly a chamber of the temple (Ne 12:44; 13:7).
3:31 room above the corner Probably a watchtower situated at the northeastern corner of the city.

4:1–23 The Jews encounter rage, mockery and the threat of physical harm from those who oppose their rebuilding of Jerusalem's walls. Confident in God and undeterred, Nehemiah arms the people and continues the work.
4:1 he became angry and was greatly incensed This phrase emphasizes the extreme anger of Sanballat at the rebuilding of Jerusalem's walls.
4:2 his associates Likely refers to Sanballat's fellow officials, including Tobiah. However, the Hebrew term used here, *echay* (literally rendered as "brothers") may indicate that Sanballat's literal brothers were present. **army** The Hebrew word used here, *chayil*, designates a group of powerful people. As such, the term may refer to an army or to a retinue of wealthy nobles. However, Sanballat more likely had military officers with him rather than the wealthy men of Samaria. **feeble** Sanballat

³Tobiah the Ammonite, who was at his side, said, "What they are building — even a fox climbing up on it would break down their wall of stones!"

⁴Hear us, our God, for we are despised. Turn their insults back on their own heads. Give them over as plunder in a land of captivity. ⁵Do not cover up their guilt or blot out their sins from your sight, for they have thrown insults in the face of[a] the builders.

⁶So we rebuilt the wall till all of it reached half its height, for the people worked with all their heart.

⁷But when Sanballat, Tobiah, the Arabs, the Ammonites and the people of Ashdod heard that the repairs to Jerusalem's walls had gone ahead and that the gaps were being closed, they were very angry. ⁸They all plotted together to come and fight against Jerusalem and stir up trouble against it. ⁹But we prayed to our God and posted a guard day and night to meet this threat.

¹⁰Meanwhile, the people in Judah said, "The strength of the laborers is giving out, and there is so much rubble that we cannot rebuild the wall."

¹¹Also our enemies said, "Before they know it or see us, we will be right there among them and will kill them and put an end to the work."

¹²Then the Jews who lived near them came and told us ten times over, "Wherever you turn, they will attack us."

¹³Therefore I stationed some of the people behind the lowest points of the wall at the exposed places, posting them by families, with their swords, spears and bows. ¹⁴After I looked things over, I stood up and said to the nobles, the officials and the rest of the people, "Don't be afraid of them. Remember the Lord, who is great and awesome, and fight for your families, your sons and your daughters, your wives and your homes."

¹⁵When our enemies heard that we were aware of their plot and that God had frustrated it, we all returned to the wall, each to our own work.

¹⁶From that day on, half of my men did the work, while the other half were equipped with spears, shields, bows and armor. The officers posted themselves behind all the people of Judah ¹⁷who were building the wall. Those who carried materials did their work with one hand and held

a 5 Or have aroused your anger before

---

seems to be describing the Jewish people as a dying people group — one that is languishing or in the last days of its existence. **Will they offer sacrifices** Sanballat may be referring to his desire to see religious activity cease in Jerusalem; sacrifices were already being offered (Ezr 6:12–18). He could also be referring to sacrifices that may be offered after the wall rebuilding project was a success (compare Ne 12:43). It could have also been that sacrifices had temporarily ceased, because of the intensity of persecution.

4:3 would break down their wall of stones Tobiah's sarcastic remark is a reference to the problems affiliated with the wall up to this point. Tobiah's statement reveals the contempt he and others have for the efforts of the Jewish people.

4:4–5 This prayer has no introductory remark about who speaks it, but the narrative implies that it is said by Nehemiah, since he is the character who has spoken in the first-person up to this point (2:9–20). This prayer is based on the promises made by God in the Abrahamic covenant — specifically, the promise to bless those who blessed Abraham's descendants and curse those who cursed them (Ge 12:1–3). Since Yahweh had already pronounced judgment on Israel's enemies (Joel 3; Jer 46–49), the prayer simply calls God to act on what he promised. This prayer is reminiscent of those found in the Prophets (Ob 15–21; Hab 2:6–17) and the Psalms (Ps 35; 58; 59; 69; 109; 137).

4:4 Turn their insults back on their own heads Describes a reversal of fortune — poetic justice.

4:5 blot out their sins from your sight A request that the adversaries of the Jewish people be shown no mercy, but instead that the punishment of their sins come upon them. Jeremiah uses the same phrase in a prayer concerning his adversaries in Jer 18:23.

4:6 we rebuilt the wall A statement that emphasizes the people's resolution in the face of opposition.

4:7 Sanballat, Tobiah, the Arabs Indicates opposition from all sides. See Ne 2:19 and note.

4:8 stir up trouble against it The enemies of the Jewish people intend to disrupt the work on the wall before it may be completed — by disorganizing or distracting them.

4:10 people in Judah said The Jewish people were lamenting their circumstances (compare note on La 1:1–5:22). Their resolve for the task of completing the wall is fading; they are in despair. **there is so much rubble** This is probably a reference to walls that were still collapsed from Nebuchadnezzar's destruction of Jerusalem in 586 BC (2Ki 25:8–12; compare Ne 2:13,17).

4:11 Before they know it or see us The enemies of the Jewish people believed they could secretly undermine the work of the Jewish people and ultimately kill them.

4:12 ten times Possibly idiomatic for a large number (Ge 31:7; Nu 14:22; Job 19:3). The people who had come in from the surrounding villages to work on the wall are being told by their friends and relatives to give up the work and protect themselves.

4:13 lowest points It seems that Nehemiah places people as military guards according to their family or tribal distinctions in locations particularly vulnerable to attack, but still sheltered.

4:14 the Lord Although the Hebrew word used here, *adon*, is the generic word for "lord" or "master" and not the divine name, the context suggests Nehemiah is talking about God (compare Ne 4:20).

4:15 returned to the wall Nehemiah's guards, and overall show of force, had the effect of not just defending the Jewish people, but also intimidating the enemy.

4:16 my men Probably refers to a group of men under the personal authority of Nehemiah as governor (5:10; 13:19). However, the Hebrew term here (*na'ar*) could refer to the Jewish returned exiles in general. **armor** It seems that these people were not just wearing armor, but were also holding armor, likely for the instance that it was needed by others.

a weapon in the other, [18]and each of the builders wore his sword at his side as he worked. But the man who sounded the trumpet stayed with me.

[19]Then I said to the nobles, the officials and the rest of the people, "The work is extensive and spread out, and we are widely separated from each other along the wall. [20]Wherever you hear the sound of the trumpet, join us there. Our God will fight for us!"

[21]So we continued the work with half the men holding spears, from the first light of dawn till the stars came out. [22]At that time I also said to the people, "Have every man and his helper stay inside Jerusalem at night, so they can serve us as guards by night and as workers by day." [23]Neither I nor my brothers nor my men nor the guards with me took off our clothes; each had his weapon, even when he went for water.[a]

Nehemiah Helps the Poor

5 Now the men and their wives raised a great outcry against their fellow Jews. [2]Some were saying, "We and our sons and daughters are nu-merous; in order for us to eat and stay alive, we must get grain."

[3]Others were saying, "We are mortgaging our fields, our vineyards and our homes to get grain during the famine."

[4]Still others were saying, "We have had to borrow money to pay the king's tax on our fields and vineyards. [5]Although we are of the same flesh and blood as our fellow Jews and though our children are as good as theirs, yet we have to subject our sons and daughters to slavery. Some of our daughters have already been enslaved, but we are powerless, because our fields and our vineyards belong to others."

[6]When I heard their outcry and these charges, I was very angry. [7]I pondered them in my mind and then accused the nobles and officials. I told them, "You are charging your own people interest!" So I called together a large meeting to deal with them [8]and said: "As far as possible, we have bought back our fellow Jews who were sold to the Gentiles. Now

[a] 23 The meaning of the Hebrew for this clause is uncertain.

4:17–18 Nehemiah notes that those who are carrying loads—either for the wall or to remove rubble—did so in a way that they could hold their weapon in one hand. Those building the wall, needing to use both hands, wore their sword on their side.

4:18 at his side These workers needed both hands free to work on the wall. **the trumpet** Refers to a ram's horn, commonly used for signal calls.

4:20 the sound of the trumpet An inventive plan to defend the city, as the people were separated over a vast area (compare Jos 6). **God will fight for us** Recalls earlier passages in which God is seen as a divine warrior (see Ex 14:14; Dt 3:22).

4:21 with half the men holding spears Probably indicates that half of the men present constantly held spears in their hands, during every waking hour.

4:22 every man and his helper stay inside Jerusalem at night If the men ventured outside the city at night, they became vulnerable to attack on the open roads. Also, if a large portion of the defenders left for the evening, those who remained in the city would be in danger of an evening assault.

4:23 each had his weapon The terse Hebrew phrase used here—*ish shilcho hammayim* (literally, "a man, his weapon, the waters")—could mean that the men did not even remove their weapons when bathing or getting a drink of water. Alternately, the Hebrew word for "water" is graphically similar to the word for "right hand," so the text may have originally indicated that they kept their weapons close at hand. Either way, they were constantly on guard.

5:1–13 In Ne 4 and 6, Nehemiah deals with external threats to the community in Jerusalem. Here, he is faced with an internal crisis: economic inequality. Two factors are explicitly blamed for economic hardships in Judah: famine (v. 3) and heavy taxation (v. 4). With a famine happening, demand for food undoubtedly would have inflated prices. The work of rebuilding the wall may also have contributed since people would have had less time for agriculture.

There are three groups negatively affected by these hardships: Those who apparently owned no land (v. 2); those who owned some land but were being forced to mortgage it (v. 3); and those who did not have the means to pay taxes (v. 4). All three groups were forced to go into debt to survive, thus putting their future in jeopardy. The wealthier members of the community were taking advantage of the situation to enrich themselves (vv. 7–8). Nehemiah orders them to stop their unfair lending practices and restore the property they acquired unethically (vv. 9–13).

5:2 we must get grain The people in this group seem to have no means of obtaining grain—perhaps because they are not land holders and thus have no way of growing food on their own.

5:3 mortgaging our fields In this time of famine, small landowners were being forced to give up their means of subsistence in order to get food in the short term. **vineyards** One of the staples of Israel's economy. The nation was famous for its wine—especially the area surrounding Gibeon, situated just north of Jerusalem. See the infographic "A Winepress in Ancient Israel" on p. 1157. **famine** Poor harvests were common in the postexilic period (Hag 1:5–6,10–11; 2:15–16,19; Mal 3:9–12).

5:4 to pay the king's tax Refers to a property or real estate tax. Persians used revenue from taxation to build their empire. The Persians were famous for wars and building projects, which drained the national treasury. Earlier empires, such as the Hittites, Assyrians and Egyptians, relied on tribute paid by conquered territories. Unwilling to rely on such an unstable practice, the Babylonians created a system of taxation. Successive empires, including the Persians, Greeks and Romans, followed Babylonian practice.

5:5 to slavery In the ancient Near East, individuals sold themselves or their children into the service of a creditor to pay off debts, a practice known as debt slavery. Old Testament law stipulated that debt slaves would be

you are selling your own people, only for them to be sold back to us!" They kept quiet, because they could find nothing to say.

⁹So I continued, "What you are doing is not right. Shouldn't you walk in the fear of our God to avoid the reproach of our Gentile enemies? ¹⁰I and my brothers and my men are also lending the people money and grain. But let us stop charging interest! ¹¹Give back to them immediately their fields, vineyards, olive groves and houses, and also the interest you are charging them — one percent of the money, grain, new wine and olive oil."

¹²"We will give it back," they said. "And we will not demand anything more from them. We will do as you say."

Then I summoned the priests and made the nobles and officials take an oath to do what they had promised. ¹³I also shook out the folds of my robe and said, "In this way may God shake out of their house and possessions anyone who does not keep this promise. So may such a person be shaken out and emptied!"

At this the whole assembly said, "Amen," and praised the LORD. And the people did as they had promised.

¹⁴Moreover, from the twentieth year of King Artaxerxes, when I was appointed to be their governor in the land of Judah, until his thirty-second year — twelve years — neither I nor my brothers ate the food allotted to the governor. ¹⁵But the earlier governors — those preceding me — placed a heavy burden on the people and took forty shekels[a] of silver from them in addition to food and wine. Their assistants also lorded it over the people. But out of reverence for God I did not act like that. ¹⁶Instead, I devoted myself to the work on this wall. All my men were assembled there for the work; we[b] did not acquire any land.

¹⁷Furthermore, a hundred and fifty Jews and officials ate at my table, as well as those who came to us from the surrounding nations. ¹⁸Each day one ox, six choice sheep and some poultry were prepared for me, and every ten days an abundant supply of wine of all kinds. In spite of all this, I never demanded the food allotted to the governor, because the demands were heavy on these people.

¹⁹Remember me with favor, my God, for all I have done for these people.

---

[a] 15 That is, about 1 pound or about 460 grams   [b] 16 Most Hebrew manuscripts; some Hebrew manuscripts, Septuagint, Vulgate and Syriac *I*

---

released from their duties when the debt was paid off or at the seventh year (Ex 21:2; Dt 15:12).

5:6 I was very angry This conflict posed a threat not only to the rebuilding project but to the unity of the community of returned exiles. Societal mistreatment originally tore the nation apart when Jeroboam led the ten northern tribes to secede from the rule of Rehoboam (1Ki 12).

5:7 accused The Hebrew term used here, *arivoh*, has legal-judicial significance. The prophets often used this term to describe Yahweh's covenantal lawsuit against those guilty of breaking his laws (e.g., Isa 3:13; Jer 2:9; Hos 4:1; Mic 6:1). **the nobles and officials** Nehemiah courageously opposes the selfish behavior of the strong in the community. This kind of unjust treatment of the weak was in part what led to the exile in the first place (Isa 5:8–10). **You are charging your own people interest** Old Testament law forbade the Israelites from charging interest when making loans to fellow Jews (Ex 22:25).

5:8 bought back our fellow Jews Wealthy Jews made an effort to buy back many of the Jewish descendants of those originally taken into slavery by the Assyrians and Babylonians. Such efforts made the return of these slaves to Jerusalem possible.

5:11 one percent of the money Probably refers to the amount of interest commonly charged by the creditors. A one percent monthly interest rate equals a 12 percent annual rate.

5:13 I also shook out the folds of my robe In ancient times, people often carried their personal belongings in the folds of their clothing. These folds essentially served as pockets. **may God shake out of their house and possessions anyone** Nehemiah's symbolic act meant to show the nation that if they disobeyed God, he would shake them out just like this garment. They would have nothing of value left after Yahweh was finished judging them.

5:14–19 Here Nehemiah reveals how he lived by example and did not take advantage of the people as previous governors had done. As governor, he was entitled to compensation derived from collection of taxes for Persia (Ne 5:14). Nehemiah indicates that while previous governors took more than their rightful compensation, he did not even take his due (v. 15). He was still able to provide food for 150 people or more, despite foregoing this official allowance (vv. 17–18).

5:14 twentieth year of King Artaxerxes Referring to 445 BC. See the timeline "Dates Related to Ezra, Nehemiah and Esther" on p. 716. **governor** This is the first indication in the text of Nehemiah's official title. **his thirty-second year** Referring to 433 BC.

5:15 the earlier governors Sheshbazzar and Zerubbabel are the only known former governors of Judah (see Ezr 5:14; Hag 1:1). However, it is not likely that Nehemiah was speaking about them; there had been a gap of some years between them and Nehemiah. **shekels** A shekel weighed 11.4 grams. Forty shekels of silver was approximately a pound of silver.

5:17 Jews and officials In the Persian custom, local nobles and officials routinely dined at the table of the king.

5:19 Remember This is the first of the prayers in which Nehemiah asks God to remember (Ne 6:14; 13:14,22,29,31). These remembrance prayers are an allusion to the curses and blessings connected to Yahweh's covenant with Israel (Lev 26; Dt 28). Here, the remembrance is positive: Nehemiah anticipates Yahweh's favor because of the good he has done on behalf of Israel (Ne 13:14,22,31). Later in the book, the negative aspect will be revealed as Nehemiah anticipates the judgment of God on those who oppose his mission (6:14; 13:29).

Further Opposition to the Rebuilding

6 When word came to Sanballat, Tobiah, Geshem the Arab and the rest of our enemies that I had rebuilt the wall and not a gap was left in it — though up to that time I had not set the doors in the gates — ²Sanballat and Geshem sent me this message: "Come, let us meet together in one of the villages*a* on the plain of Ono."

But they were scheming to harm me; ³so I sent messengers to them with this reply: "I am carrying on a great project and cannot go down. Why should the work stop while I leave it and go down to you?" ⁴Four times they sent me the same message, and each time I gave them the same answer.

⁵Then, the fifth time, Sanballat sent his aide to me with the same message, and in his hand was an unsealed letter ⁶in which was written:

"It is reported among the nations — and Geshem*b* says it is true — that you and the Jews are plotting to revolt, and therefore you are building the wall. Moreover, according to these reports you are about to become their king ⁷and have even appointed prophets to make this proclamation about you in Jerusalem: 'There is a king in Judah!' Now this report will get back to the king; so come, let us meet together."

⁸I sent him this reply: "Nothing like what you are saying is happening; you are just making it up out of your head."

⁹They were all trying to frighten us, thinking, "Their hands will get too weak for the work, and it will not be completed."

But I prayed, "Now strengthen my hands."

¹⁰One day I went to the house of Shemaiah son of Delaiah, the son of Mehetabel, who was shut in at his home. He said, "Let us meet in the house of God, inside the temple, and let us close the temple doors, because men are coming to kill you — by night they are coming to kill you."

¹¹But I said, "Should a man like me run away? Or should someone like me go into the temple to save his life? I will not go!" ¹²I realized that God had not sent him, but that he had prophesied against me because Tobiah and Sanballat had hired him. ¹³He had been hired to intimidate me so that I would commit a sin by doing this, and then they would give me a bad name to discredit me.

¹⁴Remember Tobiah and Sanballat, my God, because of what they have done; remember also the prophet Noadiah and how she and the rest of the prophets have been trying to intimidate me. ¹⁵So the wall was completed on the twenty-fifth of Elul, in fifty-two days.

Opposition to the Completed Wall

¹⁶When all our enemies heard about this, all the surrounding nations were afraid and lost their self-confidence, because they realized that this work had been done with the help of our God.

¹⁷Also, in those days the nobles of Judah were sending many letters to Tobiah, and replies from Tobiah kept coming to them. ¹⁸For many in Judah were under oath to him, since he was son-in-law to Shekaniah son of Arah, and his son Jehohanan

a 2 Or *in Kephirim*   *b* 6 Hebrew *Gashmu,* a variant of *Geshem*

6:1–14 Here the narrative returns to the external opposition to the rebuilding of Jerusalem. This time, Nehemiah's enemies try to lure him to an unsafe place outside the city (vv. 1–10), and then try to discredit him (vv. 11–14). The events of these verses likely take place near the end of the 52-day period in which the walls were rebuilt.

6:1 I had not set the doors The work on the wall was almost complete. Placing doors in the gates was the final stage of the project.

6:2 one of the villages Many English translations understand the Hebrew word used here, *kephirim,* as a proper name. In this case, Kephirim might be the same as the similar-sounding Kephirah (Jos 9:17; 18:26; Ezr 2:25). Other translations render it "[one of] the villages." **plain of Ono** Also called the Valley of Craftsmen (Ne 11:35), this place is located approximately 25 miles northwest of Jerusalem. Ono was originally a city belonging to the tribe of Benjamin (1Ch 8:1,12). **scheming to harm me** Nehemiah recognized that his enemies' invitation was insincere.

6:3 go down A topographical, not directional, reference. Jerusalem is higher in elevation than the plain of Ono.

6:5 an unsealed letter The Hebrew text here refers to an unsealed sheet of papyrus or an ostracon (a pottery shard). An open letter allowed anybody to read it and spread the rumor.

6:9 strengthen my hands This phrase is a Hebrew idiom denoting empowerment (Jer 23:14; compare Heb 12:12).

6:10 Shemaiah He is not mentioned elsewhere, but the length of Shemaiah's genealogy indicates he was probably an important person in the community.

6:11 go into the temple Laymen were not allowed to enter the temple (Nu 18:7). King Uzziah attempted it and was stricken with leprosy (2Ch 26:16–20).

6:12 Tobiah and Sanballat The first time the name of Tobiah precedes Sanballat when the two are mentioned together (Ne 2:10,19; 4:7; 6:1), suggesting that Tobiah instigated this particular plot. The phenomenon also occurs in v. 14 in Nehemiah's prayer regarding this incident.

6:14 Remember Tobiah and Sanballat The second of the remembrance prayers offered in Nehemiah (5:19; 13:14,22,29,31). See note on 5:19. **prophet Noadiah** One of four prophets mentioned by name in the OT (the others are Miriam, Deborah and Huldah; Ex 15:20; Jdg 4:4; 2Ki 22:14; compare Isa 8:3; Eze 13:17–23).

6:15–19 Even though the wall had been completed, opposition to Nehemiah from Tobiah and his allies within the city continued.

6:15 fifty-two days This building project was completed in a very short time. The later Jewish historian Josephus regarded this time frame as improbable; he refers to a period of two years and four months (Josephus, *Antiquities* 11.5.8).

had married the daughter of Meshullam son of Berekiah. [19]Moreover, they kept reporting to me his good deeds and then telling him what I said. And Tobiah sent letters to intimidate me.

7 After the wall had been rebuilt and I had set the doors in place, the gatekeepers, the musicians and the Levites were appointed. [2]I put in charge of Jerusalem my brother Hanani, along with Hananiah the commander of the citadel, because he was a man of integrity and feared God more than most people do. [3]I said to them, "The gates of Jerusalem are not to be opened until the sun is hot. While the gatekeepers are still on duty, have them shut the doors and bar them. Also appoint residents of Jerusalem as guards, some at their posts and some near their own houses."

The List of the Exiles Who Returned

7:6-73pp — Ezr 2:1-70

[4]Now the city was large and spacious, but there were few people in it, and the houses had not yet been rebuilt. [5]So my God put it into my heart to assemble the nobles, the officials and the common people for registration by families. I found the genealogical record of those who had been the first to return. This is what I found written there:

[6]These are the people of the province who came up from the captivity of the exiles whom Nebuchadnezzar king of Babylon had taken captive (they returned to Jerusalem and Judah, each to his own town, [7]in company with Zerubbabel, Joshua, Nehemiah, Azariah, Raamiah, Nahamani, Mordecai, Bilshan, Mispereth, Bigvai, Nehum and Baanah):

The list of the men of Israel:

[8]the descendants of Parosh	2,172
[9]of Shephatiah	372
[10]of Arah	652
[11]of Pahath-Moab (through the line of Jeshua and Joab)	2,818
[12]of Elam	1,254
[13]of Zattu	845
[14]of Zakkai	760
[15]of Binnui	648
[16]of Bebai	628
[17]of Azgad	2,322
[18]of Adonikam	667
[19]of Bigvai	2,067

[20]of Adin	655
[21]of Ater (through Hezekiah)	98
[22]of Hashum	328
[23]of Bezai	324
[24]of Hariph	112
[25]of Gibeon	95
[26]the men of Bethlehem and Netophah	188
[27]of Anathoth	128
[28]of Beth Azmaveth	42
[29]of Kiriath Jearim, Kephirah and Beeroth	743
[30]of Ramah and Geba	621
[31]of Mikmash	122
[32]of Bethel and Ai	123
[33]of the other Nebo	52
[34]of the other Elam	1,254
[35]of Harim	320
[36]of Jericho	345
[37]of Lod, Hadid and Ono	721
[38]of Senaah	3,930

[39]The priests:

the descendants of Jedaiah (through the family of Jeshua)	973
[40]of Immer	1,052
[41]of Pashhur	1,247
[42]of Harim	1,017

[43]The Levites:

the descendants of Jeshua (through Kadmiel through the line of Hodaviah)	74

[44]The musicians:

the descendants of Asaph	148

[45]The gatekeepers:

the descendants of Shallum, Ater, Talmon, Akkub, Hatita and Shobai	138

[46]The temple servants:

the descendants of
Ziha, Hasupha, Tabbaoth,
[47]Keros, Sia, Padon,
[48]Lebana, Hagaba, Shalmai,
[49]Hanan, Giddel, Gahar,
[50]Reaiah, Rezin, Nekoda,

7:1–4 Unfazed by continued opposition, Nehemiah continues his rebuilding efforts by appointing officers to ensure the proper functioning of the city.

7:2 Hanani The same Hanani who had given Nehemiah the bad news about Jerusalem in Ne 1:2.

7:3 until the sun is hot Normally the gates would be opened at sunrise, but this routine is altered to guard against a surprise attack.

7:5–73 This section lists the Jews who had returned to Jerusalem from Babylon years before. It is nearly identical with the list in Ezr 2. Nehemiah's purpose in presenting this genealogical information is to find out which families had returned and to encourage the people in his own day to settle in and rebuild Jerusalem (see Ne 7:4; 11:1–3). See note on Ezr 2:1–70.

51 Gazzam, Uzza, Paseah,
52 Besai, Meunim, Nephusim,
53 Bakbuk, Hakupha, Harhur,
54 Bazluth, Mehida, Harsha,
55 Barkos, Sisera, Temah,
56 Neziah and Hatipha

57 The descendants of the servants of Solomon:

the descendants of
    Sotai, Sophereth, Perida,
58 Jaala, Darkon, Giddel,
59 Shephatiah, Hattil,
    Pokereth-Hazzebaim and Amon

60 The temple servants and the
    descendants of the servants of
    Solomon   392

61 The following came up from the towns
of Tel Melah, Tel Harsha, Kerub, Addon and
Immer, but they could not show that their
families were descended from Israel:

62 the descendants of
    Delaiah, Tobiah and Nekoda   642

63 And from among the priests:

the descendants of
    Hobaiah, Hakkoz and Barzillai (a
    man who had married a daughter of
    Barzillai the Gileadite and was called
    by that name).
64 These searched for their family records,
but they could not find them and so were
excluded from the priesthood as unclean.
65 The governor, therefore, ordered them not
to eat any of the most sacred food until there
should be a priest ministering with the Urim
and Thummim.

66 The whole company numbered 42,360,
67 besides their 7,337 male and female slaves;
and they also had 245 male and female singers. 68 There were 736 horses, 245 mules,[a]
69 435 camels and 6,720 donkeys.

70 Some of the heads of the families contributed to the work. The governor gave to
the treasury 1,000 darics[b] of gold, 50 bowls
and 530 garments for priests. 71 Some of the
heads of the families gave to the treasury
for the work 20,000 darics[c] of gold and
2,200 minas[d] of silver. 72 The total given by
the rest of the people was 20,000 darics of
gold, 2,000 minas[e] of silver and 67 garments
for priests.
73 The priests, the Levites, the gatekeepers,
the musicians and the temple servants, along
with certain of the people and the rest of the
Israelites, settled in their own towns.

Ezra Reads the Law

8 When the seventh month came and the Israelites
had settled in their towns, 1 all the people came
together as one in the square before the Water Gate. They told Ezra the teacher of the Law to
bring out the Book of the Law of Moses, which the
LORD had commanded for Israel.
2 So on the first day of the seventh month Ezra
the priest brought the Law before the assembly,
which was made up of men and women and all
who were able to understand. 3 He read it aloud

a 68 Some Hebrew manuscripts (see also Ezra 2:66); most
Hebrew manuscripts do not have this verse.   *b* 70 That is,
about 19 pounds or about 8.4 kilograms   *c* 71 That is, about
375 pounds or about 170 kilograms; also in verse 72   *d* 71 That
is, about 1 1/3 tons or about 1.2 metric tons   *e* 72 That is,
about 1 1/4 tons or about 1.1 metric tons

7:64 searched for their family records Some of the
people who claimed priestly heritage were unable to prove
their ancestry (compare Ezr 2:62 and note). Proof of
proper lineage was a serious matter in postexilic Judah.
See note on 1Ch 1:1—9:44.
7:73 the seventh month Referring to the Jewish month
of Tishri. The year is still 444 BC. The last dated event
in the book was the twenty-fifth day of the sixth month,
Elul (Ne 6:15). Six days have now passed since the
completion of the wall of Jerusalem.
8:1–18 With the project to rebuild the walls of Jerusalem complete (6:15), the community turns to the task
of renewing their commitment to Yahweh. The events of
chs. 8–9 begin about a week after the rebuilding was
completed (see note on 7:73) and take place over the
span of 24 days. On the first day of the seventh month
(Lev 23:24), the people ask Ezra to read them the Law
of Moses (Ne 8:1–8). This public reading of the Torah
(or Mosaic Law) marks the moment when the people
symbolically receive God's law and commit to it just as
their forefathers had done (vv. 9–12; 9:38; compare
Ex 24:7). The reading of the Torah inspires the people
to observe the Festival of Tabernacles (or Booths) that

was prescribed for the seventh month (Ne 8:13–18; Dt
16:13–15). Illustrating how ignorant Israel had been of
Yahweh's commandments, the text observes that the
festival had not been observed properly (with the people
actually living in temporary shelters) since the time of
Joshua son of Nun (Ne 8:17).

8:1 Ezra Ezra the scribe enters the narrative of the book
of Nehemiah for the first time. See Ezr 7:6 and note.
Book of the Law of Moses The nature and content of
this Book of the Law is uncertain. One possibility is that
it contained the canonical five books of Moses (Genesis,
Exodus, Leviticus, Numbers and Deuteronomy; also called
the Pentateuch). Alternately, it may have been a copy of
the book of Deuteronomy. The practice of reading the
Torah during the Festival of Booths (or Tabernacles) is commanded in Dt 31:9–13. Similarly, some of the religious
concerns raised in Ezra and Nehemiah are grounded in
Deuteronomic law such as the conflict over intermarriage
(see Ezr 9:1—10:44 and note; compare Dt 7:1–7).
8:2 first day of the seventh month The first day of
the Jewish month of Tishri was the day of the Festival of
Trumpets (Lev 23:24). See the table "Israelite Calendar"

from daybreak till noon as he faced the square before the Water Gate in the presence of the men, women and others who could understand. And all the people listened attentively to the Book of the Law.

⁴Ezra the teacher of the Law stood on a high wooden platform built for the occasion. Beside him on his right stood Mattithiah, Shema, Anaiah, Uriah, Hilkiah and Maaseiah; and on his left were Pedaiah, Mishael, Malkijah, Hashum, Hashbaddanah, Zechariah and Meshullam.

⁵Ezra opened the book. All the people could see him because he was standing above them; and as he opened it, the people all stood up. ⁶Ezra praised the LORD, the great God; and all the people lifted their hands and responded, "Amen! Amen!" Then they bowed down and worshiped the LORD with their faces to the ground.

⁷The Levites — Jeshua, Bani, Sherebiah, Jamin, Akkub, Shabbethai, Hodiah, Maaseiah, Kelita, Azariah, Jozabad, Hanan and Pelaiah — instructed the people in the Law while the people were standing there. ⁸They read from the Book of the Law of God, making it clear*ᵃ* and giving the meaning so that the people understood what was being read.

⁹Then Nehemiah the governor, Ezra the priest and teacher of the Law, and the Levites who were instructing the people said to them all, "This day is holy to the LORD your God. Do not mourn or weep." For all the people had been weeping as they listened to the words of the Law.

¹⁰Nehemiah said, "Go and enjoy choice food and sweet drinks, and send some to those who have nothing prepared. This day is holy to our Lord. Do not grieve, for the joy of the LORD is your strength."

¹¹The Levites calmed all the people, saying, "Be still, for this is a holy day. Do not grieve."

¹²Then all the people went away to eat and drink, to send portions of food and to celebrate with great joy, because they now understood the words that had been made known to them.

¹³On the second day of the month, the heads of all the families, along with the priests and the Levites, gathered around Ezra the teacher to give attention to the words of the Law. ¹⁴They found written in the Law, which the LORD had commanded through Moses, that the Israelites were to live in temporary shelters during the festival of the seventh month ¹⁵and that they should proclaim this word and spread it throughout their towns and in Jerusalem: "Go out into the hill country and bring back branches from olive and wild olive trees, and from myrtles, palms and shade trees, to make temporary shelters" — as it is written.*ᵇ*

¹⁶So the people went out and brought back branches and built themselves temporary shelters on their own roofs, in their courtyards, in the courts of the house of God and in the square by the Water Gate and the one by the Gate of Ephraim. ¹⁷The whole company that had returned from exile built temporary shelters and lived in them. From the days of Joshua son of Nun until that day, the Israelites had not celebrated it like this. And their joy was very great.

¹⁸Day after day, from the first day to the last, Ezra read from the Book of the Law of God. They celebrated the festival for seven days, and on the eighth day, in accordance with the regulation, there was an assembly.

ᵃ 8 Or God, translating it   ᵇ 15 See Lev. 23:37-40.

---

on p. 763. **all who were able to understand** Includes children who were of sufficient age to understand the reading of the Law (compare Dt 31:12).

8:4 a high wooden platform This Hebrew term is routinely used to refer to military strongholds (or towers) in Nehemiah (Ne 3:1,11,25,26,27). This platform must have been large enough to hold Ezra and his 13 associates.

8:6 they bowed down and worshiped These Hebrew terms for bowing and worshiping are routinely linked in the OT (e.g., Ge 24:26; Ex 34:8; Nu 22:31). The people responded in worship with their voices and entire bodies.

8:7 Levites Seven of these Levites sign the pledge of Ne 10:28–39: Jeshua (10:9), Bani (10:13), Sherebiah (10:12), Hodiah (10:10), Kelita (10:10), Hanan (10:10) and Pelaiah (10:10).

8:8 making it clear The Hebrew word used here in this context can mean either reading clearly or translating the text from Hebrew into Aramaic (see Ezr 4:18; where the Aramaic cognate is used). See note on Ezr 4:7.

8:9 holy to the LORD your God The first of three times in this passage that the day is described as holy (Ne 8: 10,11; compare Lev 23:24; Nu 29:1). **Do not mourn or weep** The Festival of Trumpets was to be a joyous occasion (Dt 12:5–19; 16:9–17).

8:14 festival of the seventh month The Festival of Booths (or Tabernacles) ran for seven days (Tishri 15–22; see note on Nu 29:12–38). The observance is also commanded in Lev 23:33–43 and Dt 16:13–15. This festival is not always named explicitly; in 1Ki 8:2, it is similarly called just the festival of the seventh month. This festival is associated with two other significant events from Israel's history. The initial dedication of Solomon's temple took place in the seventh month and the festival was observed (1Ki 8). When the first group of exiles returned to Jerusalem and rebuilt the altar of the temple, they offered sacrifices and observed the Festival of Booths (Ezr 3:1–6). Both events marked the inauguration of temple worship. Here the observance marks the community's rededication of themselves to following God's law.

8:17 the Israelites had not celebrated it like this The Festival of Booths (or Tabernacles) had been celebrated on earlier occasions (see 1Ki 8:2,65; Ezr 3:4). This statement likely indicates that no previous festival had conformed as closely to the exact standards of the Law. See note on Ezr 3:4; note on 8:1–18.

8:18 an assembly The Hebrew term used here is common in Old Testament law and is used to emphasize a day on which no work was to be done (Lev 23:36; Nu 29:35; Dt 16:8).

The Israelites Confess Their Sins

9 On the twenty-fourth day of the same month, the Israelites gathered together, fasting and wearing sackcloth and putting dust on their heads. ²Those of Israelite descent had separated themselves from all foreigners. They stood in their places and confessed their sins and the sins of their ancestors. ³They stood where they were and read from the Book of the Law of the LORD their God for a quarter of the day, and spent another quarter in confession and in worshiping the LORD their God. ⁴Standing on the stairs of the Levites were Jeshua, Bani, Kadmiel, Shebaniah, Bunni, Sherebiah, Bani and Kenani. They cried out with loud voices to the LORD their God. ⁵And the Levites — Jeshua, Kadmiel, Bani, Hashabneiah, Sherebiah, Hodiah, Shebaniah and Pethahiah — said: "Stand up and praise the LORD your God, who is from everlasting to everlasting.ᵃ"

"Blessed be your glorious name, and may it be exalted above all blessing and praise. ⁶You alone are the LORD. You made the heavens, even the highest heavens, and all their starry host, the earth and all that is on it, the seas and all that is in them. You give life to everything, and the multitudes of heaven worship you.

⁷"You are the LORD God, who chose Abram and brought him out of Ur of the Chaldeans and named him Abraham. ⁸You found his heart faithful to you, and you made a covenant with him to give to his descendants the land of the Canaanites, Hittites, Amorites, Perizzites, Jebusites and Girgashites. You have kept your promise because you are righteous.

⁹"You saw the suffering of our ancestors in Egypt; you heard their cry at the Red Sea.ᵇ ¹⁰You sent signs and wonders against Pharaoh, against all his officials and all the people of his land, for you knew how arrogantly the Egyptians treated them. You made a name for yourself, which remains to this day. ¹¹You divided the sea before them, so that they passed through it on dry ground, but you hurled their pursuers into the depths, like a stone into mighty waters. ¹²By day you led them with a pillar of cloud, and by night with a pillar of fire to give them light on the way they were to take.

¹³"You came down on Mount Sinai; you spoke to them from heaven. You gave them regulations and laws that are just and right,

ᵃ 5 Or *God for ever and ever*   ᵇ 9 Or *the Sea of Reeds*

9:1–38 In this chapter, the time is now two days after the end of the Festival of Booths (or Tabernacles). Following the celebratory atmosphere of that festival, now the Jews gathered in Jerusalem adopt an attitude of repentance. The chapter closes with the community formally recommitting themselves to observe God's law and keep their part of the covenant.

The prayer recorded in Ne 9:5–37 pieces together a collection of citations from the history of Israel. However, it is more than a simple reminder of past events; it is history with an emphasis on God's faithfulness and the people's faithlessness (see the book of Judges; Ps 78; 106; compare Ac 7). Though the Israelites regularly rebelled against Yahweh, God showed compassion for his chosen people.

However, despite Yahweh's patience (Ne 9:30), the time came for him to punish the Jews by taking away their land and causing them to become slaves. Although a community of exiles returned to the land, the nation was still enslaved by foreign kings. All of this took place because of Israel's unfaithfulness (see Dt 29–30). The returned exiles expected Yahweh, who providentially cared for this generation just as he had their ancestors, to once again judge the nation if it acted unfaithfully.

9:1 On the twenty-fourth day of the same month This appears to be a unique event. There was no prescribed holiday on the twenty-fourth day of the seventh month. See the table "Israelite Calendar" on p. 763. **wearing sackcloth** Clothes typically worn as a sign of mourning. **putting dust on their heads** Although ashes typically accompanied the wearing of sackcloth, the use of dirt in mourning also seems to have been common in the ancient Near East. Dirt symbolized an identification with the dead.

SACKCLOTH
Made of goat or camel hair, sackcloth was coarse and uncomfortable to wear. In contexts of mourning, "sackcloth" usually refers to a loincloth. Sackcloth was often worn to demonstrate repentance. Jeremiah called on his generation to repent by commanding the inhabitants of Judah to put on sackcloth in mourning (Jer 6:26); Daniel used sackcloth as part of his repentance for the sins of the nation (Da 9:3); the king of Nineveh used sackcloth to demonstrate his repentance upon hearing Yahweh's announcement of imminent judgment (Jnh 3:6); Yahweh announced that Tyre and Sidon would have repented in sackcloth if they had witnessed his miracles (Mt 11:21).

9:2 Those of Israelite descent had separated themselves from all foreigners A recurring theme throughout Ezra and Nehemiah (Ezr 6:21; 10:11; Ne 10:28; 13:25).
9:3 Book of the Law As with the gathering recorded in 8:1–8, the reading of the Torah, the book of God's law, is central to the proceedings.
9:4 They cried out with loud voices Probably a cry of distress associated with the mourning described in v. 1.
9:5 the Levites The Levites may have chanted or sung the words of this psalm. **who is from everlasting to everlasting** This may indicate the audience is to bless Yahweh forever and ever, or it may describe Yahweh as the eternal God.
9:6 their starry host Probably a reference to the stars (Ps 33:6), though a reference to angels is also possible.

and decrees and commands that are good. ¹⁴You made known to them your holy Sabbath and gave them commands, decrees and laws through your servant Moses. ¹⁵In their hunger you gave them bread from heaven and in their thirst you brought them water from the rock; you told them to go in and take possession of the land you had sworn with uplifted hand to give them.

¹⁶"But they, our ancestors, became arrogant and stiff-necked, and they did not obey your commands. ¹⁷They refused to listen and failed to remember the miracles you performed among them. They became stiff-necked and in their rebellion appointed a leader in order to return to their slavery. But you are a forgiving God, gracious and compassionate, slow to anger and abounding in love. Therefore you did not desert them, ¹⁸even when they cast for themselves an image of a calf and said, 'This is your god, who brought you up out of Egypt,' or when they committed awful blasphemies.

¹⁹"Because of your great compassion you did not abandon them in the wilderness. By day the pillar of cloud did not fail to guide them on their path, nor the pillar of fire by night to shine on the way they were to take. ²⁰You gave your good Spirit to instruct them. You did not withhold your manna from their mouths, and you gave them water for their thirst. ²¹For forty years you sustained them in the wilderness; they lacked nothing, their clothes did not wear out nor did their feet become swollen.

²²"You gave them kingdoms and nations, allotting to them even the remotest frontiers. They took over the country of Sihon[a] king of Heshbon and the country of Og king of Bashan. ²³You made their children as numerous as the stars in the sky, and you brought them into the land that you told their parents to enter and possess. ²⁴Their children went in and took possession of the land. You subdued before them the Canaanites, who lived in the land; you gave the Canaanites into their hands, along with their kings and the peoples of the land, to deal with them as they pleased. ²⁵They captured fortified cities and fertile land; they took possession of houses filled with all kinds of good things, wells already dug, vineyards, olive groves and fruit trees in abundance. They ate to the full and were well-nourished; they reveled in your great goodness.

²⁶"But they were disobedient and rebelled against you; they turned their backs on your law. They killed your prophets, who had warned them in order to turn them back to you; they committed awful blasphemies. ²⁷So you delivered them into the hands of their enemies, who oppressed them. But when they were oppressed they cried out to you. From heaven you heard them, and in your great compassion you gave them deliverers, who rescued them from the hand of their enemies.

²⁸"But as soon as they were at rest, they again did what was evil in your sight. Then you abandoned them to the hand of their enemies so that they ruled over them. And when they cried out to you again, you heard from heaven, and in your compassion you delivered them time after time.

²⁹"You warned them in order to turn them back to your law, but they became arrogant and disobeyed your commands. They sinned against your ordinances, of which you said, 'The person who obeys them will live by them.' Stubbornly they turned their backs on you, became stiff-necked and refused to listen. ³⁰For many years you were patient with them. By your Spirit you warned them through your prophets. Yet they paid no attention, so you gave them into the hands of the neighboring peoples. ³¹But in your

---

[a] 22 One Hebrew manuscript and Septuagint; most Hebrew manuscripts *Sihon, that is, the country of the*

9:7 Lord The final occurrence of the name Yahweh in this psalm (Ne 9:5,6). **Abram** After recounting creation as evidence for God's greatness in v. 6, Ezra recounts God's faithfulness to his people—beginning with their ancestor Abraham—as further evidence.

9:8 the Canaanites, Hittites, Amorites, Perizzites, Jebusites and Girgashites This list is nearly identical to the list recorded in Ge 15:19–21 (only the Kenites, Kenizzites, Kadmonites and Rephaites [Rephaim] are not mentioned).

9:15 In their hunger you gave them bread from heaven God had miraculously provided manna (Ex 16:31,35) and water for his people in the wilderness (Ex 17:1–7).

9:16 stiff-necked The people are like a stubborn animal that refuses to submit to a yoke. God remained faithful in spite of the rebellious response of his people.

9:17 slow to anger and abounding in This echoes Ex 34:6–7; compare Ps 103:8; Joel 2:13; Jnh 4:2.

9:22 They took over the country When the nation defeated Sihon and Og (Nu 21:21–35), the newly conquered territory was given to the tribes of Gad, Reuben and Manasseh (Nu 32:33). The defeat of Sihon and Og is consistently used in Scripture as a reminder of Yahweh's providential deliverance of his people (e.g., Dt 31:4; Jos 2:10; Ps 135:10–11).

9:26 awful blasphemies Refers to the worship of Baal and other false gods (e.g., Eze 23; Hos 2; Mic 3).

9:28 as soon as they were at rest, they again did what was evil in your sight The pattern often repeated itself in the period of the judges, recounted in Ne 9:26–28 (Jdg 1–12).

great mercy you did not put an end to them or abandon them, for you are a gracious and merciful God.

³²"Now therefore, our God, the great God, mighty and awesome, who keeps his covenant of love, do not let all this hardship seem trifling in your eyes — the hardship that has come on us, on our kings and leaders, on our priests and prophets, on our ancestors and all your people, from the days of the kings of Assyria until today. ³³In all that has happened to us, you have remained righteous; you have acted faithfully, while we acted wickedly. ³⁴Our kings, our leaders, our priests and our ancestors did not follow your law; they did not pay attention to your commands or the statutes you warned them to keep. ³⁵Even while they were in their kingdom, enjoying your great goodness to them in the spacious and fertile land you gave them, they did not serve you or turn from their evil ways.

³⁶"But see, we are slaves today, slaves in the land you gave our ancestors so they could eat its fruit and the other good things it produces. ³⁷Because of our sins, its abundant harvest goes to the kings you have placed over us. They rule over our bodies and our cattle as they please. We are in great distress.

The Agreement of the People

³⁸"In view of all this, we are making a binding agreement, putting it in writing, and our leaders, our Levites and our priests are affixing their seals to it."ᵃ

10ᵇ Those who sealed it were:

Nehemiah the governor, the son of Hakaliah.

Zedekiah, ²Seraiah, Azariah, Jeremiah, ³Pashhur, Amariah, Malkijah,

⁴Hattush, Shebaniah, Malluk, ⁵Harim, Meremoth, Obadiah, ⁶Daniel, Ginnethon, Baruch, ⁷Meshullam, Abijah, Mijamin, ⁸Maaziah, Bilgai and Shemaiah. These were the priests.

⁹The Levites:

Jeshua son of Azaniah, Binnui of the sons of Henadad, Kadmiel, ¹⁰and their associates: Shebaniah, Hodiah, Kelita, Pelaiah, Hanan, ¹¹Mika, Rehob, Hashabiah, ¹²Zakkur, Sherebiah, Shebaniah, ¹³Hodiah, Bani and Beninu.

¹⁴The leaders of the people:

Parosh, Pahath-Moab, Elam, Zattu, Bani, ¹⁵Bunni, Azgad, Bebai, ¹⁶Adonijah, Bigvai, Adin, ¹⁷Ater, Hezekiah, Azzur, ¹⁸Hodiah, Hashum, Bezai, ¹⁹Hariph, Anathoth, Nebai, ²⁰Magpiash, Meshullam, Hezir, ²¹Meshezabel, Zadok, Jaddua, ²²Pelatiah, Hanan, Anaiah, ²³Hoshea, Hananiah, Hasshub, ²⁴Hallohesh, Pilha, Shobek, ²⁵Rehum, Hashabnah, Maaseiah, ²⁶Ahiah, Hanan, Anan, ²⁷Malluk, Harim and Baanah.

²⁸"The rest of the people — priests, Levites, gatekeepers, musicians, temple servants and all who separated themselves from the neighboring peoples for the sake of the Law of God, together with their wives and all their sons and daughters who are able to understand —

ᵃ 38 In Hebrew texts this verse (9:38) is numbered 10:1.   ᵇ In Hebrew texts 10:1-39 is numbered 10:2-40.

9:32 Now therefore This Hebrew expression marks the prayer's transition from an acknowledgment of past guilt to a present appeal for forgiveness and deliverance (compare Ex 32:30–32; 1Sa 12:10; Ezr 10:2–3). **kings of Assyria** Including Tiglath-Pileser III, Shalmaneser V, Sargon II, Sennacherib, Esarhaddon and Ashurbanipal. The phrase may also include the kings of Babylon and the Persian kings (Ezr 6:22) — those who conquered the territory previously governed by the Assyrians.
9:36 we are slaves today Although the Jews were allowed to return to their homeland, they were still subservient to the Persians.
9:37 its abundant harvest goes to the kings A reference to the oppressive Persian system of taxation.
9:38 all this Refers to the events recorded in the psalm of Ne 9:5–37. **binding agreement** This is not the regular Hebrew word for covenant (berith in Hebrew). The Hebrew word used here, amanah, emphasizes trustworthiness. However, the Hebrew verb used here, karath, suggests that a covenant is implied. Karath is closely associated

with berith in the OT (e.g., Ge 15:18; 21:27; Ex 24:8; 34:27; Dt 5:2; 1Sa 18:3; 1Ki 5:12).

10:1–27 Those who attached their names to the sealed document mentioned in Ne 9:38 would have done so by signature rather than by the stamp of their personal seals. There are a total of 84 names. First is Nehemiah (v. 1), followed by a group of priests (vv. 2–8), Levites (vv. 9–13) and leaders (vv. 14–27).

10:28–39 This covenant lists the commitments the nation was obligated to carry out. Not all of these stipulations are specifically recorded in the Law; several appear to be derived from interpretations of previously existing laws. The Jewish religious leaders here are likely adapting the Law to their contemporary setting.

The addition of the Ammonites, Moabites and Egyptians to the list of nations with whom Israel was forbidden to intermarry reflects the same type of interpretive adaptation of the Law (Ezr 9:1–2; compare Dt 7:1–4).

²⁹all these now join their fellow Israelites the nobles, and bind themselves with a curse and an oath to follow the Law of God given through Moses the servant of God and to obey carefully all the commands, regulations and decrees of the LORD our Lord.

³⁰"We promise not to give our daughters in marriage to the peoples around us or take their daughters for our sons.

³¹"When the neighboring peoples bring merchandise or grain to sell on the Sabbath, we will not buy from them on the Sabbath or on any holy day. Every seventh year we will forgo working the land and will cancel all debts.

³²"We assume the responsibility for carrying out the commands to give a third of a shekelᵃ each year for the service of the house of our God: ³³for the bread set out on the table; for the regular grain offerings and burnt offerings; for the offerings on the Sabbaths, at the New Moon feasts and at the appointed festivals; for the holy offerings; for sin offeringsᵇ to make atonement for Israel; and for all the duties of the house of our God.

³⁴"We — the priests, the Levites and the people — have cast lots to determine when each of our families is to bring to the house of our God at set times each year a contribution of wood to burn on the altar of the LORD our God, as it is written in the Law.

³⁵"We also assume responsibility for bringing to the house of the LORD each year the firstfruits of our crops and of every fruit tree.

³⁶"As it is also written in the Law, we will bring the firstborn of our sons and of our cat-

tle, of our herds and of our flocks to the house of our God, to the priests ministering there.

³⁷"Moreover, we will bring to the storerooms of the house of our God, to the priests, the first of our ground meal, of our grain offerings, of the fruit of all our trees and of our new wine and olive oil. And we will bring a tithe of our crops to the Levites, for it is the Levites who collect the tithes in all the towns where we work. ³⁸A priest descended from Aaron is to accompany the Levites when they receive the tithes, and the Levites are to bring a tenth of the tithes up to the house of our God, to the storerooms of the treasury. ³⁹The people of Israel, including the Levites, are to bring their contributions of grain, new wine and olive oil to the storerooms, where the articles for the sanctuary and for the ministering priests, the gatekeepers and the musicians are also kept.

"We will not neglect the house of our God."

The New Residents of Jerusalem
11:3-19pp — 1Ch 9:1-17

11 Now the leaders of the people settled in Jerusalem. The rest of the people cast lots to bring one out of every ten of them to live in Jerusalem, the holy city, while the remaining nine were to stay in their own towns. ²The people commended all who volunteered to live in Jerusalem. ³These are the provincial leaders who settled in Jerusalem (now some Israelites, priests, Levites, temple servants and descendants of Solomon's

---

ᵃ *32* That is, about 1/8 ounce or about 4 grams
ᵇ *33* Or *purification offerings*

10:29 a curse and an oath Throughout the OT, taking an oath was considered an indispensable part of making a covenant (e.g., Dt 29:12–14; Jos 9:15; Eze 17:13). When the nation committed to following the stipulations of the covenant, it agreed to fall under a curse if the covenant was ever broken. The curse and covenant went hand in hand: When the covenant was broken, the curse went into effect. This formula was used with the conditional Mosaic covenant (Lev 26; Dt 28). Since no specific curse is mentioned here, it is likely that the curses prescribed in Lev 26 and Dt 28 are in view.

10:31 to sell on the Sabbath Foreigners did not follow the Jewish Sabbath regulations; this practice served as a marker of Jewish identity. **we will not buy** The Mosaic Law does not specifically prohibit the purchase of food on the Sabbath. This requirement may be adapted from Ex 16:22–30. Nehemiah 13:15–16 indicates that the people soon broke their commitment to keep the Sabbath. **seventh year** The people are resolving to abide by the stipulations of Ex 23:10–11; Lev 25:2–7; and Dt 15:1–3.

10:32 a third of a shekel The Law required that all Israelites 20 years and older pay a half shekel as a temple tax (Ex 30:11–16). The oath taken in this verse mentions only a third of a shekel. This third may be in

addition to the half shekel already owed (totaling 5/6 of a shekel). Alternatively, the amount could have been intentionally changed to compensate for the poverty of some in the community (see Ne 5:1–13).

10:33 bread set out on the table Refers to the bread of the Presence. See note on Ex 25:30. **for the regular grain offerings** The grain offering was to be offered in conjunction with the burnt offering, which consisted of a one-year-old lamb each morning and evening (Ex 29:38–42). **the holy offerings** The sacred offerings associated with unique events, such as Hezekiah's restoration of worship (2Ch 29:33) and Josiah's Passover celebration (2Ch 35:1–6).

10:34 as it is written in the Law Perhaps a reference to Lev 6:12.

10:36 our sons The firstborn child could be redeemed from temple service by paying five shekels of silver (Nu 18:15–16).

11:1–24 This chapter presents the solution to the problem of Ne 7:1–4 — there were not enough people living in Jerusalem to fill and defend it.

11:1 cast lots In casting lots, the fate of each family was not up to the whim of the governor — it was the will of God. In the ancient Near East, casting lots was seen

servants lived in the towns of Judah, each on their own property in the various towns, [4]while other people from both Judah and Benjamin lived in Jerusalem):

From the descendants of Judah:

Athaiah son of Uzziah, the son of Zechariah, the son of Amariah, the son of Shephatiah, the son of Mahalalel, a descendant of Perez; [5]and Maaseiah son of Baruch, the son of Kol-Hozeh, the son of Hazaiah, the son of Adaiah, the son of Joiarib, the son of Zechariah, a descendant of Shelah. [6]The descendants of Perez who lived in Jerusalem totaled 468 men of standing.

[7]From the descendants of Benjamin:

Sallu son of Meshullam, the son of Joed, the son of Pedaiah, the son of Kolaiah, the son of Maaseiah, the son of Ithiel, the son of Jeshaiah, [8]and his followers, Gabbai and Sallai—928 men. [9]Joel son of Zikri was their chief officer, and Judah son of Hassenuah was over the New Quarter of the city.

[10]From the priests:

Jedaiah; the son of Joiarib; Jakin; [11]Seraiah son of Hilkiah, the son of Meshullam, the son of Zadok, the son of Meraioth, the son of Ahitub, the official in charge of the house of God, [12]and their associates, who carried on work for the temple—822 men; Adaiah son of Jeroham, the son of Pelaliah, the son of Amzi, the son of Zechariah, the son of Pashhur, the son of Malkijah, [13]and his associates, who were heads of families—242 men; Amashsai son of Azarel, the son of Ahzai, the son of Meshillemoth, the son of Immer, [14]and his[a] associates, who were men

of standing—128. Their chief officer was Zabdiel son of Haggedolim.

[15]From the Levites:

Shemaiah son of Hasshub, the son of Azrikam, the son of Hashabiah, the son of Bunni; [16]Shabbethai and Jozabad, two of the heads of the Levites, who had charge of the outside work of the house of God; [17]Mattaniah son of Mika, the son of Zabdi, the son of Asaph, the director who led in thanksgiving and prayer; Bakbukiah, second among his associates; and Abda son of Shammua, the son of Galal, the son of Jeduthun. [18]The Levites in the holy city totaled 284.

[19]The gatekeepers:

Akkub, Talmon and their associates, who kept watch at the gates—172 men.

[20]The rest of the Israelites, with the priests and Levites, were in all the towns of Judah, each on their ancestral property.

[21]The temple servants lived on the hill of Ophel, and Ziha and Gishpa were in charge of them.

[22]The chief officer of the Levites in Jerusalem was Uzzi son of Bani, the son of Hashabiah, the son of Mattaniah, the son of Mika. Uzzi was one of Asaph's descendants, who were the musicians responsible for the service of the house of God. [23]The musicians were under the king's orders, which regulated their daily activity.

[24]Pethahiah son of Meshezabel, one of the descendants of Zerah son of Judah, was the king's agent in all affairs relating to the people.

[25]As for the villages with their fields, some of the people of Judah lived in Kiriath Arba and its

---

[a] 14 Most Septuagint manuscripts; Hebrew *their*

---

as a way of allowing the gods to make their decisions known to people (Jnh 1:7). On multiple occasions Yahweh uses the casting of lots to reveal his will (see Pr 16:33). The lot was cast to determine which goat became the scapegoat on the Day of Atonement (Lev 16:8); which portion of the promised land was given to each tribe (Nu 26:55–56; Jos 15:1; 16:1; 17:1); to identify Saul as Yahweh's choice for Israel's king (1Sa 10:20–24); and to identify Matthias as the twelfth disciple after the suicide of Judas (Ac 1:26). The high priest's use of the Urim and Thummim was a form of casting lots to determine the judgment of God (see Ex 28:30; Ezr 2:63; Ne 7:65). **one out of every ten of them to live in Jerusalem** The nation earlier pledged a tenth of its produce to Yahweh (10:37). It now devotes a tenth of its citizens to the service of Yahweh. This repopulation effort was needed to protect the city of Jerusalem and the temple. **holy city** This epithet is found elsewhere only in v. 18; Isa 48:2; 52:1; and Da 9:24.
11:4 lived in Jerusalem Estimates of Jerusalem's population at this time range from 4,800–8,000. The list provided here is very similar to the one in 1Ch 9.

11:9 chief officer This probably refers to an administrative office subordinate to the high priest (Ne 11:14,22). It could also be a reference to military rank.
11:16 outside work This may refer to taking care of the outside walls and grounds of the temple building. It could also refer to the work of the Levites outside the temple area itself (such as collecting tithes).
11:23 the king's This probably refers to Artaxerxes, the Persian king. See note on 2:1. See the infographic "The Bowls of Darius and Artaxerxes" on p. 724.
11:25–36 Those cities south of Jerusalem were located in the territory originally given to the tribe of Judah. Nehemiah details 17 prominent villages in this region (vv. 25–30). Those cities north of Jerusalem were located in the territory originally given to the tribe of Benjamin. Nehemiah identifies 15 significant towns in this region (vv. 31–35).
11:25 Dibon This probably refers to modern ed-Dheib, located about ten miles south of Hebron. This city is to be distinguished from the Moabite Dibon (or Dimon) of Isa 15:9.

surrounding settlements, in Dibon and its settlements, in Jekabzeel and its villages, ²⁶in Jeshua, in Moladah, in Beth Pelet, ²⁷in Hazar Shual, in Beersheba and its settlements, ²⁸in Ziklag, in Mekonah and its settlements, ²⁹in En Rimmon, in Zorah, in Jarmuth, ³⁰Zanoah, Adullam and their villages, in Lachish and its fields, and in Azekah and its settlements. So they were living all the way from Beersheba to the Valley of Hinnom.

³¹The descendants of the Benjamites from Geba lived in Mikmash, Aija, Bethel and its settlements, ³²in Anathoth, Nob and Ananiah, ³³in Hazor, Ramah and Gittaim, ³⁴in Hadid, Zeboim and Neballat, ³⁵in Lod and Ono, and in Ge Harashim.

³⁶Some of the divisions of the Levites of Judah settled in Benjamin.

Priests and Levites

12 These were the priests and Levites who returned with Zerubbabel son of Shealtiel and with Joshua:

Seraiah, Jeremiah, Ezra,
²Amariah, Malluk, Hattush,
³Shekaniah, Rehum, Meremoth,
⁴Iddo, Ginnethon,^a Abijah,
⁵Mijamin,^b Moadiah, Bilgah,
⁶Shemaiah, Joiarib, Jedaiah,
⁷Sallu, Amok, Hilkiah and Jedaiah.

These were the leaders of the priests and their associates in the days of Joshua. ⁸The Levites were Jeshua, Binnui, Kadmiel, Sherebiah, Judah, and also Mattaniah, who, together with his associates, was in charge of the songs of thanksgiving. ⁹Bakbukiah and Unni, their associates, stood opposite them in the services.

¹⁰Joshua was the father of Joiakim, Joiakim the father of Eliashib, Eliashib the father of Joiada, ¹¹Joiada the father of Jonathan, and Jonathan the father of Jaddua.

¹²In the days of Joiakim, these were the heads of the priestly families:

of Seraiah's family, Meraiah;
of Jeremiah's, Hananiah;
¹³of Ezra's, Meshullam;
of Amariah's, Jehohanan;
¹⁴of Malluk's, Jonathan;
of Shekaniah's,^c Joseph;
¹⁵of Harim's, Adna;
of Meremoth's,^d Helkai;
¹⁶of Iddo's, Zechariah;
of Ginnethon's, Meshullam;
¹⁷of Abijah's, Zikri;
of Miniamin's and of Moadiah's, Piltai;
¹⁸of Bilgah's, Shammua;
of Shemaiah's, Jehonathan;
¹⁹of Joiarib's, Mattenai;
of Jedaiah's, Uzzi;
²⁰of Sallu's, Kallai;
of Amok's, Eber;
²¹of Hilkiah's, Hashabiah;
of Jedaiah's, Nethanel.

²²The family heads of the Levites in the days of Eliashib, Joiada, Johanan and Jaddua, as well as those of the priests, were recorded in the reign of Darius the Persian. ²³The family heads among the descendants of Levi up to the time of Johanan son of Eliashib were recorded in the book of the annals. ²⁴And the leaders of the Levites were Hashabiah, Sherebiah, Jeshua son of Kadmiel, and their associates, who stood opposite them to give praise and thanksgiving, one section responding to the other, as prescribed by David the man of God.

²⁵Mattaniah, Bakbukiah, Obadiah, Meshullam, Talmon and Akkub were gatekeepers who guarded

^a 4 Many Hebrew manuscripts and Vulgate (see also verse 16); most Hebrew manuscripts *Ginnethoi*   ^b 5 A variant of *Miniamin*   ^c 14 Very many Hebrew manuscripts, some Septuagint manuscripts and Syriac (see also verse 3); most Hebrew manuscripts *Shebaniah's*   ^d 15 Some Septuagint manuscripts (see also verse 3); Hebrew *Meraioth's*

11:30 Valley of Hinnom Located southwest of Jerusalem. This valley was the boundary between Judah and Benjamin (Jos 15:8).

12:1–26 This section details the priests and Levites from the time of Zerubbabel (538 BC) until the time of Nehemiah. These were the families responsible for the spiritual leadership of the nation. Nehemiah 12:1–9 is a record of priests and Levites who ministered during the time of Zerubbabel the governor and Jeshua (or Joshua) the high priest. These leaders officiated in the newly rebuilt temple, which was completed around 516 BC. The names are provided by family rather than by individual (10:2–8).

12:1 Zerubbabel Zerubbabel was an early leader of the returned exiles. See Ezr 3:2 and note. **with Joshua** Jeshua (or Joshua) was the high priest at the time of the return from exile. See Ezr 3:2 and note.

12:10–11 These verses continue the genealogy of high priests found in 1Ch 6:3–15, which ended with the

Babylonian captivity in 586 BC. The genealogy begins with Jeshua (or Joshua), the high priest during the initial return under Sheshbazzar in 538 BC, and ends with Jaddua, the high priest ca. 400 BC.

12:12–21 A record of the priests in the time of the high priest Joiakim. Joiakim was the son of Jeshua, the high priest during the time of Zerubbabel.

12:22–26 A record identifying the leadership of the land during the time of Ezra and Nehemiah. The use of titles for each of these leaders reveals the official nature of this list. Although the religious leadership was not entirely faithful around this time (see Mal 3), the Levites and priests are once again commissioned as the spiritual leaders of the nation.

12:22 Darius the Persian Refers to Darius II Nothus (424–404 BC).

12:23 book of the annals Not the canonical books of Chronicles.

the storerooms at the gates. ²⁶They served in the days of Joiakim son of Joshua, the son of Jozadak, and in the days of Nehemiah the governor and of Ezra the priest, the teacher of the Law.

Dedication of the Wall of Jerusalem

²⁷At the dedication of the wall of Jerusalem, the Levites were sought out from where they lived and were brought to Jerusalem to celebrate joyfully the dedication with songs of thanksgiving and with the music of cymbals, harps and lyres. ²⁸The musicians also were brought together from the region around Jerusalem — from the villages of the Netophathites, ²⁹from Beth Gilgal, and from the area of Geba and Azmaveth, for the musicians had built villages for themselves around Jerusalem. ³⁰When the priests and Levites had purified themselves ceremonially, they purified the people, the gates and the wall.

³¹I had the leaders of Judah go up on top of[a] the wall. I also assigned two large choirs to give thanks. One was to proceed on top of[b] the wall to the right, toward the Dung Gate. ³²Hoshaiah and half the leaders of Judah followed them, ³³along with Azariah, Ezra, Meshullam, ³⁴Judah, Benjamin, Shemaiah, Jeremiah, ³⁵as well as some priests with trumpets, and also Zechariah son of Jonathan, the son of Shemaiah, the son of Mattaniah, the son of Micaiah, the son of Zakkur, the son of Asaph, ³⁶and his associates — Shemaiah, Azarel, Milalai, Gilalai, Maai, Nethanel, Judah and Hanani — with musical instruments prescribed by David the man of God. Ezra the teacher of the Law led the procession. ³⁷At the Fountain Gate they continued directly up the steps of the City of David on the ascent to the wall and passed above the site of David's palace to the Water Gate on the east.

³⁸The second choir proceeded in the opposite direction. I followed them on top of[c] the wall, together with half the people — past the Tower of the Ovens to the Broad Wall, ³⁹over the Gate of Ephraim, the Jeshanah[d] Gate, the Fish Gate, the Tower of Hananel and the Tower of the Hundred, as far as the Sheep Gate. At the Gate of the Guard they stopped.

⁴⁰The two choirs that gave thanks then took their places in the house of God; so did I, together with half the officials, ⁴¹as well as the priests — Eliakim, Maaseiah, Miniamin, Micaiah, Elioenai, Zechariah and Hananiah with their trumpets — ⁴²and also Maaseiah, Shemaiah, Eleazar, Uzzi, Jehohanan, Malkijah, Elam and Ezer. The choirs sang under the direction of Jezrahiah. ⁴³And on that day they offered great sacrifices, rejoicing because God had given them great joy. The women and children also rejoiced. The sound of rejoicing in Jerusalem could be heard far away.

⁴⁴At that time men were appointed to be in charge of the storerooms for the contributions, firstfruits and tithes. From the fields around the towns they were to bring into the storerooms the portions required by the Law for the priests and the Levites, for Judah was pleased with the ministering priests and Levites. ⁴⁵They performed the service of their God and the service of purification, as did also the musicians and gatekeepers, according to the commands of David and his son Solomon. ⁴⁶For long ago, in the days of David and Asaph, there had been directors for the musicians and for the songs of praise and thanksgiving to God. ⁴⁷So in the days of Zerubbabel and of Nehemiah, all Israel contributed the daily portions for the musicians and the gatekeepers. They also set aside the portion for the other Levites, and the Levites set aside the portion for the descendants of Aaron.

Nehemiah's Final Reforms

13 On that day the Book of Moses was read aloud in the hearing of the people and there it was found written that no Ammonite or Moabite should ever be admitted into the assembly of God, ²because they had not met the Israelites with food and water but had hired Balaam to call

---

a 31 Or go alongside   b 31 Or proceed alongside
c 38 Or them alongside   d 39 Or Old

12:27–43 The story now picks up where Nehemiah's personal memoir left off in Ne 7:5. This dedication probably takes place within a month or two of the completion of the wall (6:15–19). The passage emphasizes the worshipful activities of the community of returned exiles: singing, thanksgiving, rejoicing and the use of musical instruments.

12:30 purified the people The process of purification included ritual bathing and shaving, putting on clean garments, fasting, abstaining from sexual intercourse and offering sacrifices (e.g., Ex 19:10,14–15; Lev 11–15; Nu 8:5–8). **the gates and the wall** The gates and walls were probably sprinkled, a practice associated with the cleansing of private houses.

12:31 two large choirs to give thanks Nehemiah divided the participants into two processions that circumnavigated the city. Each procession included the following: a thanksgiving choir (Ne 12:31,38); a prominent layperson (Hoshaiah, v. 32; Nehemiah, v. 38); half of the lay leaders of Judah (vv. 32,40); seven priests with trumpets (vv. 33–35,41); a director of music (Zechariah, v. 35; Jezrahiah, v. 42); and eight Levites with musical instruments (vv. 36,42). The first procession turned south and walked around Jerusalem in a counterclockwise direction. The second procession turned north and marched the opposite way. The assembly point was probably located opposite the temple square halfway around the city.

12:39 Gate of the Guard Possibly the Inspection (or Muster) Gate (3:31).

13:1 there it was found written See Dt 23:3–5; note on Dt 23:3.

a curse down on them. (Our God, however, turned the curse into a blessing.) ³When the people heard this law, they excluded from Israel all who were of foreign descent.

⁴Before this, Eliashib the priest had been put in charge of the storerooms of the house of our God. He was closely associated with Tobiah, ⁵and he had provided him with a large room formerly used to store the grain offerings and incense and temple articles, and also the tithes of grain, new wine and olive oil prescribed for the Levites, musicians and gatekeepers, as well as the contributions for the priests.

⁶But while all this was going on, I was not in Jerusalem, for in the thirty-second year of Artaxerxes king of Babylon I had returned to the king. Some time later I asked his permission ⁷and came back to Jerusalem. Here I learned about the evil thing Eliashib had done in providing Tobiah a room in the courts of the house of God. ⁸I was greatly displeased and threw all Tobiah's household goods out of the room. ⁹I gave orders to purify the rooms, and then I put back into them the equipment of the house of God, with the grain offerings and the incense.

¹⁰I also learned that the portions assigned to the Levites had not been given to them, and that all the Levites and musicians responsible for the service had gone back to their own fields. ¹¹So I rebuked the officials and asked them, "Why is the house of God neglected?" Then I called them together and stationed them at their posts.

¹²All Judah brought the tithes of grain, new wine and olive oil into the storerooms. ¹³I put Shelemiah the priest, Zadok the scribe, and a Levite named Pedaiah in charge of the storerooms and made Hanan son of Zakkur, the son of Mattaniah, their assistant, because they were considered trustworthy. They were made responsible for distributing the supplies to their fellow Levites.

¹⁴Remember me for this, my God, and do not blot out what I have so faithfully done for the house of my God and its services.

¹⁵In those days I saw people in Judah treading winepresses on the Sabbath and bringing in grain and loading it on donkeys, together with wine, grapes, figs and all other kinds of loads. And they were bringing all this into Jerusalem on the Sabbath. Therefore I warned them against selling food on that day. ¹⁶People from Tyre who lived in Jerusalem were bringing in fish and all kinds of merchandise and selling them in Jerusalem on the Sabbath to the people of Judah. ¹⁷I rebuked the nobles of Judah and said to them, "What is this wicked thing you are doing—desecrating the Sabbath day? ¹⁸Didn't your ancestors do the same things, so that our God brought all this calamity on us and on this city? Now you are stirring up more wrath against Israel by desecrating the Sabbath."

¹⁹When evening shadows fell on the gates of Jerusalem before the Sabbath, I ordered the doors to be shut and not opened until the Sabbath was over. I stationed some of my own men at the gates so that no load could be brought in on the Sabbath day. ²⁰Once or twice the merchants and sellers of

---

13:3 excluded from Israel all who were of foreign descent The point of separating from surrounding cultures was not racial; it was to prevent God's people from falling into idolatry (see Ex 34:11–16; Dt 7:1–6). Those foreigners who worshiped the God of Israel were welcome to become part of Israel, as Ruth the Moabite was (Ru 1:16–17; see Ezr 6:21). See note on Ezr 9:1—10:44.
13:4 Eliashib This is likely not the high priest of the same name (Ne 3:1,20). If it were the same person, it would be unusual to identify him as the priest in charge of the temple storerooms rather than as high priest. **Tobiah** The enemy of Nehemiah introduced in 2:10. He was an Ammonite who was married to a Jewish woman and had close ties in the Jewish community (6:17–19), which created trouble for Nehemiah. See 2:10 and note.
13:6 I was not in Jerusalem Nehemiah first went to Jerusalem to serve as governor in 444 BC. After 12 years, he went to Artaxerxes in 433 BC for an unspecified time before returning to Jerusalem (see note on 2:6). See the timeline "Dates Related to Ezra, Nehemiah and Esther" on p. 716. **Artaxerxes king of Babylon** Artaxerxes was a Persian king who ruled Babylon (Ezr 4:7 and note), and may have resided in Babylon at this time. See note on Ne 2:1.
13:10 portions assigned to the Levites had not been given A violation of the covenant that the community had signed (9:38; 10:28–39).
13:14 Remember me for this, my God One of the remembrance prayers offered in Nehemiah (5:19; 6:14; 13:22,29,31). See note on 5:19.

13:15 treading winepresses on the Sabbath Another violation of the commitment document signed by the remnant (10:31). **wine, grapes, figs** Suggests the time is probably somewhere between August and October—the months of the grape harvest.
13:16 People from Tyre Tyre was a Phoenician port city north of Judah that is mentioned frequently in the Bible (for example, 1Ki 5:1; Eze 26–28; Mk 7:24; Ac 21:3).

Nehemiah 13:16

TYRE
The principal city of Phoenicia (modern Lebanon) in Nehemiah's day, Tyre was located about 20 miles south of Sidon, its sister city (e.g., Jer 47:4; Joel 3:4; Mt 11:21–22; Ac 12:20). Tyre became one of the most influential trading centers of ancient times. The Phoenicians were skilled sailors who colonized villages along the Mediterranean coast (including Carthage). They became famous for their ability to trade a wide variety of goods (Isa 23:2–3,8,18; Eze 27:12–25; Am 1:9–10).

13:19 before the Sabbath About 5 p.m. on Friday. **Sabbath was over** About 11 a.m. on Sunday morning (Ne 7:3).

all kinds of goods spent the night outside Jerusalem. ²¹But I warned them and said, "Why do you spend the night by the wall? If you do this again, I will arrest you." From that time on they no longer came on the Sabbath. ²²Then I commanded the Levites to purify themselves and go and guard the gates in order to keep the Sabbath day holy.

Remember me for this also, my God, and show mercy to me according to your great love.

²³Moreover, in those days I saw men of Judah who had married women from Ashdod, Ammon and Moab. ²⁴Half of their children spoke the language of Ashdod or the language of one of the other peoples, and did not know how to speak the language of Judah. ²⁵I rebuked them and called curses down on them. I beat some of the men and pulled out their hair. I made them take an oath in God's name and said: "You are not to give your daughters in marriage to their sons, nor are you to take their daughters in marriage for your sons or for yourselves. ²⁶Was it not because of marriages like these that Solomon king of Israel sinned? Among the many nations there was no king like him. He was loved by his God, and God made him king over all Israel, but even he was led into sin by foreign women. ²⁷Must we hear now that you too are doing all this terrible wickedness and are being unfaithful to our God by marrying foreign women?"

²⁸One of the sons of Joiada son of Eliashib the high priest was son-in-law to Sanballat the Horonite. And I drove him away from me.

²⁹Remember them, my God, because they defiled the priestly office and the covenant of the priesthood and of the Levites.

³⁰So I purified the priests and the Levites of everything foreign, and assigned them duties, each to his own task. ³¹I also made provision for contributions of wood at designated times, and for the firstfruits.

Remember me with favor, my God.

13:23 who had married women from Ashdod, Ammon and Moab Another violation of the covenant signed by the community (10:30). See v. 3 and note; compare note on Ezr 9:1—10:44.

13:24 spoke the language of Ashdod Likely a Philistine dialect of Canaanite.

13:25 pulled out their hair Possibly describes the plucking of beards, a form of humiliation (see Isa 50:6; compare Ezr 9:3).

13:28 Sanballat the Horonite A leader who opposed the rebuilding of the wall of Jerusalem (see Ne 2:10 and note). The high priest was not allowed to marry a foreigner (Lev 21:14), and Sanballat was particularly hostile to Nehemiah's efforts, so this marriage is singled out as especially dangerous to the integrity of the Jewish community.

13:29 covenant of the priesthood and of the Levites The special covenant Yahweh made with the tribe of Levi, through which they were commanded to teach his laws to the rest of the nation (Lev 10:11; Dt 31:11–13; 33:10; Mal 2:4–7).

ESTHER

INTRODUCTION TO ESTHER

The book of Esther shows us that God is present even when he seems distant. In the course of the story, Esther—a Jew living during the time of the exile—becomes the queen of Persia. However, an official named Haman plots to kill the Jews throughout the empire. Esther and Mordecai, her cousin, expose the attempted genocide. Mordecai's cunning, Esther's bravery and God's unseen hand unite to save the Jewish exiles from destruction.

BACKGROUND

Esther is set about 55–65 years after the end of the Babylonian exile of the Jewish people. The narrative occurs in Susa, in the court of King Ahasuerus—better known as Xerxes, who ruled the Persian Empire from 486–465 BC. Susa was located about 150 miles north of the Persian Gulf, near the western border of modern-day Iran. Cyrus took Susa from the Elamites probably not long before he conquered Babylon in 539 BC. Darius I, father of Ahasuerus, made Susa the main capital of the Persian Empire. The book was likely composed sometime between 400–200 BC, primarily to explain the origins of the Jewish festival Purim.

STRUCTURE

Esther functions like a play, using irony, tragedy and comedy. It can be divided into two acts: In the first half of the book (Est 1–5), the danger to the Jews escalates, while in the second half (chs. 6–10), they are delivered.

At the beginning of the book, King Xerxes (Ahasuerus) sends for his wife, but she refuses to come (ch. 1). He decides to find a different wife, which leads to Esther becoming queen. Soon after, Mordecai thwarts an assassination plot against the king (ch. 2). But when Mordecai refuses to bow before Haman, a high-ranking government official, Haman is infuriated and convinces the king to sign an edict decreeing death for all Jews—claiming that they are disloyal to the crown. Haman

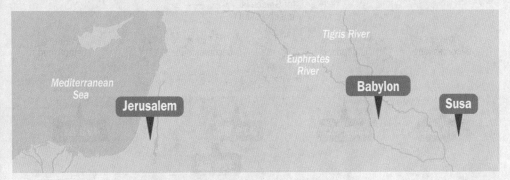

All events in the book of Esther take place in Susa, the Persian capital. Other cities on this map are given for reference.

does this slyly without naming the Jews directly (ch. 3). Learning of the plot, Mordecai pleads with Esther to speak to the king on the Jews' behalf. She initially hesitates, fearing for her life, but she ultimately agrees to approach the king (ch. 4). Esther risks her life by entering the king's inner court uninvited (4:11), but King Xerxes (Ahasuerus) responds favorably. Esther invites both him and Haman to a banquet (ch. 5). The two men attend the banquet, but Esther chooses not to reveal her request, instead inviting the men to a second banquet. The first act ends with Haman plotting the death of Mordecai.

At the beginning of the second act, the king realizes that Mordecai has not been rewarded for saving his life. Through a comical turnabout, Haman himself is forced to honor Mordecai in the public square (ch. 6). The second banquet then takes place, where Esther asks the king to save the Jews—including herself—from annihilation. When the king asks who is behind the threat, Esther identifies Haman, who is executed on the same gallows that he had built to kill Mordecai (ch. 7).

The king then gives Haman's estate to Esther and gives Mordecai the king's own signet ring, effectively allowing the Jews to strike down their enemies, who had since arisen in droves due to the genocidal edict (9:1). The entire city celebrates, and many people openly declare their Jewishness. Mordecai gains power throughout the empire, and he instructs the Jews to remember these events with an annual celebration called Purim (chs. 8–9). The book concludes with a notation that Mordecai had assumed the place of highest-ranking official to the king—Haman's former role (ch. 10).

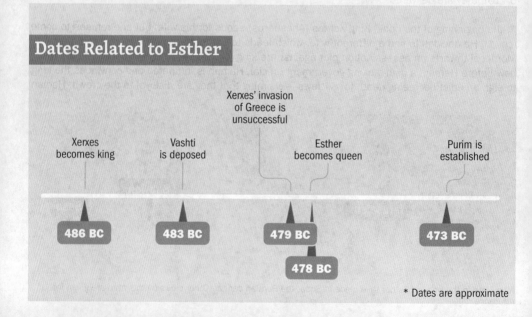

Dates Related to Esther

Xerxes becomes king — **486 BC**

Vashti is deposed — **483 BC**

Xerxes' invasion of Greece is unsuccessful

Esther becomes queen — **479 BC** / **478 BC**

Purim is established — **473 BC**

* Dates are approximate

OUTLINE

THEMES

In the book of Esther, God's people are suffering in a foreign land. God is never mentioned in the story, yet he is quietly there all along—which seems to be the point. The narrative cleverly reveals Haman's folly, the royal court's greed and the Persian law's failure. This is in direct contrast to the bravery of Esther, the wisdom of Mordecai and the courage of the Jewish people—all of which, in a way, show who God is. In addition, the unlikely turns of events in Esther suggest that God is intervening to protect his people. Esther is unexpectedly placed in a position of influence to guide the benevolent responses of the world's most powerful king.

The book of Esther also shows the interrelated nature of relationships. It gives us hope that our lives are part of an unfolding story that is infinitely greater than any one of our stories on its own. Esther embraces risks for the sake of what's right—and we are called to do the same, for the unseen God and the betterment of humanity.

Queen Vashti Deposed

1 This is what happened during the time of Xerxes,[a] the Xerxes who ruled over 127 provinces stretching from India to Cush[b]: ²At that time King Xerxes reigned from his royal throne in the citadel of Susa, ³and in the third year of his reign he gave a banquet for all his nobles and officials. The military leaders of Persia and Media, the princes, and the nobles of the provinces were present.

⁴For a full 180 days he displayed the vast wealth of his kingdom and the splendor and glory of his majesty. ⁵When these days were over, the king gave a banquet, lasting seven days, in the enclosed garden of the king's palace, for all the people from the least to the greatest who were in the citadel of Susa. ⁶The garden had hangings of white and blue linen, fastened with cords of white linen and purple material to silver rings on marble pillars. There were couches of gold and silver on a mosaic pavement of porphyry, marble, mother-of-pearl and other costly stones. ⁷Wine was served in goblets of gold, each one different from the other, and the royal wine was abundant, in keeping with the

king's liberality. ⁸By the king's command each guest was allowed to drink with no restrictions, for the king instructed all the wine stewards to serve each man what he wished.

⁹Queen Vashti also gave a banquet for the women in the royal palace of King Xerxes.

¹⁰On the seventh day, when King Xerxes was in high spirits from wine, he commanded the seven eunuchs who served him — Mehuman, Biztha, Harbona, Bigtha, Abagtha, Zethar and Karkas — ¹¹to bring before him Queen Vashti, wearing her royal crown, in order to display her beauty to the people and nobles, for she was lovely to look at. ¹²But when the attendants delivered the king's command, Queen Vashti refused to come. Then the king became furious and burned with anger.

¹³Since it was customary for the king to consult experts in matters of law and justice, he spoke with the wise men who understood the times ¹⁴and were closest to the king — Karshena, Shethar, Admatha, Tarshish, Meres, Marsena and

---

[a] 1 Hebrew *Ahasuerus*; here and throughout Esther   [b] 1 That is, the upper Nile region

---

1:1–9 The events in the book of Esther take place about 55 to 65 years after the Babylonian exile of the Jewish people had ended. The story is set in Susa, the primary capital of the Persian Empire during the reign of Ahasuerus (also known as Xerxes). Chronologically, this places it in the middle of the book of Ezra—after the second temple in Jerusalem was dedicated in 516 BC, but prior to Ezra leading a group of exiles to Jerusalem (in 458 BC). The prologue to the book of Esther details the extent of the king's reign and describes three different festivals to celebrate his reign.

The genre of the book of Esther is debated. At times, Esther seems to present itself as history. Yet there are several difficulties in aligning the narrative with other accounts of Persia's history (see note on v. 9; note on 2:3; note on 2:8). This, combined with what seems like intentional exaggeration on behalf of the narrator—the impractical size of Haman's execution device, the lavish party sequences, the absurd decrees by the king and the poetic irony—may indicate that the book is intended to function more like a play than a historical account. Regardless of how the genre issue is understood, the book was written to explain the narrative with other accounts of the origins of the Jewish festival called Purim. In the process, it emphasizes the preservation of God's people (by God's unseen hand) and addresses theologically difficult issues (9:20–32; see note on 2:10; note on 2:15).

1:1 Xerxes This Persian king was called Ahasuerus in Hebrew but is better known by his Greek name, Xerxes. See the timeline "Dates Related to Ezra, Nehemiah and Esther" on p. 716.

EVENT	DATE
Cyrus allows Jews to return to Jerusalem	538 BC
Temple is completed	516 BC
Xerxes becomes king	486 BC

1:2 Susa Located on the Shaur River, about 150 miles north of the Persian Gulf. The city became part of the Persian Empire when Cyrus took Babylon and its provinces. Darius I made Susa (also called Shushan) an administrative capital and built a palace in the city. See note on Ezr 4:9.

1:3 third year of his reign Probably sometime in 483 BC. **Persia and Media** These two nations originally allied in an effort to overthrow the Babylonians.

1:4 full 180 days While the Persians were known for extravagant celebrations, the excessive length may be an exaggeration either for comedic effect or to critique the Persians' licentious lifestyle.

1:8 allowed to drink with no restrictions The Medes and Persians had a law that whenever the king drank, everyone drank. This phrase may refer to the temporary negation of this law or to each person being allowed to drink however much he desired.

1:9 Queen Vashti Although connections at times have been made between Vashti and the Persian queen Amestris, such connections are inconclusive. Vashti is known only from the book of Esther.

1:10–22 While intoxicated, the king requests his queen come to his banquet of all men (vv. 10–11), forcing her to leave her own banquet guests (v. 9).

1:10 eunuchs Male servants or supervisory royal officials; this context implies that these men are also castrated. These particular men were likely castrated to ensure that any child born to the queen was the progeny of the king.

1:12 Queen Vashti refused to come The reason for the queen's refusal is unknown.

Esther 1:1

XERXES (AHASUERUS)
The Persian king Xerxes (Ahasuerus) reigned from 486 to 465 BC; he was the son of Darius I, who is mentioned in Ezra and Nehemiah (e.g., Ezr 4:5; Ne 12:22).

Memukan, the seven nobles of Persia and Media who had special access to the king and were highest in the kingdom.

¹⁵"According to law, what must be done to Queen Vashti?" he asked. "She has not obeyed the command of King Xerxes that the eunuchs have taken to her."

¹⁶Then Memukan replied in the presence of the king and the nobles, "Queen Vashti has done wrong, not only against the king but also against all the nobles and the peoples of all the provinces of King Xerxes. ¹⁷For the queen's conduct will become known to all the women, and so they will despise their husbands and say, 'King Xerxes commanded Queen Vashti to be brought before him, but she would not come.' ¹⁸This very day the Persian and Median women of the nobility who have heard about the queen's conduct will respond to all the king's nobles in the same way. There will be no end of disrespect and discord.

¹⁹"Therefore, if it pleases the king, let him issue a royal decree and let it be written in the laws of Persia and Media, which cannot be repealed, that Vashti is never again to enter the presence of King Xerxes. Also let the king give her royal position to someone else who is better than she. ²⁰Then when the king's edict is proclaimed throughout all his vast realm, all the women will respect their husbands, from the least to the greatest."

²¹The king and his nobles were pleased with this advice, so the king did as Memukan proposed. ²²He sent dispatches to all parts of the kingdom, to each province in its own script and to each people in their own language, proclaiming that every man should be ruler over his own household, using his native tongue.

Esther Made Queen

2 Later when King Xerxes' fury had subsided, he remembered Vashti and what she had done and what he had decreed about her. ²Then the king's personal attendants proposed, "Let a search be made for beautiful young virgins for the king. ³Let the king appoint commissioners in every province of his realm to bring all these beautiful young women into the harem at the citadel of Susa. Let them be placed under the care of Hegai, the king's eunuch, who is in charge of the women; and let beauty treatments be given to them. ⁴Then let the young woman who pleases the king be queen instead of Vashti." This advice appealed to the king, and he followed it.

⁵Now there was in the citadel of Susa a Jew of the tribe of Benjamin, named Mordecai son of Jair, the son of Shimei, the son of Kish, ⁶who had been carried into exile from Jerusalem by Nebuchadnezzar king of Babylon, among those taken captive with Jehoiachinᵃ king of Judah. ⁷Mordecai had a cousin named Hadassah, whom he had brought up because she had neither father nor mother. This young woman, who was also known as Esther, had a lovely figure and was beautiful. Mordecai had taken her as his own daughter when her father and mother died.

⁸When the king's order and edict had been

ᵃ 6 Hebrew *Jeconiah*, a variant of *Jehoiachin*

1:13–15 There may be two groups of people being consulted here (astrologers and the highest-ranking government officials) or only one group (the officials).

1:13 who understood the times This Hebrew phrase could either mean that these advisors were experts in astrology or that they were knowledgeable in the affairs of the empire and how the king's decisions would affect the people (compare 3:7; Da 2:27; 1Ch 12:32).

1:19 cannot be repealed Persian decrees could not be repealed once they became official (see Da 6:8).

2:1–18 Esther 2:12 and 2:16 indicate that about two years pass between the king's first edict in the story (1:22) and Esther becoming part of the king's harem (v. 8).

2:1 remembered Vashti It is unclear how much time passed between the decree in 1:22 and this moment.

2:2 beautiful young virgins It is not described how young the women being sought are, but according to ancient Near Eastern culture, they could have been as young as a woman in the first stages of puberty—around age 12. Had the proper requirements for seeking a Persian queen been followed, Esther would have been disqualified on the basis of her parentage. Kings of the Persian Empire of this period were supposed to only marry women from one of the seven noble Persian families (according to Greek historian Herodotus, *Histories*, 1.135; 3.84; 7.61).

2:3 the harem In Esther, this term refers generally to

the house where the women lived. The women being gathered were not yet regarded as concubines, since the concubines were specifically in the care of Shaashgaz, a different eunuch (v. 14).

2:5–6 This portion of the narrative may be intended to explain Mordecai's access to the grounds of the royal palace—a fact that becomes integral to the narrative (vv. 11,19; 4:1–2). The former empire, Babylon, intentionally utilized noble foreigners in their courts; Persia likely had similar practices (Da 1:3–5). See the timeline "Judah From the Fall of Samaria to the Exile" on p. 606.

2:5 Jew The common term for the Hebrew people after the exiles to Assyria and Babylon (compare Ezr 4:12; Ne 1:2).

2:7 a cousin Esther and Mordecai are technically first cousins, but Mordecai functions as Esther's adopted father. **was also known as Esther** Jews of the exile commonly received and used foreign names; these names were often in addition to their Hebrew names (compare Da 1:7).

2:8 Esther 2:12 indicates that twelve months pass between Esther becoming part of the harem and entering the king's private quarters. Thus, Esther became part of the king's harem in December 480 BC or January 479 BC. If the narrative of Esther is mapped to known historical events, then she becomes part of the king's harem during Persia's invasion of Greece.

proclaimed, many young women were brought to the citadel of Susa and put under the care of Hegai. Esther also was taken to the king's palace and entrusted to Hegai, who had charge of the harem. [9]She pleased him and won his favor. Immediately he provided her with her beauty treatments and special food. He assigned to her seven female attendants selected from the king's palace and moved her and her attendants into the best place in the harem.

[10]Esther had not revealed her nationality and family background, because Mordecai had forbidden her to do so. [11]Every day he walked back and forth near the courtyard of the harem to find out how Esther was and what was happening to her.

[12]Before a young woman's turn came to go in to King Xerxes, she had to complete twelve months of beauty treatments prescribed for the women, six months with oil of myrrh and six with perfumes and cosmetics. [13]And this is how she would go to the king: Anything she wanted was given her to take with her from the harem to the king's palace. [14]In the evening she would go there and in the morning return to another part of the harem to the care of Shaashgaz, the king's eunuch who was in charge of the concubines. She would not return to the king unless he was pleased with her and summoned her by name.

[15]When the turn came for Esther (the young woman Mordecai had adopted, the daughter of his uncle Abihail) to go to the king, she asked for nothing other than what Hegai, the king's eunuch who was in charge of the harem, suggested. And Esther won the favor of everyone who saw her. [16]She was taken to King Xerxes in the royal residence in the tenth month, the month of Tebeth, in the seventh year of his reign.

[17]Now the king was attracted to Esther more than to any of the other women, and she won his favor and approval more than any of the other virgins. So he set a royal crown on her head and made her queen instead of Vashti. [18]And the king gave a great banquet, Esther's banquet, for all his nobles and officials. He proclaimed a holiday throughout the provinces and distributed gifts with royal liberality.

Mordecai Uncovers a Conspiracy

[19]When the virgins were assembled a second time, Mordecai was sitting at the king's gate. [20]But Esther had kept secret her family background and nationality just as Mordecai had told her to do, for she continued to follow Mordecai's instructions as she had done when he was bringing her up.

[21]During the time Mordecai was sitting at the king's gate, Bigthana[a] and Teresh, two of the king's officers who guarded the doorway, became angry and conspired to assassinate King Xerxes. [22]But Mordecai found out about the plot and told Queen Esther, who in turn reported it to the king, giving credit to Mordecai. [23]And when the report was investigated and found to be true, the two officials were impaled on poles. All this was recorded in the book of the annals in the presence of the king.

Haman's Plot to Destroy the Jews

3 After these events, King Xerxes honored Haman son of Hammedatha, the Agagite, elevating him and giving him a seat of honor higher than that of all the other nobles. [2]All the royal officials at the king's gate knelt down and paid honor to Haman, for the king had commanded

---

[a] 21 Hebrew *Bigthan*, a variant of *Bigthana*

2:8 king's palace The women do not actually enter the king's presence at this point, but instead merely begin living in his complex (compare v. 13).

2:10 had not revealed her nationality To keep her national identity secret, Esther would have eaten unclean food, as v. 9 may be implying (Lev 11:46–47) and broken a number of other ceremonial regulations (compare Da 1:8 and Dt 7:1–6).

2:12–14 The narrative is interrupted by an excursus in Est 2:12–14 about the process of preparing virgins to visit the king.

2:14 concubines Once the king had intercourse with a woman, she was separated from the virgins, placed under the leadership of a different eunuch (Shaashgaz), and would only see the king again if he specifically asked for her.

2:15 After the interlude of vv. 12–14, the narrative transitions back to the story of Esther.

2:15 won the favor The depiction of Esther as winning everyone's favor seems to imply a further level of compromise as a Jewish person.

2:16 month of Tebeth, in the seventh year of his

reign December 479 BC or January 478 BC, about four years after Vashti had been deposed.

2:18 a great banquet The same group of people invited to the king's first festival are invited again to this festival (1:3).

2:19–23 The critical point of this passage is that Mordecai is present at the entrance of the king's compound and is free to roam about the compound as he wishes — indicating that he has an official role. It is unclear how much time elapses between when Esther becomes queen and the events of vv. 19–23 (see note on 3:1–7).

2:21 king's gate Mordecai may have stood at the gate for a variety of reasons, such as business, to exchange or overhear information (if his official role required it) or to be close to Esther without raising suspicion.

2:23 two officials were impaled on poles The Hebrew here indicates that these men were impaled, not crucified or hung with rope. Impalement was a common practice in the ancient Near East and was not necessarily how perpetrators were killed — often they would be killed beforehand. **book of the annals** The official records of the reign of Xerxes (Ahasuerus).

this concerning him. But Mordecai would not kneel down or pay him honor.

³Then the royal officials at the king's gate asked Mordecai, "Why do you disobey the king's command?" ⁴Day after day they spoke to him but he refused to comply. Therefore they told Haman about it to see whether Mordecai's behavior would be tolerated, for he had told them he was a Jew.

⁵When Haman saw that Mordecai would not kneel down or pay him honor, he was enraged. ⁶Yet having learned who Mordecai's people were, he scorned the idea of killing only Mordecai. Instead Haman looked for a way to destroy all Mordecai's people, the Jews, throughout the whole kingdom of Xerxes.

⁷In the twelfth year of King Xerxes, in the first month, the month of Nisan, the *pur* (that is, the lot) was cast in the presence of Haman to select a day and month. And the lot fell on*a* the twelfth month, the month of Adar.

a 7 Septuagint; Hebrew does not have *And the lot fell on.*

3:1–7 By the time the narrative reaches v. 7, more than four years have passed since Esther became queen (2:16). The events of 2:19–23 and 3:1–6 occur at some point during this time period.

3:1 Agagite A derogatory title that the Hebrew text uses to affiliate Haman with Agag, the Amalekite king. Agag was an enemy of Israel because of the Amalekites' attack on the Israelites when they were journeying to the promised land (Ex 17:8–14; 1Sa 15:2–3). The tension of the narrative is further enhanced by Mordecai being a Benjamite and, it seems, a descendant of Kish, Saul's father (Est 2:5). This sets up the book of Esther as the resolution to an ancient feud that Yahweh had vowed to resolve (Ex 17:14). **higher than that of all the other nobles** Haman has supreme authority among the officials, presumably second only to the king—the narrative shows that his role is a hybrid between a chief-of-staff and a general.

3:2–6 In these verses, Mordecai intentionally defies Haman, even though the king has commanded that people pay respect to Haman (v. 3). The OT contains many examples of Jewish people bowing to authority figures (e.g., Ge 33:3,6–7; 42:6; Ex 18:7; Ru 2:10; 1Sa 20:41; 24:8; 25:23; 2Sa 14:4). This suggests Mordecai's defiance could be due to antagonism between the Jews and the Amalekites (compare note on Est 3:1) or to tension between Haman and Mordecai (perhaps stemming from Haman's promotion when Mordecai was not even recognized for his service).

3:6 he scorned the idea The Hebrew text here is vague about why Haman chooses to not punish Mordecai alone. Verse 5 suggests being Jewish is Mordecai's excuse for not bowing, but that still does not justify the absurdity of Haman's logic—to punish all Jewish people for one person's decision.

3:7 In the twelfth year of King Xerxes, in the first

Israelite Calendar

MONTH	BIBLICAL NAME	MODERN EQUIVALENT	REFERENCES
1	Nisan/Aviv*	Mar–Apr	Ex 13:4; 23:15; 34:18; Dt 16:1; Ne 2:1; Est 3:7
2	Iyyar/Ziv*	Apr–May	1Ki 6:1,37
3	Sivan	May–Jun	Est 8:9
4	Tammuz	Jun–Jul	none
5	Ab	Jul–Aug	none
6	Elul	Aug–Sep	Ne 6:15
7	Tishri/Ethanim*	Sep–Oct	1Ki 8:2
8	Heshvan/Bul*	Oct–Nov	1Ki 6:38
9	Kislev	Nov–Dec	Ne 1:1; Zec 7:1
10	Tebeth	Dec–Jan	Est 2:16
11	Shebat	Jan–Feb	Zec 1:7
12	Adar	Feb–Mar	Ezr 6:15; Est 3:7,13; 8:12; 9:1,15,17,19,21
13	Second Adar†	Mar–Apr	none

* Those with two names include the Babylonian name first and Canaanite name second.

† Since the lunar calendar is 11 days shorter than the solar calendar, an extra month was added between Adar and Nisan seven times in each 19-year cycle.

⁸Then Haman said to King Xerxes, "There is a certain people dispersed among the peoples in all the provinces of your kingdom who keep themselves separate. Their customs are different from those of all other people, and they do not obey the king's laws; it is not in the king's best interest to tolerate them. ⁹If it pleases the king, let a decree be issued to destroy them, and I will give ten thousand talents*ᵃ* of silver to the king's administrators for the royal treasury."

¹⁰So the king took his signet ring from his finger and gave it to Haman son of Hammedatha, the Agagite, the enemy of the Jews. ¹¹"Keep the money," the king said to Haman, "and do with the people as you please."

¹²Then on the thirteenth day of the first month the royal secretaries were summoned. They wrote out in the script of each province and in the language of each people all Haman's orders to the king's satraps, the governors of the various provinces and the nobles of the various peoples. These were written in the name of King Xerxes himself and sealed with his own ring. ¹³Dispatches were sent by couriers to all the king's provinces with the order to destroy, kill and annihilate all the Jews — young and old, women and children — on a single day, the thirteenth day of the twelfth month, the month of Adar, and to plunder their goods. ¹⁴A copy of the text of the edict was to be issued as law in every province and made known to the people of every nationality so they would be ready for that day.

¹⁵The couriers went out, spurred on by the king's command, and the edict was issued in the citadel of Susa. The king and Haman sat down to drink, but the city of Susa was bewildered.

Mordecai Persuades Esther to Help

4 When Mordecai learned of all that had been done, he tore his clothes, put on sackcloth and ashes, and went out into the city, wailing loudly and bitterly. ²But he went only as far as the king's gate, because no one clothed in sackcloth was allowed to enter it. ³In every province to which the edict and order of the king came, there was great mourning among the Jews, with fasting, weeping and wailing. Many lay in sackcloth and ashes.

⁴When Esther's eunuchs and female attendants came and told her about Mordecai, she was in great distress. She sent clothes for him to put on instead of his sackcloth, but he would not accept them. ⁵Then Esther summoned Hathak, one of the king's eunuchs assigned to attend her, and ordered him to find out what was troubling Mordecai and why. ⁶So Hathak went out to Mordecai in the open square of the city in front of the king's gate. ⁷Mor-

ᵃ 9 That is, about 375 tons or about 340 metric tons

month, the month of Nisan March or April 474 BC. More than four years have elapsed since Esther became queen. See the table "Israelite Calendar" on p. 763; see the timeline "Dates Related to Ezra, Nehemiah and Esther" on p. 716. **pur (that is, the lot)** The Hebrew text uses the Akkadian term for casting lots, *pur*, to explain the name of the Jewish festival Purim, which will be referenced in ch. 9. The events in this verse are not occurring over a year-long period, but instead involve an elaborate game of chance occurring over multiple days to determine a specific date in the year. **month of Adar** The month that the casting of lots dictated, which is equivalent to February or March. In v. 13, it is revealed that Haman was using the casting of lots to determine the date for the destruction of the Jewish people. The date of the genocide is set for about eleven months from this moment in the narrative.

3:8–15 Now that Haman has conspired, he visits the king so that he may put his evil plan into action.

3:8 dispersed among the peoples A result of the deportation of the Jewish people by the Assyrians and Babylonians (2Ki 15; 16; 24:10–17). **they do not obey the king's laws** Haman seems to be drawing a false conclusion from his experience with Mordecai (see note on Est 3:6).

3:9 to destroy them Haman calls for the annihilation of the Jews throughout the Persian kingdom. This type of action was not without precedence in the Persian Empire. **ten thousand talents of silver** This is a ridiculous sum, equating to at least two-thirds of the annual income into the royal treasury from all tributes in the empire (compare the historian Herodotus' remarks in *Histories*, 3.95).

3:10 signet ring The imprint of the king's signet ring essentially served as his signature.

3:11 Keep the money The Hebrew text here could be interpreted as the king telling Haman that the money is unnecessary—this would be a way of bargaining with Haman (acting like the money is Haman's to do with as he wishes). This could also be a subtle way of the king acknowledging that he will receive the money later on (as a type of bribery).

3:12 the thirteenth day of the first month On the day before the Jewish Passover in 474 BC, the decree is sent to each major government leader in the Persian empire that the Jewish people were to be annihilated on a single day (compare Ex 12:6).

3:13 the twelfth month The genocide was set to happen in February or March 473 BC (9:1). The decree is sent out about eleven months before its planned fulfillment, but it would have taken approximately three to four months for it to reach the entire empire.

4:1–17 This section opens with Mordecai learning of Haman's plans to annihilate the Jews (3:12–14) and Mordecai's response of mourning.

4:1 tore his clothes This seems to have been the most commonly practiced form of visible mourning in the ancient Near East (e.g., Ge 37:34; Job 1:20; 16:15; Isa 37:1). **ashes** Another visible sign of mourning (compare Jer 6:26; Isa 58:5; 61:3; Eze 27:30).

4:4–5 There is no indication of how much time elapses between Mordecai and others learning of the edict and when Esther learns of it.

decai told him everything that had happened to him, including the exact amount of money Haman had promised to pay into the royal treasury for the destruction of the Jews. ⁸He also gave him a copy of the text of the edict for their annihilation, which had been published in Susa, to show to Esther and explain it to her, and he told him to instruct her to go into the king's presence to beg for mercy and plead with him for her people.

⁹Hathak went back and reported to Esther what Mordecai had said. ¹⁰Then she instructed him to say to Mordecai, ¹¹"All the king's officials and the people of the royal provinces know that for any man or woman who approaches the king in the inner court without being summoned the king has but one law: that they be put to death unless the king extends the gold scepter to them and spares their lives. But thirty days have passed since I was called to go to the king."

¹²When Esther's words were reported to Mordecai, ¹³he sent back this answer: "Do not think that because you are in the king's house you alone of all the Jews will escape. ¹⁴For if you remain silent at this time, relief and deliverance for the Jews will arise from another place, but you and your father's family will perish. And who knows but that you have come to your royal position for such a time as this?"

¹⁵Then Esther sent this reply to Mordecai: ¹⁶"Go, gather together all the Jews who are in Susa, and fast for me. Do not eat or drink for three days, night or day. I and my attendants will fast as you do. When this is done, I will go to the king, even though it is against the law. And if I perish, I perish."

¹⁷So Mordecai went away and carried out all of Esther's instructions.

Esther's Request to the King

5 On the third day Esther put on her royal robes and stood in the inner court of the palace, in front of the king's hall. The king was sitting on his royal throne in the hall, facing the entrance. ²When he saw Queen Esther standing in the court, he was pleased with her and held out to her the gold scepter that was in his hand. So Esther approached and touched the tip of the scepter.

³Then the king asked, "What is it, Queen Esther? What is your request? Even up to half the kingdom, it will be given you."

⁴"If it pleases the king," replied Esther, "let the king, together with Haman, come today to a banquet I have prepared for him."

⁵"Bring Haman at once," the king said, "so that we may do what Esther asks."

So the king and Haman went to the banquet Esther had prepared. ⁶As they were drinking wine, the king again asked Esther, "Now what is your petition? It will be given you. And what is your request? Even up to half the kingdom, it will be granted."

⁷Esther replied, "My petition and my request is this: ⁸If the king regards me with favor and if it pleases the king to grant my petition and fulfill my request, let the king and Haman come tomorrow to the banquet I will prepare for them. Then I will answer the king's question."

Haman's Rage Against Mordecai

⁹Haman went out that day happy and in high spirits. But when he saw Mordecai at the king's gate and observed that he neither rose nor showed fear in his presence, he was filled with rage against Mordecai. ¹⁰Nevertheless, Haman restrained himself and went home.

Calling together his friends and Zeresh, his wife, ¹¹Haman boasted to them about his vast wealth, his many sons, and all the ways the king had honored him and how he had elevated him above the other nobles and officials. ¹²"And that's not all," Haman added. "I'm the only person Queen Esther invited to accompany the king to the banquet she gave. And she has invited me along with

---

4:7 exact amount of money 10,000 talents of silver (see Est 3:9 and note).

4:8 a copy of the text of the edict Refers to the decree of 3:13.

4:14 For if you remain silent Mordecai's thinking seems to reflect that of Judaism in general—that God would find a way for his people to survive, no matter what (compare Isa 10:20). **you and your father's family will perish** Mordecai could be saying that it will be too late for the Jewish people living in Susa by the time deliverance comes or that divine retribution would come to Esther for her inaction (compare Nu 14:18).

4:16 fast for me Although God is not mentioned here, the implication is that the fasting is an observance of a time of intense prayer for the salvation of the Jewish people (compare Ps 35:13; Ezr 8:23; Ne 1:4; Jnh 3:5). **if I perish, I perish** A statement of courageous resolve, not an expression of resignation to a foregone conclusion (compare Ge 43:14).

5:1–8 On the third day of the fast of the Jewish people, Esther takes action on behalf of her people by visiting the king uninvited—it has been more than a month since she has seen him (Est 4:11).

5:2 held out to her the gold scepter A signal granting Esther permission to approach and a signal to her that she will not suffer the death penalty for this unexpected visit (4:11).

5:3 Even up to half the kingdom An idiom, not a literal statement.

5:9–14 The narrative shifts from Esther's first banquet (vv. 4–8) to the rift between Haman and Mordecai—in doing so, it circles back to the events of 3:2.

5:11 his many sons Multiple sons was a mark of greatness in the Persian empire (according to the historian Herodotus, *Histories* 1.136).

the king tomorrow. [13]But all this gives me no satisfaction as long as I see that Jew Mordecai sitting at the king's gate."

[14]His wife Zeresh and all his friends said to him, "Have a pole set up, reaching to a height of fifty cubits,[a] and ask the king in the morning to have Mordecai impaled on it. Then go with the king to the banquet and enjoy yourself." This suggestion delighted Haman, and he had the pole set up.

Mordecai Honored

6 That night the king could not sleep; so he ordered the book of the chronicles, the record of his reign, to be brought in and read to him. [2]It was found recorded there that Mordecai had exposed Bigthana and Teresh, two of the king's officers who guarded the doorway, who had conspired to assassinate King Xerxes.

[3]"What honor and recognition has Mordecai received for this?" the king asked.

"Nothing has been done for him," his attendants answered.

[4]The king said, "Who is in the court?" Now Haman had just entered the outer court of the palace to speak to the king about impaling Mordecai on the pole he had set up for him.

[5]His attendants answered, "Haman is standing in the court."

"Bring him in," the king ordered.

[6]When Haman entered, the king asked him, "What should be done for the man the king delights to honor?"

Now Haman thought to himself, "Who is there that the king would rather honor than me?" [7]So he answered the king, "For the man the king delights to honor, [8]have them bring a royal robe the king has worn and a horse the king has ridden, one with a royal crest placed on its head. [9]Then let the robe and horse be entrusted to one of the king's most noble princes. Let them robe the man the king delights to honor, and lead him on the horse through the city streets, proclaiming before

him, 'This is what is done for the man the king delights to honor!'"

[10]"Go at once," the king commanded Haman. "Get the robe and the horse and do just as you have suggested for Mordecai the Jew, who sits at the king's gate. Do not neglect anything you have recommended."

[11]So Haman got the robe and the horse. He robed Mordecai, and led him on horseback through the city streets, proclaiming before him, "This is what is done for the man the king delights to honor!"

[12]Afterward Mordecai returned to the king's gate. But Haman rushed home, with his head covered in grief, [13]and told Zeresh his wife and all his friends everything that had happened to him.

His advisers and his wife Zeresh said to him, "Since Mordecai, before whom your downfall has started, is of Jewish origin, you cannot stand against him — you will surely come to ruin!" [14]While they were still talking with him, the king's eunuchs arrived and hurried Haman away to the banquet Esther had prepared.

Haman Impaled

7 So the king and Haman went to Queen Esther's banquet, [2]and as they were drinking wine on the second day, the king again asked, "Queen Esther, what is your petition? It will be given you. What is your request? Even up to half the kingdom, it will be granted."

[3]Then Queen Esther answered, "If I have found favor with you, Your Majesty, and if it pleases you, grant me my life — this is my petition. And spare my people — this is my request. [4]For I and my people have been sold to be destroyed, killed and annihilated. If we had merely been sold as male and female slaves, I would have kept quiet, because no such distress would justify disturbing the king.[b]"

---

[a] 14 That is, about 75 feet or about 23 meters   [b] 4 Or quiet, but the compensation our adversary offers cannot be compared with the loss the king would suffer

---

5:14 a pole set up, reaching to a height of fifty cubits The planned height is completely impractical and probably intended to be hyperbole by the narrator — it would have been much taller than any structure in the city (75 to 80 feet high). See note on 2:23.

6:1–13 The narrative reintroduces Mordecai's unrecognized effort to save the king (2:21–23).

6:1 book of the chronicles, the record The records of the king's reign, which must be the same records mentioned in 2:23, based on their contents (compare Ezr 5:17; note on Est 10:2).

6:2 that Mordecai had exposed The attempted assassination is narrated in 2:21–23 — an event that could have taken place more than four years earlier.

6:8 one with a royal crest placed on its head This seems to be an expression to confirm that Haman indeed means the king's horse, not just any horse.

6:10 the Jew The emphasis on Mordecai's Jewishness shows that the king is likely still unaware that his edict will result in the death of the Jewish people (compare 3:8).

6:13 Following the public honoring of Mordecai, Haman goes home to consult with the same group of people he met with the day before (5:10).

6:13 is of Jewish origin Since Mordecai is so honored, Haman's advisors speculate that Haman's overall plot will fail.

6:14 — 7:6 The narrative changes scenes from Haman's house back to the king's palace, as Esther's second banquet for the king and Haman is about to begin.

7:1 Queen Esther's banquet This banquet could have occurred in the afternoon or evening, depending on whether Haman is executed the same day.

7:2 the second day A reference to the second banquet,

5King Xerxes asked Queen Esther, "Who is he? Where is he—the man who has dared to do such a thing?"

6Esther said, "An adversary and enemy! This vile Haman!"

Then Haman was terrified before the king and queen. 7The king got up in a rage, left his wine and went out into the palace garden. But Haman, realizing that the king had already decided his fate, stayed behind to beg Queen Esther for his life.

8Just as the king returned from the palace garden to the banquet hall, Haman was falling on the couch where Esther was reclining.

The king exclaimed, "Will he even molest the queen while she is with me in the house?"

As soon as the word left the king's mouth, they covered Haman's face. 9Then Harbona, one of the eunuchs attending the king, said, "A pole reaching to a height of fifty cubits[a] stands by Haman's house. He had it set up for Mordecai, who spoke up to help the king."

The king said, "Impale him on it!" 10So they impaled Haman on the pole he had set up for Mordecai. Then the king's fury subsided.

The King's Edict in Behalf of the Jews

8 That same day King Xerxes gave Queen Esther the estate of Haman, the enemy of the Jews. And Mordecai came into the presence of the king, for Esther had told how he was related to her. 2The king took off his signet ring, which he had reclaimed from Haman, and presented it to Mordecai. And Esther appointed him over Haman's estate.

3Esther again pleaded with the king, falling at his feet and weeping. She begged him to put an end to the evil plan of Haman the Agagite, which he had devised against the Jews. 4Then the king extended the gold scepter to Esther and she arose and stood before him.

5"If it pleases the king," she said, "and if he regards me with favor and thinks it the right thing to do, and if he is pleased with me, let an order be written overruling the dispatches that Haman son of Hammedatha, the Agagite, devised and wrote to destroy the Jews in all the king's provinces. 6For how can I bear to see disaster fall on my people? How can I bear to see the destruction of my family?"

7King Xerxes replied to Queen Esther and to Mordecai the Jew, "Because Haman attacked the Jews, I have given his estate to Esther, and they have impaled him on the pole he set up. 8Now write another decree in the king's name in behalf of the Jews as seems best to you, and seal it with the king's signet ring—for no document written in the king's name and sealed with his ring can be revoked."

9At once the royal secretaries were summoned—on the twenty-third day of the third month, the month of Sivan. They wrote out all Mordecai's orders to the Jews, and to the satraps, governors and nobles of the 127 provinces stretching from India to Cush.[b] These orders were written in the script of each province and the language of each people and also to the Jews in their own script

[a] 9 That is, about 75 feet or about 23 meters   [b] 9 That is, the upper Nile region

not a day passing. The first day was the initial feast that Esther prepared for the king and Haman (5:4–5). **Even up to half the kingdom** See note on 5:3.
7:4 been sold Likely a reference to the money Haman promised the king upon acceptance of his original proposal to annihilate the Jewish people (3:9). **merely been sold as male and female slaves** This seems to be a negotiating tactic—historically, such a situation would be unexpected and odd. **distress** The Hebrew word used here, *tsar*, could have the meaning of affliction or adversary. Affliction could refer to the possibility of slavery; adversary would be a reference to Haman (compare v. 6). **no such distress would justify disturbing the king** The Hebrew text here could refer to the empire potentially losing revenue or to a general inconvenience for the king.
7:7–10 The king may have left to determine Haman's fate or to seek the appropriate officials, so that they may arrest Haman.
7:8 falling on the couch where Esther was reclining The misdirection present throughout the narrative continues here, as Haman's begging is misunderstood as assault (compare Ge 39:7–20).
7:9 A pole Haman's plan to build his execution device had been carried out at some point during the past 24 hours or so (see note on Est 2:23). **fifty cubits** See note on 5:14.

8:1–17 Although Haman has now been executed, there is still the matter of the king's edict to annihilate the Jewish people. On the same day as Haman's execution, Esther seeks to find a resolution to this matter. Based on the formalities mentioned in this chapter, it seems that these events take place in the king's court.
8:2 his signet ring This ring allowed for someone to carry out actions on the king's behalf (see note on 3:10). **presented it to Mordecai** The king elevates Mordecai to a high position in the empire, perhaps even second in authority only to the king—essentially giving him Haman's former position (compare 10:3).
8:3 falling at his feet An act of supplication, not an act of worship or reverence (see note on 3:2–6). **Haman the Agagite** See note on 3:1.
8:4 extended the gold scepter This detail could indicate that Esther has again approached the king without an appointment (compare 4:11), which would mean that vv. 3–8 represent a different conversation than vv. 1–2, possibly on the next day.
8:5 let an order be written overruling the dispatches Since the king was unable to revoke his own decree (1:19), a new decree was necessary to counter the effects of the first one (compare Da 6:15).
8:7 the pole See note on Est 2:23.
8:9 on the twenty-third day of the third month, the

and language. ¹⁰Mordecai wrote in the name of King Xerxes, sealed the dispatches with the king's signet ring, and sent them by mounted couriers, who rode fast horses especially bred for the king.

¹¹The king's edict granted the Jews in every city the right to assemble and protect themselves; to destroy, kill and annihilate the armed men of any nationality or province who might attack them and their women and children,ᵃ and to plunder the property of their enemies. ¹²The day appointed for the Jews to do this in all the provinces of King Xerxes was the thirteenth day of the twelfth month, the month of Adar. ¹³A copy of the text of the edict was to be issued as law in every province and made known to the people of every nationality so that the Jews would be ready on that day to avenge themselves on their enemies.

¹⁴The couriers, riding the royal horses, went out, spurred on by the king's command, and the edict was issued in the citadel of Susa.

The Triumph of the Jews

¹⁵When Mordecai left the king's presence, he was wearing royal garments of blue and white, a large crown of gold and a purple robe of fine linen. And the city of Susa held a joyous celebration. ¹⁶For the Jews it was a time of happiness and joy, gladness and honor. ¹⁷In every province and in every city to which the edict of the king came, there was joy and gladness among the Jews, with feasting and celebrating. And many people of other nationalities became Jews because fear of the Jews had seized them.

9 On the thirteenth day of the twelfth month, the month of Adar, the edict commanded by the king was to be carried out. On this day the enemies of the Jews had hoped to overpower them, but now the tables were turned and the Jews got the upper hand over those who hated them. ²The Jews assembled in their cities in all the provinces of King Xerxes to attack those determined to destroy them. No one could stand against them, because the people of all the other nationalities were afraid of them. ³And all the nobles of the provinces, the satraps, the governors and the king's administrators helped the Jews, because fear of Mordecai had seized them. ⁴Mordecai was prominent in the palace; his reputation spread throughout the provinces, and he became more and more powerful.

⁵The Jews struck down all their enemies with the sword, killing and destroying them, and they

ᵃ 11 Or *province, together with their women and children, who might attack them;*

---

month of Sivan May or June 474 BC, 70 days after the original edict declaring the destruction of the Jewish people was issued (3:12). This new edict gives the Jewish people in Susa (Shushan) about eight months to prepare to defend themselves; those in the furthest parts of the empire from Susa would have four to five months to prepare by the time the edict reached them. See the table "Israelite Calendar" on p. 763.
8:11 to destroy, kill and annihilate The same words were used in Haman's original decree (3:13) and referenced by Esther in her first negotiation with the king (7:4). Since the original decree cannot be undone (1:19; 8:8), the Jewish people must be able to respond to their persecutors in kind. **women and children** This could be understood as echoing the words of Haman's edict, which granted people the right to kill Jewish men, women and children (3:13). This portion of the edict could have been included to discourage persecution of the Jewish people or to ensure that an avenger would not later on arise from their persecutors' household. When this order is actually carried out, only men are mentioned as being destroyed—women and children are not, unless Haman's sons were not adults (9:12,15; see note on 9:7–10). In theory, the persecutors of the Jewish people could have understood this new edict as cancelling out the edict to annihilate the Jews. When two laws oppose one another, both could be understood as irrelevant. **property** This additional echo of Haman's edict (3:12–13) emphasizes that the intention of Mordecai's edict could also be to practice the "eye for an eye" principle, which was allowable by Jewish law (Ex 21:24; compare Mt 5:38).
8:12 thirteenth day of the twelfth month The same day that Haman's edict was to be carried out—in February or March 473 BC.
8:14 citadel of Susa See note on Est 1:2.

8:15–17 These events could represent a continuation of the same event in vv. 9–14 or occur at some later point. Mordecai dresses in the clothing and colors of royalty.
8:15 a large crown of gold The Hebrew word used here is not the same word used for the crown (or turban) that the queen wears (1:11; 2:17), suggesting that it was a sign of Mordecai's official position—not a signal that he was acting as a king.
8:17 became Jews The Hebrew text here could indicate that non-Jewish people chose to become Jewish—meaning they made a decision to convert to Judaism; 9:27 could hint at this (compare Ru 1:16; Da 3:28–29). The non-Jewish people may also have just professed that they were Jewish, in order to ensure that they would not be on the wrong side of the coming conflict. The Hebrew text could also be interpreted as indicating that non-Jewish people chose to ally themselves with the Jewish people. **because fear of the Jews had seized them** These non-Jewish people seem to fear impending violence, which means that their concern probably stems out of the Jewish people having the backing of the king (Est 8:9–10; compare 9:2–3).

9:1–19 About eight months occur between the events of 8:9–14 and 9:1, with 8:15–16 occurring at some point in between.
9:1 Adar February or March 473 BC, the day that Haman had planned to annihilate the Jewish people (3:13; 8:12). **edict commanded by the king** Refers to the original command for people of the Persian empire to destroy the Jews (3:13). **tables were turned and the Jews got the upper hand** The Hebrew phrase used here implies a complete power or dominance—like that of a king over a land.

did what they pleased to those who hated them. ⁶In the citadel of Susa, the Jews killed and destroyed five hundred men. ⁷They also killed Parshandatha, Dalphon, Aspatha, ⁸Poratha, Adalia, Aridatha, ⁹Parmashta, Arisai, Aridai and Vaizatha, ¹⁰the ten sons of Haman son of Hammedatha, the enemy of the Jews. But they did not lay their hands on the plunder.

¹¹The number of those killed in the citadel of Susa was reported to the king that same day. ¹²The king said to Queen Esther, "The Jews have killed and destroyed five hundred men and the ten sons of Haman in the citadel of Susa. What have they done in the rest of the king's provinces? Now what is your petition? It will be given you. What is your request? It will also be granted."

¹³"If it pleases the king," Esther answered, "give the Jews in Susa permission to carry out this day's edict tomorrow also, and let Haman's ten sons be impaled on poles."

¹⁴So the king commanded that this be done. An edict was issued in Susa, and they impaled the ten sons of Haman. ¹⁵The Jews in Susa came together on the fourteenth day of the month of Adar, and they put to death in Susa three hundred men, but they did not lay their hands on the plunder.

¹⁶Meanwhile, the remainder of the Jews who were in the king's provinces also assembled to protect themselves and get relief from their enemies. They killed seventy-five thousand of them but did not lay their hands on the plunder. ¹⁷This happened on the thirteenth day of the month of Adar, and on the fourteenth they rested and made it a day of feasting and joy.

¹⁸The Jews in Susa, however, had assembled on the thirteenth and fourteenth, and then on the fifteenth they rested and made it a day of feasting and joy.

¹⁹That is why rural Jews — those living in villages — observe the fourteenth of the month of Adar as a day of joy and feasting, a day for giving presents to each other.

Purim Established

²⁰Mordecai recorded these events, and he sent letters to all the Jews throughout the provinces of King Xerxes, near and far, ²¹to have them celebrate annually the fourteenth and fifteenth days of the month of Adar ²²as the time when the Jews got relief from their enemies, and as the month when their sorrow was turned into joy and their mourning into

---

9:2 were afraid of them This fear could be the result of the Jewish people's organization, which is the emphasis of this verse, or because the government has chosen to favor the Jewish people — as v. 3 emphasizes.

9:3 all the nobles The same government officials who had received Haman's edict (3:12–13), and then Mordecai's, now choose to help the Jewish people (8:9). **fear of Mordecai had seized them** The government officials fear Mordecai because he has been appointed to a high-ranking role by the king, likely each of them.

9:5 they did what they pleased to those who hated them Mordecai's edict essentially made it possible for the Jewish people to retaliate as they saw fit (see note on 8:11).

9:6 the citadel of Susa See note on 1:2.

9:7–10 Haman's sons could have been of adult age and chose to fight against the Jewish people as an act of vengeance for their father's execution (7:10; compare note on 8:11). The narrative has already identified Haman with the derogatory term "Agagite" several times — which affiliated him with the longtime enemy of Israel, the Amalekites. Yahweh had long before declared that he would destroy the Amalekites completely (Ex 17:14) — if Haman and his sons are Amalekites, then this event has now occurred (see note on Est 3:1).

9:10 But they did not lay their hands on the plunder If the Jewish people viewed their fight as divine warfare, then the people could not keep any plunder for themselves (Jos 6:16–21; see note on Jos 6:16). If the conflict with Haman is viewed in connection with the narrative about Yahweh's command to destroy the Amalekites (1Sa 15:3), then divine war had already been declared during the reign of King Saul around 600 years earlier.

9:11–15 The narrative of Est 9:1–10 is interrupted by events back at the king's palace.

9:13 tomorrow also Mordecai's original decree limited

the Jewish retaliation to one day — the same day their enemies planned to attack them (the thirteenth of Adar; 3:13). Esther's request is that the Jewish people of Susa (or Shushan) be allowed to once again retaliate against their enemies for one more day (the fourteenth of Adar; compare v. 16). Esther's request contains no mention of imminent danger. However, Esther does specifically mention making a spectacle of Haman's sons, which may indicate that she is trying to neutralize any further threat first with fear and then with battle, if necessary. In addition, divine warfare entailed the complete destruction of an enemy (see note on v. 10; note on Jos 6:17). **poles** Haman's sons have already been killed (Est 9:7–10,12) — now Esther requests that their corpses be impaled and publicly displayed (compare note on 2:23).

9:15 month of Adar February or March 473 BC. See the table "Israelite Calendar" on p. 763. **they put to death in Susa three hundred men** Earlier v. 12 only mentioned the upper portion of Susa, but now this line focuses on either the lower portion of the city or the city in its entirety.

9:16–17 The narrative from v. 10 continues with information about the Jewish people in the remainder of the empire — who have successfully fought against those who hate them.

9:18 on the fifteenth they rested The Jewish people in Susa celebrate a day later because they had been in battle for two days — on the thirteenth and fourteenth day of the month — instead of just the thirteenth day (see vv. 11–15).

9:20–25 This passage describes how Mordecai established Purim as an ongoing observance for the Jews and lays out the expectations for the holiday (vv. 20–22). The major events of the book of Esther are also recapped (vv. 24–25).

9:20 Mordecai recorded these events Considering that Mordecai sends this information to all Jews in the empire, it seems most likely that this is a reference to

a day of celebration. He wrote them to observe the days as days of feasting and joy and giving presents of food to one another and gifts to the poor.

23 So the Jews agreed to continue the celebration they had begun, doing what Mordecai had written to them. 24 For Haman son of Hammedatha, the Agagite, the enemy of all the Jews, had plotted against the Jews to destroy them and had cast the *pur* (that is, the lot) for their ruin and destruction. 25 But when the plot came to the king's attention,*a* he issued written orders that the evil scheme Haman had devised against the Jews should come back onto his own head, and that he and his sons should be impaled on poles. 26 (Therefore these days were called Purim, from the word *pur*.) Because of everything written in this letter and because of what they had seen and what had happened to them, 27 the Jews took it on themselves to establish the custom that they and their descendants and all who join them should without fail observe these two days every year, in the way prescribed and at the time appointed. 28 These days should be remembered and observed in every generation by every family, and in every province and in every city. And these days of Purim should never fail to be celebrated by the Jews — nor should the memory of these days die out among their descendants.

29 So Queen Esther, daughter of Abihail, along with Mordecai the Jew, wrote with full authority to confirm this second letter concerning Purim. 30 And Mordecai sent letters to all the Jews in the 127 provinces of Xerxes' kingdom — words of goodwill and assurance — 31 to establish these days of Purim at their designated times, as Mordecai the Jew and Queen Esther had decreed for them, and as they had established for themselves and their descendants in regard to their times of fasting and lamentation. 32 Esther's decree confirmed these regulations about Purim, and it was written down in the records.

The Greatness of Mordecai

10 King Xerxes imposed tribute throughout the empire, to its distant shores. 2 And all his acts of power and might, together with a full account of the greatness of Mordecai, whom the king had promoted, are they not written in the book of the annals of the kings of Media and Persia? 3 Mordecai the Jew was second in rank to King Xerxes, preeminent among the Jews, and held in high esteem by his many fellow Jews, because he worked for the good of his people and spoke up for the welfare of all the Jews.

a 25 Or *when Esther came before the king*

the details in vv. 21–22 or the text of vv. 24–25 — or a combination of the two (compare v. 26).

9:21 fourteenth and fifteenth days of the month of Adar The narrative now explains why the Jewish festival of Purim is celebrated on two days — the day after the Jews in the majority of the empire overcame their enemies and the day after the Jews in the capital overcame theirs (compare vv. 17–19). See the table "Israelite Calendar" on p. 763; see the table "Israelite Festivals" on p. 200.

9:22 giving presents of food to one another This generous dimension of Purim may reflect the need for relief following a time of battle, such as the battles mentioned in this chapter (vv. 1–10). **gifts to the poor** Based on the previous phrase, the gifts to the impoverished were likely food and perhaps other provisions.

9:24 the Agagite See note on 3:1. **pur** This is cited as the reason for the festival being called Purim (v. 26). Haman had decided on what day his genocide of the Jewish people would occur by casting lots — which the narrative calls *pur* (see 3:7 and note).

9:25 he issued written orders A reference to the decree Mordecai drafted (8:9–12) to counteract the original edict that Haman issued (3:12–13).

9:26–28 The narrator concludes the synopsis of vv. 24–25 by announcing the name of the two-day Jewish festival detailed in vv. 21–22.

9:27 all who join them This is probably a reference to anyone who would become Jewish and perhaps even to those who would later live among Jewish people. **these two days** See note on v. 21.

9:29–32 The primary narrative of the book of Esther now closes with Mordecai and Esther further confirming the

holiday of Purim via a second letter. Since Purim is the only Jewish holiday up to this point in Israel's history not dictated by the Torah, the Jewish people may have needed further confirmation of its necessity.

9:31 their times of fasting and lamentation This may be a reference to regular — perhaps annual — fasting and mourning that had already been instituted prior to the time that the book of Esther was compiled (compare Zec 8:19). It could also be a reference to the fasting and mourning of the Jewish people earlier in the narrative and a request that they continue that practice (Est 4:3,16; compare 9:21–22).

9:32 it was written down in the records This could be a reference to Esther issuing a third letter, on her own accord, or just a way of closing the remarks about the second letter she issued with Mordecai (v. 29). It could also be a reference to her recording the command about Purim in some other location — perhaps some official government records.

10:1–3 In this section, the narrator seems to offer a closing epilogue. Although Esther has dealt with matters important to the Jewish people (see note on 1:1–9), God has never been mentioned and is not mentioned here in the epilogue either.

10:1 tribute This could be the king's way of recouping the costs of Mordecai's defense of the Jewish people (9:1–15) or be a restoration of the reprieve granted in 2:18.

10:2 book of the annals of the kings of Media and Persia These are likely the records mentioned in Est 2:23 and 6:1.

10:3 second in rank to King Xerxes Mordecai assumes the role that once belonged to Haman — the victim has become the victor (3:1; 9:3).

WISDOM LITERATURE

Few parts of the Bible are as theologically rich and yet largely neglected as the Wisdom Literature. While wisdom themes and language appear throughout the Old Testament, they occur in concentrated form in the books of Proverbs, Ecclesiastes and Job. Today, these books constitute the genre of Wisdom Literature in Protestant Bibles.

ANCIENT NEAR EASTERN CONTEXT

Wisdom Literature is not unique to Israel. Comparable literature is found throughout the ancient Near East, particularly in Egypt. However, Old Testament Wisdom Literature is unique in its insistence that wisdom has one source: Yahweh (Pr 3:19).

Wisdom is deeply experiential and concerned with how to live a happy and successful life amid everyday challenges. Thus, Wisdom Literature appropriately appears throughout the ancient Near East, as various cultures developed their own traditions from lived experiences. In the Bible, the experiential wisdom handed down through generations most obviously appears in the short proverbs or aphorisms found in Proverbs 10–29. Of course, we need to allow Old Testament wisdom to shape how we understand happy and successful. It is clear from Job that in order to gain wisdom, we may have to experience profound suffering. Nevertheless, the Old Testament clearly establishes that wisdom represents the path to blessing.

THE RELATIONSHIP BETWEEN PROVERBS, ECCLESIASTES AND JOB

Exploring the unique contribution of Wisdom Literature to the Bible requires an understanding of the relationship between Proverbs, Ecclesiastes and Job. The book of Proverbs is sometimes labeled "early" or "traditional wisdom." This is correct in that it serves as the foundation for wisdom theology in the Old Testament and sets out the overarching principles of wisdom (see Pr 1–9). Four categories have been identified as central to Proverbs and thus to Israel's view of wisdom:

1. Wisdom is grounded in the "fear of Yahweh."
2. Wisdom is concerned with discerning the order built into the creation by Yahweh.
3. Wisdom focuses on discerning God's ways in particular circumstances.
4. Wisdom is grounded in tradition.[1]

Given that Proverbs sets out the Israelite view of wisdom, Job and Ecclesiastes make the most sense when read against its background. These two books primarily focus on the idea that things can (and do) go wrong in life. While Proverbs also acknowledges this fact, it is not the primary focus of the book; rather, Proverbs lays the foundation for Old Testament wisdom by emphasizing proper fear of Yahweh and the relationship between a person's character and everyday consequences.

---

1 Raymond C. Van Leeuwen, "Wisdom Literature," in *Dictionary for Theological Interpretation of the Bible*, ed. Kevin J. Vanhoozer, Craig G. Bartholomew, Daniel J. Treier, and N.T. Wright (Grand Rapids, Mich: Baker, 2005), 847–50.

PROVERBS

Proverbs is not a random collection of axioms; it has been carefully edited into a literary whole, moving from the preface to its climax in the vision evoked by the valiant woman. Throughout the work, it covers key themes.

Fear of God

A central and recurring theme throughout the book of Proverbs is that the fear of Yahweh is the beginning of knowledge or wisdom (Pr 1:7,29; 2:5; 8:13; 10:27; 14:27; 15:16,33; 16:6; 19:23; 23:17; 31:30). "Fear" is best understood as holy reverence of Yahweh—the redeemer and covenant God who rescued the Israelites from slavery and brought them to himself (Ex 19:4). Such an attitude toward God represents the beginning of wisdom in two ways: It serves as the foundation on which all true wisdom and knowledge is built, and it is the starting point for the journey of life and exploration of God's world. God created the world by wisdom, and he offers this same wisdom to his people (Pr 3:19; 8:22); gaining wisdom is of surpassing value (Pr 2).

Character—Consequence

The preface to Proverbs (Pr 1:2–6) amasses a variety of terms that alerts the reader to the advantages of wisdom. Proverbs 1–9 alternates between speeches of a father to his adolescent son and speeches by Lady Wisdom, all of which emphasize the great value of pursuing and finding wisdom. Verses like Proverbs 3:9–10 indicate that wisdom results in blessing, which can include material prosperity.

Proverbs 1–9 sets out the basic principles of wisdom, central to which is the "character—consequence" theme: Those who seek wisdom and live by it can expect to flourish. God designed the world such that flourishing is a consequence of developed character. These chapters also acknowledge that wisdom involves Yahweh's discipline and reproof (see Pr 3:11–12). In later sections of the book of Proverbs, there is a greater focus on exceptions to the character—consequence theme. These exceptions are foregrounded, particularly in the "better than" proverbs (e.g., Pr 16:8; 22:1). The writer of Proverbs is well aware that in a fallen world, the wise may end up impoverished.[2]

The Valiant Woman

Proverbs culminates in Proverbs 31 with a rich evocation of lived wisdom by depicting the valiant woman. Proverbs 31:10–31 is an acrostic poem, with each verse beginning with a consecutive letter of the Hebrew alphabet. It is written in the form of a hymn—a literary style normally reserved for God or great warriors. Although there are no references to "religious" activities in her description, she is lauded as one who fears Yahweh (Pr 31:30). Her general manner of living manifests her fear of Yahweh. This shows that Old Testament wisdom did not uphold a sacred/secular dualism that pervades contemporary Christianity. Because God is the Creator, we are called to be wise in all areas of life. Thus, the valiant woman is portrayed as a wife (Pr 31:10–12), homemaker (Pr 31:13–15,21), businesswoman (she imports food from afar and trades in fabric of the highest quality; Pr 31:14,24), wine producer (Pr 31:16) and craftsperson (Pr 31:19,22,24). In addition, she performs works of charity (Pr 31:20) and teaches wisdom (Pr 31:26).

ECCLESIASTES

Both Job and Ecclesiastes deal with suffering. In Ecclesiastes, Qohelet—the Hebrew word for the name of the speaker throughout Ecclesiastes—is suffering more of an intellectual crisis, whereas

2 Raymond C. Van Leeuwen, "Wealth and Poverty: System and Contradiction in Proverbs," *Hebrew Studies* 33 (1992): 25–36.

Job suffers physical and emotional anguish. The narrator of Ecclesiastes introduces Qohelet, a figure gifted with wisdom and wealth. Ecclesiastes 1:2 summarizes Qohelet's teaching: "Meaningless! Meaningless!"—an expression of despair. A variety of translations for the Hebrew term used here, hevel, have been proposed. Hevel may be literally rendered as "vapor" or "breath." In Ecclesiastes, hevel seems to hold the metaphorical force of "enigmatic"; Qohelet has found his way into what may be called a "cloud of unknowing," and he cannot determine whether life has any meaning. His quest for meaning in life, couched in the rhetorical question of Ecclesiastes 1:3—"What do people gain from all their labors ...?"—represents a deep existential crisis and profound intellectual suffering.

Scholars are divided into two camps when it comes to the overarching message of Ecclesiastes. It could be a despairing book to which an editor added an epilogue (Ecc 12:9–14) to make the book more acceptable, or the epilogue could indicate that the overall message is positive. Either way, the struggle contained in the book and evoked by Qohelet's regular conclusions of hevel must not be downplayed.

Throughout the book of Ecclesiastes, Qohelet's hevel conclusions appear next to so-called "carpe diem sayings" (e.g., Ecc 2:24–26). These joyful passages do not reflect a despairing hedonism but a typical Old Testament celebration of the goodness of creation. They refer to eating, drinking and enjoying the pleasures of life. It is best to see these hevel and carpe diem phrases as contradictory juxtapositions. No matter what area of life he explores, Qohelet's method of exploration—which he calls "wisdom" (Ecc 1:13; 2:9)—constantly leads him to his hevel conclusion. But each time he reaches this dark point, we find a carpe diem passage juxtaposed.

This juxtaposition of contradictory views forces the reader to look closely at Qohelet's method of exploration (or epistemology). His wisdom is very different from what Proverbs calls wisdom; whereas wisdom begins with fear of Yahweh in Proverbs, Qohelet seems to rely on reason, observation and experience—fear of God is only noted in the epilogue (Ecc 12:9–14). If Ecclesiastes was written in the fourth century BC, it is possible that the author was influenced by Greek thought. In the postexilic period, it was difficult for the Jewish people to see what had happened to God's promises and purposes; in the light of Greek epistemology, Qohelet cannot find meaning anywhere in life. However, the carpe diem passages stem from his Israelite tradition. Even as he keeps coming to his hevel conclusions, he cannot deny the truth that life is good and full of things to enjoy. The heart of Ecclesiastes is the tension between these two views.

The final chapters of Ecclesiastes demonstrate how Qohelet's dilemma is resolved (Ecc 11:7—12:8). The idea of remembering and rejoicing dominate this section and provide the key to the resolution of his crisis. Ecclesiastes 12:1–7 is Qohelet's equivalent of Proverb's claim that the fear of Yahweh is the beginning of wisdom. His former epistemology is reversed; it now starts with God as Creator rather than his own experiences, reason and observations. This does not detract from the challenges of life, as the epilogue also makes clear, but it provides a foundation for living amid the mysteries of life.

JOB

In the book of Job, resolution to suffering also emerges through an encounter with God as Creator (Job 38:1—42:6). Job's suffering is clearly described; he is stripped of everything important to him and crippled with bad health (Job 1:6—2:10). Initially, he makes a remarkable confession of faith (Job 1:21). He then takes part in conversations with his friends and God before returning to

his formerly stated position of faith, now more fully embraced and understood (Job 42:5). Job's suffering is not resolved intellectually but through a remarkable encounter with God.

While the extent of suffering in Job and Ecclesiastes seems to contradict the character—consequence theme of Proverbs, these books are not really exceptions. Wisdom is not just about technique—it is about the formation of the believer at the deepest levels. This is what we witness in both Job and Ecclesiastes: Suffering is a way God makes his people truly wise.

WISDOM LITERATURE AND THE REST OF SCRIPTURE

Wisdom Literature in the Old Testament insists that creation as a whole comes from God, and that wisdom means seeking God's ways in all areas of life. Wisdom, with its robust doctrine of creation, is theologically vital for a modern Christian faith that seeks to whole-heartedly serve God. Wisdom Literature also provides an important background for the New Testament, in which Jesus is portrayed as Wisdom incarnate (Jn 1:1–2). Jesus fulfills all aspects of the Old Testament—wisdom included.

Craig G. Bartholomew

JOB

INTRODUCTION TO JOB

The book of Job explores themes of suffering and righteousness. The central question concerns the motivation behind Job's faithfulness to Yahweh (Job 1:8–9). Does Job's trust in God derive from his many God-given blessings or because he values God for being God (1:10–11)? When all of Job's blessings are stripped away, he questions God about the reason for his suffering. Job wrestles with the conflict of suffering while believing in a just God.

BACKGROUND

The author of Job is unknown, but the use of the divine name Yahweh (1:6) indicates it was written, or at least edited, by a member of God's people. Job's lifestyle reflects those of Abraham, Isaac and Jacob (Ge 12–50), indicating that it is set during the same time period (ca. 2100–2000 BC).

The story is, further, set in the land of Uz (Job 1:1), an unknown location. Lamentations 4:21 mentions both Uz and Edom, suggesting Uz could have been in (or close to) the region Edom, southeast of the Dead Sea. This possibility fits with the hometown of one Job's friends, Eliphaz the Temanite (e.g., Job 2:11); the book of Jeremiah refers to Teman as a city in Edom whose residents were known for their wisdom (Jer 49:7).

The earliest mention of Job in ancient literature comes in Ezekiel (Eze 14:14,20), which was written in the early sixth century BC. This indicates that the story of Job was known, in some form, by this time and was at least circulating as oral tradition. Literary features such as vocabulary suggest the written version of Job came to be after the Jewish exile (538 BC) and before the fourth century BC.

The book of Job functions as a dialogue with the general principles presented in Proverbs and, thus, is part of the wisdom literature genre. However, it also defies the category, containing a mix of prose and poetry, including elements of lament and legal disputation.

STRUCTURE

The book opens with a prose prologue (Job 1:1—2:13). Job is depicted as a devout father, husband and worshiper of Yahweh (1:1–5). The book then shifts to Yahweh presiding over his heavenly council. After he praises Job's upright behavior, "the *satan*" figure (Hebrew for "the accuser") asks whether

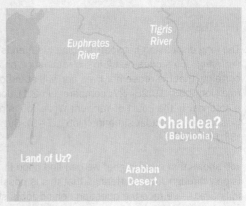

The location of the land of Uz is unknown, but it is often associated with Edom because of Lamentations 4:21.

Job's piety is because of his prosperous circumstances. To test this question, Yahweh permits the *satan* figure to strip Job of all he has (1:6–12). After losing his wealth and children, Job still does not forsake Yahweh (1:13–22). Job then loses his health, but even after this second test, he will not curse Yahweh (2:1–10). At the end of the opening prose section, Job's friends enter the narrative to console him (2:11–13).

But Job's friends don't do much consoling. Instead they argue that Job must have brought his pain on himself. Their ideas are based on a common principle of the time known as *lex talionis* ("an eye for an eye"; compare Ex 21:24). This forces Job to defend himself. The narrative cycles between the poetic speeches of Job and his friends in Job 3–27; this is followed by Job's hymn to wisdom (Job 28). Job then delivers a final defense (Job 29–31) and is rebuked by a new character, Elihu (Job 32–37).

In the climax of the book Yahweh finally speaks—from the midst of a whirlwind (Job 38–41). But instead of answering Job's questions, Yahweh articulates his unmatched power. In response, Job acquiesces to God's sovereignty (42:1–6). The epilogue (42:7–16), which shifts back to prose, describes Job's redemption: Yahweh blesses Job with abundant wealth and new family, and Job's friends—now humbled by Yahweh—sacrifice to Yahweh.

OUTLINE

- Prologue: Job's standing before God and suffering (1:1—2:13)
- Job's dialogue with his friends (3:1—27:23)
- Job's discourse on wisdom (28:1–28)
- Monologues from Job and Elihu (29:1—37:24)
- God's response to Job (38:1—42:6)
- Epilogue: Job's restoration (42:7–17)

THEMES

The long discussion between Job and his friends wrestles with the paradox of seemingly unjust suffering. Job's cries result in his requesting an advocate before Yahweh and proclaiming with certainty that his redeemer lives and will stand on the earth—lines that point forward to Jesus' role (Job 9:33; 19:25–27; compare 1Jn 2:1). Job is prosecuted by the *satan* figure and longs for a defender in the court of Yahweh. While Job is not sinless—no one is (Ro 3:23)—he is blameless in this particular situation (Job 1:7–8). But as Yahweh shows Job, he still has much to learn (38:1—40:2).

Job shows that even in grief we can find hope in a deepened relationship with Yahweh (23:10). It is only through Job's sufferings that this is possible (42:4–6). Today—with our advocate, Jesus, in heaven—we face the question behind Job's story: Will we love Yahweh, no matter what?

Prologue

1 In the land of Uz there lived a man whose name was Job. This man was blameless and upright; he feared God and shunned evil. ²He had seven sons and three daughters, ³and he owned seven thousand sheep, three thousand camels, five hundred yoke of oxen and five hundred donkeys, and had a large number of servants. He was the greatest man among all the people of the East.

⁴His sons used to hold feasts in their homes on their birthdays, and they would invite their three sisters to eat and drink with them. ⁵When a period of feasting had run its course, Job would make arrangements for them to be purified. Early in the morning he would sacrifice a burnt offering for each of them, thinking, "Perhaps my children have sinned and cursed God in their hearts." This was Job's regular custom.

⁶One day the angels*ᵃ* came to present themselves before the Lᴏʀᴅ, and Satan*ᵇ* also came with them. ⁷The Lᴏʀᴅ said to Satan, "Where have you come from?"

Satan answered the Lᴏʀᴅ, "From roaming throughout the earth, going back and forth on it."

⁸Then the Lᴏʀᴅ said to Satan, "Have you considered my servant Job? There is no one on earth like him; he is blameless and upright, a man who fears God and shuns evil."

ᵃ 6 Hebrew *the sons of God*   *ᵇ 6* Hebrew *satan* means *adversary*.

1:1—2:13 The author and date of writing for the book of Job are unknown, though the similarity of Job's lifestyle to the patriarchs of Genesis means the events of Job's life are probably set around the time of Abraham (ca. 2100–2000 BC).

The book of Job cannot be fit neatly into any one genre of literature. Aside from the narrative prologue and epilogue, the book is poetic and has some of the same concerns as the Wisdom literature found in the Bible (such as Proverbs or Ecclesiastes). However, its narrative setting distinguishes it from those other books. It also at times features elements of lament, a genre found throughout the Psalms. In addition, it contains disputation passages that make it look like a lawsuit, which is a genre that also occurs in prophetic literature. The book of Job was likely composed as a written work sometime after the Jewish exile (538 BC) and before the fourth century BC, and may have developed as oral tradition over a long period of time.

The book begins with a narrative prologue (Job 1:1—2:13). This prologue introduces Job, describes the *satan* figure's challenge, and shows Job's reaction to his suffering (see note on 1:6). It concludes with the visit of Job's friends (2:11–13). The majority of the book is composed of cycles of speeches given by Job and his friends (3:1—42:6). See the table "Cycles in Job" on p. 793.

1:1 the land of Uz The exact location of Uz is unknown. It was either near Edom (Ge 36:28; La 4:21) in the south or Aram in the north (Ge 10:22–23). **blameless** The Hebrew term used here, *tam*, indicates general purity before God, not perfection. It is used to describe the pure animals that were to be used for sacrifice (Ex 29:1; Lev 1:3). It is also a characteristic of God's work and law (Dt 32:4; Ps 19:7). Applied to people, it indicates integrity and innocence (2Sa 22:24; Ps 15:2). **upright** The Hebrew term used here, *yashar*, refers to something that is straight or level (compare Isa 26:7; Jer 31:9). It indicates honesty and righteousness (Ps 11:7; Pr 11:6). To be *yashar* is to be obedient to God (Ex 15:26; Dt 6:18). **he feared God** Describes a reverent attitude of respect, obedience and trust toward God. Fearing God is closely associated with wisdom (e.g., Pr 1:7; Ps 111:10). Job's integrity is a result of his attitude toward God. See notes on Job 1:9.

1:2 seven sons and three daughters The number seven is symbolic of completeness in the ancient world (e.g., Ge 2:2–3; 1Sa 2:5), and three was also a prominent number (e.g., Ge 6:10). The same ratio applies to Job's sheep and camels (Job 1:3).

1:3 seven thousand sheep Wealth was often measured by the number of livestock or servants (Ge 26:12–14; 30:43). Job was extremely wealthy; Nabal, who is described as being very rich, had only 3,000 sheep and 1,000 goats (1Sa 25:2).

1:5 a burnt offering Job—a pious man—was also concerned with his children's holiness. Not only were burnt offerings part of the law of Israel (Ex 29:38–41; Lev 1); they were also part of worship before the law was introduced (Ge 8:20; 22:2; Ex 10:25). **cursed God** Job was concerned that his children might have unintentionally cursed God. See note on Job 1:11. Later, this is essentially what Job's friends end up doing. In 42:7–9, God instructs Job's friends to offer burnt offerings to atone for not speaking truthfully about him. In that passage, Job offers prayers on their behalf, which God accepts. **their hearts** In ancient Israelite thought, the heart was considered the center of a person's character and primarily represented their cognitive abilities (1Sa 16:7; Ps 24:4).

1:6 angels The Hebrew phrase used here, *bene elohim*, which may be literally rendered as "sons of God," refers to spiritual beings who (in this instance) are part of God's council—the divine council. For this reason, some translations render the phrase *bene elohim* here and elsewhere as "angels." See note on Ge 6:2. **present themselves before the Lᴏʀᴅ** Portrays a divine council (Ps 82:1) with heavenly beings coming to report before the King, Yahweh. See note on Ge 1:26. **Satan** The Hebrew word used here, *satan*, literally means "the accuser" or "the adversary." He is likely acting as a prosecutor in a courtroom-like scene. In the OT, the term *satan* is often used to describe an adversary in general—whether human or divine (compare 1Ki 11:23–25). For example, in the Hebrew text of Nu 22:22, the Angel of Yahweh is also described as a *satan*. In Zec 3:1–2, the *satan* functions much like he does in Job—he stands before the angel of Yahweh and accuses the high priest, Joshua. In both Zechariah and Job, *satan* includes the definite article ("the"), which grammatically rules out its use as a proper name. Instead, it should be understood as a title ("the accuser"). By NT times, it was understood as a proper name (e.g., Mt 4:10; Lk 10:18; Ro 16:20).

1:7 roaming Elsewhere, the Hebrew term used here describes people searching for something (Jer 5:1; Am 8:12). The image of the *satan* figure wandering the earth looking for someone to accuse is similar to the NT depiction of the devil in 1Pe 5:8 (compare note on Job 1:6).

1:8 blameless and upright Mirrors the narrator's description of Job in 1:1.

⁹"Does Job fear God for nothing?" Satan replied. ¹⁰"Have you not put a hedge around him and his household and everything he has? You have blessed the work of his hands, so that his flocks and herds are spread throughout the land. ¹¹But now stretch out your hand and strike everything he has, and he will surely curse you to your face."

¹²The Lord said to Satan, "Very well, then, everything he has is in your power, but on the man himself do not lay a finger."

Then Satan went out from the presence of the Lord.

¹³One day when Job's sons and daughters were feasting and drinking wine at the oldest brother's house, ¹⁴a messenger came to Job and said, "The oxen were plowing and the donkeys were grazing nearby, ¹⁵and the Sabeans attacked and made off with them. They put the servants to the sword, and I am the only one who has escaped to tell you!"

¹⁶While he was still speaking, another messenger came and said, "The fire of God fell from the heavens and burned up the sheep and the servants, and I am the only one who has escaped to tell you!"

¹⁷While he was still speaking, another messenger came and said, "The Chaldeans formed three raiding parties and swept down on your camels and made off with them. They put the servants to the sword, and I am the only one who has escaped to tell you!"

¹⁸While he was still speaking, yet another messenger came and said, "Your sons and daughters were feasting and drinking wine at the oldest broth-er's house, ¹⁹when suddenly a mighty wind swept in from the desert and struck the four corners of the house. It collapsed on them and they are dead, and I am the only one who has escaped to tell you!"

²⁰At this, Job got up and tore his robe and shaved his head. Then he fell to the ground in worship ²¹and said:

"Naked I came from my mother's womb,
  and naked I will depart.ᵃ
The Lord gave and the Lord has taken away;
  may the name of the Lord be praised."

²²In all this, Job did not sin by charging God with wrongdoing.

2 On another day the angelsᵇ came to present themselves before the Lord, and Satan also came with them to present himself before him. ²And the Lord said to Satan, "Where have you come from?"

Satan answered the Lord, "From roaming throughout the earth, going back and forth on it."

³Then the Lord said to Satan, "Have you considered my servant Job? There is no one on earth like him; he is blameless and upright, a man who fears God and shuns evil. And he still maintains his integrity, though you incited me against him to ruin him without any reason."

⁴"Skin for skin!" Satan replied. "A man will give all he has for his own life. ⁵But now stretch out your hand and strike his flesh and bones, and he will surely curse you to your face."

ᵃ 21 Or *will return there*   ᵇ 1 Hebrew *the sons of God*

1:9 Does Job fear God for nothing The question of the source of Job's piety lies at the heart of this book's message: It may be a result of his blessing, or a response to God's character and power (chs. 38–41). The *satan* figure summarizes Job's piety with the phrase "fear God" (compare note on 1:1). Job was blameless and upright because he feared God.

1:11 curse you to your face Here and in v. 5; 2:5; and 2:9 the Hebrew text actually uses the word for bless (*barakh*), not curse. This wording is antiphrastic—using a term with the opposite of its typical meaning. The use avoids having the Biblical text explicitly say "curse God" in Hebrew. The dual usage of *barakh*, however, adds a layer of irony to the exchange since in v. 21 Job actually does bless Yahweh, even though he had lost his wealth.

1:12 everything he has God allows the *satan* figure to afflict Job, but only up to a point (compare 2:6 and note; note on 1:6). This conversation, and the real reason for his suffering, is never revealed to Job despite his many cries for an explanation (e.g., 7:20–21; 10:2–3; 23:2–7; 31:35).

1:15 Sabeans Probably the inhabitants of Sheba in Southern Arabia (1Ki 10:1–13).

1:16 While he was still speaking This phrase—repeated in Job 1:17 and 1:18—shows that Job received these catastrophic reports in sequence.

1:17 The Chaldeans The ancestors of the later Babylonian Empire. They would have most likely come from Mesopotamia toward the northeast.

1:19 a mighty wind swept in from the desert Like the second catastrophe, this final catastrophe is meteorological. Two of the devastating events were natural disasters, and two were caused by people.

1:20 tore his robe and shaved his head Typical gestures of mourning (Ge 37:34; Ezr 9:3; Jer 7:29). **worship** Job acts unexpectedly. Instead of launching into a prayer of lamentation or mourning (Jos 7:6–8), he worships God.

1:21 may the name of the Lord be praised See note on Job 1:11. Job does not bless God because he took everything away. Rather, he blesses God because he recognizes God's sovereignty. However, later Job seems to stray from this as he seeks to understand the reason for his suffering in dialog with his friends. At the book's climax, God reminds Job of his sovereignty (chs. 38–41).

1:22 Job did not sin by charging God Job unknowingly passes the *satan* figure's first challenge (compare note on 1:6). He has shown that he does not fear God just because God has blessed him.

2:1 the angels came The story returns to the scene of God's divine council. See note on 1:6.

2:3 blameless and upright Yahweh repeats his description of Job from 1:8. See note on 1:1. **maintains his integrity** The *satan* figure failed in his first challenge: Job did not curse God even though his wealth and children were taken away (compare note on 1:6).

2:4 Skin for skin This expression does not occur elsewhere in the OT. It may be related to the law of an "eye for an eye" (Ex 21:23–25).

⁶The LORD said to Satan, "Very well, then, he is in your hands; but you must spare his life."

⁷So Satan went out from the presence of the LORD and afflicted Job with painful sores from the soles of his feet to the crown of his head. ⁸Then Job took a piece of broken pottery and scraped himself with it as he sat among the ashes.

⁹His wife said to him, "Are you still maintaining your integrity? Curse God and die!"

¹⁰He replied, "You are talking like a foolish*a* woman. Shall we accept good from God, and not trouble?"

In all this, Job did not sin in what he said.

¹¹When Job's three friends, Eliphaz the Temanite, Bildad the Shuhite and Zophar the Naamathite, heard about all the troubles that had come upon him, they set out from their homes and met together by agreement to go and sympathize with him and comfort him. ¹²When they saw him from a distance, they could hardly recognize him; they began to weep aloud, and they tore their robes and sprinkled dust on their heads. ¹³Then they sat on the ground with him for seven days and seven nights. No one said a word to him, because they saw how great his suffering was.

Job Speaks

3 After this, Job opened his mouth and cursed the day of his birth. ²He said:

³"May the day of my birth perish,
  and the night that said, 'A boy is conceived!'
⁴That day — may it turn to darkness;
  may God above not care about it;
  may no light shine on it.
⁵May gloom and utter darkness claim it once more;
  may a cloud settle over it;
  may blackness overwhelm it.

a 10 The Hebrew word rendered foolish denotes moral deficiency.

2:5 strike his flesh and bones Since removing his possessions and descendants was not enough to make Job curse God, the *satan* figure suggests afflicting Job directly (compare note on 1:6). **curse you to your face** The *satan* figure still believes that if God removes his blessing, Job will curse God directly. See note on Job 1:11.

2:6 Very well, then, he is in your hands Once again, God allows the *satan* figure to afflict Job—but limits him (compare note on 1:6; note on 1:12).

2:7 painful sores The Hebrew word used here is used to describe the sixth plague on Egypt (Ex 9:9–10). A single sore also afflicted King Hezekiah (2Ki 20:7). The term can refer to a variety of illnesses. Scripture includes examples of sores that would heal (Lev 13:18) and sores that would not heal (Dt 28:27).

2:8 a piece of broken pottery and scraped himself Job may do this to relieve itching or to break open the sores (Job 7:5). **he sat among the ashes** A sign of mourning (Jer 6:26; Eze 27:30; Jnh 3:6). This also may indicate that Job is now an outcast, sitting in a trash heap outside the city.

2:9 His wife Job's wife speaks only here (she is mentioned again in Job 19:17). While her exclamation that Job should curse God reflects the *satan* figure's prediction (v. 5), she also acknowledges Job's integrity, using the same language as God (v. 3; compare note on 1:6). **Curse God and die** May reflect her desire to see her husband's misery end. Job himself wishes for death (3:20–22). She instructs Job to curse God, perhaps thinking it will lead God to kill Job and end his misery. The Hebrew word used here, *barakh* (often translated here as "curse"), actually means "bless." Since Job's previous praise of God (1:21) was not rewarded with blessing but with physical suffering, Job's wife may be sarcastically advising Job to "bless God" again—thinking this time it will result in Job's death. See note on 1:11.

2:10 like a foolish woman Job is not calling his wife a fool. Rather, he is saying her advice is foolish. **trouble** In this context, this refers to suffering or disaster (5:19; 30:26; Ecc 2:17). **Job did not sin in what he said** In Job's brief speech to his wife, he again recognizes God's sovereignty. As he did in Job 1:21, Job points out that God—as the Creator—is free to give or take. Although he does not understand it, Job views his suffering as part of God's plan. This contrasts with Job's friends who—claiming to understand God's purposes—view it as part of God's punishment.

2:11 Temanite Eliphaz is from Teman, a city in Edom associated with wisdom (Jer 49:7). **Shuhite** Bildad comes from a distant but unknown location. The term "Shuhite" may suggest a connection with Shuah, one of the sons of Abraham and Keturah (Ge 25:2). **Naamathite** Zophar is from Naamah, whose location is unknown. Naamah is listed as a female descendant of Cain (Ge 4:22). **sympathize with him** Job's friends come with the good intention of comforting him. However, their words will be of little comfort to Job (see Job 16:2; 21:34).

2:12 they tore their robes and sprinkled dust on their heads Typical gestures of mourning (1:20; 2:8).

2:13 seven days and seven nights A typical period of mourning (Ge 50:10; 1Sa 31:13). **No one said a word to him** Their silence was probably part of the mourning ritual (Eze 3:15). When they do speak, Job wishes they would remain silent (Job 13:5).

3:1–26 This chapter initiates the cycle of speeches that make up most of the book (3:1—42:6). In this first speech, Job curses the day of his birth, essentially saying, "I wish I had never been born." He expresses this wish in many different ways: wishing the day he was born never existed (vv. 3–10), wishing the night of his conception had never happened (v. 3) and lamenting that he did not die at birth (vv. 11–19). Finally, he longs for death (vv. 20–22). See the table "Cycles in Job" on p. 793.

3:1 cursed the day of his birth Instead of cursing God as the *satan* figure expected (2:5) and his wife advised (2:9), Job curses the day of his birth (vv. 1–10; compare note on 1:6). Jeremiah curses the day of his birth in a similar passage (Jer 20:14–18). The author of Ecclesiastes—when faced with the prevalence of oppression in the world—proclaims the dead more fortunate than the living, and the unborn more fortunate than both (Ecc 4:1–3).

3:4 That day — may it turn to darkness Similar to the language of Ge 1:3, but here Job wishes to reverse his own creation. In this first lament, Job introduces

⁶That night — may thick darkness seize it;
 may it not be included among the days
  of the year
 nor be entered in any of the months.
⁷May that night be barren;
 may no shout of joy be heard in it.
⁸May those who curse days[a] curse that day,
 those who are ready to rouse Leviathan.
⁹May its morning stars become dark;
 may it wait for daylight in vain
 and not see the first rays of dawn,
¹⁰for it did not shut the doors of the womb on me
 to hide trouble from my eyes.

¹¹"Why did I not perish at birth,
 and die as I came from the womb?
¹²Why were there knees to receive me
 and breasts that I might be nursed?
¹³For now I would be lying down in peace;
 I would be asleep and at rest
¹⁴with kings and rulers of the earth,
 who built for themselves places now lying
  in ruins,
¹⁵with princes who had gold,
 who filled their houses with silver.
¹⁶Or why was I not hidden away in the ground
 like a stillborn child,
 like an infant who never saw the light of day?
¹⁷There the wicked cease from turmoil,
 and there the weary are at rest.

¹⁸Captives also enjoy their ease;
 they no longer hear the slave driver's
  shout.
¹⁹The small and the great are there,
 and the slaves are freed from their owners.

²⁰"Why is light given to those in misery,
 and life to the bitter of soul,
²¹to those who long for death that does not come,
 who search for it more than for hidden
  treasure,
²²who are filled with gladness
 and rejoice when they reach the grave?
²³Why is life given to a man
 whose way is hidden,
 whom God has hedged in?
²⁴For sighing has become my daily food;
 my groans pour out like water.
²⁵What I feared has come upon me;
 what I dreaded has happened to me.
²⁶I have no peace, no quietness;
 I have no rest, but only turmoil."

Eliphaz

4 Then Eliphaz the Temanite replied:

²"If someone ventures a word with you, will
  you be impatient?
 But who can keep from speaking?

a 8 Or curse the sea

---

the themes of day and night, light and darkness (Job 3:4–10,16,20–23). These themes continue throughout his dialogue with the three friends (vv. 16,20,23; 10:21–22; 23:17). Light is a metaphor for life and what is revealed, while darkness is a metaphor for death and what is hidden or mysterious.

3:8 Leviathan A mighty sea creature (41:1; Ps 74:14; 104:26; Isa 27:1), who is also present in ancient Near Eastern mythology. In ancient Near Eastern creation stories, Leviathan represents the dark chaos of the primeval world. For creation to occur, a creator deity had to control or defeat Leviathan. In the context of Job 3, where Job wishes he had never been born (or even conceived; v. 3), his reference to rousing Leviathan represents his wish for the day of his birth to revert back to dark, primordial nonexistence. See 9:13 and note; 41:1 and note.

3:10 hide trouble from my eyes If he hadn't been born, Job would have avoided all of this misfortune (compare 5:6,7; 7:3; 11:16; 16:2).

3:11 Why did I not perish at birth Job's curse (vv. 1–10) turns to a lament (vv. 11–19) in which he does not want his misfortunes reversed, but he wishes he had never lived at all to encounter them. Lament is a common genre of Hebrew poetry. Throughout the Psalms, poets implore God to help them (e.g., Ps 12:1; 13:3–4; 17:1–2). Job does not ask for God's help; he laments that he survived to see such misfortune. The Psalms of lament frequently ask God why something is happening (e.g., Ps 10:1; 22:1); Job similarly asks five questions in this section (Job 3:11,12,16,20,23), but none of them is a cry for help out of his present distress.

3:13 I would be asleep and at rest Job wishes he were in Sheol — the OT term for the shadowy realm of

the dead (see 14:13 and note). Although he would be dead, he would no longer be tormented by his life; there would be peace among the dead (compare Job 3:17; 7:9).

3:19 The small and the great Death indiscriminately brings together rich and poor, prestigious and lowly (see vv. 14–19). Death is the great equalizer.

3:20 Why is light given to those in misery Job can find no meaning for his life. Suffering raises the difficult questions of meaning, purpose and value of life. It also brings to the surface questions about the nature of God and his involvement with his creation. The book of Job wrestles with these questions through the dialogue between Job and his friends and then through God's speech at the end of the book (chs. 41–42).

3:21 hidden treasure Extends the metaphor of darkness/death to hiddenness (see v. 4 and note) and introduces a theme of the book that ch. 28, especially, will develop.

3:23 whom God has hedged in Job feels like God has surrounded him with suffering and turmoil, leaving him with no escape (19:7–12). This phrasing is an ironic twist of the _satan_ figure's words in 1:10, where he accuses God of putting a wall of protection around Job (compare note on 1:6).

4:1 — 5:27 This is the first of three speeches by Eliphaz (compare chs. 15; 22). Eliphaz begins with a gentle and conciliatory tone (4:3–5), but quickly moves to one of his main themes: The righteous prosper while the wicked suffer (4:7–9). He describes a vision (4:12–16) in which God judges humankind (4:17–21). After extolling God's greatness (5:8–16), he closes by encouraging Job to accept God's discipline (5:17–27).

³ Think how you have instructed many,
how you have strengthened feeble hands.
⁴ Your words have supported those who
stumbled;
you have strengthened faltering knees.
⁵ But now trouble comes to you, and you are
discouraged;
it strikes you, and you are dismayed.
⁶ Should not your piety be your confidence
and your blameless ways your hope?

⁷ "Consider now: Who, being innocent, has
ever perished?
Where were the upright ever destroyed?
⁸ As I have observed, those who plow evil
and those who sow trouble reap it.
⁹ At the breath of God they perish;
at the blast of his anger they are no more.
¹⁰ The lions may roar and growl,
yet the teeth of the great lions are broken.
¹¹ The lion perishes for lack of prey,
and the cubs of the lioness are scattered.

¹² "A word was secretly brought to me,
my ears caught a whisper of it.
¹³ Amid disquieting dreams in the night,
when deep sleep falls on people,
¹⁴ fear and trembling seized me
and made all my bones shake.
¹⁵ A spirit glided past my face,
and the hair on my body stood on end.

¹⁶ It stopped,
but I could not tell what it was.
A form stood before my eyes,
and I heard a hushed voice:
¹⁷ 'Can a mortal be more righteous than God?
Can even a strong man be more pure than
his Maker?
¹⁸ If God places no trust in his servants,
if he charges his angels with error,
¹⁹ how much more those who live in houses
of clay,
whose foundations are in the dust,
who are crushed more readily than
a moth!
²⁰ Between dawn and dusk they are broken
to pieces;
unnoticed, they perish forever.
²¹ Are not the cords of their tent pulled up,
so that they die without wisdom?'

5 "Call if you will, but who will answer you?
To which of the holy ones will you turn?
² Resentment kills a fool,
and envy slays the simple.
³ I myself have seen a fool taking root,
but suddenly his house was cursed.
⁴ His children are far from safety,
crushed in court without a defender.
⁵ The hungry consume his harvest,
taking it even from among thorns,
and the thirsty pant after his wealth.

4:3 you have instructed many Eliphaz begins with affirmation of Job (compare his opening statements in 15:2 and 22:2).

4:6 your piety be your confidence Eliphaz encourages Job to take confidence in his righteousness and integrity. Ironically, Job is suffering because of his righteousness and integrity (1:8–11; 2:3–5). This is the central argument of Job's friends, which reflects a common view of divine retribution: God gives people what they deserve. According to this understanding, the righteous are rewarded while the wicked suffer (compare Pr 11:31; 13:21). Job's friends misapply this view to Job's situation; they believe his suffering is due to some sin he has committed.

4:8 As I have observed Observation of the natural world is a key characteristic of Wisdom literature (see Ecc 1:14). **reap it** The core of Job's friends' arguments: Suffering is the result of sin. While the central point is true and is echoed in Pr 22:8 (compare Gal 6:7), Job's friends apply it too broadly. In their view, all those who reap trouble must have sowed trouble. They have no room in their theology for a righteous sufferer.

4:9 blast of his anger Compare Job 1:19, where a strong wind led to the death of Job's children. Eliphaz may be subtly suggesting that sin caused their death (compare 8:4; 18:19; 27:14).

4:11 The lion perishes Eliphaz's point may be that just as the lion cannot defy natural law, so Job cannot change the way God designed the moral world to work: the sinful suffer. Alternatively, he may be using the lion as an example (v. 10) of the wicked coming to an early end (v. 7).

4:12 A word was secretly brought to me Eliphaz says

what follows came to him in a vision from God (v. 13; compare Joel 2:28; Zec 13:4). Dreams and visions in the ancient world came from the divine realm and thus carried great authority. Eliphaz claims that what he is about to say is revelation from God.

4:17 a mortal be more righteous than God Eliphaz describes the point of his vision, which he repeats in each of his speeches (Job 15:14–16; 22:2). He implies that Job is suffering because he is guilty of sin. Job agrees with Eliphaz's vision (9:2), but argues against his implication (6:10; 10:7). **a strong man be more pure than his Maker** This refers to a state of ritual cleanness achieved after a state of uncleanness (compare Lev 11:32; Nu 19:12; Ps 51:9).

4:18 he charges his angels with error Eliphaz uses a greater-to-lesser argument: If even angels cannot meet God's standards, humans have even less ability to do so (Job 4:19).

5:1 answer you Language of lament (compare Ps 3:4; 4:1; 17:6; 20:9). Eliphaz asks Job where he will turn for help. This sets up Job 5:8, where he says Job should appeal directly to God.

5:2 a fool Eliphaz does not consider Job a fool yet, but he means that if Job continues without responding appropriately to God's reproof (v. 17), he will become a fool. The notion of being foolish in the OT carries a moral component (see 2:10 and note). In Wisdom literature, the fool is contrasted with both the righteous and the wise (e.g., Pr 10:21; 12:15).

5:3 a fool taking root Eliphaz states that the success of a fool is short lived and will not last—an opinion found throughout the OT (e.g., Ps 37:35–36; Pr 1:32).

⁶For hardship does not spring from the soil,
    nor does trouble sprout from the ground.
⁷Yet man is born to trouble
    as surely as sparks fly upward.

⁸"But if I were you, I would appeal to God;
    I would lay my cause before him.
⁹He performs wonders that cannot be
        fathomed,
    miracles that cannot be counted.
¹⁰He provides rain for the earth;
    he sends water on the countryside.
¹¹The lowly he sets on high,
    and those who mourn are lifted to safety.
¹²He thwarts the plans of the crafty,
    so that their hands achieve no success.
¹³He catches the wise in their craftiness,
    and the schemes of the wily are swept away.
¹⁴Darkness comes upon them in the daytime;
    at noon they grope as in the night.
¹⁵He saves the needy from the sword in their
        mouth;
    he saves them from the clutches of the
        powerful.
¹⁶So the poor have hope,
    and injustice shuts its mouth.

¹⁷"Blessed is the one whom God corrects;
    so do not despise the discipline of the
        Almighty.ᵃ
¹⁸For he wounds, but he also binds up;
    he injures, but his hands also heal.
¹⁹From six calamities he will rescue you;
    in seven no harm will touch you.
²⁰In famine he will deliver you from death,
    and in battle from the stroke of the sword.

²¹You will be protected from the lash
        of the tongue,
    and need not fear when destruction comes.
²²You will laugh at destruction and famine,
    and need not fear the wild animals.
²³For you will have a covenant with the stones
        of the field,
    and the wild animals will be at peace
        with you.
²⁴You will know that your tent is secure;
    you will take stock of your property and
        find nothing missing.
²⁵You will know that your children will be many,
    and your descendants like the grass
        of the earth.
²⁶You will come to the grave in full vigor,
    like sheaves gathered in season.

²⁷"We have examined this, and it is true.
    So hear it and apply it to yourself."

Job

6 Then Job replied:

²"If only my anguish could be weighed
    and all my misery be placed on the scales!
³It would surely outweigh the sand
        of the seas—
    no wonder my words have been
        impetuous.
⁴The arrows of the Almighty are in me,
    my spirit drinks in their poison;
    God's terrors are marshaled against me.

ᵃ 17 Hebrew *Shaddai*; here and throughout Job

5:6 hardship does not spring from the soil The natural world does not produce punishments; people's actions do. Eliphaz reinforces his point that a person who suffers deserves it because of sin (see Job 4:6 and note).
5:7 born to trouble All people sin and deserve punishment at times in their lives.
5:8 I would appeal to God Eliphaz advises Job to appeal to God. He seems to be respectful to Job, putting himself in his friend's place, but Job's response indicates that there was condescension in Eliphaz's tone (6:15–16,24–27). Bildad makes a similar suggestion (8:5–6). Job's friends—believing that Job suffers because of divine punishment—implore Job to seek forgiveness from God. However, Job—knowing he is innocent—seeks an answer or explanation from God about the cause of his suffering (23:3–8). This verse introduces a second major theme in the book of Job (compare 4:6 and note): The desire that God himself would answer.
5:17 Blessed is the one whom God corrects A reiteration of Eliphaz's argument that Job suffers because of his guilt. Job should embrace his suffering as God's reproof and confess, and then God will restore him (compare 4:7). Eliphaz's words echo many other OT passages (e.g., Ps 94:12; Pr 3:11–12). However, his words do not apply to Job's situation—Job does not despise God's discipline, since he was not being disciplined by God. See note on Ps 1:1.
5:19 From six calamities he will rescue you; in

seven no harm Numerical sayings like this are common in Wisdom literature (e.g., Pr 6:16; 30:18,21,29; Job 40:5). Eliphaz argues that the person who turns to God will ultimately be protected from disaster.
5:25 your children will be many An insensitive comment, considering Job had lost all his children. Eventually, God blesses Job by giving him several generations of descendants (42:12–17).

6:1—7:21 In Job's first reply, he addresses both his friends and God. He first emphasizes that his complaint is justified (6:2–3). He also asserts—for the first time—that God is the cause of his suffering (6:4), while denying having done anything wrong (6:10). As earlier, Job hopes for death (6:8–9; compare 3:20–22). He also expresses disappointment at the comfort of his friends (6:14–27) and asks them for understanding (6:28–30). After lamenting his life (7:1–6) and reflecting on death (7:7–10), Job addresses God directly, demanding that he leave him alone and stop afflicting him (7:11–21).

6:2 anguish In response to Eliphaz's statement that resentment slays a fool (5:2), Job acknowledges his vexation, but not that he is a fool. **on the scales** Job uses the image of a scale to express his burden of suffering. Two trays balanced on either side of a center pole formed a scale; on one side, Job would put his misery and anguish, which would outweigh the sands of the seas on the other side (v. 3).

⁵ Does a wild donkey bray when it has grass,
  or an ox bellow when it has fodder?
⁶ Is tasteless food eaten without salt,
  or is there flavor in the sap of the mallow^a?
⁷ I refuse to touch it;
  such food makes me ill.

⁸ "Oh, that I might have my request,
  that God would grant what I hope for,
⁹ that God would be willing to crush me,
  to let loose his hand and cut off my life!
¹⁰ Then I would still have this consolation —
  my joy in unrelenting pain —
  that I had not denied the words of the
  Holy One.

¹¹ "What strength do I have, that I should still
  hope?
  What prospects, that I should be patient?
¹² Do I have the strength of stone?
  Is my flesh bronze?
¹³ Do I have any power to help myself,
  now that success has been driven from me?

¹⁴ "Anyone who withholds kindness from
  a friend
  forsakes the fear of the Almighty.
¹⁵ But my brothers are as undependable as
  intermittent streams,
  as the streams that overflow
¹⁶ when darkened by thawing ice
  and swollen with melting snow,
¹⁷ but that stop flowing in the dry season,
  and in the heat vanish from their
  channels.
¹⁸ Caravans turn aside from their routes;
  they go off into the wasteland and perish.

¹⁹ The caravans of Tema look for water,
  the traveling merchants of Sheba look
  in hope.
²⁰ They are distressed, because they had been
  confident;
  they arrive there, only to be disappointed.
²¹ Now you too have proved to be of no help;
  you see something dreadful and are afraid.
²² Have I ever said, 'Give something on my
  behalf,
  pay a ransom for me from your wealth,
²³ deliver me from the hand of the enemy,
  rescue me from the clutches of the ruthless'?

²⁴ "Teach me, and I will be quiet;
  show me where I have been wrong.
²⁵ How painful are honest words!
  But what do your arguments prove?
²⁶ Do you mean to correct what I say,
  and treat my desperate words as wind?
²⁷ You would even cast lots for the fatherless
  and barter away your friend.

²⁸ "But now be so kind as to look at me.
  Would I lie to your face?
²⁹ Relent, do not be unjust;
  reconsider, for my integrity is at stake.^b
³⁰ Is there any wickedness on my lips?
  Can my mouth not discern malice?

7 "Do not mortals have hard service on earth?
  Are not their days like those of hired
  laborers?
² Like a slave longing for the evening shadows,
  or a hired laborer waiting to be paid,

---

^a 6 The meaning of the Hebrew for this phrase is uncertain.
^b 29 Or *my righteousness still stands*

6:4 arrows of the Almighty are in me The first time Job names God as the cause of his suffering, which he will repeat throughout his speeches (e.g., 7:12–21; 9:13–35; 13:19–27).
6:5 Does a wild donkey bray when it has grass Just as animals do not cry for food when they have it, Job likewise would not lament if he had no reason to do so.
6:7 I refuse to touch Job likens his suffering to an inedible meal. The meal God has served him is too difficult to swallow.
6:8 my request Job previously wished he had never been born (3:1,3–10) or that he had died at birth (3:11–19); here he wishes to die (see v. 9).
6:10 I had not denied Rather than repent or accept God's discipline as Eliphaz suggests (5:17), Job asserts his innocence. He has done nothing to deserve his suffering. See note on 4:6; note on 4:8.
6:14 kindness from a friend Job accuses his friends of forsaking God by removing their kindness from him.
6:19 Tema Tema and Sheba were famous trade centers of Arabia.
6:20 They are distressed, because they had been confident Merchants traveling across the desert could die if they counted on water sources that turned up dry (v. 19). Job finds his friends disappointing and even dangerous in their assumptions about him.

6:21 Now you too have proved to be of no help Job likens his friends to the desert streams, which were full in the winter season (v. 16) but dry in the hot summers (v. 17). When travelers needed them most, the streams were empty and unable to help (vv. 18–20).
6:22 Have I ever said Job reminds his friends that he has never made any demands of them.
6:24 show me where I have been wrong Job has already asserted his innocence. Eliphaz suggested he accept God's discipline (5:17), but Job asks what transgression he is being disciplined for.
6:29 Relent Job pleads for compassion from his friends.
6:30 my lips Job declares his innocence. In Wisdom literature, the tongue and lips are indicators of character (e.g., Pr 10:20–21). What comes out of a person's mouth is related to that person's wisdom or righteousness (Pr 15:2; Ps 37:30). Job asserts his innocence throughout the book and insists on vindication from God (compare Job 10:5–7; 13:16–18; 27:1–6; 29:1–25; 31:1–40).

7:1–21 Job continues his response to Eliphaz and addresses God directly. He laments his life (vv. 1–6) and reflects on death (vv. 7–10). Then he demands that God leave him alone and stop afflicting him (vv. 11–21).

³ so I have been allotted months of futility,
  and nights of misery have been assigned
    to me.
⁴ When I lie down I think, 'How long before
    I get up?'
  The night drags on, and I toss and turn
    until dawn.
⁵ My body is clothed with worms and scabs,
  my skin is broken and festering.

⁶ "My days are swifter than a weaver's shuttle,
  and they come to an end without hope.
⁷ Remember, O God, that my life is but a
    breath;
  my eyes will never see happiness again.
⁸ The eye that now sees me will see me no
    longer;
  you will look for me, but I will be no more.
⁹ As a cloud vanishes and is gone,
  so one who goes down to the grave does not
    return.
¹⁰ He will never come to his house again;
  his place will know him no more.

¹¹ "Therefore I will not keep silent;
  I will speak out in the anguish of my spirit,
  I will complain in the bitterness of my
    soul.

¹² Am I the sea, or the monster of the deep,
  that you put me under guard?
¹³ When I think my bed will comfort me
  and my couch will ease my complaint,
¹⁴ even then you frighten me with dreams
  and terrify me with visions,
¹⁵ so that I prefer strangling and death,
  rather than this body of mine.
¹⁶ I despise my life; I would not live forever.
  Let me alone; my days have no
    meaning.

¹⁷ "What is mankind that you make so much
    of them,
  that you give them so much attention,
¹⁸ that you examine them every morning
  and test them every moment?
¹⁹ Will you never look away from me,
  or let me alone even for an instant?
²⁰ If I have sinned, what have I done to you,
  you who see everything we do?
  Why have you made me your target?
  Have I become a burden to you?ᵃ
²¹ Why do you not pardon my offenses
  and forgive my sins?

ᵃ 20 A few manuscripts of the Masoretic Text, an ancient Hebrew
scribal tradition and Septuagint; most manuscripts of the
Masoretic Text *I have become a burden to myself.*

7:5 my skin is broken and festering The exact nature
of Job's illness is unknown. The sores that covered
his entire body (2:7) would break open and scab over
repeatedly. His affliction made it difficult for him to sleep
(7:4)—either because of irritation (2:8) or pain (30:17).
7:6 swifter than a weaver's shuttle The shuttle on
a loom flies back and forth, and the thread is cut when
the cloth is finished. Job thinks his life is nearly finished
and he will be cut off.
7:7 Remember Job addresses God directly and asks
him to respond to his affliction—in this case, by ignoring him so that he may die (vv. 12–19). Calls for God to
remember can be found throughout the OT. These calls
sometimes appeal to God to remember his attributes—
his mercy (Ps 25:6; compare Ps 109:16), love (2Ch
6:42), word (Ne 1:8; Ps 119:49) or promises (Ex 32:13).
In some petitions, God is encouraged to remember the
actions or attitudes of his enemies (e.g., Ps 74:18).
Other times, they call God to remember and deliver the
afflicted (Jdg 16:28; Ps 106:4; Jer 15:15), to remember
his congregation (Ps 74:2) and to remember the brevity
of human life (Ps 89:47). Psalmists also ask God not
to remember their sins (Ps 25:7; 79:8). **my life is but
a breath** The Hebrew word used here, *ruach* (meaning
"wind," "breath" or "spirit"), occurs frequently in Job
(e.g., 6:4,26; 8:2; 9:18; 15:30). Job is referring to just
how short a human life is. The brevity of human life is a
theme throughout the OT. In Hebrew poetry, life is often
compared to withering grass (Ps 102:11; 103:15), a
dream (Job 20:8), a shadow (8:9; Ps 109:23; 144:4)
and a blossom (Job 14:2; Ps 103:15).
7:9 to the grave The Hebrew term used here, *she'ol*,
indicates the underworld, the place of the dead according to Hebrew thought (see note on Job 14:13).
See the infographic "Ancient Hebrew Conception of the
Universe" on p. 5.

7:11 will not keep silent Job declares that he will
continue to speak freely, which he repeats several times
throughout his speeches. See note on 10:1.
7:12 sea In the ancient Near Eastern worldview, the
sea was a force of chaos that had to be subdued by
deities. See note on Ge 1:21. **monster of the deep** In
the ancient Near Eastern worldview, sea monsters, such
as Leviathan and Rahab (see Job 3:8 and note; 9:13
and note), were viewed as threats to the created world
(see 41:1 and note; Isa 27:1 and note). Job wonders
what kind of threat he must be that God is giving him
the kind of rebuke given to these creatures (compare
Ge 18:20–21).
7:16 Let me alone Job directly demands that God leave
him alone. While God never condemns Job's speech
(Job 42:8), Job repents after God responds (42:6). **no
meaning** The Hebrew word used here, *hevel*, refers to
breath, vanity, something absurd or something meaningless. See note on Ecc 1:2.
7:17 What is mankind Echoes Ps 8:4, where the psalmist marvels that God in his majesty and glory would be
concerned with humanity. Job laments God's concern
for humanity since it is crushing him.
7:20 what have I done to you Job believes himself to
be innocent (Job 6:10); he demands to know what sin he
is guilty of that merits such devastating punishment. Job
is not claiming to be perfect, nor is he making light of sin.
He is protesting that his punishment is disproportionate
to any wrong he has done. According to the concept of
divine retribution, God gives people what they deserve,
and Job has done nothing bad enough to deserve what
he is experiencing (see 4:6 and note).
7:21 do you not pardon my offenses Job is not admitting guilt; he assumes that he is on trial and God
presumes him guilty. He wants God to stop punishing
him (compare 13:23). Job will continue to ask for a

For I will soon lie down in the dust;
  you will search for me, but I will be
    no more."

Bildad

8 Then Bildad the Shuhite replied:

2 "How long will you say such things?
  Your words are a blustering wind.
3 Does God pervert justice?
  Does the Almighty pervert what is right?
4 When your children sinned against him,
  he gave them over to the penalty of their sin.
5 But if you will seek God earnestly
  and plead with the Almighty,
6 if you are pure and upright,
  even now he will rouse himself on your
    behalf
  and restore you to your prosperous state.
7 Your beginnings will seem humble,
  so prosperous will your future be.

8 "Ask the former generation
  and find out what their ancestors learned,
9 for we were born only yesterday and know
    nothing,
  and our days on earth are but a shadow.

10 Will they not instruct you and tell you?
  Will they not bring forth words from their
    understanding?
11 Can papyrus grow tall where there is
    no marsh?
  Can reeds thrive without water?
12 While still growing and uncut,
  they wither more quickly than grass.
13 Such is the destiny of all who forget God;
  so perishes the hope of the godless.
14 What they trust in is fragile *a*;
  what they rely on is a spider's web.
15 They lean on the web, but it gives way;
  they cling to it, but it does not hold.
16 They are like a well-watered plant in the
    sunshine,
  spreading its shoots over the garden;
17 it entwines its roots around a pile of rocks
  and looks for a place among the stones.
18 But when it is torn from its spot,
  that place disowns it and says, 'I never saw
    you.'
19 Surely its life withers away,
  and *b* from the soil other plants grow.

a 14 The meaning of the Hebrew for this word is uncertain.
b 19 Or *Surely all the joy it has / is that*

fair hearing before God (9:14–20; 13:1–3,18–28; 19:7–24; 23:2–9). **I will soon lie down in the dust** Job seems to assume his request for death (6:8–9) will be granted soon.

8:1–22 In his first of his three speeches (compare 18:1–21; 25:1–6), Bildad argues that God is just (v. 3). He supports this assertion by pointing to their ancestors' teachings (vv. 8–10) and the ways of nature (vv. 11–19). Like Eliphaz (5:8), Bildad encourages Job to seek God and ask him for mercy (vv. 5–7)—then Job will be restored (vv. 20–22).

8:2 How long will you say such things Unlike Eliphaz, who responded sympathetically to Job's lament, Bildad responds to Job's protests against God (7:11–21; compare 4:3–5). He has less sympathy for Job, who has criticized God's action toward him, so he reprimands Job from the beginning of his speech.

8:3 Does God pervert justice Belief in divine justice is central to Bildad's argument. However, he mistakenly expands this to a belief in divine retribution, where any misfortune is evidence of God's judgment (see note on 4:6). The issue of God's justice and divine retribution is central to the discussion between Job and his friends. Job's friends—who hold a narrow view of divine retribution—believe any suffering is evidence of God's punishment. In their view, suffering—when it occurs—is deserved because God as a just judge would not allow the innocent to suffer. Job, however—knowing that he is innocent—recognizes exceptions to this concept.

8:4 When your children sinned Bildad's insensitive statement is based on his belief in divine justice. He believes that anyone who experiences disaster must have sinned. Since Job's children have died, he assumes they must have done something to warrant God's punishment (compare 4:8 and note).

8:6 pure and upright Job has already been described in similar terms (see 1:1 and note). Unlike Eliphaz, Bildad doubts Job's righteousness (compare 4:6; 5:17–18). **restore you to your prosperous state** According to Bildad's understanding of divine retribution, God will restore Job if he pleads for mercy and is pure and upright (compare note on 8:3).

8:7 prosperous will your future be An ironic foreshadowing of what later happens to Job, though not because he listened to Bildad's counsel (see 42:10–17).

8:8 Ask the former generation Bildad cites traditional wisdom teaching to back up his argument (compare Eliphaz, who drew on his own experiences; 4:8,12–17; 5:3).

8:9 a shadow The brevity of individual life is Bildad's rationale for adhering to wisdom passed down through the ages. Life is too short for a single person to acquire the knowledge necessary to live wisely.

8:11–19 Bildad uses three illustrations from nature to depict the fate of the ungodly in vv. 11–19. He presents his instruction as ancestral wisdom (vv. 8–10), which often uses analogies from nature. First, the godless person is like papyrus, which quickly grows to great heights (10–15 ft) under the right conditions. However, it depends on a swampy water supply and dies if the conditions change. So also the godless will perish (vv. 11–13). Second, the godless man is confident in the wrong things—like a man leaning against a spider web. Trusting in such fragility is disastrous (vv. 14–15). Finally, the godless person is like a plant in rocky soil, which has shallow roots and leaves no trace when it is easily uprooted (vv. 16–19).

8:13 who forget God Forgetting God does not simply indicate a careless lapse of memory; it implies intentional disobedience or a decision to reject God (see Dt 8:11,19; Isa 17:10; Jer 3:21).

20 "Surely God does not reject one who is
blameless
or strengthen the hands of evildoers.
21 He will yet fill your mouth with laughter
and your lips with shouts of joy.
22 Your enemies will be clothed in shame,
and the tents of the wicked will be no more."

Job

9 Then Job replied:

2 "Indeed, I know that this is true.
But how can mere mortals prove their
innocence before God?
3 Though they wished to dispute with him,
they could not answer him one time out
of a thousand.
4 His wisdom is profound, his power is vast.
Who has resisted him and come out
unscathed?
5 He moves mountains without their
knowing it
and overturns them in his anger.
6 He shakes the earth from its place
and makes its pillars tremble.
7 He speaks to the sun and it does not shine;
he seals off the light of the stars.

8 He alone stretches out the heavens
and treads on the waves of the sea.
9 He is the Maker of the Bear[a] and Orion,
the Pleiades and the constellations
of the south.
10 He performs wonders that cannot be
fathomed,
miracles that cannot be counted.
11 When he passes me, I cannot see him;
when he goes by, I cannot perceive him.
12 If he snatches away, who can stop him?
Who can say to him, 'What are you doing?'
13 God does not restrain his anger;
even the cohorts of Rahab cowered at his
feet.

14 "How then can I dispute with him?
How can I find words to argue with him?
15 Though I were innocent, I could not
answer him;
I could only plead with my Judge for mercy.
16 Even if I summoned him and he responded,
I do not believe he would give me
a hearing.
17 He would crush me with a storm
and multiply my wounds for no reason.

a 9 Or of Leo

8:20 God does not reject one who is blameless
Bildad holds to his mistaken beliefs about God's justice
and Job's status before him. He asserts that if Job is
blameless, God will restore him (compare Job 8:6).
However, God described Job as blameless before Job's
suffering (1:8).
8:22 tents of the wicked A tent was often used to
describe the welfare of a group of people (see 18:15
and note). Bildad assures Job that God will destroy the
wicked. Job later uses this same language to argue that
God does not punish the wicked (12:6).

9:1—10:22 In his second response, Job does not respond directly to Bildad's speech in the previous chapter.
Instead, he laments the way God has treated him. Job
uses legal language to express his desire to plead his
case before God and be vindicated. He first extols God's
power over creation (9:4–12), then complains about
God's seemingly unjust treatment of him (9:13–35).
Finally, he addresses God directly, complaining about
God's treatment of him (10:8–17), and asks for an explanation (10:2–7). He ends his speech by asking God
to leave him alone until his impending death (10:18–22).

9:2 can mere mortals prove their innocence This
question sets up Job's intent to contend with God (see
v. 3; 13:18; compare 29:14).
9:3 dispute with him The Hebrew word used here, *riv*,
typically refers to a legal dispute (Ex 23:2; Dt 25:1; Isa
1:17). Job uses legal language throughout this speech.
He wishes he could summon God to appear in court
(Job 9:14–16) before an arbiter (vv. 32–35) in order
to prove his innocence (10:7,14–15). Job's quest for
vindication begins here and continues through the rest
of the book (see 13:13–23; 16:18–21; 19:23–27;
23:2–14). He wants to enter into litigation with God so

he can find a way out of his situation. Job charges that
God, his adversary, is punishing him without having had
a trial. Job considers this to be a miscarriage of justice.

9:5–10 Job's hymnic words in vv. 5–10 are not used to
praise God for his greatness. Rather, he shows God's
power over creation to make his case for the futility of
contending with God. God uses his creation as a weapon
against his enemies: He overturns mountains in anger
(v. 5); he shakes the pillars of the earth (v. 6); he stops
the sun from rising (v. 7); he tramples the waves (v. 8).
His creation is helpless before him, leaving Job with no
hope of reprieve, much less vindication (vv. 12,14–20;
compare 7:17 and note).

9:5 mountains An image of stability in the ancient Near
East (Dt 33:15).
9:6 pillars Job is speaking metaphorically, but his words
reflect ancient cosmology in which the earth rests on
supporting pillars or foundations (compare Job 38:6;
Ps 74:3; 1Sa 2:8).
9:9 Bear and Orion Uncertain constellations, perhaps
Ursa Major and Orion (see note on Job 38:31; note on
38:32).
9:13 Rahab The Hebrew word here may be a proper name
referring to Rahab (26:12; Ps 89:10; Isa 51:9–10), a
mythical sea monster and symbol of chaos like Leviathan
(see Job 3:8 and note; 41:1 and note). In the ancient
Near Eastern world, creatures like these were seen as
forces of chaos that needed to be subdued. Compare
note on Gen 1:21.
9:15 Though I were innocent Job continues to use
legal terminology (see note on Job 9:3) as he laments
his inability to bring a case before God.
9:17 for no reason The Hebrew term here is the same
one used by God when talking with the *satan* figure in

18 He would not let me catch my breath
　but would overwhelm me with misery.
19 If it is a matter of strength, he is mighty!
　And if it is a matter of justice, who can
　challenge him[a]?
20 Even if I were innocent, my mouth would
　condemn me;
　if I were blameless, it would pronounce
　me guilty.

21 "Although I am blameless,
　I have no concern for myself;
　I despise my own life.
22 It is all the same; that is why I say,
　'He destroys both the blameless and
　the wicked.'
23 When a scourge brings sudden death,
　he mocks the despair of the innocent.
24 When a land falls into the hands of the
　wicked,
　he blindfolds its judges.
　If it is not he, then who is it?

25 "My days are swifter than a runner;
　they fly away without a glimpse of joy.
26 They skim past like boats of papyrus,
　like eagles swooping down on their prey.
27 If I say, 'I will forget my complaint,
　I will change my expression, and smile,'
28 I still dread all my sufferings,
　for I know you will not hold me innocent.
29 Since I am already found guilty,
　why should I struggle in vain?

30 Even if I washed myself with soap
　and my hands with cleansing powder,
31 you would plunge me into a slime pit
　so that even my clothes would detest me.

32 "He is not a mere mortal like me that I might
　answer him,
　that we might confront each other in court.
33 If only there were someone to mediate
　between us,
　someone to bring us together,
34 someone to remove God's rod from me,
　so that his terror would frighten me no
　more.
35 Then I would speak up without fear of him,
　but as it now stands with me, I cannot.

10 "I loathe my very life;
　therefore I will give free rein to my
　complaint
　and speak out in the bitterness of my soul.
2 I say to God: Do not declare me guilty,
　but tell me what charges you have
　against me.
3 Does it please you to oppress me,
　to spurn the work of your hands,
　while you smile on the plans of the
　wicked?
4 Do you have eyes of flesh?
　Do you see as a mortal sees?

[a] 19 See Septuagint; Hebrew me.

2:3 (compare note on 1:6). Job is correct that God has afflicted him without cause. The reason for Job's suffering is at the forefront of his dialogue with his friends. Job's friends believe his suffering is due to some transgression. Throughout his speeches, Job asks (and even demands) that God reveal the reason for his suffering. However, when God answers, he never gives Job an explanation (see chs. 38–41).

9:20 it would pronounce me guilty Job cries out for a hearing with God in this chapter, but he has three doubts about what would happen if he got what he wants: He would not be able to express himself adequately (v. 14); God would not listen to him (v. 16); and his words would condemn him (v. 20). These doubts lead to his despair and self-loathing (v. 21).

9:22 blameless and the wicked In contrast to his friends (4:7; 8:20), Job's experience has caused him to doubt the justice of God. Since God brought trouble on Job despite his innocence, Job assumes God punishes the innocent along with the wicked. God will eventually rebuke Job for this assumption (40:8).

9:24 he blindfolds its judges This expression refers to bribing officials (compare Ex 23:8; Ge 20:16). Job does not mean that God bribes officials, but he does imply that he can keep them from recognizing the misery of the oppressed. **If it is not he, then who** Job asks how anyone other than God could be responsible for injustice if God is sovereign and in control of creation (Job 9:5–10).

9:27 I will forget my complaint Job tries to find relief from his trouble by not thinking about his situation (compare 7:13).

9:33 to mediate Since Job doubts his ability to defend himself before God (see vv. 14,20), he desires the assistance of an arbiter—the Hebrew word used here is *mokhiach*. This theme continues through the rest of the dialogues and is especially important in 16:19–21 (see note on 16:19). The exact role of a *mokhiach* is unclear. In Am 5:10, it seems to be a person who takes up the defense of the poor or oppressed. If that is true, Job desires a *mokhiach* because he feels oppressed by God. Job's desire for an arbiter anticipates Christ's role in the NT as a mediator between God and humanity. The Septuagint (the ancient Greek translation of the OT) uses the Greek work *mesitēs* in this verse (compare 1Ti 2:5 and note).

10:1 I will give free rein to my complaint Since his attempt to forget his complaint failed (Job 9:27–28), Job declares that he must speak freely. Job's speech is at times shocking. He addresses God frankly and forcefully, accusing him of acting unjustly and demanding answers (see 7:20; 9:22–24). While Job's later response to God is much more subdued (40:3–5), God never condemns his complaint (see 42:8).

10:3 Does it please you Job sarcastically asks God if it seems good to despise his own creation. Job uses the Hebrew word *tov* here (meaning "good")—the same term God uses to describe creation in Ge 1 (see note on Ge 1:4). **you smile on the plans of the wicked** Job blatantly accuses God of injustice. Job accuses God of favoring the wicked in addition to oppressing him, an innocent man.

10:4 you see as a mortal sees Job sarcastically asks God if he is subject to human limitations. He contends

⁵Are your days like those of a mortal
  or your years like those of a strong man,
⁶that you must search out my faults
  and probe after my sin —
⁷though you know that I am not guilty
  and that no one can rescue me from your
    hand?

⁸"Your hands shaped me and made me.
  Will you now turn and destroy me?
⁹Remember that you molded me like clay.
  Will you now turn me to dust again?
¹⁰Did you not pour me out like milk
  and curdle me like cheese,
¹¹clothe me with skin and flesh
  and knit me together with bones and sinews?
¹²You gave me life and showed me kindness,
  and in your providence watched over my
    spirit.

¹³"But this is what you concealed in your heart,
  and I know that this was in your mind:
¹⁴If I sinned, you would be watching me
  and would not let my offense go unpunished.
¹⁵If I am guilty — woe to me!
  Even if I am innocent, I cannot lift my
    head,
  for I am full of shame
  and drowned in*a* my affliction.
¹⁶If I hold my head high, you stalk me like a lion
  and again display your awesome power
    against me.
¹⁷You bring new witnesses against me
  and increase your anger toward me;
  your forces come against me wave upon
    wave.

¹⁸"Why then did you bring me out of
    the womb?
  I wish I had died before any eye saw me.
¹⁹If only I had never come into being,
  or had been carried straight from the
    womb to the grave!
²⁰Are not my few days almost over?
  Turn away from me so I can have a
    moment's joy
²¹before I go to the place of no return,
  to the land of gloom and utter darkness,
²²to the land of deepest night,
  of utter darkness and disorder,
  where even the light is like darkness."

Zophar

11 Then Zophar the Naamathite replied:

²"Are all these words to go unanswered?
  Is this talker to be vindicated?
³Will your idle talk reduce others to silence?
  Will no one rebuke you when you mock?
⁴You say to God, 'My beliefs are flawless
  and I am pure in your sight.'
⁵Oh, how I wish that God would speak,
  that he would open his lips against you
⁶and disclose to you the secrets of wisdom,
  for true wisdom has two sides.
  Know this: God has even forgotten some
    of your sin.

⁷"Can you fathom the mysteries of God?
  Can you probe the limits of the Almighty?

a 15 Or and aware of

---

that God will only find iniquity or sin in him if he considers Job's situation from the limited perspective of a human being.
10:7 you know that I am not guilty Job has steadfastly maintained his innocence and accused God of not caring about his suffering (see Job 9:14,20,21). Now for the first time he asserts that God also knows that he is innocent—but he still punished him. Job cries out for a deliverer but despairs of one coming since it seems God himself is so set against him.
10:8 Your hands shaped Job appeals to God as creator (vv. 8–17). He laments that God made him only to destroy him. He contends that a creator should care for his creation, but God uses his power to show hostility and cruelty.
10:14 you would be watching me Job feels God is closely watching him, waiting for him to sin. This negative watchfulness contrasts with the positive in v. 12, where God's watchfulness protected Job.
10:15 I cannot lift my head A lifted head was a sign of pride and respect (Ge 40:20; Ps 27:6), while a lowered head signified shame and disgrace (Jdg 8:28; Zec 1:21). In the following speech, Zophar claims Job's repentance would allow him to lift his face (Job 11:15).
10:20 Turn away from me Using surprisingly direct language (see note on v. 1), Job again demands that God leave him alone (7:16). This demand follows Job's

repeated despair that he cannot have his wish never to have been born (vv. 18–19; compare 3:1–11; 7:16–17).
10:22 to the land of deepest night Expresses the deep gloom of Sheol, the realm of the dead (see 14:13 and note). Job uses five different words for darkness in vv. 21–22.

11:1–20 Zophar—Job's third friend—makes only two speeches (here and ch. 20). He offers little comfort to Job, but begins by criticizing Job's words (vv. 2–3) and asserting that Job is in fact guilty and deserving of God's punishment (vv. 4–6). He reminds Job of God's supremacy and wisdom (vv. 7–12). Finally—like Eliphaz (5:17–27) and Bildad (8:5–7,20–22)—he encourages Job to repent (vv. 13–14) and be restored (vv. 15–20).
11:2 all these words to go unanswered In Wisdom literature, speaking many words is characteristic of a fool (Pr 10:19; Ecc 5:7; 10:14).
11:4 My beliefs are flawless Job never claims this. Zophar caricatures Job's position, showing little sympathy for his agony. **in your sight** Zophar again mischaracterizes Job's claims: Job never has claimed to be completely free from sin (Job 7:21; 9:2); he only says that he has not done anything deserving of this suffering (compare 7:20; 9:20–22).
11:6 some of your sin Zophar believes God was not punishing Job as much as he deserved (compare 7:20

⁸ They are higher than the heavens above —
      what can you do?
   They are deeper than the depths below —
      what can you know?
⁹ Their measure is longer than the earth
      and wider than the sea.

¹⁰ "If he comes along and confines you in prison
      and convenes a court, who can
         oppose him?
¹¹ Surely he recognizes deceivers;
      and when he sees evil, does he not
         take note?
¹² But the witless can no more become wise
      than a wild donkey's colt can be born
         human.ᵃ

¹³ "Yet if you devote your heart to him
      and stretch out your hands to him,
¹⁴ if you put away the sin that is in your hand
      and allow no evil to dwell in your tent,
¹⁵ then, free of fault, you will lift up your face;
      you will stand firm and without fear.
¹⁶ You will surely forget your trouble,
      recalling it only as waters gone by.
¹⁷ Life will be brighter than noonday,
      and darkness will become like morning.
¹⁸ You will be secure, because there is hope;
      you will look about you and take your rest
         in safety.

¹⁹ You will lie down, with no one to make you
         afraid,
      and many will court your favor.
²⁰ But the eyes of the wicked will fail,
      and escape will elude them;
      their hope will become a dying gasp."

Job

12 Then Job replied:

² "Doubtless you are the only people who matter,
      and wisdom will die with you!
³ But I have a mind as well as you;
      I am not inferior to you.
   Who does not know all these things?

⁴ "I have become a laughingstock to my friends,
      though I called on God and he answered —
      a mere laughingstock, though righteous
         and blameless!
⁵ Those who are at ease have contempt for
         misfortune
      as the fate of those whose feet are slipping.
⁶ The tents of marauders are undisturbed,
      and those who provoke God are secure —
      those God has in his hand.ᵇ

ᵃ 12 Or *wild donkey can be born tame* ᵇ 6 Or *those whose god is in their own hand*

---

and note). Eliphaz believed Job had some small sin to confess before all was restored (4:5–6). Bildad thought Job must be righteous since he was still living, in contrast to his children (8:4–6).

11:7 mysteries of God Ironically, while Job has not claimed to understand God's work, Zophar does so by assuming Job's suffering was the result of God's punishment.

11:8 depths The Hebrew text here uses the term *she'ol*—the place of the dead according to Hebrew thought. In the ancient Near Eastern worldview, the place of the dead was believed to be below the earth. See note on 14:13.

11:11 deceivers The Hebrew word used here, *shawe*, literally rendered as "worthless," usually describes something ineffective or false. It is used elsewhere to describe a false report or false witness (Ex 23:1; Dt 5:20) and to describe other gods (Ps 31:6; Jer 18:15; Jnh 2:8).

11:12 a wild donkey's colt can be born human Zophar uses this proverb to tell Job to stop being foolish by insisting he is innocent; it will get him nowhere.

11:14 put away the sin Calls for repentance often included an appeal to put away some form of wrongdoing (1Sa 7:3).

11:15 then Zophar assures Job that restoration will follow repentance. In describing Job's possible restoration, Zophar directly contrasts some of Job's complaints.

11:17 brighter than noonday This continues the metaphor of light/life in Job (see Job 3:4 and note); it also contrasts the end of Job's last speech (see Job 10:21–22; compare Ps 37:6).

11:18 take your rest in safety Job complained that God was hunting him like a lion and attacking him relentlessly (Job 10:16–17). Zophar assures him that he will find peace when he repents.

12:1—14:22 Outside of his final speech to his friends (26:1—31:40), this is Job's longest response. In it, Job addresses his friends (12:1–13:19) and God (13:20–14:22). He begins with a sarcastic tone as he criticizes his friends (12:2–3). He continues by asserting his innocence, observing that the wicked go unpunished (12:4–6). He indicates that all creation knows God is in control (12:7–12). Job extols God's wisdom (12:13–25) before criticizing his friends again, arguing his wisdom is equal to theirs (13:1–6). Accusing them of speaking falsely for God, he states that God will rebuke them (13:7–12). After again expressing a desire to plead his case before God (13:13–19), Job addresses God directly. He uses legal terminology as he pleads with God to hear his case (13:20–27). He then discusses human suffering (13:28—14:12), ending his speech with reflections on death (14:13–22).

12:2 wisdom will die with you Job mocks his friends' certainty by saying there is no wisdom beyond theirs.

12:4 I have become a laughingstock A common theme in laments (e.g., Ps 69:10–12; Jer 20:7; La 3:14). Derision typically comes from one's enemies, but Job is speaking to friends (compare Job 19:13–15). **though righteous and blameless** Job again defends his innocence (compare 1:1). He laments that, even though he has been just and blameless (see note on 11:4), he has become an object of contempt to his friends.

12:6 The tents of marauders are undisturbed Job's friends argue that God always punishes wickedness. Job observes that wickedness often seems to go unpunished. The author of Ecclesiastes also makes this point (Ecc 7:15; 8:14). The notion of divine retribution—the idea that God repays people according to what they deserve—is central to the argument between Job and his

⁷"But ask the animals, and they will teach you,
or the birds in the sky, and they will
tell you;
⁸or speak to the earth, and it will teach you,
or let the fish in the sea inform you.
⁹Which of all these does not know
that the hand of the LORD has done this?
¹⁰In his hand is the life of every creature
and the breath of all mankind.
¹¹Does not the ear test words
as the tongue tastes food?
¹²Is not wisdom found among the aged?
Does not long life bring understanding?

¹³"To God belong wisdom and power;
counsel and understanding are his.
¹⁴What he tears down cannot be rebuilt;
those he imprisons cannot be released.
¹⁵If he holds back the waters, there is drought;
if he lets them loose, they devastate the
land.
¹⁶To him belong strength and insight;
both deceived and deceiver are his.
¹⁷He leads rulers away stripped
and makes fools of judges.
¹⁸He takes off the shackles put on by kings
and ties a loincloth*a* around their waist.
¹⁹He leads priests away stripped
and overthrows officials long established.
²⁰He silences the lips of trusted advisers
and takes away the discernment of elders.

²¹He pours contempt on nobles
and disarms the mighty.
²²He reveals the deep things of darkness
and brings utter darkness into the light.
²³He makes nations great, and destroys
them;
he enlarges nations, and disperses them.
²⁴He deprives the leaders of the earth of their
reason;
he makes them wander in a trackless
waste.
²⁵They grope in darkness with no light;
he makes them stagger like drunkards.

13 "My eyes have seen all this,
my ears have heard and understood it.
²What you know, I also know;
I am not inferior to you.
³But I desire to speak to the Almighty
and to argue my case with God.
⁴You, however, smear me with lies;
you are worthless physicians, all of you!
⁵If only you would be altogether silent!
For you, that would be wisdom.
⁶Hear now my argument;
listen to the pleas of my lips.
⁷Will you speak wickedly on God's behalf?
Will you speak deceitfully for him?
⁸Will you show him partiality?
Will you argue the case for God?

a 18 Or *shackles of kings / and ties a belt*

---

friends. Job's friends believe that the righteous always prosper while the wicked always suffer. The principle behind their point is present in wisdom literature (e.g., Pr 11:31; 13:21), but Job's friends neglect to account for any ambiguity or the idea that God's judgment may be delayed for some later time. See note on Job 4:6; note on 8:3.
12:7 they will teach you Job points to creation to show that God's control over the earth is well known.
12:9 hand of the LORD has done this This is the only occurrence of the divine name, Yahweh, in the dialogues between Job and his friends. Compare Isa 41:20.

12:13–25 In this section, Job describes the scope of God's power. He points out God's wisdom (Job 12:13) and says no one can change God's work (v. 14). He speaks of God's supremacy over several areas: the weather (v. 15), earthly leaders and authorities (vv. 17–21), light and darkness (v. 22) and the nations of the earth (v. 23). Job emphasizes the destructive nature of God's power—a direct contrast to Eliphaz's speech on God's power (5:9–14).

12:15 they devastate the land In his first speech, Eliphaz praises God as the one who sends rain to water the fields (5:10). Here, Job emphasizes that God controls both droughts and floods.
12:17 makes fools of judges Job highlights God's power to humble people and bring down those in power. Job, a formerly wealthy man (1:3), feels that God has dealt similarly with him. Eliphaz has emphasized God's ability to lift up the poor and needy (5:11,15). He, along

with Job's other friends, believes that if Job repents, God will restore him in a similar fashion.
12:22 utter darkness into the light Echoes themes of light and darkness introduced in Job's first lament (see 3:4 and note).

13:1–28 Job continues his response to his friends (chs. 12–14), arguing that he is as wise as they are (vv. 1–6). He accuses them of presumptuously speaking for God (vv. 7–9), and he says God will rebuke them (vv. 10–12). Then he asks them to be silent while he disputes his case before God (vv. 13–19). He pleads with God directly in legal terminology to hear him (vv. 20–27) before he begins a reflection on human suffering (v. 28).

13:3 to argue my case with God Instead of repenting and coming to God for mercy as his friends suggested (11:13–14), Job wishes to come before God to dispute the injustice done to him.
13:4 smear me with lies Job accuses his friends of speaking falsely. God confirms their error in 42:7.
13:7 you speak wickedly on God's behalf By claiming that Job's suffering was due to God's punishment, they attributed false reasons to God's actions.
13:8 you show him partiality Job seeks a fair hearing where he can argue his case before God (see note on 9:3). He earlier wished for the help of an arbiter (9:33 and note) and seeks impartiality. Job wanted his friends to speak truthfully (13:7) and be impartial witnesses (v. 8), but instead they made false arguments and rebuked Job without listening to him.

⁹ Would it turn out well if he examined you?
　　Could you deceive him as you might
　　　deceive a mortal?
¹⁰ He would surely call you to account
　　if you secretly showed partiality.
¹¹ Would not his splendor terrify you?
　　Would not the dread of him fall on you?
¹² Your maxims are proverbs of ashes;
　　your defenses are defenses of clay.

¹³ "Keep silent and let me speak;
　　then let come to me what may.
¹⁴ Why do I put myself in jeopardy
　　and take my life in my hands?
¹⁵ Though he slay me, yet will I hope in him;
　　I will surely[a] defend my ways to his face.
¹⁶ Indeed, this will turn out for my deliverance,
　　for no godless person would dare come
　　　before him!
¹⁷ Listen carefully to what I say;
　　let my words ring in your ears.
¹⁸ Now that I have prepared my case,
　　I know I will be vindicated.
¹⁹ Can anyone bring charges against me?
　　If so, I will be silent and die.

²⁰ "Only grant me these two things, God,
　　and then I will not hide from you:
²¹ Withdraw your hand far from me,
　　and stop frightening me with your terrors.
²² Then summon me and I will answer,
　　or let me speak, and you reply to me.
²³ How many wrongs and sins have I committed?
　　Show me my offense and my sin.

²⁴ Why do you hide your face
　　and consider me your enemy?
²⁵ Will you torment a windblown leaf?
　　Will you chase after dry chaff?
²⁶ For you write down bitter things against me
　　and make me reap the sins of my youth.
²⁷ You fasten my feet in shackles;
　　you keep close watch on all my paths
　　by putting marks on the soles of my feet.

²⁸ "So man wastes away like something rotten,
　　like a garment eaten by moths.

14 "Mortals, born of woman,
　　are of few days and full of trouble.
² They spring up like flowers and wither
　　　away;
　　like fleeting shadows, they do not endure.
³ Do you fix your eye on them?
　　Will you bring them[b] before you for
　　　judgment?
⁴ Who can bring what is pure from the
　　　impure?
　　No one!
⁵ A person's days are determined;
　　you have decreed the number of his
　　　months
　　and have set limits he cannot exceed.
⁶ So look away from him and let him alone,
　　till he has put in his time like a hired
　　　laborer.

---

[a] 15 Or *He will surely slay me; I have no hope* — / *yet I will*
[b] 3 Septuagint, Vulgate and Syriac; Hebrew *me*

13:12 maxims are proverbs of ashes Wisdom teachers in the ancient Near East often used proverbs and maxims to instruct because they are easy to remember and offer insight for many situations. These proverbs did not apply to Job's experience, and offering them was futile.
13:13 let come to me what may Job earlier declared that he would speak freely (10:1). Here, he echoes that statement and goes further—saying he will risk any consequence from demanding a hearing with God.
13:15 Though he slay me, yet will I hope Job recognizes the risk of demanding to present his case before God; God could respond by killing him. He hopes, however, that God will vindicate him.
13:16 this will turn out for my deliverance While his friends advise him to find restoration by repenting, Job believes he will find restoration by defending his innocence (compare 11:13–20).
13:19 bring charges against me Job is confident in his defense.
13:20 two things Although Job makes several requests in the following verses, his dispute with God involves two main complaints: He wants God to remove his suffering (v. 21), and he wants God to explain the reason for his suffering (vv. 22–23). **then I will not hide from you** Job has not hidden himself from God; he has spoken directly and freely to him (10:1), looking for God to answer him. Instead, God has hidden himself from Job (v. 24). The Hebrew phrase used here is similar to the phrase Cain used after God punished him for killing Abel (Ge 4:14).

Cain complained that his punishment was more than he could bear. However, while Cain was guilty of murder, Job has done nothing wrong. Job complains that not only is his suffering too great to bear—it is undeserved because he is innocent.
13:23 wrongs and sins In this verse, Job strings together several Hebrew words for sin: *awon*, *chatta'th* and *pesha'*. Whether it was a combination of sins or a specific wrongdoing, Job wants an answer.
13:27 by putting marks on the soles of my feet God has Job under constant watch, like a prisoner.
13:28 rotten The Hebrew word used here, *raqav*, is most often used to describe rottenness in the bones (see Pr 12:4; 14:30; Hab 3:16).

14:1–22 This is the last part of Job's long speech (Job 12:1—14:22). In it he reflects on human suffering (vv. 1–12) and death (vv. 13–22).
14:3 fix your eye on them Job asks God why he feels the need to watch people so closely since human life is so short and frail (compare Ps 143:2).
14:4 Who can bring what is pure from the impure Expresses an impossibility.
14:5 A person's days are determined Job seems to be indicating that humanity cannot exceed the limits placed on a human life (Ge 6:3). However, Job could also be expressing a belief that the particular length of a person's life is already decided (Ps 139:16).
14:6 let him alone Because people's time is limited

⁷"At least there is hope for a tree:
  If it is cut down, it will sprout again,
    and its new shoots will not fail.
⁸Its roots may grow old in the ground
    and its stump die in the soil,
⁹yet at the scent of water it will bud
    and put forth shoots like a plant.
¹⁰But a man dies and is laid low;
    he breathes his last and is no more.
¹¹As the water of a lake dries up
    or a riverbed becomes parched and dry,
¹²so he lies down and does not rise;
    till the heavens are no more, people will
      not awake
    or be roused from their sleep.

¹³"If only you would hide me in the grave
    and conceal me till your anger has
      passed!
  If only you would set me a time
    and then remember me!
¹⁴If someone dies, will they live again?
    All the days of my hard service
    I will wait for my renewal^a to come.
¹⁵You will call and I will answer you;
    you will long for the creature your hands
      have made.
¹⁶Surely then you will count my steps
    but not keep track of my sin.
¹⁷My offenses will be sealed up in a bag;
    you will cover over my sin.

¹⁸"But as a mountain erodes and crumbles
    and as a rock is moved from its place,
¹⁹as water wears away stones
    and torrents wash away the soil,
  so you destroy a person's hope.

²⁰You overpower them once for all, and they
      are gone;
    you change their countenance and send
      them away.
²¹If their children are honored, they do not
      know it;
    if their offspring are brought low, they do
      not see it.
²²They feel but the pain of their own bodies
    and mourn only for themselves."

Eliphaz

15 Then Eliphaz the Temanite replied:

²"Would a wise person answer with empty
      notions
    or fill their belly with the hot east wind?
³Would they argue with useless words,
    with speeches that have no value?
⁴But you even undermine piety
    and hinder devotion to God.
⁵Your sin prompts your mouth;
    you adopt the tongue of the crafty.
⁶Your own mouth condemns you, not mine;
    your own lips testify against you.

⁷"Are you the first man ever born?
    Were you brought forth before the hills?
⁸Do you listen in on God's council?
    Do you have a monopoly on wisdom?
⁹What do you know that we do not know?
    What insights do you have that we do not
      have?
¹⁰The gray-haired and the aged are on our side,
    men even older than your father.

---

^a 14 Or *release*

(Job 14:5), Job wishes God would turn his gaze away and allow people to live their lives while they can.
14:7 it will sprout again After discussing the brief nature of human life, Job considers life after death using the image of a tree. He says that trees have hope because they can grow back after being cut down, and laments that humans do not experience the same renewal (vv. 10–13).
14:12 does not rise; till the heavens are no more Job is unsure of what happens after death, but he seems to be speculating about the resurrection of the dead and perhaps even final judgment. Compare Rev 20:11–21:4.
14:13 the grave The Hebrew text here uses the word *she'ol*. This term, often transliterated in English translations as Sheol, is a reference to the underworld according to Hebrew thought, the place where the dead go (see note on 1Ki 2:6). Earlier, Job spoke of death as a place of rest, even for the wicked (Job 3:17–19). He also indicated that those who went to the realm of the dead could not return (7:9). Here, he seems to wish for a temporary asylum in Sheol. After the passing of God's wrath, then God would restore him (compare note on 14:12). See the infographic "Ancient Hebrew Conception of the Universe" on p. 5.

Job 14:13

SHEOL
The grave (sheol) was viewed as a pit in the depths of the earth (Job 11:8; Dt 32:22; Eze 31:16). It was a place of nothingness (Ecc 9:10) and decay (Isa 14:11). However, God's presence was not absent there (Ps 139:8)—he could bring people back from Sheol (1Sa 2:6; Ps 30:3; 49:15).

14:14 my renewal The Hebrew word used here, *chaliphah*, comes from the same word as Job's description of the tree's regrowth in 14:7. There, Job expressed doubt that humanity could hope to regrow like the trees. Here, he indicates that renewal from death is possible. Job may be expressing belief in the resurrection, after his visit to the realm of the dead (compare Da 12:2 and note; compare Job 14:12).
14:18 as a mountain erodes Job abandons hope for restoration, saying his hope is like the erosion of mountains (v. 19).

15:1–35 Eliphaz's second speech (compare chs. 4–5; 22) consists of rebuke and warning. He begins by criticizing

11 Are God's consolations not enough for you,
   words spoken gently to you?
12 Why has your heart carried you away,
   and why do your eyes flash,
13 so that you vent your rage against God
   and pour out such words from your mouth?

14 "What are mortals, that they could be pure,
   or those born of woman, that they could be
     righteous?
15 If God places no trust in his holy ones,
   if even the heavens are not pure in his eyes,

16 how much less mortals, who are vile and
     corrupt,
   who drink up evil like water!

17 "Listen to me and I will explain to you;
   let me tell you what I have seen,
18 what the wise have declared,
   hiding nothing received from their
     ancestors
19 (to whom alone the land was given
   when no foreigners moved among
     them):

Job (vv. 2–3) and accusing him of turning away from fearing God (vv. 4–6). He challenges Job's wisdom (vv. 7–13) and questions anyone's ability to be pure before God (vv. 14–16). He finishes by arguing that the wicked will be justly punished (vv. 17–35).

15:2 with the hot east wind A hot desert wind typically associated with destruction (e.g., Ge 41:6; Jer 18:17; Jnh 4:8).

15:8 God's council Eliphaz's sarcastic questions were meant to disparage Job's wisdom, but here he unknowingly references the divine council scene where the *satan* figure challenged God to afflict Job (Job 1:6–12; 2:1–6; compare note on 1:6). Neither Eliphaz nor Job

was present for that, so neither of them understands the true reason for Job's suffering. While trying to point out Job's lack of wisdom, Eliphaz inadvertently reveals his own lack of understanding.

15:9 What do you know Job claimed his knowledge was equal to that of his friends (12:3; 13:2). Here, Eliphaz similarly claims that their knowledge is equal to Job's.

15:11 God's consolations Eliphaz indicates that by rejecting the counsel of his friends (13:4), Job rejects the comfort of God.

15:14 that they could be pure Eliphaz reiterates the point he made from his vision (see 4:17 and note; 9:2; 25:4).

Cycles in Job

Prologue	Job 1–2	Job's Reply 3A	Job 23–24
Dialogue Cycle 1	Job 3–14	Bildad 3	Job 25
Job's Opening Lament	Job 3	Job's Reply 3B	Job 26
Eliphaz 1	Job 4–5	Job's Closing Discourse	Job 27
Job's Reply 1A	Job 6–7	Interlude on Wisdom	Job 28
Bildad 1	Job 8	Monologues	Job 29–37
Job's Reply 1B	Job 9–10	Job's Call for Vindication	Job 29–31
Zophar 1	Job 11	Elihu 1	Job 32–33
Job's Reply 1C	Job 12–14	Elihu 2	Job 34
Dialogue Cycle 2	Job 15–21	Elihu 3	Job 35
Eliphaz 2	Job 15	Elihu 4	Job 36–37
Job's Reply 2A	Job 16–17	God's Speeches	Job 38–42:6
Bildad 2	Job 18	God's First Discourse	Job 38:1–40:2
Job's Reply 2B	Job 19	Job's Response 1	Job 40:3–5
Zophar 2	Job 20	God's Second Discourse	Job 40:6–41:34
Job's Reply 2C	Job 21	Job's Response 2	Job 42:1–6
Dialogue Cycle 3	Job 22–27	Epilogue	Job 42:7–17
Eliphaz 3	Job 22		

²⁰ All his days the wicked man suffers torment,
  the ruthless man through all the years
    stored up for him.
²¹ Terrifying sounds fill his ears;
  when all seems well, marauders attack him.
²² He despairs of escaping the realm of darkness;
  he is marked for the sword.
²³ He wanders about for food like a vulture;
  he knows the day of darkness is at hand.
²⁴ Distress and anguish fill him with terror;
  troubles overwhelm him, like a king poised
    to attack,
²⁵ because he shakes his fist at God
  and vaunts himself against the Almighty,
²⁶ defiantly charging against him
  with a thick, strong shield.

²⁷ "Though his face is covered with fat
  and his waist bulges with flesh,
²⁸ he will inhabit ruined towns
  and houses where no one lives,
  houses crumbling to rubble.
²⁹ He will no longer be rich and his wealth will
    not endure,
  nor will his possessions spread over the land.
³⁰ He will not escape the darkness;
  a flame will wither his shoots,
  and the breath of God's mouth will carry
    him away.
³¹ Let him not deceive himself by trusting what
    is worthless,
  for he will get nothing in return.
³² Before his time he will wither,
  and his branches will not flourish.
³³ He will be like a vine stripped of its unripe
    grapes,
  like an olive tree shedding its blossoms.
³⁴ For the company of the godless will be
    barren,
  and fire will consume the tents of those
    who love bribes.

³⁵ They conceive trouble and give birth to evil;
  their womb fashions deceit."

Job

16 Then Job replied:

² "I have heard many things like these;
  you are miserable comforters, all of you!
³ Will your long-winded speeches never end?
  What ails you that you keep on arguing?
⁴ I also could speak like you,
  if you were in my place;
  I could make fine speeches against you
  and shake my head at you.
⁵ But my mouth would encourage you;
  comfort from my lips would bring you relief.

⁶ "Yet if I speak, my pain is not relieved;
  and if I refrain, it does not go away.
⁷ Surely, God, you have worn me out;
  you have devastated my entire household.
⁸ You have shriveled me up — and it has
    become a witness;
  my gauntness rises up and testifies
    against me.
⁹ God assails me and tears me in his anger
  and gnashes his teeth at me;
  my opponent fastens on me his piercing
    eyes.
¹⁰ People open their mouths to jeer at me;
  they strike my cheek in scorn
  and unite together against me.
¹¹ God has turned me over to the ungodly
  and thrown me into the clutches of the
    wicked.
¹² All was well with me, but he shattered me;
  he seized me by the neck and crushed me.
  He has made me his target;
¹³   his archers surround me.
  Without pity, he pierces my kidneys
  and spills my gall on the ground.

15:20 wicked man suffers torment Eliphaz vehemently argues against Job's assertion that the wicked often escape punishment (12:6; compare 5:2–5). Job's friends uphold a strict belief in divine justice with no room for exceptions (see 8:3 and note). In their view, the wicked suffer and the innocent do not. Since Job is suffering, they assume he must be guilty of some iniquity (11:6). Eliphaz spends the majority of his second speech arguing this point, hoping that Job will acknowledge his guilt and repent.
15:21 when all seems well, marauders attack While he describes the suffering of the wicked in general terms, Eliphaz mentions specific events that happened to Job. This description matches two of the tragedies that destroyed Job's wealth (1:14–15,17).
15:23 day of darkness is at hand See 3:4 and note.
15:25 he shakes his fist at God Eliphaz argues that Job suffers because he has defied God.
15:34 fire will consume Eliphaz may be alluding to the destruction of Job's sheep by fire (compare v. 30).

16:1—17:16 Job responds directly to Eliphaz's latest speech. He begins by returning Eliphaz's opening criticism (16:2–6), and then complains that God is oppressing him (16:7–17). Job briefly expresses hope of vindication (16:18–22) before turning to lament his friends (17:1–10) and the nearness of death (17:11–16).
16:2 miserable Eliphaz implied that Job brought his suffering on himself by saying he conceived trouble (15:35). Ironically, Job uses the same Hebrew term Eliphaz used, *amal*, to refer to his friends as troublesome (or miserable).
16:5 my mouth would encourage you If Job were acting as the comforter, he would use his words to strengthen and heal.
16:7 you have worn me out Job attributes his suffering directly to God. Because Job is innocent of any wrongdoing (v. 17), God has no reason to afflict him—contrary to Eliphaz's claims (15:25). Compare 6:5; 7:12–21; 9:13–35; 13:19–27.
16:9 gnashes his teeth at me Job portrays God as a wild animal tearing into its prey.

¹⁴ Again and again he bursts upon me;
　　he rushes at me like a warrior.
¹⁵ "I have sewed sackcloth over my skin
　　and buried my brow in the dust.
¹⁶ My face is red with weeping,
　　dark shadows ring my eyes;
¹⁷ yet my hands have been free of violence
　　and my prayer is pure.
¹⁸ "Earth, do not cover my blood;
　　may my cry never be laid to rest!
¹⁹ Even now my witness is in heaven;
　　my advocate is on high.
²⁰ My intercessor is my friend[a]
　　as my eyes pour out tears to God;
²¹ on behalf of a man he pleads with God
　　as one pleads for a friend.
²² "Only a few years will pass
　　before I take the path of no return.

17 ¹ My spirit is broken,
　　my days are cut short,
　　the grave awaits me.
² Surely mockers surround me;
　　my eyes must dwell on their hostility.

³ "Give me, O God, the pledge you demand.
　　Who else will put up security for me?
⁴ You have closed their minds to
　　understanding;
　　therefore you will not let them triumph.
⁵ If anyone denounces their friends for reward,
　　the eyes of their children will fail.

⁶ "God has made me a byword to everyone,
　　a man in whose face people spit.

⁷ My eyes have grown dim with grief;
　　my whole frame is but a shadow.
⁸ The upright are appalled at this;
　　the innocent are aroused against the
　　ungodly.
⁹ Nevertheless, the righteous will hold to their
　　ways,
　　and those with clean hands will grow
　　stronger.

¹⁰ "But come on, all of you, try again!
　　I will not find a wise man among you.
¹¹ My days have passed, my plans are shattered.
　　Yet the desires of my heart
¹² turn night into day;
　　in the face of the darkness light is near.
¹³ If the only home I hope for is the grave,
　　if I spread out my bed in the realm of
　　darkness,
¹⁴ if I say to corruption, 'You are my father,'
　　and to the worm, 'My mother' or 'My
　　sister,'
¹⁵ where then is my hope—
　　who can see any hope for me?
¹⁶ Will it go down to the gates of death?
　　Will we descend together into the dust?"

Bildad

18 Then Bildad the Shuhite replied:

² "When will you end these speeches?
　　Be sensible, and then we can talk.

a 20 Or My friends treat me with scorn

16:14 warrior When applied to God, the Hebrew term used here, *gibbor,* usually describes God's protection of his people (Ps 24:8; Jer 20:11; Zep 3:17). Here, Job portrays God as having the opposite intent.
16:15 I have sewed sackcloth over my skin Wearing sackcloth was a sign of mourning. The Hebrew text here seems to indicate that Job sewed it on his skin—this hyperbole is meant to indicate a permanent state of mourning.
16:18 Earth, do not cover my blood Job wishes for vindication. He hopes his blood will continue to cry out even after his death, just as Abel's blood cried out to God from the ground (Ge 4:10).
16:19 my witness is in heaven Job makes a distinction between the witness and God (Job 16:21). Job is acknowledging that there is one standing in heaven who can serve as a witness on his behalf. Cast within the larger framework of the book, this seems to be an acknowledgement that there is a prosecutor (or accuser) in heaven—who claims that Job will not fear God when everything he has is taken away (see note on 1:6)—and thus there must also be an advocate (or redeemer) in heaven. The NT writers note that Jesus has taken up this role on behalf of sinners (1Jn 2:1; Heb 4:14–15). Compare note on Job 19:25.
16:21 for a friend Job argues that just as his tears pour out before God, so he believes that his case will also be heard before God—that it will be as if a friend brought his case forward (compare Jn 15:13–15).
17:2 mockers surround me A description of Job's friends (Job 11:3; 12:4).

17:3 Give me, O God, the pledge you demand Job asks God to provide proof of his innocence to his friends (compare Ps 119:121–122).
17:6 made me a byword Rather than revealing Job's innocence, God humiliated Job before others. Job's words are echoed in several lament psalms (e.g., Ps 44:14; 69:11–12).
17:8 The upright are appalled Job suggests that, instead of mocking him or being contemptuous, his friends should be appalled at his suffering (see Job 12:4–5; 17:2).
17:12 night into day See 3:4 and note.
17:13 only home I hope for Job again hopes to find rest in death (compare 3:16–19; 17:13; see note on 3:13; note on 14:13; Ge 37:35 and note). **the grave** The Hebrew text here uses the term *she'ol,* the place of the dead according to Hebrew thought. See note on Job 14:13.
17:16 death The Hebrew text here once again uses the term *she'ol.* Here Job not only references the realm of the dead, but also references reaching its gates. God parallels this remark when he responds to Job in 38:17.

18:1–21 In his second speech, Bildad (compare chs. 8; 25) focuses on the fate of the wicked. He portrays the wicked as extinguished lamps (vv. 5–6) and someone caught in a trap (vv. 8–10). Bildad speaks of the wicked experiencing fear, calamities, disease (vv. 11–13); losing

³ Why are we regarded as cattle
and considered stupid in your sight?
⁴ You who tear yourself to pieces in your anger,
is the earth to be abandoned for your sake?
Or must the rocks be moved from their
place?

⁵ "The lamp of a wicked man is snuffed out;
the flame of his fire stops burning.
⁶ The light in his tent becomes dark;
the lamp beside him goes out.
⁷ The vigor of his step is weakened;
his own schemes throw him down.
⁸ His feet thrust him into a net;
he wanders into its mesh.
⁹ A trap seizes him by the heel;
a snare holds him fast.
¹⁰ A noose is hidden for him on the ground;
a trap lies in his path.
¹¹ Terrors startle him on every side
and dog his every step.
¹² Calamity is hungry for him;
disaster is ready for him when he falls.
¹³ It eats away parts of his skin;
death's firstborn devours his limbs.
¹⁴ He is torn from the security of his tent
and marched off to the king of terrors.
¹⁵ Fire resides*a* in his tent;
burning sulfur is scattered over his
dwelling.
¹⁶ His roots dry up below
and his branches wither above.
¹⁷ The memory of him perishes from the earth;
he has no name in the land.

¹⁸ He is driven from light into the realm of
darkness
and is banished from the world.
¹⁹ He has no offspring or descendants among
his people,
no survivor where once he lived.
²⁰ People of the west are appalled at his fate;
those of the east are seized with horror.
²¹ Surely such is the dwelling of an evil man;
such is the place of one who does not
know God."

Job

19 Then Job replied:

² "How long will you torment me
and crush me with words?
³ Ten times now you have reproached me;
shamelessly you attack me.
⁴ If it is true that I have gone astray,
my error remains my concern alone.
⁵ If indeed you would exalt yourselves
above me
and use my humiliation against me,
⁶ then know that God has wronged me
and drawn his net around me.

⁷ "Though I cry, 'Violence!' I get no
response;
though I call for help, there is no justice.
⁸ He has blocked my way so I cannot pass;
he has shrouded my paths in darkness.

a 15 Or Nothing he had remains

security and wealth (vv. 14–16); and being forgotten after death (vv. 17–19). While in his previous speech Bildad encouraged Job to repent and be restored (8:5–7,20–22), he does not acknowledge this possibility here.

18:2 Be sensible, and then we can talk Bildad previously rebuked Job for what he had said about God (8:3). Here, the purpose of his rebuke is to defend himself, Eliphaz and Zophar (v. 3).

18:4 You who tear yourself to pieces in your anger Job accused God of tearing him in his wrath (16:9). Here, Bildad turns this around, accusing Job of bringing his suffering on himself.

18:5 lamp of a wicked man is snuffed out Bildad's sentiment is reflected in several proverbs (e.g., Pr 13:9; 20:20; 24:20; compare Job 3:4 and note).

18:7 vigor of his step is weakened May refer to a failing physical condition, but more likely refers to a wicked person's actions being interrupted or stopped (compare v. 9).

18:8 thrust him into a net Bildad uses six different terms for traps or snares in vv. 8–10. He is confident that wickedness will lead to a trap—whether those who are wicked are caught in their own traps or hidden ones (compare Ps 57:6).

18:15 in his tent Tents were often used to describe the welfare of people. An enlargement of the tent signified prosperity (Isa 54:2). God protects or restores the tent of his people (see Ps 91:9–10; Jer 30:18), while thorns grow

in the tent of the wicked (see Hos 9:6). **sulfur** An instrument of divine judgment, along with fire (e.g., Ge 19:24).

18:16 His roots dry up below Job earlier used an example of a tree that could regrow after being cut down to explore the hope of renewal, and perhaps even resurrection (Job 14:7–9). A tree whose roots have dried up would have no hope of regrowth.

18:19 no offspring Not only will the wicked be destroyed, but also their entire line will be cut off (Isa 14:22). As in his first speech, Bildad is probably referencing the death of Job's children (see Job 8:4).

19:1–29 In this response, Job mostly addresses his friends. He complains about their treatment of him (vv. 1–6) and God's treatment of him (vv. 7–12). He also complains about being alienated and isolated (vv. 13–20), and he pleads with his friends for mercy and understanding (vv. 21–22). After all this complaint, Job expresses faith in his eventual vindication (vv. 23–27). He ends with a warning to his friends that their treatment of him will be judged (vv. 28–29).

19:6 God has wronged me Job wants to make it clear that God has wronged him. He uses the same Hebrew term that Bildad does in his first speech when Bildad claims God does not pervert justice (see 8:3 and note). Job believes that God has treated him unjustly. **drawn his net** In response to Bildad's claims in 18:8–10, Job argues that he has not been led into a trap by wickedness; rather, in his view, God has unjustly trapped him.

9 He has stripped me of my honor
and removed the crown from my head.
10 He tears me down on every side till I am gone;
he uproots my hope like a tree.
11 His anger burns against me;
he counts me among his enemies.
12 His troops advance in force;
they build a siege ramp against me
and encamp around my tent.

13 "He has alienated my family from me;
my acquaintances are completely
estranged from me.
14 My relatives have gone away;
my closest friends have forgotten me.
15 My guests and my female servants count me
a foreigner;
they look on me as on a stranger.
16 I summon my servant, but he does not answer,
though I beg him with my own mouth.
17 My breath is offensive to my wife;
I am loathsome to my own family.
18 Even the little boys scorn me;
when I appear, they ridicule me.
19 All my intimate friends detest me;
those I love have turned against me.
20 I am nothing but skin and bones;
I have escaped only by the skin of my teeth.ᵃ

21 "Have pity on me, my friends, have pity,
for the hand of God has struck me.
22 Why do you pursue me as God does?
Will you never get enough of my flesh?

23 "Oh, that my words were recorded,
that they were written on a scroll,
24 that they were inscribed with an iron tool
onᵇ lead,
or engraved in rock forever!
25 I know that my redeemerᶜ lives,
and that in the end he will stand on
the earth.ᵈ
26 And after my skin has been destroyed,
yetᵉ inᶠ my flesh I will see God;
27 I myself will see him
with my own eyes — I, and not another.
How my heart yearns within me!

28 "If you say, 'How we will hound him,
since the root of the trouble lies in him,ᵍ'
29 you should fear the sword yourselves;
for wrath will bring punishment by
the sword,
and then you will know that there is
judgment.ʰ"

Zophar

20 Then Zophar the Naamathite replied:

2 "My troubled thoughts prompt me to answer
because I am greatly disturbed.

ᵃ 20 Or *only by my gums*   ᵇ 24 Or *and*   ᶜ 25 Or *vindicator*
ᵈ 25 Or *on my grave*   ᵉ 26 Or *And after I awake, / though this
body has been destroyed, / then*   ᶠ 26 Or *destroyed, / apart
from*   ᵍ 28 Many Hebrew manuscripts, Septuagint and Vulgate;
most Hebrew manuscripts *me*   ʰ 29 Or *sword, / that you may
come to know the Almighty*

19:7 I cry After complaining about his friends' treatment of him, Job focuses on how God has dealt with him. Here, he specifically complains about God's silence. Job's cries for justice have gone unanswered; God has not heeded any of his calls for help.
19:8 He has blocked my way In 1:10, the *satan* figure argued that Job's faith was partly due to God's wall of protection (compare note on 1:6). Here, Job says that God has put a wall around him to prevent his escape (compare 3:23 and note).
19:12 encamp around my tent Siege ramps would normally be put up around fortified cities, not individual tents (2Sa 20:15; Da 11:15). Job emphasizes that God has taken excessive measures against him.
19:23 they were written on a scroll A written account would preserve Job's claim of innocence beyond his death. He hopes his claim will eventually be proven true so he can be vindicated. Job may be reacting to Bildad's point that the memory of the wicked perishes (Job 18:17).
19:25 redeemer Job expresses hope in his redeemer — the Hebrew word used here is *go'el*. Job has been pleading for an advocate before God, believing that he is unjustly suffering (16:11–21; 19:6), and now expresses hope in a redeemer who is alive and who will surely come to his rescue (compare 16:19,21; 1Jn 2:1). Elsewhere in the OT, God redeems his people from slavery (Ex 6:6) or exile (Isa 41:14). As a redeemer, he defends people's causes (Ps 119:154; Pr 23:11; Jer 50:34) and delivers them from death (Ps 103:4). In the law, a *go'el* (or guardian-redeemer), had several responsibilities: buying back family land that

had been sold (Lev 25:25), buying back family members who had sold themselves into slavery (Lev 25:47–49) and marrying a childless widow of a family member (Dt 25:5–10; Ru 4:5–6; see note on Ru 2:20). **stand** The Hebrew term used here, *qum*, is sometimes used as a legal term for someone standing as a witness for another (Dt 19:15–16; Ps 27:12). Job trusts that he will ultimately be vindicated, once someone is able to stand between himself and God. In Isa 53:10–12, the suffering servant is described as making intercession on behalf of humanity, for people's sins and iniquities. In the NT, John and the author of Hebrews use similar language to Isa 53:10–12 and this passage in Job to describe Jesus' role in heaven on behalf of sinners (1Jn 2:1; Heb 4:14–15).
19:26 in my flesh Job appears to be expressing hope in renewal and perhaps even in resurrection (compare Job 14:13–14).
19:29 wrath will bring punishment by the sword Confident in his eventual vindication, Job warns his friends that they will be accountable for their accusations and lack of compassion. Eventually, God shows his anger toward them and has Job pray on their behalf (42:7–9). **judgment** Job expresses hope that eventually judgment will come. While his friends see this at the end of the book (42:7–9), Job's expression here could also point to future judgment for all of humanity. Compare note on 14:12.
20:1–29 In his second and final speech (compare ch. 11), Zophar briefly rebukes Job (vv. 2–3), then spends the remainder of the speech discussing the fate of the

³ I hear a rebuke that dishonors me,
  and my understanding inspires me
    to reply.

⁴ "Surely you know how it has been from
    of old,
  ever since mankind*a* was placed on
    the earth,
⁵ that the mirth of the wicked is brief,
  the joy of the godless lasts but a moment.
⁶ Though the pride of the godless person
    reaches to the heavens
  and his head touches the clouds,
⁷ he will perish forever, like his own dung;
  those who have seen him will say, 'Where
    is he?'
⁸ Like a dream he flies away, no more to be
    found,
  banished like a vision of the night.
⁹ The eye that saw him will not see him again;
  his place will look on him no more.
¹⁰ His children must make amends to the poor;
  his own hands must give back his wealth.
¹¹ The youthful vigor that fills his bones
  will lie with him in the dust.

¹² "Though evil is sweet in his mouth
  and he hides it under his tongue,
¹³ though he cannot bear to let it go
  and lets it linger in his mouth,
¹⁴ yet his food will turn sour in his stomach;
  it will become the venom of serpents
    within him.
¹⁵ He will spit out the riches he swallowed;
  God will make his stomach vomit them up.
¹⁶ He will suck the poison of serpents;
  the fangs of an adder will kill him.
¹⁷ He will not enjoy the streams,
  the rivers flowing with honey and cream.
¹⁸ What he toiled for he must give back uneaten;
  he will not enjoy the profit from his
    trading.

¹⁹ For he has oppressed the poor and left them
    destitute;
  he has seized houses he did not build.

²⁰ "Surely he will have no respite from his
    craving;
  he cannot save himself by his treasure.
²¹ Nothing is left for him to devour;
  his prosperity will not endure.
²² In the midst of his plenty, distress will
    overtake him;
  the full force of misery will come upon him.
²³ When he has filled his belly,
  God will vent his burning anger against him
  and rain down his blows on him.
²⁴ Though he flees from an iron weapon,
  a bronze-tipped arrow pierces him.
²⁵ He pulls it out of his back,
  the gleaming point out of his liver.
  Terrors will come over him;
²⁶ total darkness lies in wait for his treasures.
  A fire unfanned will consume him
  and devour what is left in his tent.
²⁷ The heavens will expose his guilt;
  the earth will rise up against him.
²⁸ A flood will carry off his house,
  rushing waters*b* on the day of God's
    wrath.
²⁹ Such is the fate God allots the wicked,
  the heritage appointed for them by God."

Job

21
Then Job replied:

² "Listen carefully to my words;
  let this be the consolation you give me.
³ Bear with me while I speak,
  and after I have spoken, mock on.

⁴ "Is my complaint directed to a human being?
  Why should I not be impatient?

---

a 4 Or *Adam*   *b* 28 Or *The possessions in his house will be
carried off, / washed away*

---

wicked (vv. 4–29). He reiterates the destruction of the wicked (vv. 4–11), argues that wickedness will not profit (vv. 12–23) and again mentions the ultimate annihilation of the wicked (vv. 24–29). Zophar does not cover much new material here, as both Eliphaz (15:17–35) and Bildad (18:5–21) devoted large sections of their speeches to this topic.

20:6 his head touches the clouds While the wicked may reach great heights, God will bring them low (compare Isa 14:13–15; Ob 4).
20:11 will lie with him in the dust Job earlier said that his hope of vindication would go into the dust with him (Job 17:15–16). Here, Zophar argues that the punishment of the wicked will not be delayed; they will die young and go into the dust with their youthful strength.
20:17 flowing with honey and cream Describes a blessed land (Isa 7:22). The land of Israel is often described as flowing with milk and honey (Ex 3:8; Eze 20:6). Zophar argues that the wicked will not see a fruitful land.

20:20 he will have no respite Portrays the insatiable appetite of the wicked: Even if they get everything they want, the wicked are never satisfied.
20:29 God allots the wicked Zophar, along with Job's other friends, believes that any suffering is a result of divine punishment. Knowing that he is innocent, Job sees exceptions to this rule. Job's friends believe that Job is denying God's justice when he argues for his innocence in light of his suffering (Job 4:6; 8:3).

21:1–34 Each of Job's friends has argued that the wicked suffer (15:17–35; 18:5–21; 20:4–29). Here, Job responds by claiming that the wicked actually prosper. He opens by addressing his friends—asking them to listen and understand his complaint (vv. 2–6). He then argues that the wicked live long and prosperous lives (vv. 7–16) and that they are not punished (vv. 17–26). Job anticipates his friends' response and argues that travelers could support their claims (vv. 27–33). He concludes by rebuking his friends' comfort (v. 34).

⁵ Look at me and be appalled;
　clap your hand over your mouth.
⁶ When I think about this, I am terrified;
　trembling seizes my body.
⁷ Why do the wicked live on,
　growing old and increasing in power?
⁸ They see their children established around
　　them,
　their offspring before their eyes.
⁹ Their homes are safe and free from fear;
　the rod of God is not on them.
¹⁰ Their bulls never fail to breed;
　their cows calve and do not miscarry.
¹¹ They send forth their children as a flock;
　their little ones dance about.
¹² They sing to the music of timbrel and lyre;
　they make merry to the sound of the pipe.
¹³ They spend their years in prosperity
　and go down to the grave in peace.ᵃ
¹⁴ Yet they say to God, 'Leave us alone!
　We have no desire to know your ways.
¹⁵ Who is the Almighty, that we should
　　serve him?
　What would we gain by praying to him?'
¹⁶ But their prosperity is not in their own
　　hands,
　so I stand aloof from the plans of the
　　wicked.

¹⁷ "Yet how often is the lamp of the wicked
　　snuffed out?
　How often does calamity come upon them,
　the fate God allots in his anger?
¹⁸ How often are they like straw before the wind,
　like chaff swept away by a gale?
¹⁹ It is said, 'God stores up the punishment of
　　the wicked for their children.'
　Let him repay the wicked, so that they
　　themselves will experience it!
²⁰ Let their own eyes see their destruction;
　let them drink the cup of the wrath of the
　　Almighty.

²¹ For what do they care about the families they
　　leave behind
　when their allotted months come to
　　an end?

²² "Can anyone teach knowledge to God,
　since he judges even the highest?
²³ One person dies in full vigor,
　completely secure and at ease,
²⁴ well nourished in body,ᵇ
　bones rich with marrow.
²⁵ Another dies in bitterness of soul,
　never having enjoyed anything good.
²⁶ Side by side they lie in the dust,
　and worms cover them both.

²⁷ "I know full well what you are thinking,
　the schemes by which you would
　　wrong me.
²⁸ You say, 'Where now is the house of the great,
　the tents where the wicked lived?'
²⁹ Have you never questioned those who travel?
　Have you paid no regard to their
　　accounts—
³⁰ that the wicked are spared from the day
　　of calamity,
　that they are delivered fromᶜ the day
　　of wrath?
³¹ Who denounces their conduct to their face?
　Who repays them for what they have done?
³² They are carried to the grave,
　and watch is kept over their tombs.
³³ The soil in the valley is sweet to them;
　everyone follows after them,
　and a countless throng goesᵈ before them.

³⁴ "So how can you console me with your
　　nonsense?
　Nothing is left of your answers but
　　falsehood!"

ᵃ 13 Or *in an instant*　　ᵇ 24 The meaning of the Hebrew for
this word is uncertain.　　ᶜ 30 Or *wicked are reserved for the day
of calamity, / that they are brought forth to*　　ᵈ 33 Or *them, / as
a countless throng went*

21:4 my complaint directed to a human being Job's
main complaint is not against his friends; his real grievance is with God, who has afflicted him for no apparent
reason (see 9:17; 16:7).
21:8 their children established Job's friends claimed
that the wicked had no posterity (18:19; 20:21). Here,
Job argues that the wicked live to see their descendants
prosper.
21:13 They spend their years in prosperity Job argues
that the wicked live prosperous lives. This contradicts
the claims of Job's friends that the wicked do not enjoy
peaceful or prosperous lives, but undergo quick and
dramatic destruction (15:20,29; 18:18–20; 20:7–11).
the grave The Hebrew text here uses the term *she'ol*, a
reference to the realm of the dead. See note on 14:13.
**21:19 stores up the punishment of the wicked for
their children** Job seems to be quoting an opinion of
his friends or someone like them—for this reason,
many translations supply the words "you say" or "they

say" (compare 5:4; 20:10). He argues that the wicked
do not care what happens after they are gone (v. 21),
and that they should personally face God's judgment
(vv. 19–20).
21:26 Side by side they lie in the dust Job cites
examples of two different scenarios: One person dies
after living a rich and secure life (v. 23), another dies after
living a difficult and poor life (v. 25). Ultimately, both die.
Any prosperity enjoyed by the first person does not carry
beyond death. The author of Ecclesiastes also makes
this point (see Ecc 2:15–17; 6:6; 9:2).
21:32 watch is kept over their tombs Job asserts
that the wicked are honored even in death. They receive
a proper burial and are celebrated by many, contrasting
Bildad's claim that the wicked are forgotten (compare
Job 18:17 and vv. 32–33).
21:34 with your nonsense The Hebrew word used here,
hevel, also occurs in the thematic refrain of Ecclesiastes
(Ecc 1:2; 12:8).

Eliphaz

22 Then Eliphaz the Temanite replied:

2 "Can a man be of benefit to God?
　　Can even a wise person benefit him?
3 What pleasure would it give the Almighty if
　　　you were righteous?
　　What would he gain if your ways were
　　　blameless?

4 "Is it for your piety that he rebukes you
　　and brings charges against you?
5 Is not your wickedness great?
　　Are not your sins endless?
6 You demanded security from your relatives
　　　for no reason;
　　you stripped people of their clothing,
　　　leaving them naked.
7 You gave no water to the weary
　　and you withheld food from the hungry,
8 though you were a powerful man, owning
　　　land —
　　an honored man, living on it.
9 And you sent widows away empty-handed
　　and broke the strength of the fatherless.
10 That is why snares are all around you,
　　why sudden peril terrifies you,
11 why it is so dark you cannot see,
　　and why a flood of water covers you.

12 "Is not God in the heights of heaven?
　　And see how lofty are the highest stars!
13 Yet you say, 'What does God know?
　　Does he judge through such darkness?
14 Thick clouds veil him, so he does not see us
　　as he goes about in the vaulted heavens.'
15 Will you keep to the old path
　　that the wicked have trod?
16 They were carried off before their time,
　　their foundations washed away by a flood.

17 They said to God, 'Leave us alone!
　　What can the Almighty do to us?'
18 Yet it was he who filled their houses with
　　　good things,
　　so I stand aloof from the plans
　　　of the wicked.
19 The righteous see their ruin and rejoice;
　　the innocent mock them, saying,
20 'Surely our foes are destroyed,
　　and fire devours their wealth.'

21 "Submit to God and be at peace with him;
　　in this way prosperity will come to you.
22 Accept instruction from his mouth
　　and lay up his words in your heart.
23 If you return to the Almighty, you will be
　　　restored:
　　If you remove wickedness far from
　　　your tent
24 and assign your nuggets to the dust,
　　your gold of Ophir to the rocks
　　　in the ravines,
25 then the Almighty will be your gold,
　　the choicest silver for you.
26 Surely then you will find delight
　　　in the Almighty
　　and will lift up your face to God.
27 You will pray to him, and he will
　　　hear you,
　　and you will fulfill your vows.
28 What you decide on will be done,
　　and light will shine on your ways.
29 When people are brought low and you say,
　　　'Lift them up!'
　　then he will save the downcast.
30 He will deliver even one who is not
　　　innocent,
　　who will be delivered through the
　　　cleanness of your hands."

22:1–30 In his final speech (compare Job 4–5; 15), Eliphaz directly accuses Job of sinning. Eliphaz's attitude toward Job has progressed from conciliatory—gently reminding Job that God punishes the wicked, not the innocent (4:3–7)—to critical, accusing Job of violating the fear of God (15:4–6). Here, his criticism increases as he accuses Job of specific sins (vv. 2–11). He also extols God's greatness (vv. 12–20) and makes a final appeal to Job to repent (vv. 21–30). See the table "Cycles in Job" on p. 793.

22:3 pleasure would it give the Almighty Eliphaz wrongly argues that God has no stake in Job's righteousness or vindication.

22:4 for your piety that he rebukes you Eliphaz first encouraged Job to hope in his reverence for God (4:6). Later, he accused him of doing away with it (15:4). Here, he sarcastically asks if God is punishing Job because Job reveres him. Ironically, this is exactly the reason God afflicted Job. If Job did not revere God, the *satan* figure would not have challenged the reason for Job's faith (1:8–11; compare note on 1:6).

22:6–9 Eliphaz begins attributing specific sins to Job. There is no evidence of Job committing these sins; Eliphaz infers them based on Job's suffering.

22:13 What does God know Eliphaz accuses Job of limiting God. He thinks that Job, by claiming that the wicked prosper (21:14–16), is asserting that God is limited or incompetent.

22:21 Submit to God While Eliphaz now pleads with Job to repent, he previously encouraged Job to accept God's discipline (5:17). He argues that Job will only find peace after he repents.

22:24 assign your nuggets to the dust As he removed injustice from his tent (v. 23), Job would have to give up his wealth. Eliphaz attributes Job's wealth to unjust practices (vv. 6–9). **Ophir** A region known for very fine gold (Isa 13:12). Its exact location is unknown, but it is thought to have been located in the Southern Arabian Peninsula on the Red Sea. Solomon imported gold from Ophir (1Ki 9:26–28).

22:27 he will hear you Job's repentance would grant him a renewed intimacy with God. Throughout his speeches,

Job

23

Then Job replied:

2 "Even today my complaint is bitter;
    his hand[a] is heavy in spite of[b] my groaning.
3 If only I knew where to find him;
    if only I could go to his dwelling!
4 I would state my case before him
    and fill my mouth with arguments.
5 I would find out what he would answer me,
    and consider what he would say to me.
6 Would he vigorously oppose me?
    No, he would not press charges against me.
7 There the upright can establish their
        innocence before him,
    and there I would be delivered forever
        from my judge.

8 "But if I go to the east, he is not there;
    if I go to the west, I do not find him.
9 When he is at work in the north, I do not
        see him;
    when he turns to the south, I catch no
        glimpse of him.
10 But he knows the way that I take;
    when he has tested me, I will come forth
        as gold.
11 My feet have closely followed his steps;
    I have kept to his way without turning
        aside.
12 I have not departed from the commands of
        his lips;
    I have treasured the words of his mouth
        more than my daily bread.

13 "But he stands alone, and who can
        oppose him?
    He does whatever he pleases.
14 He carries out his decree against me,
    and many such plans he still has in store.
15 That is why I am terrified before him;
    when I think of all this, I fear him.
16 God has made my heart faint;
    the Almighty has terrified me.
17 Yet I am not silenced by the darkness,
    by the thick darkness that covers my face.

24

"Why does the Almighty not set times
    for judgment?
    Why must those who know him look in
        vain for such days?
2 There are those who move boundary stones;
    they pasture flocks they have stolen.
3 They drive away the orphan's donkey
    and take the widow's ox in pledge.
4 They thrust the needy from the path
    and force all the poor of the land into hiding.
5 Like wild donkeys in the desert,
    the poor go about their labor of foraging
        food;
    the wasteland provides food for their
        children.
6 They gather fodder in the fields
    and glean in the vineyards of the wicked.
7 Lacking clothes, they spend the night naked;
    they have nothing to cover themselves in
        the cold.

a 2 Septuagint and Syriac; Hebrew / the hand on me
b 2 Or heavy on me in

Job begs God for a response (Job 13:20). Ironically, Eliphaz—along with Job's other friends—will directly benefit from the acceptance of Job's prayer by God (42:8–9).

23:1—24:25 Job now returns to his legal dispute with God (see 9:13–24; 13:13–27). He wishes to bring his case before God (23:2–7), but laments that God is nowhere to be found (23:8–12). He briefly extols God's greatness (23:13–17), then complains about the prevalence of injustice: The wicked are not judged (24:1–4), and the poor are oppressed while God ignores their cries for help (24:5–12). After describing specific actions of the wicked (24:13–17), Job seems to reverse his position and argue that the wicked are punished (24:18–25).

23:3 go to his dwelling Job's primary wish is to have an audience with God where he can present his case (9:13–24; 13:13–27).
23:7 upright can establish their innocence before him While his friends have tried to convince him that he had sinned and needed to repent, Job continues to argue for his innocence. He expresses hope that an upright man such as himself (see note on 1:1) will receive a fair hearing.
23:10 he knows the way that I take While Job cannot find God, he believes that God knows him. He is confident that God will recognize that he has not followed the way of the wicked, contrary to Eliphaz's claim (22:15). **when he has tested me** Job acknowledges that his current

suffering is a test—this parallels the opening scene where the satan figure who claimed that Job would not fear God once great difficulty came his way. Job believes that his testing will have results (compare note on 1:6). He is right—it develops Job's character and results in an authentic and deep relationship with God (see note on 42:1–6).
23:13 he stands alone Job recognizes that no one can change God's mind—claiming (in the Hebrew text) that God is one. This parallels one of the primary faith statements of the Israelites from Dt 6:4.
23:15 I am terrified This Hebrew term indicates dismay or horror (Jdg 20:41; Isa 13:8). It is not the same term used for fearing God (see note on Job 1:9).
24:1 times Job laments that the wicked are not judged in the following verses. This parallel suggests that Job's question echoes the author of Ecclesiastes' complaint about evil not being punished in a timely manner (Ecc 8:11). For this reason, some translations add "of judgment" to "times" here, resulting in the rendering "times of judgment."
24:2 There are those who move boundary stones Moving boundaries—a way of illegally seizing land—was prohibited by the Law (Dt 19:14; 27:17; compare Pr 23:10–11).
24:4 force all the poor of the land into hiding Job asserts that the oppression of the poor is evidence that God's judgment is delayed, if not absent (Job 24:1).

⁸ They are drenched by mountain rains
  and hug the rocks for lack of shelter.
⁹ The fatherless child is snatched from the
    breast;
  the infant of the poor is seized for a debt.
¹⁰ Lacking clothes, they go about naked;
  they carry the sheaves, but still go hungry.
¹¹ They crush olives among the terraces ᵃ;
  they tread the winepresses, yet suffer
    thirst.
¹² The groans of the dying rise from the city,
  and the souls of the wounded cry out for
    help.
  But God charges no one with wrongdoing.

¹³ "There are those who rebel against the light,
  who do not know its ways
  or stay in its paths.
¹⁴ When daylight is gone, the murderer rises up,
  kills the poor and needy,
  and in the night steals forth like a thief.
¹⁵ The eye of the adulterer watches for dusk;
  he thinks, 'No eye will see me,'
  and he keeps his face concealed.
¹⁶ In the dark, thieves break into houses,
  but by day they shut themselves in;
  they want nothing to do with the light.
¹⁷ For all of them, midnight is their morning;
  they make friends with the terrors of
    darkness.

¹⁸ "Yet they are foam on the surface of the water;
  their portion of the land is cursed,
  so that no one goes to the vineyards.
¹⁹ As heat and drought snatch away the melted
    snow,
  so the grave snatches away those who have
    sinned.

²⁰ The womb forgets them,
  the worm feasts on them;
  the wicked are no longer remembered
  but are broken like a tree.
²¹ They prey on the barren and childless
    woman,
  and to the widow they show no kindness.
²² But God drags away the mighty by his power;
  though they become established, they have
    no assurance of life.
²³ He may let them rest in a feeling of security,
  but his eyes are on their ways.
²⁴ For a little while they are exalted, and then
    they are gone;
  they are brought low and gathered up like
    all others;
  they are cut off like heads of grain.

²⁵ "If this is not so, who can prove me false
  and reduce my words to nothing?"

Bildad

25 Then Bildad the Shuhite replied:

² "Dominion and awe belong to God;
  he establishes order in the heights of
    heaven.
³ Can his forces be numbered?
  On whom does his light not rise?
⁴ How then can a mortal be righteous
    before God?
  How can one born of woman be pure?
⁵ If even the moon is not bright
  and the stars are not pure in his eyes,

ᵃ 11 The meaning of the Hebrew for this word is uncertain.

24:10 they carry the sheaves, but still go hungry
The poor are forced to work to provide food for others
(presumably the wicked; see v. 6) while they themselves
go hungry.
24:11 they tread the winepresses The three products
Job describes—bread (from sheaves), oil and wine—were
viewed as blessings from God (see Dt 7:13; Jer 31:12).
Those who had them in abundance are described as
happy and satisfied (Ps 104:14–15; Joel 2:19). See the
infographic "A Winepress in Ancient Israel" on p. 1157.
24:12 God charges no one with wrongdoing Though
oppression is rampant, God does not rectify unjust situations.
24:13 who rebel against the light Job describes
the actions of the wicked in terms of light. Here, they
figuratively rebel against the light (compare Ps 97:11; Pr
2:13). In Job 24:14–17, darkness is a tool the wicked
use to hide their wickedness from both people and God
(compare 22:13–14).

24:18–25 In this section, Job seems to contradict his
previous statements by agreeing with his friends that the
wicked do experience punishment. Because it seems
contradictory, some translations turn this section into
a quote of Job's friends by adding "You say" at the
beginning. However, Job never explicitly says that God

never judges the wicked. He merely points out that
God's judgment is not always present or timely (21:17;
24:1). Job also argues that the wicked eventually die,
and later states that they will be cut off without hope
(21:23–26; 27:7–9). Like the author of Ecclesiastes,
Job wrestles with belief in God's justice in face of the
seemingly unjust suffering he has endured (see note on
Ecc 8:13). Despite lamenting his inability to find vindication (Job 9:15–20), Job also expresses faith that he will
be vindicated (19:25–27).

24:19 the grave The Hebrew text here refers to *she'ol*, the
underworld—the realm of the dead. See note on 14:13.

25:1–6 Bildad's brief, final speech (compare chs. 8; 18)
is the last speech of Job's friends. Bildad's main argument is that humans cannot be right before God (v. 4)—
a point made repeatedly by both Eliphaz (4:17–19;
15:14–16; 22:2) and Job (9:2). To preface this point,
Bildad extols God's greatness (vv. 2–3), which he emphasizes by arguing that even the moon and stars are
not pure before God (vv. 5–6).

25:3 does his light not rise Bildad may be referring to
Job's claims about the wicked who use darkness to hide
their sins (24:13–17). Like Eliphaz (22:12–14), Bildad
argues that God sees and judges all things.

⁶ how much less a mortal, who is but a maggot—
    a human being, who is only a worm!"

Job

26 Then Job replied:

² "How you have helped the powerless!
    How you have saved the arm that is feeble!
³ What advice you have offered to one without
        wisdom!
    And what great insight you have displayed!
⁴ Who has helped you utter these words?
    And whose spirit spoke from your mouth?

⁵ "The dead are in deep anguish,
    those beneath the waters and all that live
        in them.
⁶ The realm of the dead is naked before God;
    Destructionᵃ lies uncovered.
⁷ He spreads out the northern skies over empty
        space;
    he suspends the earth over nothing.
⁸ He wraps up the waters in his clouds,
    yet the clouds do not burst under their
        weight.
⁹ He covers the face of the full moon,
    spreading his clouds over it.
¹⁰ He marks out the horizon on the face
        of the waters
    for a boundary between light and darkness.
¹¹ The pillars of the heavens quake,
    aghast at his rebuke.

¹² By his power he churned up the sea;
    by his wisdom he cut Rahab to pieces.
¹³ By his breath the skies became fair;
    his hand pierced the gliding serpent.
¹⁴ And these are but the outer fringe of his works;
    how faint the whisper we hear of him!
    Who then can understand the thunder of
        his power?"

Job's Final Word to His Friends

27 And Job continued his discourse:

² "As surely as God lives, who has denied me
        justice,
    the Almighty, who has made my life bitter,
³ as long as I have life within me,
    the breath of God in my nostrils,
⁴ my lips will not say anything wicked,
    and my tongue will not utter lies.
⁵ I will never admit you are in the right;
    till I die, I will not deny my integrity.
⁶ I will maintain my innocence and never let go
        of it;
    my conscience will not reproach me as
        long as I live.

⁷ "May my enemy be like the wicked,
    my adversary like the unjust!
⁸ For what hope have the godless when they
        are cut off,
    when God takes away their life?

ᵃ 6 Hebrew *Abaddon*

25:4 can a mortal be righteous before God Bildad repeats his argument that no one is right before God—essentially arguing that Job cannot claim innocence (see 4:17 and note; 9:2 and note).
25:6 how much less a mortal Since even the moon and stars pale in comparison to God, no one can claim a right standing with God.
26:1–14 Job is the only named speaker from this point until Elihu responds in ch. 32. However, his speech is broken at points (27:1; 29:1), making it unclear whether 26:1—31:40 is one long speech or several separate speeches. In ch. 26, Job rebukes Bildad for not offering anything helpful or new (vv. 2–4). He then praises God's majesty and power (vv. 5–14).
26:6 realm of the dead The Hebrew text here uses the term *she'ol*, which is often transliterated in English translations as Sheol. Job has repeatedly referenced this dark, gloomy place. See note on 14:13. **Destruction** The Hebrew word used here, *avaddon*, is a synonym for the realm of the dead, *she'ol*. *Avaddon* refers to a place of destruction, perishing or ruin. Compare note on 31:12. **lies uncovered** In extolling God's greatness, Job points out that God can see all things, including the realm of the dead. See note on Pr 15:11.
26:8 the waters in his clouds Job moves from the realm of the dead (Job 26:5–7) to the sky to demonstrate that God's supremacy spans the entire creation. Compare note on Ge 1:2. See the infographic "Ancient Hebrew Conception of the Universe" on p. 5.

26:12 Rahab The Hebrew word used here, *rahav*, likely refers to a sea monster (see Job 9:13 and note; 7:12; compare Ps 89:10; Isa 51:9–10). In the ancient Near East, creatures like these were seen as forces of chaos that needed to be subdued. See note on Ge 1:21.
26:14 how faint the whisper The mighty thunder and wind is only a whisper to God. This description anticipates God's response in Job 38, where God speaks from a whirlwind. Elsewhere, God speaks in a whisper (1Ki 19:11–13).
27:1–23 This section is separated from the previous chapter by a heading (Job 27:1). Here, Job continues his final response, and again asserts his innocence (vv. 2–6). He condemns his enemies (vv. 7–10) and states his intention to teach his friends (vv. 11–12). He then discusses the fate of the wicked (vv. 13–23).
27:2 God lives Signifies an oath (1Ki 1:29–30; 22:14; Jer 5:2; 12:16). Job swears to his innocence. Making an oath on God's name was the strongest form of swearing an oath. To be proven wrong would make the oath-taker a blasphemer.
27:6 I will maintain my innocence Job finishes his oath by firmly declaring his righteousness (Job 12:4). Job is not declaring himself completely free from sin—he has acknowledged his sin in 7:21. However, he believes that he has done nothing to deserve the level of suffering God has inflicted on him. See note on 11:4.
27:8 what hope have the godless Throughout his speeches, Job has hoped for vindication. His hope is

⁹ Does God listen to their cry
    when distress comes upon them?
¹⁰ Will they find delight in the Almighty?
    Will they call on God at all times?

¹¹ "I will teach you about the power of God;
    the ways of the Almighty I will not conceal.
¹² You have all seen this yourselves.
    Why then this meaningless talk?

¹³ "Here is the fate God allots to the wicked,
    the heritage a ruthless man receives from
      the Almighty:
¹⁴ However many his children, their fate is the
      sword;
    his offspring will never have enough to eat.
¹⁵ The plague will bury those who survive him,
    and their widows will not weep for them.
¹⁶ Though he heaps up silver like dust
    and clothes like piles of clay,
¹⁷ what he lays up the righteous will wear,
    and the innocent will divide his silver.
¹⁸ The house he builds is like a moth's cocoon,
    like a hut made by a watchman.
¹⁹ He lies down wealthy, but will do so no more;
    when he opens his eyes, all is gone.
²⁰ Terrors overtake him like a flood;
    a tempest snatches him away in the night.
²¹ The east wind carries him off, and he is gone;
    it sweeps him out of his place.
²² It hurls itself against him without mercy
    as he flees headlong from its power.
²³ It claps its hands in derision
    and hisses him out of his place."

Interlude: Where Wisdom Is Found

28 There is a mine for silver
    and a place where gold is refined.
² Iron is taken from the earth,
    and copper is smelted from ore.

³ Mortals put an end to the darkness;
    they search out the farthest recesses
    for ore in the blackest darkness.
⁴ Far from human dwellings they cut a shaft,
    in places untouched by human feet;
    far from other people they dangle and
      sway.
⁵ The earth, from which food comes,
    is transformed below as by fire;
⁶ lapis lazuli comes from its rocks,
    and its dust contains nuggets of gold.
⁷ No bird of prey knows that hidden path,
    no falcon's eye has seen it.
⁸ Proud beasts do not set foot on it,
    and no lion prowls there.
⁹ People assault the flinty rock with their hands
    and lay bare the roots of the mountains.
¹⁰ They tunnel through the rock;
    their eyes see all its treasures.
¹¹ They search[a] the sources of the rivers
    and bring hidden things to light.

¹² But where can wisdom be found?
    Where does understanding dwell?
¹³ No mortal comprehends its worth;
    it cannot be found in the land of the living.
¹⁴ The deep says, "It is not in me";
    the sea says, "It is not with me."
¹⁵ It cannot be bought with the finest gold,
    nor can its price be weighed out in silver.
¹⁶ It cannot be bought with the gold of Ophir,
    with precious onyx or lapis lazuli.
¹⁷ Neither gold nor crystal can compare with it,
    nor can it be had for jewels of gold.
¹⁸ Coral and jasper are not worthy of mention;
    the price of wisdom is beyond rubies.
¹⁹ The topaz of Cush cannot compare with it;
    it cannot be bought with pure gold.

---

a 11 Septuagint, Aquila and Vulgate; Hebrew *They dam up*

---

based on his innocence and God's ultimate justice (see 19:25–26). The godless will not share in this hope because they are not innocent; instead, God will cut them off.

27:11 about the power of God Job's friends presumed to speak for God (22:26–27), and Job has already accused them of speaking falsely (13:7). Instead of presuming to know the meaning behind God's actions, they should have called out to God for understanding, like Job did (v. 10).

27:13–23 Job again speaks about the punishment of the wicked. As with 24:18–25, Job seems to contradict some of his previous speeches as he discusses the destruction of the wicked. Job may be sarcastically teaching his friends well known truths that they repeated to him. However, while Job has argued that the wicked often prosper (21:7–16) and oppress the poor without consequence (24:2–12), he never denies the judgment of the wicked. See note on 24:18–25.

28:1–28 Although this chapter is not distinguished by a heading (27:1; 29:1), it is distinguished by its subject matter: wisdom. The entire chapter asks where wisdom can be found. Because of this change in tone and topic, it is unclear whether this chapter is part of Job's words or a self-contained poem added by the narrator. The chapter includes a description of the lengths people go to when searching for gold and other valuable resources (vv. 1–11). It then turns to wisdom, showing wisdom's value and questioning its accessibility (vv. 12–22). It concludes by revealing God as the source of wisdom (vv. 23–28).

28:11 bring hidden things to light All the effort described in vv. 1–11 is for this goal.

28:12 But where can wisdom be found While people go to great lengths to find precious metals or stones, they do not know where to find wisdom. It is not found on earth (v. 13), under the earth or in the sea (v. 14).

28:16 Ophir A region known for very fine gold (Isa 13:12).

28:19 it cannot be bought with pure gold Wisdom's value is greater than all the precious stones. Proverbs also compares wisdom to precious materials (e.g., Pr 3:14–15; 16:16).

20 Where then does wisdom come from?
  Where does understanding dwell?
21 It is hidden from the eyes of every living
    thing,
  concealed even from the birds
    in the sky.
22 Destruction[a] and Death say,
  "Only a rumor of it has reached
    our ears."
23 God understands the way to it
  and he alone knows where it dwells,
24 for he views the ends of the earth
  and sees everything under the heavens.
25 When he established the force of the wind
  and measured out the waters,
26 when he made a decree for the rain
  and a path for the thunderstorm,
27 then he looked at wisdom and appraised it;
  he confirmed it and tested it.
28 And he said to the human race,
  "The fear of the Lord — that is wisdom,
  and to shun evil is understanding."

Job's Final Defense

29 Job continued his discourse:

2 "How I long for the months gone by,
  for the days when God watched over me,
3 when his lamp shone on my head
  and by his light I walked through
    darkness!
4 Oh, for the days when I was in my prime,
  when God's intimate friendship blessed my
    house,

5 when the Almighty was still with me
  and my children were around me,
6 when my path was drenched with cream
  and the rock poured out for me streams of
    olive oil.

7 "When I went to the gate of the city
  and took my seat in the public square,
8 the young men saw me and stepped aside
  and the old men rose to their feet;
9 the chief men refrained from speaking
  and covered their mouths with their
    hands;
10 the voices of the nobles were hushed,
  and their tongues stuck to the roof of their
    mouths.
11 Whoever heard me spoke well of me,
  and those who saw me commended me,
12 because I rescued the poor who cried for
    help,
  and the fatherless who had none to assist
    them.
13 The one who was dying blessed me;
  I made the widow's heart sing.
14 I put on righteousness as my clothing;
  justice was my robe and my turban.
15 I was eyes to the blind
  and feet to the lame.
16 I was a father to the needy;
  I took up the case of the stranger.
17 I broke the fangs of the wicked
  and snatched the victims from their
    teeth.

a 22 Hebrew *Abaddon*

28:22 Destruction The Hebrew text here uses the word *avaddon*; it refers to the realm of the dead, a place of ruin or destruction. Compare note on 31:12. **Death** While wisdom in its truest form is completely hidden from the living, rumors of wisdom are heard among the dead. The Hebrew term used here is *maweth*, the regular word for death, not *she'ol*, which is used in 26:6.

28:23 God understands the way to it Job finally answers the questions of vv. 12 and 20: Because God's view is all-encompassing (v. 24), he both understands how to find wisdom and knows its origin.

28:25 When he established the force of the wind Job describes the presence of wisdom at creation (vv. 25–27). Proverbs also speaks of God's use of wisdom in creation (compare Pr 3:19–20; 8:22–31).

28:28 The fear of the Lord—that is wisdom The person who searches for wisdom will develop a fear of God. Since wisdom cannot be found apart from God, the wise seeker will adopt an attitude of trust and obedience to God. A similar statement appears at the conclusion of Ecclesiastes (see Ecc 12:13).

29:1—31:40 Job's final speech is given without interruption. He looks back fondly to an earlier time in his life when he was blessed by God (Job 29:2–6) and respected in his community (29:7–17)—a time when

he anticipated a restful and prosperous end to his life (29:18–20) and was sought out as a source of wisdom and counsel (29:21–25). He then contrasts this with his current situation, where he is mocked and abused (30:1–15). He describes his suffering, attributing it to God (30:16–23), and laments (30:24–31). Job finishes his speech with an assertion of his innocence and a final plea for a hearing (31:1–40). See the table "Cycles in Job" on p. 793.

29:7 gate of the city An important social hub. It was the commercial center (2Ki 7:1), assembly place (1Ki 22:10) and place where legal rulings were made by either the city's elders or king (Dt 21:19; Ru 4:1–12; 2Sa 15:2).

29:8–10 Appropriate procedure dictated that people remain silent until the person of greater honor spoke (Job 32:4). Job says that both young and old showed him respect.

29:12–17 Job describes the basis for his good reputation. He earned respect because of his righteousness and justice: He delivered the poor, orphans and widows; he helped the sick and injured; he fought against unrighteous oppressors, even taking up the cause of strangers. Job does not speak self-righteously or arrogantly; he defends himself against Eliphaz's accusations (22:6–9) by asserting his innocence.

18 "I thought, 'I will die in my own house,
  my days as numerous as the grains of sand.
19 My roots will reach to the water,
  and the dew will lie all night on my
    branches.
20 My glory will not fade;
  the bow will be ever new in my hand.'

21 "People listened to me expectantly,
  waiting in silence for my counsel.
22 After I had spoken, they spoke no more;
  my words fell gently on their ears.
23 They waited for me as for showers
  and drank in my words as the spring rain.
24 When I smiled at them, they scarcely
    believed it;
  the light of my face was precious
    to them.*a*
25 I chose the way for them and sat as their
    chief;
  I dwelt as a king among his troops;
  I was like one who comforts mourners.

30 "But now they mock me,
  men younger than I,
  whose fathers I would have disdained
  to put with my sheep dogs.
2 Of what use was the strength of their hands
    to me,
  since their vigor had gone from them?
3 Haggard from want and hunger,
  they roamed*b* the parched land
  in desolate wastelands at night.
4 In the brush they gathered salt herbs,
  and their food*c* was the root of the broom
    bush.
5 They were banished from human society,
  shouted at as if they were thieves.
6 They were forced to live in the dry stream beds,
  among the rocks and in holes in the ground.

7 They brayed among the bushes
  and huddled in the undergrowth.
8 A base and nameless brood,
  they were driven out of the land.

9 "And now those young men mock me in song;
  I have become a byword among them.
10 They detest me and keep their distance;
  they do not hesitate to spit in my face.
11 Now that God has unstrung my bow and
    afflicted me,
  they throw off restraint in my presence.
12 On my right the tribe*d* attacks;
  they lay snares for my feet,
  they build their siege ramps against me.
13 They break up my road;
  they succeed in destroying me.
  'No one can help him,' they say.
14 They advance as through a gaping breach;
  amid the ruins they come rolling in.
15 Terrors overwhelm me;
  my dignity is driven away as by the wind,
  my safety vanishes like a cloud.

16 "And now my life ebbs away;
  days of suffering grip me.
17 Night pierces my bones;
  my gnawing pains never rest.
18 In his great power God becomes like clothing
    to me*e*;
  he binds me like the neck of my garment.
19 He throws me into the mud,
  and I am reduced to dust and ashes.

20 "I cry out to you, God, but you do not answer;
  I stand up, but you merely look at me.

a 24 The meaning of the Hebrew for this clause is uncertain.
b 3 Or *gnawed*   *c 4* Or *fuel*   *d 12* The meaning of the
Hebrew for this word is uncertain.   *e 18* Hebrew; Septuagint
power he grasps my clothing

29:18 my days as numerous Before his affliction, Job expected to live a long and prosperous life and die a peaceful death.

29:21 waiting in silence for my counsel Job longs for the former days when people respected him and listened to his advice (see vv. 7–10). Even Eliphaz has pointed out his earlier reputation for wisdom (4:3–4).

29:22 they spoke no more Contrasts his current situation, where his friends respond by rebuking him.

29:23 They waited for me as for showers People eagerly anticipated Job's insight, which would nourish and refresh them (Dt 32:2).

30:1 put with my sheep dogs Those mocking Job are not from respected families—Job would not even put his dogs in their care.

30:2–8 Job continues to portray his mockers as dog-like scavengers: They have no strength and hungrily hunt for food. People drive them out like thieves, and they live without a homeland. By describing his mockers in this way, Job emphasizes how far he has fallen. He has gone from being respected by princes and elders to being mocked by the lowest of society (compare Job 29:9–10).

30:4 salt herbs The food mentioned in this verse would be only for desperate people. The Hebrew term used here related to salt, *malluach*, does not occur elsewhere in the OT. In the rabbinic work the Talmud it is referred to as the food of the poor (Babylonian Talmud, Qiddushin 66a).

30:11 has unstrung The Hebrew word used here, *yether*, can refer to the central cord of a tent (4:21) or the string of a bow (Ps 11:2). The idea behind either option here is that Job has been humbled by God, causing people to mock and ridicule him.

30:12–14 Job portrays his mockers as an army besieging a city: They destroy his escape paths and crash through a breach in his wall. This echoes his earlier description of God's attack on him (Job 19:10–12).

30:16 my life Job moves away from his emotional suffering to describe his physical suffering. Job describes this suffering using the Hebrew word *nephesh*—a term that can mean "soul" or "life"—to indicate that he believes that he is close to death (7:21).

²¹ You turn on me ruthlessly;
  with the might of your hand you
    attack me.
²² You snatch me up and drive me before the
    wind;
  you toss me about in the storm.
²³ I know you will bring me down to death,
  to the place appointed for all the living.

²⁴ "Surely no one lays a hand on a broken man
  when he cries for help in his distress.
²⁵ Have I not wept for those in trouble?
  Has not my soul grieved for the poor?
²⁶ Yet when I hoped for good, evil came;
  when I looked for light, then came
    darkness.
²⁷ The churning inside me never stops;
  days of suffering confront me.
²⁸ I go about blackened, but not by the sun;
  I stand up in the assembly and cry for help.
²⁹ I have become a brother of jackals,
  a companion of owls.
³⁰ My skin grows black and peels;
  my body burns with fever.
³¹ My lyre is tuned to mourning,
  and my pipe to the sound of wailing.

31 "I made a covenant with my eyes
  not to look lustfully at a young woman.
² For what is our lot from God above,
  our heritage from the Almighty on high?
³ Is it not ruin for the wicked,
  disaster for those who do wrong?
⁴ Does he not see my ways
  and count my every step?

⁵ "If I have walked with falsehood
  or my foot has hurried after deceit —

⁶ let God weigh me in honest scales
  and he will know that I am blameless —
⁷ if my steps have turned from the path,
  if my heart has been led by my eyes,
  or if my hands have been defiled,
⁸ then may others eat what I have sown,
  and may my crops be uprooted.

⁹ "If my heart has been enticed by a woman,
  or if I have lurked at my neighbor's door,
¹⁰ then may my wife grind another man's grain,
  and may other men sleep with her.
¹¹ For that would have been wicked,
  a sin to be judged.
¹² It is a fire that burns to Destruction ᵃ;
  it would have uprooted my harvest.

¹³ "If I have denied justice to any of my servants,
  whether male or female,
  when they had a grievance against me,
¹⁴ what will I do when God confronts me?
  What will I answer when called to account?
¹⁵ Did not he who made me in the womb make
    them?
  Did not the same one form us both within
    our mothers?

¹⁶ "If I have denied the desires of the poor
  or let the eyes of the widow grow weary,
¹⁷ if I have kept my bread to myself,
  not sharing it with the fatherless —
¹⁸ but from my youth I reared them as a father
    would,
  and from my birth I guided the widow —
¹⁹ if I have seen anyone perishing for lack of
    clothing,
  or the needy without garments,

ᵃ 12 Hebrew *Abaddon*

30:22 You snatch me up and drive me before the wind Just like the wicked, God swept Job away with the wind (compare 27:21).
30:26 I looked for light, then came darkness Contrasts Job's former days when God lit his path (see 29:3; compare 3:4 and note).
30:29 a brother of jackals, a companion of owls Job probably likens himself to these animals because of the mournful sounds they make (compare Mic 1:8).

31:1–40 Job finishes his speech with a lengthy oath swearing his innocence. In it, he lists many specific sins: lust (Job 31:1–4), falsehood (vv. 5–8), adultery (vv. 9–12), mistreatment of servants (vv. 13–15), failure to care for the poor (vv. 16–23), trusting in wealth (vv. 24–25), idolatry (vv. 26–28), rejoicing at an enemy's misfortune (vv. 29–30), lack of generosity (vv. 31–32), hypocrisy (vv. 33–34) and abusing the land (vv. 38–40). He denies that he has committed any of them, and asks for a hearing so he can be vindicated (vv. 35–37).

31:1 covenant with my eyes Job's proclamation of his innocence includes not just his actions but his thoughts. Not only has he not committed adultery (vv. 9–12), but he has not even lusted after a woman.

31:6 let God weigh me in honest scales Since he has not practiced deceit, Job wishes to be judged by a just or truthful scale, which is described elsewhere as the delight of Yahweh (see Pr 11:1).
31:8 may others eat Job's first curse is on his work and fields. Sowing a field but having others enjoy the benefits was one of the curses on Israel for breaking the law (see Lev 26:16).
31:10 grind Job's curse here is directly related to the sin it accompanies. If Job was guilty of adultery, then he asks that his wife be taken from him. The Hebrew term used here, *tachan*, which may be literally rendered as "grind," has a double meaning. It can be a euphemism for sexual relations, or it can refer to slavery. Female slaves in Egypt were forced to grind the mill (Ex 11:5).
31:12 Destruction The Hebrew word used here, *avaddon*, often transliterated in English as Abaddon, refers to the underworld—the realm of the dead. It references a place that is dismal, characterized by ruin, perishing or destruction. For this reason, some modern translations render the Hebrew word *avaddon* "Destruction," which is how ancient translations understood it. Job is saying that adultery is like a fire that consumes everything, all the way to Abaddon.

²⁰ and their hearts did not bless me
  for warming them with the fleece from my
  sheep,
²¹ if I have raised my hand against the
  fatherless,
  knowing that I had influence in court,
²² then let my arm fall from the shoulder,
  let it be broken off at the joint.
²³ For I dreaded destruction from God,
  and for fear of his splendor I could not do
  such things.

²⁴ "If I have put my trust in gold
  or said to pure gold, 'You are my security,'
²⁵ if I have rejoiced over my great wealth,
  the fortune my hands had gained,
²⁶ if I have regarded the sun in its radiance
  or the moon moving in splendor,
²⁷ so that my heart was secretly enticed
  and my hand offered them a kiss of
  homage,
²⁸ then these also would be sins to be judged,
  for I would have been unfaithful to God on
  high.

²⁹ "If I have rejoiced at my enemy's misfortune
  or gloated over the trouble that came to
  him—
³⁰ I have not allowed my mouth to sin
  by invoking a curse against their life—
³¹ if those of my household have never said,
  'Who has not been filled with Job's
  meat?'—
³² but no stranger had to spend the night in the
  street,
  for my door was always open to the
  traveler—

³³ if I have concealed my sin as people do,ᵃ
  by hiding my guilt in my heart
³⁴ because I so feared the crowd
  and so dreaded the contempt of the clans
  that I kept silent and would not go outside—

³⁵ ("Oh, that I had someone to hear me!
  I sign now my defense—let the Almighty
  answer me;
  let my accuser put his indictment in
  writing.
³⁶ Surely I would wear it on my shoulder,
  I would put it on like a crown.
³⁷ I would give him an account of my every
  step;
  I would present it to him as to a ruler.)—

³⁸ "if my land cries out against me
  and all its furrows are wet with tears,
³⁹ if I have devoured its yield without payment
  or broken the spirit of its tenants,
⁴⁰ then let briers come up instead of wheat
  and stinkweed instead of barley."

The words of Job are ended.

Elihu

32 So these three men stopped answering Job,
because he was righteous in his own eyes.
²But Elihu son of Barakel the Buzite, of the family
of Ram, became very angry with Job for justifying
himself rather than God. ³He was also angry with
the three friends, because they had found no way
to refute Job, and yet had condemned him.ᵇ ⁴Now

ᵃ 33 Or as Adam did   ᵇ 3 Masoretic Text; an ancient Hebrew
scribal tradition Job, and so had condemned God

31:22 let it be broken off at the joint Symbolizes
destruction of strength (compare Ps 37:17; Jer 48:25).
This curse is directly related to the actions described
by Job: If he ever raised his hand against orphans (Job
31:21), his arm should be broken.
31:26 sun in its radiance Job denies ever worshiping
the sun or moon—a common form of idolatry (e.g., Dt
4:19; 2Ki 23:11; Eze 8:16).
31:35 I sign now my defense Job personally signs the
oath of innocence he has been making.
31:40 let briers come up instead of wheat Job pronounces one more curse: If he has abused the land,
the land should return the favor by producing weeds
instead of crops.

32:1—37:24 Job and his three friends have finished their
dialogue, but the speeches are not yet complete. A new
character, Elihu, is now introduced (Job 32:1–5). Elihu
claims to have been present during the earlier dialogues,
but he says that out of deference to Job's older friends, he
did not speak (32:4–14). He is angry at Job for justifying
himself against God, and he is angry with Job's three
friends for accusing Job without being able to answer
him (32:2–3). He gives a long speech divided into four
sections, each marked by a formulaic statement noting
that Elihu is answering Job (32:6; 34:1; 35:1; 36:1).

However, unlike the earlier cycle of dialogues where
Job and his friends trade speeches, Elihu is never answering anyone directly. His speech deals with three main
subjects. First, Elihu introduces himself and explains why
he has decided to speak up now (32:6–33:7). Second,
he responds to Job's assertions that he is righteous and
undeserving of such suffering (33:8–35:16). Finally, Elihu
offers his own thoughts on God's nature, his creative
activity and his ordering of the universe (36:1—37:24).
Elihu's speeches may not have been part of the earliest versions of the book. The argument that they were
added later is supported by three main considerations:
First, Elihu is not mentioned in the prologue (2:11) or the
epilogue (42:9). Second, his speeches may be left out
completely with no substantive effect on the message
or the poetic power of the book. Third, the writing style
of Elihu's speeches has a different feel from the poetry
of the other speeches. However, these reasons are
largely subjective and inconclusive, so many interpreters
address Elihu as an integral part of the book. He may
not be mentioned in the epilogue because his comments
are not new arguments but a response to and summing
up of what has gone before.

32:1 these three men stopped answering Job Job and
his three friends have reached no consensus; Job is still

Elihu had waited before speaking to Job because they were older than he. ⁵But when he saw that the three men had nothing more to say, his anger was aroused.

⁶So Elihu son of Barakel the Buzite said:

"I am young in years,
  and you are old;
that is why I was fearful,
  not daring to tell you what I know.
⁷I thought, 'Age should speak;
  advanced years should teach wisdom.'
⁸But it is the spirit^a in a person,
  the breath of the Almighty, that gives them understanding.
⁹It is not only the old^b who are wise,
  not only the aged who understand what is right.

¹⁰"Therefore I say: Listen to me;
  I too will tell you what I know.
¹¹I waited while you spoke,
  I listened to your reasoning;
while you were searching for words,
¹² I gave you my full attention.
But not one of you has proved Job wrong;
  none of you has answered his arguments.
¹³Do not say, 'We have found wisdom;
  let God, not a man, refute him.'
¹⁴But Job has not marshaled his words against me,
  and I will not answer him with your arguments.

¹⁵"They are dismayed and have no more to say;
  words have failed them.
¹⁶Must I wait, now that they are silent,
  now that they stand there with no reply?
¹⁷I too will have my say;
  I too will tell what I know.

¹⁸For I am full of words,
  and the spirit within me compels me;
¹⁹inside I am like bottled-up wine,
  like new wineskins ready to burst.
²⁰I must speak and find relief;
  I must open my lips and reply.
²¹I will show no partiality,
  nor will I flatter anyone;
²²for if I were skilled in flattery,
  my Maker would soon take me away.

33 "But now, Job, listen to my words;
  pay attention to everything I say.
²I am about to open my mouth;
  my words are on the tip of my tongue.
³My words come from an upright heart;
  my lips sincerely speak what I know.
⁴The Spirit of God has made me;
  the breath of the Almighty gives me life.
⁵Answer me then, if you can;
  stand up and argue your case before me.
⁶I am the same as you in God's sight;
  I too am a piece of clay.
⁷No fear of me should alarm you,
  nor should my hand be heavy on you.

⁸"But you have said in my hearing—
  I heard the very words—
⁹'I am pure, I have done no wrong;
  I am clean and free from sin.
¹⁰Yet God has found fault with me;
  he considers me his enemy.
¹¹He fastens my feet in shackles;
  he keeps close watch on all my paths.'

¹²"But I tell you, in this you are not right,
  for God is greater than any mortal.
¹³Why do you complain to him
  that he responds to no one's words^c?

---

^{a} 8 Or *Spirit*; also in verse 18 ^{b} 9 Or *many*; or *great*
^{c} 13 Or *that he does not answer for any of his actions*

---

convinced of his own righteousness, and his three friends remain unconvinced. Compare note on 7:20; note on 9:3.
32:2 Elihu Meaning "he is my God." Elihu is the only character introduced with a genealogy, possibly indicating that he was qualified to speak in spite of his youth.
became very angry Elihu's anger is referenced four times in this introduction. This exact phrase is later used of God (42:7). However, while God is angry only at Job's three friends, Elihu is angry at Job as well as his friends.

32:6—33:33 In the first part of his speech, Elihu gives a lengthy introduction, explaining why he has not yet spoken and defending why he should be heard (32:6–22). He then addresses Job, criticizing Job's claims and challenging his understanding of God (33:1–33).

32:7–10 Old age is typically associated with wisdom (12:12). Elihu waited to speak, hoping that the wisdom of his elders would suffice. However, he was disappointed in their inability to answer Job. Elihu points out that wisdom comes from God (compare 28:23), not old age, arguing that this gives him the right to speak.

32:14 Job has not marshaled his words against me Job has rejected his friends' comfort and accused them of falsely representing God (13:4–10). Job's friends accused him of irreverence toward God (15:4) and sinful action (22:5–9). Elihu believes that, as an impartial observer, he can respond to Job with some original arguments.
32:19 like bottled-up wine Fermenting wine generates a gas that, if not vented, bursts the wineskin. Elihu compares this to his need to speak—his body is filled with words, and he must vent by speaking.
33:4 breath of the Almighty gives me life Elihu has already argued that the breath of the Almighty gives wisdom (32:8). Here, he appeals to creation (Ge 2:7) to show that he is equal to Job (Job 33:6) and deserves to be heard.
33:9 I am pure, I have done no wrong Elihu essentially summarizes Job's position.
33:12 in this you are not right After quoting Job, Elihu states that Job is wrong and that he will present evidence showing this.
33:13 Why do you complain to him See note on 9:3.

¹⁴ For God does speak — now one way, now
another —
though no one perceives it.
¹⁵ In a dream, in a vision of the night,
when deep sleep falls on people
as they slumber in their beds,
¹⁶ he may speak in their ears
and terrify them with warnings,
¹⁷ to turn them from wrongdoing
and keep them from pride,
¹⁸ to preserve them from the pit,
their lives from perishing by the sword.ᵃ

¹⁹ "Or someone may be chastened on a bed of
pain
with constant distress in their bones,
²⁰ so that their body finds food repulsive
and their soul loathes the choicest meal.
²¹ Their flesh wastes away to nothing,
and their bones, once hidden, now
stick out.
²² They draw near to the pit,
and their life to the messengers of death.ᵇ
²³ Yet if there is an angel at their side,
a messenger, one out of a thousand,
sent to tell them how to be upright,
²⁴ and he is gracious to that person and says
to God,
'Spare them from going down to the pit;
I have found a ransom for them —
²⁵ let their flesh be renewed like a child's;
let them be restored as in the days of their
youth' —
²⁶ then that person can pray to God and find
favor with him,
they will see God's face and shout for joy;
he will restore them to full well-being.

²⁷ And they will go to others and say,
'I have sinned, I have perverted what is
right,
but I did not get what I deserved.
²⁸ God has delivered me from going down to
the pit,
and I shall live to enjoy the light of life.'

²⁹ "God does all these things to a person —
twice, even three times —
³⁰ to turn them back from the pit,
that the light of life may shine on them.

³¹ "Pay attention, Job, and listen to me;
be silent, and I will speak.
³² If you have anything to say, answer me;
speak up, for I want to vindicate you.
³³ But if not, then listen to me;
be silent, and I will teach you wisdom."

34 Then Elihu said:

² "Hear my words, you wise men;
listen to me, you men of learning.
³ For the ear tests words
as the tongue tastes food.
⁴ Let us discern for ourselves what is right;
let us learn together what is good.

⁵ "Job says, 'I am innocent,
but God denies me justice.
⁶ Although I am right,
I am considered a liar;
although I am guiltless,
his arrow inflicts an incurable wound.'
⁷ Is there anyone like Job,
who drinks scorn like water?

ᵃ 18 Or *from crossing the river*   ᵇ 22 Or *to the place of the dead*

33:15 In a dream, in a vision One of the ways God reveals himself is in dreams. Eliphaz claimed that his message came to him in a dream (4:12–16).
33:18 to preserve them from the pit The point of God communicating through dreams, according to Elihu, is to warn people away from sin and preserve their life (compare 17:14).
33:19 chastened on a bed of pain Elihu argues that God uses suffering to rebuke people.
33:22 They draw near to the pit God may afflict people so that they are close to death—just as Job is. However, he does this to redeem people from the pit of death (v. 28).
33:23 an angel at their side, a messenger, one out of a thousand Elihu may refer to Job's desire for a heavenly witness or mediator (see note on 9:33; note on 16:19). In addition to arguing the case of the suffering man, this mediator instructs the sufferer to do what is right (compare 16:21).
33:24 Spare them from going down to the pit The mediator petitions God to deliver the sufferer from death and restore his health.
33:26 pray to God and find favor with him After God speaks, Job prays for his three friends and God accepts his prayer (see 42:8–9).

33:28 God has delivered me The point of God's communication through suffering, as with dreams, is to warn sufferers away from sin and preserve their lives (v. 18).
33:29 all these things Elihu summarizes his point: At times, God in his greatness communicates elusively with humanity. He sometimes uses suffering, but does so to save people from death.

33:31–33 Elihu closes his first speech by calling on Job to hear him. He states his intention to vindicate and restore Job (v. 32) and teach him wisdom (v. 33).

34:1–37 In the second part of his speech (vv. 1–37), Elihu defends God's justice. While he addresses all the "wise men," he focuses on the claims made by Job in his speeches. After introducing his speech with a call to listen (vv. 2–4), Elihu cites Job's arguments (vv. 5–9). He spends the bulk of the chapter refuting Job's arguments (vv. 10–30) before encouraging him to repent (vv. 31–37).

34:5 God denies me justice Elihu again repeats Job's arguments with a mix of direct quotes and summarization (see 33:9–11). In this section, Elihu seems to have Job's final speech in mind (27:2–6).

8 He keeps company with evildoers;
  he associates with the wicked.
9 For he says, 'There is no profit
  in trying to please God.'

10 "So listen to me, you men of understanding.
   Far be it from God to do evil,
   from the Almighty to do wrong.
11 He repays everyone for what they have done;
   he brings on them what their conduct
     deserves.
12 It is unthinkable that God would do wrong,
   that the Almighty would pervert justice.
13 Who appointed him over the earth?
   Who put him in charge of the whole world?
14 If it were his intention
   and he withdrew his spirit[a] and breath,
15 all humanity would perish together
   and mankind would return to the dust.

16 "If you have understanding, hear this;
   listen to what I say.
17 Can someone who hates justice govern?
   Will you condemn the just and
     mighty One?
18 Is he not the One who says to kings, 'You are
     worthless,'
   and to nobles, 'You are wicked,'
19 who shows no partiality to princes
   and does not favor the rich over the poor,
   for they are all the work of his hands?
20 They die in an instant, in the middle of the
     night;
   the people are shaken and they pass away;
   the mighty are removed without human
     hand.
21 "His eyes are on the ways of mortals;
   he sees their every step.
22 There is no deep shadow, no utter darkness,
   where evildoers can hide.

23 God has no need to examine people further,
   that they should come before him for
     judgment.
24 Without inquiry he shatters the mighty
   and sets up others in their place.
25 Because he takes note of their deeds,
   he overthrows them in the night and they
     are crushed.
26 He punishes them for their wickedness
   where everyone can see them,
27 because they turned from following him
   and had no regard for any of his ways.
28 They caused the cry of the poor to come
     before him,
   so that he heard the cry of the needy.
29 But if he remains silent, who can
     condemn him?
   If he hides his face, who can see him?
   Yet he is over individual and nation alike,
30   to keep the godless from ruling,
   from laying snares for the people.

31 "Suppose someone says to God,
   'I am guilty but will offend no more.
32 Teach me what I cannot see;
   if I have done wrong, I will not do so
     again.'
33 Should God then reward you on your
     terms,
   when you refuse to repent?
   You must decide, not I;
   so tell me what you know.

34 "Men of understanding declare,
   wise men who hear me say to me,
35 'Job speaks without knowledge;
   his words lack insight.'
36 Oh, that Job might be tested to the utmost
   for answering like a wicked man!

---

[a] 14 Or *Spirit*

34:10 to do evil In Elihu's view, Job has accused God of doing wrong. Elihu uses an emphatic oath formula to argue that God has nothing to do with wickedness.
34:11 He repays everyone After arguing that God will not do wrong, Elihu turns to the topic of divine retribution. Like Job's other friends, he asserts that God repays people exactly according to their deeds. This principle—repeated throughout Proverbs (e.g., Pr 12:14; 19:17; 24:12)—does not apply to Job's situation (see note on Job 4:6; note on 5:17).
34:13 Who appointed him Elihu uses rhetorical questions to assert God's supremacy.
34:15 all humanity would perish together Elihu argues that God could destroy all humanity if he desired.
34:17–20 Elihu argues that God rules justly. He shows no preference to those in positions of power or the wealthy. All people are subject to his judgment.
34:23 God has no need to examine people further Elihu disputes Job's main complaint, arguing that God does not need to consider anyone's case. According to

Elihu, God is under no obligation to respond to Job's claims of innocence.
34:24 Without inquiry he shatters the mighty Since God sees everything, he has no need to investigate before administrating judgment.

34:26–30 Elihu argues that God judges the wicked publicly because of their wickedness in turning away from God and oppressing the poor. God also judges the wicked to prevent them from being in positions of power where they can influence people.

34:31–33 Elihu seems to be rebuking Job for dictating to God how he should judge. If Job repents, he must accept God's discipline (compare 22:22–23). Elihu leaves the choice up to Job.

34:34–37 Elihu closes his speech by rebuking Job for speaking ignorantly, and he says that any wise man would agree with him. In Elihu's view, Job should receive full punishment for his rebellious reaction to his suffering; instead of repenting, Job has spoken against God.

37 To his sin he adds rebellion;
  scornfully he claps his hands among us
  and multiplies his words against God."

35

Then Elihu said:

2 "Do you think this is just?
  You say, 'I am in the right, not God.'
3 Yet you ask him, 'What profit is it to me,[a]
  and what do I gain by not sinning?'

4 "I would like to reply to you
  and to your friends with you.
5 Look up at the heavens and see;
  gaze at the clouds so high above you.
6 If you sin, how does that affect him?
  If your sins are many, what does that do
    to him?
7 If you are righteous, what do you give to him,
  or what does he receive from your hand?
8 Your wickedness only affects humans like
    yourself,
  and your righteousness only other people.

9 "People cry out under a load of oppression;
  they plead for relief from the arm of the
    powerful.
10 But no one says, 'Where is God my Maker,
  who gives songs in the night,
11 who teaches us more than he teaches[b] the
  beasts of the earth

and makes us wiser than[c] the birds in the
    sky?'
12 He does not answer when people cry out
  because of the arrogance of the wicked.
13 Indeed, God does not listen to their empty
    plea;
  the Almighty pays no attention to it.
14 How much less, then, will he listen
  when you say that you do not see him,
    that your case is before him
    and you must wait for him,
15 and further, that his anger never punishes
  and he does not take the least notice of
    wickedness.[d]
16 So Job opens his mouth with empty talk;
  without knowledge he multiplies words."

36

Elihu continued:

2 "Bear with me a little longer and I will
    show you
  that there is more to be said in God's behalf.
3 I get my knowledge from afar;
  I will ascribe justice to my Maker.
4 Be assured that my words are not false;
  one who has perfect knowledge is
    with you.

---

a 3 Or you   b 10,11 Or night, / ¹¹who teaches us by
c 11 Or us wise by   d 15 Symmachus, Theodotion and Vulgate;
the meaning of the Hebrew for this word is uncertain.

35:1–16 In the third part of his speech (vv. 1–16), Elihu attacks Job for his claims of innocence. He begins again by quoting Job (vv. 2–3) and argues that human behavior does not concern God (vv. 4–8). Elihu then asserts that God does not listen to people who only cry out to him when they are in trouble (vv. 9–16). He includes Job in this group, arguing that God will not answer Job's arrogant demand that God respond to him.

35:2 you think this is just Elihu begins quoting Job's position by questioning whether Job really believes he is right in making the claims he has made. **I am in the right** The Hebrew word used here, *tsedeq*, can refer to justice (Lev 19:36) or righteousness (Ps 7:8). In Job 6:29, Job says that his vindication (*tsedeq*) is at stake. Elihu is troubled by Job putting his own vindication ahead of God (see 32:2 and note) and Job's statement that God has wronged him (see 19:6 and note).

35:3 by not sinning Since being righteous has provided no gain for him, Job questioned the value of righteousness (9:29–31).

35:6–8 Elihu argues that since God is transcendent, people's sins do not affect him. Likewise, their righteousness brings him no gain. Elihu asserts that an individual's righteousness or wickedness only affects that individual, presumably because God repays people according to their deeds (34:11). However, Elihu, like Eliphaz, is unaware of God's conversation with the *satan* figure (compare note on 1:6). God does have a stake in Job's righteousness, since the *satan* figure claimed that Job would curse God when afflicted (see 1:7–12; 2:2–6; note on 22:3).

35:10 who gives songs in the night In lament Psalms, singing—especially in the night—was a way for the faithful to remember God's love and protection (e.g., Ps 42:8; 77:6). **35:13 Indeed, God does not listen to their empty plea** Elihu argues that God will not respond to cries made out of pride (Job 35:12). God does not hear those who seek relief without repentance (compare Pr 1:28–31). Job, however, is not crying out only for relief—he also hopes for vindication (see Job 16:18–22; 17:15; 19:23–27). **35:14 say that you do not see him** Elihu questions how Job expects God to answer him since he has claimed that he cannot perceive him. However, while Job complains that he cannot see God (9:11; 23:8–9), he also expresses faith that God will reveal himself (19:25–27; 23:10–12).

36:1—37:24 In the fourth and final part of his speech (36:1—37:24), Elihu speaks on God's behalf, defending God's disciplinary ways and extolling his greatness. After a brief introduction where he claims to be speaking on behalf of God (36:2–4), he discusses suffering as God's discipline and the restoration that comes with repentance (36:5–15). He then applies this to Job, encouraging him to repent and not sin (36:16–21). Elihu then extols God's greatness (36:22—37:13). He again addresses Job directly, encouraging him to consider God's greatness as he makes his complaint (37:14–20). He closes with another description of God's majestic splendor (37:21–24).

36:3 my knowledge from afar As opposed to Job, who according to Elihu speaks without knowledge (34:35), Elihu claims his knowledge comes from God. **36:4 Be assured that my words are not false** Job has accused his friends of speaking falsely (13:4). Using the

5 "God is mighty, but despises no one;
    he is mighty, and firm in his purpose.
6 He does not keep the wicked alive
    but gives the afflicted their rights.
7 He does not take his eyes off the righteous;
    he enthrones them with kings
    and exalts them forever.
8 But if people are bound in chains,
    held fast by cords of affliction,
9 he tells them what they have done —
    that they have sinned arrogantly.
10 He makes them listen to correction
    and commands them to repent of their evil.
11 If they obey and serve him,
    they will spend the rest of their days in
        prosperity
    and their years in contentment.
12 But if they do not listen,
    they will perish by the sword[a]
    and die without knowledge.

13 "The godless in heart harbor resentment;
    even when he fetters them, they do not cry
        for help.
14 They die in their youth,
    among male prostitutes of the shrines.
15 But those who suffer he delivers in their
        suffering;
    he speaks to them in their affliction.

16 "He is wooing you from the jaws of distress
    to a spacious place free from restriction,
    to the comfort of your table laden with
        choice food.

17 But now you are laden with the judgment due
        the wicked;
    judgment and justice have taken hold
        of you.
18 Be careful that no one entices you by
        riches;
    do not let a large bribe turn you aside.
19 Would your wealth or even all your mighty
        efforts
    sustain you so you would not be in
        distress?
20 Do not long for the night,
    to drag people away from their homes.[b]
21 Beware of turning to evil,
    which you seem to prefer to affliction.

22 "God is exalted in his power.
    Who is a teacher like him?
23 Who has prescribed his ways for him,
    or said to him, 'You have done wrong'?
24 Remember to extol his work,
    which people have praised in song.
25 All humanity has seen it;
    mortals gaze on it from afar.
26 How great is God — beyond our
        understanding!
    The number of his years is past
        finding out.

27 "He draws up the drops of water,
    which distill as rain to the streams[c];

a 12 Or will cross the river   b 20 The meaning of the Hebrew
for verses 18-20 is uncertain.   c 27 Or distill from the mist
as rain

same Hebrew word, sheqer, Elihu assures Job that his words are true. **one who has perfect knowledge** Elihu is probably not referring to himself here, but to God, who he considers the source of his wisdom.
36:6 does not keep the wicked alive Elihu echoes the position of Job's other friends. God punishes the wicked while providing justice for the needy.
36:7 He does not take his eyes off the righteous Job earlier complained that God watched him too closely (7:20; 10:14).
36:8 bound in chains Elihu describes a situation where the righteous slip in some way, becoming chained because of sin (compare Ps 107:10–16).
36:11–12 Elihu describes two possible reactions to God's discipline. Those who listen to God's instruction and repent of their sin will be restored; they will finish life prosperous and happy. Those who do not will meet a violent death.
36:13 harbor resentment Elihu continues to describe those who do not respond to God's discipline. Instead of crying for help, they become angry.
36:14 male prostitutes of the shrines Not only does Elihu argue that the unrepentant die young, but he also suggests they die among the male cult prostitutes (in Hebrew, qedeshim) who served worshipers in temples or shrines of fertility gods (see Dt 23:18 and note; 1Ki 14:24 and note). Elihu suggests the unrepentant will die in shame.
36:15 those who suffer he delivers in their suffering God uses suffering as discipline to deliver people.

36:16–17 Elihu applies his understanding of God's discipline to Job. God has taken Job from a place of security and prosperity into judgment.
36:18 Be careful that no one entices you by riches The Hebrew text here may be understood as Elihu warning Job against responding to God's judgment with anger like the godless (Job 36:13) or a warning that wealth can be deceptive (compare 27:19–23).
36:20 Do not long for the night Elihu rebukes Job for longing for death (3:3–26; 6:8–9; 10:18–22).
36:21 which you seem to prefer Elihu warns Job to recognize the purpose of his suffering rather than choosing to sin by questioning God.
36:23 You have done wrong Because God is in an exalted position of authority, Elihu criticizes Job for questioning his justice and making demands of him (see 6:4 and note).
36:24—37:13 Elihu reminds Job to extol God's work by praising God himself. He emphasizes God's supremacy over humanity, and marvels at God's greatness as seen in a storm. By proclaiming God's greatness, Elihu hopes to show Job that he is wrong to contend with a God so much greater than humanity (33:12). Job, however, has acknowledged God's power (26:2–14). This speech anticipates God's speeches, where he proclaims his supremacy over all creation (38:2–40:2; 40:7–41:34).
36:26 beyond our understanding Such an unknowable God should be praised rather than challenged.

28 the clouds pour down their moisture
  and abundant showers fall on mankind.
29 Who can understand how he spreads out the
    clouds,
  how he thunders from his pavilion?
30 See how he scatters his lightning about him,
  bathing the depths of the sea.
31 This is the way he governs[a] the nations
  and provides food in abundance.
32 He fills his hands with lightning
  and commands it to strike its mark.
33 His thunder announces the coming storm;
  even the cattle make known its
    approach.[b]

37 "At this my heart pounds
   and leaps from its place.
2 Listen! Listen to the roar of his voice,
  to the rumbling that comes from his
    mouth.
3 He unleashes his lightning beneath the whole
    heaven
  and sends it to the ends of the earth.
4 After that comes the sound of his roar;
  he thunders with his majestic voice.
  When his voice resounds,
  he holds nothing back.
5 God's voice thunders in marvelous ways;
  he does great things beyond our
    understanding.
6 He says to the snow, 'Fall on the earth,'
  and to the rain shower, 'Be a mighty
    downpour.'
7 So that everyone he has made may know his
    work,
  he stops all people from their labor.[c]
8 The animals take cover;
  they remain in their dens.
9 The tempest comes out from its chamber,
  the cold from the driving winds.
10 The breath of God produces ice,
  and the broad waters become frozen.

11 He loads the clouds with moisture;
  he scatters his lightning through them.
12 At his direction they swirl around
  over the face of the whole earth
  to do whatever he commands them.
13 He brings the clouds to punish people,
  or to water his earth and show his love.

14 "Listen to this, Job;
  stop and consider God's wonders.
15 Do you know how God controls the clouds
  and makes his lightning flash?
16 Do you know how the clouds hang poised,
  those wonders of him who has perfect
    knowledge?
17 You who swelter in your clothes
  when the land lies hushed under the south
    wind,
18 can you join him in spreading out the skies,
  hard as a mirror of cast bronze?

19 "Tell us what we should say to him;
  we cannot draw up our case because of our
    darkness.
20 Should he be told that I want to speak?
  Would anyone ask to be swallowed up?
21 Now no one can look at the sun,
  bright as it is in the skies
  after the wind has swept them clean.
22 Out of the north he comes in golden
    splendor;
  God comes in awesome majesty.
23 The Almighty is beyond our reach and
    exalted in power;
  in his justice and great righteousness, he
    does not oppress.
24 Therefore, people revere him,
  for does he not have regard for all the wise
    in heart?[d]"

---

a 31 Or *nourishes*   *b* 33 Or *announces his coming— / the One
zealous against evil*   *c* 7 Or *work, / he fills all people with fear
by his power*   *d* 24 Or *for he does not have regard for any who
think they are wise.*

36:30 he scatters his lightning about him Lightning
represents God's power and glory (Ps 77:18).
36:31 This is the way he governs the nations Elihu
argues that God uses storms both to judge and to provide
(Job 37:13).
37:1 my heart pounds Elihu expresses how awestruck
he is at the displays of God's power.
37:7 he stops all people from their labor Probably
refers to severe snow and ice forcing people inside.
God's power over the weather allows him to force both
humanity and animals (v. 8) to take shelter.
37:12 do whatever he commands God does not exhibit control for no reason—he does it to accomplish
his goals (v. 13).
37:16 him who has perfect knowledge See note
on 36:4.
37:18 hard as a mirror of cast bronze In the ancient
Near East, mirrors were made of polished metal, usually
bronze (Ex 38:8). The description of the skies as made

of a hard substance is consistent with the language of
other ancient Near Eastern descriptions of the created
world (compare Ge 1:6–8; note on Ge 1:6).
37:19 Tell us what we should say to him Elihu sarcastically asks Job to explain how to speak to God. **we
cannot draw up our case because of our darkness**
Elihu says he—and all Job's friends—are not qualified
to bring a case before God. He sarcastically implies
that Job is arrogant to believe he can prepare a case
(compare Job 13:18).
37:23 Almighty is beyond our reach Here at the end
of his speeches, Elihu emphasizes that God is so much
greater than humanity that he cannot be found. Ironically,
God will make himself found by answering Job in the next
chapter (see 38:1).
37:24 people revere him Because of God's mighty and
awesome power, people should fear him. This matches
the description of Job's attitude toward God in the prologue (1:1,8). Elihu unknowingly alludes to the *satan*

The LORD Speaks

38 Then the LORD spoke to Job out of the storm. He said:

2 "Who is this that obscures my plans
  with words without knowledge?
3 Brace yourself like a man;
  I will question you,
  and you shall answer me.

4 "Where were you when I laid the earth's
    foundation?
  Tell me, if you understand.
5 Who marked off its dimensions? Surely you
    know!
  Who stretched a measuring line across it?
6 On what were its footings set,
  or who laid its cornerstone —

7 while the morning stars sang together
  and all the angels[a] shouted for joy?

8 "Who shut up the sea behind doors
  when it burst forth from the womb,
9 when I made the clouds its garment
  and wrapped it in thick darkness,
10 when I fixed limits for it
  and set its doors and bars in place,
11 when I said, 'This far you may come and no
    farther;
  here is where your proud waves halt'?

12 "Have you ever given orders to the morning,
  or shown the dawn its place,
13 that it might take the earth by the edges
  and shake the wicked out of it?

a 7 Hebrew *the sons of God*

figure's challenge—whether Job fears God because God had blessed him, or because God is sovereign (see 1:9 and note; note on 22:4; note on 1:6).

38:1—41:34 Throughout his speeches Job asked—even demanded—that God answer him (7:20–21; 10:2–3; 23:2–7; 31:35). Here, God responds to Job—but he does not explain his purpose in afflicting Job. God neither references Job's suffering nor his claims of innocence—but he does refer to Job's challenge (40:8). Also, God does not condemn Job as Job's friends expected. Instead, he emphasizes his power and supremacy as he sarcastically asks Job a series of questions about nature and creation—emphasizing the vast difference between himself and humanity. In answering this way, God wins his challenge with the *satan* figure (1:9; note on 1:6). Job has proven that he fears God because of who God is, and not because of how God has blessed him (see note on 1:9). God's overall point in the speech is that no one can know what God knows or do what he does—and thus Job cannot understand how the world works or his own situation for that matter. See the table "Cycles in Job" on p. 793.

38:1—40:2 God opens and closes his first speech by challenging Job (38:2–3; 40:2). Through a series of rhetorical questions, he exposes the limitations of Job's understanding and reveals his own power as Creator. He reveals his work in creation (38:4–15), shows his power and knowledge in maintaining and governing the created order (38:16–38), and shows his power in sustaining life in the animal kingdom (38:39—39:30).

38:1 LORD spoke to Job out of the storm Theophanies (appearances of God to people) often include displays of the power of nature. God's appearance at Mount Sinai was accompanied by thunder, lightning and clouds (Ex 19:16–20). Fire is also often associated with theophanies (Ex 3:2; Dt 5:24). Here, God appears to Job in a whirlwind. See the table "Old Testament Theophanies" on p. 924.

38:3 Brace yourself like a man The Hebrew phrase used here, which may be literally rendered as "gird your loins like a man," refers to how people in the ancient Near East would tie their garments into their belt to ensure that they could run quickly (compare 2Ki 4:29; Jer 1:17). **you shall answer me** Just as Job challenged God, God now challenges Job to answer his questions (compare Job 13:22). God's questions, however, are

designed to reveal his power in such a way that Job cannot answer them. Job's eventual response reflects this (see 40:4–5; 42:2–6).

38:4–7 God begins by asking Job about his role in creation. The questions are sarcastic and intend to show Job the limitation of his knowledge.

38:4 I laid the earth's foundation In ancient Near Eastern cosmology, the earth was thought to be supported by pillars sunk into the sea (e.g., 1Sa 2:8; Ps 104:5). See the infographic "Ancient Hebrew Conception of the Universe" on p. 5.

38:7 morning stars sang together Laying a foundation stone was a cause for celebration (Ezr 3:10–11). Here, God describes the heavenly celebration that accompanied the setting of the foundation of the earth. The Psalms describe scenes of the stars and angels singing praise together (e.g., Ps 19:1; 148:1–4). **angels** Refers to the members of the heavenly host. The prologue describes this same group presenting themselves to Yahweh (see Job 1:6; 2:1). Here, they rejoice at God's amazing acts of creation.

38:8–11 God continues his questions, moving to the realm of the sea. Instead of construction language, he uses birthing language to describe his creation of the seas (see Ge 1:2).

38:8 Who shut up the sea Ancient Near Eastern creation accounts, like the Enuma Elish, describe the supreme deity subduing the sea, which was depicted as a force of chaos (compare Job 7:12; 9:13). Biblical accounts of creation often allude to these accounts to show the power of Israel's God—demonstrating both his superiority over nature and other deities (e.g., Ps 77:16; 104:6–9).

38:9 I made the clouds its garment Rather than merely subduing the sea, God brought it into existence. Here, God describes caring for the mighty sea as if it were an infant, clothing it with clouds. This is likely a reference to the horizon line on a cloudy day, when it looks as if the clouds are touching the sea.

38:12–15 Moving to the creation of day and night, God continues to show his power to Job. In the ancient Near Eastern worldview, the rising of the sun occurred not because of natural laws, but by the command of God.

38:13 the earth by the edges Describes the farthest reaches of the earth (compare 37:3). People in the

¹⁴ The earth takes shape like clay under a seal;
its features stand out like those of a
garment.
¹⁵ The wicked are denied their light,
and their upraised arm is broken.

¹⁶ "Have you journeyed to the springs of the sea
or walked in the recesses of the deep?
¹⁷ Have the gates of death been shown to you?
Have you seen the gates of the deepest
darkness?
¹⁸ Have you comprehended the vast expanses of
the earth?
Tell me, if you know all this.

¹⁹ "What is the way to the abode of light?
And where does darkness reside?
²⁰ Can you take them to their places?
Do you know the paths to their dwellings?
²¹ Surely you know, for you were already born!
You have lived so many years!

²² "Have you entered the storehouses of the
snow
or seen the storehouses of the hail,
²³ which I reserve for times of trouble,
for days of war and battle?
²⁴ What is the way to the place where the
lightning is dispersed,
or the place where the east winds are
scattered over the earth?
²⁵ Who cuts a channel for the torrents of rain,
and a path for the thunderstorm,
²⁶ to water a land where no one lives,
an uninhabited desert,
²⁷ to satisfy a desolate wasteland
and make it sprout with grass?

²⁸ Does the rain have a father?
Who fathers the drops of dew?
²⁹ From whose womb comes the ice?
Who gives birth to the frost from the
heavens
³⁰ when the waters become hard as stone,
when the surface of the deep is frozen?

³¹ "Can you bind the chains^a of the Pleiades?
Can you loosen Orion's belt?
³² Can you bring forth the constellations in
their seasons^b
or lead out the Bear^c with its cubs?
³³ Do you know the laws of the heavens?
Can you set up God's^d dominion over the
earth?

³⁴ "Can you raise your voice to the clouds
and cover yourself with a flood of water?
³⁵ Do you send the lightning bolts on their way?
Do they report to you, 'Here we are'?
³⁶ Who gives the ibis wisdom^e
or gives the rooster understanding?^f
³⁷ Who has the wisdom to count the clouds?
Who can tip over the water jars of the
heavens
³⁸ when the dust becomes hard
and the clods of earth stick together?

³⁹ "Do you hunt the prey for the lioness
and satisfy the hunger of the lions
⁴⁰ when they crouch in their dens
or lie in wait in a thicket?

^a 31 Septuagint; Hebrew *beauty*   ^b 32 Or *the morning star in its season*   ^c 32 Or *out Leo*   ^d 33 Or *their*   ^e 36 That is, wisdom about the flooding of the Nile   ^f 36 That is, understanding of when to crow; the meaning of the Hebrew for this verse is uncertain.

---

ancient Near East thought the earth was spread out flat like a carpet with four corners and that the earth stood on pillars or foundations (compare Isa 11:12). **shake the wicked out of it** The image of shaking out a garment appears elsewhere in Ne 5:13 and Ac 18:6. Before God, the wicked have no dark place to hide their sins (compare Job 24:13–17).

38:16–18 The questions shift from focusing on God's acts of creation to focusing on God's unlimited knowledge of the created universe. God asks Job if he has visited the depths of the earth, the implication being that God has intimate knowledge of the universe unknown to Job.

38:16 recesses of the deep In ancient Near Eastern cosmology, the earth was thought to sit atop the deep waters (or the great deep)—this describes both this place and by extension the depths of the oceans (or seas). See Ge 7:11 and note.
38:17 the gates of death This seems to be a reference to Sheol, the place of the dead according to Hebrew thought (compare Job 3:13; 14:13 and note). **the gates of the deepest darkness** This could be a reference to Sheol or to the depths mentioned in Job 38:16. The point is that, in comparison to God, Job does not know anything about death, creation or how the world works and functions.

38:19–21 Moving from the depths of the earth to the sky, God continues to question Job's knowledge. He sarcastically proclaims that, since Job knows how to take the sun along its path, he must be very old.

38:22–24 God questions Job about his knowledge of the weather. He asks Job if he has visited the storehouses of snow and hail, or if he understands how to place lightning or wind. It was a common idea in the ancient Near East that God kept a reserve of materials for storms (Ps 135:7).

38:25–38 After questioning his knowledge, God focuses on Job's power. He asks Job if he can control the weather and meteorological phenomena. God lists several constellations, asking Job if he can keep them in place.

38:31 Orion's The Hebrew term used here, *kesil*, normally refers to a fool (e.g., Ps 49:10; Pr 1:22; 3:35), but here it probably refers to the constellation Orion (see Job 9:9; Am 5:8). For this reason, some translations refer to Orion's belt here.
38:32 constellations Since this word is parallel to "Bear" in the next line, this Hebrew word may be the name of an unknown constellation. Alternatively, it may refer to constellations in general. **the Bear** Likely refers to the constellation Ursa Major (compare Job 9:9 and note).

⁴¹ Who provides food for the raven
 when its young cry out to God
 and wander about for lack of food?

39

"Do you know when the mountain goats
 give birth?
Do you watch when the doe bears her
 fawn?
² Do you count the months till they bear?
 Do you know the time they give birth?
³ They crouch down and bring forth their
 young;
 their labor pains are ended.
⁴ Their young thrive and grow strong in the
 wilds;
 they leave and do not return.

⁵ "Who let the wild donkey go free?
 Who untied its ropes?
⁶ I gave it the wasteland as its home,
 the salt flats as its habitat.
⁷ It laughs at the commotion in the town;
 it does not hear a driver's shout.
⁸ It ranges the hills for its pasture
 and searches for any green thing.

⁹ "Will the wild ox consent to serve you?
 Will it stay by your manger at night?
¹⁰ Can you hold it to the furrow with a harness?
 Will it till the valleys behind you?
¹¹ Will you rely on it for its great strength?
 Will you leave your heavy work to it?
¹² Can you trust it to haul in your grain
 and bring it to your threshing floor?

¹³ "The wings of the ostrich flap joyfully,
 though they cannot compare
 with the wings and feathers of the stork.
¹⁴ She lays her eggs on the ground
 and lets them warm in the sand,
¹⁵ unmindful that a foot may crush them,
 that some wild animal may trample them.
¹⁶ She treats her young harshly, as if they were
 not hers;
 she cares not that her labor was in vain,

¹⁷ for God did not endow her with wisdom
 or give her a share of good sense.
¹⁸ Yet when she spreads her feathers to run,
 she laughs at horse and rider.

¹⁹ "Do you give the horse its strength
 or clothe its neck with a flowing mane?
²⁰ Do you make it leap like a locust,
 striking terror with its proud snorting?
²¹ It paws fiercely, rejoicing in its strength,
 and charges into the fray.
²² It laughs at fear, afraid of nothing;
 it does not shy away from the sword.
²³ The quiver rattles against its side,
 along with the flashing spear and lance.
²⁴ In frenzied excitement it eats up the
 ground;
 it cannot stand still when the trumpet
 sounds.
²⁵ At the blast of the trumpet it snorts, 'Aha!'
 It catches the scent of battle from afar,
 the shout of commanders and the
 battle cry.

²⁶ "Does the hawk take flight by your wisdom
 and spread its wings toward the south?
²⁷ Does the eagle soar at your command
 and build its nest on high?
²⁸ It dwells on a cliff and stays there at night;
 a rocky crag is its stronghold.
²⁹ From there it looks for food;
 its eyes detect it from afar.
³⁰ Its young ones feast on blood,
 and where the slain are, there it is."

40

The LORD said to Job:

² "Will the one who contends with the
 Almighty correct him?
 Let him who accuses God answer him!"

³ Then Job answered the LORD:

⁴ "I am unworthy — how can I reply to you?
 I put my hand over my mouth.

38:39 — 39:30 In the remainder of his speech, God questions Job's ability to provide for various aspects of the animal kingdom. God's questions point to his supremacy over animal life.

39:5 wild donkey In contrast to a domesticated donkey, the wild donkey freely wandered in the desert (Jer 2:24).
39:18 laughs at horse and rider Ostriches—which were hunted in the ancient Near East for feathers as well as food—can outrun horses.
39:19 Do you give the horse its strength Horses, which were used in warfare, were viewed as courageous (Jer 8:6), fast (Jer 4:13) and surefooted (Isa 63:13). The number of horses usually signified the strength of the army (Jos 11:4; 1Ki 4:26).
40:2 contends with the Almighty Job is now getting the day in court that he has wished for throughout the

book (see note on Job 9:3). However, instead of presenting his case, he is silent. **Let him who accuses God answer** Job demanded answers from God (7:20; 10:2; 31:35). Now, God challenges Job to answer his questions.

40:3 – 5 Job's response to God takes a much different tone than the rest of his speeches. He is more subdued and humble as he recognizes his place before God. He drops his demands for answers, and he does not follow through with his bold claims of how he would act in God's presence (23:3 – 7). Instead, he acknowledges the futility of trying to respond to God. Job's humility acknowledges that he understands at least one of God's points: Job cannot know or understand how the world works or, by extension, God's purposes in his life.

40:4 I am unworthy In comparison to the grand majesty of God, Job humbly acknowledges his own insignificance.

⁵ I spoke once, but I have no answer —
  twice, but I will say no more."

⁶ Then the LORD spoke to Job out of the storm:

⁷ "Brace yourself like a man;
  I will question you,
  and you shall answer me.

⁸ "Would you discredit my justice?
  Would you condemn me to justify yourself?
⁹ Do you have an arm like God's,
  and can your voice thunder like his?
¹⁰ Then adorn yourself with glory and splendor,
  and clothe yourself in honor and majesty.
¹¹ Unleash the fury of your wrath,
  look at all who are proud and bring
    them low,
¹² look at all who are proud and humble them,
  crush the wicked where they stand.
¹³ Bury them all in the dust together;
  shroud their faces in the grave.
¹⁴ Then I myself will admit to you
  that your own right hand can save you.

¹⁵ "Look at Behemoth,
  which I made along with you
  and which feeds on grass like an ox.
¹⁶ What strength it has in its loins,
  what power in the muscles of its belly!
¹⁷ Its tail sways like a cedar;
  the sinews of its thighs are close-knit.
¹⁸ Its bones are tubes of bronze,
  its limbs like rods of iron.
¹⁹ It ranks first among the works of God,
  yet its Maker can approach it with his
    sword.
²⁰ The hills bring it their produce,
  and all the wild animals play nearby.

²¹ Under the lotus plants it lies,
  hidden among the reeds in the marsh.
²² The lotuses conceal it in their shadow;
  the poplars by the stream surround it.
²³ A raging river does not alarm it;
  it is secure, though the Jordan should surge
    against its mouth.
²⁴ Can anyone capture it by the eyes,
  or trap it and pierce its nose?

41 ᵃ "Can you pull in Leviathan with a
  fishhook
  or tie down its tongue with a rope?
² Can you put a cord through its nose
  or pierce its jaw with a hook?
³ Will it keep begging you for mercy?
  Will it speak to you with gentle
    words?
⁴ Will it make an agreement with you
  for you to take it as your slave for life?
⁵ Can you make a pet of it like a bird
  or put it on a leash for the young women in
    your house?
⁶ Will traders barter for it?
  Will they divide it up among the
    merchants?
⁷ Can you fill its hide with harpoons
  or its head with fishing spears?
⁸ If you lay a hand on it,
  you will remember the struggle and never
    do it again!
⁹ Any hope of subduing it is false;
  the mere sight of it is overpowering.
¹⁰ No one is fierce enough to rouse it.
  Who then is able to stand against me?

ᵃ In Hebrew texts 41:1-8 is numbered 40:25-32, and 41:9-34 is
numbered 41:1-26.

40:5 I will say no more Despite Job's humility, he stops short of obeying God's command to give an answer (38:3; 40:2). God's calling Job to action a second time (v. 7) may indicate his displeasure with Job's lack of repentance (compare 42:1–6).

40:6 — 41:34 God begins his second speech by repeating his challenge to Job (40:7; see 38:3). He then addresses Job's complaints about divine justice (9:22–24; 21:7–21; 24:1–12). God sarcastically tells Job to take over managing justice by punishing the wicked (40:8–14). He follows this with a description of two powerful beasts: Behemoth (40:15–24) and Leviathan (41:1–34). By showing his control over these powerful animals, God reveals that he is the only one qualified to administer justice on earth.

40:8 justify yourself Job repeatedly claimed to be in the right (9:20; 13:18). By claiming innocence and demanding an answer from God, Job came close to justifying himself over God—an accusation made by Elihu (32:2).

40:9 have an arm like God's God responds to Job's accusation by asserting his sovereignty. God's arm was a symbol of his strength in judgment and salvation (e.g., Ex 6:6; Ps 89:13; Isa 52:10).

40:12 look at all who are proud God uses this phrase twice (compare 40:11). Here, he emphasizes the large-scale judgment that Job would be required to carry out.

40:15 Behemoth The exact identity of this animal is unknown. It most likely refers to a hippopotamus, but may refer to an elephant or even a mythical creature. The description emphasizes the animal's power and size. This strong beast is frightening and uncontrollable to humanity, but God simply considers it another one of his creatures.

40:19 ranks first among the works of God Behemoth is described as the greatest among God's creation—the first in terms of rank.

41:1 Leviathan May refer to a crocodile or a mythical sea monster. God describes the Leviathan as a mighty and fearsome creature (Job 41:12–34). This powerful creature, however, is subject to God like a pet (vv. 3–5). Biblical references to Leviathan are often symbolic references for chaos itself (3:8; 7:12; 9:13; compare Isa 27:1 and note). However, since God has described many aspects of his creation, it is best to view the reference to Leviathan—like Behemoth—as a part of his creation.

11 Who has a claim against me that I must pay?
  Everything under heaven belongs to me.

12 "I will not fail to speak of Leviathan's limbs,
  its strength and its graceful form.
13 Who can strip off its outer coat?
  Who can penetrate its double coat of
  armor ª?
14 Who dares open the doors of its mouth,
  ringed about with fearsome teeth?
15 Its back has ᵇ rows of shields
  tightly sealed together;
16 each is so close to the next
  that no air can pass between.
17 They are joined fast to one another;
  they cling together and cannot be parted.
18 Its snorting throws out flashes of light;
  its eyes are like the rays of dawn.
19 Flames stream from its mouth;
  sparks of fire shoot out.
20 Smoke pours from its nostrils
  as from a boiling pot over burning reeds.
21 Its breath sets coals ablaze,
  and flames dart from its mouth.
22 Strength resides in its neck;
  dismay goes before it.
23 The folds of its flesh are tightly joined;
  they are firm and immovable.
24 Its chest is hard as rock,
  hard as a lower millstone.
25 When it rises up, the mighty are terrified;
  they retreat before its thrashing.
26 The sword that reaches it has no effect,
  nor does the spear or the dart or the
  javelin.
27 Iron it treats like straw
  and bronze like rotten wood.
28 Arrows do not make it flee;
  slingstones are like chaff to it.
29 A club seems to it but a piece of straw;
  it laughs at the rattling of the lance.
30 Its undersides are jagged potsherds,
  leaving a trail in the mud like a threshing
  sledge.
31 It makes the depths churn like a boiling
  caldron
  and stirs up the sea like a pot of
  ointment.
32 It leaves a glistening wake behind it;
  one would think the deep had white hair.
33 Nothing on earth is its equal—
  a creature without fear.
34 It looks down on all that are haughty;
  it is king over all that are proud."

Job

42

Then Job replied to the LORD:

2 "I know that you can do all things;
  no purpose of yours can be thwarted.
3 You asked, 'Who is this that obscures my
  plans without knowledge?'
  Surely I spoke of things I did not
  understand,
  things too wonderful for me to know.

4 "You said, 'Listen now, and I will speak;
  I will question you,
  and you shall answer me.'
5 My ears had heard of you
  but now my eyes have seen you.
6 Therefore I despise myself
  and repent in dust and ashes."

Epilogue

7 After the LORD had said these things to Job, he
said to Eliphaz the Temanite, "I am angry with
you and your two friends, because you have not
spoken the truth about me, as my servant Job has.

ª 13 Septuagint; Hebrew *double bridle*   ᵇ 15 Or *Its pride is its*

41:12–34 The remainder of God's speech is a poetic description of Leviathan. God describes its great strength (Job 41:12), fearsome teeth (v. 14), impenetrable skin (vv. 15–17,23) and fiery breath (vv. 19–21). Weapons are useless against it (vv. 26–29). Just as no one is able to subdue this creature (vv. 33–34), no one can challenge the rule of Yahweh.

42:1–6 In his earlier response to God (40:4–5), Job was humble as he recognized God's greatness and his own insufficiency. Here, he acknowledges God's power and that his purposes cannot be thwarted (v. 2). He admits that he spoke ignorantly (v. 3). Finally, he repents because of the more complete understanding he has gained from seeing God (vv. 4–6).
  Job's repentance differs from what his friends implored him to do (compare 8:5–7; 11:13–15; 22:21–30). Job's friends encourage him to repent of sin—but God never accuses Job of committing any specific sin. Job's repentance occurs in response to God's character. Job

acknowledges that knowledge alone of God is insufficient and that only relationship with him counts (v. 5). Through his journey of despair, Job gains a relationship with God, and once he realizes that he repents from his demand for vindication. Job makes a statement of faith about God's sovereignty and superiority, similar to his initial response (1:21; 2:10). But this time, Job's response shows the purpose of suffering—to know God.

42:6 repent The Hebrew word used here denotes feeling sorrow. It is the same word used to describe the emotions of Job's friends in 2:11. Job has changed his attitude toward God. **dust and ashes** These words occurred earlier in 30:19. There, Job bitterly complains against God. Here, he is humbly repenting (see note on 42:1–6).

42:7–17 In the epilogue to the book of Job (42:7–17), Yahweh rebukes Job's friends for erroneously speaking about him and demands them to offer a sacrifice for themselves (42:7–8). After Job's prayer for his three

[8] So now take seven bulls and seven rams and go to my servant Job and sacrifice a burnt offering for yourselves. My servant Job will pray for you, and I will accept his prayer and not deal with you according to your folly. You have not spoken the truth about me, as my servant Job has." [9] So Eliphaz the Temanite, Bildad the Shuhite and Zophar the Naamathite did what the LORD told them; and the LORD accepted Job's prayer.

[10] After Job had prayed for his friends, the LORD restored his fortunes and gave him twice as much as he had before. [11] All his brothers and sisters and everyone who had known him before came and ate with him in his house. They comforted and consoled him over all the trouble the LORD had brought on him, and each one gave him a piece of silver[a] and a gold ring.

[12] The LORD blessed the latter part of Job's life more than the former part. He had fourteen thousand sheep, six thousand camels, a thousand yoke of oxen and a thousand donkeys. [13] And he also had seven sons and three daughters. [14] The first daughter he named Jemimah, the second Keziah and the third Keren-Happuch. [15] Nowhere in all the land were there found women as beautiful as Job's daughters, and their father granted them an inheritance along with their brothers.

[16] After this, Job lived a hundred and forty years; he saw his children and their children to the fourth generation. [17] And so Job died, an old man and full of years.

a 11 Hebrew *him a kesitah*; a kesitah was a unit of money of unknown weight and value.

---

friends is accepted by Yahweh, Job's fortunes are restored twofold, and he lives for another one hundred and forty years (42:16).

After Job's second response (42:1–6), Yahweh addresses the actions and speeches of Job's three friends. However, Yahweh does not acknowledge Elihu's speech. This could be because Elihu simply repeats the same arguments as the three friends, and thus Yahweh does not dignify him with a response. Elihu may actually be a forerunner who anticipates Yahweh's own speeches (therefore no rejection or affirmation of Elihu's speech would be expected). It is also possible that Elihu's speech is not part of the original text, and thus not mentioned in this passage (see note on 32:1—37:24).

42:7 I am angry with you God's anger is directed at Job's three friends. **as my servant Job** Job accused his friends of speaking falsely for God (13:7), arguing that God would rebuke them (13:10). Here God does exactly that—he vindicates Job by saying that Job spoke correctly of him while Job's friends did not. **42:8 sacrifice a burnt offering for yourselves** God commands Eliphaz and Job's other two friends to offer a large sacrifice in acknowledgement of their sin—they had accused Job falsely and did not speak correctly about God. **My servant Job will pray for you** While God required Job's friends to sacrifice, he wanted Job to offer a prayer on their behalf. Before his affliction,

Job offered sacrifices on behalf of his children out of a suspicion that they had done wrong (1:5). Here, out of a recognition of God's mercy, he intercedes for his friends who had definitely done wrong against him.

42:10 restored his fortunes Job is restored socially (v. 11), economically (v. 12) and also in his family (vv. 13–16). Job's restoration was not a reward for his righteousness. Instead, it was an act of grace by God. God proved his point to the *satan* figure: Job indeed feared God because of who God is—not because of God's blessing (see note on 1:9; note on 38:1—41:34; compare note on 1:6).

42:12 fourteen thousand sheep, six thousand camels Before his affliction, Job was a very wealthy man (see 1:3 and note). Now, God increases Job's wealth to double his original holdings.

42:15 an inheritance along with their brothers In addition to being beautiful, Job's daughters shared in the inheritance with their brothers. Typically, daughters did not receive any inheritance. The only other OT record of daughters receiving inheritance was when their father died without producing any sons (see Nu 27:5–8).

42:17 Job died, an old man This epitaph is similar to that of Abraham (Ge 25:8), Isaac (Ge 35:29), David (1Ch 29:28) and Jehoiada the priest (2Ch 24:15). Job's long life is another way of God vindicating Job before other people and blessing him.

WHY A GOOD GOD ALLOWS SUFFERING
by Randy Alcorn

Romans 8:28 tells us that "in all things God works for the good of those who love him, who have been called according to his purpose." Yet it is hard to believe lines like this when we witness baffling, horrific events. The primary Old Testament illustration of Romans 8:28 is Genesis 50:20. In that story, Joseph's brothers betray him and sell him into slavery. Decades later he tells them, "You intended to harm me, but God intended it for good to accomplish what is now being done, the saving of many lives" (Ge 50:20).

THE CASE OF JOSEPH

With Joseph, God does more than just make the best of a bad situation; he uses it for ultimate good (compare Eph 1:11). Five chapters before declaring that "God planned it for good," Joseph said to his brothers, "So then, it was not you who sent me here, but God. He made me father to Pharaoh, lord of his entire household and ruler of all Egypt" (Ge 45:8). We see two wills at work here: Joseph's brothers successfully perpetrated evil, and God successfully brought about good from their evil. God sovereignly worked so that the moral evil they committed—and the evils that resulted—were dramatically reversed to achieve his good purposes. As Joni Eareckson Tada puts it, "God permits what he hates to achieve what he loves."

THE GOOD OF THE CROSS

The cross is God's answer to the question, "Why don't you do something about evil?" God did do something—and what he did was so powerful that it ripped in half, from top down, the fabric of the universe itself.

God does not merely empathize with our sufferings; he inserted himself into history through Jesus. What Jesus suffered, God suffered. God ordained and allowed Jesus' temporary suffering so he could prevent our eternal suffering.

Good Friday isn't called Bad Friday, because we see it in retrospect: We know that out of the appallingly bad came inexpressible good. And that good trumps the bad: Although the bad was temporary, the good is eternal. If someone had delivered Jesus from his suffering, Jesus could not have delivered us from ours (Isa 53:10–12; Ro 6:5).

SUFFERING AND GOD'S PURPOSES

Paul wrote, "For it has been granted to you on behalf of Christ not only to believe in him, but also to suffer for him" (Php 1:29). He said, "In fact, everyone who wants to live a godly life in Christ Jesus will be persecuted" (2Ti 3:12). Jesus noted, "In this world you will have trouble" (Jn 16:33).

Abel, who pleased God, was murdered by Cain. Noah, Abraham, Joseph, Moses, nearly all the prophets and many other Biblical figures suffered (compare Heb 11). As followers of Christ, believers routinely suffer, but God has a way of using it for his purposes. Every character in God's story serves a purpose, as do all characters in his story today—believers in Jesus.

Joseph, after being sold into slavery and later sent to prison on false accusations, surely had endured enough for one life. At times, he must have felt like giving up. Talk to Job in the middle of his story—ten children dead, his body covered with excruciating boils, feeling as if God abandoned him, and friends haranguing him. Job even says: "Why did I not perish at birth?" (Job 3:11). But Job also says that God "knows the way that I take; when he has tested me, I will come forth as gold" (Job 23:10). And later on Job remarks, "My ears had heard of you but now my eyes have seen you" (Job 42:5).

WORKING TOGETHER FOR GOOD

If each of us were to list both the best and worst things that have ever happened to us, we are bound to see overlap in the two lists—especially if we have lived for a long time. God has used some of the worst things to accomplish some of the best. Like these lists already show, Romans 8:28 is true, and someday, we will see how it was true all along—each time suffering came along.

BIBLICAL POETRY

I n spite of some ambiguity about where to draw the line between Hebrew poetry and prose, traditionally roughly a third of the Old Testament has been categorized as poetry. In addition to Psalms, many of the prophetic books and most Wisdom books are written in poetic form. The books of Song of Songs and Lamentations are also poetic. This overview covers the main features and most common forms of Hebrew poetry as reflected in Psalms, Song of Songs and Lamentations.

FEATURES OF BIBLICAL POETRY

Biblical poetry is characterized by the use of parallelism, a correspondence of related clauses. This tendency to reinforce a phrase by slight modification and repetition is a common feature of Biblical style in general, not just poetry; poetic style is characterized by terse, binary sentences with a high degree of parallelism.

The relationship between parallel clauses may be semantic (having to do with meaning), syntactic (having to do with the vocabulary and phrasing), thematic, or a combination of these. The classic types of parallelism are synonymous, antithetic and synthetic. Synonymous parallelism occurs with two or more clauses that restate essentially the same information. Antithetic parallelism labels clauses that present contrasting content. Synthetic parallelism is a catchall category for instances of parallelism that do not fit either of the other types.

FORMS OF BIBLICAL POETRY

The poetry found in Psalms and Lamentations may have been used in Israelite worship and follows some fairly consistent patterns. These patterns are commonly called "types," "genres" or "forms." The main forms are lament, thanksgiving, praise and royal psalms. Some psalms are historical surveys — poetic accounts of God's interactions with Israel (e.g., Ps 78). Other psalms appear to have functioned as liturgies sung as people entered the temple for worship (e.g., Ps 15; 24). Wisdom psalms praise the benefits of righteous living (e.g., Ps 37).

Lament Psalms
A lament psalm is a cry to God brought on by hardship or despair. Sometimes the complaint is presented on behalf of the entire community, but some complaints are motivated by individual situations. Lament psalms use common themes and stereotypical language to describe the experience of suffering. A typical lament psalm (e.g., Ps 10; 28; 59) may include the following parts (though the sequence and use of each varies): an address to God; a complaint; a request for help; a reason for God to help; a statement of confidence; an assertion of innocence; a confession of sin; and an expression of praise. Sometimes a psalmist insists that his suffering is unjust because he is innocent; in other cases a psalmist confesses that he had sinned but repents. A lament may conclude with a vow of praise — a promise to praise God after deliverance from hardship.

Thanksgiving Psalms
In some ways, a thanksgiving psalm is structured as a continuation or response to a lament. The lament usually ends with a promise to praise God, and the thanksgiving psalm fulfills that promise. Some

of the common parts of a thanksgiving psalm parallel segments of a lament psalm. A thanksgiving psalm typically includes a summary of adverse circumstances and a report of God's deliverance. The lament explains the circumstances and contains a request for God to deliver. The thanksgiving psalm is an expression of praise to God motivated by a particular experience of his grace (e.g., Ps 30; 116; 124). This structural connection with lament distinguishes thanksgiving psalms from psalms of praise.

Praise Psalms

Praise psalms (or hymns) celebrate the human experience of God's goodness. While thanksgiving psalms tend to offer praise to God for specific answers to prayer, praise psalms are general expressions celebrating God's attributes and his actions in creation. Enthronement psalms (e.g., Ps 47) and Zion hymns (e.g., Ps 48) are specific types of praise psalms. The former celebrate God as king of Israel and all creation; the latter celebrate God's choice of Zion as his earthly dwelling place. Praise psalms have a simple format: a call to praise, an expression of praise and a concluding call to praise (e.g., Ps 8; 29).

Royal Psalms

Royal psalms emphasize the role of a human king as God's chosen leader for Israel (e.g., Ps 20; 45; 72). These psalms celebrate kingship while presenting the king as dependent on God for success. Royal psalms do not have a typical format or even formulaic phrases, so the identification of a psalm as a royal psalm is based only on whether its content relates to human kingship in some way.

CONTEXT AND BACKGROUND

For much of Psalms, the social and historical context of its composition is unknown. Later scribes put headings on many of the psalms to indicate their intended usage, to provide musical notation or to assign a historical setting. The headings link nearly half of the psalms to King David, and all historical headings associate the psalm with an event from David's life.

The background of Song of Songs is also unknown. Traditionally the book was associated with Solomon and thought to contain expressions of love between King Solomon and one of his wives. However, the only overt connection with Solomon is the ambiguous opening heading identifying the book as the "Solomon's Song of Songs" (SS 1:1). Further, the Hebrew used in Song of Songs contains significant features of late classical Hebrew, suggesting the book dates to the Persian period or later. Song of Songs differs from all other types of Biblical poetry, but it has significant similarities with love poetry known throughout the ancient Near East (see Pope, Song of Songs, 54–85). The question of how poetry celebrating human love and sexuality fits with the rest of the Biblical text has motivated theological traditions in both Judaism and Christianity in which the book is read as an allegory of the love between God and his people.

The historical setting for the book of Lamentations is the period of national mourning following the destruction of Jerusalem and the temple in 586 BC. The poetry of Lamentations generally follows the lament format but emphasizes the experience of grief on a greater scale. The poet dramatically describes the disaster and attempts to make sense of the horror he has witnessed. Like a lament psalm, Lamentations includes elements expressing hope and confidence that God had not completely abandoned his people despite the crisis they were presently living through.

THEOLOGICAL THEMES

Biblical poetry reveals expressions that run the gamut of human emotion—from the depth of despair to the height of happiness. While poetic language employs vivid imagery to describe events

or themes of all kinds, most Biblical poetry can be organized around two: the experience of human suffering and the assertion of divine kingship.

Human Suffering

The lament psalms, the thanksgiving psalms and the book of Lamentations reflect the common experience of sin and evil for everyone living in a fallen world. The details change, but the experience is the same. This quality gives Biblical poetry a timelessness and near-universal applicability. Everyone, at some point, experiences some unfairness or injustice; everyone comes face to face with sin and its consequences. Since many of the lament psalms are essentially prayers to God for deliverance or forgiveness, these psalms continue to influence how people pray. But these psalms can also be bold expressions of personal torment and despair, revealing that it is healthy to put such feelings into words and also comforting us with the knowledge that others have felt similar pain. Further, it is important to realize that the emphasis on suffering and injustice in many psalms is never the final word.

Divine Kingship

The theme of divine kingship encompasses the ideas of God as a warrior, as the creator and as a righteous judge. Psalms praising God for his deliverance of Israel (e.g., Ps 78) and expressions of his power over creation (e.g., Ps 104) ultimately celebrate his lordship over the universe. Imagery of God as the divine warrior marching into battle on behalf of his people (e.g., Ps 68) similarly emphasizes his kingship over his chosen ones. Overall, the theme of divine kingship brings hope that someday God's reign will be perfectly restored and the circumstances that cause suffering and pain in the world will end.

BIBLICAL POETRY AND THE NEW TESTAMENT

While poetry is less common in the New Testament, many passages allude to the poetry of the Old Testament. One of the most famous songs of the New Testament—Mary's "Magnificat" in Lk 1:46–55—closely echoes the language and themes of Hannah's song in 1 Samuel 2. Both passages address Israel's need for deliverance and allude to God's plan to raise up a deliverer. Poetry's allusiveness—its ability to evoke images and associations—enriched the interpretation of poetry as prophecy, so lines from Psalms are quoted as fulfilled in Jesus' life just as easily as Isaiah or Jeremiah (e.g., Ps 22:18 in Jn 19:24 or Ps 109:3 in Jn 15:25). Royal psalms—like Psalm 2—especially were given new significance when interpreted as references to the Messiah (e.g., Ac 13:33; Heb 5:5). Hebrews 1:5–14 links line after line of Old Testament poetry (including Ps 2:7; 45:6–7; 104:4; and 2Sa 7:14) to express the Son's superiority over all other heavenly beings and establish his right to kingship at the right hand of God. The New Testament writers make use of the poetry of the Bible to reveal that the Messiah has come, fulfilling the Old Testament longing for the restored reign of God.

Douglas Mangum

PSALMS

INTRODUCTION TO PSALMS

The book of Psalms in modern Protestant Bibles includes 150 poetic compositions meant to be sung or spoken by God's people. The psalms are directed at Yahweh as listener and are intended to express the full range of human emotion for various individual and group settings, such as praise, thanksgiving, petition and lament. Psalms was Israel's book of worship and is meant to guide God's people from generation to generation.

BACKGROUND

The English title Psalms comes from the Greek word *psalmos*—the name for the book in the Septuagint (the Greek translation of the OT). The psalms were collected over a long period and written by different people. Many include a heading, with the most common being translated as "of David." While this could indicate that David is the author of these psalms, the original Hebrew text is ambiguous; these psalms could have been written about, to, for or in honor of David.

Outside of these tributes to specific moments in Israel's history (at the beginning of some psalms), the psalms rarely mention a specific occasion affiliated with their composition. Instead, the psalms' language is open-ended, reflecting their intended ongoing use in the community—in worship gatherings, coronations, festivals and as individual prayers. Many psalms mention the specific liturgies or rituals in which they were to be used, and many contain clues that indicate they were likely used at the temple or for particular processions and sacrifices. The inclusion of musical terms in some psalms suggests that many were performed with musical accompaniment and even with particular instruments.

The titles and content of the psalms shows that they were an ongoing part of Israel's history. There are many that likely date to the united monarchy under David and Solomon (10th century BC), and some of the earliest psalms could date to the time of Moses (15th or 13th century BC; see Ps 90). There are also some that date to the Babylonian exile or a little later (sixth century BC; see Ps 137).

Various groupings within the Psalter indicate that there were collections of psalms in existence prior to the current form of the collection—such as the psalms of the sons of Korah (Ps 42–49; 84–85; 87–88), the prayers of David (72:20), and the Songs of Ascents (Ps 120–134). By the time of the Dead Sea Scrolls (ca. 250 BC–AD 50), Psalms as a collection had become part of one scroll, but the Psalms manuscripts found among the Dead Sea Scrolls show that the precise order and extent of the collection was still in flux. Jesus refers generally to "the Psalms," showing the authority of the collection in the first century AD (Lk 24:44).

STRUCTURE

The psalms are often deeply personal and are intentionally crafted literary works, not impromptu expressions. The majority of the psalms reflect ancient poetic conventions, including intricate structures and literary allusions.

As a whole, Psalms functions as an ancient book of prayers and hymns, with different kinds of songs or poetic compositions for different occasions. Liturgies were used for festivals in ancient Israel, such as Passover and the Festival of Weeks. Royal psalms celebrated the king's coronation, while other psalms honored God's kingship. There were songs of thanksgiving, as well as two kinds of laments—for individuals and for the community. Some psalms were written to be sung on pilgrimages to Jerusalem, and others were intended to celebrate Yahweh's presence in Jerusalem. Many of the psalms recall Yahweh's gracious actions toward Israel throughout its history, and some look forward to God's messiah—finding their ultimate fulfillment in Jesus.

Psalms is organized into five sections called "books." These probably were intended to mirror the Pentateuch, the first five books of the Bible. These main sections contain smaller groupings of psalms, such as the Songs of Ascents (Ps 120–134).

OUTLINE

- Book One (1–41)
- Book Two (42–72)
- Book Three (73–89)
- Book Four (90–106)
- Book Five (107–150)

Dates Related to Psalms

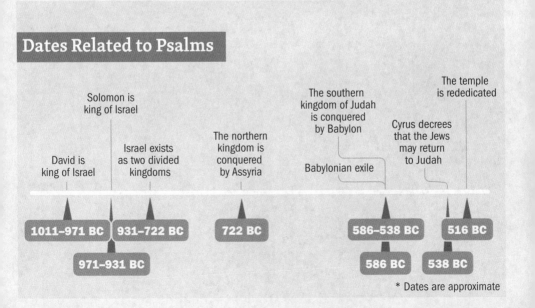

David is king of Israel — 1011–971 BC

971–931 BC

Solomon is king of Israel

Israel exists as two divided kingdoms — 931–722 BC

The northern kingdom is conquered by Assyria — 722 BC

The southern kingdom of Judah is conquered by Babylon

Babylonian exile — 586–538 BC

586 BC

Cyrus decrees that the Jews may return to Judah — 538 BC

The temple is rededicated — 516 BC

* Dates are approximate

THEMES

The psalms provide patterns of praise, worship and lament for God's people from generation to generation. As communal prayers, the psalms show worshipers how to articulate joyful praise and distressed cries — serving to teach believers and provide words for them to express their feelings to Yahweh. Hymns and temple liturgies prepare Yahweh's followers to experience the presence of the cosmic king. Laments implore Yahweh for compassion. Petitions plead with him to intervene in the world. These motifs illustrate the character of Yahweh, who involves himself in the messiness of human affairs and acts mightily on his people's behalf.

The psalms directly address Yahweh while conveying truths about him. No matter what we're experiencing, these ancient compositions provide us with powerful words, inviting us to pour out our hearts before the God of the universe.

BOOK I

Psalms 1–41

Psalm 1

¹ Blessed is the one
    who does not walk in step with the
        wicked
or stand in the way that sinners take
    or sit in the company of mockers,
² but whose delight is in the law of the Lord,
    and who meditates on his law day and
        night.
³ That person is like a tree planted by streams
        of water,
    which yields its fruit in season
and whose leaf does not wither —
    whatever they do prospers.

⁴ Not so the wicked!
    They are like chaff
    that the wind blows away.

⁵ Therefore the wicked will not stand in the
        judgment,
    nor sinners in the assembly of the
        righteous.

⁶ For the Lord watches over the way of the
        righteous,
    but the way of the wicked leads to
        destruction.

Psalm 2

¹ Why do the nations conspire[a]
    and the peoples plot in vain?
² The kings of the earth rise up
    and the rulers band together
    against the Lord and against his anointed,
        saying,
³ "Let us break their chains
    and throw off their shackles."

⁴ The One enthroned in heaven laughs;
    the Lord scoffs at them.

---

a 1 Hebrew; Septuagint *rage*

1:1–6 The book of Psalms was formed over a long period of time. Various groupings within the Psalter—such as the "Songs of Ascents" (Ps 120–134), the "psalms of the sons of Korah" (Ps 42–49; 84–85; 87–88), and the "prayers of David the son of Jesse" (72:20)—indicate that there were earlier collections before the book took its present shape. The titles and content of many psalms also hint at the long history of these songs, prayers and poems. Some may date to the time of Moses (fifteenth or thirteenth century BC; see Ps 90), many date to the united monarchy under David and Solomon (tenth century BC) and some were written during the Babylonian exile or later (sixth century BC; see Ps 137). Psalms is Israel's book of worship. See the table "Types of Psalms" on p. 830.

In its final shape, the book of Psalms is divided into five sections, the first four of which end in a similar doxology (see 41:13; 72:19; 89:52; 106:48). This first psalm, as an introduction to these "five books"—an echo of the five books of Torah or Pentateuch (the first five books of the Bible)—encourages readers to allow these songs to guide them toward wisdom and worship, granting them a place in the assembly of the righteous (1:5–6).

Psalm 1 is a wisdom psalm that describes and contrasts the way of the righteous and the way of the wicked. It first describes the character of the righteous (vv. 1–2) and their fate (v. 3), it continues with the fate of the wicked (vv. 4–5) and concludes with a statement describing Yahweh's role in their respective fates (v. 6).

1:1 Blessed The Hebrew term used here, *ashre*, describes someone who is privileged or happy. Wisdom Literature commonly uses this expression to indicate someone who is fortunate or privileged (Job 5:17; Pr 3:13; 28:14). Its Greek equivalent—*makarios*—is found in Jesus' beatitudes (Mt 5:3–11). **does not walk in step with** The three functions described here—counsel, way and seat—emphasize that the righteous avoid thinking like, behaving like and dealing with the wicked. **mockers** This common Hebrew Wisdom Literature term, *zed*, describes an arrogant fool who refuses discipline and correction (Pr 13:1; 15:12; 21:24).

1:2 meditates The Hebrew word used here, *hagah*, means "to murmur" or "read aloud." It has the connotation of pondering over something. Meditating on the Law—the first five books of the Bible—should result in obedience (Jos 1:8).

1:4 chaff The husks and stalks of wheat blown away by the wind as grain is winnowed. In contrast to the stable, flourishing tree of the righteous, the wicked are fragile and temporary (Isa 29:5; Hos 13:3).

1:6 the Lord watches over the way The way of the righteous extends beyond knowledge to a deep level of understanding (Ps 139:23–24). **the way of the wicked leads to destruction** This can refer to ultimate destruction (9:6; 37:20) or to the frustration of hopes or plans (112:10).

2:1–12 Classified as a royal psalm, Ps 2 was most likely used to celebrate the coronation of a new king. Because of its reference to the Messiah, it is quoted often in the NT. The psalmist first describes the plans the nations make against Yahweh (vv. 1–3), then shows Yahweh's mocking reaction (vv. 4–6). After presenting the decree of Yahweh as he establishes his king (vv. 7–9), the psalmist warns the plotting nations to serve Yahweh and the newly established king (vv. 10–12). See the table "Messianic Psalms" on p. 847; see the table "Types of Psalms" on p. 830.

2:1 nations Refers to hostile Gentile (non-Jewish) nations. **vain** The psalmist does not just describe the rebellious plot—he questions it and concludes it to be pointless. The Hebrew term used here, *riq*, describes a futile activity, one that expends energy without any positive result (Lev 26:16,20).

2:2 anointed This can refer to any king anointed by Yahweh. Opposing a king anointed by Yahweh amounted to opposing God himself (2Sa 14–16). The apostles apply this passage to the death of Jesus (Ac 4:25–27). The Hebrew word used here in Ps 2, *mashiach*, is the word from which the term "Messiah" is derived. It is the Hebrew equivalent of the Greek *christos*, often translated as "Christ."

5 He rebukes them in his anger
    and terrifies them in his wrath, saying,
6 "I have installed my king
    on Zion, my holy mountain."

7 I will proclaim the LORD's decree:

He said to me, "You are my son;
    today I have become your father.
8 Ask me,
    and I will make the nations your
        inheritance,
    the ends of the earth your
        possession.

9 You will break them with a rod of iron ᵃ;
    you will dash them to pieces like pottery."

10 Therefore, you kings, be wise;
    be warned, you rulers of the earth.
11 Serve the LORD with fear
    and celebrate his rule with trembling.
12 Kiss his son, or he will be angry
    and your way will lead to your
        destruction,
    for his wrath can flare up in a moment.
    Blessed are all who take refuge in him.

ᵃ 9 Or *will rule them with an iron scepter* (see Septuagint and Syriac)

2:4 One enthroned in heaven laughs Yahweh reacts to this rebellion not with concern, but with laughter. Knowing the outcome, Yahweh ridicules their efforts (Ps 37:13).
2:5 He rebukes them in his anger Disobedience triggers Yahweh's anger (Dt 11:16–17; 29:24–28; Ps 78:21–22) and often results in disaster (Dt 11:17; 2Ki 23:26–27; Ps 60:1–3).
2:6 installed my king Yahweh announces the installation of his anointed king. Compare note on 2:2. **my holy mountain** A reference to the temple mount (15:1; 24:3).
2:7 You are my son Yahweh's decree reiterates the Davidic covenant, in which Yahweh is the Davidic king's "father" (2Sa 7:14). This phrase is quoted or alluded to several times in the NT. Paul connects it to the resurrec-

tion of Jesus in Ac 13:33. The author of Hebrews quotes it twice (Heb 1:5; 5:5).
2:8 Ask me The king's privileged position enables him to ask Yahweh to extend his rule. The nations plotting together against Yahweh's king can be delivered to the king at his request.
2:9 a rod of iron Symbolizing authority and power (Ps 110:2; Ge 49:10).
2:11 Serve the LORD with fear The psalmist warns the nations (mentioned in Ps 2:1–3) to give up their futile plots and serve Yahweh.
2:12 Kiss his son An indication of allegiance (1Sa 10:1; 1Ki 19:18). **Blessed are all who take refuge** See note on Ps 1:1.

Types of Psalms

TYPE	DESCRIPTION	EXAMPLES
Enthronement	A psalm that celebrates God's kingship	Ps 24; 47; 93; 96–99
Historical	A type of praise psalm that recounts God's actions throughout history	Ps 78; 105; 106; 114; 135; 136
Corporate Lament	A cry to God from the community	Ps 12; 44; 58; 74; 80; 83; 94; 123; 126; 137
Individual Lament	A cry to God from an individual	Ps 3; 6; 13; 16; 22; 31; 57; 56; 102; 142
Pilgrimage	A psalm intended to be sung on pilgrimage to Jerusalem	Ps 120–134
Royal	A psalm on behalf of the king	Ps 2; 20; 21; 45; 72; 89; 110; 132
Song of Zion	A psalm that focuses on Yahweh's presence in Jerusalem	Ps 46; 76; 84; 87; 122
Temple Entry	A psalm intended to be sung as the worshiper enters the temple	Ps 15; 24; 26; 101
Thanksgiving	A psalm intended to express gratitude to God	Ps 18; 21; 30; 34; 40; 92; 107; 118; 138; 144
Wisdom	A psalm that shows a similarity to Wisdom literature	Ps 14; 36; 37; 49; 73; 112; 119; 127; 128; 133
Praise	A psalm intended to praise God for his attributes	Ps 8; 21; 33; 103; 111; 115; 135; 145–150

Psalm 3[a]

A psalm of David. When he fled from his son Absalom.

[1] LORD, how many are my foes!
    How many rise up against me!
[2] Many are saying of me,
    "God will not deliver him."[b]

[3] But you, LORD, are a shield around me,
    my glory, the One who lifts my head
        high.
[4] I call out to the LORD,
    and he answers me from his holy
        mountain.

[5] I lie down and sleep;
    I wake again, because the LORD
        sustains me.
[6] I will not fear though tens of thousands
    assail me on every side.

[7] Arise, LORD!
    Deliver me, my God!
  Strike all my enemies on the jaw;
    break the teeth of the wicked.

[8] From the LORD comes deliverance.
    May your blessing be on your people.

Psalm 4[c]

For the director of music. With stringed instruments. A psalm of David.

[1] Answer me when I call to you,
    my righteous God.
  Give me relief from my distress;
    have mercy on me and hear my
        prayer.

[2] How long will you people turn my glory
    into shame?
  How long will you love delusions and
    seek false gods[d]?[e]
[3] Know that the LORD has set apart his
    faithful servant for himself;
    the LORD hears when I call to him.

[4] Tremble and[f] do not sin;
    when you are on your beds,
    search your hearts and be silent.
[5] Offer the sacrifices of the righteous
    and trust in the LORD.

---

[a] In Hebrew texts 3:1-8 is numbered 3:2-9.   [b] 2 The Hebrew has *Selah* (a word of uncertain meaning) here and at the end of verses 4 and 8.   [c] In Hebrew texts 4:1-8 is numbered 4:2-9.
[d] 2 Or *seek lies*   [e] 2 The Hebrew has *Selah* (a word of uncertain meaning) here and at the end of verse 4.   [f] 4 Or *In your anger* (see Septuagint)

3:title–8 In this individual lament psalm the psalmist is someone under personal attack. The entire psalm is addressed to Yahweh. The psalmist first describes the situation (vv. 1–2), then expresses confidence in Yahweh to protect and sustain him (vv. 3–6). Finally, he petitions Yahweh to deliver him (vv. 7–8). See the table "Types of Psalms" on p. 830.

3:title A psalm The Hebrew word used here, *mizmor*, is one of several names for compositions within the psalter. A *mizmor* is a song that is usually accompanied by a musical instrument. **of David** David is associated with the authorship of the Psalms as a whole. However, the Hebrew phrase often translated as "of David" (*ledawid*) does not necessarily indicate authorship. The Hebrew preposition *lamedh* (*le-*) can mean "to," "for," "by" or "about." This makes it unclear whether the phrase "of David" in psalm titles means that the psalm was written "by David" or "for David" or was dedicated "to David." In addition, the psalm titles were most likely added later. **he fled from his son Absalom** The story of David fleeing Absalom is found in 2Sa 15–18.
3:3 a shield around me The psalmist trusts Yahweh to protect him like a shield—a common metaphor for God's protection (Ps 7:10; 18:2,30; 28:7). **One who lifts my head high** A lifted head signaled confidence and pride (27:6), while a lowered head signaled defeat and disgrace (Jdg 8:28).
3:4 his holy mountain Refers to the temple mount—Mount Zion—the place where Yahweh established his king (Ps 2:6).
3:5 I lie down and sleep The psalmist is so confident of Yahweh's protection that he leaves himself defenseless, despite his multitude of enemies.
3:7 Arise, LORD After expressing confidence in Yahweh, the psalmist petitions Yahweh to act.

4:title–8 In this individual lament psalm, the psalmist opens and closes by addressing God. He opens with a petition for God to hear his prayer (v. 1). He addresses his enemies, lamenting their treatment of him (v. 2), and he encourages them to turn to Yahweh (vv. 3–5). The psalmist concludes by addressing Yahweh and expressing trust in him (vv. 6–8).

4:title director of music The meaning of the Hebrew word used here, *menatseach*, often translated as "choirmaster," is uncertain. It derives from the verb *natsach* ("to inspect"), which is connected to the temple and its activities. **With stringed instruments** Several variations of stringed instruments were in use in the OT. See note on 92:3. **A psalm of David** See note on 3:title.
4:1 Answer me A common exclamation in the Psalms (e.g., 13:3; 27:7; 55:2; 86:1; 143:7). Appealing to God's righteousness, the psalmist finds confidence in examples of God's deliverance. **righteous** Using the Hebrew word *tsedeq*, the psalmist describes God as righteous or as the basis for his righteousness. He hopes God, as a righteous judge, will see his innocence and vindicate him.

Psalm 4:1

TSEDEQ
The word *tsedeq* refers to what is right; it can mean righteousness (132:9) or justice (Lev 19:15). Job used *tsedeq* to refer to his vindication or declaration of righteousness (Job 6:29). In the Psalms, *tsedeq* often refers to God's righteous or just judgment (Ps 9:8; 96:13).

4:2 you people These people may be causing the psalmist's distress or merely exacerbating it.

⁶ Many, Lord, are asking, "Who will bring us
  prosperity?"
Let the light of your face shine on us.
⁷ Fill my heart with joy
  when their grain and new wine
    abound.

⁸ In peace I will lie down and sleep,
  for you alone, Lord,
  make me dwell in safety.

Psalm 5ᵃ

For the director of music. For pipes. A psalm of David.

¹ Listen to my words, Lord,
  consider my lament.
² Hear my cry for help,
  my King and my God,
  for to you I pray.

³ In the morning, Lord, you hear my
    voice;
  in the morning I lay my requests
    before you
  and wait expectantly.
⁴ For you are not a God who is pleased with
    wickedness;
  with you, evil people are not welcome.

⁵ The arrogant cannot stand
  in your presence.
You hate all who do wrong;
⁶   you destroy those who tell lies.
The bloodthirsty and deceitful
  you, Lord, detest.
⁷ But I, by your great love,
  can come into your house;
in reverence I bow down
  toward your holy temple.

⁸ Lead me, Lord, in your righteousness
  because of my enemies —
  make your way straight before me.
⁹ Not a word from their mouth can be trusted;
  their heart is filled with malice.
Their throat is an open grave;
  with their tongues they tell lies.
¹⁰ Declare them guilty, O God!
  Let their intrigues be their downfall.
Banish them for their many sins,
  for they have rebelled against you.
¹¹ But let all who take refuge in you be glad;
  let them ever sing for joy.
Spread your protection over them,
  that those who love your name may rejoice
    in you.

ᵃ In Hebrew texts 5:1-12 is numbered 5:2-13.

4:3 set apart his faithful servant for himself The psalmist answers his enemies by confidently affirming that Yahweh will answer him.
4:4 Tremble The Hebrew word used here, *ragaz*, means "to tremble," usually from fear (99:1; Ex 15:14; Mic 7:17). Paul quotes the Septuagint (ancient Greek translation of the OT) version of this verse in Eph 4:26; the Septuagint uses the Greek term *orgizō,* meaning "to be angry."
4:5 Offer the sacrifices of the righteous After meditating, the psalmist's enemies should repent by offering sacrifices of righteousness and putting their trust in Yahweh. Right sacrifices—literally "sacrifices of righteousness" in the Hebrew—can refer to any sacrifices required by the law (Dt 33:19). They probably refer specifically to sacrifices accompanied by righteous behavior or obedience (Ps 51:19).
4:6 Let the light of your face shine The psalmist pleads for Yahweh to reveal himself. This reflects the priestly blessing of Nu 6:24–26. The Hebrew word used here, *paneh* (often translated as "face"), is used in this context and elsewhere in the OT to describe both the face and the presence of God: Adam and Eve hid from the presence of God in the Garden of Eden (Ge 3:8); Yahweh spoke face to face with Moses (Ex 33:11). In the Psalms, Yahweh's presence is accompanied by joy (Ps 16:11; 21:6).
4:8 In peace Just as he has in the past (v. 1), Yahweh has responded, enabling the psalmist to sleep in safety.

5:title–12 An individual lament psalm, this psalm opens with the psalmist's petition for Yahweh to hear him (vv. 1–3). He then appeals to God's justice, drawing a contrast between the wicked (vv. 4–6) and himself (v. 7). Continuing this contrast, the psalmist asks Yahweh to guide and protect him (v. 8) while destroying the wicked (vv. 9–10). He finally broadens his scope, petitioning God to protect and bless the righteous (vv. 11–12).

5:title director of music See note on 4:title. **A psalm of David** See note on 3:title.
5:1 lament The Hebrew term used here, *hagig*, occurs only here and in 39:3 in the OT. It signifies a desperate sigh or groaning, indicating the psalmist's great turmoil.
5:4 not a God who is pleased with wickedness The psalmist appeals to God's justice and describes God's negative attitude toward evil in several different ways. By not responding to the psalmist's cries, God would validate his enemies.
5:7 can come into your house In contrast to his enemies, the psalmist pledges to enter into God's presence and worship reverently in the temple. The psalmist bases this confidence on God's faithful, covenantal love (Ex 34:6). **in reverence** Fearing God in the OT describes the proper human response to God's character and holiness—showing him reverence. It includes obedience and trust (Dt 6:2; Ps 40:3).
5:8 Lead me, Lord To be led by Yahweh is to enjoy his protection and safety (23:3; Isa 42:16). The psalmists frequently appeal to Yahweh's righteousness when asking for deliverance (e.g., Ps 31:1; 71:2; 143:1), because it is often contrasted with wickedness (1:6)—showing God's hatred for evil (45:7).
5:9 Not a word from their mouth can be trusted Since God ultimately destroys those who unrepentantly live their lives as liars (v. 6), God should respond to the psalmist and deliver him from these enemies.
5:10 they have rebelled against you As he emphasizes the guilt of his enemies, the psalmist focuses on their actions toward God.
5:11 let all who take refuge in you be glad God's protection results in joy.

[12] Surely, LORD, you bless the righteous;
　　you surround them with your favor as with
　　　a shield.

Psalm 6[a]

*For the director of music. With stringed instruments.
According to sheminith.[b] A psalm of David.*

[1] LORD, do not rebuke me in your anger
　　or discipline me in your wrath.
[2] Have mercy on me, LORD, for I am faint;
　　heal me, LORD, for my bones are in agony.
[3] My soul is in deep anguish.
　　How long, LORD, how long?

[4] Turn, LORD, and deliver me;
　　save me because of your unfailing love.
[5] Among the dead no one proclaims your
　　　name.
　　Who praises you from the grave?

[6] I am worn out from my groaning.

All night long I flood my bed with weeping
　　and drench my couch with tears.

[7] My eyes grow weak with sorrow;
　　they fail because of all my foes.

[8] Away from me, all you who do evil,
　　for the LORD has heard my weeping.
[9] The LORD has heard my cry for mercy;
　　the LORD accepts my prayer.
[10] All my enemies will be overwhelmed with
　　　shame and anguish;
　　they will turn back and suddenly be put
　　　to shame.

Psalm 7[c]

*A shiggaion[d] of David, which he sang to
the LORD concerning Cush, a Benjamite.*

[1] LORD my God, I take refuge in you;
　　save and deliver me from all who pursue me,
[2] or they will tear me apart like a lion
　　and rip me to pieces with no one to
　　　rescue me.

---

[a] In Hebrew texts 6:1-10 is numbered 6:2-11.　　*[b]* Title: Probably
a musical term　　*[c]* In Hebrew texts 7:1-17 is numbered 7:2-18.
[d] Title: Probably a literary or musical term

5:12 you bless the righteous The psalmist closes with a statement upholding Yahweh's protection and blessing on the righteous, which contrast sharply with God's treatment of the psalmist's wicked enemies (vv. 4–6).

6:title–10 This individual lament psalm is also included among the seven penitential psalms, which have been popular in Christian worship since the early church (Ps 32; 38; 51; 102; 130; 143). The psalmist first appeals to Yahweh for forgiveness and grace (6:1–3). He then appeals for deliverance (vv. 4–5), and describes the intensity of his suffering (vv. 6–7). The psalm closes on a hopeful note as the psalmist rebukes his enemies, confident Yahweh has heard his cries (vv. 8–10). See the table "Types of Psalms" on p. 830.

6:title director of music See note on 4:title. **According to sheminith** The Hebrew word used here, *sheminith*, is a technical term that refers to the manner of musical accompaniment. It is related to the word *shemoneh*, meaning "eight"; it may mean an instrument with eight strings or indicate the tune or key of the psalm. **A psalm of David** See note on 3:title.

6:1 do not rebuke me in your anger The same opening phrase as Ps 38. Yahweh's discipline is usually seen in the OT as a positive way of receiving instruction (94:12; Job 5:17; Pr 3:12). However, the emphasis here is not on Yahweh's discipline in general, but on the method and severity of the discipline.

6:3 My soul The Hebrew word used here, *nephesh*, while often translated "soul" can also mean "life" (see note on Ge 1:20–25); the psalmist worried for his life. **How long** This cry is common in lament psalms (e.g., Ps 13:1; 35:17; 74:10; 90:13).

6:4 Turn, LORD The psalmist emphatically petitions Yahweh for deliverance. Using three different Hebrew terms that can be translated "turn" (*shuv*), "deliver" (*chalats*) and "save" (*yasha'*), the psalmist appeals to Yahweh to deliver his life (*nephesh* in Hebrew; see note on 6:3). The Hebrew word *shuv* ("turn") often describes Yahweh turning away from his anger (2Ki 23:26; Jnh 3:9). The

psalmist wanted Yahweh to turn his anger and discipline away and restore him.

6:5 Among the dead no one proclaims The psalmist gives a second reason for Yahweh to act: Death will prevent him from publicly proclaiming Yahweh's deliverance (Ps 30:9; 115:17). **the grave** The Hebrew text here uses *she'ol*, the Hebrew word for the realm of the dead (the underworld). See note on Job 14:13.

6:8 the LORD has heard The psalmist can rebuke his enemies because of his trust in Yahweh's response. Individual lament psalms often end with a transition from lament to praise, as the psalmist expresses confidence in God's response (Ps 22:24; 28:6; 31:21–22).

6:10 overwhelmed with shame and anguish Yahweh's restoration of the psalmist brings shame to his enemies. The great trouble that affected the psalmist's life (6:3) will now be on his enemies.

7:title–17 In this individual lament psalm, the psalmist petitions Yahweh for justice. He opens the psalm with a plea for Yahweh to deliver him from his enemies (vv. 1–2). He then claims innocence, saying if he is guilty, Yahweh should allow his enemies to destroy him (vv. 3–5). He again petitions Yahweh to deliver him by righteously administering justice (vv. 6–9). In the second half of the psalm, the psalmist discusses the righteous judgment of God (vv. 10–13) and the fate of the wicked (vv. 14–16). He concludes with a note of praise for Yahweh's righteousness (v. 17).

7:title A shiggaion The Hebrew word used here also occurs in Hab 3:1. It may come from the verb *shagah*, meaning "to wander," but its precise meaning is unknown. **of David** See note on Ps 3:title.

7:1 I take refuge in you Like many individual lament psalms, this one opens with an appeal to Yahweh (3:1; 6:1). **all who pursue me** The Hebrew word used here, *radaph*, is commonly used in the Psalms for the psalmist's opponents (31:15; 119:157).

7:2 they will tear me apart like a lion Enemies are often compared to lions in psalms (e.g., 22:13; 57:4).

³ Lord my God, if I have done this
  and there is guilt on my hands —
⁴ if I have repaid my ally with evil
  or without cause have robbed my foe —
⁵ then let my enemy pursue and overtake me;
  let him trample my life to the ground
  and make me sleep in the dust.ᵃ

⁶ Arise, Lord, in your anger;
  rise up against the rage of my enemies.
  Awake, my God; decree justice.
⁷ Let the assembled peoples gather around you,
  while you sit enthroned over them on high.
⁸   Let the Lord judge the peoples.
Vindicate me, Lord, according to my
    righteousness,
  according to my integrity, O Most High.
⁹ Bring to an end the violence of the wicked
  and make the righteous secure —
you, the righteous God
  who probes minds and hearts.

¹⁰ My shieldᵇ is God Most High,
  who saves the upright in heart.
¹¹ God is a righteous judge,
  a God who displays his wrath every day.
¹² If he does not relent,
  heᶜ will sharpen his sword;
  he will bend and string his bow.

¹³ He has prepared his deadly weapons;
  he makes ready his flaming arrows.

¹⁴ Whoever is pregnant with evil
  conceives trouble and gives birth to
    disillusionment.
¹⁵ Whoever digs a hole and scoops it out
  falls into the pit they have made.
¹⁶ The trouble they cause recoils on them;
  their violence comes down on their own
    heads.

¹⁷ I will give thanks to the Lord because of his
    righteousness;
  I will sing the praises of the name of the
    Lord Most High.

Psalm 8ᵈ

For the director of music. According to gittith.ᵉ
A psalm of David.

¹ Lord, our Lord,
  how majestic is your name in all the earth!

You have set your glory
  in the heavens.

ᵃ 5 The Hebrew has *Selah* (a word of uncertain meaning) here.
ᵇ 10 Or *sovereign*   ᶜ 12 Or *If anyone does not repent, / God*
ᵈ In Hebrew texts 8:1-9 is numbered 8:2-10.   ᵉ Title: Probably a musical term

---

Like lions, they wait eagerly for a chance to attack and destroy their prey (compare 10:9; 17:12). In the ancient Near East, lions were considered one of the mightiest animals (Pr 30:30). People who killed them were upheld as heroes (Jdg 14:5–7; 1Sa 17:34–37; 1Ch 11:22). Lions were also sometimes the agents of Yahweh's judgment (1Ki 20:36; 2Ki 17:25).

7:3 if I have done this The psalmist proclaims his innocence here and pronounces curses on himself if he is found guilty. Job—who was also unjustly afflicted—concludes his speeches with a much longer oath of innocence. See Job 31:1–40 and note.

7:5 let my enemy pursue The psalmist now pronounces his curse.

7:6 Arise, Lord, in your anger Since the psalmist believes he is innocent, he petitions Yahweh to defend him against his enemies. Yahweh's anger is usually a response to disobedience—specifically to Israel breaking the covenant (Dt 11:16–17; 29:24–28; Ps 78:21–22). It is sometimes a response to enemy nations (2:5; Jer 50:13; Na 1:2). Yahweh's anger is closely related to his righteousness and judgment since he ultimately punishes the wicked (see Ps 1:6 and note). While his anger can result in severe punishment (Dt 11:17; Ps 60:1–3), it abates quickly when the disobedient repent (Jer 3:12; Mic 7:18). **Awake, my God** Individual lament psalms often include requests for God to wake up (Ps 35:23; 44:23).

7:8 Vindicate me, Lord Having declared his innocence, the psalmist believes any judgment from Yahweh will reveal only that he, the psalmist, does not deserve the suffering he is experiencing.

7:9 make the righteous secure God's righteous judgment includes both negative and positive aspects—punishing the wicked and establishing the righteous.

7:12 he does not relent While repentance prompts Yahweh to turn away his anger (see note on 7:6), those who do not repent will feel the result of his righteous judgment (see note on 1:6).

7:15 falls into the pit The wicked are often described as victims of their own devices (57:6; 141:10; Pr 26:27; 28:10). Such results can be seen as both self-induced and as a form of judgment from God (Ps 9:15–16).

7:17 I will give thanks to the Lord because of his righteousness As with other individual lament psalms, the psalmist anticipates Yahweh's answer and favorable response (see note on 6:8). **Lord Most High** The Hebrew name for God used here, *yhwh elyon*, emphasizes Yahweh's supremacy as ruler and judge over the earth. See note on 9:2.

8:title–9 Declarations of Yahweh's majesty frame this hymn of praise (vv. 1,9). In this praise psalm, the psalmist notes God's special role for humanity in creation. He begins by proclaiming God's glory (vv. 1–2), then examines the remarkable work of God and is amazed that God even gives thought to the people he created (vv. 3–4). The psalmist then praises God for glorifying and placing humanity above the rest of creation (vv. 5–8). See the table "Types of Psalms" on p. 830.

8:title director of music See note on 4:title. *gittith* Also appears in the headings of Ps 81 and 84. It probably refers to an instrument or tune. "Gittith" may alternatively refer to a winepress (and therefore perhaps the harvest), someone or something from Gath or even a person (see 1Ch 13:13–14). **A psalm of David** See note on Ps 3:title.

8:1 Lord, our Lord The first Hebrew word used here, *yhwh*, is God's personal covenant name to Israel, Yahweh

2 Through the praise of children and
        infants
    you have established a stronghold against
        your enemies,
    to silence the foe and the avenger.
3 When I consider your heavens,
    the work of your fingers,
  the moon and the stars,
    which you have set in place,
4 what is mankind that you are mindful
        of them,
    human beings that you care for
        them?[a]

5 You have made them[b] a little lower than the
        angels[c]
    and crowned them[b] with glory and
        honor.
6 You made them rulers over the works of
        your hands;
    you put everything under their[d] feet:
7 all flocks and herds,
    and the animals of the wild,

8 the birds in the sky,
    and the fish in the sea,
    all that swim the paths of the seas.

9 LORD, our Lord,
    how majestic is your name in all the earth!

Psalm 9[e,f]

*For the director of music. To the tune of
"The Death of the Son." A psalm of David.*

1 I will give thanks to you, LORD, with all my
        heart;
    I will tell of all your wonderful deeds.
2 I will be glad and rejoice in you;
    I will sing the praises of your name,
        O Most High.

a 4 Or *what is a human being that you are mindful of him, / a
son of man that you care for him?*   b 5 Or *him*   c 5 Or *than
God*   d 6 Or *made him ruler . . . ; / . . . his*   e Psalms 9 and
10 may originally have been a single acrostic poem in which
alternating lines began with the successive letters of the Hebrew
alphabet. In the Septuagint they constitute one psalm.   f In
Hebrew texts 9:1-20 is numbered 9:2-21.

(see note on Ex 3:14). The second Hebrew word, *adon*,
conveys the sense of "master." This statement declares
that Yahweh is the master or ruler over the psalmist and
God's people. **You have set your glory in the heavens**
This Hebrew phrase used here could indicate that the
heavens are the place where God in his glory dwells or
that the heavens celebrate God's glory. It seems that
both options appear elsewhere (Ps 19:1; 113:4).
8:2 children and infants The Hebrew words used here,
olel and *yoneq*, both typically refer to nursing infants (1Ki
3:21), but can indicate children up to three years of age.
you have established a stronghold The psalmist
contrasts the weakness of infants with the enemies of
God. He declares that even the words of the most helpless about God are used by God to defend his people.
The Septuagint (the ancient Greek translation of the OT)
translates the Hebrew word *oz* used here (translated as
"strength" or "stronghold") with the Greek word *ainos*
("praise"). Jesus quotes the Greek translation of this
verse when children praise him (Mt 21:15–16).
8:3 your fingers The finger of God symbolizes his power:
Pharaoh's magicians attributed the third plague to the
finger of God (Ex 8:19); the finger of God wrote the law
on stone tablets (Ex 31:18; Dt 9:10); and in the NT,
Jesus cast out demons by the finger of God (Lk 11:20).
8:5 angels The Hebrew word used here, *elohim*, often refers to God, but it can also refer to other spiritual beings,
such as the gods or angels (Ps 82:1,6). The Septuagint
(the ancient Greek translation of the OT) translated the
term here as *angelous* (meaning "angels"). Understood
this way, the psalmist is saying that God created humanity a little lower than angels. The psalmist may also be
saying that Yahweh made humanity a little lower than
himself or a little lower than other divine beings, such as
the "sons of God" or the other members of his heavenly
host (or divine council; see Ge 6:2 and note; Ps 82:1
and note; compare Heb 1:6,14; 2:7).

8:6–8 The psalmist expounds on Yahweh's special role
for humanity. Not only does Yahweh give special attention to humanity, he also gives humanity an elevated
position: Humankind is put in charge of God's creation
(see Ge 1:28 and note). The psalmist is likely recalling

the creation account from Ge 1:26–30 as he lists the
same categories of animals—land, air and sea. See the
infographic "The Days of Creation" on p. 6.

8:6 everything under their feet Paul applies this
phrase to Christ in the NT (1Co 15:27–28). The author
of Hebrews also quotes this psalm, applying it to Jesus
(Heb 2:5–9). Both passages declare Christ's ultimate
lordship and reign, which will one day be fully realized
in the world.
8:9 LORD, our Lord See note on Ps 8:1.

9:title—10:18 Psalms 9 and 10 may have originally
been one psalm. Psalm 10 does not have a title, which
is unusual for Book One (Ps 3–41). The Septuagint
and Vulgate both list Psalms 9 and 10 as one psalm.
There is also a basic acrostic pattern—although broken
at times—where Ps 9 has lines starting with the first
half of the Hebrew alphabet and Ps 10 the second half.
    However, the content of the two psalms is very differ-
ent. Psalm 9 is a praise psalm, while Ps 10 is a lament
psalm. If they were originally one psalm, Ps 9 appears
to recount Yahweh's previous acts of deliverance in the
hope he will act similarly to rescue the afflicted in Ps
10. The praise of Yahweh's acts in Ps 9 would also give
hope to the suffering in Ps 10. See note on 10:1–18.

9:title–20 The psalmist opens this praise psalm with
the intent to praise Yahweh for his works (vv. 1–2). He
then recounts God's deliverance from enemy nations
(vv. 3–6) and describes his just and righteous rule over
the earth (vv. 7–10). He praises Yahweh for remembering the afflicted (vv. 11–12), and petitions Yahweh to
remember his, the psalmist's, affliction (vv. 13–14). The
psalmist then celebrates Yahweh allowing the destruction
of the wicked and Yahweh's preservation of the needy
(vv. 15–18). The psalmist concludes with a petition for
Yahweh to judge the nations (vv. 19–20).

9:title director of music See note on 4:title. **A psalm
of David** See note on 3:title.
9:1 all my heart The heart according to Hebrew thought
represents the center of people's character and will (e.g.,

³ My enemies turn back;
 they stumble and perish before you.
⁴ For you have upheld my right and my
 cause,
 sitting enthroned as the righteous judge.
⁵ You have rebuked the nations and destroyed
 the wicked;
 you have blotted out their name for ever
 and ever.
⁶ Endless ruin has overtaken my enemies,
 you have uprooted their cities;
 even the memory of them has perished.

⁷ The LORD reigns forever;
 he has established his throne for
 judgment.
⁸ He rules the world in righteousness
 and judges the peoples with equity.
⁹ The LORD is a refuge for the oppressed,
 a stronghold in times of trouble.
¹⁰ Those who know your name trust in you,
 for you, LORD, have never forsaken those
 who seek you.

¹¹ Sing the praises of the LORD, enthroned in
 Zion;
 proclaim among the nations what he has
 done.
¹² For he who avenges blood remembers;
 he does not ignore the cries of the afflicted.

¹³ LORD, see how my enemies persecute me!
 Have mercy and lift me up from the gates
 of death,

¹⁴ that I may declare your praises
 in the gates of Daughter Zion,
 and there rejoice in your salvation.

¹⁵ The nations have fallen into the pit they
 have dug;
 their feet are caught in the net they have
 hidden.
¹⁶ The LORD is known by his acts of justice;
 the wicked are ensnared by the work of
 their hands.ᵃ
¹⁷ The wicked go down to the realm of the dead,
 all the nations that forget God.
¹⁸ But God will never forget the needy;
 the hope of the afflicted will never perish.

¹⁹ Arise, LORD, do not let mortals triumph;
 let the nations be judged in your presence.
²⁰ Strike them with terror, LORD;
 let the nations know they are only mortal.

Psalm 10ᵇ

¹ Why, LORD, do you stand far off?
 Why do you hide yourself in times
 of trouble?

² In his arrogance the wicked man hunts down
 the weak,
 who are caught in the schemes he devises.

ᵃ 16 The Hebrew has *Higgaion* and *Selah* (words of uncertain meaning) here; *Selah* occurs also at the end of verse 20.
ᵇ Psalms 9 and 10 may originally have been a single acrostic poem in which alternating lines began with the successive letters of the Hebrew alphabet. In the Septuagint they constitute one psalm.

1Sa 2:35). **all your wonderful deeds** Praise of Yahweh in Psalms frequently remembers and describes God's past works (Ps 26:7; 40:5).
9:2 O Most High This name for God, *elyon* in Hebrew, is first used to describe Melchizedek's role as a priest of *elyon* (see Ge 14:18 and note). See the table "Names of God in the Old Testament" on p. 917.

9:3–6 The psalmist recounts Yahweh's work in delivering him from enemy nations. His enemies trip over themselves as they rush to retreat from Yahweh's presence (compare Lev 26:37). Yahweh rebukes them, and they perish (*avad* in Hebrew; this word occurs three times in these verses); even their memories perish forever. In punishing the enemy nations, God acts as a righteous judge.

9:7–10 The psalmist describes Yahweh as a king administering justice from his throne. He praises Yahweh's judgment using the Hebrew words *tsedeq* (often translated "righteous") and *mesharim* (often translated "true"). As a righteous judge, Yahweh is trustworthy. The oppressed can confidently seek refuge in him.

9:7 his throne A symbol of authority.
9:8 He rules the world The Hebrew verb related to judgment, *shaphat*, occurs six times in this psalm as the psalmist praises Yahweh for his righteous rule over the earth. **with equity** The Hebrew word used here, *mesharim*, describes equity or integrity. It often parallels righteousness and justice (Ps 99:4; Pr 2:9).
9:9 a refuge The Hebrew word used here, *misqav*, describes high walls or a rocky fortress (Isa 25:12;

33:16). When applied to Yahweh, it emphasizes the stable protection he provides for those in need (Ps 62:6–8).
9:11 Zion See 2:6 and note.

9:15–17 The psalmist describes the fate of the wicked: They are caught by their own traps. This is not by accident—it is part of Yahweh's judgment.
9:15 net The Hebrew word used here, *resheth*, describes a net that was spread over the ground or over a pit. See note on Job 18:8.
9:17 realm of the dead The Hebrew word *she'ol* is used here. See note on Job 14:13. **that forget God** Rather than a careless lapse of memory, this implies an intentional decision to reject God (Dt 8:11,19; Isa 17:10; Jer 3:21).
9:18 will never forget the needy The psalmist implies that the poor and needy are being neglected. Since this would fit with the lament of Ps 10, it gives credibility to the idea that Ps 9 and 10 were originally one psalm. See note on Ps 9:title–10:18.
9:19 Arise, LORD The psalmist has been praising God for his righteous judgment of enemy nations. He concludes by asking Yahweh to continue his judgment.

10:1–18 If Ps 10 was originally part of Ps 9 (see note on Ps 9:title—10:18), the abrupt change in tone seems strange. Psalm 9 is a praise psalm, while Ps 10 is a corporate lament psalm (for use by a group). However, the praise of Yahweh's righteous judgment in Ps 9 may be an encouragement for Yahweh to respond similarly to the cries of the afflicted in Ps 10. While Ps 9 is mostly

3 He boasts about the cravings of his heart;
  he blesses the greedy and reviles the Lord.
4 In his pride the wicked man does not seek him;
  in all his thoughts there is no room
    for God.
5 His ways are always prosperous;
  your laws are rejected by[a] him;
  he sneers at all his enemies.
6 He says to himself, "Nothing will ever
    shake me."
  He swears, "No one will ever do me harm."

7 His mouth is full of lies and threats;
  trouble and evil are under his tongue.
8 He lies in wait near the villages;
  from ambush he murders the innocent.
  His eyes watch in secret for his victims;
9   like a lion in cover he lies in wait.
  He lies in wait to catch the helpless;
  he catches the helpless and drags them off
    in his net.
10 His victims are crushed, they collapse;
  they fall under his strength.
11 He says to himself, "God will never notice;
  he covers his face and never sees."

12 Arise, Lord! Lift up your hand, O God.
  Do not forget the helpless.
13 Why does the wicked man revile God?
  Why does he say to himself,
    "He won't call me to account"?

14 But you, God, see the trouble of the afflicted;
  you consider their grief and take it in hand.
  The victims commit themselves to you;
  you are the helper of the fatherless.
15 Break the arm of the wicked man;
  call the evildoer to account for his
    wickedness
  that would not otherwise be found out.

16 The Lord is King for ever and ever;
  the nations will perish from his land.
17 You, Lord, hear the desire of the afflicted;
  you encourage them, and you listen to
    their cry,
18 defending the fatherless and the oppressed,
  so that mere earthly mortals
  will never again strike terror.

Psalm 11

For the director of music. Of David.

1 In the Lord I take refuge.
  How then can you say to me:
  "Flee like a bird to your mountain.
2 For look, the wicked bend their bows;
  they set their arrows against the strings
  to shoot from the shadows
    at the upright in heart.

a 5 See Septuagint; Hebrew / *they are haughty, and your laws are far from*

praise, there are some indications of affliction (9:13,18). There are also some verbal parallels between Ps 9 and 10. Ps 10 opens with a cry of lament to Yahweh for his seeming distance (v. 1). It then describes the boasts of the wicked (vv. 2–11) before again petitioning God to act by remembering the afflicted and punishing the wicked (vv. 12–15). It closes with a declaration of Yahweh's eternal sovereignty and a final petition for justice (vv. 16–18).

10:1 Why, Lord Lament in the OT often includes statements about Yahweh being distant (22:1; 38:21). The exclamations of Yahweh's absence do not stem from a lack of faith; rather, they come from an expectation of God's justice (10:16). Because the sufferer does not experience justice, he questions Yahweh's presence—directing his petition at the God he expects to be involved in human affairs.

10:2–11 As the psalmist describes the wicked, he emphasizes their arrogance. They oppress the impoverished and innocent, and yet they profit. In their arrogance they renounce Yahweh, believing they are safe from any judgment. The psalmist expresses concern that Yahweh seems to allow this. By standing far away, Yahweh allows the wicked to feel secure. They freely oppress others without experiencing the consequence of Yahweh's righteous judgment.

10:3 He boasts In Hebrew, "to praise" or "to boast" both come from the same word, *halal*. The wicked worship their own desires rather than Yahweh. **reviles the Lord** The Hebrew term used here, *na'ats*, may indicate disobedience (2Sa 12:14) or rejection of Yahweh (Nu 14:11). Here, it likely refers to an arrogant dismissal of Yahweh (Ps 74:10; Pr 15:5).

10:5 he sneers at The Hebrew text here could indicate an arrogant dismissal or directly speaking against Yahweh and his purposes.

10:6 Nothing will ever shake me A statement of security usually reserved for the righteous (e.g., Ps 15:5; 16:8; 21:7; 112:6).

10:11 God will never notice The psalmist reflects on the attitude of the wicked (see note on v. 1).

10:13 He won't call me to account The Hebrew verb here, *darash*, also occurs in 9:12, where the psalmist praises God for avenging the blood of the afflicted.

10:14 fatherless Referring to orphans, who were counted among the most vulnerable in ancient Israel.

10:15 Break the arm of the wicked The arm symbolized power according to Hebrew thought (Ex 15:16; Isa 51:9).

10:17 you listen to their cry Rather than being far away, Yahweh pays close attention to the cries of the afflicted (compare Ps 10:1,11).

11:title–7 While it features characteristics of individual lament psalms, this psalm lacks both a petition for help and complaints of suffering. Instead, the psalmist expresses confidence in Yahweh. The crisis is described through the advice of others, who encourage the psalmist to flee from the wicked. The psalmist opens with an affirmation that he will take refuge in Yahweh (v. 1). He then questions the advice to flee (vv. 1–3) and finally expresses confidence in Yahweh, describing him as a righteous king (vv. 4–7). See the table "Types of Psalms" on p. 830.

11:title Of David See note on 3:title.

11:1 I take refuge The Psalms often describe the happiness and joy that come from taking refuge in Yahweh

³When the foundations are being
destroyed,
what can the righteous do?"

⁴The LORD is in his holy temple;
the LORD is on his heavenly throne.
He observes everyone on earth;
his eyes examine them.
⁵The LORD examines the righteous,
but the wicked, those who love
violence,
he hates with a passion.
⁶On the wicked he will rain
fiery coals and burning sulfur;
a scorching wind will be their lot.
⁷For the LORD is righteous,
he loves justice;
the upright will see his face.

Psalm 12ᵃ

*For the director of music. According
to* sheminith.ᵇ *A psalm of David.*

¹Help, LORD, for no one is faithful anymore;
those who are loyal have vanished from
the human race.

²Everyone lies to their neighbor;
they flatter with their lips
but harbor deception in their hearts.

³May the LORD silence all flattering lips
and every boastful tongue —
⁴those who say,
"By our tongues we will prevail;
our own lips will defend us — who is lord
over us?"

⁵"Because the poor are plundered and the
needy groan,
I will now arise," says the LORD.
"I will protect them from those who
malign them."
⁶And the words of the LORD are
flawless,
like silver purified in a crucible,
like goldᶜ refined seven times.

⁷You, LORD, will keep the needy safe
and will protect us forever from the
wicked,

ᵃ In Hebrew texts 12:1-8 is numbered 12:2-9.   ᵇ Title: Probably
a musical term   ᶜ 6 Probable reading of the original Hebrew
text; Masoretic Text *earth*

(2:12; 5:11; 118:8–9). **like a bird** The psalmist rejects
the advice to flee. In parallel to the phrase used here,
taking refuge in Yahweh is often described with bird
imagery—people can take refuge under the shelter of
Yahweh's wings (36:7; 57:1; 61:4; 91:4).
11:4 The LORD is in his holy temple The earthly temple
was a representation of Yahweh's heavenly temple. The
psalmist looks to the temple as the place of Yahweh's
dwelling and a symbol of Yahweh's sovereignty over all the
earth (Hab 2:20). **his eyes examine** While the wicked
seek to hide their actions in the dark, Yahweh sees all
from his heavenly throne.
11:5 The LORD examines the righteous The Hebrew
text here could refer to Yahweh examining the state of a
person, perhaps for the purpose of judgment (compare
Ps 11:6–7), or to Yahweh testing someone. Testing
can have negative or positive implications. It is often
compared to the refining of precious metals (Pr 17:3).
The righteous may suffer or face affliction during these
periods, but such trials result in refinement or restoration
(Ps 66:10–12; Job 23:10; Zec 13:9). **he hates with
a passion** The psalmist often describes his enemies
as those who hate him (e.g., Ps 18:17; 38:19). The
Psalms provide many examples of things God despises.
To fear Yahweh is to hate evil. The prophets show how
Yahweh hates the idea of festivals and sacrifices happening while justice itself is perverted (Isa 1:14–17;
Am 5:21–24). Proverbs 6:16–19 lists several actions
Yahweh hates: injustice, lies and worshiping false gods
(Isa 61:8; Jer 44:4–5; Zec 8:17).
11:6 their lot The Hebrew word used here, *menath*,
describes the amount of punishment Yahweh has allotted the wicked (Jer 13:25). While this term can also
describe Yahweh's blessing (Ps 16:5), it is mostly
used in descriptions of Yahweh's anger (Isa 51:17;
Jer 25:15).
11:7 will see his face The psalmist can take refuge

in Yahweh because he will protect the righteous and
oppose the wicked.

12:title–8 In this corporate lament psalm, the psalmist speaks for a faithful community living in a faithless
generation. He petitions Yahweh for salvation, asking him
to destroy the liars who are prevalent (Ps 12:1–4). Then
Yahweh responds, revealing his intention to deliver the
needy (v. 5). The psalmist praises the purity of Yahweh's
promise (v. 6). He then addresses Yahweh again, expressing confidence that he will guard the faithful community
from the wicked who surround them (vv. 7–8). See the
table "Types of Psalms" on p. 830.

12:title sheminith See note on 6:title. **A psalm of
David** See note on 3:title.
12:2 lies The Hebrew word used here, *shawe*, describes
something useless or false. The psalmist's description of
the wicked emphasizes that they speak empty words or
lies (41:6). The law prohibits spreading a false report (Ex
23:1). The Hebrew word *shawe* is also used to describe
"false" or "worthless" gods (Ps 31:6; Jer 18:15). **they
flatter with their lips** The Hebrew phrase used here
describes false flattering or false speech (Isa 30:10) and
is often used in the context of tempting the righteous to
sin (Pr 5:3; Da 11:32).
12:3 silence The Hebrew word used here, *karath*, means
"to cut off," "to eradicate" or "to annihilate." It indicates
complete destruction; even the memory and posterity of
the wicked are removed (Ps 34:16; 109:15).
12:5 the poor are plundered Old Testament law required the Israelites to provide for and defend the poor
and needy (see Dt 15:11). Yahweh is often presented as
their defender and provider (Ps 35:10; 69:33; Isa 41:17).
12:6 words of the LORD In contrast with the false and
useless words of the wicked (Ps 12:2–4), Yahweh's
words—specifically his promise to act in v. 5—are
trustworthy and reliable.

⁸ who freely strut about
when what is vile is honored by the
human race.

Psalm 13ᵃ

For the director of music. A psalm of David.

¹ How long, LORD? Will you forget me forever?
How long will you hide your face
from me?
² How long must I wrestle with my thoughts
and day after day have sorrow in my heart?
How long will my enemy triumph
over me?

³ Look on me and answer, LORD my God.
Give light to my eyes, or I will sleep in
death,
⁴ and my enemy will say, "I have
overcome him,"
and my foes will rejoice when I fall.

⁵ But I trust in your unfailing love;
my heart rejoices in your salvation.
⁶ I will sing the LORD's praise,
for he has been good to me.

Psalm 14

14:1-7pp — Ps 53:1-6

For the director of music. Of David.

¹ The foolᵇ says in his heart,
"There is no God."
They are corrupt, their deeds are vile;
there is no one who does good.

² The LORD looks down from heaven
on all mankind
to see if there are any who understand,
any who seek God.
³ All have turned away, all have become
corrupt;
there is no one who does good,
not even one.

⁴ Do all these evildoers know nothing?

They devour my people as though eating
bread;
they never call on the LORD.

ᵃ In Hebrew texts 13:1-6 is numbered 13:2-6.   ᵇ 1 The Hebrew words rendered *fool* in Psalms denote one who is morally deficient.

13:title–6 This is a short individual lament psalm. In this psalm, the psalmist expresses concern with the apparent distance of Yahweh. He asks "how long" four times in the first two verses as he laments Yahweh's absence, which allows his enemies to succeed (vv. 1–2). He then petitions Yahweh to answer, asking for deliverance from death and his enemies (vv. 3–4). He concludes the psalm with a note of trust and praise to Yahweh (vv. 5–6). See the table "Types of Psalms" on p. 830.

13:title A psalm of David See note on 3:title.
13:1 How long A common cry in lament psalms. See 6:3 and note. **forget me forever** This question is answered in the psalmist's concluding note of trust and praise (vv. 5–6).
13:2 sorrow in my heart The Hebrew word used here, *yagon*, describes the opposite of joy (Jer 8:18). **will my enemy triumph over me** The psalmist laments because his enemies have been successful. While their success presents physical danger for the psalmist, this expression also presents a crisis of faith: As the righteous and just judge, Yahweh should not allow his enemies to be exalted (Ps 9:6–8).
13:3 Give light to my eyes This refers to the restoring of strength or health (1Sa 14:27).
13:4 when I fall The Hebrew word used here, *mot*, expresses a lack of security and safety.
13:5 trust in After petitioning Yahweh, the psalmist expresses his trust in Yahweh. **unfailing love** The Hebrew word used here, *chesed*, describes Yahweh's unceasing, covenantal love as seen in Yahweh's promises to his people (Ge 12:1–3; Ex 34). Here the psalmist expresses confidence despite his previous questions doubting Yahweh's presence (Ps 13:1–2). His expressions of abandonment in vv. 1–2 do not reflect a lack of faith; they reflect his concern that Yahweh is not restoring justice by defeating his enemies.

14:title–7 Nearly identical to Ps 53, Ps 14 differs in its use of God's personal name, Yahweh (*yhwh*), while Ps 53 uses the general Hebrew word *elohim* for "God." This psalm does not fit into a particular genre. It can be considered a wisdom psalm because it uses wisdom terminology including Hebrew words like *naval* (which can be translated as "fool"; 14:1) and *yada'* (which may be translated "to know"; v. 4). It also shares similarities with corporate lament psalms as a community of the faithful laments the corruption on earth (see Ps 12). The psalm opens with a description of the fool (14:1) and continues with Yahweh's perspective as he looks down on the corruption of humanity (vv. 2–3). It continues with the fate of those who do not call on Yahweh (vv. 4–6) and concludes with a statement of hope for his people (v. 7). See the table "Types of Psalms" on p. 830.

14:title Of David See note on 3:title.
14:1 The fool says A fool in the OT is primarily someone who rejects God and his ways and chooses evil (Pr 13:19). **They are corrupt** The Hebrew word used here, *shachat*, is also used to describe the earth before the flood (Ge 6:11–13).
14:2 any who understand The Hebrew verb used here, *sakhal*, can mean "to understand" or "to act wisely." Wisdom in the OT includes a religious or moral aspect since a wise person is characterized by righteousness and obedience (Ps 19:7; 37:30).
14:3 there is no one who does good Paul cites these verses (vv. 1–3)—and several others (5:9; 140:3; 10:7; 36:1; Isa 59:7–8)—in Ro 3:10–18, to show that all of humanity is sinful.
14:4 Do all these evildoers know nothing The evildoers' behavior shows their lack of knowledge. **They devour my people** This idiom refers to oppression (Ps 27:2; Pr 30:14).

5 But there they are, overwhelmed with dread,
  for God is present in the company of the
  righteous.
6 You evildoers frustrate the plans of the poor,
  but the LORD is their refuge.

7 Oh, that salvation for Israel would come out
  of Zion!
  When the LORD restores his people,
  let Jacob rejoice and Israel be glad!

Psalm 15

A psalm of David.

1 LORD, who may dwell in your sacred tent?
  Who may live on your holy mountain?

2 The one whose walk is blameless,
  who does what is righteous,
  who speaks the truth from their heart;
3 whose tongue utters no slander,
  who does no wrong to a neighbor,
  and casts no slur on others;
4 who despises a vile person
  but honors those who fear the LORD;
  who keeps an oath even when it hurts,
  and does not change their mind;

5 who lends money to the poor without
  interest;
  who does not accept a bribe against the
  innocent.

  Whoever does these things
  will never be shaken.

Psalm 16

A miktam[a] of David.

1 Keep me safe, my God,
  for in you I take refuge.

2 I say to the LORD, "You are my Lord;
  apart from you I have no good thing."
3 I say of the holy people who are in the
  land,
  "They are the noble ones in whom is all
  my delight."
4 Those who run after other gods will suffer
  more and more.
  I will not pour out libations of blood to
  such gods
  or take up their names on my lips.

a Title: Probably a literary or musical term

14:6 You evildoers The psalmist directs his comments to the foolish evildoers.
14:7 restores Refers to lifting someone up from a place of suffering or affliction to a place of prominence or wealth (Job 42:10).

15:title–5 This short temple entry psalm—a psalm used when a worshiper would enter the temple—explains Yahweh's requirements of those who worship him. It shows characteristics of wisdom psalms in prescribing a proper way of living. It can be divided into two main sections: the initial questions asking who can dwell on Yahweh's holy hill (Ps 15:1), and the remainder, which answers by describing the required characteristics (vv. 2–5). The requirements are moral conditions that involve the conscience. See the table "Types of Psalms" on p. 830.

15:title A psalm of David See note on 3:title.
15:1 in your sacred tent The Hebrew word used here, *ohel*, is a technical term referring to Yahweh's tabernacle (Ex 26:1–37; 2Sa 6:17). It is also used to refer to the Temple Mount (Ps 27:4–6). These questions were likely asked by, or of, worshipers visiting the temple or tabernacle of God. **your holy mountain** Referring to the Temple Mount, Mount Zion, which was understood to be the dwelling place of Yahweh (43:3).
15:2 blameless The Hebrew word used here, *tamim*, indicates purity or innocence (2Sa 22:24). **who speaks the truth** The Hebrew word used here, *emeth*, can mean truth or faithfulness; both are characteristics of Yahweh and his law (Ps 19:9; 25:5; 86:11; 119:142). The requirement here is not just an outward expression of truth (Pr 8:7; 12:19); it is an inward position of the heart. According to Hebrew thought, the heart was considered the center of a person's character.

15:3 After listing three things the worshiper should do (Ps 15:2), the psalm lists three things they should avoid.

15:4 those who fear the LORD Anyone desiring to enter God's tent must have a proper attitude toward others. He should despise vile people and honor those who fear Yahweh (compare note on 11:5). **who keeps an oath even when it hurts** This likely refers to a person paying what they said they would, either at Yahweh's sanctuary or to other people, even at great financial cost (see Dt 12:4–7,26).
15:5 who lends money to the poor without interest Old Testament law forbids charging interest to a fellow Israelite (see Dt 23:19–20). **who does not accept a bribe** Taking a bribe was considered a perversion of justice (Pr 17:23) and was prohibited by OT law. See Ex 23:8 and note. **never be shaken** In the Psalms, the person who is not moved or shaken is described as protected by Yahweh (e.g., Ps 16:8; 62:6; 112:6).

16:title–11 This is a psalm of confidence as the psalmist shows his trust in Yahweh. While it opens with a petition normally found in individual lament psalms, there is no mention of enemies or suffering. Instead, the psalmist shows his contentment and praises Yahweh for his blessing. After the opening petition (v. 1), the psalmist expresses contentment in Yahweh and contrasts the saints (or holy people) with those who follow another god (vv. 2–4). He confidently blesses Yahweh (vv. 5–6) and praises him for the safety and security he provides (vv. 7–11). See the table "Types of Psalms" on p. 830.

16:title A miktam The meaning of this term is uncertain. It may come from a verb meaning "to cover." **of David** See note on 3:title.
16:3 the holy people The Hebrew word used here, *qedoshim*, refers to God's chosen or set apart people (Dt 7:6). Elsewhere this phrase is used in reference to heavenly beings (Ps 89:5–7; Job 15:15). **noble ones** The Hebrew word used here, *addir*, means "mighty" or "magnificent." It is used to describe the name of Yahweh

⁵Lord, you alone are my portion and my cup;
  you make my lot secure.
⁶The boundary lines have fallen for me in
    pleasant places;
  surely I have a delightful inheritance.
⁷I will praise the Lord, who counsels me;
  even at night my heart instructs me.
⁸I keep my eyes always on the Lord.
  With him at my right hand, I will not be
    shaken.

⁹Therefore my heart is glad and my tongue
    rejoices;
  my body also will rest secure,
¹⁰because you will not abandon me to the
    realm of the dead,
  nor will you let your faithful*a* one see decay.
¹¹You make known to me the path of life;
  you will fill me with joy in your presence,
  with eternal pleasures at your right hand.

Psalm 17

A prayer of David.

¹Hear me, Lord, my plea is just;
  listen to my cry.
  Hear my prayer—
  it does not rise from deceitful lips.
²Let my vindication come from you;
  may your eyes see what is right.

³Though you probe my heart,
  though you examine me at night and
    test me,

you will find that I have planned no evil;
  my mouth has not transgressed.
⁴Though people tried to bribe me,
  I have kept myself from the ways of the
    violent
  through what your lips have commanded.
⁵My steps have held to your paths;
  my feet have not stumbled.

⁶I call on you, my God, for you will answer me;
  turn your ear to me and hear my prayer.
⁷Show me the wonders of your great love,
  you who save by your right hand
  those who take refuge in you from their
    foes.
⁸Keep me as the apple of your eye;
  hide me in the shadow of your wings
⁹from the wicked who are out to destroy me,
  from my mortal enemies who
    surround me.

¹⁰They close up their callous hearts,
  and their mouths speak with arrogance.
¹¹They have tracked me down, they now
    surround me,
  with eyes alert, to throw me to the ground.
¹²They are like a lion hungry for prey,
  like a fierce lion crouching in cover.

¹³Rise up, Lord, confront them, bring them
    down;
  with your sword rescue me from the
    wicked.

---

a 10 Or *holy*

(Ps 8:1). It can also indicate rulers or people in positions of authority (Jer 14:3; Na 3:18).
16:5 my portion The Hebrew word used here, *menath*, describes a person's allotment. The psalmist is saying Yahweh is sufficient to meet any need (Ps 73:26; La 3:24).
16:6 the boundary lines have fallen This is most likely a reference to the allotment of the promised land (Jos 14–21).
16:8 at my right hand Indicating special blessing (Ge 48:17–20).

16:10 In Acts, both Peter and Paul apply this passage to Jesus as a prophecy of his resurrection (Ac 2:24–36; 13:34–39).

16:10 realm of the dead The Hebrew word *she'ol* is used here. See note on 1Ki 2:6.

17:title–15 In this individual lament psalm—framed as a prayer—the psalmist seems to be unjustly accused of wrongdoing. He begins by petitioning Yahweh to hear him and righteously vindicate him (Ps 17:1–2). He then asserts his innocence (vv. 3–5) before again petitioning God for refuge and protection from his enemies (vv. 6–9). He describes his enemies as ravenous (vv. 10–12) and asks Yahweh to confront these wicked men and deliver him (vv. 13–14). Finally, the psalmist declares confidence that he will experience God's presence (v. 15). See the table "Types of Psalms" on p. 830.

17:title of David See note on 3:title.

17:1 Hear me, Lord, my plea is just The psalmist petitions Yahweh to hear his case, which he describes using the Hebrew word *tsedeq*, meaning "just" or "righteous."
17:2 my vindication The psalmist appeals to Yahweh, the righteous judge, to vindicate him (see 9:7–8 and notes). **from you** The Hebrew word used here, *paneh*, describes both the "face" and "presence" of God. Later the psalmist shows faith that he will look on God's face. See note on 4:6.
17:3 you will find that I have planned no evil The psalmist declares his innocence. The psalmist does not declare himself morally perfect or free from sin. He proclaims his innocence in light of his enemies' accusations (17:10–12). Compare Job 23:10–12; note on Ps 11:5.
17:6 you will answer me Already confident of his response, the psalmist calls on God to answer.
17:7 your great love The Hebrew word used here, *chesed*, refers to God's faithful, covenantal love; the psalms frequently appeal to this attribute of God when petitioning for help (5:7; 6:4; 13:5). **by your right hand** God's hand is often depicted in Psalms as a source of protection or blessing (119:173). It represents his powerful acts of creation (95:5; 102:25) as well as salvation (98:1; 109:27; 118:15–16).
17:8 the shadow of your wings A frequent image of God's protection. See note on Ru 2:12.
17:12 a lion hungry for prey See note on Ps 7:2.
17:13 Rise up, Lord Finally, the psalmist petitions Yahweh to act. The terms the psalmist uses in his petition

14 By your hand save me from such people, LORD,
 from those of this world whose reward is
 in this life.
May what you have stored up for the wicked
 fill their bellies;
 may their children gorge themselves on it,
 and may there be leftovers for their little
 ones.

15 As for me, I will be vindicated and will see
 your face;
 when I awake, I will be satisfied with
 seeing your likeness.

Psalm 18[a]

18:Title – 50pp — 2Sa 22:1-51

*For the director of music. Of David the servant
of the LORD. He sang to the LORD the words of this
song when the LORD delivered him from the hand
of all his enemies and from the hand of Saul. He said:*

1 I love you, LORD, my strength.

2 The LORD is my rock, my fortress and my
 deliverer;
 my God is my rock, in whom I take refuge,
 my shield[b] and the horn[c] of my salvation,
 my stronghold.

3 I called to the LORD, who is worthy of praise,
 and I have been saved from my enemies.

4 The cords of death entangled me;

the torrents of destruction overwhelmed me.
5 The cords of the grave coiled around me;
 the snares of death confronted me.

6 In my distress I called to the LORD;
 I cried to my God for help.
From his temple he heard my voice;
 my cry came before him, into his ears.
7 The earth trembled and quaked,
 and the foundations of the mountains
 shook;
 they trembled because he was angry.
8 Smoke rose from his nostrils;
 consuming fire came from his mouth,
 burning coals blazed out of it.
9 He parted the heavens and came down;
 dark clouds were under his feet.
10 He mounted the cherubim and flew;
 he soared on the wings of the wind.
11 He made darkness his covering, his canopy
 around him —
 the dark rain clouds of the sky.
12 Out of the brightness of his presence clouds
 advanced,
 with hailstones and bolts of lightning.
13 The LORD thundered from heaven;
 the voice of the Most High resounded.[d]

---

[a] In Hebrew texts 18:1-50 is numbered 18:2-51.
[b] 2 Or *sovereign*   [c] 2 *Horn* here symbolizes strength.
[d] 13 Some Hebrew manuscripts and Septuagint (see also
2 Samuel 22:14); most Hebrew manuscripts *resounded, / amid
hailstones and bolts of lightning*

---

indicate the urgency of the situation. **sword** The sword
is often used as a symbol of divine judgment (Lev 26:25;
Isa 66:16).
**17:14 May what you have stored up for the wicked
fill their bellies** This idiomatic phrase is most likely
meant as a contrast between the psalmist and the
wicked. The psalmist will behold the face of Yahweh (Ps
17:15), while the wicked and their offspring will receive
their treasure as their portion in this life.

18:title – 50 This royal psalm was probably used to
celebrate victories. The psalmist opens with a hymn of
praise to Yahweh for his security and salvation (vv. 1–3).
He describes his situation and his cry to Yahweh for help
(vv. 4–6), telling of a vision where Yahweh comes with
great power to deliver him from his enemies (vv. 7–19).
The psalmist ascribes Yahweh's salvation to his character: Yahweh's righteousness and blamelessness prompt
him to act (vv. 20–24). Yahweh gives justice and protection to those who take refuge in him (vv. 25–30). The
psalmist again praises Yahweh, this time for his help
and protection (vv. 31–36). He describes the defeat of
his enemies (vv. 37–42) and his rise to prominence
over them (vv. 43–45). He praises Yahweh for delivering and exalting him (vv. 46–49) and ends the psalm
by proclaiming Yahweh's faithfulness to the Davidic
royal line (v. 50).

18:title when the LORD delivered him This psalm
is almost identical to the song of David found in 2Sa
22:1–51. This does not necessarily mean David composed this psalm, although he could have — it does

means, though, that he recited it at that time. Compare
note on Ps 3:title.

18:1–3 In the opening hymn of praise, the psalmist
proclaims his love for Yahweh, who gives him strength.
He lists several terms that emphasize the stability and
security found in Yahweh.

18:2 horn A symbol of power (1Ki 22:11; Zec 1:18–21).

18:4–6 The psalmist describes his situation: He is
hunted by death with its traps, and overcome by a flood
of destruction (see note on Job 18:8). In this dire situation, he calls on Yahweh and is answered.

18:5 the grave The Hebrew word *she'ol* is used here,
which is a reference to the place of the dead (the underworld). See note on 1Ki 2:6.

18:6 From his temple Yahweh hears the psalmist's
cry from his heavenly temple. See Ps 11:4 and note.

18:7–19 This theophany, in which the psalmist describes
Yahweh acting to deliver, resembles several passages
in Exodus. The smoke and clouds surrounding Yahweh
recall the description of his appearance at Mount Sinai
in Ex 19:16–19 (see note on Ex 19:9). This passage
also reflects Moses' song after crossing the Red Sea
(Ex 15:1–18).

18:10 He mounted the cherubim Cherubim were placed
on top of the ark of the covenant — the space between
their wings symbolized where Yahweh sat, upon their
wings (Ex 25:18–20; Ps 80:1; 99:1). Cherubim also
guarded the tree of life. See Ge 3:24 and note.

14 He shot his arrows and scattered the enemy,
  with great bolts of lightning he routed
    them.
15 The valleys of the sea were exposed
  and the foundations of the earth laid bare
at your rebuke, Lord,
  at the blast of breath from your nostrils.

16 He reached down from on high and took hold
    of me;
  he drew me out of deep waters.
17 He rescued me from my powerful enemy,
  from my foes, who were too strong for me.
18 They confronted me in the day of my disaster,
  but the Lord was my support.
19 He brought me out into a spacious place;
  he rescued me because he delighted in me.

20 The Lord has dealt with me according to my
    righteousness;
  according to the cleanness of my hands he
    has rewarded me.
21 For I have kept the ways of the Lord;
  I am not guilty of turning from my God.
22 All his laws are before me;
  I have not turned away from his decrees.
23 I have been blameless before him
  and have kept myself from sin.
24 The Lord has rewarded me according to my
    righteousness,
  according to the cleanness of my hands in
    his sight.

25 To the faithful you show yourself faithful,
  to the blameless you show yourself
    blameless,
26 to the pure you show yourself pure,
  but to the devious you show yourself
    shrewd.

27 You save the humble
  but bring low those whose eyes are
    haughty.
28 You, Lord, keep my lamp burning;
  my God turns my darkness into light.
29 With your help I can advance against a troop a;
  with my God I can scale a wall.

30 As for God, his way is perfect:
  The Lord's word is flawless;
  he shields all who take refuge in him.
31 For who is God besides the Lord?
  And who is the Rock except our God?
32 It is God who arms me with strength
  and keeps my way secure.
33 He makes my feet like the feet of a deer;
  he causes me to stand on the heights.
34 He trains my hands for battle;
  my arms can bend a bow of bronze.
35 You make your saving help my shield,
  and your right hand sustains me;
  your help has made me great.
36 You provide a broad path for my feet,
  so that my ankles do not give way.

37 I pursued my enemies and overtook them;
  I did not turn back till they were destroyed.
38 I crushed them so that they could not rise;
  they fell beneath my feet.
39 You armed me with strength for battle;
  you humbled my adversaries before me.
40 You made my enemies turn their backs in
    flight,
  and I destroyed my foes.
41 They cried for help, but there was no one to
    save them—
  to the Lord, but he did not answer.

a 29 Or can run through a barricade

18:15 foundations of the earth See note on Job 38:4.

18:20–24 The psalmist ascribes his deliverance to Yahweh's righteousness. When he describes himself as righteous, the psalmist has no intention of arrogance. His righteousness allows him to hope in God, the righteous judge, for deliverance (Ps 7:3–6). Psalmists often cite the wickedness of their enemies as justification for God to destroy them (5:9–10; 10:2–15). Similarly, they cite their own righteousness as a reason for God's protection and deliverance (17:3–7).

18:20 he has rewarded me The Hebrew word used here, *shuv*—which may be literally rendered as "to return" or "bring back"—describes in this context how Yahweh returns the psalmist's righteousness by dealing righteously with him and delivering him.

18:23 I have been blameless The Hebrew word used here, *tamim*, means to be "blameless" or "upright"; it is used elsewhere to describe pure animals that were to be used for sacrifice. See note on Job 1:1.

18:25–27 Yahweh helps his people. He responds to those who are faithful, blameless, pure or humble. Anyone who is false or arrogant faces his judgment.

18:25 you show yourself faithful The Hebrew word used here, *chasid*, describes those who are faithful or godly. Elsewhere, the Hebrew text describes how Yahweh shows them *chesed*, unfailing covenantal love (see note on Ps 6:4).

18:28 You, Lord, keep my lamp burning The psalmist has confidence through Yahweh, who leads him to safety despite the circumstances (Job 29:2–3).

18:31–36 The psalmist praises Yahweh, the only true God, for strengthening and protecting him. He describes how God equips him for battle, teaching him and giving him strength to wage war (Ps 18:34). He praises God's saving protection (v. 35) and the security and stability God gives to his feet (vv. 33,36). Many terms here are repeated from the psalmist's opening hymn of praise (vv. 1–3).

18:35 your right hand Representing his powerful acts of creation (95:5; 102:25) as well as his salvation (98:1; 109:27; 118:15–16), God's hand was often seen as a source of protection or blessing.

18:41 They cried for help In contrast to the psalmist, whose cries for help are answered (v. 6), the enemies' cries are ignored.

⁴²I beat them as fine as windblown dust;
    I trampled them[a] like mud in the streets.
⁴³You have delivered me from the attacks of
        the people;
    you have made me the head of nations.
    People I did not know now serve me,
⁴⁴   foreigners cower before me;
    as soon as they hear of me, they obey me.
⁴⁵They all lose heart;
    they come trembling from their strongholds.

⁴⁶The LORD lives! Praise be to my Rock!
    Exalted be God my Savior!
⁴⁷He is the God who avenges me,
    who subdues nations under me,
⁴⁸   who saves me from my enemies.
    You exalted me above my foes;
    from a violent man you rescued me.
⁴⁹Therefore I will praise you, LORD, among the
        nations;
    I will sing the praises of your name.

⁵⁰He gives his king great victories;
    he shows unfailing love to his anointed,
    to David and to his descendants forever.

Psalm 19[b]

For the director of music. A psalm of David.

¹The heavens declare the glory of God;
    the skies proclaim the work of his hands.

²Day after day they pour forth speech;
    night after night they reveal knowledge.
³They have no speech, they use no words;
    no sound is heard from them.
⁴Yet their voice[c] goes out into all the earth,
    their words to the ends of the world.
    In the heavens God has pitched a tent for
        the sun.
⁵   It is like a bridegroom coming out of his
        chamber,
    like a champion rejoicing to run his
        course.
⁶It rises at one end of the heavens
    and makes its circuit to the other;
    nothing is deprived of its warmth.

⁷The law of the LORD is perfect,
    refreshing the soul.
    The statutes of the LORD are trustworthy,
    making wise the simple.
⁸The precepts of the LORD are right,
    giving joy to the heart.
    The commands of the LORD are radiant,
    giving light to the eyes.
⁹The fear of the LORD is pure,
    enduring forever.

[a] 42 Many Hebrew manuscripts, Septuagint, Syriac and Targum
(see also 2 Samuel 22:43); Masoretic Text *I poured them out*
[b] In Hebrew texts 19:1-14 is numbered 19:2-15.
[c] 4 Septuagint, Jerome and Syriac; Hebrew *measuring line*

18:43 you have made me the head of nations Yahweh delivers the psalmist and elevates him to a position of authority over the nations. He extends the psalmist's rule to foreign nations (2:8).
18:50 his anointed See note on 2:2. **to David and to his descendants** A reference to the Davidic covenant, where Yahweh promises to establish the offspring of David as king over his people (2Sa 7:12–16). There, Yahweh promises to never remove his *chesed* (the Hebrew word for Yahweh's faithful covenantal love; see 2Sa 7:15; note on Ps 18:25). Here, the psalmist reiterates the presence of God's *chesed* on his anointed (see note on 2:2).

19:title–14 This psalm celebrates God's Law and thus is classified as a Torah psalm. (The Torah is the Hebrew term for the first five books of the Bible.) It may combine two separate psalms, since the second half (compare 19:1–6,7–14) differs in content and tone. The first half describes how God's creation proclaims his glory (vv. 1–6). The psalmist then extols the beauty and value of God's Law (vv. 7–11), and asks Yahweh to keep him blameless and acceptable (vv. 12–14). The two halves also use different names for God. The first uses the Hebrew word *el* ("God") while the second uses *yhwh* ("Yahweh"). The difference in divine names may simply reflect the difference in content. The Hebrew name *el* emphasizes God as Creator, while *yhwh*—God's personal covenant name—relates more to the Law (see Ex 3). The psalm as a whole emphasizes that God, the supreme Creator, reveals his perfect Law to his people. See the table "Types of Psalms" on p. 830.

19:title A psalm of David See note on Ps 3:title.
19:1 the glory of God Yahweh created the heavens (referred to as *shamayim* in Hebrew) and the sky, expanse or firmament (*raqia'* in Hebrew) to reveal his glory (see Ge 1:1,6). People in the ancient Near East often worshiped the sun, moon and stars as gods—something specifically prohibited by the Law (see Dt 4:19; 17:3)—rather than the Creator whose glory they reflect.
19:2 they reveal knowledge Creation reveals the knowledge of God's supremacy.
19:4 into all the earth The expanse of the heavens declares God's glory to the entire earth. Paul may have had this psalm in mind when he spoke of God's invisible attributes (Ro 1:19–20). See the infographic "Ancient Hebrew Conception of the Universe" on p. 5.
19:5 like a bridegroom The bridegroom would be adorned with fine clothing (Isa 61:10; SS 3:11), and a joyful procession would accompany bride and bridegroom (Jer 7:34). **a champion** The Hebrew word used here, *gibor*, most likely describes an athlete who runs a race with strength and vigor.

19:7–9 The psalmist makes a series of statements using different Hebrew terms for the Law or Torah (as recorded in the first five books of the Bible). He describes the law (*torah*), testimony (*eduth*), precepts (*piqqudim*), commandment (*mitswah*), rules (*mishpat*) and fear (*yir'ah*) of Yahweh with positive attributes. The psalmist also describes the effect of the Law to revive, give wisdom, cause rejoicing and enlighten.

19:7 perfect The Hebrew word used here, *tamim*, means to be "perfect" or "blameless"; it emphasizes personal integrity.
19:8 radiant The Hebrew word used here, *bar*, emphasizes moral purity.
19:9 firm This highlights the trustworthiness of God's Law.

The decrees of the LORD are firm,
   and all of them are righteous.
[10] They are more precious than gold,
   than much pure gold;
they are sweeter than honey,
   than honey from the honeycomb.
[11] By them your servant is warned;
   in keeping them there is great reward.
[12] But who can discern their own errors?
   Forgive my hidden faults.
[13] Keep your servant also from willful sins;
   may they not rule over me.
Then I will be blameless,
   innocent of great transgression.

[14] May these words of my mouth and this
   meditation of my heart
be pleasing in your sight,
   LORD, my Rock and my Redeemer.

Psalm 20[a]

For the director of music. A psalm of David.

[1] May the LORD answer you when you are in
   distress;
may the name of the God of Jacob
   protect you.
[2] May he send you help from the sanctuary
   and grant you support from Zion.

[3] May he remember all your sacrifices
   and accept your burnt offerings.[b]
[4] May he give you the desire of your heart
   and make all your plans succeed.
[5] May we shout for joy over your victory
   and lift up our banners in the name of
   our God.

May the LORD grant all your requests.

[6] Now this I know:
   The LORD gives victory to his anointed.
He answers him from his heavenly sanctuary
   with the victorious power of his right hand.
[7] Some trust in chariots and some in horses,
   but we trust in the name of the LORD our God.
[8] They are brought to their knees and fall,
   but we rise up and stand firm.
[9] LORD, give victory to the king!
   Answer us when we call!

Psalm 21[c]

For the director of music. A psalm of David.

[1] The king rejoices in your strength, LORD.
   How great is his joy in the victories you
   give!

[a] In Hebrew texts 20:1-9 is numbered 20:2-10.   [b] 3 The Hebrew
has *Selah* (a word of uncertain meaning) here.   [c] In Hebrew
texts 21:1-13 is numbered 21:2-14.

19:11 your servant is warned The Law serves as a warning against evil (Eze 3:17–21) and brings reward for those who keep it (compare note on Ps 19:7–9).
19:13 blameless See note on Job 1:1.
19:14 pleasing The Hebrew word used here, *ratson*, often indicates God's acceptance of a sacrifice (Lev 1:3; 19:5; Isa 56:7). **my Rock** The Hebrew word used here, *tsur*, highlights the stability and protection Yahweh provides (see note on Ps 18:1–3). **my Redeemer** The Hebrew word used here, *go'el*, illustrates Yahweh's protection and care as he defends and delivers his people.

20:title–9 This royal psalm concerns Yahweh's blessing on the king, specifically his blessing in battle, seen by the reference to chariots and horses (v. 7). The psalmist's comments focus on the king, praying Yahweh will remember him and protect him (vv. 1–5). After proclaiming these hopes, the psalmist states his assurance that Yahweh saves his anointed king and protects him from his enemies (vv. 6–8). He closes with a petition to Yahweh to save the king (v. 9). This psalm should be read with Ps 21, which praises and thanks Yahweh for giving victory, offering a resolution to Ps 20. It seems that Ps 21 is either a continuation of Ps 20, or that the two were often read together. See note on 21:title–13; compare note on 21:2. See the table "Types of Psalms" on p. 830.
20:title A psalm of David See note on 3:title.
20:1 when you are in distress Most likely depicting a military concern. The king is preparing to go to battle, and the psalmist wants Yahweh's blessing to go with him. **name of the God of Jacob** Referring to Yahweh (*yhwh* in Hebrew), God's personal name in his covenant with Israel (see note on Ex 3:14). The title "God of Jacob" emphasizes Yahweh is the God of Israel's ancestors

and the founder of the nation (see Ge 32:28 and note). **protect** The Hebrew word used here, *sagav*, means "to make high." It evokes the image of God protecting his king in a strong tower or fortress (see Ps 18:1–3 and note).
20:2 from the sanctuary God's protection originates in his sanctuary (*qodesh* in Hebrew, literally meaning "holiness")—the place where his name dwelled (Dt 14:23). **Zion** Referring to the temple mount. It is also used nearly synonymously with Jerusalem. In Ps 2:6, Zion is described as the place where God has established his anointed king.
20:5 lift up our banners A sign of victory (Ex 17:15).
20:6 The LORD gives victory to his anointed Yahweh and his anointed—another name for the king—are closely associated; to oppose Yahweh's anointed is to oppose him (see Ps 2:2 and note). **victorious power of his right hand** A reference to God's protection.
20:7 Some trust in chariots The psalmist contrasts those who trust in their own military strength with those who trust in the name of Yahweh.
20:8 we rise up and stand firm Those who trust in the name of Yahweh are victorious, while those who trust in their own military strength are defeated.

21:title–13 Like Ps 20, this is a royal psalm. While Ps 20 petitions Yahweh for help in battle, Ps 21 praises him for a battle victory (compare note on Ps 20:title–9). The psalmist opens by praising Yahweh for glorifying the king and giving him salvation (21:1–6). He asserts the king's trust of Yahweh (v. 7) and describes how the king—with Yahweh's help—will defeat his enemies (vv. 8–12). The psalm ends on an enthusiastic note of praise (v. 13).

21:title A psalm of David See note on 3:title.
21:1 How great is his joy In Ps 20, the people rejoice in anticipation of Yahweh's salvation (20:5).

2 You have granted him his heart's desire
and have not withheld the request of his
lips.[a]
3 You came to greet him with rich blessings
and placed a crown of pure gold on his
head.
4 He asked you for life, and you gave it to
him—
length of days, for ever and ever.
5 Through the victories you gave, his glory is
great;
you have bestowed on him splendor and
majesty.
6 Surely you have granted him unending
blessings
and made him glad with the joy of your
presence.
7 For the king trusts in the LORD;
through the unfailing love of the Most High
he will not be shaken.

8 Your hand will lay hold on all your enemies;
your right hand will seize your foes.
9 When you appear for battle,
you will burn them up as in a blazing
furnace.
The LORD will swallow them up in his wrath,
and his fire will consume them.

10 You will destroy their descendants from the
earth,
their posterity from mankind.
11 Though they plot evil against you
and devise wicked schemes, they cannot
succeed;
12 You will make them turn their backs
when you aim at them with drawn bow.

13 Be exalted in your strength, LORD;
we will sing and praise your might.

Psalm 22[b]

*For the director of music. To the tune of
"The Doe of the Morning." A psalm of David.*

1 My God, my God, why have you forsaken me?
Why are you so far from saving me,
so far from my cries of anguish?
2 My God, I cry out by day, but you do not
answer,
by night, but I find no rest.[c]

3 Yet you are enthroned as the Holy One;
you are the one Israel praises.[d]

[a] 2 The Hebrew has *Selah* (a word of uncertain meaning) here.
[b] In Hebrew texts 22:1-31 is numbered 22:2-32.   [c] 2 Or *night,
and am not silent*   [d] 3 Or *Yet you are holy, / enthroned on the
praises of Israel*

21:2 You have granted Fulfilling the request from 20:4.
21:5 his glory is great By giving victory to his anointed
king, Yahweh shows his power over the nations (2:1–3).
21:6 unending blessings Reminiscent of the Davidic
covenant, where Yahweh promises to establish the dynasty forever (2Sa 7:16). **joy of your presence** Yahweh's
presence is a sign of his blessing. In lament psalms, the
psalmist often mourns the absence of Yahweh's
presence (see Ps 10:1 and note).

21:8–12 The first half of the psalm mostly addresses
Yahweh, praising him for blessing the king. This section
addresses the king, describing the victory he will have
over his enemies. The plans of the enemy will not succeed; Yahweh will destroy them as well as their descendants. This victory comes with Yahweh's assistance;
he will destroy the king's enemies in his wrath (21:9;
see 2:5 and note).

21:13 Be exalted in your strength, LORD Here, instead
of petitioning Yahweh for help (compare 20:9), the psalmist praises and extols him for his strength—the strength
that provided salvation (v. 1).

22:title–31 Psalm 22 stands out for its portrayal of
extreme anguish and its application to understanding
Jesus' suffering on the cross. In its OT context, it represents an individual lament psalm and portrays the
suffering of an individual waiting for God's deliverance.
 The psalmist opens with an anguished lament of being
forsaken by God (vv. 1–2). He praises God and appeals
to his past acts of deliverance (vv. 3–5). He describes
being publicly humiliated (vv. 6–8) and again appeals to
God, reminding him of his lifelong trust (vv. 9–11). He
vividly describes his suffering, portraying himself as in
physical anguish and weak (vv. 14–15) and surrounded

by enemies (vv. 12–13,16–18). He petitions God to
come quickly and deliver him (vv. 19–21). The psalmist
then turns to praise as he declares God's salvation to
the congregation of Israel (vv. 22–26). The scope of his
praise widens as he proclaims God's salvation to all the
nations and future generations (vv. 27–31).
 This psalm is used in the passion narratives of the
Gospels. Jesus quotes the opening line of this psalm
on the cross (Mt 27:46; Mk 15:34). Matthew and Mark
both allude to Ps 22:7 (Mt 27:39; Mk 15:29). Matthew
alludes to Ps 22:8 (Mt 27:43). All four gospels reflect
the dividing of garments in Ps 22:18 (Mt 27:35; Mk
15:24; Lk 23:34; Jn 19:24, which quotes the verse).
When Jesus cites the first and possibly the last verse
of this psalm (Jn 19:30), he portrays through words and
actions that he is the ultimate sufferer, the epitome of a
lament psalm incarnate (compare Isa 52:13—53:12).
See the table "Messianic Psalms" on p. 847.

22:title the director of music See note on Ps 4:title.
The Doe of the Morning Most likely the name of the
tune to which this psalm was sung. **A psalm of David**
See note on 3:title.
22:1 why have you forsaken me The feeling of being
abandoned by God causes the psalmist to despair. When
on the cross, Jesus quotes these words to communicate
a sense of abandonment by God the Father (Mt 27:46; Mk
15:34). The psalmist describes his great suffering, both
physical (Ps 22:14–15) and social (vv. 6–8), as well as
the enemies that surround him (vv. 12–13,16–18). Most
troubling to him, however, is his apparent abandonment
by God. The lifelong relationship between the psalmist
and God (vv. 9–11) deepens this pain. However, God
does not forsake his people, as the second half of the
psalm shows (vv. 22–24).

4 In you our ancestors put their trust;
  they trusted and you delivered them.
5 To you they cried out and were saved;
  in you they trusted and were not put to
    shame.

6 But I am a worm and not a man,
  scorned by everyone, despised by the
    people.
7 All who see me mock me;
  they hurl insults, shaking their heads.
8 "He trusts in the LORD," they say,
  "let the LORD rescue him.
Let him deliver him,
  since he delights in him."

9 Yet you brought me out of the womb;
  you made me trust in you, even at my
    mother's breast.
10 From birth I was cast on you;
  from my mother's womb you have been
    my God.

11 Do not be far from me,
  for trouble is near
  and there is no one to help.

12 Many bulls surround me;
  strong bulls of Bashan encircle me.
13 Roaring lions that tear their prey
  open their mouths wide against me.

22:3–5 This section of praise underscores God's silence. The psalmist's ancestors cried out to God and were delivered by him. The psalmist receives no answer to his cries. God has proven himself faithful in the past, but now appears to have forsaken the psalmist.

22:5 not put to shame The ancestors' trust in God was sure; God answered them, and they were not put to shame. In contrast, the psalmist is shamed (vv. 6–8).
22:7 they hurl insults The Hebrew phrase used here, *yaphtiru besaphah*—which may be literally rendered "they let out lips"—may indicate that people freely speak insults that would normally be held back. **shaking their heads** A gesture of derision. Matthew and Mark's ac-

count of Jesus' crucifixion refer to this verse. As Jesus hangs on the cross, people pass by shaking their heads in ridicule or mockery (Mt 27:39; Mk 15:29).
22:8 He trusts in the LORD The religious leaders repeat these words as they mock Jesus on the cross (Mt 27:43).

22:9–10 Despite his accusers' taunts, the psalmist reaffirms his trust in God. Their relationship has been close for many years—the psalmist describes God as the one who took him from the womb (Ps 71:6).

22:12 strong bulls of Bashan Refers to large and imposing creatures.
22:13 open their mouths While the Hebrew word used here, *patsah*, can indicate someone opening their mouth

Messianic Psalms

PSALM*	SPECIFIC APPLICATION TO JESUS IN NEW TESTAMENT
2	Ac 4:25–26; 13:33; Heb 1:5; 5:5; Rev 2:26–27
8	Mt 21:15–16; 1Co 15:27; Eph 1:22; Heb 2:6–8
16	Ac 2:25–31; 13:35
22	Mt 27:46; Mk 15:34; Jn 19:34; Heb 2:12
34	Jn 19:36
35	Jn 15:22
40	Heb 10:5–7
41	Jn 13:18
45	Heb 1:8–9
68	Eph 4:8
69	Jn 2:17; 15:25; Ro 15:3
89	Jn 12:34
102	Heb 1:10–12
110	Mt 22:44; 26:64; Mk 12:36; 14:62; Lk 20:42–43; Ac 2:34–35; Heb 1:13; 5:6; 7:17, 21
118	Mt 21:9,42; 23:39; Mk 12:10–11; Lk 13:35; 19:38; 20:17; Jn 12:13; Ac 4:11; 1Pe 2:7
132	Ac 2:30

* This is not a complete list; other psalms have been regarded as messianic.

¹⁴ I am poured out like water,
　and all my bones are out of joint.
My heart has turned to wax;
　it has melted within me.
¹⁵ My mouth*a* is dried up like a potsherd,
　and my tongue sticks to the roof of my
　　mouth;
you lay me in the dust of death.

¹⁶ Dogs surround me,
　a pack of villains encircles me;
　they pierce*b* my hands and my feet.
¹⁷ All my bones are on display;
　people stare and gloat over me.
¹⁸ They divide my clothes among them
　and cast lots for my garment.

¹⁹ But you, Lord, do not be far from me.
　You are my strength; come quickly to
　　help me.
²⁰ Deliver me from the sword,
　my precious life from the power of the
　　dogs.
²¹ Rescue me from the mouth of the lions;
　save me from the horns of the wild oxen.

²² I will declare your name to my people;
　in the assembly I will praise you.
²³ You who fear the Lord, praise him!
　All you descendants of Jacob, honor him!
　Revere him, all you descendants of Israel!

²⁴ For he has not despised or scorned
　the suffering of the afflicted one;
he has not hidden his face from him
　but has listened to his cry for help.

²⁵ From you comes the theme of my praise in
　　the great assembly;
before those who fear you*c* I will fulfill my
　vows.
²⁶ The poor will eat and be satisfied;
　those who seek the Lord will praise him —
　may your hearts live forever!

²⁷ All the ends of the earth
　will remember and turn to the Lord,
and all the families of the nations
　will bow down before him,
²⁸ for dominion belongs to the Lord
　and he rules over the nations.

²⁹ All the rich of the earth will feast and
　　worship;
all who go down to the dust will kneel
　before him —
　those who cannot keep themselves alive.
³⁰ Posterity will serve him;
　future generations will be told about the Lord.

a 15 Probable reading of the original Hebrew text; Masoretic Text *strength*　*b* 16 Dead Sea Scrolls and some manuscripts of the Masoretic Text, Septuagint and Syriac; most manuscripts of the Masoretic Text *me, / like a lion*　*c* 25 Hebrew *him*

to speak (Job 35:16), it often means opening a mouth to devour (Ge 4:11; La 2:16).

22:14–15 The psalmist vividly describes his suffering. The concept of being "poured out" implies weakness and instability. His heart melts like wax, possibly indicating a physical or psychological weakness (2Sa 17:10). His bones are loosened or separated (*parad* in Hebrew; see Job 41:17). He describes his strength as a dried clay pot, easily shattered (Isa 30:14). His tongue sticks to his mouth, indicating an inability to speak (Eze 3:26).

22:15 in the dust of death The psalmist's suffering, combined with God's seeming absence, leaves him without hope.

22:16 Dogs surround me Dogs were often viewed as despised scavengers in the ancient Near East (Ex 22:31; Ps 59:14–15). The psalmist's description of dogs surrounding him could indicate he was close to death, with the dogs waiting to eat him (1Ki 14:11; 2Ki 9:10). **they pierce** This line is a place where the Dead Sea Scrolls (ca. 250 BC–AD 50) illuminate the proper reading of the Hebrew text. The traditional Hebrew Bible (the Masoretic Text) reads literally "like a lion." The ancient Greek translation, the Septuagint, agrees with the Dead Sea Scrolls reading "pierce."

22:18 They divide my clothes Anticipating his death, the enemies of the psalmist are already dividing up his clothes. This is cited in the Gospels when the soldiers divide Jesus' clothes as he hangs on the cross (Jn 19:23–24; Mt 27:35; Mk 15:24; Lk 23:34).

22:19 do not be far from me The apparent distance and abandonment by God concerns the psalmist more than anything else (see note on Ps 22:1).

22:22 I will declare your name Despite his circumstances, the psalmist responds with resounding praise.

22:23–24 The psalmist encourages the community of believers to praise Yahweh. They should stand in awe of him because, contrary to the claims of vv. 1–2, God did not forsake him. Yahweh heard the psalmist's cry and responded.

22:25 my vows A vow was a promise to God, often made in times of distress (1Sa 1:10–11).

22:26 poor will eat Likely related to the thanksgiving sacrifice, which was to be shared as a meal (Lev 7:15–16; Dt 12:5–7).

22:27–28 The scope of the psalmist's praise extends beyond faithful Israelites (Ps 22:22–23) as he invites all the earth to remember and turn to Yahweh. He shows that Yahweh is not just God over Israel, but over all the nations (compare Isa 2:2–5).

22:29 All the rich Earlier, the psalmist included the afflicted in his thanksgiving banquet (see Ps 22:26 and note). Here, the wealthy (*dashen* in Hebrew, which literally means the "fat") also are invited to share in this banquet and praise Yahweh. **will kneel** The psalmist includes past generations in his thanksgiving banquet of praise. This reference to the dead praising Yahweh contrasts other statements in the Psalms where the dead do not praise God (6:5; 30:9; 115:17). However, there are similar statements elsewhere in the OT (Isa 26:19; Da 12:2). The OT view of the afterlife is difficult to discern. The realm of the dead (*she'ol* in Hebrew) was viewed as a pit of nothingness and decay (Dt 32:22; Ecc 9:10; Isa 14:11) secured by bars or gates (Job 17:16; 38:17). However, God's presence is not completely absent there

31 They will proclaim his righteousness,
  declaring to a people yet unborn:
  He has done it!

Psalm 23

A psalm of David.

1 The LORD is my shepherd, I lack nothing.
2   He makes me lie down in green
      pastures,
  he leads me beside quiet waters,
3   he refreshes my soul.
  He guides me along the right paths
    for his name's sake.
4 Even though I walk
    through the darkest valley,^a
  I will fear no evil,
    for you are with me;
  your rod and your staff,
    they comfort me.

5 You prepare a table before me
    in the presence of my enemies.
  You anoint my head with oil;
    my cup overflows.
6 Surely your goodness and love will follow me
    all the days of my life,
  and I will dwell in the house of the LORD
    forever.

Psalm 24

Of David. A psalm.

1 The earth is the LORD's, and everything in it,
    the world, and all who live in it;
2 for he founded it on the seas
    and established it on the waters.

3 Who may ascend the mountain of the LORD?
    Who may stand in his holy place?

---

^a 4 Or *the valley of the shadow of death*

(Ps 139:8). Sometimes death and *she'ol* is seen as a place of no return (Job 7:9), and other times it is viewed as a temporary location (Job 14:13).

22:30–31 The psalmist concludes his praise by including future generations. He has already broadened his scope to include the current generation—both Israelites and the nations, both rich and poor. He has also included past generations. Now, he brings past, present and future together by including the coming generations. Those not yet born will share the psalmist's story of God delivering him from the depths of suffering (compare Isa 53:10 and note; 53:12 and note).

22:31 He has done it The Hebrew phrase here, *ki asah,* can be understood as "for it is done." Jesus may have had this verse in mind when he said "It is finished" (*tetelestai* in Greek) as he died on the cross (Jn 19:30).

23:title–6 Psalm 23 is a psalm of confidence in Yahweh—showing an intimate relationship between the psalmist and Yahweh. As a hymn of trust, it expresses the psalmist's confidence in Yahweh's guidance, using images of a shepherd (vv. 1–4) and host (vv. 5–6) to portray God's care of him.

23:title A psalm of David See note on 3:title.
23:1 The LORD is my shepherd The psalmist portrays Yahweh as a shepherd, a common depiction throughout the OT. The metaphor emphasizes his care for and protection of his people (28:9; Isa 40:11). See the table "Names of God in the Old Testament" on p. 917.
23:2 green pastures This emphasizes ideas of nourishment and abundance. **quiet** The Hebrew word used here, *menuchah*, emphasizes rest and security.
23:3 right paths Describing a path of life (Pr 12:28). To be led on these paths is to enjoy Yahweh's protection (Ps 1:6). See 5:8 and note. **for his name's sake** Yahweh's protection and care of the psalmist is not only for the psalmist's sake, but for the sake of Yahweh's name (or reputation). Yahweh performs acts of deliverance to reveal his power (106:8). The destruction of his people would cause his enemies to profane (or disrespect) his name (79:9–10; Eze 20:9; 36:22–32). By saving his people, Yahweh also reveals his faithful love (Ps 109:21) through his protection (31:3–5).
23:4 darkest valley The psalmist acknowledges that

life will not always be characterized by green pastures and quiet waters (v. 2). He will walk through darkness and gloom (107:10; Job 10:22). **your rod and your staff** Tools used by shepherds to guide sheep. Having sheep pass under a rod was a way of counting them (Lev 27:32). Here, the rod symbolizes Yahweh's protection and care. Elsewhere, it serves as a symbol of divine discipline (Ps 89:32; 2Sa 7:14).
23:5 a table before me The psalmist switches from portraying Yahweh as a shepherd to portraying him as a host. Hospitality in the ancient Near East required more than providing a meal. The host was also responsible for protecting his guest (see Ge 19:8 and note). Since the psalmist, as a guest, enjoys Yahweh's protection, he can eat safely in the presence of his enemies.
23:6 Surely your goodness and love With Yahweh as his shepherd and host, the psalmist is confident that he will be protected by Yahweh's unfailing covenantal love (Ex 34:6). **forever** The Hebrew phrase used here, *le'orekh yamim*, literally means "for length of days." This does not necessarily indicate eternity; it shows the psalmist expects to be Yahweh's guest all of his life.

24:title–10 Like Ps 15, this is a temple entry psalm. Here it is not just the worshiper who enters the temple, but Yahweh himself. The psalmist begins with a statement of Yahweh's supremacy over creation (vv. 1–2), then discusses the external and internal purity requirements of the worshiper (vv. 3–6). Finally, he describes the entry of Yahweh, the victorious King (vv. 7–10). See the table "Types of Psalms" on p. 830.

24:title Of David. A psalm See note on 3:title.
24:2 on the seas Reflects the ancient Near Eastern belief that the earth was supported by pillars sunk into the sea or floated upon the sea (104:5; 1Sa 2:8). In ancient Near Eastern mythology, the sea represented chaos. The act of creation involved subduing these forces. Old Testament writers depict Yahweh as having power over the sea (Ps 77:16; Job 38:8) to show he is the supreme deity—infinitely more powerful than other ancient Near Eastern gods who continually battle the forces of chaos.
24:3 mountain of the LORD Refers to the Temple Mount in Jerusalem (Mount Zion), which Israelites believed was the dwelling place of Yahweh (Ps 43:3).

⁴ The one who has clean hands and a pure heart,
who does not trust in an idol
or swear by a false god.ᵃ

⁵ They will receive blessing from the LORD
and vindication from God their Savior.
⁶ Such is the generation of those who seek him,
who seek your face, God of Jacob.ᵇ,ᶜ

⁷ Lift up your heads, you gates;
be lifted up, you ancient doors,
that the King of glory may come in.
⁸ Who is this King of glory?
The LORD strong and mighty,
the LORD mighty in battle.
⁹ Lift up your heads, you gates;
lift them up, you ancient doors,
that the King of glory may come in.
¹⁰ Who is he, this King of glory?
The LORD Almighty—
he is the King of glory.

Psalm 25ᵈ

Of David.

¹ In you, LORD my God,
I put my trust.

² I trust in you;
do not let me be put to shame,
nor let my enemies triumph over me.

³ No one who hopes in you
will ever be put to shame,
but shame will come on those
who are treacherous without cause.

⁴ Show me your ways, LORD,
teach me your paths.
⁵ Guide me in your truth and teach me,
for you are God my Savior,
and my hope is in you all day long.
⁶ Remember, LORD, your great mercy and love,
for they are from of old.
⁷ Do not remember the sins of my youth
and my rebellious ways;
according to your love remember me,
for you, LORD, are good.

⁸ Good and upright is the LORD;
therefore he instructs sinners in his ways.
⁹ He guides the humble in what is right
and teaches them his way.
¹⁰ All the ways of the LORD are loving and
faithful
toward those who keep the demands of his
covenant.

ᵃ 4 Or *swear falsely*   ᵇ 6 Two Hebrew manuscripts and Syriac
(see also Septuagint); most Hebrew manuscripts *face, Jacob*
ᶜ 6 The Hebrew has *Selah* (a word of uncertain meaning) here
and at the end of verse 10.   ᵈ This psalm is an acrostic poem,
the verses of which begin with the successive letters of the
Hebrew alphabet.

24:4 clean hands and a pure heart The requirements
for entering the temple are both external and internal
(see 15:2 and note). The Hebrew word for "clean" (*naqi*)
means "innocent" (10:8; Job 4:7).
24:5 vindication While the description in Ps 24:4 seems
to indicate only the perfect can enter the temple, this
verse indicates the worshiper receives righteousness
and salvation from Yahweh.
24:6 who seek your face To seek God's face is to desire
to be in his presence (see note on 11:7).
24:7 Lift up your heads This psalm was most likely used
when the ark of the covenant returned from battle (see
Nu 10:35–36 and note). See the infographic "Solomon's
Temple" on p. 520; see the infographic "The Ark of the
Covenant" on p. 412.
24:8 mighty in battle The psalmist portrays Yahweh, the
King of glory, as a mighty warrior (Ex 15:3). Throughout
the OT, Biblical writers portray Yahweh going out to battle
with his people (Dt 20:2–4).
24:10 LORD Almighty The Hebrew divine title used here,
yhwh tseva'oth—which literally translates as "Yahweh of
hosts" or "Yahweh of armies"—has military connotations (1Sa 17:45). Biblical writers often used this title
in connection with the ark of the covenant (1Sa 4:4; 2Sa
6:2), which supports the idea that Israelites used this
psalm as the ark entered the temple (see note on Ps
24:7). See the table "Names of God in the Old Testament" on p. 917.
25:title–22 Psalm 25, which is probably an individual
lament psalm, is a mostly complete acrostic poem—a
poem where the lines start with consecutive letters of the
Hebrew alphabet. The psalmist emphasizes his desire
for Yahweh's guidance and deliverance. He asserts his

trust in God (vv. 1–3), then petitions Yahweh for guidance
(vv. 4–5) and forgiveness (vv. 6–7). After describing Yahweh's goodness and faithfulness (vv. 8–10), the psalmist
again seeks forgiveness (v. 11). He describes the benefits
of fearing Yahweh (vv. 12–15), and seeks his deliverance and protection (vv. 16–18,19–21). The psalmist
concludes by asking God to redeem all of Israel (v. 22).

25:title Of David See note on 3:title.
25:2 put to shame The Hebrew word used here, *bosh*,
often represents a result of misplaced trust (Job 6:20).
Here, the psalmist prays that his trust in God will be
validated.

25:4–5 The psalmist uses several Hebrew words here
for learning or instruction as he asks Yahweh to teach
(*lamad*), lead (*darakh*) and make known (*yada'*) his true
paths. The psalmist trusts in Yahweh because he guides
and protects him (Ps 23:1–3).

25:6–7 The psalmist seeks forgiveness and reminds
Yahweh of his mercy and faithful love (*chesed* in Hebrew;
see note on v. 10). He hopes Yahweh will remember these
things rather than the psalmist's sins. He contrasts
the timelessness of Yahweh's love and mercy with the
temporary sins of his youth, citing Yahweh's goodness
as his grounds for appeal (23:6).

25:8–10 After appealing to Yahweh for guidance (vv. 4–5)
and forgiveness (vv. 6–7), the psalmist praises Yahweh's
character. He trusts God (v. 2) knowing he is a good and
faithful guide who teaches the sinner and the humble.

25:10 loving The Hebrew term used here, *chesed*, is one
of Yahweh's essential characteristics. When paired with

¹¹ For the sake of your name, LORD,
  forgive my iniquity, though it is great.
¹² Who, then, are those who fear the LORD?
  He will instruct them in the ways they
    should choose.ᵃ
¹³ They will spend their days in prosperity,
  and their descendants will inherit
    the land.
¹⁴ The LORD confides in those who fear him;
  he makes his covenant known to them.
¹⁵ My eyes are ever on the LORD,
  for only he will release my feet from the
    snare.
¹⁶ Turn to me and be gracious to me,
  for I am lonely and afflicted.
¹⁷ Relieve the troubles of my heart
  and free me from my anguish.
¹⁸ Look on my affliction and my distress
  and take away all my sins.
¹⁹ See how numerous are my enemies
  and how fiercely they hate me!
²⁰ Guard my life and rescue me;
  do not let me be put to shame,
  for I take refuge in you.

²¹ May integrity and uprightness protect me,
  because my hope, LORD,ᵇ is in you.
²² Deliver Israel, O God,
  from all their troubles!

Psalm 26

Of David.

¹ Vindicate me, LORD,
  for I have led a blameless life;
I have trusted in the LORD
  and have not faltered.
² Test me, LORD, and try me,
  examine my heart and my mind;
³ for I have always been mindful of your
    unfailing love
  and have lived in reliance on your
    faithfulness.

⁴ I do not sit with the deceitful,
  nor do I associate with hypocrites.
⁵ I abhor the assembly of evildoers
  and refuse to sit with the wicked.

ᵃ 12 Or *ways he chooses*   ᵇ 21 Septuagint; Hebrew does not have LORD.

---

emeth, the Hebrew word for God's faithfulness (as it is here), *chesed* describes God as absolutely dependable to fulfill his promises (see Ex 34:6 and note).
25:11 sake of your name See note on Ps 23:3.
25:14 confides The Hebrew noun used here, *sod*, can mean "council" (Jer 23:18); it refers to a close relationship of confidence (Job 29:4; Pr 3:32).
25:15 My eyes are ever on the LORD After describing the benefits of fearing Yahweh (reverently standing in awe of him), the psalmist confirms his devotion.

25:16–20 The psalmist asks Yahweh to deliver him from his affliction and trouble. He does not specify the cause of his distress; it likely relates to his enemies (Ps 25:19–20).
25:18 Look on The Hebrew word used here, *ra'ah*, means "to consider," "to look at" or "to see." The psalmist declares that he keeps his eyes fixed on Yahweh (v. 15).
25:21 integrity and uprightness These terms, which indicate purity and honesty, are also used to describe Job (see Job 1:1 and note).
25:22 Deliver Israel, O God This closing verse is outside the acrostic pattern of the psalm (see note on 25:title–22)—which highlights it as a closing remark. The psalmist petitions God to redeem (*padah* in Hebrew) all of Israel, rather than just the psalmist.

PADAH
The Hebrew word *padah* means "to redeem." It refers to buying something back. It often occurs in the context of ransoming or delivering people from trouble or affliction. Yahweh redeems Israel from slavery in Egypt (Dt 7:8; Mic 6:4). He also redeems individuals from their enemies (2Sa 4:9; 1Ki 1:29).

26:title–12 Psalm 26 is probably a temple entry psalm—a psalm used by worshipers before entering the temple. Alternatively, it may be an individual lament psalm, in which the psalmist seeks to be vindicated from false accusations (see Ps 17), though he does not mention any affliction or specific enemies.
  The psalmist begins by asking Yahweh to vindicate or judge him. He proceeds to show his worthiness to Yahweh (26:1–3) by distancing himself from the wicked and proclaiming Yahweh's deeds (vv. 4–7). He declares his love for Yahweh's temple and petitions God not to judge him along with sinners (vv. 8–10). He closes by emphasizing his integrity and stating his intention to publicly bless Yahweh (vv. 11–12).

26:title Of David See note on 3:title.
26:1 Vindicate me The Hebrew word used here, *shaphat*, can mean specifically "to vindicate," or more generally "to judge" (Ex 18:13). The psalmist probably uses it in the sense of "to judge," as he asks Yahweh to examine him and his worth. **not faltered** The psalmist is not describing perfection; he merely indicates that his trust in Yahweh has given him security (Ps 37:31).
26:3 I have always been mindful The psalmist demonstrates his worth by showing that he pays careful attention to Yahweh's steadfast love (compare note on 25:15).

26:4–5 The psalmist expresses loyalty to Yahweh by showing his distance from those who oppose him. Like the "blessed" person of Ps 1 (see note on 1:1), the psalmist lists four types of people he does not associate with: men of falsehood, hypocrites (v. 4), evildoers and the wicked (v. 5).

26:4 deceitful The Hebrew word used here, *shawe*, describes deceptive or false people (see Job 11:11 and note). **hypocrites** The Hebrew word used here, *alam*, means "those who conceal themselves."
26:5 wicked The Hebrew word used here, *rasha'* (meaning

6 I wash my hands in innocence,
    and go about your altar, Lord,
7 proclaiming aloud your praise
    and telling of all your wonderful deeds.

8 Lord, I love the house where you live,
    the place where your glory dwells.
9 Do not take away my soul along with
        sinners,
    my life with those who are bloodthirsty,
10 in whose hands are wicked schemes,
    whose right hands are full of bribes.
11 I lead a blameless life;
    deliver me and be merciful to me.

12 My feet stand on level ground;
    in the great congregation I will praise the
        Lord.

Psalm 27

Of David.

1 The Lord is my light and my salvation —
    whom shall I fear?
The Lord is the stronghold of my life —
    of whom shall I be afraid?

2 When the wicked advance against me
    to devour[a] me,
it is my enemies and my foes
    who will stumble and fall.
3 Though an army besiege me,
    my heart will not fear;

though war break out against me,
    even then I will be confident.

4 One thing I ask from the Lord,
    this only do I seek:
that I may dwell in the house of the Lord
    all the days of my life,
to gaze on the beauty of the Lord
    and to seek him in his temple.
5 For in the day of trouble
    he will keep me safe in his dwelling;
he will hide me in the shelter of his sacred
        tent
    and set me high upon a rock.

6 Then my head will be exalted
    above the enemies who surround me;
at his sacred tent I will sacrifice with shouts
        of joy;
    I will sing and make music to the Lord.

7 Hear my voice when I call, Lord;
    be merciful to me and answer me.
8 My heart says of you, "Seek his face!"
    Your face, Lord, I will seek.
9 Do not hide your face from me,
    do not turn your servant away in anger;
    you have been my helper.
Do not reject me or forsake me,
    God my Savior.
10 Though my father and mother forsake me,
    the Lord will receive me.

a 2 Or slander

"to be guilty"), is often used in parallel with the Hebrew word for "evildoer" (Ps 10:15).

26:6 I wash my hands Those who desired to worship at the temple were required to have clean hands (see 24:4 and note; compare note on 26:title–12). **in innocence** By proclaiming his innocence, the psalmist further disassociates himself from the guilty (see note on vv. 4–5).

26:8 the house where you live The Hebrew word used here, *ma'on*—which may be literally rendered as "dwelling place" or "habitation"—could be interpreted as heaven (Dt 26:15). However, the psalmist likely refers to Yahweh's earthly dwelling place—the temple (compare note on 26:title–12). The Israelites viewed the Jerusalem temple as Yahweh's earthly dwelling place, but it was also acknowledged as only a representation of his presence (1Ki 8:27–30).

26:10 full of bribes Psalm 15 indicates that people who took bribes were forbidden from entering the temple (see 15:5 and note).

26:12 stand on level ground This aligns with the psalmist's earlier statement that he has not slipped or faltered (see note on 26:1).

27:title–14 While the first half (vv. 1–6) of this psalm resembles a psalm of confidence in Yahweh, the second half (vv. 7–14) shares features with individual lament psalms. The psalmist expresses trust that Yahweh will provide victory against his enemies (vv. 1–3). He then expresses his desire to dwell in Yahweh's presence in the temple, repeating his belief that Yahweh will give him victory (vv. 4–6). He petitions Yahweh to hear his cry,

guide him and deliver him from his enemies (vv. 7–12). He then expresses his confidence in Yahweh and encourages others to wait on him (vv. 13–14). This psalm may have been used in preparation for battle (compare Ps 20). See the table "Types of Psalms" on p. 830.

27:title Of David See note on 3:title.

27:1 The Lord is my light Represents Yahweh's guiding presence (43:3). See note on 18:28; Job 29:2–4.

27:3 besiege A siege in ancient Near Eastern warfare involved blocking off any route in or out of a city, often resulting in famine (2Ki 6:25–30).

27:4 seek The Hebrew word used here, *baqar*, means "to examine" or "to scrutinize." Here it may describe a prayerful search for Yahweh's will or a meditative reflection.

27:5 day of trouble In Ps 20, the "day of trouble" relates to a military campaign (see note on 20:1). The reference to a siege (27:3) indicates it probably has the same connotation here. **rock** The Hebrew word used here, *tsur*, refers to a secure, elevated location (see note on 18:1–3).

27:6 my head will be exalted A lifted head signaled confidence and pride. **shouts of joy** Probably describes a shout of victory. The Hebrew word used here, *teru'ah*, often appears in military contexts (2Ch 13:12). This type of shout toppled the walls of Jericho (Jos 6:5,20). It was also used to signify the presence of the ark of the covenant (1Sa 4:6; 2Sa 6:15). See the infographic "Ancient Jericho" on p. 330.

27:10 my father and mother This could be an allusion to the Davidic covenant, where Yahweh promises to be a father to the royal Davidic line. He promises to establish

¹¹ Teach me your way, LORD;
  lead me in a straight path
  because of my oppressors.
¹² Do not turn me over to the desire of
    my foes,
  for false witnesses rise up against me,
  spouting malicious accusations.

¹³ I remain confident of this:
  I will see the goodness of the LORD
  in the land of the living.
¹⁴ Wait for the LORD;
  be strong and take heart
  and wait for the LORD.

Psalm 28

Of David.

¹ To you, LORD, I call;
  you are my Rock,
  do not turn a deaf ear to me.
For if you remain silent,
  I will be like those who go down to the pit.
² Hear my cry for mercy
  as I call to you for help,
  as I lift up my hands
  toward your Most Holy Place.

³ Do not drag me away with the wicked,
  with those who do evil,
who speak cordially with their neighbors
  but harbor malice in their hearts.
⁴ Repay them for their deeds
  and for their evil work;

repay them for what their hands have done
  and bring back on them what they deserve.

⁵ Because they have no regard for the deeds of
    the LORD
  and what his hands have done,
he will tear them down
  and never build them up again.

⁶ Praise be to the LORD,
  for he has heard my cry for mercy.
⁷ The LORD is my strength and my shield;
  my heart trusts in him, and he helps me.
My heart leaps for joy,
  and with my song I praise him.

⁸ The LORD is the strength of his people,
  a fortress of salvation for his anointed one.
⁹ Save your people and bless your inheritance;
  be their shepherd and carry them forever.

Psalm 29

A psalm of David.

¹ Ascribe to the LORD, you heavenly beings,
  ascribe to the LORD glory and strength.
² Ascribe to the LORD the glory due his name;
  worship the LORD in the splendor of his^a
  holiness.

³ The voice of the LORD is over the waters;
  the God of glory thunders,
  the LORD thunders over the mighty waters.

^a *2 Or* LORD *with the splendor of*

---

the Davidic line in an eternal way (2Sa 7:14–16). See
Ps 2:7 and note; 18:50 and note.
27:12 false witnesses Implies the psalmist may be
accused of wrongdoing (see note on Ex 20:16). However,
the reference could be symbolic if this psalm was used in
preparation for battle (see Ps 27:3; note on 27:title–14).
27:14 Wait for the LORD Describes eager hope and expectation for deliverance (Ge 49:18; Isa 8:17; Isa 40:31).

28:title–9 This individual lament psalm is a plea for
justice. The psalmist opens by petitioning Yahweh to
hear his cries (Ps 28:1–2). He seeks justice, asking
Yahweh to punish the wicked and spare him (vv. 3–5).
The psalmist then expresses confidence in Yahweh by
praising him for hearing his cry (vv. 6–7). He closes by
asking Yahweh to bless and keep all his people safe
(vv. 8–9). See the table "Types of Psalms" on p. 830.

28:title Of David See note on 3:title.
28:1 my Rock See note on 27:5. **the pit** A synonym
for the Hebrew concept of *she'ol*, the realm of the dead.
See note on Job 14:13.
28:2 lift up my hands This is a posture of worship
(Ps 134:2). In parallel with this verse, at the temple's
dedication, Solomon asked Yahweh to hear any prayer for
forgiveness or deliverance that was directed toward the
temple (1Ki 8:35–45). See the infographic "Solomon's
Temple" on p. 520.
28:4 for their deeds The psalmist wants to be sure the
wicked will be punished.

28:5 they have no regard The psalmist requests that
the wicked be punished because they do not pay attention to Yahweh's deeds.
28:8 anointed one The Hebrew word used here,
mashiach, normally refers to Yahweh's anointed king (see
note on Ps 2:2). Here it represents all of God's people.

29:title–11 This praise psalm seems to draw on Canaanite
poetry in which Baal, the Canaanite god of the skies, battles
against the sea god Yam, who represents chaos (compare
note on 18:7–19). The psalmist uses this mythology to
proclaim Yahweh's glory and strength over other gods. He
begins his psalm with a call to praise Yahweh (vv. 1–2).
He praises Yahweh's voice as he describes its power
(vv. 3–9). Finally, he recognizes Yahweh as the enthroned
king and petitions him to strengthen and bless his people
(vv. 10–11). See the table "Types of Psalms" on p. 830.

29:title A psalm of David See note on 3:title.
29:1 you heavenly beings See note on Ge 6:2.
29:2 the glory due his name The psalmist encourages
his audience to give Yahweh the glory he is due. In the
psalms, Yahweh often acts to save or deliver for his
name's sake. See Ps 23:3 and note.

29:3–9 This section focuses on the Hebrew idea of *qol yhwh*
(literally the "voice of Yahweh"). The psalmist repeats the
phrase seven times—a number symbolic of completeness
(see note on Job 1:2)—to portray God's power and glory.

29:3 God of glory thunders Thunder often appears

⁴ The voice of the Lord is powerful;
  the voice of the Lord is majestic.
⁵ The voice of the Lord breaks the cedars;
  the Lord breaks in pieces the cedars of
    Lebanon.
⁶ He makes Lebanon leap like a calf,
  Sirion[a] like a young wild ox.
⁷ The voice of the Lord strikes
  with flashes of lightning.
⁸ The voice of the Lord shakes the desert;
  the Lord shakes the Desert of Kadesh.
⁹ The voice of the Lord twists the oaks[b]
  and strips the forests bare.
  And in his temple all cry, "Glory!"

¹⁰ The Lord sits enthroned over the flood;
  the Lord is enthroned as King forever.
¹¹ The Lord gives strength to his people;
  the Lord blesses his people with peace.

Psalm 30[c]

*A psalm. A song. For the dedication
of the temple.[d] Of David.*

¹ I will exalt you, Lord,
  for you lifted me out of the depths
  and did not let my enemies gloat over me.
² Lord my God, I called to you for help,
  and you healed me.
³ You, Lord, brought me up from the realm of
    the dead;
  you spared me from going down to
    the pit.

⁴ Sing the praises of the Lord, you his faithful
    people;
  praise his holy name.
⁵ For his anger lasts only a moment,
  but his favor lasts a lifetime;

weeping may stay for the night,
  but rejoicing comes in the morning.

⁶ When I felt secure, I said,
  "I will never be shaken."
⁷ Lord, when you favored me,
  you made my royal mountain[e] stand
    firm;
  but when you hid your face,
    I was dismayed.

⁸ To you, Lord, I called;
  to the Lord I cried for mercy:
⁹ "What is gained if I am silenced,
  if I go down to the pit?
  Will the dust praise you?
  Will it proclaim your faithfulness?
¹⁰ Hear, Lord, and be merciful to me;
  Lord, be my help."

¹¹ You turned my wailing into dancing;
  you removed my sackcloth and clothed me
    with joy,
¹² that my heart may sing your praises and not
    be silent.
  Lord my God, I will praise you forever.

Psalm 31[f]

31:1-4pp — Ps 71:1-3

For the director of music. A psalm of David.

¹ In you, Lord, I have taken refuge;
  let me never be put to shame;
  deliver me in your righteousness.
² Turn your ear to me,
  come quickly to my rescue;

---

[a] 6 That is, Mount Hermon   [b] 9 Or *Lord makes the deer give
birth*   [c] In Hebrew texts 30:1-12 is numbered 30:2-13.
[d] Title: Or *palace*   [e] 7 That is, Mount Zion   [f] In Hebrew texts
31:1-24 is numbered 31:2-25.

---

as a symbol or manifestation of God's voice (Ps 18:13;
Job 37:2). God answered Moses in thunder at Mount
Sinai (Ex 19:19). He used a mighty, thunderous sound
to defeat the Philistines for Samuel (1Sa 7:10). Thunder
emphasizes the power and majesty of God (Isa 30:30). It
also reveals Yahweh's superiority to Baal, the Canaanite
god of storms (1Ki 18:24–40; compare note on Ps
29:title–11).
29:6 Sirion Another name for Mount Hermon (Dt 3:9).
Both Sirion and Lebanon are mentioned in Canaanite
Baal poetry (see note on Ps 29:title–11).
29:8 Kadesh Several events during Israel's desert
wanderings occurred at Kadesh, located on the southern
border of Israel (Nu 13–14; 20:1–21).
29:10 flood The Hebrew word used here, *mabbul*, is
only used elsewhere to describe the flood in Genesis
(Ge 6:17).

30:title–12 The psalmist begins this thanksgiving
psalm—which is specifically identified as a song—with
a praise of thanks to Yahweh for rescuing him from death
(Ps 30:1–3). The psalmist then addresses the saints
(or holy ones) and encourages them to join in praising Yahweh (vv. 4–5). He briefly describes his distress

(vv. 6–7) and cries to Yahweh for help (vv. 8–10) before
concluding with thanks and praise (vv. 11–12). See the
table "Types of Psalms" on p. 830.

30:title temple The Hebrew word used here, *habbayith*,
literally means "house," and most likely refers to the
temple, God's house (5:7). The psalm itself, however,
seems to be unrelated to the temple, as it concerns
personal, not corporate (group) thanksgiving. **Of David**
See note on 3:title.
30:3 the realm of the dead The Hebrew word *she'ol* is
used here. See note on 1Ki 2:6.
30:5 comes in the morning The morning often represents restoration or blessing in the psalms (Ps 90:14;
La 3:22–23).
30:9 What is gained The psalmist argues he would
be unable to praise Yahweh or tell others of his faithful
restoration if he were dead; it would be better for Yahweh
to deliver him (see Ps 6:5 and note).
30:11 sackcloth A sign of mourning. See note on Ne 9:1.
30:12 that my heart may sing This seems to signal
that Yahweh has restored the psalmist and turned his
mourning into dancing so the psalmist could sing his
praise (see note on Ps 30:9).

be my rock of refuge,
   a strong fortress to save me.
³ Since you are my rock and my fortress,
   for the sake of your name lead and
      guide me.
⁴ Keep me free from the trap that is set for me,
   for you are my refuge.
⁵ Into your hands I commit my spirit;
   deliver me, Lord, my faithful God.

⁶ I hate those who cling to worthless idols;
   as for me, I trust in the Lord.
⁷ I will be glad and rejoice in your love,
   for you saw my affliction
   and knew the anguish of my soul.
⁸ You have not given me into the hands of the
      enemy
   but have set my feet in a spacious place.

⁹ Be merciful to me, Lord, for I am in distress;
   my eyes grow weak with sorrow,
   my soul and body with grief.
¹⁰ My life is consumed by anguish
   and my years by groaning;
   my strength fails because of my affliction,ᵃ
   and my bones grow weak.
¹¹ Because of all my enemies,
   I am the utter contempt of my neighbors
   and an object of dread to my closest friends —
   those who see me on the street flee
      from me.

¹² I am forgotten as though I were dead;
   I have become like broken pottery.
¹³ For I hear many whispering,
   "Terror on every side!"
   They conspire against me
   and plot to take my life.

¹⁴ But I trust in you, Lord;
   I say, "You are my God."
¹⁵ My times are in your hands;
   deliver me from the hands of my enemies,
   from those who pursue me.
¹⁶ Let your face shine on your servant;
   save me in your unfailing love.
¹⁷ Let me not be put to shame, Lord,
   for I have cried out to you;
   but let the wicked be put to shame
   and be silent in the realm of the dead.
¹⁸ Let their lying lips be silenced,
   for with pride and contempt
   they speak arrogantly against the righteous.

¹⁹ How abundant are the good things
   that you have stored up for those who
      fear you,
   that you bestow in the sight of all,
   on those who take refuge in you.
²⁰ In the shelter of your presence you hide them
   from all human intrigues;

ᵃ 10 Or guilt

31:title–24 Psalm 31 is an individual lament psalm with elements of a thanksgiving psalm. The psalmist opens by petitioning Yahweh to deliver him (vv. 1–2). He expresses trust in and loyalty to Yahweh (vv. 3–8) and then again petitions him for help (vv. 9–10) describing how he has been ostracized (vv. 11–13). He then again asserts trust in Yahweh and asks again for deliverance (vv. 14–18). The psalmist then turns to praise as he extols Yahweh's goodness (vv. 19–20). Finally, he addresses others who have been faithful to Yahweh as he praises Yahweh's deliverance and encourages them regarding Yahweh's faithfulness (vv. 21–24). See the table "Types of Psalms" on p. 830.

31:title director of music See note on 4:title. **A psalm of David** See note on 3:title.
31:1 let me never be put to shame The Hebrew word used here that is related to shame, *bosh*, usually comes as a result of misplaced trust (Job 6:20; Isa 1:29). However, the psalmist proclaims that the one who trusts in Yahweh will never be put to shame.
31:3 for the sake of your name See note on Ps 23:3.
31:5 I commit my spirit In the face of his troubles, which include sickness (vv. 9–10) and social alienation (vv. 11–13), the psalmist entrusts himself to Yahweh's faithful care. Jesus repeats these words as he dies on the cross (Lk 23:46). Just as the psalmist entrusts himself to God as he suffers, Jesus entrusts himself to God the Father as he dies. In Luke, this phrase emphasizes Jesus' willingness to submit himself to his Father's will (Lk 22:42; compare Isa 53:12).
31:6 I hate those The psalmist declares his loyalty to Yahweh by showing that he hates idolatry.

Psalm 31:6

SHAWE
The Hebrew word *shawe* means "worthless" or "false." It is used to describe a false witness (Dt 5:20) or a false report (Ex 23:1). It is also used to describe something that is empty or baseless (Job 35:13).

31:9–10 As he appeals to Yahweh for help, the psalmist describes his deteriorating physical condition. His description reflects other lament psalms (Ps 6:6–7; 22:14–15).

31:11 contempt The Hebrew word used here, *cherpah*, typically describes shame or disgrace that results from an action (Ge 34:14; 2Sa 13:13). The psalmist describes how his affliction has made him an object of scorn and ridicule, despite his faithfulness to Yahweh (Ps 31:6).
31:12 like broken pottery The psalmist compares himself to broken pottery, which people discard because it is useless (Jer 22:28).
31:15 in your hands Just as Job recognized that Yahweh gives and takes away (see Job 1:21 and note), the psalmist recognizes that all of his times, both good and bad, are in God's hands.
31:17 the realm of the dead The Hebrew word *she'ol* is used here. See note on Job 14:13; note on 1Ki 2:6.
31:19 good things Since he has taken refuge in Yahweh (Ps 31:1), the psalmist expects to receive Yahweh's goodness.

you keep them safe in your dwelling
　　from accusing tongues.
[21] Praise be to the LORD,
　　for he showed me the wonders of his love
　　　when I was in a city under siege.
[22] In my alarm I said,
　　"I am cut off from your sight!"
　　Yet you heard my cry for mercy
　　　when I called to you for help.

[23] Love the LORD, all his faithful people!
　　The LORD preserves those who are true
　　　to him,
　　but the proud he pays back in full.
[24] Be strong and take heart,
　　all you who hope in the LORD.

Psalm 32

Of David. A maskil.[a]

[1] Blessed is the one
　　whose transgressions are forgiven,
　　whose sins are covered.
[2] Blessed is the one
　　whose sin the LORD does not count against
　　　them
　　and in whose spirit is no deceit.

[3] When I kept silent,
　　my bones wasted away
　　through my groaning all day long.
[4] For day and night
　　your hand was heavy on me;
　　my strength was sapped
　　　as in the heat of summer.[b]
[5] Then I acknowledged my sin to you
　　and did not cover up my iniquity.

I said, "I will confess
　　my transgressions to the LORD."
And you forgave
　　the guilt of my sin.

[6] Therefore let all the faithful pray to you
　　while you may be found;
　　surely the rising of the mighty waters
　　will not reach them.
[7] You are my hiding place;
　　you will protect me from trouble
　　and surround me with songs of deliverance.

[8] I will instruct you and teach you in the way
　　　you should go;
　　I will counsel you with my loving eye
　　　on you.
[9] Do not be like the horse or the mule,
　　which have no understanding
　　but must be controlled by bit and bridle
　　or they will not come to you.
[10] Many are the woes of the wicked,
　　but the LORD's unfailing love
　　surrounds the one who trusts in him.

[11] Rejoice in the LORD and be glad, you
　　　righteous;
　　sing, all you who are upright in heart!

Psalm 33

[1] Sing joyfully to the LORD, you righteous;
　　it is fitting for the upright to praise him.
[2] Praise the LORD with the harp;
　　make music to him on the ten-stringed lyre.

a Title: Probably a literary or musical term　　*b* 4 The Hebrew
has *Selah* (a word of uncertain meaning) here and at the end of
verses 5 and 7.

31:23–24 The psalmist closes by encouraging the faithful
to love Yahweh. He assures them that Yahweh preserves
the faithful and ultimately punishes the prideful. He
encourages other sufferers by telling them to remain
strong and wait for Yahweh's deliverance.

31:24 all you who hope in the LORD Describes eager
hope and expectation for God's deliverance (Isa 40:31).

32:title–11 Used as one of the early church's penitential
psalms (Ps 6; 38; 51; 102; 130; 143), this thanksgiving
psalm focuses on the forgiveness of sins. The psalmist
begins by extolling the blessings of forgiveness (32:1–2).
He then shares how he suffered until he acknowledged
his sin and was forgiven (vv. 3–5). He encourages the
godly to pray to God, who preserved him from trouble
(vv. 6–7). Yahweh then speaks, encouraging people
to follow his instruction and teaching (vv. 8–9). The
psalmist concludes by encouraging the righteous to
rejoice in Yahweh (vv. 10–11). See the table "Types of
Psalms" on p. 830.

32:title Of David See note on 3:title. **A maskil** This
term most likely comes from the Hebrew word *sakhal*,
meaning "to have insight" or "to be skillful."

32:1–2 In this section, the psalmist uses three Hebrew
terms related to the idea of sin: *pesha'* (transgression),
chata'ah (sin) and *awon* (iniquity). Paul cites these verses
in Romans as he discusses justification (Ro 4:7–8).

32:1 Blessed See note on Ps 1:1.

32:3–5 The psalmist recounts a personal testimony
to illustrate the power of confessing sin. During a situation when he was silent and unrepentant, he suffered
and continually felt Yahweh's punishment. Only after he
acknowledged and confessed his sins to Yahweh did he
enjoy Yahweh's forgiveness.

32:6 faithful See note on 18:25.

32:8–9 In these verses, Yahweh replaces the psalmist
as speaker. In a statement reminiscent of Proverbs (Pr
1:8; 3:1; 4:1–2), Yahweh states he will instruct and
teach the people. He encourages them to accept his
instruction, and discourages them from being like a
stubborn animal that must be controlled with a bridle.

32:9 understanding The Hebrew word used here, *bin*,
meaning "to discern," describes the ability to distinguish
between right and wrong (1Ki 3:9).

3 Sing to him a new song;
   play skillfully, and shout for joy.

4 For the word of the LORD is right and true;
   he is faithful in all he does.
5 The LORD loves righteousness and justice;
   the earth is full of his unfailing love.

6 By the word of the LORD the heavens were
   made,
   their starry host by the breath of his mouth.
7 He gathers the waters of the sea into jars ᵃ;
   he puts the deep into storehouses.
8 Let all the earth fear the LORD;
   let all the people of the world revere him.
9 For he spoke, and it came to be;
   he commanded, and it stood firm.

10 The LORD foils the plans of the nations;
   he thwarts the purposes of the peoples.
11 But the plans of the LORD stand firm forever,
   the purposes of his heart through all
   generations.

12 Blessed is the nation whose God is the LORD,
   the people he chose for his inheritance.
13 From heaven the LORD looks down
   and sees all mankind;
14 from his dwelling place he watches
   all who live on earth—
15 he who forms the hearts of all,
   who considers everything they do.

16 No king is saved by the size of his army;
   no warrior escapes by his great strength.
17 A horse is a vain hope for deliverance;
   despite all its great strength it cannot save.
18 But the eyes of the LORD are on those who
   fear him,
   on those whose hope is in his unfailing love,
19 to deliver them from death
   and keep them alive in famine.

20 We wait in hope for the LORD;
   he is our help and our shield.
21 In him our hearts rejoice,
   for we trust in his holy name.
22 May your unfailing love be with us, LORD,
   even as we put our hope in you.

Psalm 34ᵇ,ᶜ

*Of David. When he pretended to be insane before
Abimelek, who drove him away, and he left.*

1 I will extol the LORD at all times;
   his praise will always be on my lips.
2 I will glory in the LORD;
   let the afflicted hear and rejoice.
3 Glorify the LORD with me;
   let us exalt his name together.

ᵃ 7 Or *sea as into a heap*   ᵇ This psalm is an acrostic poem, the
verses of which begin with the successive letters of the Hebrew
alphabet.   ᶜ In Hebrew texts 34:1-22 is numbered 34:2-23.

32:10 unfailing love surrounds See note on Ex 15:13.
32:11 Rejoice in the LORD Joy is the proper response
to Yahweh's faithful love and forgiveness.

33:1–22 In this praise psalm, the psalmist lists several
reasons Yahweh is worthy of praise. He encourages
a congregation of righteous people to sing songs of
praise and thanksgiving to Yahweh (Ps 33:1–3). He
lists Yahweh's faithfulness, righteousness and justice
as reasons to praise him (vv. 4–5). He then mentions
Yahweh's power as evidenced in creation (vv. 5–9) and
his ultimate authority over the earth (vv. 10–12). He
shows Yahweh's superiority over humanity (vv. 13–17)
before affirming his loyalty to those who fear (revere)
him (vv. 18–19). Finally, he leads the congregation in a
prayer expressing trust in Yahweh (vv. 20–22). See the
table "Types of Psalms" on p. 830.

33:1 Sing joyfully The Hebrew word used here, *ranan*
(which may be translated "to cry out" or "to exult"), describes the proper response to the greatness of Yahweh.
33:2 harp An instrument with six to eight strings, used
in celebrations, worship and prophecy (1Sa 10:5).
33:4 right The Hebrew word used here, *yashar*, may be
translated as "straight" or "level." It emphasizes that
Yahweh's word is honest and trustworthy (Pr 8:8–9).
33:8 Let all the earth fear the LORD Fearing God
involves reverently trusting and obeying him (Ps 40:3;
Dt 6:2). See note on Job 1:1.
33:12 Blessed is the nation See note on Ps 1:1.

33:16–17 The psalmist reveals that it is futile to trust
in one's own might. The strength of armies is nothing
compared to the strength of Yahweh. Those who trust in

the power of an army will not find salvation; they should
trust in Yahweh instead (v. 20). See 20:7 and note.

33:18 eyes of the LORD Describes Yahweh's protection
and care (see note on Job 36:7).
33:20 wait in hope for the LORD See note on Ps 27:14.
33:21 his holy name The name of Yahweh represents
his power and character (see Ex 3).
33:22 your unfailing love Though the psalmist has
asserted that Yahweh accompanies those who fear and
trust in him, he still petitions Yahweh to maintain his
steadfast love to them.

34:title–22 Psalm 34 is both a thanksgiving psalm and
an acrostic poem—a poem where the lines start with
consecutive letters of the Hebrew alphabet. The psalmist
opens by praising Yahweh and encouraging others to join
him (vv. 1–3). He then praises Yahweh's faithfulness,
describing a time when Yahweh delivered him (vv. 4–7).
He continues with the benefits and demands of fearing
Yahweh (vv. 8–14). Finally, the psalmist contrasts the
protection that Yahweh gives those who fear (revere)
him with the destruction that will ultimately come to the
unrepentant wicked (vv. 15–22). See the table "Types
of Psalms" on p. 830.

34:title Of David See note on 3:title. **he pretended
to be insane** See 1Sa 21:10–15. While this line could
indicate that David authored this psalm, it could also be
in recollection of this event in David's lifetime. **Abimelek**
First Samuel 21:10–15 does not mention Abimelek. The
name, which literally means "my father is king," may
have been a title for Philistine kings.
34:2 will glory The Hebrew word used here, *halal*,

⁴I sought the Lord, and he answered me;
he delivered me from all my fears.
⁵Those who look to him are radiant;
their faces are never covered with shame.
⁶This poor man called, and the Lord
heard him;
he saved him out of all his troubles.
⁷The angel of the Lord encamps around those
who fear him,
and he delivers them.

⁸Taste and see that the Lord is good;
blessed is the one who takes refuge in him.
⁹Fear the Lord, you his holy people,
for those who fear him lack nothing.
¹⁰The lions may grow weak and hungry,
but those who seek the Lord lack no good
thing.
¹¹Come, my children, listen to me;
I will teach you the fear of the Lord.
¹²Whoever of you loves life
and desires to see many good days,
¹³keep your tongue from evil
and your lips from telling lies.
¹⁴Turn from evil and do good;
seek peace and pursue it.

¹⁵The eyes of the Lord are on the righteous,
and his ears are attentive to their cry;

¹⁶but the face of the Lord is against those who
do evil,
to blot out their name from the earth.

¹⁷The righteous cry out, and the Lord hears
them;
he delivers them from all their troubles.
¹⁸The Lord is close to the brokenhearted
and saves those who are crushed in spirit.

¹⁹The righteous person may have many
troubles,
but the Lord delivers him from them all;
²⁰he protects all his bones,
not one of them will be broken.

²¹Evil will slay the wicked;
the foes of the righteous will be
condemned.
²²The Lord will rescue his servants;
no one who takes refuge in him will be
condemned.

Psalm 35

Of David.

¹Contend, Lord, with those who contend
with me;
fight against those who fight against me.

---

describes praising Yahweh proudly to others. The word *Hallelujah* (meaning "Praise Yahweh") is derived from this term.
34:3 Glorify The Hebrew word used here, *gadal*, meaning "to make great," describes declaring Yahweh's greatness.
34:7 angel of the Lord The psalmist portrays the angel of Yahweh as an army that surrounds and protects those who fear him (Zec 9:8). Also called the angel of God, the angel of Yahweh appears to be distinct from Yahweh at times (Ex 23:20–23). Other times, he appears as a visible manifestation of Yahweh (Jdg 2:1–5).

34:8–10 The psalmist encourages others to enjoy the same sort of blessings he has experienced—to "taste and see" that Yahweh is good. Those who do so will be blessed and not lack for anything (see Ps 23:1 and note). Rather than assert that those who trust Yahweh will never suffer (v. 19), the psalmist claims Yahweh will be with them and ultimately deliver them in times of suffering—one way or another.

34:8 Taste and see Describes the act of trusting, fearing and seeking Yahweh (compare note on 34:9).
34:9 Fear the Lord A reverent attitude toward Yahweh that necessitates trust and obedience (Dt 6:2). **his holy people** The Hebrew word used here, *qedoshim*, refers to Yahweh's chosen people.
34:10 lions may grow weak and hungry People in the ancient Near East thought of lions as some of the mightiest animals (Pr 30:30) and as ferocious hunters (Ps 17:12). While even these powerful animals may go hungry, those who seek Yahweh will not.
34:11–14 Like a wisdom teacher (see Pr 1:8 and note), the psalmist tells God's people that fearing Yahweh involves refraining from speaking evil or deceit—a common theme in Wisdom Literature (see Pr 4:24 and note). It also involves a turning away from evil to good (Pr 3:7–8; 8:13; 16:6).

34:16 the face of the Lord To set one's face against someone indicates hostility toward them. When used with reference to Yahweh, it usually indicates his determination to issue judgment (Lev 20:3; Jer 21:10; Eze 14:8).
34:19 righteous person may have many troubles While the psalmist indicated earlier that those who fear Yahweh will not suffer any want (Ps 34:8–10), here he indicates they should not expect a trouble-free life. They can expect that Yahweh will be with them and will deliver them from their troubles.
34:20 not one of them will be broken John cites this verse in his Gospel, saying it was fulfilled when Jesus died on the cross before his legs could be broken (Jn 19:36).
34:22 will rescue his servants Like the closing verse of Ps 35, this verse falls outside the acrostic pattern, which highlights it. See note on 25:22.

35:title–28 In this individual lament psalm, the psalmist pleads for Yahweh to vindicate him before his enemies and calls Yahweh to fight for him like a warrior (vv. 1–3). He asks Yahweh to destroy his enemies (vv. 4–8) and describes their hostility by contrasting it with the graciousness he showed them (vv. 9–16). He cries out to Yahweh, promising to offer praise and thanksgiving upon his deliverance (vv. 17–18). He asks that his enemies not be victorious (vv. 19–21). The psalmist then asks Yahweh not to be silent (vv. 22–23), pleading for vindication before his enemies (vv. 24–26). The psalmist concludes by declaring his intention to rejoice and praise Yahweh for delivering him (vv. 27–28). See the table "Types of Psalms" on p. 830.
35:title Of David See note on 3:title.
35:1 Contend The Hebrew word used here, *riv*, often appears in contexts referring to legal disputes (see Job 9:3 and note). Here it carries a meaning of going to battle (Jdg 11:25).

² Take up shield and armor;
　　arise and come to my aid.
³ Brandish spear and javelin^a
　　against those who pursue me.
　Say to me,
　　"I am your salvation."

⁴ May those who seek my life
　　be disgraced and put to shame;
　may those who plot my ruin
　　be turned back in dismay.
⁵ May they be like chaff before the wind,
　　with the angel of the Lᴏʀᴅ driving them
　　　away;
⁶ may their path be dark and slippery,
　　with the angel of the Lᴏʀᴅ pursuing them.

⁷ Since they hid their net for me without cause
　　and without cause dug a pit for me,
⁸ may ruin overtake them by surprise —
　　may the net they hid entangle them,
　　may they fall into the pit, to their ruin.
⁹ Then my soul will rejoice in the Lᴏʀᴅ
　　and delight in his salvation.
¹⁰ My whole being will exclaim,
　　"Who is like you, Lᴏʀᴅ?
　You rescue the poor from those too strong for
　　them,
　　the poor and needy from those who rob
　　them."

¹¹ Ruthless witnesses come forward;
　　they question me on things I know nothing
　　　about.
¹² They repay me evil for good
　　and leave me like one bereaved.
¹³ Yet when they were ill, I put on sackcloth
　　and humbled myself with fasting.
　When my prayers returned to me
　　unanswered,

¹⁴ 　I went about mourning
　　　as though for my friend or brother.
　I bowed my head in grief
　　　as though weeping for my mother.
¹⁵ But when I stumbled, they gathered in glee;
　　assailants gathered against me without my
　　　knowledge.
　　They slandered me without ceasing.
¹⁶ Like the ungodly they maliciously mocked;^b
　　they gnashed their teeth at me.

¹⁷ How long, Lord, will you look on?
　　Rescue me from their ravages,
　　my precious life from these lions.
¹⁸ I will give you thanks in the great assembly;
　　among the throngs I will praise you.
¹⁹ Do not let those gloat over me
　　who are my enemies without cause;
　do not let those who hate me without
　　　reason
　　maliciously wink the eye.
²⁰ They do not speak peaceably,
　　but devise false accusations
　　against those who live quietly in the land.
²¹ They sneer at me and say, "Aha! Aha!
　　With our own eyes we have seen it."

²² Lᴏʀᴅ, you have seen this; do not be silent.
　　Do not be far from me, Lord.
²³ Awake, and rise to my defense!
　　Contend for me, my God and Lord.
²⁴ Vindicate me in your righteousness, Lᴏʀᴅ
　　my God;
　　do not let them gloat over me.
²⁵ Do not let them think, "Aha, just what we
　　wanted!"
　or say, "We have swallowed him up."

^a 3 Or *and block the way*　^b 16 Septuagint; Hebrew may mean
Like an ungodly circle of mockers,

35:2 shield The shield here is not just used in defense, but in preparation for attack (Jer 46:3). See note on Ps 3:3.
35:4 May those who seek my life be disgraced The psalmist prays that his enemies will be shamed for the way they treat him.
35:5 angel of the Lᴏʀᴅ The angel of Yahweh often appears in military contexts (2Ki 19:35; see note on Ps 34:7).
35:7 they hid their net for me The psalmist emphasizes that his enemies have no reason to mistreat him. He is innocent, so he appeals to Yahweh for vindication (see note on Ps 7:3).
35:11 Ruthless witnesses The Hebrew phrase used here, *ede chamas*, often indicates a false witness (Ex 23:1), specifically one who witnesses with bad intentions against someone (Dt 19:16).
35:12 like one bereaved The Hebrew word used here, *shekhol*, usually indicates the loss of children (Isa 47:8–9).
35:13–14 The psalmist describes his response to his enemies' suffering to emphasize that they afflict him without

cause (Ps 35:7). When they were sick, he mourned with them, wearing sackcloth and fasting. He grieved with them as if they were close friends or brothers.

35:15 when I stumbled, they gathered in glee Instead of mourning with him, his enemies surround him, looking for opportunities to humiliate him further (see 17:11–12).
35:16 they gnashed their teeth at me The psalmist portrays his enemies as wild animals tearing into prey.
35:17 How long, Lord See note on 6:3.
35:18 I will give you thanks Describing public praise, a common and expected response to Yahweh's saving work (22:22).
35:19 those who hate me without reason See note on 35:7.
35:21 Aha! Aha! The Hebrew word used here, *he'ach*, is an expression of joy (Isa 44:16). The enemies take great pleasure in falsely accusing the psalmist.
35:22 Lᴏʀᴅ, you have seen The psalmist reminds Yahweh that he knows the truth. Yahweh has seen the events that have transpired and knows that the psalmist's enemies falsely accuse him.

26 May all who gloat over my distress
    be put to shame and confusion;
may all who exalt themselves over me
    be clothed with shame and disgrace.
27 May those who delight in my vindication
    shout for joy and gladness;
may they always say, "The LORD be exalted,
    who delights in the well-being of his
      servant."

28 My tongue will proclaim your righteousness,
    your praises all day long.

Psalm 36[a]

*For the director of music. Of David
the servant of the LORD.*

1 I have a message from God in my heart
    concerning the sinfulness of the wicked:[b]
There is no fear of God
    before their eyes.

2 In their own eyes they flatter themselves
    too much to detect or hate their sin.
3 The words of their mouths are wicked and
      deceitful;
    they fail to act wisely or do good.
4 Even on their beds they plot evil;
    they commit themselves to a sinful course
    and do not reject what is wrong.

5 Your love, LORD, reaches to the heavens,
    your faithfulness to the skies.

6 Your righteousness is like the highest
      mountains,
    your justice like the great deep.
You, LORD, preserve both people and
      animals.
7 How priceless is your unfailing love, O God!
    People take refuge in the shadow of your
      wings.
8 They feast on the abundance of your house;
    you give them drink from your river of
      delights.
9 For with you is the fountain of life;
    in your light we see light.

10 Continue your love to those who know you,
    your righteousness to the upright in heart.
11 May the foot of the proud not come against me,
    nor the hand of the wicked drive me away.
12 See how the evildoers lie fallen—
    thrown down, not able to rise!

Psalm 37[c]

Of David.

1 Do not fret because of those who are evil
    or be envious of those who do wrong;
2 for like the grass they will soon wither,
    like green plants they will soon die away.

[a] In Hebrew texts 36:1-12 is numbered 36:2-13.   [b] *1 Or A
message from God: The transgression of the wicked / resides in
their hearts.*   [c] This psalm is an acrostic poem, the stanzas of
which begin with the successive letters of the Hebrew alphabet.

35:27 who delight in my vindication Referring to
people who, unlike the psalmist's enemies, delighted
in his innocence. See Ps 4:1 and note.

36:title–12 Like Ps 1 and 14, this is probably a wisdom
psalm—meant to teach certain wise sayings. While it
shares certain similarities with individual lament psalms
(e.g., complaints about the wicked and petitions that
they be driven away), it contains no imminent threat. The
psalmist describes the wicked (vv. 1–4) and contrasts
them with Yahweh (vv. 5–9). Finally, he asks Yahweh to
continue to show his character and protect him from the
wicked (vv. 10–12). See the table "Types of Psalms"
on p. 830.

36:title director of music See note on 4:title. **Of David**
See note on 3:title.
36:2 they flatter The psalmist notes that flattery (*chalaq*
in Hebrew) is an empty and even destructive activity
(Pr 29:5).
36:3 The words of their mouths A person's words
reflect their character (compare Pr 15:2,28).
36:6 the highest mountains Mountains symbolize
stability (Dt 33:15) and power (Zec 4:7). **great deep**
Refers to the depths of the oceans, showing the scope
of Yahweh's judgment (Ps 36:5).
36:7 shadow of your wings This image compares
Yahweh's tender care for his people with the way a bird
protects and cares for its young (Dt 32:11).
36:8 They feast on the abundance In the ancient Near
East, hosts were responsible for protecting as well as
providing food for their guests. See note on Ps 23:5.

36:10–12 The psalmist concludes by praying that God will
continue showing his character—specifically his steadfast love and righteousness—to those who know him. He
also prays that God will protect him from the wicked. This
twofold petition summarizes the psalm, which contrasts
the wicked (vv. 1–4) with Yahweh (vv. 5–9).

37:title–40 This wisdom psalm—meant to pass on
wise sayings—focuses on the ultimate fate of the wicked
in comparison to their apparent success. The psalm is
a mostly complete acrostic poem. However, only the
odd-numbered verses fulfill the acrostic pattern of beginning a line with a letter of the Hebrew alphabet in
consecutive order. The psalm resembles a collection
of proverbs with alphabetical arrangement. Recurring
themes in this psalm include dwelling in the promised land
(vv. 3,9,11,22,29,34), the seemingly unjust prosperity
of the wicked (vv. 1,7,16,35), the ultimate destruction
of the wicked (vv. 2,10,13,17,20,36,38) and Yahweh's
protection of the righteous (vv. 4–6,11,17,18–19,22,24,
28–29,34,37–40). See the table "Types of Psalms"
on p. 830.

37:title Of David See note on 3:title.

37:1–2 This warning against envying the wicked appears throughout Proverbs (Pr 3:31–32; 23:17–18;
24:1,19–20). While the wicked achieve success and
wealth (Ps 73:3–14), their success is short lived (v. 2)
because they oppose Yahweh (Pr 3:32). He will destroy
them (Pr 24:20).

³ Trust in the LORD and do good;
    dwell in the land and enjoy safe pasture.
⁴ Take delight in the LORD,
    and he will give you the desires of your
        heart.

⁵ Commit your way to the LORD;
    trust in him and he will do this:
⁶ He will make your righteous reward shine
        like the dawn,
    your vindication like the noonday sun.

⁷ Be still before the LORD
    and wait patiently for him;
do not fret when people succeed in their ways,
    when they carry out their wicked schemes.

⁸ Refrain from anger and turn from wrath;
    do not fret — it leads only to evil.
⁹ For those who are evil will be destroyed,
    but those who hope in the LORD will
        inherit the land.

¹⁰ A little while, and the wicked will be no more;
    though you look for them, they will not be
        found.
¹¹ But the meek will inherit the land
    and enjoy peace and prosperity.

¹² The wicked plot against the righteous
    and gnash their teeth at them;
¹³ but the Lord laughs at the wicked,
    for he knows their day is coming.

¹⁴ The wicked draw the sword
    and bend the bow
to bring down the poor and needy,
    to slay those whose ways are upright.
¹⁵ But their swords will pierce their own hearts,
    and their bows will be broken.

¹⁶ Better the little that the righteous have
    than the wealth of many wicked;
¹⁷ for the power of the wicked will be broken,
    but the LORD upholds the righteous.

¹⁸ The blameless spend their days under the
        LORD's care,
    and their inheritance will endure
        forever.
¹⁹ In times of disaster they will not wither;
    in days of famine they will enjoy plenty.

²⁰ But the wicked will perish:
    Though the LORD's enemies are like the
        flowers of the field,
    they will be consumed, they will go up in
        smoke.

²¹ The wicked borrow and do not repay,
    but the righteous give generously;
²² those the LORD blesses will inherit the land,
    but those he curses will be destroyed.

²³ The LORD makes firm the steps
    of the one who delights in him;
²⁴ though he may stumble, he will not fall,
    for the LORD upholds him with his hand.

²⁵ I was young and now I am old,
    yet I have never seen the righteous
        forsaken
    or their children begging bread.
²⁶ They are always generous and lend freely;
    their children will be a blessing.ᵃ

²⁷ Turn from evil and do good;
    then you will dwell in the land forever.

ᵃ 26 Or freely; / the names of their children will be used in
blessings (see Gen. 48:20); or freely; / others will see that their
children are blessed

37:5–6 Yahweh rewards those who trust him by literally "bringing forth" (yatsa in Hebrew) their righteousness. They will be justly vindicated.

37:5 Commit your way to the LORD To commit one's way to Yahweh is to trust him with the outcome.

37:7 Be still The Hebrew word used here, damam, means "to stand still" (Jos 10:12) or "to keep quiet" (Lev 10:3). Here it indicates both; people must patiently and quietly wait for Yahweh. **do not fret** The Hebrew word used here, charah, means "to become excited" or "to be angry." The psalmist cautions against getting agitated or worried over the prosperity of the wicked.

37:9 will inherit the land Describes dwelling securely and enjoying Yahweh's blessing.

37:11 the meek will inherit the land Jesus cites this verse in his Sermon on the Mount. See Mt 5:5 and note.

37:12–13 The wicked plot against the righteous (Ps 31:13). Just as the nations plot in vain against Yahweh (2:1–3), the plots of the wicked against the righteous are also in vain.

37:14 upright The Hebrew word used here, yashar—which may be literally rendered "straight" or "level"—de-

scribes someone who is honest (1Sa 29:6) or righteous (Pr 11:6). The wicked prepare to attack the poor and needy as well as the righteous.

37:15 their bows will be broken The bow was a symbol of strength in the ancient Near East (compare Ge 49:24; Job 29:20).

37:25 yet I have never seen Drawing on personal observation, a typical characteristic of wisdom literature (compare note on 37:title–40), the author notes that he has not seen the righteous forsaken or poor. This observation directly contrasts with that of the author of Ecclesiastes (Ecc 7:15). There, the author observes that the righteous perish while the wicked prosper. However, while the author of Ecclesiastes aims to reveal the prevalence of injustice in the world (see Ecc 8:13–14), the psalmist points out the benefits of righteousness over wickedness. The psalmist could be speaking in hyperbole—emphasizing that Yahweh ultimately intercedes for the oppressed—or out of personal inexperience, as it has already been noted that the wicked are oppressive (Ps 37:14; compare 37:35).

37:27 you will dwell in the land forever Long life and success are frequently described in the OT as blessings for the righteous. See note on Pr 3:2.

28 For the LORD loves the just
and will not forsake his faithful ones.

Wrongdoers will be completely destroyed *a*;
the offspring of the wicked will perish.
29 The righteous will inherit the land
and dwell in it forever.

30 The mouths of the righteous utter wisdom,
and their tongues speak what is just.
31 The law of their God is in their hearts;
their feet do not slip.

32 The wicked lie in wait for the righteous,
intent on putting them to death;
33 but the LORD will not leave them in the power
of the wicked
or let them be condemned when brought to
trial.

34 Hope in the LORD
and keep his way.
He will exalt you to inherit the land;
when the wicked are destroyed, you will
see it.

35 I have seen a wicked and ruthless man
flourishing like a luxuriant native tree,
36 but he soon passed away and was no more;
though I looked for him, he could not be
found.

37 Consider the blameless, observe the
upright;
a future awaits those who seek peace.*b*
38 But all sinners will be destroyed;
there will be no future*c* for the wicked.

39 The salvation of the righteous comes from
the LORD;
he is their stronghold in time of trouble.

40 The LORD helps them and delivers them;
he delivers them from the wicked and
saves them,
because they take refuge in him.

Psalm 38*d*

A psalm of David. A petition.

1 LORD, do not rebuke me in your anger
or discipline me in your wrath.
2 Your arrows have pierced me,
and your hand has come down on me.
3 Because of your wrath there is no health in
my body;
there is no soundness in my bones because
of my sin.
4 My guilt has overwhelmed me
like a burden too heavy to bear.

5 My wounds fester and are loathsome
because of my sinful folly.
6 I am bowed down and brought very low;
all day long I go about mourning.
7 My back is filled with searing pain;
there is no health in my body.
8 I am feeble and utterly crushed;
I groan in anguish of heart.

9 All my longings lie open before you, Lord;
my sighing is not hidden from you.
10 My heart pounds, my strength fails me;
even the light has gone from my eyes.
11 My friends and companions avoid me
because of my wounds;
my neighbors stay far away.

a 28 See Septuagint; Hebrew *They will be protected forever*
b 37 Or *upright; / those who seek peace will have posterity*
c 38 Or *posterity*   *d* In Hebrew texts 38:1-22 is numbered 38:2-23.

37:30 their tongues speak what is just Justice, righteousness and wisdom are closely related. See Pr 1:3 and note.
37:33 when brought to trial Yahweh, as the supreme judge (Ps 9:7–10), will judge righteously and not declare the innocent to be guilty.
37:35 flourishing like a luxuriant native tree The Hebrew word used here, *ra'anan*, implies prosperity, vitality and stability (52:8; 92:14). The prosperity of the wicked is temporary, and will fade like the grass (37:2).

38:title–22 This individual lament psalm focuses on suffering caused by sin. The psalmist appears to be suffering from sickness, social alienation (v. 11) and guilt (v. 4). He asks Yahweh not to rebuke him (vv. 1–2). He describes his suffering (vv. 3–8) and complains to Yahweh about his physical (vv. 9–10) and emotional suffering (vv. 11–14). He seeks help from Yahweh as he declares his intent to wait for his answer (vv. 15–16). The psalmist then confesses and repents of his sin (vv. 17–20) before asking Yahweh not to forsake him but to save him (vv. 21–22). This was one of the early church's penitential psalms (others include Ps 6; 32; 51; 102; 130; 143). See the table "Types of Psalms" on p. 830.

38:title A psalm of David See note on 3:title. **A petition** The Hebrew word used here, *zakar*, could suggest this psalm is in remembrance of something—functioning as a type of memorial or for use with a memorial offering (see Lev 24:7).
38:2 Your arrows The psalmist attributes his suffering to Yahweh. He was likely feeling the effects of divine judgment for sin.

38:5–8 The psalmist describes the physical aspects of his suffering including festering wounds (see Job 7:5 and note), a lack of health and a sense of being feeble and crushed. He attributes this suffering to his own foolishness (107:17; see Pr 13:21 and note).

38:11 My friends and companions Social alienation appears as a common complaint in OT lament. Sufferers experienced shame and isolation because of illness, which often resulted in estrangement from friends or family (see Ps 31:11–12; Job 19:13–20). Social alienation occurred in part because Israelites often assumed there was a connection between suffering and sin. Job's friends, for example, believed Job was suffering because he had sinned. They encouraged him to repent so he would be restored (see Job 11:13–15 and notes). While

¹²Those who want to kill me set their traps,
　　those who would harm me talk of my ruin;
　　all day long they scheme and lie.

¹³I am like the deaf, who cannot hear,
　　like the mute, who cannot speak;
¹⁴I have become like one who does not hear,
　　whose mouth can offer no reply.

¹⁵LORD, I wait for you;
　　you will answer, Lord my God.

¹⁶For I said, "Do not let them gloat
　　or exalt themselves over me when my feet
　　　slip."

¹⁷For I am about to fall,
　　and my pain is ever with me.
¹⁸I confess my iniquity;
　　I am troubled by my sin.

¹⁹Many have become my enemies without
　　cause ᵃ;
　　those who hate me without reason are
　　　numerous.
²⁰Those who repay my good with evil
　　lodge accusations against me,
　　though I seek only to do what is good.

²¹LORD, do not forsake me;
　　do not be far from me, my God.
²²Come quickly to help me,
　　my Lord and my Savior.

Psalm 39ᵇ

For the director of music. For Jeduthun. A psalm of David.

¹I said, "I will watch my ways
　　and keep my tongue from sin;

I will put a muzzle on my mouth
　　while in the presence of the wicked."
²So I remained utterly silent,
　　not even saying anything good.
But my anguish increased;
³　　my heart grew hot within me.
While I meditated, the fire burned;
　　then I spoke with my tongue:

⁴"Show me, LORD, my life's end
　　and the number of my days;
　　let me know how fleeting my life is.
⁵You have made my days a mere handbreadth;
　　the span of my years is as nothing
　　　before you.
Everyone is but a breath,
　　even those who seem secure.ᶜ

⁶"Surely everyone goes around like a mere
　　phantom;
　　in vain they rush about, heaping up
　　　wealth
　　without knowing whose it will finally be.

⁷"But now, Lord, what do I look for?
　　My hope is in you.
⁸Save me from all my transgressions;
　　do not make me the scorn of fools.
⁹I was silent; I would not open my mouth,
　　for you are the one who has done this.
¹⁰Remove your scourge from me;
　　I am overcome by the blow of your hand.

ᵃ 19 One Dead Sea Scrolls manuscript; Masoretic Text *my vigorous enemies*　　ᵇ In Hebrew texts 39:1-13 is numbered 39:2-14.　　ᶜ 5 The Hebrew has *Selah* (a word of uncertain meaning) here and at the end of verse 11.

Job's suffering was not due to sin on his part (see Job 31:1–40 and note), there seems to be a connection here between the psalmist's sin and his suffering (Ps 38:3). **38:14 can offer no reply** The Hebrew word used here, *tokhachath*, can mean "argument" or "reply." Job uses it to refer to arguments for his innocence (Job 13:6; 23:4). The psalmist has no arguments here. He can only confess (Ps 38:18) and ask Yahweh not to discipline him too severely (v. 1).
38:18 I confess my iniquity The psalmist repents and confesses his sin. As in Ps 32, this represents a necessary step before restoration (see 32:3–5 and note).
38:21 do not be far from me, my God In addition to feeling isolated from society (see note on 38:11), the psalmist feels isolated from God. See 10:1 and note.
39:title–13 This individual lament psalm focuses on the brevity of human life. The psalmist suffers because of sin (see note on Ps 38:title–22; note on Ps 38:11). He intended to remain silent but was unable to do so (39:1–3). He emphasizes the brevity of life and prays for Yahweh to reveal when he will die (vv. 4–6). He affirms his trust in Yahweh and asks him for deliverance (vv. 7–8). The psalmist attributes his suffering to Yahweh's discipline (vv. 9–11) and asks him to hear him and turn his discipline away (vv. 12–13). See the table "Types of Psalms" on p. 830.

39:title director of music See note on 4:title. **For Jeduthun** The Bible includes two people named Jeduthun: a temple music leader in the time of David and Solomon (1Ch 16:41–42; 2Ch 5:12) and a prophetic figure in Josiah's time (2Ch 35:15). Jeduthun is also mentioned in Ps 62:title and 77:title. **A psalm of David** See note on 3:title.
39:1 my tongue from sin The psalmist intends to remain silent. He may have felt that he would sin by complaining about God's discipline.
39:2 anguish The Hebrew word used here, *ke'ev*, refers to pain (Jer 15:18). Job uses the same term when he states his speech cannot ease his pain (Job 16:6). The psalmist's pain increases as he refrains from speaking.
39:3 my heart grew hot This idiomatic Hebrew expression describes becoming angry (Dt 19:6). Though the psalmist tried to keep silent, his pain grew, and he became angry and exasperated.
39:4 Show me, LORD, my life's end The psalmist asks for perspective and awareness regarding the brevity of human life.
39:6 without knowing whose it will finally be Given the brevity of life, any gains people achieve must be left to others. The author of Ecclesiastes shares this lament. See Ecc 2:18 and note.
39:8 transgressions The Hebrew word used here, *pesha'*, refers to the psalmist's transgressions or wrongdoings—

¹¹ When you rebuke and discipline anyone for
their sin,
you consume their wealth like a moth —
surely everyone is but a breath.

¹² "Hear my prayer, LORD,
listen to my cry for help;
do not be deaf to my weeping.
I dwell with you as a foreigner,
a stranger, as all my ancestors were.
¹³ Look away from me, that I may enjoy life again
before I depart and am no more."

Psalm 40ᵃ

40:13-17pp — Ps 70:1-5

For the director of music. Of David. A psalm.

¹ I waited patiently for the LORD;
he turned to me and heard my cry.
² He lifted me out of the slimy pit,
out of the mud and mire;
he set my feet on a rock
and gave me a firm place to stand.
³ He put a new song in my mouth,
a hymn of praise to our God.
Many will see and fear the LORD
and put their trust in him.

⁴ Blessed is the one
who trusts in the LORD,

who does not look to the proud,
to those who turn aside to false gods.ᵇ
⁵ Many, LORD my God,
are the wonders you have done,
the things you planned for us.
None can compare with you;
were I to speak and tell of your deeds,
they would be too many to declare.

⁶ Sacrifice and offering you did not desire —
but my ears you have openedᶜ —
burnt offerings and sin offeringsᵈ you did
not require.
⁷ Then I said, "Here I am, I have come —
it is written about me in the scroll.ᵉ
⁸ I desire to do your will, my God;
your law is within my heart."

⁹ I proclaim your saving acts in the great
assembly;
I do not seal my lips, LORD,
as you know.
¹⁰ I do not hide your righteousness in
my heart;
I speak of your faithfulness and your
saving help.

ᵃ In Hebrew texts 40:1-17 is numbered 40:2-18.   ᵇ 4 Or to lies
ᶜ 6 Hebrew; some Septuagint manuscripts *but a body you have
prepared for me*   ᵈ 6 Or *purification offerings*   ᵉ 7 Or *come /
with the scroll written for me*

---

probably the cause of his suffering (Ps 39:10–11; see
note on 38:11).
39:9 you are the one who has done The psalmist
recognizes his suffering is a result of God's discipline.

39:10–11 The psalmist asks God to remove his harsh
discipline, addressing him frankly and candidly by claiming his discipline is too severe. This directness is not
unusual in the context of OT lament.

39:12 with you as a foreigner The psalmist's transgression and suffering cause him to feel estranged from
Yahweh. He considers himself a stranger or guest of
Yahweh—a contrast to the intimate personal relationship
often described in Psalms.

40:title–17 Like Ps 27, this psalm can be divided
into distinct halves. The first (vv. 1–10) is primarily a
thanksgiving psalm. The second (vv. 11–17) resembles
an individual lament psalm. The psalmist recalls an experience of Yahweh's salvation (vv. 1–3) and recounts his
protection (vv. 4–5). He lists what Yahweh desires, and
he expresses commitment to his law (vv. 6–8). He also
shows willingness to declare Yahweh's salvation before
the congregation (vv. 9–10). After describing the faithful
love and mercy of Yahweh (v. 11), the psalmist laments
the trouble that surrounds him (v. 12). He asks Yahweh
to deliver him and shame his enemies (vv. 13–15),
and he closes with the statement that all who seek
Yahweh will rejoice (vv. 16–17). See the table "Types
of Psalms" on p. 830.

40:title director of music See note on 4:title. **Of David.
A psalm** See note on 3:title.
40:1 I waited patiently The Hebrew verb form used
here indicates intensity.

40:2 slimy pit Probably refers to the bottom of a cistern.
he set my feet on a rock In contrast to the muddy
pit, a rock is a place of stability and security (see note
on 18:1–3).

40:3 new song This could refer to a change in outlook
or frame of mind rather than a written song—or to
both a change of mindset and a literal song. Instead of
mourning or lamenting, the psalmist is now prompted
to sing a song of praise.

40:4 the proud The Hebrew word used here, *rahav*, is
also the name of a mythical sea monster (see Isa 51:9
and note). In addition, in a passage showing the futility
of trusting in Egypt, Isaiah refers to Egypt with this term
(see Isa 30:7 and note).

40:5 wonders you have done, the things you planned
Describes Yahweh's past acts of deliverance and his
future plans and purposes (Ex 3:20; Mic 4:12).

40:6 Sacrifice and offering While sacrifices were a major
part of OT Law, Yahweh often states his preference for
righteousness or obedience (e.g., Mic 6:6–8). **burnt offerings** This refers to the regular daily offerings in the temple.
See Ex 29:38–42 and note. **sin offerings** An offering
intended to restore ritual purity. See Lev 4:3 and note.

40:7–8 Noting that Yahweh does not delight in sacrifice
alone, the psalmist declares that he desires to do God's
will and follow his law. His commitment to Yahweh goes
beyond outward expressions; it extends into his heart.

40:9 in the great assembly The Hebrew word used
here, *qahal*, refers to the people of Israel.
40:10 your love and your faithfulness The Hebrew
words used here, *chesed* and *emeth*, are often paired to
describe Yahweh as absolutely dependable to fulfill his
promises. See note on Ps 25:10.

I do not conceal your love and your
    faithfulness
from the great assembly.

[11] Do not withhold your mercy from me, Lord;
    may your love and faithfulness always
        protect me.
[12] For troubles without number surround me;
    my sins have overtaken me, and I
        cannot see.
They are more than the hairs of
    my head,
    and my heart fails within me.
[13] Be pleased to save me, Lord;
    come quickly, Lord, to help me.

[14] May all who want to take my life
    be put to shame and confusion;
    may all who desire my ruin
    be turned back in disgrace.
[15] May those who say to me, "Aha! Aha!"
    be appalled at their own shame.
[16] But may all who seek you
    rejoice and be glad in you;
    may those who long for your saving help
        always say,
    "The Lord is great!"

[17] But as for me, I am poor and needy;
    may the Lord think of me.
You are my help and my deliverer;
    you are my God, do not delay.

Psalm 41[a]

For the director of music. A psalm of David.

[1] Blessed are those who have regard for the
    weak;
    the Lord delivers them in times
        of trouble.
[2] The Lord protects and preserves them —
    they are counted among the blessed in the
        land —

he does not give them over to the desire of
    their foes.
[3] The Lord sustains them on their
    sickbed
    and restores them from their bed of
        illness.

[4] I said, "Have mercy on me, Lord;
    heal me, for I have sinned against you."
[5] My enemies say of me in malice,
    "When will he die and his name
        perish?"
[6] When one of them comes to see me,
    he speaks falsely, while his heart
        gathers slander;
    then he goes out and spreads it
        around.

[7] All my enemies whisper together
    against me;
    they imagine the worst for me,
        saying,
[8] "A vile disease has afflicted him;
    he will never get up from the place
        where he lies."
[9] Even my close friend,
    someone I trusted,
one who shared my bread,
    has turned[b] against me.

[10] But may you have mercy on me, Lord;
    raise me up, that I may repay them.
[11] I know that you are pleased with me,
    for my enemy does not triumph
        over me.
[12] Because of my integrity you uphold me
    and set me in your presence forever.

[13] Praise be to the Lord, the God of Israel,
    from everlasting to everlasting.
        Amen and Amen.

[a] In Hebrew texts 41:1-13 is numbered 41:2-14.   [b] 9 Hebrew *has lifted up his heel*

40:12 troubles The Hebrew word used here, *ra'ah*, can refer to both calamity and moral evil (see 15:3; Job 2:10 and note).

40:15 Aha! Aha! See note on Ps 35:21.

41:title–13 In this thanksgiving psalm, the psalmist recounts Yahweh's blessing and provision to those who are generous to the impoverished (vv. 1–4). The psalmist also recounts that when others gave up on him and offered no comfort (vv. 5–9), he asked Yahweh for help (v. 10) and was upheld (vv. 11–12). The concluding verse is most likely a doxology that concludes Book One of the Psalms (Ps 1–41; see note on 1:1–6). See the table "Types of Psalms" on p. 830.

41:title director of music See note on 4:title. **A psalm of David** See note on 3:title.

41:1 Blessed See note on 1:1.

41:3 Lord sustains them on their sickbed After describing Yahweh's protection in general terms, the

psalmist explains how he sustains and restores the sick.

41:6 he speaks falsely The visitors speak worthless and empty words (see note on 12:2) instead of comfort. Like Job's friends, they probably worsened the psalmist's suffering with accusation (Job 13:4–5; 21:34).

41:9 Even my close friend Even those close to the psalmist have abandoned him in his sickness (see Ps 55:13 and note).

41:11–12 The psalmist closes with thankfulness to Yahweh for upholding him. He attributes this to his integrity, probably in reference to his generosity toward the poor (see note on 26:1; 41:1–3).

41:13 Praise be to the Lord Each book of Psalms closes with a doxology of praise, like the one in this verse (72:18–20; 89:52; 106:48; 150:6; see note on 1:1–6). These doxologies should be viewed as independent from their respective psalms.

BOOK II

Psalms 42–72

Psalm 42[a,b]

For the director of music. A maskil[c] of the Sons of Korah.

1 As the deer pants for streams of water,
   so my soul pants for you, my God.
2 My soul thirsts for God, for the living God.
   When can I go and meet with God?
3 My tears have been my food
      day and night,
   while people say to me all day long,
      "Where is your God?"
4 These things I remember
      as I pour out my soul:
   how I used to go to the house of God
      under the protection of the Mighty One[d]
   with shouts of joy and praise
      among the festive throng.

5 Why, my soul, are you downcast?
      Why so disturbed within me?
   Put your hope in God,
      for I will yet praise him,
      my Savior and my God.

6 My soul is downcast within me;
      therefore I will remember you
   from the land of the Jordan,
      the heights of Hermon — from Mount
         Mizar.
7 Deep calls to deep
      in the roar of your waterfalls;
   all your waves and breakers
      have swept over me.

8 By day the LORD directs his love,
      at night his song is with me —
   a prayer to the God of my life.

9 I say to God my Rock,
      "Why have you forgotten me?
   Why must I go about mourning,
      oppressed by the enemy?"
10 My bones suffer mortal agony
      as my foes taunt me,
   saying to me all day long,
      "Where is your God?"

11 Why, my soul, are you downcast?
      Why so disturbed within me?

---

[a] In many Hebrew manuscripts Psalms 42 and 43 constitute one psalm.   [b] In Hebrew texts 42:1-11 is numbered 42:2-12.
[c] Title: Probably a literary or musical term   [d] 4 See Septuagint and Syriac; the meaning of the Hebrew for this line is uncertain.

42:title–43:5 Psalm 42 is the first psalm in Book Two (Ps 42–72) of the psalms (see note on 1:1–6). Psalm 42 and 43 were probably originally one psalm. They include an identical refrain (42:5,11; 43:5), in which the psalmist encourages himself to hope in God. The pair share themes of mourning, oppression (42:9; 43:2) and desiring God's presence (42:2; 43:4). In addition, Ps 43 lacks a title, which is unusual among Book Two (Ps 42–72) of the psalms. Taken together, these psalms form an individual lament psalm. The psalmist wrestles with trusting God in the midst of his suffering. He expresses his desire to appear before God and laments his suffering (42:1–4). In his downcast state (42:6–7), he takes hope in Yahweh's steadfast love (42:8) and then asks God not to forget him (42:9–10). Looking to God for vindication (43:1–2), the psalmist imagines his joy at going before God at the temple (43:3–4). See the table "Types of Psalms" on p. 830.

42:title director of music See note on 4:title. **maskil** See note on 32:title. **of the Sons of Korah** Possibly descendants of the same Korah who rebelled against Moses and Aaron (Nu 16:1–50; 26:11). However, like the affiliation of particular psalms with David, this line does not necessarily indicate that this psalm is written by Korah's descendants (see note on Ps 3:title). Korah was from the tribe of Levi; this means that he and his descendants were first set apart for service of the tabernacle, and later, the temple. More specifically, the Korahites are Kohathites, part of a clan that had the responsibility of carrying the holy items of the tabernacle during the wilderness wandering period (Nu 3:27–32; 4:1–20; 16:9). Later on, the Korahites were responsible for gatekeeping and baking functions in the temple, and were also singers (1Ch 9:17–32).

42:1 As the deer pants for streams of water The psalmist's desperation for God's sustaining presence is like a thirst for water.
42:2 living God Speaks to the presence and activity of God. See Jos 3:10 and note.
42:3 My tears have been my food Lacking the spiritual nourishment of God's presence (Ps 42:1), the psalmist feels as if he is fed only by his suffering.
42:4 These things I remember The psalmist describes past times when he would enter the temple in a festival procession to worship God (43:3). This is most likely in one of the three pilgrimage festivals (see note on Ex 23:14–17). See the table "Israelite Festivals" on p. 200.
42:5 Why, my soul, are you downcast In this refrain—repeated in Ps 42:11 and 43:5—the psalmist questions his own despair. **Put your hope** The Hebrew word used here, *yachal*, refers to hoping or waiting on God. It is not a futile activity. The psalmist has faith that God will act and bring deliverance (Pr 20:22).
42:6 land of the Jordan, the heights of Hermon Signifies the vast distance between the psalmist and God's presence in the temple in Jerusalem. It is unclear if these places refer literally to the psalmist's location or if they should be taken figuratively.
42:7 Deep The Hebrew word used here, *tehom*, refers to the deepest parts of the seas (Job 38:16). See note on Ge 1:2.
42:9 Why have you forgotten me Although he has just expressed hope (Ps 42:8), the psalmist returns to despair as he questions God's absence.
42:11 Why, my soul, are you downcast The psalmist is apparently still in despair; he closes this psalm by exhorting himself again to hope in God (see note on v. 5). Compare note on 42:title—43:5.

Put your hope in God,
for I will yet praise him,
my Savior and my God.

Psalm 43[a]

[1] Vindicate me, my God,
and plead my cause
against an unfaithful nation.
Rescue me from those who are
deceitful and wicked.
[2] You are God my stronghold.
Why have you rejected me?
Why must I go about mourning,
oppressed by the enemy?
[3] Send me your light and your faithful care,
let them lead me;
let them bring me to your holy mountain,
to the place where you dwell.
[4] Then I will go to the altar of God,
to God, my joy and my delight.
I will praise you with the lyre,
O God, my God.

[5] Why, my soul, are you downcast?
Why so disturbed within me?
Put your hope in God,
for I will yet praise him,
my Savior and my God.

Psalm 44[b]

For the director of music. Of the Sons of Korah. A maskil.[c]

[1] We have heard it with our ears, O God;
our ancestors have told us

what you did in their days,
in days long ago.
[2] With your hand you drove out the nations
and planted our ancestors;
you crushed the peoples
and made our ancestors flourish.
[3] It was not by their sword that they won the
land,
nor did their arm bring them victory;
it was your right hand, your arm,
and the light of your face, for you loved
them.

[4] You are my King and my God,
who decrees[d] victories for Jacob.
[5] Through you we push back our enemies;
through your name we trample our foes.
[6] I put no trust in my bow,
my sword does not bring me victory;
[7] but you give us victory over our enemies,
you put our adversaries to shame.
[8] In God we make our boast all day long,
and we will praise your name forever.[e]

[9] But now you have rejected and
humbled us;
you no longer go out with our armies.
[10] You made us retreat before the enemy,
and our adversaries have plundered us.
[11] You gave us up to be devoured like sheep
and have scattered us among the nations.

[a] In many Hebrew manuscripts Psalms 42 and 43 constitute one psalm.   [b] In Hebrew texts 44:1-26 is numbered 44:2-27.   [c] Title: Probably a literary or musical term   [d] 4 Septuagint, Aquila and Syriac; Hebrew *King, O God; / command*   [e] 8 The Hebrew has *Selah* (a word of uncertain meaning) here.

43:1–5 Psalm 42 and 43 were probably one psalm originally. See note on 42:title—43:5.

43:1 cause The Hebrew word used here, *riv*, typically refers to a legal dispute. See note on Job 9:3. **unfaithful nation** The Hebrew phrase used here, *lo-chasid*, refers to those who are unfaithful to Yahweh.

43:3 your light Represents Yahweh's guiding presence. **to your holy mountain, to the place where you dwell** The psalmist wants God's light and truth to lead him into God's presence at the temple, where he can quench his thirst for God (see Ps 42:1 and note).

43:4 altar The psalmist is referring to the altar in the temple (2Ch 4:1). See the infographic "Ancient Altars" on p. 127.

43:5 Why, my soul, are you downcast The psalmist closes by repeating the refrain from Ps 42 (42:5,11). See note on 42:5.

44:title–26 In this corporate lament psalm (meant to be used in a group setting), the psalmist reflects on a defeat in battle. He recounts God's previous acts of deliverance (vv. 1–3), then expresses trust that God will fight for his people (vv. 4–8). The psalmist addresses God directly as he laments that God seems to have rejected them by allowing the enemy to defeat them (vv. 9–16) when they did not deserve defeat (vv. 17–22). Finally, he asks God to come to their aid (vv. 23–26). See the table "Types of Psalms" on p. 830.

44:1 our ancestors have told us The psalmist begins by recounting stories of God passed down by his ancestors. These reminders call God to act and deliver as he had before. They also served to remind people of God's power, encouraging them to trust in him.

44:2 planted Refers to Israel inhabiting the promised land (Ex 15:17; Am 9:15).

44:3 your right hand, your arm The arm of God is a symbol of his strength in judgment as well as salvation (Ex 6:6; Isa 52:10). The right hand, specifically, represents the hand of special blessing according to Hebrew thought (Ge 48:17–20). **light of your face** The Hebrew phrase used here, *or panekha*, is similar to portions of the priestly blessing in Nu 6:24–26. See note on Ps 4:6.

44:4–8 Moving from the past to the present, the psalmist declares his current trust in God by recognizing that victory over enemies can only be achieved through God's power (see 20:7 and note). He also points to more recent times of God's protection from enemies and boasts in God (see 34:2 and note).

44:9–16 Though the psalmist trusts in God, he notes that it seems that God has abandoned his people. He declares that God has rejected them and allowed them to be disgraced by their enemies. The psalmist describes the result of God's rejection: defeat and ridicule.

44:11 devoured like sheep Rather than protect them

¹²You sold your people for a pittance,
    gaining nothing from their sale.
¹³You have made us a reproach to our neighbors,
    the scorn and derision of those
        around us.
¹⁴You have made us a byword among the
        nations;
    the peoples shake their heads at us.
¹⁵I live in disgrace all day long,
    and my face is covered with shame
¹⁶at the taunts of those who reproach and
        revile me,
    because of the enemy, who is bent on
        revenge.

¹⁷All this came upon us,
    though we had not forgotten you;
    we had not been false to your covenant.
¹⁸Our hearts had not turned back;
    our feet had not strayed from your path.
¹⁹But you crushed us and made us a haunt for
        jackals;
    you covered us over with deep darkness.

²⁰If we had forgotten the name of our God
    or spread out our hands to a foreign god,
²¹would not God have discovered it,
    since he knows the secrets of the heart?
²²Yet for your sake we face death all day long;
    we are considered as sheep to be
        slaughtered.

²³Awake, Lord! Why do you sleep?
    Rouse yourself! Do not reject us forever.
²⁴Why do you hide your face
    and forget our misery and oppression?

²⁵We are brought down to the dust;
    our bodies cling to the ground.
²⁶Rise up and help us;
    rescue us because of your unfailing love.

Psalm 45[a]

For the director of music. To the tune of "Lilies."
Of the Sons of Korah. A maskil.[b] A wedding song.

¹My heart is stirred by a noble theme
    as I recite my verses for the king;
    my tongue is the pen of a skillful writer.

²You are the most excellent of men
    and your lips have been anointed with
        grace,
    since God has blessed you forever.

³Gird your sword on your side, you
        mighty one;
    clothe yourself with splendor and majesty.
⁴In your majesty ride forth victoriously
    in the cause of truth, humility and
        justice;
    let your right hand achieve awesome
        deeds.
⁵Let your sharp arrows pierce the hearts of
        the king's enemies;
    let the nations fall beneath your feet.
⁶Your throne, O God,[c] will last for ever and
        ever;
    a scepter of justice will be the scepter of
        your kingdom.

---

[a] In Hebrew texts 45:1-17 is numbered 45:2-18.   [b] Title:
Probably a literary or musical term   [c] 6 Here the king is
addressed as God's representative.

---

like a shepherd (see 23:1 and note), God has allowed them to become like sheep ready for slaughter (see Isa 53:7 and note).
44:14 a byword The Hebrew word used here, *mashal*, refers to a proverb or saying; used in a negative context like this one, it refers to a taunt.

44:17–22 The psalmist's description of their condition in Ps 44:9–16 fits the law's description of the Israelites' punishment for disobeying God (Dt 28:15–68, especially Dt 28:25). However, the people here have not disobeyed, forgotten or broken their covenant with God. They have done nothing to deserve his rejection (Ps 44:20–21), yet God allows them to be defeated by their enemies. The psalmist freely expresses these emotions to God. This shows that whether the psalmist is right or wrong about his interpretation of recent events, he is willing to faithfully tell God what he thinks.

44:19 made us a haunt for jackals Signifies a ruined or desolate place (Isa 34:13; Jer 9:11).
44:22 for your sake we face death Paul cites this verse in Ro 8:36.
44:26 rescue us The Hebrew word used here, *padah*, (which can be rendered as "to redeem" or "buy out") often occurs in the context of ransoming people from trouble (see Dt 7:8; note on Ps 25:22).

45:title–17 This royal psalm celebrates a royal wedding. Addressing the king (v. 1), the psalmist describes his majestic appearance, focusing on his power in battle (vv. 2–5), his righteous rule and his anointing by God (vv. 6–9). The psalmist addresses the bride by encouraging her (vv. 10–12) and describing her joyful procession into the king's palace (vv. 13–15). The psalmist concludes by pronouncing a blessing on the offspring of the king and his bride (vv. 16–17). See the table "Types of Psalms" on p. 830.

45:title director of music See note on 4:title. **To the tune of "Lilies"** Lilies serve as a common metaphor in love poems (SS 2:1). As a title to this psalm, it may have connotations of love. However, since the phrase also appears in the titles of Ps 69 and 80, it may simply refer to a common tune. **Sons of Korah** See note on 42:title. *maskil* See note on 32:title.
45:2 your lips have been anointed with grace Most likely a reference to the king's speech—the king is an eloquent speaker.
45:3 mighty one The Hebrew word used here, *gibbor*, typically describes might in battle (24:8; Jer 20:11). It can also refer to a person's worth, capability or wealth (see Ru 2:1 and note).
45:6 Your throne By referring to God's throne here, the psalmist states that God establishes the king

⁷ You love righteousness and hate wickedness;
 therefore God, your God, has set you above
  your companions
 by anointing you with the oil of joy.
⁸ All your robes are fragrant with myrrh and
  aloes and cassia;
 from palaces adorned with ivory
  the music of the strings makes you glad.
⁹ Daughters of kings are among your honored
  women;
 at your right hand is the royal bride in gold
  of Ophir.

¹⁰ Listen, daughter, and pay careful attention:
 Forget your people and your father's house.
¹¹ Let the king be enthralled by your beauty;
 honor him, for he is your lord.
¹² The city of Tyre will come with a gift,^a
 people of wealth will seek your favor.
¹³ All glorious is the princess within her
  chamber;
 her gown is interwoven with gold.
¹⁴ In embroidered garments she is led to the king;
 her virgin companions follow her —
  those brought to be with her.
¹⁵ Led in with joy and gladness,
 they enter the palace of the king.

¹⁶ Your sons will take the place of your fathers;
 you will make them princes throughout
  the land.

¹⁷ I will perpetuate your memory through all
  generations;
 therefore the nations will praise you for
  ever and ever.

Psalm 46^b

*For the director of music. Of the Sons of Korah.
According to* alamoth.^c *A song.*

¹ God is our refuge and strength,
 an ever-present help in trouble.
² Therefore we will not fear, though the earth
  give way
 and the mountains fall into the heart of
  the sea,
³ though its waters roar and foam
 and the mountains quake with their
  surging.^d

⁴ There is a river whose streams make glad the
  city of God,
 the holy place where the Most High
  dwells.
⁵ God is within her, she will not fall;
 God will help her at break of day.
⁶ Nations are in uproar, kingdoms fall;
 he lifts his voice, the earth melts.

---

^a 12 Or *A Tyrian robe is among the gifts*   ^b In Hebrew texts
46:1-11 is numbered 46:2-12.   ^c Title: Probably a musical term
^d 3 The Hebrew has *Selah* (a word of uncertain meaning) here
and at the end of verses 7 and 11.

(Ps 2:7–9). **the scepter** A symbol of power or authority (110:2; Ge 49:10).
45:7 by anointing you Kings were anointed with oil upon their coronation (1Sa 10:1). Compare Ps 2:2 and note.
45:8 myrrh and aloes and cassia Fragrant spices or perfumes often used for sensual purposes. They are used frequently in the Song of Songs (see SS 3:6; 4:14 and note) and by the adulteress in Proverbs (Pr 7:17 and note).
45:9 Ophir A region known for very fine gold (Isa 13:12). See note on Job 28:16.
45:10 Forget your people and your father's house Indicates the bride is probably foreign (non-Israelite; Ge 12:1; Ru 1:16; compare 1Ki 11:1–13).
45:13–15 The psalmist describes the bride's procession to the king as joyful and extravagant. She wears beautiful and expensive robes and is accompanied by her female attendants.
45:16–17 The psalmist concludes by blessing the offspring of the newly joined king and queen. Connecting with the idea of an ongoing dynasty, the psalmist states that the king's sons will rule just as their father did. In a passage recalling the Davidic covenant (2Sa 7:16), the psalmist assures the king his name will be remembered forever.
46:title–11 Psalm 46 is the first of several songs of Zion (Ps 48; 76; 84; 87; 122) that celebrate God's presence and protection. These psalms focus on Yahweh's presence in Jerusalem (Zion is the location of the Jerusalem temple mount). After identifying God as the

Provider of refuge and strength, the psalmist celebrates his protection in natural disasters (46:1–3) and from enemy nations (vv. 4–7). The psalmist invites people to behold Yahweh's works in general. He quotes Yahweh and concludes by reaffirming his protective presence (vv. 8–11). See the table "Types of Psalms" on p. 830.

46:title director of music See note on 4:title. **Sons of Korah** See note on 42:title. **According to** *alamoth* A musical term. In 1Ch 15:20, it is related to harps.
46:1 refuge The Hebrew word used here, *machseh*, which refers to a place of refuge, creates an image of a stronghold or impenetrable fortress (Ps 61:3; 91:2). It emphasizes God's protection. **strength** The Hebrew word used here, *oz*, emphasizes God's power to protect or save (21:1; 29:11).
46:2–3 The psalmist describes natural catastrophes such as earthquakes, stormy waters and unstable mountains, which symbolized the forces of chaos in the ancient Near East (see note on 18:7–19). These verses recall God's power over chaos as evidenced in creation (see Ge 1:2 and note). The psalmist declares that he, and those speaking the psalm with him, will not fear the forces of chaos because God is their refuge and strength (Ps 46:1).
46:4 a river whose streams make glad Contrasts the chaotic waters of vv. 2–3 and symbolizes God's blessing and renewal. See Eze 47:1–12 and note. **Most High** The Hebrew name used here, *elyon*, emphasizes God's supremacy as ruler and judge over the entire earth (Ps 47:2; Dt 32:8). See the table "Names of God in the Old Testament" on p. 917.

⁷The LORD Almighty is with us;
  the God of Jacob is our fortress.

⁸Come and see what the LORD has done,
  the desolations he has brought on the earth.
⁹He makes wars cease
  to the ends of the earth.
He breaks the bow and shatters the spear;
  he burns the shields[a] with fire.
¹⁰He says, "Be still, and know that I am God;
I will be exalted among the nations,
  I will be exalted in the earth."

¹¹The LORD Almighty is with us;
  the God of Jacob is our fortress.

Psalm 47[b]

*For the director of music. Of the Sons of Korah.
A psalm.*

¹Clap your hands, all you nations;
  shout to God with cries of joy.

²For the LORD Most High is awesome,
  the great King over all the earth.
³He subdued nations under us,
  peoples under our feet.
⁴He chose our inheritance for us,
  the pride of Jacob, whom he loved.[c]

⁵God has ascended amid shouts of joy,
  the LORD amid the sounding of trumpets.
⁶Sing praises to God, sing praises;
  sing praises to our King, sing praises.
⁷For God is the King of all the earth;
  sing to him a psalm of praise.

⁸God reigns over the nations;
  God is seated on his holy throne.
⁹The nobles of the nations assemble
  as the people of the God of Abraham,
for the kings[d] of the earth belong to God;
  he is greatly exalted.

Psalm 48[e]

A song. A psalm of the Sons of Korah.

¹Great is the LORD, and most worthy of
  praise,
  in the city of our God, his holy mountain.

²Beautiful in its loftiness,
  the joy of the whole earth,
like the heights of Zaphon[f] is Mount Zion,
  the city of the Great King.

---

[a] 9 Or *chariots*   [b] In Hebrew texts 47:1-9 is numbered 47:2-10.
[c] 4 The Hebrew has *Selah* (a word of uncertain meaning) here.
[d] 9 Or *shields*   [e] In Hebrew texts 48:1-14 is numbered 48:2-15.
[f] 2 *Zaphon* was the most sacred mountain of the Canaanites.

46:7 LORD Almighty The Hebrew title used here for God, *yhwh tseva'oth*, refers to him as the commander of heavenly armies. See Ps 24:10 and note; Isa 1:9.

46:8–9 The psalmist encourages the congregation to examine the works of Yahweh. He uses imagery of weapons—bows, spears, chariots—to show Yahweh's power over enemy nations. By looking at Yahweh's military power, the people can have confidence, knowing that Yahweh is their refuge (Ps 46:1).

47:title–9 This psalm of Yahweh's kingship (or enthronement) encourages all people to loudly praise God as King over all the earth. It begins with an exhortation for all people to clap and shout loudly to God (47:1), the great and victorious King who establishes his people (vv. 2–4). The psalm describes God's ascension to the throne amid calls to praise him (vv. 5–7). The psalm then describes Yahweh's reign over the nations and the people of Israel (vv. 8–9). See the table "Types of Psalms" on p. 830.

47:title director of music See note on 4:title. **Sons of Korah** See note on 42:title. **A psalm** See note on 3:title.
47:2 Most High The Hebrew name here, *elyon*, emphasizes God's reign over all the earth—above all other powers (Dt 32:8).
47:4 inheritance The Hebrew word used here, *nachalah*, is often used to refer to the promised land (Ps 16:6). In 2:8, it is applied more broadly as God extends the heritage of the anointed king to all the nations—in recognition that Yahweh himself ultimately reigns over all the earth.
47:5 God has ascended amid shouts of joy Probably describes the procession of a victorious king, God in this instance, returning to the throne. See the infographic "The Ark of the Covenant" on p. 412.

47:9 The nobles of the nations assemble Foreign leaders, who are often opposed to God in the psalms (2:1–3; 46:6), now come together with the descendants of Abraham to praise him as King (2:10–11).

48:title–14 This song of Zion (Ps 46; 76; 84; 87; 122) focuses on praising Yahweh and his city. (Zion is the temple mount in Jerusalem and is virtually synonymous with Jerusalem itself.) The psalmist begins by asserting the greatness of Yahweh and his city, Zion (48:1–3), describing how enemy rulers turned away and fled at the sight of it (vv. 4–8). He praises God directly for his steadfast love and name (vv. 9–11). The psalmist then encourages people to examine the defenses of Zion and recognize them as a symbol of God's divine protection (vv. 12–14). See the table "Types of Psalms" on p. 830.

48:1 Great is the LORD While much of the psalm focuses on Zion, Yahweh's holy mountain, it begins with praise to Yahweh for his greatness (using the Hebrew word *gadol*).

GADOL
The term *gadol* essentially means "large" or "massive." When applied to God, it usually refers to his great power to save (Dt 4:37; Ne 1:10) or to create (Jer 27:5). It can also apply to his great love, loyalty (1Ki 3:6) or wrath (Dt 29:28). See the infographic "Jerusalem" on p. 1607.

48:2 Beautiful in its loftiness Emphasizes Zion's importance as Yahweh's chosen location rather than its

³ God is in her citadels;
he has shown himself to be her fortress.

⁴ When the kings joined forces,
when they advanced together,
⁵ they saw her and were astounded;
they fled in terror.
⁶ Trembling seized them there,
pain like that of a woman in labor.
⁷ You destroyed them like ships of Tarshish
shattered by an east wind.

⁸ As we have heard,
so we have seen
in the city of the LORD Almighty,
in the city of our God:
God makes her secure
forever.ᵃ

⁹ Within your temple, O God,
we meditate on your unfailing love.
¹⁰ Like your name, O God,
your praise reaches to the ends of the
earth;
your right hand is filled with
righteousness.
¹¹ Mount Zion rejoices,
the villages of Judah are glad
because of your judgments.

¹² Walk about Zion, go around her,
count her towers,
¹³ consider well her ramparts,
view her citadels,
that you may tell of them
to the next generation.

¹⁴ For this God is our God for ever and ever;
he will be our guide even to the end.

Psalm 49ᵇ

For the director of music. Of the Sons of Korah.
A psalm.

¹ Hear this, all you peoples;
listen, all who live in this world,
² both low and high,
rich and poor alike:
³ My mouth will speak words of wisdom;
the meditation of my heart will give you
understanding.
⁴ I will turn my ear to a proverb;
with the harp I will expound my
riddle:

⁵ Why should I fear when evil days come,
when wicked deceivers surround me —
⁶ those who trust in their wealth
and boast of their great riches?
⁷ No one can redeem the life of another
or give to God a ransom for them —
⁸ the ransom for a life is costly,
no payment is ever enough —
⁹ so that they should live on forever
and not see decay.
¹⁰ For all can see that the wise die,
that the foolish and the senseless also
perish,
leaving their wealth to others.

ᵃ 8 The Hebrew has *Selah* (a word of uncertain meaning) here.
ᵇ In Hebrew texts 49:1-20 is numbered 49:2-21.

---

actual elevation, which is not particularly impressive—several other peaks in the area are higher.

48:4–6 The psalmist describes the futile attempts of enemy nations to overthrow Zion. As soon as they see the city, they retreat in horror and amazement (Isa 13:8).

48:7 ships of Tarshish Refers to trading ships (1Ki 10:22). These ships often serve as symbols of human pride that fall under God's judgment. See Isa 2:16 and note.

48:8 LORD Almighty See note on Ps 24:10.

48:10 to the ends of the earth God's praise is not limited to Zion. Like his name, Yahweh, it extends to the ends of the earth (see note on 23:3).

48:12–14 The psalmist encourages worshipers to walk around Zion and examine its defenses—its defensive towers, fortifications and strongholds. The defenses of Zion served as symbols for God's strength and protection for his people (v. 14).

49:title–20 This wisdom psalm—meant to pass along wise sayings—focuses on earthly wealth and the fate of the wicked. The psalmist calls all people to listen to his proverb (vv. 1–4), then questions why he should fear the corrupt and powerful (vv. 5–9). Since both the wise and foolish will die and leave behind their

wealth (vv. 10–12), those who put their confidence in wealth will be consumed in the realm of the dead (*she'ol* in Hebrew; vv. 13–15). He concludes by discouraging people from fearing the wealthy, whose glory will not follow them in death (vv. 16–20). See the table "Types of Psalms" on p. 830.

49:title director of music See note on 4:title. **Sons of Korah** See note on 42:title. **A psalm** See note on 3:title.

49:1–2 The psalmist's message is intended for a wide audience, as he invites everyone to hear him. This includes people from all walks of life—the wealthy and powerful, the poor and humble.

49:4 proverb The Hebrew word used here, *mashal*, refers to a proverbial saying. It often includes comparisons or analogies. **harp** The Hebrew word used here, *kinnor*, refers to an instrument that was associated with celebration and worship.

49:7 No one can redeem the life of another The psalmist should not fear the rich and powerful because their wealth does not give them the power to buy life.

49:10 can see that the wise die The psalmist shares many observations with the author of Ecclesiastes. However, while the author of Ecclesiastes expresses frustration that there is no advantage to being wise (see Ecc 2:12–17) or wealthy (see Ecc 2:18–24), the psalmist takes comfort in knowing that those who boast

11 Their tombs will remain their houses[a]
  forever,
 their dwellings for endless generations,
 though they had[b] named lands after
  themselves.

12 People, despite their wealth, do not endure;
  they are like the beasts that perish.

13 This is the fate of those who trust in
  themselves,
 and of their followers, who approve their
  sayings.[c]

14 They are like sheep and are destined to die;
  death will be their shepherd
 (but the upright will prevail over them in
  the morning).
 Their forms will decay in the grave,
  far from their princely mansions.

15 But God will redeem me from the realm of
  the dead;
  he will surely take me to himself.

16 Do not be overawed when others grow rich,
  when the splendor of their houses
  increases;

17 for they will take nothing with them when
  they die,
  their splendor will not descend with them.

18 Though while they live they count
  themselves blessed—
 and people praise you when you prosper—

19 they will join those who have gone before
  them,
 who will never again see the light of life.

20 People who have wealth but lack
  understanding
 are like the beasts that perish.

Psalm 50

A psalm of Asaph.

1 The Mighty One, God, the LORD,
  speaks and summons the earth
 from the rising of the sun to where it sets.

2 From Zion, perfect in beauty,
  God shines forth.

3 Our God comes
  and will not be silent;
 a fire devours before him,
  and around him a tempest rages.

4 He summons the heavens above,
  and the earth, that he may judge his
  people:

5 "Gather to me this consecrated people,
  who made a covenant with me by
  sacrifice."

6 And the heavens proclaim his righteousness,
  for he is a God of justice.[d,e]

7 "Listen, my people, and I will speak;
  I will testify against you, Israel:
  I am God, your God.

---

[a] 11 Septuagint and Syriac; Hebrew *In their thoughts their houses will remain*   [b] 11 Or *generations, / for they have*   [c] 13 The Hebrew has *Selah* (a word of uncertain meaning) here and at the end of verse 15.   [d] 6 With a different word division of the Hebrew; Masoretic Text *for God himself is judge*   [e] 6 The Hebrew has *Selah* (a word of uncertain meaning) here.

---

of great wealth will ultimately take none of it with them when they die.

49:13 fate of those who trust in themselves Those who trust in their wealth (Ps 49:6) foolishly put their confidence in something that does not last and that cannot redeem or ransom them from death.

49:14 the grave The Hebrew word *she'ol* is used here, which refers to the realm of the dead (the underworld). See note on Job 14:13; note on 1Ki 2:6.

49:15 God will redeem me The psalmist concludes that he should not fear the rich or powerful on earth because he can be confident that God will redeem his life. While this could be metaphorical, for the desperate situation the psalmist is in, it could also show hope in resurrection. **the realm of the dead** In parallel with Ps 49:14, the Hebrew word *she'ol* is used here. See note on Job 14:13; note on 1Ki 2:6.

49:16 Do not be overawed The psalmist concludes that he should not fear the rich or powerful on earth because he can be confident that God will redeem his life (Ps 49:15).

49:19 those who have gone before them See note on Ge 15:15.

50:title–23 Psalm 50 functions as a prophetic oracle. God instructs and warns his people about offering sacrifices. The psalm opens with an individual announcing that God has come to speak (vv. 1–4). God calls his people to gather (vv. 5–6), and addresses them directly by warning them that he does not need animal sacrifices

(vv. 7–13). Instead, he prefers loyalty and dependence (vv. 14–15). He then rebukes the wicked for expressing false loyalty (vv. 16–21) and concludes with a final warning: His people should not forget him; but they should offer thanksgiving and live in the right way (vv. 22–23; see note on v. 14).

50:title A psalm of Asaph See note on 73:title.
50:1 The Mighty One, God, the LORD The psalmist uses three consecutive Hebrew names for God: *el*, *elohim* and *yhwh*. Taken together, the names emphasize God's supremacy as Creator of the earth and God of Israel. Because *el* and *elohim* are both usually translated as "God," most translations use "Mighty One." However, the text literally translates as "God, God, Yahweh." The first "God" (*el*) refers to God as the supreme deity.
50:3 Our God comes God appears with frightening power. Theophanies (appearances of God) typically include displays of the power of nature, like storms—showing God's ability to command these chaotic forces.
50:4 the heavens above, and the earth In the works of the prophets, God often calls heaven and earth as witnesses. See Isa 1:2 and note.
50:6 the heavens proclaim As God's witness, the heavens testify to his righteousness—showing his ability to make things right, to establish things as they should be.
50:7 Listen, my people God addresses his people; he reminds them of their covenant with him using speech similar to the covenant formula of Lev 26:12. See Eze 11:20 and note.

8 I bring no charges against you concerning
    your sacrifices
  or concerning your burnt offerings, which
    are ever before me.
9 I have no need of a bull from your stall
  or of goats from your pens,
10 for every animal of the forest is mine,
  and the cattle on a thousand hills.
11 I know every bird in the mountains,
  and the insects in the fields are mine.
12 If I were hungry I would not tell you,
  for the world is mine, and all that is in it.
13 Do I eat the flesh of bulls
  or drink the blood of goats?

14 "Sacrifice thank offerings to God,
  fulfill your vows to the Most High,
15 and call on me in the day of trouble;
  I will deliver you, and you will
    honor me."

16 But to the wicked person, God says:

"What right have you to recite my laws
  or take my covenant on your lips?
17 You hate my instruction
  and cast my words behind you.
18 When you see a thief, you join with him;
  you throw in your lot with adulterers.
19 You use your mouth for evil
  and harness your tongue to deceit.
20 You sit and testify against your brother
  and slander your own mother's son.
21 When you did these things and I kept silent,
  you thought I was exactly[a] like you.

But I now arraign you
  and set my accusations before you.
22 "Consider this, you who forget God,
  or I will tear you to pieces, with no one to
    rescue you:
23 Those who sacrifice thank offerings honor me,
  and to the blameless[b] I will show my
    salvation."

Psalm 51[c]

*For the director of music. A psalm of David. When
the prophet Nathan came to him after David
had committed adultery with Bathsheba.*

1 Have mercy on me, O God,
  according to your unfailing love;
according to your great compassion
  blot out my transgressions.
2 Wash away all my iniquity
  and cleanse me from my sin.

3 For I know my transgressions,
  and my sin is always before me.
4 Against you, you only, have I sinned
  and done what is evil in your sight;
so you are right in your verdict
  and justified when you judge.
5 Surely I was sinful at birth,
  sinful from the time my mother
    conceived me.

[a] 21 Or *thought the 'I AM' was*   [b] 23 Probable reading of the original Hebrew text; the meaning of the Masoretic Text for this phrase is uncertain.   [c] In Hebrew texts 51:1-19 is numbered 51:3-21.

50:8 I bring no charges against you concerning your sacrifices The OT consistently maintains that God does not delight in sacrifices when they are only outward expressions of religion (1Sa 15:22). See note on Ps 40:6.
50:14 thank offerings While the Hebrew term used here can indicate a specific type of thanksgiving sacrifice (Lev 7:12), here it most likely signifies that God prefers an attitude of thanksgiving over sacrifice.
50:15 in the day of trouble God desires his people to trust and rely on him—no matter what the circumstances.
50:21 you thought I was exactly like you In addition to the sins he attributes to the wicked in Ps 50:17–20, God rebukes his people for their attitude toward him. They viewed God's silence as a sign that he was unable to judge them. **set my accusations** With the heavens and earth as his witnesses (see v. 4 and note), God has given evidence for the misdeeds of the wicked.
50:22 no one to rescue Those who neglect a relationship with God find themselves with no God to rescue them during adversity (see v. 15 and note).
50:23 thank offerings See note on v. 14.

51:title–19 In Ps 51—an individual lament psalm—the psalmist, in anguish because of his sin, confesses and prays for mercy. He suffers from broken fellowship with God rather than physical affliction. He petitions God for mercy and cleansing (vv. 1–2), then acknowledges his sin (vv. 3–6). He asks God to purify and restore him (vv. 7–12), describing how he will respond to God's

forgiveness (vv. 13–15). After stating that God prefers a contrite heart over sacrifice (vv. 16–17), he concludes by petitioning God for national restoration (vv. 18–19). Psalm 51 is one of the early church's penitential psalms (or psalms of confession; Ps 6; 32; 38; 102; 130; 143). See the table "Types of Psalms" on p. 830.
51:title after David had committed adultery with Bathsheba Psalm titles were likely added later (see note on 3:title). However, the story of David's greatest failure provides a rich historical lens through which to read this psalm's appeal for forgiveness. See 2Sa 11–12.
51:1 Have mercy The Hebrew term used here, *chanan*—which may be literally rendered as "to show favor"—often appears in lament psalms as the psalmist seeks God's favor or compassion (e.g., Ps 4:1; 6:2; 41:4,10).
51:2 Wash away In his request for cleansing, the psalmist asks God to forget his sin and to purify him by removing it.
51:3–4 In confessing his sin, the psalmist recognizes that he has sinned against God himself. He acknowledges God's right to judge him. While his sin may have involved and harmed others, the psalmist is primarily concerned with his offense against God.

51:5 Surely I was sinful at birth The psalmist makes no excuses but recognizes that iniquity has been with him since birth.

⁶ Yet you desired faithfulness even in the womb;
    you taught me wisdom in that secret place.

⁷ Cleanse me with hyssop, and I will be clean;
    wash me, and I will be whiter than snow.
⁸ Let me hear joy and gladness;
    let the bones you have crushed rejoice.
⁹ Hide your face from my sins
    and blot out all my iniquity.

¹⁰ Create in me a pure heart, O God,
    and renew a steadfast spirit within me.
¹¹ Do not cast me from your presence
    or take your Holy Spirit from me.
¹² Restore to me the joy of your salvation
    and grant me a willing spirit, to sustain me.

¹³ Then I will teach transgressors your ways,
    so that sinners will turn back to you.
¹⁴ Deliver me from the guilt of bloodshed,
        O God,
    you who are God my Savior,
    and my tongue will sing of your
        righteousness.
¹⁵ Open my lips, Lord,
    and my mouth will declare your praise.
¹⁶ You do not delight in sacrifice, or I would
        bring it;
    you do not take pleasure in burnt offerings.
¹⁷ My sacrifice, O God, is*ᵃ* a broken spirit;
    a broken and contrite heart
    you, God, will not despise.

¹⁸ May it please you to prosper Zion,
    to build up the walls of Jerusalem.

¹⁹ Then you will delight in the sacrifices of the
        righteous,
    in burnt offerings offered whole;
    then bulls will be offered on your altar.

Psalm 52ᵇ

For the director of music. A maskilᶜ of David.
When Doeg the Edomite had gone to Saul and told him:
"David has gone to the house of Ahimelek."

¹ Why do you boast of evil, you mighty hero?
    Why do you boast all day long,
    you who are a disgrace in the eyes of God?
² You who practice deceit,
    your tongue plots destruction;
    it is like a sharpened razor.
³ You love evil rather than good,
    falsehood rather than speaking the truth.ᵈ
⁴ You love every harmful word,
    you deceitful tongue!

⁵ Surely God will bring you down to
        everlasting ruin:
    He will snatch you up and pluck you from
        your tent;
    he will uproot you from the land of the
        living.
⁶ The righteous will see and fear;
    they will laugh at you, saying,

ᵃ 17 Or *The sacrifices of God are*   ᵇ In Hebrew texts 52:1-9 is
numbered 52:3-11.   ᶜ Title: Probably a literary or musical term
ᵈ 3 The Hebrew has *Selah* (a word of uncertain meaning) here
and at the end of verse 5.

51:7 hyssop Israelites used hyssop branches to apply the blood of the Passover lamb to their doorposts (see Ex 12:22 and note). They were also used in other purifying rituals (Lev 14:49–53; Nu 19:18–19).

51:10 a pure heart Throughout the works of the prophets, God states he will restore his people by giving them a new heart that will enable them to return to him in obedience (see Jer 24:7; Eze 11:20 and note).

51:11 take your Holy Spirit from me The psalmist may have been thinking of when God removed his Spirit from Saul after Saul became his enemy (see 1Sa 16:14 and note).

51:14 bloodshed The Hebrew word used here, *dam*, probably refers to death in this context (see Ps 30:9). The psalmist asserts that, if God delivers him from death, he will be able to praise his righteousness and salvation. See note on 30:9.

51:16 You do not delight in sacrifice God does not delight in sacrifices that are only an outward expression of religion. See 40:6 and note.

51:17 My sacrifice, O God, is a broken spirit Instead of merely ritual sacrifice, God desires that his people trust in and rely on him. See 50:14–15 and notes.

51:18–19 The psalmist concludes with a petition for national restoration. He asks that God bestow his favor on Zion, his holy city (see 48:1–2; Isa 1:8 and note).

51:19 sacrifices of the righteous Probably refers to sacrifices that are accompanied by righteous behavior or obedience. See Ps 4:5 and note.

52:title–9 This psalm of confidence—expressing faith in God—deals with the boasting of the wicked, God's ultimate judgment of them and his steadfast love for the faithful. The psalmist first addresses the wicked, asking why they boast and accusing them of deceitful speech (vv. 1–4). He shows confidence in God's judgment (v. 5) and the response of the righteous (vv. 6–7). Finally, the psalmist expresses his confidence in God's steadfast love (vv. 8–9). See the table "Types of Psalms" on p. 830.

52:title director of music See note on 4:title. *maskil* See note on 32:title. **of David** See note on 3:title. **Doeg the Edomite had gone to Saul and told him** See 1Sa 22:6–23.

52:1 boast The Hebrew word used here, *halal*, means "to praise" (see note on Ps 10:3). The psalmist addresses those who praise evil acts instead of God. **you mighty hero** The psalmist's use of the Hebrew word *gibbor* here (meaning "strong man" or "valiant man") may indicate the wicked have become mighty because of their wealth (v. 7).

52:2–4 The use of plural words in this section of the Hebrew text indicates the psalmist is addressing a group of people. He accuses them of speaking and acting with deceit. He asserts that they love deceitful behavior, rather than what is good and right.

52:6 they will laugh at you The righteous rejoice in the downfall of the wicked. Rather than gloat over the enemy, which displeases God, they recognize God's righteous judgment (compare Pr 24:17–18 and note).

7 "Here now is the man
  who did not make God his stronghold
but trusted in his great wealth
  and grew strong by destroying others!"

8 But I am like an olive tree
  flourishing in the house of God;
I trust in God's unfailing love
  for ever and ever.
9 For what you have done I will always praise you
  in the presence of your faithful people.
And I will hope in your name,
  for your name is good.

Psalm 53[a]

53:1-6pp — Ps 14:1-7

For the director of music. According to mahalath.[b]
A maskil[c] *of David.*

1 The fool says in his heart,
  "There is no God."
They are corrupt, and their ways are vile;
  there is no one who does good.

2 God looks down from heaven
  on all mankind
to see if there are any who understand,
  any who seek God.
3 Everyone has turned away, all have become
  corrupt;
  there is no one who does good,
  not even one.

4 Do all these evildoers know nothing?

They devour my people as though eating bread;
  they never call on God.

5 But there they are, overwhelmed
  with dread,
  where there was nothing to dread.
God scattered the bones of those who
  attacked you;
  you put them to shame, for God despised
  them.

6 Oh, that salvation for Israel would come
  out of Zion!
  When God restores his people,
  let Jacob rejoice and Israel be glad!

Psalm 54[d]

*For the director of music. With stringed instruments.
A* maskil[c] *of David. When the Ziphites had gone
to Saul and said, "Is not David hiding among us?"*

1 Save me, O God, by your name;
  vindicate me by your might.
2 Hear my prayer, O God;
  listen to the words of my mouth.

3 Arrogant foes are attacking me;
  ruthless people are trying to
    kill me —
  people without regard for God.[e]

4 Surely God is my help;
  the Lord is the one who sustains me.

5 Let evil recoil on those who slander me;
  in your faithfulness destroy them.

---

[a] In Hebrew texts 53:1-6 is numbered 53:2-7.   [b] Title: Probably
a musical term   [c] Title: Probably a literary or musical term
[d] In Hebrew texts 54:1-7 is numbered 54:3-9.   [e] 3 The Hebrew
has *Selah* (a word of uncertain meaning) here.

52:8 I am like an olive tree Unlike the wicked, who
will be uprooted (Ps 52:5), the psalmist is confident and
secure in God's protection. He compares himself to a
tree, a symbol of stability and prosperity (1:3; 92:12–14).
52:9 I will always praise you God's punishment of the
wicked causes the psalmist to trust in his steadfast love
and give him thanks.
53:title–6 Psalm 53 is nearly identical to Ps 14. See
note on 14:title–7.
53:title According to *mahalath* May refer to dancing,
antiphonal singing, an instrument or sickness. ***maskil***
See note on 32:title.
53:1 fool The Hebrew word used here, *naval*, refers to
someone who rejects God and chooses evil. **are vile**
The nearly identical Ps 14:1 uses the Hebrew word
alilah ("deeds") instead of *awel* (which may be literally
rendered "iniquity"). However, both psalms emphasize
the atrocious nature of the fool's actions.
53:3 there is no one who does good See note on 14:3.
53:5 there was nothing to dread Describes an attitude of guilt and paranoia paralleled elsewhere in the
OT (Lev 26:17; see Pr 28:1 and note). **those who attacked you** In contrast to the nearly identical Ps 14,
the psalmist here addresses a person oppressed by the
fool, whereas Ps 14 addresses the fools (see 14:6 and
note). Psalm 14 emphasizes that God is the refuge to

the poor, while this verse emphasizes that God rejects
and shames the wicked.

54:title–7 In this individual lament psalm, the psalmist
emphasizes his trust in God. He begins by asking God
to deliver him (vv. 1–2), explaining how his enemies
are against him (v. 3). He then affirms his trust in God
(vv. 4–5) and concludes by giving thanks to Yahweh
for delivering him (vv. 6–7). See the table "Types of
Psalms" on p. 830.
54:title director of music See note on 4:title. ***maskil***
See note on 32:title. **of David** See note on 3:title. **Ziphites had gone to Saul and said** The Ziphites informed
Saul of David's location twice (1Sa 23:19–24; 26:1–4).
54:1 vindicate me The Hebrew word used here, *dayan*,
literally means "to judge" (Ps 50:4). When used of the
innocent, it indicates a vindication or defense of their
rights (Pr 31:8–9). See note on Ps 7:8.
54:3 people without regard for God The defining
characteristic of the psalmist's enemies. They have no
regard for God and oppress with violence. By describing
them this way, the psalmist draws a contrast between
himself and his enemies.
54:4 Surely God is my help In contrast to his enemies,
who have no regard for God, the psalmist trusts God to
help him in times of trouble.

⁶ I will sacrifice a freewill offering to you;
  I will praise your name, Lord, for it is good.
⁷ You have delivered me from all my troubles,
  and my eyes have looked in triumph on my
    foes.

Psalm 55ᵃ

For the director of music. With stringed instruments.
A maskilᵇ of David.

¹ Listen to my prayer, O God,
  do not ignore my plea;
² hear me and answer me.
  My thoughts trouble me and I am distraught
³ because of what my enemy is saying,
  because of the threats of the wicked;
  for they bring down suffering on me
  and assail me in their anger.

⁴ My heart is in anguish within me;
  the terrors of death have fallen on me.
⁵ Fear and trembling have beset me;
  horror has overwhelmed me.
⁶ I said, "Oh, that I had the wings of a dove!
  I would fly away and be at rest.
⁷ I would flee far away
  and stay in the desert;ᶜ
⁸ I would hurry to my place of shelter,
  far from the tempest and storm."

⁹ Lord, confuse the wicked, confound their
    words,
  for I see violence and strife in the city.

¹⁰ Day and night they prowl about on its walls;
  malice and abuse are within it.
¹¹ Destructive forces are at work in the city;
  threats and lies never leave its streets.

¹² If an enemy were insulting me,
  I could endure it;
  if a foe were rising against me,
  I could hide.
¹³ But it is you, a man like myself,
  my companion, my close friend,
¹⁴ with whom I once enjoyed sweet fellowship
  at the house of God,
  as we walked about
  among the worshipers.

¹⁵ Let death take my enemies by surprise;
  let them go down alive to the realm of the
    dead,
  for evil finds lodging among them.

¹⁶ As for me, I call to God,
  and the Lord saves me.
¹⁷ Evening, morning and noon
  I cry out in distress,
  and he hears my voice.
¹⁸ He rescues me unharmed
  from the battle waged against me,
  even though many oppose me.

ᵃ In Hebrew texts 55:1-23 is numbered 55:2-24.   ᵇ Title:
Probably a literary or musical term   ᶜ 7 The Hebrew has *Selah*
(a word of uncertain meaning) here and in the middle of verse 19.

54:6 I will sacrifice a freewill offering The psalmist responds to God's faithful deliverance by offering a freewill offering (*nedavah* in Hebrew)—an offering brought as an act of worship or in fulfillment of a vow (see note on Lev 7:16; 22:18).

55:title–23 In this individual lament psalm, the psalmist is not simply afflicted by enemies—he has been betrayed by a close friend. He begins by asking God to hear him and deliver him from his enemies (Ps 55:1–3). He then describes his inner anguish and expresses a desire to flee (vv. 4–8). He prays for justice as he asks God to destroy his enemies (vv. 9–11). The psalmist then explains that he suffers because of a close friend (vv. 12–14). He continues his call for justice (v. 15), confident that God will hear him and redeem him (vv. 16–19). He describes the betrayal by his friend (vv. 20–21). Finally, he encourages everyone to cast their burdens on Yahweh (v. 22) and expresses confidence that God will destroy his enemies (v. 23). See the table "Types of Psalms" on p. 830.

55:title director of music See note on 4:title. **maskil** See note on 32:title. **of David** See note on 3:title.

55:1 prayer, O God, do not ignore In OT lament, individuals often express feeling abandoned by God (44:24; Job 13:24). Their suffering leads them to feel that God is far away or distant (see Ps 10:1 and note). Rather than indicating a lack a faith, these expressions show that God's presence was believed to be accompanied by his protection (see 4:6; 13:5 and note).

55:3 assail The Hebrew word used here, *satam*, means "to hate" or "to be hostile toward."

55:4–8 The psalmist expresses his anguish, terror and fear. He voices a desire to run away and hide alone in the desert (Jer 48:28).

55:9 confound their words Possibly an allusion to the tower of Babel, where God confused the people's language (Ge 11:5–9). See the infographic "The Tower of Babel" on p. 29.

55:10 malice and abuse are within it The psalmist's enemies bring trouble to the entire city.

55:12 rising The Hebrew word used here, *gadal*, means "to exalt" or "to magnify" (see note on Ps 34:3). Here, it carries the sense of people who exalt themselves at the expense of another.

55:13 my companion The Hebrew word used here, *alluph*, refers to a close friend. The psalmist does not complain of mere abandonment; he suffers because his close friend has betrayed him. **close friend** The Hebrew word used here, *meyudda'*, can indicate a relative (Ru 2:1) or a close advisor or confidant (2Ki 10:11).

55:14 fellowship The Hebrew word used here, *sod*, can refer to a circle of confidants or a council (Ge 49:6; Job 15:8). Here, it reflects the unity between the psalmist and his friend. **at the house of God** The psalmist describes the fellowship he used to enjoy with his friend by indicating that they went to the temple together to worship at festivals (see Ps 42:4 and note).

55:15 the realm of the dead The Hebrew word *she'ol* is used here (see note on Job 14:13; note on 1Ki 2:6). The psalmist wishes his enemies would go to *she'ol* alive, which suggests that he wants them to not just experience

¹⁹ God, who is enthroned from of old,
    who does not change —
he will hear them and humble them,
    because they have no fear of God.

²⁰ My companion attacks his friends;
    he violates his covenant.
²¹ His talk is smooth as butter,
    yet war is in his heart;
his words are more soothing than oil,
    yet they are drawn swords.

²² Cast your cares on the LORD
    and he will sustain you;
he will never let
    the righteous be shaken.
²³ But you, God, will bring down the wicked
    into the pit of decay;
the bloodthirsty and deceitful
    will not live out half their days.

But as for me, I trust in you.

Psalm 56[a]

*For the director of music. To the tune of "A Dove
on Distant Oaks." Of David. A miktam.[b] When
the Philistines had seized him in Gath.*

¹ Be merciful to me, my God,
    for my enemies are in hot pursuit;
    all day long they press their attack.
² My adversaries pursue me all day long;
    in their pride many are attacking me.

³ When I am afraid, I put my trust in you.
⁴   In God, whose word I praise —
in God I trust and am not afraid.
    What can mere mortals do to me?

⁵ All day long they twist my words;
    all their schemes are for my ruin.
⁶ They conspire, they lurk,
    they watch my steps,
    hoping to take my life.
⁷ Because of their wickedness do not[c] let them
    escape;
in your anger, God, bring the nations
    down.

⁸ Record my misery;
    list my tears on your scroll[d] —
    are they not in your record?
⁹ Then my enemies will turn back
    when I call for help.
    By this I will know that God is for me.

¹⁰ In God, whose word I praise,
    in the LORD, whose word I praise —
¹¹ in God I trust and am not afraid.
    What can man do to me?

¹² I am under vows to you, my God;
    I will present my thank offerings
    to you.

---

a In Hebrew texts 56:1-13 is numbered 56:2-14.   *b* Title:
Probably a literary or musical term   *c* 7 Probable reading of
the original Hebrew text; Masoretic Text does not have *do not*.
d 8 Or *misery; / put my tears in your wineskin*

---

death but the pain of the evil they have inflicted. He wants
them to live where only death resides.
55:18 many oppose me Even though he identified an
individual as the main source of his complaint (see Ps
55:13 and note), the psalmist says that many people
are against him. While he suffers from betrayal by a
friend, he also laments those who oppress him in general (vv. 10–11).
55:21 his words are more soothing than oil The
words of the psalmist's former friend are flattering (see
Pr 5:3 and note) but destructive (see Pr 29:5 and note).
55:22 Cast your cares on the LORD Those who trust
Yahweh with their burdens can be sure God will sustain
them and protect them (Ps 37:5).

56:title–13 In this individual lament psalm, the psalmist petitions God for help (vv. 1–2) and describes his
affliction (vv. 5–6). He focuses, however, on expressing
confidence that, with God on his side, he will not fear
(vv. 3–4,8–11). Because of this, the psalm is better described as a psalm of confidence or a thanksgiving psalm.
The psalmist first asks for help (vv. 1–2), expresses
trust in God (vv. 3–4) and describes the actions of his
enemies (vv. 5–7). He reasserts his trust by declaring
that no one can harm him if God is with him (vv. 8–11).
He concludes by stating his intention to perform his vows
to God and praise God for delivering him (vv. 12–13).
See the table "Types of Psalms" on p. 830.

56:title director of music See note on 4:title. **To the
tune of "A Dove on Distant Oaks"** Most likely the name

of the tune to which this psalm was sung. **Of David** See
note on 3:title. **miktam** See note on 16:title. **When the
Philistines had seized him in Gath** Probably refers to
when David pretended to be insane before Achish the
king of Gath (1Sa 21:10–15).
56:1 hot pursuit The exact meaning of the Hebrew word
here, *sha'aph* (sometimes translated as "tramples") is
uncertain. It can indicate panting (Ps 119:131; Job 5:5;
Isa 42:14) or a longing (Job 7:2; 36:20). It may describe
how the enemies wear themselves out by attacking the
psalmist.

56:3–4 The psalmist acknowledges that he does not
need to fear his enemies because he trusts in God.

56:4 mere mortals By using the Hebrew word *basar*
(which may be literally rendered "flesh"), the psalmist
contrasts the temporary standing of his enemies (Ps
78:39) with the lasting protection of God.
56:7 in your anger, God, bring the nations down
God's anger is usually a response to disobedience.
See 7:6 and note.
56:8 my misery The Hebrew word used here, *nod*,
occurs only once in the OT. It most likely derives from
the word *nadad*, meaning "to wander"; it indicates the
psalmist's distress. **are they not in your record** The
psalmist expresses confidence that God watches over
him, even in the midst of his suffering.
56:12 vows The Hebrew word here, *neder*, refers to a
promise made to God, usually made in a time of distress.
See note on 50:14.

¹³ For you have delivered me from death
  and my feet from stumbling,
that I may walk before God
  in the light of life.

Psalm 57[a]

57:7-11pp — Ps 108:1-5

For the director of music. To the tune of "Do Not Destroy."
Of David. A miktam.[b] When he had fled
from Saul into the cave.

¹ Have mercy on me, my God, have mercy
    on me,
  for in you I take refuge.
I will take refuge in the shadow of your wings
  until the disaster has passed.

² I cry out to God Most High,
  to God, who vindicates me.
³ He sends from heaven and saves me,
  rebuking those who hotly pursue me — [c]
  God sends forth his love and his faithfulness.

⁴ I am in the midst of lions;
  I am forced to dwell among ravenous
    beasts —
men whose teeth are spears and arrows,
  whose tongues are sharp swords.

⁵ Be exalted, O God, above the heavens;
  let your glory be over all the earth.

⁶ They spread a net for my feet —
  I was bowed down in distress.

They dug a pit in my path —
  but they have fallen into it
    themselves.

⁷ My heart, O God, is steadfast,
  my heart is steadfast;
  I will sing and make music.
⁸ Awake, my soul!
  Awake, harp and lyre!
  I will awaken the dawn.

⁹ I will praise you, Lord, among the
    nations;
  I will sing of you among the peoples.
¹⁰ For great is your love, reaching to the
    heavens;
  your faithfulness reaches to the skies.

¹¹ Be exalted, O God, above the heavens;
  let your glory be over all the earth.

Psalm 58[d]

For the director of music. To the tune of "Do Not Destroy."
Of David. A miktam.[b]

¹ Do you rulers indeed speak justly?
  Do you judge people with equity?
² No, in your heart you devise injustice,
  and your hands mete out violence on
    the earth.

---

[a] In Hebrew texts 57:1-11 is numbered 57:2-12. [b] Title: Probably a literary or musical term [c] 3 The Hebrew has *Selah* (a word of uncertain meaning) here and at the end of verse 6. [d] In Hebrew texts 58:1-11 is numbered 58:2-12.

56:13 walk before God in the light Protected by God, the psalmist declares that he walks securely and safely (see 27:1 and note).

57:title–11 Psalm 57 is an individual lament psalm with an emphasis on proclaiming God's glory. The psalmist twice repeats a refrain praising God's glory (vv. 5,11). He begins by petitioning God for mercy (v. 1), then expresses confidence that God will save him (vv. 2–3). He describes his enemies (v. 4) and follows with praise (v. 5). He then continues to describe his enemies (v. 6) before praising and giving thanks for God's steadfast love (vv. 7–10). The psalm closes with a refrain of praise (v. 11). See the table "Types of Psalms" on p. 830.

57:title director of music See note on 4:title. **Do Not Destroy** This phrase appears in the titles of Ps 57–59 and Ps 75. The exact relationship to the psalm title is uncertain. It could be a tune that is supposed to fit with the words. It could also be an exhortation to protect the psalm from being destroyed. **Of David** See note on 3:title. *miktam* See note on 16:title. **had fled from Saul into the cave** David fled to a cave in both 1Sa 22:1–2 and 24:1–7.

57:1 Have mercy on me, my God A common plea in lament psalms. The Hebrew verb used here, *chanan*, refers to extending grace or compassion. See note on Ps 51:1. **in the shadow of your wings** A common image for God's protection. See note on 36:7; note on Ru 2:12. **disaster has passed** The Hebrew word here, *hawwah*, means "disaster" or "calamity" (Ps 52:2; Job 6:2). The

psalmist wants to take shelter in God's protection and wait for the destruction to pass over like a storm.

57:2 God Most High The Hebrew phrase used here, *elohim elyon*, emphasizes God's supremacy over the entire earth (Ps 47:2; Dt 32:8). **to God, who vindicates me** Given the psalmist's desire that God shame his enemies (Ps 57:3), this phrase should be understood as a call for God to bring vengeance on his behalf.

57:4 in the midst of lions Describes enemies as lions; they encircle him and wait for the chance to destroy him (17:12). See note on 7:2.

57:5 above the heavens This could refer to the highest heavens, where the Israelites believed that Yahweh dwelled, or be a general exaltation declaring that God is greater than all things.

57:7–11 This section is nearly identical to 108:1–5, which is concerned with God's military help.

57:8 Awake, harp and lyre The Hebrew text here refers to stringed instruments associated with celebration and worship. **I will awaken the dawn** Probably indicates that the psalmist woke early to praise God.

57:10 your faithfulness reaches to the skies Emphasizes the far-reaching scope of God's steadfast love and faithfulness.

58:title–11 In this corporate lament psalm (meant for group use), the psalmist curses his enemies and petitions God to punish them. He accuses the rulers of the earth of injustice (vv. 1–2), and then describes

³ Even from birth the wicked go astray;
  from the womb they are wayward,
    spreading lies.
⁴ Their venom is like the venom of a snake,
  like that of a cobra that has stopped its
    ears,
⁵ that will not heed the tune of the charmer,
  however skillful the enchanter may be.

⁶ Break the teeth in their mouths, O God;
  LORD, tear out the fangs of those lions!
⁷ Let them vanish like water that flows away;
  when they draw the bow, let their arrows
    fall short.
⁸ May they be like a slug that melts away as it
    moves along,
  like a stillborn child that never sees
    the sun.

⁹ Before your pots can feel the heat of the
    thorns —
  whether they be green or dry — the wicked
    will be swept away.^a
¹⁰ The righteous will be glad when they are
    avenged,
  when they dip their feet in the blood of the
    wicked.

¹¹ Then people will say,
  "Surely the righteous still are rewarded;
  surely there is a God who judges the
    earth."

Psalm 59^b

For the director of music. To the tune of "Do Not Destroy."
Of David. A miktam.^c When Saul had sent men
to watch David's house in order to kill him.

¹ Deliver me from my enemies, O God;
  be my fortress against those who are
    attacking me.
² Deliver me from evildoers
  and save me from those who are after my
    blood.

³ See how they lie in wait for me!
  Fierce men conspire against me
  for no offense or sin of mine, LORD.
⁴ I have done no wrong, yet they are ready to
    attack me.
  Arise to help me; look on my plight!

^a 9 The meaning of the Hebrew for this verse is uncertain.
^b In Hebrew texts 59:1-17 is numbered 59:2-18.   ^c Title:
Probably a literary or musical term

---

the actions of the wicked (vv. 3–5) and asks God to destroy them (vv. 6–9). Finally, he describes the reaction of the righteous: They will rejoice because God has carried out justice (vv. 10–11). See the table "Types of Psalms" on p. 830.

58:title director of music See note on 4:title. **Do Not Destroy** See note on 57:title. **Of David** See note on 3:title. *miktam* See note on 16:title.

58:2 in your heart you devise injustice The psalmist concludes that rulers do not judge righteously (see 58:1).

58:3–5 The wicked are characterized by deceit. The psalmist shows the extent of their wickedness by describing them as evil from birth. He describes their wickedness as poison (140:3; see note on Job 20:16): They are as dangerous as snakes that ignore their charmers (Jer 8:17).

58:6–9 In this section, the psalmist speaks graphically as he calls on God to destroy the wicked. These types of statements — common in the psalms (Ps 109:6–20; 137:8–9) — seem harsh in light of other statements about loving enemies (e.g., Pr 25:21; Mt 5:44). However, the psalmist does not merely seek revenge; he asks God to enact justice. He desires that the wicked perish so that righteousness will triumph over wickedness. If God fails to punish the wicked, his righteousness, justice and power may come into question (see Ps 10:2–11 and notes).

58:8 like a stillborn child that never sees the sun The psalmist wishes that his enemies, whom he describes as wicked from the womb (58:3), would have died there. The Hebrew word used here, *nephel* (which may be translated "stillborn child"), occurs only three times in the OT. In lamenting his own misfortune, Job wished the same thing on himself (see Job 3:16 and note). The

author of Ecclesiastes stated that an unsatisfied person is worse off than a stillborn child (see Ecc 6:3 and note).

58:10 The righteous will be glad The righteous respond to God's punishment of the wicked by rejoicing because justice has been restored (compare note on Ps 58:6–9). His vengeance on the wicked is closely tied to his vindication of the righteous (Dt 32:35–36).

58:11 Surely the righteous still are rewarded God's punishment of the wicked testifies to the reality of God's justice.

59:title–17 This individual lament psalm includes some aspects of a corporate lament psalm (meant for group use). Though the psalmist mostly speaks for himself, his enemies affect his whole city as well. He asks God for protection and deliverance from his enemies, who lie in wait for him (Ps 59:1–3). He then asserts his innocence, and restates his petition (vv. 4–5). He compares his enemies to a pack of wild dogs (vv. 6–7), expresses hope in God (vv. 8–10) and asks God to punish them (vv. 11–13). He then repeats his description from v. 6 (v. 14) and elaborates on it further (v. 15), before concluding with a song of praise (vv. 16–17). See the table "Types of Psalms" on p. 830.

59:title director of music See note on 4:title. **Do Not Destroy** See note on 57:title. **Of David** See note on 3:title. *miktam* See note on 16:title. **Saul had sent men to watch David's house** See 1Sa 19:11.

59:1 be my fortress The Hebrew word used here, *sagav*, means "to make high" (see note on Ps 20:1). Along with the other Hebrew verb used here, *natsal* ("to deliver"), these terms present an image of God removing the psalmist from a dangerous situation and placing him in a secure location.

59:4 I have done no wrong The psalmist asserts his innocence (1Sa 24:11) and appeals to God's righteousness and justice.

5 You, Lord God Almighty,
    you who are the God of Israel,
  rouse yourself to punish all the nations;
    show no mercy to wicked traitors.[a]

6 They return at evening,
    snarling like dogs,
    and prowl about the city.
7 See what they spew from their mouths —
    the words from their lips are sharp as
        swords,
    and they think, "Who can hear us?"
8 But you laugh at them, Lord;
    you scoff at all those nations.

9 You are my strength, I watch for you;
    you, God, are my fortress,
10   my God on whom I can rely.

  God will go before me
    and will let me gloat over those who
        slander me.
11 But do not kill them, Lord our shield,[b]
    or my people will forget.
  In your might uproot them
    and bring them down.
12 For the sins of their mouths,
    for the words of their lips,
    let them be caught in their pride.
  For the curses and lies they utter,
13   consume them in your wrath,
    consume them till they are no more.
  Then it will be known to the ends of the earth
    that God rules over Jacob.

14 They return at evening,
    snarling like dogs,
    and prowl about the city.
15 They wander about for food
    and howl if not satisfied.
16 But I will sing of your strength,
    in the morning I will sing of your love;
  for you are my fortress,
    my refuge in times of trouble.

17 You are my strength, I sing praise to you;
    you, God, are my fortress,
    my God on whom I can rely.

Psalm 60[c]

60:5-12pp — Ps 108:6-13

*For the director of music. To the tune of "The Lily
of the Covenant." A miktam[d] of David. For teaching.
When he fought Aram Naharaim[e] and Aram Zobah,[f]
and when Joab returned and struck down twelve thousand
Edomites in the Valley of Salt.*

1 You have rejected us, God, and burst upon us;
    you have been angry — now restore us!
2 You have shaken the land and torn it open;
    mend its fractures, for it is quaking.
3 You have shown your people desperate times;
    you have given us wine that makes us
        stagger.

---

[a] 5 The Hebrew has *Selah* (a word of uncertain meaning) here
and at the end of verse 13.   [b] 11 Or *sovereign*   [c] In Hebrew
texts 60:1-12 is numbered 60:3-14.   [d] Title: Probably a literary
or musical term   [e] Title: That is, Arameans of Northwest
Mesopotamia   [f] Title: That is, Arameans of central Syria

59:5 You, Lord God Almighty See note on Ps 24:10.
59:6 snarling like dogs Most dogs in the ancient Near
East were scavengers (Ex 22:31; 1Ki 14:11). They were
often despised and considered unclean (1Sa 17:43;
2Sa 16:9; Pr 26:17).
59:7 they spew The Hebrew word used here, *nava'* —
which may be literally rendered "to pour out" — is used
to describe people who speak with arrogance (Ps 94:4),
folly (Pr 15:2) or evil (Pr 15:28).
59:8 But you laugh at them, Lord Yahweh responds to
the arrogance and violence of the enemies of the psalmist with laughter and derision, because their efforts in
comparison to God's will are futile.
59:11 do not kill them Though the psalmist wants
God to punish his enemies, he doesn't want him to kill
them. It seems that he wants his enemies to live in a
humbled state to remind people of the consequences
of opposing God.
**59:13 it will be known to the ends of the earth that
God rules** God judges the wicked so that his power
and reign will be known throughout the earth (see 1Sa
17:45–47 and notes).
59:17 I sing praise to you Earlier, the psalmist stated
his intent to watch for God (Ps 59:9). Now he sings
praise to God, confident that he will punish his enemies.

60:title–12 In this corporate lament psalm (used for
group settings), the psalmist laments a recent military
defeat and prays that God will accompany his people in
their next battle. He describes how he feels God has

rejected them (vv. 1–3), but shows confidence in God's
deliverance (vv. 4–5). After God speaks (vv. 6–8), the
psalmist asks for his help in battle (vv. 9–11). He is
confident that, with God, they will be victorious (v. 12).
The second half of the psalm (vv. 5–12) is repeated
nearly verbatim in 108:6–13. See the table "Types of
Psalms" on p. 830.

60:title director of music See note on 4:title. **To the
tune of "The Lily of the Covenant"** The Hebrew phrase
here, *shushan eduth*, literally means "lily of the testimony."
miktam See note on 16:title. **of David** See note on
3:title. **For teaching** This seems to indicate that this
psalm was intended to help others learn about Yahweh
and his interactions with his people. The psalm inscription
seems to be particularly politically charged in comparison
to other psalms. **When he fought** This title seems to
refer to the events of 2Sa 8:1–14. However, that passage does not mention the kind of defeat described in
this psalm. Also, it mentions David striking down 18,000
Edomites rather than Joab striking down 12,000. Even
so, the Samuel narrative is probably not meant to be a
complete, detailed account of David's campaigns. First
Kings 11:15–16 provides additional detail about Joab
remaining in Edom and striking down every male.
60:1 you have been angry The psalmist thinks God
has rejected his people because of his anger. While God
is usually angered by disobedience, the psalmist does
not mention disobedience here (compare Dt 29:24–28;
see Ps 2:5 and 7:6).

⁴ But for those who fear you, you have raised a
banner
to be unfurled against the bow.ᵃ

⁵ Save us and help us with your right hand,
that those you love may be delivered.
⁶ God has spoken from his sanctuary:
"In triumph I will parcel out Shechem
and measure off the Valley of Sukkoth.
⁷ Gilead is mine, and Manasseh is mine;
Ephraim is my helmet,
Judah is my scepter.
⁸ Moab is my washbasin,
on Edom I toss my sandal;
over Philistia I shout in triumph."

⁹ Who will bring me to the fortified city?
Who will lead me to Edom?
¹⁰ Is it not you, God, you who have now
rejected us
and no longer go out with our
armies?
¹¹ Give us aid against the enemy,
for human help is worthless.
¹² With God we will gain the victory,
and he will trample down our
enemies.

Psalm 61ᵇ

For the director of music. With stringed instruments.
Of David.

¹ Hear my cry, O God;
listen to my prayer.

² From the ends of the earth I call to you,
I call as my heart grows faint;
lead me to the rock that is higher than I.
³ For you have been my refuge,
a strong tower against the foe.

⁴ I long to dwell in your tent forever
and take refuge in the shelter of your wings.ᵃ
⁵ For you, God, have heard my vows;
you have given me the heritage of those
who fear your name.

⁶ Increase the days of the king's life,
his years for many generations.
⁷ May he be enthroned in God's presence
forever;
appoint your love and faithfulness to
protect him.

ᵃ 4 The Hebrew has *Selah* (a word of uncertain meaning) here.
ᵇ In Hebrew texts 61:1-8 is numbered 61:2-9.

60:3 given us wine Biblical writers often depict God's punishment as a cup to be drunk (e.g., 75:8; Isa 51:17; Jer 25:15–16).
60:5 right hand Represents God's power: the source of his protection, blessing (Ps 119:173; Ezr 8:31) and judgment (Ps 32:4; 1Sa 5:6).

60:6–8 God speaks and reminds the people of his promises. He speaks of the division of the promised land, reminding the people that all of it belongs to him. He also mentions his ultimate power over the enemy nations of Moab, Edom and Philistia. See note on Ps 108:7–9.

60:6 Shechem A city in the tribe of Manasseh, located about 65 miles north of Jerusalem. See note on Ge 12:6. **Sukkoth** A city east of the Jordan River. See note on Ge 33:17.
60:7 Gilead A mountainous region to the east of Sukkoth. **Manasseh** A relatively large tribal allotment consisting of areas both east and west of the Jordan River. See Nu 32:33 and note. **Ephraim** A tribal allotment west of the Jordan, between Manasseh and Benjamin. See note on Ge 48:20. **Judah** A tribal allotment that included Jerusalem. Judah is often used as a designation for the entire southern kingdom.
60:8 Moab The region east of the Dead Sea. See note on Ru 1:1. **Edom** The region south of the Dead Sea. See note on Ps 108:9. **Philistia** An area along the coast of Israel to the west of Jerusalem. The Philistines oppressed Israel at multiple points in their history, and became one of the greatest enemies of Israel. Both Saul and David gained their reputations by defeating the Philistines.

60:9–11 The psalmist responds to God's speech by asking who will lead the people into battle with Edom. If God continues to reject them, going out to battle would be futile (44:9–16). The psalmist asks God to help them. See note on 108:10–13.

61:title–8 Psalm 61 combines aspects of an individual lament psalm with a royal psalm (about the king). The psalmist petitions God to hear his cry and protect him (vv. 1–2), attesting to God's past protections as he looks to the future (vv. 3–4). He shows confidence that God has heard his vows (v. 5). The psalmist then petitions God to prolong the king's life and his line (vv. 6–7), and expresses his intent to praise God's name and perform his vows (v. 8). See the table "Types of Psalms" on p. 830.

61:title director of music See note on 4:title. **stringed instruments** See note on 92:3. **Of David** See note on 3:title.
61:1 listen to my prayer The Hebrew word used here, *tephillah*, typically refers to a prayer of lament.
61:3 you have been my refuge Recalls past instances when God has protected the psalmist from his enemies (see note on 11:1). **a strong tower against the foe** Both a watchtower (2Ki 9:17) and a place of refuge (Jdg 9:51; Pr 18:10).
61:4 in your tent The Hebrew word used here, *ohel*, meaning "tent," can refer specifically to God's tabernacle (Ex 26:1–37; 2Sa 6:17) or the temple (Ps 15:1; 27:4–6). God's tent is a symbol of his presence and protection.
61:5 you have given me the heritage The Hebrew word used here, *yerushath* (often translated "heritage" or "inheritance"), describes an allotment of land given by God (Dt 2:5,12; Jos 1:15; 2Ch 20:11).
61:6 Increase the days of the king's life May indicate that the psalmist's lament involves a national crisis (see note on Ps 20:title–9).
61:7 May he be enthroned in God's presence forever Reminiscent of God's promise to establish the Davidic dynasty (2Sa 7:16; see note on Ps 21:6).

[8] Then I will ever sing in praise of your name
   and fulfill my vows day after day.

Psalm 62[a]

For the director of music. For Jeduthun.
A psalm of David.

[1] Truly my soul finds rest in God;
   my salvation comes from him.
[2] Truly he is my rock and my salvation;
   he is my fortress, I will never be shaken.

[3] How long will you assault me?
   Would all of you throw me down—
   this leaning wall, this tottering fence?
[4] Surely they intend to topple me
   from my lofty place;
   they take delight in lies.
 With their mouths they bless,
   but in their hearts they curse.[b]

[5] Yes, my soul, find rest in God;
   my hope comes from him.
[6] Truly he is my rock and my salvation;
   he is my fortress, I will not be shaken.
[7] My salvation and my honor depend on God[c];
   he is my mighty rock, my refuge.
[8] Trust in him at all times, you people;
   pour out your hearts to him,
   for God is our refuge.

[9] Surely the lowborn are but a breath,
   the highborn are but a lie.
 If weighed on a balance, they are nothing;
   together they are only a breath.
[10] Do not trust in extortion
   or put vain hope in stolen goods;
 though your riches increase,
   do not set your heart on them.

[11] One thing God has spoken,
   two things I have heard:
 "Power belongs to you, God,
[12]   and with you, Lord, is unfailing love";
 and, "You reward everyone
   according to what they have done."

Psalm 63[d]

A psalm of David. When he was in the Desert of Judah.

[1] You, God, are my God,
   earnestly I seek you;
 I thirst for you,
   my whole being longs for you,
 in a dry and parched land
   where there is no water.

---

[a] In Hebrew texts 62:1-12 is numbered 62:2-13.   [b] 4 The Hebrew has *Selah* (a word of uncertain meaning) here and at the end of verse 8.   [c] 7 Or / *God Most High is my salvation and my honor*   [d] In Hebrew texts 63:1-11 is numbered 63:2-12.

62:title–12 In this psalm of confidence (expressing faith in God), the psalmist trusts that God will preserve him in a time of distress. He begins by expressing his confidence in God, who he describes as his rock and salvation (vv. 1–2). He then addresses his enemies and describes their wickedness (vv. 3–4) before reiterating his trust in God (vv. 5–7). He encourages the congregation to put their trust in God as well (v. 8), warning them not to trust in people or in riches (vv. 9–10). The psalmist concludes by showing his confidence in God by noting God's promises (vv. 11–12). See the table "Types of Psalms" on p. 830.

62:title director of music See note on 4:title. **Jeduthun** See note on 39:title. **A psalm of David** See note on 3:title.

62:2 my rock The Hebrew word used here, *tsur*, describes a secure location and emphasizes Yahweh's protection. **my salvation** The Hebrew word used here, *yeshu'ah*—which may be rendered "salvation" or "deliverance"—refers to the liberation God provides from hazards and problems. **my fortress** The Hebrew word used here, *misgav*, describes a high wall or rocky fortress. It emphasizes the stable protection God provides for those in need. **I will never be shaken** The Hebrew verb used here, *mot*, expresses a lack of security and safety.

62:5–6 The psalmist repeats his opening words (vv. 1–2), declaring his trust in God nearly verbatim.

62:7 my honor The psalmist stakes his reputation, as well as his salvation, on his trust in God.

62:9 In Hebrew, this verse includes two phrases meaning "sons of man"—*bene-adam* and *bene ish*. Many translations

understand these to mean two different types of men. However, both phrases could be understood as synonyms, referring to humankind in general.

62:9 lowborn are but a breath Demonstrates the folly of trusting in people, who are all fleeting.

62:11 One thing God has spoken The psalmist uses a numerical saying—a literary device common in Wisdom Literature—as he looks to God's promises (see Pr 30:18 and note).

62:12 You reward everyone The psalmist upholds God's justice. He trusts that God will give to each person what they deserve, based on their deeds—and by extension, based on whether or not they repent and turn to God. This type of divine retribution is common in Wisdom Literature (see Pr 24:12; Job 34:11).

63:title–11 Psalm 63 has some characteristics of an individual lament psalm; the psalmist longs for God. However, he does not make any specific petition. Thus, this may be better classified as a psalm of confidence, expressing faith in God. The psalmist begins by expressing his longing for God as he looks to God's temple (vv. 1–2). He then praises God for his steadfast love (vv. 3–4), explaining how remembering God is enough to satisfy him (vv. 5–8). He shows confidence that God will judge his enemies (vv. 9–10) and concludes by praising God (v. 11). See the table "Types of Psalms" on p. 830.

63:title psalm of David See note on 3:title. **When he was in the Desert of Judah** May refer to David's flight from Saul (1Sa 23) or Absalom (2Sa 15:13–30).

63:1 The psalmist uses several terms to describe his longing for God: *shachar* ("seeks"), *tsama* ("thirsts") and *kamah* ("longs" or "yearns").

2 I have seen you in the sanctuary
  and beheld your power and your glory.
3 Because your love is better than life,
  my lips will glorify you.
4 I will praise you as long as I live,
  and in your name I will lift up my hands.
5 I will be fully satisfied as with the richest of
  foods;
  with singing lips my mouth will praise you.

6 On my bed I remember you;
  I think of you through the watches of the
  night.
7 Because you are my help,
  I sing in the shadow of your wings.
8 I cling to you;
  your right hand upholds me.

9 Those who want to kill me will be destroyed;
  they will go down to the depths of the earth.
10 They will be given over to the sword
  and become food for jackals.
11 But the king will rejoice in God;
  all who swear by God will glory in him,
  while the mouths of liars will be silenced.

Psalm 64ᵃ

For the director of music. A psalm of David.

1 Hear me, my God, as I voice my complaint;
  protect my life from the threat of the enemy.
2 Hide me from the conspiracy of the wicked,
  from the plots of evildoers.

3 They sharpen their tongues like
  swords
  and aim cruel words like deadly
  arrows.
4 They shoot from ambush at the
  innocent;
  they shoot suddenly, without fear.

5 They encourage each other in evil
  plans,
  they talk about hiding their snares;
  they say, "Who will see itᵇ?"
6 They plot injustice and say,
  "We have devised a perfect plan!"
  Surely the human mind and heart are
  cunning.

7 But God will shoot them with his
  arrows;
  they will suddenly be struck down.
8 He will turn their own tongues against
  them
  and bring them to ruin;
  all who see them will shake their heads
  in scorn.
9 All people will fear;
  they will proclaim the works of God
  and ponder what he has done.

10 The righteous will rejoice in the LORD
  and take refuge in him;
  all the upright in heart will glory
  in him!

ᵃ In Hebrew texts 64:1-10 is numbered 64:2-11.   ᵇ 5 Or *us*

63:2 seen you in the sanctuary The psalmist desires God because he has seen God's glory and power and knows that nothing is of greater worth.
63:3 your love is better See Ps 25:10 and note; Ex 15:13 and note.
63:4 I will lift up my hands A posture of worship (see Ps 134:2).
63:8 your right hand upholds me Represents God's power and authority. See 17:7 and note; and Isa 41:10 and note.
63:9 to the depths of the earth The underworld according to Hebrew thought, described using the Hebrew word *she'ol*, was viewed as a pit in the depths of the earth.
63:10 food for jackals Alludes to a ruined or desolate place (see Ps 44:19 and note).
63:11 the king will rejoice in God By destroying the wicked, God protects his people and his anointed king (see 20:6 and note). **who swear by God will glory in him** Swearing by God's name was a means of expressing loyalty and trust in him (see Dt 6:13 and note).
64:title–10 This individual lament psalm emphasizes divine retribution. After petitioning God for help (Ps 64:1), the psalmist describes his enemies (vv. 2–6). He then describes God's destruction of the wicked (vv. 7–8). The psalmist concludes by identifying two different responses to divine retribution: Humanity in general sees it and fears (v. 9), while the righteous see it and rejoice (v. 10). See the table "Types of Psalms" on p. 830.

64:title director of music See note on 4:title. **A psalm of David** See note on 3:title.
64:2–6 The psalmist emphasizes the secrecy and violence that are characteristic of the wicked: They plot in secret, seek to ambush the blameless and secretly set traps. He compares their words to the swords and arrows they use to attack, arguing that they seek injustice and trouble.
64:3 sharpen Treacherous people speak painful and bitter words against the blameless (see 11:2; 57:4; Pr 5:4).
64:4 They shoot from ambush at the innocent The psalms frequently depict enemies waiting to ambush the righteous (see Ps 10:8–9; 17:12).
64:5 They encourage The Hebrew word used here, *chazaq*, means "to make firm" or "to strengthen." The enemies are fully committed to doing evil.
64:7 God will shoot them with his arrows The schemes of the wicked are turned against them as God enacts divine retribution (see note on Job 4:6). The psalmist upholds the idea of *lex talionis* (often described as the principle of "an eye for an eye") where the wicked receive exactly what they had planned against others (see Dt 19:19 and note).
64:8 He will turn their own tongues against them A gesture of derision (see Ps 22:7 and note) indicating the enemies will be humiliated in their punishment.
64:9 ponder what he has done God's retribution serves as a warning to others (see 2:10–11).
64:10 The righteous will rejoice in the LORD The

Psalm 65[a]

For the director of music. A psalm of David. A song.

[1] Praise awaits[b] you, our God, in Zion;
  to you our vows will be fulfilled.
[2] You who answer prayer,
  to you all people will come.
[3] When we were overwhelmed by sins,
  you forgave[c] our transgressions.
[4] Blessed are those you choose
  and bring near to live in your courts!
We are filled with the good things of your
  house,
  of your holy temple.

[5] You answer us with awesome and righteous
  deeds,
  God our Savior,
the hope of all the ends of the earth
  and of the farthest seas,
[6] who formed the mountains by your power,
  having armed yourself with strength,
[7] who stilled the roaring of the seas,
  the roaring of their waves,
  and the turmoil of the nations.
[8] The whole earth is filled with awe at your
  wonders;
  where morning dawns, where evening fades,
  you call forth songs of joy.

[9] You care for the land and water it;
  you enrich it abundantly.

The streams of God are filled with water
  to provide the people with grain,
  for so you have ordained it.[d]
[10] You drench its furrows and level its ridges;
  you soften it with showers and bless its
  crops.
[11] You crown the year with your bounty,
  and your carts overflow with abundance.
[12] The grasslands of the wilderness overflow;
  the hills are clothed with gladness.
[13] The meadows are covered with flocks
  and the valleys are mantled with grain;
  they shout for joy and sing.

Psalm 66

For the director of music. A song. A psalm.

[1] Shout for joy to God, all the earth!
[2]   Sing the glory of his name;
  make his praise glorious.
[3] Say to God, "How awesome are your deeds!
  So great is your power
  that your enemies cringe before you.
[4] All the earth bows down to you;
  they sing praise to you,
  they sing the praises of your name."[e]

---

[a] In Hebrew texts 65:1-13 is numbered 65:2-14.   [b] 1 Or *befits*; the meaning of the Hebrew for this word is uncertain.   [c] 3 Or *made atonement for*   [d] 9 Or *for that is how you prepare the land*   [e] 4 The Hebrew has *Selah* (a word of uncertain meaning) here and at the end of verses 7 and 15.

---

righteous rejoice because God's justice gives them assurance that they can take refuge in him. See 58:10 and note.

65:title–13 This thanksgiving psalm, which is specifically described as a song, praises God for blessing the land with fertility. Israelites probably used it in a time of harvest. It may also have been a prayer asking for and anticipating God's blessing. The psalmist begins by praising God's presence and protection (vv. 1–4). He then praises God's awesome strength and sovereignty over creation (vv. 5–8), and concludes by thanking God for his provision and blessing on the land (vv. 9–13). See the table "Types of Psalms" on p. 830.

65:title director of music See note on 4:title. **psalm of David** See note on 3:title.

65:1 vows The Hebrew word used here, *neder*, usually describes a promise a person makes to God, especially during a time of distress.

65:4 to live in your courts The one who lives within the temple courts is blessed or happy (*ashre* in Hebrew) because they can be satisfied by the joy and protection of God's presence (see 1:1 and note; 27:4).

65:5 awesome and righteous deeds The Hebrew word used here, *nora'oth* ("awesome deeds"), typically refers to Yahweh's leading of his people out of Egypt and bringing them into the promised land.

65:6 who formed the mountains by your power See note on 90:2.

65:7 who stilled the roaring of the seas See 24:2 and note; Job 38:8 and note.

65:9–13 The psalmist describes how God did not just

create the earth (Ps 65:6–7); he sustains it and makes it fruitful, providing abundant water and grain. His provision reaches all types of land, including deserts and hills. The result is that the psalmist can declare that the land itself praises God.

65:9 streams of God See 46:4 and note.

65:13 they shout for joy and sing Elsewhere in the psalms, creation is shown praising God in response to God's righteous judgment (96:11–13; 98:7–9).

66:title–20 This thanksgiving psalm, which is specifically identified as a song, includes aspects of both corporate and individual praise. It begins with a call for all the earth to praise and worship God (vv. 1–4), and the psalmist celebrates God's works—specifically, the Red Sea crossing (vv. 5–7; Ex 14). The corporate call to praise continues as the psalmist describes God's deliverance and protection (Ps 66:8–12). He then moves to individual thanksgiving, declaring his intention to fulfill his vows and perform sacrifices (vv. 13–15). The psalmist invites others to listen to his personal testimony of God's deliverance and protection (vv. 16–19) and concludes by thanking God for his steadfast love (v. 20). See the table "Types of Psalms" on p. 830.

66:title director of music See note on 4:title. **A psalm** See note on 3:title.

66:1 Shout for joy The Hebrew word used here, *rua'*, is often used for a battle cry or to signify victory (41:11; 1Sa 17:20). Here, it indicates exuberant worship as the psalmist invites all the earth to praise God.

66:2 glory See note on Ps 97:6.

5 Come and see what God has done,
   his awesome deeds for mankind!
6 He turned the sea into dry land,
   they passed through the waters on foot —
   come, let us rejoice in him.
7 He rules forever by his power,
   his eyes watch the nations —
   let not the rebellious rise up against him.

8 Praise our God, all peoples,
   let the sound of his praise be heard;
9 he has preserved our lives
   and kept our feet from slipping.
10 For you, God, tested us;
   you refined us like silver.
11 You brought us into prison
   and laid burdens on our backs.
12 You let people ride over our heads;
   we went through fire and water,
   but you brought us to a place of
      abundance.

13 I will come to your temple with burnt
      offerings
   and fulfill my vows to you —
14 vows my lips promised and my mouth spoke
   when I was in trouble.
15 I will sacrifice fat animals to you
   and an offering of rams;
   I will offer bulls and goats.

16 Come and hear, all you who fear God;
   let me tell you what he has done for me.
17 I cried out to him with my mouth;
   his praise was on my tongue.
18 If I had cherished sin in my heart,
   the Lord would not have listened;

19 but God has surely listened
   and has heard my prayer.
20 Praise be to God,
   who has not rejected my prayer
   or withheld his love from me!

Psalm 67[a]

*For the director of music. With stringed instruments.
A psalm. A song.*

1 May God be gracious to us and bless us
   and make his face shine on us — [b]
2 so that your ways may be known on earth,
   your salvation among all nations.

3 May the peoples praise you, God;
   may all the peoples praise you.
4 May the nations be glad and sing for joy,
   for you rule the peoples with equity
   and guide the nations of the earth.
5 May the peoples praise you, God;
   may all the peoples praise you.

6 The land yields its harvest;
   God, our God, blesses us.
7 May God bless us still,
   so that all the ends of the earth will fear him.

Psalm 68[c]

For the director of music. Of David. A psalm. A song.

1 May God arise, may his enemies be scattered;
   may his foes flee before him.

---

[a] In Hebrew texts 67:1-7 is numbered 67:2-8.   [b] 1 The Hebrew
has *Selah* (a word of uncertain meaning) here and at the end of
verse 4.   [c] In Hebrew texts 68:1-35 is numbered 68:2-36.

66:4 All the earth bows down to you God's deeds are
so awesome that the entire earth responds with worship
and praise (22:27–28; 65:8).
66:5 Come and see what God has done The psalmist
invites people to examine God's provision for the nation
of Israel as a whole.
66:7 let not the rebellious rise up against him The
praise of God's provision for his people includes a warning to other nations.
66:13 with burnt offerings See Ex 29:36–42 and note.
66:18 If I had cherished sin in my heart The psalmist
asserts that if he had been living an unrepentant, sinful
life—or desired sin—then God would not have heard
him (Pr 28:9). However, because he was innocent, God
heard his cries and delivered him (see Ps 17:3–7).

67:title–7 Psalm 67 could be considered a thanksgiving
psalm—and is specifically identified as a song—with
the psalmist thanking God for a fruitful harvest. This is
reflected in translations of the opening line that read:
"God is gracious to us." However, the Hebrew verbs
can also be understood as petitions, with the psalmist asking God to bless them with a fruitful harvest;
this is seen in translations of the opening line that
read: "May God be gracious to us." Understood this
way, the psalm is a prayer of blessing, similar to the

priestly blessing (Nu 6:24–26). The psalmist begins
by asking God for a blessing so that God's way may be
made known (vv. 1–2). He prays that all people will praise
God, who judges the whole earth (vv. 3–5). Finally, he
prays that God would bless the harvest (vv. 6–7). See
the table "Types of Psalms" on p. 830.

67:title director of music See note on 4:title. **stringed
instruments** See note on 4:title. **A psalm** See note
on 3:title.
67:1 make his face shine on us See 4:6 and note.
67:4 equity See 9:8 and note.

68:title–35 Psalm 68 contains various themes, suggesting it is a collection of songs brought together. Israelites
most likely sang this psalm during a procession as the ark
of the covenant returned from battle. It is a praise psalm,
praising God for providing victory. The psalmist rejoices
that God will rise and scatter his enemies (vv. 1–3),
then praises God for protecting the impoverished and
helpless (vv. 4–6). The psalmist describes God's power
and provision in bringing his people through the wilderness into the promised land (vv. 7–10). He repeats
a victory song (vv. 11–14) and describes the glory of
God's mountain—Zion, the temple mount in Jerusalem
(vv. 15–18). The psalmist then blesses God for delivering

2 May you blow them away like smoke —
as wax melts before the fire,
may the wicked perish before God.
3 But may the righteous be glad
and rejoice before God;
may they be happy and joyful.

4 Sing to God, sing in praise of his name,
extol him who rides on the clouds *a*;
rejoice before him — his name is the Lord.
5 A father to the fatherless, a defender of
widows,
is God in his holy dwelling.
6 God sets the lonely in families, *b*
he leads out the prisoners with singing;
but the rebellious live in a sun-scorched
land.

7 When you, God, went out before your people,
when you marched through the
wilderness, *c*
8 the earth shook, the heavens poured down
rain,
before God, the One of Sinai,
before God, the God of Israel.
9 You gave abundant showers, O God;
you refreshed your weary inheritance.
10 Your people settled in it,
and from your bounty, God, you provided
for the poor.

11 The Lord announces the word,
and the women who proclaim it are a
mighty throng:
12 "Kings and armies flee in haste;
the women at home divide the plunder.

13 Even while you sleep among the sheep pens, *d*
the wings of my dove are sheathed with
silver,
its feathers with shining gold."
14 When the Almighty *e* scattered the kings in
the land,
it was like snow fallen on Mount Zalmon.

15 Mount Bashan, majestic mountain,
Mount Bashan, rugged mountain,
16 why gaze in envy, you rugged mountain,
at the mountain where God chooses
to reign,
where the Lord himself will dwell
forever?
17 The chariots of God are tens of thousands
and thousands of thousands;
the Lord has come from Sinai into his
sanctuary. *f*
18 When you ascended on high,
you took many captives;
you received gifts from people,
even from *g* the rebellious —
that you, *h* Lord God, might dwell there.

19 Praise be to the Lord, to God our Savior,
who daily bears our burdens.
20 Our God is a God who saves;
from the Sovereign Lord comes escape
from death.

---

a 4 Or *name, / prepare the way for him who rides through the
deserts*   *b* 6 Or *the desolate in a homeland*   *c* 7 The Hebrew
has *Selah* (a word of uncertain meaning) here and at the end of
verses 19 and 32.   *d* 13 Or *the campfires; or the saddlebags*
e 14 Hebrew *Shaddai*   *f* 17 Probable reading of the original
Hebrew text; Masoretic Text *Lord is among them at Sinai in
holiness*   *g* 18 Or *gifts for people, / even*   *h* 18 Or *they*

---

them from their enemies (vv. 19–23) and describes
the procession of the ark of the covenant (vv. 24–27).
Finally, the psalmist summons God to destroy enemy
nations (vv. 28–31) and encourages these nations to
praise God for his power and strength (vv. 32–35). See
the table "Types of Psalms" on p. 830.

68:title director of music See note on 4:title. **Of David.
A psalm** See note on 3:title.

68:1 This verse quotes the song of the ark, which the
Israelites sang whenever the ark went out (see Nu
10:35–36 and note). See the infographic "The Ark of
the Covenant" on p. 412.

68:5 A father to the fatherless Portrays God as one
who protects the most vulnerable. Old Testament Law
contained special provisions to protect orphans and
widows, who were often oppressed or mistreated (Ex
22:22–24; Dt 24:19–21).

68:7–8 The psalmist describes how God led the people
through the wilderness (Ex 13:21–22). His presence is accompanied by earthquakes and storms (see Ps 18:7–19
and note), which highlight his supremacy and power.

68:9–10 The psalmist praises God because he provides
land for his people and gives rain to make it fruitful
(65:9–13).

68:9 your weary inheritance See 47:4 and note.
68:11 the women who proclaim The OT contains
many examples of women celebrating victory with singing or dancing (Ex 15:20–21; 1Sa 18:6–7). **throng** The
women who sing here are portrayed using the Hebrew
word *tsava*, which usually describes a great host or army
(see note on Ps 103:21).

68:12 armies flee in haste The *tsava* ("host," "throng"
or "company"; see note on 68:11) of women mocks the
tseva'oth ("hosts" or "armies") of foreign kings who flee
before God's presence.

68:14 the Almighty The Hebrew term used here, *shaddai*, is used only twice in the psalms as a name for God.
See note on 91:1.

68:15 Mount Bashan Located east of the Sea of Galilee, Bashan was a noted for its fertility (see note on
22:12). In wider ancient Near Eastern religion, it was
also known as the gateway to the underworld and its
sinister inhabitants.

68:16 why gaze in envy The psalmist addresses the
mountain of Bashan, accusing it of being jealous of
Zion—the temple mount in Jerusalem (compare note
on 68:15).

68:18 When you ascended on high This seems to describe Yahweh as a victorious king returning to the throne
after battle. Paul quotes this verse in Ephesians to describe
Christ's victory over the powers of darkness, the catalyst to
the birth and empowerment of the church (see Eph 4:8).

²¹ Surely God will crush the heads of his
enemies,
the hairy crowns of those who go on in
their sins.
²² The Lord says, "I will bring them from
Bashan;
I will bring them from the depths of
the sea,
²³ that your feet may wade in the blood of your
foes,
while the tongues of your dogs have their
share."

²⁴ Your procession, God, has come into view,
the procession of my God and King into the
sanctuary.
²⁵ In front are the singers, after them the
musicians;
with them are the young women playing
the timbrels.
²⁶ Praise God in the great congregation;
praise the LORD in the assembly of Israel.
²⁷ There is the little tribe of Benjamin, leading
them,
there the great throng of Judah's princes,
and there the princes of Zebulun and of
Naphtali.

²⁸ Summon your power, God ᵃ;
show us your strength, our God, as you
have done before.
²⁹ Because of your temple at Jerusalem
kings will bring you gifts.

³⁰ Rebuke the beast among the reeds,
the herd of bulls among the calves of the
nations.
Humbled, may the beast bring bars of silver.
Scatter the nations who delight in war.
³¹ Envoys will come from Egypt;
Cushᵇ will submit herself to God.

³² Sing to God, you kingdoms of the earth,
sing praise to the Lord,
³³ to him who rides across the highest heavens,
the ancient heavens,
who thunders with mighty voice.
³⁴ Proclaim the power of God,
whose majesty is over Israel,
whose power is in the heavens.
³⁵ You, God, are awesome in your sanctuary;
the God of Israel gives power and strength
to his people.

Praise be to God!

Psalm 69ᶜ

For the director of music. To the tune of "Lilies." Of David.

¹ Save me, O God,
for the waters have come up to my neck.
² I sink in the miry depths,
where there is no foothold.

ᵃ 28 Many Hebrew manuscripts, Septuagint and Syriac; most
Hebrew manuscripts *Your God has summoned power for you*
ᵇ 31 That is, the upper Nile region   ᶜ In Hebrew texts 69:1-36 is
numbered 69:2-37.

68:20 Sovereign LORD The Hebrew phrase used here, *yhwh adonay*, combines God's personal, covenant name, Yahweh, with the general term for "master," demonstrating that Yahweh is the ultimate master or ruler. See note on Ps 8:1.

68:22–23 In this passage, God shows how he will one day completely destroy his enemies. He will not merely scatter them (vv. 1,14), but he will diligently search for them from the heights of the mountains to the depths of the sea to destroy them (see Am 9:2–3). The extent of God's destruction of his enemies reveals his power to save and protect his people (see Ps 58:10 and note).

68:24–27 A victorious procession follows God's victory. The psalmist describes the singers, musicians and young girls who take part in the celebration. Benjamin and Judah represent the southern kingdom (Judah), while Zebulun and Naphtali represent the northern kingdom (Israel).

68:28–31 The psalmist calls on God to use his strength to destroy the enemies of his people (see note on 46:1). He refers to God's past acts of salvation, encouraging God to display his power to save again. He compares their enemies to animals and describes them as loving war. He asserts that Egypt and Cush (Ethiopia) will be defeated and bring tribute.

68:31 Envoys The Hebrew word used here, *chashman-nim*, occurs only here in the OT. It could refer to people in high positions of authority, such as "nobles" or "am-

bassadors." Alternatively, it may describe some kind of tribute or gift—likely bronze articles or dyed clothing.

68:33 mighty voice See 29:3–9 and notes.

68:35 You, God, are awesome in your sanctuary God's awesome deeds originate from his sanctuary in Jerusalem—the place where his name dwells (see note on 65:5; 20:2 and note).

69:title–36 In this individual lament psalm, the faithful psalmist, whose suffering has made him an object of ridicule and scorn, prays to God for help (compare note on vv. 35–36). He describes his desperate situation (vv. 1–3), mentioning that his enemies are falsely accusing him, and asserts that God knows he is innocent (vv. 4–5). He prays that God would not let him be shamed and claims he is suffering because of his zeal for God (vv. 6–12). The psalmist asks God to deliver him (vv. 13–18), stating that God knows his affliction and his enemies (vv. 19–21). He then pronounces a curse on his enemies, asking God to destroy them (vv. 22–28). He praises God for hearing the cries of the needy (vv. 29–33) and concludes by encouraging all of creation to praise God, who he declares will save his people (vv. 34–36). See the table "Types of Psalms" on p. 830.

69:title director of music See note on 4:title. **To the tune of "Lilies"** See note on 45:title. **Of David** See note on 3:title.

69:1 waters have come up to my neck This imagery highlights the urgency of the psalmist's cry for help.

69:2 miry The Hebrew word used here, *yawen*, probably

I have come into the deep waters;
the floods engulf me.
[3] I am worn out calling for help;
my throat is parched.
My eyes fail,
looking for my God.
[4] Those who hate me without reason
outnumber the hairs of my head;
many are my enemies without cause,
those who seek to destroy me.
I am forced to restore
what I did not steal.

[5] You, God, know my folly;
my guilt is not hidden from you.

[6] Lord, the LORD Almighty,
may those who hope in you
not be disgraced because of me;
God of Israel,
may those who seek you
not be put to shame because of me.
[7] For I endure scorn for your sake,
and shame covers my face.
[8] I am a foreigner to my own family,
a stranger to my own mother's children;
[9] for zeal for your house consumes me,
and the insults of those who insult you fall
on me.
[10] When I weep and fast,
I must endure scorn;
[11] when I put on sackcloth,
people make sport of me.
[12] Those who sit at the gate mock me,
and I am the song of the drunkards.

[13] But I pray to you, LORD,
in the time of your favor;

in your great love, O God,
answer me with your sure salvation.
[14] Rescue me from the mire,
do not let me sink;
deliver me from those who hate me,
from the deep waters.
[15] Do not let the floodwaters engulf me
or the depths swallow me up
or the pit close its mouth over me.

[16] Answer me, LORD, out of the goodness of
your love;
in your great mercy turn to me.
[17] Do not hide your face from your servant;
answer me quickly, for I am in trouble.
[18] Come near and rescue me;
deliver me because of my foes.

[19] You know how I am scorned, disgraced and
shamed;
all my enemies are before you.
[20] Scorn has broken my heart
and has left me helpless;
I looked for sympathy, but there was none,
for comforters, but I found none.
[21] They put gall in my food
and gave me vinegar for my thirst.

[22] May the table set before them become a
snare;
may it become retribution and[a] a trap.
[23] May their eyes be darkened so they
cannot see,
and their backs be bent forever.
[24] Pour out your wrath on them;
let your fierce anger overtake them.

---

[a] 22 Or snare / and their fellowship become

---

refers to the muddy bottom of a cistern (see note on 40:2).
69:4 Those who hate me without reason Jesus quotes this line in John's Gospel to describe the world's hatred of him (Jn 15:25).
69:5 You, God, know my folly While his enemies' accusations were unfounded, the psalmist admits that he has done wrong. He argues that God knows his wrongdoings, which are not the cause for his current affliction (see Ps 38:13).
69:8 a foreigner to my own family Those who were close to the psalmist abandoned him because of his affliction, which they assume is a result of his sin. See note on 38:11.
69:9 zeal The Hebrew word used here, *qin'ath*, is often used to describe envy. Typically, the Bible views human envy as a negative emotion (see Pr 14:30 and note, and Ecc 4:4 and note). However, it presents zeal (*qin'ath*) on behalf of God as a positive trait (Nu 25:11–13; 1Ki 19:10).

69:10–12 The psalmist describes situations when he encountered humiliation for acting righteously. He humbled himself, fasting and mourning because of his affliction. Instead of responding with sympathy (see Ps 35:13–14), however, people responded by mocking him and singing drunken songs about him.

69:12 the song The Hebrew word used here, *neginoth*, can indicate a mocking or satirical song (see Job 30:9 and note).
69:13 I pray The Hebrew word used here, *tephillah*, is typically associated with a prayer of lament. Compare Ps 102:title–28 and note.
69:17 Do not hide your face from your servant Lament psalms often includes statements about God seeming to be distant. See 10:1 and note; compare 55:1.
69:21 gave me vinegar A metaphorical description of the people's response to the psalmist's affliction: He is thirsty, but they offer him only sour wine. The accounts of Christ's crucifixion allude to this passage (Mt 27:48; Mk 15:36; Lk 23:36). John's Gospel even states that this verse was fulfilled with Christ's suffering (Jn 19:18–29). This portrays Christ as the ultimate sufferer (compare note on Ps 22:title–31).

69:22–28 In this section, the psalmist calls on God to destroy his enemies. These types of curses—known as imprecations—are common in the psalms (58:6–9; 109:6–20; 137:8–9). They are driven by a desire for justice, rather than revenge. The psalmist looks to God to justly punish wickedness. By doing so, God would be rewarding and protecting the righteous. See note on 58:6–9.

69:23 their eyes be darkened In 69:3, the psalmist

25 May their place be deserted;
    let there be no one to dwell in their tents.
26 For they persecute those you wound
    and talk about the pain of those you hurt.
27 Charge them with crime upon crime;
    do not let them share in your salvation.
28 May they be blotted out of the book of life
    and not be listed with the righteous.

29 But as for me, afflicted and in pain —
    may your salvation, God, protect me.

30 I will praise God's name in song
    and glorify him with thanksgiving.
31 This will please the LORD more than an ox,
    more than a bull with its horns and hooves.
32 The poor will see and be glad —
    you who seek God, may your hearts live!
33 The LORD hears the needy
    and does not despise his captive people.

34 Let heaven and earth praise him,
    the seas and all that move in them,
35 for God will save Zion
    and rebuild the cities of Judah.
Then people will settle there and possess it;
36   the children of his servants will inherit it,
    and those who love his name will dwell
        there.

Psalm 70[a]

70:1-5pp — Ps 40:13-17

For the director of music. Of David. A petition.

1 Hasten, O God, to save me;
    come quickly, LORD, to help me.

2 May those who want to take my life
    be put to shame and confusion;
may all who desire my ruin
    be turned back in disgrace.
3 May those who say to me, "Aha! Aha!"
    turn back because of their shame.
4 But may all who seek you
    rejoice and be glad in you;
may those who long for your saving help
        always say,
    "The LORD is great!"

5 But as for me, I am poor and needy;
    come quickly to me, O God.
You are my help and my deliverer;
    LORD, do not delay.

Psalm 71

71:1-3pp — Ps 31:1-4

1 In you, LORD, I have taken refuge;
    let me never be put to shame.
2 In your righteousness, rescue me and
        deliver me;
    turn your ear to me and save me.
3 Be my rock of refuge,
    to which I can always go;
give the command to save me,
    for you are my rock and my fortress.
4 Deliver me, my God, from the hand of
        the wicked,
    from the grasp of those who are evil
        and cruel.

a In Hebrew texts 70:1-5 is numbered 70:2-6.

---

stated that his own eyes were failing. Here, he wishes his own suffering on his enemies.
69:28 blotted out of the book of life In the ancient Near East, belief in heavenly books or recountings was common (compare Rev 3:5 and note). The psalmist desires ultimate destruction for his enemies.
69:29 may your salvation, God, protect me Compare Ps 69:2.
69:30–31 The psalmist says that he will praise God for hearing his cries, responding with praise and thanksgiving rather than an animal sacrifice. This, he asserts, is what God would prefer. See 50:14 and note.

69:35–36 The psalmist concludes by affirming that God will protect his people. This psalm was probably part of public Israelite worship, which explains why the psalmist emphasizes national concerns. God's protection and deliverance of the psalmist confirms that God will protect and deliver his people.

70:title–5 This individual lament psalm is nearly identical to 40:13–17. It is unclear whether this psalm originally stood alone or was adapted from Ps 40. In Ps 40, it follows a section of thanksgiving where the psalmist recounts God's protection and care. Psalm 70, however, contains no thanksgiving. The psalmist prays that God would deliver him (v. 1) and shame his enemies (vv. 2–3).

He then asserts that those who seek God will rejoice in his salvation (v. 4). He concludes by repeating his petition for God to deliver him. See the table "Types of Psalms" on p. 830.

70:title director of music See note on 4:title. **Of David** See note on 3:title. **A petition** The Hebrew word used here is *zakar*. See note on 38:title.
70:1 come quickly Emphasizes the urgency of the psalmist's need. See note on 40:13–15.
70:3 Aha! Aha! The Hebrew word used here, *he'ach*, is usually an expression of joy. The psalmist's enemies have a twisted delight in his distress.

71:1–24 This individual lament psalm concludes by confidently praising God for his faithfulness and righteousness. The psalmist asks God to deliver him (vv. 1–4) and shows his trust in God, whom he has praised since birth (vv. 5–8). He prays that God would not cast him off and leave him to his enemies (vv. 9–13). He expresses his hope in God and declares that he will tell others of God's salvation (vv. 14–18). He praises God's righteousness, confident that God will restore him (vv. 19–21). The psalmist concludes by thanking God for protecting and redeeming him (vv. 22–24). See the table "Types of Psalms" on p. 830.

71:1 let me never be put to shame See note on 25:2.
71:4 evil and cruel The Hebrew words used here,

⁵ For you have been my hope, Sovereign Lord,
   my confidence since my youth.
⁶ From birth I have relied on you;
   you brought me forth from my mother's
      womb.
   I will ever praise you.
⁷ I have become a sign to many;
   you are my strong refuge.
⁸ My mouth is filled with your praise,
   declaring your splendor all day long.

⁹ Do not cast me away when I am old;
   do not forsake me when my strength is
      gone.
¹⁰ For my enemies speak against me;
   those who wait to kill me conspire
      together.
¹¹ They say, "God has forsaken him;
   pursue him and seize him,
   for no one will rescue him."
¹² Do not be far from me, my God;
   come quickly, God, to help me.
¹³ May my accusers perish in shame;
   may those who want to harm me
   be covered with scorn and disgrace.

¹⁴ As for me, I will always have hope;
   I will praise you more and more.

¹⁵ My mouth will tell of your righteous deeds,
   of your saving acts all day long—
   though I know not how to relate them all.
¹⁶ I will come and proclaim your mighty acts,
   Sovereign Lord;
   I will proclaim your righteous deeds, yours
      alone.
¹⁷ Since my youth, God, you have taught me,
   and to this day I declare your marvelous
      deeds.

¹⁸ Even when I am old and gray,
   do not forsake me, my God,
   till I declare your power to the next
      generation,
   your mighty acts to all who are
      to come.

¹⁹ Your righteousness, God, reaches to the
      heavens,
   you who have done great things.
   Who is like you, God?
²⁰ Though you have made me see troubles,
   many and bitter,
   you will restore my life again;
   from the depths of the earth
   you will again bring me up.
²¹ You will increase my honor
   and comfort me once more.

²² I will praise you with the harp
   for your faithfulness, my God;
   I will sing praise to you with the lyre,
   Holy One of Israel.
²³ My lips will shout for joy
   when I sing praise to you—
   I whom you have delivered.
²⁴ My tongue will tell of your righteous acts
   all day long,
   for those who wanted to harm me
   have been put to shame and confusion.

Psalm 72

Of Solomon.

¹ Endow the king with your justice, O God,
   the royal son with your righteousness.
² May he judge your people in righteousness,
   your afflicted ones with justice.

me'awwel (sometimes translated "evildoer") and chomets (which may be translated "oppressor"), emphasize that the psalmist's enemies are violently oppressive and unjust—a stark contrast with the lifelong faithfulness of the psalmist (vv. 5–8).

71:5 since my youth Appealing to God's righteousness, the psalmist asserts that God is his hope. He shows his loyalty to God by acknowledging that he has trusted God since he was young.

71:6 from my mother's womb The psalmist notes his lifelong faithfulness as part of his appeal for God to deliver him from his current afflictions. See 22:9–10 and note.

71:7 a sign The Hebrew word used here, mopheth, is typically used to describe a sign from God that serves as a warning (see Ex 7:3; Dt 6:22; 1Ki 13:3).

71:9 Do not cast me away The psalmist has trusted God all his life (Ps 71:5–6); he asks God not to forsake him in his old age.

71:11 God has forsaken him The psalmist's petition in v. 9 becomes more meaningful in light of his enemies' claims. They look on his suffering—concluding that God must have forsaken him—and look for an opportunity to take advantage of the situation.

71:15–16 The psalmist promises that once God delivers him, he will tell people of God's righteous deliverance and protection.

71:20 Though you have made me see troubles Even though he is not suffering because of sin, the psalmist still attributes his suffering to God—it is unclear whether the psalmist means that God has caused his suffering, allowed it or a combination of the two (see 60:1–3). **from the depths of the earth** See Ge 1:2 and note; Job 38:16 and note.

71:22 with the harp It is unclear whether the Hebrew word used here, nevel, refers precisely to a harp—it is certain that it refers to a stringed instrument. **with the lyre** The Hebrew word used here, kinnor, refers to some sort of stringed instrument associated with celebration and worship.

71:23 you have delivered The Hebrew word used here, padah—which may be rendered "to ransom" or "to redeem"—frequently refers to rescuing someone from trouble or affliction.

71:24 have been put to shame and confusion The psalmist praises God for fulfilling his earlier petition that God shame his enemies (see Ps 71:13). This could be a praise of hope, showing complete confidence in what God will do.

³ May the mountains bring prosperity to the
    people,
  the hills the fruit of righteousness.
⁴ May he defend the afflicted among the people
  and save the children of the needy;
  may he crush the oppressor.
⁵ May he endure*ᵃ* as long as the sun,
  as long as the moon, through all
    generations.
⁶ May he be like rain falling on a mown field,
  like showers watering the earth.
⁷ In his days may the righteous flourish
  and prosperity abound till the moon is no
    more.

⁸ May he rule from sea to sea
  and from the River*ᵇ* to the ends of the
    earth.
⁹ May the desert tribes bow before him
  and his enemies lick the dust.
¹⁰ May the kings of Tarshish and of distant
    shores
  bring tribute to him.
  May the kings of Sheba and Seba
    present him gifts.
¹¹ May all kings bow down to him
  and all nations serve him.

¹² For he will deliver the needy who cry out,
  the afflicted who have no one to help.
¹³ He will take pity on the weak and the needy
  and save the needy from death.

¹⁴ He will rescue them from oppression and
    violence,
  for precious is their blood in his sight.

¹⁵ Long may he live!
  May gold from Sheba be given him.
  May people ever pray for him
    and bless him all day long.
¹⁶ May grain abound throughout the land;
  on the tops of the hills may it sway.
  May the crops flourish like Lebanon
    and thrive*ᶜ* like the grass of the field.
¹⁷ May his name endure forever;
  may it continue as long as the sun.

  Then all nations will be blessed through
    him,*ᵈ*
    and they will call him blessed.

¹⁸ Praise be to the LORD God, the God of Israel,
  who alone does marvelous deeds.
¹⁹ Praise be to his glorious name forever;
  may the whole earth be filled with his
    glory.
                    Amen and Amen.

²⁰ This concludes the prayers of David son of
    Jesse.

ᵃ 5 Septuagint; Hebrew *You will be feared*   *ᵇ 8* That is, the
Euphrates   *ᶜ 16* Probable reading of the original Hebrew text;
Masoretic Text *Lebanon, / from the city*   *ᵈ 17* Or *will use his
name in blessings* (see Gen. 48:20)

72:title–20 This royal psalm is a prayer for the prosperity of God's anointed king. As he prays that God would bless the king, the psalmist also prays that God would bless the nation as a whole. He asks God to give the king the virtues of justice and righteousness so he would be able to judge the people (vv. 1–2). He prays for national prosperity, as well as justice and freedom from oppression (vv. 3–4). He also asks that the nation would fear (revere) God and that righteousness and peace will abound (vv. 5–7), then prays that the king would have military success, and finally requests that other nations would honor him with gifts and tribute (vv. 8–11). The psalmist praises the king's protection of the impoverished and needy (vv. 12–14) before concluding with a prayer for the life of the king and the prosperity of the promised land (vv. 15–17). The final section (vv. 18–20) is a doxology that concludes Book Two of the Psalms (Ps 42–72; see note on Ps 1:1–6). See the table "Types of Psalms" on p. 830.

72:title Of Solomon Two psalms are affiliated with Solomon (Ps 72 and 127). Like the psalms affiliated with David, this does not necessarily mean that Solomon authored these psalms (see note on 3:title).
72:2 May he judge your people in righteousness Since kings were responsible for judging legal disputes (see 1Ki 3:16–28), they needed to judge righteously and justly. Solomon asked Yahweh for understanding so that he could justly govern the people (1Ki 3:9).
72:3 bring prosperity The Hebrew word used here, *shalom* (which may be rendered as "prosperity" or "peace"), conveys the notion of wholeness or well-being.
72:4 May he defend the afflicted Since the king also

acted as a judge, he was responsible for enacting justice and preventing oppression. See note on Ps 72:2.
72:10 Tarshish Represents the westernmost location known to the Israelites. **May the kings of Sheba and Seba present him gifts** Associated with gold and spices, Sheba was located in the southwestern part of the Arabian Peninsula. The queen of Sheba brought gifts during Solomon's reign (see 1Ki 10:1–13).

72:12–14 The psalmist praises the king for looking after the poor and needy (see Ps 72:4 and note). A king who righteously defended the needs of the impoverished and who governed wisely would be a great benefit to his nation. He would reduce violence and oppression and build up the land (see Pr 29:4 and note).

72:16 May the crops flourish like Lebanon The trees of Lebanon were symbols of strength and prosperity.
72:17 May his name endure forever See Ps 21:6 and note. **will be blessed through him** Reflects the Abrahamic covenant, where Yahweh promised Abraham that he would bless his descendants and that they would be a blessing (Ge 12:1–3; 22:18; 26:4).

72:18–20 This section is independent from Ps 72 and represents the close of Book Two of the Psalms (see note on 1:1–6). Each book of Psalms closes with a similar doxology of praise (41:13; 89:52; 106:48; 150:6). See note on 106:48.

72:19 Praise be to his glorious name forever See note on 33:21.
72:20 the prayers of David This statement seems to refer to the psalms in Book Three (Ps 73–89) being

BOOK III

Psalms 73–89

Psalm 73

A psalm of Asaph.

¹ Surely God is good to Israel,
　to those who are pure in heart.

² But as for me, my feet had almost slipped;
　I had nearly lost my foothold.
³ For I envied the arrogant
　when I saw the prosperity of the wicked.

⁴ They have no struggles;
　their bodies are healthy and strong.ᵃ
⁵ They are free from common human burdens;
　they are not plagued by human ills.

⁶ Therefore pride is their necklace;
　they clothe themselves with violence.
⁷ From their callous hearts comes
　iniquity ᵇ;
　their evil imaginations have no limits.
⁸ They scoff, and speak with malice;
　with arrogance they threaten
　oppression.
⁹ Their mouths lay claim to heaven,
　and their tongues take possession
　of the earth.
¹⁰ Therefore their people turn to them
　and drink up waters in abundance.ᶜ
¹¹ They say, "How would God know?
　Does the Most High know anything?"

ᵃ 4 With a different word division of the Hebrew; Masoretic Text
struggles at their death; / their bodies are healthy　　ᵇ 7 Syriac
(see also Septuagint); Hebrew *Their eyes bulge with fat*
ᶜ 10 The meaning of the Hebrew for this verse is uncertain.

---

mainly associated with Asaph, while the psalms in the first two books (Ps 1–72) are mostly associated with David. There are psalms later in the book of Psalms associated with David (e.g., 101; 103; 108), but only one in Book Three (Ps 86).

73:title–28 This is the first psalm in Book Three of Psalms (Ps 73–89; see note on 1:1–6). In this wisdom psalm (meant to pass along wise sayings), the psalmist contrasts righteousness and wickedness. He begins by summarizing how God is good (73:1); he then recounts his near ruin from his fixation on the prosperity of evil people (vv. 2–3). After observing that evildoers enjoy the fruits of their wickedness without punishment (vv. 4–12), the psalmist expresses disillusionment, stating that it seems that he has followed God's way pointlessly (vv. 13–14). He looks back on his complaint (v. 15) and reevaluates his frustrations in the context of worshiping God (vv. 16–17). By doing so, he realizes God will eventually punish the wicked (vv. 18–20). The psalmist then identifies the destructive effects of his bitterness on his ability to recognize God's authority (vv. 21–22). He recalls God's help and guidance (vv. 23–24), renews his commitment to God (vv. 25–26) and reaffirms God's eventual punishment of the wicked (v. 27). He concludes by proclaiming his gladness in seeking refuge in God (v. 28).

The primary focus of Ps 73 is the internal experience of the psalmist; this is exemplified by the use of the word "heart" six times (vv. 1,7,13,21,26). The psalmist also mentions envy (v. 3) and bitterness (v. 21). In addition, this psalm also focuses on the contrast between ignorance (v. 22) and discernment (v. 17). See the table "Types of Psalms" on p. 830.

73:title A psalm See note on 3:title. **of Asaph** The first of 11 consecutive psalms attributed to Asaph. As with the affiliation of particular psalms with David, this affiliation with Asaph does not necessarily indicate authorship (see note on 3:title). Psalm 50 and Ps 73–83 are affiliated with Asaph. This, and a mention of the words of Asaph the seer in 2Ch 29:30, seems to indicate that the psalms of Asaph (at least Ps 73–83) were already a collection of psalms prior to being incorporated into the current form of the book of Psalms. Asaph the son of Berechiah was a worship leader among the Levites in King David's era. Asaph played the cymbals, sang and was in charge of music when the ark of the covenant was brought to Jerusalem (1Ch 15:17,19; 16:4–7). Asaph's

descendants had a role in both the first Jerusalem temple and the later second temple (2Ch 20:14; 29:13; 35:15; Ezr 2:41; Ne 7:44).

Psalm 73:title

ASAPH
Twelve psalms are attributed to Asaph, mostly within Book Three (Ps 50,73–83). The Bible includes several individuals named Asaph, but the psalm titles likely refer to Asaph, son of Berekiah (1Ch 6:39). He was a Levite appointed by David to worship before the ark (1Ch 16:4–7). David later established his family as temple musicians (1Ch 25:1–2). His descendants continued this role throughout the period of the kings (2Ch 35:15) and again after the exile (Ezr 3:10; Ne 11:17).

73:1–3 The opening verse of this psalm indicates it is retrospective. The psalmist presents the prosperity of the wicked as a resolved problem before he has presented the problem itself. Two structural markers also demonstrate this retrospective overview: use of the word "Truly" or "Surely" (Ps 73:1,18); the phrase "But as for me" or "But for me" (vv. 2,28).

73:1 Surely The Hebrew word used here, *akh*, expresses certainty.
73:2 my feet had almost slipped A term expressing disaster. The psalmist will identify his own envy (v. 3) and bitterness (v. 21) as the source of his near ruin.
73:3 the prosperity of the wicked Though many passages in the OT depict God punishing evildoers, OT writers often struggle when they see the wicked experience good things.
73:4–12 The psalmist leaves his retrospective viewpoint (see note on vv. 1–3) and laments in the present tense. He begins describing the benefits the wicked enjoy (vv. 4–5), but he focuses on their arrogance before God (vv. 6–12).
73:6 violence The Hebrew word used here, *chamas*, can refer to injustice or exploitation as well as physical attacks.
73:9 Their mouths lay claim to heaven The wicked openly speak against God.

¹²This is what the wicked are like —
   always free of care, they go on amassing
      wealth.
¹³Surely in vain I have kept my heart pure
   and have washed my hands in innocence.
¹⁴All day long I have been afflicted,
   and every morning brings new
      punishments.

¹⁵If I had spoken out like that,
   I would have betrayed your children.
¹⁶When I tried to understand all this,
   it troubled me deeply
¹⁷till I entered the sanctuary of God;
   then I understood their final destiny.

¹⁸Surely you place them on slippery ground;
   you cast them down to ruin.
¹⁹How suddenly are they destroyed,
   completely swept away by terrors!
²⁰They are like a dream when one awakes;
   when you arise, Lord,
   you will despise them as fantasies.

²¹When my heart was grieved
   and my spirit embittered,
²²I was senseless and ignorant;
   I was a brute beast before you.

²³Yet I am always with you;
   you hold me by my right hand.
²⁴You guide me with your counsel,
   and afterward you will take me into glory.
²⁵Whom have I in heaven but you?
   And earth has nothing I desire besides you.
²⁶My flesh and my heart may fail,
   but God is the strength of my heart
   and my portion forever.

²⁷Those who are far from you will perish;
   you destroy all who are unfaithful to you.
²⁸But as for me, it is good to be near God.
   I have made the Sovereign Lord my refuge;
   I will tell of all your deeds.

Psalm 74

A maskil*a* of Asaph.

¹O God, why have you rejected us forever?
   Why does your anger smolder against the
      sheep of your pasture?
²Remember the nation you purchased long ago,
   the people of your inheritance, whom you
      redeemed —
   Mount Zion, where you dwelt.

a Title: Probably a literary or musical term

73:14 I have been afflicted The Hebrew word used here, *naga'* (which may be rendered "to strike" or "to rebuke"), is sometimes connected to God's discipline (see Pr 3:12).

73:15–20 In this section, the psalmist presents the process of decision-making, which eventually leads to understanding. The psalmist ends his lament and identifies it as internal musing (Ps 73:15). He chooses to view the continued prosperity of the wicked through the experience of worship, where he is able to understand a bigger picture (v. 17). He then depicts the eventual punishment of the wicked (vv. 18–20).

73:15 your children The psalmist describes his complaint as a betrayal of his people — Israel. Compare 24:3–6.

73:17 till I entered the sanctuary of God Psalm 73 depicts several choices the psalmist makes in the face of his despair; the choice to worship is crucial to the new outlook he develops. **I understood their final destiny** As long as the psalmist remained bitter, he was unable to see the situation correctly (vv. 21–22).

73:18 Surely The use of the Hebrew word *akh* here echoes the opening of the psalm, where the psalmist affirms God's goodness to Israel (see v. 1 and note). **you place them on slippery ground** The psalmist expresses his conviction that God will judge evildoers.

73:21–28 Verses 21–22 could be seen as a portion of the psalmist's response following his worship experience (v. 17). However, it also marks a shift toward his renewed trust in God and his justice. This passage emphasizes the psalmist's new perspective and his expression of satisfaction with God.

73:22 I was senseless and ignorant The psalmist's resentment and mistrust had misconstrued his perceptions of God and reality.

73:24 afterward you will take me into glory The psalm-

ist may be contrasting his fate with that of the wicked, who will eventually be punished and destroyed (vv. 17–18).

73:26 portion The Hebrew word used here, *cheleq*, is also used to describe the allotment of the land of Canaan to the tribes of Israel (Jos 14:5; 18:2). The psalmist describes God as his share (or portion) in the present world.

73:28 I will tell of all your deeds The psalmist proclaims that he will publicly tell of God's works.

74:title–23 In this corporate lament psalm (meant for group settings), the psalmist focuses on the destruction of the temple and Israel's response to that devastation. The psalm opens with a pair of rhetorical questions (Ps 74:1) in which the psalmist pleads for God to protect his sanctuary and his people (vv. 2–3). He then describes the destruction of the sanctuary, and notes the defilement that the destruction caused (vv. 4–8). The psalmist then renews his plea for God's help and asks him to act to defend his honor (vv. 9–11). He recalls how God has acted in the past, recounting his mighty acts of creation as well as his actions in saving Israel (vv. 12–17). He then asks God to defend his honor as well as his people (vv. 18–23).

The psalmist repeats several Hebrew terms throughout the psalm, demonstrating his plea for God to protect his honor and his people: *zakhar* ("remember"; vv. 2,18), *qodesh* ("sanctuary"; vv. 3,7), *shemekha* ("your name"; vv. 7,10,18,21) and *'oth* ("signs"; vv. 4,9). The psalm ends with a pained request for God to act against his foes (v. 23) rather than a strong resolution of trust or confidence. See the table "Types of Psalms" on p. 830.

74:title A *maskil* See note on 32:title. **of Asaph** See note on 73:title.

74:1–3 In the opening of the psalm, the psalmist calls for God to remember his people and his commitment to them in the wake of the destruction of the temple in

³ Turn your steps toward these everlasting
  ruins,
    all this destruction the enemy has brought
      on the sanctuary.

⁴ Your foes roared in the place where you met
  with us;
    they set up their standards as signs.
⁵ They behaved like men wielding axes
    to cut through a thicket of trees.
⁶ They smashed all the carved paneling
    with their axes and hatchets.
⁷ They burned your sanctuary to the ground;
    they defiled the dwelling place of your
      Name.
⁸ They said in their hearts, "We will crush
    them completely!"
  They burned every place where God was
    worshiped in the land.

⁹ We are given no signs from God;
    no prophets are left,
  and none of us knows how long this will be.
¹⁰ How long will the enemy mock you, God?
    Will the foe revile your name forever?
¹¹ Why do you hold back your hand, your right
    hand?

Take it from the folds of your garment and
  destroy them!

¹² But God is my King from long ago;
    he brings salvation on the earth.

¹³ It was you who split open the sea by your
      power;
    you broke the heads of the monster in the
      waters.
¹⁴ It was you who crushed the heads of Leviathan
    and gave it as food to the creatures of the
      desert.
¹⁵ It was you who opened up springs and streams;
    you dried up the ever-flowing rivers.
¹⁶ The day is yours, and yours also the night;
    you established the sun and moon.
¹⁷ It was you who set all the boundaries of the
      earth;
    you made both summer and winter.

¹⁸ Remember how the enemy has mocked you,
    LORD,
  how foolish people have reviled your name.
¹⁹ Do not hand over the life of your dove to wild
    beasts;
  do not forget the lives of your afflicted
    people forever.

Jerusalem (vv. 2–7). The rhetorical questions of v. 1 connect God's inaction to judgment against his people. The temple destruction referred to is likely the destruction of the first temple by the Babylonians in 586 BC, and the psalm itself was likely written during the exilic period (586–538 BC).

74:1 why The Hebrew word used here, *lamah*, usually introduces a rhetorical question in the psalms. The question frames a confrontational idea that would be disrespectful if it were stated plainly.

74:2 purchased long ago Refers to God liberating the Hebrew people from Egypt during the Exodus event (Ex 3–13). Compare note on Ps 74:20. **Mount Zion** The temple mount in Jerusalem represented God's power, his presence and his commitment to Israel.

74:3 these everlasting ruins This line seems to place the destruction of the temple in the past. See note on vv. 1–3.

74:4–8 In addition to destroying the temple of God (vv. 3,4,7,8), God's enemies defiled it further by setting up their own signs (see note on v. 4). The psalmist describes a scene of total destruction—both physical and spiritual.

74:4 signs The Hebrew word used here, *'oth*, generally refers to some sort of distinguishing mark or proof (especially a miraculous sign). The invaders may have set up their emblems over the destroyed temple; thus their signs indicate their perceived superiority over the God of Israel, Yahweh.

74:7 your sanctuary The psalmist portrays the sanctuary's destruction as a personal insult to God.

74:8 every place The psalmist seems to describe multiple worship locations; however, Israel was supposed to have a single worship site (see Dt 12:10–14; 16:5–6; compare Ps 74:7). The Hebrew word used here, *mo'ed* (which may be rendered "meeting place" or "assembly"), could incorporate

the idea of what would later be known as synagogues. It could also reference unsanctioned worship sites.

74:9–11 In this passage, the psalmist responds to the destruction of the temple. In response to the absence of God's signs, the psalmist pleads for God to act, if only to protect his own reputation (v. 10).

74:9 We are given no signs Not only do the Israelites not see the emblems of God, but they also do not see his miraculous help.

74:11 Why do you hold back Introduces a rhetorical question (compare v. 1 and note)—the psalmist wants God to act. **your hand** Symbolizes God's power and action.

74:12–17 In this passage, the psalmist recounts God's mighty acts, which connect to the signs mentioned earlier (vv. 4,9). Although the main focus of the passage is God's acts in creation, the psalmist seems to allude to God's deliverance of Israel at the Red Sea and crossing the Jordan (v. 15; Ex 14; Jos 3).

74:13 It was you who split open the sea by your power Perhaps a reference to creation (Ge 1:6–7) or to the parting of the Red Sea (Ex 14:21).

74:14 heads of Leviathan A legendary sea monster that symbolized chaos in the ancient Near East. See Ps 104:26 and note.

74:15 It was you who opened up springs and streams May represent God's provision of water from the rock during Israel's wilderness wandering (see Ex 17:6; Nu 20:11). **you dried up the ever-flowing rivers** May refer to God stopping the Jordan River so that Joshua could lead Israel into Canaan (Jos 3; see Ps 114:3 and note).

74:18–23 The psalmist frames his plea that God honor his covenant (v. 20) by asking God to act on behalf of his own honor (vv. 18,22).

74:19 do not forget the lives of your afflicted people

²⁰ Have regard for your covenant,
    because haunts of violence fill the dark
        places of the land.
²¹ Do not let the oppressed retreat in
        disgrace;
    may the poor and needy praise your
        name.
²² Rise up, O God, and defend your cause;
    remember how fools mock you all day
        long.
²³ Do not ignore the clamor of your adversaries,
    the uproar of your enemies, which rises
        continually.

Psalm 75ᵃ

*For the director of music. To the tune of "Do Not Destroy."
A psalm of Asaph. A song.*

¹ We praise you, God,
    we praise you, for your Name is near;
    people tell of your wonderful deeds.

² You say, "I choose the appointed time;
    it is I who judge with equity.
³ When the earth and all its people quake,
    it is I who hold its pillars firm.ᵇ

⁴ To the arrogant I say, 'Boast no more,'
    and to the wicked, 'Do not lift up your
        horns.ᶜ
⁵ Do not lift your horns against heaven;
    do not speak so defiantly.'"

⁶ No one from the east or the west
    or from the desert can exalt themselves.
⁷ It is God who judges:
    He brings one down, he exalts
        another.
⁸ In the hand of the LORD is a cup
    full of foaming wine mixed with
        spices;
    he pours it out, and all the wicked
        of the earth
    drink it down to its very dregs.

⁹ As for me, I will declare this forever;
    I will sing praise to the God of Jacob,
¹⁰ who says, "I will cut off the horns of all the
        wicked,
    but the horns of the righteous will be
        lifted up."

ᵃ In Hebrew texts 75:1-10 is numbered 75:2-11.   ᵇ 3 The
Hebrew has *Selah* (a word of uncertain meaning) here.
ᶜ 4 *Horns* here symbolize strength; also in verses 5 and 10.

The psalmist portrays God's inaction as a forgetfulness of his needy people.

74:20 Have regard for your covenant Although v. 2 contains ideas and language about God's covenant with his people Israel, it does not explicitly name the covenant. Here, the psalmist appeals to God's prior commitment to Israel (Ex 24). See Ps 105:8 and note.

74:21 praise your name After God rescues them, the poor and needy will praise him.

74:23 Do not ignore the clamor of your adversaries Just as the psalmist does not want God to forget his people (v. 19), he also does not want God to overlook the insults from his enemies. The psalmist is appealing to the need for God to protect his own reputation.

75:title–10 Psalm 75 could be viewed as a corporate thanksgiving psalm (meant for group use) with a strong prophetic element. The psalmist anticipates that God's future help of Israel will resemble his past help to them. However, the anticipatory praise given to God at the end of the psalm (vv. 9–10) could suggest that it is a corporate praise psalm. The psalmist begins by thanking God for his past help to Israel and his presence with them (v. 1). He then offers a prophetic oracle, anticipating God's help for Israel (vv. 2–5). After describing God's judgment (vv. 6–8), the psalmist closes with a declaration of praise (vv. 9–10). See the table "Types of Psalms" on p. 830.

75:title director of music See note on 4:title. **Do Not Destroy** See note on 57:title. **A psalm** See note on 3:title. **of Asaph** See note on 73:title.

75:1 wonderful deeds The Hebrew word used here, *niphla'oth*, is usually associated with the events of the exodus from Egypt (see Ex 7:3).

75:2–5 This passage is best categorized as a prophetic oracle (a direct revelation from God) that anticipates God's saving help for Israel. God's words predict his

future judgment (Ps 75:2) and emphasize his ongoing support of creation (v. 3). This section closes by emphasizing humility before God (vv. 4–5).

75:3 who hold its pillars firm In addition to creating the world, God also maintains it. See the infographic "Ancient Hebrew Conception of the Universe" on p. 5.

75:4 horns A symbol of power and strength. By lifting up horns in this way (v. 5), the wicked are either standing in opposition to God or oppressing other people, or both.

75:6–8 Although this section could be read as part of the preceding words from God in vv. 2–5, the shift from the first person ("I") to the third person ("he") seems to indicate it is a response to God's words by the leader of the congregation—when this psalm was used in worship settings (see note on 75:title–10). The main theme of this section is God's future judgment, which the psalmist expresses by using metaphors for honor and humiliation (vv. 6–8).

75:8 a cup full of foaming wine The psalmist depicts judgment as becoming drunk and losing the ability to defend oneself (compare Isa 51:17–23; Jer 25:15–27).

75:9–10 The psalmist concludes by committing to praise God (Ps 75:9) and records a final statement of God's direct words to Israel (v. 10).

75:9 God of Jacob This affiliation of Israel's God, Yahweh, with Israel's patriarch, Jacob—whose name was changed to Israel (Ge 32:28)—is a way of acknowledging Yahweh's longstanding relationship with his people.

75:10 God will defeat those who arrogantly oppose him and what he represents, and uplift those who are righteous. Each person will ultimately be dealt with according to God's justice.

75:10 horns See note on Ps 75:4.

Psalm 76[a]

For the director of music. With stringed instruments.
A psalm of Asaph. A song.

[1] God is renowned in Judah;
　　in Israel his name is great.
[2] His tent is in Salem,
　　his dwelling place in Zion.
[3] There he broke the flashing arrows,
　　the shields and the swords, the weapons
　　　of war.[b]

[4] You are radiant with light,
　　more majestic than mountains rich with
　　　game.
[5] The valiant lie plundered,
　　they sleep their last sleep;
　not one of the warriors
　　can lift his hands.
[6] At your rebuke, God of Jacob,
　　both horse and chariot lie still.

[7] It is you alone who are to be feared.
　　Who can stand before you when you are
　　　angry?
[8] From heaven you pronounced judgment,
　　and the land feared and was quiet —

[9] when you, God, rose up to judge,
　　to save all the afflicted of the land.
[10] Surely your wrath against mankind brings
　　　you praise,
　　and the survivors of your wrath are
　　　restrained.[c]

[11] Make vows to the LORD your God and fulfill
　　　them;
　　let all the neighboring lands
　　bring gifts to the One to be feared.
[12] He breaks the spirit of rulers;
　　he is feared by the kings of the earth.

Psalm 77[d]

For the director of music. For Jeduthun. Of Asaph. A psalm.

[1] I cried out to God for help;
　　I cried out to God to hear me.
[2] When I was in distress, I sought the Lord;
　　at night I stretched out untiring hands,
　　and I would not be comforted.

---

[a] In Hebrew texts 76:1-12 is numbered 76:2-13.　　[b] 3 The
Hebrew has *Selah* (a word of uncertain meaning) here and at the
end of verse 9.　　[c] 10 Or *Surely the wrath of mankind brings*
you praise, / and with the remainder of wrath you arm yourself
[d] In Hebrew texts 77:1-20 is numbered 77:2-21.

76:title–12 This corporate praise psalm is associated with the songs of Zion (Ps 46; 48; 84; 87; 122). (Zion is the name of the temple mount in Jerusalem.) In this psalm, which is specifically called a song, the psalmist depicts God's greatness by recalling a time when he rescued Israel. Psalm 76 divides into four segments, each composed of three verses. The psalmist opens by focusing on God's reputation, which he defended by establishing and protecting his worship site and his people in Jerusalem (vv. 1–3). The psalmist describes enemy soldiers experiencing debilitating fear in the face of God's power (vv. 4–6). He then recalls God's role as divine king, judge and helper of his people (vv. 7–9). The psalmist concludes by responding once more to God's greatness (vv. 10–12).

Psalm 76 is thematically connected to Ps 46–48, especially in the mention of Zion (48:2,11,12), and the focus on God's acts across the whole of Israel's history. In addition, Ps 76 lacks an opening exhortation just as Ps 46 does. However, Ps 46–48 focus on viewing present events in light of the past, while Ps 76 looks beyond both the past and present into the future. See the table "Types of Psalms" on p. 830.

76:title director of music See note on 4:title. **stringed instruments** See note on 4:title. **A psalm** See note on 3:title. **of Asaph** See note on 73:title.

76:1–3 God establishing his name in Jerusalem means establishing his worship site and his people's worship of him. God protects his reputation by defending his temple and his people.

76:1 in Judah The territory surrounding Jerusalem. **Israel** Likely refers to the unified nation of Israel—which Judah was a part of.

76:3 There he broke the flashing arrows It is unclear which episode the psalmist is referring to. The OT de-

picts several sieges of Jerusalem, at least one of which included miraculous deliverance (2Ki 19:32–37).

76:6 God of Jacob A reference to the God of Israel, Yahweh. See note on Ps 75:9. **both horse and chariot lie still** This may be an allusion to God's rescue of Israel at the Red Sea (Ex 14:27,28; 15:21).

76:7–9 The psalmist depicts God as a cosmic ruler who acts on behalf of the needy.

76:7 you alone who are to be feared The Hebrew word used here, *nora*, refers to something being fearsome or awesome. See Ps 90:11 and note.

76:9 when you, God, rose up to judge God is enforcing justice against the foreign invaders. **all the afflicted of the land** The Hebrew word used here, *erets*, may refer to all land or to the land of Israel (the promised land) specifically.

76:10–12 The psalmist asserts that all people will eventually praise Yahweh (v. 10) and exhorts the faithful to worship him to their greatest capacity (v. 11). He concludes by emphasizing that all rulers and kings should fear Yahweh (v. 12).

76:11 Make vows See 116:14 and note.

77:title–20 In this individual lament psalm, the psalmist describes the comfort he has found by remembering how God helped the Israelites. The psalmist begins by depicting his anguish and pleading to God (vv. 1–3). He then describes his sleepless turmoil (v. 4) and his efforts to find some insight and resolution to his struggle (vv. 5–6). He describes a time in the past when he struggled, recalling the questions he asked regarding God's inaction (vv. 7–9). The psalmist then recalls how he focused on God's past actions on behalf of Israel (vv. 10–12). He considers God's character and shifts from an individual perspective to a corporate (group) viewpoint as he recalls

³I remembered you, God, and I groaned;
    I meditated, and my spirit grew faint.ᵃ
⁴You kept my eyes from closing;
    I was too troubled to speak.
⁵I thought about the former days,
    the years of long ago;
⁶I remembered my songs in the night.
    My heart meditated and my spirit asked:

⁷"Will the Lord reject forever?
    Will he never show his favor again?
⁸Has his unfailing love vanished forever?
    Has his promise failed for all time?
⁹Has God forgotten to be merciful?
    Has he in anger withheld his compassion?"

¹⁰Then I thought, "To this I will appeal:
    the years when the Most High stretched
        out his right hand.
¹¹I will remember the deeds of the LORD;
    yes, I will remember your miracles of
        long ago.
¹²I will consider all your works
    and meditate on all your mighty deeds."

¹³Your ways, God, are holy.
    What god is as great as our God?
¹⁴You are the God who performs miracles;
    you display your power among the
        peoples.

¹⁵With your mighty arm you redeemed your
        people,
    the descendants of Jacob and Joseph.

¹⁶The waters saw you, God,
    the waters saw you and writhed;
    the very depths were convulsed.
¹⁷The clouds poured down water,
    the heavens resounded with thunder;
    your arrows flashed back and forth.
¹⁸Your thunder was heard in the whirlwind,
    your lightning lit up the world;
    the earth trembled and quaked.
¹⁹Your path led through the sea,
    your way through the mighty waters,
    though your footprints were not seen.

²⁰You led your people like a flock
    by the hand of Moses and Aaron.

Psalm 78

A maskilᵇ of Asaph.

¹My people, hear my teaching;
    listen to the words of my mouth.

ᵃ 3 The Hebrew has *Selah* (a word of uncertain meaning) here and at the end of verses 9 and 15.   ᵇ Title: Probably a literary or musical term

---

God's actions (v. 13). He then describes God's actions across history (vv. 14–15) developing imagery about God's power (vv. 16–19). The psalmist concludes by focusing on events during the time of the exodus (v. 20). See the table "Types of Psalms" on p. 830.

77:title director of music See note on 4:title. **For Jeduthun** See note on 39:title. **Of Asaph** See note on 73:title. **A psalm** See note on 3:title.

77:1–3 Psalm 77 opens with a pained sense of desperation. The psalmist is unable to find any solace in his attempts to approach God or his examination of his personal experience of God.

77:2 I would not be comforted The situation that troubles the psalmist will not let up—he cannot get away from it.

77:3 my spirit grew faint The psalmist cannot find solace even by focusing on God.

77:4–9 The psalmist tries to understand his suffering, but he finds no relief. His reflection culminates in a series of pointed questions about his difficulties (vv. 7–9).

77:4 You kept my eyes from closing It is unclear whether the psalmist's sleeplessness results from God's direct action or from his inaction.

77:7 Will the LORD reject forever The first of a series of rhetorical questions in vv. 7–9. Yahweh will not reject the psalmist or his people forever; the psalmist implies that he finds hope by considering God's faithfulness to Israel.

77:10–15 This section is the pivot point of the psalm. The psalmist makes two significant choices: He chooses to view his difficulties in light of God's past help to Israel rather than his present anguish (vv. 10–11), and

he chooses to interpret his struggles in terms of God's relationship to the entire nation of Israel (v. 13).

77:10 the years when Refers to God's pattern of helping Israel. **the Most High** See note on 91:1.

77:12 meditate Meditation in the OT involves considering God, and then expressing the fruits of that process. See 104:34 and note.

77:13 our God The psalmist now adopts a corporate (group) perspective, speaking on behalf of God's people in general.

77:15 With your mighty arm you redeemed your people This phrase often refers to Yahweh's actions in the exodus from Egypt (e.g., Dt 4:34).

77:16–20 The psalmist concludes by describing a series of images that draw from the exodus story, especially the crossing of the Red Sea (Ex 14–15), but perhaps also the theophany at Sinai (Ex 19). The connection between this passage and the exodus story culminates in the reference to Moses and Aaron (Ps 77:20). God's rescue of Israel through the exodus is one of the strongest images of redemption in the OT and is often used in the NT. The psalmist's choice to view his personal situation through the lens of the exodus reflects his internalization of the storyline of God's involvement with his people.

77:16 waters saw you Likely refers to the crossing of the Red Sea (Ex 14).

77:17 the heavens resounded with thunder Probably alludes to the theophany at Sinai (Ex 19:16).

78:title–72 In this wisdom psalm, the psalmist recounts Israel's sacred history to exhort his audience to reflect on their behavior. He opens by identifying his psalm as a "parable" (see Ps 78:2 and note). Throughout

² I will open my mouth with a parable;
  I will utter hidden things, things from
    of old —
³ things we have heard and known,
  things our ancestors have told us.
⁴ We will not hide them from their
    descendants;
  we will tell the next generation
the praiseworthy deeds of the LORD,
  his power, and the wonders he has done.
⁵ He decreed statutes for Jacob
  and established the law in Israel,
which he commanded our ancestors
  to teach their children,

⁶ so the next generation would know them,
  even the children yet to be born,
  and they in turn would tell their children.
⁷ Then they would put their trust in God
  and would not forget his deeds
  but would keep his commands.
⁸ They would not be like their ancestors —
  a stubborn and rebellious generation,
whose hearts were not loyal to God,
  whose spirits were not faithful to him.

⁹ The men of Ephraim, though armed with
    bows,
  turned back on the day of battle;

---

the psalm, the psalmist focuses on Israel (vv. 5,21,71) and their journey with God. However, in v. 9, he more specifically mentions the Ephraimites to introduce his overview of Israel's pattern of unfaithfulness during the exodus and wilderness wanderings (vv. 9–16). The psalmist then presents the episode of the manna and quail (vv. 17–31), portraying it as a sign of their faithlessness (vv. 17–20). He also describes God's provision of manna (vv. 21–25) and mentions God's punishment of Israel with a plague (vv. 26–31).

The psalmist then depicts the pattern of Israel's waywardness and God's subsequent punishment of them during the wilderness wanderings (vv. 32–37). This time was also marked by God's compassion, but Israel never changed (vv. 38–41). The psalmist then discusses Israel's failure to remember the plagues against Egypt and God's subsequent deliverance of his people (vv. 42–53). This section concludes with Israel's entry into and settlement in the promised land (vv. 54–55). The psalmist then briefly portrays Israel's history within the promised land (vv. 56–64), depicting their idolatry (v. 57), which prompted God to punish them (v. 62). He recounts God's eventual rescue of Israel, describing how God has rejected Ephraim and selected Judah to house his temple (vv. 65–72). The psalmist concludes by emphasizing David's faithfulness and skill in guiding Israel (v. 72).

Psalm 78 is the second longest psalm (after Ps 119), and is one of several historical psalms that make use of extended presentations of Israel's history (compare Ps 105; 106). The psalm can also be categorized as a wisdom psalm since it is an exhortation framed as a story (see v. 2), and aims to prompt people to reflect on their relationship with God. See the table "Types of Psalms" on p. 830.

78:title *maskil* See note on 32:title. **of Asaph** See note on 73:title.

78:1–8 The introduction to Ps 78 explains that it is a "parable" (v. 2) intended to exhort the Israelites to not be like their forefathers (v. 8).

78:1–4 The opening of the psalm mentions that Israel's history will be used as a parable (see v. 2 and note). God's discipline of Israel seems to be described as part of his wondrous works.

78:2 a parable The Hebrew term used here, *mashal*, can refer to a saying or a proverb (see Pr 1:6), but it can also be an extended figurative comparison or story like what is depicted in this psalm. **hidden things** The

Hebrew word used here, *chidah*, refers to a riddle or enigmatic saying.

78:4 We will not hide them from their descendants Israel failed to follow God throughout its history. The psalmist seems to be saying that he will not hide the past from God's people but instead use it for teaching. **wonders** The Hebrew word used here, *niphla'oth*, is usually associated with the events of the exodus from Egypt (see Ex 7:3).

78:5–8 The psalmist describes how God (Ps 78:5) demanded that Israel not only recount his laws and instructions, but also remember the good and bad parts of their history. The Israelites should teach God's laws and Israel's history so that each new generation would know not to go astray (v. 8).

78:5 for Jacob The ancestor of the Israelites whose name was changed to "Israel" (see Ge 32:22–28). **to teach their children** God commanded Israel to teach his law to the children of the next generation (see Dt 6:6–7).

78:8 stubborn and rebellious generation Israel's record of faithlessness spanned the length of its history, and the psalmist may be referring to Israel's idolatry and apostasy within the promised land or more specifically to the events recorded in Nu 14:22–23.

78:9–16 This section is the first of two thematic overviews in Ps 78 (see vv. 32–41). This section summarizes Israel's interaction with God during the exodus (Ex 6–12) and then in the wilderness (Ex 14–40; Nu 11–25).

78:9 This verse could have been inserted by a later editor since the depiction of Israel's faithlessness would have continued unbroken without it—instead this comment about Ephraim is inserted. However, the subsequent mention of Ephraim and Judah in Ps 78:67–68 indicates that v. 9 is not purposeless. In Ps 78, Ephraim functions as a contrast to Judah (and David), and the story of Ephraim seems to be central to the psalmist's overall point.

78:9 Ephraim A tribe of Israel and also representative of the northern kingdom of Israel (Hos 4:17; 2Ch 25:7). Shiloh, which was in Ephraim, could have been the central place of worship for the entire nation (1Sa 1:24; compare Jos 18:1; 22:12), but instead Jerusalem was selected (see Ps 78:60–69). Ephraim also served as a general symbol of idolatry in Israel's history, primarily because of their early affiliation with idolatry (Jdg 18:31). In the current form of the psalm, Ephraim seems to be symbolic of the overall disobedience of God's people, but especially of the disobedience of the northern tribes. See note on Ps 78:10; compare note on v. 60.

10 they did not keep God's covenant
    and refused to live by his law.
11 They forgot what he had done,
    the wonders he had shown them.
12 He did miracles in the sight of their ancestors
    in the land of Egypt, in the region of Zoan.
13 He divided the sea and led them through;
    he made the water stand up like a wall.
14 He guided them with the cloud by day
    and with light from the fire all night.
15 He split the rocks in the wilderness
    and gave them water as abundant as the
        seas;
16 he brought streams out of a rocky crag
    and made water flow down like rivers.

17 But they continued to sin against him,
    rebelling in the wilderness against the
        Most High.
18 They willfully put God to the test
    by demanding the food they craved.
19 They spoke against God;
    they said, "Can God really
        spread a table in the wilderness?
20 True, he struck the rock,
    and water gushed out,
    streams flowed abundantly,
but can he also give us bread?
    Can he supply meat for his people?"

21 When the LORD heard them, he was furious;
    his fire broke out against Jacob,
    and his wrath rose against Israel,
22 for they did not believe in God
    or trust in his deliverance.
23 Yet he gave a command to the skies above
    and opened the doors of the heavens;
24 he rained down manna for the people to eat,
    he gave them the grain of heaven.
25 Human beings ate the bread of angels;
    he sent them all the food they could eat.
26 He let loose the east wind from the heavens
    and by his power made the south wind
        blow.
27 He rained meat down on them like dust,
    birds like sand on the seashore.
28 He made them come down inside their camp,
    all around their tents.
29 They ate till they were gorged —
    he had given them what they craved.
30 But before they turned from what they
        craved,
    even while the food was still in their mouths,
31 God's anger rose against them;
    he put to death the sturdiest among them,
    cutting down the young men of Israel.

32 In spite of all this, they kept on sinning;
    in spite of his wonders, they did not believe.

78:10 they did not keep God's covenant The Ephraimites did not keep God's law or drive out the Canaanites
from their portion of the promised land as they were
supposed to (Jdg 1:29). After Israel entered the promised
land, the Ephraimites, and the Israelite people in general,
primarily sinned against God by participating in idolatry
(see Jdg 18:31). Compare note on Ps 78:9.
78:11 wonders he had shown them Identification
with the events of the exodus was a feature of Israel's
ongoing religious life (see Dt 5:1–5; 11:7).
78:13 he made the water stand up like a wall See
Ex 15:8, compare Jos 3:16.
78:14 He guided them with the cloud See Ex
13:21–22; 40:34–38.
78:15 He split the rocks in the wilderness See Ex
17:1–7; Nu 20:2–13.

78:17–20 Israel's main fault in the episode recalled here
was their demand for meat (see Nu 11:4–6); however, the
psalmist implies that Israel complained against God on a
regular basis (compare Ex 16–17; Nu 11; Ps 78:19–20).

**78:17 rebelling in the wilderness against the Most
High** The psalmist seems to be specifically referring
to Israel's dissatisfaction with God's provision in Nu
11:1–6, not Israel's later refusal to enter into Canaan
(Nu 14:1–4). **the Most High** See note on Ps 91:1.
78:19 a table in the wilderness This portrayal of rebellion is a condensed account of Israel's complaining.
Israel had eaten manna from before the time that they
arrived at Sinai (see Ex 16).
78:20 struck the rock, and water gushed out See
Nu 20:11. **can he also give us bread? Can he supply
meat** The issue was not God's ability to provide, but
rather Israel's impatience and insolence.

78:21–25 In this section, the psalmist focuses on God's
anger and his provision of manna to Israel. He implies
that, although God was furious with Israel, he did not stop
providing food for them. This section may be a stylized
review of the wilderness journey of Israel, contrasting the
reality of God's continual provision of manna (Ex 16:35)
with Israel's general disloyalty to God.

78:22 they did not believe in God Israel commonly
longed for Egypt when facing difficulties in the wilderness
(see Ex 16:3; Nu 11:1–6).
78:24 he rained down manna for the people to eat
See Ex 16:4.
78:25 the bread of angels A poetic way of emphasizing
the miraculous nature of God's provision.
78:27 He rained meat down on them like dust See
Nu 11:31.
78:29 he had given them what they craved See
Nu 11:4,34.
78:30 food was still in their mouths See Nu 11:33.
78:31 he put to death the sturdiest among them The
account of Nu 11 does not include this specific detail,
but it does note that a plague came upon the people (Nu
11:33) and earlier in Nu 11 death does come to some
people as a result of God's anger (Nu 11:1). For God to
strike down Israel's strongest young people indicates
that God is not restraining himself—these strong people
are crucial for Israel's continued survival.

78:32–41 This section is the second of two thematic
overviews in Ps 78 (see vv. 9–16). In v. 32, the psalmist views the history of Israel in the wilderness through
the lens of events recounted in Nu 11–21 and Nu 25.

78:32 In spite of all this The psalmist uses the story
of the manna and quail (Nu 11) to introduce the entire

³³ So he ended their days in futility
  and their years in terror.
³⁴ Whenever God slew them, they would
  seek him;
  they eagerly turned to him again.
³⁵ They remembered that God was their Rock,
  that God Most High was their Redeemer.
³⁶ But then they would flatter him with their
  mouths,
  lying to him with their tongues;
³⁷ their hearts were not loyal to him,
  they were not faithful to his covenant.
³⁸ Yet he was merciful;
  he forgave their iniquities
  and did not destroy them.
  Time after time he restrained his anger
  and did not stir up his full wrath.
³⁹ He remembered that they were but flesh,
  a passing breeze that does not return.

⁴⁰ How often they rebelled against him in the
  wilderness
  and grieved him in the wasteland!
⁴¹ Again and again they put God to the test;
  they vexed the Holy One of Israel.
⁴² They did not remember his power —
  the day he redeemed them from the
  oppressor,
⁴³ the day he displayed his signs in Egypt,
  his wonders in the region of Zoan.
⁴⁴ He turned their river into blood;
  they could not drink from their streams.
⁴⁵ He sent swarms of flies that devoured them,
  and frogs that devastated them.

⁴⁶ He gave their crops to the grasshopper,
  their produce to the locust.
⁴⁷ He destroyed their vines with hail
  and their sycamore-figs with sleet.
⁴⁸ He gave over their cattle to the hail,
  their livestock to bolts of lightning.
⁴⁹ He unleashed against them his hot
  anger,
  his wrath, indignation and hostility —
  a band of destroying angels.
⁵⁰ He prepared a path for his anger;
  he did not spare them from death
  but gave them over to the plague.
⁵¹ He struck down all the firstborn of
  Egypt,
  the firstfruits of manhood in the
  tents of Ham.
⁵² But he brought his people out like
  a flock;
  he led them like sheep through the
  wilderness.
⁵³ He guided them safely, so they were
  unafraid;
  but the sea engulfed their enemies.
⁵⁴ And so he brought them to the border of his
  holy land,
  to the hill country his right hand had
  taken.
⁵⁵ He drove out nations before them
  and allotted their lands to them as an
  inheritance;
  he settled the tribes of Israel in their
  homes.

story of Israel's faithlessness in the wilderness. The psalmist excludes the story of Israel's rebellion after hearing from the spies that went to Canaan (Nu 13–14). This was the occasion that prompted God to prohibit the wilderness generation from ever entering Canaan (see Nu 14:20–38, especially Nu 14:20–25).

78:34 slew them, they would seek him After receiving God's punishment for rebellion, the Israelites would turn to him again—but only temporarily.

78:36 But then they would flatter him The people did not keep their promise to remain faithful to God.

78:37 they were not faithful to his covenant In the wilderness, Israel sinned by complaining about God's provision for them (Nu 11), committing idolatry (Ex 32) and refusing to enter the promised land (Nu 13–14). See Ps 105:8 and note.

78:38 he forgave The Hebrew word used here, *kaphar*, means "to cover." It has the sense of covering iniquities or sin to avert punishment. **Time after time he restrained his anger** God did not completely destroy Israel on the many occasions when he could have.

78:42–55 In this section, the psalmist summarizes God's actions on behalf of Israel from the events of the exodus from Egypt to the entry into the promised land. The presentation is focused almost entirely on the plagues against Egypt (vv. 42–53) with a short segment devoted to entry into Canaan and the allotment of the land to the tribes of Israel (vv. 54–55).

78:42–43 God's demonstration of his power against Egypt is the template for redemption in the OT. The psalmist revisits the events of the exodus and portrays Israel's failure in the wilderness as a failure to remember God's previous rescue of them and trust him accordingly.

78:44–53 In this passage, the psalmist selectively overviews the plagues against Egypt, giving great weight to the tenth plague—the death of the firstborn (Ex 12:29–32)—and the subsequent departure of Israel from Egypt. The psalmist also includes the events at the Red Sea, but doesn't emphasize them.

78:44 He turned their river into blood The first plague (Ex 7:14–25).

78:45 flies The fourth plague (Ex 8:20–32). **frogs** The second plague (Ex 8:1–15).

78:46 grasshopper The eighth plague (Ex 10:1–20).

78:47 hail The seventh plague (Ex 9:13–25).

78:48 He gave over their cattle to the hail See Ex 9:19,25. **their livestock to bolts of lightning** See Ex 9:24.

78:49 destroying angels The agents of God's destruction during the tenth plague (see Ex 12:29–32).

78:51 He struck down all the firstborn of Egypt See Ex 12:29. **the tents of Ham** Ham was one of Noah's sons. His descendants are described as settling in the regions of Egypt and Canaan (Ge 10:6–20). See Ps 105:23 and note.

⁵⁶ But they put God to the test
  and rebelled against the Most High;
  they did not keep his statutes.
⁵⁷ Like their ancestors they were disloyal
    and faithless,
  as unreliable as a faulty bow.
⁵⁸ They angered him with their high places;
  they aroused his jealousy with their
    idols.
⁵⁹ When God heard them, he was furious;
  he rejected Israel completely.
⁶⁰ He abandoned the tabernacle of Shiloh,
  the tent he had set up among humans.
⁶¹ He sent the ark of his might into
    captivity,
  his splendor into the hands of the
    enemy.
⁶² He gave his people over to the sword;
  he was furious with his inheritance.
⁶³ Fire consumed their young men,
  and their young women had no wedding
    songs;

⁶⁴ their priests were put to the sword,
  and their widows could not weep.

⁶⁵ Then the Lord awoke as from sleep,
  as a warrior wakes from the stupor of
    wine.
⁶⁶ He beat back his enemies;
  he put them to everlasting shame.
⁶⁷ Then he rejected the tents of Joseph,
  he did not choose the tribe of Ephraim;
⁶⁸ but he chose the tribe of Judah,
  Mount Zion, which he loved.
⁶⁹ He built his sanctuary like the heights,
  like the earth that he established
    forever.
⁷⁰ He chose David his servant
  and took him from the sheep pens;
⁷¹ from tending the sheep he brought him
  to be the shepherd of his people Jacob,
  of Israel his inheritance.
⁷² And David shepherded them with integrity
    of heart;
  with skillful hands he led them.

78:53 the sea engulfed their enemies See Ex 14:21–31; 15:21.
78:55 allotted their lands to them as an inheritance See Jos 13–21.

78:56–64 This section may depict the period of the judges prior to the establishment of the monarchy (see the book of Judges). The psalmist connects Israel's unfaithfulness within the promised land (Canaan) to their unfaithfulness during the time in the wilderness. For the psalmist, the primary sin of Israel at this time was idolatry (Ps 78:58). See note on vv. 59–64.
78:57 as unreliable as a faulty bow An arrow shot from a warped bow will not fly straight.
78:58 high places Ancient worship sites were usually located on hills because of the ancient Near Eastern belief that they were connected to heaven and deities. Though the Law prohibited high places, many Israelites still participated in idolatrous worship at them (see Dt 12:10–14; 16:5–6). **their idols** Although Israel had previously fallen into idolatry (e.g., Ex 32:1–10; Nu 25:1–9), the psalmist focuses on idolatry within the land of Israel specifically, probably because it was viewed as defiling both the land and the people. See Ps 96:5 and note.

78:59–64 The psalmist continues to examine Israel's unfaithfulness within the land of Israel and focuses on the sanctuary at Shiloh (see 1Sa 1–4). The precise agent of God's judgment in this section (Ps 78:62) and the timing of his rescue of Israel (v. 66) is ambiguous.
78:59 he rejected Israel completely This seems to refer to just the northern kingdom or northern tribes of Israel (see v. 67). The psalmist portrays God's focus on Judah (v. 68) and David (v. 70) after this point. Compare vv. 65–72 and note.
78:60 Shiloh The location of the ark of the covenant and the center of worship in 1Sa 1–4 (compare Ps 132:8). Shiloh was the center of Israelite worship before Jerusalem (and David) rose to prominence (ca. 1004 BC).
78:62 He gave his people over to the sword See 1Sa 4:1–11; note on Ps 78:59–64. **his inheritance** Probably

refers to the people of Israel, especially Ephraim and the other northern tribes. See note v. 59; note on 47:4.

78:65–72 In this final section, the psalmist depicts God's deliverance of Israel (78:65–66)—showing that the northern tribes were not rejected completely (v. 59)—and his selection of Jerusalem as his worship site (v. 68). A part of the selection of the worship site of Mount Zion in Jerusalem is the choice of David as God's appointed leader (vv. 70–72).
78:66 He beat back his enemies See 1Sa 5; compare Ps 78:62 and note; note on vv. 59–64.
78:67–72 The closing emphasis of this psalm on David offers an exhortation to hope in the Davidic covenant (see 2Sa 7), but the rest of the psalm issues a word of caution encouraging the Israelites to trust in God alone. Just as God shifted his favor from Ephraim (Ps 78:9,67) to Judah (v. 68), he can continue to punish unfaithfulness while keeping his promises to Israel.
78:67 he rejected the tents of Joseph Because of the tribal allotment of his sons (Ephraim and Manasseh), Joseph is associated with the northern kingdom of Israel, which was united under David (1004 BC) but later split with Judah (930 BC). Compare 105:17 and note. **Ephraim** See note on 78:9.
78:68 chose the tribe of Judah The tribal allotment to Judah included Jerusalem (compare 97:8). Most of the area of Judah was located south and southwest of Jerusalem. Judah was later the center of the southern kingdom after the kingdom split (see note on 78:67). David was also one of the descendants of the patriarch Judah. **Mount Zion** The temple mount in Jerusalem and often used synonymously for Jerusalem in general. See 20:2 and note.
78:69 He built his sanctuary like the heights The Israelites considered the temple on Mount Zion to be the location of God's presence on earth.
78:71 his people Jacob, of Israel his inheritance The psalmist identifies David as the leader of all Israel, not just the southern kingdom of Judah.

Psalm 79

A psalm of Asaph.

[1] O God, the nations have invaded your
  inheritance;
  they have defiled your holy temple,
  they have reduced Jerusalem to rubble.
[2] They have left the dead bodies of your
  servants
  as food for the birds of the sky,
  the flesh of your own people for the
  animals of the wild.
[3] They have poured out blood like water
  all around Jerusalem,
  and there is no one to bury the dead.
[4] We are objects of contempt to our neighbors,
  of scorn and derision to those around us.

[5] How long, Lord? Will you be angry forever?
  How long will your jealousy burn like fire?
[6] Pour out your wrath on the nations
  that do not acknowledge you,
  on the kingdoms
  that do not call on your name;
[7] for they have devoured Jacob
  and devastated his homeland.

[8] Do not hold against us the sins of past
  generations;
  may your mercy come quickly to meet us,
  for we are in desperate need.
[9] Help us, God our Savior,
  for the glory of your name;

deliver us and forgive our sins
  for your name's sake.
[10] Why should the nations say,
  "Where is their God?"

Before our eyes, make known among the
  nations
  that you avenge the outpoured blood of
  your servants.
[11] May the groans of the prisoners come
  before you;
  with your strong arm preserve those
  condemned to die.
[12] Pay back into the laps of our neighbors seven
  times
  the contempt they have hurled at you, Lord.
[13] Then we your people, the sheep of your
  pasture,
  will praise you forever;
from generation to generation
  we will proclaim your praise.

Psalm 80[a]

*For the director of music. To the tune of "The Lilies
of the Covenant." Of Asaph. A psalm.*

[1] Hear us, Shepherd of Israel,
  you who lead Joseph like a flock.
You who sit enthroned between the
  cherubim,
  shine forth [2] before Ephraim, Benjamin and
  Manasseh.

[a] In Hebrew texts 80:1-19 is numbered 80:2-20.

79:title–13 This corporate lament psalm (meant for group settings) depicts the destruction of the temple (ca. 586 BC; v. 1) and the captivity (exile) of the people of Israel (v. 11). The psalmist opens by describing the destruction of the Jerusalem temple and its defilement (v. 1), which is a result of the Israelite corpses strewn across the area (vv. 2–3). He describes how the neighboring nations mock Israel (v. 4). The psalmist then calls for God to defend his people (vv. 5–7) and his reputation (vv. 8–10) by punishing the surrounding nations who have destroyed Israel. He asks God to avenge his people (vv. 10–11) and punish those who mock him and his people (v. 12). The psalmist concludes by committing to praise God after he rescues Israel. See the table "Types of Psalms" on p. 830.

79:title A psalm See note on 3:title. **of Asaph** See note on 73:title.

79:1–4 This passage presents a stark picture of the destruction of Jerusalem and the temple. The psalmist focuses on the ruined buildings (v. 1) and the defilement of the ground from Israelite corpses and bloodshed (vv. 2–3). He then recounts the mocking taunts from Israel's enemies (v. 4).

79:1 the nations Throughout this psalm, the psalmist focuses on foreign powers around Israel (vv. 6,12). **your inheritance** This may refer to God's temple, the land of Israel or the people of Israel (compare 94:5,14).

79:2 bodies of your servants Unburied corpses represented total military defeat.

79:5 Will you be angry forever The psalmist views God's failure to punish Israel's enemies as his displeasure and judgment (Dt 28:15–68).

79:7 devastated his homeland The psalmist could be depicting Jerusalem as Israel's residence (compare Ps 79:1) or be referring to the destruction of the nation in general.

79:8–10 The psalmist portrays God's inaction as evidence of his judgment of Israel (v. 8). Rather than asking God to defend his people, the psalmist asks God to defend his own honor and reputation.

79:8 sins of past generations The psalmist depicts Israel's suffering at the hands of foreigners as God's judgment on their sins. See Dt 5:8–10.

79:9 for your name's sake The psalmist pleads that God defend his reputation by delivering his people.

79:10 Where is their God A claim that Israel's God is powerless.

79:11 groans of the prisoners Although the psalmist has not yet mentioned exile or captivity, this verse indicates that God's people find themselves in captivity away from the land of Israel. This exile occurred ca. 586–538 BC.

80:title–19 In this corporate lament psalm (meant for group settings), the psalmist focuses on the northern tribes of Israel. He opens by asking God to save his

Awaken your might;
come and save us.

³ Restore us, O God;
make your face shine on us,
that we may be saved.

⁴ How long, Lᴏʀᴅ God Almighty,
will your anger smolder
against the prayers of your people?
⁵ You have fed them with the bread of tears;
you have made them drink tears by the
bowlful.
⁶ You have made us an object of derision*ᵃ* to
our neighbors,
and our enemies mock us.

⁷ Restore us, God Almighty;
make your face shine on us,
that we may be saved.

⁸ You transplanted a vine from Egypt;
you drove out the nations and planted it.
⁹ You cleared the ground for it,
and it took root and filled the land.

¹⁰ The mountains were covered with its shade,
the mighty cedars with its branches.
¹¹ Its branches reached as far as the Sea,*ᵇ*
its shoots as far as the River.*ᶜ*

¹² Why have you broken down its walls
so that all who pass by pick its grapes?
¹³ Boars from the forest ravage it,
and insects from the fields feed on it.
¹⁴ Return to us, God Almighty!
Look down from heaven and see!
Watch over this vine,
¹⁵ the root your right hand has planted,
the son*ᵈ* you have raised up for yourself.

¹⁶ Your vine is cut down, it is burned with fire;
at your rebuke your people perish.
¹⁷ Let your hand rest on the man at your right
hand,
the son of man you have raised up for
yourself.

---

*ᵃ 6 Probable reading of the original Hebrew text; Masoretic Text
contention   ᵇ 11 Probably the Mediterranean   ᶜ 11 That is,
the Euphrates   ᵈ 15 Or branch*

---

northern tribes (vv. 1–2). He then begs God to restore the nation—a plea that he repeats three times throughout the psalm (vv. 3,7,19). The psalmist begs God to relent from punishing his people (vv. 4–5), and describes how the foreign nations mock Israel as a result of his inaction (v. 6). He then describes Israel as a vine (v. 8) that God brought out of Egypt and established in Canaan (vv. 9–11). He laments that God has allowed his vine to be attacked by those around it (vv. 12–13), begging God to reconsider his vine and care for it again (vv. 14–15). He describes the vine as damaged and suffering, but asserts that God can still help it (vv. 16–17). The psalmist then promises that Israel will praise God if he will save them (v. 18). He concludes by repeating his plea for restoration (v. 19). See the table "Types of Psalms" on p. 830.

80:title director of music See note on 4:title. **To the tune of "The Lilies of the Covenant"** The headings of Ps 45, 60, and 69 also mention lilies. See note on 60:title; compare note on 45:title. **Of Asaph** See note on 73:title. **A psalm** See note on 3:title.

80:1–2 The tribes mentioned in these verses are associated with the northern kingdom of Israel, with the exception of Benjamin. Although Joseph never had a tribal allotment in Canaan, the tribes named after his two children, Ephraim and Manasseh, were given land, as was his brother Benjamin. All three tribes were centrally located in the overall allotment of the land of Canaan.

80:1 You who sit enthroned between the cherubim A reference to the golden cherubim on the ark of the covenant. See note on 18:10.
80:2 Ephraim One of Joseph's sons (Ge 48:1) who was numbered among the tribes of Israel. His name was sometimes used to refer to the northern kingdom after the split of the kingdom of Israel into Judah in the south and Israel in the north (ca. 930 BC; e.g., Hos 5:3–5). See note on Ps 78:9. **Benjamin** Joseph's brother who was also specially favored by Jacob (Ge 42:2). **Manasseh** One of Joseph's sons (Ge 48:1) whose tribe was allotted a very large inheritance of land in Canaan.

80:3 This line is repeated in Ps 80:7 and v. 19, but the name of God is expanded each time. Here in v. 3, the generic name for God as creator is used in Hebrew: *elohim*. In v. 7 and v. 14, the Hebrew text uses *elohim tseva'oth*, which may be rendered "God of hosts" or "God of armies." Finally, in v. 19, *yhwh elohim tseva'oth* is used, which means "Yahweh God of hosts"; this is an echo of v. 4, which also uses this title.

80:3 Restore us The Hebrew word used here, *shuv*, has the basic meaning of "turn" or "return"; here and in v. 3 and v. 19, it literally means "cause to return." Compare v. 14. **make your face shine** The psalmist asks God to show his power or glory (compare v. 16; Dt 33:2). See Ps 4:6 and note.
80:4 Lᴏʀᴅ God Almighty The Hebrew text here uses the expression *yhwh elohim tseva'oth* (see note on 80:3). This is an expression indicating that Yahweh is the supreme deity who has the power to control heavenly and cosmic forces.

80:7–13 The psalmist figuratively depicts Israel as a vine.

80:8 You transplanted a vine from Egypt The psalmist identifies the vine with Israel by referring to the exodus from Egypt.

80:10–11 Several expressions in vv. 10–11 are meant to indicate the geographical extent of Israel. At its widest point, the kingdom of Israel (under David and Solomon) extended over the land of Canaan from the Mediterranean Sea to the Euphrates River.

80:11 the Sea Refers to the Mediterranean Sea. **the River** Refers to the Euphrates River.
80:12 its walls Vineyards usually had protective walls. Broken-down walls indicated the vine keeper's neglect.
80:15 the son The psalmist shifts from portraying Israel as a vine to portraying Israel as a son (*ben* in Hebrew).
80:17 man at your right hand A position of privilege and responsibility. The psalmist is probably referring to the king of Israel. **the son of man** Likely refers to the human king of Israel.

¹⁸ Then we will not turn away from you;
　　revive us, and we will call on your name.

¹⁹ Restore us, LORD God Almighty;
　　make your face shine on us,
　　that we may be saved.

Psalm 81[a]

For the director of music. According to gittith.[b] Of Asaph.

¹ Sing for joy to God our strength;
　　shout aloud to the God of Jacob!
² Begin the music, strike the timbrel,
　　play the melodious harp and lyre.

³ Sound the ram's horn at the New Moon,
　　and when the moon is full, on the day of
　　　our festival;
⁴ this is a decree for Israel,
　　an ordinance of the God of Jacob.
⁵ When God went out against Egypt,
　　he established it as a statute for Joseph.

I heard an unknown voice say:

⁶ "I removed the burden from their shoulders;
　　their hands were set free from the basket.

⁷ In your distress you called and I rescued you,
　　I answered you out of a thundercloud;
　　I tested you at the waters of Meribah.[c]
⁸ Hear me, my people, and I will warn you —
　　if you would only listen to me, Israel!
⁹ You shall have no foreign god among you;
　　you shall not worship any god other
　　　than me.
¹⁰ I am the LORD your God,
　　who brought you up out of Egypt.
　　Open wide your mouth and I will fill it.

¹¹ "But my people would not listen to me;
　　Israel would not submit to me.
¹² So I gave them over to their stubborn hearts
　　to follow their own devices.

¹³ "If my people would only listen to me,
　　if Israel would only follow my ways,
¹⁴ how quickly I would subdue their enemies
　　and turn my hand against their foes!
¹⁵ Those who hate the LORD would cringe
　　before him,
　　and their punishment would last forever.

---

a In Hebrew texts 81:1-16 is numbered 81:2-17.　b Title: Probably a musical term　c 7 The Hebrew has Selah (a word of uncertain meaning) here.

80:18 Then we will not turn away from you The psalmist commits on behalf of God's people that they will be faithful to God after he rescues Israel.
80:19 LORD God Almighty See v. 3 and note.

81:title–16 The psalmist opens this corporate praise psalm (meant for group settings) by calling the nation to praise God with song and instruments (vv. 1–2). Verse 3 indicates that this psalm was meant to be used at the time of a new moon feast (see v. 3 and note), which God commanded when he rescued Israel from Egypt (vv. 4–5). The psalmist then depicts God's direct address to Israel, in which he alludes to the exodus from Egypt (vv. 6–7), the revelation at Sinai (v. 7) and Israel's idolatry in the wilderness (v. 9). God expresses his concern for Israel by stating that he desires for them to obey him (v. 8) and desires to care for them (v. 10). God then speaks about Israel, saying that they would not listen to him (v. 11), so he let them choose their own path (v. 12). God again expresses his desire that Israel listen to him (v. 13), and states that he would help them against their enemies if they would follow his ways (vv. 14–15). God ends by repeating his desire to provide for Israel (v. 16).

　While this psalm is probably best classified as a corporate praise psalm, it contains a strong prophetic element. The prophetic element is not a prediction, but rather an exhortation in the form of a direct address from God through a human speaker (vv. 6–16). In addition, the psalm seems to contain some directions for its use in a public liturgical setting (vv. 1–5). See the table "Types of Psalms" on p. 830.

81:title director of music See note on 4:title. **gittith** See note on 8:title. **Of Asaph** See note on 73:title.

81:1–5 The exhortation to praise God with singing and instruments (vv. 1–2) culminates in a call to blow trumpets at a festival occasion (v. 3).

81:1 God of Jacob This phrase is used again in v. 4, and may simply be a poetic variation on the name for the

God of Israel. However, since Jacob was a pivotal figure in the history of the nation, the reference may contain an allusion to some element of Jacob's story, such as his renaming by God (see Ge 32:28). See Ps 105:6 and note.

81:3 ram's horn The Hebrew word used here, *shophar* — which refers to a trumpet made from a ram's horn — was used to rally troops for battle and to call people to worship. **on the day of our festival** May refer to the New Year (Festival of Trumpets; Lev 23:23–25), the Day of Atonement (Lev 23:26–32) or the Festival of Booths (or Tabernacles; see Lev 23:33–43).

81:6–10 God recounts his actions on behalf of Israel — specifically how he freed them from slavery in Egypt (Ps 81:6–7). He then refers to the events at Sinai and Meribah (v. 7). God then recounts his longing that Israel would listen to him (v. 8), that they refrain from idolatrous worship (v. 9) and that they would let him provide for their needs (v. 10).

81:6 I removed the burden from their shoulders A poetic way to refer to the hard labor God delivered Israel from while they were enslaved in Egypt (compare Ex 5:1–21).
81:7 In your distress you called See Ex 3:7. **a thundercloud** See Ex 19:18–19. **waters of Meribah** See Ex 17:7.

81:11–16 God now speaks about Israel rather than speaking to Israel. He describes how Israel was stubborn, so he released them to go their own way (Ps 81:11–12). He then repeats his longing for Israel to listen to him and follow him so that he will subdue Israel's enemies forever (vv. 13–15). The psalm closes with God expressing his desire to help Israel (v. 16).

81:11 my people would not listen God has listened to Israel and rescued them (v. 7), but Israel refused to listen (v. 8). Since Israel would not listen to God, he let them fall into disaster so that they would come to their senses.
81:14 how quickly I would subdue their enemies Until this point, the psalmist has only implied that Israel is being oppressed.

16 But you would be fed with the finest of
   wheat;
   with honey from the rock I would
   satisfy you."

Psalm 82

A psalm of Asaph.

1 God presides in the great assembly;
   he renders judgment among the "gods":

2 "How long will you[a] defend the unjust
   and show partiality to the wicked?[b]
3 Defend the weak and the fatherless;
   uphold the cause of the poor and the
   oppressed.

4 Rescue the weak and the needy;
   deliver them from the hand of the wicked.

5 "The 'gods' know nothing, they understand
   nothing.
   They walk about in darkness;
   all the foundations of the earth are shaken.

6 "I said, 'You are "gods";
   you are all sons of the Most High.'
7 But you will die like mere mortals;
   you will fall like every other ruler."

8 Rise up, O God, judge the earth,
   for all the nations are your inheritance.

[a] 2 The Hebrew is plural.   [b] 2 The Hebrew has *Selah* (a word of uncertain meaning) here.

81:15 Those who hate the Lᴏʀᴅ Since Yahweh is Israel's God, the foreign nations oppressing Israel are showing that they hate Yahweh.

82:title–8 Psalm 82 is unusual in that God serves as the main speaker. It sets the scene with God taking his place in the divine council (v. 1). God then speaks and rebukes the gods as he commands them to act justly toward the weak and needy (vv. 2–4). The psalmist continues by describing the gods as ignorant (v. 5) before God again speaks and condemns them to die like men (vv. 6–7). The psalmist concludes by petitioning God to judge the earth (v. 8).

82:title A psalm See note on 4:title. **of Asaph** See note on 73:title.

82:1 presides The Hebrew word used here, *nitsav*, is a singular verbal form, which means that its subject, which is *elohim* in Hebrew—and could be translated as "God" or "gods"—should be translated in the singular as "God." The imagery that extends from this verb is one of presiding, since the setting is a formal council meeting. **great assembly** A descriptive phrase used of the heavenly host. Like other ancient Near Eastern cultures, the psalmist conceived of God as directing the affairs of the unseen world through an administration of divine beings. The members of the heavenly host are often referred to as a "council" or "assembly" (see 1Ki 22:19–23). **among the "gods"** The Hebrew preposition used here, *qerev*, requires the Hebrew word *elohim* to be translated as a plural here—as "gods." The gods in the verse are the council members, the heavenly host (see Ps 82:6). A council of divine beings is also mentioned in 89:5–7, where they are depicted as in heaven or the skies. In 1Ki 22:19–23 the members of the heavenly host are called *ruach* (often translated "spirit"). Old Testament writers use the Hebrew word *elohim* to refer to divine beings other than the God of Israel (like demons in Dt 32:17 or the spirits of the human dead in 1Sa 28:13). These *elohim* were never considered equal to the God of Israel, Yahweh—who is superior and the Creator of all (see Ps 89:6–8; 95:3).

82:2 How long The affairs of the nations of the world are supposed to be judged according to divine law and justice; furthermore, the spiritual authorities involved in the affairs of the nations (the gods; see note on 82:1) must observe divine law and justice. However, the divine beings God addresses have perverted justice (see Dt 32:8–9; note on 32:8). **show partiality to the wicked** The gods (*elohim* in Hebrew) have failed in their administrative duties involving humanity; they are

corrupt and will be judged (compare note on Ps 82:1). In this psalm, they are on trial before God, who is their judge—he is speaking to them. The concept of divine beings being authoritatively involved in the affairs of the nations comes from Dt 32:8–9, where Yahweh notes that he chose Israel as his own people and allowed other nations to be under the dominion of the "sons of God" (see note on Dt 32:8).

82:3–4 The four nouns used in the Hebrew text of Ps 82:3–4 commonly occur in the OT to refer to the socially marginalized. The language the psalmist uses emphasizes the need for the wicked (who could be rich or poor) to be prevented from mistreating the lower social classes. The lowest classes—which were commonly neglected in ancient Near Eastern cultures—were to be protected. The divine order God commands would remedy this situation.

82:4 deliver them from the hand of the wicked In God's ultimatum to the corrupt gods (*elohim* in Hebrew; see note on v. 1), God calls for the wicked to be stripped of power and for true justice to be restored.

82:5 the foundations of the earth The Hebrew phrase used here, *mosde erets*, reflects ancient Near Eastern (and Israelite) cosmology. The ancient Israelites believed the world rested on pillars or a foundation. See the infographic "Ancient Hebrew Conception of the Universe" on p. 5. **are shaken** The psalmist describes the failure of the gods (*elohim* in Hebrew) as having cosmic consequences. The very stability of all life was threatened when the gods were disloyal to God (Yahweh).

82:6 you are all A plural pronoun is used here in Hebrew. **sons of the Most High** The Hebrew phrase used here is a synonym for the more common Hebrew phrase *bene elohim* (usually translated "sons of God"). It denotes divine beings (see Ge 6:2,4; Job 1:6; 2:1; 38:7; Dt 32:8).

82:7 you will die like mere mortals Although the gods (*elohim* in Hebrew) are not people, they will die like people do (compare note on Ps 82:1). By definition, no created thing is truly eternal unless Yahweh makes it such; as a result, even divine beings have conditional immortality—they don't have a lifespan, but their life depends on God's will and discretion.

82:8 Rise up, O God The singular Hebrew imperative used here, *qumah*, indicates that the Hebrew word *elohim* is singular here and should be translated as "God" (compare note on v. 1). The psalmist calls on God to rise up and judge the whole earth, reclaiming the nations he disinherited and allowed to come under the jurisdiction

Psalm 83[a]

A song. A psalm of Asaph.

[1] O God, do not remain silent;
do not turn a deaf ear,
do not stand aloof, O God.
[2] See how your enemies growl,
how your foes rear their heads.
[3] With cunning they conspire against your people;
they plot against those you cherish.
[4] "Come," they say, "let us destroy them as a nation,
so that Israel's name is remembered no more."

[5] With one mind they plot together;
they form an alliance against you —
[6] the tents of Edom and the Ishmaelites,
of Moab and the Hagrites,
[7] Byblos, Ammon and Amalek,
Philistia, with the people of Tyre.
[8] Even Assyria has joined them
to reinforce Lot's descendants.[b]

[9] Do to them as you did to Midian,
as you did to Sisera and Jabin at the river Kishon,
[10] who perished at Endor
and became like dung on the ground.
[11] Make their nobles like Oreb and Zeeb,
all their princes like Zebah and Zalmunna,
[12] who said, "Let us take possession
of the pasturelands of God."

[a] In Hebrew texts 83:1-18 is numbered 83:2-19.   [b] 8 The Hebrew has *Selah* (a word of uncertain meaning) here.

---

of other gods at Babel (see note on Dt 32:8; note on 32:9). Some of the earliest poetry in the OT presents the idea of Yahweh's global kingly reign (see Ps 29:10; Ex 15:18; compare Dt 2:9,19).

83:title–18 In this corporate lament psalm (meant for group settings)—which is specifically identified as a song—the psalmist focuses on Israel's neighbors and requests that God act against them as he did against Israel's enemies in the past. He opens by requesting that God act in response to the uproar that Israel's enemies make (Ps 83:1–2) because those enemies have banded together to destroy his people (vv. 3–4). The psalmist lists those nations that have conspired against God himself (vv. 5–7), ending with the powerful kingdom of Assyria (v. 8). He then recalls God's past rescues of Israel, listing several enemies who attempted to destroy Israel (vv. 9–11) to obtain their land (v. 12). The psalmist asks God to totally destroy them (vv. 13–15) and humiliate them so that his reputation would be supreme (vv. 16–18). The psalm contains many names of nations in the psalmist's time as well as several instances of deliverance in Israel's history. See the table "Types of Psalms" on p. 830.

83:title A psalm See note on 3:title. **of Asaph** See note on 73:title.

83:1–4 The psalmist opens by focusing on the concepts of speech and noise, and requests that God speak against Israel's enemies (v. 1). Here, the psalmist describes the enemies of Israel (vv. 2–4); later, he depicts them as enemies of God himself (v. 5).

83:1–2 These verses portray the interaction between God and the nations in terms of speech.

83:2 growl The Hebrew word used here, *hamah*, portrays noisy rebellion and chaos.

83:3 against your people The enemies initially focus on his people; later, the psalmist will portray them opposing God directly (v. 5).

83:4 Israel's name God will protect the name of Israel when he forces Israel's enemies to recognize his name (vv. 16,18).

83:5–8 The psalmist depicts the adversaries of Israel as enemies of God (v. 5). When viewed on a map, the enemies almost totally surround Israel (vv. 6–7). The

superpower of Assyria is the final enemy on the list, and it is depicted in terms of the regional rivalries that trouble Israel (v. 8).

83:5 an alliance The psalmist may be contrasting the foreign nations' plan to destroy Israel with God's covenant to protect Israel (Dt 28–30).

83:6 Edom Descendants of Jacob's half brother Esau. See Ps 108:9 and note. **Ishmaelites** Ishmael was the half brother of Isaac (see Ge 16:1–16; 21:8–21); the Ishmaelites became an ancient rival of the nation of Israel. **Moab** Illegitimate descendants of Lot, the nephew of Abraham. See note on Ru 1:1. **Hagrites** Probably the descendants of Ishmael's mother, Hagar (see Ge 16; compare 1Ch 5:10,19–20).

83:7 Byblos May refer to a city in the territory of Edom or a port city on the coast north of Israel. **Ammon** One of the children of Lot (see Ge 19:30–38). His descendants, along with Moab, became an ancient rival of Israel. **Amalek** The Amalekites were the first enemies that Israel faced after they left Egypt (Ex 17:8–16). They became symbolic of any enemy that sought to destroy Israel (Ex 17:16). **Philistia** The Philistines were bitter enemies against Israel, especially during the time of Saul and David. **Tyre** An important trading center north of Israel on the Mediterranean coast. The trading activities of Tyre involved settling port cities around the Mediterranean, possibly resulting in religious syncretism that influenced Israel.

83:8 to reinforce Lot's descendants The psalmist depicts the military power of the Assyrian Empire in terms of the regional rivalries of Israel. He implies that Moab and Ammon have entered into a military alliance with Assyria against Israel.

83:9–12 In response to the enemies that Israel faces, the psalmist recounts past instances when God has delivered Israel when they were vulnerable (Ps 83:9–11). He petitions that Israel not be separated from the land that God has given them (v. 12).

83:9 Midian An enemy of Israel at several points in their history (e.g., Jdg 6–7). **Sisera** During the time of the Judges, Sisera was commander of Jabin's army, which oppressed Israel (Jdg 4:2–3). **Jabin** A king in the northern part of Canaan who oppressed Israel during the time of the Judges (see Jdg 4:2,24).

13 Make them like tumbleweed, my God,
    like chaff before the wind.
14 As fire consumes the forest
    or a flame sets the mountains ablaze,
15 so pursue them with your tempest
    and terrify them with your storm.
16 Cover their faces with shame, LORD,
    so that they will seek your name.

17 May they ever be ashamed and dismayed;
    may they perish in disgrace.
18 Let them know that you, whose name is the
    LORD —
    that you alone are the Most High over all
    the earth.

Psalm 84[a]

For the director of music. According to gittith.[b]
Of the Sons of Korah. A psalm.

1 How lovely is your dwelling place,
    LORD Almighty!
2 My soul yearns, even faints,
    for the courts of the LORD;

my heart and my flesh cry out
    for the living God.
3 Even the sparrow has found a home,
    and the swallow a nest for herself,
    where she may have her young —
a place near your altar,
    LORD Almighty, my King and my God.
4 Blessed are those who dwell in your house;
    they are ever praising you.[c]

5 Blessed are those whose strength is in you,
    whose hearts are set on pilgrimage.
6 As they pass through the Valley of Baka,
    they make it a place of springs;
    the autumn rains also cover it with pools.[d]
7 They go from strength to strength,
    till each appears before God in Zion.

8 Hear my prayer, LORD God Almighty;
    listen to me, God of Jacob.
9 Look on our shield,[e] O God;
    look with favor on your anointed one.

a In Hebrew texts 84:1-12 is numbered 84:2-13.   b Title:
Probably a musical term   c 4 The Hebrew has *Selah* (a word of
uncertain meaning) here and at the end of verse 8.
d 6 Or *blessings*   e 9 Or *sovereign*

83:11 Oreb and Zeeb Princes of Midian from the story of Gideon (see Jdg 7:25). **Zebah and Zalmunna** Enemies of Israel from the story of Gideon (see Jdg 8:1–21).
83:12 the pasturelands of God Refers to the land of Israel; the enemies implicitly identify Israel as sheep and God as their shepherd. Their statement thus mocks God because it implies that the divine shepherd cannot protect his sheep.

83:13–18 After recounting past events when God delivered his people, the psalmist requests that God destroy his enemies (Ps 83:13–15). The psalmist hopes that his enemies will be humiliated and forced to recognize God's supreme power (vv. 17–18).

83:16 so that they will seek your name The psalmist seems to indicate that God's enemies will plead for mercy in desperation after they are defeated.
83:18 Let them know Knowledge of God can have both positive and negative ramifications. Here the sense is that God's enemies will know his power as he decisively judges them.

84:title–12 In this song of Zion—the psalms that focus on Yahweh's presence in the temple in Jerusalem (compare Ps 46; 48; 76; 84; 87; 122)—the psalmist emphasizes the joyful experience of the worshipers within the temple. He opens by admiring Yahweh's temple and then expresses joy in Yahweh (84:1–2). The psalmist describes how Yahweh cares for his creatures by providing a place for all of them at the temple (v. 3) so that they might be blessed in their worship of God (v. 4). He develops the theme of blessing at the worship site by depicting how Yahweh enables all those who desire to worship him to make their way to Zion, the temple mount (vv. 5–7). He then alludes to the anointed ruler of Israel and asks that Yahweh help him (vv. 8–9). The psalmist returns to the theme of blessing and emphasizes the joy that comes from being in the temple (v. 10) because of Yahweh's generosity to those who are faithful to him (vv. 11–12). See the table "Types of Psalms" on p. 830.

84:title director of music See note on 4:title. **gittith** See note on 8:title. **Sons of Korah** See note on 42:title. **A psalm** See note on 3:title.

84:1–4 The psalmist emphasizes his joy in worshiping Yahweh (vv. 1–2). He describes how Yahweh cares for those who worship him by providing a place for all creation to worship him at the temple (v. 3).

84:1 LORD Almighty The Hebrew text here uses the phrase *yhwh tseva'oth*. See note on 24:10.
84:2 my heart and my flesh cry out Other psalms speak highly of the temple (e.g., 138:2), but the psalmist's focus on the joy of the worship experience at the Jerusalem temple is a special feature of Ps 84.
84:3 my God In the Hebrew text, Yahweh (*yhwh*) is specifically identified as the God and king of the worshiper.
84:4 those who dwell in your house This may refer to the literal servants in the temple or it may be a depiction of people who are so consumed by the experience of worship that they are almost always worshiping at the temple.

84:5–7 The psalmist envisions Yahweh's help to those who are traveling to Zion (v. 5). Yahweh provides for them (v. 6) until they are finally able to appear before him in worship (v. 7).

84:7 appears before God in Zion Three annual festivals in Israel were called pilgrimage festivals because worshipers were required to travel to Jerusalem to come before Yahweh in worship at the temple (see Dt 16:1–17).

84:8–9 The psalmist draws attention to the role of the king in Israel's welfare and asks Yahweh to help his human representative on earth (Ps 84:9).

84:9 our shield The Hebrew word used here, *magen*, seems to refer to God's anointed ruler in this instance, the king, who was also Israel's military leader. In v. 11, the Hebrew word used here, *magen*, refers to God himself. Compare 115:9 and note.

¹⁰ Better is one day in your courts
    than a thousand elsewhere;
I would rather be a doorkeeper in the house
        of my God
    than dwell in the tents of the wicked.
¹¹ For the LORD God is a sun and shield;
    the LORD bestows favor and honor;
no good thing does he withhold
    from those whose walk is blameless.

¹² LORD Almighty,
    blessed is the one who trusts in you.

Psalm 85^a

For the director of music. Of the Sons of Korah.
A psalm.

¹ You, LORD, showed favor to your land;
    you restored the fortunes of Jacob.
² You forgave the iniquity of your people
    and covered all their sins.^b
³ You set aside all your wrath
    and turned from your fierce anger.

⁴ Restore us again, God our Savior,
    and put away your displeasure toward us.
⁵ Will you be angry with us forever?
    Will you prolong your anger through all
        generations?
⁶ Will you not revive us again,
    that your people may rejoice in you?
⁷ Show us your unfailing love, LORD,
    and grant us your salvation.

⁸ I will listen to what God the LORD says;
    he promises peace to his people, his
        faithful servants —
    but let them not turn to folly.
⁹ Surely his salvation is near those who
        fear him,
    that his glory may dwell in our land.

¹⁰ Love and faithfulness meet together;
    righteousness and peace kiss each other.
¹¹ Faithfulness springs forth from the earth,
    and righteousness looks down from heaven.

^a In Hebrew texts 85:1-13 is numbered 85:2-14.   ^b 2 The
Hebrew has *Selah* (a word of uncertain meaning) here.

84:10–12 The psalmist returns to praising Yahweh's temple (v. 10) because of Yahweh's care for those who honor him and trust him (vv. 11–12).

84:10 a doorkeeper The psalmist states that simply being close to Yahweh's temple is better than being in any other place.

85:title–13 This corporate lament psalm (meant for group settings) contains a prophetic element—focusing on hope in God's future help. The psalmist opens by recounting Yahweh's past restoration of Israel (v. 1), especially his forgiveness of their sins (vv. 2–3). He then pleads for God to restore Israel again and begs that he set aside his anger at his people (vv. 4–5), show his love to them and rescue them (vv. 6–7). The psalmist (or the people present) then requests to hear what Yahweh will say to Israel when he rescues them (v. 8) and emphasizes trust in God's loyalty to those who honor and love him (v. 9). The final section of the psalm is a prophecy portraying love and faithfulness between God and Israel (vv. 10–11). Yahweh will provide good things for his people who are faithful, in accordance with his character (vv. 12–13). See the table "Types of Psalms" on p. 830.

85:title director of music See note on 4:title. **Sons of Korah** See note on 42:title. **A psalm** See note on 6:title.

85:1–3 The psalmist begins by recounting God's past restoration of Israel after he has punished their unfaithfulness (see Dt 28–30).

85:1 your land Yahweh's purposes for Israel meant both them inhabiting Canaan and being faithful to his covenant with them (see Jos 1:1–9).

85:2 You forgave The Hebrew verb used here, *nasa*, means to "lift" or "take away." God removes the ramifications of iniquities.

85:4–7 The psalmist pleads for God to restore Israel as he did before (Ps 85:4). He identifies the situation

the people are in as God's punishment for their sin (v. 5) and pleads for God to forgive Israel and help his people (vv. 6–7).

85:6 Will you not revive us again Portrays Israel's captivity and separation from the promised land as death for the nation (compare vv. 1,9,12). **that your people may rejoice in you** The psalmist implicitly commits to praising God after he rescues Israel. The purpose of God's rescue would be that his reputation would be honored.

85:8–9 The identity of the voice in vv. 8–9 is unclear; it may be the individual psalmist or the nation as a group. This unit may portray a liturgical statement that the people of Israel would speak during the performance of the psalm. Compare note on 85:title–13.

85:8 peace The Hebrew word *shalom* can refer to overall well-being and wholeness. See note on 120:6. **let them not turn to folly** By Yahweh being faithful to Israel, he will enable his people to be faithful to him in return (see Jer 31:31–34; compare Jer 32:36–41).

85:9 in our land Although the psalmist does not specifically mention the captivity or exile of God's people, he seems to imply it by stating that glory does not presently dwell in the land of Israel.

85:10–13 This passage is a prophetic statement of hope in Yahweh's future mercy. It is unclear whether Yahweh speaks directly in Ps 85:10–11. Essentially, vv. 10–11 state that Israel will be faithful to Yahweh and Yahweh will love Israel.

Verses 12–13 may be part of the preceding prophetic statement, but they might also be a concluding expression of hope in response to the prediction of future harmony between God and Israel.

85:10 Love and faithfulness meet together The psalmist portrays mutual faithfulness between Yahweh and Israel. **righteousness and peace** Israel's unfaithfulness has made it impossible for righteousness and peace to exist together because Yahweh's righteousness could not tolerate Israel's waywardness (see v. 8).

¹²The Lᴏʀᴅ will indeed give what is good,
and our land will yield its harvest.
¹³Righteousness goes before him
and prepares the way for his steps.

Psalm 86

A prayer of David.

¹Hear me, Lᴏʀᴅ, and answer me,
for I am poor and needy.
²Guard my life, for I am faithful to you;
save your servant who trusts in you.
You are my God; ³have mercy on me, Lord,
for I call to you all day long.
⁴Bring joy to your servant, Lord,
for I put my trust in you.

⁵You, Lord, are forgiving and good,
abounding in love to all who call to you.

⁶Hear my prayer, Lᴏʀᴅ;
listen to my cry for mercy.
⁷When I am in distress, I call to you,
because you answer me.

⁸Among the gods there is none like you, Lord;
no deeds can compare with yours.
⁹All the nations you have made
will come and worship before you, Lord;
they will bring glory to your name.
¹⁰For you are great and do marvelous deeds;
you alone are God.

¹¹Teach me your way, Lᴏʀᴅ,
that I may rely on your faithfulness;
give me an undivided heart,
that I may fear your name.
¹²I will praise you, Lord my God, with all my
heart;
I will glorify your name forever.

85:13 Righteousness goes before him This phrase may have an intentional double meaning: God's righteousness (*tsedeq* in Hebrew) enables Israel's faithfulness, and Israel's righteousness makes it so that Yahweh can express his love without violating his character (compare vv. 10–11).

86:title–17 In this individual lament psalm, the psalmist—a servant of God (vv. 2,4,16)—pleads for God's help against ruthless enemies (v. 14). The psalmist begins by asking Yahweh to help him, distinguishing himself by his faithfulness and great need (vv. 1–2). He lifts his soul in desperation (vv. 3–4), calling on God because of his kind nature (v. 5) and history of helping him (vv. 6–7). The psalmist recalls Yahweh's superiority over all other deities (v. 8) and predicts that someday all nations will worship him (vv. 9–10). He then asks God to instruct him and transform him (v. 11) so that he might praise him (vv. 12–13). The psalmist focuses on his enemies again, noting their ruthlessness and their dishonor of God (v. 14). He concludes by noting God's loving nature (v. 15) and pleads that God will rescue him (v. 16) and put his enemies to shame (v. 17).

Psalm 86 is characterized by the psalmist's distinguishing between names for God that are almost synonymous in other parts of the Bible. The psalmist sets the Hebrew names *yhwh* (Yahweh; vv. 1,6,11,17) and *adonay* ("my Lord" or "my master"; vv. 3,4,5,8,9,12,15) beside each other to emphasize his personal commitment to God. He also uses the general Hebrew title *elohim* ("God"; vv. 2,10,12,14,15) to portray his interaction with God, the object of his personal loyalty and the supreme Deity. See the table "Types of Psalms" on p. 830.

86:title A prayer The Hebrew word used here, *tephillah*, may indicate a prayer of supplication that would characterize a lament psalm. **of David** Psalm 86 is the only psalm affiliated with David in Book Three of the Psalms (Ps 73–89; see note on 1:1–6; compare note on 72:20).

86:1–7 In the opening passage, the psalmist identifies his role as Yahweh's servant (vv. 2,4) and, in the Hebrew text, introduces the personal name *yhwh* (Yahweh; vv. 1,6) and the title *adonay* ("my Lord"; vv. 3,4,5).

86:1 Lᴏʀᴅ The Hebrew word *yhwh* (Yahweh) is the personal name God revealed to Moses in Ex 3:13–15. **poor and needy** The Hebrew words used here, *ani* and *evyon*,

often occur together. While both are associated with poverty and need, *evyon* seems to particularly convey misery that results from oppression.

86:2 your servant The psalmist identifies himself as Yahweh's servant (*eved* in Hebrew; see Ps 86:3,4,16), possibly indicating a special relationship with Yahweh beyond general submission (compare Dt 34:5; Jos 24:29). **my God** Although the psalmist uses several terms for God, he only uses the Hebrew term *elohay* here and in Ps 86:12.

86:3 Lord The Hebrew word used here, *adonay* (which literally means "my master"), occurs as a title for God more often in Ps 86 than any other psalm (vv. 4,5,8,9,12,15). It refers to God as divine master.

86:5 in love The psalmist connects God's love (*chesed* in Hebrew) to anyone who calls upon him. Later, the psalmist declares how God's love has been personally expressed to him (v. 13). In v. 15, the psalmist appeals to God's love. See note on 25:10.

86:8–13 In this passage, the psalmist describes God's worthiness and God's personal commitment to him. He anticipates that all the nations will one day recognize God's excellence and come to worship him (vv. 8–10). In response, he asks that God teach him and change him (v. 11) so that he might praise him (v. 12). The psalmist closes by asserting that God will rescue him, portraying his deliverance as already complete (v. 13).

86:8 Among the gods The God of Israel, Yahweh—whom the psalmist also calls his Lord (or master)—is superior to all other divine beings (*elohim* in Hebrew). He demonstrates this by being creator of all nations (v. 11). Compare Ps 82:1 and note; 136:2 and note; compare 138:1.

86:9 All the nations you have made The nations that are under the jurisdiction of other gods will break free of them and come and worship their creator, the God of Israel. Compare 82:2 and note.

86:10 you alone are God The Hebrew word used here, *elohim*, often emphasizes God's status as the supreme deity; he is the creator of all, including other spiritual beings.

86:11 that I may fear your name Refers to revering, honoring and obeying God (see 90:11 and note). God's name (*yhwh* in Hebrew) represents his reputation.

¹³ For great is your love toward me;
　　you have delivered me from the depths,
　　from the realm of the dead.

¹⁴ Arrogant foes are attacking me, O God;
　　ruthless people are trying to kill me —
　　they have no regard for you.

¹⁵ But you, Lord, are a compassionate and
　　gracious God,
　　slow to anger, abounding in love and
　　faithfulness.

¹⁶ Turn to me and have mercy on me;
　　show your strength in behalf of your
　　servant;
save me, because I serve you
　　just as my mother did.

¹⁷ Give me a sign of your goodness,
　　that my enemies may see it and be put
　　to shame,
for you, LORD, have helped me and
　　comforted me.

Psalm 87

Of the Sons of Korah. A psalm. A song.

¹ He has founded his city on the holy mountain.
² The LORD loves the gates of Zion
　　more than all the other dwellings of Jacob.

³ Glorious things are said of you,
　　city of God:ᵃ

⁴ "I will record Rahabᵇ and Babylon
　　among those who acknowledge me —
　　Philistia too, and Tyre, along with Cushᶜ —
　　and will say, 'This one was born in Zion.'"ᵈ
⁵ Indeed, of Zion it will be said,
　　"This one and that one were born in her,
　　and the Most High himself will
　　establish her."
⁶ The LORD will write in the register of the
　　peoples:
　　"This one was born in Zion."

⁷ As they make music they will sing,
　　"All my fountains are in you."

Psalm 88ᵉ

*A song. A psalm of the Sons of Korah. For the director
of music. According to* mahalath leannoth.ᶠ
*A maskil*ᵍ *of Heman the Ezrahite.*

¹ LORD, you are the God who saves me;
　　day and night I cry out to you.
² May my prayer come before you;
　　turn your ear to my cry.

ᵃ 3 The Hebrew has *Selah* (a word of uncertain meaning) here
and at the end of verse 6.　　ᵇ 4 A poetic name for Egypt
ᶜ 4 That is, the upper Nile region　　ᵈ 4 Or *"I will record
concerning those who acknowledge me: / 'This one was born in
Zion.' / Hear this, Rahab and Babylon, / and you too, Philistia,
Tyre and Cush."*　　ᵉ In Hebrew texts 88:1-18 is numbered 88:2-
19.　　ᶠ Title: Possibly a tune, "The Suffering of Affliction"
ᵍ Title: Probably a literary or musical term

86:13 the realm of the dead The Hebrew word *she'ol*
is used here (see note on Job 14:13; note on 1Ki 2:6).
The psalmist equates God's work in his life as equivalent to being redeemed from the underworld. In ancient
Hebrew thought, *she'ol* was believed to be below the
earth. See the infographic "Ancient Hebrew Conception
of the Universe" on p. 5.

86:14–17 Up to this point, the psalmist has not given
much attention to his enemies. Even now, he mainly
characterizes his enemies by their impiety—they are
insolent and do not honor God (v. 14). The psalmist
emphasizes the goodness of God's nature in traditional—
but personalized—terms (v. 15; compare Ex 34:6), and
closes by emphasizing his role as a servant of God (Ps
86:16) who is asking for a sign of God's favor (v. 17).

87:title–7 This is a psalm of Zion—one of the psalms
that celebrates Yahweh's presence at the temple mount
in Jerusalem (compare Ps 46; 48; 76; 84; 122). It
includes a prophetic vision of foreign nations coming to
worship in Jerusalem. The psalmist opens by focusing on
Zion—which is virtually synonymous with Jerusalem—as
the city of God, emphasizing Yahweh's care and attention
(87:1–3). He then portrays the foreign nations coming to
worship God and honoring those originally from Jerusalem
(v. 4). This focus on the residents of Zion continues even
as Yahweh records the foreigners who come to Jerusalem
(vv. 5–6). These original residents dance and sing in
honor of the sacred city (v. 7). See the table "Types of
Psalms" on p. 830.

87:title Sons of Korah See note on 42:title. **A psalm**
See note on 3:title.

87:1–3 The psalmist begins by focusing on Jerusalem;
his devotion to the city is symbolic of his loyalty to Yahweh.

87:1 the holy mountain Refers to Mount Zion, the
temple mount in Jerusalem.

87:3 city of God Zion and Jerusalem are often used
interchangeably as names for God's sacred city. Jerusalem was associated with God's presence because the
temple was located there on Mount Zion.

87:4 The psalmist speaks in the persona of Israel and
depicts conversation between Israel and the surrounding
nations. The neighboring nations focus on Jerusalem and
emphasize Israel's unique relationship to the holy city
(and the God who dwells there).

87:4 Rahab Refers to Egypt, an international power
and ancient enemy of Israel (see Isa 30:7). **Babylon** An
international power that eventually destroyed the southern
kingdom of Judah (586 BC) and became a symbol of
wickedness and animosity toward God. **Philistia too,
and Tyre** See note on Ps 83:7. **Cush** The precise location
is uncertain, but it probably refers to the region south
of Egypt. **This one was born** The nations give special
honor to Israel because of its original association with
the sacred city of Jerusalem and the temple there.

87:5–7 The close of Ps 87 maintains the special honor
God gives to Israel—the residents of Zion (v.5) prior to the
events recorded in v. 4—as he writes down the names
of the newcomers to Jerusalem (v. 6). Verse 7 closes
the psalm with worshipers praising Yahweh's presence
in Zion as that which sustains them.

87:6 The LORD will write in the register of the peoples

³ I am overwhelmed with troubles
and my life draws near to death.
⁴ I am counted among those who go down to
the pit;
I am like one without strength.
⁵ I am set apart with the dead,
like the slain who lie in the grave,
whom you remember no more,
who are cut off from your care.

⁶ You have put me in the lowest pit,
in the darkest depths.
⁷ Your wrath lies heavily on me;
you have overwhelmed me with all your
waves.ᵃ
⁸ You have taken from me my closest friends
and have made me repulsive to them.
I am confined and cannot escape;
⁹   my eyes are dim with grief.

I call to you, LORD, every day;
I spread out my hands to you.
¹⁰ Do you show your wonders to the dead?
Do their spirits rise up and praise you?
¹¹ Is your love declared in the grave,
your faithfulness in Destructionᵇ?
¹² Are your wonders known in the place of
darkness,
or your righteous deeds in the land of
oblivion?

¹³ But I cry to you for help, LORD;
in the morning my prayer comes
before you.
¹⁴ Why, LORD, do you reject me
and hide your face from me?

ᵃ 7 The Hebrew has *Selah* (a word of uncertain meaning) here
and at the end of verse 10.   ᵇ 11 Hebrew *Abaddon*

The psalmist portrays Yahweh as recording those coming to Jerusalem in a ledger. **This one was born** This line shows Yahweh's focus, and acknowledgement of, those who were originally connected to Jerusalem.
87:7 As they make music they will sing This could refer to skilled people, perhaps temple personnel, or more generally to the people coming to Jerusalem to worship. **my fountains** Symbolic of life and God's provision.

88:title–18 Psalm 88, which is specifically identified as a song, is an unusually despairing individual lament psalm; it does not include the customary sense of trust or hope that usually closes such psalms. The psalmist first describes his ceaseless desperation as he pleads to Yahweh (vv. 1–2). He sees himself as virtually dead (vv. 3–5) and views his agonizing situation as the result of God's judgment (vv. 6–7). He is so afflicted that his friends avoid him (v. 8) and he has no way to escape (v. 9). He then describes his pleas (v. 9) and asks a series of rhetorical questions that function as requests for Yahweh to rescue him (vv. 10–12). The psalmist refers to his ongoing pleas for help (v. 13) and expresses his anguish before Yahweh (v. 14) as he depicts the nearness of his pain (v. 15). He finds his affliction to be overwhelming (vv. 16–17) and concludes by saying that he is utterly alone except for his suffering (v. 18). Compare note on vv. 13–18. See the table "Types of Psalms" on p. 830.

88:title psalm See note on 3:title. **Sons of Korah** See note on 42:title. **director of music** See note on 4:title. **mahalath** See note on 53:title. **leannoth** The Hebrew term used here is a form of the Hebrew verb *anah* (meaning "to afflict"). It may refer to the affliction that the psalm portrays. Alternatively, it could be read in connection with the preceding term, *mahalath*. **maskil** See note on 32:title. **Heman the Ezrahite** Compare 1Ki 4:31; 1Ch 2:6.

88:1–9 The psalmist recounts his troubles and takes them to Yahweh, whom he views as the ultimate source of his trouble and also its ultimate solution. He sees his rescue as coming from God's attention and direct help (Ps 88:5).

88:1 day and night I cry out The psalmist emphasizes his constant pleading.
88:3 death The Hebrew word *she'ol* is used here. See note on Job 14:13; note on 1Ki 2:6.
88:4 pit The Hebrew word used here, *bor*, can refer to a pit or a cistern. It is used metaphorically to refer to the grave.
88:5 I am set apart with the dead One of many Hebrew images of death.
88:7 Your wrath lies heavily on me The psalmist attributes his suffering to God's judgment.
88:8 You have taken from me my closest friends It is unclear whether the psalmist's isolation is a result of God's direct action or a result of the psalmist's disturbing, possibly repulsive condition. Compare Ps 88:18.

88:9–12 In the second half of v. 9, the psalmist re-emphasizes his continual pleading; he then presents a series of questions that function as requests for Yahweh's help (vv. 10–12). The psalmist appeals to Yahweh's reputation, emphasizing that dead people cannot praise God and declare his wonders and thus Yahweh should help him. In his suffering, the psalmist stops short of extending these questions to a sense of hope and trust.

88:10 spirits The psalmist shows no hope in death; for him, in his current emotional state, it seems like the end.
88:11 Destruction The Hebrew word used here, *avaddon*, is sometimes used synonymously with the Hebrew word *she'ol*, the term for the realm of the dead (Job 26:6). *Avaddon* refers to a place of perishing, ruin or destruction. See note on Job 31:12.
88:12 darkness A symbol of death (compare Ps 107:18 and note; 88:18). **land of oblivion** A Hebrew image for death. Other psalms reflect the opposite belief—that God's presence is even known in the realm of the dead (see 22:29 and note).

88:13–18 The psalmist resumes his pleading (v. 13) and accuses Yahweh of afflicting him through neglect (v. 14). He sees himself as helpless and overwhelmed before God (vv. 15–17). The psalmist concludes with an especially bleak note of loneliness (v. 18). Psalms such as this one, despite being accusatory of Yahweh, actually express faith in him by directing concerns to him. The accusations of Yahweh do not necessarily accurately depict Yahweh's character or his actual role in the psalmist's life—instead, they express the emotion of the psalmist toward Yahweh. In this regard, psalms like this one show that Yahweh is willing to listen to any and all prayers directed faithfully to him.

88:14 hide your face Yahweh's face symbolizes his attention, representing his presence and relationship with

¹⁵ From my youth I have suffered and been
close to death;
I have borne your terrors and am in
despair.
¹⁶ Your wrath has swept over me;
your terrors have destroyed me.
¹⁷ All day long they surround me like a flood;
they have completely engulfed me.
¹⁸ You have taken from me friend and
neighbor —
darkness is my closest friend.

Psalm 89 *ᵃ*

A maskil ᵇ of Ethan the Ezrahite.

¹ I will sing of the LORD's great love forever;
with my mouth I will make your
faithfulness known
through all generations.
² I will declare that your love stands firm
forever,
that you have established your faithfulness
in heaven itself.
³ You said, "I have made a covenant with my
chosen one,
I have sworn to David my servant,
⁴ 'I will establish your line forever
and make your throne firm through all
generations.'" ᶜ

⁵ The heavens praise your wonders, LORD,
your faithfulness too, in the assembly of
the holy ones.
⁶ For who in the skies above can compare with
the LORD?
Who is like the LORD among the heavenly
beings?
⁷ In the council of the holy ones God is greatly
feared;
he is more awesome than all who
surround him.
⁸ Who is like you, LORD God Almighty?
You, LORD, are mighty, and your
faithfulness surrounds you.

⁹ You rule over the surging sea;
when its waves mount up, you still them.
¹⁰ You crushed Rahab like one of the slain;
with your strong arm you scattered your
enemies.
¹¹ The heavens are yours, and yours also the
earth;
you founded the world and all that is in it.
¹² You created the north and the south;
Tabor and Hermon sing for joy at your
name.

ᵃ In Hebrew texts 89:1-52 is numbered 89:2-53.   *ᵇ* Title:
Probably a literary or musical term   *ᶜ 4* The Hebrew has *Selah*
(a word of uncertain meaning) here and at the end of verses 37,
45 and 48.

---

him. Even though the psalmist attributes his suffering to God's actions, he also portrays his suffering as a result of God's neglect. Compare note on vv. 13–18.

89:title–52 Psalm 89 combines aspects of royal psalms (in honor of the king) and corporate lament psalms. It has three clearly marked sections. The first section (vv. 1–18) is a hymn to Yahweh's kingship. The second (vv. 19–37) is a divine oracle in which Yahweh restates the Davidic covenant. The third (vv. 38–51) is a lament in which the psalmist mourns the fact that Yahweh seems to have rejected his people. The first two sections assert Yahweh's power and offer a reminder of his promises. The psalmist uses these assertions as motivation for his lament as he cries out to Yahweh to fulfill his promise to his people (v. 49). The final verse (v. 52) is a doxology that concludes Book Three of the psalms (Ps 73–89; see 1:1–6). See the table "Types of Psalms" on p. 830.

89:title *maskil* See note on 32:title. **Ethan the Ezrahite** One of David's singers along with Asaph (1Ch 15:19).
89:2 love stands firm forever Yahweh's steadfast love and faithfulness provides the basis for the psalmist's desire to sing (Ps 89:1).

89:3–4 The theme of Yahweh's covenant with David (see 2Sa 7:1–17 and note) runs throughout Ps 89, especially in vv. 19–37. The psalmist bases his lament on Yahweh's apparent abandonment of his covenant (vv. 39,49).

89:5 The heavens praise your wonders, LORD Other psalms likewise personify the heavens as praising Yahweh (19:1; 50:6). **in the assembly of the holy ones** A reference to Yahweh's divine council or heavenly host (see 89:7), who assist him in administering the affairs

of heaven and earth (compare 1Ki 22:19–23). The Hebrew term used here, *qedoshim* ("holy ones"), is also used elsewhere to speak of divine beings (Dt 33:2–3; Job 5:1; 15:15; Zec 14:5; Da 4:17). Psalm 82 focuses on God's divine council (see note on 82:1).

89:6 heavenly beings The Hebrew phrase used here, *bene' elim* — which can be literally rendered as "sons of God" — refers to the divine beings of the heavenly host (see note on 82:1).

89:7 the council of the holy ones See note on 89:5.
all who surround him Refers to the holy ones (*qedoshim* in Hebrew) or heavenly beings (*bene' elim* in Hebrew). No other divine being is comparable to Yahweh, the God of Israel, for he created everything. Compare v. 8.

89:9 surging sea A common ancient Near Eastern image of disorder and cosmic chaos. Only the God of Israel, Yahweh, can truly restrain this force (see Ge 1:2). In Ps 89:25, Yahweh extends this power to the anointed, Davidic king. See the infographic "Ancient Hebrew Conception of the Universe" on p. 5.

89:10 Rahab A mythical sea monster akin to Leviathan (see 74:13–14), which symbolized the forces of chaos (see v. 9). (This monster is not related to the Rahab of Jos 2.) Some ancient Near Eastern creation traditions described the gods subduing an original primeval chaos to bring about an orderly world for humans to live in. This psalm and others (e.g., Ps 74:12–17) reflect a similar conception of the world (see Ge 1:2), but show that Yahweh is the one who created order out of chaos — demonstrating his vast superiority to all other deities.

89:11–12 The psalmist points to Yahweh's work of creation and illustrates his sovereignty over all of the heavens and earth.

13 Your arm is endowed with power;
    your hand is strong, your right hand exalted.

14 Righteousness and justice are the foundation
        of your throne;
    love and faithfulness go before you.

15 Blessed are those who have learned to
        acclaim you,
    who walk in the light of your presence,
        LORD.

16 They rejoice in your name all day long;
    they celebrate your righteousness.

17 For you are their glory and strength,
    and by your favor you exalt our horn.[a]

18 Indeed, our shield[b] belongs to the LORD,
    our king to the Holy One of Israel.

19 Once you spoke in a vision,
    to your faithful people you said:
"I have bestowed strength on a warrior;
    I have raised up a young man from among
        the people.

20 I have found David my servant;
    with my sacred oil I have anointed him.

21 My hand will sustain him;
    surely my arm will strengthen him.

22 The enemy will not get the better of him;
    the wicked will not oppress him.

23 I will crush his foes before him
    and strike down his adversaries.

24 My faithful love will be with him,
    and through my name his horn[c] will be
        exalted.

25 I will set his hand over the sea,
    his right hand over the rivers.

26 He will call out to me, 'You are my Father,
    my God, the Rock my Savior.'

27 And I will appoint him to be my firstborn,
    the most exalted of the kings of the earth.

28 I will maintain my love to him forever,
    and my covenant with him will never fail.

29 I will establish his line forever,
    his throne as long as the heavens endure.

30 "If his sons forsake my law
    and do not follow my statutes,

31 if they violate my decrees
    and fail to keep my commands,

32 I will punish their sin with the rod,
    their iniquity with flogging;

33 but I will not take my love from him,
    nor will I ever betray my faithfulness.

34 I will not violate my covenant
    or alter what my lips have uttered.

35 Once for all, I have sworn by my holiness—
    and I will not lie to David—

36 that his line will continue forever
    and his throne endure before me like
        the sun;

37 it will be established forever like the moon,
    the faithful witness in the sky."

38 But you have rejected, you have spurned,
    you have been very angry with your
        anointed one.

39 You have renounced the covenant with your
        servant
    and have defiled his crown in the dust.

---

a 17 *Horn* here symbolizes strong one.   *b* 18 Or *sovereign*
c 24 *Horn* here symbolizes strength.

89:13 Your arm is endowed with power A symbol of Yahweh's strength. See Ps 44:3 and note.

89:17 horn A symbol of power and strength. Yahweh's favor exalts his people to a position of power.

89:19–37 The psalmist presents a divine oracle in which Yahweh affirms the promise he made to David to establish his kingdom forever. This section uses many of the same terms as vv. 1–18 and makes several allusions to the Davidic covenant of 2Sa 7:1–17.

89:20 I have found David my servant Yahweh chose David after rejecting Saul as king (see 1Sa 13:14 and note). **I have anointed** The Hebrew verb used here, *mashach*, refers to the process of officially installing a king in Israel. See note on Ps 2:2.

89:23 I will crush his foes before him Yahweh promised David rest from his enemies. See 2Sa 7:11 and note.

89:25 I will set his hand over the sea Refers to Yahweh giving power to the Davidic king that resembles Yahweh's very strength. Compare Ps 89:9 and note.

89:26 You are my Father, my God A reference to the covenant promised to David. See 2Sa 7:14 and note. **Rock** A common image of Yahweh's protection. See note on Ps 18:1–3.

89:27 I will appoint him to be my firstborn Yahweh also refers to the entire nation of Israel as his firstborn (see Ex 4:22 and note).

89:28 my love Reminiscent of Yahweh's promise to

David (see 2Sa 7:15 and note). Yahweh reiterates that he is absolutely faithful in fulfilling his promises.

89:29 I will establish his line forever Yahweh promised to establish David's throne and offspring forever. See 2Sa 7:13 and note.

89:30–32 Just as in the Davidic covenant, Yahweh establishes that he will punish the Davidic line if they forsake him (see 2Sa 7:14 and note). He reaffirmed this warning to Solomon at the dedication of the temple (see 1Ki 9:6–9).

89:33–51 In this third section of the psalm (see note on 89:title–52) the psalmist laments that Yahweh has carried out the actions he described that he would in vv. 30–32.

89:33 nor will I ever betray my faithfulness This promise is especially important in the final section of the psalm (Ps 89:38–51). As the psalmist laments Yahweh's apparent abandonment, he appeals to Yahweh's steadfast love and faithfulness (see v. 49 and note).

89:35 by my holiness Possibly a reference to the temple.

89:38 But you have rejected The psalmist draws an emphatic contrast between Yahweh's promise to establish the Davidic kingdom forever and Israel's current state.

89:39 defiled his crown in the dust Rather than lifting up his horn (v. 24), Yahweh has thrown down the crown of the Davidic dynasty.

⁴⁰You have broken through all his walls
and reduced his strongholds to ruins.
⁴¹All who pass by have plundered him;
he has become the scorn of his neighbors.
⁴²You have exalted the right hand of his foes;
you have made all his enemies rejoice.
⁴³Indeed, you have turned back the edge of his
sword
and have not supported him in battle.
⁴⁴You have put an end to his splendor
and cast his throne to the ground.
⁴⁵You have cut short the days of his youth;
you have covered him with a mantle of
shame.

⁴⁶How long, LORD? Will you hide yourself
forever?
How long will your wrath burn like fire?
⁴⁷Remember how fleeting is my life.
For what futility you have created all
humanity!
⁴⁸Who can live and not see death,
or who can escape the power of the
grave?
⁴⁹Lord, where is your former great love,
which in your faithfulness you swore to
David?
⁵⁰Remember, Lord, how your servant hasᵃ been
mocked,
how I bear in my heart the taunts of all the
nations,

⁵¹the taunts with which your enemies, LORD,
have mocked,
with which they have mocked every step
of your anointed one.

⁵²Praise be to the LORD forever!
Amen and Amen.

BOOK IV

Psalms 90–106

Psalm 90

A prayer of Moses the man of God.

¹Lord, you have been our dwelling place
throughout all generations.
²Before the mountains were born
or you brought forth the whole world,
from everlasting to everlasting you
are God.

³You turn people back to dust,
saying, "Return to dust, you
mortals."
⁴A thousand years in your sight
are like a day that has just gone by,
or like a watch in the night.

ᵃ 50 Or your servants have

89:40 reduced his strongholds to ruins Yahweh had promised to be Israel's protection (v. 26). Instead, in the psalmist's view, Yahweh has destroyed the stronghold of his people.

89:42–43 Instead of exalting his chosen king and giving him victory over his enemies (vv. 22–23), Yahweh has exalted the enemies of the king and given them victory. Compare note on vv. 33–51.

89:45 you have covered him with a mantle of shame The psalmist feels that his trust in Yahweh's promises has been misplaced because of his suffering. See note on 25:2.

89:47 Remember how fleeting is my life The psalmist calls attention to the brevity of human life to convince Yahweh to act.

89:48 the grave The Hebrew word *she'ol* is used here, which refers to the realm of the dead (the underworld; see note on Job 14:13; note on 1Ki 2:6).

89:49 where is your former great love The psalmist appeals to Yahweh's steadfast love and faithfulness (see Ps 89:1; compare 25:10 and note).

89:50 Remember Petitions for remembrance (*zakhar* in Hebrew) are common in laments. See note on Job 10:9. **your servant** The psalmist emphasizes that the nations are mocking Yahweh's own servants, which reflects poorly on Yahweh's reputation (see Ps 74:title–23 and note).

89:52 Like the other books in the psalms, this Third Book of Psalms closes with a doxology that should be viewed as independent from the psalm itself (compare 41:13; 72:18–20; 106:48; 150:6; see note on 1:1–6).

90:title–17 Psalm 90—the first psalm in Book Four of the Psalms (see note on 1:1–6)—is a corporate lament psalm (meant for group settings) that emphasizes the frailty of human life. The psalmist compares people to God, and encourages them to follow God and obey his commands. The psalmist begins by focusing on God's unchanging nature (vv. 1–2), then contrasts God's nature with the frailty of humanity (vv. 3–12). Finally, the psalmist petitions God to satisfy his people and give them his favor (vv. 13–17). The psalmist aims to call people to recognize God and follow his ways; in this way, the psalm also functions as a wisdom psalm. See the table "Types of Psalms" on p. 830.

90:title A prayer of Moses Psalm 90 is the only psalm affiliated with Moses, possibly suggesting it should be read in view of Israel's wilderness experience (see the book of Numbers). The wilderness journey was characterized by Israel's repetitive unfaithfulness and God's subsequent punishment. **man of God** The Hebrew phrase used here, *ish-ha'elohim*, likely has a prophetic connotation (see Dt 18:15; 34:10). Moses is called *eved-yhwh* ("the servant of Yahweh") in Dt 34:5.

90:1–3 Psalm 90 opens by comparing God's permanence with the frailty of humankind.

90:2 were born or you brought forth The Hebrew words used here, *yalad* ("give birth") and *chil* ("bring forth"), hold connotations of birth, indicating an element of tension in the creative process. The created world is, in a way, unstable, while God is constant. Biblical depictions of creation are not limited to Ge 1–2. Genesis 9 views

⁵ Yet you sweep people away in the sleep of
 death —
 they are like the new grass of the
 morning:
⁶ In the morning it springs up new,
 but by evening it is dry and withered.

⁷ We are consumed by your anger
 and terrified by your indignation.
⁸ You have set our iniquities before you,
 our secret sins in the light of your
 presence.
⁹ All our days pass away under your
 wrath;
 we finish our years with a moan.
¹⁰ Our days may come to seventy years,
 or eighty, if our strength endures;
 yet the best of them are but trouble and
 sorrow,
 for they quickly pass, and we fly away.
¹¹ If only we knew the power of your anger!
 Your wrath is as great as the fear that is
 your due.

¹² Teach us to number our days,
 that we may gain a heart of wisdom.

¹³ Relent, Lᴏʀᴅ! How long will it be?
 Have compassion on your servants.
¹⁴ Satisfy us in the morning with your
 unfailing love,
 that we may sing for joy and be glad all
 our days.
¹⁵ Make us glad for as many days as you have
 afflicted us,
 for as many years as we have seen
 trouble.
¹⁶ May your deeds be shown to your
 servants,
 your splendor to their children.

¹⁷ May the favor*ᵃ* of the Lord our God rest
 on us;
 establish the work of our hands
 for us —
 yes, establish the work of our hands.

ᵃ 17 Or *beauty*

---

the post-flood restoration of the world as re-creation; Isa 40–55 describes God's promise of redemption to those in the Babylonian exile in terms of creation imagery. Other Biblical books also contain elements of creation, such as Job 38–41. Creation is developed as a major theme in the psalms (Ps 8; 19; 104; 139; 148). See the infographic "The Days of Creation" on p. 6.
90:3 You turn people back This phrase is used here and at the close of the psalm (90:13), to provide a bookend structure to the psalm. **to dust** The Hebrew word used here, *dakka* (meaning "something crushed"), emphasizes the fragility of people before the Creator. This is not the same word that appears in Ge 2:7 (*aphar* in Hebrew).

90:4–6 These verses focus on the human condition in general, describing the fragility of humanity — human life doesn't last very long (Ps 90:4) and is easily destroyed (vv. 5–6).
90:4 or like a watch in the night The Hebrew word used here, *ashmurah*, refers to a length of time during the night, when most people are asleep and unaware.
90:6 by evening it is dry and withered See v. 14.

90:7–8 Verse 5 introduced God's destructive power, but didn't describe his motive for sweeping humans away (see v. 5). These verses indicate that God's anger and judgment upon humanity is a result of human sin. People are not only mortal and fragile, they are also accountable to God and liable to judgment.
90:7 We are consumed God's anger and subsequent judgment are a response to sin (compare v. 8). Here, divine judgment — not natural aging — is the main component in human mortality (see v. 10 and note).
90:8 iniquities The Hebrew word used here, *awon*, can refer to misdeeds or the guilt and punishment that come from the misdeeds.
90:9–12 This section of the psalm reflects on the realities of life before God. Since people are weak and liable to judgment, they should respond with obedience and submission to God.

90:9 All our days Compare v. 15.
90:10 seventy years, or eighty, if our strength endures Describes an average life span; this is the first identification in the psalm of normal human aging being a cause of death (compare vv. 7–8,9). **trouble and sorrow** The psalmist directly relates the difficulty of life to judgment from God.
90:11 the fear Fearing God means placing all other potential objects of fear or reverence in perspective and revering him above else. Fearing God can be described as giving him respect or honor. Psalm 90:12 advocates a response to God's power and wrath.
90:12 Teach us to number our days A response to God's power and wrath — emphasizing that people should pay attention to God's ways each day and appreciate the life given to them. **a heart of wisdom** Wisdom starts with being properly oriented to God.

90:13–17 This final section presents the foremost element of Biblical wisdom: submission to God. Wisdom is expressed in an impassioned plea to God for mercy, not a detached, analytical stance.

90:14 Satisfy us in the morning In contrast to the withering grass of vv. 5–6, those satisfied by God from the moment they wake can withstand adversity. See v. 5 and note. **all our days** In v. 6, the grass is described as withering after a single hot day; in contrast, people whom God helps look forward to long life.
90:16 your deeds Refers to God's reaction to the previous pleas for compassion, satisfaction and joy (vv. 13–15). **their children** The psalmist wants God's blessing to extend beyond the present generation to later generations of God's people. See v. 17 and note.
90:17 establish the work of our hands This could refer generally to obedience and faithfulness to God (the wisdom described in v. 12). More specifically, if Moses is the psalmist (see 90:title and note), the work described here may be defined by passages like Dt 6:1–15, and describe Israel's faithfulness to the covenant while in the promised land.

Psalm 91

[1] Whoever dwells in the shelter of the Most
High
will rest in the shadow of the Almighty.[a]
[2] I will say of the LORD, "He is my refuge and
my fortress,
my God, in whom I trust."

[3] Surely he will save you
from the fowler's snare
and from the deadly pestilence.
[4] He will cover you with his feathers,
and under his wings you will find refuge;
his faithfulness will be your shield and
rampart.
[5] You will not fear the terror of night,
nor the arrow that flies by day,
[6] nor the pestilence that stalks in the darkness,
nor the plague that destroys at midday.
[7] A thousand may fall at your side,
ten thousand at your right hand,
but it will not come near you.
[8] You will only observe with your eyes
and see the punishment of the wicked.

[9] If you say, "The LORD is my refuge,"
and you make the Most High your
dwelling,
[10] no harm will overtake you,
no disaster will come near your
tent.
[11] For he will command his angels
concerning you
to guard you in all your ways;
[12] they will lift you up in their hands,
so that you will not strike your foot against
a stone.
[13] You will tread on the lion and the cobra;
you will trample the great lion and the
serpent.

[14] "Because he[b] loves me," says the LORD, "I will
rescue him;
I will protect him, for he acknowledges my
name.
[15] He will call on me, and I will answer him;
I will be with him in trouble,
I will deliver him and honor him.

---

[a] 1 Hebrew *Shaddai*   [b] 14 That is, probably the king

91:1–16 A psalm of confidence, Ps 91 is sometimes called "The Soldier's Psalm" because it emphasizes Yahweh's protection of people in times of crisis. Three voices speak in succession. The psalm opens with an individual proclaiming his trust in Yahweh (vv. 1–8). An audience then speaks to that individual, and describes Yahweh's protection and care (vv. 9–13). The psalm concludes with Yahweh speaking about the faithful person; he promises to protect him (vv. 14–16). See the table "Types of Psalms" on p. 830.

91:1–2 Psalm 91 first examines the idea of living in the presence of Yahweh, then personalizes it. The first-person perspective does not return until v. 9 (compare vv. 14–16). Verses 1–2 use four different names for God. The different names for God could represent various approaches to understanding him (or various traditions being brought together). Alternatively, the different names of God could emphasize different aspects of his nature or character.

91:1 Most High The Hebrew word used here, *elyon*, which is a name for God, means "upper" or "most high." Compare note on Ge 14:18. See the table "Names of God in the Old Testament" on p. 917. **Almighty** The Hebrew word used here, *shaddai*, is a name for God, and likely refers to him being a God of the mountain (Sinai and later Zion) or of the mountainous wilderness (see note on Ge 17:1).
91:2 the LORD The Hebrew text here used the word *yhwh* (Yahweh), which is the personal name God revealed to Moses in Ex 3:13–15. **God** The Hebrew text here uses the word *eloha*, a form of God's general name *elohim*, which is often used in contexts that refer to him as creator. The psalmist here refers to Yahweh—who has also been identified with two other names in 91:1—as his God.

91:3–6 The psalmist initially focuses on the image of a bird protecting its young. He then introduces images of military armor and weapons.

91:4 He will cover The Hebrew word used here, *sakhakh*, means to "shut off" or "make inaccessible," for the purpose of protection. **under his wings** Yahweh's care and actions are combined in the picture of a bird caring for its young. See note on 17:8; note on Ru 2:12.
91:5 the terror The Hebrew word used here, *pachad*, describes a debilitating fear.

91:7–8 These verses portray some sort of chaotic situation—perhaps a battle. Though thousands of people are dying, the faithful person doesn't need to fear harm. The psalm later identifies that these people are dying as a result of Yahweh's judgment.

91:9–10 These verses offer a strong statement about the absolute nature of God's protection.

91:11–12 Satan quotes Ps 91:11–12 during the temptation of Christ (Mt 4:6; Lk 4:10–11). Jesus captures the true sense of Ps 91 when he responds by quoting Dt 6:16. Psalm 91 ultimately emphasizes total trust in Yahweh and loyalty to him (see v. 2).

91:11–13 This passage envisions personally appointed spiritual bodyguards for the faithful person. Yahweh's emissaries will advocate for the faithful person.

91:14–16 The psalm now returns to the theme of trust; this time, however, Yahweh addresses the faithful person (compare v. 2). Yahweh personally assures the trusting follower and promises future help and blessings.

91:14 he acknowledges my name Emphasizes intimate knowledge of God rather than a particular label for God. Verses 1–2 demonstrates that the psalmist knows several names for God, but none are repeated here. Instead, the idea behind knowing God's name is having a deep love for him and an awareness of his character and nature.
91:15 honor him The psalmist draws a connection between faithfulness to Yahweh and honor from him.

¹⁶With long life I will satisfy him
    and show him my salvation."

Psalm 92[a]

A psalm. A song. For the Sabbath day.

¹It is good to praise the Lord
    and make music to your name, O Most High,
²proclaiming your love in the morning

and your faithfulness at night,
³to the music of the ten-stringed lyre
    and the melody of the harp.

⁴For you make me glad by your deeds, Lord;
    I sing for joy at what your hands have done.
⁵How great are your works, Lord,
    how profound your thoughts!

[a] In Hebrew texts 92:1-15 is numbered 92:2-16.

91:16 long life Long life is often associated with Yahweh's blessing in the OT (e.g., Ge 35:28; 47:29). **show him** A future-oriented promise. The faithful person will be shown God's blessings and experience what it means to be in his presence and protection (Ps 91:9–13). **my salvation** The Hebrew word used here, *yeshu'ah*, refers to help or deliverance. God's *yeshu'ah* here is viewed as deliverance from hazards and problems.

92:title–15 Psalm 92 is a thanksgiving psalm. It focuses on a contrast between the righteous and the wicked, sometimes called the "two ways" motif (see 1:1–6). After opening with a general proclamation of worship

Names of God in the Old Testament

NAME	REFERENCE*
Adonai	Ex 4:13; Jos 3:11; 1Ki 22:6; Zec 9:4
Adonai Yahweh	Ge 15:2; 2 Sam 7:18–19; Isa 61:1; Ezek 25:3; 37:3; Am 7:1
El	Ge 46:3; 2Sa 22:33; Ne 1:5; Job 9:2; Isa 9:6
El Bethel	Ge 31:13; 35:7
El Elyon	Ge 14:18–22
El Olam	Ge 21:33
El Ro'i	Ge 16:13
El Shaddai	Ge 17:1; Ex 6:3; Ru 1:20; Job 5:17; Ps 68:14; Isa 13:6; Joel 1:15
Eloah	Dt 32:15; Job 12:6; Pr 30:5; Isa 44:8; Hab 3:3
Elohim	Ge 1:1; 17:3; Ex 3:1; Dt 5:26; Ps 7:9
Elyon	Dt 32:8; Ps 9:2; 78:17; Isa 14:14; La 3:38
Yahweh	Ge 4:1; Ex 3:15; 6:3; 1Sa 12:22; Isa 42:8
Yahweh Elohim	Ge 2:4; 3:1; Ex 9:30; Ezr 9:15; Ps 72:18
Yahweh Elyon	Ps 7:17; 47:2; 91:1; 97:9
Yahweh Yir'eh	Ge 22:14
Yahweh Meqaddish	Lev 20:8
Yahweh Nissi	Ex 17:15
Yahweh Rohi	Ps 23:1
Yahweh Rophe	Ex 15:26
Yahweh Shalom	Jdg 6:24
Yahweh Shammah	Eze 48:35
Yahweh Tseva'oth	1Sa 1:3; 1Ki 18:15; Ps 24:10; Isa 1:9; Zec 1:3
Yahweh Tsidqenu	Jer 23:6

*Not an exhaustive list.

⁶ Senseless people do not know,
    fools do not understand,
⁷ that though the wicked spring up like grass
    and all evildoers flourish,
    they will be destroyed forever.

⁸ But you, LORD, are forever exalted.

⁹ For surely your enemies, LORD,
    surely your enemies will perish;
    all evildoers will be scattered.
¹⁰ You have exalted my horn*ᵃ* like that of a
    wild ox;
    fine oils have been poured on me.
¹¹ My eyes have seen the defeat of my
    adversaries;
    my ears have heard the rout of my wicked
    foes.

¹² The righteous will flourish like a palm tree,
    they will grow like a cedar of Lebanon;
¹³ planted in the house of the LORD,
    they will flourish in the courts of our God.
¹⁴ They will still bear fruit in old age,
    they will stay fresh and green,
¹⁵ proclaiming, "The LORD is upright;
    he is my Rock, and there is no wickedness
    in him."

Psalm 93

¹ The LORD reigns, he is robed in majesty;
    the LORD is robed in majesty and armed
    with strength;
    indeed, the world is established, firm
    and secure.
² Your throne was established long ago;
    you are from all eternity.

ᵃ *10* *Horn* here symbolizes strength.

(vv. 1–5), the psalmist describes the wicked and characterizes them as enemies of God (vv. 5–9). He then describes the victory of the righteous (vv. 10–11) and elaborates on the benefits they receive from their loyalty to Yahweh (vv. 12–15). See the table "Types of Psalms" on p. 830.

92:title psalm See note on 3:title. **A song. For the Sabbath day** This is the only psalm specifically associated with the Sabbath, the seventh day of the week and the Israelite day of rest. This suggests that this psalm was meant to be used for thanking God for the day of rest.

92:1–4 The psalm opens with thanksgiving to Yahweh using various musical instruments. The psalmist praises Yahweh because he has personally experienced his works.

92:1 Although Israelite worship centered on sacrifice, internal attitudes played a significant role. Giving thanks for Yahweh's actions and praising Yahweh's excellence were thus central; these activities affected emotions and attitudes. Several OT passages emphasize the importance of a right mindset in worship and life (e.g., Mic 6:6–8; Ps 69:30–31).

92:1 Most High The Hebrew word used here, *elyon*, is a relatively common name for God. See note on 91:1.
92:2 proclaiming The psalmist advocates declaring God's love and faithfulness. In v. 15, he declares Yahweh's moral goodness. This verse and v. 15 function as structural bookends for the psalm.

92:3 ten-stringed lyre The Hebrew word used here, *asor*, could describe a lute or a harp. **the harp** The Hebrew word used here, *kinnor*, describes a stringed instrument of some sort, possibly a lyre, zither or harp.

92:5–9 Here, the psalmist focuses on Yahweh's thoughts rather than his works. Yahweh's thoughts contrast with the foolishness of the wicked. Verse 9 names and identifies the wicked as the enemies of Yahweh. The psalmist predicts that all evildoers will eventually be scattered and destroyed.

92:6 fools Describes people who have a disrespectful attitude toward Yahweh and his instruction.

92:10–11 The psalmist recounts how Yahweh has exalted him and allowed him to see his enemies fall.

92:10 my horn A symbol of strength and power. **fine oils** This signifies that Yahweh has blessed the psalmist.

92:12–15 The psalm closes by listing blessings that the righteous will experience. Because of the benefits of being near God, the righteous are described as remaining healthy and productive even as they grow old. The final statement of the psalm praises Yahweh's moral goodness.

92:12 a palm tree Palm trees require a lot of water to thrive. Here, they symbolize lavish abundance and provision from proximity to God. **a cedar of Lebanon** A symbol of strength and prosperity.

92:13 The image of Yahweh as a king with a court appears throughout the OT and reflects the ancient Near Eastern practice of depicting deities as kings. People in the ancient Near East considered temples to be the palaces of deities; they would go there to worship and make requests of the divine king. As king, a deity would have an entourage, which would meet in his court. Compare Ps 82.

92:13 house of the LORD Refers to the Jerusalem temple.
92:14 They will still bear fruit in old age The psalmist envisions the righteous living long and productive lives beyond normal expectations. Compare 92:7.
92:15 my Rock A symbol of Yahweh's faithfulness and constancy.

93:1–5 Like Ps 47, Ps 93 is a psalm of Yahweh's kingship (or enthronement) that praises Yahweh as King over all the earth. In Ps 93, the psalmist portrays Yahweh as a powerful ruler (vv. 1–2) and describes how Yahweh easily overpowers his enemy, the primordial waters (the seas; vv. 4–5). He concludes by emphasizing Yahweh's decrees and encouraging loyalty to him (v. 5). See the table "Types of Psalms" on p. 830.

93:1–2 Verses 1–2 envisions Yahweh as an awesome king enthroned over the world. These verses emphasize the stability of his reign, as well as his great age—that he is eternal.

93:1 The LORD reigns This typifies the main theme and contents of the psalms of Yahweh's kingship or enthronement, which are also sometimes called theocratic psalms (Ps 47; 93; 95–99). Psalms 95–99 form a collection; Ps 93 is sometimes included in this grouping because

³ The seas have lifted up, LORD,
  the seas have lifted up their voice;
  the seas have lifted up their pounding waves.
⁴ Mightier than the thunder of the great waters,
  mightier than the breakers of the sea —
  the LORD on high is mighty.

⁵ Your statutes, LORD, stand firm;
  holiness adorns your house
  for endless days.

Psalm 94

¹ The LORD is a God who avenges.
  O God who avenges, shine forth.
² Rise up, Judge of the earth;
  pay back to the proud what they deserve.
³ How long, LORD, will the wicked,
  how long will the wicked be jubilant?

⁴ They pour out arrogant words;
  all the evildoers are full of boasting.
⁵ They crush your people, LORD;
  they oppress your inheritance.
⁶ They slay the widow and the foreigner;
  they murder the fatherless.
⁷ They say, "The LORD does not see;
  the God of Jacob takes no notice."

⁸ Take notice, you senseless ones among the
    people;
  you fools, when will you become wise?
⁹ Does he who fashioned the ear not hear?
  Does he who formed the eye not see?
¹⁰ Does he who disciplines nations not punish?
  Does he who teaches mankind lack
    knowledge?
¹¹ The LORD knows all human plans;
  he knows that they are futile.

---

of its close proximity and content. (Psalm 47 is included because of its similarities in content.) Several blocks of psalms seem to have existed as separate collections before they were incorporated into the book of Psalms (see note on 1:1–6). **the world** Refers to the dry land Yahweh created in the beginning, as opposed to the seas (vv. 3–4; Ge 1:6–10; compare Isa 14:17).

93:3–4 The image of Yahweh's secure reign serves as a reference point when the chaotic floodwaters of Ps 93:3–4 are introduced. Yahweh is not in a struggle against the waters, like the gods in other ancient Near Eastern literature—he is already established securely as ruler. In its ancient Near Eastern context, this psalm would have emphasized Yahweh as superior God and King of all.

93:5 The psalmist shifts from focusing on Yahweh's power and splendor to his instruction and character. Yahweh's ability to stand against the symbol of chaos in the ancient Near East—the waters (the seas and rivers)—establishes his right to reign over the earth and dictate truth.

93:5 holiness This can refer to moral purity or being set apart for Yahweh, or both. The psalmist indicates that Yahweh's magnificence is supported by his character; he deserves the splendid distinctiveness that typifies him. Like Yahweh himself, his house (the heavens)—and the Jerusalem temple like it (the symbol of his presence on earth)—is set apart as sacred (compare Ex 19:22).

94:1–23 Psalm 94 is a corporate lament psalm (meant for group settings) that calls for Yahweh's retribution against the oppressors of his people. The psalmist begins by petitioning Yahweh to take vengeance on the proud (vv. 1–2). He describes the wicked oppressors, who are part of Yahweh's people, who exploit their fellow Israelites (vv. 3–7). The psalmist expresses outrage regarding this injustice, and he criticizes the belief of the oppressors that they will escape Yahweh's punishment (vv. 8–11). The psalmist then extols Yahweh's discipline (vv. 12–13) and asserts that Yahweh will bring justice (vv. 14–15). Finally, he shows confidence that Yahweh knows about the evil of the wicked, and that he will eventually destroy them (vv. 16–23). See the table "Types of Psalms" on p. 830.

94:1–3 The psalmist begs Yahweh to act in retribution against the wicked.

94:2 Judge The psalmist is appealing to Yahweh's perfect justice, requesting that it come soon.
94:3 How long The psalmist employs a rhetorical question to appeal to Yahweh's justice.

94:4–7 Not only do the wicked defy Yahweh's laws, they mock Yahweh's ability to punish them.

94:4 arrogant The Hebrew word used here, *athaq*, describes speaking in an unrestrained or impudent manner.
94:5 your inheritance Since the people of Israel belong to Yahweh (see Ex 3), mistreating them is an especially serious offense. See note on Ps 47:4.

94:6 The OT presents widows, sojourners (foreigners) and orphans as particularly vulnerable to exploitation (Ex 22:21–24; Dt 14:29; 16:11; compare Jer 7:6). Since these groups are not included in the patrilineal system, they had no property rights and lacked many legal rights but were to be protected, in line with Yahweh's values (e.g., Dt 10:18–19; 14:28–29; 16:11–12; 24:17). The Israelites' treatment of these vulnerable people represented the ethical health of the nation.

94:6 foreigner The Hebrew word used here, *ger*, describes a resident alien in Israel; as non-Israelites, foreigners were outside of social power structures and vulnerable to injustice. **fatherless** Orphans were cut off from inheritance rights in a patriarchal society if they were not of age to take over the estate.
94:7 takes no notice This verb sets up a rhetorical wordplay with the very beginning of Ps 94:8.

94:8–11 The psalmist warns the evildoers that Yahweh knows everything they do and that he will eventually hold them accountable for their actions.

94:8 Take notice The psalmist reverses the insult of v. 7 and turns it against the wicked. Compare note on v. 7. **fools** Refers to people characterized by insolence toward Yahweh.
94:9 hear The psalmist further responds to the insult that Yahweh does not perceive what the evildoers do (v. 7); Yahweh, the Creator of the ear and eyes, hears and sees everything.

¹²Blessed is the one you discipline, Lord,
  the one you teach from your law;
¹³you grant them relief from days of trouble,
  till a pit is dug for the wicked.
¹⁴For the Lord will not reject his people;
  he will never forsake his inheritance.
¹⁵Judgment will again be founded on
    righteousness,
  and all the upright in heart will follow it.

¹⁶Who will rise up for me against the wicked?
  Who will take a stand for me against
    evildoers?
¹⁷Unless the Lord had given me help,
  I would soon have dwelt in the silence
    of death.
¹⁸When I said, "My foot is slipping,"
  your unfailing love, Lord, supported me.
¹⁹When anxiety was great within me,
  your consolation brought me joy.

²⁰Can a corrupt throne be allied with you—
  a throne that brings on misery by its
    decrees?
²¹The wicked band together against the righteous
  and condemn the innocent to death.

²²But the Lord has become my fortress,
  and my God the rock in whom I take
    refuge.
²³He will repay them for their sins
  and destroy them for their wickedness;
  the Lord our God will destroy them.

Psalm 95

¹Come, let us sing for joy to the Lord;
  let us shout aloud to the Rock of our
    salvation.
²Let us come before him with thanksgiving
  and extol him with music and song.

³For the Lord is the great God,
  the great King above all gods.
⁴In his hand are the depths of the earth,
  and the mountain peaks belong
    to him.
⁵The sea is his, for he made it,
  and his hands formed the dry land.

⁶Come, let us bow down in worship,
  let us kneel before the Lord our Maker;

94:12 law The Hebrew word used here, *torah*, can refer either to the OT law or to instruction in general.

94:14 his inheritance The Hebrew word used here, *nachalah*, refers to the people of Israel. See note on 47:4.

94:16–23 These verses compose a statement of trust in Yahweh and predict Yahweh's vengeance on wicked rulers. The final section of the psalm depicts incredibly corrupt rulers.

94:21 the innocent The psalmist portrays the injustice against the innocent in the strongest possible terms: The Hebrew phrase used here, *dam naqi*, literally means "innocent blood."

94:22 rock in whom I take refuge The psalmist uses the metaphors in this verse to emphasize Yahweh's strength against the wicked.

94:23 destroy them The Hebrew word used here, *tsamat*, emphasizes the certainty of the future destruction of the wicked rulers.

95:1–11 While it is more of a general praise psalm, Ps 95 is often included among the psalms of Yahweh's kingship or enthronement (see note on 93:1), because it refers to Yahweh with the Hebrew term *melekh gadol* ("great King"; v. 3). However, Ps 95 is mostly a call to worship and a historical reflection on Israel's rebellion in the wilderness. The psalmist begins by calling people to worship Yahweh and sing to him as the sovereign King over all creation (vv. 1–5). He encourages his fellow Israelites to worship Yahweh because they are his people (vv. 6–7). The psalmist then admonishes his audience to remain responsive to Yahweh, and he warns them not to rebel against him as the Israelites did in the wilderness—that pattern of rebellion eventually brought Yahweh's wrath upon Israel (vv. 8–11). See the table "Types of Psalms" on p. 830.

95:1 the Rock The Hebrew word used here, *tsur*, highlights the stability and protection Yahweh provides.

95:3–5 Verses 4–5 have a cosmic scope, emphasizing Yahweh's power over everything. This passage contains parallel descriptions that emphasize Yahweh's power over the totality of the created world: depths and heights; sea and dry land. In its original ancient Near Eastern context, these descriptions show, as v. 3 emphasizes, Yahweh's power over all other gods (*elohim* in Hebrew).

95:3 great God The Hebrew phrase used here, *gadol el*, refers to Yahweh being the God who is greater than all others divine beings (gods)—for he created them too. *El* is the common Semitic word for "God." This phrase declares Yahweh as greater than the gods of the foreign pantheons and any other spiritual beings. **great King** Yahweh is the cosmic king—all must ultimately report and answer to him. Compare Ps 82. **gods** The Hebrew word used here, *elohim*, emphasizes that Yahweh is not just the superior power in the earthly realm (vv. 4–5) but also in the spiritual realm. He is king of all (see note on 82:1; note on 93:1; compare 98:6 and note).

95:4 The psalmist portrays the whole world as under the jurisdiction of Yahweh, the God who created it. Compare note on 95:3–5.

95:5 The sea was the symbol of primordial chaos in the ancient Near East. Yahweh's power over it shows that he is truly the great God (see note on 95:3). Compare note on 95:3–5.

95:6–7 The psalmist calls the people to worship Yahweh, their Creator and sustainer. He focuses on the image of shepherd and sheep, which sets up the focus on Yahweh's guidance in the second half of v. 7 and vv. 10–11.

95:6 The psalmist uses three different Hebrew terms to describe bowing down, the foundational action of worship in the OT: *chawah* (which denotes bowing), *kara'* (which refers to bending a person's knees or kneeling) and *barakh* (which derives from the word for "knee" and means "to kneel").

95:6 our Maker The psalmist now further emphasizes Yahweh's superiority—he is the one who made humanity.

⁷for he is our God
and we are the people of his
pasture,
the flock under his care.

Today, if only you would hear his
voice,
⁸ "Do not harden your hearts as you did
at Meribah,ᵃ
as you did that day at Massahᵇ in the
wilderness,
⁹ where your ancestors tested me;
they tried me, though they had seen
what I did.
¹⁰ For forty years I was angry with that
generation;
I said, 'They are a people whose hearts
go astray,
and they have not known my
ways.'
¹¹ So I declared on oath in my anger,
'They shall never enter my
rest.'"

Psalm 96

96:1-13pp — 1Ch 16:23-33

¹ Sing to the LORD a new song;
sing to the LORD, all the earth.
² Sing to the LORD, praise his name;
proclaim his salvation day after day.
³ Declare his glory among the nations,
his marvelous deeds among all
peoples.

⁴ For great is the LORD and most worthy of
praise;
he is to be feared above all gods.
⁵ For all the gods of the nations are idols,
but the LORD made the heavens.
⁶ Splendor and majesty are before him;
strength and glory are in his sanctuary.

⁷ Ascribe to the LORD, all you families
of nations,
ascribe to the LORD glory and strength.

ᵃ 8 Meribah means quarreling.   ᵇ 8 Massah means testing.

95:7–11 In the second half of v. 7 and vv. 10–11, the psalmist exhorts the people to trust Yahweh and follow him and his ways. He emphasizes Yahweh's guidance by rehearsing the story of Israel in the wilderness and urges his audience to be receptive to Yahweh's leadership.

95:7 the flock under his care The psalmist depicts Yahweh as the shepherd who watches over, guides and protects the Israelites.

95:8 harden The Israelites stubbornly refused to follow Yahweh even after he, their Creator, rescued them (v. 6). **Meribah** A reference to the location where the Israelites quarreled with Moses and tested Yahweh. See Ex 17:1–7. **the wilderness** The Israelites wandered in the wilderness—uninhabited land—between the exodus and their entry into the promised land.

95:9 what I did This probably refers to Yahweh's work in the exodus.

95:10 my ways The Hebrew word used here, derekh, literally means "path," but by extension can also refer to behavior or conduct. The Israelites were resisting Yahweh's spiritual guidance even as they followed him in the wilderness. Compare Jer 50:6; Pr 3:6.

95:11 my rest The Hebrew word used here, menuchah—which can mean "resting place" or "place of quiet"—probably refers to the promised land and Yahweh's purposes for Israel.

96:1–13 Psalm 96 is a psalm of Yahweh's kingship or enthronement (see note on 93:1). In it, the psalmist calls all the earth to declare Yahweh's excellence (vv. 1–3). He encourages Israel to tell the surrounding nations—and the entire created world—of Yahweh's worthiness (vv. 4–6), which will draw them to worship the true God (vv. 7–10). The psalmist concludes by describing the earth's joyous anticipation of Yahweh's rule being fully established over everything (see vv. 11–13 and note). See the table "Types of Psalms" on p. 830.

96:1–3 The psalmist repeats the Hebrew phrase shiru layhwh ("sing to Yahweh") three times in vv. 1–2. The earth is the only identified audience of the series of commands.

The psalmist then commands Yahweh's people, the Israelites, to declare his miraculous actions to the foreign peoples (or nations) around them.

96:2 his name This phrase emphasizes intimate knowledge of God rather than a particular name as multiple names are used for God. See note on 91:14. **salvation** The Hebrew word used here, yeshu'ah, refers in the psalms to Yahweh's deliverance from whatever hazards the psalmist is experiencing. See 91:16 and note.

96:3 peoples Refers to people groups other than the Israelites (vv. 3,5,7,10,13).

96:4–6 The psalmist asserts that people should declare God's glory because he is the only deity worth praising. He made the heavens, and his greatness and beauty are obvious.

96:4 to be feared See 90:11 and note. **gods** The Hebrew word used here, elohim—which is plural in form—is sometimes used in reference to Yahweh, but here it refers to deities worshiped by the nations surrounding Israel (96:5).

96:5 gods See note on 96:4. **idols** The Hebrew word used here, elil—which can be rendered as "insignificant," "vain" or "weak"—describes foreign gods in a derogatory sense, portraying them as nonentities. **the LORD made the heavens** The psalmist argues that other rival deities are worthless because Yahweh made the place where the other gods supposedly live, the heavens. Yahweh is the Creator of all.

96:6 in his sanctuary Yahweh is set apart from all the foreign gods—he dwells in his holy place. This could be a reference to the heavens or to the Jerusalem temple. Considering that vv. 8–10 envision people coming to Yahweh from around the world, the Jerusalem temple is likely being referenced here. Compare 93:5 and note.

96:7–10 The psalmist issues a series of commands about what should be ascribed to Yahweh—what belongs to him (vv. 7–8, compare vv. 1–3). In doing so, he asserts Yahweh's superiority over all the earth and that all should worship him. The psalmist seems to envision people from other nations coming to Jerusalem to worship Yahweh.

⁸Ascribe to the LORD the glory due his name;
   bring an offering and come into his courts.
⁹Worship the LORD in the splendor of his*a*
      holiness;
   tremble before him, all the earth.
¹⁰Say among the nations, "The LORD reigns."
   The world is firmly established, it cannot
      be moved;
   he will judge the peoples with equity.
¹¹Let the heavens rejoice, let the earth be glad;
   let the sea resound, and all that is in it.
¹²Let the fields be jubilant, and everything in
      them;
   let all the trees of the forest sing for joy.
¹³Let all creation rejoice before the LORD, for
   he comes,
   he comes to judge the earth.
   He will judge the world in righteousness
   and the peoples in his faithfulness.

Psalm 97

¹The LORD reigns, let the earth be glad;
   let the distant shores rejoice.

²Clouds and thick darkness surround him;
   righteousness and justice are the
      foundation of his throne.
³Fire goes before him
   and consumes his foes on every side.
⁴His lightning lights up the world;
   the earth sees and trembles.
⁵The mountains melt like wax before the
      LORD,
   before the Lord of all the earth.
⁶The heavens proclaim his righteousness,
   and all peoples see his glory.

⁷All who worship images are put to shame,
   those who boast in idols —
   worship him, all you gods!

⁸Zion hears and rejoices
   and the villages of Judah are glad
   because of your judgments, LORD.
⁹For you, LORD, are the Most High over all
      the earth;
   you are exalted far above all gods.

a 9 Or LORD *with the splendor of*

96:8 offering The Hebrew word used here, *minchah*, refers in general to a gift, present or tribute — specifically a food or grain offering (see Lev 2:1 and note).

96:10 The psalmist uses language reminiscent of Yahweh's actions as Creator to show his superiority. Compare note on 95:3–5.

96:10 among the nations The message of Yahweh's kingdom was not to be restricted to Israel, but instead was to reach the entire world. This represents a reclaiming of the nations of the earth by Yahweh (compare note on Ps 82:2). **The LORD reigns** See note on Ps 93:1. **with equity** The psalmist declares that Yahweh will judge all people with fairness or integrity.

96:11–13 The psalmist describes personified creation as looking forward to Yahweh's judgment, which will be right and fair. As Yahweh's reign is fully established over everything in the way that it should be — with justice and equality (righteousness) — everything on heaven and earth that knows Yahweh will rejoice.

97:1–12 As a psalm of Yahweh's kingship (or enthronement), Ps 97 praises Yahweh's glorious reign (see note on 93:1). The psalmist begins by depicting Yahweh's power over all creation (vv. 1–7). His description of Yahweh echoes Ex 19–20, where Yahweh appears to Israel at Sinai. Yahweh's appearance here is oriented toward the rescue of his loyal people (Ps 97:8–9) and he rebukes those who do not worship him (v. 7). The psalmist concludes by calling Israel to continue to trust Yahweh and remain loyal to him while they wait for his deliverance (vv. 10–12). See the table "Types of Psalms" on p. 830.

97:1–6 The psalmist begins by asserting Yahweh's power and authority over all creation. He depicts Yahweh as terrifying and dangerous as he proceeds through the world.

97:2 Clouds and thick darkness Describes a tumultuous cloak of ominous clouds and darkness like what accompanied the appearance of Yahweh at Sinai (see Ex 19:16–19). Yahweh's self-manifestation takes several

forms in the OT. At Sinai, Yahweh was veiled in thick clouds, accompanied by thunder and lightning. In Ex 20:19, the Israelites tell Moses that they do not want to speak directly to God, lest they die. Both the Sinai theophany and Ps 97 focus on Yahweh's role as supreme ruler. See the table "Old Testament Theophanies" on p. 924. **righteousness** Yahweh's rule is based on what is right. **foundation** Yahweh's reign is established on the basis of his right actions and ability to bring about justice.

97:5 The mountains melt like wax People in the ancient Near East believed mountains were the places where deities, who came from the heavens, came to earth and communed with people. The psalmist is taunting foreign gods with this description — showing that the earthly dwellings of other deities cannot compare to Yahweh's strength (v. 9).

97:6–7 The personified heavens announce Yahweh's importance before the entire world, and they proclaim him as the only deity worthy of worship.

97:6 his glory The Hebrew word used here, *kavod* — which can be rendered as "splendor" or "honor" — literally refers to the heaviness of Yahweh's reputation. That it is greater in weight than anything else. Yahweh's glory is paralleled by his righteousness and justice (v. 6). See note on Ex 16:10.

97:7 All who worship images Those who are idolatrous should feel shame since they worship that which is false. **idols** See note on 96:5. **gods** The Hebrew word used here, *elohim* — which is plural in form and is sometimes used to refer to the God of Israel — refers to foreign deities in this instance. It is not just the people but also the deities of foreign nations who are called upon to proclaim the truth — that Yahweh, the Creator and Judge of all — is superior to all and the true God. He is the only one worthy of worship. Compare Ps 82; note on 82:2.

97:8–9 The psalmist describes how Yahweh's people rejoice in him as the only worthy God.

97:9 Most High See note on 91:1. **you are exalted far above all gods** Just as Yahweh is high over the earth, he is

¹⁰ Let those who love the LORD hate evil,
for he guards the lives of his faithful ones
and delivers them from the hand of the
wicked.
¹¹ Light shines*a* on the righteous
and joy on the upright in heart.
¹² Rejoice in the LORD, you who are righteous,
and praise his holy name.

Psalm 98

A psalm.

¹ Sing to the LORD a new song,
for he has done marvelous things;
his right hand and his holy arm
have worked salvation for him.
² The LORD has made his salvation known
and revealed his righteousness to the
nations.
³ He has remembered his love
and his faithfulness to Israel;
all the ends of the earth have seen
the salvation of our God.

⁴ Shout for joy to the LORD, all the earth,
burst into jubilant song with music;
⁵ make music to the LORD with the harp,
with the harp and the sound of singing,
⁶ with trumpets and the blast of the ram's
horn—
shout for joy before the LORD, the King.

⁷ Let the sea resound, and everything in it,
the world, and all who live in it.
⁸ Let the rivers clap their hands,
let the mountains sing together for joy;
⁹ let them sing before the LORD,
for he comes to judge the earth.
He will judge the world in righteousness
and the peoples with equity.

Psalm 99

¹ The LORD reigns,
let the nations tremble;
he sits enthroned between the cherubim,
let the earth shake.

a 11 One Hebrew manuscript and ancient versions (see also
112:4); most Hebrew manuscripts *Light is sown*

also above the foreign gods. People in the ancient Near East believed the gods belonged to the realm of the heavens, but here Yahweh is depicted as even above the place where they dwelled (compare note on 97:5). See note on v. 7.

97:10–12 The psalmist calls Yahweh's people to remain loyal to him and trust in his future help and blessings. The psalmist asserts that people should demonstrate loyalty to Yahweh through outward acts as well as inward allegiance; all people should praise Yahweh in all that they do.

98:title–9 In this psalm of Yahweh's kingship (or enthronement) the psalmist calls Israel to sing a new and joyful song to Yahweh because he has helped them (vv. 1–3; see note on 93:1). He then extends that call to all the people of the earth and eventually the earth itself (vv. 4–6). The psalmist concludes by describing how all of creation joyfully anticipates the full establishment of Yahweh's righteous reign (vv. 7–9). See the table "Types of Psalms" on p. 830.

98:title A psalm See note on 3:title.

98:1–3 Through his actions, Yahweh has displayed his righteousness and his faithfulness to Israel. The watching world has seen Yahweh's salvation. The psalmist may be considering a new perspective on Israel's history, or he may have new instances of Yahweh's help to Israel in mind. This section of Ps 98 reflects parts of Ps 96 and 100.

98:1 holy arm See note on 44:3.
98:2 his salvation See note on 91:16. **the nations** Refers to people groups outside Israel. Yahweh expresses concern for the entirety of humanity throughout the OT, with Israel playing a central role in his purpose of redemption.
98:3 his love See note on 25:10.
98:4–6 The psalmist exhorts his audience to sing praises to Yahweh and celebrate him as King.

98:6 trumpets Refers to a long, metallic trumpet used for giving a signal call. **horn** The Hebrew word here, *shophar*, refers to a ram's horn used mainly as a signaling device, such as a call to war (Nu 31:6). **the LORD, the King** Emphasizes Yahweh's theocratic rule over the earth. See note on Ps 93:1.

98:7–9 The psalmist describes personified creation rejoicing at Yahweh's arrival to judge the earth, because his arrival means the restoration of justice. This section reflects 96:11–13.

98:7 Let the sea resound The sea rejoices at Yahweh's approach (compare 93:3–4). The psalms portray the natural world's two main responses to Yahweh's rule over all creation: The earth either shakes in terror or responds in joyous anticipation of Yahweh's righteous reign. **the world** The Hebrew word used here, *tevel*, often refers specifically to the inhabited world. See note on 90:2.

99:1–9 This final psalm of Yahweh's kingship (or enthronement) reflects on Yahweh's position as ruler of everything, enthroned above the world (see note on 93:1). The picture of Yahweh's throne fuses elements of heaven and earth; this psalm paints a portrait of Yahweh's throne that exists simultaneously in heaven and in the Jerusalem temple (99:1–5). The psalmist then focuses on Yahweh's guidance through his servants and his appearances in Israel's history (vv. 6–7). The psalmist concludes by calling Israel to worship Yahweh at his holy mountain—the temple in Jerusalem (vv. 8–9). See the table "Types of Psalms" on p. 830.

99:1–3 The psalmist describes how Yahweh, who is powerful and holy, is the ultimate ruler of the whole world.

99:1 the nations See 96:3 and note. **cherubim** This refers to the golden cherubim on the ark of the covenant. See note on 18:10.

Old Testament Theophanies

TYPE OF THEOPHANY*	REFERENCE	NOTES
God appears to Adam and Eve in the Garden of Eden	Ge 3:8 – 13	—
God appears to Cain	Ge 4:1 – 16 (e.g. Ge 4:16)	—
God appears to Abram	Ge 12:6 – 7; 17:1 – 21	—
God comes to Abram	Ge 15:1 – 21	Vision fused with actions
Appearance to Hagar by a spring	Ge 16:7 – 14	Angel of Yahweh
Abraham's three visitors	Ge 18:1 – 33 (18:10, 22, 33)	—
Binding of Isaac	Ge 22	Angel of Yahweh (Ge 22:11,15)
Isaac at Gerar	Ge 26:2 – 5, 24, 25	—
Jacob's dream of angels at Bethel	Ge 28:10 – 22	Dream
Jacob wrestles with God	Ge 32:22 – 32	—
God renames Jacob	Ge 35:1 – 15	—
God tells Jacob to move to Egypt	Ge 46:2 – 7	Vision
The Burning Bush	Ex 3:1 – 4:17	Angel of Yahweh (Ex 3:2)
God tells Moses to return to Egypt; "bridegroom of blood"	Ex 4:19 – 26	—
God's glory passes by Moses	Ex 33:17 – 23	—
Commissioning of Joshua	Dt 31:14 – 15	—
Call of Gideon	Judg 6:11 – 24	Angel of Yahweh (Jdg 6:12)
Solomon's prayer for wisdom	1Ki 3:3 – 15; 2Ch 1:7 – 13	Dream
God speaks to Elijah	1Ki 19:9 – 18	—
God speaks to Job	Job 38:1; 40:6; 42:7 – 9	—
Call of Isaiah	Isa 6:1 – 13	Vision
Call of Jeremiah	Jer 1:4 – 10 (see Jer 1:9)	Word of Yahweh (Jer 1:4)
God appears to Ezekiel	Eze 1:4 – 28	—
Ezekiel's vision of God leaving the temple	Eze 10:1 – 22	Vision (see Eze 8:1 – 4)
Nebuchadnezzar's furnace	Da 3:24 – 25	"Angel" (Da 3:28)
Handwriting on the wall	Da 5:1 – 31	Hand sent from presence of God (Da 5:24)
The pillar of fire and cloud that led Israel in the wilderness	Ex 13:21 – 22; Nu 9:15 – 23; 10:11 – 12, 34	—
The pillar of fire and cloud between Israel and Egypt	Ex 14:19 – 20, 24 – 25	Angel of God (Ex 14:19)
The glory of Yahweh appears in a cloud	Ex 16:10	—
Revelation at Mt. Sinai†	Ex 19:16 – 20; Dt 4:9 – 14	—

² Great is the Lᴏʀᴅ in Zion;
    he is exalted over all the nations.
³ Let them praise your great and awesome
        name —
    he is holy.

⁴ The King is mighty, he loves justice —
    you have established equity;
  in Jacob you have done
    what is just and right.
⁵ Exalt the Lᴏʀᴅ our God

and worship at his footstool;
    he is holy.

⁶ Moses and Aaron were among his priests,
    Samuel was among those who called on his
        name;
  they called on the Lᴏʀᴅ
    and he answered them.
⁷ He spoke to them from the pillar of cloud;
    they kept his statutes and the decrees he
        gave them.

99:2 Zion The temple mount in Jerusalem, which is virtually synonymous with Jerusalem itself. From Jerusalem, Yahweh sits as the ruler who is above all rulers and powers of the earth. See note on 20:2.
99:3 name See 91:14 and note. **he is holy** See 93:5 and note.
99:4–5 The psalmist describes Yahweh's holiness and strength, which is based on his justice—that he brings about equality.
99:4 Jacob Refers here to the nation of Israel. The patriarch Jacob's name was changed by God to Israel (see Ge 32:28). **just and right** The psalmist uses the justice and righteousness that Yahweh has brought to Israel as support for why everyone should praise Yahweh (Ps 99:3).
99:5 Lᴏʀᴅ our God Yahweh is specifically called the God of Israel. This wording is repeated a total of three times (vv. 5,8,9). **his footstool** This refers to the earth in Isa 66:1, the ark of the covenant in 1Ch 28:2 and Zion (the temple mount) in La 2:1. Here, it probably refers to the temple mount in Jerusalem.
99:6–9 Elaborating on the ideas of Ps 99:4, the psalmist describes how Yahweh has proven his character through his faithfulness to Israel and his discipline of Israel when it does wrong.

99:6 Moses and Aaron See Ex 7:1–2. **his priests** Refers to someone with the authority to minister before Yahweh in sacred space, such as the tabernacle and temple. **Samuel** A prominent leader of Israel during the transition from the time of the Judges into the monarchy. The psalmist may be drawing from the episode of Samuel's calling in 1Sa 3.

PRIESTS
Priests served as mediators between God and the people of Israel; the office was hereditary. Though Moses' duties didn't involve regular priestly activity, he served as mediator between God and the people. The priest's main role in the OT was applying the blood of sacrifices and offering worship to God in the tabernacle and temple. The Levites were responsible for handling the sacred items of God's tabernacle during transport, and they performed certain duties within the temple after it was built.

99:7 the pillar of cloud During Israel's time in the

Old Testament Theophanies (continued)

TYPE OF THEOPHANY*	REFERENCE	NOTES
The glory of God appears in a cloud on Mt. Sinai	Ex 24:15–18	—
Cloud over tent of meeting with Moses (before tabernacle)	Ex 33:7–11	—
Cloud over tent of meeting; glory of God in tabernacle	Ex 40:34–38	—
The 70 elders	Nu 11:24–25	—
Judgment on Miriam and Aaron	Nu 12:5	—
Glory of God fills Solomon's temple	1Ki 8:1–11; 2Ch 5:13–14; 7:1–3	—

*Theophanies are special manifestations of God that are accompanied by acute awareness of his presence. Prophetic dialogue (compare Ex 6–14) is not a theophany.

†The revelation at Sinai became the template for theophanic depictions of God at Mt. Zion/Jerusalem (e.g. Pss 18:7–20, 29:1–11, 97:1–5, 144:5–6; Mic 1:2–4).

8 LORD our God,
   you answered them;
you were to Israel a forgiving God,
   though you punished their misdeeds.[a]
9 Exalt the LORD our God
   and worship at his holy mountain,
   for the LORD our God is holy.

Psalm 100

A psalm. For giving grateful praise.

1 Shout for joy to the LORD, all the earth.
2   Worship the LORD with gladness;
   come before him with joyful songs.
3 Know that the LORD is God.
   It is he who made us, and we are his [b];
   we are his people, the sheep of his pasture.

4 Enter his gates with thanksgiving
   and his courts with praise;
   give thanks to him and praise his name.
5 For the LORD is good and his love endures
      forever;
   his faithfulness continues through all
      generations.

Psalm 101

Of David. A psalm.

1 I will sing of your love and justice;
   to you, LORD, I will sing praise.
2 I will be careful to lead a blameless life —
   when will you come to me?

I will conduct the affairs of my house
   with a blameless heart.
3 I will not look with approval
   on anything that is vile.

I hate what faithless people do;
   I will have no part in it.
4 The perverse of heart shall be far from me;
   I will have nothing to do with what is evil.

5 Whoever slanders their neighbor in secret,
   I will put to silence;
whoever has haughty eyes and a proud heart,
   I will not tolerate.

6 My eyes will be on the faithful in the land,
   that they may dwell with me;

---

[a] 8 Or *God, / an avenger of the wrongs done to them*
[b] 3 Or *and not we ourselves*

---

wilderness, Yahweh appeared in a pillar of cloud. See Ex 19:9; 40:34–38.
99:8 forgiving The Hebrew word used here, *nasa*—which may be literally rendered as "to carry" or "to lift up"—describes how Yahweh removes sin or iniquity.
99:9 holy mountain Refers to mount Zion, the temple mount in Jerusalem. **the LORD our God is holy** The psalmist concludes by combining the Hebrew phrases *yhwh elohenu* ("Yahweh our God") and *hu qadosh* ("holy is he"). This acts as a closing proclamation about the character of Yahweh—that he is set apart from everything else.

100:title–5 Psalm 100 is not strictly a psalm of Yahweh's kingship (or enthronement) since it doesn't explicitly identify Yahweh as King (see 93:1 and note). However, it does follow immediately after a collection of enthronement psalms (Ps 95–99) and echoes some of their language and themes. In this short praise psalm, the psalmist calls the entire earth to worship Yahweh with joy (100:1–2). He emphasizes gratitude (vv. 3–4) and loyalty to the good God who cares for his people (v. 5). See the table "Types of Psalms" on p. 830.

100:title A psalm See note on 3:title. **For giving grateful praise** Psalm 100 is specifically described as a hymn, or a song devoted to praising Yahweh.
100:2 Worship The Hebrew word used here, *a'vad*, can describe work or service in general, or refer to honoring Yahweh in formal worship.
100:3 made The psalmist is probably referring to Yahweh's activity in making Israel into a people for himself, though the psalmist could also be referring to Yahweh as the creator of humanity. **the sheep of his pasture** Compare 95:7 and note.
100:4 his courts See note on 92:13. **his name** See note on 91:14.
100:5 his love See note on 25:10.

101:title–8 The specific genre of Ps 101 is difficult to determine. It most likely belongs with the temple entry psalms as the psalmist declares his worthiness to enter the temple (see Ps 15:title–5 and note). The psalmist shows his commitment to faithfulness, justice and integrity (101:1–2) and his rejection of evil (vv. 3–4). He extends his personal righteousness to others as he expresses his intention to expel the wicked and corrupt and look favorably on the faithful (vv. 5–8). See the table "Types of Psalms" on p. 830.

101:title Of David. A psalm See note on 3:title.

101:1–2 The psalmist commits himself and his house to integrity and obedience (Dt 17:14–20) as he looks to worship at the temple. Compare Ps 15:1–2.

101:2 I will be careful The psalmist hopes to gain wisdom and insight through thoughtful reflection; he wants to find out how to obey. **to lead a blameless life** The Hebrew phrase used here is *derekh tamim*. The Hebrew word *tamim* has a sense of "faultlessness," and indicates a high degree of integrity and honesty. The psalmist needs to demonstrate faultless piety in order to fulfill his function well (compare Dt 17:14–20). The OT concept of *tamim* refers to a person living in a state in which no obvious charge or ready accusation could be brought against him or her. It usually describes loyalty to Yahweh and passion for him and observing his commands. When the psalmist states in the Hebrew text that he will ponder *derekh tamim* (which may be literally rendered as "the blameless way"), he is declaring that he is looking for ways that he (and Israel) can better follow Yahweh. Compare Ps 101:6.

101:3–5 The psalmist extends his commitment to personal integrity by rejecting evil, including the evil behavior of others. Compare Ps 15:3–5.

101:5 Whoever slanders See Lev 19:16 and note.

the one whose walk is blameless
will minister to me.

⁷No one who practices deceit
will dwell in my house;
no one who speaks falsely
will stand in my presence.

⁸Every morning I will put to silence
all the wicked in the land;
I will cut off every evildoer
from the city of the LORD.

Psalm 102ᵃ

*A prayer of an afflicted person who has grown weak
and pours out a lament before the LORD.*

¹Hear my prayer, LORD;
let my cry for help come to you.
²Do not hide your face from me
when I am in distress.
Turn your ear to me;
when I call, answer me quickly.

³For my days vanish like smoke;
my bones burn like glowing embers.

⁴My heart is blighted and withered like
grass;
I forget to eat my food.
⁵In my distress I groan aloud
and am reduced to skin and bones.
⁶I am like a desert owl,
like an owl among the ruins.
⁷I lie awake; I have become
like a bird alone on a roof.
⁸All day long my enemies taunt me;
those who rail against me use my name as
a curse.
⁹For I eat ashes as my food
and mingle my drink with tears
¹⁰because of your great wrath,
for you have taken me up and thrown me
aside.
¹¹My days are like the evening shadow;
I wither away like grass.

¹²But you, LORD, sit enthroned forever;
your renown endures through all
generations.

ᵃ In Hebrew texts 102:1-28 is numbered 102:2-29.

101:6–8 In these verses, the psalmist describes his intention to support the faithful, remove wicked people from the land and remove any evil from his own house. This implies that the author is in a position of authority, such as that of a king.

101:6 minister Describes the service that priests perform before Yahweh, as well as the work servants do before a human king (Est 1:10).
101:8 city of the LORD Refers to Jerusalem, which seems to be an emblem for the whole nation since it includes the palace of the Davidic king, a larger area around it and the temple (once it was built). The statement in this verse implies that the psalmist views Jerusalem, and the land of Israel in general, as sacred. See note on Ps 20:2. See the infographic "Jerusalem" on p. 1607.

102:title–28 Psalm 102 is explicitly identified as an individual lament psalm. It alternates between the psalmist's personal expression and his focus on the entire community of Israel. The psalmist uses his personal suffering as a window into the national situation; he pleads for Yahweh's help at both a personal and national level.

After a petition for help (vv. 1–2), the psalmist describes his affliction (vv. 3–11). He describes Yahweh's sovereign power, confident that he hears the prayers of the afflicted (vv. 12–17). Assuming Yahweh's help, the psalmist desires his situation to be remembered by future generations (vv. 18–22). He again laments his affliction (vv. 23–24) before concluding by praising God (vv. 25–28). See the table "Types of Psalms" on p. 830.

102:title afflicted This title specifically identifies the psalm as an individual lament psalm as it describes the psalmist using the Hebrew word *ani* (which may be literally rendered "poor" or "needy"). **a lament** The Hebrew word used here, *siach*, refers to lament or anxiety. In addition to communicating the psalmists' distress, lament psalms also include requests for Yahweh's action.

102:1–2 The psalmist begins with an impassioned plea that Yahweh would listen to his plight. This individual focus remains until v. 13, when the psalmist addresses concerns beyond himself.

102:3–8 The psalmist describes the details of the suffering he is experiencing. He feels physical and emotional pain, as well as social ridicule.

102:3 my bones burn This could indicate the depth of the feeling the psalmist is experiencing, since bones are the most durable parts of the body (compare Jer 20:9; Job 30:30).
102:6 a desert owl Owls were associated with barren places, and they eat unclean prey.

102:9–11 The psalmist interprets his difficulties as being the result of divine action. He struggles because of God's anger. See note on Ps 88:13–18.

102:9 eat ashes A symbol of destitution and mourning. The psalmist may be indicating repentance by mentioning his close association with ashes. In ancient Israel, the ritual actions connected with mourning and repentance often overlapped, since sorrow was an element in both. Israelites mourned by adopting a posture of destitution, which included fasting, rubbing ashes on one's body, wearing ragged clothing and separating themselves from normal living situations.

102:12–17 The psalmist now presents a communal expression of hope. He is confident that Yahweh will help Israel so that other nations will eventually honor him. Like the psalms of Yahweh's kingship (see note on 93:1), the psalmist specifically mentions Yahweh's enthronement.

102:12 endures through all generations Compare 102:18,24.

¹³ You will arise and have compassion on Zion,
  for it is time to show favor to her;
  the appointed time has come.
¹⁴ For her stones are dear to your servants;
  her very dust moves them to pity.
¹⁵ The nations will fear the name of the LORD,
  all the kings of the earth will revere your
    glory.
¹⁶ For the LORD will rebuild Zion
  and appear in his glory.
¹⁷ He will respond to the prayer of the destitute;
  he will not despise their plea.

¹⁸ Let this be written for a future generation,
  that a people not yet created may praise
    the LORD:
¹⁹ "The LORD looked down from his sanctuary
    on high,
  from heaven he viewed the earth,
²⁰ to hear the groans of the prisoners
  and release those condemned to death."
²¹ So the name of the LORD will be declared in
    Zion
  and his praise in Jerusalem
²² when the peoples and the kingdoms
  assemble to worship the LORD.

²³ In the course of my life*ᵃ* he broke my
    strength;
  he cut short my days.

²⁴ So I said:
  "Do not take me away, my God, in the midst
    of my days;
  your years go on through all generations.
²⁵ In the beginning you laid the foundations of
    the earth,
  and the heavens are the work of your
    hands.
²⁶ They will perish, but you remain;
  they will all wear out like a garment.
Like clothing you will change them
  and they will be discarded.
²⁷ But you remain the same,
  and your years will never end.
²⁸ The children of your servants will live in
    your presence;
  their descendants will be established
    before you."

Psalm 103

Of David.

¹ Praise the LORD, my soul;
  all my inmost being, praise his holy name.
² Praise the LORD, my soul,
  and forget not all his benefits —

ᵃ 23 Or By his power

102:13 Zion Refers to the temple mount in Jerusalem, from which Yahweh was understood to rule the earth; but this verse reflects that Yahweh rules even if his temple is in ruin (v. 16). This is because Yahweh also rules from heaven. See note on 20:2.
102:14 your servants The psalmist implies that Israel is loyal to Yahweh and his holy city (Jerusalem). As his loyal servants, they wait for him to help them.
102:15 fear the name of the LORD Describes a reverence for Yahweh's character and nature. See 91:14 and note.
102:16 rebuild Zion The psalmist believes Yahweh's action on behalf of Zion (see note on 102:13) will enhance his reputation.
102:17 the prayer of the destitute Psalm 102 is the prayer of a suffering person; here, the psalmist references a prayer within his prayer.

102:18–22 The psalmist shifts to a future time, anticipating that future generations will worship Yahweh when they remember how he helped Israel in the past.

102:20 groans of the prisoners This echoes the Israelites' struggle before the exodus from Egypt (compare Ex 2:23–25), but probably more directly refers to their time in Babylonian exile (586–538 BC; compare note on Ps 102:13).
102:21 in Jerusalem The terms Zion and Jerusalem are nearly synonymous. See 101:8 and note; 20:2 and note.

102:22 The psalmist envisions people from around the world coming to worship Yahweh in Jerusalem (compare Isa 2:1–4).

102:23–24 The psalmist now shifts back to an individual

perspective. He emphasizes that, in his perspective, Yahweh was involved in his suffering and pleads for mercy from God. See Dt 28–30.

102:23 he broke The Hebrew word used here, *anah*, indicates a violent action, an overpowering blow.

102:25–28 The psalmist now connects Yahweh's unchanging nature to Israel's hope for stability in the future. Because Yahweh never changes, Israel can trust that those who serve him will be able to be in his presence. The psalmist particularly envisions this for the descendants of the Israelites on whose behalf he speaks.

102:25 This verse emphasizes that Yahweh is the one who rightfully reigns over everything, for he created it.

102:26 They will perish Since Yahweh, who is eternal, will outlast any of his creations, he forms the basis of Israel's hope.
102:28 The children of your servants The psalmist emphasizes the hope that God's people can have long into the future. Compare Ps 90:16 and 103:17.

103:title–22 In this thanksgiving psalm, the psalmist reflects on Yahweh's compassion and the good things he does for those who trust him. The psalmist fuses statements about Yahweh's actions and character to portray Yahweh's love and loyalty. He responds to who Yahweh is with worship and trust. He begins by blessing Yahweh and extolling his character (vv. 1–5). He then reflects on Yahweh's loving disposition toward Israel (v. 6–14) as he compares the brevity of human life to the everlasting love of God (vv. 15–19). The psalmist concludes by calling everyone to bless (or praise) Yahweh (vv. 20–22). See the table "Types of Psalms" on p. 830.

³ who forgives all your sins
  and heals all your diseases,
⁴ who redeems your life from the pit
  and crowns you with love and compassion,
⁵ who satisfies your desires with good things
  so that your youth is renewed like the
    eagle's.

⁶ The LORD works righteousness
  and justice for all the oppressed.

⁷ He made known his ways to Moses,
  his deeds to the people of Israel:
⁸ The LORD is compassionate and gracious,
  slow to anger, abounding in love.
⁹ He will not always accuse,
  nor will he harbor his anger forever;
¹⁰ he does not treat us as our sins deserve
  or repay us according to our iniquities.
¹¹ For as high as the heavens are above the
    earth,
  so great is his love for those who fear him;
¹² as far as the east is from the west,
  so far has he removed our transgressions
    from us.

¹³ As a father has compassion on his children,
  so the LORD has compassion on those who
    fear him;

¹⁴ for he knows how we are formed,
  he remembers that we are dust.
¹⁵ The life of mortals is like grass,
  they flourish like a flower
    of the field;
¹⁶ the wind blows over it and it is gone,
  and its place remembers it no more.
¹⁷ But from everlasting to everlasting
  the LORD's love is with those who
    fear him,
  and his righteousness with their
    children's children —
¹⁸ with those who keep his covenant
  and remember to obey his precepts.

¹⁹ The LORD has established his throne in
    heaven,
  and his kingdom rules over all.

²⁰ Praise the LORD, you his angels,
  you mighty ones who do his bidding,
  who obey his word.
²¹ Praise the LORD, all his heavenly
    hosts,
  you his servants who do his will.
²² Praise the LORD, all his works
  everywhere in his dominion.

  Praise the LORD, my soul.

103:title Of David See note on 3:title.

103:1–5 The psalmist opens with the command to bless (or praise) Yahweh, and then lists the many good things that Yahweh does for his people. For more than half of the psalm, he focuses on these benefits (v. 2) and Yahweh's loving nature.

103:1 Praise the LORD The psalmist repeats this command six times (vv. 1,2,20,21,22). The Hebrew word used here, *barakh* (which may be literally rendered as "to bless"), describes bestowing someone with special power or declaring Yahweh to be the source of special power. In that regard, it means praising Yahweh for who he is. Compare 106:48 and note. **name** This refers primarily to the essential character and nature of Yahweh.

103:4 who redeems The Hebrew word used here, *go'el*, refers to a person who rescues another from a form of bondage through outside help. The term is applied to situations ranging from physical harm, to slavery, to debt. See note on Job 19:25. **love** See note on 25:10. **compassion** The Hebrew word used here, *rachamim*, describes a deeply felt care or mercy.

103:5 eagle's Symbolic of strength and speed, perhaps because of its ability to attack quickly from above.

103:6–10 The psalmist now focuses on Yahweh's character. Because of his loving nature, Yahweh acts on behalf of Israel (v. 7). He is merciful, and therefore he cares for Israel.

103:6 righteousness The psalmist associates Yahweh's righteousness with his care and help of the oppressed. Yahweh is a God of right actions. See 97:2 and note.

103:7 his deeds Probably refers to Yahweh's work during the exodus—likely the plagues against Egypt and the crossing of the Red Sea (Ex 7–12; 14–15).

103:11–14 The psalmist connects Yahweh's compassion to knowing him. While Yahweh does show love to those who fear him, his love is not dependent on their faultless observance. He is aware of human weakness, and loves people even though they sin.

103:11 those who fear him See note on Ps 90:11.

103:15–19 The psalmist describes Yahweh's permanence and reign over creation. His love sustains his people as they seek and follow his commands. While obedience matters to Yahweh, it is his care that sustains people, not their efforts at obedience. The images of vv. 15–16 resemble 90:5–6.

103:17 his righteousness See 103:6 and note. **with their children's children** This multi-generational relationship between Yahweh and Israel is a feature of Yahweh's covenant relationship with his people (see v. 18).

103:18 his covenant Refers to the relationship between Yahweh and Israel. See 105:8 and note.

103:20–22 The psalmist concludes with a series of commands to bless (or praise) Yahweh that echo the opening of the psalm. He closes the psalm by reaffirming his devotion to Yahweh.

103:21 his heavenly hosts The Hebrew word used here, *tsava*, may refer to military armies or to Yahweh's heavenly host; when referring to the heavenly realm, it can also refer to stars and other heavenly bodies. People can also be a part of Yahweh's hosts. **his servants** This can refer to the service priests do before Yahweh, but here it seems to refer broadly to those who follow Yahweh. Compare Ex 19:6.

103:22 Praise the LORD, my soul See Ps 103:1 and note.

Psalm 104

¹ Praise the LORD, my soul.

LORD my God, you are very great;
  you are clothed with splendor and
    majesty.

² The LORD wraps himself in light as with a
    garment;
  he stretches out the heavens like a tent
³   and lays the beams of his upper chambers
      on their waters.
  He makes the clouds his chariot
    and rides on the wings of the wind.
⁴ He makes winds his messengers,ᵃ
    flames of fire his servants.

⁵ He set the earth on its foundations;
    it can never be moved.
⁶ You covered it with the watery depths as
      with a garment;
    the waters stood above the mountains.

⁷ But at your rebuke the waters fled,
    at the sound of your thunder they took to
      flight;
⁸ they flowed over the mountains,
    they went down into the valleys,
    to the place you assigned for them.
⁹ You set a boundary they cannot cross;
    never again will they cover the earth.

¹⁰ He makes springs pour water into the
      ravines;
    it flows between the mountains.
¹¹ They give water to all the beasts of the field;
    the wild donkeys quench their thirst.
¹² The birds of the sky nest by the waters;
    they sing among the branches.
¹³ He waters the mountains from his upper
      chambers;
    the land is satisfied by the fruit of his
      work.

ᵃ 4 Or angels

104:1–35 In this praise psalm, the psalmist explores Yahweh's work in creating and sustaining the world. The psalmist intertwines these two emphases, indicating that Yahweh continues to support the world because he made it in the first place. The psalmist begins by praising Yahweh for his splendor and majesty (vv. 1–4). He then describes Yahweh's work in creation (vv. 5–9). As he praises Yahweh for sustaining creation, he turns specifically to Yahweh's work in providing water (vv. 10–13), fertility for crops (vv. 14–15) and dwelling places for animals (vv. 16–18). He describes Yahweh's power over the sun and moon (vv. 19–23)—which were often worshiped as gods in the ancient Near East—and shows how creation reveals Yahweh's glory (vv. 24–26). He then praises Yahweh's provision again (vv. 27–30). The psalmist concludes by praising Yahweh because he is sovereign over creation (vv. 31–35).

Two texts are usually compared with Ps 104: the ancient Egyptian "Great Hymn to Aten" and the creation account of Ge 1:1—2:4. However, neither parallel is exact. This psalm shows that Yahweh is intimately connected to sustaining the created order—is powerful over all of it—and that his work at the creation is only the beginning. See the table "Types of Psalms" on p. 830.

104:1–4 Psalm 104 begins and closes with the psalmist commanding his soul (*nephesh* in Hebrew) to bless (praise) Yahweh (vv. 1,35; compare 103:1,22). The opening verses of Ps 104 offer praise for the full breadth of creation.

104:1 Praise The Hebrew text here uses the word *barakh*. See 103:1 and note.

104:2–4 If Ps 104 is read in terms of Ge 1:1—2:4, the Hebrew word *or* ("light") in Ps 104:2 corresponds to day one of creation. In this case, vv. 2–4 correspond to the separation of the waters above from the waters below in day two of creation. See the infographic "The Days of Creation" on p. 6.

104:3 on their waters Reflects a cosmology similar to Ge 1:6–7, where the primordial world was a mass of water that God began to build within. See the infographic "Ancient Hebrew Conception of the Universe" on p. 5.

his chariot People in the ancient Near East sometimes depicted deities riding on storms or in the sky.

104:4 flames of fire The elements under Yahweh's command.

104:5–13 If Ps 104 is read in terms of Ge 1:1—2:4, then Ps 104:5–13 corresponds to the creation of dry land in day three of creation. However, the psalmist views the primordial state of the world somewhat differently than the author of Ge 1, since he explicitly states that God founded the earth under the depths before he uncovered it (compare Ge 1:1–2; Ps 104:6), which Ge 1:1–2 does not describe.

104:5–9 The psalmist focuses primarily on Yahweh's establishment of the terrestrial realm. Yahweh establishes a stable stage for the rest of his creative work.

104:6 above the mountains In its original state, land was submerged under the waters. Thus, the psalmist describes Yahweh's immense power. The psalmist might also be subtly criticizing the ancient Near Eastern understanding of mountains as places where people could commune with divine beings—Yahweh is the one who made these mountains visible and thus is far superior. See Ps 90:2 and note.

104:7 your thunder Reflects theophany imagery similar to Yahweh's appearance at Sinai (see Ex 19:18–20). See Ps 97:2 and note. See the table "Old Testament Theophanies" on p. 924.

104:10–13 The psalmist focuses on how Yahweh provides water for all creatures. In juxtaposition to ancient Near Eastern beliefs, he portrays Yahweh as living above the mountains, not on them (v. 13; see note on v. 6).

104:11 beasts The Hebrew word used here, *chayyah*, is a general term for wild animals.

104:13 from his upper chambers This reflects ancient Near Eastern cosmology, which held that it was through windows in the heavens that water came to the earth. See 90:2 and note.

¹⁴ He makes grass grow for the cattle,
   and plants for people to cultivate —
   bringing forth food from the earth:
¹⁵ wine that gladdens human hearts,
   oil to make their faces shine,
   and bread that sustains their hearts.
¹⁶ The trees of the Lord are well watered,
   the cedars of Lebanon that he planted.
¹⁷ There the birds make their nests;
   the stork has its home in the junipers.
¹⁸ The high mountains belong to the wild goats;
   the crags are a refuge for the hyrax.

¹⁹ He made the moon to mark the seasons,
   and the sun knows when to go down.
²⁰ You bring darkness, it becomes night,
   and all the beasts of the forest prowl.
²¹ The lions roar for their prey
   and seek their food from God.
²² The sun rises, and they steal away;
   they return and lie down in their dens.
²³ Then people go out to their work,
   to their labor until evening.

²⁴ How many are your works, Lord!
   In wisdom you made them all;
   the earth is full of your creatures.
²⁵ There is the sea, vast and spacious,
   teeming with creatures beyond number —
   living things both large and small.
²⁶ There the ships go to and fro,
   and Leviathan, which you formed to frolic
      there.

²⁷ All creatures look to you
   to give them their food at the proper time.
²⁸ When you give it to them,
   they gather it up;
   when you open your hand,
   they are satisfied with good things.
²⁹ When you hide your face,
   they are terrified;
   when you take away their breath,
   they die and return to the dust.
³⁰ When you send your Spirit,
   they are created,
   and you renew the face of the ground.

104:14-18 Read in terms of Ge 1:1—2:4, Ps 104:14-18 corresponds to the creation of plants and trees in day three of creation. See the infographic "The Days of Creation" on p. 6.

104:14-15 The psalmist now focuses on how Yahweh provides for plants and people.

104:14 cattle The Hebrew word used here, *behemah*, can refer to animals in general, but it can also refer specifically to cattle or other domestic animals. **for people to cultivate** See v. 23 and note.
104:15 wine that gladdens Yahweh doesn't just provide bare necessities; he also provides pleasant gifts. **oil** Ancients used various oils and remedies to counteract the weathering effects of the hot climate on their skin. Having the resources and opportunity to care for oneself this way was a sign of prosperity.

104:16-18 The psalmist explains how not all of Yahweh's creation exists for the sake of people; some of the world exists to please Yahweh alone.

104:16 the cedars of Lebanon The cedars in the mountain forests of Lebanon were famous in ancient Israel for their size and strength.

104:19-23 The psalmist describes that Yahweh created the world in a way that allows for all of his creatures to survive.

104:20-24 Read in terms of Ge 1:1—2:4, Ps 104:21-24 corresponds to the creation of land animals and humans in day six of creation. Psalm 104 doesn't follow the exact order of creation in Genesis. Part of what was created in day six (land animals and humans) comes before what was created in day five (sea creatures). See the infographic "The Days of Creation" on p. 6.

104:23 work The Hebrew word used here, *po'al*—which can be rendered "deed," "work," "action" or "accomplishment"—does not necessarily have a negative connotation.

104:24-26 The psalmist ascribes the vast scope of the sea as proof of Yahweh's great power and skill. The primordial waters represented chaos in the ancient Near East—Yahweh subdues them with ease.

104:24 wisdom The Hebrew word used here, *chokhmah*—meaning "skill," "experience" and "shrewdness"—is often used of human wisdom. Yahweh's *chokhmah* is marked by his insight and foresight.

104:25-26 Read in terms of Ge 1:1—2:4, Ps 104:25-26 corresponds to the creation of the sea creatures in day five of creation. Verse 24 is part of the previous section of the psalm because it mentions all of the creatures of the earth.

104:26 Leviathan A legendary sea monster in the ancient Near East. Several OT passages mention ancient monsters to make a theological point (e.g., Job 3:8). However, even when the monsters receive full attention in a passage, they remain mysterious (e.g., Job 40:15—41:34). While large, powerful creatures do exist in the world, the portrayals of the ancient monsters are primarily meant to be symbols of the uncontrollable power of nature. Unlike the gods of the ancient Near East, Yahweh does not need to battle these primordial monsters to gain control of creation; instead he effortlessly controls them because he created them.

104:27-30 The psalmist indicates that Yahweh not only gives food to his creatures, but he also gives them their very life-breath—which he will eventually take away. Read in terms of Ge 1:1—2:4, Ps 104:27-30 corresponds to Yahweh's provision of food for all creatures in day six of creation.

104:29 hide your face When God hides his face, he has withdrawn his care and help. **breath** The Hebrew word used here, *ruach*, is often used to signify a person's spirit or to denote their life-breath or vitality. **dust** The Hebrew word here, *aphar*, is also used in Ge 2:7.

³¹ May the glory of the LORD endure forever;
    may the LORD rejoice in his works —
³² he who looks at the earth, and it trembles,
    who touches the mountains, and they
    smoke.

³³ I will sing to the LORD all my life;
    I will sing praise to my God as long as I live.
³⁴ May my meditation be pleasing to him,
    as I rejoice in the LORD.
³⁵ But may sinners vanish from the earth
    and the wicked be no more.

Praise the LORD, my soul.

Praise the LORD.ᵃ

Psalm 105

105:1-15pp — 1Ch 16:8-22

¹ Give praise to the LORD, proclaim his name;
    make known among the nations what he
    has done.

² Sing to him, sing praise to him;
    tell of all his wonderful acts.
³ Glory in his holy name;
    let the hearts of those who seek the LORD
    rejoice.
⁴ Look to the LORD and his strength;
    seek his face always.

⁵ Remember the wonders he has done,
    his miracles, and the judgments he
    pronounced,
⁶ you his servants, the descendants of
    Abraham,
    his chosen ones, the children
    of Jacob.
⁷ He is the LORD our God;
    his judgments are in all the earth.

⁸ He remembers his covenant forever,
    the promise he made, for a thousand
    generations,

ᵃ 35 Hebrew *Hallelu Yah*; in the Septuagint this line stands at the beginning of Psalm 105.

104:31–35 The psalmist introduces several new emphases in his conclusion, broadening the view of Yahweh's work in the world to reemphasize the absolute need for people to praise him (compare Ps 104:1). To this point, the psalmist has focused on creation and Yahweh's role as ongoing provider for creation; he now shifts to emphasize Yahweh's overwhelming might. The psalmist expresses his desire that the wicked be removed from the earth, implying that Yahweh is the lawgiver as well as Creator. This also shows the psalmist's recognition that sinful behavior disturbs the very order Yahweh intended. The Hebrew text of this psalm concludes with the psalmist commanding his audience to bless (*barakh* in Hebrew) and praise (*halal* in Hebrew) Yahweh.

104:32 they smoke This seems to evoke theophany imagery. See v. 7 and note.
104:34 my meditation Meditation in the psalms involves considering Yahweh, and then expressing the results of that process. The psalms portray meditation as a sort of worship (see Ps 1).
104:35 Praise the LORD The Hebrew text here uses the phrase *hallu-yah*. In the psalms, the Hebrew term *hallu-yah* appears only in Ps 104–106; 111–117; 135; and 146–150 (Ps 120–134—the psalms of ascent—do not contain the phrase *hallu-yah*). The term *hallu-yah* means "praise Yah," using a shortened form of the name *yhwh* (Yahweh).

105:1–45 This praise psalm recounts Yahweh's work on behalf of Israel from a very positive standpoint—in this regard, it could be classified as a historical psalm. After an introductory note of praise (vv. 1–6), the psalmist follows the events from the Pentateuch, beginning with Yahweh's covenant with Abraham (vv. 7–15). He describes how Israel came to Egypt and grew in number (vv. 16–25), and emphasizes Yahweh's miraculous signs as he describes the exodus (vv. 26–38). He shows how Yahweh protected the Israelites during the wilderness years (vv. 39–42), and concludes with Israel's entry into the promised land (vv. 43–44). See the table "Types of Psalms" on p. 830.

105:1–6 The psalmist begins by calling the audience to proclaim Yahweh's wondrous deeds so that both Israel and the surrounding peoples will recall them. He mentions Israel's special status as Yahweh's chosen people, and specifically names the patriarchs Abraham and Jacob (see Ge 12:1–3; 32:28) in anticipation of the historical summary that will follow.

105:1 Give praise Refers to glad remembrance of Yahweh's actions.
105:2 tell of all his wonderful acts Focuses on Yahweh's excellence and moral goodness displayed in his actions.
105:5 his miracles The Hebrew word used here, *mopheth* (which can be rendered as "wonder" or "sign"), is used in connection with Moses' signs (Ex 4:21; 11:10).
105:6 descendants of Abraham By identifying Israel as Abraham's offspring, the psalmist anticipates the discussion of the Abrahamic covenant in Ps 105:8–10 (compare Ge 17). **chosen ones** The Hebrew word used here, *bachir*, can refer to one who is chosen or pious. **children of Jacob** Refers to the people of Israel, emphasizing their heritage as descendants of a special series of promises begun with Abraham. See Ge 48–49.

105:7–11 The psalmist continues to rehearse Israel's sacred history by mentioning the patriarchs as well as Yahweh's covenant with Israel. He mentions all three patriarchs, as well as the anticipation of future possession of the land of Canaan. This section corresponds to Ge 12–36.

105:8 his covenant Refers to the set of stipulations that governs the relationship between Yahweh and Israel. The OT describes four main Biblical covenants, including Yahweh's covenant with Noah (Ge 9), Abraham (Ge 15; 17), Moses and the people at Sinai (Ex 19–34) and Moab (Dt 29–30), and David (2Sa 7). The prophet Jeremiah explicitly mentions a "new covenant" (Jer 31:31–34; compare 32:36–41). Hosea 6:7 may also imply a covenant with Adam. The Biblical covenants ultimately depict Yahweh seeking to bring Israel and the rest of the world to himself. Yahweh initiates all of the Biblical covenants between him and people; the directives he gives in the covenants are aimed at maintaining relationship with him, rather than creating that relationship.

⁹the covenant he made with Abraham,
   the oath he swore to Isaac.
¹⁰He confirmed it to Jacob as a decree,
   to Israel as an everlasting covenant:
¹¹"To you I will give the land of Canaan
   as the portion you will inherit."

¹²When they were but few in number,
   few indeed, and strangers in it,
¹³they wandered from nation to nation,
   from one kingdom to another.
¹⁴He allowed no one to oppress them;
   for their sake he rebuked kings:
¹⁵"Do not touch my anointed ones;
   do my prophets no harm."

¹⁶He called down famine on the land
   and destroyed all their supplies of food;
¹⁷and he sent a man before them —
   Joseph, sold as a slave.
¹⁸They bruised his feet with shackles,
   his neck was put in irons,
¹⁹till what he foretold came to pass,
   till the word of the LORD proved
      him true.
²⁰The king sent and released him,
   the ruler of peoples set him free.

²¹He made him master of his household,
   ruler over all he possessed,
²²to instruct his princes as he pleased
   and teach his elders wisdom.

²³Then Israel entered Egypt;
   Jacob resided as a foreigner in the land
      of Ham.
²⁴The LORD made his people very fruitful;
   he made them too numerous for their foes,
²⁵whose hearts he turned to hate his people,
   to conspire against his servants.
²⁶He sent Moses his servant,
   and Aaron, whom he had chosen.
²⁷They performed his signs among them,
   his wonders in the land of Ham.
²⁸He sent darkness and made the land dark —
   for had they not rebelled against his
      words?
²⁹He turned their waters into blood,
   causing their fish to die.
³⁰Their land teemed with frogs,
   which went up into the bedrooms of their
      rulers.
³¹He spoke, and there came swarms of flies,
   and gnats throughout their country.

105:9 Abraham Yahweh interacted with Abraham in a series of promises and agreements culminating in a covenant (Ge 12:1–7; 13:14–17; 15:1–21; 17:1–27; 22:15–18). **Isaac** The son of Abraham and Israel's second patriarch. Yahweh extended the promises and covenant with Abraham to Isaac in Ge 26:1–5.
105:10 He confirmed Yahweh extended the promises and covenant that he made with Abraham and Isaac to Jacob in Ge 28:13–15 and Ge 35:9–12. Isaac's blessing to Jacob also mentioned elements of these promises (see Ge 27:27–29). **to Israel** When used in this way, the name Israel naturally extends from the person Jacob (renamed Israel) to the entire people of Israel who are descended from Jacob. **everlasting covenant** The Hebrew phrase used here, berith olam, is used with reference to Abraham in Ge 17:1–27. The expression is first used in Ge 9:16 to describe Yahweh's covenant with humankind after the flood.
105:11 the land of Canaan The original object of Yahweh's promises to Abraham (see Ps 105:6 and note). It may relate to the land reference in v. 44.

105:12–15 In this interlude, the psalmist reflects on the period when the patriarchs were wandering in the land of Canaan (and the surrounding region). His description of the events is very general; he may be drawing from the three episodes where a patriarch's wife was in danger of being violated by a foreign ruler (see Ge 12:10–20; 20:1–18; 26:6–11).

105:15 my anointed ones The act of anointing included smearing an object or person with liquid (such as oil or dye), and thereby set them apart as special. **my prophets** Refers specifically to Abraham (see Ge 20:7). In the OT the Hebrew term used here, navi, typically refers to someone who hears from Yahweh by means of special communication or visions and then speaks on Yahweh's behalf. Here the psalmist appears to be using it in a general sense to reflect the wording of Ge 20:7.

105:16–22 The psalmist recounts the story of Joseph's imprisonment and rise to power in Egypt (Ge 37; 39–41).

105:17 Joseph The son of Jacob who was sold into slavery by his envious brothers (see Ge 37:26–28). Although he was a pivotal figure in Israel's history, he is not usually described as a patriarch of Israel.

105:19 proved The Hebrew word used here, tsaraph — which generally refers to smelting or refining metals — might have the sense of proving or demonstrating value.

105:23–36 The psalmist recounts the story of Israel's enslavement in Egypt and their deliverance through Moses. He mentions eight out of the ten plagues against Egypt, culminating in the first Passover and the death of the firstborn of Egypt (Ex 1–12).

105:23 entered Egypt Corresponds to Ge 46:3–7. **Ham** One of Noah's sons who helped repopulate the world following the great flood (Ge 6–9; see 10:1,6–14). Ham and his sons settled in the area around Egypt and the coastland that would later be called Canaan.
105:24 fruitful Corresponds to Ex 1:7, where Egypt became fearful of the numerous people of Israel and enslaved them. **their foes** This is a retrospective evaluation. Before Egypt had enslaved Israel, they were not enemies (see Ge 47:5–6; Ex 1:8).
105:25 whose hearts he turned Yahweh's work against the nation of Egypt is a prominent theme of the exodus story. The psalmist views Egypt as a collective unit.
105:27 his signs Refers to the plagues against Egypt in the book of Exodus. See Ex 4:1–9; 7:8–12.
105:29 waters into blood The first plague (see Ex 7:14–25).
105:30 frogs The second plague (see Ex 8:1–15).
105:31 flies The fourth plague (see Ex 8:20–32). **gnats** The third plague (see Ex 8:16–19).

³²He turned their rain into hail,
    with lightning throughout their land;
³³he struck down their vines and fig trees
    and shattered the trees of their country.
³⁴He spoke, and the locusts came,
    grasshoppers without number;
³⁵they ate up every green thing in their land,
    ate up the produce of their soil.
³⁶Then he struck down all the firstborn in their
    land,
    the firstfruits of all their manhood.
³⁷He brought out Israel, laden with silver and
    gold,
    and from among their tribes no one
    faltered.
³⁸Egypt was glad when they left,
    because dread of Israel had fallen on them.

³⁹He spread out a cloud as a covering,
    and a fire to give light at night.
⁴⁰They asked, and he brought them quail;
    he fed them well with the bread of heaven.
⁴¹He opened the rock, and water gushed out;
    it flowed like a river in the desert.

⁴²For he remembered his holy promise
    given to his servant Abraham.
⁴³He brought out his people with rejoicing,
    his chosen ones with shouts of joy;
⁴⁴he gave them the lands of the nations,
    and they fell heir to what others had toiled
    for—
⁴⁵that they might keep his precepts
    and observe his laws.

Praise the LORD.[a]

Psalm 106

106:1,47-48pp — 1Ch 16:34-36

¹Praise the LORD.[b]

Give thanks to the LORD, for he is good;
    his love endures forever.

²Who can proclaim the mighty acts of the LORD
    or fully declare his praise?

[a] 45 Hebrew *Hallelu Yah*   [b] 1 Hebrew *Hallelu Yah*; also in
verse 48

105:32 hail The seventh plague (see Ex 9:13–25). The psalmist does not list plagues five and six (dead livestock and boils).
105:33 struck The psalmist elaborates on the disaster brought on by the plague of hail.
105:34 locusts The eighth plague (see Ex 10:1–20).
105:36 firstborn The tenth plague against Egypt, which coincides with the first Passover (Ex 11:1–10; 12:29–32). **firstfruits** The Hebrew word used here, *reshith*, is associated with the first products of harvest and the first offspring of animals and people. Israelites associated firstfruits with the choicest and best of something, and therefore considered them to have special value.

105:37–42 The psalmist briefly recounts the time of Israel's journey in the wilderness (Ex 12—Nu 36). He presents the events in a positive light and doesn't mention Israel's rebellion.

105:37 with silver and gold See Ex 12:35–36. **faltered** Implies that no one fell and stayed down.
105:39 cloud Indicated Yahweh's presence with Israel (see Ex 13:21–22).
105:40 quail Yahweh's provision of the quail during the wilderness journey eventually developed into an example of Israel's failure (see Ex 16:13; Nu 11:31–34). **bread of heaven** Refers to manna (see Ex 16:1–35).
105:41 He opened the rock May refer to Ex 17:1–7 or Nu 20:2–13. The psalmist doesn't mention Moses' failure in Nu 20.
105:42 his holy promise Refers to the covenantal promises made to Abraham. See Ps 103:18 and note; 105:6 and note; v. 9 and note.

105:43–45 The psalmist concludes by summarizing the exodus from Egypt to the entry into the promised land. He asserts that Yahweh brought Israel out of Egypt and into Canaan so that they would obey him and his commands.

105:43 with rejoicing This may be an echo of the joyful songs of Moses and Miriam (see Ex 15:1–18,21).
105:44 the lands of the nations Probably refers to the land Yahweh promised to Abraham, Canaan (see Ps 105:11 and note).
105:45 keep his precepts The psalmist clarifies that Yahweh delivered Israel and brought them into the promised land so that they might obey him. **Praise the LORD** This closing statement is repeated at the beginning and end of Ps 106 (106:1,48), and seems to form a connection with that psalm. See 104:35 and note.

106:1–48 Like Ps 105, Ps 106 is a praise psalm that reflects on Israel's history. However, the psalmist reflects on Israel's sacred history from the perspective of exile—being scattered among foreign nations as a punishment for unfaithfulness to Yahweh. This is almost certainly a reference to the Babylonian exile (ca. 586–538 BC). After a call to praise Yahweh (vv. 1–3), the psalmist petitions Yahweh to remember his people (vv. 4–5). He identifies with past generations by admitting guilt (v. 6). He describes Yahweh's provision for them (vv. 7–12) and their disobedience of Yahweh (vv. 13–43). The psalmist describes Yahweh's faithfulness to them and expresses hope in Yahweh's mercy (vv. 45–47). The psalmist expresses that, even though Israel deserves their punishment, they hope that Yahweh will have mercy on them again. This is the last psalm in Book Four of the Psalms (see note on 1:1–6); in that regard, 106:48 is a doxology, closing Book Four, and likely not originally part of the psalm itself. See the table "Types of Psalms" on p. 830.

106:1–3 The psalmist begins by praising Yahweh for his steadfast love, mentioning his mighty works and affirming the importance of keeping Yahweh's commands. These themes form a backdrop for the rest of the psalm.

106:1 Praise the LORD The psalm opens and closes with the Hebrew phrase *hallu-yah* (v. 48). See note on 104:35; note on 105:45. **Give thanks to the LORD, for he is good; his love endures forever** In the Hebrew text, this phrase is repeated verbatim in 107:1, creating a connection between Ps 106 and 107.

³ Blessed are those who act justly,
  who always do what is right.

⁴ Remember me, LORD, when you show favor
    to your people,
  come to my aid when you save them,
⁵ that I may enjoy the prosperity of your
    chosen ones,
  that I may share in the joy of your nation
  and join your inheritance in giving praise.

⁶ We have sinned, even as our ancestors did;
  we have done wrong and acted wickedly.
⁷ When our ancestors were in Egypt,
  they gave no thought to your miracles;
  they did not remember your many
    kindnesses,
  and they rebelled by the sea, the Red Sea.ᵃ
⁸ Yet he saved them for his name's sake,
  to make his mighty power known.
⁹ He rebuked the Red Sea, and it dried up;
  he led them through the depths as through
    a desert.
¹⁰ He saved them from the hand of the foe;
  from the hand of the enemy he redeemed
    them.
¹¹ The waters covered their adversaries;
  not one of them survived.
¹² Then they believed his promises
  and sang his praise.

¹³ But they soon forgot what he had done
  and did not wait for his plan to unfold.
¹⁴ In the desert they gave in to their craving;
  in the wilderness they put God to the test.
¹⁵ So he gave them what they asked for,
  but sent a wasting disease among them.

¹⁶ In the camp they grew envious of Moses
  and of Aaron, who was consecrated
    to the LORD.
¹⁷ The earth opened up and swallowed Dathan;
  it buried the company of Abiram.
¹⁸ Fire blazed among their followers;
  a flame consumed the wicked.
¹⁹ At Horeb they made a calf
  and worshiped an idol cast from metal.
²⁰ They exchanged their glorious God
  for an image of a bull, which eats grass.
²¹ They forgot the God who saved them,
  who had done great things in Egypt,
²² miracles in the land of Ham
  and awesome deeds by the Red Sea.
²³ So he said he would destroy them —
  had not Moses, his chosen one,
  stood in the breach before him
  to keep his wrath from destroying them.

²⁴ Then they despised the pleasant land;
  they did not believe his promise.

ᵃ 7 Or *the Sea of Reeds*; also in verses 9 and 22

106:2 Questions such as the one in this verse could have had a liturgical function in a public worship setting.

106:3 In this verse, the psalmist answers the question he posed in v. 2.

106:4–5 The psalmist personally identifies himself with Israel's communal hope in Yahweh's love and saving help. The mention of Yahweh's chosen ones and his inheritance (v. 5) anticipates the mention of the covenant in v. 45.

106:4 your people The psalmist now begins to identify himself and his people with his ancestors (see vv. 6,47).
106:5 your inheritance The Hebrew word used here, *nachalah*, often references the land of Israel and also can refer to the people of Israel as a nation. Compare v. 40.

106:6–12 The psalmist equates the current generation with their ancestors. He recalls the incident at the Red Sea, where Israel failed to trust Yahweh following the plagues against Egypt (see Ex 14–15). The psalmist recounts episodes from the Pentateuch until Ps 106:34.

106:6 We have sinned, even as our ancestors did The psalmist asserts that, just as Israel sinned in times past, the current generation of Israel has sinned in the present.
106:7 in Egypt The psalmist may refer to the Israelites' enslavement in Egypt, or the miraculous events of the exodus. **rebelled** Refers to the events by the Red Sea in Ex 14:10–14. The psalmist describes Israel's complaining and lack of faith as rebellion.
106:8 for his name's sake The revelation of Yahweh's name—that is, his character and nature—is often related to Yahweh's salvific action. See Ps 91:14 and note; 23:3 and note; compare Ex 3.

106:10 redeemed them Refers to rescue from a form of bondage through outside help. See Ps 103:4 and note.
106:12 sang See Ex 15.

106:13–15 The psalmist recounts how Israel complained about meat, and Yahweh punished them with an overabundance of quail and a plague (see Nu 11:4,13,31–34).

106:13 forgot Refers to failing to trust and remain loyal. **did not wait** See Nu 11:1–6,31–35.
106:14 they gave in to their craving See Nu 11:1–4,13,31–35; compare Ps 105:40 and note.

106:16–18 The psalmist recounts Korah's rebellion in Nu 16.

106:17 The earth opened While the psalmist doesn't mention Korah by name, he identifies his subordinates, Dathan and Abiram (see Nu 16:32). These types of omissions can indicate intense disapproval on the part of an ancient author; the author may not even want to mention the offensive person or thing.
106:18 Fire blazed See Nu 16:35.

106:19–23 The psalmist recounts the story of the golden calf in Ex 32:1–6.

106:19 Horeb Another name for Sinai, where God revealed the Ten Commandments to Moses.
106:22 Ham One of Noah's sons; here his name is used to refer to Egypt (see Ge 10:6). Compare Ps 105:23 and note.
106:23 he would destroy them Recounts the exchange between Yahweh and Moses in Ex 32:7–14.

106:24–27 The psalmist recounts how Israel refused to trust Yahweh and enter Canaan in Nu 13–14.

25 They grumbled in their tents
	and did not obey the Lord.
26 So he swore to them with uplifted hand
	that he would make them fall in the
		wilderness,
27 make their descendants fall among the nations
	and scatter them throughout the lands.

28 They yoked themselves to the Baal of Peor
	and ate sacrifices offered to lifeless gods;
29 they aroused the Lord's anger by their
		wicked deeds,
	and a plague broke out among them.
30 But Phinehas stood up and intervened,
	and the plague was checked.
31 This was credited to him as righteousness
	for endless generations to come.
32 By the waters of Meribah they angered the
		Lord,
	and trouble came to Moses because of them;
33 for they rebelled against the Spirit of God,
	and rash words came from Moses' lips.ᵃ

34 They did not destroy the peoples
	as the Lord had commanded them,
35 but they mingled with the nations
	and adopted their customs.
36 They worshiped their idols,
	which became a snare to them.
37 They sacrificed their sons
	and their daughters to false gods.
38 They shed innocent blood,
	the blood of their sons and daughters,
	whom they sacrificed to the idols of
		Canaan,
	and the land was desecrated by their
		blood.
39 They defiled themselves by what they did;
	by their deeds they prostituted
		themselves.

40 Therefore the Lord was angry with his people
	and abhorred his inheritance.

ᵃ 33 Or *against his spirit, / and rash words came from his lips*

106:24 they despised The Hebrew word used here, *ma'as*, can mean "to refuse" or "to reject," and by extension means "to despise" that which is given. **his promise** This refers to Yahweh's words in Ex 33:1–2. Yahweh's promise can be traced as far back as Ge 12:1–3.
106:25 grumbled See Nu 14:1–12.
106:26 swore to them See Nu 14:20–23; Ps 95:11 and note. **that he would make them fall in the wilderness** See Nu 14:20–38.
106:27 among the nations The psalmist is probably reflecting on the condition of the Israelites at the time of writing this psalm (see Ps 106:47) rather than drawing from a specific episode in history. Just as the rebellious generation of Israelites died off in the wilderness, many Israelites may have been dying outside of Israel, scattered in foreign nations. See note on 106:1–48.

106:28–31 The psalmist recounts the wilderness generation's final rebellion with Baal of Peor in Nu 25.

106:28 They yoked themselves This refers to the Israelites' unfaithfulness and worship of other gods in terms of sexual infidelity (see Nu 25:1–5). The events of Nu 25 represent a definitive act of betrayal. **ate sacrifices offered to lifeless gods** Numbers 25 does not mention this ritual. The psalmist might be alluding to practices elsewhere in Israel's history or to events not recorded in Nu 25.
106:30 Phinehas A priest who impaled a couple for ritually defiling the tabernacle sanctuary. See Nu 25:7–8.
106:31 credited to him as righteousness This statement reflects the words of Ge 15:6.
106:32–33 The psalmist describes Nu 20:10–13 where Moses drew water from the rock at Meribah by striking it instead of speaking to it as Yahweh had commanded (Nu 20:8). Following this incident, Yahweh prohibited Moses from entering the promised land (Nu 20:12).

106:33 rash words came from Moses' lips The psalmist suggests that Yahweh punished Moses for his words but there is no record of this in Numbers. The psalmist could be using Moses to represent how the people of Israel spoke against Yahweh and his purposes or be alluding to a tradition not recorded in Numbers.

106:34–39 The psalmist now considers the time after Israel entered into Canaan (the promised land). He relates a general historical survey, and seems to depict the overall degeneration of Israel during the period of the book of Judges. Psalm 106:39 ends the list of the crimes of Israel's ancestors.

106:34 They did not destroy the peoples Probably recounts Jdg 2:11—3:6, where the Israelites allowed some of the Canaanites to remain in the promised land after they took possession. This led to some Israelites following Canaanite practices. **as the Lord had commanded them** In general, Israel attempted to interact peacefully with their neighbors. Yahweh commanded the Israelites to eradicate the inhabitants of Canaan as a judgment against those people groups and because he knew that the Israelites would eventually worship the gods of the Canaanites otherwise. See Dt 7:1–5; note on Jos 6:16; note on 6:17.
106:37 They sacrificed The use of the Hebrew word *zavach* here may be figurative, referring to the Israelites leading their children to fatal error. However, the reference to blood (Ps 106:38) suggests that the psalmist is referring to actual child sacrifice, which is mentioned at several points. For example, Ahaz and Manasseh sacrificed their sons during national crises (2Ki 16:3; 21:6; compare Jdg 11:28–40), apparently in an attempt to win favor with a foreign deity. Child sacrifice is specifically prohibited in OT law and was a capital crime (Lev 18:21; 20:2–5). **false gods** The Hebrew word used here, *shedim*, occurs only in the plural in the OT (compare Dt 32:17). It seems to refer to malevolent spirits as a group.
106:38 innocent blood The Hebrew expression used here can extend beyond the literal shedding of blood to include any act of injustice. Compare Ps 94:21. **desecrated by their blood** See Eze 22.

106:40–43 The psalmist depicts how Yahweh punished Israel for its disobedience and unfaithfulness. The precise episode of punishment he describes is unclear. It may have occurred during the period of the Judges (Ps 106:43); however, the reference to the nations (v. 41) seems to go beyond the regional conflicts of the Judges period, and anticipates the exile and hope of restoration (v. 47).

BOOK V

Psalms 107–150

Psalm 107

41 He gave them into the hands of the
    nations,
    and their foes ruled over them.
42 Their enemies oppressed them
    and subjected them to their
    power.
43 Many times he delivered them,
    but they were bent on rebellion
    and they wasted away in their sin.
44 Yet he took note of their distress
    when he heard their cry;
45 for their sake he remembered his
    covenant
    and out of his great love he relented.
46 He caused all who held them captive
    to show them mercy.

47 Save us, LORD our God,
    and gather us from the nations,
  that we may give thanks to your holy
    name
    and glory in your praise.

48 Praise be to the LORD, the God of Israel,
    from everlasting to everlasting.

Let all the people say, "Amen!"

Praise the LORD.

1 Give thanks to the LORD, for he is good;
    his love endures forever.

2 Let the redeemed of the LORD tell their
    story —
    those he redeemed from the hand
    of the foe,
3 those he gathered from the lands,
    from east and west, from north and south.[a]

4 Some wandered in desert wastelands,
    finding no way to a city where they could
    settle.
5 They were hungry and thirsty,
    and their lives ebbed away.
6 Then they cried out to the LORD in their
    trouble,
    and he delivered them from their
    distress.
7 He led them by a straight way
    to a city where they could settle.

a 3 Hebrew *north and the sea*

106:40 his inheritance Compare v. 5.
106:43 Many times he delivered them Probably refers to the cycle of the book of Judges (see Jdg 2:11–23).

106:44–46 In this section, the psalmist mentions the covenant, through which Yahweh showed his consistent concern for Israel's welfare. Yahweh always remembered his commitment to Israel; therefore, he always helped them. In these verses, the psalmist anticipates that Yahweh will continue to help them. He seems to meld several of Israel's experiences of oppression into a single expression, such as their enslavement in Egypt and various times of oppression during the time of the Judges.

106:44 he heard their cry Part of the pattern in the book of Judges (e.g., Jdg 3:15).

106:47–48 The psalmist asks Yahweh to help Israel and gather them from their scattered locations in exile (see note on Ps 106:1–48). The psalm closes by blessing Yahweh and repeating the opening command of v. 1.

106:48 This verse functions as a doxology or closing to Book Four of Psalms (see note on 1:1–6). The closing verses of each book of Psalms contain statements of blessing to Yahweh. Such formulaic statements of praise to Yahweh are usually called doxologies, and point to some level of intentional arrangement of each book of the Psalms. However, the precise nature of that arrangement is unclear. These statements could indicate that the psalms were collected into these books in stages; they could also indicate that the psalms were transmitted for a time in the form of these books.

107:1–43 Psalm 107 is the first psalm in the final book of Psalms—Book Five (see note on 1:1–6). Like Ps 106, Ps 107 is a praise psalm that looks back on Israel's history.

In it, the psalmist recalls how Yahweh has redeemed portions of his people from various locations and difficult situations. He first recounts the locations and situations of difficulty (vv. 1–32), then describes Yahweh's power (vv. 33–43). He implies that any ruler who attempts to oppress Yahweh's people will experience the difficulty that they try to bring upon Israel. This psalm seems to reflect the context of Israelite life after the Babylonian exile (after 538 BC) as it mentions Yahweh gathering his people from around the world (v. 3), and more specifically, the context after the second temple was made and rededicated (after 516 BC). See the table "Types of Psalms" on p. 830.

107:1–3 The psalmist calls his audience to thank Yahweh for rescuing his people from trouble. He describes the gathering of Israel from the four points of the compass, which would correspond to Israel's experience of dispersion in the exile. See note on Ps 107:1–43.

107:1 his love See note on 25:10.
107:2 redeemed See note on 103:4.
107:3 those he gathered The psalmist is probably considering the past experience of exile. See note on 107:1–43.

107:4–9 The psalmist envisions Israelites who wander in the wilderness without direction until Yahweh guides them.

107:4 desert wastelands See note on Ps 95:8. **to a city** In the harsh climate of the ancient Near East, cities were sources of life, protection and economic activity since they were located near sources of water and food.

107:6 The psalmist repeats this verse nearly verbatim three additional times (vv. 13,19,28).

8 Let them give thanks to the LORD for his
   unfailing love
   and his wonderful deeds for mankind,
9 for he satisfies the thirsty
   and fills the hungry with good things.

10 Some sat in darkness, in utter darkness,
    prisoners suffering in iron chains,
11 because they rebelled against God's
    commands
    and despised the plans of the Most High.
12 So he subjected them to bitter labor;
    they stumbled, and there was no one to
    help.
13 Then they cried to the LORD in their trouble,
    and he saved them from their distress.
14 He brought them out of darkness, the utter
    darkness,
    and broke away their chains.
15 Let them give thanks to the LORD for his
    unfailing love
    and his wonderful deeds for mankind,
16 for he breaks down gates of bronze
    and cuts through bars of iron.

17 Some became fools through their rebellious
    ways
    and suffered affliction because of their
    iniquities.
18 They loathed all food
    and drew near the gates of death.
19 Then they cried to the LORD in their
    trouble,
    and he saved them from their distress.
20 He sent out his word and healed them;
    he rescued them from the grave.

21 Let them give thanks to the LORD for his
    unfailing love
    and his wonderful deeds for mankind.
22 Let them sacrifice thank offerings
    and tell of his works with songs of joy.

23 Some went out on the sea in ships;
    they were merchants on the mighty
    waters.
24 They saw the works of the LORD,
    his wonderful deeds in the deep.
25 For he spoke and stirred up a tempest
    that lifted high the waves.
26 They mounted up to the heavens and went
    down to the depths;
    in their peril their courage melted away.
27 They reeled and staggered like drunkards;
    they were at their wits' end.
28 Then they cried out to the LORD in their
    trouble,
    and he brought them out of their distress.
29 He stilled the storm to a whisper;
    the waves of the sea[a] were hushed.
30 They were glad when it grew calm,
    and he guided them to their desired haven.
31 Let them give thanks to the LORD for his
    unfailing love
    and his wonderful deeds for mankind.
32 Let them exalt him in the assembly of the
    people
    and praise him in the council of the elders.

33 He turned rivers into a desert,
    flowing springs into thirsty ground,

a 29 Dead Sea Scrolls; Masoretic Text / their waves

107:8 The psalmist repeats this verse verbatim three additional times (vv. 15,21,31).

107:8 mankind Probably refers specifically to the people of Israel who have been gathered from dispersion in exile (v. 3) and worship in the assembly of Israel (v. 32).

107:10–16 The psalmist envisions Israelites who are imprisoned until Yahweh frees them—this language reflects the Israelites' time in Babylonian exile (586–538 BC). While the language is generally figurative, for some Israelites the language here reflects a real experience.

107:10 in utter darkness See note on 23:4.

107:11 God's commands The psalmist indicates they suffered because they broke Yahweh's covenant.

107:16 gates of bronze The psalmist describes a strong prison that would be difficult to escape. Bronze and iron were the hardest metals in the ancient Near East.

107:17–22 The psalmist describes Israelites who suffer illness because of their own sin. They are near death until Yahweh heals them. Compare Dt 28–30.

107:18 the gates of death The Hebrew phrase used here, *sha'arei maweth*, is possibly related to the Hebrew word *tsalmaweth* (meaning "deep darkness" or "shadow of death") used in Ps 107:10 and v. 14. The Bible con-

tains a rich vocabulary and set of images for death, which illuminate the OT view of the afterlife (see note on 116:3). The OT presents death as the natural end of life, and perhaps as the unnatural result of sin (see note on Ge 3:22).

107:20 his word In Ps 107:17, the psalmist implied that Yahweh's action—as a response to the people's sin—caused (or at least allowed) the affliction of the people; here, he explicitly attributes their healing to Yahweh.

107:22 thank offerings See note on 96:8.

107:23–32 The psalmist envisions Israelites encountering storms at sea in the course of their business. They fear for their lives until Yahweh calms the seas. The seas (or the waters) represented chaos in the ancient Near East and are described as being held back by Yahweh (see 104:6–8).

107:23 the sea The psalmist may mention the sea to connect this scene to the previous episodes in Ps 107; the sea is another sphere in which Yahweh's power is necessary for people to survive. **they were merchants** Describes a trade mission or business journey.

107:26 depths See note on Ge 1:2.

107:30 their desired haven The sea is the ultimate trackless wilderness. Just as Yahweh brought the wandering people of Ps 107:7 to a safe city, he brought the sailors to a safe harbor.

³⁴ and fruitful land into a salt waste,
  because of the wickedness of those who
    lived there.
³⁵ He turned the desert into pools of water
  and the parched ground into flowing
    springs;
³⁶ there he brought the hungry to live,
  and they founded a city where they could
    settle.
³⁷ They sowed fields and planted vineyards
  that yielded a fruitful harvest;
³⁸ he blessed them, and their numbers greatly
    increased,
  and he did not let their herds diminish.

³⁹ Then their numbers decreased, and they
    were humbled
  by oppression, calamity and sorrow;
⁴⁰ he who pours contempt on nobles
  made them wander in a trackless waste.
⁴¹ But he lifted the needy out of their affliction
  and increased their families like flocks.
⁴² The upright see and rejoice,
  but all the wicked shut their mouths.

⁴³ Let the one who is wise heed these things
  and ponder the loving deeds of the Lord.

Psalm 108ᵃ

108:1-5pp — Ps 57:7-11
108:6-13pp — Ps 60:5-12

A song. A psalm of David.

¹ My heart, O God, is steadfast;
  I will sing and make music with all
    my soul.
² Awake, harp and lyre!
  I will awaken the dawn.
³ I will praise you, Lord, among
    the nations;
  I will sing of you among the peoples.
⁴ For great is your love, higher than the
    heavens;
  your faithfulness reaches to the skies.
⁵ Be exalted, O God, above the heavens;
  let your glory be over all the earth.

ᵃ In Hebrew texts 108:1-13 is numbered 108:2-14.

107:33-38 The psalmist emphasizes that, although Yahweh brings hardship because of people's sin, he also brings blessings (see Dt 28–30). The psalmist reflects in a way that signals that the time of Yahweh's punishment is over (see Ps 107:20,34; see note on vv. 1–43). The psalmist concentrates on the wilderness motifs of vv. 4–9, which are tangible elements that everyone hearing the psalm could identify with. By developing the topics of water and cities in relation to Yahweh's power, the psalmist is able to focus on Yahweh's work to reestablish Israel.

107:34 a salt waste The Hebrew word used here, *melechah*, refers to salted land, which cannot produce vegetation.
107:36 city The people establish a city, which begins a new focus in Ps 107 (compare vv. 4,7). This could refer to the reestablishment of Jerusalem after the exile.
107:38 their numbers greatly increased Yahweh's provision remains the ultimate source of prosperity.

107:39-43 In this closing passage, the psalmist implies that Yahweh protects Israel after he has restored them. He will afflict any rulers attacking Israel, and his ongoing care for those who have suffered will encourage those faithful to him.

107:40 on nobles Yahweh reverses the oppression that his people suffer. **waste** The Hebrew word used here, *tohu*, describes substance lacking boundary, order and definition. See note on Ge 1:2.
107:42 wicked The psalmist seems to refer to those inside and outside of Israel who oppose Yahweh's ways and oppress others.
107:43 wise See note on Ps 104:24. **ponder** The psalmist implies that the key to wisdom is a steady focus on Yahweh's steadfast love.

108:title-13 Psalm 108 is a corporate lament psalm (meant for group settings) that combines sections from Ps 57 and 60. The psalmist expresses concern that God has stopped helping Israel as he promised. He combines his personal relationship with God with his participation in the people of Israel, and pleads with God to help Israel triumph over local enemies. He quotes 57:7–11 as he praises God's steadfast love (108:1–5). He then quotes 60:5–12 as he asks God to fulfill his promises and give them victory over their enemies (108:6–13). See the table "Types of Psalms" on p. 830.

108:title A song The Hebrew word used here, *shir*, may refer to a song that is meant to be chanted, not accompanied by musical instrumentation. **A psalm of David** See note on 3:title.

108:1-5 The psalm begins by focusing on personal worship of God. While he is likely addressing an Israelite audience, he still envisions proclaiming God's goodness to the surrounding nations (v. 3). Verses 1–5 reproduce 57:7–11, which is connected by its inscription to an episode when David hid from King Saul in a cave (see 57:title and note).

108:1 This verse essentially quotes 57:7.

108:2 This verse essentially quotes 57:8.

108:2 I will awaken the dawn This probably indicates that the psalmist woke early to praise God.

108:3 This verse quotes 57:9 verbatim.

108:3 among the peoples The Hebrew word used here, *ummim*, is a term for ethnic groups other than the Israelites; *goyim* is the more common Hebrew term (see 96:3 and note).

108:4 This verse quotes 57:10 verbatim.

108:5-6 The psalmist continues to worship God personally, but introduces his request for help and deliverance. He urgently wants an answer from God (v. 6).

108:5 This verse quotes 57:11 verbatim.

108:5 above the heavens The psalmist notes that God is above the heavens; this shows that God is above everything in terms of fame and power.

⁶Save us and help us with your right hand,
  that those you love may be delivered.
⁷God has spoken from his sanctuary:
  "In triumph I will parcel out Shechem
  and measure off the Valley of Sukkoth.
⁸Gilead is mine, Manasseh is mine;
  Ephraim is my helmet,
  Judah is my scepter.
⁹Moab is my washbasin,
  on Edom I toss my sandal;
  over Philistia I shout in triumph."

¹⁰Who will bring me to the fortified city?
  Who will lead me to Edom?
¹¹Is it not you, God, you who have rejected us
  and no longer go out with our armies?
¹²Give us aid against the enemy,
  for human help is worthless.
¹³With God we will gain the victory,
  and he will trample down our enemies.

Psalm 109

For the director of music. Of David. A psalm.

¹My God, whom I praise,
  do not remain silent,
²for people who are wicked and deceitful
  have opened their mouths against me;
  they have spoken against me with lying
    tongues.
³With words of hatred they surround me;
  they attack me without cause.
⁴In return for my friendship they
    accuse me,
  but I am a man of prayer.
⁵They repay me evil for good,
  and hatred for my friendship.

⁶Appoint someone evil to oppose my enemy;
  let an accuser stand at his right hand.

108:6 This verse quotes 60:5 verbatim.

108:7–9 The psalmist reminds God of his promises to Israel in a roundabout way. He takes himself and Israel out of the picture and speaks only of God's words regarding what he will do for himself. The places he mentions are adjacent to or very near Jerusalem, forming a circle around it.

108:7 This verse quotes 60:6 verbatim.

108:8 This verse quotes 60:7 verbatim.

108:8 scepter The Hebrew word used here, *mechoqeq*, is also used in Ge 49:10, where the tribe of Judah is associated with the royal line in Israel. Judah's descendants are traced in Ge 38:29–30 and Ru 4:18, ultimately tying Judah and King David together. As anointed king over Israel (see 2Sa 7), David became the prototype of the Messianic expectation in Israel. As Israel endured various judgments that eventually culminated in exile (586 BC), the hope for restoration of Israel included the reinstatement of a king in the model of David. For Christians, the fulfillment of that hope is Jesus, who is descended from David (see Mt 1:1–17).

108:9 This verse quotes Ps 60:8 verbatim.

108:9 Moab An enemy of Israel in much of the OT (see note on Ru 1:1). **my washbasin** God is simultaneously claiming the lands of Israel's traditional enemies and demeaning them. The lands of Moab and Edom belong to God, who is described as using them like the furniture in his palace—a palace which emerges from Jerusalem. **Edom** An area south of the Dead Sea.

Psalm 108:9

EDOM
The Edomites were thought to have descended from Jacob's brother Esau; the relationship between the two nations reflects the relationship of the two brothers (compare Ge 27). Israel and Edom were never at peace. The Edomites later assisted the Babylonians' invasion of Judah (see the book of Obadiah).

108:10–13 The psalmist reemerges as the military leader of Israel rather than its worship leader. He specifically identifies Israel's enemy (Ps 108:10) and his request for God's presence (v. 11). The psalmist ends by implying that Israel will triumph only with God's help.

108:10 This verse quotes 60:9 verbatim.

108:11 This verse quotes 60:10 verbatim.

108:12 This verse quotes 60:11 verbatim.

108:13 This verse quotes 60:12 verbatim.

109:title–31 In Ps 109, an individual lament psalm, the psalmist complains to God and requests his help as he experiences opposition from personal enemies. After crying out to God (v. 1), the psalmist describes the actions of his enemies (vv. 2–5). He then calls curses or imprecations on them (vv. 6–15). He continues to describe his enemies and ask Yahweh to punish them (vv. 16–20). He laments his condition (vv. 21–25) and again cries out to Yahweh for help (vv. 26–29). Finally, he concludes by giving thanks to Yahweh in anticipation of Yahweh's deliverance (vv. 30–31). See the table "Types of Psalms" on p. 830.

109:title director of music See note on 4:title. **Of David. A psalm** See note on 3:title.

109:1–5 The psalmist describes his general situation as he faces social opposition. He proclaims that he has not done wrong (v. 3), and asserts that he has been good and kind to those who now attack him (vv. 4–5). The psalmist chooses to address the matter in prayer to God rather than attack in return (v. 4).

109:4 accuse The Hebrew word used here, *satan*, means "to be hostile toward" (see v. 6). The technical term for "adversary" or "accuser" was *satan*. This basic meaning seems to be the basis for the characterization of Satan as the primary enemy of God and the accuser of his people. **prayer** The Hebrew word used here, *tephillah*, refers to a prayer associated with a concern or need.

109:6–15 The psalmist curses his adversaries. He wants his enemies to be annihilated and his enemies' descendants to be destroyed as well. These harsh words

⁷ When he is tried, let him be found guilty,
    and may his prayers condemn him.
⁸ May his days be few;
    may another take his place of leadership.
⁹ May his children be fatherless
    and his wife a widow.
¹⁰ May his children be wandering beggars;
    may they be driven*ᵃ* from their ruined
      homes.
¹¹ May a creditor seize all he has;
    may strangers plunder the fruits of his
      labor.
¹² May no one extend kindness to him
    or take pity on his fatherless children.
¹³ May his descendants be cut off,
    their names blotted out from the next
      generation.
¹⁴ May the iniquity of his fathers be
      remembered before the Lord;
    may the sin of his mother never be
      blotted out.
¹⁵ May their sins always remain before the
      Lord,
    that he may blot out their name from the
      earth.

¹⁶ For he never thought of doing a kindness,
    but hounded to death the poor
    and the needy and the brokenhearted.
¹⁷ He loved to pronounce a curse —
    may it come back on him.

He found no pleasure in blessing —
    may it be far from him.
¹⁸ He wore cursing as his garment;
    it entered into his body like water,
    into his bones like oil.
¹⁹ May it be like a cloak wrapped about him,
    like a belt tied forever around him.
²⁰ May this be the Lord's payment to my
      accusers,
    to those who speak evil of me.

²¹ But you, Sovereign Lord,
    help me for your name's sake;
    out of the goodness of your love,
      deliver me.
²² For I am poor and needy,
    and my heart is wounded within me.
²³ I fade away like an evening shadow;
    I am shaken off like a locust.
²⁴ My knees give way from fasting;
    my body is thin and gaunt.
²⁵ I am an object of scorn to my accusers;
    when they see me, they shake their heads.

²⁶ Help me, Lord my God;
    save me according to your unfailing love.
²⁷ Let them know that it is your hand,
    that you, Lord, have done it.
²⁸ While they curse, may you bless;
    may those who attack me be put to shame,
    but may your servant rejoice.

ᵃ 10 Septuagint; Hebrew *sought*

---

seem to reflect the concept of *lex talionis* (often described as an "eye for an eye"), which was common in the ancient Near East. It seems that the difficulties that have befallen the psalmist he wishes upon his enemies, who have caused his difficulties.

109:6 at his right hand A position of influence and honor. In court, both accusers and defenders are portrayed as standing at the right hand of a person. Compare v. 31.
109:10 ruined homes A picture of utter destitution.
109:11 a creditor The psalmist envisions complete financial collapse for his enemies' surviving families. See note on 109:6–15.
109:12 kindness Compare v. 16.
109:13 next generation The psalmist wants the family line of his enemies to end, which in the ancient Near East is the conceptual equivalent of having never lived.
109:14 the iniquity of his fathers In Ex 34:6–7, Yahweh promised that he will not extend punishment for crimes from generation to generation. However, elsewhere sins are depicted as passing from generation to generation, suggesting that the effects of sin did transmit from one generation to the next (e.g., Nu 14:18).

109:16–20 The psalmist presents the rationale for his anger toward his enemies by personifying them as a single person. Not only are the psalmist's enemies cruel toward him, but they also treat other people badly and harm the needy.

109:16 doing a kindness Connected to the punishment in Ps 109:12. **poor and the needy** The Hebrew words

used here, *ani* and *evyon*, often occur together and are both associated with poverty and need in general. The word *evyon* might also include misery that comes from oppression. Compare vv. 22,31.
109:17 to pronounce a curse The Hebrew word used here, *qelalah*, is used in a curse formula in which someone or something is declared to have bad things come upon them. The psalmist may be describing poetic justice: arrogant presumption meets a fitting end. Compare note on vv. 6–15. **blessing** Though the Hebrew word used here, *berakhah*, can refer to a blessing that someone can seek and receive, it is also a formula for blessing (in contrast to cursing). See 103:1 and note.
109:18 his bones The psalmist is describing accursedness that sinks into his enemies as deep as possible.

109:21–25 The psalmist identifies himself as part of the needy people his enemies enjoy harming. The psalmist's suffering is both emotional and physical, and he begs Yahweh for help.

109:26–29 The psalmist connects his request for Yahweh's help to Yahweh's love and his good reputation. The psalmist wants Yahweh's help not only for his personal vindication, but also because he wants Yahweh's character to be displayed.

109:28 put to shame Just as the psalmist's complaint is located in his social context, this punishment needs a social context to have any force (see v. 25). Compare note on 109:6–15.

²⁹ May my accusers be clothed with disgrace
and wrapped in shame as in a cloak.

³⁰ With my mouth I will greatly extol the LORD;
in the great throng of worshipers I will
praise him.

³¹ For he stands at the right hand of the needy,
to save their lives from those who would
condemn them.

Psalm 110

Of David. A psalm.

¹ The LORD says to my lord:ᵃ

"Sit at my right hand
until I make your enemies
a footstool for your feet."

² The LORD will extend your mighty scepter
from Zion, saying,
"Rule in the midst of your enemies!"

³ Your troops will be willing
on your day of battle.
Arrayed in holy splendor,
your young men will come to you
like dew from the morning's womb.ᵇ

⁴ The LORD has sworn
and will not change his mind:
"You are a priest forever,
in the order of Melchizedek."

⁵ The Lord is at your right hand ᶜ;
he will crush kings on the day of his wrath.

⁶ He will judge the nations, heaping up the
dead
and crushing the rulers of the whole
earth.

⁷ He will drink from a brook along the way,ᵈ
and so he will lift his head high.

ᵃ 1 Or *Lord*   ᵇ 3 The meaning of the Hebrew for this sentence
is uncertain.   ᶜ 5 Or *My lord is at your right hand*, LORD
ᵈ 7 The meaning of the Hebrew for this clause is uncertain.

109:30–31 The psalmist concludes by committing to praise Yahweh after deliverance. He describes how Yahweh helps the needy and rescues them from accusers who unjustly attack them.

109:30 With my mouth This contrasts with the wicked lies of the psalmist's enemies (see vv. 2–4); the psalmist will express his confidence in Yahweh's help.

110:title–7 Psalm 110 is a royal psalm (about kingship) that is structured around two statements from Yahweh. The first is a prophetic oracle (vv. 1–3), and the second is a divine oath (vv. 4–7). Psalm 110 is connected to the Messianic understanding of Jesus and his work. New Testament writers quote material from both halves of Ps 110 to support an understanding of Jesus as Messiah. See the table "Types of Psalms" on p. 830.

110:title Of David. A psalm See note on 3:title.

110:1–3 New Testament writers quote the opening line of this prophetic oracle four times (Mt 22:44; Mk 12:36; Lk 20:42; Ac 2:34). This passage proclaims that a Davidic figure, acting as Yahweh's military representative on earth, will expand Yahweh's influence to the surrounding nations. In addition, parts of v. 1 are quoted in 1Co 15:25 and Heb 1:13.

110:1 The LORD says The Hebrew phrase used here, *ne'um yhwh*, refers to an announcement of Yahweh; the word *ne'um* can mean "oracle" or "utterance." The expression is common in the prophetic books and marks Ps 110:1–3 as a prophetic utterance. Textual parallels from Assyrian royal prophecies and other Assyrian coronation texts show that such divine endorsements for kings were standard in the ancient Near East. **my lord** The identification of *adoni* ("my lord") is crucial to the psalm, and it determines how the psalm is used in a worship context. David may prophetically see himself as carrying on a divinely appointed role; in this case, he composed it as a song that the people sing regarding him as they celebrate in worship of God. Alternatively, David may prophetically see a future individual within his lineage receiving a divinely appointed role; in this case, he composed the psalm in his own voice in anticipation of that person. Jesus quotes from v. 1 in reference to

himself (Mt 22:44; Mk 12:36; Lk 20:42–43). He portrays the speaker of Ps 110:1 as David, and asks why David would refer to his son as lord. Jesus seems to understand the verse as a direct prophecy concerning himself, and not one that is mediated by David's self-understanding as a ruler within a specially chosen lineage. **Sit** God, seated as a divine ruler, tells his chosen representative to sit beside him in a place of honor and authority while he arranges everything. **at my right hand** A position of honor and authority. See v. 5. **footstool** Portrays great humiliation for the king's enemies. See 99:5 and note.

110:4–7 In this divine oath, God endorses his earthly representative as a priest in addition to his role as king. This fusion of king and priest is distinctive to the Davidic ruler, since the laws concerning priests in the OT strictly separate the offices of king and priest (see 99:6 and note). The author of Hebrews uses this connection to articulate Jesus' role (see note on 110:4).

110:4 a priest A priest was one with the proper authority to minister before God in his sacred places. **Melchizedek** A priest of God from before the time of Moses and Aaron, and thus outside of the hereditary framework of the priesthood (see 99:6 and note). He blessed Abraham and also received a tithe from him (see Ge 14:18–20). Melchizedek is central to the discussion of Christ as priest in Hebrews (Heb 4:14—5:10; 6:13—8:13).

110:5 The perspective of the psalm changes from Yahweh speaking to the psalmist speaking. The third-person references in Ps 110:5–7 are ambiguous. They may be referring to Yahweh, or to Yahweh's chosen ruler—the Lord referenced in v. 1. They likely refer to Yahweh's chosen ruler (see note on v. 7).

110:5 at your right hand This seems to refer to the Lord referenced in v. 1 being at the right hand of Yahweh—a point which has already been made in v. 1.
110:7 He will drink This seems to indicate that the third-person pronouns in vv. 5–7 refer to God's chosen ruler, not Yahweh himself. Yahweh provides water for his chosen agent as he proceeds on his mission. **he will lift his head high** A lifted head was symbolic of both victory and God's favor.

Psalm 111[a]

[1] Praise the LORD.[b]

I will extol the LORD with all my heart
    in the council of the upright and in the
    assembly.

[2] Great are the works of the LORD;
    they are pondered by all who delight in
    them.
[3] Glorious and majestic are his deeds,
    and his righteousness endures forever.
[4] He has caused his wonders to be
    remembered;
    the LORD is gracious and compassionate.
[5] He provides food for those who fear him;
    he remembers his covenant forever.

[6] He has shown his people the power of his
    works,
    giving them the lands of other nations.
[7] The works of his hands are faithful and just;
    all his precepts are trustworthy.

[8] They are established for ever and ever,
    enacted in faithfulness and uprightness.
[9] He provided redemption for his people;
    he ordained his covenant forever —
    holy and awesome is his name.

[10] The fear of the LORD is the beginning of
    wisdom;
    all who follow his precepts have good
    understanding.
To him belongs eternal praise.

Psalm 112[a]

[1] Praise the LORD.[b]

Blessed are those who fear the LORD,
    who find great delight in his commands.

[2] Their children will be mighty in the land;
    the generation of the upright will be blessed.

[a] This psalm is an acrostic poem, the lines of which begin with
the successive letters of the Hebrew alphabet.   [b] 1 Hebrew
Hallelu Yah

111:1–10 Psalm 111 is a praise psalm celebrating Yahweh's work and commands. After an introductory statement praising Yahweh (v. 1), it has two main sections. The first section focuses on Yahweh's works and his character (vv. 2–6). The second section focuses on Yahweh's covenants and commands (vv. 7–9). The final verse of the psalm combines these concerns into a subtle call for obedience and loyalty to Yahweh (v. 10).

Psalm 111 is an alphabetic acrostic psalm, in which each line of the psalm begins with the next letter of the Hebrew alphabet. The pattern begins after the opening phrase in Hebrew, *hallu-yah* ("praise Yahweh"); when the lines are divided according to the Hebrew letters, there are 22 lines. See the table "Types of Psalms" on p. 830.

111:1 Praise the LORD See note on 104:35.

111:2–6 The psalmist reflects on Yahweh's works, which reveal his character. Yahweh is not simply powerful, he is also compassionate toward his people and faithful to his commitments to them.

111:2 the works of the LORD. The Hebrew phrase used here, *ma'aseh yhwh*, often refers to the events in the book of Exodus.

111:3 forever The Hebrew word used here, *ad* (which refers to "a lasting future time"), is synonymous with *olam* ("long time" or "future time"; vv. 5,9). In Ps 111, these terms convey the meaning of "forever." The word *ad* serves as a structural bookend in Ps 111. The verses between these bookends use the term *olam*, describing how Yahweh remembers his covenant until *olam* (v. 5) and has commanded his covenant until *olam* (v. 9). In v. 8, the psalmist combines the two terms, emphasizing the eternality of Yahweh's precepts (v. 8). This pattern draws attention to Yahweh's precepts, which are trustworthy (v. 7) and to be performed faithfully (v. 8).

111:6 the lands of other nations The psalmist describes how Yahweh took the inheritance from the nations and gave it to Israel (see note on 47:5; 96:3 and note).

111:7–10 The psalmist reflects on Yahweh's commands in the light of his good record in caring for his people.

Yahweh's requirements are not based on the threat of violence, but on the history of his provision for Israel. The psalmist expands the sense of fear of Yahweh beyond terror of punishment, presenting it as trust in Yahweh's provision and character (v. 10).

111:9 his name See 91:14 and note.

111:10 The psalmist's assertion in this verse is similar to statements in Proverbs and Job (e.g., Pr 1:7; 9:10; Job 28:28). The Hebrew idea of *yir'ah* (fear of Yahweh) referenced here seems to lie somewhere between "respect" and "terror." Wisdom is a practically focused skill in living. Fear of God and wisdom are frequently combined, and are thus viewed as synonyms. Wisdom is always connected to ethical responsibilities before God.

111:10 beginning of wisdom The primary prerequisite of OT wisdom is the proper stance toward God and his requirements.

112:1–10 Psalm 112 is structured as an alphabetic acrostic, in which each line begins with a successive letter of the Hebrew alphabet (see 111:1–10 and note). It is a wisdom psalm—meant to pass along wise sayings—that, like Ps 1, contrasts the path of the righteous with the path of the wicked. The psalmist first describes the character of the righteous (v. 1), then recalls the blessings that come to them (vv. 2–5). He shows that the righteous are secure because they can trust in Yahweh (vv. 6–9). The psalmist concludes by mentioning the ultimate fate of the wicked (v. 10). See the table "Types of Psalms" on p. 830.

112:1–4 After commanding his audience to praise Yahweh, the psalmist lists the bountiful blessings of the righteous person who follows Yahweh. The Hebrew word *ashre* used in these verses (meaning "blessed" or "fortunate") occurs frequently in the psalms to highlight the state of the righteous person (e.g., 1:1; 41:1; 106:3).

112:1 Blessed The Hebrew word used here, *ashre*, occurs more than 25 times in the psalms. It is connected with the idea of wisdom and what is commonly called the "two

³ Wealth and riches are in their houses,
  and their righteousness endures forever.
⁴ Even in darkness light dawns for the upright,
  for those who are gracious and
    compassionate and righteous.
⁵ Good will come to those who are generous
  and lend freely,
  who conduct their affairs with justice.

⁶ Surely the righteous will never be shaken;
  they will be remembered forever.
⁷ They will have no fear of bad news;
  their hearts are steadfast, trusting in the
    Lord.
⁸ Their hearts are secure, they will have no
    fear;
  in the end they will look in triumph on
    their foes.
⁹ They have freely scattered their gifts to the
    poor,
  their righteousness endures forever;
  their horn[a] will be lifted high in honor.

¹⁰ The wicked will see and be vexed,
  they will gnash their teeth and waste away;
  the longings of the wicked will come to
    nothing.

Psalm 113

¹ Praise the Lord.[b]

Praise the Lord, you his servants;
  praise the name of the Lord.
² Let the name of the Lord be praised,
  both now and forevermore.
³ From the rising of the sun to the place where
    it sets,
  the name of the Lord is to be praised.

⁴ The Lord is exalted over all the nations,
  his glory above the heavens.
⁵ Who is like the Lord our God,
  the One who sits enthroned on high,

---

a 9 *Horn* here symbolizes dignity.   *b* 1 Hebrew *Hallelu Yah*;
also in verse 9

---

ways" motif—referring to the way of wickedness versus God's ways—prevalent in Wisdom Literature (see Ps 1). Jesus alludes to the term *ashre* in the Beatitudes (Mt 5:2–12; Lk 6:20–23). See note on Ps 1:1. **who fear the Lord** See note on 90:11.

112:2 the land Though the Hebrew word used here, *erets*, can refer to ground or territory in general, it often refers more specifically to the land of Israel, as it probably does here.

112:3 righteousness The Hebrew word used here, *tsedaqah*, refers to right actions, which can be loyalty or acting justly. In this context, it likely refers to actual deeds of loyalty or justice done for the community (compare 112:9). For the OT authors, righteousness (*tsedaqah*) is connected to a right attitude toward God and right deeds in light of God's commands. The OT speaks of genuinely pious actions as having some sort of lasting component because they are connected to real deeds, just as God's righteousness is connected to real deeds.

112:5–9 In this passage, the psalmist specifies the ethics of the righteous person—especially in relationship to the impoverished. He also describes the inner life of the righteous. Because righteous people trust Yahweh and deal with others justly, they will enjoy Yahweh's help.

112:5 who are generous The Hebrew word used here, *chanan*, means "to favor," "to have compassion" or "to be gracious"—referring generally to a generous attitude. In the ancient Near East, the impoverished relied on generosity to survive. Although OT law required that the Israelites be generous, Yahweh reassured those who gave to the needy that he would bless them (see Dt 15:7–11; Pr 19:17).

112:6 remembered forever This description of the righteous (*tsaddiq* in Hebrew) mirrors Ps 111's description of Yahweh's righteousness (*tsedaqah* in Hebrew). See 111:3.

112:8 they will have no fear The psalmist indicates that righteous people—who fear Yahweh (112:1)—will never need to fear because they will always have Yahweh's help when faced with enemies.

112:9 their horn A symbol of strength and power.

112:10 they will gnash their teeth A gesture of rage

associated with clenched jaws, such as speaking through clenched teeth or grinding one's teeth.

113:1–9 A praise psalm, Ps 113 is a hymn or song praising Yahweh's nature and character. The psalmist begins by calling his audience to praise Yahweh (vv. 1–3). He then describes Yahweh's position over the created world (vv. 4–6), concluding with examples of Yahweh's help for those in need (vv. 7–9). Psalms 113–118 are a collection within the book of Psalms known as the Egyptian Hallel, which Israelites traditionally recited at Passover. These psalms derive their name from the prevalence of the Hebrew term *hallu-yah* and their use in the annual Passover ritual, which commemorates the exodus from Egypt. (The Hebrew term *hall-el*, meaning "praise God," is related to the Hebrew term *hallu-yah* meaning "praise Yah"—*yah* is the shortened form of the divine name Yahweh.) See the table "Types of Psalms" on p. 830.

113:1–3 After calling his audience to praise Yahweh, the psalmist focuses on the name of Yahweh as an emblem of his worthiness.

113:1 Praise the Lord See note on 104:35.
113:2 praised See note on 106:48.

113:4–6 The psalmist focuses on Yahweh's power and authority over everything. He implies that Yahweh deserves that position of authority because of his glorious character.

113:4 his glory above the heavens Just as Yahweh is above the nations and has authority over them, he has authority over the heavens as well. Yahweh is not bounded by the heavens—as other ancient Near Eastern gods were generally believed to be—and he is above any other beings that inhabit the heavenly realm.

113:5 the Lord our God The Hebrew text here uses the phrase *yhwh eloheinu*, which may be rendered "Yahweh our God." This combination of names for Yahweh originated in the exodus story, where God reveals his personal name (Ex 3:14; 6:2,8) and enters into a covenant with Israel (Ex 19:5–6). **enthroned on high** The image of a seated king implies stable authority and rule—the king, Yahweh,

6 who stoops down to look
  on the heavens and the earth?

7 He raises the poor from the dust
  and lifts the needy from the ash heap;
8 he seats them with princes,
  with the princes of his people.
9 He settles the childless woman in her home
  as a happy mother of children.

  Praise the LORD.

Psalm 114

1 When Israel came out of Egypt,
  Jacob from a people of foreign tongue,
2 Judah became God's sanctuary,
  Israel his dominion.

3 The sea looked and fled,
  the Jordan turned back;
4 the mountains leaped like rams,
  the hills like lambs.

5 Why was it, sea, that you fled?
  Why, Jordan, did you turn back?
6 Why, mountains, did you leap like rams,
  you hills, like lambs?

7 Tremble, earth, at the presence of the Lord,
  at the presence of the God of Jacob,
8 who turned the rock into a pool,
  the hard rock into springs of water.

Psalm 115

115:4-11pp — Ps 135:15-20

1 Not to us, LORD, not to us
  but to your name be the glory,
  because of your love and faithfulness.

2 Why do the nations say,
  "Where is their God?"
3 Our God is in heaven;
  he does whatever pleases him.

---

is not away from his throne in an effort to subdue his kingdom, but rules it from the splendor of his palace. **113:6 who stoops down to look** This phrase further emphasizes Yahweh's position above everything (see Ps 113:4 and note). He rules over the entire created order (including heaven), and his nature and capacity cannot be contained within that created order.

113:7–9 The psalmist concludes by illustrating the ways that Yahweh helps those in need. He presents Yahweh as merciful in addition to powerful. The psalmist describes Yahweh's magnificent justice (vv. 4–6) and specific care (vv. 7–9).

113:7 needy See note on 109:16. **ash heap** The Hebrew word used here, *ashpoth*, refers to a heap of ash, garbage or manure.

113:8 princes of his people Yahweh helps with the physical needs of people, and also alleviates social stigma and shame.

113:9 childless woman Israelites often interpreted childlessness as divine punishment that could lead to divorce (Ex 23:26; Dt 7:14). Further, children were a source of pride and satisfaction and could provide for their aged parents. Several OT narratives focus on God's miraculous provision of children (e.g., Sarah in Ge 21:1–7; Rachel in 30:22–24; Hannah in 1Sa 1:19–20).

114:1–8 Psalm 114 is a praise psalm included among the collection of psalms known as the Egyptian Hallel (see note on 113:1–9). Psalm 114 is a brief, stylized presentation of a pivotal phase in Israel's history. The psalmist praises God for his works during the exodus (Ex 1–15) and the Israelite people's subsequent entry into the promised land of Canaan (Jos 1–4). He focuses on God's power over water and earth, drawing from Israel's miraculous passages through bodies of water. The psalmist also examines God's power over the land, possibly drawing from Israel's time in the wilderness. He closes by fusing the motifs of water and earth, recounting how God miraculously provided for the Israelites with water during their time in the wilderness. See the table "Types of Psalms" on p. 830.

114:1–2 The opening verses of Ps 114 locate the psalm in the time of the exodus. The psalmist emphasizes the intimate nature of God's relationship with Israel; the people of Israel are described as like a residence for God.

114:1 Egypt The exodus story is a pattern for the rest of the biblical narrative, and is the prototype for God's rescue of humanity. **Jacob** See note on 105:6. **foreign tongue** The psalmist might be using the Hebrew word *lo'ez* here—meaning "to speak a foreign or incomprehensible language"—as an insult.

114:2–6 In this symmetrically structured passage, the psalmist describes the personified responses to God of the Red Sea, the Jordan River, the mountains and the hills. He first lists their fearful responses, then asks why they reacted as they did.

114:2 Judah Jacob's son, Judah, became the namesake of a tribe of descendants which included David and Jesus. Jerusalem was also located in the land allotted to Judah (see 97:8; 108:8). **sanctuary** See note on 96:6.

114:3 The sea looked and fled Refers to the events of Ex 14, where God parted the waters of the Red Sea so that the Israelites could walk across on dry land. **Jordan turned back** Refers to the events of Jos 3, where the waters of the Jordan River miraculously stopped so that Joshua could lead the people of Israel into the promised land.

114:4 leaped like rams This has no direct parallel in the story of the exodus, but God is portrayed as shaking the earth in the theophany at Sinai (see Ps 97:2 and note).

114:7–8 The psalmist concludes by emphasizing God's power, which he uses for Israel's benefit. The earth should fear God because he can make it do anything that he wants for his people.

114:7 the God of Jacob See Ex 3:6 and note.

114:8 who turned the rock into a pool This refers to the events of Ex 17:1–7 (and perhaps Nu 20:2–13), when God provided water for Israel from a rock.

115:1–18 Psalm 115, a psalm of confidence—expressing faith in God—is included in the collection of psalms known as the Egyptian Hallel (see note on 113:1–9). It

⁴ But their idols are silver and gold,
    made by human hands.
⁵ They have mouths, but cannot
    speak,
    eyes, but cannot see.
⁶ They have ears, but cannot hear,
    noses, but cannot smell.
⁷ They have hands, but cannot feel,
    feet, but cannot walk,
    nor can they utter a sound with their
    throats.
⁸ Those who make them will be like
    them,
    and so will all who trust in them.

⁹ All you Israelites, trust in the LORD —
    he is their help and shield.
¹⁰ House of Aaron, trust in the LORD —
    he is their help and shield.
¹¹ You who fear him, trust in the LORD —
    he is their help and shield.

¹² The LORD remembers us and will
    bless us:
    He will bless his people Israel,
    he will bless the house of Aaron,
¹³ he will bless those who fear the LORD —
    small and great alike.

¹⁴ May the LORD cause you to flourish,
    both you and your children.
¹⁵ May you be blessed by the LORD,
    the Maker of heaven and earth.

¹⁶ The highest heavens belong to the LORD,
    but the earth he has given to mankind.
¹⁷ It is not the dead who praise the LORD,
    those who go down to the place of
    silence;
¹⁸ it is we who extol the LORD,
    both now and forevermore.

Praise the LORD.ᵃ

ᵃ 18 Hebrew *Hallelu Yah*

portrays a community of worshipers declaring hope in God as they contrast the powerless, dead idols of the nations with their powerful, living God. The psalmist begins with a prayer for Yahweh's help (vv. 1–2). He then contrasts Yahweh's sovereign power with the useless-ness of idols (vv. 3–8). He encourages Israel to trust in Yahweh (vv. 9–11), who will remember them and bless them (vv. 12–15). He concludes by emphasizing Israel's living hope in the living God (vv. 16–18). See the table "Types of Psalms" on p. 830.

115:1–3 The psalmist begins by implicitly calling for Yahweh to act on Israel's behalf in order to glorify himself in the sight of the surrounding nations.
115:1 your name See note on 91:14.
115:3 Our God The psalmist is not asking God to prove himself so that Israel will remain loyal, but so that the other nations will see his power and recognize him. **in heaven** See note on 108:5.
115:4–8 The psalmist discusses the dead idols of the nations who can do nothing for those who trust in them. The idols are powerless; as a result, the nations have no power, and won't be able to do anything. Through his taunts, the psalmist seems to alternate between criticizing the powerlessness of the idols and critiquing the fact that they are represented in images.
115:5 They have mouths, but cannot speak Implies that the idol does not reveal anything to those who worship it. **eyes, but cannot see** Implies that the idol is not aware of anything, and will never help those who worship it (compare Ex 3:7).
115:6 ears, but cannot hear Implies that the idol can-not respond to requests, and will never help those who worship it (contrast Ps 91:15; 99:6; 102:2; 2Ch 7:14; Isa 65:24). **noses, but cannot smell** The psalmist may be mocking sacrifices being offered to idols. In contrast, Leviticus often describes sacrifices offered to God as a pleasing aroma (e.g., Lev 1:13).
115:8 will be like them The psalmist implies that the people who look to powerless idols will be powerless and helpless when crisis comes upon them. **trust in**

them Trusting a deity meant worshiping it and attending to its requirements.

115:9–15 The psalmist calls Israel to trust in Yahweh, implying that Yahweh is powerful and willing to help them. He first mentions Israel as a unit, then splits the people into priests and worshipers. The psalmist calls all Israel to trust in the God who is not created by human hands or controlled by human intermediaries. This passage also reflects on the pivotal role of priests in the life of Israel, and the psalmist affirms Yahweh's care for all of the people of Israel, whether modest or wealthy.

115:9–11 This series of three addressees — Israel, priests and all believers (Ps 115:9–11) — is repeated in vv. 12–13.
115:9 shield Refers to Yahweh's protection.
115:10 House of Aaron Refers to the priests, the lead-ers of Israel's worship. See note on 99:6.
115:11 You who fear See note on 90:11.
115:12 remembers us The Hebrew verb used here, *zakhar*, refers to a calling to mind that occurs in conjunc-tion with some activity. See note on Ex 2:24. **will bless** Yahweh's blessing of Israel is a continuation of the sort of blessing that is inherent in creating and sustaining the world; it is also dependent on Israel's obedience within the context of Yahweh's covenant. See Dt 28–30.

115:16–18 The psalmist concludes by affirming the crucial role of Israel's praise of Yahweh. Since Yahweh has given stewardship of the earth to people (see Ge 1:28), it is critical that Israel honor Yahweh's will.
115:16 mankind The Hebrew phrase used here, *bene-adam*, is a term for people that are not connected to any particular national group — here it refers to humanity in general.
115:17 who go down to the place of silence The OT understanding of the state of people after death is unclear. Many passages depict the dead descending to *she'ol* (a Hebrew term referring to the realm of the dead). This verse seems to depict the after-death state as a mysterious, silent underworld. Alternatively, it may depict a soundless grave holding a corpse.

Psalm 116

[1] I love the LORD, for he heard my voice;
he heard my cry for mercy.
[2] Because he turned his ear to me,
I will call on him as long as I live.

[3] The cords of death entangled me,
the anguish of the grave came over me;
I was overcome by distress and sorrow.
[4] Then I called on the name of the LORD:
"LORD, save me!"

[5] The LORD is gracious and righteous;
our God is full of compassion.
[6] The LORD protects the unwary;
when I was brought low, he saved me.

[7] Return to your rest, my soul,
for the LORD has been good to you.

[8] For you, LORD, have delivered me from death,
my eyes from tears,
my feet from stumbling,
[9] that I may walk before the LORD
in the land of the living.

[10] I trusted in the LORD when I said,
"I am greatly afflicted";
[11] in my alarm I said,
"Everyone is a liar."

[12] What shall I return to the LORD
for all his goodness to me?

[13] I will lift up the cup of salvation
and call on the name of the LORD.
[14] I will fulfill my vows to the LORD
in the presence of all his people.

[15] Precious in the sight of the LORD
is the death of his faithful servants.
[16] Truly I am your servant, LORD;
I serve you just as my mother did;
you have freed me from my chains.

[17] I will sacrifice a thank offering to you
and call on the name of the LORD.
[18] I will fulfill my vows to the LORD
in the presence of all his people,
[19] in the courts of the house of the
LORD —
in your midst, Jerusalem.

Praise the LORD.[a]

Psalm 117

[1] Praise the LORD, all you nations;
extol him, all you peoples.
[2] For great is his love toward us,
and the faithfulness of the LORD endures
forever.

Praise the LORD.[a]

[a] 19,2 Hebrew *Hallelu Yah*

116:1–19 The fourth of the Egyptian Hallel psalms (see note on Ps 113:1–9), Ps 116 is a thanksgiving psalm in which the psalmist reflects on a time when Yahweh helped him, and he responds with gratitude and loyalty. Yahweh heard the psalmist's plea for help and delivered him from danger (vv. 1–4). The psalmist then proclaims Yahweh's goodness and deliverance (vv. 5–11). Looking to repay Yahweh, he states his intention to pay his vows and offer sacrifices of thanksgiving (vv. 12–19). See the table "Types of Psalms" on p. 830.

116:1–4 The psalmist is motivated to worship because he is grateful that Yahweh helped him during his crisis.

116:1 he heard The psalmist indicates that Yahweh granted his request.
116:2 I will call An implicit expression of trust.
116:3 grave The Hebrew word *she'ol* is used here, which refers to the realm of the dead (the underworld; see note on Job 14:13; note on 1Ki 2:6). The psalmist notes that his anguish is so great that it is as if the realm of the dead has visited him in life.

116:5–7 The psalmist praises Yahweh's nature and character after being delivered. The psalmist calms himself by recalling Yahweh's action on his behalf.

116:6 the unwary The psalmist implies that Yahweh saves those who cannot save themselves.

116:8–11 The psalmist returns to addressing Yahweh personally before making a further commitment to obey him. The psalmist reflects a pivotal moment of trust in the midst of crisis.

116:8 In this verse, the psalmist lists things Yahweh has delivered him from. Each of these expressions portrays disastrous experiences from which there seemed to be no escape.

116:8 my eyes from tears Describes deep, irreversible loss rather than casual grief.
116:9 I may walk before the LORD The psalmist asserts that he will live in continual obedience to Yahweh.

116:12–14 The psalmist describes how he will worship in response to Yahweh's help.

116:13–14 Ps 116:13–14 are repeated in vv. 17–18; both passages describe public actions of worship.

116:13 the cup of salvation The psalmist may be referring to a ritual involving a cup of wine as a libation (or drink offering).
116:14 my vows Reflects a custom of making promises to Yahweh in gratitude or making a promise to repay in return for divine help. See note on Ecc 5:4. **in the presence of all his people** A public display of gratitude meant to bolster Yahweh's reputation.

116:15–19 The psalmist emphasizes his loyalty to Yahweh after deliverance. Heartfelt gratitude is at the center of his public worship.

116:17 a thank offering See note on Ps 107:22.
116:19 house of the LORD See note on 92:13; note on 99:6. **Jerusalem** The center of worship in ancient Israel, which was subsequently seen as a holy city.

117:1–2 This brief praise psalm makes a distinctive statement by echoing the great theme of Yahweh's

Psalm 118

[1] Give thanks to the LORD, for he is
  good;
  his love endures forever.

[2] Let Israel say:
  "His love endures forever."
[3] Let the house of Aaron say:
  "His love endures forever."
[4] Let those who fear the LORD say:
  "His love endures forever."

[5] When hard pressed, I cried to the LORD;
  he brought me into a spacious place.
[6] The LORD is with me; I will not be afraid.
  What can mere mortals do to me?
[7] The LORD is with me; he is my helper.
  I look in triumph on my enemies.

[8] It is better to take refuge in the LORD
  than to trust in humans.

[9] It is better to take refuge in the LORD
  than to trust in princes.
[10] All the nations surrounded me,
  but in the name of the LORD I cut them
    down.
[11] They surrounded me on every side,
  but in the name of the LORD I cut them
    down.
[12] They swarmed around me like bees,
  but they were consumed as quickly as
    burning thorns;
  in the name of the LORD I cut them down.
[13] I was pushed back and about to fall,
  but the LORD helped me.
[14] The LORD is my strength and my defense [a];
  he has become my salvation.

[15] Shouts of joy and victory
  resound in the tents of the righteous:

[a] 14 Or song

---

steadfast love toward Israel, orienting it toward the foreign nations and calling them to praise Yahweh (compare Isa 2:1–4). This psalm is included in the collection of psalms known as the Egyptian Hallel psalms (see note on Ps 113:1–9).

117:1 nations The Hebrew word used here, *goy*, refers to geographic territories or people groups outside of Israel. **peoples** See note on 108:3.

117:2 The Hebrew words used in this verse, *chesed* (which may be rendered "steadfast love" or "graciousness"), and *emeth* (which may be rendered as "trustworthiness," "constancy" or even 'faithfulness') are often paired together to describe Yahweh as absolutely dependable to fulfill his promises.

117:2 forever See note on 111:3. **Praise the LORD** See note on 104:35.

118:1–29 Psalm 118, which could be considered a praise psalm or thanksgiving psalm, concludes the collection of Egyptian Hallel psalms (see note on 113:1–9). After an introductory exhortation (vv. 1–4), it alternates between personal testimony from a first-person singular perspective ("I"; "my") and a communal liturgy first-person plural perspective ("we"; "us"). The psalmist describes Yahweh's deliverance (vv. 5–7,10–15,17–21) as the congregation responds to that testimony (vv. 8–9,22–27). The psalm closes as both the psalmist (v. 28) and congregation (v. 29) praise Yahweh. Psalm 118 held particular importance for the NT authors who quoted from it often (focusing especially on vv. 22–23,25–26). See the table "Types of Psalms" on p. 830.

118:1–4 Psalm 118 begins and ends with a call to give thanks to Yahweh (vv. 1,29). The speaker may be a minister in a liturgical setting, or the psalmist might be providing a bookend structure to frame the psalm. Verses 1 and 29 are verbatim repetitions of 106:1 and 107:1.
  Following the opening line, the psalmist exhorts three addressees (Israel, priests and believers in general) to confess Yahweh's faithful love (compare 115:9–13). This repetitive opening series introduces the rest of Ps 118 and establishes the focus on Yahweh's faithfulness that continues through the psalm.

118:1 See note on vv. 1–4.

118:3 house of Aaron Refers to the priests.
118:4 those who fear the LORD Refers to faithful worshipers. See note on 90:11.

118:5–7 The individual testimony of a king figure is the main focus of roughly the first half of this psalm. This short passage begins the testimony of the king figure, which continues further in vv. 10–18.

118:8–9 The psalmist interrupts the testimony of the king figure with a brief statement of a general principle. The speaker may be the community participating in a liturgy, or it may be a minister.

118:8 to trust See note on 115:8.
118:9 princes The situation of the king in 118:10–13 indicates that trusting princes may refer to making political alliances.

118:10–13 Although vv. 10–18 occurs in the first-person singular perspective, the passage can be divided further. Verses 10–13 indicate that the speaker is a king, since he is surrounded by other nations and he cuts them off in the name of Yahweh. This passage depicts a battle situation in which the king emerges victorious with Yahweh's help.

118:10 the name of the LORD The king's actions were based on Yahweh's authority and enabled by Yahweh's power. See note on 91:14. **I cut them down** The Hebrew word used here, *mul*, usually means "to circumcise" (see Ge 17:1–14). The psalmist may be employing a play on words: Not only are the unclean enemies of God struck down by the covenant-keeping Yahweh—whose covenant is symbolized by the cutting of circumcision—but they are cut down while encircling Yahweh's servant (see Ps 118:10–12).
118:12 like bees In parts of the ancient Near East, bees were a symbol of relentless pursuit.

118:14–18 This group of affirmations of Yahweh's deliverance echoes both the exodus story and other psalms (e.g., 60:12; 108:13). These verses emphasize that Yahweh's deliverance has saved the king figure.

"The LORD's right hand has done mighty
  things!
16 The LORD's right hand is lifted high;
  the LORD's right hand has done mighty
    things!"
17 I will not die but live,
  and will proclaim what the LORD has done.
18 The LORD has chastened me severely,
  but he has not given me over to death.
19 Open for me the gates of the righteous;
  I will enter and give thanks to
    the LORD.
20 This is the gate of the LORD
  through which the righteous may
    enter.
21 I will give you thanks, for you
    answered me;
  you have become my salvation.

22 The stone the builders rejected
  has become the cornerstone;
23 the LORD has done this,
  and it is marvelous in our eyes.

24 The LORD has done it this very day;
  let us rejoice today and be glad.

25 LORD, save us!
  LORD, grant us success!

26 Blessed is he who comes in the name
    of the LORD.
  From the house of the LORD we
    bless you.*a*
27 The LORD is God,
  and he has made his light shine
    on us.
  With boughs in hand, join in the festal
    procession
  up*b* to the horns of the altar.

28 You are my God, and I will praise you;
  you are my God, and I will exalt you.

29 Give thanks to the LORD, for he is good;
  his love endures forever.

a 26 The Hebrew is plural.   *b 27* Or *Bind the festal sacrifice with ropes / and take it*

118:14 This verse quotes Ex 15:2, part of the Song of Moses that immediately follows the narrative account of Israel's deliverance at the Red Sea in Ex 14.

118:14 he has become my salvation Yahweh's saving acts are centered in who he is, not merely his deeds.

118:18 has chastened me severely The psalmist may be describing strenuous training or some sort of punishment. In the OT, God is never disinterested or distant from his people; he corrects them and guides them.

118:19–21 Following the king figure's testimony, the psalm presents what seems to be a formalized dialogue involving the king and another voice. The king requests entry into what seems to be the temple, and a voice (either the community or minister) explains the requirements. The king figure then shifts into direct address, and expresses thanks to Yahweh. This direct address resumes briefly in Ps 118:28.

118:20 the gate of the LORD Refers to the entrance to the temple in Jerusalem.

118:22–27 This section, which seems to be spoken by the community, is mostly oriented toward the king figure and Yahweh's deliverance of him. Verses 22–24 is a unit, but vv. 25,26, and 27 could all be analyzed separately as successive stages in the community's response to Yahweh.

118:22–24 This section is the worshiping community's initial response to the king figure's deliverance.

118:22 This verse is a sort of proverb or truism that is applied to Israel's king. The sense is that a stone that is rejected for one purpose can be used for another one. Jesus quotes vv. 22–23 in Mt 21:42–43 and Mk 12:10–11 in the context of his parable of the tenants and the vineyard.

118:22 the cornerstone Illustrates that an unwanted stone has been reused and placed in a position of importance. The Hebrew phrase used here, *rosh*

pinnah—which may be literally rendered "head of the corner"—could refer to a cornerstone, located at the bottom of a structure, or a capstone, which is located at the top of a structure. The Messianic interpretation of the cornerstone of Ps 118:22 seems to have its roots in the use of Ps 118 as part of the Hallel psalms used in the annual Passover celebration (see note on 113:1–9). Jews of the Second Temple period (516 BC–AD 70) primarily associated Ps 118 with the Davidic king and the Messianic hopes surrounding him. However, Ps 118 is not the only source for the Messianic stone imagery. Isaiah 8:14 and 28:16 can also be associated with messianic imagery of a stumbling stone or a stone that gave offense.

118:25 This counterintuitive interjection by the community here may be a strong affirmation that Israel trusts in Yahweh alone and not the king. Alternatively, the psalm may be reliving the experience of crisis and deliverance; however, nothing in the psalm indicates such a shift in agenda.

118:26 The psalm resumes a sense of joy after the brief interlude of Ps 118:25. The congregation seems to turn its attention to welcoming the vindicated king. The blessing comes from the house of Yahweh (*beth yhwh* in Hebrew), not the congregation's authority. All four gospels quote v. 26 within the context of Christ's Triumphal Entry into Jerusalem (Mt 21:9; Mk 11:9; Lk 19:38; Jn 12:13).

118:28–29 Psalm 118:28 resumes both the first-person singular perspective and direct address to Yahweh that last appeared in v. 21. After a personal commitment to praise Yahweh, the psalm closes by restating the first verse of the psalm, a call to give thanks to Yahweh (vv. 1,29). See note on vv. 1–4.

118:28 You are my God The king figure concludes with a statement of loyalty following his deliverance from danger.

118:29 The psalmist closes by repeating his call for the audience to remember Yahweh's actions. See v. 1.

Psalm 119[a]

א Aleph

[1] Blessed are those whose ways are blameless,
who walk according to the law of the LORD.
[2] Blessed are those who keep his statutes
and seek him with all their heart—
[3] they do no wrong
but follow his ways.
[4] You have laid down precepts
that are to be fully obeyed.
[5] Oh, that my ways were steadfast
in obeying your decrees!
[6] Then I would not be put to shame
when I consider all your commands.

[7] I will praise you with an upright heart
as I learn your righteous laws.
[8] I will obey your decrees;
do not utterly forsake me.

ב Beth

[9] How can a young person stay on the path of
purity?
By living according to your word.
[10] I seek you with all my heart;
do not let me stray from your commands.

[a] This psalm is an acrostic poem, the stanzas of which begin
with successive letters of the Hebrew alphabet; moreover, the
verses of each stanza begin with the same letter of the Hebrew
alphabet.

119:1–176 Psalm 119 is an extended alphabet acrostic that combines elements of a wisdom psalm and an individual lament psalm. Each stanza of the psalm contains lines that in the Hebrew text all start with the same Hebrew letter. This continues until all 22 letters of the Hebrew alphabet are used. It focuses on the two-ways motif—the concept of following Yahweh's ways or the way of wickedness—and the transformative role of submission to Yahweh's instruction, and the desperate need for Yahweh's help. Although the alphabet acrostic is the most prominent feature of the psalm in Hebrew, the most prominent theme is Yahweh's directions—as seen by the repetition of eight Hebrew words for his instructions: *torah* (see note on v. 1), *imrah* (see note on v. 11), *davar* (see note on v. 9), *mishpat* (see note on v. 7), *eduth* (see note on v. 22), *mitswah* (see note on v. 6), *choq* (see note on v. 5) and *piqqudim* (see note on v. 4). The meanings of these words tend to overlap. See the table "Types of Psalms" on p. 830.

119:1–8 Stanza 1, *Aleph*, is an introduction to the entire psalm, similar to how Ps 1 introduces the psalter. The repetition of the Hebrew word *ashre* (often translated "blessed") in 119:1–2 echoes 1:1. This stanza includes images of walking a right path (which also echoes 1:1; see 119:1,3–4) and diligently keeping Yahweh's statutes (vv. 4,8). The Hebrew word *derekh* ("way"; see note on v. 1) occurs in both halves of the unit (vv. 1,3,5), as does the idea of keeping Yahweh's directions (vv. 4,5,8).

This stanza divides into two four-verse segments. The psalmist begins by emphasizing the blessings that result from living according to Yahweh's directions (vv. 1–3). He then addresses Yahweh in response to his directions (v. 4). In the second half, the psalmist asserts that he will aspire to keep Yahweh's directions loyally (vv. 5–6). He pledges to praise Yahweh with pure motives once he is transformed by Yahweh's directions, and commits to keeping Yahweh's directions. He concludes by asking Yahweh not to abandon him (vv. 7–8).

119:1 ways The Hebrew word used here, *derekh*, and the related word *orach* (both of which may be rendered as "path" or "way") evoke a sense of conduct, or acting on Yahweh's directions (compare v. 9). **blameless** The Hebrew word used here, *tamim*, emphasizes a high degree of integrity and honesty rather than absolute perfection. See 101:2 and note. **law** The Hebrew term used here, *torah*, is one of the eight words used for Yahweh's directions in Ps 119 (see note on vv. 1–176). The word *torah* is also the most frequently used of the eight

terms, probably indicating that it should be understood as capturing the essence of Yahweh's directions.
119:3 wrong The Hebrew word used here, *awlah*, may denote well-established patterns of willful behavior with a corresponding stance toward Yahweh.
119:4 precepts The Hebrew word used here, *piqqudim*, is one of the eight terms for Yahweh's directions in Ps 119. It comes from the word *paqad*, which can be translated "inspect" or "command." The word *paqad* can also have the sense of entrusting something for safe keeping.
119:5 decrees The Hebrew word used here, *choq*, refers to a prescribed boundary; in Ps 119, it always appears in the plural form (*chuqqim*). It is one of the eight terms for Yahweh's directions in Ps 119.
119:6 commands The Hebrew word used here, *mitswah*, one of the eight terms for Yahweh's directions in Ps 119, comes from the verb meaning "to command." The term occurs only in the plural in Ps 119, and has a collective sense of all of the specific commandments that can—and should—be observed.
119:7 as I learn Teaching and learning is one of the major themes of Ps 119; the psalmist often pleads for Yahweh to teach him his directions. Here, the psalmist anticipates that learning Yahweh's directions will transform him. Three Hebrew expressions for teaching and learning occur throughout Ps 119: *lamad* (vv. 7,71,73), *limmad* and *hevin* (see v. 34 and note). **laws** The Hebrew word used here, *mishpat*, is one of the eight terms for Yahweh's directions in Ps 119. It has the sense of a legal ruling or decision.

119:9–16 Stanza 2, *Beth*, explores the theme of keeping pure conduct by internalizing Yahweh's word and responding to it verbally. The Hebrew concept of *derekh* or *orach*, which occurs three times in this stanza (vv. 9,14,15), connects back to Stanza 1 (vv. 1–8). Yahweh's *davar* (see note on v. 9) appears at the beginning and end of Stanza 2 (vv. 9,16). This stanza divides into two four-verse segments. The psalmist asserts that people can keep their ways pure (v. 9) by seeking Yahweh and internalizing his word (vv. 10–11). He then asks Yahweh to teach him (v. 12). In the second half, the psalmist expresses his response to his internalization of Yahweh's directions (vv. 13–16).

119:9 word The Hebrew word used here, *davar*, one of the eight terms for Yahweh's directions in Ps 119, is generally translated as "word." In Ps 119, it appears approximately 19 times in the singular. Two patterned expressions in the psalm give it slightly different meanings. It is the object of the verb "to hope" five times (119:81),

¹¹ I have hidden your word in my heart
    that I might not sin against you.
¹² Praise be to you, LORD;
    teach me your decrees.
¹³ With my lips I recount
    all the laws that come from your mouth.
¹⁴ I rejoice in following your statutes
    as one rejoices in great riches.
¹⁵ I meditate on your precepts
    and consider your ways.
¹⁶ I delight in your decrees;
    I will not neglect your word.

ג Gimel

¹⁷ Be good to your servant while I live,
    that I may obey your word.
¹⁸ Open my eyes that I may see
    wonderful things in your law.
¹⁹ I am a stranger on earth;
    do not hide your commands from me.
²⁰ My soul is consumed with longing
    for your laws at all times.
²¹ You rebuke the arrogant, who are accursed,
    those who stray from your commands.
²² Remove from me their scorn and contempt,
    for I keep your statutes.

²³ Though rulers sit together and slander me,
    your servant will meditate on your
        decrees.
²⁴ Your statutes are my delight;
    they are my counselors.

ד Daleth

²⁵ I am laid low in the dust;
    preserve my life according to your word.
²⁶ I gave an account of my ways and you
        answered me;
    teach me your decrees.
²⁷ Cause me to understand the way of your
        precepts,
    that I may meditate on your wonderful
        deeds.
²⁸ My soul is weary with sorrow;
    strengthen me according to your word.
²⁹ Keep me from deceitful ways;
    be gracious to me and teach me your law.
³⁰ I have chosen the way of faithfulness;
    I have set my heart on your laws.
³¹ I hold fast to your statutes, LORD;
    do not let me be put to shame.
³² I run in the path of your commands,
    for you have broadened my understanding.

---

and is preceded by the Hebrew word *ke-* ("according to") five times, which may give it a sense of ethical obedience (e.g., 119:105).

119:11 word The Hebrew word used here, *imrah*, is one of the eight terms for Yahweh's directions in Ps 119. It often describes a pledge or promise, and can also refer to a word that should be obeyed (see vv. 67,133,158). The psalmist portrays himself as having internalized Yahweh's directions at a deep level, which results in a consuming loyalty that envelops his will and his emotions.

119:12 teach me The psalmists repeats this request 11 times in Ps 119; in eight of those instances, he asks Yahweh to teach him his statutes.

119:17–24 Stanza 3, *Gimel*, introduces the theme of hostility or opposition that is prevalent throughout the psalm (see v. 21 and note). The psalmist identifies himself as Yahweh's servant (vv. 17,24) and views Yahweh's directions as his primary way of navigating the opposition he faces (vv. 19,24). The psalmist begins by identifying himself as Yahweh's *eved* ("servant"; see note on v. 17). He then emphasizes his need for Yahweh's help in understanding his directions (v. 18) and his longing for those directions (v. 20). As a displaced person (v. 19), the psalmist is vulnerable to attack (vv. 21–24). In the second half, the psalmist depicts the hostility he faces from those who are opposed to Yahweh and his directions. He describes them as insolent and wayward (v. 21), stating that they treat him with contempt (vv. 22–23). Nevertheless, the psalmist resolves to keep focusing on Yahweh and his directions (vv. 23–24).

119:17 servant The Hebrew word used here, *eved*, conveys the sense of being a servant. The psalmist may be alluding to the special status other servants of Yahweh have had. See 86:2 and note.

119:18 wonderful things The Hebrew word used here,

niphla'oth, is usually associated with Yahweh's mighty actions on behalf of Israel during the exodus (see Ex 7:3).

119:21 those who stray The Hebrew word used here, *shagah*, implies unintentionally doing wrong. The psalmist may be attributing his enemies' accursedness to their ignorance—they simply don't know enough to understand that they need Yahweh's guidance.

119:22 statutes The Hebrew word used here, *eduth*, is one of the eight words for Yahweh's directions in Ps 119. It has the sense of treaty stipulations that are handed down by a superior to a subordinate.

119:25–32 Stanza 4, *Daleth*, depicts the psalmist's pain and his decision to remain loyal to Yahweh's directions. The stanza is marked by the five occurrences of the Hebrew term *derekh* ("way"; see v. 1 and note). This stanza divides into two four-verse segments. The psalmist begins by crying out in suffering and begging Yahweh to enliven him (v. 25). He then portrays the cooperation between his loyalty and Yahweh's help and again asks Yahweh to strengthen him (v. 28). In the second half, the psalmist asks Yahweh to keep him from false or evil ways (see v. 29) and expresses that he has chosen Yahweh's way (v. 30). He determines to cling to Yahweh's directions in hope of eventual vindication (v. 31). He concludes by emphasizing that Yahweh's work of transforming him will help him follow Yahweh's way (v. 32).

119:25–28 Verses 25 and 28 both begin with the Hebrew word *naphshi* and end with *kidvarekha*. These parallels establish them as bookends for the first half of Stanza 4. The ideas v. 25 and v. 28 express also resemble each other. Verses 26–27 emphasize the cooperation between the psalmist's loyalty and Yahweh's help: as the speaker proclaims his loyalty, Yahweh enables him to understand; as Yahweh enables him to understand, the speaker proclaims his loyalty (vv. 26–27).

ה He

³³ Teach me, LORD, the way of your decrees,
that I may follow it to the end.ᵃ
³⁴ Give me understanding, so that I may keep
your law
and obey it with all my heart.
³⁵ Direct me in the path of your commands,
for there I find delight.
³⁶ Turn my heart toward your statutes
and not toward selfish gain.
³⁷ Turn my eyes away from worthless things;
preserve my life according to your word.ᵇ
³⁸ Fulfill your promise to your servant,
so that you may be feared.
³⁹ Take away the disgrace I dread,
for your laws are good.
⁴⁰ How I long for your precepts!
In your righteousness preserve my life.

ו Waw

⁴¹ May your unfailing love come to me, LORD,
your salvation, according to your promise;

⁴² then I can answer anyone who taunts me,
for I trust in your word.
⁴³ Never take your word of truth from my
mouth,
for I have put my hope in your laws.
⁴⁴ I will always obey your law,
for ever and ever.
⁴⁵ I will walk about in freedom,
for I have sought out your precepts.
⁴⁶ I will speak of your statutes before kings
and will not be put to shame,
⁴⁷ for I delight in your commands
because I love them.
⁴⁸ I reach out for your commands, which
I love,
that I may meditate on your decrees.

ז Zayin

⁴⁹ Remember your word to your servant,
for you have given me hope.

ᵃ 33 Or *follow it for its reward*   ᵇ 37 Two manuscripts of the
Masoretic Text and Dead Sea Scrolls; most manuscripts of the
Masoretic Text *life in your way*

119:33–40 In Stanza 5, *He,* the psalmist asks Yahweh to change him so that he might keep Yahweh's directions. The first five verses of this stanza open with this request. The psalmist wants Yahweh to transform him so that he can avoid being seduced by unjust gain (v. 36), continue to worship Yahweh (v. 38), receive protection from attack (v. 39) and receive sustenance (vv. 37,40). Verses 33–40 are best read as two four-verse sections. The psalmist begins by asking Yahweh to teach him the way (v. 33), repeating this request three additional times (vv. 34,35,36). As a result, the psalmist will be able to attend to his directions rather than unjust gain (v. 36). In the second half, the psalmist continues to ask Yahweh to change him (v. 37), hoping to find sustenance in the face of reproach (v. 39) and other difficulties (vv. 37–40).

119:34 Give me understanding This request occurs six times in the psalm (vv. 27,34,73,125,144,169), but never twice in the same stanza. The Hebrew verb used here, *bin,* is synonymous with teaching (see v. 12 and note).

119:41–48 Stanza 6, *Waw,* is the first of five stanzas to contain all eight of the Hebrew words for Yahweh's directions (see note on vv. 1–176). This stanza focuses on words and speaking. For example, it includes three occurrences of the Hebrew word *davar* ("word"). Likewise, the psalmist portrays Yahweh's word as being in his mouth (v. 43).

This stanza divides into two units of four verses each. The psalmist begins by mentioning Yahweh's steadfast love and salvation (v. 41). He then implies that his response to those who oppose him comes from Yahweh's word (v. 42), the object of his hope (v. 43). He pledges to keep Yahweh's directions faithfully (v. 44). In the second half, the psalmist anticipates the help he hopes to receive from Yahweh (vv. 45–46). He concludes by emphasizing his delight in Yahweh's directions (vv. 47–48).

119:41–44 The mention of Yahweh's steadfast love and salvation (v. 41) seems to point beyond the boundaries

of what is described in Ps 119 and may be alluding to more than the psalmist's experience of Yahweh's directions (see note on v. 7).

119:48 I reach out Throughout Ps 119, the psalmist addresses Yahweh's directions in terms usually reserved for Yahweh alone in the OT. For example, the psalmist expresses love for Yahweh's directions, saying that he loves (*ahav* in Hebrew) God's *torah,* God's *mitswah,* God's *davar,* God's *piqqudim* and God's *eduth* (see note on vv. 1–176). The combination of love with these terms is unique to Ps 119. The psalmist also positions himself toward Yahweh's directions in ways usually reserved for Yahweh. The speaker clings (*davaq* in Hebrew) to God's directions (v. 31; compare Dt 11:22); he trusts in (*batach;* Ps 119:42; compare 2Ki 18:5,20,22,30) and fears (*yare*) them (Ps 119:120). He even raises his hands to them (v. 48). **I may meditate** This indicates verbal rumination over Yahweh's directions, not just silent reflection. See 104:34 and note.

119:49–56 Stanza 7, *Zayin,* focuses on the themes of remembering (vv. 49,52,55) and Yahweh's comfort (vv. 50,52). It is also characterized by the triple mention in the Hebrew text of Yahweh's *torah* ("law"; vv. 51,53,55). The Hebrew words *davar* (v. 49) and *imrah* (v. 50) are paired in successive verses in this stanza (see v. 1 and note).

When analyzed according to the progression of its themes, this stanza divides into four couplets. The psalmist begins by begging Yahweh to remember his word (v. 49), which provides hope and comfort to the psalmist (v. 50) who is afflicted by insolent mockers. The psalmist remains loyal to Yahweh's *torah* (v. 51) and takes comfort when he remembers Yahweh's judgments from ancient times (v. 52). In the second half, the psalmist expresses anger at those who turn away from Yahweh's *torah* (v. 53), describing Yahweh's directions as his songs (v. 54). The psalmist then recounts how he remembers Yahweh's name at night and keeps his laws (v. 55). He concludes by portraying the keeping of Yahweh's directions as his possession—it is a blessing that belongs to him (v. 56).

⁵⁰ My comfort in my suffering is this:
    Your promise preserves my life.
⁵¹ The arrogant mock me unmercifully,
    but I do not turn from your law.
⁵² I remember, LORD, your ancient laws,
    and I find comfort in them.
⁵³ Indignation grips me because of the wicked,
    who have forsaken your law.
⁵⁴ Your decrees are the theme of my song
    wherever I lodge.
⁵⁵ In the night, LORD, I remember your name,
    that I may keep your law.
⁵⁶ This has been my practice:
    I obey your precepts.

ח Heth

⁵⁷ You are my portion, LORD;
    I have promised to obey your words.
⁵⁸ I have sought your face with all my heart;
    be gracious to me according to your
        promise.
⁵⁹ I have considered my ways
    and have turned my steps to your statutes.
⁶⁰ I will hasten and not delay
    to obey your commands.
⁶¹ Though the wicked bind me with ropes,
    I will not forget your law.

⁶² At midnight I rise to give you thanks
    for your righteous laws.
⁶³ I am a friend to all who fear you,
    to all who follow your precepts.
⁶⁴ The earth is filled with your love, LORD;
    teach me your decrees.

ט Teth

⁶⁵ Do good to your servant
    according to your word, LORD.
⁶⁶ Teach me knowledge and good judgment,
    for I trust your commands.
⁶⁷ Before I was afflicted I went astray,
    but now I obey your word.
⁶⁸ You are good, and what you do is good;
    teach me your decrees.
⁶⁹ Though the arrogant have smeared me with
        lies,
    I keep your precepts with all my heart.
⁷⁰ Their hearts are callous and unfeeling,
    but I delight in your law.
⁷¹ It was good for me to be afflicted
    so that I might learn your decrees.
⁷² The law from your mouth is more precious
        to me
    than thousands of pieces of silver
        and gold.

119:53–56 Even though this passage opens by focusing on the wicked (v. 53), the psalmist quickly returns to his delight in Yahweh and his directions (vv. 54–55). His remembrance of Yahweh's name marks the final two verses as a separate couplet and reinforces this stanza's connection to the sacred history of Israel. Everything that the psalmist remembers in Stanza 7 seems to point to Yahweh's commitment to Israel and his deliverance of them (see v. 55). The final verse of the stanza concludes the final couplet, the second half of the stanza, and the stanza as a whole. The psalmist sees Yahweh's directions and keeping them as his special possession (v. 56).

119:57–64 Stanza 8, *Heth*, is the second of five stanzas that contains all eight of the words used for Yahweh's directions (see vv. 1–176 and note). This stanza emphasizes that Yahweh's directions are an expression of Yahweh himself; the psalmist portrays keeping Yahweh's directions as the way to draw near to him. This section can be divided into two four-verse units with a contrast between private and social settings, or into four two-verse couplets with slightly separate focuses. The psalmist begins by identifying Yahweh as his portion and then commits to keep his directions (v. 57) and seek Yahweh's favor (v. 58). He portrays his self-examination as turning upon a path (v. 59) and making haste to keep Yahweh's directions (v. 60).

In the second half of this stanza, the psalmist describes the social implications of his allegiance to Yahweh's directions. He observes Yahweh's directions even though he suffers because of wicked people (v. 61), and praises Yahweh late at night because of his just decrees (v. 62). The psalmist also mentions those who fear Yahweh and keep his directions (v. 63). He concludes by recognizing Yahweh's presence in all of creation (v. 64).

119:65–72 Stanza 9, *Teth*, explores what is good when viewed through the experience of affliction (vv. 67,71). Yahweh's goodness and the goodness of his directions are the reference point for the psalmist as he reflects on how he has learned from his suffering. Five of the eight verses in this stanza begin with the Hebrew word *tov*, often translated "good." (vv. 65,66,68,71,72). While this repetition may have been the result of the sparse options for words starting with the Hebrew letter *teth*, it still establishes the theme of goodness.

This section could be divided into two four-verse sections; however, the mention of the psalmist's affliction splits each section, so the stanza is better divided into four pairs of couplets. The psalmist begins by proclaiming Yahweh's goodness (v. 65) and asking Yahweh to teach him good judgment (v. 66). He then emphasizes that the affliction he has experienced has made him loyal to Yahweh's directions (v. 67). He reaffirms the goodness of Yahweh's character and actions, and asks Yahweh to teach him (v. 68).

In the second half of the stanza, the psalmist describes how the *zed* (a Hebrew word often rendered as "arrogant" or "presumptuous") spread lies that harm him (v. 69); their loyalties are opposed to the psalmist's loyalty to Yahweh's directions (v. 70). However, his affliction increases his loyalty to Yahweh's directions (v. 71). He closes by proclaiming the deep value that Yahweh's directions have to him (v. 72).

119:67 I went astray The Hebrew word used here, *shagag*, implies going astray or making a mistake. The affliction the psalmist experienced after going astray prompted him to learn Yahweh's directions and become more capable of following them (see v. 71).

׳ Yodh

73 Your hands made me and formed me;
    give me understanding to learn your
        commands.
74 May those who fear you rejoice when they
        see me,
    for I have put my hope in your word.
75 I know, LORD, that your laws are
        righteous,
    and that in faithfulness you have
        afflicted me.
76 May your unfailing love be my comfort,
    according to your promise to your
        servant.
77 Let your compassion come to me that I may
        live,
    for your law is my delight.
78 May the arrogant be put to shame for
        wronging me without cause;
    but I will meditate on your precepts.
79 May those who fear you turn to me,
    those who understand your statutes.
80 May I wholeheartedly follow your decrees,
    that I may not be put to shame.

כ Kaph

81 My soul faints with longing for your
        salvation,
    but I have put my hope in your word.
82 My eyes fail, looking for your promise;
    I say, "When will you comfort me?"
83 Though I am like a wineskin in the smoke,
    I do not forget your decrees.
84 How long must your servant wait?
    When will you punish my persecutors?
85 The arrogant dig pits to trap me,
    contrary to your law.
86 All your commands are trustworthy;
    help me, for I am being persecuted without
        cause.
87 They almost wiped me from the earth,
    but I have not forsaken your precepts.
88 In your unfailing love preserve my life,
    that I may obey the statutes of your mouth.

ל Lamedh

89 Your word, LORD, is eternal;
    it stands firm in the heavens.

119:73–80 Stanza 10, *Yodh*, reflects on the psalmist's experience of affliction in terms of how other faithful people perceive it. Although v. 63 mentioned others who fear Yahweh, the psalmist's interaction with them is not developed until now (vv. 74,79). Unlike previous stanzas, this section does not have formal structural markers that divide it into segments. A chiastic structure does appear in the dual references to those who fear Yahweh (vv. 74,79) and the connections between Yahweh's comfort (v. 76) and his mercy (v. 77). However, reading it in this way doesn't provide any further insight. Furthermore, the psalmist's pleas that he would live (v. 77) and not suffer shame (v. 80) do not have parallels in the first half of the stanza.

The psalmist begins by asserting that he needs Yahweh, who created him, to help him understand his commandments (v. 73). He anticipates that the hope he develops will encourage others (v. 74), even though he is suffering affliction (v. 75). He interprets Yahweh's affliction as something constructive (v. 75), and asks Yahweh to comfort him (v. 76) so that he can hope in Yahweh's compassion and rescue (v. 77). He also wishes for vindication, asserting that, unlike him, the lying wrongdoers will be the ones who experience shame (vv. 78–80). He asserts that, in the midst of this vindication, those who fear Yahweh will learn Yahweh's directions more fully (v. 79).

119:81–88 Stanza 11, *Kaph*, focuses on the psalmist's sense of longing and desperation. He asks Yahweh to help him escape his persecutors (vv. 84,86), but emphasizes that he has not stopped following Yahweh's directions even though he is suffering (vv. 83,87). Verses 81–88 could be divided two ways. It could be divided into three units: two triplets (vv. 81–83 and vv. 84–86; one of which is marked by the Hebrew word *radaph*) with a couplet at the end (marked by the Hebrew word *kalah*; vv. 87–88). Alternatively, it could be read as four couplets. This approach depends on the thematic parallel between v. 83

and v. 87. By using the idea of the psalmist's faithfulness as an entry point in both v. 83 and v. 87, the persecution in v. 84 can be contrasted with Yahweh's help in v. 88. The repeated Hebrew word *kalah* in v. 87 also fits with dividing Stanza 11 into four couplets.

The psalmist begins by stating his desire for Yahweh's directions, which will provide him with help and comfort (vv. 81–82). He then describes the destructive effects of his suffering, yet emphasizes his loyalty to Yahweh's directions (v. 83). In v. 84, the psalmist depicts his suffering in terms of his persecutors (vv. 84–85). He indicates that Yahweh's directions are trustworthy, but he needs Yahweh to help him escape his persecutors (v. 86). Even though he has almost perished, he has not stopped following Yahweh's directions (v. 87), and he pleads once more for Yahweh to help him (v. 88).

119:89–96 Stanza 12, *Lamedh*, marks the midpoint of Ps 119 and reintroduces a positive tone of trust in the eventual triumph of Yahweh's directions. The psalmist emphasizes the role that Yahweh's word has in establishing the cosmos (vv. 89–91) and compares that to the way that Yahweh's directions establish and protect him (vv. 92–95). This section divides into two units of four verses each, marked by the Hebrew word *le'olam* (implying permanence; see vv. 89,93).

The psalmist begins this stanza by emphasizing the role of Yahweh's word in establishing and supporting the created order (vv. 89–91). He then depicts the central role of Yahweh's directions in preserving him in his time of crisis (v. 92). The second half of Stanza 12 is a sort of inversion of the first half. The psalmist focuses on the role of Yahweh's directions for him at a personal level for three lines (vv. 93–95), and then shifts to a very broad consideration of Yahweh's directions (v. 96).

119:89–92 As the start of the second half of Ps 119, Stanza 12 may be mimicking the opening of the psalm. The first three verses connect with the broad theme of

90 Your faithfulness continues through all
      generations;
   you established the earth, and it endures.
91 Your laws endure to this day,
   for all things serve you.
92 If your law had not been my delight,
   I would have perished in my affliction.
93 I will never forget your precepts,
   for by them you have preserved my life.
94 Save me, for I am yours;
   I have sought out your precepts.
95 The wicked are waiting to destroy me,
   but I will ponder your statutes.
96 To all perfection I see a limit,
   but your commands are boundless.

‫מ‬ Mem

97 Oh, how I love your law!
   I meditate on it all day long.
98 Your commands are always with me
   and make me wiser than my enemies.
99 I have more insight than all my teachers,
   for I meditate on your statutes.
100 I have more understanding than the elders,
    for I obey your precepts.
101 I have kept my feet from every evil path
    so that I might obey your word.
102 I have not departed from your laws,
    for you yourself have taught me.

103 How sweet are your words to my taste,
    sweeter than honey to my mouth!
104 I gain understanding from your precepts;
    therefore I hate every wrong path.

‫נ‬ Nun

105 Your word is a lamp for my feet,
    a light on my path.
106 I have taken an oath and confirmed it,
    that I will follow your righteous laws.
107 I have suffered much;
    preserve my life, LORD, according to your
       word.
108 Accept, LORD, the willing praise of my
       mouth,
    and teach me your laws.
109 Though I constantly take my life in my hands,
    I will not forget your law.
110 The wicked have set a snare for me,
    but I have not strayed from your precepts.
111 Your statutes are my heritage forever;
    they are the joy of my heart.
112 My heart is set on keeping your decrees
    to the very end.[a]

‫ס‬ Samekh

113 I hate double-minded people,
    but I love your law.

a 112 Or *decrees / for their enduring reward*

---

emphasizing Yahweh's authority—v. 92 is a personal response to the truth the opening three verses present. The mention of heavens and earth establishes a cosmic scope for the stanza, where Yahweh's directions establish and then maintain the created order.

119:93–96 The psalmist stresses the personal focus of this unit of poetry by mentioning Yahweh's *piqqudim* in the Hebrew text (see note on v. 4) and their role in enlivening him (vv. 93–94). He then implicitly contrasts the help that Yahweh's precepts bring with the destruction that the wicked plan (v. 95). He closes by considering Yahweh's directions on a cosmic scale (v. 96).

119:96 perfection The Hebrew word used here, *tikhlah*, conveys completeness or totality in the sense of being totally comprehensive. Even the most perfectly complete thing has a limit.

119:97–104 Stanza 13, *Mem*, focuses on two main themes—understanding and action. The psalmist explains the insight that his attention to Yahweh's directions has given him. He also explains the central role that following Yahweh's directions has for him. This stanza divides into two sections of four verses each. The psalmist proclaims his love for Yahweh's *torah* ("law" or "instruction"; v. 97), and then makes three successive comparisons between his understanding and the understanding of those around him (vv. 98–100). In the second half of the stanza, he focuses on abstaining from evil ways (vv. 101,104) and following Yahweh's directions (vv. 102–103).

119:100 for I obey your precepts The psalmist has more insight than his elders because of his conduct. In this psalm, knowledge includes a person's actions and affections in addition to thoughts.

119:105–112 Stanza 14, *Nun*, focuses on the psalmist's commitment to Yahweh's directions in the face of affliction—perhaps even mortal danger (v. 109). He has sworn (v. 106) to follow Yahweh's directions and is determined to continue in that direction (v. 112). This stanza divides into four pairs of verses. The first two pairs are marked by the Hebrew words *davar* (vv. 105,107) and *mishpat* (vv. 106,108). The second two pairs are separated thematically: the first pair emphasizes the danger that the psalmist faces (v. 110), and the second pair emphasizes his commitment to—and delight in—Yahweh's directions.

The psalmist expresses his commitment to Yahweh's directions (vv. 105–106). Even though he is suffering, he worships Yahweh out of a sense of joy (vv. 107–108). The psalmist then identifies the wicked as the source of his suffering, but remains faithful to Yahweh's directions (vv. 109–110). He concludes by expressing joy in following Yahweh's directions and committing to remain loyal to them (vv. 111–112).

119:111 my heritage The Hebrew word used here, *nachal*, indicates the possession of inalienable, inherited property.

119:113–120 Stanza 15, *Samekh*, contrasts the psalmist's love of Yahweh's directions with his hatred of the "divided" or "double-minded" (*se'eph* in Hebrew; v. 113). However, the psalmist does not take pleasure in the destruction of the wicked, but dreads their fate (v. 120).

114 You are my refuge and my shield;
    I have put my hope in your word.
115 Away from me, you evildoers,
    that I may keep the commands of my God!
116 Sustain me, my God, according to your
        promise, and I will live;
    do not let my hopes be dashed.
117 Uphold me, and I will be delivered;
    I will always have regard for your decrees.
118 You reject all who stray from your decrees,
    for their delusions come to nothing.
119 All the wicked of the earth you discard like
        dross;
    therefore I love your statutes.
120 My flesh trembles in fear of you;
    I stand in awe of your laws.

ע Ayin

121 I have done what is righteous and just;
    do not leave me to my oppressors.
122 Ensure your servant's well-being;
    do not let the arrogant oppress me.

123 My eyes fail, looking for your salvation,
    looking for your righteous promise.
124 Deal with your servant according to
        your love
    and teach me your decrees.
125 I am your servant; give me discernment
    that I may understand your statutes.
126 It is time for you to act, LORD;
    your law is being broken.
127 Because I love your commands
    more than gold, more than pure gold,
128 and because I consider all your precepts
        right,
    I hate every wrong path.

פ Pe

129 Your statutes are wonderful;
    therefore I obey them.
130 The unfolding of your words gives light;
    it gives understanding to the simple.
131 I open my mouth and pant,
    longing for your commands.

He emphasizes that those who are loyal to Yahweh's directions will be upheld (vv. 116–117), while those who turn away will be discarded (vv. 118–119).

Unlike most other stanzas of the psalm, Stanza 15 does not divide into four-verse segments or multiple pairs of lines. It is best understood according to its thematic content, which separates Stanza 15 into a 3–2–3 structure, with two three-verse units separated by a pair of verses. The psalmist begins by expressing his desire to withdraw from the wicked so that he might keep Yahweh's directions fully (vv. 113–115). He then asks Yahweh to help him and sustain him so that he can continue keeping his directions (vv. 116–117). In the final verses, the psalmist focuses on the fate of the wicked (v. 118). Though he is pleased that justice is done (v. 119), he is terrified by the reality of that judgment (v. 120).

119:113 double-minded people The Hebrew word used here, se'eph—which generally means "divided"—may refer to people, or it may be related to "that which is divided." In this regard, it could be meant as a contrast with Yahweh's directions. The best parallel with the term se'eph is se'ippim in 1Ki 18:21, where Elijah challenges Israel to no longer serve both Yahweh and Baal.

119:121–128 Stanza 16, Ayin, develops the theme of loyalty (see note on Ps 119:113–120) and develops it into a plea for Yahweh to act to validate his directions. In v. 121, v. 124, and v. 126, the psalmist focuses on his actions and Yahweh's actions, using the Hebrew word asah. By portraying himself as Yahweh's servant (vv. 122,124,125) the psalmist attaches himself to Yahweh's pattern of action in the history of Israel. The psalmist anticipates Yahweh's faithful action (vv. 123,126) and continues to express his devotion to Yahweh's direction as he waits for Yahweh to rescue him and vindicate Yahweh's directions (vv. 127–128).

This stanza best divides into two four-verse sections. The psalmist begins by begging Yahweh to rescue his faithful servant (vv. 121–124). As Yahweh's servant, he longs for Yahweh's help in terms of his promise (v. 123)

and his steadfast love (v. 124). In the second half of the stanza, the psalmist asks Yahweh to teach him more (v. 125). He then directly asks Yahweh to act to validate his directions and his authority (v. 126). The psalmist closes by expressing his love and commitment to Yahweh's directions, seemingly in anticipation of Yahweh's action (vv. 127–128).

119:125–128 In this passage, the psalmist emphasizes his loyalty to Yahweh's directions with his anticipation of Yahweh's action. Though the psalmist emphasized his just and right actions (v. 121), he still wants to know more of Yahweh's directions (v. 125). He boldly calls Yahweh to act to defend his own directions (v. 126). While he waits, he proclaims his loyalty to Yahweh's directions and his pleasure in keeping them (vv. 127–128).

119:126 your law is being broken Yahweh's torah ("law" or "instruction") is connected to his reputation. The psalmist suggests that if Yahweh does not maintain justice, his claim to authority is undermined.

119:129–136 Stanza 17, Pe, focuses on the theme of the transformative effect that Yahweh's directions have on the psalmist (v. 130) and the harmful effects of sin and human opposition (vv. 133–134). The psalmist longs for Yahweh's directions because of their wonderful quality (vv. 129–131). He weeps because others do not follow Yahweh's directions (v. 136).

This stanza divides into four pairs of verses, but they cohere as two four-verse units as well. The psalmist begins by praising Yahweh's directions and their power to enlighten the pethi (a Hebrew term meaning a naïve or gullible person; see vv. 129–130). He then describes his desire for Yahweh's directions, and pleads that Yahweh will impart them to him (vv. 131–132). In the second half, the psalmist describes the hazards of sin and human opposition, and asks Yahweh to help him remain faithful in following his directions (vv. 133–134). He concludes by asking Yahweh to show favor and teach him, expressing his sorrow over those who do not follow Yahweh's directions (vv. 135–136).

132 Turn to me and have mercy on me,
　　as you always do to those who love your
　　　name.
133 Direct my footsteps according to your word;
　　let no sin rule over me.
134 Redeem me from human oppression,
　　that I may obey your precepts.
135 Make your face shine on your servant
　　and teach me your decrees.
136 Streams of tears flow from my eyes,
　　for your law is not obeyed.

צ Tsadhe

137 You are righteous, Lord,
　　and your laws are right.
138 The statutes you have laid down are
　　righteous;
　　they are fully trustworthy.
139 My zeal wears me out,
　　for my enemies ignore your words.
140 Your promises have been thoroughly tested,
　　and your servant loves them.
141 Though I am lowly and despised,
　　I do not forget your precepts.
142 Your righteousness is everlasting
　　and your law is true.
143 Trouble and distress have come upon me,
　　but your commands give me delight.

144 Your statutes are always righteous;
　　give me understanding that I may live.

ק Qoph

145 I call with all my heart; answer me, Lord,
　　and I will obey your decrees.
146 I call out to you; save me
　　and I will keep your statutes.
147 I rise before dawn and cry for help;
　　I have put my hope in your word.
148 My eyes stay open through the watches of
　　the night,
　　that I may meditate on your promises.
149 Hear my voice in accordance with your love;
　　preserve my life, Lord, according to your
　　　laws.
150 Those who devise wicked schemes are near,
　　but they are far from your law.
151 Yet you are near, Lord,
　　and all your commands are true.
152 Long ago I learned from your statutes
　　that you established them to last
　　　forever.

ר Resh

153 Look on my suffering and deliver me,
　　for I have not forgotten your law.

119:137–144 Stanza 18, *Tsadhe*, focuses on the righteousness of Yahweh's directions; the Hebrew words *tsaddiq* or *tsedeq* (both of which denote righteousness) appear five times in this stanza (vv. 137,138,142,144). The psalmist emphasizes that Yahweh's righteousness and directions are based in his character. Because he is trustworthy and righteous (v. 138), his directions are also righteous and trustworthy (vv. 137,142).

This stanza divides into four pairs of verses. The main shift in focus is between "you" (v. 137) and "I" (v. 141)—the psalmist does not discuss his situation until the second half of the stanza. He begins by connecting Yahweh's righteousness with the reliability of his directions (vv. 137–138), and describes his indignation as others ignore Yahweh's directions (v. 139). The psalmist then explains that his love for Yahweh's directions comes from their trustworthiness (v. 140).

In the second half of the stanza, the psalmist focuses on his personal situation. Even though he is lowly, he maintains his loyalty to Yahweh's directions (v. 141). He explains that Yahweh's righteousness will endure without compromise (v. 142) and will continue to validate his directions. The psalmist remains loyal to Yahweh's directions in spite of his afflictions (v. 143), and he concludes by pleading that Yahweh give him insight into his directions (v. 144).

119:145–152 Stanza 19, *Qoph*, focuses on the psalmist's cries to Yahweh and his anticipation of Yahweh's faithfulness to his promise (v. 148) and testimonies (v. 152). The psalmist can hope (vv. 147,151) in Yahweh and his directions (v. 151) because of Yahweh's nearness.

This stanza divides into two halves; vv. 145–148 divides further into two pairs of verses. The psalmist begins by crying to Yahweh and expressing his commitment to keep Yahweh's directions (vv. 145–146). He then portrays his sleeplessness, stating that he arises day and night to consider Yahweh's directions (vv. 147–148). In the second half of the stanza, the psalmist pleads for Yahweh's rescue (v. 149) and portrays the nearness of both Yahweh and his enemies (vv. 150–151). He concludes by expressing trust in the reliability of Yahweh's directions (v. 152).

119:153–160 Stanza 20, *Resh*, focuses on the psalmist's plea that Yahweh will save him. Three times he repeats his request for his life to be preserved (vv. 154,156,159), and also asks Yahweh to deliver (v. 153) and redeem him (v. 154). The psalmist also contrasts the greatness of Yahweh's mercy (v. 156) with his numerous enemies (v. 157), using the Hebrew word *rav* ("many" or "much") in both verses. The contrast between Yahweh's great mercy and the numerous enemies gives some unity to the motif of sight in Stanza 20.

This stanza divides clearly in the center, with two pairs of verses beginning the unit. The second half of the stanza does not divide into pairs, but presents a final verse as a summary statement (v. 160). The psalmist begins by repeating his request for Yahweh to look on him and rescue him (vv. 153–154). He then points to the wicked who have separated themselves from Yahweh's mercy by ignoring his directions (vv. 155–156).

In the second half of the stanza, the psalmist focuses on the wicked people's hostility toward Yahweh and himself (v. 157). Rather than expressing fear, he expresses disgust for the wicked (v. 158) and asks Yahweh to enliven him according to his *chesed* (Yahweh's unfailing, covenantal love; v. 159). In v. 160, the psalmist emphasizes his trust in Yahweh and his directions (v. 160).

154 Defend my cause and redeem me;
 preserve my life according to your
 promise.
155 Salvation is far from the wicked,
 for they do not seek out your decrees.
156 Your compassion, LORD, is great;
 preserve my life according to your laws.
157 Many are the foes who persecute me,
 but I have not turned from your statutes.
158 I look on the faithless with loathing,
 for they do not obey your word.
159 See how I love your precepts;
 preserve my life, LORD, in accordance with
 your love.
160 All your words are true;
 all your righteous laws are eternal.

ש Sin and Shin

161 Rulers persecute me without cause,
 but my heart trembles at your word.
162 I rejoice in your promise
 like one who finds great spoil.
163 I hate and detest falsehood
 but I love your law.
164 Seven times a day I praise you
 for your righteous laws.
165 Great peace have those who love your law,
 and nothing can make them stumble.
166 I wait for your salvation, LORD,
 and I follow your commands.
167 I obey your statutes,
 for I love them greatly.

168 I obey your precepts and your statutes,
 for all my ways are known to you.

ת Taw

169 May my cry come before you, LORD;
 give me understanding according to your
 word.
170 May my supplication come before you;
 deliver me according to your promise.
171 May my lips overflow with praise,
 for you teach me your decrees.
172 May my tongue sing of your word,
 for all your commands are righteous.
173 May your hand be ready to help me,
 for I have chosen your precepts.
174 I long for your salvation, LORD,
 and your law gives me delight.
175 Let me live that I may praise you,
 and may your laws sustain me.
176 I have strayed like a lost sheep.
 Seek your servant,
 for I have not forgotten your
 commands.

Psalm 120

A song of ascents.

1 I call on the LORD in my distress,
 and he answers me.
2 Save me, LORD,
 from lying lips
 and from deceitful tongues.

119:161–168 Stanza 21, *Sin/Shin*, demonstrates a sense of hope in Yahweh's *yeshu'ah* (a Hebrew word implying salvation or deliverance; see v. 166). In this stanza, the psalmist emphasizes his love for Yahweh's directions (vv. 163,165,167). He also mentions the joy (v. 162) and peace (v. 165) that he finds from Yahweh's directions.

This stanza divides into four couplets by theme. The psalmist opens by describing the opposition that he faces (v. 161), and how he is in awe of Yahweh's directions rather than his powerful opponents. He asserts that Yahweh's direction is like treasure to him (v. 162). He then contrasts his hatred of falsehood with his love for Yahweh's directions (v. 163), and describes that he regularly praises Yahweh for his direction (v. 164).

In the second half of the stanza, the psalmist implicitly contrasts the peace of those who love Yahweh's directions with the persecution from human princes (v. 165). He expresses his hope in Yahweh's salvation, and notes that he follows Yahweh's directions (v. 166). In the final pair of verses, the psalmist asserts that he keeps Yahweh's directions because he loves them and his life is completely open to Yahweh (vv. 167–168).

119:169–176 Stanza 22, *Taw*, closes the psalm by emphasizing the psalmist's love for Yahweh's directions and his need of Yahweh's help and the transforming power of Yahweh's directions. The final verse (v. 176) expresses a tension, but ultimately establishes that

even the most devoted people need Yahweh to help them remain devoted to him.

This stanza divides into four couplets that shift in perspective as they proceed. The stanza opens with the psalmist's plea that Yahweh will hear him, give him insight and rescue him (vv. 169–170). He then shifts to praising Yahweh and his directions (vv. 171–172). In vv. 173–174, the psalmist returns to pleading for Yahweh's help, and expresses his commitment to Yahweh and his directions (vv. 173–174). In the final couplet, the psalmist pleads that Yahweh's directions will help him survive (v. 175). The psalmist concludes by confessing that he has gone astray like a lost sheep and asks for Yahweh to seek him so that he may continue to follow Yahweh's directions (v. 176).

120:title–7 This individual lament psalm—which is part of the pilgrimage psalms (Ps 120–134; see note on 120:title)—focuses on the trouble the psalmist faces. The psalm opens by presenting a resolution to his trouble before he even requests deliverance. The psalmist cries directly to Yahweh for help (vv. 1–2). He focuses on his lying adversaries and wishes for their destruction (vv. 3–4). He then returns to his own predicament, regretting that he is distant from the land of Israel (vv. 5–6). The final verse restates the psalmist's problem in terms of the foreigners he lives with—they are incompatible with his beliefs (v. 7). Unlike most lament psalms, the psalmist ends without resolving the matter with an expression

³ What will he do to you,
  and what more besides,
  you deceitful tongue?
⁴ He will punish you with a warrior's sharp
    arrows,
  with burning coals of the broom bush.

⁵ Woe to me that I dwell in Meshek,
  that I live among the tents of Kedar!
⁶ Too long have I lived
  among those who hate peace.
⁷ I am for peace;
  but when I speak, they are for war.

Psalm 121

A song of ascents.

¹ I lift up my eyes to the mountains —
  where does my help come from?
² My help comes from the LORD,
  the Maker of heaven and earth.

³ He will not let your foot slip —
  he who watches over you will
    not slumber;
⁴ indeed, he who watches over Israel
  will neither slumber nor sleep.

---

of hope. Most laments in the psalms conclude with an element of trust and hope. This psalm may lack that feature because it is included in the subsection of the Psalms called the Songs of Ascents or pilgrimage psalms (Ps 120–134). Later psalms in this series may provide the turn toward trust and hope that Ps 120 lacks. See the table "Types of Psalms" on p. 830.

120:title A song of ascents Psalms 120–134 each include the title *shir hamma'aloth* (usually translated "Song of Ascents"). They may be called Songs of Ascents because they frequently reference Jerusalem and Zion (the temple mount in Jerusalem); Biblical writers regularly describe individuals as going up to Jerusalem, no matter where the people are located in relationship to the city. The Songs of Ascents were traditionally sung during the Jewish Festival of Booths or Tabernacles in autumn (see Lev 23:33–44 and note). They also seem to have been sung during pilgrimages to Jerusalem in general. In Jewish tradition, the Festival of Tabernacles commemorates Israel's wanderings in the wilderness. The pilgrimage theme of the Songs of Ascents resonates with the wilderness theme of the festival. Another possible theme of the Songs of Ascents is the mention of foreign peoples. Psalms 120–134 may be connected with the dispersion of the Jews following the time of the Babylonian exile (after 538 BC), which could also resonate with the idea of wandering without a permanent home. See the table "Types of Psalms" on p. 830.

120:1–2 Psalm 120 opens with a call and answer statement, which seems to resolve the psalmist's problem almost before the psalm begins. Usually, Yahweh's help is the answer to a psalmist's cry, and it comes at the end of the psalm. However, v. 2 continues to portray the psalmist's cry for help.

120:4 burning coals Probably describes burning arrows. People in the ancient Near East often used burning arrows in warfare, shooting them into walled cities to set them on fire.

120:5–7 The psalmist concludes by returning to the discussion of his problem. He is in a foreign place with people who have different beliefs and values than him. Although he wants to coexist, the residents of his temporary home want only strife.

120:5 The place names in v. 5 are in opposite directions, and are probably meant to symbolize a general reality of living far from home.

120:5 in Meshek Located northwest of Canaan, in modern-day Turkey (compare Eze 27:13). **Kedar** A nomadic shepherding tribe that lived to the southeast of Canaan (compare Isa 21:13–17).

120:6 peace The Hebrew word used here, *shalom*, has a wide range of meanings; it can refer to the absence of war or an all-encompassing sense of well-being and wholeness.

120:7 war The Hebrew word used here, *milchamah*, describes close combat involving hand-to-hand fighting and intense struggle.

121:title–8 Psalm 121 is a part of the pilgrimage psalms intended to be sung during pilgrimage to Jerusalem (Ps 120–134; see note on 120:title). This individual psalm of confidence (a psalm that faithfully expresses trust in Yahweh) presents a series of statements of trust in Yahweh's protection and help. The psalm opens with a personal question-and-answer segment that establishes that the psalmist's help comes from Yahweh himself (Ps 121:1–2). The psalmist then addresses his audience as he explores the different ways that Yahweh guards his people. First, he emphasizes that Yahweh never gets tired, but is always alert and vigilant in protecting his people (vv. 3–4). He then shows that Yahweh's protection covers his people at all times, guarding them from danger, day and night (vv. 5–6). He concludes by asserting that Yahweh's protection accompanies them in all movements of their daily life (vv. 7–8). See the table "Types of Psalms" on p. 830.

121:title A song of ascents See note on 120:title.

121:1–2 The opening two verses are in the form of question and answer; they establish the central idea that the psalmist's help will come directly from Yahweh.

121:1 I lift up my eyes to the mountains The psalmist may be indicating that some sort of danger comes from the hills, or could be referencing mountains and hills as places for hiding and protection. Alternatively, this may be a reference to Zion, God's dwelling place on earth (compare 48:1–3; 87:1–2; 133:3). It could also be a general reference to the ancient Near Eastern belief that the gods often dwelled on mountain tops; in this case, the psalmist is indicating that his help does not come from where people usually expect it (the gods) but from Yahweh (121:2). **where does my help come from** The psalmist seems to be looking to the hills so that he can consider whether they will be a source of help to him.

121:2 My help comes from the LORD In contrast to the help that natural defenses could provide (such as the mountains around Jerusalem; see 125:2), the psalmist believes that his help comes directly from Yahweh.

121:3–4 Here, the psalm shifts dramatically to the second-person perspective, which can include the psalmist and anyone else who would hear the psalm. These verses explore the way that Yahweh guards his people constantly.

⁵The LORD watches over you —
　　the LORD is your shade at your right hand;
⁶the sun will not harm you by day,
　　nor the moon by night.

⁷The LORD will keep you from all harm —
　　he will watch over your life;
⁸the LORD will watch over your coming and
　　going
　　both now and forevermore.

Psalm 122

A song of ascents. Of David.

¹I rejoiced with those who said to me,
　　"Let us go to the house of the LORD."
²Our feet are standing
　　in your gates, Jerusalem.

³Jerusalem is built like a city
　　that is closely compacted together.
⁴That is where the tribes go up —
　　the tribes of the LORD —

to praise the name of the LORD
　　according to the statute given to Israel.
⁵There stand the thrones for judgment,
　　the thrones of the house of David.

⁶Pray for the peace of Jerusalem:
　　"May those who love you be secure.
⁷May there be peace within your walls
　　and security within your citadels."
⁸For the sake of my family and friends,
　　I will say, "Peace be within you."
⁹For the sake of the house of the LORD our God,
　　I will seek your prosperity.

Psalm 123

A song of ascents.

¹I lift up my eyes to you,
　　to you who sit enthroned in heaven.
²As the eyes of slaves look to the hand of their
　　master,
　　as the eyes of a female slave look to the
　　hand of her mistress,

121:5–6 These verses continue to emphasize Yahweh's protection by depicting him covering his people constantly.

121:5 the LORD is your shade Shade is usually a positive image of protection in the OT, and it portrays enveloping safety and refreshment from the heat.
121:6 the sun will not harm you by day In the harsh climate of the ancient Near East, shade from the heat could be the difference between life and death. **the moon by night** The psalmist envisions day-and-night protection. Unlike many gods of the ancient Near East who were believed to descend to the underworld at night, Yahweh is constantly available and vigilant.

121:7–8 These verses portray Yahweh's protection as something that moves around with the psalmist — Yahweh's protection is not just a stationary hideout or only in Jerusalem. Yahweh is present everywhere with his people.

121:8 your coming and going Yahweh's protection moves with the psalmist; Yahweh is not just a hideout, but a bodyguard.

122:title–9 Psalm 122 is a song of Zion, meaning that it focuses on Jerusalem as the primary location of Yahweh's presence in Israel (compare Ps 46; 48; 76; 84; 87). Psalm 122 is also one of the pilgrimage psalms intended to be sung during pilgrimage to Jerusalem (Ps 120–134; see note on 120:title). The psalmist opens by focusing on Jerusalem as the site of worship (vv. 1–2). He then develops the idea of Jerusalem as the emblem of Israel's unity through its government (vv. 3–5). The psalmist concludes by exhorting his listeners to pray for Jerusalem's security and prosperity because it is a pivotal element in the continued well-being of Israel (vv. 6–9). See the table "Types of Psalms" on p. 830.

122:title A song of ascents See note on 120:title. **Of David** See note on 3:title.

122:1–2 Psalm 122 opens with the psalmist's statement of love for the house of Yahweh and Jerusalem as its home.

122:1 house of the LORD Refers to the Jerusalem temple.

122:3–5 Jerusalem is a meeting place not only between Yahweh and Israel, but also between the tribes of Israel. The psalmist places the government of Israel at the center of this interaction between Yahweh and the people.

122:4 tribes of the LORD Refers to the tribes of Israel (see Ge 35:10,22–26). Each tribe was allotted its own land (see Jos 14:1–5).
122:5 thrones for judgment Indicates a context where regular legal judgments are given. Yahweh is the source of such authority; he delegated authority to his representative, the Davidic king.

122:6–9 Because Jerusalem is such a crucial site of worship and unity, it needs to remain stable and prosperous. The psalmist encourages the people to pray for the peace and security of Jerusalem.

122:7 peace Although the Hebrew word used here, *shalom* (often translated "peace"), seems to primarily describe safety from military attack here, the psalmist is probably also using it in the sense of justice and righteousness (Ps 122:8).
122:9 house of the LORD our God For Jerusalem to prosper, it must stay centered on worship of Yahweh, the God of Israel.

123:title–4 This corporate lament psalm — which is also one of the pilgrimage psalms (Ps 120–134) meant to be sung during pilgrimage to Jerusalem (see note on 120:title) — depicts Israel waiting for Yahweh, the enthroned king in heaven, to act on their behalf. The psalm opens with an individual voice addressing Yahweh (v. 1). It then shifts into a corporate voice, which portrays the people's anticipation of Yahweh's action (v. 2). The community pleads for Yahweh's mercy and action in the face of the scorn of the surrounding people (vv. 3–4). See the table "Types of Psalms" on p. 830.

123:title A song of ascents See note on 120:title.

so our eyes look to the LORD our God,
 till he shows us his mercy.

[3] Have mercy on us, LORD, have mercy on us,
 for we have endured no end of contempt.
[4] We have endured no end
 of ridicule from the arrogant,
 of contempt from the proud.

Psalm 124

A song of ascents. Of David.

[1] If the LORD had not been on our side —
 let Israel say —
[2] if the LORD had not been on our side
 when people attacked us,
[3] they would have swallowed us alive
 when their anger flared against us;
[4] the flood would have engulfed us,
 the torrent would have swept over us,

[5] the raging waters
 would have swept us away.

[6] Praise be to the LORD,
 who has not let us be torn by their
 teeth.
[7] We have escaped like a bird
 from the fowler's snare;
 the snare has been broken,
 and we have escaped.
[8] Our help is in the name of the LORD,
 the Maker of heaven and earth.

Psalm 125

A song of ascents.

[1] Those who trust in the LORD are like
 Mount Zion,
 which cannot be shaken but endures
 forever.

123:1 I lift up my eyes The psalmist places his hope in Yahweh as the source of his assistance.

123:2 This verse describes Israel's anticipation of Yahweh's action by comparing it to the way servants wait for their masters.

123:3–4 The psalm moves from a general expression of hopeful anticipation to explaining Israel's complaint. The community finds itself in an environment where they are despised, and they want Yahweh's help.

123:4 contempt from the proud Contrasts proud people (who trust in themselves) and Israel, who places trust in Yahweh. The psalmist implies that, by showing contempt for Israel, the proud are showing contempt for Yahweh.

124:title–8 In this corporate thanksgiving psalm (meant for group settings)—which is also one of the pilgrimage psalms (Ps 120–134) intended to be sung during pilgrimage to Jerusalem (see note on 120:title)—Israel thanks God for his help during a crisis involving other nations. Each half of the psalm begins by mentioning Yahweh and then develops a central image of the crisis Israel faces. The first section compares the enemy's anger to an overwhelming flood (vv. 1–5). The second describes them as hunters pursuing Israel, who is portrayed as a bird that has barely escaped capture (vv. 6–8). Although the various expressions mentioning Yahweh do not occur in a single recurring pattern, a specific reference to Yahweh opens the psalm (in a repeated line), begins the second major section, and then occurs in the closing verse. This structural emphasis on Yahweh's name reinforces the psalm's focus on thanking God for his help. See the table "Types of Psalms" on p. 830.

124:title A song of ascents See note on 120:title. **Of David** See note on 3:title.

124:1–5 The first two verses contain the same phrase. These repetitions establish that Ps 124 will focus on Yahweh's work on behalf of Israel. The psalmist then uses graphic flood imagery to describe the crisis, depicting Israel's enemies as an overpowering flood that threatens to destroy Israel.

124:3 swallowed us alive Here and in v. 6, the psalmist

portrays the nations as a mouth that wants to consume Israel.

124:4–5 The psalmist portrays the nations using several images of dangerous waters that threaten to cover Israel and sweep it away. Such flood imagery is usually connected to Yahweh's subordination of chaos during creation and reflects his power over the whole world (see 93:3–4). Yahweh, Israel's Creator, will provide his people with an escape (see vv. 6–8).

124:6–8 The psalmist mentions Yahweh by name again and introduces a new image for the crisis threatening Israel. The enemies of Israel are like deadly hunters who will capture Israel and consume it. The closing verse of Ps 124 mentions Yahweh again, forming a bookend structure that emphasizes Yahweh's help as the object of Israel's thanksgiving (v. 8).

124:8 Our help is in the name The psalmist concludes by mentioning that Yahweh is the only reason Israel has survived. Yahweh's name refers to his reputation or fame; the psalmist mentions Yahweh's name to testify that he is reliable and faithful. Yahweh has come through again because he always comes through.

125:title–5 Psalm 125 is a corporate psalm of confidence—meant for a group to use to express trust in Yahweh. Psalm 125 is also one of the pilgrimage psalms (Ps 120–134), intended to be during pilgrimage to Jerusalem (see note on 120:title). Psalm 125 combines themes of trust in Yahweh and observance of Yahweh's covenant with his protection of Jerusalem. The psalm opens by describing the interplay between Israel's trust in Yahweh and his protection of Israel and Jerusalem (vv. 1–2), and explains Yahweh's protection of Israel from foreign rule as a concern to protect the purity of Israel (vv. 1–3). Then, the psalm begins a new section by addressing Yahweh in a direct request to protect the righteous, punish evildoers and bring peace upon Israel (vv. 4–5). See the table "Types of Psalms" on p. 830.

125:title A song of ascents See note on 120:title.

125:1–3 The opening verses establish the psalm's theme of trust. Yahweh will protect his people so that they might remain pure from the influence of corrupt rule.

² As the mountains surround Jerusalem,
  so the LORD surrounds his people
  both now and forevermore.

³ The scepter of the wicked will not remain
  over the land allotted to the righteous,
  for then the righteous might use
  their hands to do evil.

⁴ LORD, do good to those who are good,
  to those who are upright in heart.
⁵ But those who turn to crooked ways
  the LORD will banish with the evildoers.

Peace be on Israel.

Psalm 126

A song of ascents.

¹ When the LORD restored the fortunes of*ᵃ*
  Zion,
  we were like those who dreamed.*ᵇ*
² Our mouths were filled with laughter,
  our tongues with songs of joy.

Then it was said among the nations,
  "The LORD has done great things for
  them."
³ The LORD has done great things for us,
  and we are filled with joy.

⁴ Restore our fortunes,*ᶜ* LORD,
  like streams in the Negev.
⁵ Those who sow with tears
  will reap with songs of joy.
⁶ Those who go out weeping,
  carrying seed to sow,
will return with songs of joy,
  carrying sheaves with them.

Psalm 127

A song of ascents. Of Solomon.

¹ Unless the LORD builds the house,
  the builders labor in vain.

ᵃ 1 Or LORD *brought back the captives to*   *ᵇ 1* Or *those restored to health*   *ᶜ 4* Or *Bring back our captives*

125:1 trust The Hebrew word used here, *batach*, implies security or confidence. Israel's trust in Yahweh implies their loyalty to Yahweh and his commands. **Mount Zion** Refers to the temple mount in Jerusalem.

125:4–5 The psalmist addresses Yahweh directly and pleads for him to protect his people and punish the wicked. This request fits with v. 3's concern for purity and loyalty to Yahweh. Verse 3 and vv. 4–5 seem to anticipate difficulties in the future rather than describe a present crisis of corruption within Israel.

125:5 will banish Suggests invasion and deportation, which Judah experienced during the Babylonian exile (ca. 586–538 BC). **Peace** For Israel to experience *shalom* (the Hebrew word used here) the people must remain loyal to Yahweh and in right relationship with each other (see note on 120:6).

126:title–6 This corporate lament pleads for Yahweh to restore Israel as he has in the past. It is also one of the pilgrimage psalms (Ps 120–134) intended to be sung during pilgrimage to Jerusalem (see note on 120:title). The psalmist begins Ps 126 by recalling a time when Yahweh restored the nation, describing the Israelites' joy and the surrounding nations' awareness of Yahweh's power as a result of the event (vv. 1–3). The psalmist then presents the request of corporate Israel for Yahweh to restore Israel again, anticipating new joy following Yahweh's help (vv. 4–6). See the table "Types of Psalms" on p. 830.

126:title A song of ascents See note on 120:title.

126:1–3 The first half of Ps 126 describes a previous time when Yahweh had restored Israel, apparently unexpectedly. After an initial period of quiet, Israel is joyful, and even the surrounding nations notice Yahweh's help.

126:1 restored the fortunes The Hebrew word used here, *shivah*, implies captivity when it occurs by itself, but often occurs in the expression *shuv shivah*, as it does here, which literally means "restore the captivity of." The

expression essentially indicates that Yahweh is returning something to the way it was before calamity happened. It probably indicates that Yahweh had returned the Israelites to Jerusalem after a period of exile (likely a reference to the events following 538 BC). **like those who dreamed** Indicates that the Israelites were in a daze, as though awakened by surprise.

126:2 The LORD has done great things for them Corporate Israel repeats this line almost verbatim in v. 3. The nations acknowledge Yahweh's greatness because of his actions on behalf of Israel.

126:4–6 In the second half of Ps 126, the Israelites beg Yahweh for help in their present situation. The psalmist depicts the restoration in terms of ample water in the desert and a bountiful harvest that prompts new joy.

126:4 Restore This plea expresses a current request. Israel now finds itself in a situation of great crisis and needs God to rescue and restore them. Compare v. 1.

126:5 sow with tears The motif of sorrowful planting and joyful harvest occurs twice in vv. 5–6. The verses focus on the sorrow of the planter, which may reflect Israel's captivity. **will reap with songs of joy** While v. 5 emphasizes the joy of the harvest, v. 6 adds the element of a very bountiful harvest. The joyful harvest probably reflects the exiles' return to Jerusalem (v. 2) being accompanied by security in Jerusalem and Yahweh's presence.

127:title–5 This wisdom psalm—meant for passing along wise teachings—shows how God is involved in all aspects of life. Rather than contrasting the way of the wicked with those who follow God—commonly called the "two ways" motif—it focuses on Yahweh's provision in terms of protection (vv. 1–2) and progeny (vv. 3–5). The psalm may have been originally composed for a king, though its contents make it applicable to all of Yahweh's people. Psalm 127 is part of the pilgrimage psalms (Ps 120–134), intended to be used during pilgrimage to Jerusalem (see note on 120:title). See the table "Types of Psalms" on p. 830.

Unless the Lord watches over
   the city,
      the guards stand watch in vain.
² In vain you rise early
      and stay up late,
   toiling for food to eat —
      for he grants sleep to^a those he loves.

³ Children are a heritage from
      the Lord,
      offspring a reward from him.
⁴ Like arrows in the hands of a
      warrior
   are children born in one's youth.
⁵ Blessed is the man
      whose quiver is full of them.
   They will not be put to shame
      when they contend with their
         opponents in court.

Psalm 128

A song of ascents.

¹ Blessed are all who fear the Lord,
   who walk in obedience to him.
² You will eat the fruit of your labor;
   blessings and prosperity will be yours.
³ Your wife will be like a fruitful vine
      within your house;
   your children will be like olive shoots
      around your table.
⁴ Yes, this will be the blessing
   for the man who fears the Lord.

⁵ May the Lord bless you from Zion;
   may you see the prosperity of Jerusalem
      all the days of your life.

^a 2 Or *eat— / for while they sleep he provides for*

127:title A song of ascents See note on 120:title.
Of Solomon One of two psalms that are affiliated with Solomon (Ps 72 and 127). See note on 72:title.

127:1–2 Psalm 127 opens with several statements of truth that relate to building and protecting a house. Since the concern for protection involves watchmen over a city (v. 1), the likely setting is of a king who diligently strives to develop and protect his kingdom. However, the main point for the owner of the house is that Yahweh allows the owner to rest securely without anxiety (v. 2).

127:1 Unless the Lord builds the house Probably refers to a dynasty—the parallel reference to watching over a city creates a wider context than an individual who owns a house.

127:2 In this verse and v. 1, the psalmist seems to be speaking to people who are troubled and restless.

127:2 he grants sleep to those he loves The psalmist may describe people as a collective group here, or he may be urging the people to accept the king's role as Yahweh's chosen leader. If the people trust Yahweh and his representative (the king), they can rest at ease.

127:3–5 These verses seem to be disconnected from the opening section of the psalm. However, *banim* in the Hebrew text ("children") may be connected with *bayith* ("house") in v. 1 in the sense that residents of a kingdom are metaphorically children of a king. This conclusion is supported by the idea of children being like a warrior's arrows in v. 4 and the reference to city gates. See note on v. 3.

127:3 Children are a heritage from the Lord A large family was understood to be a blessing in ancient Near Eastern thought. Taken by itself, v. 3 is a truism, but the reference to *yad-gibbor* in the Hebrew text ("the hand of a warrior") in v. 4 indicates that *banim* ("children") could refer figuratively to subjects of the king.
127:4 Like arrows in the hands of a warrior The addition of the warrior image to the ancient Near Eastern ideal of a large family creates a pattern that fits with a metaphorical use of family as subjects of the king. Compare note on v. 3; note on vv. 3–5.
127:5 court The Hebrew text here uses the word *sa'ar*, which may be literally rendered "gate." In time of war, gates were the weak spots in city walls, and therefore

the location of much of the armed conflict when a city was attacked. However, a king with many subjects is able to protect his city gates.

128:title–6 In this wisdom psalm—meant for passing on wise teachings—the psalmist asserts that fear (reverence) of Yahweh is the foundation for Yahweh's subsequent blessing. The psalmist begins by connecting Yahweh's blessing—mainly in the form of numerous progeny—with fear of Yahweh and right conduct (vv. 1–2). He then connects the theme of abundant children to multi-generational stability within Jerusalem (vv. 5–6). The focus on peace within Jerusalem may connect thematically to the psalm's opening emphasis on right worship and conduct, since stability within the land of Israel is often connected to covenant faithfulness in the OT (see Dt 28). Psalm 128 is also one of the pilgrimage psalms (Ps 120–134) that were intended to be used during pilgrimage to Jerusalem (see note on 120:title). See the table "Types of Psalms" on p. 830.

128:title A song of ascents See note on 120:title.

128:1–2 The psalmist begins with a general statement connecting obedience and blessing. He then addresses the audience in personal terms to draw them toward obedience to Yahweh.

128:3–4 The psalmist describes the benefits of obedience primarily in terms of a prosperous and happy family. He addresses the recipient in personal terms before shifting back, restating the connection between obedience and blessing.

128:3 Your wife will be like a fruitful vine The psalmist employs the motif of family as a fruitful plant to depict the success of the pious person because of his blessed life. The pious man's family will be fruitful like a garden or orchard. (Large families were viewed as a tremendous blessing in the ancient Near East.)
128:4 the blessing The Hebrew word used here, *barakh*, describes Yahweh's granting prosperity to the pious man in this instance. It is the usual word for the extension of good wishes or special enablement.
128:5 bless you from Zion It is from Yahweh's dwelling place in Jerusalem—the proper place of worship— that he is depicted as blessing people. This hints at the idea that blessing can only be fully established as

⁶ May you live to see your children's children —
   peace be on Israel.

Psalm 129

A song of ascents.

¹ "They have greatly oppressed me from my
      youth,"
   let Israel say;
² "they have greatly oppressed me from my
      youth,
   but they have not gained the victory
      over me.
³ Plowmen have plowed my back
   and made their furrows long.
⁴ But the LORD is righteous;
   he has cut me free from the cords of the
      wicked."

⁵ May all who hate Zion
   be turned back in shame.
⁶ May they be like grass on the roof,
   which withers before it can grow;
⁷ a reaper cannot fill his hands with it,
   nor one who gathers fill his arms.
⁸ May those who pass by not say to them,
   "The blessing of the LORD be
      on you;
   we bless you in the name of the LORD."

Psalm 130

A song of ascents.

¹ Out of the depths I cry to you, LORD;
²   Lord, hear my voice.
   Let your ears be attentive
   to my cry for mercy.

---

the entire nation worships Yahweh appropriately in his chosen place. **prosperity of Jerusalem** The blessing of Jerusalem is symbolic here of the condition of the people of Israel in general. This prosperity includes right corporate (group) worship, economic stability and freedom from attack.

128:6 to see your children's children The blessing includes long life and numerous progeny. Long life and many children were key tenants of Yahweh's blessing in ancient Israelite thought. **peace** See note on 125:5. **Israel** This probably refers to the people of the nation and the promised land—especially Jerusalem.

129:title–8 Psalm 129 does not fit a specific structural pattern, and its themes allow it to fit into several categories. The psalmist begins by recalling affliction from oppressors (vv. 1–3); he then describes how the situation was resolved when Yahweh freed Israel from its bonds (v. 4). The psalmist then focuses on all enemies who hate Zion (v. 5)—symbolic of God's people in general—and requests that Yahweh block their efforts and reduce them to nothing (vv. 6–8).

Verses 1–4 focus on recalling Yahweh's deliverance, allowing this psalm to be classified as a corporate (group) thanksgiving psalm; however, vv. 5–8 emphasize a request for deliverance, allowing for the classification of a corporate lament psalm. It could also be viewed as a corporate psalm of confidence—meant to articulate trust in God—in which Israel recalls Yahweh's deliverance (vv. 1–4) and then trusts Yahweh to repeat that deliverance in the future (vv. 5–8). Psalm 129 is also part of the collection of pilgrimage psalms (Ps 120–134) intended to be used during pilgrimage to Jerusalem (see note on 120:title). See the table "Types of Psalms" on p. 830.

129:title A song of ascents See note on 120:title.

129:1–4 Israel recounts its past affliction. Although their suffering was awful (v. 3), Yahweh freed them from oppressive rulers and gave them hope.

129:1 They have greatly oppressed me from my youth Although this opening line is presented in an individual voice, it is meant to express the collective viewpoint of the entire nation of Israel.

129:2 they have not gained the victory Israel's tormenters have not been completely victorious.

129:3 Plowmen have plowed my back This may in-

dicate that Israel had been enslaved, or that Israel had been physically tortured.

129:4 cords of the wicked This could refer to harness-like restraints for an enslaved people, or restraints within a prison. Compare v. 3 and note.

129:5–8 The psalmist addresses present and future enemies of Israel, predicting or wishing for their eventual downfall. Verse 5 seems to have a military attack of Jerusalem in view; vv. 6–7 depicts Israel's enemies quickly disappearing.

129:6 on the roof Refers to the practice of building structures with flat earthen roofs. People in the ancient Near East placed soil on rooftops over planks and rolled it flat, then grew grass on top of the flat roof. See the infographic "Ancient Israelite House" on p. 1205.

129:8 The blessing of the LORD The enemies of Israel have not been able to subdue the nation (v. 2) and do not experience Yahweh's blessing because they do not know him.

130:title–8 This individual lament psalm—which is also part of the pilgrimage psalms (Ps 120–134) that were meant to be used during pilgrimage to Jerusalem (see note on 120:title)—focuses on the psalmist's internal experience. He begins by crying for help and pleading for Yahweh's mercy (vv. 1–2). He then implicitly asks forgiveness by stating that no one could endure Yahweh's scrutiny for sins, but Yahweh forgives in order that he might be worshiped (vv. 3–4). The psalmist then describes his hope and anticipation of Yahweh's help in terms of night watchmen yearning for morning light (vv. 5–6). He concludes by exhorting all Israel to hope in Yahweh because he will redeem Israel (vv. 7–8). See the table "Types of Psalms" on p. 830.

130:title A song of ascents See note on 120:title.

130:1–2 The psalmist begins by pleading with Yahweh for help. The psalmist may feel that his difficulties result from his sins, as indicated by his later mention of iniquities (vv. 3,8).

130:1 the depths The Hebrew word used here, *ma'amaqqim*, usually refers to the depths of the sea (see Isa 51:10). While Israelites did engage in sea travel and trade (compare Ps 107:23), the sea was usually viewed as a symbol of chaos and danger. Thus, *ma'amaqqim*

³ If you, Lord, kept a record of sins,
Lord, who could stand?
⁴ But with you there is forgiveness,
so that we can, with reverence, serve you.

⁵ I wait for the Lord, my whole being waits,
and in his word I put my hope.
⁶ I wait for the Lord
more than watchmen wait for the
morning,
more than watchmen wait for the
morning.

⁷ Israel, put your hope in the Lord,
for with the Lord is unfailing love
and with him is full redemption.
⁸ He himself will redeem Israel
from all their sins.

Psalm 131

A song of ascents. Of David.

¹ My heart is not proud, Lord,
my eyes are not haughty;

I do not concern myself with great matters
or things too wonderful for me.
² But I have calmed and quieted myself,
I am like a weaned child with its mother;
like a weaned child I am content.

³ Israel, put your hope in the Lord
both now and forevermore.

Psalm 132

132:8-10pp — 2Ch 6:41-42

A song of ascents.

¹ Lord, remember David
and all his self-denial.

² He swore an oath to the Lord,
he made a vow to the Mighty One of Jacob:
³ "I will not enter my house
or go to my bed,
⁴ I will allow no sleep to my eyes
or slumber to my eyelids,
⁵ till I find a place for the Lord,
a dwelling for the Mighty One of Jacob."

---

may be a figurative expression for guilty feelings or some sort of literal imprisonment.

130:3–4 The psalmist seems to connect his suffering to possible punishment for sin, but he emphasizes Yahweh's forgiving nature. He asserts that Yahweh forgives so that he might be worshiped; thus, the psalmist implies that he will worship Yahweh if Yahweh rescues him.

130:3 a record of sins The Hebrew word used here, *awon*, can refer to a misdeed itself, the guilt caused by the misdeed or even the punishment for the misdeed. Here, the term is plural and likely refers to the guilt that misdeeds accrue. **who could stand** The psalmist is aware that no one lives perfectly before Yahweh and that no one can withstand close scrutiny by Yahweh for misdeeds and mistakes.

130:4 forgiveness This type of pardon goes beyond a strictly legal context to include the general stance of trust in Yahweh (compare Nu 14:19–20).

130:5–6 The psalmist waits for Yahweh's help.

130:5 I put my hope The Hebrew word used here, *yachal*, is synonymous with *qawah* (often rendered "wait"), which is used twice earlier in this verse. Both terms indicate waiting with anticipation (compare Ps 130:7).

130:7–8 The psalmist exhorts all Israel to hope in Yahweh's redemption from sin. His ability to present his psalm is implicit proof of Yahweh's redemption.

130:8 will redeem The Hebrew verb used here, *padah*, has the sense of ransoming or releasing from imprisonment. This depicts iniquities as creating guilt that must be offset by some sort of recompense (see v. 3 and note; v. 7).

131:title–3 This individual psalm of confidence—expressing trust in God—focuses on the experience of internal calm. The psalmist begins by addressing Yahweh personally and stating his submission to Yahweh's order, declaring that he does not seek to understand things

that are closed to him or too hard for him to comprehend (v. 1). He then describes his inner discipline and compares his soul to a weaned child content to be with its mother (132:2). The psalmist concludes by exhorting Israel to hope in Yahweh like he does (130:3). Psalm 131 is also part of the collection of pilgrimage psalms (Ps 120–134) meant to be used during pilgrimage to Jerusalem (see note on 120:title). See the table "Types of Psalms" on p. 830.

131:title A song of ascents See note on 120:title. **Of David** One of four psalms of ascents affiliated with David (compare Ps 124; 131; 133; see note on 3:title). **131:1 great matters or things too wonderful for me** Instead of striving to understand things that are outside his understanding, the psalmist continues to trust Yahweh.

131:2 like a weaned child The psalmist uses a description that describes increasing maturity; the child no longer needs the mother's milk and shows maturity in its ability to wait.

132:title–18 The psalmist opens this royal psalm (about kingship) by begging Yahweh to remember David's loyalty and his desire to build the temple (vv. 1–5). He then describes how the surrounding residents of Judah respond by coming to worship in Jerusalem (vv. 6–7). The psalmist addresses Yahweh directly as he requests that Yahweh inhabit the worship site because of his promise to David (vv. 8–10). He then recounts Yahweh's promise to David (vv. 11–12) and proclaims that Yahweh has indeed chosen Jerusalem as his site of worship. He concludes by asserting that Yahweh will bless the city and David (or the Davidic king) while thwarting his enemies (vv. 13–18).

Though Ps 132 is a royal psalm, it could also be a liturgy of the Davidic covenant because of its back-and-forth sequence of perspectives. The psalm focuses on the Davidic covenant (see 2Sa 7:1–17 and note) and looks back on Yahweh's promise to David in hope that Yahweh

⁶ We heard it in Ephrathah,
 we came upon it in the fields of Jaar:ᵃ
⁷ "Let us go to his dwelling place,
 let us worship at his footstool, saying,
⁸ 'Arise, LORD, and come to your resting place,
 you and the ark of your might.
⁹ May your priests be clothed with your
 righteousness;
 may your faithful people sing for joy.'"

¹⁰ For the sake of your servant David,
 do not reject your anointed one.

¹¹ The LORD swore an oath to David,
 a sure oath he will not revoke:
"One of your own descendants
 I will place on your throne.
¹² If your sons keep my covenant
 and the statutes I teach them,
 then their sons will sit
 on your throne for ever and ever."

¹³ For the LORD has chosen Zion,
 he has desired it for his dwelling, saying,
¹⁴ "This is my resting place for ever and ever;
 here I will sit enthroned, for I have desired it.

¹⁵ I will bless her with abundant provisions;
 her poor I will satisfy with food.
¹⁶ I will clothe her priests with salvation,
 and her faithful people will ever sing for joy.

¹⁷ "Here I will make a hornᵇ grow for David
 and set up a lamp for my anointed one.
¹⁸ I will clothe his enemies with shame,
 but his head will be adorned with a radiant
 crown."

Psalm 133

A song of ascents. Of David.

¹ How good and pleasant it is
 when God's people live together in unity!

² It is like precious oil poured on the head,
 running down on the beard,
 running down on Aaron's beard,
 down on the collar of his robe.

ᵃ 6 Or *heard of it in Ephrathah, / we found it in the fields of Jearim.* (See 1 Chron. 13:5,6) (And no quotation marks around verses 7-9)   ᵇ 17 *Horn* here symbolizes strong one, that is, king.

---

will act on Israel's behalf again in the present time. In addition, Ps 132 is also one of the pilgrimage psalms (Ps 120–134) intended to be used during pilgrimage to Jerusalem (see note on 120:title). See the table "Types of Psalms" on p. 830.

132:title A song of ascents See note on 120:title.

132:1–5 After requesting that Yahweh remember David's hardships and loyalty, the psalmist describes David's desire to build the temple (see 2Sa 7:1–3; 1Ch 17:1–2). While Yahweh did not allow David to build the temple, David did move the ark of the covenant to Jerusalem.

132:2 He swore an oath to the LORD A structural marker in this psalm; David swears an oath in Ps 132:2, and Yahweh swears an oath in v. 11.

132:6 Ephrathah This refers to the district of Judah where David was from (1Sa 17:12). It contained several villages, including Bethlehem and Kiriath Jearim (where the ark of the covenant was housed for a time; see 1Sa 7:1–2).

132:7 footstool The meaning of the Hebrew phrase used here, *hadom regel*, varies according to its context. Here, it probably refers to the ark of the covenant (Ps 132:8; 1Ch 28:2).

132:8–10 The psalmist implores Yahweh to inhabit the worship site (in Jerusalem) and remember the descendant of David who now rules.

132:9 your priests The priests are distinguished by qualities such as moral purity, ethical integrity and loyalty to both Yahweh and the nation of Israel. See note on Ps 4:1. **your faithful** The Hebrew word used here, *chasid*, refers to people who are faithful or pious in a way that is similar to Yahweh's *chesed* (his unfailing, covenantal love; see note on 25:10).

132:10 your anointed one Refers to the chosen ruler presently on the throne. The psalmist asks Yahweh to help the Davidic heir.

132:11–12 Psalm 132 focuses on Yahweh's promise to David (see 2Sa 7). Yahweh promises to keep subsequent descendants of David in dynastic power as long as they remain faithful in keeping his covenant.

132:11 your own descendants I will place In 2Sa 7:12–16, Yahweh promises that a physical descendant of David will remain on Israel's throne.

132:12 If your sons keep my covenant The Davidic covenant was conditional; it required that David's descendants continue to show loyalty to Yahweh.

132:13–18 The psalmist concludes by emphasizing that Yahweh has chosen Jerusalem as his worship site and that he will bless the city—and by extension all of Israel—and keep his promise to David.

132:13 the LORD has chosen Zion Texts such as Dt 12:5 and Dt 11 indicate that Yahweh would choose a central worship site in the future. In 2Sa 6:12, David moved the ark to Jerusalem, establishing it as the city where central worship would take place. Second Samuel 7:13 and 1Ki 6:12–13 locate Yahweh's choice of a dwelling place on Mount Zion where Solomon's temple was built.

132:17 horn A symbol of strength and help. **a lamp for my anointed** Mirrors the sacred light in the tent of meeting of the tabernacle (Lev 24:1–4), which was to be a perpetual signal of Yahweh's presence. The symbolism here is probably related to Yahweh's perpetual commitment to his promise to David.

133:title–3 Psalm 133 is a wisdom psalm (meant to pass on wise teachings) or a corporate psalm of confidence (meant to help a group express trust in God). It is also part of the pilgrimage psalms (Ps 120–134) that were intended to be used during pilgrimage to Jerusalem (see note on 120:title).

The opening of Ps 133 forms the basis for the other comparisons in the psalm. The psalmist comments on the blessing of unity. He then compares this blessing to the anointing oil of Aaron, the first high priest—probably

³ It is as if the dew of Hermon
    were falling on Mount Zion.
For there the Lord bestows his blessing,
    even life forevermore.

Psalm 134

A song of ascents.

¹ Praise the Lord, all you servants
    of the Lord
who minister by night in the house of the
    Lord.
² Lift up your hands in the sanctuary
    and praise the Lord.

³ May the Lord bless you from Zion,
    he who is the Maker of heaven and earth.

Psalm 135

135:15-20pp — Ps 115:4-11

¹ Praise the Lord.ᵃ

Praise the name of the Lord;
    praise him, you servants of the Lord,
² you who minister in the house of the Lord,
    in the courts of the house of our God.

³ Praise the Lord, for the Lord is good;
    sing praise to his name, for that is pleasant.
⁴ For the Lord has chosen Jacob to be his own,
    Israel to be his treasured possession.

⁵ I know that the Lord is great,
    that our Lord is greater than all gods.

ᵃ 1 Hebrew *Hallelu Yah*; also in verses 3 and 21

---

signifying that right worship is symbolic of the connection between God and Israel (v. 2). The psalmist compares the blessing of v. 1 to dew that collects on the hills of Israel (see v. 3 and note). He concludes by reemphasizing that Jerusalem is the central location to worship Yahweh and receive his blessing (v. 3).

Psalm 133 could be classified as either a wisdom psalm or a corporate psalm of confidence, depending on how much emphasis is placed on the thematic elements of the psalm. The language of blessing and prosperity occupies most of Ps 133, indicating that it is connected to ideas of blessings for keeping covenant (e.g., Dt 28). Psalm 133 layers many images and similes, making interpretation challenging. See the table "Types of Psalms" on p. 830.

133:title A song of ascents See note on 120:title. **Of David** See note on 3:title.
133:1 when God's people live together in unity This expression probably reflects statements like those in Ge 13:6 or 36:7, where extended families are described as being unable to dwell peaceably together because the land could not support them.
133:2 precious oil poured on the head Implies God's presence. God's provision and presence enable Israel to dwell together in Jerusalem. **on Aaron's beard** Compare Ex 29:1–9.
133:3 as if the dew of Hermon Symbolizes Yahweh's provision for the land of Israel. Dew was often a crucial source of water. **bestows his blessing** Yahweh's presence was understood to dwell on the temple mount, Mount Zion, in the Jerusalem temple. This made it possible for the people of Israel to live together there (see Dt 12:5–7; compare Ps 133:1).

134:title–3 Psalm 134 concludes the Songs of Ascents or pilgrimage psalms (Ps 120–134), which were intended to be used during pilgrimage to Jerusalem (see note on 120:title). It is a corporate praise psalm (meant for group settings) in which those who serve Yahweh in the temple are called to bless him. The psalmist opens by calling Yahweh's servants within the temple to bless him as well as the temple itself (vv. 1–2). He then extends Yahweh's blessing to every worshiper at the temple (v. 3). See the table "Types of Psalms" on p. 830.

134:title A song of ascents See note on 120:title.
134:1 in the house of the Lord Identifies the previously

mentioned servants as attendants within the temple — night watchmen.
134:2 Lift up your hands in the sanctuary A figure of speech called metonymy — the lifting up of hands signals praise of Yahweh.
134:3 he who is the Maker of heaven and earth The psalmist portrays Yahweh as living in Jerusalem and describes him as the Creator. The psalmist seems to marvel that cosmic power is located within the holy city.

135:1–21 This corporate praise psalm (meant for group settings) proclaims Yahweh's greatness in terms of his power over the cosmos and his actions on behalf of his people. The psalmist begins by calling Yahweh's servants to praise him because he is good and because he has chosen Israel as his own (vv. 1–4). The psalmist then introduces the theme of Yahweh's great power over other gods and all of the created order (vv. 5–7). The psalmist illustrates this by recalling events like the exodus and Israel's entry into the promised land (vv. 8–12). The psalmist discusses Yahweh's reputation and its connection to his care for his people (vv. 13–14), then reconsiders the powerlessness of foreign idols and the futility of the foreigners' trust in them (vv. 15–18). He concludes by calling all of Yahweh's people to praise him (vv. 19–21). See the table "Types of Psalms" on p. 830.

135:1–4 The opening call to praise takes place within the Jerusalem temple (vv. 1–2). Yahweh deserves praise for his moral goodness and his help of Israel (vv. 3–4).

135:1 Praise the Lord The Hebrew phrase used here *hallu-yah* occurs only in the last third of the psalms (Ps 104–150). See note on 104:35.
135:4 possession Describes Yahweh's special relationship with Israel. At the time of the Sinai covenant, Yahweh refers to Israel using the same Hebrew word used here, *segullah* (see Ex 19:5).

135:5–7 The psalmist first praises Yahweh's superiority over foreign gods, then focuses on Yahweh's power over all creation.

135:5 gods The Hebrew word used here, *elohim*, while it can refer to the God of Israel, refers here to the deities worshiped by other nations. The Psalmist proclaims that *adone* ("our Lord"), the God of Israel (Yahweh), is greater than all other spiritual beings. Compare Ps 82; note on 82:2.

⁶ The LORD does whatever pleases him,
  in the heavens and on the earth,
  in the seas and all their depths.
⁷ He makes clouds rise from the ends
    of the earth;
  he sends lightning with the rain
  and brings out the wind from his
    storehouses.

⁸ He struck down the firstborn of Egypt,
  the firstborn of people and animals.
⁹ He sent his signs and wonders into your
    midst, Egypt,
  against Pharaoh and all his servants.
¹⁰ He struck down many nations
  and killed mighty kings —
¹¹ Sihon king of the Amorites,
  Og king of Bashan,
  and all the kings of Canaan —
¹² and he gave their land as an
    inheritance,
  an inheritance to his people Israel.

¹³ Your name, LORD, endures forever,
  your renown, LORD, through all
    generations.

¹⁴ For the LORD will vindicate his people
  and have compassion on his servants.

¹⁵ The idols of the nations are silver and gold,
  made by human hands.
¹⁶ They have mouths, but cannot speak,
  eyes, but cannot see.
¹⁷ They have ears, but cannot hear,
  nor is there breath in their mouths.
¹⁸ Those who make them will be like them,
  and so will all who trust in them.

¹⁹ All you Israelites, praise the LORD;
  house of Aaron, praise the LORD;
²⁰ house of Levi, praise the LORD;
  you who fear him, praise the LORD.
²¹ Praise be to the LORD from Zion,
  to him who dwells in Jerusalem.

Praise the LORD.

Psalm 136

¹ Give thanks to the LORD, for he is good.
  His love endures forever.
² Give thanks to the God of gods.
  His love endures forever.

135:6 in the seas and all their depths Though the pairing of heaven and earth usually means everything, the seas are specifically mentioned here because the seas were viewed in the ancient Near East as a primordial power that a god had to subdue (compare Ps 93:3–4; 107:23–30). Unlike foreign gods, Yahweh is not in a battle with the forces of nature but instead completely and easily rules over them.

135:7 the wind from his storehouses Several OT passages depict Yahweh controlling the elements — rain, snow, hail and wind — by storing them in chambers (e.g., Job 38:22).

135:8–12 The psalmist draws from two events from Israel's history that emphasize Yahweh's power: the plagues against Egypt during the exodus and Yahweh's action against the Canaanites during Israel's entry into the promised land. This rehearsal reflects Ps 105 (compare 135:12; 105:43–44). However, while the plagues are a common theme in the psalms, the mention of Sihon and Og is relatively distinctive (compare 136:17–22).

135:10 He struck down many nations Israel first overcame resistance on the east side of the Jordan River before crossing the Jordan and overcoming the nations there. Compare note on Jos 6:16; note on 6:17.

135:11 Sihon king of the Amorites, Og king of Bashan The first enemies that the new generation of Israelites defeated after the wilderness wanderings (Nu 21:21–35). See the infographic "Ancient Jericho" on p. 330.

135:12 inheritance The Hebrew word used here, *nachalah*, describes inalienable, inherited property. Yahweh judged the nations of Canaan in part by taking away their right to the land (Dt 9:4–6).

135:13–14 This section focuses on Yahweh's reputation and connects it to his continued faithfulness to his commitment to his people. This sets up the extended treatment of the powerless idols in Ps 135:15–18.

135:14 This verse is quoted in Heb 10:30.

135:14 will vindicate The Hebrew word used here, *dayan*, often refers in legal contexts to pleading or deciding a legal dispute. Israel is experiencing injustice, and Yahweh will judge the matter and execute justice against those who are oppressing Israel.

135:15–18 In this passage, the psalmist denounces foreign idols as powerless and worthless, stating that they will eventually bring about the downfall of those who trust in them. This section reflects Ps 115:4–8; 135:18 essentially repeats 115:8.

135:15 idols of the nations See 96:5 and note.

135:19–21 The psalmist concludes by calling all Israel to praise Yahweh. He centers the call within the context of worship at the Jerusalem temple (as seen in vv. 1–2).

135:19 house of Aaron Aaron was the first high priest; the duties of the priests were separate from the duties of the Levites.

135:20 house of Levi The Levites were authorized to manage many of the sacred items and tasks in Israel's ritual worship, but not all Levites were priests. Compare note on v. 19. **you who fear** This probably refers to the Israelites in general (v. 19). It could also include anyone who is loyal to Yahweh and observes his commands.

136:1–26 In this corporate praise psalm (meant for use in group settings), the psalmist rehearses Israel's sacred history, focusing on the events of the exodus and entry into the promised land. The psalmist begins by calling his audience to praise God for his goodness and his power over all that exists (vv. 1–3), and he emphasizes God's work in creating the cosmos (vv. 4–9). He then focuses on God's relationship with Israel, describing how he delivered Israel from slavery in Egypt and guided them through the wilderness (vv. 10–16). The psalmist depicts Israel's entry into the promised land (vv. 17–22)

³ Give thanks to the Lord of lords:
His love endures forever.

⁴ to him who alone does great wonders,
His love endures forever.

⁵ who by his understanding made the heavens,
His love endures forever.

⁶ who spread out the earth upon the waters,
His love endures forever.

⁷ who made the great lights —
His love endures forever.

⁸ the sun to govern the day,
His love endures forever.

⁹ the moon and stars to govern the night;
His love endures forever.

¹⁰ to him who struck down the firstborn of Egypt
His love endures forever.

¹¹ and brought Israel out from among them
His love endures forever.

¹² with a mighty hand and outstretched arm;
His love endures forever.

¹³ to him who divided the Red Sea[a] asunder
His love endures forever.

¹⁴ and brought Israel through the midst of it,
His love endures forever.

¹⁵ but swept Pharaoh and his army into
the Red Sea;
His love endures forever.

¹⁶ to him who led his people through
the wilderness;
His love endures forever.

¹⁷ to him who struck down great kings,
His love endures forever.

¹⁸ and killed mighty kings —
His love endures forever.

¹⁹ Sihon king of the Amorites
His love endures forever.

²⁰ and Og king of Bashan —
His love endures forever.

²¹ and gave their land as an inheritance,
His love endures forever.

²² an inheritance to his servant Israel.
His love endures forever.

²³ He remembered us in our low estate
His love endures forever.

²⁴ and freed us from our enemies.
His love endures forever.

ᵃ 13 Or *the Sea of Reeds*; also in verse 15

---

and closes with a brief series of statements that echo the various themes of each of the major sections of the psalm (vv. 23–26). See the table "Types of Psalms" on p. 830.

136:1–3 After an initial statement of thanksgiving for God's goodness, the psalmist exhorts his audience to give thanks to Israel's God as the supreme God and Lord over all creation (see Dt 10:17).

136:1 The second half of Ps 136:1 is repeated verbatim throughout the psalm.

136:1 love The Hebrew word used here, *chesed*—which refers to God's covenantal love (see note on 25:10)—is rooted in his commitment to Israel that developed in a series of promises given to Israel's great leaders. **forever** The Hebrew expression used here, *le'olam*, conveys the unceasing nature of God's commitment over the course of Israel's history.

136:2 God of gods The Hebrew phrase used here, *elohe ha'elohim*, communicates God's supremacy over foreign deities. Compare Ps 82:1 and note; 82:2 and note.

136:3 Lord of lords The Hebrew phrase used here, *adone haadonim*, is probably meant to communicate God's power over the human sphere, especially when paralleled with *elohe ha'elohim* (see note on 136:2), which emphasizes God's power over the spiritual realm.

136:4–9 The psalmist focuses on God's activity in creation. The creation of heavens, earth and the celestial bodies all point to God's insight, skill and power.

136:4 great wonders The Hebrew word used here, *niphla'oth*, is most commonly associated with the events of the exodus (see Ex 7:3).

136:6 who spread out the earth upon the waters This reflects ancient Near Eastern cosmology, which understood the earth as a platform sitting upon waters and supported by pillars. See the infographic "Ancient Hebrew Conception of the Universe" on p. 5.

136:8–9 The depiction of the sun and moon ruling over the day and night (respectively) reflects the creation account of Ge 1. Both instances use the Hebrew word *mashal*, which means to rule or exercise dominion (see Ge 1:18). See the infographic "The Days of Creation" on p. 6.

136:10–16 In his depiction of the exodus, the psalmist highlights the most spectacular of God's mighty works—the final plague of the death of the firstborn of Egypt (Ex 12:29–32) and the crossing of the Red Sea (Ex 14–15).

136:10 struck down the firstborn The tenth plague against Egypt (see Ex 12:29–32).
136:16 led his people through the wilderness The events of Israel's wilderness journey begin after crossing the Red Sea (Ex 15:22) and continue through the book of Numbers.

136:17–22 Like Ps 135:10–12, these verses depict the defeat of the Amorites as a decisive event in God's provision for Israel. Psalm 136:21–22 depicts Israel's entry into Canaan as an act of power and a transfer of ownership, calling Canaan a heritage given to Israel.

136:17 him who struck down great kings Although the psalmist specifically mentions Sihon and Og (vv. 19–20), he may have all of the events of the conquest of Canaan in mind (see vv. 21–22).
136:21 gave their land as an inheritance See 135:12 and note.

136:23–26 In this closing section, the psalmist reiterates the major emphases of the other sections of the psalm, but not in the order he originally presented them. Verse 23 seems to refer to the Israelites' time in Egypt, while v. 24 seems to refer to their victory over the Amorites. In v. 25, the psalmist discusses God's provision of food, which is likely an echo of the creation theme of vv. 4–9. The use of the Hebrew phrase *el hashamayim* (meaning "God of heaven"; v. 26) echoes the introduction of the psalm, especially v. 2.

25 He gives food to every creature.
His love endures forever.

26 Give thanks to the God of heaven.
His love endures forever.

Psalm 137

1 By the rivers of Babylon we sat and wept
when we remembered Zion.
2 There on the poplars
we hung our harps,
3 for there our captors asked us for songs,
our tormentors demanded songs of joy;
they said, "Sing us one of the songs of Zion!"

4 How can we sing the songs of the LORD
while in a foreign land?
5 If I forget you, Jerusalem,
may my right hand forget its skill.
6 May my tongue cling to the roof of my mouth
if I do not remember you,

if I do not consider Jerusalem
my highest joy.

7 Remember, LORD, what the Edomites did
on the day Jerusalem fell.
"Tear it down," they cried,
"tear it down to its foundations!"
8 Daughter Babylon, doomed to destruction,
happy is the one who repays you
according to what you have done to us.
9 Happy is the one who seizes your infants
and dashes them against the rocks.

Psalm 138

Of David.

1 I will praise you, LORD, with all my heart;
before the "gods" I will sing your praise.
2 I will bow down toward your holy temple
and will praise your name
for your unfailing love and your faithfulness,

136:23 remembered us in our low estate This probably refers to Israel's enslavement in Egypt (see Ex 3:7).
136:26 Give thanks to the God of heaven This echoes Ps 136:1–3 and encapsulates the other titles given to Yahweh there. As the ruler of heaven, he is ultimately sovereign over everything else.

137:1–9 This corporate lament psalm (meant for group settings) depicts Israel's despair during the Babylonian exile (ca. 586–538 BC). The psalmist focuses on the destruction of Jerusalem (586 BC). The psalm opens with a picture of despair, in which the exiles of Israel are being taunted with requests to sing songs from their homeland (vv. 1–3). The psalmist then clarifies their sense of despair, explaining the connection between worship of Yahweh and the worship site in Jerusalem; to sing to Yahweh in a foreign land would be like forgetting the humiliation that has been heaped on Jerusalem (vv. 4–6). The psalmist concludes by wishing for vengeance on Edom and Babylon, who destroyed Jerusalem and its people (vv. 7–9). See the table "Types of Psalms" on p. 830.

137:1 By the rivers of Babylon This places readers in the midst of the sorrow of the Israelites who have been deported.
137:3 songs of Zion Any song of praise would include references to Yahweh's special relationship to Israel and his commitment to protect them. Compare Dt 28–30.
137:4–6 This section is highly emotional, but the thought that the Hebrew text expresses is not entirely clear. It seems to emphasize Yahweh's connection to his temple in Jerusalem—perhaps indicating that praising Yahweh outside of Jerusalem before he has vindicated himself before the world would be like acknowledging his defeat.

137:5 If I forget you, Jerusalem The psalmist refuses to move past the destruction of Jerusalem and refit his praise of Yahweh for the new situation. **may my right hand forget** This may be a poetic way for the psalmist to say that he will never play music again.
137:6 May my tongue cling to the roof of my mouth This could be a poetic way of the psalmist saying he will never sing again. **if I do not remember you** The Hebrew word used here, *zakhar*—which could be translated as

"cause to remember," "make known" or "profess"—suggests that the psalmist will never sing again if he forgets Yahweh.

137:7–9 The psalmist concludes by cursing the Edomites and the Babylonians—especially the Babylonians. The curse implies that in addition to destroying Jerusalem and the temple, the Babylonians slaughtered the Israelites (possibly the Israelite children; see v. 9 and note).

137:8 Daughter Babylon The Hebrew phrase here, *bath-bavel*, refers to the capital city of Babylon, which is contrasted with Jerusalem throughout this psalm.
137:9 Happy The Hebrew word used here, *ashre*, implies blessing and connects the violent actions in v. 9 to the path of deep loyalty to God. **infants** While the Hebrew word used here, *olal*, can indicate an infant, it can also refer more generally to a child. The children of *bath-bavel* (see note on v. 8) could simply refer to the people of Babylon, but this could also be a request for Yahweh to evoke the ancient Near Eastern principle of *lex talionis* (commonly referred to as "an eye for an eye").

138:title–8 In this individual thanksgiving psalm, the psalmist begins by praising Yahweh and thanking him for his help (vv. 1–3). He then widens his viewpoint and looks at the whole world, saying that all world rulers will eventually praise Yahweh for the way he helps the needy (vv. 4–6). The psalmist concludes by expressing his trust and confidence in Yahweh and asking for his continued protection (vv. 7–8). See the table "Types of Psalms" on p. 830.

138:title Of David Psalms 138–145 are the last psalms affiliated with David and make up roughly half of the psalms affiliated with David in Book Five of the Psalms (Ps 107–150). Since Ps 146–150 are collectively a conclusion to the entire Psalter, this final block of Davidic psalms (Ps 138–145) adds weight to the traditional view of the entire Psalter as "The Psalms of David." See note on 3:title.

138:1–3 The psalmist thanks Yahweh for his help and praises his reputation and character. His praise portrays a strong sense of personal gratitude.

for you have so exalted your solemn decree
  that it surpasses your fame.
³ When I called, you answered me;
  you greatly emboldened me.

⁴ May all the kings of the earth praise you, LORD,
  when they hear what you have decreed.
⁵ May they sing of the ways of the LORD,
  for the glory of the LORD is great.

⁶ Though the LORD is exalted, he looks kindly
    on the lowly;
  though lofty, he sees them from afar.
⁷ Though I walk in the midst of trouble,
  you preserve my life.
  You stretch out your hand against the anger
    of my foes;
  with your right hand you save me.
⁸ The LORD will vindicate me;
  your love, LORD, endures forever —
  do not abandon the works of your hands.

Psalm 139

For the director of music. Of David. A psalm.

¹ You have searched me, LORD,
  and you know me.
² You know when I sit and when I rise;
  you perceive my thoughts from afar.
³ You discern my going out and my lying down;
  you are familiar with all my ways.
⁴ Before a word is on my tongue
  you, LORD, know it completely.
⁵ You hem me in behind and before,
  and you lay your hand upon me.
⁶ Such knowledge is too wonderful for me,
  too lofty for me to attain.

⁷ Where can I go from your Spirit?
  Where can I flee from your presence?
⁸ If I go up to the heavens, you are there;
  if I make my bed in the depths, you are there.

138:1 the "gods" While the Hebrew word used here, *elohim*, can sometimes refer to the God of Israel, it is plural in form and here refers to foreign deities. **I will sing your praise** The psalmist is apparently in some sort of international context, where he praises Yahweh at the expense of the deities of the foreign nations.
138:2 I will bow down toward your holy temple The psalmist honors the temple because it is Yahweh's residence on earth.

138:4–6 The psalmist widens his view to the international stage, and he seems to imply that Yahweh will gain fame because he helped him. He implies that Yahweh's personal help for the psalmist will eventually translate into a more prominent place for Israel among the nations, which other kings will notice.

138:4 all the kings of the earth This explicitly identifies the international context of the psalm (compare note on 138:1).
138:5 May they sing The psalmist anticipates that the foreign kings will sing (*shir* in Hebrew) of the ways of Yahweh, which seems to indicate that they will come to worship the God of Israel, Yahweh, at some point.

138:7–8 The psalmist returns to a personalized address to Yahweh. The psalmist seems to have his role as king in view, since he mentions deliverance from his enemies as well as Yahweh's purpose for him. The final statement of v. 8 might refer personally to the psalmist, or it might refer to Israel as a whole. Compare note on v. 7.

138:7 I walk in the midst of trouble The international scope of the psalm (e.g., v. 4) and the psalmist's strong sense of mission (v. 8) suggest he is speaking as a king navigating the perils of international relations as a believer in Yahweh.

139:title–24 Psalm 139 is a wisdom psalm—meant to pass along wise teachings—that has the features of a hymn and lament. These various features are expressed in the themes of the psalm rather than its structure; the hymn-like elements focus on Yahweh's greatness (especially his knowledge), while the lament-like elements focus on Yahweh's power over the psalmist. However, the contrast between the way of the wicked (vv. 19–22) and

the way of God (v. 24) creates the "two ways" motif that characterizes Biblical wisdom; this becomes the dominant feature of the psalm since the psalmist's response to God's greatness and power is the primary issue.
  The psalmist begins by affirming that Yahweh already knows him thoroughly (vv. 1–4). He emphasizes Yahweh's power over him (v. 5) and his great insight (v. 6). The psalmist then develops the fusion of Yahweh's knowledge and power in three ways. The psalmist depicts the comprehensive scope of Yahweh's presence (vv. 7–12); he depicts God's intimate knowledge of him (vv. 13–16); and he depicts his response to God's knowledge and power (vv. 17–22). The psalmist concludes by echoing the beginning of the psalm, now in light of his response to God. The psalmist wants God to examine him and try him afresh so that his entire being may be secured in loyalty to God (vv. 23–24). See the table "Types of Psalms" on p. 830.

139:title director of music See note on 4:title. **Of David. A psalm** See note on 3:title; note on 138:title.

139:1–6 In these verses, the psalmist emphasizes Yahweh's knowledge of him and ultimate power over him. Verse 5 and 6 combine the hymn and lament themes that will be developed later in the psalm.

139:2 thoughts The Hebrew word used here, *rea'*, is one of the most common Hebrew words in the OT for thinking.
139:5 You hem me in It is unclear what connotation the psalmist intends when using the Hebrew word *tsur* here; it can mean "to bind," "encircle" or "lay siege to." In v. 6, the psalmist indicates that he accepts close scrutiny from God, but that he does not understand it.
139:7 Spirit The Hebrew word used here, *ruach*, referring to God's Spirit, is held parallel to God's *paneh* (his "face" or "presence") in the second part of the verse. In the OT, the portrayal of God's Spirit has two main features: The Spirit of God was usually sent upon someone for a short time to accomplish a specific task (e.g., Jdg 6:34; 1Sa 19:23), and the Spirit of God was localized as an expression of God's presence. However, the psalmist's experience of God's Spirit is unusual for the OT in that the Spirit of God came upon him and did not leave (1Sa 16:13).
139:8 the depths The Hebrew word *she'ol* is used here, which refers to the realm of the dead (the underworld;

⁹ If I rise on the wings of the dawn,
　if I settle on the far side of the sea,
¹⁰ even there your hand will guide me,
　your right hand will hold me fast.
¹¹ If I say, "Surely the darkness will hide me
　and the light become night around me,"
¹² even the darkness will not be dark to you;
　the night will shine like the day,
　for darkness is as light to you.

¹³ For you created my inmost being;
　you knit me together in my mother's womb.
¹⁴ I praise you because I am fearfully and
　　wonderfully made;
　your works are wonderful,
　I know that full well.
¹⁵ My frame was not hidden from you
　when I was made in the secret place,
　when I was woven together in the depths
　　of the earth.
¹⁶ Your eyes saw my unformed body;
　all the days ordained for me were written
　　in your book
　before one of them came to be.
¹⁷ How precious to me are your thoughts,ᵃ God!
　How vast is the sum of them!
¹⁸ Were I to count them,
　they would outnumber the grains of sand—
　when I awake, I am still with you.

¹⁹ If only you, God, would slay the wicked!
　Away from me, you who are bloodthirsty!
²⁰ They speak of you with evil intent;
　your adversaries misuse your name.
²¹ Do I not hate those who hate you, LORD,
　and abhor those who are in rebellion
　　against you?
²² I have nothing but hatred for them;
　I count them my enemies.
²³ Search me, God, and know my heart;
　test me and know my anxious
　　thoughts.
²⁴ See if there is any offensive way in me,
　and lead me in the way everlasting.

Psalm 140ᵇ

For the director of music. A psalm of David.

¹ Rescue me, LORD, from evildoers;
　protect me from the violent,
² who devise evil plans in their hearts
　and stir up war every day.
³ They make their tongues as sharp as a
　　serpent's;
　the poison of vipers is on their lips.ᶜ

ᵃ 17 Or *How amazing are your thoughts concerning me*　　ᵇ In Hebrew texts 140:1-13 is numbered 140:2-14.　　ᶜ 3 The Hebrew has *Selah* (a word of uncertain meaning) here and at the end of verses 5 and 8.

---

see note on Job 14:13; note on 1Ki 2:6). The psalmist believes that there is no place where God's presence cannot be experienced—it can be known in the heavens, where Yahweh was thought to reside, or in the underworld if Yahweh so chooses. The point is that there is no place off limits to Yahweh—a person cannot escape him or his judgment.

139:9 the dawn The Hebrew word used here, *shachar*, refers to the sunrise or the morning light. This is possibly a poetic description of the east. It parallels the Hebrew word *yam* in the next line—likely referring to the west.
139:10 your right hand Implies God's care and action to protect the psalmist.
139:11 will hide me The psalmist probably is not thinking of intentionally hiding from God. Rather, the Hebrew word used here, *choshekh*, seems to indicate some sort of peril that will separate him from God.

139:13–16 The psalmist praises God's total knowledge of him in intimate and comprehensive terms. God has always known the psalmist (almost from before the womb; see Ps 139:13,15), and he knows the psalmist's future before it happens (v. 16).

139:13 my inmost being The Hebrew word used here, *kilyah*, can refer to organs like kidneys in sacrificial animals. It is also used metaphorically for one's inner self and is often used parallel to the heart (see Jer 11:20).
139:15 My frame People in the ancient Near East considered bones to be particularly indicative of a person's nature because they were the deepest and longest-lasting part of a person.
139:16 my unformed body The Hebrew word used here, *golem*, refers to a formless mass or incomplete vessel and is sometimes thought to indicate an embryo or fetus.

139:19–22 The psalmist's response to God continues as his passion for God translates into enmity for God's opponents. He expresses his loyalty to God by aligning himself against God's enemies. The psalmist makes two requests as he responds to God's power and knowledge: He asks that God use his power to slay the wicked (Ps 139:19) and that God examine him afresh (v. 23).

139:23–24 Several key terms from vv. 1–3 are repeated in vv. 23–24 (see note on vv. 1–6). In response to God's knowledge and power, the psalmist desires for God to examine him afresh (v. 23).

140:title–13 In this individual lament psalm, the psalmist pleads for Yahweh to help him as he faces the schemes of his enemies. He opens by requesting that Yahweh protect him from evil men (v. 1) who plan wicked things (v. 2) and speak hurtful things (v. 3). He then specifically asks for protection from those who have been planning traps for him (vv. 4–5) and denounces them as arrogant (v. 5). He asks Yahweh for mercy (v. 6), remembering Yahweh's help in past times of war (v. 7). He asks that the plans of the wicked would fail so that they would not be exalted to positions of prominence or power (v. 8; compare v. 11). The psalmist then continues to employ the battle motif and requests Yahweh's help against those who surround him (vv. 9–11). He is especially concerned that those slandering him would not be established in power (v. 11). The psalmist closes by stating his confidence that Yahweh helps the afflicted (v. 12) so that they might thank him (v. 13). See the table "Types of Psalms" on p. 830.

140:title director of music See note on 4:title. **A psalm of David** See note on 3:title; note on 138:title.

⁴ Keep me safe, LORD, from the hands of the
  wicked;
 protect me from the violent,
  who devise ways to trip my feet.
⁵ The arrogant have hidden a snare for me;
 they have spread out the cords of their net
 and have set traps for me along my path.

⁶ I say to the LORD, "You are my God."
 Hear, LORD, my cry for mercy.
⁷ Sovereign LORD, my strong deliverer,
 you shield my head in the day of battle.
⁸ Do not grant the wicked their desires, LORD;
 do not let their plans succeed.

⁹ Those who surround me proudly rear their
  heads;
 may the mischief of their lips engulf them.
¹⁰ May burning coals fall on them;
 may they be thrown into the fire,
 into miry pits, never to rise.

¹¹ May slanderers not be established in the
  land;
 may disaster hunt down the violent.
¹² I know that the LORD secures justice for the
  poor
 and upholds the cause of the needy.
¹³ Surely the righteous will praise your name,
 and the upright will live in your presence.

Psalm 141

A psalm of David.

¹ I call to you, LORD, come quickly to me;
 hear me when I call to you.
² May my prayer be set before you like incense;
 may the lifting up of my hands be like the
  evening sacrifice.

³ Set a guard over my mouth, LORD;
 keep watch over the door of my lips.

140:1–5 The repeated Hebrew phrase *me'ish chamasim tintsereni* (a petition to be saved from evil enemies; vv. 1,4) summarizes the first section of Ps 140. The psalmist faces his opponents' evil schemes, traps (vv. 2,4,5) and harmful words (v. 3; compare vv. 9,11).

140:2 war The Hebrew word used here, *milchamah*, refers literally to close fighting or struggle, like hand-to-hand combat.

140:3 They make their tongues as sharp as a serpent's The words of the psalmist's opponents are compared to poison or venom (*chemah* in Hebrew).

140:4–5 The psalmist focuses on his opponents' actions, particularly their traps (vv. 4–5). These traps are most likely metaphorical (see v. 5); the verbal traps may refer to harmful attacks on the psalmist's reputation and status.

140:5 The arrogant Refers to those who disregard or oppose Yahweh's purposes.

140:6–8 The psalmist remembers Yahweh's past help in battle (v. 7) and pleads for him to block his enemies' schemes so they will not gain power (v. 8).

140:7 you shield my head in the day of battle The psalmist depicts Yahweh acting as his helmet in past battles.

140:9–11 The psalmist portrays Yahweh's help in terms of deliverance from enemies who surround him (v. 9), and he prays that the schemes and slander his enemies have brought against him (vv. 9,11) will be turned back on them (v. 10).

140:10 May burning coals fall on them Though this may describe divine judgment (fire from heaven), it is probably an image of battle that included burning arrows and throwing coals at enemies.

140:12–13 The psalmist casts his confidence in terms of Yahweh's general help for the afflicted, who praise Yahweh when he aids them. While the psalmist certainly presents himself as afflicted in Ps 140, his portrayal of a wider view of Yahweh's justice is more than humble self-effacement. The closing statement (v. 13) portrays

the just society that the psalmist desires for all Israel in contrast to the evil system that would result if the wicked gained power (see vv. 8,11).

140:12 justice for the poor This expression reaches as far back as the exodus (see Ex 3:7), and it usually has the corporate (group) situation of Israel in view.

141:title–10 In this individual lament psalm, the psalmist requests Yahweh's help in maintaining his personal integrity as he seeks to avoid any traps that evil people might set for him. He does not seem to have a specific situation in mind, but he expresses a desire for Yahweh to guard him from any impropriety or harm. The psalmist opens by asking Yahweh to hear his calls and regard his personal prayer and worship as equivalent to sacrifice (Ps 141:1–2). He asks Yahweh to guard his behavior (vv. 3–4) and hopes to find people who will rebuke him honestly should he go astray (v. 5). He then prays against evildoers, anticipates their downfall (vv. 6–7) and asks that Yahweh protect him from their schemes, entrapping them in their own tricks instead (vv. 8–10). See the table "Types of Psalms" on p. 830.

141:title A psalm of David See note on 3:title; note on 138:title.

141:1–2 The psalmist's request for Yahweh's presence reflects his close relationship with God. He perceives that his prayer and personal worship is on par with sacrifice and incense as a means of approaching Yahweh.

141:2 May my prayer be set before you like incense The psalmist asks Yahweh to accept his personal worship as if it were incense and sacrifice—the mainstays of ritual worship in Israel.

141:3–5 The psalmist is primarily concerned with his personal integrity; protection from enemies is a secondary thought. He asks Yahweh to help him manage himself and provide other people of good character to help him so that he won't be led astray.

141:3 Set a guard over my mouth, LORD The psalmist recognizes the influence of speech as well as the difficulty of controlling it.

⁴Do not let my heart be drawn to what is evil
  so that I take part in wicked deeds
along with those who are evildoers;
  do not let me eat their delicacies.

⁵Let a righteous man strike me — that is a
    kindness;
  let him rebuke me — that is oil on my head.
My head will not refuse it,
  for my prayer will still be against the deeds
    of evildoers.

⁶Their rulers will be thrown down from the
    cliffs,
  and the wicked will learn that my words
    were well spoken.
⁷They will say, "As one plows and breaks up
    the earth,
  so our bones have been scattered at the
    mouth of the grave."

⁸But my eyes are fixed on you, Sovereign
  Lord;
  in you I take refuge — do not give me over
    to death.
⁹Keep me safe from the traps set by evildoers,
  from the snares they have laid for me.
¹⁰Let the wicked fall into their own nets,
  while I pass by in safety.

Psalm 142ᵃ

A maskilᵇ of David. When he was in the cave. A prayer.

¹I cry aloud to the Lord;
  I lift up my voice to the Lord for mercy.
²I pour out before him my complaint;
  before him I tell my trouble.

³When my spirit grows faint within me,
  it is you who watch over my way.
In the path where I walk
  people have hidden a snare for me.
⁴Look and see, there is no one at my right
    hand;
  no one is concerned for me.
I have no refuge;
  no one cares for my life.

⁵I cry to you, Lord;
  I say, "You are my refuge,
  my portion in the land of the living."

⁶Listen to my cry,
  for I am in desperate need;
rescue me from those who pursue me,
  for they are too strong for me.

ᵃ In Hebrew texts 142:1-7 are numbered 142:2-8.   ᵇ Title:
Probably a literary or musical term

141:4 along with those who are evildoers The
psalmist recognizes the influence friends and associates can have. **delicacies** The Hebrew word used here,
man'ammim, does not occur very often in the OT and
derives from a word meaning "lovely" or "kind." The
psalmist may anticipate that these enticing things will entangle him or make him dependent on those who do evil.
141:5 Let a righteous man strike me In Proverbs, a
wise person is someone who accepts rebuke or correction
(e.g., Pr 9:8; 17:10). **oil on my head** Anointing oil was a
sign of honor reserved primarily for guests or someone
in a place of honor or authority (see Ps 23:5 and note).

141:6–7 The precise meaning of the Hebrew text of
vv. 6–7 is uncertain. Verse 6 focuses on corrupt judges
(or perhaps influential people in general). The meaning
of v. 7 depends on whose bones are in question. The
psalmist seems to be talking about the suffering of Israel
under corrupt government.

141:7 the grave The Hebrew word *she'ol* is used here,
which refers to the realm of the dead (the underworld).
See note on Job 14:13; note on 1Ki 2:6.

141:8–10 Although individual lament psalms often
focus on enemies and their wickedness, the psalmist
here focuses on Yahweh, believing that this action (v. 8)
will guide him past the traps that the wicked have set
for him (vv. 9–10).

142:title–7 In this individual lament psalm, the psalmist
asks Yahweh to deliver him from those pursuing him. He
begins by expressing anguish as he cries out to Yahweh
for relief from his trouble (vv. 1–2). Recognizing that
Yahweh has previously guarded his way, the psalmist
laments that he is alone and that his enemies have set
a trap in his way (vv. 3–4). He then describes Yahweh as
his protection and help, and he begs Yahweh to save him

from the strong people who are pursuing him (vv. 5–6).
The psalmist concludes with a final request for Yahweh
to bring him out of the place where he is trapped, and
expresses his hope that he will eventually be surrounded
by likeminded people who follow Yahweh (v. 7). See the
table "Types of Psalms" on p. 830.

142:title *maskil* See note on 32:title. **of David** See
note on 3:title; note on 138:title. **When he was in the
cave** See note on 57:title. **A prayer** See note on 86:title.

142:1–2 The repeated words and ideas throughout this
section highlight the psalmist's anguish.

142:2 complaint The Hebrew word used here, *sich*, usually indicates verbal lamenting or complaining.

142:3–4 The psalmist expresses that he trusts in Yahweh's help even though he is terrified and anticipates
that his pursuers will catch him (v. 3). He sees Yahweh
as his last hiding place and the only one who can help
him (v. 4).

142:3 you who watch over my way The psalmist
portrays himself in a life-or-death situation, and he needs
Yahweh to guide him out of it.

142:5–7 The psalmist begs Yahweh for help and portrays
him as a hiding place and ally (v. 5). He begs Yahweh to
help him in this desperate moment and save him from
the powerful people chasing him (v. 6). The psalmist then
closes with a final request for help and an expression of
confidence that he will be rescued and eventually find
himself among godly friends (v. 7).

142:5 my portion The Hebrew word used here, *cheleq*, is
related to the verb used to describe the apportionment of
the land of Canaan to the tribes of Israel (Jos 14:5; 18:2).

⁷Set me free from my prison,
    that I may praise your name.
Then the righteous will gather about me
    because of your goodness to me.

Psalm 143

A psalm of David.

¹LORD, hear my prayer,
    listen to my cry for mercy;
in your faithfulness and righteousness
    come to my relief.
²Do not bring your servant into judgment,
    for no one living is righteous before you.
³The enemy pursues me,
    he crushes me to the ground;
he makes me dwell in the darkness
    like those long dead.
⁴So my spirit grows faint within me;
    my heart within me is dismayed.
⁵I remember the days of long ago;
    I meditate on all your works
    and consider what your hands have done.

⁶I spread out my hands to you;
    I thirst for you like a parched land.ᵃ

⁷Answer me quickly, LORD;
    my spirit fails.
Do not hide your face from me
    or I will be like those who go down to
        the pit.
⁸Let the morning bring me word of your
        unfailing love,
    for I have put my trust in you.
Show me the way I should go,
    for to you I entrust my life.
⁹Rescue me from my enemies, LORD,
    for I hide myself in you.
¹⁰Teach me to do your will,
    for you are my God;
may your good Spirit
    lead me on level ground.

¹¹For your name's sake, LORD, preserve my life;
    in your righteousness, bring me out of
        trouble.

ᵃ 6 The Hebrew has *Selah* (a word of uncertain meaning) here.

142:7 prison The Hebrew word used here, *masger*, comes from a word meaning "to shut in." The psalmist feels trapped and powerless. **that I may praise your name** Psalmists in lament psalms often commit to give thanks after being rescued (see Ps 22:22 and note).

143:title–12 In this individual lament psalm, the psalmist begs Yahweh to rescue him from his enemies. He begins by asking Yahweh to listen to him and rescue him rather than judge him (vv. 1–2), explaining that his enemies have pursued him and he fears for his life (vv. 3–4). He recalls Yahweh's past deeds of rescue and reaches out to him in his desperation (vv. 5–6), requesting Yahweh to rescue him so that he does not die (v. 7). The psalmist desperately pleads that he might see the next morning because of Yahweh's help, and he asks that Yahweh guide him out of the crisis he now faces (v. 8). He then restates his request for deliverance and implies his hope in Yahweh (v. 9). He commits himself to doing God's will in the future (v. 10) and connects his request for help to Yahweh's reputation and character (v. 11). The psalmist closes by reaffirming his relationship with Yahweh and emphasizing his trust that Yahweh will destroy the enemies of his servant (v. 12). See the table "Types of Psalms" on p. 830.

143:title A psalm of David See note on 3:title; note on 138:title.

143:1–2 By connecting the present crisis with Yahweh's mercy toward sinners, the psalmist adds an unexpected depth to his plea for help. Though he fears his enemies, he also sees himself as open to Yahweh's judgment; he addresses things that might be between him and Yahweh before he describes his crisis.

143:2 Do not bring your servant into judgment The psalmist does not equate his crisis with judgment, but he sees the outcome of it as either punishment or vindication. Therefore, he pleads that his present crisis would not become a means of punishment, even though Yahweh would be justified if he chose to punish him.

143:3–4 The psalmist describes the crisis he faces in dire terms. He believes he is facing death, and he is terrified.

143:5–6 The psalmist recalls Yahweh's past deeds (probably Yahweh's many rescues). He yearns for Yahweh's presence as well as deliverance.

143:5 I meditate Meditation in the OT involves thinking about Yahweh and expressing those thoughts. See note on 104:34.

143:6 I thirst for you The Hebrew phrase used here may be literally rendered "my soul is as parched earth for you." The Hebrew word *nephesh* is used here, which has a variety of meanings. It may refer to a person's soul, life or throat. Thus, this verse employs a clever wordplay; the psalmist could be describing either a parched throat longing for water, or the inner longing of his soul to be with Yahweh.

143:7–8 The psalmist hopes to live through the night and hear of Yahweh's faithfulness in the morning.

143:7 the pit The Hebrew word used here, *bor*, refers to a cistern for storing water. The *bor* is often used metaphorically in the psalms to refer to the grave or the realm of the dead (compare 143:3).

143:9–10 In his request for deliverance, the psalmist implies that he will follow God's ways faithfully (v. 10). His concern for his relationship with God is connected to his initial request for God's mercy and forgiveness (v. 2).

143:10 Spirit See 139:7 and note.

143:11–12 The final portion of Ps 143 implies the psalmist and Yahweh's commitment to each other. Since the psalmist is Yahweh's servant (v. 12), he trusts that Yahweh will deliver him according to his prior commitments and his reputation (v. 11).

143:11 For your name's sake The psalmist appeals to Yahweh's own reputation as the reason for why Yahweh should deliver him. Compare 124:8 and note.

¹²In your unfailing love, silence my enemies;
destroy all my foes,
for I am your servant.

Psalm 144

Of David.

¹Praise be to the LORD my Rock,
who trains my hands for war,
my fingers for battle.
²He is my loving God and my fortress,
my stronghold and my deliverer,
my shield, in whom I take refuge,
who subdues peoples*ᵃ* under me.

³LORD, what are human beings that you care
for them,
mere mortals that you think of them?
⁴They are like a breath;
their days are like a fleeting shadow.

⁵Part your heavens, LORD, and come down;
touch the mountains, so that they smoke.
⁶Send forth lightning and scatter the enemy;
shoot your arrows and rout them.
⁷Reach down your hand from on high;
deliver me and rescue me

from the mighty waters,
from the hands of foreigners
⁸whose mouths are full of lies,
whose right hands are deceitful.

⁹I will sing a new song to you, my God;
on the ten-stringed lyre I will make music
to you,
¹⁰to the One who gives victory to kings,
who delivers his servant David.

From the deadly sword ¹¹deliver me;
rescue me from the hands of foreigners
whose mouths are full of lies,
whose right hands are deceitful.

¹²Then our sons in their youth
will be like well-nurtured plants,
and our daughters will be like pillars
carved to adorn a palace.
¹³Our barns will be filled
with every kind of provision.
Our sheep will increase by thousands,
by tens of thousands in our fields;
¹⁴   our oxen will draw heavy loads.*ᵇ*

ᵃ 2 Many manuscripts of the Masoretic Text, Dead Sea Scrolls, Aquila, Jerome and Syriac; most manuscripts of the Masoretic Text *subdues my people*   *ᵇ 14* Or *our chieftains will be firmly established*

144:title–15 In this royal psalm (about kingship), the psalmist first addresses Yahweh individually, then participates in a communal address. He begins by blessing Yahweh as the one who prepares him for battle, protects him during battle, and places him in his role as king (vv. 1–2). The psalmist then speaks as a representative of the entire nation of Israel and highlights his (and their) insignificance before Yahweh (vv. 3–4). He fuses theophany imagery and creation imagery as he pleads with Yahweh to deliver him (and all of Israel) from foreign enemies (vv. 5–8). The psalmist depicts the praise of Yahweh following a victory, and does so in personal terms, emphasizing his role as Yahweh's servant (vv. 9–10). His individual voice then disappears from the psalm, as the remainder of the psalm presents a series of communal requests for blessing: sons and daughters (v. 12), food and livestock (v. 13) and social stability (v. 14). The psalm closes with a blessing on both the people and God (v. 15). See the table "Types of Psalms" on p. 830.

144:title Of David See note on 3:title; note on 138:title.

144:1–2 The psalmist depicts Yahweh's preparation and protection of him.

144:1 Rock The Hebrew word used here, *tsur*, highlights the stability and protection that Yahweh provides. See note on 18:1–3.

144:3–4 Although this text seems to portray the psalmist as an individual, he seems to be referring to Yahweh's relationship with Israel in anticipation of vv. 12–15, with himself in a representative role.

144:4 a breath The Hebrew word used here, *hevel*, occurs frequently in Ecclesiastes and is often translated "vanity" and sometimes as "meaningless" (see Ecc 1:2 and note).

144:5–8 In these verses, the psalmist fuses theophany imagery (compare Ex 19:16) and creation imagery to portray Yahweh's defeat of foreign powers (Ps 144:7–8; compare Ex 19:16; Ps 93:3–4). He describes the foreign enemies as a flood (144:7). Verse 11 repeats most of vv. 7–8.

144:5 Part your heavens The Hebrew word used here, *natah*, means to "bow down," "stretch" or "spread." The phrase illustrates Yahweh splitting the heavens so that he can descend. Compare Isa 64:1. **touch the mountains, so that they smoke** Recalls Yahweh's appearance at Sinai (Ex 19:18).

144:8 right hands are deceitful Refers to betrayal or failure. People in the ancient Near East would raise their right hands when taking an oath (compare Dt 32:40), and also make a commitment by shaking hands. The foreigners either failed to follow through on their promises or were simply not powerful enough to honor them.

144:9–11 The psalmist anticipates praising Yahweh, emphasizing his role as king. He repeats much of his earlier request for deliverance (Ps 144:7–8,11), which lacks the reference to the foreigners as flood waters (v. 7).

144:11 This verse is essentially the same as the second half of v. 7 and v. 8.

144:12–15 The psalm now shifts to a communal request for blessing; it presents a list of good things that culminate in worship. The Israelites see their greatest blessing as Yahweh himself (v. 15).

144:12 pillars Probably a symbol of fertility, though stability is also possible. Their fruitfulness will be the pillars of the community.

144:14 no cry of distress The Hebrew word used here,

There will be no breaching of walls,
no going into captivity,
no cry of distress in our streets.
¹⁵ Blessed is the people of whom this is true;
blessed is the people whose God is the LORD.

Psalm 145^a

A psalm of praise. Of David.

¹ I will exalt you, my God the King;
I will praise your name for ever and ever.
² Every day I will praise you
and extol your name for ever and ever.

³ Great is the LORD and most worthy of praise;
his greatness no one can fathom.
⁴ One generation commends your works to
another;
they tell of your mighty acts.
⁵ They speak of the glorious splendor of your
majesty —
and I will meditate on your wonderful
works.^b
⁶ They tell of the power of your awesome
works —
and I will proclaim your great deeds.
⁷ They celebrate your abundant goodness
and joyfully sing of your righteousness.

⁸ The LORD is gracious and compassionate,
slow to anger and rich in love.
⁹ The LORD is good to all;
he has compassion on all he has made.
¹⁰ All your works praise you, LORD;
your faithful people extol you.
¹¹ They tell of the glory of your kingdom
and speak of your might,
¹² so that all people may know of your mighty
acts
and the glorious splendor of your kingdom.
¹³ Your kingdom is an everlasting kingdom,
and your dominion endures through all
generations.

The LORD is trustworthy in all he promises
and faithful in all he does.^c
¹⁴ The LORD upholds all who fall
and lifts up all who are bowed down.
¹⁵ The eyes of all look to you,
and you give them their food at the proper
time.

---

^a This psalm is an acrostic poem, the verses of which (including verse 13b) begin with the successive letters of the Hebrew alphabet. ^b 5 Dead Sea Scrolls and Syriac (see also Septuagint); Masoretic Text *On the glorious splendor of your majesty / and on your wonderful works I will meditate* ^c 13 One manuscript of the Masoretic Text, Dead Sea Scrolls and Syriac (see also Septuagint); most manuscripts of the Masoretic Text do not have the last two lines of verse 13.

---

tsewachah, refers to a cry of lament. It may imply the presence of justice, meaning there is no violence, or indicate overflowing prosperity, because no one is begging.
144:15 Blessed The Hebrew word used here, *ashre*, is the first word of the psalter (1:1).

145:title–21 Psalm 145—which is specifically identified as a praise psalm—is an individual praise psalm with an acrostic structure, meaning that each line starts with a consecutive letter of the Hebrew alphabet (see note on vv. 13–20). The psalmist addresses God personally, listing many ways in which he will praise God and his fame (vv. 1–3). He then envisions multiple generations recounting God's mighty deeds to the next generation, praising God and his reputation (vv. 4–7). The psalmist recounts Yahweh's excellent character, focusing on his love and mercy (vv. 8–9). He then brings several of the previous elements of the psalm together by depicting the Israelites' praise of Yahweh and his deeds, teaching successive generations to do likewise (vv. 10–13). He praises Yahweh's kind and loving nature, which cares for the needy and sustains the world (vv. 13–16). He also praises Yahweh for his care of all who call on him and his punishment of the wicked (vv. 17–20). The psalmist concludes by committing to praise Yahweh and calling everyone to praise him (v. 21). See the table "Types of Psalms" on p. 830.

145:title Of David The final psalm affiliated with David. See note on 3:title; note on 138:title.
145:1 I will praise your name Refers to God's reputation for faithful care of Israel.

145:4–7 The psalmist portrays multiple generations rehearsing God's deeds on behalf of Israel, depicting himself participating as well (see vv. 5,6).

145:4 mighty acts This term usually refers to God's rescue of Israel from enslavement in Egypt (see Ex 7:1–5).
145:5 I will meditate See note on Ps 104:34.
145:8–9 The psalmist uses familiar language to describe God (Ex 34:6) and depicts him as sustaining his creation.

145:8 rich in love While God's unfailing love (*chesed* in Hebrew) is often defined as his covenant love, this verse locates it within God's nature, not just in his commitments and actions. See note on Ps 25:10.

145:10–13 In this section, the psalmist fuses his praise (vv. 1–3) and the multigenerational rehearsal of Yahweh's deeds (vv. 4–7). This section extends through the first half of v. 13.

145:13–20 The second half of v. 13 is absent in the traditional Hebrew text. However, it is found in the Septuagint as well as in the Biblical Dead Sea Scrolls (ca. 250 BC–AD 50). It completes the acrostic pattern by supplying the missing verse beginning with the Hebrew letter *nun*. The similarity with v. 17 provides a way to divide the segments of the psalm, and the mention that Yahweh is faithful fits thematically with Yahweh's provision in vv. 14–16. The second half of v. 13 and vv. 14–16 emphasize Yahweh's care and work in sustaining the world, while vv. 17–20 emphasize his care for those loyal to him and his work in giving them justice.

145:15 at the proper time The psalmist portrays the seasonal cycle of growth and harvest as Yahweh's direct provision.

16 You open your hand
  and satisfy the desires of every living thing.

17 The LORD is righteous in all his ways
  and faithful in all he does.
18 The LORD is near to all who call on him,
  to all who call on him in truth.
19 He fulfills the desires of those who fear him;
  he hears their cry and saves them.
20 The LORD watches over all who love him,
  but all the wicked he will destroy.

21 My mouth will speak in praise of the LORD.
  Let every creature praise his holy name
  for ever and ever.

Psalm 146

1 Praise the LORD.[a]

Praise the LORD, my soul.

2 I will praise the LORD all my life;
  I will sing praise to my God as long as I live.
3 Do not put your trust in princes,
  in human beings, who cannot save.
4 When their spirit departs, they return to the
    ground;
  on that very day their plans come to
    nothing.

5 Blessed are those whose help is the God of
    Jacob,
  whose hope is in the LORD their God.
6 He is the Maker of heaven and earth,
  the sea, and everything in them —
  he remains faithful forever.
7 He upholds the cause of the oppressed
  and gives food to the hungry.
  The LORD sets prisoners free,
8   the LORD gives sight to the blind,
  the LORD lifts up those who are bowed down,
  the LORD loves the righteous.
9 The LORD watches over the foreigner
  and sustains the fatherless and the widow,
  but he frustrates the ways of the wicked.

10 The LORD reigns forever,
  your God, O Zion, for all generations.

Praise the LORD.

Psalm 147

1 Praise the LORD.[b]

How good it is to sing praises to our God,
  how pleasant and fitting to praise him!

---

[a] 1 Hebrew *Hallelu Yah*; also in verse 10   [b] 1 Hebrew *Hallelu Yah*; also in verse 20

145:16 You open your hand Yahweh ultimately provides the food for the entire world.
145:19 those who fear him See 90:11 and note.

146:1–10 The psalmist opens this praise psalm by exhorting his audience to praise Yahweh; he also describes his intention to praise Yahweh himself (vv. 1–2). He then exhorts his audience to place trust in Yahweh alone (vv. 3–4). The psalmist states that the blessed people in the world are those who hope in the God who created everything (v. 5), helps the oppressed, feeds the hungry (v. 7), heals the suffering, loves the righteous (v. 8) and protects the vulnerable (v. 9). He also states that Yahweh opposes the wicked (v. 9). He concludes by praising Yahweh, who will reign forever (v. 10).

This praise psalm features multiple commands to praise Yahweh (*hallu-yah* in Hebrew) and multiple references to Yahweh. This distinctive language is echoed throughout Ps 146–150, and these final five psalms can be seen as a doxology for the psalter as a whole. See the table "Types of Psalms" on p. 830.

146:1–2 The opening exhortation to praise Yahweh is coupled with the psalmist's commitment to praise Yahweh as long as he is able.

146:1 Praise the LORD See 135:1 and note.

146:3–4 The psalmist exhorts his audience to avoid trusting powerful human rulers, implying that Yahweh is the only one worthy of being trusted.

146:5–9 This lengthy list of Yahweh's deeds reflects his excellent character. By referring to those who are loyal to Yahweh using the Hebrew word *ashre* (often translated "blessed"), Ps 146 connects with the psalms that are often called wisdom psalms and portray a stark choice

between two paths in life—righteousness and wickedness (e.g., 1:1). While the primary focus is Yahweh's greatness, the contrast between righteousness and wickedness is implied in v. 9.

146:5 God of Jacob See Ex 3:6 and note.
146:7 the cause The Hebrew word used here, *mishpat*, can refer to the general concept of justice or a specific legal decision. **sets prisoners free** The psalmist is probably referring to the exodus from Egypt (see Ex 6:1–9).
146:8 the righteous The Hebrew word used here, *tsaddiq*, refers to people who are marked by loyalty to God through keeping his covenant. See Dt 28–30.
146:9 the foreigner The Hebrew word used here, *ger*, refers to resident aliens who were outside of social power structures and vulnerable to injustice.
146:10 Praise the LORD See Ps 135:1 and note.

147:1–20 This corporate praise psalm (meant for group settings) intertwines Yahweh's special relationship with Israel and his work in creating and sustaining the world. The psalmist begins by exhorting the Israelites to praise Yahweh for his tender care of them and his control over the cosmos (vv. 1–6). He then connects Yahweh's continuing sustenance of the world (vv. 8–9) to his ongoing protection of faithful Israel (vv. 10–11). The psalmist continues to focus on the protection of Israel by presenting the peace and stability of Jerusalem as a symbol of the nation (vv. 12–14). He then revisits Yahweh's power over creation as proof of his ability to protect Israel (vv. 15–18). The psalmist concludes by articulating that Yahweh has a special relationship with the Israelites because he has revealed himself and his word to them (vv. 19–20). The command to praise Yahweh (*hallu-yah*) opens and closes the psalm, but it is not given special emphasis beyond that (see note on 146:1–10). See the table "Types of Psalms" on p. 830.

²The LORD builds up Jerusalem;
  he gathers the exiles of Israel.
³He heals the brokenhearted
  and binds up their wounds.
⁴He determines the number of the stars
  and calls them each by name.
⁵Great is our Lord and mighty in power;
  his understanding has no limit.
⁶The LORD sustains the humble
  but casts the wicked to the ground.

⁷Sing to the LORD with grateful praise;
  make music to our God on the harp.

⁸He covers the sky with clouds;
  he supplies the earth with rain
  and makes grass grow on the hills.
⁹He provides food for the cattle
  and for the young ravens when they call.

¹⁰His pleasure is not in the strength of the
    horse,
  nor his delight in the legs of the warrior;
¹¹the LORD delights in those who fear him,
  who put their hope in his unfailing love.

¹²Extol the LORD, Jerusalem;
  praise your God, Zion.

¹³He strengthens the bars of your gates
  and blesses your people within you.

¹⁴He grants peace to your borders
  and satisfies you with the finest
    of wheat.

¹⁵He sends his command to the earth;
  his word runs swiftly.
¹⁶He spreads the snow like wool
  and scatters the frost like ashes.
¹⁷He hurls down his hail like pebbles.
  Who can withstand his icy blast?
¹⁸He sends his word and melts them;
  he stirs up his breezes, and the
    waters flow.

¹⁹He has revealed his word to Jacob,
  his laws and decrees to Israel.
²⁰He has done this for no other nation;
  they do not know his laws.^a

Praise the LORD.

Psalm 148

¹Praise the LORD.^b

Praise the LORD from the heavens;
  praise him in the heights above.

^a 20 Masoretic Text; Dead Sea Scrolls and Septuagint *nation; / he
has not made his laws known to them*   ^b 1 Hebrew *Hallelu
Yah*; also in verse 14

147:1–6 In the Hebrew text, the psalmist begins by exhorting the nation to sing praises to *elohenu* (often translated as "our God"; 147:1) for his work in building the nation by bringing the Israelites back to Jerusalem (v. 2) and caring for them (v. 3). He highlights this special care for Israel by mentioning Yahweh's power over the cosmos (vv. 4–5) and concern to protect the humble while punishing the wicked (v. 6).

147:1 Praise the LORD See 135:1 and note.
147:2 exiles of Israel The main way that Israel's people were scattered was through invasion and exile. This line seems to specifically refer to the Babylonian exile (ca. 586–538 BC).
147:4 stars The psalmist references stars (see Ge 1:16) to parallel Yahweh's cosmic power with his meticulous attention to detail.
147:6 humble The Hebrew word used here, *anaw*, can depict dejection or piety.

147:7–11 In these verses, the psalmist exhorts the Israelites to sing in thanksgiving (Ps 147:7), emphasizing Yahweh's provision for the created order (vv. 8–9). He also returns to the theme of accountability (from v. 6) as he exhorts the Israelites to trust Yahweh and remain loyal to him rather than hoping for military strength (vv. 10–11).

147:9 He provides food for the cattle Although people are near the pinnacle of the created order (Ge 1:26,28), they are not the only creatures that Yahweh cares about and sustains (compare Job 39).
147:10 legs of the warrior If the horse of Ps 147:10 is meant to represent military strength, this phrase probably indicates the physical power of warriors.

147:12–20 In this segment, the psalmist fuses Yahweh's care for Jerusalem (and all of Israel) with his power over the whole world. He begins by depicting the stability and health of Jerusalem (vv. 12–14) and concludes by describing Yahweh's choice of Israel and revelation of himself to them (vv. 19–20). The focus on the power of Yahweh's word shows his ability to accomplish his plans for Israel (see note on 119:1–176; 119:9 and note).

147:12 Extol the LORD The Hebrew word used here, *shavach yhwh*, is a poetic variation of *hallu-yah*, which is a common exhortation in Ps 147 to praise Yahweh.
147:14 peace The Hebrew word used here, *shalom*, is portrayed as the foundation of Israel's prosperity.
147:19 his laws and decrees The psalmist may be associating Yahweh's word with the revelation that he has already given (Ex 20) and his ongoing legal judgments (compare Ps 147:20).
147:20 He has done this for no other nation Although the OT sometimes indicates that Yahweh has given revelation to the wider world (see 19:1), he has only given Israel his specific legal revelation and ongoing provision. **Praise the LORD** See 135:1 and note.

148:1–14 This corporate praise psalm (meant for group settings) fuses Yahweh's role as Israel's God with his power over all of the created order. The psalmist opens by exhorting heaven, all of the angels and spiritual beings, and all the celestial bodies to praise Yahweh (vv. 1–4), emphasizing that they only exist because Yahweh has created them (vv. 5–6). The psalmist then focuses on the world beneath heaven, and he exhorts the earth and all of the animals and people to praise Yahweh (vv. 7–12). He concludes by emphasizing the central place of Israel within Yahweh's concern, noting that Yahweh has placed himself as the central source of Israel's help (v. 14).

2 Praise him, all his angels;
   praise him, all his heavenly hosts.
3 Praise him, sun and moon;
   praise him, all you shining stars.
4 Praise him, you highest heavens
   and you waters above the skies.

5 Let them praise the name of the LORD,
   for at his command they were created,
6 and he established them for ever and ever —
   he issued a decree that will never pass
   away.

7 Praise the LORD from the earth,
   you great sea creatures and all ocean
   depths,
8 lightning and hail, snow and clouds,
   stormy winds that do his bidding,
9 you mountains and all hills,
   fruit trees and all cedars,
10 wild animals and all cattle,
   small creatures and flying birds,

11 kings of the earth and all nations,
   you princes and all rulers on earth,
12 young men and women,
   old men and children.

13 Let them praise the name of the LORD,
   for his name alone is exalted;
   his splendor is above the earth and the
   heavens.
14 And he has raised up for his people a horn,[a]
   the praise of all his faithful servants,
   of Israel, the people close to his heart.

Praise the LORD.

Psalm 149

1 Praise the LORD.[b]

Sing to the LORD a new song,
   his praise in the assembly of his faithful
   people.

[a] 14 Horn here symbolizes strength.   [b] 1 Hebrew Hallelu Yah;
also in verse 9

This psalm is marked by the repetition of the Hebrew phrases hallu eth-yhwh ("praise Yahweh") and halluhu ("praise him"). The twin commands to praise Yahweh from hashamayim ("the heavens"; v. 1) and from ha'arets ("the earth"; v. 7) divide the focus of the psalm between heaven and earth. The subsequent repetition of calling for praise of Yahweh's name (vv. 5,13) reinforces the psalmist's transition between heaven and earth. Compare note on 146:1–10. See the table "Types of Psalms" on p. 830.

148:1–4 The psalmist commands heavenly beings and celestial bodies to praise Yahweh, emphasizing their subordinate status. This series of commands anticipates the explicit focus on Yahweh as Creator in vv. 5–6. This emphasizes that all the powers that were worshiped in the ancient Near East are actually subordinate to the God of Israel, Yahweh, and owe him their allegiance.

148:1 Praise the LORD See 135:1 and note.
148:2 heavenly hosts The Hebrew word used here, tsava', can refer to troops or an army and here seems to reference all spiritual beings.
148:4 highest heavens Ancient Near Eastern cosmology sometimes included a concept of levels of ascent in the heavens, with the highest level being the residence of Yahweh. **waters above the skies** In the ancient Hebrew conception of the universe, there were waters above a dome-like firmament. See the infographic "Ancient Hebrew Conception of the Universe" on p. 5.

148:5–6 The exhortation to praise the name (shem in Hebrew) of Yahweh occurs twice in Ps 148 and marks the places where the psalmist closes one topic and shifts to another (vv. 5,13). This section emphasizes the subordinate status of the heavenly creatures to Yahweh. Following this section, the psalmist will focus on the created order beneath heaven (below the spiritual realm).

148:5 name of the LORD See 135:1 and note.
148:6 for ever and ever The seeming permanence of the celestial bodies is based on Yahweh's permanence.

148:7–12 The list of earthly creatures that the psalmist exhorts to praise Yahweh eventually culminates with people (vv. 11–12). This emphasizes that everything Yahweh created should praise him as powerful and superior to all, because he is.

148:7 you great sea creatures and all ocean depths The oceans (or seas) were symbolic of chaos in the ancient Near East, and the great sea monsters were their most terrifying and uncontrollable inhabitants. To summon the sea monsters to praise God is to proclaim Yahweh's power over absolutely everything. Unlike the gods of the ancient Near East, Yahweh is not in a battle with these creatures but instead they are simply commanded to praise him. Yahweh is already in power; there is no real struggle.

148:13–14 The psalmist repeats the call to praise the name of Yahweh, combining his focus on heaven and earth and emphasizing the subordinate status of all of Yahweh's creatures (v. 13). He concludes by placing Yahweh himself at the center of Israel's attention and hope (v. 14).

148:14 a horn A symbol of power and strength. **Praise the LORD** See 135:1 and note.

149:1–9 In this corporate praise psalm (meant for group settings), the congregation of Israel praises Yahweh and envisions their place in Yahweh's future judgment of the foreign nations. The psalmist begins by calling the Israelites to praise Yahweh and rejoice in him, probably within the context of temple worship in Jerusalem (vv. 1–2). He exhorts the people to praise Yahweh with dancing and music because the recollection of his help brings him fame (vv. 3–4). The psalm then portrays the Israelites' response to their worship of Yahweh. The psalmist envisions the Israelites as having a central role in God's future judgment of wicked nations, stating that they will wield swords even as they praise God (vv. 5–7). The psalmist sees this role as an honor for those faithful to God — they will imprison the rulers of wicked nations and thus justice will come (vv. 8–9). The psalm opens and closes with the exhortation to praise Yahweh (hallu-yah in Hebrew; vv. 1,9). Compare note on 146:1–10. See the table "Types of Psalms" on p. 830.

² Let Israel rejoice in their Maker;
　let the people of Zion be glad in their King.
³ Let them praise his name with dancing
　and make music to him with timbrel and
　　harp.
⁴ For the LORD takes delight in his people;
　he crowns the humble with victory.
⁵ Let his faithful people rejoice in this honor
　and sing for joy on their beds.

⁶ May the praise of God be in their mouths
　and a double-edged sword in their hands,
⁷ to inflict vengeance on the nations
　and punishment on the peoples,
⁸ to bind their kings with fetters,
　their nobles with shackles of iron,
⁹ to carry out the sentence written against
　them—
　this is the glory of all his faithful people.

Praise the LORD.

Psalm 150

¹ Praise the LORD.ᵃ

Praise God in his sanctuary;
　praise him in his mighty heavens.
² Praise him for his acts of power;
　praise him for his surpassing greatness.
³ Praise him with the sounding of
　　the trumpet,
　praise him with the harp and lyre,
⁴ praise him with timbrel and dancing,
　praise him with the strings and pipe,
⁵ praise him with the clash of cymbals,
　praise him with resounding cymbals.

⁶ Let everything that has breath praise the
　LORD.

Praise the LORD.

ᵃ 1 Hebrew *Hallelu Yah*; also in verse 6

149:1–4 The psalmist calls the Israelites to praise Yahweh as Creator and King in response to his help of them (v. 4). He calls the people to express joyful, exuberant praise with dancing and music.

149:1 Praise the LORD See 135:1 and note. **Sing to the LORD a new song** The exhortation to sing a new song might accompany what the psalmist sees as a new act of deliverance by Yahweh (e.g., 144:9). Alternatively, the psalmist may be expressing hope that Yahweh will act again on behalf of Israel.
149:2 let the people of Zion be glad in their King Although the psalms of David often portray Yahweh's help of Israel as mediated through the human king, a few psalms portray Yahweh as King without the mediation of a human ruler, such as this one. The most prominent of these psalms are the enthronement psalms (Ps 93; 95–99).
149:3 praise his name with dancing Dancing was a part of worship in ancient Israel; for example, David danced when the ark of the covenant was brought to Jerusalem (2Sa 6:16).
149:4 the humble The Hebrew word used here, *anaw*, refers to people partly defined by their piety, in which they are submissive before Yahweh (see Ps 147:6 and note).
149:5–9 The psalmist portrays the Israelites as the primary human agents in God's judgment of wicked nations. The Israelites are not taking revenge for anything that they have experienced, but executing judgment on behalf of God's justice (v. 9; compare Dt 9:4–6).

149:7 vengeance The Hebrew word used here, *neqamah*, portrays justified retribution.
149:8 to bind their kings with fetters Although there is some symmetry between chaining the kings and the way that the Israelites were carried into exile (compare 2Ki 25:7), this psalm does not explicitly make that connection.
149:9 glory The Hebrew word used here, *hadar*, is probably descriptive of the closeness to God that the faithful Israelites enjoy. **Praise the LORD** See note on 104:35.

150:1–6 This corporate praise psalm functions as the concluding doxology for the psalter. The psalm opens with a series of exhortations to praise Yahweh because of who he is. The psalmist wants Yahweh to be praised in the temple—the place that signified his dwelling place on earth—and in heaven, where the fullness of his glory dwells, for his deeds and character (vv. 1–2). He then exhorts the Israelites to praise Yahweh with a series of musical instruments, which implies great enthusiasm and joy (vv. 3–5). The psalm and psalter concludes with a final call for everything to praise Yahweh (v. 6). An exhortation to praise Yahweh occurs at least twice in every verse of Ps 150. The common command to praise Yahweh (*halluyah*) opens and closes the psalm and the final book of Psalms, Book Five (see note on 1:1–6). Compare note on 146:1–10. See the table "Types of Psalms" on p. 830.

150:1–2 The exhortations to praise Yahweh cover the widest possible range; Yahweh is to be praised on earth, in heaven, for his past deeds in rescuing Israel and for his character.

150:1 Praise the LORD See 135:1 and note. **praise him** The Hebrew exhortation used here, *halluhu* (commonly translated "praise him"), occurs nine times in Ps 150. **heavens** The Hebrew word used here, *raqia'*, also occurs in Ge 1:6 to describe the vaulted dome that separates the waters above from the waters below. The psalmist may be envisioning praise from both earth and heaven.
150:2 for his acts of power This often refers to Yahweh's actions on behalf of the Israelites when he rescues them (compare Ps 145:4–7).

150:3–6 The list of musical instruments here has a cumulative effect, which culminates in the call for everything to praise Yahweh.

150:3 with the sounding of the trumpet See note on 1Ki 1:34. **with the harp and lyre** See note on Ps 92:3.
150:6 everything that has breath Everything that can breathe is called upon to praise Yahweh. **Praise the LORD** The call to praise Yahweh concludes both the psalm and the book of Psalms.

WORSHIP IN THE OLD TESTAMENT
by Chelle Stearns

Worship in the Old Testament, as now, is relational. The condition of a person's heart—which is the center of his or her being in ancient Israelite thought—was the most critical aspect of the worship relationship (Ps 40:6–8). The religion of Israel was established for the sake of Yahweh's presence in the midst of his people (Lev 26:11–13). Yahweh was not some distant god to be appeased, nor was he pleased by empty ritual; rather, he sought relationship with his people and welcomed it in many forms, including petition (Ps 13), pilgrimage (Ps 122:1–4), thanksgiving (Ps 9:1–6), playing instruments (Ps 150) obedience (Ps 119), complaint (Job 16:7–14), lamentation (Jer 20:14), repentance (Ps 51) and remembrance (Dt 6:4–8)—all of which took both verbal and physical form (Ex 15:1–21; Est 4:1–3; Ps 6:6; 121).

Yahweh's presence with his people begins intimately with the breath that gives life to Adam and Eve (Ge 2:7). They remain in full communion with their creator until they eat the fruit of the forbidden tree (Ge 3:6–7) and discover their nakedness and vulnerability. They can do nothing to restore their relationship with Yahweh themselves. Yahweh sacrifices animals (Ge 3:21) to clothe and cover their shame, thus resolving their alienation and preserving his relational presence by means of atonement (Isa 40:1–2; Ro 5:12; 1Co 15:22,45). It is this active redemption that defines Yahweh's relationship with all of creation (Ge 9:8–16; Ro 8:18–23).

Yahweh's initiative in redeeming his people for worship can be seen in the lives of Abram and Sarai. Their story marks a shift in the divine-human relationship: It signals the beginning of a clearly defined community of human beings who embody a restored relationship with their Creator. Yahweh approaches Abram (before changing his name to Abraham; Ge 17:5) and not only promises to make him into a great nation but to bless all people through him (Ge 12:2–3). Thus God chooses one man (and one woman, Sarai, renamed Sarah; Ge 17:15–16) to establish a nation through which all nations will ultimately be blessed (Isa 2:2–4; 9:1–10; 49:5–6; 65:17–25).

This pattern of redemption continues through the calling and naming of the patriarchs—Abraham (Ge 22), Isaac (Ge 26:24–25) and Jacob (Ge 28:10–22)—but it is through Moses that the Israelite religion is established. The law, the priests, the tabernacle, the atonement rites, the Sabbath day of rest—all of this acknowledged Yahweh's presence dwelling among his people.

However, the Israelites feared Yahweh's presence, as when they were confronted with the voice of Yahweh at the base of God's holy mountain, Mount Sinai (see Ex 19); they begged Moses to intercede on their behalf (Ex 20:18–21). Yahweh chose to dwell with them, but did so at a slight distance, providing a means of mediation through the tabernacle and the rituals maintained by the priests. The rituals and tabernacle served as a means for the people to commune with—worship—Yahweh (Ex 40:34–35; Eze 43:1–5; 1Co 3:16; Heb 10:19–23).

Idolatry, the worship of other gods, was the greatest strain on the relationship between Israel and Yahweh after this relationship was established. Yahweh commanded his people not to put any other god before him (Ex 20:3; Isa 42:8), but the Israelites—beginning with their fashioning of the golden calf while Moses was on Mount Sinai (Ex 32)—repeatedly turned away from Yahweh

to idols. Even their leaders were involved (Ex 32:1; compare Isa 65:1–2; Jer 2:11–13). Despite Israel's waywardness (Hos 2:13–23; Am 9:11–15), the prophets testify to Yahweh's continued faithfulness: "I will be your God and you will be my people" (Jer 7:23; 11:4; 30:22; Eze 36:28). He promises a new covenant—one that will be written on their hearts rather than on stone (Jer 31:31–34; compare 2Co 3:3; Heb 8–9).

The NT depicts this new covenant as inaugurated by Jesus, the embodied presence of God and the ultimate faithful worshiper—and therefore the only one through whom the worshiper is ultimately transformed (1Co 13:12). Ultimately, all those who belong to Jesus will gather around the throne and worship God together—with all creation—forever (Rev 5).

PROVERBS

INTRODUCTION TO PROVERBS

Proverbs consists of many wise sayings, compiled into a book. These sayings offer practical advice for daily life and vary widely in their content—ranging from work and money to speech, integrity and discipline. But the wisdom in Proverbs is not just about practical advice; Proverbs reminds us that true wisdom derives from the fear of Yahweh and has its source in him (Pr 1:7; 2:6; 9:10).

BACKGROUND

Although the first line of Proverbs associates the entire book with Solomon, the content is ascribed to at least three authors: Solomon (Pr 1:1; 10:1; 25:1), Agur (Pr 30:1) and Lemuel (Pr 31:1). Agur and Lemuel are unknown outside the book. But Solomon, the son of King David, reigned over Israel in the 10th century BC and was renowned for speaking proverbs (1Ki 4:32). It is possible that Solomon wrote the proverbs attributed to him, or he might have sponsored their collection. The work of collecting wise teachings was likely ongoing in Israel, but it is mentioned explicitly in Proverbs 25:1 as occurring during the reign of King Hezekiah—who ruled the southern kingdom of Israel, known as Judah, about 200 years after Solomon. Collectively, this evidence seems to indicate that the book of Proverbs was composed over time with multiple contributors—which aligns with how proverbs were handed down in the ancient world. They usually circulated orally long before they were collected in written form. Proverbs likely has roots during Solomon's reign, but might not have reached its final form until the Persian period (ca. 540–332 BC) or the early Hellenistic era (ca. fourth to third centuries BC).

Proverbs is the prime Biblical example of wisdom literature; other examples include Job, Ecclesiastes and possibly Song of Songs. Wisdom literature is interested in giving its readers, especially young people, advice on how to cultivate virtue, avoid foolishness and gain divine favor. The people groups surrounding Israel had their own versions of wisdom literature, which provided a background for Israelite sages and might have been adapted by them. Israel's recorded history compares Solomon's wisdom to that of nearby cultures, proclaiming his wisdom to be greater than that of Egypt and all the peoples of the east (1Ki 4:30). *The Instruction of Amenemope*, an Egyptian collection of sayings that dates to the 12th century BC, bears a resemblance to Proverbs 22:17–24:22. Collections of Mesopotamian proverbs likewise bear similarities to the genre of Proverbs.

STRUCTURE

Although the sayings in Proverbs may seem like a random assortment, the collection is actually a curated, unified literary work. The text includes seven distinct groups of proverbs, some of which are attributed to different authors and exhibit two styles of writing. Notably, the first collection's long discourses on wisdom (Pr 1:1—9:18) contrast with the other six collections' much shorter sayings (Pr 10:1—31:31). Multiple topics are scattered across these collections. Advice regarding subjects such as laziness (Pr 6:6–11; 10:4; 24:30–34; 26:13), sexual immorality (Pr 5:1–23; 23:26–28; 29:3), humility (Pr 11:2; 25:6–7; 29:23), and friendship (Pr 13:20; 22:24–25; 27:17) can be found throughout the book.

OUTLINE

- Instructions from teacher to student (Pr 1:1—9:18)
- The proverbs of Solomon (Pr 10:1—22:16)
- The words of the wise (Pr 22:17—24:22)
- Further words of the wise (Pr 24:23–34)
- The proverbs of Solomon collected by Hezekiah's men (Pr 25:1—29:27)
- The words of Agur (Pr 30:1–33)
- The words of Lemuel (Pr 31:1–31)

THEMES

The main theme of Proverbs is that wisdom proceeds from revering and trusting God. Our actions reflect our inner character, and vice versa; by honoring God with our lives and following his wisdom, we can expect to experience the blessing of God's goodness. In the natural order of God's world, good character produces a life that will flourish, though Proverbs is also clear that the natural order does not always win; sometimes, against all logic, evil and folly thrive.

The primary concern of Proverbs, like other wisdom literature from the ancient Near East, is instruction: Younger generations need such wisdom to live well. But the book of Proverbs is also unique among its contemporaries in its emphasis on worshiping Yahweh—the only true source of such wisdom and fullness of life (Pr 3:19). Proverbs repeatedly shows us that we must live according to Yahweh's ways—by living ethically, representing justice and caring for the weak and impoverished—even when society at large tells us otherwise.

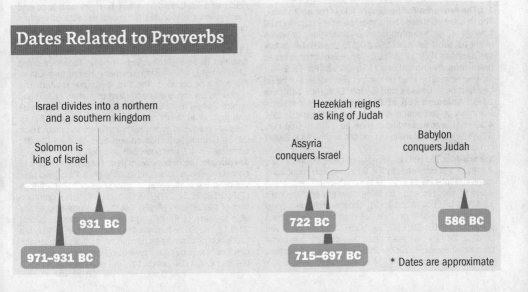

Dates Related to Proverbs

Israel divides into a northern
and a southern kingdom

Hezekiah reigns
as king of Judah

Solomon is
king of Israel

Assyria
conquers Israel

Babylon
conquers Judah

931 BC

722 BC

586 BC

971–931 BC

715–697 BC

* Dates are approximate

Purpose and Theme

1 The proverbs of Solomon son of David, king of Israel:

² for gaining wisdom and instruction;
  for understanding words of insight;
³ for receiving instruction in prudent
    behavior,
  doing what is right and just and fair;
⁴ for giving prudence to those who are simple,ᵃ
  knowledge and discretion to the young —
⁵ let the wise listen and add to their learning,
  and let the discerning get guidance —
⁶ for understanding proverbs and parables,
  the sayings and riddles of the wise.ᵇ

⁷ The fear of the LORD is the beginning of
    knowledge,
  but foolsᶜ despise wisdom and instruction.

Prologue: Exhortations to Embrace Wisdom

Warning Against the Invitation of Sinful Men

⁸ Listen, my son, to your father's instruction
  and do not forsake your mother's
    teaching.
⁹ They are a garland to grace your head
  and a chain to adorn your neck.

¹⁰ My son, if sinful men entice you,
  do not give in to them.

ᵃ 4 The Hebrew word rendered *simple* in Proverbs denotes a person who is gullible, without moral direction and inclined to evil.   ᵇ 6 Or *understanding a proverb, namely, a parable, / and the sayings of the wise, their riddles*   ᶜ 7 The Hebrew words rendered *fool* in Proverbs, and often elsewhere in the Old Testament, denote a person who is morally deficient.

1:1–7 Proverbs is a series of wise sayings for a wide audience — the young and simple (Pr 1:4) to the already wise (vv. 5–6). The book presents itself as for everyone willing to learn but not for the fool who will despise what it offers (v. 7). Particular proverbs are affiliated with Solomon (v. 1; 10:1; 25:1), Agur (30:1), Lemuel (31:1), men during Hezekiah's lifetime (25:1) and the "wise" in general (22:17; 24:23). While some proverbs may have originated with King Solomon (tenth century BC), the reference to the gathering of proverbs during King Hezekiah's lifetime (ca. 715–697 BC) suggests a deliberate effort to preserve Israel and Judah's literary tradition following the fall of the northern kingdom of Israel in 722 BC. This effort of collecting, recopying and perhaps editing may have taken place all the way up to the third century BC.

The opening verses act as an introduction to the entire book. After the title (1:1), the intention of the book is given (vv. 2–6): to provide the reader with wisdom, knowledge, instruction and understanding. Verse 7 then presents the motto of the book and of Wisdom Literature.

1:1 The proverbs The heading or title of the entire book. The Hebrew word used here, *mashal*, refers to proverbial sayings. Usually comparisons or analogies, proverbs might be short sayings (1Sa 10:12; Eze 16:44) or longer parables (Eze 17:2–10). They were often passed down through generations (1Sa 24:13; Ps 78:2–4). They were mostly used to instruct (Ecc 12:9) but could be used negatively as taunts (Job 17:6; Isa 14:4; Jer 24:9). **Solomon son of David** First Kings presents Solomon as the wisest man in the whole earth (1Ki 4:29–31), whose wisdom comes as a gift of God (1Ki 3:3–15; 4:29). Solomon is credited with writing 3,000 proverbs (1Ki 4:32).

1:2 wisdom The Hebrew word used here, *chokhmah*, is a key term in Proverbs. In the OT *chokhmah* most commonly describes wise judgment or decision making, which leads to success and can bring strength and favor (Pr 13:10; 14:8; Ecc 8:5; 10:12). *Chokhmah* is also used to describe the skill or ability of craftsmen and artists (Ex 28:3; 35:10; 36:1–2; Jer 10:9). Animals can even be described as very wise when they cleverly overcome their weaknesses (Pr 30:24–28). The wise avoid reckless or angry behavior (14:35; 24:5; Ecc 7:19; compare Pr

14:16; 16:14; 29:8,11). **instruction** The Hebrew word used here, *musar*, is another key term in Proverbs. It can refer to instruction or discipline dispensed by either people or God (Dt 11:2; Job 5:17; Pr 3:11; Isa 26:16; compare Pr 1:8; 4:1). Those who follow instruction find wisdom and life (1:3; 19:20), but the foolish and the wicked hate instruction and pay the price (Ps 50:17; Pr 4:13; 6:23; 10:17; 15:5; compare 5:23; 13:18; 15:32). **insight** The Hebrew word used here, *binah*, refers to understanding or discernment and is also a key term in Proverbs. It often occurs in parallel with wisdom (Job 12:12; Pr 2:2; 4:5–7), and it describes the ability to understand things like righteousness, justice and piety (2:5,9; 28:5). The insightful person is not gullible (14:15), carefully considers his or her actions (21:29; 23:1) and has the ability to discern between options (1Ki 3:9; Job 32:9; Pr 14:8). A related word, *tevunah*, is also used in Proverbs (e.g., 2:2–3).

1:3 prudent People who act wisely or prudently work hard and exercise restraint in their speech (Ps 36:3; Pr 10:5,19). They find favor with others (14:35; 17:2), and they seek God, finding his blessing as well (Ps 14:2; 53:2; Pr 15:24; 16:20). **what is right and just and fair** Proverbs elaborates the moral aspects of wisdom and its relationship to righteousness, justice and equity. The wise walk in the path of righteousness and justice (8:20). Wisdom enables people to understand these qualities (2:9). Righteousness (*tsedeq*) describes doing what is right, while justice (*mishpat*) refers to a just or fair ruling or decision. The two ideas are related. The righteous person is characterized by justice (12:5) and rejoices when justice is done (21:15). Righteousness and justice are both associated with truth (12:5,17). They are preferred over wealth and even sacrifice (15:8; 21:3). Ultimately, justice comes from Yahweh (29:26; compare Ps 4:1 and note; 5:8 and note).

1:4 simple The Hebrew word used here, *pethi*, refers to someone who is naïve and gullible (Pr 14:15) and falls victim to temptation out of ignorance or obliviousness (7:7; 9:16; 22:3; 27:12). In Proverbs folly is a common trait of the simple (14:18). Yet these same people are able to learn (1:4; 9:6) and accept discipline (19:25; 21:11); they are described as being able to acquire prudence or cleverness (*ormah*, v. 4). Although *ormah* can indicate a negative trait (i.e., the crafty; compare Ge 3:1; Ex 21:14; Job 5:12), in Proverbs it describes

¹¹ If they say, "Come along with us;
　　let's lie in wait for innocent blood,
　　let's ambush some harmless soul;
¹² let's swallow them alive, like the grave,
　　and whole, like those who go down to
　　　the pit;
¹³ we will get all sorts of valuable things
　　and fill our houses with plunder;

¹⁴ cast lots with us;
　　we will all share the loot" —
¹⁵ my son, do not go along with them,
　　do not set foot on their paths;
¹⁶ for their feet rush into evil,
　　they are swift to shed blood.
¹⁷ How useless to spread a net
　　where every bird can see it!

---

those whose shrewdness protects them from danger (Pr 22:3; 27:12). In contrast to the way it treats the fool or scoffer, Proverbs presents its instruction as palatable to the simple or naïve person. **knowledge** The Hebrew word used here, *da'ath*, is similar to wisdom (10:14; 18:15). It both comes from God (1:7; 2:6) and can be learned through instruction or discipline (12:1; 19:25; 21:11). The person with knowledge shows restraint and experiences success (4:4–5; 11:9; 17:27; 19:2; Ecc 7:12). **discretion** The Hebrew term used here, *mezimmah*, has both positive and negative connotations. In Proverbs it is typically positive, but elsewhere it often describes negative plans or schemes (Job 21:27; Ps 21:11; 37:7; Pr 12:2; 14:17; 24:8). In Proverbs *mezimmah* is often used in the context of having the understanding to discern a situation and thus make the right, godly decision (5:1–4; 8:12–13). **the young** The Hebrew word used here, *na'ar*, indicates a youth, a child or a young man. This type of person may act foolishly (22:15), but is not necessarily a fool. Instead, this young person lacks sense (7:7) and needs instruction and discipline so that a fool's life may be prevented (22:6,15; 23:13–14).

1:5 learning The ability to increase in knowledge by listening to instruction is characteristic of the wise (9:9; compare 1:2). **guidance** The Hebrew word used here, *tachbuloth*, refers to strategies for navigating life, which can be used for good or evil (11:14; 12:5; 24:6). Proverbs promises that an intelligent person can learn them by reading the book.

1:6 The author describes four kinds of teachings the reader should understand: proverbs (*mashal*; see note on v. 1); sayings or parables (*melitsah*), which can be mocking or satirical (Hab 2:6); words of the wise or wisdom sayings in general (*divre chakhamim*, see Ecc 12:11); and riddles (*chidah*)—ambiguous sayings that require interpretation (Jdg 14:12–14).

1:7 fear of the Lᴏʀᴅ A reverent attitude toward Yahweh. The fear of Yahweh is an important concept in Proverbs and the OT. It indicates awe for God (compare Job 1:1, 1:8; 2:3; Ecc 12:13). A person fears God by being loyal to him and faithful to his covenant—obedient to his commands. The fear of Yahweh involves humility and righteous living (Pr 3:7; 8:13; 14:2; 16:6; 22:4). Its benefits can include blessing, Yahweh's protection and long life (10:27; 14:26–27; 19:23; 28:14). In Proverbs the fear of Yahweh is where wisdom begins (1:7; 9:10; compare Ps 111:10; Pr 15:33). However, there is a reciprocal relationship between the two: Fearing Yahweh is the beginning of wisdom, but receiving wisdom helps people better understand the fear of Yahweh (2:1–5). Those who do not fear Yahweh are said to hate knowledge, and they will eventually come to ruin (1:29–33). Piety is an important virtue in wisdom literature of the ancient world, but Proverbs is alone in its assertion that the fear of Yahweh is where wisdom begins. Fear of Yahweh motivates wise behavior

and is required to gain what the book promises. **fools** Fools arrogantly reject teaching because they believe themselves to be wise (12:15). Proverbs uses two main Hebrew words to refer to the fool: *kesil* and *ewil*. There is no significant difference in meaning between the two; this verse uses *ewil*. (A third word referring to a fool, *naval*, only occurs three times in Proverbs). Proverbs 12:23 and 13:16 link the two main terms by saying fools (*kesil*) produce folly (*iwweleth*, from the word *ewil*). The fool hates wisdom and knowledge (1:7,22) and refuses instruction and discipline (15:5; 16:22; 17:10). Instead, the fool prefers evil (10:23; 13:19) and rejects God (Ps 14:1). This attitude, as well as his rejection of repentance (Pr 14:12), assures the fool's destructive fate (10:14,21; compare 10:8). Fools recklessly get themselves into trouble (14:16; 18:6), are arrogant (12:15) and untrustworthy (26:6), and speak impulsively and argumentatively (20:3; 29:9,11; compare 17:27). Because of fools' destructive nature, Proverbs advises avoiding them so as not to become like them and share their fate (13:20; 14:7). Several other terms in Proverbs describe people similar to the fool. The most common are the scoffer (see 1:22 and note), the lazy person (see 6:9 and note), the person who lacks sense and the simple (see 1:4 and note).

1:8 — 9:18 The opening chapters of Proverbs are lectures from a father to his son. In these longer speeches, the father admonishes his son to choose the path of wisdom over the path of folly. The personified figures of wisdom and folly also try to persuade the son (1:20–33; 9:1–18). These chapters contrast with the rest of the book of Proverbs, which mostly consists of collections of short sayings. By beginning the book with the father's instruction, Proverbs establishes the importance of wisdom and creates the context in which to read the shorter proverbs and aphorisms that make up the rest of the book.

1:8 Listen, my son, to your father's instruction The wisdom of Proverbs is presented as a father teaching his son (2:1; 3:1; 4:10; 5:1; 6:20). Passed down through generations (4:3–4), these teachings resemble the commands of the law (Dt 6:7).

1:9 a garland to grace your head Just as adorning oneself with jewelry enhances physical beauty, obtaining wisdom enhances character (Pr 3:22; 4:9).

1:10 sinful men entice you The ability to withstand temptation is characteristic of the wise; in contrast, the fool enjoys doing wrong (10:23).

1:12 grave The Hebrew term used here, *she'ol*, generally refers to the place of the dead (see note on Job 14:13; compare Ge 37:35).

1:15 do not go along with them To accompany sinful people is to associate with and behave like them (Pr 1:10). See Ps 1:1 and note.

1:17 where every bird can see Birds who see a trap being set do not fall into it.

¹⁸ These men lie in wait for their own blood;
  they ambush only themselves!
¹⁹ Such are the paths of all who go after ill-
    gotten gain;
  it takes away the life of those who get it.

Wisdom's Rebuke

²⁰ Out in the open wisdom calls aloud,
  she raises her voice in the public square;
²¹ on top of the wallᵃ she cries out,
  at the city gate she makes her speech:

²² "How long will you who are simple love your
    simple ways?
  How long will mockers delight in mockery
    and fools hate knowledge?
²³ Repent at my rebuke!
  Then I will pour out my thoughts to you,
  I will make known to you my teachings.
²⁴ But since you refuse to listen when I call
  and no one pays attention when I stretch
    out my hand,
²⁵ since you disregard all my advice
  and do not accept my rebuke,
²⁶ I in turn will laugh when disaster strikes you;
  I will mock when calamity overtakes you —
²⁷ when calamity overtakes you like a storm,
  when disaster sweeps over you like a
    whirlwind,
  when distress and trouble overwhelm you.

²⁸ "Then they will call to me but I will not
    answer;
  they will look for me but will not find me,
²⁹ since they hated knowledge
  and did not choose to fear the LORD.
³⁰ Since they would not accept my advice
  and spurned my rebuke,
³¹ they will eat the fruit of their ways
  and be filled with the fruit of their
    schemes.
³² For the waywardness of the simple will kill
    them,
  and the complacency of fools will destroy
    them;
³³ but whoever listens to me will live
    in safety
  and be at ease, without fear of harm."

Moral Benefits of Wisdom

2 My son, if you accept my words
  and store up my commands within you,
² turning your ear to wisdom
  and applying your heart to
    understanding —
³ indeed, if you call out for insight
  and cry aloud for understanding,
⁴ and if you look for it as for silver
  and search for it as for hidden treasure,

ᵃ 21 Septuagint; Hebrew / at noisy street corners

1:18 they ambush only themselves In contrast to the birds of Pr 1:17, the sinner sets a trap, then foolishly falls into it. Compare Ps 7:15 and note.
1:19 it takes away the life of those who get it Throughout Proverbs, wickedness and folly always lead to disaster (Pr 13:21; compare Job 4:6 and note; 8:3 and note).
1:20–33 In this passage, wisdom is personified as a woman who urges the simple to heed her words. Crying in the streets (Pr 1:20–21), she admonishes the simple, scoffers and fools to listen to her words (vv. 22–23; see note on v. 4). She describes the disastrous consequences of ignoring her call (vv. 24–27). Wisdom will not respond to those who reject her (vv. 28–30); those who ignore her will eventually be destroyed by their folly (vv. 31–32). Wisdom concludes by encouraging people to heed her call and secure themselves from disaster (v. 33).
1:20 wisdom calls aloud Wisdom calls throughout the city. In the street, markets and city gates, wisdom makes her call available to anyone who will listen. See note on 8:1–36. **her voice** Wisdom is personified as a woman because the Hebrew word for wisdom, *chokhmah*, is feminine.
1:22 How long Wisdom addresses her call to three types of people: the simple, the scoffer and the fool (see 1:4 and note). Scoffers hate discipline (9:7–8; 13:1; 15:12), cause strife and conflict (22:10; 29:8) and do not find wisdom because their arrogance prevents it (21:24; 14:6). God scorns and eventually condemns them (3:33–34; 19:29).

1:28 I will not answer Once the fool rejects wisdom, wisdom rejects the fool (1Sa 8:18).
1:29 did not choose to fear the LORD Emphasizes the religious aspect of wisdom: To reject knowledge is to reject the fear of Yahweh (see note on Pr 1:7).
1:31 they will eat the fruit of their ways Foolishness leads to destruction (10:8). This destruction can be the natural result of folly (26:27) or a divine punishment (Jer 6:19).
1:33 whoever listens to me will live in safety Those who heed wisdom's call find security just as those who trust in Yahweh have security (Ps 4:8; 16:8–9; 25:12–13). Wisdom Literature operates on the principle that God designed the world so that people would get what they deserve: If they are righteous, they are blessed; if they are wicked, they are punished. See note on Pr 3:2.

2:1–22 This chapter contains a paternal call regarding wisdom. It begins with a series of "if" statements that describe the search for wisdom (vv. 1–4), and it continues with several "then" statements about the results of wisdom. Wisdom provides an understanding of the fear of Yahweh (v. 5) as well as righteousness and justice (v. 9). It also delivers from evil, as the wise person can withstand temptation (vv. 11–19). The person who seeks and finds wisdom walks in righteousness and avoids the judgment of the wicked (vv. 20–22).

2:1 My son See 1:8; note on 1:8—9:18.
2:4 you look for it as for silver Job 28 describes wisdom as something that cannot be found, unlike silver and other precious metals or stones. See Job 28:1–28 and note.

⁵then you will understand the fear
of the LORD
and find the knowledge of God.
⁶For the LORD gives wisdom;
from his mouth come knowledge and
understanding.
⁷He holds success in store for the upright,
he is a shield to those whose walk is
blameless,
⁸for he guards the course of the just
and protects the way of his
faithful ones.

⁹Then you will understand what is right
and just
and fair—every good path.
¹⁰For wisdom will enter your heart,
and knowledge will be pleasant to your
soul.
¹¹Discretion will protect you,
and understanding will guard you.

¹²Wisdom will save you from the ways of
wicked men,
from men whose words are perverse,
¹³who have left the straight paths
to walk in dark ways,
¹⁴who delight in doing wrong
and rejoice in the perverseness of evil,

¹⁵whose paths are crooked
and who are devious in their ways.

¹⁶Wisdom will save you also from the
adulterous woman,
from the wayward woman with her
seductive words,
¹⁷who has left the partner of her youth
and ignored the covenant she made before
God.ᵃ
¹⁸Surely her house leads down to death
and her paths to the spirits of the dead.
¹⁹None who go to her return
or attain the paths of life.

²⁰Thus you will walk in the ways of the good
and keep to the paths of the righteous.
²¹For the upright will live in the land,
and the blameless will remain in it;
²²but the wicked will be cut off from the land,
and the unfaithful will be torn from it.

Wisdom Bestows Well-Being

3 My son, do not forget my teaching,
but keep my commands in your heart,
²for they will prolong your life many years
and bring you peace and prosperity.

ᵃ 17 Or *covenant of her God*

2:5 fear of the LORD Searching for wisdom results in a better understanding of the fear of Yahweh (see note on Pr 1:7). Wisdom and the fear of Yahweh are closely connected; elsewhere, the fear of Yahweh gives wisdom (15:33).
2:6 the LORD gives wisdom Wisdom comes from Yahweh, the only one who fully understands it and knows its origins (Job 28:23–28).
2:7 for the upright Yahweh gives wisdom to the upright, who live with integrity. These terms are also used to describe Job. See Job 1:1 and note.
2:8 faithful ones The Hebrew word used here, *chasid,* comes from the word *chesed,* which describes a faithful, covenantal love (compare 1Sa 2:9; Ps 86:2; Ex 20:6 and note).
2:9 what is right and just and fair Wisdom enables people to understand and walk in these qualities. See note on Pr 1:3.
2:11 Discretion will protect you Discretion and understanding serve as defenses against evil. See v. 2; note on 1:2; note on 1:4.
2:12 perverse The Hebrew word used here describes dishonest and wicked speech (10:32; 16:28). Perverted speech—the enemy of wisdom and Yahweh (8:13)—will ultimately be cut off (10:31).
2:14 who delight in doing wrong The foolish and wicked enjoy evil (10:23).
2:16 adulterous woman Wisdom preserves its keepers from the temptations of the forbidden woman and the adulteress. While elsewhere in the OT these terms can describe strange or foreign people (2Sa 15:19; Isa 61:5), in Proverbs they refer to married women who act unfaithfully (Pr 2:17; 7:18–20). Though the speech of the adulteress is smooth or seductive (6:24; 7:5,21), readers should answer the call of wisdom (8:1–3) rather

than follow the adulteress's call (7:6–12). Proverbs warns against associating with the adulteress (5:8; 6:25; 7:25), who takes advantage of the simple (7:6–9; see note on 1:4). Following her can result in death (2:18–19; 5:5; 7:27).
2:17 ignored the covenant she made before God In violating her commitment to her husband, the adulteress violates the covenant of God (Ex 20:14; Mal 2:14). See the table "Covenants in the Old Testament" on p. 469.
2:18 the spirits The Hebrew word used here, *repha'im,* refers to the spirits of the dead in the underworld, where they have a shadowy existence (compare Pr 21:16; Job 26:5; Ps 88:11; Isa 14:9). See note on Job 14:13.

2:21–22 Proverbs 2 concludes by describing the results of following wisdom. The upright and those with integrity (see note on v. 7) inhabit the land, while the wicked are cut off. To inhabit the land means to live in safety and enjoy Yahweh's blessing (10:30; Ps 37:3–4). While "the land" can refer specifically to Israel (Dt 4:1), here it is best understood as meaning the earth in general.

3:1–12 In this section, a father encourages his son to remember his teaching, including love and faithfulness (Pr 3:1,3). In doing so, the son will be ensured a long and successful life (vv. 2,4). The father also tells his son to trust in and acknowledge Yahweh rather than his own wisdom (vv. 5–8), to honor Yahweh with his wealth (vv. 9–10) and to accept Yahweh's discipline (vv. 11–12).

3:1 My son See 1:8; note on 1:8—9:18.
3:2 they will prolong your life many years Proverbs ascribes blessings to those who are wise, righteous and faithful: They can find long life and success (3:4; 10:2,27; 12:28; 16:22) while the wicked will be destroyed (10:30; 11:19). However, these statements are general

³ Let love and faithfulness never leave you;
  bind them around your neck,
  write them on the tablet of your heart.
⁴ Then you will win favor and a good name
  in the sight of God and man.

⁵ Trust in the Lᴏʀᴅ with all your heart
  and lean not on your own understanding;
⁶ in all your ways submit to him,
  and he will make your paths straight.ᵃ

⁷ Do not be wise in your own eyes;
  fear the Lᴏʀᴅ and shun evil.
⁸ This will bring health to your body
  and nourishment to your bones.

⁹ Honor the Lᴏʀᴅ with your wealth,
  with the firstfruits of all your crops;
¹⁰ then your barns will be filled to overflowing,
  and your vats will brim over with new wine.

¹¹ My son, do not despise the Lᴏʀᴅ's discipline,
  and do not resent his rebuke,
¹² because the Lᴏʀᴅ disciplines those he loves,
  as a father the son he delights in.ᵇ

¹³ Blessed are those who find wisdom,
  those who gain understanding,
¹⁴ for she is more profitable than silver
  and yields better returns than gold.
¹⁵ She is more precious than rubies;
  nothing you desire can compare with her.
¹⁶ Long life is in her right hand;
  in her left hand are riches and honor.
¹⁷ Her ways are pleasant ways,
  and all her paths are peace.
¹⁸ She is a tree of life to those who take hold
  of her;
  those who hold her fast will be blessed.

¹⁹ By wisdom the Lᴏʀᴅ laid the earth's
  foundations,
  by understanding he set the heavens in
  place;
²⁰ by his knowledge the watery depths were
  divided,
  and the clouds let drop the dew.

ᵃ 6 Or *will direct your paths*   ᵇ 12 Hebrew; Septuagint *loves, /
and he chastens everyone he accepts as his child*

---

principles, not promises. Often, success and failure can be attributed to natural results. The wise (17:27; 19:2) avoid trouble by practicing caution and restraint, while the fool's recklessness leads to trouble (14:16; 18:6). The lazy attitude of the sluggard results in less success than the hard-working wise person (6:9–11; 10:4; 12:27; 13:4; 21:25). While some proverbs show the wise and righteous enjoying wealth (8:18; 13:22; 14:24), others show the wicked as wealthy (16:8, 16:19; 28:6). Overall, Proverbs emphasizes that wisdom and righteousness are preferable to wealth (17:1; 19:22; 22:1). The blessings ascribed to the wise and righteous in Proverbs are not guarantees. As other examples from Wisdom Literature demonstrate, at times the righteous suffer and the wicked prosper (Job 12:6; Ecc 7:15).
3:3 love The Hebrew word used here, *chesed*, describes a faithful covenantal love. The characteristics in this verse are later spoken of as preserving the rule of a king (Pr 20:28). **bind them around your neck** A way to keep them close and ensure they will not be forgotten (Dt 6:8–9). Compare Ex 13:9 and note.
3:5 Trust in the Lᴏʀᴅ Since wisdom comes from Yahweh (Pr 2:6), he must be trusted. This often involves relying on God's wisdom rather than human wisdom (3:7). It involves doing the right thing when a situation presents itself and trusting God as guide; it involves morality and the process of discernment. God has given people rational ability, and Proverbs assumes people will use it to make good decisions. However, the book cautions against depending on rational abilities alone. Proverbs urges everyone to keep God in mind in everything they do (v. 6); this is how a person's life progresses toward God's goals.
3:7 Do not be wise in your own eyes Humility is a characteristic of the wise, while arrogance is an attribute of the fool (12:15; 21:24). **fear the Lᴏʀᴅ** Refers to having a correct and reverent attitude toward Yahweh. See note on 1:7. **shun evil** Refers to both rejecting wickedness and pursuing good (Ps 34:14; 37:27).
3:9 with the firstfruits of all your crops The law required that the Israelites give the firstfruits of their

harvest to Yahweh (see Ex 23:16–19; note on Pr 23:26; Lev 23:10–11; Dt 26:2).
3:10 your vats will brim over with new wine Wine was considered a blessing from God and a symbol of abundance. Compare Dt 7:13; Ps 104:14–15; and note on Job 24:11.
3:11 do not despise the Lᴏʀᴅ's discipline Willingness to accept discipline is a characteristic of the wise. The author of Hebrews quotes these verses when encouraging readers to endure through life's struggles (Heb 12:5–6).

3:13–20 This brief hymn extolling wisdom begins by asserting that the one who finds wisdom and understanding is blessed or happy (Pr 3:13). Wisdom is then compared to silver, gold and precious stones (vv. 14–15). Wisdom is more valuable than any of these substances (Job 28:15–19) because of its benefits, which can include long life, riches, honor and peace (Pr 3:15–18). Finally, the hymn describes how Yahweh used wisdom in creation (vv. 19–20).

3:13 Blessed The Hebrew word used here, *ashre*, can indicate being happy or blessed (see note on Ps 1:1).
3:17 all her paths are peace Describes a path of safety and security.
3:18 tree of life A symbol of renewal and life. In Proverbs, the tree of life is equated with a fulfilled desire (Pr 13:12), a gentle tongue (15:4) and the fruit of the righteous (11:30). References to the fountain of life are used in a similar way (13:14; 14:27; 16:22). The tree of life is contrasted with a broken spirit (15:4) and a sick heart (13:12). With this contrast in mind, the tree of life may be a symbol of physical or spiritual renewal. The creation language of 3:19–20 resembles Ge 2:9, where the tree of life represents eternal life (Ge 3:22; see note on 2:9).
3:19 By wisdom the Lᴏʀᴅ laid the earth's foundations God used wisdom in laying the foundation of the earth. See Job 38:4 and note; and Pr 8:22 and note.
3:20 depths Refers to the primordial sea (see Ge 1:2 and note). See the infographic "Ancient Hebrew Conception of the Universe" on p. 5.

²¹ My son, do not let wisdom and
   understanding out of your sight,
   preserve sound judgment and discretion;
²² they will be life for you,
   an ornament to grace your neck.
²³ Then you will go on your way in safety,
   and your foot will not stumble.
²⁴ When you lie down, you will not be afraid;
   when you lie down, your sleep will be sweet.
²⁵ Have no fear of sudden disaster
   or of the ruin that overtakes the wicked,
²⁶ for the LORD will be at your side
   and will keep your foot from being snared.

²⁷ Do not withhold good from those to whom it
   is due,
   when it is in your power to act.
²⁸ Do not say to your neighbor,
   "Come back tomorrow and I'll give it to
   you" —
   when you already have it with you.
²⁹ Do not plot harm against your neighbor,
   who lives trustfully near you.
³⁰ Do not accuse anyone for no reason —
   when they have done you no harm.

³¹ Do not envy the violent
   or choose any of their ways.

³² For the LORD detests the perverse
   but takes the upright into his confidence.
³³ The LORD's curse is on the house of the wicked,
   but he blesses the home of the righteous.
³⁴ He mocks proud mockers
   but shows favor to the humble and
   oppressed.

³⁵ The wise inherit honor,
   but fools get only shame.

Get Wisdom at Any Cost

4 Listen, my sons, to a father's instruction;
   pay attention and gain understanding.
² I give you sound learning,
   so do not forsake my teaching.
³ For I too was a son to my father,
   still tender, and cherished by my mother.
⁴ Then he taught me, and he said to me,
   "Take hold of my words with all your
   heart;
   keep my commands, and you will live.
⁵ Get wisdom, get understanding;
   do not forget my words or turn away from
   them.
⁶ Do not forsake wisdom, and she will
   protect you;
   love her, and she will watch over you.
⁷ The beginning of wisdom is this: Get[a]
   wisdom.
   Though it cost all you have,[b] get
   understanding.
⁸ Cherish her, and she will exalt you;
   embrace her, and she will honor you.
⁹ She will give you a garland to grace your
   head
   and present you with a glorious crown."

¹⁰ Listen, my son, accept what I say,
   and the years of your life will be many.

---

[a] 7 Or *Wisdom is supreme; therefore get*   [b] 7 Or *wisdom. /
Whatever else you get*

3:21–35 In this section, the father encourages his son to keep wisdom close. He describes the safety and security that comes from a life lived in wisdom (Pr 3:23–26). He then gives a series of commands pertaining to the treatment of others (vv. 27–31). Finally, he describes Yahweh's attitude toward the wicked and the righteous (vv. 32–35).

3:21 My son See 1:8; note on 1:8—9:18.
3:22 an ornament to grace your neck Wisdom enhances character just as jewelry enhances physical beauty.
3:24 your sleep will be sweet Those with wisdom sleep peacefully, confident in the protection of Yahweh (Ps 4:8; Jer 31:26).
3:27 Do not withhold good Emphasizes the moral or ethical aspect of wisdom; the wise person learns righteousness and justice. See Pr 1:3 and note.
3:29 harm The Hebrew word used here, *ra'ah*, can refer to harm or calamity, as well as to evil. See note on Ps 15:3.
3:31 Do not envy the violent Refers to the envy that comes when wicked people achieve success (Ps 73:3–14).
3:32 the LORD detests The wise should not envy people of violence because—while they may be successful—they represent an abomination to Yahweh. Under the curse of Yahweh, the wicked only achieve temporary success. Ultimately, their end is ruin (Ps 73:16–20).
3:33 The LORD's curse is on the house of the wicked

Yahweh will ultimately send punishment on the wicked and his family (compare Pr 28:27; Dt 28:20; Mal 2:2). In the OT the family is a unit and shares the fate of the family's head (Jos 7:24–25; Nu 16:32).
3:34 He mocks proud mockers In Proverbs, the scorners or scoffers are similar to the fools. See note on Pr 1:7; and note on 1:22.

4:1–27 Chapter 4 consists of three sets of paternal instructions. In the first, the father encourages his sons to listen to wisdom (vv. 1–2) and quotes the teachings of his own father (vv. 3–9). In the second, he urges his son to keep hold of his instruction (vv. 10–13) and warns him not to follow the path of the wicked (vv. 14–19). In the third, he advises his son to continue on the path of wisdom and not turn aside from it (vv. 20–27).

4:1 Listen, my sons, to a father's instruction See 1:8; note on 1:8—9:18.
4:3 a son to my father The father presents the teaching of his father. Traditionally, wisdom passed down through generations was considered more authoritative (Job 8:8–10; 15:18).
4:5 get understanding Discernment is closely related to wisdom in Proverbs. See note on Pr 1:2.
4:10 Listen, my son See note on 1:8. **years of your life will be many** Long life is considered a reward for wisdom and righteousness. See note on 3:2.

¹¹ I instruct you in the way of wisdom
　　and lead you along straight paths.
¹² When you walk, your steps will not be
　　　hampered;
　　when you run, you will not stumble.
¹³ Hold on to instruction, do not let it go;
　　guard it well, for it is your life.
¹⁴ Do not set foot on the path of the wicked
　　or walk in the way of evildoers.
¹⁵ Avoid it, do not travel on it;
　　turn from it and go on your way.
¹⁶ For they cannot rest until they do evil;
　　they are robbed of sleep till they make
　　　someone stumble.
¹⁷ They eat the bread of wickedness
　　and drink the wine of violence.

¹⁸ The path of the righteous is like the
　　　morning sun,
　　shining ever brighter till the full light
　　　of day.
¹⁹ But the way of the wicked is like deep
　　　darkness;
　　they do not know what makes them
　　　stumble.

²⁰ My son, pay attention to what I say;
　　turn your ear to my words.
²¹ Do not let them out of your sight,
　　keep them within your heart;

²² for they are life to those who find them
　　and health to one's whole body.
²³ Above all else, guard your heart,
　　for everything you do flows from it.
²⁴ Keep your mouth free of perversity;
　　keep corrupt talk far from your lips.
²⁵ Let your eyes look straight ahead;
　　fix your gaze directly before you.
²⁶ Give careful thought to theᵃ paths for
　　　your feet
　　and be steadfast in all your ways.
²⁷ Do not turn to the right or the left;
　　keep your foot from evil.

Warning Against Adultery

5 My son, pay attention to my wisdom,
　　turn your ear to my words of insight,
² that you may maintain discretion
　　and your lips may preserve
　　　knowledge.
³ For the lips of the adulterous woman drip
　　　honey,
　　and her speech is smoother than oil;
⁴ but in the end she is bitter as gall,
　　sharp as a double-edged sword.
⁵ Her feet go down to death;
　　her steps lead straight to the grave.

ᵃ 26 Or *Make level*

4:11 straight paths Wisdom is paralleled with honest and righteous living. See note on 2:7.
4:13 Hold on to instruction Wisdom should be protected because of its great value and the effort required to obtain and maintain it (2:4; 3:13–15).
4:14 Do not set foot on the path of the wicked While the way of wisdom is safe and peaceful (3:17; 4:12), the way of the wicked is dark and crooked (2:15; 4:19). See Ps 1:1–6.
4:16 they cannot rest In contrast to the restful, easy sleep of the wise (Pr 3:24), the wicked cannot even go to sleep before they commit evil.
4:17 eat the bread of wickedness The wicked feed on evil. It is their source of strength and motivation.
4:18–19 These verses contrast the paths of the righteous and the wicked. The righteous follow a bright path, which allows them to see and proceed in safety (Job 29:2–3). In contrast, the wicked take a dark path, which prevents them from seeing traps or obstacles, causing them to stumble (Job 12:24–25; 18:10).

4:20 My son, pay attention to what I say See Pr 1:8; note on 1:8—9:18.

4:23–27 The father encourages his son to keep wisdom by guarding various aspects of his body. His heart should be vigilant (v. 23), his mouth should avoid falsehood (v. 24) and his eyes should be directed forward (v. 25). Finally, he should keep the path of his feet clear and not turn toward evil (vv. 26–27).

4:23 Above all else, guard your heart Appropriate speech and the state of the heart are closely associated in vv. 20–24. Restrained speech is a common

theme in Wisdom Literature (e.g., 10:19; 16:23; 17:27; 21:23). **everything you do flows** The speech of the wise benefits the speaker and the listener (10:20,31; 12:18; 15:2,4; 18:21).
4:24 Keep your mouth free of perversity The Hebrew phrase used here for a kind of sinful speech literally means "falseness of mouth." In Proverbs, the mouth reflects a person's character (15:2,28).
4:26 Give careful thought The Hebrew word used here indicates clearing a way (Isa 26:7). Here, the father encourages his son to intentionally remain on the path of wisdom and righteousness (Pr 4:11).

5:1–23 This lengthy warning against adultery begins with a typical exhortation for the son to pay attention to the wisdom of his father (vv. 1–2). The father warns that although the forbidden woman may be alluring, she is deadly (vv. 3–6). He warns his sons to avoid her and notes the consequences of not doing so, including economic ruin and social shame (vv. 7–14). He then prescribes fidelity in marriage as the proper outlet for sexual expression (vv. 15–20). He concludes with a more general warning about the fate of the wicked (vv. 21–23).

5:1 My son, pay attention to my wisdom See note on 1:8; note on 1:8—9:18.
5:3 the lips of the adulterous woman Described as smoother than oil and sweet like honey, both of which were signs of luxury. The forbidden woman appears as an alluring and flattering temptress. See note on 2:16.
5:4 gall While the adulteress's speech may be sweet and appealing, in the end it becomes bitter and painful in the end.
a double-edged sword Used to wound by stabbing, a two-edged sword could also be concealed (Jdg 3:16–22).

⁶ She gives no thought to the way of life;
　　her paths wander aimlessly, but she does
　　　not know it.

⁷ Now then, my sons, listen to me;
　　do not turn aside from what I say.
⁸ Keep to a path far from her,
　　do not go near the door of her house,
⁹ lest you lose your honor to others
　　and your dignity*ᵃ* to one who is cruel,
¹⁰ lest strangers feast on your wealth
　　and your toil enrich the house of another.
¹¹ At the end of your life you will groan,
　　when your flesh and body are spent.
¹² You will say, "How I hated discipline!
　　How my heart spurned correction!
¹³ I would not obey my teachers
　　or turn my ear to my instructors.
¹⁴ And I was soon in serious trouble
　　in the assembly of God's people."

¹⁵ Drink water from your own cistern,
　　running water from your own well.
¹⁶ Should your springs overflow in the streets,
　　your streams of water in the public
　　　squares?
¹⁷ Let them be yours alone,
　　never to be shared with strangers.
¹⁸ May your fountain be blessed,
　　and may you rejoice in the wife of your
　　　youth.

¹⁹ A loving doe, a graceful deer —
　　may her breasts satisfy you always,
　　may you ever be intoxicated with
　　　her love.
²⁰ Why, my son, be intoxicated with another
　　man's wife?
　　Why embrace the bosom of a wayward
　　woman?

²¹ For your ways are in full view of the LORD,
　　and he examines all your paths.
²² The evil deeds of the wicked ensnare them;
　　the cords of their sins hold them fast.
²³ For lack of discipline they will die,
　　led astray by their own great folly.

Warnings Against Folly

6 My son, if you have put up security for your
　　neighbor,
　　if you have shaken hands in pledge for a
　　　stranger,
² you have been trapped by what you said,
　　ensnared by the words of your mouth.
³ So do this, my son, to free yourself,
　　since you have fallen into your neighbor's
　　　hands:
　　Go — to the point of exhaustion —ᵇ
　　and give your neighbor no rest!

ᵃ 9 Or *years*　ᵇ 3 Or *Go and humble yourself,*

Elsewhere, it represents a tool of God's punishment (Ps 149:6–9).

5:6 She gives no thought to the way of life Unlike the wise, the adulteress does not carefully consider her path. See Pr 4:26 and note. **her paths wander aimlessly** In v. 27, the father encouraged his son to carefully avoid swerving from the path of wisdom and righteousness.

5:7 sons, listen to me See 1:8; note on 1:8—9:18.

5:8 Keep to a path far from her The father encourages his sons to keep distance between themselves and the adulteress. Their way (2:8,20; 4:11–14) should not even approach her.

5:10 strangers feast on your wealth The words that describe the people who will take wealth in this verse are the same words used in 2:16 to describe the adulteress.

5:12 How I hated discipline In Proverbs, a fool or scoffer hates discipline (9:7–8; 15:5) while the wise love it (9:8–9; 12:1).

5:15 Drink water from your own cistern A euphemism for sexual relations. The son is encouraged to find sexual satisfaction with his wife. The man in the Song of Songs also uses water as a euphemism; he describes his beloved as a sealed spring or fountain (SS 4:12,15).

5:17 never to be shared with strangers Considering the next verse, this phrase is probably an encouragement to the son to only share sexual pleasures with his wife. The Hebrew word used here, *zar* ("stranger"), probably is a reference to the woman of Pr 2:16 and 5:3,20, who is described with the same word.

5:18 wife of your youth That is, the woman whom the son married when he was young (2:17; compare Mal 2:14).

5:21 he examines all your paths See note on Pr 4:26.

5:22 cords This refers to a cord used in a trap (Ps 140:5). The wicked are caught in their own traps. See note on Job 18:8.

5:23 For lack of discipline they will die Lack of discipline is associated with folly. This lack of discipline allows the fool to fall into temptation.

6:1–19 In Pr 6, the father gives his son a series of practical warnings. He begins with instructions on giving a pledge for someone (vv. 1–5). He then uses the example of an ant to warn against slothfulness (vv. 6–11). Finally, he describes the fate of the wicked (vv. 12–15) and lists traits hated by Yahweh (vv. 16–19).

6:1 My son See 1:8; note on 1:8—9:18. **you have put up security for your neighbor** A pledge or security was collateral taken for a loan. Wisdom Literature speaks strongly against putting up security or pledges (11:15; 22:26); the one putting up security would be held responsible if the debtor defaulted on his loan. The law allowed for a creditor to require a pledge or security when offering a loan. Garments often served as this security. Any garment taken as a pledge had to be returned before nightfall (Ex 22:26–27). The law prohibited taking any pledges that would damage the debtor's ability to make a living (Dt 24:6). It also prohibited forcefully taking pledges from debtors (Dt 24:10). See note on Ex 22:21–25.

6:3 give your neighbor no rest Emphasizes the urgency of the situation. The debtor should quickly go and petition the creditor for mercy. The Hebrew phrase used here indicates a fervent, continued pleading. This idea is also seen in the parable of the widow and the unjust judge (Lk 18:1–5).

⁴Allow no sleep to your eyes,
    no slumber to your eyelids.
⁵Free yourself, like a gazelle from the hand
        of the hunter,
    like a bird from the snare of the fowler.

⁶Go to the ant, you sluggard;
    consider its ways and be wise!
⁷It has no commander,
    no overseer or ruler,
⁸yet it stores its provisions in summer
    and gathers its food at harvest.

⁹How long will you lie there, you
        sluggard?
    When will you get up from your
        sleep?
¹⁰A little sleep, a little slumber,
    a little folding of the hands to rest—
¹¹and poverty will come on you like
        a thief
    and scarcity like an armed man.

¹²A troublemaker and a villain,
    who goes about with a corrupt mouth,
¹³   who winks maliciously with his eye,
    signals with his feet
    and motions with his fingers,
¹⁴   who plots evil with deceit in his heart—
    he always stirs up conflict.

¹⁵Therefore disaster will overtake him in
        an instant;
    he will suddenly be destroyed—without
        remedy.

¹⁶There are six things the Lord hates,
    seven that are detestable to him:
¹⁷   haughty eyes,
        a lying tongue,
        hands that shed innocent blood,
¹⁸   a heart that devises wicked schemes,
        feet that are quick to rush into evil,
¹⁹   a false witness who pours out lies
        and a person who stirs up conflict in the
            community.

Warning Against Adultery

²⁰My son, keep your father's command
    and do not forsake your mother's teaching.
²¹Bind them always on your heart;
    fasten them around your neck.
²²When you walk, they will guide you;
    when you sleep, they will watch over you;
    when you awake, they will speak to you.
²³For this command is a lamp,
    this teaching is a light,
    and correction and instruction
    are the way to life,

6:6 Go to the ant, you sluggard The ant appears only twice in the Bible—here and in Pr 30:25. In both places, it appears as an example of wisdom and prudence, since ants work hard to store up food (compare note on 6:9).
6:7 It has no commander The ant has enough initiative and discipline to work hard without any supervision. The argument moves from lesser to greater: The idea is that if the seemingly inconsequential ant can do this, then a human must be able to do more.
6:9 sluggard A recurring character in Proverbs, who stands in sharp contrast here to the industrious ant (vv. 6–8). The Hebrew word used here, *atsel*, appears only in Proverbs. It describes a person who is too lazy to work (21:25) and finds any excuse to stay in bed (26:13–14). The sluggard's land becomes overgrown (24:30) and the sluggard ends up with nothing and in poverty (6:9–11; 10:4; 13:4; 20:4). The sluggard and the slothful man (*remiyyah*) contrast with the diligent or hardworking person (10:4; 13:4). Like the fool and scoffer, the sluggard believes himself to be wise (26:16), and like the fool, the sluggard's life will end in destruction because of laziness (21:25).
6:10 folding of the hands Indicates a refusal to work (Ecc 4:5). The sluggard's hands are often mentioned in Proverbs (Pr 10:4; 19:24; 21:25).
6:11 will come on you like a thief For the sluggard, poverty comes suddenly and ruthlessly like a thief or armed man. The onset of poverty should be obvious for sluggards since they do not work (20:4). However, their arrogance (26:16) may blind them to this.
6:12 A troublemaker This quality is closely associated with evil (16:27) and rebellion (1Sa 2:12). In the NT, a version of the Hebrew term used here, *beliyya'al*, is mentioned as being the opposite of Christ (2Co 6:15). **with a corrupt mouth** Indicates deceit. See note on Pr 4:24.

6:13 who winks maliciously with his eye The exact meanings of the three gestures described here are uncertain. They are most likely associated with the deceit mentioned in 6:12. The wicked do not just lie with their mouths, but use many parts of their bodies—eyes, feet, fingers—to carry out their deceit.
6:14 evil The Hebrew word used here can refer to harm or trouble as well as to evil. See note on Ps 15:3.
6:16 There are six things This does not suggest that Yahweh hates only six things while considering seven an abomination. Here, the author uses a literary device to show that the following list of traits is both hated by and an abomination to God. Numerical sayings are a common literary device in wisdom literature. The formula "number … number+1" is used throughout Proverbs (see Pr 30:18 and note; compare 30:15,21; Job 5:19).
6:19 false witness The law prohibits bearing false witness (Ex 20:16). The person who gives a false testimony faces the same punishment as the accused (Dt 19:18–19).

6:20–35 The father gives another warning against adultery (Pr 5:1–23). He begins by encouraging his son to keep his teaching close (6:20–21). His commandment and teaching will lead his son and guard him from the temptation of the adulteress (vv. 22–24). He warns his son against desiring her beauty (vv. 25–28). Comparing adultery to theft, he describes the specific consequences that will be taken against him by the woman's husband (vv. 29–35).

6:20 My son, keep your father's command See 1:8; note on 1:8—9:18.
6:21 Bind them always on your heart The son is charged to keep his parents' commandments close and ensure they will not be forgotten. Compare Ex 13:9.

²⁴keeping you from your neighbor's wife,
from the smooth talk of a wayward
woman.

²⁵Do not lust in your heart after her beauty
or let her captivate you with her eyes.

²⁶For a prostitute can be had for a loaf of bread,
but another man's wife preys on your very
life.
²⁷Can a man scoop fire into his lap
without his clothes being burned?
²⁸Can a man walk on hot coals
without his feet being scorched?
²⁹So is he who sleeps with another man's wife;
no one who touches her will go
unpunished.

³⁰People do not despise a thief if he steals
to satisfy his hunger when he is starving.
³¹Yet if he is caught, he must pay sevenfold,
though it costs him all the wealth of his
house.
³²But a man who commits adultery has no
sense;
whoever does so destroys himself.
³³Blows and disgrace are his lot,
and his shame will never be wiped away.

³⁴For jealousy arouses a husband's fury,
and he will show no mercy when he takes
revenge.
³⁵He will not accept any compensation;
he will refuse a bribe, however great it is.

Warning Against the Adulterous Woman

7 My son, keep my words
and store up my commands within you.
²Keep my commands and you will live;
guard my teachings as the apple of
your eye.
³Bind them on your fingers;
write them on the tablet of your heart.
⁴Say to wisdom, "You are my sister,"
and to insight, "You are my relative."
⁵They will keep you from the adulterous
woman,
from the wayward woman with her
seductive words.

⁶At the window of my house
I looked down through the lattice.
⁷I saw among the simple,
I noticed among the young men,
a youth who had no sense.

6:24 neighbor's wife See note on Pr 2:16. **from the smooth talk** See 5:3 and note.
6:25 Do not lust in your heart after her beauty Previously, the father mentioned only the flattering and seductive speech of the adulteress. Here, he describes her physical appeal as he warns his son to avoid her.
6:26 a loaf of bread Translations of this verse vary, but its most likely meaning is that a prostitute is far less costly—the price of a meal—than an adulterous relationship, which costs the son his life. This comparison does not endorse prostitution, just as the comparison to theft does not endorse stealing (6:30). Prostitution is condemned elsewhere in Proverbs (23:27; 29:3).
6:29 no one who touches her will go unpunished In the law, the punishment for adultery was death for both the man and the woman (Lev 20:10; Dt 22:22).
6:30 People do not despise a thief May be a relative statement; people do despise thieves, but not as much as adulterers (Pr 6:33). A hungry thief can elicit sympathy.
6:32 no sense The Hebrew term used here, *chasar-lev*, suggests a lack of good sense. The person who lacks sense is lazy like the sluggard and pursues worthless things instead of working (12:11; 24:30). His unwise decisions and enjoyment of folly get him into trouble (compare 17:18; 15:21; 10:13; see note on 1:4). Like the fool and scoffer, he commits adultery, but his motivations are not the same (3:33–34; 6:32; 10:23; 13:19). He succumbs to the adulteress because he is gullible and weak (7:7; 9:4, 9:16). **destroys himself** The negative consequences of sin or folly in Proverbs are often attributed to natural results rather than divine punishment (see note on 3:2). Here, the consequence for adultery is death.
6:34 jealousy arouses a husband's fury The husband of the adulteress will ensure that retribution will be made.
6:35 He will not accept any compensation As opposed

to the lender in 6:1–5, who could be petitioned for mercy, the jealous husband will not accept any compensation (see note on v. 3).

7:1–27 The father again gives an extended warning about adultery (compare 5:1–23). He encourages his son to keep his teaching close (7:1–3). If his son keeps wisdom as a close friend—perhaps alluding to wisdom personified as a woman in ch. 2; 8:1—9:9—he can avoid the temptation of the adulteress (7:4–5). The father then focuses on the aggressive tactics the adulteress uses to seduce those he calls the simple (vv. 6–21). He describes the consequences of being seduced by her (vv. 22–23) and issues a final warning to avoid her (vv. 24–27).

7:1 My son, keep my words See 1:8; note on 1:8—9:18.
7:2 apple The Hebrew word used here, *ishon*, seems to refer to the small reflection seen in the pupil of someone's eye. The phrase describes keeping something close and carefully watching over it (Dt 32:10; Ps 17:8).
7:3 Bind them on your fingers A way to ensure the commands would not be forgotten.
7:4 sister The Hebrew word used here, *achoth*, does not always indicate a sibling relationship; it can also refer to a bride (SS 4:9–10; 5:1–2), which is probably its meaning here. The father advises his son to take wisdom, rather than the adulteress, as his intimate companion.
7:5 from the adulterous woman Wisdom preserves the wise from the temptations of the adulteress. See note on Pr 2:16. **her seductive words** See 5:3 and note.
7:7 among the simple In Proverbs, the simple person and the person who lacks sense represent those who are gullible and easily fall into temptation. Unlike the fool, the simple person can learn to respond to discipline (19:25; 21:11; see note on 1:4; note on 6:32).

⁸ He was going down the street near her
  corner,
    walking along in the direction of her house
⁹ at twilight, as the day was fading,
    as the dark of night set in.

¹⁰ Then out came a woman to meet him,
    dressed like a prostitute and with crafty
      intent.
¹¹ (She is unruly and defiant,
    her feet never stay at home;
¹² now in the street, now in the squares,
    at every corner she lurks.)
¹³ She took hold of him and kissed him
    and with a brazen face she said:

¹⁴ "Today I fulfilled my vows,
    and I have food from my fellowship
      offering at home.
¹⁵ So I came out to meet you;
    I looked for you and have found you!
¹⁶ I have covered my bed
    with colored linens from Egypt.
¹⁷ I have perfumed my bed
    with myrrh, aloes and cinnamon.
¹⁸ Come, let's drink deeply of love till morning;
    let's enjoy ourselves with love!
¹⁹ My husband is not at home;
    he has gone on a long journey.
²⁰ He took his purse filled with money
    and will not be home till full moon."

²¹ With persuasive words she led him astray;
    she seduced him with her smooth talk.
²² All at once he followed her
    like an ox going to the slaughter,
    like a deer^a stepping into a noose^b
²³   till an arrow pierces his liver,
    like a bird darting into a snare,
    little knowing it will cost him his life.

²⁴ Now then, my sons, listen to me;
    pay attention to what I say.
²⁵ Do not let your heart turn to her ways
    or stray into her paths.
²⁶ Many are the victims she has brought down;
    her slain are a mighty throng.
²⁷ Her house is a highway to the grave,
    leading down to the chambers of death.

Wisdom's Call

8 Does not wisdom call out?
    Does not understanding raise her voice?
² At the highest point along the way,
    where the paths meet, she takes
      her stand;
³ beside the gate leading into the city,
    at the entrance, she cries aloud:
⁴ "To you, O people, I call out;
    I raise my voice to all mankind.

---

^{a} 22 Syriac (see also Septuagint); Hebrew *fool*
^{b} 22 The meaning of the Hebrew for this line is uncertain.

7:10 crafty intent The Hebrew phrase used here, which is literally rendered as "guarded of heart," probably indicates that this woman acts carefully to avoid being caught (7:19).
7:13 a brazen face Refers to the adulteress's impudence and defiance of social appropriateness. Compare Dt 28:50; Jer 3:3; Eze 3:7–9.
7:17 myrrh A fragrant gum native to Arabia. It was used in incense (Ex 30:23) and as a perfume (Ps 45:8; SS 1:13). The adulteress makes her bed more alluring by perfuming it with precious, pleasant-smelling spices. **aloes** A spice used in perfumes. In the OT, it is paralleled with myrrh (Ps 45:8; SS 4:14). **cinnamon** A fragrant luxury item (SS 4:14) used in incense (Ex 30:23).
7:21 persuasive words The Hebrew word used here, *leqach*, also appears in Pr 5:1 and 5:13 to indicate a person listening to wise instruction or understanding. In this instance, the speech of the adulteress, rather than the father's teaching, is what is listened to.
7:23 liver People in the ancient Near East viewed the liver as the seat of life. **like a bird darting into a snare** Depicts sin and its consequences as a bird foolishly falling into a trap (1:17–19). Compare Ps 7:15 and note. **it will cost him his life** The punishment for adultery under the law was death for both the man and the woman (Lev 20:10; Dt 22:22). Compare note on Pr 6:29.
7:24 sons See Pr 1:8; note on 1:8—9:18.
7:26 a mighty throng The Hebrew word used here, *atsum*, implies a great number of mighty men. A single adulteress can bring down an entire army.
7:27 chambers Here, the rooms in the realm of the dead contrast with the alluring and luxurious room the adulteress describes (7:16–17).

8:1–36 In this chapter, wisdom is personified as a woman who calls all of humanity to heed her voice (see 1:20–33 and note; 8:1–5). She describes her speech as noble and righteous (vv. 6–11). She continues by contrasting herself with pride, evil and deception (vv. 12–14) and explaining her benefits to rulers (vv. 15–21). She also describes her role in creation (vv. 22–31). Finally, wisdom repeats her call, encouraging all to find life by keeping her ways (vv. 32–36).

8:1 wisdom The Hebrew word used here, *chokhmah*, generally refers to instructions or teachings—practical precepts useful for living (1:2 and note; 1:7; 2:2,6,10; 4:5,7; 14:1). In Proverbs, these precepts come from God (2:6) and are connected to the fear of Yahweh (1:7; 9:10). In certain contexts, wisdom is personified (see note on 1:20–33). At times, the character wisdom appears divine (8:22–31). The author of Proverbs may intend this as a literary device without any theological implications. Alternatively, wisdom may point to an early idea of the Godhead. See v. 22 and note. **Does not understanding raise her voice** See note on 1:20.
8:2 highest point along the way Refers to the high ground within a city.
8:3 gate leading into the city City gates consisted of a towered entrance and a large open area where people gathered, similar to a civic or community center. Citizens often conducted business there (compare Ru 4:1). **at the entrance** Refers to the outer opening of the gateway where people came and went. Wisdom cries aloud at this busy hub of the city where she can be readily heard. She raises her voice at locations within the city (Pr 8:2),

5 You who are simple, gain prudence;
     you who are foolish, set your hearts on it.[a]
6 Listen, for I have trustworthy things to say;
     I open my lips to speak what is right.
7 My mouth speaks what is true,
     for my lips detest wickedness.
8 All the words of my mouth are just;
     none of them is crooked or perverse.
9 To the discerning all of them are right;
     they are upright to those who have found
        knowledge.
10 Choose my instruction instead of silver,
     knowledge rather than choice gold,
11 for wisdom is more precious than rubies,
     and nothing you desire can compare
        with her.

12 "I, wisdom, dwell together with
        prudence;
     I possess knowledge and discretion.

13 To fear the LORD is to hate evil;
     I hate pride and arrogance,
     evil behavior and perverse speech.
14 Counsel and sound judgment are mine;
     I have insight, I have power.
15 By me kings reign
     and rulers issue decrees that are just;
16 by me princes govern,
     and nobles — all who rule on earth.[b]
17 I love those who love me,
     and those who seek me find me.
18 With me are riches and honor,
     enduring wealth and prosperity.
19 My fruit is better than fine gold;
     what I yield surpasses choice silver.
20 I walk in the way of righteousness,
     along the paths of justice,

a 5 Septuagint; Hebrew *foolish, instruct your minds*
b 16 Some Hebrew manuscripts and Septuagint; other Hebrew
manuscripts *all righteous rulers*

---

crying out at the city gates (v. 3). Wisdom preaches in two distinct areas, maximizing her opportunity for being heard. Her choice of locations highlights the importance of her message.
8:4 my voice to all mankind Wisdom calls to all of humanity. She exhorts her audience to pay close attention to her words three times in this chapter.
8:5 You who are simple The Hebrew word used here refers to people who are naïve and easily led astray. See note on 1:4. **you who are foolish** The fool is different from the simple person (compare note on 7:7; note on 1:4). It describes someone who not only is unable to follow instruction but actively rebels against it (10:23). See note on 1:7. **set your hearts on it** The Hebrew phrase used here, *havinu lev*, refers to understanding the heart. The ancient Israelites understood a person's heart to be the seat of cognition and memory.
8:6 open my lips to speak what is right Refers to being forthright and honest, having no veiled intention.
8:7 my lips detest wickedness Wise speech—that which true wisdom speaks—is incompatible with evil words (8:8; Job 6:30).
8:8 none of them is crooked or perverse Crookedness indicates falseness (see note on Pr 4:24). While honesty is straight and direct, dishonesty or deception is twisted or crooked. The wording describes the human condition (Job 5:13), which God must deal with. At times, God even uses deception to judge the wicked—answering the wicked by utilizing their own methods against them (2Sa 22:27; 1Sa 16:1–5; Jos 8:1–2).
8:9 they are upright to those who have found knowledge True knowledge results in straightness or right conduct.
8:10 my instruction The Hebrew word used here, *musar*, indicates correction or education. See note on Pr 1:2.
8:12 I, wisdom Wisdom is cast as a person or entity speaking in her own right. See note on 8:1. **prudence** The Hebrew word used here refers to cunning. See note on 1:4. **knowledge** The Hebrew word used here, *da'ath*, refers to a broad range of things that can be known, including the acquisition and retention of specific facts, assertions or concepts (which can be either good or evil; compare Ge 2:9). It can also refer more generally to God's instructions for living (Isa 58:2; Job 21:14). **discre-**

tion** The Hebrew word used here, *mezimmah*, describes shrewdness or skills of perception. It is also paired with *da'ath* ("knowledge") in Pr 1:4 (see note on 1:4).
8:13 To fear the LORD Wisdom does not stand alone. It is closely connected with fearing Yahweh, which means having a proper attitude of respect for him and obedience to him. See note on 1:7. **pride and arrogance** Pride is a characteristic of the fool (12:15) and scoffer (21:24). **evil behavior** Refers to a disposition; wisdom rejects evil dispositions or behaviors. The wise do not exhibit an evil disposition. See 8:20. **perverse speech** The Hebrew phrase used here describes speech that is dishonest or wicked.
8:14 Counsel Refers to advice or sound planning. **sound judgment** Refers to resourcefulness or competence. **I have insight** Refers to keen understanding and discernment. See note on 1:2.
8:15–16 A wise ruler governs with justice. He righteously judges the wicked (see 20:8 and note) and has his throne established (16:12; 20:28). In contrast, a foolish king is a burden to his people (see 28:16 and note). Ultimately, the king's heart is directed by Yahweh (21:1).
8:17 those who seek me Both statements in this verse aim to motivate the reader to seek wisdom (compare 8:18–19). The vocabulary of love suggests that in the pursuit of wisdom, there is a need not just for an emotional commitment, not just a pragmatic vision. Its attainment therefore involves heartfelt satisfaction.
8:18 enduring wealth and prosperity The pairings in this verse speak of honorable wealth. While unprincipled people may possess certain characteristics of wisdom, their wealth is not the kind described here because it lacks honor (see v. 20). Wealth and power are neither indications of the kind of wisdom God desires, nor are they necessarily indications of divine blessing. The writer avoids blessing wealth for its own sake.
8:19 My fruit is better than fine gold Wisdom is often depicted as preferable to gold or other precious metals (3:14–15).
8:20 I walk Indicates a habitual activity. **paths of justice** The Hebrew word used here, *mishpat*, refers to a fair ruling or decision. It is associated with truth and righteousness. See note on 1:3.

²¹ bestowing a rich inheritance on those who
love me
and making their treasuries full.

²² "The LORD brought me forth as the first of
his works,ᵃ,ᵇ
before his deeds of old;
²³ I was formed long ages ago,
at the very beginning, when the world
came to be.
²⁴ When there were no watery depths, I was
given birth,
when there were no springs overflowing
with water;
²⁵ before the mountains were settled in place,
before the hills, I was given birth,
²⁶ before he made the world or its fields
or any of the dust of the earth.

²⁷ I was there when he set the heavens in place,
when he marked out the horizon on the
face of the deep,
²⁸ when he established the clouds above
and fixed securely the fountains of the
deep,
²⁹ when he gave the sea its boundary
so the waters would not overstep his
command,
and when he marked out the foundations of
the earth.
³⁰ Then I was constantlyᶜ at his side.
I was filled with delight day after day,
rejoicing always in his presence,

ᵃ 22 Or way; or dominion   ᵇ 22 Or The LORD possessed me at
the beginning of his work; or The LORD brought me forth at the
beginning of his work   ᶜ 30 Or was the artisan; or was a little
child

8:21 making their treasuries full Wisdom promises rewards of permanence and continuity across generations (13:22). See note on 3:2.

8:22 brought me forth The Hebrew word used here, *qanah*, has a wide range of meanings. It can describe buying (Ge 47:22; Ex 21:2; Pr 20:14), acquiring (Ru 4:8; Isa 11:11; Ps 78:54; Pr 1:5; 4:5,7), bringing forth or giving birth (Ge 4:1) and creating (Ge 14:19,22; Dt 32:6; Ps 139:13). However *qanah* is understood here, it is clear that wisdom is being utilized at the beginning of the world. **as the first of his works** If the Hebrew word *qanah* in the previous line is taken as "created," this line refers to wisdom as God's first act of creation, before all other things. But if the word *qanah* is understood as "brought forth," this line portrays wisdom as an instrument of God during creation. Wisdom then would be the first primary instrument used in the act of creation and preexistent before the world (compare 8:23–24). This second interpretation aligns well with the NT depiction of Jesus as the agent of creation (Col 1:16; 1Co 8:6) who is referred to as "the wisdom of God" (1Co 1:24,30; compare Mt 23:29–36; Lk 11:45–52; Heb 1:1–3).

8:23 I was formed The Hebrew word used here could be related to the Hebrew verb *nasakh* or *sakhakh*. If it is related to *nasakh*, then the Hebrew text could indicate that wisdom was put in place or established, not created. Psalm 2:6 uses the verb *nasakh* when it refers to God putting in place a king — God does not create the king in that moment, but instead selects him and puts him in his place as ruler. If Proverbs is using the verb *sakhakh* here then it seems that this refers to the weaving together, fashioning or forming of wisdom, before the world existed. In Ps 139:13 God forms (*qanah*) and knits together (*sakhakh*) a baby in the mother's womb (compare Job 10:11). Under both interpretations, the point of this line is that wisdom played a critical role during the creation of the world. **ages ago** Wisdom has existed for a very long time — this could even imply that wisdom has always existed. **when the world came** The interpretation of this phrase depends on how the first part of this verse and 8:22 is understood. This line could be understood as referring to wisdom being created and put together before the creation of the earth — as the first act of creation (see note on v. 22). It could also refer to wisdom as the agent of the creation of the world. The NT picks up on this language when it depicts Jesus as personified wisdom, who was preexistent with God the

Father before the creation of the world; it is through Jesus that creation comes to be (see Jn 1:1–18 and note).

8:24 depths The Hebrew word used here alludes to the beginning of God's creative activity in Ge 1:2. **I was given birth** The Hebrew word used here, *chil*, can indicate bringing forth or being in labor. The interpretation of this phrase, which also occurs in Pr 8:25, is affected by the interpretation of the vocabulary of vv. 22–23. Either way this verse is understood, it indicates that wisdom existed before the world.

8:26 before he made This language alludes to the description of creation in Ge 1, once again indicating that wisdom was there before creation took place.

8:27 I was there Wisdom is cast as a person or entity speaking in her own right (see v. 1 and note). She says that she was present with God when he established the heavens. **when he set the heavens in place** Refers to God's creative act in Ge 1:1 (compare Pr 1:6–10). See the infographic "The Days of Creation" on p. 6. **he marked out the horizon** Describes the visible horizon line — the place where the sun rises and sets (compare Job 26:10). This language reflects the ancient Near Eastern belief that the horizon line, where the ocean and sky meet, is the start of a solid dome that surrounds the skies and holds in place the waters above the skies (8:28–29; compare Ge 1:6 and note). See the infographic "Ancient Hebrew Conception of the Universe" on p. 5.

8:28 he established the clouds above People in the ancient Near East believed that above the skies was a solid dome covering the earth. This phrase either refers to the area above the dome (or firmament) or to the dome itself. **fountains of the deep** This reflects the ancient Near Eastern belief that there were foundations or pillars holding up a firmament (or dome) between the skies and the waters above them. See Ge 7:11 and note.

8:29 waters would not overstep his command Conveys the ancient Near Eastern belief that the waters are stopped at the horizon by the barrier, the dome or firmament, that God put in place and that they could not go past it (compare Ge 1:6). Waters, like the seas and oceans, were a symbol of chaos in the ancient Near East; Yahweh's ultimate power is shown by his ability to simply speak and put chaos under his jurisdiction. **foundations of the earth** People in the ancient Near East believed the earth stood on foundations that went down to the depths of the waters below. See note on Job 38:4.

8:30 at his side Wisdom explicitly claims she was pres-

³¹ rejoicing in his whole world
    and delighting in mankind.
³² "Now then, my children, listen to me;
    blessed are those who keep my ways.
³³ Listen to my instruction and be wise;
    do not disregard it.
³⁴ Blessed are those who listen to me,
    watching daily at my doors,
    waiting at my doorway.
³⁵ For those who find me find life
    and receive favor from the Lᴏʀᴅ.
³⁶ But those who fail to find me harm themselves;
    all who hate me love death."

Invitations of Wisdom and Folly

9 Wisdom has built her house;
    she has set up*ᵃ* its seven pillars.
² She has prepared her meat and mixed her
    wine;
    she has also set her table.
³ She has sent out her servants, and she calls
    from the highest point of the city,
⁴ "Let all who are simple come to my house!"
    To those who have no sense she says,

⁵ "Come, eat my food
    and drink the wine I have mixed.
⁶ Leave your simple ways and you will live;
    walk in the way of insight."

⁷ Whoever corrects a mocker invites insults;
    whoever rebukes the wicked incurs abuse.
⁸ Do not rebuke mockers or they will hate you;
    rebuke the wise and they will love you.
⁹ Instruct the wise and they will be wiser still;
    teach the righteous and they will add to
    their learning.

¹⁰ The fear of the Lᴏʀᴅ is the beginning of
    wisdom,
    and knowledge of the Holy One is
    understanding.
¹¹ For through wisdom*ᵇ* your days will be many,
    and years will be added to your life.
¹² If you are wise, your wisdom will reward you;
    if you are a mocker, you alone will suffer.

¹³ Folly is an unruly woman;
    she is simple and knows nothing.

ᵃ 1 Septuagint, Syriac and Targum; Hebrew *has hewn out*
ᵇ 11 Septuagint, Syriac and Targum; Hebrew *me*

---

ent with God when heaven and earth were created. This parallels Jesus being present at creation (see Jn 1:1 and note; note on 1:2). **rejoicing always in his presence** The Hebrew word used here indicates playing or frolicking in a way that causes merriment for those watching. The word refers to things that give God amusement, such as creation (Ps 104:31) or the Leviathan (Ps 104:26). **8:31 delighting in mankind** The Hebrew phrase used here could be understood as wisdom finding delight in humankind, or humankind finding delight in wisdom. It is more likely that wisdom is finding delight in humanity since this strikes a parallel: Just as God is delighted by wisdom, wisdom is delighted by humanity.
8:34 Blessed are those who listen to me Proverbs ascribes blessings as coming to those who are wise. See note on Pr 3:2.
8:35 those who find me Life is the reward for those who pursue wisdom (compare 3:18; 4:22). This probably indicates a fullness of life, as it is life according to God's ways. **favor** The person who seeks to do good is pleasing to Yahweh (see note on 12:2).
8:36 those who fail to find me harm themselves Choosing to reject wisdom is portrayed as self-destructive (compare 15:32). **all who hate me love death** Rejecting wisdom can ultimately result in death (14:12; 16:25; 21:6), whereas righteousness and wisdom can save from death (14:27,32).

9:1–18 In ch. 9, wisdom and folly offer competing feasts. In the first section, wisdom prepares for the feast (vv. 1–6). She sets the table and sends out women to invite the simple people, encouraging them to come, feast and learn to walk with insight (see note on 7:7; note on 1:4). Wisdom then compares the reactions of the scoffer and the wise to reproof and instruction (9:7–12). The final section parallels the first, as folly prepares a feast (vv. 13–18). She loudly calls to whomever passes by, inviting the simple people, who unknowingly enter the realm of the dead.

9:1 Wisdom has built her house Wisdom is presented as industrious and hard working. In contrast, folly merely sits at the door of her house (vv. 13–14). **seven** Symbolic of perfection or completeness.
9:2 She has prepared her meat The Hebrew phrase used here does not designate any specific animal but does indicate preparation for a feast (Ge 43:16). **mixed her wine** Sometimes spices were added to wine to improve its taste (SS 8:2). The banquet of wisdom is far more appealing than the water and bread offered by folly (Pr 9:17).
9:3 She has sent out her servants Wisdom sends out female servants to invite people to come to her banquet. This description resembles Jesus' parable of the wedding feast (Mt 22:1–14).
9:4 all who are simple Wisdom invites the simple person and the person who lacks sense to come learn. See note on Pr 1:4.
9:7 Whoever corrects a mocker In Proverbs, scoffers refuse correction. Their arrogance (21:24) prevents them from obtaining wisdom (14:6). See note on 1:22.
9:8 rebuke the wise In contrast to the scoffer, the wise person accepts rebuke. Throughout Proverbs, the wise person exhibits wisdom by humbly looking to increase in wisdom (12:15; 21:11).
9:10 fear of the Lᴏʀᴅ Reverence for Yahweh. See note on 1:7.
9:11 years will be added to your life In Proverbs, one reward for wisdom is long life. See note on 3:2.
9:12 your wisdom will reward you Elsewhere, wisdom and folly are said to affect others (10:1). This passage emphasizes the responsibility of the individual to accept or reject wisdom. The verse essentially warns that rejecting reproof occurs at one's own peril.
9:13 Folly is an unruly woman Here, folly resembles the adulteress of 7:11. Quietness is characteristic of the wise because strife and arguing often accompany loudness (17:1; 29:9). **simple** The Hebrew word used here, *pethayyuth*, only occurs here in the OT. It is likely related to the Hebrew word *pethi* ("simple"; see note on 1:4).

¹⁴ She sits at the door of her house,
   on a seat at the highest point of the city,
¹⁵ calling out to those who pass by,
   who go straight on their way,
¹⁶ "Let all who are simple come to my house!"
   To those who have no sense she says,
¹⁷ "Stolen water is sweet;
   food eaten in secret is delicious!"
¹⁸ But little do they know that the dead are there,
   that her guests are deep in the realm of the
   dead.

Proverbs of Solomon

10 The proverbs of Solomon:

A wise son brings joy to his father,
   but a foolish son brings grief to his mother.

² Ill-gotten treasures have no lasting value,
   but righteousness delivers from death.

³ The LORD does not let the righteous go
      hungry,
   but he thwarts the craving of the wicked.

⁴ Lazy hands make for poverty,
   but diligent hands bring wealth.

⁵ He who gathers crops in summer is a
      prudent son,
   but he who sleeps during harvest is a
      disgraceful son.

⁶ Blessings crown the head of the righteous,
   but violence overwhelms the mouth of the
      wicked.ᵃ

⁷ The name of the righteous is used in
      blessings,ᵇ
   but the name of the wicked will rot.

⁸ The wise in heart accept commands,
   but a chattering fool comes to ruin.

⁹ Whoever walks in integrity walks securely,
   but whoever takes crooked paths will be
      found out.

¹⁰ Whoever winks maliciously causes grief,
   and a chattering fool comes to ruin.

¹¹ The mouth of the righteous is a fountain
      of life,
   but the mouth of the wicked conceals
      violence.

¹² Hatred stirs up conflict,
   but love covers over all wrongs.

¹³ Wisdom is found on the lips of the discerning,
   but a rod is for the back of one who has
      no sense.

¹⁴ The wise store up knowledge,
   but the mouth of a fool invites ruin.

ᵃ 6 Or *righteous, / but the mouth of the wicked conceals violence*
ᵇ 7 See Gen. 48:20.

9:14 sits at the door of her house The picture of folly contrasts with that of wisdom. See note on 9:1.
9:16 all who are simple Folly's invitation is the same as wisdom's. See note on v. 4.
9:17 Stolen water is sweet Possibly a euphemism for forbidden sexual relations. See 5:15 and note.
9:18 little do they know The simple person ignorantly follows after folly, not realizing where it leads (7:21–23; see note on 1:4). **the dead are there** Proverbs consistently presents death as the consequences of folly (5:5; 7:27). See note on 3:2.

10:1—22:16 Proverbs 10:1—22:16 is a collection of short sayings that are often clustered together to treat particular topics, such as wealth and poverty (10:12–18), speech (11:9–12), diligence and sloth (12:24–28), and pride and humility (15:25–33).

10:1 The proverbs of Solomon See note on 1:1. **A wise son brings joy to his father** A recurring theme in Proverbs (15:20; 17:21; 23:15). A person's wisdom or folly affects their parents. The wise son pursues righteousness and keeps the law (23:24; 28:7), while the foolish son engages in immorality and violence (19:26; 29:3).

10:2–3 These two proverbs uphold the value of righteousness over wickedness. The first proverb states that while the wicked may obtain wealth, it ultimately does not profit them. Instead, righteousness—not earthly wealth—protects a person's life. The second proverb asserts that Yahweh protects the righteous.

10:2 righteousness delivers from death See note on 3:2.

10:3 thwarts The Hebrew word used here indicates pushing (Dt 6:19). Yahweh pushes away the things desired by the wicked.
10:5 he who sleeps during harvest Indicates laziness. Like the foolish son (Pr 10:1), the lazy son also brings shame to his parents.
10:8 wise in heart accept commands Describes obedience, a characteristic of the wise. **a chattering fool** The Hebrew expression used here literally means "foolish lips." The fool's lips (speech) are depicted as the cause of the fool's trouble throughout Proverbs (14:3; 18:6).
10:9 integrity The Hebrew word used here, *tom*, indicates purity or innocence (2Sa 22:24). Those who walk with integrity do what is right both outwardly and inwardly (compare Ps 15:2 and note). Walking with integrity is to be preferred over riches (Pr 19:1; 28:6). Those who walk with integrity walk securely because Yahweh protects them (2:7). This does not mean they will never encounter trouble; Job, a man of integrity, experienced much suffering (see Job 1:1 and note). Instead, this statement expresses confidence that God protects those who walk blamelessly (see note on Pr 3:2).
10:10 Whoever winks maliciously The exact meaning of this gesture is unknown. It is likely an indication of deceitfulness. See note on 6:13.
10:12 love covers over all wrongs The Hebrew word used here, *kasah*, indicates covering (Ge 7:19) or concealing (Pr 10:11). It can also refer to forgiving (Ps 32:1; 85:2).
10:14 store up knowledge The Hebrew word used here, *tsaphan*, means "to store" (Pr 2:7), indicating the wise have an abundance of knowledge (*da'ath*, see note on 1:4).

15 The wealth of the rich is their fortified city,
  but poverty is the ruin of the poor.

16 The wages of the righteous is life,
  but the earnings of the wicked are sin and
    death.

17 Whoever heeds discipline shows the way to
    life,
  but whoever ignores correction leads
    others astray.

18 Whoever conceals hatred with lying lips
  and spreads slander is a fool.

19 Sin is not ended by multiplying words,
  but the prudent hold their tongues.

20 The tongue of the righteous is choice silver,
  but the heart of the wicked is of little
    value.

21 The lips of the righteous nourish many,
  but fools die for lack of sense.

22 The blessing of the LORD brings wealth,
  without painful toil for it.

23 A fool finds pleasure in wicked schemes,
  but a person of understanding delights in
    wisdom.

24 What the wicked dread will overtake them;
  what the righteous desire will be granted.

25 When the storm has swept by, the wicked are
    gone,
  but the righteous stand firm forever.

26 As vinegar to the teeth and smoke to the eyes,
  so are sluggards to those who send them.

27 The fear of the LORD adds length to life,
  but the years of the wicked are cut short.

28 The prospect of the righteous is joy,
  but the hopes of the wicked come to
    nothing.

29 The way of the LORD is a refuge for the
    blameless,
  but it is the ruin of those who do evil.

30 The righteous will never be uprooted,
  but the wicked will not remain in the land.

31 From the mouth of the righteous comes the
    fruit of wisdom,
  but a perverse tongue will be silenced.

32 The lips of the righteous know what finds
    favor,
  but the mouth of the wicked only what is
    perverse.

11 The LORD detests dishonest scales,
  but accurate weights find favor with him.

2 When pride comes, then comes disgrace,
  but with humility comes wisdom.

3 The integrity of the upright guides them,
  but the unfaithful are destroyed by their
    duplicity.

4 Wealth is worthless in the day of wrath,
  but righteousness delivers from death.

5 The righteousness of the blameless makes
    their paths straight,
  but the wicked are brought down by their
    own wickedness.

6 The righteousness of the upright delivers
    them,
  but the unfaithful are trapped by evil
    desires.

10:18 Whoever conceals hatred In 10:12, the Hebrew word used here, *kasah*, was used with the sense of "to forgive." Here, it is used with the more deceptive sense of "to conceal." The person described here tries to hide hatred.

10:19 by multiplying words Restraint in speech is advocated throughout Proverbs. While a fool's speech leads to ruin (18:6–7), keeping quiet can help avoid trouble (21:23). A fool's silence may even make the fool seem wise (17:28).

10:22 The blessing of the LORD brings wealth This does not mean that wealth always accompanies wise or righteous people, or that possessing wealth always indicates wisdom and righteousness. Elsewhere, Proverbs warns against seeking wealth (23:4; 28:20). Here, riches represent a blessing from God because God serves as the source of all things—both good and bad (1Sa 2:7; Job 2:10). See note on Pr 3:2.

10:23 A fool finds pleasure The Hebrew word used here, *sechoq*, indicates laughter (Job 8:21; Ps 126:2). The fool finds enjoyment in doing wrong. In contrast, the wise person finds pleasure in wisdom.

10:27 fear of the LORD adds length to life Proverbs consistently holds up long life as a blessing for those

who have reverence for Yahweh. See note on Pr 1:7; and see note on 3:2.

10:30 the land Can refer to Israel specifically or the earth in general. See 2:21–22 and note.

11:1 dishonest scales Dishonest scales were prohibited by the law (Lev 19:35–36; Dt 25:13–16). Merchants used weights to measure out money or produce. Dishonest merchants used faulty scales or weights to cheat their customers. This practice was prohibited by the law and condemned by the prophets (Am 8:5; Mic 6:11) because it was used to oppress the impoverished (Hos 12:7).

11:2 pride comes Arrogance is a trait of the fool (Pr 12:15; 21:24).

11:3–9 These proverbs contrast the security enjoyed by the righteous with the inevitable destruction of the wicked. The righteous enjoy deliverance from trouble (v. 8) and have security because of their integrity (v. 3), righteousness (vv. 5–6) and wisdom (v. 9). In contrast, the wicked's actions ultimately lead to destruction, because of their perverseness (v. 3), overall wickedness (v. 5) and lust (v. 6). Instead of avoiding trouble, the wicked walk into it (v. 8). Riches cannot preserve the wicked (v. 4); when they die, their hope and wealth die with them (v. 6).

[7] Hopes placed in mortals die with them;
all the promise of[a] their power comes to
nothing.

[8] The righteous person is rescued from
trouble,
and it falls on the wicked instead.

[9] With their mouths the godless destroy their
neighbors,
but through knowledge the righteous
escape.

[10] When the righteous prosper, the city rejoices;
when the wicked perish, there are shouts
of joy.

[11] Through the blessing of the upright a city is
exalted,
but by the mouth of the wicked it is
destroyed.

[12] Whoever derides their neighbor has no sense,
but the one who has understanding holds
their tongue.

[13] A gossip betrays a confidence,
but a trustworthy person keeps a secret.

[14] For lack of guidance a nation falls,
but victory is won through many advisers.

[15] Whoever puts up security for a stranger will
surely suffer,
but whoever refuses to shake hands in
pledge is safe.

[16] A kindhearted woman gains honor,
but ruthless men gain only wealth.

[17] Those who are kind benefit themselves,
but the cruel bring ruin on themselves.

[18] A wicked person earns deceptive wages,
but the one who sows righteousness reaps
a sure reward.

[19] Truly the righteous attain life,
but whoever pursues evil finds death.

[20] The LORD detests those whose hearts are
perverse,
but he delights in those whose ways are
blameless.

[21] Be sure of this: The wicked will not go
unpunished,
but those who are righteous will go free.

[22] Like a gold ring in a pig's snout
is a beautiful woman who shows no
discretion.

[23] The desire of the righteous ends only in good,
but the hope of the wicked only in wrath.

[24] One person gives freely, yet gains even more;
another withholds unduly, but comes to
poverty.

[25] A generous person will prosper;
whoever refreshes others will be refreshed.

[26] People curse the one who hoards grain,
but they pray God's blessing on the one
who is willing to sell.

[a] 7 Two Hebrew manuscripts; most Hebrew manuscripts,
Vulgate, Syriac and Targum *When the wicked die, their hope
perishes; / all they expected from*

11:9 through knowledge the righteous escape
Knowledge (see note on 1:4) helps the righteous get
themselves out of trouble created by the godless person.

11:10–11 These proverbs describe reactions to the fate
of the righteous and the wicked. The whole city rejoices
when the righteous prosper; they also rejoice when the
wicked perish. Verse 11 offers the reason for these
reactions: The righteous bring blessing to the city, while
the wicked destroy it. The righteous are characterized
by justice and fairness (1:3; 21:15; 29:4), while the
wicked are characterized by violence and oppression
(4:17; 17:23; 21:10).

11:12 one who has understanding holds their tongue
Like the prudent (10:19; compare 1:3 and note), those
with understanding wisely restrain their speech (compare 11:9).

11:14 For lack of guidance Can refer to either guidance
or strategy. Compare 1:5, where the book promises its
reader guidance.

11:15 Whoever puts up security for a stranger
Proverbs 6:1–5 warns against putting up security for a
neighbor (see note on 6:1).

11:16 but ruthless men gain only wealth This could
be viewed as contradicting other statements about wealth
(10:22; 14:24), but Proverbs never denies that the wicked
can obtain wealth. Instead, Proverbs shows that a proper

attitude of righteousness and humility is preferable to
wealth—especially wealth earned through injustice or
wickedness (16:8, 16:19; 28:6).

11:18 deceptive wages Wealth obtained by the wicked
(11:16) does not last (v. 4). In contrast, the righteous
obtain a wage that leads to life, characterized by a relationship with God (10:16).

11:21 The wicked will not go unpunished The ultimate punishment of the wicked is referenced throughout
Proverbs (10:30; 12:7). These references serve as expressions of faith in God's justice (compare Ecc 8:13).

11:22 a gold ring in a pig's snout A metaphor of
mismatched things. The matching of the gold ring and
the pig is paired with the remainder of the proverb about
a beautiful woman without discretion. The pig could
represent the beautiful woman who lacks good sense.
However, in the structure of the metaphor, the gold
ring may represent the woman, while the pig is the one
wearing her—that is, her husband. Rather than having a
wife who is his crown (Pr 12:4), he has an empty-headed
wife who makes him look foolish. Either interpretation
admonishes men to choose prudent wives.

11:24 yet gains Rather than a promise that generosity
will yield financial profit, this verse reflects the general
principle that kindness or stinginess will be reciprocated
(11:26). See note on 3:2.

²⁷ Whoever seeks good finds favor,
but evil comes to one who searches for it.

²⁸ Those who trust in their riches will fall,
but the righteous will thrive like a green
leaf.

²⁹ Whoever brings ruin on their family will
inherit only wind,
and the fool will be servant to the wise.

³⁰ The fruit of the righteous is a tree of life,
and the one who is wise saves lives.

³¹ If the righteous receive their due on earth,
how much more the ungodly and the
sinner!

12 Whoever loves discipline loves
knowledge,
but whoever hates correction is stupid.

² Good people obtain favor from the LORD,
but he condemns those who devise wicked
schemes.

³ No one can be established through
wickedness,
but the righteous cannot be uprooted.

⁴ A wife of noble character is her husband's
crown,
but a disgraceful wife is like decay in his
bones.

⁵ The plans of the righteous are just,
but the advice of the wicked is deceitful.

⁶ The words of the wicked lie in wait for blood,
but the speech of the upright rescues them.

⁷ The wicked are overthrown and are no more,
but the house of the righteous stands firm.

⁸ A person is praised according to their
prudence,
and one with a warped mind is despised.

⁹ Better to be a nobody and yet have a servant
than pretend to be somebody and have no
food.

¹⁰ The righteous care for the needs of their
animals,
but the kindest acts of the wicked are
cruel.

¹¹ Those who work their land will have
abundant food,
but those who chase fantasies have no
sense.

¹² The wicked desire the stronghold of
evildoers,
but the root of the righteous endures.

¹³ Evildoers are trapped by their sinful talk,
and so the innocent escape trouble.

¹⁴ From the fruit of their lips people are filled
with good things,
and the work of their hands brings them
reward.

¹⁵ The way of fools seems right to them,
but the wise listen to advice.

11:27 evil comes to one who searches for it The person who goes looking for trouble (*ra'ah*; see note on 3:29) will find it.

11:28 will thrive like a green leaf An image of prosperity. Elsewhere, the righteous are compared to a stable and fruitful tree (Ps 1:3; Jer 17:8).

11:30 fruit of the righteous is a tree of life Earlier, wisdom was called a tree of life. See Pr 3:18 and note.

12:1 Whoever loves discipline loves knowledge The wise love discipline because it increases their knowledge (9:8; 21:11). **stupid** The Hebrew term used here, *ba'ar*, refers to someone who hates correction. This term only occurs twice in Proverbs (see 30:2–3). It seems to refer to someone who despises discipline and so lacks wisdom and knowledge, especially about God. The hatred of reproof can ultimately lead to death (15:10). In Psalms, the stupid person is depicted as lacking understanding about Yahweh's works (Ps 92:5–7).

12:2 favor The Hebrew word used here refers to what is pleasing or acceptable (Pr 10:32; 11:1). The person who seeks to do good is pleasing to Yahweh (11:27).

12:3 No one can be established through wickedness Rather than claiming that wicked people cannot prosper, this principle points to the preference of righteousness over wickedness and expresses a belief in the ultimate judgment of the wicked (compare 11:21 and note). Elsewhere in Proverbs, Yahweh establishes people's steps (16:9).

12:4 A wife of noble character The Hebrew phrase

used here, referring to an excellent wife or a woman of character, is used to describe Ruth (Ru 3:11). Compare Pr 31:10 and note.

12:9 and yet have a servant The Hebrew text here could be understood as speaking about a servant or a person working for himself. Either way, the proverb asserts that it is better to live humbly but comfortably than to make a false, superficial show of wealth.

12:10 animals The Hebrew term used here generally refers to domestic animals (Lev 25:7; 2Ki 3:17). While the righteous care for their animals, the wicked act cruelly even when they attempt to be merciful or compassionate.

12:11 Those who work their land Hard work is a characteristic of the wise throughout Proverbs (Pr 10:5); laziness is a characteristic of the fool (24:30–34).

12:12 the root of the righteous endures This verse contrasts the covetousness of the wicked with the productivity (or endurance) of the righteous.

12:13 by their sinful talk The wicked are caught by their own speech. This may indicate someone being caught in a lie or falling victim to their own rash or foolish words (1Sa 25:10–13). Foolish or sinful speech ultimately harms the speaker (Pr 18:7; Ps 64:8). **innocent escape trouble** Rather than claiming that the righteous never encounter trouble, this phrase indicates that the righteous avoid the trouble that comes to the person who lies or speaks foolishly.

12:15 wise listen to advice This contrasts with the stupid person, who hates correction. See note on Pr 12:1.

[16] Fools show their annoyance at once,
  but the prudent overlook an insult.

[17] An honest witness tells the truth,
  but a false witness tells lies.

[18] The words of the reckless pierce like swords,
  but the tongue of the wise brings healing.

[19] Truthful lips endure forever,
  but a lying tongue lasts only a moment.

[20] Deceit is in the hearts of those who plot evil,
  but those who promote peace have joy.

[21] No harm overtakes the righteous,
  but the wicked have their fill of trouble.

[22] The LORD detests lying lips,
  but he delights in people who are
  trustworthy.

[23] The prudent keep their knowledge to
  themselves,
  but a fool's heart blurts out folly.

[24] Diligent hands will rule,
  but laziness ends in forced labor.

[25] Anxiety weighs down the heart,
  but a kind word cheers it up.

[26] The righteous choose their friends carefully,
  but the way of the wicked leads them
  astray.

[27] The lazy do not roast[a] any game,
  but the diligent feed on the riches of the
  hunt.

[28] In the way of righteousness there is life;
  along that path is immortality.

13 A wise son heeds his father's instruction,
  but a mocker does not respond to
  rebukes.

[2] From the fruit of their lips people enjoy good
  things,
  but the unfaithful have an appetite for
  violence.

[3] Those who guard their lips preserve their
  lives,
  but those who speak rashly will come to
  ruin.

[4] A sluggard's appetite is never filled,
  but the desires of the diligent are fully
  satisfied.

[5] The righteous hate what is false,
  but the wicked make themselves a stench
  and bring shame on themselves.

[6] Righteousness guards the person of integrity,
  but wickedness overthrows the sinner.

[7] One person pretends to be rich, yet has
  nothing;
  another pretends to be poor, yet has great
  wealth.

[8] A person's riches may ransom their life,
  but the poor cannot respond to threatening
  rebukes.

[9] The light of the righteous shines brightly,
  but the lamp of the wicked is snuffed out.

[10] Where there is strife, there is pride,
  but wisdom is found in those who take
  advice.

[11] Dishonest money dwindles away,
  but whoever gathers money little by little
  makes it grow.

[12] Hope deferred makes the heart sick,
  but a longing fulfilled is a tree of life.

[a] 27 The meaning of the Hebrew for this word is uncertain.

12:16 overlook This may refer to forgiving an offense or to overlooking the offense completely. **insult** The Hebrew word used here, *qalon*, often refers to shame or disgrace. Elsewhere, disgrace accompanies pride (11:2), wickedness (18:3) and an arrogant refusal to heed instruction (13:18).

12:18 pierce like swords Emphasizes the potential damage of speech. This may indicate those who speak without thinking (Lev 5:4), damaging both themselves and others. Elsewhere, a false accusation is compared to a sword (Pr 25:18). The speech of the forbidden woman is also compared to a sword (5:3–4).

12:24 Diligent hands will rule The benefit of hard work is emphasized throughout Proverbs. The diligent person becomes wealthy (10:4; 12:27). The diligent person's life is abundantly supplied (13:4; 21:5). Here, hard work puts the diligent person in a position of authority over the lazy person.

12:26 leads them astray The ways of both the righteous and the wicked influence those whom they associate with. See note on 11:10–11.

13:1 A wise son heeds his father's instruction See note on 1:8; 1:8—9:18. **a mocker does not respond to rebukes** See 1:22; 12:1 and note.

13:3 Those who guard their lips preserve their lives Restraint in speech is a recurring theme in Proverbs. See note on 10:19.

13:4 A sluggard's appetite This phrase describes someone who refuses to work (20:4). The sluggard looks for excuses to stay in bed and ends up in poverty (26:13–14; 10:4). See note on 6:9.

13:8 A person's riches may ransom their life The rich may be able to buy their way out of trouble, using their wealth to protect themselves. But the impoverished have far fewer concerns because they have nothing worth protecting.

13:9 light A metaphor for life and the quality of life (compare Job 18:5–6). The lamp carries the same connotation. The righteous rejoice, while the wicked die prematurely (compare Job 18:18; Ecc 6:4).

13:12 Hope deferred Hope can be negative or positive depending on who is doing the hoping (Pr 10:28; 11:7).

¹³ Whoever scorns instruction will pay for it,
  but whoever respects a command is
    rewarded.

¹⁴ The teaching of the wise is a fountain of life,
  turning a person from the snares of death.

¹⁵ Good judgment wins favor,
  but the way of the unfaithful leads to their
    destruction.ᵃ

¹⁶ All who are prudent act withᵇ knowledge,
  but fools expose their folly.

¹⁷ A wicked messenger falls into trouble,
  but a trustworthy envoy brings healing.

¹⁸ Whoever disregards discipline comes to
    poverty and shame,
  but whoever heeds correction is honored.

¹⁹ A longing fulfilled is sweet to the soul,
  but fools detest turning from evil.

²⁰ Walk with the wise and become wise,
  for a companion of fools suffers harm.

²¹ Trouble pursues the sinner,
  but the righteous are rewarded with good
    things.

²² A good person leaves an inheritance for their
    children's children,
  but a sinner's wealth is stored up for the
    righteous.

²³ An unplowed field produces food for the
    poor,
  but injustice sweeps it away.

²⁴ Whoever spares the rod hates their
    children,
  but the one who loves their children is
    careful to discipline them.

²⁵ The righteous eat to their hearts'
    content,
  but the stomach of the wicked goes
    hungry.

14 The wise woman builds her house,
  but with her own hands the foolish one
    tears hers down.

² Whoever fears the LORD walks uprightly,
  but those who despise him are devious in
    their ways.

ᵃ 15 Septuagint and Syriac; the meaning of the Hebrew for this phrase is uncertain. ᵇ 16 Or *prudent protect themselves through*

Here, it speaks to the discouragement people feel when their hopes are frustrated. **a longing fulfilled** Like hopes, desires can be negative or positive. The desire of the sluggard ends in the sluggard's death (21:25), while the desire of the righteous results in good (11:23). The fulfilling of desire is a refreshing encouragement (13:19). **a tree of life** A symbol of renewal and life. See note on 3:18.

13:13 command The Hebrew word used here, *mitswah*, can refer to the law (Ex 24:12), but in Proverbs it typically refers to wisdom teaching in general (Pr 2:1; 3:1; 4:4; 6:20). The commandments serve as protection from sin (6:23–24). Benefits for keeping the commandments can include a long and peaceful life (see 3:2 and note).

13:14 teaching Wisdom Literature uses the Hebrew word *torah* to refer simply to instruction or teaching, not the Law (i.e., the Pentateuch) or legal stipulations. **a fountain of life** A source of life for the wise and those who learn from them.

13:16 All who are prudent act with knowledge The prudent person is clever and acts intelligently (see note on 1:4; compare 12:23; 22:3; 27:12).

13:18 whoever heeds correction is honored Acceptance of discipline or reproof is a trait of the wise person. See note on 12:1.

13:19 turning from evil Implies a rejection of wickedness and a pursuit of good (Ps 34:14). The fool enjoys evil (Pr 10:23).

13:20 become wise Like the righteous, the wise bless those around them (see 12:26 and note). In contrast, those who associate with fools experience harm.

13:21 Trouble pursues the sinner In 11:27, evil comes to the person who searches for it. Here, the sinner does not search for evil, but evil or disaster pursues the sinner. Disaster can refer to the practical results of sin or folly (12:13; 18:6) or to the ultimate punishment (11:21).

13:23 injustice sweeps it away Suggests that at least in some cases, poverty results from injustice. Poverty can also result from laziness (6:9–11).

13:24 Whoever spares the rod hates their children Proverbs emphasizes the importance of discipline, viewing it as a matter of life or death (19:18; 23:13–14). Since children are characterized by folly in Proverbs (22:15), proper training and discipline ensure they will remain on the right path throughout their lives (22:6). In Wisdom Literature, broad statements and intentional exaggerations are often chosen for effect and memorability. Thus, it's possible to read this verse as hyperbolic (hence the mention of hating), stressing the idea of discipline and not necessarily physical punishment.

In its original, ancient Near Eastern context, Proverbs was probably understood as advocating for physical discipline of children (22:15; 23:13), but it seems to only do so for times when discipline by teaching is insufficient (compare 29:19). Proverbs makes the reason for discipline as important as the discipline itself: The discipline of parents, like the discipline of Yahweh, should be done to benefit the child and should not be too severe (6:23; 19:18; compare Dt 8:5; Pr 3:11; Ps 6:1 and note). **discipline** The Hebrew word used here, *musar*, emphasizes teaching or instructing (Pr 1:2 and note; 1:8; 4:1; 19:20).

14:1 house Refers to the wise woman's household (compare 24:3–4; 31:10–31). This woman is described as building her household, which in the ancient Near East would have involved having children, raising a family and caring for the household economy.

14:2 Whoever fears the LORD The fear of Yahweh is an important concept in both Wisdom Literature and the OT as a whole. It describes a reverent attitude toward Yahweh, one that both acknowledges his full power and involves obedience to him. In Proverbs, the fear of Yahweh is recognized as the beginning of wisdom (see 1:7 and note; 9:10). The person who gains wisdom better understands the fear of Yahweh (2:5).

³ A fool's mouth lashes out with pride,
  but the lips of the wise protect them.

⁴ Where there are no oxen, the manger is
    empty,
  but from the strength of an ox come
    abundant harvests.

⁵ An honest witness does not deceive,
  but a false witness pours out lies.

⁶ The mocker seeks wisdom and finds none,
  but knowledge comes easily to the
    discerning.

⁷ Stay away from a fool,
  for you will not find knowledge on their
    lips.

⁸ The wisdom of the prudent is to give thought
    to their ways,
  but the folly of fools is deception.

⁹ Fools mock at making amends for sin,
  but goodwill is found among the upright.

¹⁰ Each heart knows its own bitterness,
  and no one else can share its joy.

¹¹ The house of the wicked will be destroyed,
  but the tent of the upright will flourish.

¹² There is a way that appears to be right,
  but in the end it leads to death.

¹³ Even in laughter the heart may ache,
  and rejoicing may end in grief.

¹⁴ The faithless will be fully repaid for their
    ways,
  and the good rewarded for theirs.

¹⁵ The simple believe anything,
  but the prudent give thought to their steps.

¹⁶ The wise fear the Lᴏʀᴅ and shun evil,
  but a fool is hotheaded and yet feels secure.

¹⁷ A quick-tempered person does foolish things,
  and the one who devises evil schemes is
    hated.

¹⁸ The simple inherit folly,
  but the prudent are crowned with
    knowledge.

¹⁹ Evildoers will bow down in the presence of
    the good,
  and the wicked at the gates of the
    righteous.

²⁰ The poor are shunned even by their
    neighbors,
  but the rich have many friends.

²¹ It is a sin to despise one's neighbor,
  but blessed is the one who is kind to the
    needy.

²² Do not those who plot evil go astray?
  But those who plan what is good find*ᵃ* love
    and faithfulness.

ᵃ 22 Or *show*

14:3 A fool's mouth A fool gets into trouble by speaking impulsively (29:11) and argumentatively (20:3). By contrast, the restrained (10:19; 17:27) and careful speech of the wise acts as a type of protection (compare 11:9,12–13).

14:4 the manger is empty The stalls will be clean if the farmer has no oxen, but the farmer will not have any food either. Unpleasant work is necessary for a harvest.

14:6 mocker seeks wisdom Scoffers cannot gain wisdom because they despise correction (13:1; 15:12; see 1:22 and note).

14:8 to give thought to their ways The wise benefit practically from their pursuit of wisdom. Here, wisdom helps people make careful decisions (21:29).

14:9 making amends for sin The Hebrew word used here, *asham*, can describe the guilt offering (a specific kind of sacrifice; Lev 5:14–19) or guilt in general (Ge 26:10). The implication is that fools are proud and refuse to admit wrongdoing or seek reconciliation. Their arrogance (Pr 21:24) and preference for evil (10:23; 13:19) cause them to reject responsibility for their sin.

14:11 tent of the upright will flourish A tent often was used to represent a person's welfare (compare Job 8:22 and note). Proverbs views a successful life as one of the rewards of wisdom and righteousness (see note on Pr 3:2).

14:12 a way that appears to be right Repeated in 16:25, this proverb reflects the way of the forbidden woman that can ultimately end in death (5:3–6; 7:25–27). In contrast, the way of wisdom leads to pleasantness and peace (3:17–18).

14:13 Even in laughter the heart may ache This seemingly pessimistic proverb highlights the joys and sorrows of life. It also highlights the ultimate end of humanity (Ecc 7:2–4).

14:14 faithless The Hebrew word used here, *sug*, indicates turning back. It is often used in the sense of turning away from God (Ps 44:18; 53:3; Isa 59:13).

14:15 simple The Hebrew word used here, *pethi*, describes someone who is ignorant or oblivious. Unlike the fool, a simple person has the ability to learn (Pr 21:11; see 1:4 and note).

14:16 shun evil Refers both to rejecting wickedness and pursuing good (Ps 34:14; 37:27).

14:18 crowned with knowledge Knowledge or wisdom are rewards in themselves (compare Pr 12:4; 14:24; 16:31; 17:6), and the simple should strive to gain them (see note on 1:4).

14:19 Evildoers will bow down in the presence of the good Describes the ultimate victory of good over evil. Conquered people demonstrated their submission by bowing down before their victors (Ge 37:7–8; Isa 60:14).

14:20 poor are shunned even by their neighbors People more often exhibit friendliness to those who can benefit them. Proverbs 14:21 corrects this notion.

14:21 the one who is kind to the needy People are more likely to befriend the rich than the impoverished (v. 20). However, generosity to the poor results in blessing and happiness (Ps 1:1) and honors God (Pr 14:31).

²³ All hard work brings a profit,
    but mere talk leads only to poverty.

²⁴ The wealth of the wise is their crown,
    but the folly of fools yields folly.

²⁵ A truthful witness saves lives,
    but a false witness is deceitful.

²⁶ Whoever fears the LORD has a secure
    fortress,
    and for their children it will be a refuge.

²⁷ The fear of the LORD is a fountain of life,
    turning a person from the snares of death.

²⁸ A large population is a king's glory,
    but without subjects a prince is ruined.

²⁹ Whoever is patient has great understanding,
    but one who is quick-tempered displays
    folly.

³⁰ A heart at peace gives life to the body,
    but envy rots the bones.

³¹ Whoever oppresses the poor shows contempt
    for their Maker,
    but whoever is kind to the needy
    honors God.

³² When calamity comes, the wicked are
    brought down,
    but even in death the righteous seek refuge
    in God.

³³ Wisdom reposes in the heart of the
    discerning
    and even among fools she lets herself be
    known.ᵃ

³⁴ Righteousness exalts a nation,
    but sin condemns any people.

³⁵ A king delights in a wise servant,
    but a shameful servant arouses his fury.

15 A gentle answer turns away wrath,
    but a harsh word stirs up anger.

² The tongue of the wise adorns knowledge,
    but the mouth of the fool gushes folly.

³ The eyes of the LORD are everywhere,
    keeping watch on the wicked and the good.

⁴ The soothing tongue is a tree of life,
    but a perverse tongue crushes the spirit.

⁵ A fool spurns a parent's discipline,
    but whoever heeds correction shows
    prudence.

⁶ The house of the righteous contains great
    treasure,
    but the income of the wicked brings ruin.

⁷ The lips of the wise spread knowledge,
    but the hearts of fools are not upright.

⁸ The LORD detests the sacrifice of the wicked,
    but the prayer of the upright pleases him.

⁹ The LORD detests the way of the wicked,
    but he loves those who pursue righteousness.

¹⁰ Stern discipline awaits anyone who leaves
    the path;
    the one who hates correction will die.

ᵃ 33 Hebrew; Septuagint and Syriac *discerning / but in the heart of fools she is not known*

14:23 All hard work brings a profit Advocates hard work. For the temporary aspect of this profit, see Ecc 2:22 and note.

14:27 a fountain of life Compare Pr 13:14, where the teaching of the wise is a source of life.

14:30 envy The Hebrew word used here, *qin'ah*, refers to a sin considered worse than anger (27:4) and thus strongly condemned.

14:31 Whoever oppresses the poor shows contempt for their Maker Yahweh is the maker of both the rich and the impoverished (22:2). Oppression of the poor—usually for financial gain (22:16)—is an offense to God, who will one day execute justice on behalf of the impoverished (Ps 146:7).

14:34 Righteousness exalts a nation All of society feels the benefits of righteousness. See Pr 11:10–11 and note.

14:35 A king delights in a wise servant Caution before rulers is a recurring theme in Wisdom Literature (23:1). Ecclesiastes advocates caution before the king because of the king's authority (Ecc 8:2–5).

15:1 A gentle answer A patient or gentle answer (Pr 14:3; 25:15) defuses anger (e.g., Gideon's response to the men of Ephraim in Jdg 8:1–3). In contrast, a harsh answer escalates a situation (e.g., Nabal's response to David in 1Sa 25:10–13 ["Nabal" means "fool"]).

15:3 keeping watch on the wicked and the good

Yahweh sees the ways of all people (Pr 5:21). The Psalms portray him as examining humanity from his heavenly throne (Ps 11:4–5). He watches so he can eventually bring all actions under his judgment (Ecc 12:14).

15:4 The soothing tongue is a tree of life Because it defuses anger, a gentle tongue is portrayed as a tree of life—a symbol of renewal (Pr 15:1; see note on 3:18).

15:5 A fool spurns a parent's discipline The fool is characterized by rejection of instruction and correction. See 1:7 and note; compare 15:20; 23:22.

15:6 great treasure Proverbs consistently holds up long life and success as rewards for wisdom. See note on 3:2.

15:7 The lips of the wise spread knowledge The wise benefit those around them, while the fool should be avoided (13:20; 14:7).

15:8 sacrifice of the wicked Describes a sacrifice made insincerely or for the purpose of appearing righteous. God condemns insincere sacrifices throughout the OT. He prefers righteousness and justice over outward displays of religion (21:3; Isa 1:11–17). God also values faithfulness and obedience over sacrifice (1Sa 15:22; Hos 6:6). Even unintentionally faulty sacrifices are condemned (compare Ecc 5:1 and note).

15:9 The LORD detests In addition to their sacrifices, Yahweh considers the lives of wicked people—and even their thoughts—an abomination (Pr 15:26).

¹¹ Death and Destruction[a] lie open before the
  LORD —
how much more do human hearts!

¹² Mockers resent correction,
  so they avoid the wise.

¹³ A happy heart makes the face cheerful,
  but heartache crushes the spirit.

¹⁴ The discerning heart seeks knowledge,
  but the mouth of a fool feeds on folly.

¹⁵ All the days of the oppressed are wretched,
  but the cheerful heart has a continual
  feast.

¹⁶ Better a little with the fear of the LORD
  than great wealth with turmoil.

¹⁷ Better a small serving of vegetables
  with love
than a fattened calf with hatred.

¹⁸ A hot-tempered person stirs up conflict,
  but the one who is patient calms a quarrel.

¹⁹ The way of the sluggard is blocked with
  thorns,
but the path of the upright is a highway.

²⁰ A wise son brings joy to his father,
  but a foolish man despises his mother.

²¹ Folly brings joy to one who has no sense,
  but whoever has understanding keeps a
  straight course.

[a] 11 Hebrew *Abaddon*

15:11 Death The scope of God's watch stretches even to the realm of the dead. The Hebrew word used here, *she'ol*, refers to the shadowy underworld of the dead (see note on Job 3:13; note on 14:13; note on 26:6). **Destruction** The Hebrew word used here, *avad,* refers to perishing or going to ruin — like *she'ol,* it describes the underworld (Pr 27:20; Ps 88:10–12; compare Rev 9:11).

15:12 Mockers resent correction Scoffers are characterized by their attitude, which prevents them from finding wisdom (see Pr 1:22 and note; 9:7–8; 13:1; 14:6; 21:24).

15:16–17 These two proverbs promote godliness and contentment over material wealth — a common theme in Wisdom Literature. An impoverished but peaceful home is preferred over one that is wealthy but contentious (17:1). The author of Ecclesiastes also promotes a restful life over the pursuit of profit (Ecc 4:6).

15:16 Better a little Wealth is a good thing, but its value is negated by trouble. Many proverbs follow the "better ... than ..." pattern (e.g., Pr 12:9; 15:16–17; 16:8,19; 17:1; 19:1; 21:9,19; 25:24; 27:5; 28:6). These proverbs assert the relative value of one thing over another, inviting the reader to consider the options. The most common themes in "better than" proverbs are wealth and poverty (e.g., 15:16–17; 16:8,16; 17:1) and humility and greatness (e.g., 12:9; 16:19; 25:7). By requiring a person to weigh the value of different options, "better than" proverbs illustrate wisdom in action.

15:18 A hot-tempered person stirs up conflict Like hard words, someone quick to anger only causes problems; in contrast, the level-headed person defuses anger (see 15:1 and note).

15:19 way of the sluggard Idleness makes the lazy person's way more difficult. See 6:9 and note.

15:21 Folly brings joy The fool enjoys folly and sees no need to become wise.

Parallelism in Hebrew Poetry

TYPE	DESCRIPTION	EXAMPLE
Number Parallelism	First a number (*n*) is mentioned, then a higher number (*n + 1*)	For three sins of Damascus, | even for four, I will not relent. (Am 1:3)
Synonymous Parallelism	The second line of poetry restates or supports the idea of the first line	**Statement A:** My people, hear my teaching; | **Reiteration A':** listen to the words of my mouth (Ps 78:1)
Antithetic Parallelism	The second line of poetry contrasts the idea of the first line	**Statement A:** The tongue of the wise adorns knowledge, | **Contrast B:** but the mouth of fool gushes folly (Pr 15:2)
Developmental Parallelism	The second line of poetry extends or builds upon the idea of the first line	**Statement A:** That person is like a tree | **Development A':** planted by streams of water | **Development A'':** which yields its fruit in season | **Development A''':** and whose leaf does not wither. | **Development A'''':** whatever they do prospers (Ps 1:3)

²² Plans fail for lack of counsel,
   but with many advisers they succeed.

²³ A person finds joy in giving an apt reply —
   and how good is a timely word!

²⁴ The path of life leads upward for
      the prudent
   to keep them from going down to the realm
      of the dead.

²⁵ The LORD tears down the house of the proud,
   but he sets the widow's boundary stones in
      place.

²⁶ The LORD detests the thoughts of the wicked,
   but gracious words are pure in his sight.

²⁷ The greedy bring ruin to their households,
   but the one who hates bribes will live.

²⁸ The heart of the righteous weighs its
      answers,
   but the mouth of the wicked gushes evil.

²⁹ The LORD is far from the wicked,
   but he hears the prayer of the righteous.

³⁰ Light in a messenger's eyes brings joy to the
      heart,
   and good news gives health to the bones.

³¹ Whoever heeds life-giving correction
   will be at home among the wise.

³² Those who disregard discipline despise
      themselves,
   but the one who heeds correction gains
      understanding.

³³ Wisdom's instruction is to fear the LORD,
   and humility comes before honor.

16 To humans belong the plans of the heart,
   but from the LORD comes the proper
      answer of the tongue.

² All a person's ways seem pure to them,
   but motives are weighed by the LORD.

³ Commit to the LORD whatever you do,
   and he will establish your plans.

⁴ The LORD works out everything to its proper
      end —
   even the wicked for a day of disaster.

⁵ The LORD detests all the proud of heart.
   Be sure of this: They will not go
      unpunished.

⁶ Through love and faithfulness sin is
      atoned for;
   through the fear of the LORD evil is
      avoided.

⁷ When the LORD takes pleasure in
      anyone's way,
   he causes their enemies to make peace
      with them.

⁸ Better a little with righteousness
   than much gain with injustice.

⁹ In their hearts humans plan their course,
   but the LORD establishes their steps.

¹⁰ The lips of a king speak as an oracle,
   and his mouth does not betray justice.

15:22 Plans fail for lack of counsel The wise person seeks advice from others before acting. An abundance of counselors ensures that any foolish decisions are noticed and prevented (11:14; 24:6).

15:24 going down to the realm of the dead Prudence protects a person's life from the realm of the dead, called *she'ol* in Hebrew (see note on 3:2; Ge 37:35 and note; compare Job 3:13; 14:13; 26:6).

15:25 widow's boundary stones Widows were among the most impoverished people in the ancient Near East. The law included special protections for widows so that they would not be exploited (Ex 22:22–24; see note on Ru 1:5). Moving another person's boundary marker amounts to theft and thus is condemned.

15:33 to fear the LORD Denotes reverence for Yahweh (see note on 1:7).

16:1–9 This section is framed by a comparison of the plans of people's hearts and the direction of Yahweh (vv. 1,9). Yahweh establishes the plans of those who seek him and follow him; he causes their enemies to be at peace with them (vv. 3,7). Yahweh looks at the heart of humankind (v. 2) and punishes the arrogant (v. 5). Yahweh has created everything—even the wicked—for a purpose (v. 4).

16:2 seem pure to them People tend to rationalize their motives and behavior (compare 14:12), but God discerns both.

16:5 They will not go unpunished An expression of faith in God's justice (see note on Ecc 8:13).

16:6 love and faithfulness The Hebrew text here uses the word pairing of *chesed* and *emet*, which also occurs in Pr 3:3–4, which says that the person who keeps *chesed* and *emeth* finds the favor of Yahweh (see note on 3:3). **sin is atoned for** The OT sacrificial system required that an offering or sacrifice be made to signify atonement (see note on Lev 4:20). This proverb is not intended to negate this idea but instead note that it is only through faith and love that atonement can come. **through the fear of the LORD** The fear of Yahweh—a proper attitude of reverence—serves as a protection from sin. See Pr 1:7 and note.

16:8 Better a little with righteousness Emphasizes that righteousness is better than material wealth (see note on 1:3; note on 15:16).

16:10–15 These proverbs address the monarchy. The first involves the judgment of the wise king (v. 10). Since justice originates from Yahweh (v. 11), the righteous king will have his throne established (v. 12). Verse 13 notes that the king delights in righteous advisors. Finally, two proverbs encourage seeking the king's favor and appeasing his anger (vv. 14–15).

16:10 his mouth does not betray justice The king in this proverb is most likely righteous and wise (20:28). Other proverbs address the reigns of wicked kings (28:15–16).

¹¹ Honest scales and balances belong to the
    LORD;
    all the weights in the bag are of his making.

¹² Kings detest wrongdoing,
    for a throne is established through
    righteousness.

¹³ Kings take pleasure in honest lips;
    they value the one who speaks what is right.

¹⁴ A king's wrath is a messenger of death,
    but the wise will appease it.

¹⁵ When a king's face brightens, it means life;
    his favor is like a rain cloud in spring.

¹⁶ How much better to get wisdom than gold,
    to get insight rather than silver!

¹⁷ The highway of the upright avoids evil;
    those who guard their ways preserve their
    lives.

¹⁸ Pride goes before destruction,
    a haughty spirit before a fall.

¹⁹ Better to be lowly in spirit along with the
    oppressed
    than to share plunder with the proud.

²⁰ Whoever gives heed to instruction prospers,ᵃ
    and blessed is the one who trusts in the
    LORD.

²¹ The wise in heart are called discerning,
    and gracious words promote instruction.ᵇ

²² Prudence is a fountain of life to the prudent,
    but folly brings punishment to fools.

²³ The hearts of the wise make their mouths
    prudent,
    and their lips promote instruction.ᶜ

²⁴ Gracious words are a honeycomb,
    sweet to the soul and healing to the bones.

²⁵ There is a way that appears to be right,
    but in the end it leads to death.

²⁶ The appetite of laborers works for them;
    their hunger drives them on.

²⁷ A scoundrel plots evil,
    and on their lips it is like a scorching fire.

²⁸ A perverse person stirs up conflict,
    and a gossip separates close friends.

²⁹ A violent person entices their neighbor
    and leads them down a path that is not
    good.

³⁰ Whoever winks with their eye is plotting
    perversity;
    whoever purses their lips is bent on evil.

³¹ Gray hair is a crown of splendor;
    it is attained in the way of righteousness.

³² Better a patient person than a warrior,
    one with self-control than one who takes a
    city.

³³ The lot is cast into the lap,
    but its every decision is from the LORD.

ᵃ 20 Or *whoever speaks prudently finds what is good*
ᵇ 21 Or *words make a person persuasive*   ᶜ 23 Or *prudent /
and make their lips persuasive*

**16:11 Honest scales and balances belong to the
LORD** See 11:1 and note.
16:14 A king's wrath An angry king is unpredictable,
unleashing his wrath in any direction he pleases. The
wise person tries to assuage the anger (19:12; 20:2;
24:21–22).
16:15 a king's face brightens Refers to the king's
favor or friendliness (compare Ps 4:6; 44:3; 89:15).
like a rain cloud in spring Those who wisely appease
the king's wrath obtain his favor. Compare Pr 14:35.
16:16 How much better to get wisdom than gold
Wisdom is also shown to be preferable to precious
metals in 3:13–15 and Job 28:15–19.
16:18 Pride goes before destruction Pride, a characteristic of fools, leads to disgrace (Pr 11:2; 29:23).
a haughty spirit The Hebrew word used here, *govah*,
literally refers to height (Job 11:8) and figuratively refers
to pride (Ps 10:4; Jer 48:29). While the proud may find
some success (Pr 16:19), they will eventually be brought
low—often through their own stupidity and refusal to
listen to instruction.
16:19 Better to be lowly in spirit Humility, like righteousness, is preferable to wealth (compare v. 8; 15:16
and note).
16:20 blessed The Hebrew word used here designates
someone who is fortunate or privileged. See note on
Ps 1:1.

16:21 discerning The ability to make wise choices (to
use discernment) is closely related to wisdom (compare
Pr 1:2 and note; 8:12 and note).
16:23 make their mouths prudent The Hebrew word
used here, *sakhal*, indicates acting wisely (14:35; 17:2).
People's actions or speech reveal their wisdom.
16:25 a way that appears to be right See note on
14:12.

16:27–30 These proverbs address people who cause
problems. People who are worthless (v. 27), dishonest
(vv. 28,30) or violent (v. 29) negatively affect those around
them. They bring evil by tempting and dividing those who
associate with them.

16:27 A scoundrel The Hebrew word used here,
beliyya'al, can refer to worthlessness or wickedness.
Throughout Proverbs, this type of person is frequently
characterized by dishonest speech. Compare 6:12 and
note.
16:28 a gossip The Hebrew word used here refers to
grumbling or slanderous talk (Dt 1:27).
16:30 Whoever winks with their eye A characteristic
of a worthless person (Pr 6:12–15). See note on 6:13.
16:31 Gray hair is a crown of splendor In the ancient
Near East, old age was typically associated with wisdom
(Job 12:12).
16:33 lot is cast Ancient Israelites cast lots to determine

17 Better a dry crust with peace and quiet
than a house full of feasting, with strife.

2 A prudent servant will rule over a
disgraceful son
and will share the inheritance as one
of the family.

3 The crucible for silver and the furnace for gold,
but the LORD tests the heart.

4 A wicked person listens to deceitful lips;
a liar pays attention to a destructive
tongue.

5 Whoever mocks the poor shows contempt for
their Maker;
whoever gloats over disaster will not go
unpunished.

6 Children's children are a crown to the aged,
and parents are the pride of their children.

7 Eloquent lips are unsuited to a godless fool —
how much worse lying lips to a ruler!

8 A bribe is seen as a charm by the one who
gives it;
they think success will come at every turn.

9 Whoever would foster love covers over an
offense,
but whoever repeats the matter separates
close friends.

10 A rebuke impresses a discerning person
more than a hundred lashes a fool.

11 Evildoers foster rebellion against God;
the messenger of death will be sent against
them.

12 Better to meet a bear robbed of her cubs
than a fool bent on folly.

13 Evil will never leave the house
of one who pays back evil for good.

14 Starting a quarrel is like breaching a dam;
so drop the matter before a dispute
breaks out.

15 Acquitting the guilty and condemning the
innocent —
the LORD detests them both.

16 Why should fools have money in hand to buy
wisdom,
when they are not able to understand it?

17 A friend loves at all times,
and a brother is born for a time of
adversity.

18 One who has no sense shakes hands in pledge
and puts up security for a neighbor.

19 Whoever loves a quarrel loves sin;
whoever builds a high gate invites
destruction.

20 One whose heart is corrupt does not prosper;
one whose tongue is perverse falls into
trouble.

---

action or responsibility (1Ch 25:8; Jos 14:2; compare Ne 11:1 and note). While casting lots amounts to a game of chance, Yahweh can determine the outcome (1Sa 14:41–42; compare Jnh 1:7).

17:1 Better a dry crust with peace and quiet Wisdom Literature commonly promotes contentment and peace over material wealth. See note on Pr 15:16. **feasting** The Hebrew word used here refers to animal sacrifices. In the ancient Near East, sacrifices were understood as occasions for fellowship between people and their gods or between the people offering the sacrifice. Such sacrifices required a certain amount of wealth. The idea of this proverb seems to be that it is better to have a life of poverty than a life of lavish wealth that involves conflict.

17:3 the LORD tests the heart Throughout the OT, testing is often compared to refining precious metals (Mal 3:3; compare Ps 11:5 and note).

17:5 shows contempt for their Maker Mocking the impoverished is an offense to God, who is the creator of both the mocker and the person being mocked (compare 1Sa 2:7; Dt 8:17–18; Pr 14:31 and note). The person who mocks the poor presumes that the impoverished are responsible for their unfortunate circumstances: Either they are suffering punishment for wrongdoing (compare Job's friends; see note on Job 4:6), or they brought hard times on themselves through their folly. However, it is not possible to understand all the reasons why people suffer and it is an affront to God to presume otherwise. Compare Pr 19:17; 22:2.

17:7 fool The Hebrew term used here is the same word used for the godless person in Ps 14:1 (see note on Pr 1:7).

17:8 a charm The Hebrew phrase used here, literally rendered as "stone of favor," does not occur elsewhere in the OT. It probably refers to a stone that was supposed to bring fortune, like a good luck charm.

17:9 covers The Hebrew word used here, which signifies covering or forgiving, implies that love can overcome a past wrongdoing and bridge an estranged relationship. See note on 10:12.

17:11 Evildoers foster rebellion The evil person never has good motives and will eventually be punished.

17:12 a bear robbed of her cubs An encounter of this type would likely result in death (compare 2Ki 2:23–25). Elsewhere, this image describes an angry and destructive force (2Sa 17:8; Hos 13:8).

17:15 Acquitting the guilty The author of Ecclesiastes also laments this kind of injustice (compare Ecc 8:14 and note).

17:16 when they are not able to understand it Wisdom cannot be purchased (Job 28:15–19); it is obtained through discipline and the fear of Yahweh (Pr 1:28–33).

17:17 brother The poetic parallelism of friend with brother indicates that the brother here is not necessarily a family member. It describes a close friend — one who stands with his friend through times of trouble. See the table "Parallelism in Hebrew Poetry" on p. 1008. **adversity** The Hebrew word used here can indicate adversity, distress (as in Ge 35:3) or trouble (as in Ps 142:2).

17:18 shakes hands in pledge This phrase refers to

²¹ To have a fool for a child brings grief;
    there is no joy for the parent of a godless
    fool.

²² A cheerful heart is good medicine,
    but a crushed spirit dries up the bones.

²³ The wicked accept bribes in secret
    to pervert the course of justice.

²⁴ A discerning person keeps wisdom in view,
    but a fool's eyes wander to the ends of the
    earth.

²⁵ A foolish son brings grief to his father
    and bitterness to the mother who bore him.

²⁶ If imposing a fine on the innocent is not good,
    surely to flog honest officials is not right.

²⁷ The one who has knowledge uses words with
    restraint,
    and whoever has understanding is even-
    tempered.

²⁸ Even fools are thought wise if they keep
    silent,
    and discerning if they hold their tongues.

18 An unfriendly person pursues selfish ends
    and against all sound judgment starts
    quarrels.

² Fools find no pleasure in understanding
    but delight in airing their own opinions.

³ When wickedness comes, so does contempt,
    and with shame comes reproach.

⁴ The words of the mouth are deep waters,
    but the fountain of wisdom is a rushing
    stream.

⁵ It is not good to be partial to the wicked
    and so deprive the innocent of justice.

⁶ The lips of fools bring them strife,
    and their mouths invite a beating.

⁷ The mouths of fools are their undoing,
    and their lips are a snare to their
    very lives.

⁸ The words of a gossip are like choice morsels;
    they go down to the inmost parts.

⁹ One who is slack in his work
    is brother to one who destroys.

¹⁰ The name of the LORD is a fortified tower;
    the righteous run to it and are safe.

¹¹ The wealth of the rich is their fortified city;
    they imagine it a wall too high to scale.

¹² Before a downfall the heart is haughty,
    but humility comes before honor.

¹³ To answer before listening —
    that is folly and shame.

¹⁴ The human spirit can endure in sickness,
    but a crushed spirit who can bear?

¹⁵ The heart of the discerning acquires
    knowledge,
    for the ears of the wise seek it out.

---

foolishly assuming responsibility for someone else's debt (see Pr 6:1 and note).

17:21 To have a fool for a child brings grief Wise children make their parents proud, and fools bring shame. See note on 10:1; compare 15:20; 23:15.

17:22 cheerful heart is good medicine Proverbs often speaks of the benefits of a happy frame of mind. Joy is encouraged, while anxiety and discouragement only weigh a person down (12:25; 15:13,15; 18:14).

17:24 A discerning person keeps wisdom in view Wisdom is close at hand, and the discerning person will find it because the discerning person is receptive to it. **ends of the earth** The fool will never gain wisdom because the fool looks for the wrong things (compare Job 28; Dt 30:11–14).

17:27 one who has knowledge uses words with restraint Restraint of speech is a characteristic of the wise. See note on Pr 10:19; compare 15:1,18; 14:29. **even-tempered** In contrast to a hot-tempered person, an even-tempered person is self-controlled and slow to anger (compare 15:18).

18:1 selfish ends The Hebrew word used here refers to separation (compare Ge 13:11). Here, it describes those who willfully alienate themselves from society.

18:2 in airing their own opinions The fool has no regard for the wisdom of others (Pr 15:5).

18:4 deep waters Proverbs 20:5 uses a similar expression to indicate that a person's mind (or heart) is hard for another to understand. This could mean that this proverb indicates that the place words come from—a

person's character—is also difficult to understand. As a whole, this proverb seems to indicate that wisdom is an ongoing, life-giving source.

18:5 It is not good to be partial to the wicked Yahweh considers the preferential treatment of the wicked and the unjust treatment of the righteous to be an abomination— a horrible thing that goes against his purposes (17:15).

18:6 their mouths invite a beating The fool gets into trouble through recklessness (14:16) and unrestrained speech (29:11).

18:8 like choice morsels This proverb—repeated verbatim in 26:22—does not encourage gossip. Instead, it reflects reality: People greedily devour gossip, always looking for more. The idea that the belly stores thoughts comes from ancient Egypt: Thoughts reside in the belly until people decide which ones are worth speaking (compare 20:27,30; 22:18; Job 15:2; 32:18–19).

18:9 is brother to one who destroys Laziness is a destructive attitude. The sluggard ends up in poverty (Pr 6:9–11; 10:4); rather than maintain a field, the sluggard ruins it (24:30–34).

18:10 a fortified tower Both a watchtower (2Ki 9:17) and a place of refuge (Jdg 9:51). The Psalms often compare God to a tower of refuge (Ps 18:2; 61:3; see note on 18:1–3).

18:11 wealth of the rich The righteous trust in the name of Yahweh for protection, but here the rich trust in wealth. However, this security is a delusion or folly that cannot provide the protection of the name of Yahweh (Pr 11:28).

¹⁶ A gift opens the way
   and ushers the giver into the presence of
   the great.

¹⁷ In a lawsuit the first to speak seems right,
   until someone comes forward and cross-
   examines.

¹⁸ Casting the lot settles disputes
   and keeps strong opponents apart.

¹⁹ A brother wronged is more unyielding than a
   fortified city;
   disputes are like the barred gates of a
   citadel.

²⁰ From the fruit of their mouth a person's
   stomach is filled;
   with the harvest of their lips they are
   satisfied.

²¹ The tongue has the power of life and death,
   and those who love it will eat its fruit.

²² He who finds a wife finds what is good
   and receives favor from the LORD.

²³ The poor plead for mercy,
   but the rich answer harshly.

²⁴ One who has unreliable friends soon comes
   to ruin,
   but there is a friend who sticks closer than
   a brother.

19

¹ Better the poor whose walk is blameless
   than a fool whose lips are perverse.

² Desire without knowledge is not good —
   how much more will hasty feet miss
   the way!

³ A person's own folly leads to their ruin,
   yet their heart rages against the LORD.

⁴ Wealth attracts many friends,
   but even the closest friend of the poor
   person deserts them.

⁵ A false witness will not go unpunished,
   and whoever pours out lies will not go free.

⁶ Many curry favor with a ruler,
   and everyone is the friend of one who
   gives gifts.

⁷ The poor are shunned by all their relatives —
   how much more do their friends avoid them!
Though the poor pursue them with pleading,
   they are nowhere to be found.[a]

⁸ The one who gets wisdom loves life;
   the one who cherishes understanding will
   soon prosper.

⁹ A false witness will not go unpunished,
   and whoever pours out lies will perish.

[a] 7 The meaning of the Hebrew for this sentence is uncertain.

18:13 folly and shame A person who gives answers without listening is like the fool who only seeks to express his or her opinion (18:2).

18:16 gift The Hebrew word used here, *mattan*, differs from the term for a bribe (*shochad*; 17:8). Here, the gift is meant more innocently to appease or curry favor (19:6; 21:14).

18:18 Casting the lot settles disputes When used to determine responsibility, casting lots ended arguments (Jnh 1:7; see note on Pr 16:33).

18:19 A brother wronged Illustrates the divisive nature of arguments. Like a heavily fortified city, an offended person is difficult to reach.

18:20–21 These two proverbs show the power of speech, to be life giving or taking. See note on 12:13.

18:20 they are satisfied The Hebrew text here could be understood as indicating a positive or negative result, meaning that speech can affect a person's life for good or bad.

18:21 will eat its fruit It is unclear whether this is positive or negative. The ambiguity is likely intentional and probably meant to indicate the need to use caution both when speaking and listening.

18:22 He who finds a wife Proverbs makes both positive and negative statements about wives: It is better to live alone than with a quarrelsome wife (19:13; 21:9; 25:24), but a prudent wife is a gift from Yahweh (19:14) — she is the glory of her husband (12:4).

18:24 One who has unreliable friends One close friend is more valuable than many friends. A close friend will stick by someone who faces adversity (17:17).

19:1 Better the poor Poverty with integrity is better than wealth gained deceitfully (16:8; 28:6; see note on 15:16). **whose lips are perverse** Proverbs frequently connects a person's speech and character (e.g., 14:25; 16:23; 17:27). The contrast in this proverb implies that wealth does not always go to people who deserve it.

19:2 how much more will hasty feet miss the way Acting impulsively or recklessly causes mistakes. Instead, Proverbs encourages caution and restraint (14:16; 17:27).

19:3 their heart rages against the LORD Rather than accept responsibility for their actions, fools blame God for their mistakes (compare 1:7 and note).

19:4 Wealth attracts many friends Riches bring the numerous superficial friends described in 18:24. **the closest friend of the poor person deserts them** Even close friends may abandon a person who becomes impoverished (compare 14:20; 19:7).

19:5 A false witness will not go unpunished A person who gave false testimony was to receive the same punishment as the accused (Dt 19:18–19).

19:6 a ruler The Hebrew term used here refers to a man with high standing who may also be generous. The second line of this proverb confirms that he is a man who gives gifts. However, the proverb is ambiguous about whether this is a truly generous man or someone who gives gifts for self-serving purposes. **gifts** The Hebrew word used here, *mattan*, differs from the term for bribe (*shochad*; Pr 17:8) and is intended more innocently to appease or gain favor. Compare 18:16 and note.

19:7 shunned by all their relatives Expands the idea of 19:4. A brother should be faithful, but Proverbs relates

¹⁰ It is not fitting for a fool to live in luxury —
how much worse for a slave to rule over
princes!

¹¹ A person's wisdom yields patience;
it is to one's glory to overlook an
offense.

¹² A king's rage is like the roar of a lion,
but his favor is like dew on the grass.

¹³ A foolish child is a father's ruin,
and a quarrelsome wife is like
the constant dripping of a leaky roof.

¹⁴ Houses and wealth are inherited from
parents,
but a prudent wife is from the Lord.

¹⁵ Laziness brings on deep sleep,
and the shiftless go hungry.

¹⁶ Whoever keeps commandments keeps
their life,
but whoever shows contempt for their
ways will die.

¹⁷ Whoever is kind to the poor lends to the
Lord,
and he will reward them for what they
have done.

¹⁸ Discipline your children, for in that there is
hope;
do not be a willing party to their death.

¹⁹ A hot-tempered person must pay
the penalty;
rescue them, and you will have to do it
again.

²⁰ Listen to advice and accept discipline,
and at the end you will be counted among
the wise.

²¹ Many are the plans in a person's heart,
but it is the Lord's purpose that prevails.

²² What a person desires is unfailing love ᵃ;
better to be poor than a liar.

²³ The fear of the Lord leads to life;
then one rests content, untouched by
trouble.

²⁴ A sluggard buries his hand in the dish;
he will not even bring it back to
his mouth!

²⁵ Flog a mocker, and the simple will learn
prudence;
rebuke the discerning, and they will gain
knowledge.

²⁶ Whoever robs their father and drives out
their mother
is a child who brings shame and
disgrace.

²⁷ Stop listening to instruction, my son,
and you will stray from the words of
knowledge.

²⁸ A corrupt witness mocks at justice,
and the mouth of the wicked gulps
down evil.

²⁹ Penalties are prepared for mockers,
and beatings for the backs of fools.

ᵃ 22 Or *Greed is a person's shame*

---

life as it really is—i.e., people are fickle and relationships often go awry.

19:10 for a slave to rule over princes In the ancient Near East, a slave was viewed as the lowest person in the social structure and as having no rights. A slave coming into power would be so improbable that it would seem absurd. This proverb is not arguing against slaves obtaining an elevated status, but instead showing the absurdity of a fool becoming wealthy (compare Ecc 10:6–7 and note).

19:11 wisdom The Hebrew word used here, *sekhel*, refers to good sense or discretion, a characteristic of the wise. A person with good sense is level headed and can defuse conflict (Pr 15:18). Elsewhere, the person who is patient or self-controlled is said to be better than the mighty (16:32). **to overlook an offense** Wise people do not hold grudges, which only cause strife (10:12) and ruin relationships (18:19).

19:12 roar of a lion An ominous sign of coming disaster. An angry ruler is an unpredictable threat (see 16:14 and note).

19:16 commandments In Proverbs, this word typically refers to wisdom teaching in general (see note on 13:13). The reward for following the commandment here is life (see note on 3:2).

19:17 lends to the Lord Those who give generously to the impoverished are being generous with God. Previ-

ously, oppression of the poor has been called an insult to God, the Creator of both the rich and poor (see 17:5 and note; compare 14:31; 22:2).

19:18 do not be a willing party to their death Discipline must be an act of love because it is life-saving (23:13–14; see note on 13:24).

19:19 you will have to do it again Seems to contradict the advice in 10:12 and 19:11 to forgive offenses. However, proverbs are not rules or promises, but general principles that require wise application to different situations. See note on 26:4–5.

19:24 he will not even bring it back to his mouth Comically portrays the destructive nature of exaggerated laziness: The sluggard is too lazy to even feed himself. See 6:9 and note.

19:25 Flog a mocker, and the simple will learn While scoffers do not learn from discipline, the simple learn from their example (compare 13:1; 21:11; see 1:4 and note; 1:22 and note). **they will gain knowledge** See note on 9:8.

19:27 my son See 1:8 and note; note on 1:8—9:18.

19:28 A corrupt witness Someone who is false, rebellious or evil (see 6:12 and note; note on 6:19).

19:29 beatings for the backs of fools See note on 14:3.

20 Wine is a mocker and beer a brawler;
whoever is led astray by them is not
wise.

² A king's wrath strikes terror like the roar of a
lion;
those who anger him forfeit their lives.

³ It is to one's honor to avoid strife,
but every fool is quick to quarrel.

⁴ Sluggards do not plow in season;
so at harvest time they look but find
nothing.

⁵ The purposes of a person's heart are deep
waters,
but one who has insight draws them out.

⁶ Many claim to have unfailing love,
but a faithful person who can find?

⁷ The righteous lead blameless lives;
blessed are their children after them.

⁸ When a king sits on his throne to judge,
he winnows out all evil with his eyes.

⁹ Who can say, "I have kept my heart pure;
I am clean and without sin"?

¹⁰ Differing weights and differing measures —
the Lord detests them both.

¹¹ Even small children are known by their
actions,
so is their conduct really pure and upright?

¹² Ears that hear and eyes that see —
the Lord has made them both.

¹³ Do not love sleep or you will grow poor;
stay awake and you will have food
to spare.

¹⁴ "It's no good, it's no good!" says the buyer —
then goes off and boasts about the
purchase.

¹⁵ Gold there is, and rubies in abundance,
but lips that speak knowledge are a rare
jewel.

¹⁶ Take the garment of one who puts up
security for a stranger;
hold it in pledge if it is done for an
outsider.

¹⁷ Food gained by fraud tastes sweet,
but one ends up with a mouth full
of gravel.

¹⁸ Plans are established by seeking advice;
so if you wage war, obtain guidance.

¹⁹ A gossip betrays a confidence;
so avoid anyone who talks too much.

²⁰ If someone curses their father or
mother,
their lamp will be snuffed out in pitch
darkness.

²¹ An inheritance claimed too soon
will not be blessed at the end.

20:1 Wine is a mocker Warns against the over consumption of alcohol. Drunkenness should be avoided because it causes strife—a theme expounded upon in 23:29–35.
20:2 king's wrath Guarding against the king's anger is a recurring theme in Proverbs. Compare 16:14; 19:12.
20:4 Sluggards do not plow in season See 6:9 and note; 13:4 and note.
20:8 winnows Kings were responsible for judging legal disputes (1Ki 3:16–28). This word refers to the process of separating grain from plant stalks (see note on Ru 3:2). It is often used figuratively to describe judgment (Isa 41:15–16; Jer 15:8; 51:2). Jesus uses similar terminology when he speaks of the wicked (the chaff or stalks) being separated from the righteous (grain) and destroyed (Mt 3:12). See the infographic "A Threshing Floor" on p. 497.
20:9 I have kept my heart pure The rhetorical questions in this proverb illustrate that no one is completely guiltless (1Ki 8:46; Ps 143:2; Job 4:17–19).
20:10 Differing weights and differing measures Dishonest merchants would often use faulty scales and weights to cheat their customers. See note on Pr 11:1.
20:11 Even small children are known This phrase is ambiguous. Either the child pretends to be good but really is not, or the child's actions will indicate how he or she will act as an adult.
20:12 Ears that hear and eyes that see Indicates perceptive listening and seeing, not just sensory ability.
20:13 Do not love sleep Laziness is condemned as a path to poverty (6:9–11; 19:15; 20:4).

20:14 "It's no good, it's no good!" says the buyer Describes a negotiating tactic: A buyer claims a deal is no good to get a lower price, then the buyer boasts about the great deal that has been secured. It is unclear whether this proverb condemns this practice or merely reflects upon it.
20:15 lips that speak knowledge are a rare jewel Wisdom is better than precious stones, gold and silver (3:14–15; 16:16; Job 28:15–19).
20:16 Take the garment Advocates holding people responsible for their obligations. Proverbs earlier warned against putting up security for others to avoid becoming responsible if they defaulted (see Pr 6:1 and note). Taking a person's garment was a common form of security or collateral for a loan. However, the law required that it be returned to a person before nightfall (Ex 22:26–27; Dt 24:10–13).
20:17 ends up with a mouth full of gravel Highlights the ultimate reward of deceit: Its gain may be sweet, but it is fleeting.
20:18 if you wage war, obtain guidance Rather than encouraging war, this proverb reflects the reality of war and prescribes the proper way to wage it (compare Pr 20:3). A careful and wise leader will be more successful in war than a powerful but reckless one (24:5–6; Ecc 9:13–18).
20:19 anyone who talks too much Describes those who speak too much and talk foolishly about things they should not. Unlike the slanderer, the simple babbler may not be malicious.

²² Do not say, "I'll pay you back for this wrong!"
　　Wait for the Lord, and he will avenge you.

²³ The Lord detests differing weights,
　　and dishonest scales do not please him.

²⁴ A person's steps are directed by the Lord.
　　How then can anyone understand their
　　own way?

²⁵ It is a trap to dedicate something rashly
　　and only later to consider one's vows.

²⁶ A wise king winnows out the wicked;
　　he drives the threshing wheel over them.

²⁷ The human spirit is^a the lamp of the Lord
　　that sheds light on one's inmost being.

²⁸ Love and faithfulness keep a king safe;
　　through love his throne is made secure.

²⁹ The glory of young men is their strength,
　　gray hair the splendor of the old.

³⁰ Blows and wounds scrub away evil,
　　and beatings purge the inmost being.

21 In the Lord's hand the king's heart is a
　　stream of water
　that he channels toward all who
　　please him.

² A person may think their own ways
　　are right,
　but the Lord weighs the heart.

³ To do what is right and just
　　is more acceptable to the Lord than
　　sacrifice.

⁴ Haughty eyes and a proud heart —
　　the unplowed field of the wicked —
　　produce sin.

⁵ The plans of the diligent lead to profit
　　as surely as haste leads to poverty.

⁶ A fortune made by a lying tongue
　　is a fleeting vapor and a deadly snare.^b

⁷ The violence of the wicked will drag them
　　away,
　　for they refuse to do what is right.

⁸ The way of the guilty is devious,
　　but the conduct of the innocent is upright.

⁹ Better to live on a corner of the roof
　　than share a house with a quarrelsome
　　wife.

¹⁰ The wicked crave evil;
　　their neighbors get no mercy from them.

¹¹ When a mocker is punished, the simple gain
　　wisdom;
　　by paying attention to the wise they get
　　knowledge.

---

^a 27 Or *A person's words are*　^b 6 Some Hebrew manuscripts, Septuagint and Vulgate; most Hebrew manuscripts *vapor for those who seek death*

20:20 If someone curses their father or mother This refers to acting contemptuously (Pr 30:11,17; compare Ex 21:17; Lev 20:9).

20:22 Wait for the Lord Encourages people to patiently trust in Yahweh instead of taking matters into their own hands. David exemplified this patience in his situation with Saul (1Sa 26:8–11).

20:24 A person's steps are directed by the Lord People are responsible for their own actions, but Yahweh is ultimately over all of human life and has his own plans that cannot be thwarted (compare Pr 16:9). Proverbs affirms God's plans and following them (compare 14:12; 16:9; 19:21) and in doing so holds people responsible to live well. The goal of the book is to help people learn how to navigate life in the fear of Yahweh (1:1–7).

20:25 only later to consider one's vows While the law did not require making vows, it considered leaving a vow unfulfilled a serious offense (Nu 30:2; Dt 23:21–23). The author of Ecclesiastes warns against making a rash vow, arguing it is better to refrain from making them (see Ecc 5:4–6 and note).

20:26 he drives the threshing wheel over them Grain could be threshed by rolling a wheel over it to crack the husk. Here it signifies the king's ability to identify and remove evil from society.

20:29 splendor of the old In the ancient Near East, old age was a sign of wisdom (Job 12:12; 32:6–7); in Israel, old age was also considered a sign of God's favor or a reward for obedience (Ge 15:15; Dt 30:19–20).

21:1 In the Lord's hand Even though kings hold great power (Pr 14:28; 16:15; 20:2), they are ultimately under the jurisdiction of God's power over the entire earth. See note on 29:26.

21:2 but the Lord weighs the heart Ancients considered the heart to be the center of a person's character (1Sa 16:7).

21:3 more acceptable to the Lord than sacrifice Yahweh's preference for righteousness over sacrifice is well attested in the OT (1Sa 15:22; Jer 7:22–23; Hos 6:6). The prophets echo this emphasis on justice over sacrifice (Isa 1:11–17; Mic 6:6–8). Proverbs condemns the faulty sacrifices of the wicked (Pr 15:8).

21:4 unplowed field The Hebrew word used here may refer either to a lamp or plowing. If it signifies a lamp, the verse says that the very life of the wicked is sin. If it indicates plowing, it indicates that the wicked produce sin.

21:6 a fleeting vapor and a deadly snare Proverbs indicates that any wealth obtained through dubious measures is fleeting (10:2; 11:18; 20:17). Here, this kind of wealth is not just fleeting; it is destructive.

21:9 a corner of the roof Probably refers to a small guestroom on a flat roof (1Ki 17:19; 2Ki 4:10). It is better to live in isolation—separated from family—than to share a house with a quarrelsome wife. Proverbs 21:19 takes isolation even further and suggests that living in the desert is preferable to living with a quarrelsome woman.

21:10 evil The Hebrew word used here can refer to trouble or harm. The wicked person wishes harm on people (6:14; 11:27).

21:11 simple gain wisdom The scoffer's punishment serves as a warning to the simple. However, in contrast

¹² The Righteous One[a] takes note of the house
    of the wicked
  and brings the wicked to ruin.

¹³ Whoever shuts their ears to the cry of the
    poor
  will also cry out and not be answered.

¹⁴ A gift given in secret soothes anger,
  and a bribe concealed in the cloak pacifies
    great wrath.

¹⁵ When justice is done, it brings joy to the
    righteous
  but terror to evildoers.

¹⁶ Whoever strays from the path
    of prudence
  comes to rest in the company of
    the dead.

¹⁷ Whoever loves pleasure will become
    poor;
  whoever loves wine and olive oil will
    never be rich.

¹⁸ The wicked become a ransom for the
    righteous,
  and the unfaithful for the upright.

¹⁹ Better to live in a desert
  than with a quarrelsome and nagging wife.

²⁰ The wise store up choice food and olive oil,
  but fools gulp theirs down.

²¹ Whoever pursues righteousness and love
  finds life, prosperity[b] and honor.

²² One who is wise can go up against the city of
    the mighty
  and pull down the stronghold in which
    they trust.

²³ Those who guard their mouths and their
    tongues
  keep themselves from calamity.

²⁴ The proud and arrogant person — "Mocker"
    is his name —
  behaves with insolent fury.

²⁵ The craving of a sluggard will be the death
    of him,
  because his hands refuse to work.
²⁶ All day long he craves for more,
  but the righteous give without sparing.

²⁷ The sacrifice of the wicked is detestable —
  how much more so when brought with evil
    intent!

²⁸ A false witness will perish,
  but a careful listener will testify
    successfully.

²⁹ The wicked put up a bold front,
  but the upright give thought to their ways.

³⁰ There is no wisdom, no insight, no plan
  that can succeed against the Lord.

³¹ The horse is made ready for the day of battle,
  but victory rests with the Lord.

___

a 12 Or *The righteous person*   *b* 21 Or *righteousness*

___

to the simple, scoffers do not respond (13:1; see note on 1:4; note on 1:22).

21:12 The Righteous One The Hebrew expression used here may refer to God or to a righteous person who sees the wicked and declares that God will overthrow them. Compare Eliphaz in Job 5:3–4.

21:13 will also cry out and not be answered Yahweh will repay generosity to the impoverished (Pr 14:21; 19:17). However, those who oppress the poor insult God (14:31; 17:5 and note); they will not receive any mercy.

21:14 A gift given in secret soothes anger See note on 18:16.

21:16 company of the dead The consequences for straying from the way of wisdom are more dire than they might seem in the moment. See 2:18 and note.

21:17 whoever loves wine and olive oil Condemns gluttony and a life of self-indulgent consumption (21:20). This proverb does not condemn wine or oil, which were considered blessings from God (Dt 7:13; Ps 104:14–15). Likewise, it does not condemn pleasure, also seen as a gift of God (compare note on Ecc 9:7–10).

21:19 to live in a desert Whereas other proverbs (Pr 21:9; 25:24) state that it is better to live on a rooftop than with a contentious wife, this proverbs intensifies the image by saying it is better to live in a desert or wilderness.

21:21 Whoever pursues righteousness Just as the person who pursues evil will find it (11:27), the person who seeks righteousness will find it. **finds life** The reward

for wisdom and righteousness is long life and success. See note on 3:2.

21:22 One who is wise can go up against the city of the mighty Wisdom is better than might and military strength (compare 11:14; 20:18; 24:5–6; Ecc 9:16,18).

21:24 behaves with insolent fury The scoffer or mocker acts with overwhelming pride that is infuriating. See note on Pr 1:22.

21:25 The craving of a sluggard will be the death of him Sluggards place preference on their sleep and prefer to be lazy (6:9–11). They refuse to work and look for excuses to stay inside (20:4; 26:13–14). Their laziness is depicted as ultimately leading to poverty and their death (10:4; see note on 6:9).

21:27 sacrifice of the wicked A sacrifice that is insincere or made only to appear righteous. See note on 15:8.

21:28 A false witness will perish A false witness was to receive the same punishment as the accused (Dt 19:18–19).

21:30 that can succeed against the Lord All human wisdom is frail and useless before Yahweh and his wisdom. The book of Proverbs promotes human wisdom and considers it worthwhile for righteousness (Pr 11:14; 15:22; 20:18). However, it puts human wisdom in proper perspective: It is only found in the fear of Yahweh and it is always subject to God's higher wisdom (1:7; 20:24).

21:31 but victory rests with the Lord Yahweh—not human preparation—determines outcomes. See note on 20:24; note on Ps 20:7.

22

A good name is more desirable than
    great riches;
  to be esteemed is better than silver or gold.

2 Rich and poor have this in common:
  The LORD is the Maker of them all.

3 The prudent see danger and take refuge,
  but the simple keep going and pay the
    penalty.

4 Humility is the fear of the LORD;
  its wages are riches and honor and life.

5 In the paths of the wicked are snares and
    pitfalls,
  but those who would preserve their life
    stay far from them.

6 Start children off on the way they should go,
  and even when they are old they will not
    turn from it.

7 The rich rule over the poor,
  and the borrower is slave to the lender.

8 Whoever sows injustice reaps calamity,
  and the rod they wield in fury will be
    broken.

9 The generous will themselves be blessed,
  for they share their food with the poor.

10 Drive out the mocker, and out goes strife;
  quarrels and insults are ended.

11 One who loves a pure heart and who speaks
    with grace
  will have the king for a friend.

12 The eyes of the LORD keep watch over
    knowledge,
  but he frustrates the words of the
    unfaithful.

13 The sluggard says, "There's a lion outside!
  I'll be killed in the public square!"

14 The mouth of an adulterous woman is a
    deep pit;
  a man who is under the LORD's wrath falls
    into it.

15 Folly is bound up in the heart of a child,
  but the rod of discipline will drive it far
    away.

16 One who oppresses the poor to increase his
    wealth
  and one who gives gifts to the rich — both
    come to poverty.

Thirty Sayings of the Wise

Saying 1

17 Pay attention and turn your ear to the
    sayings of the wise;
  apply your heart to what I teach,

22:1 A good name is more desirable than great riches Stresses the value of a good reputation (Ecc 7:1). Like wisdom, a good reputation is more valuable than material wealth (Pr 3:13–15; 16:16).

22:2 Rich and poor have this in common All people are equally created by God, regardless of wealth or status. Other proverbs cite this as a reason to avoid oppressing the impoverished (14:31; 17:5).

22:3 the simple keep going The simple are characterized by a lack of concern for danger. See 1:4 and note.

22:4 fear of the LORD Describes a pious attitude toward Yahweh (see note on 1:7). **riches and honor and life** Proverbs notes that blessings often come to the wise and faithful. See note on 3:2.

22:6 the way they should go Refers to moral education, the way that is proper for a child (compare 23:19; Job 31:7). **they will not turn from it** Describes a pattern, not a promise. Children are responsible for their choices, regardless of their parents' training. See note on Pr 3:2.

22:7 The rich rule over the poor Rather than encourage the subjugation of the impoverished, this proverb reflects upon the fact that the rich have prominence while the poor have to depend on others. It also serves as a warning to live wisely (21:17,20). Proverbs 22:2 stresses the equality of the poor and rich before Yahweh.

22:9 generous will themselves be blessed Generous people will be blessed because Yahweh will repay them (see 19:17 and note).

22:10 Drive out the mocker Scoffers cause contention and arguments; removing them yields a more peaceful situation. Proverbs 21:24 used three terms to describe the arrogance of the scoffer (see note on 21:24; compare note on 1:22). Here, three terms are used to show the trouble scoffers bring. The first describes arguments stirred up by anger or slanderous accusations (15:18; 16:28); the second can refer to a legal dispute (Dt 17:8); and the third refers to shame or disgrace (Pr 11:2).

22:13 I'll be killed in the public square The sluggard's words are meant to be an absurd excuse for laziness. This proverb is repeated in a larger section condemning the sluggard (26:13–16; see 6:9 and note).

22:14 The mouth of an adulterous woman See note on 2:16.

22:15 in the heart of a child In Proverbs, the child represents someone in need of instruction or discipline. While the child may act foolishly or without sense (7:7), the child willingly accepts discipline in order to learn (22:6)—the child is thus distinguished from the fool. **discipline** The Hebrew word used here, *musar*, emphasizes teaching or instruction. The intent of discipline should be for the instruction and benefit of the child. See note on 13:24; compare note on 1:2.

22:17—24:22 The first section of Solomon's proverbs (10:1—22:16) now comes to an end. The proverbs in this section are attributed to "the wise" in general, not to a specific author. Longer than those in 10:1—22:16, these proverbs sometimes span several verses (23:29–35). A short prologue (22:17–21) instructs the reader to listen to the words of the wise, which are true and pleasant (22:18,21).

The writings of other ancient sages apparently influenced this section of Proverbs; it shows particular similarities to the Egyptian work *Instruction of Amenemope*.

¹⁸ for it is pleasing when you keep them in your
heart
and have all of them ready on your lips.
¹⁹ So that your trust may be in the LORD,
I teach you today, even you.
²⁰ Have I not written thirty sayings for you,
sayings of counsel and knowledge,
²¹ teaching you to be honest and to speak the
truth,
so that you bring back truthful reports
to those you serve?

Saying 2

²² Do not exploit the poor because they
are poor
and do not crush the needy in court,
²³ for the LORD will take up their case
and will exact life for life.

Saying 3

²⁴ Do not make friends with a hot-tempered
person,
do not associate with one easily
angered,
²⁵ or you may learn their ways
and get yourself ensnared.

Saying 4

²⁶ Do not be one who shakes hands in pledge
or puts up security for debts;

²⁷ if you lack the means to pay,
your very bed will be snatched from
under you.

Saying 5

²⁸ Do not move an ancient boundary stone
set up by your ancestors.

Saying 6

²⁹ Do you see someone skilled in their work?
They will serve before kings;
they will not serve before officials of low
rank.

Saying 7

23 When you sit to dine with a ruler,
note well what*ᵃ* is before you,
² and put a knife to your throat
if you are given to gluttony.
³ Do not crave his delicacies,
for that food is deceptive.

Saying 8

⁴ Do not wear yourself out to get rich;
do not trust your own cleverness.
⁵ Cast but a glance at riches, and they are gone,
for they will surely sprout wings
and fly off to the sky like an eagle.

ᵃ 1 Or *who*

The compilers of Proverbs did not copy ancient Near Eastern counterparts, but they likely used other writings as the basis for the structure and content of this collection (see note on 22:20). The most notable difference between other ancient Near Eastern wisdom literature and Hebrew wisdom is that Hebrew wisdom begins with the fear of Yahweh (see 1:7 and note).

22:18 in your heart The Hebrew phrase used here literally means "in your belly." In the ancient Near East, thoughts were sometimes believed to be stored in the belly (see 18:8 and note).
22:20 thirty sayings The remainder of this section (22:22—24:22) divides into roughly 30 paragraphs. There are different ways to divide this section of Proverbs, ranging from 28 to 31 sayings. The collection is modeled after the structure of other ancient Near Eastern wisdom literature, where 30 sayings was a common format. The Egyptian work *Instruction of Amenemope*—which has many similarities to this section—includes 30 chapters.

22:22–23 This proverb addresses the exploitation of the impoverished. Because they are unable to protect their legal rights, the poor are an easy target for the rich and powerful. The rationale given here for not robbing them is that Yahweh defends them.

22:22 do not crush the needy in court The gate of a city was often the center of commercial and legal activity (see Ru 4:1 and note).
22:23 the LORD will take up their case Previous proverbs showed that the oppression of the poor insults God, the Maker of both rich and poor (14:31; 17:5). This proverb goes further, stating Yahweh will come to

the defense of the impoverished and carry out justice for the oppressed.

22:24–25 This proverb exhorts the reader to avoid chronically angry people (15:18; 27:3; 29:22). While quarrelsome people bring destruction, the greatest danger of associating with them is becoming like them. This threat of corruption is also a common theme in Egyptian wisdom literature.

22:26–27 This proverb warns against putting up security or pledges. It echoes a common theme in Proverbs (e.g., 6:1–5; 11:15; 17:18; 20:16; see note on 6:1).

22:28 Do not move an ancient boundary stone Moving boundaries was a way to illegally seize land. It was prohibited by the law (Dt 19:14; 27:17). This proverb is expounded on in Pr 23:10–11.

23:1–3 This proverb advises caution when eating with someone in a position of authority. It specifically warns against overindulging. Rulers might notice such behavior and think less of a person. Alternatively, rulers might have ulterior motives—like the stingy man of vv. 6–7—and use the indulgence as an opportunity to require something from a guest.

23:2 put a knife to your throat The Hebrew phrase used here refers to exercising self-control.
23:3 food is deceptive May indicate that the ruler has a hidden motive for the feast (see note on vv. 1–3).

23:4–5 This proverb does not condemn wealth; it warns against the pursuit of wealth. Ecclesiastes also warns about pursuit of wealth and its inability to satisfy (Ecc 5:10).

Saying 9

[6] Do not eat the food of a begrudging host,
  do not crave his delicacies;
[7] for he is the kind of person
  who is always thinking about the cost.[a]
"Eat and drink," he says to you,
  but his heart is not with you.
[8] You will vomit up the little you have eaten
  and will have wasted your compliments.

Saying 10

[9] Do not speak to fools,
  for they will scorn your prudent words.

Saying 11

[10] Do not move an ancient boundary stone
  or encroach on the fields of the fatherless,
[11] for their Defender is strong;
  he will take up their case against you.

Saying 12

[12] Apply your heart to instruction
  and your ears to words of knowledge.

Saying 13

[13] Do not withhold discipline from a child;
  if you punish them with the rod, they will
    not die.
[14] Punish them with the rod
  and save them from death.

Saying 14

[15] My son, if your heart is wise,
  then my heart will be glad indeed;
[16] my inmost being will rejoice
  when your lips speak what is right.

Saying 15

[17] Do not let your heart envy sinners,
  but always be zealous for the fear of the
    LORD.
[18] There is surely a future hope for you,
  and your hope will not be cut off.

Saying 16

[19] Listen, my son, and be wise,
  and set your heart on the right path:
[20] Do not join those who drink too much wine
  or gorge themselves on meat,
[21] for drunkards and gluttons become poor,
  and drowsiness clothes them in rags.

Saying 17

[22] Listen to your father, who gave you life,
  and do not despise your mother when she
    is old.
[23] Buy the truth and do not sell it —
  wisdom, instruction and insight as well.

---

[a] 7 Or *for as he thinks within himself, / so he is*; or *for as he puts on a feast, / so he is*

It describes two situations: In one, a person pursues wealth but never enjoys it or finds satisfaction (Ecc 4:7–8). In the second, someone loses all their wealth and is left with nothing (Ecc 5:13–17).

23:6–8 This proverb warns against eating with a stingy person. The stingy person may appear hospitable and generous on the outside but is resentful and calculating inside (Pr 23:7).

23:6 a begrudging host The Hebrew expression used here, *ra' ayin*, describes those who are duplicitous and only interested in their own wealth. In contrast, the term *tov ayin* (22:9) describes a generous person.

23:9 Do not speak to fools Warns against wasting words on a fool. Fools are not interested in instruction or wisdom (1:7; 15:5); instead, they only flaunt their folly (13:16).

23:10–11 This proverb warns against taking advantage of widows and orphans by seizing their property. Widows were especially vulnerable and depended on relatives to protect them, and this proverb asserts that God himself will take up their case (Dt 10:18; Ps 68:6).

23:10 Do not move an ancient boundary stone Prohibited by the law (Dt 19:14; 27:17), moving boundaries was a way to seize land illegally. See note on Pr 22:28.

23:11 Defender The Hebrew word used here, *go'el*, most likely refers to God (see Job 19:25 and note). God defends the cause of the oppressed or afflicted (Ps 119:154; Jer 50:34). Proverbs 22:22–23 indicates that God advocates for the impoverished and oppressed while punishing their oppressors.

23:12–14 This proverb admonishes the reader to take discipline to heart and also to administer it to children. Discipline given now can keep children from later peril.

23:12 instruction The Hebrew word used here can refer to discipline (23:13) or teaching (4:1; see 1:2 and note).

23:13 you punish them with the rod Proverbs consistently emphasizes the importance of discipline. See note on 13:24.

23:14 death The Hebrew word used here, *she'ol*, refers to the realm of the dead (see note on Ge 37:35; note on Job 14:13). Discipline, as well as wisdom, is seen as a life-saving exercise (see note on Pr 3:2).

23:15–16 This proverb encourages a son to learn wisdom and in doing so make his parents happy. See 10:1.

23:15 My son See note on 1:8.

23:17–18 This proverb warns against envying the wicked and encourages the righteous to look to the future instead. In doing so, it implies that sinners sometimes find success. This proverb resembles Ps 73, where the Psalmist feels envious of the success of the wicked (Ps 73:2–3) but regains confidence when witnessing their ultimate fate (Ps 73:16–17) and destruction (Ps 73:27).

23:19–21 This proverb warns against dissipation, specifically drunkenness and gluttony (compare Dt 21:20). The son has two ways he can go, and choosing the wrong one will land him among drunkards and gluttons—a sure path to ruin. The theme of drunkenness is continued later in Pr 23:29–35.

²⁴ The father of a righteous child has great joy;
　　a man who fathers a wise son rejoices
　　　　in him.
²⁵ May your father and mother rejoice;
　　may she who gave you birth be joyful!

Saying 18

²⁶ My son, give me your heart
　　and let your eyes delight in my ways,
²⁷ for an adulterous woman is a deep pit,
　　and a wayward wife is a narrow well.
²⁸ Like a bandit she lies in wait
　　and multiplies the unfaithful among men.

Saying 19

²⁹ Who has woe? Who has sorrow?
　　Who has strife? Who has complaints?
　　Who has needless bruises? Who has
　　　　bloodshot eyes?
³⁰ Those who linger over wine,
　　who go to sample bowls of mixed wine.
³¹ Do not gaze at wine when it is red,
　　when it sparkles in the cup,
　　when it goes down smoothly!
³² In the end it bites like a snake
　　and poisons like a viper.
³³ Your eyes will see strange sights,
　　and your mind will imagine confusing
　　　　things.
³⁴ You will be like one sleeping on the
　　　　high seas,
　　lying on top of the rigging.

³⁵ "They hit me," you will say, "but I'm not hurt!
　　They beat me, but I don't feel it!
　　When will I wake up
　　　　so I can find another drink?"

Saying 20

24 Do not envy the wicked,
　　do not desire their company;
² for their hearts plot violence,
　　and their lips talk about making trouble.

Saying 21

³ By wisdom a house is built,
　　and through understanding it is established;
⁴ through knowledge its rooms are filled
　　with rare and beautiful treasures.

Saying 22

⁵ The wise prevail through great power,
　　and those who have knowledge muster
　　　　their strength.
⁶ Surely you need guidance to wage war,
　　and victory is won through many advisers.

Saying 23

⁷ Wisdom is too high for fools;
　　in the assembly at the gate they must not
　　　　open their mouths.

Saying 24

⁸ Whoever plots evil
　　will be known as a schemer.

23:22–25 This proverb encourages the son to accept his parents' instruction and to pursue wisdom. He will then gain wisdom and make his parents rejoice (see 10:1; 23:15–16).
23:22 Listen to your father, who gave you life See note on 1:8.
23:23 Buy the truth Rather than implying that truth, wisdom, instruction or understanding can be purchased, this proverb encourages those who are wise to obtain truth and wisdom and to not give them up. Elsewhere, wisdom cannot be purchased by gold, silver or any precious stones (Job 28:15–19).
23:26–28 This proverb warns about the destructive nature of the adulteress—a theme throughout Proverbs (e.g., Pr 2:16–19; 5:3–23; 6:23–35; 7:4–27; see note on 2:16).
23:28 lies in wait The adulteress is an active danger as well as a passive one—i.e., a pit or well to fall into (23:27).
23:29–35 This longer proverb addresses problems associated with drunkenness. It begins with a series of questions that list the issues faced by those who linger over wine (vv. 29–30). It warns against the initial allure of wine (v. 31) before describing the results of drunkenness. Verse 32 compares the effects of drunkenness to the bite of a snake. In v. 33, drunkenness affects people's vision and causes them to stagger as if they

were on a ship (v. 34). Oblivious to surroundings, the drunk foolishly seeks another drink (v. 35).
23:30 who go to sample bowls of mixed wine Sometimes spices were added to wine to improve its taste.
24:1–2 This proverb advises against envying wicked people, perhaps for the success and prosperity they enjoy (3:31; 23:17; 24:19; Ps 37:1). They are intent on destruction and deceit, and Proverbs makes clear elsewhere what happens to such people (Pr 1:10–15; 3:31–33; 23:17–18).
24:3–4 This proverb describes the constructive nature of wisdom. Proverbs elsewhere personifies wisdom as an industrious woman who builds her house (9:1). Here, wisdom does not just build the house; she fills it with prosperity and happiness (see note on 3:2).
24:5–6 This proverb praises the power of wisdom. It is more powerful than physical strength and military prowess, a common theme in Proverbs (compare 11:14; 15:22; 20:18).
24:6 Surely you need guidance to wage war While not encouraging war, Proverbs recognizes the reality of war and prescribes the proper way to wage it (24:5–6; compare 20:18; Ecc 9:13–18).
24:7 in the assembly at the gate The place of gathering where civic and commercial business were often conducted. See note on Pr 8:3.

⁹ The schemes of folly are sin,
and people detest a mocker.

Saying 25

¹⁰ If you falter in a time of trouble,
how small is your strength!
¹¹ Rescue those being led away to death;
hold back those staggering toward
slaughter.
¹² If you say, "But we knew nothing about this,"
does not he who weighs the heart
perceive it?
Does not he who guards your life know it?
Will he not repay everyone according to
what they have done?

Saying 26

¹³ Eat honey, my son, for it is good;
honey from the comb is sweet to your
taste.
¹⁴ Know also that wisdom is like honey for you:
If you find it, there is a future hope
for you,
and your hope will not be cut off.

Saying 27

¹⁵ Do not lurk like a thief near the house of the
righteous,
do not plunder their dwelling place;
¹⁶ for though the righteous fall seven times,
they rise again,
but the wicked stumble when calamity
strikes.

Saying 28

¹⁷ Do not gloat when your enemy falls;
when they stumble, do not let your heart
rejoice,
¹⁸ or the LORD will see and disapprove
and turn his wrath away from them.

Saying 29

¹⁹ Do not fret because of evildoers
or be envious of the wicked,
²⁰ for the evildoer has no future hope,
and the lamp of the wicked will be
snuffed out.

Saying 30

²¹ Fear the LORD and the king, my son,
and do not join with rebellious officials,
²² for those two will send sudden destruction
on them,
and who knows what calamities they can
bring?

Further Sayings of the Wise

²³ These also are sayings of the wise:

To show partiality in judging is not good:
²⁴ Whoever says to the guilty, "You are
innocent,"
will be cursed by peoples and denounced
by nations.
²⁵ But it will go well with those who convict the
guilty,
and rich blessing will come on them.

24:8–9 This proverb describes someone who schemes and says the schemer will acquire a reputation that invites hatred.

24:10–12 This proverb calls for the rescue of people threatened by death. This may refer to instructing people in life-saving wisdom or righteousness—helping others avoid the path that ultimately leads to death (13:14; 14:12). Alternatively, it may instruct that people condemned to execution not be abandoned. The proverb warns against ignoring such people and later claiming ignorance; God weighs the heart and knows the truth.

24:13–14 This proverb compares the sweetness of honey to the sweetness of wisdom. Just as honey is sweet to the mouth, wisdom is sweet to a person's whole life. Elsewhere, the law is compared to honey (Ps 19:10–11).

24:15–16 This proverb warns that trying to destroy the righteous is futile. While the righteous may be defeated temporarily, ultimately the wicked will be destroyed (Pr 14:32).

24:16 seven times Symbolizes perfection or completeness. Here, the number seven illustrates that no matter how many times the righteous fall, their defeat is temporary; they will rise again.

24:17–18 Following the warning about trying to destroy the righteous (vv. 15–16), this proverb warns against

gloating at the fall of an enemy. Proverbs 20:22 warns against revenge, encouraging the wise to wait for Yahweh. Here, readers are advised not to rejoice when their enemy falls because God may end up having mercy on the enemy.

24:19–20 This proverb warns against envying the wicked (compare vv. 1–2). They will die and may not leave any descendants (13:9; 20:20; 23:18).

24:19 or be envious of the wicked Proverbs teaches that the success of the wicked will be short-lived (24:20); therefore, the wise should not envy the wicked. See note on 23:17–18.

24:21–22 This proverb admonishes the son to respect divine and human authority and to avoid those who disregard their authority. Both God and the king have the power to destroy (14:35; 16:14; 19:12; 20:2).

24:23–34 This section of the sayings of the wise is the shortest collection of proverbs (see 22:17—24:22 and note). It addresses the topics of justice in the courts (24:23–26,28–29) and hard work in the home (vv. 27,30–34).

24:23 To show partiality in judging Forbidden by the law (Dt 1:17).
24:24 Whoever says to the guilty, "You are innocent" Declaring the guilty to be innocent offends God as well as people. The person who does so is abhorred by the nations and is an abomination to God (Pr 17:15).

26 An honest answer
　　is like a kiss on the lips.

27 Put your outdoor work in order
　　and get your fields ready;
　　after that, build your house.

28 Do not testify against your neighbor without
　　cause —
　　would you use your lips to mislead?
29 Do not say, "I'll do to them as they have done
　　to me;
　　I'll pay them back for what they did."

30 I went past the field of a sluggard,
　　past the vineyard of someone who has no
　　　sense;
31 thorns had come up everywhere,
　　the ground was covered with weeds,
　　and the stone wall was in ruins.
32 I applied my heart to what I observed
　　and learned a lesson from what I saw:
33 A little sleep, a little slumber,
　　a little folding of the hands to rest —
34 and poverty will come on you like a thief
　　and scarcity like an armed man.

More Proverbs of Solomon

25 These are more proverbs of Solomon,
　　compiled by the men of Hezekiah king
of Judah:

2 It is the glory of God to conceal a matter;
　　to search out a matter is the glory of kings.
3 As the heavens are high and the earth is deep,
　　so the hearts of kings are unsearchable.

4 Remove the dross from the silver,
　　and a silversmith can produce a vessel;
5 remove wicked officials from the king's
　　presence,
　　and his throne will be established through
　　righteousness.

6 Do not exalt yourself in the king's presence,
　　and do not claim a place among his
　　great men;
7 it is better for him to say to you, "Come up
　　here,"
　　than for him to humiliate you before his
　　nobles.

What you have seen with your eyes
8 　do not bring[a] hastily to court,
　for what will you do in the end
　　if your neighbor puts you to shame?

9 If you take your neighbor to court,
　　do not betray another's confidence,
10 or the one who hears it may shame you
　　and the charge against you will stand.

11 Like apples[b] of gold in settings of silver
　　is a ruling rightly given.
12 Like an earring of gold or an ornament of
　　fine gold
　　is the rebuke of a wise judge to a
　　listening ear.

13 Like a snow-cooled drink at harvest time
　　is a trustworthy messenger to the one who
　　sends him;
　　he refreshes the spirit of his master.

---

a 7,8 Or nobles / on whom you had set your eyes. / 8Do not go
b 11 Or possibly apricots

24:26 a kiss on the lips A sign of homage or friendship (2Sa 15:5; 1Ki 19:18; 1Sa 20:41). An honest person shows respect to others by telling the truth.
24:29 as they have done to me In Proverbs, the wise are encouraged to trust Yahweh to correct the wrongs done to them. See note on Pr 20:22.
24:30–34 This proverb describes the consequences of laziness. The sluggard's laziness results in an overgrown field and broken down wall. This leads to the sluggard being poor and in need. See note on 21:25.
25:1—29:27 Men during Hezekiah's reign copied this second and final collection of proverbs attributed to Solomon (see 10:1). Hezekiah reigned for 29 years as a righteous and prosperous king. He is credited with a religious revival in Israel (2Ki 18:2–8; 2Ch 29:3—31:21). See the timeline "The Divided Kingdom" on p. 536.
25:1 proverbs of Solomon See note on Pr 1:1. **compiled** The Hebrew word used here, literally meaning "to move," is used in the sense of moving from one book to another.
25:2 It is the glory of God to conceal a matter This enigmatic proverb contrasts God and the king. God shows his glory by his great and unknowable power, specifically in creation (Job 11:7; 26:14). In contrast, the glory of

the king is to know and understand in order to rightly govern his people (1Ki 3:9).
25:6–7 This proverb warns against self-promotion: It is better to remain humble and be promoted than to be presumptuous and be rebuked. Jesus teaches a similar lesson in Lk 14:7–11, applying it to all of life.
25:9 If you take your neighbor to court Recommends dealing with conflicts tactfully to preserve the reputation of both parties from damage caused by misinformed gossip. Jesus gives more explicit instructions on dealing with conflict among God's people (Mt 18:15–17). He advises first going to someone alone to raise issues of fault. By doing this, there is an opportunity for an apology and the restoration of the relationship. But if the person the conflict is brought to does not listen, Jesus suggests confronting the person again in the presence of others who act as witnesses (Dt 19:15). If the person still refuses to listen, then the fault should be brought before the church. Barring repentance, the friend should be excluded from fellowship. Paul also echoes this manner of approaching disputes (Titus 3:10).
25:11 apples of gold A decorative motif used in jewelry. Compare to the pomegranate in Ex 39:24–25; 1Ki 7:18.
25:13 snow-cooled Likely indicates a cool or refreshing break from the heat of summer, since literal snowfall

¹⁴ Like clouds and wind without rain
    is one who boasts of gifts never given.

¹⁵ Through patience a ruler can be persuaded,
    and a gentle tongue can break a bone.

¹⁶ If you find honey, eat just enough —
    too much of it, and you will vomit.
¹⁷ Seldom set foot in your neighbor's house —
    too much of you, and they will hate you.

¹⁸ Like a club or a sword or a sharp arrow
    is one who gives false testimony against a
      neighbor.
¹⁹ Like a broken tooth or a lame foot
    is reliance on the unfaithful in a time of
      trouble.
²⁰ Like one who takes away a garment on a
      cold day,
    or like vinegar poured on a wound,
    is one who sings songs to a heavy heart.

²¹ If your enemy is hungry, give him food to eat;
    if he is thirsty, give him water to drink.
²² In doing this, you will heap burning coals on
      his head,
    and the LORD will reward you.

²³ Like a north wind that brings unexpected
      rain
    is a sly tongue — which provokes a
      horrified look.

²⁴ Better to live on a corner of the roof
    than share a house with a quarrelsome
      wife.

²⁵ Like cold water to a weary soul
    is good news from a distant land.
²⁶ Like a muddied spring or a polluted well
    are the righteous who give way to the
      wicked.

²⁷ It is not good to eat too much honey,
    nor is it honorable to search out matters
      that are too deep.

²⁸ Like a city whose walls are broken through
    is a person who lacks self-control.

26 Like snow in summer or rain in
      harvest,
    honor is not fitting for a fool.
² Like a fluttering sparrow or a darting
      swallow,
    an undeserved curse does not come
      to rest.
³ A whip for the horse, a bridle for
      the donkey,
    and a rod for the backs of fools!
⁴ Do not answer a fool according to his folly,
    or you yourself will be just like him.
⁵ Answer a fool according to his folly,
    or he will be wise in his own eyes.
⁶ Sending a message by the hands of a fool
    is like cutting off one's feet or drinking
      poison.
⁷ Like the useless legs of one who is lame
    is a proverb in the mouth of a fool.
⁸ Like tying a stone in a sling
    is the giving of honor to a fool.

---

would devastate the crops. **harvest time** Typically April (for grain or barley) through September (for grapes or olives).

25:16 eat just enough Proverbs 24:13–14 compares honey's sweetness to the sweetness of wisdom. This proverb warns against gluttony and over-consumption (23:20–21).

25:17 too much of you A satirical reference to the previous proverb (25:16). Just as the glutton gets sick from eating too much honey, someone can get too much of a guest; in both instances the Hebrew word *sava'* is used.

25:18 gives false testimony against a neighbor In the law, a false witness was given the same punishment as the accused (Dt 19:18–19; see note on Pr 6:19).

25:20 a wound The Septuagint (the ancient Greek translation of the OT) translates the Hebrew word used here, *nether* (literally rendered as "soda"), with the Greek word *helkos*, meaning "wound." In this sense, acting joyfully toward someone in sorrow is like pouring vinegar on a wound — a painful act. Alternatively, if the reference to soda is retained, the image is one of counter-productivity: vinegar and soda neutralize and destroy each other.

25:21–22 Earlier proverbs warned against revenge (Pr 20:22; 24:29) or rejoicing at an enemy's defeat (24:17–18). This proverb goes further, encouraging readers to show generosity to their enemies; generosity shames the enemy and hopefully encourages repentance. Paul quotes this proverb in Romans when he encourages his readers to overcome evil with good (Ro 12:17–21).

25:24 Better to live on a corner of the roof See note on Pr 21:9.

25:27 It is not good to eat too much honey The emphasis of this proverb is different than 25:16. While the first proverb focused on gluttony (see note on v. 16), this proverb addresses humility (vv. 6–7; 27:2).

26:3 a rod for the backs of fools Like a horse or donkey, a fool must be restrained or controlled. This proverb is a reminder of the importance of accepting instruction or discipline (Ps 32:8–9).

26:4–5 These two proverbs seem to contradict each other. The first one warns not to answer a fool according to his folly, while the second encourages answering a fool according to his folly. However, the book of Proverbs is not a list of rules; it is a collection of general principles for life — principles which must be applied carefully to relevant situations. For example, Pr 19:11 says it is a glory to overlook someone's offense. However, 19:19 says not to spare a man of great wrath. In certain situations, the offense should be overlooked, but in other situations, it should not.

When understood this way, these verses do not contradict each other; rather, they complement each other by providing different reasoning for engaging or not engaging with a fool. The fools should not be responded to in certain situations because fools only bring down the one answering. In other situations, however, the fool needs a response because he will think he is correct if no one contradicts him.

⁹ Like a thornbush in a drunkard's hand
  is a proverb in the mouth of a fool.
¹⁰ Like an archer who wounds at random
  is one who hires a fool or any passer-by.
¹¹ As a dog returns to its vomit,
  so fools repeat their folly.
¹² Do you see a person wise in their own eyes?
  There is more hope for a fool than for them.

¹³ A sluggard says, "There's a lion in the road,
  a fierce lion roaming the streets!"
¹⁴ As a door turns on its hinges,
  so a sluggard turns on his bed.
¹⁵ A sluggard buries his hand in the dish;
  he is too lazy to bring it back to his mouth.
¹⁶ A sluggard is wiser in his own eyes
  than seven people who answer discreetly.

¹⁷ Like one who grabs a stray dog by the ears
  is someone who rushes into a quarrel not
    their own.

¹⁸ Like a maniac shooting
  flaming arrows of death
¹⁹ is one who deceives their neighbor
  and says, "I was only joking!"

²⁰ Without wood a fire goes out;
  without a gossip a quarrel dies down.
²¹ As charcoal to embers and as wood to fire,
  so is a quarrelsome person for kindling
    strife.

²² The words of a gossip are like choice morsels;
  they go down to the inmost parts.

²³ Like a coating of silver dross on earthenware
  are fervent[a] lips with an evil heart.
²⁴ Enemies disguise themselves with their lips,
  but in their hearts they harbor deceit.
²⁵ Though their speech is charming, do not
    believe them,
  for seven abominations fill their hearts.
²⁶ Their malice may be concealed by deception,
  but their wickedness will be exposed in the
    assembly.
²⁷ Whoever digs a pit will fall into it;
  if someone rolls a stone, it will roll back on
    them.

²⁸ A lying tongue hates those it hurts,
  and a flattering mouth works ruin.

27 Do not boast about tomorrow,
  for you do not know what a day may
    bring.

² Let someone else praise you, and not your
    own mouth;
  an outsider, and not your own lips.

³ Stone is heavy and sand a burden,
  but a fool's provocation is heavier than
    both.

a 23 Hebrew; Septuagint *smooth*

26:7–12 This series of proverbs makes various comparisons that show the worthlessness of the fool: A proverb is useless (v. 7) and painful (v. 9) in the mouth of a fool. Giving a fool honor is pointless and absurd, like tying a stone into a sling (v. 8). Hiring a fool is a dangerous gamble (v. 10). Finally, the fool's inability to learn is highlighted as the fool returns to folly like a dog to vomit (v. 11). The proverbs strongly emphasize the negative aspects of the fool. However, v. 12 changes focus to show that the person who is wise in his own eyes is even worse than the fool.

26:9 Like a thornbush While anyone can speak proverbs, their power comes from knowing the meaning and how to apply it. When fools speak proverbs, they can injure themselves and others. By contrast, proverbs in the mouth of the wise bring healing. Compare 10:32; 11:9; 12:18; 14:3.

26:13–16 These proverbs are about the sluggard (see note on 6:9). They ridicule the person too lazy to protect themselves (26:13), get out of bed (v. 14) and bother to eat (v. 15). The sluggard's most destructive trait is that he considers himself wise (v. 16; compare vv. 5,12); thus, the sluggard will never change.

26:13 There's a lion in the road Making absurd excuses for laziness, the sluggard is characterized by a lack of responsibility (22:13).

26:15 A sluggard buries his hand in the dish A comical portrayal of the sluggard's laziness (19:24).

26:16 than seven people who answer discreetly As in 24:16, seven should not be taken literally. It symbolizes completeness (compare note on 24:15–16).

26:17–22 These proverbs warn against careless speech that provokes quarrels. They remind the reader that butting into other people's arguments is dangerous, and they compare the person who deceives and claims to be joking to someone who recklessly throws around deadly flaming arrows (vv. 18–19). Three proverbs warn of the damage caused by slander and quarrels (vv. 20–22).

26:20 a quarrel dies down Slander or whispering fuels quarreling (v. 21; see note on 16:28). When it is stopped, quarreling often ends.

26:22 like choice morsels This proverb describes the reality that people devour gossip like delicacies. See 18:8 and note.

26:23–28 This section concerns a dishonest or deceitful person who disguises evil intentions with gracious speech. However, the person's wickedness will eventually be exposed. Ultimately, the sins of the deceitful person will lead to destruction, like someone who falls into their own pit (v. 27).

26:23 silver dross Just as a covering of silver (some translations have "glaze") hides the clay of a pot, speech can hide a person's true feelings or intentions.

26:25 seven abominations fill their hearts The number seven indicates completeness. Despite having gracious speech, this person's heart is utterly abominable.

27:1 Do not boast about tomorrow Warns against making presumptions about the future. James develops this theme further (Jas 4:13–17).

27:2 Let someone else praise you A warning against self-promotion (compare Pr 25:6–7 and note; and 25:27 and note).

4 Anger is cruel and fury overwhelming,
  but who can stand before jealousy?

5 Better is open rebuke
  than hidden love.

6 Wounds from a friend can be trusted,
  but an enemy multiplies kisses.

7 One who is full loathes honey from the comb,
  but to the hungry even what is bitter tastes
    sweet.

8 Like a bird that flees its nest
  is anyone who flees from home.

9 Perfume and incense bring joy to the heart,
  and the pleasantness of a friend
    springs from their heartfelt advice.

10 Do not forsake your friend or a friend of your
    family,
  and do not go to your relative's house when
    disaster strikes you —
  better a neighbor nearby than a relative far
    away.

11 Be wise, my son, and bring joy to my heart;
  then I can answer anyone who treats me
    with contempt.

12 The prudent see danger and take refuge,
  but the simple keep going and pay the
    penalty.

13 Take the garment of one who puts up
    security for a stranger;
  hold it in pledge if it is done for an
    outsider.

14 If anyone loudly blesses their neighbor early
    in the morning,
  it will be taken as a curse.

15 A quarrelsome wife is like the dripping
  of a leaky roof in a rainstorm;

16 restraining her is like restraining the wind
  or grasping oil with the hand.

17 As iron sharpens iron,
  so one person sharpens another.

18 The one who guards a fig tree will eat its
    fruit,
  and whoever protects their master will be
    honored.

19 As water reflects the face,
  so one's life reflects the heart.[a]

20 Death and Destruction[b] are never satisfied,
  and neither are human eyes.

21 The crucible for silver and the furnace for
    gold,
  but people are tested by their praise.

22 Though you grind a fool in a mortar,
  grinding them like grain with a pestle,
  you will not remove their folly
    from them.

23 Be sure you know the condition of your
    flocks,
  give careful attention to your herds;

24 for riches do not endure forever,
  and a crown is not secure for all
    generations.

25 When the hay is removed and new growth
    appears
  and the grass from the hills is gathered in,

26 the lambs will provide you with clothing,
  and the goats with the price of a field.

a 19 Or so others reflect your heart back to you   b 20 Hebrew
Abaddon

27:5 Better is open rebuke Rebuke is shown to be an active form of love (3:12). Throughout Proverbs, rebuke is seen as a valuable form of teaching. Those who heed rebuke are prudent and wise (9:8; 15:5; 17:10). Rebuke serves as a life-giving tool (10:17), whereas ignoring a problem can lead to death (15:10). Poverty and disgrace come to the person who ignores rebuke, while the person who accepts it finds honor (13:18). Yahweh rebukes those he loves (3:12).

27:10 do not go to your relative's house A statement on the comparative value of friendship, not a disparaging remark about family. Some friends stick closer than brothers (compare 18:24). **better a neighbor nearby** It is better to seek help from someone close to you when in need. A faraway relative may not be in a position to help.

27:12 the simple keep going The prudent demonstrate caution and avoid danger or temptation. In contrast, the simple are gullible (14:15; see 1:4 and note) and susceptible to temptation (7:6–9; 9:16–17).

27:13 if it is done for an outsider See note on 20:16, which is nearly identical to this proverb.

27:15 A quarrelsome wife Proverbs frequently warns against the frustration caused by a quarrelsome marriage. See note on 21:9.

27:17 iron sharpens iron Close friends provide constructive criticism and accountability. Just as sharpening an iron blade makes it more effective, close friends sharpen one another's character.

27:19 one's life reflects the heart This phrase could refer to a person's heart reflecting his or her behavior (compare 16:2; Jer 17:9)—people gain insight about themselves by considering their actions. This phrase could also indicate that a person understands their own character better by observing another person's heart—meaning that people learn about themselves from the compliments and criticisms of other people (compare Pr 27:2).

27:20 Death and Destruction See note on 15:11.

27:23–27 This proverb discusses the fleeting nature of wealth. Proverbs 23:4–5 warned against wasting effort on acquiring wealth (see 23:4–5 and note). Here, the proverb emphasizes being wise with wealth by preparing for lean days. People should pay careful attention to their flocks so that when conditions deteriorate, they will not be in need.

27 You will have plenty of goats' milk to feed
  your family
  and to nourish your female servants.

28 The wicked flee though no one
  pursues,
  but the righteous are as bold as a lion.

2 When a country is rebellious, it has many
  rulers,
  but a ruler with discernment and
  knowledge maintains order.

3 A ruler[a] who oppresses the poor
  is like a driving rain that leaves no
  crops.

4 Those who forsake instruction praise
  the wicked,
  but those who heed it resist them.

5 Evildoers do not understand what
  is right,
  but those who seek the LORD understand
  it fully.

6 Better the poor whose walk is blameless
  than the rich whose ways are perverse.

7 A discerning son heeds instruction,
  but a companion of gluttons disgraces
  his father.

8 Whoever increases wealth by taking interest
  or profit from the poor
  amasses it for another, who will be kind to
  the poor.

9 If anyone turns a deaf ear to my instruction,
  even their prayers are detestable.

10 Whoever leads the upright along an
  evil path
  will fall into their own trap,
  but the blameless will receive a good
  inheritance.

11 The rich are wise in their own eyes;
  one who is poor and discerning sees
  how deluded they are.

12 When the righteous triumph, there is great
  elation;
  but when the wicked rise to power, people
  go into hiding.

13 Whoever conceals their sins does not
  prosper,
  but the one who confesses and renounces
  them finds mercy.

14 Blessed is the one who always trembles
  before God,
  but whoever hardens their heart falls
  into trouble.

15 Like a roaring lion or a charging bear
  is a wicked ruler over a helpless
  people.

16 A tyrannical ruler practices extortion,
  but one who hates ill-gotten gain will
  enjoy a long reign.

17 Anyone tormented by the guilt of
  murder
  will seek refuge in the grave;
  let no one hold them back.

a 3 Or A poor person

28:1 The wicked flee Describes an attitude of guilty paranoia. This statement echoes one of the judgments of disobeying the law (Lev 26:17). Psalm 53:5 ascribes a similar attitude of fear and paranoia to the fool. **lion** Considered a mighty and courageous animal by the ancients.
28:4 Those who forsake instruction praise the wicked Likens disobedience to praising the wicked. Keeping the law is a way of combating the wicked. God does not accept the prayer of the person who rejects the law (Pr 28:9), but he blesses the person who keeps it (29:18).
28:5 Evildoers do not understand what is right Evil people do not understand justice, but those who seek Yahweh do. Elsewhere in Proverbs, wisdom is closely related to justice (1:3; 2:6–10; 8:20).
28:6 whose walk is blameless Like 19:1, this proverb shows that integrity is more valuable than wealth (see 10:9 and note). The crooked will be destroyed, while those who walk with integrity find deliverance (28:18).
28:7 a companion of gluttons disgraces his father Those who associate with gluttons not only shame their fathers, they also risk destruction (23:20–21).
28:8 by taking interest or profit from the poor The law prohibited charging interest to a fellow Israelite (Ex 22:25; Lev 25:36–37). Those who increased their wealth through these measures would be illegally oppressing the impoverished, which is an insult to God (Pr 14:31).

28:10 will fall into their own trap Ultimately, the sin of the wicked will be exposed and will cause their own destruction. See note on 26:23–28.
28:11 The rich are wise in their own eyes Proverbs 26:12 declares that people who are wise in their own eyes are worse off than the fool. This phrase describes the arrogance of a person who does not take advice (12:15). At times in Proverbs, wealth is seen to accompany wisdom (14:24), but this is not always the case (v. 6; see 15:16–17 and note).
28:12 When the righteous triumph Implies that the welfare of society often rises or falls with the character of its leadership. See note on 11:10–11.
28:16 A tyrannical ruler The ruler was responsible for judging legal matters as well as governing the land (see 20:8 and note). A just king would benefit the land (29:4; see note on Ecc 10:16–17). Understanding often parallels wisdom in Proverbs. It describes the ability to discern between right and wrong (1Ki 3:9). Believed to be from God (Pr 2:6), understanding is related to justice and righteousness (2:9; 28:5). A ruler without understanding lacks the ability to righteously administer justice.
28:17 tormented The Hebrew word used here, *ashaq*, refers to oppression or extortion. In this instance, it most likely refers to a guilty conscience (v. 1).

¹⁸ The one whose walk is blameless is kept safe,
  but the one whose ways are perverse will
    fall into the pit.ᵃ

¹⁹ Those who work their land will have
    abundant food,
  but those who chase fantasies will have
    their fill of poverty.

²⁰ A faithful person will be richly blessed,
  but one eager to get rich will not go
    unpunished.

²¹ To show partiality is not good —
  yet a person will do wrong for a piece
    of bread.

²² The stingy are eager to get rich
  and are unaware that poverty awaits them.

²³ Whoever rebukes a person will in the end
    gain favor
  rather than one who has a flattering
    tongue.

²⁴ Whoever robs their father or mother
  and says, "It's not wrong,"
  is partner to one who destroys.

²⁵ The greedy stir up conflict,
  but those who trust in the Lord will
    prosper.

²⁶ Those who trust in themselves are fools,
  but those who walk in wisdom are kept
    safe.

²⁷ Those who give to the poor will lack nothing,
  but those who close their eyes to them
    receive many curses.

²⁸ When the wicked rise to power, people go
    into hiding;
  but when the wicked perish, the righteous
    thrive.

29 Whoever remains stiff-necked after
    many rebukes
  will suddenly be destroyed — without
    remedy.

² When the righteous thrive, the people
    rejoice;
  when the wicked rule, the people groan.

³ A man who loves wisdom brings joy to his
    father,
  but a companion of prostitutes squanders
    his wealth.

⁴ By justice a king gives a country stability,
  but those who are greedy forᵇ bribes tear it
    down.

⁵ Those who flatter their neighbors
  are spreading nets for their feet.

⁶ Evildoers are snared by their own sin,
  but the righteous shout for joy and are glad.

⁷ The righteous care about justice for the poor,
  but the wicked have no such concern.

⁸ Mockers stir up a city,
  but the wise turn away anger.

⁹ If a wise person goes to court with a fool,
  the fool rages and scoffs, and there is no
    peace.

ᵃ 18 Syriac (see Septuagint); Hebrew *into one*   ᵇ 4 Or *who give*

28:18 one whose walk is blameless is kept safe Those who walk with integrity walk securely because Yahweh protects them, but that does not mean they will never encounter trouble. See 10:9 and note. **one whose ways are perverse will fall** Wickedness is seen as a path of destruction throughout Proverbs, whereas the righteous and wise live peacefully and successfully. See note on 3:2.
28:19 will have their fill of poverty The hard worker will usually have plenty to eat, but the lazy or undisciplined person will be poor (24:30–34).
28:20 one eager to get rich This verse does not condemn wealth. The contrasting parallel with the faithful person indicates that this wealth was probably obtained unfairly (28:8). It may also indicate that the person seeking wealth does so for personal glory (23:4–5; 28:11). Other proverbs indicate that the person who lives wisely will be wealthy (21:20) and that hard work leads to wealth (10:4; 12:27).
28:21 To show partiality is not good The law prohibits partiality in judgment (Lev 19:15; Dt 1:17). This verse compares partiality with bribes — both are perversions of justice (Pr 17:23).
28:23 Whoever rebukes a person In Proverbs, rebuke is considered a valuable form of teaching and an active display of love. See note on 27:5.

28:27 Those who give to the poor will lack nothing Proverbs upholds the general principle that both kindness and stinginess will be reciprocated. See note on 3:2.
28:28 When the wicked rise to power, people go into hiding The nation suffers when the wicked — characterized by oppression and injustice — rise to positions of authority (see 29:2; see note on 11:10–11).
29:1 remains stiff-necked Describes someone who stubbornly refuses to accept direction or reproof (see Ex 32:9 and note). **will suddenly be destroyed — without remedy** Emphasizes the severe consequence of ignoring reproof (Pr 13:18; 15:10).
29:2 When the righteous thrive, the people rejoice The righteous are characterized by justice and fairness. Righteous leaders cause a nation to rejoice. See note on 11:10–11.
29:4 bribes The Hebrew word used here, *terumah*, refers to a contribution or tribute (Ex 25:2; Nu 31:41). This proverb may be describing a king who takes bribes or a king who oppresses his subjects with heavy taxes (1Ki 12:13–15).
29:5 spreading nets for their feet Portrays flattery as empty and even destructive (compare Pr 28:23).
29:6 Evildoers are snared by their own sin As elsewhere, the wicked are portrayed as falling into their own traps (Ps 9:15; Job 18:8–10).

¹⁰ The bloodthirsty hate a person of integrity
    and seek to kill the upright.

¹¹ Fools give full vent to their rage,
    but the wise bring calm in the end.

¹² If a ruler listens to lies,
    all his officials become wicked.

¹³ The poor and the oppressor have this in
        common:
    The LORD gives sight to the eyes of both.

¹⁴ If a king judges the poor with fairness,
    his throne will be established forever.

¹⁵ A rod and a reprimand impart wisdom,
    but a child left undisciplined disgraces its
        mother.

¹⁶ When the wicked thrive, so does sin,
    but the righteous will see their downfall.

¹⁷ Discipline your children, and they will give
        you peace;
    they will bring you the delights you desire.

¹⁸ Where there is no revelation, people cast off
        restraint;
    but blessed is the one who heeds wisdom's
        instruction.

¹⁹ Servants cannot be corrected by mere words;
    though they understand, they will not
        respond.

²⁰ Do you see someone who speaks in haste?
    There is more hope for a fool than for them.

²¹ A servant pampered from youth
    will turn out to be insolent.

²² An angry person stirs up conflict,
    and a hot-tempered person commits many
        sins.

²³ Pride brings a person low,
    but the lowly in spirit gain honor.

²⁴ The accomplices of thieves are their own
        enemies;
    they are put under oath and dare not
        testify.

²⁵ Fear of man will prove to be a snare,
    but whoever trusts in the LORD is kept
        safe.

²⁶ Many seek an audience with a ruler,
    but it is from the LORD that one gets justice.

²⁷ The righteous detest the dishonest;
    the wicked detest the upright.

Sayings of Agur

30 The sayings of Agur son of Jakeh — an
inspired utterance.

This man's utterance to Ithiel:

"I am weary, God,
    but I can prevail.ᵃ

ᵃ 1 With a different word division of the Hebrew; Masoretic Text
utterance to Ithiel, / to Ithiel and Ukal:

29:9 rages and scoffs Arguing with a fool is a futile task (Pr 20:3); rather than listening, they despise any reproof or instruction (15:5).
29:13 The LORD gives sight to the eyes of both God makes both the impoverished person and the oppressor. The proverb implies that since both are dependent on God for life, the oppressor should treat the poor person justly.
29:14 a king judges the poor with fairness A king's throne is established by righteousness (16:12), faithful love (20:28) and justice (29:4). Evil and oppression (28:15–16) will destroy it.
29:15 a child left undisciplined disgraces Proverbs emphasizes discipline because a child needs instruction to avoid folly (22:15; see note on 13:24).
29:17 they will give you peace Not only does discipline help a child (19:18; 23:13–14), it brings rest and delight — rather than shame — to parents (10:1; 27:11; compare 29:15).
29:18 Where there is no revelation Emphasizes the importance of divine revelation for a nation's well-being. Without it, the people make serious mistakes (Ex 32:25). Similarly, Amos warns of a coming judgment where Yahweh will send a famine of the words of Yahweh, meaning Yahweh's words would no longer be heard (Am 8:11–12). Lamentations includes a lament about the lack of prophetic vision (La 2:9). Psalm 74 includes a similar lament (Ps 74:9). The story of God's call on Samuel begins by explaining that visions were not frequent in those days (1Sa 3:1). **instruction** The Hebrew word used here, *torah*, may refer simply to instruction,

as elsewhere in Proverbs (e.g., Pr 1:8; 3:1; 4:2; 6:20), or it may refer to God's law.
29:19 Servants In the ancient Near East, servants were part of the household in which they worked and were viewed as the responsibility of the household head (the oldest male). **by mere words** This proverb does not advocate abuse. It also does not necessarily advocate for physical discipline; this line could be understood as suggesting seriousness (or be hyperbolic). See note on 13:24. People are instructed to discipline their servants as they would their children, to remove folly (13:24; 22:15; compare 29:17). This is done for the purposes of delivering someone from the path that can lead to death (23:13–14; compare 29:18).
29:23 Pride brings a person low Pride is seen as a destructive attitude throughout Proverbs (11:2; 16:18). Pride prevents people from accepting reproof or advice (12:15; 13:18).
29:24 accomplices of thieves are their own enemies Because they endanger themselves by keeping company with those who break the law. Proverbs warns against keeping company with several types of people. Besides thieves, righteous people should avoid the company of sinners (1:10–16), fools (13:20; 14:7), slanderers (20:19) and gluttons (28:7).
29:25 Fear of man Refers to trusting in human power. In juxtaposition to Yahweh's lasting security, people can only provide temporary security.
29:26 Many seek an audience with a ruler Kings administer justice on earth (see note on 20:8), but ultimately, justice comes from God (16:11; 28:5).

² Surely I am only a brute, not a man;
  I do not have human understanding.
³ I have not learned wisdom,
  nor have I attained to the knowledge of the
    Holy One.
⁴ Who has gone up to heaven and come down?
  Whose hands have gathered up the wind?
  Who has wrapped up the waters in a cloak?
  Who has established all the ends of the
    earth?
  What is his name, and what is the name
    of his son?
  Surely you know!

⁵ "Every word of God is flawless;
  he is a shield to those who take refuge
    in him.
⁶ Do not add to his words,
  or he will rebuke you and prove you a liar.

⁷ "Two things I ask of you, LORD;
  do not refuse me before I die:
⁸ Keep falsehood and lies far from me;
  give me neither poverty nor riches,
  but give me only my daily bread.
⁹ Otherwise, I may have too much and
    disown you
  and say, 'Who is the LORD?'
  Or I may become poor and steal,
    and so dishonor the name of my God.

¹⁰ "Do not slander a servant to their master,
  or they will curse you, and you will pay
    for it.

¹¹ "There are those who curse their fathers
  and do not bless their mothers;
¹² those who are pure in their own eyes
  and yet are not cleansed of their
    filth;

30:1–33 This section of proverbs is attributed to Agur son of Jakeh (see note on v. 1). Noticeably different in style than other sections of Proverbs, it begins with a confession of ignorance (vv. 2–4), an assertion of the truth of God's word (vv. 5–6) and a prayer that God will keep him from falsehood (vv. 7–9). Agur follows this first-person introduction with a series of proverbs (vv. 10–33), many in the form of numerical sayings (see v. 18 and note).

30:1 Agur son of Jakeh The identity of Agur son of Jakeh is unknown. The name does not occur elsewhere in the Bible. Agur may be a pseudonym for Solomon as the one who stores up (*agar*) wisdom, but there is no evidence for this. Agur is best understood as an otherwise unnamed wise man. **an inspired utterance** The Hebrew word used here, *massa*, can refer to an oracle, or it can be a proper noun. Typically an oracle is a prophetic pronouncement, often of judgment—something generally out of place in Wisdom Literature (compare Nu 24:3; Isa 13:1; Mal 1:1). As a proper noun, *Massa* refers to a tribe in Northern Arabia associated with a son of Ishmael (Ge 25:14; 1Ch 1:30). Its presence here may indicate that Agur was from Massa. **I am weary, God, but I can prevail** The meaning of the Hebrew phrase used here, *le'ithi'el le'ithi'el we'ukhal*, is uncertain. It could refer to the recipients of Agur's words: Ithiel, Ithiel and Ucal. It could also be understood as indicating that Agur, the speaker, calls out to God about his weariness, using the same exact phrase twice. It may also be that Agur first addresses Ithiel and then calls out to God about his weariness.

30:2–3 Wisdom teaching often begins with a statement encouraging readers to heed the wisdom about to be spoken (Pr 1:8–9; 22:17–21). Usually, these statements display the wisdom of the speaker and show the value of heeding his words. The author of Ecclesiastes states his wisdom unequivocally as he gives authority to his words (see Ecc 1:16 and note). Here, Agur's words begin with a very striking statement of ignorance. He intends to show the limitation of human wisdom when compared to God's wisdom (Pr 30:5–6).

30:3 Holy One This title for God emphasizes that he is set apart from humanity and is great. See note on Isa 1:4.
30:4 Whose hands have gathered up the wind The

implied answer to these questions is God. Similar rhetorical questions appear in Job (Job 38–41) and Isaiah (Isa 40:12–14). Questions like these emphasize God's greatness, especially in comparison to the limited knowledge of humankind. See note on Job 38:1—41:34. **wrapped up the waters in a cloak** This indicates God's supreme power. This could indicate Yahweh's care for the sea—that he clothes it—or simply his ability to overcome it, in that he is so powerful that he could wrap the sea in a piece of clothing (compare note on Job 38:9; note on Pr 8:28). The piece of clothing could be the clouds—in God's speech to Job, the clouds are described as a garment for the sea (Job 38:9). In the ancient Near Eastern creation accounts, the sea is depicted as a force of chaos which deities subdue to demonstrate their might. Wisdom Literature often alludes to these accounts to show the power and greatness of Yahweh (e.g., Job 26:7–14). **established all the ends of the earth** People in the ancient Near East viewed the earth as a flat surface (Job 38:13; Isa 11:12; see note on Pr 8:29) supported by pillars (Job 38:4–7; Ps 104:5). See the infographic "Ancient Hebrew Conception of the Universe" on p. 5. **what is the name of his son** The meaning of this question is unclear. In Proverbs, a son is always the recipient of the father's teaching (see 1:8 and note). Elsewhere in the OT, God refers to the nation Israel as his son (Ex 4:22; Hos 11:1). God's son is left unnamed here, leaving open the possibility that this is an early allusion to the forthcoming Messiah (compare Lk 1:31–33).

30:6 Do not add to his words This warning to not alter God's words is appropriate in light of the limitation of human wisdom when compared to God's wisdom (Pr 30:2–4). The law also includes a warning not to add to or take away from God's word (Dt 4:2; 12:32). In the NT, John concludes the book of Revelation with a warning against adding or taking away from his prophecy (Rev 22:18–19).

30:7–9 Agur makes two requests of God. First, he asks God to keep him from falsehood (see Ps 19:13 and note). Falsehood stands in contrast to the true words of God (Pr 30:5). Second, Agur asks God for a life of moderation that includes neither wealth nor poverty. He asks for this in order to keep from profaning God's name by stealing or being too satisfied with his wealth (Dt 8:11–14).

¹³ those whose eyes are ever so haughty,
    whose glances are so disdainful;
¹⁴ those whose teeth are swords
    and whose jaws are set with knives
to devour the poor from the earth
    and the needy from among mankind.

¹⁵ "The leech has two daughters.
    'Give! Give!' they cry.

"There are three things that are never
    satisfied,
    four that never say, 'Enough!':
¹⁶ the grave, the barren womb,
    land, which is never satisfied with water,
    and fire, which never says, 'Enough!'

¹⁷ "The eye that mocks a father,
    that scorns an aged mother,
will be pecked out by the ravens of the valley,
    will be eaten by the vultures.

¹⁸ "There are three things that are too amazing
    for me,
    four that I do not understand:
¹⁹ the way of an eagle in the sky,
    the way of a snake on a rock,
the way of a ship on the high seas,
    and the way of a man with a young woman.

²⁰ "This is the way of an adulterous woman:
    She eats and wipes her mouth
    and says, 'I've done nothing wrong.'

²¹ "Under three things the earth trembles,
    under four it cannot bear up:
²² a servant who becomes king,
    a godless fool who gets plenty to eat,

²³ a contemptible woman who gets married,
    and a servant who displaces her mistress.

²⁴ "Four things on earth are small,
    yet they are extremely wise:
²⁵ Ants are creatures of little strength,
    yet they store up their food in the summer;
²⁶ hyraxes are creatures of little power,
    yet they make their home in the crags;
²⁷ locusts have no king,
    yet they advance together in ranks;
²⁸ a lizard can be caught with the hand,
    yet it is found in kings' palaces.

²⁹ "There are three things that are stately in
    their stride,
    four that move with stately bearing:
³⁰ a lion, mighty among beasts,
    who retreats before nothing;
³¹ a strutting rooster, a he-goat,
    and a king secure against revolt.^a

³² "If you play the fool and exalt yourself,
    or if you plan evil,
    clap your hand over your mouth!
³³ For as churning cream produces butter,
    and as twisting the nose produces blood,
    so stirring up anger produces strife."

Sayings of King Lemuel

31 The sayings of King Lemuel—an inspired
utterance his mother taught him.

² Listen, my son! Listen, son of my womb!
    Listen, my son, the answer to my prayers!

^a 31 The meaning of the Hebrew for this phrase is uncertain.

30:12 pure The Hebrew word used here, *tahor*, indicates ceremonial purity (Lev 10:10). Agur describes those who believe themselves to be righteous because they act righteously. These people, however, are hypocrites and an abomination to God (see Pr 15:8 and note; Isa 1:12–17).

30:15–16 These verses include a numerical saying (see note on Pr 30:18) with examples of the insatiable nature of gluttony.

30:15 leech Since leeches attach themselves to people or animals to suck blood, the usage here symbolizes greed. **two daughters** The two daughters of the leech probably represent its two suckers.

30:16 grave This is a reference to the realm of the dead, called *she'ol* in Hebrew (compare Ge 37:35 and note; Job 14:13 and note). Elsewhere, *she'ol* is portrayed as greedy and insatiable (Pr 27:20; Hab 2:5).

30:18 There are three things that are too amazing for me It is not clear what makes the three things described in Pr 30:19 amazing. Many interpreters think it is that none of them is taught their ways: Eagles fly, snakes slither and ships sail without instruction. **four that I do not understand** The formula "number ... number+1" is a common literary device in Wisdom Literature. Rather than indicate that three of the listed items are too wonderful, while four are not understood,

it means that the listed items are characterized by both of these descriptions. Compare 6:16.

30:19 the way of a man with a young woman A euphemism for sexual intercourse. Romantic love is wondrous and mysterious.

30:21 under four The four things described in 30:22–23 are upsetting because they are inversions of the proper order of things. See v. 18 and note.

30:22 a servant who becomes king This proverb seems to refer to a servant usurping the throne. A similar idea is discussed in Ecclesiastes (see Ecc 10:6–7 and note).

30:24 they are extremely wise Agur lists several small creatures that exemplify wisdom. The clever ways in which they overcome weakness demonstrate their wisdom.

30:29 four that move with stately bearing The confident strides of the lion, the rooster and the he-goat illustrate the majesty and power of a king. See Pr 30:18 and note.

30:32 clap your hand over your mouth Indicates silence (compare Jdg 18:19; Job 21:5).

31:1–31 This final section of Proverbs is attributed to King Lemuel. It is presented as a teaching from his mother and can be divided into two sections: advice for the king related to his rule and administration of justice (Pr 31:2–9) and a description of an excellent wife in the form of an acrostic poem (vv. 10–21).

3 Do not spend your strength[a] on women,
   your vigor on those who ruin kings.

4 It is not for kings, Lemuel—
   it is not for kings to drink wine,
   not for rulers to crave beer,
5 lest they drink and forget what has been
      decreed,
   and deprive all the oppressed of their
      rights.
6 Let beer be for those who are perishing,
   wine for those who are in anguish!
7 Let them drink and forget their poverty
   and remember their misery no more.

8 Speak up for those who cannot speak for
      themselves,
   for the rights of all who are destitute.
9 Speak up and judge fairly;
   defend the rights of the poor and needy.

Epilogue: The Wife of Noble Character

10 [b] A wife of noble character who can find?
   She is worth far more than rubies.
11 Her husband has full confidence in her
   and lacks nothing of value.
12 She brings him good, not harm,
   all the days of her life.

13 She selects wool and flax
   and works with eager hands.
14 She is like the merchant ships,
   bringing her food from afar.
15 She gets up while it is still night;
   she provides food for her family
   and portions for her female servants.
16 She considers a field and buys it;
   out of her earnings she plants a vineyard.
17 She sets about her work vigorously;
   her arms are strong for her tasks.
18 She sees that her trading is profitable,
   and her lamp does not go out at night.
19 In her hand she holds the distaff
   and grasps the spindle with her
      fingers.
20 She opens her arms to the poor
   and extends her hands to the needy.
21 When it snows, she has no fear for her
      household;
   for all of them are clothed in scarlet.
22 She makes coverings for her bed;
   she is clothed in fine linen and purple.
23 Her husband is respected at the city gate,
   where he takes his seat among the elders
      of the land.

a 3 Or wealth   b 10 Verses 10-31 are an acrostic poem, the
verses of which begin with the successive letters of the Hebrew
alphabet.

31:1 King Lemuel Lemuel means "belonging to God."
This is the only mention of King Lemuel in the Bible.
31:3 strength The Hebrew word used here, *chayil*, is
the same term used to describe the wife in v. 10. Here
it emphasizes virility or energy. Lemuel's mother does
not have all women in mind, as the description of the
wife shows. She may be thinking of the adulteress or
forbidden woman (see note on 2:16) warned against
throughout Proverbs (2:18–19; 5:5; 7:27). She may also
be warning against a large harem of concubines. This
practice, prohibited by the law (Dt 17:17), contributed to
King Solomon's downfall (1Ki 11:11; Ne 13:26).

31:4–5 Lemuel's mother warns him to avoid alcohol. A
drunken and self-indulgent king would likely ignore the
needs of his people. See note on Ecc 10:16–17.

31:4 it is not for kings to drink wine Not an absolute
prohibition, since wine was a staple of normal diets
and royal banquets. Proverbs condemns drunkenness
(Pr 21:17; 23:29–35), a particular liability in a ruler
responsible for maintaining law and order.

31:8–9 The king was responsible for administering justice
in legal disputes. King Lemuel's mother encourages him
to take up the cause of the impoverished and needy. He
should judge his kingdom righteously, just as God judges
the world (compare Ps 9:7–8 and note).

31:10–31 Proverbs closes with an acrostic poem describing an excellent wife. The woman is married and
seeks the best for her husband (Pr 31:11–12). Industrious and hard-working, she takes care of her household
(vv. 15,21–22,27) and finds success in a variety of fields
(vv. 13–14,16–19). She is generous to the impoverished

(v. 20) and teaches wisdom (v. 26). Her children and
husband praise her because her excellence surpasses
other women (vv. 28–29). Most importantly, she fears
Yahweh (v. 30) and should be publicly recognized and
praised (v. 31).

31:10 wife of noble character This Hebrew phrase,
esheth chayil, is also used to describe Ruth (Ru 3:11), who
fits many of the characteristics of the ideal wife described
in this section. She was hard-working and took initiative
(Ru 2:2), and she was praised in the gates (Ru 4:11).
The word *chayil* can also indicate strength (Pr 31:3),
wealth (Ge 34:29) or courage (1Sa 16:8).

31:13 She selects wool and flax The excellent wife has
skill with a variety of materials used to make linen—this
would have been a highly valued skill in the ancient Near
East (Pr 31:21–22,24). Flax is a plant that would be dried
(see Jos 2:6) and spun into linen. Wool, which comes
from sheep, was spun into yarn (Ex 35:25).

31:17 She sets about her work vigorously She has
physical strength and stamina and is prepared to work
hard. This Hebrew expression used here refers to tuck-
ing the tunic into the belt so it is not in the way during
intense activity.

31:19 In her hand she holds the distaff The distaff
and spindle were tools used to make linen, which the
excellent wife used to make clothing for her household
(Pr 31:21–22) and to sell for profit (v. 24).

31:21 clothed in scarlet Expensive material typically
worn by the wealthy (2Sa 1:24; Isa 1:18; Jer 4:30).
She provides clothes that are both luxurious and warm.

31:23 Her husband is respected at the city gate City
gates were the social and economic hub of the city. The
elders were the leaders responsible for legal rulings (see

²⁴ She makes linen garments and sells them,
and supplies the merchants with sashes.
²⁵ She is clothed with strength and dignity;
she can laugh at the days to come.
²⁶ She speaks with wisdom,
and faithful instruction is on her
tongue.
²⁷ She watches over the affairs of her
household
and does not eat the bread of idleness.

²⁸ Her children arise and call her blessed;
her husband also, and he praises her:
²⁹ "Many women do noble things,
but you surpass them all."
³⁰ Charm is deceptive, and beauty is fleeting;
but a woman who fears the Lord is to be
praised.
³¹ Honor her for all that her hands have done,
and let her works bring her praise at the
city gate.

note on Ru 4:1). The husband of the excellent wife was known and respected among the leaders of the town. Job describes how he was respected by all at the city gate before his suffering (Job 29:7–11).

31:25 She is clothed with strength and dignity While the excellent wife produces clothing from fine linen (Pr 31:22), she is better known for her character.

31:30 fleeting The Hebrew word used here, *hevel*, is used figuratively to describe things that are brief and transitory (see Ecc 1:2 and note). Here, it speaks to the fleeting nature of physical beauty. **a woman who fears the Lord** More than her charm or beauty, the excellent wife is characterized by her fear of Yahweh. This pious attitude of obedience toward God is closely related to wisdom in Proverbs (Pr 1:7; 2:5; 9:10; 15:33).

31:31 let her works bring her praise at the city gate Just as her husband is known in the gates (see 31:23), the works of an excellent wife should be known and praised by the people.

ECCLESIASTES

INTRODUCTION TO ECCLESIASTES

Ecclesiastes addresses the times when life doesn't make sense—when it seems that wisdom cannot offer any satisfactory answers. The author takes an honest, unflinching look at wealth and labor, pleasure and wisdom. The speaker finally decides that they are ultimately meaningless in themselves. But the book also concludes that realizing such limitations should encourage us to approach God with awe (Ecc 12:9–14).

BACKGROUND

The title "Ecclesiastes" comes from the Latin translation of the Hebrew term *qoheleth* in the opening verse. This word, which refers to someone who assembles a group, is often translated as "teacher" or "preacher" and sometimes just transliterated by interpreters as *Qoheleth*. Because the speaker describes himself as David's son and the king in Jerusalem over all Israel (1:1,12), Ecclesiastes has been attributed to Solomon, who was known for his wisdom and wealth (compare 1:16; 2:1–11; 12:9). This would indicate a 10th-century BC date for the work.

Yet the general perspective and vocabulary of Ecclesiastes could suggest another author. When speaking of injustice, the author does not speak as someone who can do something about it, yet a king could (3:16; 4:1; 5:8–9; 7:7; 8:9). Also, the inclusion of Aramaic and Persian words—not in usage in Hebrew texts until around 539 BC—suggests a date after that time, perhaps as late as the third century BC. If the work is not composed by Solomon, then the speaker's remarks that make him sound like Solomon are meant to place the work within the tradition of Solomon's wisdom. There is also the possibility that some of the content originated with Solomon and later composers or editors were involved in the final form.

STRUCTURE

Ecclesiastes is a journey. It begins with a prologue (1:1–11) that introduces the Teacher (or Preacher) and his theme: Life is mysterious and seems to make no difference at all. The Teacher then describes his search for wisdom and meaning in life—a quest that ends in frustration (1:12—6:12). The second half of the book focuses on wisdom, as the Teacher begins to shift from relying primarily on reason to trusting in the personhood and ways of God (7:1—12:7). Like all things in life, wisdom ultimately comes from the Creator. An epilogue (12:9–14) sums up the words of the Teacher and the main lesson of his quest: Fear God, and obey his commandments.

The idea of fearing God—viewing him with reverence and awe—is a key part of Proverbs. Both Ecclesiastes and Proverbs are part of the genre of OT Wisdom Literature, which involves an examination of how life works and offers guiding principles for navigating it.

OUTLINE

- Introduction: The theme of emptiness (1:1–11)
- The search for meaning (1:12—6:12)
- The Teacher's advice (7:1—12:8)
- Conclusion: Fear God, and obey his commands (12:9–14)

THEMES

Ecclesiastes makes a point of showing that life is perplexing and short (1:2–11). It also illustrates the confusion of life, questioning why the wicked prosper and injustice abounds (3:16; 4:1–5). The author shows the limitations of wisdom while affirming its importance (2:12–17; 7:1–13).

Absurdity will figure prominently in life because no one can really control their life. Human life involves mourning and dancing, silence and speaking, death and healing—and true wisdom is finding contentment in all of these times (5:20).

Ecclesiastes exposes the utter emptiness of life without God. The pursuits often thought to give life meaning—wealth, work, power, knowledge and pleasure—are all fleeting. They are ultimately poor substitutes for serving God (Ecc 12). Likewise, learning cannot result in a meaningful life,

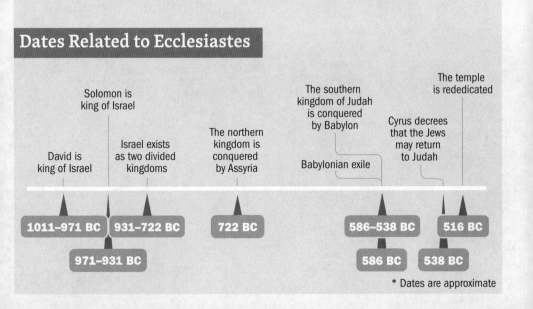

Dates Related to Ecclesiastes

David is king of Israel	Solomon is king of Israel	Israel exists as two divided kingdoms	The northern kingdom is conquered by Assyria	The southern kingdom of Judah is conquered by Babylon	Babylonian exile	Cyrus decrees that the Jews may return to Judah	The temple is rededicated
1011–971 BC	**971–931 BC**	**931–722 BC**	**722 BC**	**586–538 BC** / **586 BC**		**538 BC**	**516 BC**

* Dates are approximate

because there will always be something that doesn't make sense. As the author discovers, self-reliance and reason are deceptive devices. The pain of our struggles with futility and injustice should rightly prompt us to go to God. We must acknowledge that we cannot understand life, God or God's ways (3:11; 8:17).

Ecclesiastes highlights the incredible peace that comes with entrusting our lives to God (3:12–14; 12:9–14). The best a person can do is to enjoy what is given to them (3:13,22), fear and obey the God who gives life (8:10–13), and stand alongside other people (4:9–12).

The results a person can achieve offer them no real advantage (5:8–20). Nothing can help a person escape the frailty of human existence—everyone dies (9:1–6). Only God can offer anything lasting (8:10–13). This point shows how desperately we need eternal relationship with God through Jesus (Jn 3:16–17). Everything else is just a part of the journey—and for that reason, it is always worth taking risks for God, knowing that he is the ultimate judge of everything (Ecc 11).

Everything Is Meaningless

1 The words of the Teacher,[a] son of David, king in Jerusalem:

² "Meaningless! Meaningless!"
    says the Teacher.
  "Utterly meaningless!
    Everything is meaningless."

³ What do people gain from all their labors
    at which they toil under the sun?
⁴ Generations come and generations go,
    but the earth remains forever.
⁵ The sun rises and the sun sets,
    and hurries back to where it rises.
⁶ The wind blows to the south
    and turns to the north;
  round and round it goes,
    ever returning on its course.
⁷ All streams flow into the sea,
    yet the sea is never full.
  To the place the streams come from,
    there they return again.
⁸ All things are wearisome,
    more than one can say.
  The eye never has enough of seeing,
    nor the ear its fill of hearing.
⁹ What has been will be again,
    what has been done will be done again;
    there is nothing new under the sun.

¹⁰ Is there anything of which one can say,
    "Look! This is something new"?
  It was here already, long ago;
    it was here before our time.
¹¹ No one remembers the former generations,
    and even those yet to come
  will not be remembered
    by those who follow them.

Wisdom Is Meaningless

¹² I, the Teacher, was king over Israel in Jerusalem. ¹³ I applied my mind to study and to explore by wisdom all that is done under the heavens. What a heavy burden God has laid on mankind! ¹⁴ I have seen all the things that are done under the sun; all of them are meaningless, a chasing after the wind.

¹⁵ What is crooked cannot be straightened;
    what is lacking cannot be counted.

¹⁶ I said to myself, "Look, I have increased in wisdom more than anyone who has ruled over Jerusalem before me; I have experienced much of wisdom and knowledge." ¹⁷ Then I applied myself to the understanding of wisdom, and also of madness and folly, but I learned that this, too, is a chasing after the wind.

---

[a] 1 Or *the leader of the assembly*; also in verses 2 and 12

1:1 Ecclesiastes is a book of wisdom sayings that examines the meaning of life's endeavors, the value of common wisdom and the problem of injustice. The opening verse presents the speaker as a member of David's royal family, but his name is not mentioned. Solomon was the only son of David who was king in Jerusalem and over all of Israel (Ecc 1:12). This has contributed to the view that Solomon wrote the book in the 10th century BC. Also contributing to this view is Solomon's reputation for wisdom and the description of the wealth amassed in 2:1–11. But these factors could point to the book being in the tradition of Solomon's wisdom, rather than by him. There are several factors that point to Ecclesiastes being compiled or edited after Solomon's lifetime (12:9–10). For example, when the author speaks of injustice or oppression, he does not speak from a kingly perspective, as someone who has the power to do something about it (3:16; 4:1; 5:8–9; 7:7; 8:9). Also, there are Aramaic and Persian words in the book, which were not in usage by Jewish people until their encounter with the Persians (see note on 2:5; note on 2:8; note on 8:11). These factors point to a compilation date of the book after 539 BC and perhaps as late as the third century BC.

1:1 Teacher The Hebrew word used here, *qoheleth*, often translated "Preacher," is unique to Ecclesiastes and can also be translated "Teacher," "Speaker" or "Leader of the Assembly." The origin of the term *qoheleth* is uncertain. It most likely derives from the Hebrew word *qahal* (meaning "to assemble"); thus, it is usually connected to someone who would lead an assembly, like a speaker or preacher.
1:2 Utterly meaningless The Hebrew word used here, *hevel*, is often translated as "vanity," "absurd " or "senseless."

Ecclesiastes 1:2

HEVEL
The Hebrew word *hevel* occurs more times in Ecclesiastes than in all other OT books combined. It literally means "breath" or "vapor," but it can be understood as "vanity," "meaninglessness," "absurdity" or "senselessness." The author of Ecclesiastes uses the word to describe frustrating or unfair situations.

1:3–11 This poem illustrates the futility and brevity of life—key themes in Ecclesiastes. By showing that life is a continuing cycle, the author demonstrates how little an individual's life affects the world (v. 3). Verse 4 highlights the brevity of human life. Verses 5–7 describe the ongoing and unchanging cycles of the sun (v. 5), wind (v. 6) and water (v. 7). Verses 8–10 reveal the futility of searching for satisfaction, especially in work. Verse 11 illustrates how little individual lives matter.

1:3 What do people gain Throughout the book, the author points out the limited ability of people to achieve any real gain or advantage (2:11; 3:9; 5:16; 6:8,11; 10:11). Any gains achieved by hard work are eventually negated by death. **under the sun** Similar to "under heaven" (2:3; Dt 7:24), this phrase describes the entirety of life on earth.
1:5 The sun rises The author uses examples from the natural world to show that life involves cycles.
1:7 sea is never full Just as the sea is never full, people struggle to be filled or find satisfaction in life (compare 6:7 and note).

¹⁸ For with much wisdom comes much sorrow;
the more knowledge, the more grief.

Pleasures Are Meaningless

2 I said to myself, "Come now, I will test you with pleasure to find out what is good." But that also proved to be meaningless. ²"Laughter," I said, "is madness. And what does pleasure accomplish?" ³I tried cheering myself with wine, and embracing folly — my mind still guiding me with wisdom. I wanted to see what was good for people to do under the heavens during the few days of their lives.

⁴I undertook great projects: I built houses for myself and planted vineyards. ⁵I made gardens and parks and planted all kinds of fruit trees in them. ⁶I made reservoirs to water groves of flourishing trees. ⁷I bought male and female slaves and had other slaves who were born in my house. I also owned more herds and flocks than anyone in Jerusalem before me. ⁸I amassed silver and gold for myself, and the treasure of kings and provinces. I acquired male and female singers, and a harem^a as well — the delights of a man's heart. ⁹I became greater by far than anyone in Jerusalem before me. In all this my wisdom stayed with me.

¹⁰I denied myself nothing my eyes desired;
I refused my heart no pleasure.
My heart took delight in all my labor,
and this was the reward for all my toil.

¹¹Yet when I surveyed all that my hands had done
and what I had toiled to achieve,
everything was meaningless, a chasing after the wind;
nothing was gained under the sun.

Wisdom and Folly Are Meaningless

¹²Then I turned my thoughts to consider wisdom,
and also madness and folly.
What more can the king's successor do
than what has already been done?
¹³I saw that wisdom is better than folly,
just as light is better than darkness.
¹⁴The wise have eyes in their heads,
while the fool walks in the darkness;
but I came to realize
that the same fate overtakes them both.

¹⁵Then I said to myself,

"The fate of the fool will overtake me also.
What then do I gain by being wise?"
I said to myself,
"This too is meaningless."
¹⁶For the wise, like the fool, will not be long remembered;
the days have already come when both have been forgotten.
Like the fool, the wise too must die!

^a 8 The meaning of the Hebrew for this phrase is uncertain.

1:11 No one remembers Only a handful of people are remembered for more than a generation.

1:12–18 After the opening poem highlighting the themes of life's futility and brevity (vv. 3–11), the author describes his search for understanding. He explains that he applied himself to understand every aspect of life on earth, concluding that life is absurd and senseless (vv. 13–14). By presenting himself as the model of wisdom (v. 16), he gives legitimacy to his conclusion.

1:12 king over Israel in Jerusalem See note on v. 1.
1:15 cannot be straightened This phrase can be understood in a moral sense as a reference to injustice; it can also be understood as a reference to the limitations of human intellect.
1:16 I have increased in wisdom This claim is not meant to be boastful but to add legitimacy to the author's message. If this extremely wise person cannot fully understand the work of God (8:16–17), then no one can.
1:17 a chasing after the wind Even though the author has acquired much wisdom and knowledge (v. 16), he recognizes the limitations of human intellect. See note on 2:17.
1:18 much sorrow Wisdom produces vexation or grief in that it fails to provide any satisfying answers to life's frustrating or unfair situations (8:16–17).

2:1–26 In ch. 2, the author considers three areas of life: pleasure and wealth (vv. 1–11), wisdom (vv. 12–17), and work (vv. 18–23). He concludes that all of these are senseless.

2:1–11 In this section, the author examines the value of pleasure and wealth. In his attempt to examine all of life for value, he withholds nothing from himself by adding many possessions and pleasures. He concludes that pleasure itself is the only reward, and that it adds no gain.

2:2 what does pleasure accomplish While here the author deems pleasure useless, he encourages enjoyment of life throughout the book (vv. 24–26; 3:12–13,22; 5:18–20; 8:15; 9:7–10; 11:8–10). These calls to joy do not contradict this passage. While pleasure for the sake of pleasure provides no gain, the ability to enjoy work is perceived as a gift of God.
2:5 parks The word used here, *pardes*, comes from a Persian term. Its presence here may indicate that Ecclesiastes was written or at least edited after the Babylonian exile (post 538 BC), when such words were more common.
2:8 provinces The word used here, *medinah*, comes from an Aramaic root. Like the word *pardes* (see note on v. 5), it may indicate a date for Ecclesiastes after the exile.
2:10 reward for all my toil See note on v. 2.
2:11 what I had toiled Great effort was put forth to amass all the wealth and possessions. **everything was meaningless** See note on v. 17. **under the sun** Refers to the entirety of life on earth.
2:13 wisdom is better than See note on v. 26.
2:14 same fate Even though it is better to be wise, both the wise and the foolish share the same fate: death.
2:15 will overtake me also Any advantage gained by living with wisdom is lost in death.

Toil Is Meaningless

[17] So I hated life, because the work that is done under the sun was grievous to me. All of it is meaningless, a chasing after the wind. [18] I hated all the things I had toiled for under the sun, because I must leave them to the one who comes after me. [19] And who knows whether that person will be wise or foolish? Yet they will have control over all the fruit of my toil into which I have poured my effort and skill under the sun. This too is meaningless. [20] So my heart began to despair over all my toilsome labor under the sun. [21] For a person may labor with wisdom, knowledge and skill, and then they must leave all they own to another who has not toiled for it. This too is meaningless and a great misfortune. [22] What do people get for all the toil and anxious striving with which they labor under the sun? [23] All their days their work is grief and pain; even at night their minds do not rest. This too is meaningless.

[24] A person can do nothing better than to eat and drink and find satisfaction in their own toil. This too, I see, is from the hand of God, [25] for without him, who can eat or find enjoyment? [26] To the person who pleases him, God gives wisdom, knowledge and happiness, but to the sinner he gives the task of gathering and storing up wealth to hand it over to the one who pleases God. This too is meaningless, a chasing after the wind.

A Time for Everything

3 There is a time for everything,
and a season for every activity under the heavens:

[2] a time to be born and a time to die,
a time to plant and a time to uproot,
[3] a time to kill and a time to heal,
a time to tear down and a time to build,
[4] a time to weep and a time to laugh,
a time to mourn and a time to dance,
[5] a time to scatter stones and a time to gather them,
a time to embrace and a time to refrain from embracing,
[6] a time to search and a time to give up,
a time to keep and a time to throw away,
[7] a time to tear and a time to mend,
a time to be silent and a time to speak,
[8] a time to love and a time to hate,
a time for war and a time for peace.

[9] What do workers gain from their toil? [10] I have seen the burden God has laid on the human race.

2:17 I hated life The author despairs because wisdom promises no better fate than folly. **chasing after the wind** This Hebrew phrase occurs only in Ecclesiastes, although a similar phrase occurs in Hos 12:1. In Ecclesiastes, it almost always appears in parallel to the Hebrew word *hevel* (see note on Ecc 1:2). It refers to a senseless or futile activity where nothing can be gained. Just like trying to catch the wind, these efforts are unending and ineffective.

2:18–24 In this section, the author laments the fact that all of the fruits of his labor will be left to the enjoyment of someone who did not earn them and may not be worthy of them.

2:18 one who comes after It is not the work itself that the author hates; he hates the fact that he must leave his profit to someone who did not work for it.
2:21 meaningless and a great misfortune The Hebrew word used here, *ra'ah*, is paired with the Hebrew word *hevel* (which can be rendered as "meaningless" or "vanity"; see note on 1:2) several times in Ecclesiastes (4:8; 6:2). It emphasizes the unfairness or injustice of the situations the author describes.

RA'AH
While the word *ra'ah* is often translated as "evil," it can also indicate misfortune, disaster, harm or trouble. Job responds to his wife by saying they should accept the "evil" or "disaster" that God brings along with the good things (see Job 2:10 and note). Proverbs and Psalms both warn against planning "evil" or "harm" against a neighbor (e.g., Pr 3:29; Ps 15:3).

2:22 all the toil As with wisdom, death cancels out any profit gained by a person's efforts (vv. 15–16; 1:3).

2:24–26 The author finishes his examination of pleasure, wisdom and work (vv. 1–26). He finds none of these things satisfactory, so he concludes by encouraging people to find enjoyment in life (see note on 9:7–10).

2:24 find satisfaction in their own toil Since any profit from work is temporary, people should look for enjoyment, not wealth (see ch. 1). **from the hand of God** See note on 9:7–10.
2:26 gives wisdom While wisdom, knowledge and joy are fleeting, they are still a gift from God.

3:1–8 This poem illustrates that there is an appropriate time for all activities that constitute human life. Positive events are paralleled with negative ones to reflect reality.

3:3 a time to kill The author is not advocating murder or capital punishment. Instead, he is reflecting on the reality of life, which includes both killing and healing.
3:4 a time to weep Mourning rituals were common in the ancient Near East. The statement here is reminiscent of Paul's later encouragement for believers to rejoice with those who rejoice and weep with those who weep (Ro 12:15).
3:5 a time to scatter stones Most likely a reference to putting stones on a field to ruin it (see 2Ki 3:19,25) and clearing stones from a field to cultivate it. It may also refer to demolishing or constructing a building or represent a euphemism for sexual relations.
3:7 a time to be silent Restraint in speech is a recurring theme in Wisdom Literature.
3:8 a time to hate While hate is commonly used in reference to enemies (Ps 18:17; 38:19), it can also indicate a lack of love (Ge 29:31).

¹¹He has made everything beautiful in its time. He has also set eternity in the human heart; yet*ᵃ* no one can fathom what God has done from beginning to end. ¹²I know that there is nothing better for people than to be happy and to do good while they live. ¹³That each of them may eat and drink, and find satisfaction in all their toil — this is the gift of God. ¹⁴I know that everything God does will endure forever; nothing can be added to it and nothing taken from it. God does it so that people will fear him.

¹⁵ Whatever is has already been,
  and what will be has been before;
  and God will call the past to account.*ᵇ*

¹⁶And I saw something else under the sun:

In the place of judgment — wickedness was
    there,
  in the place of justice — wickedness was
    there.

¹⁷I said to myself,

"God will bring into judgment
  both the righteous and the wicked,
for there will be a time for every activity,
  a time to judge every deed."

¹⁸I also said to myself, "As for humans, God tests them so that they may see that they are like the animals. ¹⁹Surely the fate of human beings is like that of the animals; the same fate awaits them both: As one dies, so dies the other. All have the same breath*ᶜ*; humans have no advantage over animals. Everything is meaningless. ²⁰All go to the same place; all come from dust, and to dust all return. ²¹Who knows if the human spirit rises upward and if the spirit of the animal goes down into the earth?"

²²So I saw that there is nothing better for a person than to enjoy their work, because that is their lot. For who can bring them to see what will happen after them?

Oppression, Toil, Friendlessness

4 Again I looked and saw all the oppression that was taking place under the sun:

I saw the tears of the oppressed —
    and they have no comforter;
power was on the side of their oppressors —
    and they have no comforter.
² And I declared that the dead,
    who had already died,
  are happier than the living,
    who are still alive.
³ But better than both
  is the one who has never been born,
who has not seen the evil
    that is done under the sun.

ᵃ 11 Or *also placed ignorance in the human heart, so that*
ᵇ 15 Or *God calls back the past*   *ᶜ 19* Or *spirit*

3:9–15 In this section the author draws out the implications of the poem of "times" (Ecc 3:1–8). While there is an appropriate time for all things, it is God who establishes these times (see v. 11 and note), and his work is fixed so it cannot be changed (v. 14). Because humanity cannot fully discern God's appointed times (v. 11), the author encourages people to enjoy life and be content (see note on 9:7–10).

3:9 What do workers gain See note on 1:3.
3:11 beautiful in its time The Hebrew word used here, *yapheh*, is often translated "beautiful," but it can also be understood as "appropriate" or "good." God has placed in order all human activity—both positive and negative. The description of this order as "appropriate" or "good" recalls the description of creation in Ge 1 as "good" (e.g., Ge 1:4,10,12,18,21,25,31). **eternity** People have a desire to understand how they fit into the plan of life—which the author attempts to explain in this book (Ecc 1:13; 8:16–17). In Ecclesiastes, this Hebrew word (*olam*) often occurs in passages that contrast it with the brevity of human life. Here it probably refers to a desire in people to understand the eternity of God's work (v. 14). **yet no one can fathom what God has done** While God has set the appropriate time for everything, he has not revealed this to humanity.
3:13 this is the gift of God See note on 9:7–10.
3:14 will endure forever Not only is God's work good or appropriate (see note on v. 11), it is also unchanging. **nothing can be added** God's work cannot be improved. **will fear him** Fearing God does not mean being terrified by him; rather, fear describes a reverent posture taken toward God—the proper human response to his greatness and holiness. It relates to obeying and serving God (Ge 22:12; Dt 6:2,13) as well as trusting him (Ps 40:3; 115:11). It is also closely associated with wisdom (Pr 1:7; Ps 111:10).
3:16 under the sun See note on Ecc 1:3.
3:17 I said to myself Confronted with the observation ("I saw . . .") of injustice in v. 16, the author demonstrates faith in the ultimate justice of God. See note on 8:13.
3:19 no advantage over animals See note on 1:3–11.
3:20 and to dust all return This same language is used in Ge 3:19 when God curses Adam.
3:21 human spirit rises This verse is not meant to be a definitive statement concerning what happens after death (compare Ecc 12:7). Rather, it emphasizes the limitation of human knowledge.
3:22 enjoy their work God gives humanity the ability to enjoy life (5:19), and he also prevents them from enjoying it (6:1–2). All aspects of life—both good and bad—are in the hands of God (9:1). The author encourages people to enjoy life whenever they can while recognizing that both prosperity and adversity come from God (7:14). See note on 9:7–10. **what will happen after them** All should trust God and accept their lot because humanity's wisdom is limited—especially given God's supremacy. See 12:13 and note.

4:1–12 This passage is similar to lamentations made by Job and Jeremiah (Job 3:3–26; Jer 20:14–18). However, Job and Jeremiah lamented their own suffering, whereas the author of Ecclesiastes laments oppression and injustice in general.

⁴And I saw that all toil and all achievement spring from one person's envy of another. This too is meaningless, a chasing after the wind.

⁵Fools fold their hands
    and ruin themselves.
⁶Better one handful with tranquillity
    than two handfuls with toil
    and chasing after the wind.

⁷Again I saw something meaningless under the sun:

⁸There was a man all alone;
    he had neither son nor brother.
There was no end to his toil,
    yet his eyes were not content with his
        wealth.
"For whom am I toiling," he asked,
    "and why am I depriving myself of
        enjoyment?"
This too is meaningless—
    a miserable business!

⁹Two are better than one,
    because they have a good return for their
        labor:
¹⁰If either of them falls down,
    one can help the other up.
But pity anyone who falls
    and has no one to help them up.
¹¹Also, if two lie down together, they will keep
        warm.
    But how can one keep warm alone?
¹²Though one may be overpowered,
    two can defend themselves.
A cord of three strands is not quickly broken.

Advancement Is Meaningless

¹³Better a poor but wise youth than an old but foolish king who no longer knows how to heed a warning. ¹⁴The youth may have come from prison to the kingship, or he may have been born in poverty within his kingdom. ¹⁵I saw that all who lived and walked under the sun followed the youth, the king's successor. ¹⁶There was no end to all the people who were before them. But those who came later were not pleased with the successor. This too is meaningless, a chasing after the wind.

Fulfill Your Vow to God

5 ᵃ Guard your steps when you go to the house of God. Go near to listen rather than to offer the sacrifice of fools, who do not know that they do wrong.

²Do not be quick with your mouth,
    do not be hasty in your heart
    to utter anything before God.
God is in heaven
    and you are on earth,
    so let your words be few.
³A dream comes when there are many cares,
    and many words mark the speech of a fool.

⁴When you make a vow to God, do not delay to fulfill it. He has no pleasure in fools; fulfill your vow. ⁵It is better not to make a vow than to make one and not fulfill it. ⁶Do not let your mouth lead you into sin. And do not protest to the temple messenger, "My vow was a mistake." Why should God be angry at what you say and destroy the work of your hands? ⁷Much dreaming and many words are meaningless. Therefore fear God.

Riches Are Meaningless

⁸If you see the poor oppressed in a district, and justice and rights denied, do not be surprised at

ᵃ In Hebrew texts 5:1 is numbered 4:17, and 5:2-20 is numbered 5:1-19.

4:4 from one person's envy of another In the OT, human envy (*qin'ah*) is negative when directed toward others. It is described as a destructive emotion (Job 5:2; Pr 14:30) that is more powerful than anger (Pr 6:34; 27:4). **meaningless, a chasing after the wind** Envy prevents people from finding satisfaction in their work. Compare Ecc 1:2 and note; and 2:17 and note.
4:5 Fools fold their hands Refers to someone who refuses to work.
4:6 two handfuls with toil Just as laziness is harmful and should be avoided, so is working without the ability to enjoy one's work.
4:8 meaningless—a miserable business The Hebrew text here uses a pairing of words similar to those used in 2:21 (see note on 2:21). This emphasizes the frustration of laboring for what seems like little to no purpose.
4:11 But how can one keep warm People who work with others are more effective than they can be alone.
4:13 old but foolish king While old age is typically associated with wisdom (Job 12:12), here the old king is a fool.
4:16 were not pleased with the successor Even

though the wise youth ascended to the throne, he is eventually despised, rendering his wisdom useless.
5:1 Guard your steps People should approach God's presence carefully and with humility. **to offer the sacrifice of fools** Refers to sacrifices or any other outward expression of religion done without obedience (1Sa 15:22; Pr 21:27; Isa 1:11–20). God's preference for obedience over sacrifice appears throughout the OT (Pr 21:3; Jer 7:22–23). Jesus emphasizes this theme in the Gospels (Mt 9:13; 23:23; Mk 12:29–34).
5:2 God is in heaven and you are on earth Instead of asserting divine indifference, this image serves to contrast God's authority with human limitations.
5:3 speech of a fool See note on Ecc 3:7.
5:4 do not delay to fulfill it Leaving a vow unfulfilled was a serious offense. See Nu 30:2; Pr 20:25, and Dt 23:21–23, each of which closely resemble this passage.
5:6 a mistake The Hebrew word used here, *shegagah*, refers to an unintentional or inadvertent sin (see Lev 4:2 and note).
5:7 fear God See Ecc 3:14 and note.
5:8 justice and rights denied Unfairness, oppression

such things; for one official is eyed by a higher one, and over them both are others higher still. [9]The increase from the land is taken by all; the king himself profits from the fields.

[10]Whoever loves money never has enough;
whoever loves wealth is never satisfied
with their income.
This too is meaningless.

[11]As goods increase,
so do those who consume them.
And what benefit are they to the owners
except to feast their eyes on them?

[12]The sleep of a laborer is sweet,
whether they eat little or much,
but as for the rich, their abundance
permits them no sleep.

[13]I have seen a grievous evil under the sun:

wealth hoarded to the harm of its owners,
[14]   or wealth lost through some misfortune,
so that when they have children
there is nothing left for them to inherit.
[15]Everyone comes naked from their mother's
womb,
and as everyone comes, so they depart.
They take nothing from their toil
that they can carry in their hands.

[16]This too is a grievous evil:

As everyone comes, so they depart,
and what do they gain,
since they toil for the wind?

[17]All their days they eat in darkness,
with great frustration, affliction and
anger.

[18]This is what I have observed to be good: that it is appropriate for a person to eat, to drink and to find satisfaction in their toilsome labor under the sun during the few days of life God has given them — for this is their lot. [19]Moreover, when God gives someone wealth and possessions, and the ability to enjoy them, to accept their lot and be happy in their toil — this is a gift of God. [20]They seldom reflect on the days of their life, because God keeps them occupied with gladness of heart.

6 I have seen another evil under the sun, and it weighs heavily on mankind: [2]God gives some people wealth, possessions and honor, so that they lack nothing their hearts desire, but God does not grant them the ability to enjoy them, and strangers enjoy them instead. This is meaningless, a grievous evil.

[3]A man may have a hundred children and live many years; yet no matter how long he lives, if he cannot enjoy his prosperity and does not receive proper burial, I say that a stillborn child is better off than he. [4]It comes without meaning, it departs in darkness, and in darkness its name is shrouded. [5]Though it never saw the sun or knew anything, it has more rest than does that man — [6]even if he lives a thousand years twice over but fails to enjoy his prosperity. Do not all go to the same place?

[7]Everyone's toil is for their mouth,
yet their appetite is never satisfied.

---

and injustice constitute a large part of what makes life senseless (see note on 1:2). This description of injustice contributes to debates about whether Solomon wrote Ecclesiastes. The idea is that, as king, Solomon would have had power to do something about oppression of the poor and other injustices, whereas the author does not appear to be in such a position. See note on 1:1.
5:9 the king himself profits from the fields See note on 10:16.
5:11 so do those who consume them Material wealth does not satisfy because consumption or appetite increases as much as goods increase.
5:12 permits them no sleep The desire for wealth is portrayed as a worrying and unsatisfying quest (2:23; 4:4,8; 5:17; 6:7). Compare 2:17 and note.
5:13–14 In this passage, the author describes someone who loses his wealth due to a bad investment and dies with nothing—a senseless and evil (or bad) scenario. Ecclesiastes presents several similar situations in which labor fails to satisfy: 4:4 depicts working from jealousy as senseless and futile; 4:7–8 presents working alone without the ability to share one's wealth as unsatisfying; 2:18–23 laments leaving the efforts of labor to someone who did not earn them.
5:15 naked from their mother's womb Similar to the statement Job makes after losing his wealth and children (Job 1:21).
5:16 what do they gain The difficulty of producing a

profit through hard work especially troubles the author. See note on Ecc 1:3. **toil for the wind** See note on 2:17.
5:18 find satisfaction in their toilsome labor See note on 9:7–10. **this is their lot** See note on 3:22.
5:19 ability to enjoy them God does not simply give away wealth and possessions; instead, he gives the ability to enjoy them and be satisfied. **accept their lot and be happy in their toil** Since their lives are in God's hand (9:1) and human wisdom is limited (8:16–17), people should be satisfied with God's provision—whether good or bad (7:14).
6:1 I have seen another evil See note on 2:21. **under the sun** Refers to all life on the earth.
6:2 strangers The Hebrew word used here, *nokhri*, typically refers to a foreigner or non-Israelite (1Ki 8:41). It is most likely used here to refer to someone outside of a person's family.
6:3 a hundred children See Ps 127:3 and note. **does not receive proper burial** See note on Ecc 8:10. **stillborn child** The Hebrew word used here, *nephel*, occurs only three times in the OT. The psalmist of Ps 58 curses his enemies, wishing they would be like a stillborn child (Ps 58:8). Job, when lamenting his own suffering, wishes he had died as a stillborn (Job 3:16).
6:5 rest See note on Job 3:13.
6:6 same place See note on Ecc 2:15; see note on 3:20.
6:7 appetite is never satisfied Laboring for things to consume and to accumulate wealth are portrayed as unsatisfying throughout Ecclesiastes (e.g., 5:10–12,17;

⁸ What advantage have the wise over fools?
What do the poor gain
by knowing how to conduct themselves
before others?
⁹ Better what the eye sees
than the roving of the appetite.
This too is meaningless,
a chasing after the wind.

¹⁰ Whatever exists has already been named,
and what humanity is has been known;
no one can contend
with someone who is stronger.
¹¹ The more the words,
the less the meaning,
and how does that profit anyone?

¹² For who knows what is good for a person in life, during the few and meaningless days they pass through like a shadow? Who can tell them what will happen under the sun after they are gone?

Wisdom

7 A good name is better than fine perfume,
and the day of death better than the day of
birth.
² It is better to go to a house of mourning
than to go to a house of feasting,
for death is the destiny of everyone;
the living should take this to heart.
³ Frustration is better than laughter,
because a sad face is good for the heart.
⁴ The heart of the wise is in the house of
mourning,
but the heart of fools is in the house of
pleasure.

⁵ It is better to heed the rebuke of a wise
person
than to listen to the song of fools.
⁶ Like the crackling of thorns under the pot,
so is the laughter of fools.
This too is meaningless.

⁷ Extortion turns a wise person into a fool,
and a bribe corrupts the heart.

⁸ The end of a matter is better than its
beginning,
and patience is better than pride.
⁹ Do not be quickly provoked in your spirit,
for anger resides in the lap of fools.

¹⁰ Do not say, "Why were the old days better
than these?"
For it is not wise to ask such questions.

¹¹ Wisdom, like an inheritance, is a good
thing
and benefits those who see the sun.
¹² Wisdom is a shelter
as money is a shelter,
but the advantage of knowledge is this:
Wisdom preserves those who have it.

¹³ Consider what God has done:

Who can straighten
what he has made crooked?
¹⁴ When times are good, be happy;
but when times are bad, consider this:
God has made the one
as well as the other.
Therefore, no one can discover
anything about their future.

4:7–8; 6:2). These statements seem to contradict others from Proverbs that characterize the profits of hard work as satisfying (Pr 12:14; 18:20). This apparent contradiction results from the different emphases of each book. Proverbs explains why hard work is superior to laziness—which the author of Ecclesiastes agrees with (Ecc 4:5). The author of Ecclesiastes, however, points out that we keep wanting more and all profits are lost in death (5:16). The author of Ecclesiastes considers the ability to enjoy one's labor an example of true satisfaction (5:18–19).
6:8 wise over fools Since both wisdom and folly end in death, the wise have no advantage over fools (2:12–17).
6:9 meaningless, a chasing after the wind See 1:2 and note; 2:17 and note.
6:11 The more the words, the less the meaning Since human wisdom is limited, the more words are spoken, the more senseless they are in trying to understand the work of God (3:11; 8:17).
6:12 like a shadow A common expression used to illustrate the brevity of life (Job 8:9; 14:2; Ps 102:11; 109:23; 144:4).
7:1 better than fine perfume In the ancient world, an abundance of oil was a sign of wealth (Job 29:6; Pr 21:20; Mt 26:7).
7:2 a house of mourning The Hebrew word used here,

beth-evel, only occurs this one time in the Bible, although a similar phrase (*beth marzeach*) appears in Jeremiah (see Jer 16:5 and note). The phrase emphasizes the mortality that comes with being human (compare note on Ecc 4:2). **should take this to heart** People should live in a manner that recognizes their mortality.
7:4 heart of the wise "Heart" in the OT refers to the essential character of a person, not just the center of emotions (1Sa 16:7). **pleasure** See Ecc 2:2 and note.
7:6 crackling of thorns Just as thorns burn quickly and provide little heat, foolish laughter is short-lived and accomplishes little.
7:9 anger resides in the lap of fools Proverbs often describes fools as having quick tempers (Pr 14:17,29), while the wise are slow to anger (Pr 16:32; 19:11).
7:12 money is a shelter Both wisdom and wealth provide value—but with limitation.
7:13 what he has made crooked Echoes the earlier proclamation that God makes everything "beautiful," "good" or "appropriate" in its time (see Ecc 3:11 and note).
7:14 the one as well as the other People should accept both good and bad situations in life, recognizing that they are dependent on God, not their circumstances (3:11). See note on 9:7–10. **no one can discover anything** God's work is unknowable (3:11–14).

15 In this meaningless life of mine I have seen both of these:

the righteous perishing in their
righteousness,
and the wicked living long in their
wickedness.
16 Do not be overrighteous,
neither be overwise —
why destroy yourself?
17 Do not be overwicked,
and do not be a fool —
why die before your time?
18 It is good to grasp the one
and not let go of the other.
Whoever fears God will avoid all extremes.[a]

19 Wisdom makes one wise person more
powerful
than ten rulers in a city.

20 Indeed, there is no one on earth who is
righteous,
no one who does what is right and never
sins.

21 Do not pay attention to every word
people say,
or you may hear your servant cursing you —
22 for you know in your heart
that many times you yourself have cursed
others.

23 All this I tested by wisdom and I said,

"I am determined to be wise" —
but this was beyond me.
24 Whatever exists is far off and most
profound —
who can discover it?
25 So I turned my mind to understand,
to investigate and to search out wisdom
and the scheme of things
and to understand the stupidity of
wickedness
and the madness of folly.

26 I find more bitter than death
the woman who is a snare,
whose heart is a trap
and whose hands are chains.
The man who pleases God will escape her,
but the sinner she will ensnare.

27 "Look," says the Teacher,[b] "this is what I have discovered:

"Adding one thing to another to discover the
scheme of things —
28 while I was still searching
but not finding —
I found one upright man among a thousand,
but not one upright woman among
them all.
29 This only have I found:
God created mankind upright,
but they have gone in search of many
schemes."

8 Who is like the wise?
Who knows the explanation of things?
A person's wisdom brightens their face
and changes its hard appearance.

Obey the King

2 Obey the king's command, I say, because you took an oath before God. 3 Do not be in a hurry to leave the king's presence. Do not stand up for a bad cause, for he will do whatever he pleases. 4 Since a king's word is supreme, who can say to him, "What are you doing?"

5 Whoever obeys his command will come to no
harm,
and the wise heart will know the proper
time and procedure.
6 For there is a proper time and procedure for
every matter,
though a person may be weighed down by
misery.

a 18 Or will follow them both   b 27 Or the leader of the assembly

---

7:15 righteous perishing See note on 8:13.
7:16 Do not be overrighteous A warning against relying on wisdom and righteousness for prolonged life or happiness (vv. 15; 2:15). destroy The person who relies on his or her own wisdom or righteousness for a happy, prosperous life will be disappointed.
7:17 Do not be overwicked Not permission to be somewhat wicked, but a warning against wickedness that recognizes it cannot be completely avoided (v. 20). die before your time Wickedness and folly were commonly believed to result in premature death (Ps 37:10; Pr 6:12–15; 10:8,27).
7:18 Whoever fears God The person who fears God recognizes the limitation of human wisdom and righteousness, while also being aware of the results of wickedness and folly. See Ecc 3:14 and note.
7:23 this was beyond me Reflects the limitation of human wisdom.

7:26 woman This may evoke a common feature of Wisdom Literature: its personification of wisdom and foolishness as two women (see Pr 9:1–18 and note).
7:27 says the Teacher See note on Ecc 1:1.
7:29 God created mankind upright Probably a reference to the first chapters of Genesis (see Ecc 3:11 and note; and 3:20 and note). God created humanity "good," but Adam and Eve sinned by seeking their own wisdom apart from God (Ge 3:5).
8:1 brightens their face A person's wisdom (or folly) will be evident (10:3). its hard appearance This is probably a reference to stubborn arrogance (Dt 28:50).
8:2 Obey the king's command See note on Ecc 10:20.
8:4 What are you doing Just as no one can legitimately challenge divine authority (3:14; 7:13–14), no one can challenge the authority of the king.
8:6 a proper time and procedure See note on 3:9–15.

⁷Since no one knows the future,
who can tell someone else what is to come?
⁸As no one has power over the wind to
contain it,
so*ᵃ* no one has power over the time of their
death.
As no one is discharged in time of war,
so wickedness will not release those who
practice it.

⁹All this I saw, as I applied my mind to every-thing done under the sun. There is a time when a man lords it over others to his own*ᵇ* hurt. ¹⁰Then too, I saw the wicked buried—those who used to come and go from the holy place and receive praise*ᶜ* in the city where they did this. This too is meaningless.

¹¹When the sentence for a crime is not quickly carried out, people's hearts are filled with schemes to do wrong. ¹²Although a wicked person who commits a hundred crimes may live a long time, I know that it will go better with those who fear God, who are reverent before him. ¹³Yet because the wicked do not fear God, it will not go well with them, and their days will not lengthen like a shadow.

¹⁴There is something else meaningless that oc-curs on earth: the righteous who get what the wicked deserve, and the wicked who get what the righteous deserve. This too, I say, is meaningless. ¹⁵So I commend the enjoyment of life, because there is nothing better for a person under the sun than to eat and drink and be glad. Then joy will accompany them in their toil all the days of the life God has given them under the sun.

¹⁶When I applied my mind to know wisdom and to observe the labor that is done on earth—people getting no sleep day or night— ¹⁷then I saw all that God has done. No one can comprehend what goes on under the sun. Despite all their efforts to search it out, no one can discover its meaning. Even if the wise claim they know, they cannot really comprehend it.

A Common Destiny for All

9 So I reflected on all this and concluded that the righteous and the wise and what they do are in God's hands, but no one knows whether love or hate awaits them. ²All share a common destiny—the righteous and the wicked, the good and the bad,*ᵈ* the clean and the unclean, those who offer sacrifices and those who do not.

As it is with the good,
so with the sinful;
as it is with those who take oaths,
so with those who are afraid to take them.

³This is the evil in everything that happens under the sun: The same destiny overtakes all. The hearts of people, moreover, are full of evil and there is madness in their hearts while they live, and afterward they join the dead. ⁴Anyone who is among the living has hope*ᵉ*—even a live dog is better off than a dead lion!

⁵For the living know that they will die,
but the dead know nothing;
they have no further reward,
and even their name is forgotten.
⁶Their love, their hate
and their jealousy have long since vanished;

ᵃ 8 Or over the human spirit to retain it, / and so ᵇ 9 Or to their ᶜ 10 Some Hebrew manuscripts and Septuagint (Aquila); most Hebrew manuscripts and are forgotten ᵈ 2 Septuagint (Aquila), Vulgate and Syriac; Hebrew does not have and the bad. ᵉ 4 Or What then is to be chosen? With all who live, there is hope

8:7 no one knows the future A similar statement is made in the book of James, which bears many similarities to OT Wisdom Literature (see Jas 4:14).
8:8 wickedness will not release those who prac-tice it See note on Ecc 8:14.
8:9 under the sun See note on 1:3.
8:10 I saw the wicked buried Receiving a proper burial was important in the OT (1Sa 31:11–13; 2Ki 9:10). In addition, celebrating a wicked person in death while forgetting the righteous was considered an injustice (Ecc 4:16; 9:15). **holy place** Possibly a reference to the temple (Ps 24:3) or to the burial place of the wicked. See the infographic "Temple Comparison" on p. 1558.
8:11 sentence The word used here, *pithgam*, is a Persian term. Its presence in Ecclesiastes suggests the book was written or edited after the exile when Persian terms were more commonly used by Jewish people (post-538 BC; see note on Ecc 1:1).
8:13 their days will not lengthen This seems to con-tradict the claims of v. 12 and v. 14. However, as in 3:16–17, the author contrasts his observation of the prevalence of injustice with his belief that God's justice will prevail.

8:14 the righteous who get what the wicked deserve The author laments that the wicked and the righteous get the opposite of what they deserve. Wisdom Litera-ture traditionally teaches that the righteous will prosper while the wicked perish. While the author of Ecclesiastes upholds that God's justice will prevail, he expresses frustration that this justice is perverted.
8:15 I commend the enjoyment See note on 9:7–10.
8:17 wise claim they know No matter the effort, hu-man wisdom is limited (12:12).
9:1 no one knows Since human wisdom is limited, people must recognize God's sovereignty whether the future brings adversity or prosperity.
9:2 All share a common destiny See note on 2:14. **the clean and the unclean** Normally refers to ritual cleanliness. See note on Lev 11:1–47. **so with those who are afraid to take them** See note on Ecc 5:4.
9:4 a live dog is better off than a dead lion Lions were respected as majestic, powerful predators (Ge 49:9; 2Sa 17:10; Pr 28:1; 30:30; Mic 5:8). Dogs were looked down upon as despised scavengers (Ex 22:31; 1Sa 17:43; 2Sa 16:9; 1Ki 14:11; Ps 59:14–15; Pr 26:11).
9:5 they have no further reward The dead—unlike the living—can no longer enjoy life.

never again will they have a part
in anything that happens under the sun.

⁷Go, eat your food with gladness, and drink your wine with a joyful heart, for God has already approved what you do. ⁸Always be clothed in white, and always anoint your head with oil. ⁹Enjoy life with your wife, whom you love, all the days of this meaningless life that God has given you under the sun—all your meaningless days. For this is your lot in life and in your toilsome labor under the sun. ¹⁰Whatever your hand finds to do, do it with all your might, for in the realm of the dead, where you are going, there is neither working nor planning nor knowledge nor wisdom.

¹¹I have seen something else under the sun:

The race is not to the swift
    or the battle to the strong,
nor does food come to the wise
    or wealth to the brilliant
    or favor to the learned;
but time and chance happen to them all.

¹²Moreover, no one knows when their hour will come:

As fish are caught in a cruel net,
    or birds are taken in a snare,
so people are trapped by evil times
    that fall unexpectedly upon them.

Wisdom Better Than Folly

¹³I also saw under the sun this example of wisdom that greatly impressed me: ¹⁴There was once a small city with only a few people in it. And a powerful king came against it, surrounded it and built huge siege works against it. ¹⁵Now there lived in that city a man poor but wise, and he saved the city by his wisdom. But nobody remembered that poor man. ¹⁶So I said, "Wisdom is better than strength." But the poor man's wisdom is despised, and his words are no longer heeded.

¹⁷The quiet words of the wise are more to
    be heeded
    than the shouts of a ruler of fools.
¹⁸Wisdom is better than weapons of war,
    but one sinner destroys much good.

10 As dead flies give perfume a bad smell,
    so a little folly outweighs wisdom and
    honor.
²The heart of the wise inclines to the right,
    but the heart of the fool to the left.
³Even as fools walk along the road,
    they lack sense
    and show everyone how stupid they are.
⁴If a ruler's anger rises against you,
    do not leave your post;
    calmness can lay great offenses to rest.

⁵There is an evil I have seen under the sun,
    the sort of error that arises from a ruler:
⁶Fools are put in many high positions,
    while the rich occupy the low ones.
⁷I have seen slaves on horseback,
    while princes go on foot like slaves.

⁸Whoever digs a pit may fall into it;
    whoever breaks through a wall may be
    bitten by a snake.
⁹Whoever quarries stones may be injured
    by them;
    whoever splits logs may be endangered by
    them.

9:7–10 This is the longest of the author's calls to enjoy life (see Ecc 2:24–26; 3:12–13,22; 5:18–20; 8:15; 11:8–10). Some believe these passages advocate self-indulgent and pleasure-seeking behavior. Others believe they advocate enjoyment as kind of a precarious possibility given life's difficulties. However, in all of these passages, the enjoyment of life is seen as a gift from God.
    Ultimately, the author's calls to enjoy life do not grant permission to live in self-indulgence. Rather, they encourage enjoying life to its fullest while being content with what God has given—all the while recognizing God's supremacy and human limitation (3:11; 7:14).

9:7 eat your food with gladness Bread, wine and oil (v. 8) were considered blessings from God and often used in celebrations (Dt 7:13; Ps 104:14–15; Jer 31:12; Joel 2:19). **God has already approved what you do** The ability to enjoy life is not just a gift from God; it is his desire.
9:9 meaningless Normally the author uses this term to indicate senselessness or absurdity (see note on Ecc 1:2). Here, however, the author seems to use its literal meaning to emphasize the brevity of life (Job 7:16; Ps 39:5; 78:33).
9:10 in the realm of the dead See note on Ge 37:35; note on 1Ki 2:6.
9:11 time and chance Often, timing and chance affect the outcome more than skill or ability.

9:12 taken in a snare See note on Job 18:8.

9:13–16 This story of the poor, wise man who saved the city illustrates the author's opinion of wisdom. The wisdom of the poor man saved an entire city from a powerful king, which illustrates wisdom's value. However, despite the greatness of his wisdom, it provided little value—the poor man was not remembered for saving the city, and he was even despised. Just as in Ecc 2:12–17, wisdom is valuable, but it can be undermined and negated by foolishness.

9:18 one sinner destroys much good Possibly a reference to the fall in Ge 3 (see note on Ecc 7:29).
10:1 perfume The addition of something small, such as a dead fly, would ruin the perfume.
10:4 a ruler's anger See note on v. 16; and note on v. 20.
10:5 under the sun See note on 1:3.

10:6–7 These verses describe situations where people have been placed in inappropriate positions. Fools and slaves are elevated to positions of authority and respect while the rich and powerful are put in positions of servitude. Here, the author is concerned with unfair or unjust situations.

¹⁰ If the ax is dull
    and its edge unsharpened,
more strength is needed,
    but skill will bring success.

¹¹ If a snake bites before it is charmed,
    the charmer receives no fee.

¹² Words from the mouth of the wise are
      gracious,
    but fools are consumed by their own lips.
¹³ At the beginning their words are folly;
    at the end they are wicked madness —
¹⁴   and fools multiply words.

No one knows what is coming —
    who can tell someone else what will
      happen after them?

¹⁵ The toil of fools wearies them;
    they do not know the way to town.

¹⁶ Woe to the land whose king was a servant^a
    and whose princes feast in the morning.
¹⁷ Blessed is the land whose king is of noble
      birth
    and whose princes eat at a proper time —
    for strength and not for drunkenness.

¹⁸ Through laziness, the rafters sag;
    because of idle hands, the house leaks.

¹⁹ A feast is made for laughter,
    wine makes life merry,
    and money is the answer for everything.

²⁰ Do not revile the king even in your thoughts,
    or curse the rich in your bedroom,
because a bird in the sky may carry your
      words,
    and a bird on the wing may report what
    you say.

Invest in Many Ventures

11 Ship your grain across the sea;
    after many days you may receive a return.
² Invest in seven ventures, yes, in eight;
    you do not know what disaster may come
      upon the land.

³ If clouds are full of water,
    they pour rain on the earth.
Whether a tree falls to the south or to the
      north,
    in the place where it falls, there it will lie.
⁴ Whoever watches the wind will not plant;
    whoever looks at the clouds will not reap.

⁵ As you do not know the path of the wind,
    or how the body is formed^b in a mother's
      womb,
so you cannot understand the work of God,
    the Maker of all things.

⁶ Sow your seed in the morning,
    and at evening let your hands not be idle,
for you do not know which will succeed,
    whether this or that,
    or whether both will do equally well.

Remember Your Creator While Young

⁷ Light is sweet,
    and it pleases the eyes to see the sun.
⁸ However many years anyone may live,
    let them enjoy them all.
But let them remember the days of darkness,
    for there will be many.
    Everything to come is meaningless.

^a 16 Or *king is a child*   ^b 5 Or *know how life* (or *the spirit*) /
enters the body being formed

10:8–9 These verses describe situations where time and chance (9:11) negatively affect people. In each instance, normal day to day activities — digging a pit, tearing down a wall, breaking rocks or cutting wood — are interrupted by some sort of accident, illustrating humanity's limited ability to know or control future circumstances.

10:12–15 The speech of the wise and the fool is a common theme in Wisdom Literature. Proverbs often upholds wise speech as beneficial (Pr 16:23) while condemning the speech of the fool (18:7). Ecclesiastes 10:15 speaks about the fools' actions rather than their speech.

10:16 king was a servant The fate of a nation depends on the quality of its leadership. Foolish rulers who live self-indulgent lives often neglect the needs of their subjects, whereas rulers who exercise proper self-restraint can greatly benefit their nations (1Ki 3:9–14,28).

10:17 Blessed See note on Ps 1:1. **drunkenness** Rulers should not indulge in drunken behavior because it can impair their ability to rule justly (Pr 31:4–5) — and even put them at risk of assassination (1Ki 16:8–10).

10:18–19 These verses may be stand-alone proverbs or they may connect to Ecc 10:16–17. If the latter is true,

then v. 18 describes the effect of an incompetent ruler (v. 16) while v. 19 describes the land of a competent ruler (v. 17).

10:19 A feast See note on 9:7.
10:20 Do not revile the king The author warns against cursing a king regardless of his competence (vv. 16–17). Compare note on v. 16.

11:1–6 In this section, the author gives advice on how to live while recognizing the limitations of human wisdom and knowledge. Since it is difficult to know what will be profitable and what will fall victim to "time and chance," people should work hard in a variety of areas.

11:1 Ship your grain across the sea Possibly an idiom encouraging the reader to be generous, but given the context of vv. 1–6, it likely refers to taking calculated risks in commercial endeavors.
11:2 Invest in seven ventures, yes, in eight Because the future cannot be known, the author encourages people to make diverse investments.
11:4 will not plant Taking time to try to determine the future accomplishes nothing.
11:8 enjoy them all See note on 9:7–10. **remember**

⁹You who are young, be happy while you are
young,
and let your heart give you joy in the days
of your youth.
Follow the ways of your heart
and whatever your eyes see,
but know that for all these things
God will bring you into judgment.
¹⁰So then, banish anxiety from your heart
and cast off the troubles of your body,
for youth and vigor are meaningless.

12 Remember your Creator
in the days of your youth,
before the days of trouble come
and the years approach when you
will say,
"I find no pleasure in them" —
²before the sun and the light
and the moon and the stars grow dark,
and the clouds return after the rain;
³when the keepers of the house tremble,
and the strong men stoop,
when the grinders cease because they
are few,
and those looking through the windows
grow dim;
⁴when the doors to the street are closed
and the sound of grinding fades;
when people rise up at the sound of birds,

but all their songs grow faint;
⁵when people are afraid of heights
and of dangers in the streets;
when the almond tree blossoms
and the grasshopper drags itself along
and desire no longer is stirred.
Then people go to their eternal home
and mourners go about the streets.

⁶Remember him — before the silver cord is
severed,
and the golden bowl is broken;
before the pitcher is shattered at the
spring,
and the wheel broken at the well,
⁷and the dust returns to the ground it came
from,
and the spirit returns to God who
gave it.

⁸"Meaningless! Meaningless!" says the
Teacher.ᵃ
"Everything is meaningless!"

The Conclusion of the Matter

⁹Not only was the Teacher wise, but he also
imparted knowledge to the people. He pondered
and searched out and set in order many prov-

ᵃ 8 Or *the leader of the assembly*; also in verses 9 and 10

---

the days of darkness Recalling one's mortality yields better appreciation and enjoyment of life.

11:9 bring you into judgment Throughout Ecclesiastes, the author expresses faith in God's justice. This belief is the reason for the book's final appeal to fear God and obey his commandments (12:13–14).

11:10 vigor The Hebrew word used here, *shacharuth*, literally rendered "blackness," most likely refers to the dark hair of youth in contrast with the gray hair of old age (Pr 20:29; Isa 46:4). **meaningless** Youth is fleeting (see note on Ecc 9:9). The work of removing anxiety and frustration from the heart should begin early in life.

12:1–8 In this remaining section (before the book's epilogue), the author reflects on old age and death—an appropriate conclusion considering his focus on human limitation, the brevity of life and death as the ultimate fate (1:3–11). Using a variety of metaphors, he describes how the body breaks down as one gets older.

12:1 Creator Emphasizes God's sovereignty in relation to the limits of human wisdom (see note on Job 38:1—41:34). **the days of trouble** The author encourages people to enjoy life while they are young—before the troubles of old age described in Ecc 12:2–7.

12:2 grow dark Best understood as a metaphor for failing eyesight due to aging or a general statement about the coming storm that represents death.

12:3 This is likely a list of various metaphors for the physical decline of old age: trembling hands, weakened muscles or a stooped back, lost teeth and failing eyesight.

12:4 doors to the street are closed Possibly a general reference to the dimming of the senses or a metaphor for

hearing loss. **sound of grinding fades** May describe a loss of hearing or teeth (v. 3), or an inability to work. **rise up at the sound of birds** Probably refers to loss of sleep. **12:5 almond tree blossoms** Since the almond tree's flowers were white, this likely refers to hair turning white. **grasshopper drags itself along** Possibly a metaphor for the decreased mobility of old age.

12:6–7 The metaphors of these verses refer to death, not aging.

12:6 broken Several vessels are broken that are meant to hold water, which is a symbol of life (2Sa 14:14). **12:7 dust returns to the ground** Dust returning to the earth calls to mind the curse of Ge 3:19. **12:8 the Teacher** See note on 1:1. **Everything is meaningless** See note on Ecc 1:2.

12:9–14 The book closes with an epilogue written in third-person voice. This conclusion and the opening verses (1:1–2) provide a frame around the "words of qoheleth" (1:3—12:7; see note on 1:1). By organizing the book this way, the author provides a framework to understanding the "words of qoheleth" (see note on 12:1). The epilogue first describes the author, praising his wisdom and the integrity of his words (vv. 9–10). It then warns against trusting human wisdom to provide satisfying explanations for the difficult situations of life under the sun (vv. 11–12). The epilogue ends with a concluding exhortation: Fear God and keep his commandments (vv. 13–14).

12:9 he also imparted knowledge to the people The author was not simply a wise man; he was also an educator and writer.

erbs. [10]The Teacher searched to find just the right words, and what he wrote was upright and true.

[11]The words of the wise are like goads, their collected sayings like firmly embedded nails — given by one shepherd.[a] [12]Be warned, my son, of anything in addition to them.

Of making many books there is no end, and much study wearies the body.

[13]Now all has been heard;
here is the conclusion of the matter:
Fear God and keep his commandments,
for this is the duty of all mankind.
[14]For God will bring every deed into judgment,
including every hidden thing,
whether it is good or evil.

[a] 11 Or *Shepherd*

12:10 just the right words While the author desired to write pleasing words as he examined life, he discovered that life often fails to allow for them. The author calls these words in Hebrew, *divre-chephets*, which may be literally rendered as "words of joy." But instead of writing these words, the author focused on writing an honest description of life that addresses its difficulties. The author calls these words in Hebrew *yosher divre emeth*; literally "honest words of truth."

12:11 goads Pointed sticks used to drive or guide cattle.

12:12 my son Wisdom literature was traditionally pre-sented as a father's teachings to his son (Pr 1:8; 2:1; 3:1; 4:10; 5:1). **making many books** Refers to a human search for wisdom.

12:13 Fear God and keep his commandments In light of humanity's limitation and God's supremacy as seen throughout the book, the only proper attitude in life is one of trust and obedience to God. See note on 3:14.

12:14 every deed into judgment Faith in God's justice leads the author to encourage people to fear God and keep his commandments.

SONG OF SONGS

INTRODUCTION TO SONG OF SONGS

Song of Songs, or Song of Solomon, is a group of poems celebrating romantic love between a man and woman. With extended metaphors—many of which seem odd today but were fitting in the ancient Near East—the book upholds the goodness of all God's creation, including sexuality (compare Ge 1:31; 2:18). Marriage is celebrated as a full and rich expression of God's love, meant to be pursued with longing and held onto tightly.

BACKGROUND

King Solomon has been identified as the author of the work because he is named in the book's inscription. However, like the heading attached to many psalms, the original Hebrew text is ambiguous and might not be identifying the author. Instead, the book could be written about, to, for or in honor of Solomon. Even if some of the poems in the Song did originate with Solomon, several places in the text refer to him as the subject, not the author (SS 3:6–11; 8:11–12).

If the Song was written by or about Solomon, the relationship it describes would have to be his first marriage. As 1 Kings 11 relates, Solomon eventually married 700 wives and had 300 concubines, which would undermine the book's affirmation of monogamy (compare SS 3:11). Nevertheless, the Song uses so many metaphors related to Solomon's kingdom—including signs of Israel's prosperity—some connection to him must be intended, perhaps just for setting.

To illustrate God's point of view, the Song uses cultural references and imagery that occur in other ancient Near Eastern literature—similar to much of the Old Testament. There are also linguistic parallels to poetry of the second century BC. This means the Song could date as late as the second century BC or as early as Solomon's era, the 10th century BC (with later editing or development of the content being involved).

The Song was likely meant to be sung aloud and could have functioned like a play—there are multiple speakers. It could also be an allegory or simply poetry. The allegory viewpoint usually designates the man as God and the woman as Israel, as the husband-wife metaphor for God and his people occurs elsewhere in the Old Testament (e.g., Isa 54:5; Hos 2:16). In Christian interpretation, the man is sometimes described as Christ and the woman

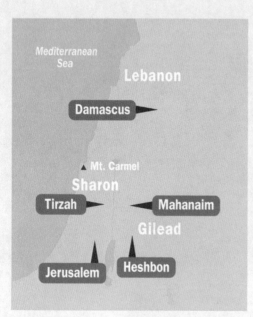

This map depicts places named in the book of Song of Songs.

the church, based on New Testament usage of similar metaphors (e.g., 2Co 11:2; Eph 5:24,32; Rev 19:7; 22:17). But the sexual language of the Song makes this application difficult and often problematic, and nothing within the text itself indicates that such an interpretation is intended.

STRUCTURE

The Song contains several poems, perhaps six in all (SS 1:2—2:7; 2:8—3:5; 3:6—5:1; 5:2—6:3; 6:4—8:4; 8:5–14). However, the precise number of poems is difficult to trace, as is the precise number of characters. Like a play, the text switches speakers, develops over a series of dramatic scenes and includes refrains. To make these transitions easier, English translations often add headings that indicate the speaker, but these headings are not part of the original Hebrew text and represent the interpretation of modern translators.

The poems seem to trace the development of the two main characters' relationship—from courtship, to wedding, to marriage. The work concludes with an epilogue that functions as a summary of the love between the couple.

OUTLINE

- Courtship (1:1—3:5)
- Wedding (3:6—5:1)
- Marriage (5:2—8:4)
- Epilogue (8:5–14)

THEMES

Although God is never explicitly mentioned in the Song, the work celebrates God's work in the world by reflecting on his creation. In this regard, these ancient love poems articulate an ethic for wisely stewarding God's creation.

By recording ancient Near Eastern compliments about the body, the Song affirms the human body as good and worthy of admiration (2:9–10; 4:1–4,7). The Song affirms intimacy as part of God's creative work and embraces it as good. From the Bible's larger perspective, this means intimacy in marriage (Pr 5:18; Eph 5:23–33; Heb 13:4). The Song recognizes the longing a person feels when falling in love, and rather than shunning such emotions, it progresses toward marriage—the intended application of such thoughts (compare 1Co 6:12–20).

In celebrating love, the Song uses figurative language intended to kindle all of the senses. The Song shows that God cherishes all that he has made and intends romance and sexual love to be good. It affirms this integral aspect of our humanity, calling us to recognize its value and embrace it in marriage when it is our calling (compare 1Co 7:8–9).

The fallen societies we live in are filled with distorted portrayals of romance and sexuality, reflecting passions that are selfish and exploitative. The love poetry of the Song challenges this broken mindset and celebrates our Creator's beautiful design: human love as it was meant to be.

1 Solomon's Song of Songs.

She[a]

[2] Let him kiss me with the kisses of his
    mouth —
    for your love is more delightful than wine.
[3] Pleasing is the fragrance of your perfumes;
    your name is like perfume poured out.
    No wonder the young women love you!
[4] Take me away with you — let us hurry!
    Let the king bring me into his chambers.

Friends

We rejoice and delight in you [b];
    we will praise your love more than wine.

She

How right they are to adore you!

[5] Dark am I, yet lovely,
    daughters of Jerusalem,
    dark like the tents of Kedar,
    like the tent curtains of Solomon.[c]
[6] Do not stare at me because I am dark,
    because I am darkened by the sun.

My mother's sons were angry with me
    and made me take care of the vineyards;
    my own vineyard I had to neglect.
[7] Tell me, you whom I love,
    where you graze your flock
    and where you rest your sheep at midday.
    Why should I be like a veiled woman
    beside the flocks of your friends?

Friends

[8] If you do not know, most beautiful
    of women,
    follow the tracks of the sheep
and graze your young goats
    by the tents of the shepherds.

He

[9] I liken you, my darling, to a mare
    among Pharaoh's chariot horses.

---

[a] The main male and female speakers (identified primarily on the basis of the gender of the relevant Hebrew forms) are indicated by the captions *He* and *She* respectively. The words of others are marked *Friends*. In some instances the divisions and their captions are debatable.   [b] 4 The Hebrew is masculine singular.   [c] 5 Or *Salma*

1:1–4 The Song, likely meant to be sung aloud, represents the love between a man and a woman. It opens with words from a woman. The Song could be an allegory, function like a play or be poetry. If an allegory, the man represents God and the woman is Israel. However, the sexual language in the book makes this application difficult. If a play or poetry, the man could be Israel's King Solomon and the woman his first wife. The man and woman could also refer to an unnamed couple (compare 3:6–11 and note). However, Solomon notoriously grew his number of wives and concubines (1Ki 11:1–4; compare Dt 17:17), which is in sharp contrast to the exclusive relationship between the two lovers (see SS 8:11–12 and note).

The Song could date to the 10th century BC, Solomon's era, or as late as the second century BC (there are some linguistic parallels to poetry of that era).

The only indication of a speaker in the Hebrew text of the Song comes from the Hebrew verbs, which designate a singular male or female speaker or a plural ("we") speaker. Some translations provide headings like "She" or "Young Woman"; however, these headings are not part of the Hebrew text.

1:1 Solomon's The Hebrew preposition used here, *le-*, can mean "to," "for," "by" or "about." The relationship between the Song and Solomon is unclear. Solomon may have been the author of the book, the book may have been written for or dedicated to him, or it could be in the tradition of Solomon (in his honor or as a critique of him; compare SS 8:11–12 and note). **Song of Songs** The Hebrew word used here, *shir*, which opens Song of Songs, most often indicates a happy or joyful song (Ps 28:7; Pr 25:20; Isa 30:29). The full Hebrew phrase used here, *shir hashirim*, literally means "song of songs," but idiomatically may be understood as "the greatest song." This superscription may also indicate that the book is a series of songs or poems that make up a single song or poem.
1:2 kiss me While kissing was used in greetings and as a sign of respect (Ge 29:13; 1Sa 10:1), it was also used

to express romantic love (Pr 7:13). **your love is more delightful than wine** The Hebrew word used here, *dod*, most likely indicates sexual love (Pr 7:18; Eze 23:17). The woman describes her lover as more pleasing and intoxicating than wine.
1:3 your name is like perfume poured out "Name" here indicates the man's reputation (Ecc 7:1). **young women** See note on Isa 7:14. **love you** In contrast to the earlier Hebrew word used for love (*dod*; SS 1:2), the Hebrew word used here, *ahev*, better describes general attraction or care.
1:4 the king Though the designation "king" may indicate literal royalty, it may be a term of endearment for the lover. **We rejoice and delight in you** The second half of v. 4 is a summarizing refrain or chorus. While the identity of the singers is uncertain, they are likely the "daughters of Jerusalem" from v. 5.
1:5 Dark am I, yet lovely In ancient Near Eastern culture, light skin was considered an indicator of beauty. Women in working-class families became darkened by the sun since they worked outside in the fields (v. 6), so light skin may have been more desirable because dark skin often indicated a lower social class. **daughters of Jerusalem** The identity of the daughters of Jerusalem is disputed. Within the book, their words function as a chorus. **Kedar** The Kedar—most likely nomadic shepherds (Isa 60:7; Jer 49:28–29)—were an Arabian tribe descended from Ishmael (Ge 25:13).
1:6 angry The Hebrew word used here, *charah*, literally means "to become hot." It may be a play on words; her brothers' anger or heat caused her to be burned by the sun. **my own vineyard** A metaphor for physical appearance.
1:7 you whom I love See note on SS 3:1. **a veiled woman** The reference to a veil probably indicates that by searching for him, she would have looked like a cult prostitute (see Dt 23:17–18; compare the story of Tamar in Ge 38:14–19).
1:8 graze your young goats The speaker seems to advise the woman to disguise herself and her reasons

¹⁰ Your cheeks are beautiful with earrings,
  your neck with strings of jewels.
¹¹ We will make you earrings of gold,
  studded with silver.

She

¹² While the king was at his table,
  my perfume spread its fragrance.
¹³ My beloved is to me a sachet of myrrh
  resting between my breasts.
¹⁴ My beloved is to me a cluster of henna
  blossoms
  from the vineyards of En Gedi.

He

¹⁵ How beautiful you are, my darling!
  Oh, how beautiful!
  Your eyes are doves.

She

¹⁶ How handsome you are, my beloved!
  Oh, how charming!
  And our bed is verdant.

He

¹⁷ The beams of our house are cedars;
  our rafters are firs.

She[a]

2 I am a rose[b] of Sharon,
  a lily of the valleys.

He

² Like a lily among thorns
  is my darling among the young women.

She

³ Like an apple[c] tree among the trees of the
  forest
  is my beloved among the young men.
  I delight to sit in his shade,
  and his fruit is sweet to my taste.
⁴ Let him lead me to the banquet hall,
  and let his banner over me be love.
⁵ Strengthen me with raisins,
  refresh me with apples,
  for I am faint with love.
⁶ His left arm is under my head,
  and his right arm embraces me.
⁷ Daughters of Jerusalem, I charge you
  by the gazelles and by the does
  of the field:
Do not arouse or awaken love
  until it so desires.

⁸ Listen! My beloved!
  Look! Here he comes,
leaping across the mountains,
  bounding over the hills.
⁹ My beloved is like a gazelle or a young stag.
  Look! There he stands behind our wall,

---

[a] Or *He*   [b] 1 Probably a member of the crocus family   [c] 3 Or possibly *apricot*; here and elsewhere in Song of Songs

---

for being out. In this way, she can still search for her lover without looking like a cult prostitute (compare note on SS 1:7).

1:9 a mare among Pharaoh's chariot horses In the ancient Near East, only stallions were used to pull chariots. Releasing a mare among chariots would excite and distract the stallions.

1:12 king See note on 1:4. **perfume** An expensive ointment extracted from a plant found in the Himalayan Mountains. A woman (identified as Mary the sister of Lazarus in Jn 12:3) used it to anoint Jesus (Mk 14:3–9).

1:13 a sachet of myrrh A fragrant gum used in anointing oil (Ex 30:23), as well as a perfume (Ps 45:8). **resting between my breasts** The Hebrew word used here, *lin*, means "to stay the night" (Ge 28:11).

1:14 henna blossoms When crushed, henna blossoms produce a reddish dye used to color hair or skin. They are referred to here for their fragrant qualities. **En Gedi** A fertile oasis located along the western shore of the Dead Sea.

1:15 Your eyes are doves Since doves were not a common symbol of beauty (Hos 7:11), the reason for this comparison is unclear. The twofold statement of the woman's beauty indicates it is a compliment. It may describe gentleness or softness.

1:16 bed is verdant The Hebrew word used here, *ra'anan* (meaning "leafy" or "luxuriant"), is meant to evoke an outdoor garden or forest location.

1:17 beams of our house are cedars The woman is not describing a literal house; she poetically describes the outdoor location of their lovemaking.

2:1 Sharon A plain along the Mediterranean coast, known for its beauty and fertility (1Ch 5:16; Isa 35:2).

2:3 to sit in his shade An image of safety and protection. **his fruit is sweet** Likely a sexual euphemism.

2:4 his banner Banners were used for military purposes. Here, the man's banner represents a declaration of his love.

2:6 embraces The Hebrew word used here, *chavaq*, can have either friendly (Ge 48:10) or sexual (Pr 5:20) implications. Here, it indicates a sexual union as the woman describes her encounter with her beloved.

2:7 I charge you The woman is encouraging the daughters of Jerusalem to swear an oath that they will refrain from love until the appropriate time. This verse is repeated in SS 3:5; 8:4. **gazelles and by the does** Symbols of beauty (4:5; Pr 5:19). **until it so desires** In light of the all-consuming nature of love as described in SS 2:3–6, the woman warns the daughters not to hurry love but to wait for it to blossom. Expressing this kind of love requires a proper context and occasion.

2:8–17 In this section, the woman describes the coming of her beloved with great anticipation (vv. 8–9). He arrives and invites her to go away with him (v. 10). Winter gives way to spring as their love flourishes and grows (vv. 11–15). Then the beloved leaves, and she again longs for his return (v. 17).

2:8 leaping across the mountains May indicate the urgency of his approach. It may also indicate that he had to overcome certain obstacles to reach her.

2:9 our wall The pronoun "our" is probably meant to include the woman's mother.

gazing through the windows,
  peering through the lattice.
[10] My beloved spoke and said to me,
  "Arise, my darling,
  my beautiful one, come with me.
[11] See! The winter is past;
  the rains are over and gone.
[12] Flowers appear on the earth;
  the season of singing has come,
  the cooing of doves
  is heard in our land.
[13] The fig tree forms its early fruit;
  the blossoming vines spread their
    fragrance.
  Arise, come, my darling;
  my beautiful one, come with me."

He

[14] My dove in the clefts of the rock,
  in the hiding places on the mountainside,
show me your face,
  let me hear your voice;
for your voice is sweet,
  and your face is lovely.
[15] Catch for us the foxes,
  the little foxes
that ruin the vineyards,
  our vineyards that are in bloom.

She

[16] My beloved is mine and I am his;
  he browses among the lilies.

[17] Until the day breaks
  and the shadows flee,
turn, my beloved,
  and be like a gazelle
or like a young stag
  on the rugged hills.[a]

3 All night long on my bed
  I looked for the one my heart loves;
  I looked for him but did not find him.
[2] I will get up now and go about the city,
  through its streets and squares;
I will search for the one my heart loves.
  So I looked for him but did not find him.
[3] The watchmen found me
  as they made their rounds in the city.
  "Have you seen the one my heart loves?"
[4] Scarcely had I passed them
  when I found the one my heart loves.
I held him and would not let him go
  till I had brought him to my mother's
    house,
  to the room of the one who conceived me.
[5] Daughters of Jerusalem, I charge you
  by the gazelles and by the does of the field:
Do not arouse or awaken love
  until it so desires.

[6] Who is this coming up from the wilderness
  like a column of smoke,
perfumed with myrrh and incense
  made from all the spices of the merchant?

---

a 17 Or the hills of Bether

2:11–13 The ending of winter and beginning of spring marks the perfect time to leave. This has both practical and symbolic meaning. The winter's cold temperature and heavy rains made traveling more difficult. In addition, the blooming flowers and ripening fruit symbolically speak of the blossoming love between the woman and her beloved.

2:12 singing This word can refer either to "pruning" or to "a song." It may describe the singing of birds who returned after migrating for the winter.

2:14 My dove See note on 1:15. **show me your face** The second half of this verse contains striking poetic parallelism: two requests (face, voice) are followed by two descriptions (voice, face). See the table "Parallelism in Hebrew Poetry" on p. 1008.

2:15 Catch for us the foxes Elsewhere in Song of Songs, the vineyard represents the woman (1:6) or a place of sexual union (6:11–12); the foxes probably represent some kind of hindrance to their love. Alternatively, the foxes may represent rival young men or unwanted suitors. By referring to the blossoming of the vineyards, the woman may also be saying that she and her beloved should take advantage of their love while the time is right.

2:16 he browses among the lilies The image here probably indicates physical intimacy as the beloved finds refreshment and nourishment via his love.

3:1–5 In this poem, the woman wakes in the night and searches carefully for her beloved. She finds him and brings him back to her mother's house. While the meaning

behind this poem is unclear, it likely describes a dream or fantasy that takes place in the woman's imagination. Taken this way, it expresses the woman's longing and desire for her beloved; he consumes her thoughts.

3:1 my heart The Hebrew word used here, *nephesh* (often rendered as "soul" or "life"), can carry the sense of "appetite" (compare Ecc 6:9). Here, it indicates the woman's desire for her beloved; she loves him with her entire being.

3:2 through its streets Since the city at night would not be a safe or respectable place for a young woman (Pr 7:10–12), she likely dreams or imagines this scenario.

3:4 brought him to my mother's house Indicates the woman's intention to enjoy intimacy in a secure, private place (compare SS 8:2).

3:6–11 This poem describes a wedding processional. It is unclear whether it refers to a real event or takes place in the woman's imagination (see note on vv. 1–5). Most likely, the woman is imagining the wedding processional or her beloved. The reference to King Solomon is most likely symbolic, as Solomon is known for his great wealth.

3:6 a column of smoke It may refer to plumes of dust being kicked up by the procession. It is also possible that the smoke emanates from the burning of fragrant incense. **myrrh** See note on 1:13. **incense** The Hebrew text here refers to a fragrant resin used as incense (Ex 30:34) and in other offerings (Lev 2:1; 24:7).

7 Look! It is Solomon's carriage,
  escorted by sixty warriors,
  the noblest of Israel,
8 all of them wearing the sword,
  all experienced in battle,
  each with his sword at his side,
  prepared for the terrors of the night.
9 King Solomon made for himself the carriage;
  he made it of wood from Lebanon.
10 Its posts he made of silver,
  its base of gold.
  Its seat was upholstered with purple,
  its interior inlaid with love.
  Daughters of Jerusalem, 11 come out,
  and look, you daughters of Zion.
  Look[a] on King Solomon wearing a crown,
  the crown with which his mother
    crowned him
  on the day of his wedding,
  the day his heart rejoiced.

He

4 How beautiful you are, my darling!
  Oh, how beautiful!
  Your eyes behind your veil are doves.
  Your hair is like a flock of goats
  descending from the hills of Gilead.
2 Your teeth are like a flock of sheep just shorn,
  coming up from the washing.
  Each has its twin;
  not one of them is alone.
3 Your lips are like a scarlet ribbon;
  your mouth is lovely.
  Your temples behind your veil
  are like the halves of a pomegranate.
4 Your neck is like the tower of David,
  built with courses of stone[b];

on it hang a thousand shields,
  all of them shields of warriors.
5 Your breasts are like two fawns,
  like twin fawns of a gazelle
  that browse among the lilies.
6 Until the day breaks
  and the shadows flee,
  I will go to the mountain of myrrh
  and to the hill of incense.
7 You are altogether beautiful, my
    darling;
  there is no flaw in you.

8 Come with me from Lebanon, my bride,
  come with me from Lebanon.
  Descend from the crest of Amana,
  from the top of Senir, the summit of
    Hermon,
  from the lions' dens
  and the mountain haunts of leopards.
9 You have stolen my heart, my sister, my
    bride;
  you have stolen my heart
  with one glance of your eyes,
  with one jewel of your necklace.
10 How delightful is your love, my sister,
    my bride!
  How much more pleasing is your love
    than wine,
  and the fragrance of your perfume
  more than any spice!
11 Your lips drop sweetness as the honeycomb,
    my bride;
  milk and honey are under your tongue.

[a] 10,11 Or *interior lovingly inlaid / by the daughters of Jerusalem. / 11Come out, you daughters of Zion, / and look* [b] 4 The meaning of the Hebrew for this phrase is uncertain.

3:9 Lebanon See Ezr 3:7 and note; Isa 60:13 and note.
3:10 inlaid with love This could indicate that it was made lovingly or with care.
3:11 you daughters of Zion The woman encourages the daughters of Zion—who should be identified with the daughters of Jerusalem—to go out and look upon her king dressed in wedding garments. Compare note on SS 2:7.

4:1—5:1 The man is the only speaker in this section until the second half of v. 16. He describes the woman in sensuous detail, starting with her head—describing her eyes, hair, teeth, lips, temples and neck—then moving to her breasts (vv. 1–7). Inviting her to join him (vv. 8–9), he continues describing her, focusing on her love (vv. 10–16). Finally, the woman responds by inviting him to eat of her garden (v. 16). The man responds by describing their sexual union (5:1). The poem concludes with a chorus calling for celebration (5:1).

4:1 flock of goats Her hair is lush and flowing, like black goats spread out over a hillside. **Gilead** A mountainous region east of the Jordan River.
4:2 coming up from the washing The man emphasizes the whiteness and purity of her teeth. **Each has its twin** Probably indicates that the top and bottom rows of her teeth were complete. In the ancient world, a mouth full of perfect, healthy teeth was rare.

4:3 a scarlet ribbon May indicate that she used cosmetics to paint her lips.
4:4 like the tower of David Likely emphasizes that her neck was tall and slender, like a strong tower. **hang a thousand shields** May refer to necklaces adorning the woman's neck.
4:5 like two fawns By repeating "two" and "twins," the man emphasizes the symmetry of the woman's breasts. The reference to fawns and gazelles could emphasize the softness of her breasts, or her youthfulness.
4:6 mountain of myrrh A euphemism for the woman's breasts (1:13).
4:8 bride The man refers to the woman as his bride for the first time. This section (4:1—5:1) is the only one in the book that uses this word. **Senir, the summit of Hermon** Mountains located in Lebanon.
4:9 my sister A common term of endearment; it does not indicate that the man and woman have any family relationship.
4:10 How much more pleasing is your love than wine This probably refers to sexual love. See note on 1:2; note on 1:3.
4:11 milk and honey are under your tongue Milk and honey represent abundance and wealth (Ex 3:8; Dt 6:3). Their presence under her tongue may be intended to evoke an image of passionate kissing.

The fragrance of your garments
    is like the fragrance of Lebanon.
¹² You are a garden locked up, my sister, my
      bride;
    you are a spring enclosed, a sealed
      fountain.
¹³ Your plants are an orchard of pomegranates
    with choice fruits,
    with henna and nard,
¹⁴   nard and saffron,
    calamus and cinnamon,
    with every kind of incense tree,
    with myrrh and aloes
    and all the finest spices.
¹⁵ You are*a* a garden fountain,
    a well of flowing water
    streaming down from Lebanon.

She

¹⁶ Awake, north wind,
    and come, south wind!
Blow on my garden,
    that its fragrance may spread everywhere.
Let my beloved come into his garden
    and taste its choice fruits.

He

5 I have come into my garden, my sister, my
      bride;
    I have gathered my myrrh with my spice.
I have eaten my honeycomb and my honey;
    I have drunk my wine and my milk.

Friends

Eat, friends, and drink;
    drink your fill of love.

She

² I slept but my heart was awake.
    Listen! My beloved is knocking:
"Open to me, my sister, my darling,
    my dove, my flawless one.
My head is drenched with dew,
    my hair with the dampness of the night."
³ I have taken off my robe —
    must I put it on again?
I have washed my feet —
    must I soil them again?
⁴ My beloved thrust his hand through the
      latch-opening;
    my heart began to pound for him.
⁵ I arose to open for my beloved,
    and my hands dripped with myrrh,
my fingers with flowing myrrh,
    on the handles of the bolt.
⁶ I opened for my beloved,
    but my beloved had left; he was gone.
    My heart sank at his departure.*b*
I looked for him but did not find him.
    I called him but he did not answer.
⁷ The watchmen found me
    as they made their rounds in the city.

a 15 Or *I am* (spoken by *She*)   *b* 6 Or *heart had gone out to him when he spoke*

4:12 a garden locked up The garden may be a euphemism for the woman's sexuality; the fact that it is locked or secure may indicate her virginity. It may also mean that she is reserved for him alone—she is his private garden. **a spring enclosed** See Pr 5:15 and note.
4:13 with henna See SS 1:14 and note.
4:14 The man's description of the woman continues as he lists many different exotic and precious fruits and spices. These items were fragrant and sensual. Several of them—cinnamon, myrrh and aloe—were used by the adulteress to lure the simple in Proverbs (see Pr 7:17 and note). The image is meant to portray the woman as exotic, beautiful and satisfying.
4:15 a well of flowing water The description of the water as "living" or "flowing" emphasizes freshness and cleanness, as well as abundance (see Pr 5:15 and note; compare Jer 2:13).
4:16 Awake The beginning of this verse may be attributed to the man who has been speaking (SS 4:1–15) or to the woman who speaks in the second half of this verse. This Hebrew word can mean "to stir up" or "to arouse." **Blow on my garden** Either the man or the woman asks the wind to blow open the woman's garden (see note on v. 12) to make it available for the man. **Let my beloved come into his garden** The woman speaks here, inviting her beloved to come and share sexual intimacy with her.
5:1 I have come into my garden This section (4:1—5:1) climaxes as the man and woman consummate their love. The man responds to the woman's invitation (4:16) by partaking of the sensual pleasures of her garden (4:10–15). **I have eaten my honeycomb and my honey** Earlier, the man used honey to describe the sweetness of the woman's kiss (4:11). Here, he states that he ate the honeycomb along with the honey—most likely emphasizing the totality of his sexual intimacy with her. **Eat, friends** The speaker in this section (4:1—5:1) could be the man inviting others to celebrate their love, or, more likely, the lover's companions—perhaps the daughters of Jerusalem—celebrating with and encouraging them to enjoy their love.

5:2–8 In what is likely another dream scene (like 3:1–5), the woman wakes to the sound of her beloved knocking and looking for her love. She is unprepared for his arrival, but still goes to open the door for him. However, when she does, he is no longer there. As in 3:2, she goes out looking for him. She encounters watchmen again (3:3), but this time they treat her harshly, beating her and taking her veil. This section may describe a temporary difficulty in the man and woman's relationship, possibly a situation where their sexual desires do not align or where they had to be separated for some reason.

5:2 I slept but my heart was awake Possibly indicates that this section is a dream. See 4:16 and note. **my sister** See note on 4:9. **dampness of the night** The man has endured discomfort to be with the woman, adding to the urgency of his request. This phrase may be a euphemism for the man's desire for sexual release; Deuteronomy uses a similar phrase to refer to a nocturnal emission (Dt 23:10).

They beat me, they bruised me;
   they took away my cloak,
   those watchmen of the walls!
⁸ Daughters of Jerusalem, I charge you —
   if you find my beloved,
   what will you tell him?
   Tell him I am faint with love.

Friends

⁹ How is your beloved better than others,
   most beautiful of women?
How is your beloved better than others,
   that you so charge us?

She

¹⁰ My beloved is radiant and ruddy,
   outstanding among ten thousand.
¹¹ His head is purest gold;
   his hair is wavy
   and black as a raven.
¹² His eyes are like doves
   by the water streams,
   washed in milk,
   mounted like jewels.
¹³ His cheeks are like beds of spice
   yielding perfume.
His lips are like lilies
   dripping with myrrh.
¹⁴ His arms are rods of gold
   set with topaz.

His body is like polished ivory
   decorated with lapis lazuli.
¹⁵ His legs are pillars of marble
   set on bases of pure gold.
His appearance is like Lebanon,
   choice as its cedars.
¹⁶ His mouth is sweetness itself;
   he is altogether lovely.
This is my beloved, this is my friend,
   daughters of Jerusalem.

Friends

6 Where has your beloved gone,
   most beautiful of women?
Which way did your beloved turn,
   that we may look for him with you?

She

² My beloved has gone down to his garden,
   to the beds of spices,
to browse in the gardens
   and to gather lilies.
³ I am my beloved's and my beloved is
     mine;
   he browses among the lilies.

He

⁴ You are as beautiful as Tirzah, my darling,
   as lovely as Jerusalem,
   as majestic as troops with banners.

5:3 I have taken off my robe Her excuse of not being dressed is probably a playful excuse; given his intentions, her lack of a garment is a feeble reason for not allowing the man inside.

5:4 thrust his hand through the latch-opening This phrase may describe the man finding a way to open the door—or, on a metaphorical level, the man initiating sex with the woman.

5:5 open for my beloved The woman grants the man's earlier request. See SS 5:2.

5:6 but my beloved had left Since this scene is most likely a dream, the man's absence when his beloved opens the door probably symbolizes some kind of break in the relationship or the woman's longing and desire for her beloved (compare 3:1–5).

5:7 They beat me The woman's encounter with the watchmen here starkly contrasts her encounter with them in 3:3. Here, they beat her and strip her of her garment. This encounter may symbolize an obstacle to intimacy between the lovers or some kind of division in the relationship.

5:9 your beloved In response to the woman's plea for help in finding her beloved (v. 8), the daughters of Jerusalem ask what makes her beloved superior to other men. This chorus serves as a transition from the dream/nightmare of vv. 2–8 to the woman's description of her beloved in vv. 10–16.

5:10–16 In this section, the woman describes her beloved's appearance in great detail. The description acts as a parallel to the man's description of her in ch. 4. In 4:1–7, however, the man directed his comments toward the woman. Here, she directs her comments toward the daughters of Jerusalem.

5:10 ruddy The Hebrew word used here (which may be translated "red"; see Ge 25:30) could indicate a brownish red skin color. It may also indicate that the man was healthy or fit.

5:11 black as a raven Emphasizes his youth—his hair is black, as opposed to gray (Pr 20:29).

5:12 washed in milk May indicate the whiteness of his eyes, or symbolize wealth and abundance (Ex 3:8; Job 29:6).

5:13 His cheeks are like beds of spice Since most men wore beards (Lev 19:27), the woman probably has the man's beard in mind here.

5:14 His arms are rods of gold Since gold is not a particularly strong metal, the comparison here emphasizes the beauty and value of the man's arms. **His body** The Hebrew word used here often refers to intestines (2Sa 20:10), which were metaphorically affiliated with emotions (Isa 16:11). It can also refer to loins (Ge 15:4), which is probably intended here.

5:15 His legs are pillars of marble The woman's description of the man's legs emphasizes their strength as well as their value.

6:1 Where has your beloved gone In SS 5:9, the daughters of Jerusalem asked why the woman's beloved was worth seeking. Now, after she has described him, they express their desire to seek him with her.

6:2–3 In this short poem, the woman describes sexual intimacy with the man. As she describes their intimacy, the woman emphasizes that they completely belong to each other.

6:2 to his garden See note on 4:12.

⁵Turn your eyes from me;
    they overwhelm me.
Your hair is like a flock of goats
    descending from Gilead.
⁶Your teeth are like a flock of sheep
    coming up from the washing.
Each has its twin,
    not one of them is missing.
⁷Your temples behind your veil
    are like the halves of a pomegranate.
⁸Sixty queens there may be,
    and eighty concubines,
    and virgins beyond number;
⁹but my dove, my perfect one, is unique,
    the only daughter of her mother,
    the favorite of the one who bore her.
The young women saw her and called her
        blessed;
    the queens and concubines praised her.

Friends

¹⁰Who is this that appears like the dawn,
    fair as the moon, bright as the sun,
    majestic as the stars in procession?

He

¹¹I went down to the grove of nut trees
    to look at the new growth in the
        valley,
    to see if the vines had budded
    or the pomegranates were in bloom.

¹²Before I realized it,
    my desire set me among the royal chariots
        of my people.ᵃ

Friends

¹³Come back, come back, O Shulammite;
    come back, come back, that we may gaze
        on you!

He

Why would you gaze on the Shulammite
    as on the dance of Mahanaim?ᵇ

7ᶜ How beautiful your sandaled feet,
    O prince's daughter!
Your graceful legs are like jewels,
    the work of an artist's hands.
²Your navel is a rounded goblet
    that never lacks blended wine.
Your waist is a mound of wheat
    encircled by lilies.
³Your breasts are like two fawns,
    like twin fawns of a gazelle.
⁴Your neck is like an ivory tower.
Your eyes are the pools of Heshbon
    by the gate of Bath Rabbim.
Your nose is like the tower of Lebanon
    looking toward Damascus.

ᵃ 12 Or *among the chariots of Amminadab*; or *among the chariots of the people of the prince*   ᵇ 13 In Hebrew texts this verse (6:13) is numbered 7:1.   ᶜ In Hebrew texts 7:1-13 is numbered 7:2-14.

6:4–10 In this section, the man describes the woman's beauty. Many of his descriptions echo 4:1–7. This section also includes the responses of other women as they praise her for her perfect beauty.

6:4 beautiful as Tirzah Tirzah was the capital of the northern kingdom ca. 920–880 BC (1Ki 15:33). Jerusalem was the capital of the southern kingdom and of united Israel.

6:6 not one of them is missing See note on SS 4:2.

6:8 Sixty queens there may be, and eighty concubines, and virgins The man lists three royal classes of women to show the superiority of his woman. Concubines were considered the king's secondary wives; their status was below that of the queen. The Hebrew word used here, *almah* (often translated "virgin" or "maiden"), refers to any unmarried woman. Here, the virgins were likely young female royal attendants. See the table "Parallelism in Hebrew Poetry" on p. 1008.

6:9 favorite of the one who bore her Could indicate that the woman was favored by her mother.

6:10 Who is this This verse most likely presents the praise given by the women of v. 9 toward the woman.

6:11–12 The speaker in these verses is unclear. Also, the Hebrew phrasing used in v. 12 is very difficult, which means that an exact translation cannot be rendered. The scene seems to present some kind of rendezvous between the man and woman in a garden setting. It could be real or imaginary, like the woman's search for the man in 3:1–5.

6:13 Shulammite This term only appears here in the OT. It may be a feminine form of the name Solomon—implying a woman affiliated with him. It could also be a name that associates the woman with Shunem, a town in the tribe of Issachar (Jos 19:17–18; 1Ki 1:3–4).

7:1–5 The man again describes the woman's beauty in detail. In SS 4:1–7, his description started with her head and worked down to her breasts. Here, he begins with her feet and works up to her head.

7:1 O prince's daughter Like the Hebrew word *melekh* (meaning "king"; see note on 1:4), this is probably a symbolic term of respect or endearment. The woman most likely does not come from a noble or privileged family, as shown by her work in the fields (see 1:5 and note; 1:6 and note). **legs are like jewels** This analogy emphasizes the beauty and value of the woman's thighs; they were crafted with care, much like the rings were crafted by master jewelers.

7:2 navel is a rounded goblet The Hebrew word used here, *shor*, refers to the umbilical cord in Ezekiel (Eze 16:4). Here, it is probably a sexual euphemism. **that never lacks blended wine** Elsewhere, wine is compared to sexual love (see 1:2 and note). **Your waist is a mound of wheat** This image evokes fertility.

7:3 like two fawns See note on 4:5.

7:4 ivory tower See note on 4:4. **pools of Heshbon** Heshbon, a city in Moab, may be referred to here because of its pools and water reservoirs (Nu 21:25–30). Or, it may be a wordplay since Heshbon sounds very similar to the word for ivory in Hebrew, *hashshen*.

⁵Your head crowns you like Mount Carmel.
  Your hair is like royal tapestry;
    the king is held captive by its tresses.
⁶How beautiful you are and how pleasing,
  my love, with your delights!
⁷Your stature is like that of the palm,
  and your breasts like clusters of fruit.
⁸I said, "I will climb the palm tree;
  I will take hold of its fruit."
May your breasts be like clusters of grapes
    on the vine,
  the fragrance of your breath like apples,
⁹ and your mouth like the best wine.

She

May the wine go straight to my beloved,
  flowing gently over lips and teeth.ᵃ
¹⁰I belong to my beloved,
  and his desire is for me.
¹¹Come, my beloved, let us go to the countryside,
  let us spend the night in the villages.ᵇ
¹²Let us go early to the vineyards
  to see if the vines have budded,
if their blossoms have opened,
  and if the pomegranates are in bloom—
    there I will give you my love.
¹³The mandrakes send out their fragrance,
  and at our door is every delicacy,
both new and old,
  that I have stored up for you, my beloved.

8 If only you were to me like a brother,
  who was nursed at my mother's breasts!
Then, if I found you outside,
  I would kiss you,
    and no one would despise me.
²I would lead you
  and bring you to my mother's house—
    she who has taught me.
I would give you spiced wine to drink,
  the nectar of my pomegranates.
³His left arm is under my head
  and his right arm embraces me.
⁴Daughters of Jerusalem, I charge you:
  Do not arouse or awaken love
    until it so desires.

Friends

⁵Who is this coming up from the
    wilderness
  leaning on her beloved?

She

Under the apple tree I roused you;
  there your mother conceived you,
    there she who was in labor gave you
      birth.
⁶Place me like a seal over your heart,
  like a seal on your arm;
for love is as strong as death,
  its jealousyᶜ unyielding as the grave.

ᵃ 9 Septuagint, Aquila, Vulgate and Syriac; Hebrew *lips of sleepers*   ᵇ 11 Or *the henna bushes*   ᶜ 6 Or *ardor*

7:5 Your head crowns you like Mount Carmel Probably indicating that her head was beautiful or majestic (Isa 35:2). **royal tapestry** Earlier descriptions indicate that the woman's hair was black (see SS 4:1 and note; 6:5). The Hebrew word used here, *argaman*, means "purple." In the ancient world, purple dye was extracted from snails, and it was very expensive and rare. Clothes dyed with purple were signs of wealth or royalty (Jdg 8:26; Est 1:6; Da 5:29). By describing her hair as purple, the man most likely compares her worth to royalty (compare note on SS 7:1). **the king** This could indicate that even the king is held captive by the woman's beauty, or it could be a reference to the term of endearment the woman uses for her lover (compare note on 1:4).
7:7 your breasts like clusters of fruit The comparison here most likely relates to the sweet and desirable taste of the date palm.
7:9 your mouth like the best wine See 1:2; compare 4:11 and note. **May the wine go straight to my beloved** It is unclear whether the woman starts speaking here or in v. 10. Either way, the speaker here describes the pleasure of their passionate kiss.
7:12 vineyards Earlier, this word was used to describe the woman's body (see 1:6 and note) or the love between the man and woman (see 2:15 and note). **blossoms have opened** Represents the readiness of the man and woman to fulfill their sexual desires (6:11; see note on 2:11–13). **love** See note on 1:2.
7:13 I have stored up for you The woman has saved her fruits—a symbol of sexual activity (see note on v. 7)—for her beloved.

8:1 like a brother The woman does not wish that she and her beloved were siblings—sexual relations between siblings were prohibited by the Law (Lev 20:17). Rather, she wishes that they could express physical love more openly. See note on SS 4:9.
8:2 my mother's house See note on 3:4. **wine to drink** A euphemism for sexual activity. See 1:2; compare 5:1 and note. **nectar of my pomegranates** Indicates the woman's sexuality (see 4:13). In 6:11 and 7:12, the woman uses the image of blooming pomegranates to describe readiness for sexual activity.
8:3 his right arm embraces me See 2:6 and note.
8:4 I charge you See note on 2:7.
8:5 Who is this This phrase is identical to the opening of the royal wedding procession (see 3:6–11). This time, however, the woman and her beloved are together. It is unclear whether the woman or the daughters of Jerusalem speak here. **Under the apple tree I roused you** Apples have already been used with erotic connotations (see 2:3; 7:8).
8:6 love is as strong as death Just as people cannot avoid death, a woman cannot ignore or avoid the love she feels for her beloved. **jealousy** Here, jealousy positively depicts a desire for exclusivity. Just as Yahweh jealously desires his people (Ex 20:5), the woman is jealous for her beloved. **unyielding as the grave** The comparison of jealousy to the grave probably indicates the insatiable nature of death (see Pr 30:16 and note). **flame** The Hebrew word used here, *shalhevethyah*, occurs only once in the Bible. It may be a combination of *shalheveth* ("flame" or "fire") and *yah* (the abbreviated form of Yahweh). If so,

It burns like blazing fire,
like a mighty flame.[a]
[7] Many waters cannot quench love;
rivers cannot sweep it away.
If one were to give
all the wealth of one's house for love,
it[b] would be utterly scorned.

Friends

[8] We have a little sister,
and her breasts are not yet grown.
What shall we do for our sister
on the day she is spoken for?
[9] If she is a wall,
we will build towers of silver on her.
If she is a door,
we will enclose her with panels of cedar.

She

[10] I am a wall,
and my breasts are like towers.
Thus I have become in his eyes
like one bringing contentment.

[11] Solomon had a vineyard in Baal Hamon;
he let out his vineyard to tenants.
Each was to bring for its fruit
a thousand shekels[c] of silver.
[12] But my own vineyard is mine to give;
the thousand shekels are for you, Solomon,
and two hundred[d] are for those who tend
its fruit.

He

[13] You who dwell in the gardens
with friends in attendance,
let me hear your voice!

She

[14] Come away, my beloved,
and be like a gazelle
or like a young stag
on the spice-laden mountains.

---

[a] 6 Or *fire, / like the very flame of the* LORD   [b] 7 Or *he*
[c] 11 That is, about 25 pounds or about 12 kilograms; also in
verse 12   [d] 12 That is, about 5 pounds or about 2.3
kilograms

---

this is the only mention of God in Song of Songs. This form may act as a superlative—"the fiercest flame."

8:8 We have a little sister The woman's brothers (SS 1:6) speak here for the first time. In the ancient Near East, brothers often played a role in the marriage of their sister (Ge 24:29–69; Jdg 21:22). **her breasts are not** She has not reached sexual maturity (Eze 16:7–8). **on the day she is spoken for** Most likely a reference to her future marriage. The brothers here ask how to protect their sister and prepare her for her future wedding.

8:9 she is a wall The images of a wall and closed doors demonstrate the brothers' desire to protect their sister's virginity. The reactions of the brothers of Dinah and Tamar to their rapes demonstrate this desire for protection (Ge 34:1–30; 2Sa 13:1–33).

8:10 my breasts are like towers The woman responds to her brothers by stating that she is now sexually mature. She has kept herself chaste and is now ready for an intimate relationship.

8:11–12 The speaker could be either the man or the woman. Solomon is mentioned here in a seemingly negative light (compare 3:6–11 and note). If the man is speaking, then he seems to be comparing the abundant wives and concubines of Solomon (1Ki 11:3) to the monogamous love he shares with the woman. While Solomon may have a great number of lovers, the man is fully satisfied with his single lover.

8:11 vineyard Elsewhere in the book, vineyards symbolize the couple's relationship (2:15) or the woman's appearance (1:6). **Baal Hamon** This place name is otherwise unknown. Since the name literally means "lord of a crowd," it may symbolize the number of wives and concubines Solomon had. **he let out his vineyard to tenants** The reference to Solomon letting out his vineyard shows the lack of an intimate relationship between Solomon and his harem.

8:12 mine to give The exclusive and intimate relationship between the man and woman (2:16; 6:3) sharply contrasts Solomon and his vast harem.

8:14 spice-laden mountains A reference to the woman herself. Earlier, the man used a similar phrase to refer to the woman's breasts (see 4:6 and note). The book closes with the woman expressing her desire for her beloved to come quickly and be with her.

THE MAJOR PROPHETS

I n English Bibles, the books that belong to the Major Prophets are Isaiah, Jeremiah, Ezekiel and Daniel. This grouping stems from the Septuagint, the ancient Greek translation of the Hebrew Bible, which became the Scriptures most often used by the early church. Unlike the first three books, however, Daniel is a work of apocalyptic literature (like the New Testament book of Revelation). While apocalypses resemble prophecy, these genres have significant differences; for this reason both Daniel and Revelation are discussed in the article "Apocalyptic Literature." This article focuses on Isaiah, Jeremiah and Ezekiel.

HISTORICAL AND SOCIAL CONTEXTS

The books of Isaiah, Jeremiah and Ezekiel span Israel's all-important historical hinge: the exiles of Judah to Babylon (597 and 586 BC) and the people's subsequent returns to their homeland (beginning in 538 BC). Each book sounds God's warning of impending judgment while foreseeing the hope of restoration. The decimation of Israel's temple, the deposing of their king and loss of nationhood, and their deportation to a foreign land would spell the end of most peoples and their religion, but the messages of Isaiah, Jeremiah and Ezekiel made clear that Yahweh's purposes will prevail, and that through these events he will demonstrate his justice and mercy.

Isaiah

The scope of Isaiah is enormous, both in length and time period. The subject matter of the book spans the pre-exilic (Isa 1–39), exilic (Isa 40–55) and postexilic (Isa 56–66) periods. Isaiah's ministry takes place in late eighth-century Jerusalem before the exile, and begins by focusing on King David and Mount Zion, the sacred mountain of God's temple.

In the chapter closing this first section, Isaiah warns king Hezekiah that "The time will surely come when everything in your palace ... will be carried off to Babylon" (Isa 39:6). The next chapter leaps about 150 years forward, addressing God's people in Babylonian exile (see Isa 48:20) and offering comfort to Jerusalem by announcing that its term of punishment has come to an end (Isa 40:1–2). Thus, Isaiah 1–39 predicts the exile, and Isaiah 40–55 predicts Israel's return. Signaling another shift in audience, Isaiah 56 refers to Yahweh's altar and temple on Mount Zion, which points to the Second Temple period after the exiles have returned from Babylon.

Jeremiah

Jeremiah appears roughly two generations after Isaiah (ca. 627 BC). While his hometown, Anathoth, was within walking distance of Jerusalem, it lay within the territory of Benjamin in a world more at home with the traditions inherited from northern Israel. Jeremiah's ministry began in the waning years of the Assyrian Empire, when Judah enjoyed a brief generation of independence. The discovery of "the Book of the Law" (likely an early version of the book of Deuteronomy) within the temple archives led to the reforms of King Josiah: the centralization of the nation's worship at the Jerusalem temple, the elimination of idols, and the promotion of the worship of Yahweh alone (2Ki 22–23). Many of Jeremiah's oracles echo these themes.

After Josiah's death, Jeremiah delivered his well-known temple sermon (Jer 7:1–15; 26:1–6), indicting the people for falling away from Yahweh's law and threatening both the temple's

destruction and the people's exile from the land. A few years later Nebuchadnezzar and the Babylonians became the new superpower in the Fertile Crescent, and Jeremiah warned Judah that God would use Babylon to enact his judgment on the nation's faithlessness. Because Jeremiah advocated surrender, Judah's political and military authorities accused him of treachery. Even after the Babylonian invasion vindicated his message, he was forced to flee to Egypt.

Ezekiel

Given his occupation as a priest (Eze 1:3), Ezekiel's social and religious world centers on Israel's priestly traditions. The word of Yahweh first came to him while he was exiled in Babylon. Part of the first group to be deported from Jerusalem in 597 BC (2Ki 24:10–16), Ezekiel decried the idolatry practiced in the Jerusalem temple and predicted Jerusalem's captivity. On hearing that the city had fallen to the Babylonians (Eze 33:21), his message turned to one of hope and restoration.

THEOLOGICAL PERSPECTIVES IN THE PROPHETS

The Character of Yahweh

Each book presents a distinctive perspective on Yahweh's character. For Isaiah, Yahweh is, above all, "the Holy One of Israel," a title that prevails throughout the book. In his powerful vision (Isa 6), he hears the seraphim singing, "Holy, holy, holy is the LORD Almighty!" This divine title reflects the tension conveyed in his prophecies, namely that Yahweh is the Almighty Creator who is free and sovereign, yet he has chosen to bind himself to Israel with a covenant. Israel shows itself to be untrusting and faithless to the covenant, and thus deserving of Yahweh's anger.

In Isaiah 40–55, the section addressed to the exiles in Babylon, there is a remarkable development in Israel's understanding of Yahweh: the monotheism (belief in only one God) implicit in Israel's religion now takes center stage. Given the hopeless situation of the Jewish exiles living in the shadow of a world superpower, they could have never imagined that another foreign conqueror would "shepherd" them back to their homeland and underwrite the rebuilding of their temple. Yahweh's use of Cyrus the Great, king of Persia, indicates his sovereignty over all nations (Isa 44:24—45:7). As argued in the trial speeches against the nations in Isaiah, the rise of Cyrus was unforeseen by the royal counselors and diviners of the Babylonian court, thus rendering their so-called gods speechless, useless nothings (e.g., Isa 41:21–29; 44:6–8; 45:18–25).

More so than the other Major Prophets, Jeremiah entwines his theology with his own life story. From the moment of his call he understands himself to be a prophetic ambassador—even if sent with an unpopular message (Jer 1:1–11). While other "prophets" had messages the people wanted to hear, Jeremiah was uniquely privy to Yahweh's council (Jer 23:9–22). This situation bred conflict, including opposition from kings, prophets and the people—and especially struggles with Yahweh himself. Adopting the lament form (as in the Psalms), Jeremiah expresses his disappointment in no uncertain terms. While he discovers Yahweh to be true, he also learns that being his servant—especially in the troubling times of Babylonian invasion—is difficult (see Jer 12:1–6; 15:10–21). In his message for the people Jeremiah presents Yahweh as their liberator, as the exodus shows, but by their repeated faithlessness they forfeit his protection and incur his judgment (Jer 2:4–19). Nevertheless, he later declares Yahweh's ultimate intention: "'I know the plans I have for you,' declares the LORD, 'plans to prosper you and not to harm you, plans to give you hope and a future'" (Jer 29:11).

As a priest, Ezekiel's theology centers on God's presence in sacred space. While Jeremiah, along with the book of Deuteronomy, speaks of the temple as the place where Yahweh's "Name" dwells

(Jer 7:10–14), Ezekiel prefers to speak of the temple as the place where Yahweh's "glory" manifests itself. As Isaiah's vision of Yahweh's heavenly court defined his theology (Isa 6), so Ezekiel's opening vision of the "appearance of the likeness of the glory of the LORD" (Eze 1:28) defines his theology and ministry. Foregrounded in this vision is the good news that Yahweh, unlike other ancient Near Eastern deities, is transcendent and not obliged to a particular place. The ominous news is that he is free to move away from rebellious Jerusalem.

Israel's Sin and Yahweh's Judgment

The Major Prophets regularly address the sin of God's people and the nature of his judgment. Early in his ministry, Isaiah denounced social abuses, but his vision of the Holy One of Israel in his heavenly court (Isa 6) reveals a strange commission to harden the hearts of the people until the time of the exile. The meaning of this saying unfolds within a literary unit known as "Isaiah's Memoirs" (Isa 6:1—8:18, dating to around 742–733 BC). Isaiah begins to execute this commission by offering an oracle of salvation conditional on trusting in Yahweh. King Ahaz, who simply feigns piety, chooses rather to trust in a political means of "salvation": He calls on Assyria to rescue him from the two kings threatening to invade and depose him (see also 2Ki 16). As a result, the kingdom of Judah becomes a vassal to the Assyrian Empire.

For Isaiah, however, once a person has "seen" the Lord of Hosts and the Holy One of Israel, all other fears pale in comparison to the fear of God (Isa 8:12–13). Thus, by offering a promise of salvation that the house of David rejects, "the heart of this people" is hardened to the prophetic word (Isa 6:10). He then seals his memoirs as "testimony" and a "sign" (Isa 8:16–18). The remainder of his ministry focuses on the issue of trust: He promotes patiently trusting in the God whose temple resides on Mount Zion over against the leadership's anxious trust in political and military alliances formed against the Assyrian Empire (e.g., Isa 8:18).

Roughly 20 years later, the next phase of Isaiah's ministry (713–711 BC) addresses the possibility of Jerusalem joining a coalition with Ashdod and Egypt in order to rebel against the Assyrian Empire. Once again, Isaiah urges the Jerusalem leadership to resist this political means of deliverance and instead trust that the God of Zion will protect Jerusalem (e.g., Isa 14:28–32; 18:1–7; 20:1–6).

The final phase of Isaiah's ministry focuses on trying to dissuade the Jerusalem leadership from joining yet another rebel alliance against Assyria after the death of their king, Sargon II, in 705 BC (e.g., Isa 30:1–17; 31:1–9). King Hezekiah evidently rejects Isaiah's counsel and champions the rebellion. After King Sennacherib retaliates in 701 BC with an invasion of Judah and threatens to overtake Jerusalem, Isaiah steps forth and offers Yahweh's 11th-hour oracle of rescue that Jerusalem will be spared (Isa 37:21–35). In the end, however, Hezekiah's courting of Babylonian ambassadors during this Assyrian crisis results in Yahweh's subsequent judgment of exile to Babylon (Isa 39:1–8).

Being more at home with traditions popular among the northern tribes, Jeremiah addresses the sin of God's people differently than Isaiah. He interprets events through the lens of Yahweh's providence during the exodus and wilderness periods (e.g., Jer 2:1–8) and Yahweh's revelation of the law (e.g., Jer 7:8–10). Jeremiah indicts Judah for their faithlessness to "the spring of living water," (Yahweh) and their defection to "broken cisterns" (other gods and their idols; Jer 2:13). While Isaiah charged his generation with their failure to trust God in the face of Assyrian imperialism, Jeremiah charges his generation living on the eve of Babylonian rule with misplaced trust in the temple of Yahweh on Mount Zion, presuming that it should guarantee refuge from foreign

invasion (Jer 7:1–11). Mount Zion cannot provide refuge if the people continue to disregard the laws given by Yahweh on Mount Sinai, including the Ten Commandments and others found in the book of Deuteronomy. While Jeremiah endorses the Davidic covenant, he clearly understands it to be conditional and for the purpose of ensuring social justice, especially for "the foreigner, the fatherless or the widow" (Jer 22:1–5). His "report card" on the recent Davidic kings is particularly scathing—with the exception of Josiah—and signals the end of the Davidic dynasty (Jer 22:11–30). Because Jeremiah understands Babylon to be Yahweh's agent of judgment on Judah, he advocates surrender, rather than resistance, and so is labeled a traitor (Jer 27:1–15).

While Ezekiel indicts the people of Judah for social injustices, he particularly focuses on their "profaning" what is holy, as he assesses them from his priestly perspective. Idolatry stands center stage as the sin of Judah, found even at the temple itself (e.g., Eze 6; 8–9; 14; 20; 23). In addition, there is profanation of Sabbath observance (e.g., Eze 20:12–24; 22:8,26; 23:38). Yahweh's judgment, therefore, takes the form of the departure of his glory from the temple (Eze 10:1–22).

Israel's Future Hope

A remaining concern of the Major Prophets is Israel's future hope. Isaiah's vision for Israel's future in Isaiah 1–39 foresees an exalted Mount Zion, to which all nations make pilgrimage (Isa 2:1–5), and a new David, who will actually uphold the kingdom "with justice and righteousness" (Isa 9:6–7; see 11:1–5). In Isa 40–55, the promises originally given to David are transferred to the people of Zion (Isa 55:3–5; 52:1–2), and Yahweh's designated "messiah" (or "anointed one") and "shepherd" is Cyrus, a Persian king (Isa 44:28—45:1). While Cyrus is Yahweh's agent for the restoration of Jerusalem and its temple, his agent for the spiritual restoration of Israel is a figure named "my servant," as described in the Servant Songs (Isa 42:1–9; 49:1–12; 50:4–11; 52:13—53:12). Unlike Cyrus who will "tread on rulers ... as if he were a potter treading the clay" (Isa 41:25), this Servant will not even crush "a bruised reed" (Isa 42:3). He will even suffer rejection and abuse, and bear "the sin of many" (Isa 53:12). Moreover, his mission is not only to bring Israel back to Yahweh; Yahweh promises, "I will also make you a light for the Gentiles, that my salvation may reach to the ends of the earth" (Isa 49:6).

The New Testament applies these Servant passages to both Jesus (Mt 8:17; 12:18–21; Lk 22:37; Jn 12:38; Ac 8:32–33; 1Pe 2:22–25) and the church (Ac 13:47; Ro 8:33–34). The audience of Isaiah 40–55 must have wondered how they could ever return to their homeland while captives in the land of Babylon. And so the prophet appeals to the precedent of the exodus: As Yahweh delivered the Hebrew slaves from the superpower of their time, so he will do again in a glorious second exodus. In the third section of the book of Isaiah, Isaiah 56–66, the prophet envisions a new identity for the people of God, defined not by ethnicity but by keeping Sabbath and Yahweh's covenant (Isa 56:1–8). As a result, Yahweh declares that his "house will be called a house of prayer for all nations," thus including Gentiles. The prophet also relativizes the centrality of the temple by noting that Yahweh specially dwells with those who are humble and contrite of spirit (Isa 56:7; 57:15; see 66:1–2).

Like Isaiah, Jeremiah foresees a new David as a key agent bringing Israel's restoration (Jer 23:1–8). But as the Sinai covenant was his principal criterion for assessing the people's sin, so a new covenant is central to his vision of the future (Jer 31:31–34). Yahweh takes the initiative to remedy the catch-22 of the human condition: Although the human "heart is deceitful above all things and beyond cure" (Jer 17:9) and the people of God have broken Yahweh's covenant (Jer 11:10), Yahweh freely decrees a new covenant (Jer 31:31–34). What is distinctly new is not its contents but its medium: "I will put my law in their minds and write it on their hearts" (Jer 31:33).

Here is the clearest statement in the Hebrew Bible that God's instruction can be interiorized by God himself, resulting in true inner transformation.

A new temple occupies the center stage of Ezekiel's vision for restoration (Eze 40–48), just as might be expected based on his priestly background. Unlike Isaiah 56, however, Ezekiel's vision excludes "foreigners uncircumcised in heart and flesh" (Eze 44:6–9). Like Isaiah and Jeremiah, Ezekiel foresees a new David in Israel's restoration (Eze 34:20–24; 37:24–28). While he does call this ruler "king," his preferred titles reflect subordination: "servant," "shepherd" and "prince." Similar to Jeremiah, Ezekiel also promises a new covenant (Eze 36:24–29), though his articulation uses priestly images ("I will sprinkle clean water on you," Eze 36:25). Not only will Yahweh put his law on his people's heart, he will replace the heart of stone with a heart of flesh and his spirit within will ensure that they walk in his statutes, thus making them truly human.

ANTICIPATION OF A NEW AND BETTER COVENANT

In anticipation of the destruction of Jerusalem, the Major Prophets deconstruct the ancient Near Eastern cultural assumption that the patron deity of Israel is in any way beholden to his people or subject to their fate. Yahweh is free, yet he has chosen to pledge himself to his people in a covenant relationship. Yahweh expects a just society of authentic worshipers—a nation that expresses worship through obedience to Yahweh's moral and spiritual instruction, not through mere ritual observance. Even though his people violate these agreements, Yahweh freely decrees comfort and restoration. And this restoration does not merely reinstate the original promises and conditions—it heightens them. He promises a new and better "David," a Servant who will suffer and bear the sin of many, a new and better covenant, and divine presence that dwells immediately with those who have contrite and renewed hearts. The Prophets also clarify that Yahweh is not simply the God of Israel but the only true God and thus the God of all peoples. In turn, "the people of God" are redefined to include any—including Gentiles—who would embrace Yahweh's gracious covenant promises.

Craig C. Broyles

ISAIAH

INTRODUCTION TO ISAIAH

The book of Isaiah addresses the problem of sin, showing the need for salvation. Isaiah is called by God to speak to the people of Judah and call attention to their wrongdoings—and the resulting judgment. But judgment is not the end of the story; the book also prophesies salvation and restoration. This hopeful picture is what made Isaiah such a compelling book to early Christians, who saw its ultimate fulfillment in Jesus.

BACKGROUND

Isaiah's ministry spanned the reigns of four kings of Judah during the eighth century BC. Little is known about his life, although the book does allude to him being a husband and father (Isa 8:3).

Much of Isaiah's prophetic activity, recorded in Isaiah 1–39, relates to the Syro-Ephraimite War during the reign of King Ahaz (ca. 735 BC) or to the Assyrian king Sennacherib's invasion of Judah during Hezekiah's reign (701 BC). In 722 BC Assyria conquered the northern kingdom of Israel, representing an imminent threat to the southern kingdom of Judah. Isaiah warned that a similar judgment would come to Judah.

Isaiah 40–66 addresses the period of the exile of God's people, after Judah fell to Babylon in 586 BC, and the following return of God's people. The shift in focus in these later chapters may indicate that a different author (or perhaps several authors) wrote or reworked them.

STRUCTURE

The book of Isaiah can be divided into three sections. The first section (1:1—39:8) includes a list of Judah's sins and God's plans for judgment (3:1–26) and describes Isaiah's commission as a prophet with a vision of Yahweh (6:1–13). Following this, Isaiah issues judgments against Judah,

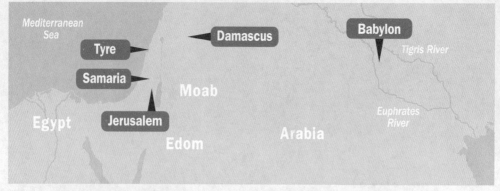

This map depicts some of the major locations related to the book of Isaiah.

the Assyrian invaders, Israel and other nations—specifically for their pride in their own strength, their failure to recognize Yahweh's hand behind their success (ch. 10), and Israel and Judah's failure to seek Yahweh for help, instead of trusting in earthly allies (chs. 7–8; 28–31). But this section also foretells hope. Salvation is coming through the Prince of Peace, and the Spirit of Yahweh shall rest upon this "shoot" from the stump of Jesse (see 9:1–7; 11:1–10). The narrative near the end of the first section records Sennacherib's invasion of Judah, King Hezekiah's prayer for deliverance and the eventual defeat of Sennacherib (36:1—38:22; compare 2Ki 18–20; 2Ch 29–32). Isaiah then prophesizes concerning the rise of the kingdom of Babylon and the destruction of Judah (Isa 39:1–8).

The middle section (40:1—55:13) conveys how the anointed one of God, the Messiah, will come as a suffering servant who will die and rise for humanity (see 52:13—53:12). Ultimately, Babylon will receive judgment for its oppression of God's people, and one day God's people will celebrate and have peace. As a sign of this hopeful future, God's people return from exile.

The final section (56:1—66:24) centers on the themes of salvation and judgment, which include the restoration of God's people, Yahweh's judgment of the nations, and the creation of a new heaven and earth where Yahweh will be worshiped by all.

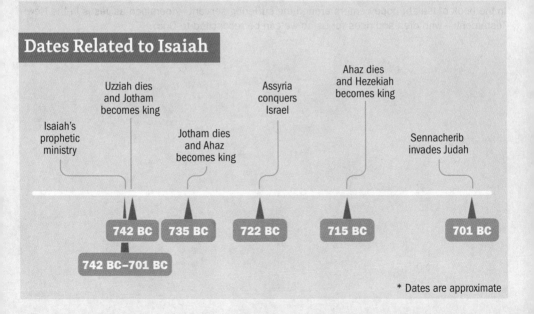

Dates Related to Isaiah

	Uzziah dies and Jotham becomes king		Assyria conquers Israel	Ahaz dies and Hezekiah becomes king	
Isaiah's prophetic ministry		Jotham dies and Ahaz becomes king			Sennacherib invades Judah
	742 BC	735 BC	722 BC	715 BC	701 BC

742 BC–701 BC

* Dates are approximate

OUTLINE

- The judgment of God's people and the nations (1:1—39:8)
- The restoration and salvation of God's people (40:1—55:13)
- The future of God's people (56:1—66:24)

THEMES

The book of Isaiah highlights the problem of sin but also offers a message of salvation. Yahweh is both just and merciful. He is the true God who created everything, and when people seek salvation in foreign nations and their gods, it is a denial of what he can and will do for his people. Idolatry leads to judgment.

After judgment there is a new era of comfort. Yahweh will bring his people back from exile and send a servant. This future servant—also referred to as the Messiah—will suffer, die and rise again so that people can have a relationship with God. The servant carries the sin of many and intercedes for transgressors. He will redeem God's people and bring about worship of Yahweh by all the nations.

Isaiah's message of mercy, justice and salvation makes it the prophetic book most commonly cited in the New Testament. In particular, the Gospel writers point to Isaiah's promise of a Messiah and its fulfillment in Jesus, born of a virgin in the lineage of King David (for example, compare 7:14; 9:6; 11:1–2 with Mt 1; also see Mt 4:14–16; 8:17; 12:17–21; Lk 4:17–21; Jn 12:41). In the book of Isaiah, hope centers around the suffering servant—identified as Jesus in the New Testament—who dies and rises for us so we can be reconciled to God.

1

The vision concerning Judah and Jerusalem that Isaiah son of Amoz saw during the reigns of Uzziah, Jotham, Ahaz and Hezekiah, kings of Judah.

A Rebellious Nation

2 Hear me, you heavens! Listen, earth!
  For the LORD has spoken:
"I reared children and brought them up,
  but they have rebelled against me.
3 The ox knows its master,
  the donkey its owner's manger,
but Israel does not know,
  my people do not understand."

4 Woe to the sinful nation,
  a people whose guilt is great,
a brood of evildoers,
  children given to corruption!
They have forsaken the LORD;
  they have spurned the Holy One of Israel
  and turned their backs on him.

5 Why should you be beaten anymore?
  Why do you persist in rebellion?
Your whole head is injured,
  your whole heart afflicted.
6 From the sole of your foot to the top of your
    head
  there is no soundness —
only wounds and welts
  and open sores,
not cleansed or bandaged
  or soothed with olive oil.

7 Your country is desolate,
  your cities burned with fire;
your fields are being stripped by
    foreigners
  right before you,
laid waste as when overthrown by
    strangers.
8 Daughter Zion is left
  like a shelter in a vineyard,
like a hut in a cucumber field,
like a city under siege.

1:1–31 The first chapter of Isaiah serves as a summary vision and presents the major themes of the book: judgment on Judah for rebelliousness and hope for the future restoration of Zion. Isaiah's prophetic ministry occurred during the eighth century BC.

1:1 The vision concerning Judah and Jerusalem that Isaiah This opening heading (or superscription) identifies the book as prophetic revelation associated with Isaiah the prophet. The books of Nahum and Obadiah are also identified as visions. Headings like this are common in OT poetry. **Judah and Jerusalem** The northern kingdom of Israel fell to Assyria in 722 BC, during Isaiah's lifetime. This and other traumatic events provide the dramatic backdrop for Isaiah's warning of impending judgment against the southern kingdom of Judah. **Isaiah** The prophet's name means "Yahweh is salvation." See the timeline "Approximate Dates of Old Testament Prophets" on p. 1070. **kings of Judah** The full reigns of all four kings covers a period of about a century (792–697 BC). The reference to Uzziah's death in Isa 6:1 suggests Isaiah's ministry started around 742 BC. Compare Hos 1:1 and note.

ISAIAH
Isaiah's ministry spans the reigns of four kings of Judah over a period of around 60 years, but most of his prophetic activity relates to the Syro-Ephraimite crisis during the reign of Ahaz (ca. 732 BC) or the Assyrian king Sennacherib's invasion and siege of Jerusalem during the reign of Hezekiah (701 BC). Tradition holds that Isaiah was of royal descent, a cousin of King Uzziah.

1:2–20 Yahweh formally brings a legal suit against Judah for a breach of contract (breaking their covenant with him). The accusation appears in Isa 1:2–3, followed by a direct address to the people outlining the charges detailed in vv. 4–20.

1:2 you heavens! Listen, earth Heaven and earth are called to witness God's accusation against Israel. The word pair can be read as figure of speech (a merism) invoking all of creation. The language also echoes Dt 30:19 and 31:28, where heaven and earth witness the formal acceptance of the covenant between God and Israel. **rebelled** The Hebrew word for "rebel" is elsewhere used to describe political rebellion (see 2Ki 3:5–7). It indicates a breach of contract—when someone has not fulfilled his or her contractual obligation. In this case, the Israelites are accused of breaking their agreement to obey God.

1:3 Israel Here, "Israel" refers to God's people generally, not just the northern kingdom. The vision is addressed to Judah and Jerusalem, the southern kingdom.

1:4 Holy One of Israel This title for God is frequently used in Isaiah to emphasize the holiness of God.

1:6 sole of your foot to the top of your head All levels of society will be affected by this judgment—from leadership to the common people.

1:7 cities burned with fire Assyrian annals indicate that Sennacherib's invasion of Judah in 701 BC left 46 cities under siege or destroyed.

1:8 Daughter Zion Refers to Jerusalem. The city surrounded Zion and the temple—Yahweh's dwelling place in their midst. Personifying the city as a daughter continues the parent-child metaphor of Isa 1:2; it may also signify God's affection. At various points throughout the book, the "daughter of Zion" metaphor is applied to the city as a geographic location, the female inhabitants of the city and the displaced people of God. See 3:16–17; 4:4; 10:32; 16:1; 37:22; 52:2; 62:11. **Zion** Another name for Jerusalem, "Zion" symbolized God's choice of the city as his dwelling. God's care for Zion is a major theme in Isaiah. Isaiah addresses the question of whether God will preserve the city precisely because it is his special dwelling, or whether he will allow it to be purged and purified through judgment. **a shelter in a vineyard** The image of a temporary structure alone in the middle of a field emphasizes Jerusalem's precarious position: after Assyria's campaign against Judah in 701 BC, Jerusalem was weakened—but still standing. See the infographic "Sennacherib's Prism" on p. 597.

⁹Unless the LORD Almighty
   had left us some survivors,
we would have become like Sodom,
   we would have been like Gomorrah.

¹⁰Hear the word of the LORD,
   you rulers of Sodom;

listen to the instruction of our God,
   you people of Gomorrah!
¹¹"The multitude of your sacrifices —
   what are they to me?" says the LORD.
"I have more than enough of burnt offerings,
   of rams and the fat of fattened animals;

1:9 LORD Almighty This is a common title for God in Isaiah. It occurs over 50 times. God is commander-in-chief of the heavenly armies. This title reinforces the metaphor of Yahweh as a warrior who leads armies on behalf of or against his people. In Isaiah, God is depicted both as leader of the heavenly armies coming to rescue Israel (42:13) and as the unseen hand guiding foreign armies that besiege Israel and Judah as instruments of divine judgment (10:5). **survivors** The fate of Judah's survivors is a key theme of Isaiah (see 4:2; 10:20). Isaiah emphasizes that a remnant of Israel is left only because of God's grace. **like Sodom** God destroyed Sodom and Gomorrah for their wickedness (Ge 19). The prophets frequently referenced the cities to illustrate what God's judgment looks like (see Isa 13:19; Jer 49:18; Am 4:11; Zep 2:9).

1:10 word of the LORD The prophets frequently used this phrase to legitimize their message: It is from God, not of their own making.

1:11–14 The prophets often criticized outward observance of rites and rituals when the people used it to mask inward rebellion, defiance or disloyalty to Yahweh (compare 1Sa 15:22; Am 4:4–5; Mic 6:6–8).

1:11 multitude of your sacrifices An increase in offerings is meaningless without a change in attitude. The sacrifice represented Israel's relationship of dependence on Yahweh. There was no point in going through the motions if they had abandoned that dependence — either through idolatry or pride in their self-sufficiency. The substitution of an animal whose blood atoned for their

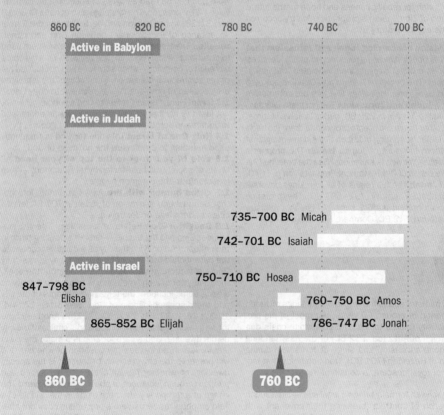

Approximate Dates of Old Testament Prophets

| 860 BC | 820 BC | 780 BC | 740 BC | 700 BC |

Active in Babylon

Active in Judah

735–700 BC Micah
742–701 BC Isaiah

Active in Israel

750–710 BC Hosea

847–798 BC
Elisha

760–750 BC Amos

865–852 BC Elijah

786–747 BC Jonah

860 BC

760 BC

* Or possibly 845–830 BC, † Or possibly 825–810 BC, ‡ Or possibly 500–460 BC
All dates are approximate

I have no pleasure
　in the blood of bulls and lambs and goats.
[12] When you come to appear before me,
　who has asked this of you,
　this trampling of my courts?
[13] Stop bringing meaningless offerings!
　Your incense is detestable to me.

New Moons, Sabbaths and convocations —
　I cannot bear your worthless assemblies.
[14] Your New Moon feasts and your appointed
　festivals
　I hate with all my being.
They have become a burden to me;
　I am weary of bearing them.

---

sins was ineffective if the people were not sincere in their repentance. **burnt offerings** God's insistence that he does not want burnt offerings would be surprising to the people of Judah. Leviticus 1 praises the burnt offering as a pleasing aroma to Yahweh (Lev 1:9). The significance of this offering is that it was a gift totally devoted to Yahweh. Other offerings were only partially burned up, and could be consumed by the priests and Levites. See note on Lev 1:3.

1:12 this of you, this trampling of my courts Ironically, the people of Judah believed God required the elaborate sacrificial system now being condemned.

1:13 New Moons Israel's holy days included sacrifices for the new moon (Nu 28:11–15). The new moon also represented an occasion for ritual feasting (1Sa 20:5,24). Work and travel was prohibited, similar to a Sabbath observance (2Ki 4:23). **Sabbaths** The weekly Sabbath was the central observance of sacred time in ancient Israel. Leviticus specifically commands that no work is to be done on the Sabbath (Lev 23:3). See the infographic "The Days of Creation" on p. 6. **convocations** Biblical law required three major festivals or convocations where all of Israel gathered to worship Yahweh. Leviticus 23:4–44 describes these festivals: the Festival of Unleavened Bread, the Festival of Weeks and the Festival of Booths (Festival of Tabernacles).

1:14 hate with all my being God hates Israel's empty religiosity in the very core of his being. The Hebrew

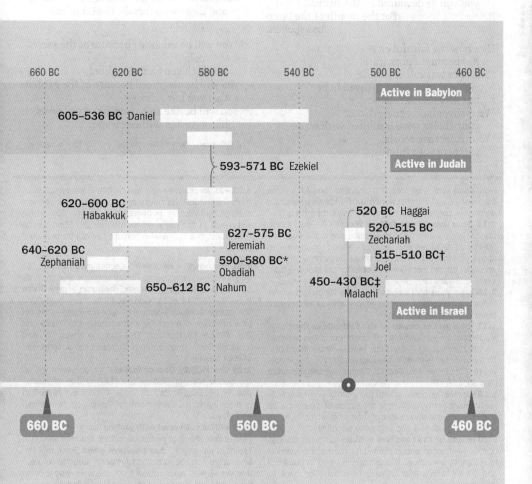

| 660 BC | 620 BC | 580 BC | 540 BC | 500 BC | 460 BC |

Active in Babylon

605–536 BC Daniel

593–571 BC Ezekiel

Active in Judah

620–600 BC
Habakkuk

520 BC Haggai

520–515 BC
Zechariah

627–575 BC
Jeremiah

640–620 BC
Zephaniah

590–580 BC*
Obadiah

515–510 BC†
Joel

650–612 BC Nahum

450–430 BC‡
Malachi

Active in Israel

660 BC　　　　**560 BC**　　　　**460 BC**

¹⁵ When you spread out your hands in prayer,
   I hide my eyes from you;
even when you offer many prayers,
   I am not listening.

Your hands are full of blood!

¹⁶ Wash and make yourselves clean.
   Take your evil deeds out of my sight;
   stop doing wrong.
¹⁷ Learn to do right; seek justice.
   Defend the oppressed.ᵃ
Take up the cause of the fatherless;
   plead the case of the widow.

¹⁸ "Come now, let us settle the matter,"
   says the LORD.
"Though your sins are like scarlet,
   they shall be as white as snow;
though they are red as crimson,
   they shall be like wool.
¹⁹ If you are willing and obedient,
   you will eat the good things of the land;
²⁰ but if you resist and rebel,
   you will be devoured by the sword."
            For the mouth of the LORD
                       has spoken.

²¹ See how the faithful city
   has become a prostitute!
She once was full of justice;
   righteousness used to dwell in her—
   but now murderers!
²² Your silver has become dross,
   your choice wine is diluted with water.
²³ Your rulers are rebels,
   partners with thieves;

they all love bribes
   and chase after gifts.
They do not defend the cause of the
      fatherless;
   the widow's case does not come before
      them.

²⁴ Therefore the Lord, the LORD Almighty,
   the Mighty One of Israel, declares:
"Ah! I will vent my wrath on my foes
   and avenge myself on my enemies.
²⁵ I will turn my hand against you;ᵇ
   I will thoroughly purge away your dross
   and remove all your impurities.
²⁶ I will restore your leaders as in days
      of old,
   your rulers as at the beginning.
Afterward you will be called
   the City of Righteousness,
   the Faithful City."

²⁷ Zion will be delivered with justice,
   her penitent ones with righteousness.
²⁸ But rebels and sinners will both be broken,
   and those who forsake the LORD will
      perish.

²⁹ "You will be ashamed because of the sacred
      oaks
   in which you have delighted;
you will be disgraced because of the gardens
   that you have chosen.
³⁰ You will be like an oak with fading leaves,
   like a garden without water.

ᵃ 17 Or justice. / Correct the oppressor   ᵇ 25 That is, against
Jerusalem

---

word used here is commonly translated "soul" but more frequently used with reference to the life essence of a person. In some cases, "my soul" can simply mean "I."
1:15 Your hands are full of blood Like sacrifices, prayers are pointless and ineffective due to the people's rebellious attitudes and actions. "Blood" may refer to literal violence and murder, ritual uncleanness from improper animal sacrifice or metaphorical staining from sinful attitudes (compare Isa 59:3).
1:16 Take your evil deeds God calls for inward repentance after condemning the empty efforts of outward observance in vv. 11–15.
1:17 Take up the cause of the fatherless Righteous leadership always involves fair treatment of the weakest members of society—orphans, widows and immigrants. This concern is evident in the Law (Dt 24:17), the Prophets (Isa 1:17; Jer 7:6; Zec 7:10) and Wisdom literature (Job 31:16–18).
1:18 scarlet The contrast with the white of snow and wool (symbolizing purity) reinforces the status of the people as impure and unclean because of their sins, which included injustice, bloodshed and improper sacrifice.
1:20 mouth of the LORD has spoken Indicates the end of this section of accusation, and marks a transition to a lament over Zion. The phrase is used in Isa 40:5 and 58:14 to link later oracles of restoration back to this choice.

1:21–31 Jerusalem—the faithful city—has turned away from God (v. 21). Its rulers and its riches have become corrupt and require purification by fire (v. 25), which will result in the city's restoration (v. 26). Zion will be redeemed, but those who corrupt her will be punished (vv. 27–31).

1:21 See how The Hebrew interjection here indicates the beginning of a new poem. The interjection also formally marks the poem as a "lament." **become a prostitute** Israel's unfaithfulness to God was tantamount to adultery. The prophets regularly compare God's covenant with Israel to a marriage contract between husband and wife (Jer 3:6–10; Eze 16; Hos 1:2). This image was typically used to shock God's people into recognizing the seriousness of their rebellion.
1:24 the Mighty One of Israel A unique variation on the poetic title for God as the "Mighty One of Jacob" (Isa 49:26; 60:16; Ps 132:2; Ge 49:24). **my foes** God is referring to his own unfaithful people as "enemies" and "foes."
1:27 will be delivered with justice Isaiah 4:4 suggests God is the agent of redemption that comes through a "spirit of judgment." **her penitent ones** Since this Hebrew word can mean both "to repent" and "to return," this verse may refer either to those who repent or to those who have returned to Jerusalem after the exile.

³¹ The mighty man will become tinder
    and his work a spark;
both will burn together,
    with no one to quench the fire."

The Mountain of the LORD

2:1-4pp — Mic 4:1-3

2 This is what Isaiah son of Amoz saw concerning Judah and Jerusalem:

² In the last days

the mountain of the LORD's temple will be
    established
    as the highest of the mountains;
it will be exalted above the hills,
    and all nations will stream to it.

³ Many peoples will come and say,

"Come, let us go up to the mountain of the
    LORD,
    to the temple of the God of Jacob.
He will teach us his ways,
    so that we may walk in his paths."
The law will go out from Zion,
    the word of the LORD from Jerusalem.

⁴ He will judge between the nations
    and will settle disputes for many peoples.
They will beat their swords into plowshares
    and their spears into pruning hooks.
Nation will not take up sword against
    nation,
    nor will they train for war anymore.

⁵ Come, descendants of Jacob,
    let us walk in the light of the LORD.

The Day of the LORD

⁶ You, LORD, have abandoned your people,
    the descendants of Jacob.
They are full of superstitions from the East;
    they practice divination like the
        Philistines
    and embrace pagan customs.
⁷ Their land is full of silver and gold;
    there is no end to their treasures.
Their land is full of horses;
    there is no end to their chariots.
⁸ Their land is full of idols;
    they bow down to the work of their hands,
    to what their fingers have made.

1:29 the gardens The references to oak or terebinth trees and gardens likely allude to Canaanite religious practices, possibly including the Asherah poles that Hezekiah cut down in 2Ki 18:4.

1:31 with no one to quench the fire Both the rebellious leaders of Judah and the product of their labor (idols for worship) will be destroyed in the judgment to come.

2:1–5 The prophecy in Isa 2:2–5 is virtually identical to Mic 4:1–3. Some overlap in the prophetic books is not unusual because of shared themes of judgment, usually followed by future reconciliation and restoration. However, the overlap in this case is so close that it is likely that either Micah quoted Isaiah or both Micah and Isaiah used a psalm well-known among the prophets.

2:1 This is what Prophets were messengers or ambassadors who brought a word from God to the people. Similarly, messengers from a king would travel to a subject kingdom and recite the words given to them by their masters. **This is what Isaiah son of Amoz saw** May refer to all of Isa 2:2, the poetic section in 2:2–4:6, or to chs. 2–12 as a whole.

2:2 last days While this can refer to an indeterminate future time, the prophets often used this term to refer to a time when the world would be set right and people would begin worshiping the one true God again (see Jer 48:47; 49:39; Eze 38:16; Hos 3:5). **mountain of the LORD's temple** Refers to Mount Zion as God's abode (see note on Isa 1:8). Ancient mythology often depicted gods living on sacred mountains. Hebrew poets often applied familiar Canaanite imagery to Yahweh to assert his superiority. The imagery of the holy mountain subtly contrasts with traditions about the god Baal. The Canaanites viewed Mount Zaphon as the home of Baal. Isaiah may be pushing Judah to recognize that Yahweh alone is God. **highest of the mountains** Psalm 48:1–2 refers to Zion as God's holy mountain and praises its height. The image of Jerusalem or Zion as a very high mountain

also occurs in Ps 78:68–69; Eze 40:2; and Zec 14:10. **all nations will stream to it** While Isaiah's message was directed at Judah, he looks ahead to a day when God's salvation will be for all the nations, not just Israel.

2:3 He will teach us his ways Judah has turned away from God's teaching, but one day all the nations will seek it eagerly. The Hebrew word for "teach" is a verbal form of the word "Torah," meaning "law" or "instruction." The book of Proverbs teaches that right living comes from following God's ways or moral and ethical principles for living (Pr 3:6; 20:24).

2:4 They will beat their swords into plowshares Judah has been under threat of war for years; one day, God's righteous reign on earth will be accompanied by international peace. Weapons of war will be refashioned into agricultural implements. Joel 3 includes a similar scene of God judging the nations, but it employs images of war and wrath rather than peace. Joel 3:10 reverses this imagery, calling on the nations to beat their plowshares into swords and their pruning hooks into spears.

2:6–22 When God's judgment comes, all the things people arrogantly rely on — military might, foreign alliances, economic strength and religious ritual — will fall short. God alone will be recognized as the one who can be relied upon.

2:6 they practice divination like the Philistines The Philistines used signs, omens and other natural phenomena to foretell the future. Israel's reliance on magic and divination violated their covenant with Yahweh. The Philistines were Israel's neighbors to the west on the Mediterranean coast.

2:7 land is full Their economic and military strength is emphasized with silver, gold, treasures, horses and chariots — typical worldly resources in which people put their faith. Under King Uzziah, Judah experienced a period of great prosperity. This period of economic and military

⁹ So people will be brought low
    and everyone humbled —
  do not forgive them.ᵃ

¹⁰ Go into the rocks, hide in the ground
    from the fearful presence of the Lᴏʀᴅ
    and the splendor of his majesty!
¹¹ The eyes of the arrogant will be humbled
    and human pride brought low;
  the Lᴏʀᴅ alone will be exalted in that day.

¹² The Lᴏʀᴅ Almighty has a day in store
    for all the proud and lofty,
  for all that is exalted
    (and they will be humbled),
¹³ for all the cedars of Lebanon, tall
    and lofty,
  and all the oaks of Bashan,
¹⁴ for all the towering mountains
    and all the high hills,
¹⁵ for every lofty tower
    and every fortified wall,
¹⁶ for every trading shipᵇ
    and every stately vessel.
¹⁷ The arrogance of man will be brought low
    and human pride humbled;
  the Lᴏʀᴅ alone will be exalted in that day,
¹⁸   and the idols will totally disappear.

¹⁹ People will flee to caves in the rocks
    and to holes in the ground
  from the fearful presence of the Lᴏʀᴅ
    and the splendor of his majesty,
  when he rises to shake the earth.

²⁰ In that day people will throw away
    to the moles and bats
  their idols of silver and idols of gold,
    which they made to worship.
²¹ They will flee to caverns in the rocks
    and to the overhanging crags
  from the fearful presence of the Lᴏʀᴅ
    and the splendor of his majesty,
  when he rises to shake the earth.

²² Stop trusting in mere humans,
    who have but a breath in their nostrils.
  Why hold them in esteem?

Judgment on Jerusalem and Judah

3 See now, the Lord,
    the Lᴏʀᴅ Almighty,
  is about to take from Jerusalem and Judah
    both supply and support:
  all supplies of food and all supplies of water,
²   the hero and the warrior,
  the judge and the prophet,
    the diviner and the elder,
³ the captain of fifty and the man of rank,
    the counselor, skilled craftsman and clever
    enchanter.

⁴ "I will make mere youths their officials;
    children will rule over them."

⁵ People will oppress each other —
    man against man, neighbor against
    neighbor.

ᵃ 9 Or *not raise them up*   ᵇ 16 Hebrew *every ship of Tarshish*

---

strength (during the early eighth century BC) paralleled a similar time of prosperity and strength in the northern kingdom under Jeroboam II. See the timeline "The Divided Kingdom" on p. 536.

2:9 do not forgive them Isaiah interjects with a very human response: Those who reject God should get what they deserve. The prophets recognized that some of their oracles of judgment were conditioned on the response of the people. If they repented, God relented. Their strong sense of justice sometimes led them to object to God's apparent change of plan and insist on judgment rather than mercy.

2:10 hide in the ground The time for repentance has passed—all the people can do is take cover in the rocks, dust, caverns and cliffs. **fearful presence of the Lord** The earthly presence of Yahweh is terrifying, even when he is not mobilized for judgment (see Isa 6; Ex 20:18–19).

2:12–18 Pride ultimately results in judgment. Isaiah opens with a general statement about the universal nature of pride in Isa 2:12, and expands with nine examples of natural and human-made symbols that often are lifted up as replacements for God.

2:13 cedars of Lebanon A highly prized building material symbolizing earthly wealth and splendor (1Ki 5:6; Eze 27:5). **oaks of Bashan** Another prized building resource symbolic of material wealth and power (Eze 27:6).

2:16 trading ship Symbolic of wealth produced by economic trade. The references in Isa 2:13–14 to Lebanon

Bashan and the trading ship from Tarshish (see text note) focus on the primary wealth-building industries for the nations around Israel and Judah.

2:22 Stop trusting in mere humans This section opens in v. 5 with an appeal for Israel to repent and turn to God. It ends with an appeal to turn away from people who cannot do what God can—truly help them.

3:1—4:1 This warning of judgment first focuses on the effect of a military defeat—where all traditional leadership has been removed. It then focuses on the social ramifications of the loss. The message of 3:1–15 is directed toward the leaders of Judah, who are responsible for leading the people away from God. The focus of 3:16—4:1 is on the "daughters of Zion" and their financial and social loss in light of the removal of male leadership and husbands.

3:1 Lord Almighty This title emphasizes God's military role in light of the siege imagery that follows. See note on 1:9. **food** Under siege, the supply of food and water is of utmost importance (see 2Ki 6:24—7:20). Like many cities, Jerusalem's water supply was just outside the city until 701 BC, when Hezekiah had a tunnel dug to bring water into the city in preparation for siege (see 2Ch 32:30). See the infographic "Inscription From Hezekiah's Tunnel" on p. 599.

3:2 hero and the warrior The prophet lists 11 leadership roles that cover the traditional areas of influence—politi-

The young will rise up against the old,
    the nobody against the honored.

⁶ A man will seize one of his brothers
    in his father's house, and say,
"You have a cloak, you be our leader;
    take charge of this heap of ruins!"
⁷ But in that day he will cry out,
    "I have no remedy.
I have no food or clothing in my house;
    do not make me the leader of the people."

⁸ Jerusalem staggers,
    Judah is falling;
their words and deeds are against the LORD,
    defying his glorious presence.
⁹ The look on their faces testifies against them;
    they parade their sin like Sodom;
    they do not hide it.
Woe to them!
    They have brought disaster upon
        themselves.

¹⁰ Tell the righteous it will be well with them,
    for they will enjoy the fruit of their deeds.
¹¹ Woe to the wicked!
    Disaster is upon them!
They will be paid back
    for what their hands have done.

¹² Youths oppress my people,
    women rule over them.
My people, your guides lead you astray;
    they turn you from the path.

¹³ The LORD takes his place in court;
    he rises to judge the people.
¹⁴ The LORD enters into judgment
    against the elders and leaders of his people:
"It is you who have ruined my vineyard;
    the plunder from the poor is in your
        houses.

¹⁵ What do you mean by crushing my people
    and grinding the faces of the poor?"
        declares the Lord, the LORD Almighty.

¹⁶ The LORD says,
    "The women of Zion are haughty,
walking along with outstretched necks,
    flirting with their eyes,
strutting along with swaying hips,
    with ornaments jingling on their
        ankles.
¹⁷ Therefore the Lord will bring sores on
        the heads of the women of Zion;
    the LORD will make their scalps bald."

¹⁸ In that day the Lord will snatch away their
finery: the bangles and headbands and crescent
necklaces, ¹⁹ the earrings and bracelets and veils,
²⁰ the headdresses and anklets and sashes, the
perfume bottles and charms, ²¹ the signet rings
and nose rings, ²² the fine robes and the capes and
cloaks, the purses ²³ and mirrors, and the linen
garments and tiaras and shawls.

²⁴ Instead of fragrance there will be
        a stench;
    instead of a sash, a rope;
instead of well-dressed hair, baldness;
    instead of fine clothing, sackcloth;
    instead of beauty, branding.
²⁵ Your men will fall by the sword,
    your warriors in battle.
²⁶ The gates of Zion will lament and mourn;
    destitute, she will sit on the ground.

4 ¹ In that day seven women
    will take hold of one man
and say, "We will eat our own food
    and provide our own clothes;
only let us be called by your name.
    Take away our disgrace!"

cal, judicial, religious and military—to stress that the
support being removed is greater than mere food and
water. The entire leadership structure of Judah will be
forfeited.
3:4 I will make mere youths their officials When
the generation of leaders is removed, only children will
be left to fill the traditional male leadership positions.
3:5 oppress each other Suggests a return to the anarchy of the days before Israel had a king. See Jdg 17:6.
3:6 You have a cloak The qualifications for leadership
are minimal; people without qualifications other than
clothing will be designated as leaders.
3:7 I have no remedy No one wants to be in charge
because there is nothing left for a leader to do except
tend to the wounded.
3:9 Sodom See note on Isa 1:9.
3:11 Woe to the wicked While it may look like the wicked
have prospered, God will ultimately save the righteous
and punish the wicked (see Ecc 8:12–13).
3:12 Youths oppress my people May imply that only
women and children will be left to rule (see Isa 3:4
and note).

3:14 elders Members of the ruling upper class. God
will judge the officials of Judah for their mistreatment
of the poor. **my vineyard** A metaphor for Israel and
Judah. See 5:1–7.

3:16—4:1 The imagery from 3:16—4:1 depicts Judah
as vain girls more concerned with how they look than with
how they act. Though the prophet may be condemning
actual practices, he may also be metaphorically presenting the pride and idolatry of Judah in social terms.

3:16 women of Zion The prophets often use feminine
imagery for Israel and Judah—sometimes as a wife
breaking the marriage covenant, and sometimes as a
daughter disobeying the father. See note on 1:8.
3:17 will bring sores on the heads of the women God
will take away the physical beauty, clothing and jewelry
that they value most.
3:26 gates of Zion Now Jerusalem itself is personified
as the woman being humiliated.
4:1 seven women The male population will be severely
reduced, resulting in a shortage of eligible husbands.

The Branch of the Lord

²In that day the Branch of the Lord will be beautiful and glorious, and the fruit of the land will be the pride and glory of the survivors in Israel. ³Those who are left in Zion, who remain in Jerusalem, will be called holy, all who are recorded among the living in Jerusalem. ⁴The Lord will wash away the filth of the women of Zion; he will cleanse the bloodstains from Jerusalem by a spirit^a of judgment and a spirit^a of fire. ⁵Then the Lord will create over all of Mount Zion and over those who assemble there a cloud of smoke by day and a glow of flaming fire by night; over everything the glory^b will be a canopy. ⁶It will be a shelter and shade from the heat of the day, and a refuge and hiding place from the storm and rain.

The Song of the Vineyard

5 I will sing for the one I love
  a song about his vineyard:
My loved one had a vineyard
  on a fertile hillside.
²He dug it up and cleared it of stones
  and planted it with the choicest vines.

He built a watchtower in it
  and cut out a winepress as well.
Then he looked for a crop of good grapes,
  but it yielded only bad fruit.

³"Now you dwellers in Jerusalem and people
    of Judah,
  judge between me and my vineyard.
⁴What more could have been done for my
    vineyard
  than I have done for it?
When I looked for good grapes,
  why did it yield only bad?
⁵Now I will tell you
  what I am going to do to my vineyard:
I will take away its hedge,
  and it will be destroyed;
I will break down its wall,
  and it will be trampled.
⁶I will make it a wasteland,
  neither pruned nor cultivated,
  and briers and thorns will grow there.
I will command the clouds
  not to rain on it."

---

^a 4 Or the Spirit   ^b 5 Or over all the glory there

4:2 In that day Previously in Isaiah, "that day" referred to the day of judgment (see 3:7; 4:1). Here, it refers to the day of ultimate restoration in the Messianic age. **Branch of the Lord** A metaphor referring to the Messiah, as indicated by Jer 23:5, 33:15; and Zec 6:12. In Zec 3:8, God's heir—being the Messianic Branch (which can also be rendered as "sprout" or "shoot")—is further identified as Yahweh's "servant." This links the messiah to the servant imagery of Isa 40—55 (compare 11:1 for a similar metaphor). The "branch of Yahweh" may also identify the believing remnant (based on the reference to the survivors of Israel), but the Messianic imagery in Jeremiah and Zechariah makes this less plausible. The context makes the branch something valued by the remnant, not the remnant themselves.
4:3 Those who are left in Zion, who remain in Jerusalem Refers to the remnant after the act of judgment. That the entire remnant is now "holy" suggests the future fulfillment of a Messianic Zion, not the near fulfillment of a rebuilt and repopulated city. This also reinforces the identification of the "branch" as the Messiah (see note on v. 2). **who are recorded among the living** This reference suggests a future period of total reconciliation between God and his people.
4:4 the women of Zion See note on 1:8. **a spirit of fire** Fire is a theological symbol associated with judgment, purification and divine presence. Divine judgment often comes by a purifying fire—as in 1:25, where the cleansing of sin by judgment is compared to the removal of impurity in the smelting process (compare Mal 3:2–5). Fire symbolizes Yahweh's presence in Isa 4:5, so the image of burning here bridges the related associations of divine judgment and presence.
4:5 flaming fire by night God's presence in Zion will be as it was with Israel in the wilderness (see Ex 13:21–22; 40:34–38; Nu 9:15–23): He will dwell visibly in their midst. Israel's covenant with Yahweh had three major parts: He would be their God, they would be his people

and he would dwell among them (Ex 6:7; 25:8; 33:14; 40:34; Jer 30:22). Sin required God to turn his face away or remove his presence (Lev 17:10; 20:3; Eze 14:8; 15:7). See the infographic "The Tabernacle" on p. 138.

5:1–7 Though this poem calls itself a love song (Isa 5:1), it more closely resembles a parable. The poet uses the metaphor of a vineyard to describe God's care for Israel. The symbolic meaning, which is initially shrouded in figurative language (vv. 1–6), will be drawn out explicitly in v. 7. As a parable, it resembles the NT parable of the tenants in Mt 21:33–41.
5:1 one I love The prophet writes from the perspective of one who is in right relationship with Yahweh. **vineyard** Garden or vineyard imagery for a beloved figure are also found in Song of Songs (see SS 2:15; 4:16; 8:11–12). The metaphor appears to symbolize the potential for fertility. The vineyard motif is also present in Isa 27:2–5.
5:2 He dug it up God's handiwork in creating Israel as a people for himself is compared to the hard work of preparing the rocky, hilly soil of Judah for farming. If God owns the vineyard, it is his to do with as he pleases. **bad fruit** The Hebrew expression implies that the vineyard produced stinking, inedible fruit, not just sour or uncultivated grapes.
5:4 When I looked for good grapes Yahweh had every reason to expect his creation would produce fruit. He prepared the soil, cultivated the vines and protected the vineyard. The metaphor of a divine planting and a failure of humanity to provide for the crop is known elsewhere in ancient Near Eastern literature. In the Akkadian myth of *Erra and Ishum*, the god Marduk laments how he planted Babylon like an orchard, but never got any fruit.
5:5 break down its wall A subtle indication that this vineyard metaphorically represents a city, since the wall of the vineyard was usually just the hedgerow. The imagery foreshadows the siege and invasion of Jerusalem where the country is trampled by foreign armies.

⁷ The vineyard of the LORD Almighty
    is the nation of Israel,
and the people of Judah
    are the vines he delighted in.
And he looked for justice, but saw
        bloodshed;
    for righteousness, but heard cries of
        distress.

Woes and Judgments

⁸ Woe to you who add house to house
    and join field to field
till no space is left
    and you live alone in the land.

⁹ The LORD Almighty has declared in my hearing:

"Surely the great houses will become
        desolate,
    the fine mansions left without occupants.
¹⁰ A ten-acre vineyard will produce only a bath[a]
        of wine;
    a homer[b] of seed will yield only an ephah[c]
        of grain."

¹¹ Woe to those who rise early in the morning
    to run after their drinks,
who stay up late at night
    till they are inflamed with wine.
¹² They have harps and lyres at their banquets,
    pipes and timbrels and wine,
but they have no regard for the deeds
        of the LORD,
    no respect for the work of his hands.
¹³ Therefore my people will go into exile
    for lack of understanding;

those of high rank will die of hunger
    and the common people will be parched
        with thirst.
¹⁴ Therefore Death expands its jaws,
    opening wide its mouth;
into it will descend their nobles and
        masses
    with all their brawlers and revelers.
¹⁵ So people will be brought low
    and everyone humbled,
    the eyes of the arrogant humbled.
¹⁶ But the LORD Almighty will be exalted by his
        justice,
    and the holy God will be proved holy by his
        righteous acts.
¹⁷ Then sheep will graze as in their own
        pasture;
    lambs will feed[d] among the ruins of the
        rich.

¹⁸ Woe to those who draw sin along with cords
    of deceit,
    and wickedness as with cart ropes,
¹⁹ to those who say, "Let God hurry;
    let him hasten his work
    so we may see it.
The plan of the Holy One of Israel —
    let it approach, let it come into view,
    so we may know it."

²⁰ Woe to those who call evil good
    and good evil,
who put darkness for light
    and light for darkness,

---

[a] 10 That is, about 6 gallons or about 22 liters   [b] 10 That is, probably about 360 pounds or about 160 kilograms   [c] 10 That is, probably about 36 pounds or about 16 kilograms   [d] 17 Septuagint; Hebrew / strangers will eat

---

5:7 is the nation of Israel The prophet reveals that vv. 3–6 is actually a metaphorical indictment against Judah and Jerusalem. **justice, but saw bloodshed** Wordplay in Hebrew poetry is difficult to reproduce in translation. The Hebrew words contrasted in this closing stanza sound similar: *mishpat* ("justice") and *mispach* ("bloodshed"), *tsedaqah* ("righteousness") and *tse'aqah* ("call for help"). The central ethical principles of the OT are justice and righteousness. Justice involves both a concern for punishment and a concern for fairness. Righteousness is regularly paired with justice in the prophetic writings (Am 5:24; Isa 32:16; Hos 2:19).

5:8–30 The reality behind the vineyard metaphor is brought to light with six woes found in Isa 5:8,11,18, and 20–22. The woes highlight various ways that injustice and unrighteousness have overtaken the land.

5:8 join field to field Refers to rich people systematically taking land from the poor. Their behavior violates the regulations about property ownership found in the Pentateuch, especially Lev 25 and Nu 26:55 and 33:54 (compare 1Ki 21:1–3; Mic 2:2). **the land** Israel's continued possession of the land is conditional on their obedience (Dt 4:26).

5:10 will yield only an ephah of grain Roughly 10 percent of the initial investment will be recouped at harvest. The expectation was a tenfold yield or more, not a 90 percent loss (compare Mt 13:8).

5:12 at their banquets, pipes and timbrels and wine The second woe is directed at those who have essentially made a religion out of drunken partying. This woe is likely also intended for the rich and prosperous of society, accusing them of ignoring the real political, social and religious issues that should command their attention.

5:15 the eyes of the arrogant Isaiah continually focuses on pride as the fundamental sin of humanity. This reflects a strong current of thought throughout the OT: The ultimate sin is to exalt oneself, while the ultimate virtue is humility.

5:16 LORD Almighty will be exalted The exaltation of Yahweh occurs when people enact justice and righteousness.

5:19 let him hasten his work The people's prideful and haughty attitude comes into focus as they express a mocking desire to see God bring about the day of judgment that the prophet is warning them of.

5:20 evil good and good evil As Isa 5:21 makes clear, relying on our own wisdom leads to a distorted view of the world and a skewed perspective on right and wrong.

who put bitter for sweet
and sweet for bitter.

21 Woe to those who are wise in their own eyes
and clever in their own sight.

22 Woe to those who are heroes at drinking
wine
and champions at mixing drinks,
23 who acquit the guilty for a bribe,
but deny justice to the innocent.
24 Therefore, as tongues of fire lick up straw
and as dry grass sinks down in the flames,
so their roots will decay
and their flowers blow away like dust;
for they have rejected the law of the LORD
Almighty
and spurned the word of the Holy One of
Israel.
25 Therefore the LORD's anger burns against his
people;
his hand is raised and he strikes them
down.
The mountains shake,
and the dead bodies are like refuse in the
streets.

Yet for all this, his anger is not turned away,
his hand is still upraised.

26 He lifts up a banner for the distant nations,
he whistles for those at the ends of the
earth.
Here they come,
swiftly and speedily!

27 Not one of them grows tired or stumbles,
not one slumbers or sleeps;
not a belt is loosened at the waist,
not a sandal strap is broken.
28 Their arrows are sharp,
all their bows are strung;
their horses' hooves seem like flint,
their chariot wheels like a whirlwind.
29 Their roar is like that of the lion,
they roar like young lions;
they growl as they seize their prey
and carry it off with no one to rescue.
30 In that day they will roar over it
like the roaring of the sea.
And if one looks at the land,
there is only darkness and distress;
even the sun will be darkened by clouds.

Isaiah's Commission

6 In the year that King Uzziah died, I saw the
Lord, high and exalted, seated on a throne;
and the train of his robe filled the temple. 2 Above
him were seraphim, each with six wings: With
two wings they covered their faces, with two they
covered their feet, and with two they were flying.
3 And they were calling to one another:

"Holy, holy, holy is the LORD Almighty;
the whole earth is full of his glory."

4 At the sound of their voices the doorposts and
thresholds shook and the temple was filled with
smoke.

5:23 acquit the guilty Refers to corruption in court
and echoes 1:23.
5:25 his hand is still upraised This line is reused as
a refrain in chs. 9–10 (9:12,17,21; 10:4).
5:26 he whistles for those God uses the nations as
instruments of judgment. This is in contrast with 2:2–4,
where the nations come to Jerusalem to worship and
learn from Yahweh. See 7:18.
5:27 Not one of them grows tired The advancing
armies of Assyria are described in almost superhuman
fashion.

6:1–7 Isaiah's throne-room vision of Yahweh changes the
way he represents God's sovereignty and glory in the rest
of the book. The placement of this account six chapters
into the book may indicate that it is not Isaiah's initial
commissioning as a prophet of God (compare Ezekiel's
vision of Yahweh in Eze 1), but rather his commissioning
for a special task or mission. This fits the specific message he is given in Isa 6:9–10. Alternatively, chs. 1–5
may be a prologue to the book as a whole; those chapters
introduce key ideas and themes present throughout
chs. 1–66. In that case, the vision in ch. 6 could be an
account of Isaiah's initial prophetic commissioning—a
common motif in God's interactions with the prophets
(see Ex 3 or Eze 1).

6:1 In the year that King Uzziah died Uzziah probably
died around 742 BC. Isaiah 1:1 says Isaiah was active
in the reign of Uzziah, but Uzziah may only be included

there because Isaiah's ministry began in the last year of
Uzziah's life. See the timeline "The Divided Kingdom" on
p. 536. **seated on a throne** Isaiah sees the heavenly
throne room of Yahweh. The Israelites understood the
temple in Jerusalem to be Yahweh's earthly dwelling.
Thus, Isaiah's vision links Yahweh's heavenly throne
with his divine residence in the temple (compare Ps
11:4; Isa 66:1). **the train of his robe** With God on his
throne in heaven, the temple only contains the very bottom of God's robe. The Hebrew here refers to the edge
of the skirt or hem. See the infographic "The Ark of the
Covenant" on p. 412.
6:2 seraphim These heavenly beings attending to Yahweh
are only mentioned here. Their name is derived from a
Hebrew term that indicates some sort of serpent. The
related Hebrew verb denotes burning, so the seraphim
are sometimes considered fiery serpents. **each with six
wings** Spiritual beings are often depicted with sets of
wings. The cherubim in Eze 1 have four wings each. The
greater number of wings of the seraphim may indicate
their higher status in the heavenly hierarchy. **two wings
they covered their faces** The seraphim likely had to
protect themselves from the brightness of the glory of
Yahweh. The seraphim cover their bodies with four wings
and fly with two.
6:3 Holy, holy, holy The threefold repetition intensifies
the superlative. See the infographic "The Most Holy
Place" on p. 525. **his glory** The glory of Yahweh is his
visible earthly presence. Isaiah's vision recalls a past

5 "Woe to me!" I cried. "I am ruined! For I am a man of unclean lips, and I live among a people of unclean lips, and my eyes have seen the King, the Lord Almighty."

6 Then one of the seraphim flew to me with a live coal in his hand, which he had taken with tongs from the altar. 7 With it he touched my mouth and said, "See, this has touched your lips; your guilt is taken away and your sin atoned for."

8 Then I heard the voice of the Lord saying, "Whom shall I send? And who will go for us?"

And I said, "Here am I. Send me!"

9 He said, "Go and tell this people:

" 'Be ever hearing, but never
understanding;
be ever seeing, but never perceiving.'
10 Make the heart of this people calloused;
make their ears dull
and close their eyes.[a]
Otherwise they might see with their eyes,
hear with their ears,
understand with their hearts,
and turn and be healed."

11 Then I said, "For how long, Lord?"

And he answered:

"Until the cities lie ruined
and without inhabitant,
until the houses are left deserted
and the fields ruined and ravaged,
12 until the Lord has sent everyone
far away
and the land is utterly forsaken.
13 And though a tenth remains in the land,
it will again be laid waste.

But as the terebinth and oak
leave stumps when they are cut
down,
so the holy seed will be the stump in
the land."

The Sign of Immanuel

7 When Ahaz son of Jotham, the son of Uzziah, was king of Judah, King Rezin of Aram and Pekah son of Remaliah king of Israel marched up to fight against Jerusalem, but they could not overpower it.

2 Now the house of David was told, "Aram has allied itself with[b] Ephraim"; so the hearts of Ahaz and his people were shaken, as the trees of the forest are shaken by the wind.

3 Then the Lord said to Isaiah, "Go out, you and your son Shear-Jashub,[c] to meet Ahaz at the end of the aqueduct of the Upper Pool, on the road to the Launderer's Field. 4 Say to him, 'Be careful, keep calm and don't be afraid. Do not lose heart because of these two smoldering stubs of firewood — because of the fierce anger of Rezin and Aram and of the son of Remaliah. 5 Aram, Ephraim and Remaliah's son have plotted your ruin, saying, 6 "Let us invade Judah; let us tear it apart and divide it among ourselves, and make the son of Tabeel king over it." 7 Yet this is what the Sovereign Lord says:

a 9,10 Hebrew; Septuagint 'You will be ever hearing, but never understanding; / you will be ever seeing, but never perceiving.' / 10This people's heart has become calloused; / they hardly hear with their ears, / and they have closed their eyes   b 2 Or has set up camp in   c 3 Shear-Jashub means a remnant will return.

---

time in Israel's history when Yahweh was visibly present among them (see Ex 16:7–10; 29:43; 40:34–35; 1Ki 8:11; Ps 26:8; 63:2).

6:5 Woe to me Appearing improperly before a king could lead to death. See Ex 33:20; Est 4:11.

6:7 your guilt is taken away Isaiah is cleansed of sin so that he can remain in the divine presence and live to tell about it. **atoned for** Atonement achieved a ritual cleansing of sin, usually by means of blood sacrifice. Isaiah's atonement without sacrifice illustrates God's freedom to extend mercy by his grace (see Ex 33:19).

6:8–13 Isaiah is now ready to receive the divine message, or at least to overhear the deliberations in the divine council.

6:8 who will go for us A mark of a true prophet was that he had stood in the divine council and received his mission directly from God. See Ge 1:26 and note; Jer 23:18; 1Ki 22:19–23.

6:9–10 God orders Isaiah to make sure the people do not repent and thus avoid judgment. The prophet is essentially being asked to allow the people to continue along the same path of disobedience they have been on. The passage is quoted numerous times in the NT to support the general lack of a positive response among

the Jewish people to Jesus as the Messiah. See Mt 13:14–15; Jn 12:40; Ac 28:25–29.

6:12 Lord has sent everyone far away Destruction and exile are the instruments of God's judgment.

6:13 though a tenth remains in the land A hint that a small group of people will survive. From that remnant, God will rebuild his people. See note on Isa 1:9. **holy seed will be the stump in the land** A foreshadowing of the Messianic promise of 11:1.

7:1 When Ahaz son of Jotham, the son of Uzziah The events of ch. 7 take place around 735 BC (see 2Ki 15:37 — 16:8). Aram (also known as Syria) and Israel have joined forces to rebel against the Assyrian Empire. They are trying to force Judah to join their rebellion.

7:2 house of David The address highlights God's promise to preserve David's family on the throne of Jerusalem (2Sa 7:8–17). See the infographic "The Tel Dan Stele" on p. 1080.

7:3 your son Shear-Jashub Isaiah's sons are given symbolic names as living reminders of God's message (compare Hos 1:4–9). "Shear-Jashub" refers to the return of the remnant, which symbolized both judgment and the hope of future restoration. See the table "Symbolic Names of People in Hebrew" on p. 1388.

7:6 son of Tabeel Probably a puppet ruler to replace Ahaz and bring Judah into their alliance.

"'It will not take place,
it will not happen,
⁸for the head of Aram is Damascus,
and the head of Damascus is only Rezin.
Within sixty-five years
Ephraim will be too shattered to be a
people.
⁹The head of Ephraim is Samaria,
and the head of Samaria is only
Remaliah's son.

If you do not stand firm in your faith,
you will not stand at all.'"

¹⁰Again the LORD spoke to Ahaz, ¹¹"Ask the LORD your God for a sign, whether in the deepest depths or in the highest heights."

¹²But Ahaz said, "I will not ask; I will not put the LORD to the test."

¹³Then Isaiah said, "Hear now, you house of David! Is it not enough to try the patience of hu-

---

7:8 Within sixty-five years When Israel was conquered by Assyria in 722 BC, a large part of the population was taken into exile. Assyria then resettled the land with exiles from other areas they conquered. The resulting mixed population within two generations could be referred to here.

7:10–25 Isaiah's meeting with Ahaz should have encouraged his faith in Yahweh to deliver Judah from its present predicament. Instead, Ahaz discounts the reassurance

Yahweh offers, and compounds his sin by refusing a divine sign. The sign of Immanuel has implications for the immediate future: Within a year or two—the time it would take for a woman to conceive, give birth and rear a young boy—the threat from the Syro-Ephraimite alliance will have passed. The ultimate fulfillment of the sign points to the future restoration of God's relationship with his people through the miraculous birth of God in human form (Mt 1:23).

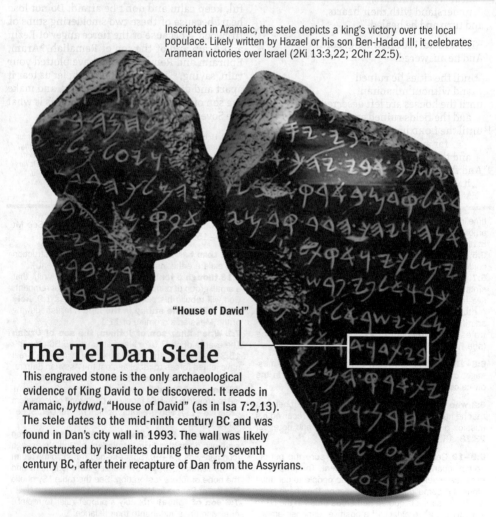

Inscripted in Aramaic, the stele depicts a king's victory over the local populace. Likely written by Hazael or his son Ben-Hadad III, it celebrates Aramean victories over Israel (2Ki 13:3,22; 2Chr 22:5).

"House of David"

The Tel Dan Stele

This engraved stone is the only archaeological evidence of King David to be discovered. It reads in Aramaic, *bytdwd*, "House of David" (as in Isa 7:2,13). The stele dates to the mid-ninth century BC and was found in Dan's city wall in 1993. The wall was likely reconstructed by Israelites during the early seventh century BC, after their recapture of Dan from the Assyrians.

mans? Will you try the patience of my God also? [14]Therefore the Lord himself will give you[a] a sign: The virgin[b] will conceive and give birth to a son, and[c] will call him Immanuel.[d] [15]He will be eating curds and honey when he knows enough to reject the wrong and choose the right, [16]for before the boy knows enough to reject the wrong and choose the right, the land of the two kings you dread will be laid waste. [17]The Lord will bring on you and on your people and on the house of your father a time unlike any since Ephraim broke away from Judah — he will bring the king of Assyria."

Assyria, the Lord's Instrument

[18]In that day the Lord will whistle for flies from the Nile delta in Egypt and for bees from the land of Assyria. [19]They will all come and settle in the steep ravines and in the crevices in the rocks, on all the thornbushes and at all the water holes. [20]In that day the Lord will use a razor hired from beyond the Euphrates River — the king of Assyria — to shave your head and private parts, and to cut off your beard also. [21]In that day, a person will keep alive a young cow and two goats. [22]And because of the abundance of the milk they give, there will be curds to eat. All who remain in the land will eat curds and honey. [23]In that day, in every place where there were a thousand vines worth a thousand silver shekels,[e] there will be only briers and thorns. [24]Hunters will go there with bow and arrow, for the land will be covered with briers and thorns. [25]As for all the hills once cultivated by the hoe, you will no longer go there for fear of the briers and thorns; they will become places where cattle are turned loose and where sheep run.

Isaiah and His Children as Signs

8 The Lord said to me, "Take a large scroll and write on it with an ordinary pen: Maher-Shal-al-Hash-Baz."[f] [2]So I called in Uriah the priest and Zechariah son of Jeberekiah as reliable witnesses for me. [3]Then I made love to the prophetess, and she conceived and gave birth to a son. And the Lord said to me, "Name him Maher-Shalal-Hash-Baz. [4]For before the boy knows how to say 'My father' or 'My mother,' the wealth of Damascus and the plunder of Samaria will be carried off by the king of Assyria."

[a] 14 The Hebrew is plural.   [b] 14 Or *young woman*
[c] 14 Masoretic Text; Dead Sea Scrolls *son, and he* or *son, and they*   [d] 14 *Immanuel* means *God with us.*   [e] 23 That is, about 25 pounds or about 12 kilograms   [f] 1 *Maher-Shalal-Hash-Baz* means *quick to the plunder, swift to the spoil*; also in verse 3.

7:12 I will not put the Lord to the test Ahaz's refusal to ask for a sign is rebellious, not pious.
7:14 The virgin The Hebrew term here, *almah,* indicates a young woman of marriageable age. In the ancient world, a young unmarried woman who had reached puberty could reasonably be assumed to be a virgin because of the close social and familial restrictions on her activities. There is ongoing debate about whether *almah* technically denotes a virgin, since the Hebrew term *bethulah* is the more precise word for "virgin." If *almah* does not denote virginity, the implication would be that the NT interpretation of the virgin birth is mistaken (see note on Mt 1:23). The overlapping use of *almah* and *bethulah* in Ge 24 to refer to the unmarried Rebekah demonstrates that these terms were considered to be interchangeable (see Ge 24:16,43). The Septuagint uses the Greek term *parthenos* to translate *almah* in Isa 7:14 and Ge 24:43. Drawing on the Septuagint, the NT interpretation is based on the Greek word *parthenos,* also a more precise word for "virgin." The NT describes the fulfillment of Isa 7:14 with the birth of Jesus in Mt 1:18–23. **Immanuel** Means "God with us." The three symbolic names of these children point to the three phases of God's future work: imminent judgment, coming restoration and future redemption (compare Isa 7:3; 8:1). God's presence among his people was an important theological symbol for Israel (the presence of Yahweh enters the temple in 1Ki 8:10–11). The people's sinfulness puts that privilege in jeopardy. The name Immanuel symbolizes the full restoration of Yahweh's broken relationship with his people. While the immediate context of the sign itself points to a short-term fulfillment (see note on Isa 7:10–25), the larger context of Isaiah heavily stresses the future time of redemption and reconciliation between Yahweh and

Israel. The close relationship between Messianic and divine roles and titles supports the understanding of Immanuel as a Messianic figure. In 11:1–10, the Messiah is given the divine right to judge the nations; his reign inaugurates an era of worldwide peace.
7:18 bees from the land God will use the nations to judge Israel and Judah. Their soldiers will swarm over the land like insects.
7:20 private parts The Hebrew term here is sometimes used as a euphemism for genitalia.
8:1 with an ordinary pen Written with an ordinary writing instrument so all could understand. **Maher-Shalal-Hash-Baz** This Hebrew name means "spoil speeds, prey hastens," symbolizing the rapidly approaching defeat of Israel and Aram (also known as Syria). See 7:3 and note; 7:14 and note. See the table "Symbolic Names of People in Hebrew" on p. 1388.
8:2 reliable witnesses Since Ahaz rebuffed Isaiah's call for him to trust in Yahweh, witnesses will verify the authenticity of this new sign. Isaiah's instructions are typical of prophetic sign-acts. The prophet is instructed to carry out certain actions as a concrete reminder to the people of Yahweh's involvement. See Eze 4–5 or Isa 20 for similar sign-acts.
8:3 the prophetess Being called a "prophetess" likely indicates some status greater than simply "wife of a prophet." It is a rare distinction to be identified as a female prophet in the OT. Aside from this unnamed woman, only four women are identified as prophetesses in the OT: Miriam, Moses' sister (Ex 15:20); Deborah (Jdg 4:4); Huldah (2Ki 22:14; 2Ch 34:22); and Noadiah (Ne 6:14).
8:4 plunder of Samaria Loss of wealth to the spoils of war is the fate symbolized by the boy's name.

⁵The LORD spoke to me again:

⁶ "Because this people has rejected
  the gently flowing waters of Shiloah
and rejoices over Rezin
  and the son of Remaliah,
⁷ therefore the Lord is about to bring against
    them
  the mighty floodwaters of the Euphrates —
  the king of Assyria with all his pomp.
It will overflow all its channels,
  run over all its banks
⁸ and sweep on into Judah, swirling over it,
  passing through it and reaching up to the
    neck.
Its outspread wings will cover the breadth of
    your land,
  Immanuel*ᵃ!"

⁹ Raise the war cry,ᵇ you nations, and be
    shattered!
  Listen, all you distant lands.
Prepare for battle, and be shattered!
  Prepare for battle, and be shattered!
¹⁰ Devise your strategy, but it will be
    thwarted;
  propose your plan, but it will not stand,
  for God is with us.ᶜ

¹¹ This is what the LORD says to me with his
strong hand upon me, warning me not to follow
the way of this people:

¹² "Do not call conspiracy
  everything this people calls a conspiracy;
do not fear what they fear,
  and do not dread it.
¹³ The LORD Almighty is the one you are to
    regard as holy,
  he is the one you are to fear,
  he is the one you are to dread.
¹⁴ He will be a holy place;
  for both Israel and Judah he will be
a stone that causes people to stumble
  and a rock that makes them fall.

And for the people of Jerusalem he will be
  a trap and a snare.
¹⁵ Many of them will stumble;
  they will fall and be broken,
  they will be snared and captured."

¹⁶ Bind up this testimony of warning
  and seal up God's instruction among my
    disciples.
¹⁷ I will wait for the LORD,
  who is hiding his face from the
    descendants of Jacob.
I will put my trust in him.

¹⁸ Here am I, and the children the LORD has giv-
en me. We are signs and symbols in Israel from
the LORD Almighty, who dwells on Mount Zion.

The Darkness Turns to Light

¹⁹ When someone tells you to consult mediums
and spiritists, who whisper and mutter, should
not a people inquire of their God? Why consult
the dead on behalf of the living? ²⁰ Consult God's
instruction and the testimony of warning. If anyone does not speak according to this word, they
have no light of dawn. ²¹ Distressed and hungry,
they will roam through the land; when they are
famished, they will become enraged and, looking upward, will curse their king and their God.
²² Then they will look toward the earth and see
only distress and darkness and fearful gloom, and
they will be thrust into utter darkness.

9 ᵈ Nevertheless, there will be no more gloom
for those who were in distress. In the past
he humbled the land of Zebulun and the land of
Naphtali, but in the future he will honor Galilee
of the nations, by the Way of the Sea, beyond the
Jordan —

² The people walking in darkness
  have seen a great light;

ᵃ 8 *Immanuel* means *God with us.*   ᵇ 9 Or *Do your worst*
ᶜ 10 Hebrew *Immanuel*   ᵈ In Hebrew texts 9:1 is numbered
8:23, and 9:2-21 is numbered 9:1-20.

8:7 floodwaters of the Euphrates The coming invasion
is visualized as a flood from the Euphrates south through
Aram (Syria), Israel and Judah. The metaphor is developed
through Isa 8:6–8 until Judah is left up to her neck in
floodwaters, barely surviving the onslaught (see v. 8).
8:8 Its outspread wings Usually an image of divine
protection (see Dt 32:11; Ps 17:8), the wings here
describe the flood spread over the entire land as divine
judgment. **Immanuel** The re-use of the name "God with
us" links the judgment back to the sign of Isa 7:14 and
points ahead to the future victory of Immanuel (see
vv. 9–10; note on 7:14).
**8:11 This is what the LORD says to me with his strong
hand upon me** The prophets sometimes describe a very
tangible experience of the divine presence.
8:14 a stone that causes people to stumble Paul
quotes from this verse in Ro 9:33.

8:16 my disciples The consistency of the message and
vocabulary of Isaiah suggests that his prophecies were
preserved by disciples.
8:19 mediums and spiritists The people will turn to
magic and idol worship instead of seeking Yahweh.

9:1–7 The poetry of Isa 9:1–7 blends elements of
thanksgiving and royal psalms to emphasize the ideals
of Davidic kingship. Isaiah 11:1–9 similarly emphasizes
a future idealistic rule of a Davidic king. Later Christian
interpretation has understood both chs. 9 and 11 as
Messianic prophecies awaiting perfect fulfillment in
Christ's second coming; no historical Davidic king fits
the picture of the ideal ruler described here.

9:1 Zebulun and the land of Naphtali As the two
northernmost tribes in Israel, they would have been the
first to fall in an invasion from Mesopotamia.

on those living in the land of deep darkness
　a light has dawned.
³ You have enlarged the nation
　and increased their joy;
they rejoice before you
　as people rejoice at the harvest,
as warriors rejoice
　when dividing the plunder.
⁴ For as in the day of Midian's defeat,
　you have shattered
the yoke that burdens them,
　the bar across their shoulders,
　the rod of their oppressor.
⁵ Every warrior's boot used in battle
　and every garment rolled in blood
will be destined for burning,
　will be fuel for the fire.
⁶ For to us a child is born,
　to us a son is given,
　and the government will be on his
　　shoulders.
And he will be called
　Wonderful Counselor, Mighty God,
　Everlasting Father, Prince of Peace.
⁷ Of the greatness of his government and
　　peace
　there will be no end.
He will reign on David's throne
　and over his kingdom,
establishing and upholding it
　with justice and righteousness
from that time on and forever.
The zeal of the LORD Almighty
　will accomplish this.

The LORD's Anger Against Israel

⁸ The Lord has sent a message against Jacob;
　it will fall on Israel.

⁹ All the people will know it—
　Ephraim and the inhabitants of Samaria—
who say with pride
　and arrogance of heart,
¹⁰ "The bricks have fallen down,
　but we will rebuild with dressed stone;
the fig trees have been felled,
　but we will replace them with cedars."
¹¹ But the LORD has strengthened Rezin's foes
　　against them
　and has spurred their enemies on.
¹² Arameans from the east and Philistines from
　　the west
　have devoured Israel with open mouth.

Yet for all this, his anger is not turned away,
　his hand is still upraised.

¹³ But the people have not returned to him who
　　struck them,
　nor have they sought the LORD Almighty.
¹⁴ So the LORD will cut off from Israel both head
　　and tail,
　both palm branch and reed in a single day;
¹⁵ the elders and dignitaries are the head,
　the prophets who teach lies are the tail.
¹⁶ Those who guide this people mislead them,
　and those who are guided are led astray.
¹⁷ Therefore the Lord will take no pleasure in
　　the young men,
　nor will he pity the fatherless and widows,
for everyone is ungodly and wicked,
　every mouth speaks folly.

Yet for all this, his anger is not turned away,
　his hand is still upraised.

¹⁸ Surely wickedness burns like a fire;
　it consumes briers and thorns,

9:6 to us a son is given The promise of hope through a future Davidic king. Attempts to connect this promise to a ruler of Isaiah's day usually focus on Hezekiah, son and successor of Ahaz, the king to whom Isaiah delivered his warnings and who rejected his offer to provide a sign in 7:12. The sign provided in 7:14 and the prediction of a future ideal Davidic ruler point ultimately to the Messiah, but immediate hopes for Judah's future would have been directed at the Davidic line, continued through Hezekiah. **Wonderful Counselor, Mighty God** This list of titles or attributes for the future king includes divine titles that would be unusual if referring to a human Davidic king.

9:8—10:4 This oracle of judgment against the northern kingdom of Israel is punctuated by the repetition of the phrase about God's anger in vv. 12,17,21; and 10:4. Israel's main sin was their trust in their own power instead of seeking and trusting God.

9:9 pride and arrogance of heart Israel's pride in their own success and confidence that they will recover under their own power will be their downfall.
9:11 Rezin's foes Assyria, the power to whom Ahaz appealed for help against the alliance of Aram (also

called Syria) and Israel. Rezin was king of Aram, north of Israel, and so first to experience Assyria's invasion.
9:12 his anger is not turned away This refrain, which first occurs in 5:25, supports the increasing intensity of judgment against Israel, which will reach all levels of society.
9:13 nor have they sought the LORD Almighty Judgment was inevitable once Israel chose not to ask for Yahweh's deliverance.
9:14 in a single day God will judge Assyria in one day, just as he uses Assyria to punish Israel in one day. See 10:17.
9:17 fatherless and widows Orphans and widows are usually afforded special care and protection in Biblical law. However, the judgment is so thorough that all levels of society are affected.
9:18 in a column of smoke Yahweh's judgment comes by fire and is symbolized by a column of smoke. Isaiah also envisioned Zion covered by God's protective presence as a cloud and smoke in 4:5–6. The column of smoke symbolizes God's presence, either for protection or judgment.

it sets the forest thickets ablaze,
  so that it rolls upward in a column of
    smoke.
[19] By the wrath of the LORD Almighty
  the land will be scorched
and the people will be fuel for the fire;
  they will not spare one another.
[20] On the right they will devour,
  but still be hungry;
on the left they will eat,
  but not be satisfied.
Each will feed on the flesh of their own
    offspring [a]:
[21]   Manasseh will feed on Ephraim, and
    Ephraim on Manasseh;
  together they will turn against Judah.

Yet for all this, his anger is not turned away,
  his hand is still upraised.

10

Woe to those who make unjust laws,
  to those who issue oppressive decrees,
[2] to deprive the poor of their rights
  and withhold justice from the oppressed of
    my people,
making widows their prey
  and robbing the fatherless.
[3] What will you do on the day of reckoning,
  when disaster comes from afar?
To whom will you run for help?
  Where will you leave your riches?
[4] Nothing will remain but to cringe among the
    captives
  or fall among the slain.

Yet for all this, his anger is not turned away,
  his hand is still upraised.

God's Judgment on Assyria

[5] "Woe to the Assyrian, the rod of my anger,
  in whose hand is the club of my wrath!

[6] I send him against a godless nation,
  I dispatch him against a people who
    anger me,
to seize loot and snatch plunder,
  and to trample them down like mud in the
    streets.
[7] But this is not what he intends,
  this is not what he has in mind;
his purpose is to destroy,
  to put an end to many nations.
[8] 'Are not my commanders all kings?' he says.
[9]   'Has not Kalno fared like Carchemish?
Is not Hamath like Arpad,
  and Samaria like Damascus?
[10] As my hand seized the kingdoms of the idols,
  kingdoms whose images excelled those of
    Jerusalem and Samaria —
[11] shall I not deal with Jerusalem and her
    images
  as I dealt with Samaria and her idols?'"

[12] When the Lord has finished all his work
against Mount Zion and Jerusalem, he will say,
"I will punish the king of Assyria for the willful
pride of his heart and the haughty look in his
eyes. [13] For he says:

"'By the strength of my hand I have done
    this,
  and by my wisdom, because I have
    understanding.
I removed the boundaries of nations,
  I plundered their treasures;
like a mighty one I subdued [b] their
    kings.
[14] As one reaches into a nest,
  so my hand reached for the wealth of the
    nations;
as people gather abandoned eggs,
  so I gathered all the countries;

---

[a] 20 Or arm   [b] 13 Or treasures; / I subdued the mighty,

9:20 will feed on the flesh of their own offspring
The horrors of a drawn-out siege are used metaphorically
to depict the people turning on each other.
9:21 Manasseh will feed on Ephraim The tribes of
Manasseh and Ephraim were named after the two sons of
Joseph. The metaphor suggests a lack of unity among the
northern tribes, even as God used them to punish Judah.
10:2 to deprive the poor of their rights Refers to
the injustice of the rich and powerful exploiting the
poor and weak.
10:5 Assyrian, the rod of my anger Yahweh used Assyria to punish Israel. Victory in the ancient world was
often attributed to the superiority of one's god. Yahweh
is thus presented as truly superior—he, not Assyria's
god, is behind their success. The foreign nations are
simply tools in the hands of Yahweh. See the timeline
"Dates Related to Isaiah and 2 Kings" on p. 1116; see
the infographic "Sennacherib's Prism" on p. 597.
10:6 godless nation Israel is considered godless since
it had turned away from Yahweh.

10:8–14 Assyria's arrogance is revealed in this self-
confident speech. The king of Assyria believes his military
victories represent spiritual victories over the idols of
the cities he has conquered. He also elevates himself
to demigod status, boasting in his own strength, wisdom
and understanding.
10:8 not my commanders all kings The Assyrian Empire
turned conquered kings into subject vassals, so the king
of Assyria could rightly boast that his subject commanders
were kings in their own right. Many ancient inscriptions
from this period attest to this practice, including the
Bar-Rakib stele, where the king of Sam'al declares his
loyalty to Tiglath-Pileser, king of Assyria.
**10:9 not Hamath like Arpad, and Samaria like Damas-
cus** The king boasts over the cities he has conquered.
Each pair moves geographically closer to Israel.
10:12 Mount Zion See note on 1:8; note on 2:2. **I will
punish** Assyria will also be judged for pride and arrogance
once Israel's punishment is complete. See note on v. 5.

not one flapped a wing,
  or opened its mouth to chirp.'"

15 Does the ax raise itself above the person who
      swings it,
  or the saw boast against the one who
      uses it?
As if a rod were to wield the person who lifts
      it up,
  or a club brandish the one who is not
      wood!
16 Therefore, the Lord, the LORD Almighty,
  will send a wasting disease upon his sturdy
      warriors;
under his pomp a fire will be kindled
  like a blazing flame.
17 The Light of Israel will become a fire,
  their Holy One a flame;
in a single day it will burn and consume
  his thorns and his briers.
18 The splendor of his forests and fertile
      fields
  it will completely destroy,
  as when a sick person wastes away.
19 And the remaining trees of his forests will be
      so few
  that a child could write them down.

The Remnant of Israel

20 In that day the remnant of Israel,
  the survivors of Jacob,
will no longer rely on him
  who struck them down
but will truly rely on the LORD,
  the Holy One of Israel.
21 A remnant will return,ᵃ a remnant
      of Jacob
will return to the Mighty God.
22 Though your people be like the sand by
      the sea, Israel,
  only a remnant will return.
Destruction has been decreed,
  overwhelming and righteous.

23 The Lord, the LORD Almighty, will carry out
  the destruction decreed upon the whole
      land.

24 Therefore this is what the Lord, the LORD
Almighty, says:

  "My people who live in Zion,
      do not be afraid of the Assyrians,
  who beat you with a rod
      and lift up a club against you, as Egypt did.
25 Very soon my anger against you will end
      and my wrath will be directed to their
          destruction."

26 The LORD Almighty will lash them with a
      whip,
  as when he struck down Midian at the rock
      of Oreb;
and he will raise his staff over the waters,
  as he did in Egypt.
27 In that day their burden will be lifted from
      your shoulders,
  their yoke from your neck;
the yoke will be broken
  because you have grown so fat.ᵇ

28 They enter Aiath;
  they pass through Migron;
  they store supplies at Mikmash.
29 They go over the pass, and say,
  "We will camp overnight at Geba."
Ramah trembles;
  Gibeah of Saul flees.
30 Cry out, Daughter Gallim!
  Listen, Laishah!
  Poor Anathoth!
31 Madmenah is in flight;
  the people of Gebim take cover.
32 This day they will halt at Nob;
  they will shake their fist
at the mount of Daughter Zion,
  at the hill of Jerusalem.

ᵃ 21 Hebrew *shear-jashub* (see 7:3 and note); also in verse 22
ᵇ 27 Hebrew; Septuagint *broken / from your shoulders*

10:15 ax raise itself above the person who swings
A tool is useless on its own. Assyria is judged for not
recognizing that it is only a tool in the hand of God.
10:20 remnant of Israel Contrasts with the imagery in
v. 19, which depicts the destruction of Assyria until only
a remnant of forest remains. See note on 1:9.
10:21 A remnant will return Refers to a spiritual, not
necessarily physical, return.
10:22 like the sand by the sea The apostle Paul quotes
this verse in Ro 9:27–28.
10:24 the Assyrians This people group came from
central Mesopotamia on the Tigris River. They were the
dominant power in the ancient Near East during the
eighth and seventh centuries BC.

Isaiah 10:24

ASSYRIANS
The land of Assyria straddled the upper Tigris River. It
was almost completely surrounded by mountains: the
Zagros in the east, the Armenian in the north, the Ham-
rin Hills in the south and a low-lying ridge in the west
that separated the Assyrian heartland from the Jazira
steppe. Assyria was governed by a collection of powerful city-states, including Ashur (sometimes spelled
"Asshur"), Calah and Nineveh. The Assyrian religion
was polytheistic. Ashur, Adad, Sin, Shamash and Ishtar
were the chief deities of the Assyrian pantheon, but
Ashur was regarded as the most powerful.

33 See, the Lord, the LORD Almighty,
　　will lop off the boughs with great power.
The lofty trees will be felled,
　　the tall ones will be brought low.
34 He will cut down the forest thickets with
　　　an ax;
　　Lebanon will fall before the Mighty One.

The Branch From Jesse

11 A shoot will come up from the stump of
　　　Jesse;
　　from his roots a Branch will bear fruit.
2 The Spirit of the LORD will rest on him —
　　the Spirit of wisdom and of
　　　understanding,
　　the Spirit of counsel and of might,
　　the Spirit of the knowledge and fear of the
　　　LORD —
3 and he will delight in the fear of the LORD.

He will not judge by what he sees with his
　　　eyes,
　　or decide by what he hears with his ears;
4 but with righteousness he will judge the
　　　needy,
　　with justice he will give decisions for the
　　　poor of the earth.
He will strike the earth with the rod of his
　　　mouth;
　　with the breath of his lips he will slay the
　　　wicked.
5 Righteousness will be his belt
　　and faithfulness the sash around his waist.

6 The wolf will live with the lamb,
　　the leopard will lie down with the goat,
　　the calf and the lion and the yearling[a]
　　　together;
　　and a little child will lead them.
7 The cow will feed with the bear,
　　their young will lie down together,
　　and the lion will eat straw like the ox.
8 The infant will play near the cobra's den,
　　and the young child will put its hand into
　　　the viper's nest.
9 They will neither harm nor destroy
　　on all my holy mountain,
　　for the earth will be filled with the
　　　knowledge of the LORD
　　as the waters cover the sea.

10 In that day the Root of Jesse will stand as a
banner for the peoples; the nations will rally to
him, and his resting place will be glorious. 11 In
that day the Lord will reach out his hand a second time to reclaim the surviving remnant of
his people from Assyria, from Lower Egypt, from
Upper Egypt, from Cush,[b] from Elam, from Babylonia,[c] from Hamath and from the islands of the
Mediterranean.

12 He will raise a banner for the nations
　　and gather the exiles of Israel;
　　he will assemble the scattered people of
　　　Judah
　　from the four quarters of the earth.

---

a 6 Hebrew; Septuagint *lion will feed*　　b 11 That is, the upper
Nile region　　c 11 Hebrew *Shinar*

10:28–32 The path of the Assyrian invaders is laid out from the northeast part of Judah to the vicinity of Jerusalem. The place names are mentioned in order, drawing geographically closer and closer to the immediate vicinity of Jerusalem.

10:32 they will shake their fist at the mount Assyria gets close enough to threaten Jerusalem, but does not conquer her. **Zion** Refers to Jerusalem. See note on Isa 1:8.

10:33 will lop off the boughs with great power Assyria was metaphorically depicted as a tool in the hand of God in vv. 14–15. In vv. 33–34 that metaphor is turned about as the tool is cut down to size.

11:1–16 This passage closely connects to 2:2–4 and 9:1–7 in its depiction of the future peaceful rule of Yahweh through his ideal David-like king, the Messiah.

11:1 A shoot will come up from the stump of Jesse The stump is a metaphor for the remnant of the royal family of David. The kingly line is all but eliminated in the invasions and deportations by the Babylonians (see 6:13). The shoot is a metaphor for restoration of the line in the Messiah. Compare 53:2. **from his roots a Branch will bear fruit** The branch is again a metaphor for the Messiah. See Zec 3:8 and note.

11:2 This verse describes the characteristics of an ideal ruler (see 1Sa 16:13; Dt 1:13; 1Ki 3:9). Wisdom, understanding, knowledge and fear of Yahweh were key components of righteous living (see Pr 1:7; 2:5; Ps 14:4).

11:4 rod of his mouth The power of the Messiah is evident through his words. See Isa 49:2 and note.

11:5 Righteousness will be his belt The NT imagery of the "armor of God" in Eph 6:11–17 builds on this image of the righteousness and faithfulness clothing the Messiah, along with the image of the divine armor in Isa 59:17.

11:6 wolf will live with the lamb The predator and prey relationship is negated in vv. 6–9 to symbolize the peace of a renewed creation. This is often connected with end-times or millennial expectations, such as in Ro 8:19–22 and Rev 20:1–6. Compare Isa 2:4. **a little child will lead them** In the utopian conditions of the Messiah's rule, all dangers of the animal kingdom are removed.

11:10 Root of Jesse An allusion to the Messiah. See vv. 1; Ro 15:12. **a banner for the peoples** The image of a signal for the other nations of the world reappears in Isa 49:22 and 62:10, where the signal also indicates that the time has come for God's people to return to their land.

11:11 his hand a second time The first time was the exodus from Egypt. See Ex 13–15. **from Assyria, from Lower Egypt** The list of nations in the verse gives a sense of how widely dispersed the remnant is across the known world.

13 Ephraim's jealousy will vanish,
  and Judah's enemies[a] will be destroyed;
Ephraim will not be jealous of Judah,
  nor Judah hostile toward Ephraim.
14 They will swoop down on the slopes of
    Philistia to the west;
  together they will plunder the people to
    the east.
They will subdue Edom and Moab,
  and the Ammonites will be subject
    to them.
15 The LORD will dry up
  the gulf of the Egyptian sea;
with a scorching wind he will sweep
  his hand
  over the Euphrates River.
He will break it up into seven streams
  so that anyone can cross over in sandals.
16 There will be a highway for the remnant of
    his people
  that is left from Assyria,
as there was for Israel
  when they came up from Egypt.

Songs of Praise

12 In that day you will say:

"I will praise you, LORD.
  Although you were angry with me,
your anger has turned away
  and you have comforted me.
2 Surely God is my salvation;
  I will trust and not be afraid.

The LORD, the LORD himself, is my strength
  and my defense [b];
  he has become my salvation."
3 With joy you will draw water
  from the wells of salvation.

4 In that day you will say:

"Give praise to the LORD, proclaim
    his name;
  make known among the nations what he
    has done,
  and proclaim that his name is exalted.
5 Sing to the LORD, for he has done glorious
    things;
  let this be known to all the world.
6 Shout aloud and sing for joy, people of Zion,
  for great is the Holy One of Israel among
    you."

A Prophecy Against Babylon

13 A prophecy against Babylon that Isaiah son
of Amoz saw:

2 Raise a banner on a bare hilltop,
  shout to them;
beckon to them
  to enter the gates of the nobles.
3 I have commanded those I prepared for
    battle;
  I have summoned my warriors to carry out
    my wrath —
  those who rejoice in my triumph.

---

[a] 13 Or hostility   [b] 2 Or song

11:12 He will raise a banner for the nations The signal notifies the nations that it is time to bring Israel back to her homeland. See Isa 11:10 and note.
11:13 Ephraim will not be jealous of Judah Israel and Judah will be reunited.
11:15 will dry up the gulf of the Egyptian sea Echoes the miracle of the parting of the Red Sea in Ex 14:15–29, where Israel crosses on dry ground.
11:16 a highway Illustrates the easy path Israel should have once God restores them. Compare to Isa 35:8–10; 40:3.

12:1–6 Verses 1–6 are a thanksgiving song indicating the people's change of attitude toward Yahweh after the judgment and restoration of the remnant. The formulaic language is similar to many psalms; it includes phrases reminiscent of Ps 46:5; 98:1; 105:1; and 118:14.

12:1 I will praise you, LORD Reflects elements of praise hymns and thanksgiving songs found in the book of Psalms. The first-person address is typical of thanksgiving songs that reflect an individual's grateful response to God for his deliverance.
12:2 Surely God is my salvation Isaiah 12 praises God for the salvation promised through the Messiah in ch. 11. The hymn in Ex 15:1–18 similarly focuses on salvation brought about by Yahweh. The poetic parallels of Isa 12 and Ex 15 suggest a connection between the deliverance promised in Isaiah, and the deliverance

already accomplished through the exodus. The exodus motif appears prominently in Isa 40–55 where the return of the exiles from Babylon is envisioned as a second miraculous redemption—like the exodus. **LORD, the LORD himself** The Hebrew name for God here—literally Yah Yahweh—is unusual. The shortened form "Yah" is common in poetry and is used in Ex 15:2 in addition to numerous psalms.

12:4 Give praise to the LORD Psalm 105:1 reflects this same poetic formula: Give thanks to Yahweh, call on his name, and make known his deeds among the people. The poetry of Isaiah reflects a level of exalted style rarely matched in the OT outside of the book of Psalms.
12:6 great is the Holy One of Israel among you Psalm 46:4–5 similarly declares that God is in the midst of Zion and will bring joy and salvation to the city.
13:1 A prophecy against Babylon This heading begins a series of prophecies directed against the nations (Isa 13–27). The peoples of the earth will one day recognize Yahweh's sovereignty and be held accountable to him for their actions. Similar prophecies against the nations are common in other prophetic books. See the table "Oracles Against the Nations" on p. 1244.
13:2 Raise a banner on a bare hilltop A banner is used as a signal to gather the army through which Yahweh will bring judgment on Babylon. See vv. 4, 17.
13:3 those I prepared for battle The Hebrew word here comes from the verb qadash, which describes setting

⁴Listen, a noise on the mountains,
  like that of a great multitude!
Listen, an uproar among the kingdoms,
  like nations massing together!
The Lord Almighty is mustering
  an army for war.
⁵They come from faraway lands,
  from the ends of the heavens—
the Lord and the weapons of his wrath—
  to destroy the whole country.

⁶Wail, for the day of the Lord is near;
  it will come like destruction from the
    Almighty.ᵃ
⁷Because of this, all hands will go limp,
  every heart will melt with fear.
⁸Terror will seize them,
  pain and anguish will grip them;
  they will writhe like a woman in labor.
They will look aghast at each other,
  their faces aflame.

⁹See, the day of the Lord is coming
  —a cruel day, with wrath and fierce
    anger—
to make the land desolate
  and destroy the sinners within it.
¹⁰The stars of heaven and their constellations
  will not show their light.
The rising sun will be darkened
  and the moon will not give its light.
¹¹I will punish the world for its evil,
  the wicked for their sins.
I will put an end to the arrogance of the
    haughty
  and will humble the pride of the
    ruthless.
¹²I will make people scarcer than pure gold,
  more rare than the gold of Ophir.

¹³Therefore I will make the heavens tremble;
  and the earth will shake from its place
at the wrath of the Lord Almighty,
  in the day of his burning anger.

¹⁴Like a hunted gazelle,
  like sheep without a shepherd,
they will all return to their own people,
  they will flee to their native land.
¹⁵Whoever is captured will be thrust through;
  all who are caught will fall by the sword.
¹⁶Their infants will be dashed to pieces before
    their eyes;
  their houses will be looted and their wives
    violated.

¹⁷See, I will stir up against them the Medes,
  who do not care for silver
  and have no delight in gold.
¹⁸Their bows will strike down the young men;
  they will have no mercy on infants,
  nor will they look with compassion on
    children.
¹⁹Babylon, the jewel of kingdoms,
  the pride and glory of the Babylonians,ᵇ
will be overthrown by God
  like Sodom and Gomorrah.
²⁰She will never be inhabited
  or lived in through all generations;
there no nomads will pitch their tents,
  there no shepherds will rest their flocks.
²¹But desert creatures will lie there,
  jackals will fill her houses;
there the owls will dwell,
  and there the wild goats will leap about.
²²Hyenas will inhabit her strongholds,
  jackals her luxurious palaces.

ᵃ 6 Hebrew *Shaddai*   ᵇ 19 Or *Chaldeans*

---

apart for a specific use. Its appearance here indicates that this non-Israelite army—as the instrument of Yahweh's judgment—is set apart for a divine purpose.

13:4 nations massing together The army assembling against Babylon will consist of multiple nations and kingdoms. The empire that overthrew Babylon in 539 BC was a combination of the Medes and the Persians.

Lord Almighty is mustering an army Yahweh even commands foreign armies. The Assyrian commander acknowledges that they were directed by Yahweh to punish Israel and Judah in 36:10, though this acknowledgement may simply be rhetorical.

13:6 the day of the Lord is near The day of God's judgment takes several forms throughout the OT. It finds partial fulfillment in the divinely ordained destructions of 722 BC and 586 BC, which are likely most pertinent here. References to the day of Yahweh can also have an apocalyptic or eschatological orientation, referring to the end of time.

13:10 will not show their light God rules even over the stars, constellations, sun and moon—all of which played an important role in ancient religious practices, especially as divine signs or omens.

13:11 I will punish the world The imagery of judgment alternates between a localized punishment of a particular nation (i.e., Babylon) and a global punishment of all evil. The prophecies in ch. 23 also mix this imagery of punishment against the nations and destruction against the entire world. Chapters 24–27 then contains images of global destruction, which are comparable to vv. 11–13.

13:13 I will make the heavens tremble The coming of Yahweh was often accompanied by cosmic upheaval: The earth shakes, and the heavens tremble. A manifestation of God's presence (or theophany) was often accompanied by imagery like this (see 2Sa 22:8; Job 26:11; Joel 2:10).

13:15 will be thrust through The invaders will take no prisoners or leave any alive—not even the women and children, who are often claimed as spoils of war.

13:17 the Medes The Medo-Persian Empire conquered Babylon in 539 BC. See Da 5:30–31.

13:20 She will never be inhabited Babylon never regained its position of prominence in the ancient world after 539 BC. See Jer 50:39–40.

13:21 desert creatures will lie there The undoing of human civilization and return to a state of wilderness is

Her time is at hand,
 and her days will not be prolonged.

14 The Lord will have compassion on Jacob;
 once again he will choose Israel
and will settle them in their own land.
Foreigners will join them
 and unite with the descendants of Jacob.
² Nations will take them
 and bring them to their own place.
And Israel will take possession of the nations
 and make them male and female servants
 in the Lord's land.
They will make captives of their captors
 and rule over their oppressors.

³ On the day the Lord gives you relief from your
suffering and turmoil and from the harsh labor
forced on you, ⁴ you will take up this taunt against
the king of Babylon:

How the oppressor has come to an end!
 How his fury*ᵃ* has ended!
⁵ The Lord has broken the rod of the wicked,
 the scepter of the rulers,
⁶ which in anger struck down peoples
 with unceasing blows,
and in fury subdued nations
 with relentless aggression.
⁷ All the lands are at rest and at peace;
 they break into singing.

⁸ Even the junipers and the cedars of Lebanon
 gloat over you and say,
"Now that you have been laid low,
 no one comes to cut us down."

⁹ The realm of the dead below is all astir
 to meet you at your coming;
it rouses the spirits of the departed to greet
 you —
all those who were leaders in the world;
it makes them rise from their thrones —
 all those who were kings over the nations.
¹⁰ They will all respond,
 they will say to you,
"You also have become weak, as we are;
 you have become like us."
¹¹ All your pomp has been brought down to the
 grave,
 along with the noise of your harps;
maggots are spread out beneath you
 and worms cover you.

¹² How you have fallen from heaven,
 morning star, son of the dawn!
You have been cast down to the earth,
 you who once laid low the nations!
¹³ You said in your heart,
 "I will ascend to the heavens;

ᵃ 4 Dead Sea Scrolls, Septuagint and Syriac; the meaning of the word in the Masoretic Text is uncertain.

a popular image in Isaiah for what will follow the coming day of Yahweh. Compare Isa 34:11–15.

14:1–2 Following the oracle of destruction against Babylon and the world at large in ch. 13, this short section reiterates God's promises of restoration following his judgment. The chapter continues with poetic pronouncements of doom against Babylon, Assyria and Philistia. Cosmic imagery is mixed in; the account in vv. 12–15 is often thought to describe Satan's fall from heaven.

14:1 their own land Possession of the land was a key part of the covenant between God and Israel. If Israel was obedient, they would continue to possess the land. However, disobedience would lead to exile. See Dt 4:1; 28.
14:2 Israel will take possession of the nations The restored house of Israel will take a preeminent place among the cultures of the world.
14:3 harsh labor The same phrase is used in Ex 1:14 to describe the Israelites' slavery in Egypt. Israel's restoration is envisioned in Isaiah as a second exodus.
14:4 this taunt The Hebrew word here denotes a proverb. It can also carry the sense of a mocking song, such as in Jer 24:9; Mic 2:4; and Hab 2:6, where the taunt is also directed at the Babylonians. **the king of Babylon** Babylon is the future oppressor of Judah. The eventual fall of Jerusalem and the exile to Babylon is foreshadowed throughout the book of Isaiah; the envisioned restoration focuses on a return from exile. See the timeline "Dates Related to Isaiah and 2 Kings" on p. 1116.
14:8 cedars of Lebanon The region of Lebanon was famous for abundance and natural beauty, which centered on the highly prized cedars in great demand as building

materials. In 2Ki 19:23, the king of Assyria is said to have boasted over his victory, cutting down the cedars and cypresses (or junipers) of the forest. This standard boast is inverted here, where the cedars boast that no one comes to cut them down.
14:9 realm of the dead below is all astir The underworld welcomes the now-fallen king. **the spirits of the departed** The Hebrew term *repha'im* ("shades") refers to the dead in their shadowy existence in the afterlife (compare Ps 88:10).
14:12 morning star This Hebrew word referring to Venus as the morning star is translated into Latin as "Lucifer," which later made its way into some English translations. **son of the dawn** The human king is mocked for his arrogance in believing himself to be like one of the gods. The Hebrew word *shachar* ("dawn") is known from Canaanite mythology as the name of a deity. Ezekiel uses similar imagery in his lament over the king of Tyre (see Eze 28).
14:13 I will ascend to the heavens The king of Babylon's arrogance reflects the same pride as the people who built the tower of Babel (Ge 11:4). See the infographic "The Tower of Babel" on p. 29. **above the stars of God** This phrase describes heavenly beings (see Job 38:7–8 and note). In this verse it serves to identify the pride of both the king of Babylon and the original divine being whose story serves as the backdrop. **the utmost heights of Mount Zaphon** Canaanite mythology depicted a northern mountain as the seat of the gods. The sacred mountain was called Zaphon—the same as the Hebrew word for north. Hebrew poetry often uses similar imagery to Canaanite poetry, but in a

I will raise my throne
    above the stars of God;
I will sit enthroned on the mount of
    assembly,
    on the utmost heights of Mount Zaphon.[a]
[14] I will ascend above the tops of the clouds;
    I will make myself like the Most High."
[15] But you are brought down to the realm of the
    dead,
    to the depths of the pit.

[16] Those who see you stare at you,
    they ponder your fate:
"Is this the man who shook the earth
    and made kingdoms tremble,
[17] the man who made the world a wilderness,
    who overthrew its cities
    and would not let his captives go home?"

[18] All the kings of the nations lie in state,
    each in his own tomb.
[19] But you are cast out of your tomb
    like a rejected branch;
you are covered with the slain,
    with those pierced by the sword,
    those who descend to the stones of the pit.
Like a corpse trampled underfoot,
[20]   you will not join them in burial,
for you have destroyed your land
    and killed your people.

Let the offspring of the wicked
    never be mentioned again.
[21] Prepare a place to slaughter his children
    for the sins of their ancestors;
they are not to rise to inherit the land
    and cover the earth with their cities.

[22] "I will rise up against them,"
    declares the LORD Almighty.
"I will wipe out Babylon's name and
    survivors,
    her offspring and descendants,"
            declares the LORD.

[23] "I will turn her into a place for owls
    and into swampland;
I will sweep her with the broom of
    destruction,"
    declares the LORD Almighty.

[24] The LORD Almighty has sworn,

"Surely, as I have planned, so it will be,
    and as I have purposed, so it will happen.
[25] I will crush the Assyrian in my land;
    on my mountains I will trample him down.
His yoke will be taken from my people,
    and his burden removed from their
    shoulders."

[26] This is the plan determined for the whole
    world;
    this is the hand stretched out over all
    nations.
[27] For the LORD Almighty has purposed, and
    who can thwart him?
    His hand is stretched out, and who can
    turn it back?

A Prophecy Against the Philistines

[28] This prophecy came in the year King Ahaz
died:

[29] Do not rejoice, all you Philistines,
    that the rod that struck you is broken;
from the root of that snake will spring up a
    viper,
    its fruit will be a darting, venomous
    serpent.
[30] The poorest of the poor will find pasture,
    and the needy will lie down in safety.
But your root I will destroy by famine;
    it will slay your survivors.

[31] Wail, you gate! Howl, you city!
    Melt away, all you Philistines!

[a] 13 Or *of the north*; Zaphon was the most sacred mountain of
the Canaanites.

---

polemical way. For example, in Ps 48:1–2, Yahweh's holy mountain—Zion—is said to be in the far north (that is, Zaphon). Since Zion is actually located in the southern part of Israel, the identification with Zaphon should be understood as an intentional move to assert Yahweh's superiority over Canaanite gods.

14:21 to inherit the land A similar concern is expressed in Ge 11:6 before God confounds the speech of those building the Tower of Babel.

14:22 name and survivors In contrast to God's promise to preserve a remnant for Israel, no remnant will be preserved for Babylon.

14:25 I will crush the Assyrian in my land This pronouncement of judgment against Assyria is similar to that found in Isa 10:12–19. Assyria turns back before conquering Jerusalem. See the infographic "Sennacherib's Prism" on p. 597.

14:28 in the year King Ahaz died About 715 BC. Isaiah's prophetic ministry covered parts of the reigns of four kings of Judah. See 1:1.

14:29 the rod that struck you is broken May refer to the Davidic dynasty that had asserted dominance over the Philistines. The rod could also refer to Assyria (see 10:5,24): Sargon II made Philistia into an Assyrian province in 711 BC. **will be a darting, venomous serpent** The singular of the Hebrew term used to describe the heavenly beings in 6:2 (seraphim). This reference is likely a metaphor for a coming Assyrian king. Tiglath-Pileser had brought Philistia under Assyrian control in 734 BC. His successors, Sargon II and Sennacherib, both suppressed rebellions in Philistia in 720, 712 and 701 BC.

14:30 it will slay your survivors Only Israel is promised a remnant. See v. 22.

A cloud of smoke comes from the north,
    and there is not a straggler in its ranks.
³² What answer shall be given
    to the envoys of that nation?
"The Lord has established Zion,
    and in her his afflicted people will find
        refuge."

A Prophecy Against Moab

16:6-12pp — Jer 48:29-36

15 A prophecy against Moab:

Ar in Moab is ruined,
    destroyed in a night!
Kir in Moab is ruined,
    destroyed in a night!
² Dibon goes up to its temple,
    to its high places to weep;
Moab wails over Nebo and Medeba.
Every head is shaved
    and every beard cut off.
³ In the streets they wear sackcloth;
    on the roofs and in the public squares
they all wail,
    prostrate with weeping.
⁴ Heshbon and Elealeh cry out,
    their voices are heard all the way to Jahaz.
Therefore the armed men of Moab cry out,
    and their hearts are faint.
⁵ My heart cries out over Moab;
    her fugitives flee as far as Zoar,
    as far as Eglath Shelishiyah.

They go up the hill to Luhith,
    weeping as they go;
on the road to Horonaim
    they lament their destruction.
⁶ The waters of Nimrim are dried up
    and the grass is withered;
the vegetation is gone
    and nothing green is left.
⁷ So the wealth they have acquired and
        stored up
    they carry away over the Ravine of the
        Poplars.
⁸ Their outcry echoes along the border of
        Moab;
    their wailing reaches as far as Eglaim,
    their lamentation as far as Beer Elim.
⁹ The waters of Dimon*ᵃ* are full of blood,
    but I will bring still more upon Dimon*ᵃ* —
a lion upon the fugitives of Moab
    and upon those who remain in the land.

16 Send lambs as tribute
    to the ruler of the land,
from Sela, across the desert,
    to the mount of Daughter Zion.
² Like fluttering birds
    pushed from the nest,
so are the women of Moab
    at the fords of the Arnon.

³ "Make up your mind," Moab says.
    "Render a decision.

ᵃ 9 Dimon, a wordplay on Dibon (see verse 2), sounds like the Hebrew for blood.

14:32 his afflicted people will find refuge The oracle against the Philistines ends with an assurance of protection from Zion.

15:1 — 16:14 Unlike most of the other oracles against the nations, which gloat over their eventual downfall, this oracle about Moab is sympathetic. In 15:5 and 16:9–11, Yahweh laments over the misfortune of Moab. Still, the same sin of pride and arrogance requires judgment. Jeremiah offers a similar prophecy against Moab in Jer 48.

15:1 A prophecy against Moab In many oracles against the nations, a heading like this indicates a specific recipient (see Isa 13:1). See the table "Oracles Against the Nations" on p. 1244. **Ar in Moab is ruined** The northern cities of Moab are destroyed; the southern cities are depicted mourning over the loss, while fugitives flee southward.

MOAB
Moab was Israel and Judah's neighbor to the east across the Jordan River. Many of the northern Moabite cities described in this passage were once possessed by Israel. Several of them—such as Heshbon and Elealeh—were built by Israelites (Nu 32:37). When Israel

and Judah were strong, they dominated and controlled this area of the Transjordan. During Isaiah's day, Moab—along with all the other countries in the region—was subject to Assyrian invasion.

15:2 high places The temple and high places indicate sites of worship for Chemosh, the god of Moab. He is mentioned in 1Ki 11:7,33 as one of the foreign deities whose worship was promoted in Israel. The deity is mentioned outside the Bible in an inscription attributed to Mesha, king of Moab (see 2Ki 3:4–5). See the infographic "The Mesha Stele" on p. 565.

15:5 on the road to Horonaim The fugitives are fleeing from the destroyed northern cities and heading south.

15:6 waters of Nimrim Likely refers to a stream running along the southwest edge of the Moabite plateau and into the Dead Sea, modern Seil en Numera.

15:7 the wealth they have acquired and stored up they carry away The wealth and supplies of the kingdom are carried off as spoils of war.

15:9 a lion upon the fugitives of Moab The few who escape the invaders will have to contend with an untamed wilderness, where even the beasts are under God's command to destroy them in judgment.

16:1 Send lambs Moab, in distress, sends a gift to Judah along with a request for asylum.

16:2 at the fords of the Arnon The Arnon River, the primary river in the region, formed a large canyon that created a natural boundary for Moab. It would have

Make your shadow like night —
    at high noon.
Hide the fugitives,
    do not betray the refugees.
⁴ Let the Moabite fugitives stay with you;
    be their shelter from the destroyer."

The oppressor will come to an end,
    and destruction will cease;
    the aggressor will vanish from
      the land.
⁵ In love a throne will be established;
    in faithfulness a man will sit on it —
    one from the house*ᵃ* of David —
one who in judging seeks justice
    and speeds the cause of righteousness.

⁶ We have heard of Moab's pride —
    how great is her arrogance! —
of her conceit, her pride and her insolence;
    but her boasts are empty.
⁷ Therefore the Moabites wail,
    they wail together for Moab.
Lament and grieve
    for the raisin cakes of Kir Hareseth.
⁸ The fields of Heshbon wither,
    the vines of Sibmah also.
The rulers of the nations
    have trampled down the choicest
      vines,
which once reached Jazer
    and spread toward the desert.
Their shoots spread out
    and went as far as the sea.*ᵇ*
⁹ So I weep, as Jazer weeps,
    for the vines of Sibmah.

Heshbon and Elealeh,
    I drench you with tears!
The shouts of joy over your ripened
      fruit
    and over your harvests have been
      stilled.
¹⁰ Joy and gladness are taken away from
      the orchards;
    no one sings or shouts in the vineyards;
no one treads out wine at the presses,
    for I have put an end to the shouting.
¹¹ My heart laments for Moab like a harp,
    my inmost being for Kir Hareseth.
¹² When Moab appears at her high place,
    she only wears herself out;
when she goes to her shrine to pray,
    it is to no avail.

¹³ This is the word the Lᴏʀᴅ has already spoken concerning Moab. ¹⁴ But now the Lᴏʀᴅ says: "Within three years, as a servant bound by contract would count them, Moab's splendor and all her many people will be despised, and her survivors will be very few and feeble."

A Prophecy Against Damascus

17 A prophecy against Damascus:

"See, Damascus will no longer be a city
    but will become a heap of ruins.
² The cities of Aroer will be deserted
    and left to flocks, which will lie down,
    with no one to make them afraid.

ᵃ 5 Hebrew *tent*   *ᵇ* 8 Probably the Dead Sea

---

presented a difficult obstacle for fleeing refugees to bypass. See the infographic "The Mesha Stele" on p. 565.
16:3 Make up your mind The daughters of Moab appeal to standards of social justice in requesting protection in Zion.
16:4 Let the Moabite fugitives stay with you In the book of Ruth, a family from Judah sojourns in Moab during a famine (see Ru 1:1–4). In 1Sa 22:3, David leaves his parents with the king of Moab. As distant relatives, the Moabite refugees may have expected a reciprocal welcome.
16:8 fields of Heshbon wither Focuses on the physical and economic ruin of the northern part of Moab. Heshbon was a city near the northern border of Moab. Sibmah was likely in the same general region as Heshbon. **rulers of the nations** The oracle never explicitly identifies the invaders, which allows the prophecy to be applicable in future eras.
16:9 I weep, as Jazer weeps Yahweh empathizes with Moab in Isa 16:9–11, even though he is responsible for bringing the destruction (v. 10). See 15:5. **Jazer** A city north of Heshbon.
16:11 My heart The Hebrew term here refers to the belly, which is associated with emotions in Hebrew. Translations may render it as "heart," the part of the body associated with emotions in English.

16:12 at her high place, she only wears herself out The lament over Moab begins and ends with a thematic inclusio (a bracketing by repetition) focused on the futility of worshiping any gods but Yahweh. See 15:1–2.
16:13 is the word the Lᴏʀᴅ has already spoken A short prose appendix is added to what was expressed poetically. The introductory phrase marks this as new and more immediately relevant information.
16:14 Within three years Moab's destruction is imminent and will occur in a few years' time. This may refer to the Assyrian campaigns that came around 715 BC.

17:1–14 This oracle — which focuses on Damascus, the capital of Aram (also called Syria) — recalls the crisis of chs. 7–8 (ca. 735 BC), where Aram and Israel jointly rebelled against Assyria and besieged Judah in an attempt to force them into their alliance. The overlapping imagery connecting Israel and Aram, and at times portraying Aram as almost part of Israel itself, is likely meant to emphasize the intertwined nature of these two powers at this time due to their alliance.

17:2 cities of Aroer A common place name. One town named Aroer was located on the border of Moab with Ammon (Dt 2:36; Jos 13:16). This context might indicate that another Aroer may have been located near Damascus. See the table "Parallelism in Hebrew Poetry" on p. 1008.

3 The fortified city will disappear from
    Ephraim,
  and royal power from Damascus;
the remnant of Aram will be
  like the glory of the Israelites,"
               declares the LORD Almighty.

4 "In that day the glory of Jacob will fade;
  the fat of his body will waste away.
5 It will be as when reapers harvest the
    standing grain,
  gathering the grain in their arms —
as when someone gleans heads of grain
  in the Valley of Rephaim.
6 Yet some gleanings will remain,
  as when an olive tree is beaten,
leaving two or three olives on the topmost
    branches,
  four or five on the fruitful boughs,"
        declares the LORD, the God of Israel.

7 In that day people will look to their Maker
  and turn their eyes to the Holy One of
    Israel.
8 They will not look to the altars,
  the work of their hands,
and they will have no regard for the Asherah
  poles[a]
and the incense altars their fingers have
  made.

9 In that day their strong cities, which they left because of the Israelites, will be like places abandoned to thickets and undergrowth. And all will be desolation.

10 You have forgotten God your Savior;
  you have not remembered the Rock, your
    fortress.
Therefore, though you set out the finest plants
  and plant imported vines,

11 though on the day you set them out, you
    make them grow,
  and on the morning when you plant them,
    you bring them to bud,
yet the harvest will be as nothing
  in the day of disease and incurable pain.

12 Woe to the many nations that rage —
  they rage like the raging sea!
Woe to the peoples who roar —
  they roar like the roaring of great waters!
13 Although the peoples roar like the roar of
    surging waters,
  when he rebukes them they flee far away,
driven before the wind like chaff on the hills,
  like tumbleweed before a gale.
14 In the evening, sudden terror!
  Before the morning, they are gone!
This is the portion of those who loot us,
  the lot of those who plunder us.

A Prophecy Against Cush

18 Woe to the land of whirring wings[b]
    along the rivers of Cush,[c]
2 which sends envoys by sea
  in papyrus boats over the water.

Go, swift messengers,
to a people tall and smooth-skinned,
  to a people feared far and wide,
an aggressive nation of strange speech,
  whose land is divided by rivers.

3 All you people of the world,
  you who live on the earth,
when a banner is raised on the mountains,
  you will see it,

---

a 8 That is, wooden symbols of the goddess Asherah   b 1 Or of locusts   c 1 That is, the upper Nile region

---

17:3 will disappear from Ephraim Following the initial pronouncement against Damascus, Israel and Aram (Syria) are blurred together. Ephraim was commonly used to refer to the entire northern kingdom of Israel. **the remnant of Aram** Allied in rebellion, the remnant of Aram (Syria) will receive the same fate as Israel. **declares the LORD Almighty** This formula often concluded a prophetic oracle — giving the sense that the oracle against Damascus is complete and has ended with a glimmer of hope.
17:4 In that day the glory of Jacob will fade The "glory" appeared to be a positive attribute in Isa 17:3, but is now revealed to be a representation of their pride.
17:6 some gleanings will remain, as when an olive tree is beaten An allusion to the remnant of Israel, similar to 24:13.
17:8 Asherah poles Wooden poles erected to worship the Canaanite goddess Asherah, possibly representing sacred trees or groves.
17:10 You have forgotten God your Savior When Israel trusted God, he gave them victory. Perhaps meant to recall the conquest successes.

17:12 roaring of great waters A combination of images in vv. 12–14 presents the nations initially as instruments of God's wrath (compare 13:3) — harbingers of watery chaos. It quickly inverts that image with an oracle of supernatural salvation reminiscent of God's actions on behalf of Israel in the exodus (see Ex 14) and the conquest of the promised land (e.g., Jos 6).
17:14 the portion of those who loot us The oracles against the nations were likely intended to give Judah hope in the midst of destruction and chaos.

18:1–7 Though no heading indicates a shift (compare Isa 17:1), the focus moves to an oracle against Cush (also called "Ethiopia"). The oracle describes a distant land desperately sending out envoys to find allies. See the table "Oracles Against the Nations" on p. 1244.
18:1 Woe This Hebrew interjection expresses pity, sympathy or disappointment. **rivers of Cush** The Hebrew name here "Cush" (*kush*) is used in the OT to designate a region of East Africa that likely included southern Egypt and northern Sudan. The rivers may be the headwaters of the Nile. The Greek Septuagint used "Ethiopia" to translate

and when a trumpet sounds,
  you will hear it.
⁴ This is what the LORD says to me:
  "I will remain quiet and will look on from
    my dwelling place,
  like shimmering heat in the sunshine,
  like a cloud of dew in the heat of harvest."
⁵ For, before the harvest, when the blossom is
    gone
  and the flower becomes a ripening
    grape,
  he will cut off the shoots with pruning
    knives,
  and cut down and take away the spreading
    branches.
⁶ They will all be left to the mountain birds of
    prey
  and to the wild animals;
  the birds will feed on them all summer,
  the wild animals all winter.

⁷ At that time gifts will be brought to the LORD
Almighty

from a people tall and smooth-skinned,
  from a people feared far and wide,
an aggressive nation of strange speech,
  whose land is divided by rivers —

the gifts will be brought to Mount Zion, the place
of the Name of the LORD Almighty.

A Prophecy Against Egypt

19 A prophecy against Egypt:

See, the LORD rides on a swift cloud
  and is coming to Egypt.

The idols of Egypt tremble before him,
  and the hearts of the Egyptians melt with
    fear.

² "I will stir up Egyptian against Egyptian —
  brother will fight against brother,
  neighbor against neighbor,
  city against city,
  kingdom against kingdom.
³ The Egyptians will lose heart,
  and I will bring their plans to nothing;
  they will consult the idols and the spirits of
    the dead,
  the mediums and the spiritists.
⁴ I will hand the Egyptians over
  to the power of a cruel master,
  and a fierce king will rule over them,"
  declares the Lord, the LORD Almighty.

⁵ The waters of the river will dry up,
  and the riverbed will be parched and dry.
⁶ The canals will stink;
  the streams of Egypt will dwindle and
    dry up.
The reeds and rushes will wither,
⁷ also the plants along the Nile,
  at the mouth of the river.
Every sown field along the Nile
  will become parched, will blow away and
    be no more.
⁸ The fishermen will groan and lament,
  all who cast hooks into the Nile;
  those who throw nets on the water
  will pine away.
⁹ Those who work with combed flax will
    despair,
  the weavers of fine linen will lose hope.

Hebrew "Cush," as do some modern translations. The
Biblical region was further north than modern Ethiopia.
18:2 swift messengers The mission is urgent—the
messengers are traveling light and fast on the papyrus
boats.
18:5 he will cut off the shoots The judgment is likened
to a premature harvest. See 17:5–6.
18:6 birds will feed on them all summer Reveals
that death is behind the harvest metaphor; the dead
will become carrion for wild animals.
18:7 gifts will be brought Along with the other nations,
the unknown superpower to whom the ambassadors fled
will one day bring tribute to Yahweh (see 2:2–4; 11:12).
Since tribute payment was a symbol of subjugation and
surrender, the nations ultimately acknowledge Yahweh's
sovereignty by bringing him tribute
19:1 A prophecy against Egypt A typical heading
for oracles against the nations (see 13:1; 15:1; 17:1;
21:1,11,13; 22:1; 23:1). See the table "Oracles Against
the Nations" on p. 1244. **LORD rides on a swift cloud**
The image of Yahweh riding on a cloud is a stock poetic
motif also found in Ugaritic literature, where the god Baal
is called the "rider of the clouds." The Biblical writers
assert Yahweh's superiority over Baal by appropriating
Baal's titles and storm-god imagery.

EGYPTIANS
Egypt is sometimes identified as the land of Ham in the
OT (Ps 78:51; 105:23,27; 106:22). It is located at the
northeastern tip of Africa, forming a land bridge to the
continent of Asia. The Nile River is the defining feature
of Egypt. Because the Nile flows from south to north,
southern Egypt is known as Upper Egypt, while northern
Egypt is known as Lower Egypt.

Ra, the sun god, was the chief god of the ancient
Egyptians. However, many other gods were routinely
worshiped, including Osiris, god of the Nile, and Isis,
goddess of children. A significant aspect of Egyptian
religion was that the pharaoh was considered a god.

19:3 consult the idols and the spirits of the dead
When the traditional counsel fails, the Egyptians will
seek out supernatural advice from every possible source.
19:4 I will hand the Egyptians over While Egypt is
weakened by internal conflict, they will fall to a strong
foreign power. Assyria invaded Egypt under Esarhaddon

¹⁰ The workers in cloth will be dejected,
  and all the wage earners will be sick at
    heart.

¹¹ The officials of Zoan are nothing but fools;
  the wise counselors of Pharaoh give
    senseless advice.
How can you say to Pharaoh,
  "I am one of the wise men,
  a disciple of the ancient kings"?

¹² Where are your wise men now?
  Let them show you and make known
what the Lord Almighty
  has planned against Egypt.
¹³ The officials of Zoan have become fools,
  the leaders of Memphis are deceived;
  the cornerstones of her peoples
  have led Egypt astray.
¹⁴ The Lord has poured into them
  a spirit of dizziness;
they make Egypt stagger in all that she does,
  as a drunkard staggers around in his
    vomit.
¹⁵ There is nothing Egypt can do —
  head or tail, palm branch or reed.

¹⁶ In that day the Egyptians will become weaklings. They will shudder with fear at the uplifted hand that the Lord Almighty raises against them. ¹⁷ And the land of Judah will bring terror to the Egyptians; everyone to whom Judah is mentioned will be terrified, because of what the Lord Almighty is planning against them.

¹⁸ In that day five cities in Egypt will speak the language of Canaan and swear allegiance to the Lord Almighty. One of them will be called the City of the Sun.ᵃ

¹⁹ In that day there will be an altar to the Lord in the heart of Egypt, and a monument to the Lord at its border. ²⁰ It will be a sign and witness to the Lord Almighty in the land of Egypt. When they cry out to the Lord because of their oppressors, he will send them a savior and defender, and he will rescue them. ²¹ So the Lord will make himself known to the Egyptians, and in that day they will acknowledge the Lord. They will worship with sacrifices and grain offerings; they will make vows to the Lord and keep them. ²² The Lord will strike Egypt with a plague; he will strike them and heal them. They will turn to the Lord, and he will respond to their pleas and heal them.

²³ In that day there will be a highway from Egypt to Assyria. The Assyrians will go to Egypt and the Egyptians to Assyria. The Egyptians and Assyrians will worship together. ²⁴ In that day Israel will be the third, along with Egypt and Assyria, a blessingᵇ on the earth. ²⁵ The Lord Almighty will bless

ᵃ 18 Some manuscripts of the Masoretic Text, Dead Sea Scrolls, Symmachus and Vulgate; most manuscripts of the Masoretic Text *City of Destruction*   ᵇ 24 Or *Assyria, whose names will be used in blessings* (see Gen. 48:20); or *Assyria, who will be seen by others as blessed*

---

in the seventh century BC and subjugated the Egyptians for a short time.

19:6 will dwindle and dry up Without the flooding of the Nile, Egypt would quickly revert to a harsh, uninhabitable desert.

19:11 Zoan Capital of Egypt during the time of the Israelite monarchy—until ca. 725 BC. The city was located in the northern delta region. Egypt was renowned in the ancient world for its wisdom teaching. Outside of the Bible, ancient Egypt provides the most Wisdom literature from the ancient Near East.

19:13 Memphis The city of Memphis, called Noph in Hebrew, was a prominent political and religious center for northern Egypt.

19:15 head or tail, palm branch or reed The same sequence is found in 9:14–15; the metaphor represents the political and religious elite.

19:16–25 This passage—punctuated by the sixfold repetition of "in that day"—contains another prophetic announcement of the coming day of Yahweh. Fear turns to repentance and repentance to deliverance with the startling adoption of Egypt and Assyria into Yahweh's chosen people.

19:16 Egyptians will become weaklings The previous oracle in vv. 1–15 relentlessly mocked the Egyptians for their reliance on sources of power that will ultimately prove worthless when Yahweh comes in judgment. The insult invokes gender stereotypes to call into question Egypt's confidence in their military strength (compare Na 3:13; Jer 50:37; Jer 51:30).

19:18 five cities in Egypt The worship of Yahweh will spread from five cities to the entire land of Egypt—it will even include Assyria, symbolizing its spread to the entire world. Jeremiah 44:1 mentions four cities inhabited by Jewish refugees. **speak the language of Canaan** Possibly symbolizes the future prestige of Israel in that the Egyptians—who were prejudiced against Canaanites—will be speaking a Canaanite language.

19:19 in the heart of Egypt Worship of Yahweh was not bound to the land of Israel. At least two Jewish temples were built in Egypt during the exilic period and later. The Jewish colony at Elephantine in southern Egypt had a temple. Many documents have been preserved from the colony detailing political, religious, civil and economic issues in the fifth century BC.

19:21 they will acknowledge the Lord A continuation of the theme that all the nations will one day worship Yahweh and acknowledge him as the true God (see Isa 2:2–4).

19:22 he will strike them and heal them The striking was evident in the first half of the oracle (vv. 1–15). Discipline and judgment precedes mercy.

19:23 Egyptians and Assyrians will worship together The two competing superpowers of the day will one day achieve world peace. The imagery presents the world as perfect and ideal after the cleansing judgment of the day of Yahweh.

19:25 The threefold blessing in this verse connects Egypt, Assyria and Israel, emphasizing a complete and total peace. In this passage, Egypt and Assyria appear to be on par with Israel as God's chosen ones. However, the two nations represent the ultimate acceptance of all peoples to the possibility of peace with God.

them, saying, "Blessed be Egypt my people, Assyria my handiwork, and Israel my inheritance."

A Prophecy Against Egypt and Cush

20 In the year that the supreme commander, sent by Sargon king of Assyria, came to Ashdod and attacked and captured it — ²at that time the LORD spoke through Isaiah son of Amoz. He said to him, "Take off the sackcloth from your body and the sandals from your feet." And he did so, going around stripped and barefoot.

³Then the LORD said, "Just as my servant Isaiah has gone stripped and barefoot for three years, as a sign and portent against Egypt and Cush,ᵃ ⁴so the king of Assyria will lead away stripped and barefoot the Egyptian captives and Cushite exiles, young and old, with buttocks bared — to Egypt's shame. ⁵Those who trusted in Cush and boasted in Egypt will be dismayed and put to shame. ⁶In that day the people who live on this coast will say, 'See what has happened to those we relied on, those we fled to for help and deliverance from the king of Assyria! How then can we escape?'"

A Prophecy Against Babylon

21 A prophecy against the Desert by the Sea:

Like whirlwinds sweeping through the
   southland,
an invader comes from the desert,
   from a land of terror.

²A dire vision has been shown to me:
   The traitor betrays, the looter takes loot.
Elam, attack! Media, lay siege!
   I will bring to an end all the groaning she
      caused.

³At this my body is racked with pain,
   pangs seize me, like those of a woman in
      labor;
I am staggered by what I hear,
   I am bewildered by what I see.
⁴My heart falters,
   fear makes me tremble;
the twilight I longed for
   has become a horror to me.

⁵They set the tables,
   they spread the rugs,
   they eat, they drink!
Get up, you officers,
   oil the shields!

⁶This is what the Lord says to me:

"Go, post a lookout
   and have him report what he sees.
⁷When he sees chariots
   with teams of horses,
riders on donkeys
   or riders on camels,
let him be alert,
   fully alert."

ᵃ 3 That is, the upper Nile region; also in verse 5

20:1–6 The oracles against the nations are interrupted for this narrative account. Here, Isaiah carries out a prophetic act as a sign against Egypt and Cush (also called "Ethiopia"). Isaiah is commanded to walk around naked and barefoot like a prisoner of war being led into captivity.

20:1 Sargon king of Assyria Sargon II was king of Assyria from 722–705 BC. This campaign in 711 BC was recorded in Sargon's official annals. See the timeline "Dates Related to Isaiah and 2 Kings" on p. 1116.
20:2 Isaiah son of Amoz Unlike the first-person account in chs. 6–8, the prophet is referred to in the third person in this narrative. **Take off the sackcloth from your body** Isaiah apparently was already dressed for mourning in sackcloth—perhaps symbolizing the national mourning to come from the looming threat of Assyria and Ahaz's refusal to turn to Yahweh for help. See the table "Symbolic Actions of the Prophets" on p. 1195.
20:3 my servant Isaiah Yahweh often refers to his prophets as his "servant." In chs. 40–55, the role of the servant of Yahweh is associated with the nation of Israel (41:8–9; 42:1; 44:1), and then to an individual servant (especially in chs. 49–55). See note on 42:1–9.
portent against Egypt and Cush Ashdod would appeal to Egypt and Cush (also rendered "Ethiopia") for help. The warning seems more immediately relevant for the Philistines (see v. 6), who had hoped for aid from Egypt, but will instead see Egypt humiliated. At this time, Egypt was ruled by Cushite (or Nubian) pharaohs. After Ashdod falls, the pharaoh turns the rebellious Philistine king over

to Sargon II. The humiliation of Egypt would come later when Esarhaddon controlled Memphis and part of Egypt for two years in the seventh century (see note on 19:4).
20:5 Those who trusted in Cush and boasted in Egypt will be dismayed and put to shame Judah must learn from Ashdod's example: Their neighbors sought an alliance with Egypt against Assyria and it didn't work out in their favor.

21:1–17 This section is another oracle against Babylon (v. 9). Chapter 21 also contains two short oracles against Edom (vv. 11–12) and Arabia (vv. 13–17). The first-person account of the revelation and the prophet's emotional reaction to the vision (vv. 3–4) creates a more vivid scene than the other oracles against the nations.

21:1 against the Desert by the Sea Unlike earlier oracles against specific nations, this heading is ambiguous and mysterious. It may describe the watery wilderness created by the marshes of the Tigris and Euphrates delta where they enter the Persian Gulf. **the southland** A dry region of Palestine south of the hill country of Judah. The territory formed a natural southern boundary for Judah.
21:2 Media, lay siege See 13:17, which foreshadows Yahweh's purpose for the Medes to conquer Babylon.
21:3 my body is racked with pain It is unclear why the prophet reacts with such anguish and dismay to the fall of Babylon (v. 9). His vision may be so vivid, and the exposure to human suffering so great, that he is overwhelmed.

[8] And the lookout[a] shouted,

"Day after day, my lord, I stand on the
watchtower;
every night I stay at my post.
[9] Look, here comes a man in a chariot
with a team of horses.
And he gives back the answer:
'Babylon has fallen, has fallen!
All the images of its gods
lie shattered on the ground!'"

[10] My people who are crushed on the threshing
floor,
I tell you what I have heard
from the LORD Almighty,
from the God of Israel.

A Prophecy Against Edom

[11] A prophecy against Dumah [b]:

Someone calls to me from Seir,
"Watchman, what is left of the night?
Watchman, what is left of the night?"
[12] The watchman replies,
"Morning is coming, but also the night.
If you would ask, then ask;
and come back yet again."

A Prophecy Against Arabia

[13] A prophecy against Arabia:

You caravans of Dedanites,
who camp in the thickets of Arabia,
[14]   bring water for the thirsty;
you who live in Tema,
bring food for the fugitives.
[15] They flee from the sword,
from the drawn sword,

from the bent bow
and from the heat of battle.

[16] This is what the Lord says to me: "Within one
year, as a servant bound by contract would count it,
all the splendor of Kedar will come to an end. [17] The
survivors of the archers, the warriors of Kedar, will
be few." The LORD, the God of Israel, has spoken.

A Prophecy About Jerusalem

22 A prophecy against the Valley of Vision:

What troubles you now,
that you have all gone up on the roofs,
[2] you town so full of commotion,
you city of tumult and revelry?
Your slain were not killed by the sword,
nor did they die in battle.
[3] All your leaders have fled together;
they have been captured without using
the bow.
All you who were caught were taken prisoner
together,
having fled while the enemy was still far
away.
[4] Therefore I said, "Turn away from me;
let me weep bitterly.
Do not try to console me
over the destruction of my people."

[5] The Lord, the LORD Almighty, has a day
of tumult and trampling and terror
in the Valley of Vision,
a day of battering down walls
and of crying out to the mountains.

[a] 8 Dead Sea Scrolls and Syriac; Masoretic Text *A lion*
[b] 11 *Dumah*, a wordplay on *Edom*, means *silence* or *stillness*.

21:5 They set the tables Unaware that disaster is
almost upon them, the Babylonians continue eating
and drinking.
21:6 post a lookout Portrays the prophet as a watchman, warning the people of the judgment to come (compare Hab 2:1; Eze 3:17).
21:9 Babylon has fallen The seat of Mesopotamian
culture and influence is destroyed. In later literature,
Babylon symbolizes all wicked worldly power opposed
to God (e.g., Rev 14:8; 18:2).
21:11 A prophecy against Dumah The Hebrew term
dumah ("silence") refers to the silence of the underworld
in Ps 115:17. The parallel reference here to Seir indicates
the name is either a corruption of Edom or a wordplay
on the name Edom and the eerie nighttime stillness of
the oracle's content. See the table "Oracles Against the
Nations" on p. 1244.
21:13 caravans of Dedanites The inhabitants of Arabia
(including Dedanites and Ishmaelites) were primarily
known to the rest of the Middle East by their reputation
as traders (see Eze 27:20; Ge 37:25). Dedanites were
descendants of Abraham by Keturah (see Ge 25:3).
21:14 in Tema The refugees from the overthrow of
Babylon would flee as far as Arabia. The last king of
Babylon, Nabonidus, spent 10 years of his reign at the

Arabian oasis of Tema, leaving his son, Belshazzar, to
rule Babylon. See Da 5:1–31.
21:16 Kedar Kedar is another name for the Ishmaelites
(see Ge 25:13). Kedar was in the northern part of the
Arabian desert, east of the Jordan River and east of Syria.

22:1–25 Having focused on surrounding peoples, the
oracles of judgment finally return to address Jerusalem
and Judah. This shift emphasizes for Judah that ultimately
all talk of Yahweh's ordained judgment on their neighbors
culminates in a warning for them — as God's people — to
repent. Their status as God's chosen people is not to be
taken lightly; greater knowledge of the truth demands
greater accountability.

22:1 A prophecy against the Valley of Vision While
this heading is cryptic, Isa 22:8–10 reveals it refers to
Jerusalem and its inhabitants. "Valley of Vision" implies
that they had opportunity to see and respond to God.
22:3 All your leaders have fled together When Babylon
took Jerusalem in 586 BC, the warriors of Judah fled by
night (see 2Ki 25:1–7).
22:5 a day of tumult and trampling and terror The
day of Yahweh is a terrifying day of judgment (compare Isa
2:12; Mic 7:14). **Valley of Vision** Refers to Jerusalem
(see note on Isa 22:8). While Jerusalem is built on a

⁶Elam takes up the quiver,
  with her charioteers and horses;
  Kir uncovers the shield.
⁷Your choicest valleys are full of chariots,
  and horsemen are posted at the city gates.

⁸The Lord stripped away the defenses of
  Judah,
  and you looked in that day
  to the weapons in the Palace of the Forest.
⁹You saw that the walls of the City of David
  were broken through in many places;
you stored up water
  in the Lower Pool.
¹⁰You counted the buildings in Jerusalem
  and tore down houses to strengthen the
  wall.
¹¹You built a reservoir between the two walls
  for the water of the Old Pool,
but you did not look to the One who made it,
  or have regard for the One who planned it
  long ago.

¹²The Lord, the LORD Almighty,
  called you on that day
to weep and to wail,
  to tear out your hair and put on sackcloth.
¹³But see, there is joy and revelry,
  slaughtering of cattle and killing of sheep,
  eating of meat and drinking of wine!
"Let us eat and drink," you say,
  "for tomorrow we die!"

¹⁴The LORD Almighty has revealed this in my
hearing: "Till your dying day this sin will not be
atoned for," says the Lord, the LORD Almighty.

¹⁵This is what the Lord, the LORD Almighty,
says:

"Go, say to this steward,
  to Shebna the palace administrator:
¹⁶What are you doing here and who gave you
  permission
  to cut out a grave for yourself here,
hewing your grave on the height
  and chiseling your resting place in the rock?

¹⁷"Beware, the LORD is about to take firm hold
  of you
  and hurl you away, you mighty man.
¹⁸He will roll you up tightly like a ball
  and throw you into a large country.
There you will die
  and there the chariots you were so
  proud of
  will become a disgrace to your master's
  house.
¹⁹I will depose you from your office,
  and you will be ousted from your position.

²⁰"In that day I will summon my servant, Eliakim son of Hilkiah. ²¹I will clothe him with your
robe and fasten your sash around him and hand
your authority over to him. He will be a father to
those who live in Jerusalem and to the people of
Judah. ²²I will place on his shoulder the key to the
house of David; what he opens no one can shut,
and what he shuts no one can open. ²³I will drive
him like a peg into a firm place; he will become
a seat[a] of honor for the house of his father. ²⁴All

---

[a] 23 Or throne

"mount" like most ancient cities, it does not have high
ground in its immediate surroundings.
22:6 Elam takes up the quiver, with her charioteers
Elam is also invoked as an invader against Babylon in
21:2. Elam may have been allied with Assyria or Babylon;
Elamites may have also served one of those empires as
mercenaries. The reference to Kir in the second half of
the verse suggests the mercenary option is most likely.
Kir uncovers the shield The precise location of Kir is
unknown. Assyria exiled Syrian captives to Kir (2Ki 16:9),
suggesting it was part of Mesopotamia.
22:8 stripped away the defenses of Judah Reveals
the "Valley of Vision" is Judah and Jerusalem. Yahweh
has exposed Judah in judgment. **in the Palace of the
Forest** Part of the palace complex in Jerusalem that
Solomon built (1Ki 7:2–5). It may have served as an
armory (1Ki 10:16–17).
22:9 you stored up water in the Lower Pool Under
Hezekiah, Jerusalem made elaborate preparations for
an Assyrian siege by reinforcing its walls (Isa 22:10)
and establishing a water supply (see 2Ch 32:30). See
note on Isa 3:1. See the infographic "Inscription From
Hezekiah's Tunnel" on p. 599.
22:11 you did not look to the One who made it All
of their preparations are worthless; they are not seeking
God's help through the crisis.
22:13 tomorrow we die Resigned to their fate and

unwilling to repent, they focus on enjoying worldly pleasures to the end (see 1Co 15:32, where this is quoted).
22:15 Shebna He appears again in Isa 36–39, but
is demoted in rank to "secretary" or scribe. **palace
administrator** A title for a steward—the equivalent of
a modern president's chief of staff.
22:16 hewing your grave on the height A royal steward's tomb was found carved in the rocks outside of
Jerusalem in the late 1800s. While the name on the
tomb is damaged, it may be the tomb of the steward
criticized here.
22:18 will become a disgrace to your master's house
Shebna is condemned strongly and removed from his
position of power. He may have been condemned for his
pride and taking royal privileges for himself.
22:20 Eliakim son of Hilkiah The steward in the encounter with Assyria described in 36:3, where he is
accompanied by Shebna the scribe. Shebna may have
been demoted and replaced by Eliakim, but still retained
on staff.
22:22 the key to the house of David Eliakim will
receive Shebna's position of power and influence. The
key is a symbol of royal authority held by the steward.
Revelation 3:7 alludes to this verse, understanding the
key of the house of David to refer to the royal authority
invested in the Messiah.

the glory of his family will hang on him: its offspring and offshoots — all its lesser vessels, from
the bowls to all the jars.

25 "In that day," declares the LORD Almighty,
"the peg driven into the firm place will give way;
it will be sheared off and will fall, and the load
hanging on it will be cut down." The LORD has
spoken.

A Prophecy Against Tyre

23 A prophecy against Tyre:

Wail, you ships of Tarshish!
    For Tyre is destroyed
    and left without house or harbor.
From the land of Cyprus
    word has come to them.

2 Be silent, you people of the island
    and you merchants of Sidon,
    whom the seafarers have enriched.
3 On the great waters
    came the grain of the Shihor;
the harvest of the Nile*a* was the revenue of
        Tyre,
    and she became the marketplace of the
        nations.

4 Be ashamed, Sidon, and you fortress of the sea,
    for the sea has spoken:
    "I have neither been in labor nor given birth;
    I have neither reared sons nor brought up
        daughters."
5 When word comes to Egypt,
    they will be in anguish at the report from
        Tyre.

6 Cross over to Tarshish;
    wail, you people of the island.
7 Is this your city of revelry,
    the old, old city,
whose feet have taken her
    to settle in far-off lands?
8 Who planned this against Tyre,
    the bestower of crowns,
whose merchants are princes,
    whose traders are renowned in the earth?
9 The LORD Almighty planned it,
    to bring down her pride in all her splendor
    and to humble all who are renowned on
        the earth.

10 Till*b* your land as they do along the Nile,
    Daughter Tarshish,
    for you no longer have a harbor.
11 The LORD has stretched out his hand over the
        sea
    and made its kingdoms tremble.
He has given an order concerning Phoenicia
    that her fortresses be destroyed.
12 He said, "No more of your reveling,
    Virgin Daughter Sidon, now crushed!

"Up, cross over to Cyprus;
    even there you will find no rest."
13 Look at the land of the Babylonians,*c*
    this people that is now of no account!
The Assyrians have made it
    a place for desert creatures;

a 2,3 Masoretic Text; Dead Sea Scrolls *Sidon, / who cross over the
sea; / your envoys 3are on the great waters. / The grain of the
Shihor, / the harvest of the Nile,*   *b 10* Dead Sea Scrolls and
some Septuagint manuscripts; Masoretic Text *Go through*
c 13 Or *Chaldeans*

22:25 driven into the firm place will give way For a
time, Eliakim's leadership will be solid and stable. But
even the stability of the later reign of Hezekiah (post 701
BC) will not last; the day of Yahweh's judgment will come.

23:1–18 The Phoenician cites of Tyre and Sidon, Israel's
near neighbors to the northwest, were popular targets
in prophetic oracles against surrounding nations (e.g.,
Eze 26:2—28:24; Joel 3:4–8; Am 1:9,10; Zec 9:2–4).
The Phoenicians were a major influence on Canaanite
idolatry, which may explain the prophets' indignation.
King Ahab, one of Israel's most powerful kings during
the divided monarchy, married Jezebel, a princess of
Sidon. First Kings 16:31 describes the role played by
Baal worship in this alliance.

23:1 A prophecy against Tyre Unlike Isa 21:1 and
22:1, the oracle about Tyre resumes the pattern seen in
19:1; 17:1; 15:1; and 13:1, where the city or nation is
explicitly identified. Tyre is a seaport; the Phoenicians
were well-established seafaring traders. See the table
"Oracles Against the Nations" on p. 1244. **Tarshish** A
distant port where the Phoenicians traded. The oracle
begins by addressing those who conduct business with
Tyre, drawing their attention to the destruction of the
city (see 2:16 and note; Jnh 1:3 and note). See the
infographic "Ancient Phoenician Ship" on p. 1317.

23:2 you merchants of Sidon Sidon was another
prominent Phoenician city-state located north of Tyre
along the Mediterranean coast.
23:3 marketplace of the nations The Phoenicians
were international traders. Their economic influence
encouraged most nations around the Mediterranean to
maintain positive relations with them.
23:5 When word comes to Egypt The news of Tyre's
destruction will spread to her main trading partners—
Egypt and Tarshish (see Isa 23:6).
**23:7 whose feet have taken her to settle in far-off
lands** Tyre founded Phoenician colonies around the
Mediterranean, such as Carthage.
23:9 her pride in all her splendor The prestige of their
status as international merchants manifested in pride. As
with other pronouncements of judgment in Isaiah, pride
is the chief sin that demands punishment.
23:11 stretched out his hand over the sea Echoing
the actions of Moses in Ex 14:21, Yahweh's hand is
stretched out in an act of judgment and an assertion
of power over the chaotic ancient and primeval forces
represented by the sea (see Isa 10:4; 9:12).
23:13 Look at the land of the Babylonians Babylon
is presented to Tyre as an example. This may be a recommendation to watch the fate of another power that
rebelled against Assyria, or a warning to indicate the
direction this prophesied destruction will come from.

they raised up their siege towers,
they stripped its fortresses bare
and turned it into a ruin.

[14] Wail, you ships of Tarshish;
your fortress is destroyed!

[15] At that time Tyre will be forgotten for seventy years, the span of a king's life. But at the end of these seventy years, it will happen to Tyre as in the song of the prostitute:

[16] "Take up a harp, walk through the city,
you forgotten prostitute;
play the harp well, sing many a song,
so that you will be remembered."

[17] At the end of seventy years, the LORD will deal with Tyre. She will return to her lucrative prostitution and will ply her trade with all the kingdoms on the face of the earth. [18] Yet her profit and her earnings will be set apart for the LORD; they will not be stored up or hoarded. Her profits will go to those who live before the LORD, for abundant food and fine clothes.

The LORD's Devastation of the Earth

24 See, the LORD is going to lay waste
the earth
and devastate it;
he will ruin its face
and scatter its inhabitants —
[2] it will be the same
for priest as for people,
for the master as for his servant,
for the mistress as for her servant,
for seller as for buyer,
for borrower as for lender,
for debtor as for creditor.

[3] The earth will be completely laid waste
and totally plundered.
The LORD has spoken this word.

[4] The earth dries up and withers,
the world languishes and withers,
the heavens languish with the earth.
[5] The earth is defiled by its people;
they have disobeyed the laws,
violated the statutes
and broken the everlasting covenant.
[6] Therefore a curse consumes the earth;
its people must bear their guilt.
Therefore earth's inhabitants are
burned up,
and very few are left.
[7] The new wine dries up and the vine
withers;
all the merrymakers groan.
[8] The joyful timbrels are stilled,
the noise of the revelers has stopped,
the joyful harp is silent.
[9] No longer do they drink wine with a song;
the beer is bitter to its drinkers.
[10] The ruined city lies desolate;
the entrance to every house is barred.
[11] In the streets they cry out for wine;
all joy turns to gloom,
all joyful sounds are banished from
the earth.
[12] The city is left in ruins,
its gate is battered to pieces.
[13] So will it be on the earth
and among the nations,
as when an olive tree is beaten,
or as when gleanings are left after the
grape harvest.

See the timeline "Dates Related to Isaiah and 2 Kings" on p. 1116. **Assyrians have made it a place for desert creatures** Assyria violently put down a rebellion and nearly destroyed Babylon in 689 BC.
23:15 At that time Tyre will be forgotten Tyre will experience 70 years of decline. The time of this period of decline is unknown; 70 years may be a symbolic number indicating the complete loss of a generation.
23:18 her profit and her earnings will be set apart The scene shifts to a future time when the nations all serve Yahweh (see 2:2–4). Tyre is back in the trading business, but now serves the true God.

24:1–23 The oracles against the nations culminate in a pronouncement of cosmic judgment against the whole earth. Worldwide disaster, sitting in the background of the oracles presented in chs. 13–23, now comes to the fore in chs. 24–27. The scene of judgment evokes imagery from the ancient stories of Ge 1–11—especially the flood story and the Tower of Babel incident.

24:1 he will ruin its face In the oracles against the nations, other nations often serve as the agents of God's judgment. In this cosmic judgment, the earth itself becomes the agent via an earthquake. **scatter its inhabitants** The same Hebrew word for scattering

is also used in Ge 11:9, where God judges the people for building the Tower of Babel. See the infographic "The Tower of Babel" on p. 29.
24:2 same for priest as for people All levels of society—weak to powerful, rich to poor—will be affected by this judgment.
24:5 The earth is defiled by its people God brought about the flood in Ge 6:5–7 because of the general wickedness infecting the entire creation. **broken the everlasting covenant** If only Judah or Israel are in view, the covenant refers to the Mosaic covenant—the Israelites have failed to keep the law. However, the larger context of Isa 13–23 suggests the indictment here is against all peoples, not just Judah.
24:6 very few are left Judgment leaves only a small remnant—just as in the flood story, where only Noah and seven others survived on the ark. See 1:9. See the infographic "Inside Noah's Ark" on p. 19.
24:10 ruined city lies desolate The identity of the city or town is unclear. The nameless city can symbolically represent urban human civilization. The use of the Hebrew word *tohu* ("emptiness") recalls the description of the earth as *tohu* and *bohu* in Ge 1:2 (see note on Ge 1:2).
24:13 as when an olive tree is beaten Using the same

¹⁴ They raise their voices, they shout for joy;
  from the west they acclaim the LORD's
    majesty.
¹⁵ Therefore in the east give glory to the LORD;
  exalt the name of the LORD, the God of
    Israel,
  in the islands of the sea.
¹⁶ From the ends of the earth we hear
    singing:
  "Glory to the Righteous One."

But I said, "I waste away, I waste away!
  Woe to me!
The treacherous betray!
  With treachery the treacherous betray!"
¹⁷ Terror and pit and snare await you,
  people of the earth.
¹⁸ Whoever flees at the sound of terror
  will fall into a pit;
whoever climbs out of the pit
  will be caught in a snare.

The floodgates of the heavens are opened,
  the foundations of the earth shake.
¹⁹ The earth is broken up,
  the earth is split asunder,
  the earth is violently shaken.
²⁰ The earth reels like a drunkard,
  it sways like a hut in the wind;
so heavy upon it is the guilt of its rebellion
  that it falls — never to rise again.

²¹ In that day the LORD will punish
  the powers in the heavens above
  and the kings on the earth below.
²² They will be herded together
  like prisoners bound in a dungeon;
they will be shut up in prison
  and be punished[a] after many days.
²³ The moon will be dismayed,
  the sun ashamed;

for the LORD Almighty will reign
  on Mount Zion and in Jerusalem,
  and before its elders — with great glory.

Praise to the LORD

25 LORD, you are my God;
  I will exalt you and praise your name,
for in perfect faithfulness
  you have done wonderful things,
  things planned long ago.
² You have made the city a heap of rubble,
  the fortified town a ruin,
the foreigners' stronghold a city no more;
  it will never be rebuilt.
³ Therefore strong peoples will honor you;
  cities of ruthless nations will revere you.
⁴ You have been a refuge for the poor,
  a refuge for the needy in their distress,
a shelter from the storm
  and a shade from the heat.
For the breath of the ruthless
  is like a storm driving against a wall
⁵   and like the heat of the desert.
You silence the uproar of foreigners;
  as heat is reduced by the shadow of a cloud,
  so the song of the ruthless is stilled.

⁶ On this mountain the LORD Almighty will
    prepare
  a feast of rich food for all peoples,
a banquet of aged wine —
  the best of meats and the finest of wines.
⁷ On this mountain he will destroy
  the shroud that enfolds all peoples,
the sheet that covers all nations;
⁸   he will swallow up death forever.
The Sovereign LORD will wipe away the tears
  from all faces;

---

[a] 22 Or *released*

---

agricultural imagery of Isa 17:6, this invokes the futile attempt to find any fruit after the harvest was complete. **24:16 treacherous betray** Compare the prophet's reaction to his vision in 21:2–4. The same image of betrayal and destruction is found in 21:2–4 and 33:1. **24:18 will fall into a pit** Describes inescapable judgment. The terror, pit and snare create a poetic image of God's judgment (compare Jer 48:43–44). **floodgates of the heavens are opened** In Ge 7:11, the flood begins when the windows (or floodgates) of heaven are opened. The flood itself and the image of water as a destructive force allude to the chaotic conditions of creation before God brought order by dividing the waters in Ge 1:6. **24:21 In that day** Alludes to the coming day of Yahweh in total judgment over first earth, then heaven. The phrase is common in Isaiah, giving a repetitive cadence to oracles of judgment. The phrase is used seven times from Isa 24–27 (25:9; 26:1; 27:1–2,12–13). **powers in the heavens above** Possibly a reference to fallen angels or to the idolatrous worship of celestial bodies outlawed in Dt 17:3.

24:23 The moon will be dismayed The moon is likely referenced as a heavenly body that was worshiped idolatrously. See Isa 24:21 and note.

25:1–12 A hymn of praise to Yahweh, presumably placed as a response to the apocalyptic judgment of ch. 24. The poem seems to be a reaction to the reign of Yahweh foretold in 24:23.

25:2 city a heap Apparently the same unnamed city mentioned in 24:10–12; 26:5 (see 24:10 and note). **25:6 On this mountain the LORD Almighty** Compare the nations' trek to the mountain of Yahweh in 2:2–4 and its establishment in 11:9. Yahweh will dwell visibly again on his mountain (4:5). He will teach them (2:3), judge them (2:4) and provide richly for them. The mountain is Zion, Yahweh's dwelling in Jerusalem. See note on 1:8. **25:8 he will swallow up death forever** Ironically, death or the underworld is often pictured as the swallower of life (e.g., 5:14).

he will remove his people's disgrace
    from all the earth.
                  The LORD has spoken.

9 In that day they will say,

"Surely this is our God;
    we trusted in him, and he saved us.
This is the LORD, we trusted in him;
    let us rejoice and be glad in his salvation."

10 The hand of the LORD will rest on this
    mountain;
    but Moab will be trampled in their land
    as straw is trampled down in the manure.
11 They will stretch out their hands in it,
    as swimmers stretch out their hands to
        swim.
God will bring down their pride
    despite the cleverness[a] of their hands.
12 He will bring down your high fortified walls
    and lay them low;
he will bring them down to the ground,
    to the very dust.

A Song of Praise

26 In that day this song will be sung in the land of Judah:

We have a strong city;
    God makes salvation
    its walls and ramparts.
2 Open the gates
    that the righteous nation may enter,
    the nation that keeps faith.
3 You will keep in perfect peace
    those whose minds are steadfast,
    because they trust in you.
4 Trust in the LORD forever,
    for the LORD, the LORD himself, is the Rock
        eternal.
5 He humbles those who dwell on high,
    he lays the lofty city low;

he levels it to the ground
    and casts it down to the dust.
6 Feet trample it down —
    the feet of the oppressed,
    the footsteps of the poor.

7 The path of the righteous is level;
    you, the Upright One, make the way of the
        righteous smooth.
8 Yes, LORD, walking in the way of your laws,[b]
    we wait for you;
your name and renown
    are the desire of our hearts.
9 My soul yearns for you in the night;
    in the morning my spirit longs for you.
When your judgments come upon the earth,
    the people of the world learn
        righteousness.
10 But when grace is shown to the wicked,
    they do not learn righteousness;
even in a land of uprightness they go on
        doing evil
    and do not regard the majesty of the LORD.
11 LORD, your hand is lifted high,
    but they do not see it.
Let them see your zeal for your people and be
        put to shame;
    let the fire reserved for your enemies
        consume them.

12 LORD, you establish peace for us;
    all that we have accomplished you have
        done for us.
13 LORD our God, other lords besides you have
        ruled over us,
    but your name alone do we honor.
14 They are now dead, they live no more;
    their spirits do not rise.
You punished them and brought them to
        ruin;
    you wiped out all memory of them.

---

[a] 11 The meaning of the Hebrew for this word is uncertain.
[b] 8 Or judgments

25:9 his salvation Refers to the victory over death and the establishment of Yahweh's earthly reign.
25:10 hand of the LORD Symbolizes his presence for protection and blessing. The hand of God—representing power—can come down in blessing or judgment. **Moab will be trampled** This hymn of victory and salvation ends with a reiteration of the judgment and victory that Yahweh will bring over the nations. Moab is representative of all the nations who are awaiting judgment for their pride and arrogance (compare 15:1; 16:6).
26:1 In that day Prophecies about the day of judgment and the day of ultimate salvation are both introduced with the phrase "on/in that day." The reference to a song to be sung echoes 12:1, where a hymn of thanksgiving follows the foretelling of an ideal age of Messianic justice. Compare 11:11; 12:1. **in the land of Judah** The global disaster (or apocalypse) of ch. 24 recedes, and Yahweh's special relationship with Judah and his dwelling in Jerusalem comes into focus. The entire world will

experience blessing through God's relationship with his covenant people (Ge 12:2–3).
26:2 Open the gates The gates of the metaphorical city were in ruins in Isa 24:12.
26:3 You will keep in perfect peace The righteous can count on peace instead of war, destruction and judgment as long as they continue to trust in Yahweh.
26:4 the Rock eternal The image of a rock is a common metaphor for God in Biblical poetry (see Ps 18:1–3; 31:3; 71:3; Dt 32:30–31).
26:5 He humbles those who dwell on high A common image of judgment: God humbles those who exalt themselves (see Isa 2:9–12).
26:7 you, the Upright One, make the way of the righteous smooth The tone in Isa 26:7–10 is reminiscent of a wisdom psalm or proverb focused on how suffering produces character and teaches righteousness. See Pr 3:5–6.
26:12 you establish peace for us The focus shifts

15 You have enlarged the nation, LORD;
 you have enlarged the nation.
You have gained glory for yourself;
 you have extended all the borders of the
 land.

16 LORD, they came to you in their distress;
 when you disciplined them,
 they could barely whisper a prayer.*a*
17 As a pregnant woman about to give birth
 writhes and cries out in her pain,
 so were we in your presence, LORD.
18 We were with child, we writhed in labor,
 but we gave birth to wind.
We have not brought salvation to
 the earth,
 and the people of the world have not
 come to life.

19 But your dead will live, LORD;
 their bodies will rise —
let those who dwell in the dust
 wake up and shout for joy —
your dew is like the dew of the morning;
 the earth will give birth to her dead.

20 Go, my people, enter your rooms
 and shut the doors behind you;
hide yourselves for a little while
 until his wrath has passed by.
21 See, the LORD is coming out of his
 dwelling
 to punish the people of the earth for
 their sins.
The earth will disclose the blood shed on it;
 the earth will conceal its slain no longer.

Deliverance of Israel

27 In that day,

the LORD will punish with his sword —
 his fierce, great and powerful sword —
Leviathan the gliding serpent,
 Leviathan the coiling serpent;
he will slay the monster of the sea.

2 In that day —

"Sing about a fruitful vineyard:
3 I, the LORD, watch over it;
 I water it continually.
I guard it day and night
 so that no one may harm it.
4 I am not angry.
If only there were briers and thorns
 confronting me!
 I would march against them in battle;
 I would set them all on fire.
5 Or else let them come to me for refuge;
 let them make peace with me,
 yes, let them make peace with me."

6 In days to come Jacob will take root,
 Israel will bud and blossom
 and fill all the world with fruit.

7 Has the LORD struck her
 as he struck down those who struck
 her?
Has she been killed
 as those were killed who killed her?

a 16 The meaning of the Hebrew for this clause is uncertain.

---

to the peace that will come in the Messianic age (see 9:7; Mic 5:5).
26:16 they could barely whisper Acknowledges the pattern of disbelief, oppression and deliverance experienced through Israel and Judah's history. The current generation is confessing to the sins of their ancestors.
26:19 your dead will live Restoration and resurrection is coming, but judgment must be completed first (see Isa 26:20–21). Resurrection of the dead sometimes appears to be a metaphor for national restoration, as in Eze 37:1–14. The announcement that Israel's dead will live, but the dead of the foreign oppressors will not rise again (Isa 26:14), suggests a contrast between the future glorification of Israel and the ultimate judgment of the nations. However, the bodily resurrection of the dead is implied by the larger context of this verse. The NT understands the resurrection of Christ as the precursor to the future bodily resurrection of all people.
26:21 punish the people of the earth Returns to the theme of cosmic judgment deserved because of excessive bloodshed (see 24:1–6). Isaiah 24:5 indicates that the earth will be punished for violating the statutes of God's everlasting covenant. The only covenant that was incumbent on all humanity was God's covenant with Noah. The primary statute of that covenant was a commandment against bloodshed (Ge 9:6). The statement that the earth "will disclose the blood shed on it"

reinforces the conclusion that bloodshed is the primary sin for which humanity is to be punished.
27:1 Leviathan the coiling serpent While the apocalyptic imagery in Isa 25 alluded to the watery chaos of the flood and victory as swallowing death (25:8), here Yahweh's ultimate victory is represented as an assault on the serpent — invoking an ancient theme of gods bringing order by subduing the chaos monster (see note on Ge 1:21; note on Job 41:1). The battle with the dragon appears in Rev 12:3–9, where he is identified with Satan himself. In the OT references, God brings order to the universe by slaying a primeval dragon symbolizing chaos (compare Isa 51:9; Ps 74:14; 89:10; Job 9:13; 26:12; 41:1). The motif of divine combat with a serpent or dragon was found in Mesopotamian and Canaanite mythology. The Biblical theme inspired apocalyptic writers in Jewish and Christian literature, especially the books of 1 Enoch and Revelation.
27:4 If only there were briers and thorns confronting me! I would march against them in battle God's protection is so thorough that there are no longer any enemies coming against his vineyard, but he longs for some to show the extent of his protection. Compare Isa 10:17, where Yahweh burns up the metaphorical thrones and briers of Assyria.
27:6 fill all the world with fruit Israel will be a blessing to the entire world (see Ge 12:2–3).

8 By warfare[a] and exile you contend with
    her —
  with his fierce blast he drives her out,
    as on a day the east wind blows.
9 By this, then, will Jacob's guilt be atoned for,
    and this will be the full fruit of the removal
      of his sin:
When he makes all the altar stones
    to be like limestone crushed to pieces,
no Asherah poles[b] or incense altars
    will be left standing.
10 The fortified city stands desolate,
    an abandoned settlement, forsaken like the
      wilderness;
there the calves graze,
    there they lie down;
    they strip its branches bare.
11 When its twigs are dry, they are broken off
    and women come and make fires with
      them.
For this is a people without understanding;
    so their Maker has no compassion on
      them,
    and their Creator shows them no favor.

12 In that day the LORD will thresh from the flowing Euphrates to the Wadi of Egypt, and you, Israel, will be gathered up one by one. 13 And in that day a great trumpet will sound. Those who were perishing in Assyria and those who were exiled in Egypt will come and worship the LORD on the holy mountain in Jerusalem.

Woe to the Leaders of Ephraim and Judah

28 Woe to that wreath, the pride of
    Ephraim's drunkards,
  to the fading flower, his glorious beauty,
  set on the head of a fertile valley —
    to that city, the pride of those laid low by
      wine!
2 See, the Lord has one who is powerful and
    strong.
Like a hailstorm and a destructive wind,
like a driving rain and a flooding downpour,
    he will throw it forcefully to the ground.
3 That wreath, the pride of Ephraim's
    drunkards,
  will be trampled underfoot.
4 That fading flower, his glorious beauty,
    set on the head of a fertile valley,
will be like figs ripe before harvest —
    as soon as people see them and take them
      in hand,
    they swallow them.

5 In that day the LORD Almighty
    will be a glorious crown,
a beautiful wreath
    for the remnant of his people.
6 He will be a spirit of justice
    to the one who sits in judgment,
a source of strength
    to those who turn back the battle at the gate.

7 And these also stagger from wine
    and reel from beer:
Priests and prophets stagger from beer
    and are befuddled with wine;
they reel from beer,
    they stagger when seeing visions,
    they stumble when rendering decisions.
8 All the tables are covered with vomit
    and there is not a spot without filth.

---

[a] 8 See Septuagint; the meaning of the Hebrew for this word is uncertain.   [b] 9 That is, wooden symbols of the goddess Asherah

---

27:9 Asherah poles Wooden poles symbolizing worship of the goddess Asherah. See note on Ex 34:13.
27:12 In that day The day of Yahweh imagery is used to point both to the coming day of judgment and the ultimate day of God's salvation. See note on Isa 4:2. **flowing Euphrates to the Wadi of Egypt** The judgment will extend from one end of the promised land to the other (Ge 15:18) when the day of Yahweh comes.
27:13 Assyria Located in central Mesopotamia. Assyria and Egypt were the opposing superpowers of the day. **the holy mountain in Jerusalem** Mount Zion was seen as Yahweh's dwelling place. See Isa 2:2 and note.

28:1–13 The prophet's attention returns to the present crisis, where Israel's rebellion against Assyria will soon result in—or perhaps has already resulted in—destruction and exile. Assyria conquered Samaria in 722 BC. Isaiah uses the exile of the northern kingdom to warn Judah to return to Yahweh before they suffer the same fate. Chapters 28–39 remain primarily focused on the historical situation of the late eighth century BC.
  In addition, this section marks the beginning of the six "woes" pronounced in chs. 28–33. Chapter 5 contains a similar section of "woes"; this segment may be structured to mirror chs. 5–8, which also focuses on a political crisis of the day.

28:1 Ephraim's drunkards In Hos 7:5, the prophet describes the leaders of Israel getting drunk instead of attending to affairs of state. **to the fading flower, his glorious beauty** Refers to Samaria, the capital of Israel (here called Ephraim)—a once powerful city that is about to be subdued.
28:2 a driving rain and a flooding downpour Assyria is depicted as an unstoppable onslaught of floodwaters (see Isa 8:7–8).
28:4 figs ripe before harvest Describes something very desirable and quickly taken.
28:7 Priests and prophets stagger from beer May shift focus from the political leaders in v. 1 to religious leaders; or the referent was deliberately left ambiguous, and it is now revealed that religious mismanagement—not just political—is being condemned.
28:8 tables are covered with vomit and there is not a spot without filth Everything that comes out

9 "Who is it he is trying to teach?
    To whom is he explaining his
        message?
To children weaned from their milk,
    to those just taken from the breast?
10 For it is:
    Do this, do that,
    a rule for this, a rule for that [a];
    a little here, a little there."

11 Very well then, with foreign lips and strange
        tongues
    God will speak to this people,
12 to whom he said,
    "This is the resting place, let the weary
        rest";
    and, "This is the place of repose" —
    but they would not listen.
13 So then, the word of the LORD to them will
        become:
    Do this, do that,
    a rule for this, a rule for that;
    a little here, a little there —
so that as they go they will fall backward;
    they will be injured and snared and
        captured.

14 Therefore hear the word of the LORD, you
        scoffers
    who rule this people in Jerusalem.
15 You boast, "We have entered into a covenant
        with death,
    with the realm of the dead we have made
        an agreement.
When an overwhelming scourge sweeps by,
    it cannot touch us,

for we have made a lie our refuge
    and falsehood [b] our hiding place."

16 So this is what the Sovereign LORD says:

"See, I lay a stone in Zion, a tested stone,
    a precious cornerstone for a sure
        foundation;
the one who relies on it
    will never be stricken with panic.
17 I will make justice the measuring line
    and righteousness the plumb line;
hail will sweep away your refuge, the lie,
    and water will overflow your hiding place.
18 Your covenant with death will be annulled;
    your agreement with the realm of the dead
        will not stand.
When the overwhelming scourge sweeps by,
    you will be beaten down by it.
19 As often as it comes it will carry you away;
    morning after morning, by day and by
        night,
    it will sweep through."

The understanding of this message
    will bring sheer terror.
20 The bed is too short to stretch out on,
    the blanket too narrow to wrap around
        you.
21 The LORD will rise up as he did at Mount
        Perazim,
    he will rouse himself as in the Valley of
        Gibeon —

[a] 10 Hebrew / *sav lasav sav lasav* / *kav lakav kav lakav*
(probably meaningless sounds mimicking the prophet's words);
also in verse 13   [b] 15 Or *false gods*

---

of the mouths of the drunken priests and prophets is
equivalent to vomit.
28:9 Who is it he is trying to teach The spiritual
leaders show no interest in hearing from Yahweh (see
Jer 6:10). In Isa 53:11, Yahweh is able to save through
the knowledge he imparted to the Servant. Yahweh's
knowledge is often contrasted with the limited knowledge
of arrogant people. Even though people now have access
to knowledge that would make them "like God" (Ge 3:5),
Yahweh's knowledge is unmatched—people are unable
to rightly handle it without him (see Isa 47:10; Pr 1:7;
3:20; Nu 24:16). **To children weaned from their milk**
Children have a better chance of understanding the message than the drunken leaders. See Isa 28:19 and 53:1.
28:10 Do this, do that The saying here (repeated in
v. 13) is difficult to understand due to its singsong and
nonsensical nature. Considering Isaiah's love of poetic
wordplay, it is likely meant to be gibberish, reflecting
either the drunken speech of the priests and prophets,
the baby-talk alluded to in v. 9 or the barbarian speech
of v. 11. Its placement in v. 10 suggests it is meant to
evoke all three.
28:11 foreign lips Refers to foreign invaders whose
native language would be unintelligible to the people
of Israel and Judah—either the Assyrians, or foreign
mercenaries serving the Assyrian army.

28:14–29 The failure of the leaders of both Israel and
Judah is answered by the faithfulness of Yahweh to his
own redemptive plan regarding Zion (v. 16). The judgment
on Israel is turned into a warning to Judah whose leaders
are on the same path of disobedience.

28:14 you scoffers The leaders refuse to take seriously
the counsel and signs given by Yahweh. The judgment he
will bring puts an end to all scoffing (see vv. 22; 29:20).
**28:15 with the realm of the dead we have made
an agreement** An ironic characterization: The alliance
Judah sought with Egypt against Assyria is depicted as an
agreement with death itself (see 2Ki 18:21; Isa 30:1–5).
28:16 lay a stone in Zion The theme of God's care and
concern for Zion is a unifying feature of chs. 28–39. There
is a tension in the presentation of the theme between
protection and punishment. God ultimately protects Jerusalem from Assyria, but later uses Babylon to punish
them. Some leaders understood the promises of protection for Zion as unconditional indicators that Jerusalem
and the temple would be preserved no matter what; God
chose Zion for his dwelling. The tension is ultimately
resolved when the cornerstone of Zion is revealed to
metaphorically point to the stability of God's redemptive
plan through the Messiah (see 8:14; Ro 9:33; 10:11).
28:17 I will make justice the measuring line As in Isa
28:10 and 28:13, the Hebrew term denotes a measuring

to do his work, his strange work,
  and perform his task, his alien task.
[22] Now stop your mocking,
  or your chains will become heavier;
the Lord, the LORD Almighty, has told me
  of the destruction decreed against the
    whole land.

[23] Listen and hear my voice;
  pay attention and hear what I say.
[24] When a farmer plows for planting, does he
    plow continually?
Does he keep on breaking up and working
    the soil?
[25] When he has leveled the surface,
  does he not sow caraway and scatter
    cumin?
Does he not plant wheat in its place,[a]
  barley in its plot,[a]
  and spelt in its field?
[26] His God instructs him
  and teaches him the right way.

[27] Caraway is not threshed with a sledge,
  nor is the wheel of a cart rolled over
    cumin;
caraway is beaten out with a rod,
  and cumin with a stick.
[28] Grain must be ground to make bread;
  so one does not go on threshing it
    forever.
The wheels of a threshing cart may be rolled
    over it,
  but one does not use horses to grind
    grain.
[29] All this also comes from the LORD Almighty,
  whose plan is wonderful,
  whose wisdom is magnificent.

Woe to David's City

29 Woe to you, Ariel, Ariel,
  the city where David settled!
Add year to year
  and let your cycle of festivals go on.
[2] Yet I will besiege Ariel;
  she will mourn and lament,
  she will be to me like an altar hearth.[b]
[3] I will encamp against you on all sides;
  I will encircle you with towers
  and set up my siege works against you.
[4] Brought low, you will speak from
    the ground;
  your speech will mumble out of the dust.
Your voice will come ghostlike from the
    earth;
  out of the dust your speech will whisper.

[5] But your many enemies will become like fine
    dust,
  the ruthless hordes like blown chaff.
Suddenly, in an instant,
[6] the LORD Almighty will come
with thunder and earthquake and great
    noise,
  with windstorm and tempest and flames of
    a devouring fire.
[7] Then the hordes of all the nations that fight
    against Ariel,
  that attack her and her fortress and
    besiege her,
will be as it is with a dream,
  with a vision in the night—
[8] as when a hungry person dreams of eating,
  but awakens hungry still;

---

[a] 25 The meaning of the Hebrew for this word is uncertain.
[b] 2 The Hebrew for *altar hearth* sounds like the Hebrew for *Ariel*.

---

line. An attention to justice and righteousness similar to the concerns of wisdom teaching can be seen in parts of chs. 28–33.
28:21 Mount Perazim The site of one of David's early victories against the Philistines as king of Israel (2Sa 5:20). **as in the Valley of Gibeon** Likely refers to the miracle of the sun standing still in Joshua's victory in Jos 10:12; may also refer to one of David's victories (e.g., 1Ch 14:13).
28:24 a farmer plows for planting The work of God against his people is metaphorically pictured as plowing, harvest and threshing.
28:27 a sledge An agricultural implement that consisted of a board pulled by oxen. A driver would stand on the board to add weight, and stones were embedded in the underside. The sledge was then driven over the harvested grain stalks to separate the heads of grain from the grass and chaff.

29:1–24 This poetic lament over the siege of Jerusalem alternates between grief over the punishment that must be brought on Judah for their religious complacency, judgment on the nations and defense of Zion because of God's covenant fidelity.

29:1 Ariel The following phrases suggest this is a poetic reference to Jerusalem; the usage here is unusual. Ariel may be a name meaning "lion of God" since the Hebrew word *ari* means "lion" and *el* means "god." Other usages suggest the term may refer to an altar hearth (Eze 43:15–16; Mesha Stele, line 12) or a warrior (2Sa 23:20). See the infographic "The Mesha Stele" on p. 565.
29:2 she will be to me like an altar hearth This context suggests the term here is referring to an altar hearth. The other possible translations make little sense here, as an ironic reference to Jerusalem's former glory seems out of place. See note on Isa 29:1.
29:3 I will encamp against you The coming siege is the work of Yahweh himself, commander in chief of all armies—heavenly and human (see v. 6 and note).
29:5 in an instant The Assyrians depart suddenly after divine intervention in 37:36–37 (compare 2Ki 19:35).
29:6 LORD Almighty This title refers to God as the leader of the heavenly armies. See note on Isa 1:9. **thunder** Natural events like thunder and earthquake often accompany a theophany or appearance of God (see 6:4; 30:30; 1Ki 19:11–12; Ex 19:16–20).

29:9 drunk, but not from wine What appears to be

as when a thirsty person dreams of drinking,
  but awakens faint and thirsty still.
So will it be with the hordes of all the nations
  that fight against Mount Zion.

⁹ Be stunned and amazed,
  blind yourselves and be sightless;
be drunk, but not from wine,
  stagger, but not from beer.
¹⁰ The LORD has brought over you a deep sleep:
  He has sealed your eyes (the prophets);
  he has covered your heads (the seers).

¹¹ For you this whole vision is nothing but words sealed in a scroll. And if you give the scroll to someone who can read, and say, "Read this, please," they will answer, "I can't; it is sealed." ¹² Or if you give the scroll to someone who cannot read, and say, "Read this, please," they will answer, "I don't know how to read."

¹³ The Lord says:

"These people come near to me with their
    mouth
  and honor me with their lips,
    but their hearts are far from me.
Their worship of me
  is based on merely human rules they have
    been taught.ᵃ
¹⁴ Therefore once more I will astound these
    people
  with wonder upon wonder;
the wisdom of the wise will perish,
  the intelligence of the intelligent will
    vanish."
¹⁵ Woe to those who go to great depths
  to hide their plans from the LORD,
who do their work in darkness and think,
  "Who sees us? Who will know?"

¹⁶ You turn things upside down,
  as if the potter were thought to be like
    the clay!
Shall what is formed say to the one who
    formed it,
  "You did not make me"?
Can the pot say to the potter,
  "You know nothing"?

¹⁷ In a very short time, will not Lebanon
    be turned into a fertile field
  and the fertile field seem like a
    forest?
¹⁸ In that day the deaf will hear the words
    of the scroll,
  and out of gloom and darkness
    the eyes of the blind will see.
¹⁹ Once more the humble will rejoice in
    the LORD;
  the needy will rejoice in the Holy One
    of Israel.
²⁰ The ruthless will vanish,
  the mockers will disappear,
  and all who have an eye for evil will be
    cut down —
²¹ those who with a word make someone out to
    be guilty,
  who ensnare the defender in court
  and with false testimony deprive the
    innocent of justice.

²² Therefore this is what the LORD, who redeemed Abraham, says to the descendants of Jacob:

"No longer will Jacob be ashamed;
  no longer will their faces grow pale.

ᵃ 13 Hebrew; Septuagint *They worship me in vain; / their teachings are merely human rules*

---

a depiction of the staggering blindness of the nations defeated by Yahweh turns into an indictment of Judah's religious leaders in v. 10.

29:11 words sealed in a scroll The prophet's message is like a document sealed up for a future audience that will be able to understand it. A seal could only be broken by one with the proper authority—breaking it was akin to opening mail not addressed to you (compare 8:16; Da 12:4).

29:13 their hearts are far from me The people appeared to be following Yahweh, but it was only mechanical rituals—their hearts weren't in it (see Isa 1:10–17). The people display a similar attitude in Eze 33:31. In the future, the repentant remnant will reverse their attitudes (see Isa 58:2). This verse is quoted in Mt 15:8–9 as an example of how far away the people of Jesus' day had wandered from true worship.

29:15 to those who go to great depths to hide their plans from the LORD An expression of grief alluding to the leaders of Judah's plans to ally with Egypt (see Isa 30:1–5). **from the LORD, who do their work in darkness** The elders of Israel are similarly

depicted as conducting sinful business in the dark in Eze 8:12.

29:16 potter were thought to be like the clay Isa 10:15 describes a tool, which is useless without one to wield it, to illustrate God's sovereignty over all contemporary powers. Here, Yahweh's sovereignty is illustrated by the image of a potter and clay. Just like the tool has no say in how it is used, the pot has no right to question the design of the potter. The potter and clay image is reused in 45:9; Isa 64:8; and Jer 18:4–6. The theme is also applied in Ro 9:20–22.

29:17 Lebanon A region north of Israel (Ps 72:16; Hos 14:5,7; Zec 10:10; SS 4:15). The image of the lush fertile land led to the occasional metaphorical use of Lebanon for Judah, either in images of God undoing or restoring the fertile land (Isa 33:9; Jer 22:6; Na 1:4).

29:18 deaf will hear the words Contrasts Isa 29:9–12, where no one could decipher or understand the message. Now, the deaf and blind shall miraculously hear and see the message.

29:19 needy will rejoice The meek and the poor are depicted exhibiting a proper attitude of worship and dependence on God (compare 61:1).

²³ When they see among them their children,
the work of my hands,
they will keep my name holy;
they will acknowledge the holiness of the
Holy One of Jacob,
and will stand in awe of the God of Israel.
²⁴ Those who are wayward in spirit will gain
understanding;
those who complain will accept
instruction."

Woe to the Obstinate Nation

30 "Woe to the obstinate children,"
declares the LORD,
"to those who carry out plans that are not
mine,
forming an alliance, but not by my Spirit,
heaping sin upon sin;
² who go down to Egypt
without consulting me;
who look for help to Pharaoh's protection,
to Egypt's shade for refuge.
³ But Pharaoh's protection will be to your
shame,
Egypt's shade will bring you disgrace.
⁴ Though they have officials in Zoan
and their envoys have arrived in Hanes,
⁵ everyone will be put to shame
because of a people useless to them,
who bring neither help nor advantage,
but only shame and disgrace."

⁶ A prophecy concerning the animals of the
Negev:

Through a land of hardship and distress,
of lions and lionesses,
of adders and darting snakes,
the envoys carry their riches on donkeys'
backs,
their treasures on the humps of camels,
to that unprofitable nation,
⁷ to Egypt, whose help is utterly useless.
Therefore I call her
Rahab the Do-Nothing.

⁸ Go now, write it on a tablet for them,
inscribe it on a scroll,
that for the days to come
it may be an everlasting witness.
⁹ For these are rebellious people, deceitful
children,
children unwilling to listen to the LORD's
instruction.
¹⁰ They say to the seers,
"See no more visions!"
and to the prophets,
"Give us no more visions of what is
right!
Tell us pleasant things,
prophesy illusions.
¹¹ Leave this way,
get off this path,
and stop confronting us
with the Holy One of Israel!"

29:23 their children, the work of my hands God's chosen are also referred to as the work of his hands in 60:21. In 19:25, Assyria and Egypt are folded into the chosen people (symbolizing salvation extending to the nations).
29:24 will accept instruction Understanding and accepting instruction are prerequisites of true wisdom (see Pr 1:1–7; 9:9).

30:1–7 Judah sought an alliance with Egypt to strengthen their position against Assyrian invasion (see Isa 36:6). Isaiah's critique of that plan is focused on the people's failure to seek Yahweh's counsel on the matter before carrying out their own plans. They looked for human help instead of relying on God. The criticism of an alliance with Egypt does not suggest that submission to Assyria represented the correct path, only that God should have been consulted before they decided which path to take.

30:2 without consulting me In the ancient Near East, it was customary to seek guidance of a deity in political matters of this magnitude. The Israelites' failure to ask for Yahweh's guidance reflects a dangerous level of pride and self-sufficiency (see 29:15).
30:3 Pharaoh's protection Egypt gave the appearance of being able to protect others, but they had little influence outside their own borders.
30:4 Zoan See note on 19:11. **Hanes** Probably a city in the south central Nile delta region, Egypt's main power center.
30:6 A prophecy concerning the animals of the

Negev Reminiscent of the oracles against the nations in chs. 13–27. The Negev was a desert region south of Palestine bordering on Egyptian territory in the Sinai Peninsula. **darting snakes** See Dt 8:15 for the characterization of the wilderness as the land of such serpents. Imagery of a flying serpent was known from Egyptian art (see note on Isa 6:2).
30:7 Rahab A mythological beast (like the serpent Leviathan) whose defeat brought order to the universe. Rahab may be a poetic name for Egypt in Ps 87:4. The image portrays a former formidable enemy that now sits powerless.

30:8–17 The people's rebellious attitudes are revealed in their blatant refusal to hear the truth from God's prophets. Instead, they insist on hearing only good news — even if it's false. The satirical depiction of Judah's people asking for illusions (Isa 30:10) instead of the truth confirms the mockery they are making of their faith (29:13).

30:8 write it on a tablet for them Isaiah records the message for posterity, just as in 8:16–18. The people may be unwilling to listen at the present time, but it will be preserved for the time when they are ready to repent (see Hab 2:2).
30:10 Tell us pleasant things The people only want to hear of blessing and prosperity — fantasy instead of reality. In 1Ki 22, King Ahab prefers the favorable counsel of false prophets and initially avoids inquiring of the prophet Micaiah because he never gave him good news (1Ki 22:18). **prophesy illusions** The people

12 Therefore this is what the Holy One of Israel says:

"Because you have rejected this message,
    relied on oppression
    and depended on deceit,
13 this sin will become for you
    like a high wall, cracked and bulging,
    that collapses suddenly, in an instant.
14 It will break in pieces like pottery,
    shattered so mercilessly
that among its pieces not a fragment will be
        found
    for taking coals from a hearth
    or scooping water out of a cistern."

15 This is what the Sovereign LORD, the Holy
One of Israel, says:

"In repentance and rest is your salvation,
    in quietness and trust is your strength,
    but you would have none of it.
16 You said, 'No, we will flee on horses.'
    Therefore you will flee!
You said, 'We will ride off on swift horses.'
    Therefore your pursuers will be swift!
17 A thousand will flee
    at the threat of one;
at the threat of five
    you will all flee away,
till you are left
    like a flagstaff on a mountaintop,
    like a banner on a hill."

18 Yet the LORD longs to be gracious to you;
    therefore he will rise up to show you
        compassion.
For the LORD is a God of justice.
    Blessed are all who wait for him!

19 People of Zion, who live in Jerusalem, you will
weep no more. How gracious he will be when you
cry for help! As soon as he hears, he will answer
you. 20 Although the Lord gives you the bread of
adversity and the water of affliction, your teachers
will be hidden no more; with your own eyes you
will see them. 21 Whether you turn to the right or
to the left, your ears will hear a voice behind you,
saying, "This is the way; walk in it." 22 Then you
will desecrate your idols overlaid with silver and
your images covered with gold; you will throw
them away like a menstrual cloth and say to them,
"Away with you!"

23 He will also send you rain for the seed you sow
in the ground, and the food that comes from the
land will be rich and plentiful. In that day your
cattle will graze in broad meadows. 24 The oxen
and donkeys that work the soil will eat fodder
and mash, spread out with fork and shovel. 25 In
the day of great slaughter, when the towers fall,
streams of water will flow on every high mountain and every lofty hill. 26 The moon will shine
like the sun, and the sunlight will be seven times
brighter, like the light of seven full days, when
the LORD binds up the bruises of his people and
heals the wounds he inflicted.

27 See, the Name of the LORD comes from afar,
    with burning anger and dense clouds of
        smoke;
his lips are full of wrath,
    and his tongue is a consuming fire.
28 His breath is like a rushing torrent,
    rising up to the neck.
He shakes the nations in the sieve of
        destruction;
    he places in the jaws of the peoples
    a bit that leads them astray.
29 And you will sing
    as on the night you celebrate a holy
        festival;

---

prefer false prophets. The true prophets of Yahweh are
consistently at odds with others falsely claiming to speak
on Yahweh's behalf.

30:14 not a fragment will be found Broken pottery
could be reused—sometimes as writing material. This
metaphor indicates nothing useful will be gained from
an alliance with Egypt.

30:16 we will flee on horses Cavalry and chariots were
likely a part of any military assistance sent by Egypt (see
Isa 31:1–3). The Assyrian general who mocks Judah's
efforts at resistance refers to their need for horses from
Egypt, and even offers to provide Judah with horses if they
can provide riders to put up a fight (see 2Ki 18:23–24).

30:17 A thousand Alludes to Dt 32:30, where a thousand are chased away by one because Yahweh had given
them over for judgment.

30:18–33 The tension between divine justice and divine
mercy requires God to restrain his grace for a time. The
people ignored God and sought salvation from a human
power that ultimately failed, but God waits to restore
them to true salvation.

30:22 you will desecrate your idols Full repentance
required a clean break from idolatry. Israelite worship
had become a blend of Yahweh worship and worship
of Canaanite, Ammonite and Moabite deities (see 1Ki
11:1–8; 2Ki 23:4–14). Isaiah 2:20 also depicts people
throwing away their idols.

30:25 every high mountain and every lofty hill After
Israel abandons its idols, Yahweh restores the abundance
and fertility of the land. His anger against every lofty
mountain and high hill has also subsided (see 2:14).

30:27 his tongue is a consuming fire Yahweh comes
with typical divine theophanic imagery (see 29:6 and note).

30:28 His breath The same Hebrew word for "breath,"
ruach, can refer to "wind" or "spirit." Lips, tongue and
breath are Yahweh's offensive weapons. Compare 11:4
where the Messiah will destroy the wicked with his breath.

a rushing torrent, rising up to the neck Before, Assyria
came down like a flood against Israel, leaving Judah up
to the neck in water (8:7–8). Now the image is reversed:
Yahweh is coming to punish Assyria.

30:29 mountain of the LORD Refers to Mount Zion as
God's dwelling place. See note on 2:2.

your hearts will rejoice
　　as when people playing pipes go up
to the mountain of the LORD,
　　to the Rock of Israel.
30 The LORD will cause people to hear his
　　　majestic voice
　　and will make them see his arm coming
　　　down
with raging anger and consuming fire,
　　with cloudburst, thunderstorm and hail.
31 The voice of the LORD will shatter Assyria;
　　with his rod he will strike them down.
32 Every stroke the LORD lays on them
　　with his punishing club
will be to the music of timbrels and harps,
　　as he fights them in battle with the blows
　　　of his arm.
33 Topheth has long been prepared;
　　it has been made ready for the king.
Its fire pit has been made deep and wide,
　　with an abundance of fire and wood;
the breath of the LORD,
　　like a stream of burning sulfur,
　　sets it ablaze.

Woe to Those Who Rely on Egypt

31 Woe to those who go down to Egypt for
　　help,
　　who rely on horses,
who trust in the multitude of their chariots
　　and in the great strength of their
　　　horsemen,
but do not look to the Holy One of Israel,
　　or seek help from the LORD.
2 Yet he too is wise and can bring disaster;
　　he does not take back his words.
He will rise up against that wicked nation,
　　against those who help evildoers.
3 But the Egyptians are mere mortals and not
　　God;
　　their horses are flesh and not spirit.

When the LORD stretches out his hand,
　　those who help will stumble,
　　those who are helped will fall;
　　all will perish together.

4 This is what the LORD says to me:

"As a lion growls,
　　a great lion over its prey —
and though a whole band of shepherds
　　is called together against it,
it is not frightened by their shouts
　　or disturbed by their clamor —
so the LORD Almighty will come down
　　to do battle on Mount Zion and on its
　　　heights.
5 Like birds hovering overhead,
　　the LORD Almighty will shield Jerusalem;
he will shield it and deliver it,
　　he will 'pass over' it and will rescue it."

6 Return, you Israelites, to the One you have so
greatly revolted against. 7 For in that day every
one of you will reject the idols of silver and gold
your sinful hands have made.

8 "Assyria will fall by no human sword;
　　a sword, not of mortals, will devour them.
They will flee before the sword
　　and their young men will be put to forced
　　　labor.
9 Their stronghold will fall because of terror;
　　at the sight of the battle standard their
　　　commanders will panic,"
declares the LORD,
　　whose fire is in Zion,
　　whose furnace is in Jerusalem.

The Kingdom of Righteousness

32 See, a king will reign in righteousness
　　and rulers will rule with justice.
2 Each one will be like a shelter from the wind
　　and a refuge from the storm,

30:31 with his rod he will strike them down A reversal of 10:5, where Assyria was the rod. Now, they are struck by it.
30:33 Topheth This Hebrew term, *tophteh,* is a variation on Topheth, a name for a religious site near Jerusalem where child sacrifice was performed (2Ki 23:10; Jer 7:31–32).

31:1–9 This chapter briefly reiterates the folly of seeking help from Egypt. It uses imagery from Isa 29–30, including the reliance on Egyptian horses and Yahweh's siege and rescue of Jerusalem.

31:1 do not look to the Holy One When threatened by Assyria, the people of Judah sought help from Egypt instead of God (see 30:2).
31:3 all will perish together Judah and Egypt both suffered from Assyrian domination and destruction. Sennacherib destroyed many cities of Judah (701 BC). His son, Esarhaddon, conquered the Egyptian city of

Memphis (671 BC). See the timeline "Dates Related to Isaiah and 2 Kings" on p. 1116.
31:4 As a lion growls, a great lion Like a lion, Yahweh comes down to Zion. But while they expect him to defend his holy mountain, he comes to fight against it: Zion is the fallen prey. God offers judgment, then mercy. He besieges Zion, then rescues it. **LORD Almighty** A title referring to God as the leader of the heavenly armies. See note on 1:9.
31:5 Like birds hovering overhead God besieges, then rescues Zion. The imagery here is of a bird hovering over its nest to protect; such imagery is also found in Dt 32:11 and Ps 91:4.
31:8 by no human sword God fights for Israel—no human alliance was necessary (see Isa 37:36–38). The deliverance is conditional on repentance. Hezekiah intercedes on behalf of the people in 37:14–20, right before the promised rescue.

like streams of water in the desert
    and the shadow of a great rock in a thirsty
        land.

³ Then the eyes of those who see will no longer
        be closed,
    and the ears of those who hear will listen.
⁴ The fearful heart will know and understand,
    and the stammering tongue will be fluent
        and clear.
⁵ No longer will the fool be called noble
    nor the scoundrel be highly respected.
⁶ For fools speak folly,
    their hearts are bent on evil:
They practice ungodliness
    and spread error concerning the LORD;
the hungry they leave empty
    and from the thirsty they withhold water.
⁷ Scoundrels use wicked methods,
    they make up evil schemes
to destroy the poor with lies,
    even when the plea of the needy is just.
⁸ But the noble make noble plans,
    and by noble deeds they stand.

The Women of Jerusalem

⁹ You women who are so complacent,
    rise up and listen to me;
you daughters who feel secure,
    hear what I have to say!
¹⁰ In little more than a year
    you who feel secure will tremble;
the grape harvest will fail,
    and the harvest of fruit will not come.

¹¹ Tremble, you complacent women;
    shudder, you daughters who feel
        secure!
Strip off your fine clothes
    and wrap yourselves in rags.
¹² Beat your breasts for the pleasant fields,
    for the fruitful vines
¹³ and for the land of my people,
    a land overgrown with thorns and briers —
yes, mourn for all houses of merriment
    and for this city of revelry.
¹⁴ The fortress will be abandoned,
    the noisy city deserted;
citadel and watchtower will become a
        wasteland forever,
    the delight of donkeys, a pasture for flocks,
¹⁵ till the Spirit is poured on us from on high,
    and the desert becomes a fertile field,
    and the fertile field seems like a forest.
¹⁶ The LORD's justice will dwell in the desert,
    his righteousness live in the fertile field.
¹⁷ The fruit of that righteousness will be peace;
    its effect will be quietness and confidence
        forever.
¹⁸ My people will live in peaceful dwelling
        places,
    in secure homes,
    in undisturbed places of rest.
¹⁹ Though hail flattens the forest
    and the city is leveled completely,
²⁰ how blessed you will be,
    sowing your seed by every stream,
    and letting your cattle and donkeys range
        free.

32:1–8 The series of six "woe" sayings (see note on 28:1–13) is interrupted by a vision of future calm under the reign of a righteous king. This placement emphasizes the future deliverance of Jerusalem and the peace that will follow if they return and repent as in 30:15 and 31:6.

32:1 a king will reign in righteousness May refer to the Messiah (see 11:1–4) or a repentant king of Judah. Hezekiah's repentance in 37:14–20 contrasts the unrepentant Ahaz of 7:12–13. Psalm 72 praises David's successors, urging them to rule in righteousness and justice. Hezekiah is portrayed as one of the most godly kings of Judah, who removed idolatrous worship from Judah and followed Yahweh like David (see 2Ki 18:3–7).
32:3 the eyes of those who see See note on Isa 29:18. Once again, the message will finally be received, understood and accepted.
32:4 stammering tongue Compare the gibberish spoken in 28:10–11 (see note on 28:10).
32:6 their hearts are bent on evil Isaiah criticizes the arrogance and injustice of the leaders (as in 5:8–20), the false prophecies (30:10) and the failure of leaders to provide for the less fortunate (1:16–17).

32:9–20 The women of Judah—more concerned with their physical appearance—have also lost their way spiritually (see 3:16–4:1). The call to repent in 31:6 is re-emphasized and addressed beyond the leadership of

Israel to the entire population; repentance must be more than the lone act of a humbled king (see note on v. 1). Images of desolation intertwine with glimpses of future renewal and deliverance.

32:10 In little more than a year The Assyrian invasion occurred in 701 BC.
32:11 Strip off your fine clothes Refers to actions of grief, distress and mourning. The actions foreshadow the humiliation of invasion and exile, or may be outward signs of humility and repentance. Babylon receives a similar humiliation in 47:2–3.
32:14 the delight of donkeys Nature overruns what was formerly a civilized, populous city (see 27:10; 34:11–15).
32:15 Spirit is poured on us from on high Future reversal and restoration is enabled by an outpouring of God's Spirit (see Joel 2:28).
32:17 will be quietness and confidence forever This same effect was predicted in Isa 30:15. The false ease and security of the women in v. 9 is replaced by genuine rest and security that comes from the righteousness of God.

32:20 Describes the return to an Eden-like ecological peace (see 30:23–24). The domesticated ox and the donkey were usually kept penned in so they would not wander into danger or off the owner's property (see Ex 21:33; 23:4).

Distress and Help

33 Woe to you, destroyer,
you who have not been destroyed!
Woe to you, betrayer,
you who have not been betrayed!
When you stop destroying,
you will be destroyed;
when you stop betraying,
you will be betrayed.

[2] Lord, be gracious to us;
we long for you.
Be our strength every morning,
our salvation in time of distress.
[3] At the uproar of your army, the peoples flee;
when you rise up, the nations scatter.
[4] Your plunder, O nations, is harvested as by
young locusts;
like a swarm of locusts people pounce
on it.

[5] The Lord is exalted, for he dwells on high;
he will fill Zion with his justice and
righteousness.
[6] He will be the sure foundation for your times,
a rich store of salvation and wisdom and
knowledge;
the fear of the Lord is the key to this
treasure.[a]

[7] Look, their brave men cry aloud in the
streets;
the envoys of peace weep bitterly.
[8] The highways are deserted,
no travelers are on the roads.
The treaty is broken,
its witnesses[b] are despised,
no one is respected.
[9] The land dries up and wastes away,
Lebanon is ashamed and withers;
Sharon is like the Arabah,
and Bashan and Carmel drop their leaves.

[10] "Now will I arise," says the Lord.
"Now will I be exalted;
now will I be lifted up.
[11] You conceive chaff,
you give birth to straw;
your breath is a fire that consumes you.
[12] The peoples will be burned to ashes;
like cut thornbushes they will be set
ablaze."

[13] You who are far away, hear what I have done;
you who are near, acknowledge my power!
[14] The sinners in Zion are terrified;
trembling grips the godless:
"Who of us can dwell with the consuming
fire?
Who of us can dwell with everlasting
burning?"
[15] Those who walk righteously
and speak what is right,
who reject gain from extortion
and keep their hands from accepting
bribes,
who stop their ears against plots of murder
and shut their eyes against contemplating
evil—
[16] they are the ones who will dwell on the
heights,
whose refuge will be the mountain
fortress.
Their bread will be supplied,
and water will not fail them.

[17] Your eyes will see the king in his beauty
and view a land that stretches afar.
[18] In your thoughts you will ponder the former
terror:
"Where is that chief officer?
Where is the one who took the revenue?
Where is the officer in charge of the
towers?"

---

[a] 6 Or *is a treasure from him*   [b] 8 Dead Sea Scrolls; Masoretic
Text / *the cities*

33:1–24 This chapter is a final "woe" on the oppressors of Judah, presenting the judgment Yahweh will bring on them in defense of his people (compare Isa 31:8–9). The themes of judgment on the nations and exaltation of God mix together against the backdrop of Judah's repentance (v. 2).

33:1 to you, destroyer The crisis of 701 BC and the narrative account of that incident in chs. 36–39 suggest this refers to Assyria.

33:2 Lord, be gracious to us A psalm-like appeal to Yahweh, and a sign of the repentance of the people who wait on God's salvation (see 25:9; compare 36:18).

33:5 he will fill Zion with his justice and righteousness The prophet is confident in God's plan to rise up and save Zion, especially after the repentant appeal of v. 2.

33:8 treaty is broken Hezekiah paid tribute to Assyria (see 2Ki 18:14–17), but Assyria attacked anyway. The invasion was a breach of their agreement.

33:9 The land dries up and wastes away The land is experiencing the decline that accompanied judgment (see Isa 32:10 and note). **Sharon** A coastal plain northwest of Jerusalem that served as a prime transportation route from the north to the region of Judah.

33:10 will I arise God arises to bring justice as promised. See note on v. 5.

33:11 a fire that consumes you The image of fire used in judgment against Assyria is familiar from 10:16–17.

33:12 burned to ashes Burning human bones to make lime from their ashes showed disrespect for the body of the dead (see note on Am 2:1; compare Isa 10:17).

33:16 water will not fail them Contrasts with the bread of adversity and water of affliction in 30:20—after judgment, mercy and provision.

33:17 will see the king in his beauty Either a reference to God himself as in 6:5, or an allusion to the righteous king of 32:1–8 (see note on 32:1). The image of king is directly appropriated for Yahweh in v. 22.

¹⁹ You will see those arrogant people no more,
  people whose speech is obscure,
  whose language is strange and
   incomprehensible.

²⁰ Look on Zion, the city of our festivals;
  your eyes will see Jerusalem,
  a peaceful abode, a tent that will not be
   moved;
 its stakes will never be pulled up,
  nor any of its ropes broken.
²¹ There the LORD will be our Mighty One.
  It will be like a place of broad rivers and
   streams.
 No galley with oars will ride them,
  no mighty ship will sail them.
²² For the LORD is our judge,
  the LORD is our lawgiver,
  the LORD is our king;
  it is he who will save us.

²³ Your rigging hangs loose:
  The mast is not held secure,
  the sail is not spread.
 Then an abundance of spoils will be divided
  and even the lame will carry off plunder.
²⁴ No one living in Zion will say, "I am ill";
  and the sins of those who dwell there will
   be forgiven.

Judgment Against the Nations

34 Come near, you nations, and listen;
  pay attention, you peoples!
 Let the earth hear, and all that is in it,
  the world, and all that comes out of it!

² The LORD is angry with all nations;
  his wrath is on all their armies.
 He will totally destroy[a] them,
  he will give them over to slaughter.
³ Their slain will be thrown out,
  their dead bodies will stink;
  the mountains will be soaked with their
   blood.
⁴ All the stars in the sky will be dissolved
  and the heavens rolled up like a scroll;
 all the starry host will fall
  like withered leaves from the vine,
  like shriveled figs from the fig tree.

⁵ My sword has drunk its fill in the heavens;
  see, it descends in judgment on Edom,
  the people I have totally destroyed.
⁶ The sword of the LORD is bathed in blood,
  it is covered with fat —
 the blood of lambs and goats,
  fat from the kidneys of rams.
 For the LORD has a sacrifice in Bozrah
  and a great slaughter in the land of Edom.
⁷ And the wild oxen will fall with them,
  the bull calves and the great bulls.
 Their land will be drenched with blood,
  and the dust will be soaked with fat.

⁸ For the LORD has a day of vengeance,
  a year of retribution, to uphold Zion's cause.
⁹ Edom's streams will be turned into pitch,
  her dust into burning sulfur;
  her land will become blazing pitch!

[a] 2 The Hebrew term refers to the irrevocable giving over of things or persons to the LORD, often by totally destroying them; also in verse 5.

33:19 arrogant people Refers to the arrogant Assyrians as in 10:12–14. See 28:11.
33:20 our festivals The Hebrew term here is singular, so it likely denotes a specific feast or festival. Jerusalem is the focal point where sacred time was observed. See the table "Israelite Festivals" on p. 200. **a peaceful abode** Reverses the image of distress in vv. 7–9. Like most oracles of salvation and restoration in Isaiah, this idyllic view of the future of Zion best fits in the future reign of the Messianic king when all the nations have acknowledged Yahweh's sovereignty (see 2:2–4; 11:1–16).
33:22 LORD is our judge Yahweh's ultimate sovereignty is acknowledged as the people realize he is the only righteous judge, lawgiver and rightful king.
33:24 sins of those who dwell there will be forgiven The remnant will be forgiven based on the redemptive work of Yahweh (compare Jer 50:20; Isa 1:26). Also note the redemptive role of the Servant in 53:11.

34:1–17 Isaiah returns to the theme of cosmic judgment (using language reminiscent of chs. 24–27) as a reminder that the deliverance foreshadowed in ch. 33 is part of Yahweh's larger plan of judgment against the nations (chs. 13–27).

34:1 Come near, you nations, and listen The invocation calls all peoples to attention in order to contrast the folly of human pride with the wisdom of trusting in God.

34:2 angry with all nations Describes a disaster like the global destruction of 24:1–6, but with the added element of rage. Rage and anger in the OT have a connotation of heat and fire (see Dt 29:27–28), hinting at the fiery destruction promised to the nations in Isa 33:10–12. **He will totally destroy them** In war, items devoted to destruction were under a sacred ban (see Lev 27:28 and note). The destruction in this context was like an act of sacrifice, set apart to please God (see Jos 6:17–18; Dt 7:2; 20:17).
34:4 All the stars in the sky will be dissolved Images of cosmic destruction beyond the scope of the slaughter of the nations' armies.
34:5 judgment on Edom All the nations were devoted to destruction in Isa 34:2 (see note on v. 2). Now, Edom receives the brunt of God's wrath as representative of all the enemies of Yahweh. The absence of Edom in Isaiah's earlier cycle of oracles is likely deliberate, setting up Edom as the nation to receive God's wrath against all the earth. Later Jewish and Christian texts use "Edom" as a cipher for Rome, the ultimate enemy.
34:6 it is covered with fat—the blood Biblical sacrifice required blood and fat—especially the fat around organs like the kidneys. The imagery sets up the announcement in the next line that Yahweh has a sacrifice (see Lev 3:1–17).
34:8 retribution, to uphold Zion's cause The people expected God to defend Zion, but misunderstood that

¹⁰ It will not be quenched night or day;
    its smoke will rise forever.
From generation to generation it will lie
    desolate;
    no one will ever pass through it again.
¹¹ The desert owlᵃ and screech owlᵃ will
    possess it;
    the great owlᵃ and the raven will nest
    there.
God will stretch out over Edom
    the measuring line of chaos
    and the plumb line of desolation.
¹² Her nobles will have nothing there to be
    called a kingdom,
    all her princes will vanish away.
¹³ Thorns will overrun her citadels,
    nettles and brambles her strongholds.
She will become a haunt for jackals,
    a home for owls.
¹⁴ Desert creatures will meet with hyenas,
    and wild goats will bleat to each other;
there the night creatures will also lie down
    and find for themselves places of rest.
¹⁵ The owl will nest there and lay eggs,
    she will hatch them, and care for her
    young
    under the shadow of her wings;
there also the falcons will gather,
    each with its mate.

¹⁶ Look in the scroll of the LORD and read:

None of these will be missing,
    not one will lack her mate.
For it is his mouth that has given the order,
    and his Spirit will gather them together.
¹⁷ He allots their portions;
    his hand distributes them by measure.

They will possess it forever
    and dwell there from generation to
    generation.

Joy of the Redeemed

35 The desert and the parched land will
    be glad;
    the wilderness will rejoice and
    blossom.
Like the crocus, ²it will burst into bloom;
    it will rejoice greatly and shout for joy.
The glory of Lebanon will be given to it,
    the splendor of Carmel and
    Sharon;
they will see the glory of the LORD,
    the splendor of our God.

³ Strengthen the feeble hands,
    steady the knees that give way;
⁴ say to those with fearful hearts,
    "Be strong, do not fear;
your God will come,
    he will come with vengeance;
with divine retribution
    he will come to save you."

⁵ Then will the eyes of the blind be opened
    and the ears of the deaf unstopped.
⁶ Then will the lame leap like a deer,
    and the mute tongue shout for joy.
Water will gush forth in the wilderness
    and streams in the desert.
⁷ The burning sand will become a pool,
    the thirsty ground bubbling springs.
In the haunts where jackals once lay,
    grass and reeds and papyrus will grow.

ᵃ 11 The precise identification of these birds is uncertain.

---

his concern was unconditional and temporal. Rather than preach repentance, many false prophets advocated complacency: Surely God would not allow harm to come to Zion. But judgment and repentance were necessary before God would arise (see Isa 33:2–10; 30:10 and note).
34:10 It will not be quenched night or day Edom is turned into a perpetual place of burning pitch and sulfur, similar to NT images of the lake of fire (Rev 14:11; 20:10).
34:11 over Edom the measuring line of chaos Alludes to the return to ancient primeval chaos through the rare combination of the Hebrew words *tohu* and *bohu* ("emptiness" and "nothing"). In Ge 1:2, the earth was similarly *tohu* and *bohu* (see note on Ge 1:2). Note a similar allusion to the undoing of creation in Jer 4:23.
34:14 night creatures The Hebrew noun *lilith* appears only here in the Bible and may be related to the Hebrew word for "night" (*laylah*). The surrounding references to wildlife suggest the possibility that "Lilith" is a nocturnal animal. In Mesopotamian mythology, Lilith was the name of a demon.
34:16 in the scroll of the LORD A hint that God's commands and prophecies (probably those recorded in Isaiah) exist in some written form. Note the command to bind the testimony in Isa 8:16 and record the prophecy in 30:8.

35:1–10 The undoing of creation through judgment in 34:4–15 is reversed; a rejuvenation and renewal of the created order heralds the return of the righteous remnant to Zion.

35:1 wilderness will rejoice The return of God's people is cast as a second exodus—this time through a wilderness filled with gladness, rejoicing and singing (contrast the harsh and terrifying wilderness of Ex 15:22; Dt 1:19).

35:2 This verse references the lush, fertile regions on the edge of Israel and Judah's territories. The image directly contrasts the withering away of Lebanon, Carmel and Sharon (see 33:9 and note).

35:5 will the eyes of the blind be opened Symbolizes the coming of God's salvation—blind see, deaf hear, lame walk and mute sing (compare 29:18; 32:3–4; 42:7; and Jesus's allusion in Lk 7:22).

35:7 thirsty ground bubbling springs The renewal of a desert into a waterway echoes the exodus events of water bursting from the desert rocks (see Nu 20:2–13); it is used again in Isa 48:20–21 and 49:10.

8 And a highway will be there;
    it will be called the Way of Holiness;
    it will be for those who walk on that Way.
    The unclean will not journey on it;
    wicked fools will not go about on it.
9 No lion will be there,
    nor any ravenous beast;
    they will not be found there.
    But only the redeemed will walk there,
10   and those the LORD has rescued will
        return.
    They will enter Zion with singing;
    everlasting joy will crown their heads.
    Gladness and joy will overtake them,
    and sorrow and sighing will flee away.

Sennacherib Threatens Jerusalem

36:1-22pp — 2Ki 18:13,17-37; 2Ch 32:9-19

36 In the fourteenth year of King Hezekiah's reign, Sennacherib king of Assyria attacked all the fortified cities of Judah and captured them. 2 Then the king of Assyria sent his field commander with a large army from Lachish to King Hezekiah at Jerusalem. When the commander stopped at the aqueduct of the Upper Pool, on the road to the Launderer's Field, 3 Eliakim son of Hilkiah the palace administrator, Shebna the secretary, and Joah son of Asaph the recorder went out to him.

4 The field commander said to them, "Tell Hezekiah:

"'This is what the great king, the king of Assyria, says: On what are you basing this confidence of yours? 5 You say you have counsel and might for war — but you speak only empty words. On whom are you depending, that you rebel against me? 6 Look, I know you are depending on Egypt, that splintered reed of a staff, which pierces the hand of anyone who leans on it! Such is Pharaoh king of Egypt to all who depend on him. 7 But if you say to me, "We are depending on the LORD our God" — isn't he the one whose high places and altars Hezekiah removed, saying to Judah

35:8 a highway will be there See 40:3. **The unclean will not journey on it** The idea of a righteous remnant that returns to Zion is implied by the designation of this highway as sacred—the Way of Holiness. Those who are ritually unclean cannot travel along this route. The imagery gives hope to those suffering under the threat of exile in Isaiah's day. Its ultimate fulfillment points to the future state of Zion under the Messiah's rule, where all who inhabit Zion are called "holy" (see 4:3–4).
35:9 No lion will be there Describes the peace in the natural world that accompanies the Messiah's reign (see 11:6–8).
35:10 those the LORD has rescued will return Illustrates the ultimate future triumph of Yahweh and the deliverance of his people through their return. Their return foreshadows the establishment of salvation under a new covenant based on the atonement of Christ (see Heb 12:22–24).
36:1–22 While most of the book of Isaiah is poetic, the narratives of Isa 6–8 and Isa 36–39 provide a historical setting for the two major crises that form the background of Isaiah's message. This narrative focuses on the Assyrian crisis faced by King Hezekiah of Judah around 701 BC. These chapters cover the same events as 2Ki 18:13—20:19. The overlap suggests the two books may have common authorship or a common source. Other Biblical passages give Isaiah a role in writing the court histories of Uzziah and Hezekiah (2Ch 26:22; 32:32). See the timeline "Judah From the Fall of Samaria to the Exile" on p. 606; see the timeline "Dates Related to Isaiah and 2 Kings" on p. 1116.

36:1 fourteenth year of King Hezekiah's reign 701 BC; see 2Ki 18:13. Second Kings indicates that Hezekiah rebelled against Assyria (2Ki 18:7), causing Sennacherib to invade. However, Hezekiah's religious reform and strict observance of Yahweh worship is praised in 2 Kings; his ability to stand up to Assyria was connected to divine blessing in 2Ki 18:7.
36:2 a large army While the Assyrian king besieges Lachish, he sends a high-ranking official to pressure Hezekiah into surrender. This official's title translates as "chief cupbearer." The siege of Lachish was well-documented in a series of reliefs decorating a room of Sennacherib's palace in Nineveh. **the road to the Launderer's Field** The Assyrian official meets the envoys of Hezekiah at the very place where Isaiah met Ahaz (Isa 7:3).
36:3 Eliakim son of Hilkiah Eliakim was promoted to chief steward, an office formerly held by Shebna. See 22:15–25. **Shebna the secretary** Shebna was formerly the one "over the household" (the chief steward), but was demoted by God for his pride. See 22:15. **Joah** Means "Yahweh is brother." Joah's presence in the embassy to the Assyrian official suggests he is an important member of the court.
36:4 This is what the great king, the king of Assyria, says The Assyrian official's speech in vv. 4–20 matches 2Ki 18:19–35 almost verbatim, suggesting an official record of his words existed.
36:5 On whom are you depending Trust is a repeated theme in the Assyrian official's speech; it highlights the message of Isaiah all along—that Judah should trust in Yahweh alone, not Egypt, human wisdom or military strength. The Assyrian's speech mocks the idea that Egypt can be trusted, or that trust in Yahweh will bring success. He claims that Yahweh himself sent Assyria against Judah (see Isa 36:10).
36:6 Pharaoh king of Egypt to all Shabaka, the pharaoh at this time, handed over former allies in 712 BC after Ashdod fell to Assyria.
36:7 high places See note on 57:7.

DATE	EVENT
725–722 BC	Assyrians besiege Samaria. The Israelites are defeated and sent into exile.
705 BC	Sennacherib becomes king.
701 BC	Sennacherib invades Judah.
681 BC	Sennacherib is assassinated by two of his sons.

and Jerusalem, "You must worship before this altar"?

8 "Come now, make a bargain with my master, the king of Assyria: I will give you two thousand horses — if you can put riders on them! 9How then can you repulse one officer of the least of my master's officials, even though you are depending on Egypt for chariots and horsemen[a]? 10Furthermore, have I come to attack and destroy this land

[a] 9 Or charioteers

36:10 have I come to attack and destroy this land without the LORD Isaiah 10:5–6 indicates this is a true assertion: Yahweh sent Assyria to judge Israel and Judah.

Dates Related to Isaiah and 2 Kings

740 BC   720 BC   700 BC   680 BC

717 BC Sargon II defeats the Philistine city of Ashdod and deposes its king (Isa 20:1).

705 BC Sennacherib, son of Sargon, becomes king and moves the Assyrian capital to Nineveh.

701 BC Sennacherib invades Judah but returns to Assyria without conquering Jerusalem (2Ki 18:13–19:36; 2Ch 32:1–32:20; Isa 36:1–37:35).

689 BC Sennacherib sacks Babylon.

681 BC Sennacherib is assassinated by two of his sons. Esarhaddon becomes king (2Ki 19:37; 2Ch 32:21; Isa 37:38).

725–722 BC Shalmaneser begins a three-year siege of Samaria. The Israelites are defeated and sent into exile by the new king, Sargon II (2Ki 17:4–6; 2Ki 18:9–10).

727 BC Shalmaneser V becomes king.

734 BC Tiglath-Pileser defeats Pekah king of Israel (2Ki 15:29; 1Ch 5:26).

734 BC Ahaz king of Judah becomes vassal of Tiglath-Pileser (2Ki 16:7–9; 2Ch 28:16–21).

738 BC Menahem king of Israel becomes vassal of Tiglath-Pileser (2Ki 15:19–20).

745 BC Tiglath-Pileser III, son of Adad-nirari III, becomes king.

740 BC   720 BC   700 BC   680 BC

All dates are approximate

without the LORD? The LORD himself told me to march against this country and destroy it.'"

¹¹Then Eliakim, Shebna and Joah said to the field commander, "Please speak to your servants in Aramaic, since we understand it. Don't speak to us in Hebrew in the hearing of the people on the wall."

¹²But the commander replied, "Was it only to your master and you that my master sent me to say these things, and not to the people sitting on

---

36:11 Please speak to your servants in Aramaic The Judean officials ask to conduct their negotiations in Aramaic—the international language of business and diplomacy at this time—rather than Hebrew. They fear that a general panic might set in among the people of Jerusalem if they hear the threats directly.

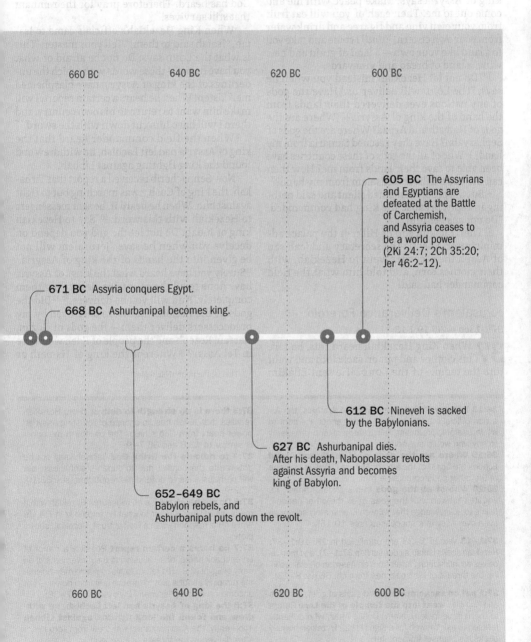

660 BC   640 BC   620 BC   600 BC

605 BC The Assyrians and Egyptians are defeated at the Battle of Carchemish, and Assyria ceases to be a world power (2Ki 24:7; 2Ch 35:20; Jer 46:2-12).

671 BC Assyria conquers Egypt.

668 BC Ashurbanipal becomes king.

612 BC Nineveh is sacked by the Babylonians.

627 BC Ashurbanipal dies. After his death, Nabopolassar revolts against Assyria and becomes king of Babylon.

652-649 BC Babylon rebels, and Ashurbanipal puts down the revolt.

660 BC   640 BC   620 BC   600 BC

the wall—who, like you, will have to eat their own excrement and drink their own urine?"

¹³Then the commander stood and called out in Hebrew, "Hear the words of the great king, the king of Assyria! ¹⁴This is what the king says: Do not let Hezekiah deceive you. He cannot deliver you! ¹⁵Do not let Hezekiah persuade you to trust in the Lord when he says, 'The Lord will surely deliver us; this city will not be given into the hand of the king of Assyria.'

¹⁶"Do not listen to Hezekiah. This is what the king of Assyria says: Make peace with me and come out to me. Then each of you will eat fruit from your own vine and fig tree and drink water from your own cistern, ¹⁷until I come and take you to a land like your own—a land of grain and new wine, a land of bread and vineyards.

¹⁸"Do not let Hezekiah mislead you when he says, 'The Lord will deliver us.' Have the gods of any nations ever delivered their lands from the hand of the king of Assyria? ¹⁹Where are the gods of Hamath and Arpad? Where are the gods of Sepharvaim? Have they rescued Samaria from my hand? ²⁰Who of all the gods of these countries have been able to save their lands from me? How then can the Lord deliver Jerusalem from my hand?"

²¹But the people remained silent and said nothing in reply, because the king had commanded, "Do not answer him."

²²Then Eliakim son of Hilkiah the palace administrator, Shebna the secretary and Joah son of Asaph the recorder went to Hezekiah, with their clothes torn, and told him what the field commander had said.

Jerusalem's Deliverance Foretold

37:1-13pp — 2Ki 19:1-13

37 When King Hezekiah heard this, he tore his clothes and put on sackcloth and went into the temple of the Lord. ²He sent Eliakim the palace administrator, Shebna the secretary, and the leading priests, all wearing sackcloth, to the prophet Isaiah son of Amoz. ³They told him, "This is what Hezekiah says: This day is a day of distress and rebuke and disgrace, as when children come to the moment of birth and there is no strength to deliver them. ⁴It may be that the Lord your God will hear the words of the field commander, whom his master, the king of Assyria, has sent to ridicule the living God, and that he will rebuke him for the words the Lord your God has heard. Therefore pray for the remnant that still survives."

⁵When King Hezekiah's officials came to Isaiah, ⁶Isaiah said to them, "Tell your master, 'This is what the Lord says: Do not be afraid of what you have heard—those words with which the underlings of the king of Assyria have blasphemed me. ⁷Listen! When he hears a certain report, I will make him want to return to his own country, and there I will have him cut down with the sword.'"

⁸When the field commander heard that the king of Assyria had left Lachish, he withdrew and found the king fighting against Libnah.

⁹Now Sennacherib received a report that Tirhakah, the king of Cush,ᵃ was marching out to fight against him. When he heard it, he sent messengers to Hezekiah with this word: ¹⁰"Say to Hezekiah king of Judah: Do not let the god you depend on deceive you when he says, 'Jerusalem will not be given into the hands of the king of Assyria.' ¹¹Surely you have heard what the kings of Assyria have done to all the countries, destroying them completely. And will you be delivered? ¹²Did the gods of the nations that were destroyed by my predecessors deliver them—the gods of Gozan, Harran, Rezeph and the people of Eden who were in Tel Assar? ¹³Where is the king of Hamath or

ᵃ 9 That is, the upper Nile region

36:13 Hebrew Rather than switch to Aramaic, the Assyrian official makes an even bolder announcement to all Jerusalem, promising fair treatment and prosperity to any who would surrender.

36:19 Where are the gods of Hamath and Arpad Echoes the boast of the king of Assyria (10:8–11). None of the other gods could save their cities.

36:20 Who of all the gods In his prideful boast, he equates Yahweh with the gods of all the other nations, failing to acknowledge that Yahweh is ultimately sovereign even over Assyria's successes (see 10:15).

37:1–13 Verses 1–38 are paralleled in 2Ki 19:1–37. Hezekiah seeks Isaiah's counsel (Isa 37:1–7), and then receives an intimidating letter from an Assyrian official, echoing the threats of his speeches from ch. 36 (vv. 8–13).

37:1 put on sackcloth Outward signs of grief, distress and humility. **went into the temple of the Lord** Refers to the temple in Jerusalem. Unlike Ahaz, who defiantly refused to ask Yahweh for a sign (7:12), Hezekiah humbly seeks his counsel immediately.

37:3 there is no strength to deliver them Hezekiah realizes that Judah has no chance of resisting Assyrian power apart from God's help. The childbirth metaphor is similar to 13:8 and 66:7–9.

37:4 to ridicule the living God Yahweh may not be drawn into the conflict due to Judah's sinfulness, but will perhaps arise to defend his reputation (see 33:10; 37:35).

37:6 Do not be afraid Isaiah reassures Hezekiah with a message of trust similar to what he told Ahaz in 7:4–5. While Ahaz responds with a lack of trust, Hezekiah shows piety.

37:7 he hears a certain report Possibly a rumor of unrest back home, or an allusion to the movements of an army of Egypt (v. 9). His return to his own land may indicate the rumor is about a plot to remove him from power—not uncommon among Assyrian kings (see vv. 37–38).

37:8 the king of Assyria had left Lachish, he withdrew and found the king fighting against Libnah Apparently, the Assyrian army withdrew from Jerusalem after delivering the threats to Hezekiah.

the king of Arpad? Where are the kings of Lair, Sepharvaim, Hena and Ivvah?"

Hezekiah's Prayer

37:14-20pp — 2Ki 19:14-19

[14]Hezekiah received the letter from the messengers and read it. Then he went up to the temple of the LORD and spread it out before the LORD. [15]And Hezekiah prayed to the LORD: [16]"LORD Almighty, the God of Israel, enthroned between the cherubim, you alone are God over all the kingdoms of the earth. You have made heaven and earth. [17]Give ear, LORD, and hear; open your eyes, LORD, and see; listen to all the words Sennacherib has sent to ridicule the living God.

[18]"It is true, LORD, that the Assyrian kings have laid waste all these peoples and their lands. [19]They have thrown their gods into the fire and destroyed them, for they were not gods but only wood and stone, fashioned by human hands. [20]Now, LORD our God, deliver us from his hand, so that all the kingdoms of the earth may know that you, LORD, are the only God. *[a]*"

Sennacherib's Fall

37:21-38pp — 2Ki 19:20-37; 2Ch 32:20-21

[21]Then Isaiah son of Amoz sent a message to Hezekiah: "This is what the LORD, the God of Israel, says: Because you have prayed to me concerning Sennacherib king of Assyria, [22]this is the word the LORD has spoken against him:

"Virgin Daughter Zion
    despises and mocks you.
Daughter Jerusalem
    tosses her head as you flee.
[23]Who is it you have ridiculed and blasphemed?
    Against whom have you raised your voice
and lifted your eyes in pride?
    Against the Holy One of Israel!

[24]By your messengers
    you have ridiculed the Lord.
And you have said,
    'With my many chariots
I have ascended the heights of the mountains,
    the utmost heights of Lebanon.
I have cut down its tallest cedars,
    the choicest of its junipers.
I have reached its remotest heights,
    the finest of its forests.
[25]I have dug wells in foreign lands*[b]*
    and drunk the water there.
With the soles of my feet
    I have dried up all the streams of Egypt.'

[26]"Have you not heard?
    Long ago I ordained it.
In days of old I planned it;
    now I have brought it to pass,
that you have turned fortified cities
    into piles of stone.
[27]Their people, drained of power,
    are dismayed and put to shame.
They are like plants in the field,
    like tender green shoots,
like grass sprouting on the roof,
    scorched*[c]* before it grows up.

[28]"But I know where you are
    and when you come and go
    and how you rage against me.
[29]Because you rage against me
    and because your insolence has reached my ears,
I will put my hook in your nose
    and my bit in your mouth,

[a] 20 Dead Sea Scrolls (see also 2 Kings 19:19); Masoretic Text *you alone are the LORD*   *[b]* 25 Dead Sea Scrolls (see also 2 Kings 19:24); Masoretic Text does not have *in foreign lands.*   *[c]* 27 Some manuscripts of the Masoretic Text, Dead Sea Scrolls and some Septuagint manuscripts (see also 2 Kings 19:26); most manuscripts of the Masoretic Text *roof / and terraced fields*

37:9 Tirhakah, the king of Cush The younger brother of the pharaoh Shabaka. Egypt usually remained neutral in Assyrian conflicts in Syria-Palestine, but Judah's tribute (see 30:6) must have inspired them to at least make a nominal attempt to assist Judah.
37:12 that were destroyed by my predecessors Familiar rhetoric from arrogant Assyria (see 10:10–11; 36:18–20).
37:13 king See 10:9.
37:14 Hezekiah received the letter Diplomatic correspondence was common in the ancient Near East. Many archives of letters have been discovered from ancient Egypt, Mesopotamia and Syria-Palestine. **he went up** The king gives no immediate reply to the messengers, but sets the letter before Yahweh to ask for deliverance (see note on v. 1).
37:16 enthroned between the cherubim Yahweh's presence in the temple was above the cherubim on top of

the ark of the covenant (see Ex 25:22; Nu 7:89; 1Sa 4:4). See the infographic "The Ark of the Covenant" on p. 412.
37:19 fashioned by human hands While the gods of the nations were unable to deliver them, Hezekiah serves the true God—not an idol made by human hands (see Isa 41:23,29; 44:9–20).
37:20 kingdoms of the earth may know Yahweh would prove himself in the eyes of the nations if he delivered them when all other deities failed. The ultimate recognition of Yahweh by all the nations is a central theme of Isaiah (see 2:2–4).
37:22 the word the LORD has spoken A prophecy of judgment for Sennacherib's arrogance, similar to the downfall of Assyria predicted in 10:12–27 and 31:8–9.
37:29 my hook The Assyrians used hooks on their prisoners (see 2Ch 33:11; Eze 19:9). **my bit in your mouth** Just as a bit and bridle gives control over a horse, God can easily turn Assyria's course. See Isa 30:28.

and I will make you return
by the way you came.

30 "This will be the sign for you, Hezekiah:

"This year you will eat what grows by itself,
and the second year what springs from
that.
But in the third year sow and reap,
plant vineyards and eat their fruit.
31 Once more a remnant of the kingdom of
Judah
will take root below and bear fruit above.
32 For out of Jerusalem will come a remnant,
and out of Mount Zion a band of
survivors.
The zeal of the LORD Almighty
will accomplish this.

33 "Therefore this is what the LORD says concerning the king of Assyria:

"He will not enter this city
or shoot an arrow here.
He will not come before it with shield
or build a siege ramp against it.
34 By the way that he came he will return;
he will not enter this city,"
declares the LORD.
35 "I will defend this city and save it,
for my sake and for the sake of David my
servant!"

36 Then the angel of the LORD went out and put
to death a hundred and eighty-five thousand in
the Assyrian camp. When the people got up the
next morning — there were all the dead bodies!

37 So Sennacherib king of Assyria broke camp and
withdrew. He returned to Nineveh and stayed
there.

38 One day, while he was worshiping in the temple of his god Nisrok, his sons Adrammelek and
Sharezer killed him with the sword, and they
escaped to the land of Ararat. And Esarhaddon
his son succeeded him as king.

Hezekiah's Illness

38:1-8pp — 2Ki 20:1-11; 2Ch 32:24-26

38 In those days Hezekiah became ill and was
at the point of death. The prophet Isaiah
son of Amoz went to him and said, "This is what
the LORD says: Put your house in order, because
you are going to die; you will not recover."
2 Hezekiah turned his face to the wall and
prayed to the LORD, 3 "Remember, LORD, how I
have walked before you faithfully and with wholehearted devotion and have done what is good in
your eyes." And Hezekiah wept bitterly.
4 Then the word of the LORD came to Isaiah:
5 "Go and tell Hezekiah, 'This is what the LORD,
the God of your father David, says: I have heard
your prayer and seen your tears; I will add fifteen
years to your life. 6 And I will deliver you and this
city from the hand of the king of Assyria. I will
defend this city.
7 "'This is the LORD's sign to you that the LORD
will do what he has promised: 8 I will make the
shadow cast by the sun go back the ten steps it
has gone down on the stairway of Ahaz.'" So
the sunlight went back the ten steps it had gone
down.

37:35 for my sake Hezekiah's prayer has resulted in
Jerusalem's salvation as the remnant of Judah. But
Judah will not be saved because they are Yahweh's
chosen people, or because Jerusalem is his dwelling.
Yahweh will save Jerusalem for his own reputation and
his covenant with David.
37:36 the angel of the LORD Appearances of the "angel
of Yahweh" in the OT often blur the distinction between
Yahweh and the angel. The angel's appearance symbolized both judgment (2Sa 24:16) and deliverance or
protection (Ex 14:19). **put to death a hundred and
eighty-five thousand** A miraculous delivery, and the
fulfillment of Isa 31:8 and 10:16.
**37:37 Sennacherib king of Assyria broke camp
and withdrew** The official annals of Sennacherib give
no details as to why he left Judah without conquering
Jerusalem. He simply says he left Hezekiah cooped up
"like a bird in a cage." See the infographic "Sennacherib's
Prism" on p. 597.
37:38 worshiping in the temple of his god Nisrok Sennacherib's assassination occurred much later — in 681
BC. Omitting the time-lapse in the Biblical narrative gives
a greater sense of immediacy between God's prophecy
that Sennacherib would die in his own land (v. 7) and the
fulfillment in v. 38. See the timeline "Dates Related to
Isaiah and 2 Kings" on p. 1116. **Esarhaddon his son**
King of Assyria from 681–669 BC.

38:1–22 Hezekiah's illness and recovery seems to
be set just before the events of 37:36 — when Yahweh
delivered Jerusalem from Assyria. Verse 6 indicates
that Hezekiah's life will be spared and the city will be
delivered. The narrative in vv. 1–8 is paralleled by the
account in 2Ki 20:1–11. While the two accounts have
minor variations, the most significant difference is the
hymn of Hezekiah in Isa 38:9–20, which does not appear in Second Kings.
38:1 you will not recover The news that he won't
recover from the illness tests his faith and gives him a
chance to pray and rely on God even more. Prophets'
warnings of impending disaster were often implicit calls
for repentance as a way to avert disaster (see Jnh 3:4).
38:3 I have walked before you faithfully Hezekiah's
prayer focuses on his general positive stance toward
Yahweh (seen in 2Ki 18:6–7).
38:5 I have heard your prayer Hezekiah's repentance
was the desired result of the pronouncement in Isa 38:1.
The king's repentance opens the way for God's mercy, and
mirrors the national repentance that Isaiah encouraged
as a prerequisite to national deliverance (see 33:2–9).
**38:8 will make the shadow cast by the sun go back
the ten steps it has gone down on the stairway of
Ahaz** Represents the extension of Hezekiah's life — he
is further away from death than before.

⁹A writing of Hezekiah king of Judah after his illness and recovery:

¹⁰I said, "In the prime of my life
must I go through the gates of death
and be robbed of the rest of my years?"
¹¹I said, "I will not again see the LORD himself
in the land of the living;
no longer will I look on my fellow man,
or be with those who now dwell in this
world.
¹²Like a shepherd's tent my house
has been pulled down and taken from me.
Like a weaver I have rolled up my life,
and he has cut me off from the loom;
day and night you made an end of me.
¹³I waited patiently till dawn,
but like a lion he broke all my bones;
day and night you made an end of me.
¹⁴I cried like a swift or thrush,
I moaned like a mourning dove.
My eyes grew weak as I looked to the
heavens.
I am being threatened; Lord, come to my
aid!"

¹⁵But what can I say?
He has spoken to me, and he himself has
done this.
I will walk humbly all my years
because of this anguish of my soul.
¹⁶Lord, by such things people live;
and my spirit finds life in them too.
You restored me to health
and let me live.

¹⁷Surely it was for my benefit
that I suffered such anguish.
In your love you kept me
from the pit of destruction;
you have put all my sins
behind your back.
¹⁸For the grave cannot praise you,
death cannot sing your praise;
those who go down to the pit
cannot hope for your faithfulness.
¹⁹The living, the living — they praise you,
as I am doing today;
parents tell their children
about your faithfulness.

²⁰The LORD will save me,
and we will sing with stringed instruments
all the days of our lives
in the temple of the LORD.

²¹Isaiah had said, "Prepare a poultice of figs and apply it to the boil, and he will recover."

²²Hezekiah had asked, "What will be the sign that I will go up to the temple of the LORD?"

Envoys From Babylon

39:1-8pp — 2Ki 20:12-19

39 At that time Marduk-Baladan son of Baladan king of Babylon sent Hezekiah letters and a gift, because he had heard of his illness and recovery. ²Hezekiah received the envoys gladly and showed them what was in his storehouses — the silver, the gold, the spices, the fine olive oil — his entire armory and everything found among his

---

38:9 A writing of Hezekiah king of Judah Reminiscent of the historical headings on many psalms (e.g., Ps 3:title; 18:title).

38:10 In the prime of my life Hezekiah was only 25 when he began to reign (2Ki 18:2). The invasion occurred in his fourteenth year (Isa 36:1), so Hezekiah was only 39 years old at the time of this life-threatening illness.

38:12 he has cut me off from the loom The metaphor of the weaver illustrates Hezekiah's acknowledgment that God would decide when and how he — as the weaver's creation — will be used or discarded.

38:18 grave The underworld, the place of the dead. See note on Ge 37:35.

38:20 in the temple of the LORD Contrasting the gates of death (Sheol) in Isa 38:10, he will now spend his days at the house of God.

38:22 temple of the LORD If he is healed, his first task will be to go to the temple to thank Yahweh.

39:1-8 Hezekiah's interaction with ambassadors from Babylon foreshadows the future threat of conquest and exile at the hands of the Babylonians. Up to this point, the Assyrian crisis has provided the primary historical background of the book. Moving forward, the focus shifts to the plight of Judah in exile in Babylon. This brief account provides a structural bridge between the two major sections of Isaiah by pointing ahead to the Babylonian exile. The parallel account appears in 2Ki 20:12-21.

39:1 Marduk-Baladan son of Baladan A Babylonian chieftain who represented an ongoing threat to Assyrian domination by taking power in Babylon and organizing effective defense against Assyria. He contacted Hezekiah in order to win his support against Assyria — their mutual enemy. **he had heard of his illness** See Isa 38:1–8, 21.

DATE	EVENT
704 BC	Merodach-Baladan (Marduk-Baladan) sends envoys to Hezekiah
626 BC	Nabopolassar rebels against Assyria and becomes king of Babylon
605 BC	Nebuchadnezzar defeats Egypt and Assyria
597 BC	Nebuchadnezzar besieges Jerusalem

39:2 showed them what was in his storehouses Hezekiah naively welcomes the Babylonians as friends, and openly shows them his remaining wealth. He may have been trying to impress potential allies, and thought Babylon would conquer Assyria. But he too quickly moved away from the humble faith in Yahweh demonstrated during the Assyrian crisis. **did not show them** The writer goes to extra lengths to emphasize that Hezekiah showed them everything and had no suspicion of their motives.

treasures. There was nothing in his palace or in all his kingdom that Hezekiah did not show them.

³Then Isaiah the prophet went to King Hezekiah and asked, "What did those men say, and where did they come from?"

"From a distant land," Hezekiah replied. "They came to me from Babylon."

⁴The prophet asked, "What did they see in your palace?"

"They saw everything in my palace," Hezekiah said. "There is nothing among my treasures that I did not show them."

⁵Then Isaiah said to Hezekiah, "Hear the word of the Lord Almighty: ⁶The time will surely come when everything in your palace, and all that your predecessors have stored up until this day, will be carried off to Babylon. Nothing will be left, says the Lord. ⁷And some of your descendants, your own flesh and blood who will be born to you, will be taken away, and they will become eunuchs in the palace of the king of Babylon."

⁸"The word of the Lord you have spoken is good," Hezekiah replied. For he thought, "There will be peace and security in my lifetime."

Comfort for God's People

40 Comfort, comfort my people,
    says your God.
²Speak tenderly to Jerusalem,
    and proclaim to her

that her hard service has been completed,
    that her sin has been paid for,
that she has received from the Lord's hand
    double for all her sins.

³A voice of one calling:
"In the wilderness prepare
    the way for the Lord ª;
make straight in the desert
    a highway for our God.ᵇ
⁴Every valley shall be raised up,
    every mountain and hill made low;
the rough ground shall become level,
    the rugged places a plain.
⁵And the glory of the Lord will be revealed,
    and all people will see it together.
            For the mouth of the Lord
                    has spoken."

⁶A voice says, "Cry out."
    And I said, "What shall I cry?"

"All people are like grass,
    and all their faithfulness is like the flowers
        of the field.
⁷The grass withers and the flowers fall,
    because the breath of the Lord blows on
        them.
    Surely the people are grass.

ª 3 Or A voice of one calling in the wilderness: / "Prepare the way for the Lord   ᵇ 3 Hebrew; Septuagint make straight the paths of our God

39:3 where did they come from Isaiah shows the cautious, guarded attitude that Hezekiah should have had. **39:6 will be carried off to Babylon** This is fulfilled in 2Ki 24:10–14.
39:7 will be taken away Hezekiah's descendant Jehoiachin is taken into exile (see 2Ki 24:15).
39:8 peace and security in my lifetime Hezekiah's selfish resignation shows he did not take to heart his vow to pass on the praise of Yahweh as promised in Isa 38:19. While Hezekiah is one of the good kings in Judah's history, he fails to pass on piety for Yahweh to his son Manasseh, who leads the people back to idolatry after Hezekiah's death.

40:1—55:13 The authorship of the later chapters of Isaiah is debated; the geographical and historical perspective of these chapters shifts from Jerusalem at the turn of the seventh century BC to Babylon in the mid-sixth century BC. As a prophet, Isaiah could have been shown circumstances and events 150 years in the future. But the tone of the speeches in this later section suggests they were written by a contemporary of the events, who pleads with the people to trust God for restoration.

Regardless of the setting and identity of the human author, these chapters have much in common with chs. 1–39. They show a well-planned development of Isaiah's concerns for Yahweh's holiness, sovereignty and plans for restoration of Judah.

40:1 comfort my people The consolation and comfort of Israel is a key theme of chs. 40–55. While oracles of restoration and salvation are interspersed with oracles of judgment throughout chs. 1–39, this part of the books

is characterized by a reduced focus on judgment; the prophet's words of comfort are directed at those who have already been punished (see v. 2).
40:2 her hard service has been completed The Hebrew term tsava can indicate armed service or servitude. The following assertion that she has paid "double" for her sins suggests the context is a prison sentence or penal servitude. **double for all her sins** The Hebrew term used here (meaning "double" or "two") only occurs here and in Job 11:6. This context suggests a meaning of "more than enough" rather than specifically "double."
40:3 In the wilderness prepare the way God will lead the remnant through the wilderness from Babylon to Zion, just like the exodus from Egypt. This verse is quoted in all four Gospels in connection with John the Baptist, who prepares the way for Jesus. A different understanding of syntax (how the phrases were related) has led to the NT (and Septuagint) understanding of "the voice of one crying in the wilderness" versus "in the wilderness prepare." The Hebrew parallelism connects the phrase with "make straight in the desert." See the table "Parallelism in Hebrew Poetry" on p. 1008.
40:4 every mountain and hill made low Similar imagery to the trembling of the natural world that accompanies an appearance of God (or theophany).
40:5 mouth of the Lord has spoken The opening poem of Isaiah concludes with the same formula (see Isa 1:20).

40:6–8 This scene echoes Isaiah's commission in 6:1–13.

40:6 A voice says, "Cry out" Just as in 6:11, the prophet receives a message to proclaim and asks for clarification.

⁸ The grass withers and the flowers fall,
　　but the word of our God endures forever."

⁹ You who bring good news to Zion,
　　go up on a high mountain.
　You who bring good news to Jerusalem,ᵃ
　　lift up your voice with a shout,
　lift it up, do not be afraid;
　　say to the towns of Judah,
　　"Here is your God!"
¹⁰ See, the Sovereign LORD comes with power,
　　and he rules with a mighty arm.
　See, his reward is with him,
　　and his recompense accompanies him.
¹¹ He tends his flock like a shepherd:
　　He gathers the lambs in his arms
　and carries them close to his heart;
　　he gently leads those that have young.

¹² Who has measured the waters in the hollow
　　　of his hand,
　　or with the breadth of his hand marked off
　　　the heavens?
　Who has held the dust of the earth in a basket,
　　or weighed the mountains on the scales
　　and the hills in a balance?
¹³ Who can fathom the Spiritᵇ of the LORD,
　　or instruct the LORD as his counselor?
¹⁴ Whom did the LORD consult to enlighten
　　　him,
　　and who taught him the right way?
　Who was it that taught him knowledge,
　　or showed him the path of understanding?

¹⁵ Surely the nations are like a drop in a bucket;
　　they are regarded as dust on the scales;
　　he weighs the islands as though they were
　　　fine dust.
¹⁶ Lebanon is not sufficient for altar fires,
　　nor its animals enough for burnt offerings.
¹⁷ Before him all the nations are as nothing;
　　they are regarded by him as worthless
　　and less than nothing.

¹⁸ With whom, then, will you compare God?
　　To what image will you liken him?
¹⁹ As for an idol, a metalworker casts it,
　　and a goldsmith overlays it with gold
　　and fashions silver chains for it.
²⁰ A person too poor to present such an offering
　　selects wood that will not rot;
　they look for a skilled worker
　　to set up an idol that will not topple.

²¹ Do you not know?
　　Have you not heard?
　Has it not been told you from the beginning?
　　Have you not understood since the earth
　　　was founded?
²² He sits enthroned above the circle of the
　　　earth,
　　and its people are like grasshoppers.
　He stretches out the heavens like a canopy,
　　and spreads them out like a tent to live in.

ᵃ 9 Or Zion, bringer of good news, / go up on a high mountain. /
Jerusalem, bringer of good news　　ᵇ 13 Or mind

40:9–31 The message for the prophet concludes in v. 9 with a charge to carry the news to Judah. The rest of the section provides an epic poetic description of the greatness of God, fulfilling the charge of v. 9 to proclaim good news to the cities of Judah.

40:9 You who bring good news to Zion Rather than identifying Zion or Jerusalem as the herald, the Hebrew allows for the reading "herald of good news for Zion" and "herald of good news for Jerusalem" in the parallel line. In the context of the prophet's message and charge to preach, it is reasonable to read v. 9 as addressed to him along with v. 8.

40:10 See, his reward is with him The phrase occurs again in 62:11. The reuse of particular phrases such as this provides stylistic unity in the book. **his recompense** God will come with payback—either Judah's repayment, compensation for service or the repayment demanded against the nations in judgment as in 34:8 and 35:4.

40:11 He tends his flock like a shepherd Illustrates God's care for his people, and is also found in Ps 23:1–6 and as an image of Christ in Jn 10:22–29.

40:12 Who has measured the waters Creation imagery affirms Yahweh's sovereignty; he is the only Creator. These questions, which reflect Job 38, are designed to illustrate the finite nature of the created world compared to the infinite God who created it. **the hollow of his hand** An image of the sheer immensity of God in his power over the universe. The imagery of God holding the oceans in the hollow of his hand and covering the

heavens with the width of his hand sets up the later contrast with humanity—where the nations are little more than a drop of water or a speck of dust (see Isa 40:15 and note).

40:15 like a drop in a bucket Compared to the greatness of God, all the power of earthly nations is next to nothing—a drop of water or a speck of dust. See note on v. 12.

40:16 Lebanon is not sufficient for altar fires Lebanon had a reputation for its timber. Those who truly wanted to make an altar and a sacrifice worthy of Yahweh would not find enough trees or animals even in this tree-dominated region to provide a sufficient fire and sacrifice.

40:17 worthless and less than nothing The Hebrew term used here, *tohu* ("emptiness," also in v. 23), describes the disorder of the earth at the beginning of its creation (see note on Ge 1:2).

40:19 As for an idol, a metalworker casts All idols made by human hands are powerless. The argument against idolatry continues in Isa 40:25 and 46:5.

40:21 since the earth was founded Creation itself should have been enough of a witness for people to understand there was a Creator (see Ro 1:19–20).

40:22 circle of the earth Likely refers to the ancient Hebrew idea of a dome or vault over the earth (Ge 1:6–7). The poetic reference also occurs in Job 22:14 and Pr 8:27 with reference to God's creative power. See the infographic "Ancient Hebrew Conception of the Universe" on p. 5.

²³ He brings princes to naught
　　and reduces the rulers of this world to
　　　nothing.
²⁴ No sooner are they planted,
　　no sooner are they sown,
　　no sooner do they take root in the
　　　ground,
　than he blows on them and they wither,
　　and a whirlwind sweeps them away like
　　　chaff.

²⁵ "To whom will you compare me?
　　Or who is my equal?" says the Holy One.
²⁶ Lift up your eyes and look to the heavens:
　　Who created all these?
　He who brings out the starry host one by one
　　and calls forth each of them by name.
　Because of his great power and mighty
　　　strength,
　　not one of them is missing.

²⁷ Why do you complain, Jacob?
　　Why do you say, Israel,
　"My way is hidden from the LORD;
　　my cause is disregarded by my God"?
²⁸ Do you not know?
　　Have you not heard?
　The LORD is the everlasting God,
　　the Creator of the ends of the earth.
　He will not grow tired or weary,
　　and his understanding no one can
　　　fathom.
²⁹ He gives strength to the weary
　　and increases the power of the weak.
³⁰ Even youths grow tired and weary,
　　and young men stumble and fall;
³¹ but those who hope in the LORD
　　will renew their strength.
　They will soar on wings like eagles;
　　they will run and not grow weary,
　　they will walk and not be faint.

The Helper of Israel

41 "Be silent before me, you islands!
　　Let the nations renew their strength!
　Let them come forward and speak;
　　let us meet together at the place of
　　　judgment.

² "Who has stirred up one from the east,
　　calling him in righteousness to his
　　　service[a]?
　He hands nations over to him
　　and subdues kings before him.
　He turns them to dust with his sword,
　　to windblown chaff with his bow.
³ He pursues them and moves on unscathed,
　　by a path his feet have not traveled before.
⁴ Who has done this and carried it through,
　　calling forth the generations from the
　　　beginning?
　I, the LORD — with the first of them
　　and with the last — I am he."

⁵ The islands have seen it and fear;
　　the ends of the earth tremble.
　They approach and come forward;
⁶ 　they help each other
　　and say to their companions, "Be strong!"
⁷ The metalworker encourages the
　　　goldsmith,
　　and the one who smooths with the
　　　hammer
　spurs on the one who strikes the anvil.
　One says of the welding, "It is good."
　　The other nails down the idol so it will not
　　　topple.

⁸ "But you, Israel, my servant,
　　Jacob, whom I have chosen,
　　you descendants of Abraham my friend,

---

[a] 2 Or east, / whom victory meets at every step

40:23 He brings princes to naught God's sovereignty is expressed in his ultimate power over all the so-called powerful of the earth (see Job 12:21; Ps 107:40).
40:26 Who created all these As in Ge 1:1, the Hebrew term *bara* is always a divine prerogative. See note on Ge 1:1.
40:28 Creator of the ends of the earth The focus on God as Creator and totally "other" than his creation answers the statements of Isa 40:27. Since God's ways are unknowable, they have no grounds to make such a claim.
40:30 Even youths grow tired God's store of energy and power exhausts even the seemingly endless supply of a young person's energy.
40:31 They will soar on wings like eagles Alludes to the exodus miracle (Ex 19:4); the poet casts the vision for a new exodus led by God (Isa 40:3) from Babylon.

41:1–20 Yahweh acts in history, proving his sovereignty over the nations. He also reassures his people that, just as he acted on their behalf before, he will do so again.

41:1 let us meet together at the place of judgment Yahweh summons the nations to a courtroom scene where he is both the judge and the defendant. The trial determines who really is the true God — Yahweh or the idols of the nations.
41:2 Who has stirred up one from the east Yahweh raised up Assyria (10:5–6) and Babylon (39:6) to be his agents of judgment. He also raised up Cyrus of Persia, whose rising empire will soon defeat Babylon and take over most of the ancient Near East.
41:4 I, the LORD — with the first A polarity emphasizing Yahweh's sole right to be worshiped as God. The theme also appears in 43:10–11; 48:12; and 44:6 — where the context of idolatry is more explicit. The NT also uses this imagery (see Rev 22:13).
41:8 Israel, my servant, Jacob The Servant — chosen by God — is an important figure in Isa 40–55. It emphasizes the special covenant relationship between Yahweh and his chosen people. Here, "my servant" refers to Israel — the entire nation as the patriarch Jacob or Israel. The names are inverted with the same image in 44:1–2.

⁹ I took you from the ends of the earth,
  from its farthest corners I called you.
I said, 'You are my servant';
  I have chosen you and have not rejected
    you.
¹⁰ So do not fear, for I am with you;
  do not be dismayed, for I am your God.
I will strengthen you and help you;
  I will uphold you with my righteous right
    hand.

¹¹ "All who rage against you
  will surely be ashamed and disgraced;
those who oppose you
  will be as nothing and perish.
¹² Though you search for your enemies,
  you will not find them.
Those who wage war against you
  will be as nothing at all.
¹³ For I am the LORD your God
  who takes hold of your right hand
and says to you, Do not fear;
  I will help you.
¹⁴ Do not be afraid, you worm Jacob,
  little Israel, do not fear,
for I myself will help you," declares
    the LORD,
  your Redeemer, the Holy One of Israel.
¹⁵ "See, I will make you into a threshing sledge,
  new and sharp, with many teeth.
You will thresh the mountains and crush
    them,
  and reduce the hills to chaff.
¹⁶ You will winnow them, the wind will pick
    them up,
  and a gale will blow them away.
But you will rejoice in the LORD
  and glory in the Holy One of Israel.

¹⁷ "The poor and needy search for water,
  but there is none;
  their tongues are parched with thirst.
But I the LORD will answer them;
  I, the God of Israel, will not forsake
    them.
¹⁸ I will make rivers flow on barren heights,
  and springs within the valleys.
I will turn the desert into pools of water,
  and the parched ground into springs.
¹⁹ I will put in the desert
  the cedar and the acacia, the myrtle and
    the olive.
I will set junipers in the wasteland,
  the fir and the cypress together,
²⁰ so that people may see and know,
  may consider and understand,
that the hand of the LORD has done this,
  that the Holy One of Israel has created it.

²¹ "Present your case," says the LORD.
  "Set forth your arguments," says Jacob's
    King.
²² "Tell us, you idols,
  what is going to happen.
Tell us what the former things were,
  so that we may consider them
  and know their final outcome.
Or declare to us the things to come,
²³ tell us what the future holds,
  so we may know that you are gods.
Do something, whether good or bad,
  so that we will be dismayed and filled
    with fear.
²⁴ But you are less than nothing
  and your works are utterly worthless;
  whoever chooses you is detestable.

41:9 from the ends of the earth An allusion to the exodus story and Israel's bondage in Egypt, figuratively referred to as "the ends of the earth" (see Ex 1–15).

41:10 right hand Symbolic of his power and authority. Being at the right hand of a leader symbolized the power and authority of that leader. Placing Jesus at the right hand of God is another frequent way the NT asserts his unique authority (see Mt 26:64; Ac 2:33; 5:31; Ro 8:34; Eph 1:20).

41:14 your Redeemer, the Holy One of Israel The holy God they rejected now redeems them. See Isa 1:4 and note.

41:15 You will thresh the mountains Bringing low the lofty mountains and hills as promised in 2:14.

41:18 I will turn the desert into pools Chapter 35 illustrates the same motif of the renewal of creation—the flowering of the desert so the exiles can return across it (see 35:1,6).

41:20 the Holy One of Israel has created it Invoking Yahweh's creative power with bara (see Ge 1:1 and note). His restoration of the wilderness to an Edenic state is proof of his power.

41:21 Set forth your arguments Yahweh proved his power by freeing Israel from Egypt, and by bringing life to the desert (an allusion both to what was described in Isa 41:18–20 and to Israel in the wilderness in Nu 20:11). Now he calls on the nations to bring their idols to provide evidence of their power (see note on Isa 41:1).

41:22 Tell us, you idols, what is going to happen Predictive prophecy is proof of real divine power. **the former things** Refers to earlier prophecies and the ability to explain their fulfillment. The contrast between "first" and "last"—or "former things" and "latter things"—is prominent in chs. 40–48. The "former things" sometimes seem to refer to God's earlier words of judgment in chs. 1–39, while the "latter things" are the new pronouncements in chs. 40–48 that emphasize consolation and restoration. Ultimately, the words illustrate that formerly, judgment would take place, but now salvation is coming.

41:23 Do something, whether good or bad The appeal is for the idols to doing anything at all—good or bad—to prove they are real.

41:24 whoever chooses you is detestable A strong denunciation of any idolater. The Hebrew term here may refer to what is physically, ritually or ethically abhorrent. In 2Ki 23:13, the word refers to the gods of the surrounding nations. Both the idol and the idolater are an abomination.

²⁵ "I have stirred up one from the north, and he
  comes —
  one from the rising sun who calls on my
    name.
He treads on rulers as if they were mortar,
  as if he were a potter treading the clay.
²⁶ Who told of this from the beginning, so we
    could know,
  or beforehand, so we could say, 'He was
    right'?
No one told of this,
  no one foretold it,
  no one heard any words from you.
²⁷ I was the first to tell Zion, 'Look, here they
    are!'
  I gave to Jerusalem a messenger of good
    news.
²⁸ I look but there is no one —
  no one among the gods to give counsel,
  no one to give answer when I ask them.
²⁹ See, they are all false!
  Their deeds amount to nothing;
  their images are but wind and
    confusion.

The Servant of the Lord

42 "Here is my servant, whom I uphold,
  my chosen one in whom I delight;
I will put my Spirit on him,
  and he will bring justice to the nations.

² He will not shout or cry out,
  or raise his voice in the streets.
³ A bruised reed he will not break,
  and a smoldering wick he will not snuff
    out.
In faithfulness he will bring forth justice;
⁴ he will not falter or be discouraged
  till he establishes justice on earth.
  In his teaching the islands will put their
    hope."

⁵ This is what God the Lord says —
  the Creator of the heavens, who stretches
    them out,
  who spreads out the earth with all that
    springs from it,
  who gives breath to its people,
  and life to those who walk on it:
⁶ "I, the Lord, have called you in
    righteousness;
  I will take hold of your hand.
I will keep you and will make you
  to be a covenant for the people
  and a light for the Gentiles,
⁷ to open eyes that are blind,
  to free captives from prison
  and to release from the dungeon those who
    sit in darkness.

⁸ "I am the Lord; that is my name!
  I will not yield my glory to another
  or my praise to idols.

41:25 I have stirred up one from the north Refers to Cyrus (see note on Isa 41:2). The references to north and east may indicate the two parts of his empire—Media was north of Persia. Jeremiah frequently described disaster coming from the north (see note on Jer 50:3).
41:26 No one told of this Yahweh claims the credit for raising up Cyrus for his own purposes; he points out the failure of the idols of the nations to declare these events.
41:27 to Jerusalem a messenger of good news The prophet was sent as the herald to declare the return to Zion. See Isa 40:9.
41:29 Their deeds amount to nothing The futility of idolatry is emphasized through the repeated focus on their inability to do anything.

42:1–9 This is the first of four poems in chs. 40–55 focused on the figure of the servant of Yahweh. The first half (vv. 1–4) describes a servant, while the second half (vv. 5–9) turns to the topic of Yahweh's superiority over idols—a theme continued in vv. 10–17. The four servant songs are found in vv. 1–9; 49:1–7; 50:4–9; and 52:13—53:12. The transition in identity of the servant figure from corporate Israel to an individual acting on Israel's behalf in chs. 40–55 complicates the understanding of these passages.
  This first servant song may be addressed to corporate Israel while the second servant song in 49:1–7 may mark the transition of the role to an individual. However, all references to a servant in chs. 40–48 (with the notable exception of 42:1–9) explicitly identify the servant as corporate Israel (41:8–9; 42:18–25; 43:1–10; 44:1–2,21; 45:4; 48:20). If this passage is about Israel

as a people, then vv. 6–7 reflect their corporate calling to be a blessing to the peoples of the world (compare Ge 12:3). Their inability to fulfill their calling results in the mission being reassigned to an individual servant (Isa 49:6). Alternately, the lack of explicit identification of this servant as Israel in vv. 1–9 along with the strong literary connections to the Messianic imagery in 11:1–10 supports understanding the servant as a representative of Israel as a whole—as the Davidic king who represents the people before God. The Gospel of Matthew sees the fulfillment of this prophecy in Jesus Christ (Mt 12:18–21).

42:1 my servant Identified as "Israel" in Isa 41:8, also having been "chosen." The servant here may also be a Messianic figure (compare with 11:2–4). **I will put my Spirit on him** The servant is described with language similar to the Davidic Messiah from 11:2; he receives the Spirit of God, which enables him to act with wisdom and justice.
42:4 he establishes justice on earth One of the hallmarks of the Messiah's reign is the establishment of perfect justice on earth (see vv. 1; 11:1–10).
42:6 a covenant for the people and a light Compare 49:6–8, which reinforces the identification of the individual servant as the light for the nations and the covenant for the people.
42:7 to open eyes that are blind The restoration of Israel and the advent of the Messiah is accompanied by miraculous signs (see 35:5). **free captives from prison and to release** The exiles are essentially imprisoned in a foreign land. The prophet's message is meant to reassure them that God—through his servant—will

⁹ See, the former things have taken place,
   and new things I declare;
before they spring into being
   I announce them to you."

Song of Praise to the LORD

¹⁰ Sing to the LORD a new song,
   his praise from the ends of the earth,
you who go down to the sea, and all that is
   in it,
   you islands, and all who live in them.
¹¹ Let the wilderness and its towns raise their
   voices;
   let the settlements where Kedar lives rejoice.
Let the people of Sela sing for joy;
   let them shout from the mountaintops.
¹² Let them give glory to the LORD
   and proclaim his praise in the islands.
¹³ The LORD will march out like a champion,
   like a warrior he will stir up his zeal;
with a shout he will raise the battle cry
   and will triumph over his enemies.

¹⁴ "For a long time I have kept silent,
   I have been quiet and held myself back.
But now, like a woman in childbirth,
   I cry out, I gasp and pant.
¹⁵ I will lay waste the mountains and hills
   and dry up all their vegetation;
I will turn rivers into islands
   and dry up the pools.
¹⁶ I will lead the blind by ways they have not
   known,
   along unfamiliar paths I will guide them;
I will turn the darkness into light before them
   and make the rough places smooth.
These are the things I will do;
   I will not forsake them.
¹⁷ But those who trust in idols,
   who say to images, 'You are our gods,'
   will be turned back in utter shame.

Israel Blind and Deaf

¹⁸ "Hear, you deaf;
   look, you blind, and see!
¹⁹ Who is blind but my servant,
   and deaf like the messenger I send?
Who is blind like the one in covenant
   with me,
   blind like the servant of the LORD?
²⁰ You have seen many things, but you pay no
   attention;
   your ears are open, but you do not listen."
²¹ It pleased the LORD
   for the sake of his righteousness
to make his law great and glorious.
²² But this is a people plundered and looted,
   all of them trapped in pits
   or hidden away in prisons.
They have become plunder,
   with no one to rescue them;
they have been made loot,
   with no one to say, "Send them back."

²³ Which of you will listen to this
   or pay close attention in time to come?
²⁴ Who handed Jacob over to become loot,
   and Israel to the plunderers?
Was it not the LORD,
   against whom we have sinned?
For they would not follow his ways;
   they did not obey his law.
²⁵ So he poured out on them his burning anger,
   the violence of war.
It enveloped them in flames, yet they did not
   understand;
   it consumed them, but they did not take it
   to heart.

Israel's Only Savior

43 But now, this is what the LORD says —
   he who created you, Jacob,
   he who formed you, Israel:

---

lead them to salvation. The fulfillment comes in stages. The prophet was looking to the immediate return from Babylon, but the ultimate fulfillment was Messianic.
42:9 the former things have taken place The things Yahweh predicted through his prophets have happened — proof of his deity (v. 8).

42:10–17 A praise psalm rejoicing over the salvation and victory of Yahweh described in vv. 1–9. The polemic against idolatry is also a key theme of this song.

42:10 to the LORD a new song The "new song" is in praise of the "new things" Yahweh declared in v. 9. Compare Ps 33:3.
42:13 LORD will march out like a champion The praise in Isa 42:10–12 preceded Yahweh's arrival; he arrives prepared to do battle on behalf of his people (see 40:10; 59:17). Isaiah's poetic imagery of Creator, Sustainer and Warrior is meant to reassure the people in exile that their God still has power to save them.

42:15 I will lay waste the mountains and hills Reversing the imagery of a revived wilderness in 41:18–19.
42:19 blind but my servant Here, the servant is used to describe wayward, sinful Israel in language reminiscent of 1:3 and 6:9–10. A comparison with the servant description in 41:8–10 suggests a contrast between the servant figures: collective Israel in need of salvation and the individual Servant through whom salvation will be accomplished.

43:1–28 The return of the exiles from all corners of the earth is promised, and the themes of creation, divine kingship, election and the futility of idols are revisited as reassurance of Yahweh's power to save.

43:1 he who created you, Jacob Yahweh is responsible for both Israel's creation as living beings and their formation as a nation. **I have redeemed you** God already identified himself as their redeemer in 41:14. Now, he reminds them of the relationship between redeemer and

"Do not fear, for I have redeemed you;
　　I have summoned you by name; you are
　　　mine.
2 When you pass through the waters,
　　I will be with you;
and when you pass through the rivers,
　　they will not sweep over you.
When you walk through the fire,
　　you will not be burned;
　　the flames will not set you ablaze.
3 For I am the LORD your God,
　　the Holy One of Israel, your Savior;
I give Egypt for your ransom,
　　Cush[a] and Seba in your stead.
4 Since you are precious and honored in my
　　　sight,
　　and because I love you,
I will give people in exchange for you,
　　nations in exchange for your life.
5 Do not be afraid, for I am with you;
　　I will bring your children from the east
　　and gather you from the west.
6 I will say to the north, 'Give them up!'
　　and to the south, 'Do not hold them back.'
Bring my sons from afar
　　and my daughters from the ends of the
　　　earth —
7 everyone who is called by my name,
　　whom I created for my glory,
　　whom I formed and made."

8 Lead out those who have eyes but are blind,
　　who have ears but are deaf.
9 All the nations gather together
　　and the peoples assemble.
Which of their gods foretold this
　　and proclaimed to us the former things?
Let them bring in their witnesses to prove
　　they were right,
　　so that others may hear and say, "It is
　　　true."

10 "You are my witnesses," declares the LORD,
　　"and my servant whom I have chosen,
so that you may know and believe me
　　and understand that I am he.
Before me no god was formed,
　　nor will there be one after me.
11 I, even I, am the LORD,
　　and apart from me there is no savior.
12 I have revealed and saved and proclaimed —
　　I, and not some foreign god among you.
You are my witnesses," declares the LORD,
　　"that I am God.
13 　Yes, and from ancient days I am he.
No one can deliver out of my hand.
　　When I act, who can reverse it?"

God's Mercy and Israel's Unfaithfulness

14 This is what the LORD says —
　　your Redeemer, the Holy One of Israel:
"For your sake I will send to Babylon
　　and bring down as fugitives all the
　　　Babylonians,[b]
in the ships in which they took pride.
15 I am the LORD, your Holy One,
　　Israel's Creator, your King."

16 This is what the LORD says —
　　he who made a way through the sea,
　　a path through the mighty waters,
17 who drew out the chariots and horses,
　　the army and reinforcements together,
and they lay there, never to rise again,
　　extinguished, snuffed out like a wick:
18 "Forget the former things;
　　do not dwell on the past.
19 See, I am doing a new thing!
　　Now it springs up; do you not perceive it?
I am making a way in the wilderness
　　and streams in the wasteland.

[a] 3 That is, the upper Nile region　　[b] 14 Or Chaldeans

redeemed. The exiles have no reason to fear, because
salvation is assured.
43:2 you pass through the waters Continuing the
poet's emphasis on the return as a second exodus,
this is likely an allusion to Israel's passing through the
Red Sea. See Ex 14.
43:3 I am the LORD your God Echoes God's pronouncement at the opening of the Ten Commandments in Ex
20:2.
43:6 from the ends of the earth God will bring back his
people from all points of the compass and the farthest
regions of the known world. While ancient deities were
often considered to have merely local power and influence, God's power has no geographical limit. The prophets reacting to Israel and Judah's oppression by foreign
powers stressed Yahweh as a global, not local, deity.
43:7 everyone who is called by my name Echoes Isa
43:1; the phrase rounds off the poetic section in vv. 1–7
and signals a shift of focus in the following section away
from the election and creation themes back to the idolatry
and trial motif in vv. 8–13.

43:9 All the nations gather together Reconvening the
assembly of 41:1 and 41:21–24 where the nations were
challenged to bring proof of their gods' power.
43:10 my servant whom I have chosen Refers to
corporate Israel, as in 41:8 and 42:19. **Before me no
god was formed** No other deity existed before Yahweh.
See 41:4; 47:8.
43:11 apart from me there is no savior This assertion is repeated in 45:21 again in the context of a strong
polemic against idolatry.
43:14 For your sake I will send to Babylon Yahweh
will redeem them from Babylon just as he brought them
out of Egypt (Ex 6:6). **Babylonians** Chaldea was an
area of southern Mesopotamia associated with Babylon.
The names "Chaldeans" and "Babylonians" are usually
synonymous.
43:16 a way through the sea Allusions to the exodus from Egypt inspire Israel to remember how Yahweh
formerly accomplished their salvation with great power,
especially as evidenced by the crossing of the Red Sea
(see Ex 14:21–31).

20 The wild animals honor me,
  the jackals and the owls,
because I provide water in the wilderness
  and streams in the wasteland,
to give drink to my people, my chosen,
21 the people I formed for myself
  that they may proclaim my praise.

22 "Yet you have not called on me, Jacob,
  you have not wearied yourselves for[a] me,
    Israel.
23 You have not brought me sheep for burnt
    offerings,
  nor honored me with your sacrifices.
I have not burdened you with grain offerings
  nor wearied you with demands for
    incense.
24 You have not bought any fragrant calamus
    for me,
  or lavished on me the fat of your sacrifices.
But you have burdened me with your sins
  and wearied me with your offenses.

25 "I, even I, am he who blots out
  your transgressions, for my own sake,
  and remembers your sins no more.
26 Review the past for me,
  let us argue the matter together;
  state the case for your innocence.
27 Your first father sinned;
  those I sent to teach you rebelled
    against me.
28 So I disgraced the dignitaries of your temple;
  I consigned Jacob to destruction[b]
  and Israel to scorn.

Israel the Chosen

44 "But now listen, Jacob, my servant,
  Israel, whom I have chosen.
2 This is what the LORD says —

he who made you, who formed you in the
    womb,
  and who will help you:
Do not be afraid, Jacob, my servant,
  Jeshurun,[c] whom I have chosen.
3 For I will pour water on the thirsty land,
  and streams on the dry ground;
I will pour out my Spirit on your offspring,
  and my blessing on your descendants.
4 They will spring up like grass in a meadow,
  like poplar trees by flowing streams.
5 Some will say, 'I belong to the LORD';
  others will call themselves by the name of
    Jacob;
still others will write on their hand, 'The
    LORD's,'
  and will take the name Israel.

The LORD, Not Idols

6 "This is what the LORD says —
  Israel's King and Redeemer, the LORD
    Almighty:
I am the first and I am the last;
  apart from me there is no God.
7 Who then is like me? Let him proclaim it.
  Let him declare and lay out before me
what has happened since I established my
    ancient people,
  and what is yet to come —
  yes, let them foretell what will come.
8 Do not tremble, do not be afraid.
  Did I not proclaim this and foretell it
    long ago?
You are my witnesses. Is there any God
    besides me?
  No, there is no other Rock; I know not one."

---

a 22 Or *Jacob; / surely you have grown weary of*   *b 28* The
Hebrew term refers to the irrevocable giving over of things or
persons to the LORD, often by totally destroying them.
c 2 Jeshurun means *the upright one,* that is, Israel.

43:18 Forget the former things After evoking strong
memories of the exodus event in Isa 43:16–17, God
instructs the exiles to stop dwelling on the past.
43:19 I am making a way in the wilderness Compare
40:3–4; 35:5–8.
43:21 that they may proclaim my praise Yahweh saves,
and expects to be praised for it. But instead of receiving
praise and sacrifices, he was burdened by sins (see v. 24).
**43:25 who blots out your transgressions, for my
own sake** Since Israel failed to worship properly and
bring proper sacrifices, Yahweh forgives their sins out
of his own grace.
43:27 Your first father sinned Perhaps an allusion to
Adam as the one through whom sin entered the world (see
Ro 5:12–14). **those I sent to teach you** Refers to the
religious leaders. Since they also failed to lead Israel into
proper relationship with Yahweh, a savior was still needed.
44:1–5 After the reminder in Isa 43:2–28 that Israel
deserved judgment for idolatry, the tone of Yahweh's
message shifts back to that of hope and restoration.

44:1 Israel, whom I have chosen The servant here is
corporate Israel, as in 41:8 and 43:10.
44:2 Jeshurun A poetic name for Israel, found otherwise
only in the two poems attributed to Moses (Dt 32:15;
33:5,26). See the table "Symbolic Names of People in
Hebrew" on p. 1388.
44:3 my Spirit on your offspring Salvation comes
with the promise of the Spirit, which will enable
their descendants to enjoy the promised blessing
because they will be wholly devoted to Yahweh (see
Joel 2:28–29).
44:6–8 Yahweh's status as true God, King, Redeemer
and Deliverer of Israel is declared again, and compared
with the utter futility of belief in handmade idols.
44:6 apart from me there is no God See Isa 43:10
and note; compare Dt 4:35,39.
44:8 You are my witnesses God continues to call on
Israel as his witnesses that he alone is God. See Isa
43:10 and note.

⁹All who make idols are nothing,
  and the things they treasure are worthless.
Those who would speak up for them are
    blind;
  they are ignorant, to their own shame.
¹⁰Who shapes a god and casts an idol,
  which can profit nothing?
¹¹People who do that will be put to shame;
  such craftsmen are only human beings.
Let them all come together and take their
    stand;
  they will be brought down to terror and
    shame.

¹²The blacksmith takes a tool
  and works with it in the coals;
he shapes an idol with hammers,
  he forges it with the might of his arm.
He gets hungry and loses his strength;
  he drinks no water and grows faint.
¹³The carpenter measures with a line
  and makes an outline with a marker;
he roughs it out with chisels
  and marks it with compasses.
He shapes it in human form,
  human form in all its glory,
  that it may dwell in a shrine.
¹⁴He cut down cedars,
  or perhaps took a cypress or oak.
He let it grow among the trees of the forest,
  or planted a pine, and the rain made it
    grow.
¹⁵It is used as fuel for burning;
  some of it he takes and warms himself,
  he kindles a fire and bakes bread.
But he also fashions a god and worships it;
  he makes an idol and bows down to it.
¹⁶Half of the wood he burns in the fire;
  over it he prepares his meal,
  he roasts his meat and eats his fill.
He also warms himself and says,
  "Ah! I am warm; I see the fire."
¹⁷From the rest he makes a god, his idol;
  he bows down to it and worships.
He prays to it and says,
  "Save me! You are my god!"

¹⁸They know nothing, they understand
    nothing;
  their eyes are plastered over so they cannot
    see,
  and their minds closed so they cannot
    understand.
¹⁹No one stops to think,
  no one has the knowledge or
    understanding to say,
"Half of it I used for fuel;
  I even baked bread over its coals,
  I roasted meat and I ate.
Shall I make a detestable thing from what is
    left?
  Shall I bow down to a block of wood?"
²⁰Such a person feeds on ashes; a deluded heart
    misleads him;
  he cannot save himself, or say,
  "Is not this thing in my right hand a lie?"

²¹"Remember these things, Jacob,
  for you, Israel, are my servant.
I have made you, you are my servant;
  Israel, I will not forget you.
²²I have swept away your offenses like a cloud,
  your sins like the morning mist.
Return to me,
  for I have redeemed you."

²³Sing for joy, you heavens, for the LORD has
    done this;
  shout aloud, you earth beneath.
Burst into song, you mountains,
  you forests and all your trees,
for the LORD has redeemed Jacob,
  he displays his glory in Israel.

Jerusalem to Be Inhabited

²⁴"This is what the LORD says —
  your Redeemer, who formed you in the
    womb:

I am the LORD,
  the Maker of all things,
  who stretches out the heavens,
  who spreads out the earth by myself,

44:9 All who make idols are nothing The idol-makers are *tohu*; the same Hebrew word is used in Ge 1:2 to describe the formless state of the world at the beginning of creation. Those who "create" other gods are not creators in the same sense of Yahweh, who formed order from chaos. **Those who would speak up for them** Contrasted with Israel as God's witnesses in Isa 43:10. **44:15 bows down to it** The irony is intentional: The same wood used for cooking is used to carve an idol. The imagery highlights the absurdity of worshiping something made by human hands. The creation cannot be greater than the creator. The so-called god would not exist without the human responsible for creating it. **44:18 They know nothing** Those who practice idol

worship do not recognize its absurdity in part because they have been blinded to the truth (see 6:9–10). The made-up speech of the craftsman in v. 19 articulates the ridiculous inner monologue an idol-worshipper might have if he was conscious of the reality behind his actions.

44:21–28 Another speech of redemption and salvation, which repeats themes from earlier speeches (see 42:15; 43:11–21,25–26; 44:1–8). The passage culminates in the revelation that Yahweh has raised up Cyrus to bring about the promised restoration of Judah.

44:24 who stretches out the heavens Yahweh's work as Creator of all the earth supports his ability to form Israel as a people and secure the promised redemption.

25 who foils the signs of false prophets
  and makes fools of diviners,
who overthrows the learning of the wise
  and turns it into nonsense,
26 who carries out the words of his servants
  and fulfills the predictions of his
    messengers,

who says of Jerusalem, 'It shall be inhabited,'
  of the towns of Judah, 'They shall be
    rebuilt,'
  and of their ruins, 'I will restore them,'
27 who says to the watery deep, 'Be dry,
  and I will dry up your streams,'
28 who says of Cyrus, 'He is my shepherd
  and will accomplish all that I please;
he will say of Jerusalem, "Let it be rebuilt,"
  and of the temple, "Let its foundations be
    laid."'

45 "This is what the LORD says to his
    anointed,
  to Cyrus, whose right hand I take hold of
to subdue nations before him
  and to strip kings of their armor,
to open doors before him
  so that gates will not be shut:
2 I will go before you
  and will level the mountains a;
I will break down gates of bronze
  and cut through bars of iron.
3 I will give you hidden treasures,
  riches stored in secret places,

so that you may know that I am the LORD,
  the God of Israel, who summons you by
    name.
4 For the sake of Jacob my servant,
  of Israel my chosen,
I summon you by name
  and bestow on you a title of honor,
  though you do not acknowledge me.
5 I am the LORD, and there is no other;
  apart from me there is no God.
I will strengthen you,
  though you have not acknowledged me,
6 so that from the rising of the sun
  to the place of its setting
people may know there is none besides me.
  I am the LORD, and there is no other.
7 I form the light and create darkness,
  I bring prosperity and create disaster;
  I, the LORD, do all these things.

8 "You heavens above, rain down my
    righteousness;
  let the clouds shower it down.
Let the earth open wide,
  let salvation spring up,
let righteousness flourish with it;
  I, the LORD, have created it.

9 "Woe to those who quarrel with their Maker,
  those who are nothing but potsherds
  among the potsherds on the ground.

a 2 Dead Sea Scrolls and Septuagint; the meaning of the word in the Masoretic Text is uncertain.

44:26 the towns of Judah Jeremiah 32:15 and 32:44 contain a similar promise that Judah will be rebuilt and inhabited.
44:28 Cyrus See note on Isa 45:1. **my shepherd** The Davidic kings should have held the role of shepherd of God's people. Instead, it goes to a foreign conqueror (compare Eze 34:1–10).

45:1–13 God's plan will be accomplished through Cyrus, a foreign king. Yahweh first took credit for this chain of events in Isa 41:2–4. But now, Cyrus is identified explicitly by name (first in the preceding verse, 44:28). The prophet emphasizes Yahweh's power over all things—even the actions of foreign kings who unknowingly do his bidding (v. 5)—and the darkness and calamity that plague the world order (v. 7).

45:1 his anointed Refers to Cyrus' selection for a specific purpose—saving Israel. The Hebrew term *mashiach* ("anointed one") reflects the tradition of selecting and equipping for service—e.g., kings were anointed by the prophets in 1Sa 10:1; 16:13; and 1Ki 19:15–16. The term later takes on overt Messianic connotations (see Da 9:25–26). **Cyrus** Cyrus conquered Babylon in 539 BC and decreed that the Jewish exiles could return to their homeland (see Isa 44:28; 41:2–4).
45:3 you may know that I am the LORD Yahweh's actions in history are expected to bring the foreign king to an acknowledgment of his power (see Ex 12:31–32; Da 3:28–29; 4:34).

45:4 Israel my chosen God forgives Israel's sin for his own sake in Isa 43:25; they had not repented, but he still delivers them because of their status as his chosen. See 41:8 and note. **though you do not acknowledge me** Cyrus should know it is Yahweh's hand guiding him (see v. 3 and note).
45:6 from the rising of the sun Even if Cyrus does not know or acknowledge Yahweh, his acts in history will eventually prove his power to the entire world.
45:7 I form the light and create darkness In Ge 1:3–4, God creates light and separates the darkness. This assertion indicates that the darkness, too, was God's creation—it was not just there to begin with. In the same way, God is described as creating both well-being and calamity. The reference here indicates Yahweh's superiority to both light and dark. The opposition between light and darkness also becomes a prominent theme in Jewish and Christian thought, especially in the Gospel of John and the War Scroll from the Dead Sea Scrolls.
45:9 potsherds among the potsherds on the ground The potter and clay image projects a powerful view of God's sovereignty, creativity and right to do as he wishes with his creation (see Isa 29:16 and note). **Does the clay say to the potter** The ridiculousness of a lump of clay talking back to the potter highlights the futility of people—who were made from dust (Ge 2:7) by God himself—questioning God's purposes.

Does the clay say to the potter,
  'What are you making?'
Does your work say,
  'The potter has no hands'?
[10] Woe to the one who says to a father,
  'What have you begotten?'
or to a mother,
  'What have you brought to birth?'

[11] "This is what the Lord says—
  the Holy One of Israel, and its Maker:
Concerning things to come,
  do you question me about my children,
  or give me orders about the work of my
    hands?
[12] It is I who made the earth
  and created mankind on it.
My own hands stretched out the heavens;
  I marshaled their starry hosts.
[13] I will raise up Cyrus[a] in my righteousness:
  I will make all his ways straight.
He will rebuild my city
  and set my exiles free,
but not for a price or reward,
  says the Lord Almighty."

[14] This is what the Lord says:

"The products of Egypt and the merchandise
    of Cush,[b]
  and those tall Sabeans—
they will come over to you
  and will be yours;
they will trudge behind you,
  coming over to you in chains.
They will bow down before you
  and plead with you, saying,
'Surely God is with you, and there is no other;
  there is no other god.'"

[15] Truly you are a God who has been hiding
    himself,
  the God and Savior of Israel.

[16] All the makers of idols will be put to shame
    and disgraced;
  they will go off into disgrace together.
[17] But Israel will be saved by the Lord
  with an everlasting salvation;
you will never be put to shame or
    disgraced,
  to ages everlasting.

[18] For this is what the Lord says—
he who created the heavens,
  he is God;
he who fashioned and made the earth,
  he founded it;
he did not create it to be empty,
  but formed it to be inhabited—
he says:
"I am the Lord,
  and there is no other.
[19] I have not spoken in secret,
  from somewhere in a land of darkness;
I have not said to Jacob's descendants,
  'Seek me in vain.'
I, the Lord, speak the truth;
  I declare what is right.

[20] "Gather together and come;
  assemble, you fugitives from the
    nations.
Ignorant are those who carry about idols
    of wood,
  who pray to gods that cannot save.
[21] Declare what is to be, present it—
  let them take counsel together.
Who foretold this long ago,
  who declared it from the distant past?
Was it not I, the Lord?
  And there is no God apart from me,
a righteous God and a Savior;
  there is none but me.

[a] 13 Hebrew *him*   [b] 14 That is, the upper Nile region

45:11 Concerning things to come, do you question me
Accurate prophecy is the distinguishing mark of the true God. The mock trial against the gods of the nations also challenges them to demonstrate their power (see Isa 41:23). **45:12 It is I who made the earth** Yahweh's rightful place as ruler over all events and people is regularly supported in chs. 40–48 by his position as Creator of all things (compare vv. 7,9). See the infographic "The Days of Creation" on p. 6. **45:13 my exiles free** An inscription attributed to Cyrus shows that his policy toward exiled populations such as the Jews allowed them to repatriate to their ancestral homelands. See the infographic "The Cyrus Cylinder" on p. 714. **not for a price or reward** Cyrus had no financial incentive to allow the Jews to return, rebuild their city and restore their temple. **45:14 The products of Egypt** Now the nations are depicted as willfully subjecting themselves to the rule of Jerusalem and Yahweh (see note on 60:5). **45:18 he did not create it to be empty** The Hebrew

term *tohu* ("emptiness") here may indicate that God did not create without a purpose. In v. 19, the same word connotes futility. The references to *tohu* in this passage may be allusions to Ge 1:2, where the earth prior to creation is described as *tohu* and *bohu* ("empty" and "nothing"). **formed it to be inhabited** The statement that Yahweh intended the world for inhabitants gives a purpose behind his act of creation—he did not create without a master plan. **45:19 Seek me in vain** Just as God had a purpose behind creating the world, he also had a purpose behind calling Israel his people. **45:20 gods that cannot save** The futility of idolatry ultimately boils down to the contrast between the living God—Yahweh—who will rise to redeem his people, and the dead gods made by people who cannot redeem, save or even respond to those who worship them. **45:21 there is no God apart from me** Yahweh alone is capable of saving; he alone is righteous. See Isa 43:10; 44:6.

22 "Turn to me and be saved,
all you ends of the earth;
for I am God, and there is no other.
23 By myself I have sworn,
my mouth has uttered in all integrity
a word that will not be revoked:
Before me every knee will bow;
by me every tongue will swear.
24 They will say of me, 'In the LORD alone
are deliverance and strength.'"
All who have raged against him
will come to him and be put to shame.
25 But all the descendants of Israel
will find deliverance in the LORD
and will make their boast in him.

Gods of Babylon

46 Bel bows down, Nebo stoops low;
their idols are borne by beasts of
burden.[a]
The images that are carried about are
burdensome,
a burden for the weary.
2 They stoop and bow down together;
unable to rescue the burden,
they themselves go off into captivity.

3 "Listen to me, you descendants of Jacob,
all the remnant of the people of Israel,
you whom I have upheld since your birth,
and have carried since you were born.
4 Even to your old age and gray hairs
I am he, I am he who will sustain you.
I have made you and I will carry you;
I will sustain you and I will rescue you.

5 "With whom will you compare me or count
me equal?
To whom will you liken me that we may be
compared?
6 Some pour out gold from their bags
and weigh out silver on the scales;
they hire a goldsmith to make it into a god,
and they bow down and worship it.
7 They lift it to their shoulders and carry it;
they set it up in its place, and there it
stands.
From that spot it cannot move.
Even though someone cries out to it, it cannot
answer;
it cannot save them from their troubles.

8 "Remember this, keep it in mind,
take it to heart, you rebels.
9 Remember the former things, those of long
ago;
I am God, and there is no other;
I am God, and there is none like me.
10 I make known the end from the beginning,
from ancient times, what is still to come.
I say, 'My purpose will stand,
and I will do all that I please.'
11 From the east I summon a bird of prey;
from a far-off land, a man to fulfill my
purpose.
What I have said, that I will bring about;
what I have planned, that I will do.
12 Listen to me, you stubborn-hearted,
you who are now far from my
righteousness.

a 1 Or *are but beasts and cattle*

45:23 By myself I have sworn Normally oaths are sworn by a greater power. Since there is no greater power, Yahweh swears on his own reputation. **Before me every knee will bow** Quoted in Ro 14:11 and alluded to in Php 2:10–11 with a reapplication to Jesus.

46:1–13 Isaiah's polemic against foreign idols reaches a dramatic climax as he satirizes Babylonian processional imagery, ridiculing the powerlessness of the man-made statues. Mesopotamian deities were associated with certain cities. During a god's festival, it was a sign of honor for the deity of a neighboring city to visit. To symbolize the movement of the god, his statue was carried from one city to the other in a ritual procession. Isaiah mocks the ritual by pointing out that the beasts of burden carrying the idols have more life and power than the idols themselves.

46:1 Bel Another name for Marduk, the chief god in the Babylonian hierarchy of gods (see note on Jer 50:2). The Babylonian creation epic *Enuma Elish* depicts Marduk as the creator. Isaiah's focus on Yahweh's role as Creator may subtly interact with myths about Marduk. See the table "Pagan Deities of the Old Testament" on p. 1287. **Nebo** The son of Bel or Marduk and the patron deity of the city of Borsippa, south of Babylon.
46:2 they themselves go off into captivity The idols from conquered peoples would be carried into exile along with the deported people.

46:3 carried since you were born Yahweh has carried Israel from the beginning, even if they did not recognize his presence (see Dt 1:31).
46:4 I will carry you; I will sustain you and I will rescue Contrasts with the idols who are themselves borne and carried by others and definitely cannot save (see Isa 46:1–2). This passage plays off the Hebrew words for "carry" and "save" to demonstrate the superiority of Yahweh over the idols.
46:5 or count me equal No gods can compare with Yahweh—the only God. The parallel with Marduk is striking; *Enuma Elish* declares that no god can equal Marduk (see note on v. 1). Yahweh has argued throughout this section (chs. 40–48) that no god can equal him or be compared to him (see 40:18).
46:6 to make it into a god The irony of the craftsmen making their own gods is highlighted in 44:10–20. Now, the focus shifts to others who bring their precious metals to another person to pay him to make a god for them.
46:7 they set it up in its place Isaiah is mocking the fact that the attendants are the ones doing all the work—their gods can do nothing without them.
46:9 the former things, those of long ago Yahweh predicted events in the past, so Israel should be confident that he will act again (see 42:9).
46:12 you stubborn-hearted Refers to those who doubt Yahweh is willing or able to save them. He refutes their doubts in v. 13 by declaring the salvation will come soon.

[13] I am bringing my righteousness near,
    it is not far away;
    and my salvation will not be delayed.
I will grant salvation to Zion,
    my splendor to Israel.

The Fall of Babylon

47 "Go down, sit in the dust,
    Virgin Daughter Babylon;
sit on the ground without a throne,
    queen city of the Babylonians.[a]
No more will you be called
    tender or delicate.
[2] Take millstones and grind flour;
    take off your veil.
Lift up your skirts, bare your legs,
    and wade through the streams.
[3] Your nakedness will be exposed
    and your shame uncovered.
I will take vengeance;
    I will spare no one."

[4] Our Redeemer — the LORD Almighty is his
    name —
is the Holy One of Israel.

[5] "Sit in silence, go into darkness,
    queen city of the Babylonians;
no more will you be called
    queen of kingdoms.
[6] I was angry with my people
    and desecrated my inheritance;
I gave them into your hand,
    and you showed them no mercy.

Even on the aged
    you laid a very heavy yoke.
[7] You said, 'I am forever —
    the eternal queen!'
But you did not consider these things
    or reflect on what might happen.

[8] "Now then, listen, you lover of pleasure,
    lounging in your security
and saying to yourself,
    'I am, and there is none besides me.
I will never be a widow
    or suffer the loss of children.'
[9] Both of these will overtake you
    in a moment, on a single day:
    loss of children and widowhood.
They will come upon you in full
    measure,
in spite of your many sorceries
    and all your potent spells.
[10] You have trusted in your wickedness
    and have said, 'No one sees me.'
Your wisdom and knowledge mislead you
    when you say to yourself,
    'I am, and there is none besides me.'
[11] Disaster will come upon you,
    and you will not know how to conjure
    it away.
A calamity will fall upon you
    that you cannot ward off with a
    ransom;
a catastrophe you cannot foresee
    will suddenly come upon you.

[a] 1 Or Chaldeans; also in verse 5

46:13 my salvation will not be delayed Cyrus' victory comes in 539 BC.

47:1–15 The humiliation of Babylon's gods in 46:1–2 is followed by a poetic description of the humiliation of Babylon. The city is personified as a woman—both virgin daughter and mother to her inhabitants. The imagery is reminiscent of descriptions of Jerusalem as a virgin daughter or unfaithful wife in 1:21; 37:22; and Eze 16:15–34.

47:1 Virgin Daughter Babylon The prophets referred to cities in danger of judgment as virgin daughters (see Isa 23:12). The image reflects the sheer helplessness of unmarried girls in an invasion; they faced the loss of potential husbands and their own virginity in a military defeat.

47:2 Take millstones and grind flour Grinding grain for flour was one of the most menial jobs for a slave girl, symbolizing the complete reversal of her status in society. **bare your legs** Slave girls or prisoners were depicted in ancient Near Eastern art with bared legs, while upper class women wore long skirts. The personified city is being exposed and humiliated. The Hebrew word for legs (*shoq*) may more accurately refer to the upper leg or thigh in this case, highlighting the sexual connotation of her nakedness.

47:3 Your nakedness The Hebrew term *erwah* ("naked-

ness") often indicates a shameful exposure of a sexual nature (see Ge 9:22–23; La 1:8; Eze 16:37).

47:5 queen of kingdoms The Babylonian Empire controlled a large swath of the Fertile Crescent that included many formerly independent powerful kingdoms such as Assyria, Aram (Syria), Phoenicia, Philistia, Israel and Judah.

47:6 I was angry with my people Yahweh used Babylon to punish his own people. But like Assyria (Isa 10:12–15), they will be held accountable and judged for their arrogant, self-sufficient attitudes.

47:7 I am forever—the eternal queen Babylon is condemned by her own arrogant words—just as the king of Assyria was judged for his haughty claims in 10:8–11,13–14.

47:8 I am, and there is none besides Babylon's prideful claim to unique authority and status echoes Yahweh's in 45:5–6 (compare Ex 3:14). Babylon is not claiming that no other cities exist on earth; rather, she is claiming that no other cities can compare to her.

47:9 loss of children and widowhood In the extended metaphor of Babylon as queen mother, the loss of children refers to the death or capture of the city's inhabitants in an invasion. **in spite of your many sorceries** Babylon had a reputation for magic and divination in the ancient Near East.

47:11 you cannot foresee Despite their reputation for fortune-telling and sorcery, Babylon's overthrow would

12 "Keep on, then, with your magic spells
    and with your many sorceries,
    which you have labored at since childhood.
Perhaps you will succeed,
    perhaps you will cause terror.
13 All the counsel you have received has only
        worn you out!
Let your astrologers come forward,
    those stargazers who make predictions
        month by month,
    let them save you from what is coming
        upon you.
14 Surely they are like stubble;
    the fire will burn them up.
They cannot even save themselves
    from the power of the flame.
These are not coals for warmth;
    this is not a fire to sit by.
15 That is all they are to you —
    these you have dealt with
    and labored with since childhood.
All of them go on in their error;
    there is not one that can save you.

Stubborn Israel

48 "Listen to this, you descendants of Jacob,
    you who are called by the name of Israel
    and come from the line of Judah,
you who take oaths in the name of the LORD
    and invoke the God of Israel —
    but not in truth or righteousness —
2 you who call yourselves citizens of the holy
        city
    and claim to rely on the God of Israel —
    the LORD Almighty is his name:

3 I foretold the former things long ago,
    my mouth announced them and I made
        them known;
    then suddenly I acted, and they came to
        pass.
4 For I knew how stubborn you were;
    your neck muscles were iron,
    your forehead was bronze.
5 Therefore I told you these things long ago;
    before they happened I announced them to
        you
so that you could not say,
    'My images brought them about;
    my wooden image and metal god ordained
        them.'
6 You have heard these things; look at them all.
    Will you not admit them?

"From now on I will tell you of new things,
    of hidden things unknown to you.
7 They are created now, and not long ago;
    you have not heard of them before today.
So you cannot say,
    'Yes, I knew of them.'
8 You have neither heard nor understood;
    from of old your ears have not been open.
Well do I know how treacherous you are;
    you were called a rebel from birth.
9 For my own name's sake I delay my wrath;
    for the sake of my praise I hold it back
        from you,
    so as not to destroy you completely.
10 See, I have refined you, though not as
        silver;
    I have tested you in the furnace of
        affliction.

---

come unexpectedly and without warning. The Persian army takes the city in 539 BC with very little resistance.
47:13 those stargazers Refers to astrology, a form of divination that looked for omens of future events in the movements of the stars and planets. Ancient Mesopotamian archives contain many records of observed celestial phenomena, from the recurring new moons to the rarer solar eclipses.

48:1–11 The themes of Yahweh's sovereignty, Israel's sinful stubbornness and the futility of idol worship are reinforced here. Ultimately, Isaiah's message is directed at the exiles to explain the purpose behind their present sufferings. Despite appearances, Yahweh sovereignly ordained all the events that led to Judah's fall, the destruction of Jerusalem, the loss of the temple and the scattering of the exiles.

48:1 come from the line of Judah Isaiah 40–48 refers to Judah as Jacob and Israel regularly (see 43:1), but only here are those names explicitly linked with Judah. The use of all three titles may hint at a reunited Israel.
invoke the God of Israel Israel's greatest sin was not simply abandoning Yahweh to serve other gods. The sin was in elevating the worship of other gods alongside worship of Yahweh. Religious blending (or syncretism) in ancient Israel primarily involved the worship of other West

Semitic deities like Asherah, Baal, Chemosh or Milcom, or the adaptation of Canaanite religious symbols, myths and rituals to the worship of Yahweh.
48:3 I foretold the former things long ago Yahweh's sovereignty and power is proven by prophecy.
48:4 For I knew how stubborn you were The proof of past prophecy was necessary due to the people's stubbornness.
48:5 My images brought them about Yahweh's announcement was meant to prevent them from mistakenly attributing any events to the power or prediction of their idols. Many ancient inscriptions show evidence that the people in the ancient Near East attributed their successes and failures to blessing and affliction from divine forces.
48:6 new things, of hidden things God's past faithfulness should encourage Israel to have faith in what he says will happen in the future.
48:8 you were called a rebel Israel's persistent rebellion in turning away from Yahweh is a recurring theme throughout the history of Israel as a nation in the books of Exodus, Numbers, Judges and 1–2 Kings.
48:9 For my own name's sake I delay my wrath God's compassion toward Israel in restraining his anger is for his sake, not theirs.
48:10 See, I have refined you The punishment of invasion and exile is compared to the smelting process

¹¹ For my own sake, for my own sake, I do this.
How can I let myself be defamed?
I will not yield my glory to another.

Israel Freed

¹² "Listen to me, Jacob,
Israel, whom I have called:
I am he;
I am the first and I am the last.
¹³ My own hand laid the foundations of the
earth,
and my right hand spread out the heavens;
when I summon them,
they all stand up together.

¹⁴ "Come together, all of you, and listen:
Which of the idols has foretold these
things?
The LORD's chosen ally
will carry out his purpose against
Babylon;
his arm will be against the Babylonians.^a
¹⁵ I, even I, have spoken;
yes, I have called him.
I will bring him,
and he will succeed in his mission.

¹⁶ "Come near me and listen to this:

"From the first announcement I have not
spoken in secret;
at the time it happens, I am there."

And now the Sovereign LORD has sent me,
endowed with his Spirit.

¹⁷ This is what the LORD says —
your Redeemer, the Holy One of Israel:
"I am the LORD your God,
who teaches you what is best for you,
who directs you in the way you should go.
¹⁸ If only you had paid attention to my
commands,
your peace would have been like a river,
your well-being like the waves of the sea.
¹⁹ Your descendants would have been like
the sand,
your children like its numberless
grains;
their name would never be blotted out
nor destroyed from before me."

²⁰ Leave Babylon,
flee from the Babylonians!
Announce this with shouts of joy
and proclaim it.
Send it out to the ends of the earth;
say, "The LORD has redeemed his servant
Jacob."
²¹ They did not thirst when he led them
through the deserts;
he made water flow for them from
the rock;
he split the rock
and water gushed out.

²² "There is no peace," says the LORD, "for
the wicked."

^a 14 Or *Chaldeans*; also in verse 20

---

designed to remove impurities from fine metals like silver. The refining should remove the impurity of their past sins and restore their relationship with God (see 1:22,25).

48:12–22 Yahweh again appeals to Israel to recognize his ability to redeem them based on his power shown through creation and his provision shown through fulfilled prophecy.

48:12 the first and I am the last An appeal to his unique divinity (see note on 41:22). Yahweh's claim to be first and last is an assertion that he is neither created by another god nor has he begotten lesser divine beings after him.

48:13 laid the foundations of the earth Yahweh's creative power is frequently summarized with references to setting the earth on its foundations and spreading out the heavens (see Job 38:4; Pr 8:29; Isa 51:13; Ps 102:25). See the infographic "Ancient Hebrew Conception of the Universe" on p. 5.

48:14 Which of the idols has foretold these things Yahweh asks if any of their idols predicted Cyrus' rise as he has (see Isa 41:26).

48:16 Sovereign LORD has sent me, endowed with his Spirit The first-person speaker in vv. 15–16a is Yahweh himself. The speaker switches here without warning, as God is now referred to in the third person and the speaker refers to himself in the first person. The speaker may be the prophet, or it may be the Servant of Yahweh called

by God in 49:1–3, who is also the first-person speaker in that passage.

48:18 you had paid attention to my commands Neither the judgment of exile nor the invasion would have been necessary if Israel had kept the commandments and held up their end of the covenant agreement.

48:19 name would never be blotted out "Name" has an idiomatic sense of legacy or reputation. Cutting off the name of a people or family meant all the members were dead and no one was left to carry on the legacy or memory of the family (see Jer 11:19). The self-worth and identity of a person was intimately connected to their name. It carries the connotation of honor and reputation. In that sense, a name is used by Yahweh to justify his actions — he will act to save his reputation (Isa 48:9).

48:20 Announce this with shouts of joy and proclaim it Contrasts with the exodus from Egypt, which occurred in haste and at night (Ex 12:31–42). The joyfulness of the departure from Babylon also contrasts with the fearfulness of the exodus from Egypt (Ex 14:10).

48:21 led them through the deserts The renewal of life in the desert symbolized by the presence of water is a familiar motif in Isaiah's oracles of restoration (see Isa 35:6; 44:3; compare Ps 105:41).

48:22 "There is no peace," says the LORD This statement is repeated in Isa 57:21; it may serve here as a refrain ending the section of chs. 40–48. That section began with a call for comfort and ends with this statement that peace and righteousness are connected (see v. 18).

The Servant of the LORD

49 Listen to me, you islands;
hear this, you distant nations:
Before I was born the LORD called me;
from my mother's womb he has spoken my
name.
[2] He made my mouth like a sharpened sword,
in the shadow of his hand he hid me;
he made me into a polished arrow
and concealed me in his quiver.
[3] He said to me, "You are my servant,
Israel, in whom I will display my
splendor."
[4] But I said, "I have labored in vain;
I have spent my strength for nothing at all.
Yet what is due me is in the LORD's hand,
and my reward is with my God."

[5] And now the LORD says —
he who formed me in the womb to be his
servant
to bring Jacob back to him
and gather Israel to himself,
for I am[a] honored in the eyes of the LORD
and my God has been my strength —
[6] he says:
"It is too small a thing for you to be my servant
to restore the tribes of Jacob
and bring back those of Israel I have kept.

I will also make you a light for the Gentiles,
that my salvation may reach to the ends
of the earth."

[7] This is what the LORD says —
the Redeemer and Holy One of Israel —
to him who was despised and abhorred by
the nation,
to the servant of rulers:
"Kings will see you and stand up,
princes will see and bow down,
because of the LORD, who is faithful,
the Holy One of Israel, who has chosen
you."

Restoration of Israel

[8] This is what the LORD says:

"In the time of my favor I will answer you,
and in the day of salvation I will
help you;
I will keep you and will make you
to be a covenant for the people,
to restore the land
and to reassign its desolate inheritances,
[9] to say to the captives, 'Come out,'
and to those in darkness, 'Be free!'

[a] 5 Or *him, / but Israel would not be gathered; / yet I will be*

49:1–7 This is the second of four passages focused on the figure of the servant of Yahweh, often called servant songs (see note on 42:1–9). While the "servant" references in chs. 40–48 refer mainly to Israel as a nation, the remaining references in chs. 49–55 seem to focus on an individual servant with a mission to save Israel. The servant songs are full of Messianic imagery—the servant suffers and dies on behalf of Israel. This passage highlights the servant's call and commission by God to save Israel and be a light to the nations (49:6).

49:1 Before I was born the LORD called me Reflects the servant's prophetic call as in Jer 1:5 (compare Ps 22:9). The image of calling before birth is associated with Israel in Isa 44:2.

49:2 He made my mouth like a sharpened sword God raised up Cyrus, who conquered by his military strength. The servant conquers by the power of his word, just like the Messiah who strikes with the "rod of his mouth" in 11:4. Since the Hebrew word for "mouth" is also used idiomatically for the "edge" of a sword (see Jdg 3:16; Pr 5:4), a play on words here is possible. The power of speech as an offensive weapon like a sword is reflected also in Hos 6:5.

49:3 my servant, Israel The individual servant now embodies and represents corporate Israel. In Isa 44:1, Israel was explicitly called the servant, but v. 5 makes it clear that the servant is distinct from corporate Israel and sent to save Israel. Yahweh will use the servant to display his glory. The servant's work will fulfill everything the nation of Israel was supposed to have done to glorify Yahweh, but failed to do.

49:5 gather Israel The servant's mission was to restore Israel's relationship with Yahweh. See note on v. 3.

49:6 It is too small a thing for you The servant announced his mission to Israel in v. 5. Now, Yahweh reveals that the mission is not to Israel only, but to all the nations of the world. Redeeming Israel alone was too easy; Yahweh wishes for a greater display of his sovereignty. **a light for the Gentiles** Compare 42:6, where Israel may be given this mission to be a light to the nations (see note on 42:1–9). The mission that was Israel's corporately is reassigned to the servant individually, who fulfills Israel's obligations to Yahweh in order to restore their relationship. **may reach to the ends of the earth** The entire world—not just Israel—will have access to Yahweh's salvation through the servant (see Ac 13:47). Isaiah has elsewhere hinted that nations would one day be included in the people of God (see Isa 2:2–4).

49:7 Kings will see you and stand up First, the servant is despised, then honored by kings. Compare the silent astonishment of the kings before the Servant in 52:15 and the humility of royalty in the imagery of kings carrying the exiles back to Jerusalem in v. 23.

49:8–26 The restoration and return of Israel is described again as a second exodus, led by the Messiah or servant figure. The theme of supernatural renewal of the desert and miraculous provision for the people is again prominent as in 35:1–10; 41:17–20; and 43:19–20.

49:8 time of my favor The arrival of the promised salvation is partially fulfilled in the return from exile but described in idealistic terms that reflect the future rule of the Messiah. **a covenant for the people** Israel was commissioned to be a covenant for the people and a light for the nations. Compare 42:6.

49:9 to the captives Compare the release of captives in 42:7. Prosperity and the release of prisoners were

"They will feed beside the roads
  and find pasture on every barren hill.
¹⁰ They will neither hunger nor thirst,
  nor will the desert heat or the sun beat
    down on them.
He who has compassion on them will guide
    them
  and lead them beside springs of water.
¹¹ I will turn all my mountains into roads,
  and my highways will be raised up.
¹² See, they will come from afar—
  some from the north, some from the west,
  some from the region of Aswan.ᵃ"

¹³ Shout for joy, you heavens;
  rejoice, you earth;
  burst into song, you mountains!
For the Lord comforts his people
  and will have compassion on his
    afflicted ones.

¹⁴ But Zion said, "The Lord has forsaken me,
  the Lord has forgotten me."

¹⁵ "Can a mother forget the baby at her
    breast
  and have no compassion on the child she
    has borne?
Though she may forget,
  I will not forget you!
¹⁶ See, I have engraved you on the palms of my
    hands;
  your walls are ever before me.
¹⁷ Your children hasten back,
  and those who laid you waste depart
    from you.

¹⁸ Lift up your eyes and look around;
  all your children gather and come to you.
As surely as I live," declares the Lord,
  "you will wear them all as ornaments;
  you will put them on, like a bride.

¹⁹ "Though you were ruined and made desolate
  and your land laid waste,
now you will be too small for your people,
  and those who devoured you will be far
    away.
²⁰ The children born during your bereavement
  will yet say in your hearing,
'This place is too small for us;
  give us more space to live in.'
²¹ Then you will say in your heart,
  'Who bore me these?
I was bereaved and barren;
  I was exiled and rejected.
Who brought these up?
I was left all alone,
  but these—where have they come from?'"

²² This is what the Sovereign Lord says:

"See, I will beckon to the nations,
  I will lift up my banner to the peoples;
they will bring your sons in their arms
  and carry your daughters on their hips.
²³ Kings will be your foster fathers,
  and their queens your nursing mothers.
They will bow down before you with their
    faces to the ground;
  they will lick the dust at your feet.

ᵃ 12 Dead Sea Scrolls; Masoretic Text *Sinim*

---

considered hallmarks of the reign of a righteous and just king. Those attributes become part of the ideal future envisioned under the reign of the Messiah.

49:12 region of Aswan The Hebrew text has "land of Sinim," which is believed to be a reference to Syene, a settlement at the first cataract of the Nile in Egypt and the location of modern-day Aswan. A Jewish settlement was nearby that seems to have been established during the exile. Syene was a settlement neighboring the Jewish military colony at Elephantine. A large archive of documents written in Aramaic from this period was discovered at Elephantine, and provides a remarkable window into Jewish life outside of Palestine (in the Diaspora) during the postexilic period.

49:13 Lord comforts his people God called for someone to comfort Israel; now he comforts them himself. See 40:3.

49:14 Lord has forsaken me Despite the repeated assurances that redemption is coming, the exiles are still feeling abandoned. They should be responding with joy as the prophet has in v. 13, but they resist, denying the reality behind the message of comfort and hope. Yahweh addresses Zion directly in vv. 15–21 to reassure her of his care.

49:15 a mother forget the baby at her breast Both masculine and feminine metaphors are used to describe Yahweh and his relationship with people. He is described as both mother (66:13), father (63:16) and sometimes husband to Israel (54:6). **I will not forget you** It is not possible for Yahweh to forget or fail to fully love his children.

49:16 I have engraved you on the palms of my hands The second person address is directed at Zion or Jerusalem in vv. 15–21. The reference to "walls" suggests that what was engraved was a plan for restoring the city.

49:19 you will be too small for your people The magnitude of the return will be so great that Zion will be too small for all who want to live there. Since the historical return was a small band of exiles, the reference either points to a future restoration or functions as hyperbole to emphasize that Jerusalem will be inhabited, not forgotten.

49:21 Who bore me these Zion is astonished at the restoration of her population.

49:22 I will lift up my banner to the peoples This return was foreshadowed in 11:10–12. The signal was used to summon nations for judgment in 5:26. Now, it is used to signal the time for God's people to be brought home.

49:23 you will know that I am the Lord Yahweh's sovereignty over the nations is demonstrated by his power even over kings and queens who bring the exiles home personally. The theme that the foreign nations would eventually acknowledge Yahweh's sovereignty is found in 2:2–5.

Then you will know that I am the LORD;
  those who hope in me will not be
  disappointed."

²⁴ Can plunder be taken from warriors,
  or captives be rescued from the fierce[a]?

²⁵ But this is what the LORD says:

"Yes, captives will be taken from warriors,
  and plunder retrieved from the fierce;
I will contend with those who contend
  with you,
  and your children I will save.
²⁶ I will make your oppressors eat their own
  flesh;
  they will be drunk on their own blood, as
  with wine.
Then all mankind will know
  that I, the LORD, am your Savior,
  your Redeemer, the Mighty One of Jacob."

Israel's Sin and the Servant's Obedience

50 This is what the LORD says:

"Where is your mother's certificate of divorce
  with which I sent her away?
Or to which of my creditors
  did I sell you?
Because of your sins you were sold;
  because of your transgressions your
  mother was sent away.

² When I came, why was there no one?
  When I called, why was there no one to
  answer?
Was my arm too short to deliver you?
  Do I lack the strength to rescue you?
By a mere rebuke I dry up the sea,
  I turn rivers into a desert;
their fish rot for lack of water
  and die of thirst.
³ I clothe the heavens with darkness
  and make sackcloth its covering."

⁴ The Sovereign LORD has given me a well-
  instructed tongue,
  to know the word that sustains the weary.
He wakens me morning by morning,
  wakens my ear to listen like one being
  instructed.
⁵ The Sovereign LORD has opened my ears;
  I have not been rebellious,
  I have not turned away.
⁶ I offered my back to those who beat me,
  my cheeks to those who pulled out my
  beard;
I did not hide my face
  from mocking and spitting.
⁷ Because the Sovereign LORD helps me,
  I will not be disgraced.
Therefore have I set my face like flint,
  and I know I will not be put to shame.

---

a 24 Dead Sea Scrolls, Vulgate and Syriac (see also Septuagint and verse 25); Masoretic Text *righteous*

49:25 captives will be taken from warriors Returning from exile or imprisonment in the ancient world was unusual; it was rare for prisoners to be rescued. But these obstacles are no problem for Yahweh.

49:26 Then all mankind will know Yahweh's victory will prove that he is the true God of Israel. The use of this recognition formula is likely meant to evoke the traditions of the first exodus, where it was used extensively (e.g., Ex 6:7; 14:18; 29:46). The formula is also used by Isaiah in Isa 49:23 and 45:3, and becomes a central part of Ezekiel's message (used more than 60 times including Eze 12:15; Eze 21:5; see note on Eze 5:13).

50:1–11 Yahweh declares to the exiles that their punishment is only temporary, and that they will soon be redeemed—though they doubt his power to redeem. The third servant song in Isa 50:4–9 contrasts the servant's obedience in the face of suffering with Israel's doubts and fears.

50:1 your mother's certificate of divorce The rhetorical question indicates the absence of a certificate of divorce; therefore, Yahweh had not divorced Israel. Yahweh is reassuring the exiles that he has not permanently abandoned them. **to which of my creditors did I sell you** Israelites could sell themselves or their children into slavery to pay off debt. Yahweh uses the metaphor of slavery to indicate that, although they were sent away temporarily, they can and will be redeemed. **50:2 no one to answer** Yahweh calls out for his people, but encounters silence. Israel was blind and deaf to the

seriousness of their sins in 42:18–23. They felt abandoned by God, and doubted his ability to save them (49:14). **By a mere rebuke I dry up the sea** Yahweh alludes to his power demonstrated against Egypt in the exodus when he made a dry path through the Red Sea (see Ex 14:21–22).

50:4–9 Isaiah 50:4–9 is the third servant song. The song focuses on the obedient attention and unwavering trust the servant has in Yahweh, which contrasts with the failure of Israel to respond to Yahweh's call in v. 2.

50:4 me The first-person speaker changes from Yahweh to the servant. The shift in speaker is marked by the reference to Yahweh now in the third person. **a well-instructed tongue** The servant claims he is a disciple of God himself and credits God for his knowledgeable speech. A disciple's role was to learn from his master and accurately transmit the traditions learned from him. The servant learns from God—as Israel should have—and is capable of passing on God's word (again, as Israel should have). **word that sustains the weary** The power in the servant's word is comparable to the promised renewal coming to those who waited on Yahweh in 40:31. **50:6 my back to those who beat me** The account of the rejection and abuse of the servant intensifies (see 49:7), and will climax in the final servant song (52:13–53:12). His attitude contrasts with the nation that complains of being forsaken by Yahweh after being taken captive and likely mistreated. **50:7 I set my face like flint** The servant's faith in Yahweh will not be shaken, and is just as strong as Israel's stubborn unwillingness to repent (48:4).

⁸He who vindicates me is near.
　Who then will bring charges against me?
　Let us face each other!
　Who is my accuser?
　Let him confront me!
⁹It is the Sovereign LORD who helps me.
　Who will condemn me?
　They will all wear out like a garment;
　the moths will eat them up.

¹⁰Who among you fears the LORD
　and obeys the word of his servant?
　Let the one who walks in the dark,
　who has no light,
　trust in the name of the LORD
　and rely on their God.
¹¹But now, all you who light fires
　and provide yourselves with flaming
　　torches,
　go, walk in the light of your fires
　and of the torches you have set ablaze.
　This is what you shall receive from my hand:
　You will lie down in torment.

Everlasting Salvation for Zion

51 "Listen to me, you who pursue
　righteousness
　and who seek the LORD:
　Look to the rock from which you were cut
　and to the quarry from which you were
　　hewn;

²look to Abraham, your father,
　and to Sarah, who gave you birth.
　When I called him he was only one man,
　and I blessed him and made him many.
³The LORD will surely comfort Zion
　and will look with compassion on all her
　　ruins;
　he will make her deserts like Eden,
　her wastelands like the garden of the
　　LORD.
　Joy and gladness will be found in her,
　thanksgiving and the sound of singing.

⁴"Listen to me, my people;
　hear me, my nation:
　Instruction will go out from me;
　my justice will become a light to the
　　nations.
⁵My righteousness draws near speedily,
　my salvation is on the way,
　and my arm will bring justice to the
　　nations.
　The islands will look to me
　and wait in hope for my arm.
⁶Lift up your eyes to the heavens,
　look at the earth beneath;
　the heavens will vanish like smoke,
　the earth will wear out like a garment
　and its inhabitants die like flies.
　But my salvation will last forever,
　my righteousness will never fail.

50:8 He who vindicates me is near The servant's sufferings are the result of the guilt of others. He will be vindicated once the truth is known.

50:10 Who among you fears the LORD True wisdom is found in fearing Yahweh (Pr 1:7). Since the servant has been taught the proper way to live to please God (Isa 50:4), his words should be obeyed. **Let the one who walks in the dark** Those in darkness should wait for the light of the Messiah. Human attempts to conquer the darkness are condemned in v. 11. Compare 9:2.

51:1 to the rock Invokes the imagery of highly valued, quarried and dressed stone used in building projects.

51:2 Abraham, your father Abraham was the founder of the Hebrew nation, the forefather of God's chosen people. Yahweh promised to make Abraham a great nation and bless the entire world through him (see Ge 12:2–3; 15:5; 18:18; 22:17–18). **he was only one man** Yahweh's miraculous work in taking one man and creating a nation of chosen people should be proof of his power to provide for Israel (compare Eze 33:24).

51:3 Zion The name of Yahweh's earthly dwelling and holy mountain, figuratively used to represent Jerusalem and, by extension, the nation of Israel. **he will make her deserts like Eden** The perfection of Eden and God's original plan for the earth became the ideal image for the restoration of God's people in the land he promised them. In prophetic literature, the return to Eden is a powerful metaphor for the hope of ultimate restoration of the divine-human relationship. Eden imagery is also found in Joel 2:3, and is used extensively by Ezekiel (Eze 28:13; 31:9,16,18; 36:35).

51:4 Instruction will go out from me The parallelism in the next line indicates this law will be used to promote justice and righteousness. The link to exodus traditions in Isa 51:3 suggests the return to Zion from Babylonian exile will play out as a second exodus, complete with wilderness wanderings, and the receiving of the law directly from Yahweh as at Mt. Sinai (see Ex 19–20). Israel's condemnation by the prophets is often about the people's interest in following the letter of the law while ignoring the spirit of the law. Isaiah 1:11–17 criticizes Israel for depending on empty religious rituals instead of practicing righteousness and justice. Similarly, Micah 6:6–8 points out the futility of following the rituals when the proper attitude and behavior is not there. **a light to the nations** Yahweh's justice and righteousness will be displayed through the work of the servant, who will be held up as a light to the peoples (compare Isa 49:6). The coming of the Messiah is described as a light that replaces the people's spiritual darkness in 9:2, and the servant is sent as a light to the nations (49:6). The light metaphor emphasizes the servant's role in embodying God's presence, power and knowledge to the nations.

51:5 my arm will bring justice to the nations The arm of Yahweh symbolizes the earthly manifestation of his power (compare Ex 6:6; Isa 51:9). In this case, his power will be manifested through the servant (53:1). The Messiah judges the nations on behalf of Yahweh in 11:3–5,10.

51:6 my salvation will last forever Though the heavens may vanish, the earth wear out, and all life on earth die, Yahweh's salvation will endure. The imagery is not

7 "Hear me, you who know what is right,
you people who have taken my instruction
to heart:
Do not fear the reproach of mere mortals
or be terrified by their insults.
8 For the moth will eat them up like a garment;
the worm will devour them like wool.
But my righteousness will last forever,
my salvation through all generations."

9 Awake, awake, arm of the Lord,
clothe yourself with strength!
Awake, as in days gone by,
as in generations of old.
Was it not you who cut Rahab to pieces,
who pierced that monster through?
10 Was it not you who dried up the sea,
the waters of the great deep,
who made a road in the depths of the sea
so that the redeemed might cross over?
11 Those the Lord has rescued will return.
They will enter Zion with singing;
everlasting joy will crown their heads.
Gladness and joy will overtake them,
and sorrow and sighing will flee away.

12 "I, even I, am he who comforts you.
Who are you that you fear mere mortals,
human beings who are but grass,
13 that you forget the Lord your Maker,
who stretches out the heavens
and who lays the foundations of the earth,
that you live in constant terror every day
because of the wrath of the oppressor,
who is bent on destruction?
For where is the wrath of the oppressor?
14 The cowering prisoners will soon be set
free;
they will not die in their dungeon,
nor will they lack bread.
15 For I am the Lord your God,
who stirs up the sea so that its waves
roar —
the Lord Almighty is his name.
16 I have put my words in your mouth
and covered you with the shadow of my
hand —
I who set the heavens in place,
who laid the foundations of the earth,
and who say to Zion, 'You are my people.'"

referring to a literal end to heaven and earth. Rather, the language contrasts the enduring nature of God's plan of salvation with the temporary nature of his creation.
51:7 you people who have taken my instruction to heart One aspect of God's renewed covenant with Israel was that true worshipers had a heart focused on obeying him. In Jeremiah, God promises to write his Law on their hearts (Jer 31:33); Ezekiel describes it as a heart transplant, where God replaces our stubborn hearts of stone with receptive hearts of flesh (Eze 11:19; 36:26).
51:9 Awake, as in days gone by The prophet begs Yahweh to bring the promised salvation now by reminding him of his past act of deliverance. The phrasing used here refers to the time of the exodus, made clear by the references to God's power over the sea in the following lines. **Rahab** One of the names for the mythological dragon from Yahweh's primordial battle with the forces of chaos. In Isa 30:7, Rahab is figuratively used to represent Egypt. The usage here is appropriate as an allusion to the exodus from Egypt. Biblical references to the sea monster Rahab fall into two groups: allusions to the dragon defeated at the time of creation (Ps 89:10; Job 9:13; 26:12), and metaphorical references to Egypt (Ps 87:4; Isa 30:7). The use here seems to blend the two images, invoking the creation motif of God's victory over the sea monster with the Red Sea victory over Egypt.
51:10 dried up the sea Alludes to the Israelites' crossing of the Red Sea on dry ground in Ex 14:21–22. The story of Israel's founding as a nation is intimately tied to creation imagery, which depicts God's creative energy as binding the forces of chaos, symbolized by the untamed and awesome power of the sea. The triumph of Yahweh over the sea in the exodus is likened to the mythological battle between the god Baal and the sea god Yam in Ugaritic literature. Baal's victory in the myth establishes his kingship over the Canaanite gods. Yahweh's victory over the sea establishes him as the supreme power of the universe, able to subdue the mighty forces of chaos.
51:11 Those the Lord has rescued This wording also

occurs in Isa 35:10, summarizing the miraculous work of Yahweh leading the exiles back to Zion through the wilderness.
51:12 I, even I, am he who comforts you Yahweh responds to the prophet's summons of v. 9. In 40:1, Yahweh calls for someone to come and comfort his people. Now, he responds that he is the Comforter. His comfort is again expressed in 66:13. **mere mortals** Yahweh is highlighting the oddity of their fear of mortal man while forgetting the immortal God.
51:13 who stretches out the heavens Yahweh identifies himself as the Creator using common poetic images for creation (compare 40:22; 48:13). The use of creation imagery is concentrated in chs. 40–48. Here, it serves the same purpose: proof of Yahweh's ultimate sovereignty over all things by virtue of his creation of all things.
51:14 bread As an essential staple of people's diet in Biblical times, bread was often used to represent food in general (e.g., Dt 8:3; Eze 5:16). Yahweh's assurance that bread will be provided to the exiles invokes the exodus image of manna—the miraculous bread Yahweh provided daily to Israel in the wilderness (see Ex 16:4). The return from exile will be a second exodus in nearly every way.
51:15 I am the Lord your God The speaker from Isa 51:12 now specifically identifies himself as Yahweh. This identification formula brings to the fore the covenantal basis of Israel and Yahweh's relationship. In Ex 6:7, Yahweh makes an agreement with Israel where he takes them as his people and they accept him as their God. This is then followed by Yahweh's declaration that "I am Yahweh your God."
51:16 put my words in your mouth A common way for God to refer to his prophets. The second-person pronoun is singular. Yahweh may be speaking to the prophet Isaiah or to the Servant. The language is reminiscent of Dt 18:18, where Yahweh will put his words in the mouth of the promised prophet like Moses. The predominance of exodus imagery in this part of Isaiah—combined with the presentation of the Servant as another Moses—suggests God is speaking to the Servant here.

The Cup of the LORD's Wrath

[17] Awake, awake!
  Rise up, Jerusalem,
you who have drunk from the hand of the
  LORD
  the cup of his wrath,
you who have drained to its dregs
  the goblet that makes people stagger.
[18] Among all the children she bore
  there was none to guide her;
among all the children she reared
  there was none to take her by the hand.
[19] These double calamities have come upon
  you—
  who can comfort you?—
ruin and destruction, famine and sword—
  who can[a] console you?
[20] Your children have fainted;
  they lie at every street corner,
  like antelope caught in a net.
They are filled with the wrath of the LORD,
  with the rebuke of your God.

[21] Therefore hear this, you afflicted one,
  made drunk, but not with wine.
[22] This is what your Sovereign LORD says,
  your God, who defends his people:
"See, I have taken out of your hand
  the cup that made you stagger;
from that cup, the goblet of my wrath,
  you will never drink again.
[23] I will put it into the hands of your
    tormentors,
  who said to you,
  'Fall prostrate that we may walk on you.'
And you made your back like the ground,
  like a street to be walked on."

52 Awake, awake, Zion,
  clothe yourself with strength!
Put on your garments of splendor,
  Jerusalem, the holy city.
The uncircumcised and defiled
  will not enter you again.
[2] Shake off your dust;
  rise up, sit enthroned, Jerusalem.
Free yourself from the chains on your neck,
  Daughter Zion, now a captive.

[3] For this is what the LORD says:

"You were sold for nothing,
  and without money you will be redeemed."

[4] For this is what the Sovereign LORD says:

"At first my people went down to Egypt to
    live;
  lately, Assyria has oppressed them.

[5] "And now what do I have here?" declares the
LORD.

"For my people have been taken away for
    nothing,
  and those who rule them mock,[b]"
                        declares the LORD.
"And all day long
  my name is constantly blasphemed.
[6] Therefore my people will know my name;
  therefore in that day they will know
that it is I who foretold it.
  Yes, it is I."

[7] How beautiful on the mountains
  are the feet of those who bring good news,

---

[a] 19 Dead Sea Scrolls, Septuagint, Vulgate and Syriac; Masoretic Text / how can I   [b] 5 Dead Sea Scrolls and Vulgate; Masoretic Text wail

---

51:17 Jerusalem Jerusalem and Zion can figuratively refer to the entire nation of God's chosen people. In Isa 51:9, the prophet called on Yahweh to awaken and show his power. Now Yahweh calls on them to wake up and be attentive to the fact that he has judged them, but now he will redeem them.

51:22 who defends Yahweh acts on their behalf. Compare Jer 50:34.

52:1–12 Yahweh calls on Jerusalem to prepare to receive the returning exiles. The time of salvation is drawing near. The passage idealizes the return by picturing Jerusalem in a future state of perfect holiness.

52:1 your garments of splendor Representative of ritual purity and preparation to experience the return of the divine presence (see Ex 28:2; Zec 3:1–4). The image of Jerusalem dressed in pure garments reverses the image of stripped and destitute Babylon in Isa 47:1–2. **will not enter you again** The sanctity of the land and restoration to ritual purity worthy of the presence of Yahweh is a common motif in oracles of salvation (see 35:8; Joel 3:17). The Biblical writers were very concerned about defilement of the land where Yahweh's presence was to dwell. The holiness of the land increased as one

moved closer to the Holy of Holies (most Holy Place) in the temple—the site of God's earthly presence.

52:3 without money you will be redeemed The redemption of property—including persons sold into slavery—usually required some kind of financial exchange. God did not have to provide anything in exchange. It was his prerogative to redeem.

52:4 At first my people went down to Egypt A brief overview of Israel's history of oppression: enslaved in Egypt, then exiled by Assyria and Babylon (see Ge 46:6; Ex 1:11–14; 2Ki 17:3–6; 24:10–16). See the timeline "Dates Related to Isaiah and 2 Kings" on p. 1116.

52:5 my name is constantly blasphemed Yahweh is concerned with his own reputation. The same concern is evident in Isa 48:11, where Yahweh declares he will save for the sake of his name and his glory. See note on 48:19.

52:7 those who bring good news The messenger usually brought news of a victory (compare 2Sa 18:24–27). This verse is quoted in support of preaching the gospel in Ro 10:15. **Your God reigns** May signify the restored reign of Yahweh in his temple. The watchmen in Isa 52:8 are looking for this messenger and his announcement that Yahweh is returning to his holy mountain.

who proclaim peace,
    who bring good tidings,
    who proclaim salvation,
who say to Zion,
    "Your God reigns!"
[8] Listen! Your watchmen lift up their voices;
    together they shout for joy.
When the LORD returns to Zion,
    they will see it with their own eyes.
[9] Burst into songs of joy together,
    you ruins of Jerusalem,
for the LORD has comforted his people,
    he has redeemed Jerusalem.
[10] The LORD will lay bare his holy arm
    in the sight of all the nations,
and all the ends of the earth will see
    the salvation of our God.

[11] Depart, depart, go out from there!
    Touch no unclean thing!
Come out from it and be pure,
    you who carry the articles of the LORD's
    house.
[12] But you will not leave in haste
    or go in flight;
for the LORD will go before you,
    the God of Israel will be your rear guard.

The Suffering and Glory of the Servant

[13] See, my servant will act wisely [a];
    he will be raised and lifted up and highly
    exalted.
[14] Just as there were many who were appalled
    at him [b] —
    his appearance was so disfigured beyond
    that of any human being
    and his form marred beyond human
    likeness —
[15] so he will sprinkle many nations, [c]
    and kings will shut their mouths because
    of him.
For what they were not told, they will
    see,
and what they have not heard, they will
    understand.

53 Who has believed our message
    and to whom has the arm of the LORD
    been revealed?
[2] He grew up before him like a tender
    shoot,
    and like a root out of dry ground.

---

[a] 13 Or *will prosper*   [b] 14 Hebrew *you*   [c] 15 Or *so will many nations be amazed at him* (see also Septuagint)

52:9 LORD has comforted his people See note on 51:12.

52:10 the ends of the earth God's act of saving Israel will have worldwide impact: All will see it and recognize his power (see Ps 98:3).

52:11 the articles of the LORD's In 2Ki 24:13, Nebuchadnezzar is depicted carrying off the treasures of the temple and the royal palace. In Ezr 1:7–11, the temple vessels are returned to the exiles to bring back with them for the temple they plan to rebuild.

52:12 your rear guard In the exodus, Yahweh moved behind Israel to guard the rear from Pharaoh's attack during the crossing of the Red Sea (see Ex 14:19). He also led the way ahead of them through the wilderness. Compare Isa 58:8.

52:13—53:12 This is the last of the four servant songs in chs. 40–55. Here the power of Yahweh—represented by his arm—is revealed in his servant. Here, the speaker realizes that he, and everyone else, has gone astray (53:6) and that the servant represents Yahweh's way to bring them back into relationship with him—he is Yahweh's will in action (53:1). After a long battle as Yahweh's warrior, the servant vicariously suffers and dies (53:10). He is then resurrected (at the end of 53:10). The servant's death as a guilt offering (called an *asham* in Hebrew; see note on Lev 5:14—6:7) carried the sin of his "offspring," and (possibly) restored them to their land. He then witnesses their relationship with Yahweh subsequently reconciled (53:10–12).

52:13 servant In 49:3, the servant of Yahweh has inherited the role of God's people, the entire identity of the people of Israel. He is acting on their behalf—carrying out their vocation. **and lifted up** The servant shares in Yahweh's role as the restorer of his people and—within the larger context of Isaiah—is the way Yahweh brings reconciliation.

52:14 appalled at him Some manuscripts read "him," while most read "you." If the reading "him" is selected, people are astonished at what the servant is capable of. But if the reading "you" is chosen, people are surprised by what Zion is doing. **so disfigured beyond that of any human being** He will not look like other men once he suffers—his physical appearance will be disfigured.

52:15 sprinkle many nations The Hebrew verb used here, *nazah*, typically refers to sprinkling (Ex 29:21; Lev 4:6,17; 5:9; 6:27). The translator of the Greek Septuagint, however, used a Greek verb denoting astonishment or surprise (*thaumazō*). The Greek translator may have inferred this meaning for the Hebrew word *nazah* based on the following parallel phrase about the kings' silence. However, the translator may also have known of a Hebrew homonym for *nazah* meaning "startle" since Arabic (a Semitic language related to Hebrew) attests *nazah* with that meaning. **many nations** Or "many peoples"—not just the Israelites, but people from all over the earth. **shut their mouths** Foreshadows Isa 53:7. The graciousness of the servant's response to the unjust pain inflicted upon him will shut the mouths of kings. **they will see** Prior to the servant, the kings had not "seen" in the prophetic sense—they had not understood, or perceived, what God was doing among them. Now, the servant brings Yahweh's work to the forefront of their thought: They are confronted with who he is and what he is doing among them.

53:1 Who has believed A rhetorical question referring to the prophet's consistent message of redemption and salvation (compare 52:7,10). **our** The identification of this first-person plural group is debated. The suggestions are the Gentile nations from v. 12, the nation of Israel or the Israelite prophets collectively. The best option in context is that the group is the nation of Israel, the same group that has gone astray (v. 6). **arm of the LORD** Symbolizes the earthly manifestation of Yahweh's power (see 51:5 and note). Here the servant becomes Yahweh's divine

He had no beauty or majesty to attract us to
  him,
    nothing in his appearance that we should
      desire him.
[3] He was despised and rejected by mankind,
    a man of suffering, and familiar with pain.
  Like one from whom people hide their faces
    he was despised, and we held him in low
      esteem.

[4] Surely he took up our pain
    and bore our suffering,
  yet we considered him punished by God,
    stricken by him, and afflicted.
[5] But he was pierced for our transgressions,
    he was crushed for our iniquities;
  the punishment that brought us peace was
    on him,
    and by his wounds we are healed.
[6] We all, like sheep, have gone astray,
    each of us has turned to our own way;

and the LORD has laid on him
    the iniquity of us all.
[7] He was oppressed and afflicted,
    yet he did not open his mouth;
  he was led like a lamb to the slaughter,
    and as a sheep before its shearers
      is silent,
    so he did not open his mouth.
[8] By oppression[a] and judgment he was taken
      away.
    Yet who of his generation protested?
  For he was cut off from the land of the
      living;
    for the transgression of my people he was
      punished.[b]
[9] He was assigned a grave with the wicked,
    and with the rich in his death,

[a] 8 Or From arrest   [b] 8 Or generation considered / that he was
cut off from the land of the living, / that he was punished for the
transgression of my people?

---

warrior in battle—an integral part in Yahweh's fight to reclaim his people. The phrase "Yahweh's arm" is used in Ex 15:16 to describe Yahweh's victory over the Egyptians and his future victories over Edom, Moab and Canaan.

53:2–11 The prophet describes *how* God will restore and reconcile his people. The oracle both critiques the people and tells what will come to pass. The final servant song in Isa 52:13—53:12 fulfills many of the obligations of the previous servants—making him the servant *par excellence*. The servant in 52:13—53:12 becomes the one who finally, and ultimately, accomplishes what Yahweh deemed necessary to restore and reconcile his people to himself.

53:2 like a tender shoot The shoot's role in 11:1–12 parallels that of the servant. In both passages, Yahweh is appointing a leader to bring about change in the land and the people. The shoot in 11:1–12 and the branch in Zec 3:8–9 are both bringers of the divine will of Yahweh. The servant's divinely appointed role in Zec 3:8–9 also parallels the vocation of the servant in Isa 52:13—53:12.

53:3 despised and rejected The servant is considered worthless, not worthy of attention. **people hide their faces** Parallels the servant being despised and rejected. People look away to symbolize their dissociation with the servant (compare note on 59:2). The NT events surrounding Jesus' betrayal exemplify this imagery of total rejection and dissociation. After Judas betrays Jesus (Lk 22:47–53), he feels so guilty that he commits suicide (Mt 27:3–10). Also, Peter rejects Jesus on the night he is delivered into the hands of his enemies (Mk 14:66–72); Jesus even prophesies that this will happen (Mk 14:26–30). **we held him in low esteem** As in Isa 53:1, the "we" here must refer to the nation of Israel. This rejection of the servant by his own people is likely echoed in Jn 1:10–11.

53:4 took up our pain The Hebrew word *choli* is frequently used for serious illness or injury (Dt 7:15; 2Ki 1:2; 2Ki 13:14). Its use here likely indicates that the servant had the ability to heal—this is linked to his willingness to die on behalf of the people. This verse is applied to Jesus in Mt 8:17.

53:5 pierced for our transgressions The people real-

ize that the servant is suffering for their wrongdoing, not being punished for his own sin. John likely alludes to this passage when he describes how Jesus is pierced in the side with a spear (Jn 19:34). **peace** The servant brings people into right relationship with God (Isa 53:11–12) and others. **by his wounds we are healed** The servant is able to heal people—metaphorically and physically—because he is willing to follow the will of Yahweh—even though it results in his suffering.

53:6 We all, like sheep The metaphor of wayward Israel as a flock of sheep without a shepherd is a common motif used in prophetic literature (see 56:11; Jer 13:20; 23:1; 49:20; Eze 34:1–10; Zec 10:2). This imagery emphasizes Israel's willful wandering from Yahweh, their punishment of scattering through exile, and the future hope of the ingathering under a new divinely appointed shepherd (see Isa 40:11 and note, and note on Eze 34:11).

53:7 slaughter Possibly alludes to sacrifice since sheep were important sacrificial animals. Lambs were used in the offering made on the Day of Atonement (Nu 29:8). Lambs were also sacrificed on Passover (Ex 12:3–6).

53:8 By oppression and judgment The implication is that the servant's treatment was completely unjust. The phrase is best understood as indicating oppressive legal treatment leading to an undeserved death sentence. The servant has not died yet in this poem—instead, the prophet is foreshadowing the servant's death by suggesting that it seemed improbable that the servant would die. The servant being cut off from the "land of the living" is symbolic of the exile of God's people in Babylon. The servant, in his death, takes upon himself the very reason why the Israelites went into exile: their iniquities. In doing so, he takes upon himself the symbolic punishment of exile as well.

53:9 a grave with the wicked The intention of those making the servant suffer is for him to die as a wicked person next to wicked people. A connection to this prophecy can be made when Jesus is crucified next to two criminals (Mk 15:27; Lk 23:32–33). **rich in his death** The narratives of the NT Gospels suggest that the manner of Jesus' burial fulfills the prophecy of the suffering servant in Isa 53:9 (see Mk 15:43–46; Lk 23:50–56).

though he had done no violence,
nor was any deceit in his mouth.

¹⁰ Yet it was the LORD's will to crush him and
cause him to suffer,
and though the LORD makes^a his life an
offering for sin,
he will see his offspring and prolong his days,
and the will of the LORD will prosper in his
hand.
¹¹ After he has suffered,
he will see the light of life^b and be
satisfied ^c;
by his knowledge^d my righteous servant will
justify many,
and he will bear their iniquities.
¹² Therefore I will give him a portion among the
great,^e
and he will divide the spoils with the
strong,^f
because he poured out his life unto death,
and was numbered with the transgressors.
For he bore the sin of many,
and made intercession for the
transgressors.

The Future Glory of Zion

54 "Sing, barren woman,
you who never bore a child;
burst into song, shout for joy,
you who were never in labor;
because more are the children of the
desolate woman
than of her who has a husband,"
says the LORD.
² "Enlarge the place of your tent,
stretch your tent curtains wide,
do not hold back;
lengthen your cords,
strengthen your stakes.
³ For you will spread out to the right and
to the left;
your descendants will dispossess
nations
and settle in their desolate
cities.

^a 10 Hebrew *though you make*   ^b 11 Dead Sea Scrolls (see also
Septuagint); Masoretic Text does not have *the light of life.*
^c 11 Or (with Masoretic Text) ¹¹*He will see the fruit of his suffering
/ and will be satisfied*   ^d 11 Or *by knowledge of him*
^e 12 Or *many*   ^f 12 Or *numerous*

53:10 it was the LORD's will People may be the instruments of the servant's death, but it is ultimately
Yahweh's will that he suffers, dies and is resurrected.
Not only are the events leading up the servant's death in
Yahweh's will, but so is his death. Via Yahweh's triumph
over the servant's death, he will create a new way for
the sins of many to be carried (Isa 53:12). **makes his
life an offering for sin** The servant dies as a guilt
offering. A guilt offering was required in cases when a
wrong was unintentionally or unknowingly committed.
Once the guilt was known, the offering was necessary
to atone for the sin (Lev 5:14–19). **he will see his
offspring** The servant is resurrected; people only "see
[their] offspring" in life. **prolong his days** The servant
will live a long life after he is made a guilt offering. Because of the servant's obedience to Yahweh's will, he
is resurrected and blessed. He is blessed with perhaps
the two most desired things in the ancient Near East:
long life and the ability to see descendants (either his
own or simply that of his people). **in his hand** God's
will is now in the hands of the servant. He has been
empowered by Yahweh.
53:11 he will see All intact Dead Sea Scrolls manuscripts and the Septuagint (the ancient Greek translation
of the Bible) contain the word "light"; the Masoretic Text
simply reads "he will see." The most probable original
text is "he will see light" (Dead Sea Scrolls) or "he will
show him light" (Septuagint). The word "light" is required
for the text to make sense poetically. **my righteous servant** Yahweh begins speaking again. **will justify many**
Like Israel—as Yahweh's servant—was commanded
to bring forth justice to the nations, the servant makes
many righteous. **bear their iniquities** The iniquities of
the people are placed upon the Servant (similar to the
goat on the Day of Atonement in Lev 16:22).

53:12 This verse is an epilogue to Isa 53:1–11. The
servant has suffered, died and is resurrected. Now, the
prophet—via the voice of Yahweh—tells us more about
the results of the servant's actions.

53:12 a portion The servant is given a portion of that
which he regained for the people—perhaps their land,
or perhaps their reconciled relationship with Yahweh (or
both). **he will divide the spoils** Yahweh's servant is a
warrior whose suffering involves a triumphant battle over
death, resulting in resurrection. This triumph results in
Yahweh's people being made righteous (v. 11)—a victory
that likely results in the reclaiming of their relationship
with Yahweh and their land. The servant then shares
in the bounty of his victory. **bore the sin of many** The
servant does not just bear people's iniquities (their
culpability or guilt); he also carries their sin—their
actual wrongdoings. The servant takes responsibility
for all the things that people have done wrong against
God and one another. **made intercession for the
transgressors** The servant vicariously suffers for the
people by bearing their iniquities and carrying their
sin through becoming their guilt offering. His actions
are somewhat akin to—though not entirely the same
as—the role of the priests in Leviticus (vv. 10–12;
compare Lev 10:17).
54:1 Sing Using the imperative verb forms, the prophet
commands Zion to rejoice and celebrate in light of the
redemptive work of the servant in Isa 53. **barren woman**
Refers to Zion's loss of inhabitants. The city is metaphorically depicted as abandoned, deserted and vacant
in 49:19–21 and 51:2–3. Personified Zion describes
herself as one barren and bereaved of children in 49:21.
The analogy also points to the reference to Abraham and
Sarah in 51:2—the nation of Israel was built on the
promise of offspring to one who was barren.
54:2 Enlarge the place of your tent Zion needs to
prepare for a growth in population.
54:3 your descendants God promised Abraham that all
the nations would be blessed through his descendants
(Ge 12:3; 28:14). Israel's possession of the nations
should be understood in light of this idea of blessing,
especially the spread of the knowledge of God throughout
the world (Isa 11:10).

4 "Do not be afraid; you will not be put to shame.
  Do not fear disgrace; you will not be
    humiliated.
You will forget the shame of your youth
  and remember no more the reproach of
    your widowhood.
5 For your Maker is your husband—
  the LORD Almighty is his name—
the Holy One of Israel is your Redeemer;
  he is called the God of all the earth.
6 The LORD will call you back
  as if you were a wife deserted and
    distressed in spirit—
a wife who married young,
  only to be rejected," says your God.
7 "For a brief moment I abandoned you,
  but with deep compassion I will bring you
    back.
8 In a surge of anger
  I hid my face from you for a moment,
but with everlasting kindness
  I will have compassion on you,"
says the LORD your Redeemer.

9 "To me this is like the days of Noah,
  when I swore that the waters of Noah
    would never again cover the earth.
So now I have sworn not to be angry with
    you,
  never to rebuke you again.
10 Though the mountains be shaken
  and the hills be removed,
yet my unfailing love for you will not be
    shaken
  nor my covenant of peace be removed,"
says the LORD, who has compassion on
    you.

11 "Afflicted city, lashed by storms and not
    comforted,
  I will rebuild you with stones of
    turquoise,[a]
  your foundations with lapis lazuli.
12 I will make your battlements of rubies,
  your gates of sparkling jewels,
  and all your walls of precious
    stones.
13 All your children will be taught by
    the LORD,
  and great will be their peace.
14 In righteousness you will be established:
  Tyranny will be far from you;
    you will have nothing to fear.
  Terror will be far removed;
    it will not come near you.
15 If anyone does attack you, it will not be
    my doing;
  whoever attacks you will surrender
    to you.

16 "See, it is I who created the blacksmith
  who fans the coals into flame
  and forges a weapon fit for its work.
And it is I who have created the destroyer
    to wreak havoc;
17   no weapon forged against you will
    prevail,
  and you will refute every tongue that
    accuses you.
This is the heritage of the servants of
    the LORD,
  and this is their vindication from me,"
    declares the LORD.

a 11 The meaning of the Hebrew for this word is uncertain.

54:4 shame of your youth Refers to Israel's idolatry (see 42:17; 45:16). Jeremiah also acknowledges this shameful behavior had begun in Israel's earliest days (see Jer 3:24–25).

54:5 your Maker is your husband Zion's shame and widowhood are removed—she is once again reunited with her husband, God. In Isa 50:1, Yahweh insists he did not divorce Israel but that they would be reconciled soon (compare 62:4–5; Hos 2:7).

54:7 For a brief moment Though God describes the exile as a "brief moment," time did not pass quickly for the exiles—they viewed their punishment as endless (see Ps 74:1). But in God's timing—especially compared to the eternal nature of his covenant (Isa 54:10)—the span of a generation was only a short time.

54:9 Noah God used Noah to preserve life during the great flood (Ge 6–9). This analogy involves both God's just requirement to punish human wickedness as he did in the flood of Ge 6–9 and his assurances of future grace and restoration after the flood (Ge 8:21; 9:11). The judgment brought against Israel by foreign invasion is metaphorically depicted as an overwhelming flood in Isa 8:5–8. See the infographic "Inside Noah's Ark" on p. 19.

54:10 my unfailing love for you will not be shaken Alludes to the ultimate fulfillment of the salvation accom-

plished by the Messiah (see 16:5; 55:3). The Hebrew word *chesed* ("love; kindness") often describes Yahweh's attitude of covenant love or loyalty toward Israel. The Hebrew word encompasses the concepts of loyalty, faithfulness, benevolence and kindness. **my covenant of peace** The renewed covenant with Israel is unlike the first covenant; it will be eternal and permanent. Jeremiah describes God establishing an entirely new covenant (Jer 31:31–33), and Ezekiel uses the same term—a covenant of peace—to describe the future peace of the Messiah's reign (Eze 34:25–31).

54:13 will be taught by the LORD Yahweh's direct instruction of the people will ensure the future blessing he has promised. Learning from God contrasts with the empty religiosity taught by people (Isa 29:13). Not only Israel, but all the nations, will one day seek Yahweh to learn from him (2:3). The concept of learning directly from God through the Holy Spirit is also found in 1Co 2:13 and 1Th 4:9.

54:17 the servants of the LORD Refers to Yahweh's true followers who will receive the benefits of all the promises in Isa 54:1–17. The role of the servant transitions from the individual servant of chs. 49–53 to a group of faithful followers awaiting the promised salvation in chs. 56–66.

Invitation to the Thirsty

55 "Come, all you who are thirsty,
come to the waters;
and you who have no money,
come, buy and eat!
Come, buy wine and milk
without money and without cost.
2 Why spend money on what is not bread,
and your labor on what does not
satisfy?
Listen, listen to me, and eat what is
good,
and you will delight in the richest
of fare.
3 Give ear and come to me;
listen, that you may live.
I will make an everlasting covenant
with you,
my faithful love promised to David.
4 See, I have made him a witness to the
peoples,
a ruler and commander of the peoples.
5 Surely you will summon nations you know
not,
and nations you do not know will come
running to you,
because of the LORD your God,
the Holy One of Israel,
for he has endowed you with splendor."

6 Seek the LORD while he may be found;
call on him while he is near.
7 Let the wicked forsake their ways
and the unrighteous their thoughts.

Let them turn to the LORD, and he will have
mercy on them,
and to our God, for he will freely pardon.

8 "For my thoughts are not your thoughts,
neither are your ways my ways,"
declares the LORD.
9 "As the heavens are higher than the earth,
so are my ways higher than your ways
and my thoughts than your thoughts.
10 As the rain and the snow
come down from heaven,
and do not return to it
without watering the earth
and making it bud and flourish,
so that it yields seed for the sower and
bread for the eater,
11 so is my word that goes out from my mouth:
It will not return to me empty,
but will accomplish what I desire
and achieve the purpose for which I
sent it.
12 You will go out in joy
and be led forth in peace;
the mountains and hills
will burst into song before you,
and all the trees of the field
will clap their hands.
13 Instead of the thornbush will grow the
juniper,
and instead of briers the myrtle will grow.
This will be for the LORD's renown,
for an everlasting sign,
that will endure forever."

55:1 come to the waters In 44:3, Yahweh's blessing is likened to the renewing power of water. Likewise, the promised salvation provides satisfaction for all the exiles' spiritual needs. Jesus alludes to this verse in Jn 7:37–38; the people's response in Jn 7:40–41 demonstrates his allusion was understood as a Messianic reference.

55:3 everlasting covenant The renewal of a covenant relationship between Yahweh and his people will be enduring and based on his promises to David (see Ps 89:33–35). The restored covenant is an everlasting covenant (Isa 61:8), a covenant of peace (54:10; Eze 37:26) and a new covenant (Jer 31:31). This new covenant replaces the conditional and temporary covenant God made with Israel—which they had broken (see note on Isa 54:10).

55:4 a witness to the peoples Yahweh's relationship with David and the establishment of David's earthly power was a symbol foreshadowing the power and reign of the Davidic Messiah. The Messiah would rule the world with complete authority (see 11:1–10).

55:5 you will summon nations In v. 3, "you" is plural and refers to the people with whom Yahweh will establish a new covenant. Here, "you" is singular, suggesting it refers to an individual. Since the person has been glorified, it may refer to the Messianic servant (compare 4:2).

55:7 he will freely pardon All that is necessary to receive forgiveness is repentance—there is no mention

of ritual or sacrifice. Attitude, not action, is central to restoring the relationship between God and humankind. Only God can forgive sins. The OT usage of the Hebrew word *salach* ("forgive, pardon") may lie behind the story in Mk 2:5–12 where Jesus heals a paralytic but first announces his sins are forgiven, raising the ire of the religious leaders who insist only God can forgive sins (Mk 2:7).

55:8 my thoughts are not your thoughts Invites trust in Yahweh's ability to accomplish everything he has promised for his people if they repent. While people may fail in their plans or promises, God can be trusted to keep his word.

55:11 It will not return to me empty Yahweh's word cannot fail to bring about the desired results (compare Isa 40:8). The word of God contains very real power to accomplish his will. Creation happened through divine speech in Ge 1 (compare Ps 33:6,9), and Yahweh brought life back into lifeless bones through the prophetic words of Ezekiel (Eze 37:1–14).

55:12 trees of the field will clap their hands Creation itself cannot help but praise God for the triumphant success of his word (compare Lk 19:40).

55:13 everlasting sign The renewal of creation—undoing the negative effects of sin from the fall—will be established as a permanent monument to God's glory. The prophet's vision of the future renewal and restoration of creation runs throughout Isa 40–55.

Salvation for Others

56 This is what the LORD says:

"Maintain justice
and do what is right,
for my salvation is close at hand
and my righteousness will soon be
revealed.
[2] Blessed is the one who does this —
the person who holds it fast,
who keeps the Sabbath without
desecrating it,
and keeps their hands from doing any
evil."

[3] Let no foreigner who is bound to the LORD say,
"The LORD will surely exclude me from his
people."
And let no eunuch complain,
"I am only a dry tree."

[4] For this is what the LORD says:

"To the eunuchs who keep my Sabbaths,
who choose what pleases me
and hold fast to my covenant —
[5] to them I will give within my temple and its
walls
a memorial and a name
better than sons and daughters;

I will give them an everlasting name
that will endure forever.
[6] And foreigners who bind themselves to
the LORD
to minister to him,
to love the name of the LORD,
and to be his servants,
all who keep the Sabbath without
desecrating it
and who hold fast to my covenant —
[7] these I will bring to my holy mountain
and give them joy in my house
of prayer.
Their burnt offerings and sacrifices
will be accepted on my altar;
for my house will be called
a house of prayer for all nations."
[8] The Sovereign LORD declares —
he who gathers the exiles of Israel:
"I will gather still others to them
besides those already gathered."

God's Accusation Against the Wicked

[9] Come, all you beasts of the field,
come and devour, all you beasts of the
forest!
[10] Israel's watchmen are blind,
they all lack knowledge;

56:1–8 Yahweh advises Israel on how to behave while they wait for the promised salvation. After painting a glorious picture of what Yahweh's salvation will look like in chs. 40–55, Isaiah must address the more practical reality of living righteously in the present.

The exiles who returned from Babylon did not experience the full blessing of redemption promised in chs. 40–55. Therefore, chs. 56–66 serve to contextualize their experience within God's larger plan of salvation and the glorious future reign of the Messiah. Since the prophets expressed their revelation in a way that mixed immediate and future elements of God's plan, it was understandable that the people would be disillusioned if the fulfillment they hoped for would only be experienced by future generations.

In this section, Yahweh reveals that salvation is available for all who would follow him and keep the covenant, even non-Israelites and those previously excluded by the Law.

56:1 Maintain justice and do what is right Justice and righteousness are the fundamental virtues embodying the ideal standards of God, both legal and ethical. Waiting in anticipation for the coming deliverance of the Messiah does not replace the people's responsibility to live rightly. The Hebrew terms here are paired throughout Isaiah as the two central elements of redemption (e.g., 1:27; 5:7; 5:16; 32:16–17). The pairing may reflect the spectrum of right behavior toward both God and other people.

56:2 Blessed is the one A "blessed is" or "happy is" statement was a common formula for wisdom teaching in the ancient world—especially Biblical poetry and Wisdom literature in the OT (e.g., Ps 1:1; Pr 3:13).

56:4 the eunuchs who keep my Sabbaths A eunuch was often (though not always) a castrated male official. The prohibition against emasculated men entering the assembly of God in Dt 23:1 would have excluded them from worship. The image of the eunuch as a "dry tree" in Isa 56:3 probably alludes to his inability to have children. The most important element of worship is having an attitude that will lead one to choose what pleases God. The intentional observance of the Sabbath is more important than being able to enter the temple for sacrifice.

56:5 a memorial and a name Yahweh's offer would have had a significant cultural impact. While the memories of most people were kept alive after death by their family, a eunuch would have no offspring. A high-ranking eunuch might earn the right to construct a monument to commemorate his accomplishments. David's son Absalom builds himself a monument because he has no son to carry on his legacy (2Sa 18:18).

56:6 foreigners The grandchildren of foreigners who joined Israel were given the right to enter the assembly of Yahweh (Dt 23:7–8). Yahweh now emphasizes that his true servants are those who follow the covenant and love him, not necessarily those linked to Israel by blood. **servants** The singular "servant" motif in Isa 40–55 is replaced by an emphasis on Yahweh's true followers as his servants. The atoning work of the Servant in ch. 53 makes salvation accessible to all who genuinely follow Yahweh.

56:7 a house of prayer for all nations The idea that foreigners would pray to Yahweh is found in Solomon's prayer dedicating the temple in 1Ki 8:41–43. The motif of Gentile nations coming to acknowledge Yahweh and worship him alongside the people of Israel is found throughout Isaiah (see Isa 2:2–5; 19:19–25; 42:6; 49:6; 60:5).

they are all mute dogs,
    they cannot bark;
they lie around and dream,
    they love to sleep.
[11] They are dogs with mighty appetites;
    they never have enough.
They are shepherds who lack understanding;
    they all turn to their own way,
    they seek their own gain.
[12] "Come," each one cries, "let me get wine!
    Let us drink our fill of beer!
And tomorrow will be like today,
    or even far better."

57

The righteous perish,
    and no one takes it to heart;
the devout are taken away,
    and no one understands
that the righteous are taken away
    to be spared from evil.
[2] Those who walk uprightly
    enter into peace;
    they find rest as they lie in death.

[3] "But you—come here, you children of a
    sorceress,
    you offspring of adulterers and prostitutes!
[4] Who are you mocking?
    At whom do you sneer
    and stick out your tongue?
Are you not a brood of rebels,
    the offspring of liars?
[5] You burn with lust among the oaks
    and under every spreading tree;
you sacrifice your children in the ravines
    and under the overhanging crags.

[6] The idols among the smooth stones of the
    ravines are your portion;
    indeed, they are your lot.
Yes, to them you have poured out drink
    offerings
    and offered grain offerings.
    In view of all this, should I relent?
[7] You have made your bed on a high and lofty
    hill;
    there you went up to offer your sacrifices.
[8] Behind your doors and your doorposts
    you have put your pagan symbols.
Forsaking me, you uncovered your bed,
    you climbed into it and opened it wide;
you made a pact with those whose beds you
    love,
    and you looked with lust on their naked
    bodies.
[9] You went to Molek[a] with olive oil
    and increased your perfumes.
You sent your ambassadors[b] far away;
    you descended to the very realm of the
    dead!
[10] You wearied yourself by such going about,
    but you would not say, 'It is hopeless.'
You found renewal of your strength,
    and so you did not faint.

[11] "Whom have you so dreaded and feared
    that you have not been true to me,
and have neither remembered me
    nor taken this to heart?
Is it not because I have long been silent
    that you do not fear me?

---

[a] 9 Or *to the king*   [b] 9 Or *idols*

56:11 shepherds Represents the rulers of Israel who seek their own gain instead of the welfare of the people. The metaphor is developed further in Eze 34:1–10.

57:1 The righteous perish Surrounded by wickedness, the few remaining righteous people would welcome death as a merciful release. These verses invert the stereotypical understanding that death is a punishment or judgment for wickedness.

57:3 you offspring of adulterers Refers to illegitimate children born out of an immoral union. In Jesus' day, the Jewish religious leaders protest that they are not children of immorality (see Jn 8:41).

57:5 among the oaks A site of idolatrous worship; see note on Isa 1:29. **you sacrifice your children** Child sacrifice appears to have been one of the idolatrous practices of the Canaanites. Ezekiel also accuses Israel of participating in these sacrifices (see Eze 16:20–21). Leviticus 18:21 suggests worship of Molech (also rendered "Molek"), the Canaanite god, involved child sacrifice. The Valley of Hinnom outside of Jerusalem was also associated with child sacrifice (see 2Ki 23:10; Jer 7:31–32).

57:6 smooth stones of the ravines Refers to the smooth stones found at the bottom of a dry riverbed or wadi. Since wadis were also preferred burial areas, these stones may refer to the tombs cut in the rock cliffs. The pagan religious practice of child sacrifice was

also conducted in the wadi, especially the Hinnom Valley (see note on Jer 7:31).

57:7 a high and lofty hill Ancients believed the gods lived on high mountains, so shrines to worship the various gods of the Canaanites were often set up on hills and mountains. Religious sites devoted to idol worship are often referred to as high places. Occurrences in the OT and in the Mesha Stele (or Moabite Stone) demonstrate the term refers to religious locations. Prior to the building of the temple, worship of Yahweh at local shrines such as these was apparently permissible, as the prophet Samuel presided over sacrifices at the high place (1Sa 9:13–19). Later, sacrifice was centralized at the temple only, and the high places were removed (2Ki 18:4). See the infographic "The Mesha Stele" on p. 565.

57:8 you uncovered your bed Israel is depicted as an unfaithful wife—a common prophetic motif (see Eze 16:24–25). **you looked with lust on their naked bodies** The Hebrew phrase here reads "looked on a hand." The Hebrew word for "hand" (*yad*) is a euphemism for male genitalia.

57:11 and have neither remembered me Throughout the book of Deuteronomy, Moses appealed to Israel to "remember" Yahweh and his mighty acts by which he saved them from Egypt. Yahweh asks why they did not remember, when it was so strongly emphasized that they must.

12 I will expose your righteousness and your
   works,
   and they will not benefit you.
13 When you cry out for help,
   let your collection of idols save you!
   The wind will carry all of them off,
   a mere breath will blow them away.
   But whoever takes refuge in me
   will inherit the land
   and possess my holy mountain."

Comfort for the Contrite

14 And it will be said:

"Build up, build up, prepare the road!
   Remove the obstacles out of the way of my
   people."
15 For this is what the high and exalted One
   says —
   he who lives forever, whose name is holy:
"I live in a high and holy place,
   but also with the one who is contrite and
   lowly in spirit,
to revive the spirit of the lowly
   and to revive the heart of the contrite.
16 I will not accuse them forever,
   nor will I always be angry,
   for then they would faint away because of
   me —
   the very people I have created.
17 I was enraged by their sinful greed;
   I punished them, and hid my face in
   anger,
   yet they kept on in their willful ways.
18 I have seen their ways, but I will heal them;
   I will guide them and restore comfort to
   Israel's mourners,
19   creating praise on their lips.
   Peace, peace, to those far and near,"
   says the LORD. "And I will heal them."
20 But the wicked are like the tossing sea,
   which cannot rest,
   whose waves cast up mire and mud.
21 "There is no peace," says my God, "for the
   wicked."

True Fasting

58 "Shout it aloud, do not hold back.
   Raise your voice like a trumpet.
   Declare to my people their rebellion
   and to the descendants of Jacob their sins.
2 For day after day they seek me out;
   they seem eager to know my ways,
   as if they were a nation that does what is
   right
   and has not forsaken the commands of its
   God.
They ask me for just decisions
   and seem eager for God to come near them.
3 'Why have we fasted,' they say,
   'and you have not seen it?
Why have we humbled ourselves,
   and you have not noticed?'

"Yet on the day of your fasting, you do as you
   please
   and exploit all your workers.
4 Your fasting ends in quarreling and strife,
   and in striking each other with wicked
   fists.
You cannot fast as you do today
   and expect your voice to be heard on high.
5 Is this the kind of fast I have chosen,
   only a day for people to humble
   themselves?
Is it only for bowing one's head like a reed
   and for lying in sackcloth and ashes?
Is that what you call a fast,
   a day acceptable to the LORD?

6 "Is not this the kind of fasting I have chosen:
   to loose the chains of injustice
   and untie the cords of the yoke,
to set the oppressed free
   and break every yoke?
7 Is it not to share your food with the hungry
   and to provide the poor wanderer with
   shelter —
when you see the naked, to clothe them,
   and not to turn away from your own flesh
   and blood?

57:15 the high and exalted One Echoes the vision of God in Isa 6:1, and the exaltation of the Servant in 52:13. **the one who is contrite and lowly in spirit** While God's dwelling is high and separate, his presence can still be found among the humble (compare Ps 138:6). **57:16 the very people** Yahweh's unending wrath would extinguish all life that he had created; his anger is temporary (see 1Pe 5:10; compare Ge 2:7). **57:21 There is no peace** See the earlier occurrence of this phrase in Isa 48:22. Here the wicked are unable to respond to the offer of peace.

58:1–14 Religious rituals done irresponsibly and with improper motives do not gain divine favor. The criticism of empty rituals echoes the indictment of 1:10–20.

58:2 a nation that does what is right Israel was going through the motions of religious rituals they believed God required. They were being righteous by their standards, but the empty ritualism displeased God. **58:3 on the day of your fasting** While fasting was an appropriate act of worship, their motives for fasting were self-serving. They claimed to have humbled themselves, but their actions are motivated by pride. The only fast day prescribed by OT law was on the Day of Atonement (see Lev 16:29), but other fasts could be declared for a variety of reasons (1Sa 14:24). **and exploit all your workers** Their outward religious observances were meaningless if they did not experience the change of heart that would inspire them to treat others justly. Compare Isa 1:11–17.

8 Then your light will break forth like the
    dawn,
  and your healing will quickly appear;
then your righteousness[a] will go before you,
  and the glory of the LORD will be your rear
    guard.
9 Then you will call, and the LORD will
    answer;
  you will cry for help, and he will say: Here
    am I.

"If you do away with the yoke of oppression,
  with the pointing finger and malicious
    talk,
10 and if you spend yourselves in behalf of the
    hungry
  and satisfy the needs of the oppressed,
then your light will rise in the darkness,
  and your night will become like the
    noonday.
11 The LORD will guide you always;
  he will satisfy your needs in a sun-
    scorched land
  and will strengthen your frame.
You will be like a well-watered garden,
  like a spring whose waters never fail.
12 Your people will rebuild the ancient ruins
  and will raise up the age-old
    foundations;
you will be called Repairer of Broken
    Walls,
  Restorer of Streets with Dwellings.

13 "If you keep your feet from breaking the
    Sabbath
  and from doing as you please on my holy
    day,
if you call the Sabbath a delight
  and the LORD's holy day honorable,
and if you honor it by not going your own
    way
  and not doing as you please or speaking
    idle words,

14 then you will find your joy in the LORD,
  and I will cause you to ride in triumph on
    the heights of the land
  and to feast on the inheritance of your
    father Jacob."
For the mouth of the LORD
              has spoken.

Sin, Confession and Redemption

59 Surely the arm of the LORD is not too
    short to save,
  nor his ear too dull to hear.
2 But your iniquities have separated
    you from your God;
  your sins have hidden his face from you,
    so that he will not hear.
3 For your hands are stained with blood,
    your fingers with guilt.
Your lips have spoken falsely,
    and your tongue mutters wicked things.
4 No one calls for justice;
    no one pleads a case with integrity.
They rely on empty arguments, they utter
    lies;
  they conceive trouble and give birth to evil.
5 They hatch the eggs of vipers
    and spin a spider's web.
Whoever eats their eggs will die,
    and when one is broken, an adder is
      hatched.
6 Their cobwebs are useless for clothing;
    they cannot cover themselves with what
      they make.
Their deeds are evil deeds,
    and acts of violence are in their hands.
7 Their feet rush into sin;
    they are swift to shed innocent blood.
They pursue evil schemes;
    acts of violence mark their ways.

a 8 Or your righteous One

58:9 and the LORD will answer Genuine repentance is evidenced by their behavior—how they treat the poor and hungry. Fasting without genuine repentance was useless (see note on v. 3).
58:10 your light will rise in the darkness Overcoming darkness with light was a motif connected with the rise of the Messiah (see 9:1–7; 51:4 and note).
58:12 will rebuild the ancient ruins Destruction caused by war regularly necessitated that ruined cities be rebuilt. The restoration of Jerusalem is promised also in 44:28 and 61:4. City sites were selected for their strategic locations, usually on hills or other high ground. Since the location was desirable, a destroyed city would often be rebuilt directly on top of the previous city.
58:13 you keep your feet from breaking the Sabbath The people were accustomed to going about their own business on the Sabbath, essentially trampling over the sanctity of the day (see 56:2). See the infographic "A Winepress in Ancient Israel" on p. 1157.

58:14 I will cause you to ride in triumph on the heights of the land Alludes to the miraculous provision of exodus, using the same poetic image as Dt 32:12–13.
the mouth of the LORD has spoken Echoes the end of the opening poem of Isa 1 (see 1:20).
59:2 iniquities have separated you Sin strains Israel's relationship with God to the point of total separation. Israel's actions required the separation—it was not what God wanted. **hidden his face** Symbolizes a break in communication and a denial of physical presence. People hid their faces from the Servant in 53:3 as a sign of rejection. Here, Yahweh is forced to turn his face away from them because he cannot look on sin (Hab 1:13).
59:3 your hands are stained with blood See Isa 1:15 and note.
59:5 an adder is hatched The Hebrew term here is a very rare word for a poisonous serpent. The only other occurrences are in Job 20:16 and Isa 30:6.

⁸ The way of peace they do not know;
  there is no justice in their paths.
They have turned them into crooked roads;
  no one who walks along them will know
    peace.

⁹ So justice is far from us,
  and righteousness does not reach us.
We look for light, but all is darkness;
  for brightness, but we walk in deep
    shadows.
¹⁰ Like the blind we grope along the wall,
  feeling our way like people without eyes.
At midday we stumble as if it were twilight;
  among the strong, we are like the dead.
¹¹ We all growl like bears;
  we moan mournfully like doves.
We look for justice, but find none;
  for deliverance, but it is far away.

¹² For our offenses are many in your sight,
  and our sins testify against us.
Our offenses are ever with us,
  and we acknowledge our iniquities:
¹³ rebellion and treachery against the LORD,
  turning our backs on our God,
inciting revolt and oppression,
  uttering lies our hearts have conceived.
¹⁴ So justice is driven back,
  and righteousness stands at a distance;
truth has stumbled in the streets,
  honesty cannot enter.
¹⁵ Truth is nowhere to be found,
  and whoever shuns evil becomes a prey.

The LORD looked and was displeased
  that there was no justice.
¹⁶ He saw that there was no one,
  he was appalled that there was no one to
    intervene;

so his own arm achieved salvation for him,
  and his own righteousness sustained him.
¹⁷ He put on righteousness as his breastplate,
  and the helmet of salvation on his head;
he put on the garments of vengeance
  and wrapped himself in zeal as in
    a cloak.
¹⁸ According to what they have done,
  so will he repay
wrath to his enemies
  and retribution to his foes;
  he will repay the islands their due.
¹⁹ From the west, people will fear the name of
    the LORD,
  and from the rising of the sun, they will
    revere his glory.
For he will come like a pent-up flood
  that the breath of the LORD drives along.ᵃ

²⁰ "The Redeemer will come to Zion,
  to those in Jacob who repent of their sins,"
    declares the LORD.

²¹ "As for me, this is my covenant with them,"
says the LORD. "My Spirit, who is on you, will
not depart from you, and my words that I have
put in your mouth will always be on your lips, on
the lips of your children and on the lips of their
descendants — from this time on and forever,"
says the LORD.

The Glory of Zion

60 "Arise, shine, for your light has come,
    and the glory of the LORD rises upon
      you.
² See, darkness covers the earth
    and thick darkness is over the peoples,

ᵃ 19 Or *When enemies come in like a flood, / the Spirit of the
LORD will put them to flight*

59:8 They have turned them into crooked roads The
Hebrew verb used here, *aqash*, denotes twisting and is
always used to describe turning away from what is considered good or right (Mic 3:9; Job 9:20). Deviating from
righteousness is often described with the metaphor of a
twisted path or crooked road (Pr 10:9; 28:18).
59:10 At midday we stumble as if it were twilight
The metaphor of blindness reflects the people's spiritual
blindness and inability to find their way back to God.
59:14 justice is driven back The expectation was
set up in Isa 51:4–6 that salvation — symbolized by
Yahweh's justice and righteousness — was on its way;
they only needed to wait on it. Their lack of faith has
prevented them from experiencing the full blessing that
was promised.
59:16 so his own arm achieved salvation for him
The people's inability to turn back to God on their own
displeased God, but he knew that he alone was able to
bring salvation.
59:17 righteousness as his breastplate Evokes the
image of God as the Divine Warrior, arising to do battle
on behalf of his people. His armor is symbolic and based

on his attributes of righteousness and holiness. The
armor of God imagery from Eph 6:13–17 develops these
concepts further.
59:20 Redeemer will come to Zion Yahweh identifies
himself as Israel's redeemer in Isa 43:14. This is either a
third-person reference to himself or a reference to another
sent as Yahweh's agent to be the redeemer. The apostle
Paul identifies this redeemer with Christ (Ro 11:25–26).
59:21 My Spirit, who is on you The Spirit is upon the
redeemer — the Messiah. The pronoun "you" is singular.
Similar language is used to describe the Messiah in Isa
11:2. **that I have put in your mouth** A standard formula
referring to God's communication with his prophets. See
note on 51:16.
60:1–22 This passage emphasizes the motif of the nations bringing tribute to Yahweh introduced in 18:7. This
motif appears more prominently in these last chapters of
Isaiah (see chs. 60–61; 66). When the ultimate redemption of Israel is accomplished, the glory of Yahweh will
visibly dwell in Zion as a light (vv. 1–2) so bright that the
sun and moon will not be needed (vv. 19–20), drawing
the nations *en masse* (v. 3). The nations will bring their

but the LORD rises upon you
    and his glory appears over you.
³ Nations will come to your light,
    and kings to the brightness of your dawn.

⁴ "Lift up your eyes and look about you:
    All assemble and come to you;
your sons come from afar,
    and your daughters are carried on the hip.
⁵ Then you will look and be radiant,
    your heart will throb and swell with joy;
the wealth on the seas will be brought to you,
    to you the riches of the nations will come.
⁶ Herds of camels will cover your land,
    young camels of Midian and Ephah.
And all from Sheba will come,
    bearing gold and incense
    and proclaiming the praise of the LORD.
⁷ All Kedar's flocks will be gathered to you,
    the rams of Nebaioth will serve you;
they will be accepted as offerings on my altar,
    and I will adorn my glorious temple.

⁸ "Who are these that fly along like clouds,
    like doves to their nests?
⁹ Surely the islands look to me;
    in the lead are the ships of Tarshish,ᵃ
bringing your children from afar,
    with their silver and gold,
to the honor of the LORD your God,
    the Holy One of Israel,
    for he has endowed you with splendor.

¹⁰ "Foreigners will rebuild your walls,
    and their kings will serve you.

Though in anger I struck you,
    in favor I will show you compassion.
¹¹ Your gates will always stand open,
    they will never be shut, day or night,
so that people may bring you the wealth of
    the nations —
    their kings led in triumphal procession.
¹² For the nation or kingdom that will not serve
    you will perish;
    it will be utterly ruined.

¹³ "The glory of Lebanon will come to you,
    the juniper, the fir and the cypress
    together,
to adorn my sanctuary;
    and I will glorify the place for my feet.
¹⁴ The children of your oppressors will come
    bowing before you;
all who despise you will bow down at your
    feet
and will call you the City of the LORD,
    Zion of the Holy One of Israel.

¹⁵ "Although you have been forsaken and
    hated,
    with no one traveling through,
I will make you the everlasting pride
    and the joy of all generations.
¹⁶ You will drink the milk of nations
    and be nursed at royal breasts.
Then you will know that I, the LORD, am your
    Savior,
    your Redeemer, the Mighty One of Jacob.

ᵃ 9 Or *the trading ships*

---

wealth to Yahweh in response to the inexorable draw to the light (vv. 5–6,11). In addition to their wealth, the nations will bring the children of Israel back (v. 4). Israel will have a special status in this new era of peace as a priestly class (61:6); they and the temple will be the primary beneficiaries of the material tribute from the nations (v. 7,13; 66:12,18–20).

60:1 your light has come Light is a metaphor for the salvation and spiritual awakening brought by the Messiah (see note on 51:4). **upon you** The second-person pronouns in this passage are feminine and singular. They refer to Zion/Jerusalem, which is personified as female (see 49:21–22; 51:18–20; 52:1–2).
60:3 Nations will come to your light In 42:6, Israel was sent as a light to the nations. That role was transferred to the Servant-Messiah in 49:6. Nations are described streaming to Zion in 2:2–5 and 11:10.
60:5 riches of the nations Refers to tribute brought to Yahweh. The conquering powers in the ancient Near East would exact tribute or tax payments on people they conquered. Isaiah envisions a reversal where the nations now pay tribute to Jerusalem (see note on 18:7).
60:6 gold and incense Gold was associated with riches and power. Frankincense—a tree resin imported from Arabia—was highly prized as a spice and perfume.
60:7 they will be accepted as offerings on my altar See note on 56:7.

60:9 Tarshish A seaport city presumed to be in the western Mediterranean. See Ge 10:4 and note; Isa 2:16 and note; Jnh 1:3 and note.
60:10 Foreigners will rebuild your walls May allude to Persian support for the rebuilding of Jerusalem (see Isa 45:13; Ne 2:1–9). More directly, it refers to the honor and assistance that will come from all nations when redemption comes.
60:11 they will never be shut Zion's future will be so peaceful and prosperous that they will never need to lock the gates against any enemies or thieves.
60:13 The glory of Lebanon Because of its abundance, fertility, and rugged beauty, the Lebanon region is a standard image for earthly majesty and glory in the OT (see Isa 14:8 and note; 29:17 and note). The value placed on the cedars of Lebanon and the wealth associated with the Phoenicians likely resulted in the widespread use of Lebanon as a literary image symbolizing prosperity and stability (Hos 14:5–7; Ps 92:12; Isa 35:2). **I will glorify the place for my feet** The temple was described as Yahweh's footstool (Ps 99:5; 132:7; Eze 43:7; compare note on Isa 6:1).
60:14 the City of the LORD Isaiah 62:2 indicates that God will give Jerusalem a new name. Here, the city is named "City of Yahweh."
60:16 be nursed at royal breasts Ancient Near Eastern imagery frequently depicted kings or gods suckling the breast of a goddess. The image symbolized

17 Instead of bronze I will bring you gold,
  and silver in place of iron.
Instead of wood I will bring you bronze,
  and iron in place of stones.
I will make peace your governor
  and well-being your ruler.
18 No longer will violence be heard in your
    land,
  nor ruin or destruction within your
    borders,
but you will call your walls Salvation
  and your gates Praise.
19 The sun will no more be your light by day,
  nor will the brightness of the moon shine
    on you,
for the LORD will be your everlasting light,
  and your God will be your glory.
20 Your sun will never set again,
  and your moon will wane no more;
the LORD will be your everlasting light,
  and your days of sorrow will end.
21 Then all your people will be righteous
  and they will possess the land forever.
They are the shoot I have planted,
  the work of my hands,
for the display of my splendor.
22 The least of you will become a thousand,
  the smallest a mighty nation.
I am the LORD;
  in its time I will do this swiftly."

The Year of the LORD's Favor

61 The Spirit of the Sovereign LORD is
    on me,
  because the LORD has anointed me
to proclaim good news to the poor.

He has sent me to bind up the brokenhearted,
  to proclaim freedom for the captives
  and release from darkness for the
    prisoners,[a]
2 to proclaim the year of the LORD's favor
  and the day of vengeance of our God,
to comfort all who mourn,
3   and provide for those who grieve in Zion—
to bestow on them a crown of beauty
  instead of ashes,
the oil of joy
  instead of mourning,
and a garment of praise
  instead of a spirit of despair.
They will be called oaks of righteousness,
  a planting of the LORD
  for the display of his splendor.

4 They will rebuild the ancient ruins
  and restore the places long devastated;
they will renew the ruined cities
  that have been devastated for generations.
5 Strangers will shepherd your flocks;
  foreigners will work your fields and
    vineyards.
6 And you will be called priests of the LORD,
  you will be named ministers of our God.
You will feed on the wealth of nations,
  and in their riches you will boast.

7 Instead of your shame
  you will receive a double portion,
and instead of disgrace
  you will rejoice in your inheritance.
And so you will inherit a double portion in
    your land,
  and everlasting joy will be yours.

a 1 Hebrew; Septuagint the blind

---

that the god or king was receiving the best possible care and attention. Here, the nursing imagery reflects how Israel will receive the best of what all the nations have to offer.
60:17 I will bring you gold, and silver in place of iron While iron represents swords and spears, silver represents the wealth of nations (see v. 5 and note).
60:19 LORD will be your everlasting light See note on 51:4.
60:21 the shoot The planting consists of the true followers of Yahweh (61:3). The branch is a Messianic image in 4:2 and 11:1 (see note on 4:2).
61:1 The Spirit of the Sovereign LORD The language echoes the Messianic description of 11:2 and resembles the Servant language of 42:1 and 48:16 (compare 59:21). Jesus inaugurates his public ministry in the Gospel of Luke with a reading from this passage (Lk 4:18–22). By invoking this passage of Scripture, Jesus identifies himself as the Messianic Servant and takes up the role of a prophet to announce the good news of salvation (see Isa 52:7). **LORD has anointed me** Anointing symbolized conferring of holiness and authority. Kings, prophets and priests could all be anointed to signify that they had been set apart and selected for that specific role.

proclaim good news Connotes a messenger bringing a favorable announcement. Isaiah 41:27 announces that God would send a herald of good news.
61:2 the year of the LORD's favor Refers to the year when slaves were freed and land was returned to its original owners. It was supposed to occur every fiftieth year, and was announced by a trumpet blast on the Day of Atonement (Lev 25:9). **comfort all who mourn** In Isa 40:1, Yahweh calls out for someone to comfort Zion. The Messianic Servant has answered that call. See note on 40:1.
61:3 oaks of righteousness Alludes to the planting of 60:21, and reverses the oak imagery of 1:29. Instead of worshiping oaks as symbols of idolatry, God's people will be established and planted as symbols of righteousness.
61:5 foreigners will work your fields Compare 14:2, where Israel's former foreign oppressors will one day serve them as slaves.
61:6 priests of the LORD Yahweh had initially established Israel to be a "kingdom of priests" (Ex 19:5–6). God's chosen people were to serve as mediators between God and the nations. Israel's failure to keep the covenant had impeded their ability to fulfill that role. Their redemption restores their status and reaffirms their calling. **the**

8 "For I, the LORD, love justice;
    I hate robbery and wrongdoing.
In my faithfulness I will reward my people
    and make an everlasting covenant with
        them.
9 Their descendants will be known among the
        nations
    and their offspring among the peoples.
All who see them will acknowledge
    that they are a people the LORD has
        blessed."

10 I delight greatly in the LORD;
    my soul rejoices in my God.
For he has clothed me with garments of
        salvation
    and arrayed me in a robe of his
        righteousness,
as a bridegroom adorns his head like a priest,
    and as a bride adorns herself with her
        jewels.
11 For as the soil makes the sprout come up
    and a garden causes seeds to grow,
so the Sovereign LORD will make
        righteousness
    and praise spring up before all nations.

Zion's New Name

62 For Zion's sake I will not keep silent,
    for Jerusalem's sake I will not remain
        quiet,
till her vindication shines out like the dawn,
    her salvation like a blazing torch.
2 The nations will see your vindication,
    and all kings your glory;

you will be called by a new name
    that the mouth of the LORD will bestow.
3 You will be a crown of splendor in the LORD's
        hand,
    a royal diadem in the hand of your God.
4 No longer will they call you Deserted,
    or name your land Desolate.
But you will be called Hephzibah,[a]
    and your land Beulah[b];
for the LORD will take delight in you,
    and your land will be married.
5 As a young man marries a young woman,
    so will your Builder marry you;
as a bridegroom rejoices over his bride,
    so will your God rejoice over you.

6 I have posted watchmen on your walls,
        Jerusalem;
    they will never be silent day or night.
You who call on the LORD,
    give yourselves no rest,
7 and give him no rest till he establishes
        Jerusalem
    and makes her the praise of the earth.

8 The LORD has sworn by his right hand
    and by his mighty arm:
"Never again will I give your grain
    as food for your enemies,
and never again will foreigners drink the
        new wine
    for which you have toiled;
9 but those who harvest it will eat it
    and praise the LORD,

---

[a] 4 Hephzibah means *my delight is in her.*   [b] 4 Beulah means *married.*

---

wealth of nations Tribute brought to Yahweh, reversing the history of Israel and Judah paying tribute to foreign nations. See note on Isa 60:5.

61:8 I, the LORD, love justice The lack of justice in Israel is a central element of the indictment against them in 1:23. Yahweh has established his concern for justice repeatedly in Isaiah (e.g., 1:27; 5:7,16; 28:17; 30:18; 42:1). **everlasting covenant** See note on 55:3.

61:10 I delight greatly in the LORD The speaker shifts from Yahweh to either Zion or the Servant. If it is Zion, it is rejoicing in the salvation Yahweh has brought. If the Servant, he is rejoicing over the salvation made possible through him.

61:11 causes seeds to grow An allusion to the Messianic title of "branch," "shoot" or "sprout." See 4:2; 11:1.

62:2 The nations will see your vindication Yahweh's redemption of Israel created a righteous remnant. They are righteous because of God's forgiveness, not because of their merit or ability to keep the covenant on their own. The nations eventually see and respond to the righteousness established by God's salvation. See note on 2:2; note on 56:7. **you will be called by a new name** Jerusalem is named "City of Yahweh" in 60:14. Isaiah 1:26 also predicts Jerusalem will be called the "City of Righteousness," and Zec 8:3 names it the "Faithful City." In Isa 62:4, the city is

called Hephzibah or "My Delight is in Her," which may be the new name indicated here. The renaming of locations and individuals is a common motif for declaring change. The name captures the essence of the person or place, so renaming signifies a fundamental change of purpose or status.

62:4 No longer will they call you Deserted Zion lamented that God had forsaken her in 49:14, using the same Hebrew verb; the reversal of that status was announced in 60:15. **name your land Desolate** In 54:1, Zion is called "desolate." **Hephzibah** See note on v. 2. See the table "Symbolic Names of People in Hebrew" on p. 1388. **your land Beulah** The name *be'ulah* is Hebrew for "married." This marriage represents a restoration of the covenant that had been broken. Yahweh explicitly pointed out that he had not divorced them in 50:1. The marriage imagery in vv. 4–5 foreshadows the NT metaphor for the church as the Bride of Christ (see 2Co 11:2; Eph 5:25–27; Rev 19:7–9). This NT metaphor is based on the OT representations of Yahweh's relationship with Israel as a marriage.

62:8 LORD has sworn An oath is sworn invoking the witness of one greater than the one swearing. Since no one is greater than Yahweh, he must swear on himself.

and those who gather the grapes will drink it
in the courts of my sanctuary."

10 Pass through, pass through the gates!
Prepare the way for the people.
Build up, build up the highway!
Remove the stones.
Raise a banner for the nations.

11 The LORD has made proclamation
to the ends of the earth:
"Say to Daughter Zion,
'See, your Savior comes!
See, his reward is with him,
and his recompense accompanies him.'"
12 They will be called the Holy People,
the Redeemed of the LORD;
and you will be called Sought After,
the City No Longer Deserted.

God's Day of Vengeance and Redemption

63 Who is this coming from Edom,
from Bozrah, with his garments stained
crimson?
Who is this, robed in splendor,
striding forward in the greatness of his
strength?

"It is I, proclaiming victory,
mighty to save."

2 Why are your garments red,
like those of one treading the winepress?

3 "I have trodden the winepress alone;
from the nations no one was with me.
I trampled them in my anger
and trod them down in my wrath;
their blood spattered my garments,
and I stained all my clothing.

4 It was for me the day of vengeance;
the year for me to redeem had come.
5 I looked, but there was no one to help,
I was appalled that no one gave support;
so my own arm achieved salvation for me,
and my own wrath sustained me.
6 I trampled the nations in my anger;
in my wrath I made them drunk
and poured their blood on the ground."

Praise and Prayer

7 I will tell of the kindnesses of the LORD,
the deeds for which he is to be praised,
according to all the LORD has done for us —
yes, the many good things
he has done for Israel,
according to his compassion and many
kindnesses.
8 He said, "Surely they are my people,
children who will be true to me";
and so he became their Savior.
9 In all their distress he too was distressed,
and the angel of his presence saved them.[a]
In his love and mercy he redeemed them;
he lifted them up and carried them
all the days of old.
10 Yet they rebelled
and grieved his Holy Spirit.
So he turned and became their enemy
and he himself fought against them.

11 Then his people recalled[b] the days of old,
the days of Moses and his people —
where is he who brought them through the
sea,
with the shepherd of his flock?
Where is he who set
his Holy Spirit among them,

---

[a] 9 Or Savior 9in their distress. / It was no envoy or angel / but
his own presence that saved them   [b] 11 Or But may he recall

---

62:10 Prepare the way for the people Echoes Isa 40:3 and 57:14, preparing for the coming salvation. **a banner for the nations** The signal indicates it was time to return to Zion (see 11:10,12; 49:22 and note).
62:11 Daughter Zion Refers to Jerusalem. See note on 1:8. **his reward** An echo of 40:10. These repetitions were likely used to evoke thematic and textual connections throughout all the prophetic material connected with Isaiah.
62:12 Sought After, the City No Longer Deserted The nations will all seek Yahweh at Zion and be attracted to the righteousness of the city (see v. 2 and note; v. 4 and note).
63:1 Who is this coming from Edom The prophet now sees a vision of Yahweh as the Divine Warrior returning to Zion after vanquishing the nations. The OT often depicts Yahweh coming from the south — probably following the exodus route and associating him with Mount Sinai in the wilderness far south of Israel. See note on 34:5. **with his garments stained crimson** Compare the blood-dipped robe of the conquering Christ in Rev 19:13.
63:3 their blood spattered my garments The Hebrew

word used here and in Isa 63:6 refers literally to the juice of the trampled grape, and metaphorically to blood. Isaiah's imagery mixes that of the farmer stained with grape juice from trampling his harvest and that of the warrior returning from battle with blood-stained garments.
63:5 my own arm achieved salvation for me See 59:16.
63:9 In all their distress he too was distressed Refers to Yahweh's empathy in seeing the plight of his people (compare Ex 2:23 – 25). **the angel of his presence** Echoes Ex 23:20 – 23 and the symbol of Yahweh's presence with Israel during the exodus. Allusions to the exodus permeate the imagery of Isa 63:7 – 14.
63:10 grieved his Holy Spirit There are few references to the "Holy Spirit" in the OT. Only here is there a hint of his existence as a distinct person with attributes such as the emotion of grief. Compare Paul's warning against grieving the Holy Spirit in Eph 4:30.
63:11 shepherd of his flock Refers to the leaders of Israel in the exodus — Moses and Aaron. See note on Isa 40:11.

¹² who sent his glorious arm of power
   to be at Moses' right hand,
who divided the waters before them,
   to gain for himself everlasting
      renown,
¹³ who led them through the depths?
Like a horse in open country,
   they did not stumble;
¹⁴ like cattle that go down to the plain,
   they were given rest by the Spirit of
      the LORD.

This is how you guided your people
   to make for yourself a glorious name.

¹⁵ Look down from heaven and see,
   from your lofty throne, holy and glorious.
Where are your zeal and your might?
   Your tenderness and compassion are
      withheld from us.
¹⁶ But you are our Father,
   though Abraham does not know us
   or Israel acknowledge us;

63:12 to gain for himself everlasting renown Alludes to Ex 14:21. God's mighty acts were meant to establish his power and authority in the eyes of Israel and the nations (see Ne 9:10).

63:16 Abraham does not know us Abraham would not recognize his own descendants because of how far off the path they've wandered from following Yahweh (see Ge 15:6 on Abraham's faith).

A Winepress in Ancient Israel

An ancient winepress was a rock-hewn open-air system. Grapes were pressed by being trodden underfoot in a treading floor. The juice would pour through a channel into a vat, where it would ferment. It would then be collected in jars.

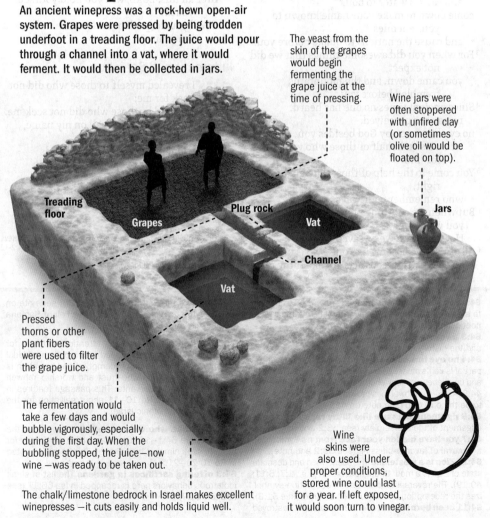

The yeast from the skin of the grapes would begin fermenting the grape juice at the time of pressing.

Wine jars were often stoppered with unfired clay (or sometimes olive oil would be floated on top).

Treading floor

Grapes

Plug rock

Vat

Jars

Channel

Vat

Pressed thorns or other plant fibers were used to filter the grape juice.

The fermentation would take a few days and would bubble vigorously, especially during the first day. When the bubbling stopped, the juice—now wine—was ready to be taken out.

Wine skins were also used. Under proper conditions, stored wine could last for a year. If left exposed, it would soon turn to vinegar.

The chalk/limestone bedrock in Israel makes excellent winepresses—it cuts easily and holds liquid well.

you, LORD, are our Father,
  our Redeemer from of old is your name.
[17] Why, LORD, do you make us wander from
    your ways
  and harden our hearts so we do not revere
    you?
Return for the sake of your servants,
  the tribes that are your inheritance.
[18] For a little while your people possessed your
    holy place,
  but now our enemies have trampled down
    your sanctuary.
[19] We are yours from of old;
  but you have not ruled over them,
  they have not been called[a] by your name.

64 [b] Oh, that you would rend the heavens
    and come down,
  that the mountains would tremble before
    you!
[2] As when fire sets twigs ablaze
    and causes water to boil,
  come down to make your name known to
    your enemies
  and cause the nations to quake before you!
[3] For when you did awesome things that we did
    not expect,
  you came down, and the mountains
    trembled before you.
[4] Since ancient times no one has heard,
  no ear has perceived,
no eye has seen any God besides you,
  who acts on behalf of those who wait
    for him.
[5] You come to the help of those who gladly do
    right,
  who remember your ways.
But when we continued to sin against them,
  you were angry.
How then can we be saved?
[6] All of us have become like one who is unclean,
  and all our righteous acts are like filthy rags;

we all shrivel up like a leaf,
  and like the wind our sins sweep us away.
[7] No one calls on your name
    or strives to lay hold of you;
for you have hidden your face from us
  and have given us over to[c] our sins.

[8] Yet you, LORD, are our Father.
  We are the clay, you are the potter;
  we are all the work of your hand.
[9] Do not be angry beyond measure, LORD;
  do not remember our sins forever.
Oh, look on us, we pray,
  for we are all your people.
[10] Your sacred cities have become a wasteland;
  even Zion is a wasteland, Jerusalem a
    desolation.
[11] Our holy and glorious temple, where our
    ancestors praised you,
  has been burned with fire,
  and all that we treasured lies in ruins.
[12] After all this, LORD, will you hold yourself
    back?
  Will you keep silent and punish us beyond
    measure?

Judgment and Salvation

65 "I revealed myself to those who did not
    ask for me;
  I was found by those who did not seek me.
To a nation that did not call on my name,
  I said, 'Here am I, here am I.'
[2] All day long I have held out my hands
    to an obstinate people,
who walk in ways not good,
    pursuing their own imaginations—
[3] a people who continually provoke me
    to my very face,

[a] 19 Or *We are like those you have never ruled, / like those never called*   [b] In Hebrew texts 64:1 is numbered 63:19b, and 64:2-12 is numbered 64:1-11.   [c] 7 Septuagint, Syriac and Targum; Hebrew *have made us melt because of*

64:1 you would rend the heavens An appeal to Yahweh to step down from heaven and intervene. Compare the poetic language of Ps 18:9 and 144:5.
64:3 awesome things Alludes to the exodus miracles and the history recapped in Isa 63:7–14.
64:4 no eye has seen any God besides you A central part of Isaiah's message is asserting the total sovereignty and uniqueness of Yahweh, the only true God (see 43:11; 44:6; 45:5–6). Yahweh has proven himself through action to be the only God (see note on 41:21).
64:6 righteous acts are like filthy rags An acknowledgement of their false piety (see 58:2 and note).
64:7 you have hidden your face from us Symbolizes a removal of favor or blessing (see 59:2 and note).
64:10 Zion is a wasteland The abandoned and desolate state of Zion is a motif throughout Isaiah (e.g., 1:7; 6:11; 49:19). The reversal of this state of desolation symbolizes the redemption and restoration of Israel (see 51:3).
64:11 been burned with fire The temple was destroyed

completely by the Babylonians in 586 BC; see note on 4:4. See the timeline "Judah From the Fall of Samaria to the Exile" on p. 606.

65:1–16 Yahweh recounts his attention and care for Israel, and how Israel responded with rebellion and idol worship. The plan to bring redemption and salvation is directed toward those who trust and worship Yahweh faithfully—his true servants. This passage features in Paul's argument in Ro 10–11 about salvation for the Gentiles, not just ethnic Israel.
65:1 to those who did not ask A response to the appeal of Isa 64:1–12. God was willing and ready for them to seek him, but they did not. This verse is quoted in Ro 10:20–21.
65:3 offering sacrifices in gardens The list of sinful idolatrous behaviors here is recapped in Isa 66:17 (see note on 1:29).

offering sacrifices in gardens
  and burning incense on altars of brick;
[4] who sit among the graves
  and spend their nights keeping secret vigil;
who eat the flesh of pigs,
  and whose pots hold broth of impure meat;
[5] who say, 'Keep away; don't come near me,
  for I am too sacred for you!'
Such people are smoke in my nostrils,
  a fire that keeps burning all day.

[6] "See, it stands written before me:
  I will not keep silent but will pay back in full;
  I will pay it back into their laps—
[7] both your sins and the sins of your ancestors,"
  says the LORD.
"Because they burned sacrifices on the
    mountains
  and defied me on the hills,
I will measure into their laps
  the full payment for their former deeds."

[8] This is what the LORD says:

"As when juice is still found in a cluster of
    grapes
  and people say, 'Don't destroy it,
    there is still a blessing in it,'
so will I do in behalf of my servants;
  I will not destroy them all.
[9] I will bring forth descendants from Jacob,
  and from Judah those who will possess my
    mountains;
my chosen people will inherit them,
  and there will my servants live.
[10] Sharon will become a pasture for flocks,
  and the Valley of Achor a resting place for
    herds,
  for my people who seek me.

[11] "But as for you who forsake the LORD
  and forget my holy mountain,
who spread a table for Fortune
  and fill bowls of mixed wine for Destiny,
[12] I will destine you for the sword,
  and all of you will fall in the slaughter;

for I called but you did not answer,
  I spoke but you did not listen.
You did evil in my sight
  and chose what displeases me."

[13] Therefore this is what the Sovereign LORD says:

"My servants will eat,
  but you will go hungry;
my servants will drink,
  but you will go thirsty;
my servants will rejoice,
  but you will be put to shame.
[14] My servants will sing
  out of the joy of their hearts,
but you will cry out
  from anguish of heart
  and wail in brokenness of spirit.
[15] You will leave your name
  for my chosen ones to use in their curses;
the Sovereign LORD will put you to death,
  but to his servants he will give another
    name.
[16] Whoever invokes a blessing in the land
  will do so by the one true God;
whoever takes an oath in the land
  will swear by the one true God.
For the past troubles will be forgotten
  and hidden from my eyes.

New Heavens and a New Earth

[17] "See, I will create
  new heavens and a new earth.
The former things will not be remembered,
  nor will they come to mind.
[18] But be glad and rejoice forever
  in what I will create,
for I will create Jerusalem to be a delight
  and its people a joy.
[19] I will rejoice over Jerusalem
  and take delight in my people;
the sound of weeping and of crying
  will be heard in it no more.

65:4 who eat the flesh of pigs Their eating pig's flesh was symbolic of the people's failure to observe the Biblical dietary laws (see Lev 11:7 and note).
65:5 smoke in my nostrils Those who think themselves holy without Yahweh's favor can expect judgment. Compare Isa 1:31 and 9:18.
65:7 your sins and the sins of your ancestors Unlike the warning of Ex 20:5 that the children would be punished for their parents' sins, the judgment comes on them for their own sins compounded by the legacy of the sinful attitudes and practices passed on by their parents. **on the mountains** The high places. See note on Isa 57:7; compare Eze 20:28.
65:8 in behalf of my servants Judgment is required as punishment for sin, but God has mercy for the sake of his true followers.
65:10 Sharon The coastal plain between the hills of Judah and the Mediterranean Sea, forming the western

border of Judah. **Valley of Achor** A valley near Jericho, northeast of Jerusalem, that forms the northern border of Judah (Jos 7:26; 15:7).
65:11 who spread a table for Fortune The Hebrew term for "fortune" (gad) appears as a name for the god of fortune in Canaanite literature. **fill bowls of mixed wine for Destiny** The Hebrew term for "destiny" (meni) apparently refers to a god of fate or destiny unknown in extra-Biblical sources. References to Fortune and Destiny indicate that idol worship was still a problem in Judah after the return from exile.
65:13 My servants will eat Those who truly seek Yahweh will eat and drink while the idol worshipers go without.
65:17 new heavens and a new earth Represents the culmination of Isaiah's visions for an idealized future ruled by the Messiah (11:1–11). **will not be remembered** Compare 43:10–11.

20 "Never again will there be in it
    an infant who lives but a few days,
    or an old man who does not live out his
        years;
the one who dies at a hundred
    will be thought a mere child;
the one who fails to reach[a] a hundred
    will be considered accursed.
21 They will build houses and dwell in them;
    they will plant vineyards and eat their fruit.
22 No longer will they build houses and others
        live in them,
    or plant and others eat.
For as the days of a tree,
    so will be the days of my people;
my chosen ones will long enjoy
    the work of their hands.
23 They will not labor in vain,
    nor will they bear children doomed to
        misfortune;
for they will be a people blessed by the LORD,
    they and their descendants with them.
24 Before they call I will answer;
    while they are still speaking I will hear.
25 The wolf and the lamb will feed together,
    and the lion will eat straw like the ox,
    and dust will be the serpent's food.
They will neither harm nor destroy
    on all my holy mountain,"
                            says the LORD.

Judgment and Hope

66 This is what the LORD says:

"Heaven is my throne,
    and the earth is my footstool.
Where is the house you will build for me?
    Where will my resting place be?
2 Has not my hand made all these things,
    and so they came into being?"
                        declares the LORD.

"These are the ones I look on with favor:
    those who are humble and contrite in spirit,
    and who tremble at my word.
3 But whoever sacrifices a bull
    is like one who kills a person,
and whoever offers a lamb
    is like one who breaks a dog's neck;

whoever makes a grain offering
    is like one who presents pig's blood,
and whoever burns memorial incense
    is like one who worships an idol.
They have chosen their own ways,
    and they delight in their abominations;
4 so I also will choose harsh treatment for them
    and will bring on them what they dread.
For when I called, no one answered,
    when I spoke, no one listened.
They did evil in my sight
    and chose what displeases me."

5 Hear the word of the LORD,
    you who tremble at his word:
"Your own people who hate you,
    and exclude you because of my name, have
        said,
'Let the LORD be glorified,
    that we may see your joy!'
    Yet they will be put to shame.
6 Hear that uproar from the city,
    hear that noise from the temple!
It is the sound of the LORD
    repaying his enemies all they deserve.

7 "Before she goes into labor,
    she gives birth;
before the pains come upon her,
    she delivers a son.
8 Who has ever heard of such things?
    Who has ever seen things like this?
Can a country be born in a day
    or a nation be brought forth in a moment?
Yet no sooner is Zion in labor
    than she gives birth to her children.
9 Do I bring to the moment of birth
    and not give delivery?" says the LORD.
"Do I close up the womb
    when I bring to delivery?" says your God.
10 "Rejoice with Jerusalem and be glad for her,
    all you who love her;
rejoice greatly with her,
    all you who mourn over her.
11 For you will nurse and be satisfied
    at her comforting breasts;
you will drink deeply
    and delight in her overflowing abundance."

---

[a] 20 Or the sinner who reaches

65:25 wolf and the lamb will feed together See 11:6 and note; 11:7. **dust will be the serpent's food** An allusion to Ge 3:14–15. The salvation prefigured there will be accomplished by the Messiah.
66:1 Heaven is my throne Isaiah saw God's heavenly throne in his vision in the temple in Isa 6 (see 6:1 and note). **earth is my footstool** Compare Ps 99:5, where the temple is envisioned as God's footstool.
66:2 those who are humble and contrite God chooses to dwell among the humble because they have the proper attitude of reverence toward him (see Isa 57:15).

66:3 whoever sacrifices a bull The prophet again focuses on the futility of rituals done with improper attitude (see 1:10–17). **pig's blood** Offering an unclean animal like a pig (see Lev 11:7) on the altar would profane the altar. The right rituals with the wrong attitude are tantamount to sacrilege and idol worship.
66:6 hear that noise from the temple Yahweh responds to their empty religiosity with judgment.
66:8 she gives birth to her children Compare Isa 49:19–21; 54:1–3.

¹²For this is what the LORD says:

"I will extend peace to her like a river,
  and the wealth of nations like a flooding
    stream;
you will nurse and be carried on her arm
  and dandled on her knees.
¹³ As a mother comforts her child,
  so will I comfort you;
  and you will be comforted over Jerusalem."

¹⁴ When you see this, your heart will rejoice
  and you will flourish like grass;
  the hand of the LORD will be made known to
    his servants,
  but his fury will be shown to his foes.
¹⁵ See, the LORD is coming with fire,
  and his chariots are like a whirlwind;
he will bring down his anger with fury,
  and his rebuke with flames of fire.
¹⁶ For with fire and with his sword
  the LORD will execute judgment on all
    people,
  and many will be those slain by the LORD.

¹⁷"Those who consecrate and purify themselves
to go into the gardens, following one who is among
those who eat the flesh of pigs, rats and other unclean things — they will meet their end together
with the one they follow," declares the LORD.

¹⁸"And I, because of what they have planned and
done, am about to come[a] and gather the people
of all nations and languages, and they will come
and see my glory.

¹⁹"I will set a sign among them, and I will send
some of those who survive to the nations — to
Tarshish, to the Libyans[b] and Lydians (famous as
archers), to Tubal and Greece, and to the distant
islands that have not heard of my fame or seen my
glory. They will proclaim my glory among the nations. ²⁰And they will bring all your people, from
all the nations, to my holy mountain in Jerusalem as
an offering to the LORD — on horses, in chariots and
wagons, and on mules and camels," says the LORD.
"They will bring them, as the Israelites bring their
grain offerings, to the temple of the LORD in ceremonially clean vessels. ²¹And I will select some of
them also to be priests and Levites," says the LORD.

²²"As the new heavens and the new earth that
I make will endure before me," declares the
LORD, "so will your name and descendants endure. ²³From one New Moon to another and from
one Sabbath to another, all mankind will come
and bow down before me," says the LORD. ²⁴"And
they will go out and look on the dead bodies of
those who rebelled against me; the worms that
eat them will not die, the fire that burns them
will not be quenched, and they will be loathsome
to all mankind."

---

a 18 The meaning of the Hebrew for this clause is uncertain.
b 19 Some Septuagint manuscripts *Put* (Libyans); Hebrew *Pul*

66:12 peace to her like a river See 48:18. **like a flooding stream; you will nurse** Similar imagery as 60:16, but
applied to Jerusalem personified as a mother (see v. 8).
**66:15 LORD is coming with fire, and his chariots are
like a whirlwind** Fire and whirlwind are frequently associated with the presence of Yahweh and encounters
with Yahweh (e.g., Ex 3:1–12; Job 38:1; 40:6).
**66:17 Those who consecrate and purify themselves
to go into the gardens** See Isa 65:3 and note. **those
who eat the flesh of pigs** See 65:4 and note.
66:18 gather the people of all nations and languages
An event foreshadowed throughout Isaiah (e.g., 2:2–4;
11:10; 45:23). For an initial NT fulfillment, see Ac 2.

66:19 The locations on this list symbolize the far reaches
of the known world.

66:19 Tarshish Probably a Phoenician colony in Spain
(see Isa 23:1 and note; Jnh 1:3 and note). **to the Libyans** Hebrew *pul* occurs only in this verse and may be a
copyist's error for *put*. Put was a region in North Africa,
roughly corresponding to Libya. This idea is the basis for
English translations referring to Put or Libya. **Lydians**
Lud or Lydia is in Asia Minor (modern Turkey). **Tubal** In
Asia Minor (modern Turkey). **Greece** Greece is understood as the land of the descendants of Javan, Noah's
grandson (Ge 10:2).
66:20 camels One-humped camels. See note on Ge 12:16.
66:22 new heavens and the new earth See note
on Isa 65:17.
66:23 all mankind See 49:26 and note.
66:24 go out and look The setting may be the Valley of
Hinnom outside of Jerusalem based on Jeremiah's identification of that site as the location of future judgment for

the wicked (see Jer 7:30–34; 19:6–7). The valley was
condemned in the OT as a site of human sacrifice (see
note on Jer 7:31; compare 2Ki 23:10). **dead bodies** The
corpses are left exposed to view, depriving them of the
honor of burial. This exposure provides another link to the
imagery of Jer 7 where the dead are left and became food
for wild animals (see Jer 7:33 and note). The corpses of
Gog's army were also initially left exposed in the open field
as food for scavenging wild animals (see Eze 39:4–5).
worms that eat them will not die Possibly implying
that there are so many corpses that the worms eating
the bodies will never run out of food (compare Isa 14:11).
In Ezekiel 39, the great size of Gog's army was implied
by stating that the people of Israel would need seven
months to bury all of the bodies and that their weapons
would provide fuel for Israel's fires for seven years (see
Eze 39:9–16). These final lines of Isaiah contributed to
the ancient conception of eternal punishment by fire and
worms: The pairing was used as an image of unending
torment in ancient Jewish literature (see Sirach 7:17;
Judith 16:17). This verse also influenced later depictions of the Valley of Hinnom or Gehenna as hell. See Mt
5:22,29–30; Mk 9:43–48; compare Rev 21:8. **not be
quenched** This final verse in Isaiah echoes the sentiment
of Isa 1:27–31, the closing verses of the first chapter.
These literary connections tie the book of Isaiah together
as a unified composition. Just as v. 24 declares the fire
will not be quenched, so 1:27–31 announces that those
who rebel against Yahweh will be consumed and burn with
no one to quench them. The warning in 1:27–31 indicated
that repentance was still possible. This closing verse may
also serve as a warning that when Yahweh's final judgment comes, there will be no more time for repentance.

SALVATION, THE SPIRIT AND THE RESURRECTED SERVANT IN ISAIAH
by John D. Barry

O ver 500 years before Jesus, there was a prophecy that an innocent servant would suffer and die on behalf of the sins of others—but also be raised to life again (Isa 53:10–12). At the time Isaiah 52:13—53:12 was written, there was no precedent for such a radical idea, which makes this passage all the more shocking and profound.

THE IDENTITY OF THE SERVANT IN ISAIAH

Is the servant the nation of Israel or an individual? We can't assume it's always one or always the other in Isaiah; both generalizations are problematic. The identities of the various "servants" in Isaiah are:

CHARACTER(S) REFERRED TO AS "MY SERVANT(S)"	PASSAGE
Isaiah	Isa 20:3
Eliakim, son of Hilkiah	Isa 22:20
Israel	Isa 41:8–9; 42:1,19; 43:10; 44:1–2,21; 45:4; (compare Jer 30:10; 46:27–28; Eze 28:25; 37:25)
An individual servant	Isa 49:3; Isa 52:13; 53:12
Israel (plural—"my servants")	Isa 65:8–9,13–14

Not counting early references to the prophet himself or to Eliakim, an official under King Hezekiah, the servant in the book of Isaiah is always Israel (or, synonymously, Jacob) prior to Isaiah 49:

> But you, *Israel, my servant, Jacob*, whom I have chosen, you descendants of Abraham my friend, I took you from the ends of the earth, from its farthest corners I called you. I said, "You are *my servant*"; I have chosen you and have not rejected you (Isa 41:8–9, emphasis added in this and the following examples).

> "*You [Israel]* are *my witnesses* ["you" is plural in the Hebrew]," declares the LORD, "and *my servant* whom I have chosen, so that you may know and believe me and understand that I am he. Before me no god was formed, nor will there be one after me" (Isa 43:10).

> "But now listen, *Jacob, my servant, Israel,* whom I have chosen. This is what the LORD says— he who made you, who formed you in the womb, and who will help you: Do not be afraid, *Jacob, my servant,* Jeshurun, whom I have chosen (Isa 44:1–2).

> "Remember these things, *Jacob,* for you, *Israel,* are *my servant*. I have made you, you are my servant; *Israel*, I will not forget you (Isa 44:21).

> For the sake of *Jacob my servant*, of *Israel my chosen*, I summon you by name and bestow on you a title of honor, though you do not acknowledge me (Isa 45:4).

In these examples, the servant is the people or nation of Israel—likely the second generation of Israelites living in Babylon during the exile.

But this collective identity shifts in Isaiah 49. Note the first-person language for the servant in Isaiah 49:1–4:

> Listen to me, you islands; hear this, you distant nations: Before *I* was born the LORD called *me*; from *my* mother's womb he has spoken *my* name. He made *my* mouth like a sharpened sword, in the shadow of his hand he hid *me*; he made *me* into a polished arrow and concealed *me* in his quiver. He said to *me*, "You are my servant, *Israel*, in whom I will display my splendor." But *I* said, "*I* have labored in vain; *I* have spent my strength for nothing at all. Yet what is due *me* is in the LORD's hand, and *my* reward is with *my* God."

At first glance, the line "You are my servant, Israel" suggests that Israel remains synonymous with Yahweh's servant; but one verse later, in Isaiah 49:5, there is a clear distinction between Israel and the servant:

> And now the LORD says—he who formed me in the womb to be his servant *to bring Jacob back to him* and *gather Israel to himself*, for I am honored in the eyes of the LORD and my God has been my strength.

Isaiah 49:6 also makes this distinction:

> He [Yahweh] says: "It is too small a thing for you to be my servant *to restore the tribes of Jacob* and *bring back those of Israel I have kept*. I will also make you a light for the Gentiles, that my salvation may reach to the ends of the earth."

The juxtaposition of Israel against the servant suggests that we should understand Isaiah 49:3—"You are my servant, Israel"—as the introduction of a new servant, who will go on to fulfill all or part of Israel's role in bringing God's salvation to the ends of the earth (compare Lk 3:22).

INTERPRETING ISAIAH 52:13—53:12

The individual in Isaiah 52:13—53:12 has taken up Israel's commission as God's chosen servant. It is his duty to reconcile God and humanity. But how will he do this? Who causes the servant's suffering? Who kills him? The Hebrew of Isa 53:10–12 is filled with textual difficulties (such as the subject of the verb translated "makes" below), but when we identify the referents for the pronouns (she, he, you) in our passage, four major players emerge: the prophet, Zion/Jerusalem (Isa 51:3–23; 52:7), the servant, and Yahweh. In light of this, the following rendering of Isaiah 53:10–12 includes the names of the main players in square brackets instead of some of the pronouns.

> [The prophet says,] "Yet Yahweh was pleased to crush [the servant]; he afflicted [the servant] (with sickness). If [Zion/Jerusalem] makes [the servant's] life a guilt offering, [the servant] will see offspring, [the servant] will prolong days. And the will of Yahweh is in [the servant's] hand; it will succeed. Out of trouble of his life [the servant] will see light; [the servant] will be satisfied by his knowledge." [Yahweh says,] "My righteous servant will bring justice to many and he will bear their iniquities. Therefore I [Yahweh] will divide

to [the servant] a portion among the many, and with the strong ones [the servant] shall divide bounty, because he exposed his life to death and was counted with transgressors, and he carried the sin of the many and will intercede for transgressors.

Yahweh is the ultimate cause behind the servant's suffering (Isa 53:12)—it was in his will (Isa 53:10)—but Zion or Jerusalem (symbolizing Yahweh's people) makes the servant a guilt offering (reading the verb as "she makes").

In ancient Israel, a "guilt offering" was made by someone who had deceived, robbed, defrauded, lied or sworn falsely. In addition to making things right with other people, the Israelites needed to make things right with Yahweh (Lev 5:14–19; 7:7; compare Lev 16:22). Guilt offerings of bulls (or goats) died when offered; so the servant, as the guilt offering for God's people, must die (Isa 53:10).

But something miraculous happens: The servant is alive—he is resurrected. The passage promises that he will see offspring and prolong days, both of which can only happen in life (e.g., Ge 48:11; Isa 61:9; Ex 20:12; Dt 4:40; 5:16; 17:20; 25:15; Jos 24:31; Jdg 2:7; Pr 3:1–2). Following the text of the Dead Sea Scrolls and Septuagint, Isaiah 53:11 also implies resurrection: "he will see light" (compare Isa 9:6; Ps 36:10; 49:20; Job 3:16; 33:28).

Because the servant "poured out his life unto death" and was resurrected, he is able to carry the "sin of many" and continue to intercede for transgressors (Isa 53:12). It is because of the servant's death and resurrection that God's relationship with Israel, and with all people, is restored.

From the larger perspective of the book of Isaiah as a whole, the Suffering Servant is also connected with the Messiah figure of Isaiah 11, who judges rightly, helps the impoverished and has the very Spirit of Yahweh upon him (compare Isa 11:1–2; 53:2; Zec 3:8–9).

THE SERVANT AND OUR RESURRECTION

The Suffering Servant, as the saving grace of humanity, is both resurrected and the bringer of resurrection. Picking up on the language of Isaiah 52:13 and Isaiah 53:11, Daniel 12:1–4 speaks of a corporate resurrection of many people. Daniel 12:2 says: "Multitudes who sleep in the dust of the earth will awake: some to everlasting life, others to shame and everlasting contempt."

Theologically, this link suggests that it is because of the Suffering Servant that the resurrection of humanity is possible. The apostle Paul takes up this language when he speaks of the importance of Jesus' resurrection, its connection to our salvation and the power it gives us to overcome sin (Ro 6:5–14). The resurrection of Jesus, the Suffering Servant, has radical implications for all of humanity.

This connection is also made in Revelation 20:11–15, which speaks of the resurrection of the dead and the judgment of humanity during the end times. This act is directly tied to the personhood of Jesus, who is referred to as the Lamb who is slain and who appears as a rider—clothed

in a robe dipped in blood—on a white horse battling evil (Rev 5:12; 19:11–21). The Suffering Servant is likewise prophesied using the language of a divine warrior, equating him with Yahweh (Isa 52:15—53:1,12).

THE SERVANT, JUSTICE AND THE HOLY SPIRIT

The Suffering Servant prophecy is so powerful that it is understandable why Jesus casts his entire ministry in terms of it, proclaiming his authority to bring Good News to the impoverished and freedom to the oppressed, and to heal; he reads from Isaiah and says it is about him (Lk 4:18; Isa 61:1–2). The portion he reads evokes the messianic language of Isa 11:2; 48:16; and 52:7 as well as the Suffering Servant language of Isa 42:1. The Suffering Servant, Jesus, is not just about salvation or even just about resurrection—he is about new life for all of humanity. The cry of justice and longing for restoration is integral to what it means to be a Christian.

The Spirit of Yahweh is upon Jesus, as he proclaims in Luke; and it because of Jesus that the Holy Spirit is with believers today. The trajectory of Luke's Gospel—and Luke's second volume, Acts—is that the Good News of Jesus will reach the entire world via the Holy Spirit's work among his people (Lk 24:45–49; Ac 2). In Luke, Jesus shows that the Scriptures point to him and specifically to his death and subsequent glory (Lk 24:26–27,44). And this grounds the mission of Jesus' people today: to set the captives free through the work of the Spirit, to raise up the impoverished and oppressed, and to proclaim that salvation has come to the world. Yahweh's favor and Spirit have reached the world via the Suffering Servant. Jesus, the one prophesied so powerfully centuries before in the book of Isaiah, is still seen among us via the work of the Holy Spirit (Jn 14:15–31). Jesus is God with us (Isa 7:14).

(This article was adapted in part from The Resurrected Servant in Isaiah *by John D. Barry.)*

JEREMIAH

INTRODUCTION TO JEREMIAH

The book of Jeremiah is about Yahweh's goodness and his people's refusal to follow his ways (Jer 6:16). It also portrays Jeremiah's persistence in following his prophetic call despite indifference and opposition. Jeremiah warned Judah, the southern kingdom of Israel, of God's judgment—which culminated in 586 BC with the destruction of Jerusalem and the temple. But Yahweh ultimately provides hope, promising to renew his covenant with his people (31:31–34). Jeremiah proclaims that God had long ago established a contractual agreement with them and will restore that relationship (compare Ex 24:1–8).

BACKGROUND

We have more information about Jeremiah than any of the other writing prophets. He was born near the middle of the seventh century BC in Anathoth, a town three miles northeast of Jerusalem. He was from a priestly family and may have been a descendant of Abiathar, the high priest under David whom Solomon had banished to Anathoth (1Ki 2:26). Jeremiah was called to be a prophet during Josiah's reign, around 627 BC (Jer 1:2,6). However, most of his known prophetic ministry occurred after approximately 605 BC, as Judah declined and then fell to the Babylonians under King Nebuchadnezzar.

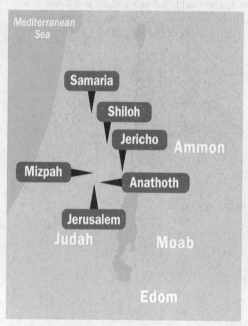

This map depicts some of the major locations related to the book of Jeremiah.

Jeremiah experienced opposition throughout his ministry. King Jehoiakim (609–597 BC) burned a scroll of Jeremiah's prophecies to indicate his contempt (ch. 36). During the siege of Jerusalem, Jeremiah was accused of treason and imprisoned because of his preaching (ch. 37). After Jerusalem fell, Jeremiah chose to remain (40:1–6), but he was still taken to Egypt against his will around 585 BC (43:4–7).

STRUCTURE

The book of Jeremiah can be divided into six major sections. The prologue (1:1–19) relates Jeremiah's call to be a prophet. The second section (2:1—25:38) contains judgment oracles against Judah and Jerusalem (chs. 2–20), as well as three collections of oracles and prose sermons concerning Jerusalem and the kings there (21:1—23:8), the lying prophets (23:9–40) and Nebuchadnezzar and Babylon (24:1—25:38).

The third section (26:1—39:18) corresponds to Jeremiah's life before the fall of Jerusalem. It begins with various prose narratives illustrating the unpopularity of Jeremiah's message (chs. 26–29). The next section is the "Book of Comfort" (chs. 30–33), which describes the future restoration of Israel and Judah, as well as the new covenant that Yahweh establishes with his people (31:31–34). More narratives follow in Jeremiah 34–39: the release and re-enslavement of all the slaves in Jerusalem (ch. 34), Jeremiah's interactions with the Rekabites (ch. 35), the burning of Jeremiah's prophetic scroll by King Jehoiakim (ch. 36) and the events immediately before the fall of Jerusalem (37:3—39:18).

The fourth section (40:1—45:5) records events after Jerusalem is captured by the Babylonians: Jeremiah's decision to stay in the land (40:1–6), Gedaliah's brief rule as governor and his assassination (40:7—41:18), Jeremiah's forced journey to Egypt (chs. 42–44) and Jeremiah's closing words to his scribe, Baruch (45:1–5).

The fifth section (chs. 46–51) contains Jeremiah's oracles against the nations. The final chapter serves as an epilogue and is substantially the same as 2 Kings 24:18—25:30; it describes the fall of Jerusalem, the three deportations of the people of Judah and King Jehoiachin's release from prison in Babylon (Jer 52).

OUTLINE

- Jeremiah's call (1:1–19)
- Judgment on Judah (2:1—25:38)
- Jeremiah's life before the fall of Jerusalem (26:1—39:18)
- Jeremiah's life after the fall of Jerusalem (40:1—45:5)
- Oracles against the nations (46:1—51:64)
- Historical appendix (52:1–34)

THEMES

Jeremiah had a clear calling, but he also experienced the sadness and loneliness of speaking to an unrepentant people. He told God's people that their approaching exile was a consequence of their disregard for God's law. They would not be protected by their political alliances or their cultural markers, but only by a return to God.

Although Jeremiah prophesied impending disaster, he also prophesied hope. The disaster was not averted, but God would restore his people and form a new covenant with them—his law would be written on their hearts. This covenant is linked to the new covenant in Christ in the New Testament (Heb 8:8–12; 10:16–17). Jeremiah continued to share the word of Yahweh in a hopeless situation, knowing that God would remain faithful. Jeremiah offers us a model of what it means to be faithful despite opposition and disaster.

1 The words of Jeremiah son of Hilkiah, one of the priests at Anathoth in the territory of Benjamin. [2]The word of the LORD came to him in the thirteenth year of the reign of Josiah son of Amon king of Judah, [3]and through the reign of Jehoiakim son of Josiah king of Judah, down to the fifth month of the eleventh year of Zedekiah son of Josiah king of Judah, when the people of Jerusalem went into exile.

The Call of Jeremiah

[4]The word of the LORD came to me, saying,

[5] "Before I formed you in the womb I knew[a] you,
    before you were born I set you apart;
    I appointed you as a prophet to the nations."

[6]"Alas, Sovereign LORD," I said, "I do not know how to speak; I am too young."

[7]But the LORD said to me, "Do not say, 'I am too young.' You must go to everyone I send you to and say whatever I command you. [8]Do not be afraid of them, for I am with you and will rescue you," declares the LORD.

[9]Then the LORD reached out his hand and touched my mouth and said to me, "I have put my words in your mouth. [10]See, today I appoint you over nations and kingdoms to uproot and tear down, to destroy and overthrow, to build and to plant."

[11]The word of the LORD came to me: "What do you see, Jeremiah?"

a 5 Or *chose*

1:1–3 Jeremiah begins by identifying the prophet and placing his career during the reigns of the last few kings of Judah (627–587 BC). See the timeline "Approximate Dates of Old Testament Prophets" on p. 1070.

1:1 Jeremiah A popular name in Israel belonging to 10 OT figures. The Hebrew name *yirmeyahu* used here can be translated as "may Yahweh lift up" or, to capitalize on the perception of Yahweh as a divine warrior, "may Yahweh cast" (see Ex 15:1,21). Also, the name sounds like a phrase in the ancient Akkadian language that could mean "may Yahweh loosen the womb" and adds significance to his calling "in the womb" in Jer 1:5. **Anathoth** A village a few kilometers north of Jerusalem. Abiathar, one of the two officiating high priests of King David, was exiled there with his family after Solomon was installed as king over Israel (1Ki 2:26–27). The priests of Anathoth were most likely a clan that claimed descent from the Davidic high priest, Abiathar, who was the last survivor of the house of Eli (compare 1Sa 2:27–36). Eli officiated at the sanctuary in Shiloh before the construction of Solomon's temple (1Sa 1:3). As a boy, Jeremiah would have been raised, educated and trained by the priests of Anathoth in the religious traditions of Shiloh. Jeremiah is the only prophet to draw references to the Shiloh sanctuary (Jer 7:12,14; 26:6,9) and to the prophet, Samuel (15:1), who also was associated with the house of Eli. **territory of Benjamin** In his preaching, Jeremiah occasionally refers to his tribal affiliation. He calls the Benjamites to leave Jerusalem in an oracle of destruction (6:1). Jeremiah 31:15 portrays the mother of Benjamin, Rachel, weeping for her children in Ramah.

Jeremiah 1:1

THE TRIBE OF BENJAMIN
One of the 12 tribes of ancient Israel. Their territory bordered Judah to the north, not far from Jerusalem. When the northern tribes led by Jeroboam rebelled against Rehoboam, the son of Solomon, David's heir, at least some of the tribe of Benjamin remained loyal to Rehoboam (1Ki 12:21). During the period of the divided kingdom, Benjamin's national allegiance wavered between Israel and Judah. The border between the northern and southern kingdoms cut through the territory allotted to the tribe of Benjamin.

1:2 The word of the LORD came to him The English translation "came" could be misleading. In Hebrew, the word of Yahweh is an event, not merely an audible message. The word of Yahweh here is identified specifically as Yahweh in vv. 6, 7 and 9. **thirteenth year of the reign of Josiah** Approximately 628–626 BC. See the timeline "Life of Jeremiah" on p. 1170. **Josiah** Josiah was the last of the "good kings" in the Deuteronomistic History; he had a considerable effect on the life and theology of Jeremiah (2Ki 22–23).

1:3 Jehoiakim Ruled from 609–597 BC. In contrast to his opinions of Josiah, Jeremiah is highly critical of Jehoiakim, who reversed the religious reforms of his father and went against Yahweh (2Ki 23:37). This indictment is usually reserved for those Judean kings who supported sites of worship and sacrifice outside of Jerusalem, but Jehoiakim is censured for the grievousness of the sins of Manasseh, his grandfather. Also, Jehoiakim was a willing vassal of Necho, the pharaoh in Egypt. Jeremiah would have seen an alliance with Egypt as akin to high treason (see Dt 17:16; 28:63–68). His opposition to Jehoiakim's pro-Egyptian sympathies is a major theme throughout this book. See the timeline "The Divided Kingdom" on p. 536. **fifth month** The fall of Jerusalem occurred on the ninth day of the month of Tammuz, 586 BC. See the table "Israelite Calendar" on p. 763; see the timeline "Judah From the Fall of Samaria to the Exile" on p. 606. **Zedekiah** A puppet king installed by Nebuchadnezzar II as a vassal of Babylon. He ruled from 597–586 BC. The prophet is less severe in his criticism of Zedekiah than in his criticism of Jehoiakim.

1:4–19 Isaiah, Jeremiah and Ezekiel each record an experience of calling or commissioning by Yahweh. This calling identifies their mission and message.

1:4 word The Hebrew term here can be translated as "word," "event" or "matter." In the context of the prophetic experience, the word of Yahweh is experienced as a real auditory, visual and physical event.

1:5 in the womb The idea that God created Jeremiah for a specific purpose forms a play on words with Jeremiah's name, which could mean "may Yahweh loosen the womb" (see note on Jer 1:1). If this is the case, then Jeremiah's prophetic call begins at birth. The apostle Paul seems to have applied this aspect of Jeremiah's ministry to himself in Gal 1:14–16. **knew** The Hebrew verb for "to know" is used to describe the most intimate of relationships. **I set you apart** Jeremiah has been set apart or consecrated for a special purpose or task. This phrase completes a triad,

"I see the branch of an almond tree," I replied. ¹²The LORD said to me, "You have seen correctly, for I am watchingᵃ to see that my word is fulfilled."

¹³The word of the LORD came to me again: "What do you see?"

"I see a pot that is boiling," I answered. "It is tilting toward us from the north."

¹⁴The LORD said to me, "From the north disaster will be poured out on all who live in the land. ¹⁵I am about to summon all the peoples of the northern kingdoms," declares the LORD.

"Their kings will come and set up their
    thrones
  in the entrance of the gates of Jerusalem;
they will come against all her surrounding
    walls
  and against all the towns of Judah.

¹⁶I will pronounce my judgments on my people
  because of their wickedness in
    forsaking me,
in burning incense to other gods
  and in worshiping what their hands have
    made.

¹⁷"Get yourself ready! Stand up and say to them whatever I command you. Do not be terrified by them, or I will terrify you before them. ¹⁸Today I have made you a fortified city, an iron pillar and a bronze wall to stand against the whole land — against the kings of Judah, its officials, its priests and the people of the land. ¹⁹They will fight against you but will not overcome you, for I am with you and will rescue you," declares the LORD.

ᵃ 12 The Hebrew for *watching* sounds like the Hebrew for *almond tree*.

"I formed you ... I knew you ... I consecrated you," which defines what it means for Jeremiah to be a prophet to the nations. **prophet to the nations** Jeremiah's distinction as a prophet to the nations required special emphasis. He was called not only to deliver God's message to the people in Israel and Judah, but also to confront kings and emperors with Yahweh's divine justice. The specific language used to describe Jeremiah's call closely corresponds to royal birth announcements from Mesopotamia and Egypt. Jeremiah is called to address the kings and rulers of the foreign nations as an equal; just as they are born to office, he is born to be Yahweh's prophet.

1:6 I am too young His objection is that he is not yet a man according to ancient Israelite standards; he is still under 20, quite likely 12–16 years old at the time of his calling. Jeremiah's protestation that he does not know how to speak parallels Moses' objection in Ex 3:11. His distinction as a boy is similar to Samuel's call in 1Sa 3:1–14.

1:8 I am with you Yahweh's reassurance of his presence is a common theme throughout the OT (Ex 3:12; Jos 1:5; Jdg 6:16). The very name of Yahweh, disclosed to Moses in Ex 3:14, means "I AM WHO I AM." It contains an implicit promise of his presence. In Moses' call in Ex 6:1–8, the promise of deliverance accompanies Yahweh's presence.

1:9 my words The prophet's role as a messenger involved faithfully communicating the words of the one who sent him. The parallels between Moses and Jeremiah inform the entire call narrative, and it seems that Jeremiah — and the compilers of the book after him — envisioned himself as a new Moses whose words would echo the fulfillment of Moses' prediction of destruction and exile in Dt 28:47–68.

1:10 to build and to plant While Jeremiah's ministry is destructive, it contains constructive elements, as well (compare Jer 29:1–28; 31:4–5).

1:11 word of the LORD A common introduction to a prophetic oracle of Yahweh. **branch of an almond tree** The blossoming almond branch indicates that Yahweh's words are about to take place.

1:12 my word is fulfilled The first oracle in vv. 5–10. It has been spoken, but its fulfillment lies in the future.

1:13 a pot that is boiling Compare the metaphor of the cooking pot in Eze 11:11–12.

1:14 From the north A looming disaster from the north is a common image in Jeremiah and is symbolic of Babylon (compare Jer 50:9). While the Babylonian Empire lay directly east of Jerusalem, any militarized force proceeded around the Arabian Desert and entered the Palestinian region from the north before moving southward to Jerusalem. **who live in the land** The residents of Jerusalem and the surrounding region.

1:15 all the peoples Not the 10 tribes of the now-extinct kingdom of Israel; rather, a coalition of foreign nations subservient to Babylon through treaties (25:8–9). **the gates of Jerusalem** In the ancient Near East, the city gates functioned as a civic center where city officials, merchants and leaders met to discuss politics and business, and where rulers administered judgment (e.g., Dt 16:18; 17:5). If foreign invaders possessed the city gates, it meant that the city had been conquered (see Ge 22:17; 24:60). After the siege of Jerusalem, the officials of Babylon took seats of judgment in the city gates (Jer 39:3). **against all the towns of Judah** The people depend on fortified cities, such as Gezer and Lachish in the Judean hill country, for safety and preservation.

1:16 judgments The word here refers to judgments rendered in a court. The laws Moses gives to Israel in the Book of the Covenant related to the regulation of civil and social order are introduced with this Hebrew term (Ex 21–23). This word is often used in conjunction with other legal terms (see Lev 26:46; Dt 4:8,44; 6:1; 1Ki 9:4). The appearance of these terms together reinforces the distinction of the civil law from the religious and ceremonial laws of Israel. **in forsaking me** This is a summary of the following indictments. The charge of desertion is a major theme in the book of Deuteronomy (Dt 28:20; 31:16). It appears frequently in the oracles of Jeremiah (Jer 2:13,17,19; 5:7,19). **what their hands have made** Accusations of idolatry form the basis for many of Jeremiah's oracles (7:8–10; 11:10; 19:4,13; 25:6; 44:3–15). Yahweh's desertion often accompanies the Israelites' religious infidelity. The same phrasing in 2Ki 22:17 appears to describe the sins of previous generations, prior to Josiah's reforms (see note on Jer 1:2). These themes link the oracles of Jeremiah, the book of Deuteronomy, and the religious reforms of Josiah.

1:17 Get yourself ready A phrase that denotes preparation for a strenuous task.

1:18 made The Hebrew wording here is the same as that used to describe Jeremiah's appointment as a prophet in vv. 5 and 9. The promise to strengthen Jeremiah is directly connected to the call narrative in vv. 4–10; for Jeremiah, it functions as an arsenal of reinforcements

Life of Jeremiah

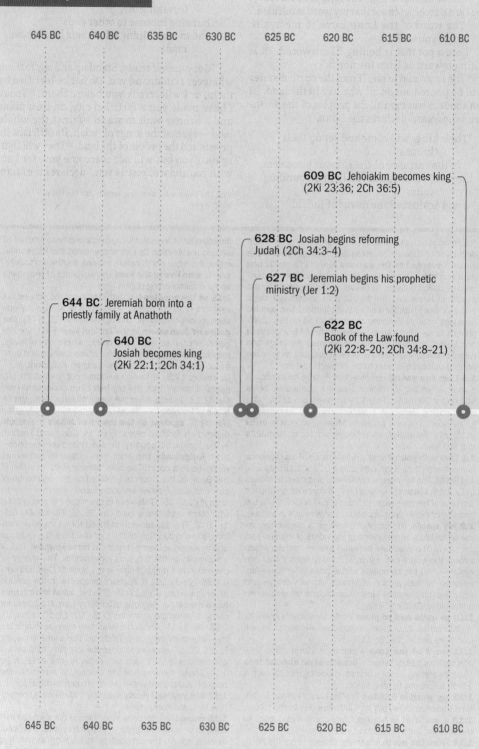

645 BC   640 BC   635 BC   630 BC   625 BC   620 BC   615 BC   610 BC

609 BC Jehoiakim becomes king (2Ki 23:36; 2Ch 36:5)

628 BC Josiah begins reforming Judah (2Ch 34:3–4)

627 BC Jeremiah begins his prophetic ministry (Jer 1:2)

644 BC Jeremiah born into a priestly family at Anathoth

640 BC Josiah becomes king (2Ki 22:1; 2Ch 34:1)

622 BC Book of the Law found (2Ki 22:8–20; 2Ch 34:8–21)

645 BC   640 BC   635 BC   630 BC   625 BC   620 BC   615 BC   610 BC

All dates are approximate

605 BC 600 BC 595 BC 590 BC 585 BC 580 BC

589 BC Zedekiah's request for God's help rejected (Jer 21)

588 BC Siege of Jerusalem begins (Jer 39:1; 52:4)

588 BC The Babylonians withdraw for a short time; Jeremiah is put in prison (Jer 37:5–15)

588 BC The people of Jerusalem free their slaves, then enslave them again (Jer 34:8–22)

588 BC Jeremiah buys a field (Jer 32)

587 BC Jeremiah prophesies Israel's restoration (Jer 33)

587 BC Jeremiah is transferred to the court of the guard (Jer 37:16–21)

586 BC Jerusalem falls (Jer 39:2–7; 52:6–11)

586 BC The temple is destroyed and the people taken into exile (Jer 39:8–10; 52:12–30)

586 BC Jeremiah is freed (Jer 40)

585 BC Gedaliah, governor of Judah, is assassinated (Jer 40:7—41:15)

585 BC Jeremiah is taken to Egypt (Jer 41:16—43:13)

581 BC Nebuzaradan deports 745 Jews to Babylon (Jer 52:30)

605 BC Nebuchadnezzar becomes king of Babylon

605 BC Jeremiah delivers his Temple Sermon (Jer 7:1–15; 26)

605 BC Baruch reads Jeremiah's scroll in the temple; Jehoiakim burns it (Jer 36)

605 BC Jeremiah consoles Baruch (Jer 45:1–5)

594 BC Jeremiah writes a letter to the Babylonian exiles (Jer 29)

594 BC Hananiah prophesies falsely; Jeremiah rebukes him (Jer 28)

594 BC Jeremiah urges Zedekiah to submit to Babylon's yoke (Jer 27)

597 BC Jehoiachin becomes king (2Ki 24:8; 2Ch 36:9)

597 BC Jeremiah prophesies that Jehoiachin will be taken to Babylon (Jer 13:18–19; 22:24–30)

597 BC Zedekiah becomes king (Jer 52:1)

599 BC Jeremiah contrasts Judah with the Rekabites (Jer 35)

601 BC Jehoiakim rebels against Babylon (2Ki 24:1)

604 BC Jehoiakim becomes vassal of Babylon (2Ki 24:1; 2Ch 36:6–7)

605 BC 600 BC 595 BC 590 BC 585 BC 580 BC

Israel Forsakes God

2 The word of the LORD came to me: [2]"Go and proclaim in the hearing of Jerusalem:

"This is what the LORD says:

"'I remember the devotion of your youth,
how as a bride you loved me
and followed me through the wilderness,
through a land not sown.
[3] Israel was holy to the LORD,
the firstfruits of his harvest;
all who devoured her were held guilty,
and disaster overtook them,'"
declares the LORD.

[4] Hear the word of the LORD, you descendants
of Jacob,
all you clans of Israel.

[5] This is what the LORD says:

"What fault did your ancestors find in me,
that they strayed so far from me?
They followed worthless idols
and became worthless themselves.
[6] They did not ask, 'Where is the LORD,
who brought us up out of Egypt
and led us through the barren
wilderness,
through a land of deserts and
ravines,
a land of drought and utter darkness,
a land where no one travels and no one
lives?'
[7] I brought you into a fertile land
to eat its fruit and rich produce.
But you came and defiled my land
and made my inheritance detestable.
[8] The priests did not ask,
'Where is the LORD?'
Those who deal with the law did not
know me;
the leaders rebelled against me.
The prophets prophesied by Baal,
following worthless idols.

for his mission. **a fortified city, an iron pillar** Images of a siege campaign. **kings of Judah** The triad of kings, officials (or princes) and priests parallels the call of Jeremiah to prophesy against nations in v. 10. Throughout the ancient Near East, there was an insoluble bond between religious and political institutions. Jeremiah frequently counts the priests in Jerusalem among his opponents (see 20:1–6; 26:7–19; 29:24–28).

1:19 declares the LORD The Hebrew expression here commonly indicates a divine declaration; the promise is a confirmation of God's earlier pledge to be with Jeremiah. See v. 8 and note.

2:1—3:5 This section of oracles is part of an early collection that includes 3:6—4:4. It centers on the themes of apostasy and repentance. The first group of oracles, 2:1—3:5, focuses on the religious infidelity of Judah and the Jerusalem temple. This religious criticism is coupled with an equally strong disparagement of King Jehoiakim's foreign policy.

2:2 in the hearing of Jerusalem Jeremiah is commanded to walk through Jerusalem, broadcasting his message so all the residents of the city will hear it. **This is what the LORD says** A frequently recurring phrase for the beginning of a prophetic proclamation; it appears nearly 300 times in the OT (Ex 7:17; Jos 24:2; 1Sa 10:18; 1Ki 13:2; 2Ki 20:1; Isa 31:4; Am 1:3). More than half the occurrences of this phrase are found in the book of Jeremiah. **remember** Implies Yahweh is recalling the distant past—times and circumstances that have long since come to an end. Yahweh is laying a civil charge against Israel. While a charge of idolatry against the nation might well be construed as a religious offense, Yahweh's indictment is presented as a civil dispute. See note on Jer 1:16. **your youth** The word here is from the same root as the word Jeremiah used to describe his own adolescence in 1:6. While the word itself is masculine, in this context it can be translated "girlhood." **how as a bride** This is the only occurrence of this Hebrew word in the OT. The term may refer to either the time of engagement or marriage, but the sense conveys the early love of Israel, the young bride of Yahweh. **followed me** This

verb, which has the core meaning "to walk," is frequently used to describe religious devotion. In Deuteronomy, Israel is frequently commanded to walk after Yahweh, and to abstain from walking after other gods (see Dt 5:31; 6:14; 8:6). **through the wilderness** Alludes to the wilderness wanderings of the Israelites after the exodus. **2:3 holy to the LORD** The separation of Israel as a chosen nation is a recurring theme in Deuteronomy, and it likely influenced Jeremiah's understanding of Israel's relationship to God (Dt 7:6; 14:2). **the firstfruits** The concept of firstfruits is most commonly associated with the temple services and the practice of worshiping Yahweh. The sense is that Israel is a special gift or offering to Yahweh. **declares the LORD** This recurring phrase here marks the conclusion of the first oracle.
2:4 you clans of Israel Jeremiah's first oracle corresponds to a time when the kingdom of Israel, composed of the 10 northern tribes, had ceased to exist after the Assyrian invasion 734–721 BC. See the timeline "The Divided Kingdom" on p. 536.
2:6 out of Egypt Alludes to the exodus. **utter darkness** This Hebrew phrasing appears in Ps 23:4; it can also be translated "the shadow of death."
2:7 a fertile land This term is commonly associated with Mount Carmel on the Mediterranean coast where Elijah faced the prophets of Baal (1Ki 18). **defiled my land** Like the Song of Moses in Deuteronomy, Jeremiah shows the sins of Israel occurring immediately after their settlement in Canaan (Dt 32:15–18). **my inheritance** The heritage or inheritance of Yahweh is the promised land as well as the people of Israel themselves (Dt 4:20–21; 32:9; Jer 3:19; 10:16). **detestable** Refers to idolatrous practices in the OT (Dt 12:31; 13:14; 2Ki 16:3; 2Ch 28:3; Eze 16:50; Mal 2:11). See note on Eze 5:9.
2:8 The priests The first of the national leaders condemned for abandoning Yahweh and supporting other gods. **Where is the LORD** A refrain repeated from Jer 2:6. **Those who deal with** By the time of Josiah's reforms, the vocation of priest had come to include the proper interpretation and instruction of the Law—usually called the torah (Eze 7:26; 22:26; Hos 4:6; Zep 3:4; Hag 2:11; Mal 2:7). **the law** The Hebrew word used here, torah,

⁹ "Therefore I bring charges against you
        again,"
                                declares the LORD.
    "And I will bring charges against your
        children's children.
¹⁰ Cross over to the coasts of Cyprus and look,
        send to Kedarᵃ and observe closely;
    see if there has ever been anything like
        this:
¹¹ Has a nation ever changed its gods?
        (Yet they are not gods at all.)
    But my people have exchanged their glorious
        God
        for worthless idols.
¹² Be appalled at this, you heavens,
        and shudder with great horror,"
                                declares the LORD.
¹³ "My people have committed two sins:
    They have forsaken me,
        the spring of living water,
    and have dug their own cisterns,
        broken cisterns that cannot hold
        water.
¹⁴ Is Israel a servant, a slave by birth?
        Why then has he become plunder?

¹⁵ Lions have roared;
        they have growled at him.
    They have laid waste his land;
        his towns are burned and deserted.
¹⁶ Also, the men of Memphis and Tahpanhes
        have cracked your skull.
¹⁷ Have you not brought this on yourselves
        by forsaking the LORD your God
        when he led you in the way?
¹⁸ Now why go to Egypt
        to drink water from the Nileᵇ?
    And why go to Assyria
        to drink water from the Euphrates?
¹⁹ Your wickedness will punish you;
        your backsliding will rebuke you.
    Consider then and realize
        how evil and bitter it is for you
    when you forsake the LORD your God
        and have no awe of me,"
                declares the Lord, the LORD Almighty.

²⁰ "Long ago you broke off your yoke
        and tore off your bonds;
    you said, 'I will not serve you!'

ᵃ 10 In the Syro-Arabian desert   ᵇ 18 Hebrew *Shihor*; that is, a
branch of the Nile

means "instruction" or "teaching" and refers to the Law
that eventually comprised the entire Pentateuch. Most
likely, Jeremiah considers the *torah* to be the book of
Deuteronomy. See note on Jer 1:1. **the leaders** The
leaders are called *ro'im* ("shepherds") in Hebrew, using a metaphor for kings or aristocratic rulers common
throughout the ancient Near East (compare 3:15 and
note). Here, the term includes "kings" and "princes"
(see 1:18 and note; compare 23:1–4). **The prophets**
Jeremiah's contentious conflict with rival prophets in
and around Jerusalem is a prevalent theme throughout
the book (see 23:9–40; 27:9–15). **Baal** A Canaanite
god. See the table "Pagan Deities of the Old Testament"
on p. 1287.
2:9 I bring charges against you again Yahweh presents his case against Israel for breaking the covenant
relationship. **declares the LORD** A phrase which marks
the end of this oracle (see v. 3 and note).
2:13 that cannot hold water Foreign gods are broken
containers; they cannot produce water, and they cannot
hold the water poured into them.
2:14 a slave by birth Refers to slaves born of the
household, not acquired through purchase (see Ge 14:14;
17:13,23,27; Lev 22:11). Israel is referred to more
honorably elsewhere as a slave of Yahweh (compare Isa
42:1; 43:10; 44:1,21). **plunder** The idea here is that
Israel is plunder taken after a battle. It was common
practice throughout the ancient Near East to enslave
foreigners as spoils of war (compare Nu 14:3,31; Dt
1:39; Isa 42:22; Eze 34:8,22).
2:15 Lions Represents the coalition of nations that
composed the Babylonian Empire. For most of Jeremiah's
ministry, Judah was under the constant threat of conquest
and occupation, first from Assyria, then Egypt and finally
Babylon. Josiah was killed in 609 BC in battle against the
Egyptians at Megiddo; Egypt was conquered by Babylon
at Carchemish in 605 BC. From the time of Josiah's
death, Jeremiah foresaw that Babylon would eventually

dominate Egypt. Babylonian forces were crouching at
the borders of Judah like roaring lions; their strike was
imminent. **waste** Refers to the Babylonian campaign and
eventual destruction of Jerusalem between 604–586
BC. **deserted** The exile to Babylon and the destruction
of Jerusalem left the region desolate. In Deuteronomy
29:21–29, Yahweh threatens Israel with exile as punishment for their abandonment and idolatry.
2:16 Memphis Cities in Egypt. Tahpanhes becomes home
to Jeremiah and the remaining Jews after the exile (Jer
43:7–9). This oracle anticipates the defeat of Judah at
the hands of Egypt and Babylon.
2:17 by forsaking the LORD your God The culmination
of the oracle predicts judgment on Israel for their apostasy. The people's abandonment of Yahweh in spite of
his protection stands in stark contrast with the promise
made in Dt 31:6–8. **the way** A phrase used throughout
the OT to describe the covenant-based relationship the
people ought to have with Yahweh (compare Dt 5:33;
9:12; Ps 32:8; 143:8; Isa 48:17; Jer 7:23; 42:3).
2:18 water from the Nile Contrasts with the image of
Yahweh as the spring of living waters in v. 13.
2:19 your backsliding This verse uses the Hebrew word
shuv, which can mean both "to turn" and "to repent."
Rather than turning back to Yahweh in contrition, Israel
has turned away in rebellion (compare 3:22–4:2). **no
awe of me** As a sign of their devotion to God, people
are called to be fearers of Yahweh (compare Dt 14:23;
17:19; Ps 15:4; 22:23; 112:1; Isa 50:10; Mal 3:16).
Jeremiah uses a word meaning "to tremble" or "to be in
dread," which may be an echo of Hos 3:5.
2:20 your yoke A familiar image for Jeremiah (Jer 5:5;
28:2,4,11; 30:8). The image of a domesticated pack
animal in the context of oracles on marriage and fidelity
may be due to ancient Near Eastern perspectives on
gender roles. The spurned husband appears to equate
Israel's failed marriage obligation to that of a stubborn
and useless draft animal. **not** In contrast with Israel's

Indeed, on every high hill
  and under every spreading tree
  you lay down as a prostitute.
21 I had planted you like a choice vine
  of sound and reliable stock.
How then did you turn against me
  into a corrupt, wild vine?
22 Although you wash yourself with soap
  and use an abundance of cleansing
    powder,
  the stain of your guilt is still before me,"
    declares the Sovereign LORD.
23 "How can you say, 'I am not defiled;
  I have not run after the Baals'?
See how you behaved in the valley;
  consider what you have done.
You are a swift she-camel
  running here and there,
24 a wild donkey accustomed to the desert,
  sniffing the wind in her craving—
  in her heat who can restrain her?

Any males that pursue her need not tire
    themselves;
  at mating time they will find her.
25 Do not run until your feet are bare
  and your throat is dry.
But you said, 'It's no use!
  I love foreign gods,
  and I must go after them.'

26 "As a thief is disgraced when he is
    caught,
  so the people of Israel are disgraced—
they, their kings and their officials,
  their priests and their prophets.
27 They say to wood, 'You are my father,'
  and to stone, 'You gave me birth.'
They have turned their backs to me
  and not their faces;
yet when they are in trouble,
  they say,
  'Come and save us!'

ideal depiction as the servant of Yahweh (v. 14 and note), the rebellious nation refuses to acknowledge its master. **on every high hill** Hills were sites of pagan religious activity in the OT (1Ki 14:23; 2Ki 16:4; 17:10 Isa 65:7; Eze 6:13). Jeremiah uses this term in his own oracles, berating Israel for idolatrous practices (Jer 3:23; 13:27; 17:2). **under every spreading tree** Frequently indicates a place of pagan religious activity in the OT (Dt 12:2; 1Ki 14:23; 2Ki 16:4; Isa 57:5). In the ancient Near East, trees were symbols for fertility and were frequently associated with the Canaanite goddess, Asherah. Jeremiah likely refers to shrines designated specifically for the worship of fertility goddesses.

2:21 a choice vine The metaphor depicts a vine of high quality and good stock. In Isa 5:1–7, Israel is depicted as a fertile, well-tended vineyard. In Dt 32:32, the enemies of Israel are portrayed as a poisonous vine that has sprouted from the vine of Sodom. **wild vine** Used in the OT to refer to non-Israelite people and lands. The image here reinforces the idea that Israel—Yahweh's property, his spouse—has been seduced and ruined.

2:22 guilt The word here is frequently translated as "iniquity" or "sin." The reference to a stain or mark may be euphemistic for bloodstains on a woman's clothes. However, this imagery more likely derives from Isa 1:15–20: Stains of blood on the worshiper's hands prevent him from entering God's presence. The context equates the offending stains with religious violations.

2:23 I am not defiled Judah's response to Yahweh's accusations of infidelity. **I have not run after the Baals** One may choose either to walk after Yahweh or to walk after foreign gods, as Judah is accused of doing. **See how you behaved** An allusion to conduct (see Jer 2:17 and note): By following after false gods, Judah's conduct is marked by failure and treachery. The implication that Judah can see evidence of its journey may suggest it is leaving traces of uncleanness behind (see v. 22 and note). **the valley** Compare with the high hills in v. 20. This may be the valley of Beth Peor from Dt 4:46 and Nu 25:1–5, where Israel began to whore with the daughters of Moab, worshiping foreign gods. Alternatively, it may be the Valley of Ben Hinnom (or valley of Gehenna; see Jer 7:31 and note; compare Mt 5:22; 5:29–30; 10:28;

Mk 9:43–47; Lk 12:5). The Valley of Ben Hinnom was notorious in the Biblical period as a place of child sacrifice to the Canaanite deity Molek (see Lev 20:2–5; 2Ki 23:10; Jer 32:35). **a swift she-camel** Young camels are notoriously unreliable; they wander off with no provocation. It is characteristic for adult camels to walk no more than three steps in any direction. **running here and there** The camel tracks aimlessly back and forth. This metaphor describes Judah's wavering between foreign alliances with Egypt and Assyria. In the context of a marriage covenant, the young, fickle animal represents the promiscuous wife who wanders from the embrace of one lover to another.

2:24 accustomed to the desert Wild donkeys do not stay in one place. The animal represents the faithless Judah, who is fickle in her commitments. **they will find her** Judah's religious debauchery is so pronounced that it is a willing partner for any. The image of the two fickle animals—one ruled by indecisiveness, the other by irrepressible desire—depicts Judah's religious indiscretions.

2:25 Do not run until your feet are bare In conjunction with its parallel in the next phrase, the expression serves as a humorous barb directed at the animals' handlers in the previous verse. Attempts to control the camel and donkey are futile. **I love foreign gods** Refers to enemies of Israel and Judah (Hos 7:9; Isa 1:7; 25:2; Jer 5:19; 30:8; Eze 7:21; 11:9). In Dt 32:16, Yahweh's jealousy is kindled by Israel's association with foreigners. **I must go after them** The nation will either walk after Yahweh or the gods of foreign nations.

2:27 This verse reflects Jeremiah's belief in monotheism. While trees and stones were common religious objects in the ancient Near East, Jeremiah characterizes them as lifeless representations of non-existent gods.

2:27 to wood The leafy tree was a common representation of the Canaanite female deity, Asherah, the female consort of the chief god in the pantheon, El (see Jer 2:20 and note). **You are my father** In Canaanite worship, Asherah was the mother of the gods and all the living. Ancients would have praised her for giving birth, and they acknowledged the male deity as their father.

28 Where then are the gods you made for
   yourselves?
     Let them come if they can save you
       when you are in trouble!
   For you, Judah, have as many gods
     as you have towns.

29 "Why do you bring charges against me?
     You have all rebelled against me,"
                         declares the LORD.
30 "In vain I punished your people;
     they did not respond to correction.
   Your sword has devoured your prophets
     like a ravenous lion.

31 "You of this generation, consider the word
of the LORD:

   "Have I been a desert to Israel
     or a land of great darkness?
   Why do my people say, 'We are free
     to roam;
     we will come to you no more'?
32 Does a young woman forget her jewelry,
     a bride her wedding ornaments?
   Yet my people have forgotten me,
     days without number.

33 How skilled you are at pursuing love!
     Even the worst of women can learn from
       your ways.
34 On your clothes is found
     the lifeblood of the innocent poor,
       though you did not catch them breaking in.
   Yet in spite of all this
35   you say, 'I am innocent;
     he is not angry with me.'
   But I will pass judgment on you
     because you say, 'I have not sinned.'
36 Why do you go about so much,
     changing your ways?
   You will be disappointed by Egypt
     as you were by Assyria.
37 You will also leave that place
     with your hands on your head,
   for the LORD has rejected those you trust;
     you will not be helped by them.

3 "If a man divorces his wife
   and she leaves him and marries another
     man,
   should he return to her again?
     Would not the land be completely
       defiled?

Jeremiah's ironic reversal cleverly emphasizes the lunacy of worshiping lifeless objects.

2:30 your prophets It is unclear which prophets are the subject here. Jeremiah 26:20–23, which records the death of the prophet, Uriah (also rendered "Urijah"), at the hands of King Jehoiakim, may be the background for this claim.

2:31 this generation From 2:31—3:5, the address shifts to the present residents of Jerusalem. Earlier oracles in this group addressed a personified nation (either Judah, Israel or both) and concerned past sins.

2:32 her jewelry Refers to bridal ornaments of silver and gold. See 2Sa 1:24; Isa 49:18; Eze 16:10–13. **wedding ornaments** The Hebrew term here refers to bands or knotted cords. A betrothed girl would keep such a cord, untying a single knot each day until the day of her wedding. **days without number** Likely in reference to the knotted cord. As the witless bride has forgotten to untie the knots in her cord, so Israel has forgotten Yahweh.

2:33 at pursuing love Faithless Israel has already confessed to loving strangers (see Jer 2:25 and note).

2:34 On your clothes This appears to be an echo of the earlier charge that the unfaithful Israel's bloodstains are still visible on its garment. See v. 22 and note. **lifeblood of the innocent poor** In 22:3 and 22:17, the prophet criticizes Jehoiakim specifically for his treatment of the resident alien, the fatherless and the widow and for shedding innocent blood. **breaking in** According to ancient Israelite law, those who caught thieves in the act could execute them without fear of incurring blood guilt. See Ex 22:2–3.

2:36 changing your ways Recalls Jer 2:23, where Israel is depicted as a wandering camel. See v. 23 and note. **by Egypt** Perhaps a prediction of the defeat of Israel by Egypt at Megiddo in 609 BC, but more likely a warning of the dire outcome of Jehoiakim's pro-Egyptian policies. See 1:3 and note. **by Assyria** A recollection of the col-

lapse of the northern kingdom (Israel) at the hands of Assyria (2Ki 17:6; 2Ch 28:16–21). The pronouncement of Israel's shame is a fulfillment of the oracle in Jer 2:26. **2:37 your hands on your head** A sign of shame. **rejected those you trust** Refers to allies that Jehoiakim made in Egypt in a futile effort to overcome the Babylonian threat (see 1:3 and note).

3:1–5 This oracle may belong to the previous section, or it may begin a new collection. Based on the similarity in theme and content between the two passages, it is likely part of the same cycle.

3:1 divorces The term here, with the core meaning "to send," is based on the divorce procedures in Dt 24:1–4. **she leaves him** The familiar theme of walking after Yahweh or foreign gods is repeated here to help reinforce the connection of this oracle to the collection in Jer 2:1–37. See Dt 5:33; 6:14; 8:6; Jer 2:2 and note; 2:8. **return** The Hebrew term used here, *shuv*, means "to turn" or "to return," and is used throughout the OT for "to repent." The principle issue in this oracle is the law recorded in Dt 24:4 that prohibits a man who divorces his wife from remarrying her if she divorces again or if she is widowed and wishes to return to him. The reversal of the actions in this verse is striking, especially set against an ancient Near Eastern context in which women had very few rights. In this unprecedented case, Yahweh is portrayed as the jilted spouse who might return to Israel, the faithless wife. Such an image evokes a strong sense of God's longsuffering and mercy. **land** The metaphor is made explicit here: The land has been polluted just as the adulterous wife incurs pollution and filth (see Jer 2:22 and note; 2:34 and note). **many lovers** The relationships that Israel has with its numerous partners are casual and fickle. **declares the LORD** The familiar phrase concludes the oracle (2:3,9,12,19,22,29).

But you have lived as a prostitute with many
　　lovers—
　　would you now return to me?"
　　　　　　　　　　declares the LORD.
² "Look up to the barren heights and see.
　　Is there any place where you have not been
　　　　ravished?
By the roadside you sat waiting for
　　lovers,
　　sat like a nomad in the desert.
You have defiled the land
　　with your prostitution and wickedness.
³ Therefore the showers have been withheld,
　　and no spring rains have fallen.
Yet you have the brazen look of
　　a prostitute;
　　you refuse to blush with shame.
⁴ Have you not just called to me:
　　'My Father, my friend from my youth,
⁵ will you always be angry?
　　Will your wrath continue forever?'
This is how you talk,
　　but you do all the evil you can."

Unfaithful Israel

⁶During the reign of King Josiah, the LORD said
to me, "Have you seen what faithless Israel has
done? She has gone up on every high hill and under every spreading tree and has committed adultery there. ⁷I thought that after she had done all
this she would return to me but she did not, and
her unfaithful sister Judah saw it. ⁸I gave faithless
Israel her certificate of divorce and sent her away
because of all her adulteries. Yet I saw that her
unfaithful sister Judah had no fear; she also went
out and committed adultery. ⁹Because Israel's
immorality mattered so little to her, she defiled
the land and committed adultery with stone and
wood. ¹⁰In spite of all this, her unfaithful sister
Judah did not return to me with all her heart, but
only in pretense," declares the LORD.

¹¹The LORD said to me, "Faithless Israel is more
righteous than unfaithful Judah. ¹²Go, proclaim
this message toward the north:

"'Return, faithless Israel,' declares the LORD,
　　'I will frown on you no longer,

3:2 to the barren heights The Hebrew text refers to "high hills" or "high places"—sites of idol worship (see 2:20 and note). **not been ravished** Refers to aggressive sexual contact outside of marriage. The word was considered crude and too direct for the Jewish scribes who preserved the OT (Masoretes). In the Masoretic Text, the verb meaning "to lie with" was substituted as a euphemism for sexual matters. This same word appears in three other places in the OT: Dt 28:30; Isa 13:16; and Zec 14:2, which all refer to rape. **By the roadside** See Jer 2:17 and note; 2:23 and note; Isa 49:9. **a nomad in the desert** A reference to the nomadic tribes who engaged in trade and commerce with those who passed by on roads between settlements. The phrase might allude to waylaying people for financial gain, as either a trader or a roadside bandit. **You have defiled the land** In the book of Deuteronomy—and for Jeremiah—the crime of prostitution threatens to incur guilt that will defile the nation, rendering it impure and worthless. See Dt 24:4; Jer 3:1 and note. **with your prostitution and wickedness** The double adjective describes extremely offensive and excessive promiscuity.

3:3 showers have been withheld Suggests Israel's sinfulness has caused the drought. **the brazen look of a prostitute** The Hebrew text uses a common idiom for stubbornness and obstinate rebellion (Eze 3:7–8; Isa 48:4). Israel is adulterous and blatantly promiscuous despite stern warnings.

3:4 My Father Jeremiah likely is recalling Yahweh's self-designation as Israel's father in the Song of Moses (Dt 32:6). Ironically, the same cry appears on the lips of those who worship at the fertility pole in Jer 2:27. **my friend** The term here often is used to indicate an especially close friend. It can be distinguished from Yahweh's charge that Israel has adulterated itself with many companions (see v. 1 and note). The covenant relationship that exists between Israel and Yahweh is especially intimate, which intensifies the gravity of the offense.

3:5 always This word implies bearing a grudge: Yahweh's anger is not eternal, and he is not begrudging (Ps 103:9; Mic 7:18).

3:6—4:4 The second series of oracles in Jeremiah is distinguished from the first by its preoccupation with the northern kingdom, Israel. Jeremiah 3:6–11 serves as an introduction to the oracles that follow and provides a connection to the first section with its comparison to Judah. Jeremiah 3:12—4:4 is a series of sayings and prophecies Jeremiah likely uttered over the course of his career. They have been collected here on the basis of their common subject: the desired return of Israel as an idealized united kingdom in the future.

3:6 During the reign of King Josiah This would be very early in the prophetic career of Jeremiah. See 1:2 and note. **faithless** The Hebrew word used here, *meshuvah*, derives from the Hebrew word *shuv*, meaning "to turn." Here (as in 2:19) it implies turning away. Compare v. 7 and note.

3:7 she would return to me Recalls the theme of the final oracle in the previous sequence, in which Yahweh compares himself to a jilted husband who has divorced his wife (compare Dt 24:1–4). In the previous oracle, the answer to the question "Will he return to her?" is an emphatic, rhetorical "No!" Here, there seems to be a possibility that Israel might return to Yahweh. **her unfaithful sister Judah** Polygamy was the norm among wealthy land owners and rulers in the ancient Near East, including Biblical Israel. In this oracle, Jeremiah tells the story of Yahweh's two adulterous wives and how each responds to the gravity of their infidelity. Compare Eze 23.

3:8 sent her away In Hosea 2:2, Yahweh threatens to divorce Israel for its adulterous ways; he drives Israel out of his house (Hos 9:15). Jeremiah echoes Hosea's prophetic description of Israel's exile in 722 BC.

3:9 the land See Jer 3:1 and note; 3:2 and note. **stone and wood** Recalls Jeremiah's amusing and ironic taunt in 2:27.

3:10 with all her heart The condition of the "heart" is an integral theme in Deuteronomy and frequently appears in the book of Jeremiah (compare Dt 4:9; 5:29; 6:5; 26:16). **pretense** Jeremiah refers to Josiah's religious reforms (see Jer 1:2 and note). While Josiah's official

for I am faithful,' declares the LORD,
'I will not be angry forever.
¹³ Only acknowledge your guilt —
you have rebelled against the LORD your
God,
you have scattered your favors to foreign
gods
under every spreading tree,
and have not obeyed me,'"
declares the LORD.

¹⁴"Return, faithless people," declares the LORD,
"for I am your husband. I will choose you — one
from a town and two from a clan — and bring you
to Zion. ¹⁵Then I will give you shepherds after my
own heart, who will lead you with knowledge and
understanding. ¹⁶In those days, when your numbers have increased greatly in the land," declares

the LORD, "people will no longer say, 'The ark of
the covenant of the LORD.' It will never enter their
minds or be remembered; it will not be missed,
nor will another one be made. ¹⁷At that time they
will call Jerusalem The Throne of the LORD, and
all nations will gather in Jerusalem to honor the
name of the LORD. No longer will they follow the
stubbornness of their evil hearts. ¹⁸In those days
the people of Judah will join the people of Israel,
and together they will come from a northern land
to the land I gave your ancestors as an inheritance.
¹⁹"I myself said,

"'How gladly would I treat you like my
children
and give you a pleasant land,
the most beautiful inheritance of any
nation.'

---

commitment to the "Yahweh-only" movement yields some fleeting positive results, in the end it is a fruitless and hollow gesture.
3:12 the north Refers to the former kingdom of Israel, not the encroaching threat from Babylon and its allies as in 1:14–15 and 2:14–15. At the time of Jeremiah's ministry, more than 100 years had elapsed since the capture of Samaria and Assyria's occupation of the northern kingdom. As part of its policy of assimilation, Assyria had transplanted its own citizens to Israel in great numbers in order to eliminate the Israelite population through interbreeding (2Ki 17:24–41). Consequently, the Judaeans regarded the present inhabitants north of Judah (formerly Israel) as impure "half breeds" at best and repulsive foreigners at worst (Ezr 4:1–6; Ne 4:1–3; 10:28–31; 13:23–30). Amid this hostility between northerners and southerners, Jeremiah hoped for a new, united kingdom as part of a highly anticipated future Messianic age (Jer 31:31–34). **Return, faithless Israel** The Hebrew phrase here translates literally as "return, turned away Israel." **declares the LORD** The prophetic phrase appears twice in this single verse, marking the presence of short, individual oracles strung together on the common theme of Yahweh's invitation for reconcilia-tion to the former northern kingdom. **I will not be angry forever** Echoes v. 5.
3:13 under every spreading tree Trees were common fertility symbols of the Canaanite goddess, Asherah. See 2:20 and note; 3:6; Isa 1:29.
3:14 Return, faithless people As in Jer 3:12, the concept conveyed here is "turning away." **I am your husband** The Hebrew word used here, *ba'alti*, denotes "your lord" or "your husband." It might be a wordplay on the Canaanite deity, Baal. **one from a town and two from a clan** Reflects the Hebrew poetic technique of number parallelism (compare Am 1:3; Hos 6:2; Dt 32:30; Pr 6:16). The parallel structure is inverted, with one being saved from the large population of a city and two being saved from the smaller unit of the clan. The poetic effect highlights the small size of the remnant drawn from different parts of society. **bring you to Zion** The word "Zion" appears frequently in Hebrew poetic literature as a designation of the city Jerusalem or the Jerusalem temple (Isa 4:3; 30:19; Mic 3:10; Zep 3:16; Zec 1:14; Ps 51:18).
3:15 shepherds after my own heart The leaders of Israel and the aristocracy are called *ro'im* ("shepherds")

in Jer 2:8. The reference to seeking Yahweh's heart con-trasts the rebelliousness of Judah, who did not return with her whole heart (see v. 10 and note). The metaphor of the shepherd as ideal ruler is also applied to the Davidic messiah (see Eze 34:23 and note).
3:16 In those days A prophecy of prediction; a hopeful expectation for the future restoration of Israel. **The ark of the covenant** Symbolic of Yahweh's presence and divine throne (see Nu 14:44; 2Ki 19:15). The ark of the covenant has special significance for Jeremiah because of its association with the ancient religious shrine at Shiloh and its connection to the priestly lineage of Eli living at Anathoth (see Jer 1:1 and note). Prior to the ark's permanent placement in Jerusalem, it was housed in the sanctuary at Shiloh under the care of Eli (Jos 18:1). In Shiloh, the ark was first described as the ark of Yahweh of the armies, enthroned on cherubim (1Sa 4:4). While the ark was there, the Shiloh sanctuary featured an annual festival that was celebrated through a massive pilgrimage (see Jdg 21:19; 1Sa 1:3). See the infographic "The Ark of the Covenant" on p. 412.
3:17 Throne of the LORD The ark of the covenant was considered the place where Yahweh sat like a king, receiving tribute and dispensing justice (1Ki 8:6; 2Ki 19:15). In Jeremiah's oracle of the future kingdom and new covenant of Yahweh, there would be no more need for a representative throne for God. Jerusalem itself would become the new dwelling place of God, who would permanently be in the midst of his people. **the name of the LORD** In Deuteronomy, the presence of Yahweh is manifested; his "name" dwells (Dt 12:11; 14:23; 16:6; 26:2). **their evil hearts** Jeremiah frequently uses this phrase, which recalls Dt 29:18, to describe the treach-erous disobedience of those who breached Yahweh's covenant (Jer 7:24; 9:14; 11:8). The familiar pattern from Deuteronomy and Jeremiah is repeated: A person's deepest thoughts and intentions are manifested in the "heart" (v. 10 and note).
3:18 people of Judah will join Intended to evoke thoughts of a hopeful reunification of the Davidic kingdom (see note on v. 12). **from a northern land** The kingdom of Israel disappeared after its war with Assyria, and the kingdom of Judah ended with the destruction of Jerusa-lem and the deportation of its citizens to Babylon. The reference here is to exiles returning from both Assyria and Babylon to the promised land.

I thought you would call me 'Father'
and not turn away from following me.
20 But like a woman unfaithful to her husband,
so you, Israel, have been unfaithful
to me,"
declares the LORD.

21 A cry is heard on the barren heights,
the weeping and pleading of the people of
Israel,
because they have perverted their ways
and have forgotten the LORD their God.

22 "Return, faithless people;
I will cure you of backsliding."

"Yes, we will come to you,
for you are the LORD our God.
23 Surely the idolatrous commotion on
the hills
and mountains is a deception;
surely in the LORD our God
is the salvation of Israel.
24 From our youth shameful gods have
consumed
the fruits of our ancestors' labor —
their flocks and herds,
their sons and daughters.
25 Let us lie down in our shame,
and let our disgrace cover us.
We have sinned against the LORD our God,
both we and our ancestors;
from our youth till this day
we have not obeyed the LORD our God."

4 "If you, Israel, will return,
then return to me,"
declares the LORD.

"If you put your detestable idols out of my
sight
and no longer go astray,
2 and if in a truthful, just and righteous way
you swear, 'As surely as the LORD lives,'
then the nations will invoke blessings
by him
and in him they will boast."

3 This is what the LORD says to the people of
Judah and to Jerusalem:

"Break up your unplowed ground
and do not sow among thorns.
4 Circumcise yourselves to the LORD,
circumcise your hearts,
you people of Judah and inhabitants of
Jerusalem,
or my wrath will flare up and burn like fire
because of the evil you have done —
burn with no one to quench it.

Disaster From the North

5 "Announce in Judah and proclaim in
Jerusalem and say:
'Sound the trumpet throughout
the land!'
Cry aloud and say:
'Gather together!
Let us flee to the fortified cities!'
6 Raise the signal to go to Zion!
Flee for safety without delay!
For I am bringing disaster from
the north,
even terrible destruction."

3:20 Israel Likely refers to the former northern kingdom of Israel.

3:21 on the barren heights This alludes to the pagan religious high places (see 2:20 and note; 3:2). It also might refer to the prostitute or the bartering nomad along the road.

3:22 you are the LORD In v. 21, the people have forgotten their God. This is the beginning of Israel's confession that forms vv. 22–25.

3:23 idolatrous commotion on the hills and mountains Likely alludes to the practice of cultic prostitution, which is forbidden in Dt 23:17. **a deception** Refers to the object of pagan worship on the high places (see v. 10 and note).

4:1 If you, Israel, will return Likely infers a condition: If the people of Israel would repent, they could return to Yahweh. **your detestable idols** The Hebrew word used here, *shiqquts*, refers to abominable religious practices. Repentance involves a clean break with idolatry. In 1Ki 11:5–7, the term describes the gods of Israel's neighbors. Referring to foreign deities with a word for repulsive objects was intended to discourage Israel from worshiping those deities. The word can refer to anything detestable from the perspective of proper Yahweh worship—anything violating standards of holiness, exclusive worship and ritual purity.

4:3 Break up your unplowed ground An agricultural metaphor urging Judah to prepare themselves to accept God's message and repent.

4:4 circumcise your hearts Circumcision was the sign of Israel's covenant devotion to Yahweh, the outward symbol that identified them as a people set apart. Physical circumcision was intended to be an external sign of a changed heart. The concept of circumcision of the heart highlights both the intent of the external circumcision and Israel's failure to actually give Yahweh the devotion represented by the act. Compare Dt 10:16; Ro 2:28–29.

4:5–18 Jeremiah warns of the impending judgment coming on Judah from the Babylonian invasion. He issues an appeal for Judah to repent and perhaps be spared from judgment (Jer 4:14).

4:5 Sound the trumpet throughout the land The trumpet was blown by the watchman, whose job was to warn the people of incoming danger. See 6:17; Eze 33:3–6. **fortified cities** A century before Jeremiah, the Assyrian king, Sennacherib, boasted that he had defeated 46 fortified cities in Judah. A list of fortified cities in Judah is given in 2Ch 11:5–12. According to Jeremiah, Lachish and Azekah are two of the last fortified cities to hold out against Babylon (see Jer 34:7

7 A lion has come out of his lair;
　　a destroyer of nations has set out.
He has left his place
　　to lay waste your land.
Your towns will lie in ruins
　　without inhabitant.
8 So put on sackcloth,
　　lament and wail,
for the fierce anger of the LORD
　　has not turned away from us.

9 "In that day," declares the LORD,
　　"the king and the officials will lose
　　　　heart,
the priests will be horrified,
　　and the prophets will be appalled."

10 Then I said, "Alas, Sovereign LORD! How completely you have deceived this people and Jerusalem by saying, 'You will have peace,' when the sword is at our throats!"

11 At that time this people and Jerusalem will be told, "A scorching wind from the barren heights in the desert blows toward my people, but not to winnow or cleanse; 12 a wind too strong for that comes from me. Now I pronounce my judgments against them."

13 Look! He advances like the clouds,
　　his chariots come like a whirlwind,
his horses are swifter than eagles.
　　Woe to us! We are ruined!

14 Jerusalem, wash the evil from your heart and
　　be saved.
How long will you harbor wicked
　　thoughts?
15 A voice is announcing from Dan,
　　proclaiming disaster from the hills of
　　　　Ephraim.
16 "Tell this to the nations,
　　proclaim concerning Jerusalem:
'A besieging army is coming from a distant
　　land,
raising a war cry against the cities
　　of Judah.
17 They surround her like men guarding
　　a field,
because she has rebelled against me,'"
　　　　　　　　　　　declares the LORD.
18 "Your own conduct and actions
　　have brought this on you.
This is your punishment.
　　How bitter it is!
　　How it pierces to the heart!"

19 Oh, my anguish, my anguish!
　　I writhe in pain.
Oh, the agony of my heart!
　　My heart pounds within me,
　　I cannot keep silent.
For I have heard the sound of the
　　trumpet;
　　I have heard the battle cry.

and note). See the infographic "The Lachish Letters" on p. 1228.

4:6 Zion Another name for Jerusalem, often signifying the Temple Mount. **disaster from the north** Babylon would attack from the north. See 1:13–16 and note on 1:14.

4:7 A lion has come out of his lair The invader from the north is metaphorically depicted as a lion, just as Babylon is in 2:15.

4:8 sackcloth Wearing sackcloth, a coarse material, symbolized despair, humiliation, mourning, sorrow and distress.

4:9 In that day Refers to the coming day of judgment and divine wrath. The prophets often interweave imagery of immediate judgment (the Babylonian invasion) with future, final eschatological judgment.

4:10 This verse records Jeremiah's emotional reaction to the divine revelation he has just received. Jeremiah's accusation of deceit on Yahweh's part appears blasphemous and dangerous, but it must be understood in the context of the false prophecies of peace that had been circulating in Yahweh's name (see 14:13; 23:16–17). Jeremiah is dismayed to realize that those comforting words were not from God.

4:11 A scorching wind Describes a harsh desert wind that is too strong for winnowing because both grain and chaff would be blown away. The metaphor implies that Yahweh's judgment will sweep over all people equally.

4:15 Dan The warning comes from the far northern part of Israel. The phrase "from Dan to Beersheba" was used to refer to all Israel, using the northernmost and south-ernmost cities to represent the whole (a figure of speech called a merism; e.g., 1Sa 3:20). The tribe of Dan was allotted territory just north of Judah and Jerusalem (Jos 19:40–46). When they were unable to conquer it (Jdg 1:34), they resettled to the northern Canaanite city of Laish (or Leshem) and renamed it "Dan" (see Jos 19:47; Jdg 18:1–31). **hills of Ephraim** The phrase here refers to the entire hill country in central Palestine occupied by Ephraim and extending north into territory assigned to the tribe of Manasseh. The geographic progression from Dan to the hills of Ephraim depicts the alarm being sounded throughout the land and the warning being rushed to Jerusalem. Fire signals were most likely used to pass on the warning (see v. 5 and note; 6:1).

4:19–31 In this passage, an unnamed speaker (or speakers) expresses great sorrow and anguish over the coming desolation of Judah. The voice could belong to Jeremiah himself, to Jerusalem personified, to Yahweh, or to the prophet as a representative for the community. The speaking voice might switch among those options, adding to the ambiguity to the passage.

4:19 my anguish, my anguish The word here refers to the internal organs, usually digestive organs such as intestines or stomach. Metaphorically, the term is used for one's inner being, especially the seat of emotions (Job 30:27). The metaphor is used in reference to Yahweh, describing his anguish over carrying out judgment (Jer 31:20; Isa 16:11), and in reference to Zion lamenting her losses (La 1:20).

20 Disaster follows disaster;
    the whole land lies in ruins.
In an instant my tents are destroyed,
    my shelter in a moment.
21 How long must I see the battle standard
    and hear the sound of the trumpet?

22 "My people are fools;
    they do not know me.
They are senseless children;
    they have no understanding.
They are skilled in doing evil;
    they know not how to do good."

23 I looked at the earth,
    and it was formless and empty;
and at the heavens,
    and their light was gone.
24 I looked at the mountains,
    and they were quaking;
all the hills were swaying.
25 I looked, and there were no people;
    every bird in the sky had flown away.
26 I looked, and the fruitful land was a desert;
    all its towns lay in ruins
    before the LORD, before his fierce anger.

27 This is what the LORD says:

"The whole land will be ruined,
    though I will not destroy it completely.
28 Therefore the earth will mourn
    and the heavens above grow dark,
because I have spoken and will not relent,
    I have decided and will not turn back."

29 At the sound of horsemen and archers
    every town takes to flight.
Some go into the thickets;
    some climb up among the rocks.

All the towns are deserted;
    no one lives in them.

30 What are you doing, you devastated one?
    Why dress yourself in scarlet
    and put on jewels of gold?
Why highlight your eyes with makeup?
    You adorn yourself in vain.
Your lovers despise you;
    they want to kill you.

31 I hear a cry as of a woman in labor,
    a groan as of one bearing her first child —
the cry of Daughter Zion gasping for breath,
    stretching out her hands and saying,
"Alas! I am fainting;
    my life is given over to murderers."

Not One Is Upright

5 "Go up and down the streets of Jerusalem,
    look around and consider,
    search through her squares.
If you can find but one person
    who deals honestly and seeks the truth,
    I will forgive this city.
2 Although they say, 'As surely as the LORD
        lives,'
    still they are swearing falsely."

3 LORD, do not your eyes look for truth?
    You struck them, but they felt no pain;
    you crushed them, but they refused
        correction.
They made their faces harder than stone
    and refused to repent.
4 I thought, "These are only the poor;
    they are foolish,
for they do not know the way of the LORD,
    the requirements of their God.

4:23–26 This short poem has strong literary overtones of the creation account from Ge 1, which focuses on Yahweh's role of bringing form and structure to the universe. The imagery of creation is reversed to describe divine judgment as an unmaking of the created order. The devastation from invasion brings an end to Judah's world and way of life. See the infographic "The Days of Creation" on p. 6.

4:23 formless and empty A rare combination of the uncommon terms *tohu* and *bohu*, alluding directly to the creation imagery in Genesis (see Ge 1:2 and note). Judgment may be seen as an undoing of creation, a return to primordial chaos (compare Isa 34:11 and note). **their light was gone** Alludes to Ge 1:2–3.
4:25 there were no people See Ge 1:26–27. **bird in the sky** See Ge 1:20–22.
4:26 the fruitful land was a desert See Ge 1:11.
4:30 dress yourself in scarlet Personified Jerusalem is depicted as a woman desperate to save her life by currying favor with her former lovers. The description is reminiscent of depictions of Israel as an unfaithful wife. Compare Eze 16:15–18.

4:31 Daughter Zion Refers to Jerusalem, which surrounded the temple and Mount Zion. The metaphor continues the personification of the city as a woman from Jer 4:30.

5:1–13 Jeremiah depicts a scene where he desperately tries to find one righteous person whose presence might persuade Yahweh to postpone punishment. The scene resembles Abraham's attempt to save Sodom and Gomorrah for the sake of 10 righteous people (Ge 18:22–33). As is the case with Abraham, Jeremiah is unable to find the required number of righteous people. Ezekiel later overturns this concept, arguing that the righteousness of a few would not save the many, who must be punished for their own sins (Eze 14:12–14).

5:3 correction The Hebrew words used here refer to instruction. Compare Pr 1:7. **They made their faces harder than stone** Discipline has inspired more stubbornness, not repentance. Compare Jer 2:30; Eze 3:8. **refused to repent** Jeremiah does not present Israel as passive or ignorant; they willfully and knowingly refuse to repent even in the face of judgment and punishment.

⁵ So I will go to the leaders
and speak to them;
surely they know the way of the LORD,
the requirements of their God."
But with one accord they too had broken off
the yoke
and torn off the bonds.
⁶ Therefore a lion from the forest will attack
them,
a wolf from the desert will ravage them,
a leopard will lie in wait near their towns
to tear to pieces any who venture out,
for their rebellion is great
and their backslidings many.

⁷ "Why should I forgive you?
Your children have forsaken me
and sworn by gods that are not gods.
I supplied all their needs,
yet they committed adultery
and thronged to the houses of prostitutes.
⁸ They are well-fed, lusty stallions,
each neighing for another man's wife.
⁹ Should I not punish them for this?"
declares the LORD.
"Should I not avenge myself
on such a nation as this?

¹⁰ "Go through her vineyards and ravage them,
but do not destroy them completely.
Strip off her branches,
for these people do not belong to the LORD.
¹¹ The people of Israel and the people of Judah
have been utterly unfaithful to me,"
declares the LORD.

¹² They have lied about the LORD;
they said, "He will do nothing!
No harm will come to us;
we will never see sword or famine.
¹³ The prophets are but wind
and the word is not in them;
so let what they say be done to them."

¹⁴ Therefore this is what the LORD God Almighty
says:

"Because the people have spoken these
words,
I will make my words in your mouth a fire
and these people the wood it consumes.
¹⁵ People of Israel," declares the LORD,
"I am bringing a distant nation against
you —
an ancient and enduring nation,
a people whose language you do
not know,
whose speech you do not understand.
¹⁶ Their quivers are like an open grave;
all of them are mighty warriors.
¹⁷ They will devour your harvests and food,
devour your sons and daughters;
they will devour your flocks and herds,
devour your vines and fig trees.
With the sword they will destroy
the fortified cities in which you trust.

¹⁸ "Yet even in those days," declares the LORD,
"I will not destroy you completely. ¹⁹ And when
the people ask, 'Why has the LORD our God done
all this to us?' you will tell them, 'As you have forsaken me and served foreign gods in your own
land, so now you will serve foreigners in a land
not your own.'

²⁰ "Announce this to the descendants of Jacob
and proclaim it in Judah:
²¹ Hear this, you foolish and senseless people,
who have eyes but do not see,
who have ears but do not hear:

5:5 had broken off the yoke Symbolic of Israel's rejection of Yahweh's rule through their rejection of his law. Compare the imagery of Jer 2:20. The image of a yoke is often used metaphorically to indicate a burden, obligation or slavery, so the image is positive in 2:20 where Yahweh reminds Israel that he broke the yoke of their slavery to Egypt (compare Lev 26:13). Jeremiah subtly undermines the usual expectation of the metaphor in a way that foreshadows the NT depiction of the law as a burden (Ac 15:10). Yahweh's real expectation was not external observance but internal obedience and true faith (Mic 6:8). The contrast comes out in Jesus' use of the metaphor in Mt 11:29–30.

5:6 a lion from the forest Compare the image of the enemy from the north as a lion in Jer 4:7. Judgment by attack from wild beasts was part of the punishment curses built into the Sinai covenant (see Lev 26:22; compare Eze 5:17; Dt 32:24). **their backslidings** The Hebrew word here means "turning" and uses the same root for turning or returning as words indicating repentance (see Jer 2:19). Jeremiah frequently plays on the ambiguity of this word for denoting both physical movement (toward or away) and religious inclination (toward or away).

5:7 the houses of prostitutes Symbolic of the temples of idols. See 2:20 and note.

5:10 do not destroy them completely Foreshadows Yahweh's plan to preserve a remnant (see 31:31–34). **these people do not belong to the LORD** Yahweh disavows ownership of Israel. He no longer recognizes them because of their apostasy.

5:13 prophets are but wind Their prophecies will be proven false — empty words with no effect.

5:14–31 Yahweh declares judgment against Israel for its complacency and its foolish assurance that he would not act. The proclamation has three parts: describing the invasion and exile (vv. 14–19), asserting Yahweh's sovereignty and Israel's foolishness not to fear him (vv. 20–24) and reiterating Israel's sin with an emphasis on social injustice and hypocritical worship (vv. 25–31).

5:15 a distant nation Namely, Babylon. See note on 1:3.
5:18 I will not destroy you completely God will preserve a remnant.
5:21 who have eyes but do not see Compare Isa 6:9–10.

22 Should you not fear me?" declares the LORD.
  "Should you not tremble in my presence?
I made the sand a boundary for the sea,
  an everlasting barrier it cannot cross.
The waves may roll, but they cannot prevail;
  they may roar, but they cannot cross it.
23 But these people have stubborn and
    rebellious hearts;
  they have turned aside and gone away.
24 They do not say to themselves,
  'Let us fear the LORD our God,
who gives autumn and spring rains in season,
  who assures us of the regular weeks of
    harvest.'
25 Your wrongdoings have kept these away;
  your sins have deprived you of good.

26 "Among my people are the wicked
  who lie in wait like men who snare birds
  and like those who set traps to catch
    people.
27 Like cages full of birds,
  their houses are full of deceit;
they have become rich and powerful
28 and have grown fat and sleek.
Their evil deeds have no limit;
  they do not seek justice.
They do not promote the case of the
    fatherless;
  they do not defend the just cause of the
    poor.
29 Should I not punish them for this?"
  declares the LORD.

"Should I not avenge myself
  on such a nation as this?

30 "A horrible and shocking thing
  has happened in the land:
31 The prophets prophesy lies,
  the priests rule by their own
    authority,
and my people love it this way.
  But what will you do in the end?

Jerusalem Under Siege

6 "Flee for safety, people of Benjamin!
  Flee from Jerusalem!
Sound the trumpet in Tekoa!
  Raise the signal over Beth Hakkerem!
For disaster looms out of the north,
  even terrible destruction.
2 I will destroy Daughter Zion,
  so beautiful and delicate.
3 Shepherds with their flocks will come
    against her;
  they will pitch their tents around her,
  each tending his own portion."

4 "Prepare for battle against her!
  Arise, let us attack at noon!
But, alas, the daylight is fading,
  and the shadows of evening grow
    long.
5 So arise, let us attack at night
  and destroy her fortresses!"

5:22 Should you not fear me Yahweh's power over creation and acts of subduing the forces of chaos should inspire reverence, not apathy. **I made the sand a boundary** Jeremiah uses poetic creation language that echoes parts of Job, Proverbs, Isaiah and Psalms. Yahweh's active restraint of the sea is a common motif in creation poetry (see Ps 104:9; Job 38:10–11; Pr 8:29). The sea (called *yam* in Hebrew) symbolized chaos and disorder. In Canaanite mythology, the god Yam ("Sea") battled against the storm god, Baal, for supremacy. OT descriptions of Yahweh taming the sea or restraining stormy waters likely bear traces of this ancient myth, symbolizing the struggle to bring order from chaos. The depth to which this mythological imagery was ingrained in the Israelite worldview is reflected in the disciples' reaction to Jesus calming a storm on the Sea of Galilee in Mt 8:23–27. See note on Ge 1:2.
5:24 who gives autumn and spring rains in season Yahweh's role as provider through the agricultural cycle is highlighted as further reason for Israel to respect and worship him. Canaanite religion attributed the control of the rains to Baal.
5:28 they do not seek justice Jeremiah now connects the wicked of Jer 5:26 with the leaders of Israelite society. Criticizing the leaders for failing to observe their obligations for social justice is a common prophetic indictment. See Isa 1:16–23; Am 4:1–5. See note on Ex 22:21–27.
5:31 The prophets prophesy lies The religious leaders have failed just as thoroughly as the civil leaders (see Jer 5:26–28).

6:1–30 The end referenced in 5:31 is now described as imminent and in progress. Yahweh's judgment is poured out on all of Judah (v. 11) as the prophet warns them to flee from the coming invasion (v. 1).
6:1 people of Benjamin Jeremiah warns his own tribe to flee Jerusalem first. **trumpet** The ram's horn was often used as a trumpet to signal a warning. See 1Ki 1:34 and note. **Tekoa** A town in the highlands of southern Judah, about 10 miles south of Jerusalem. Tekoa was one of the fortified cities of Judah (2Ch 11:6; see note on Jer 4:5) and the hometown of the prophet Amos (see Am 1:1). The location had strategic importance as a military outpost protecting Jerusalem. The city was at an elevation of about 2,800 feet, with a view of Bethlehem, the Mount of Olives, the Jordan Valley and the Transjordan. **Beth Hakkerem** A city on a hill south of Jerusalem, probably modern Ramat Rachel (Khirbet es-Sallah) located three miles southwest of Jerusalem. The location would have been well-suited for a fire signal like the one at Lachish or Azekah (see note on Jer 34:7). **disaster looms out of the north** Invasions by Mesopotamian empires always came from the north (see 1:14 and note).
6:2 Daughter Zion A metaphor describing Jerusalem. See note on 4:31.
6:3 Shepherds with their flocks A metaphorical depiction of the invading armies and their commanders.
6:5 let us attack at night A night attack was unusual; Jeremiah's contrast between a noon and a night attack simply underscores Jerusalem's weakness. A night attack would be just as effective as a daytime attack.

⁶This is what the LORD Almighty says:

"Cut down the trees
　and build siege ramps against Jerusalem.
This city must be punished;
　it is filled with oppression.
⁷As a well pours out its water,
　so she pours out her wickedness.
Violence and destruction resound in her;
　her sickness and wounds are ever
　　before me.
⁸Take warning, Jerusalem,
　or I will turn away from you
and make your land desolate
　so no one can live in it."

⁹This is what the LORD Almighty says:

"Let them glean the remnant of Israel
　as thoroughly as a vine;
pass your hand over the branches again,
　like one gathering grapes."

¹⁰To whom can I speak and give warning?
　Who will listen to me?
Their ears are closed[a]
　so they cannot hear.
The word of the LORD is offensive to them;
　they find no pleasure in it.
¹¹But I am full of the wrath of the LORD,
　and I cannot hold it in.

"Pour it out on the children in the street
　and on the young men gathered together;
both husband and wife will be caught in it,
　and the old, those weighed down with
　　years.
¹²Their houses will be turned over to others,
　together with their fields and their wives,

when I stretch out my hand
　against those who live in the land,"
　　　　　　　　declares the LORD.
¹³"From the least to the greatest,
　all are greedy for gain;
prophets and priests alike,
　all practice deceit.
¹⁴They dress the wound of my people
　as though it were not serious.
'Peace, peace,' they say,
　when there is no peace.
¹⁵Are they ashamed of their detestable
　　conduct?
No, they have no shame at all;
　they do not even know how to blush.
So they will fall among the fallen;
　they will be brought down when I punish
　　them,"
　　　　　　　　says the LORD.

¹⁶This is what the LORD says:

"Stand at the crossroads and look;
　ask for the ancient paths,
ask where the good way is, and walk in it,
　and you will find rest for your souls.
But you said, 'We will not walk in it.'
¹⁷I appointed watchmen over you and said,
　'Listen to the sound of the trumpet!'
But you said, 'We will not listen.'
¹⁸Therefore hear, you nations;
　you who are witnesses,
　observe what will happen to them.
¹⁹Hear, you earth:
　I am bringing disaster on this people,
　the fruit of their schemes,

---

a 10 Hebrew *uncircumcised*

6:6 LORD Almighty The use of this title reinforces Yahweh's role as commander-in-chief over the invading foreign army that is following his will by besieging and destroying Judah. **Cut down the trees** Presumably to make battering rams for the siege. The battering ram was a long wooden beam that was usually metal tipped and protected by a frame on four or six wheels. The battering ram was only effective when brought close to the city wall. **build siege ramps against Jerusalem** A fortified city was usually surrounded by a dry moat and protected by a steep rampart. Invading armies built a ramp or mound to give the battering ram access to the wall. See note on Eze 4:2.

6:9 the remnant of Israel Refers to those who have survived the judgment. The implication here, however, is not escape and safety, but judgment returning even for those who thought they had escaped.

6:10 Their ears are closed The Hebrew text uses circumcision language to describe ears that are not open to hearing Yahweh's message. The metaphor of circumcision is more commonly used of the uncircumcised heart (Jer 4:4). Compare 7:26; Ac 7:51.

6:14 Peace, peace The basic message of the false prophets was that no judgment or disaster was imminent. Jeremiah repeats this in Jer 8:11 and has a similar senti-

ment in 14:13 and 23:17. Compare Eze 13:10; Mic 3:5; and note on Jer 4:10.

6:15 their detestable conduct The Hebrew word used here, *to'evah*, refers to anything that might be culturally or socially offensive, but the term often carries a specifically religious sense. Anything that offends Yahweh's sense of purity and holiness can be *to'evah* and jeopardize Israel's relationship to Yahweh. References to "abominations" or "detestable practices" can include idolatrous religious practices, but the context here is ambiguous, as the previous verses emphasize economic injustice and false prophecy (vv. 13–14). An abomination threatened the very existence of Israel, since breaking the covenant with Yahweh brought on the destructive judgments outlined in the covenant curses (see Dt 28).

6:16 ancient paths A metaphor for the proper way to worship Yahweh according to the laws of the Pentateuch. Compare Jer 18:15. **We will not walk** The people's refusal is direct and explicit; it is open rebellion against following Yahweh.

6:17 watchmen A metaphor for the prophets. See note on Eze 3:17.

6:18 hear, you nations Yahweh calls on the nations to witness his indictment and judgment against Israel.

6:19 my law The Hebrew word used here, *torah*, generally

because they have not listened to my words
and have rejected my law.
20 What do I care about incense from Sheba
or sweet calamus from a distant land?
Your burnt offerings are not acceptable;
your sacrifices do not please me."

21 Therefore this is what the LORD says:

"I will put obstacles before this people.
Parents and children alike will stumble
over them;
neighbors and friends will perish."

22 This is what the LORD says:

"Look, an army is coming
from the land of the north;
a great nation is being stirred up
from the ends of the earth.
23 They are armed with bow and spear;
they are cruel and show no mercy.
They sound like the roaring sea
as they ride on their horses;
they come like men in battle formation
to attack you, Daughter Zion."

24 We have heard reports about them,
and our hands hang limp.
Anguish has gripped us,
pain like that of a woman in labor.
25 Do not go out to the fields
or walk on the roads,

for the enemy has a sword,
and there is terror on every side.
26 Put on sackcloth, my people,
and roll in ashes;
mourn with bitter wailing
as for an only son,
for suddenly the destroyer
will come upon us.

27 "I have made you a tester of metals
and my people the ore,
that you may observe
and test their ways.
28 They are all hardened rebels,
going about to slander.
They are bronze and iron;
they all act corruptly.
29 The bellows blow fiercely
to burn away the lead with fire,
but the refining goes on in vain;
the wicked are not purged out.
30 They are called rejected silver,
because the LORD has rejected them."

False Religion Worthless

7 This is the word that came to Jeremiah from
the LORD: 2 "Stand at the gate of the LORD's
house and there proclaim this message:

"'Hear the word of the LORD, all you people of
Judah who come through these gates to worship
the LORD. 3 This is what the LORD Almighty, the God
of Israel, says: Reform your ways and your actions,

---

refers to "teaching" or "instruction" but can take on
the more specialized sense of God's law. Compare Pr
1:8; Dt 30:10.
6:20 incense An aromatic tree resin imported from Arabia
and highly valued as a spice and perfume. Frankincense
was used in grain offerings (Lev 2:1–2) and was the
primary ingredient in the incense that was burned in
Yahweh's temple (Ex 30:34). The rejection of Israel's
empty religious ritualism is a prominent theme in the
prophetic literature (see Isa 1:11–17; Am 5:21–23; Mic
6:6–8). **Sheba** An important trading center in southwest
Arabia. **sweet calamus** Likely the same aromatic cane
mentioned in Ex 30:23. The sweet cane would have been
imported from India, Arabia or Ethiopia, probably also by
way of caravans from Sheba. **Your burnt offerings** The
most common type of sacrifice in ancient Israel. In this
offering, the entire animal was burned on the altar. See
note on Lev 1:3. **your sacrifices** The term here denotes
an animal sacrifice in which only the inedible parts of
the animal were totally burned, the rest being consumed
by the participants in the sacrifice. Burnt offerings and
sacrifices are often paired, likely to indicate the totality
of animal sacrifices (compare Hos 6:6).
6:26 Put on sackcloth A coarse garment symbolic of
mourning. See note on Jer 4:8. **roll in ashes** Also part
of rituals for mourning. See Eze 27:30.
6:28 bronze and iron The pairing of bronze and iron
often symbolizes strength (see Jer 1:18; 15:12), but
here it denotes Israel's stubbornness.
6:29 to burn away the lead with fire Refining silver
from lead ore and testing silver for quality involved heating
large amounts of lead. The lead would draw impurities out

of the silver, or the lead would separate from the silver so
that it could be skimmed off. If the ore contained metals
other than lead and silver, the silver would end up an
unusable mixture. These useless byproducts from failed
refining are likely what is meant by rejected silver in v. 30.
**6:29 refining goes on in vain; the wicked are not
purged out** The refining was designed to remove the
wicked from the midst of the repentant righteous. The
process failed because none repented.
6:30 rejected silver The prophets frequently depict Yahweh's judgment as a refining fire, with his people coming
through the process as dross, the rejected byproduct.
See Isa 1:22; Eze 22:19–20.

7:1–15 This passage is known as Jeremiah's "temple sermon" because he is commanded to deliver the
message in the temple gate. The narrative section of
Jeremiah (mainly Jer 26–45) picks up with this event
in 26:1–15, albeit with an abbreviated version of the
message (26:4–6). The general message carries deep
theological relevance for the community and reflects a
time prior to the destruction and judgment of 586 BC
(see chs. 5–6). The scene in ch. 26 is dated to the
reign of Jehoiakim (609–597 BC). Jeremiah highlights
the people's failure to keep the letter and intent of the
law, and he declares that their confidence in Yahweh's
protection is a false hope since they have broken the
covenant. See the timeline "Life of Jeremiah" on p. 1170.

7:2 the gate of the LORD's house A high traffic area.
Jeremiah's audience would be everyone coming and
going from the temple for worship or sacrifice.

and I will let you live in this place. ⁴Do not trust in deceptive words and say, "This is the temple of the LORD, the temple of the LORD, the temple of the LORD!" ⁵If you really change your ways and your actions and deal with each other justly, ⁶if you do not oppress the foreigner, the fatherless or the widow and do not shed innocent blood in this place, and if you do not follow other gods to your own harm, ⁷then I will let you live in this place, in the land I gave your ancestors for ever and ever. ⁸But look, you are trusting in deceptive words that are worthless.

⁹"'Will you steal and murder, commit adultery and perjury,ᵃ burn incense to Baal and follow other gods you have not known, ¹⁰and then come and stand before me in this house, which bears my Name, and say, "We are safe" — safe to do all these detestable things? ¹¹Has this house, which bears my Name, become a den of robbers to you? But I have been watching! declares the LORD.

¹²"'Go now to the place in Shiloh where I first made a dwelling for my Name, and see what I did to it because of the wickedness of my people Israel. ¹³While you were doing all these things, declares the LORD, I spoke to you again and again, but you did not listen; I called you, but you did not answer.

¹⁴Therefore, what I did to Shiloh I will now do to the house that bears my Name, the temple you trust in, the place I gave to you and your ancestors. ¹⁵I will thrust you from my presence, just as I did all your fellow Israelites, the people of Ephraim.'

¹⁶"So do not pray for this people nor offer any plea or petition for them; do not plead with me, for I will not listen to you. ¹⁷Do you not see what they are doing in the towns of Judah and in the streets of Jerusalem? ¹⁸The children gather wood, the fathers light the fire, and the women knead the dough and make cakes to offer to the Queen of Heaven. They pour out drink offerings to other gods to arouse my anger. ¹⁹But am I the one they are provoking? declares the LORD. Are they not rather harming themselves, to their own shame?

²⁰"Therefore this is what the Sovereign LORD says: My anger and my wrath will be poured out on this place — on man and beast, on the trees of the field and on the crops of your land — and it will burn and not be quenched.

²¹"This is what the LORD Almighty, the God of Israel, says: Go ahead, add your burnt offerings to your other sacrifices and eat the meat yourselves!

ᵃ 9 Or *and swear by false gods*

7:3 LORD Almighty See note on 6:6. **I will let you live in this place** Reflects the conditional nature of the covenant between Yahweh and the Israelites: They possessed the land as long as they kept the covenant law (see Dt 28; Lev 26).

7:4 the temple of the LORD The repetition might reflect a liturgical formula, a protective incantation or an emphatic declaration. Triple repetition appears in Babylonian incantation texts and is a common feature of liturgy. The triple repetition in Isa 6:3 ("holy, holy, holy") seems to have a superlative or emphatic effect.

7:6 the foreigner, the fatherless or the widow Symbolic of the most vulnerable of society.

7:9 you steal and murder, commit adultery and perjury The accusations reflect behaviors prohibited in the Ten Commandments. See Dt 5:6–21.

7:10 this house The temple.

7:11 a den of robbers Alludes to the stealing noted in Jer 7:9. This phrase is used in the Gospels to highlight the injustice taking place in the temple (see Mt 21:13). Jesus quotes Isa 56:7 and Jer 7:11.

7:12 Shiloh where I first made a dwelling for my Name Shiloh was located in the hill country of Ephraim, north of Bethel. It was the main religious center for Israel before the monarchy. Shiloh served as a central gathering point for Israel during the conquest prior to the allotment of the land among the 12 tribes (see Jos 18:1; 19:51). The tabernacle was set up there and the ark of the covenant, symbolizing Yahweh's presence among his people, was kept there. Shiloh remained the central place for worshiping Yahweh through the time of the judges. **see what I did to it** The religious center at Shiloh apparently was overrun after the Battle of Aphek (1Sa 4:1–11), when the Philistines defeated Israel and captured the ark of the covenant. The disaster is portrayed as judgment against the priestly family of Eli for failing to properly carry out their responsibilities toward Yahweh (1Sa 3:10–15).

7:15 just as I did all your fellow Israelites Judah would experience the same fate as the northern kingdom of Israel. See 2Ki 17:6.

7:16–29 The prophets usually were mediators of a message from God to the people, but they also could intercede with God on behalf of the people. Moses exemplifies the role of mediator in Ex 32:10–14. Yahweh explicitly commands Jeremiah not to intercede on the people's behalf because it is too late to turn back the judgment (compare Jer 11:14; 14:11; 15:1); their idolatry is too great (v. 18).

7:16 do not pray for this people Praying to God on behalf of others was a common part of a prophet's ministry. See Ge 20:7; Nu 21:7; 1Sa 12:19.

7:18 The children gather wood Idol-worship is a family affair, as children, father and mother are all involved. They likely practice Canaanite fertility rituals designed to invoke divine blessing on their crops to produce a good harvest. Ancients thought of divine blessing as a force that they could tap by observing the proper rituals at the right time. Yahweh's anger at the people's worship practices stems from their belief that he could be mechanically manipulated alongside these foreign deities and that they expected him to bless them even when their behavior did not warrant it. **make cakes to offer to the Queen of Heaven** The Hebrew word used here, *kawwanim*, is borrowed from the ancient Akkadian language; it refers to a cake used in the worship of the goddess Ishtar. Offering cakes to deities was common in Mesopotamia. Many cake molds representing a goddess were found at Mari in northeast Syria. Ishtar, who may be the queen of heaven referenced here, was the principal goddess of ancient Mesopotamia. In the OT and Canaanite texts, she is known as Astarte or Ashtoreth (see 2Ki 23:13).

7:21 add your burnt offerings to your other sacrifices See Jer 6:20 and note. The multiplication of sacrifices is pointless without an attitude of obedience.

22For when I brought your ancestors out of Egypt and spoke to them, I did not just give them commands about burnt offerings and sacrifices, 23but I gave them this command: Obey me, and I will be your God and you will be my people. Walk in obedience to all I command you, that it may go well with you. 24But they did not listen or pay attention; instead, they followed the stubborn inclinations of their evil hearts. They went backward and not forward. 25From the time your ancestors left Egypt until now, day after day, again and again I sent you my servants the prophets. 26But they did not listen to me or pay attention. They were stiff-necked and did more evil than their ancestors.'

27"When you tell them all this, they will not listen to you; when you call to them, they will not answer. 28Therefore say to them, 'This is the nation that has not obeyed the LORD its God or responded to correction. Truth has perished; it has vanished from their lips.

29"'Cut off your hair and throw it away; take up a lament on the barren heights, for the LORD has rejected and abandoned this generation that is under his wrath.

The Valley of Slaughter

30"'The people of Judah have done evil in my eyes, declares the LORD. They have set up their detestable idols in the house that bears my Name and have defiled it. 31They have built the high places of Topheth in the Valley of Ben Hinnom to burn their sons and daughters in the fire — something I did not command, nor did it enter my mind. 32So beware, the days are coming, declares the LORD, when people will no longer call it Topheth or the Valley of Ben Hinnom, but the Valley of Slaughter, for they will bury the dead in Topheth until there is no more room. 33Then the carcasses of this people will become food for the birds and the wild animals, and there will be no one to frighten them away. 34I will bring an end to the sounds of joy and gladness and to the voices of bride and bridegroom in the towns of Judah and the streets of Jerusalem, for the land will become desolate.

8 "'At that time, declares the LORD, the bones of the kings and officials of Judah, the bones of the priests and prophets, and the bones of the people of Jerusalem will be removed from their graves. 2They will be exposed to the sun and the moon and all the stars of the heavens, which they have loved and served and which they have followed and consulted and worshiped. They will not be gathered up or buried, but will be like dung lying on the ground. 3Wherever I banish them, all the survivors of this evil nation will prefer death to life, declares the LORD Almighty.'

7:25 my servants the prophets Jeremiah is the latest of a long tradition of prophets whom Yahweh sent to warn Israel to turn back to him.

7:26 did more evil than their ancestors The history of Israel is succinctly described as one of continual decline and disobedience. Despite the occasional renewals of righteousness, the overall trajectory was continually away from Yahweh.

7:29 Cut off your hair A sign of mourning.

7:30—8:3 Yahweh condemns the mixed worship going on in his temple as well as the Canaanite practice of child sacrifice, which Judah apparently adopted and conducted in the Valley of Ben Hinnom just outside Jerusalem. The message of judgment pronounces a sentence of death on all of Judah (8:1).

7:30 their detestable idols Manasseh had placed Canaanite idols and altars in the temple (see 2Ki 21:2–7). Josiah destroyed all of them during his religious reforms (see 2Ki 23:4–20). **house that bears my Name** The temple.

7:31 the Valley of Ben Hinnom This site of ritual child sacrifice also is mentioned in Jer 19 and 2Ki 23:10. Also called "Gehenna," the valley curved along the south and west sides of Jerusalem (see Jos 15:8 and note). In literature from the Second Temple period, including the NT, this valley represents the site of the future, final eschatological judgment on the wicked. The infamy of this valley as a place of child sacrifice allowed Jeremiah to simply allude to it as "the valley" in Jer 2:23. Isaiah likely is making the same allusion in Isa 57:5–6. Worship of the Canaanite deity Molek is connected with child sacrifice in Lev 18:21. Archaeological evidence for the Canaanite practice has been found at the site of ancient Carthage, a Phoenician colony in north Africa.

7:32 the Valley of Slaughter The valley where the people of Judah massacred their children in defiance of Yahweh will be the site of their massacre in judgment.

7:33 food for the birds Part of the curse for breaking the covenant (see Dt 28:26). Proper burial was important in the ancient Near East, based on beliefs of the ongoing relationship between the living and the dead. Exposure of corpses was a common practice for the Assyrians, who would exhume the corpses of leaders when the vassals violated the treaty. The act was believed to disrupt the rest of their spirits and deprive them of the offerings given to the cult of the dead.

8:1 the bones of the kings and officials of Judah See note on Jer 7:33. Exposure of the bones defiled the valley from ritual use. Compare 2Ki 23:16, where Josiah exhumes the tombs around the Bethel shrine and burns the bones on the altar.

8:2 all the stars of the heavens The sun, moon and stars were associated with divine beings in the ancient Near East. The prophets of Yahweh often condemned worship of the planets, the sun, the moon and the stars (astral worship; see 2Ki 17:16; 21:5). The Babylonians developed the practice of using celestial phenomena as divine signs or omens for predicting and directing human destiny. Later Judaism adapted the well-developed astrology of the Hellenistic period (derived from the older Babylonian versions), equating the 12 sons of Jacob (the tribes of Israel) with the 12 signs of the zodiac. This practice was reconciled with Jewish monotheism by considering the stars and their movements as simply part of Yahweh's creation through which he could communicate human destiny if he chose.

8:3 all the survivors Surviving the massacre is depicted as a fate worse than death. **LORD Almighty** See note on Jer 6:6.

Sin and Punishment

⁴"Say to them, 'This is what the LORD says:

"'When people fall down, do they not get up?
    When someone turns away, do they not
        return?
⁵ Why then have these people turned away?
    Why does Jerusalem always turn away?
They cling to deceit;
    they refuse to return.
⁶ I have listened attentively,
    but they do not say what is right.
None of them repent of their wickedness,
    saying, "What have I done?"
Each pursues their own course
    like a horse charging into battle.
⁷ Even the stork in the sky
    knows her appointed seasons,
and the dove, the swift and the thrush
    observe the time of their migration.
But my people do not know
    the requirements of the LORD.

⁸"'How can you say, "We are wise,
    for we have the law of the LORD,"
when actually the lying pen of the scribes
    has handled it falsely?
⁹ The wise will be put to shame;
    they will be dismayed and trapped.
Since they have rejected the word of the
        LORD,
    what kind of wisdom do they have?
¹⁰ Therefore I will give their wives to other men
    and their fields to new owners.
From the least to the greatest,
    all are greedy for gain;
prophets and priests alike,
    all practice deceit.
¹¹ They dress the wound of my people
    as though it were not serious.
"Peace, peace," they say,
    when there is no peace.

¹² Are they ashamed of their detestable conduct?
    No, they have no shame at all;
    they do not even know how to blush.
So they will fall among the fallen;
    they will be brought down when they are
        punished,
                        says the LORD.

¹³ "'I will take away their harvest,
                        declares the LORD.
    There will be no grapes on the vine.
There will be no figs on the tree,
    and their leaves will wither.
What I have given them
    will be taken from them.ᵃ'"

¹⁴ Why are we sitting here?
    Gather together!
Let us flee to the fortified cities
    and perish there!
For the LORD our God has doomed us to
        perish
    and given us poisoned water to drink,
    because we have sinned against him.
¹⁵ We hoped for peace
    but no good has come,
for a time of healing
    but there is only terror.
¹⁶ The snorting of the enemy's horses
    is heard from Dan;
at the neighing of their stallions
    the whole land trembles.
They have come to devour
    the land and everything in it,
    the city and all who live there.

¹⁷ "See, I will send venomous snakes among
        you,
    vipers that cannot be charmed,
    and they will bite you,"
                        declares the LORD.

ᵃ 13 The meaning of the Hebrew for this sentence is uncertain.

8:4–17 The people's failure to repent and impending judgment are common recurring themes in Jeremiah. The central section of this passage in vv. 10–12 repeats many of the details of judgment expressed previously in 6:12–15. Rejecting the word of Yahweh is the ultimate act of foolishness, but the people believed they were following what their prophets and priests had presented as the word of Yahweh (vv. 8–9). Jeremiah rejects their appeal, asserting that those prophets and scribes had not really heard from God.

8:8 we have the law of the LORD Jeremiah rebukes Israel for claiming to have the law since they don't obey it or follow Yahweh (v. 7). **lying pen of the scribes** Jeremiah accuses the scribes—the official teachers and transmitters of the written word of God—of passing on a corrupted interpretation of the divine message.

8:13 no grapes on the vine The metaphor of Judah as a vineyard with no fruit echoes the imagery of 5:10 and

Isa 5:1–7. **There will be no figs on the tree** Compare Jesus' parable of the Barren Fig Tree in Lk 13:6–9. There should have been fruit, but there was not, so the fig tree and vineyard should be destroyed to make room for a plant or field that truly will bear fruit.

8:14 poisoned water A metaphor for shortening the siege. A city under siege could not last long without a protected water supply. If the water supply was tainted, the city would have to surrender.

8:16 Dan The northernmost city in Israel. See note on Jer 4:15.

8:17 venomous snakes among you, vipers that cannot be charmed Metaphors for the invading Babylonians. Snakes were feared in the ancient world, and ancient Near Eastern literature contains many incantations against snakes and snakebites. The implication here is that those types of incantations are ineffective against these snakes. Judah can do nothing to guard against this imminent attack.

¹⁸ You who are my Comforterᵃ in sorrow,
  my heart is faint within me.
¹⁹ Listen to the cry of my people
  from a land far away:
  "Is the Lord not in Zion?
  Is her King no longer there?"

  "Why have they aroused my anger with their
    images,
  with their worthless foreign idols?"

²⁰ "The harvest is past,
  the summer has ended,
  and we are not saved."

²¹ Since my people are crushed, I am crushed;
  I mourn, and horror grips me.
²² Is there no balm in Gilead?
  Is there no physician there?
  Why then is there no healing
  for the wound of my people?

9 ᵇ ¹ Oh, that my head were a spring of water
  and my eyes a fountain of tears!
I would weep day and night
  for the slain of my people.
² Oh, that I had in the desert
  a lodging place for travelers,
so that I might leave my people
  and go away from them;
for they are all adulterers,
  a crowd of unfaithful people.

³ "They make ready their tongue
  like a bow, to shoot lies;
it is not by truth
  that they triumphᶜ in the land.
They go from one sin to another;
  they do not acknowledge me,"
        declares the Lord.
⁴ "Beware of your friends;
  do not trust anyone in your clan.

For every one of them is a deceiver,ᵈ
  and every friend a slanderer.
⁵ Friend deceives friend,
  and no one speaks the truth.
They have taught their tongues to lie;
  they weary themselves with sinning.
⁶ Youᵉ live in the midst of deception;
  in their deceit they refuse to
    acknowledge me,"
        declares the Lord.

⁷ Therefore this is what the Lord Almighty says:

"See, I will refine and test them,
  for what else can I do
because of the sin of my people?
⁸ Their tongue is a deadly arrow;
  it speaks deceitfully.
With their mouths they all speak cordially to
    their neighbors,
but in their hearts they set traps for them.
⁹ Should I not punish them for this?"
        declares the Lord.
"Should I not avenge myself
  on such a nation as this?"

¹⁰ I will weep and wail for the mountains
  and take up a lament concerning the
    wilderness grasslands.
They are desolate and untraveled,
  and the lowing of cattle is not heard.
The birds have all fled
  and the animals are gone.

¹¹ "I will make Jerusalem a heap of ruins,
  a haunt of jackals;
and I will lay waste the towns of Judah
  so no one can live there."

ᵃ 18 The meaning of the Hebrew for this word is uncertain.
ᵇ In Hebrew texts 9:1 is numbered 8:23, and 9:2-26 is numbered
9:1-25.   ᶜ 3 Or lies; / they are not valiant for truth   ᵈ 4 Or a
deceiving Jacob   ᵉ 6 That is, Jeremiah (the Hebrew is singular)

8:19 my people An expression for Judah used primarily
in Jeremiah and Lamentations. **Zion** Refers to Jerusalem.
See note on 3:14. **her King** Refers to Yahweh, Zion's
divine king.
8:22 Gilead A region on the eastern side of the Jordan
River allotted to the tribes of Reuben, Manasseh and
Gad. The area was well forested and fertile, producing
grapes, olives and fruit trees. The area was also known
for its balm, an aromatic tree resin (see Ge 37:25).
9:1 my eyes a fountain of tears The strong emotion of
this verse has often been attributed to Jeremiah, giving
him his reputation as the "weeping prophet." However,
the poetic language leaves the speaker ambiguous.
Regardless of the referent, the action signifies Yahweh's
rejection of his people through his agent, the prophet,
or through removing his presence.
**9:3 They make ready their tongue like a bow, to
shoot** A metaphor depicting speech as a dangerous
weapon. **declares the Lord** Marks the preceding as
divine speech. This phrase is the only clue to the identity
of the speaker in 8:18—9:3.

9:4–26 Accusations of idolatry, commands to mourn and
pronouncements of judgment are interwoven in a series
of oracles that either begin or end with "says Yahweh" or
"thus says Yahweh." The theme of testing, lament and
punishment run throughout. Most of the text is likely
attributable to Yahweh via the prophet, but the identity
of the speaker is ambiguous at times (e.g., vv. 10,12).
9:7 Lord Almighty See note on 6:6. **I will refine and
test them** The judgment of Yahweh is metaphorically
described as a refining fire. Compare 6:27; Isa 1:25.
9:10 weep and wail for the mountains Yahweh describes his grief over the judgment that he must carry
out against the land of Israel. **a lament** A lament was
used to express mourning or distress over the loss of
an individual, community or city.
9:11 I will make Jerusalem a heap of ruins Depicting
the city as a ruin or desolate waste was a common motif
for the aftermath of divine judgment. Compare Isa 25:2.
a haunt of jackals Compare Isa 34:13. The jackal was
a scavenger, and its presence symbolizes desolation.

¹²Who is wise enough to understand this? Who has been instructed by the LORD and can explain it? Why has the land been ruined and laid waste like a desert that no one can cross?

¹³The LORD said, "It is because they have forsaken my law, which I set before them; they have not obeyed me or followed my law. ¹⁴Instead, they have followed the stubbornness of their hearts; they have followed the Baals, as their ancestors taught them." ¹⁵Therefore this is what the LORD Almighty, the God of Israel, says: "See, I will make this people eat bitter food and drink poisoned water. ¹⁶I will scatter them among nations that neither they nor their ancestors have known, and I will pursue them with the sword until I have made an end of them."

¹⁷This is what the LORD Almighty says:

"Consider now! Call for the wailing women to
    come;
  send for the most skillful of them.
¹⁸Let them come quickly
    and wail over us
till our eyes overflow with tears
    and water streams from our eyelids.
¹⁹The sound of wailing is heard from Zion:
  'How ruined we are!
  How great is our shame!
We must leave our land
    because our houses are in ruins.'"

²⁰Now, you women, hear the word of
    the LORD;
  open your ears to the words of his mouth.
Teach your daughters how to wail;
    teach one another a lament.
²¹Death has climbed in through our windows
    and has entered our fortresses;
it has removed the children from the streets
    and the young men from the public
      squares.

²²Say, "This is what the LORD declares:

"'Dead bodies will lie
    like dung on the open field,
like cut grain behind the reaper,
    with no one to gather them.'"

²³This is what the LORD says:

"Let not the wise boast of their wisdom
    or the strong boast of their strength
    or the rich boast of their riches,
²⁴but let the one who boasts boast about
    this:
  that they have the understanding to
      know me,
that I am the LORD, who exercises kindness,
    justice and righteousness on earth,
  for in these I delight,"

                declares the LORD.

²⁵"The days are coming," declares the LORD, "when I will punish all who are circumcised only in the flesh— ²⁶Egypt, Judah, Edom, Ammon, Moab and all who live in the wilderness in distant places.[a] For all these nations are really uncircumcised, and even the whole house of Israel is uncircumcised in heart."

God and Idols

10:12-16pp — Jer 51:15-19

10 Hear what the LORD says to you, people of Israel. ²This is what the LORD says:

"Do not learn the ways of the nations
    or be terrified by signs in the heavens,
    though the nations are terrified by them.
³For the practices of the peoples are
      worthless;
  they cut a tree out of the forest,
    and a craftsman shapes it with his chisel.

---

[a] 26 Or *wilderness and who clip the hair by their foreheads*

9:14 the Baals Usually a reference to the chief Canaanite deity, Baal Hadad, but here it is used in the plural as generic term for Canaanite idols.

9:15 poisoned water A metaphor for judgment. See note on Jer 8:14.

9:16 I will scatter them among nations The penalty for breaking the covenant (Lev 26:33; Dt 28:64).

9:17 the wailing women Yahweh is hiring professional mourners to lament over Zion, reflecting a common custom in the ancient Near East.

9:19 Zion Jerusalem. See note on Jer 4:6.

9:22 will lie like dung on the open field There will be so many dead that their bodies will be left unburied. See 7:33 and note.

9:24 that they have the understanding to know me Knowing what Yahweh wants and doing it is the essence of true wisdom and proper worship. Yahweh wants his people to emulate him in practicing kindness, justice and righteousness. Israel had fundamentally failed to emulate these aspects of God's character.

9:25 who are circumcised only in the flesh Transformation of the heart was more important than physical change. See 4:4.

10:2 Do not learn the ways of the nations Specifically, their religious practices. Compare 7:18. **signs in the heavens** Alludes to the practice of astrology. See note on 8:2.

10:3 a craftsman shapes it The prophets emphasized the ridiculous reality behind idol-worship. Someone cuts down a tree, fashions an image, overlays it with gold, nails it down and calls it a god. Compare Isa 40:19; 41:7; 44:9–20. The belief system of the ancient idol-worshiper was slightly more nuanced than the prophets' depiction. Similar to the OT account of Yahweh's presence entering the temple (see 1Ki 8:10–11), ancients believed that the presence of the deity came into the idol—if the god chose to favor the worshiper. Spells, incantations and other magical practices were intended to manipulate the deity to enter the idol; other rituals were designed to care for the deity and its image. The control over the

4 They adorn it with silver and gold;
    they fasten it with hammer and nails
      so it will not totter.
5 Like a scarecrow in a cucumber field,
    their idols cannot speak;
they must be carried
    because they cannot walk.
Do not fear them;
    they can do no harm
      nor can they do any good."

6 No one is like you, LORD;
    you are great,
    and your name is mighty in power.
7 Who should not fear you,
    King of the nations?
    This is your due.
Among all the wise leaders of the nations
    and in all their kingdoms,
    there is no one like you.

8 They are all senseless and foolish;
    they are taught by worthless wooden idols.
9 Hammered silver is brought from Tarshish
    and gold from Uphaz.
What the craftsman and goldsmith have made
    is then dressed in blue and purple —
    all made by skilled workers.
10 But the LORD is the true God;
    he is the living God, the eternal King.
When he is angry, the earth trembles;
    the nations cannot endure his wrath.

11 "Tell them this: 'These gods, who did not make the heavens and the earth, will perish from the earth and from under the heavens.'" [a]

12 But God made the earth by his power;
    he founded the world by his wisdom
    and stretched out the heavens by his
      understanding.
13 When he thunders, the waters in the heavens
    roar;
    he makes clouds rise from the ends of the
      earth.
He sends lightning with the rain
    and brings out the wind from his
      storehouses.
14 Everyone is senseless and without
      knowledge;
    every goldsmith is shamed by his idols.
The images he makes are a fraud;
    they have no breath in them.
15 They are worthless, the objects of mockery;
    when their judgment comes, they will
      perish.
16 He who is the Portion of Jacob is not like
      these,
    for he is the Maker of all things,
including Israel, the people of his
      inheritance —
    the LORD Almighty is his name.

Coming Destruction

17 Gather up your belongings to leave the land,
    you who live under siege.
18 For this is what the LORD says:
    "At this time I will hurl out
    those who live in this land;

a 11 The text of this verse is in Aramaic.

---

deity through ritual and magic represents a concept of deity that is inconsistent with worship of Yahweh, who cannot be compelled to act based on human expressions of worship.

10:5 they must be carried Mesopotamians dressed, washed and fed their idols. On special occasions, they would transport an idol from its home city to another city to honor the celebration for another deity. See note on Isa 46:1–13.

10:6 No one is like you, LORD The ultimate purpose of prophetic attacks against idolatry is to assert the uniqueness of Yahweh. Compare Isa 40:18–19.

10:9 Hammered silver is brought from Tarshish A distant trading port; likely a Phoenician colony in Spain. See note on Jnh 1:3. **gold from Uphaz** The location of Uphaz is unknown. It is mentioned again in Da 10:5, also in connection with high-quality gold. **blue and purple** The high cost of purple dye made wearing the color too expensive for any but the most wealthy, so it came to be associated with the high status of royalty and divinity.

10:11 The poetry in Jer 10:10 and 10:12 is interrupted by this prose verse in Aramaic. Most of the OT is written in ancient Hebrew, with a few extended passages in Aramaic. While the switch to Aramaic here is unexpected and unusual, the chiasm (an inverted parallel pattern, like A-B-B-A) in the sentence suggests that it might convey a popular saying, using wordplay that would not have been possible in Hebrew. Aramaic was in use at the time as an international diplomatic language (see Isa 36:11) and was known by the educated elite of Judah.

10:12 made the earth by his power The poetry in Jer 10:12–16 is repeated in 51:15–19.

10:13 He sends lightning with the rain While Biblical poetry commonly appropriates Semitic storm god imagery for Yahweh, the idea that he maintains storehouses of water for rain, hail and snow is not a common ancient Near Eastern motif. It is a common Biblical motif, however. The imagery closely echoes Dt 28:12; Ps 33:7; 135:7; and Job 38:22.

10:14 senseless and without knowledge Recalls the sentiment of Jer 9:12,23, where abandoning Yahweh is the ultimate folly, and true wisdom comes from recognizing and acknowledging his sovereignty. **shamed by his idols** Compare Isa 42:17. **no breath in them** The *ruach* is the animating life force absent from the idols. See note on Eze 37:5.

10:16 He who is the Portion of Jacob Refers to Yahweh himself as the Israelites' inheritance. **LORD Almighty** A title identifying God as leader of the heavenly armies — and also ultimately in authority over earthly armies — See note on Jer 6:6.

I will bring distress on them
    so that they may be captured."

[19] Woe to me because of my injury!
    My wound is incurable!
    Yet I said to myself,
      "This is my sickness, and I must endure it."
[20] My tent is destroyed;
    all its ropes are snapped.
    My children are gone from me and are no more;
    no one is left now to pitch my tent
    or to set up my shelter.
[21] The shepherds are senseless
    and do not inquire of the Lord;
  so they do not prosper
    and all their flock is scattered.
[22] Listen! The report is coming —
    a great commotion from the land of the
      north!
  It will make the towns of Judah desolate,
    a haunt of jackals.

Jeremiah's Prayer

[23] Lord, I know that people's lives are not their
    own;
    it is not for them to direct their steps.

[24] Discipline me, Lord, but only in due
      measure —
    not in your anger,
    or you will reduce me to nothing.
[25] Pour out your wrath on the nations
    that do not acknowledge you,
    on the peoples who do not call on your name.
  For they have devoured Jacob;
    they have devoured him completely
    and destroyed his homeland.

The Covenant Is Broken

11 This is the word that came to Jeremiah from the Lord: [2] "Listen to the terms of this covenant and tell them to the people of Judah and to those who live in Jerusalem. [3] Tell them that this is what the Lord, the God of Israel, says: 'Cursed is the one who does not obey the terms of this covenant — [4] the terms I commanded your ancestors when I brought them out of Egypt, out of the iron-smelting furnace.' I said, 'Obey me and do everything I command you, and you will be my people, and I will be your God. [5] Then I will fulfill the oath I swore to your ancestors, to give them a land flowing with milk and honey' — the land you possess today."

10:19–21 Jeremiah's poetic style is heavy on figurative use of the first person, a feature that has led many interpreters to equate the first-person voice of the poetic laments with the prophet himself. Here, the most straightforward understanding of the speaker is Zion (Jerusalem) personified, a prominent feature in Lamentations (La 1:11b–16,17–22; 2:11,20–22).

10:19 Woe to me because of my injury Jerusalem expresses grief over her loss.
10:21 The shepherds are senseless Judah's leaders are metaphorically depicted as shepherds who should be caring for their flock, the people. **do not inquire of the Lord** Compare 1Ki 22:5, where Jehoshaphat of Judah is portrayed as the faithful king who wants to inquire of Yahweh as opposed to Ahab, who does not want to hear the true message. On Jehoshaphat, see 2Ch 17:3. The Hebrew verb *darash* is often used with the sense of consulting divine or supernatural powers (e.g., 1Ki 22:5; 2Ki 1:3; 1Sa 28:7; Eze 14:3).
10:22 land of the north See note on Jer 6:1. The motif of disaster from the north also appears in 1:13–15; 4:6; and 6:1–9. **a haunt of jackals** The presence of scavengers like jackals indicates desolation. Compare 9:11; Isa 34:13.

10:23–25 Now the prophet himself appears to respond to the disaster envisioned in Jer 10:22 by offering an intercessory prayer on behalf of Israel.

10:25 Pour out your wrath on the nations The language resembles imprecatory psalms that ask Yahweh for vengeance on enemies. See note on Ps 109:1–31.

11:1—20:18 This section of the book contains prophetic pronouncements against Judah that reflect the themes of impending military defeat and subsequent devastation of the land of Judah. The theme of conflict unifies the oracles, manifesting in two ways: as the individual conflict of the prophet, reflected in his response to his role and message; and as the communal conflict of Israel, reflected in the focus on impending national doom. At the most basic level, the conflict expresses the spiritual and social aspects of the broken relationship between Israel and Yahweh. Despite the eclectic mix of material in these chapters — poetic laments, prose narrative, oracles of judgment and oracles of salvation — the theme of lament and complaint dominates the section, which features laments from Jeremiah, Yahweh and the people of Judah.

11:1–23 This passage refers back to the exodus and Yahweh's selection of Israel as a people. The concept of the covenant explains the nature of Israel's broken relationship with Yahweh, since both sides had obligations to keep for the covenant to remain in force. The disaster that comes on the Israelites can be explained as the inevitable result of their failure to keep the covenant.

11:2 this covenant Refers back to the Mosaic covenant, as indicated by the allusions to the exodus in Jer 11:4,7. The ancient covenant treaty format — found in Assyrian and Hittite vassal treaties and reflected in the structure of Deuteronomy — is reproduced in miniature in the summary of the covenant found in vv. 3–13. The covenant consisted of a historical prologue recounting Yahweh's acts of salvation on their behalf (vv. 4–5) and the legal details — what they had to do to keep the covenant (vv. 3,7), blessings for keeping the covenant (v. 5) and curses for breaking it (vv. 3,8–13).
11:4 iron-smelting furnace A direct allusion to Dt 4:20, connecting the historical summary here with the historical prologue from the Deuteronomic version of the covenant. Compare also 1Ki 8:51. **Obey me** Reminiscent of the language of covenant blessing for Lev 26:3. **I will be your God** Compare Lev 26:12.

I answered, "Amen, LORD."

⁶The LORD said to me, "Proclaim all these words in the towns of Judah and in the streets of Jerusalem: 'Listen to the terms of this covenant and follow them. ⁷From the time I brought your ancestors up from Egypt until today, I warned them again and again, saying, "Obey me." ⁸But they did not listen or pay attention; instead, they followed the stubbornness of their evil hearts. So I brought on them all the curses of the covenant I had commanded them to follow but that they did not keep.'"

⁹Then the LORD said to me, "There is a conspiracy among the people of Judah and those who live in Jerusalem. ¹⁰They have returned to the sins of their ancestors, who refused to listen to my words. They have followed other gods to serve them. Both Israel and Judah have broken the covenant I made with their ancestors. ¹¹Therefore this is what the LORD says: 'I will bring on them a disaster they cannot escape. Although they cry out to me, I will not listen to them. ¹²The towns of Judah and the people of Jerusalem will go and cry out to the gods to whom they burn incense, but they will not help them at all when disaster strikes. ¹³You, Judah, have as many gods as you have towns; and the altars you have set up to burn incense to that shameful god Baal are as many as the streets of Jerusalem.'

¹⁴"Do not pray for this people or offer any plea or petition for them, because I will not listen when they call to me in the time of their distress.

¹⁵ "What is my beloved doing in my temple
     as she, with many others, works out her
          evil schemes?
  Can consecrated meat avert your
          punishment?
  When you engage in your wickedness,
     then you rejoice.ᵃ"

¹⁶ The LORD called you a thriving olive tree
     with fruit beautiful in form.
  But with the roar of a mighty storm
     he will set it on fire,
     and its branches will be broken.

¹⁷The LORD Almighty, who planted you, has decreed disaster for you, because the people of both Israel and Judah have done evil and aroused my anger by burning incense to Baal.

Plot Against Jeremiah

¹⁸Because the LORD revealed their plot to me, I knew it, for at that time he showed me what they were doing. ¹⁹I had been like a gentle lamb led to the slaughter; I did not realize that they had plotted against me, saying,

"Let us destroy the tree and its fruit;
     let us cut him off from the land of the
          living,
     that his name be remembered no more."
²⁰ But you, LORD Almighty, who judge
          righteously
     and test the heart and mind,
  let me see your vengeance on them,
     for to you I have committed my cause.

²¹Therefore this is what the LORD says about the people of Anathoth who are threatening to kill you, saying, "Do not prophesy in the name of the LORD or you will die by our hands" — ²²therefore this is what the LORD Almighty says: "I will punish them. Their young men will die by the sword, their sons and daughters by famine. ²³Not even a remnant will be left to them, because I will bring disaster on the people of Anathoth in the year of their punishment."

Jeremiah's Complaint

12 You are always righteous, LORD,
     when I bring a case before you.
  Yet I would speak with you about your
          justice:
     Why does the way of the wicked prosper?
     Why do all the faithless live at ease?

ᵃ 15 Or Could consecrated meat avert your punishment? / Then you would rejoice

---

11:5 the oath I swore to your ancestors Yahweh connects the earlier promises he made to the patriarchs to give their descendants the land of Canaan (see Ge 15:7; 17:8; 26:4; 28:13) with the promise to bring Israel out of Egypt (Ex 3:8). **a land flowing with milk and honey** An image of fertility and abundance applied to the land of Canaan, especially in connection with the exodus and conquest narratives (see Ex 3:8; 13:5; Dt 6:3).
11:13 Baal The chief Canaanite deity and the main opponent of Yahweh in the Biblical accounts of ancient Israel's idolatry. See 1Ki 16:31–32.
11:14 Do not pray for this people See note on Jer 7:16. Yahweh reminds Jeremiah to abstain from interceding on behalf of the people (compare 14:11). The reference to "this people" instead of "my people" now that the covenant has been broken and revoked.
11:15 my beloved Subtly invokes the image of Israel

as the unfaithful wife. **consecrated meat** It is too late to start offering sacrifices to Yahweh; the punishment is inevitable. They sealed their fate with too many offerings to Baal (v. 17).
11:17 LORD Almighty See note on 6:6.

11:18–23 The first lament has two parts: Jeremiah's complaint over an apparent attempt on his life, and Yahweh's response. Based on the response, the antagonists were the people of Jeremiah's hometown in Anathoth, possibly even his own family.

11:19 like a gentle lamb led to the slaughter Compare Isa 53:7.
11:20 let me see your vengeance on them See note on Jer 10:25. The request for punishment of one's enemies is a common feature of individual laments.
11:21 the people of Anathoth Jeremiah's hometown. See 1:1 and note.

2 You have planted them, and they have taken
root;
they grow and bear fruit.
You are always on their lips
but far from their hearts.
3 Yet you know me, LORD;
you see me and test my thoughts about
you.
Drag them off like sheep to be butchered!
Set them apart for the day of slaughter!
4 How long will the land lie parched
and the grass in every field be withered?
Because those who live in it are wicked,
the animals and birds have perished.
Moreover, the people are saying,
"He will not see what happens to us."

God's Answer

5 "If you have raced with men on foot
and they have worn you out,
how can you compete with horses?
If you stumble[a] in safe country,
how will you manage in the thickets by[b]
the Jordan?
6 Your relatives, members of your own
family—
even they have betrayed you;
they have raised a loud cry against you.
Do not trust them,
though they speak well of you.

7 "I will forsake my house,
abandon my inheritance;
I will give the one I love
into the hands of her enemies.

8 My inheritance has become to me
like a lion in the forest.
She roars at me;
therefore I hate her.
9 Has not my inheritance become to me
like a speckled bird of prey
that other birds of prey surround and
attack?
Go and gather all the wild beasts;
bring them to devour.
10 Many shepherds will ruin my vineyard
and trample down my field;
they will turn my pleasant field
into a desolate wasteland.
11 It will be made a wasteland,
parched and desolate before me;
the whole land will be laid waste
because there is no one who cares.
12 Over all the barren heights in the desert
destroyers will swarm,
for the sword of the LORD will devour
from one end of the land to the other;
no one will be safe.
13 They will sow wheat but reap thorns;
they will wear themselves out but gain
nothing.
They will bear the shame of their harvest
because of the LORD's fierce anger."

14 This is what the LORD says: "As for all my wicked neighbors who seize the inheritance I gave my people Israel, I will uproot them from their lands and I will uproot the people of Judah from among them. 15 But after I uproot them, I will again have

a 5 Or *you feel secure only*   b 5 Or *the flooding of*

12:1–6 Jeremiah's second complaint or lament addresses the apparent injustice of a world where the wicked prosper while the righteous suffer. Jeremiah affirms Yahweh's righteousness but implies that he suffers unjustly for the wickedness of the people (v. 3). Yahweh's response (vv. 5–6) is a reminder that he never promised Jeremiah an easy path, and that things are about to get worse.

12:1 Why does the way of the wicked prosper? Why do all the faithless live at ease Jeremiah has been announcing God's judgment on Judah, yet the judgment has not come, and injustice and oppression continue. Numerous Biblical writers echoed Jeremiah's frustration over the worldly success of the wicked, in part because one of the teaching methods of OT ethics (e.g., in Proverbs and other Wisdom texts) was to encourage obedience by promising rewards and to discourage disobedience by warning of destruction. Compare Job 12:6; 21:7–15; Ps 92:7; Mal 3:15.

12:3 and test my thoughts about you By asking Yahweh to test him, Jeremiah is setting himself up as the righteous sufferer in contrast with the prosperous wicked (Jer 12:1). **Drag them off like sheep** The prophet asks Yahweh to set things right and punish the wicked.

12:6 Your relatives, members of your own family The lament in 11:18–23 alludes to an attempt on Jeremiah's life originating with the people of Anathoth, his hometown. Yahweh's reference to treachery on the part of his own family may be connected to that earlier attempt.

12:7–13 Yahweh's lament over his people subtly responds to Jeremiah's complaint over his personal suffering; he emphasizes that he, too, has suffered great loss. In fact, his loss is greater than Jeremiah's because he was compelled by Israel's sin to hand them over for judgment.

12:8 I hate her Conveys rejection because of unreciprocated love (see Ge 29:31). Compare Hos 9:15.

12:10 shepherds The metaphor of the shepherds could point to the failure of Judah's leaders (see Jer 10:21 and note) or the invasion of Babylon (see 6:3 and note).

12:12 the sword of the LORD The invaders are Yahweh's agents for judgment. Compare Isa 10:5–6.

12:14–17 Jeremiah adds an oracle of salvation, offering a glimmer of hope to Judah and a glimpse at the future judgment to come against Israel's enemies. Even though Yahweh may use foreign nations to judge Israel, he will judge those nations in turn for their wickedness (compare Isa 10:12; 14:22–25).

compassion and will bring each of them back to their own inheritance and their own country. [16]And if they learn well the ways of my people and swear by my name, saying, 'As surely as the LORD lives'—even as they once taught my people to swear by Baal—then they will be established among my people. [17]But if any nation does not listen, I will completely uproot and destroy it," declares the LORD.

A Linen Belt

13 This is what the LORD said to me: "Go and buy a linen belt and put it around your waist, but do not let it touch water." [2]So I bought a belt, as the LORD directed, and put it around my waist.

[3]Then the word of the LORD came to me a second time: [4]"Take the belt you bought and are wearing around your waist, and go now to Perath[a] and hide it there in a crevice in the rocks." [5]So I went and hid it at Perath, as the LORD told me.

[6]Many days later the LORD said to me, "Go now to Perath and get the belt I told you to hide there." [7]So I went to Perath and dug up the belt and took it from the place where I had hidden it, but now it was ruined and completely useless.

[8]Then the word of the LORD came to me: [9]"This is what the LORD says: 'In the same way I will ruin the pride of Judah and the great pride of Jerusalem.

[10]These wicked people, who refuse to listen to my words, who follow the stubbornness of their hearts and go after other gods to serve and worship them, will be like this belt—completely useless! [11]For as a belt is bound around the waist, so I bound all the people of Israel and all the people of Judah to me,' declares the LORD, 'to be my people for my renown and praise and honor. But they have not listened.'

Wineskins

[12]"Say to them: 'This is what the LORD, the God of Israel, says: Every wineskin should be filled with wine.' And if they say to you, 'Don't we know that every wineskin should be filled with wine?' [13]then tell them, 'This is what the LORD says: I am going to fill with drunkenness all who live in this land, including the kings who sit on David's throne, the priests, the prophets and all those living in Jerusalem. [14]I will smash them one against the other, parents and children alike, declares the LORD. I will allow no pity or mercy or compassion to keep me from destroying them.'"

Threat of Captivity

[15]Hear and pay attention,
do not be arrogant,
for the LORD has spoken.

[a] 4 Or possibly *to the Euphrates*; similarly in verses 5-7

12:16 they learn well the ways of my people Salvation is offered to the nations if they will acknowledge Yahweh's sovereignty. Compare Isa 2:2–3.

13:1–11 Jeremiah performs a symbolic action designed to illustrate how Israel's once intimate relationship with Yahweh had been spoiled. See the table "Symbolic Actions of the Prophets" on p. 1195.

13:1 a linen belt The use of linen is significant since priestly garments were to be made only of linen (Lev 16:4). If this article of clothing is an undergarment, the symbolism may suggest a level of intimacy. The Hebrew word used here, *ezor*, is often understood as a loincloth or undergarment, but it also could refer to a type of girdle or sash worn around the waist to hold other garments in place. Other Biblical uses of *ezor* suggest it was an outwardly visible piece of clothing (Eze 23:15; 2Ki 1:8). **do not let it touch water** The command to keep the garment out of water is enigmatic and open to a variety of interpretations. Most likely, the command means that the garment should be left in its original condition. This would enhance the contrast between the condition before and after Jeremiah's act of placing the garment where it could be ruined.

13:4 Perath The location of the Euphrates (*perath*) affects the understanding of Jeremiah's action. Normally, the Hebrew word used here, *perath*, refers to the Euphrates River, which was more than 350 miles away—a journey of six to eight weeks (one way). The location was symbolic of the Babylonians as those who would ruin the land of Judah. While a straightforward reading of this passage suggests that Jeremiah traveled several months

to the Euphrates and back and repeated the trip again later, a literal journey is not necessary to understand the symbolism. A prophetic sign-act was symbolic, and even locations could be symbolized instead of literally visited (see Eze 4:1–3). Jeremiah is fond of wordplay, so Parah (a site four miles northeast of Anathoth) could have been a symbolic location for the Euphrates (*perath*). **13:9 the pride of Judah** The garment is revealed to be symbolic of Judah.

13:11 a belt is bound around the waist See note on Jer 13:1. The analogy here comparing the garment with the prestige and glory of the one wearing it suggests it is an externally visible garment, like a sash around the waist. **people for my renown** Yahweh had invested a great deal in Israel as his people, and his reputation was closely tied to their fate. See 33:9.

13:12–14 An oracle of judgment, introduced by an enigmatic saying about jars of wine, is pronounced against the leaders of Judah and all the people. The saying likely expresses a popular proverb or aphorism.

13:12 Every wineskin should be filled with wine The same consonants denote the Hebrew words for "jar" (*nevel*) and "fool" (*naval*). The wordplay recasts the proverb as "every fool will be filled with wine." This is either a comment on the triteness of the proverb or a critique of complacency and misplaced confidence.

13:15–27 This oracle first calls for repentance (vv. 15–17). It then addresses the downfall of the king (vv. 18–19) and highlights how Judah's idolatry has led to destruction (vv. 20–27). See the timeline "Life of Jeremiah" on p. 1170.

¹⁶Give glory to the LORD your God
before he brings the darkness,
before your feet stumble
on the darkening hills.
You hope for light,
but he will turn it to utter darkness
and change it to deep gloom.
¹⁷If you do not listen,
I will weep in secret
because of your pride;
my eyes will weep bitterly,
overflowing with tears,
because the LORD's flock will be taken
captive.

¹⁸Say to the king and to the queen mother,
"Come down from your thrones,

for your glorious crowns
will fall from your heads."
¹⁹The cities in the Negev will be shut up,
and there will be no one to open them.
All Judah will be carried into exile,
carried completely away.

²⁰Look up and see
those who are coming from the north.
Where is the flock that was entrusted to you,
the sheep of which you boasted?
²¹What will you say when the LORD sets over you
those you cultivated as your special allies?
Will not pain grip you
like that of a woman in labor?
²²And if you ask yourself,
"Why has this happened to me?" —

13:18 the king and to the queen mother See 2Ki 24:8. Jehoiachin was taken into exile in 597 BC. Jeremiah likely is alluding to the loss of royal power at that time. Most of the ruling class went into exile with Jehoiachin. **13:19 Negev** The region south of Jerusalem, the southern extent of Judah's territory.

13:20 those who are coming from the north The invaders. See Jer 1:14 and note. **the flock** Alludes to the metaphor of the king as shepherd and the people as his flock. See 10:21 and note.
13:22 Why has this happened to me Judah is depicted as playing innocent, questioning the disaster as unjust

---

Symbolic Actions of the Prophets

ACTION	REFERENCE
Isaiah walks naked through Jerusalem	Isa 20:2-6
Jeremiah's ruined loincloth	Jer 13:1-11
Jeremiah does not marry	Jer 16:1-9
Jeremiah goes to the potter's house	Jer 18:1-12
Jeremiah breaks a jar in the Valley of Ben Hinnom	Jer 19:1-13
Jeremiah wears a yoke	Jer 27:1-22
Jeremiah buys a field	Jer 32:1-44
Jeremiah offers wine to the Rekabites	Jer 35:1-19
Jeremiah hides stones	Jer 43:8-13
Seraiah throws Jeremiah's scroll into the Euphrates	Jer 51:59-64
Ezekiel acts out the siege and destruction of Jerusalem	Eze 4:1—5:17
Ezekiel acts out the exile	Eze 12:1-16
Ezekiel eats nervously	Eze 12:17-20
Ezekiel does not mourn his wife	Eze 24:15-27
Ezekiel uses sticks to symbolize the reunification of Israel	Eze 37:15-28
Hosea marries Gomer	Hos 1:2-3
Hosea redeems his wife	Hos 3:1-5
Zechariah crowns Joshua the high priest	Zec 6:9-15
Zechariah acts out the role of shepherd	Zec 11:4-17

it is because of your many sins
  that your skirts have been torn off
  and your body mistreated.
²³ Can an Ethiopian[a] change his skin
  or a leopard its spots?
Neither can you do good
  who are accustomed to doing evil.

²⁴ "I will scatter you like chaff
  driven by the desert wind.
²⁵ This is your lot,
  the portion I have decreed for you,"
                                          declares the Lord,
"because you have forgotten me
  and trusted in false gods.
²⁶ I will pull up your skirts over your face
  that your shame may be seen —
²⁷ your adulteries and lustful neighings,
  your shameless prostitution!
I have seen your detestable acts
  on the hills and in the fields.
Woe to you, Jerusalem!
  How long will you be unclean?"

Drought, Famine, Sword

14 This is the word of the Lord that came to
Jeremiah concerning the drought:

² "Judah mourns,
  her cities languish;
they wail for the land,
  and a cry goes up from Jerusalem.
³ The nobles send their servants for water;
  they go to the cisterns
  but find no water.
They return with their jars unfilled;
  dismayed and despairing,
  they cover their heads.

⁴ The ground is cracked
  because there is no rain in the land;
the farmers are dismayed
  and cover their heads.
⁵ Even the doe in the field
  deserts her newborn fawn
  because there is no grass.
⁶ Wild donkeys stand on the barren heights
  and pant like jackals;
their eyes fail
  for lack of food."

⁷ Although our sins testify against us,
  do something, Lord, for the sake of your
    name.
For we have often rebelled;
  we have sinned against you.
⁸ You who are the hope of Israel,
  its Savior in times of distress,
why are you like a stranger in the land,
  like a traveler who stays only a night?
⁹ Why are you like a man taken by surprise,
  like a warrior powerless to save?
You are among us, Lord,
  and we bear your name;
  do not forsake us!

¹⁰ This is what the Lord says about this people:

"They greatly love to wander;
  they do not restrain their feet.
So the Lord does not accept them;
  he will now remember their wickedness
  and punish them for their sins."

¹¹ Then the Lord said to me, "Do not pray for
the well-being of this people. ¹² Although they

a 23 Hebrew *Cushite* (probably a person from the upper Nile region)

---

and inexplicable. Yahweh's reply indicates they should have known better and should have expected retribution. **that your skirts have been torn off** A symbol of humiliation and public shame. Being unclothed or stripped metaphorically depicts them being exposed to the judgment of God. See Isa 47:3; Na 3:5; La 1:8.
13:24 I will scatter you like chaff A standard depiction of judgment by exile. See Lev 26:33.
13:27 your adulteries and lustful neighings, your shameless prostitution! I have seen your detestable acts Imagery of idolatry and sexual infidelity are intertwined. Compare Eze 16:1–58 and note on Eze 16:15.

14:1–12 Yahweh's judgment against Judah is metaphorically depicted as a drought affecting the entire land. Jeremiah describes the conditions of the drought (Jer 14:1–6) and prays to Yahweh, acknowledging the people's sin and begging for deliverance (vv. 7–9). Yahweh responds that they've brought this punishment on themselves and that it's too late to change (vv. 10–12).

14:1 the drought One of the punishments for breaking the covenant (see Dt 28:22–24; Lev 26:18–19). Jeremiah has already likened national distress to a severe

drought (see Jer 3:3; 12:4). Ancients understood drought as a sign of divine displeasure.
14:3 cover their heads A symbol of communal lament and mourning.
14:7 our sins testify against us This communal lament could record the people's genuine repentance, but it more likely shows Jeremiah interceding on their behalf. See v. 11 and note.
14:8 its Savior in times of distress Under the terms of the covenant, Yahweh should save. The implicit criticism in this appeal ignores the fact that the covenant was broken by the people when they disobeyed Yahweh and turned to other gods (see 11:14 and note).
14:9 like a warrior powerless to save The standard explanation for defeat in the ancient Near East was that the local deity was not strong enough to save his people. Compare Eze 8:12 and note. In this regard, the prophets' assertions that Yahweh had allowed the Israelites' defeat and even orchestrated it to judge them was an unorthodox concept (see Isa 59:1). **bear your name** Appeals to Yahweh's reputation and reminds him that he will look weak for not saving his people. See previous note; Eze 36:12 and note.
14:11 Do not pray for the well-being See Jer 7:16

fast, I will not listen to their cry; though they offer burnt offerings and grain offerings, I will not accept them. Instead, I will destroy them with the sword, famine and plague."

¹³But I said, "Alas, Sovereign LORD! The prophets keep telling them, 'You will not see the sword or suffer famine. Indeed, I will give you lasting peace in this place.'"

¹⁴Then the LORD said to me, "The prophets are prophesying lies in my name. I have not sent them or appointed them or spoken to them. They are prophesying to you false visions, divinations, idolatries[a] and the delusions of their own minds. ¹⁵Therefore this is what the LORD says about the prophets who are prophesying in my name: I did not send them, yet they are saying, 'No sword or famine will touch this land.' Those same prophets will perish by sword and famine. ¹⁶And the people they are prophesying to will be thrown out into the streets of Jerusalem because of the famine and sword. There will be no one to bury them, their wives, their sons and their daughters. I will pour out on them the calamity they deserve.

¹⁷"Speak this word to them:

"'Let my eyes overflow with tears
    night and day without ceasing;
for the Virgin Daughter, my people,
    has suffered a grievous wound,
    a crushing blow.
¹⁸If I go into the country,
    I see those slain by the sword;
if I go into the city,
    I see the ravages of famine.
Both prophet and priest
    have gone to a land they know not.'"

¹⁹Have you rejected Judah completely?
    Do you despise Zion?
Why have you afflicted us
    so that we cannot be healed?
We hoped for peace
    but no good has come,
for a time of healing
    but there is only terror.
²⁰We acknowledge our wickedness, LORD,
    and the guilt of our ancestors;
    we have indeed sinned against you.
²¹For the sake of your name do not
        despise us;
    do not dishonor your glorious throne.
Remember your covenant with us
    and do not break it.
²²Do any of the worthless idols of the nations
        bring rain?
    Do the skies themselves send down
        showers?
No, it is you, LORD our God.
    Therefore our hope is in you,
    for you are the one who does all this.

15 Then the LORD said to me: "Even if Moses and Samuel were to stand before me, my heart would not go out to this people. Send them away from my presence! Let them go! ²And if they ask you, 'Where shall we go?' tell them, 'This is what the LORD says:

"'Those destined for death, to death;
    those for the sword, to the sword;
    those for starvation, to starvation;
    those for captivity, to captivity.'

---

[a] 14 Or *visions, worthless divinations*

---

and note; 11:14 and note. Yahweh reminds Jeremiah that he is not to intercede on behalf of the people. This suggests that vv. 7–9 reflects Jeremiah's prayer on the people's behalf, not their genuine repentance.

14:12 burnt offerings and grain offerings See 6:20 and note. Outward obedience to the rituals was meaningless without a change of heart. Compare Isa 1:13–15. **with the sword, famine and plague** Three major disasters that would affect the entire land were invasion, drought and the resulting famine, and disease. Jeremiah and Ezekiel use this triad of disasters as an image of divine judgment (see Jer 16:4; 24:10; 32:24; Eze 5:12; 6:11; 7:15). It likely reflects the covenant curses (see Lev 26:25–26; Dt 28:21–25).

14:13–18 Jeremiah protests that the people have simply been deceived by prophets promising peace and security. Yahweh harshly condemns those prophets as speaking lies in his name, and he pronounces judgment upon them.

14:17 Let my eyes overflow with tears The true word from Yahweh is that he must judge, though it grieves him to punish his people. Compare Jer 12:7–11.

14:19–22 Jeremiah records another communal confession, acknowledging the people's sinfulness and begging Yahweh to intervene. As in vv. 7–9, Jeremiah likely is offering this lament on behalf of the people, who remain unrepentant. He still holds out hope that, as representative of Judah before Yahweh, he can confess their sins and beg Yahweh's forgiveness.

14:21 For the sake of your name See note on v. 9. If Yahweh cannot save for the sake of his people or Zion, he might be motivated to save to preserve his reputation. Compare Isa 51:9–10. **do not dishonor your glorious throne** He appeals to Yahweh to save his temple since it represents his earthly presence. See Jer 3:17 and note. **your covenant** It was not Yahweh who was guilty of breaking the covenant, yet the people appeal to him to keep his side of the agreement.

15:1–9 Yahweh responds to the people's lament and confession in 14:19–22, emphasizing again that the time for prophetic intercession has passed. Nothing can avert the coming destruction.

15:1 Moses and Samuel Examples of prophetic intercessors. See Nu 21:7; 1Sa 12:19. Moses and Samuel also represent a time in Israel's history when the prophet was a political leader who kept Israel on the right path of serving Yahweh.

15:2 Those destined for death, to death Pestilence,

³"I will send four kinds of destroyers against them," declares the LORD, "the sword to kill and the dogs to drag away and the birds and the wild animals to devour and destroy. ⁴I will make them abhorrent to all the kingdoms of the earth because of what Manasseh son of Hezekiah king of Judah did in Jerusalem.

⁵"Who will have pity on you, Jerusalem?
    Who will mourn for you?
    Who will stop to ask how you are?
⁶You have rejected me," declares the LORD.
    "You keep on backsliding.
So I will reach out and destroy you;
    I am tired of holding back.
⁷I will winnow them with a winnowing fork
    at the city gates of the land.
I will bring bereavement and destruction on
        my people,
    for they have not changed their ways.
⁸I will make their widows more numerous
    than the sand of the sea.
At midday I will bring a destroyer
    against the mothers of their young men;
suddenly I will bring down on them
    anguish and terror.
⁹The mother of seven will grow faint
    and breathe her last.
Her sun will set while it is still day;
    she will be disgraced and humiliated.
I will put the survivors to the sword
    before their enemies,"
                    declares the LORD.

¹⁰Alas, my mother, that you gave me birth,
    a man with whom the whole land strives
        and contends!

I have neither lent nor borrowed,
    yet everyone curses me.

¹¹The LORD said,

"Surely I will deliver you for a good purpose;
    surely I will make your enemies plead with
        you
    in times of disaster and times of distress.

¹²"Can a man break iron —
    iron from the north — or bronze?

¹³"Your wealth and your treasures
    I will give as plunder, without charge,
because of all your sins
    throughout your country.
¹⁴I will enslave you to your enemies
    inᵃ a land you do not know,
for my anger will kindle a fire
    that will burn against you."

¹⁵LORD, you understand;
    remember me and care for me.
    Avenge me on my persecutors.
You are long-suffering — do not take me
        away;
    think of how I suffer reproach for your
        sake.
¹⁶When your words came, I ate them;
    they were my joy and my heart's delight,
for I bear your name,
    LORD God Almighty.
¹⁷I never sat in the company of revelers,
    never made merry with them;

ᵃ 14 Some Hebrew manuscripts, Septuagint and Syriac (see also 17:4); most Hebrew manuscripts *I will cause your enemies to bring you / into*

---

famine and sword form an image of divine judgment. Sometimes exile (Jer 15:2b) and wild beasts (v. 3) were added to the list of punishments. See note on 14:12; compare Eze 6:11–12.

15:4 Manasseh Judah's most wicked king (see note on 2Ch 33:1).

MANASSEH

Manasseh was the son of the righteous King Hezekiah and grandfather of King Josiah. He ruled Judah 697–642 BC. The Biblical history records Manasseh's reign as one of unprecedented idolatry and apostasy (2Ki 21; 2Ch 33). His father, Hezekiah, had destroyed the high places and attempted to wipe out idolatry (2Ki 18:4), but Manasseh rebuilt the high places, set up altars for the Canaanite deities (Baal, Asherah) engaged in child sacrifice and witchcraft, and set up an Asherah pole in the temple of Yahweh (2Ki 21:3–7). Manasseh's evil was so great that even Josiah's reforms (2Ki 23:4–25)—removing all those idols, and destroying altars and local shrines—were not

enough to prevent Yahweh from bringing judgment on Judah (2Ki 23:26–27). Second Kings explicitly blames the destruction of Jerusalem and the temple in 586 BC on the sins of Manasseh (2Ki 24:3–4).

15:7 winnowing fork A six-pronged fork for tossing harvested grain into the air so the wind could blow away the lightweight chaff, while the heavier grain kernels fell to the ground. Winnowing can metaphorically represent the way God deals with people and nations, separating the worthless chaff from the grain worth saving. Compare Isa 41:15–16.

15:9 mother of seven A sign of divine blessing, since seven symbolizes completeness.

15:10–21 Jeremiah's third complaint reflects his despair over the double disaster he will experience—the persecution from his own people and the horrors of enemy attack and exile. The complaint consists of Jeremiah's lament (Jer 15:10–18) and Yahweh's reply (vv. 19–21).

15:12 iron Alludes to the divine strengthening that Yahweh gave Jeremiah in 1:17–19.

15:16 I ate them A poetic reference to Yahweh putting his words in Jeremiah's mouth for him to speak. Compare 1:9; Eze 2:8—3:3.

I sat alone because your hand was on me
    and you had filled me with indignation.
[18] Why is my pain unending
    and my wound grievous and incurable?
You are to me like a deceptive brook,
    like a spring that fails.

[19] Therefore this is what the LORD says:

"If you repent, I will restore you
    that you may serve me;
if you utter worthy, not worthless, words,
    you will be my spokesman.
Let this people turn to you,
    but you must not turn to them.
[20] I will make you a wall to this people,
    a fortified wall of bronze;
they will fight against you
    but will not overcome you,
for I am with you
    to rescue and save you,"
                declares the LORD.
[21] "I will save you from the hands of the wicked
    and deliver you from the grasp of the
        cruel.'"

Day of Disaster

16 Then the word of the LORD came to me: [2]"You must not marry and have sons or daughters in this place." [3] For this is what the LORD says about the sons and daughters born in this land and about the women who are their mothers and the men who are their fathers: [4]"They will die of deadly diseases. They will not be mourned or buried but will be like dung lying on the ground. They will perish

by sword and famine, and their dead bodies will become food for the birds and the wild animals."

[5] For this is what the LORD says: "Do not enter a house where there is a funeral meal; do not go to mourn or show sympathy, because I have withdrawn my blessing, my love and my pity from this people," declares the LORD. [6]"Both high and low will die in this land. They will not be buried or mourned, and no one will cut themselves or shave their head for the dead. [7] No one will offer food to comfort those who mourn for the dead — not even for a father or a mother — nor will anyone give them a drink to console them.

[8]"And do not enter a house where there is feasting and sit down to eat and drink. [9] For this is what the LORD Almighty, the God of Israel, says: Before your eyes and in your days I will bring an end to the sounds of joy and gladness and to the voices of bride and bridegroom in this place.

[10]"When you tell these people all this and they ask you, 'Why has the LORD decreed such a great disaster against us? What wrong have we done? What sin have we committed against the LORD our God?' [11] then say to them, 'It is because your ancestors forsook me,' declares the LORD, 'and followed other gods and served and worshiped them. They forsook me and did not keep my law. [12] But you have behaved more wickedly than your ancestors. See how all of you are following the stubbornness of your evil hearts instead of obeying me. [13] So I will throw you out of this land into a land neither you nor your ancestors have known, and there you will serve other gods day and night, for I will show you no favor.'

[14]"However, the days are coming," declares the LORD, "when it will no longer be said, 'As surely

---

15:17 your hand A prophet's experience of Yahweh's power is often described as the hand of God (compare Isa 8:11; Eze 3:14). See Eze 1:3 and note.

15:19 If you repent Yahweh's response to Jeremiah implies that he has wandered away from his prophetic responsibilities, perhaps siding too much with the people under judgment. Yahweh is calling him to repent or return — both possible meanings of the Hebrew word — so he can be reinstated as Yahweh's spokesman.

16:1–13 The familiar motif of divine judgment via sword, famine and disease is combined with a command to Jeremiah to remain unmarried. Jeremiah's lack of a family underscores the coming loss of family which the inhabitants of Judah face (Jer 16:3–4). So many people will die that the dead cannot be given a proper burial. The imagery closely parallels 7:33—8:3.

16:2 You must not marry With an instruction suggesting a symbolic act, Yahweh commands Jeremiah not to marry. See note on 13:1–11. See the table "Symbolic Actions of the Prophets" on p. 1195.

16:4 for the birds See 7:33 and note.

16:5 a house where there is a funeral meal Jeremiah is not to participate in typical mourning rituals to symbolize how the devastated population of Judah will be unable to give the dead a proper burial (see v. 6). The Hebrew term used here, *marzeach*, often refers to

a funeral banquet. It might imply an ongoing cult of the dead, alluded to in passages such as Dt 26:14; Isa 57:6–8; and Ps 106:28. This ritual drinking feast was mentioned in ancient Semitic texts extending over a period of 3,000 years. The basic idea is that of a drinking club, usually with religious connotations, sometimes with funerary associations. Biblical law explicitly forbids the mourning practices of cutting oneself and shaving one's head. See Dt 14:1; Lev 19:28.

16:8 a house where there is feasting The *beth mishteh*, sometimes translated as "house of feasting," refers to a celebratory feast; it is the opposite of the *beth marzeach*, which may be translated as "house of mourning" (Jer 16:5). Yahweh commands Jeremiah to break all social obligations; he cannot attend funerals or feasts (such as the wedding banquet indicated in v. 9).

16:13 neither you nor your ancestors have known Fulfills the covenant curse of Dt 28:64 to scatter Israel to foreign lands, where they will worship foreign gods.

16:14–21 This oracle of restoration depicts the return of the exiles to Israel as a reenactment of the exodus. This exodus surpasses the first exodus because Yahweh will gather his people from all around the world, instead of from Egypt alone. The theme of restoration from exile as a second exodus is common in the book of Isaiah (see Isa 14:3; 35:1; 48:21) and found in the book of Ezekiel (see Eze 20:33–49 and note).

as the LORD lives, who brought the Israelites up out of Egypt,' [15]but it will be said, 'As surely as the LORD lives, who brought the Israelites up out of the land of the north and out of all the countries where he had banished them.' For I will restore them to the land I gave their ancestors.

[16]"But now I will send for many fishermen," declares the LORD, "and they will catch them. After that I will send for many hunters, and they will hunt them down on every mountain and hill and from the crevices of the rocks. [17]My eyes are on all their ways; they are not hidden from me, nor is their sin concealed from my eyes. [18]I will repay them double for their wickedness and their sin, because they have defiled my land with the lifeless forms of their vile images and have filled my inheritance with their detestable idols."

[19] LORD, my strength and my fortress,
my refuge in time of distress,
to you the nations will come
from the ends of the earth and say,
"Our ancestors possessed nothing but false
gods,
worthless idols that did them no good.
[20] Do people make their own gods?
Yes, but they are not gods!"

[21] "Therefore I will teach them —
this time I will teach them
my power and might.
Then they will know
that my name is the LORD.

17 "Judah's sin is engraved with an iron tool,
inscribed with a flint point,
on the tablets of their hearts
and on the horns of their altars.
[2] Even their children remember
their altars and Asherah poles[a]

beside the spreading trees
and on the high hills.
[3] My mountain in the land
and your[b] wealth and all your treasures
I will give away as plunder,
together with your high places,
because of sin throughout your country.
[4] Through your own fault you will lose
the inheritance I gave you.
I will enslave you to your enemies
in a land you do not know,
for you have kindled my anger,
and it will burn forever."

[5] This is what the LORD says:

"Cursed is the one who trusts in man,
who draws strength from mere flesh
and whose heart turns away from the LORD.
[6] That person will be like a bush in the
wastelands;
they will not see prosperity when it comes.
They will dwell in the parched places of the
desert,
in a salt land where no one lives.

[7] "But blessed is the one who trusts in the LORD,
whose confidence is in him.
[8] They will be like a tree planted by the water
that sends out its roots by the stream.
It does not fear when heat comes;
its leaves are always green.
It has no worries in a year of drought
and never fails to bear fruit."

[9] The heart is deceitful above all things
and beyond cure.
Who can understand it?

---

[a] 2 That is, wooden symbols of the goddess Asherah
[b] 2,3 Or hills / [3]and the mountains of the land. / Your

16:14 out of Egypt Yahweh's redemption of Israel from slavery in Egypt was an important component of his identity and how he revealed himself to Israel (see Jer 2:6; Lev 11:45; Dt 6:12; 2Ki 17:36). The previous manifestations of his power will pale in comparison with the coming salvation.

16:19–20 Jeremiah responds to Yahweh with praise and repents as he had commanded (see Jer 15:19–21).

16:21 they will know that my name is the LORD A divine recognition formula that connects Yahweh's acts with the people's acknowledgement of him as God. See Eze 5:13 and note.

17:1–4 This section continues the theme of divine judgment from the previous chapter. The passage reiterates Judah's sins, emphasizing idolatry.

17:1 an iron tool A stylus used for inscribing wood, metal or stone. Such engravings were meant to be permanent; unlike writings on scrolls (using ink), they were not easily changed, removed or damaged. The metaphor thus emphasizes the severity of Judah's sin. **the horns of their altars** Projections at the corners of the altar; used for both ritual and practical purposes. See note on Ex 27:2.

17:2 Asherah poles Carved wooden poles (Jdg 6:25) or living trees (Dt 16:21) used as symbols of fertility; connected with worship of the goddess Asherah. See note on Dt 16:21. **spreading trees and on the high hills** A standard phrase indicating sites devoted to Canaanite gods. The "high hills" likely refer to high places, which are mentioned explicitly in Jer 17:3 (see 2:20 and note).

17:5–13 This poetic section consists of a wisdom poem that concludes with a praise hymn. The wisdom sayings are reminiscent of Ps 1, with an emphasis on trusting Yahweh and avoiding wickedness.

17:6 the wastelands The arid wasteland around the Dead Sea.

17:9 The heart is deceitful above all things The Hebrew term for the heart metaphorically refers to a person's inner life—the will, thoughts, motivations and emotions. This is a different understanding than "heart" in modern Western thinking, which primarily indicates the seat of emotions.

¹⁰ "I the Lord search the heart
and examine the mind,
to reward each person according to their
conduct,
according to what their deeds deserve."

¹¹ Like a partridge that hatches eggs it did not
lay
are those who gain riches by unjust means.
When their lives are half gone, their riches
will desert them,
and in the end they will prove to be fools.

¹² A glorious throne, exalted from the
beginning,
is the place of our sanctuary.
¹³ Lord, you are the hope of Israel;
all who forsake you will be put to shame.
Those who turn away from you will be
written in the dust
because they have forsaken the Lord,
the spring of living water.

¹⁴ Heal me, Lord, and I will be healed;
save me and I will be saved,
for you are the one I praise.
¹⁵ They keep saying to me,
"Where is the word of the Lord?
Let it now be fulfilled!"
¹⁶ I have not run away from being your
shepherd;
you know I have not desired the day of
despair.
What passes my lips is open before you.
¹⁷ Do not be a terror to me;
you are my refuge in the day of disaster.
¹⁸ Let my persecutors be put to shame,
but keep me from shame;
let them be terrified,
but keep me from terror.

Bring on them the day of disaster;
destroy them with double destruction.

Keeping the Sabbath Day Holy

¹⁹ This is what the Lord said to me: "Go and
stand at the Gate of the People,ᵃ through which
the kings of Judah go in and out; stand also at
all the other gates of Jerusalem. ²⁰ Say to them,
'Hear the word of the Lord, you kings of Judah
and all people of Judah and everyone living in
Jerusalem who come through these gates. ²¹ This
is what the Lord says: Be careful not to carry a
load on the Sabbath day or bring it through the
gates of Jerusalem. ²² Do not bring a load out of
your houses or do any work on the Sabbath, but
keep the Sabbath day holy, as I commanded your
ancestors. ²³ Yet they did not listen or pay attention; they were stiff-necked and would not listen
or respond to discipline. ²⁴ But if you are careful
to obey me, declares the Lord, and bring no load
through the gates of this city on the Sabbath, but
keep the Sabbath day holy by not doing any work
on it, ²⁵ then kings who sit on David's throne will
come through the gates of this city with their officials. They and their officials will come riding in
chariots and on horses, accompanied by the men
of Judah and those living in Jerusalem, and this
city will be inhabited forever. ²⁶ People will come
from the towns of Judah and the villages around
Jerusalem, from the territory of Benjamin and the
western foothills, from the hill country and the
Negev, bringing burnt offerings and sacrifices,
grain offerings and incense, and bringing thank
offerings to the house of the Lord. ²⁷ But if you do
not obey me to keep the Sabbath day holy by not
carrying any load as you come through the gates
of Jerusalem on the Sabbath day, then I will kindle

ᵃ 19 Or Army

17:12 A glorious throne Refers to the temple. See
note on Jer 14:21.

17:14–18 Unlike previous laments, Jeremiah's fourth
lament (see note on 11:1—20:18) does not include a
response from Yahweh. Jeremiah asks for healing and
salvation; the healing refers to forgiveness of his sins and
repairing his relationship with Yahweh (compare Ps 41:4).
Jeremiah has faithfully carried out his prophetic mission
by calling Israel to repentance, but he still experiences
persecution. The lament ends with his wish for Yahweh's
judgment on his enemies (see note on Jer 10:25).

17:15 Where is the word of the Lord Jeremiah's persecutors mock him because the disaster he prophesied
has not yet come.

17:19–27 Yahweh commands Jeremiah to preach to
all Judah, admonishing them for breaking the Sabbath
and appealing to them to start observing it properly.
The message promises restoration of Judah's monarchy
if the people repent, but threatens destruction if they
continue in disobedience.

17:19 Gate of the People Jeremiah is to start at this
gate and continue to *all* of Jerusalem's gates—areas
with high traffic and commercial activity.

17:21 not to carry a load on the Sabbath day Work
was forbidden on the Sabbath (Ex 20:10; 31:14–15;
Lev 23:3). The penalty for working on the Sabbath was
death. See Nu 15:32–36. **gates of Jerusalem** Jeremiah
is criticizing people for working on the Sabbath. Compare
Nehemiah's distress at the blatant commercial activity
conducted on the Sabbath in postexilic Jerusalem (see
Ne 13:15–19).

17:26 around Jerusalem The geographical areas mentioned here are those closest to Jerusalem, giving them
the easiest access to the temple for worship. **territory
of Benjamin** The area just north of Jerusalem. Technically, the city of Jerusalem itself was in land allotted to
Benjamin. **western foothills** The low hills separating
the coastal plain from the central hill country. **Negev**
The southern region of Judah. See note on Jer 13:19.
offerings This verse lists the full range of offerings
brought to the temple. On burnt offerings, sacrifices and

an unquenchable fire in the gates of Jerusalem that will consume her fortresses.'"

At the Potter's House

18 This is the word that came to Jeremiah from the LORD: ²"Go down to the potter's house, and there I will give you my message." ³So I went down to the potter's house, and I saw him working at the wheel. ⁴But the pot he was shaping from the clay was marred in his hands; so the potter formed it into another pot, shaping it as seemed best to him.

⁵Then the word of the LORD came to me. ⁶He said, "Can I not do with you, Israel, as this potter does?" declares the LORD. "Like clay in the hand of the potter, so are you in my hand, Israel. ⁷If at any time I announce that a nation or kingdom is to be uprooted, torn down and destroyed, ⁸and if that nation I warned repents of its evil, then I will relent and not inflict on it the disaster I had planned. ⁹And if at another time I announce that a nation or kingdom is to be built up and planted, ¹⁰and if it does evil in my sight and does not obey me, then I will reconsider the good I had intended to do for it.

¹¹"Now therefore say to the people of Judah and those living in Jerusalem, 'This is what the LORD says: Look! I am preparing a disaster for you and devising a plan against you. So turn from your evil ways, each one of you, and reform your ways and your actions.' ¹²But they will reply, 'It's no use. We will continue with our own plans; we will all follow the stubbornness of our evil hearts.'"

¹³Therefore this is what the LORD says:

"Inquire among the nations:
  Who has ever heard anything like this?
A most horrible thing has been done
  by Virgin Israel.
¹⁴Does the snow of Lebanon
  ever vanish from its rocky slopes?
Do its cool waters from distant sources
  ever stop flowing?ᵃ
¹⁵Yet my people have forgotten me;
  they burn incense to worthless idols,
which made them stumble in their ways,
  in the ancient paths.
They made them walk in byways,
  on roads not built up.
¹⁶Their land will be an object of horror
  and of lasting scorn;
all who pass by will be appalled
  and will shake their heads.
¹⁷Like a wind from the east,
  I will scatter them before their enemies;
I will show them my back and not my
      face
  in the day of their disaster."

¹⁸They said, "Come, let's make plans against Jeremiah; for the teaching of the law by the priest will not cease, nor will counsel from the wise, nor the word from the prophets. So come, let's attack him with our tongues and pay no attention to anything he says."

ᵃ 14 The meaning of the Hebrew for this sentence is uncertain.

---

frankincense, see note on 6:20; compare note on Lev 1:2; note on 1:3; note on 2:1; note on 3:1.

18:1–12 Jeremiah receives divine instructions for another symbolic action (compare Jer 13:1–11 and note); this time, he is to observe the local potter at work and remind Israel that Yahweh's role is analogous to the potter, who does as he wishes with the clay. See the table "Symbolic Actions of the Prophets" on p. 1195.

18:2 potter's house The Hebrew word used here means "shaper" and is related to one of the terms used to describe Yahweh's creative activity. In Genesis 2:7, Yahweh shapes Adam from the dust; this act is likely the basis for the potter metaphor for God.

18:4 potter formed it into another pot Reworking the same clay into a new vessel creates an added layer to the metaphor: Yahweh might reshape a new Israel, foreshadowing Jer 31.

18:6 do with you, Israel, as this potter God as potter and his creation as clay is a common symbol for his sovereignty (see Isa 29:16 and note; Isa 45:9; Isa 64:8; Ro 9:20–23).

18:8 that nation The hypothetical conditions offered here are similar to Ezekiel's discussion of moral responsibility in Eze 18 (compare especially Eze 18:21). **I will relent** The Hebrew verb here has a wide and nuanced range of meaning. It can be translated as "be sorry," "show regret," "show compassion" or "be comforted," and it can convey the sense of changing one's mind based

on circumstances or behavior. It is not too late for the people to repent. While judgment oracles often include a call for the people to repent, the people rarely respond positively to the prophets. Jeremiah, Ezekiel and Isaiah all portray Israel as being almost beyond hope because of their rebellion and refusal to repent.

18:13–17 An oracle of judgment, again focusing on Israel's apostasy and idol worship.

18:14 snow of Lebanon Both rhetorical questions anticipate a negative answer; a positive answer would defy the natural order. The reference here is to Mount Hermon (also called "Sirion"), which is more than 9,000 feet high.

18:15 They made them walk in byways, on roads not built up A metaphor for Israel wandering from the path Yahweh prepared for them. See Jer 6:16 and note.

18:17 Like a wind from the east, I will scatter An east wind is often a scorching, violent windstorm (compare 4:11; Isa 27:8; Job 15:2; Ge 41:6; Jnh 4:8). Judgment by scattering is a common image based on the covenant curses. See Lev 26:33. **I will show them my back** Symbolizes rejection, a removal of divine favor and presence.

18:18–23 In his fifth lament, Jeremiah describes the hostile response his prophetic ministry has received from the people of Judah, and he appeals to Yahweh to intervene and judge his persecutors.

18:18 plans against Jeremiah Jeremiah's first two laments similarly focused on attempts on his life. See

¹⁹ Listen to me, LORD;
  hear what my accusers are saying!
²⁰ Should good be repaid with evil?
  Yet they have dug a pit for me.
Remember that I stood before you
  and spoke in their behalf
  to turn your wrath away from them.
²¹ So give their children over to famine;
  hand them over to the power of the sword.
Let their wives be made childless and
    widows;
  let their men be put to death,
  their young men slain by the sword in
    battle.
²² Let a cry be heard from their houses
  when you suddenly bring invaders against
    them,
for they have dug a pit to capture me
  and have hidden snares for my feet.
²³ But you, LORD, know
  all their plots to kill me.
Do not forgive their crimes
  or blot out their sins from your sight.
Let them be overthrown before you;
  deal with them in the time of your anger.

19 This is what the LORD says: "Go and buy a clay jar from a potter. Take along some of the elders of the people and of the priests ² and go out to the Valley of Ben Hinnom, near the entrance of the Potsherd Gate. There proclaim the words I tell you, ³ and say, 'Hear the word of the LORD, you kings of Judah and people of Jerusalem. This is what the LORD Almighty, the God of Israel, says: Listen! I am going to bring a disaster on this place that will make the ears of everyone who hears of it tingle. ⁴ For they have forsaken me and made this a place of foreign gods; they have burned incense in it to gods that neither they nor their

ancestors nor the kings of Judah ever knew, and they have filled this place with the blood of the innocent. ⁵ They have built the high places of Baal to burn their children in the fire as offerings to Baal — something I did not command or mention, nor did it enter my mind. ⁶ So beware, the days are coming, declares the LORD, when people will no longer call this place Topheth or the Valley of Ben Hinnom, but the Valley of Slaughter.

⁷ "'In this place I will ruin^a the plans of Judah and Jerusalem. I will make them fall by the sword before their enemies, at the hands of those who want to kill them, and I will give their carcasses as food to the birds and the wild animals. ⁸ I will devastate this city and make it an object of horror and scorn; all who pass by will be appalled and will scoff because of all its wounds. ⁹ I will make them eat the flesh of their sons and daughters, and they will eat one another's flesh because their enemies will press the siege so hard against them to destroy them.'

¹⁰ "Then break the jar while those who go with you are watching, ¹¹ and say to them, 'This is what the LORD Almighty says: I will smash this nation and this city just as this potter's jar is smashed and cannot be repaired. They will bury the dead in Topheth until there is no more room. ¹² This is what I will do to this place and to those who live here, declares the LORD. I will make this city like Topheth. ¹³ The houses in Jerusalem and those of the kings of Judah will be defiled like this place, Topheth — all the houses where they burned incense on the roofs to all the starry hosts and poured out drink offerings to other gods.'"

¹⁴ Jeremiah then returned from Topheth, where the LORD had sent him to prophesy, and stood in the court of the LORD's temple and said to all the

---

^a 7 The Hebrew for *ruin* sounds like the Hebrew for *jar* (see verses 1 and 10).

Jer 11:18–23 and note; 12:1–6 and note. **teaching of the law by the priest will not cease, nor will** The people's reaction depicts their defense of the three central and official religious offices — priest, prophet and sage. The people believe Jeremiah is at odds with the will of Yahweh as revealed through his priests, his prophets and the royal counselors. The people refused to believe Jeremiah was right and that their leaders were wrong (compare ch. 28; Eze 7:26).
18:21 give their children over to famine The people for whom Jeremiah had interceded now reject him (Jer 18:20), so he asks God to bring judgment.

19:1–15 Jeremiah receives instructions to carry out another sign-act, again using pottery as a symbol of Judah. His actions echo the symbolism from 18:1–12. In this sign-act, Jeremiah smashes the pot representing Judah to symbolize its imminent destruction at the hands of the Babylonians. The judgment oracle accompanying the sign-act repeats the indictments against Israel for idol worship and child sacrifice (see 1:16; 2:20–37; 7:30—8:3). See the table "Symbolic Actions of the Prophets" on p. 1195.

19:2 Valley of Ben Hinnom A site where child sacrifices took place. Also called "Gehenna." See note on 7:31. **Potsherd Gate** The location is uncertain since this name is used only here. It is probably to be identified with the Dung Gate, which was used for taking refuse out of Jerusalem. See Ne 2:13 and note.
19:3 LORD Almighty See note on Jer 6:6.
19:5 high places of Baal Shrines devoted to Baal-worship. See note on Ps 78:58. **burn their children in the fire** See Jer 7:31 and note. Compare 32:35; Lev 18:21.
19:9 eat the flesh of their sons They will resort to cannibalism due to the shortage of food from the siege (see Eze 5:10 and note; compare La 2:20; 4:10; Isa 9:20). **siege** See Jer 6:6 and note; Eze 4:2 and note.
19:13 where they burned incense on the roofs The roof was the site of sacrifice to astral deities represented by sun, moon and stars (see 2Ki 23:12; Zep 1:5). During Biblical times, roofs were usually flat and had a variety of uses, including guest quarters (2Ki 4:10), sleeping (1Sa 9:25), mourning (Isa 15:3), storage (Jos 2:6), and religious worship and sacrifices. See Jer 8:2 and note. See the infographic "Ancient Israelite House" on p. 1205.

people, ¹⁵"This is what the LORD Almighty, the God of Israel, says: 'Listen! I am going to bring on this city and all the villages around it every disaster I pronounced against them, because they were stiff-necked and would not listen to my words.'"

Jeremiah and Pashhur

20 When the priest Pashhur son of Immer, the official in charge of the temple of the LORD, heard Jeremiah prophesying these things, ²he had Jeremiah the prophet beaten and put in the stocks at the Upper Gate of Benjamin at the LORD's temple. ³The next day, when Pashhur released him from the stocks, Jeremiah said to him, "The LORD's name for you is not Pashhur, but Terror on Every Side. ⁴For this is what the LORD says: 'I will make you a terror to yourself and to all your friends; with your own eyes you will see them fall by the sword of their enemies. I will give all Judah into the hands of the king of Babylon, who will carry them away to Babylon or put them to the sword. ⁵I will deliver all the wealth of this city into the hands of their enemies — all its products, all its valuables and all the treasures of the kings of Judah. They will take it away as plunder and carry it off to Babylon. ⁶And you, Pashhur, and all who live in your house will go into exile to Babylon. There you will die and be buried, you and all your friends to whom you have prophesied lies.'"

Jeremiah's Complaint

⁷You deceived*ᵃ* me, LORD, and I was deceived*ᵃ*;
  you overpowered me and prevailed.
I am ridiculed all day long;
  everyone mocks me.
⁸Whenever I speak, I cry out
  proclaiming violence and destruction.
So the word of the LORD has brought me
  insult and reproach all day long.
⁹But if I say, "I will not mention his word
  or speak anymore in his name,"
his word is in my heart like a fire,
  a fire shut up in my bones.
I am weary of holding it in;
  indeed, I cannot.
¹⁰I hear many whispering,
  "Terror on every side!
  Denounce him! Let's denounce him!"
All my friends
  are waiting for me to slip, saying,
"Perhaps he will be deceived;
  then we will prevail over him
  and take our revenge on him."

¹¹But the LORD is with me like a mighty warrior;
  so my persecutors will stumble and not prevail.
They will fail and be thoroughly disgraced;
  their dishonor will never be forgotten.

ᵃ 7 Or *persuaded*

20:1–6 Jeremiah's prophecy, which he delivered in the temple court (Jer 19:14–15), elicits a strong reaction from the priest, Pashhur, who was responsible for maintaining order in the temple. Jeremiah is beaten and put in stocks overnight, resulting in a strong denunciation of Pashhur the next morning. The incident provides an example of the persecution Jeremiah received and leads into his final two laments in vv. 7–18.

20:1 priest Pashhur son of Immer Pashhur was a common name at this time. Jeremiah's narrative mentions three individuals with this name. This individual is not the same as the Pashhur named in 21:1 or 38:1. **official in charge of the temple of the LORD** The chief officer was probably charged with maintaining order in the temple area (compare 29:26). Jeremiah was disturbing the peace.

20:2 the stocks Refers to some instrument or place of restraint and punishment, a confinement that limited movement. The exact meaning of the term here is unclear. It also occurs in 29:26 and 2Ch 16:10 and is almost always translated "stocks." The Hebrew root has the basic sense of "turn, overturn." Jeremiah might have been confined to a small jail cell or placed in a device that kept the body in a stooped position. The reference in 2Ch 16:10 suggests a prison or building with a phrase that can be translated as "house of the stocks." **Upper Gate of Benjamin** The Benjamin Gate was the northern exit from the city (see Jer 37:13). This gate was likely the northern gate of the temple complex, facing the territory of Benjamin.

20:3 Terror on Every Side Pashhur's new name is *magor missaviv*, a Hebrew phrase used several times

in Jeremiah to depict the people's dismay at the impending Babylonian invasion (see 6:25; 46:5; 49:29). Instead of meting out punishment, Pashhur will experience divine wrath. The phrase may be borrowed from poetic language such as Ps 31:13. The Hebrew phrase *magor missaviv* can be construed in three different ways, and the detailed explanation of Pashhur's punishment seems to invoke all of them. *Magor* can mean "terror," "attack" and "place of sojourning." These three senses correspond to the punishments described in Jer 20:4–6. Pashhur will be a terror to his friends, who will suffer death from the Babylonian attack while he is taken into exile. The addition of *missaviv*, sometimes translated as "all around," gives Jeremiah's pun the added sense that Pashhur will be *magor* in every sense of the word. See the table "Symbolic Names of People in Hebrew" on p. 1388.

20:6 you have prophesied lies Classifies Pashhur among the lying prophets who will be judged for prophesying peace (see 14:13–16).

20:7–13 Jeremiah's sixth lament channels his frustration into an accusation against God for deliberately leading him into difficult circumstances. The language of this lament is bold and direct, leaving a clear view of the distress experienced by the prophet and his ambivalence toward Yahweh.

20:8 insult and reproach all day long Jeremiah's experience of proclaiming God's word has been overwhelmingly negative, filled with humiliation and mockery.

20:10 Terror on every side See note on v. 3. Now the phrase *magor missaviv* is used to depict Jeremiah's enemies plotting against him.

¹² Lord Almighty, you who examine the
righteous
and probe the heart and mind,
let me see your vengeance on them,
for to you I have committed my
cause.

¹³ Sing to the Lord!
Give praise to the Lord!
He rescues the life of the needy
from the hands of the wicked.

¹⁴ Cursed be the day I was born!
May the day my mother bore me not be
blessed!

¹⁵ Cursed be the man who brought my father
the news,
who made him very glad, saying,
"A child is born to you — a son!"
¹⁶ May that man be like the towns
the Lord overthrew without pity.
May he hear wailing in the morning,
a battle cry at noon.
¹⁷ For he did not kill me in the womb,
with my mother as my grave,
her womb enlarged forever.
¹⁸ Why did I ever come out of the womb
to see trouble and sorrow
and to end my days in shame?

20:13 Sing to the Lord The lament ends in thanksgiving and praise. Lament psalms often contain expressions of praise and trust, anticipating Yahweh's deliverance in response to the psalmist's complaint.

20:14—18 With his seventh lament, Jeremiah concludes the series that dominates 11:1—20:18 by complaining about his very existence. Like Job, he wishes he'd never been born to experience such misery (compare Job 3).

20:14 Cursed be the day Jeremiah's curse of his own birth may be an intentional rejection of his prophetic call (see Jer 1:5). He lamented his own birth before, but less harshly (15:10). See Job 3:3 and note on Job 3:1.
20:17 he did not kill me in the womb Yahweh won't let Jeremiah stop prophesying (Jer 20:9), so he wishes instead that he had never been born.

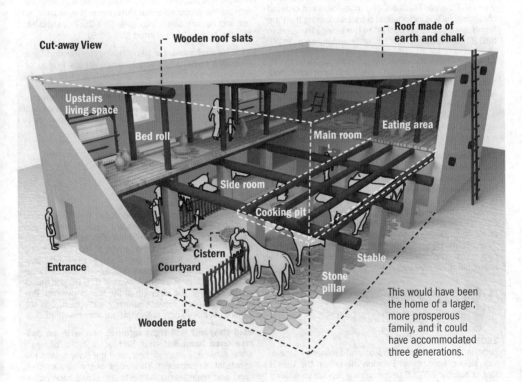

Cut-away View

Wooden roof slats

Roof made of
earth and chalk

Upstairs
living space

Bed roll

Main room

Eating area

Side room

Cooking pit

Cistern

Stable

Entrance

Courtyard

Stone
pillar

This would have been
the home of a larger,
more prosperous
family, and it could
have accommodated
three generations.

Wooden gate

Ancient Israelite House

For more than 600 years—ca. 1500 BC–500 BC—nearly all Israelite houses were built with the same distinctive layout. While surrounding cultures used other house plans, the Israelites even used this one for wealthy homes and public buildings. Its usage disappeared during the Babylonian exile.

God Rejects Zedekiah's Request

21 The word came to Jeremiah from the LORD when King Zedekiah sent to him Pashhur son of Malkijah and the priest Zephaniah son of Maaseiah. They said: [2]"Inquire now of the LORD for us because Nebuchadnezzar[a] king of Babylon is attacking us. Perhaps the LORD will perform wonders for us as in times past so that he will withdraw from us."

[3]But Jeremiah answered them, "Tell Zedekiah, [4]'This is what the LORD, the God of Israel, says: I am about to turn against you the weapons of war that are in your hands, which you are using to fight the king of Babylon and the Babylonians[b] who are outside the wall besieging you. And I will gather them inside this city. [5]I myself will fight against you with an outstretched hand and a mighty arm in furious anger and in great wrath. [6]I will strike down those who live in this city — both man and beast — and they will die of a terrible plague. [7]After that, declares the LORD, I will give Zedekiah king of Judah, his officials and the people in this city who survive the plague, sword and famine, into the hands of Nebuchadnezzar king of Babylon and to their enemies who want to kill them. He will put them to the sword; he will show them no mercy or pity or compassion.'

[8]"Furthermore, tell the people, 'This is what the

---

[a] 2 Hebrew *Nebuchadrezzar*, of which *Nebuchadnezzar* is a variant; here and often in Jeremiah and Ezekiel
[b] 4 Or *Chaldeans*; also in verse 9

21:1—23:8 This section has a collection of prophecies oriented around the theme of Davidic kingship. The unifying feature of this eclectic collection is the announcement of inevitable judgment on Judah, Jerusalem, the Davidic dynasty and specific kings. The leaders' failure to uphold proper standards for social justice and worship of Yahweh is a central factor in the coming judgment. The oracles also include a glimpse at future restoration under the Davidic Messiah. The material is not ordered chronologically; it includes references covering the time from Josiah's death in 609 BC to the fall of Jerusalem in 586 BC. See the timeline "Life of Jeremiah" on p. 1170.

21:1–10 Zedekiah sends his officials to Jeremiah to inquire whether Yahweh will save them from Nebuchadnezzar and the Babylonians (Chaldeans). The historical situation must have been in 588 or 587 BC, after Nebuchadnezzar had begun his invasion. The tone of the inquiry shows that Zedekiah is holding out hope for a miraculous deliverance on par with Hezekiah's escape from the Assyrian siege in 701 BC (see Isa 37:36 and note).

21:1 Zedekiah Judah's last Davidic ruler (597–586 BC). Jeremiah depicts Zedekiah as a weak ruler who is pushed around by his advisers (see Jer 38:16–27). **Pashhur son of Malkijah** A royal official also mentioned in 38:1. This is not the Pashhur of 20:1. Malkijah is called the king's son in 38:6, but Pashhur's relation to Zedekiah is unclear. **priest Zephaniah** A high-ranking priest and possible relative of Jeremiah (see 29:24–27; 32:7; 35:4). He was called second priest (52:24), the rank below chief priest. Zephaniah was executed by the Babylonians (see 2Ki 25:18–21).

ZEDEKIAH
Zedekiah was the son of Josiah and brother of Jehoiakim. Nebuchadnezzar of Babylon made him the vassal king of Judah in 597 BC following King Jehoiakim's failed rebellion against Babylonian rule (see 2Ki 24:1–17). Nebuchadnezzar took Jehoiachin, Jehoiakim's son and successor, into exile and left Zedekiah to rule as a puppet king in his place. Unfortunately, most of the ruling class of Judah was carried into exile with Jehoiachin, leaving young Zedekiah with naïve and inexperienced advisers. Initially, Zedekiah was loyal to Nebuchadnezzar, but internal pressure from his advisers led him to rebel

against Babylon and rely on Egypt for military assistance (see Jer 37:5 and note on Eze 17:1–24). The Babylonians besieged Jerusalem beginning in the ninth year of Zedekiah's reign (588 or 587 BC; 2Ki 25:1). The siege lasted about 18 months until the eleventh year of Zedekiah's reign (586 BC; 2Ki 25:2). The Babylonians captured Zedekiah when he attempted to flee the city at night (2Ki 25:4–6). As punishment, he was forced to witness the execution of his sons; then his eyes were put out and he was taken into exile (2Ki 25:7). Jerusalem and the temple were burned (2Ki 25:9).

21:2 Nebuchadnezzar Nebuchadnezzar invaded Syria-Palestine three times when vassal states like Judah refused to pay tribute. The Hebrew text of Jer 21–52 mainly uses the proper Akkadian form of his name, Nebuchadrezzar. On the different meanings of his name, see note on Eze 26:7. **he will withdraw from us** Just as the Assyrian King Sennacherib had withdrawn more than a century before. See Isa 37:36–38.

NEBUCHADNEZZAR
Nebuchadnezzar (or Nebuchadrezzar) was the second king of the Chaldean (Babylonian) dynasty, which ruled the ancient Near East from Babylon for almost a century. The Neo-Babylonian Empire was at its height during Nebuchadnezzar's long rule (43 years, 605–562 BC). He was the son of Nabopolassar, a Chaldean who declared independence from Assyria in 626 BC and founded the dynasty. The strength of the Neo-Babylonian Empire was primarily Nebuchadnezzar's creation, and the empire collapsed only a generation after his death.

21:5 I myself will fight against you with an outstretched hand Resisting Babylon is futile for Israel since Yahweh is against them, and the Babylonians are agents of his judgment. The image of the outstretched hand and mighty arm subverts the usual redemptive associations of the phrase (see Dt 4:34).
21:7 the plague, sword and famine These disasters probably reflect the curses for violating the covenant. See note on Jer 14:12.
21:8 and the way of death Reminds the people of Judah that they had a choice to follow Yahweh. This either/or formula is common in Jeremiah's rhetoric (see 7:1–15; 22:1–5) and seems to be based on Dt 30:15.

LORD says: See, I am setting before you the way of life and the way of death. ⁹Whoever stays in this city will die by the sword, famine or plague. But whoever goes out and surrenders to the Babylonians who are besieging you will live; they will escape with their lives. ¹⁰I have determined to do this city harm and not good, declares the LORD. It will be given into the hands of the king of Babylon, and he will destroy it with fire.'

¹¹"Moreover, say to the royal house of Judah, 'Hear the word of the LORD. ¹²This is what the LORD says to you, house of David:

"'Administer justice every morning;
   rescue from the hand of the oppressor
   the one who has been robbed,
or my wrath will break out and burn
   like fire
   because of the evil you have done —
   burn with no one to quench it.
¹³ I am against you, Jerusalem,
   you who live above this valley
   on the rocky plateau, declares
      the LORD —
you who say, "Who can come against us?
   Who can enter our refuge?"
¹⁴ I will punish you as your deeds deserve,
   declares the LORD.
I will kindle a fire in your forests
   that will consume everything around you.'"

Judgment Against Wicked Kings

22 This is what the LORD says: "Go down to the palace of the king of Judah and proclaim this message there: ²'Hear the word of the LORD to you, king of Judah, you who sit on David's throne — you, your officials and your people who come through these gates. ³This is what the LORD says: Do what is just and right. Rescue from the hand of the oppressor the one who has been robbed. Do no wrong or violence to the foreigner, the fatherless or the widow, and do not shed innocent blood in this place. ⁴For if you are careful to carry out these commands, then kings who sit on David's throne will come through the gates of this palace, riding in chariots and on horses, accompanied by their officials and their people. ⁵But if you do not obey these commands, declares the LORD, I swear by myself that this palace will become a ruin.'"

⁶For this is what the LORD says about the palace of the king of Judah:

"Though you are like Gilead to me,
   like the summit of Lebanon,
I will surely make you like a wasteland,
   like towns not inhabited.
⁷ I will send destroyers against you,
   each man with his weapons,

21:11–14 A poetic oracle that admonishes the Davidic kings for their unjust rule and pronounces fiery judgment on Jerusalem for their failure.

21:11 the royal house of Judah Zedekiah is king, but the oracle is directed against the royal house in a general way, speaking to the injustice of current and prior rulers.
21:12 Administer justice One of the basic responsibilities of kingship was defending the weak from oppression. See Pr 31:5.
21:14 your deeds deserve Refers to Judah's continual idolatry and refusal to repent. See Jer 6:19. **I will kindle a fire in your forests** Fire is a common symbol of divine wrath and judgment (compare Isa 5:24; Eze 20:47).

22:1–30 With the exception of Jer 22:20–23, this section contains a series of messages concerning the last few kings of Judah. Jeremiah urges Zedekiah to repent, rule justly and live up to the Biblical standard for a Davidic king. The messages concerning previous kings are intended to defuse political rhetoric that looks to the past and hopes to restore Judah's status with support from Egypt. Jeremiah opposes the attitude of the leaders, who believe that Yahweh will save Jerusalem again because of his concern for the Davidic dynasty (compare 21:2; 2Ki 19:34). For Jeremiah, the presence of a Davidic king is not a sure sign of Yahweh's favor. The people have mistakenly placed their faith in the institution of kingship instead of in Yahweh. Even a Davidic king cannot expect divine blessing when he oppresses his people (Jer 22:3).

22:2 to you, king of Judah The address is likely to King Zedekiah (see note on 21:1).

22:3 what is just and right Represents the ideal standards for legal and ethical behavior and an ideal for kingship modeled on the righteousness of Yahweh (Dt 10:18). Justice and righteousness function as a pair of concepts to encompass correct behavior toward God and man: to act with integrity toward others and correctly observe the laws of God. The Hebrew term for justice carries a legal sense; the Hebrew term for righteousness reflects an ethical concern. See Isa 1:17 and note. **the foreigner, the fatherless or the widow** Immigrants, orphans and widows were to be protected, not oppressed. The laws of Deuteronomy especially emphasize the obligation for just treatment of foreigners, orphans and widows (see Dt 14:29; 24:17,19–21; 26:12–13; 27:19). These three groups represent the most vulnerable people of society who have no clan or family structure to defend their rights. See note on Jer 5:28, and note on Ps 94:5.
22:5 I swear by myself An oath was validated by invoking a deity as a witness. Yahweh swears on himself, since there is no other greater power to swear by.
22:6 Gilead A fertile region east of the Jordan River. Metaphorically, Gilead and Lebanon represent desirable and profitable property. See note on Jer 8:22. **the summit of Lebanon** A heavily forested mountainous region north of Israel that was famous for its abundance of natural resources (especially timber) and rugged beauty. See Isa 29:17 and note; Isa 60:13 and note.
22:7 they will cut up your fine cedar beams Compare 2Ki 19:23. Here, Lebanon is a metaphor for Judah, and cutting down the best cedar trees represents the destruction of its most cherished institutions—the royal line of David and the temple of Yahweh.

and they will cut up your fine cedar beams
and throw them into the fire.

⁸"People from many nations will pass by this
city and will ask one another, 'Why has the LORD
done such a thing to this great city?' ⁹And the
answer will be: 'Because they have forsaken the
covenant of the LORD their God and have worshiped and served other gods.'"

¹⁰ Do not weep for the dead king or mourn his
    loss;
  rather, weep bitterly for him who is
    exiled,
because he will never return
  nor see his native land again.

¹¹For this is what the LORD says about Shallumᵃ
son of Josiah, who succeeded his father as king of
Judah but has gone from this place: "He will never
return. ¹²He will die in the place where they have
led him captive; he will not see this land again."

¹³ "Woe to him who builds his palace by
    unrighteousness,
  his upper rooms by injustice,
making his own people work for
    nothing,
  not paying them for their labor.
¹⁴ He says, 'I will build myself a great palace
    with spacious upper rooms.'
So he makes large windows in it,
  panels it with cedar
  and decorates it in red.

¹⁵ "Does it make you a king
  to have more and more cedar?
Did not your father have food and
    drink?
He did what was right and just,
  so all went well with him.
¹⁶ He defended the cause of the poor
    and needy,
  and so all went well.
Is that not what it means to know me?"
  declares the LORD.
¹⁷ "But your eyes and your heart
  are set only on dishonest gain,
on shedding innocent blood
  and on oppression and extortion."

¹⁸Therefore this is what the LORD says about
Jehoiakim son of Josiah king of Judah:

"They will not mourn for him:
  'Alas, my brother! Alas, my sister!'
They will not mourn for him:
  'Alas, my master! Alas, his
    splendor!'
¹⁹ He will have the burial of a donkey —
  dragged away and thrown
  outside the gates of Jerusalem."

²⁰ "Go up to Lebanon and cry out,
  let your voice be heard in Bashan,
cry out from Abarim,
  for all your allies are crushed.

ᵃ 11 Also called Jehoahaz

22:10 Do not weep for the dead king Refers to King Josiah, who died in battle with the Egyptians in 609 BC. Josiah's death brought an end to his nationalistic plan of expansion, which was centered on a reunited Israel free from foreign domination. Jeremiah is subtly indicating that there will be no restoration of the independence of Josiah's kingdom. **weep bitterly for him who is exiled** Refers to Jehoahaz, who succeeded Josiah as king for three months in 609 BC. He was exiled to Egypt by Pharaoh Necho, who replaced him on the throne with Jehoiakim. Jehoahaz, or Shallum, was Josiah's fourth son (1Ch 3:15; see note on Jer 22:11). His choice as king by the people of the land likely indicates he shared Josiah's political outlook concerning Babylon and Egypt and thus enjoyed the support of those with anti-Egyptian interests. Necho's move to quickly depose Jehoahaz and replace him with the pro-Egyptian Jehoiakim likely also testifies to Jehoahaz's anti-Egyptian loyalties. See the timeline "Judah From the Fall of Samaria to the Exile" on p. 606; see the timeline "The Divided Kingdom" on p. 536. **he will never return nor see his native land again** Jehoahaz died in Egypt (2Ki 23:34). If any political factions in Judah held out hope for his restoration to the throne, Jeremiah is telling them unequivocally that their hope is misplaced; he will not return.
22:11 Shallum son of Josiah, who succeeded his father as king of Judah The personal name of King Jehoahaz. The name means "payment" or "recompense." See 1Ch 3:15; see note on Jer 22:10.

22:13–19 This passage is a poetic woe oracle critical of Jehoiakim, especially his lavish building projects and oppressive use of forced labor. Jeremiah pronounces a disgraceful end for the king without proper mourning or burial. The exact details of Jehoiakim's death are unknown, though he appears to have died prior to Nebuchadnezzar's siege of Jerusalem. The Biblical writers give no account of his burial.
22:14 a great palace with spacious upper rooms The depiction of Jehoiakim in this section suggests he patterned himself as a ruler like Solomon.
22:15 make you a king to have more and more cedar A mocking rhetorical question. Using Jehoiakim's father, Josiah, as a favorable example, Jeremiah asserts that one is a king by virtue of character, not by virtue of construction projects.
22:16 to know me Knowledge of Yahweh comes through emulating him in the attributes of justice, righteousness and care for the oppressed and less fortunate. Compare Dt 10:18.
22:18 Jehoiakim son of Josiah king of Judah Second son of Josiah (see 1Ch 3:15). He was appointed king in 609 BC by Pharaoh Necho and ruled until 597 BC. Jehoiakim was a vassal of Egypt until Nebuchadnezzar defeated them at Carchemish in 605 BC (see Jer 46:2), ending Egyptian power and influence in Syria-Palestine. Nebuchadnezzar records that he received tribute from all the kings of this region in 604 BC.
22:19 He will have the burial of a donkey A dis-

²¹ I warned you when you felt secure,
  but you said, 'I will not listen!'
This has been your way from your youth;
  you have not obeyed me.
²² The wind will drive all your shepherds away,
  and your allies will go into exile.
Then you will be ashamed and disgraced
  because of all your wickedness.
²³ You who live in 'Lebanon,ᵃ'
  who are nestled in cedar buildings,
how you will groan when pangs come upon
      you,
  pain like that of a woman in labor!

²⁴ "As surely as I live," declares the LORD, "even if you, Jehoiachinᵇ son of Jehoiakim king of Judah, were a signet ring on my right hand, I would still pull you off. ²⁵ I will deliver you into the hands of those who want to kill you, those you fear — Nebuchadnezzar king of Babylon and the Babylonians.ᶜ ²⁶ I will hurl you and the mother who gave you birth into another country, where neither of you was born, and there you both will die. ²⁷ You will never come back to the land you long to return to."

²⁸ Is this man Jehoiachin a despised, broken pot,
  an object no one wants?
Why will he and his children be hurled out,
  cast into a land they do not know?
²⁹ O land, land, land,
  hear the word of the LORD!

³⁰ This is what the LORD says:
"Record this man as if childless,
  a man who will not prosper in his lifetime,
for none of his offspring will prosper,
  none will sit on the throne of David
  or rule anymore in Judah."

The Righteous Branch

23 "Woe to the shepherds who are destroying and scattering the sheep of my pasture!" declares the LORD. ² Therefore this is what the LORD, the God of Israel, says to the shepherds who tend my people: "Because you have scattered my flock and driven them away and have not bestowed care on them, I will bestow punishment on you for the evil you have done," declares the LORD. ³ "I myself will gather the remnant of my flock out of all the countries where I have driven them and will bring them back to their pasture, where they will be fruitful and increase in number. ⁴ I will place shepherds over them who will tend them, and they will no longer be afraid or terrified, nor will any be missing," declares the LORD.

⁵ "The days are coming," declares the LORD,
  "when I will raise up for Davidᵈ a righteous
      Branch,

ᵃ 23 That is, the palace in Jerusalem (see 1 Kings 7:2)
ᵇ 24 Hebrew *Koniah*, a variant of *Jehoiachin*; also in verse 28
ᶜ 25 Or *Chaldeans* ᵈ 5 Or *up from David's line*

---

honorable burial, not one fit for a king. The details of Jehoiakim's burial are unknown.

22:20–23 This oracle pronouncing judgment on Jerusalem interrupts the series of oracles directed at the final kings of Judah. Jerusalem is personified as an adulterous wife who should lament over her coming punishment. The references to "shepherds" and "cedar" link the oracle to themes related to the royal house of David (see 2:8 and note; 3:15; 10:21; 22:6–7,14; Isa 56:11; Eze 34:1–10 and note).

22:20 Lebanon See note on Jer 22:6. **Bashan** A fertile plateau east of the Sea of Galilee and south of Mount Hermon. It was north of the region of Gilead mentioned in v. 6. **Abarim** A mountain range northeast of the Dead Sea. See Dt 32:49. **all your allies are crushed** In the metaphor of Israel as an unfaithful wife, her lovers can either be political allies (see Eze 23:5–9) or foreign deities (Hos 2:1–13).
22:22 your shepherds Refers to the leaders of Judah. See note on Jer 3:15.
22:23 You who live in 'Lebanon,' who are nestled in cedar buildings A metaphor for Jerusalem. The reference to cedars alludes to the extensive use of cedar in the building of the royal palace and the temple.

22:24–30 An oracle of judgment against Jehoiachin, who was king of Judah for only three months before being taken into exile by Nebuchadnezzar in 597 BC.

22:24 Jehoiachin In the Hebrew Bible, the name of this king appears in several forms, leading to various English renderings: Jehoiachin, Jeconiah and Coniah. The

name means "Yahweh establishes." **a signet ring on my right hand** The signet ring was a stamp seal used to mark ownership. It was a symbol of royal authority. The right hand was a symbol of power. See note on Est 3:10, and note on Ge 41:42. See note on Isa 41:10. See the infographic "Royal Seals of Judah" on p. 593.
22:27 You will never come back Jeremiah addresses the hopes of people who still considered Jehoiachin the rightful king of Judah and looked for his return. Jehoiachin's exile to Babylon is permanent; there will be no restoration. Babylonian administrative records actually treat him as a king in exile, and the prophet Ezekiel never refers to his successor, Zedekiah, as king (*melekh*). See note on Eze 1:2.
22:30 none of his offspring will prosper, none Not only will Jehoiachin die in exile, but his descendants will not regain the Davidic throne. He may as well have died childless, since his children will not inherit the kingdom.

23:1–8 An oracle of restoration looking ahead to the future reign of the Messiah, who will live up to the ideals of Davidic kingship. This oracle concludes the series of prophecies against the house of David with a hopeful outlook. While the last few kings have deserved the judgment they received, Yahweh will raise up a righteous ruler and bring Judah back from exile.

23:1 the shepherds who are destroying and scattering A metaphor for the rulers of Judah.
23:5 I will raise up for David a righteous Branch The Hebrew word used here, *tsemach*, often translated "branch," is a metaphor referring to the Messiah (see Isa 4:2 and note). **what is just and right** The Messiah will fulfill the ideal that Zedekiah could not live up to. See Jer 22:3 and note.

a King who will reign wisely
   and do what is just and right in the land.
⁶ In his days Judah will be saved
   and Israel will live in safety.
This is the name by which he will be called:
   The LORD Our Righteous Savior.

⁷"So then, the days are coming," declares the LORD, "when people will no longer say, 'As surely as the LORD lives, who brought the Israelites up out of Egypt,' ⁸but they will say, 'As surely as the LORD lives, who brought the descendants of Israel up out of the land of the north and out of all the countries where he had banished them.' Then they will live in their own land."

Lying Prophets

⁹Concerning the prophets:

My heart is broken within me;
   all my bones tremble.
I am like a drunken man,
   like a strong man overcome by wine,
because of the LORD
   and his holy words.
¹⁰ The land is full of adulterers;
   because of the curse^a the land lies parched
   and the pastures in the wilderness are withered.
The prophets follow an evil course
   and use their power unjustly.

¹¹ "Both prophet and priest are godless;
   even in my temple I find their wickedness,"
                 declares the LORD.
¹² "Therefore their path will become slippery;
   they will be banished to darkness
   and there they will fall.
I will bring disaster on them
   in the year they are punished,"
                 declares the LORD.

¹³ "Among the prophets of Samaria
   I saw this repulsive thing:

They prophesied by Baal
   and led my people Israel astray.
¹⁴ And among the prophets of Jerusalem
   I have seen something horrible:
   They commit adultery and live a lie.
They strengthen the hands of evildoers,
   so that not one of them turns from their wickedness.
They are all like Sodom to me;
   the people of Jerusalem are like Gomorrah."

¹⁵Therefore this is what the LORD Almighty says concerning the prophets:

"I will make them eat bitter food
   and drink poisoned water,
because from the prophets of Jerusalem
   ungodliness has spread throughout the land."

¹⁶This is what the LORD Almighty says:

"Do not listen to what the prophets are prophesying to you;
   they fill you with false hopes.
They speak visions from their own minds,
   not from the mouth of the LORD.
¹⁷They keep saying to those who despise me,
   'The LORD says: You will have peace.'
And to all who follow the stubbornness of their hearts
   they say, 'No harm will come to you.'
¹⁸ But which of them has stood in the council of the LORD
   to see or to hear his word?
   Who has listened and heard his word?
¹⁹ See, the storm of the LORD
   will burst out in wrath,
a whirlwind swirling down
   on the heads of the wicked.
²⁰ The anger of the LORD will not turn back
   until he fully accomplishes
   the purposes of his heart.

^a 10 Or because of these things

23:6 LORD Our Righteous Savior A play on Zedekiah's name, which means "Yahweh is my righteousness." The Messiah fulfills the expectation for the Davidic king. While earlier passages (e.g., 21:11–14) encouraged Zedekiah to repent and, in effect, live up to his name, this passage uses his name as a prophecy pointing to a future king who will fulfill all the ideals embodied in the role of the Davidic king. See the table "Names of God in the Old Testament" on p. 917.

23:7 out of Egypt See note on 16:14.

23:9–40 Jeremiah follows the collection of oracles against the royal house with a collection of oracles against false prophets. The overall sentiment is similar to 14:13–18. These oracles are general in their accusations of idolatry and immorality. Specific incidents involving false prophets are recorded in chs. 28–29.

23:10 The land is full of adulterers Refers metaphorically to idolatry.

23:11 I find their wickedness Idol-worship was occurring in the temple of Yahweh according to 2Ki 23:4 and Eze 8.

23:13 the prophets of Samaria Refers to the prophets of the northern kingdom of Israel. Apparently, these were prophets of Baal, not Yahweh (see 1Ki 18:20–40). **Baal** The Canaanite storm god and Yahweh's leading rival for Israel's worship.

23:14 the prophets of Jerusalem Jeremiah accuses the prophets of Judah of promoting injustice as well as idolatry. **like Sodom** Yahweh's destruction of Sodom and Gomorrah (see Ge 18–19) typified the devastating effects of his wrath. See note on Isa 1:9.

23:15 LORD Almighty A title identifying God as leader of

In days to come
  you will understand it clearly.
²¹ I did not send these prophets,
  yet they have run with their message;
I did not speak to them,
  yet they have prophesied.
²² But if they had stood in my council,
  they would have proclaimed my words to
    my people
and would have turned them from their evil
    ways
and from their evil deeds.

²³ "Am I only a God nearby,"
                              declares the LORD,
  "and not a God far away?
²⁴ Who can hide in secret places
  so that I cannot see them?"
                              declares the LORD.
  "Do not I fill heaven and earth?"
                              declares the LORD.

²⁵ "I have heard what the prophets say who prophesy lies in my name. They say, 'I had a dream! I had a dream!' ²⁶ How long will this continue in the hearts of these lying prophets, who prophesy the delusions of their own minds? ²⁷ They think the dreams they tell one another will make my people forget my name, just as their ancestors forgot my name through Baal worship. ²⁸ Let the prophet who has a dream recount the dream, but let the one who has my word speak it faithfully. For what has straw to do with grain?" declares the LORD. ²⁹ "Is not my word like fire," declares the LORD, "and like a hammer that breaks a rock in pieces?

³⁰ "Therefore," declares the LORD, "I am against the prophets who steal from one another words supposedly from me. ³¹ Yes," declares the LORD, "I am against the prophets who wag their own tongues and yet declare, 'The LORD declares.'

³² Indeed, I am against those who prophesy false dreams," declares the LORD. "They tell them and lead my people astray with their reckless lies, yet I did not send or appoint them. They do not benefit these people in the least," declares the LORD.

False Prophecy

³³ "When these people, or a prophet or a priest, ask you, 'What is the message from the LORD?' say to them, 'What message? I will forsake you, declares the LORD.' ³⁴ If a prophet or a priest or anyone else claims, 'This is a message from the LORD,' I will punish them and their household. ³⁵ This is what each of you keeps saying to your friends and other Israelites: 'What is the LORD's answer?' or 'What has the LORD spoken?' ³⁶ But you must not mention 'a message from the LORD' again, because each one's word becomes their own message. So you distort the words of the living God, the LORD Almighty, our God. ³⁷ This is what you keep saying to a prophet: 'What is the LORD's answer to you?' or 'What has the LORD spoken?' ³⁸ Although you claim, 'This is a message from the LORD,' this is what the LORD says: You used the words, 'This is a message from the LORD,' even though I told you that you must not claim, 'This is a message from the LORD.' ³⁹ Therefore, I will surely forget you and cast you out of my presence along with the city I gave to you and your ancestors. ⁴⁰ I will bring on you everlasting disgrace — everlasting shame that will not be forgotten."

Two Baskets of Figs

24 After Jehoiachin[a] son of Jehoiakim king of Judah and the officials, the skilled workers and the artisans of Judah were carried into exile

---

ᵃ 1 Hebrew *Jeconiah*, a variant of *Jehoiachin*

---

the heavenly armies. See note on Jer 6:6. **bitter food** A metaphor for judgment.
23:23 a God nearby The rhetorical questions in vv. 23–24 emphasize Yahweh's presence everywhere (his omnipresence). He is well aware of the abuses carried on in his name by the prophets.
23:28 what has straw to do with grain Contrasts the valuable grain (true prophecy) with the worthless chaff (false prophecy).
23:29 my word like fire Which will consume the straw of v. 28.
23:32 false dreams While Yahweh could communicate through dreams (e.g., Ge 28:12), these prophets were falsely claiming to have received divine revelation through dreams. Dreams were a commonly accepted means of communication from the gods in the ancient Near East (e.g., Jacob in Ge 28:12; Joseph in Ge 37:5–11; Pharaoh in Ge 41:1–8; Nebuchadnezzar in Da 2; 4; Joseph in Mt 1:20). Dreams usually were viewed positively, but Jeremiah's opposition is based on their misuse. Ancient Near Eastern texts include reports of dreams that were taken seriously and studied for their value as omens for

predicting the future. In the dream of Gudea of Lagash (2150 BC), the god, Ningirsu, sends a figure who commands Gudea to build a temple. This mysterious figure is reminiscent of the apocalyptic figures described in Daniel and Ezekiel (Da 7; Eze 1:25–28).

23:33–40 Jeremiah condemns the false prophets who are passing off their messages of good news — as though they are reporting messages from God himself. Because of the many false prophecies, Jeremiah prohibits use of the Hebrew word *massa*, which indicates a divine communication.

23:33 message The Hebrew Masoretic text reads *eth-mah-massa* ("what burden?"), but the Greek Septuagint understood the phrase as *attem hamassa* ("you are the burden") — which makes better sense of the Hebrew grammar. Following the Septuagint reading, the prophet's response plays on the double meaning of *massa*, which can denote a prophetic oracle or a physical burden. Jeremiah declares that the very people who are asking for the *massa* ("message") are themselves the *massa* ("burden") that Yahweh is about to throw away.

from Jerusalem to Babylon by Nebuchadnezzar king of Babylon, the LORD showed me two baskets of figs placed in front of the temple of the LORD. ²One basket had very good figs, like those that ripen early; the other basket had very bad figs, so bad they could not be eaten.

³Then the LORD asked me, "What do you see, Jeremiah?"

"Figs," I answered. "The good ones are very good, but the bad ones are so bad they cannot be eaten."

⁴Then the word of the LORD came to me: ⁵"This is what the LORD, the God of Israel, says: 'Like these good figs, I regard as good the exiles from Judah, whom I sent away from this place to the land of the Babylonians.ᵃ ⁶My eyes will watch over them for their good, and I will bring them back to this land. I will build them up and not tear them down; I will plant them and not uproot them. ⁷I will give them a heart to know me, that I am the LORD. They will be my people, and I will be their God, for they will return to me with all their heart.

⁸"'But like the bad figs, which are so bad they cannot be eaten,' says the LORD, 'so will I deal with Zedekiah king of Judah, his officials and the survivors from Jerusalem, whether they remain in this land or live in Egypt. ⁹I will make them

abhorrent and an offense to all the kingdoms of the earth, a reproach and a byword, a curseᵇ and an object of ridicule, wherever I banish them. ¹⁰I will send the sword, famine and plague against them until they are destroyed from the land I gave to them and their ancestors.'"

Seventy Years of Captivity

25 The word came to Jeremiah concerning all the people of Judah in the fourth year of Jehoiakim son of Josiah king of Judah, which was the first year of Nebuchadnezzar king of Babylon. ²So Jeremiah the prophet said to all the people of Judah and to all those living in Jerusalem: ³For twenty-three years — from the thirteenth year of Josiah son of Amon king of Judah until this very day — the word of the LORD has come to me and I have spoken to you again and again, but you have not listened.

⁴And though the LORD has sent all his servants the prophets to you again and again, you have not listened or paid any attention. ⁵They said, "Turn now, each of you, from your evil ways and your evil practices, and you can stay in the land the LORD gave to you and your ancestors for ever

ᵃ 5 Or *Chaldeans*   ᵇ 9 That is, their names will be used in cursing (see 29:22); or, others will see that they are cursed.

24:1–10 Jeremiah reports a vision in which he saw two baskets of figs—one good and one bad—before the temple of Yahweh. The interpretation of the vision looks ahead to Yahweh's plan to bring his people back from Babylonian exile. Those who remain in the land or flee to Egypt are seen as opposing Yahweh's plan. The vision is dated to the time after Jehoiachin and the upper class of Judah were taken into exile in Babylon (597 BC). The comparison of the good and bad figs likely is a critique on the poor quality of the leadership left behind in Judah. Jeremiah is generally critical of the bad leadership advice that King Zedekiah received from his inept advisers. See the timeline "Life of Jeremiah" on p. 1170.

24:1 Jehoiachin See note on 22:24. **king of Judah and the officials, the skilled workers and the artisans of Judah** Compare 2Ki 24:12–16. All the experienced and skilled people were taken to Babylon. **Nebuchadnezzar** See note on Jer 21:2. **figs** A sweet, succulent fruit that is common in Biblical imagery as a symbol of prosperity and security (see 1Ki 4:25; Mic 4:4). The fig tree and its fruit could also be symbols of judgment; failure to keep the covenant meant a loss of prosperity and fruitfulness (see Jer 5:17; 8:13; Isa 34:4; Joel 1:7). A fruitless fig tree is used as a metaphor for spiritual fruitlessness in the NT (Mt 21:19–21; Lk 13:6–9).

24:5 to the land of the Babylonians Describes exile in Babylon. "Chaldean" and "Babylonian" are generally synonymous in Biblical usage (see note on Isa 43:14).

24:8 Zedekiah See note on Jer 21:1. The people who remained were likely rejected because they did not repent after seeing the fate of the first group of exiles in 597 BC. **the survivors from Jerusalem** The contrast between the good and bad figs demonstrates the positive and negative functions of the Biblical image of the remnant. In 8:3,

the remnant that escapes the first round of judgment will still be punished (compare Eze 6:8 and note; 6:9 and note). The remnant often is a positive image pointing to Yahweh's gathering of his people and the return of the exiles from Babylon. Isaiah explicitly develops this theme into the idea of the "righteous remnant" (see Isa 62:2 and note). Here, the good figs represent the righteous remnant that will be restored. The bad figs represent the part of the remnant that will still be judged. **live in Egypt** Jews who emigrated to Egypt in response to the Babylonian invasion in 597 BC. Jeremiah is forced to accompany a group fleeing to Egypt after the destruction of Jerusalem in 586 BC (Jer 43–44).

24:10 sword, famine and plague These disasters probably reflect the curses for disobeying the covenant given in Leviticus and Deuteronomy. See note on 14:12.

25:1–14 This passage summarizes the main themes of Jeremiah's preaching up to this point: Judah's idolatry, the coming judgment, Babylonian exile and judgment on other foreign nations.

25:1 the fourth year of Jehoiakim 605 BC. See note on 22:18. See the timeline "Life of Jeremiah" on p. 1170. **the first year of Nebuchadnezzar** Likely a reference to the accession year of Nebuchadnezzar, which also was 605 BC. See note on Eze 24:1.

25:3 twenty-three years—from the thirteenth year of Josiah 627–605 BC. See note on Jer 1:2.

25:4 all his servants the prophets Judah has a long history of ignoring God's messengers, as the nation rejected Jeremiah and all the prophets who came before him. Compare 2Ki 17:13–14.

25:5 Turn The call for Judah to repent is a central part of Jeremiah's prophecies (see Jer 3:1—4:4). **you can stay in the land** Continued possession of the land was

and ever. ⁶Do not follow other gods to serve and worship them; do not arouse my anger with what your hands have made. Then I will not harm you."

⁷"But you did not listen to me," declares the LORD, "and you have aroused my anger with what your hands have made, and you have brought harm to yourselves."

⁸Therefore the LORD Almighty says this: "Because you have not listened to my words, ⁹I will summon all the peoples of the north and my servant Nebuchadnezzar king of Babylon," declares the LORD, "and I will bring them against this land and its inhabitants and against all the surrounding nations. I will completely destroyᵃ them and make them an object of horror and scorn, and an everlasting ruin. ¹⁰I will banish from them the sounds of joy and gladness, the voices of bride and bridegroom, the sound of millstones and the light of the lamp. ¹¹This whole country will become a desolate wasteland, and these nations will serve the king of Babylon seventy years.

¹²"But when the seventy years are fulfilled, I will punish the king of Babylon and his nation, the land of the Babylonians,ᵇ for their guilt," declares the LORD, "and will make it desolate forever. ¹³I will bring on that land all the things I have spoken against it, all that are written in this book and prophesied by Jeremiah against all the nations. ¹⁴They themselves will be enslaved by many nations and great kings; I will repay them according to their deeds and the work of their hands."

The Cup of God's Wrath

¹⁵This is what the LORD, the God of Israel, said to me: "Take from my hand this cup filled with the wine of my wrath and make all the nations to whom I send you drink it. ¹⁶When they drink it, they will stagger and go mad because of the sword I will send among them."

¹⁷So I took the cup from the LORD's hand and made all the nations to whom he sent me drink it: ¹⁸Jerusalem and the towns of Judah, its kings and officials, to make them a ruin and an object of horror and scorn, a curseᶜ — as they are today; ¹⁹Pharaoh king of Egypt, his attendants, his officials and all his people, ²⁰and all the foreign people there; all the kings of Uz; all the kings of the Philistines (those of Ashkelon, Gaza, Ekron, and the people left at Ashdod); ²¹Edom, Moab and Ammon; ²²all the kings of Tyre and Sidon; the kings of the coastlands across the sea; ²³Dedan,

ᵃ 9 The Hebrew term refers to the irrevocable giving over of things or persons to the LORD, often by totally destroying them.   ᵇ 12 Or *Chaldeans*   ᶜ 18 That is, their names to be used in cursing (see 29:22); or, to be seen by others as cursed

conditional on their repentance and obedience (see Dt 8:1 and note).

25:9 all the peoples of the north Alludes to the enemy from the north (see Jer 1:15 and note). **my servant Nebuchadnezzar king of Babylon** Explicitly identifies the enemy from the north as the invading Babylonians. The reference to Nebuchadnezzar as Yahweh's servant identifies him as the agent of judgment (see note on 21:2). Compare Isa 10:5; 44:28—45:1.

25:10 the sound of millstones Used to grind grain into flour. All normal daily activity will cease.

25:11 seventy years A symbolic number, possibly representing a single lifetime (see Ps 90:10 and note; Isa 23:15). The period from 605–539 BC was 66 years. The first return from exile was sometime between 539 and 535 BC. Aligning the prediction of 70 years of exile with a historical 70-year period is complicated. The year 605 BC did not mark a significant exile of Jews. More Jews were taken into exile in 597 and 586 BC. Jeremiah views the 597 BC exile as more significant because of who was taken (see Jer 24:5). The closest alignment with 70 years comes by reckoning the period from the destruction of the temple in 586 BC to the completion of the second temple in 516 BC. The reference to a 70-year exile also appears in 2Ch 36:21 and Zec 1:12. The author of Chronicles interprets the 70-year period as the time of an overdue Sabbath rest for the land. This prophecy is developed further in Da 9 (see Da 9:24 and note).

25:15–38 An oracle of judgment depicting Yahweh's wrath as a cup of wine. Jeremiah is to take the cup to the nations. The first half of the oracle is a prose narrative listing the nations to be judged (Jer 25:15–29). The second half is a poetic description of Yahweh's judgment on the earth (vv. 30–38).

25:15 this cup filled with the wine of my wrath A cup of wine as a metaphor for divine punishment appears several times in the OT (see Isa 51:17; Ps 75:8; Jer 49:12; Hab 2:15–16). Isaiah's use of the image shows that the cup results in drunkenness and loss of physical and mental awareness, not death. **all the nations** This cup of wrath is to be distributed to all the nations, not just Israel. The imagery of judgment against foreign nations is more prominent in Jer 46–51.

25:20 Uz The exact location of Uz is unknown. It is referenced as the homeland of Job in Job 1:1. It also is mentioned in parallel with Edom in La 4:21, which suggests Uz is located south or southeast of the Dead Sea, in the northwest corner of the Arabian Peninsula. **the Philistines** Israel's enemy on the coastal plain west of Judah (see Ge 21:32 and note; Jos 13:3 and note). Their civilization was concentrated in five main cities—Ashkelon, Gaza, Ekron, Ashdod and Gath. Ashkelon was a seaport on the Mediterranean coast, and Gaza and Ashdod were located near the coast. Ekron and Gath were near the border with Judah. The reference to the remnants of Ashdod reflects the writer's knowledge that Ashdod was destroyed in 610 BC by the Egyptians. Gath may have been destroyed in 715 BC by Sargon of Assyria. Like Jeremiah, most of the prophets omit Gath from their oracles announcing judgment on the other four Philistine cities (e.g., Am 1:6–8; Zep 2:4–6).

25:21 Edom Judgment started with Judah and gradually spiraled outward. The first nations mentioned are Israel's closest neighbors and oldest enemies. Edom was Judah's neighbor to the southeast on the southeastern corner of the Dead Sea. The Edomites were descendants of Jacob's brother, Esau (see note on Ge 25:25). **Moab** Judah's neighbor east of the Jordan River. The Moabites were descended from Abraham's nephew, Lot

Tema, Buz and all who are in distant places[a]; [24]all the kings of Arabia and all the kings of the foreign people who live in the wilderness; [25]all the kings of Zimri, Elam and Media; [26]and all the kings of the north, near and far, one after the other — all the kingdoms on the face of the earth. And after all of them, the king of Sheshak[b] will drink it too.

[27]"Then tell them, 'This is what the LORD Almighty, the God of Israel, says: Drink, get drunk and vomit, and fall to rise no more because of the sword I will send among you.' [28]But if they refuse to take the cup from your hand and drink, tell them, 'This is what the LORD Almighty says: You must drink it! [29]See, I am beginning to bring disaster on the city that bears my Name, and will you indeed go unpunished? You will not go unpunished, for I am calling down a sword on all who live on the earth, declares the LORD Almighty.'

[30]"Now prophesy all these words against them and say to them:

"'The LORD will roar from on high;
he will thunder from his holy dwelling
and roar mightily against his land.
He will shout like those who tread the grapes,
shout against all who live on the earth.
[31]The tumult will resound to the ends of the earth,
for the LORD will bring charges against the nations;
he will bring judgment on all mankind
and put the wicked to the sword,'"

declares the LORD.

[32]This is what the LORD Almighty says:

"Look! Disaster is spreading
from nation to nation;
a mighty storm is rising
from the ends of the earth."

[33]At that time those slain by the LORD will be everywhere — from one end of the earth to the other. They will not be mourned or gathered up or buried, but will be like dung lying on the ground.

[34]Weep and wail, you shepherds;
roll in the dust, you leaders of the flock.
For your time to be slaughtered has come;
you will fall like the best of the rams.[c]
[35]The shepherds will have nowhere to flee,
the leaders of the flock no place to escape.
[36]Hear the cry of the shepherds,
the wailing of the leaders of the flock,
for the LORD is destroying their pasture.
[37]The peaceful meadows will be laid waste
because of the fierce anger of the LORD.
[38]Like a lion he will leave his lair,
and their land will become desolate
because of the sword[d] of the oppressor
and because of the LORD's fierce anger.

Jeremiah Threatened With Death

26 Early in the reign of Jehoiakim son of Josiah king of Judah, this word came from the LORD: [2]"This is what the LORD says: Stand in

[a] 23 Or who clip the hair by their foreheads   [b] 26 Sheshak is a cryptogram for Babylon.   [c] 34 Septuagint; Hebrew fall and be shattered like fine pottery   [d] 38 Some Hebrew manuscripts and Septuagint (see also 46:16 and 50:16); most Hebrew manuscripts anger

(see Ge 19:30–38). **Ammon** Judah and Israel's neighbor east of the Jordan and north of Moab. The Ammonites were also descended from Lot (see Ge 19:30–38).
25:22 Tyre The leading city of the Phoenicians (see note on Eze 26:1—28:19). It was located on the Mediterranean coast northwest of Israel (see note on Eze 26:2). **Sidon** An important Phoenician city about 25 miles north of Tyre on the coast. **the coastlands across the sea** Likely refers to Phoenician colonies around the Mediterranean coast.
25:23 Dedan A trading center in north central Arabia. See note on Eze 27:15. **Tema** An Arabian oasis (see note on Isa 21:14). **Buz** This location is unknown.
25:25 Zimri An unknown location. It is paralleled with references in Persia, east of Babylon. **Elam** A mountainous region east of Babylon and north of the Persian Gulf (see note on Eze 32:24). Elam is in the southern area of the Iranian plateau in the Zagros Mountains. **Media** The northwest area of the Zagros Mountains and Iranian Plateau, roughly corresponding to the northwest region of modern Iran.
25:26 all the kingdoms Yahweh's cup of wrath is extended to all the nations of the earth. Jeremiah's role in symbolically bringing this cup of wrath to the nations fulfills his commission as a "prophet to the nations" (Jer 1:5). **king of Sheshak** The list ends with Judah's current enemy. Following the Hebrew text, many English transla-

tions refer to Babylon as Sheshach (Sheshak), which is an athbash cryptogram (also used in 51:41). An athbash cipher is based on a simple alphabetic substitution; the first letter of the alphabet is replaced with the last, and so on. There may have been some double meaning or wordplay involved, though the significance is now lost.
25:30 LORD will roar from on high A poetic expression of Yahweh's appearing in judgment (compare Joel 3:16; Am 1:2).

26:1—29:32 This section narrates three incidents in which Jeremiah comes into conflict with the priests, prophets and civil authorities in Jerusalem because of his preaching, which they take to be blasphemous and treasonous.

26:1–15 Jeremiah delivers his "temple sermon" (see Jer 7:1–15 and note), which is not received well by the people of Judah. His assertion that the temple is likely to be destroyed if they don't repent undermines their belief in Yahweh's special election of Jerusalem and the temple. The content of Jeremiah's message in vv. 4–6 is an abbreviated version of the sermon from 7:3–15.

26:1 Early in the reign of Jehoiakim Jehoiakim began to reign in 609 BC (see note on 22:18). This likely refers to the year he took the throne, from autumn 609 to April 608 BC (see note on 25:1). See the timeline "Life of Jeremiah" on p. 1170.

the courtyard of the Lord's house and speak to all the people of the towns of Judah who come to worship in the house of the Lord. Tell them everything I command you; do not omit a word. ³Perhaps they will listen and each will turn from their evil ways. Then I will relent and not inflict on them the disaster I was planning because of the evil they have done. ⁴Say to them, 'This is what the Lord says: If you do not listen to me and follow my law, which I have set before you, ⁵and if you do not listen to the words of my servants the prophets, whom I have sent to you again and again (though you have not listened), ⁶then I will make this house like Shiloh and this city a curse^a among all the nations of the earth.'"

⁷The priests, the prophets and all the people heard Jeremiah speak these words in the house of the Lord. ⁸But as soon as Jeremiah finished telling all the people everything the Lord had commanded him to say, the priests, the prophets and all the people seized him and said, "You must die! ⁹Why do you prophesy in the Lord's name that this house will be like Shiloh and this city will be desolate and deserted?" And all the people crowded around Jeremiah in the house of the Lord.

¹⁰When the officials of Judah heard about these things, they went up from the royal palace to the house of the Lord and took their places at the entrance of the New Gate of the Lord's house. ¹¹Then the priests and the prophets said to the officials and all the people, "This man should be sentenced to death because he has prophesied against this city. You have heard it with your own ears!"

¹²Then Jeremiah said to all the officials and all the people: "The Lord sent me to prophesy against this house and this city all the things you have heard. ¹³Now reform your ways and your actions and obey the Lord your God. Then the Lord will relent and not bring the disaster he has pronounced against you. ¹⁴As for me, I am in your hands; do with me whatever you think is good and right. ¹⁵Be assured, however, that if you put me to death, you will bring the guilt of innocent blood on yourselves and on this city and on those who live in it, for in truth the Lord has sent me to you to speak all these words in your hearing."

¹⁶Then the officials and all the people said to the priests and the prophets, "This man should not be sentenced to death! He has spoken to us in the name of the Lord our God."

¹⁷Some of the elders of the land stepped forward and said to the entire assembly of people, ¹⁸"Micah of Moresheth prophesied in the days of Hezekiah king of Judah. He told all the people of Judah, 'This is what the Lord Almighty says:

"'Zion will be plowed like a field,
    Jerusalem will become a heap of rubble,
    the temple hill a mound overgrown with
        thickets.'^{b}

¹⁹"Did Hezekiah king of Judah or anyone else in Judah put him to death? Did not Hezekiah fear the Lord and seek his favor? And did not the Lord relent, so that he did not bring the disaster he pronounced against them? We are about to bring a terrible disaster on ourselves!"

²⁰(Now Uriah son of Shemaiah from Kiriath Jearim was another man who prophesied in the name of the Lord; he prophesied the same things against this city and this land as Jeremiah did. ²¹When King Jehoiakim and all his officers and officials heard his words, the king was determined

---

^{a} 6 That is, its name will be used in cursing (see 29:22); or, others will see that it is cursed. ^{b} 18 Micah 3:12

26:6 Shiloh Israel's main religious center before the monarchy. See note on Jer 7:12.

26:8 You must die The penalty for false prophecy was death (see Dt 18:15–22).

26:9 Why do you prophesy Reflects the people's belief that Jeremiah's very act of speaking such a message could bring about the disaster he predicted. This superstition was common in the ancient world, where prophets were believed to not only proclaim the divine message but also unleash the prophesied divine action through their speech.

26:10 at the entrance of the New Gate The gate complex functioned as a local court (see Am 5:10–15). This scene provides one of the most complete accounts of a trial found in the OT. **the New Gate of the Lord's house** Also mentioned in Jer 36:10. Since the royal palace was on the south side of the temple, the New Gate is probably the gate on the south side of the inner court. It may be the same as the Upper Gate rebuilt by King Jotham (2Ki 15:35).

26:13 obey Jeremiah's defense is that Yahweh sent him and that his message is conditional on their repentance.

26:15 innocent blood Refers to wrongful deaths brought about by a corrupt legal system. Jeremiah has regularly included shedding innocent blood in his lists of injustices (see Jer 2:34; 7:6; 19:4; 22:3,17; compare note on Eze 22:9).

26:17 the elders of the land Refers to local leaders, the heads of clans or tribes. Moses appointed elders to help oversee the judicial aspects of local government (see Nu 11:16–30).

26:18 Micah of Moresheth The Biblical prophet (see Mic 1:1 and note). **Hezekiah king of Judah** Reigned 715–697 BC (see 2Ki 18–20). **Zion will be plowed** This quote from Mic 3:12 predicts judgment on Judah and Jerusalem for their injustice and their complacent assumption that Yahweh would save Zion no matter what. The themes of Jeremiah's preaching are the same as the warning preached by Micah a century earlier (see Mic 3:9–12).

26:20 Uriah son of Shemaiah This prophet is otherwise unknown. His story is added here to emphasize the grave danger Jeremiah was in. **Kiriath Jearim** A city about eight miles northwest of Jerusalem.

26:21 King Jehoiakim See note on Jer 22:18. Since the current incident is said to be at the beginning of Jehoiakim's reign, the execution of Uriah (also rendered "Urijah") must have been fairly recent. The ease with which Uriah is recovered from Egypt (vv. 22–23) suggests

to put him to death. But Uriah heard of it and fled in fear to Egypt. [22]King Jehoiakim, however, sent Elnathan son of Akbor to Egypt, along with some other men. [23]They brought Uriah out of Egypt and took him to King Jehoiakim, who had him struck down with a sword and his body thrown into the burial place of the common people.)

[24]Furthermore, Ahikam son of Shaphan supported Jeremiah, and so he was not handed over to the people to be put to death.

Judah to Serve Nebuchadnezzar

27 Early in the reign of Zedekiah[a] son of Josiah king of Judah, this word came to Jeremiah from the LORD: [2]This is what the LORD said to me: "Make a yoke out of straps and crossbars and put it on your neck. [3]Then send word to the kings of Edom, Moab, Ammon, Tyre and Sidon through the envoys who have come to Jerusalem to Zedekiah king of Judah. [4]Give them a message for their masters and say, 'This is what the LORD Almighty, the God of Israel, says: "Tell this to your masters: [5]With my great power and outstretched arm I made the earth and its people and the animals that are on it, and I give it to anyone I please. [6]Now I will give all your countries into the hands of my servant Nebuchadnezzar king of Babylon; I will make even the wild animals subject to him. [7]All nations will serve him and his son and his grandson until the time for his land comes; then many nations and great kings will subjugate him.

[8]"'If, however, any nation or kingdom will not serve Nebuchadnezzar king of Babylon or bow its neck under his yoke, I will punish that nation with the sword, famine and plague, declares the LORD, until I destroy it by his hand. [9]So do not listen to your prophets, your diviners, your interpreters of dreams, your mediums or your sorcerers who tell you, 'You will not serve the king of Babylon.' [10]They prophesy lies to you that will only serve to remove you far from your lands; I will banish you and you will perish. [11]But if any nation will bow its neck under the yoke of the king of Babylon and serve him, I will let that nation remain in its own land to till it and to live there, declares the LORD."'"

[12]I gave the same message to Zedekiah king of Judah. I said, "Bow your neck under the yoke of the king of Babylon; serve him and his people, and you will live. [13]Why will you and your people

---

a 1 A few Hebrew manuscripts and Syriac (see also 27:3,12 and 28:1); most Hebrew manuscripts *Jehoiakim* (Most Septuagint manuscripts do not have this verse.)

---

that he was killed while Jehoiakim was still a vassal of Egypt (609–605 BC).

26:22 Elnathan son of Akbor One of the officials present when the contents of Jeremiah's scroll were reported in 36:11–13. He may have been the son of one of the officials of Josiah mentioned in 2Ki 22:12. Despite his role in retrieving Uriah (also rendered "Urijah") for execution, he may have been sympathetic to Jeremiah's message since he attempts to prevent the king from burning the scroll in Jer 36:25.

26:24 Ahikam son of Shaphan Jeremiah owed his vindication in this incident to the influence of Ahikam, who had also served Josiah and had been part of Josiah's religious reforms (see 2Ki 22:12–14). His father, Shaphan, was the scribe responsible for bringing the scroll of the Law to Josiah's attention (2Ki 22:3–14). The support of the family of Shaphan was instrumental in Jeremiah's survival during this period (see Jer 36:10, 25; 39:14; 40:5–16).

27:1–22 This narrative reports Jeremiah's symbolic action of wearing a yoke, which represents how Judah and the neighboring nations in Syria-Palestine should yield to the rule of Babylon. See the table "Symbolic Actions of the Prophets" on p. 1195.

27:1 Early in the reign of Zedekiah Reigned 597–586 BC. According to 28:1, this was the fourth year of his reign (594/593 BC; see note on 21:1). Most Hebrew manuscripts read "reign of Jehoiakim" here, but this appears to be a scribal error. In v. 3 and 27:12, Jeremiah refers to Zedekiah as the king at the time of this incident. See the timeline "Life of Jeremiah" on p. 1170.

27:2 a yoke out of straps and crossbars A yoke consisted of a wooden crossbar laid across the necks of a team of oxen and attached with leather straps. See note on Na 1:13.

27:3 Judah's closest neighbors have sent envoys to Jerusalem to convince Zedekiah to join them in rebellion against Babylon. On the nations listed here, see note on Jer 25:21; note on 25:22. This conspiracy probably was motivated by a revolt in the Babylonian army in December 595 and January 594 BC. While Nebuchadnezzar was busy holding onto power at home, his vassals in Syria-Palestine plotted their own rebellion, hoping to regain their independence. In addition, the pharaoh Psammetichus II came to power in 595 BC, perhaps reviving hopes of Egyptian support in Syria-Palestine.

27:6 my servant Nebuchadnezzar king of Babylon Identifies Nebuchadnezzar as Yahweh's agent who is carrying out God's will (see 25:9 and note).

27:7 him and his son and his grandson Likely a generic image simply indicating that Babylon's power would not endure long after Nebuchadnezzar. The Babylonian Empire was at its height under Nebuchadnezzar and fell to Persia only a generation after his death. Three of his descendants succeeded him on the throne, but they ruled for a total of only six years. The last king of the empire was Nabonidus, who claimed to be a legitimate successor of Nebuchadnezzar but likely was a usurper. He reigned for 17 years and was on the throne when the Persian ruler Cyrus the Great conquered Babylon in 539 BC.

27:8 with the sword, famine and plague See 14:12 and note.

27:9 do not listen to your prophets Connecting the prophets with diviners and fortune-tellers, as this verse does, was a means of disparaging their advice. Deuteronomy forbids Israel from participating in divination or fortune-telling, which it describes as the abominable practices of their neighbors (Dt 18:9–12).

27:9 You will not serve the king of Babylon The other prophets are telling the kings what they want to hear: that their rebellion will be successful (compare 1Ki 22:5–6).

die by the sword, famine and plague with which the LORD has threatened any nation that will not serve the king of Babylon? ¹⁴Do not listen to the words of the prophets who say to you, 'You will not serve the king of Babylon,' for they are prophesying lies to you. ¹⁵'I have not sent them,' declares the LORD. 'They are prophesying lies in my name. Therefore, I will banish you and you will perish, both you and the prophets who prophesy to you.'"

¹⁶Then I said to the priests and all these people, "This is what the LORD says: Do not listen to the prophets who say, 'Very soon now the articles from the LORD's house will be brought back from Babylon.' They are prophesying lies to you. ¹⁷Do not listen to them. Serve the king of Babylon, and you will live. Why should this city become a ruin? ¹⁸If they are prophets and have the word of the LORD, let them plead with the LORD Almighty that the articles remaining in the house of the LORD and in the palace of the king of Judah and in Jerusalem be not taken to Babylon. ¹⁹For this is what the LORD Almighty says about the pillars, the bronze Sea, the movable stands and the other articles that are left in this city, ²⁰which Nebuchadnezzar king of Babylon did not take away when he carried Jehoiachin*ᵃ* son of Jehoiakim king of Judah into exile from Jerusalem to Babylon, along with all the nobles of Judah and Jerusalem— ²¹yes, this is what the LORD Almighty, the God of Israel, says about the things that are left in the house of the LORD and in the palace of the king of Judah and in Jerusalem: ²²'They will be taken to Babylon and there they will remain until the day I come for them,' declares the LORD. 'Then I will bring them back and restore them to this place.'"

The False Prophet Hananiah

28 In the fifth month of that same year, the fourth year, early in the reign of Zedekiah king of Judah, the prophet Hananiah son of Azzur, who was from Gibeon, said to me in the house of the LORD in the presence of the priests and all the people: ²"This is what the LORD Almighty, the God of Israel, says: 'I will break the yoke of the king of Babylon. ³Within two years I will bring back to this place all the articles of the LORD's house that Nebuchadnezzar king of Babylon removed from here and took to Babylon. ⁴I will also bring back to this place Jehoiachin*ᵃ* son of Jehoiakim king of Judah and all the other exiles from Judah who went to Babylon,' declares the LORD, 'for I will break the yoke of the king of Babylon.'"

⁵Then the prophet Jeremiah replied to the prophet Hananiah before the priests and all the people who were standing in the house of the LORD. ⁶He said, "Amen! May the LORD do so! May the LORD fulfill the words you have prophesied by bringing the articles of the LORD's house and all the exiles back to this place from Babylon. ⁷Nevertheless, listen to what I have to say in your hearing and in the hearing of all the people: ⁸From early times the prophets who preceded you and me have prophesied war, disaster and plague against many countries and great kingdoms. ⁹But the prophet who prophesies peace will be recognized as one truly sent by the LORD only if his prediction comes true."

¹⁰Then the prophet Hananiah took the yoke off the neck of the prophet Jeremiah and broke it,

ᵃ 20,4 Hebrew Jeconiah, a variant of Jehoiachin

27:16 the articles from the LORD's house Refers to the temple utensils and other portable objects that Nebuchadnezzar carried off in 597 BC (see 2Ki 24:8–13).
27:19 about the pillars The front of the temple had two bronze pillars and a huge cast-bronze basin (called the "sea"). The stands also were bronze and held wash basins. All of these things and more miscellaneous bronze items would be taken to Babylon in 586 BC (see 2Ki 25:13–18).
27:20 Jehoiachin The Hebrew here is *yekhonyah* (often rendered in English as Jeconiah), which is another name for Jehoiachin. See note on Jer 22:24.
28:1–17 The narrative provides a specific incident that exemplifies the kind of opposition Jeremiah faced from other prophets—who also were claiming to represent Yahweh. The story also reflects the potential for confusion among prophets, priests and royal officials, who were unsure which side represented the true will of Yahweh. The truth became clear only in retrospect, after the prophet's message had come to pass (or not).
28:1 In the fifth month of that same year Refers back to the events of 27:1–22, so 594/593 BC (see note on 27:1). **Zedekiah** See note on 21:1. **the prophet Hananiah son of Azzur, who was from Gibeon** Like

Jeremiah, Hananiah was from the territory of Benjamin. Gibeon was about six miles northwest of Jerusalem.
28:2 LORD Almighty, the God of Israel To introduce his message, Hananiah uses the same prophetic formula as Jeremiah (27:4). He, too, claims that he speaks for Yahweh. **I will break the yoke of the king of Babylon** Hananiah gives an oracle of salvation. His message is typical of the standard prophetic propaganda of the time (compare 5:13; 6:14). On the yoke as a symbol of submission, see note on Na 1:13.
28:3 will bring back to this place all the articles Hananiah's message is exactly what Jeremiah warned against in Jer 27:16. **Nebuchadnezzar** See note on 21:2.
28:4 Jehoiachin Hananiah also predicts the return of King Jehoiachin (Jeconiah) from exile, directly contradicting the oracle in 22:24–27, in which Jeremiah insisted that they should not expect Jehoiachin's return (see note on 22:27).
28:9 as one truly sent by the LORD Jeremiah openly questions Hananiah's calling as a prophet, intimating that his lies will be known when peace does not come about within two years.
28:10 took the yoke off the neck In response to Jeremiah's doubts about his message, Hananiah performs a symbolic action of his own, repeating his prediction

[11]and he said before all the people, "This is what the LORD says: 'In the same way I will break the yoke of Nebuchadnezzar king of Babylon off the neck of all the nations within two years.'" At this, the prophet Jeremiah went on his way.

[12]After the prophet Hananiah had broken the yoke off the neck of the prophet Jeremiah, the word of the LORD came to Jeremiah: [13]"Go and tell Hananiah, 'This is what the LORD says: You have broken a wooden yoke, but in its place you will get a yoke of iron. [14]This is what the LORD Almighty, the God of Israel, says: I will put an iron yoke on the necks of all these nations to make them serve Nebuchadnezzar king of Babylon, and they will serve him. I will even give him control over the wild animals.'"

[15]Then the prophet Jeremiah said to Hananiah the prophet, "Listen, Hananiah! The LORD has not sent you, yet you have persuaded this nation to trust in lies. [16]Therefore this is what the LORD says: 'I am about to remove you from the face of the earth. This very year you are going to die, because you have preached rebellion against the LORD.'"

[17]In the seventh month of that same year, Hananiah the prophet died.

A Letter to the Exiles

29 This is the text of the letter that the prophet Jeremiah sent from Jerusalem to the surviving elders among the exiles and to the priests, the prophets and all the other people Nebuchadnezzar had carried into exile from Jerusalem to Babylon. [2](This was after King Jehoiachin[a] and the queen mother, the court officials and the leaders of Judah and Jerusalem, the skilled workers and the artisans had gone into exile from Jerusalem.) [3]He entrusted the letter to Elasah son of Shaphan and to Gemariah son of Hilkiah, whom Zedekiah king of Judah sent to King Nebuchadnezzar in Babylon. It said:

[4]This is what the LORD Almighty, the God of Israel, says to all those I carried into exile from Jerusalem to Babylon: [5]"Build houses and settle down; plant gardens and eat what they produce. [6]Marry and have sons and daughters; find wives for your sons and give your daughters in marriage, so that they too may have sons and daughters. Increase in number there; do not decrease. [7]Also, seek the peace and prosperity of the city to which I have carried you into exile. Pray to the LORD for it, because if it prospers, you too will prosper." [8]Yes, this is what the LORD Almighty, the God of Israel, says: "Do not let the prophets and diviners among you deceive you. Do not listen to the dreams you encourage them to have. [9]They are prophesying lies to you in my name. I have not sent them," declares the LORD.

[10]This is what the LORD says: "When seventy years are completed for Babylon, I will come to you and fulfill my good promise to bring you back to this place. [11]For I know the plans I have for you," declares the LORD, "plans to prosper you and not to harm you, plans to give you hope and a future. [12]Then you will call on me and come and pray to me, and I will listen to you. [13]You will seek me

[a] 2 Hebrew *Jeconiah*, a variant of *Jehoiachin*

---

from v. 2 and dramatically breaking Jeremiah's yoke, which symbolized submission to Babylon.

28:14 an iron yoke Symbolic of a yoke that could not be easily broken. A literal yoke would not have been made of iron because the weight would have been impractical.

28:16 you have preached rebellion against the LORD Inciting rebellion against Nebuchadnezzar was equivalent to rebelling against Yahweh, who had given Babylon dominion for the time being. Nebuchadnezzar was Yahweh's agent of judgment on Judah and the nations.

28:17 Hananiah the prophet died In addition to fulfilling Jeremiah's prediction in the previous verse, Hananiah's death reflects the penalty for false prophecy (Dt 18:15–22).

29:1–32 Jeremiah's conflict with false prophets extended even to the exilic community in Babylon. This passage records the contents of a letter Jeremiah sent to the exiles encouraging them to settle in for the long haul and ignore their prophets, who preached a short exile and an imminent return home. Jeremiah tells the exiles to build houses, plant crops, carry on with their lives and even pray for the peace and prosperity of the foreign cities where they live. This advice elicits a strong reaction from another prophet in exile named Shemaiah; his letter to the priest Zephaniah, demanding Jeremiah's

punishment, also is recorded here. Jeremiah's response to Shemaiah is the same as his response to Hananiah (Jer 28:15–16): Jeremiah accuses him of rebelling against Yahweh and making the people of Judah trust in a lie.

29:1 the text of the letter Jeremiah's letter—probably a papyrus scroll—is delivered by envoys dispatched to Babylon by King Zedekiah. It is addressed to the entire community that was taken into exile in 597 BC. See the timeline "Life of Jeremiah" on p. 1170.

29:2 Jehoiachin The Hebrew here is *yekhonyah* (often translated as Jeconiah), which is another name for Jehoiachin. See note on 22:24. **the court officials** The Hebrew text refers here to castrated men, who often served as government officials in the ancient Near East. See note on Ne 1:11; and note on Est 1:10.

29:3 Zedekiah See note on Jer 21:1. **Nebuchadnezzar** See note on 21:2.

29:5 Build houses The exiles should treat their situation as a permanent move.

29:8 prophets and diviners There were prophets in exile, but Yahweh insists that he did not speak through them to promise peace and restoration (v. 9). **dreams** See note on 23:32.

29:10 seventy years A period of time symbolic of a human lifespan (see note on 25:11).

and find me when you seek me with all your heart. [14]I will be found by you," declares the LORD, "and will bring you back from captivity.[a] I will gather you from all the nations and places where I have banished you," declares the LORD, "and will bring you back to the place from which I carried you into exile."

[15]You may say, "The LORD has raised up prophets for us in Babylon," [16]but this is what the LORD says about the king who sits on David's throne and all the people who remain in this city, your fellow citizens who did not go with you into exile — [17]yes, this is what the LORD Almighty says: "I will send the sword, famine and plague against them and I will make them like figs that are so bad they cannot be eaten. [18]I will pursue them with the sword, famine and plague and will make them abhorrent to all the kingdoms of the earth, a curse[b] and an object of horror, of scorn and reproach, among all the nations where I drive them. [19]For they have not listened to my words," declares the LORD, "words that I sent to them again and again by my servants the prophets. And you exiles have not listened either," declares the LORD.

[20]Therefore, hear the word of the LORD, all you exiles whom I have sent away from Jerusalem to Babylon. [21]This is what the LORD Almighty, the God of Israel, says about Ahab son of Kolaiah and Zedekiah son of Maaseiah, who are prophesying lies to you in my name: "I will deliver them into the hands of Nebuchadnezzar king of Babylon, and he will put them to death before your very eyes. [22]Because of them, all the exiles from Judah who are in Babylon will use this curse: 'May the LORD treat you like Zedekiah and Ahab, whom the king of Babylon burned in the fire.' [23]For they have done outrageous things in Israel; they have committed adultery with their neighbors' wives, and in my name they have uttered lies — which I did not authorize. I know it and am a witness to it," declares the LORD.

Message to Shemaiah

[24]Tell Shemaiah the Nehelamite, [25]"This is what the LORD Almighty, the God of Israel, says: You sent letters in your own name to all the people in Jerusalem, to the priest Zephaniah son of Maaseiah, and to all the other priests. You said to Zephaniah, [26]'The LORD has appointed you priest in place of Jehoiada to be in charge of the house of the LORD; you should put any maniac who acts like a prophet into the stocks and neck-irons. [27]So why have you not reprimanded Jeremiah from Anathoth, who poses as a prophet among you? [28]He has sent this message to us in Babylon: It will be a long time. Therefore build houses and settle down; plant gardens and eat what they produce.'"

[29]Zephaniah the priest, however, read the letter to Jeremiah the prophet. [30]Then the word of the LORD came to Jeremiah: [31]"Send this message to all the exiles: 'This is what the LORD says about Shemaiah the Nehelamite: Because Shemaiah has prophesied to you, even though I did not send him, and has persuaded you to trust in lies, [32]this is what the LORD says: I will surely punish Shemaiah the Nehelamite and his descendants. He will have no one left among this people, nor will he see the good things I will do for my people, declares the LORD, because he has preached rebellion against me.'"

Restoration of Israel

30 This is the word that came to Jeremiah from the LORD: [2]"This is what the LORD, the God of Israel, says: 'Write in a book all the words I have spoken to you. [3]The days are coming,' declares the LORD, 'when I will bring my people Israel and Judah back from captivity[c] and restore

---

[a] 14 Or *will restore your fortunes*   [b] 18 That is, their names will be used in cursing (see verse 22); or, others will see that they are cursed.   [c] 3 Or *will restore the fortunes of my people Israel and Judah*

29:14 will bring you back A promise of salvation based on Dt 30:3 and a common image in the prophetic books (Jer 30:3; 33:7; Isa 1:26; Eze 16:53; 39:25).

29:15 raised up prophets for us in Babylon See Jer 29:8 and note. Their statement indicates doubt about which prophets to believe.

29:17 sword, famine and plague See 14:12 and note. **figs** Alludes to Jeremiah's vision in 24:1–10 (see note on 24:1).

29:21 Ahab son of Kolaiah and Zedekiah Jeremiah calls out two of the prophets in exile mentioned in v. 15.

29:23 they have committed adultery with their neighbors' wives Likely a metaphor for idolatry (see 23:13–15).

29:24 Shemaiah Jeremiah's correspondence includes a reply to Shemaiah, who is otherwise unmentioned in the Bible. The location of Nehelam is unknown.

29:25 Zephaniah The letter is addressed primarily to the priest in charge of the temple courts. The sender inquires why Jeremiah has not been arrested for his insurrection (see note on 21:1).

29:26 into the stocks and neck-irons This verse probably reflects duties of the temple's chief officer. See 20:1 and note; 20:2 and note.

30:1—33:26 This collection of oracles is often called the "book of consolation" because it expresses hope for Israel's future. These salvation oracles show that judgment was not the end of Yahweh's plan; rather, judgment brought Israel to a new level of commitment and relationship with him. The climax of this hopeful message comes in 31:31–34, where Yahweh describes their new covenant relationship. These promises also address themes of national restoration, return from exile and the reign of the Messiah.

them to the land I gave their ancestors to possess,'
says the LORD."

⁴These are the words the LORD spoke concerning Israel and Judah: ⁵"This is what the LORD says:

"'Cries of fear are heard —
    terror, not peace.
⁶ Ask and see:
    Can a man bear children?
Then why do I see every strong man
    with his hands on his stomach like a
        woman in labor,
    every face turned deathly pale?
⁷ How awful that day will be!
    No other will be like it.
It will be a time of trouble for Jacob,
    but he will be saved out of it.

⁸ "'In that day,' declares the LORD Almighty,
    'I will break the yoke off their necks
and will tear off their bonds;
    no longer will foreigners enslave them.
⁹ Instead, they will serve the LORD their God
    and David their king,
    whom I will raise up for them.

¹⁰ "'So do not be afraid, Jacob my servant;
    do not be dismayed, Israel,'
                    declares the LORD.
'I will surely save you out of a distant place,
    your descendants from the land of their
        exile.
Jacob will again have peace and security,
    and no one will make him afraid.
¹¹ I am with you and will save you,'
    declares the LORD.
'Though I completely destroy all the nations
    among which I scatter you,
    I will not completely destroy you.
I will discipline you but only in due measure;
    I will not let you go entirely unpunished.'

¹² "This is what the LORD says:

"'Your wound is incurable,
    your injury beyond healing.

¹³ There is no one to plead your cause,
    no remedy for your sore,
    no healing for you.
¹⁴ All your allies have forgotten you;
    they care nothing for you.
I have struck you as an enemy would
    and punished you as would the cruel,
because your guilt is so great
    and your sins so many.
¹⁵ Why do you cry out over your wound,
    your pain that has no cure?
Because of your great guilt and many sins
    I have done these things to you.

¹⁶ "'But all who devour you will be
        devoured;
    all your enemies will go into exile.
Those who plunder you will be plundered;
    all who make spoil of you I will despoil.
¹⁷ But I will restore you to health
    and heal your wounds,'
                    declares the LORD,
'because you are called an outcast,
    Zion for whom no one cares.'

¹⁸ "This is what the LORD says:

"'I will restore the fortunes of Jacob's tents
    and have compassion on his dwellings;
the city will be rebuilt on her ruins,
    and the palace will stand in its proper
        place.
¹⁹ From them will come songs of thanksgiving
    and the sound of rejoicing.
I will add to their numbers,
    and they will not be decreased;
I will bring them honor,
    and they will not be disdained.
²⁰ Their children will be as in days of old,
    and their community will be established
        before me;
    I will punish all who oppress them.
²¹ Their leader will be one of their own;
    their ruler will arise from among them.

30:1–24 The opening oracle focuses on the restoration of Israel and Judah. After they experience judgment through invasion and exile, they will be rebuilt and repopulated.

30:2 Write in a book all the words Yahweh commands Jeremiah to write down his prophecies so that the message of judgment followed by restoration will be preserved for future generations (compare 36:2). The Hebrew word *sepher*, used here, is a general term for a written document. It can be a scroll, a letter or an inscription. See note on Eze 2:9.

30:3 I will bring my people Israel and Judah back from captivity See Jer 29:14 and note. This national restoration includes both Israel and Judah. Compare Ezekiel's vision of restoration of all Israel in Eze 37:11–14.

30:8 In that day Alludes to the day of salvation (see note on Isa 26:1). **yoke** Refers to the rule of Babylon (see Jer 27:8–12).

30:9 David their king, whom I will raise up A reference to the Davidic Messiah. Compare Eze 34:23–24; 37:24–25.

30:11 I will not completely destroy you Compare Jer 46:28. The entire world is subject to Yahweh's wrath, but only Israel was promised a remnant (see Isa 14:22 and note; 14:30 and note; compare note on Isa 1:9).

30:14 allies have forgotten you The Hebrew text here uses a word for love (*ahav*) that serves to metaphorically present Judah's political allies as lovers (compare Eze 23:5). The prophets frequently use a metaphor of marital infidelity to criticize Israel and Judah for seeking assistance from other gods or other nations instead of returning to Yahweh (22:20–22; Eze 16:23–41; 23:5–27; Hos 2:7–15; La 1:19).

30:17 Zion Refers to Jerusalem (see note on Isa 1:8). Yahweh's promise to restore Jerusalem is meant to counter the popular notion that he had abandoned the city.

I will bring him near and he will come close
to me —
for who is he who will devote himself
to be close to me?'
declares the LORD.

²² "'So you will be my people,
and I will be your God.'"

²³ See, the storm of the LORD
will burst out in wrath,
a driving wind swirling down
on the heads of the wicked.
²⁴ The fierce anger of the LORD will not turn
back
until he fully accomplishes
the purposes of his heart.
In days to come
you will understand this.

31

"At that time," declares the LORD, "I will be
the God of all the families of Israel, and they
will be my people."
²This is what the LORD says:

"The people who survive the sword
will find favor in the wilderness;
I will come to give rest to Israel."

³The LORD appeared to us in the past,ᵃ saying:

"I have loved you with an everlasting love;
I have drawn you with unfailing kindness.
⁴ I will build you up again,
and you, Virgin Israel, will be rebuilt.

Again you will take up your timbrels
and go out to dance with the joyful.
⁵ Again you will plant vineyards
on the hills of Samaria;
the farmers will plant them
and enjoy their fruit.
⁶ There will be a day when watchmen cry out
on the hills of Ephraim,
'Come, let us go up to Zion,
to the LORD our God.'"

⁷This is what the LORD says:

"Sing with joy for Jacob;
shout for the foremost of the nations.
Make your praises heard, and say,
'LORD, save your people,
the remnant of Israel.'
⁸ See, I will bring them from the land of the
north
and gather them from the ends of the earth.
Among them will be the blind and the lame,
expectant mothers and women in labor;
a great throng will return.
⁹ They will come with weeping;
they will pray as I bring them back.
I will lead them beside streams of water
on a level path where they will not
stumble,
because I am Israel's father,
and Ephraim is my firstborn son.

ᵃ 3 Or LORD has appeared to us from afar

30:21 leader will be one of their own In other words, they will not be subject to foreign domination.
30:22 So you will be my people A covenant formula expressing Israel's relationship with Yahweh (see Jer 24:7; 31:33; Lev 26:12; Eze 11:20; Zec 8:8).

31:1–30 This oracle of salvation continues the theme of rebuilding Israel and reestablishing the people. The oracle uses references to Israel, Ephraim and Samaria—names for the northern kingdom—in an inclusive way to emphasize the total restoration of Israel and Judah. The promised restoration is grounded fully in the love of Yahweh for his people (Jer 31:3,20). The poetic imagery is reminiscent of the exodus story, the Israelites' wilderness wandering and their establishment as a nation in the land of Canaan.

31:1 all the families of Israel Emphasizes the complete restoration of all 12 tribes of Israel—both Israel and Judah. The northern kingdom was defeated and its 10 tribes taken into exile in 722 BC, nearly a century before Jeremiah was born.
31:4 Again you will take up your timbrels Alludes to the exodus traditions—when Yahweh established Israel—to encourage their faith in his plan to rebuild Israel (compare Ex 15:20).
31:5 the hills of Samaria Refers to the northern kingdom of Israel. Samaria was the former capital city of Israel, and the place-name was also applied to the surrounding region. During the Israelite monarchy, this region was known by the Israelite tribal name Ephraim

(used frequently in the prophetic books of Isaiah and Hosea). After the fall of the northern kingdom, the terms Samaria and Ephraim could be used to designate the northern region that was formerly part of Israel. See note on 1Ki 16:24.
31:6 the hills of Ephraim A reference to the northern kingdom of Israel. See note on Eze 37:16. **Zion** Refers to the Temple Mount in Jerusalem (see note on Isa 1:8). The depiction of the northern kingdom seeking Yahweh at Zion—located in the southern kingdom of Judah—is a surprising reversal of the north's earlier rejection of Zion (1Ki 12:26–33) and a statement of Israel and Judah's reunification. Compare Isa 2:3.
31:7 Jacob A poetic reference to all Israel. Jacob's 12 sons founded the 12 tribes of Israel (see Ge 35:22–27; 49:2–28). **the remnant of Israel** In salvation oracles, the remnant often refers to the scattered survivors of judgment who will be gathered back to Israel through Yahweh's act of redemption (compare Isa 4:2; 11:11; 49:22). See note on Isa 1:9; note on Jer 24:8.
31:8 land of the north The exiles were taken north as the invaders returned the way they came. The motif of invasion from the north (see 1:14 and note) is reversed to depict the exiles returning from the north. **the blind and the lame** Physical infirmities will not hinder the return (compare Isa 35:5–6).
31:9 with weeping Symbolizes genuine repentance (see Jer 31:30–34). **I will lead them beside streams of water** Imagery reminiscent of Isa 35:6–8. Salvation oracles often use images of a renewed creation.

10 "Hear the word of the LORD, you nations;
    proclaim it in distant coastlands:
'He who scattered Israel will gather them
    and will watch over his flock like a
    shepherd.'
11 For the LORD will deliver Jacob
    and redeem them from the hand of those
    stronger than they.
12 They will come and shout for joy on the
    heights of Zion;
    they will rejoice in the bounty of the
    LORD—
the grain, the new wine and the olive oil,
    the young of the flocks and herds.
They will be like a well-watered garden,
    and they will sorrow no more.
13 Then young women will dance and
    be glad,
    young men and old as well.
I will turn their mourning into gladness;
    I will give them comfort and joy instead
    of sorrow.
14 I will satisfy the priests with abundance,
    and my people will be filled with my
    bounty,"
                        declares the LORD.

15 This is what the LORD says:

"A voice is heard in Ramah,
    mourning and great weeping,
Rachel weeping for her children
    and refusing to be comforted,
    because they are no more."

16 This is what the LORD says:

"Restrain your voice from weeping
    and your eyes from tears,
for your work will be rewarded,"
                        declares the LORD.
"They will return from the land of the
    enemy.

17 So there is hope for your descendants,"
                        declares the LORD.
"Your children will return to their own
    land.

18 "I have surely heard Ephraim's moaning:
'You disciplined me like an unruly calf,
    and I have been disciplined.
Restore me, and I will return,
    because you are the LORD my God.
19 After I strayed,
    I repented;
after I came to understand,
    I beat my breast.
I was ashamed and humiliated
    because I bore the disgrace of my youth.'
20 Is not Ephraim my dear son,
    the child in whom I delight?
Though I often speak against him,
    I still remember him.
Therefore my heart yearns for him;
    I have great compassion for him,"
                        declares the LORD.

21 "Set up road signs;
    put up guideposts.
Take note of the highway,
    the road that you take.
Return, Virgin Israel,
    return to your towns.
22 How long will you wander,
    unfaithful Daughter Israel?
The LORD will create a new thing on earth—
    the woman will return to*a* the man."

23 This is what the LORD Almighty, the God
of Israel, says: "When I bring them back from
captivity,*b* the people in the land of Judah and in
its towns will once again use these words: 'The
LORD bless you, you prosperous city, you sacred

a 22 Or *will protect*   *b 23* Or *I restore their fortunes*

31:10 He who scattered Israel will gather them The scattering was part of the covenant curses (Lev 26:33), but the restoration and gathering also was promised (Dt 30:1–4). Compare Jer 9:16; 10:21; 30:11; Eze 36:19,24.
31:15 A voice is heard in Ramah Quoted in Mt 2:18. **Ramah** A village in the territory of Benjamin, about 8 miles north of Jerusalem and a few miles northwest of Anathoth. The town was located close to the main north–south highway and appears to be the site where the captives were assembled for exile after the fall of Jerusalem (see Jer 40:1). **Rachel weeping for her children** Rachel was Jacob's favorite wife (Ge 29:30) and the mother of Joseph and Benjamin. According to one Israelite tradition, her tomb was in Benjamite territory, north of Jerusalem (1Sa 10:2).
31:19 I beat my breast A gesture of distress and mourning (see Eze 21:12).
31:21 Return, Virgin Israel Encourages the exiles to prepare for return.

31:22 LORD will create a new thing Asserts that the people can trust Yahweh, even though their present circumstances had overturned their understanding of him and his relationship with them. **woman will return to the man** This phrase is open to many translations and interpretations. It might reflect a proverbial saying whose precise nuance has been lost. The form of the Hebrew verb used here, *savav*, seems to mean "surround," "encompass" or "encircle." It likely means that Israel embraces Yahweh. The imagery would fit with the metaphor of Israel as Yahweh's unfaithful wife, which is common in the prophets (Eze 16; Hos 2; Jer 2). This interpretation also fits with the imagery in this part of Jeremiah, as repentant Israel turns back to God (see v. 9). Another option is that this points to Israel's hope for a future (v. 17) by alluding to virgin Israel (v. 21) having a son.
31:23 Judah and in its towns An oracle affirming the restoration of Judah with imagery similar to that for the restoration of Israel in vv. 2–6.

mountain.' ²⁴People will live together in Judah and all its towns — farmers and those who move about with their flocks. ²⁵I will refresh the weary and satisfy the faint."

²⁶At this I awoke and looked around. My sleep had been pleasant to me.

²⁷"The days are coming," declares the LORD, "when I will plant the kingdoms of Israel and Judah with the offspring of people and of animals. ²⁸Just as I watched over them to uproot and tear down, and to overthrow, destroy and bring disaster, so I will watch over them to build and to plant," declares the LORD. ²⁹"In those days people will no longer say,

'The parents have eaten sour grapes,
　and the children's teeth are set on edge.'

³⁰Instead, everyone will die for their own sin; whoever eats sour grapes — their own teeth will be set on edge.

³¹"The days are coming," declares the LORD,
　"when I will make a new covenant
with the people of Israel
　and with the people of Judah.
³²It will not be like the covenant
　I made with their ancestors
when I took them by the hand
　to lead them out of Egypt,
because they broke my covenant,
　though I was a husband to*ᵃ* them,*ᵇ*"
　　　　　　　　declares the LORD.

³³"This is the covenant I will make with the
　　people of Israel
　after that time," declares the LORD.
"I will put my law in their minds
　and write it on their hearts.
I will be their God,
　and they will be my people.
³⁴No longer will they teach their neighbor,
　or say to one another, 'Know the LORD,'
because they will all know me,
　from the least of them to the greatest,"
　　　　　　　　declares the LORD.
"For I will forgive their wickedness
　and will remember their sins no more."

³⁵This is what the LORD says,

he who appoints the sun
　to shine by day,
who decrees the moon and stars
　to shine by night,
who stirs up the sea
　so that its waves roar —
the LORD Almighty is his name:
³⁶"Only if these decrees vanish from
　　my sight,"
　declares the LORD,
"will Israel ever cease
　being a nation before me."

³⁷This is what the LORD says:

ᵃ 32 Hebrew; Septuagint and Syriac / *and I turned away from*
ᵇ 32 Or *was their master*

31:26 My sleep had been pleasant to me A first-person reaction to the vision of restoration, suggesting that Jeremiah received the revelation through a dream. The statement has interesting parallels in Assyrian dream-reports, which often include the dreamer's reaction. In one Assyrian text, King Ashurbanipal hears good news from the battlefront and says: "My dreams were very pleasant, and, in the morning, I overheard only nice words."

31:27 with the offspring of people Compare Eze 36:9–11.

31:29 parents have eaten sour grapes This proverb, which also appears in Eze 18:2, carries an implicit criticism of Yahweh for punishing people for the sins of others. The proverb is succinctly refuted in Jer 31:30 with the assertion that everyone is punished for their individual sin. Ezekiel might be quoting from Jeremiah here and expanding on the concept more fully. See note on Eze 18:2; compare Eze 18:1–32 and note.

31:30 everyone will die for their own sin Compare Eze 18:4.

31:31–34 A new covenant is necessary because Israel's sin invalidated the Mosaic covenant (see note on Jer 11:2). The internal transformation of the people makes it possible for them to obey the law and live righteously. Compare Eze 11:19; 36:26–28.

31:31 I will make a new covenant The new covenant involves an internalization of Yahweh's law. The law will be written on their minds and hearts, so there will be

no need to teach the people about Yahweh or about the law. The phrase in Hebrew expresses the idea of making a covenant with the idiom cut a covenant (see note on 1Sa 11:1). Yahweh will give his people the inner ability to obey his righteous standards and fulfill the requirement of covenant obedience; the whole earth will be full of his knowledge as result (Isa 11:9). With this new covenant, Yahweh will forgive Israel's iniquity and forget their sins (Jer 31:34). This forgiveness is based on Yahweh's grace and sovereign choice (33:6–8), but it involves Israel's repentance (36:3), which is made possible through substitutionary atonement (Isa 53:4–6). In the NT, Christ teaches that the new covenant would be inaugurated by his blood (Mt 26:27–28; Lk 22:20). The writer of Hebrews develops the idea of a new covenant mediated through Christ that replaces the Sinai covenant (see Heb 8:6–13; 9:1—10:18). The ultimate fulfillment of the new covenant will come during the millennial reign of the Messiah.

31:33 on their hearts. I will be their God A common covenant formula (see Jer 30:22 and note).

31:35–40 Yahweh's power is manifested in his act of creation, establishing and maintaining the natural order. His sovereignty over all things offers assurance that the promised salvation will come to pass. This passage contains a hymn-like oracle of salvation that emphasizes God's creative power followed by a declaration that Jerusalem will be rebuilt, expanded and purified. See Ge 1:16. See the infographic "The Days of Creation" on p. 6.

"Only if the heavens above can be measured
and the foundations of the earth below be
searched out
will I reject all the descendants of Israel
because of all they have done,"
                                    declares the LORD.

38 "The days are coming," declares the LORD,
"when this city will be rebuilt for me from the
Tower of Hananel to the Corner Gate. 39 The measuring line will stretch from there straight to the
hill of Gareb and then turn to Goah. 40 The whole
valley where dead bodies and ashes are thrown,
and all the terraces out to the Kidron Valley on the
east as far as the corner of the Horse Gate, will
be holy to the LORD. The city will never again be
uprooted or demolished."

Jeremiah Buys a Field

32 This is the word that came to Jeremiah from
the LORD in the tenth year of Zedekiah
king of Judah, which was the eighteenth year of
Nebuchadnezzar. 2 The army of the king of Babylon was then besieging Jerusalem, and Jeremiah
the prophet was confined in the courtyard of the
guard in the royal palace of Judah.

3 Now Zedekiah king of Judah had imprisoned
him there, saying, "Why do you prophesy as you
do? You say, 'This is what the LORD says: I am about
to give this city into the hands of the king of Babylon, and he will capture it. 4 Zedekiah king of
Judah will not escape the Babylonians[a] but will
certainly be given into the hands of the king of

Babylon, and will speak with him face to face and
see him with his own eyes. 5 He will take Zedekiah
to Babylon, where he will remain until I deal with
him, declares the LORD. If you fight against the
Babylonians, you will not succeed.'"

6 Jeremiah said, "The word of the LORD came to
me: 7 Hanamel son of Shallum your uncle is going
to come to you and say, 'Buy my field at Anathoth,
because as nearest relative it is your right and
duty to buy it.'

8 "Then, just as the LORD had said, my cousin
Hanamel came to me in the courtyard of the guard
and said, 'Buy my field at Anathoth in the territory of Benjamin. Since it is your right to redeem it
and possess it, buy it for yourself.'

"I knew that this was the word of the LORD;
9 so I bought the field at Anathoth from my cousin Hanamel and weighed out for him seventeen
shekels[b] of silver. 10 I signed and sealed the deed,
had it witnessed, and weighed out the silver on the
scales. 11 I took the deed of purchase — the sealed
copy containing the terms and conditions, as well
as the unsealed copy — 12 and I gave this deed to
Baruch son of Neriah, the son of Mahseiah, in
the presence of my cousin Hanamel and of the
witnesses who had signed the deed and of all the
Jews sitting in the courtyard of the guard.

13 "In their presence I gave Baruch these instructions: 14 'This is what the LORD Almighty, the God
of Israel, says: Take these documents, both the
sealed and unsealed copies of the deed of pur-

---

[a] 4 Or Chaldeans; also in verses 5, 24, 25, 28, 29 and 43
[b] 9 That is, about 7 ounces or about 200 grams

31:38 Tower of Hananel to the Corner Gate Locations
on the northern and western sides of the city. The description of the boundaries of Jerusalem (Jer 31:38–40)
starts on the north side and moves counterclockwise.
31:39 the hill of Gareb An unknown location. **Goah**
Also unknown.
**31:40 valley where dead bodies and ashes are
thrown** Refers to the Hinnom Valley, where child sacrifices
to the Canaanite deity Molek were performed (see note
on 7:31). This valley bordered Jerusalem to the west
and south. **Kidron Valley** The Kidron Valley bordered
Jerusalem on the east. **corner of the Horse Gate** The
southeast corner of the city. See Ne 3:28 and note.

32:1–15 In another symbolic action, Jeremiah purchases
a field (compare Jer 13:1–11). Despite the present
siege of Jerusalem and the imminent exile of much of
the population, he depicts his faith in Yahweh's plans
for Israel's future. See the table "Symbolic Actions of
the Prophets" on p. 1195.

32:1 tenth year of Zedekiah 587 BC. The city had
been under siege for at least several months (2Ki 25:1).
On the difficulty in reconciling Israelite and Babylonian
dates, see note on Eze 24:1. See the timeline "Life of
Jeremiah" on p. 1170.
32:3 Zedekiah Judah's last Davidic ruler. See note
on Jer 21:1.
32:4 the Babylonians The Hebrew text uses "Bab-

ylonians" and "Chaldeans" interchangeably. See note
on Isa 43:14.
32:7 Hanamel Jeremiah's cousin is mentioned only in
this passage. **Anathoth** Jeremiah's hometown (see note
on Jer 1:1). **as nearest relative it is your right and
duty to buy** The transaction is conducted according to
the laws for property redemption. See Lev 25:25.
32:9 seventeen shekels of silver A measurement
by weight, not a coin. A shekel was 0.4 ounces or 11.6
grams. This amount of silver was about 7 ounces.
32:10 on the scales Stone weights were balanced
against the silver on a scale to determine the correct
price. Biblical law and prophetic indictments of unjust
behavior both draw attention to the practice of fraud —
using weights that were either too light or too heavy (Dt
25:13–16; Lev 19:35–36; Eze 45:10; Am 8:5; Mic
6:11). A dishonest merchant would use lighter weights
for selling and heavier ones for buying.
32:11 the deed of purchase — the sealed copy The
original document was sealed and stored to provide a
permanent record of the terms and conditions at the
time of sale. In a land transaction, the deed was written, signed by the principles and the witnesses, sealed
with wax, and stored in a clay jar. A second copy was
written and signed but left unsealed for reference. All
the steps of this process are detailed in this transaction
(Jer 32:9–15).
32:12 Baruch Jeremiah's scribe and close companion.

chase, and put them in a clay jar so they will last a long time. ¹⁵For this is what the LORD Almighty, the God of Israel, says: Houses, fields and vineyards will again be bought in this land.'

¹⁶"After I had given the deed of purchase to Baruch son of Neriah, I prayed to the LORD:

¹⁷"Ah, Sovereign LORD, you have made the heavens and the earth by your great power and outstretched arm. Nothing is too hard for you. ¹⁸You show love to thousands but bring the punishment for the parents' sins into the laps of their children after them. Great and mighty God, whose name is the LORD Almighty, ¹⁹great are your purposes and mighty are your deeds. Your eyes are open to the ways of all mankind; you reward each person according to their conduct and as their deeds deserve. ²⁰You performed signs and wonders in Egypt and have continued them to this day, in Israel and among all mankind, and have gained the renown that is still yours. ²¹You brought your people Israel out of Egypt with signs and wonders, by a mighty hand and an outstretched arm and with great terror. ²²You gave them this land you had sworn to give their ancestors, a land flowing with milk and honey. ²³They came in and took possession of it, but they did not obey you or follow your law; they did not do what you commanded them to do. So you brought all this disaster on them.

²⁴"See how the siege ramps are built up to take the city. Because of the sword, famine and plague, the city will be given into the hands of the Babylonians who are attacking it. What you said has happened, as you now see. ²⁵And though the city will be given into the hands of the Babylonians, you, Sovereign LORD, say to me, 'Buy the field with silver and have the transaction witnessed.'"

²⁶Then the word of the LORD came to Jeremiah: ²⁷"I am the LORD, the God of all mankind. Is anything too hard for me? ²⁸Therefore this is what the LORD says: I am about to give this city into the hands of the Babylonians and to Nebuchadnezzar king of Babylon, who will capture it. ²⁹The Babylonians who are attacking this city will come in and set it on fire; they will burn it down, along with the houses where the people aroused my anger by burning incense on the roofs to Baal and by pouring out drink offerings to other gods.

³⁰"The people of Israel and Judah have done nothing but evil in my sight from their youth; indeed, the people of Israel have done nothing but arouse my anger with what their hands have made, declares the LORD. ³¹From the day it was built until now, this city has so aroused my anger and wrath that I must remove it from my sight. ³²The people of Israel and Judah have provoked me by all the evil they have done — they, their kings and officials, their priests and prophets, the people of Judah and those living in Jerusalem. ³³They turned their backs to me and not their faces; though I taught them again and again, they would not listen or respond to discipline. ³⁴They set up their vile images in the house that bears my Name and defiled it. ³⁵They built high places for Baal in the Valley of Ben Hinnom to sacrifice

---

Jeremiah 32:12

BARUCH
Jeremiah's scribe, who recorded oracles at his dictation. Baruch also appears as Jeremiah's close associate and companion (Jer 43:1–7; 45:1–5). Jeremiah seems to have needed a scribe initially only because he was no longer allowed into the temple court and required someone who could read his prophecies there (36:5).

A seventh-century BC seal impression has been found with the name "Berechiah son of Neriah, the scribe," which likely refers to the Biblical Baruch. ("Berechiah" is the full form of the name "Baruch.") The use of a double patronym (listing the name of his father and grandfather) in 32:12 probably indicates Baruch was part of a prominent scribal family serving the royal house of Judah. His brother, Seraiah, was an official of King Zedekiah and accompanied the king on a trip to Babylon in 593 BC (see 51:59 and note on 51:59–64).

32:15 will again be bought in this land The purpose of the symbolic actions is stated explicitly here and in vv. 43–44. Jeremiah's purchase is designed to emphasize his faith in Yahweh's promised restoration.

32:16–25 Following his purchase, Jeremiah offers a prayer affirming his faith in Yahweh but expressing his doubts over the purchase due to the city's imminent fall to the Babylonians. The prayer follows the pattern of other Biblical prayers from after the exile (compare Da 9:4–19; Ezr 9:6–15; Ne 9:6–37). It opens with praise (Jer 32:17–19), which is followed by a historical summary highlighting Yahweh's power to save and Israel's choice to rebel, culminating in their present circumstance under Babylonian siege (vv. 20–24). Jeremiah doesn't mention the reason for his prayer—questioning the land purchase—until the very end (v. 25).

32:18 LORD Almighty See note on 6:6.
32:24 the siege ramps See 6:6 and note; see note on Eze 4:2. **sword, famine and plague** See note on Jer 14:12.

32:26–35 Yahweh responds to Jeremiah, assuring him of the eventual restoration of Judah and reiterating his plan to judge Judah and Jerusalem using the Babylonians. Yahweh's response also repeats the charges of idolatry from earlier in the book (e.g., 3:6–11; 7:30–32; 19:13).

32:28 Nebuchadnezzar See note on 21:2.
32:29 where the people aroused my anger by burning incense on the roofs See note on 19:13. **Baal** The main Canaanite god.

their sons and daughters to Molek, though I never commanded — nor did it enter my mind — that they should do such a detestable thing and so make Judah sin.

³⁶"You are saying about this city, 'By the sword, famine and plague it will be given into the hands of the king of Babylon'; but this is what the LORD, the God of Israel, says: ³⁷I will surely gather them from all the lands where I banish them in my furious anger and great wrath; I will bring them back to this place and let them live in safety. ³⁸They will be my people, and I will be their God. ³⁹I will give them singleness of heart and action, so that they will always fear me and that all will then go well for them and for their children after them. ⁴⁰I will make an everlasting covenant with them: I will never stop doing good to them, and I will inspire them to fear me, so that they will never turn away from me. ⁴¹I will rejoice in doing them good and will assuredly plant them in this land with all my heart and soul.

⁴²"This is what the LORD says: As I have brought all this great calamity on this people, so I will give them all the prosperity I have promised them. ⁴³Once more fields will be bought in this land of which you say, 'It is a desolate waste, without people or animals, for it has been given into the hands of the Babylonians.' ⁴⁴Fields will be bought for silver, and deeds will be signed, sealed and witnessed in the territory of Benjamin, in the villages around Jerusalem, in the towns of Judah and in the towns of the hill country, of the western foothills and of the Negev, because I will restore their fortunes,^a declares the LORD."

Promise of Restoration

33 While Jeremiah was still confined in the courtyard of the guard, the word of the LORD came to him a second time: ²"This is what the LORD says, he who made the earth, the LORD who formed it and established it — the LORD is his name: ³'Call to me and I will answer you and tell you great and unsearchable things you do not know.' ⁴For this is what the LORD, the God of Israel, says about the houses in this city and the royal palaces of Judah that have been torn down to be used against the siege ramps and the sword ⁵in the fight with the Babylonians^b: 'They will be filled with the dead bodies of the people I will slay in my anger and wrath. I will hide my face from this city because of all its wickedness.

⁶"'Nevertheless, I will bring health and healing to it; I will heal my people and will let them enjoy abundant peace and security. ⁷I will bring Judah and Israel back from captivity^c and will rebuild them as they were before. ⁸I will cleanse them from all the sin they have committed against me and will forgive all their sins of rebellion against me. ⁹Then this city will bring me renown, joy, praise and honor before all nations on earth that hear of all the good things I do for it; and they will be in awe and will tremble at the abundant prosperity and peace I provide for it.'

¹⁰"This is what the LORD says: 'You say about this place, "It is a desolate waste, without people or animals." Yet in the towns of Judah and the streets of

---

^a 44 Or will bring them back from captivity ^b 5 Or Chaldeans ^c 7 Or will restore the fortunes of Judah and Israel

---

32:34 their vile images Refers to idols in the Jerusalem temple (see note on Eze 5:9; compare Eze 8:5–18; 2Ki 23:4).

32:35 Valley of Ben Hinnom A site where child sacrifices took place. See note on Jer 7:31. **their sons and daughters to Molek** Forbidden in Lev 18:21 (see note on Jer 7:31; compare 2Ki 23:10). Molek was commonly understood to be a Canaanite deity whose worship required child sacrifice (see note on Lev 18:21). See the table "Pagan Deities of the Old Testament" on p. 1287.

32:36–44 Yahweh's response to Jeremiah's prayer concludes with an emphasis on the renewed covenant, future restoration of the land and the future prosperity of the people.

32:38 They will be my people The covenant formula. See note on Jer 30:22.

32:39 singleness of heart and action Compare Eze 11:19–20.

32:40 everlasting covenant A renewed covenant to replace the covenant that Israel had broken. Compare Isa 55:3 and note.

32:43 fields will be bought in this land See Jer 32:15 and note.

32:44 The geographic references here cover the primary regions inhabited by the Israelites, including: Jeremiah's home territory where he bought the field (Benjamin); Jerusalem and its vicinity; the northern hill country (Ephraim); the foothills west of Jerusalem (Shephelah); and the southern desert (Negev).

33:1–13 This passage contains several oracles promising future restoration of Judah and Jerusalem and describing the rebuilding of Jerusalem and the return of human and animal populations. The images that were used to describe the downfall of human civilization in Judah are now used to describe the restoration (compare 7:34 with v. 11).

33:1 the courtyard of the guard See 32:2–3.

33:3 great and unsearchable things When the announcement of salvation follows promises of judgment, it is often presented as something new and hidden (compare Isa 42:9).

33:4 that have been torn down Houses were built into the city wall. The defensive preparations for the siege required that these houses be used for military purposes.

33:5 I will hide my face from this city Yahweh has turned away from the city and empowered the invaders to triumph.

33:7 I will bring Judah and Israel back from captivity Restoration for both kingdoms.

33:8 will forgive all their sins See note on Jer 31:31; compare 31:34.

Jerusalem that are deserted, inhabited by neither people nor animals, there will be heard once more [11]the sounds of joy and gladness, the voices of bride and bridegroom, and the voices of those who bring thank offerings to the house of the LORD, saying,

"Give thanks to the LORD Almighty,
 for the LORD is good;
 his love endures forever."

For I will restore the fortunes of the land as they were before,' says the LORD.

[12]"This is what the LORD Almighty says: 'In this place, desolate and without people or animals — in all its towns there will again be pastures for shepherds to rest their flocks. [13]In the towns of the hill country, of the western foothills and of the Negev, in the territory of Benjamin, in the villages around Jerusalem and in the towns of Judah, flocks will again pass under the hand of the one who counts them,' says the LORD.

[14]"The days are coming,' declares the LORD, 'when I will fulfill the good promise I made to the people of Israel and Judah.

[15] "'In those days and at that time
 I will make a righteous Branch sprout from
  David's line;
 he will do what is just and right in the
  land.
[16] In those days Judah will be saved
 and Jerusalem will live in safety.
 This is the name by which it[a] will be called:
  The LORD Our Righteous Savior.'

[17]For this is what the LORD says: 'David will never fail to have a man to sit on the throne of Israel, [18]nor will the Levitical priests ever fail to have a man to stand before me continually to offer burnt

offerings, to burn grain offerings and to present sacrifices.'"

[19]The word of the LORD came to Jeremiah: [20]"This is what the LORD says: 'If you can break my covenant with the day and my covenant with the night, so that day and night no longer come at their appointed time, [21]then my covenant with David my servant — and my covenant with the Levites who are priests ministering before me — can be broken and David will no longer have a descendant to reign on his throne. [22]I will make the descendants of David my servant and the Levites who minister before me as countless as the stars in the sky and as measureless as the sand on the seashore.'"

[23]The word of the LORD came to Jeremiah: [24]"Have you not noticed that these people are saying, 'The LORD has rejected the two kingdoms[b] he chose'? So they despise my people and no longer regard them as a nation. [25]This is what the LORD says: 'If I have not made my covenant with day and night and established the laws of heaven and earth, [26]then I will reject the descendants of Jacob and David my servant and will not choose one of his sons to rule over the descendants of Abraham, Isaac and Jacob. For I will restore their fortunes[c] and have compassion on them.'"

Warning to Zedekiah

34 While Nebuchadnezzar king of Babylon and all his army and all the kingdoms and peoples in the empire he ruled were fighting against Jerusalem and all its surrounding towns, this word came to Jeremiah from the LORD: [2]"This is what the

---

[a] 16 Or he   [b] 24 Or families   [c] 26 Or will bring them back from captivity

---

33:11 the sounds of joy Reverses the imagery of destruction repeated in 7:34; 16:9; and 25:10.
33:13 In the towns of the hill country See 32:44 and note.
33:14–26 This passage begins with a near quote of the "righteous Branch" passage from 23:5–6 and continues with an expansion of the theme of future righteous leadership for Israel. This section concludes the "book of consolation" in chs. 30–33 by looking ahead to the ultimate time of peace and prosperity for Israel under the rule of the Davidic Messiah.
33:14 days are coming Jeremiah frequently uses this phrase (15 times) to indicate future judgment (e.g., 7:32) as well as future restoration (e.g., 30:3).
33:15 a righteous Branch A metaphor for the Messiah. See 23:5 and note. **what is just and right** Ideals that Zedekiah neglected; see 22:3 and note.
33:17 David will never fail to have a man Connects the promise given to David of an eternal dynasty (2Sa 7:16) with its ultimate fulfillment in the reign of the Messiah.
33:18 the Levitical priests The promise of restoration involves the reestablishment of both royal and priestly institutions. The priest, Phinehas, was promised a per-

petual priesthood in Nu 25:11–13. **to offer burnt offerings** See note on Lev 1:3.
33:20 my covenant with the day Yahweh's promises to David and to the priests will be as certain and predictable as the movements of the earth around the sun.
33:22 as countless as the stars in the sky and as measureless as the sand The language of blessing to Abraham in Ge 22:17–18 is extended to David and the Levitical priests.
33:24 these people Refers to the surrounding nations, who view the destruction of Israel and Judah as God's rejection of his people.
33:26 the descendants of Jacob and David my servant Israel and Judah are not rejected or forgotten. Yahweh's relationship with creation itself would have to cease before he would reject or forget his people.

34:1–22 An oracle of judgment against Zedekiah and the people of Jerusalem that reflects conditions in the city during the siege and predicts Zedekiah's ultimate fate.

34:1 Nebuchadnezzar See note on Jer 21:2. Nebuchadnezzar's invasion of Judah, including the siege of Jerusalem (v. 7), is underway at this time.
34:2 Zedekiah Judah's last Davidic king. See note on 21:1.

LORD, the God of Israel, says: Go to Zedekiah king of Judah and tell him, 'This is what the LORD says: I am about to give this city into the hands of the king of Babylon, and he will burn it down. ³You will not escape from his grasp but will surely be captured and given into his hands. You will see the king of Babylon with your own eyes, and he will speak with you face to face. And you will go to Babylon.

⁴"'Yet hear the LORD's promise to you, Zedekiah king of Judah. This is what the LORD says concerning you: You will not die by the sword; ⁵you will die peacefully. As people made a funeral fire in honor of your predecessors, the kings who ruled before you, so they will make a fire in your honor and lament, "Alas, master!" I myself make this promise, declares the LORD.'"

⁶Then Jeremiah the prophet told all this to Zedekiah king of Judah, in Jerusalem, ⁷while the army of the king of Babylon was fighting against Jerusalem and the other cities of Judah that were still holding out—Lachish and Azekah. These were the only fortified cities left in Judah.

34:3 see the king of Babylon Later, Zedekiah is indeed brought before Nebuchadnezzar at Riblah, where he is forced to watch the execution of his sons before being blinded and taken to Babylon (see 2Ki 25:6–7).
34:7 Lachish and Azekah Border fortresses in the hill country of Judah, southwest of Jerusalem. Letters recovered from the ruins of Lachish provide evidence of the military correspondence at the time of the Babylonian invasion. One letter is from a sentry on the lookout for signal fires from both Lachish and Azekah. His ominous comment that he can no longer see the signal from Azekah suggests that the city had finally fallen to Babylon and supports the depiction here of Lachish and Azekah as the last two fortifications holding out against the invaders. See the infographic "The Lachish Letters" below. **fortified cities** See note on Jer 4:5.

The Lachish Letters

An ostracon is a piece of broken pottery used as a writing surface. These ostraca are named for the city of Lachish, where they were found. They seem to have been written just before the Babylonian captivity, in the days before Nebuchadnezzar's troops conquered Lachish and the rest of Judah.

Mediterranean Sea — ISRAEL (PRESENT DAY) — Dead Sea — Lachish — JORDAN (PRESENT DAY) — EGYPT

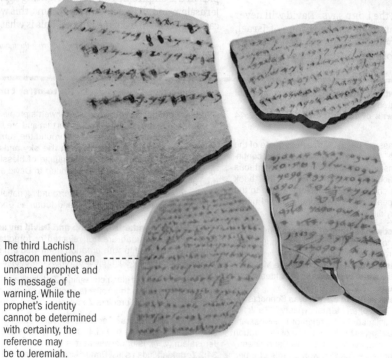

The third Lachish ostracon mentions an unnamed prophet and his message of warning. While the prophet's identity cannot be determined with certainty, the reference may be to Jeremiah.

Freedom for Slaves

⁸The word came to Jeremiah from the LORD after King Zedekiah had made a covenant with all the people in Jerusalem to proclaim freedom for the slaves. ⁹Everyone was to free their Hebrew slaves, both male and female; no one was to hold a fellow Hebrew in bondage. ¹⁰So all the officials and people who entered into this covenant agreed that they would free their male and female slaves and no longer hold them in bondage. They agreed, and set them free. ¹¹But afterward they changed their minds and took back the slaves they had freed and enslaved them again.

¹²Then the word of the LORD came to Jeremiah: ¹³"This is what the LORD, the God of Israel, says: I made a covenant with your ancestors when I brought them out of Egypt, out of the land of slavery. I said, ¹⁴'Every seventh year each of you must free any fellow Hebrews who have sold themselves to you. After they have served you six years, you must let them go free.'ᵃ Your ancestors, however, did not listen to me or pay attention to me. ¹⁵Recently you repented and did what is right in my sight: Each of you proclaimed freedom to your own people. You even made a covenant before me in the house that bears my Name. ¹⁶But now you have turned around and profaned my name; each of you has taken back the male and female slaves you had set free to go where they wished. You have forced them to become your slaves again.

¹⁷"Therefore this is what the LORD says: You have not obeyed me; you have not proclaimed freedom to your own people. So I now proclaim 'freedom' for you, declares the LORD — 'freedom' to fall by the sword, plague and famine. I will make you abhorrent to all the kingdoms of the earth. ¹⁸Those who have violated my covenant and have not fulfilled the terms of the covenant they made before me, I will treat like the calf they cut in two and then walked between its pieces. ¹⁹The leaders of Judah and Jerusalem, the court officials, the priests and all the people of the land who walked between the pieces of the calf, ²⁰I will deliver into the hands of their enemies who want to kill them. Their dead bodies will become food for the birds and the wild animals.

²¹"I will deliver Zedekiah king of Judah and his officials into the hands of their enemies who want to kill them, to the army of the king of Babylon, which has withdrawn from you. ²²I am going to give the order, declares the LORD, and I will bring them back to this city. They will fight against it, take it and burn it down. And I will lay waste the towns of Judah so no one can live there."

The Rekabites

35 This is the word that came to Jeremiah from the LORD during the reign of Jehoiakim son of Josiah king of Judah: ²"Go to the Rekabite family and invite them to come to one of the side rooms of the house of the LORD and give them wine to drink."

ᵃ 14 Deut. 15:12

34:8–22 Sometime during the siege of Jerusalem, Zedekiah apparently decreed that all Hebrew slaves should be set free. This decision might have been motivated by a need for more defenders or as an attempt to please Yahweh by enacting a long-overdue enforcement of the law (Ex 21:2; Dt 15:12). The Egyptian advance forced Babylon to temporarily lift the siege (Jer 37:6–15), which resulted in all the slave owners in Jerusalem reneging on their commitment to free their slaves. This act of injustice forms the basis of the judgment oracle pronounced against Jerusalem in 34:13–22, appealing to the law (Ex 21:2; Dt 15:12) and criticizing the people for repenting and then backsliding so quickly (Jer 34:15–16). See the table "Covenants in the Old Testament" on p. 469.

34:9 to free their Hebrew slaves The law provided only for indentured servitude of fellow Israelites, not for long-term slavery (see Ex 21:2 and note).

34:11 afterward they changed their minds Jeremiah uses the Hebrew word for "turn" repeatedly in this passage to describe the people wavering between doing the right thing and returning to their wicked ways.

34:14 Every seventh year Paraphrases the legal stipulation from Ex 21:2 and Dt 15:12.

34:15 Recently you repented Here, the Hebrew word for "turn" indicates repenting. **proclaimed freedom** Alludes to the Year of Jubilee, during which property was to revert to its original owner and slaves were to be set free (see Lev 25:10 and note on Lev 25:1–7). **made a covenant before me** The covenant to free the slaves

must have invoked Yahweh as a witness. His act of punishment is an appropriate response to the breaking of the covenant, since he was made guarantor by their oaths in his name.

34:16 profaned my name They did so by breaking the promise that was sworn in Yahweh's name (see Jer 34:15 and note).

34:17 to fall by the sword, plague and famine An ironic reversal: Yahweh frees his people from the covenant with him, releasing them to judgment by the sword, pestilence and famine. On this triad of punishments, see note on 14:12.

34:18 I will treat like the calf They had ratified the covenant by passing through the parts of a sacrificial animal cut in half (Ge 15:7–21; see Ge 15:10 and note; 1Sa 11:1 and note).

34:20 food for the birds Part of the curse for breaking the covenant. See Jer 7:33 and note.

34:21 king of Babylon, which has withdrawn Indicates that this incident occurred while Babylon had lifted the siege to face Egypt in battle. See 37:6–15.

34:22 will bring them back to this city The Babylonians' siege of Jerusalem was, in fact, lifted only temporarily.

35:1–19 This narrative dates from the time of Jehoiakim (reigned 609–597 BC) and is not chronologically sequential with the preceding narrative from the time of Zedekiah and the siege of Jerusalem (587 BC). The narrative probably is placed here intentionally, following the depiction of Jerusalem's unfaithfulness in 34:8–22,

³So I went to get Jaazaniah son of Jeremiah, the son of Habazziniah, and his brothers and all his sons — the whole family of the Rekabites. ⁴I brought them into the house of the Lord, into the room of the sons of Hanan son of Igdaliah the man of God. It was next to the room of the officials, which was over that of Maaseiah son of Shallum the doorkeeper. ⁵Then I set bowls full of wine and some cups before the Rekabites and said to them, "Drink some wine."

⁶But they replied, "We do not drink wine, because our forefather Jehonadab[a] son of Rekab gave us this command: 'Neither you nor your descendants must ever drink wine. ⁷Also you must never build houses, sow seed or plant vineyards; you must never have any of these things, but must always live in tents. Then you will live a long time in the land where you are nomads.' ⁸We have obeyed everything our forefather Jehonadab son of Rekab commanded us. Neither we nor our wives nor our sons and daughters have ever drunk wine ⁹or built houses to live in or had vineyards, fields or crops. ¹⁰We have lived in tents and have fully obeyed everything our forefather Jehonadab commanded us. ¹¹But when Nebuchadnezzar king of Babylon invaded this land, we said, 'Come, we must go to Jerusalem to escape the Babylonian[b] and Aramean armies.' So we have remained in Jerusalem."

¹²Then the word of the Lord came to Jeremiah, saying: ¹³"This is what the Lord Almighty, the God of Israel, says: Go and tell the people of Judah and those living in Jerusalem, 'Will you not learn a lesson and obey my words?' declares the Lord. ¹⁴Jehonadab son of Rekab ordered his descendants not to drink wine and this command has been kept. To this day they do not drink wine, because they obey their forefather's command. But I have spoken to you again and again, yet you have not obeyed me. ¹⁵Again and again I sent all my servants the prophets to you. They said, "Each of you must turn from your wicked ways and reform your actions; do not follow other gods to serve them. Then you will live in the land I have given to you and your ancestors." But you have not paid attention or listened to me. ¹⁶The descendants of Jehonadab son of Rekab have carried out the command their forefather gave them, but these people have not obeyed me.'

¹⁷"Therefore this is what the Lord God Almighty, the God of Israel, says: 'Listen! I am going to bring on Judah and on everyone living in Jerusalem every disaster I pronounced against them. I spoke to them, but they did not listen; I called to them, but they did not answer.'"

¹⁸Then Jeremiah said to the family of the Rekabites, "This is what the Lord Almighty, the God of Israel, says: 'You have obeyed the command of your forefather Jehonadab and have followed all his instructions and have done everything he ordered.' ¹⁹Therefore this is what the Lord Al-

---

[a] 6 Hebrew Jonadab, a variant of Jehonadab; here and often in this chapter   [b] 11 Or Chaldean

---

in order to draw an explicit contrast between the faithfulness of the sect of Rekabites and the unfaithfulness of the leaders of Judah. Jeremiah carried out a symbolic action designed to test the Rekabites' observance of the traditional prohibitions peculiar to their clan. He visited the Rekabites, brought them to the temple, and offered them wine, which their ancestor had forbidden. Their faithfulness to family traditions observed over a period of two centuries provides a lesson for the people of Judah, who should have had similar devotion to the laws of Yahweh. See the table "Symbolic Actions of the Prophets" on p. 1195; See the timeline "Life of Jeremiah" on p. 1170.

35:1 Jehoiakim See note on 22:18.
35:2 the Rekabite A nomadic tribe apparently related to the Kenites (1Ch 2:55) and descended from Jonadab (Jehonadab), son of Rekab (2Ki 10:15). The Rekabites also could have been a guild of traveling craftsmen associated with metalwork and chariot-making. The genealogy in 1Ch 2:55 connects them with the Kenites, who were known for their metalwork. The Semitic name Rekab appears in Aramaic and Ugaritic texts, where it is associated with chariot makers or drivers. The scene from 2Ki 10 also involves a chariot, assuming that Jehonadab's relationship to Jehu was based on the business of chariot-making.
35:4 the room of the officials Priestly families and royal officials had rooms in the temple complex where they may have conducted business or shared sacrificial meals. **doorkeeper** A priestly office responsible for overseeing the collection of temple taxes and guarding the entrances to the temple (see Jer 52:24; 2Ki 12:9; 22:4; 23:4; 25:18).
35:5 Drink some wine Jeremiah sets out wine before the Rekabites, knowing they will not drink it. The action takes place in the temple chambers, providing a public audience for Jeremiah's contrasting examples of covenant loyalty.
35:6 Jehonadab See 2Ki 10:15–23. He actively supported Jehu's purge of the supporters of Baal, suggesting that he may have been a committed follower of Yahweh.
35:7 you must never build houses Jehonadab's rules required abstaining from alcohol, agriculture and permanent housing. The purpose behind these rules is unclear, but Jeremiah is concerned not with why the Rekabites obey—simply that they do. The clan has kept these rules for a period of at least 200 years. The story of Jehu's rebellion, in which Jehonadab plays a minor part, takes place around 840 BC. The rules might be designed to keep the clan separate from Israelite society and untainted by Canaanite religious practices. The unsettled lifestyle suited the Rekabites' work as metalworkers, allowing them to move as needed for work. The prohibition against alcohol is unusual as a trait of a nomadic society or as a religious observance (for the time), but a restriction on drinking makes sense in a family of craftsmen where the secrets of the trade would have been closely guarded.
35:19 to serve me The Hebrew expression here signifies worshiping in Yahweh's presence in the temple. Despite the coming judgment, a remnant will be preserved from the Rekabites.

mighty, the God of Israel, says: 'Jehonadab son of Rekab will never fail to have a descendant to serve me.'"

Jehoiakim Burns Jeremiah's Scroll

36 In the fourth year of Jehoiakim son of Josiah king of Judah, this word came to Jeremiah from the LORD: ²"Take a scroll and write on it all the words I have spoken to you concerning Israel, Judah and all the other nations from the time I began speaking to you in the reign of Josiah till now. ³Perhaps when the people of Judah hear about every disaster I plan to inflict on them, they will each turn from their wicked ways; then I will forgive their wickedness and their sin."

⁴So Jeremiah called Baruch son of Neriah, and while Jeremiah dictated all the words the LORD had spoken to him, Baruch wrote them on the scroll. ⁵Then Jeremiah told Baruch, "I am restricted; I am not allowed to go to the LORD's temple. ⁶So you go to the house of the LORD on a day of fasting and read to the people from the scroll the words of the LORD that you wrote as I dictated. Read them to all the people of Judah who come in from their towns. ⁷Perhaps they will bring their petition before the LORD and will each turn from their wicked ways, for the anger and wrath pronounced against this people by the LORD are great."

⁸Baruch son of Neriah did everything Jeremiah the prophet told him to do; at the LORD's temple he read the words of the LORD from the scroll. ⁹In the ninth month of the fifth year of Jehoiakim son of Josiah king of Judah, a time of fasting before the LORD was proclaimed for all the people in Jerusalem and those who had come from the towns of Judah. ¹⁰From the room of Gemariah son of Shaphan the secretary, which was in the upper courtyard at the entrance of the New Gate of the temple, Baruch read to all the people at the LORD's temple the words of Jeremiah from the scroll.

¹¹When Micaiah son of Gemariah, the son of Shaphan, heard all the words of the LORD from the scroll, ¹²he went down to the secretary's room in the royal palace, where all the officials were sitting: Elishama the secretary, Delaiah son of Shemaiah, Elnathan son of Akbor, Gemariah son of Shaphan, Zedekiah son of Hananiah, and all the other officials. ¹³After Micaiah told them everything he had heard Baruch read to the people from the scroll, ¹⁴all the officials sent Jehudi son of Nethaniah, the son of Shelemiah, the son of Cushi, to say to Baruch, "Bring the scroll from which you have read to the people and come." So Baruch son of Neriah went to them with the scroll in his hand. ¹⁵They said to him, "Sit down, please, and read it to us."

So Baruch read it to them. ¹⁶When they heard all these words, they looked at each other in fear and said to Baruch, "We must report all these words to the king." ¹⁷Then they asked Baruch, "Tell us, how did you come to write all this? Did Jeremiah dictate it?"

¹⁸"Yes," Baruch replied, "he dictated all these words to me, and I wrote them in ink on the scroll."

36:1–32 This chapter describes the composition of two scrolls containing the prophecies of Jeremiah. After the scribe Baruch delivers the first scroll to the palace, King Jehoiakim disregards the message and burns it. His blatant rejection of Yahweh's message alarms his officials, several of whom had responded positively to Jeremiah's preaching and assisted Baruch and Jeremiah in avoiding arrest. The scene may have been intended to evoke a contrast between Josiah's positive response to hearing God's words (2Ki 22) and Jehoiakim's negative response.

36:1 fourth year of Jehoiakim 605 BC. See note on Jer 22:18. See the timeline "Life of Jeremiah" on p. 1170.
36:2 in the reign of Josiah till now This first scroll contains the prophecies of Jeremiah from the beginning of his career in 627 BC until the present day, 605 BC. See note on 1:2.
36:4 Baruch See note on 32:12. **while Jeremiah dictated all the words the LORD had spoken to him, Baruch wrote them** Emphasizes that the words are Jeremiah's, a fact that vv. 17–18 specifically mentions.
36:5 I am restricted Jeremiah was likely restricted from going into the temple as a result of the events surrounding the temple sermon in 26:1–24.
36:6 a day of fasting Since everyone is required to gather in Jerusalem in the temple on the day of fasting (see v. 10), a substantial audience will be present to hear the scroll's contents. The Day of Atonement is the only fast prescribed in the Biblical law (Lev 16). More holidays are designated as days of fasting after the exile (Zec 8:19; Est 4:16). See note on Isa 58:3.
36:9 In the ninth month of the fifth year of Jehoiakim 604 BC, the year Nebuchadnezzar destroyed the Philistine city of Ashkelon and about the time Jehoiakim became a vassal of Babylon. The fast may have been called as a response to the national emergency posed by the destruction of nearby Ashkelon.
36:10 Gemariah A son of Josiah's secretary, Shaphan. He is probably the brother of Ahikam, who assisted Jeremiah in Jer 26:24 (see note on 26:24). **the upper courtyard** Likely indicates he is addressing the people from above. **the New Gate of the temple** See 26:10 and note.
36:12 to the secretary's room Micaiah (also rendered "Michaiah") is apparently staffing the chamber of Gemariah in the temple complex. He brings the message of Jeremiah's scroll to the attention of his father, Gemariah, and other royal officials. The secretary and the officials with him probably are royal scribes. **Elnathan** See note on 26:22.
36:16 they looked at each other in fear Their reaction reveals that they understand the importance of the prophetic charges against Judah. They may have hoped that the king would respond positively to the call for repentance.
36:17 Jeremiah dictate it See v. 4 and note. The officials want to be certain that the words came from Jeremiah himself.

¹⁹Then the officials said to Baruch, "You and Jeremiah, go and hide. Don't let anyone know where you are."

²⁰After they put the scroll in the room of Elishama the secretary, they went to the king in the courtyard and reported everything to him. ²¹The king sent Jehudi to get the scroll, and Jehudi brought it from the room of Elishama the secretary and read it to the king and all the officials standing beside him. ²²It was the ninth month and the king was sitting in the winter apartment, with a fire burning in the firepot in front of him. ²³Whenever Jehudi had read three or four columns of the scroll, the king cut them off with a scribe's knife and threw them into the firepot, until the entire scroll was burned in the fire. ²⁴The king and all his attendants who heard all these words showed no fear, nor did they tear their clothes. ²⁵Even though Elnathan, Delaiah and Gemariah urged the king not to burn the scroll, he would not listen to them. ²⁶Instead, the king commanded Jerahmeel, a son of the king, Seraiah son of Azriel and Shelemiah son of Abdeel to arrest Baruch the scribe and Jeremiah the prophet. But the LORD had hidden them.

²⁷After the king burned the scroll containing the words that Baruch had written at Jeremiah's dictation, the word of the LORD came to Jeremiah: ²⁸"Take another scroll and write on it all the words that were on the first scroll, which Jehoiakim king of Judah burned up. ²⁹Also tell Jehoiakim king of Judah, 'This is what the LORD says: You burned that scroll and said, "Why did you write on it that the king of Babylon would certainly come and destroy this land and wipe from it both man and beast?" ³⁰Therefore this is what the LORD says about Jehoiakim king of Judah: He will have no one to sit on the throne of David; his body will be thrown out and exposed to the heat by day and the frost by night. ³¹I will punish him and his children and his attendants for their wickedness; I will bring on them and those living in Jerusalem and the people of Judah every disaster I pronounced against them, because they have not listened.'"

³²So Jeremiah took another scroll and gave it to the scribe Baruch son of Neriah, and as Jeremiah dictated, Baruch wrote on it all the words of the scroll that Jehoiakim king of Judah had burned in the fire. And many similar words were added to them.

Jeremiah in Prison

37 Zedekiah son of Josiah was made king of Judah by Nebuchadnezzar king of Babylon; he reigned in place of Jehoiachin[a] son of Jehoiakim. ²Neither he nor his attendants nor the people of the land paid any attention to the words the LORD had spoken through Jeremiah the prophet.

³King Zedekiah, however, sent Jehukal son of Shelemiah with the priest Zephaniah son of Maaseiah to Jeremiah the prophet with this message: "Please pray to the LORD our God for us."

⁴Now Jeremiah was free to come and go among the people, for he had not yet been put in prison. ⁵Pharaoh's army had marched out of Egypt, and

─────────

ᵃ 1 Hebrew *Koniah*, a variant of *Jehoiachin*

36:19 You and Jeremiah, go and hide The officials believe that the message is important enough to bring to the king, but they also are aware that a negative reaction by the king would endanger both Baruch and Jeremiah. Their advice to hide proves to be appropriate (see v. 26).
36:21 The king sent Jehudi to get the scroll Jehoiakim's request to hear the words directly from the scroll is a ploy to get his hands on the scroll to burn it.
36:22 ninth month December. See the table "Israelite Calendar" on p. 763.
36:23 scroll was burned in the fire In the ancient Near East, people believed that words had the power to bring about the events they foretold (see note on 26:9). By destroying the scroll, Jehoiakim attempts to destroy the words themselves and the potential they represent.
36:24 The king and all his attendants Alludes to 2Ki 22:11 and Josiah's repentant reaction to hearing the Torah scroll.
36:25 Elnathan, Delaiah and Gemariah Elnathan, son of Achbor (also rendered "Akbor"), and Gemariah, son of Shaphan, are descended from officials of Josiah who were present when the Torah scroll was read in 622 BC (see 2Ki 22:12).
36:30 no one to sit on the throne of David Compare Jer 22:30, where the same is promised to Jehoiakim's son, Jehoiachin, who reigned for only three months in 597 BC. **his body will be thrown out** Compare the woe oracle against Jehoiakim in 22:13–19.

36:32 many similar words were added The second edition of the scroll was expanded.

37:1—39:18 These chapters return to the time of the Babylonian siege of Jerusalem (see 34:1). Zedekiah consults with Jeremiah several times. He hopes for a positive word from Yahweh but receives only continued warnings. Jeremiah's enemies at the royal court conspire to have him imprisoned and then left to die in a muddy cistern. The section ends with the fall of Jerusalem to Nebuchadnezzar.

37:1–10 Jeremiah warns Zedekiah that the Babylonian siege has been lifted only temporarily (see note on 34:8–22). The advance of the Egyptian army under Pharaoh Hophra (see note on Eze 29:2) gave Zedekiah and the people of Jerusalem a false hope that the city would be delivered. Zedekiah sends two officials to Jeremiah, to ask him to intercede with Yahweh on their behalf. Instead, Jeremiah offers an oracle of judgment indicating that Egypt's army will soon be defeated and the Babylonians will return.

37:1 Zedekiah See note on Jer 21:1. **Nebuchadnezzar** See note on 21:2. **Jehoiachin** See note on 22:24.
37:4 had not yet been put in prison The events that follow (up to 38:28) explain why Jeremiah was imprisoned in 32:1–3.
37:5 Pharaoh's army had marched Hophra led a

when the Babylonians*a* who were besieging Jerusalem heard the report about them, they withdrew from Jerusalem.

⁶Then the word of the LORD came to Jeremiah the prophet: ⁷"This is what the LORD, the God of Israel, says: Tell the king of Judah, who sent you to inquire of me, 'Pharaoh's army, which has marched out to support you, will go back to its own land, to Egypt. ⁸Then the Babylonians will return and attack this city; they will capture it and burn it down.' ⁹"This is what the LORD says: Do not deceive yourselves, thinking, 'The Babylonians will surely leave us.' They will not! ¹⁰Even if you were to defeat the entire Babylonian*b* army that is attacking you and only wounded men were left in their tents, they would come out and burn this city down."

¹¹After the Babylonian army had withdrawn from Jerusalem because of Pharaoh's army, ¹²Jeremiah started to leave the city to go to the territory of Benjamin to get his share of the property among the people there. ¹³But when he reached the Benjamin Gate, the captain of the guard, whose name was Irijah son of Shelemiah, the son of Hananiah, arrested him and said, "You are deserting to the Babylonians!"

¹⁴"That's not true!" Jeremiah said. "I am not deserting to the Babylonians." But Irijah would not listen to him; instead, he arrested Jeremiah and brought him to the officials. ¹⁵They were angry with Jeremiah and had him beaten and imprisoned in the house of Jonathan the secretary, which they had made into a prison.

¹⁶Jeremiah was put into a vaulted cell in a dungeon, where he remained a long time. ¹⁷Then King Zedekiah sent for him and had him brought to the palace, where he asked him privately, "Is there any word from the LORD?"

"Yes," Jeremiah replied, "you will be delivered into the hands of the king of Babylon."

¹⁸Then Jeremiah said to King Zedekiah, "What crime have I committed against you or your attendants or this people, that you have put me in prison? ¹⁹Where are your prophets who prophesied to you, 'The king of Babylon will not attack you or this land'? ²⁰But now, my lord the king, please listen. Let me bring my petition before you: Do not send me back to the house of Jonathan the secretary, or I will die there."

²¹King Zedekiah then gave orders for Jeremiah to be placed in the courtyard of the guard and given a loaf of bread from the street of the bakers each day until all the bread in the city was gone. So Jeremiah remained in the courtyard of the guard.

Jeremiah Thrown Into a Cistern

38 Shephatiah son of Mattan, Gedaliah son of Pashhur, Jehukal*c* son of Shelemiah, and Pashhur son of Malkijah heard what Jeremiah was telling all the people when he said, ²"This is what the LORD says: 'Whoever stays in this city will die by the sword, famine or plague, but whoever goes over to the Babylonians*d* will live. They will escape with their lives; they will live.' ³And this is what the LORD says: 'This city will certainly be given into the hands of the army of the king of Babylon, who will capture it.'"

⁴Then the officials said to the king, "This man

a 5 Or *Chaldeans*; also in verses 8, 9, 13 and 14   *b* 10 Or *Chaldean*; also in verse 11   *c* 1 Hebrew *Jukal*, a variant of *Jehukal*   *d* 2 Or *Chaldeans*; also in verses 18, 19 and 23

campaign into Palestine in the summer of 587 BC to oppose Nebuchadnezzar and come to the aid of Judah (see note on Eze 29:2).
37:8 the Babylonians will return Jeremiah's warning is unequivocally clear: Egyptian intervention will fail, the Babylonians (Chaldeans) will return and the city will burn. There is no hope of escape or victory.
37:10 you were to defeat the entire Babylonian army Even if Judah does prevail against the Babylonian army, Yahweh's judgment against Jerusalem will still occur.
37:11–21 Jeremiah attempts to leave the city during the short time the siege is lifted, but he is detained at the city gate and accused of deserting to the Babylonians. Since he has urged surrender to Babylon (see Jer 27), he is viewed as a traitor. Jeremiah is beaten and imprisoned; he remains in jail until the fall of Jerusalem.
37:12 territory of Benjamin Jeremiah's home territory. **get his share of the property among the people there** Refers to his share of the family's land (see Ge 31:14; 33:19).
37:13 Benjamin Gate See note on Jer 20:2. **You are deserting to the Babylonians** Irijah has good cause to suspect desertion, since Jeremiah has preached that the people should surrender to Babylon (21:9).

37:15 They were angry with Jeremiah They may have been looking for an excuse to arrest him, perhaps connecting their present circumstance with his prophecies of destruction (see note on 36:23).
37:16 dungeon The Hebrew expression here means "house of the cistern." Apparently Jonathan's house had cisterns that could be used as cells.
37:17 asked him privately Zedekiah, still hoping for divine intervention, exercises caution due to Jeremiah's unpopularity.
37:19 Where are your prophets Jeremiah has been vindicated in his conflict with the false prophets who preached peace and security (e.g., ch. 28). Their predictions of Babylon's fall have failed to come true.
38:1–6 A group of royal officials demand that Jeremiah be executed because of his pro-Babylonian prophecies. Zedekiah appears unable to intervene, even conceding to the officials that he is powerless against them (v. 5). The officials throw Jeremiah into a muddy cistern in the court of the guard and leave him to die.
38:2 will die by the sword, famine or plague Quotes the prophecy from 21:9. See note on 14:12.
38:4 He is discouraging The officials perceive that Jeremiah's prophecies of imminent defeat are bad for morale.

should be put to death. He is discouraging the soldiers who are left in this city, as well as all the people, by the things he is saying to them. This man is not seeking the good of these people but their ruin."

⁵"He is in your hands," King Zedekiah answered. "The king can do nothing to oppose you."

⁶So they took Jeremiah and put him into the cistern of Malkijah, the king's son, which was in the courtyard of the guard. They lowered Jeremiah by ropes into the cistern; it had no water in it, only mud, and Jeremiah sank down into the mud.

⁷But Ebed-Melek, a Cushite,ᵃ an officialᵇ in the royal palace, heard that they had put Jeremiah into the cistern. While the king was sitting in the Benjamin Gate, ⁸Ebed-Melek went out of the palace and said to him, ⁹"My lord the king, these men have acted wickedly in all they have done to Jeremiah the prophet. They have thrown him into a cistern, where he will starve to death when there is no longer any bread in the city."

¹⁰Then the king commanded Ebed-Melek the Cushite, "Take thirty men from here with you and lift Jeremiah the prophet out of the cistern before he dies."

¹¹So Ebed-Melek took the men with him and went to a room under the treasury in the palace. He took some old rags and worn-out clothes from there and let them down with ropes to Jeremiah in the cistern. ¹²Ebed-Melek the Cushite said to Jeremiah, "Put these old rags and worn-out clothes under your arms to pad the ropes." Jeremiah did so, ¹³and they pulled him up with the ropes and lifted him out of the cistern. And Jeremiah remained in the courtyard of the guard.

Zedekiah Questions Jeremiah Again

¹⁴Then King Zedekiah sent for Jeremiah the prophet and had him brought to the third entrance to the temple of the LORD. "I am going to ask you something," the king said to Jeremiah. "Do not hide anything from me."

¹⁵Jeremiah said to Zedekiah, "If I give you an answer, will you not kill me? Even if I did give you counsel, you would not listen to me."

¹⁶But King Zedekiah swore this oath secretly to Jeremiah: "As surely as the LORD lives, who has given us breath, I will neither kill you nor hand you over to those who want to kill you."

¹⁷Then Jeremiah said to Zedekiah, "This is what the LORD God Almighty, the God of Israel, says: 'If you surrender to the officers of the king of Babylon, your life will be spared and this city will not be burned down; you and your family will live. ¹⁸But if you will not surrender to the officers of the king of Babylon, this city will be given into the hands of the Babylonians and they will burn it down; you yourself will not escape from them.'"

¹⁹King Zedekiah said to Jeremiah, "I am afraid of the Jews who have gone over to the Babylonians, for the Babylonians may hand me over to them and they will mistreat me."

²⁰"They will not hand you over," Jeremiah replied. "Obey the LORD by doing what I tell you. Then it will go well with you, and your life will be spared. ²¹But if you refuse to surrender, this is what the LORD has revealed to me: ²²All the women left in the palace of the king of Judah will be brought out to the officials of the king of Babylon. Those women will say to you:

"'They misled you and overcame you—
    those trusted friends of yours.
Your feet are sunk in the mud;
    your friends have deserted you.'

²³"All your wives and children will be brought out to the Babylonians. You yourself will not escape from their hands but will be captured by

ᵃ 7 Probably from the upper Nile region   ᵇ 7 Or a eunuch

38:5 king can do nothing to oppose you Emphasizes how much influence the officials had over the decisions of the king. Zedekiah fears both the pro-Egyptian (vv. 4–5) and pro-Babylonian (v. 19) factions in his government.

38:6 cistern of Malkijah, the king's son A cistern was a bottle-shaped pit dug out of rock and used to store water. Cisterns varied in size, with some as deep as 120 feet; a typical cistern had a mouth about 2 feet across and was 15–20 feet deep. Cisterns full of rainwater were important for a city under siege. The fact that this cistern is empty might indicate that the city is running low on supplies. On Malkijah, see note on 21:1.

38:7–13 Jeremiah is rescued from the cistern by Zedekiah's non-Israelite servant. While the king cannot prevent his officials from mistreating Jeremiah, he can allow his men to save him.

38:7 Ebed-Melek, a Cushite, an official His name means "servant of the king." His title, *saris,* can be used generally for a court official (Ge 37:36; 2Ki 23:11) or

specifically for a eunuch (Est 2:3; see note on Est 1:10). The text connects him with the region of Cush, located south of Egypt, roughly in the area of modern Ethiopia.

38:14–28 Zedekiah again summons Jeremiah, hoping for a new message of hope from Yahweh. Since the king is afraid of the group that tried to kill Jeremiah, he meets the prophet secretly and makes him swear not to tell the officials about their conversation (Jer 38:26–27). Jeremiah's message is the same: either surrender to Babylon and spare the city, or continue to fight and the city will burn.

38:14 the third entrance to the temple Refers to an unknown location.

38:18 the Babylonians The Hebrew text uses "Babylonians" and "Chaldeans" interchangeably. See note on Isa 43:14.

38:22 Your feet are sunk in the mud Turns Jeremiah's experience in the muddy cistern into an object lesson: Jeremiah was stuck, but his friends helped him escape; Zedekiah's friends will desert him.

the king of Babylon; and this city will^a be burned down."

²⁴Then Zedekiah said to Jeremiah, "Do not let anyone know about this conversation, or you may die. ²⁵If the officials hear that I talked with you, and they come to you and say, 'Tell us what you said to the king and what the king said to you; do not hide it from us or we will kill you,' ²⁶then tell them, 'I was pleading with the king not to send me back to Jonathan's house to die there.'"

²⁷All the officials did come to Jeremiah and question him, and he told them everything the king had ordered him to say. So they said no more to him, for no one had heard his conversation with the king.

²⁸And Jeremiah remained in the courtyard of the guard until the day Jerusalem was captured.

The Fall of Jerusalem

39:1-10pp — 2Ki 25:1-12; Jer 52:4-16

39 This is how Jerusalem was taken: ¹In the ninth year of Zedekiah king of Judah, in the tenth month, Nebuchadnezzar king of Babylon marched against Jerusalem with his whole army and laid siege to it. ²And on the ninth day of the fourth month of Zedekiah's eleventh year, the city wall was broken through. ³Then all the officials of the king of Babylon came and took seats in the Middle Gate: Nergal-Sharezer of Samgar, Nebo-Sarsekim a chief officer, Nergal-Sharezer a high official and all the other officials of the king of Babylon. ⁴When Zedekiah king of Judah and all the soldiers saw them, they fled; they left the city

at night by way of the king's garden, through the gate between the two walls, and headed toward the Arabah.^b

⁵But the Babylonian^c army pursued them and overtook Zedekiah in the plains of Jericho. They captured him and took him to Nebuchadnezzar king of Babylon at Riblah in the land of Hamath, where he pronounced sentence on him. ⁶There at Riblah the king of Babylon slaughtered the sons of Zedekiah before his eyes and also killed all the nobles of Judah. ⁷Then he put out Zedekiah's eyes and bound him with bronze shackles to take him to Babylon.

⁸The Babylonians^d set fire to the royal palace and the houses of the people and broke down the walls of Jerusalem. ⁹Nebuzaradan commander of the imperial guard carried into exile to Babylon the people who remained in the city, along with those who had gone over to him, and the rest of the people. ¹⁰But Nebuzaradan the commander of the guard left behind in the land of Judah some of the poor people, who owned nothing; and at that time he gave them vineyards and fields.

¹¹Now Nebuchadnezzar king of Babylon had given these orders about Jeremiah through Nebuzaradan commander of the imperial guard: ¹²"Take him and look after him; don't harm him but do for him whatever he asks." ¹³So Nebuzaradan the commander of the guard, Nebushazban a chief officer, Nergal-Sharezer a high official and all the other officers of the king of Babylon ¹⁴sent and

---

^a 23 Or *and you will cause this city to*   ^b 4 Or *the Jordan Valley*
^c 5 Or *Chaldean*   ^d 8 Or *Chaldeans*

38:26 not to send me back Compare Jer 37:20. The content of the conversation is accurate but for a different occasion. Zedekiah is afraid of the officials who want to kill Jeremiah (see v. 4; v. 5 and note).

39:1–18 Jerusalem falls to Babylon, and Zedekiah is taken captive. Apart from the details about the treatment of Jeremiah and a prophecy (vv. 11–18), the narrative closely parallels the accounts in 52:4–16 and 2Ki 25:1–12.

39:1 the ninth year of Zedekiah Probably 587 BC. The full date of the beginning of the siege is given in 2Ki 25:1 and Eze 24:1; it was the tenth day of the tenth month. See note on Eze 24:1. See the timeline "Life of Jeremiah" on p. 1170; see the table "Israelite Calendar" on p. 763. **Zedekiah king of Judah** See note on Jer 21:1. **Nebuchadnezzar king of Babylon** See note on 21:2.
39:2 the fourth month of Zedekiah's eleventh year The siege lasted about a year and a half, until July of 586 BC.
39:3 Middle Gate The gate is mentioned only here, but archaeological evidence suggests it was the north-facing gate, perhaps the same as the Fish Gate mentioned in Ne 3:3. Sitting in the gate asserted Babylonian rule over the city. **Nergal-Sharezer of Samgar, Nebo-Sarsekim** The list of names presented in this verse can be construed as the names *or* titles of six officials, or as the names *and* titles of three officials. The Hebrew scribes preserv-

ing the OT text had difficulty distinguishing names from titles and properly dividing the Babylonian syllables. The names and titles appear differently in various English translations, and their meanings are unclear.
39:4 they left the city at night See 2Ki 25:4 and note on Eze 12:4. **toward the Arabah** The wilderness east of Jerusalem around the Dead Sea.
39:5 the plains of Jericho The area just east of Jerusalem. Zedekiah didn't get very far. **at Riblah in the land of Hamath** The city in northern Syria where Nebuchadnezzar was headquartered during his campaign in Palestine. Compare Eze 6:14.
39:6 king of Babylon slaughtered the sons of Zedekiah See 2Ki 25:7.
39:9 Nebuzaradan commander The commander of the forces that conquered Jerusalem. He is also responsible for the destruction and plunder of the city and the organization of the captives for exile. His name means "[the god] Nabu has given me offspring." His Hebrew title, *rav-tabbachim*, must be an archaic term for a high-powered military commander. See 2Ki 25:8–12.
39:10 poor people, who owned nothing The poor people were not deported; since they had no property, they posed no threat to Babylon. Giving fields and vineyards to the poor was a means of developing a positive relationship with them and restoring agriculture in the region.
39:13 Nebushazban a chief officer See note on Jer 39:3.
39:14 Gedaliah The governor of Judah after the Babylonian exile.

had Jeremiah taken out of the courtyard of the guard. They turned him over to Gedaliah son of Ahikam, the son of Shaphan, to take him back to his home. So he remained among his own people.

[15]While Jeremiah had been confined in the courtyard of the guard, the word of the LORD came to him: [16]"Go and tell Ebed-Melek the Cushite, 'This is what the LORD Almighty, the God of Israel, says: I am about to fulfill my words against this city — words concerning disaster, not prosperity. At that time they will be fulfilled before your eyes. [17]But I will rescue you on that day, declares the LORD; you will not be given into the hands of those you fear. [18]I will save you; you will not fall by the sword but will escape with your life, because you trust in me, declares the LORD.'"

Jeremiah Freed

40 The word came to Jeremiah from the LORD after Nebuzaradan commander of the imperial guard had released him at Ramah. He had found Jeremiah bound in chains among all the captives from Jerusalem and Judah who were being carried into exile to Babylon. [2]When the commander of the guard found Jeremiah, he said to him, "The LORD your God decreed this disaster for this place. [3]And now the LORD has brought it about; he has done just as he said he would. All this happened because you people sinned against the LORD and did not obey him. [4]But today I am freeing you from the chains on your wrists. Come with me to Babylon, if you like, and I will look after you; but if you do not want to, then don't come. Look, the whole country lies before you; go wherever you please." [5]However, before Jeremiah turned to go,[a] Nebuzaradan added, "Go back to Gedaliah son of Ahikam, the son of Shaphan, whom the king of Babylon has appointed over the towns of Judah, and live with him among the people, or go anywhere else you please."

Then the commander gave him provisions and a present and let him go. [6]So Jeremiah went to Gedaliah son of Ahikam at Mizpah and stayed with him among the people who were left behind in the land.

Gedaliah Assassinated

40:7-9; 41:1-3pp — 2Ki 25:22-26

[7]When all the army officers and their men who were still in the open country heard that the king

a 5 Or Jeremiah answered

GEDALIAH
Gedaliah's name means "Yahweh is great." his introduction with a double patronym (listing the names of both his father and grandfather) in Jer 39:14 clarifies his association with the prominent family of royal scribes descended from Shaphan (see 2 Kgs 22). Several members of this family are depicted as offering support for Jeremiah (see Jer 26:24; 36:10,25). After the destruction of Jerusalem and the exile of most of the population to Babylon, Gedaliah was appointed governor over the remaining population of poor farmers. His governorship ended when he was assassinated by Ishmael son of Nethaniah (41:2–3).

39:16 Ebed-Melek the Cushite See 38:7 and note.

40:1 — 44:30 These chapters record the events of the aftermath of Jerusalem's destruction. Gedaliah (see note on 39:14) is appointed governor by Babylon, but a rebellious faction among the survivors of Judah plots his assassination. Gedaliah's supporters still fear Babylonian reprisal for his death, so they flee to Egypt, taking Jeremiah and Baruch with them despite Jeremiah's insistence that Yahweh's will is for them to remain in Judah and rebuild. Once in Egypt, Jeremiah prophesies against idolatry and criticizes the Jewish refugees settling in Egypt for abandoning their country and their God.

40:1 — 41:18 This section describes Gedaliah's short rule as governor and his attempt at reconstructing the country and Judean society before his assassination. Compare 2Ki 25:22–26.

40:1 Nebuzaradan commander of the imperial guard See note on Jer 39:9. **Ramah** See note on 31:15. **all the captives** Jeremiah apparently accompanied Nebuzaradan to Ramah with the exiles being prepared for deportation to Babylon. Compare 39:11–12.

40:5 Gedaliah See note on 39:14.

40:6 Mizpah A city about eight miles north of Jerusalem on the northern border of the territory of Benjamin. Most of the southern cities of Judah had been left uninhabitable by the Babylonian invasion. Biblical Mizpah is usually identified with the site of Tell en-Nasbeh.

MIZPAH
Mizpah was a border fortress with massive fortifications, including a wall that was roughly 13 feet thick. The archaeological site of Tell en-Nasbeh is most likely Mizpah. The town was built up by King Asa to defend the northern border of Judah from Israelite incursions (1Ki 15:16–22). Before the monarchy, the location had served as a rallying point for the tribes of Israel. All Israel gathered there before confronting the Benjamites over the rape and murder of the Levite's concubine (Jdg 20–21). The site also is mentioned as a place for sacred assemblies under Samuel (1Sa 7:5–12). After the exile, Mizpah became a regional capital in the province of Yehud (Judea; Ne 3:15). Northern Judah was still inhabitable after the Babylonian invasion. The fortresses to the south were largely destroyed in 586 BC, but sites to the north of Jerusalem, like Tell en-Nasbeh, were not.

40:7 all the army officers Refers to the remnants of Judah's army that had scattered after Jerusalem fell. Compare 52:8.

of Babylon had appointed Gedaliah son of Ahikam as governor over the land and had put him in charge of the men, women and children who were the poorest in the land and who had not been carried into exile to Babylon, ⁸they came to Gedaliah at Mizpah—Ishmael son of Nethaniah, Johanan and Jonathan the sons of Kareah, Seraiah son of Tanhumeth, the sons of Ephai the Netophathite, and Jaazaniah*a* the son of the Maakathite, and their men. ⁹Gedaliah son of Ahikam, the son of Shaphan, took an oath to reassure them and their men. "Do not be afraid to serve the Babylonians,*b*" he said. "Settle down in the land and serve the king of Babylon, and it will go well with you. ¹⁰I myself will stay at Mizpah to represent you before the Babylonians who come to us, but you are to harvest the wine, summer fruit and olive oil, and put them in your storage jars, and live in the towns you have taken over."

¹¹When all the Jews in Moab, Ammon, Edom and all the other countries heard that the king of Babylon had left a remnant in Judah and had appointed Gedaliah son of Ahikam, the son of Shaphan, as governor over them, ¹²they all came back to the land of Judah, to Gedaliah at Mizpah, from all the countries where they had been scattered. And they harvested an abundance of wine and summer fruit.

¹³Johanan son of Kareah and all the army officers still in the open country came to Gedaliah at Mizpah ¹⁴and said to him, "Don't you know that Baalis king of the Ammonites has sent Ishmael son of Nethaniah to take your life?" But Gedaliah son of Ahikam did not believe them.

¹⁵Then Johanan son of Kareah said privately to Gedaliah in Mizpah, "Let me go and kill Ishmael son of Nethaniah, and no one will know it. Why should he take your life and cause all the Jews who are gathered around you to be scattered and the remnant of Judah to perish?"

¹⁶But Gedaliah son of Ahikam said to Johanan son of Kareah, "Don't do such a thing! What you are saying about Ishmael is not true."

41 In the seventh month Ishmael son of Nethaniah, the son of Elishama, who was of royal blood and had been one of the king's officers, came with ten men to Gedaliah son of Ahikam at Mizpah. While they were eating together there, ²Ishmael son of Nethaniah and the ten men who were with him got up and struck down Gedaliah son of Ahikam, the son of Shaphan, with the sword, killing the one whom the king of Babylon had appointed as governor over the land. ³Ishmael also killed all the men of Judah who were with Gedaliah at Mizpah, as well as the Babylonian*c* soldiers who were there.

⁴The day after Gedaliah's assassination, before anyone knew about it, ⁵eighty men who had shaved off their beards, torn their clothes and cut themselves came from Shechem, Shiloh and Samaria, bringing grain offerings and incense with them to the house of the LORD. ⁶Ishmael son of Nethaniah went out from Mizpah to meet them, weeping as he went. When he met them, he said, "Come to Gedaliah son of Ahikam." ⁷When they went into the city, Ishmael son of Nethaniah and the men who were with him slaughtered them and threw them into a cistern. ⁸But ten of them said to Ishmael, "Don't kill us! We have wheat and barley, olive oil and honey, hidden in a field." So he let them alone and did not kill them with the others. ⁹Now the cistern where he threw all the

---

a 8 Hebrew *Jezaniah*, a variant of *Jaazaniah*
b 9 Or *Chaldeans*; also in verse 10   *c 3* Or *Chaldean*

40:8 Ishmael According to 41:1, Ishmael is a member of the royal family. He leads the faction plotting against Gedaliah. **Jonathan** A troop commander supporting Gedaliah. Later, he leads a group of Jews to Egypt after Gedaliah is assassinated.

40:14 Baalis A seal from the sixth century BC confirms the existence of this king, who is mentioned only here in the Bible. His motivation for orchestrating Gedaliah's assassination is unknown. Ammon was the territory east of the Jordan River and north of Moab. See note on 25:21. **did not believe them** Gedaliah cannot accept that Ishmael would betray him. This misplaced trust soon costs Gedaliah and dozens of others their lives (41:1–8).

41:1–18 Gedaliah, the Judean governor appointed by Babylon, is assassinated, and Mizpah becomes the scene of a chaotic massacre. Ishmael lures 80 pilgrims into the city, where he and his men slaughter 70 of them—sparing 10 who bribe them with the promise of food. The people who remained in Mizpah under Gedaliah's protection are then taken hostage as Ishmael flees to the Ammonites. Johanan pursues, overtaking the group and recovering the hostages, but Ishmael escapes with eight men.

41:1 In the seventh month Autumn. The year is often assumed to be 586 BC, the same year as the fall of Jerusalem. See the timeline "Life of Jeremiah" on p. 1170; see the table "Israelite Calendar" on p. 763. **Ishmael** See 40:8 and note. **Gedaliah** See note on 39:14. **Mizpah** See note on 40:6. **While they were eating together there** Describes a traditional offer of hospitality. Gedaliah trusted Ishmael, refusing to believe Johanan's report that Ishmael intended to kill him (40:16).

41:5 cut themselves Shaving, tearing clothes and cutting the body were practices involved in mourning rituals. The pilgrims might have been lamenting the destruction of Jerusalem and the loss of the temple. See note on Dt 14:1. **from Shechem, Shiloh and Samaria** Religious pilgrims from three Israelite cities. The seventh month was the time of the Festival of Tabernacles. **grain offerings and incense** The site of the temple was still considered holy and continued to be used for worship. On grain offerings and incense, see Lev 2:1–16 and note. **41:6 weeping as he went** Ishmael mimics their mournful attitude, giving the impression that like-minded mourners are to be found in Mizpah.

41:7 a cistern The site of Tell en-Nasbeh (probably Biblical Mizpah) was honeycombed with cisterns dug into the rock. See note on 38:6.

bodies of the men he had killed along with Gedaliah was the one King Asa had made as part of his defense against Baasha king of Israel. Ishmael son of Nethaniah filled it with the dead.

[10]Ishmael made captives of all the rest of the people who were in Mizpah—the king's daughters along with all the others who were left there, over whom Nebuzaradan commander of the imperial guard had appointed Gedaliah son of Ahikam. Ishmael son of Nethaniah took them captive and set out to cross over to the Ammonites.

[11]When Johanan son of Kareah and all the army officers who were with him heard about all the crimes Ishmael son of Nethaniah had committed, [12]they took all their men and went to fight Ishmael son of Nethaniah. They caught up with him near the great pool in Gibeon. [13]When all the people Ishmael had with him saw Johanan son of Kareah and the army officers who were with him, they were glad. [14]All the people Ishmael had taken captive at Mizpah turned and went over to Johanan son of Kareah. [15]But Ishmael son of Nethaniah and eight of his men escaped from Johanan and fled to the Ammonites.

Flight to Egypt

[16]Then Johanan son of Kareah and all the army officers who were with him led away all the people of Mizpah who had survived, whom Johanan had recovered from Ishmael son of Nethaniah after Ishmael had assassinated Gedaliah son of Ahikam—the soldiers, women, children and court officials he had recovered from Gibeon. [17]And they went on, stopping at Geruth Kimham near Bethlehem on their way to Egypt [18]to escape the Babylonians.[a] They were afraid of them because Ishmael son of Nethaniah had killed Gedaliah son of Ahikam, whom the king of Babylon had appointed as governor over the land.

42 Then all the army officers, including Johanan son of Kareah and Jezaniah[b] son of Hoshaiah, and all the people from the least to the greatest approached [2]Jeremiah the prophet and said to him, "Please hear our petition and pray to the LORD your God for this entire remnant. For as you now see, though we were once many, now only a few are left. [3]Pray that the LORD your God will tell us where we should go and what we should do."

[4]"I have heard you," replied Jeremiah the prophet. "I will certainly pray to the LORD your God as you have requested; I will tell you everything the LORD says and will keep nothing back from you."

[5]Then they said to Jeremiah, "May the LORD be a true and faithful witness against us if we do not act in accordance with everything the LORD your God sends you to tell us. [6]Whether it is favorable or unfavorable, we will obey the LORD our God, to whom we are sending you, so that it will go well with us, for we will obey the LORD our God."

[7]Ten days later the word of the LORD came to Jeremiah. [8]So he called together Johanan son of Kareah and all the army officers who were with him and all the people from the least to the greatest. [9]He said to them, "This is what the LORD, the God of Israel, to whom you sent me to present your petition, says: [10]'If you stay in this land, I will build you up and not tear you down; I will plant you and not uproot you, for I have relented concerning the disaster I have inflicted on you. [11]Do not be afraid of the king of Babylon, whom you now fear. Do not be afraid of him, declares the LORD, for I am with you and will save you and deliver you from his hands. [12]I will show you compassion so that he will have compassion on you and restore you to your land.'

[13]"However, if you say, 'We will not stay in this land,' and so disobey the LORD your God, [14]and if you say, 'No, we will go and live in Egypt, where we will not see war or hear the trumpet or be hungry for bread,' [15]then hear the word of the

---

[a] 18 Or Chaldeans   [b] 1 Hebrew; Septuagint (see also 43:2) Azariah

---

41:10 the king's daughters The Babylonians apparently had left some princesses of the royal house of David alive and in Judah under Gedaliah's care. The Hebrew terminology here could refer to women of royal descent, not necessarily the daughters of Zedekiah directly. Since Ishmael belonged to the royal family, he would have been interested in keeping them alive. **Nebuzaradan** The Babylonian official who organized the deportation. See note on 39:9. **the Ammonites** Ishmael's assassination plot was backed by the king of the Ammonites. See 40:14 and note.
41:18 They were afraid of them The flight to Egypt is motivated by fear that the Babylonians' response to Gedaliah's assassination will involve more violence.
42:1–22 Before continuing on to Egypt (41:17), the refugees from Mizpah ask Jeremiah to seek Yahweh's will regarding whether they should stay or go. Jeremiah warns strenuously against the trip to Egypt, insisting that

Yahweh will not bless the refugees there, but they ignore the warning and proceed with the journey (43:1–7).
42:1 Johanan The leader of the group fleeing Mizpah after Gedaliah's death. **Jezaniah** Another troop commander.
42:2 pray to the LORD your God for this entire remnant One of the roles of a prophet was to serve as intercessor and mediator between Yahweh and the people.
42:5 May the LORD be a true and faithful witness against us The people formally swear to abide by the word they receive from Yahweh, invoking Yahweh as witness to their oath.
42:10 I will build you up The time of judgment has passed. The time for renewal and restoration is beginning. Compare 24:6; 31:28.
42:11 Do not be afraid of the king of Babylon The reprisal they feared over Gedaliah's assassination would not come (see 41:18 and note).

LORD, you remnant of Judah. This is what the LORD Almighty, the God of Israel, says: 'If you are determined to go to Egypt and you do go to settle there, ¹⁶then the sword you fear will overtake you there, and the famine you dread will follow you into Egypt, and there you will die. ¹⁷Indeed, all who are determined to go to Egypt to settle there will die by the sword, famine and plague; not one of them will survive or escape the disaster I will bring on them.' ¹⁸This is what the LORD Almighty, the God of Israel, says: 'As my anger and wrath have been poured out on those who lived in Jerusalem, so will my wrath be poured out on you when you go to Egypt. You will be a curse*a* and an object of horror, a curse*a* and an object of reproach; you will never see this place again.'

¹⁹"Remnant of Judah, the LORD has told you, 'Do not go to Egypt.' Be sure of this: I warn you today ²⁰that you made a fatal mistake when you sent me to the LORD your God and said, 'Pray to the LORD our God for us; tell us everything he says and we will do it.' ²¹I have told you today, but you still have not obeyed the LORD your God in all he sent me to tell you. ²²So now, be sure of this: You will die by the sword, famine and plague in the place where you want to go to settle."

43 When Jeremiah had finished telling the people all the words of the LORD their God — everything the LORD had sent him to tell them — ²Azariah son of Hoshaiah and Johanan son of Kareah and all the arrogant men said to Jeremiah, "You are lying! The LORD our God has not sent you to say, 'You must not go to Egypt to settle there.' ³But Baruch son of Neriah is inciting you against us to hand us over to the Babylonians,*b* so they may kill us or carry us into exile to Babylon."

⁴So Johanan son of Kareah and all the army officers and all the people disobeyed the LORD's command to stay in the land of Judah. ⁵Instead, Johanan son of Kareah and all the army officers led away all the remnant of Judah who had come back to live in the land of Judah from all the nations where they had been scattered. ⁶They also led away all those whom Nebuzaradan commander of the imperial guard had left with Gedaliah son of Ahikam, the son of Shaphan — the men, the women, the children and the king's daughters. And they took Jeremiah the prophet and Baruch son of Neriah along with them. ⁷So they entered Egypt in disobedience to the LORD and went as far as Tahpanhes.

⁸In Tahpanhes the word of the LORD came to Jeremiah: ⁹"While the Jews are watching, take some large stones with you and bury them in clay in the brick pavement at the entrance to Pharaoh's palace in Tahpanhes. ¹⁰Then say to them, 'This is what the LORD Almighty, the God of Israel, says: I will send for my servant Nebuchadnezzar king of Babylon, and I will set his throne over these stones I have buried here; he will spread his royal canopy above them. ¹¹He will come and attack Egypt, bringing death to those destined for death, captivity to those destined for captivity, and the sword to those destined for the sword. ¹²He will set fire to the temples of the gods of Egypt; he will burn their temples and take their gods captive. As a shepherd picks his garment clean of lice, so he will pick Egypt clean and depart. ¹³There in the temple of the sun*c* in Egypt he will demolish the sacred pillars and will burn down the temples of the gods of Egypt.'"

a 18 That is, your name will be used in cursing (see 29:22); or, others will see that you are cursed.   *b 3* Or *Chaldeans*
c 13 Or *in Heliopolis*

42:17 by the sword, famine and plague These disasters probably reflect the curses for violating the covenant. See note on 14:12.

42:21 you still have not obeyed the LORD Jeremiah knows that even though they asked for the message from Yahweh, they will not listen or obey it. Compare 38:15. Zedekiah also asked for Yahweh's message and similarly chose to ignore it.

43:1–13 Just as Jeremiah predicted (42:21), the people do not listen to him. They accuse him of lying in order to persuade them to wait around for punishment from Babylon. They also implicate Baruch in their conspiracy theory. Even though Jeremiah's prophecies about Babylon had proven true, here he is accused of false prophecy. He and Baruch perhaps were distrusted because of their pro-Babylonian and anti-Egyptian politics.

43:2 Azariah Mentioned only here. **Johanan** Leader of the Judean refugees from Mizpah (see chs. 40–41).
43:3 Baruch See note on 32:12.
43:5 all the remnant of Judah The entire group of refugees heads to Egypt, taking Baruch and Jeremiah with them.

43:6 Nebuzaradan See note on 39:9. **Gedaliah** See note on 39:14. **the king's daughters** See note on 41:10.
43:7 Tahpanhes A village in the eastern Nile delta region of Egypt. See 2:16.
43:9 take some large stones with you A symbolic action (compare 13:1–14; 19:1–15) in which Jeremiah places two stones near a palace of Pharaoh to symbolize where Nebuchadnezzar's throne will be set up after he conquers Egypt. See the table "Symbolic Actions of the Prophets" on p. 1195.
43:10 Nebuchadnezzar See 21:2 and note; 25:9 and note.
43:12 and take their gods captive A nation's gods could be taken into exile by a conqueror. The carved image usually was placed in the temple of the conquering deity, symbolizing the defeated god's inferiority.
43:13 in the temple of the sun in Egypt he will demolish the sacred pillars See note on Eze 30:17. The four-sided pillars known as obelisks were common monuments in ancient Egypt. **will burn down** Just as the Jerusalem temple was burned, so too will the temples of Egypt burn.

Disaster Because of Idolatry

44 This word came to Jeremiah concerning all the Jews living in Lower Egypt — in Migdol, Tahpanhes and Memphis — and in Upper Egypt: ²"This is what the LORD Almighty, the God of Israel, says: You saw the great disaster I brought on Jerusalem and on all the towns of Judah. Today they lie deserted and in ruins ³because of the evil they have done. They aroused my anger by burning incense to and worshiping other gods that neither they nor you nor your ancestors ever knew. ⁴Again and again I sent my servants the prophets, who said, 'Do not do this detestable thing that I hate!' ⁵But they did not listen or pay attention; they did not turn from their wickedness or stop burning incense to other gods. ⁶Therefore, my fierce anger was poured out; it raged against the towns of Judah and the streets of Jerusalem and made them the desolate ruins they are today.

⁷"Now this is what the LORD God Almighty, the God of Israel, says: Why bring such great disaster on yourselves by cutting off from Judah the men and women, the children and infants, and so leave yourselves without a remnant? ⁸Why arouse my anger with what your hands have made, burning incense to other gods in Egypt, where you have come to live? You will destroy yourselves and make yourselves a curse*a* and an object of reproach among all the nations on earth. ⁹Have you forgotten the wickedness committed by your ancestors and by the kings and queens of Judah and the wickedness committed by you and your wives in the land of Judah and the streets of Je-

rusalem? ¹⁰To this day they have not humbled themselves or shown reverence, nor have they followed my law and the decrees I set before you and your ancestors.

¹¹"Therefore this is what the LORD Almighty, the God of Israel, says: I am determined to bring disaster on you and to destroy all Judah. ¹²I will take away the remnant of Judah who were determined to go to Egypt to settle there. They will all perish in Egypt; they will fall by the sword or die from famine. From the least to the greatest, they will die by sword or famine. They will become a curse and an object of horror, a curse and an object of reproach. ¹³I will punish those who live in Egypt with the sword, famine and plague, as I punished Jerusalem. ¹⁴None of the remnant of Judah who have gone to live in Egypt will escape or survive to return to the land of Judah, to which they long to return and live; none will return except a few fugitives."

¹⁵Then all the men who knew that their wives were burning incense to other gods, along with all the women who were present — a large assembly — and all the people living in Lower and Upper Egypt, said to Jeremiah, ¹⁶"We will not listen to the message you have spoken to us in the name of the LORD! ¹⁷We will certainly do everything we said we would: We will burn incense to the Queen of Heaven and will pour out drink offerings to her just as we and our ancestors, our kings and

---

a 8 That is, your name will be used in cursing (see 29:22); or, others will see that you are cursed; also in verse 12; similarly in verse 22.

44:1–30 Jeremiah prophesies against the entire population of Jews who fled to Egypt after the Babylonian invasion. He warns them against idolatry, using the destruction of Jerusalem to underscore the dire consequences of abandoning Yahweh again. The people's defiant response (Jer 44:15–19) follows their usual pattern of ignoring Jeremiah's prophecies, but they also offer a surprisingly different interpretation of their present circumstances, blaming the national disaster not on Yahweh's judgment but on the displeasure of the "Queen of Heaven." Jeremiah turns their explanation back on them, declaring that the idol-worship occurring in Judah was the reason for Yahweh's wrath. If they persist in idolatry in Egypt, they will again suffer the punishment of Yahweh by sword and famine.

44:1 Jews living in Lower Egypt Archaeological evidence supports an increase in the population of Jewish communities in Egypt around this time. The most important evidence of Jewish daily life in Egypt comes from the colony at Elephantine. See note on Isa 49:12. **Migdol** In the northeast of Egypt. See note on Eze 29:10. **Tahpanhes** A city in the eastern delta region. **Memphis** A city at the entrance of the delta region. See note on Eze 30:13. **Upper Egypt** The southern region of Egypt. See note on Eze 29:14.

44:3 by burning incense to and worshiping other gods The fundamental sin of Judah was idolatry. Compare Jer 1:16; 7:9; 18:15; 19:4.

44:4 this detestable thing The Hebrew word can refer to anything offensive but often refers specifically to something that offends Yahweh's sense of holiness. See 6:15 and note.

44:7 so leave yourselves without a remnant A serious consequence, symbolizing a complete and final break with Yahweh. See note on Isa 1:9. Compare Isa 14:22 and note.

44:11 to destroy all Judah The remnant that escaped to Egypt is under the same indictment of judgment for idolatry. Unless they repent, the punishment will follow them wherever they flee.

44:15 their wives were burning incense to other gods The comparison with the rituals for the Queen of Heaven in Jer 7:18–20 indicate the idolatry was a family affair.

44:16 We will not listen to Their defiant response and persistent rebellion serves to justify Yahweh's judgment. Ezekiel says the behavior of the fugitives will help explain Yahweh's anger (see Eze 12:16 and note; 14:22 and note).

44:17 the Queen of Heaven See note on Jer 7:18. Probably a reference to the goddess Ishtar or Astarte. See the table "Pagan Deities of the Old Testament" on p. 1287. **we had plenty of food** An idealized recollection of their prosperity in Judah prior to the Babylonian invasion, implying that the disaster came only after they stopped making offerings to the Queen of Heaven.

our officials did in the towns of Judah and in the streets of Jerusalem. At that time we had plenty of food and were well off and suffered no harm. [18]But ever since we stopped burning incense to the Queen of Heaven and pouring out drink offerings to her, we have had nothing and have been perishing by sword and famine."

[19]The women added, "When we burned incense to the Queen of Heaven and poured out drink offerings to her, did not our husbands know that we were making cakes impressed with her image and pouring out drink offerings to her?"

[20]Then Jeremiah said to all the people, both men and women, who were answering him, [21]"Did not the LORD remember and call to mind the incense burned in the towns of Judah and the streets of Jerusalem by you and your ancestors, your kings and your officials and the people of the land? [22]When the LORD could no longer endure your wicked actions and the detestable things you did, your land became a curse and a desolate waste without inhabitants, as it is today. [23]Because you have burned incense and have sinned against the LORD and have not obeyed him or followed his law or his decrees or his stipulations, this disaster has come upon you, as you now see."

[24]Then Jeremiah said to all the people, including the women, "Hear the word of the LORD, all you people of Judah in Egypt. [25]This is what the LORD Almighty, the God of Israel, says: You and your wives have done what you said you would do when you promised, 'We will certainly carry out the vows we made to burn incense and pour out drink offerings to the Queen of Heaven.'

"Go ahead then, do what you promised! Keep your vows! [26]But hear the word of the LORD, all you Jews living in Egypt: 'I swear by my great name,' says the LORD, 'that no one from Judah living anywhere in Egypt will ever again invoke my name or swear, "As surely as the Sovereign LORD lives." [27]For I am watching over them for harm, not for good; the Jews in Egypt will perish by sword and famine until they are all destroyed. [28]Those who escape the sword and return to the land of Judah from Egypt will be very few. Then the whole remnant of Judah who came to live in Egypt will know whose word will stand — mine or theirs.

[29]"'This will be the sign to you that I will punish you in this place,' declares the LORD, 'so that you will know that my threats of harm against you will surely stand.' [30]This is what the LORD says: 'I am going to deliver Pharaoh Hophra king of Egypt into the hands of his enemies who want to kill him, just as I gave Zedekiah king of Judah into the hands of Nebuchadnezzar king of Babylon, the enemy who wanted to kill him.'"

A Message to Baruch

45 When Baruch son of Neriah wrote on a scroll the words Jeremiah the prophet dictated in the fourth year of Jehoiakim son of Josiah king of Judah, Jeremiah said this to Baruch: [2]"This is what the LORD, the God of Israel, says to you, Baruch: [3]You said, 'Woe to me! The LORD has added sorrow to my pain; I am worn out with groaning and find no rest.' [4]But the LORD has told me to say to you, 'This is what the LORD says: I will overthrow what I have built and uproot what I have planted, throughout the earth. [5]Should you then seek great things for yourself? Do not seek them. For I will bring disaster on all people, declares the LORD, but wherever you go I will let you escape with your life.'"

A Message About Egypt

46 This is the word of the LORD that came to Jeremiah the prophet concerning the nations:

[2]Concerning Egypt:

This is the message against the army of Pharaoh Necho king of Egypt, which was defeated

---

44:22 LORD could no longer endure your wicked Jeremiah challenges their explanation. Their prosperity was from Yahweh, who was patiently tolerating their evil, giving them a chance to repent. Eventually, he could no longer bear it and had to punish them.
44:30 Pharaoh Hophra Reigned 589–570 BC. Hophra was the Egyptian king who led the army attempting to save Judah from Nebuchadnezzar's siege (see 37:5). The downfall of Hophra will be a sign to the remnant of coming judgment and of Yahweh's sovereignty. Hophra was killed in a coup in 570 BC. See note on Eze 29:2. **Zedekiah** See note on Jer 21:1. **Nebuchadnezzar** See note on 21:2.

45:1–5 This individual salvation oracle addressed to Baruch is dated to 605 BC and alludes to the events of ch. 36. Baruch's lament (45:3) reveals his feelings of persecution following that incident and his subsequent unpopular association with Jeremiah (compare Jeremiah's laments in 11:18—20:18). As consolation for his suffering,

Yahweh assures him that he will survive the destruction of Jerusalem. The passage alludes to Baruch seeking great things for himself, but there is no indication in the book as to what his ambitions might have been. See the timeline "Life of Jeremiah" on p. 1170.

45:1 Baruch Jeremiah's scribe and companion. See note on 32:12. **Jeremiah the prophet dictated** See 36:4. **the fourth year of Jehoiakim** 605 BC.
45:3 Woe to me Perhaps lamenting his status as a fugitive after reading Jeremiah's scroll. See 36:26.
45:5 I will let you escape with your life A common idiom in Jeremiah referring to survival of the invasion, grounded in trusting Yahweh. See 29:1; 39:18.

46:1—51:64 Oracles announcing judgment on foreign nations are common in the Prophetic books. These oracles assert Yahweh's sovereignty and right to judge the nations. This section of Jeremiah appears to have existed as a separate collection of oracles compiled later, along

at Carchemish on the Euphrates River by Nebuchadnezzar king of Babylon in the fourth year of Jehoiakim son of Josiah king of Judah:

³ "Prepare your shields, both large and small,
and march out for battle!
⁴ Harness the horses,
mount the steeds!
Take your positions
with helmets on!
Polish your spears,
put on your armor!
⁵ What do I see?
They are terrified,
they are retreating,
their warriors are defeated.
They flee in haste
without looking back,
and there is terror on every side,"
declares the LORD.
⁶ "The swift cannot flee
nor the strong escape.
In the north by the River Euphrates
they stumble and fall.

⁷ "Who is this that rises like the Nile,
like rivers of surging waters?
⁸ Egypt rises like the Nile,
like rivers of surging waters.
She says, 'I will rise and cover the earth;
I will destroy cities and their people.'
⁹ Charge, you horses!
Drive furiously, you charioteers!
March on, you warriors — men of Cush[a] and
Put who carry shields,
men of Lydia who draw the bow.

¹⁰ But that day belongs to the Lord, the LORD Almighty —
a day of vengeance, for vengeance on his foes.
The sword will devour till it is satisfied,
till it has quenched its thirst with blood.
For the Lord, the LORD Almighty, will offer sacrifice
in the land of the north by the River Euphrates.

¹¹ "Go up to Gilead and get balm,
Virgin Daughter Egypt.
But you try many medicines in vain;
there is no healing for you.
¹² The nations will hear of your shame;
your cries will fill the earth.
One warrior will stumble over another;
both will fall down together."

¹³ This is the message the LORD spoke to Jeremiah the prophet about the coming of Nebuchadnezzar king of Babylon to attack Egypt:

¹⁴ "Announce this in Egypt, and proclaim it in Migdol;
proclaim it also in Memphis and Tahpanhes:
'Take your positions and get ready,
for the sword devours those around you.'
¹⁵ Why will your warriors be laid low?
They cannot stand, for the LORD will push them down.

[a] 9 That is, the upper Nile region

---

with other prophetic material from Jeremiah; the ancient Greek translation known as the Septuagint has the entire section in a different location. All the traditional enemies of Israel are mentioned in these oracles. The last two chapters of the section contain lengthy denunciations of Babylon, emphasizing their eventual demise after Yahweh has finished using them as his agents of judgment. See the table "Oracles Against the Nations" on p. 1244.

46:1–28 Jeremiah's oracle of judgment on Egypt focuses on two events: Egypt's defeat at the battle of Carchemish in 605 BC and Nebuchadnezzar's later invasion of Egypt around 569–68 BC.

46:2 Pharaoh Necho Egyptian ruler whose reign corresponded with the reigns of Josiah, Jehoahaz and Jehoiakim in Judah. **Carchemish** A city in northern Syria. It was the site of a major battle in 605 BC in which the Babylonians defeated the remnants of the Assyrian army and its Egyptian allies. The Battle of Carchemish marks a major turning point in the history of the ancient Near East. Although the Babylonians had destroyed the Assyrian city of Nineveh in 612 BC, the battle at Carchemish signals the final demise of the Assyrian Empire, which had been the largest empire of its time. The Babylonian victory also laid the foundation for the emergence of the Medo-Persian Empire less than a century later.

Nebuchadnezzar See note on 21:2. **the fourth year of Jehoiakim** 605 BC.

Jeremiah 46:2

PHARAOH NECHO
Necho II (or Neco) ruled in Egypt from 609–595 BC. He was part of the Saite (or 26th) Dynasty and the son of Psammetichus I, who founded the dynasty (663–609 BC). Necho was heavily invested in the foreign affairs of Syria-Palestine and Mesopotamia. His military activities in the region had a significant impact on the history of Judah. King Josiah of Judah opposed Necho as Necho was passing through Israelite territory on his way to aid Assyria. Josiah was killed in the ensuing battle at Megiddo in 609 BC (2Ki 23:28–30). On his return from Assyria, Necho asserted Egyptian control over Judah by deposing Josiah's successor, Jehoahaz, and replacing him with another son of Josiah, Jehoiakim (2Ki 23:31–35). Jehoiakim was a loyal vassal of Egypt until 604 BC, when Nebuchadnezzar took control of the area after defeating Necho in 605 BC at the Battle of Carchemish. Necho was able to keep Nebuchadnezzar out of Egypt in 601 BC, but Necho's role in the politics of Syria-Palestine was finished (2Ki 24:7).

¹⁶ They will stumble repeatedly;
  they will fall over each other.
They will say, 'Get up, let us go back
  to our own people and our native lands,
  away from the sword of the oppressor.'
¹⁷ There they will exclaim,
  'Pharaoh king of Egypt is only a loud noise;
  he has missed his opportunity.'

¹⁸ "As surely as I live," declares the King,
  whose name is the LORD Almighty,
"one will come who is like Tabor among the
  mountains,
  like Carmel by the sea.
¹⁹ Pack your belongings for exile,
  you who live in Egypt,
for Memphis will be laid waste
  and lie in ruins without inhabitant.

²⁰ "Egypt is a beautiful heifer,
  but a gadfly is coming
  against her from the north.
²¹ The mercenaries in her ranks
  are like fattened calves.
They too will turn and flee together,
  they will not stand their ground,
for the day of disaster is coming upon them,
  the time for them to be punished.
²² Egypt will hiss like a fleeing serpent
  as the enemy advances in force;
they will come against her with axes,
  like men who cut down trees.
²³ They will chop down her forest,"
                    declares the LORD,
  "dense though it be.

They are more numerous than locusts,
  they cannot be counted.
²⁴ Daughter Egypt will be put to shame,
  given into the hands of the people of the
  north."

²⁵ The LORD Almighty, the God of Israel, says: "I am about to bring punishment on Amon god of Thebes, on Pharaoh, on Egypt and her gods and her kings, and on those who rely on Pharaoh. ²⁶ I will give them into the hands of those who want to kill them — Nebuchadnezzar king of Babylon and his officers. Later, however, Egypt will be inhabited as in times past," declares the LORD.

²⁷ "Do not be afraid, Jacob my servant;
  do not be dismayed, Israel.
I will surely save you out of a distant place,
  your descendants from the land of their
  exile.
Jacob will again have peace and security,
  and no one will make him afraid.
²⁸ Do not be afraid, Jacob my servant,
  for I am with you," declares the LORD.
"Though I completely destroy all the nations
  among which I scatter you,
  I will not completely destroy you.
I will discipline you but only in due measure;
  I will not let you go entirely unpunished."

A Message About the Philistines

47 This is the word of the LORD that came to Jeremiah the prophet concerning the Philistines before Pharaoh attacked Gaza:

46:3 your shields, both large and small The Hebrew words used here, *magen* and *tsinnah*, refer to two sizes of shields.

46:5 there is terror on every side The Hebrew phrase used here, *magor missaviv*, appears several times in Jeremiah to describe imminent judgment. See note on 20:3.

46:7 Who is this that rises like the Nile Jeremiah depicts Egypt's ambitions of world conquest with the image of rising floodwaters. The annual flood of the Nile was an essential component of Egyptian agriculture.

46:9 Cush and Put Cush (Ethiopia) and Put (Libya) were Egypt's neighbors to the south and west. See note on Eze 38:5. **men of Lydia** The kingdom of Lud (Lydia) was located in central Turkey. See note on Eze 27:10.

46:10 belongs to the Lord, the LORD Almighty The ultimate day of judgment against the nations.

46:11 Gilead A region east of the Jordan known for its balm. See Jer 8:22 and note. After defeating Egypt and Assyria at Carchemish, Nebuchadnezzar consolidated his power in Syria-Palestine and exerted control over the region down to the border of Egypt. Necho was able to repel his attack in 601 BC. There also is evidence that Nebuchadnezzar mounted another attempt to invade Egypt toward the end of his reign in 568 BC.

46:14 Migdol On Egypt's northeastern frontier. See note on Eze 29:10. **Memphis and Tahpanhes** Cities in the Nile delta region. See note on Jer 43:7; note on 44:1; note on Eze 30:13.

46:17 a loud noise; he has missed his opportunity This statement derides Egypt for bragging but failing to act. The phrase might involve a Hebrew pun on the name of Pharaoh Hophra. This second judgment oracle is concerned with a later period in Egyptian history. Pharaoh Hophra was the king who attempted to help Judah during Nebuchadnezzar's siege of Jerusalem in 587 BC. His assistance was too little too late. See Jer 44:30 and note; compare note on Eze 29:2.

46:18 Tabor among the mountains A prominent mountain on the north side of the Jezreel Valley. Both Tabor and Carmel are important and easily distinguished landmarks. **Carmel by the sea** A mountain range on the Mediterranean coast that divided Israel, with the plain of Acco to the north and the plain of Sharon to the south.

46:19 Pack your belongings for exile Compare Eze 12:3. Egypt is warned to expect the same fate as Jerusalem.

46:20 a gadfly is coming against her from the north A metaphor for Babylon. Compare Isa 7:18.

46:21 like fattened calves Ready for slaughter. Compare 1Sa 28:24.

46:25 Amon god of Thebes Amon was an Egyptian sun god whose temple was at Thebes (called "No" in Hebrew). See note on Eze 30:14. See the table "Pagan Deities of the Old Testament" on p. 1287.

46:27 Do not be afraid, Jacob my servant A promise of future restoration for Israel and Judah is inserted here to remind Israel that its discipline is temporary.

²This is what the LORD says:

"See how the waters are rising in the north;
    they will become an overflowing torrent.
They will overflow the land and everything
    in it,
    the towns and those who live in them.
The people will cry out;
    all who dwell in the land will wail
³ at the sound of the hooves of galloping steeds,
    at the noise of enemy chariots
    and the rumble of their wheels.

Parents will not turn to help their children;
    their hands will hang limp.
⁴ For the day has come
    to destroy all the Philistines
and to remove all survivors
    who could help Tyre and Sidon.
The LORD is about to destroy the Philistines,
    the remnant from the coasts of Caphtor.ᵃ
⁵ Gaza will shave her head in mourning;
    Ashkelon will be silenced.

ᵃ 4 That is, Crete

47:1–7 This oracle of judgment against the Philistines is probably connected to Nebuchadnezzar's destruction of Ashkelon in 604 BC, though the editorial heading in Jer 47:1 connects it with an Egyptian campaign against Gaza. However, the region of Philistia was the battleground for part of the confrontation between Babylon and Egypt in 601 BC. See the table "Oracles Against the Nations" below.

47:1 the Philistines Inhabitants of the coastal plain west of Judah. See note on Eze 25:15–17. **Pharaoh attacked Gaza** Herodotus records that, after repelling Nebuchadnezzar's invasion in 601 BC, Necho continued north and captured the Philistine city of Gaza. On Gaza, see note on Jer 25:20; on Necho, see note on 46:2.

47:2 See how the waters are rising in the north The image of rising waters is used for Egypt in 46:7–8, but the warning of danger from the north suggests Babylonian attack.

47:4 Tyre and Sidon Phoenician cities, presumably mentioned because they are allies of the Philistines. On the Phoenicians, see note on Eze 26:1—28:26. **from the coasts of Caphtor** Usually identified with Crete, the homeland of the Philistines according to Am 9:7. Archaeological artifacts from the Philistines bear similarities to those found on Crete. The Philistines usually are associated with the Sea Peoples, who entered Syria-Palestine by land and sea through the Aegean basin and Asia Minor around 1200 BC.

47:5 will shave her head in mourning Probably

Oracles Against the Nations

NATION	ISAIAH	JEREMIAH	EZEKIEL	MINOR PROPHETS
Assyria	Isa 14:24–27	—	—	Na; Zep 2:13–15
Babylon	Isa 13:1–14; 21:1–10	Jer 50:1–51:	—	—
Egypt	Isa 19:1–25	Jer 25:19; 46:1–26	Eze 29:1–32; 32	Joel 3:19
Ammon	—	Jer 25:21; 49:1–6	Eze 25:1–7	Am 1:13–15; Zep 2:8–11
Moab	Isa 15:1–16:14	Jer 25:21; 48:1–47	Eze 25:8–11	Am 2:1–3; Zep 2:8–11
Syria/Damascus	Isa 17:1–6	Jer 49:23–27	—	Am 1:3–5
Tyre/Sidon	Isa 23:1–18	Jer 25:22	Eze 26:1–28:26	Joel 3:4; Am 1:9–10
Philistia	Isa 14:28–32	Jer 25:20; 47:1–7	Eze 25:15–17	Joel 3:4; Am 1:6–8; Zep 2:4–7
Cush	Isa 18:1–7	—	—	Zep 2:12
Edom	Isa 21:11–12; 34:5–17	Jer 25:20–21; 49:7–22	Eze 25:12–14	Ob; Joel 3:19; Am 1:11–12
Arabia/Kedar	Isa 21:13–17	Jer 25:23–24; 49:28–33	—	—
Elam/Media	—	Jer 25:25; 49:34–39	—	—

You remnant on the plain,
how long will you cut yourselves?

[6] "'Alas, sword of the LORD,
how long till you rest?
Return to your sheath;
cease and be still.'
[7] But how can it rest
when the LORD has commanded it,
when he has ordered it
to attack Ashkelon and the coast?"

A Message About Moab

48:29-36pp — Isa 16:6-12

48 Concerning Moab:

This is what the LORD Almighty, the God of Israel, says:

"Woe to Nebo, for it will be ruined.
Kiriathaim will be disgraced and captured;
the stronghold[a] will be disgraced and
shattered.
[2] Moab will be praised no more;
in Heshbon[b] people will plot her downfall:
'Come, let us put an end to that nation.'
You, the people of Madmen,[c] will also be
silenced;
the sword will pursue you.
[3] Cries of anguish arise from Horonaim,
cries of great havoc and destruction.
[4] Moab will be broken;
her little ones will cry out.[d]
[5] They go up the hill to Luhith,
weeping bitterly as they go;
on the road down to Horonaim
anguished cries over the destruction are
heard.

[6] Flee! Run for your lives;
become like a bush[e] in the desert.
[7] Since you trust in your deeds and riches,
you too will be taken captive,
and Chemosh will go into exile,
together with his priests and officials.
[8] The destroyer will come against every town,
and not a town will escape.
The valley will be ruined
and the plateau destroyed,
because the LORD has spoken.
[9] Put salt on Moab,
for she will be laid waste[f];
her towns will become desolate,
with no one to live in them.

[10] "A curse on anyone who is lax in doing the
LORD's work!
A curse on anyone who keeps their sword
from bloodshed!

[11] "Moab has been at rest from youth,
like wine left on its dregs,
not poured from one jar to another —
she has not gone into exile.
So she tastes as she did,
and her aroma is unchanged.
[12] But days are coming,"
declares the LORD,
"when I will send men who pour from
pitchers,
and they will pour her out;
they will empty her pitchers
and smash her jars.

---

[a] *1* Or *captured; / Misgab*   [b] *2* The Hebrew for *Heshbon*
sounds like the Hebrew for *plot*.   [c] *2* The name of the Moabite
town Madmen sounds like the Hebrew for *be silenced*.
[d] *4* Hebrew; Septuagint / *proclaim it to Zoar*   [e] *6* Or *like Aroer*
[f] *9* Or *Give wings to Moab, / for she will fly away*

---

alluding to mourning rituals accompanying national distress. **Ashkelon** A Philistine seaport that was destroyed by Nebuchadnezzar in 604 BC. See note on Jer 47:1-7. **will you cut yourselves** Refers to mourning rituals. See note on 41:5.

Jeremiah 47:5

ASHKELON

Ashkelon was an ancient Canaanite city-state on the Mediterranean coast. Joshua 13:3 lists it as one of the five cities of the Philistines, and it was captured by Judah during the conquest (Jdg 1:18). Most likely, the Canaanite city was settled by the Philistines after the Sea Peoples failed to conquer Egypt around 1190 BC. Ashkelon did not yield to Babylonian rule after the Battle of Carchemish, so Nebuchadnezzar destroyed the city in 604 BC. It was rebuilt into a thriving port in the Persian period and continued to be an important regional city until 1270 AD.

48:1-47 Moab was a close neighbor of Judah, located across the Jordan east of the Dead Sea. It also was a traditional enemy of Israel and Judah (Nu 22-24; 2Ki 3). This oracle describes the distress of a foreign invasion sweeping across Moab. Many of the locations mentioned are unknown.

48:1 Moab The nation was related to Israel through Abraham's nephew, Lot (Ge 19:37). See note on Isa 15:1. **Nebo** Probably referring to Mount Nebo in northern Moab. See Dt 32:49. **Kiriathaim** A Moabite city near Mount Nebo assigned to the Israelite tribe of Reuben (Nu 32:37).

48:2 Heshbon A city in northern Moab, in an area sometimes controlled by Israel (Nu 32:37). **Madmen** Location unknown.

48:3 Horonaim Location unknown.

48:5 Luhith In southwest Moab.

48:7 Chemosh Moab's patron deity (see note on Nu 21:29). The idol of a conquered people was sometimes carried off as part of the spoil (see note on Jer 43:12; Isa 46:2 and note).

48:8 The destroyer will come against every town Nebuchadnezzar campaigned in Moab in 582 BC.

13 Then Moab will be ashamed of Chemosh,
  as Israel was ashamed
  when they trusted in Bethel.

14 "How can you say, 'We are warriors,
  men valiant in battle'?
15 Moab will be destroyed and her towns
    invaded;
  her finest young men will go down in the
    slaughter,"
  declares the King, whose name is the LORD
    Almighty.
16 "The fall of Moab is at hand;
  her calamity will come quickly.
17 Mourn for her, all who live around her,
  all who know her fame;
  say, 'How broken is the mighty scepter,
  how broken the glorious staff!'

18 "Come down from your glory
  and sit on the parched ground,
  you inhabitants of Daughter Dibon,
  for the one who destroys Moab
  will come up against you
  and ruin your fortified cities.
19 Stand by the road and watch,
  you who live in Aroer.
  Ask the man fleeing and the woman
    escaping,
  ask them, 'What has happened?'
20 Moab is disgraced, for she is shattered.
  Wail and cry out!
  Announce by the Arnon
  that Moab is destroyed.
21 Judgment has come to the plateau —
  to Holon, Jahzah and Mephaath,
22   to Dibon, Nebo and Beth Diblathaim,
23   to Kiriathaim, Beth Gamul and Beth Meon,
24   to Kerioth and Bozrah —
  to all the towns of Moab, far and near.
25 Moab's horn[a] is cut off;
  her arm is broken,"
                          declares the LORD.

26 "Make her drunk,
  for she has defied the LORD.
  Let Moab wallow in her vomit;
  let her be an object of ridicule.
27 Was not Israel the object of your ridicule?
  Was she caught among thieves,

that you shake your head in scorn
  whenever you speak of her?
28 Abandon your towns and dwell among the
    rocks,
  you who live in Moab.
  Be like a dove that makes its nest
  at the mouth of a cave.

29 "We have heard of Moab's pride —
  how great is her arrogance! —
  of her insolence, her pride, her conceit
  and the haughtiness of her heart.
30 I know her insolence but it is futile,"
                          declares the LORD,
  "and her boasts accomplish nothing.
31 Therefore I wail over Moab,
  for all Moab I cry out,
  I moan for the people of Kir Hareseth.
32 I weep for you, as Jazer weeps,
  you vines of Sibmah.
  Your branches spread as far as the sea[b];
  they reached as far as[c] Jazer.
  The destroyer has fallen
  on your ripened fruit and grapes.
33 Joy and gladness are gone
  from the orchards and fields of Moab.
  I have stopped the flow of wine from the
    presses;
  no one treads them with shouts of joy.
  Although there are shouts,
  they are not shouts of joy.

34 "The sound of their cry rises
  from Heshbon to Elealeh and Jahaz,
  from Zoar as far as Horonaim and Eglath
    Shelishiyah,
  for even the waters of Nimrim are dried up.
35 In Moab I will put an end
  to those who make offerings on the high
    places
  and burn incense to their gods,"
                          declares the LORD.
36 "So my heart laments for Moab like the music
    of a pipe;
  it laments like a pipe for the people of Kir
    Hareseth.
  The wealth they acquired is gone.

---

[a] 25 Horn here symbolizes strength.   [b] 32 Probably the Dead
Sea   [c] 32 Two Hebrew manuscripts and Septuagint; most
Hebrew manuscripts as far as the Sea of

48:13 Then Moab will be ashamed of Chemosh
Moab's fundamental sin was also idolatry, just as Israel's
and Judah's had been before their destruction.
48:18 Dibon A city in the Transjordan east of the Dead
Sea and north of the Arnon River. See Jos 13:9 and note.
48:19 Aroer A city just southeast of Dibon.
48:20 by the Arnon A river flowing into the east side of
the Dead Sea. See note on Isa 16:2.

48:21–24 The judgment on Moab is emphasized through
a list of 12 locations, but the identification of most of
them is speculative—even for those mentioned else-

where in the OT. The point is that the entire territory is
affected. Compare the lengthy list of nations to experience Yahweh's wrath, given in Jer 25:19–26.

48:25 Moab's horn is cut off In the Hebrew text, the
reference to Moab's "horn" invokes a symbol of strength
and royal or divine power. See note on Eze 29:21; compare note on Da 7:7.
48:32 I weep for you, as Jazer See Isa 16:9 and note.
48:34 Eglath Shelishiyah In southern Moab. **even the
waters of Nimrim are dried up** See Isa 15:6 and note.

³⁷Every head is shaved
    and every beard cut off;
  every hand is slashed
    and every waist is covered with sackcloth.
³⁸On all the roofs in Moab
    and in the public squares
  there is nothing but mourning,
    for I have broken Moab
    like a jar that no one wants,"
                                declares the LORD.
³⁹"How shattered she is! How they wail!
    How Moab turns her back in shame!
  Moab has become an object of ridicule,
    an object of horror to all those around
      her."

⁴⁰This is what the LORD says:

  "Look! An eagle is swooping down,
    spreading its wings over Moab.
⁴¹Kerioth*ᵃ will be captured
    and the strongholds taken.
  In that day the hearts of Moab's warriors
    will be like the heart of a woman in labor.
⁴²Moab will be destroyed as a nation
    because she defied the LORD.
⁴³Terror and pit and snare await you,
    you people of Moab,"
                                declares the LORD.
⁴⁴"Whoever flees from the terror
    will fall into a pit,
  whoever climbs out of the pit
    will be caught in a snare;
  for I will bring on Moab
    the year of her punishment,"
                                declares the LORD.
⁴⁵"In the shadow of Heshbon
    the fugitives stand helpless,
  for a fire has gone out from Heshbon,
    a blaze from the midst of Sihon;

  it burns the foreheads of Moab,
    the skulls of the noisy boasters.
⁴⁶Woe to you, Moab!
    The people of Chemosh are destroyed;
  your sons are taken into exile
    and your daughters into captivity.

⁴⁷"Yet I will restore the fortunes of Moab
    in days to come,"
                                declares the LORD.

Here ends the judgment on Moab.

A Message About Ammon

49 Concerning the Ammonites:

This is what the LORD says:

  "Has Israel no sons?
    Has Israel no heir?
  Why then has Molek*ᵇ taken possession of
      Gad?
    Why do his people live in its towns?
²But the days are coming,"
    declares the LORD,
  "when I will sound the battle cry
    against Rabbah of the Ammonites;
  it will become a mound of ruins,
    and its surrounding villages will be set on
      fire.
  Then Israel will drive out
    those who drove her out,"
                                says the LORD.
³"Wail, Heshbon, for Ai is destroyed!
    Cry out, you inhabitants of Rabbah!
  Put on sackcloth and mourn;
    rush here and there inside the walls,
  for Molek will go into exile,
    together with his priests and officials.

ᵃ 41 Or *The cities*   ᵇ 1 Or *their king*; also in verse 3

48:37 Every head is shaved The practices described in this verse reflect mourning rituals over the national distress. See Jer 41:5 and note; compare Isa 15:2–3. **48:45 from the midst of Sihon** An Amorite king who opposed Israel. Heshbon was his city. See Nu 21:21–26.

49:1–6 An oracle of judgment on Ammon, Israel's neighbor east of the Jordan River and north of Moab. A traditional enemy of Judah and Israel, Ammon supported Ishmael in his plot to assassinate Gedaliah. See Jer 40:13—41:15. See the table "Oracles Against the Nations" on p. 1244.

49:1 Molek The Hebrew text says *malkam* ("their king") but the reference could also be taken as *milkom*, the name of the patron god of the Ammonites. Here, a reference to Ammon's god would be symbolic of the kingdom of Ammon itself, so either reading is possible. The Ammonite god may also have been known by the name Molek (see 1Ki 11:5,7) The Hebrew spelling of the deity name Milcom was easily misread as "their king" in

ancient Hebrew manuscripts, which were written without vowels to distinguish the words. The ancient translations of the OT read the name Milcom in several cases (including this verse) where the Hebrew text reads a form of "king." The deity name Milcom is also attested on the Amman Citadel inscription from the ninth century BC. **Gad** An Israelite tribe with territory east of the Jordan River, bordering Ammon. Israel and Ammon regularly disputed possession of the territory (Jdg 11:12–27; 2Sa 12:26–31). **49:2 Rabbah** Capital of Ammon. The site is in the middle of modern-day Amman, the capital of Jordan. See Eze 21:20 and note. **49:3 Heshbon** A city in northern Moab in the territory disputed among Israel, Moab and Ammon. **Ai is destroyed** The identification of Ai is uncertain. It is not the city mentioned in Joshua's conquests (Jos 7). The Hebrew word means "heap of ruins" (see Jer 26:18), so it might not refer to a specific location. **Molek will go into exile** The same fate as the god of Moab. See 48:7 and note.

⁴ Why do you boast of your valleys,
    boast of your valleys so fruitful?
Unfaithful Daughter Ammon,
    you trust in your riches and say,
    'Who will attack me?'
⁵ I will bring terror on you
    from all those around you,"
        declares the Lord, the LORD Almighty.
"Every one of you will be driven away,
    and no one will gather the fugitives.

⁶ "Yet afterward, I will restore the fortunes
    of the Ammonites,"
        declares the LORD.

A Message About Edom

49:9-10pp — Ob 5-6
49:14-16pp — Ob 1-4

⁷ Concerning Edom:

This is what the LORD Almighty says:

"Is there no longer wisdom in Teman?
    Has counsel perished from the prudent?
    Has their wisdom decayed?
⁸ Turn and flee, hide in deep caves,
    you who live in Dedan,
for I will bring disaster on Esau
    at the time when I punish him.
⁹ If grape pickers came to you,
    would they not leave a few grapes?
If thieves came during the night,
    would they not steal only as much as they
        wanted?
¹⁰ But I will strip Esau bare;
    I will uncover his hiding places,
    so that he cannot conceal himself.
His armed men are destroyed,
    also his allies and neighbors,
    so there is no one to say,
¹¹ 'Leave your fatherless children; I will keep
        them alive.
    Your widows too can depend on me.'"

¹² This is what the LORD says: "If those who do
not deserve to drink the cup must drink it, why
should you go unpunished? You will not go unpunished, but must drink it. ¹³ I swear by myself,"
declares the LORD, "that Bozrah will become a ruin
and a curse,ᵃ an object of horror and reproach; and
all its towns will be in ruins forever."

¹⁴ I have heard a message from the LORD;
    an envoy was sent to the nations to say,
"Assemble yourselves to attack it!
    Rise up for battle!"

¹⁵ "Now I will make you small among the
        nations,
    despised by mankind.
¹⁶ The terror you inspire
    and the pride of your heart have
        deceived you,
you who live in the clefts of the rocks,
    who occupy the heights of the hill.
Though you build your nest as high as the
        eagle's,
    from there I will bring you down,"
        declares the LORD.
¹⁷ "Edom will become an object of horror;
    all who pass by will be appalled and will
        scoff
    because of all its wounds.
¹⁸ As Sodom and Gomorrah were overthrown,
    along with their neighboring towns,"
        says the LORD,
"so no one will live there;
    no people will dwell in it.

¹⁹ "Like a lion coming up from Jordan's thickets
    to a rich pastureland,
I will chase Edom from its land in an instant.
    Who is the chosen one I will appoint for
        this?
Who is like me and who can challenge me?
    And what shepherd can stand against me?"

ᵃ 13 That is, its name will be used in cursing (see 29:22); or,
others will see that it is cursed.

49:7–22 An oracle of judgment against Edom, Judah's neighbor southeast of the Dead Sea. Edom was one of Israel's most bitter enemies. Compare Isa 21:11–12; Eze 25:12–14.

49:7 no longer wisdom in Teman Edom had a reputation for wisdom (Ob 8). **Teman** An important city in Edom, often used to refer to the entire territory.

49:8 Dedan A trading center in Arabia, southeast of Edom. The warning may be for Dedanites to avoid Edom because it will soon be judged. **disaster on Esau** Edomites descended from Esau, Israel's brother. See note on Ge 25:25.

49:9 If grape pickers came to you, would they not leave a few grapes? If thieves came during the night, would they not steal only as much as they wanted This verse is nearly identical to Ob 5. The book of Obadiah consists entirely of a judgment oracle against Edom.

49:11 Your widows too can depend on me The rest of Edom receives judgment, but Yahweh cares for the orphans and widows. See Dt 10:18; Ps 68:5.

49:12 do not deserve to drink the cup must drink See Jer 25:15 and note. Yahweh did not spare his own people from his wrath, so other nations should not expect to escape.

49:13 Bozrah will become a ruin and a curse, an object of horror Bozrah, Edom's capital, will experience the same fate as Judah (24:9).

49:14–16 The poem in these three verses is essentially identical to that in Ob 1–4.

49:18 Sodom and Gomorrah were overthrown, along with their neighboring towns Places destroyed by Yahweh for wickedness (Ge 19). The traditional location of Sodom and Gomorrah is either within or very close to Edomite territory. See note on Isa 1:9.

20 Therefore, hear what the LORD has planned
     against Edom,
   what he has purposed against those who
     live in Teman:
   The young of the flock will be dragged away;
     their pasture will be appalled at their fate.
21 At the sound of their fall the earth will
     tremble;
   their cry will resound to the Red Sea.[a]
22 Look! An eagle will soar and swoop down,
     spreading its wings over Bozrah.
   In that day the hearts of Edom's warriors
     will be like the heart of a woman in labor.

A Message About Damascus

23 Concerning Damascus:

   "Hamath and Arpad are dismayed,
     for they have heard bad news.
   They are disheartened,
     troubled like[b] the restless sea.
24 Damascus has become feeble,
     she has turned to flee
     and panic has gripped her;
   anguish and pain have seized her,
     pain like that of a woman in labor.
25 Why has the city of renown not been
     abandoned,
     the town in which I delight?
26 Surely, her young men will fall in the streets;
     all her soldiers will be silenced in that day,"
             declares the LORD Almighty.
27 "I will set fire to the walls of Damascus;
     it will consume the fortresses of Ben-Hadad."

A Message About Kedar and Hazor

28 Concerning Kedar and the kingdoms of Hazor,
   which Nebuchadnezzar king of Babylon attacked:

   This is what the LORD says:

   "Arise, and attack Kedar
     and destroy the people of the East.
29 Their tents and their flocks will be taken;
     their shelters will be carried off
     with all their goods and camels.
   People will shout to them,
     'Terror on every side!'

30 "Flee quickly away!
     Stay in deep caves, you who live in
       Hazor,"
                     declares the LORD.
   "Nebuchadnezzar king of Babylon has
     plotted against you;
     he has devised a plan against you.

31 "Arise and attack a nation at ease,
     which lives in confidence,"
                     declares the LORD,
   "a nation that has neither gates nor bars;
     its people live far from danger.
32 Their camels will become plunder,
     and their large herds will be spoils
       of war.
   I will scatter to the winds those who are in
     distant places[c]
   and will bring disaster on them from every
     side,"
                     declares the LORD.
33 "Hazor will become a haunt of jackals,
     a desolate place forever.
   No one will live there;
     no people will dwell in it."

A Message About Elam

34 This is the word of the LORD that came to
Jeremiah the prophet concerning Elam, early in
the reign of Zedekiah king of Judah:

35 This is what the LORD Almighty says:

   "See, I will break the bow of Elam,
     the mainstay of their might.

a 21 Or the Sea of Reeds   b 23 Hebrew on or by   c 32 Or who
clip the hair by their foreheads

49:20 young of the flock will be dragged away Refers
to the exile of the people. The imagery portrays the people
as sheep and their leaders as shepherds.
49:21 to the Red Sea A significant distance away.

49:23–27 A judgment oracle against Damascus, the
capital of Syria (Aram)—Israel's neighbor to the north and
another traditional enemy (1Ki 11:24–25; 2Ki 8:7–9).
Damascus and most of the Aramean city-states were dominated by the imperial powers of Assyria and Babylonia.

49:23 Hamath and Arpad Hamath was a city on the
Orontes River in central Syria, about 132 miles north
of Damascus. Arpad was a regional center in northern
Syria. Hamath and Arpad are mentioned as a pair in the
Bible and in ancient Assyrian texts. See Isa 10:9; 36:19.
49:24 a woman in labor A typical metaphor for anguish
and pain. See Jer 4:31; 48:41; 49:22.
49:27 Ben-Hadad A name for several Aramean kings.
See 1Ki 15:18–20; 2Ki 13:24.

49:28–33 Judgment against Arabian tribes. Compare
Isa 21:13–17.
49:28 Kedar Refers to the northern region of Arabia.
See note on Isa 21:16. **Hazor** An otherwise unknown
settlement in northern Arabia. **Nebuchadnezzar** See
note on Jer 21:2.
49:29 Terror on every side See note on 20:3.

49:34–39 This judgment oracle moves out of Judah's
immediate sphere of neighbors all the way to Elam, a
distant region on the east side of Mesopotamia. Elam had
been conquered by the Assyrians and ruled by Babylon
and later Persia.

49:34 Elam The region east of the Tigris River on the
north side of the Persian Gulf. **early in the reign of
Zedekiah** 597 BC. On Zedekiah, see note on 21:1.
49:35 the bow of Elam See Isa 22:6 and note.

³⁶ I will bring against Elam the four winds
  from the four quarters of heaven;
I will scatter them to the four winds,
  and there will not be a nation
where Elam's exiles do not go.
³⁷ I will shatter Elam before their foes,
  before those who want to kill them;
I will bring disaster on them,
  even my fierce anger,"
             declares the LORD.
"I will pursue them with the sword
  until I have made an end of them.
³⁸ I will set my throne in Elam
  and destroy her king and officials,"
             declares the LORD.

³⁹ "Yet I will restore the fortunes of Elam
  in days to come,"
             declares the LORD.

A Message About Babylon

51:15-19pp — Jer 10:12-16

50 This is the word the LORD spoke through
Jeremiah the prophet concerning Babylon
and the land of the Babylonians ᵃ:

² "Announce and proclaim among
    the nations,
  lift up a banner and proclaim it;
  keep nothing back, but say,
'Babylon will be captured;
  Bel will be put to shame,
  Marduk filled with terror.
Her images will be put to shame
  and her idols filled with terror.'
³ A nation from the north will attack her
  and lay waste her land.
No one will live in it;
  both people and animals will flee away.

⁴ "In those days, at that time,"
             declares the LORD,
"the people of Israel and the people of Judah
    together
  will go in tears to seek the LORD their God.
⁵ They will ask the way to Zion
  and turn their faces toward it.
They will come and bind themselves to the
    LORD
  in an everlasting covenant
  that will not be forgotten.

⁶ "My people have been lost sheep;
  their shepherds have led them astray
  and caused them to roam on the
    mountains.
They wandered over mountain and hill
  and forgot their own resting place.
⁷ Whoever found them devoured them;
  their enemies said, 'We are not guilty,
for they sinned against the LORD, their
    verdant pasture,
  the LORD, the hope of their ancestors.'

⁸ "Flee out of Babylon;
  leave the land of the Babylonians,
  and be like the goats that lead the flock.
⁹ For I will stir up and bring against Babylon
  an alliance of great nations from the land
    of the north.
They will take up their positions against her,
  and from the north she will be captured.
Their arrows will be like skilled warriors
  who do not return empty-handed.
¹⁰ So Babylonia ᵇ will be plundered;
  all who plunder her will have their fill,"
             declares the LORD.

ᵃ 1 Or *Chaldeans*; also in verses 8, 25, 35 and 45
ᵇ 10 Or *Chaldea*

50:1 — 51:64 The oracles against the nations culminate in this lengthy prophecy against Babylon. The message is simple: Babylon will be defeated and destroyed. However, this message is detailed through short, poetic prophecies, ending with a report of a sign-act symbolizing Babylon's demise. Jeremiah's message of submission to Babylon in the present (see Jer 27:17) is made more palatable to his exilic audience by emphasizing the certainty of Babylon's eventual fall and the subordination of its power to the sovereignty of Yahweh. See the table "Oracles Against the Nations" on p. 1244.

50:1 Babylon The dominant world power of Jeremiah's day. See 21:2 and note. **the land of the Babylonians** Many English translations follow the Hebrew text and refer to the Babylonians as Chaldeans. See note on Isa 43:14.
50:2 Bel will be put to shame "Bel" and "Marduk" ("Merodach") refer to the same Babylonian god.

Jeremiah 50:2

MARDUK
Also known as Bel (see Isa 46:1 and note), Marduk was the chief god of all the Babylonian gods. The Babylonian creation epic *Enuma Elish* recounts how Marduk ascended to the kingship of the gods. Marduk was a storm god associated with fertility and creation. The deity name is seen in the Biblical names "Marduk-Baladan" (Isa 39:1; also rendered "Merodach-Baladan") and "Awel-Marduk" (Jer 52:31; also rendered "Evil-Merodach"). See the table "Pagan Deities of the Old Testament" on p. 1287.

50:3 from the north Jeremiah's standard motif of disaster coming from the north (e.g., Jer 1:14; 4:6; 6:1; 10:22). In the earlier examples, the Babylonians are the invaders; now they are the prey. Compare v. 9.

50:4-7 An oracle of salvation for Israel, emphasizing reunification and a return to Zion.

¹¹ "Because you rejoice and are glad,
    you who pillage my inheritance,
because you frolic like a heifer threshing
        grain
    and neigh like stallions,
¹² your mother will be greatly ashamed;
    she who gave you birth will be disgraced.
She will be the least of the nations —
    a wilderness, a dry land, a desert.
¹³ Because of the Lord's anger she will not be
        inhabited
    but will be completely desolate.
All who pass Babylon will be appalled;
    they will scoff because of all her wounds.

¹⁴ "Take up your positions around Babylon,
    all you who draw the bow.
Shoot at her! Spare no arrows,
    for she has sinned against the Lord.
¹⁵ Shout against her on every side!
    She surrenders, her towers fall,
    her walls are torn down.
Since this is the vengeance of the Lord,
    take vengeance on her;
    do to her as she has done to others.
¹⁶ Cut off from Babylon the sower,
    and the reaper with his sickle at harvest.
Because of the sword of the oppressor
    let everyone return to their own people,
    let everyone flee to their own land.

¹⁷ "Israel is a scattered flock
    that lions have chased away.
The first to devour them
    was the king of Assyria;
the last to crush their bones
    was Nebuchadnezzar king of Babylon."

¹⁸ Therefore this is what the Lord Almighty, the
God of Israel, says:

"I will punish the king of Babylon and his land
    as I punished the king of Assyria.
¹⁹ But I will bring Israel back to their own
        pasture,
    and they will graze on Carmel and Bashan;

their appetite will be satisfied
    on the hills of Ephraim and Gilead.
²⁰ In those days, at that time,"
    declares the Lord,
"search will be made for Israel's guilt,
    but there will be none,
and for the sins of Judah,
    but none will be found,
    for I will forgive the remnant I spare.

²¹ "Attack the land of Merathaim
    and those who live in Pekod.
Pursue, kill and completely destroy^a them,"
        declares the Lord.
    "Do everything I have commanded you.
²² The noise of battle is in the land,
    the noise of great destruction!
²³ How broken and shattered
    is the hammer of the whole earth!
How desolate is Babylon
    among the nations!
²⁴ I set a trap for you, Babylon,
    and you were caught before you knew it;
you were found and captured
    because you opposed the Lord.
²⁵ The Lord has opened his arsenal
    and brought out the weapons of his
        wrath,
for the Sovereign Lord Almighty has work
        to do
    in the land of the Babylonians.
²⁶ Come against her from afar.
    Break open her granaries;
    pile her up like heaps of grain.
Completely destroy her
    and leave her no remnant.
²⁷ Kill all her young bulls;
    let them go down to the slaughter!
Woe to them! For their day has come,
    the time for them to be punished.

---

^a 21 The Hebrew term refers to the irrevocable giving over of
things or persons to the Lord, often by totally destroying them;
also in verse 26.

50:4 will go in tears Compare 31:7–9.
50:6 lost sheep Compare 13:20; Isa 53:6; Zec 10:2.
their shepherds Refers to Israel's leaders, who led the
people away from Yahweh.
50:9 an alliance of great nations Babylon was conquered by an alliance of the Medes and Persians led by
Cyrus the Great in 539 BC. **from the land of the north**
See Jer 50:3 and note. The homeland of the Medes was
north and east of Babylon.
50:10 Babylonia See v. 1 and note.
50:12 your mother A representation of the city of
Babylon.
50:17 the king of Assyria Conquered the northern
kingdom of Israel in 722 BC. See 2Ki 17:6; see note
on Isa 10:5. **to crush their bones** Nebuchadnezzar
completed the destruction of Israel and Judah begun
by Assyria. **Nebuchadnezzar** See note on Jer 21:2.

50:19 I will bring Israel back to their own pasture
The locations mentioned here indicate that the prophet
envisions the restoration of the northern kingdom. **Carmel** See note on 46:18. **Bashan** See note on 22:20.
the hills of Ephraim See note on 4:15. **Gilead** See
note on 22:6.
50:20 there will be none Compare 31:34; Isa 40:2.
50:21 Merathaim Means "double rebellion" and is a
pun on the Akkadian word *marratum*, which refers to the
marshy region where the Tigris—Euphrates delta merges
with the Persian Gulf. See the table "Symbolic Names
of People in Hebrew" on p. 1388.
Pekod A region in southeastern Mesopotamia, part of
the territory of Babylon. The word means "punishment"
in Hebrew and might be another wordplay.
destroy them Compare Isa 34:2 and note. See note
on Ex 22:20.

28 Listen to the fugitives and refugees from
      Babylon
    declaring in Zion
  how the LORD our God has taken vengeance,
    vengeance for his temple.

29 "Summon archers against Babylon,
    all those who draw the bow.
  Encamp all around her;
    let no one escape.
  Repay her for her deeds;
    do to her as she has done.
  For she has defied the LORD,
    the Holy One of Israel.
30 Therefore, her young men will fall in the
      streets;
  all her soldiers will be silenced in that day,"
                              declares the LORD.

31 "See, I am against you, you arrogant one,"
    declares the Lord, the LORD Almighty,
  "for your day has come,
    the time for you to be punished.
32 The arrogant one will stumble and fall
    and no one will help her up;
  I will kindle a fire in her towns
    that will consume all who are around her."

33 This is what the LORD Almighty says:

  "The people of Israel are oppressed,
    and the people of Judah as well.
  All their captors hold them fast,
    refusing to let them go.
34 Yet their Redeemer is strong;
    the LORD Almighty is his name.
  He will vigorously defend their cause
    so that he may bring rest to their land,
  but unrest to those who live in Babylon.

35 "A sword against the Babylonians!"
    declares the LORD —
  "against those who live in Babylon
    and against her officials and wise men!
36 A sword against her false prophets!
    They will become fools.
  A sword against her warriors!
    They will be filled with terror.

37 A sword against her horses and chariots
    and all the foreigners in her ranks!
    They will become weaklings.
  A sword against her treasures!
    They will be plundered.
38 A drought on[a] her waters!
    They will dry up.
  For it is a land of idols,
    idols that will go mad with terror.

39 "So desert creatures and hyenas will live
      there,
    and there the owl will dwell.
  It will never again be inhabited
    or lived in from generation to generation.
40 As I overthrew Sodom and Gomorrah
    along with their neighboring towns,"
                              declares the LORD,
  "so no one will live there;
    no people will dwell in it.

41 "Look! An army is coming from the north;
    a great nation and many kings
    are being stirred up from the ends of the
      earth.
42 They are armed with bows and spears;
    they are cruel and without mercy.
  They sound like the roaring sea
    as they ride on their horses;
  they come like men in battle formation
    to attack you, Daughter Babylon.
43 The king of Babylon has heard reports about
      them,
    and his hands hang limp.
  Anguish has gripped him,
    pain like that of a woman in labor.
44 Like a lion coming up from Jordan's thickets
    to a rich pastureland,
  I will chase Babylon from its land in an
      instant.
  Who is the chosen one I will appoint for
      this?
  Who is like me and who can challenge me?
    And what shepherd can stand
      against me?"

    [a] 38 Or A sword against

50:28 fugitives and refugees Since the fugitives escaped to announce Yahweh's judgment on Babylon in Jerusalem, the image is probably of Jewish exiles returning home after Babylon is destroyed.

50:33–40 The imagery of judgment on Babylon in this passage emphasizes reversals—rest for the earth but unrest for Babylon, the wise are made foolish, the strong are made weak, treasure becomes plunder and water dries up.

50:34 Redeemer Compare Isa 41:14. Yahweh is frequently pictured as redeemer in Isa 40–66.
50:37 They will become weaklings A reversal where the strong will become weak. The Hebrew text pre-

sents the reversal using the image that mighty warriors will become "women" (nashim). The statement was an intentional insult invoking gender stereotypes to connote weakness (compare Jer 51:30; Isa 19:16; Na 3:13).
50:40 Sodom and Gomorrah along with their neighboring towns A standard Biblical example of divine judgment. See Jer 49:18 and note; compare Isa 13:19.

50:44–46 The imagery here is identical to Jer 49:19–21. There are numerous parallels in imagery between the oracle against Edom in ch. 49 and the oracle against Babylon in ch. 50.

45 Therefore, hear what the LORD has planned
against Babylon,
what he has purposed against the land of
the Babylonians:
The young of the flock will be dragged away;
their pasture will be appalled at their fate.
46 At the sound of Babylon's capture the earth
will tremble;
its cry will resound among the nations.

51 This is what the LORD says:

"See, I will stir up the spirit of a destroyer
against Babylon and the people of Leb
Kamai.[a]
2 I will send foreigners to Babylon
to winnow her and to devastate
her land;
they will oppose her on every side
in the day of her disaster.
3 Let not the archer string his bow,
nor let him put on his armor.
Do not spare her young men;
completely destroy[b] her army.
4 They will fall down slain in Babylon,[c]
fatally wounded in her streets.
5 For Israel and Judah have not been
forsaken
by their God, the LORD Almighty,
though their land[d] is full of guilt
before the Holy One of Israel.

6 "Flee from Babylon!
Run for your lives!
Do not be destroyed because of her sins.
It is time for the LORD's vengeance;
he will repay her what she deserves.
7 Babylon was a gold cup in the LORD's hand;
she made the whole earth drunk.
The nations drank her wine;
therefore they have now gone mad.
8 Babylon will suddenly fall and be broken.
Wail over her!
Get balm for her pain;
perhaps she can be healed.
9 "We would have healed Babylon,
but she cannot be healed;

let us leave her and each go to our own land,
for her judgment reaches to the skies,
it rises as high as the heavens.'

10 "'The LORD has vindicated us;
come, let us tell in Zion
what the LORD our God has done.'

11 "Sharpen the arrows,
take up the shields!
The LORD has stirred up the kings of the
Medes,
because his purpose is to destroy Babylon.
The LORD will take vengeance,
vengeance for his temple.
12 Lift up a banner against the walls of Babylon!
Reinforce the guard,
station the watchmen,
prepare an ambush!
The LORD will carry out his purpose,
his decree against the people of Babylon.
13 You who live by many waters
and are rich in treasures,
your end has come,
the time for you to be destroyed.
14 The LORD Almighty has sworn by himself:
I will surely fill you with troops, as with a
swarm of locusts,
and they will shout in triumph over you.

15 "He made the earth by his power;
he founded the world by his wisdom
and stretched out the heavens by his
understanding.
16 When he thunders, the waters in the heavens
roar;
he makes clouds rise from the ends of the
earth.
He sends lightning with the rain
and brings out the wind from his
storehouses.

17 "Everyone is senseless and without
knowledge;
every goldsmith is shamed by his idols.

---

[a] 1 Leb Kamai is a cryptogram for Chaldea, that is, Babylonia.
[b] 3 The Hebrew term refers to the irrevocable giving over of
things or persons to the LORD, often by totally destroying them.
[c] 4 Or Chaldea   [d] 5 Or Almighty, / and the land of the
Babylonians

50:45 young of the flock will be dragged away See
49:20 and note.

51:1–64 The judgment oracle against Babylon continues,
focusing on Babylon's ultimate destruction. The poetic
oracles of judgment are concluded with an account of
a symbolic action representing Babylon's demise in
vv. 59–64.

51:1 Leb Kamai This Hebrew expression means "heart
of one who rises against me." It probably is a coded
reference and not a place-name.

51:7 a gold cup in the LORD's hand Babylon was Yahweh's tool to judge the nations. Compare the imagery

of the cup of wrath in 25:15–29 and the depiction of
Assyria as Yahweh's tool of judgment in Isa 10:5.

51:11 the kings of the Medes Media was in northwest
Iran, the region to the north and east of Babylon. The
Medes became a province of Persia in 549 BC and participated
in Persia's takeover of the Babylonian Empire in 539 BC.

51:14 LORD Almighty has sworn by himself See Jer
22:5 and note.

51:15–19 This passage is essentially identical to
10:12–16 and makes use of stock poetic imagery about
Yahweh as Creator. See note on 10:12; note on 10:13;
note on 10:14; note on 10:16.

The images he makes are a fraud;
　they have no breath in them.
[18] They are worthless, the objects of mockery;
　when their judgment comes, they will
　　perish.
[19] He who is the Portion of Jacob is not like
　　these,
　for he is the Maker of all things,
including the people of his inheritance —
　the LORD Almighty is his name.

[20] "You are my war club,
　my weapon for battle —
with you I shatter nations,
　with you I destroy kingdoms,
[21] with you I shatter horse and rider,
　with you I shatter chariot and driver,
[22] with you I shatter man and woman,
　with you I shatter old man and youth,
　with you I shatter young man and young
　　woman,
[23] with you I shatter shepherd and flock,
　with you I shatter farmer and oxen,
　with you I shatter governors and
　　officials.

[24]"Before your eyes I will repay Babylon and all
who live in Babylonia[a] for all the wrong they have
done in Zion," declares the LORD.

[25]"I am against you, you destroying mountain,
　you who destroy the whole earth,"
　　　　　　　　　　declares the LORD.
"I will stretch out my hand against you,
　roll you off the cliffs,
　and make you a burned-out mountain.
[26] No rock will be taken from you for a
　　cornerstone,
　nor any stone for a foundation,
　for you will be desolate forever,"
　　　　　　　　　　declares the LORD.

[27]"Lift up a banner in the land!
　Blow the trumpet among the nations!
Prepare the nations for battle against her;
　summon against her these kingdoms:
　Ararat, Minni and Ashkenaz.
Appoint a commander against her;
　send up horses like a swarm of locusts.
[28] Prepare the nations for battle against her —
　the kings of the Medes,
　their governors and all their officials,
　and all the countries they rule.

[29] The land trembles and writhes,
　for the LORD's purposes against Babylon
　　stand —
to lay waste the land of Babylon
　so that no one will live there.
[30] Babylon's warriors have stopped fighting;
　they remain in their strongholds.
Their strength is exhausted;
　they have become weaklings.
Her dwellings are set on fire;
　the bars of her gates are broken.
[31] One courier follows another
　and messenger follows messenger
to announce to the king of Babylon
　that his entire city is captured,
[32] the river crossings seized,
　the marshes set on fire,
　and the soldiers terrified."

[33] This is what the LORD Almighty, the God of
Israel, says:

"Daughter Babylon is like a threshing floor
　at the time it is trampled;
　the time to harvest her will soon come."

[34] "Nebuchadnezzar king of Babylon has
　　devoured us,
　he has thrown us into confusion,
　he has made us an empty jar.
Like a serpent he has swallowed us
　and filled his stomach with our
　　delicacies,
　and then has spewed us out.
[35] May the violence done to our flesh[b] be on
　　Babylon,"
　say the inhabitants of Zion.
"May our blood be on those who live in
　　Babylonia,"
　says Jerusalem.

[36] Therefore this is what the LORD says:

"See, I will defend your cause
　and avenge you;
I will dry up her sea
　and make her springs dry.
[37] Babylon will be a heap of ruins,
　a haunt of jackals,
an object of horror and scorn,
　a place where no one lives.

---

[a] 24 Or *Chaldea*; also in verse 35　　[b] 35 Or *done to us and to our children*

51:24 wrong they have done in Zion Namely, the destruction of the temple. Compare 50:28; 51:11.
51:25 you destroying mountain For the image of Babylon as a mountain, see Da 2:35.
51:27 Ararat, Minni and Ashkenaz Regions of eastern Turkey, northwest Iran and the Caucasus—all part of the territory controlled by the Medes (see Jer 51:28). The peoples of these lands had participated in ending Assyrian rule; now they are being summoned to assist in toppling Babylon.
51:30 they have become weaklings See 50:37 and note.
51:33 like a threshing floor See note on 1Sa 23:1; note on Isa 28:27. See the infographic "A Threshing Floor" on p. 497.
51:34 Nebuchadnezzar See note on Jer 21:2.

38 Her people all roar like young lions,
    they growl like lion cubs.
39 But while they are aroused,
    I will set out a feast for them
    and make them drunk,
  so that they shout with laughter —
    then sleep forever and not awake,"
                    declares the LORD.
40 "I will bring them down
    like lambs to the slaughter,
    like rams and goats.

41 "How Sheshak[a] will be captured,
    the boast of the whole earth seized!
  How desolate Babylon will be
    among the nations!
42 The sea will rise over Babylon;
    its roaring waves will cover her.
43 Her towns will be desolate,
    a dry and desert land,
  a land where no one lives,
    through which no one travels.
44 I will punish Bel in Babylon
    and make him spew out what he has
      swallowed.
  The nations will no longer stream to him.
  And the wall of Babylon will fall.

45 "Come out of her, my people!
    Run for your lives!
    Run from the fierce anger of the LORD.
46 Do not lose heart or be afraid
    when rumors are heard in the land;
  one rumor comes this year, another the next,
    rumors of violence in the land
    and of ruler against ruler.
47 For the time will surely come
    when I will punish the idols of Babylon;
  her whole land will be disgraced
    and her slain will all lie fallen within her.
48 Then heaven and earth and all that is in them
    will shout for joy over Babylon,
  for out of the north
    destroyers will attack her,"
                    declares the LORD.

49 "Babylon must fall because of Israel's slain,
    just as the slain in all the earth
    have fallen because of Babylon.
50 You who have escaped the sword,
    leave and do not linger!

Remember the LORD in a distant land,
    and call to mind Jerusalem."

51 "We are disgraced,
    for we have been insulted
    and shame covers our faces,
  because foreigners have entered
    the holy places of the LORD's house."

52 "But days are coming," declares the LORD,
    "when I will punish her idols,
  and throughout her land
    the wounded will groan.
53 Even if Babylon ascends to the heavens
    and fortifies her lofty stronghold,
  I will send destroyers against her,"
                    declares the LORD.

54 "The sound of a cry comes from Babylon,
    the sound of great destruction
    from the land of the Babylonians.[b]
55 The LORD will destroy Babylon;
    he will silence her noisy din.
  Waves of enemies will rage like great waters;
    the roar of their voices will resound.
56 A destroyer will come against Babylon;
    her warriors will be captured,
    and their bows will be broken.
  For the LORD is a God of retribution;
    he will repay in full.
57 I will make her officials and wise men drunk,
    her governors, officers and warriors as
      well;
  they will sleep forever and not awake,"
    declares the King, whose name is the LORD
      Almighty.

58 This is what the LORD Almighty says:

"Babylon's thick wall will be leveled
    and her high gates set on fire;
  the peoples exhaust themselves for nothing,
    the nations' labor is only fuel for the
      flames."

59 This is the message Jeremiah the prophet gave to the staff officer Seraiah son of Neriah, the son of Mahseiah, when he went to Babylon with Zedekiah king of Judah in the fourth year of his reign. 60 Jeremiah had written on a scroll about all the disasters that would come upon Babylon — all that

[a] 41 Sheshak is a cryptogram for Babylon.   [b] 54 Or Chaldeans

51:41 Sheshak The Hebrew text uses *sheshakh* for "Babylon" (see 25:26 and note).
51:44 Bel Babylon's chief deity (called both "Bel" and "Marduk"). See note on 50:2.
51:59–64 The lengthy oracle condemning Babylon concludes with a final symbolic action that Jeremiah performs vicariously through the royal official Seraiah, brother of Baruch (see note on 32:12). Seraiah is part of the delegation accompanying King Zedekiah to Babylon in 593 BC.

Jeremiah gives Seraiah a scroll listing the disasters that will befall Babylon. He commands Seraiah to read the scroll aloud in Babylon, then tie it to a rock and throw it into the Euphrates River. The action symbolizes that the list will come true; the same thing that happened to the scroll will happen to Babylon. See the table "Symbolic Actions of the Prophets" on p. 1195.

51:59 Zedekiah See note on 21:1. **fourth year of his reign** 593 BC. See note on 27:1.

had been recorded concerning Babylon. ⁶¹He said to Seraiah, "When you get to Babylon, see that you read all these words aloud. ⁶²Then say, 'LORD, you have said you will destroy this place, so that neither people nor animals will live in it; it will be desolate forever.' ⁶³When you finish reading this scroll, tie a stone to it and throw it into the Euphrates. ⁶⁴Then say, 'So will Babylon sink to rise no more because of the disaster I will bring on her. And her people will fall.'"

The words of Jeremiah end here.

The Fall of Jerusalem

52:1-3pp — 2Ki 24:18-20; 2Ch 36:11-16
52:4-16pp — Jer 39:1-10
52:4-21pp — 2Ki 25:1-21; 2Ch 36:17-20

52 Zedekiah was twenty-one years old when he became king, and he reigned in Jerusalem eleven years. His mother's name was Hamutal daughter of Jeremiah; she was from Libnah. ²He did evil in the eyes of the LORD, just as Jehoiakim had done. ³It was because of the LORD's anger that all this happened to Jerusalem and Judah, and in the end he thrust them from his presence.

Now Zedekiah rebelled against the king of Babylon.

⁴So in the ninth year of Zedekiah's reign, on the tenth day of the tenth month, Nebuchadnezzar king of Babylon marched against Jerusalem with his whole army. They encamped outside the city and built siege works all around it. ⁵The city was kept under siege until the eleventh year of King Zedekiah.

⁶By the ninth day of the fourth month the famine in the city had become so severe that there was no food for the people to eat. ⁷Then the city wall was broken through, and the whole army fled. They left the city at night through the gate between the two walls near the king's garden, though the Babylonians[a] were surrounding the city. They fled toward the Arabah,[b] ⁸but the Babylonian[c] army pursued King Zedekiah and overtook him in the plains of Jericho. All his soldiers were separated from him and scattered, ⁹and he was captured.

He was taken to the king of Babylon at Riblah in the land of Hamath, where he pronounced sentence on him. ¹⁰There at Riblah the king of Babylon killed the sons of Zedekiah before his eyes; he also killed all the officials of Judah. ¹¹Then he put out Zedekiah's eyes, bound him with bronze shackles and took him to Babylon, where he put him in prison till the day of his death.

¹²On the tenth day of the fifth month, in the nineteenth year of Nebuchadnezzar king of Babylon, Nebuzaradan commander of the imperial guard, who served the king of Babylon, came to Jerusalem. ¹³He set fire to the temple of the LORD, the royal palace and all the houses of Jerusalem. Every important building he burned down. ¹⁴The whole Babylonian army, under the commander of the imperial guard, broke down all the walls around Jerusalem. ¹⁵Nebuzaradan the commander of the guard carried into exile some of the poorest people and those who remained in the city, along with the rest of the craftsmen[d] and those who had deserted to the king of Babylon. ¹⁶But Nebuzaradan left behind the rest of the poorest people of the land to work the vineyards and fields.

¹⁷The Babylonians broke up the bronze pillars, the movable stands and the bronze Sea that were at the temple of the LORD and they carried all the bronze to Babylon. ¹⁸They also took away the pots, shovels, wick trimmers, sprinkling bowls, dishes and all the bronze articles used in the temple service. ¹⁹The commander of the imperial

---

[a] 7 Or *Chaldeans*; also in verse 17   [b] 7 Or *the Jordan Valley*
[c] 8 Or *Chaldean*; also in verse 14   [d] 15 Or *the populace*

52:1–34 The book of Jeremiah concludes with a historical appendix that closely parallels the conclusion of 2 Kings (see 2Ki 24:18—25:30). Jeremiah is unique among the Prophetic books because it essentially borrows its ending from another Biblical book. The effect is that the book of Jeremiah and the Deuteronomistic History (i.e., Joshua through Kings) have virtually the same ending. This connection suggests that the editors who compiled the historical books might have had a hand in the compilation of Jeremiah's prophecies.

52:2 Jehoiakim See note on Jer 22:18.
52:4 in the ninth year of Zedekiah's reign See note on 39:1. The events described in vv. 4–16 also are recounted in 39:1–10. **siege works** See Eze 4:2 and note.
52:5 eleventh year of King Zedekiah The siege lasted about a year and a half, until July of 586 BC. Compare Jer 39:2.
52:7 the Arabah Refers to the desert area around the Dead Sea. Compare 39:4; see note on 17:6.
52:8 the plains of Jericho See note on 39:5.
52:9 Riblah in the land of Hamath See note on 39:5.

52:10 he also killed all the officials of Judah See vv. 24–27.
52:11 prison till the day of his death Zedekiah's imprisonment and death are additional details not found in the 2 Kings account. See 2Ki 25:7.
52:12 On the tenth day of the fifth month A month after the city walls were breached (Jer 52:6), the temple and palace were burned down, the city walls were torn down, and all the other large houses of the city were burned. See the timeline "Life of Jeremiah" on p. 1170; see the table "Israelite Calendar" on p. 763. **Nebuzaradan** See note on 39:9.
52:16 to work the vineyards and fields See 39:10 and note.

52:17–23 Before the temple was burned, its valuables were plundered, including the large pillars and basins of bronze and all the gold and silver. The list of temple furnishings here is based on the description of the furnishings in 1Ki 7:13–39 and is more detailed than the parallel passage in 2Ki 25:13–17. See the infographic "Solomon's Temple" on p. 520.

guard took away the basins, censers, sprinkling bowls, pots, lampstands, dishes and bowls used for drink offerings — all that were made of pure gold or silver.

²⁰The bronze from the two pillars, the Sea and the twelve bronze bulls under it, and the movable stands, which King Solomon had made for the temple of the LORD, was more than could be weighed. ²¹Each pillar was eighteen cubits high and twelve cubits in circumference*a*; each was four fingers thick, and hollow. ²²The bronze capital on top of one pillar was five cubits*b* high and was decorated with a network and pomegranates of bronze all around. The other pillar, with its pomegranates, was similar. ²³There were ninety-six pomegranates on the sides; the total number of pomegranates above the surrounding network was a hundred.

²⁴The commander of the guard took as prisoners Seraiah the chief priest, Zephaniah the priest next in rank and the three doorkeepers. ²⁵Of those still in the city, he took the officer in charge of the fighting men, and seven royal advisers. He also took the secretary who was chief officer in charge of conscripting the people of the land, sixty of whom were found in the city. ²⁶Nebuzaradan the commander took them all and brought them to the king of Babylon at Riblah. ²⁷There at Riblah, in the land of Hamath, the king had them executed.

So Judah went into captivity, away from her land. ²⁸This is the number of the people Nebuchadnezzar carried into exile:

in the seventh year, 3,023 Jews;
²⁹ in Nebuchadnezzar's eighteenth year,
832 people from Jerusalem;
³⁰ in his twenty-third year,
745 Jews taken into exile by Nebuzaradan the commander of the imperial guard.

There were 4,600 people in all.

Jehoiachin Released
52:31-34pp — 2Ki 25:27-30

³¹In the thirty-seventh year of the exile of Jehoiachin king of Judah, in the year Awel-Marduk became king of Babylon, on the twenty-fifth day of the twelfth month, he released Jehoiachin king of Judah and freed him from prison. ³²He spoke kindly to him and gave him a seat of honor higher than those of the other kings who were with him in Babylon. ³³So Jehoiachin put aside his prison clothes and for the rest of his life ate regularly at the king's table. ³⁴Day by day the king of Babylon gave Jehoiachin a regular allowance as long as he lived, till the day of his death.

a 21 That is, about 27 feet high and 18 feet in circumference or about 8.1 meters high and 5.4 meters in circumference
b 22 That is, about 7 1/2 feet or about 2.3 meters

52:24 three doorkeepers See note on Jer 35:4.

52:28-30 One of the main differences between Jeremiah's account and that of 2Ki 25 is this report of three deportations to Babylon. The first correlates with the deportation of Jehoiachin in 597 BC; the second is the deportation from the destruction of Jerusalem in 586 BC; and the third is an otherwise unknown deportation conducted in 582 BC (perhaps connected with the assassination of Gedaliah; see Jer 41:2; note on 41:1–18). See the timeline "Life of Jeremiah" on p. 1170.

52:31-34 This account is identical to that in 2Ki 25:27-30. Nebuchadnezzar's successor, Awel-Marduk (also rendered "Evil-Merodach"), frees Jehoiachin (also called Jeconiah and Coniah) from imprisonment and gives him an honored status as a king in exile.

52:31 In the thirty-seventh year 560 BC. This date suggests that both the OT historical books and the book of Jeremiah were edited sometime after 560 BC. **Awel-Marduk** Son and successor of Nebuchadnezzar II. Reigned 562–560 BC.

LAMENTATIONS

INTRODUCTION TO LAMENTATIONS

Lamentations is set just after Jerusalem's destruction by the Babylonians in 586 BC. The book is composed of five poems that mourn the catastrophe. In Lamentations, the poet grieves, yet still has faith—crying out to God for mercy.

BACKGROUND

Although the Hebrew text of Lamentations is anonymous, tradition attributes the book to the prophet Jeremiah. Second Chronicles records that Jeremiah composed a lament for King Josiah, which indicates that he was familiar with this literary form (2Ch 35:25).

The author of Lamentations appears to have been a witness to the Babylonians' siege of Jerusalem (see 2Ki 25; Jer 52). The eyewitness account emphasizes the book's message with vivid images of the temple's destruction and the suffering of God's people. The author makes clear that although the Babylonians are the cause of the suffering depicted in the book, Yahweh has allowed this to happen because his people have abandoned his ways. Although Yahweh had long held back the negative consequences of forsaking his covenant (his contract), the people refused to change their ways and chose to live outside of relationship with him (compare Ex 24:1–8).

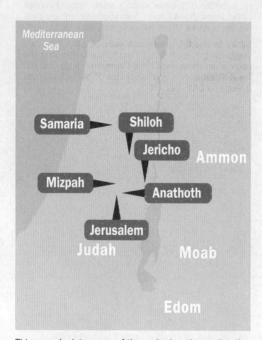

This map depicts some of the major locations related to the book of Lamentations.

STRUCTURE

The first four of Lamentations' five poems exhibit an acrostic structure, with each line beginning with a different letter of the Hebrew alphabet, in alphabetical order. The opening poem (La 1:1–22) includes multiple voices expressing the hardships faced in Jerusalem, personified as "Daughter Zion." In the second poem (2:1–22), the poet cries out to God and declares the destruction of the city to be the result of God's judgment (see 2:1). In the third poem (3:1–66), the tone changes to one of acceptance and repentance. We see here that God's promises and compassion will eventually bring restoration to his people, and the invaders will be cursed (3:21–33,64–66). However, despite this hope, the next chapter returns to sorrow, which continues to the end of the book.

The fourth poem (4:1–22) acknowledges the trauma experienced by the people as they

were stripped of their humanity during the invasion. The poet identifies the cause of this suffering as the sinfulness and guilt of Jerusalem's prophets and priests, again noting that God was justified in his judgment against his people (4:11,13,16). The fifth and final poem (5:1–22) offers a summary of the people's sin and suffering and includes a plea that God restore them, bringing renewal (see 5:21).

OUTLINE

- The desolation of Jerusalem (1:1–22)
- God's judgment on Jerusalem (2:1–22)
- Hope in God's faithfulness in the midst of disaster (3:1–66)
- Jerusalem before and after the siege (4:1–22)
- A prayer for restoration (5:1–22)

THEMES

The book of Lamentations confirms that the world, sadly, is full of suffering due to sin's presence. The full effect of sin, and thus suffering, is held back only by God's intercession. When God removes his hand of protection from Jerusalem, after years of waiting for the people to turn to him, the city falls. And in its destruction is a glimpse of what it is like to live without God's protection.

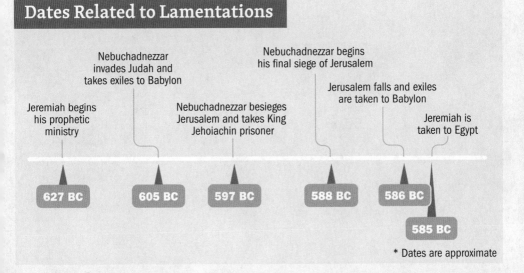

Dates Related to Lamentations

Nebuchadnezzar invades Judah and takes exiles to Babylon

Nebuchadnezzar begins his final siege of Jerusalem

Jerusalem falls and exiles are taken to Babylon

Jeremiah begins his prophetic ministry

Nebuchadnezzar besieges Jerusalem and takes King Jehoiachin prisoner

Jeremiah is taken to Egypt

627 BC

605 BC

597 BC

588 BC

586 BC

585 BC

* Dates are approximate

Lamentations does not explain away tragedy; it confronts it. Lamentations portrays the raw experience of humanity by expressing loss with full force and then mourning it. The pain is so vivid and fresh that the book ends in devastation. For those who had experienced the invasion of Jerusalem and the destruction of the temple, a hopeful future was nowhere on the horizon.

Lamentations shows the need for all people to turn to Yahweh; he is our hope. This is the only sort of resolution that Lamentations offers. The book's final verse can be translated as a question: "Have you abandoned us, and are you angry with us beyond measure?" There is no answer, but the poet still expects to hear from God someday. In times of suffering and despair, we wait upon Yahweh—even when the way forward is unclear.

1 ^a How deserted lies the city,
   once so full of people!
How like a widow is she,
   who once was great among the nations!
She who was queen among the provinces
   has now become a slave.

² Bitterly she weeps at night,
   tears are on her cheeks.
Among all her lovers
   there is no one to comfort her.
All her friends have betrayed her;
   they have become her enemies.

³ After affliction and harsh labor,
   Judah has gone into exile.
She dwells among the nations;
   she finds no resting place.

All who pursue her have overtaken her
   in the midst of her distress.

⁴ The roads to Zion mourn,
   for no one comes to her appointed
       festivals.
All her gateways are desolate,
   her priests groan,
her young women grieve,
   and she is in bitter anguish.

⁵ Her foes have become her masters;
   her enemies are at ease.
The LORD has brought her grief
   because of her many sins.

^a This chapter is an acrostic poem, the verses of which begin with the successive letters of the Hebrew alphabet.

1:1—5:22 The book of Lamentations consists of a series of five poetic laments mourning the national disaster of 586 BC when the Babylonians destroyed Jerusalem, including the temple, and took many of the people into exile. The poems were likely composed soon after that, during the exilic period (compare Ps 137). Ancient tradition connects Lamentations with the prophet Jeremiah (based on 2Ch 35:25), but the book itself does not identify its author or provide many clues as to its date or place of writing. There are similarities with some language and themes of Jeremiah, but these likely reflect the writer's agreement with Jeremiah's theological assessment of the causes for Jerusalem's destruction and the shared genre of lament psalm used both by Jeremiah and the writer of Lamentations. The poetry of Lamentations reflects the work of a highly skilled poet or poets, making full use of poetic techniques like parallelism, meter, acrostic and metaphor.

1:1–22 The first lament focuses on Zion, personified as a grieving widow. The first half of the lament describes Zion and her downfall primarily in the third person (La 1:1–11), while the second half is an individual lament in the first person spoken by the personified city (vv. 12–22).

1:1 How deserted lies the city The Hebrew title of the book comes from its opening word, *ekhah* ("how"). The grief over the destruction of the city is similar to the genre of "city lament" in Mesopotamian literature, where the destruction of a city is mourned and attributed to divine judgment and abandonment. *Ekhah* starts with the first letter of the Hebrew alphabet, *aleph*. Most of the poems in Lamentations follow the acrostic pattern. The alphabetic acrostic is the most prominent literary device in the book of Lamentations, but it is difficult to represent in translation. Each successive verse in chs. 1–2 and ch. 4 begins with the next letter of the 22-letter Hebrew alphabet. In ch. 3, each letter is used for three successive verses. Chapter 5 does not use an acrostic, though it also contains 22 verses. The acrostic device may have been employed simply to highlight the writer's poetic skill in aligning his thoughts with the literary form. Other acrostics in the OT include Ps 34, 111 and 119.
full of people The Hebrew poetry of La 1–4 reflects a deliberate style and structure known as a *qinah*. This poetic form deploys intentionally unbalanced lines. This line in Lamentations, for example, uses two words in Hebrew, following the three words in the first line. The *qinah* meter

is a word-stress rhythm with a longer half line followed by a shorter half line, usually three words in the first and two in the second. It was named after its use in formal lament poetry (*qinah* means "lament"), but the meter is not exclusive to laments, nor do all laments use the meter. For example, Isa 40:9–11 and SS 1:9–11 use the meter, though they are not laments, and 2Sa 1:17–27 does not use it, though it is a lament. The book of Lamentations, like most Hebrew poetry, is not consistent in using the pattern. **like a widow** Bereaved of inhabitants (children) and husband (Yahweh). Compare Isa 54:1–7. Depicting the city as a widow reflects Jerusalem's overall loss of status. Everything that provided prestige and stability in ancient Near Eastern society has been taken away. Widowhood symbolized vulnerability and poverty in ancient Near Eastern society. The fact that male-dominated social structures left widows and others without a legal advocate seems to have been recognized by ancient writers, who encouraged the powerful to deal justly with them (see Code of Hammurabi; compare Lk 18:1–8). **queen among the provinces** Laments Jerusalem's fall from past glory. Compare La 5:16 and Eze 16:10–14. The transformation from princess to slave represents Jerusalem's utter humiliation. The imagery of this lament is similar to Isa 47:1–15, which personifies Babylon as a royal woman brought to ruin, including widowhood (compare Isa 47:1,8).
1:2 her lovers Former allies. The prophets depicted Israel's political and spiritual abandonment of Yahweh as adultery. See Jer 3:1; 4:30; 22:20–22; 30:14; Eze 16:26–37; 23:22–27. See note on Isa 1:21.
1:3 Judah has gone into exile Deportation was a common practice for the Assyrians and Babylonians, but it was also the ultimate punishment for breaking the covenant with Yahweh (Dt 28:64–68). Judah experienced three deportations to Babylon. See Jer 52:28–30 and note.
1:4 Zion Another name for Jerusalem, referring to the Temple Mount as the center for worship in Israel. The population has been decimated or deported and the temple destroyed, so no worshipers are coming.
1:5 LORD has brought her grief Judgment has come from Yahweh as a result of their sin. Compare Jer 30:14–15. Before the exile, the prophets warned Judah in vain that judgment was imminent because the people had turned away from God (e.g., Jer 11:1–13; 17:1–4). They had been warned that one of the consequences of breaking faith with Yahweh would be exile (Lev 26:33; Dt 28:36). The purpose of the discipline is correction, not destruction (compare Pr 3:11–12).

Her children have gone into exile,
captive before the foe.

6 All the splendor has departed
from Daughter Zion.
Her princes are like deer
that find no pasture;
in weakness they have fled
before the pursuer.

7 In the days of her affliction and wandering
Jerusalem remembers all the treasures
that were hers in days of old.
When her people fell into enemy hands,
there was no one to help her.
Her enemies looked at her
and laughed at her destruction.

8 Jerusalem has sinned greatly
and so has become unclean.
All who honored her despise her,
for they have all seen her naked;
she herself groans
and turns away.

9 Her filthiness clung to her skirts;
she did not consider her future.
Her fall was astounding;
there was none to comfort her.
"Look, LORD, on my affliction,
for the enemy has triumphed."

10 The enemy laid hands
on all her treasures;
she saw pagan nations
enter her sanctuary—
those you had forbidden
to enter your assembly.

11 All her people groan
as they search for bread;
they barter their treasures for food
to keep themselves alive.
"Look, LORD, and consider,
for I am despised."

12 "Is it nothing to you, all you who pass by?
Look around and see.
Is any suffering like my suffering
that was inflicted on me,
that the LORD brought on me
in the day of his fierce anger?

13 "From on high he sent fire,
sent it down into my bones.
He spread a net for my feet
and turned me back.
He made me desolate,
faint all the day long.

14 "My sins have been bound into a yoke a;
by his hands they were woven
together.
They have been hung on my neck,
and the Lord has sapped my strength.
He has given me into the hands
of those I cannot withstand.

15 "The Lord has rejected
all the warriors in my midst;
he has summoned an army against me
to b crush my young men.
In his winepress the Lord has trampled
Virgin Daughter Judah.

16 "This is why I weep
and my eyes overflow with tears.
No one is near to comfort me,
no one to restore my spirit.
My children are destitute
because the enemy has prevailed."

17 Zion stretches out her hands,
but there is no one to comfort her.
The LORD has decreed for Jacob
that his neighbors become his foes;

---

a 14 Most Hebrew manuscripts; many Hebrew manuscripts and Septuagint *He kept watch over my sins*   b 15 Or *has set a time for me / when he will*

1:6 Daughter Zion A metaphor for Jerusalem. See note on Isa 1:8. **in weakness they have fled before the pursuer** These lines may be alluding to the events described in 2Ki 25:3–6 when King Zedekiah and his officials fled besieged Jerusalem by night, only to be captured by the Babylonians.
1:8 they have all seen her naked Alluding to adultery and public shame. The language of La 1:8–9 presents public exposure as the humiliating punishment for sexual infidelity. Similar language serves the same function in Isa 47:3, Jer 13:22 (and 13:26), Eze 16:37 and Na 3:5–6.
1:9 she did not consider her future The parallel imagery from Jer 13:22 suggests personified Zion feigned ignorance that her sin was the cause of the disaster that struck her. See Jer 13:22 and note. **Look, LORD, on my affliction** The woman who personifies Zion now interjects with a cry to Yahweh. Many first-person laments in both the books of Jeremiah and Lamentations reflect the voice of personified Zion. See Jer 10:19–21 and note.

1:10 pagan nations enter her sanctuary The Babylonians plundered the temple before burning it down (see 2Ki 25:9–17). **to enter your assembly** Compare Dt 23:3–6.
1:11 Look, LORD Personified Zion speaks. See note on La 1:9.
1:14 My sins have been bound into a yoke The yoke was a symbol of judgment. See Dt 28:48. In other contexts, the yoke represents subjection to a stronger power or authority (see Isa 9:4; 58:6; Jer 5:5; 27:8). See note on Jer 5:5.
1:15 In his winepress the Lord has trampled Judah is like the grapes smashed underfoot in a winepress. Compare Isa 63:2–3. See the infographic "A Winepress in Ancient Israel" on p. 1157.
1:17 Zion stretches out her hands The first-person lament of personified Zion is interrupted with a comment from the narrator, describing the scene. Zion is looking for help and comfort.

Jerusalem has become
 an unclean thing among them.

18 "The LORD is righteous,
 yet I rebelled against his command.
Listen, all you peoples;
 look on my suffering.
My young men and young women
 have gone into exile.

19 "I called to my allies
 but they betrayed me.
My priests and my elders
 perished in the city
while they searched for food
 to keep themselves alive.

20 "See, LORD, how distressed I am!
 I am in torment within,
and in my heart I am disturbed,
 for I have been most rebellious.
Outside, the sword bereaves;
 inside, there is only death.

21 "People have heard my groaning,
 but there is no one to comfort me.
All my enemies have heard of my distress;
 they rejoice at what you have done.
May you bring the day you have announced
 so they may become like me.

22 "Let all their wickedness come before you;
 deal with them
as you have dealt with me
 because of all my sins.
My groans are many
 and my heart is faint."

2 [a] How the Lord has covered Daughter Zion
 with the cloud of his anger[b]!
He has hurled down the splendor of Israel
 from heaven to earth;
he has not remembered his footstool
 in the day of his anger.

2 Without pity the Lord has swallowed up
 all the dwellings of Jacob;
in his wrath he has torn down
 the strongholds of Daughter Judah.
He has brought her kingdom and its princes
 down to the ground in dishonor.

3 In fierce anger he has cut off
 every horn[c,d] of Israel.
He has withdrawn his right hand
 at the approach of the enemy.
He has burned in Jacob like a flaming fire
 that consumes everything around it.

4 Like an enemy he has strung his bow;
 his right hand is ready.
Like a foe he has slain
 all who were pleasing to the eye;
he has poured out his wrath like fire
 on the tent of Daughter Zion.

5 The Lord is like an enemy;
 he has swallowed up Israel.
He has swallowed up all her palaces
 and destroyed her strongholds.

[a] This chapter is an acrostic poem, the verses of which begin with the successive letters of the Hebrew alphabet. [b] 1 Or How the Lord in his anger / has treated Daughter Zion with contempt [c] 3 Or off / all the strength; or every king [d] 3 Horn here symbolizes strength.

1:18 I rebelled against his command Jerusalem confesses that she was justly punished on account of her rebellion. Compare Jer 14:7,20.
1:19 My priests and my elders perished in the city The religious and civil leaders who led Israel astray (see Jer 2:8 and note; compare Eze 7:26–27).
1:20 within The Hebrew word refers to internal digestive organs. See note on Jer 4:19.
1:22 deal with them The poetry of the OT often contains calls like this for Yahweh to judge enemies (e.g., Ps 28:4; 35:1–28). Now that judgment has come on Jerusalem, the city longs that Yahweh's promised day of judgment would come on the other nations (compare Isa 47:11; Jer 30:16).

2:1–22 This second lament focuses on the great suffering inflicted on Zion when Yahweh became like an enemy (La 2:5). The emphasis is on the wrath of the Divine Warrior unleashed against his people, but the poet has no illusions that Yahweh's anger is unwarranted or unjustified (v. 17; compare Jer 7:18). While the Divine Warrior imagery can be found throughout Lamentations, it is especially emphasized in La 2.

2:1 Daughter Zion Identifying Jerusalem by the name of its most sacred space and personifying the city as a woman. See note on Isa 1:8. **the splendor of Israel** Referring to Jerusalem or the temple (compare Isa 13:19;

64:11; Ps 78:59–61). **his footstool** A metaphor used for the temple as the site of Yahweh's earthly dwelling. See Ps 99:5 and note. Compare Isa 60:13; Eze 43:7. **the day of his anger** Referring to the day of Yahweh that the prophets warned Israel about, when Yahweh would come to judge Israel and the nations. There are more than 200 instances of the prophets referring to the day of Yahweh either directly or with a Hebrew phrase literally translated as "on that day." See Isa 2:12; 13:6; 19:16–25; 22:5; Jer 4:9; 30:5–7; 46:10; Eze 7:1–27; 30:3; 39:8; Joel 1:15; La 2:1,11; 3:4; 4:14; Am 5:18–20; Ob 15; Zep 1:7,14; Mal 3:2.
2:2 the dwellings of Jacob Referring to the nation of Israel by the name of their ancestor Jacob (see Ge 25–49). **strongholds of Daughter Judah** The fortified cities of Judah. See note on Jer 4:5.
2:3 horn The Hebrew here emphasizes the idea of power by using the Hebrew word for "horn," which was symbolic of power itself. See note on Eze 29:21. **his right hand** The right hand symbolized presence, power and protection (see Ex 15:6). See note on Isa 41:10.
2:4 Like an enemy he has strung his bow Imagery of the Divine Warrior, coming in wrath, fighting against Israel. See Isa 29:3 and note. Technically, the Babylonians wielded the weaponry that cut down Jerusalem, but their success was due to Yahweh's posture of judgment against his people (compare Isa 10:5 and note).

He has multiplied mourning and
  lamentation
    for Daughter Judah.

⁶ He has laid waste his dwelling like a garden;
  he has destroyed his place of meeting.
The LORD has made Zion forget
  her appointed festivals and her Sabbaths;
in his fierce anger he has spurned
  both king and priest.

⁷ The Lord has rejected his altar
  and abandoned his sanctuary.
He has given the walls of her palaces
  into the hands of the enemy;
they have raised a shout in the house
    of the LORD
  as on the day of an appointed festival.

⁸ The LORD determined to tear down
  the wall around Daughter Zion.
He stretched out a measuring line
  and did not withhold his hand from
    destroying.
He made ramparts and walls lament;
  together they wasted away.

⁹ Her gates have sunk into the ground;
  their bars he has broken and destroyed.
Her king and her princes are exiled among
    the nations,
  the law is no more,
and her prophets no longer find
  visions from the LORD.

¹⁰ The elders of Daughter Zion
  sit on the ground in silence;
they have sprinkled dust on their heads
  and put on sackcloth.
The young women of Jerusalem
  have bowed their heads to the ground.

¹¹ My eyes fail from weeping,
  I am in torment within;
my heart is poured out on the ground
  because my people are destroyed,
because children and infants faint
  in the streets of the city.

¹² They say to their mothers,
  "Where is bread and wine?"
as they faint like the wounded
  in the streets of the city,
as their lives ebb away
  in their mothers' arms.

¹³ What can I say for you?
  With what can I compare you,
    Daughter Jerusalem?
To what can I liken you,
  that I may comfort you,
    Virgin Daughter Zion?
Your wound is as deep as the sea.
  Who can heal you?

¹⁴ The visions of your prophets
  were false and worthless;
they did not expose your sin
  to ward off your captivity.

The presentation of Yahweh as the Divine Warrior is a
key theme in Lamentations. According to Deuteronomy
28, the Divine Warrior would fight for Israel, not against
them, if they remained obedient (Dt 28:7). However, if
they rebelled against Yahweh, they would be as one of
his enemies (Dt 28:25). Lamentations uses that contrast to explain how and why Jerusalem fell. **Like a foe**
Compare Jer 30:14.
2:6 his dwelling This a metaphor for the temple. Compare Isa 1:8; 5:5–6. **Zion** Another name for Jerusalem.
See note on Isa 1:8. **appointed festivals and her
Sabbaths** Regular religious observances have been
neglected. Regarding the Sabbath, see note on Ge 2:3.
king and priest Yahweh has abandoned both royal and
religious institutions.
2:7 Lord has rejected his altar Yahweh has rejected
his dwelling because of Israel's idolatry (Eze 8–11).
Compare Eze 24:21; Ps 78:60; Jer 7:12.
2:8 He stretched out a measuring line Used in both
construction and demolition and here as a metaphor for
judgment. See 2Ki 21:13; Isa 34:11; Zec 1:16.
**2:9 Her king and her princes are exiled among the
nations** The upper classes of Judah were taken into
exile by Babylon, including both King Jehoiachin in 597
BC and King Zedekiah in 586 BC (2Ki 24:12–16; Jer
52:11). See the timeline "Judah From the Fall of Samaria
to the Exile" on p. 606. **law is no more** Referring to
priestly teaching. **prophets no longer find visions from
the LORD** The failure of the prophets who claimed to be
preaching peace in the name of Yahweh is a prominent

theme in Jeremiah (see Jer 5:31; 14:13; 23:16–17;
28:1–17). Despite their claims, they had not really heard
from Yahweh (see La 2:14).
2:10 The elders of Daughter Zion Local leaders. The
national institutions of political and religious power have
fallen (compare Jer 4:9). On elders, see note on Jer
26:17. **they have sprinkled dust on their heads** A
traditional sign of mourning (Jos 7:6; Job 2:12). **put on
sackcloth** Another traditional part of mourning rituals,
which were done in times of national distress, not just
personal loss. On sackcloth, see Isa 15:2; Jer 4:8; 6:26.
See note on Jer 6:26.

2:11–19 An account of an individual's emotional reaction
to the great suffering of Zion. The poet addresses Zion
directly (La 2:13) and laments her fate, but ultimately
urges her to look to Yahweh for salvation (vv. 18–19).

2:11 My eyes fail from weeping The individual lament
is similar to that of personified Zion in 1:12–22. **I am in
torment within** See note on 1:20; Jer 4:19. **my heart**
The Hebrew word here refers to the liver; this expression
is often translated "heart" or "bile." The expression is
a metaphor for inner emotional turmoil. **my people** A
term for Jerusalem used frequently in Jeremiah and
Lamentations (e.g., Jer 8:21; 14:17).
2:14 false and worthless See La 2:9 and note. **to
ward off your captivity** The Hebrew phrase used here
commonly denotes future salvation in Biblical poetry, especially in Jeremiah and Psalms (see Jer 29:14; 30:3,18;
33:7; compare Dt 30:3; Ps 14:7; 126:1).

The prophecies they gave you
  were false and misleading.

¹⁵ All who pass your way
    clap their hands at you;
  they scoff and shake their heads
    at Daughter Jerusalem:
  "Is this the city that was called
    the perfection of beauty,
    the joy of the whole earth?"

¹⁶ All your enemies open their mouths
    wide against you;
  they scoff and gnash their teeth
    and say, "We have swallowed her up.
  This is the day we have waited for;
    we have lived to see it."

¹⁷ The LORD has done what he planned;
    he has fulfilled his word,
    which he decreed long ago.
  He has overthrown you without pity,
    he has let the enemy gloat over you,
    he has exalted the horn[a] of your foes.

¹⁸ The hearts of the people
    cry out to the Lord.
  You walls of Daughter Zion,
    let your tears flow like a river
    day and night;
  give yourself no relief,
    your eyes no rest.

¹⁹ Arise, cry out in the night,
    as the watches of the night begin;
  pour out your heart like water
    in the presence of the Lord.
  Lift up your hands to him
    for the lives of your children,

who faint from hunger
    at every street corner.

²⁰ "Look, LORD, and consider:
    Whom have you ever treated like this?
  Should women eat their offspring,
    the children they have cared for?
  Should priest and prophet be killed
    in the sanctuary of the Lord?

²¹ "Young and old lie together
    in the dust of the streets;
  my young men and young women
    have fallen by the sword.
  You have slain them in the day of your anger;
    you have slaughtered them without pity.

²² "As you summon to a feast day,
    so you summoned against me terrors on
      every side.
  In the day of the LORD's anger
    no one escaped or survived;
  those I cared for and reared
    my enemy has destroyed."

3 [b] I am the man who has seen affliction
    by the rod of the LORD's wrath.
² He has driven me away and made me walk
    in darkness rather than light;
³ indeed, he has turned his hand against me
    again and again, all day long.

⁴ He has made my skin and my flesh grow old
    and has broken my bones.

---

a 17 Horn here symbolizes strength.   *b* This chapter is an acrostic poem; the verses of each stanza begin with the successive letters of the Hebrew alphabet, and the verses within each stanza begin with the same letter.

2:15 All who pass your way Passersby scoff at the once-great city of Jerusalem. Compare Jer 18:16; 19:8.
2:17 LORD has done what he planned The judgment described in La 2:1–8 was part of Yahweh's plan, carrying out the punishment necessary for Israel's breaking of the covenant (see Dt 28:15–68).
2:18 let your tears flow like a river Zion is urged to pray and turn back to Yahweh. Compare Jer 13:17; 14:17.
2:20 Look, LORD Zion responds to the exhortation to pray in La 2:18–19 by offering this appeal to Yahweh, emphasizing the great suffering from which none could escape. Young and old, male and female, all suffered alike. **eat their offspring** Meaning the people would resort to cannibalism due to the shortage of food (see Eze 5:10 and note; compare La 4:10; Isa 9:20; Jer 19:9).
2:22 terrors on every side Another phrase reminiscent of Jeremiah. See Jer 6:25; note on Jer 20:3. **the day of the LORD's anger** When Yahweh could come to judge Israel and the nations. See La 2:1 and note.

3:1–66 In this third lament, the acrostic (see note on 1:1) starts three successive verses with each letter of the Hebrew alphabet. The poem can be divided into an individual complaint (vv. 1–18), a transition from despair to hope (vv. 19–24), a contemplation of Yahweh's sovereignty over suffering (vv. 25–39), a communal lament (vv. 40–47) and a renewed individual lament (vv. 48–66). The opening lament acknowledges the sufferer is experiencing the wrath of Yahweh, but the central section emphasizes that this situation is temporary and urges hope in Yahweh based on his faithfulness and steadfast love. The communal lament urges repentance and confesses guilt but laments the severity of the divine wrath and the humiliation of Israel in the eyes of her enemies. The concluding complaint emphasizes suffering caused by enemies and implores Yahweh to intervene to punish the sufferer's enemies, a common pattern in traditional laments found in the Psalms.

3:1 man The speaker in this individual lament (vv. 1–18) is male, contrasting with the female voice of personified Zion's lament in 1:12–22. This term for "man" frequently occurs in wisdom contexts (15 times in Job; four times in wisdom psalms), linking this opening lament with the sage-like teaching in vv. 25–39. **who has seen affliction by the rod of the LORD's wrath** The speaker claims to have firsthand experience of the suffering inflicted on Israel because of Yahweh's wrath. His personal experience adds credibility and authority to the exhortation to hope and trust Yahweh in vv. 21–39. At many points, the speaker's description of his suffering in vv. 1–19 echoes various complaints from the book of Job.

⁵He has besieged me and surrounded me
  with bitterness and hardship.
⁶He has made me dwell in darkness
  like those long dead.

⁷He has walled me in so I cannot escape;
  he has weighed me down with chains.
⁸Even when I call out or cry for help,
  he shuts out my prayer.
⁹He has barred my way with blocks of stone;
  he has made my paths crooked.

¹⁰Like a bear lying in wait,
  like a lion in hiding,
¹¹he dragged me from the path and
  mangled me
  and left me without help.
¹²He drew his bow
  and made me the target for his arrows.

¹³He pierced my heart
  with arrows from his quiver.
¹⁴I became the laughingstock of all my people;
  they mock me in song all day long.
¹⁵He has filled me with bitter herbs
  and given me gall to drink.

¹⁶He has broken my teeth with gravel;
  he has trampled me in the dust.
¹⁷I have been deprived of peace;
  I have forgotten what prosperity is.
¹⁸So I say, "My splendor is gone
  and all that I had hoped from the LORD."

¹⁹I remember my affliction and my
  wandering,
  the bitterness and the gall.
²⁰I well remember them,
  and my soul is downcast within me.
²¹Yet this I call to mind
  and therefore I have hope:

²²Because of the LORD's great love we are not
  consumed,
  for his compassions never fail.
²³They are new every morning;
  great is your faithfulness.
²⁴I say to myself, "The LORD is my portion;
  therefore I will wait for him."

²⁵The LORD is good to those whose hope is in
  him,
  to the one who seeks him;

3:4 He has made my skin and my flesh grow old The imagery of this lament is generic and stereotypical, following the conventions of the lament genre to describe the sufferer's experience (compare Ps 38:2–3; 32:4). The generic language helps readers identify with the person's suffering, which is likely described in exaggerated figurative terms using traditional motifs (Job 13:28; Mic 3:2–3). The stereotypical nature of the descriptions makes any attempt to identify the speaker speculative. The language is very similar to parts of Job and Psalms (especially Job 19; Ps 38). **broken my bones** A traditional image of punishment (Isa 38:13; Ps 34:20; Mic 3:3).
3:5 He has besieged me and surrounded Jerusalem was besieged, and the sufferer describes his experience as God's siege against him personally. Compare Job 19:12 and note.
3:6 like those long dead Being left in total darkness is comparable to being abandoned in Sheol—the place of the dead. Compare Ps 143:3.
3:7 He has walled me in As though in a prison. Compare Job 19:8 and note.
3:8 Even when I call out or cry for help The sufferer complains that his cries for help are ignored by God. Compare Job 19:7 and note.
3:10 a bear lying in wait Enemies are often depicted in poetry as wild animals waiting to attack (see Ps 7:2; 17:12; 22:12–13,16). The enemy here is Yahweh (compare Hos 13:8; Job 10:16; Am 5:19).
3:12 He drew his bow Returning to the imagery of the Divine Warrior unleashing arrows on his enemy (La 3:13). Compare 2:4 and note. **made me the target** Compare Job 16:12–13.
3:13 He pierced my heart with arrows from his quiver Compare Job 6:4; Ps 38:2.
3:14 laughingstock of all my people Echoes of Jeremiah's lament in Jer 20:7 and the enemies gloating over Jerusalem in La 1:7.
3:15 given me gall to drink A bitter plant metaphorically

reflecting sorrow and emotional bitterness (Pr 5:4; Am 5:7; 6:12; Jer 9:15; 23:15).

3:19–24 The individual lament draws to a close in La 3:19–21. The last phrase of v. 21 begins the transition toward the more hopeful outlook expressed in vv. 22–24. These three verses provide the only glimmer of hope in the entire book; they reveal that even in the midst of despair, all hope is not lost.

3:22 LORD's great love we are not consumed The speaker appeals to Yahweh's covenant love to justify his hope. The Hebrew term used here for Yahweh's covenant love is *chesed*. This phrase could be referring to the eternal nature of Yahweh's *chesed* or to *chesed* as the essential quality of Yahweh's nature that allows him to restrain his wrath and justice from bringing a total end. Some English translations follow the ancient Aramaic versions here, which read "The kindnesses of Yahweh never cease"; others follow the traditional Hebrew text, which says "Because of Yahweh's mercies [or great love], we are not consumed." Deciding which reading to follow is part of the task of a field of study known as textual criticism. The difference between what the Hebrew reads and what the Aramaic translators may have read is only one letter. The poetic parallelism with the rest of the line (which reads literally, "his mercies never come to an end") supports following the Aramaic reading. See the table "Parallelism in Hebrew Poetry" on p. 1008.
3:24 LORD is my portion This phrase refers to the Israelite's land allotment (see note on Eze 45:7). The priests and Levites had no land portion because Yahweh was their portion (Nu 18:20). Compare Ps 16:5; 73:26.

3:25–39 The lament in La 3:1–21 served as an introduction to the speaker's teaching about trust in Yahweh's goodness and sovereignty in this section. Here he adopts the tone of a wisdom teacher, encouraging the sufferers to learn to wait patiently through their suffering and look forward to the future salvation of Yahweh.

²⁶it is good to wait quietly
  for the salvation of the LORD.
²⁷It is good for a man to bear the yoke
  while he is young.

²⁸Let him sit alone in silence,
  for the LORD has laid it on him.
²⁹Let him bury his face in the dust—
  there may yet be hope.
³⁰Let him offer his cheek to one who would
  strike him,
  and let him be filled with disgrace.

³¹For no one is cast off
  by the Lord forever.
³²Though he brings grief, he will show
  compassion,
  so great is his unfailing love.
³³For he does not willingly bring affliction
  or grief to anyone.

³⁴To crush underfoot
  all prisoners in the land,
³⁵to deny people their rights
  before the Most High,
³⁶to deprive them of justice—
  would not the Lord see such things?

³⁷Who can speak and have it happen
  if the Lord has not decreed it?
³⁸Is it not from the mouth of the Most High
  that both calamities and good things come?
³⁹Why should the living complain
  when punished for their sins?

⁴⁰Let us examine our ways and test them,
  and let us return to the LORD.
⁴¹Let us lift up our hearts and our hands
  to God in heaven, and say:
⁴²"We have sinned and rebelled
  and you have not forgiven.

⁴³"You have covered yourself with anger and
  pursued us;
  you have slain without pity.
⁴⁴You have covered yourself with a cloud
  so that no prayer can get through.
⁴⁵You have made us scum and refuse
  among the nations.

⁴⁶"All our enemies have opened their mouths
  wide against us.
⁴⁷We have suffered terror and pitfalls,
  ruin and destruction."
⁴⁸Streams of tears flow from my eyes
  because my people are destroyed.

⁴⁹My eyes will flow unceasingly,
  without relief,
⁵⁰until the LORD looks down
  from heaven and sees.
⁵¹What I see brings grief to my soul
  because of all the women of my city.

⁵²Those who were my enemies without cause
  hunted me like a bird.
⁵³They tried to end my life in a pit
  and threw stones at me;
⁵⁴the waters closed over my head,
  and I thought I was about to perish.

3:25 good to those whose hope Reminiscent of the statements of praise and assurance found in thanksgiving psalms (such as Ps 34:8). Yahweh's goodness is an essential part of his nature, manifested toward those who seek him (compare Ps 86:5; Ro 8:28).
3:26 to wait quietly for the salvation of the LORD Compare Mic 7:7.
3:27 to bear the yoke while he is young Implying the present suffering is valuable as discipline (compare Pr 23:13–14).
3:30 Let him offer his cheek to one who would strike Imagery reminiscent of the suffering servant in Isaiah (compare Isa 50:6).
3:31 no one is cast off by the Lord forever Yahweh's wrath is temporary, not a defining quality of who he is. Compare Ps 103:9.
3:36 would not the Lord see Though some translations take this phrase as a statement, it should probably be understood as an example of rhetoric, like the questions that follow in La 3:37–39. The idea of this phrase is rendered well in English by: "Does the Lord not see?" The rhetoric implies that he does see; nothing happens without his sanction.
3:38 both calamities and good things Blessing and judgment both come from God. Compare Isa 45:7 and note.
3:39 their sins Judgment is deserved punishment for sin, not malicious affliction arbitrarily inflicted by a vindictive God. The writer is not implying that all suffering is punishment for sin (see Job 4:6 and note; Job 22:5 and note). In their present circumstance, Judah's disfavor with Yahweh was the result of their sin. None of them has the right to complain about their punishment because it was well-deserved.
3:40–47 This language shifts to involve the rest of the community in this lament, confessing their sin and seeking forgiveness and renewal from Yahweh. The introspective confession in La 3:40–42 acts almost like a response to the teaching of vv. 25–39.
3:41 Let us lift up our hearts and our hands An appeal to internal transformation not just outward obeisance.
3:44 You have covered yourself with a cloud Yahweh has made himself inaccessible. The cloud was also a symbol of his presence (Ex 14:19; 19:16; 1Ki 8:10).
3:48–66 A renewed individual lament, but the speaker now seems to be speaking as a representative of the community. The language is similar to traditional laments in the Psalms that emphasize suffering caused by human enemies and call on Yahweh to aid his people against their enemies.
3:48 Streams of tears flow from my eyes Compare La 1:16; 2:11; 2:18; Jer 13:17; 14:17. **my people are destroyed** Refers to Jerusalem. See La 2:11 and note.
3:52 my enemies This lament focuses on oppression from external enemies, not Yahweh's judgment.
3:54 waters closed over my head Drowning was associated with the underworld (Sheol) and reflected a deep-seated cultural fear. Compare Jnh 2:2–5; Ps 69:1–2,14–15; 88:17.

55 I called on your name, Lord,
   from the depths of the pit.
56 You heard my plea: "Do not close your ears
   to my cry for relief."
57 You came near when I called you,
   and you said, "Do not fear."

58 You, Lord, took up my case;
   you redeemed my life.
59 Lord, you have seen the wrong done to me.
   Uphold my cause!
60 You have seen the depth of their vengeance,
   all their plots against me.

61 Lord, you have heard their insults,
   all their plots against me —
62 what my enemies whisper and mutter
   against me all day long.
63 Look at them! Sitting or standing,
   they mock me in their songs.

64 Pay them back what they deserve, Lord,
   for what their hands have done.
65 Put a veil over their hearts,
   and may your curse be on them!
66 Pursue them in anger and destroy them
   from under the heavens of the Lord.

4 ᵃ How the gold has lost its luster,
   the fine gold become dull!
   The sacred gems are scattered
   at every street corner.

2 How the precious children of Zion,
   once worth their weight in gold,
   are now considered as pots of clay,
   the work of a potter's hands!

3 Even jackals offer their breasts
   to nurse their young,
   but my people have become
      heartless
   like ostriches in the desert.

4 Because of thirst the infant's
      tongue
   sticks to the roof of its mouth;
   the children beg for bread,
   but no one gives it to them.

5 Those who once ate delicacies
   are destitute in the streets.
   Those brought up in royal purple
   now lie on ash heaps.

6 The punishment of my people
   is greater than that of Sodom,
   which was overthrown in a moment
   without a hand turned to help her.

7 Their princes were brighter than
      snow
   and whiter than milk,

ᵃ This chapter is an acrostic poem, the verses of which begin
with the successive letters of the Hebrew alphabet.

3:55 the depths of the pit A metaphor for Sheol but often used to express the sentiment that the sufferer has reached bottom, the breaking point. Only God can save them from their distress.

3:56 You heard my plea A statement of assurance similar to that found in thanksgiving psalms (compare Ps 18:6). The statements in La 3:55–61 reflect the speaker's confidence that Yahweh will respond to his prayer. It is possible that the Hebrew verbs in vv. 56–66 could be read not as statements of assurance in past actions, but as requests for Yahweh's intervention. The difference depends on whether this lament is read as closing with a statement of trust and assurance in Yahweh's intervention (speaking as if it has already happened) or as a prayer requesting that intervention in the future.

3:64 Pay them back what they deserve, Lord The verb forms of the Hebrew in vv. 64–66 could be read as declarations about God's future actions or as requests. See note on v. 56.

4:1–22 The fourth lament reports the suffering of the people of Jerusalem during the final days of the Babylonian siege. The poet describes a scene of death by famine, a fate worse than death by the sword. This poem has the two clearest historical allusions in the book: Judah's expectation of Egyptian assistance during the siege (v. 17) and Zedekiah's ill-fated flight from Jerusalem (vv. 18–20). The short passage with these allusions (vv. 17–20) is also marked by a shift to first-person plural from the detached third-person reporting of the rest of the lament. The lament ends with one of the few references to foreign nations in the book, condemning Edom for rejoicing over Yahweh's punishment of Zion (vv. 21–22).

4:1 How the gold has lost its luster This verse begins with the Hebrew word *ekhah* just like the acrostic laments in 1:1 and 2:1. See note on 1:1. **the fine gold** The gold and precious stones metaphorically represent the inhabitants of the city, emphasizing the value of human life and lamenting its loss.

4:2 pots of clay Easily broken and discarded. The people were more precious than gold, but they were thrown out like broken dishes. Compare Jer 18:6 and Jeremiah's symbolic action breaking a clay pot in Jer 19:10–11.

4:3 Even jackals offer their breasts Wild animals care for their young, but mothers in Jerusalem are unable to feed their children because there is no food. The jackal was a scavenger often associated with deserted and desolated ruins (see Ps 44:19; Isa 34:13; Jer 9:11). See Ps 63:10 and note. Jackals and ostriches (or "owls" in some translations) are mentioned frequently as a poetic word pair in the OT (Isa 34:13; 43:20; Job 30:29; Mic 1:8). **my people** Refers to Jerusalem. See La 2:11 and note. **have become heartless** The ostrich is a symbol of a senseless beast that does not care for its young in Job 39:13–18.

4:5 purple A symbol of their wealthy and privileged upbringing. See note on Jer 10:9.

4:6 The punishment The Hebrew term here can refer to the sin or the punishment for the sin. **that of Sodom** The poet laments that Zion's punishment was harsher than that of Sodom. The contrast is focused on the length of the punishment. The people of Jerusalem languished under a lengthy siege and died slowly of hunger compared with the people of Sodom, who were punished quickly with fire and brimstone. On Sodom, see Ge 19.

4:7 princes were brighter than snow The metaphor means they were in good health and handsome.

their bodies more ruddy than rubies,
their appearance like lapis lazuli.

8 But now they are blacker than soot;
they are not recognized in the streets.
Their skin has shriveled on their bones;
it has become as dry as a stick.

9 Those killed by the sword are better off
than those who die of famine;
racked with hunger, they waste away
for lack of food from the field.

10 With their own hands compassionate
women
have cooked their own children,
who became their food
when my people were destroyed.

11 The LORD has given full vent to his
wrath;
he has poured out his fierce anger.
He kindled a fire in Zion
that consumed her foundations.

12 The kings of the earth did not believe,
nor did any of the peoples of
the world,
that enemies and foes could enter
the gates of Jerusalem.

13 But it happened because of the sins of her
prophets
and the iniquities of her priests,
who shed within her
the blood of the righteous.

14 Now they grope through the streets
as if they were blind.
They are so defiled with blood
that no one dares to touch their
garments.

15 "Go away! You are unclean!" people cry to
them.
"Away! Away! Don't touch us!"
When they flee and wander about,
people among the nations say,
"They can stay here no longer."

16 The LORD himself has scattered them;
he no longer watches over them.
The priests are shown no honor,
the elders no favor.

17 Moreover, our eyes failed,
looking in vain for help;
from our towers we watched
for a nation that could not save us.

18 People stalked us at every step,
so we could not walk in our streets.
Our end was near, our days were numbered,
for our end had come.

19 Our pursuers were swifter
than eagles in the sky;
they chased us over the mountains
and lay in wait for us in the desert.

20 The LORD's anointed, our very life
breath,
was caught in their traps.
We thought that under his shadow
we would live among the nations.

21 Rejoice and be glad, Daughter Edom,
you who live in the land of Uz.
But to you also the cup will be passed;
you will be drunk and stripped naked.

22 Your punishment will end, Daughter Zion;
he will not prolong your exile.
But he will punish your sin, Daughter Edom,
and expose your wickedness.

4:8 blacker than soot A darkened face was an image of poor health due to famine (see La 5:10; compare Job 30:28).

4:9 Those killed by the sword Better to have died in battle, since it was quick, than to die slowly of hunger.

4:10 cooked their own children The food shortage caused by siege led people to unthinkable measures of cannibalism to survive. See La 2:20; 2Ki 6:29; and note on Jer 19:9.

4:11 LORD has given full vent to his wrath Compare Eze 5:13. **He kindled a fire in Zion** Reminiscent of Jer 17:27. Fire was a standard image of divine judgment, fulfilled literally when Babylon burned the city and the temple (Jer 52:13). See Jer 21:14 and note.

4:12 foes could enter the gates of Jerusalem Referring to the belief that Yahweh would not allow Zion to be taken. A belief grounded in Yahweh's past deliverance of the city, especially from Assyria in 701 BC. See note on Jer 21:2. Compare Ps 48:1–8; Isa 37:36–38.

4:13 of the sins of her prophets Compare La 2:20; Jer 5:31. Judah's religious leaders had led her astray. **blood of the righteous** Shedding innocent blood was one of the indictments against Judah's leaders highlighted by Jeremiah. See note on Jer 26:15.

4:15 "Go away! You are unclean!" people cry to them Treating the leaders as if they were lepers. See Lev 13:45.

4:16 The LORD The attention of Yahweh turned toward them in disapproval and judgment (see Lev 26:17; Ps 34:16).

4:17 a nation that could not save In rebelling against Babylon, Zedekiah had banked heavily on the expectation of Egyptian military aid (see note on Eze 17:7). The army sent by Egypt was ultimately unable to overcome Babylonian power (Jer 34:21–22; 37:5–10). On Zedekiah, see note on Jer 21:1.

4:19 in the desert When the walls of Jerusalem were breached, Zedekiah fled by night. The Babylonians overtook their party on the plains of Jericho, an open wilderness area a few miles east of Jerusalem. See Jer 39:4–5.

4:20 LORD's anointed Referring to Zedekiah the king, who was captured by the Babylonians (2Ki 25:5–6). See La 4:19 and note.

4:21 Edom Judah's neighbor to the southeast, who escaped destruction in 586 BC, probably by allying with

5 Remember, Lord, what has happened to us;
  look, and see our disgrace.
2 Our inheritance has been turned over to
  strangers,
  our homes to foreigners.
3 We have become fatherless,
  our mothers are widows.
4 We must buy the water we drink;
  our wood can be had only at
  a price.
5 Those who pursue us are at our
  heels;
  we are weary and find no rest.
6 We submitted to Egypt and Assyria
  to get enough bread.
7 Our ancestors sinned and are no more,
  and we bear their punishment.
8 Slaves rule over us,
  and there is no one to free us from their
  hands.
9 We get our bread at the risk of our
  lives
  because of the sword in the
  desert.

10 Our skin is hot as an oven,
  feverish from hunger.
11 Women have been violated in Zion,
  and virgins in the towns of Judah.
12 Princes have been hung up by their
  hands;
  elders are shown no respect.
13 Young men toil at the millstones;
  boys stagger under loads of wood.
14 The elders are gone from the city gate;
  the young men have stopped their
  music.
15 Joy is gone from our hearts;
  our dancing has turned to
  mourning.
16 The crown has fallen from our head.
  Woe to us, for we have sinned!
17 Because of this our hearts are faint,
  because of these things our eyes
  grow dim
18 for Mount Zion, which lies
  desolate,
  with jackals prowling over it.

Babylon. See note on Eze 35:5, and note on Jer 25:21. Edom is singled out for judgment because they gloated over Jerusalem's downfall (see Ob 10–12; Ps 137:7; Jer 49:7–22). **the land of Uz** Its parallel mention with Edom in this verse may indicate that Uz was in the vicinity of Edom, southeast of Israel. See note on Jer 25:20. **to you also the cup will be passed** Referring to the cup of Yahweh's wrath, a metaphor developed in Jer 25:15–29 and applied again to Edom in Jer 49:12. See note on Jer 25:15.

4:22 This verse foreshadows future restoration for Zion. While Zion can look forward to restoration, Edom has no future. Compare Isa 40:1–4; note on Isa 40:3.

5:1–22 The final lament is the only one that does not follow the acrostic format (see note on La 1:1). This poem describes the plight of Judah, overrun by invaders and oppressed by her conquerors. The imagery highlights the chaos and anarchy accompanying invasion, where the strong oppress the weak, land and property are seized, women raped and leaders executed or humiliated. The poet acknowledges the sin of the nation's ancestors but protests bearing the punishment (v. 7). The poem ends with a heartfelt plea to Yahweh for restoration but concludes pessimistically, fearing Yahweh has totally rejected Israel (vv. 19–22).

5:1 Remember, Lord, what has happened to us An address typical of a lament (see Ps 89:50).
5:2 Our inheritance The land. See note on Eze 36:12.
5:3 widows Widows and orphans were among the most vulnerable groups in ancient Near Eastern society. Biblical law made special allowances for their care (Dt 24:19–21), and their oppression was symptomatic of a society that had lost sight of God's ethical ideals (Isa 1:23). The losses inflicted on Judah through destruction and exile have reduced the people to a vulnerable state. Compare Isa 9:17 and note.
5:6 Egypt and Assyria Implying the need to seek help

from their former enemies and oppressors. Assyria and Egypt represent the two dominant empires on either side of Syria-Palestine. The empires of Mesopotamia and Egypt frequently clashed over control of the area in between them. Compare Hos 12:1.

5:7 their punishment The Hebrew term here can indicate either the sin or the punishment for it. The sentiment can be read as either an acknowledgment of the principle of transgenerational punishment (see Ex 20:5) or as a protest of that principle (see Eze 18:2; Jer 31:29–30). Yahweh had patiently withheld judgment for generations, waiting for his people to repent. This principle offers justification for bringing judgment, but the generation experiencing the judgment would legitimately wonder why they appeared to be suffering for the sins of others. Two prophets from the time of the exile, Jeremiah and Ezekiel, directly refuted this charge that their generation suffered unjustly. They argued that their contemporaries were suffering from the consequences of their own sins. See note on Eze 18:1–32.
5:8 Slaves rule over us Emphasizing the total upheaval of society (Pr 19:10; 30:21–23; Ecc 10:5–7).
5:12 Princes have been hung up by their hands Likely referring to impaling on a stake after execution, used as a terror tactic and means of public disgrace (1Sa 31:10; 2Sa 21:12). Some upper-class officials were found and executed after the 586 BC destruction of Jerusalem (2Ki 25:19–21). **elders are shown no respect** See La 4:16.
5:13 Young men toil Forced to perform manual labor usually done by slaves (see Ex 11:5; Jdg 16:21).
5:14 elders are gone from the city gate The elders are no longer in charge of local affairs. The contrast of old men and young men in this verse reflects a situation where everyone's usual activities and responsibilities have been disrupted.
5:18 Mount Zion, which lies desolate Referring to the Temple Mount in Jerusalem. **with jackals prowling over it** The temple site is like a deserted ruin, where wild animals prowl. See note on La 4:3.

¹⁹ You, Lᴏʀᴅ, reign forever;
　　your throne endures from generation to
　　generation.
²⁰ Why do you always forget us?
　　Why do you forsake us so long?

²¹ Restore us to yourself, Lᴏʀᴅ, that we may
　　return;
　　renew our days as of old
²² unless you have utterly rejected us
　　and are angry with us beyond measure.

5:19–22 A final appeal to Yahweh, opening with praise and ending with pessimism. The ambivalence of this prayer echoes that of communal laments such as Ps 44, where the speaker alternates from a statement of trust (see Ps 44:1–8) to a dejected pessimism, certain that Yahweh has abandoned them and only cautiously hopeful that the appeal for help will be heard (see Ps 44:9–26).

5:19 You, Lᴏʀᴅ, reign forever Formulaic praise language. Compare Ps 9:7.
5:20 Why do you always forget us Laments often

express the feeling that God has abandoned the person or community, but by continuing to appeal to God, they demonstrate a belief that God is still there and listening. Compare Ps 13:1.
5:21 Restore us to yourself, Lᴏʀᴅ Reminiscent of the refrain in Ps 80 (compare Ps 80:3). The hopeful note sounded by this appeal for restoration is dulled by the pessimism of La 5:22.
5:22 you have utterly rejected us Expressing the fear that has already been acknowledged and answered by 3:31, which asserted that Yahweh's wrath was only temporary. See 3:31 and note.

EZEKIEL

INTRODUCTION TO EZEKIEL

Ezekiel prophesied while living in Babylon. He explained that God's people had experienced Yahweh's judgment—seen in their Babylonian exile—because they had worshiped idols and turned away from Yahweh. Ezekiel sees God's glory depart from Jerusalem but also envisions the hope of its return. There is judgment and mercy throughout the book; there is pain and new life.

BACKGROUND

Since Ezekiel's prophecies were directed not just toward Judah, but also toward nations including Babylon, Egypt and Tyre, many can be linked with historical events and placed on a timeline. Ezekiel was probably a young man when King Josiah reigned and implemented religious reforms (640–609 BC), so while he saw a glimmer of what Judah could be, he would live to see the most tragic of its days.

Ezekiel's prophetic ministry (593–571 BC) took place during the reign of Nebuchadnezzar of the Neo-Babylonian Empire. In 597 BC, Nebuchadnezzar had besieged Jerusalem, plundering the temple and taking more than 10,000 captives to Babylon, including officials, craftsmen and nobles. This deportation included the priest Ezekiel (2Ki 24:10–16; Eze 1:2). Ezekiel lived far from his home country of Judah, which was subservient to Babylon.

A few years after the beginning of Ezekiel's ministry, Judah's King Zedekiah rebelled against Nebuchadnezzar, who retaliated by destroying Jerusalem after two more years of brutal attack (2Ki 25; Jer 39:1–10). By 586 BC, both the city and the temple were in shambles. Some months later, the Jews living in Babylon heard the news (Eze 33:21–22).

The exiled Jews were assimilated into Babylonian life (Dan 1:1–9). Some bought homes (Eze 33:30), and many eventually chose not to return to their homeland, but to remain in Babylon

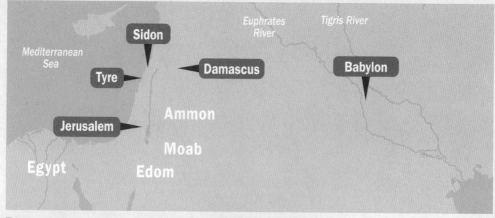

This map depicts some of the major locations mentioned in Ezekiel.

instead (compare Ezr 2:64–65). Ezekiel's last recorded oracle, dated April of 571 BC (Eze 29:17), describes Nebuchadnezzar attacking Egypt after his siege of Tyre.

STRUCTURE

The book of Ezekiel can be divided into four main sections. The first 24 chapters describe the beginning of the prophet's ministry and include his oracles against Judah and Jerusalem. After receiving his first vision (chs. 1–3), Ezekiel prophesies the destruction of Jerusalem by using symbolic actions (chs. 4–7). Other visions reveal the abominations taking place at the temple of Yahweh and the departure of his glory (chs. 8–11). The people's sins against Yahweh led to prophecies of judgment against Jerusalem (chs. 12–24).

In chapters 25–32, Ezekiel prophesies judgment against other nations. Chapters 33–39 focus on the theme of Israel's restoration, including the famous vision of the valley of dry bones coming to life (ch. 37). In the final section (chs. 40–48) the prophet's elaborate vision reveals a new temple that is cleansed so that Yahweh's glory may return.

OUTLINE

- Oracles against Judah and Jerusalem (1:1—24:27)
- Oracles against foreign nations (25:1—32:32)
- Prophecies of restoration (33:1—39:29)
- A restored temple (40:1—48:35)

THEMES

In Ezekiel, we see the large-scale ramifications of disobedience to Yahweh. The people of Judah had turned their backs on God. After abundant pleas and warnings, Yahweh eventually allowed the Babylonians to inflict pain on his people—an act meant to cause the people to acknowledge their sin and turn to Yahweh.

Ezekiel also portrays the gravity of sin and the severity of the judgment that it warranted. In the sins of Judah, we see our own sins reflected—we, too, lose the power of God's presence in our lives when we turn away from him.

Ezekiel also shows the people that restoration and reconciliation can follow judgment; they can return to Yahweh. Once Jerusalem was destroyed, Ezekiel changed his tone from one of warning to one of hope. Yahweh brings resurrection and new life: He can even raise dry bones in a desert and offer them new life, a prophecy the New Testament implicitly connects with the resurrection of the dead that Jesus' own death and resurrection makes possible (ch. 37; Jn 5:25–29; compare Ro 6:1–13; 1Co 15:12–34). Ezekiel's language of a good shepherd—of Yahweh himself seeking his people and strengthening them—is picked up in the New Testament when Jesus says, "I am the good shepherd" (Eze 34:11–16; Jn 10:11).

Ezekiel's Inaugural Vision

1 In my thirtieth year, in the fourth month on the fifth day, while I was among the exiles by the Kebar River, the heavens were opened and I saw visions of God.

²On the fifth of the month — it was the fifth year of the exile of King Jehoiachin — ³the word of the LORD came to Ezekiel the priest, the son of Buzi, by the Kebar River in the land of the Babylonians.ᵃ There the hand of the LORD was on him.

⁴I looked, and I saw a windstorm coming out of the north — an immense cloud with flashing lightning and surrounded by brilliant light. The center of the fire looked like glowing metal, ⁵and in the fire was what looked like four living crea-

ᵃ 3 Or *Chaldeans*

1:1–3 The book of Ezekiel begins with a series of chronological and geographical statements identifying the time and place of Ezekiel's ministry (during the exile in Babylon in the early sixth century BC). Ezekiel is more meticulous than most of the prophets in attaching a particular date to his oracles. See the timeline "Approximate Dates of Old Testament Prophets" on p. 1070.

1:1 thirtieth year Date phrases usually originate from important events, such as the reference to the fifth year of Jehoiachin's exile in Eze 1:2. Since Ezekiel was a priest, the most likely explanation for the year reference is his thirtieth year of age, the time when a priest began official service in the temple (see Nu 4:30). **fourth month on the fifth day** The fourth month corresponds to late June and early July in the modern calendar. The year is the fifth year from King Jehoiachin's exile, or 593 BC (Eze 1:2). Biblical dates are typically calculated using a lunisolar calendar based on a combination of the movements of the sun and moon, the most common calendar in the ancient Near East and Mediterranean. The month begins with the new moon and lasts 29 or 30 days. After the Babylonian exile, the Jews adopted the Babylonian names for the months; the fourth month was known as Tammuz. See the timeline "Dates in Ezekiel" on p. 1276; see the table "Israelite Calendar" on p. 763. **Kebar River** Ezekiel lived in a Jewish settlement near Nippur, east of Babylon. The Kebar (also rendered "Chebar") was an aqueduct that diverted water from the Euphrates River through the city of Nippur. Two Babylonian tablets containing the name "Chebar canal" were unearthed in Nippur, establishing Ezekiel's settlement in the vicinity. **the heavens were opened** A common phrase in NT visionary texts, which were heavily influenced by Ezekiel's visions (see Mt 3:16; Jn 1:51; Ac 7:56; 10:11; Rev 19:11).

1:2 fifth year of the exile Nebuchadnezzar, the crown prince of Babylon, took Jehoiachin and the leading officials of Judah into exile in 597 BC (see 2Ki 24:10–16). This vision would have occurred in 593 BC, prior to Nebuchadnezzar's destruction of Jerusalem and the temple in 586 BC. Jehoiachin's father, Jehoiakim, was made a vassal of Babylon in 605 BC. He revolted against Babylon in 601 BC (see 2Ki 24:1), resulting in another Babylonian invasion in 598 BC. Jehoiakim died at the beginning of this invasion, and Jehoiachin (also called Jeconiah or Coniah) reigned for three months before surrendering to Nebuchadnezzar (2Ki 24:8,12). Jehoiachin was taken into exile and his uncle, Zedekiah, was named regent prince in Jerusalem. Administrative documents show that Babylon considered Jehoiachin to be Judah's rightful king — even while Zedekiah ruled. Ezekiel dates most of his oracles from Jehoiachin's exile, and he never uses the title *melekh* ("king") for Zedekiah.

1:3 the word of the LORD See note on Isa 1:10. **Ezekiel the priest, the son of Buzi** Like Jeremiah, Ezekiel is among the priestly elite. His prophecies share many of

a priest's typical concerns, such as purity and holiness. **the land of the Babylonians** The Hebrew text uses "Babylonians" and "Chaldeans" interchangeably. See note on Isa 43:14. **the hand of the LORD** Symbolizes a physical manifestation of his power and presence. Yahweh's hand comes on the prophet Elijah giving him physical power to outrun King Ahab's chariot in 1Ki 18:46. The phrase also describes the power of prophecy coming on the prophet Elisha in 2Ki 3:15. Ezekiel experiences the power of Yahweh's hand (see Eze 2:2,9; 3:14; 8:3).

1:4–28 Unlike Isaiah, who seems to have encountered Yahweh in the Jerusalem temple (see Isa 6), Ezekiel is visited in Babylon by Yahweh's chariot-throne. His description of the throne, heavenly beings and the wheels transporting it likely reflects his own limited ability to describe what he saw; thus he uses metaphors and analogies.

1:4 a windstorm coming out of the north A divine appearance or theophany was characterized by storm, wind, thunder, cloud, lightning and earthquake imagery (compare Job 38:1). The description of storm wind from the north is most likely an intentional allusion to Semitic storm-god imagery. The Semitic god, Hadad, was associated with both life-giving rains and the destructive power of storms, especially through strong winds and lightning. In the Ugaritic texts, Hadad was another name for Baal. Biblical writers never refer to Hadad, but they regularly reference the Canaanite god, Baal. See the table "Old Testament Theophanies" on p. 924. **glowing metal** Ezekiel is the only author to use the Hebrew word here, *chashmal*. While the precise meaning of the word is obscure, context and etymology suggest it was a bright yellow substance, probably amber.

1:5 what looked like The Hebrew word used here, *demuth* (which may be translated "likeness"), occurs 25 times in the OT — 16 times in Ezekiel alone. Ezekiel uses this word 10 times in Eze 1 and 4 times in ch. 10 to describe the living beings and the divine chariot. *Demuth* denotes a simple comparison, and Ezekiel uses it to distance himself as he describes the indescribable divine manifestation. A distinctive meaning of *demuth* is to describe a model, representation, form or image of something. For example, King Ahaz sends a *demuth* of the altar he sees in Damascus to the Jerusalem temple for the priest, Uriah (also rendered "Urijah"), to use in constructing a full-sized version (2Ki 16:10). The word is also used to describe the impossibility of finding a deity to compare to Yahweh (Isa 40:18). **four living creatures** Ezekiel uses the nondescript Hebrew word *chayyah* for a living being here rather than a more specific term for heavenly beings such as *keruvim* ("cherubim"; see Ge 3:24 and note) or *seraphim* (see Isa 6:2 and note). The term emphasizes that Ezekiel is uncertain as to what he's seeing, since *chayyah* most simply means "animate being." Ezekiel's second encounter with the

tures. In appearance their form was human, ⁶but each of them had four faces and four wings. ⁷Their legs were straight; their feet were like those of a calf and gleamed like burnished bronze. ⁸Under their wings on their four sides they had human hands. All four of them had faces and wings, ⁹and the wings of one touched the wings of another. Each one went straight ahead; they did not turn as they moved.

¹⁰Their faces looked like this: Each of the four had the face of a human being, and on the right side each had the face of a lion, and on the left the face of an ox; each also had the face of an eagle. ¹¹Such were their faces. They each had two wings spreading out upward, each wing touching that of the creature on either side; and each had two other wings covering its body. ¹²Each one went straight ahead. Wherever the spirit would go, they would go, without turning as they went. ¹³The appearance of the living creatures was like burning coals of fire or like torches. Fire moved back and forth among the creatures; it was bright, and lightning flashed out of it. ¹⁴The creatures sped back and forth like flashes of lightning.

¹⁵As I looked at the living creatures, I saw a wheel on the ground beside each creature with its four faces. ¹⁶This was the appearance and structure of the wheels: They sparkled like topaz, and all four looked alike. Each appeared to be made like a wheel intersecting a wheel. ¹⁷As they moved, they would go in any one of the four directions the creatures faced; the wheels did not change direction as the creatures went. ¹⁸Their rims were high and awesome, and all four rims were full of eyes all around.

¹⁹When the living creatures moved, the wheels beside them moved; and when the living creatures rose from the ground, the wheels also rose. ²⁰Wherever the spirit would go, they would go, and the wheels would rise along with them, because the spirit of the living creatures was in the wheels. ²¹When the creatures moved, they also moved; when the creatures stood still, they also stood still; and when the creatures rose from the ground, the wheels rose along with them, because the spirit of the living creatures was in the wheels.

²²Spread out above the heads of the living creatures was what looked something like a vault, sparkling like crystal, and awesome. ²³Under the vault their wings were stretched out one toward the other, and each had two wings covering its body. ²⁴When the creatures moved, I heard the

---

divine chariot in Eze 10 specifically refers to the beings as cherubim, fitting with imagery of Yahweh riding a cherub in Ps 18:10. Ezekiel's depiction resembles the apostle John's vision in Rev 4:6–8, which describes four living creatures surrounding the throne. Statues of composite creatures guarding throne rooms have been found in excavations of Assyrian cities such as Nineveh and Nimrud. They often had human heads on the bodies of lions or bulls. Similar figures have been found in Syro-Phoenician and Persian art with eagle's heads, wings or bull's legs. Ezekiel's creatures are winged with bovine legs and four faces—human, lion, ox and eagle (see Eze 1:9–10).

1:7 burnished bronze Compare to the description of the Son of God with feet of burnished bronze in Rev 1:15 and 2:18. Apocalyptic imagery in the books of Daniel and Revelation strongly echoes Ezekiel's depictions.

1:9 wings of one touched the wings of another See 1Ki 6:27. See the infographic "Solomon's Temple" on p. 560.

1:12 spirit The Hebrew word used here, *ruach,* seems to refer to an external spirit or force directing the movements of the living creatures. The word often refers to the Spirit of God and may refer to the empowering of the Holy Spirit, as in Eze 3:12.

1:13 appearance The Hebrew word used here, *mar'eh,* occurs seven times in this vision. The word denotes outward appearance but can also connote a pattern or image (Nu 8:4). Here, the term parallels Ezekiel's careful phrasing in Eze 1:26, showing an intentional avoidance of concrete descriptions (see note on v. 5).

1:16 the wheels Ezekiel uses ambiguous language in describing the wheels (called *ophanim* in Hebrew) just as he did in depicting the living creatures. The Hebrew word *ophan* is a term for a typical chariot wheel (see Ex 14:25). Compare Daniel's description of the divine chariot

throne in Da 7:9. **They sparkled like topaz** The wheels shine like a precious stone (called *tarshish* in Hebrew), but the precise identification of the stone is uncertain. Beryl, golden topaz, yellow jasper and chrysolite are possible suggestions. The same word is used to describe a heavenly being in Da 10:6. **a wheel intersecting a wheel** This phrase could refer to concentric circles (i.e., the hub to which the spokes attach in an ordinary wheel), but Ezekiel's careful description seems to defy such a simple explanation. Another possibility is a gyroscope-like apparatus with wheels at right angles to one another. The latter option provides the possibility of multidirectional travel without turning.

1:18 full of eyes all around The eyes may be metaphors for lights or precious stones covering the wheels, or they may indicate literal eyes, suggesting the wheels themselves were living creatures. Compare John's vision in Rev 4:6–8, where he describes the living creatures covered in eyes (see note on Rev 4:7).

1:20 the spirit See note on Eze 1:12. **the spirit of the living creatures** The spirit was in the wheels (i.e., an animating force). The Hebrew uses the singular *chayyah* ("living thing"), just as wind or breath is the animating force in the creation of Adam (see Ge 2:7).

1:22 a vault The Hebrew term used here is the same term used for the dome of the sky in Ge 1:6. This is an appropriate connection given that the expanse divided heaven and earth, with Yahweh dwelling above the expanse (see note on Ge 1:6–10). **sparkling like** Ezekiel continues to use ambiguous language (see note on Eze 1:5). **crystal** Compare John's vision in Rev 4:6 of a solid crystal surface before the divine throne.

1:24 roar of rushing waters A roaring sound like rushing water accompanies Yahweh's arrival (see Eze 43:2). Compare the coming of the Son of Man in Rev 1:15. **Almighty** The Hebrew word used here, *shadday*, is a

sound of their wings, like the roar of rushing waters, like the voice of the Almighty,[a] like the tumult of an army. When they stood still, they lowered their wings.

[25] Then there came a voice from above the vault over their heads as they stood with lowered wings. [26] Above the vault over their heads was what looked like a throne of lapis lazuli, and

[a] 24 Hebrew *Shaddai*

common name for God (often rendered "Shaddai") used most frequently in the books of Genesis (see Ge 17:1 and note) and Job (see Job 6:4). Ezekiel uses it only here and in the parallel passage in Eze 10:5 to describe the sound of the divine chariot. The precise origin and etymology of *shadday* is unclear. English renderings as "Almighty" are likely derived from the use of Greek word *pantokratōr*, meaning "almighty," to represent *shadday* in the Greek Septuagint. The Latin Vulgate uses *omnipotens*, meaning

"almighty," for *shadday*. The Greek translator may have understood the Hebrew word to be related to the verb *shadad*, which means "to destroy violently." Shaddai as a deity's name probably means "he of the Mountain," based on the Akkadian word *šadû*, meaning "mountain." The name is used for deities in Ugaritic, Phoenician and Egyptian sources.

1:26 was what looked like a throne See note on v. 5.
what looked like a throne of lapis lazuli See note on

Dates in Ezekiel

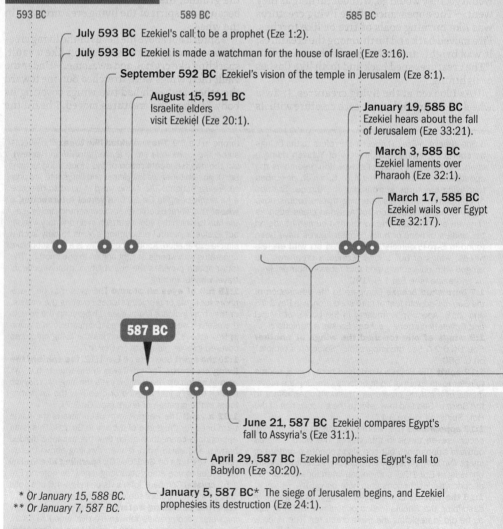

593 BC   589 BC   585 BC

July 593 BC Ezekiel's call to be a prophet (Eze 1:2).

July 593 BC Ezekiel is made a watchman for the house of Israel (Eze 3:16).

September 592 BC Ezekiel's vision of the temple in Jerusalem (Eze 8:1).

August 15, 591 BC
Israelite elders
visit Ezekiel (Eze 20:1).

January 19, 585 BC
Ezekiel hears about the fall
of Jerusalem (Eze 33:21).

March 3, 585 BC
Ezekiel laments over
Pharaoh (Eze 32:1).

March 17, 585 BC
Ezekiel wails over Egypt
(Eze 32:17).

587 BC

June 21, 587 BC Ezekiel compares Egypt's
fall to Assyria's (Eze 31:1).

April 29, 587 BC Ezekiel prophesies Egypt's fall to
Babylon (Eze 30:20).

* Or January 15, 588 BC.
** Or January 7, 587 BC.

January 5, 587 BC* The siege of Jerusalem begins, and Ezekiel
prophesies its destruction (Eze 24:1).

593 BC   589 BC   585 BC

high above on the throne was a figure like that of a man. ²⁷I saw that from what appeared to be his waist up he looked like glowing metal, as if full of fire, and that from there down he looked like fire; and brilliant light surrounded him. ²⁸Like the appearance of a rainbow in the clouds on a rainy day, so was the radiance around him.

This was the appearance of the likeness of the glory of the LORD. When I saw it, I fell facedown, and I heard the voice of one speaking.

v. 13. The descriptive Hebrew word used here, *sappir*, indicates sapphire stone or lapis lazuli, a bright blue semiprecious stone that was highly prized in the ancient world. Compare the sapphire pavement under God's feet in Ex 24:10. **a figure like that of a man** Ezekiel sees a figure that resembles a person, but he avoids saying that he sees a human being by using terms that convey likeness (see note on Eze 1:5) and appearance (see note on v. 13) in his descriptions.

1:27 what appeared to be his waist Ezekiel believes he sees the figure of a man with a waist, but he avoids stating so with certainty. Previous appearances of Yahweh in human form have been more subtle, such as his appearance to Abraham in Ge 18:1. Here, Yahweh's human-like form is obscured by the brightness of his glory. **1:28 appearance of a rainbow** Compare Rev 4:3. **likeness of the glory of the LORD** Ezekiel acknowledges that he's been describing a vision of Yahweh in his glory

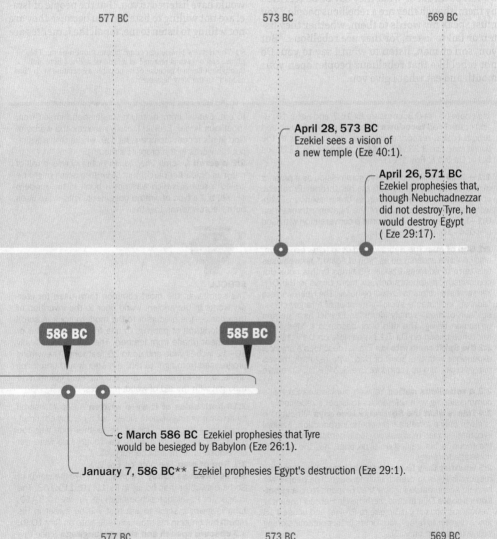

577 BC   573 BC   569 BC

April 28, 573 BC
Ezekiel sees a vision of a new temple (Eze 40:1).

April 26, 571 BC
Ezekiel prophesies that, though Nebuchadnezzar did not destroy Tyre, he would destroy Egypt (Eze 29:17).

586 BC

585 BC

c March 586 BC Ezekiel prophesies that Tyre would be besieged by Babylon (Eze 26:1).

January 7, 586 BC** Ezekiel prophesies Egypt's destruction (Eze 29:1).

Ezekiel's Call to Be a Prophet

2 He said to me, "Son of man,[a] stand up on your feet and I will speak to you." [2]As he spoke, the Spirit came into me and raised me to my feet, and I heard him speaking to me.

[3]He said: "Son of man, I am sending you to the Israelites, to a rebellious nation that has rebelled against me; they and their ancestors have been in revolt against me to this very day. [4]The people to whom I am sending you are obstinate and stubborn. Say to them, 'This is what the Sovereign Lord says.' [5]And whether they listen or fail to listen — for they are a rebellious people — they will know that a prophet has been among them. [6]And you, son of man, do not be afraid of them or their words. Do not be afraid, though briers and thorns are all around you and you live among scorpions. Do not be afraid of what they say or be terrified by them, though they are a rebellious people. [7]You must speak my words to them, whether they listen or fail to listen, for they are rebellious. [8]But you, son of man, listen to what I say to you. Do not rebel like that rebellious people; open your mouth and eat what I give you."

[9]Then I looked, and I saw a hand stretched out to me. In it was a scroll, [10]which he unrolled before me. On both sides of it were written words of lament and mourning and woe.

3 And he said to me, "Son of man, eat what is before you, eat this scroll; then go and speak to the people of Israel." [2]So I opened my mouth, and he gave me the scroll to eat.

[3]Then he said to me, "Son of man, eat this scroll I am giving you and fill your stomach with it." So I ate it, and it tasted as sweet as honey in my mouth.

[4]He then said to me: "Son of man, go now to the people of Israel and speak my words to them. [5]You are not being sent to a people of obscure speech and strange language, but to the people of Israel — [6]not to many peoples of obscure speech and strange language, whose words you cannot understand. Surely if I had sent you to them, they would have listened to you. [7]But the people of Israel are not willing to listen to you because they are not willing to listen to me, for all the Israelites are

[a] 1 The Hebrew phrase *ben adam* means *human being*. The phrase *son of man* is retained as a form of address here and throughout Ezekiel because of its possible association with "Son of Man" in the New Testament.

(see note on Isa 6:3; compare Ex 16:7 and note; 16:10 and note). **I fell facedown** He acts out of reverence and fear, a typical response in human encounters with the divine (see Eze 3:23; 43:3; 44:4; compare Ge 17:3; Jos 5:14; Da 8:17; Rev 1:17).

2:1—3:15 Ezekiel receives his commission as a prophet in the presence of Yahweh on his throne. Prophetic commissions always happen in the presence of Yahweh: Isaiah sees a vision of the heavenly throne (Isa 6:1–11), and Jeremiah records a conversation with God (Jer 1:4–10; compare Ex 4).

2:1 Son of man The Hebrew word used here, *ben-adam*, also could be understood as "son of Adam." Yahweh uses this term to address Ezekiel 93 times in this book (for comparison, it appears only six more times in the OT). Yahweh never refers to Ezekiel by name. The Hebrew idiom "son of" indicates a specific member of a larger class, so "son of man" simply identifies Ezekiel as a person or human being. The title later becomes a Messianic reference based on Da 7:13 (see note on Da 7:13).

2:2 the Spirit came into me Ezekiel describes a physical experience with the Spirit of God, who regularly moves him or picks him up (compare Eze 3:24; 8:3). Compare note on 1:3.

2:3 a rebellious nation Yahweh punctuates Ezekiel's commissioning with references to Israel's rebellion.

2:4 This is what the Sovereign Lord says Although he is given only a formulaic prophetic introduction, Ezekiel is commissioned to speak on God's behalf. At this point, the focus is his calling as a prophet, not the specific message to Israel.

2:5 whether they listen or fail to listen The prophet's responsibility is to preach the message. The people will be held accountable for how they respond to it. **a rebellious people** This phrase, *beth meri* in Hebrew (meaning "rebellious house"), is unique to Ezekiel and is used 15 times to refer to Israel, four times in this commissioning scene (see note on v. 3).

2:8 eat what I give you By obeying Yahweh's command

to eat, Ezekiel immediately distinguishes himself from rebellious Israel. Ezekiel literally receives the words of God in his mouth (compare Jer 1:9, where God says he put his words in the prophet's mouth).

2:9 a scroll A scroll (*megillah* in Hebrew) was a roll of papyrus or leather parchment. A written scroll might be called a *sepher*, which was not a book in the modern sense, but a type of written document. This verse uses both Hebrew terms together.

SCROLL

The scroll was the most common form used for literary works in the ancient world prior to the invention of the codex—the precursor to the modern book. A scroll was a long roll of papyrus (made from reed plants) or parchment (made from leather). The rolls were usually 10–12 inches wide and up to 35 feet long. The writing progressed from right to left; a reader would unroll columns to the left and roll up the completed columns to the right with the aid of wooden rollers.

2:10 both sides of it were written A papyrus scroll could have writing on both sides, but a parchment scroll could not—the hairy side of the leather hide was too rough. Techniques to smooth the rough side were not developed until the first century AD.

3:1 Son of man See note on Eze 2:1.

3:3 as sweet as honey The psalmist says the words of God are sweeter than honey in Ps 19:10; 119:103. The imagery of Revelation echoes Ezekiel. In Rev 10:9–10, John is given a scroll to eat that will be sweet in his mouth but bitter in his stomach (see note on Rev 10:9).

3:5 obscure speech and strange language Since this phrase refers to languages that Ezekiel does not know,

hardened and obstinate. ⁸But I will make you as unyielding and hardened as they are. ⁹I will make your forehead like the hardest stone, harder than flint. Do not be afraid of them or terrified by them, though they are a rebellious people."

¹⁰And he said to me, "Son of man, listen carefully and take to heart all the words I speak to you. ¹¹Go now to your people in exile and speak to them. Say to them, 'This is what the Sovereign Lord says,' whether they listen or fail to listen."

¹²Then the Spirit lifted me up, and I heard behind me a loud rumbling sound as the glory of the Lord rose from the place where it was standing.ᵃ ¹³It was the sound of the wings of the living creatures brushing against each other and the sound of the wheels beside them, a loud rumbling sound. ¹⁴The Spirit then lifted me up and took me away, and I went in bitterness and in the anger of my spirit, with the strong hand of the Lord on me. ¹⁵I came to the exiles who lived at Tel Aviv near the Kebar River. And there, where they were living, I sat among them for seven days — deeply distressed.

Ezekiel's Task as Watchman

¹⁶At the end of seven days the word of the Lord came to me: ¹⁷"Son of man, I have made you a watchman for the people of Israel; so hear the word I speak and give them warning from me. ¹⁸When I say to a wicked person, 'You will surely die,' and you do not warn them or speak out to dissuade them from their evil ways in order to save their life, that wicked person will die forᵇ their sin, and I will hold you accountable for their blood. ¹⁹But if you do warn the wicked person and they do not turn from their wickedness or from their evil ways, they will die for their sin; but you will have saved yourself.

²⁰"Again, when a righteous person turns from their righteousness and does evil, and I put a stumbling block before them, they will die. Since you did not warn them, they will die for their sin. The righteous things that person did will not be remembered, and I will hold you accountable for their blood. ²¹But if you do warn the righteous person not to sin and they do not sin, they will surely live because they took warning, and you will have saved yourself."

²²The hand of the Lord was on me there, and he said to me, "Get up and go out to the plain, and there I will speak to you." ²³So I got up and went out to the plain. And the glory of the Lord was standing there, like the glory I had seen by the Kebar River, and I fell facedown.

ᵃ 12 Probable reading of the original Hebrew text; Masoretic Text *sound — may the glory of the Lord be praised from his place*
ᵇ 18 Or *in*; also in verses 19 and 20

---

it emphasizes his commission as a prophet to Israel in exile, not to the people of Babylon.
3:6 they would have listened to you Compare the success of Jonah's preaching to Nineveh in Jnh 3:4–5.
3:8 I will make you as unyielding Compare Jer 1:18–19. Yahweh promises Ezekiel a divine strength in proclaiming the message that is equal to Israel's stubborn resistance.
3:11 Go now to your people in exile Ezekiel's ministry is specifically intended for the Jews exiled in Babylon. His message addresses their crisis of faith after exile and helps explain Yahweh's judgment of idolatry.
3:12 Then the Spirit lifted me up See note on Eze 2:2.
a loud rumbling sound See note on 1:4.
3:14 in bitterness and in the anger of my spirit Ezekiel is likely describing his excitement following an intense spiritual encounter, not a bitter anger. In Hebrew, heat is associated with a highly emotional state—hot with excitement, hot with anger. Likewise, the Hebrew word for "bitterness" carries the sense of emotional agony. It seems that through his experience of the Spirit of Yahweh, Ezekiel is overcome by emotion or altered consciousness. The early prophets would prophesy while in this state (see 1Sa 10:5–12; 19:20–24). **the strong hand of the Lord** Represents a physical manifestation of God's power and presence. See note on Eze 1:3.
3:15 Tel Aviv The settlement of Jewish exiles where Ezekiel lived. It was apparently located near Nippur on the Kebar River (also rendered "Chebar canal"). The name is modified from its Babylonian name meaning "mound produced by a great flood." It likely refers to the abandoned mound of an ancient city where the Babylonians settled the Jewish deportees. It is the only mention of the place name in the Biblical text. **Kebar River** Located in Babylon. See note on 1:1. **seven days** The priestly ordination ritual in Lev 8:33 required a specific length of time. Leviticus

specifies seven days as the period for ritual purity. Elsewhere in the OT, it reflects time allotted for mourning (Ge 50:10; 1Sa 31:13). Job sits for seven days and nights after the tragic loss of family and property in Job 2:13.

3:16–27 Ezekiel receives his first specific instructions for his role as prophet. This passage and its parallel passage in Eze 33:1–20 form literary bookends (called an inclusio) around Ezekiel's prophecies prior to the account of Jerusalem's fall (33:21).
3:16 the word of the Lord came to me The prophet's standard introduction to his prophecies. While not unique to Ezekiel, the phrase is distinctive of his style.
3:17 watchman The Hebrew word used here, *tsopheh,* refers to a lookout or sentry whose job was to warn the settlement of coming danger. The image illustrates the prophet's role to remind the people of God's impending judgment if they fail to repent. The metaphor appears in Hos 9:8; Jer 6:17; and Isa 56:10, depicting the false prophets of Israel as blind watchmen. Ezekiel's use of the image implies a more concrete role for his ministry.
3:18 dissuade them from their evil ways Ezekiel's responsibility ends with providing the warning. He is given the same obligation to warn the wicked to repent and the righteous not to stray into wickedness. **wicked person will die for their sin** The consequences for sin are the same whether a person has lived a wicked life or a righteous life (see Eze 3:20; compare Ro 6:23). **I will hold you accountable for their blood** Ezekiel will face consequences if he fails to carry out his duties. Based on similar phrasing in 2Sa 4:11 and Ge 9:5–6, it appears Ezekiel's punishment will also be death. If his failure to warn is equated with murder, then Biblical law would require the death penalty (see Ex 21:12; Lev 24:17; Nu 35:31–33).
3:20 I put a stumbling block before them The sequence of events is the focus here. Yahweh lays the stumbling

²⁴Then the Spirit came into me and raised me to my feet. He spoke to me and said: "Go, shut yourself inside your house. ²⁵And you, son of man, they will tie with ropes; you will be bound so that you cannot go out among the people. ²⁶I will make your tongue stick to the roof of your mouth so that you will be silent and unable to rebuke them, for they are a rebellious people. ²⁷But when I speak to you, I will open your mouth and you shall say to them, 'This is what the Sovereign Lord says.' Whoever will listen let them listen, and whoever will refuse let them refuse; for they are a rebellious people.

Siege of Jerusalem Symbolized

4 "Now, son of man, take a block of clay, put it in front of you and draw the city of Jerusalem on it. ²Then lay siege to it: Erect siege works against it, build a ramp up to it, set up camps against it and put battering rams around it. ³Then take an iron pan, place it as an iron wall between you and the city and turn your face toward it. It will be under siege, and you shall besiege it. This will be a sign to the people of Israel.

⁴"Then lie on your left side and put the sin of the people of Israel upon yourself.ᵃ You are to bear their sin for the number of days you lie on your side. ⁵I have assigned you the same number of days as the years of their sin. So for 390 days you will bear the sin of the people of Israel.

⁶"After you have finished this, lie down again, this time on your right side, and bear the sin of the people of Judah. I have assigned you 40 days, a day for each year. ⁷Turn your face toward the siege of Jerusalem and with bared arm prophesy

ᵃ 4 Or upon your side

block only after the righteous person has already turned to injustice. The idea here is that a figurative obstacle blocks the path of a rebellious person. It symbolizes the judgment of God, but stumbling blocks are not always placed by God. They can be something that tempts a person to sin, such as gold or silver in Eze 7:19. The idols Israel worshiped are called stumbling blocks in 14:3–4; they led Israel away from Yahweh and into sin. Jeremiah uses the same imagery of God's judgment (Jer 6:21) when Israel failed to heed the watchmen's warning (Jer 6:17; compare Eze 3:17). The NT presents the concept of the stumbling block as something that causes a person to sin (1Co 8:9; Ro 11:9). **3:22 hand of the Lord was on me** See Eze 1:3 and note. **the plain** The Hebrew term here almost always indicates a broad, smooth plain in a valley, not a narrow, mountainous valley. This reference is to the river valley of southern Mesopotamia.
3:23 I had seen by the Kebar River Ezekiel's initial vision and commissioning ends as it started: with a vision of the glory of Yahweh, described in detail in 1:1—2:2. On the Kebar River (also rendered "Chebar canal"), see note on 1:1.
3:24 Then the Spirit came into me See 2:2 and note. The sequence of events is identical to the earlier vision.
3:26 you will be silent In the ancient world, paralysis and muteness were common symptoms of being overcome by a supernatural power. It is unclear how long Ezekiel is mute. The next reference to his muteness is 24:27, where he learns he will regain his speech when the messenger arrives with news of Jerusalem falling. That event does not occur until 33:21–22. If Ezekiel is mute from his initial vision until the fall of Jerusalem, he would have been silent nearly seven years. Ezekiel's inability to speak may be compared to the reaction of Daniel in Da 10:15 and the divinely imposed muteness of Zechariah in Lk 1:20.

4:1–17 Ezekiel enacts a symbolic siege of Jerusalem. Prophetic sign-acts are powerful visual representations of God's message. See the table "Symbolic Actions of the Prophets" on p. 1195.
4:1 take a block of clay It is probably engraved with a city plan to symbolize a city under siege. **son of man** See note on Eze 2:1. **city of Jerusalem** Ezekiel's drama illustrates the siege predicted against Jerusalem. The scene's climax reveals that Jerusalem is under siege in v. 7; the delayed identification makes the image more

powerful. People observing the prophet may have hoped his actions represented a siege of Babylon, the overthrow of their oppressors.

SYMBOLIC ACTIONS OF EZEKIEL	REFERENCE
Acts out the siege and destruction of Jerusalem	Eze 4:1—5:17
Acts out the exile	Eze 12:1–20
Does not mourn his wife	Eze 24:15–27
Uses sticks to symbolize the reunification of Israel	Eze 37:15–28

4:2 lay siege to it Literally fulfilled in 2Ki 25:1. Compare Yahweh's declaration that he will place siege works around Jerusalem in Isa 29:3. Ezekiel's role in this drama is to represent Yahweh, the ultimate orchestrator. **build a ramp up** The Hebrew wording specifically indicates a siege ramp. An attacking army would construct a large earthen ramp to bridge the dry moat surrounding fortified cities. The structure would provide access to the city wall for the battering rams. The Assyrians and Babylonians left behind well-documented accounts of siege methods involving towers, ramps and battering rams.
4:3 an iron pan This type of dish had a specific priestly use for preparing grain offerings (Lev 2:5). **as an iron wall** Represents the barrier Israel's sin has raised between them and Yahweh. **turn your face toward it** Ezekiel is acting out Yahweh's promise from Lev 26:17 to set his face against (to act against) Israel if they disobey his laws (see note on Eze 4:2). **sign** The prophet's symbolic actions provide a tangible reminder for Israel of his prophetic prediction (compare 12:6; Isa 8:18; 20:3–6).
4:4 You are to bear their sin Used with the Hebrew verb *nasa*, meaning "bear," the noun *awon* usually carries the sense of "sin" or "iniquity" (e.g., Lev 10:17). The image of the prophet bearing the punishment deserved by the people prefigures the NT representation of Christ bearing the sin of all people (see 1Pe 2:24; compare Isa 53:12).
4:5 the years of their sin Ezekiel spends 390 days bound and lying on his left side. This second phase of the sign-act represents the prophet bearing the punishment of Israel. The significance of 390 years is unclear.
4:6 again Ezekiel will repeat the action but on his other side to symbolize the punishment of Judah. **40 days** An allusion to Nu 14:34, where, after spying out the land of Canaan for 40 days, Israel is punished with 40 years of

against her. ⁸I will tie you up with ropes so that you cannot turn from one side to the other until you have finished the days of your siege.

⁹"Take wheat and barley, beans and lentils, millet and spelt; put them in a storage jar and use them to make bread for yourself. You are to eat it during the 390 days you lie on your side. ¹⁰Weigh out twenty shekels*a* of food to eat each day and eat it at set times. ¹¹Also measure out a sixth of a hin*b* of water and drink it at set times. ¹²Eat the food as you would a loaf of barley bread; bake it in the sight of the people, using human excrement for fuel." ¹³The Lᴏʀᴅ said, "In this way the people of Israel will eat defiled food among the nations where I will drive them."

¹⁴Then I said, "Not so, Sovereign Lᴏʀᴅ! I have never defiled myself. From my youth until now I have never eaten anything found dead or torn by wild animals. No impure meat has ever entered my mouth."

¹⁵"Very well," he said, "I will let you bake your bread over cow dung instead of human excrement."

¹⁶He then said to me: "Son of man, I am about to cut off the food supply in Jerusalem. The people will eat rationed food in anxiety and drink rationed water in despair, ¹⁷for food and water will be scarce. They will be appalled at the sight of each other and will waste away because of*c* their sin.

God's Razor of Judgment

5 "Now, son of man, take a sharp sword and use it as a barber's razor to shave your head and your beard. Then take a set of scales and divide up the hair. ²When the days of your siege come to an end, burn a third of the hair inside the city. Take a third and strike it with the sword all around the city. And scatter a third to the wind. For I will pursue them with drawn sword. ³But take a few hairs and tuck them away in the folds of your garment. ⁴Again, take a few of these and throw them into the fire and burn them up. A fire will spread from there to all Israel.

⁵"This is what the Sovereign Lᴏʀᴅ says: This is Jerusalem, which I have set in the center of the nations, with countries all around her. ⁶Yet in her wickedness she has rebelled against my laws and decrees more than the nations and countries around her. She has rejected my laws and has not followed my decrees.

a 10 That is, about 8 ounces or about 230 grams   *b 11* That is, about 2/3 quart or about 0.6 liter   *c 17* Or *away in*

---

wandering in the wilderness to atone for their unbelief. A year for each day is reversed to a day for each year in Ezekiel's sign-act. If Ezekiel performed the sign-act as described, he would have been lying bound for nearly 14 months. The text provides no insight about how Ezekiel was to perform the sign-act. He might have performed it daily for only a set period of time.

4:7 and with bared arm To symbolize Yahweh's preparation to act in judgment (see Isa 52:10).

4:8 from one side to the other Ezekiel now represents the besieged people. In a city under siege, people lose all freedom of movement.

4:9 wheat and barley These ingredients are typically used for bread, but most of the other ingredients mentioned are unusual. The combination of ingredients suggests that Ezekiel's bread represents a siege bread created from whatever remained from a dwindling food supply.

4:10 Weigh out twenty shekels of food to eat each day The small quantity of food allotted to Ezekiel also mimics siege conditions. His rations of about eight ounces were barely enough to avoid starvation.

4:11 a sixth of a hin As with food, strict water rationing was necessary during a siege.

4:12 human excrement Animal dung was a common fuel for cooking fires in the ancient Near East, as wood was too valuable to use for these purposes. Human dung, however, was considered unclean, and using it would make a person ritually impure (see Dt 23:12–14; see note on Lev 11:1–47).

4:14 I have never defiled myself As a priest, Ezekiel is acutely aware of issues of ritual purity, and he reacts strongly to Yahweh's command to use human dung to bake the bread (see note on Eze 5:11). Peter's objection to obeying God's command to eat unclean animals (Ac 10:14) reflects Ezekiel's reaction here.

4:15 bake your bread over cow dung instead of human excrement Honoring Ezekiel's scruples, Yahweh creates a compromise (see note on Eze 4:14).

4:16 cut off the food supply The Hebrew phrase used here likely reflects Ezekiel's priestly background since one of the only uses of this phrase outside of Ezekiel is in Lev 26:26, also in the context of siege as punishment for disobedience.

5:1–17 Ezekiel performs another sign-act symbolizing the destruction of Jerusalem and the scattering of Judah into exile.

5:1 son of man See note on Eze 2:1. **a sharp sword** A sword in the ancient Near East could range from 18 inches to 3 feet long, much larger than the shorter blade typically used for shaving. The sword underscores the symbolism of judgment by military defeat. **barber's razor** Shaving was not a typical practice among the Israelites and was a sign of mourning (Jer 7:29) or purification (Nu 8:7; Lev 14:9). Forced shaving of the hair and beard was a means of humiliating one's enemies (see Isa 7:20 and note). **a set of scales** This act has parallels in Babylonian magical texts where hair was to be weighed on scales.

5:2 burn a third of the hair Division into thirds is imagery used for destruction or salvation in Zec 13:8–9. The symbolic actions mimic the retributions promised for iniquity and rebellion in the book of Leviticus. Burning is the punishment prescribed for certain sexual offenses in Lev 20:14 and 21:9. **strike it with the sword** Destruction by sword is promised in Lev 26:25. **scatter a third to the wind** Punishment by scattering is promised in Lev 26:33. **I will pursue them with drawn sword** Echoes Lev 26:33, where Yahweh warned Israel that he would scatter them and unsheathe the sword after them if they disobeyed.

5:3 a few hairs A small amount of hair is kept back, representing preservation of a remnant. See note on Isa 1:9.

5:6 in her wickedness she has rebelled against my laws and decrees more than the nations Ezekiel typically presents Israel as more rebellious and wicked than Gentile nations (see Eze 16:47–48). The rationale for

7"Therefore this is what the Sovereign LORD says: You have been more unruly than the nations around you and have not followed my decrees or kept my laws. You have not even[a] conformed to the standards of the nations around you.

8"Therefore this is what the Sovereign LORD says: I myself am against you, Jerusalem, and I will inflict punishment on you in the sight of the nations. 9Because of all your detestable idols, I will do to you what I have never done before and will never do again. 10Therefore in your midst parents will eat their children, and children will eat their parents. I will inflict punishment on you and will scatter all your survivors to the winds. 11Therefore as surely as I live, declares the Sovereign LORD, because you have defiled my sanctuary with all your vile images and detestable practices, I myself will shave you; I will not look on you with pity or spare you. 12A third of your people will die of the plague or perish by famine inside you; a third will fall by the sword outside your walls; and a third I will scatter to the winds and pursue with drawn sword.

13"Then my anger will cease and my wrath against them will subside, and I will be avenged. And when I have spent my wrath on them, they will know that I the LORD have spoken in my zeal.

14"I will make you a ruin and a reproach among the nations around you, in the sight of all who pass by. 15You will be a reproach and a taunt, a warning and an object of horror to the nations around you when I inflict punishment on you in anger and in wrath and with stinging rebuke. I the LORD have spoken. 16When I shoot at you with my deadly and destructive arrows of famine, I will shoot to destroy you. I will bring more and more famine upon you and cut off your supply of food. 17I will send famine and wild beasts against you, and they will leave you childless. Plague and bloodshed will sweep through you, and I will bring the sword against you. I the LORD have spoken."

Doom for the Mountains of Israel

6 The word of the LORD came to me: 2"Son of man, set your face against the mountains of Israel; prophesy against them 3and say: 'You mountains of Israel, hear the word of the Sovereign LORD. This is what the Sovereign LORD says to the mountains and hills, to the ravines and valleys: I am about to bring a sword against you, and I will destroy your high places. 4Your altars will be demolished and your incense altars will be smashed; and I will slay your people in front of your idols. 5I will lay the dead bodies of the Israelites in front of their idols, and I will scatter your bones around your altars. 6Wherever you live, the towns will be laid waste and the high places demolished, so that your altars will be laid waste and devastated, your idols smashed and ruined,

[a] 7 Most Hebrew manuscripts; some Hebrew manuscripts and Syriac *You have*

this comparison is likely based on Israel's accountability to Yahweh because of the covenant.

5:9 your detestable idols The Hebrew term refers to anything that might be found culturally or socially offensive (see note on Ex 8:26). In context, the term applies to sacrilegious offenses, especially anything that offends Yahweh's sense of purity or holiness. An abomination represented a threat to the very existence of Israel, since breaking the covenant with Yahweh would lead to judgments outlined in the covenant curses (see Lev 26; Dt 28).

5:10 parents will eat their children Cannibalism was one of the covenant curses in both Leviticus and Deuteronomy (see Lev 26:29; Dt 28:53). A long siege could result in food shortages, leading desperate people to resort to cannibalism (see 2Ki 6:28–29).

5:11 you have defiled my sanctuary The Hebrew word used here, *tame*, meaning "defiled," generally refers to a state of ceremonial uncleanness. Israel's idolatry had polluted Yahweh's temple. The usage of *tame* is concentrated in Ezekiel, Leviticus and passages in Numbers concerned with priestly regulations (see note on Eze 1:3). Yahweh's presence eventually departs from the temple because the site is ritually impure. Ritual purity must be restored before Yahweh's presence would return (see Isa 52:1 and note). **your vile images** The Hebrew term here is a synonym for the term meaning "abomination," and refers more specifically to abhorrent religious practices (see note on Eze 5:9). **or spare** The time for mercy has passed, and Israel's sin has made judgment inevitable.

5:12 will die of the plague The Hebrew word used here,

dever ("pestilence"), is one of the punishments promised in Lev 26 for breaking the covenant (see Lev 26:25).

5:13 they will know that I the LORD Yahweh's deeds reveal him as the true God. This phrasing announcing how people will come to recognize Yahweh through his deeds is called the "recognition formula." It is often used in contexts where God intentionally acts to prove his power to his people or the surrounding nations (compare Ex 16:12; 1Ki 20:13). See note on Isa 49:26.

6:1–14 Ezekiel receives another message from Yahweh that is focused on impending judgment of Israel's idolatry. The covenant curses of Lev 26 are coming into effect because of Israel's sin. The sign-act of Eze 5 visualized how Israel would be punished and invoked the curses of wild beasts, pestilence, famine, sword and scattering from Leviticus. The fourfold use of the recognition formula—"then they/you will know that I am Yahweh" (see note on 5:13)—emphasizes Yahweh's role in the judgment he is about to unleash against Israel (vv. 7,10,13,14).

6:2 the mountains of Israel Ezekiel is commanded to prophesy against the mountains, but the indictment is directed at people who created mountain shrines for idol worship (see 1Ki 14:23).

6:3 your high places The Hebrew word used here, *bamah*, refers to a religious shrine; such shrines are frequently associated with idolatry.

6:5 scatter your bones around your altars The presence of dead bodies and bones would have defiled those high places and made them unfit for further religious activity.

your incense altars broken down, and what you have made wiped out. ⁷Your people will fall slain among you, and you will know that I am the LORD.

⁸"'But I will spare some, for some of you will escape the sword when you are scattered among the lands and nations. ⁹Then in the nations where they have been carried captive, those who escape will remember me — how I have been grieved by their adulterous hearts, which have turned away from me, and by their eyes, which have lusted after their idols. They will loathe themselves for the evil they have done and for all their detestable practices. ¹⁰And they will know that I am the LORD; I did not threaten in vain to bring this calamity on them.

¹¹"'This is what the Sovereign LORD says: Strike your hands together and stamp your feet and cry out "Alas!" because of all the wicked and detestable practices of the people of Israel, for they will fall by the sword, famine and plague. ¹²One who is far away will die of the plague, and one who is near will fall by the sword, and anyone who survives and is spared will die of famine. So will I pour out my wrath on them. ¹³And they will know that I am the LORD, when their people lie slain among their idols around their altars, on every high hill and on all the mountaintops, under every spreading tree and every leafy oak — places where they offered fragrant incense to all their idols. ¹⁴And I will stretch out my hand against them and make the land a desolate waste from the desert to Diblah[a] — wherever they live. Then they will know that I am the LORD.'"

The End Has Come

7 The word of the LORD came to me: ²"Son of man, this is what the Sovereign LORD says to the land of Israel:

"'The end! The end has come
  upon the four corners of the land!
³The end is now upon you,
  and I will unleash my anger against you.
I will judge you according to your conduct
  and repay you for all your detestable
    practices.
⁴I will not look on you with pity;
  I will not spare you.
I will surely repay you for your conduct
  and for the detestable practices among
    you.

"'Then you will know that I am the LORD.'

⁵"This is what the Sovereign LORD says:

"'Disaster! Unheard-of[b] disaster!
  See, it comes!
⁶The end has come!
  The end has come!
It has roused itself against you.
  See, it comes!
⁷Doom has come upon you,
  upon you who dwell in the land.
The time has come! The day is near!
  There is panic, not joy, on the mountains.

---

a 14 Most Hebrew manuscripts; a few Hebrew manuscripts *Riblah*   b 5 Most Hebrew manuscripts; some Hebrew manuscripts and Syriac *Disaster after*

6:8 I will spare some The preservation of a remnant was promised in Eze 5:3. Yahweh's plan to save a remnant of his people and bring them safely out of judgment is a prominent theme throughout the Bible (see note on Isa 1:9). The remnant is preserved solely based on Yahweh's grace and sovereign choice. Total annihilation of the people might satisfy God's zeal for justice, but his compassion for them and his desire to be glorified motivates him to preserve a remnant. **scattered among the lands** The scattering was promised in Lev 26:33. Ezekiel's reliance on the Leviticus curses illustrates his intention to remind the Israelites that they were warned of the consequences of breaking the covenant.
6:9 in the nations where they have been carried captive, those who escape will remember me Israel's punishment was intended to inspire repentance and true faith in those who survived. **adulterous** The prophets often depict Israel's idolatry as marital infidelity (compare Jer 2:20; see note on Isa 1:21).
6:13 under every spreading tree and every leafy oak Idolatrous practices were associated with trees, especially oaks (compare 1Ki 14:23; Isa 1:29 and note; 57:5; Jer 2:20 and note).
6:14 to Diblah Most Hebrew manuscripts read "Diblah" for this place name, but Diblah is an otherwise unknown location. Some Hebrew manuscripts read "Riblah," a location north of Damascus. The Hebrew letters for "D" (*dalet*) and "R" (*resh*) are visually similar and often

confused in Hebrew manuscripts. A reference to Riblah fits the imagery of this verse about the entire land being made desolate since Nu 34:11 identifies Riblah as one of the cities on the far northeastern border of the land allotted to Israel. The Sinai wilderness or desert mentioned here in Eze 6:14 forms the southwest border. Riblah was also the site where Zedekiah lost his sight and his sons were executed by King Nebuchadnezzar (see 2Ki 25:6–7).

7:1–27 The judgment Ezekiel prophesied culminates in a rhythmic, almost poetic declaration that the promised end is near. The prophets describe this judgment as the "Day of Yahweh" because the focus is on Yahweh's climactic intervention in Israel's daily life. He comes to punish iniquity after he patiently waited for repentance. "Day of Yahweh" and related phrases such as "that day" occur some 200 times in prophetic literature.

7:2 land of Israel Ezekiel's prophecy of destruction against Judah is addressed to the land itself, though the punishment is meant for the inhabitants.
7:3 your detestable practices See note on Eze 5:9.
7:6 end has come This verse exemplifies Ezekiel's wordplay in this chapter. In Hebrew, the full verse reads *qets ba ba haqqets heqits elayikh hinneh ba'ah*. The repetition emphasizes the word *qets* ("end") and forms of the verb *bo* ("come").

8 I am about to pour out my wrath on you
and spend my anger against you.
I will judge you according to your conduct
and repay you for all your detestable
practices.
9 I will not look on you with pity;
I will not spare you.
I will repay you for your conduct
and for the detestable practices among you.

"Then you will know that it is I the Lord who
strikes you.

10 "'See, the day!
See, it comes!
Doom has burst forth,
the rod has budded,
arrogance has blossomed!
11 Violence has arisen,[a]
a rod to punish the wicked.
None of the people will be left,
none of that crowd —
none of their wealth,
nothing of value.
12 The time has come!
The day has arrived!
Let not the buyer rejoice
nor the seller grieve,
for my wrath is on the whole crowd.
13 The seller will not recover
the property that was sold —
as long as both buyer and seller live.
For the vision concerning the whole crowd
will not be reversed.
Because of their sins, not one of them
will preserve their life.
14 "'They have blown the trumpet,
they have made all things ready,
but no one will go into battle,
for my wrath is on the whole crowd.
15 Outside is the sword;
inside are plague and famine.
Those in the country
will die by the sword;
those in the city
will be devoured by famine and plague.
16 The fugitives who escape
will flee to the mountains.

Like doves of the valleys,
they will all moan,
each for their own sins.
17 Every hand will go limp;
every leg will be wet with urine.
18 They will put on sackcloth
and be clothed with terror.
Every face will be covered with shame,
and every head will be shaved.

19 "'They will throw their silver into the streets,
and their gold will be treated as a thing
unclean.
Their silver and gold
will not be able to deliver them
in the day of the Lord's wrath.
It will not satisfy their hunger
or fill their stomachs,
for it has caused them to stumble into sin.
20 They took pride in their beautiful jewelry
and used it to make their detestable idols.
They made it into vile images;
therefore I will make it a thing unclean for
them.
21 I will give their wealth as plunder to
foreigners
and as loot to the wicked of the earth,
who will defile it.
22 I will turn my face away from the people,
and robbers will desecrate the place I
treasure.
They will enter it
and will defile it.

23 "'Prepare chains!
For the land is full of bloodshed,
and the city is full of violence.
24 I will bring the most wicked of nations
to take possession of their houses.
I will put an end to the pride of the mighty,
and their sanctuaries will be desecrated.
25 When terror comes,
they will seek peace in vain.
26 Calamity upon calamity will come,
and rumor upon rumor.

[a] 11 Or The violent one has become

7:11 arisen, a rod to punish the wicked The violence
of the people is turned on them in judgment.
7:15 inside are plague and famine These disasters—
invasion, disease and hunger—appear in 5:2,12; 6:11.
They allude to the covenant curses of Lev 26.
7:16 fugitives who escape The remnant that survives
the judgment. See Eze 6:8 and note; 6:9 and note.
7:18 They will put on sackcloth Sackcloth and baldness were signs of mourning (see Isa 22:12; and see
note on Job 16:15).
7:19 throw their silver into the streets When disaster
comes, the desire to survive overcomes that of keeping
valuable possessions, especially heavy precious metals.

silver and gold will not be able to deliver Ezekiel's
reference is more likely to idols of silver and gold than
to economic status (see Zep 1:18).
7:20 their beautiful jewelry Likely refers to the decorations in the temple; used to represent the temple itself
(compare Isa 64:11). **their detestable idols** See note
on Eze 5:11.
7:22 I will turn my face away from the people The
"face" symbolizes presence. **place I treasure** The
Jerusalem temple.
7:26 priestly instruction in the law will cease In Jer
18:18, the people confidently express that the law would
never perish from the priest.

They will go searching for a vision from the prophet,
> priestly instruction in the law will cease,
> the counsel of the elders will come to an end.
27 The king will mourn,
> the prince will be clothed with despair,
> and the hands of the people of the land will tremble.
> I will deal with them according to their conduct,
> and by their own standards I will judge them.

"'Then they will know that I am the LORD.'"

Idolatry in the Temple

8 In the sixth year, in the sixth month on the fifth day, while I was sitting in my house and the elders of Judah were sitting before me, the hand of the Sovereign LORD came on me there. ²I looked, and I saw a figure like that of a man.ᵃ From what appeared to be his waist down he was like fire, and from there up his appearance was as bright as glowing metal. ³He stretched out what looked like a hand and took me by the hair of my head. The Spirit lifted me up between earth and heaven and in visions of God he took me to Jerusalem, to the entrance of the north gate of the inner court, where the idol that provokes to jealousy stood. ⁴And there before me was the glory of the God of Israel, as in the vision I had seen in the plain.

⁵Then he said to me, "Son of man, look toward the north." So I looked, and in the entrance north of the gate of the altar I saw this idol of jealousy.

⁶And he said to me, "Son of man, do you see what they are doing — the utterly detestable things the Israelites are doing here, things that will drive me far from my sanctuary? But you will see things that are even more detestable."

⁷Then he brought me to the entrance to the court. I looked, and I saw a hole in the wall. ⁸He said to me, "Son of man, now dig into the wall." So I dug into the wall and saw a doorway there.

⁹And he said to me, "Go in and see the wicked and detestable things they are doing here." ¹⁰So I went in and looked, and I saw portrayed all over the walls all kinds of crawling things and unclean animals and all the idols of Israel. ¹¹In front of them stood seventy elders of Israel, and Jaazaniah son of Shaphan was standing among them. Each

---

ᵃ 2 Or saw a fiery figure

8:1–18 Ezekiel's vision of the temple in Jerusalem picks up on themes and imagery from his inaugural vision in Eze 1–3. The vision of the defiled temple extends through chs. 8–11 and foreshadows the end of the book. The prophet describes a vision of a restored and rebuilt temple in chs. 40–48. The vision in this chapter takes Ezekiel through the temple to witness scenes of idolatry that his divine guide promises will escalate in severity. These abominations in the temple are Yahweh's justification for rejecting Israel, removing his presence and punishing his people.

8:1 on the fifth day Ezekiel's inaugural vision also occurred on the fifth day of a month (see 1:1–2). The sixth year refers to the years of King Jehoiachin's exile, the typical reference for Ezekiel's dating scheme (see note on 1:2). This event occurs in mid-September 592 BC, a year and two months after the vision in chs. 1–3. See the timeline "Dates in Ezekiel" on p. 1276. **the elders of Judah** The leaders of the exiled community are with Ezekiel in his home when he is overcome by the vision from God. The exact nature of the leaders' business with the prophet is unstated. **hand of the Sovereign LORD came on me** Ezekiel frequently describes his interaction with God in very physical, anthropomorphic language (see note on 1:3). **8:2 like that** The same human-like divine form Ezekiel describes in 1:26–27. He remains cautious in his descriptions (see note on 1:13). **glowing metal** See note on 1:4. **8:3 what looked like** The Hebrew word used here, *tavnith,* indicates a pattern for construction (2Ki 16:10). Ezekiel uses the word synonymously with words for likeness and appearance (see note on Eze 1:5; and note on 1:13). **in visions of God he took me to Jerusalem** Ezekiel describes a supernatural, dream-like experience in which God shows him what is happening in Judah. The detailed nature of Ezekiel's description has led to

speculation that he traveled to Jerusalem during his exile. However, he would have had intimate knowledge of the temple layout from his priestly education. Further, his vision does not necessarily reflect the physical reality of events in Jerusalem. The vision is concerned with depicting the sin of Israel in a tangible way that justifies Yahweh's punishment. See the infographic "Solomon's Temple" on p. 520. **idol that provokes to jealousy** The reference is clearly to an idol at the entrance to the inner court of the temple, but the identification is left ambiguous. Idol worship provoked Yahweh's jealousy (see Dt 32:16). **8:4 glory of the God of Israel** Ezekiel connects his vision to what he saw before in Eze 1:28. **in the vision I had seen in the plain** Points back to his second encounter with Yahweh in 3:23. **8:6 utterly detestable things** Ezekiel sees for himself the abominations declared in 5:11 (see note on 5:11). **will drive me far from my sanctuary** This is the essence of Ezekiel's vision: The idolatry in the temple has driven Yahweh away. **you will see things that are even more detestable** This assurance is repeated after each scene of idolatry (see vv. 13,15). The first example is the image outside the inner court, where Ezekiel was dropped first. The next one will be even worse. **8:9 detestable things they are doing here** Characterizing idols as abominations is one of Ezekiel's most common descriptive techniques (see note on 5:11). **8:10 crawling things and unclean animals** The carvings Ezekiel sees violate the command prohibiting the creation of graven images (Ex 20:4). The laws of Deuteronomy also explicitly forbade the people from carving of images of humans, animals, birds or fish (see Dt 4:15–18). Further, animals categorized as creeping things are unclean (Lev 11:44). **8:11 seventy elders** The number of elders signifies the upper level of leadership in Israel (compare Moses' selection

had a censer in his hand, and a fragrant cloud of incense was rising.

¹²He said to me, "Son of man, have you seen what the elders of Israel are doing in the darkness, each at the shrine of his own idol? They say, 'The Lord does not see us; the Lord has forsaken the land.'" ¹³Again, he said, "You will see them doing things that are even more detestable."

¹⁴Then he brought me to the entrance of the north gate of the house of the Lord, and I saw women sitting there, mourning the god Tammuz. ¹⁵He said to me, "Do you see this, son of man? You will see things that are even more detestable than this."

¹⁶He then brought me into the inner court of the house of the Lord, and there at the entrance to the temple, between the portico and the altar, were about twenty-five men. With their backs toward the temple of the Lord and their faces toward the east, they were bowing down to the sun in the east.

¹⁷He said to me, "Have you seen this, son of man? Is it a trivial matter for the people of Judah to do the detestable things they are doing here? Must they also fill the land with violence and con-

tinually arouse my anger? Look at them putting the branch to their nose! ¹⁸Therefore I will deal with them in anger; I will not look on them with pity or spare them. Although they shout in my ears, I will not listen to them."

Judgment on the Idolaters

9 Then I heard him call out in a loud voice, "Bring near those who are appointed to execute judgment on the city, each with a weapon in his hand." ²And I saw six men coming from the direction of the upper gate, which faces north, each with a deadly weapon in his hand. With them was a man clothed in linen who had a writing kit at his side. They came in and stood beside the bronze altar.

³Now the glory of the God of Israel went up from above the cherubim, where it had been, and moved to the threshold of the temple. Then the Lord called to the man clothed in linen who had the writing kit at his side ⁴and said to him, "Go throughout the city of Jerusalem and put a mark on the foreheads of those who grieve and lament over all the detestable things that are done in it."

---

of 70 elders in Nu 11:24 and the presence of 70 elders in Ex 24:1). **Jaazaniah son of Shaphan** Shaphan was the scribe of Josiah during religious reforms described in 2Ki 22:8—23:30. Shaphan's family members are mentioned favorably in the book of Jeremiah and seem to have been loyal followers of Yahweh (Jer 26:24; 29:3; 36:11–19). The family's positive reputation may explain the specific mention here of one member involved in idol worship. **had a censer** A pan with a handle used for removing ashes from an altar or burning incense over hot coals. **a fragrant cloud of incense** The priests created a cloud of incense on the Day of Atonement to screen the high priest from the divine presence in the Holy of Holies (the most Holy Place; Ex 26:33). Ironically, the cloud Ezekiel sees is created for idols and separates people from Yahweh.

8:12 shrine of his own idol This description suggests that elders were burning incense at carved niches around the temple complex.

8:14 mourning the god Tammuz Tammuz (Dumuzi) was a Sumerian deity and part of the dying-and-rising-god mythology connected to fertility rituals. During the dry, unproductive season, Tammuz inhabited the underworld. Rituals of mourning for Tammuz—the apparent scene described here—were intended to restore Tammuz to life and thus restore the land's fertility. The worship of Tammuz at the Jerusalem temple adds an element of Mesopotamian idolatry to the Canaanite idolatry already present. See the table "Pagan Deities of the Old Testament" on p. 1287.

8:16 twenty-five men The number of men present varies from 20–25 based on different OT versions. The Greek text reads 20; the Hebrew reads 25. The Mesopotamian sun god Shamash is associated with the number 20. **With their backs toward the temple of the Lord** Turning their backs shows great disrespect to Yahweh. In ancient cultures, turning one's back on the king was tantamount to treason and worthy of death. **bowing down to the sun** The sun, or *shemesh*, was worshiped as a deity named Shamash. Mesopotamian texts depict Shamash and Tammuz as temple guardians.

8:17 them putting the branch to their nose This probably refers to a Mesopotamian religious practice. Cedar branches were associated with the deity Tammuz (see Eze 8:14). Some depictions of Assyrian kings before their gods show a branch held in front of their faces—apparently a gesture of entreaty.

9:1–11 Ezekiel witnesses the execution of the idolaters observed in ch. 8. Yahweh himself orders the massacre as punishment for their sin. Only a small remnant who disapproved of the idolatry survives. The scene graphically depicts Yahweh's role in the destruction that comes upon Judah.

9:1 those who are appointed to execute judgment The Hebrew expression here can refer to those who administer punishment or vengeance, so "punishers" or "avengers" would be appropriate English equivalents. While the avengers are identified as men in v. 2, their role in carrying out Yahweh's judgment combined with the visionary backdrop of the scene suggests they might be heavenly beings.

9:2 six men Those mentioned in v. 1. Ezekiel sees a total of seven men, a significant Biblical number indicating completeness. Babylonian mythology depicts a group of seven deities under the command of the god, Erra, whose primary function is punishment and destruction. The Aramaic inscription from Sefire contains curses invoking the wrath of "the Seven" if the treaty provisions are broken. **man clothed in linen** The seventh figure, whose role is to save, not destroy. Compare Daniel's description of his angelic guide as a man clothed in linen (Da 10:5; 12:6–7). **a writing kit** Since Ezekiel's audience is exiled in Babylonia, the heavenly figure carrying a scribal writing kit likely would have reminded them of the Babylonian god Nabu, the scribe of the gods and the patron god of scribes. Nabu was responsible for recording people's destinies.

9:4 put a mark on the foreheads The mark was probably the Hebrew letter *taw*, which in the ancient script was shaped like an X or a plus sign (+). *Taw* was the last

Pagan Deities of the Old Testament

DEITY	WORSHIPED IN	REFERENCES
Adrammelek	Sepharvaim	2Ki 17:31
Amon	Egypt	Jer 46:25; Na 3:8
Anammelek	Sepharvaim	2Ki 17:31
Apis	Egypt	Jer 46:15
Asherah	Canaan	Dt 7:5; 16:21; Jdg 6:25–30; 1Ki 15:13; 16:33; 18:19; 2Ki 13:6; 17:16; 18:4; 21:3,7; 23:4–15; 2Ch 15:16, etc.
Ashima	Hamath	2Ki 17:30
Ashtoreth/Astarte/Ishtar/"Queen of Heaven"	Assyria, Babylon, Canaan, Egypt, Phoenicia	Jdg 2:13; 10:6; 1Sa 7:3–4; 12:10; 31:10; 1Ki 11:5,33; 2Ki 11:5; Jer 7:18; 44:17–19, 25
Baal	Canaan	Nu 22:41; 25:3; Jdg 2:11; 6:25–32; 1Sa 7:4; 12:10; 1Ki 16:31–32; 18:25–26; 2Ki 3:2; 10:26–28; 2Ch 17:3; 23:17; Jer 2:8; 7:9; 19:5; Hos 2:8,13; 11:2; Zep 1:4, etc.
Baal-Zebub	Philistia	2Ki 1:2,3,6,16
Bel/Marduk	Babylon	Isa 46:1; Jer 50:2; 51:44
Chemosh	Moab	Nu 21:29; Jdg 11:24; 1Ki 11:7, 33; 2Ki 23:13; Jer 48:7,13,46
Dagon	Philistia	Jdg 16:23; 1Sa 5:2–7; 1Ch 10:10
Kaiwan	Babylon	Am 5:26
Milcom	Ammon	1Ki 11:5,33; 2Ki 23:13; Jer 49:1, 3; Zep 1:5
Molek	Ammon	Lev 18:21; 20:2–5; 1Ki 11:7; 2Ki 23:10; Jer 32:35
Nebo	Babylon	Isa 46:1
Nergal	Cuth	2Ki 17:30
Nibhaz	Ivvah	2Ki 17:31
Nisrok	Assyria	2Ki 19:37; Isa 37:38
Rimmon/Hadad-rimmon	Aram	2Ki 5:18; Zec 12:11
Sakkuth	Babylon	Am 5:26
SukkothBenoth	Babylon	2Ki 17:30
Tammuz	Babylon, Sumer	Eze 8:14
Tartak	Ivvah	2Ki 17:31

⁵As I listened, he said to the others, "Follow him through the city and kill, without showing pity or compassion. ⁶Slaughter the old men, the young men and women, the mothers and children, but do not touch anyone who has the mark. Begin at my sanctuary." So they began with the old men who were in front of the temple.

⁷Then he said to them, "Defile the temple and fill the courts with the slain. Go!" So they went out and began killing throughout the city. ⁸While they were killing and I was left alone, I fell face-down, crying out, "Alas, Sovereign LORD! Are you going to destroy the entire remnant of Israel in this outpouring of your wrath on Jerusalem?"

⁹He answered me, "The sin of the people of Israel and Judah is exceedingly great; the land is full of bloodshed and the city is full of injustice. They say, 'The LORD has forsaken the land; the LORD does not see.' ¹⁰So I will not look on them with pity or spare them, but I will bring down on their own heads what they have done."

¹¹Then the man in linen with the writing kit at his side brought back word, saying, "I have done as you commanded."

God's Glory Departs From the Temple

10 I looked, and I saw the likeness of a throne of lapis lazuli above the vault that was over the heads of the cherubim. ²The LORD said to the man clothed in linen, "Go in among the wheels beneath the cherubim. Fill your hands with burning coals from among the cherubim and scatter them over the city." And as I watched, he went in.

³Now the cherubim were standing on the south side of the temple when the man went in, and a cloud filled the inner court. ⁴Then the glory of the LORD rose from above the cherubim and moved to the threshold of the temple. The cloud filled the temple, and the court was full of the radiance of the glory of the LORD. ⁵The sound of the wings of the cherubim could be heard as far away as the outer court, like the voice of God Almighty[a] when he speaks.

⁶When the LORD commanded the man in linen, "Take fire from among the wheels, from among the cherubim," the man went in and stood beside a wheel. ⁷Then one of the cherubim reached out his hand to the fire that was among them. He took up some of it and put it into the hands of the man in linen, who took it and went out. ⁸(Under the wings of the cherubim could be seen what looked like human hands.)

⁹I looked, and I saw beside the cherubim four wheels, one beside each of the cherubim; the wheels sparkled like topaz. ¹⁰As for their appearance, the four of them looked alike; each was like a wheel intersecting a wheel. ¹¹As they moved, they would go in any one of the four directions the cherubim faced; the wheels did not turn about[b] as the cherubim went. The cherubim went in whatever direction the head faced, without turning as they went. ¹²Their entire bodies, including their backs, their hands and their wings, were completely full of eyes, as were their four wheels. ¹³I heard the wheels being called "the whirling wheels." ¹⁴Each of the cherubim had four faces: One face was that of a cherub, the second the face of a human being, the third the face of a lion, and the fourth the face of an eagle.

¹⁵Then the cherubim rose upward. These were the living creatures I had seen by the Kebar River. ¹⁶When the cherubim moved, the wheels beside them moved; and when the cherubim spread their wings to rise from the ground, the wheels did not leave their side. ¹⁷When the cherubim stood still,

---

a 5 Hebrew *El-Shaddai*   *b 11* Or *aside*

---

letter in the Hebrew alphabet, and Jewish groups in the Second Temple period and Late Antiquity continued to use it as a mark of righteousness until its similarity with the Christian cross made it unpopular in rabbinic Judaism.
9:6 do not touch anyone who has the mark Compare the adoption of this imagery in Rev 9:4.
9:7 Defile the temple The temple, which already has been defiled by idolatry, will now be further defiled by dead bodies (see Eze 7:21–22).
9:9 LORD does not see Ironically, he did see and came to punish them for their behavior (see 8:12).

10:1–22 Ezekiel describes his vision of Yahweh on his chariot-throne with many of the same images and phrases from his inaugural vision in ch. 1. This vision focuses on Yahweh's departure from his temple. In the ancient world, gods were believed to have a limited range or sphere of influence. Ezekiel's vision shows that Yahweh is free to leave his chosen earthly dwelling without his power being diminished. Yahweh was not conquered or overcome by the foreign invaders or their gods; he chose to leave the temple because Israel defiled it and abandoned the covenant.

10:1 the vault A dome or platform held up by the cherubim (see 1:22 and note).
10:2 the man clothed in linen The scribe who marked the remnant for salvation obeys Yahweh's command to enact judgment of the city by fire (see 9:2 and note).
the wheels See note on 1:16. **the cherubim** The living creatures from Ezekiel's earlier vision are now explicitly identified as cherubim (see 1:5 and note).
10:4 The cloud filled the temple The divine presence first entered the temple accompanied by a cloud (1Ki 8:10).
10:10 like a wheel intersecting a wheel See note on Eze 1:16.
10:11 did not turn about as the cherubim went With four faces, they had no need to turn.
10:14 four faces In 1:10, the four faces are identified slightly differently.
10:15 living creatures The prophet clarifies that these cherubim are the living creatures he observed in his inaugural vision (see note on 1:5).

they also stood still; and when the cherubim rose, they rose with them, because the spirit of the living creatures was in them.

¹⁸Then the glory of the LORD departed from over the threshold of the temple and stopped above the cherubim. ¹⁹While I watched, the cherubim spread their wings and rose from the ground, and as they went, the wheels went with them. They stopped at the entrance of the east gate of the LORD's house, and the glory of the God of Israel was above them.

²⁰These were the living creatures I had seen beneath the God of Israel by the Kebar River, and I realized that they were cherubim. ²¹Each had four faces and four wings, and under their wings was what looked like human hands. ²²Their faces had the same appearance as those I had seen by the Kebar River. Each one went straight ahead.

God's Sure Judgment on Jerusalem

11 Then the Spirit lifted me up and brought me to the gate of the house of the LORD that faces east. There at the entrance of the gate were twenty-five men, and I saw among them Jaazaniah son of Azzur and Pelatiah son of Benaiah, leaders of the people. ²The LORD said to me, "Son of man, these are the men who are plotting evil and giving wicked advice in this city. ³They say, 'Haven't our houses been recently rebuilt? This city is a pot, and we are the meat in it.' ⁴Therefore prophesy against them; prophesy, son of man."

⁵Then the Spirit of the LORD came on me, and he told me to say: "This is what the LORD says: That is what you are saying, you leaders in Israel, but I know what is going through your mind. ⁶You have killed many people in this city and filled its streets with the dead.

⁷"Therefore this is what the Sovereign LORD says: The bodies you have thrown there are the meat and this city is the pot, but I will drive you out of it. ⁸You fear the sword, and the sword is what I will bring against you, declares the Sovereign LORD. ⁹I will drive you out of the city and deliver you into the hands of foreigners and inflict punishment on you. ¹⁰You will fall by the sword, and I will execute judgment on you at the borders of Israel. Then you will know that I am the LORD.

11:1–13 The final scene of Ezekiel's vision appears to depict a time prior to the scene in 9:1–11 when the wicked of Jerusalem are destroyed in judgment. The prophet observes a council of Judah's leaders who apparently are deliberating about their course of action in light of Babylonian oppression. The reign of Zedekiah, Judah's last Davidic king (597–586 BC), serves as the historical backdrop for this scene and the oracles in chs. 12–14. Zedekiah, Josiah's brother, was installed as a puppet ruler by Nebuchadnezzar after the failed rebellions of Josiah's son and grandson, Jehoiakim and Jehoiachin (sometimes called Jeconiah). Zedekiah, who initially was loyal to Babylon, faced mounting pressure from influential leaders who favored rebellion against Babylon and alliance with Egypt. Help from an Egyptian alliance failed to materialize. As a result, Zedekiah was captured, Jerusalem was destroyed and the temple was burned. Ezekiel's vision comes before the destruction and addresses the leaders' failure to discern the true cause of the disaster.

11:1 twenty-five men Perhaps the same men who had been worshiping the sun in 8:16. **Jaazaniah son of Azzur and Pelatiah** Ezekiel calls attention to two of the men, identifying them with the Hebrew title *sar*. The title can indicate any high-ranking officer or official, but it also can designate a member of the aristocracy.
11:3 Haven't our houses been recently rebuilt It may be that the leaders are expressing confidence in their safety and hope for a prosperous future. Alternatively, their counsel could be construed negatively, expressing their sense of the impending doom from Babylonian invasion. The response could also express general ambivalence. **This city is a pot** This seems to refer to a standard cooking pot. The cooking pot (or cauldron) could symbolize protection. However, a cooking pot would be an unusual symbol of protection since the contents are about to be cooked. Further examples of this metaphor in ch. 11 do little to clarify the sense (see vv. 7,11) since they play on the ambiguity of safety and danger to those in or out of the pot. The metaphor is expanded in ch. 24.

11:5 Spirit of the LORD came on me When Ezekiel refers to the Spirit or hand of Yahweh coming upon him, it indicates the onset of a Spirit-inspired, trance-like state. Ezekiel is overcome with emotion or experiencing altered consciousness through his connection with the divine. This prophetic state was brought on by an intensely overwhelming experience of the Spirit of Yahweh. This experience is most commonly depicted for the early prophets in the historical books 1 Samuel–2 Kings (see 1Sa 10:5–12; 19:20–24). **what is going through your mind** Yahweh knows their plans, even those they have thought but have not stated (compare Eze 20:32; Isa 29:15).
11:6 You have killed many people in this city Warns that the destruction depicted in Eze 9:7 is their own responsibility, even though it is divinely mandated. Their sin has made the judgment inevitable.
11:7 bodies you have thrown there are the meat The prophecy reverses the saying attributed to the leaders in v. 3. They may have thought that being in the city (metaphorically the pot or cauldron) meant protection, but their poor choice of analogy prompts associations of dead meat cooking. The metaphor seems to imply that the leaders have first, through their poor judgment, multiplied those who will be slain in the city (cooked in the pot), and now the leaders themselves will be taken from the city for judgment (see v. 9). The English idiom out of the pot and into the frying pan is similar to this metaphor.
11:9 I will drive you out A contrast between the high-ranking officials who will be brought out and the common people who will be slain in the city. Second Kings 25:4–7 records how Zedekiah and his officers made a breach in the city wall and escaped at night, leaving the city to Nebuchadnezzar's destruction. Their eleventh-hour escape was part of Yahweh's plan to separate them for special judgment. **into the hands of foreigners** Zedekiah and his officials were quickly caught by the Babylonians and brought before Nebuchadnezzar.
11:10 I will execute judgment on you at the borders of Israel A reference to Riblah, located on the Orontes River in northern Syria, where Nebuchadnezzar was

¹¹This city will not be a pot for you, nor will you be the meat in it; I will execute judgment on you at the borders of Israel. ¹²And you will know that I am the Lord, for you have not followed my decrees or kept my laws but have conformed to the standards of the nations around you."

¹³Now as I was prophesying, Pelatiah son of Benaiah died. Then I fell facedown and cried out in a loud voice, "Alas, Sovereign Lord! Will you completely destroy the remnant of Israel?"

The Promise of Israel's Return

¹⁴The word of the Lord came to me: ¹⁵"Son of man, the people of Jerusalem have said of your fellow exiles and all the other Israelites, 'They are far away from the Lord; this land was given to us as our possession.'

¹⁶"Therefore say: 'This is what the Sovereign Lord says: Although I sent them far away among the nations and scattered them among the countries, yet for a little while I have been a sanctuary for them in the countries where they have gone.'

¹⁷"Therefore say: 'This is what the Sovereign Lord says: I will gather you from the nations and bring you back from the countries where you have been scattered, and I will give you back the land of Israel again.'

¹⁸"They will return to it and remove all its vile images and detestable idols. ¹⁹I will give them an undivided heart and put a new spirit in them; I will remove from them their heart of stone and give them a heart of flesh. ²⁰Then they will follow my decrees and be careful to keep my laws. They will be my people, and I will be their God. ²¹But as for those whose hearts are devoted to their vile images and detestable idols, I will bring down on their own heads what they have done, declares the Sovereign Lord."

²²Then the cherubim, with the wheels beside them, spread their wings, and the glory of the God of Israel was above them. ²³The glory of the Lord went up from within the city and stopped above the mountain east of it. ²⁴The Spirit lifted me up and brought me to the exiles in Babylonia[a] in the vision given by the Spirit of God.

Then the vision I had seen went up from me, ²⁵and I told the exiles everything the Lord had shown me.

The Exile Symbolized

12 The word of the Lord came to me: ²"Son of man, you are living among a rebellious people. They have eyes to see but do not see and

[a] 24 Or Chaldea

headquartered during his campaign into Palestine (see 2Ki 25:6,20–21; compare Eze 6:14 and note). **you will know that I am the Lord** The recognition formula (see note on Eze 5:13). The delay between past prophecy and enacted judgment may have given people time to doubt that Yahweh would do as he threatened. This formula underscores that his actions will remove any doubt about his power or deity.
11:12 standards of the nations Refers to the idolatrous practices Ezekiel witnessed in 8:5–16 (i.e., mixed religious practices of the Canaanites, Egyptians and Babylonians).
11:13 Pelatiah son of Benaiah died One of the two individuals recognized and named by Ezekiel drops dead during the prophecy, upsetting Ezekiel greatly.
11:14–25 Here, Yahweh gives Ezekiel the first glimpse of his plan for future salvation and restoration. God himself enables the people to respond to him by replacing their rebellious hearts of stone with hearts of flesh (v. 19).
11:15 They are far away from the Lord The people have lost sight of the connection between their obedience to Yahweh and their continued possession of the land God gave them. The prevailing understanding in the ancient world was that deities had power and influence over specific territories. This belief extends to the exiles, who complained that they were unable to sing worship to Yahweh when they were in a foreign land (see Ps 137:4). Ezekiel's description of Yahweh's presence outside the land and his graphic depiction of Yahweh's mobility attempt to break this limited understanding of his power.
11:16 scattered them among the countries A familiar part of Yahweh's plan for judgment, enacted in the sign from Eze 5:2 and promised again in 6:8. The emphasis on the scattering of Israel is based on the covenant curse

from Lev 26:33. **sanctuary** Worship or access to the divine presence is not limited to the temple in Jerusalem. Yahweh asserts that he has been present among the exiles, and his presence makes any land a sanctuary. The Hebrew word used here, *miqdash*, refers to a sacred place. It is used specifically of the early sanctuaries at Shechem (Jos 24:26), the tabernacle (Ex 25:8) and the Jerusalem temple (1Ch 22:19).
11:17 I will gather you from the nations Yahweh's action in gathering Israel from exile and returning them to the land is a frequent prophetic image of salvation (compare Isa 54:7; Mic 2:12; Jer 23:3; 32:37).
11:19 put a new spirit in Anticipates the more developed salvation oracle in Eze 36:26 that also promises the new spirit and the heart of flesh. **heart of stone** The heart of stone symbolizes a stubborn rejection of Yahweh.
11:20 my people, and I will be their God Based on the covenant formula of Lev 26:12. Relationship between God and his people is possible only through proper observance of the covenant. Exodus 6:7 combines a similar statement of covenant relationship with a version of the recognition formula (see note on Eze 5:13).
11:22 cherubim, with the wheels beside them, spread their wings The prophetic word ends, and Ezekiel resumes his description of what he sees. The divine chariot-throne that had been on the temple's threshold slowly departs and begins to move eastward out of the city.
11:23 mountain See the infographic "Jerusalem" on p. 1607.
11:24 The Spirit lifted me up Compare 8:3. Ezekiel is returned home in the same way he was transported to Jerusalem.
11:25 I told the exiles The narrative ends by linking back to the original scene of 8:1: Ezekiel is in his house

ears to hear but do not hear, for they are a rebellious people.

[3] "Therefore, son of man, pack your belongings for exile and in the daytime, as they watch, set out and go from where you are to another place. Perhaps they will understand, though they are a rebellious people. [4]During the daytime, while they watch, bring out your belongings packed for exile. Then in the evening, while they are watching, go out like those who go into exile. [5]While they watch, dig through the wall and take your belongings out through it. [6]Put them on your shoulder as they are watching and carry them out at dusk. Cover your face so that you cannot see the land, for I have made you a sign to the Israelites."

[7]So I did as I was commanded. During the day I brought out my things packed for exile. Then in the evening I dug through the wall with my hands. I took my belongings out at dusk, carrying them on my shoulders while they watched.

[8]In the morning the word of the LORD came to me: [9]"Son of man, did not the Israelites, that rebellious people, ask you, 'What are you doing?'

[10]Say to them, 'This is what the Sovereign LORD says: This prophecy concerns the prince in Jerusalem and all the Israelites who are there.' [11]Say to them, 'I am a sign to you.'

"As I have done, so it will be done to them. They will go into exile as captives.

[12]"The prince among them will put his things on his shoulder at dusk and leave, and a hole will be dug in the wall for him to go through. He will cover his face so that he cannot see the land. [13]I will spread my net for him, and he will be caught in my snare; I will bring him to Babylonia, the land of the Chaldeans, but he will not see it, and there he will die. [14]I will scatter to the winds all those around him — his staff and all his troops — and I will pursue them with drawn sword.

[15]"They will know that I am the LORD, when I disperse them among the nations and scatter them through the countries. [16]But I will spare a few of them from the sword, famine and plague, so that in the nations where they go they may acknowledge all their detestable practices. Then they will know that I am the LORD."

[17]The word of the LORD came to me: [18]"Son of man, tremble as you eat your food, and shudder in fear as you drink your water. [19]Say to the people of the land: 'This is what the Sovereign LORD says about those living in Jerusalem and in the land of Israel: They will eat their food in anxiety and drink their water in despair, for their land will be stripped of everything in it because of the violence of all who live there. [20]The inhabited towns will be laid waste and the land will be desolate. Then you will know that I am the LORD.'"

There Will Be No Delay

[21]The word of the LORD came to me: [22]"Son of man, what is this proverb you have in the land of Israel: 'The days go by and every vision comes to nothing'? [23]Say to them, 'This is what the Sovereign LORD says: I am going to put an end to this proverb, and they will no longer quote it in Israel.' Say to them, 'The days are near when every vision will be fulfilled. [24]For there will be no more false visions or flattering divinations among the people of Israel. [25]But I the LORD will speak what I will, and it shall be fulfilled without delay. For in your

---

with the elders of Judah. Now he reports the vision to them in detail.

12:1–28 Ezekiel is commanded to stage another scene, which symbolizes the exile and punishment of Judah. The dramatization of prophecy is a well-developed practice for Ezekiel, begun in the sign-acts of chs. 4–5. See note on 4:1–17. See the table "Symbolic Actions of the Prophets" on p. 1195.

12:2 Son of man See note on 2:1.

12:3 pack your belongings for exile Assyrian reliefs depict prisoners being deported and carrying large bags on their shoulders. The Talmud claimed that the baggage consisted of a sleeping mat, a lamp and a bowl. Ezekiel was part of the first group of exiles, along with King Jehoiachin, in 597 BC (see note on 1:2).

12:4 in the evening, while they are watching, go out Ezekiel's departure at evening is unusual since night would not seem to be the optimal time to begin a long journey. The darkness may symbolize the exiles' desire to avoid capture. The timing makes sense if Ezekiel's act is understood as mirroring what happens to Zedekiah, who flees besieged Jerusalem at night (see 2Ki 25:4).

12:6 Cover your face Perhaps symbolizing the exiles' ignorance of their destination or grief over the loss of the land (see 2Sa 19:4–5). **a sign to the Israelites**

Ezekiel's actions make him a sign (*mopheth* in Hebrew), a living reminder of God's prophetic word.

12:10 prophecy concerns the prince in Jerusalem Refers to Zedekiah. Ezekiel uses the title *nasi*, or "prince," for Zedekiah, brother of Josiah and uncle to the rightful king, Jehoiachin. Ezekiel never refers to Zedekiah as king or *melekh* since the status of "king in exile" was still afforded to Jehoiachin, who was living in Babylon.

12:13 but he will not see it Possibly an allusion to Zedekiah being blinded by the Babylonians (see 2Ki 25:7).

12:16 they may acknowledge all their detestable practices A group of survivors is preserved precisely so they can acknowledge Israel's guilt to the nations.

12:18 tremble as you eat your food Reminiscent of the siege rations from Eze 4:10–11. Ezekiel now depicts either the rations of a prisoner heading into exile or the plight of someone left in the land after invaders have destroyed nearly everything. See the table "Symbolic Actions of the Prophets" on p. 1195.

12:19 will be stripped of everything in it Invading armies often took the crops and livestock of the inhabitants.

12:22 every vision comes to nothing The people have become complacent in light of repeated prophecies of judgment that have not been fulfilled.

12:24 false visions False prophecy was a problem during

days, you rebellious people, I will fulfill whatever I say, declares the Sovereign LORD.'"

²⁶The word of the LORD came to me: ²⁷"Son of man, the Israelites are saying, 'The vision he sees is for many years from now, and he prophesies about the distant future.'

²⁸"Therefore say to them, 'This is what the Sovereign LORD says: None of my words will be delayed any longer; whatever I say will be fulfilled, declares the Sovereign LORD.'"

False Prophets Condemned

13 The word of the LORD came to me: ²"Son of man, prophesy against the prophets of Israel who are now prophesying. Say to those who prophesy out of their own imagination: 'Hear the word of the LORD! ³This is what the Sovereign LORD says: Woe to the foolish^a prophets who follow their own spirit and have seen nothing! ⁴Your prophets, Israel, are like jackals among ruins. ⁵You have not gone up to the breaches in the wall to repair it for the people of Israel so that it will stand firm in the battle on the day of the LORD. ⁶Their visions are false and their divinations a lie. Even though the LORD has not sent them, they say, "The LORD declares," and expect him to fulfill their words. ⁷Have you not seen false visions and uttered lying divinations when you say, "The LORD declares," though I have not spoken?

⁸"'Therefore this is what the Sovereign LORD says: Because of your false words and lying visions, I am against you, declares the Sovereign LORD. ⁹My hand will be against the prophets who see false visions and utter lying divinations. They will not belong to the council of my people or be listed in the records of Israel, nor will they enter the land of Israel. Then you will know that I am the Sovereign LORD.

¹⁰"'Because they lead my people astray, saying, "Peace," when there is no peace, and because, when a flimsy wall is built, they cover it with whitewash, ¹¹therefore tell those who cover it with whitewash that it is going to fall. Rain will come in torrents, and I will send hailstones hurtling down, and violent winds will burst forth. ¹²When the wall collapses, will people not ask you, "Where is the whitewash you covered it with?"

¹³"'Therefore this is what the Sovereign LORD says: In my wrath I will unleash a violent wind, and in my anger hailstones and torrents of rain will fall with destructive fury. ¹⁴I will tear down the wall you have covered with whitewash and will level it to the ground so that its foundation will be laid bare. When it^b falls, you will be destroyed in it; and you will know that I am the LORD. ¹⁵So I will pour out my wrath against the wall and against those who covered it with whitewash. I will say to you, "The wall is gone and so are those who whitewashed it, ¹⁶those prophets of Israel who prophesied to Jerusalem and saw visions of peace for her when there was no peace, declares the Sovereign LORD."'

¹⁷"Now, son of man, set your face against the daughters of your people who prophesy out of their own imagination. Prophesy against them ¹⁸and say, 'This is what the Sovereign LORD says: Woe to the women who sew magic charms on all their wrists and make veils of various lengths for their heads in order to ensnare people. Will you

---

^a 3 Or *wicked*   ^b 14 Or *the city*

Ezekiel's day—especially in Jerusalem, where prophets promoted a false sense of security (compare Jer 28–29).

13:1–23 Following the condemnation of false visions in Eze 12:21–28, Ezekiel receives an oracle directed at false prophets. The oracle addresses male prophets who lie about having received a divine word and female prophets who engage in obscure magical practices.

13:3 Woe to the foolish prophets The interjection *hoy* ("woe") expresses pity, pain or disappointment and marks this as a particular type of prophetic saying. The woe oracle is a common genre in prophetic literature (e.g., Isa 5:8; Mic 2:1). The pronouncement of woe accompanies an accusation or a description of the condemned behavior and is followed by a declaration of judgment. Here, the accusation is in Eze 13:3–7, and the judgment is pronounced in vv. 8–9. This prophetic style also appears in the NT, most notably in the sayings of Jesus (see Lk 10:13; Mt 18:7).

13:4 like jackals among ruins The prophets were cunning, motivated by their own self-interest.

13:5 You have not gone up to the breaches The prophets neglected their responsibility to serve as watchmen and warn of impending danger (see note on Eze 3:17).

the day of the LORD See note on 7:1–27.

13:6 expect him to fulfill their words Prophecy and divination in the ancient world had manipulative overtones. Incantations and rituals were designed to manipulate the deity into fulfilling requests. These false prophets believed that God would be bound to honor their utterances made on his behalf.

13:9 the council Refers to the community's assembly of leaders.

13:10 saying, "Peace," when there is no peace The declaration that peace and prosperity were on the way (see Jer 6:14) was a false but popular message at the time. The dislike of a prophet such as Jeremiah (who is arrested for preaching doom and destruction) reflects that he was not telling the people what they wanted to hear. The true prophet preaches the message without regard for whether it will be popular or well-received.

whitewash The metaphor of the whitewashed wall refers to the strong, sturdy appearance given to the fake, flimsy message of the false prophets.

13:14 you will know that I am the LORD See note on Eze 5:13.

13:17 the daughters The female prophets involved in magic. Ezekiel carefully avoids calling them "prophetesses."

13:18 magic charms The Hebrew word used here, *keseth,* is likely related to an Akkadian term for magic that used bindings. Babylonian incantations involved magical

ensnare the lives of my people but preserve your own? ¹⁹You have profaned me among my people for a few handfuls of barley and scraps of bread. By lying to my people, who listen to lies, you have killed those who should not have died and have spared those who should not live.

²⁰"Therefore this is what the Sovereign Lord says: I am against your magic charms with which you ensnare people like birds and I will tear them from your arms; I will set free the people that you ensnare like birds. ²¹I will tear off your veils and save my people from your hands, and they will no longer fall prey to your power. Then you will know that I am the Lord. ²²Because you disheartened the righteous with your lies, when I had brought them no grief, and because you encouraged the wicked not to turn from their evil ways and so save their lives, ²³therefore you will no longer see false visions or practice divination. I will save my people from your hands. And then you will know that I am the Lord.'"

Idolaters Condemned

14 Some of the elders of Israel came to me and sat down in front of me. ²Then the word of the Lord came to me: ³"Son of man, these men have set up idols in their hearts and put wicked stumbling blocks before their faces. Should I let them inquire of me at all? ⁴Therefore speak to them and tell them, 'This is what the Sovereign Lord says: When any of the Israelites set up idols in their hearts and put a wicked stumbling block before their faces and then go to a prophet, I the Lord will answer them myself in keeping with their great idolatry. ⁵I will do this to recapture the hearts of the people of Israel, who have all deserted me for their idols.'

⁶"Therefore say to the people of Israel, 'This is what the Sovereign Lord says: Repent! Turn from your idols and renounce all your detestable practices!

⁷"'When any of the Israelites or any foreigner residing in Israel separate themselves from me and set up idols in their hearts and put a wicked stumbling block before their faces and then go to a prophet to inquire of me, I the Lord will answer them myself. ⁸I will set my face against them and make them an example and a byword. I will remove them from my people. Then you will know that I am the Lord.

⁹"'And if the prophet is enticed to utter a prophecy, I the Lord have enticed that prophet, and I will stretch out my hand against him and destroy him from among my people Israel. ¹⁰They will bear their guilt—the prophet will be as guilty as the one who consults him. ¹¹Then the people of Israel will no longer stray from me, nor will they defile themselves anymore with all their sins. They will be my people, and I will be their God, declares the Sovereign Lord.'"

Jerusalem's Judgment Inescapable

¹²The word of the Lord came to me: ¹³"Son of man, if a country sins against me by being

---

knots and bonds. **veils** The rare Hebrew word used here, *mispachah*, is used instead of the normal word for veil, suggesting a special type of head-covering used in magical rituals. **ensnare people** The Hebrew phrase used here likely refers to necromancy, the practice of attempting to communicate with the dead (see Isa 8:19 and note).

14:1–11 The theme of false Yahweh worship continues from Eze 13 but with a shift in focus to the people, represented by the elders rather than the false prophets. Yahweh is incredulous that these elders would seek a genuine word from him through Ezekiel because of their involvement in idol worship.

14:1 elders of Israel came to me The leaders of the exiled community may have visited Ezekiel on a regular basis, acknowledging his role of spiritual leadership as prophet and priest of Yahweh. Whether they fully accepted Ezekiel's authority is unclear, since he criticizes them for their lack of total commitment to Yahweh.

14:3 idols in their hearts The Hebrew word used here, *gillulim*, appears only in the plural in the OT and always in reference to idols. The Biblical use is intentionally insulting and disparaging because *gillulim* is based on the word *gel*, meaning "dung" (see 4:12; Job 20:7).

The phrase *gilluleihem al-libbam*, can be taken literally or metaphorically. The elders might be literally guilty by wearing some sort of magical amulet around their necks, or they may simply be guilty of devotion to other gods. Wearing protective amulets was a common practice

among the Babylonians. They wore amulets to protect against demons, ensure a safe pregnancy and birth, facilitate romantic attraction or protect themselves from destruction and disease. **wicked stumbling blocks** The connection with Eze 7:19 suggests the people in exile are being condemned for idolatry in the same terms as those in Judah (see note on 3:20). **I let them inquire of me at all** The rhetorical question highlights the spiritual unworthiness of the elders. They seek the guidance of Yahweh, but they hedge their bets with their devotion to other gods.

14:4 go to a prophet The answer to the question in v. 3 appears to be "yes." The people can come and inquire of Yahweh—even in the midst of their idolatry.

14:6 your detestable practices See note on 5:9.

14:8 I will set my face against them That is, Yahweh will turn in judgment on them and pronounce a sentence. Likely an allusion to Lev 20:6, where one who seeks guidance through magic is cut off from the people after Yahweh sets his face against them. **an example and a byword** See note on Job 17:6.

14:9 I the Lord have enticed that prophet Ezekiel's rhetoric seems to be based on 1Ki 22, where all the prophets declaring victory for Ahab, king of Israel, have been misled by a lying spirit. Only the prophet Micaiah declares the truth—that Israel will be defeated and Ahab will die (see 1Ki 22:13–23). **I will stretch out my hand** A common idiom for divine judgment. It is used most frequently by Ezekiel but is based on Ex 7:5.

unfaithful and I stretch out my hand against it to cut off its food supply and send famine upon it and kill its people and their animals, ¹⁴even if these three men — Noah, Daniel[a] and Job — were in it, they could save only themselves by their righteousness, declares the Sovereign LORD.

¹⁵"Or if I send wild beasts through that country and they leave it childless and it becomes desolate so that no one can pass through it because of the beasts, ¹⁶as surely as I live, declares the Sovereign LORD, even if these three men were in it, they could not save their own sons or daughters. They alone would be saved, but the land would be desolate.

¹⁷"Or if I bring a sword against that country and say, 'Let the sword pass throughout the land,' and I kill its people and their animals, ¹⁸as surely as I live, declares the Sovereign LORD, even if these three men were in it, they could not save their own sons or daughters. They alone would be saved.

¹⁹"Or if I send a plague into that land and pour out my wrath on it through bloodshed, killing its people and their animals, ²⁰as surely as I live, declares the Sovereign LORD, even if Noah, Daniel and Job were in it, they could save neither son nor daughter. They would save only themselves by their righteousness.

²¹"For this is what the Sovereign LORD says: How much worse will it be when I send against Jerusalem my four dreadful judgments — sword and famine and wild beasts and plague — to kill its men and their animals! ²²Yet there will be some survivors — sons and daughters who will be brought out of it. They will come to you, and when you see their conduct and their actions, you will be consoled regarding the disaster I have brought on Jerusalem — every disaster I have brought on it. ²³You will be consoled when you see their conduct and their actions, for you will know that I have done nothing in it without cause, declares the Sovereign LORD."

Jerusalem as a Useless Vine

15 The word of the LORD came to me: ²"Son of man, how is the wood of a vine different from that of a branch from any of the trees in the forest? ³Is wood ever taken from it to make anything useful? Do they make pegs from it to hang things on? ⁴And after it is thrown on the fire as fuel and the fire burns both ends and chars the middle, is it then useful for anything? ⁵If it was not useful for anything when it was whole, how much less can it be made into something useful when the fire has burned it and it is charred?

⁶"Therefore this is what the Sovereign LORD says: As I have given the wood of the vine among the trees of the forest as fuel for the fire, so will I treat the people living in Jerusalem. ⁷I will set my face against them. Although they have come out of the fire, the fire will yet consume them. And when I set my face against them, you will know that I am the LORD. ⁸I will make the land desolate because they have been unfaithful, declares the Sovereign LORD."

[a] 14 Or Danel, a man of renown in ancient literature; also in verse 20

14:12–23 This passage returns to imagery of punishment by sword, famine, pestilence and wild beasts from Eze 5–7 (especially see 5:17; 6:11; 7:15). The sayings are structured as case law (if X, then Y), which is prominent in Lev 17–26 (see Lev 17:10; 20:6,10 for examples).

The underlying theological issue is whether the righteousness of a few can delay the judgment of many. Ezekiel's answer is "no," while in Genesis God answered "maybe" to Abraham's intercession for Sodom (see Ge 18:23–33).

14:13 to cut off its food See note on Eze 4:16.
14:14 Noah, Daniel and Job The theme is similar to Abraham's plea to Yahweh to spare Sodom for the sake of 10 righteous men (Ge 18:32); but here, even the presence of three legendary, righteous men would not be enough to spare anyone else (compare Jer 15:1). The identity of Daniel here is disputed. Biblical Daniel was Ezekiel's contemporary; he, too, was part of the first deportation to Babylon, but he settled in the royal court. The reference to a contemporary Jewish figure (Daniel) between two ancient non-Israelites (Noah and Job) seems out of place. This Daniel might refer to an ancient non-Israelite known for his righteousness. The mention of Daniel in Eze 28:3 — in the context of an oracle against the Canaanite city of Tyre — strengthens this possibility because Canaanite literature describes a character named Daniel as a wise judge similar to Job. Ezekiel's mention of three non-Israelite examples fits his rhetoric that Israel had become even worse than the Gentile nations around her (see 5:6–7).

14:22 there will be some survivors See note on Isa 1:9. **you will be consoled regarding the disaster I have brought** In this case, the remnant was preserved to provide justification for the judgment. Once the exiles see how bad the people really were, they will understand why judgment was necessary.

15:1–8 This is the first of a series of parables and extended metaphors that characterize Eze 15:1—24:14. The prophet uses a variety of poetic images to describe Israel and recount its history of rebellion against Yahweh. This metaphor describes Israel as a vine branch—good for nothing except fuel for the fire. The parables in chs. 17 and 19 continue the vine imagery. The vine is a traditional image associated with Judah (based on Ge 49:11–12) that symbolized life and fertile growth. Isaiah uses those associations to present Judah as a vineyard (Isa 5:1–7). Jeremiah uses the image to describe Israel's decline from a choice vine to a wild vine (Jer 2:21). Ezekiel extends that association further: Even the wild vine is now nothing but a dead vine. The OT imagery of the vine finds new life in Jesus' characterization of himself as the true vine in Jn 15:1–17.

15:3 Do they make pegs from it While the vine symbolized life and agricultural growth, once the plant itself had died, the wood was useless for making even the most basic of tools.

Jerusalem as an Adulterous Wife

16 The word of the LORD came to me: [2]"Son of man, confront Jerusalem with her detestable practices [3]and say, 'This is what the Sovereign LORD says to Jerusalem: Your ancestry and birth were in the land of the Canaanites; your father was an Amorite and your mother a Hittite. [4]On the day you were born your cord was not cut, nor were you washed with water to make you clean, nor were you rubbed with salt or wrapped in cloths. [5]No one looked on you with pity or had compassion enough to do any of these things for you. Rather, you were thrown out into the open field, for on the day you were born you were despised.

[6]"'Then I passed by and saw you kicking about in your blood, and as you lay there in your blood I said to you, "Live!"[a] [7]I made you grow like a plant of the field. You grew and developed and entered puberty. Your breasts had formed and your hair had grown, yet you were stark naked.

[8]"'Later I passed by, and when I looked at you and saw that you were old enough for love, I spread the corner of my garment over you and covered your naked body. I gave you my solemn oath and entered into a covenant with you, declares the Sovereign LORD, and you became mine.

[9]"'I bathed you with water and washed the blood from you and put ointments on you. [10]I clothed you with an embroidered dress and put sandals of fine leather on you. I dressed you in fine linen and covered you with costly garments. [11]I adorned you with jewelry: I put bracelets on your arms and a necklace around your neck, [12]and I put a ring on your nose, earrings on your ears and a beautiful crown on your head. [13]So you were adorned with gold and silver; your clothes were of fine linen and costly fabric and embroidered cloth. Your food was honey, olive oil and the finest flour. You became very beautiful and rose to be a queen. [14]And your fame spread among the nations on account of your beauty, because the splendor I had given you made your beauty perfect, declares the Sovereign LORD.

[15]"'But you trusted in your beauty and used your

---

[a] 6 A few Hebrew manuscripts, Septuagint and Syriac; most Hebrew manuscripts repeat *and as you lay there in your blood I said to you, "Live!"*

15:7 set my face against them A posture of judgment (see Eze 14:8 and note).

16:1–58 Ezekiel expands the traditional prophetic motif of Israel as Yahweh's unfaithful bride into a graphic symbolic story (or allegory), depicting Israel's political and religious activities as brazen infidelity. Ezekiel's language is crude and explicit, characterizing Israel as an adulteress with an insatiable sexual appetite. The overall meaning of the metaphor is clear, but the specific details are complicated; the boundary between literal and figurative is often blurred. The extended metaphor covers the full range of Israel's history, presenting Israel as an abandoned infant, an attractive young woman, a radiant bride and a married seductress. Yahweh narrates the story in the first person, with himself in the role of king and husband. Like any metaphor, the comparisons break down when pressed in the details. The depictions of violent humiliation and punishment against the unfaithful bride should be read as symbolic of the Babylonian invasion and destruction of Judah, not as a model for the literal treatment of an adulterous wife.

16:2 with her detestable practices See note on 5:9.
16:3 land of the Canaanites The city of Jerusalem represents the land of Judah, and by extension, God's chosen people. Jerusalem was a Canaanite city before David conquered it and made it his capital (2Sa 5:6–9). **your father was an Amorite and your mother a Hittite** The Amorites and Hittites were pre-Israelite inhabitants of Canaan. The emphasis on Jerusalem's Canaanite ancestry would have been insulting to Ezekiel's Israelite audience.
16:4 nor were you rubbed with salt An ancient practice still performed by Palestinian Arab mothers, who believe it to be beneficial. **wrapped in cloths** The sequence of actions—cutting the umbilical cord, washing the baby, rubbing with salt and wrapping in cloth—would have been performed by a midwife attending the birth. The symbolism emphasizes that no one who cared about the child was present.

16:5 you were thrown out into the open field Infanticide was practiced in the ancient world, usually involving unwanted females or deformed infants. It also was a means of population control, usually out of economic necessity; some villages had trouble supporting their existing children. The implication of casting the child into the open field meant that the parents were renouncing all legal claims on the child and leaving its survival in the hands of God or a passerby who might adopt the baby and save its life.
16:6 in your blood I said to you, "Live!" Ancient Near Eastern texts use phrasing related to birth fluid and blood in legal adoption formulas. Yahweh is declaring his intent to adopt the baby, simultaneously claiming all legal right to the child. The adoption regulations of the Code of Hammurabi (17th century BC) literally state, "If a man has adopted an infant still in his amniotic fluid."
16:7 your hair had grown Juxtaposed with the statement about developed breasts, the reference to hair likely refers to pubic hair. The young woman was now ready for marriage and sexuality. Almost identical phrasing can be seen in a Sumerian hymn to the goddess Ishtar, where the young women declare their breasts and pubic hair have grown, so they can now have sex.
16:8 Later I passed by The first time, he formally adopted her as a daughter; this time, their relationship becomes a marriage arrangement. **you were old enough for love** The Hebrew word used here for love, *dodim*, refers specifically to sexual love (see SS 5:1). **I spread the corner of my garment over you** Signifies the intent to marry the woman (compare Ru 3:9). **I gave you my solemn oath** Entering into a marriage covenant with her.

16:10–13 Having taken Jerusalem as wife, Yahweh provides her with clothing and food, advancing her status to that of a queen. The list of jewelry is reminiscent of that in Isa 3:18–23.

16:15–21 The tale now turns from the woman's rise to royal status to her misuse of that status. She misappropriates all the good things Yahweh has given her and

fame to become a prostitute. You lavished your favors on anyone who passed by and your beauty became his. ¹⁶You took some of your garments to make gaudy high places, where you carried on your prostitution. You went to him, and he possessed your beauty.ᵃ ¹⁷You also took the fine jewelry I gave you, the jewelry made of my gold and silver, and you made for yourself male idols and engaged in prostitution with them. ¹⁸And you took your embroidered clothes to put on them, and you offered my oil and incense before them. ¹⁹Also the food I provided for you — the flour, olive oil and honey I gave you to eat — you offered as fragrant incense before them. That is what happened, declares the Sovereign LORD.

²⁰"'And you took your sons and daughters whom you bore to me and sacrificed them as food to the idols. Was your prostitution not enough? ²¹You slaughtered my children and sacrificed them to the idols. ²²In all your detestable practices and your prostitution you did not remember the days of your youth, when you were naked and bare, kicking about in your blood.

²³"'Woe! Woe to you, declares the Sovereign LORD. In addition to all your other wickedness, ²⁴you built a mound for yourself and made a lofty shrine in every public square. ²⁵At every street corner you built your lofty shrines and degraded your beauty, spreading your legs with increasing promiscuity to anyone who passed by. ²⁶You en-

gaged in prostitution with the Egyptians, your neighbors with large genitals, and aroused my anger with your increasing promiscuity. ²⁷So I stretched out my hand against you and reduced your territory; I gave you over to the greed of your enemies, the daughters of the Philistines, who were shocked by your lewd conduct. ²⁸You engaged in prostitution with the Assyrians too, because you were insatiable; and even after that, you still were not satisfied. ²⁹Then you increased your promiscuity to include Babylonia,ᵇ a land of merchants, but even with this you were not satisfied.

³⁰"'I am filled with fury against you,ᶜ declares the Sovereign LORD, when you do all these things, acting like a brazen prostitute! ³¹When you built your mounds at every street corner and made your lofty shrines in every public square, you were unlike a prostitute, because you scorned payment.

³²"'You adulterous wife! You prefer strangers to your own husband! ³³All prostitutes receive gifts, but you give gifts to all your lovers, bribing them to come to you from everywhere for your illicit favors. ³⁴So in your prostitution you are the opposite of others; no one runs after you for your favors. You are the very opposite, for you give payment and none is given to you.

³⁵"'Therefore, you prostitute, hear the word of

ᵃ 16 The meaning of the Hebrew for this sentence is uncertain.
ᵇ 29 Or *Chaldea*   ᶜ 30 Or *How feverish is your heart,*

---

uses them for the benefit of her lovers (symbolizing idols). She uses her fine clothes to make shelters where she meets her lovers, and she refashions her jewelry into images of men. The mixture of images shifts between sexual and religious, highlighting the difficulty of separating the literal and figurative aspects of the metaphor.

16:15 used your fame to become a prostitute The Hebrew verb *zanah*, meaning "to play the whore" and the related noun *taznuth*, meaning "whoring," appear throughout this passage to characterize the idolatrous behavior of Israel. Adultery breaks the marriage covenant in the same way idolatry broke the covenant requirement to worship only Yahweh. The Hebrew word is the same for prostitution. The possible practice of cult prostitution connected to idol worship blurs the distinction between literal and figurative in this accusation.

16:16 gaudy high places Represents the high places where Israel engaged in idol worship alongside worship of Yahweh. It also carries the double meaning of the colorfully decorated bed of a prostitute (compare Pr 7:16–17; see note on Isa 57:7).

16:17 male idols and engaged in prostitution with them Metaphorically represents idol worship. The symbolism weaves together images of idolatry and sexuality.

16:19 fragrant incense See note on Eze 20:28.

16:20 your sons and daughters Refers to the inhabitants of Judah. **sacrificed them as food to the idols** Possibly an allusion to child sacrifice (see note on 20:26).

16:24 mound A dome or elevated platform for ritual prostitution.

16:25 spreading your legs The Hebrew is quite ex-

plicit. She offers herself by indecently spreading her legs. The literal Hebrew phrase here reads "you spread your feet wide."

16:26 the Egyptians Jerusalem's illicit relationships involved the surrounding major powers: Egyptians, Assyrians and Babylonians. Judah sought political and military support from Egypt to oppose both the Assyrians (see note on Isa 30:1–7) and the Babylonians (see note on Eze 17:7). **with large genitals** Another of Ezekiel's sexually charged images that is often toned down in translation. The Hebrew phrase used here, *gidle vasar*, means "great of flesh."

16:27 I stretched out my hand against you See note on 14:9; compare Isa 5:25 and note. **reduced your territory** An allusion to the husband's responsibility to provide for his wife outlined in Ex 21:10. If a husband took a second wife, the law prevented him from diminishing the portion of his first wife; however, in the case of adultery, he was no longer responsible for the wife's well-being. Legally, the penalty for adultery was death (see Lev 20:10). **the Philistines** Israel's traditional enemies to the west, on the coastal plain.

16:28 the Assyrians King Ahaz of Judah had appealed to Assyria for assistance against Israel and Syria around 734 BC (see note on Isa 7:1).

16:29 Babylonia The Bible sometimes uses "Babylon" and "Chaldea" interchangeably.

16:31 unlike a prostitute, because you scorned payment Cultic and commercial prostitutes accepted payment for their services. However, Jerusalem's adulterous liaisons gained her nothing and gave away everything.

the LORD! ³⁶This is what the Sovereign LORD says: Because you poured out your lust and exposed your naked body in your promiscuity with your lovers, and because of all your detestable idols, and because you gave them your children's blood, ³⁷therefore I am going to gather all your lovers, with whom you found pleasure, those you loved as well as those you hated. I will gather them against you from all around and will strip you in front of them, and they will see you stark naked. ³⁸I will sentence you to the punishment of women who commit adultery and who shed blood; I will bring on you the blood vengeance of my wrath and jealous anger. ³⁹Then I will deliver you into the hands of your lovers, and they will tear down your mounds and destroy your lofty shrines. They will strip you of your clothes and take your fine jewelry and leave you stark naked. ⁴⁰They will bring a mob against you, who will stone you and hack you to pieces with their swords. ⁴¹They will burn down your houses and inflict punishment on you in the sight of many women. I will put a stop to your prostitution, and you will no longer pay your lovers. ⁴²Then my wrath against you will subside and my jealous anger will turn away from you; I will be calm and no longer angry.

⁴³"Because you did not remember the days of your youth but enraged me with all these things, I will surely bring down on your head what you have done, declares the Sovereign LORD. Did you not add lewdness to all your other detestable practices?

⁴⁴"Everyone who quotes proverbs will quote this proverb about you: "Like mother, like daughter." ⁴⁵You are a true daughter of your mother, who despised her husband and her children; and you are a true sister of your sisters, who despised their husbands and their children. Your mother was a Hittite and your father an Amorite. ⁴⁶Your older sister was Samaria, who lived to the north of you with her daughters; and your younger sister, who lived to the south of you with her daughters, was Sodom. ⁴⁷You not only followed their ways and copied their detestable practices, but in all your ways you soon became more depraved than they. ⁴⁸As surely as I live, declares the Sovereign LORD, your sister Sodom and her daughters never did what you and your daughters have done.

⁴⁹"'Now this was the sin of your sister Sodom: She and her daughters were arrogant, overfed and unconcerned; they did not help the poor and needy. ⁵⁰They were haughty and did detestable things before me. Therefore I did away with them as you have seen. ⁵¹Samaria did not commit half the sins you did. You have done more detestable things than they, and have made your sisters seem righteous by all these things you have done. ⁵²Bear your disgrace, for you have furnished some justification for your sisters. Because your sins were more vile than theirs, they appear more righteous than you. So then, be ashamed and bear your disgrace, for you have made your sisters appear righteous.

⁵³"However, I will restore the fortunes of Sodom and her daughters and of Samaria and her daughters, and your fortunes along with them, ⁵⁴so that you may bear your disgrace and be ashamed of all you have done in giving them comfort. ⁵⁵And your sisters, Sodom with her daughters and Samaria with her daughters, will return to what they were before; and you and your daughters will return to what you were before. ⁵⁶You would not even mention your sister Sodom in the day of your pride, ⁵⁷before your wickedness was uncovered. Even so, you are now scorned by the daughters of Edom*ᵃ* and all her neighbors

---

ᵃ *57* Many Hebrew manuscripts and Syriac; most Hebrew manuscripts, Septuagint and Vulgate *Aram*

16:36 exposed your naked body The Hebrew idiom used here — *galah erwah*, meaning "expose nakedness" — is a common euphemism for sexual activity (see Lev 18:6 and note).

16:37–43 The focus shifts from a detailed description of the woman's infidelity to an explicit account of her public humiliation and punishment. The details of the metaphor should not be pressed at this point, since the literal destruction of Jerusalem by the Babylonians seems to underlie the violent depiction of physical and sexual abuse. Ancient Near Eastern law codes, however, allowed the husband to punish his adulterous wife as he pleased, depending on the circumstances.

16:38 the punishment of women who commit adultery Both adultery and murder were capital offenses (see Lev 20:10; Dt 19:11–12).

16:40 hack you to pieces with their swords A description more appropriate for an invasion than capital punishment.

16:41 They will burn down your houses The judgment in Eze 16:39–41 starts with the woman's shelter and clothing being removed and shifts to a depiction of the city's destruction.

16:44 Like mother, like daughter Jerusalem's mother was a Hittite (v. 3). The comparison means that Judahite Jerusalem was just as guilty of idolatry as Canaanite Jerusalem.

16:46 older sister was Samaria Foreshadowing the similar tale of two sisters in ch. 23, the prophet describes Jerusalem and her behavior in light of Samaria, the capital city of Israel, and Sodom, an ancient Canaanite city on the Dead Sea. By this time, both of these cities had long been destroyed. **Sodom** A proverbial example of divine judgment (Ge 19).

16:49 they did not help the poor Sodom's great crime is categorized as social injustice, adding a new level of critique to the accusation of idolatry.

16:52 Bear your disgrace That is, accept the shame of punishment (see note on Eze 22:4).

16:56 You would not even mention your sister Sodom Alluding to Sodom's reputation as the ultimate example of a wicked city that received Yahweh's destruction.

16:57 you are now scorned by See note on 22:4.

and the daughters of the Philistines — all those around you who despise you. [58]You will bear the consequences of your lewdness and your detestable practices, declares the LORD.

[59]"'This is what the Sovereign LORD says: I will deal with you as you deserve, because you have despised my oath by breaking the covenant. [60]Yet I will remember the covenant I made with you in the days of your youth, and I will establish an everlasting covenant with you. [61]Then you will remember your ways and be ashamed when you receive your sisters, both those who are older than you and those who are younger. I will give them to you as daughters, but not on the basis of my covenant with you. [62]So I will establish my covenant with you, and you will know that I am the LORD. [63]Then, when I make atonement for you for all you have done, you will remember and be ashamed and never again open your mouth because of your humiliation, declares the Sovereign LORD.'"

Two Eagles and a Vine

17 The word of the LORD came to me: [2]"Son of man, set forth an allegory and tell it to the Israelites as a parable. [3]Say to them, 'This is what the Sovereign LORD says: A great eagle with powerful wings, long feathers and full plumage

of varied colors came to Lebanon. Taking hold of the top of a cedar, [4]he broke off its topmost shoot and carried it away to a land of merchants, where he planted it in a city of traders.

[5]"'He took one of the seedlings of the land and put it in fertile soil. He planted it like a willow by abundant water, [6]and it sprouted and became a low, spreading vine. Its branches turned toward him, but its roots remained under it. So it became a vine and produced branches and put out leafy boughs.

[7]"'But there was another great eagle with powerful wings and full plumage. The vine now sent out its roots toward him from the plot where it was planted and stretched out its branches to him for water. [8]It had been planted in good soil by abundant water so that it would produce branches, bear fruit and become a splendid vine.'

[9]"Say to them, 'This is what the Sovereign LORD says: Will it thrive? Will it not be uprooted and stripped of its fruit so that it withers? All its new growth will wither. It will not take a strong arm or many people to pull it up by the roots. [10]It has been planted, but will it thrive? Will it not wither completely when the east wind strikes it — wither away in the plot where it grew?'"

[11]Then the word of the LORD came to me: [12]"Say to this rebellious people, 'Do you not know what these

---

16:59–63 The lengthy oracle concludes with a hint of the future restoration of Israel under a new, everlasting covenant.

16:59 because you have despised my oath A covenant was ratified with an oath, so breaking the covenant broke the solemn oath as well.

16:60 everlasting covenant This future hope is an important part of prophetic oracles of salvation (see 37:26; Isa 55:3 and note; 61:8; Jer 32:40).

16:61 give them to you as daughters Symbolizes the relative status of Samaria and Sodom as lower than that of Jerusalem.

17:1–24 Ezekiel retells Judah's recent history as a parable about two eagles and a vine. The story resembles NT parables, in that it is told and then explained for a puzzled audience (compare Mt 13:1–23). The parable addresses the folly of rebelling against Babylon and seeking help from Egypt.

17:2 an allegory Indicates an enigmatic saying that requires explanation to be understood (see Jdg 14:12–14). Learning to understand such sayings was considered a quality of gaining wisdom (see Pr 1:6). **tell it to the Israelites as a parable** A saying or story teaching a moral lesson (see note on Pr 1:1). Parables and proverbs make full use of metaphorical comparisons and figurative language. Ezekiel apparently has a reputation for using parables (see Eze 20:49). Teaching through parables and riddles was characteristic of the OT sage. Ezekiel's propensity for these wisdom genres reflects his status as priest, prophet and sage.

17:3 eagle This bird can represent both swift strength and ominous destructive power (see Hab 1:8; La 4:19;

Job 9:26). This first eagle stands for Nebuchadnezzar, king of Babylon, who campaigned in Judah in 598 BC and took King Jehoiachin into exile (see note on Eze 1:2).

17:4 its topmost shoot The cedar represents Judah, and the topmost twig (or branch or shoot) refers to King Jehoiachin, who was taken by Nebuchadnezzar into exile in Babylon.

17:5 the seedlings of the land The planting by Nebuchadnezzar alludes to his maneuver to reestablish the kingdom of Judah by installing Jehoiachin's uncle Zedekiah as king. The coronation of Zedekiah restored Judah's political status as a subservient state of Babylon. **fertile soil** Depicts Judah's potential to become a flourishing society.

17:6 a low, spreading vine Represents Judah (see 15:1–8 and note). **Its branches turned toward him** Initially, Zedekiah was loyal to Nebuchadnezzar.

17:7 another great eagle The second eagle is less grand and powerful, but it is still formidable. This eagle likely represents Pharaoh Psammetichus II of Egypt. When Psammetichus came to power in 595 BC, several nations in Syria-Palestine (including Moab, Ammon, Edom, Tyre and Sidon) saw an opportunity to rebel against Babylon (see Jer 27:1–11). In 591 BC, Psammetichus entered Palestine, challenging Babylonian power there. **vine now sent out its roots toward him** Zedekiah was caught between political factions in Jerusalem. One group advocated continued loyalty to Babylon; the other promoted rebellion and alliance with Egypt. Eventually, Zedekiah was convinced to rebel with the promise of Egyptian support.

17:9 Will it not be uprooted The rhetorical question directs the audience's attention to the dangerous circumstances. Once Judah has rebelled, there will be little to stop Nebuchadnezzar from destroying it.

things mean?' Say to them: 'The king of Babylon went to Jerusalem and carried off her king and her nobles, bringing them back with him to Babylon. [13]Then he took a member of the royal family and made a treaty with him, putting him under oath. He also carried away the leading men of the land, [14]so that the kingdom would be brought low, unable to rise again, surviving only by keeping his treaty. [15]But the king rebelled against him by sending his envoys to Egypt to get horses and a large army. Will he succeed? Will he who does such things escape? Will he break the treaty and yet escape?

[16]"'As surely as I live, declares the Sovereign LORD, he shall die in Babylon, in the land of the king who put him on the throne, whose oath he despised and whose treaty he broke. [17]Pharaoh with his mighty army and great horde will be of no help to him in war, when ramps are built and siege works erected to destroy many lives. [18]He despised the oath by breaking the covenant. Because he had given his hand in pledge and yet did all these things, he shall not escape.

[19]"'Therefore this is what the Sovereign LORD says: As surely as I live, I will repay him for despising my oath and breaking my covenant. [20]I will spread my net for him, and he will be caught in my snare. I will bring him to Babylon and execute judgment on him there because he was unfaithful to me. [21]All his choice troops will fall by the sword,

and the survivors will be scattered to the winds. Then you will know that I the LORD have spoken.

[22]"'This is what the Sovereign LORD says: I myself will take a shoot from the very top of a cedar and plant it; I will break off a tender sprig from its topmost shoots and plant it on a high and lofty mountain. [23]On the mountain heights of Israel I will plant it; it will produce branches and bear fruit and become a splendid cedar. Birds of every kind will nest in it; they will find shelter in the shade of its branches. [24]All the trees of the forest will know that I the LORD bring down the tall tree and make the low tree grow tall. I dry up the green tree and make the dry tree flourish.

"'I the LORD have spoken, and I will do it.'"

The One Who Sins Will Die

18 The word of the LORD came to me: [2]"What do you people mean by quoting this proverb about the land of Israel:

"'The parents eat sour grapes,
    and the children's teeth are set on edge'?

[3]"As surely as I live, declares the Sovereign LORD, you will no longer quote this proverb in Israel. [4]For everyone belongs to me, the parent as well as the child — both alike belong to me. The one who sins is the one who will die.

17:12 this rebellious people One of Ezekiel's favorite expressions for Judah (see note on Eze 2:5).
17:13 royal family Refers to Zedekiah; see v. 5 and note. **and made a treaty with him** The agreement between Zedekiah and Nebuchadnezzar is described as an oath and a covenant. Suzerain-vassal treaties in the ancient Near East were ratified by invoking the native deities of both parties as witnesses. Zedekiah's rebellion against Nebuchadnezzar resulted in breaking an oath he had called on Yahweh to guarantee (see 2Ch 36:13). This explains Yahweh's role in bringing judgment against Zedekiah for rebelling against Babylon (see Eze 17:19–20). See the table "Covenants in the Old Testament" on p. 469. **He also carried away the leading men of the land** The new king had few experienced advisers since most of the leading men were deported along with Jehoiachin (see 2Ki 24:14–15).
17:16 he shall die in Babylon The Babylonians ultimately killed Zedekiah's sons in front of him, blinded him and took him into captivity (2Ki 25:7).
17:17 siege works Zedekiah can expect no help from Egypt when it really counts. On siege warfare, see note on Eze 4:2.
17:22 a shoot from the very top Symbolizes a new beginning and Yahweh's plan to restore his people. The imagery brings the elements of the parable into an oracle of hope and future salvation. **a tender sprig** From the cedar symbolizing Judah comes the tender topmost twig (or shoot or branch) symbolizing the Messiah. Compare Isa 11:1. **a high and lofty mountain** Zion, Yahweh's holy mountain. See Ps 2:6 and Isa 2:2.
18:1–32 As in Eze 12:22, a proverb representing the people's attitudes is presented and then refuted. Ezekiel's

concern here is addressing the second-generation exiles' bitterness over suffering for what they perceive as their parents' sins. While Biblical law justified punishment across generations (see Ex 20:5 and note), Ezekiel focuses on the reality of each individual's accountability for sin and practical rebellion against God.

18:2 proverb Proverbs could be wise, enigmatic sayings by important teachers, as well as conventional adages by common people (see note on Eze 17:2). **children's teeth are set on edge** Depicts a person's involuntary reaction to an extremely unpleasant taste. Since experience cannot be transferred, the saying implies that the children's suffering for their parents' sin is unnatural. Their criticism of Yahweh is later illustrated in a false proverb in v. 25, which expresses that the way of Yahweh is not right. The popularity of the saying here in v. 2 is shown by the parallel in Jer 31:29–30, which also rejects the saying and promotes individual responsibility.
18:4 The one who sins is the one who will die The statement here (and a similar remark in Jer 31:30) offers a contrast to Ex 20:5, which declares that Yahweh will punish sin across generations, sometimes delaying judgment for future generations. The idea of punishment across generations was well-established in the culture of the Biblical world. This concept corresponds with Yahweh's great patience as he withholds punishment and hopes for Israel and Judah to repent. A delay in full-blown judgment, however, did not imply that earlier generations went unpunished or that the current generation is without guilt. Many of the behaviors listed here focus on things that a righteous person avoids. This type of negative confession was common in the ancient

5 "Suppose there is a righteous man
  who does what is just and right.
6 He does not eat at the mountain shrines
  or look to the idols of Israel.
He does not defile his neighbor's wife
  or have sexual relations with a woman
    during her period.
7 He does not oppress anyone,
  but returns what he took in pledge for a
    loan.
He does not commit robbery
  but gives his food to the hungry
  and provides clothing for the naked.
8 He does not lend to them at interest
  or take a profit from them.
He withholds his hand from doing wrong
  and judges fairly between two parties.
9 He follows my decrees
  and faithfully keeps my laws.
That man is righteous;
  he will surely live,
                declares the Sovereign LORD.

10 "Suppose he has a violent son, who sheds blood or does any of these other things[a] 11 (though the father has done none of them):

"He eats at the mountain shrines.
He defiles his neighbor's wife.
12 He oppresses the poor and needy.
He commits robbery.
He does not return what he took in pledge.
He looks to the idols.
He does detestable things.
13 He lends at interest and takes a profit.

Will such a man live? He will not! Because he has done all these detestable things, he is to be put to death; his blood will be on his own head.

14 "But suppose this son has a son who sees all the sins his father commits, and though he sees them, he does not do such things:

15 "He does not eat at the mountain shrines
  or look to the idols of Israel.
He does not defile his neighbor's wife.
16 He does not oppress anyone
  or require a pledge for a loan.
He does not commit robbery
  but gives his food to the hungry
  and provides clothing for the naked.
17 He withholds his hand from mistreating
    the poor
  and takes no interest or profit from them.
He keeps my laws and follows my decrees.

He will not die for his father's sin; he will surely live. 18 But his father will die for his own sin, because he practiced extortion, robbed his brother and did what was wrong among his people.

19 "Yet you ask, 'Why does the son not share the guilt of his father?' Since the son has done what is just and right and has been careful to keep all my decrees, he will surely live. 20 The one who sins is the one who will die. The child will not share the guilt of the parent, nor will the parent share the guilt of the child. The righteousness of the righteous will be credited to them, and the wickedness of the wicked will be charged against them.

21 "But if a wicked person turns away from all the sins they have committed and keeps all my decrees and does what is just and right, that person will surely live; they will not die. 22 None of the offenses they have committed will be remembered against them. Because of the righteous things they have done, they will live. 23 Do I take any pleasure in the death of the wicked? declares the Sovereign

---

[a] 10 Or things to a brother

Near East. For example, the Egyptian Book of the Dead contained negative confessions designed to satisfy the gods about a person's moral character and secure entry into the afterlife. The lists of moral and immoral behaviors emphasized the ideals of kingship and leadership in the ancient Near Eastern culture.

18:6 He does not eat at the mountain shrines Probably an indirect reference to idol-worship on the mountain shrines called high places (see note on Isa 57:7). **the idols of Israel** This phrase also occurs in Eze 8:10, referring to idolatry in the Jerusalem temple. See note on 14:3. **He does not defile his neighbor's wife** Forbidden in Lev 18:20. **sexual relations with a woman during her period** Forbidden in Lev 18:19.
18:7 returns what he took in pledge for a loan A requirement of Ex 22:26. **He does not commit robbery** See Lev 6:1–7 and Ex 20:15. **gives his food to the hungry** Caring for the poor was an ideal moral virtue (see Isa 58:7).
18:8 He does not lend to them at interest Forbidden in Ex 22:25 and Lev 25:36.
18:9 he will surely live The granting of life sums up

the positive blessings for covenant obedience found in Lev 26:3–13 (compare Eze 20:11; Am 5:4).
18:10 Suppose he has a violent son Ezekiel's test cases run through three generations: a righteous man who fathers a wicked son, who in turn fathers a righteous son. The relative merit and punishment warranted to each for their behavior does not cross generational lines.
18:17 will not die for his father's sin His righteous behavior preserves his life just as it had for his grandfather.
18:19 does the son not share the guilt of his father They expected the descendants to suffer the consequences of their ancestors' sin, even though their proverb (see Eze 18:2) expressed that such an arrangement was unfair. Ezekiel anticipates their objection and answers by reiterating that all are responsible for their own behavior, good or bad.
18:21 if a wicked person turns away The wicked are not excluded from possible salvation. Full repentance also leads to life.
18:23 turn from their ways and live Yahweh prefers repentance to punishment.

LORD. Rather, am I not pleased when they turn from their ways and live? ²⁴"But if a righteous person turns from their righteousness and commits sin and does the same detestable things the wicked person does, will they live? None of the righteous things that person has done will be remembered. Because of the unfaithfulness they are guilty of and because of the sins they have committed, they will die. ²⁵"Yet you say, 'The way of the Lord is not just.' Hear, you Israelites: Is my way unjust? Is it not your ways that are unjust? ²⁶If a righteous person turns from their righteousness and commits sin, they will die for it; because of the sin they have committed they will die. ²⁷But if a wicked person turns away from the wickedness they have committed and does what is just and right, they will save their life. ²⁸Because they consider all the offenses they have committed and turn away from them, that person will surely live; they will not die. ²⁹Yet the Israelites say, 'The way of the Lord is not just.' Are my ways unjust, people of Israel? Is it not your ways that are unjust?

³⁰"Therefore, you Israelites, I will judge each of you according to your own ways, declares the Sovereign LORD. Repent! Turn away from all your offenses; then sin will not be your downfall. ³¹Rid yourselves of all the offenses you have committed, and get a new heart and a new spirit. Why will you die, people of Israel? ³²For I take no pleasure in the death of anyone, declares the Sovereign LORD. Repent and live!

A Lament Over Israel's Princes

19 "Take up a lament concerning the princes of Israel ²and say:

"'What a lioness was your mother
among the lions!

She lay down among them
and reared her cubs.
³She brought up one of her cubs,
and he became a strong lion.
He learned to tear the prey
and he became a man-eater.
⁴The nations heard about him,
and he was trapped in their pit.
They led him with hooks
to the land of Egypt.

⁵"'When she saw her hope unfulfilled,
her expectation gone,
she took another of her cubs
and made him a strong lion.
⁶He prowled among the lions,
for he was now a strong lion.
He learned to tear the prey
and he became a man-eater.
⁷He broke down^a their strongholds
and devastated their towns.
The land and all who were in it
were terrified by his roaring.
⁸Then the nations came against him,
those from regions round about.
They spread their net for him,
and he was trapped in their pit.
⁹With hooks they pulled him into a cage
and brought him to the king
of Babylon.
They put him in prison,
so his roar was heard no longer
on the mountains of Israel.

¹⁰"'Your mother was like a vine in your
vineyard^b
planted by the water;

---

^a 7 Targum (see Septuagint); Hebrew *He knew*   ^b 10 Two Hebrew manuscripts; most Hebrew manuscripts *your blood*

18:25 The way of the Lord is not just See note on v. 2. An explicit objection to Yahweh's sovereignty, repeated in v. 29.

19:1–14 Ezekiel continues his string of metaphors and parables with another historical allegory (or symbolic story), similar to ch. 17. The form of lamentation emphasized mourning over the imminent disaster coming upon Judah, as well as disappointment in Judah's behavior. Unlike the parable in ch. 17, the imagery here is unexplained and the symbolism is not always clear.

19:1 lament A lamentation (or lament) is a specific genre of Hebrew poetry, identified as a *qinah*. The *qinah* was characterized by an unbalanced poetic line — usually a line of three accented words followed by a line of two accents. This pattern was frequently used in funeral dirges. The lament form was one of the most common in Hebrew poetry, found in David's lament at the death of Saul and Jonathan in 2Sa 1:19–27, the book of Lamentations, and numerous psalms (e.g., Ps 3; 44; 137). **the princes of Israel** Likely symbolizing the final rulers of Judah — Jehoahaz, Jehoiakim, Jehoiachin and Zedekiah. **19:2 What a lioness was your mother** The lion was a

traditional symbol of Judah (see Ge 49:9). The reference to a mother could be literal (Josiah's Queen Hamutal, mother of Jehoahaz and Zedekiah; 2Ki 23:32; 24:18) or metaphorical for the nation of Judah (based on Ge 49:9). **her cubs** Refers to the princes of Israel.

19:3 one of her cubs If the image of the lioness symbolizes the queen mother, then this likely refers to Jehoahaz, who briefly was king in 609 BC before being deposed by Pharaoh Neco and taken captive to Egypt (Eze 19:4; compare 2Ki 23:31–35). Jehoahaz's full brother Zedekiah, who ruled Judah 597–586 BC, would be the second cub (v. 5). The symbolism of vv. 8–9 fits with events from Zedekiah's reign.

19:4 to the land of Egypt See note on v. 3.
19:5 another of her cubs See note on v. 3.
19:7 He broke down their strongholds The Hebrew wording is difficult. The verse is clear in presenting this king in a negative light, but his precise offenses are open to interpretation.
19:8 the nations came against him Jeremiah 27:1–11 records ambassadors from Moab, Ammon, Edom, Tyre and Sidon (nations surrounding Judah) coming to convince Zedekiah to join them in rebellion against Babylon.

it was fruitful and full of branches
because of abundant water.
¹¹ Its branches were strong,
fit for a ruler's scepter.
It towered high
above the thick foliage,
conspicuous for its height
and for its many branches.
¹² But it was uprooted in fury
and thrown to the ground.
The east wind made it shrivel,
it was stripped of its fruit;
its strong branches withered
and fire consumed them.
¹³ Now it is planted in the desert,
in a dry and thirsty land.
¹⁴ Fire spread from one of its main[a] branches
and consumed its fruit.
No strong branch is left on it
fit for a ruler's scepter.'

"This is a lament and is to be used as a lament."

Rebellious Israel Purged

20 In the seventh year, in the fifth month on the tenth day, some of the elders of Israel came to inquire of the LORD, and they sat down in front of me.

² Then the word of the LORD came to me: ³ "Son of man, speak to the elders of Israel and say to them, 'This is what the Sovereign LORD says: Have you come to inquire of me? As surely as I live, I will not let you inquire of me, declares the Sovereign LORD.'

⁴ "Will you judge them? Will you judge them,

son of man? Then confront them with the detestable practices of their ancestors ⁵ and say to them: 'This is what the Sovereign LORD says: On the day I chose Israel, I swore with uplifted hand to the descendants of Jacob and revealed myself to them in Egypt. With uplifted hand I said to them, "I am the LORD your God." ⁶ On that day I swore to them that I would bring them out of Egypt into a land I had searched out for them, a land flowing with milk and honey, the most beautiful of all lands. ⁷ And I said to them, "Each of you, get rid of the vile images you have set your eyes on, and do not defile yourselves with the idols of Egypt. I am the LORD your God."

⁸ "'But they rebelled against me and would not listen to me; they did not get rid of the vile images they had set their eyes on, nor did they forsake the idols of Egypt. So I said I would pour out my wrath on them and spend my anger against them in Egypt. ⁹ But for the sake of my name, I brought them out of Egypt. I did it to keep my name from being profaned in the eyes of the nations among whom they lived and in whose sight I had revealed myself to the Israelites. ¹⁰ Therefore I led them out of Egypt and brought them into the wilderness. ¹¹ I gave them my decrees and made known to them my laws, by which the person who obeys them will live. ¹² Also I gave them my Sabbaths as a sign between us, so they would know that I the LORD made them holy.

¹³ "'Yet the people of Israel rebelled against me in the wilderness. They did not follow my decrees but rejected my laws — by which the person who

---

[a] 14 Or *from under its*

19:10 Your mother was like a vine This imagery recalls the parable of Eze 15:1–8.
19:11 branches were strong, fit for a ruler's scepter The vine and stems symbolize the royal dynasty of Judah and the kings of Judah.
19:12 its strong branches Refers to Zedekiah, the ruler when the vine was uprooted.
19:14 No strong branch is left on it fit for a ruler's scepter Refers to the loss of the Davidic kingship. The lament over the lack of a strong stem or branch may hint at Messianic expectation (compare Isa 11:1).

20:1–32 Inspired by another visit from Israel's elders, Ezekiel recaps Israel's idolatry, describing a history of almost constant rebellion. His summary focuses on the people's responsibility for their sin and omits reference to prominent figures like Moses or to non-Israelite enticements to sin. It also emphasizes events outside the promised land, a historical situation that would have new significance for the exiles' current situation.

20:1 seventh year, in the fifth month Calculating from the start of Jehoiachin's exile (as Ezekiel usually does; see note on Eze 1:2), this oracle dates to August 15, 591 BC. See the timeline "Dates in Ezekiel" on p. 1276.
20:3 I will not let you inquire of me In ch. 14, Yahweh allowed them to inquire of him primarily to give them a

chance to repent. The time for repentance has passed, and now judgment must be completed.
20:4 Will you judge them, son of man Ezekiel judges them by declaring their abominations, advising them of both charge and verdict. **the detestable practices of their ancestors** Refers to Israel's past history of idolatry (see 16:2; compare note on 5:9).
20:7 the vile images A reference to idolatry (see note on 5:11).
20:8 spend my anger against them Ezekiel chronologically moves up Yahweh's command against idolatry, so that Israel's history of rebellion begins while they are still in Egypt.
20:9 for the sake of my name Yahweh's forbearance is based solely on his sovereign choice. Concerned with preserving his reputation, he delays judgment for a time. The same theme appears in Isa 48:9–11. The emphasis on God acting for the sake of his own reputation is significant to Ezekiel in light of his assertion of individual responsibility in Eze 18. Judgment was deferred to preserve Yahweh's reputation, not to pass on the punishment to the next generation.
20:11 I gave them my decrees Refers to the law God gave to Israel at Sinai; see Ex 19–20.
20:12 I gave them my Sabbaths See Ex 20:8–11. A main focus of the Ten Commandments is the Sabbath,

obeys them will live — and they utterly desecrated my Sabbaths. So I said I would pour out my wrath on them and destroy them in the wilderness. [14]But for the sake of my name I did what would keep it from being profaned in the eyes of the nations in whose sight I had brought them out. [15]Also with uplifted hand I swore to them in the wilderness that I would not bring them into the land I had given them — a land flowing with milk and honey, the most beautiful of all lands — [16]because they rejected my laws and did not follow my decrees and desecrated my Sabbaths. For their hearts were devoted to their idols. [17]Yet I looked on them with pity and did not destroy them or put an end to them in the wilderness. [18]I said to their children in the wilderness, "Do not follow the statutes of your parents or keep their laws or defile yourselves with their idols. [19]I am the Lord your God; follow my decrees and be careful to keep my laws. [20]Keep my Sabbaths holy, that they may be a sign between us. Then you will know that I am the Lord your God."

[21]"But the children rebelled against me: They did not follow my decrees, they were not careful to keep my laws, of which I said, "The person who obeys them will live by them," and they desecrated my Sabbaths. So I said I would pour out my wrath on them and spend my anger against them in the wilderness. [22]But I withheld my hand, and for the sake of my name I did what would keep it from being profaned in the eyes of the nations in whose sight I had brought them out. [23]Also with uplifted hand I swore to them in the wilderness that I would disperse them among the nations and scatter them through the countries, [24]because they had not obeyed my laws but had rejected my decrees and desecrated my Sabbaths, and their eyes lusted after their parents' idols. [25]So I gave them other statutes that were not good and laws through which they could not live; [26]I defiled them through their gifts — the sacrifice of every firstborn — that I might fill them with horror so they would know that I am the Lord.'

[27]"Therefore, son of man, speak to the people of Israel and say to them, 'This is what the Sovereign Lord says: In this also your ancestors blasphemed me by being unfaithful to me: [28]When I brought them into the land I had sworn to give them and they saw any high hill or any leafy tree, there they offered their sacrifices, made offerings that aroused my anger, presented their fragrant incense and poured out their drink offerings. [29]Then I said to them: What is this high place you go to?'" (It is called Bamah[a] to this day.)

Rebellious Israel Renewed

[30]"Therefore say to the Israelites: 'This is what the Sovereign Lord says: Will you defile yourselves the way your ancestors did and lust after their vile images? [31]When you offer your gifts — the sacrifice of your children in the fire — you continue to defile yourselves with all your idols to this day. Am I to let you inquire of me, you Israelites? As surely as I live, declares the Sovereign Lord, I will not let you inquire of me.

---

[a] 29 Bamah means high place.

---

because proper Sabbath observance is an acknowledgment of the relationship between Yahweh and the people.
20:23 I would disperse them among the nations One of the curses for violating the covenant (see Dt 28:64; Lev 26:33).
20:25 I gave them other statutes that were not good The laws and rules were deemed not good in that the people were unable to meet the standard they set. The people's failure placed them under the condemnation of the law rather than the blessings of the covenant. Ezekiel's bold assertion that the law was not good and brought death must be understood in the sense of a community deeply affected by the loss and collapse of their religious worldview. They were considering the mystery of divine punishment while suffering the consequences clearly laid out in the law itself. The apostle Paul also wrestles with this theological issue and offers the nuanced understanding that it was the sin brought to light by the law that brought death, not the law itself (see Ro 7:7–25). Elsewhere in the OT, the law is celebrated (see Ps 19; 119). Ezekiel's undermining of that imagery served to shock his audience into a realization of what they had done.
20:26 sacrifice of every firstborn The law required that all firstborn be given to Yahweh — meaning they were consecrated to him (an acknowledgment that he created them) — but the law also provided for the immediate redemption of firstborn children (see Lev 2:12 and note). If the terms of the law to redeem these

children were not followed, this accusation may refer to the practice of child sacrifice, which is opposed in the OT (see Dt 12:31). Child sacrifice was a practice of Israel's neighboring nation Canaan. OT references to the practice condemn Israel for participating in such a heinous practice that was never sanctioned by Yahweh (Jer 7:31). Two kings of Judah may have been guilty of child sacrifice (2Ki 16:3; 21:6). Levitical law explicitly forbids the practice, and the OT consistently associates it with worship of the Canaanite deity Molek (Lev 18:21; 20:2–5; compare 2Ki 23:10; Jer 7:28–34; 32:35; also rendered "Molech").
20:28 any high hill or any leafy tree An allusion to Israel's local shrines (see note on Eze 6:13 and note on Isa 57:7). **offerings that aroused my anger** Compare Eze 8:17; 2Ki 23:26. Judah's idolatry offended God and provoked his anger. **their fragrant incense** Refers to the belief that the aroma of the sacrifice satisfied the deity. **their drink offerings** Sacrificial rituals involved liquid and grain offerings in addition to animal sacrifice. The liquid was usually wine (see Ex 29:40–41; Nu 15:1–10).
20:29 Bamah This name means "high place" and was probably used initially to refer to hilltop shrines, though later "high places" were built on lower ground. The word eventually became a generic term to denote a local religious shrine.
20:31 your children in the fire See note on Eze 20:26. The OT frequently condemns the practice of child sacrifice (see Dt 12:31 and note).

32 "'You say, "We want to be like the nations, like the peoples of the world, who serve wood and stone." But what you have in mind will never happen. 33 As surely as I live, declares the Sovereign LORD, I will reign over you with a mighty hand and an outstretched arm and with outpoured wrath. 34 I will bring you from the nations and gather you from the countries where you have been scattered — with a mighty hand and an outstretched arm and with outpoured wrath. 35 I will bring you into the wilderness of the nations and there, face to face, I will execute judgment upon you. 36 As I judged your ancestors in the wilderness of the land of Egypt, so I will judge you, declares the Sovereign LORD. 37 I will take note of you as you pass under my rod, and I will bring you into the bond of the covenant. 38 I will purge you of those who revolt and rebel against me. Although I will bring them out of the land where they are living, yet they will not enter the land of Israel. Then you will know that I am the LORD.

39 "'As for you, people of Israel, this is what the Sovereign LORD says: Go and serve your idols, every one of you! But afterward you will surely listen to me and no longer profane my holy name with your gifts and idols. 40 For on my holy mountain, the high mountain of Israel, declares the Sovereign LORD, there in the land all the people of Israel will serve me, and there I will accept them. There I will require your offerings and your choice gifts,[a] along with all your holy sacrifices. 41 I will accept you as fragrant incense when I bring you out from the nations and gather you from the countries where you have been scattered, and I will be proved holy through you in the sight of the nations. 42 Then you will know that I am the LORD, when I bring you into the land of Israel, the land I had sworn with uplifted hand to give to your ancestors. 43 There you will remember your conduct and all the actions by which you have defiled yourselves, and you will loathe yourselves for all the evil you have done. 44 You will know that I am the LORD, when I deal with you for my name's sake and not according to your evil ways and your corrupt practices, you people of Israel, declares the Sovereign LORD.'"

Prophecy Against the South

45 The word of the LORD came to me: 46 "Son of man, set your face toward the south; preach against the south and prophesy against the forest of the southland. 47 Say to the southern forest: 'Hear the word of the LORD. This is what the Sovereign LORD says: I am about to set fire to you, and it will consume all your trees, both green and dry. The blazing flame will not be quenched, and every face from south to north will be scorched by it. 48 Everyone will see that I the LORD have kindled it; it will not be quenched.'"

49 Then I said, "Sovereign LORD, they are saying of me, 'Isn't he just telling parables?'"[b]

Babylon as God's Sword of Judgment

21[c] The word of the LORD came to me: 2 "Son of man, set your face against Jerusalem and preach against the sanctuary. Prophesy against the land of Israel 3 and say to her: 'This is what the LORD says: I am against you. I will draw my sword from its sheath and cut off from you both the righteous and the wicked. 4 Because I am going to cut off the righ-

[a] 40 Or and the gifts of your firstfruits   [b] 49 In Hebrew texts 20:45-49 is numbered 21:1-5.   [c] In Hebrew texts 21:1-32 is numbered 21:6-37.

20:33–49 Yahweh promises to restore Israel, gathering the people and bringing them out of foreign lands in a sort of second exodus. The prophet's reuse of exodus and wilderness imagery applies the primary salvation event of Israel's past to the anticipated salvation event of Israel's future. Similar imagery appears throughout the book of Isaiah (see Isa 14; 35; 43).

20:35 face to face An intimate meeting, recalling the way Moses met with Yahweh (Ex 33:11; Dt 34:10). The last time Israel met God face to face was at Sinai (see Dt 5:4).

20:37 I will take note of you as you pass under my rod An idiom indicating selection (see Lev 27:32). Those selected will be set apart to accept the obligation of the covenant. Those who are not selected will be punished (see Eze 20:38).

20:38 they will not enter the land of Israel Entering the land is a privilege for those who keep faith with Yahweh.

20:39 Go and serve your idols, every one of you An ironic and sarcastic statement, similar to those in Am 4:4 and Jer 44:25. **no longer profane my holy name** Implies that Israel was offering Yahweh rituals and religious practices that had been created for Canaanite idols.

20:40 on my holy mountain Refers to Zion, Yahweh's holy mountain (see note on Isa 2:2).

20:41 I will accept you as fragrant incense The obedience and devotion of restored Israel is as pleasing to Yahweh as sacrifice.

20:44 for my name's sake Yahweh didn't punish them according to what they deserved for their sin. He punished but then saved for the sake of his reputation (see note on Eze 20:9).

20:46 set your face toward An expression indicating Ezekiel's act of turning his attention toward his intended audience. Many of the oracles in Ezekiel open with this phrase (e.g., 6:2; 13:17; 21:2; 25:2; 28:21; 29:2; 35:2; 38:2). **south** The Hebrew word used here, *teman*, was used for the direction south and as a name for a place in Edom, southeast of Judah. **southland** The Hebrew word used here, *negev* (sometimes rendered "Negeb"), can be a term for "south." Its specific application to the wilderness region known as the Negev is unlikely here, since the Negev was not a forested area.

20:48 I the LORD have kindled it The power of the fire will reveal its divine origin (see Isa 40:5).

20:49 they are saying of me Ezekiel wonders whether his parables and metaphors are getting through to his audience.

teous and the wicked, my sword will be unsheathed against everyone from south to north. ⁵Then all people will know that I the Lᴏʀᴅ have drawn my sword from its sheath; it will not return again.'

⁶"Therefore groan, son of man! Groan before them with broken heart and bitter grief. ⁷And when they ask you, 'Why are you groaning?' you shall say, 'Because of the news that is coming. Every heart will melt with fear and every hand go limp; every spirit will become faint and every leg will be wet with urine.' It is coming! It will surely take place, declares the Sovereign Lᴏʀᴅ."

⁸The word of the Lᴏʀᴅ came to me: ⁹"Son of man, prophesy and say, 'This is what the Lord says:

"'A sword, a sword,
    sharpened and polished—
¹⁰ sharpened for the slaughter,
    polished to flash like lightning!

"'Shall we rejoice in the scepter of my royal son? The sword despises every such stick.

¹¹ "'The sword is appointed to be polished,
    to be grasped with the hand;
it is sharpened and polished,
    made ready for the hand of the slayer.
¹² Cry out and wail, son of man,
    for it is against my people;
    it is against all the princes of Israel.
They are thrown to the sword
    along with my people.
Therefore beat your breast.

¹³ "'Testing will surely come. And what if even the scepter, which the sword despises, does not continue? declares the Sovereign Lᴏʀᴅ.'

¹⁴ "So then, son of man, prophesy
    and strike your hands together.
Let the sword strike twice,
    even three times.
It is a sword for slaughter—
    a sword for great slaughter,
    closing in on them from every side.
¹⁵ So that hearts may melt with fear
    and the fallen be many,
I have stationed the sword for slaughterᵃ
    at all their gates.
Look! It is forged to strike like lightning,
    it is grasped for slaughter.
¹⁶ Slash to the right, you sword,
    then to the left,
    wherever your blade is turned.
¹⁷ I too will strike my hands together,
    and my wrath will subside.
I the Lᴏʀᴅ have spoken."

¹⁸The word of the Lᴏʀᴅ came to me: ¹⁹"Son of man, mark out two roads for the sword of the king of Babylon to take, both starting from the same country. Make a signpost where the road branches off to the city. ²⁰Mark out one road for the sword to come against Rabbah of the Ammonites and another against Judah and fortified Jerusalem. ²¹For the king of Babylon will stop at the fork in the road, at the junction of the two roads, to seek an omen: He will cast lots with arrows, he will consult his idols, he will examine the liver. ²²Into his right hand will come the lot for Jerusalem, where he is to set up battering rams, to give the command to slaughter, to sound the battle cry,

ᵃ 15 Septuagint; the meaning of the Hebrew for this word is uncertain.

21:2 set your face against Jerusalem Ezekiel's customary way to indicate the recipient of his oracle (see note on Eze 20:46). **the sanctuary** The Hebrew word used here, *miqdash*, is usually singular and refers to the Jerusalem temple; however, in this verse it is plural in most Hebrew manuscripts. If the plural was intended, Ezekiel likely is pronouncing judgment on the many local shrines used for idol worship in the area. **the land of Israel** One of Ezekiel's characteristic phrases for referring to the people of Israel (see note on 7:2).
21:3 my sword The imagery of vv. 1–32 is structured as three separate oracles linked by a catchword, "sword." **the righteous and the wicked** A figure of speech (called a merism) indicating judgment against everyone.
21:7 the news that is coming Refers to the coming judgment, the Day of Yahweh from 7:5–6.
21:12 the princes of Israel Ezekiel is lamenting the death of the royal house of David (see 2Ki 25:6–7). **Therefore beat your breast** A gesture of mourning and lament (compare Jer 31:19).
21:14 strike your hands together Suggests the prophet was acting out his prophecy in some way (compare Eze 6:11 and 5:1–2, where Ezekiel uses a sword in his sign-act).
21:16 Slash to the right Like in v. 14, this implies that Ezekiel is miming the actions described here: brandishing

a sharp sword, cutting both directions and acting out the judgment to come.
21:19 mark out two roads Possibly another sign-act; he may have created a model highway with two paths for the king to choose between, complete with road signs describing where each path leads. **the sword of the king of Babylon** The sword of divine judgment is revealed as the sword of the king of Babylon. **the road branches off** The sign indicates one route leading to Rabbah and another leading to Jerusalem.
21:20 Rabbah of the Ammonites Rabbah was the capital of Ammon, Judah's neighbor to the northeast. Ancient Rabbah is in the middle of modern Amman in Jordan.
21:21 to seek an omen The king will engage in various forms of divination, attempting to determine whether a course of action would have a favorable outcome. Divination was a means for discerning the divine, so the result was interpreted as the desire of the gods. One of the primary forms of divination practiced by the Babylonians was studying the liver of sacrificed animals. Other methods mentioned in the Bible include casting lots (Ac 1:26) and observing water in a cup (Ge 44:1–5). **He will cast lots with arrows** A form of divination where one arrow is picked from a group (like drawing straws). **his idols** Images of dead ancestors. See note on Ge 31:19.
21:22 set battering rams against the gates This verse

to set battering rams against the gates, to build a ramp and to erect siege works. ²³It will seem like a false omen to those who have sworn allegiance to him, but he will remind them of their guilt and take them captive.

²⁴"Therefore this is what the Sovereign LORD says: 'Because you people have brought to mind your guilt by your open rebellion, revealing your sins in all that you do—because you have done this, you will be taken captive.

²⁵"'You profane and wicked prince of Israel, whose day has come, whose time of punishment has reached its climax, ²⁶this is what the Sovereign LORD says: Take off the turban, remove the crown. It will not be as it was: The lowly will be exalted and the exalted will be brought low. ²⁷A ruin! A ruin! I will make it a ruin! The crown will not be restored until he to whom it rightfully belongs shall come; to him I will give it.'

²⁸"And you, son of man, prophesy and say, 'This is what the Sovereign LORD says about the Ammonites and their insults:

"'A sword, a sword,
    drawn for the slaughter,
polished to consume
    and to flash like lightning!
²⁹Despite false visions concerning you
    and lying divinations about you,
it will be laid on the necks
    of the wicked who are to be slain,
whose day has come,
    whose time of punishment has reached its
        climax.

³⁰"'Let the sword return to its sheath.
    In the place where you were created,
in the land of your ancestry,
    I will judge you.
³¹I will pour out my wrath on you
    and breathe out my fiery anger against
        you;

I will deliver you into the hands of brutal
        men,
    men skilled in destruction.
³²You will be fuel for the fire,
    your blood will be shed in your land,
you will be remembered no more;
    for I the LORD have spoken.'"

Judgment on Jerusalem's Sins

22 The word of the LORD came to me:

²"Son of man, will you judge her? Will you judge this city of bloodshed? Then confront her with all her detestable practices ³and say: 'This is what the Sovereign LORD says: You city that brings on herself doom by shedding blood in her midst and defiles herself by making idols, ⁴you have become guilty because of the blood you have shed and have become defiled by the idols you have made. You have brought your days to a close, and the end of your years has come. Therefore I will make you an object of scorn to the nations and a laughing-stock to all the countries. ⁵Those who are near and those who are far away will mock you, you infamous city, full of turmoil.

⁶"'See how each of the princes of Israel who are in you uses his power to shed blood. ⁷In you they have treated father and mother with contempt; in you they have oppressed the foreigner and mistreated the fatherless and the widow. ⁸You have despised my holy things and desecrated my Sabbaths. ⁹In you are slanderers who are bent on shedding blood; in you are those who eat at the mountain shrines and commit lewd acts. ¹⁰In you are those who dishonor their father's bed; in you are those who violate women during their period, when they are ceremonially unclean. ¹¹In you one man commits a detestable offense with his neighbor's wife, another shamefully defiles his daughter-in-law, and another violates his sister,

---

lists implements of siege warfare, an art which the Assyrians and Babylonians mastered. See note on Eze 4:2.
21:25 prince of Israel A reference to Zedekiah, whose foolish rebellion against Nebuchadnezzar initiated this invasion. Ezekiel never refers to Zedekiah as king (see note on 12:10).
21:26 Take off the turban, remove the crown Refers to the visible tokens of Zedekiah's authority. Artistic renderings found in Mesopotamia indicate that crowns in ancient Near Eastern kingdoms more closely resembled turbans.
21:28 about the Ammonites The oracle ends with an assurance to Ammon that, while the first lot fell to Jerusalem for judgment, the sword is still ready and can bring judgment on them.
21:29 false visions Predictions that the Ammonites have escaped judgment are false.
21:32 You will be fuel for the fire Babylon itself will be judged. The Babylonian Empire would fall to Persia in 539 BC.

22:1–31 Ezekiel's statement about the word of God coming to him (vv. 1,17,23) marks off three separate discourses devoted to indicting Jerusalem and the inhabitants of Judah for their corruption. The prophet's responsibilities included raising the people's awareness of God's perspective on their conduct. The specific accusations reflect Ezekiel's detailed knowledge of Biblical law, especially Leviticus, and invoke the same behaviors criticized hypothetically in ch. 18. The prophet identifies sinful Judah with the wicked son who was held responsible for his own sinful behavior (see 18:10–13; 18:10 and note). Despite clear connections to legal prohibitions, Ezekiel's condemnation focuses on issues of bloodshed and ritual impurity or defilement.

22:2 Will you judge this city of bloodshed Yahweh commands Ezekiel to judge, which appears to involve delivering an accusation rather than a verdict (see 20:4 and note). **her detestable practices** See note on 5:9.
22:4 an object of scorn to the nations The Hebrew

his own father's daughter. ¹²In you are people who accept bribes to shed blood; you take interest and make a profit from the poor. You extort unjust gain from your neighbors. And you have forgotten me, declares the Sovereign LORD.

¹³"'I will surely strike my hands together at the unjust gain you have made and at the blood you have shed in your midst. ¹⁴Will your courage endure or your hands be strong in the day I deal with you? I the LORD have spoken, and I will do it. ¹⁵I will disperse you among the nations and scatter you through the countries; and I will put an end to your uncleanness. ¹⁶When you have been defiled⁰ in the eyes of the nations, you will know that I am the LORD.'"

¹⁷Then the word of the LORD came to me: ¹⁸"Son of man, the people of Israel have become dross to me; all of them are the copper, tin, iron and lead left inside a furnace. They are but the dross of silver. ¹⁹Therefore this is what the Sovereign LORD says: 'Because you have all become dross, I will gather you into Jerusalem. ²⁰As silver, copper, iron, lead and tin are gathered into a furnace to be melted with a fiery blast, so will I gather you in my anger and my wrath and put you inside the city and melt you. ²¹I will gather you and I will blow on you with my fiery wrath, and you will be melted inside her. ²²As silver is melted in a furnace, so you will be melted inside her, and you will know that I the LORD have poured out my wrath on you.'"

²³Again the word of the LORD came to me: ²⁴"Son of man, say to the land, 'You are a land that has not been cleansed or rained on in the day of wrath.' ²⁵There is a conspiracy of her princes⁰ within her like a roaring lion tearing its prey; they devour people, take treasures and precious things and make many widows within her. ²⁶Her priests do violence to my law and profane my holy things; they do not distinguish between the holy and the common; they teach that there is no difference between the unclean and the clean; and they shut their eyes to the keeping of my Sabbaths, so that I am profaned among them. ²⁷Her officials within her are like wolves tearing their prey; they shed blood and kill people to make unjust gain. ²⁸Her prophets whitewash these deeds for them by false visions and lying divinations. They say, 'This is what the Sovereign LORD says' — when the LORD has not spoken. ²⁹The people of the land practice extortion and commit robbery; they oppress the poor and needy and mistreat the foreigner, denying them justice.

³⁰"I looked for someone among them who would build up the wall and stand before me in the gap on behalf of the land so I would not have to destroy it, but I found no one. ³¹So I will pour out my wrath on them and consume them with my fiery anger, bringing down on their own heads all they have done, declares the Sovereign LORD."

---

a 16 Or *When I have allotted you your inheritance*
b 25 Septuagint; Hebrew *prophets*

---

word used here, *cherpah,* refers to a condition of shame or disgrace. Israel will be shamed before the nations. Ancient societies placed a high value on honor and shame as markers of social status. Codes of honor and shame governed behavior, since the reputation of an entire family or clan could be tainted by association with one immoral or shameless member. Social pressure to avoid the stigma of shame or loss of honor would have motivated people to do everything they could to avoid being a public reproach.
22:6 princes of Israel Refers to Jerusalem's ruling class.
22:7 father and mother with contempt Violates Ex 20:12; Dt 27:16. **they have oppressed the foreigner** Violates Ex 22:21–22. **mistreated the fatherless and the widow** The laws in Exodus awarded protected status to foreigners, widows and orphans (see Ex 22:21–27).
22:8 You have despised my holy things An indictment directed toward priests for failing to observe proper rituals for maintaining the sanctuary's purity.
22:9 In you are slanderers who are bent on shedding blood Presumably indicates that false accusations have led to wrongful deaths. The legal basis is Lev 19:16, which connects the concept of slander with shedding blood (*dam* in Hebrew; sometimes translated "life"). **those who eat at the mountain shrines** Compare Eze 18:6. An unusual phrase Ezekiel uses to refer to idol worship at the high places. **lewd acts** See 16:43.
22:10 those who dishonor their father's bed The list of sexual sins in vv. 10–11 covers most of the prohibited sexual unions recorded in Lev 18:6–20. This verse uses a

Hebrew euphemism for sexuality that concerns the mother or stepmother to the men (see note on Ge 9:22–24).
22:12 people who accept bribes to shed blood See Dt 27:25. Ezekiel's accusations leave little room for Israel to protest their punishment, since he draws on a wide range of legal traditions to show their failure to honor the covenant. **you take interest and make a profit** Part of the hypothetical sins in Eze 18:8, but specifically forbidden by Lev 25:36.
22:15 I will disperse you among the nations Part of Ezekiel's goal is to explain the reason for the Jews' exile to Babylon. He repeatedly reminds them of Yahweh's promise to scatter them if they failed to keep the covenant (see Lev 26:33).
22:16 you will know that I am the LORD See note on Eze 5:13.
22:18 dross This symbolizes impurity, a key theme in Ezekiel—the Hebrew term here refers to the waste material left after metals are purified by the process of smelting.
22:26 they do not distinguish between the holy Violates the command of Lev 10:10.
22:27 Her officials A different Hebrew title than is used for the royal princes in Eze 19:2 and 22:6. *Sar* (used here) simply denotes a ranking official.
22:28 Her prophets whitewash The depiction of false prophecy as whitewash, covering the reality of imminent judgment, reflects 13:10–12.
22:30 someone among them who would build up Yahweh cannot find even one righteous person to justify deferring his judgment a little longer (compare Jer 5:1; Isa 59:16).

Two Adulterous Sisters

23 The word of the Lord came to me: ²"Son of man, there were two women, daughters of the same mother. ³They became prostitutes in Egypt, engaging in prostitution from their youth. In that land their breasts were fondled and their virgin bosoms caressed. ⁴The older was named Oholah, and her sister was Oholibah. They were mine and gave birth to sons and daughters. Oholah is Samaria, and Oholibah is Jerusalem.

⁵"Oholah engaged in prostitution while she was still mine; and she lusted after her lovers, the Assyrians — warriors ⁶clothed in blue, governors and commanders, all of them handsome young men, and mounted horsemen. ⁷She gave herself as a prostitute to all the elite of the Assyrians and defiled herself with all the idols of everyone she lusted after. ⁸She did not give up the prostitution she began in Egypt, when during her youth men slept with her, caressed her virgin bosom and poured out their lust on her.

⁹"Therefore I delivered her into the hands of her lovers, the Assyrians, for whom she lusted. ¹⁰They stripped her naked, took away her sons and daughters and killed her with the sword. She became a byword among women, and punishment was inflicted on her.

¹¹"Her sister Oholibah saw this, yet in her lust and prostitution she was more depraved than her sister. ¹²She too lusted after the Assyrians — governors and commanders, warriors in full dress, mounted horsemen, all handsome young men. ¹³I saw that she too defiled herself; both of them went the same way.

¹⁴"But she carried her prostitution still further. She saw men portrayed on a wall, figures of Chaldeans*a* portrayed in red, ¹⁵with belts around their waists and flowing turbans on their heads; all of them looked like Babylonian chariot officers, natives of Chaldea.*b* ¹⁶As soon as she saw them, she lusted after them and sent messengers to them in Chaldea. ¹⁷Then the Babylonians came to her, to the bed of love, and in their lust they defiled her. After she had been defiled by them, she turned away from them in disgust. ¹⁸When she carried on her prostitution openly and exposed her naked body, I turned away from her in disgust, just as I had turned away from her sister. ¹⁹Yet she became more and more promiscuous as she recalled the days of her youth, when she was a prostitute in Egypt. ²⁰There she lusted after her lovers, whose genitals were like those of donkeys and whose emission was like that of horses. ²¹So you longed for the lewdness of your

a 14 Or Babylonians   b 15 Or Babylonia; also in verse 16

23:1–49 Ezekiel returns to the metaphor of Israel as an unfaithful wife—graphically developed in Eze 16—and recasts it as an allegory (or symbolic story) about Israel and Judah. He also picks up the image of Samaria as Jerusalem's sister presented in 16:44–53. The political oppression of Israel and Judah is portrayed in explicit terms of sexual abuse and molestation. Just like the unfaithful wife in ch. 16, both sisters are judged and punished for their infidelity.

23:2 two women, daughters of the same mother The references to having the same mother and to their early life together in Egypt point to the time when Israel was unified. The two women represent the divided kingdoms of Israel and Judah. See 16:44 and note.

23:3 They became prostitutes in Egypt Compare 20:5–8, which links Israel's history of idolatry to its time in Egypt. On the prostitution imagery, see note on 16:15. **their breasts were fondled** Israel's slavery and oppression in Egypt is metaphorically likened to sexual abuse.

23:4 Oholah Meaning "her tent." **Oholibah** Meaning "my tent in her." See the table "Symbolic Names of People in Hebrew" on p. 1388. **They were mine** Symbolizing marriage (compare 16:8). **gave birth to sons and daughters** Refers to the inhabitants of the cities (see 16:20 and note). **Oholah is Samaria, and Oholibah is Jerusalem** Samaria was the capital of the northern kingdom of Israel; Jerusalem was the capital of the southern kingdom of Judah.

23:6 clothed in blue Due to the high cost of the dye, fabric of this color was too expensive for all but the wealthiest and most powerful officials.

23:7 the elite of the Assyrians Alludes to Israel's submission to Assyrian dominance by paying tribute (see

2Ki 15:19; 17:3). **defiled herself with all the idols** Connects political and religious submission. Acknowledging the gods of one's overlords was likely part of expressing submission to their rule.

23:9 the Assyrians, for whom she lusted Samaria was destroyed by Assyria in 722 BC. With irony or poetic justice, the objects of her lust become the agents of divinely decreed destruction.

23:10 They stripped her naked A metaphor for the land being stripped bare by an invading army; also suggestive of rape by foreign soldiers (see note on Eze 16:36). **took away her sons and daughters** The northern tribes of Israel were taken into exile by Assyria.

23:11–13 Even after observing Oholah's behavior and ultimate demise, Oholibah follows her older sister's example, failing to reflect even slightly on the lesson to be learned from her sister's punishment.

23:11 in her lust and prostitution she was more depraved than her sister Compare 16:47–52, which similarly emphasizes the greater depravity of Judah .

23:12 lusted after the Assyrians Alludes to Judah's acceptance of Assyria as overlord after the fall of Samaria.

23:14 figures of Chaldeans portrayed in red While still subject to Assyria, King Hezekiah entertained envoys from Babylon (also called Chaldea) (see 2Ki 20:12–13).

23:17 came to her, to the bed of love Babylon succeeded Assyria as the ruling empire in the Near East. The Babylonian king, Nebuchadnezzar, conducted three campaigns into Palestine, deporting most of Judah's population. **turned away from them in disgust** Alludes to Judah's changing political positions from loyalty to Babylon under Hezekiah and Josiah to rebellion against Babylon under Jehoiakim and Zedekiah.

youth, when in Egypt your bosom was caressed and your young breasts fondled.[a]

[22]"Therefore, Oholibah, this is what the Sovereign LORD says: I will stir up your lovers against you, those you turned away from in disgust, and I will bring them against you from every side — [23]the Babylonians and all the Chaldeans, the men of Pekod and Shoa and Koa, and all the Assyrians with them, handsome young men, all of them governors and commanders, chariot officers and men of high rank, all mounted on horses. [24]They will come against you with weapons,[b] chariots and wagons and with a throng of people; they will take up positions against you on every side with large and small shields and with helmets. I will turn you over to them for punishment, and they will punish you according to their standards. [25]I will direct my jealous anger against you, and they will deal with you in fury. They will cut off your noses and your ears, and those of you who are left will fall by the sword. They will take away your sons and daughters, and those of you who are left will be consumed by fire. [26]They will also strip you of your clothes and take your fine jewelry. [27]So I will put a stop to the lewdness and prostitution you began in Egypt. You will not look on these things with longing or remember Egypt anymore.

[28]"For this is what the Sovereign LORD says: I am about to deliver you into the hands of those you hate, to those you turned away from in disgust. [29]They will deal with you in hatred and take away everything you have worked for. They will leave you stark naked, and the shame of your prostitution will be exposed. Your lewdness and promiscuity [30]have brought this on you, because you lusted after the nations and defiled yourself with their idols. [31]You have gone the way of your sister; so I will put her cup into your hand.

[32]"This is what the Sovereign LORD says:

"You will drink your sister's cup,
　a cup large and deep;
it will bring scorn and derision,
　for it holds so much.
[33]You will be filled with drunkenness and
　　sorrow,
　the cup of ruin and desolation,
　the cup of your sister Samaria.
[34]You will drink it and drain it dry
　and chew on its pieces —
　and you will tear your breasts.

I have spoken, declares the Sovereign LORD.

[35]"Therefore this is what the Sovereign LORD says: Since you have forgotten me and turned your back on me, you must bear the consequences of your lewdness and prostitution."

[36]The LORD said to me: "Son of man, will you judge Oholah and Oholibah? Then confront them with their detestable practices, [37]for they have committed adultery and blood is on their hands. They committed adultery with their idols; they even sacrificed their children, whom they bore to me, as food for them. [38]They have also done this to me: At that same time they defiled my sanctuary and desecrated my Sabbaths. [39]On the very day they sacrificed their children to their idols, they entered my sanctuary and desecrated it. That is what they did in my house.

[40]"They even sent messengers for men who came from far away, and when they arrived you bathed yourself for them, applied eye makeup and put on your jewelry. [41]You sat on an elegant

---

[a] 21 Syriac (see also verse 3); Hebrew caressed because of your young breasts　　[b] 24 The meaning of the Hebrew for this word is uncertain.

23:19–21 Oholibah now lusts for Egypt, her first love (Eze 23:3). The shift in attention from Babylon to Egypt mirrors the shift in political alliance during Ezekiel's time. Zedekiah's alliance with Egypt in support of his rebellion against Babylon is depicted in 17:15. While Assyria and Babylon are depicted as virile, powerful young men, Egypt is portrayed as interested in hedonistic debauchery.

23:20 donkeys See 16:26 and note.
23:22 lovers against you, those you turned away from in disgust The Babylonians (see v. 17 and note). Zedekiah's rebellion against Babylon leads to the destruction of Jerusalem and the temple in 586 BC.
23:23 Pekod and Shoa and Koa Most likely refers to Aramean or Amorite tribes allied with the Babylonians. **all the Assyrians** Babylon put an end to Assyrian power in 605 BC. If Assyrians participated in the invasion of Judah, they must have been mercenaries of Babylon.
23:24 with large and small shields and with helmets The Hebrew terms here denote a large shield, a standard shield and a helmet or turban. **I will turn you over to them for punishment** The Babylonians carry out the divinely ordained judgment on Jerusalem.

23:25 They will cut off your noses and your ears Permitted under Mesopotamian laws as punishment for adultery.
23:31 I will put her cup into your hand Warns that Judah will experience the same fate as Israel. The cup symbolizes divine wrath in Jer 25:15 and Isa 51:17.
23:36–49 The story of Oholah and Oholibah concludes in Eze 23:35. The oracle shifts in v. 36, with a familiar call for Ezekiel to pronounce judgment and announce the sentence of Yahweh (see 20:4; 22:2). The judgment oracle more clearly relates Judah's punishment with her failure to worship Yahweh properly and exclusively.

23:36 you judge Oholah and Oholibah See 20:4 and note.
23:37 blood is on their hands See Isa 1:15 and note. **They committed adultery with their idols** See Eze 16:17 and note. **they even sacrificed their children, whom they bore to me, as food for them** An allusion to child sacrifice (see 16:20).
23:40 applied eye makeup Eye makeup was customary in the ancient Near East.

couch, with a table spread before it on which you had placed the incense and olive oil that belonged to me.

⁴²"The noise of a carefree crowd was around her; drunkards were brought from the desert along with men from the rabble, and they put bracelets on the wrists of the woman and her sister and beautiful crowns on their heads. ⁴³Then I said about the one worn out by adultery, 'Now let them use her as a prostitute, for that is all she is.' ⁴⁴And they slept with her. As men sleep with a prostitute, so they slept with those lewd women, Oholah and Oholibah. ⁴⁵But righteous judges will sentence them to the punishment of women who commit adultery and shed blood, because they are adulterous and blood is on their hands.

⁴⁶"This is what the Sovereign LORD says: Bring a mob against them and give them over to terror and plunder. ⁴⁷The mob will stone them and cut them down with their swords; they will kill their sons and daughters and burn down their houses.

⁴⁸"So I will put an end to lewdness in the land, that all women may take warning and not imitate you. ⁴⁹You will suffer the penalty for your lewdness and bear the consequences of your sins of idolatry. Then you will know that I am the Sovereign LORD."

Jerusalem as a Cooking Pot

24 In the ninth year, in the tenth month on the tenth day, the word of the LORD came to me: ²"Son of man, record this date, this very date, because the king of Babylon has laid siege to Jerusalem this very day. ³Tell this rebellious people a parable and say to them: 'This is what the Sovereign LORD says:

"'Put on the cooking pot; put it on
    and pour water into it.
⁴ Put into it the pieces of meat,
    all the choice pieces — the leg and the
        shoulder.
Fill it with the best of these bones;
⁵   take the pick of the flock.
Pile wood beneath it for the bones;
    bring it to a boil
    and cook the bones in it.

⁶"'For this is what the Sovereign LORD says:

"'Woe to the city of bloodshed,
    to the pot now encrusted,
    whose deposit will not go away!
Take the meat out piece by piece
    in whatever order it comes.

⁷"'For the blood she shed is in her
        midst:
    She poured it on the bare rock;
she did not pour it on the ground,
    where the dust would cover it.
⁸ To stir up wrath and take revenge
    I put her blood on the bare rock,
    so that it would not be covered.

⁹"'Therefore this is what the Sovereign LORD says:

"'Woe to the city of bloodshed!
    I, too, will pile the wood high.
¹⁰ So heap on the wood
    and kindle the fire.

23:42 noise of a carefree crowd was around her An enigmatic phrase perhaps implying that she is drawn to debauchery and has no concern for the company she keeps.

23:45 to the punishment of women who commit adultery Compare 16:38.

23:46–49 The end of the passage closely parallels 16:38–41, mixing the metaphorical judgment for sexual immorality with the literal judgment of the city's destruction. Punishment comes by stoning, sword and burning, just as in 16:40–41.

24:1–14 Ezekiel's series of parables throughout 15:1—24:14 culminates in a return to the enigmatic cooking pot (or cauldron) reference from 11:3. Here, Yahweh again commands the prophet to use a symbolic parable to warn rebellious Israel of imminent destruction through siege. The parable itself is a short poem in vv. 3–5; it is followed by further explanation of the imagery in vv. 6–14.

24:1 In the ninth year, in the tenth month This date formula is based on 2Ki 25:1, which records the beginning of Nebuchadnezzar's siege in the ninth year of Zedekiah's reign. The date correlates to January 5, 587 BC. Ezekiel usually dates his oracles based on the year of King Jehoiachin's exile (see Eze 1:2 and note). Here he adopts the standard practice of reckoning dates

counting from the king's first full year on the throne. See the timeline "Dates in Ezekiel" on p. 1276.

24:3–5 This short poem describes a cook preparing a stew. The reference to choice cuts of meat from the best of the flock suggests that this is not symbolizing an everyday meal. The image of a pot and meat represented Jerusalem and its inhabitants in 11:2–7.

24:3 Tell this rebellious people a parable See note on 17:2.

24:6 Woe to the city of bloodshed Ezekiel is concerned with impurity, which is symbolized by bloodshed. **encrusted** The impurity is inside the pot (or cauldron), suggesting that it may refer to the choice cuts of meat. If so, this implies that rather than being Yahweh's chosen, Jerusalem's inhabitants are viewed as contaminated and will be discarded. In the context of Ezekiel's parable, this line might mean that the inhabitants of Jerusalem would be expelled from the city haphazardly.

24:7 not pour it on the ground As prescribed by Mosaic Law in Lev 17:13 (compare Dt 12:16). The metaphor suggests that the sins by which Jerusalem became impure were done in the open, with no attempt to hide the behavior.

24:8 so that it would not be covered It remains exposed as a visible testimony to Jerusalem's sinful behavior.

24:9 I, too, will pile the wood high Yahweh takes on the role of cook from the proverb in Eze 24:3–5.

Cook the meat well,
    mixing in the spices;
    and let the bones be charred.
[11] Then set the empty pot on the coals
    till it becomes hot and its copper glows,
so that its impurities may be melted
    and its deposit burned away.
[12] It has frustrated all efforts;
    its heavy deposit has not been removed,
    not even by fire.

[13] "'Now your impurity is lewdness. Because I tried to cleanse you but you would not be cleansed from your impurity, you will not be clean again until my wrath against you has subsided.

[14] "'I the LORD have spoken. The time has come for me to act. I will not hold back; I will not have pity, nor will I relent. You will be judged according to your conduct and your actions, declares the Sovereign LORD.'"

Ezekiel's Wife Dies

[15] The word of the LORD came to me: [16] "Son of man, with one blow I am about to take away from you the delight of your eyes. Yet do not lament or weep or shed any tears. [17] Groan quietly; do not mourn for the dead. Keep your turban fastened and your sandals on your feet; do not cover your mustache and beard or eat the customary food of mourners."

[18] So I spoke to the people in the morning, and in the evening my wife died. The next morning I did as I had been commanded.

[19] Then the people asked me, "Won't you tell us what these things have to do with us? Why are you acting like this?"

[20] So I said to them, "The word of the LORD came to me: [21] Say to the people of Israel, 'This is what the Sovereign LORD says: I am about to desecrate my sanctuary — the stronghold in which you take pride, the delight of your eyes, the object of your affection. The sons and daughters you left behind will fall by the sword. [22] And you will do as I have done. You will not cover your mustache and beard or eat the customary food of mourners. [23] You will keep your turbans on your heads and your sandals on your feet. You will not mourn or weep but will waste away because of[a] your sins and groan among yourselves. [24] Ezekiel will be a sign to you; you will do just as he has done. When this happens, you will know that I am the Sovereign LORD.'

[25] "And you, son of man, on the day I take away their stronghold, their joy and glory, the delight of their eyes, their heart's desire, and their sons and daughters as well — [26] on that day a fugitive will come to tell you the news. [27] At that time your mouth will be opened; you will speak with him and will no longer be silent. So you will be a sign to them, and they will know that I am the LORD."

A Prophecy Against Ammon

25 The word of the LORD came to me: [2] "Son of man, set your face against the Ammonites and prophesy against them. [3] Say to them, 'Hear the word of the Sovereign LORD. This is what the Sovereign LORD says: Because you said "Aha!" over my sanctuary when it was desecrated and over the

a 23 Or away in

24:15–27 Yahweh again commands Ezekiel to perform symbolic acts, just as in chs. 4; 5; 12. He informs the prophet that his wife will die, but that he must not mourn. See the table "Symbolic Actions of the Prophets" on p. 1195.

24:16 delight of your eyes Refers to Ezekiel's wife (v. 18).

24:17 Keep your turban fastened and your sandals on Ezekiel must dress normally, as if nothing out of the ordinary has occurred. **or eat the customary food of mourners** Apparently an idiom for the bread used in mourning rituals (see vv. 22; Hos 9:4).

24:18 spoke to the people in the morning He may have delivered the parable and interpretation from Eze 24:1–14 (see note on vv. 15–27).

24:21 my sanctuary — the stronghold in which you take pride The death of Ezekiel's wife symbolizes Judah's loss when the temple is destroyed.

24:22–24 The importance of the temple ultimately is overshadowed by the revelation of Yahweh through his acts of judgment (v. 24). The people respond to this imminent national tragedy, recognizing that they have no right to mourn when their collective sin has brought this judgment upon their nation, their temple and their children.

24:27 your mouth will be opened; you will speak with him The day the exiles receive the message that Jerusalem has fallen will inaugurate a new phase in Ezekiel's ministry (see 33:21–22, where this event is fulfilled). Ezekiel's prophecies in chs. 34–48 are oriented toward Israel's future salvation and restoration. **will no longer be silent** See 3:26–27. The details of his muteness are open to interpretation.

25:1—32:32 Chapters 1–24 focused on Jerusalem's impending judgment at the hands of the Babylonians. The oracles now turn toward judgment against foreign nations, first the immediate neighbors of Judah and then the major powers in the ancient Near East, especially Egypt. The relationship between Egypt and Judah was strained at this time, as Judah's hopes for Egyptian help in opposing Babylon proved false.

25:1–7 Ammon, mentioned in the sign-act of the signpost in 21:19–20, receives the first prophetic critique. The signpost marked Nebuchadnezzar's choice of whether to move his invading army against Judah or Ammon; the choice fell on Judah. This first oracle against the nations expands on 21:28–29, in which Ammon was warned not to gloat over its escape because judgment was still to come. See the table "Oracles Against the Nations" on p. 1244.

land of Israel when it was laid waste and over the people of Judah when they went into exile, [4]therefore I am going to give you to the people of the East as a possession. They will set up their camps and pitch their tents among you; they will eat your fruit and drink your milk. [5]I will turn Rabbah into a pasture for camels and Ammon into a resting place for sheep. Then you will know that I am the LORD. [6]For this is what the Sovereign LORD says: Because you have clapped your hands and stamped your feet, rejoicing with all the malice of your heart against the land of Israel, [7]therefore I will stretch out my hand against you and give you as plunder to the nations. I will wipe you out from among the nations and exterminate you from the countries. I will destroy you, and you will know that I am the LORD.'"

A Prophecy Against Moab

[8]"This is what the Sovereign LORD says: 'Because Moab and Seir said, "Look, Judah has become like all the other nations," [9]therefore I will expose the flank of Moab, beginning at its frontier towns — Beth Jeshimoth, Baal Meon and Kiriathaim — the glory of that land. [10]I will give Moab along with the Ammonites to the people of the East as a possession, so that the Ammonites will not be remembered among the nations; [11]and I will inflict punishment on Moab. Then they will know that I am the LORD.'"

A Prophecy Against Edom

[12]"This is what the Sovereign LORD says: 'Because Edom took revenge on Judah and became

very guilty by doing so, [13]therefore this is what the Sovereign LORD says: I will stretch out my hand against Edom and kill both man and beast. I will lay it waste, and from Teman to Dedan they will fall by the sword. [14]I will take vengeance on Edom by the hand of my people Israel, and they will deal with Edom in accordance with my anger and my wrath; they will know my vengeance, declares the Sovereign LORD.'"

A Prophecy Against Philistia

[15]"This is what the Sovereign LORD says: 'Because the Philistines acted in vengeance and took revenge with malice in their hearts, and with ancient hostility sought to destroy Judah, [16]therefore this is what the Sovereign LORD says: I am about to stretch out my hand against the Philistines, and I will wipe out the Kerethites and destroy those remaining along the coast. [17]I will carry out great vengeance on them and punish them in my wrath. Then they will know that I am the LORD, when I take vengeance on them.'"

A Prophecy Against Tyre

26 In the eleventh month of the twelfth[a] year, on the first day of the month, the word of the LORD came to me: [2]"Son of man, because Tyre has said of Jerusalem, 'Aha! The gate to the nations is broken, and its doors have swung open to me; now

---

[a] 1 Probable reading of the original Hebrew text; Masoretic Text does not have *month of the twelfth*.

25:2 the Ammonites Israel and Judah's neighbor to the east of the Jordan River. Their territory was northeast of the Dead Sea. Israel and Ammon fought over control of the fertile region of Gilead that lay between them. According to Ge 19:38, the Ammonites were distantly related to Israel through Abraham's nephew, Lot.
25:3 Aha Ammon is depicted as rejoicing over Judah's downfall. The Hebrew term expresses a cry of satisfaction over an enemy's misfortune. See Ps 35:21.
25:4 the people of the East A reference to nomadic desert tribes who would take advantage of Ammon's defeat and move into the area. See Jdg 6:3.
25:5 Rabbah The capital city of Ammon (see note on Eze 21:20). **a pasture for camels** Nomadic desert tribes would tend their flocks in pastures on the outskirts of a city. **you will know that I am the LORD** The recognition formula also applies to foreign nations, who will acknowledge Yahweh after experiencing his punishment. See note on 5:13.
25:7 I will stretch out my hand against you See note on 14:9.

25:8–11 The second oracle addresses Moab, Ammon's neighbor to the south. Moab also was a traditional enemy of Israel and Judah. The nation was related to Israel through Lot (see Ge 19:37).
25:8 Moab and Seir Some renderings of this verse refer only to Moab; others include a reference to Seir (also known as Edom). The Septuagint (the Greek translation of the OT) does not mention Seir. Since the subsequent

oracle (Eze 25:12–14) is addressed to Seir, the Septuagint reading is most likely original, and this oracle is intended for Moab alone.
25:9 Beth Jeshimoth, Baal Meon and Kiriathaim All three cities were along Moab's western line of defense.
25:10 the people of the East Nebuchadnezzar eventually returned to conquer Ammon in 582 BC.

25:12–14 Edom was Judah's neighbor to the southeast, located on the southeastern corner of the Dead Sea. According to the Bible, they were related to Israel through Esau (Ge 36).
25:12 on Judah Suggests that Edom was allied with Babylon in the conflict that led to Judah's destruction.

25:15–17 The Philistines were Judah's neighbor to the west. These Mediterranean people, possibly from the Aegean, settled in the region along the coast.
25:16 the Kerethites An Aegean-based people related to the Philistines.

26:1—28:19 Ezekiel directs his series of three oracles and prophecies in 26:1—28:19 toward the entire Phoenician civilization, Israel's neighbors to the northwest. They are represented in the oracles by their most powerful city-states, Tyre and Sidon. With great rhetorical skill, Ezekiel blurs reality with myth and metaphor to exaggerate Tyre's glory and announce its coming destruction. See the table "Oracles Against the Nations" on p. 1244.

that she lies in ruins I will prosper,' ³therefore this is what the Sovereign LORD says: I am against you, Tyre, and I will bring many nations against you, like the sea casting up its waves. ⁴They will destroy the walls of Tyre and pull down her towers; I will scrape away her rubble and make her a bare rock. ⁵Out in the sea she will become a place to spread fishnets, for I have spoken, declares the Sovereign LORD. She will become plunder for the nations, ⁶and her settlements on the mainland will be ravaged by the sword. Then they will know that I am the LORD.

⁷"For this is what the Sovereign LORD says: From the north I am going to bring against Tyre Nebuchadnezzar[a] king of Babylon, king of kings, with horses and chariots, with horsemen and a great army. ⁸He will ravage your settlements on the mainland with the sword; he will set up siege works against you, build a ramp up to your walls and raise his shields against you. ⁹He will direct the blows of his battering rams against your walls and demolish your towers with his weapons. ¹⁰His horses will be so many that they will cover you with dust. Your walls will tremble at the noise of the warhorses, wagons and chariots when he enters your gates as men enter a city whose walls have been broken through. ¹¹The hooves of his horses will trample all your streets; he will kill your people with the sword, and your strong pillars will fall to the ground. ¹²They will plunder your wealth and loot your merchandise; they will

---

[a] 7 Hebrew *Nebuchadrezzar*, of which *Nebuchadnezzar* is a variant; here and often in Ezekiel and Jeremiah

---

26:1–21 Like Ammon in 25:3–7, Tyre is initially condemned for gloating over Jerusalem's destruction. The oracle in vv. 2–6 follows the pattern of short pronouncements against the nations used in ch. 25. Ezekiel goes on to expand the prophecy, outlining in detail how judgment will come on Tyre (vv. 7–14), then lamenting Tyre's fate (vv. 15–21). The usual prophetic attacks on Tyre are motivated by the influence that Phoenician religion had on Israelite idolatry (see note on Isa 23:1–18).

26:1 on the first day of the month The Hebrew text does not indicate the month (it may have been omitted by scribal error), so a precise date is uncertain. The text likely referred to the eleventh or twelfth year and the eleventh or twelfth month. The repetition of numbers would have made it easy to overlook one in copying; also eleven and twelve are spelled similarly. If the timing correlates with Nebuchadnezzar's historical siege of Tyre, that event began in 586 or 585 BC. The year seems to follow Ezekiel's standard of dating from Jehoiachin's exile (see note on Eze 1:2). See the timeline "Dates in Ezekiel" on p. 1276.
26:2 Tyre The most powerful and influential of Phoenicia's city-states, located along the Mediterranean coast. Tyre was occupied continuously throughout the Biblical period. **Aha** See 25:3 and note.

TYRE
A Phoenician city-state whose main city was an island approximately a half-mile wide, located about a half-mile off the coast. The island location saved the main city from total destruction by Nebuchadnezzar, who razed the portion of the city on the coast. Nebuchadnezzar turned to besiege Tyre after the destruction of Jerusalem in 586 BC. His siege of Tyre carried on for 13 years. Nebuchadnezzar couldn't reach Tyre because he lacked a fleet, and the island city was able to maintain food and water supplies through its maritime network.

26:3 many nations The Babylonian army included mercenaries and soldiers from other nations.
26:5 a place to spread fishnets Tyre will be razed until the island is barren—useless for anything except drying fishnets.

26:6 settlements on the mainland The coastal portion of the city, the surrounding villages and their inhabitants.
26:7 Nebuchadnezzar The Hebrew text reflects the king's proper Akkadian name, Nebuchadrezzar, meaning "Nabu, protect the eldest son." Nabu was a popular Babylonian deity. Most Biblical texts substitute the name Nebuchadnezzar, a disparaging pun meaning "Nabu, protect the mule." A mule was incapable of having offspring, so the name expresses the opposite hope of the king's true name. Ancient Near Eastern curse formulas often invoked an absence of any descendants. **king of kings** A title used by Assyrian and Persian kings. Its use by Neo-Babylonian kings such as Nebuchadnezzar is unattested outside the Bible (compare Ezr 7:12; Da 2:37).

26:8–12 Ezekiel accurately depicts standard siege tactics in the ancient Near East. A siege wall protects the attackers below. The mound or ramp gives battering rams and troops access to the city wall. Siege towers give the attackers a high vantage point, so that archers could protect the soldiers who were building the siege ramp or manning the battering rams. Shields protect the siege engines. Once the city was breached, the inhabitants would be killed by the sword or rounded up for slavery or deportation. The city's wealth was plundered and the walls and houses were demolished.

26:8 he will set up siege works against you Nebuchadnezzar besieged Tyre for 13 years, from 586–573 BC. He was able to destroy the coastal city and villages but couldn't reach the main island city. The siege finally ended when a treaty was negotiated and Tyre's royal house was deported. Although the city was significantly weakened, it remained standing. While Nebuchadnezzar eventually achieved the submission of Tyre, he did not physically invade the main city, trampling its streets and reducing it to rubble. Ezekiel points out this failure in Eze 29:18. Here, his description goes beyond the facts of the siege of Tyre. This suggests that he is following the pattern of royal inscriptions describing a king's exploits in highly exaggerated and stereotyped formulas. For example, Ezekiel accurately describes the stages of a siege, but a siege mound would have been logistically impossible at Tyre. One possibility is that different elements of Ezekiel's siege vision were fulfilled during different sieges. Alexander the Great also besieged Tyre (in 332 BC). **against you, build a ramp up to your walls** See note on 4:2.
26:12 throw your stones, timber and rubble Alexander

break down your walls and demolish your fine houses and throw your stones, timber and rubble into the sea. [13]I will put an end to your noisy songs, and the music of your harps will be heard no more. [14]I will make you a bare rock, and you will become a place to spread fishnets. You will never be rebuilt, for I the LORD have spoken, declares the Sovereign LORD.

[15]"This is what the Sovereign LORD says to Tyre: Will not the coastlands tremble at the sound of your fall, when the wounded groan and the slaughter takes place in you? [16]Then all the princes of the coast will step down from their thrones and lay aside their robes and take off their embroidered garments. Clothed with terror, they will sit on the ground, trembling every moment, appalled at you. [17]Then they will take up a lament concerning you and say to you:

"'How you are destroyed, city of renown,
   peopled by men of the sea!
You were a power on the seas,
   you and your citizens;
you put your terror
   on all who lived there.
[18]Now the coastlands tremble
   on the day of your fall;
the islands in the sea
   are terrified at your collapse.'

[19]"This is what the Sovereign LORD says: When I make you a desolate city, like cities no longer inhabited, and when I bring the ocean depths over you and its vast waters cover you, [20]then I will bring you down with those who go down to the pit, to the people of long ago. I will make you dwell in the earth below, as in ancient ruins, with those who go down to the pit, and you will not return or take your place[a] in the land of the living. [21]I will bring you to a horrible end and you will be no more. You will be sought, but you will never again be found, declares the Sovereign LORD."

A Lament Over Tyre

27 The word of the LORD came to me: [2]"Son of man, take up a lament concerning Tyre. [3]Say to Tyre, situated at the gateway to the sea, merchant of peoples on many coasts, 'This is what the Sovereign LORD says:

"'You say, Tyre,
   "I am perfect in beauty."
[4]Your domain was on the high seas;
   your builders brought your beauty to
      perfection.
[5]They made all your timbers
   of juniper from Senir[b];
they took a cedar from Lebanon
   to make a mast for you.
[6]Of oaks from Bashan
   they made your oars;
of cypress wood[c] from the coasts of Cyprus
   they made your deck, adorned with
      ivory.

[a] 20 Septuagint; Hebrew *return, and I will give glory*   [b] 5 That is, Mount Hermon   [c] 6 Targum; the Masoretic Text has a different division of the consonants.

---

the Great used the rubble from the mainland city of Tyre to build a causeway out to the island city to conquer it.
26:14 You will never be rebuilt Ezekiel's vision of a decisive victory should be understood as rhetorical exaggeration (or hyperbole) based on the symbolism of v. 5. Based on 29:18, Ezekiel was aware that Nebuchadnezzar's siege was less successful than anticipated.
26:15 coastlands The prophets often use this word (*iyyim*, meaning "island" or "coastland" in Hebrew) to refer to the known reaches of the inhabited world (compare Isa 11:11; 40:15; Jer 31:10).
26:16 all the princes of the coast Refers to the wealthy merchants of Tyre (see Isa 23:8).
26:17 lament See note on Eze 19:1.
26:19 and its vast waters cover you Tyre was master of the sea, but the sea has washed away all trace of the city. This exaggeration emphasizes the poetic justice of Tyre's judgment.
26:20 with those who go down to the pit Depicts Tyre's arrival in the underworld.

27:1–36 Ezekiel's second lamentation for Tyre depicts the city as one of its grand merchant vessels, heavily laden with products for trade and shipwrecked on the high seas. Ezekiel's emphasis on commerce and seafaring calls for many technical expressions whose nuances are uncertain; this is the only time they appear in the OT. While the details may be partly obscured by the difficult language, the overall message is clear: Tyre's worldwide

influence and reputation is meaningless when divine judgment comes. Ezekiel emphasizes Tyre's wide sphere of influence with a lengthy list of nations and peoples that traded with the city. Many of the names are rarely mentioned in the Bible, as shown in the Table of Nations in Ge 10 (see note on Ge 10:1–32). For further background on Tyre, see note on Eze 26:1—28:19.

27:2 lament See note on 19:1.
27:3 many coasts See note on 26:15. **You say, Tyre, "I am perfect"** The prophet commonly recites the nation's own words before pronouncing judgment against it (see 25:3; 26:2).

27:4–7 The metaphor of Tyre as a ship begins. The vessel is built from local timber, but additional materials are imported from Cyprus, Egypt and elsewhere.

27:5 juniper from Senir Another name for Mount Hermon, the highest peak at the southern end of the Anti-Lebanon Mountains located between Tyre and Damascus (see Dt 3:8–9; Jos 11:17). **a cedar from Lebanon** One of the Phoenicians' primary exports (see note on Isa 14:8).
27:6 oaks from Bashan Another valuable commodity. Bashan was a fertile plateau east of the Sea of Galilee and south of Mount Hermon (or Senir; see note on Eze 27:5). **cypress wood from the coasts of Cyprus** Imports from the Mediterranean island. The Phoenician colony of Kition was on the southeast coast of Cyprus.

7 Fine embroidered linen from Egypt was
    your sail
  and served as your banner;
your awnings were of blue and purple
    from the coasts of Elishah.
8 Men of Sidon and Arvad were your oarsmen;
  your skilled men, Tyre, were aboard as
    your sailors.
9 Veteran craftsmen of Byblos were on board
  as shipwrights to caulk your seams.
All the ships of the sea and their sailors
  came alongside to trade for your wares.

10 "'Men of Persia, Lydia and Put
  served as soldiers in your army.
They hung their shields and helmets on
    your walls,
  bringing you splendor.
11 Men of Arvad and Helek
  guarded your walls on every side;
men of Gammad
  were in your towers.
They hung their shields around your walls;
  they brought your beauty to perfection.

12 "'Tarshish did business with you because of
your great wealth of goods; they exchanged silver,
iron, tin and lead for your merchandise.
13 "'Greece, Tubal and Meshek did business with
you; they traded human beings and articles of
bronze for your wares.

14 "'Men of Beth Togarmah exchanged chariot
horses, cavalry horses and mules for your merchandise.
15 "'The men of Rhodes[a] traded with you, and
many coastlands were your customers; they paid
you with ivory tusks and ebony.
16 "'Aram[b] did business with you because of your
many products; they exchanged turquoise, purple
fabric, embroidered work, fine linen, coral and
rubies for your merchandise.
17 "'Judah and Israel traded with you; they exchanged wheat from Minnith and confections,[c]
honey, olive oil and balm for your wares.
18 "'Damascus did business with you because of
your many products and great wealth of goods.
They offered wine from Helbon, wool from Zahar
19 and casks of wine from Izal in exchange for your
wares: wrought iron, cassia and calamus.
20 "'Dedan traded in saddle blankets with you.
21 "'Arabia and all the princes of Kedar were
your customers; they did business with you in
lambs, rams and goats.
22 "'The merchants of Sheba and Raamah traded
with you; for your merchandise they exchanged
the finest of all kinds of spices and precious
stones, and gold.
23 "'Harran, Kanneh and Eden and merchants

---

a 15 Septuagint; Hebrew *Dedan*   *b 16* Most Hebrew
manuscripts; some Hebrew manuscripts and Syriac *Edom*
c 17 The meaning of the Hebrew for this word is uncertain.

27:7 Fine embroidered linen from Egypt A sign of
luxury (see 16:10). **blue and purple** The Phoenicians
had an advanced textile industry and created blue and
purple dye from the mucus of Mediterranean sea snails.
Compare note on 23:6.

27:8–9 The oracle shifts focus to the crew, which includes sailors from several Phoenician cities. The clearly
defined hierarchy of roles includes oarsmen, navigators,
sailors and shipwrights.

27:8 Sidon and Arvad Phoenician cities on the Mediterranean coast north of Tyre.

27:9 Byblos Another Phoenician coastal city.

27:10 Men of Persia, Lydia and Put Ezekiel refers to
these nations to highlight Tyre's far-reaching influence
in the ancient world—far to the east, to the northwest
and to the southwest.

27:11 Helek A place called Helek is not mentioned
elsewhere in the OT, but Assyrian annals mention a place
known as Hilakku in southeastern Turkey. Alternately, the
Hebrew word could be understood as a common noun
with a suffix, so *helekh* could mean "your army." **men
of Gammad** The location of Gammad (also rendered
"Gamad") is uncertain. It could be in southeastern Turkey
or north along the Mediterranean coast.

27:12–25 Highlighting the Phoenicians' impressive
commercial network, Ezekiel provides an extensive list
of Tyre's trading partners and their commodities.

27:12 Tarshish Tarshish represents the furthest extent
of the known world to the west (see note on Jnh 1:3).

27:13 Greece, Tubal and Meshek These names are
mentioned in Ge 10:2 as sons of Japheth (Noah's

son). Javan was the Biblical name for Greece. Tubal
and Meshech (also rendered "Meshek") likely were locations in central and northeastern Turkey, respectively.

27:14 Beth Togarmah Another name from the Table
of Nations (see Ge 10:3). Assyrian records suggest the
location was in the area of modern Armenia.

27:15 Rhodes Either a reference to an oasis and trading center in north central Arabia (see Ge 10:7) or to
an island in the Aegean Sea. The Hebrew text reads
Dedan—a location in Arabia. The Greek Septuagint
reads Rhodes—the island in the Aegean.

27:16 Aram Israel's neighbor northeast of the Sea of
Galilee and Phoenicia's neighbor to the east.

27:17 wheat from Minnith Possibly referring to wheat
exported from Ammon. Minnith appears in Jdg 11:33,
apparently as one of the 20 Ammonite towns. Its precise
location is uncertain.

27:18 Damascus Capital city of Syria (Aram), located
roughly 60 miles northeast of Tyre (see note on Eze
27:16). **wine from Helbon, wool from Zahar** Probably
goods from Syria, northwest of Damascus.

27:19 cassia An aromatic herb used to make perfume;
likely imported from India by way of south Arabia. **calamus** A reed used for making spices; probably the same
as the aromatic cane mentioned in Ex 30:23.

27:21 Kedar An important nomadic tribe based in northwest Arabia. See note on Isa 21:16.

27:22 Sheba and Raamah Sheba was an important
trading center in southwestern Arabia. The only other
mention of Raamah in the OT is the Table of Nations in
Ge 10:7, also associated with Sheba.

27:23 Harran An Aramaean city in upper Mesopotamia
on the Balikh River. Abram's family settled there after

of Sheba, Ashur and Kilmad traded with you. ²⁴In
your marketplace they traded with you beautiful
garments, blue fabric, embroidered work and multi-
colored rugs with cords twisted and tightly knotted.

²⁵ "'The ships of Tarshish serve
    as carriers for your wares.
You are filled with heavy cargo
    as you sail the sea.
²⁶ Your oarsmen take you
    out to the high seas.
But the east wind will break you to pieces
    far out at sea.
²⁷ Your wealth, merchandise and wares,
    your mariners, sailors and shipwrights,
your merchants and all your soldiers,
    and everyone else on board
will sink into the heart of the sea
    on the day of your shipwreck.
²⁸ The shorelands will quake
    when your sailors cry out.
²⁹ All who handle the oars
    will abandon their ships;
the mariners and all the sailors
    will stand on the shore.
³⁰ They will raise their voice
    and cry bitterly over you;
they will sprinkle dust on their heads
    and roll in ashes.
³¹ They will shave their heads because of you
    and will put on sackcloth.
They will weep over you with anguish of soul
    and with bitter mourning.
³² As they wail and mourn over you,
    they will take up a lament concerning you:

"Who was ever silenced like Tyre,
    surrounded by the sea?"
³³ When your merchandise went out on the seas,
    you satisfied many nations;
with your great wealth and your wares
    you enriched the kings of the earth.
³⁴ Now you are shattered by the sea
    in the depths of the waters;
your wares and all your company
    have gone down with you.
³⁵ All who live in the coastlands
    are appalled at you;
their kings shudder with horror
    and their faces are distorted with fear.
³⁶ The merchants among the nations scoff at you;
    you have come to a horrible end
    and will be no more.'"

A Prophecy Against the King of Tyre

28 The word of the LORD came to me: ²"Son of man, say to the ruler of Tyre, 'This is what the Sovereign LORD says:

"'In the pride of your heart
    you say, "I am a god;
I sit on the throne of a god
    in the heart of the seas."
But you are a mere mortal and not a god,
    though you think you are as wise as a god.
³ Are you wiser than Daniel^a?
    Is no secret hidden from you?
⁴ By your wisdom and understanding
    you have gained wealth for yourself

^a 3 Or *Danel*, a man of renown in ancient literature

---

leaving Ur (see Ge 11:31). **Kanneh** Probably the same as Assyrian Kannu, but the precise location is unknown. **Eden** Referring to an Aramaean state west of Haran (also rendered "Harran") known in Assyrian sources as Bit Adini. **Ashur** Ashur (also rendered "Asshur") was the original capital city of Assyria, as well as the name of its primary deity. **Kilmad** Unknown outside this reference. **27:25 The ships of Tarshish** See Eze 27:12 and note. The phrase could refer to Phoenician ships bound for Tarshish, though it is likely that Tarshish was a Phoenician colony. See note on Isa 2:16. See the infographic "Ancient Phoenician Ship" on p. 1317.

27:26–36 Tyre's doom is pictured as a massive shipwreck, with all hands lost and all wealth sunk to the bottom of the sea. As Tyre sinks, the rest of Phoenicia, symbolized by sailors on their own ships, watches in horror and mourns bitterly for their loss.

27:30 they will sprinkle dust on their heads and roll in ashes Symbolic mourning rituals (see Job 30:19). **27:31 They will shave their heads** Part of mourning rituals (see Eze 7:18 and note).

28:1–10 Ezekiel's final oracle against Tyre focuses on the city's leadership. The prophet uses a rhetorical device in which the indictment against the king or prince reflects an indictment against the entire people, based on their

pride in their own wealth. The oracle is divided into two parts (vv. 1–10 and vv. 11–19): the first is addressed to the ruler and takes the form of an indictment followed by a verdict and sentence; the second part is a lamentation.

28:2 the ruler of Tyre The king of Tyre at this time was Ethbaal III, but no details of the oracle relate specifically to him. **I am a god** Indicts the prince with his own words (see note on 27:3). The ruler of Tyre appears to be equating himself with Melqart, Tyre's patron deity. Connections between deity and kingship were common in the ancient Near East. Kings often held ritual roles establishing their status as living representatives of the local deity. In Canaanite religion, Melqart was a city god whose myths depict him as a hero similar to the Greek demigod Hercules. He may have originated as a deified hero or king, just as the king of Tyre in this oracle is claiming divinity. **on the throne of a god in the heart of the seas** The motif of a divine abode surrounded by water was common in ancient Near Eastern literature. **28:3 Daniel** See note on 14:14. The figure mentioned here might be the Biblical Daniel who was known for his wisdom (see Da 1:17; 4:6). Since this oracle has distinct mythological overtones, the reference also could be to the character Danel from the Ugaritic Tale of Aqhat, who by Ezekiel's time might have acquired a reputation for wisdom.

and amassed gold and silver
   in your treasuries.
⁵ By your great skill in trading
   you have increased your wealth,
and because of your wealth
   your heart has grown proud.

⁶ "'Therefore this is what the Sovereign LORD
says:

   "'Because you think you are wise,
      as wise as a god,
⁷ I am going to bring foreigners against you,
   the most ruthless of nations;

28:7 foreigners These foreigners are identified in Eze 26:7 as the Babylonians.

Ancient Phoenician Ship

The Phoenicians were the greatest traders of the ancient world. They bartered goods throughout the Mediterranean, traveling as far as Spain and the West African coast—incredible distances for small ships with rudimentary maps and no more than the stars to guide them.

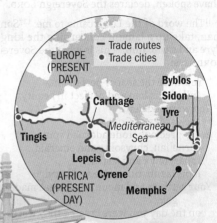

The three greatest Phoenician cities were Sidon, Byblos and Tyre. The Bible often presents Tyre as an example of wealth and influence.

A Phoenician shipwreck from the 14th century BC was discovered off the coast of Turkey. It was carrying 10 tons of copper, one ton of tin, nearly a ton of terebinth resin (for incense) in 150 jars, a large quantity of raw glass and many other precious goods.

Mortise-and-tenon construction

Builders would chisel matching square holes (mortises) into the edges of the boards and insert square lengths of oak (tenons).

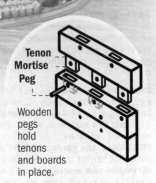

Wooden pegs hold tenons and boards in place.

they will draw their swords against your
beauty and wisdom
and pierce your shining splendor.
⁸ They will bring you down to the pit,
and you will die a violent death
in the heart of the seas.
⁹ Will you then say, "I am a god,"
in the presence of those who kill you?
You will be but a mortal, not a god,
in the hands of those who slay you.
¹⁰ You will die the death of the uncircumcised
at the hands of foreigners.

I have spoken, declares the Sovereign LORD.'"

¹¹The word of the LORD came to me: ¹²"Son of
man, take up a lament concerning the king of
Tyre and say to him: 'This is what the Sovereign
LORD says:

"'You were the seal of perfection,
full of wisdom and perfect in beauty.
¹³ You were in Eden,
the garden of God;
every precious stone adorned you:
carnelian, chrysolite and emerald,
topaz, onyx and jasper,
lapis lazuli, turquoise and beryl.ᵃ
Your settings and mountingsᵇ were made of
gold;
on the day you were created they were
prepared.
¹⁴ You were anointed as a guardian cherub,
for so I ordained you.
You were on the holy mount of God;
you walked among the fiery stones.
¹⁵ You were blameless in your ways
from the day you were created
till wickedness was found in you.

¹⁶ Through your widespread trade
you were filled with violence,
and you sinned.
So I drove you in disgrace from the mount
of God,
and I expelled you, guardian cherub,
from among the fiery stones.
¹⁷ Your heart became proud
on account of your beauty,
and you corrupted your wisdom
because of your splendor.
So I threw you to the earth;
I made a spectacle of you before kings.
¹⁸ By your many sins and dishonest trade
you have desecrated your sanctuaries.
So I made a fire come out from you,
and it consumed you,
and I reduced you to ashes on the ground
in the sight of all who were watching.
¹⁹ All the nations who knew you
are appalled at you;
you have come to a horrible end
and will be no more.'"

A Prophecy Against Sidon

²⁰The word of the LORD came to me: ²¹"Son of
man, set your face against Sidon; prophesy against
her ²²and say: 'This is what the Sovereign LORD says:

"'I am against you, Sidon,
and among you I will display my glory.
You will know that I am the LORD,
when I inflict punishment on you
and within you am proved to be holy.

ᵃ 13 The precise identification of some of these precious stones is
uncertain.   ᵇ 13 The meaning of the Hebrew for this phrase is
uncertain.

28:10 the death of the uncircumcised The Israelites considered it a disgrace to be uncircumcised. The
Egyptians, who also practiced circumcision, held the
same belief. According to Greek historian Herodotus,
the Phoenicians adopted the practice from the Egyptians.
Referring to the king of Tyre as uncircumcised may have
been intentionally insulting.

28:11–19 The second section of the oracle is described
as a lamentation addressed to the king of Tyre. The
imagery draws on mythological motifs to attribute primordial and angelic traits to the king: He is placed in the
garden of Eden (compare Ge 2–3) and called a guardian
cherub (Eze 28:14).

28:12 lament See note on 19:1. This lament is a mocking, sarcastic modification of the genre, similar to the
taunt song in Isa 14:4–23. **seal of perfection** The king
is likened to a royal seal, which often were made from
semiprecious stones.
28:13 Eden, the garden of God Places the king in the
primordial, perfect creation (see Ge 2:8–10). **carnelian,
chrysolite and emerald** These precious stones likely
allude to the priestly attire described in Ex 28:17–20.
28:14 anointed as a guardian cherub Cherubim (plural)

were divine guardians of the throne room in Babylon. This
cherub, associated with Eden, is not specifically identified.
The reference might be to the cherubim guarding Eden
in Ge 3:24. The difficulty with this possibility is that the
cherub here in Eze 28 is said to have been blameless
before becoming corrupt (Eze 28:15); no such wording
in Ge 3:24 aligns with this description. Another possibility is that the cherub here refers to an unnamed divine
throne guardian in Eden who became corrupt (see note
on Isa 14:12). In any case, the cherub is cast out of
Eden, the mountain of God (compare Eze 28:13,16),
and Ezekiel refers to this event to describe the fate of
the prince of Tyre. **holy mount of God** The placement
of the king as guardian cherub on the divine mountain
equates him with a divine being serving God in his holy
dwelling (see note on Isa 2:2).

28:20–24 The oracles against Judah's neighbors end
with judgment against Sidon, another prominent Phoenician city. The format follows that of the short oracles
against the nations, as in Eze 25:1–17.

28:21 set your face against Sidon Compare 25:2, and
note on 20:46. Sidon was located on the Mediterranean
coast, about 25 miles north of Tyre.

23 I will send a plague upon you
    and make blood flow in your streets.
The slain will fall within you,
    with the sword against you on every side.
Then you will know that I am the LORD.

24 "'No longer will the people of Israel have malicious neighbors who are painful briers and sharp thorns. Then they will know that I am the Sovereign LORD. 25 "This is what the Sovereign LORD says: When I gather the people of Israel from the nations where they have been scattered, I will be proved holy through them in the sight of the nations. Then they will live in their own land, which I gave to my servant Jacob. 26 They will live there in safety and will build houses and plant vineyards; they will live in safety when I inflict punishment on all their neighbors who maligned them. Then they will know that I am the LORD their God.'"

A Prophecy Against Egypt

Judgment on Pharaoh

29 In the tenth year, in the tenth month on the twelfth day, the word of the LORD came to me: 2 "Son of man, set your face against Pharaoh king of Egypt and prophesy against him and against all Egypt. 3 Speak to him and say: 'This is what the Sovereign LORD says:

"'I am against you, Pharaoh king of Egypt,
    you great monster lying among your
        streams.
You say, "The Nile belongs to me;
    I made it for myself."
4 But I will put hooks in your jaws
    and make the fish of your streams stick to
        your scales.
I will pull you out from among your streams,
    with all the fish sticking to your scales.
5 I will leave you in the desert,
    you and all the fish of your streams.
You will fall on the open field
    and not be gathered or picked up.
I will give you as food
    to the beasts of the earth and the birds of
        the sky.
6 Then all who live in Egypt will know that I am the LORD.

"'You have been a staff of reed for the people of Israel. 7 When they grasped you with their hands, you splintered and you tore open their shoulders; when they leaned on you, you broke and their backs were wrenched.[a]

8 "'Therefore this is what the Sovereign LORD

---

[a] 7 Syriac (see also Septuagint and Vulgate); Hebrew *and you caused their backs to stand*

28:23 plague Reflects the judgment by pestilence, blood and sword that was directed against Judah in 5:17.
28:24 malicious neighbors who are painful briers and sharp thorns The prophetic oracles against the nations seem to be meant to encourage Israel or Judah that the nations who have oppressed them will be judged eventually. They also seem to proclaim Yahweh's power to bring the nations to recognize his sovereignty.

28:25–26 This interlude serves to remind Israel that they can look forward to a time of restoration brought about by Yahweh's defeat of their enemies.

28:25 When I gather the people of Israel The scattering of God's people is a standard punishment invoked by Ezekiel and based on the covenant curse of Lev 26:33 (see Eze 20:23).

29:1—32:32 Ezekiel now turns his attention to Egypt, leveling critique and pronouncements of doom in a sequence of seven oracles. Egypt is the seventh and final nation to be addressed in the prophet's oracles against foreign nations. His attention on Egypt is likely due to the disastrous consequences that resulted from Egypt's involvement in Judah's affairs during the reign of Zedekiah. See note on 17:1–24. See the table "Oracles Against the Nations" on p. 1244.

29:1–21 The first oracle is directed at the pharaoh. The indictment centers on Egypt's pride and arrogance—along with its inability to help Judah as promised, which ultimately led to Jerusalem's destruction by the Babylonians.

29:1 tenth year, in the tenth month If the date is rendered by years of exile (as Ezekiel usually does), this

oracle dates to January 7, 587 BC—just two days after the siege of Jerusalem began. If the date is determined by the years of Zedekiah's reign (as in 24:1), this would be a year later (see 24:1 and note). See the timeline "Dates in Ezekiel" on p. 1276.
29:2 set your face See note on 20:46. **Pharaoh king of Egypt** Refers to Hophra, who ruled 589–570 BC. Hophra was ambitious and inclined to involve Egypt in the affairs of Palestine. His military response to Zedekiah's call for aid forced Nebuchadnezzar to temporarily lift the siege of Jerusalem (Jer 37:5). The attempted intervention failed, as Hophra either withdrew or was driven out by the Babylonians.
29:3 you great monster The Hebrew term means "serpent," "dragon" or "sea monster." Here, the word describes a crocodile in the Nile River, but it frequently appears in OT passages with mythological overtones (e.g., Isa 51:9). In Ps 74:13 and Isa 30:7, Egypt is linked to mythology of divine combat with a serpentine chaos monster. Both passages use the Hebrew terminology in parallel with "Rahab," one of the names given for the chaos monster (see note on Isa 51:9). The reference here, however, has been thoroughly demythologized. See note on Isa 27:1. **Nile belongs to me; I made it for myself** An arrogant claim implying divinity (compare Eze 28:2 and note). From earliest Egyptian history, it appears the Egyptians believed the pharaoh was the living incarnation of a deity. Over time, that status diminished into the pharaoh's role as the gods' human representative.
29:6 a staff of reed A metaphor highlighting their weakness and their failure to support Israel as promised.
29:8 I will bring a sword against you Compare 14:17. The nations experience the same types of judgments prophesied against Judah earlier in the book.

says: I will bring a sword against you and kill both man and beast. ⁹Egypt will become a desolate wasteland. Then they will know that I am the LORD.

"'Because you said, "The Nile is mine; I made it," ¹⁰therefore I am against you and against your streams, and I will make the land of Egypt a ruin and a desolate waste from Migdol to Aswan, as far as the border of Cush.ᵃ ¹¹The foot of neither man nor beast will pass through it; no one will live there for forty years. ¹²I will make the land of Egypt desolate among devastated lands, and her cities will lie desolate forty years among ruined cities. And I will disperse the Egyptians among the nations and scatter them through the countries.

¹³"'Yet this is what the Sovereign LORD says: At the end of forty years I will gather the Egyptians from the nations where they were scattered. ¹⁴I will bring them back from captivity and return them to Upper Egypt, the land of their ancestry. There they will be a lowly kingdom. ¹⁵It will be the lowliest of kingdoms and will never again exalt itself above the other nations. I will make it so weak that it will never again rule over the nations. ¹⁶Egypt will no longer be a source of confidence for the people of Israel but will be a reminder of their sin in turning to her for help. Then they will know that I am the Sovereign LORD.'"

Nebuchadnezzar's Reward

¹⁷In the twenty-seventh year, in the first month on the first day, the word of the LORD came to me:

¹⁸"Son of man, Nebuchadnezzar king of Babylon drove his army in a hard campaign against Tyre; every head was rubbed bare and every shoulder made raw. Yet he and his army got no reward from the campaign he led against Tyre. ¹⁹Therefore this is what the Sovereign LORD says: I am going to give Egypt to Nebuchadnezzar king of Babylon, and he will carry off its wealth. He will loot and plunder the land as pay for his army. ²⁰I have given him Egypt as a reward for his efforts because he and his army did it for me, declares the Sovereign LORD. ²¹On that day I will make a hornᵇ grow for the Israelites, and I will open your mouth among them. Then they will know that I am the LORD."

A Lament Over Egypt

30 The word of the LORD came to me: ²"Son of man, prophesy and say: 'This is what the Sovereign LORD says:

"'Wail and say,
  "Alas for that day!"
³ For the day is near,
  the day of the LORD is near —
a day of clouds,
  a time of doom for the nations.
⁴ A sword will come against Egypt,
  and anguish will come upon Cush.ᶜ

ᵃ 10 That is, the upper Nile region   ᵇ 21 Horn here symbolizes strength.   ᶜ 4 That is, the upper Nile region; also in verses 5 and 9

29:10 Migdol From the Canaanite word for "tower" or "fortress." Used as a proper name for several Egyptian military installations on the northeast frontier of Egypt. **to Aswan** One of the main towns in southern Egypt; located at the first cataract of the Nile. The site marks the southern frontier of Egypt (see note on Isa 49:12). **the border of Cush** The region of the upper Nile south of Egypt; also called Nubia, Cush or Ethiopia. Syene (Aswan) was the last Egyptian town before the border. Geographic references here cover the length of Egypt from its northeastern frontier to its southern border.

29:11 no one will live there for forty years Rather than being a specific time period, a period of 40 years was symbolic of a temporary national punishment, representing the passing of one generation.

29:12 I will disperse the Egyptians among the nations The same judgment declared for Israel. Echoes the curses of the covenant from Lev 26:33. See Eze 11:16 and note.

29:14 I will bring them back from captivity and return them to Upper Egypt Compare 16:53 and 39:25. **Upper Egypt** A name for the southern half of Egypt. This region borders Cush (compare Isa 11:11). Ezekiel's reference to the region as the Egyptians' land of origin accurately reflects the Egyptians' own traditions.

29:17 twenty-seventh year, in the first month The oracle dates to April 26, 571 BC, making this the latest-dated oracle of the book. See the timeline "Dates in Ezekiel" on p. 1276.

29:18 drove his army in a hard campaign against

Tyre The Babylonians besieged Tyre for 13 years (see note on Eze 26:8). **he and his army got no reward from the campaign he led against Tyre** The long siege was ended diplomatically. Tyre submitted to Babylonian rule, but the city was not destroyed.

29:19 am going to give Egypt to Nebuchadnezzar Nebuchadnezzar apparently invaded Egypt in 568 BC, but few details of the campaign are known. A fragment from his annals and the Greek historian Herodotus mention that the campaign occurred.

29:21 I will make a horn grow The horn could refer to a restoration of Israel's power or symbolize a king (compare Da 7:7). The horn of an animal was a token of its power. The symbolism likely points to the restoration of Davidic kingship through the Messiah. See Ps 132:17.

30:1–19 This third oracle against Egypt is the only one without a date. It consists of four segments, each introduced by the Hebrew formula *koh amar adonay yhwh* ("thus says the Lord Yahweh"). The oracle reuses the imagery of Eze 29:1–21, pronouncing judgment on Egypt and expanding on the earlier oracle. Ezekiel's use of "Day of Yahweh" imagery echoes 7:10–27.

30:3 day of the LORD See note on 7:1–27. **a day of clouds** Depictions of clouds or thick darkness is a common part of the Day of Yahweh motif (compare Joel 2:2; Zep 1:15). **a time of doom for the nations** The Hebrew text reads "a time for the nations," implying the Day of Yahweh is ultimately about judgment against all the nations, not just Egypt.

When the slain fall in Egypt,
   her wealth will be carried away
   and her foundations torn down.

⁵Cush and Libya, Lydia and all Arabia, Kub and the people of the covenant land will fall by the sword along with Egypt.

⁶"This is what the LORD says:

"The allies of Egypt will fall
   and her proud strength will fail.
From Migdol to Aswan
   they will fall by the sword within her,
         declares the Sovereign LORD.
⁷"They will be desolate
   among desolate lands,
and their cities will lie
   among ruined cities.
⁸Then they will know that I am the LORD,
   when I set fire to Egypt
   and all her helpers are crushed.

⁹"On that day messengers will go out from me in ships to frighten Cush out of her complacency. Anguish will take hold of them on the day of Egypt's doom, for it is sure to come.

¹⁰"This is what the Sovereign LORD says:

"I will put an end to the hordes of Egypt
   by the hand of Nebuchadnezzar king of
      Babylon.
¹¹He and his army — the most ruthless of
      nations —
will be brought in to destroy the land.
They will draw their swords against Egypt
   and fill the land with the slain.
¹²I will dry up the waters of the Nile
   and sell the land to an evil nation;

by the hand of foreigners
   I will lay waste the land and everything
      in it.

I the LORD have spoken.

¹³"This is what the Sovereign LORD says:

"I will destroy the idols
   and put an end to the images in Memphis.
No longer will there be a prince in Egypt,
   and I will spread fear throughout the land.
¹⁴I will lay waste Upper Egypt,
   set fire to Zoan
   and inflict punishment on Thebes.
¹⁵I will pour out my wrath on Pelusium,
   the stronghold of Egypt,
   and wipe out the hordes of Thebes.
¹⁶I will set fire to Egypt;
   Pelusium will writhe in agony.
Thebes will be taken by storm;
   Memphis will be in constant distress.
¹⁷The young men of Heliopolis and Bubastis
   will fall by the sword,
   and the cities themselves will go into
      captivity.
¹⁸Dark will be the day at Tahpanhes
   when I break the yoke of Egypt;
   there her proud strength will come to an
      end.
She will be covered with clouds,
   and her villages will go into captivity.
¹⁹So I will inflict punishment on Egypt,
   and they will know that I am the LORD.'"

Pharaoh's Arms Are Broken

²⁰In the eleventh year, in the first month on the seventh day, the word of the LORD came to me:

30:5 Cush and Libya, Lydia Identifies the nations referenced in Eze 30:3. They are major allies and neighbors of Egypt, including: Cush (Nubia or Ethiopia; see note on 29:10); the peoples of the Arabian Peninsula; Lydia in central Asia Minor (see note on 27:10); and two regions of Libya.

30:13 images in Memphis The city of Memphis (called "Noph" in Hebrew) was one of the ancient capitals of Lower Egypt, located near the beginning of the delta region. Pharaoh Hophra (see note on 29:2) had a palace at Memphis, but it also was an important religious center with temples to many Egyptian gods. **No longer will there be a prince** Pronounces an end to religious and royal institutions. The pharaoh at this time was Hophra, one of the last kings of the Saite Dynasty in Egypt. After the Saite Dynasty, Egypt was dominated by a succession of foreign empires. The country was annexed by Cambyses of Persia starting in 525 BC, then by Alexander the Great in 332 BC and Rome in 30 BC.

30:14 Upper Egypt See note on 29:14. **Zoan** An important city in the northeastern delta region of Egypt. Also known as Tanis, it was the capital city of Egypt during the Israelite monarchy. **Thebes** Thebes (called "No" in Hebrew) was the ancient capital city of Upper Egypt and the site of two large temples to the god Amon. It was an

important religious center with many other temples and tombs of the kings. Some of the best-preserved monuments in Egypt are in this area, including the temples at Karnak, Luxor and Medinet Habu.

30:15 Pelusium, the stronghold of Egypt Pelusium (called "Sin" in Hebrew) was the official entry point into Egypt on the northeastern frontier, located on the Mediterranean coast at the far eastern edge of the Delta region.

30:17 Heliopolis and Bubastis These cities are in Lower Egypt in the Nile Delta region. On (Heliopolis) was an important center for worship of the sun god Re. Ezekiel writes the name of Heliopolis as *awen* ("iniquity" or "wickedness"), a possible pun on the Egyptian name On. The goddess Bastet was worshiped in Pi-beseth, which means "house of Bastet." Pi-beseth increased in status as a religious center after the Assyrians destroyed Thebes in 663 BC.

30:18 Tahpanhes A village and border outpost in the eastern Nile Delta.

30:20–26 This oracle can be read as a response to Egypt's attempted involvement in Judean affairs in 587 BC. While the Egyptian attack forces the Babylonians to leave Jerusalem, it is not the sign of deliverance that the people of Judah hoped for. Ezekiel warns them against such hopes because Egypt will soon fall.

²¹"Son of man, I have broken the arm of Pharaoh king of Egypt. It has not been bound up to be healed or put in a splint so that it may become strong enough to hold a sword. ²²Therefore this is what the Sovereign LORD says: I am against Pharaoh king of Egypt. I will break both his arms, the good arm as well as the broken one, and make the sword fall from his hand. ²³I will disperse the Egyptians among the nations and scatter them through the countries. ²⁴I will strengthen the arms of the king of Babylon and put my sword in his hand, but I will break the arms of Pharaoh, and he will groan before him like a mortally wounded man. ²⁵I will strengthen the arms of the king of Babylon, but the arms of Pharaoh will fall limp. Then they will know that I am the LORD, when I put my sword into the hand of the king of Babylon and he brandishes it against Egypt. ²⁶I will disperse the Egyptians among the nations and scatter them through the countries. Then they will know that I am the LORD."

Pharaoh as a Felled Cedar of Lebanon

31 In the eleventh year, in the third month on the first day, the word of the LORD came to me: ²"Son of man, say to Pharaoh king of Egypt and to his hordes:

"'Who can be compared with you in majesty?
³ Consider Assyria, once a cedar in Lebanon,
  with beautiful branches overshadowing
    the forest;
  it towered on high,
    its top above the thick foliage.
⁴ The waters nourished it,
    deep springs made it grow tall;
  their streams flowed
    all around its base
  and sent their channels
    to all the trees of the field.
⁵ So it towered higher
    than all the trees of the field;
  its boughs increased
    and its branches grew long,
  spreading because of abundant
    waters.
⁶ All the birds of the sky
    nested in its boughs,
  all the animals of the wild
    gave birth under its branches;
  all the great nations
    lived in its shade.
⁷ It was majestic in beauty,
    with its spreading boughs,
  for its roots went down
    to abundant waters.
⁸ The cedars in the garden of God
    could not rival it,
  nor could the junipers
    equal its boughs,
  nor could the plane trees
    compare with its branches —
  no tree in the garden of God
    could match its beauty.
⁹ I made it beautiful
    with abundant branches,
  the envy of all the trees of Eden
    in the garden of God.

¹⁰"'Therefore this is what the Sovereign LORD says: Because the great cedar towered over the

---

30:20 eleventh year, in the first month The date corresponds to April 29, 587 BC, close to the time when Egypt's invasion of Palestine forced Nebuchadnezzar to temporarily lift the siege of Jerusalem. See the timeline "Dates in Ezekiel" on p. 1276.

30:21 I have broken the arm of Pharaoh The arm symbolizes strength and the ability to wage war.

31:1–18 This fifth oracle against Egypt draws on the historical glory and downfall of Assyria and mythological "cosmic tree" imagery to depict the coming downfall of the pharaoh and the decline of Egypt.

31:1 eleventh year, in the third month Dates to June 21, 587 BC, almost two months after the previous prophecy (30:20–26).

31:2 Pharaoh king of Egypt See note on 29:2.

31:3–9 Ezekiel presents a symbolic story or allegory about a cedar, which denotes Assyria but stands for the most powerful nation of the time. By doing so, he teaches that even the mightiest of nations eventually falls to a greater power. In the ancient Near East, the cedar symbolized majesty, but Ezekiel's description bears striking parallels with the Mesopotamian myth of a cosmic tree whose roots reach to the underworld and whose top reaches to the heavens. Presenting the fall of Assyria as the felling of a great tree echoes the denunciation of Assyria for their pride in Isa 10:5–19.

31:3 Assyria, once a cedar in Lebanon The Lebanese cedars were highly prized building materials in the ancient world (see note on Isa 14:8).

31:6 all the great nations lived in its shade The image of a "cosmic tree" or "world tree" (see note on Eze 31:3–9) represented world order, connecting the human world with the heavens and the netherworld. The tree is often depicted as sheltering animals or people. Ezekiel has thoroughly politicized the image, however, since Assyria dominated all neighboring nations, generating fear with their cruel and harsh military reprisals for rebellion.

31:8 the garden of God Mentioned three times in vv. 8–9 and equated with Eden in v. 9. Comparison to the ideal garden paradise of Ge 2 emphasizes the greatness of the Assyrian cedar. Mesopotamian mythology also depicts a garden reserved for the gods' enjoyment and off limits to humans.

31:10–18 Ezekiel describes the great cedar's fall. Although the allegory initially referred to Assyria, the indictment intentionally blurs the distinctions between past judgment on Assyria and future judgment on Egypt, alternating between second- and third-person pronouns to address the judgment's subject. Assyria's fall serves as a warning to Egypt, which will suffer the same fate.

thick foliage, and because it was proud of its height, ¹¹I gave it into the hands of the ruler of the nations, for him to deal with according to its wickedness. I cast it aside, ¹²and the most ruthless of foreign nations cut it down and left it. Its boughs fell on the mountains and in all the valleys; its branches lay broken in all the ravines of the land. All the nations of the earth came out from under its shade and left it. ¹³All the birds settled on the fallen tree, and all the wild animals lived among its branches. ¹⁴Therefore no other trees by the waters are ever to tower proudly on high, lifting their tops above the thick foliage. No other trees so well-watered are ever to reach such a height; they are all destined for death, for the earth below, among mortals who go down to the realm of the dead.

¹⁵"'This is what the Sovereign LORD says: On the day it was brought down to the realm of the dead I covered the deep springs with mourning for it; I held back its streams, and its abundant waters were restrained. Because of it I clothed Lebanon with gloom, and all the trees of the field withered away. ¹⁶I made the nations tremble at the sound of its fall when I brought it down to the realm of the dead to be with those who go down to the pit. Then all the trees of Eden, the choicest and best of Lebanon, the well-watered trees, were consoled in the earth below. ¹⁷They too, like the great cedar, had gone down to the realm of the dead, to those killed by the sword, along with the armed men who lived in its shade among the nations.

¹⁸"'Which of the trees of Eden can be compared with you in splendor and majesty? Yet you, too, will be brought down with the trees of Eden to the earth below; you will lie among the uncircumcised, with those killed by the sword.

"'This is Pharaoh and all his hordes, declares the Sovereign LORD.'"

A Lament Over Pharaoh

32 In the twelfth year, in the twelfth month on the first day, the word of the LORD came to me: ²"Son of man, take up a lament concerning Pharaoh king of Egypt and say to him:

"'You are like a lion among the
        nations;
    you are like a monster in the seas
thrashing about in your streams,
    churning the water with your feet
    and muddying the streams.

³"'This is what the Sovereign LORD says:

"'With a great throng of people
    I will cast my net over you,
    and they will haul you up in my net.
⁴I will throw you on the land
    and hurl you on the open field.
I will let all the birds of the sky settle
        on you
    and all the animals of the wild gorge
        themselves on you.
⁵I will spread your flesh on the mountains
    and fill the valleys with your
        remains.
⁶I will drench the land with your flowing
        blood
    all the way to the mountains,
    and the ravines will be filled with your
        flesh.
⁷When I snuff you out, I will cover the
        heavens
    and darken their stars;
I will cover the sun with a cloud,
    and the moon will not give its light.
⁸All the shining lights in the heavens
    I will darken over you;
I will bring darkness over your land,
        declares the Sovereign LORD.

31:11 into the hands of the ruler Assyria had been a world power for nearly three centuries before falling to Babylon about 25 years before Ezekiel's time. At the time of Assyria's decline, Egypt had been allied with Assyria and had sent an army to help oppose Babylon in 609 BC. Babylon had already overrun the Assyrian capital of Nineveh in 612 BC and left the Assyrian army in tatters. In 605 BC, Nebuchadnezzar defeated the combined forces at the Battle of Carchemish. Egypt's influence in Syria-Palestine was severely diminished after that defeat. In a sense, Egypt and Assyria fell to Babylon at the same time. One was completely destroyed, while the other returned home with no ability to exert any influence on foreign affairs.

31:12 most ruthless of foreign nations A reference to Babylon (see Eze 28:7).

31:14 who go down to the realm of the dead An image of descent into the underworld (see 26:20; and see note on Job 14:13).

31:15 it was brought down to the realm of the dead The Hebrew text here uses the word *she'ol*. This term is often transliterated in English translations as Sheol as the Biblical name for the domain of the dead (see note on Ge 37:35).

31:18 lie among the uncircumcised The Egyptians also practiced circumcision and abhorred the uncircumcised, making this characterization an intentional insult. See note on Eze 28:10.

32:1–16 The sixth oracle against Egypt is characterized as a lament (like that against Tyre in 27:1). The judgments depicted here are reused from previous oracles against Egypt in chs. 29–31 and, in Ezekiel's typical style, blur metaphorical and literal imagery.

32:1 on the first day March 3, 585 BC, about two months after news of Jerusalem's fall had reached Ezekiel (see 33:21). See the timeline "Dates in Ezekiel" on p. 1276.

32:2 lament See note on 19:1. **a monster in the seas** See 29:3 and note.

⁹I will trouble the hearts of many peoples
  when I bring about your destruction
      among the nations,
    among[a] lands you have not known.
¹⁰I will cause many peoples to be appalled at
      you,
  and their kings will shudder with horror
      because of you
  when I brandish my sword before them.
On the day of your downfall
  each of them will tremble
  every moment for his life.

¹¹"'For this is what the Sovereign Lord says:

"'The sword of the king of Babylon
  will come against you.
¹²I will cause your hordes to fall
  by the swords of mighty men —
    the most ruthless of all nations.
They will shatter the pride of Egypt,
  and all her hordes will be overthrown.
¹³I will destroy all her cattle
  from beside abundant waters
no longer to be stirred by the foot of man
  or muddied by the hooves of cattle.
¹⁴Then I will let her waters settle
  and make her streams flow like oil,
      declares the Sovereign Lord.
¹⁵When I make Egypt desolate
  and strip the land of everything in it,
when I strike down all who live there,
  then they will know that I am the Lord.'

¹⁶"This is the lament they will chant for her. The daughters of the nations will chant it; for Egypt and all her hordes they will chant it, declares the Sovereign Lord."

Egypt's Descent Into the Realm of the Dead

¹⁷In the twelfth year, on the fifteenth day of the month, the word of the Lord came to me: ¹⁸"Son of man, wail for the hordes of Egypt and consign to the earth below both her and the daughters of mighty nations, along with those who go down to the pit. ¹⁹Say to them, 'Are you more favored than others? Go down and be laid among the uncircum-

cised.' ²⁰They will fall among those killed by the sword. The sword is drawn; let her be dragged off with all her hordes. ²¹From within the realm of the dead the mighty leaders will say of Egypt and her allies, 'They have come down and they lie with the uncircumcised, with those killed by the sword.'

²²"Assyria is there with her whole army; she is surrounded by the graves of all her slain, all who have fallen by the sword. ²³Their graves are in the depths of the pit and her army lies around her grave. All who had spread terror in the land of the living are slain, fallen by the sword.

²⁴"Elam is there, with all her hordes around her grave. All of them are slain, fallen by the sword. All who had spread terror in the land of the living went down uncircumcised to the earth below. They bear their shame with those who go down to the pit. ²⁵A bed is made for her among the slain, with all her hordes around her grave. All of them are uncircumcised, killed by the sword. Because their terror had spread in the land of the living, they bear their shame with those who go down to the pit; they are laid among the slain.

²⁶"Meshek and Tubal are there, with all their hordes around their graves. All of them are uncircumcised, killed by the sword because they spread their terror in the land of the living. ²⁷But they do not lie with the fallen warriors of old,[b] who went down to the realm of the dead with their weapons of war — their swords placed under their heads and their shields[c] resting on their bones — though these warriors also had terrorized the land of the living.

²⁸"You too, Pharaoh, will be broken and will lie among the uncircumcised, with those killed by the sword.

²⁹"Edom is there, her kings and all her princes; despite their power, they are laid with those killed by the sword. They lie with the uncircumcised, with those who go down to the pit.

³⁰"All the princes of the north and all the Sidonians are there; they went down with the slain in

---

[a] 9 Hebrew; Septuagint *bring you into captivity among the nations, / to*   [b] 27 Septuagint; Hebrew *warriors who were uncircumcised*   [c] 27 Probable reading of the original Hebrew text; Masoretic Text *punishment*

32:12 most ruthless of all nations See 28:7.

32:17–32 This seventh oracle depicts Egypt's descent into the underworld. Many other nations are already there to greet Egypt, echoing the scene from Isa 14:9–15. The image of the descent to the underworld was used previously for Tyre (Eze 26:20) and Egypt (31:16). While they may have been powerful and feared on earth, they all must bear the shame of their defeat and descent into death. Egypt's fate will be just like theirs, providing a small measure of consolation for Pharaoh (see v. 31).

32:17 fifteenth day of the month Two weeks after the previous oracle (see note on v. 1). See the timeline "Dates in Ezekiel" on p. 1276.

32:19 uncircumcised See 31:18 and note.

32:24 Elam Located east of Babylon and just north of the Persian Gulf in southwestern Iran. Elam was absorbed into the Persian Empire.

32:26 Meshek and Tubal A region of central Turkey (see note on 27:13).

32:29 Edom is there Judah's neighbor to the southeast (see note on 25:12–14).

32:30 the princes of the north Possibly a reference to Aram or Syria, Israel's immediate neighbor to the north.

all the Sidonians Refers to the Phoenicians, Israel's neighbor to the northwest (see note on 26:1—28:19).

disgrace despite the terror caused by their power. They lie uncircumcised with those killed by the sword and bear their shame with those who go down to the pit.

³¹"Pharaoh — he and all his army — will see them and he will be consoled for all his hordes that were killed by the sword, declares the Sovereign LORD. ³²Although I had him spread terror in the land of the living, Pharaoh and all his hordes will be laid among the uncircumcised, with those killed by the sword, declares the Sovereign LORD."

Renewal of Ezekiel's Call as Watchman

33 The word of the LORD came to me: ²"Son of man, speak to your people and say to them: 'When I bring the sword against a land, and the people of the land choose one of their men and make him their watchman, ³and he sees the sword coming against the land and blows the trumpet to warn the people, ⁴then if anyone hears the trumpet but does not heed the warning and the sword comes and takes their life, their blood will be on their own head. ⁵Since they heard the sound of the trumpet but did not heed the warning, their blood will be on their own head. If they had heeded the warning, they would have saved themselves. ⁶But if the watchman sees the sword coming and does not blow the trumpet to warn the people and the sword comes and takes someone's life, that person's life will be taken because of their sin, but I will hold the watchman accountable for their blood.'

⁷"Son of man, I have made you a watchman for the people of Israel; so hear the word I speak and give them warning from me. ⁸When I say to the wicked, 'You wicked person, you will surely die,' and you do not speak out to dissuade them from their ways, that wicked person will die forᵃ their sin, and I will hold you accountable for their blood. ⁹But if you do warn the wicked person to turn from their ways and they do not do so, they will die for their sin, though you yourself will be saved.

¹⁰"Son of man, say to the Israelites, 'This is what you are saying: "Our offenses and sins weigh us down, and we are wasting away because ofᵇ them. How then can we live?"' ¹¹Say to them, 'As surely as I live, declares the Sovereign LORD, I take no pleasure in the death of the wicked, but rather that they turn from their ways and live. Turn! Turn from your evil ways! Why will you die, people of Israel?'

¹²"Therefore, son of man, say to your people, 'If someone who is righteous disobeys, that person's former righteousness will count for nothing. And if someone who is wicked repents, that person's former wickedness will not bring condemnation. The righteous person who sins will not be allowed to live even though they were formerly righteous.' ¹³If I tell a righteous person that they will surely live, but then they trust in their righteousness and do evil, none of the righteous things that person has done will be remembered; they will die for the evil they have done. ¹⁴And if I say to a wicked person, 'You will surely die,' but they then turn away from their sin and do what is just and right— ¹⁵if they give back what they took in pledge for a loan, return what they have stolen, follow the decrees that give life, and do no evil— that person will surely live; they will not die. ¹⁶None of the sins that person has committed will be remembered against them. They have done what is just and right; they will surely live.

¹⁷"Yet your people say, 'The way of the Lord is not just.' But it is their way that is not just. ¹⁸If a righteous person turns from their righteousness and does evil, they will die for it. ¹⁹And if a wicked person turns away from their wickedness and does what is just and right, they will live by doing so. ²⁰Yet you Israelites say, 'The way of the Lord is not just.' But I will judge each of you according to your own ways."

Jerusalem's Fall Explained

²¹In the twelfth year of our exile, in the tenth month on the fifth day, a man who had escaped from Jerusalem came to me and said, "The city

ᵃ 8 Or in; also in verse 9   ᵇ 10 Or away in

33:1–9 Ezekiel's role as watchman for God's people, first assigned in 3:16–21, is revisited here. If the watchman sounds a warning and the people fail to act, the people are responsible for their own fate.

33:2 When I bring the sword against See 14:17; 21:3 and note on 6:1–14.

33:10–20 Ezekiel revisits the topic of individual responsibility for sin that was presented in 18:20–32. He emphasizes the need to repent and affirms Yahweh's just decisions to save or punish depending on the individual's choice to live righteously or wickedly.

33:21–33 Ezekiel has revisited two prominent theological themes in vv. 1–20: his role in warning Israel of judgment, and individual accountability for sin. These reminders are important, considering the immediate need to offer theological justification for Jerusalem's fall. Here, Ezekiel receives official word of the destruction of Jerusalem (vv. 21–22), gives his prophecy (vv. 23–33), then summarizes the many abominations Israel was condemned for in chs. 5–24. While the earlier parts of his book contained glimmers of a future hope for Israel, judgment was the primary focus. Now attention gradually shifts toward restoration of the land, the people, the kingship and the temple in chs. 34–48.

33:21 tenth month on the fifth day The date is January 19, 585 BC, about five months after the fall of Jerusalem. The journey from Palestine to Babylonia took four to five months (see Ezr 7:9). See the timeline "Dates in Ezekiel" on p. 1276; see the timeline "Judah From

has fallen!" 22Now the evening before the man arrived, the hand of the LORD was on me, and he opened my mouth before the man came to me in the morning. So my mouth was opened and I was no longer silent.

23Then the word of the LORD came to me: 24"Son of man, the people living in those ruins in the land of Israel are saying, 'Abraham was only one man, yet he possessed the land. But we are many; surely the land has been given to us as our possession.' 25Therefore say to them, 'This is what the Sovereign LORD says: Since you eat meat with the blood still in it and look to your idols and shed blood, should you then possess the land? 26You rely on your sword, you do detestable things, and each of you defiles his neighbor's wife. Should you then possess the land?'

27"Say this to them: 'This is what the Sovereign LORD says: As surely as I live, those who are left in the ruins will fall by the sword, those out in the country I will give to the wild animals to be devoured, and those in strongholds and caves will die of a plague. 28I will make the land a desolate waste, and her proud strength will come to an end, and the mountains of Israel will become desolate so that no one will cross them. 29Then they will know that I am the LORD, when I have made the land a desolate waste because of all the detestable things they have done.'

30"As for you, son of man, your people are talking together about you by the walls and at the doors of the houses, saying to each other, 'Come and hear the message that has come from the LORD.' 31My people come to you, as they usually do, and sit before you to hear your words, but they do not put them into practice. Their mouths speak of love, but their hearts are greedy for unjust gain. 32Indeed, to them you are nothing more than one who sings love songs with a beautiful voice and plays an instrument well, for they hear your words but do not put them into practice.

33"When all this comes true — and it surely will — then they will know that a prophet has been among them."

The LORD Will Be Israel's Shepherd

34 The word of the LORD came to me: 2"Son of man, prophesy against the shepherds of Israel; prophesy and say to them: 'This is what the Sovereign LORD says: Woe to you shepherds of Israel who only take care of yourselves! Should not shepherds take care of the flock? 3You eat the curds, clothe yourselves with the wool and slaughter the choice animals, but you do not take care of the flock. 4You have not strengthened the weak or healed the sick or bound up the injured. You have

---

the Fall of Samaria to the Exile" on p. 606. **a man who had escaped** Also appears in Eze 24:26. This fugitive probably was not a survivor who escaped the destruction and brought word to the community. He more likely was an exile brought with those deported by Babylon in 586 BC. For Ezekiel, the Hebrew term *palit*—which can be translated "fugitive," "escapee" or "survivor"—had great theological significance. He reacted strongly in 11:13 when a man named Pelatiah (whose name means "Yahweh rescues") died during his prophecy. Ezekiel took it as a sign that perhaps Yahweh would decide to not leave any survivors. According to 6:8–9 and 14:22–23, survivors would escape divine judgment only to be scattered among the nations. Ezekiel's and Isaiah's views of the remnant are very different. Isaiah focuses on the eventual repentance and righteousness of the remnant that emerges from the judgment of exile (see Isa 26:2; 28:5). Ezekiel emphasizes the survivor's role as witness to vindicate Yahweh's judgment. **33:22 the hand of the LORD** See note on Eze 1:3. **33:24 Abraham was only one man** Appeals to Yahweh's promise to Abraham in Ge 15:18 and 17:8 as a basis for their right to the land. Possession of the land had been made conditional by the Sinai covenant, whose laws Israel had flagrantly ignored. Their argument from the lesser to the greater is flawed by the unequal comparison of the two covenants. The Gospels also record Jewish confidence in their descent from Abraham in Mt 3:9 and Lk 3:8. Keeping the law was much more about holiness and godly, righteous living than about observing the minute details of each regulation. Both OT and NT writers condemn this empty legalism as something outside the true faith that Yahweh wants from his followers. **33:25 you eat meat with the blood** Prohibited in God's covenant with Noah (see Ge 9:4 and note; compare Lev 3:17; 19:26). **shed blood** See Eze 22:3. The sin

of bloodshed was often used as a catch-all condemnation that could apply to both religious impropriety and social injustice. **33:26 you do detestable things** See note on 5:9.

33:30–33 Ezekiel's audience in Babylon easily could have felt far removed from his pronouncements of doom. Here, he describes the people gathering to hear him, apparently to hear the divine word. Their true motivation is later revealed to be mere entertainment.

33:33 a prophet has been among them The statement alludes to his commissioning scene (see 2:5) and structures the content of chs. 1–33 as a distinct unit of the book.

34:1–10 Ezekiel uses the metaphor of a shepherd leading his sheep to condemn Israel's leaders for misleading God's people. The shepherd metaphor draws on the ideal of Davidic kingship, alluding to David's boyhood role as shepherd (see 2Sa 5:2). The kings should have shepherded Yahweh's sheep faithfully, but instead they neglected the sheep and provided for themselves.

34:2 the shepherds of Israel The leaders should have guided Israel to Yahweh, but instead they led Israel astray (compare Isa 56:11; Jer 2:8). The association of kingship with shepherding was a common metaphor in ancient Mesopotamia. The people or sheep were the property of the gods, and the king was entrusted with their care. Ezekiel's condemnation of the shepherds of Israel illustrates the failure of Israel's kings to fulfill their divinely ordained responsibility to care for the people. **who only take care** The shepherds exploit the privilege of their position without consideration for their responsibility. They focus on their own gain, not the well-being of the flock.

not brought back the strays or searched for the lost. You have ruled them harshly and brutally. [5]So they were scattered because there was no shepherd, and when they were scattered they became food for all the wild animals. [6]My sheep wandered over all the mountains and on every high hill. They were scattered over the whole earth, and no one searched or looked for them.

[7]"'Therefore, you shepherds, hear the word of the LORD: [8]As surely as I live, declares the Sovereign LORD, because my flock lacks a shepherd and so has been plundered and has become food for all the wild animals, and because my shepherds did not search for my flock but cared for themselves rather than for my flock, [9]therefore, you shepherds, hear the word of the LORD: [10]This is what the Sovereign LORD says: I am against the shepherds and will hold them accountable for my flock. I will remove them from tending the flock so that the shepherds can no longer feed themselves. I will rescue my flock from their mouths, and it will no longer be food for them.

[11]"'For this is what the Sovereign LORD says: I myself will search for my sheep and look after them. [12]As a shepherd looks after his scattered flock when he is with them, so will I look after my sheep. I will rescue them from all the places where they were scattered on a day of clouds and darkness. [13]I will bring them out from the nations and gather them from the countries, and I will bring them into their own land. I will pasture them on the mountains of Israel, in the ravines and in all the settlements in the land. [14]I will tend them in a good pasture, and the mountain heights of Israel will be their grazing land. There they will lie down in good grazing land, and there they will feed in a rich pasture on the mountains of Israel. [15]I myself will tend my sheep and have them lie down, declares the Sovereign LORD. [16]I will search for the lost and bring back the strays. I will bind

up the injured and strengthen the weak, but the sleek and the strong I will destroy. I will shepherd the flock with justice.

[17]"'As for you, my flock, this is what the Sovereign LORD says: I will judge between one sheep and another, and between rams and goats. [18]Is it not enough for you to feed on the good pasture? Must you also trample the rest of your pasture with your feet? Is it not enough for you to drink clear water? Must you also muddy the rest with your feet? [19]Must my flock feed on what you have trampled and drink what you have muddied with your feet?

[20]"'Therefore this is what the Sovereign LORD says to them: See, I myself will judge between the fat sheep and the lean sheep. [21]Because you shove with flank and shoulder, butting all the weak sheep with your horns until you have driven them away, [22]I will save my flock, and they will no longer be plundered. I will judge between one sheep and another. [23]I will place over them one shepherd, my servant David, and he will tend them; he will tend them and be their shepherd. [24]I the LORD will be their God, and my servant David will be prince among them. I the LORD have spoken.

[25]"'I will make a covenant of peace with them and rid the land of savage beasts so that they may live in the wilderness and sleep in the forests in safety. [26]I will make them and the places surrounding my hill a blessing.[a] I will send down showers in season; there will be showers of blessing. [27]The trees will yield their fruit and the ground will yield its crops; the people will be secure in their land. They will know that I am the LORD, when I break the bars of their yoke and rescue them from

[a] 26 Or I will cause them and the places surrounding my hill to be named in blessings (see Gen. 48:20); or I will cause them and the places surrounding my hill to be seen as blessed

---

34:5 they were scattered Ezekiel often uses scattering to depict punishment for breaking the covenant (see also Lev 26:33).

34:11–24 Yahweh takes over the role of shepherd to rescue and restore his sheep. This metaphor also appears in Isa 40:11. The imagery is similar to Ps 23.

34:11 I myself will search for my sheep Since the shepherds would not search for the sheep (Eze 34:8), Yahweh must do so himself. Yahweh is described as a shepherd to Jacob in Ge 48:15. In ancient Mesopotamia, the gods' association with shepherding was just as prominent as the king's (see note on Eze 34:2). For example, the Babylonian god Marduk is known by the divine title (or epithet), "the shepherd of the people." A divine epithet identifies Yahweh as shepherd in Ge 49:24. His role as the ultimate "Good Shepherd" is seen through the many actions he undertakes on behalf of his flock (e.g., feeding, leading, watching over, seeking, rescuing, gathering; see Isa 40:11; Ps 23; 95:7; 100:3; Mic 7:14; Zec 10:3; 11:7).

34:12 a day of clouds and darkness A reference to the Day of Yahweh, the time of his wrath and judgment. See Eze 30:3 and note.

34:17 I will judge between one sheep and another Yahweh condemns inequities within the flock. Not only are the leaders to blame for mismanagement, but the people themselves are to blame for their mistreatment of each other.

34:22 I will save my flock Yahweh's true flock is a distinct, smaller part of the larger flock. He will recognize and save those who are his (compare Jn 10:14).

34:23 one shepherd, my servant David The role of shepherd will be returned to the Davidic Messiah, who will care for God's sheep properly. Jesus fulfills that role and alludes to the imagery of Eze 34 in Jn 10:1–18. Compare Jer 23:3–6.

34:25–31 Restoration of Israel's relationship with Yahweh brings the covenant blessings promised in Lev 26:3–13. Ezekiel has skillfully reworked the blessings from Lev 26:3–13 into a future picture of hope for Israel.

the hands of those who enslaved them. ²⁸They will no longer be plundered by the nations, nor will wild animals devour them. They will live in safety, and no one will make them afraid. ²⁹I will provide for them a land renowned for its crops, and they will no longer be victims of famine in the land or bear the scorn of the nations. ³⁰Then they will know that I, the LORD their God, am with them and that they, the Israelites, are my people, declares the Sovereign LORD. ³¹You are my sheep, the sheep of my pasture, and I am your God, declares the Sovereign LORD.'"

A Prophecy Against Edom

35 The word of the LORD came to me: ²"Son of man, set your face against Mount Seir; prophesy against it ³and say: 'This is what the Sovereign LORD says: I am against you, Mount Seir, and I will stretch out my hand against you and make you a desolate waste. ⁴I will turn your towns into ruins and you will be desolate. Then you will know that I am the LORD.

⁵"'Because you harbored an ancient hostility and delivered the Israelites over to the sword at the time of their calamity, the time their punishment reached its climax, ⁶therefore as surely as I live, declares the Sovereign LORD, I will give you over to bloodshed and it will pursue you. Since you did not hate bloodshed, bloodshed will pursue you. ⁷I will make Mount Seir a desolate waste and cut off from it all who come and go. ⁸I will fill your mountains with the slain; those killed by the sword will fall on your hills and in your valleys and in all your ravines. ⁹I will make you desolate forever; your towns will not be inhabited. Then you will know that I am the LORD.

¹⁰"'Because you have said, "These two nations and countries will be ours and we will take possession of them," even though I the LORD was there, ¹¹therefore as surely as I live, declares the Sovereign LORD, I will treat you in accordance with the anger and jealousy you showed in your hatred of them and I will make myself known among them when I judge you. ¹²Then you will know that I the LORD have heard all the contemptible things you have said against the mountains of Israel. You said, "They have been laid waste and have been given over to us to devour." ¹³You boasted against me and spoke against me without restraint, and I heard it. ¹⁴This is what the Sovereign LORD says: While the whole earth rejoices, I will make you desolate. ¹⁵Because you rejoiced when the inheritance of Israel became desolate, that is how I will treat you. You will be desolate, Mount Seir, you and all of Edom. Then they will know that I am the LORD.'"

Hope for the Mountains of Israel

36 "Son of man, prophesy to the mountains of Israel and say, 'Mountains of Israel, hear the word of the LORD. ²This is what the Sovereign LORD says: The enemy said of you,

---

34:29 the scorn of the nations A reversal of Yahweh's prior judgment. See Eze 22:4 and note.

35:1–15 This appendix to the oracles against the nations revisits the judgment of Edom (25:12–14). The style and rhetoric are familiar, borrowing themes and images from Ezekiel's earlier oracles.

35:2 set your face against See note on 20:46. **Mount Seir** Refers to the region south of the Dead Sea; used as a synonym for Edom (see Ge 32:3).

35:3 the Sovereign LORD says: I am against you A common introduction to Yahweh's pronouncements against those under judgment. It is used in oracles against the nations as well as against Israel (see Eze 13:8; 21:3; 26:3; 28:22; 29:3; 29:10). **I will stretch out my hand against you** A typical image of divine judgment. **a desolate waste** The Hebrew uses two related words, giving the pronouncement a poetic assonance: *shemamah umeshammah*. Compare 29:9; 33:28–29.

35:5 ancient hostility Edom was regularly in conflict with Judah and Israel during the time of the monarchy. Their hostility is explained through the sibling rivalry between Jacob and Esau that began even before their birth (see Ge 25:22–23). Jacob is the forebear of the Israelites, as Esau is of the Edomites. Due to their close geographic proximity, Edom is regularly included in prophetic indictments of Israel's neighbors (see Am 1:11–12; Jer 49:7–22; Isa 34:5–10; Joel 3:19; Ob 1–21). **at the time of their calamity** See Eze 25:12. Edom may have been allied with Babylon against Judah.

35:10 These two nations and countries will be ours Edom is condemned for coveting the territory of Israel and Judah after their downfall. Edom had no right to the land, which still belonged to Yahweh even though he had displaced his people. Archaeological evidence from the end of the Judean monarchy supports the accusation of Edom's gradual encroachment into Judah's territory south of Jerusalem. **I the LORD was there** Edom assumed that Yahweh had abandoned Judah, since the land lay in ruins and most of the people had been deported.

36:1–15 The judgment against the mountains of Seir in 35:1–15 contrasts with the renewal of the mountains of Israel predicted here. The two prophecies are related by their focus on mountains, and the prophecy to the mountains of Israel refers back to Edom and its desire to take Judah's land (35:10). This prophecy reflects a reversal of the judgment and destruction pronounced in ch. 6.

36:1 the mountains of Israel The mountains were condemned earlier in Ezekiel as sites for idol worship. See 6:2.

36:2–7 The declaration of renewal to the mountains of Israel is preceded by a complicated series of statements punctuated with the phrase *koh amar adonay yhwh* (which may be rendered as "thus says the Lord Yahweh" or "this is what the Sovereign Lord says"). The repetition of key words and phrases also obscures the simple function of the passage, which is a succinct summary of the book's previous chapters. Israel was judged and became an example to the nations. The nations gloated over Israel's downfall instead of learning from its mistake, so they will be judged in turn.

"Aha! The ancient heights have become our possession."' ³Therefore prophesy and say, 'This is what the Sovereign Lord says: Because they ravaged and crushed you from every side so that you became the possession of the rest of the nations and the object of people's malicious talk and slander, ⁴therefore, mountains of Israel, hear the word of the Sovereign Lord: This is what the Sovereign Lord says to the mountains and hills, to the ravines and valleys, to the desolate ruins and the deserted towns that have been plundered and ridiculed by the rest of the nations around you — ⁵this is what the Sovereign Lord says: In my burning zeal I have spoken against the rest of the nations, and against all Edom, for with glee and with malice in their hearts they made my land their own possession so that they might plunder its pastureland.' ⁶Therefore prophesy concerning the land of Israel and say to the mountains and hills, to the ravines and valleys: 'This is what the Sovereign Lord says: I speak in my jealous wrath because you have suffered the scorn of the nations. ⁷Therefore this is what the Sovereign Lord says: I swear with uplifted hand that the nations around you will also suffer scorn.

⁸"But you, mountains of Israel, will produce branches and fruit for my people Israel, for they will soon come home. ⁹I am concerned for you and will look on you with favor; you will be plowed and sown, ¹⁰and I will cause many people to live on you — yes, all of Israel. The towns will be inhabited and the ruins rebuilt. ¹¹I will increase the number of people and animals living on you, and they will be fruitful and become numerous. I will settle people on you as in the past and will make you prosper more than before. Then you will know that I am the Lord. ¹²I will cause people, my people Israel, to live on you. They will possess you, and you will be their inheritance; you will never again deprive them of their children.

¹³"This is what the Sovereign Lord says: Because some say to you, "You devour people and deprive your nation of its children," ¹⁴therefore you will no longer devour people or make your nation childless, declares the Sovereign Lord. ¹⁵No longer will I make you hear the taunts of the nations, and no longer will you suffer the scorn of the peoples or cause your nation to fall, declares the Sovereign Lord.'"

Israel's Restoration Assured

¹⁶Again the word of the Lord came to me: ¹⁷"Son of man, when the people of Israel were living in their own land, they defiled it by their conduct and their actions. Their conduct was like a woman's monthly uncleanness in my sight. ¹⁸So I poured out my wrath on them because they had shed blood in the land and because they had defiled it with their idols. ¹⁹I dispersed them among the nations, and they were scattered through the countries; I judged them according to their conduct and their actions. ²⁰And wherever they went among the nations they profaned my holy name, for it was said of them, 'These are the Lord's people, and yet they had to leave his land.' ²¹I had concern for my holy name, which the people of Israel profaned among the nations where they had gone.

36:2 Aha Refers to Edom's reaction in 35:10–12 (see note on 25:3).

36:8–15 In v. 8, the focus shifts from Israel's past shame to a hopeful future, repeating the imagery of renewal connected to the covenant of peace in 34:25–30.

36:9 I am concerned for you In this context, Yahweh's words — *hineni alekhem* in Hebrew — represent a reversal of his previous position and an intentional allusion to the familiar challenge formula — *hineni elekha* ("I am against you"; see note on 35:3).

36:11 I will increase the number of people and animals living on you Reverses the language of judgment from 14:13–21.

36:12 you will be their inheritance Refers to traditions about Israel's inheritance of the land, a focal theme of the books of Numbers and Joshua. Israel's restored relationship with Yahweh includes their possession of the promised land. The Hebrew word used here, *nachalah* ("inheritance"), carries great theological significance in its use to designate Israel's claim to the land of Canaan. Priestly regulations about the distribution of the land among the tribes of Israel frequently use *nachalah* (see Nu 26:52–56; 33:50—34:29). This language of inheritance carried the implication of permanent possession. Yahweh gave Palestine to the Israelites as their *nachalah*. Yahweh's grant of this land often is linked back to his promises to the patriarchs and their descendants (see Dt 6:10). While motivated by concern for his own reputation, Yahweh's unilateral act of restoration also could be understood in light of his unconditional promises to Abraham (Ge 15:18–21), Isaac (Ge 26:3) and Jacob (Ge 28:13).

36:16–21 Ezekiel summarizes Israel's history in terms of the broken covenant, the defiled land and the wrath of God. Themes of idolatry, bloodshed and scattering connect the summary with earlier parts of Ezekiel and with Leviticus. Yahweh's grace and concern for his own reputation bring an end to the time of judgment.

36:17 a woman's monthly uncleanness See Lev 15:19–24. Menstrual impurity could be used metaphorically to indicate extreme pollution.

36:20 they had to leave his land Reflects the ancient Near Eastern understanding of the connection between a god, his nation and their possession of the land. According to the prevailing wisdom, a dispossessed people driven off their land had been abandoned by their god.

36:21 my holy name Yahweh's concern for his name focuses on his character and reputation (see Eze 20:9 and note).

²²"Therefore say to the Israelites, 'This is what the Sovereign Lord says: It is not for your sake, people of Israel, that I am going to do these things, but for the sake of my holy name, which you have profaned among the nations where you have gone. ²³I will show the holiness of my great name, which has been profaned among the nations, the name you have profaned among them. Then the nations will know that I am the Lord, declares the Sovereign Lord, when I am proved holy through you before their eyes.

²⁴"'For I will take you out of the nations; I will gather you from all the countries and bring you back into your own land. ²⁵I will sprinkle clean water on you, and you will be clean; I will cleanse you from all your impurities and from all your idols. ²⁶I will give you a new heart and put a new spirit in you; I will remove from you your heart of stone and give you a heart of flesh. ²⁷And I will put my Spirit in you and move you to follow my decrees and be careful to keep my laws. ²⁸Then you will live in the land I gave your ancestors; you will be my people, and I will be your God. ²⁹I will save you from all your uncleanness. I will call for the grain and make it plentiful and will not bring famine upon you. ³⁰I will increase the fruit of the trees and the crops of the field, so that you will no longer suffer disgrace among the nations because of famine. ³¹Then you will remember your evil ways and wicked deeds, and you will loathe yourselves for your sins and detestable practices. ³²I want you to know that I am not doing this for your sake, declares the Sovereign Lord. Be ashamed and disgraced for your conduct, people of Israel!

³³"'This is what the Sovereign Lord says: On the day I cleanse you from all your sins, I will resettle your towns, and the ruins will be rebuilt. ³⁴The desolate land will be cultivated instead of lying desolate in the sight of all who pass through it. ³⁵They will say, "This land that was laid waste has become like the garden of Eden; the cities that were lying in ruins, desolate and destroyed, are now fortified and inhabited." ³⁶Then the nations around you that remain will know that I the Lord have rebuilt what was destroyed and have replanted what was desolate. I the Lord have spoken, and I will do it.'

³⁷"This is what the Sovereign Lord says: Once again I will yield to Israel's plea and do this for them: I will make their people as numerous as sheep, ³⁸as numerous as the flocks for offerings at Jerusalem during her appointed festivals. So will the ruined cities be filled with flocks of people. Then they will know that I am the Lord."

The Valley of Dry Bones

37 The hand of the Lord was on me, and he brought me out by the Spirit of the Lord and set me in the middle of a valley; it was full of bones. ²He led me back and forth among them, and I saw a great many bones on the floor of the valley, bones that were very dry. ³He asked me, "Son of man, can these bones live?"

36:22–38 This passage uses the priestly concept of ritual purity to introduce Yahweh's plan of redemption, just as Jeremiah uses political and legal imagery (see Jer 31–32). Yahweh's direct role in providing the people with a new heart and new spirit holds theological significance (see Eze 36:26–27). Only Yahweh's action—not the people's—can cleanse, purify and prepare Israel for true relationship with him.

36:23 I will show the holiness of my great name Israel's behavior tarnished Yahweh's reputation and required his judgment, but the nations interpreted that judgment as weakness (see v. 20). He acts to restore his reputation, not because Israel had done anything to deserve salvation.

36:25 I will sprinkle clean water on you Refers to ritual purity and cleanness (e.g., Lev 15:19–24; Nu 19:20).

36:26 a new heart and put a new spirit From a Biblical perspective, the heart was the seat of the mind and will, not just emotion. Ezekiel seems to use heart and spirit in tandem to refer to a person's whole being (compare Eze 18:31).

36:27 I will put my Spirit in you Total transformation from rebellion to obedience requires divine intervention. Acts 2:4 and Ro 8:9 give a more concrete example, with God's Holy Spirit dwelling in those who believe in Christ. An immediate application demonstrating the life-giving effects of Yahweh's Spirit comes in Eze 37:1–14 (Ezekiel's vision of the valley of dry bones).

36:29 I will call for the grain The renewed relationship between Yahweh and his people allows him to bless the land and increase its produce (compare Lev 26:4–5).

36:38 the flocks for offerings at Jerusalem during her appointed festivals The people were to gather in Jerusalem three times a year for a weeklong religious observance. The city would swell with people during these feasts, and a greater quantity of livestock would be necessary for sacrifices.

37:1–14 Ezekiel follows the prophecy of salvation and new life in Eze 36:22–38 with a vivid description of another visionary experience that is similar to his encounters with Yahweh in chs. 1–3 and 8–11. He is transported from a vision of life (the renewed creation of 36:33–38) to one of death and desolation in a valley full of dry bones. The theme of death and new life dominates the vision, building on the imagery of 36:16–32. Ezekiel's active participation and obedience result in an immediate and miraculous fulfillment of his prophecy. The passage consists of the vision report (vv. 1–10) and an interpretation of the vision (vv. 11–14). The revival of life in dry bones demonstrates Yahweh's power to restore the community of Judah and offers hope to the exiles.

37:1 The hand of the Lord was on me See note on 1:3; compare 8:1. **the Spirit of the Lord** See 11:5 and note. **full of bones** Ezekiel does not see corpses of people who died recently (those from the siege of Jerusalem, for example; see 33:21–22). Instead, he sees a wide plain filled with dry bones—apparently randomly strewn human bones, not skeletons. The scene resembles a

I said, "Sovereign Lord, you alone know."

⁴Then he said to me, "Prophesy to these bones and say to them, 'Dry bones, hear the word of the Lord! ⁵This is what the Sovereign Lord says to these bones: I will make breath[a] enter you, and you will come to life. ⁶I will attach tendons to you and make flesh come upon you and cover you with skin; I will put breath in you, and you will come to life. Then you will know that I am the Lord.'"

⁷So I prophesied as I was commanded. And as I was prophesying, there was a noise, a rattling sound, and the bones came together, bone to bone. ⁸I looked, and tendons and flesh appeared on them and skin covered them, but there was no breath in them.

⁹Then he said to me, "Prophesy to the breath; prophesy, son of man, and say to it, 'This is what the Sovereign Lord says: Come, breath, from the four winds and breathe into these slain, that they may live.'" ¹⁰So I prophesied as he commanded me, and breath entered them; they came to life and stood up on their feet—a vast army.

¹¹Then he said to me: "Son of man, these bones are the people of Israel. They say, 'Our bones are dried up and our hope is gone; we are cut off.' ¹²Therefore prophesy and say to them: 'This is what the Sovereign Lord says: My people, I am going to open your graves and bring you up from them; I will bring you back to the land of Israel.

¹³Then you, my people, will know that I am the Lord, when I open your graves and bring you up from them. ¹⁴I will put my Spirit in you and you will live, and I will settle you in your own land. Then you will know that I the Lord have spoken, and I have done it, declares the Lord.'"

One Nation Under One King

¹⁵The word of the Lord came to me: ¹⁶"Son of man, take a stick of wood and write on it, 'Belonging to Judah and the Israelites associated with him.' Then take another stick of wood, and write on it, 'Belonging to Joseph (that is, to Ephraim) and all the Israelites associated with him.' ¹⁷Join them together into one stick so that they will become one in your hand.

¹⁸"When your people ask you, 'Won't you tell us what you mean by this?' ¹⁹say to them, 'This is what the Sovereign Lord says: I am going to take the stick of Joseph—which is in Ephraim's hand—and of the Israelite tribes associated with him, and join it to Judah's stick. I will make them into a single stick of wood, and they will become one in my hand.' ²⁰Hold before their eyes the sticks you have written on ²¹and say to them, 'This is what the Sovereign Lord says: I will take the Israelites

___

ᵃ 5 The Hebrew for this word can also mean *wind* or *spirit* (see verses 6-14).

___

long-forgotten battlefield, where two armies fought and died with no one left to bury them.

37:3 these bones live Yahweh is not asking Ezekiel for his opinion on whether people can be brought back to life. The prophet would have been familiar with that possibility based on the experiences of the prophets Elijah (1Ki 17:17–24) and Elisha (2Ki 4:32–37), and perhaps Isa 53:10–11. Ezekiel's response indicates his understanding that the possibility depended entirely on Yahweh's actions. The prophetic stories of resurrection focus on the recently dead, not the long dead. Ezekiel may have had no expectation of any resurrection for those whose corpses had decayed to such a state. Ezekiel's response reflects his faith in Yahweh's power, but he likely did not have a well-developed sense of physical resurrection at the end of days such as that seen in Da 12:1–2. Several OT passages hint at physical resurrection, including Isa 26:19 and Hos 6:2. The concept also exists in ancient Zoroastrian beliefs about a physical resurrection.

37:5 I will make breath enter you The Hebrew word used here, *ruach*, means "wind," "spirit," or "breath," depending on the context. It is used to refer to the "breath of life" in Ge 6:17 and often carries the sense of a living being's animating force (as in Ecc 3:21).

37:9 Prophesy to the breath The second command emphasizes that life had not yet been restored. The two levels of prophecy and fulfillment in Eze 37:1–10 provide an element of dramatic suspense and highlight the importance of the "breath" (compare Ge 2:7). **four winds** The word is the same for "wind" and "breath." See note on Eze 37:5.

37:10 and breath entered them The essence of life enters after the body is created, just as when God cre-

ated Adam in Ge 2:7. This vision of resurrection likely influenced the apostle John (see Rev 11:11 and note).

37:11 these bones are the people of Israel The dry bones represent the nation of Israel collectively and throughout history—not just the recent victims of invasion and exile. Even the northern tribes, exiled much earlier by the Assyrians in 722 BC, are included, as explained by the following oracle in Eze 37:15–28.

37:12 My people, I am going to open your graves Resurrection of the dead metaphorically illustrates Israel's restoration as a nation. The concept of bodily resurrection was not well developed during Ezekiel's day (see note on v. 3).

37:15–28 Ezekiel performs a sign-act depicting the reunification of Israel and Judah. As before, his symbolic actions illicit a confused response from the people, resulting in two prophecies that explain his actions. See the table "Symbolic Actions of the Prophets" on p. 1195.

37:16 a stick of wood The same phrase is used in vv. 17,19,20. Perhaps Ezekiel was using wooden writing tablets. Wooden boards covered in wax were used for temporary writing purposes. **Belonging to Judah** The first piece of wood symbolizes Judah, the southern kingdom. **Belonging to Joseph (that is, to Ephraim)** The second piece of wood symbolizes the northern kingdom of Israel. Ephraim was Joseph's son, and the tribe named after him became the most powerful in the northern kingdom. Due to the tribe's dominance, Biblical writers commonly use the name Ephraim to refer to the northern kingdom as a whole.

37:17 they will become one Ezekiel's sign-act predicts a future restoration of Israel and Judah into a unified kingdom.

out of the nations where they have gone. I will gather them from all around and bring them back into their own land. ²²I will make them one nation in the land, on the mountains of Israel. There will be one king over all of them and they will never again be two nations or be divided into two kingdoms. ²³They will no longer defile themselves with their idols and vile images or with any of their offenses, for I will save them from all their sinful backsliding,ᵃ and I will cleanse them. They will be my people, and I will be their God.

²⁴"'My servant David will be king over them, and they will all have one shepherd. They will follow my laws and be careful to keep my decrees. ²⁵They will live in the land I gave to my servant Jacob, the land where your ancestors lived. They and their children and their children's children will live there forever, and David my servant will be their prince forever. ²⁶I will make a covenant of peace with them; it will be an everlasting covenant. I will establish them and increase their numbers, and I will put my sanctuary among them forever. ²⁷My dwelling place will be with them; I will be their God, and they will be my people. ²⁸Then the nations will know that I the LORD make Israel holy, when my sanctuary is among them forever.'"

The LORD's Great Victory Over the Nations

38 The word of the LORD came to me: ²"Son of man, set your face against Gog, of the land of Magog, the chief prince ofᵇ Meshek and Tubal; prophesy against him ³and say: 'This is what the Sovereign LORD says: I am against you, Gog, chief prince ofᶜ Meshek and Tubal. ⁴I will turn you around, put hooks in your jaws and bring you out with your whole army — your horses, your horsemen fully armed, and a great horde with large and small shields, all of them brandishing their swords. ⁵Persia, Cushᵈ and Put will be with them, all with shields and helmets, ⁶also Gomer with all its troops, and Beth Togarmah from the far north with all its troops — the many nations with you.

ᵃ 23 Many Hebrew manuscripts (see also Septuagint); most Hebrew manuscripts *all their dwelling places where they sinned* ᵇ 2 Or *the prince of Rosh,* ᶜ 3 Or *Gog, prince of Rosh,* ᵈ 5 That is, the upper Nile region

---

37:21–28 This further explanation of the sign-act goes beyond the prediction of unity for Israel and Judah to the ultimate expectation of a Messiah, in the role of a Davidic king ruling over a new united monarchy. Ezekiel's special concerns for ritual purity, covenant obedience and the divine presence continue to dominate his vision of the Messianic age. Ezekiel also reuses imagery from his salvation oracle in ch. 34 and paints a picture similar to Isa 11:1–9.

37:23 their idols and vile images The Hebrew word here refers to abhorrent, offensive or vile religious practices. See note on Eze 5:11. **They will be my people** Reactivates the covenant promise of Lev 26:12.
37:24 David will be king over them An allusion to the Messiah. Compare Jer 23:5. **they will all have one shepherd** Compare Eze 34:23.
37:26 covenant of peace See 34:25. **everlasting covenant** See 16:60. The everlasting covenant is the culmination of Yahweh's plan for salvation.
37:27 My dwelling place will be with them The divine presence returns to his people. Ezekiel described Yahweh's departure from his dwelling in 10:18.

38:1—39:24 The prophecy against Gog interrupts the restorative vision of ch. 37 with the onslaught of a vast army. While the structure follows that of an oracle of judgment against a foreign nation, the location of the land of Magog is uncertain. As in earlier oracles against the nations (such as ch. 27), Ezekiel uses geographic references from the Table of Nations in Ge 10 to give a global scope to his apocalyptic vision. This perplexing oracle of the last days has inspired extensive speculation. Interpreters have strained to explain the symbolism in historical, eschatological or metaphorical terms. The primary antagonist's identity is perhaps the most elusive detail. A northern prince leads a great horde of soldiers south against a peaceful Israel. Yahweh thwarts the invasion, rising to defend his people and their land.

Ezekiel's rhetoric often uses themes of Yahweh's holiness and his desire to vindicate his reputation through judgment. The imagery recalls the motif of disaster from the north (Jer 4:6) as well as Isaiah's vision of Yahweh defeating Israel's enemies on the mountains (Isa 14:25) and the end-of-days global battle envisioned in Zec 14. The later use of "Gog and Magog" in apocalyptic texts demonstrates Ezekiel's influence on Jewish and Christian literature. The phrase has become a cipher for the evil enemy of God's people in the end times (e.g., Rev 20).

38:2 Gog The identity of Gog is uncertain. Ezekiel does not seem to attach any particular significance to the figure beyond using it as a symbol for human pride subject to divine judgment. In the eschatological framework of the oracle, an attempt to connect Gog with a historical figure would be misguided. The most common historical identification of Gog focuses on Gyges, king of Lydia in central Asia Minor. Problems with this identification include the lack of hostility between Lydia and Judah and the 50-year period between the reign of Gyges and the time of Ezekiel. The creation of the name as a symbolic enemy is more likely, especially considering the graphic similarities in Hebrew between the name Gog and names of ancient enemies of Israel, Og (Nu 21:33) and Agag (Nu 24:7; 1Sa 15:8–33). The regular interchange of Og, Agag and Gog in copies of the Greek translation of the Bible (the Septuagint) strengthens the suggestion that these mysterious figures blended into an archetypal enemy of Israel. **land of Magog** Most likely a Hebrew form of the Akkadian name Mat Gugu, meaning "land of Gog." **the chief prince of Meshek and Tubal** Meshech (also rendered "Meshek") and Tubal are mentioned in the Table of Nations in Ge 10:2. Their location in central Asia Minor supports a connection between Magog and Lydia. See note on Eze 27:13.
38:4 I will turn you around, put hooks in your jaws See 29:4. **with large and small shields** See note on 23:24.

⁷"'Get ready; be prepared, you and all the hordes gathered about you, and take command of them. ⁸After many days you will be called to arms. In future years you will invade a land that has recovered from war, whose people were gathered from many nations to the mountains of Israel, which had long been desolate. They had been brought out from the nations, and now all of them live in safety. ⁹You and all your troops and the many nations with you will go up, advancing like a storm; you will be like a cloud covering the land.

¹⁰"'This is what the Sovereign Lord says: On that day thoughts will come into your mind and you will devise an evil scheme. ¹¹You will say, "I will invade a land of unwalled villages; I will attack a peaceful and unsuspecting people — all of them living without walls and without gates and bars. ¹²I will plunder and loot and turn my hand against the resettled ruins and the people gathered from the nations, rich in livestock and goods, living at the center of the land.ᵃ" ¹³Sheba and Dedan and the merchants of Tarshish and all her villagesᵇ will say to you, "Have you come to plunder? Have you gathered your hordes to loot, to carry off silver and gold, to take away livestock and goods and to seize much plunder?"'

¹⁴"Therefore, son of man, prophesy and say to Gog: 'This is what the Sovereign Lord says: In that day, when my people Israel are living in safety, will you not take notice of it? ¹⁵You will come from your place in the far north, you and many nations with you, all of them riding on horses, a great horde, a mighty army. ¹⁶You will advance against my people Israel like a cloud that covers the land. In days to come, Gog, I will bring you against my land, so that the nations may know me when I am proved holy through you before their eyes.

¹⁷"This is what the Sovereign Lord says: You are the one I spoke of in former days by my servants the prophets of Israel. At that time they prophesied for years that I would bring you against them. ¹⁸This is what will happen in that day: When Gog attacks the land of Israel, my hot anger will be aroused, declares the Sovereign Lord. ¹⁹In my zeal and fiery wrath I declare that at that time there shall be a great earthquake in the land of Israel. ²⁰The fish in the sea, the birds in the sky, the beasts of the field, every creature that moves along the ground, and all the people on the face of the earth will tremble at my presence. The mountains will be overturned, the cliffs will crumble and every wall will fall to the ground. ²¹I will summon a sword against Gog on all my mountains, declares the Sovereign Lord. Every man's sword will be against his brother. ²²I will execute judgment on him with plague and bloodshed; I will pour down torrents of rain, hailstones and burning sulfur on him and on his troops and on the many nations with him. ²³And so I will show my greatness and my holiness, and I will make myself known in the sight of many nations. Then they will know that I am the Lord.'

39 "Son of man, prophesy against Gog and say: 'This is what the Sovereign Lord says: I am against you, Gog, chief prince ofᶜ Meshek and Tubal. ²I will turn you around and drag you along. I will bring you from the far north and send you against the mountains of Israel. ³Then I will strike your bow from your left hand and make your arrows drop from your right hand. ⁴On the mountains of Israel you will fall, you and all your troops and the nations with you. I will give you as food to all kinds of carrion birds and to the wild animals. ⁵You will fall in the open field, for I have spoken, declares the Sovereign Lord. ⁶I will send fire on Magog and on those who live in safety in the coastlands, and they will know that I am the Lord.

⁷"'I will make known my holy name among my people Israel. I will no longer let my holy name be profaned, and the nations will know that I the Lord am the Holy One in Israel. ⁸It is coming!

ᵃ 12 The Hebrew for this phrase means *the navel of the earth.*
ᵇ 13 Or *her strong lions*   ᶜ 1 Or *Gog, prince of Rosh,*

38:5–6 Gog's vast army includes soldiers from a range of territories. The geographic extent of his connections is reminiscent of those of Tyre from ch. 27. As in ch. 27, the names of Gog's allies come from the Table of Nations in Ge 10.

38:5 Persia, Cush and Put Imagery echoing Eze 27:10. Persia was the country east of Babylon (modern Iran). Cush was the country south of Egypt, also known as Ethiopia or Nubia. Put was a name for Libya, west of Egypt in North Africa.

38:6 Gomer Likely a name for the people known as Gimirrai to the Assyrians and Cimmerians to the Greeks. They lived in northern Anatolia (modern Turkey) near the Black Sea and were historical enemies of Lydia. If Magog is a name for Lydia, then Ezekiel depicts them as allies. **Beth Togarmah** Ge 10:3 lists Togarmah as a son of Gomer. They were likely from the same general area as Gomer (see note on Eze 27:14).

38:13 Sheba and Dedan Centers of trade in Arabia. See note on 27:15. **Tarshish** A Phoenician trading port, probably in Spain. See note on Jnh 1:3.

38:16 so that the nations may know me when I am proved holy Yahweh's purpose in summoning Gog becomes clear. Once again, he must repair his reputation in the eyes of the nations by showing himself powerful enough to defend his people.

38:17 I spoke of in former days Likely alludes to the prophetic motif of invasion from the north (see Jer 6:22).

38:19 great earthquake The appearance of God (a theophany) caused extensive upheaval and cosmic disturbances (compare Jer 4:23–26).

39:1 Gog See note on Eze 38:2.

39:3 strike your bow from your left hand Yahweh alone defeats Gog; Israel is not involved until the battle is over.

39:8 the day I have spoken An allusion to the Day of Yahweh, a motif in prophetic literature about a future

It will surely take place, declares the Sovereign Lord. This is the day I have spoken of.

9 "Then those who live in the towns of Israel will go out and use the weapons for fuel and burn them up — the small and large shields, the bows and arrows, the war clubs and spears. For seven years they will use them for fuel. 10 They will not need to gather wood from the fields or cut it from the forests, because they will use the weapons for fuel. And they will plunder those who plundered them and loot those who looted them, declares the Sovereign Lord.

11 "On that day I will give Gog a burial place in Israel, in the valley of those who travel east of the Sea. It will block the way of travelers, because Gog and all his hordes will be buried there. So it will be called the Valley of Hamon Gog.ᵃ

12 "For seven months the Israelites will be burying them in order to cleanse the land. 13 All the people of the land will bury them, and the day I display my glory will be a memorable day for them, declares the Sovereign Lord. 14 People will be continually employed in cleansing the land. They will spread out across the land and, along with others, they will bury any bodies that are lying on the ground.

"After the seven months they will carry out a more detailed search. 15 As they go through the land, anyone who sees a human bone will leave a marker beside it until the gravediggers bury it in the Valley of Hamon Gog, 16 near a town called Hamonah.ᵇ And so they will cleanse the land.'

17 "Son of man, this is what the Sovereign Lord says: Call out to every kind of bird and all the wild animals: 'Assemble and come together from all around to the sacrifice I am preparing for you, the great sacrifice on the mountains of Israel. There you will eat flesh and drink blood. 18 You will eat the flesh of mighty men and drink the blood of the princes of the earth as if they were rams and lambs, goats and bulls — all of them fattened animals from Bashan. 19 At the sacrifice I am preparing for you, you will eat fat till you are glutted and drink blood till you are drunk. 20 At my table you will eat your fill of horses and riders, mighty men and soldiers of every kind,' declares the Sovereign Lord.

21 "I will display my glory among the nations, and all the nations will see the punishment I inflict and the hand I lay on them. 22 From that day forward the people of Israel will know that I am the Lord their God. 23 And the nations will know that the people of Israel went into exile for their sin, because they were unfaithful to me. So I hid my face from them and handed them over to their enemies, and they all fell by the sword. 24 I dealt with them according to their uncleanness and their offenses, and I hid my face from them.

25 "Therefore this is what the Sovereign Lord says: I will now restore the fortunes of Jacobᶜ and will have compassion on all the people of Israel, and I will be zealous for my holy name. 26 They will forget their shame and all the unfaithfulness they showed toward me when they lived in safety in their land with no one to make them afraid. 27 When I have brought them back from the nations and have gathered them from the countries of their enemies, I will be proved holy through them in the sight of many nations. 28 Then they will know that I am the Lord their God, for though I sent them into exile among the nations, I will gather them to their own land, not leaving any behind. 29 I will no longer hide my face from them, for I will pour out my Spirit on the people of Israel, declares the Sovereign Lord."

The Temple Area Restored

40 In the twenty-fifth year of our exile, at the beginning of the year, on the tenth of the month, in the fourteenth year after the fall of the city — on that very day the hand of the Lord was on me and he took me there. 2 In visions of God he took me to the land of Israel and set me on a very high mountain, on whose south side were some buildings that looked like a city. 3 He took me

---

ᵃ 11 Hamon Gog means hordes of Gog. ᵇ 16 Hamonah means horde. ᶜ 25 Or now bring Jacob back from captivity

---

day of judgment against Israel and all nations (see note on 7:1–27).

39:9 For seven years The hordes of Gog were so great that their equipment provided fuel to supply Israel for seven years. This duration of the fires is symbolic.

39:11 in the valley of those who travel Variously translated as the valley of "those who have passed on," "passersby," "travelers" or "passengers," possibly alluding to the underworld. Compare Isa 14:9–21. **Valley of Hamon Gog** Meaning the "valley of the multitude of Gog." Possibly a wordplay on the Valley of Gehenna, or Ben Hinnom.

39:12 For seven months The span of time is symbolic, just as the seven years of burning are symbolic in Eze 39:9. There also are seven nations mentioned as allies of Gog. **to cleanse the land** Dead bodies caused ritual impurity.

39:17–20 Yahweh summons the birds and beasts to a feast where the sacrifices are Gog's slain warriors. The imagery appears also in Rev 19:17–21.

39:18 Bashan A fertile region northeast of the Sea of Galilee.

39:25–29 The oracle of the distant future ends with an affirmation of the hope promised for the immediate future. Yahweh gathers the exiles and restores the community in Judah. The imagery recalls the depiction of salvation and renewal in Eze 36–37.

40:1—48:35 The final section of Ezekiel centers on his vision of a new temple, an important next step in Yahweh's plan to dwell in the midst of his people (see 37:26–28). Ezekiel's vision is structured as a guided tour, just as in chs. 8–11. Instead of witnessing the

there, and I saw a man whose appearance was like bronze; he was standing in the gateway with a linen cord and a measuring rod in his hand. [4]The man said to me, "Son of man, look carefully and listen closely and pay attention to everything I am going to show you, for that is why you have been brought here. Tell the people of Israel everything you see."

The East Gate to the Outer Court

[5]I saw a wall completely surrounding the temple area. The length of the measuring rod in the man's hand was six long cubits,[a] each of which was a cubit and a handbreadth. He measured the wall; it was one measuring rod thick and one rod high. [6]Then he went to the east gate. He climbed its steps and measured the threshold of the gate; it was one rod deep. [7]The alcoves for the guards were one rod long and one rod wide, and the projecting walls between the alcoves were five cubits[b] thick. And the threshold of the gate next to the portico facing the temple was one rod deep.

[8]Then he measured the portico of the gateway; [9]it[c] was eight cubits[d] deep and its jambs were two cubits[e] thick. The portico of the gateway faced the temple.

[10]Inside the east gate were three alcoves on each side; the three had the same measurements, and the faces of the projecting walls on each side had the same measurements. [11]Then he measured the width of the entrance of the gateway; it was ten cubits and its length was thirteen cubits.[f] [12]In front of each alcove was a wall one cubit high, and the alcoves were six cubits square. [13]Then he measured the gateway from the top of the rear wall of one alcove to the top of the opposite one; the distance was twenty-five cubits[g] from one parapet opening to the opposite one. [14]He measured along the faces of the projecting walls all around the inside of the gateway — sixty cubits.[h] The measurement was up to the portico[i] facing the courtyard.[j] [15]The distance from the entrance of the gateway to the far end of its portico was fifty cubits.[k] [16]The alcoves and the projecting walls inside the gateway were surmounted by narrow parapet

[a] 5 That is, about 11 feet or about 3.2 meters; also in verse 12. The long cubit of about 21 inches or about 53 centimeters is the basic unit of measurement of length throughout chapters 40–48.
[b] 7 That is, about 8 3/4 feet or about 2.7 meters; also in verse 48
[c] 8,9 Many Hebrew manuscripts, Septuagint, Vulgate and Syriac; most Hebrew manuscripts *gateway facing the temple; it was one rod deep.* [9]*Then he measured the portico of the gateway; it*
[d] 9 That is, about 14 feet or about 4.2 meters
[e] 9 That is, about 3 1/2 feet or about 1 meter
[f] 11 That is, about 18 feet wide and 23 feet long or about 5.3 meters wide and 6.9 meters long
[g] 13 That is, about 44 feet or about 13 meters; also in verses 21, 25, 29, 30, 33 and 36
[h] 14 That is, about 105 feet or about 32 meters
[i] 14 Septuagint; Hebrew *projecting wall*
[j] 14 The meaning of the Hebrew for this verse is uncertain.
[k] 15 That is, about 88 feet or about 27 meters; also in verses 21, 25, 29, 33 and 36

abominations of idolatry in the temple, he sees a new and improved temple that is ready for the return of Yahweh's presence.

The detailed description of the temple layout and measurements in 40:1—43:27 recalls the narrative of the tabernacle's construction in Ex 36–40, which also culminated in the indwelling of the divine presence. Regulations for temple service and proper worship in Eze 44:1—46:24 reflect legal sections of the OT, especially Lev 1–7; Ex 21–23 and Dt 12–26.

The temple and regulations envisioned by Ezekiel were not fulfilled by the completion of the second temple in 516 BC. His visions typically use concrete images and vivid metaphors to teach a theological point. The temple vision can be interpreted as an extended metaphor reflecting an ideal of holiness and purity abandoned by Judah before the exile. In Ezekiel's temple, the distinction between sacred and profane, clean and unclean, is perfectly maintained—and more strictly than with previous regulations. The theological importance of this plan is to prevent any further defilement of the temple. Ezekiel's plan for a new temple was intended to focus on Yahweh's holiness and sovereignty and to bring the people hope during their time of despair. See the infographic "Ezekiel's Temple" on p. 1336.

40:1–4 Ezekiel revisits Israel in a vision as in Eze 8:1. The earlier vision showed Ezekiel how the temple had been defiled. This vision brings him to a future temple where the sanctity of Yahweh's dwelling is perfectly maintained.

40:1 on the tenth of the month Dates to April 28, 573 BC. The tenth day of the first month was the date the lamb was to be selected for Passover (see Ex 12:3). See the timeline "Dates in Ezekiel" on p. 1276. **the hand of the LORD** See Eze 1:3 and note.

40:2 visions of God Links this vision to the earlier experiences in 1:1 and 8:3. **on a very high mountain** Compare John's vision of the new Jerusalem in Rev 21:10.

40:3 whose appearance was like bronze Compare the description of the divine guide in Eze 8:2, which uses a different word. The distinction may be Ezekiel's attempt to clarify that the two figures are not the same. **with a linen cord and a measuring rod** The cord and the reed were both measuring tools. The cord was for longer measurements, the reed for shorter lengths. The prophet Zechariah also sees an angel with a measuring line in Zec 2:1–2.

40:4 Son of man The man uses the same form of address that Yahweh uses for Ezekiel throughout the book (see note on Eze 2:1).

40:5–37 Ezekiel's tour begins at the outer wall and the eastern gateway and continues through the outer court, the southern and northern gateways, and the inner court, which has three gateways identical to those for the outer court. The east gate is important, as it is the gate through which Yahweh departed the temple in 10:19.

40:5 a wall completely surrounding The wall separated the sacred area of the temple from the profane (not sacred) area outside the temple. The wall was 10.5 feet wide and 10.5 feet tall. The city-gate style described here far exceeds the usual gate plan for a temple. Ezekiel's temple is built like a fortress, with imposing gates and guardrooms designed to protect the sanctity of the site from the ritually impure. **six long cubits** A standard cubit was about 18 inches, and a handbreadth was about 3 inches. The long cubit was about 21 inches or 1.75 feet, making the length of the measurement 10.5 feet. The measurements in chs. 40–48 are likely all based on this long cubit.

40:16 palm trees The doorways of the first temple also were decorated with palm trees (see 1Ki 6:32).

openings all around, as was the portico; the openings all around faced inward. The faces of the projecting walls were decorated with palm trees.

The Outer Court

[17]Then he brought me into the outer court. There I saw some rooms and a pavement that had been constructed all around the court; there were thirty rooms along the pavement. [18]It abutted the sides of the gateways and was as wide as they were long; this was the lower pavement. [19]Then he measured the distance from the inside of the lower gateway to the outside of the inner court; it was a hundred cubits[a] on the east side as well as on the north.

The North Gate

[20]Then he measured the length and width of the north gate, leading into the outer court. [21]Its alcoves—three on each side—its projecting walls and its portico had the same measurements as those of the first gateway. It was fifty cubits long and twenty-five cubits wide. [22]Its openings, its portico and its

[a] 19 That is, about 175 feet or about 53 meters; also in verses 23, 27 and 47

40:17 thirty rooms along the pavement The purpose of these chambers is not explained.

40:19 a hundred cubits Since the long cubit was about 1.75 feet, this length was 175 feet (see note on v. 5).

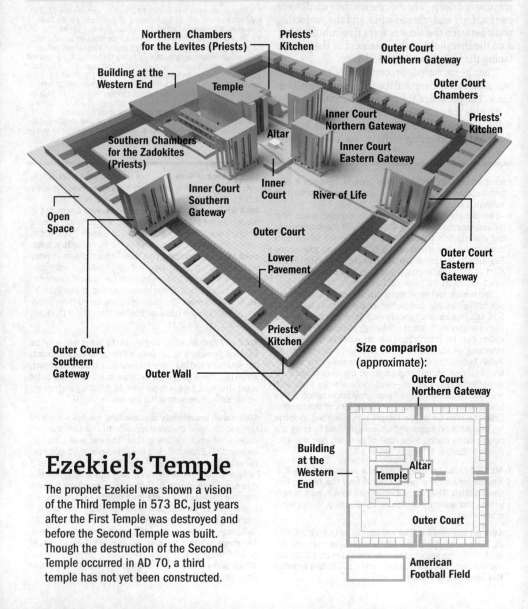

Northern Chambers for the Levites (Priests)
Priests' Kitchen
Building at the Western End
Temple
Outer Court Northern Gateway
Outer Court Chambers
Priests' Kitchen
Inner Court Northern Gateway
Altar
Southern Chambers for the Zadokites (Priests)
Inner Court Eastern Gateway
Inner Court Southern Gateway
Inner Court
River of Life
Open Space
Outer Court
Outer Court Eastern Gateway
Lower Pavement
Priests' Kitchen
Outer Court Southern Gateway
Outer Wall

Size comparison (approximate):

Outer Court Northern Gateway

Building at the Western End
Temple
Altar
Outer Court

American Football Field

Ezekiel's Temple

The prophet Ezekiel was shown a vision of the Third Temple in 573 BC, just years after the First Temple was destroyed and before the Second Temple was built. Though the destruction of the Second Temple occurred in AD 70, a third temple has not yet been constructed.

palm tree decorations had the same measurements as those of the gate facing east. Seven steps led up to it, with its portico opposite them. [23]There was a gate to the inner court facing the north gate, just as there was on the east. He measured from one gate to the opposite one; it was a hundred cubits.

The South Gate

[24]Then he led me to the south side and I saw the south gate. He measured its jambs and its portico, and they had the same measurements as the others. [25]The gateway and its portico had narrow openings all around, like the openings of the others. It was fifty cubits long and twenty-five cubits wide. [26]Seven steps led up to it, with its portico opposite them; it had palm tree decorations on the faces of the projecting walls on each side. [27]The inner court also had a gate facing south, and he measured from this gate to the outer gate on the south side; it was a hundred cubits.

The Gates to the Inner Court

[28]Then he brought me into the inner court through the south gate, and he measured the south gate; it had the same measurements as the others. [29]Its alcoves, its projecting walls and its portico had the same measurements as the others. The gateway and its portico had openings all around. It was fifty cubits long and twenty-five cubits wide. [30](The porticoes of the gateways around the inner court were twenty-five cubits wide and five cubits deep.) [31]Its portico faced the outer court; palm trees decorated its jambs, and eight steps led up to it.

[32]Then he brought me to the inner court on the east side, and he measured the gateway; it had the same measurements as the others. [33]Its alcoves, its projecting walls and its portico had the same measurements as the others. The gateway and its portico had openings all around. It was fifty cubits long and twenty-five cubits wide. [34]Its portico faced the outer court; palm trees decorated the jambs on either side, and eight steps led up to it.

[35]Then he brought me to the north gate and measured it. It had the same measurements as the others, [36]as did its alcoves, its projecting walls and its portico, and it had openings all around. It was fifty cubits long and twenty-five cubits wide. [37]Its portico[a] faced the outer court; palm trees decorated the jambs on either side, and eight steps led up to it.

The Rooms for Preparing Sacrifices

[38]A room with a doorway was by the portico in each of the inner gateways, where the burnt offerings were washed. [39]In the portico of the gateway were two tables on each side, on which the burnt offerings, sin offerings[b] and guilt offerings were slaughtered. [40]By the outside wall of the portico of the gateway, near the steps at the entrance of the north gateway were two tables, and on the other side of the steps were two tables. [41]So there were four tables on one side of the gateway and four on the other—eight tables in all—on which the sacrifices were slaughtered. [42]There were also four tables of dressed stone for the burnt offerings, each a cubit and a half long, a cubit and a half wide and a cubit high.[c] On them were placed the utensils for slaughtering the burnt offerings and the other sacrifices. [43]And double-pronged hooks, each a handbreadth[d] long, were attached to the wall all around. The tables were for the flesh of the offerings.

The Rooms for the Priests

[44]Outside the inner gate, within the inner court, were two rooms, one[e] at the side of the north gate and facing south, and another at the side of the south[f] gate and facing north. [45]He said to me, "The room facing south is for the priests who guard the temple, [46]and the room facing north is for the

---

[a] 37 Septuagint (see also verses 31 and 34); Hebrew *jambs*
[b] 39 Or *purification offerings*   [c] 42 That is, about 2 2/3 feet long and wide and 21 inches high or about 80 centimetres long and wide and 53 centimetres high   [d] 43 That is, about 3 1/2 inches or about 9 centimetres   [e] 44 Septuagint; Hebrew *were rooms for singers, which were*   [f] 44 Septuagint; Hebrew *east*

40:21 same measurements as those of the first gateway Few details are given for the other gates, since they match the first.

40:22 Seven steps led up to it The elevation of the interior of the temple complex increased to accompany the increase in levels of holiness. The number seven symbolizes completeness.

40:31 eight steps The inner courtyard is elevated above the outer court by eight steps. The additional step symbolizes the increased holiness of this inner court (see Eze 40:22 and note).

40:38 A room with a doorway was by the portico Ezekiel sees a room devoted to the slaughter and preparation of sacrificial animals.

40:39 burnt offerings, sin offerings and guilt offerings These three types of sacrifice are described in detail in Leviticus. On burnt offerings, see note on Lev 1:3. On sin offerings, see note on Lev 4:3. On guilt offerings, see note on Lev 5:14—6:7.

40:45 priests who guard the temple The Hebrew expression here connotes guard duty (see 2Ki 11:4–7). Priestly service involved defending the sanctity of temple space.

40:46 the priests who guard the altar They were responsible for guarding the sacred space of the altar. **These are the sons of Zadok** Likely referring to both groups of priests as Zadokites.

Ezekiel 40:46

ZADOK
Zadok was high priest under David (2Sa 8:17), and his family dominated the priesthood until the exile. Claims of Zadokite descent played a major part in conflicts over control of the priesthood during the Second Temple period (ca. 516 BC–AD 70).

priests who guard the altar. These are the sons of Zadok, who are the only Levites who may draw near to the LORD to minister before him."

⁴⁷Then he measured the court: It was square — a hundred cubits long and a hundred cubits wide. And the altar was in front of the temple.

The New Temple

⁴⁸He brought me to the portico of the temple and measured the jambs of the portico; they were five cubits wide on either side. The width of the entrance was fourteen cubitsᵃ and its projecting walls wereᵇ three cubitsᶜ wide on either side. ⁴⁹The portico was twenty cubitsᵈ wide, and twelveᵉ cubitsᶠ from front to back. It was reached by a flight of stairs,ᵍ and there were pillars on each side of the jambs.

41 Then the man brought me to the main hall and measured the jambs; the width of the jambs was six cubitsʰ on each side.ⁱ ²The entrance was ten cubitsʲ wide, and the projecting walls on each side of it were five cubitsᵏ wide. He also measured the main hall; it was forty cubits long and twenty cubits wide.ˡ

³Then he went into the inner sanctuary and measured the jambs of the entrance; each was two cubitsᵐ wide. The entrance was six cubits wide, and the projecting walls on each side of it were seven cubitsⁿ wide. ⁴And he measured the length of the inner sanctuary; it was twenty cubits, and its width was twenty cubits across the end of the main hall. He said to me, "This is the Most Holy Place."

⁵Then he measured the wall of the temple; it was six cubits thick, and each side room around the temple was four cubitsᵒ wide. ⁶The side rooms were on three levels, one above another, thirty on each level. There were ledges all around the wall of the temple to serve as supports for the side rooms, so that the supports were not inserted into the wall of the temple. ⁷The side rooms all around the temple were wider at each successive level. The structure surrounding the temple was built in ascending stages, so that the rooms widened as one went upward. A stairway went up from the lowest floor to the top floor through the middle floor.

⁸I saw that the temple had a raised base all around it, forming the foundation of the side rooms. It was the length of the rod, six long cubits. ⁹The outer wall of the side rooms was five cubits thick. The open area between the side rooms of the temple ¹⁰and the priests' rooms was twenty cubits wide all around the temple. ¹¹There were

---

ᵃ 48 That is, about 25 feet or about 7.4 meters   ᵇ 48 Septuagint; Hebrew *entrance was*   ᶜ 48 That is, about 5 1/4 feet or about 1.6 meters   ᵈ 49 That is, about 35 feet or about 11 meters   ᵉ 49 Septuagint; Hebrew *eleven*   ᶠ 49 That is, about 21 feet or about 6.4 meters   ᵍ 49 Hebrew; Septuagint *Ten steps led up to it*   ʰ 1 That is, about 11 feet or about 3.2 meters; also in verses 3, 5 and 8   ⁱ 1 One Hebrew manuscript and Septuagint; most Hebrew manuscripts *side, the width of the tent*   ʲ 2 That is, about 18 feet or about 5.3 meters   ᵏ 2 That is, about 8 3/4 feet or about 2.7 meters; also in verses 9, 11 and 12   ˡ 2 That is, about 70 feet long and 35 feet wide or about 21 meters long and 11 meters wide   ᵐ 3 That is, about 3 1/2 feet or about 1.1 meters; also in verse 22   ⁿ 3 That is, about 12 feet or about 3.7 meters   ᵒ 5 That is, about 7 feet or about 2.1 meters

---

40:47 a hundred cubits See note on Eze 40:19.

40:48–49 Ezekiel now moves to the temple itself, which is elevated 10 steps above the inner courtyard. The greater levels of holiness throughout the temple are accompanied by increases in elevation.

40:48 the portico of the temple The Hebrew expression here refers to the temple's entry room. Ezekiel's temple is a three-room structure just as Solomon's temple was. The three-room style used for Solomon's temple and Ezekiel's temple was a well-established style for temples in the ancient Near East, especially in the area of Syria-Palestine. Similar structures have been excavated from the Late Bronze Age cities of Megiddo and Hazor (pre-Israelite Canaanite cities).

41:1–26 Ezekiel's tour continues through the interior of the temple. Some of the architectural terms are difficult to define, but the general plan is similar to Solomon's temple described in 1Ki 6:1–37. The combination of detailed measurements with scarce information about furnishings and function for some temple areas suggests that Ezekiel's primary concern was marking off the sacred space, not providing a building plan for future construction. Throughout his description of the temple and the land, Ezekiel's overriding concern is maintaining sanctity at all costs. See the infographic "Solomon's Temple" on p. 520; see the infographic "Ezekiel's Temple" on p. 1336.

41:1 the main hall The Hebrew word used here, *hekhal*, refers to the residence of a divine or earthly ruler. Its use in reference to the temple highlights its role as the palace of Yahweh.

41:2 The entrance was ten cubits wide The increasing levels of holiness are signified by the incremental reduction in the size of entryways between rooms as they progress deeper into the temple. The initial entrance was 14 cubits (see Eze 40:48; the cubit in chs. 40–48 is about 1.75 feet). The entrance from the first room to the second is 10 cubits. The doorway between the second and third rooms is similarly reduced by four cubits to six (see v. 3).

41:4 the Most Holy Place Ezekiel's guide pauses to confirm his understanding of this inner room as the Holy of Holies (*qodesh haqqodashim*) — the Most Holy Place of the temple. Note that only the guide enters the room. Ezekiel was in the second room — which he, as a priest, would have been allowed to enter in the earlier temples. Only the high priest was allowed to enter the Most Holy Place, and then only once a year on the Day of Atonement (see Lev 16). The Most Holy Place was where the ark of the covenant was kept. Yahweh's presence there was symbolized by the atonement cover (or mercy seat), where he sat on a throne above the cherubim (Lev 16:2; Ps 99:1). The atonement cover (mercy seat) was the focus of the Day of Atonement ceremony (Lev 16:13–15). See the infographic "The Ark of the Covenant" on p. 412; see the infographic "The Most Holy Place" on p. 525.

41:6 The side rooms were on three levels The purpose of these 90 side rooms is not specified.

entrances to the side rooms from the open area, one on the north and another on the south; and the base adjoining the open area was five cubits wide all around.

[12] The building facing the temple courtyard on the west side was seventy cubits[a] wide. The wall of the building was five cubits thick all around, and its length was ninety cubits.[b]

[13] Then he measured the temple; it was a hundred cubits[c] long, and the temple courtyard and the building with its walls were also a hundred cubits long. [14] The width of the temple courtyard on the east, including the front of the temple, was a hundred cubits.

[15] Then he measured the length of the building facing the courtyard at the rear of the temple, including its galleries on each side; it was a hundred cubits.

The main hall, the inner sanctuary and the portico facing the court, [16] as well as the thresholds and the narrow windows and galleries around the three of them — everything beyond and including the threshold was covered with wood. The floor, the wall up to the windows, and the windows were covered. [17] In the space above the outside of the entrance to the inner sanctuary and on the walls at regular intervals all around the inner and outer sanctuary [18] were carved cherubim and palm trees. Palm trees alternated with cherubim. Each cherub had two faces: [19] the face of a human being toward the palm tree on one side and the face of a lion toward the palm tree on the other. They were carved all around the whole temple. [20] From the floor to the area above the entrance, cherubim and palm trees were carved on the wall of the main hall.

[21] The main hall had a rectangular doorframe, and the one at the front of the Most Holy Place was similar. [22] There was a wooden altar three cubits[d] high and two cubits square[e]; its corners, its base[f] and its sides were of wood. The man said to me, "This is the table that is before the LORD." [23] Both the main hall and the Most Holy Place had double doors. [24] Each door had two leaves — two hinged leaves for each door. [25] And on the doors of the main hall were carved cherubim and palm trees like those carved on the walls, and there was

a wooden overhang on the front of the portico. [26] On the sidewalls of the portico were narrow windows with palm trees carved on each side. The side rooms of the temple also had overhangs.

The Rooms for the Priests

42 Then the man led me northward into the outer court and brought me to the rooms opposite the temple courtyard and opposite the outer wall on the north side. [2] The building whose door faced north was a hundred cubits long and fifty cubits wide.[g] [3] Both in the section twenty cubits[h] from the inner court and in the section opposite the pavement of the outer court, gallery faced gallery at the three levels. [4] In front of the rooms was an inner passageway ten cubits wide and a hundred cubits[i] long.[j] Their doors were on the north. [5] Now the upper rooms were narrower, for the galleries took more space from them than from the rooms on the lower and middle floors of the building. [6] The rooms on the top floor had no pillars, as the courts had; so they were smaller in floor space than those on the lower and middle floors. [7] There was an outer wall parallel to the rooms and the outer court; it extended in front of the rooms for fifty cubits. [8] While the row of rooms on the side next to the outer court was fifty cubits long, the row on the side nearest the sanctuary was a hundred cubits long. [9] The lower rooms had an entrance on the east side as one enters them from the outer court.

[10] On the south side[k] along the length of the wall of the outer court, adjoining the temple courtyard and opposite the outer wall, were rooms [11] with a passageway in front of them. These were like the rooms on the north; they had the same length and width, with similar exits and dimensions. Similar to the doorways on the north [12] were the doorways

---

[a] 12 That is, about 123 feet or about 37 meters   [b] 12 That is, about 158 feet or about 48 meters   [c] 13 That is, about 175 feet or about 53 meters; also in verses 14 and 15   [d] 22 That is, about 5 1/4 feet or about 1.5 meters   [e] 22 Septuagint; Hebrew long   [f] 22 Septuagint; Hebrew length   [g] 2 That is, about 175 feet long and 88 feet wide or about 53 meters long and 27 meters wide   [h] 3 That is, about 35 feet or about 11 meters   [i] 4 Septuagint and Syriac; Hebrew and one cubit   [j] 4 That is, about 18 feet wide and 175 feet long or about 5.3 meters wide and 53 meters long   [k] 10 Septuagint; Hebrew Eastward

---

41:12 The building facing the temple courtyard Instead of a western gate, a large building sat directly behind the temple. This location suggests that it was meant to block rear access to the temple. Other than its size, no other details on the building are given.

41:18 cherubim and palm trees Refers to the cherubim and palm trees decorating the first temple (see 1Ki 6:29–36).

41:22 table that is before the LORD Likely represents the table for the bread of the Presence; see Ex 25:23–30.

42:1–20 Ezekiel leaves the main temple building and describes two buildings to the north and south of the

inner court complex. These three-story buildings contained chambers for the priests and can be understood as transitional areas, where holy things such as sacrificial offerings, clothes and equipment were stored to separate them from the less-holy outer court. After Ezekiel describes the chambers, his guide measures the perimeter of the temple complex.

42:1 the rooms The purpose of the chambers is made clear in Eze 42:13–14. They functioned as vestries or sacristies where the priests could change from their inner-court garments into their outer-court garments.

of the rooms on the south. There was a doorway at the beginning of the passageway that was parallel to the corresponding wall extending eastward, by which one enters the rooms.

¹³Then he said to me, "The north and south rooms facing the temple courtyard are the priests' rooms, where the priests who approach the LORD will eat the most holy offerings. There they will put the most holy offerings — the grain offerings, the sin offerings^a and the guilt offerings — for the place is holy. ¹⁴Once the priests enter the holy precincts, they are not to go into the outer court until they leave behind the garments in which they minister, for these are holy. They are to put on other clothes before they go near the places that are for the people."

¹⁵When he had finished measuring what was inside the temple area, he led me out by the east gate and measured the area all around: ¹⁶He measured the east side with the measuring rod; it was five hundred cubits.^b,c ¹⁷He measured the north side; it was five hundred cubits^d by the measuring rod. ¹⁸He measured the south side; it was five hundred cubits by the measuring rod. ¹⁹Then he turned to the west side and measured; it was five hundred cubits by the measuring rod. ²⁰So he measured the area on all four sides. It had a wall around it, five hundred cubits long and five hundred cubits wide, to separate the holy from the common.

God's Glory Returns to the Temple

43 Then the man brought me to the gate facing east, ²and I saw the glory of the God of Israel coming from the east. His voice was like the roar of rushing waters, and the land was radiant with his glory. ³The vision I saw was like the vision I had seen when he^e came to destroy the city and

like the visions I had seen by the Kebar River, and I fell facedown. ⁴The glory of the LORD entered the temple through the gate facing east. ⁵Then the Spirit lifted me up and brought me into the inner court, and the glory of the LORD filled the temple.

⁶While the man was standing beside me, I heard someone speaking to me from inside the temple. ⁷He said: "Son of man, this is the place of my throne and the place for the soles of my feet. This is where I will live among the Israelites forever. The people of Israel will never again defile my holy name — neither they nor their kings — by their prostitution and the funeral offerings^f for their kings at their death.^g ⁸When they placed their threshold next to my threshold and their doorposts beside my doorposts, with only a wall between me and them, they defiled my holy name by their detestable practices. So I destroyed them in my anger. ⁹Now let them put away from me their prostitution and the funeral offerings for their kings, and I will live among them forever.

¹⁰"Son of man, describe the temple to the people of Israel, that they may be ashamed of their sins. Let them consider its perfection, ¹¹and if they are ashamed of all they have done, make known to them the design of the temple — its arrangement, its exits and entrances — its whole design and all its regulations^h and laws. Write these down before them so that they may be faithful to its design and follow all its regulations.

^a 13 Or *purification offerings*   ^b 16 See Septuagint of verse 17; Hebrew *rods*; also in verses 18 and 19.   ^c 16 Five hundred cubits equal about 875 feet or about 265 meters; also in verses 17, 18 and 19.   ^d 17 Septuagint; Hebrew *rods*   ^e 3 Some Hebrew manuscripts and Vulgate; most Hebrew manuscripts *I*   ^f 7 Or *the memorial monuments*; also in verse 9   ^g 7 Or *their high places*   ^h 11 Some Hebrew manuscripts and Septuagint; most Hebrew manuscripts *regulations and its whole design*

42:13 the priests' rooms The sacrifices and the holy garments must remain in these chambers and not be taken into the outer court.

42:15 the east gate Ezekiel's tour of the temple complex's interior ends where it began, at the outer eastern gate (see 40:6).

42:16 five hundred cubits The temple is a perfect square, each side measuring 500 cubits or 875 feet. The entire temple complex covered an area of about 17.5 acres (71,129 square meters). Ezekiel's temple is significantly larger than Solomon's temple. See the infographic "Ezekiel's Temple" on p. 1336; see the infographic "Solomon's Temple" on p. 520.

43:1–12 Ezekiel's guide returns him to the outer eastern gate of the temple, where the tour began, to witness Yahweh's return to dwell in the temple. The scene is the reverse of 10:15–22, in which Yahweh's chariot-throne departed through the east gate. Ezekiel now describes the return of Yahweh's glory in much the same terms, emphasizing that what he sees is identical to the earlier visions (v. 3). After Yahweh returns, he declares to Ezekiel that he will remain there. He stresses the need for Israel to treat his name and his temple with proper respect and maintain the absolute holiness of the area.

43:2 the glory of the God of Israel The visible presence of Yahweh (see note on Isa 6:3).

43:3 when he came to destroy the city Alludes to Ezekiel's earlier vision of the temple and city (see Eze 9:3).

by the Kebar River Alludes to Ezekiel's inaugural vision (see 1:1—3:15). **I fell facedown** A typical response of reverence and fear. See note on 1:28.

43:5 the glory of the LORD filled the temple Compare 1Ki 8:10–11 when the divine presence entered Solomon's temple. The language is similar in Isa 6:1 and Eze 10:4.

43:6 someone speaking to me from inside the temple Recalls Ezekiel's inaugural vision (see 1:28).

43:7 I will live among the Israelites Fulfills the promise of 37:26–28.

43:8 placed their threshold next to my threshold Refers to the mixed use of the earlier temple, where idol-worship was conducted side by side with sacrifices to Yahweh (see chs. 8–11). **their detestable practices** The Hebrew word used here, *to'evah*, can refer to anything offensive. In this context, it refers to sacrilegious offenses. See note on 5:9.

¹²"This is the law of the temple: All the surrounding area on top of the mountain will be most holy. Such is the law of the temple.

The Great Altar Restored

¹³"These are the measurements of the altar in long cubits,ᵃ that cubit being a cubit and a handbreadth: Its gutter is a cubit deep and a cubit wide, with a rim of one spanᵇ around the edge. And this is the height of the altar: ¹⁴From the gutter on the ground up to the lower ledge that goes around the altar it is two cubits high, and the ledge is a cubit wide.ᶜ From this lower ledge to the upper ledge that goes around the altar it is four cubits high, and that ledge is also a cubit wide.ᵈ ¹⁵Above that, the altar hearth is four cubits high, and four horns project upward from the hearth. ¹⁶The altar hearth is square, twelve cubitsᵉ long and twelve cubits wide. ¹⁷The upper ledge also is square, fourteen cubitsᶠ long and fourteen cubits wide. All around the altar is a gutter of one cubit with a rim of half a cubit.ᵇ The steps of the altar face east."

¹⁸Then he said to me, "Son of man, this is what the Sovereign LORD says: These will be the regulations for sacrificing burnt offerings and splashing blood against the altar when it is built: ¹⁹You are to give a young bull as a sin offeringᵍ to the Levitical priests of the family of Zadok, who come near to minister before me, declares the Sovereign LORD. ²⁰You are to take some of its blood and put it on the four horns of the altar and on the four corners of the upper ledge and all around the rim, and so purify the altar and make atonement for it. ²¹You are to take the bull for the sin offering and burn it in the designated part of the temple area outside the sanctuary.

²²"On the second day you are to offer a male goat without defect for a sin offering, and the altar is to be purified as it was purified with the bull. ²³When you have finished purifying it, you are to offer a young bull and a ram from the flock, both without defect. ²⁴You are to offer them before the LORD, and the priests are to sprinkle salt on them and sacrifice them as a burnt offering to the LORD.

²⁵"For seven days you are to provide a male goat daily for a sin offering; you are also to provide a young bull and a ram from the flock, both without defect. ²⁶For seven days they are to make atonement for the altar and cleanse it; thus they will dedicate it. ²⁷At the end of these days, from the eighth day on, the priests are to present your burnt offerings and fellowship offerings on the altar. Then I will accept you, declares the Sovereign LORD."

The Priesthood Restored

44 Then the man brought me back to the outer gate of the sanctuary, the one facing east, and it was shut. ²The LORD said to me, "This gate is to remain shut. It must not be opened; no one may enter through it. It is to remain shut because the LORD, the God of Israel, has entered through it. ³The prince himself is the only one who may sit inside the gateway to eat in the presence of the

---

ᵃ *13* That is, about 21 inches or about 53 centimeters; also in verses 14 and 17. The long cubit is the basic unit for linear measurement throughout Ezekiel 40–48.   ᵇ *13,17* That is, about 11 inches or about 27 centimeters   ᶜ *14* That is, about 3 1/2 feet high and 1 3/4 feet wide or about 105 centimeters high and 53 centimeters wide   ᵈ *14* That is, about 7 feet high and 1 3/4 feet wide or about 2.1 meters high and 53 centimeters wide   ᵉ *16* That is, about 21 feet or about 6.4 meters   ᶠ *17* That is, about 25 feet or about 7.4 meters   ᵍ *19* Or *purification offering*; also in verses 21, 22 and 25

43:13—46:24 Ezekiel's focus shifts to the rules and procedures regulating the activities of this new temple. Yahweh presents the laws to Ezekiel in a scene reminiscent of Moses at Sinai (compare Ex 19–24). Just as Moses received laws directly from Yahweh at his holy mountain, so Ezekiel receives a new set of laws directly from Yahweh at the top of the high mountain where the new temple is located. Ezekiel's laws do not harmonize with the legal sections of the Pentateuch (the first five books of the Bible) because the new temple is accompanied by a new set of regulations. In general, the laws are directed at maintaining a greater level of sanctity and a stricter form of ritual purity than the laws in the Pentateuch.

43:13–27 Ezekiel describes the altar for burnt offerings in the inner court of the temple. Its design is similar to the one built by Solomon (2Ch 4:1); both are elevated, four-horned altars, but Solomon's was solid bronze and larger than Ezekiel's. The material of Ezekiel's altar can be inferred as tiered stone, but the text does not explicitly discuss the composition of material, unlike the altar description in Ex 20:22–26. See the infographic "Ezekiel's Altar" on p. 1342; see the infographic "Ancient Altars" on p. 127; see the table "Altars in the Old Testament" on p. 249.

43:19 the family of Zadok Zadok was the high priest under David. See note on Eze 40:46.

43:20 four horns of the altar Examples of four-horned stone altars have been unearthed in Palestine at Arad and Beersheba, both from sites dating to the Israelite monarchy.

44:1–14 The eastern gate by which Yahweh had entered the temple is now permanently closed. Only the temple's northern and southern gates remain open. In the hall of the eastern gateway, the *nasi* ("prince" or "ruler") eats a ceremonial meal in the presence of Yahweh, but the gate remains closed. Ezekiel also summarizes Israel's failure to worship Yahweh properly, specifically condemning the Levites for leading Israel astray.

44:3 The prince The precise nature of this office is unclear. Typically, the Hebrew word *nasi* denotes a political role: the leader of the Jewish community. Elsewhere Ezekiel uses the term to refer to the Davidic Messiah (34:24; 37:25). Here his role is religious, but it is not clearly cultic or priestly.

LORD. He is to enter by way of the portico of the gateway and go out the same way."

⁴Then the man brought me by way of the north gate to the front of the temple. I looked and saw the glory of the LORD filling the temple of the LORD, and I fell facedown.

⁵The LORD said to me, "Son of man, look carefully, listen closely and give attention to everything I tell you concerning all the regulations and instructions regarding the temple of the LORD. Give attention to the entrance to the temple and all the exits of the sanctuary. ⁶Say to rebellious Israel, 'This is what the Sovereign LORD says: Enough of your detestable practices, people of Israel! ⁷In addition to all your other detestable practices, you brought foreigners uncircumcised in heart and flesh into my sanctuary, desecrating my temple while you offered me food, fat and blood, and you broke my covenant. ⁸Instead of carrying out your duty in regard to my holy things, you put others in charge of my sanctuary. ⁹This is what the Sovereign LORD says: No foreigner uncircumcised in heart and flesh is to enter my sanctuary, not even the foreigners who live among the Israelites.

¹⁰"The Levites who went far from me when Israel went astray and who wandered from me after their idols must bear the consequences of their sin. ¹¹They may serve in my sanctuary, having charge of the gates of the temple and serving in it; they may slaughter the burnt offerings

---

44:4 glory of the LORD filling the temple See 43:5 and note.

44:9 No foreigner uncircumcised in heart and flesh Israel's past idolatry can be summarized as one offense: They violated Yahweh's sacred space. Stricter observance

of procedures and regulations designed to protect the sacred space will prevent future violation.

44:10 must bear the consequences of their sin See note on 4:4.

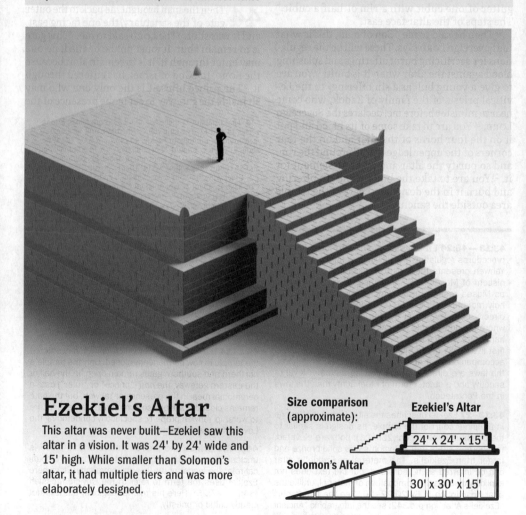

Ezekiel's Altar

This altar was never built—Ezekiel saw this altar in a vision. It was 24' by 24' wide and 15' high. While smaller than Solomon's altar, it had multiple tiers and was more elaborately designed.

Size comparison (approximate):

Ezekiel's Altar
24' x 24' x 15'

Solomon's Altar
30' x 30' x 15'

and sacrifices for the people and stand before the people and serve them. [12]But because they served them in the presence of their idols and made the people of Israel fall into sin, therefore I have sworn with uplifted hand that they must bear the consequences of their sin, declares the Sovereign LORD. [13]They are not to come near to serve me as priests or come near any of my holy things or my most holy offerings; they must bear the shame of their detestable practices. [14]And I will appoint them to guard the temple for all the work that is to be done in it.

[15]"'But the Levitical priests, who are descendants of Zadok and who guarded my sanctuary when the Israelites went astray from me, are to come near to minister before me; they are to stand before me to offer sacrifices of fat and blood, declares the Sovereign LORD. [16]They alone are to enter my sanctuary; they alone are to come near my table to minister before me and serve me as guards.

[17]"'When they enter the gates of the inner court, they are to wear linen clothes; they must not wear any woolen garment while ministering at the gates of the inner court or inside the temple. [18]They are to wear linen turbans on their heads and linen undergarments around their waists. They must not wear anything that makes them perspire. [19]When they go out into the outer court where the people are, they are to take off the clothes they have been ministering in and are to leave them in the sacred rooms, and put on other clothes, so that the people are not consecrated through contact with their garments.

[20]"'They must not shave their heads or let their hair grow long, but they are to keep the hair of their heads trimmed. [21]No priest is to drink wine when he enters the inner court. [22]They must not marry widows or divorced women; they may marry only virgins of Israelite descent or widows of priests. [23]They are to teach my people the difference be-

tween the holy and the common and show them how to distinguish between the unclean and the clean.

[24]"'In any dispute, the priests are to serve as judges and decide it according to my ordinances. They are to keep my laws and my decrees for all my appointed festivals, and they are to keep my Sabbaths holy.

[25]"'A priest must not defile himself by going near a dead person; however, if the dead person was his father or mother, son or daughter, brother or unmarried sister, then he may defile himself. [26]After he is cleansed, he must wait seven days. [27]On the day he goes into the inner court of the sanctuary to minister in the sanctuary, he is to offer a sin offering[a] for himself, declares the Sovereign LORD.

[28]"'I am to be the only inheritance the priests have. You are to give them no possession in Israel; I will be their possession. [29]They will eat the grain offerings, the sin offerings and the guilt offerings; and everything in Israel devoted[b] to the LORD will belong to them. [30]The best of all the firstfruits and of all your special gifts will belong to the priests. You are to give them the first portion of your ground meal so that a blessing may rest on your household. [31]The priests must not eat anything, whether bird or animal, found dead or torn by wild animals.

Israel Fully Restored

45 "'When you allot the land as an inheritance, you are to present to the LORD a portion of the land as a sacred district, 25,000 cubits[c] long and 20,000[d] cubits[e] wide; the entire area will be holy. [2]Of this, a section 500 cubits[f]

[a] 27 Or purification offering; also in verse 29   [b] 29 The Hebrew term refers to the irrevocable giving over of things or persons to the LORD.   [e] 1 That is, about 8 miles or about 13 kilometers; also in verses 3, 5 and 6   [d] 1 Septuagint (see also verses 3 and 5 and 48:9); Hebrew 10,000   [e] 1 That is, about 6 1/2 miles or about 11 kilometers   [f] 2 That is, about 875 feet or about 265 meters

44:12 made the people of Israel fall into sin One of Ezekiel's characteristic phrases to describe idolatry (see 7:19; 14:3–7).

44:15–31 While Yahweh criticizes the Levites for their role in Israel's idolatry, he praises the Zadokite priests for their faithfulness. This section lays out the rules and procedures priests must follow to maintain their ritual purity.

44:15 descendants of Zadok See note on 40:46.
44:17 linen clothes The command to wear linen rather than wool prevents ritual defilement through excessive sweating (see v. 18).
44:19 people are not consecrated through contact with their garments See 42:13–14. Priests were required to change clothes in the holy chambers. Holiness was thought to be a transferrable force—potentially deadly if handled improperly.
44:23 They are to teach my people According to 22:26, one of the priests' primary failures before the

exile was in not teaching the distinction between sacred and profane, pure and impure.
44:28 only inheritance the priests have See note on 36:12. The Levites received no allotment of land within Israel.

45:1–6 Ezekiel's concern for the sanctity of the temple area extends to the land surrounding it, which is set aside as a sacred district.

45:1 inheritance Refers to traditions about Israel's inheritance of the land. See note on 36:12. **portion** The Hebrew word used here, terumah, denotes something set apart as a contribution or offering, often for food offerings designated for the priests. **25,000 cubits long** Assuming Ezekiel's measurements are still based on the long cubit (about 21 inches or 1.75 feet), this holy district is roughly 8.3 miles by 6.6 miles, an area of nearly 55 square miles or 35,200 acres. See note on 40:5.
45:2 a section 500 cubits square As in 42:16–20.
50 cubits around it for open land A buffer zone to

square is to be for the sanctuary, with 50 cubits[a] around it for open land. ³In the sacred district, measure off a section 25,000 cubits long and 10,000 cubits[b] wide. In it will be the sanctuary, the Most Holy Place. ⁴It will be the sacred portion of the land for the priests, who minister in the sanctuary and who draw near to minister before the LORD. It will be a place for their houses as well as a holy place for the sanctuary. ⁵An area 25,000 cubits long and 10,000 cubits wide will belong to the Levites, who serve in the temple, as their possession for towns to live in.[c]

⁶"'You are to give the city as its property an area 5,000 cubits[d] wide and 25,000 cubits long, adjoining the sacred portion; it will belong to all Israel.

⁷"'The prince will have the land bordering each side of the area formed by the sacred district and the property of the city. It will extend westward from the west side and eastward from the east side, running lengthwise from the western to the eastern border parallel to one of the tribal portions. ⁸This land will be his possession in Israel. And my princes will no longer oppress my people but will allow the people of Israel to possess the land according to their tribes.

⁹"'This is what the Sovereign LORD says: You have gone far enough, princes of Israel! Give up your violence and oppression and do what is just and right. Stop dispossessing my people, declares the Sovereign LORD. ¹⁰You are to use accurate scales, an accurate ephah[e] and an accurate bath.[f] ¹¹The ephah and the bath are to be the same size, the bath containing a tenth of a homer and the ephah a tenth of a homer; the homer is to be the standard measure for both. ¹²The shekel[g] is to consist of twenty gerahs. Twenty shekels plus twenty-five shekels plus fifteen shekels equal one mina.[h]

¹³"'This is the special gift you are to offer: a sixth of an ephah[i] from each homer of wheat and a sixth of an ephah[j] from each homer of barley. ¹⁴The prescribed portion of olive oil, measured by the bath, is a tenth of a bath[k] from each cor (which consists of ten baths or one homer, for ten baths are equivalent to a homer). ¹⁵Also one sheep is to be taken from every flock of two hundred from the well-watered pastures of Israel. These will be used for the grain offerings, burnt offerings and fellowship offerings to make atonement for the people, declares the Sovereign LORD. ¹⁶All the people of the land will be required to give this special offering to the prince in Israel. ¹⁷It will be the duty of the prince to provide the burnt offerings, grain offerings and drink offerings at the festivals, the New Moons and the Sabbaths — at all the appointed festivals of Israel. He will provide the sin offerings,[l] grain offerings, burnt offerings and fellowship offerings to make atonement for the Israelites.

¹⁸"'This is what the Sovereign LORD says: In the first month on the first day you are to take a young bull without defect and purify the sanctuary. ¹⁹The priest is to take some of the blood of the sin offering and put it on the doorposts of the temple, on the four corners of the upper ledge of the altar and on the gateposts of the inner court. ²⁰You are to do the same on the seventh day of the month for anyone who sins unintentionally or through ignorance; so you are to make atonement for the temple.

²¹"'In the first month on the fourteenth day you are to observe the Passover, a festival lasting seven days, during which you shall eat bread made without yeast. ²²On that day the prince is to provide

---

[a] 2 That is, about 88 feet or about 27 meters   [b] 3 That is, about 3 1/3 miles or about 5.3 kilometers; also in verse 5
[c] 5 Septuagint; Hebrew *temple; they will have as their possession 20 rooms*   [d] 6 That is, about 1 2/3 miles or about 2.7 kilometers   [e] 10 An ephah was a dry measure having the capacity of about 3/5 bushel or about 22 liters.   [f] 10 A bath was a liquid measure equaling about 6 gallons or about 22 liters.   [g] 12 A shekel weighed about 2/5 ounce or about 12 grams.   [h] 12 That is, 60 shekels; the common mina was 50 shekels. Sixty shekels were about 1 1/2 pounds or about 690 grams.   [i] 13 That is, probably about 6 pounds or about 2.7 kilograms   [j] 13 That is, probably about 5 pounds or about 2.3 kilograms   [k] 14 That is, about 2 1/2 quarts or about 2.2 liters   [l] 17 Or *purification offerings*; also in verses 19, 22, 23 and 25

prevent the temple from being defiled by anyone who was not ritually pure.

45:7—46:18 The special status that Ezekiel describes for the *nasi* ("prince" or "ruler"; see 44:3 and note) includes the grant of two large tracts of land on either side of the sacred district. As a civil leader of the community, the prince has specific responsibilities, which are described here. Yahweh's primary concern is social justice—fair trade and an end to economic oppression (compare Isa 5:8; see note on Isa 1:17). The prophets' accusations against Israel focused on social injustice, idolatry and empty ritualism in their worship of Yahweh. Civil and religious leaders were held responsible for leading Israel astray (see Eze 22:26–28).

45:7 the tribal portions The Hebrew word used here, *cheleq* (plural *chalaqim*), can describe the land given as the inheritance (see note on 36:12). The word refers to portions of land allotted to the tribes of Israel after the conquest (e.g., Jos 19:9). The tribal allotments are outlined in Eze 48:1–7.

45:10 an accurate ephah and an accurate bath Compare Lev 19:35–36. An ephah was a dry measure (3/5 of a bushel; 22 liters), while a bath was a liquid measure (about 6 gallons; 22 liters).

45:11 a homer About 6 bushels or 220 liters.

45:12 The shekel is to consist of twenty gerahs The shekel was a standard for measuring weight, approximately 11 grams. The gerah was 0.6 grams. **mina** A larger unit for measuring weight, approximately 60 shekels or about 1.25 pounds.

45:17 burnt offerings, grain offerings and drink offerings See note on Eze 40:39. **the festivals, the New Moons and the Sabbaths** See note on Isa 1:13. **45:21 the Passover, a festival** See Ex 12; Dt 16.

a bull as a sin offering for himself and for all the people of the land. [23]Every day during the seven days of the festival he is to provide seven bulls and seven rams without defect as a burnt offering to the LORD, and a male goat for a sin offering. [24]He is to provide as a grain offering an ephah for each bull and an ephah for each ram, along with a hin[a] of olive oil for each ephah.

[25]"During the seven days of the festival, which begins in the seventh month on the fifteenth day, he is to make the same provision for sin offerings, burnt offerings, grain offerings and oil.

46 "'This is what the Sovereign LORD says: The gate of the inner court facing east is to be shut on the six working days, but on the Sabbath day and on the day of the New Moon it is to be opened. [2]The prince is to enter from the outside through the portico of the gateway and stand by the gatepost. The priests are to sacrifice his burnt offering and his fellowship offerings. He is to bow down in worship at the threshold of the gateway and then go out, but the gate will not be shut until evening. [3]On the Sabbaths and New Moons the people of the land are to worship in the presence of the LORD at the entrance of that gateway. [4]The burnt offering the prince brings to the LORD on the Sabbath day is to be six male lambs and a ram, all without defect. [5]The grain offering given with the ram is to be an ephah,[b] and the grain offering with the lambs is to be as much as he pleases, along with a hin[c] of olive oil for each ephah. [6]On the day of the New Moon he is to offer a young bull, six lambs and a ram, all without defect. [7]He is to provide as a grain offering one ephah with the bull, one ephah with the ram, and with the lambs as much as he wants to give, along with a hin of oil for each ephah. [8]When the prince enters, he is to go in through the portico of the gateway, and he is to come out the same way.

[9]"'When the people of the land come before the LORD at the appointed festivals, whoever enters by the north gate to worship is to go out the south gate; and whoever enters by the south gate is to go out the north gate. No one is to return through the gate by which they entered, but each is to go out the opposite gate. [10]The prince is to be among them, going in when they go in and going out when they go out. [11]At the feasts and the appointed festivals, the grain offering is to be an ephah with a bull, an ephah with a ram, and with the lambs as much as he pleases, along with a hin of oil for each ephah.

[12]"'When the prince provides a freewill offering to the LORD — whether a burnt offering or fellowship offerings — the gate facing east is to be opened for him. He shall offer his burnt offering or his fellowship offerings as he does on the Sabbath day. Then he shall go out, and after he has gone out, the gate will be shut.

[13]"'Every day you are to provide a year-old lamb without defect for a burnt offering to the LORD; morning by morning you shall provide it. [14]You are also to provide with it morning by morning a grain offering, consisting of a sixth of an ephah[d] with a third of a hin[e] of oil to moisten the flour. The presenting of this grain offering to the LORD is a lasting ordinance. [15]So the lamb and the grain offering and the oil shall be provided morning by morning for a regular burnt offering.

[16]"'This is what the Sovereign LORD says: If the prince makes a gift from his inheritance to one of his sons, it will also belong to his descendants; it is to be their property by inheritance. [17]If, however, he makes a gift from his inheritance to one of his servants, the servant may keep it until the year of freedom; then it will revert to the prince. His inheritance belongs to his sons only; it is theirs. [18]The prince must not take any of the inheritance

---

a 24 That is, about 1 gallon or about 3.8 liters   *b 5* That is, probably about 35 pounds or about 16 kilograms; also in verses 7 and 11   *c 5* That is, about 1 gallon or about 3.8 liters; also in verses 7 and 11   *d 14* That is, probably about 6 pounds or about 2.7 kilograms   *e 14* That is, about 1 1/2 quarts or about 1.3 liters

---

45:25 in the seventh month on the fifteenth day The feast is not named here, but the date coincides with the Festival of Tabernacles (or Booths; see Lev 23:34 and note).

46:1–18 Ezekiel provides additional details on sacrifice procedures. The prince plays a central role in these rituals, which also involve the people and the priests. Ezekiel shows a particular concern for the sanctity of the gates, dictating when they must be opened and closed and detailing the procedure for entering and exiting.

46:1 The gate of the inner court The temple building itself faces this gate, which symbolizes direct access to the temple.

46:3 the people of the land are to worship When the eastern gate was open, the people could look from the outer court into the inner court toward the temple itself. This was the closest they could come to the divine presence.

46:5 a hin of olive oil for each ephah The grain offering consisted of about 3/5 of a bushel of grain with four quarts of oil.

46:10 The prince is to be among them, going in when they go in The prince holds the same level of sanctity as the people. He is not a priest and does not have access to the inner court or the temple building.

46:16–18 The final stipulation in this section provides direction for the prince to prevent him and his family from unjustly acquiring land. The prince may permanently give land to his sons, but a land grant to a servant will last only until the Year of Jubilee. As shown in Eze 46:18, the stipulation removes any incentive for the prince to take other people's land. See note on 45:7—46:18.

46:17 the year of freedom The Year of Jubilee as commanded in Lev 25:10.

of the people, driving them off their property. He is to give his sons their inheritance out of his own property, so that not one of my people will be separated from their property.'"

¹⁹Then the man brought me through the entrance at the side of the gate to the sacred rooms facing north, which belonged to the priests, and showed me a place at the western end. ²⁰He said to me, "This is the place where the priests are to cook the guilt offering and the sin offering[a] and bake the grain offering, to avoid bringing them into the outer court and consecrating the people."

²¹He then brought me to the outer court and led me around to its four corners, and I saw in each corner another court. ²²In the four corners of the outer court were enclosed[b] courts, forty cubits long and thirty cubits wide;[c] each of the courts in the four corners was the same size. ²³Around the inside of each of the four courts was a ledge of stone, with places for fire built all around under the ledge. ²⁴He said to me, "These are the kitchens where those who minister at the temple are to cook the sacrifices of the people."

The River From the Temple

47 The man brought me back to the entrance to the temple, and I saw water coming out from under the threshold of the temple toward the east (for the temple faced east). The water was coming down from under the south side of the temple, south of the altar. ²He then brought me out through the north gate and led me around the outside to the outer gate facing east, and the water was trickling from the south side.

³As the man went eastward with a measuring line in his hand, he measured off a thousand cubits[d] and then led me through water that was ankle-deep. ⁴He measured off another thousand cubits and led me through water that was knee-deep. He measured off another thousand and led me through water that was up to the waist. ⁵He measured off another thousand, but now it was a river that I could not cross, because the water had risen and was deep enough to swim in — a river that no one could cross. ⁶He asked me, "Son of man, do you see this?"

Then he led me back to the bank of the river. ⁷When I arrived there, I saw a great number of trees on each side of the river. ⁸He said to me, "This water flows toward the eastern region and goes down into the Arabah,[e] where it enters the Dead Sea. When it empties into the sea, the salty water there becomes fresh. ⁹Swarms of living creatures will live wherever the river flows. There will be large numbers of fish, because this water flows there and makes the salt water fresh; so where the river flows everything will live. ¹⁰Fishermen will stand along the shore; from En Gedi to En Eglaim there will be places for spreading nets. The fish will be of many kinds — like the fish of the Mediterranean Sea. ¹¹But the swamps and marshes will not become fresh; they will be left for salt. ¹²Fruit trees of all kinds will grow on both banks of the river. Their leaves will not wither, nor will their fruit fail. Every month they will bear fruit, because the water from the sanctuary flows to them. Their fruit will serve for food and their leaves for healing."

The Boundaries of the Land

¹³This is what the Sovereign LORD says: "These are the boundaries of the land that you will divide among the twelve tribes of Israel as their

---

[a] 20 Or *purification offering*   [b] 22 The meaning of the Hebrew for this word is uncertain.   [c] 22 That is, about 70 feet long and 53 feet wide or about 21 meters long and 16 meters wide   [d] 3 That is, about 1,700 feet or about 530 meters   [e] 8 Or *the Jordan Valley*

46:19–24 Ezekiel's tour of the temple complex continues to a kitchen area in the inner court where the priests were to prepare offerings too holy to risk contact with the people in the outer court. Next, he is shown four kitchens for preparing sacrifices for the common people. Kitchens were necessary because sacrifices were sacred meals in which the priests participated with the community.

47:1–12 Ezekiel's temple tour concludes at the entrance of the temple proper, where he finds a stream of water coming from beneath the temple and flowing east. Ezekiel's guide walks him through the water, measuring the growing river and testing the depth until it becomes impassable just over a mile from the temple. The water flowing from the temple gives life and renews the land it flows through. If this holy district and sacred city represents Jerusalem, the life-giving power of the river would be significant in restoring the region east of Jerusalem—a dry, lifeless wilderness approaching the salty waters of the Dead Sea. Ezekiel seems to envision a river of life that heals the waters of the Dead Sea and turns the wilderness into a lush orchard. This imagery recalls the book of Isaiah, where the deserts bloom under Yahweh's redemptive hand (see Isa 35:1).

47:3 a thousand cubits Many English translations follow the Hebrew text and give the distance in cubits; others convert the cubits to feet. Assuming that Ezekiel is using the long cubit (1.75 feet), 1,000 cubits is 1,750 feet, and the total distance covered through Eze 47:5 is more than 1.3 miles.

47:8 the Arabah Refers to the rift valley of the Jordan River, including the Sea of Galilee and the Dead Sea. **the Dead Sea** The Hebrew text refers to the Dead Sea simply as "the sea." **into the sea, the salty water there becomes fresh** The high concentration of salt in the Dead Sea prevents all life.

47:10 from En Gedi to En Eglaim Locations on the shore of the Dead Sea. **the Mediterranean Sea** The Hebrew text refers to the Mediterranean Sea as the "great sea."

47:13–23 Ezekiel outlines the boundaries of the land allotted to Israel in detail. The assignment resembles the boundary lists from Nu 34 and Jos 13–19.

inheritance, with two portions for Joseph. [14]You are to divide it equally among them. Because I swore with uplifted hand to give it to your ancestors, this land will become your inheritance.

[15]"This is to be the boundary of the land:

"On the north side it will run from the Mediterranean Sea by the Hethlon road past Lebo Hamath to Zedad, [16]Berothah[a] and Sibraim (which lies on the border between Damascus and Hamath), as far as Hazer Hattikon, which is on the border of Hauran. [17]The boundary will extend from the sea to Hazar Enan,[b] along the northern border of Damascus, with the border of Hamath to the north. This will be the northern boundary.

[18]"On the east side the boundary will run between Hauran and Damascus, along the Jordan between Gilead and the land of Israel, to the Dead Sea and as far as Tamar.[c] This will be the eastern boundary.

[19]"On the south side it will run from Tamar as far as the waters of Meribah Kadesh, then along the Wadi of Egypt to the Mediterranean Sea. This will be the southern boundary.

[20]"On the west side, the Mediterranean Sea will be the boundary to a point opposite Lebo Hamath. This will be the western boundary.

[21]"You are to distribute this land among yourselves according to the tribes of Israel. [22]You are to allot it as an inheritance for yourselves and for the foreigners residing among you and who have children. You are to consider them as native-born Israelites; along with you they are to be allotted an inheritance among the tribes of Israel. [23]In whatever tribe a foreigner resides, there you are to give them their inheritance," declares the Sovereign LORD.

The Division of the Land

48 "These are the tribes, listed by name: At the northern frontier, Dan will have one portion; it will follow the Hethlon road to Lebo Hamath; Hazar Enan and the northern border of Damascus next to Hamath will be part of its border from the east side to the west side.

[2]"Asher will have one portion; it will border the territory of Dan from east to west.

[3]"Naphtali will have one portion; it will border the territory of Asher from east to west.

[4]"Manasseh will have one portion; it will border the territory of Naphtali from east to west.

[5]"Ephraim will have one portion; it will border the territory of Manasseh from east to west.

[6]"Reuben will have one portion; it will border the territory of Ephraim from east to west.

[7]"Judah will have one portion; it will border the territory of Reuben from east to west.

[8]"Bordering the territory of Judah from east to west will be the portion you are to present as a special gift. It will be 25,000 cubits[d] wide, and its length from east to west will equal one of the tribal portions; the sanctuary will be in the center of it.

[9]"The special portion you are to offer to the LORD will be 25,000 cubits long and 10,000 cubits[e] wide. [10]This will be the sacred portion for the priests. It will be 25,000 cubits long on the north side, 10,000 cubits wide on the west side, 10,000 cubits wide on the east side and 25,000 cubits long on the south side. In the center of it will be the sanctuary of the LORD. [11]This will be for the consecrated priests, the Zadokites, who were faithful in serving me and did not go astray as the Levites did when the Israelites went astray. [12]It will be a special gift to them from the sacred portion of the land, a most holy portion, bordering the territory of the Levites.

[13]"Alongside the territory of the priests, the Levites will have an allotment 25,000 cubits long and 10,000 cubits wide. Its total length will be

---

[a] 15,16 See Septuagint and 48:1; Hebrew *road to go into Zedad,* [16]*Hamath, Berothah.*   [b] 17 Hebrew *Enon,* a variant of *Enan*
[c] 18 See Syriac; Hebrew *Israel. You will measure to the Dead Sea.*
[d] 8 That is, about 8 miles or about 13 kilometers; also in verses 9, 10, 13, 15, 20 and 21   [e] 9 That is, about 3 1/3 miles or about 5.3 kilometers; also in verses 10, 13 and 18

47:15 Hethlon This location is uncertain. **Zedad** A village in northeastern Syria.
47:16 Berothah A city in Syria. See 2Sa 8:8. **Sibraim** This location is unknown. **Damascus** A prominent city in southern Syria. **Hazer Hattikon** A village in northeast Syria. **the border of Hauran** The region south of Damascus and east of the Sea of Galilee.
47:17 Hazar Enan A village in northeast Syria.
47:19 Meribah Kadesh Also known as Kadesh Barnea, an area in the northeast Sinai desert. **then along the Wadi of Egypt** A dry riverbed in the northeast Sinai desert.
47:20 Lebo Hamath See Eze 47:15. The complete perimeter of the border was described.

48:1–29 Here Ezekiel describes the divisions of the land by tribe and specifies how the portion of land allotted for the city will be subdivided. The passage resembles the division of the land after the conquest in Jos 13–19 where twelve tribes were allotted territory. The tribe of Levi (including the priests) originally received no land inheritance (Nu 18:20–24; Jos 13:14). In Ezekiel's vision of the restored land, the priests and Levites also receive an allotment (see Eze 48:8–15 and note).

48:1 the tribes, listed by name The tribes of Israel are named after the sons of Jacob (see Ge 49:1–28). The descendants of Jacob's son Joseph made up two tribes—Ephraim and Manasseh (Ge 48)—because Jacob had adopted them as his own (Ge 48:5).

48:8–15 Ezekiel gives the details of the sacred district again. The dimensions and uses are the same as outlined previously (see note on Eze 45:1–6; note on 45:1).

48:11 the Zadokites Zadok was high priest under David. See note on 40:46.

25,000 cubits and its width 10,000 cubits. ¹⁴They must not sell or exchange any of it. This is the best of the land and must not pass into other hands, because it is holy to the Lord.

¹⁵"The remaining area, 5,000 cubits[a] wide and 25,000 cubits long, will be for the common use of the city, for houses and for pastureland. The city will be in the center of it ¹⁶and will have these measurements: the north side 4,500 cubits,[b] the south side 4,500 cubits, the east side 4,500 cubits, and the west side 4,500 cubits. ¹⁷The pastureland for the city will be 250 cubits[c] on the north, 250 cubits on the south, 250 cubits on the east, and 250 cubits on the west. ¹⁸What remains of the area, bordering on the sacred portion and running the length of it, will be 10,000 cubits on the east side and 10,000 cubits on the west side. Its produce will supply food for the workers of the city. ¹⁹The workers from the city who farm it will come from all the tribes of Israel. ²⁰The entire portion will be a square, 25,000 cubits on each side. As a special gift you will set aside the sacred portion, along with the property of the city.

²¹"What remains on both sides of the area formed by the sacred portion and the property of the city will belong to the prince. It will extend eastward from the 25,000 cubits of the sacred portion to the eastern border, and westward from the 25,000 cubits to the western border. Both these areas running the length of the tribal portions will belong to the prince, and the sacred portion with the temple sanctuary will be in the center of them. ²²So the property of the Levites and the property of the city will lie in the center of the area that belongs to the prince. The area belonging to the prince will lie between the border of Judah and the border of Benjamin.

²³"As for the rest of the tribes: Benjamin will have one portion; it will extend from the east side to the west side.

²⁴"Simeon will have one portion; it will border the territory of Benjamin from east to west.

²⁵"Issachar will have one portion; it will border the territory of Simeon from east to west.

²⁶"Zebulun will have one portion; it will border the territory of Issachar from east to west.

²⁷"Gad will have one portion; it will border the territory of Zebulun from east to west.

²⁸"The southern boundary of Gad will run south from Tamar to the waters of Meribah Kadesh, then along the Wadi of Egypt to the Mediterranean Sea.

²⁹"This is the land you are to allot as an inheritance to the tribes of Israel, and these will be their portions," declares the Sovereign Lord.

The Gates of the New City

³⁰"These will be the exits of the city: Beginning on the north side, which is 4,500 cubits long, ³¹the gates of the city will be named after the tribes of Israel. The three gates on the north side will be the gate of Reuben, the gate of Judah and the gate of Levi.

³²"On the east side, which is 4,500 cubits long, will be three gates: the gate of Joseph, the gate of Benjamin and the gate of Dan.

³³"On the south side, which measures 4,500 cubits, will be three gates: the gate of Simeon, the gate of Issachar and the gate of Zebulun.

³⁴"On the west side, which is 4,500 cubits long, will be three gates: the gate of Gad, the gate of Asher and the gate of Naphtali.

³⁵"The distance all around will be 18,000 cubits.[d]

"And the name of the city from that time on will be:

the Lord is there."

[a] 15 That is, about 1 2/3 miles or about 2.7 kilometers
[b] 16 That is, about 1 1/2 miles or about 2.4 kilometers; also in verses 30, 32, 33 and 34   [c] 17 That is, about 440 feet or about 135 meters   [d] 35 That is, about 6 miles or about 9.5 kilometers

48:15–19 Ezekiel outlines the dimensions of the city and the assigned use for the rest of the city's allotment of land. The city will be a square covering approximately 2.2 square miles (4,500 cubits each side). The land immediately surrounding the city will be pastureland, a band 250 cubits wide. The city and the pastureland together form a square with each side measuring 5,000 cubits—the entire width of the city's land allotment. The city occupies the center of the land, and the remaining 10,000 cubits on either side are designated as farmland to grow food for the city's inhabitants.

48:19 all the tribes of Israel While each tribe has an allotment of land, the city itself includes inhabitants from all 12 tribes.

48:21 to the prince Reiterating the assignment from 45:7.

48:30–35 Access to the city comes through 12 gates, three on each side. They are named for each of the 12 tribes.

48:35 the Lord is there The Hebrew name of the city will be *yhwh shammah*, or "Yahweh is Here"—symbolizing Yahweh's promise to dwell among his people. See the table "Names of God in the Old Testament" on p. 917.

DANIEL

INTRODUCTION TO DANIEL

The stories of Daniel show that God will look after his people. The first half of the book records events — set in Babylon, when God's people were facing laws that opposed their faith — that demonstrate God's care for and response to his people as they face hardships. The second half includes visions that communicate a broader view of God's plan and his sovereignty over all nations. The book of Daniel gives comfort to those who are oppressed and dealing with tragedies.

BACKGROUND

The book of Daniel is set during the Babylonian exile (Da 1:1–3). When King Nebuchadnezzar of Babylon defeated the Egyptians at the battle of Carchemish (605 BC), Judah came under his authority. He then entered Jerusalem and took many prominent citizens to Babylon, including Daniel and three of his friends. Several years later, Nebuchadnezzar again deported people from Judah to Babylon (597 BC; see 2Ki 24:11–16). These captives included the prophet Ezekiel. A decade after that, a final rebellion by King Zedekiah brought the full weight of Nebuchadnezzar's wrath against Judah. Jerusalem and its temple were destroyed, and the remaining population was taken to Babylon (586 BC; see 2Ki 24:18—25:21). Daniel spent his entire adult life in Babylon — even after the Babylonians were conquered by the Persians in 539 BC (Da 1:21; 10:1).

The date of the book of Daniel's composition is debated, with some arguing for a sixth-century BC date and others arguing for a date as late as the second century BC. It could be that Daniel recorded at least the visions in the latter half of the book (which are narrated in the first person) in the sixth century BC and the complete book did not reach its current form until much later. Reasons often given for the later date include the book's language and its detailed account of events that occurred in the second century.

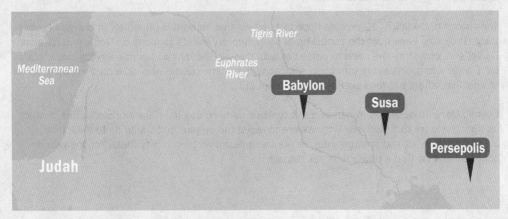

This map depicts some of the major locations mentioned in Daniel.

STRUCTURE

The book of Daniel can be divided into two sections. The first contains a series of tales from the Babylonian court in which Daniel and his friends navigate life as exiles in a foreign land (chs. 1–6). This includes the famous stories of Daniel's friends in the fiery furnace (ch. 3) and Daniel in the lions' den (ch. 6). Amid pressure to compromise, Daniel and his friends stay true to worshiping only the King of kings, Yahweh—not Nebuchadnezzar and Belshazzar of Babylon, or Darius the Mede. This section shows how Yahweh protects his people, despite what earthly kings may do. Interestingly, part of the book is recorded in Aramaic and part in Hebrew. However, this language division does not correspond to the genre division between Daniel 1–6 and 7–12. The Aramaic portion of the book is Daniel 2:4—7:28.

The second section (chs. 7–12) is set later in Daniel's career. Unlike the first section, Daniel himself narrates most of the content, describing a series of symbolic visions and their interpretations. Each vision is intended to inspire God's people during difficult times.

OUTLINE

- Daniel's experiences in Babylon (1:1—6:28)
- Daniel's visions of future events (7:1—12:13)

THEMES

Living in a culture hostile to Yahweh, Daniel shows that courageous faith in Yahweh—along with personal integrity and persistent prayer—is the way to live. The stories of Daniel 1–6 demonstrate how the people of God can live righteously, even in a culture that opposes their faith. Daniel and his three friends ask Yahweh to deliver them from life-threatening danger and impossible dilemmas, and he is faithful to answer.

The visions of Daniel 7–12 provide hope by teaching that Yahweh is ultimately in charge of everything. They step back from the confusion of contemporary events to focus on God's greater plan. Daniel's visions show the need to persist in faith through the messiness of everyday circumstances. Daniel also proclaims resurrection, indicating that some people who have died will wake up to eternal life; others will face everlasting contempt (12:2).

Overall, Daniel teaches us to persevere. It teaches us to refuse to let the world's stories distract us from the story that God is telling. We are to resist the empire that wants us to think that actions like praying and showing integrity are insignificant when in reality these actions provide opportunities for God's power to break through.

Daniel's Training in Babylon

1 In the third year of the reign of Jehoiakim king of Judah, Nebuchadnezzar king of Babylon came to Jerusalem and besieged it. ²And the Lord delivered Jehoiakim king of Judah into his hand, along with some of the articles from the temple of God. These he carried off to the temple of his god in Babylonia^a and put in the treasure house of his god.

³Then the king ordered Ashpenaz, chief of his court officials, to bring into the king's service some of the Israelites from the royal family and the nobility — ⁴young men without any physical defect, handsome, showing aptitude for every kind of learning, well informed, quick to understand, and qualified to serve in the king's palace. He was to teach them the language and literature of the Babylonians.^b ⁵The king assigned them a daily amount of food and wine from the king's table. They were to be trained for three years, and after that they were to enter the king's service.

⁶Among those who were chosen were some from Judah: Daniel, Hananiah, Mishael and Azariah. ⁷The chief official gave them new names: to Daniel, the name Belteshazzar; to Hananiah, Shadrach; to Mishael, Meshach; and to Azariah, Abednego.

^a 2 Hebrew *Shinar*   ^b 4 Or *Chaldeans*

1:1–7 The book of Daniel opens with a brief review of the subjugation of Jerusalem by King Nebuchadnezzar, setting the stage for the narratives that follow. The protagonists of the story are introduced by their Hebrew names: Daniel, Hananiah, Mishael and Azariah (Da 1:6). Their names are changed in v. 7, signaling a shift in place from Jerusalem to Babylon. See the timeline "Approximate Dates of Old Testament Prophets" on p. 1070.

1:1 third year The third year of Jehoiakim's reign (606 BC) does not coincide with the known siege of Jerusalem by Nebuchadnezzar in 597 BC (compare v. 1 with 2Ki 24:10–12; 2Ch 36:9–10)—a discrepancy that makes it difficult to determine when Daniel was taken to Babylon. Daniel 1:1 claims that a siege occurred in 606 BC—during the third year of Jehoiakim's reign (609–597 BC). The Babylonian Chronicles—which are tablets that record the history of Babylon—report a siege that occurred during the reign of Jehoiachin in 597 BC, but this was *after* the death of Jehoiakim (compare 2Ki 24:10–17). While 2Ch 36:5–10 records that Nebuchadnezzar came to Jerusalem twice in a brief period, other ancient documents do not mention an earlier siege. It may be that the event mentioned here was not a formal siege, or Nebuchadnezzar may have sent others to deal with Jehoiakim (compare 2Ki 18:13–37, where both kings are represented by others). See the infographic "The Babylonian Chronicles" on p. 605. **Nebuchadnezzar** King of Babylon from 605 to 562 BC. According to the Babylonian Chronicles, Nebuchadnezzar's siege of Jerusalem occurred in 597 BC. The Babylonian Chronicles are a series of tablets discovered in the late 19th century. They present a selective series of accounts about Babylonian history covering the period from around 625–225 BC. Unlike other historical documents from the ancient Near East, these texts reflect an accurate catalog of historical events and omit the self-aggrandizing qualities often found in Egyptian texts. For example, they chronicle defeats as well as victories—a practice almost without parallel in antiquity—making them one of the earliest attempts at historiography. They assist in our understanding of the Biblical record, particularly the book of Daniel, and cover some of the events leading up to (and including) Judah's exile to Babylon.

REGNAL CHRONOLOGY	
Accession Year System	Length of reign begins at New Year
Non-Accession Year System	Length of reign begins at coronation
Postdating System	Length of reign begins after first full year

NEBUCHADNEZZAR
Known as a master builder and military architect, Nebuchadnezzar was the pride of the Neo-Babylonian Empire. He ruled for 43 years (605–562 BC) and gained fame by defeating the Egyptians at the Battle of Carchemish in 605 BC just before ascending the throne. Historical sources emphasize his vast army and warring tendencies, portraying him as a king obsessed with conquest and power. He is portrayed similarly in Daniel but is used to make a theological point: The power of earthly rulers comes from God.

1:2 into his hand Expresses the sovereignty of God over the nations—a theme repeated throughout the book. The setting for the book of Daniel is the deportation of Judah to Babylon, or the Babylonian exile. When Nebuchadnezzar defeated the Egyptians at the Battle of Carchemish and subsequently became king in 605 BC, Judah fell under Babylonian control. Jehoiakim, then king of Judah, was a submissive vassal for three years, then rebelled. The court tales of Daniel and his three friends (Da 1–6) are placed within this setting of living under Babylonian domination. The latter half of the book—chs. 7–12—deals with a later persecution. The arguments over when the book of Daniel was written involve this change of setting halfway through the book. Traditionally, Daniel is considered the author, so the book must have been written in his lifetime (sixth century BC). The stories in chs. 1–6 relate to Daniel and his friends in sixth-century Babylon. The change in style and character of chs. 7–12—with its focus on future events, especially those of the early second century BC—have led some to conclude that the book was written after Daniel's lifetime. **in Babylonia** The ancient Hebrew name for Babylon, used here, was "Shinar" (see Ge 11:2 and note). **put in** In ancient Near Eastern warfare, placing the objects of a defeated enemy in the temple of one's god was a common practice. See the table "Pagan Deities of the Old Testament" on p. 1287.

1:3 officials The Hebrew word here *saris* (often translated "eunuch" or simply "official") is used to designate a trusted royal official (Ge 37:36; 2Ki 23:11). A *saris* may have been a eunuch or castrated male (Isa 56:3; 2Ki 20:18). While castration of palace officials was common in the ancient Near East (primarily during the Persian period), it is unknown whether it was practiced

⁸But Daniel resolved not to defile himself with the royal food and wine, and he asked the chief official for permission not to defile himself this way. ⁹Now God had caused the official to show favor and compassion to Daniel, ¹⁰but the official told Daniel, "I am afraid of my lord the king, who has assigned your*ᵃ* food and drink. Why should he see you looking worse than the other young men your age? The king would then have my head because of you."

¹¹Daniel then said to the guard whom the chief official had appointed over Daniel, Hananiah, Mishael and Azariah, ¹²"Please test your servants for ten days: Give us nothing but vegetables to eat

ᵃ 10 The Hebrew for *your* and *you* in this verse is plural.

in Nebuchadnezzar's Babylon. **some of the Israelites** Babylonians often detained and educated royal captives. These captives could later be returned to their homeland as influential sympathizers to their overlords.
1:4 teach them the language and literature Indoctrination was the key to successfully integrating captives into their new homeland. The incorporation of political, cultural and religious education made captives look favorably upon those who conquered them.
1:6 Daniel Means "God is my judge." **Hananiah, Mishael and Azariah** These Hebrew names identify the three young men with the God of Israel: Hananiah ("Yahweh has acted graciously"); Mishael (may mean "Who is what God is"); and Azariah ("Yahweh has helped").

Daniel 1:6

DANIEL
Little is known of Daniel outside of the Biblical book bearing his name. At some point in Nebuchadnezzar's conquest of Palestine, Daniel was taken captive to Babylon and served in the king's court. He is renowned for his wisdom and ability to interpret dreams and omens. Portrayed as the quintessential Jewish sage, he serves as a model of covenant fidelity and righteousness (see Da 2:14 and note).

Life of Daniel

620 BC   600 BC   580 BC

605 BC Nebuchadnezzar becomes king of Babylon

598/7 BC* Daniel and his friends are taken to Babylon (Da 1:1–2)

597–595 BC** Daniel and his friends are trained to serve Nebuchadnezzar (Da 1:3–20)

620 BC Daniel is born

595 BC* Nebuchadnezzar's dream of a statue (Da 2)

593 BC Ezekiel begins his prophetic ministry in Babylon

586 BC Jerusalem falls to Babylon

620 BC   600 BC   580 BC

*All dates are approximate *Or 605 BC, ** Or 605–603 BC, ***or 603 BC*

and water to drink. ¹³Then compare our appearance with that of the young men who eat the royal food, and treat your servants in accordance with what you see." ¹⁴So he agreed to this and tested them for ten days.

¹⁵At the end of the ten days they looked healthier and better nourished than any of the young men who ate the royal food. ¹⁶So the guard took away their choice food and the wine they were to drink and gave them vegetables instead.

¹⁷To these four young men God gave knowledge and understanding of all kinds of literature and

1:7 gave them new names A common custom in this time period was that a king would rename foreigners who were brought to the king's court as captives. For Daniel and Azariah, the Hebrew references to God in their names (-el for God or -iah for Yahweh) are replaced with references to Babylonian deities like Nabu or Marduk (also called Bel). Their new names symbolized serving Babylon. Daniel's new name, Belteshazzar, probably means "Bel protect the prince" (see 4:8). Azariah's new name, Abednego, is probably a misspelling of Abed-Nabu, meaning "servant of Nabu." The meanings of Shadrach and Meshach are uncertain, and the deity references may be missing from their names. The purpose of renaming was to completely disassociate captives from their former way of life.

JEWISH AND BABYLONIAN NAMES	
Daniel	Belteshazzar
Hananiah	Shadrach
Mishael	Meshach
Azariah	Abednego

1:8–21 Now that the Jews are in Babylon, they need leaders who will act and speak on behalf of God. The four youths from Da 1:6 fill this role. Verses 8–21 provide the first demonstration of God's favor on the exiles. Daniel and his friends determine to eat according to the standards of the Law, and God provides for them by granting them success in a challenge to the palace master.

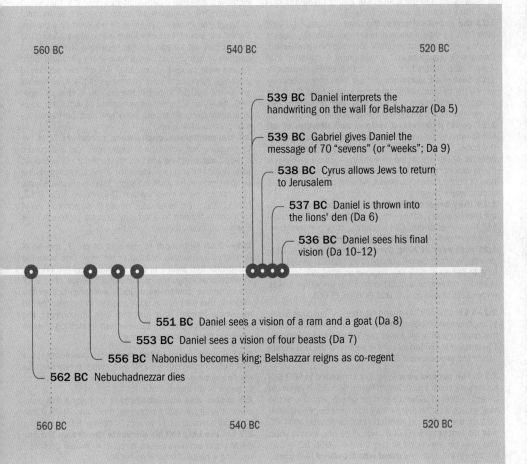

560 BC   540 BC   520 BC

539 BC Daniel interprets the handwriting on the wall for Belshazzar (Da 5)

539 BC Gabriel gives Daniel the message of 70 "sevens" (or "weeks"; Da 9)

538 BC Cyrus allows Jews to return to Jerusalem

537 BC Daniel is thrown into the lions' den (Da 6)

536 BC Daniel sees his final vision (Da 10–12)

551 BC Daniel sees a vision of a ram and a goat (Da 8)

553 BC Daniel sees a vision of four beasts (Da 7)

556 BC Nabonidus becomes king; Belshazzar reigns as co-regent

562 BC Nebuchadnezzar dies

560 BC   540 BC   520 BC

learning. And Daniel could understand visions and dreams of all kinds.

¹⁸At the end of the time set by the king to bring them into his service, the chief official presented them to Nebuchadnezzar. ¹⁹The king talked with them, and he found none equal to Daniel, Hananiah, Mishael and Azariah; so they entered the king's service. ²⁰In every matter of wisdom and understanding about which the king questioned them, he found them ten times better than all the magicians and enchanters in his whole kingdom. ²¹And Daniel remained there until the first year of King Cyrus.

Nebuchadnezzar's Dream

2 In the second year of his reign, Nebuchadnezzar had dreams; his mind was troubled and he could not sleep. ²So the king summoned the magicians, enchanters, sorcerers and astrologers[a] to tell him what he had dreamed. When they came in and stood before the king, ³he said to them, "I

have had a dream that troubles me and I want to know what it means.[b]"

⁴Then the astrologers answered the king,[c] "May the king live forever! Tell your servants the dream, and we will interpret it."

⁵The king replied to the astrologers, "This is what I have firmly decided: If you do not tell me what my dream was and interpret it, I will have you cut into pieces and your houses turned into piles of rubble. ⁶But if you tell me the dream and explain it, you will receive from me gifts and rewards and great honor. So tell me the dream and interpret it for me."

⁷Once more they replied, "Let the king tell his servants the dream, and we will interpret it."

⁸Then the king answered, "I am certain that you are trying to gain time, because you realize that this is what I have firmly decided: ⁹If you do not tell me the dream, there is only one penalty for you. You have conspired to tell me misleading and

---

[a] 2 Or *Chaldeans*; also in verses 4, 5 and 10   [b] 3 Or *was*
[c] 4 At this point the Hebrew text has *in Aramaic*, indicating that the text from here through the end of chapter 7 is in Aramaic.

1:8 not to defile himself The defilement spoken of here is likely related to the concept of eating unclean foods (i.e., ritual impurity; see Lev 7:19–27).

1:11 the guard Ashpenaz, the chief official of the king (see Da 1:3), defers some of his responsibility by placing the four Hebrew youths under the care of his steward. Daniel receives favor and compassion, suggesting that Ashpenaz probably found a way to honor his request.

1:12 test your servants Rather than risk appearing unhealthy by abstaining from the king's food for three years, Daniel suggests a brief test. His deferential language makes the request more palatable.

1:17 could understand visions and dreams of all kinds Introduces a motif that will resurface throughout the book. The Hebrew words used here for visions and dreams designate divine revelation. A vision involves a divine experience that occurs while awake, as an interruption of normal consciousness, while a prophetic dream occurs while sleeping.

1:19 they entered the king's service God blessed the four Hebrew youths—they are noticeably more qualified than their peers. Consequently, they are assigned prominent positions in the king's court.

1:21 first year of King Cyrus Refers to the year Babylon came under Cyrus' control (539 BC). Cyrus became king of Persia in 559 BC. This verse gives the span of Daniel's career as a courtier in Babylon when it was under Babylonian control (ca. 606–539 BC).

2:1–16 Following Daniel and his friends' success in ch. 1, another test comes their way. The Hebrew youths pass this challenge through prayer and Yahweh's intervention. The chapter is divided into three sections; the first establishes the predicament Daniel and his friends will face.

2:1 In the second year Probably sometime in 603 BC. Nebuchadnezzar's reign began late in 605 BC. Babylonian records usually followed a system where year one of the king's reign was the first full calendar year beginning after he took the throne. In Nebuchadnezzar's case, 604 BC was his first year, so 603 BC would be his second year. The year he ascended to the throne—605 BC—was his accession year. **his mind was troubled** Nebuchad-

nezzar's anxiety is accompanied by sleeplessness. The Hebrew phrase used here indicates a turmoil that would disrupt normal sleeping patterns. In Ge 41:8, the ruler of Egypt (the Pharaoh) is similarly troubled by a dream. Daniel will assist Nebuchadnezzar in understanding the dream just as Joseph did for Pharaoh. The lives and careers of Joseph and Daniel have many parallels: Both figures were carried against their will into the service of a foreign ruler; both were viewed as pious, God-fearing Jews who sought to live righteously in a strange land; both have been upheld as paragons of virtue for Jews in similar circumstances; both are also portrayed as interpreters of dreams.

2:2 the magicians, enchanters, sorcerers Titles belonging to members of the priestly class who interpreted omens. **astrologers** The Hebrew term for "Chaldeans" was originally a designation for an Aramaic-speaking people-group in Babylon, so some biblical passages use "Chaldean" as a synonym for "Babylonian" (Ezr 5:12; Eze 12:13). The label later became a technical term for people trained in astrology and so is sometimes translated "astrologers" "or "diviners."

2:4—7:28 From here to the end of ch. 7, the book is written in Aramaic instead of Hebrew. One possible reason for this switch is that Aramaic was the primary international language of the period. Since chs. 2–7 are meant to demonstrate God's sovereignty over the nations, this part of the book needed to be readable to the whole empire—not just the Jews. In contrast, the apocalypses of chs. 8–12—written in Hebrew—were intended for a Jewish audience.

2:4 Tell your servants the dream The advisors expect that Nebuchadnezzar will follow standard procedure: He will describe his dream, and then they will confer together to arrive at an interpretation.

2:5 dream was and interpret it In making this command, the king intends to prevent the Babylonians (Chaldeans) from deceiving him with a fictional interpretation.

2:7 Let the king tell his servants the dream The magicians and advisors desire a return to proper protocol; the king's request was impossible.

wicked things, hoping the situation will change. So then, tell me the dream, and I will know that you can interpret it for me."

[10]The astrologers answered the king, "There is no one on earth who can do what the king asks! No king, however great and mighty, has ever asked such a thing of any magician or enchanter or astrologer. [11]What the king asks is too difficult. No one can reveal it to the king except the gods, and they do not live among humans."

[12]This made the king so angry and furious that he ordered the execution of all the wise men of Babylon. [13]So the decree was issued to put the wise men to death, and men were sent to look for Daniel and his friends to put them to death.

[14]When Arioch, the commander of the king's guard, had gone out to put to death the wise men of Babylon, Daniel spoke to him with wisdom and tact. [15]He asked the king's officer, "Why did the king issue such a harsh decree?" Arioch then explained the matter to Daniel. [16]At this, Daniel went in to the king and asked for time, so that he might interpret the dream for him.

[17]Then Daniel returned to his house and explained the matter to his friends Hananiah, Mishael and Azariah. [18]He urged them to plead for mercy from the God of heaven concerning this mystery, so that he and his friends might not be executed with the rest of the wise men of Babylon. [19]During the night the mystery was revealed to Daniel in a vision. Then Daniel praised the God of heaven [20]and said:

"Praise be to the name of God for ever and ever;
    wisdom and power are his.
[21]He changes times and seasons;
    he deposes kings and raises up others.
He gives wisdom to the wise
    and knowledge to the discerning.
[22]He reveals deep and hidden things;
    he knows what lies in darkness,
    and light dwells with him.
[23]I thank and praise you, God of my ancestors:
    You have given me wisdom and power,
you have made known to me what we asked
    of you,
    you have made known to us the dream of
    the king."

Daniel Interprets the Dream

[24]Then Daniel went to Arioch, whom the king had appointed to execute the wise men of Babylon, and said to him, "Do not execute the wise men of Babylon. Take me to the king, and I will interpret his dream for him."

[25]Arioch took Daniel to the king at once and said, "I have found a man among the exiles from Judah who can tell the king what his dream means."

[26]The king asked Daniel (also called Belteshazzar), "Are you able to tell me what I saw in my dream and interpret it?"

[27]Daniel replied, "No wise man, enchanter, magician or diviner can explain to the king the

---

2:11 the gods, and they do not live among humans Daniel is later said to have the spirit of the holy gods (or Holy God) in him (see 4:8–9). A deliberate contrast is being set up between the impotent Babylonian religious figures and the competent Daniel. More specifically, it is a contrast between the powerless Babylonian gods and the all-powerful God of Israel.

2:12 all the wise men of Babylon Furious that they could not retell and explain his dream, Nebuchadnezzar commands that the whole pagan priestly class be killed. Daniel and his friends are included in this group.

2:14 with wisdom and tact Daniel is presented as the ideal Jewish sage, a teacher of wisdom in the Biblical period. In the Jewish tradition, sages (or wise men) were typically measured against the example of Solomon, upon whom God bestowed great wisdom (see 1Ki 3:5–14). Sages were skilled in communication and rhetoric, and their observations and moral teachings generally ran counter to the accepted norms of the day (e.g., Jesus' command to love one's enemies).

2:15 Arioch then explained the matter Daniel is apparently unaware of the king's initial request. It is unclear why he would have been excluded from the original audience of Da 2:2—perhaps the Babylonians (Chaldeans) considered him and his friends too young and inexperienced.

2:17–30 After hearing of the king's harsh edict, Daniel immediately enlists the prayer support of his three friends. God is pleased to honor their request, and the mystery of the king's dream is revealed to Daniel through a vision in the night. Daniel prays and acknowledges God's power, then approaches the king with confidence.

The king questions Daniel—but Daniel is quick to defer all glory to God.

2:18 plead for mercy from the God Not only is Daniel quick to give God the glory for the eventual outcome (see vv. 27–28), he also hurriedly seeks God's help through prayer.

2:21 he deposes kings and raises up others A prominent theme throughout the book: God is sovereign over all nations and their rulers. This is one of the two primary themes of the book of Daniel (see v. 47 and note). The book was written to give hope and instruction to the exiles. However, its court tales and visions also demonstrate God's sovereignty over kings, kingdoms and mysteries.

2:22 reveals deep and hidden things God as revealer is the second major theme of the book (see vv. 21,47). God's revelatory work through Daniel distinguishes him from the other sages in Nebuchadnezzar's service.

2:23 God of my ancestors Similar to refusing the king's food in ch. 1, this phrase connects Daniel to the worship of the God of Abraham, Isaac and Jacob and shows resistance to the Babylonian policy of religious pluralism and idol worship (see 1:8 and note).

2:24 Take me to the king The proper method for approaching the king. In the ancient Near East, a person could not approach the king's throne uninvited. The details are not recorded, but Daniel may have violated protocol in v. 16, similar to Esther (Est 4:10—5:2). If so, he was apparently granted leniency, perhaps due to his position in the king's court.

2:26 Belteshazzar Daniel's Babylonian name. See Da 1:7 and note.

2:27 No wise man Daniel agrees with the Babylonians'

mystery he has asked about, 28but there is a God in heaven who reveals mysteries. He has shown King Nebuchadnezzar what will happen in days to come. Your dream and the visions that passed through your mind as you were lying in bed are these:

29"As Your Majesty was lying there, your mind turned to things to come, and the revealer of mysteries showed you what is going to happen. 30As for me, this mystery has been revealed to me, not because I have greater wisdom than anyone else alive, but so that Your Majesty may know the interpretation and that you may understand what went through your mind.

31"Your Majesty looked, and there before you stood a large statue — an enormous, dazzling statue, awesome in appearance. 32The head of the statue was made of pure gold, its chest and arms of silver, its belly and thighs of bronze, 33its legs of iron, its feet partly of iron and partly of baked clay. 34While you were watching, a rock was cut out, but not by human hands. It struck the statue on its feet of iron and clay and smashed them. 35Then the iron, the clay, the bronze, the silver and the gold were all broken to pieces and became like chaff on a threshing floor in the summer. The wind swept them away without leaving a trace. But the rock that struck the statue became a huge mountain and filled the whole earth.

36"This was the dream, and now we will interpret it to the king. 37Your Majesty, you are the king of kings. The God of heaven has given you dominion and power and might and glory; 38in your hands he has placed all mankind and the beasts of the field and the birds in the sky. Wherever they live, he has made you ruler over them all. You are that head of gold.

39"After you, another kingdom will arise, inferior to yours. Next, a third kingdom, one of bronze, will rule over the whole earth. 40Finally, there will be a fourth kingdom, strong as iron — for iron breaks and smashes everything — and as iron breaks things to pieces, so it will crush and break all the others. 41Just as you saw that the feet and toes were partly of baked clay and partly of iron, so this will be a divided kingdom; yet it will have some of the strength of iron in it, even as you saw iron mixed with clay. 42As the toes were partly iron and partly clay, so this kingdom will be partly strong and partly brittle. 43And just as you saw the iron mixed with baked clay, so the people will be a mixture and will not remain united, any more than iron mixes with clay.

44"In the time of those kings, the God of heaven will set up a kingdom that will never be destroyed, nor will it be left to another people. It will crush all those kingdoms and bring them to an end, but it will itself endure forever. 45This is the meaning of the vision of the rock cut out of a mountain, but not by human hands — a rock that broke the iron, the bronze, the clay, the silver and the gold to pieces.

"The great God has shown the king what will take place in the future. The dream is true and its interpretation is trustworthy."

46Then King Nebuchadnezzar fell prostrate before Daniel and paid him honor and ordered that an offering and incense be presented to him. 47The

---

(Chaldeans') earlier statement. Apart from God's revelation, no man can interpret the dream.

2:28 there is a God Daniel gives the credit to Yahweh, even before he addresses the king's dream. He recognizes that Nebuchadnezzar's request is impossible, but God reveals the meaning of the dream to him through prayer.

2:31–45 With the court formalities out of the way, Daniel proceeds to tell the king his dream and its interpretation. The king saw a massive statue, indicative of his kingdom and the future kingdoms of the world. The contents of the vision come up again in the latter portion of the book (chs. 7–12), where several of Daniel's visions are recorded.

2:31 awesome in appearance The statue was massive and alarming in appearance. It was composed of varying materials — from gold to clay — that represent a progressive decline in value.

2:35 became like chaff In the ancient Near East, harvesters would throw wheat into the air to remove its seed coverings. The wind would carry off the debris while the good grain fell to the ground.

2:38 head of gold Nebuchadnezzar — representative of the Babylonian Empire — is the head of the statue. The fact that he is "gold" may indicate that subsequent kingdoms will be inferior until the kingdom of the Messiah is established (see v. 31 and note).

PART OF STATUE	KINGDOM
Head of Gold	Babylon
Chest and Arms of Silver	Media or Media-Persia
Middle and Thighs of Bronze	Persia or Greece
Legs of Iron, Feet of Iron and Clay	Greece or Rome

2:39 This verse references two kingdoms, and there are two main options for interpreting them. One interpretation sees the first as the Medo-Persian Empire (see 5:28) and the second as the Greek Empire. The other sees the first as the Median Empire and the second as the Persian Empire.

2:40 fourth kingdom This could be either Rome or Greece, depending on how the two kingdoms in v. 39 are interpreted.

2:41 divided kingdom At his death, Alexander's empire was divided among four of his generals.

2:44 will never be destroyed The fifth and final kingdom in Nebuchadnezzar's dream is the kingdom God himself will establish universally. This is the great hope for Daniel's readers.

2:45 rock While this refers to the destruction of the empires represented by the statue, its precise meaning is uncertain.

king said to Daniel, "Surely your God is the God of gods and the Lord of kings and a revealer of mysteries, for you were able to reveal this mystery."

⁴⁸Then the king placed Daniel in a high position and lavished many gifts on him. He made him ruler over the entire province of Babylon and placed him in charge of all its wise men. ⁴⁹Moreover, at Daniel's request the king appointed Shadrach, Meshach and Abednego administrators over the province of Babylon, while Daniel himself remained at the royal court.

The Image of Gold and the Blazing Furnace

3 King Nebuchadnezzar made an image of gold, sixty cubits high and six cubits wide,ᵃ and set it up on the plain of Dura in the province of Babylon. ²He then summoned the satraps, prefects, governors, advisers, treasurers, judges, magistrates and all the other provincial officials to come to the dedication of the image he had set up. ³So the satraps, prefects, governors, advisers, treasurers, judges, magistrates and all the other provincial officials assembled for the dedication of the image that King Nebuchadnezzar had set up, and they stood before it.

⁴Then the herald loudly proclaimed, "Nations and peoples of every language, this is what you are commanded to do: ⁵As soon as you hear the sound of the horn, flute, zither, lyre, harp, pipe and all kinds of music, you must fall down and worship the image of gold that King Nebuchadnezzar has set up. ⁶Whoever does not fall down and worship will immediately be thrown into a blazing furnace."

⁷Therefore, as soon as they heard the sound of the horn, flute, zither, lyre, harp and all kinds of music, all the nations and peoples of every language fell down and worshiped the image of gold that King Nebuchadnezzar had set up.

⁸At this time some astrologersᵇ came forward and denounced the Jews. ⁹They said to King Nebuchadnezzar, "May the king live forever! ¹⁰Your Majesty has issued a decree that everyone who hears the sound of the horn, flute, zither, lyre, harp, pipe and all kinds of music must fall down and worship the image of gold, ¹¹and that whoever does not fall down and worship will be thrown into a blazing furnace. ¹²But there are some Jews whom you have set over the affairs of the province

---

ᵃ 1 That is, about 90 feet high and 9 feet wide or about 27 meters high and 2.7 meters wide   ᵇ 8 Or *Chaldeans*

2:46–49 After Daniel discloses the dream and its meaning, Nebuchadnezzar promotes him and his three friends. Ironically, those who were excluded from the initial audience in v. 2 are set over all the other wise men in positions of leadership. The king's actions in v. 46 symbolize the point of the book: The kings of the earth must bow to the sovereignty of God.

2:46 fell prostrate No king would ever bow down and pay homage to a slave in the ancient Near East. This action would have shocked everyone present.

2:47 Lord of kings and a revealer of mysteries The two primary themes of Daniel (see v. 21 and note; v. 22 and note).

2:48 the entire province of Babylon Daniel was likely made a chief administrator of a region and placed over the council of the wise men.

3:1–7 Following Daniel's successful interpretation of his dream, Nebuchadnezzar erects a massive statue in tribute to himself, his kingdom and his god or gods. In this chapter, Yahweh once again demonstrates his power, revealing to Nebuchadnezzar and his attendants that he is the one true God. See the table "Miracles of the Prophets" on p. 1366.

3:1 made an image of gold Nebuchadnezzar creates a massive statue, showing that his pride trumps his momentary humiliation in 2:46–47. The statue's identity is unknown. Daniel's flattering statement in 2:38 may have prompted Nebuchadnezzar to erect a statue of himself. Alternatively, the image may have been a likeness of his god, Marduk/Bel (see "gods" in vv. 12,14).

3:2 and all the other provincial officials The group is composed of the leaders of the empire. Their veneration of the image was a reflection of their loyalty to the crown. The presence of Persian titles like "satrap" (as opposed

to Babylonian ones) in this list of officials is sometimes taken as evidence suggesting that Daniel might not have been written during the sixth century BC. However, like most OT books, Daniel likely underwent subsequent editing, during which some Persian or Greek loan-words could have been added for clarification.

3:5 horn, flute The names of the instruments come from a period after the Babylonian Empire, but the inclusion of Greek names here may be due to later editing for clarification (see v. 2 and note).

3:6 fall down The Aramaic word used here indicates an act of homage and total subservience. **a blazing furnace** Those who do not prostrate themselves and worship will be given this death penalty. Fire is used for execution throughout the OT. Death by fire was a particularly brutal, painful method of killing; it was employed to invoke horror and command obedience.

3:8–30 The account in the remainder of the chapter stands as an example of faith, religious fidelity and courage. Shadrach, Meshach and Abednego refuse to compromise their convictions by conforming to the religious practices of Babylon; God subsequently brings about a great deliverance.

3:12 Shadrach, Meshach and Abednego These men are representative of a particular group, district or locale, as were the others in attendance. They may have been the only Jews present. Daniel's absence in this narrative is unexplained. However, since the group that gathered for the ceremony was representative of the entire empire, Daniel's three friends may represent his administration (see 2:49). Alternatively, he could have been excused based upon the piety he expressed before Nebuchadnezzar in 2:27–30. **pay no attention** When it came to religious observance, they gave heed to God's commands and proscriptions rather than those of the king.

of Babylon — Shadrach, Meshach and Abednego — who pay no attention to you, Your Majesty. They neither serve your gods nor worship the image of gold you have set up."

[13]Furious with rage, Nebuchadnezzar summoned Shadrach, Meshach and Abednego. So these men were brought before the king, [14]and Nebuchadnezzar said to them, "Is it true, Shadrach, Meshach and Abednego, that you do not serve my gods or worship the image of gold I have set up? [15]Now when you hear the sound of the horn, flute, zither, lyre, harp, pipe and all kinds of music, if you are ready to fall down and worship the image I made, very good. But if you do not worship it, you will be thrown immediately into a blazing furnace. Then what god will be able to rescue you from my hand?"

[16]Shadrach, Meshach and Abednego replied to him, "King Nebuchadnezzar, we do not need to defend ourselves before you in this matter. [17]If we are thrown into the blazing furnace, the God we serve is able to deliver us from it, and he will deliver us[a] from Your Majesty's hand. [18]But even if he does not, we want you to know, Your Majesty, that we will not serve your gods or worship the image of gold you have set up."

[19]Then Nebuchadnezzar was furious with Shadrach, Meshach and Abednego, and his attitude toward them changed. He ordered the furnace heated seven times hotter than usual [20]and commanded some of the strongest soldiers in his army to tie up Shadrach, Meshach and Abednego and throw them into the blazing furnace. [21]So these men, wearing their robes, trousers, turbans and other clothes, were bound and thrown into the blazing furnace. [22]The king's command was so urgent and the furnace so hot that the flames of the fire killed the soldiers who took up Shadrach, Meshach and Abednego, [23]and these three men, firmly tied, fell into the blazing furnace.

[24]Then King Nebuchadnezzar leaped to his feet in amazement and asked his advisers, "Weren't there three men that we tied up and threw into the fire?"

They replied, "Certainly, Your Majesty."

[25]He said, "Look! I see four men walking around in the fire, unbound and unharmed, and the fourth looks like a son of the gods."

[26]Nebuchadnezzar then approached the opening of the blazing furnace and shouted, "Shadrach, Meshach and Abednego, servants of the Most High God, come out! Come here!"

So Shadrach, Meshach and Abednego came out of the fire, [27]and the satraps, prefects, governors and royal advisers crowded around them. They saw that the fire had not harmed their bodies, nor was a hair of their heads singed; their robes were not scorched, and there was no smell of fire on them.

[28]Then Nebuchadnezzar said, "Praise be to the God of Shadrach, Meshach and Abednego, who has sent his angel and rescued his servants! They trusted in him and defied the king's command and were willing to give up their lives rather than serve or worship any god except their own God. [29]Therefore I decree that the people of any nation or language who say anything against the God of Shadrach, Meshach and Abednego be cut into pieces and their houses be turned into piles of rubble, for no other god can save in this way."

[30]Then the king promoted Shadrach, Meshach and Abednego in the province of Babylon.

Nebuchadnezzar's Dream of a Tree

4[b] King Nebuchadnezzar,

To the nations and peoples of every language, who live in all the earth:

---

[a] 17 Or *If the God we serve is able to deliver us, then he will deliver us from the blazing furnace and*   [b] In Aramaic texts 4:1-3 is numbered 3:31-33, and 4:4-37 is numbered 4:1-34.

3:15 what god Reminiscent of Pharaoh's response in Ex 5:2. Nebuchadnezzar underestimates the power of Israel's God, despite having had firsthand experience of it (see Da 2).

3:17 If we are thrown into the blazing furnace, the God we serve is able Even if death is the consequence of noncompliance, they will still hold fast to their religious commitments and trust God for deliverance.

3:18 But even if he does not If God elects not to deliver them from death, they will not regret their decision to stand firm.

3:19 seven times An idiomatic Aramaic phrase expressing the king's desire to have the furnace as hot as possible.

3:20 strongest soldiers This designation is applied to the top soldiers in the king's employ (e.g., David's mighty men in 2Sa 23:8–39).

3:22 killed the soldiers In his rage, Nebuchadnezzar thinks nothing of the lives of some of his best soldiers.

3:23 fell The same Aramaic word here is also used in Da 3:6 (see note on v. 6) to indicate an act of worship.

The three Hebrew youths fall into the fire because they would not bow before the image.

3:25 four men Set in opposition to the deliberate specification of three men in v. 23. **a son of the gods** The Aramaic phrase here for "son of the gods" is akin to the Hebrew phrase "son of God/the gods," which is generally a reference to spiritual beings sent from God. The man was a divine being sent to render service to the three Hebrew youths. The fourth man in the furnace has been variously identified as an unidentified angel, Gabriel, the preincarnate Christ or God himself.

3:26 Most High God Similar to his declaration to Daniel in 2:47 that his God is above all other gods. The king realizes that not even his gods could have performed such a feat.

3:28 trusted in him Demonstrates the point of this passage: Those who trust in Yahweh and do not conform to the religious standards of pagan kings will be delivered.

3:29 Therefore I decree Rulers often issued decrees that protected various religious groups within their jurisdiction.

May you prosper greatly!

²It is my pleasure to tell you about the miraculous signs and wonders that the Most High God has performed for me.

³How great are his signs,
how mighty his wonders!
His kingdom is an eternal kingdom;
his dominion endures from
generation to generation.

⁴I, Nebuchadnezzar, was at home in my palace, contented and prosperous. ⁵I had a dream that made me afraid. As I was lying in bed, the images and visions that passed through my mind terrified me. ⁶So I commanded that all the wise men of Babylon be brought before me to interpret the dream for me. ⁷When the magicians, enchanters, astrologers*ᵃ* and diviners came, I told them the dream, but they could not interpret it for me. ⁸Finally, Daniel came into my presence and I told him the dream. (He is called Belteshazzar, after the name of my god, and the spirit of the holy gods is in him.)

⁹I said, "Belteshazzar, chief of the magicians, I know that the spirit of the holy gods is in you, and no mystery is too difficult for you. Here is my dream; interpret it for me. ¹⁰These are the visions I saw while lying in bed: I looked, and there before me stood a tree in the middle of the land. Its height was enormous. ¹¹The tree grew large and strong and its top touched the sky; it was visible to the ends of the earth. ¹²Its leaves were beautiful, its fruit abundant, and on it was food for all. Under it the wild animals found shelter, and the birds lived in its branches; from it every creature was fed.

¹³"In the visions I saw while lying in bed, I looked, and there before me was a holy one, a messenger,ᵇ coming down from heaven. ¹⁴He called in a loud voice: 'Cut down the tree and trim off its branches; strip off its leaves and scatter its fruit. Let the animals flee from under it and the birds from its branches. ¹⁵But let the stump and its roots, bound with iron and bronze, remain in the ground, in the grass of the field.

"'Let him be drenched with the dew of heaven, and let him live with the animals among the plants of the earth. ¹⁶Let his mind be changed from that of a man and let him be given the mind of an animal, till seven timesᶜ pass by for him.

¹⁷"'The decision is announced by messengers, the holy ones declare the verdict, so that the living may know that the Most High is sovereign over all kingdoms on earth and gives them to anyone he wishes and sets over them the lowliest of people.'

ᵃ 7 Or *Chaldeans*   ᵇ 13 Or *watchman*; also in verses 17 and 23
ᶜ 16 Or *years*; also in verses 23, 25 and 32

4:1–37 Chapter 4 is written in the form of a letter. Written primarily from the first-person perspective of Nebuchadnezzar, ch. 4 was to be distributed throughout the world as a testimony to the power of the Most High God.

4:1 nations and peoples of every language Representative of the whole empire (see 3:4,7,12 and note; 3:29).

4:2 signs and wonders On three occasions, the king witnessed the miraculous power of Israel's God.

4:3 How great are his signs Expressions of praise are a common feature in neo-Babylonian and Persian letters. This phrase parallels the Psalms and NT letters.

4:4–18 Nebuchadnezzar recounts the circumstances surrounding his dream. After yet another failed attempt at explanation by the king's advisors, he calls for Daniel—whose success is guaranteed by Yahweh.

4:4 was at home in my palace, contented In contrast to the Jewish captives. Nebuchadnezzar receives a vision of condemnation while enjoying the opulence and splendor of palace life.

4:5 I had a dream Nebuchadnezzar's second dream.

4:6 all the wise men of Babylon Does not include Daniel—he will be summoned later. As is typical in court tales, the contrast between the protagonist and the antagonists must be established. **to interpret** The king reveals his dream to the wise men—unlike 2:2, where he demands they recount it.

4:7 they could not interpret it The sages' failure is typical; only Daniel—through God's assistance—can interpret dreams.

4:8 spirit of the holy gods The Aramaic phrase here is probably meant to include both the gods of Babylon and Daniel's God (see vv. 9,18; 5:11,14). The phrase has been variously interpreted as "Spirit of the Holy God," "Holy Spirit" or "spirit of the holy gods." Since the Babylonians had a very limited understanding of Israel's God—and their religion was polytheistic—"spirit of the holy gods" is appropriate. Nebuchadnezzar comes to recognize the superiority of Israel's God over the gods of Babylon.

4:10 tree Tree imagery was common in the ancient Near East. Parallels can be seen with the tree of Eze 31. The interpretation of the vision and its symbols occurs in Da 4:20–27.

4:11 the ends of the earth The tree was visible globally.

4:12 food for all Not only was it visible throughout the earth, it also provided for the whole world.

4:13 a messenger The Aramaic term used here is a term for a watchman (or watcher) related to a verb for being awake and alert. In Second Temple Judaism, the "Watchers" were fallen angels (see 1 Enoch 1–36). The being here is identified as a "holy one" coming down from heaven, indicating this figure is an angel acting as a messenger of Yahweh.

4:14 Cut down The angel decrees that the tree be dismantled. Its power and glory are to be removed, and those who are reliant on it are encouraged to flee from its presence.

4:16 times The Aramaic wording here is ambiguous about how long this time period is.

4:17 announced by messengers The members of

¹⁸"This is the dream that I, King Nebuchadnezzar, had. Now, Belteshazzar, tell me what it means, for none of the wise men in my kingdom can interpret it for me. But you can, because the spirit of the holy gods is in you."

Daniel Interprets the Dream

¹⁹Then Daniel (also called Belteshazzar) was greatly perplexed for a time, and his thoughts terrified him. So the king said, "Belteshazzar, do not let the dream or its meaning alarm you."

Belteshazzar answered, "My lord, if only the dream applied to your enemies and its meaning to your adversaries! ²⁰The tree you saw, which grew large and strong, with its top touching the sky, visible to the whole earth, ²¹with beautiful leaves and abundant fruit, providing food for all, giving shelter to the wild animals, and having nesting places in its branches for the birds — ²²Your Majesty, you are that tree! You have become great and strong; your greatness has grown until it reaches the sky, and your dominion extends to distant parts of the earth.

²³"Your Majesty saw a holy one, a messenger, coming down from heaven and saying, 'Cut down the tree and destroy it, but leave the stump, bound with iron and bronze, in the grass of the field, while its roots remain in the ground. Let him be drenched with the dew of heaven; let him live with the wild animals, until seven times pass by for him.'

²⁴"This is the interpretation, Your Majesty, and this is the decree the Most High has issued against my lord the king: ²⁵You will be driven away from people and will live with the wild animals; you will eat grass like the ox and be drenched with the dew of heaven. Seven times will pass by for you until you acknowledge that the Most High is sovereign over all kingdoms on earth and gives them to anyone he wishes. ²⁶The command to leave the stump of the tree with its roots means that your kingdom will be restored to you when you acknowledge that Heaven rules. ²⁷Therefore, Your Majesty, be pleased to accept my advice: Renounce your sins by doing what is right, and your wickedness by being kind to the oppressed. It may be that then your prosperity will continue."

The Dream Is Fulfilled

²⁸All this happened to King Nebuchadnezzar. ²⁹Twelve months later, as the king was walking on the roof of the royal palace of Babylon, ³⁰he said, "Is not this the great Babylon I have built as the royal residence, by my mighty power and for the glory of my majesty?"

³¹Even as the words were on his lips, a voice came from heaven, "This is what is decreed for you, King Nebuchadnezzar: Your royal authority has been taken from you. ³²You will be driven away from people and will live with the wild animals; you will eat grass like the ox. Seven times will pass by for you until you acknowledge that the Most High is sovereign over all kingdoms on earth and gives them to anyone he wishes."

³³Immediately what had been said about Nebuchadnezzar was fulfilled. He was driven away from people and ate grass like the ox. His body was drenched with the dew of heaven until his hair grew like the feathers of an eagle and his nails like the claws of a bird.

God's heavenly host participate in God's rule by carrying out God's decree (v. 24). **the Most High** One of two primary themes in Daniel (see note on 2:47). This is the lesson the king failed to learn from his first two divine encounters.

4:19–27 Reluctantly, Daniel interprets Nebuchadnezzar's vision. Although it will ultimately result in good, he is hesitant and fearful to pass judgment on the king.

4:19 terrified Daniel has to deliver a message of impending disaster to the world's most powerful king—fear is a natural response. **to your adversaries** Distressed by the dream's meaning, Daniel wishes it applied to someone else.

4:20 its top touching the sky Refers to the king's rebellious arrogance; pride was the reason for his temporary downfall. This phrase reflects the language of Ge 11:4 and Isa 14:13.

4:24 decree The decree originates from the Most High, but the heavenly messenger (Da 4:13) carries out the verdict.

4:25 driven away from people Daniel tells Nebuchadnezzar that he will lose his senses (v. 16) and become like an animal for a period of seven "times" (probably seven years). He will no longer enjoy the luxuries of the palace, but will live with animals, experiencing the same diet and exposure to the elements as they do. Through this mental and physical banishment, the king must learn who is truly sovereign—God.

4:27 your prosperity will continue Daniel instructs the king to atone for his sins by pursuing righteousness and mercy. Although the decree is firm, he sees the possibility of postponing its fulfillment through repentance.

4:28–33 That which was decreed by God and carried out by the angel finally came to pass. Nebuchadnezzar, the pride of Babylon, was reduced to a mere animal and forced to live outside like a beast.

4:30 by my mighty power If Nebuchadnezzar did repent (see v. 29), he returned to his former prideful disposition. The king is surveying his accomplishments and boasting about them.

4:31 Even as the words were on his lips Nebuchadnezzar barely finishes his thought before the judgment is imposed, indicating the swift nature of God's chastisement.

[34] At the end of that time, I, Nebuchadnezzar, raised my eyes toward heaven, and my sanity was restored. Then I praised the Most High; I honored and glorified him who lives forever.

His dominion is an eternal dominion;
    his kingdom endures from generation to
        generation.
[35] All the peoples of the earth
    are regarded as nothing.
He does as he pleases
    with the powers of heaven
    and the peoples of the earth.
No one can hold back his hand
    or say to him: "What have you done?"

[36] At the same time that my sanity was restored, my honor and splendor were returned to me for the glory of my kingdom. My advisers and nobles sought me out, and I was restored to my throne and became even greater than before. [37] Now I, Nebuchadnezzar, praise and exalt and glorify the King of heaven, because everything he does is right and all his ways are just. And those who walk in pride he is able to humble.

The Writing on the Wall

5 King Belshazzar gave a great banquet for a thousand of his nobles and drank wine with them. [2] While Belshazzar was drinking his wine,

he gave orders to bring in the gold and silver goblets that Nebuchadnezzar his father[a] had taken from the temple in Jerusalem, so that the king and his nobles, his wives and his concubines might drink from them. [3] So they brought in the gold goblets that had been taken from the temple of God in Jerusalem, and the king and his nobles, his wives and his concubines drank from them. [4] As they drank the wine, they praised the gods of gold and silver, of bronze, iron, wood and stone.

[5] Suddenly the fingers of a human hand appeared and wrote on the plaster of the wall, near the lampstand in the royal palace. The king watched the hand as it wrote. [6] His face turned pale and he was so frightened that his legs became weak and his knees were knocking.

[7] The king summoned the enchanters, astrologers[b] and diviners. Then he said to these wise men of Babylon, "Whoever reads this writing and tells me what it means will be clothed in purple and have a gold chain placed around his neck, and he will be made the third highest ruler in the kingdom."

[8] Then all the king's wise men came in, but they could not read the writing or tell the king what it meant. [9] So King Belshazzar became even more terrified and his face grew more pale. His nobles were baffled.

[10] The queen,[c] hearing the voices of the king and his nobles, came into the banquet hall. "May

---

[a] 2 Or *ancestor*; or *predecessor*; also in verses 11, 13 and 18   [b] 7 Or *Chaldeans*; also in verse 11   [c] 10 Or *queen mother*

4:34–37 This final section is the impetus for the king's letter: The God of the Jews demonstrated his sovereignty and power to Nebuchadnezzar in judgment, but he graciously restored him after a period of humiliation.

4:34 I praised The point of the king's insanity and banishment (see v. 25) was to elicit the response of vv. 34–35.
4:36 became even greater than before In comparable stories from antiquity, the protagonist is often elevated to a higher state of blessedness or privilege (e.g., Job 42:10,12).

5:1–12 Nebuchadnezzar fades from the storyline at the close of ch. 4, and a new king—Belshazzar (not to be confused with "Belteshazzar," Daniel's Babylonian name)—comes onto the scene. In the first part of ch. 5, a hand appears and writes a cryptic message on the wall of the banqueting hall after Belshazzar acts irreverently toward Israel's God. When the Babylonian wise men once again fail to be of use, the queen mother informs Belshazzar of a certain man that previously handled such matters—Daniel.

5:1 King Belshazzar The son of King Nabonidus and crown prince of Babylon. King Nabonidus spent 10 years in Teima and set Belshazzar over the affairs of Babylon while he was gone. Belshazzar served as *de facto* king until the threat of impending invasion brought Nabonidus back. Until the discovery of additional ancient Babylonian records like The Babylonian Chronicles—which are tablets that record the history of Babylon—the depiction of

Belshazzar as the last king of Babylon was sometimes used as an example of Daniel's historical inaccuracy. The Babylonian texts revealed that Nabonidus had made his son Belshazzar co-regent and ruler of Babylon. See the infographic "The Babylonian Chronicles" on p. 605.
5:2 While Belshazzar was drinking his wine Indicates drunkenness. Belshazzar acts ignorantly due to his intoxication. **his father** Nebuchadnezzar was Belshazzar's "father" as the founder of their empire and his predecessor as king. It is also possible that his father Nabonidus had married a daughter of Nebuchadnezzar to legitimize his claim to the throne—making Nebuchadnezzar his grandfather. **might drink from them** A disrespectful act. In ancient Near Eastern warfare, placing vessels in the temple of one's god—as Nebuchadnezzar did—was a sign of defeat over an enemy (see 1:2). But to use them in revelry was sacrilegious; it would demand God's immediate retribution.
5:5 fingers of a human hand Details about the detached hand are unknown; it stands as one of the most eerie images in the Bible. It may allude to Ex 8:19; 31:18, and therefore represent the hand of God.
5:6 His face turned pale This verse describes the physical responses of the king as terror gripped him. **he was so frightened** Similar to Nebuchadnezzar's initial reaction to his dreams in Da 2:1.
5:7 he will be made the third highest ruler in the kingdom He would rule behind Nabonidus and the crown prince, Belshazzar (see v. 1 and note).
5:10 The queen Her familiarity with the events of a

the king live forever!" she said. "Don't be alarmed! Don't look so pale! ¹¹There is a man in your kingdom who has the spirit of the holy gods in him. In the time of your father he was found to have insight and intelligence and wisdom like that of the gods. Your father, King Nebuchadnezzar, appointed him chief of the magicians, enchanters, astrologers and diviners. ¹²He did this because Daniel, whom the king called Belteshazzar, was found to have a keen mind and knowledge and understanding, and also the ability to interpret dreams, explain riddles and solve difficult problems. Call for Daniel, and he will tell you what the writing means."

¹³So Daniel was brought before the king, and the king said to him, "Are you Daniel, one of the exiles my father the king brought from Judah? ¹⁴I have heard that the spirit of the gods is in you and that you have insight, intelligence and outstanding wisdom. ¹⁵The wise men and enchanters were brought before me to read this writing and tell me what it means, but they could not explain it. ¹⁶Now I have heard that you are able to give interpretations and to solve difficult problems. If you can read this writing and tell me what it means, you will be clothed in purple and have a gold chain placed around your neck, and you will be made the third highest ruler in the kingdom."

¹⁷Then Daniel answered the king, "You may keep your gifts for yourself and give your rewards to someone else. Nevertheless, I will read the writing for the king and tell him what it means.

¹⁸"Your Majesty, the Most High God gave your father Nebuchadnezzar sovereignty and greatness and glory and splendor. ¹⁹Because of the high position he gave him, all the nations and peoples of every language dreaded and feared him. Those the king wanted to put to death, he put to death; those he wanted to spare, he spared; those he wanted to promote, he promoted; and those he wanted to humble, he humbled. ²⁰But when his heart became arrogant and hardened with pride, he was deposed from his royal throne and stripped of his glory. ²¹He was driven away from people and given the mind of an animal; he lived with the wild donkeys and ate grass like the ox; and his body was drenched with the dew of heaven, until he acknowledged that the Most High God is sovereign over all kingdoms on earth and sets over them anyone he wishes.

²²"But you, Belshazzar, his son,[a] have not humbled yourself, though you knew all this. ²³Instead, you have set yourself up against the Lord of heaven. You had the goblets from his temple brought to you, and you and your nobles, your wives and your concubines drank wine from them. You praised the gods of silver and gold, of bronze, iron, wood and stone, which cannot see or hear or understand. But you did not honor the God who holds in his hand your life and all your ways. ²⁴Therefore he sent the hand that wrote the inscription.

²⁵"This is the inscription that was written:

MENE, MENE, TEKEL, PARSIN

²⁶"Here is what these words mean:

Mene[b]: God has numbered the days of your reign and brought it to an end.
²⁷Tekel[c]: You have been weighed on the scales and found wanting.

---

[a] 22 Or descendant; or successor   [b] 26 Mene can mean numbered or mina (a unit of money).   [c] 27 Tekel can mean weighed or shekel.

previous king suggests that she is likely the queen mother, possibly a daughter of Nebuchadnezzar (see note on v. 2).

5:11 the spirit of the holy gods See 4:8 and note.
Your father, King Nebuchadnezzar The emphasis upon the royalty of Belshazzar's father (or predecessor; see v. 2 and note) prompts him to act similarly.

5:12 Belteshazzar Daniel's court name is invoked because of its meaning ("Bel protect the prince," see 1:7 and note). **ability to interpret dreams, explain riddles and solve difficult problems** The queen extends Daniel's skills beyond merely dream interpretation; she reestablishes him as a valuable advisor.

5:13–31 Daniel enters the narrative after having received an introduction from the queen mother. Unlike the other court tales, Daniel rebukes the king, interprets the writing, pronounces the judgment, and leaves. God's retribution on the sacrilege of Belshazzar is dealt with swiftly.

5:13 was brought Following accepted protocol (see 2:16; 2:24 and note).

5:17 You may keep your gifts for yourself In contrast to his deferential politeness toward Nebuchadnezzar, Daniel rebukes Belshazzar. While Nebuchadnezzar repented from his folly and recognized God's supremacy, Belshazzar will have no such opportunity—his offenses are so significant that God chooses to deal with him swiftly and finally.

5:18 Most High God Daniel affirms the superiority of his God over the Babylonian gods (see 3:26 and note).

5:22 have not humbled yourself Like Nebuchadnezzar, pride is the ultimate cause of Belshazzar's downfall. Unlike Nebuchadnezzar, however, Belshazzar will not be restored (see note on v. 17). **you knew all this** Though Belshazzar apparently knew of this incident, he was unaware that Daniel—Nebuchadnezzar's most trusted advisor—had informed him of his fate.

5:25 MENE, MENE, TEKEL, PARSIN The enigmatic message is "a mina, a mina, a shekel, and two halves" (either a half-mina or a half-shekel) and refers to units of measure. The related verbal forms (used in vv. 26–28) mean "to number, to weigh, to divide," respectively. The puzzle is the significance of the words for Belshazzar and his guests. Daniel explains the message by playing on the verbal meanings: being numbered, being weighed, being divided.

5:26 what these words mean God has appraised Belshazzar and found him to be an insufficient ruler. As a result, he will strip the kingdom from him and divide it among the Medes and Persians.

28 *Peres*ᵃ: Your kingdom is divided and given to the Medes and Persians."

29 Then at Belshazzar's command, Daniel was clothed in purple, a gold chain was placed around his neck, and he was proclaimed the third highest ruler in the kingdom.

30 That very night Belshazzar, king of the Babylonians,ᵇ was slain, 31 and Darius the Mede took over the kingdom, at the age of sixty-two.ᶜ

Daniel in the Den of Lions

6 ᵈ It pleased Darius to appoint 120 satraps to rule throughout the kingdom, 2 with three administrators over them, one of whom was Daniel. The satraps were made accountable to them so that the king might not suffer loss. 3 Now Daniel so distinguished himself among the administrators and the satraps by his exceptional qualities that the king planned to set him over the whole kingdom. 4 At this, the administrators and the satraps tried to find grounds for charges against Daniel in his conduct of government affairs, but they were unable to do so. They could find no corruption in him, because he was trustworthy and neither corrupt nor negligent. 5 Finally these men said, "We will never find any basis for charges against this man Daniel unless it has something to do with the law of his God."

6 So these administrators and satraps went as a group to the king and said: "May King Darius live forever! 7 The royal administrators, prefects, satraps, advisers and governors have all agreed that the king should issue an edict and enforce the decree that anyone who prays to any god or human being during the next thirty days, except to you, Your Majesty, shall be thrown into the lions'

den. 8 Now, Your Majesty, issue the decree and put it in writing so that it cannot be altered — in accordance with the law of the Medes and Persians, which cannot be repealed." 9 So King Darius put the decree in writing.

10 Now when Daniel learned that the decree had been published, he went home to his upstairs room where the windows opened toward Jerusalem. Three times a day he got down on his knees and prayed, giving thanks to his God, just as he had done before. 11 Then these men went as a group and found Daniel praying and asking God for help. 12 So they went to the king and spoke to him about his royal decree: "Did you not publish a decree that during the next thirty days anyone who prays to any god or human being except to you, Your Majesty, would be thrown into the lions' den?"

The king answered, "The decree stands — in accordance with the law of the Medes and Persians, which cannot be repealed."

13 Then they said to the king, "Daniel, who is one of the exiles from Judah, pays no attention to you, Your Majesty, or to the decree you put in writing. He still prays three times a day." 14 When the king heard this, he was greatly distressed; he was determined to rescue Daniel and made every effort until sundown to save him.

15 Then the men went as a group to King Darius and said to him, "Remember, Your Majesty, that according to the law of the Medes and Persians no decree or edict that the king issues can be changed."

ᵃ 28 *Peres* (the singular of *Parsin*) can mean *divided* or *Persia* or *a half mina* or *a half shekel.*   ᵇ 30 Or *Chaldeans*   ᶜ 31 In Aramaic texts this verse (5:31) is numbered 6:1.   ᵈ In Aramaic texts 6:1-28 is numbered 6:2-29.

5:29 at Belshazzar's command Despite the unfavorable interpretation, Belshazzar promotes Daniel as promised (see v. 16).

5:31 Darius The identity of this king is unknown. Most likely, Darius the Mede can be equated with Gubaru, the governor of Babylon appointed by Cyrus. Gubaru ruled Babylon for 14 years (539–525 BC) and is mentioned frequently in cuneiform tablets as the supreme authority in Babylonia for crimes committed — unlike Cyrus or Cambyses, who are never mentioned in the same legal capacity.

6:1–28 In ch. 6, Darius the Mede is ruler of Babylon. Due to the cunning of some jealous courtiers, Darius becomes trapped by his own command and is forced to throw Daniel, his most trusted advisor, into a den of lions. In his sovereignty, God spares Daniel's life, and Darius restores him to his position. Daniel's enemies meet their demise at the mouths of the lions.

6:1 Darius Darius the Mede might have been in charge only of Babylonia, not the entire Persian empire. See note on 5:31. **120 satraps** These government officials were responsible for collecting tribute and maintaining security throughout the kingdom.

6:4 they were unable to do so Daniel maintained his

integrity in every facet of life. Darius' jealous counselors attempt to discredit Daniel, but he lives blamelessly before God. Daniel is upheld as the model of virtue among Jewish sages (see 2:14 and note). His character served as the supreme example of fidelity and excellence for exiled Jews or those living under foreign governments.

6:5 with the law of his God In order to find fault with Daniel, his opponents have to make his religion temporarily illegal.

6:7 the lions' den Lions were placed in a large pit, which was then sealed with a rock.

6:8 the law of the Medes and Persians, which cannot be repealed A written legal decree was considered permanent or unalterable (see Est 1:19; 8:8).

6:10 Now when Daniel learned Daniel chooses to obey God's command to worship him alone (see Ex 20:3) over the king's edict.

6:13 one of the exiles from Judah Ethnic distinction was commonplace; this is to be understood as an insult (see Da 2:25; 5:13). Their envy is partly due to his being a foreigner and an exile.

6:14 he was greatly distressed Darius realizes that he has been tricked by his advisors. **made every effort until sundown** Darius pursues extreme measures in an effort to free Daniel.

16So the king gave the order, and they brought Daniel and threw him into the lions' den. The king said to Daniel, "May your God, whom you serve continually, rescue you!"

17A stone was brought and placed over the mouth of the den, and the king sealed it with his own signet ring and with the rings of his nobles, so that Daniel's situation might not be changed. 18Then the king returned to his palace and spent the night without eating and without any entertainment being brought to him. And he could not sleep.

19At the first light of dawn, the king got up and hurried to the lions' den. 20When he came near the den, he called to Daniel in an anguished voice, "Daniel, servant of the living God, has your God, whom you serve continually, been able to rescue you from the lions?"

21Daniel answered, "May the king live forever! 22My God sent his angel, and he shut the mouths of the lions. They have not hurt me, because I was found innocent in his sight. Nor have I ever done any wrong before you, Your Majesty."

23The king was overjoyed and gave orders to lift Daniel out of the den. And when Daniel was lifted from the den, no wound was found on him, because he had trusted in his God.

24At the king's command, the men who had falsely accused Daniel were brought in and thrown into the lions' den, along with their wives and children. And before they reached the floor of the den, the lions overpowered them and crushed all their bones.

25Then King Darius wrote to all the nations and peoples of every language in all the earth:

"May you prosper greatly!

26"I issue a decree that in every part of my kingdom people must fear and reverence the God of Daniel.

"For he is the living God
   and he endures forever;
his kingdom will not be destroyed,
   his dominion will never end.
27He rescues and he saves;
   he performs signs and wonders
   in the heavens and on the earth.
He has rescued Daniel
   from the power of the lions."

28So Daniel prospered during the reign of Darius and the reign of Cyrus[a] the Persian.

Daniel's Dream of Four Beasts

7 In the first year of Belshazzar king of Babylon, Daniel had a dream, and visions passed through his mind as he was lying in bed. He wrote down the substance of his dream.

2Daniel said: "In my vision at night I looked, and there before me were the four winds of heaven churning up the great sea. 3Four great beasts, each different from the others, came up out of the sea.

4"The first was like a lion, and it had the wings of an eagle. I watched until its wings were torn off

---

a 28 Or *Darius, that is, the reign of Cyrus*

6:16 your God The king calls upon Daniel's God rather than his own.

6:17 sealed it with his own signet ring A broken seal would alert the authorities that the den had been opened during the night. The seal also testified to the issuance, authority and approval of the decree.

6:20 an anguished voice The king was deeply troubled at the prospect of killing a righteous man and losing his most trusted advisor.

6:22 My God sent his angel We are given no details about what took place in the den, only that God sent his angel to close the lions' mouths.

6:23 trusted in his God When faced with the pressure of religious conformity in a foreign land, Daniel acted righteously and God delivered him (see 3:28).

6:24 men who had falsely accused Daniel In addition to plotting against Daniel, the men lied to the king and tricked him into condemning his most trusted advisor (v. 7). **thrown into the lions' den, along with their wives and children** The king also kills the families of those who accused Daniel. The OT contains both the concept of individual responsibility and corporate guilt. In this instance, corporate guilt links the fate of the entire family to the activity of the family leader, the father. Darius chooses to rid his empire of the conspirators and those related to them. In addition to eliminating the guilty parties, this would also prevent future retaliation against the throne by children whose fathers had been executed by royal decree. **the lions overpowered them** Lest anyone deny the miraculous power of Daniel's God, the narrator is quick to show the ferocity and tenacious appetite of the lions on the same day Daniel was removed from the den. He was not spared on account of the lions' lack of hunger; he was spared because of God's intervention.

6:28 Daniel prospered This verse bookends 1:21 and closes out the narrative portion of Daniel. The connection to Cyrus from 1:21 may suggest that the court narratives found in chs. 1–6 originally existed independently of the record of the visions in chs. 7–12. Eventually, later editors may have combined various scriptural traditions related to Daniel. **Cyrus** The same Cyrus who decreed the Jews could return home from exile in 538 BC (see Ezr 1:1–4). See the infographic "The Cyrus Cylinder" on p. 714.

7:1–8 While chs. 1–6 are narrative, chs. 7–12 are categorized as apocalyptic literature. The remainder of the book presents a series of Daniel's visions and their interpretations. The future focus of Daniel's visions, emphasizing events surrounding the persecution of the Jews by Antiochus IV Epiphanes in the second century BC, is a key part of the debate over when Daniel was written. On one hand, it is unremarkable that an inspired prophet could provide testimony of events yet to come. On the other hand, the level of historical detail of some of the visions, especially ch. 11, is unusual for Biblical prophecy.

and it was lifted from the ground so that it stood on two feet like a human being, and the mind of a human was given to it.

⁵"And there before me was a second beast, which looked like a bear. It was raised up on one of its sides, and it had three ribs in its mouth between its teeth. It was told, 'Get up and eat your fill of flesh!'

⁶"After that, I looked, and there before me was another beast, one that looked like a leopard. And on its back it had four wings like those of a bird. This beast had four heads, and it was given authority to rule.

⁷"After that, in my vision at night I looked, and there before me was a fourth beast — terrifying and frightening and very powerful. It had large iron teeth; it crushed and devoured its victims and trampled underfoot whatever was left. It was different from all the former beasts, and it had ten horns.

⁸"While I was thinking about the horns, there before me was another horn, a little one, which came up among them; and three of the first horns were uprooted before it. This horn had eyes like the eyes of a human being and a mouth that spoke boastfully.

⁹"As I looked,

"thrones were set in place,
    and the Ancient of Days took his seat.
His clothing was as white as snow;
    the hair of his head was white like wool.
His throne was flaming with fire,
    and its wheels were all ablaze.
¹⁰ A river of fire was flowing,
    coming out from before him.

Daniel 7:1-8

ANTIOCHUS
Antiochus is a villainous figure in Jewish history. After coming to power as a king of the Greek Seleucid Empire that grew out of Alexander's conquests, he attacked Jerusalem on the Sabbath. He killed the males of the city and carried the women and children into slavery. Antiochus also outlawed Jewish customs and practices and profaned the temple by dedicating it to Zeus. The dedicatory sacrifice in 167 BC is referred to as the abomination that causes desolation in Da 11:31; 12:11 and Mk 13:14. His terrorizing of the Jews prompted the Maccabee Revolt in 166–160 BC (compare 1 Maccabees 1:54).

7:1 first year of Belshazzar Approximately 550 BC. See 5:1 and note.
7:2 In my vision at night I looked One major difference between the narratives and the visions is that Daniel is mentioned in third-person voice in the stories, but the visions are told from a first-person perspective. **four winds of heaven** Indicative of the four points on a compass: north, south, east and west. The imagery is apparently borrowed from Zec 6:5–7. **the great sea** The sea is often used throughout the Hebrew Bible as a symbol of turmoil and chaos.
7:3 Four great beasts This first vision recasts the components of the statue from Nebuchadnezzar's vision in ch. 2 as four beasts, symbolizing four kingdoms. As in ch. 2, the four kingdoms can be interpreted as either Babylon, Media, Persia and Greece, or Babylon, Media-Persia, Greece and Rome. See note on 2:31–45.

BEASTS	KINGDOMS FROM DANIEL 2
Lion with Eagle's Wings	Babylon, head of Gold
Bear	Media (or Media-Persia), Chest and Arms of Silver
Leopard with Four Wings and Heads	Persia (or Greece), Middle and Thighs of Bronze
Ten-horned Beast with Iron Teeth	Greece (or Rome), Legs and Feet of Iron and Clay

7:4 first was like a lion Corresponds to the head of gold in 2:32,37–38, representing Babylon or Nebuchadnezzar.
7:5 a second beast Corresponds to the chest and arms of silver in 2:32,39 and could refer to the Median Empire. Alternatively, this may be a combination of two empires (Medo-Persia). Under the Medo-Persia, Greece and Rome view, distinctions are made between the "horn" imagery in ch. 7 and 8. Also, under this view, the material of the vision is often applied to the last days of the church rather than the anticipated conclusion of persecution suffered by the Jews (see 8:17 and note). **It was raised up on one of its sides** May indicate some sort of physical anomaly or posture — the beast was raised up on its hind feet in a fighting position. If this beast represents the combined Medo-Persian Empire, the phrase may indicate the strength of the Persians over the Medes. **it had three ribs** May refer to tusks or fangs. This makes sense in light of the command to arise and devour.
7:6 like a leopard Corresponds to the middle and thighs of bronze in 2:32,39.
7:7 a fourth beast — terrifying and frightening Corresponds to the legs and feet in 2:33,40–43. Most likely a reference to Greece, though Rome is also possible (see 2:40 and note). **ten horns** Identified as 10 kings (see v. 24 and note). Horns symbolized might and power in antiquity (e.g., Dt 33:17; 2Sa 22:3; Ps 18:2; Zec 1:18–21; compare 1 Enoch 90:9; and the Rule of Blessings [1QSb] 5.26 from the Dead Sea Scrolls).
7:8 another horn, a little one The descriptor "little" is derogatory. The close recounting of the deeds of Antiochus IV throughout the remaining visions suggests that the little horn likely refers to him. However, if Rome is the fourth beast, this horn may alternatively represent the antichrist.

7:9–12 The description of the beasts and the little horn prompts the arrival of the Ancient of Days. He passes judgment and makes way for "one like a son of man" (7:13).
7:9 Ancient of Days A reference to God. Compare Job 36:26. **clothing was as white as snow** The typical color of the clothing of heavenly beings (see Mt 28:3; Mk 9:2–3; Rev 3:5).
7:10 The court was seated God sitting as judge over creation is a common Biblical motif (e.g., 1Sa 2:10; 1Ch 16:14; Ps 94:2; 96:13). **and the books were opened** Books containing records of human deeds are common throughout the Bible (e.g., Ps 69:28; Isa 65:6; Mal 3:16; Rev 20:12).

Miracles of the Prophets

PROPHET/HERO	MIRACLE	REFERENCE
Moses/Aaron	Aaron's rod becomes a serpent	Ex 7:10 – 12
Moses	The Ten Plagues	Ex 7:20 – 8:12:30
Moses	The Red Sea/Sea of Reeds parts	Ex 14:21 – 31
Moses	Waters of Marah made drinkable	Ex 15:23 – 25
Moses	Manna	Ex 16:14 – 35
Moses	Water from the rock	Ex 17:5 – 7; compare Nu 20:7 – 11
Moses	Aaron's rod sprouts	Nu 17:5 – 7
Moses	Fire at Taberah	Nu 11:1 – 3
Moses	The ground opens beneath Korah and his followers	Nu 16:30 – 33
Moses	The bronze serpent	Num 21:8 – 9
Joshua	The Jordan is divided	Jos 3:14 – 17
Joshua	The walls of Jericho fall	Jos 6:6 – 20
Joshua	The sun and moon stand still	Jos 10:12 – 14
Samson	Water from the hollow at Lehi	Jdg 15:19
Samuel	As Samuel sacrifices, Yahweh destroys the Philistines with thunder	1Sa 7:10 – 12
Samuel	Samuel calls Yahweh to send rain and thunder	1Sa 12:18
An unnamed prophet	Jeroboam's hand is withered and restored	1Ki 13:4 – 6
Elijah	Elijah fed by ravens	1Ki 17:4 – 6
Elijah	The widow of Zarephath is provided with food	1Ki 17:10 – 16
Elijah	The widow of Zarephath's son is revived	1Ki 17:17 – 24
Elijah	Mount Carmel and the prophets of Baal	1Ki 18:30 – 38
Elijah	Fire consumes Ahab's captain and fifty men	2Ki 1:10 – 12
Elijah	The Jordan is divided	2Ki 2:8
Elisha	The Jordan is divided	2Ki 2:14
Elisha	The water of Jericho is made drinkable	2Ki 2:19 – 22
Elisha	Mocking children are mauled by bears	2Ki 2:23 – 24
Elisha	Water comes for Jehoshaphat's army	2Ki 3:16 – 20
Elisha	The widow's oil is multiplied	2Ki 4:2 – 7
Elisha	The Shunnamite woman bears a son	2Ki 4:1 – 17
Elisha	Elisha revives the Shunnamite woman's son	2Ki 4:18 – 37
Elisha	Poison stew is un-poisoned	2Ki 4:38 – 41
Elisha	One hundred men fed with 20 loaves	2Ki 4:42 – 44
Elisha	Naaman cured of leprosy	2Ki 5:1 – 19a

Thousands upon thousands attended him;
  ten thousand times ten thousand stood
    before him.
The court was seated,
  and the books were opened.

¹¹"Then I continued to watch because of the boastful words the horn was speaking. I kept looking until the beast was slain and its body destroyed and thrown into the blazing fire. ¹²(The other beasts had been stripped of their authority, but were allowed to live for a period of time.)

¹³"In my vision at night I looked, and there before me was one like a son of man,ᵃ coming with the clouds of heaven. He approached the Ancient of Days and was led into his presence. ¹⁴He was given authority, glory and sovereign power; all nations and peoples of every language worshiped him. His dominion is an everlasting dominion that will not pass away, and his kingdom is one that will never be destroyed.

The Interpretation of the Dream

¹⁵"I, Daniel, was troubled in spirit, and the visions that passed through my mind disturbed me. ¹⁶I approached one of those standing there and asked him the meaning of all this.

"So he told me and gave me the interpretation of these things: ¹⁷'The four great beasts are four kings that will rise from the earth. ¹⁸But the holy people of the Most High will receive the kingdom and will possess it forever — yes, for ever and ever.'

¹⁹"Then I wanted to know the meaning of the fourth beast, which was different from all the others and most terrifying, with its iron teeth and bronze claws — the beast that crushed and devoured its victims and trampled underfoot whatever was left. ²⁰I also wanted to know about the ten horns on its head and about the other horn that

ᵃ 13 The Aramaic phrase *bar enash* means *human being*. The phrase *son of man* is retained here because of its use in the New Testament as a title of Jesus, probably based largely on this verse.

7:13–14 Following the judgment by the Ancient of Days, a human Messianic figure appears. He is presented before the Ancient One and given a dominion that will never pass away.

7:13 one like a son of man The Aramaic phrase used here is an idiom that can be translated as "one like a human being." Jesus adopts this phrase as a title ("Son of Man"). "One like a son of man" is probably best understood as a Messianic reference—which makes the most sense in light of Da 7:14. If the vision of ch. 7 parallels that of ch. 2, the figure refers to the fifth kingdom (2:44). Messianic expectations of the time anticipated one who would drive out foreign enemies, legitimize the temple religion and usher in a period of utopia for the people of Israel.

7:15–28 For the first time in the book, Daniel could not make sense of a vision and needed someone to explain it to him. He questions one of the throne room attendants, who clarifies the meaning of the beasts and the little horn. The account ends with the anticipation of God's kingdom and a glimmer of hope. The vision will be expanded upon in later chapters.

7:16 I approached one of those standing there Perhaps Gabriel (see 9:21).
7:17 four great beasts are four kings The four kings represent four kingdoms (see v. 3 and note).
7:18 the holy people of the Most High The Aramaic word used here is probably an inclusive term referring to saints and angels.

Miracles of the Prophets (continued)

PROPHET/HERO	MIRACLE	REFERENCE
Elisha	Gehazi is struck with Naaman's leprosy	2Ki 5:19b – 27
Elisha	The floating iron axhead	2Ki 6:1 – 7
Elisha	Elisha surrounded by horses and chariots of fire	2Ki 6:17
Elisha	The Syrian army is struck blind	2Ki 6:18 – 20
Elisha	Elisha's bones revive a dead man	2Ki 13:21
Isaiah	Hezekiah is healed	2Ki 20:7
Isaiah	The sun retreats	2Ki 20:9 – 11
Shadrach, Meshach, Abednego	Rescued from the furnace	Da 3:1 – 30
Daniel	Rescued from the lion's den	Da 6:10 – 23
Jonah	Rescued from the belly of the fish	Jnh 1:17 – 2:10

came up, before which three of them fell—the horn that looked more imposing than the others and that had eyes and a mouth that spoke boastfully. [21]As I watched, this horn was waging war against the holy people and defeating them, [22]until the Ancient of Days came and pronounced judgment in favor of the holy people of the Most High, and the time came when they possessed the kingdom.

[23]"He gave me this explanation: 'The fourth beast is a fourth kingdom that will appear on earth. It will be different from all the other kingdoms and will devour the whole earth, trampling it down and crushing it. [24]The ten horns are ten kings who will come from this kingdom. After them another king will arise, different from the earlier ones; he will subdue three kings. [25]He will speak against the Most High and oppress his holy people and try to change the set times and the laws. The holy people will be delivered into his hands for a time, times and half a time.[a]

[26]"'But the court will sit, and his power will be taken away and completely destroyed forever. [27]Then the sovereignty, power and greatness of all the kingdoms under heaven will be handed over to the holy people of the Most High. His kingdom will be an everlasting kingdom, and all rulers will worship and obey him.'

[28]"This is the end of the matter. I, Daniel, was deeply troubled by my thoughts, and my face turned pale, but I kept the matter to myself."

Daniel's Vision of a Ram and a Goat

8 In the third year of King Belshazzar's reign, I, Daniel, had a vision, after the one that had already appeared to me. [2]In my vision I saw myself in the citadel of Susa in the province of Elam; in the vision I was beside the Ulai Canal. [3]I looked up, and there before me was a ram with two horns, standing beside the canal, and the horns were long. One of the horns was longer than the other but grew up later. [4]I watched the ram as it charged toward the west and the north and the south. No animal could stand against it, and none could rescue from its power. It did as it pleased and became great.

[5]As I was thinking about this, suddenly a goat with a prominent horn between its eyes came from the west, crossing the whole earth without touching the ground. [6]It came toward the two-horned ram I had seen standing beside the canal and charged at it in great rage. [7]I saw it attack the ram furiously, striking the ram and shattering its two horns. The ram was powerless to stand against it; the goat knocked it to the ground and trampled on it, and none could rescue the ram from its power. [8]The goat became very great, but at the height of its power the large horn was broken off, and in its place four prominent horns grew up toward the four winds of heaven.

[a] 25 Or for a year, two years and half a year

7:23 fourth kingdom See v. 7 and note.

7:24 ten kings who will come These may be ten Seleucid rulers. While seven of these rulers are easily identifiable, the other three are unknown. The number ten may also be a round symbolic number, which is a common feature in apocalyptic literature. For those who believe the fourth beast is Rome, the ten horns may represent a ten-nation confederation that will arise during a seven-year tribulation period preceding Christ's return. **After them another king will arise** The "little horn" (see v. 8). **subdue three kings** In an effort to attain the throne, the "little horn" will be instrumental in removing three other kings. Following the death of his father—Antiochus III—Antiochus IV was fourth in line to inherit the throne. His brother, Seleucus IV, and his brother's two sons were rightful heirs ahead of him. However, all three were murdered, allowing Antiochus to assume the throne.

7:25 for a time, times and half a time The approximate duration of Antiochus' Jewish persecution—three-and-a-half years. If the little horn is the antichrist, this is the final three-and-a-half years of the tribulation period.

7:27 an everlasting kingdom Daniel does not elaborate on the details of this kingdom. His focus is not on the kingdom itself; it is on the fact that the Gentile kingdoms and the persecution associated with them will come to an end.

8:1–14 While 2:4—7:28 was originally written in Aramaic, the language in ch. 8 returns to Hebrew (see note on 2:4—7:28). The vision of ch. 8 builds upon ch. 7, taking the portrayal of the tyrannical Antiochus even further. Chapter 8 occurs two years after ch. 7 (see note on 8:1), and it gives greater insight into what will happen during the transition from the Persian to the Greek Empire.

LINGUISTIC STRUCTURE OF DANIEL

| Hebrew: 1:1—2:3 | Aramaic: 2:4—7:28 | Hebrew: 8:1—12:13 |

8:1 third year of King Belshazzar's reign Daniel places his second vision in the reign of Belshazzar, around 548 BC (see 5:1; 7:1). See the timeline "Life of Daniel" on p. 1352.

8:3 ram Perhaps an astrological symbol. A first-century BC zodiac list identifies Persia as a ram. **two horns** The kings of Media and Persia (see v. 20). Media and Persia existed as separate kingdoms until Media conquered Persia under Cyrus the Great. Media and Persia—though two distinct kingdoms—are often correlated in antiquity. **One of the horns was longer than the other** Persia, under Cyrus, absorbed the Median Empire and seized control of its army. See 7:5 and note.

8:5 a goat May also be an astrological symbol (see note on v. 3). The zodiac sign Capricorn is a horned goat. The male goat represents Greece (v. 21). **a prominent horn between its eyes** A reference to Alexander the Great (see v. 21) and his dominance of the other Greek rulers.

8:7 shattering its two horns Alexander savagely attacked and defeated the Medo-Persian Empire during the reign of Darius III.

⁹Out of one of them came another horn, which started small but grew in power to the south and to the east and toward the Beautiful Land. ¹⁰It grew until it reached the host of the heavens, and it threw some of the starry host down to the earth and trampled on them. ¹¹It set itself up to be as great as the commander of the army of the LORD; it took away the daily sacrifice from the LORD, and his sanctuary was thrown down. ¹²Because of rebellion, the LORD's peopleᵃ and the daily sacrifice were given over to it. It prospered in everything it did, and truth was thrown to the ground.

¹³Then I heard a holy one speaking, and another holy one said to him, "How long will it take for the vision to be fulfilled — the vision concerning the daily sacrifice, the rebellion that causes desolation, the surrender of the sanctuary and the trampling underfoot of the LORD's people?"

¹⁴He said to me, "It will take 2,300 evenings and mornings; then the sanctuary will be reconsecrated."

The Interpretation of the Vision

¹⁵While I, Daniel, was watching the vision and trying to understand it, there before me stood one who looked like a man. ¹⁶And I heard a man's voice from the Ulai calling, "Gabriel, tell this man the meaning of the vision."

¹⁷As he came near the place where I was standing, I was terrified and fell prostrate. "Son of man,"ᵇ he said to me, "understand that the vision concerns the time of the end."

¹⁸While he was speaking to me, I was in a deep sleep, with my face to the ground. Then he touched me and raised me to my feet.

¹⁹He said: "I am going to tell you what will happen later in the time of wrath, because the vision concerns the appointed time of the end.ᶜ ²⁰The two-horned ram that you saw represents the kings of Media and Persia. ²¹The shaggy goat is the king of Greece, and the large horn between its eyes is the first king. ²²The four horns that replaced the one that was broken off represent four kingdoms that will emerge from his nation but will not have the same power.

²³"In the latter part of their reign, when rebels have become completely wicked, a fierce-looking king, a master of intrigue, will arise. ²⁴He will become very strong, but not by his own power. He will cause astounding devastation and will succeed in whatever he does. He will destroy those who are mighty, the holy people. ²⁵He will cause deceit to prosper, and he will consider himself superior. When they feel secure, he will destroy many and take his stand against the Prince of princes. Yet he will be destroyed, but not by human power.

ᵃ 12 Or rebellion, the armies   ᵇ 17 The Hebrew phrase ben adam means human being. The phrase son of man is retained as a form of address here because of its possible association with "Son of Man" in the New Testament.   ᶜ 19 Or because the end will be at the appointed time

---

8:8 at the height of its power the large horn was broken off Alexander died unexpectedly at the height of his power in 323 BC. **four prominent horns** At his death, Alexander divided his empire among four of his generals. War broke out among the generals (often referred to as the *Diadochoi* from the Greek word for "successors") within two years.

8:9 came another horn, which started small Seleucus received part of Alexander's empire; Antiochus IV Epiphanes came from his line. The same imagery of the "little horn" from ch. 7 is used again of Antiochus IV (see 7:8 and note). Because the book addresses Jews undergoing persecution (especially during the reign of Antiochus), it is likely that the little horn represents Antiochus throughout and that the fourth empire is Greece. If the fourth beast represents Rome, the identity of the little horn is more difficult to establish. **Beautiful Land** Jerusalem (see Eze 20:6,15).

8:11 commander of the army of the LORD A reference either to God or the angelic prince who is Yahweh in the OT — that is, the Angel of Yahweh (compare the nearly identical phrase in Jos 5:14). The divine name Yahweh does not appear in the Hebrew for this verse (see note on 9:2). **it took away** Antiochus outlawed Jewish religious practices, and dedicated worship to Zeus instead of Yahweh (see 1 Maccabees 1:44–50; 2 Maccabees 6:2).

8:12 Because of rebellion Perhaps a reference to the Jews who adopted Antiochus' immoral Hellenistic lifestyle (see Da 8:10; compare 1 Maccabees 1:43; 2 Maccabees 6:12).

8:13 rebellion that causes desolation Antiochus IV

erected an altar to Zeus over the existing altar in the temple (see 1 Maccabees 1:54; 2 Maccabees 6:2).

8:14 It will take 2,300 evenings and mornings The angel measures the length of time that the sanctuary would remain defiled by the number of missed sacrifices. The number 2,300 describes the total number of evening and morning sacrifices that would be missed (compare to Da 7:25 and note). In total, 2,300 sacrifices — one in the evening and one in the morning — would take 1,150 days to complete.

8:15–27 In the last portion of this chapter, the angel Gabriel arrives to help Daniel understand the vision. Gabriel identifies the ram and the goat and describes the exploits of Antiochus in summary fashion.

8:15 one who looked like a man In this instance, an angel.

8:16 Gabriel An angel who delivers important messages in the Bible (see 9:21; Lk 1:19,26). See the table "Angels in the Bible" on p. 2120.

8:17 time of the end Refers to times when suffering will be replaced by restoration to instill hope in oppressed Jews. In apocalyptic literature, references to end times can connote the cessation of a particular activity, a future period of God's wrath manifested in judgment, or the end of time. The usage of the phrase here encompasses all three aspects, indicating an end to suffering and the termination of foreign kingdoms.

8:22 represent four kingdoms that will emerge from his nation See Da 8:8 and note.

8:23 a master of intrigue This ability implies wisdom in the ancient Near East (see 5:12).

26"The vision of the evenings and mornings that has been given you is true, but seal up the vision, for it concerns the distant future."

27I, Daniel, was worn out. I lay exhausted for several days. Then I got up and went about the king's business. I was appalled by the vision; it was beyond understanding.

Daniel's Prayer

9 In the first year of Darius son of Xerxes[a] (a Mede by descent), who was made ruler over the Babylonian[b] kingdom — 2in the first year of his reign, I, Daniel, understood from the Scriptures, according to the word of the LORD given to Jeremiah the prophet, that the desolation of Jerusalem would last seventy years. 3So I turned to the Lord God and pleaded with him in prayer and petition, in fasting, and in sackcloth and ashes.

4I prayed to the LORD my God and confessed:

"Lord, the great and awesome God, who keeps his covenant of love with those who love him and keep his commandments, 5we have sinned and done wrong. We have been wicked and have rebelled; we have turned away from your commands and laws. 6We have not listened to your servants the prophets, who spoke in your name to our kings, our princes and our ancestors, and to all the people of the land.

7"Lord, you are righteous, but this day we are covered with shame — the people of Judah and the inhabitants of Jerusalem and all Israel, both near and far, in all the countries where you have scattered us because of our unfaithfulness to you. 8We and our kings, our princes and our ancestors are covered

with shame, LORD, because we have sinned against you. 9The Lord our God is merciful and forgiving, even though we have rebelled against him; 10we have not obeyed the LORD our God or kept the laws he gave us through his servants the prophets. 11All Israel has transgressed your law and turned away, refusing to obey you.

"Therefore the curses and sworn judgments written in the Law of Moses, the servant of God, have been poured out on us, because we have sinned against you. 12You have fulfilled the words spoken against us and against our rulers by bringing on us great disaster. Under the whole heaven nothing has ever been done like what has been done to Jerusalem. 13Just as it is written in the Law of Moses, all this disaster has come on us, yet we have not sought the favor of the LORD our God by turning from our sins and giving attention to your truth. 14The LORD did not hesitate to bring the disaster on us, for the LORD our God is righteous in everything he does; yet we have not obeyed him.

15"Now, Lord our God, who brought your people out of Egypt with a mighty hand and who made for yourself a name that endures to this day, we have sinned, we have done wrong. 16Lord, in keeping with all your righteous acts, turn away your anger and your wrath from Jerusalem, your city, your holy hill. Our sins and the iniquities of our ancestors have made Jerusalem and your people an object of scorn to all those around us.

17"Now, our God, hear the prayers and

---

[a] 1 Hebrew *Ahasuerus*   [b] 1 Or *Chaldean*

8:26 it concerns the distant future Though thematically relevant to those in the Babylonian exile, the vision was specifically intended for those who would undergo future persecution.

9:1–19 Chapter 9 occurs during the first year of Darius (see ch. 6). Here, Daniel comes across a passage in the book of Jeremiah that speaks of the restoration of the Jews from exile. Daniel pleads with God for forgiveness on behalf of his people.

9:2 the Scriptures The Prophets of the OT. In this verse, the prophet appears to be meditating on the book of Jeremiah and realizes that the matters about which Jeremiah spoke are due to be fulfilled. **LORD** This is the first instance in the book of Daniel where "Yahweh," the proper Hebrew name of God, is used. The other occurrences of the divine name in Daniel appear in the prayer in vv. 4–19. **seventy years** Jeremiah prophesied that Judah would be captive in Babylon for 70 years (see Jer 25:11 and note; 29:10–14). This is probably a round number that is representative of a lifetime rather than an exact figure (see Ps 90:9–10; Isa 23:15). The beginning date may refer to Nebuchadnezzar's first capture of Jerusalem or his final destruction of the city in 586 BC.

The ending date may refer to the decree of Cyrus that Jews may return to Jerusalem in 538 BC or the rebuilding of the temple in 516 BC.

9:3 fasting, and in sackcloth and ashes A customary sign of grief (see Est 4:1,3; Jnh 3:6).

9:4 who keeps his covenant In contrast to rebellious Israel—for whom Daniel seeks forgiveness and restoration—God keeps his covenant and is faithful concerning his promises.

9:7 Lord, you are righteous God acted within his covenant stipulations and is therefore justified in punishing Israel for disobedience (see Da 9:11 and note). Daniel recognizes this and juxtaposes God's righteousness with Israel's shame.

9:11 refusing to obey you The Israelites acted with stubborn defiance; they knew the right thing to do, but intentionally chose the opposite. **the curses and sworn judgments written** References the curses found in Dt 28:15–68. When Yahweh made his covenant with Israel, he warned them of the consequences of disobedience. Daniel recognizes that Israel broke its covenant agreement with Yahweh and is being punished.

9:15 out of Egypt Appealing to the exodus foreshadows Daniel's forthcoming request for restoration through forgiveness.

petitions of your servant. For your sake, Lord, look with favor on your desolate sanctuary. [18]Give ear, our God, and hear; open your eyes and see the desolation of the city that bears your Name. We do not make requests of you because we are righteous, but because of your great mercy. [19]Lord, listen! Lord, forgive! Lord, hear and act! For your sake, my God, do not delay, because your city and your people bear your Name."

The Seventy "Sevens"

[20]While I was speaking and praying, confessing my sin and the sin of my people Israel and making my request to the LORD my God for his holy hill— [21]while I was still in prayer, Gabriel, the man I had seen in the earlier vision, came to me in swift flight about the time of the evening sacrifice. [22]He instructed me and said to me, "Daniel, I have now come to give you insight and understanding. [23]As soon as you began to pray, a word went out, which I have come to tell you, for you are highly esteemed. Therefore, consider the word and understand the vision:

[24]"Seventy 'sevens'[a] are decreed for your people and your holy city to finish[b] transgression, to put an end to sin, to atone for wickedness, to bring in everlasting righteousness, to seal up vision and prophecy and to anoint the Most Holy Place.[c]

[25]"Know and understand this: From the time the word goes out to restore and rebuild Jerusalem until the Anointed One,[d] the ruler, comes, there will be seven 'sevens,' and sixty-two 'sevens.' It will be rebuilt with streets and a trench, but in times of trouble. [26]After the sixty-two 'sevens,' the Anointed One will be put to death and will have nothing.[e] The people of the ruler who will come will destroy the city and the sanctuary. The end

[a] 24 Or 'weeks'; also in verses 25 and 26   [b] 24 Or restrain
[c] 24 Or the most holy One   [d] 25 Or an anointed one; also in verse 26   [e] 26 Or death and will have no one; or death, but not for himself

9:19 Lord, listen! Lord, forgive! Lord, hear and act! For your sake, my God Daniel's prayer reaches its peak with four imperatives asking Yahweh to forgive and take swift action. **bear your Name** The condition of God's city—the temple—and his people reflects on him. Daniel pleads for their restoration so that the greatness of God's name might be restored, not defamed. Daniel is concerned with God's reputation among the nations; he does not want to bring any reproach on his name.

9:20–23 While Daniel is still praying, the angel Gabriel appears. He announces his mission and God's favor to the aging prophet.

9:20 the sin of my people Israel Daniel functions representatively in this passage: He identifies himself with sinful Israel and prays on their behalf.

9:21 Gabriel, the man Elsewhere, Gabriel is identified as an angel (Lk 1:19,26). He has the form or appearance of a human (see Da 7:13 and note; 8:15–16).

9:23 for you are highly esteemed Daniel's prayer will not be answered in the way he wants. However, Gabriel will give him an explanation because of his favor with Yahweh. **consider the word and understand the vision** Gabriel structures his speech around this phrase, which identifies the two parts of his revelation: word and vision. The word is the revelation that follows in v. 24. After explaining it, he tells Daniel to know and understand the vision he is about to give in vv. 25–27.

9:24–27 Gabriel elaborates on the word and vision from v. 23. He tells Daniel what God has decreed: a set time frame for judgment that will not be altered. In ch. 7, Daniel learned about the rise and fall of four kingdoms and the little horn. In ch. 8, the conflict between Persia and Greece was elaborated upon, as was the profaning activities of the little horn. In this chapter, Daniel gets a glimpse into the desolating actions of the one previously identified as the little horn. This sets up the final vision in chs. 10–12.

This prophecy about the 70 sevens (or weeks) is notoriously difficult to understand. The main interpretive issue is identifying the time when the prophecy is to be fulfilled. The most common suggestions relate the fulfillment to the time of Antiochus, the time of Christ, the destruction of the second temple in AD 70 or some unspecified future eschatological event.

9:24 Seventy 'sevens' The Hebrew phrase used here ("seventy sevens") is sometimes translated "seventy weeks" (see v. 2 and note). These words together likely represent "weeks" of years—70 periods of seven, or 490 years (e.g., Lev 25:8). Gabriel reinterprets Jeremiah's prophecy about the 70 years of exile in Babylon (see Jer 25:11–12; 29:10–14). **to finish transgression** The six consecutive infinitives describe what will take place by the end of the 70 weeks. While some believe the events refer to Jesus and his first and second comings, others argue that these events took place before the time of Christ. **to anoint the Most Holy Place** In the context of Antiochus' offense and the ensuing rebellion, this phrase likely refers to the cleansing and rededication of the temple by Judas Maccabeus in 164 BC (see 1 Maccabees 4:36–59). Others take this as a foreshadowing of an eschatological event.

9:25 to restore and rebuild Jerusalem The Hebrew word translated here as "to restore" can also be translated "to return"—a reference to the fact that the Israelites will return from captivity. **Anointed One, the ruler** Likely refers to Joshua, the postexilic high priest. He and Zerubbabel are identified as anointed ones (see Zec 4:14). Joshua and Zerubbabel led the rebuilding efforts in Jerusalem and restored temple worship. Others believe this language and imagery refers to the Messianic arrival of Jesus, the great high priest of New Testament theology. **seven 'sevens'** In the traditional Hebrew Masoretic Text, punctuation clearly separates the seven weeks from the 62 weeks. This would require that the two periods of weeks not be read together—the anointed one does not come after a total of 69 weeks (thus identifying him with the same anointed one in Da 9:26); rather, he comes after the first seven weeks. There are, therefore, two anointed ones in this passage.

9:26 Anointed One The identification of the anointed one depends on how the timing of the 70 weeks is interpreted. In the second century BC context, the anointed one could be the high priest Onias III, who was murdered in 171 BC (see 2 Maccabees 4:30–38).

will come like a flood: War will continue until the end, and desolations have been decreed. ²⁷He will confirm a covenant with many for one 'seven.'ᵃ In the middle of the 'seven'ᵃ he will put an end to sacrifice and offering. And at the templeᵇ he will set up an abomination that causes desolation, until the end that is decreed is poured out on him.ᶜ"ᵈ

Daniel's Vision of a Man

10 In the third year of Cyrus king of Persia, a revelation was given to Daniel (who was called Belteshazzar). Its message was true and it concerned a great war.ᵉ The understanding of the message came to him in a vision.

²At that time I, Daniel, mourned for three weeks. ³I ate no choice food; no meat or wine touched my lips; and I used no lotions at all until the three weeks were over.

⁴On the twenty-fourth day of the first month, as I was standing on the bank of the great river, the Tigris, ⁵I looked up and there before me was a man dressed in linen, with a belt of fine gold from Uphaz around his waist. ⁶His body was like topaz, his face like lightning, his eyes like flaming torches, his arms and legs like the gleam of burnished bronze, and his voice like the sound of a multitude.

⁷I, Daniel, was the only one who saw the vision; those who were with me did not see it, but such terror overwhelmed them that they fled and hid themselves. ⁸So I was left alone, gazing at this great vision; I had no strength left, my face turned deathly pale and I was helpless. ⁹Then I heard him speaking, and as I listened to him, I fell into a deep sleep, my face to the ground.

¹⁰A hand touched me and set me trembling on my hands and knees. ¹¹He said, "Daniel, you who

are highly esteemed, consider carefully the words I am about to speak to you, and stand up, for I have now been sent to you." And when he said this to me, I stood up trembling.

¹²Then he continued, "Do not be afraid, Daniel. Since the first day that you set your mind to gain understanding and to humble yourself before your God, your words were heard, and I have come in response to them. ¹³But the prince of the Persian kingdom resisted me twenty-one days. Then Michael, one of the chief princes, came to help me, because I was detained there with the king of Persia. ¹⁴Now I have come to explain to you what will happen to your people in the future, for the vision concerns a time yet to come."

¹⁵While he was saying this to me, I bowed with my face toward the ground and was speechless. ¹⁶Then one who looked like a manᶠ touched my lips, and I opened my mouth and began to speak. I said to the one standing before me, "I am overcome with anguish because of the vision, my lord, and I feel very weak. ¹⁷How can I, your servant, talk with you, my lord? My strength is gone and I can hardly breathe."

¹⁸Again the one who looked like a man touched me and gave me strength. ¹⁹"Do not be afraid, you who are highly esteemed," he said. "Peace! Be strong now; be strong."

When he spoke to me, I was strengthened and said, "Speak, my lord, since you have given me strength."

²⁰So he said, "Do you know why I have come to

ᵃ 27 Or 'week'   ᵇ 27 Septuagint and Theodotion; Hebrew wing
ᶜ 27 Or it   ᵈ 27 Or And one who causes desolation will come upon the wing of the abominable temple, until the end that is decreed is poured out on the desolated city   ᵉ 1 Or true and burdensome   ᶠ 16 Most manuscripts of the Masoretic Text; one manuscript of the Masoretic Text, Dead Sea Scrolls and Septuagint Then something that looked like a human hand

---

9:27 an abomination that causes desolation See Da 8:13 and note.

10:1–21 This final revelation in chs. 10–12 is a further elaboration upon the visions of chs. 7–9 (see passage overview in 9:24–27).

This chapter recounts Daniel's encounter with an angelic figure. The angel touches him and gives him strength before proceeding with the revelation, which is recounted in chs. 11–12.

10:1 third year of Cyrus king of Persia 536 BC (see 1:21 and note).

10:4 twenty-fourth day of the first month Refers to the month of Nisan; Daniel was fasting through the Passover festival. See the table "Israelite Calendar" on p. 763; see the table "Israelite Festivals" on p. 200.

10:5 dressed in linen Typical clothing for angelic figures (see 12:6–7; Eze 9:2; 10:2).

10:7 the only one who saw the vision Reminiscent of Saul's (Paul) experience on the road to Damascus (see Ac 9:3–7). Those who were with Daniel could not see what was taking place, but they fled out of terror.

10:13 the prince of the Persian kingdom The angelic

custodian of Persia. The notion of patron angels and gods is a derivative of the ancient Near Eastern understanding of a divine assembly or council that would periodically convene to decide the outcome of world events (see Dt 32:8 and note). The Biblical authors use this same imagery. For example, in Job 1, Israel's God sits as president over the assembly with all others subservient to him. **Michael, one of the chief princes** Possibly the patron angel of Israel. Michael is depicted as warring on behalf of Israel (see Rev 12:7) and is called Israel's protector (Da 12:1).

10:14 future See 8:17 and note.

10:16 one who looked like a man A common way to refer to angels in Daniel—they appear in human form. **touched my lips** Reminiscent of Isa 6:7 and Jer 1:9. When a prophet's lips were touched by Yahweh, an angel or another divine being, they were cleaned and commissioned. In each case, the prophet or priest is given the right to speak on behalf of the deity they represent.

10:20 the prince of Greece will come After he finishes battling with the prince of Persia, the angel will have to battle with the prince of Greece. The sequence of Persia through Greece is reflected in the visions in Daniel (particularly ch. 8), including chs. 11–12.

you? Soon I will return to fight against the prince of Persia, and when I go, the prince of Greece will come; ²¹but first I will tell you what is written in the Book of Truth. (No one supports me against

11 them except Michael, your prince. ¹And in the first year of Darius the Mede, I took my stand to support and protect him.)

The Kings of the South and the North

²"Now then, I tell you the truth: Three more kings will arise in Persia, and then a fourth, who will be far richer than all the others. When he has gained power by his wealth, he will stir up everyone against the kingdom of Greece. ³Then a mighty king will arise, who will rule with great power and do as he pleases. ⁴After he has arisen, his empire will be broken up and parceled out toward the four winds of heaven. It will not go to his descendants, nor will it have the power he exercised, because his empire will be uprooted and given to others.

⁵"The king of the South will become strong, but one of his commanders will become even stronger than he and will rule his own kingdom with great power. ⁶After some years, they will become allies. The daughter of the king of the South will go to the king of the North to make an alliance, but she will not retain her power, and he and his power*ᵃ* will not last. In those days she will be betrayed,

together with her royal escort and her father*ᵇ* and the one who supported her.

⁷"One from her family line will arise to take her place. He will attack the forces of the king of the North and enter his fortress; he will fight against them and be victorious. ⁸He will also seize their gods, their metal images and their valuable articles of silver and gold and carry them off to Egypt. For some years he will leave the king of the North alone. ⁹Then the king of the North will invade the realm of the king of the South but will retreat to his own country. ¹⁰His sons will prepare for war and assemble a great army, which will sweep on like an irresistible flood and carry the battle as far as his fortress.

¹¹"Then the king of the South will march out in a rage and fight against the king of the North, who will raise a large army, but it will be defeated. ¹²When the army is carried off, the king of the South will be filled with pride and will slaughter many thousands, yet he will not remain triumphant. ¹³For the king of the North will muster another army, larger than the first; and after several years, he will advance with a huge army fully equipped.

¹⁴"In those times many will rise against the king of the South. Those who are violent among your own people will rebel in fulfillment of the vision,

ᵃ 6 Or offspring   ᵇ 6 Or child (see Vulgate and Syriac)

10:21 the Book of Truth Not the books referenced in 7:10; 12:1. This book apparently contains the unfolding of history. **Michael, your prince** The concept of Michael's princeship originates with this reference. He occurs frequently in extra-Biblical literature of the Hellenistic period and in the Biblical corpus (vv. 13; 12:1; Jude 9; Rev 12:7).

11:1–45 This section outlines the succession of kings during the transition period from Persian dominance to Greek dominance—represented by the third and fourth beasts of Da 7, and the ram and goat in ch. 8. The struggle for control of Palestine between the rival Hellenistic Greek kingdoms of the Ptolemies and Seleucids also receives attention. The career of the little horn of chs. 7–8 also receives greater detail.

11:2 Three more kings The identities of the three kings (in addition to Cyrus; see 10:1) are uncertain. They may be Darius, Xerxes (also known as Ahasuerus) and Artaxerxes. Chapter 11 closely tracks events associated with ancient Persia and Greece until late in the chapter, when correlations become less transparent. **a fourth** Likely Darius III Codomannus (336–330 BC). This king could alternatively be Xerxes I, but the connection with the fall of Persia to Alexander in the next verse makes Darius III more likely. See the infographic "The Bowls of Darius and Artaxerxes" on p. 724.

11:3 mighty king Alexander. The Hebrew phrase here can be translated as "warrior king," which describes well the career of Alexander.

11:4 his empire will be broken up See 8:8 and note. **It will not go to his descendants** Alexander's kingdom was passed to his generals, not his children.

11:5 king of the South Ptolemy I, who gained control of Egypt following the death of Alexander. **one of his commanders** Seleucus I began to govern Babylon after Alexander's death but was forced out by Antigonus, another one of Alexander's generals. He later regained control of Babylon and expanded his empire to include Syria and Media.

11:6 they will become allies Seleucus' grandson, Antiochus II, married Ptolemy's granddaughter, Bernice. **she will not retain her power** Antiochus II and Bernice had a child, but Antiochus reconciled with his former wife, Laodice. She poisoned him and was also responsible for the deaths of Bernice, her child and her entourage.

11:7 her family line Bernice's brother, Ptolemy III, successfully attacked the Seleucids.

11:9 will invade the realm The son of Laodice, Seleucus II, reclaimed what Ptolemy III took.

11:10 His sons will prepare for war Seleucus III and Antiochus III. The latter became a mighty force from 223–187 BC.

11:11 king of the South will march out in a rage Ptolemy IV countered Antiochus III and defeated him at Raphia in 217 BC.

11:13 the king of the North will muster From 212–205 BC, Antiochus III conducted many successful campaigns. He eventually gained full control of Judea in 200 BC at the Battle of Paneas (the city called Caesarea Philippi in the New Testament).

11:14 will rise against the king of the South Philip V of Macedon joined forces with Antiochus III to crush Egypt and the Ptolemaic dynasty. **Those who are violent among your own people** May refer to Jewish supporters of the Seleucids.

but without success. ¹⁵Then the king of the North will come and build up siege ramps and will capture a fortified city. The forces of the South will be powerless to resist; even their best troops will not have the strength to stand. ¹⁶The invader will do as he pleases; no one will be able to stand against him. He will establish himself in the Beautiful Land and will have the power to destroy it. ¹⁷He will determine to come with the might of his entire kingdom and will make an alliance with the king of the South. And he will give him a daughter in marriage in order to overthrow the kingdom, but his plans*ᵃ* will not succeed or help him. ¹⁸Then he will turn his attention to the coastlands and will take many of them, but a commander will put an end to his insolence and will turn his insolence back on him. ¹⁹After this, he will turn back toward the fortresses of his own country but will stumble and fall, to be seen no more.

²⁰"His successor will send out a tax collector to maintain the royal splendor. In a few years, however, he will be destroyed, yet not in anger or in battle.

²¹"He will be succeeded by a contemptible person who has not been given the honor of royalty. He will invade the kingdom when its people feel secure, and he will seize it through intrigue. ²²Then an overwhelming army will be swept away before him; both it and a prince of the covenant will be destroyed. ²³After coming to an agreement with him, he will act deceitfully, and with only a few people he will rise to power. ²⁴When the richest provinces feel secure, he will invade them and will achieve what neither his fathers nor his forefathers did. He will distribute plunder, loot and wealth among his followers. He will plot the overthrow of fortresses—but only for a time.

²⁵"With a large army he will stir up his strength and courage against the king of the South. The king of the South will wage war with a large and very powerful army, but he will not be able to stand because of the plots devised against him. ²⁶Those who eat from the king's provisions will try to destroy him; his army will be swept away, and many will fall in battle. ²⁷The two kings, with their hearts bent on evil, will sit at the same table and lie to each other, but to no avail, because an end will still come at the appointed time. ²⁸The king of the North will return to his own country with great wealth, but his heart will be set against the holy covenant. He will take action against it and then return to his own country.

²⁹"At the appointed time he will invade the South again, but this time the outcome will be different from what it was before. ³⁰Ships of the western coastlands will oppose him, and he will lose heart. Then he will turn back and vent his fury against the holy covenant. He will return and show favor to those who forsake the holy covenant.

³¹"His armed forces will rise up to desecrate the temple fortress and will abolish the daily sacrifice. Then they will set up the abomination that causes desolation. ³²With flattery he will corrupt those who have violated the covenant, but the people who know their God will firmly resist him.

³³"Those who are wise will instruct many, though for a time they will fall by the sword or be burned or captured or plundered. ³⁴When they fall, they will receive a little help, and many who are not sincere will join them. ³⁵Some of the wise

---

ᵃ 17 Or but she

11:17 will make an alliance with the king of the South Antiochus III betrothed Cleopatra I, his daughter, to Ptolemy V as a peace settlement.

11:18 to the coastlands Refers to Greece. Rome warned Antiochus III to leave Greece alone, but he did not listen. **a commander** The Roman Lucius Cornelius Scipio. Antiochus III lost two decisive battles to Scipio at Thermopylae (191 BC) and Magnesia (190 BC).

11:19 will stumble and fall Rome imposed heavy tribute upon Antiochus III as a result of his Greek adventures. In an effort to pay, Antiochus III attempted to sack the temple of Bel at Elymais and was killed in 187 BC.

11:20 His successor Refers to Seleucus IV, the son of Antiochus III. **a tax collector** Refers to Heliodorus, who was sent to the Jerusalem temple to confiscate its treasury (see 2 Maccabees 3). **not in anger or in battle** Seleucus IV was killed in 175 BC as a result of a plot hatched by Heliodorus.

11:21 a contemptible person Antiochus IV (see Da 7:8 and note).

11:22 a prince of the covenant Likely refers to the high priest Onias III, who was murdered in the time of Antiochus IV (see 9:26 and note).

11:25 king of the South Ptolemy VI. Antiochus attacked Egypt in 170 BC.

11:27 lie to each other Ptolemy VI's mother was Cleopatra Syra, Antiochus' sister. Ptolemy agreed to meet with his uncle in Memphis. Antiochus IV feigned friendship and allegedly took control of his nephew's kingdom.

11:28 against the holy covenant On his way back from Egypt, Antiochus was short on funds and plundered the gold of the Jerusalem temple.

11:29 he will invade Antiochus IV invaded Egypt for a second time in 168 BC.

11:30 Ships of the western coastlands A Roman envoy. The Roman consul Popillius Laenas stipulated that Antiochus IV must withdraw from Egypt or face the Roman army. Knowing that he could not defeat Rome, Antiochus complied. Humiliated and enraged, he headed home seeking an outlet for his wrath.

11:31 the abomination that causes desolation See 8:13 and note.

11:33 Those who are wise Refers to wise men who taught the apocalyptic wisdom of Daniel and lived righteously in the midst of turmoil. The language is borrowed from Isaiah's "Suffering Servant" motif (see 12:3; Isa 52:13; 53:11).

11:34 little help Probably a veiled reference to the Maccabees, who relied on armed resistance rather than the wise men's approach to suffering and injustice. Daniel

will stumble, so that they may be refined, purified and made spotless until the time of the end, for it will still come at the appointed time.

The King Who Exalts Himself

³⁶"The king will do as he pleases. He will exalt and magnify himself above every god and will say unheard-of things against the God of gods. He will be successful until the time of wrath is completed, for what has been determined must take place. ³⁷He will show no regard for the gods of his ancestors or for the one desired by women, nor will he regard any god, but will exalt himself above them all. ³⁸Instead of them, he will honor a god of fortresses; a god unknown to his ancestors he will honor with gold and silver, with precious stones and costly gifts. ³⁹He will attack the mightiest fortresses with the help of a foreign god and will greatly honor those who acknowledge him. He will make them rulers over many people and will distribute the land at a price.ᵃ

⁴⁰"At the time of the end the king of the South will engage him in battle, and the king of the North will storm out against him with chariots and cavalry and a great fleet of ships. He will invade many countries and sweep through them like a flood. ⁴¹He will also invade the Beautiful Land. Many countries will fall, but Edom, Moab and the leaders of Ammon will be delivered from his hand. ⁴²He will extend his power over many countries; Egypt will not escape. ⁴³He will gain control of the treasures of gold and silver and all the riches of Egypt, with the Libyans and Cushitesᵇ in submission. ⁴⁴But reports from the east and the north will alarm him, and he will set out in a great rage to destroy and annihilate many. ⁴⁵He will pitch his royal tents between the seas atᶜ the beautiful holy mountain. Yet he will come to his end, and no one will help him.

The End Times

12 "At that time Michael, the great prince who protects your people, will arise. There will be a time of distress such as has not happened from the beginning of nations until then. But at that time your people — everyone whose name is found written in the book — will be delivered. ²Multitudes who sleep in the dust of the earth will awake: some to everlasting life, others to shame and everlasting contempt. ³Those who are wiseᵈ will shine like the brightness of the heavens, and those who lead many to righteousness, like the stars for ever and ever. ⁴But you, Daniel, roll up

ᵃ 39 Or *land for a reward*   ᵇ 43 That is, people from the upper Nile region   ᶜ 45 Or *the sea and*   ᵈ 3 Or *who impart wisdom*

---

apparently thought little of responding to conflict with conflict (see Da 11:32).

11:36 will do as he This verse presents a divergence between the options for identifying the four kingdoms discussed in ch. 7 (see 7:3 and note). Up to this point, the historical events in the vision are quite clear. However, some hold that from here the text is no longer talking about Antiochus IV, but a later antichrist figure (see 7:8 and note). It is difficult to reconcile the events of vv. 36–45 with the life and reign of Antiochus IV. On the other hand, the text presents no change in characters or leadership.

11:37 will exalt himself above them all Antiochus' surname ("Epiphanes") means "manifest." He considered himself to be a god in the flesh.

11:38 god of fortresses If this refers to Antiochus IV, it may indicate his rededication of the Jerusalem temple to Olympian Zeus (2 Maccabees 6:2).

11:44 east and the north Likely refers to reports received from elsewhere in the Seleucid Empire. If Antiochus IV was fighting in Egypt when these reports came (see Da 11:42), then most of his territory was located to the north and east of his location.

11:45 between the seas at the beautiful holy mountain Refers to Jerusalem. **Yet he will come to his end** Stationing himself in Palestine in v. 44 due to the "reports" does not necessarily mean that he died there. Daniel does not say where or how, just that his death would not be "by human power" (8:25). Antiochus IV did not die in Palestine but during a campaign in Persia in 164 BC (see 1 Maccabees 6:1–17; 2 Maccabees 1:14–16; 9:1–29).

12:1–13 Chapter 12 details the much anticipated "time of the end" (see 8:17). There will be an increase in lawlessness and persecution for the Jews during the reign of Antiochus, but those whose names are found in the book will be delivered. Chapter 12 also contains a message of resurrection for those who will die during the persecution.

12:1 At that time Possibly referring to the death of Antiochus IV (see 11:45 and note). **Michael, the great prince** See 10:13 and note; 10:21 and note. **a time of distress** Describes the persecution under Antiochus IV (e.g., 1 Maccabees 1:54–64; 2 Maccabees 6:7–11). In this verse, Michael arises to the Israelites' defense, particularly in response to Antiochus' return from battle to quell a rebellion (see Da 11:44–45).

12:2–3 In Hebrew, significant allusions to the Servant Song in Isa 52:13—53:12 are evident. These linguistic links reflect a conscious understanding of Isa 53 as a text about resurrection. Just as the suffering servant figure is resurrected and restored to a relationship with God, his people also will be resurrected and restored to a relationship with him. The allusions serve to connect God's people in Da 12:2–3 with the suffering servant, so that God's servant—Israel (the "people" in v. 1)—is resurrected.

12:2 some to everlasting life Daniel is expounding on Isaiah's framework for resurrection. This fits with the reconciliation and restoration promised to Israel through the Servant figure in Isa 52:13—53:12. Resurrection accounts also occur in Isa 26:19; Eze 37:1–14.

12:3 Those who are wise See Da 11:33 and note. **those who lead many to righteousness** In 11:33, wise men are said to give understanding. Here, they turn many to righteousness. The description of those who lead

and seal the words of the scroll until the time of the end. Many will go here and there to increase knowledge."

⁵Then I, Daniel, looked, and there before me stood two others, one on this bank of the river and one on the opposite bank. ⁶One of them said to the man clothed in linen, who was above the waters of the river, "How long will it be before these astonishing things are fulfilled?"

⁷The man clothed in linen, who was above the waters of the river, lifted his right hand and his left hand toward heaven, and I heard him swear by him who lives forever, saying, "It will be for a time, times and half a time.ᵃ When the power of the holy people has been finally broken, all these things will be completed."

⁸I heard, but I did not understand. So I asked, "My lord, what will the outcome of all this be?"

⁹He replied, "Go your way, Daniel, because the words are rolled up and sealed until the time of the end. ¹⁰Many will be purified, made spotless and refined, but the wicked will continue to be wicked. None of the wicked will understand, but those who are wise will understand.

¹¹"From the time that the daily sacrifice is abolished and the abomination that causes desolation is set up, there will be 1,290 days. ¹²Blessed is the one who waits for and reaches the end of the 1,335 days.

¹³"As for you, go your way till the end. You will rest, and then at the end of the days you will rise to receive your allotted inheritance."

ᵃ 7 Or a year, two years and half a year

---

people to righteousness in this verse echoes language about the righteous servant from Isa 53:11 — solidifying the relationship between these passages.

12:4 seal the words of the scroll The scroll (or book) here refers to the book of Daniel, not the book mentioned in v. 1. As is typical of apocalyptic literature, the book containing the vision is sealed until its contents become pertinent to the time at hand. See Da 7:10 and note. **knowledge** The intended reading of the Hebrew text here is debated. The words for "knowledge" and "evil" only differ by one letter in Hebrew. The difference is whether a Hebrew "d" or "r" is read and those letters look very similar; both are represented in the various manuscripts and versions.

12:7 a time, times and half a time Echoes 7:25 (see 7:25 and note). This refers to the last half of the week in 9:27.

12:9 Go Daniel would receive no further revelation on the matter, thus leaving his question in v. 8 unanswered. He — and those for whom the vision was recorded — had all of the information needed to persevere in righteousness through persecution.

12:11 1,290 days Verses 11–12 present two seemingly irreconcilable time frames for Antiochus' desecration of the sanctuary to the end times. In 8:13–14, an angel confirms that 2,300 evening and morning sacrifices (or 1,150 days) will elapse as the sanctuary lies desolate (see note on 8:14). Immediately following this time, the temple would be cleansed (see 8:14). But in v. 11, the figure from 8:14 is extended by 140 days. The two figures (1,150 days and 1,290 days) may represent approximations. Additionally, something else of great importance may have been anticipated 40 days after the 1,290 days (the 1,335 days of v. 12). However, if the dating of the desolation and later cleansing in 1 Maccabees is accepted, the elapsed time was actually closer to 1,100 days (see 1 Maccabees 1:54; 4:52). Ultimately, the exact referents are unknown. In part, this is why they have been applied to a future eschatological timetable.

12:13 the end of the days When all that was predicted in Da 10–12 and chs. 7–9 takes place, Daniel will arise with those of v. 2 to his everlasting life (see 8:17 and note; v. 1 and note). Since the end of days is in view throughout the persecution, it is a fitting theme with which to close the book.

THE MINOR PROPHETS

The 12 books of the Minor Prophets cover a period of roughly 300 years, approximately from 760 BC (Amos) to 450 BC (Malachi). Except for Jonah, the books all identify the author in a heading. The arrangement of the books in the Biblical canon is chronological, with the exception of Joel and Obadiah.

DATES OF THE MINOR PROPHETS	
Eighth Century BC	Hosea, Amos, Jonah and Micah
Seventh Century BC	Nahum, Habakkuk and Zephaniah
Sixth Century BC	Joel, Obadiah, Haggai and Zechariah
Fifth Century BC	Malachi

Although it's possible that Joel and Obadiah, which flank the book of Amos, were written early—following the canonical order (in the ninth century)—evidence in the books themselves points to a later date for both, probably the sixth century BC. Both Joel and Obadiah speak of the exile of Judah in 586 BC as a past event (e.g., Joel 3:1–3,6; Ob 10–16). Their placement with Amos is likely due to their similar themes. Joel and Amos picture Yahweh roaring like a lion from Zion (Joel 3:16; Am 1:2). Obadiah prophesies the conquest of Edom, an event anticipated in Amos 9:12. As for the book of Jonah, it's uncertain when or by whom it was written—but its title character, the prophet Jonah, lived in the first half of the eighth century (2Ki 14:25).

In the Hebrew Bible, the Minor Prophets are treated as a unit referred to as The Twelve. While they share similar themes, these 12 books are distinct literary units with distinct messages.

CONTEXTS AND THEMES

Hosea

Hosea prophesied during the eighth century BC, an eventful period in the history of Israel and Judah. In 722 BC, the Assyrians conquered the northern kingdom of Israel and took the people into exile.

Hosea's message focuses on the northern kingdom, especially their idolatry. In an effort to produce children and enjoy agricultural abundance, the people worshiped the Canaanite fertility god Baal. Yahweh compares Israel's unfaithfulness to adultery. As a living symbol of their lack of fidelity, he commanded Hosea to marry Gomer, a woman who was unfaithful to him. To illustrate his determination to win back Israel, he required Hosea to reclaim his adulterous wife.

The book of Hosea paints vivid portraits of Yahweh as a moth, bone decay, a hunter, a lion, a leopard and a bear. Yahweh threatens to kill his people's children, rip the people open and tear them apart (Hos 9:11–17; 13:7–8). At the same time, in contrast to these disturbing images Yahweh is depicted as a lover who romantically pursues his wayward first love (Hos 2:14). We glimpse the heart of God and view his great compassion for his people. As he contemplates his severe

judgment upon Israel, his heart goes out to them, and he relents from sending calamity in its full force (Hos 11:8–9).

Joel

The occasion for the prophecy was a locust invasion in the promised land that had devastated their crops. The destruction was a foreshadowing of a worse judgment to come if the people did not repent of their sin. Apparently they did change their ways; Yahweh relented from judgment and promised to restore the people. He envisioned a day when he would pour out his Spirit upon the entire covenant community.

Amos

Amos delivered his message to the northern kingdom of Israel around 760 BC, warning them of impending judgment because they had violated Yahweh's covenant. Focusing his message on the socioeconomic oppression prevalent in Israelite society, Amos is the first prophet to speak of the day of Yahweh (Am 5:18–20). The people expected it to be a time when Yahweh would defeat their enemies and usher in a new era of blessing; but Amos talks about a day of dark judgment for the people themselves as well. The book ends on a positive note, with the promise of a renewed Davidic dynasty and restored blessing.

Obadiah

The date of this short prophecy is debated, but the disaster described in Obadiah 10–14 appears to be Judah's exile in 586 BC, which the Edomites exploited to their advantage. Obadiah announced Yahweh would avenge his people by judging Edom as well as other nations, for their mistreatment of Judah. He would also restore a remnant of his exiled people to their city and land.

Jonah

The book of Jonah is distinctive among the Minor Prophets; there is no heading identifying its author, and the book is a biographical narrative of God's dealings with Jonah rather than a collection of speeches by the prophet. We cannot be sure what historical or social conditions prompted this book, but it depicts a disobedient, reluctant prophet who stands in contrast to the sinful but ultimately repentant foreigners described in the book. Unlike Jonah, the sailors and the Ninevites responded humbly to Yahweh. The book shows how the sovereign God, before whom all nations are morally responsible, does not wish to destroy sinners but offers them an opportunity to repent and experience his mercy.

Micah

A contemporary of Isaiah, Micah prophesied during the second half of the eighth century BC. His message is an accusation of social injustice committed by the southern kingdom of Judah. Micah announced that Jerusalem would be destroyed, but this doom was postponed because of Hezekiah's repentance (compare Mic 3:12; Jer 26:17–19). The people would be exiled to Babylon, but Yahweh, in fulfillment of his promise to Abraham, would eventually forgive and restore his exiled people (Ge 12). He would also reestablish David's dynasty under an ideal Davidic ruler (2Sa 7), who would protect the covenant community from all would-be conquerors.

Nahum

Nahum prophesied sometime between the fall of Thebes in 663 BC, which had already occurred (Na 3:8–10), and the fall of Nineveh in 612 BC, which he anticipated. Yahweh would bring about the fall of Nineveh, and the whole Assyrian empire, because of its violent imperialism (Na 3:1).

Habakkuk

Habakkuk prophesied around the late seventh century BC, prior to the downfall of Jerusalem in 586 BC. In a dialogue with Yahweh, Habakkuk lamented the injustice he saw in Judah; Yahweh announced he would use the Babylonians as his instrument of judgment. Habakkuk called Babylon an arrogant, cruel nation, but Yahweh assured Habakkuk that his justice would be satisfied and Babylon would be punished. After receiving a vision, the prophet expressed faith in Yahweh's ability to sustain his followers through difficult times.

Zephaniah

Zephaniah prophesied in the late seventh century, prior to the fall of Nineveh in 612 BC, an event he anticipated (Zep 2:13–15). His message focuses on the "day of Yahweh," a day of judgment against both Judah and the nations, with a purification that culminates in worldwide worship of Yahweh and the restoration and moral transformation of the covenant community.

Haggai

Haggai's four messages are dated to 520 BC, the second year of the reign of the Persian king Darius. Yahweh challenged those who had returned from exile to rebuild the temple, and he promised to glorify the temple, provide agricultural abundance and restore the Davidic dynasty (compare 2Sa 7).

Zechariah

The authorship and unity of the book of Zechariah is a matter of debate. The three messages in Zechariah 1–8 are specifically dated to 520–518 BC and attributed to Zechariah (Zec 1:1,7; 7:1). However, the headings of the two oracles in Zechariah 9–14 do not identify the author; both say "the word of the LORD," the same phrase that appears at the beginning of the book of Malachi (Mal 1:1). These chapters may have been written by an anonymous author as a bridge between Zechariah and Malachi.[1] Given their canonical placement, however, it seems more likely these oracles come from later in Zechariah's ministry.[2]

Zechariah urged those who had returned from exile to show their repentance through obedience, reminding them that Yahweh places a higher priority on obedience than on religious ritual. The prophet envisioned a time when Yahweh would gather all of the exiles, make Jerusalem the center of his worldwide rule and restore the Davidic dynasty. In the era to come, the king and the priesthood would cooperate fully in carrying out Yahweh's purposes for the covenant community.

Malachi

The date of Malachi is not certain, but the reference to a governor places the book in the period of Persian rule (Mal 1:8). Parallels with Ezra—Nehemiah (references to marriages with foreigners, failure to pay tithes and social injustice) suggest Malachi prophesied in the mid-fifth century.

The book contains six disputations in which Yahweh addresses complaints from his people. Malachi emphasizes Yahweh's commitment to his people and the obedience he expects from them. Yahweh promises to eliminate the wicked and to form the righteous remnant into a purified covenant community.

CONTRIBUTION TO THE CANON

While the Minor Prophets are 12 distinct books, several major themes emerge from the corpus as a whole and contribute to the larger Biblical narrative.

1 Ralph L. Smith, *Micah–Malachi*, WBC (Waco, TX: Word Books, 1984), 169–73, 242–49. 2 C. Hassell Bullock, *Introduction to the Old Testament Prophetic Books* (Chicago: Moody, 1986), 316–17.

The Minor Prophets assume that Yahweh of Israel is the king of the world and has absolute authority over the nations of the earth. He uses some nations (such as Assyria and Babylon) as his instruments of judgment, yet he also holds them accountable for their mistreatment of his people (Am 1–2). Yet he displays great concern for even the most evil of nations, and will ultimately include all nations within his earthly kingdom (Isa 2:1–4; compare the themes of Jonah and Zephaniah).

Yahweh's covenant relationship with his people is also a major theme in the Minor Prophets. The eighth-century prophets accused the people of breaking the law established by Moses and threatened them with judgment based on the covenant curses (Dt 28). The eighth-century prophets also anticipated a time when Yahweh would reestablish the Davidic dynasty and restore its former glory (Hos 3:5; Amos 9:12; Mic 5:2; compare Hag 2:23; Zec 3:8; 6:12; 12:8–10; Jer 23:5; 33:15). The postexilic prophets made it clear that Yahweh was still faithful to his covenant promises established with Abraham (Ge 12)—and that the returning exiles were called to be faithful in return. While Micah is the only one of the 12 books to refer directly to the Abrahamic promise, other prophets picture the ultimate fulfillment of its blessings (Hos 1:10; Am 9:15; Mic 7:18–20; Zec 8:13).

Robert Chisholm

HOSEA

INTRODUCTION TO HOSEA

The prophet Hosea intentionally marries an unfaithful woman to symbolically portray God's relationship with unfaithful Israel. Hosea's prophecies elaborate on this metaphor, calling Israel to account for idolatry and foretelling judgment, but also promising God's faithfulness despite Israel's mistakes.

BACKGROUND

Hosea is the first of 12 short prophetic books known as the Minor Prophets. In the Hebrew Bible version of the Old Testament, these are collected into a single work called "The Book of the Twelve" (or simply "The Twelve") because they were originally contained together on one scroll.

Hosea prophesied in the northern kingdom of Israel from approximately 750 to 715 BC. This was a time of upheaval and uncertainty. Hosea prophesies the fall of Israel but does not report the fulfillment of the prophecy—which came in 722 BC when the Assyrian Empire conquered Israel's capital, Samaria. Although Hosea's proclamations are directed mostly at Israel, the book probably was compiled in Judah (the southern kingdom). This is suggested by the rulers listed in Hosea 1:1, most of whom are kings of Judah; the only king of Israel mentioned here is Jeroboam II (ca. 786–746 BC; 2Ki 14:23–29).

STRUCTURE

There are two major sections in Hosea. The first section (Hos 1–3) is Hosea's symbolic enactment of God's relationship with Israel by his marriage with an adulterous woman, Gomer. This marriage takes place at God's direction and results in three children who are given symbolic names (1:4,6,9). After Gomer leaves Hosea for another man, Hosea is told to once again love an adulterous woman, possibly indicating that he is to reconcile with Gomer and redeem her from slavery (3:1–2). Hosea's marriage represents God's relationship with Israel, while Gomer's adultery represents Israel's idolatry.

The second section of Hosea (chs. 4–14) is a collection of prophecies articulating the message behind Hosea's actions. The prophecies of this section are largely delivered in

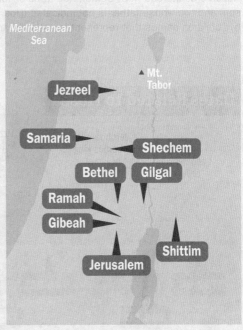

This map depicts many of the locations related to the book of Hosea.

the voice of Yahweh. They use a variety of metaphors to portray the Israelites' unfaithfulness and God's judgment against their disobedience, as well as God's unrelenting love for his people and his promise to restore them.

OUTLINE

- Hosea's symbolic family (1:1—3:5)
- Prophecies revealing the message behind the symbols (4:1—14:9)

THEMES

The main concern of Hosea is Israel's unfaithfulness and God's faithful response. Portraying idolatry as adultery is not unique to Hosea; other biblical books represent God's relationship with Israel as a marriage and depict idol worship as an adulterous violation of the covenant—the contractual agreement—between God and his people (Ex 24:1–8). Hosea explains this symbolism in greater depth than usual—especially in the book's first section, where the metaphors become realities in Hosea's own family.

Hosea's adulterous wife, Gomer, has three children—one (Jezreel) who is identified as Hosea's son, and two whose father is not indicated (Hos 1:4–9). God commands Hosea to give the latter two children names that represent Israel's distance from God: *lo-ruchamah* (translated as "not

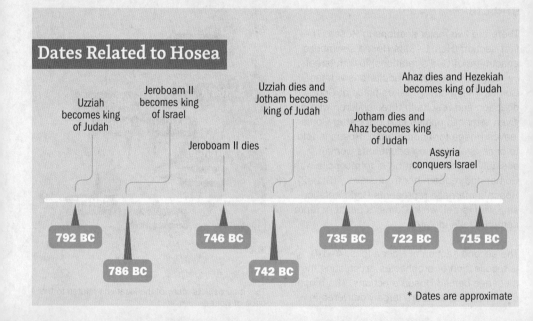

Dates Related to Hosea

Uzziah becomes king of Judah — 792 BC

Jeroboam II becomes king of Israel — 786 BC

Jeroboam II dies — 746 BC

Uzziah dies and Jotham becomes king of Judah — 742 BC

Jotham dies and Ahaz becomes king of Judah — 735 BC

Ahaz dies and Hezekiah becomes king of Judah

Assyria conquers Israel — 722 BC

715 BC

* Dates are approximate

pitied" or "not loved") and *lo-ammi* (literally, "not my people"). Just as Hosea's commitment to Gomer shows God's ongoing love for Israel, the children's names ultimately demonstrate covenant renewal: God says he will have pity on "Not Pitied" and will say "you are my people" to "Not My People" (2:23).

The second section of Hosea uses other images for Israel's unfaithfulness to God. For example, Israel is like a calf that needs to be tamed (10:11), and Israel is God's wayward son (11:1–4). But even amid Israel's disobedience and Hosea's warnings of judgment, the book's ultimate message is a promise of God's love: He will continue to cherish his people—and when they return to him, he will restore them.

Hosea's hard-hitting depiction of Israel as a cheating wife reveals the depth of God's pain—and his love. More than anything, he wants intimacy with his people, but they continually reject him. The metaphor challenges us to consider our own unfaithfulness to God; it asks us to seriously examine the ways in which we cheat on God. The metaphor also reveals God's enduring faithfulness toward us: He calls us back to him and to a more fulfilling life marked by faithfulness.

1 The word of the Lord that came to Hosea son of Beeri during the reigns of Uzziah, Jotham, Ahaz and Hezekiah, kings of Judah, and during the reign of Jeroboam son of Jehoash[a] king of Israel:

Hosea's Wife and Children

²When the Lord began to speak through Hosea, the Lord said to him, "Go, marry a promiscuous woman and have children with her, for like an adulterous wife this land is guilty of unfaithfulness to the Lord." ³So he married Gomer daughter of Diblaim, and she conceived and bore him a son.

⁴Then the Lord said to Hosea, "Call him Jezreel, because I will soon punish the house of Jehu for the massacre at Jezreel, and I will put an end to the kingdom of Israel. ⁵In that day I will break Israel's bow in the Valley of Jezreel."

⁶Gomer conceived again and gave birth to a daughter. Then the Lord said to Hosea, "Call her Lo-Ruhamah (which means "not loved"), for I will no longer show love to Israel, that I should at all forgive them. ⁷Yet I will show love to Judah; and I will save them — not by bow, sword or battle, or by horses and horsemen, but I, the Lord their God, will save them."

⁸After she had weaned Lo-Ruhamah, Gomer had another son. ⁹Then the Lord said, "Call him Lo-Ammi (which means "not my people"), for you are not my people, and I am not your God.[b]

¹⁰"Yet the Israelites will be like the sand on the seashore, which cannot be measured or counted. In the place where it was said to them, 'You are not my people,' they will be called 'children of the

---

[a] 1 Hebrew *Joash*, a variant of *Jehoash*   [b] 9 Or *your I AM*

1:1 Hosea is the first of the 12 Minor Prophets (named for the relative brevity of their prophecies). The heading introduces the prophet Hosea and orients his ministry to the eighth-century BC reigns of four kings of Judah and the king of Israel, Jeroboam II. Hosea prophesied to the northern kingdom of Israel in the years leading up to its fall to Assyria in 722 BC. The main theme of Hosea's prophecy is Israel's unfaithfulness to Yahweh, which he depicts through numerous metaphors, including Israel as an unfaithful wife and as a rebellious child. The central act emphasizing Israel's adultery is Hosea's experience with his own unfaithful wife, Gomer. See the timeline "Approximate Dates of Old Testament Prophets" on p. 1070.

1:1 The word of the Lord A standard prophetic phrase for introducing divine revelation (compare Joel 1:1; Mic 1:1; Zep 1:1). **Hosea** Literally "he has delivered." Hosea's name is a shortened form of Hoshaiah (compare Jer 42:1), which means "Yahweh has delivered." **Beeri** A Hittite name (Ge 26:34). Rabbinic tradition connects him with the Beerah mentioned in 1Ch 5:6. **during the reigns** The reigns mentioned here cover a large portion of the eighth century. Hosea was a contemporary of Amos, Jonah, Isaiah and Micah. Uzziah and Jeroboam were contemporaries in the first half of the eighth century BC. Hezekiah reigned until the early seventh century BC. Hosea's ministry could have lasted 20–45 years, but most of his prophecies are relevant for the years just before Assyria conquered Israel (722 BC). **Uzziah** See note on 2Ch 26:1. **kings of Judah** Israel had not heeded Hosea's warnings to Israel, and God judged them as a result. Judah needed to hear the same message and repent before it was too late. Since Hosea was from the north (Israel) and ministered to the northern kingdom (Israel), the opening reference to four Judean kings probably indicates that Hosea's prophecies were compiled and transmitted for a Judean audience. **during the reign of Jeroboam** Hosea mentions only Jeroboam II as king of Israel, suggesting he didn't view the weak kings who ruled after him as significant. During Jeroboam's reign from 786–746 BC, Israel experienced a period of great prosperity, peace and stability. The assassination of Jeroboam's son and successor, Zechariah, brought an end to the dynasty of Jehu in 745 BC (2Ki 15:8–12). The ensuing political instability in Israel accompanied a rebirth of Assyrian power, ultimately leading to the destruction of Samaria and the deportation of the Israelites in 722 BC.

Hosea 1:1

JEROBOAM II

Jeroboam, son of Joash, was Israel's most successful king since Solomon, expanding Israelite control into the Transjordan and north into Aramean territory (2Ki 14:23–29). His 41-year reign was characterized by unprecedented peace and economic prosperity. Jeroboam's success was largely the result of a temporary power vacuum in the ancient Near East that allowed both Israel and Judah to assert more control over the region. Aram, also called Syria, was Israel's main enemy through the late ninth century BC. By the time of Jeroboam, Aram had been weakened by conflicts with Assyria. As a result, Jeroboam was able to conquer territory formerly under the control of Aram, such as Damascus, Hamath and the Transjordan. The Assyrian Empire didn't oppose this expansion until the end of Jeroboam's reign. In the early eighth century BC, Assyrian power waned because of internal conflicts over succession and external threats from north of Mesopotamia; as a result, they paid little attention to the affairs of Syria-Palestine. Egypt was also weak during this time, consumed by civil war.

1:2–11 Isaiah, Jeremiah and Ezekiel each use the image of Israel as an unfaithful wife, emphasizing that the severity of Israel's idolatry was tantamount to adultery. Hosea takes this metaphorical comparison and turns it into a literal symbolic act, marrying a woman who is continually unfaithful to him. This passage introduces Hosea's family — his wife, Gomer, and the three children she bears. He takes her as a wife following Yahweh's explicit command. See the table "Symbolic Actions of the Prophets" on p. 1195.

1:2 a promiscuous woman The Hebrew term here, *zenunim*, refers broadly to extramarital sex, including adultery and prostitution. The text does not explain how Gomer fits this description. The main impact of the metaphor and symbolic action comes from the image of adultery, not necessarily prostitution. It also is possible that she was not a prostitute or adulteress at all; the reference to her unfaithfulness could be indicating idolatry. In that case, Gomer could fit the criterion solely

living God.' ¹¹The people of Judah and the people of Israel will come together; they will appoint one leader and will come up out of the land, for great will be the day of Jezreel.ᵃ

2 ᵇ "Say of your brothers, 'My people,' and of your sisters, 'My loved one.'

Israel Punished and Restored

² "Rebuke your mother, rebuke her,
   for she is not my wife,
   and I am not her husband.

Let her remove the adulterous look from her
      face
   and the unfaithfulness from between her
      breasts.
³ Otherwise I will strip her naked
   and make her as bare as on the day she was
      born;
I will make her like a desert,
   turn her into a parched land,
   and slay her with thirst.

ᵃ 11 In Hebrew texts 1:10,11 is numbered 2:1,2.   ᵇ In Hebrew texts 2:1-23 is numbered 2:3-25.

---

in the sense that she worshiped idols, just as others in Israel did at this time. **children** The Hebrew expression refers to illegitimate children. The text hints that Gomer's first child is Hosea's, while the second and third may have been fathered by her other lovers. It is also possible that Gomer already had children from prostitution or a previous marriage. **this land is guilty of unfaithfulness** The prophet equates widespread idol worship in Israel with adultery. Breaking the covenant with Yahweh was like breaking a marriage covenant.

1:3 bore him a son The text explicitly indicates that the first child is born to Hosea. However, it does not make the same statement for the other two, possibly indicating that only the first child was legitimate (see note on Hos 1:2).

1:4 Jezreel A symbolic name referring to the valley where Jehu overthrew the Omride dynasty (2Ki 9–10) and founded the current dynasty ruled by Jeroboam II. The name Jezreel means "God sows" or "God scatters." Hosea's prophecies often contain wordplays connected to reversals of fortune. This name can have positive or negative connotations, depending on whether the scattering is punishment or planting. The prophet Isaiah also gives symbolic names to his children (compare Isa 7–8). See the table "Symbolic Names of People in Hebrew" on p. 1388. **house of Jehu** The current dynasty of Israelite kings. King Jeroboam II was the fourth king of the dynasty. **massacre at Jezreel** The Israelite general Jehu seized power in a bloody coup in 841 BC, which began when the prophet Elisha, following Yahweh's command, anointed Jehu as king (2Ki 9:1–13). Jehu then killed Israel's reigning king, Joram, on the plain of Jezreel (see 2Ki 9:14–26). Jehu also was responsible for the death of Ahaziah, king of Judah (2Ki 9:27–28)— something Yahweh had not commanded. In this case, God may be punishing the house of Jehu because Jehu had murdered the Davidic king of Judah (compare 1Sa 24:6 and note). **put an end to the kingdom** In 722 BC, Assyria conquered the kingdom of Israel. Since this occurred approximately 25 years after the fall of the house of Jehu, the punishment and reference to Jehu here may refer to the northern kingdom in general, not Jehu's dynasty specifically.

1:6 Call her Lo-Ruhamah The name used here, *lo-ruchamah* (which in Hebrew means "not pitied" or "unloved"), could symbolize Hosea's denial of fatherhood. The name comes from the Hebrew verb *racham*, which signifies having compassion or showing love and tender affection. Hosea's rejection of the child reflects Yahweh's rejection of Israel. See the table "Symbolic Names of People in Hebrew" on p. 1388.

1:9 Call him Lo-Ammi The symbolic Hebrew name *lo-ammi*, which means "not my people," here is a direct refutation of the covenant formula, the most basic statement of Israel's relationship with Yahweh (see Ex 6:7; Jer 30:22 and note).

1:10 — 2:1 This section foreshadows the future restoration of Israel and the reversal of its rejection, symbolized by the naming of Hosea's children. The harsh rejection in Hos 1:9 is tempered by an appeal to Yahweh's covenant with Abraham (Ge 22:17) in Hos 1:10. The rejected children of Israel will one day be restored to the family of God.

1:10 like the sand on the seashore Following the rejection of Israel (implied by the naming of *lo-ammi*, v.9), Yahweh invokes the language of the covenant with Abraham (Ge 22:17) to express his plan for the future restoration of his people. **children of the living God** The Hebrew phrase used here, *bene el-chay*, meaning "sons of the living God," represents Israel as Yahweh's covenant community. The phrasing recalls the OT description of Yahweh's heavenly assembly as "sons of God" (*bene elohim* in Hebrew; see Ge 6:2 and note; compare Job 1:6; Ps 29:1). Yahweh's heavenly assembly is also described as a divine council (*adath el*) in the Hebrew text (see Ps 82:1 and note). The exodus story transfers that image of God's assembly from heaven to history by referring to the Israelites as the assembly of Yahweh (*adath yhwh* in Hebrew; Nu 27:17) and the assembly of the sons of Israel (*adath bene-yisra'el* in Hebrew; Ex 16:1). The reference here in Hos 1:10 to the *bene el-chay* similarly represents Israel as God's chosen community.

2:1 This verse belongs with the oracle of restoration in Hos 1:10–11. In the Hebrew text, ch. 2 begins at 1:10.

2:1 My people The Hebrew word here, *ammi*, reverses the name of Hosea's son in 1:9, symbolically affirming him as "my people." **My loved one** The Hebrew word used here, *ruchamah*, reverses the name of Hosea's daughter, showing that she is loved.

2:2–13 This poetic description of Israel's idolatry as marital infidelity expands the theme of the unfaithful wife symbolized by Hosea's marriage in 1:2. The prophets regularly employed the analogy of marital unfaithfulness (compare Eze 16; 23; Jer 2–3; Isa 1:21). Here, the prophet depicts Yahweh as the betrayed husband and Israel (both the people and the land) as his unfaithful wife. The imagery of unfaithfulness and punishment is similar to other applications of this metaphor in the OT, especially Eze 16, which may be expanding on Hosea's allegory.

2:2 she is not my wife An accusation of infidelity. Israel has wandered away, and Yahweh suspends his marital obligation to care for her. Through this statement, Yahweh acknowledges their estrangement and threatens divorce. One of the methods of divorce in the ancient Near East was to speak a legal formula similar to this declaration. However, if Yahweh is divorcing Israel here, there would be no basis for the threats of punishment to follow or the renewed commitment in Hos 2:16.

⁴I will not show my love to her children,
   because they are the children of adultery.
⁵Their mother has been unfaithful
   and has conceived them in disgrace.
She said, 'I will go after my lovers,
   who give me my food and my water,
   my wool and my linen, my olive oil and my
      drink.'
⁶Therefore I will block her path with
      thornbushes;
   I will wall her in so that she cannot find
      her way.
⁷She will chase after her lovers but not catch
      them;
   she will look for them but not find them.
Then she will say,
   'I will go back to my husband as at first,
   for then I was better off than now.'
⁸She has not acknowledged that I was the one
   who gave her the grain, the new wine and
      oil,
who lavished on her the silver and gold—
   which they used for Baal.

⁹"Therefore I will take away my grain when it
      ripens,
   and my new wine when it is ready.

I will take back my wool and my linen,
   intended to cover her naked body.
¹⁰So now I will expose her lewdness
   before the eyes of her lovers;
   no one will take her out of my hands.
¹¹I will stop all her celebrations:
   her yearly festivals, her New Moons,
   her Sabbath days—all her appointed
      festivals.
¹²I will ruin her vines and her fig trees,
   which she said were her pay from her lovers;
I will make them a thicket,
   and wild animals will devour them.
¹³I will punish her for the days
   she burned incense to the Baals;
she decked herself with rings and jewelry,
   and went after her lovers,
   but me she forgot,"
                              declares the LORD.

¹⁴"Therefore I am now going to allure her;
   I will lead her into the wilderness
   and speak tenderly to her.
¹⁵There I will give her back her vineyards,
   and will make the Valley of Achor*a* a door
      of hope.

a 15 *Achor* means *trouble*.

2:3 I will strip her naked Describes punishment by public humiliation. Wills from the ancient Near East attest to this treatment of a woman who chooses to remarry after her husband's death. The act symbolizes the removal of property rights from the woman so that her former husband's property does not transfer to her new husband. This aligns with Israel, who, by her infidelity with other gods, is renouncing her claims of ownership on the land Yahweh gave her. In an Old Babylonian divorce declaration, the ex-wife is to go out naked following the divorce, probably also symbolizing the end of the husband's responsibility to provide for her. Being stripped naked was also part of the standard curse language used in ancient Near Eastern treaties for what would be done to whoever broke the treaty.

2:5 I will go after my lovers Refers to the Canaanite idols that Israel worshiped and actively pursued. Her lovers could be political or religious—anything that Israel places faith in for deliverance other than Yahweh. Ezekiel 16 interweaves both ideas, criticizing unfaithful Israel first for idol worship (Eze 16:15–21), then for seeking political support from Egypt and Assyria (Eze 16:26–28; see La 1:2 and note). **who give me my food** Illustrates that Israel accepted the Canaanite understanding that the god Baal was responsible for agricultural fertility, a notion Yahweh rejects in Hos 2:8.

2:7 back to my husband as at first Her decision to return signifies reconciliation that wouldn't have been possible if there had been a formal divorce (Dt 24:1–4).

2:8 Baal The Canaanite storm god. See note on 1Ki 18:18.

2:10 I will expose her lewdness Describes public humiliation—likely a reference to exposure of the genitalia (compare Isa 3:18–26; La 1:8 and note; Jer 13:22 and note). Ezekiel similarly depicts Israel being exposed to her former lovers (Eze 16:37).

2:11 her yearly festivals, her New Moons, her Sabbath days Refers to times set aside for religious observances. Yahweh is unhappy with Israel's worship because it has been blended with worship of Canaanite gods. See Isa 1:13 and note; 1:14 and note.

2:12 her vines and her fig trees Symbols of agricultural and economic well-being. See note on Eze 15:1–8. **her pay from her lovers** The phrasing casts Israel's economic produce as the earnings of a prostitute. Yahweh provided these things (v. 8), but Israel gives the credit to Baal (v. 13).

2:13 the Baals The word *ba'al* simply means "lord" or "master" and could be used to refer to any number of various local Canaanite deities. Besides the main Canaanite god known as Baal (technically, Baal-Hadad), the OT records several other local Canaanite deities that use *ba'al* as part of their name. Nine are attested only as place-names but likely derive from references to local deities. Apart from the place-names, the most important examples include: Baal of Peor (Nu 25:3); Baal-Zebub, god of Ekron (2Ki 1:2–4); Baal-Berith, "lord of the covenant" (Jdg 8:33); and Baal Zaphon, "lord of the mountain," which was an epithet of Baal-Hadad that appears as a place name in the OT (Nu 33:7). The name Baal-Shamem, or "Lord of Heaven," is prominent in Phoenician and Aramaic inscriptions, but it does not appear in the OT. See the table "Pagan Deities of the Old Testament" on p. 1287.

2:14–23 Yahweh describes his plan for wooing Israel back and restoring their relationship.

2:14 I will lead her into the wilderness Alludes to the wilderness wanderings—Israel was more dependent on Yahweh before being settled in the land of Canaan (see the book of Numbers).

There she will respond[a] as in the days of her
youth,
as in the day she came up out of Egypt.
[16] "In that day," declares the LORD,
"you will call me 'my husband';
you will no longer call me 'my master.[b]'
[17] I will remove the names of the Baals from her
lips;
no longer will their names be invoked.
[18] In that day I will make a covenant for them
with the beasts of the field, the birds in the
sky
and the creatures that move along the
ground.
Bow and sword and battle
I will abolish from the land,
so that all may lie down in safety.
[19] I will betroth you to me forever;
I will betroth you in[c] righteousness and
justice,
in[c] love and compassion.
[20] I will betroth you in[c] faithfulness,
and you will acknowledge the LORD.

[21] "In that day I will respond,"
declares the LORD —
"I will respond to the skies,
and they will respond to the earth;

[22] and the earth will respond to the grain,
the new wine and the olive oil,
and they will respond to Jezreel.[d]
[23] I will plant her for myself in the land;
I will show my love to the one I called 'Not
my loved one.[e]'
I will say to those called 'Not my people,[f]'
'You are my people';
and they will say, 'You are my God.'"

Hosea's Reconciliation With His Wife

3 The LORD said to me, "Go, show your love to
your wife again, though she is loved by another man and is an adulteress. Love her as the LORD
loves the Israelites, though they turn to other gods
and love the sacred raisin cakes."

[2] So I bought her for fifteen shekels[g] of silver
and about a homer and a lethek[h] of barley. [3] Then
I told her, "You are to live with me many days; you
must not be a prostitute or be intimate with any
man, and I will behave the same way toward you."

[4] For the Israelites will live many days without
king or prince, without sacrifice or sacred stones,

---

[a] 15 Or *sing*   [b] 16 Hebrew *baal*   [c] 19,20 Or *with*
[d] 22 *Jezreel* means *God plants.*   [e] 23 Hebrew *Lo-Ruhamah* (see
1:6)   [f] 23 Hebrew *Lo-Ammi* (see 1:9)   [g] 2 That is, about
6 ounces or about 170 grams   [h] 2 A homer and a lethek
possibly weighed about 430 pounds or about 195 kilograms.

2:15 Valley of Achor Means "valley of trouble." The
site east of the Dead Sea where Israel was in trouble for
disobedience during the early days of the conquest of
Canaan (Jos 7:22–26). See the table "Symbolic Names
of People in Hebrew" on p. 1388. **came up out of Egypt**
Refers to the exodus and Yahweh's act of salvation, in
which he brought Israel out of slavery (Ex 1–15). The text
depicts the restoration as a reenactment of this central
salvation event from the formation of Israel as a nation.
2:16 'my husband' The Hebrew text here can be literally
rendered, "my man." In Hebrew, a woman's husband can
be described as her man. The verse contrasts this term
with the Hebrew word *ba'al*, meaning "lord" or "master,"
which also can refer to a woman's husband. **'my master'**
The Hebrew text here uses the term *ba'al*. If Israel used
the generic title *ba'al* for Yahweh, this would have caused
confusion about which deity they were worshiping.
2:18 make a covenant for them The renewal of the
covenant restores the relationship between Yahweh and
Israel. Jeremiah takes this idea further, emphasizing the
need for a completely new covenant (see note on Jer
31:31). **Bow and sword and battle I will abolish** The
restoration is accompanied by total peace in the human
and natural world. Compare Isa 2:4; 11:6–9.

2:19 The four virtues listed in this verse, combined with
the faithfulness mentioned in Hos 2:20, form the essence
of Yahweh's character. Biblical writers frequently mention these virtues together (Ex 34:6; Ps 33:5; 86:15;
89:14; Jer 9:24).

2:19 in righteousness and justice The central ethical
principles of the OT. See note on Isa 5:7.

2:20 you will acknowledge the LORD In the book of
Jeremiah, the imagery of restoration is developed further
(compare Jer 31:31–34).

2:22 Jezreel Meaning "God will sow"; the symbolic
name of Hosea's first child.
2:23 I will plant her for myself in the land Earlier, the
name "Jezreel" telegraphed disaster and destruction (see
note on 1:4). Now, the image is positive: God will plant
and rebuild Israel. **I will show my love to the one I
called 'Not my loved one'** See 1:6 and note; v. 1 and
note. **to those called 'Not my people,' 'You are my
people'** Reverses the earlier repudiation of the covenant
formula. See 1:9 and note; v. 1 and note.

3:1–5 Yahweh commands Hosea to love an adulteress
again, probably indicating that he should reclaim his wife.
Hosea obeys and takes back Gomer, his unfaithful wife,
just as Yahweh will take back unfaithful Israel. The conditions of her return, however, involve a lengthy period of
abstinence. This symbolizes that Israel will go through a
time without royal or religious leadership until it repents
and Yahweh restores it fully in the latter days. See the
table "Symbolic Actions of the Prophets" on p. 1195.

3:1 wife again, though she is loved by another man
The Hebrew text doesn't explicitly identify the woman,
but the symbolism of the action requires it to refer to
Hosea's wife, Gomer. The language seems to imply that
she is committing adultery by living with another man as
if she were his wife, not that she is living as a prostitute.
as the LORD loves the Israelites The analogy is spelled
out clearly: Hosea is to redeem his unfaithful wife, just as
Yahweh will redeem his idolatrous people. **sacred raisin
cakes** Signifies some sort of food offering presented to
idols. Compare Jer 7:18 and note. **3:2 I bought her** Suggests that Gomer had come under
some kind of debt-slavery. **fifteen shekels of silver and
about a homer and a lethek of barley** The combined

Symbolic Names of People in Hebrew

NAME IN HEBREW*	MEANING	REFERENCE
Ishmael	God hears	Ge 16:11
Abraham	Father of a multitude	Ge 17:5
Sarah	Princess	Ge 17:15
Isaac	He laughs	Ge 17:19
Jacob	He grabs by the heel, or He deceives	Ge 25:26
Edom	Red	Ge 25:30
Reuben	See, a son	Ge 29:32
Naphtali	My struggle	Ge 30:8
Gad	Good fortune, or A Troop	Ge 30:11
Asher	Happy	Ge 30:13
Joseph	May he add	Ge 30:24
Israel	He struggles with God, or God strives	Ge 32:28
Benjamin	Son of my right hand	Ge 35:18
Perez	Breaking out	Ge 38:29
Eliezer	My God is helper	Ex 18:4
Jerub-Baal	Let Baal contend	Jdg 6:28–32 (compare 2Sa 11:21)
Ichabod	Glory has departed, or No glory	1Sa 4:19–22
Shear-Jashub	A remnant shall return	Isa 7:3
Immanuel	God with us	Isa 7:14
Maher-Shalal-Hash-Baz	Quick to the plunder, swift to the spoil	Isa 8:1–4
Ariel	Lion of God, or Altar hearth	Isa 29:1,2,7 (compare Eze 43:15–16)
Rahab	Arrogant/Raging	Isa 30:7; 51:9
Jeshurun	Upright one	Isa 44:2 (compare Dt 32:15; 33:5)
Hephzibah	My delight is in her	Isa 62:4
Beulah	Married	Isa 62:4
Merathaim	Double rebellion	Jer 50:21
Pekod	Punishment	Jer 50:21
Oholah	Her tent	Eze 23
Oholibah	perhaps "My tent (is) in her"	Eze 23
Jezreel	[Predicts defeat at Jezreel]; God plants	Hos 1:4; 2:22
Lo-Ruhamah	She has not received mercy (or Not loved)	Hos 1:6; 2:23 (compare Hos 2:1)
Lo-Ammi	Not my people	Hos 1:9; 2:23 (compare Hos 2:1)
Achor	Trouble	Hos 2:15 (compare Jos 7:22–26)
Malachi	My messenger	Mal 1:1

* Although almost any Hebrew name can be interpreted as a sentence or label with an external referent (see Ru 1:20), symbolic names are meant to warn or encourage a wide audience with reference to God's purposes.

without ephod or household gods. ⁵Afterward the Israelites will return and seek the Lord their God and David their king. They will come trembling to the Lord and to his blessings in the last days.

The Charge Against Israel

4 Hear the word of the Lord, you
Israelites,
because the Lord has a charge to bring
against you who live in the land:
"There is no faithfulness, no love,
no acknowledgment of God in the land.
² There is only cursing,ᵃ lying and murder,
stealing and adultery;
they break all bounds,
and bloodshed follows bloodshed.
³ Because of this the land dries up,
and all who live in it waste away;
the beasts of the field, the birds in the sky
and the fish in the sea are swept away.

⁴ "But let no one bring a charge,
let no one accuse another,
for your people are like those
who bring charges against a priest.
⁵ You stumble day and night,
and the prophets stumble with you.
So I will destroy your mother —
⁶ my people are destroyed from lack
of knowledge.

"Because you have rejected
knowledge,
I also reject you as my priests;
because you have ignored the law of
your God,
I also will ignore your children.
⁷ The more priests there were,
the more they sinned against me;
they exchanged their glorious Godᵇ
for something disgraceful.
⁸ They feed on the sins of my people
and relish their wickedness.
⁹ And it will be: Like people, like priests.
I will punish both of them for their ways
and repay them for their deeds.

¹⁰ "They will eat but not have enough;
they will engage in prostitution but not
flourish,
because they have deserted the Lord
to give themselves ¹¹to prostitution;
old wine and new wine
take away their understanding.
¹² My people consult a wooden idol,
and a diviner's rod speaks to them.
A spirit of prostitution leads them astray;
they are unfaithful to their God.
¹³ They sacrifice on the mountaintops
and burn offerings on the hills,

ᵃ 2 That is, to pronounce a curse on   ᵇ 7 Syriac (see also an ancient Hebrew scribal tradition); Masoretic Text *me; / I will exchange their glory*

---

price of silver and barley was roughly equivalent to 30 shekels, which the Law prescribes as compensation for the loss of a slave (Ex 21:32).
3:3 many days An indeterminate period of time. Gomer (Israel) must remain faithful indefinitely in order to maintain the conditions necessary to fully restore the relationship.
3:4 household gods The meaning of the Hebrew word *teraphim* is somewhat uncertain. See note on Ge 31:19.
3:5 David their king Signals a reunification of the northern and southern kingdoms. The reference to latter days also marks this as a Messianic expectation (compare Eze 34:23; Jer 23:5). **last days** The prophets often use this phrase to refer to a time when the world would be set right. See note on Isa 2:2.

4:1—14:9 The rest of the book of Hosea is prophetic poetry condemning Israel for wandering away from Yahweh, warning of the coming judgment, and calling Israel to repent. The oracles are strung together without the opening or closing formulas typical of the Major Prophets (i.e., phrases like "thus says Yahweh"). The prophetic indictment centers on economic inequalities, injustice, oppression and idol worship. The book ends with a call to repentance and a promise of forgiveness. The style differs from Hos 1–3, which focuses on Hosea and his family as symbolic of Israel.

4:1–19 Yahweh brings a formal legal indictment against Israel for its general breakdown in morality and for losing all knowledge of God. The indictment focuses on the priests' failure to lead Israel in appropriately following Yahweh's Law. Compare Mic 6:2.

4:1 Hear the word of the Lord Prophets commonly use this phrase to emphasize that their message comes from Yahweh. See Isa 1:10 and note; compare Jer 2:4; 7:2; Eze 13:2. **acknowledgment of God** Produces behavior emulating God. See note on 2:19; compare Jer 31:34.
4:2 cursing, lying and murder, stealing and adultery The offenses listed here are violations of the Ten Commandments, especially Ex 20:13–16. **bloodshed follows bloodshed** Compare Jer 7:6; 22:3,17.
4:3 the land dries up The curses of the covenant affected the entire land, and by extension, all life dependent on that land (Dt 28:18,23–24).
4:5 the prophets stumble with you Describes false prophecy (compare Jer 14:13–16; 23:9–40). **your mother** Probably a metaphorical reference to Israel (compare Hos 2:2).
4:6 destroyed from lack of knowledge The priests were responsible for teaching the Law to the people (see Lev 10:11).
4:8 They feed on the sins of my people The Hebrew word here can refer to sin itself or a sin offering. The priests benefited directly from the sacrificial system, which was their source of food (see Lev 6:25–26). It was in their own self-interest to allow the people to sin more and more.
4:10 they will engage in prostitution but not flourish The prophet draws on the metaphor of idol-worship as adultery: The people will not receive any benefit from their infidelity. Compare note on Hos 1:2–11; 2:5 and note.
4:12 a wooden idol Refers to an idol carved of wood (compare Isa 44:15) or an Asherah pole (see note on Isa 17:8).
4:13 They sacrifice on the mountaintops and burn

under oak, poplar and terebinth,
where the shade is pleasant.
Therefore your daughters turn to prostitution
and your daughters-in-law to adultery.

¹⁴ "I will not punish your daughters
when they turn to prostitution,
nor your daughters-in-law
when they commit adultery,
because the men themselves consort with
harlots
and sacrifice with shrine prostitutes —
a people without understanding will come
to ruin!

¹⁵ "Though you, Israel, commit adultery,
do not let Judah become guilty.

"Do not go to Gilgal;
do not go up to Beth Aven.ᵃ
And do not swear, 'As surely as the LORD
lives!'

¹⁶ The Israelites are stubborn,
like a stubborn heifer.

How then can the LORD pasture
them
like lambs in a meadow?
¹⁷ Ephraim is joined to idols;
leave him alone!
¹⁸ Even when their drinks are gone,
they continue their prostitution;
their rulers dearly love shameful
ways.
¹⁹ A whirlwind will sweep them away,
and their sacrifices will bring them
shame.

Judgment Against Israel

5 "Hear this, you priests!
Pay attention, you Israelites!
Listen, royal house!
This judgment is against you:
You have been a snare at Mizpah,
a net spread out on Tabor.

ᵃ 15 Beth Aven means house of wickedness (a derogatory name for Bethel, which means house of God).

offerings on the hills The prophet is probably referring to mountain shrines called high places (see note on Eze 20:29; note on Isa 57:7). Prophets frequently attack these local shrines as the sites for Israel's idolatrous worship (e.g., Isa 2:14; Jer 3:23; Eze 6:13). **oak, poplar and terebinth** Idolatrous practices were associated with trees. See note on Eze 6:13.
4:14 men themselves consort with harlots The Hebrew verb in this verse means "divide" or "spread" and could be a euphemism for sexual intercourse. **sacrifice with shrine prostitutes** The references to prostitution in the context of idol worship (Hos 4:12–14) suggests that sexual practices were part of Canaanite fertility rituals. Mesopotamian culture seems to have distinguished between commercial prostitution and temple prostitution. The sexual rites conducted at the temple were connected to rituals that ensured fertility for the land. Payment to a temple prostitute went to support the temple and was an offering to the deity. Commercial prostitution occurred near temples solely because the temple was a high-traffic area where prostitutes could find many customers. The evidence for cultic prostitution in ancient Israel and the ancient Near East is inconclusive. Canaanite and Akkadian texts mention people who were serving the gods as prostitutes.
4:15 Gilgal Probably a reference to the Gilgal near Jericho, where Israel camped during the conquest. Joshua had set up 12 stones there as a memorial (Jos 4:1–8,19–24). The site later became an important religious center (1Sa 7:16; 10:8; 11:14–15). The prophet Amos also criticizes Gilgal for religious infidelity (Am 4:4; 5:5). **to Beth Aven** The prophet may be referring to a city in the territory of Benjamin, located near the border with Ephraim. Or he may be making an indirect and derogatory reference to the Israelite shrine at Bethel, located in the territory of Ephraim (see Am 5:5). In Hebrew, this name could be vocalized as Beth-on, meaning "House of Wealth," or Beth-aven, meaning "House of Wickedness." The name always occurs as Beth-aven in the Masoretic Text, the traditional Hebrew text. Hosea is likely making a pun on the name of Bethel, meaning "House of God," by revocalizing the name of the nearby village Beth-on as Beth Aven.

4:17 Ephraim Hosea uses the name Ephraim to refer to the whole northern kingdom of Israel 37 times. The hill country of Ephraim was the core of Israelite territory; it was where Samaria, the capital, and the important city of Shechem were located. Ephraim was traditionally one of the strongest tribes of the northern kingdom. The prophets Isaiah, Jeremiah and Ezekiel also use Ephraim to represent Israel (compare Isa 7:2–17; 9:8; Jer 31:9; Eze 37:16).

Hosea 4:17

EPHRAIM
Ephraim primarily refers to the central hill country of Palestine, including the tribal territory of both Ephraim and Manasseh. Ephraim was the name of Joseph's second son (Ge 41:52). Jacob adopted Ephraim (Ge 48:5) and his brother, Manasseh, and allotted them full status among his sons. Joshua 16:5–10 describes the borders of Ephraim's allotted territory in the promised land, but their central area of control was the hill country of Ephraim, sometimes mentioned jointly with the territory of Manasseh (see Dt 34:2). This region encompassed the western section of the Jordanian mountainous area from around Bethel in the south to the plain of Jezreel in the north. The tribe of Ephraim settled in the more fertile southern part of this region. The cities of Shechem and Samaria are in the center of this region. See the map "Tribal Distribution of Palestine" on p. 2253.

4:19 A whirlwind will sweep them away See note on Hos 5:4.

5:1–15 The indictment that the prophet presented in Hos 4 now culminates in a guilty verdict directed at the priest and the king, who have led Israel into idolatry. The prophet then focuses on the divine wrath coming on both Israel and Judah. The historical setting seems to relate to the time of the Syro-Ephraimite War (ca. 735–732 BC). See note on Isa 7:1.

² The rebels are knee-deep in slaughter.
  I will discipline all of them.
³ I know all about Ephraim;
  Israel is not hidden from me.
Ephraim, you have now turned to
    prostitution;
  Israel is corrupt.

⁴ "Their deeds do not permit them
  to return to their God.
A spirit of prostitution is in their heart;
  they do not acknowledge the LORD.
⁵ Israel's arrogance testifies against them;
  the Israelites, even Ephraim, stumble in
    their sin;
  Judah also stumbles with them.
⁶ When they go with their flocks and herds
  to seek the LORD,
they will not find him;
  he has withdrawn himself from them.
⁷ They are unfaithful to the LORD;
  they give birth to illegitimate children.
When they celebrate their New Moon
    feasts,
  he will devour^a their fields.

⁸ "Sound the trumpet in Gibeah,
  the horn in Ramah.
Raise the battle cry in Beth Aven ^b;
  lead on, Benjamin.

⁹ Ephraim will be laid waste
  on the day of reckoning.
Among the tribes of Israel
  I proclaim what is certain.
¹⁰ Judah's leaders are like those
  who move boundary stones.
I will pour out my wrath on them
  like a flood of water.
¹¹ Ephraim is oppressed,
  trampled in judgment,
  intent on pursuing idols.^c
¹² I am like a moth to Ephraim,
  like rot to the people of Judah.

¹³ "When Ephraim saw his sickness,
  and Judah his sores,
then Ephraim turned to Assyria,
  and sent to the great king for help.
But he is not able to cure you,
  not able to heal your sores.
¹⁴ For I will be like a lion to Ephraim,
  like a great lion to Judah.
I will tear them to pieces and go away;
  I will carry them off, with no one to rescue
    them.

---

^a 7 Or Now their New Moon feasts / will devour them and
^b 8 Beth Aven means house of wickedness (a derogatory name for
Bethel, which means house of God).   ^c 11 The meaning of the
Hebrew for this word is uncertain.

5:1 judgment Used in the sense of a legal verdict and
sentence. **Mizpah** A city in the territory of Benjamin on
the border with Israel. See note on Jer 40:6. **Tabor** A
mountain on the northern side of the Jezreel Valley. See
note on Jer 46:18.
5:3 I know Contrasts with Hos 5:4. Yahweh knows Israel and its actions, but it does not know him. **Ephraim**
Refers here to the whole northern kingdom. See note
on 4:17. **you have now turned to prostitution** Hosea
uses this idiom nine times to describe Israel's idolatry.
5:4 A spirit of prostitution Refers to the spirit of
idolatry that has become so pervasive in the land. The
reference to a ruach (wind or spirit) in 4:19 probably also
reflects this idea.
5:6 he has withdrawn himself from them The worship
at Israel's local shrines will be fruitless, since there is
no divine power there. The people mistook Yahweh's
blessing for that of their idols, so he will withdraw that
blessing (compare 2:5,8).
5:7 illegitimate children These children are unknown
to Yahweh, who renounces any responsibility to care for
them. Reflects Hosea's situation with his younger two
children. See note on 1:2. **New Moon feasts** Probably
indicates that Israel's observance of new moon festivals
in honor of Baal will lead to their downfall. The new moon
was a traditional day for sacrifice and ritual feasting (Nu
28:11–15; 1Sa 20:5,26). The celebration of the appearance of the new moon, starting the new month, was also
important in Canaanite religion. See note on Isa 1:13.

5:8 All the locations mentioned in Hos 5:8 are along
the north—south route that a Judean army moving
to invade Israel would have followed. Israel and Judah
regularly disputed over control of the northern part of
Benjamin's territory.

5:8 Gibeah A city in the territory of Benjamin, the home-
town of King Saul (1Sa 10:26). Gibeah was at the center
of the conflict described in Jdg 19–21, in which the men
of that city rape and murder a Levite's concubine (see
note on Jdg 19:13). **Ramah** A city in the territory of
Benjamin, not far from Gibeah (see note on Jer 31:15).
Ramah (or Ramathaim) was the home of the prophet
Samuel (see 1Sa 1:1 and note). **Raise the battle cry**
Probably a call to arms, mobilizing Benjamin against
Israel. **in Beth Aven** See note on Hos 4:15. **Benjamin**
Gibeah, Ramah and possibly Beth Aven were in the territory of Benjamin.
5:10 like those who move boundary stones Possibly
indicating an attack on Ephraim by Judah. The law forbids
moving a boundary stone to steal property (Dt 19:14).
Judah's aggression is akin to theft. In the Dead Sea
Scrolls, this phrase is used as a metaphor for people
who led Israel astray from rightful worship of Yahweh.
5:13 Ephraim turned to Assyria Likely alludes to tribute
or payment that the king of Israel gave to Assyria for
mercenary assistance. Menahem (reigned 746–737
BC) paid Tiglath-Pileser III to help him consolidate his
power after assassinating the previous king, Shallum
(2Ki 15:13–20). Shallum had, in turn, assassinated
Zechariah, son of Jeroboam II, ending the dynasty of
Jehu (see note on Hos 1:1). The reference could also
relate to Israel's status as vassal of Assyria following
the rebellion of the Syro-Ephraimite War (735–732 BC).
Hoshea had overthrown Pekah, the Israelite king who
had rebelled against Tiglath-Pileser (2Ki 15:29–30).
Hoshea, who was the last king of Israel, had paid tribute
to Assyria and been a vassal of Assyria before rebelling
himself (2Ki 17:1–6).

¹⁵ Then I will return to my lair
    until they have borne their guilt
    and seek my face —
in their misery
    they will earnestly seek me."

Israel Unrepentant

6 "Come, let us return to the LORD.
    He has torn us to pieces
    but he will heal us;
he has injured us
    but he will bind up our wounds.
² After two days he will revive us;
    on the third day he will restore us,
    that we may live in his presence.
³ Let us acknowledge the LORD;
    let us press on to acknowledge him.
As surely as the sun rises,
    he will appear;
he will come to us like the winter rains,
    like the spring rains that water the earth."

⁴ "What can I do with you, Ephraim?
    What can I do with you, Judah?
Your love is like the morning mist,
    like the early dew that disappears.
⁵ Therefore I cut you in pieces with my
    prophets,
    I killed you with the words of my mouth —
    then my judgments go forth like the sun.ᵃ

⁶ For I desire mercy, not sacrifice,
    and acknowledgment of God rather than
    burnt offerings.
⁷ As at Adam,ᵇ they have broken the covenant;
    they were unfaithful to me there.
⁸ Gilead is a city of evildoers,
    stained with footprints of blood.
⁹ As marauders lie in ambush for a victim,
    so do bands of priests;
they murder on the road to Shechem,
    carrying out their wicked schemes.
¹⁰ I have seen a horrible thing in Israel:
    There Ephraim is given to prostitution,
    Israel is defiled.

¹¹ "Also for you, Judah,
    a harvest is appointed.

"Whenever I would restore the fortunes of
    my people,
7 ¹ whenever I would heal Israel,
    the sins of Ephraim are exposed
    and the crimes of Samaria revealed.
They practice deceit,
    thieves break into houses,
    bandits rob in the streets;
² but they do not realize
    that I remember all their evil deeds.

ᵃ 5 The meaning of the Hebrew for this line is uncertain.
ᵇ 7 Or *Like Adam*; or *Like human beings*

6:1 — 7:16 This passage emphasizes Israel's sin and injustice, especially its failure to truly repent, acknowledge its guilt and seek Yahweh for help.

6:1 he will bind up our wounds The people seek Yahweh to save them from judgment (Hos 5:6), but their repentance is not genuine.

6:2 After two days he will revive us The Israelites perceive that judgment will last only for a short time.

6:4 like the morning mist Illustrates that their love is not genuine; it is self-serving. As soon as trouble has passed, they will go back to their old habits.

6:5 with the words of my mouth Portrays Yahweh's speech as power — an offensive weapon. **judgments go forth like the sun** The prophet is playing on the imagery of Hos 6:3, which indicates that Yahweh's coming to save is as certain as the coming of the dawn. He indicates that the light comes, but in judgment.

6:6 mercy, not sacrifice This verse summarizes a central teaching of the OT prophets: Yahweh desires and values internal commitment and character transformation over external ritual observances (compare note on La 3:22). The prophets regularly condemn Israel for attending to the letter of the law while ignoring the spirit of the law (compare Isa 1:11–17; Am 4:4–5; Mic 6:6–8; note on Isa 51:4). Jesus incorporates this teaching into his criticism of the religious leaders of his time, quoting this part of Hos 6:6 twice in an attempt to get the Pharisees to understand that intentions are more important than actions (see Mt 9:13 and note; 12:7). **acknowledgment of God** Knowledge is exemplified by having a right relationship with Yahweh, showing true faith, loyalty and obedience. Those who know Yahweh emulate his behav-

ior, which is characterized by steadfast love, justice and righteousness (Jer 9:23–24). The indictment against Israel stems from a lack of knowledge (Hos 4:1,6). The prophet contrasts Yahweh's knowledge of Israel with Israel's ignorance of Yahweh (5:3–4). Israel pretends to attempt to know God (6:3), but it does not realize that its ritual actions are empty. The people's failure to attain true knowledge of God will ultimately lead to judgment (8:1–7) because they substituted knowledge of an idol for knowledge of Yahweh. See note on 2:19. **burnt offerings** See note on Isa 1:11.

6:7 As at Adam, they have broken the covenant The prophet compares Israel's breaking faith with Yahweh to Adam's failure to keep Yahweh's single command in the garden of Eden (Ge 2:16–17; 3:17). Israel transgressed the Mosaic covenant (compare Hos 8:1), while Adam broke the relationship Yahweh had established in Ge 1–3. The reference to Adam is sometimes understood as a place, based on the statement that the people dealt faithlessly with God "there." However, there is no known tradition of Israel breaking the covenant with Yahweh at a place called Adam. The only time "Adam" occurs as a place-name in the OT is Jos 3:16.

6:8 Gilead A region on the eastern side of the Jordan River (see note on Jer 8:22), which was sometimes controlled by Israel but taken by Assyria in 733–732 BC (2Ki 15:29).

6:9 Shechem A city in the hill country of Ephraim (see note on Hos 4:17). Abraham built an altar there (Ge 12:6–7), and it was one of the Levitical cities of refuge (Jos 20:7–9).

7:1 Samaria The capital of the northern kingdom. See note on Jer 31:5.

Their sins engulf them;
they are always before me.

3 "They delight the king with their wickedness,
the princes with their lies.
4 They are all adulterers,
burning like an oven
whose fire the baker need not stir
from the kneading of the dough till it rises.
5 On the day of the festival of our king
the princes become inflamed with wine,
and he joins hands with the mockers.
6 Their hearts are like an oven;
they approach him with intrigue.
Their passion smolders all night;
in the morning it blazes like a flaming fire.
7 All of them are hot as an oven;
they devour their rulers.
All their kings fall,
and none of them calls on me.

8 "Ephraim mixes with the nations;
Ephraim is a flat loaf not turned over.
9 Foreigners sap his strength,
but he does not realize it.
His hair is sprinkled with gray,
but he does not notice.
10 Israel's arrogance testifies against him,
but despite all this
he does not return to the LORD his God
or search for him.

11 "Ephraim is like a dove,
easily deceived and senseless —
now calling to Egypt,
now turning to Assyria.
12 When they go, I will throw my net over them;
I will pull them down like the birds in the
sky.

When I hear them flocking together,
I will catch them.
13 Woe to them,
because they have strayed from me!
Destruction to them,
because they have rebelled against me!
I long to redeem them
but they speak about me falsely.
14 They do not cry out to me from their hearts
but wail on their beds.
They slash themselves,[a] appealing to their
gods
for grain and new wine,
but they turn away from me.
15 I trained them and strengthened their arms,
but they plot evil against me.
16 They do not turn to the Most High;
they are like a faulty bow.
Their leaders will fall by the sword
because of their insolent words.
For this they will be ridiculed
in the land of Egypt.

Israel to Reap the Whirlwind

8 "Put the trumpet to your lips!
An eagle is over the house of the LORD
because the people have broken my covenant
and rebelled against my law.
2 Israel cries out to me,
'Our God, we acknowledge you!'
3 But Israel has rejected what is good;
an enemy will pursue him.
4 They set up kings without my consent;
they choose princes without my approval.

a 14 Some Hebrew manuscripts and Septuagint; most Hebrew
manuscripts *They gather together*

7:4 burning like an oven Hosea uses the image of an earthenware bread oven to describe Israel's simmering political situation. The heat from the oven metaphorically represents drunkenness, anger, treachery and destruction. References to rulers being devoured (Hos 7:7) and seeking help from Egypt or Assyria (v. 11) suggest the similes in this chapter are designed to reflect the political intrigue that characterized Israel's closing years. Four of the final six kings of Israel were assassinated, and the final king, Hoshea, shifted between accepting Assyrian rule and seeking Egyptian assistance to oppose Assyria.
7:8 mixes with the nations Israel was weakened from reliance on foreign aid (v. 9). **Ephraim is a flat loaf not turned over** Perhaps alluding to Israel's inconsistent and ineffective foreign policies: Their plans are only half-baked.
7:11 like a dove, easily deceived and senseless The dove is a symbol of ignorant innocence (Mt 10:16). Instead of seeking Yahweh (Hos 7:10), Israel foolishly gambled on foreign alliances, wavering between Assyrian and Egyptian loyalties (2Ki 17:1–5).
7:14 They slash themselves Symbolic of national mourning and distress. See note on Dt 14:1.
7:16 a faulty bow The prophet literally describes the bow as slack or loose—useless for its intended purpose.

8:1–14 This chapter contains a collection of poetic sayings reiterating how the Israelites have strayed from Yahweh in their choice of rulers, their religious practices and their foreign policy.
8:1 trumpet to your lips Ancients used trumpets to sound an alarm or gather the people. See note on Hos 5:8. **eagle** The Hebrew word refers to any large bird of prey and is often translated as "eagle" or "vulture" (see note on Eze 17:3). Here, the bird symbolizes a foreign invader—probably Assyria. **house of the LORD** Though this phrase usually refers to the temple in Jerusalem, Hosea uses it more generically to refer to the land of Israel (see Hos 9:4,15). **broken my covenant** Compare 6:7 and note.
8:2 Israel cries out to me, 'Our God, we acknowledge you!' The Israelites are bewildered that Yahweh is not responding to their cry, even though they are simply going through the motions of legalistic ritual. Their outward ritualism conceals an inward rebellion (compare 6:6 and note).
8:4 They set up kings The kingship in Israel had passed through the hands of numerous usurpers since the time of Jeroboam I (1Ki 11–12). Few of those kings were divinely appointed. The only notable exceptions were

With their silver and gold
    they make idols for themselves
    to their own destruction.
5 Samaria, throw out your calf-idol!
    My anger burns against them.
How long will they be incapable of purity?
6   They are from Israel!
This calf — a metalworker has made it;
    it is not God.
It will be broken in pieces,
    that calf of Samaria.

7 "They sow the wind
    and reap the whirlwind.
The stalk has no head;
    it will produce no flour.
Were it to yield grain,
    foreigners would swallow it up.
8 Israel is swallowed up;
    now she is among the nations
    like something no one wants.
9 For they have gone up to Assyria
    like a wild donkey wandering alone.
Ephraim has sold herself to lovers.
10 Although they have sold themselves among
    the nations,
    I will now gather them together.
They will begin to waste away
    under the oppression of the mighty king.

11 "Though Ephraim built many altars for sin
    offerings,
    these have become altars for sinning.

12 I wrote for them the many things of my law,
    but they regarded them as something
    foreign.
13 Though they offer sacrifices as gifts
    to me,
    and though they eat the meat,
    the Lord is not pleased with them.
Now he will remember their wickedness
    and punish their sins:
    They will return to Egypt.
14 Israel has forgotten their Maker
    and built palaces;
Judah has fortified many towns.
But I will send fire on their cities
    that will consume their fortresses."

Punishment for Israel

9 Do not rejoice, Israel;
    do not be jubilant like the other nations.
For you have been unfaithful to your God;
    you love the wages of a prostitute
    at every threshing floor.
2 Threshing floors and winepresses will not
    feed the people;
    the new wine will fail them.
3 They will not remain in the Lord's land;
    Ephraim will return to Egypt
    and eat unclean food in Assyria.
4 They will not pour out wine offerings to the
    Lord,
    nor will their sacrifices please him.

Jeroboam (1Ki 11:29–40) and Jehu (2Ki 9:1–3). The political turmoil of the last two decades of Israel's existence resulted in part from the rule of weak, illegitimate kings after the dynasty of Jehu was eliminated in 745 BC. See note on Hos 1:1. See the timeline "The Divided Kingdom" on p. 536. **With their silver and gold they make idols** Jeroboam made two golden calves and established shrines at Bethel and Dan so the northern Israelites would not need to travel to Jerusalem for sacrifices. See 1Ki 12:28–30.

8:6 calf of Samaria Refers to the calf idol at Bethel (1Ki 12:28–29). Samaria refers to Israel in general. Canaanite religion often used bull and calf images, as demonstrated by the discovery of bovine figurines at Ugarit, Tyre and Hazor. The god El was also known as "Bull El," and Near Eastern storm gods, such as Baal, are often depicted riding a bull. Jeroboam's golden calves were probably a representation of Yahweh's mount, with Yahweh riding a bull like other storm gods. Hosea condemns these idols as reflections of the sort of religious blending (syncretism) that Yahweh disapproved of. By Hosea's time, Assyria had probably taken control of the northern region, including Dan, so only the shrine at Bethel would have remained.

8:9 Ephraim has sold herself to lovers Refers to political allies. See note on Hos 2:5.

8:10 under the oppression The heavy tribute Assyria exacted was a major factor inspiring rebellion in Israel and surrounding kingdoms.

8:13 They will return to Egypt Reverses the deliverance from Egypt as punishment. See Dt 28:68.

8:14 built palaces In their prosperity, the people of Israel have neglected to acknowledge Yahweh as the one responsible for blessing them.

9:1—10:15 Hosea 9 and 10 continue the prophet's poetic account of Israel's spiritual history, focusing on the religious unfaithfulness and moral injustice that characterized their most prosperous period since King Solomon. The prophet looks back on Israel's sin and lack of repentance, and he warns of imminent judgment.

9:1 you love the wages of a prostitute Israel's produce is again portrayed as a prostitute's wages. Compare 2:12 and note. **every threshing floor** The site where ancients brought grain and processed it after the harvest. This location was probably connected with festivals celebrating the harvest, which could have involved prostitution. See the infographic "A Threshing Floor" on p. 497.

9:2 will not feed In punishment, they will lose the material provision that they had attributed to their idols. See 2:5 and note.

9:3 They will not remain in the Lord's land Punishment involves removal from the land. **Ephraim will return to Egypt** The mention of Egypt and Assyria reflects Israel's changing political alliances. See 8:13 and note.

9:4 wine offerings See note on Eze 20:28. **bread of mourners** Anyone who had contact with a dead body became ritually unclean for seven days (Nu 19:11). By extension, their food was also unclean and could not be used for religious offerings.

Such sacrifices will be to them like the bread
of mourners;
all who eat them will be unclean.
This food will be for themselves;
it will not come into the temple
of the LORD.

5 What will you do on the day of your
appointed festivals,
on the feast days of the LORD?
6 Even if they escape from destruction,
Egypt will gather them,
and Memphis will bury them.
Their treasures of silver will be taken over
by briers,
and thorns will overrun their tents.
7 The days of punishment are coming,
the days of reckoning are at hand.
Let Israel know this.
Because your sins are so many
and your hostility so great,
the prophet is considered a fool,
the inspired person a maniac.
8 The prophet, along with my God,
is the watchman over Ephraim,[a]
yet snares await him on all his paths,
and hostility in the house of his God.
9 They have sunk deep into corruption,
as in the days of Gibeah.
God will remember their wickedness
and punish them for their sins.

10 "When I found Israel,
it was like finding grapes in the desert;
when I saw your ancestors,
it was like seeing the early fruit on the
fig tree.
But when they came to Baal Peor,
they consecrated themselves to that
shameful idol
and became as vile as the thing they loved.
11 Ephraim's glory will fly away like a bird —
no birth, no pregnancy, no conception.
12 Even if they rear children,
I will bereave them of every one.
Woe to them
when I turn away from them!

13 I have seen Ephraim, like Tyre,
planted in a pleasant place.
But Ephraim will bring out
their children to the slayer."

14 Give them, LORD —
what will you give them?
Give them wombs that miscarry
and breasts that are dry.

15 "Because of all their wickedness in Gilgal,
I hated them there.
Because of their sinful deeds,
I will drive them out of my house.
I will no longer love them;
all their leaders are rebellious.
16 Ephraim is blighted,
their root is withered,
they yield no fruit.
Even if they bear children,
I will slay their cherished offspring."

17 My God will reject them
because they have not obeyed him;
they will be wanderers among the nations.

10 Israel was a spreading vine;
he brought forth fruit for himself.
As his fruit increased,
he built more altars;
as his land prospered,
he adorned his sacred stones.
2 Their heart is deceitful,
and now they must bear their guilt.
The LORD will demolish their altars
and destroy their sacred stones.

3 Then they will say, "We have no king
because we did not revere the LORD.
But even if we had a king,
what could he do for us?"
4 They make many promises,
take false oaths
and make agreements;
therefore lawsuits spring up
like poisonous weeds in a plowed field.

---

a 8 Or *The prophet is the watchman over Ephraim, / the people of my God*

9:6 Memphis will bury them A capital of Egypt. See note on Eze 30:13.
9:7 your sins are so many and your hostility so great Israel never repented from iniquity, making the prophet's conditional message of restoration appear foolish. **inspired person** Refers to the prophet who experienced God's revelation through his spirit. These lines about the prophet being a fool and a madman likely reflect Israel's reaction to the prophet's preaching.
9:8 The prophet, along with my God, is the watchman over Ephraim A prophet, like a watchman, was responsible for giving warnings about danger. See note on Eze 3:17.
9:9 in the days of Gibeah Refers to the events of Jdg 19–21. See note on Hos 5:8.
9:10 early fruit on the fig tree Figs symbolized prosperity and security. See note on Jer 24:1. **Baal Peor** Refers to an occasion during the exodus when Israel committed idolatry. See Nu 25:1–18 and note.
9:15 Gilgal A site near Jericho that was an important religious center in the time of Samuel. See note on Hos 4:15.
10:1 Israel was a spreading vine For related vine metaphors, see Eze 15:1–8 and note. **he built more altars** Israel's prosperity only inspired further idolatry. Compare Dt 8:11–14.
10:3 We have no king Foreshadows the end of the northern kingdom.

5 The people who live in Samaria fear
  for the calf-idol of Beth Aven.*
Its people will mourn over it,
  and so will its idolatrous priests,
those who had rejoiced over its splendor,
  because it is taken from them into exile.
6 It will be carried to Assyria
  as tribute for the great king.
Ephraim will be disgraced;
  Israel will be ashamed of its foreign
    alliances.
7 Samaria's king will be destroyed,
  swept away like a twig on the surface of
    the waters.
8 The high places of wickedness* will be
    destroyed—
  it is the sin of Israel.
Thorns and thistles will grow up
  and cover their altars.
Then they will say to the mountains,
  "Cover us!"
  and to the hills, "Fall on us!"

9 "Since the days of Gibeah, you have sinned,
    Israel,
  and there you have remained.*
Will not war again overtake
  the evildoers in Gibeah?
10 When I please, I will punish them;
  nations will be gathered against them
to put them in bonds for their double sin.
11 Ephraim is a trained heifer
  that loves to thresh;
so I will put a yoke
  on her fair neck.
I will drive Ephraim,
  Judah must plow,
  and Jacob must break up the ground.
12 Sow righteousness for yourselves,
  reap the fruit of unfailing love,

and break up your unplowed ground;
  for it is time to seek the LORD,
until he comes
  and showers his righteousness on you.
13 But you have planted wickedness,
  you have reaped evil,
  you have eaten the fruit of deception.
Because you have depended on your own
    strength
  and on your many warriors,
14 the roar of battle will rise against your
    people,
  so that all your fortresses will be
    devastated—
as Shalman devastated Beth Arbel on the day
    of battle,
  when mothers were dashed to the ground
    with their children.
15 So will it happen to you, Bethel,
  because your wickedness is great.
When that day dawns,
  the king of Israel will be completely
    destroyed.

God's Love for Israel

11 "When Israel was a child, I loved him,
  and out of Egypt I called my son.
2 But the more they were called,
  the more they went away from me.*
They sacrificed to the Baals
  and they burned incense to images.
3 It was I who taught Ephraim to walk,
  taking them by the arms;
but they did not realize
  it was I who healed them.

---

a 5 Beth Aven means *house of wickedness* (a derogatory name for
Bethel, which means *house of God*). *b 8* Hebrew *aven,* a
reference to Beth Aven (a derogatory name for Bethel); see verse 5.
c 9 Or *there a stand was taken* *d 2* Septuagint; Hebrew *them*

10:5 Samaria The capital city of the northern kingdom.
See note on Jer 31:5. **calf-idol of Beth Aven** Refers
to the golden calf set up at Bethel. See Hos 4:15 and
note; 8:6 and note. **it is taken from them into exile**
In applying the punishment of exile to the calf (compare
Jer 48:7 and note), the Hebrew text reflects the ancient
Near Eastern practice of deporting the idols of conquered
cities (see note on Isa 46:1–13).
10:6 Israel will be ashamed of its foreign alliances
Because this false god was unable to save the nation.
10:8 high places Local religious shrines. See note on Isa
57:7. **wickedness** Refers to Beth Aven; "Aven" means
"wickedness." See note on Hos 4:15.
10:9 Gibeah Refers to the events of Jdg 19–21. See
note on Hos 5:8
10:10 their double sin An allusion to the two golden
calves set up by Jeroboam (1Ki 12:28).
10:12 break up your unplowed ground An agricultural
metaphor urging the people to prepare themselves to
accept God's message and repent.
10:14 Shalman devastated Beth Arbel The reference

here is uncertain. The prophet might be alluding to a
campaign of an Assyrian king named Shalmaneser.
10:15 Bethel Location of the Israelite shrine with the
golden calf. See note on Hos 8:6.

11:1–11 This oracle of compassion and restoration highlights Yahweh's love for his people even as they continue
to stray and rebel. Though their rebellion requires him
to judge them (vv. 5–7), his compassion will ultimately
overcome his wrath. He will renew his relationship with
Israel, restoring its people to their land and their homes.

11:1 out of Egypt I called my son Refers to the events
of the exodus (see Ex 1–15). The Gospel of Matthew
cites this phrase in connection with Jesus' return from
Egypt (Mt 2:14–15). Hosea is alluding to the exodus,
but Matthew understands the verse as pointing forward
to future Messianic fulfillment. He takes the historical
events symbolically as a typology where Jesus fulfills
the mission to obey and keep the Law in a literal way
that Israel could not.
11:2 the more they went away from me See Isa
1:2–4. **Baals** See note on Hos 2:13.

⁴ I led them with cords of human kindness,
with ties of love.
To them I was like one who lifts
a little child to the cheek,
and I bent down to feed them.

⁵ "Will they not return to Egypt
and will not Assyria rule over them
because they refuse to repent?
⁶ A sword will flash in their cities;
it will devour their false prophets
and put an end to their plans.
⁷ My people are determined to turn from me.
Even though they call me God Most High,
I will by no means exalt them.

⁸ "How can I give you up, Ephraim?
How can I hand you over, Israel?
How can I treat you like Admah?
How can I make you like Zeboyim?
My heart is changed within me;
all my compassion is aroused.
⁹ I will not carry out my fierce anger,
nor will I devastate Ephraim again.
For I am God, and not a man—
the Holy One among you.
I will not come against their cities.
¹⁰ They will follow the LORD;
he will roar like a lion.
When he roars,
his children will come trembling from the
west.
¹¹ They will come from Egypt,
trembling like sparrows,
from Assyria, fluttering like doves.

I will settle them in their homes,"
declares the LORD.

Israel's Sin

¹² Ephraim has surrounded me with lies,
Israel with deceit.
And Judah is unruly against God,
even against the faithful Holy One.^a

12 ^b ¹ Ephraim feeds on the wind;
he pursues the east wind all day
and multiplies lies and violence.
He makes a treaty with Assyria
and sends olive oil to Egypt.
² The LORD has a charge to bring against Judah;
he will punish Jacob^c according to his ways
and repay him according to his deeds.
³ In the womb he grasped his brother's heel;
as a man he struggled with God.
⁴ He struggled with the angel and overcame
him;
he wept and begged for his favor.
He found him at Bethel
and talked with him there—
⁵ the LORD God Almighty,
the LORD is his name!
⁶ But you must return to your God;
maintain love and justice,
and wait for your God always.

⁷ The merchant uses dishonest scales
and loves to defraud.

^a 12 In Hebrew texts this verse (11:12) is numbered 12:1. ^b In Hebrew texts 12:1-14 is numbered 12:2-15. ^c 2 Jacob means *he grasps the heel*, a Hebrew idiom for *he takes advantage of* or *he deceives*.

11:4 cords of human kindness The prophet uses imagery of a farmer caring for his livestock. **one who lifts a little child** Yahweh used cords, bands and the yoke for gentle guidance—not oppression.
11:5 Will they not return to Egypt English translations have produced contradictory readings of this phrase. Some translations read, "shall return" or "surely shall return," which would parallel the punishment described in 8:13. Other translations say "shall not return," perhaps indicating a change in the punishment (from returning to slavery in Egypt to domination by Assyria; compare 9:3). Another approach is to read the opening part of the verse as a rhetorical question: "Will they not return …?" **Assyria rule over them** After Israel (the northern kingdom) falls in 722 BC, the region becomes a province of Assyria. The Assyrians take the Israelites into exile.
11:8 How can I give you up, Ephraim Jeremiah 31:20 and Isa 49:15 contain similar expressions of Yahweh's love for Israel. **Admah** A proverbial image of a city destroyed by divine wrath. Admah is one of the cities of the plain associated with Sodom and Gomorrah in Genesis (Ge 10:19; 14:2). **Zeboyim** The sister city of Admah; destroyed along with Sodom and Gomorrah (Ge 10:19; 19:29).
11:10 he will roar like a lion A common image for Yahweh that emphasizes his strength (compare Am 1:2; Joel 3:16; Jer 25:30). **will come trembling from the**

west Illustrates Yahweh bringing a group of survivors of Israel (the remnant) back to the land (compare Isa 11:11–16; 35:10; 60:4; Jer 16:15).
12:1 feeds on the wind Refers to Israel's idolatry and ill-advised alliances. Such efforts are ultimately unsatisfying because they do not involve trusting in Yahweh. **makes a treaty with Assyria** Probably alludes to King Hoshea's shifting alliances (2Ki 17:3–4).
12:2–14 Hosea continues to emphasize Israel's religious and political failings, using traditions about the patriarch Jacob to parallel Israel's wanderings. The comparison with Jacob emphasizes his reputation for deceit and desire for personal gain.
12:2 Jacob Refers to Israel, using the name of the nation's ancestor (Ge 32:28).
12:3 he grasped his brother's heel Alludes to Jacob's birth and the act that earned him the name "Jacob," which means "he supplants" (Ge 25:26). **as a man he struggled with God** Alludes to the event where God renames Jacob as "Israel" (Ge 32:28).
12:4 He found him at Bethel Alludes to the events of Ge 28:10–22, where Yahweh passes the promises he made with Abraham and Isaac to Jacob.
12:7 uses dishonest scales Incorrect weights used in dishonest trade. See note on Jer 32:10.

8 Ephraim boasts,
"I am very rich; I have become wealthy.
With all my wealth they will not find in me
any iniquity or sin."

9 "I have been the LORD your God
ever since you came out of Egypt;
I will make you live in tents again,
as in the days of your appointed festivals.
10 I spoke to the prophets,
gave them many visions
and told parables through them."

11 Is Gilead wicked?
Its people are worthless!
Do they sacrifice bulls in Gilgal?
Their altars will be like piles of stones
on a plowed field.
12 Jacob fled to the country of Aram a;
Israel served to get a wife,
and to pay for her he tended sheep.
13 The LORD used a prophet to bring Israel up
from Egypt,
by a prophet he cared for him.
14 But Ephraim has aroused his bitter anger;
his Lord will leave on him the guilt of his
bloodshed
and will repay him for his contempt.

The LORD's Anger Against Israel

13 When Ephraim spoke, people trembled;
he was exalted in Israel.
But he became guilty of Baal worship and
died.
2 Now they sin more and more;
they make idols for themselves from their
silver,
cleverly fashioned images,
all of them the work of craftsmen.

It is said of these people,
"They offer human sacrifices!
They kiss b calf-idols!"
3 Therefore they will be like the morning mist,
like the early dew that disappears,
like chaff swirling from a threshing floor,
like smoke escaping through a window.

4 "But I have been the LORD your God
ever since you came out of Egypt.
You shall acknowledge no God but me,
no Savior except me.
5 I cared for you in the wilderness,
in the land of burning heat.
6 When I fed them, they were satisfied;
when they were satisfied, they became
proud;
then they forgot me.
7 So I will be like a lion to them,
like a leopard I will lurk by the path.
8 Like a bear robbed of her cubs,
I will attack them and rip them open;
like a lion I will devour them —
a wild animal will tear them apart.

9 "You are destroyed, Israel,
because you are against me, against your
helper.
10 Where is your king, that he may save you?
Where are your rulers in all your towns,
of whom you said,
'Give me a king and princes'?
11 So in my anger I gave you a king,
and in my wrath I took him away.
12 The guilt of Ephraim is stored up,
his sins are kept on record.

a 12 That is, Northwest Mesopotamia   b 2 Or "Men who sacrifice / kiss

---

12:8 they will not find in me any iniquity or sin Ephraim understands material prosperity as the result of divine blessing; they follow a stereotypical way of thinking, equating blessing with righteousness and suffering with sin. See note on Jer 12:1.
12:9 I will make you live in tents again Alludes to the Festival of Tabernacles (Lev 23:39–43). Apparently, the Israelites had been neglecting this observance (Ne 8:13–18). See the table "Israelite Festivals" on p. 200.
12:10 told parables through them Although the word for "parable" does not appear in the Hebrew text, the verb used here implies speaking in metaphorical language.
12:11 Gilead A region east of the Jordan River. See note on Hos 6:8. **Gilgal** A site near Jericho that was an important religious center in the time of Samuel. See note on 4:15.
12:12 Jacob fled to the country of Aram Alludes to the events of Ge 28–29. The allusion also invokes hope of restoration because Jacob eventually returned to Palestine.
12:13 LORD used a prophet The prophet shifts from relating traditions about Jacob to alluding to Moses leading Israel (Dt 18:15).

13:1–16 This collection of prophetic sayings reiterates the main accusations against Israel and interweaves them with images of Yahweh's judgment. The imagery is familiar and continues to utilize Hosea's poetic style of using word pictures. Hosea's confident certainty in Israel's sin and Yahweh's coming judgment unify the diverse material in these sayings.

13:1 When Ephraim spoke, people trembled Emphasizes Ephraim's former place of prominence among the tribes of Israel. **Baal** The chief god of the Canaanites.
13:2 human sacrifices Baal-worship involved child sacrifice. See note on Isa 57:5; compare note on Jer 7:31. **They kiss** A sign of respect or devotion (1Ki 19:18). **calf-idols** Likely referring to a calf idol connected with Baal-worship (see note on Hos 8:6).
13:3 like the morning mist Compare 6:4.
13:4 no Savior except me The prophet invokes the exodus traditions to assert Yahweh's sovereignty. Compare Isa 43:11.
13:7 So I will be like a lion to them The prophets regularly used wild animals to symbolize divine judgment (Eze 5:17; see Jer 5:6 and note; compare Hos 5:14).
13:10 your king See 8:4 and note.

[13] Pains as of a woman in childbirth come to
him,
but he is a child without wisdom;
when the time arrives,
he doesn't have the sense to come out of
the womb.

[14] "I will deliver this people from the power of
the grave;
I will redeem them from death.
Where, O death, are your plagues?
Where, O grave, is your destruction?

"I will have no compassion,
[15]   even though he thrives among his
brothers.
An east wind from the LORD will come,
blowing in from the desert;
his spring will fail
and his well dry up.
His storehouse will be plundered
of all its treasures.
[16] The people of Samaria must bear their guilt,
because they have rebelled against their
God.
They will fall by the sword;
their little ones will be dashed to the
ground,
their pregnant women ripped open."[a]

Repentance to Bring Blessing

14 [b] Return, Israel, to the LORD your God.
Your sins have been your downfall!
[2] Take words with you
and return to the LORD.
Say to him:
"Forgive all our sins

and receive us graciously,
that we may offer the fruit of our lips.[c]
[3] Assyria cannot save us;
we will not mount warhorses.
We will never again say 'Our gods'
to what our own hands have made,
for in you the fatherless find compassion."

[4] "I will heal their waywardness
and love them freely,
for my anger has turned away from them.
[5] I will be like the dew to Israel;
he will blossom like a lily.
Like a cedar of Lebanon
he will send down his roots;
[6]   his young shoots will grow.
His splendor will be like an olive tree,
his fragrance like a cedar of Lebanon.
[7] People will dwell again in his shade;
they will flourish like the grain,
they will blossom like the vine —
Israel's fame will be like the wine of
Lebanon.
[8] Ephraim, what more have I[d] to do with
idols?
I will answer him and care for him.
I am like a flourishing juniper;
your fruitfulness comes from me."

[9] Who is wise? Let them realize these things.
Who is discerning? Let them understand.
The ways of the LORD are right;
the righteous walk in them,
but the rebellious stumble in them.

---

[a] 16 In Hebrew texts this verse (13:16) is numbered 14:1.   [b] In
Hebrew texts 14:1-9 is numbered 14:2-10.   [c] 2 Or offer our lips
as sacrifices of bulls   [d] 8 Or Hebrew; Septuagint What more
has Ephraim

13:14 power of the grave Refers to death and the afterlife. See note on Job 14:13. **Where, O grave, is your
destruction** Quoted by the apostle Paul in 1Co 15:55.
13:15 east A symbol of divine judgment. Compare Jer
18:17 and note.
13:16 Samaria The capital of the northern kingdom
Israel. See note on Jer 31:5.

14:1–9 Hosea concludes with a call for Israel to repent and a promise of Yahweh's forgiveness and future
restoration.

14:2 fruit of our lips Probably refers to Israel's verbal
confession, which is more important than actual sacrifices
(compare Ps 50:7–23).
14:3 Assyria cannot save us Israel's confession includes an acknowledgement of its two main failings:

seeking foreign political aid and serving manmade idols.
The confession also alludes to past injustice by mentioning Yahweh's concern for the orphan (Ex 22:22–23).
14:4 I will heal their waywardness Yahweh responds
to Israel's confession.
14:5 he will blossom like a lily Oracles of salvation
regularly employ imagery of renewed fertility and natural
abundance. Compare Isa 27:6. **cedar of Lebanon** See
note on Isa 2:13.
14:8 your fruitfulness comes from me Yahweh has
always provided, but Ephraim needs to acknowledge
him instead of attributing success to the worship of
Baal. Compare 2:8.
14:9 Who is wise Hosea concludes with a Proverbs-like
exhortation to seek true wisdom in following the ways
of Yahweh (compare Ps 107:43; Jer 9:21; Pr 10:29).

JOEL

INTRODUCTION TO JOEL

The book of Joel is concerned with the Day of Yahweh, a coming time when God will judge the world and make all things right. Joel draws on a real-life catastrophe—a swarm of locusts devastating the land of Judah—to warn of the disaster that the Day of Yahweh will bring to those who do not repent. He also promises that God will save the people of Judah and Jerusalem who call on him (Joel 2:32).

BACKGROUND

The Bible does not provide any biographical information about the prophet Joel (other than his father's name, Pethuel; 1:1). Since the book addresses a situation in Judah, Joel probably prophesied in this region rather than in the northern territory of Israel.

The date of Joel is uncertain, but the book could have been written during the period when Judah was an independent kingdom, as early as the late ninth century BC. It also could have been composed after the Babylonian exile, during the sixth century BC, when Judah was a province of the Persian Empire. Based on Joel 1:13 and 2:17, the temple clearly was functioning when the book was written, but this could have been Solomon's temple (before the exile) or Zerubbabel's temple (after the exile).

This map depicts many of the locations related to the book of Joel.

STRUCTURE

The first half of the book (1:1—2:17) focuses on disaster and judgment for Judah, while the second half (2:18—3:21) focuses on God's restoration of Judah and judgment of Judah's enemies. Each half can be divided into two sections.

The first section (ch. 1) describes a plague of locusts that brings about a famine. In response, Joel calls the people to repent in preparation for the Day of Yahweh (1:13–16). The second section (2:1–17) warns of judgment on the Day of Yahweh. It portrays an attacking army as if it were a locust invasion; this is the army of Yahweh (2:11). Again, the section ends with a call to repentance and an affirmation of God's mercy and love (2:12–14).

In the book's latter half, the third section (2:18–32) describes God restoring the land and bringing blessing—following the judgment and destruction described in the previous sections. God not only will restore the land's fertility (2:19–27), but also will pour out his Spirit upon all people (2:28–29). The fourth section (ch. 3) describes God's coming judgment on the nations that have been oppressing Judah. It ends with a portrayal of Judah's future glory, with God dwelling on Mount Zion (3:17–21).

OUTLINE

- The locust invasion (1:1–20)
- Judgment on God's people (2:1–17)
- Consolation for God's people (2:18–32)
- Judgment on the nations (3:1–21)

THEMES

The main theme of Joel is the approaching Day of Yahweh, which initially brings pain for God's people (the first half of the book) but ultimately leads to their renewal and vindication (the second half). In a locust plague, Joel sees just how frail humanity is and just how chaotic the world really is—emphasizing how desperately we need God. In the plague, Joel also sees a glimpse of what it will be like when Yahweh's heavenly army invades the world to bring about order and

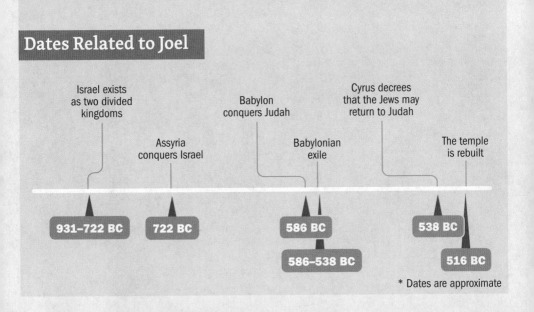

Dates Related to Joel

Israel exists as two divided kingdoms

Assyria conquers Israel

Babylon conquers Judah

Babylonian exile

Cyrus decrees that the Jews may return to Judah

The temple is rebuilt

931–722 BC   722 BC   586 BC   538 BC

586–538 BC   516 BC

* Dates are approximate

peace: It will be grim before it gets better, because the evil that pervades much of humanity must be removed.

The forthcoming Day of Yahweh is meant to prompt God's people to change their ways. The locust plague serves as a warning (e.g., 1:14): People should turn to God with their whole hearts now, while there is still opportunity (2:12–13).

Joel emphasizes that God's mercy will only extend so far before he returns to make all things right. And on that day, like locusts eat a field, God's judgment will consume the evil of the world (chs. 1–2; compare 2Pe 3:10). God will have pity on repentant people and save those who call on his name, which is what all are called to do now (Joel 2:18–19,32). Joel reminds us that God is present and active in the world, working toward a difficult but beautiful end—the restoration of peace and justice throughout the world.

1

The word of the LORD that came to Joel son of Pethuel.

An Invasion of Locusts

2 Hear this, you elders;
  listen, all who live in the land.
Has anything like this ever happened in your
    days
  or in the days of your ancestors?
3 Tell it to your children,
    and let your children tell it to their
      children,
    and their children to the next generation.
4 What the locust swarm has left
    the great locusts have eaten;
  what the great locusts have left
    the young locusts have eaten;
  what the young locusts have left
    other locusts*a* have eaten.

5 Wake up, you drunkards, and weep!
  Wail, all you drinkers of wine;
  wail because of the new wine,
    for it has been snatched from your lips.
6 A nation has invaded my land,
    a mighty army without number;
  it has the teeth of a lion,
    the fangs of a lioness.
7 It has laid waste my vines
    and ruined my fig trees.
  It has stripped off their bark
    and thrown it away,
    leaving their branches white.

8 Mourn like a virgin in sackcloth
    grieving for the betrothed of her youth.
9 Grain offerings and drink offerings
    are cut off from the house of the LORD.

a 4 The precise meaning of the four Hebrew words used here for locusts is uncertain.

1:1 Nothing is known about the prophet Joel aside from his name and his father's name. Joel, meaning "Yahweh is God," was a common first name in ancient Israel, with some 15 Biblical figures bearing the name. Joel's language reflects traditional prophetic forms of speech and phrasing. Like the other prophets, he shows a level of familiarity with temple worship and ritual. His references to Zion (2:1,15,32) and Jerusalem (2:32; 3:1) suggest that he prophesied in Judah, the southern kingdom. The dating of his prophecies hinges on which invasion is linked to his metaphor of the locust plague; options range from the late eighth century BC to the postexilic period (fifth or fourth century BC).

The central theme of his short message is the coming Day of Yahweh. Joel's prophecies can be divided into thematic halves. The first half is focused on judgment and repentance (vv. 1:1—2:17); the second half represents Yahweh's response to the people, promising future restoration and judgment on the nations (2:18—3:21). See the timeline "Approximate Dates of Old Testament Prophets" on p. 1070.

1:1 word of the LORD A common introductory phrase (see Hos 1:1 and note). **Joel son of Pethuel** Joel's name means "Yahweh is God." The meaning of his father's name is uncertain, perhaps "young man of God."

1:2–20 Joel opens by calling the people to realize that the national calamity upon them—an invasion of locusts—is a precursor of the military invasion they can expect as judgment unless they repent. The first section describes the coming locust invasion. It ends with a call for repentance that links the locust disaster to the coming Day of Yahweh.

1:2 Hear this, you elders A standard phrase prophets used to call their audiences to attention (compare Hos 4:1). **elders** Chief leaders of the people (see note on Jer 26:17). The address to the elders may imply there is no longer a king. This could point to a postexilic date for the book. The elders were important leaders during the exile and the Second Temple community. Compare Eze 8:1; Ezr 5:5. **or in the days of your ancestors** Evokes the imagery of the plague of locusts on Egypt (see Ex 10:4–6).

1:4 the locust swarm Joel used four different Hebrew words for "locust" to emphasize the extreme nature of the ecological disaster. Locusts came in swarms, consuming all plant growth (see Ex 10:4–6). The locust swarm was part of the curse for breaking the covenant (see Dt 28:38). The four terms for locusts probably do not designate different species of locust or different stages in the locusts' development. The terms are regularly used in parallel throughout Biblical poetry. Joel is likely describing four successive waves of locusts that wreak total havoc on the agriculture and plant life of the region. Apocalyptic imagery uses the motif of four destroyers predominantly to emphasize total destruction and judgment (compare Eze 14:21; Da 7:1–7; Rev 6:1–8; 9:15).

1:5 it has been snatched from your lips The devastation of the vineyards will mean no more wine for the drunkards.

1:6 A nation has invaded my land Comparing an invading army to locusts is a common motif in the Bible and ancient Near Eastern literature (Jdg 6:5; Jer 5:15–17; 46:23; 51:14). Joel reverses the image, comparing the swarm of locusts to an invading army (Joel 2:4–5).

1:7 It has laid waste my vines Lush vineyards and fig trees symbolize an ideal of prosperous peace (1Ki 4:25; Isa 36:16–17; Mic 4:4). The devastation of vines and figs is a common symbol of judgment (see Jer 8:13 and note). The reference to vines and fig trees also signifies the extent of the devastation—locusts tend to attack vines and fig trees only after they have consumed everything else.

1:8 like a virgin in sackcloth The metaphor evokes the depth of mourning of a young woman who has lost her fiancé and her security for the future. **in sackcloth** A coarse garment symbolic of mourning. Sackcloth was often made of camel or goat hair.

1:9 Grain offerings and drink offerings Because of the devastation from the locusts, neither grain nor wine were available to use in the daily offerings at the temple (Ex 29:38–41; Lev 23:13). An Akkadian hymn from the time of Sargon II (722–705 BC) similarly laments that a locust plague threatens to cut off the regular offerings of god and goddess. **the house of the LORD** Joel's references to the temple and temple worship suggest he is not writing during the exile when the temple was destroyed. Solomon's temple was destroyed in 586 BC

The priests are in mourning,
    those who minister before the Lord.
¹⁰ The fields are ruined,
    the ground is dried up;
the grain is destroyed,
    the new wine is dried up,
    the olive oil fails.

¹¹ Despair, you farmers,
    wail, you vine growers;
grieve for the wheat and the barley,
    because the harvest of the field is
      destroyed.
¹² The vine is dried up
    and the fig tree is withered;
the pomegranate, the palm and the apple*ᵃ*
    tree —
    all the trees of the field — are dried up.
Surely the people's joy
    is withered away.

A Call to Lamentation

¹³ Put on sackcloth, you priests, and mourn;
    wail, you who minister before the altar.
Come, spend the night in sackcloth,
    you who minister before my God;
for the grain offerings and drink offerings
    are withheld from the house of your God.
¹⁴ Declare a holy fast;
    call a sacred assembly.
Summon the elders
    and all who live in the land
to the house of the Lord your God,
    and cry out to the Lord.

¹⁵ Alas for that day!
    For the day of the Lord is near;
    it will come like destruction from the
      Almighty.*ᵇ*

¹⁶ Has not the food been cut off
    before our very eyes —
joy and gladness
    from the house of our God?
¹⁷ The seeds are shriveled
    beneath the clods.*ᶜ*
The storehouses are in ruins,
    the granaries have been broken down,
    for the grain has dried up.
¹⁸ How the cattle moan!
    The herds mill about
because they have no pasture;
    even the flocks of sheep are suffering.

¹⁹ To you, Lord, I call,
    for fire has devoured the pastures in the
      wilderness
    and flames have burned up all the trees of
      the field.
²⁰ Even the wild animals pant for you;
    the streams of water have dried up
    and fire has devoured the pastures in the
      wilderness.

An Army of Locusts

2 Blow the trumpet in Zion;
    sound the alarm on my holy hill.

Let all who live in the land tremble,
    for the day of the Lord is coming.
It is close at hand —
²   a day of darkness and gloom,
    a day of clouds and blackness.
Like dawn spreading across the mountains
    a large and mighty army comes,
such as never was in ancient times
    nor ever will be in ages to come.

ᵃ 12 Or possibly *apricot*   *ᵇ 15* Hebrew *Shaddai*
ᶜ 17 The meaning of the Hebrew for this word is uncertain.

(2Ki 25:9). The second temple was completed around 516 BC (Ezr 6:14–15.).

1:10 fields are ruined The destructive effects from a locust attack affected economic growth for many years, not just the current growing season. The devastation of plant life could reduce the fertility of the fields, increase topsoil erosion and turn the region into a wasteland. Some fruit trees take years to mature before they produce fruit.

1:12 people's joy is withered away Harvest was a time of joy, so a ruined harvest was a time of grief. Compare Jer 48:33.

1:13 you priests, and mourn The disaster is interpreted as divine judgment. Joel calls on the priests to lead the people in mourning and repentance. The prophet's commands to the priests are found in Joel 1:13–14, while vv. 15–20 reflect the content of the prayer on behalf of the people.

1:14 a holy fast The practice of fasting is generally connected with mourning and repentance in the OT. The fast was part of the communal preparation that was necessary for seeking Yahweh's intervention in their situation.

1:15 day of the Lord is near Warning of the coming day of Yahweh's judgment is a prominent theme in the

OT prophets. The phrasing here is nearly identical to Isa 13:6 (see note on Isa 13:6). The Day of Yahweh is the main theme in the book of Joel. It can refer to two events: Yahweh's coming in judgment against Israel or the nations, or his coming to save his people. Joel uses the image in both ways, signifying both judgment and salvation.

1:19 fire has devoured the pastures Fire is a common image for divine judgment (see note on Isa 4:4).

2:1–17 The prophet continues to describe the chaos and cosmic upheaval accompanying the Day of Yahweh, depicting the invading locusts as an unstoppable army led by Yahweh. The terrifying judgment elicits another call for repentance as the priests intervene with Yahweh, pleading that the people be spared.

2:1 Blow the trumpet The trumpet was blown to warn of impending danger (see note on Jer 4:5). **Zion** Refers to the Temple Mount and, by extension, Jerusalem. Zion was envisioned as Yahweh's sacred dwelling (see note on Isa 2:2). **day of the Lord** See note on Joel 1:15.

2:2 a day of darkness and gloom Darkness is a typical element in the description of the Day of Yahweh (see

³ Before them fire devours,
  behind them a flame blazes.
Before them the land is like the garden of Eden,
  behind them, a desert waste —
  nothing escapes them.
⁴ They have the appearance of horses;
  they gallop along like cavalry.
⁵ With a noise like that of chariots
  they leap over the mountaintops,
like a crackling fire consuming stubble,
  like a mighty army drawn up for battle.

⁶ At the sight of them, nations are in anguish;
  every face turns pale.
⁷ They charge like warriors;
  they scale walls like soldiers.
They all march in line,
  not swerving from their course.
⁸ They do not jostle each other;
  each marches straight ahead.
They plunge through defenses
  without breaking ranks.
⁹ They rush upon the city;
  they run along the wall.
They climb into the houses;
  like thieves they enter through the windows.

¹⁰ Before them the earth shakes,
  the heavens tremble,
the sun and moon are darkened,
  and the stars no longer shine.
¹¹ The Lord thunders
  at the head of his army;
his forces are beyond number,
  and mighty is the army that obeys his
  command.

The day of the Lord is great;
  it is dreadful.
Who can endure it?

Rend Your Heart

¹² "Even now," declares the Lord,
  "return to me with all your heart,
  with fasting and weeping and mourning."

¹³ Rend your heart
  and not your garments.
Return to the Lord your God,
  for he is gracious and compassionate,
slow to anger and abounding in love,
  and he relents from sending calamity.
¹⁴ Who knows? He may turn and relent
  and leave behind a blessing —
grain offerings and drink offerings
  for the Lord your God.

¹⁵ Blow the trumpet in Zion,
  declare a holy fast,
  call a sacred assembly.
¹⁶ Gather the people,
  consecrate the assembly;
bring together the elders,
  gather the children,
  those nursing at the breast.
Let the bridegroom leave his room
  and the bride her chamber.
¹⁷ Let the priests, who minister before the Lord,
  weep between the portico and the altar.
Let them say, "Spare your people, Lord.
  Do not make your inheritance an object
  of scorn,
  a byword among the nations.

---

note on Eze 30:3; compare Zep 1:15; Am 5:18–20). Clouds and darkness accompany divine appearances, also called theophanies (see note on Ex 19:9). The imagery recalls the appearance of Yahweh to Israel on Mount Sinai (Ex 19:9–20; Dt 4:11). Here, the dark cloud of invading locusts mirrors the traditional imagery of divine judgment at the Day of Yahweh. See the table "Old Testament Theophanies" on p. 924.
2:3 Before them fire devours Fire is a common image for divine judgment (see note on Isa 4:4). **garden of Eden** Alludes to the lush, verdant growth of Yahweh's initial creation (Ge 2:8–9; see Isa 51:3 and note). Compared to the devastated land the locusts left behind, the land they have not yet touched looks as perfect as Eden.
2:5 like a mighty army Invading armies are often likened to locusts; here, locusts are instead compared to an army. See Joel 1:6 and note.
2:10 Before them the earth shakes Imagery of cosmic upheaval accompanies many descriptions of a theophany (compare Isa 13:13 and note).
2:11 The Lord thunders at the head of his army Placing Yahweh at the head of the locust army connects the natural disaster with divine judgment. **Who can endure it** Compare Mal 3:2.
2:12 return to me with all your heart Yahweh calls on his people to return and give him undivided devotion (compare Joel 1:13–14). Even in the face of impending

doom, the prophets regularly called for repentance with the hope that God would relent from the predicted judgment (compare Jer 4:1; Hos 12:6).
2:13 Rend your heart and not your garments Internal spiritual brokenness is more important than the outward act of tearing one's clothes, which was a sign of mourning (see Ge 37:29; compare Jer 4:4 and note). **gracious and compassionate** The second half of this verse is a formulaic description of Yahweh's character, highlighting grace, mercy, patience and loving kindness as the attributes by which he defines himself (Ex 34:6). This language is prominent in OT prayers that appeal to Yahweh's character to justify mercy when Israel deserved punishment (Nu 14:18; Ne 9:17; Ps 86:15; 103:8; 145:8; Jnh 4:2). The prophets also invoke this description when they are appealing to God to relent from disaster.
2:14 Who knows Reflects hope that there was still time to avoid judgment (compare Jnh 3:9).
2:15 Blow the trumpet in Zion Unlike Joel 2:1, the signal is calling for an assembly, not warning of danger. **declare a holy fast** Compare 1:14.
2:16 Gather the people, consecrate the assembly Everyone is called out for this assembly. See 2Ch 20:13.
2:17 the priests The temple priests are the ones offering the prayer of intercession on behalf of the people. **between the portico and the altar** The court in front of the temple. The location described is the traditional

Why should they say among the peoples,
  'Where is their God?'"

The LORD's Answer

¹⁸ Then the LORD was jealous for his land
  and took pity on his people.

¹⁹ The LORD replied^a to them:

"I am sending you grain, new wine and olive
    oil,
  enough to satisfy you fully;
never again will I make you
  an object of scorn to the nations.

²⁰ "I will drive the northern horde far from you,
    pushing it into a parched and barren land;
  its eastern ranks will drown in the Dead Sea
    and its western ranks will rise in the
      Mediterranean Sea.
  And its stench will go up;
    its smell will rise."

Surely he has done great things!
²¹   Do not be afraid, land of Judah;
    be glad and rejoice.
  Surely the LORD has done great things!
²²   Do not be afraid, you wild animals,
    for the pastures in the wilderness are
      becoming green.
  The trees are bearing their fruit;
    the fig tree and the vine yield their riches.
²³ Be glad, people of Zion,
    rejoice in the LORD your God,
  for he has given you the autumn rains
    because he is faithful.
  He sends you abundant showers,
    both autumn and spring rains, as before.
²⁴ The threshing floors will be filled with grain;
    the vats will overflow with new wine and
      oil.

^a 18,19 Or LORD will be jealous . . . / and take pity . . . / ¹⁹The
LORD will reply

---

spot for interceding before Yahweh (see 1Ki 8:22). **Where is their God** The disaster that befell Israel would make the surrounding nations believe that Yahweh had abandoned them. This language is typical of laments (Ps 42:3; 79:10; 115:2).

2:18—3:21 Yahweh answers the people's prayers in the second half of the book (see note on Joel 1:1). The promised restoration reverses the economic devastation from the locust invasion and offers assurance of a future day of judgment when Yahweh will punish the nations and renew Israel. The shift from a plea for deliverance to a statement of assurance is typical in lament psalms.

2:18 Then the LORD was jealous The transition in v. 18 is marked by the use of the Hebrew narrative past tense to introduce Yahweh's answer. **jealous for his land** In this context, Yahweh's jealousy is in concern for his own reputation. The nations questioned his ability to take care of his people in v. 17 (compare Eze 39:25; see note on Isa 48:19; note on Eze 20:9).

2:19 grain, new wine and olive oil Responds directly to the lament in Joel 1:16–17 about the crop failure caused by the locusts. **an object of scorn to the nations** This is a response to the plea in v. 17. The two verses are linked by their use of the Hebrew word *cherpah*, often translated as "disgrace," "reproach" or "scorn." See note on Eze 22:4.

2:20 northern The identity of the northerner is unclear; it may be locusts or an invading army. The enemy being driven into the sea is consistent with the image of the invaders as locusts, but locust swarms usually originate in the south around the Red Sea and the Arabian Peninsula. The motif of an invading enemy from the north is prominent in the books of Jeremiah and Ezekiel (see Jer 1:14 and note; Eze 38–39). Palestine was regularly invaded from the north by the Mesopotamian empires (Assyria, Babylon), so the image of a northern invader became prototypical for apocalyptic visions of a future enemy (Eze 38–39; Rev 20:8). Joel mixes the imagery of a northern invader with that of the locust swarm. **the Dead Sea** The Hebrew expression here may refer to the Dead Sea on the southeast side of Judah or the Persian Gulf on the eastern side of the Arabian Peninsula. **the**

Mediterranean Sea The Mediterranean Sea is described in Hebrew as the western sea. Locust swarms were often pushed out to sea by powerful eastern winds coming off the desert—the same prevailing winds that pushed them into Palestine in the first place. **stench** The smell of millions of dead locusts is likened to the stench of corpses from Yahweh's defeat of Israel's enemies (compare Isa 34:3).

2:22 pastures in the wilderness are becoming green The renewal of creation is a common element in oracles of restoration. Salvation is envisioned as a reestablishment of the ideal conditions of Yahweh's initial act of creation (compare Isa 35:1–10 and note). **fig tree and the vine yield their riches** A reversal of the destruction described in Joel 1:7. Compare Zec 8:12.

2:23 the autumn rains because he is faithful The Hebrew term used here primarily expresses righteousness, and can sometimes also express related concepts such as vindication. Context suggests Yahweh's generosity and faithfulness in renewing the usual cycle of rain (compare Hos 10:12). The word *moreh* is used only twice in the sense of "early rain" (Ps 84:6). The full phrase here is *hammoreh litsdaqah*. Disregarding the larger context of the verse, a Jewish sect understood this phrase as a reference to "the teacher of righteousness" since *moreh* is also a word for "teacher." They were expecting a leader who would "teach justice at the end of days" (Damascus Document 6.10–11). Their spiritual leader is frequently described with the title *hammoreh hatsedeq* in the Dead Sea Scrolls. **autumn and spring rains** The rainy season in Palestine begins in the autumn and runs until spring. In Hebrew, the term for autumn rains means the "early rain," and the term for spring rains means the "latter rain." These rainy seasons were crucial for the agricultural cycle. Grain was harvested in the spring and processed in the summer.

2:24 threshing floors Areas for removing kernels of grain from their stalks and husks. See the infographic "A Threshing Floor" on p. 497. **vats will overflow with new wine and oil** Grapes were harvested in the fall; olives were harvested in the fall and early winter. See the infographic "A Winepress in Ancient Israel" on p. 1157.

25 "I will repay you for the years the locusts
　　　have eaten —
　　the great locust and the young locust,
　　the other locusts and the locust swarm[a] —
　my great army that I sent among you.
26 You will have plenty to eat, until you are full,
　　　and you will praise the name of the Lord
　　　　your God,
　　who has worked wonders for you;
　never again will my people be shamed.
27 Then you will know that I am in Israel,
　　that I am the Lord your God,
　　　and that there is no other;
　never again will my people be shamed.

The Day of the Lord

28 "And afterward,
　　I will pour out my Spirit on all people.
　Your sons and daughters will prophesy,
　　your old men will dream dreams,
　　your young men will see visions.
29 Even on my servants, both men and women,
　　I will pour out my Spirit in those days.
30 I will show wonders in the heavens
　　and on the earth,
　　blood and fire and billows of smoke.
31 The sun will be turned to darkness
　　and the moon to blood
　　before the coming of the great and
　　　dreadful day of the Lord.

32 And everyone who calls
　　　on the name of the Lord will be
　　　　saved;
　for on Mount Zion and in Jerusalem
　　there will be deliverance,
　　as the Lord has said,
　even among the survivors
　　whom the Lord calls.[b]

The Nations Judged

3[c] "In those days and at that time,
　　when I restore the fortunes of Judah and
　　　Jerusalem,
2 I will gather all nations
　　and bring them down to the Valley of
　　　Jehoshaphat.[d]
　There I will put them on trial
　　for what they did to my inheritance, my
　　　people Israel,
　because they scattered my people among
　　　the nations
　　and divided up my land.
3 They cast lots for my people
　　and traded boys for prostitutes;
　　they sold girls for wine to drink.

---

[a] 25 The precise meaning of the four Hebrew words used here
for locusts is uncertain.　[b] 32 In Hebrew texts 2:28-32 is
numbered 3:1-5.　[c] In Hebrew texts 3:1-21 is numbered 4:1-21.
[d] 2 Jehoshaphat means the Lord judges; also in verse 12.

2:25 the locust swarm The same Hebrew word for
locusts as used in Joel 1:4 (see note on 1:4).

2:28–32 This five-verse section stands as a separate
chapter in the Hebrew text. The abundance promised with
Yahweh's restoration in vv. 18–27 is amplified through
a promise that all of God's people will receive the blessing of his Spirit and witness his coming on the future
Day of Yahweh, when he comes to judge all people. The
apostle Peter quotes this entire passage in his sermon
at Pentecost, when the Holy Spirit is poured out on the
followers of Jesus (Ac 2:17–21).

2:28 pour out my Spirit The Spirit of Yahweh was an
expected part of future redemption. Compare Isa 32:15;
Eze 39:29. **Your sons and daughters will prophesy**
Alludes to a state of prophetic exhilaration brought on
by the Spirit of Yahweh. See note on Eze 11:5.

2:30 I will show wonders in the heavens Echoes
earlier descriptions of the cosmic upheaval that will
accompany the Day of Yahweh (see note on Joel 2:10).

2:32 everyone who calls on the name Quoted by the
apostle Paul in Ro 10:13. **there will be deliverance**
Compare Ob 17.

3:1–21 Joel concludes his oracle of salvation by assuring
Judah of divine judgment on its enemies. The purpose
seems to be the same as that of the oracles against
the nations found in Isaiah, Jeremiah and Ezekiel, but
Joel's scope broadly encompasses all nations and refers to specific enemies of Judah only in passing. The
image of Judah's glorious future that ends the oracle
(Joel 3:17–21) reflects similar accounts of ideal restoration found near the end of other prophetic books (Isa
66:10–14; Hos 14:4–9; Am 9:11–15).

3:1 In those days and at that time A common prophetic
phrase alluding to the future day of salvation (compare Jer
33:15). **I restore the fortunes** See note on Jer 29:14.
3:2 all nations Compare Jer 25:31; Eze 39:21; Zep
3:8. **Valley of Jehoshaphat** An unknown location with
a symbolic name that means "the Valley where Yahweh
will judge." This is the place where Yahweh gathers the
nations for judgment. Judaism, Christianity and Islam
all include a tradition of a final divine judgment in this
valley. The traditional identification connects the site
with the part of the Kidron Valley just east of Jerusalem.
The pseudepigraphal book of First Enoch also describes
a final judgment taking place in a deep valley (1 Enoch
53:1; 54:1). **they scattered my people among the
nations** Both Assyria and Babylon were responsible
for deporting Israelites. The scattering was one of the
punishments emphasized in the covenant curses (see
Lev 26:33). **divided up my land** Israel became an Assyrian province after 722 BC. Judah was a province of
Babylon and Persia (586 BC and 539 BC). Judah had no
independent political existence until after the Maccabean
revolt (ca. 167–160 BC). See the timeline "Dates Related
to Isaiah and 2 Kings" on p. 1116.

3:3 They cast lots for my people Casting lots was
a form of divination. People determined the will of the
gods through the ancient equivalent of throwing dice.
Here, it refers to the method of dividing up the spoils
of conquest (compare Ob 11). Unlike most forms of
divination, casting lots was not forbidden in the OT and
was even promoted as a means of determining Yahweh's
will (see Pr 16:33). The priestly Urim and Thummim (see
Ex 28:30) were used to inquire of Yahweh for requests
requiring a simple yes or no answer (see Lev 16:7–10).

⁴"Now what have you against me, Tyre and Sidon and all you regions of Philistia? Are you repaying me for something I have done? If you are paying me back, I will swiftly and speedily return on your own heads what you have done. ⁵For you took my silver and my gold and carried off my finest treasures to your temples.ᵃ ⁶You sold the people of Judah and Jerusalem to the Greeks, that you might send them far from their homeland.

⁷"See, I am going to rouse them out of the places to which you sold them, and I will return on your own heads what you have done. ⁸I will sell your sons and daughters to the people of Judah, and they will sell them to the Sabeans, a nation far away." The LORD has spoken.

⁹Proclaim this among the nations:
　Prepare for war!
Rouse the warriors!
　Let all the fighting men draw near and
　　attack.
¹⁰Beat your plowshares into swords
　and your pruning hooks into spears.
Let the weakling say,
　"I am strong!"
¹¹Come quickly, all you nations from every
　side,
　and assemble there.

Bring down your warriors, LORD!

¹²"Let the nations be roused;
　let them advance into the Valley of
　　Jehoshaphat,
for there I will sit
　to judge all the nations on every side.

¹³Swing the sickle,
　for the harvest is ripe.
Come, trample the grapes,
　for the winepress is full
　and the vats overflow—
so great is their wickedness!"

¹⁴Multitudes, multitudes
　in the valley of decision!
For the day of the LORD is near
　in the valley of decision.
¹⁵The sun and moon will be
　darkened,
　and the stars no longer shine.
¹⁶The LORD will roar from Zion
　and thunder from Jerusalem;
　the earth and the heavens will
　　tremble.
But the LORD will be a refuge for his
　people,
　a stronghold for the people of
　Israel.

Blessings for God's People

¹⁷"Then you will know that I, the LORD your
　God,
　dwell in Zion, my holy hill.
Jerusalem will be holy;
　never again will foreigners invade her.

¹⁸"In that day the mountains will drip new
　wine,
　and the hills will flow with milk;
　all the ravines of Judah will run with
　water.

ᵃ 5 Or palaces

3:4 Tyre and Sidon Prominent Phoenician cities on the Mediterranean coast, northwest of Israel (see note on Eze 26:1—28:19). On Tyre, see note on Eze 26:2. **Philistia** The territory of the coastal plain southwest of Judah (see note on 1Sa 4:1).
3:6 the Greeks The Hebrew term used here is derived from Javan, the usual designation for Greeks in both Greece and Asia Minor (see Ge 10:2; Isa 66:19). Ezekiel also mentions trade of human slaves between Tyre and Javan (see Eze 27:13 and note).
3:8 the Sabeans Probably referring to the people of Sheba or Saba from southern Arabia (see 1Ki 10:1 and note).
3:10 Beat your plowshares into swords The imagery here is an exact reversal of Isa 2:4 (compare Mic 4:3), where the final judgment is described as a time of peaceful gathering. Here, the nations are called out to war, but their opponent is Yahweh arrayed for judgment. Compare Isa 8:9–10.
3:13 Swing the sickle A tool with a curved blade used for harvesting. This imagery of judgment as a harvest is expanded in Rev 14:14–20. **winepress is full** Compare Isa 63:1–6 for the image of judgment as Yahweh treading grapes in a winepress. See the infographic "A Winepress in Ancient Israel" on p. 1157.

3:14 the valley of decision Probably refers to the Valley of Jehoshaphat (see note on Joel 3:2). The name is likely a play on words with the image of a sickle, because the Hebrew term usually translated as "decision" comes from a verb meaning "sharpen" or "decide." **day of the LORD** See note on 1:15.
3:16 The LORD will roar from Zion Joel seems to be quoting from Am 1:2. Compare Jer 25:30 and note. **the earth and the heavens will tremble** Compare Joel 2:10–11. **LORD will be a refuge for his people** Emphasizes that Yahweh's wrath is now directed at the nations, not Israel (compare Ps 37:39; Isa 25:4).
3:17 Zion, my holy hill The Temple Mount in Jerusalem. See note on Isa 2:2. **never again will foreigners invade her** See note on Isa 52:1.
3:18 the mountains will drip new wine Compare Am 9:13. **A fountain will flow** Compare Eze 47:1–12 and note. **valley of acacias** The Hebrew name for this site, shittim, comes from the word shittah, meaning acacia bush. The site was the site of Israel's last encampment in the Transjordan before entering the land of Canaan (see Nu 25:1; Jos 2:1). The site is also connected with the idolatrous worship of the Baal of Peor (see Nu 25:1–9). Joel's image of a fountain watering the valley depicts irrigation in the desert, similar to that in Eze 47.

A fountain will flow out of the Lord's
   house
   and will water the valley of acacias.[a]
[19] But Egypt will be desolate,
   Edom a desert waste,
because of violence done to the people of
   Judah,
   in whose land they shed innocent
   blood.

[20] Judah will be inhabited forever
   and Jerusalem through all
   generations.
[21] Shall I leave their innocent blood
   unavenged?
   No, I will not."

   The Lord dwells in Zion!

[a] 18 Or *Valley of Shittim*

3:19 Egypt will be desolate Egypt's interference in the affairs of Israel and Judah earned them frequent condemnation in the prophetic oracles against the nations (see Isa 19; Jer 46; Eze 29–32). **Edom a desert waste** A traditional enemy of Judah condemned for gloating over Jerusalem's destruction. See Eze 25:12–14 and note. **violence done to the people of Judah** Compare the similar accusation against Edom in Ob 10. **innocent blood** Likely an allusion to the punishment for blood guilt

(Dt 19:10). Widespread injustice is often summarized under the crime of shedding innocent blood (see Isa 59:7; Jer 7:6; 2Ki 21:16). **3:21 Shall I leave their innocent blood unavenged** Likely draws on the traditions of the avenger of blood as in Joel 3:19 (see Dt 19:1–13). **The Lord dwells in Zion** The concluding statement emphasizes Yahweh's presence among his people.

AMOS

INTRODUCTION TO AMOS

The prophet Amos rebukes injustice wherever it is found—even among God's chosen people. Amos mostly presents oracles of judgment and disaster, but these end with a promise: After judgment, God will restore Israel. Amos calls on God's people to repent of their sin against him and others.

BACKGROUND

Although Amos appears toward the middle of the Prophetic books, he is likely the earliest of the "writing prophets" (that is, prophets who have biblical books named after them). Amos came from the town of Tekoa in Judah and had a brief prophetic ministry directed at the northern kingdom of Israel during the reigns of King Jeroboam II in Israel and King Uzziah (Azariah) in Judah (the southern kingdom). Both kings reigned from the 780s to the 740s BC. Amos' ministry probably dates somewhat later in their reigns, perhaps sometime between 760 and 750 BC.

While Jeroboam II did evil in the northern kingdom of Israel, leading God's people astray (2Ki 14:24), Uzziah in the southern kingdom of Judah did what was right in Yahweh's eyes—for a time (2Ki 15:3; 2Ch 26). Uzziah had a fruitful reign until his strength led to pride, and his pride to his downfall (2Ch 26:16–21). Within this context, Amos speaks his words of truth.

Amos was not a professional prophet and did not come from a prophetic background. He was a shepherd and likely was the owner of his flock, not merely a hired hand. He also tended sycamore figs (Am 1:1; 7:14–15). Little else is known about him.

This map depicts the recipients of Amos's prophecies.

STRUCTURE

The book of Amos can be divided into three sections. The first (chs. 1–2) briefly introduces the prophet and conveys eight messages of judgment, each introduced with a phrase stating the words belong to Yahweh. The first six messages condemn foreign nations for injustice and oppression (1:3—2:3). The seventh tells of judgment against Judah for rejecting God's law (2:4–5), while the eighth message—the longest—takes aim at Israel (2:6–16). The kingdom is judged for injustice, sexual immorality and rejection of God's guidance, including a rejection of his prophets.

The second section (chs. 3–6) includes three messages of judgment introduced by a command to hear this word. These messages are all directed at the northern kingdom of Israel. Amos accuses them of oppressing the poor (e.g., 4:1; 5:11) and worshiping improperly, especially at the wrong place—Bethel, rather than Yahweh's ordained place of Jerusalem in Judah (e.g., 4:4–5). King Jeroboam II of Israel, and most of the kings of Israel before him, encouraged worship of Yahweh at Bethel rather than Jerusalem—this politically motivated decision was tantamount to heresy. But despite the words of rebuke and discipline, Israel refused to turn back to God (e.g., 4:6–11).

The third section of Amos (chs. 7–9) presents three visions of the judgment that awaits Israel. Between the first and second visions, a brief narrative episode tells of a priest from Bethel who attempts to stop Amos from prophesying in Israel (7:10–17). Here, we see the pitiful effects of the disunity among God's people, created from selfish ambition and spurred by the separation of worship sites. The third vision tells of what will come after judgment (9:11–15).

OUTLINE

- Indictments against the nations, Judah and Israel (1:1—2:16)
- Judgment on Israel (3:1—6:14)
- Visions of judgment and restoration (7:1—9:15)

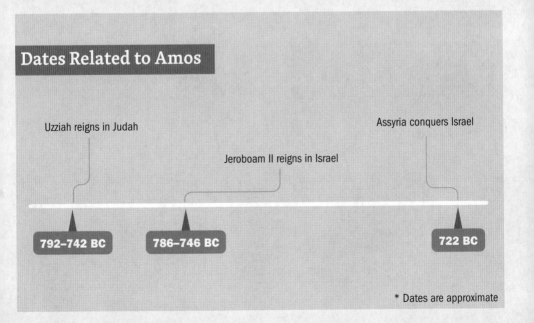

Dates Related to Amos

Uzziah reigns in Judah

Jeroboam II reigns in Israel

Assyria conquers Israel

792–742 BC

786–746 BC

722 BC

* Dates are approximate

THEMES

Amos focuses on God's concern for justice. The nations surrounding Israel are judged and will suffer for their oppressive actions. However, contrary to what the Israelites might have expected, their position as God's chosen people will not protect them from disaster. In fact, their relationship with God sets a higher standard for them (3:1–2). If they persist in their injustice, they will suffer just like the other nations (6:1–3,11–14).

Amos also critiques the people of Israel for improper worship. Their rituals are worthless if the worshipers do not also seek justice (5:21–24). In addition, Israel's worship involves improper sacrifices (such as leavened bread) being offered at improper worship sites (such as Bethel and Gilgal; 4:4–5). Amos' warnings of judgment do not merely proclaim disaster; they also invite repentance.

The message of Amos is a call to reflect on our interactions with other people. Regardless of our place in the world, all of us enjoy some degree of privilege over others, and we need God to help us recognize how our attitudes and behaviors might be unfair, unjust or even oppressive. Without committed action that advances God's justice, anything we do to worship him will amount to an empty ritual. But when we turn to God in repentance and seek his ways, we will encounter his transforming presence dwelling among us. This is the promise in the closing images of Amos: God will lift up his people and give them a beautiful and fruitful future (9:11–15).

1 The words of Amos, one of the shepherds of Tekoa — the vision he saw concerning Israel two years before the earthquake, when Uzziah was king of Judah and Jeroboam son of Jehoash[a] was king of Israel.

²He said:

"The Lord roars from Zion
and thunders from Jerusalem;
the pastures of the shepherds dry up,
and the top of Carmel withers."

Judgment on Israel's Neighbors

³This is what the Lord says:

"For three sins of Damascus,
even for four, I will not relent.
Because she threshed Gilead
with sledges having iron teeth,
⁴I will send fire on the house of Hazael
that will consume the fortresses of
Ben-Hadad.
⁵I will break down the gate of Damascus;
I will destroy the king who is in[b] the Valley
of Aven[c]

and the one who holds the scepter in Beth Eden.
The people of Aram will go into exile to Kir,"
says the Lord.

⁶This is what the Lord says:

"For three sins of Gaza,
even for four, I will not relent.
Because she took captive whole communities
and sold them to Edom,
⁷I will send fire on the walls of Gaza
that will consume her fortresses.
⁸I will destroy the king[d] of Ashdod
and the one who holds the scepter in
Ashkelon.
I will turn my hand against Ekron,
till the last of the Philistines are dead,"
says the Sovereign Lord.

⁹This is what the Lord says:

"For three sins of Tyre,
even for four, I will not relent.

---

a 1 Hebrew *Joash,* a variant of *Jehoash*   *b 5* Or *the inhabitants of*   *c 5 Aven* means *wickedness.*   *d 8* Or *inhabitants*

1:1 The opening verse places Amos' ministry in the eighth century BC, contemporary with Hosea, Isaiah and Micah. Amos is probably the earliest of these prophets, since his ministry is oriented to the roughly contemporaneous reigns of Uzziah of Judah and Jeroboam II of Israel in the first half of the century. This would also make Amos the first of the writing prophets. Amos was from the southern kingdom of Judah, but his ministry was directed at the idolatry of the northern kingdom of Israel. See the timeline "Approximate Dates of Old Testament Prophets" on p. 1070.

1:1 Amos Means "burdensome" or "burden-bearer." **the shepherds** Amos is no ordinary shepherd. The Hebrew term used here occurs only one other time in the OT, where it refers to Mesha, king of Moab, as someone who bred sheep (2Ki 3:4). Mesha's substantial tribute and his status as king of Moab indicate that a *noqed* was a large-scale livestock breeder, not a poor, common shepherd watching someone else's flocks. **Tekoa** A town in the hill country of Judah about 10 miles south of Jerusalem. See note on Jer 6:1. **two years before the earthquake** The reference to Amos' ministry occurring "two years before the earthquake" was likely intended to more firmly orient his preaching to a memorable event. Earthquakes are not rare in Israel, so this particular earthquake must have been especially damaging or violent. Excavations at Hazor attest to a powerful earthquake around 760 BC. The archaeological evidence, however, could be dated a decade in either direction, still placing Amos's ministry within the same general range provided by the dates of the royal reigns. This event is undoubtedly the same as that mentioned in Zec 14:5, some 250 years later. Amos' ministry probably dates sometime between 760–750 BC, but his ministry may have lasted only several months to two years. **when Uzziah was king of Judah** Though the precise dates of Uzziah's reign are debated, he ruled in the first half of the eighth century, roughly 792–742 BC. **Jeroboam son of Jehoash was king of Israel** Reigned 786–746 BC. See note on Hos 1:1.

AMOS
Nothing is known about the prophet Amos apart from what can be learned from the book bearing his name. He was from the village of Tekoa, south of Jerusalem in the territory of Judah, but his ministry took him north to the Israelite shrine at Bethel (Am 7:10). His preaching is focused primarily on the excesses and injustices of the northern kingdom. His own descriptions of himself as a sheepherder, a cattleman and a grower of figs in Am 7:14 point to his agricultural background, but not necessarily to the popular image of him as a poor farmer and laborer called out of the fields to prophesy against Israel. His withering critiques of the injustice of the wealthy have also lent weight to the assumption that Amos was among the poor. The terminology used for Amos' agricultural work, however, lends itself to the image of a wealthy breeder of flocks and herds.

1:2 — 2:3 Amos opens with an oracle of judgment against Israel's neighbors. The prophets regularly use oracles against the nations to emphasize Yahweh's judgment coming on Israel's enemies. These oracles are often placed after emphatic pronouncements of doom on Israel and Judah, reassuring Israel that the nations used to judge them will in turn be judged by Yahweh. Amos uses the rhetoric of judgment against the nations to the opposite effect, lulling his audience into complacent agreement with his introductory vision and shocking them when it culminates in an oracle of doom for Israel and Judah, using the same formulaic imagery (Am 2:4–6).

1:2 Lord roars from Zion An image of divine wrath emphasizing Yahweh's dwelling place was Mount Zion, the Temple Mount in Jerusalem. The imagery of thunder and cosmic quaking also often accompanies a theophany

Because she sold whole communities of
  captives to Edom,
disregarding a treaty of brotherhood,
¹⁰ I will send fire on the walls of Tyre
  that will consume her fortresses."

¹¹This is what the LORD says:

"For three sins of Edom,
  even for four, I will not relent.
Because he pursued his brother with a sword
  and slaughtered the women of the land,
because his anger raged continually
  and his fury flamed unchecked,
¹² I will send fire on Teman
  that will consume the fortresses of
    Bozrah."

¹³This is what the LORD says:

"For three sins of Ammon,
  even for four, I will not relent.

Because he ripped open the pregnant
  women of Gilead
in order to extend his borders,
¹⁴ I will set fire to the walls of Rabbah
  that will consume her fortresses
amid war cries on the day of
    battle,
  amid violent winds on a stormy
    day.
¹⁵ Her king*ᵃ* will go into exile,
  he and his officials together,"
                                    says the LORD.

2 This is what the LORD says:

"For three sins of Moab,
  even for four, I will not relent.
Because he burned to ashes
  the bones of Edom's king,

ᵃ 15 Or / Molek

(e.g., Joel 3:16). The metaphor of Yahweh as an unstoppable lion on the attack is common in descriptions of divine judgment (e.g., Isa 31:4; Jer 25:38; Hos 11:10; Am 3:8). **Carmel** Likely referring to Mount Carmel, which marked the northwest border of Israel. The mountain was the setting for Elijah's confrontation with the prophets of Baal in 1Ki 18. See note on Jer 46:18.
1:3 For three sins of Damascus, even for four This formula, with different cities mentioned, functions as a refrain throughout this section (Am 1:6,9,11,13; 2:1,4,6). The formula uses number juxtaposition parallelism (n, n+1) to represent an increasing but indefinite number of offenses. The number four can represent completeness, especially in reference to judgment. See note on Joel 1:4. See the table "Parallelism in Hebrew Poetry" on p. 1008. **Damascus** The chief city of Aram (also called Syria), the nation north of Israel. It was the capital during the tenth–eighth centuries BC before falling to Assyria in 732 BC. Aram was one of Israel's main enemies during the monarchy (1Ki 11:23–25; 15:16–20; 20:1—22:40) except when they allied to oppose Assyria (2Ki 16:5–9). **Gilead** A fertile region of the northern Transjordan, one of the areas of Israel closest to Damascus. See note on Jer 8:22. **sledges having iron teeth** Driven over harvested grain to separate the kernels from the stalks and chaff. See note on Isa 28:27.
1:4 house of Hazael An Aramean king who founded a new dynasty by assassinating the previous king in 842 BC (2Ki 8:7–15). Hazael was Aram's most powerful king and frequently threatened Israel and Judah (2Ki 12:17–18; 13:3). **Ben-Hadad** The name of at least two kings of Damascus. This reference probably applies to the Ben-Hadad who was the son and successor of Hazael (2Ki 13:24–25).
1:5 Valley of Aven Possibly refers to the plain in Syria between the Lebanon and Anti-Lebanon mountain ranges. **Beth Eden** An Aramean state west of Harran known in Assyrian sources as Bit Adini. Compare Eze 27:23. **Aram** The names Aram and Syria both refer primarily to the region controlled by Damascus. The Arameans were the inhabitants of the territory roughly included in modern Lebanon and Syria. They were organized in a number of small city-states including Damascus, Beth-Eden and Hamath. **Kir** Probably a location in Mesopotamia. Ac-

cording to Am 9:7, the Arameans originated in Kir. See note on Isa 22:6.
1:6 Gaza One of the five cities of the Philistines. Three more cities from the Philistine pentapolis are mentioned in Am 1:8—Ashdod, Ashkelon and Ekron. See note on Jer 25:20, and note on 1Sa 4:1. **took captive** Probably alluding to Philistine involvement in the slave trade, though the precise historical background is uncertain. **Edom** Judah's neighbor to the southeast. See note on Jer 25:21.
1:9 sins of Tyre A Phoenician seaport located northwest of Israel. See note on Eze 26:2. **sold whole communities of captives to Edom** The same accusation as that against Gaza in Am 1:6. Likely also refers to Tyre's involvement in the slave trade (compare Eze 27:3). See note on Am 1:6. **a treaty of brotherhood** Possibly refers to the treaty between King Solomon and King Hiram of Tyre (1Ki 5:12). Other ties between Israel and Phoenicia included the marriage of King Ahab to Jezebel, daughter of Ethbaal, king of Sidon (1Ki 16:31). Tyre is known to have had a king named Ethbaal during the time of Ezekiel (see note on Eze 28:2).
1:11 he pursued his brother with a sword Edom's ancestor, Esau, and Israel's ancestor, Jacob, were brothers (see Ge 25:25–26). The two nations were frequently at war with one another (see 2Ch 28:17), so there is no need to identify a specific historical reference here. Edom receives special condemnation in Ob 1–14, the book following Amos in the 12 Minor Prophets. Other oracles against Edom are found in Isa 34; Eze 35; Jer 49. **his fury flamed unchecked** Edom's transgression is slightly different as they are condemned for harboring a grudge against Israel.
1:12 Teman An important Edomite city. See note on Jer 49:7. **the fortresses of Bozrah** The ancient capital of Edom. See note on Jer 49:13.
1:13 Ammon Israel's neighbor to the east in the Transjordan. See note on Eze 25:2. **ripped open the pregnant women** An image of vicious destruction. Compare Hos 13:16. **extend his borders** Ammon regularly fought over territory with Israel and Judah.
1:14 Rabbah The capital of Ammon. See note on Eze 21:20.
1:15 king will go into exile The Hebrew text here

[2] I will send fire on Moab
    that will consume the fortresses of
        Kerioth.[a]
Moab will go down in great tumult
    amid war cries and the blast of the
        trumpet.
[3] I will destroy her ruler
    and kill all her officials with him,"
                says the LORD.

[4] This is what the LORD says:

"For three sins of Judah,
    even for four, I will not relent.
Because they have rejected the law
        of the LORD
    and have not kept his decrees,
because they have been led astray by
        false gods,[b]
    the gods[c] their ancestors followed,
[5] I will send fire on Judah
    that will consume the fortresses of
        Jerusalem."

Judgment on Israel

[6] This is what the LORD says:

"For three sins of Israel,
    even for four, I will not relent.
They sell the innocent for silver,
    and the needy for a pair of sandals.
[7] They trample on the heads of the poor
    as on the dust of the ground
    and deny justice to the oppressed.
Father and son use the same girl
    and so profane my holy name.
[8] They lie down beside every altar
    on garments taken in pledge.
In the house of their god
    they drink wine taken as fines.

[9] "Yet I destroyed the Amorites before them,
    though they were tall as the cedars
    and strong as the oaks.

[a] 2 Or of her cities   [b] 4 Or by lies   [c] 4 Or lies

---

could mean "their king"; it also could be the name of the Ammonite deity Molek (compare Jer 49:3 and note). **2:1 For three sins of Moab, even for four** See note on Am 1:3. **Moab** Judah's neighbor in the Transjordan, east of the Dead Sea and south of Ammon. See Jer 48:1–47 and note. **burned to ashes the bones** Moab will be judged not for offenses against Israel or Judah but for desecrating the corpse of an Edomite king, implying judgment is based on some universal ethic of divine justice. Edom was Moab's neighbor to the south. Burning bones to make lime was a way of removing all honor and respect from the body of the deceased. Lime was used to make the whitewash, mortar and plaster that coated walls and floors (Dt 27:2–4). The lime was made from calcium oxide obtained by burning shells or animal bones at an extreme temperature. The accusation here makes it seem that burning human bones was unusual and abhorrent. For the same image used for burning in judgment, see Isa 33:12. **2:2 Kerioth** An uncertain location in Moab, also mentioned in Jer 48:24. The Hebrew term used here means "cities." Here and in Jer 48:41, this word appears with the definite article, so it may refer to the location of Kerioth or to Moab's fortified cities in general. The site is also mentioned in an inscription from the Moabite king, Mesha. See the infographic "The Mesha Stele" on p. 565.

2:4–5 The accusations now move closer to home with a condemnation of Judah. The indictment against Judah has a different tone than those focused on the nations. The earlier condemnations emphasized offenses on an international scale, invading and enslaving neighboring peoples. The condemnation of Judah centers on their rejection of Yahweh's law, a concept developed in the covenant language of Leviticus, Deuteronomy and the Deuteronomistic History (Lev 26:14–15; Dt 5:1; 28:15; 2Ki 17:15). The formulaic language follows the pattern Amos started, but the change of tone might suggest this accusation was added later, especially since Israel is the primary target in most of Amos' preaching.

2:4 Judah Referring to the southern Israelite kingdom whose capital was Jerusalem. See note on Ge 49:8.

rejected the law of the LORD A common indictment in the Prophets. Compare Isa 24:5; 42:24; Jer 6:19; 44:10. **2:5 I will send fire on Judah** Compare Hos 8:14.

2:6–16 The real target of Amos' critique finally comes into focus with a denunciation of Israel using the same formulaic indictment as before. The initial accusation in Am 2:6–8 focuses on acts of social injustice—exploitation of the poor and needy. The oracle then expands by recounting Yahweh's provision for Israel in the exodus and conquest. Their rejection of Yahweh's caring guidance will result in judgment through a disastrous military defeat.

2:6 They sell the innocent for silver Refers to debt slavery. The parallel with "sandals" suggests the indebtedness was not very great in proportion to the punishment (compare the parable of the Unforgiving Servant in Mt 18:21–35). **2:7 use the same girl** The offense may be the exploitation of the girl or may allude to laws about incest (Lev 18:6–18; 20:12). **profane my holy name** The injustice of his people and lack of concern in following Yahweh's standards reflects poorly on his character or reputation. On "name" in the sense of "reputation," see note on Isa 48:19. **2:8 garments taken in pledge** Referring to the practice of taking a garment as security for a loan. That they were lying on these garments likely points to a violation of the Biblical law (Ex 22:26–27). A garment taken in pledge was not to be kept overnight. An ancient Hebrew letter from the late seventh century BC was excavated at a Judean fortress on the Mediterranean coast south of Yavneh-Yam. The letter attests to this practice of taking garments in pledge; it is a formal complaint lodged by an average laborer who protests the unlawful seizure of his cloak by his immediate superior. **the house of their god** Probably refers to idolatrous shrines. The Hebrew phrase used here can be read as "their God" or "their gods." **wine taken as fines** Refers to wine provided as payment for a fine. **2:9 Amorites** The name is frequently used in the OT to refer to the inhabitants of the land of Canaan before Israel's conquest (Ge 15:19–21). Israel faced opposition from two Amorite kings in the Transjordan; they defeated

I destroyed their fruit above
and their roots below.
[10] I brought you up out of Egypt
and led you forty years in the wilderness
to give you the land of the Amorites.

[11] "I also raised up prophets from among your children
and Nazirites from among your youths.
Is this not true, people of Israel?"

declares the LORD.

[12] "But you made the Nazirites drink wine
and commanded the prophets not to
prophesy.

[13] "Now then, I will crush you
as a cart crushes when loaded with grain.
[14] The swift will not escape,
the strong will not muster their strength,
and the warrior will not save his life.
[15] The archer will not stand his ground,
the fleet-footed soldier will not get away,
and the horseman will not save his life.
[16] Even the bravest warriors
will flee naked on that day,"

declares the LORD.

Witnesses Summoned Against Israel

3 Hear this word, people of Israel, the word the
LORD has spoken against you — against the
whole family I brought up out of Egypt:

[2] "You only have I chosen
of all the families of the earth;
therefore I will punish you
for all your sins."

[3] Do two walk together
unless they have agreed to do so?
[4] Does a lion roar in the thicket
when it has no prey?
Does it growl in its den
when it has caught nothing?
[5] Does a bird swoop down to a trap on the ground
when no bait is there?
Does a trap spring up from the ground
if it has not caught anything?
[6] When a trumpet sounds in a city,
do not the people tremble?
When disaster comes to a city,
has not the LORD caused it?

[7] Surely the Sovereign LORD does nothing
without revealing his plan
to his servants the prophets.

[8] The lion has roared —
who will not fear?
The Sovereign LORD has spoken —
who can but prophesy?

[9] Proclaim to the fortresses of Ashdod
and to the fortresses of Egypt:

---

the kings Sihon and Og (Nu 21:21–35; Dt 3). **they were tall as the cedars** Alluding to the tradition that giants were among the Canaanites and Amorites before the Israelite conquest (Nu 13:32–33; Dt 3:1–11; compare note on Ge 6:4). Deuteronomy 3:11 specifically identified the Amorite king, Og, as a descendant of the Rephaim who had an iron bed that measured nine cubits by four cubits (13.5 feet by 6 feet).
2:10 out of Egypt Alludes to the exodus as the prime example of Yahweh's commitment to save his people. Yahweh emphasizes his active role in bringing Israel out of Egypt and into the land (compare Ex 12:17). **led you forty years in the wilderness** See Dt 8:2. **to give you the land of the Amorites** See Nu 21:25.
2:11 I also raised up prophets from among your children Yahweh continually raised up prophets to call Israel to repentance. Compare Jer 7:25 and note. **Nazirites** People set apart for God through a vow (see Nu 6:1–21 and note). The Nazirite was dedicated to divine service for a temporary period of time. Samuel and Samson are devoted to Yahweh's service as Nazirites, but their commitment was permanent (1Sa 1:11; Jdg 13:3–5). Nazirite service was marked by the vow and specific practices that separated that person from normal society. For example, Nazirites were forbidden to drink wine or any fermented beverage. They also were prohibited from shaving or cutting their hair. Other regulations, such as the prohibition of coming in contact with a corpse, were designed to maintain the ritual purity of the devotee.
2:12 you made the Nazirites drink wine Violating the prohibition in Nu 6:3. **commanded the prophets not to prophesy** Compare Isa 30:10.

2:14 the warrior The Hebrew word used here, *gibbor*, refers to a powerful warrior (see note on 1Ch 26:6). The imagery here is one of military defeat. Israel fell to Assyria in 722 BC.
2:16 on that day Referring to the Day of Yahweh. See note on Joel 1:15.

3:1—5:17 Amos continues his criticism of Israel through three oracles of judgment, each beginning with the phrase "Hear this word" (Am 3:1; 4:1; 5:1). The rhetoric alternates between detailing Israel's specific sins and revealing the divine plan for judgment, with a few appeals for repentance interspersed.

3:1 Hear this word This formulaic introduction opens the oracles in v. 1; 4:1; 5:1. **out of Egypt** See 2:10 and note.
3:2 You only have I chosen Israel's status as Yahweh's chosen people means they are held to a higher standard (see note on Hos 6:6). Knowledge, in this context, refers to their covenant relationship.

3:3–8 Yahweh uses a series of rhetorical questions, where the expected answer is "no," to emphasize that judgment is just as certain as the predictable reactions evoked by the questions. Seven questions in Am 3:3–6 are interrupted by the acknowledgment of Yahweh's sovereignty required by the question in v. 6. The final questions in v. 8 emphasize the prophet's role as a mere messenger for God who is unable to resist the call to preach (compare Jer 20:8–9).

3:4 a lion See Am 1:2 and note.
3:6 a trumpet sounds in a city An alarm sounded by the watchman to warn of danger. See note on Jer

"Assemble yourselves on the mountains of
Samaria;
see the great unrest within her
and the oppression among her people."

10 "They do not know how to do right," declares
the Lord,
"who store up in their fortresses
what they have plundered and looted."

11 Therefore this is what the Sovereign Lord says:

"An enemy will overrun your land,
pull down your strongholds
and plunder your fortresses."

12 This is what the Lord says:

"As a shepherd rescues from the lion's mouth
only two leg bones or a piece of an ear,
so will the Israelites living in Samaria be
rescued,
with only the head of a bed
and a piece of fabric[a] from a couch. [b]"

13 "Hear this and testify against the descendants
of Jacob," declares the Lord, the Lord God Almighty.

14 "On the day I punish Israel for her sins,
I will destroy the altars of Bethel;
the horns of the altar will be cut off
and fall to the ground.

15 I will tear down the winter house
along with the summer house;
the houses adorned with ivory will be
destroyed
and the mansions will be demolished,"
declares the Lord.

Israel Has Not Returned to God

4 Hear this word, you cows of Bashan on
Mount Samaria,
you women who oppress the poor and
crush the needy
and say to your husbands, "Bring us some
drinks!"
2 The Sovereign Lord has sworn by his
holiness:
"The time will surely come
when you will be taken away with hooks,
the last of you with fishhooks.[c]
3 You will each go straight out
through breaches in the wall,
and you will be cast out toward Harmon,[d]"
declares the Lord.

---

a 12 The meaning of the Hebrew for this phrase is uncertain.
b 12 Or Israelites be rescued, / those who sit in Samaria / on the
edge of their beds / and in Damascus on their couches.
c 2 Or away in baskets, / the last of you in fish baskets
d 3 Masoretic Text; with a different word division of the Hebrew
(see Septuagint) out, you mountain of oppression

4:5. **disaster** The Biblical writers were secure in their
understanding that Yahweh was the ultimate agent behind all events. See La 3:38; Mic 1:12; compare Isa
45:7 and note.
**3:7 Sovereign Lord does nothing without revealing
his plan** Qualifies the statement in Am 3:6 by emphasizing that Yahweh does reveal his plans and his demands
to his people through the prophets. **his servants the
prophets** A common phrase in Jeremiah and Kings to
refer to the prophets (Jer 7:25; 25:4; 2Ki 9:7; 17:13).
3:9 Ashdod One of the main cities of the Philistines.
See note on Am 1:6. **Egypt** Both Ashdod and Egypt are
south of Israel and would be threatened by the advance of
any Mesopotamian power past Samaria, Israel's capital.
Having a vested interest in Samaria's stability, these
nations are called to witness the corruption that will
lead to Israel's downfall. **Samaria** The capital of Israel.
See note on Jer 31:5.
3:11 An enemy will overrun your land Fulfilled by
Assyria in 722 BC. See 2Ki 18:9–12.
3:12 two leg bones or a piece of an ear If a shepherd
could provide proof that an animal was destroyed by a
predator, he would be absolved of responsibility for the
loss and not be suspected of theft. The attempt to retrieve
some evidence of destruction informs the metaphor here.
The rescue is not a hopeful image. Only broken pieces
will remain of Samaria as evidence of the destruction.
3:14 the altars of Bethel An ancient sanctuary turned
into one of the primary religious centers of the northern
kingdom (see 1Ki 12:25–33; note on Hos 8:6). **the
horns of the altar** The horns of the altar represented
the place where people could seek refuge and protection
(Ex 21:14; 1Ki 1:50–51; 2:28–29). Cutting off the horns
desecrated the altar, transforming it from a sacred site
to an ordinary object. See note on Ex 27:2.

3:15 winter house along with the summer house The
ability to maintain two residences was a symbol of the
extravagance of the rich in Samaria. A summer residence
would likely have been in the cooler area of the central
hill country. A winter home might have been located in
the warmer Jezreel Valley. **the houses adorned with
ivory** King Ahab built a house heavily decorated with
ivory, a symbol of lavish wealth (see 1Ki 22:39 and note;
compare Ps 45:8). Ivory inlays were used to decorate
wood furniture and buildings.
4:1 Hear this word The same formulaic introduction
used in Am 3:1; 5:1. **cows of Bashan** A derogatory label
ridiculing the wealthy women of Samaria. Bashan was
the fertile plateau east of the Sea of Galilee and south
of Mount Hermon. The region was known for its livestock,
especially cattle (Ps 22:12; Eze 39:18). **Samaria** The
capital of Israel (the northern kingdom). See note on Jer
31:5. **you women who oppress the poor** The women
are guilty of self-indulgence at the expense of the poor
and powerless of society.
4:3 Harmon This word occurs only here and is probably
the name of a place. If this is a place, it likely refers
to a location where the Israelites would be exiled. The
location is unknown. The ancient Bible translations similarly had difficulty understanding this term.
The Septuagint, the ancient Greek translation, reads
"mountain of Remman," and the Targum, the Aramaic
translation, has "mountains of Armenia." The Hebrew
consonants could also be representing the word "Hermon," a reference to Mount Hermon north of Bashan,
symbolizing deportation to the north. A slight change in
the Hebrew yields a word meaning "to the dung heap,"
which fits the context of defeat and is related to a term
always used to describe corpses left unburied (e.g.,
Jer 9:22; 16:4).

⁴ "Go to Bethel and sin;
  go to Gilgal and sin yet more.
Bring your sacrifices every morning,
  your tithes every three years.ᵃ
⁵ Burn leavened bread as a thank offering
  and brag about your freewill offerings —
  boast about them, you Israelites,
  for this is what you love to do,"
            declares the Sovereign LORD.

⁶ "I gave you empty stomachs in every city
  and lack of bread in every town,
  yet you have not returned to me,"
            declares the LORD.

⁷ "I also withheld rain from you
  when the harvest was still three months
    away.
I sent rain on one town,
  but withheld it from another.
One field had rain;
  another had none and dried up.
⁸ People staggered from town to town for water
  but did not get enough to drink,
  yet you have not returned to me,"
            declares the LORD.

⁹ "Many times I struck your gardens and
    vineyards,
  destroying them with blight and mildew.
Locusts devoured your fig and olive trees,
  yet you have not returned to me,"
            declares the LORD.

¹⁰ "I sent plagues among you
  as I did to Egypt.

I killed your young men with the sword,
  along with your captured horses.
I filled your nostrils with the stench of your
    camps,
  yet you have not returned to me,"
            declares the LORD.

¹¹ "I overthrew some of you
  as I overthrew Sodom and Gomorrah.
You were like a burning stick snatched from
    the fire,
  yet you have not returned to me,"
            declares the LORD.

¹² "Therefore this is what I will do to you, Israel,
  and because I will do this to you, Israel,
  prepare to meet your God."

¹³ He who forms the mountains,
  who creates the wind,
  and who reveals his thoughts to mankind,
who turns dawn to darkness,
  and treads on the heights of the earth —
  the LORD God Almighty is his name.

A Lament and Call to Repentance

5 Hear this word, Israel, this lament I take up
  concerning you:

² "Fallen is Virgin Israel,
  never to rise again,
deserted in her own land,
  with no one to lift her up."

ᵃ 4 Or days

4:4 Bethel One of the worship centers of the northern kingdom. See note on Am 3:14. **Gilgal** An Israelite sanctuary near Jericho. See note on Hos 4:15. **Bring your sacrifices every morning** Amos offers a satirical critique of Israelite worship, mockingly encouraging them to continue in religious rituals that he has identified as "transgression." Frequency of offerings is meaningless without genuine obedience.
4:5 thank offering Compare Lev 7:13. **freewill offerings** Compare Dt 12:6; Lev 22:18.

4:6–13 Despite past discipline and divine judgment, Israel has not returned to following Yahweh. Amos recounts the past disasters that served as divine warnings, and he foreshadows a coming final judgment when Israel will come face to face with Yahweh (Am 4:12). Drought, famine, blight, mildew and pestilence are all part of the curses for breaking the Mosaic covenant (Dt 28:15–24).

4:6 empty stomachs The Hebrew text uses an idiom meaning "empty teeth" as a metaphor for famine. The people had no food to stick to their teeth. **yet you have not returned to me** This refrain is repeated throughout this series and reflects the prophetic expectation that warnings should inspire repentance. See Joel 2:12 and note.
4:7 I also withheld rain Referring to God's judgment through drought. By causing the crops to fail, the drought created the famine. Compare 1Ki 17:1; Jer 14:1 and note.
4:9 your gardens and vineyards The culture of the

Biblical world was thoroughly agrarian. Grapes, figs and olives were primary crops (compare Joel 2:19–24; Hab 3:17). Drought, disease (blight) and locusts were the main dangers to the agricultural economy of Israel. **blight and mildew** Both were damaging to the crops. See Dt 28:22. **Locusts** Part of the curse for breaking the covenant. See Dt 28:38; note on Joel 1:4.
4:10 plagues among you as I did to Egypt Compare Dt 28:27. **the stench of your camps** The smell of death from the corpses of the young men. Compare Joel 2:20 and note.
4:11 Sodom and Gomorrah Proverbial examples of divine judgment. See note on Isa 1:9.
4:12 Israel, prepare to meet your God Alluding cryptically to future judgment.
4:13 He who forms the mountains The oracle concludes with a doxology (a declaration of praise) that praises Yahweh as Creator using standard hymnic language common in Biblical poetry (compare Am 5:8; 9:6; Isa 40:12; Ps 104; Job 9). **treads on the heights of the earth** Compare Mic 1:3.

5:1–17 Amos presents Israel with a funeral dirge lamenting its future destruction (Am 5:1–3). He follows the lament with a renewed call to repentance, which is filled with warnings of judgment and accusations of sin.

5:1 Hear this word This formulaic introduction also appears in 3:1; 4:1. **lament** The Hebrew word used

³This is what the Sovereign Lᴏʀᴅ says to Israel:

"Your city that marches out a thousand strong
  will have only a hundred left;
your town that marches out a hundred strong
  will have only ten left."

⁴This is what the Lᴏʀᴅ says to Israel:

"Seek me and live;
5   do not seek Bethel,
do not go to Gilgal,
  do not journey to Beersheba.
For Gilgal will surely go into exile,
  and Bethel will be reduced to nothing. ᵃ"
⁶Seek the Lᴏʀᴅ and live,
  or he will sweep through the tribes of
    Joseph like a fire;
it will devour them,
  and Bethel will have no one to quench it.

⁷There are those who turn justice into
    bitterness
  and cast righteousness to the ground.

⁸He who made the Pleiades and Orion,
  who turns midnight into dawn
  and darkens day into night,

who calls for the waters of the sea
  and pours them out over the face of the
    land—
  the Lᴏʀᴅ is his name.
⁹With a blinding flash he destroys the
    stronghold
  and brings the fortified city to ruin.

¹⁰There are those who hate the one who
    upholds justice in court
  and detest the one who tells the truth.

¹¹You levy a straw tax on the poor
  and impose a tax on their grain.
Therefore, though you have built stone
    mansions,
  you will not live in them;
though you have planted lush vineyards,
  you will not drink their wine.
¹²For I know how many are your offenses
  and how great your sins.

There are those who oppress the innocent
    and take bribes
  and deprive the poor of justice in the
    courts.

ᵃ 5 Hebrew *aven*, a reference to Beth Aven (a derogatory name for Bethel); see Hosea 4:15.

---

here is *qinah*, referring to a specific kind of poetry. See note on Eze 19:1.
5:2 Virgin Israel An image expressing Israel's helplessness and vulnerability (see Jer 18:13; 31:4,21; compare Isa 47:1 and note).
5:3 only a hundred left Israel's military defeat is envisioned as the loss of 90 percent of their soldiers. The small remnant symbolizes evidence of destruction, not hope for the future, similar to the imagery in Am 3:12.
5:4 Seek me and live Israel has one chance to survive this massive defeat through genuine repentance.
5:5 Bethel One of the northern kingdom's major centers of worship. See note on 3:14. **Gilgal** An Israelite sanctuary near Jericho. See note on Hos 4:15. **Beersheba** A location in southern Judah, perhaps mentioned as a site of pilgrimage for Israelites from the northern kingdom.

BEERSHEBA
Beersheba was a town in the southern Judean desert associated with the patriarchs Abraham, Isaac and Jacob. The Hebrew name means "well of seven" or "well of oath," and the patriarchal stories involving the name invoke both meanings (Ge 21:28–31; 26:30–33). The name appears in the phrase "from Dan to Beersheba" to represent all Israel by referring to the northern and southern frontiers (see Jdg 20:1 and note). The site may have had importance as a local religious center based on its association with the patriarchs. Jacob offered sacrifices there before leaving the promised land for Egypt, suggesting there might have been an altar or monument left there (Ge 46:1–4). The religious sites at Bethel and Gilgal also were associated with altars or monuments from Israel's past.

5:6 the tribes of Joseph Refers to the northern kingdom. See note on Ob 18.
5:7 justice Frequently mentioned together with righteousness in Amos (e.g., Am 5:24; compare note on Isa 5:7). **bitterness** See note on La 3:15.

5:8–9 This hymn, which emphasizes Yahweh's great power as Creator of the universe, punctuates the call for repentance. It reminds Israel of the true glory and grandeur of Yahweh in contrast to the geographical constraints of the shrines at Bethel and Gilgal.

5:8 the Pleiades and Orion The Hebrew words used here are the names of constellations—usually identified as the Pleiades and Orion. The two are commonly paired in the OT (e.g., Job 9:9; 38:31). The Greek writers Homer and Hesiod and Mesopotamian writers also mention the Pleiades and Orion together. The Biblical passages using this pair are all depictions of Yahweh's awesome power as the sovereign lord over nature. The reference may also be an implicit polemic against astral worship—the worship of the sun, moon and stars (see note on Jer 8:2).
5:10 those who hate the one who upholds justice in court The elders of a city would hold court in the gate. The wickedness of Israel's upper class is evident in their hatred for any leader who dares to oppose their interests and side with truth and justice. Compare Isa 10:2; 29:21.
5:11 You levy a straw tax on the poor A specific example of their injustice is oppressing the poor and taking more than their share of the land's produce. Compare Isa 10:2 and note. **you will not live in them** Part of the curses for breaking the covenant law (Dt 28:30). **lush vineyards** Compare Dt 28:39.
5:12 bribes See Eze 22:12 and note; compare Dt 16:19.

13 Therefore the prudent keep quiet in such
    times,
  for the times are evil.

14 Seek good, not evil,
    that you may live.
  Then the Lord God Almighty will be with
    you,
  just as you say he is.
15 Hate evil, love good;
    maintain justice in the courts.
  Perhaps the Lord God Almighty will have
    mercy
    on the remnant of Joseph.

16 Therefore this is what the Lord, the Lord God
Almighty, says:

"There will be wailing in all the streets
    and cries of anguish in every public
      square.
  The farmers will be summoned to weep
    and the mourners to wail.
17 There will be wailing in all the vineyards,
    for I will pass through your midst,"
                                says the Lord.

The Day of the Lord

18 Woe to you who long
    for the day of the Lord!
  Why do you long for the day of the Lord?
    That day will be darkness, not light.
19 It will be as though a man fled from
      a lion
    only to meet a bear,
  as though he entered his house
    and rested his hand on the wall
    only to have a snake bite him.

20 Will not the day of the Lord be darkness, not
      light—
    pitch-dark, without a ray of brightness?

21 "I hate, I despise your religious festivals;
    your assemblies are a stench to me.
22 Even though you bring me burnt offerings
      and grain offerings,
    I will not accept them.
  Though you bring choice fellowship
      offerings,
    I will have no regard for them.
23 Away with the noise of your songs!
    I will not listen to the music of your harps.
24 But let justice roll on like a river,
    righteousness like a never-failing stream!

25 "Did you bring me sacrifices and offerings
    forty years in the wilderness, people of
      Israel?
26 You have lifted up the shrine of your king,
    the pedestal of your idols,
    the star of your god[a]—
    which you made for yourselves.
27 Therefore I will send you into exile beyond
      Damascus,"
  says the Lord, whose name is God
    Almighty.

Woe to the Complacent

6 Woe to you who are complacent in Zion,
    and to you who feel secure on Mount
      Samaria,
  you notable men of the foremost nation,
    to whom the people of Israel come!

a 26 Or lifted up Sakkuth your king / and Kaiwan your idols, /
your star-gods; Septuagint lifted up the shrine of Molek / and the
star of your god Rephan, / their idols

5:14 Seek good, not evil Reiterates the appeal to
repent.
5:15 will have mercy on the remnant of Joseph The
prophets preached repentance in the hope that there
was still a chance to avert divine wrath. See note on
Joel 2:12. the remnant of Joseph Those who remain
from the northern kingdom after the judgment. See
note on Isa 1:9.
5:16 There will be wailing Returns to the image of lament over national disaster, as in Am 5:1–3. If they fail
to heed the call to repent, they will experience judgment.

5:18—6:14 Amos presents a series of "woe" sayings
in which he strongly condemns Israel for injustice and
false worship and promises divine judgment. The description of Israel's sinfulness in 5:18—6:7 provides
the justification for the judgment outlined in 6:8–14.
Compare Isa 5:8–30.

5:18 the day of the Lord Amos is the earliest prophet
to introduce the motif of the "Day of Yahweh." His criticism shows that Israel expected the Day of Yahweh to
be a time of vindication and victory over their enemies.
Amos warns them to be careful what they wish for, since
the Day of Yahweh is a day of disaster. See note on Joel

1:15. darkness, not light A typical element of the Day
of Yahweh. See Joel 2:2 and note.
5:21 I despise your religious festivals Yahweh hates
outward ritual observance that hides inward rebellion
and failure to live up to his standards for justice and
righteousness (see Isa 1:11–14 and note; compare
note on Hos 6:6).
5:22 I will not accept Compare Jer 6:20.
5:26 shrine of your king, the pedestal of your idols,
the star of your god The rare Hebrew words used here—
sikkuth and kiyyun—may have been names for Babylonian
deities. Sikkuth (Sakkuth) may refer to the obscure Babylonian god, Sakkut. Kiyyun (Kaiwan; Chiun) is a Babylonian
name for the planet Saturn, which was worshiped as a god.
Some translations read these names as common nouns
related to idolatry. The verse is probably denouncing the
worship of heavenly bodies like the sun, stars and the
planets (known as astral worship; see note on Jer 8:2). See
the table "Pagan Deities of the Old Testament" on p. 1287.
5:27 I will send you into exile beyond Damascus
Israel was deported by Assyria and resettled in Mesopotamia. See 2Ki 17:6.
6:1 Woe to you who are complacent The next woe
oracle (Am 6:1–3) attacks the leaders of Israel and Judah

² Go to Kalneh and look at it;
  go from there to great Hamath,
  and then go down to Gath in Philistia.
Are they better off than your two kingdoms?
  Is their land larger than yours?
³ You put off the day of disaster
  and bring near a reign of terror.
⁴ You lie on beds adorned with ivory
  and lounge on your couches.
You dine on choice lambs
  and fattened calves.
⁵ You strum away on your harps like David
  and improvise on musical instruments.
⁶ You drink wine by the bowlful
  and use the finest lotions,
  but you do not grieve over the ruin of Joseph.
⁷ Therefore you will be among the first to go
    into exile;
  your feasting and lounging will end.

The LORD Abhors the Pride of Israel

⁸ The Sovereign LORD has sworn by himself —
the LORD God Almighty declares:

"I abhor the pride of Jacob
  and detest his fortresses;
I will deliver up the city
  and everything in it."

⁹ If ten people are left in one house, they too will die. ¹⁰ And if the relative who comes to carry the bodies out of the house to burn them[a] asks anyone who might be hiding there, "Is anyone else with you?" and he says, "No," then he will go on to say, "Hush! We must not mention the name of the LORD."

¹¹ For the LORD has given the command,
  and he will smash the great house into
    pieces
  and the small house into bits.

¹² Do horses run on the rocky crags?
  Does one plow the sea[b] with oxen?
But you have turned justice into poison
  and the fruit of righteousness into
    bitterness —
¹³ you who rejoice in the conquest of Lo Debar[c]
  and say, "Did we not take Karnaim[d] by our
    own strength?"

¹⁴ For the LORD God Almighty declares,
"I will stir up a nation against you, Israel,
  that will oppress you all the way
    from Lebo Hamath to the valley of the
      Arabah."

Locusts, Fire and a Plumb Line

7 This is what the Sovereign LORD showed me: He was preparing swarms of locusts after the king's share had been harvested and just as the late crops were coming up. ² When they had stripped

---

a 10 Or *to make a funeral fire in honor of the dead*   *b 12* With a different word division of the Hebrew; Masoretic Text *plow there*   *c 13* *Lo Debar* means *nothing.*   *d 13* *Karnaim* means *horns; horn* here symbolizes strength.

---

who have grown complacent with a false sense of security. **Zion** Refers to the Temple Mount in Jerusalem. Amos is critical of the leaders of Judah as well as the leaders of Israel. **Samaria** Capital of the northern kingdom (see note on Jer 31:5); likely home to a religious shrine based on Mic 1:6–7; Isa 10:11.
6:2 Kalneh A city in northern Syria that was destroyed by Assyria in 738 BC. Compare Isa 10:9. **Hamath** An important city in northern Syria. See note on Jer 49:23. **to Gath in Philistia** One of the five cities of the Philistines, possibly destroyed by Assyria in 715 BC. None of the later prophets mention Gath by name when they list the cities of the Philistines (see note on Jer 25:20). **Are they better off than your two kingdoms** These surrounding nations north and south of Israel and Judah will fall to Assyria, so Israel should expect nothing different.
6:4 You lie on beds A woe oracle (Am 6:4–7) criticizing the sloth, gluttony and drunkenness of the wealthy. **beds adorned with ivory** According to Assyrian records, a couch with ivory inlay was part of the tribute the Judean King Hezekiah delivered to Sennacherib (2Ki 18:13–16). More than 500 ivory fragments dating to the ninth and eighth centuries BC have been found in excavations at Samaria. See note on Am 3:15.
6:6 you do not grieve over the ruin of Joseph The leaders are consumed with self-indulgent pleasures. They ignore the rampant injustice and impending national disaster.
6:8–14 Israel's sin leads to inevitable judgment. Yahweh's wrath will bring a total end to Israel.

6:8 the pride of Jacob Israel's self-sufficient attitude and refusal to repent are signs of the great pride that will lead to their downfall.
6:10 We must not mention the name of the LORD Out of fear of calling down further judgment from an angry deity.
6:12 Do horses run on the rocky crags These animal metaphors highlight the unnatural nature of Israel's rejection of Yahweh's justice and righteousness. **bitterness** See note on La 3:15.
6:13 Lo Debar A town in the northern part of the Transjordan, close to where the Yarmuk River joins the Jordan River. It may have been part of the territory recovered by Jeroboam II (2Ki 14:25). The location is likely the same as Debir in Jos 13:26, and the name is probably a derivation of a foreign word since it is spelled inconsistently in Hebrew in 2Sa 9:4–5 and 2Sa 17:27. Amos uses the ambiguity to make a play on words. The term *lo* means "no," and *dabar* means "thing"; Amos accuses them of rejoicing in "nothing." **Karnaim** A city in Gilead east of the Sea of Galilee. It is mentioned in the OT only here and in Ge 14:5. Karnaim may have been part of the area that Jeroboam II reconquered (2Ki 14:25). The name Karnaim means "two horns." The horn was a symbol of power, and Amos is forming a pun on the symbolic associations with the horn.
6:14 Lebo Hamath to the valley of the Arabah Encompasses the full length of Israel's territory. The same locations are used to show how Jeroboam II expanded Israel's borders in 2Ki 14:25. Under Jeroboam II, Israel controlled territory from northern Syria (Hamath) to the southeast end of the Dead Sea (the Arabah).

the land clean, I cried out, "Sovereign Lord, forgive! How can Jacob survive? He is so small!"
³So the Lord relented.

"This will not happen," the Lord said.

⁴This is what the Sovereign Lord showed me: The Sovereign Lord was calling for judgment by fire; it dried up the great deep and devoured the land. ⁵Then I cried out, "Sovereign Lord, I beg you, stop! How can Jacob survive? He is so small!"
⁶So the Lord relented.

"This will not happen either," the Sovereign Lord said.

⁷This is what he showed me: The Lord was standing by a wall that had been built true to plumb,ᵃ with a plumb lineᵇ in his hand. ⁸And the Lord asked me, "What do you see, Amos?"

"A plumb line," I replied.

Then the Lord said, "Look, I am setting a plumb line among my people Israel; I will spare them no longer.

⁹"The high places of Isaac will be destroyed
 and the sanctuaries of Israel will be ruined;
with my sword I will rise against the house
 of Jeroboam."

Amos and Amaziah

¹⁰Then Amaziah the priest of Bethel sent a message to Jeroboam king of Israel: "Amos is raising a conspiracy against you in the very heart of Israel. The land cannot bear all his words. ¹¹For this is what Amos is saying:

"'Jeroboam will die by the sword,
 and Israel will surely go into exile,
 away from their native land.'"

¹²Then Amaziah said to Amos, "Get out, you seer! Go back to the land of Judah. Earn your bread

---

ᵃ 7 The meaning of the Hebrew for this phrase is uncertain.
ᵇ 7 The meaning of the Hebrew for this phrase is uncertain; also in verse 8.

7:1—9:4 This section is shaped by reports of five visions that symbolize judgment on Israel. At first, Amos intercedes on behalf of the people, and the judgment is delayed. The section also includes the confrontation between Amos and Amaziah, the priest at Bethel (Am 7:10–17). The "vision report" is a common genre that the prophets use to describe their eyewitness interaction with Yahweh (see Eze 1–3; Isa 6).

7:1 Sovereign Lord showed me A characteristic opening for Amos' vision reports (e.g., Am 7:6–7; 8:1). The usual pattern for Amos' vision report has three sections: Yahweh initiating the vision, Amos seeing or responding, and Yahweh explaining the vision or responding to Amos. **locusts** A migratory insect that travels in swarms. A swarm of locusts can be devastating to the crops. See note on Joel 1:4. **king's share** The king apparently received a large portion of the first crop, so the locusts threatened the second crop that was probably the share of the average farmer. **had been harvested and just as the late crops were coming up** Israel's growing season had two main crops. The first was planted in autumn and harvested in the spring. The second was planted during the winter and harvested in early summer. The growth was supported by the early and late rain cycle. See note on Joel 2:23.

7:2 they had stripped the land clean The locust plague had progressed before Amos intervened. **Sovereign Lord, forgive** The prophet intercedes, asking Yahweh to relent from judgment (compare Eze 9:8; 11:13; note on Jer 7:16–29).

7:3 Lord relented Yahweh relents from total judgment in these first two visions. This sets up a pattern of expectation that if the people repent or the prophet intercedes, they may avert judgment. Compare Jer 15:1 and note.

7:4 judgment by fire The second vision is of judgment coming by fire, which is a common agent of divine punishment (see note on Isa 4:4).

7:5 Sovereign Lord, I beg you, stop Amos intercedes a second time. See Am 7:2 and note.

7:7 a wall that had been built true to plumb The third vision involves a metaphor for construction or demolition. The Hebrew word translated "plumb line" is unique to this

passage, so the precise meaning is uncertain. Related words in other Semitic languages suggest a meaning of "lead" or "tin." The association of the word with a wall in this context supports the meaning of "plumb line," where a small metal weight is attached to a string to determine whether a wall is straight. The plumb line metaphorically represents an external standard to distinguish right from wrong.

7:9 high places Local religious shrines. See note on Isa 57:7. **the house of Jeroboam** Probably a reference to the current king, Jeroboam II (see note on Hos 1:1). However, the criticism of illicit sanctuaries may indicate this reference does double duty: It alludes to Jeroboam, the son of Nebat, who established the Israelite shrines at Dan and Bethel, as well as the current king.

7:10–17 This account of a confrontation between Amos and the priest Amaziah provides what little biographical information we have on Amos (apart from Am 1:1). The priest objects to Amos' message of doom and destruction and orders him to leave Bethel. Amos answers with a prophecy of judgment against Amaziah and his family.

7:10 Amaziah the priest of Bethel Likely the chief priest of the shrine at Bethel. See note on 3:14. **Jeroboam king of Israel** Jeroboam II reigned 786–746 BC. See note on Hos 1:1. **Amos is raising a conspiracy against you** His prophecy in Am 7:8–9 was interpreted as a threat against the king. Amaziah's report of Amos' words, however, doesn't align with anything specific that Amos has said thus far in the book. **cannot bear all his words** Compare Jer 38:4.

7:11 Jeroboam will die by the sword An interpretation of Am 7:9. **Israel will surely go into exile** Exile has been foreshadowed as punishment throughout the book of Amos. See 4:2–3; 5:5,27; 6:7.

7:12 seer Amaziah may be intentionally avoiding calling Amos a prophet by using the Hebrew word that means "seer." Amaziah is more concerned with the location where Amos is prophesying than with the fact that he is prophesying at all. He orders Amos to return to Judah and prophesy there. **Earn your bread there** Alludes to the prophets who earn their livelihood by prophesying (compare Mic 3:5).

there and do your prophesying there. ¹³Don't prophesy anymore at Bethel, because this is the king's sanctuary and the temple of the kingdom."

¹⁴Amos answered Amaziah, "I was neither a prophet nor the son of a prophet, but I was a shepherd, and I also took care of sycamore-fig trees. ¹⁵But the Lord took me from tending the flock and said to me, 'Go, prophesy to my people Israel.' ¹⁶Now then, hear the word of the Lord. You say,

"'Do not prophesy against Israel,
    and stop preaching against the
        descendants of Isaac.'

¹⁷"Therefore this is what the Lord says:

"'Your wife will become a prostitute in
        the city,
    and your sons and daughters will fall by
        the sword.
Your land will be measured and divided up,
    and you yourself will die in a pagan[a]
        country.
And Israel will surely go into exile,
    away from their native land.'"

A Basket of Ripe Fruit

8 This is what the Sovereign Lord showed me: a basket of ripe fruit. ²"What do you see, Amos?" he asked.

"A basket of ripe fruit," I answered.

Then the Lord said to me, "The time is ripe for my people Israel; I will spare them no longer.

³"In that day," declares the Sovereign Lord, "the songs in the temple will turn to wailing.[b] Many, many bodies — flung everywhere! Silence!"

⁴Hear this, you who trample the needy
    and do away with the poor of the land,

⁵saying,

"When will the New Moon be over
    that we may sell grain,
and the Sabbath be ended
    that we may market wheat?" —
skimping on the measure,
    boosting the price
    and cheating with dishonest scales,
⁶buying the poor with silver
    and the needy for a pair of sandals,
    selling even the sweepings with
        the wheat.

⁷The Lord has sworn by himself, the Pride of Jacob: "I will never forget anything they have done.

⁸"Will not the land tremble for this,
    and all who live in it mourn?
The whole land will rise like the Nile;
    it will be stirred up and then sink
    like the river of Egypt.

⁹"In that day," declares the Sovereign Lord,

"I will make the sun go down at noon
    and darken the earth in broad
        daylight.
¹⁰I will turn your religious festivals into
        mourning
    and all your singing into weeping.
I will make all of you wear sackcloth
    and shave your heads.

---

a 17 Hebrew *an unclean*   *b 3* Or *"the temple singers will wail*

7:13 king's sanctuary He does not identify it as Yahweh's sanctuary. This confrontation may have been recorded to emphasize how far Israel had strayed from truly following Yahweh.

7:14 I was neither a prophet Amos insists that he is a layman, not a professional prophet. He does not earn his keep through prophecy. **son of a prophet** Possibly alludes to the prophetic guild mentioned in 1–2 Kings. See note on 2Ki 2:3. **I was a shepherd, and I also took care of sycamore-fig trees** See note on Am 1:1.

7:17 Your wife will become a prostitute Amaziah's punishment is the loss of his family and standing in society. He will lose his wife, children, property and purity. The Hebrew verbs here could be understood as expressing a wish or pronouncing a curse.

8:1–14 The fourth vision report again emphasizes divine judgment (vv. 1–3). Amos renews the accusations of injustice (vv. 4–6) before transitioning to an expansion on the Day of Yahweh imagery (vv. 7–14) introduced in 5:18–20.

8:1 Sovereign Lord showed me See note on 7:1.
8:2 The time is ripe The Hebrew word for "end" sounds like the word for "summer fruit." These two words, *qets* and *qayits*, were likely identical in the Israelite dialect of Hebrew. Inscriptions from Samaria have revealed that, in the northern dialect, both words would have been

written and pronounced *qets*. Biblical Hebrew generally represents the dialect of Judah, where there would have been a difference between *qayits* and *qets*.

8:3 Many, many bodies Dead bodies in the temple would defile it. Compare Eze 9:7 and note.
8:4 you who trample the needy Reiterates the accusations of injustice. Compare Am 5:11 and note.
8:5 the New Moon The merchants have no respect for the sacred day. They only want it to end so they can return to their unjust business practices. See note on Isa 1:13. **the Sabbath** See note on Ex 20:8–11. **with dishonest scales** God reveals how the merchants' thoughts revolve around greed and fraud. They cheated the people into giving more money for less grain by using weights skewed in the merchants' favor. See note on Jer 32:10; compare Eze 45:10; Mic 6:11.
8:6 the needy for a pair of sandals Repeats the accusation from Am 2:6.
8:7 the Pride of Jacob Compare 6:8 and note.
8:8 whole land will rise like the Nile The Nile River was Egypt's primary source of water. The river usually followed a predictable cycle of rising to flood the fields before receding again. Here Amos refers to the annual flooding cycle to depict the inevitability of divine judgment. Compare 9:5.
8:9 In that day Refers to the Day of Yahweh, the time of judgment. See 5:18–20.

I will make that time like mourning for an
    only son
  and the end of it like a bitter day.

¹¹ "The days are coming," declares the
    Sovereign LORD,
  "when I will send a famine through the
    land—
not a famine of food or a thirst for water,
  but a famine of hearing the words of the
    LORD.
¹² People will stagger from sea to sea
  and wander from north to east,
searching for the word of the LORD,
  but they will not find it.

¹³ "In that day

"the lovely young women and strong young
    men
  will faint because of thirst.
¹⁴ Those who swear by the sin of Samaria—
  who say, 'As surely as your god lives, Dan,'
  or, 'As surely as the god^a of Beersheba
    lives'—
  they will fall, never to rise again."

Israel to Be Destroyed

9 I saw the Lord standing by the altar, and he
said:

"Strike the tops of the pillars
  so that the thresholds shake.
Bring them down on the heads of all the people;
  those who are left I will kill with the sword.

Not one will get away,
  none will escape.
² Though they dig down to the depths below,
  from there my hand will take them.
Though they climb up to the heavens above,
  from there I will bring them down.
³ Though they hide themselves on the top of
    Carmel,
  there I will hunt them down and seize
    them.
Though they hide from my eyes at the bottom
    of the sea,
  there I will command the serpent to bite
    them.
⁴ Though they are driven into exile by their
    enemies,
  there I will command the sword to slay them.

"I will keep my eye on them
  for harm and not for good."

⁵ The Lord, the LORD Almighty—
  he touches the earth and it melts,
  and all who live in it mourn;
the whole land rises like the Nile,
  then sinks like the river of Egypt;
⁶ he builds his lofty palace^b in the heavens
  and sets its foundation^c on the earth;
he calls for the waters of the sea
  and pours them out over the face of the
    land—
  the LORD is his name.

---

^a 14 Hebrew *the way*   ^b 6 The meaning of the Hebrew for this
phrase is uncertain.   ^c 6 The meaning of the Hebrew for this
word is uncertain.

8:11 a famine of hearing the words of the LORD Since
Israel was happy to reject Yahweh's message when it was
available to them, Yahweh will withdraw the revelation.
8:14 the sin of Samaria Another likely wordplay alluding
to the idolatry of Israel. The Hebrew word here—usually
translated as "sin" or "guilt"—sounds similar to the
name of the Canaanite goddess, Asherah. King Ahab had
erected an Asherah image in Samaria (1Ki 16:32–33; 2Ki
13:6). Some English translations convey this idea directly
by referring to the "idol" or "goddess" of Samaria. **Dan**
One of the religious locations established by Jeroboam.
See note on Hos 8:4. **as the god of Beersheba lives**
An unusual formula for an oath, but possibly alluding to
some otherwise unknown local worship practices connected with Beersheba. See Am 5:5 and note.

9:1–10 The fifth vision report (vv. 1–4) consists of Amos'
vision of Yahweh, who describes in detail how thoroughly
he will exact judgment on Israel. To emphasize the totality
of Yahweh's sovereignty, the imagery employs several
merisms—figures of speech that use two components
to refer to a whole (e.g., "from head to toe" describes
the entire body). Amos follows this report with another
hymnic interruption (vv. 5–6), as if the wrathful rhetoric
of the vision report needed to be placed in context of
the wrath of the Creator of the cosmos, who can do
as he pleases with his creation. Yahweh declares his
concern for his people and that he will punish them for
their sin (vv. 7–10).

9:1 LORD standing by the altar Amos offers no further
detail about the location of this altar. He could be at
the shrine in Bethel, about to destroy it. Alternatively,
Yahweh could be in his heavenly palace, after which
the earthly temples were modeled, or he could be
in his earthly dwelling at the Jerusalem temple. See
the infographic "Ancient Altars" on p. 127. **so that
the thresholds shake** An image of destruction for a
temple or palace. The tops of the pillars are often called
"capitals" (e.g., 1Ki 7:16), and the thresholds are the
bottoms. The merism indicates the total destruction
of the structure.
9:2 depths below Refers to the underworld. The contrast
between this place (also called Sheol; see note on Ge
37:35) and heaven reinforces that there is nowhere for
anyone to escape. See the infographic "Ancient Hebrew
Conception of the Universe" on p. 5.
9:3 Carmel A high mountain near the Mediterranean
coast (see note on Am 1:2). The merism between the
mountain and the bottom of the sea emphasizes that
there is no earthly hiding place to escape Yahweh.
9:4 for harm and not for good Yahweh's wrath is not
malevolent; it should be expected based on Israel's failure
to keep even the most basic aspects of the covenant
(Dt 28:15–68).
9:5 sinks like the river of Egypt The Nile had an annual flood cycle. See Am 8:8 and note.

⁷"Are not you Israelites
  the same to me as the Cushites[a]?"
                declares the LORD.
  "Did I not bring Israel up from Egypt,
  the Philistines from Caphtor[b]
  and the Arameans from Kir?

⁸"Surely the eyes of the Sovereign LORD
  are on the sinful kingdom.
I will destroy it
  from the face of the earth.
Yet I will not totally destroy
  the descendants of Jacob,"
                declares the LORD.
⁹"For I will give the command,
  and I will shake the people of Israel
  among all the nations
as grain is shaken in a sieve,
  and not a pebble will reach the ground.
¹⁰All the sinners among my people
  will die by the sword,
all those who say,
  'Disaster will not overtake or meet us.'

Israel's Restoration

¹¹"In that day

"I will restore David's fallen shelter —
  I will repair its broken walls
  and restore its ruins —
  and will rebuild it as it used to be,

¹²so that they may possess the remnant of
  Edom
  and all the nations that bear my name, [c]"
                declares the LORD,
                who will do these things.

¹³"The days are coming," declares the LORD,

"when the reaper will be overtaken by the
  plowman
  and the planter by the one treading
  grapes.
New wine will drip from the mountains
  and flow from all the hills,
¹⁴ and I will bring my people Israel back from
  exile.[d]

"They will rebuild the ruined cities and live
  in them.
They will plant vineyards and drink their
  wine;
they will make gardens and eat their
  fruit.
¹⁵I will plant Israel in their own land,
  never again to be uprooted
  from the land I have given them,"

                says the LORD your God.

[a] 7 That is, people from the upper Nile region   [b] 7 That is,
Crete   [c] 12 Hebrew; Septuagint *so that the remnant of people /
and all the nations that bear my name may seek me*   [d] 14 Or
will restore the fortunes of my people Israel

9:7 Are not you Israelites the same to me as the Cushites Yahweh reveals to Israel that, despite Israel's election as his chosen people, he still cares for all people. The area south of Egypt was at the far end of the known world for the Israelites at this time. See note on Isa 18:1. **Philistines from Caphtor and the Arameans from Kir** Yahweh claims responsibility not only for the movement of Israel from Egypt to Canaan but also for the migrations of the Philistines and the Arameans (Syrians). **Caphtor** Usually identified with Crete. See note on Jer 47:4. **Kir** Likely a place in Mesopotamia.
9:8 I will not totally destroy the descendants of Jacob Foreshadows the future restoration described in Am 9:11–15. **the descendants of Jacob** Refers to Israel.

9:11–15 Amos ends with a salvation oracle. He follows the pattern of Hosea and Joel by ending with a vision of an ideal future in which Israel is restored and the broken relationship with Yahweh is repaired.

9:11 In that day Points to the day of salvation. See note on Isa 27:12. **David's fallen shelter** Reminds Israel, which had rejected the Davidic dynasty, of Yahweh's promises to David.
9:12 the remnant of Edom Compare Ob 19.
9:13 the reaper will be overtaken by the plowman The imagery here is of a blessed creation where the land is continually fertile and the growing season is continuous. As soon as the harvest is complete, the land can be plowed to plant again. **New wine will drip from the mountains** Compare Joel 3:18.
9:14 I will bring my people Israel back from exile The restoration involves the reversal of the curses about vineyards and houses (Am 5:11). See note on Jer 29:14.

OBADIAH

INTRODUCTION TO OBADIAH

Obadiah is the shortest book in the Old Testament. It tells of Yahweh's judgment on Judah's neighbor, Edom. Injustice does not go unrecognized by Yahweh. In the case of Edom, their injustice—tormenting the people of Judah while Judah was invaded by other nations—meant their coming downfall. Obadiah also envisions that Judah itself will be restored. This theme of the coming Day of Yahweh, when God will execute judgment and fulfill his promises, is common among other Prophetic Books—especially Joel and Amos.

BACKGROUND

The first line of Obadiah identifies the book as the vision of Obadiah, whose name means "servant of Yahweh." Several people named Obadiah are mentioned in the Old Testament, but it is unclear whether any of them may be identified as the prophet of this text. It also is unclear when the book was written.

The Israelites had a long and checkered history with their neighbors the Edomites, the descendants of Jacob's brother Esau (see Ge 25:23; 27:41; Nu 20:14–21). The events mentioned in Obadiah could have occurred in several different time periods. The invasion of Jerusalem in Obadiah 11, for example, could point to the total destruction of Jerusalem by the Babylonians in 586 BC. This date is supported by the record of the Edomites joining in the looting and committing violence against the inhabitants of Jerusalem (Ps 137:7; La 4:21). In addition, the literary style of Obadiah 1–9 is similar to that of Jeremiah 49:7–16, which was written around the fall of Jerusalem. However, it remains possible that Obadiah was written earlier and Jeremiah may have borrowed from Obadiah. The possibility of a ninth-century BC date is based on 2 Kings 8:20–22 and 2 Chronicles 21:8–10, which record Edom's revolt against Judah during the reign of King Jehoram. Whenever the events of Obadiah took place, the main issue is that the Edomites viewed the suffering of the people of Judah as an opportunity for gain instead of a time for grieving.

This map depicts many of the locations related to the book of Obadiah—though Edom is the main focus of the book.

STRUCTURE

The book of Obadiah begins with a report of judgment against Edom (Ob 1–9). Yahweh will bring about destruction for Edom. The Edomites' tactical advantage of living in the hard-to-reach mountains will not protect them from Yahweh's judgment—their place of pride will lead to their downfall. The prophet then

turns to the reason for this judgment: Edom gloated over the destruction of Judah and even participated in its downfall (vv. 10–14).

The prophet steps back, in Obadiah 15–21, to speak of the coming Day of Yahweh, on which multiple nations—not just Edom—will be judged. However, the Day of Yahweh is not only about judgment: God will also deliver his people and fulfill his promises to them (vv. 19–21).

OUTLINE

- Judgment against Edom (vv. 1–9)
- Edom's sins (vv. 10–14)
- Reversal of fates on the Day of Yahweh (vv. 15–21)

THEMES

The three main themes of the book of Obadiah include the folly of pride, reaping what you sow and loving your enemies. Obadiah accuses Edom of being self-aggrandizing: Because Edom is lofty, God pulls it to the ground (vv. 2–3). The Edomites' arrogance makes them oblivious to the truth that their allies are really their enemies (v. 7). In addition, those who should be their friends and brothers—their relatives in Judah—have become their enemies.

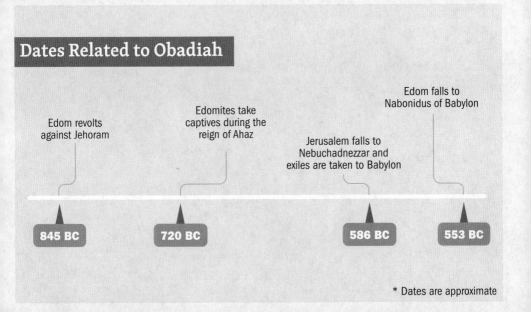

Dates Related to Obadiah

Edom revolts against Jehoram — **845 BC**

Edomites take captives during the reign of Ahaz — **720 BC**

Jerusalem falls to Nebuchadnezzar and exiles are taken to Babylon — **586 BC**

Edom falls to Nabonidus of Babylon — **553 BC**

* Dates are approximate

The Edomites also reap the violence they sowed when they gloated over Jerusalem's invasion (vv. 10–14). In response to the Edomites' rejoicing, God will topple Edom and give their land to his people (vv. 19–21). Through Obadiah, Yahweh assures Judah that he will judge Edom for its crimes and that his people will eventually triumph.

Obadiah also shows us how to treat our enemies. At the time Obadiah was written, Judah and Edom were two nations, but they were descended from twin brothers, Jacob and Esau. As nations with such a connection, they should have protected each other like brothers (v. 12). Obadiah shows us that we can trust God to bring justice and right our wrongs—even when people as close to us as relatives turn into enemies and encroach upon us. In its cries against Edom, Obadiah also shows us that we should love and forgive all, regardless of racial, ethnic or religious boundaries. Obadiah demonstrates that we can rest in God at all times—knowing that he will enact justice, in his way and his time.

Obadiah's Vision

1–4pp — Jer 49:14-16
5–6pp — Jer 49:9-10

¹The vision of Obadiah.

This is what the Sovereign Lord says about Edom —

We have heard a message from the Lord:
    An envoy was sent to the nations to say,
    "Rise, let us go against her for battle" —

² "See, I will make you small among the
        nations;
    you will be utterly despised.
³ The pride of your heart has deceived you,
    you who live in the clefts of the rocks[a]
    and make your home on the heights,
you who say to yourself,
    'Who can bring me down to the
        ground?'

⁴ Though you soar like the eagle
    and make your nest among the stars,
    from there I will bring you down,"
                declares the Lord.
⁵ "If thieves came to you,
    if robbers in the night —
oh, what a disaster awaits you! —
    would they not steal only as much as they
        wanted?
If grape pickers came to you,
    would they not leave a few grapes?
⁶ But how Esau will be ransacked,
    his hidden treasures pillaged!
⁷ All your allies will force you to the border;
    your friends will deceive and
        overpower you;
those who eat your bread will set
        a trap for you,[b]
but you will not detect it.

[a] 3 Or of Sela   [b] 7 The meaning of the Hebrew for this clause is uncertain.

1–14 The short book of Obadiah divides into two main sections: vv. 1–14 and 15–21. The first follows the typical prophetic genre of an oracle against the nations. This oracle is directed entirely against Edom, Judah's neighbor to the southeast. The picture of Edom gloating over Jerusalem's downfall — probably at the hands of the Babylonians in 586 BC — is similarly criticized in oracles of Ezekiel (Eze 25:12–14; 35:1–15). Isaiah and Jeremiah also include oracles of judgment against Edom (Isa 34:5–17; Jer 49:7–22). See the timeline "Approximate Dates of Old Testament Prophets" on p. 1070; see the table "Oracles Against the Nations" on p. 1244.

1 vision Signifies a revelation given by Yahweh; a common phrase used by the prophets. See note on Isa 1:1. **Obadiah** Meaning "servant of Yahweh"; fitting for his prophetic service to his people. Obadiah the prophet is unknown outside of the book bearing his name. The name Obadiah is fairly common in the OT, and no additional personal details such as a title, tribal affiliation or father's name are provided. Any of those details would help link Obadiah with one of the other 11 people in the OT with that name (e.g., 1Ki 18:3; 1Ch 3:21; 7:3; 2Ch 17:7; 34:12; Ezr 8:9; Ne 10:5). The most popular suggestion about Obadiah's identity is that he was one of the royal officials of that name, serving either under Ahab of Israel (1Ki 18:1–16) or Jehoshaphat of Judah (2Ch 17:7). Both of these kings reigned in the ninth century BC, one of the possible time periods for Obadiah's ministry. However, the content of Obadiah's message concerning Edom's transgressions against the southern kingdom of Judah suggests his ministry could also have followed the fall of Jerusalem to Babylon in 586 BC. This would make Jeremiah his contemporary (compare Ob 1–4; Jer 49:14–16). Like Jeremiah, Obadiah refers to the Day of Yahweh as the time when God will come to judge the nations for their mistreatment of his people (Ob 15). **about Edom** Obadiah is commanded to bring forth a message of judgment on one of Judah's closest neighbors. See Jer 49:7 and note. **We have heard a message** Obadiah's phrasing in Ob 1–4 is substantially similar to Jer 49:14–16. Obadiah also shares common Hebrew phrases as well as concepts with Joel, Amos and

Ezekiel (compare Joel 2:32; 3:19–20; Am 9:12; Eze 35), so there may have been a common stock of prophetic phrases that Jeremiah and Obadiah both adapted for their oracles against Edom. Based on other connections between the imagery in Obadiah and Jeremiah (see Ob 7 and Jer 38:22), it seems likely that Obadiah adapted content from Jeremiah. However, Jeremiah's prophecies are also often reminiscent of the work of earlier prophets. **An envoy** Judah has received information from Yahweh concerning Edom and has obediently sent out a messenger. **the nations** The Hebrew term here is commonly used for non-Jewish people (Gentiles). Yahweh calls for Judah to send out a messenger to other nations so they can help destroy Edom. **let us go against her for battle** The message to the nations involves two aspects of faith: rising to action and following through with the commandment (up to and including battle).

2 small among the nations; you will be utterly despised Edom was never very large in terms of population or territory. This proclamation emphasizes their general insignificance on the larger world stage. Not only will they be insignificant but others will also look on them with contempt.

3 pride of your heart Pride is often emphasized as the cardinal sin of the nations, resting in their own power and opposing Yahweh (e.g., Isa 14:13–15; Jer 48:29; Eze 28:1; compare note on Isa 2:12–18). **the clefts of the rocks** Edom was a mountainous region south and east of the Dead Sea. The Hebrew word for "rock" or "cliff" also is the name of an Edomite fortress (Sela; see 2Ki 14:7). **Who can bring me down to the ground** A rhetorical question highlighting Edom's complacent trust in their impregnable mountain security. Yahweh will answer the rhetorical question in Ob 4.

5 thieves came to you Obadiah appears to be expanding on Jer 49:9, reversing the references — first thieves, then grape gatherers — and inserting the line about plunderers.

6 Esau will be ransacked Using the name of Esau to stand for the entire country of Edom (compare Jer 49:10), just like the name of Jacob is often used to refer to Israel (e.g., Hos 12:2). On Esau, see note on Ge 25:25.

7 your friends will deceive and overpower you Compare Jer 38:22.

8 "In that day," declares the LORD,
      "will I not destroy the wise men of Edom,
      those of understanding in the mountains
         of Esau?
9 Your warriors, Teman, will be terrified,
      and everyone in Esau's mountains
      will be cut down in the slaughter.
10 Because of the violence against your brother
         Jacob,
      you will be covered with shame;
      you will be destroyed forever.
11 On the day you stood aloof
      while strangers carried off his wealth
   and foreigners entered his gates
      and cast lots for Jerusalem,
      you were like one of them.
12 You should not gloat over your brother
      in the day of his misfortune,
   nor rejoice over the people of Judah
      in the day of their destruction,
   nor boast so much
      in the day of their trouble.
13 You should not march through the gates of
         my people
      in the day of their disaster,
   nor gloat over them in their calamity
      in the day of their disaster,
   nor seize their wealth
      in the day of their disaster.
14 You should not wait at the crossroads
      to cut down their fugitives,
   nor hand over their survivors
      in the day of their trouble.

15 "The day of the LORD is near
      for all nations.
   As you have done, it will be done to you;
      your deeds will return upon your own
         head.
16 Just as you drank on my holy hill,
      so all the nations will drink continually;
   they will drink and drink
      and be as if they had never been.
17 But on Mount Zion will be deliverance;
      it will be holy,
      and Jacob will possess his inheritance.
18 Jacob will be a fire
      and Joseph a flame;
   Esau will be stubble,
      and they will set him on fire and destroy
         him.
   There will be no survivors
      from Esau."
                        The LORD has spoken.

19 People from the Negev will occupy
      the mountains of Esau,

---

8 the wise men of Edom Edom had a reputation for wisdom. Compare Jer 49:7. **mountains of Esau** Referring to Edom in this way is unique to Obadiah (Ob 9,19,21). Edom's terrain was mountainous (compare v. 4; Mal 1:3) and the name of their traditional founding father, Esau, has already been used to refer to the entire country (see note on Ob 6). Another common name for Edom is "Seir" or "Mount Seir" (see Eze 35:2 and note). Obadiah could be substituting "Mount Esau" for "Mount Seir." Ezekiel's oracle against Edom in Eze 35 is addressed to Mount Seir. Obadiah never uses Seir to refer to Edom.
9 Teman An important Edomite city. See Jer 49:7 and note.
10 Because of the violence Probably alludes to the destruction of Jerusalem and the temple in 586 BC, but the narrative of this event in 2Ki 25 doesn't mention the Edomites being involved. They are likely being criticized for their inaction (see Ob 11 and note).
11 On the day you stood aloof Biblical tradition blames Edom for cruelly gloating over Jerusalem's demise (Ps 137:7; Eze 25:12–14; 35:12–14; La 4:21–22). Here, their offense appears to be standing idly by and not attempting to assist Judah. **strangers carried off his wealth** The Babylonians took the treasures from the temple before they burned it down (2Ki 25:13–17). **cast lots for Jerusalem** The practice of casting lots was used to divide the spoils of war. See note on Joel 3:3. **like one of them** In terms of guilt, Edom may as well have actively assisted Babylon. Their inaction and gloating over their neighbor's fall made them complicit in the greater crimes.

12–14 The series of eight statements in Ob 12–14 are worded as divine prohibitions that Edom should obey. The detail describing the actions suggests this is a literary device referring to past offenses and framing them as divine prohibitions to emphasize Edom's guilt. An alternative way of understanding the eight "do not" statements is translating them as "you should not have"—scolding them for past mistakes instead of commanding future obedience.

12 nor boast so much in the day of their trouble Compare Ps 137:7.
13 nor seize their wealth Edom did expand into some of the former territory of southern Judah after 586 BC. Compare Eze 35:10 and note.
14 to cut down their fugitives Instead of offering a safe refuge for the survivors of Judah, Edom apparently killed or captured them.

15–21 The second part of Obadiah focuses on Yahweh's final judgment of the nations and the corresponding restoration of his chosen people.

15 The day of the LORD The Day of Yahweh is a time of judgment against the nations of the world for their opposition to his rule. See note on Joel 1:15. **As you have done, it will be done to you** Compare Eze 35:15.
16 my holy hill A reference to Zion, the Temple Mount in Jerusalem. **all the nations will drink continually** Obadiah's language here presupposes the fully developed metaphor of the cup of wrath from Jer 25:15–29; 49:12 (see note on Jer 25:15).
17 Mount Zion will be deliverance Compare Joel 2:32.
18 Jacob will be a fire Referring to Israel as the agent of judgment against Edom. Compare the wording of Isa 10:17. **Joseph** Referring to Israel as a whole. Joseph was a son of Jacob and father of Ephraim and Manasseh. The territories of Ephraim and Manasseh formed the core of the northern kingdom's territory. See note on Hos 4:17.

and people from the foothills will possess
the land of the Philistines.
They will occupy the fields of Ephraim and
Samaria,
and Benjamin will possess Gilead.
20 This company of Israelite exiles who are in
Canaan
will possess the land as far as Zarephath;

the exiles from Jerusalem who are in
Sepharad
will possess the towns of the Negev.
21 Deliverers will go up on[a] Mount Zion
to govern the mountains of Esau.
And the kingdom will be the LORD's.

[a] 21 Or *from*

19 the Negev Each region of Israel is depicted as taking possession of the nearest disputed territory or enemy territory. See note on Isa 21:1; note on Jer 32:44. **the foothills** The Shephelah consisted of the western foothills of Judah on the border of the coastal plain, which was primarily the territory of the Philistines. See Jer 32:44 and note. **the Philistines** See note on 1Sa 4:1. **Ephraim** See note on Hos 4:17. **Samaria** See note on Jer 31:5. **Benjamin** The tribal territory between Judah and Ephraim. Benjamin was usually part of the southern kingdom. Here, the tribe is allotted the fertile Gilead region, across the Jordan to the northeast. **Gilead** A region east of the Jordan River. See note on Jer 8:22. **20 Zarephath** A Phoenician coastal village in the region of Sidon (see 1Ki 17:9). See note on Eze 26:1—28:19. **Sepharad** Probably Sardis in western Asia Minor. Exiles from distant lands will return to reclaim their share of the promised land.

JONAH

INTRODUCTION TO JONAH

Jonah is the only narrative included in the books of the Minor Prophets. It tells the story of God commanding the prophet Jonah to preach in Nineveh, but Jonah decides to run the other way by boarding a ship. After God orchestrates a storm and a great fish swallows Jonah, he obeys God's command. But when Nineveh—a major city of the Assyrian Empire and Israel's enemy—repents after listening to Jonah, he is infuriated. The book's lesson becomes clear in the end: God's care extends to all who call on him—even those who previously stood against his people. His mercy is truly for all.

BACKGROUND

The book of Jonah does not name its author. The title character is a prophet—Jonah, son of Amittai—who was active in Israel during the reign of Jeroboam II (ca. 786–746 BC; 2Ki 14:25).

The main question complicating the interpretation of Jonah is that of genre: whether the book should be read as a historical narrative or a satiric parable. Some ancient sources, including the New Testament, could be understood as interpreting the narrative as historical (e.g., Mt 12:39–42; 3 Maccabees 6:8; Josephus, *Antiquities* 9.208). However, the same question of genre affects how those references should be interpreted. The primary issue is not whether the events in the story could have happened. A God who performs miracles could certainly cause a great fish to swallow a human being (Jnh 1:17) or cause a vine to grow and wither in a matter of hours (4:6–7). Instead, the issue is what the author intended. Those who argue that the book is a satirical parable interpret its exaggerated elements as comic devices used to lampoon the Israelites, who take pride in their privileged status but do not respond to God's prophets. These exaggerations include the huge size of Nineveh, the short sermon Jonah gives, and that even the animals

This map depicts many of the locations related to the book of Jonah. Though Jonah's hometown is not mentioned in this book, it is named in 2 Kings 14:25 as Gath Hepher, which is located just north of Samaria.

of Nineveh repent in sackcloth and ashes (3:8). Whatever the story's genre, the theological lesson remains the same: God's love and mercy extend to all people who trust in him.

STRUCTURE

The book of Jonah has four chapters, which correspond to its four sections. In Jonah 1, God orders Jonah to preach to Nineveh, but Jonah flees aboard a boat to Tarshish. When a storm surrounds the ship at Yahweh's command, the sailors choose to throw Jonah into the sea and a huge fish swallows him.

In Jonah 2, Jonah recites a poetic prayer inside the fish, acknowledging that Yahweh heard his call and rescued him. Jonah promises to obey God's command. God then orders the fish to vomit Jonah on dry land.

Jonah 3 takes Jonah to Nineveh, where he proclaims, without elegance or tact, that the city will be demolished after 40 days (3:4). Surprisingly, the Ninevites' response is repentance and belief in God—and Yahweh decides not to destroy the city (3:10).

In Jonah 4, Yahweh's compassion incites anger in Jonah, who focuses on his own life difficulties, like his lack of shade in the heat of the day. In response, Yahweh makes a plant for shade grow and then die. Jonah complains, and Yahweh reminds him of the great irony of the situation. Jonah

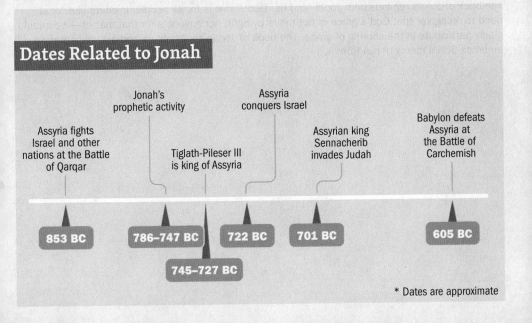

Dates Related to Jonah

| 853 BC | 786–747 BC | 745–727 BC | 722 BC | 701 BC | 605 BC |

Assyria fights Israel and other nations at the Battle of Qarqar

Jonah's prophetic activity

Tiglath-Pileser III is king of Assyria

Assyria conquers Israel

Assyrian king Sennacherib invades Judah

Babylon defeats Assyria at the Battle of Carchemish

* Dates are approximate

mourns a plant, for which he did not labor or make grow, but he does not care for the great city of Nineveh (4:10–11).

OUTLINE

- God calls and Jonah flees (1:1–17)
- Jonah's prayer in the fish (2:1–10)
- Nineveh repents at Jonah's preaching (3:1–10)
- Jonah's anger and God's response (4:1–11)

THEMES

The main theme of Jonah is that God's grace and love extends to outsiders and even oppressors. The Israelites, as God's people, should regard the love of God not as something earned, but as something gifted by God.

Jonah also illustrates the narrowness of nationalistic pride and the wideness of God's mercy. Jonah begrudges God's grace to Nineveh; many of us have similar, despicable feelings, which must be dealt with and changed. Jonah complains to the God who saved him from the depths of the ocean—while ultimately being forced to recognize his own lowly place before the Maker of all. Being judgmental and the need to find humility often go hand in hand.

The book of Jonah reminds both Jonah and us: God's love is for all people. Insiders like Jonah need to recognize that God's grace is not theirs by right, nor anyone's for that matter—we should gladly participate in the sharing of grace. The book of Jonah confronts us and asks whether we will embrace God's mercy or run from it.

Jonah Flees From the LORD

1 The word of the LORD came to Jonah son of Amittai: ²"Go to the great city of Nineveh and preach against it, because its wickedness has come up before me."

³But Jonah ran away from the LORD and headed for Tarshish. He went down to Joppa, where he found a ship bound for that port. After paying the fare, he went aboard and sailed for Tarshish to flee from the LORD.

⁴Then the LORD sent a great wind on the sea, and such a violent storm arose that the ship threatened to break up. ⁵All the sailors were afraid and each cried out to his own god. And they threw the cargo into the sea to lighten the ship.

But Jonah had gone below deck, where he lay down and fell into a deep sleep. ⁶The captain went to him and said, "How can you sleep? Get up and call on your god! Maybe he will take notice of us so that we will not perish."

⁷Then the sailors said to each other, "Come, let us cast lots to find out who is responsible for this calamity." They cast lots and the lot fell on Jonah. ⁸So they asked him, "Tell us, who is responsible

---

1:1–6 The book of Jonah contains one of the most beloved stories in the Bible; however, its unique style contrasts with the books of the Prophets and raises questions about how this book should be read. The main approaches to interpretation differ on whether to read Jonah as history or as a symbolic story like a parable or allegory.

A historical reading accepts the events described in the book of Jonah as having occurred just as described. According to 2Ki 14:25, the prophet Jonah, son of Amittai, lived during the reign of Jeroboam II in Israel (ca. 786–746 BC). Ancient Jewish writings may have regarded Jonah as history, but this is not certain (see Josephus, *Antiquities* 9.208; 3 Maccabees 6:8; compare Mt 12:39–42). Interpretations that read the story as a parable or allegory emphasize its theological message and literary features. See the timeline "Approximate Dates of Old Testament Prophets" on p. 1070.

1:1 word of the LORD The book of Jonah opens with a traditional Hebrew formula meaning "now it came about" (compare Jos 1:1; Jdg 1:1; Ru 1:1; 1Sa 1:1; 2Sa 1:1; Est 1:1). Ezekiel is the only other Prophetic book to begin this way (Ez 1:1). **Jonah** The name Jonah means "dove." **Amittai** Means "truth" or "faithfulness."

JONAH
Jonah was from Gath Hepher (meaning "winepress of the pit"), a town in lower Galilee near Nazareth (2Ki 14:25). The town has been identified with the modern village of el-Meshhed, where the tomb of Jonah is still shown. Gath Hepher was within the tribal territory given to Zebulun (see Jos 19:10,13), so it is likely that Jonah belonged to that tribe.

1:2 the great city of Nineveh Nineveh was a major metropolis, one of four great cities of Assyria. Compare Jnh 4:11. **preach against it** The message that Jonah is to preach is supplied in 3:4. **its wickedness** A general reference to the city's violence, immorality and idolatry. Assyria was a militaristic society with a reputation for violence and cruelty in warfare. Their religion was polytheistic. Ashur, Adad, Sin, Shamash and Ishtar were the chief deities of the Assyrian pantheon, Ashur being regarded as the most powerful. The Assyrian gods were patron gods, worshiped for their blessing and protection of specific cities. The patron deity of Nineveh was Ishtar, goddess of love and war. **1:3 Tarshish** Probably Tartessus in southern Spain, perhaps the most distant city known to Israel. Tartessus was a Phoenician colony. At this time, Phoenicia was a close ally of Israel, an alliance solidified with the marriage between King Ahab of Israel and Jezebel, a Phoenician princess. See note on Isa 23:1. **Joppa** The closest port to Jerusalem.

JOPPA
Joppa, meaning "beauty," was located about 30 miles northwest of Jerusalem on the shores of the Mediterranean Sea. The port at Joppa was where Solomon received the shipments of cedar logs for the Jerusalem temple (2Ch 2:16). The members of the Jewish community who returned from exile likewise used Joppa as a port to receive cedar logs from Lebanon for the rebuilding of the temple (Ezr 3:7). The port was likely controlled by the Philistines or Phoenicians in the eighth to sixth centuries BC.

1:4 the sea The Mediterranean Sea.
1:5 All the sailors were afraid If these sailors were Phoenicians, then the storm must have been terrible indeed. The Phoenicians were legendary for their seamanship and navigating skills. See the infographic "Ancient Phoenician Ship" on p. 1317. **his own god** At this time, individuals often had their own personal god that they worshiped above all others. **to lighten the ship** A lighter ship is easier to control in the midst of a storm.
1:6 How can you sleep The captain cannot believe Jonah is sleeping; he calls him to wake up and pray for Yahweh to calm the storm.
1:7 let us cast lots The casting of lots was common throughout the ancient Near East as a way of allowing the gods to make their decisions known to people (see Est 3:7). The Bible regularly depicts faithful followers of Yahweh using lots to discover God's will (Pr 16:33). The lot was cast to determine which goat became the scapegoat on the Day of Atonement (see Lev 16:8), to indicate which portion of the promised land was given to each tribe (see Nu 26:55–56; Jos 15:1; 16:1; 17:1) and to identify Saul as Yahweh's choice for Israel's king (1Sa 10:20–24). Lots were also cast to determine which families would live in Jerusalem (Ne 11:1) and to identify Matthias as the twelfth disciple after Judas committed suicide (Ac 1:26). In fact, the Urim and Thummim used by the high priest was a form of casting lots to determine the judgment of God (compare Ex 28:30; Ezr 2:63; Ne 7:65). **this calamity** The Hebrew term for evil is used here in the sense of calamity or disaster.

for making all this trouble for us? What kind of work do you do? Where do you come from? What is your country? From what people are you?"

⁹He answered, "I am a Hebrew and I worship the LORD, the God of heaven, who made the sea and the dry land."

¹⁰This terrified them and they asked, "What have you done?" (They knew he was running away from the LORD, because he had already told them so.)

¹¹The sea was getting rougher and rougher. So they asked him, "What should we do to you to make the sea calm down for us?"

¹²"Pick me up and throw me into the sea," he replied, "and it will become calm. I know that it is my fault that this great storm has come upon you."

¹³Instead, the men did their best to row back to land. But they could not, for the sea grew even wilder than before. ¹⁴Then they cried out to the LORD, "Please, LORD, do not let us die for taking this man's life. Do not hold us accountable for killing an innocent man, for you, LORD, have done as you pleased." ¹⁵Then they took Jonah and threw him overboard, and the raging sea grew calm. ¹⁶At this the men greatly feared the LORD, and they offered a sacrifice to the LORD and made vows to him.

Jonah's Prayer

¹⁷Now the LORD provided a huge fish to swallow Jonah, and Jonah was in the belly of the fish three days and three nights. ¹From inside the fish Jonah prayed to the LORD his God. ²He said:

"In my distress I called to the LORD,
　and he answered me.
From deep in the realm of the dead I called
　for help,
　and you listened to my cry.
³ You hurled me into the depths,
　into the very heart of the seas,
　and the currents swirled about me;
　all your waves and breakers
　swept over me.
⁴ I said, 'I have been banished
　from your sight;
yet I will look again
　toward your holy temple.'
⁵ The engulfing waters threatened me,ᵇ
　the deep surrounded me;
　seaweed was wrapped around my head.

ᵃ In Hebrew texts 2:1 is numbered 1:17, and 2:1-10 is numbered 2:2-11.　ᵇ 5 Or *waters were at my throat*

1:9 I am a Hebrew This title first appears in Ge 14:13 to differentiate Abram from the Amorites among whom he lived. The term always appears in interaction with foreigners, being used by foreigners to describe Israelites or by Israelites to describe themselves to foreigners. **I worship the LORD** The Hebrew term used here can be translated as "fear" or "worship," which is the connotation here. **the God of heaven** This title is rarely used prior to the exile (see Ge 24:3,7; Ezr 1:2; 5:11,12; 6:9,10). **the sea and the dry land** A figure of speech indicating totality (called a merism) acknowledging Yahweh's sovereignty over all creation.

1:10 from the LORD Literally, "from the face of Yahweh." Jonah's claim that he serves Yahweh, the supreme Creator God, is ironic in the context of his attempted flight from the presence of the Creator. Jonah's attitude seems casual and almost flippant. The sailors respond with appropriate fear and horror at his foolish actions in angering a powerful deity.

1:12 throw me into the sea The Hebrew term here is the same word used in Jnh 1:4 to describe Yahweh causing the great storm.

1:14 Do not hold us accountable for killing an innocent man The sailors do not want to be held guilty for killing Jonah.

1:16 At this the men greatly feared the LORD Jonah claimed to fear Yahweh, but the non-Jewish sailors are the ones who actually show him proper reverence. See note on v. 5. **vows** A solemn promise to God to do something or to abstain from something. In this instance, the sailors might have vowed to worship Yahweh and forsake all other gods.

1:17 provided This term is used repeatedly in Jonah to emphasize Yahweh's sovereignty (see 4:6–8). **fish** This is the general term for all kinds of fish; it does not refer specifically to a whale. **three days and three nights** This phrase can refer to a full day and parts of two others (see Mt 12:40).

2:1–10 The prayer in Jnh 2:2–9 resembles the psalms of thanksgiving from the book of Psalms (compare Ps 18:6; 120:1). The use of this type of psalm is another example of the narrative's penchant for ironic reversal. A thanksgiving psalm typically recounts a past danger, describes God's deliverance and offers thanks. Jonah is still in the belly of the fish, not yet fully out of danger. His situation calls for a lament psalm—a confession of sin or cry of distress punctuated by a hope in God's future deliverance.

2:1 Jonah prayed to the LORD The prayer that follows is a prayer of thanksgiving and trust. While Jonah appears thankful that the fish has saved him, he doesn't actually acknowledge his sin or explicitly repent of his actions. He is only thankful that he did not drown (see Jnh 2:3,5–6). **2:2 he answered** Yahweh responded to Jonah's distress by sending the fish to swallow him. **deep in the realm of the dead** A figure of speech referring to the depths of the ocean. The chaos of the sea was associated with drawing closer to the underworld (*she'ol* in Hebrew; see note on Ge 37:35). See the infographic "Ancient Hebrew Conception of the Universe" on p. 5.

2:4 banished from your sight Jonah felt that God no longer looked on him with favor since he was descending to the depths of the ocean. Therefore, he cried out (past tense) in the midst of his distress (v. 2). **I will look again toward your holy temple** This is a present-tense statement of faith as Jonah reflects on his situation in the belly of the whale. **your holy temple** Meaning the temple in Jerusalem. The Hebrew phrase here is rarely used in the OT. It appears elsewhere only in the Psalms (Ps 5:7; 11:4; 65:4; 79:1; 138:2), in Micah (Mic 1:2) and in Habakkuk (Hab 2:20).

2:5 threatened me The Hebrew term used here has a variety of meanings, all of which illustrate the extent to which the waters closed over Jonah.

⁶ To the roots of the mountains I sank down;
　the earth beneath barred me in forever.
　But you, LORD my God,
　　brought my life up from the pit.

⁷ "When my life was ebbing away,
　　I remembered you, LORD,
　and my prayer rose to you,
　　to your holy temple.

⁸ "Those who cling to worthless idols
　　turn away from God's love for them.
⁹ But I, with shouts of grateful praise,
　　will sacrifice to you.
　What I have vowed I will make good.
　　I will say, 'Salvation comes from the LORD.'"

¹⁰ And the LORD commanded the fish, and it vomited Jonah onto dry land.

Jonah Goes to Nineveh

3 Then the word of the LORD came to Jonah a second time: ²"Go to the great city of Nineveh and proclaim to it the message I give you."

³ Jonah obeyed the word of the LORD and went to Nineveh. Now Nineveh was a very large city; it took three days to go through it. ⁴ Jonah began by going a day's journey into the city, proclaiming, "Forty more days and Nineveh will be overthrown." ⁵ The Ninevites believed God. A fast was proclaimed, and all of them, from the greatest to the least, put on sackcloth.

2:6 roots of the mountains The lowest parts of the ocean floor. See note on Jnh 2:2. **barred me in** Bars were used on city gates and prisons as locks. Jonah is picturing himself locked inside the earth. **you, LORD my God, brought my life up from the pit** Another statement of faith (compare v. 4). **from the pit** That is, Sheol (see v. 2), used figuratively of the depths of the ocean. The Hebrew term here is also used as a synonym for Sheol in Job 33:18.
2:7 When my life was ebbing away Meaning that Jonah was losing hope. The Hebrew word translated as "life" or "soul" is used here to describe Jonah's mental state. **remembered** The Hebrew word used here most often occurs in the context of prayer (see 1Sa 1:11; 2Ki 20:3; 2Ch 6:42; Ne 5:19).
2:8 Those who cling to worthless idols A reference to the Israelites, the audience of the book of Jonah. The Israelites refused to repent of their idolatry and eventually were sent to Assyria as exiles. **worthless idols** The Hebrew word here is used to denote falsehood or lack of value. **love for** The Hebrew term used here is often used in reference to Yahweh's covenant with Israel (see Dt 7:9,12; 1Ki 8:23; Ne 1:5).
2:9 What I have vowed I will make good Jonah may have vowed to offer a sacrifice to Yahweh when he prayed for deliverance (see Jnh 2:2), or the reference may be to the first half of the verse and Jonah is at that moment making a vow to Yahweh. **Salvation comes from the LORD** The Hebrew word used here, yeshu'a, meaning "salvation," is used in the sense of deliverance.
2:10 it vomited Jonah onto dry land The fish likely deposited Jonah somewhere along the eastern Mediterranean coast, perhaps near Joppa itself. See the table "Miracles of the Prophets" on p. 1366.

3:1–5 This brief account of Jonah's ministry illustrates the challenges faced by literal versus figurative interpretations of the book (see note on 1:1–6). Jonah is sent again to Nineveh and obeys this time. The city is described as great (as in 1:2)—a common mark of exaggeration (hyperbole) in Jonah with the great wind (1:4), the great storm (1:12) and the great fish (1:17). The further enigmatic detail that the city is a three-day journey seems to refer to how long it would take to walk across the city. The explanation that Jonah preached for three days in the city is difficult in light of vv. 4–5, where Jonah walks a day's journey into the city, preaches his brief oracle of doom, and everyone repents.
　The narrative's penchant for ironic reversal can be seen most fully here. The typical Israelite prophet accepted Yahweh's call, preached to God's people and was met with stubborn resistance (compare Isa 6:8; 7:9–13; Jer 5:1–3). Here, the Israelite prophet initially rejects Yahweh's call, begrudgingly preaches to a foreign people and meets universal repentance. These narrative details fit well with understanding Jonah as a non-literal story, a satirical critique of Israel's failure to repent after God's repeated attempts to reach them through his prophets (Jer 7:25–26).
3:2 Go to the great city of Nineveh See note on 1:2. **proclaim to it** If Jonah delivered a literal message to Nineveh, he probably would have spoken Aramaic, a common language used in trade and diplomacy in the ancient Near East. Isaiah 36:11 indicates that the educated elite in Israel and Judah could speak Aramaic in the late eighth century BC.
3:3 it took three days to go through it The Hebrew phrase used here describes highways or straight passages (compare Eze 42:4; Isa 35:8), suggesting that this refers to the diameter of the city. However, the phrase also can refer to the length of a journey, regardless of whether the route is direct or circuitous (Ne 2:6). Excavations of Nineveh indicate that the circumference of the city walls at the height of Nineveh's power as the Assyrian capital was about 7.75 miles. A person could easily walk 15–20 miles a day in ancient times. Either the writer has employed hyperbole to deliberately exaggerate the size of Nineveh (45–60 miles across), or this phrase indicates something other than the width of the city. It also can be understood as a reference to Jonah preaching throughout the city over the course of three days; however, since Nineveh repents immediately after the first day of preaching (Jnh 3:5), it is unlikely that Jonah continued preaching for two more days.
3:4 a day's journey A total of about 15 miles. Jonah travels about a third of the way into the city and delivers his message. See note on v. 3. **will be overthrown** The Hebrew term used here (haphak) has a wide range of meaning depending on context. The basic meaning is "turn," but the word is used for both destruction (Ge 19:21) and transformation (Ps 66:6). Jonah's oracle is ambiguous, proclaiming 40 days until Nineveh is changed. The nature of the change depends on the people of Nineveh. If the people do not change, they will experience God's judgment. If the people change, they will experience God's mercy (Jnh 4:2).
3:5 fast A time set aside for abstaining from food. **put on sackcloth** Sackcloth was fabric made of goat or camel hair, which made it coarse and uncomfortable.

⁶When Jonah's warning reached the king of Nineveh, he rose from his throne, took off his royal robes, covered himself with sackcloth and sat down in the dust. ⁷This is the proclamation he issued in Nineveh:

"By the decree of the king and his nobles:

Do not let people or animals, herds or flocks, taste anything; do not let them eat or drink. ⁸But let people and animals be covered with sackcloth. Let everyone call urgently on God. Let them give up their evil ways and their violence. ⁹Who knows? God may yet relent and with compassion turn from his fierce anger so that we will not perish."

¹⁰When God saw what they did and how they turned from their evil ways, he relented and did not bring on them the destruction he had threatened.

Jonah's Anger at the LORD's Compassion

4 But to Jonah this seemed very wrong, and he became angry. ²He prayed to the LORD, "Isn't this what I said, LORD, when I was still at home? That is what I tried to forestall by fleeing to Tarshish. I knew that you are a gracious and compassionate God, slow to anger and abounding in love, a God who relents from sending calamity. ³Now, LORD, take away my life, for it is better for me to die than to live."

⁴But the LORD replied, "Is it right for you to be angry?"

⁵Jonah had gone out and sat down at a place east of the city. There he made himself a shelter, sat in its shade and waited to see what would happen to the city. ⁶Then the LORD God provided a leafy plantᵃ and made it grow up over Jonah to give shade for his head to ease his discomfort, and Jonah was very happy about the plant. ⁷But at dawn the next day God provided a worm, which chewed the plant so that it withered. ⁸When the sun rose, God provided a scorching east wind, and the sun blazed on Jonah's head so that he grew faint. He wanted to die, and said, "It would be better for me to die than to live."

⁹But God said to Jonah, "Is it right for you to be angry about the plant?"

"It is," he said. "And I'm so angry I wish I were dead."

ᵃ 6 The precise identification of this plant is uncertain; also in verses 7, 9 and 10.

The piece of sackcloth used in mourning usually took the form of a loincloth. The custom of wearing sackcloth usually demonstrated an individual's act of repentance. The king of Nineveh wore sackcloth to demonstrate his repentance upon hearing Yahweh's announcement of imminent judgment (see Jnh 3:6).

3:6 king of Nineveh The king of Assyria in Jonah's day was probably Assur-dan III (772–755 BC). However, Nineveh was not the capital of Assyria at this time, and it would be unusual for the king of Assyria to be identified as "king of Nineveh." **his royal robes** A symbol of the king's exalted position. The robes of kings were usually made out of the finest material and were quite ornate. **and sat down in the dust** Ash was used to identify with the dead. Sitting in ashes was commonly associated with the wearing of sackcloth (see Est 4:1; Jer 6:26; Da 9:3; Mt 11:21).

3:7 his nobles Representing the most important families in Nineveh. **taste anything** Refers to fasting. See note on Jnh 3:5. **drink** This fast could have lasted only about three days if people and animals refrained from drinking water.

3:8 Let them give up The Hebrew term here has the core sense of turning around. Here and elsewhere it is used with the idea of repentance. This contrasts sharply with the adamant refusal to repent that is the typical response that Israelite prophets received at home (compare Jer 5:3 and note).

3:9 his fierce anger Literally, "anger of nose." In modern usage, it might be rendered "flaring nostrils."

4:1–11 The final scene finds Jonah sulking outside of Nineveh, angry over God's compassion on the city following the universal repentance of man and beast (3:7–10). Jonah appears to be waiting in hope that God will destroy the city (v. 5). To teach Jonah a lesson, God sends a leafy plant to provide him with shade but then destroys the plant by means of a worm. Jonah's grief-filled reaction to the loss of the plant reflects how he should have responded to the very idea that the entire population of a city was about to be wiped out by God's wrath. The narrative has focused on Jonah almost exclusively—his call, his flight, his punishment and his preaching. The portrait of the prophet that emerges goes against all expectations for a Biblical prophet. Prophets plead for God to have mercy despite Israel's failure to repent (see note on Jer 7:16); Jonah complains about God's mercy and wishes Nineveh had not repented. He reluctantly obeyed Yahweh and then preached only the bare minimum (Jnh 3:4). The story does not say he repeated the message, just that he went into the city and spoke a brief oracle that inspired unprecedented repentance. In this passage, he explains his motivation: He knew God would show mercy and he doesn't think Nineveh deserves it.

4:1 to Jonah this seemed very wrong The Hebrew term used here to refer to evil or wrong is the same word used in 1:2 and 3:8 to describe the wickedness of the Assyrians.

4:2 Jonah's description of Yahweh follows a typical formulaic pattern in Hebrew similar to Ex 34:6 and Joel 2:13. The phrasing is prominent in OT prayers for mercy. See note on Joel 2:13.

4:2 home Refers to Israel. **fleeing to Tarshish** See note on 1:3.

4:5 shelter A makeshift shelter. The term also is used to describe the temporary shelters that the Israelites built during the Festival of Tabernacles (Lev 23:40–42). **waited to see what would happen to the city** Jonah was likely still hoping that God would destroy the city.

4:6 a leafy plant Possibly the castor oil plant, a gourd that grows quite rapidly in hot climates. This plant grows

¹⁰But the LORD said, "You have been concerned about this plant, though you did not tend it or make it grow. It sprang up overnight and died overnight. ¹¹And should I not have concern for the great city of Nineveh, in which there are more than a hundred and twenty thousand people who cannot tell their right hand from their left — and also many animals?"

---

to a height of 12 feet and has large leaves. **his discomfort** Jonah's discomfort was caused by the heat typically associated with the region of Nineveh.

4:8 scorching east wind This hot wind would have come off the Arabian Desert. Technically, this wind would have come from the southwest when it hit the region of Nineveh. However, Jonah is written from the perspective of his audience, the nation Israel. In Israel, the wind from the Arabian Desert would have come from the east. **the sun blazed** In the region of Nineveh, it easily could have been more than 120 degrees Fahrenheit in the sun.

4:11 a hundred and twenty thousand people Population estimates for the ancient city vary and depend on whether the surrounding countryside is included in addition to the city proper. The estimated population for Nineveh and its surrounding areas is around 300,000 for the seventh century BC, a century after Jonah. Much of the population of Nineveh lived in the countryside outside the city walls (e.g., farmers, herdsmen and fishermen). The mention of a great number of animals indicates the reference is to more than those inside the city walls. The figure of 120,000 is reasonable for the city's population. **cannot tell their right hand from their left** This phrase may be a figure of speech for those who have no knowledge of God, indicating spiritual and moral ignorance.

MICAH

INTRODUCTION TO MICAH

Micah has been called a "miniature Isaiah" because of its similarities to that book. Both prophets spoke to the same audience from the same city during roughly the same historical period: Jerusalem in the eighth century BC. During Micah's ministry, the northern kingdom of Israel fell to the Assyrian Empire (722 BC), and the southern kingdom of Judah came close to the same fate in 701 BC (see 2Ki 17–20). According to Micah, who prophesied to both kingdoms, the reason for these attacks was the abuse of prosperity by God's people. He gives both warnings and oracles of hope—looking forward to a day of judgment leading to peace (Mic 4:2–5).

BACKGROUND

Micah was from Judah and prophesied during the reigns of Jotham, Ahaz and Hezekiah (1:1; ca. 740–700 BC). Jeremiah 26:18 also mentions the prophet Micah: About 100 years after Micah, Jeremiah records that Micah of Moresheth prophesied during Hezekiah's time. It seems that Micah's hometown, also called Moresheth Gath, was located about 25 miles southwest of Jerusalem—an area through which Assyrian forces often traveled (Mic 1:1,14). Therefore, Micah may have been an eyewitness to Assyria's invasion of Judah.

The biblical account of Assyria's siege of Jerusalem states that Yahweh killed 185,000 Assyrian soldiers while they slept just outside the city (2Ki 19:35–36; 2Ch 32:21). Consequently, the Assyrian king Sennacherib and his army were forced to retreat. An inscription found in Sennacherib's palace admits the defeat, saying that Hezekiah "did not submit to my yoke." By the end of Hezekiah's reign, Assyria's successor—the Babylonian Empire—was gaining power (Mic 4:10; 2Ki 20:12–21). Micah views Assyria and Babylon as instruments of divine judgment for the unfaithfulness of God's people. He focuses his prophecies on his own people, condemning their idolatry, oppression of the poor and greed (Mic 1:7; 2:1–2; 3:11).

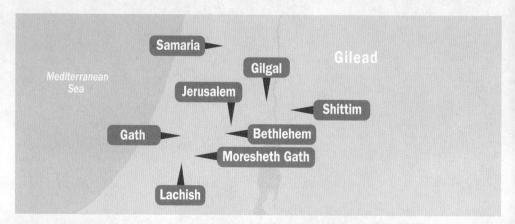

This map depicts many of the locations related to the book of Micah.

STRUCTURE

Although Micah predicts the fall of Samaria (the capital of Israel at the time; 1:6) at the beginning of the book and the Babylonian captivity near the end (7:8–9), most of the material is not arranged chronologically. Instead, the book is organized around three major prophetic oracles, each opening with a call to listen to (or hear) the word of Yahweh (1:2; 3:1; 6:1). The first oracle (1:2—2:13) announces Yahweh's judgment on Israel and Judah—particularly on their selfish leaders. The second oracle contrasts the ungodly leaders in Jerusalem (3:1–12) and the future Messiah (4:1—5:15). Micah 4–5 offers hope that Yahweh will bring about a time of peace and prosperity. The third oracle begins with an accusation (6:1–16) and a lament (7:1–7). Judah is accused of acting in an ungodly way, like Israel, the northern kingdom. The book concludes with a promise of forgiveness and future restoration (7:8–20).

OUTLINE

- Judgment is coming (1:1—2:13)
- Restoration follows judgment (3:1—5:15)
- Charge against Israel and promise of salvation (6:1—7:20)

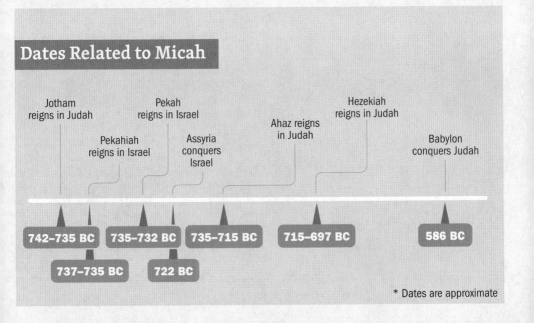

Dates Related to Micah

Jotham reigns in Judah — 742–735 BC

Pekahiah reigns in Israel — 737–735 BC

Pekah reigns in Israel — 735–732 BC

Assyria conquers Israel — 722 BC

Assyria conquers Israel — 735–715 BC

Ahaz reigns in Judah — 715–697 BC

Hezekiah reigns in Judah

Babylon conquers Judah — 586 BC

* Dates are approximate

THEMES

The two main themes of Micah are God's judgment against idolatry and injustice, and hope that God's people will return to him and be restored. Micah warns the people of Judah that if they behave as the northern kingdom of Israel did, they will face the same kind of divine judgment that befell Israel (1:5; 3:1; 6:16). But Micah 4–5 speaks of forgiveness and hope. Micah proclaims that this salvation will emerge through a ruler from Bethlehem; Micah boldly claims this ruler will shepherd the people of Israel and judge between people and nations (5:1–6). This prophecy ultimately points to Jesus (Mt 2:1–12; compare Lk 2:1–20).

The book of Micah is a call to repent and authentically worship Yahweh. Worship is not an activity that can be tacked on a life of self-absorption; it is a total reorienting of our lives around God. Instead of acting like Israel's selfish leaders (Mic 3:1–12), we should model what he truly desires: justice, mercy and humility (6:8). Although people continue to walk in the name of their own gods, Micah tells us that we should live differently: We must walk in the name of our God, Yahweh (4:5).

1

The word of the LORD that came to Micah of Moresheth during the reigns of Jotham, Ahaz and Hezekiah, kings of Judah — the vision he saw concerning Samaria and Jerusalem.

² Hear, you peoples, all of you,
  listen, earth and all who live in it,
that the Sovereign LORD may bear witness
    against you,
  the Lord from his holy temple.

Judgment Against Samaria and Jerusalem

³ Look! The LORD is coming from his dwelling
    place;
  he comes down and treads on the heights
    of the earth.
⁴ The mountains melt beneath him
  and the valleys split apart,
like wax before the fire,
  like water rushing down a slope.
⁵ All this is because of Jacob's transgression,
  because of the sins of the people of Israel.
What is Jacob's transgression?
  Is it not Samaria?

What is Judah's high place?
  Is it not Jerusalem?

⁶ "Therefore I will make Samaria a heap of
    rubble,
  a place for planting vineyards.
I will pour her stones into the valley
  and lay bare her foundations.
⁷ All her idols will be broken to pieces;
  all her temple gifts will be burned with fire;
  I will destroy all her images.
Since she gathered her gifts from the wages
    of prostitutes,
  as the wages of prostitutes they will again
    be used."

Weeping and Mourning

⁸ Because of this I will weep and wail;
  I will go about barefoot and naked.
I will howl like a jackal
  and moan like an owl.
⁹ For Samaria's plague is incurable;
  it has spread to Judah.
It has reached the very gate of my people,
  even to Jerusalem itself.

1:1 Micah ministered to Jerusalem in the eighth century BC, making him a contemporary of Isaiah. One notable difference between the two is that Isaiah directs his prophecies toward the royal family while Micah appears to focus on commoners. Micah is quoted two times in the NT (5:2 in Mt 2:5–6; Mic 7:6 in Mt 10:35–36). The book consists of three prophetic oracles (beginning at Mic 1:2; 3:1; 6:1) that announce judgment on Samaria and Judah and look forward to a future restoration. See the timeline "Approximate Dates of Old Testament Prophets" on p. 1070.

1:1 word of the LORD A common introductory formula. See Hos 1:1 and note. **Micah** One of the few writing prophets to be mentioned by name in another prophetic book (see Jer 26:18; compare Jeremiah in Da 9:2). When Jehoiakim came to the throne, Jeremiah's life was threatened because he prophesied the destruction of Jerusalem. The elders interceded for him, reminding the people that Micah had predicted the same thing (see Mic 3:12; Jer 26:18). That the elders remembered Micah's prophecies 100 years after he delivered them speaks to Micah's influence. **Moresheth** Micah's hometown, Moresheth, was near the Philistine city of Gath (see v. 10 and note; v. 14). Its residents were called Morashtites. **during the reigns of Jotham, Ahaz and Hezekiah** Jotham reigned from 742–735 BC. Ahaz reigned from 735–715 BC. Hezekiah reigned from 715–697 BC. Since Micah does not mention Uzziah, it can be assumed the king died prior to the beginning of the prophet's ministry. Since Uzziah died in 740 BC, Micah's ministry began between 740 and 733 BC. The prophet ministered until at least the Assyrian invasion of Judah in 701 BC because he records the distress that accompanied that invasion (1:10–16; 5:6). **kings of Judah** Judah was the southern kingdom of Israel. **Samaria and Jerusalem** The capitals of Israel and Judah, respectively. See the infographic "Jerusalem" on p. 1607.

MICAH
Micah means "Who is like Yahweh?" and is a shortened form of the name Micaiah (see 1Ki 22:8). Micah's hometown is mentioned in Mic 1:1 to identify him since the name Micah was fairly common (e.g., Jdg 17:1; 1Ch 8:34; 2Ch 34:20). The identification of the prophet's hometown also indicates that his ministry probably took place in another city, likely Jerusalem. The city and its temple are emphasized throughout the book (e.g., Mic 1:2,5; 3:12—4:2).

1:2 Hear The Hebrew word used here distinguishes the three major divisions of the book (see Mic 3:1; 6:1). It also reveals that what follows is an oracle. **you peoples, all of you** Micah's prophetic oracle is addressed to the entire earth. **holy temple** Yahweh's heavenly abode, as opposed to the temple in Jerusalem. The Hebrew phrase used here appears elsewhere only in Psalms (Ps 5:7; 11:4; 65:4; 79:1; 138:2), Jonah (Jnh 2:4,7), and Habakkuk (Hab 2:20).

1:3 the earth Likely refers to both the mountains and the cultic high places, the idolatrous centers of pagan worship. See note on Isa 57:7. Treading upon them indicates Yahweh's sovereign omnipotence (see Am 4:13). High places were elevated religious shrines used in the worship of storm gods such as Baal. Israel was responsible for destroying the high places of Canaan (see Nu 33:52; Dt 12:2–3; 33:29). However, rather than destroy these sites, the nation occupied and used them and even built more of their own (see 1Ki 12:32; 14:23).

1:5 All this Refers to the coming of Yahweh in judgment as described in Mic 1:3–4. **Jacob's** Jacob is used as a

¹⁰ Tell it not in Gath ᵃ;
   weep not at all.
In Beth Ophrah ᵇ
   roll in the dust.
¹¹ Pass by naked and in shame,
   you who live in Shaphir.ᶜ
Those who live in Zaananᵈ
   will not come out.
Beth Ezel is in mourning;
   it no longer protects you.
¹² Those who live in Marothᵉ writhe in pain,
   waiting for relief,
because disaster has come from the LORD,
   even to the gate of Jerusalem.
¹³ You who live in Lachish,
   harness fast horses to the chariot.
You are where the sin of Daughter Zion began,
   for the transgressions of Israel were found
      in you.
¹⁴ Therefore you will give parting gifts
   to Moresheth Gath.
The town of Akzibᶠ will prove deceptive
   to the kings of Israel.
¹⁵ I will bring a conqueror against you
   who live in Mareshah.ᵍ

The nobles of Israel
   will flee to Adullam.
¹⁶ Shave your head in mourning
   for the children in whom you delight;
make yourself as bald as the vulture,
   for they will go from you into exile.

Human Plans and God's Plans

2 Woe to those who plan iniquity,
   to those who plot evil on their beds!
At morning's light they carry it out
   because it is in their power to do it.
² They covet fields and seize them,
   and houses, and take them.
They defraud people of their homes,
   they rob them of their inheritance.

³ Therefore, the LORD says:

"I am planning disaster against this people,
   from which you cannot save yourselves.

ᵃ 10 Gath sounds like the Hebrew for tell.   ᵇ 10 Beth Ophrah
means house of dust.   ᶜ 11 Shaphir means pleasant.
ᵈ 11 Zaanan sounds like the Hebrew for come out.   ᵉ 12 Maroth
sounds like the Hebrew for bitter.   ᶠ 14 Akzib means deception.
ᵍ 15 Mareshah sounds like the Hebrew for conqueror.

---

synonym for the people of Israel. Israel's original name was Jacob (see Ge 32:28).
1:6 I will make Samaria a heap Yahweh's judgment on Samaria was fulfilled in 722 BC when the city was destroyed by the Assyrians.
1:7 her images Images or statues of a deity. These idols were worshiped as the visible manifestation of the god. Yahweh strongly condemned this practice in the Ten Commandments (see Ex 20:4). **the wages of prostitutes** The idols of Israel are compared to the wages of a harlot. They had been made from the metal given to the temple by worshipers. Israel had accumulated wealth by engaging in idolatry, an act God regarded as adultery. These same wages will return to pay a harlot—the enemy soldiers who plunder the city will spend their loot on prostitutes.
1:8 a jackal Known for their loud, mournful wails.
1:9 It has reached the very gate of my people When the Assyrian king Sennacherib invaded Jerusalem in 701 BC, he surrounded the city of Jerusalem. See the infographic "Sennacherib's Prism" on p. 597.
1:10 Gath One of the most prominent cities in Philistia. **weep not at all** The nation was commanded not to weep because their mourning would bring joy to the Philistines. **dust** Rolling in the dust was a form of mourning designed to identify oneself with the dead.

📍   Micah 1:10

GATH
A Philistine city located in the low hill country west of Jerusalem, near the border of Judah. It was one of the so-called Philistine Pentapolis city-states along with Ashdod, Ashkelon, Ekron and Gaza (see 1Sa 6:17). Gath was particularly famous for being the birthplace of Goliath (1Sa 17:4). It is probably to be identified with the modern-day Tell es-Safi.

1:11 Shaphir Means "beautiful." Shaphir was probably located in the Philistine plain. **Zaanan** Means "place of flocks." An unidentified city located in the Judean hill country. It is probably modern-day Zenan (Jos 15:37). **Beth Ezel is in mourning** Means "house of the leader." Located in southern Judah, Beth Ezel is probably modern day Deir el-Asal.
1:13 Lachish Means "impregnable." Lachish was located about 30 miles southwest of Jerusalem and 15 miles west of Hebron. The city is identified with the modern Tell ed-Duweir. **Daughter Zion** A title routinely used for Jerusalem in the OT (see 2Ki 19:21; Isa 10:32; La 2:13; Zep 3:14; Zec 9:9). The term Zion is frequently used for the whole of Jerusalem. See note on Isa 1:8.
1:15 a conqueror Refers to the Assyrian king Sennacherib (see note on Mic 1:9). **Adullam** David fled to the cave of Adullam after leaving Gath (1Sa 22:1). The leaders of the nation will now flee there from the Assyrian invasion.
1:16 Shave your head in mourning Removing hair was a sign of mourning (see Ezr 9:3; Jer 7:29).
2:1 Woe The Hebrew term is used here as a divine threat. In this form, the prophetic oracle is called a "woe pronouncement." See note on Eze 13:3. **plot evil on their beds** These wicked individuals lay on their beds at night thinking of evil plots. They cannot sleep because they are consumed with wickedness. **power** The Hebrew word used here typically means "god"; however, when used of people it denotes strength or might. These evildoers were powerful, wealthy people with the ability to carry out their schemes and profit by them (see Mic 2:2).
2:2 defraud people of their homes, they rob them of their inheritance An example of poetic synonymous parallelism. See the table "Parallelism in Hebrew Poetry" on p. 1008.
2:3 You will no longer walk proudly The mistreatment of others (see v. 2) has given these evildoers the impression that they are better than those upon whom they prey.

You will no longer walk proudly,
for it will be a time of calamity.
⁴ In that day people will ridicule you;
they will taunt you with this mournful
song:
'We are utterly ruined;
my people's possession is divided up.
He takes it from me!
He assigns our fields to traitors.'"

⁵ Therefore you will have no one in the
assembly of the LORD
to divide the land by lot.

False Prophets

⁶ "Do not prophesy," their prophets say.
"Do not prophesy about these things;
disgrace will not overtake us."
⁷ You descendants of Jacob, should it be said,
"Does the LORD become^a impatient?
Does he do such things?"

"Do not my words do good
to the one whose ways are upright?
⁸ Lately my people have risen up
like an enemy.
You strip off the rich robe
from those who pass by without a care,
like men returning from battle.
⁹ You drive the women of my people
from their pleasant homes.
You take away my blessing
from their children forever.

¹⁰ Get up, go away!
For this is not your resting place,
because it is defiled,
it is ruined, beyond all remedy.
¹¹ If a liar and deceiver comes and says,
'I will prophesy for you plenty of wine and
beer,'
that would be just the prophet for this
people!

Deliverance Promised

¹² "I will surely gather all of you, Jacob;
I will surely bring together the remnant of
Israel.
I will bring them together like sheep in
a pen,
like a flock in its pasture;
the place will throng with people.
¹³ The One who breaks open the way will go up
before them;
they will break through the gate and go
out.
Their King will pass through before them,
the LORD at their head."

Leaders and Prophets Rebuked

3 Then I said,

"Listen, you leaders of Jacob,
you rulers of Israel.

^a 7 Or Is the Spirit of the LORD

2:4 that day The "Day of Yahweh," a day of divine judgment (see Joel 2:1; Am 5:18; Ob 15). **people will ridicule you** The Hebrew text uses a term that usually refers to a proverb. In this context it is best seen as a derogatory proverbial chant against an object of scorn and ridicule, such as the foreign nations (see Dt 28:37; Isa 14:4; Jer 24:9; Hab 2:6; compare note on Pr 1:1). **He assigns our fields to traitors** The land of Israel will be given to a foreign nation that does not worship Yahweh (see Dt 28:49).
2:5 assembly of the LORD The nation of Israel. **by lot** The casting of lots was seen throughout the ancient Near East as a way of allowing the gods to make their decisions known to people (see Est 3:7). Both Herodotus (*Histories* 3.128) and Xenophon (*Cyropaedia* 1.6.46; 4.5.55) mention the custom of casting lots. Yahweh himself often employed the lot as the method by which to make his will known (see Pr 16:33).
2:6 Do not prophesy about these things The false prophets of the land were encouraging Micah not to prophesy such harsh words. Isaiah encountered the same type of antagonism at this time (Isa 30:10). **disgrace will not overtake us** The false prophets claimed Yahweh would not send judgment on Israel.
2:7 You descendants of Jacob That is, Israel. See note on Mic 1:5. **to the one whose ways are upright** Micah reminds the nation that the words of the true prophets of God benefit the righteous.
2:8 risen up like an enemy Instead of walking uprightly

(see v. 7), the nation had become violent and oppressive in their actions toward each other.
2:9 from their children The children of these defenseless women would have been deeply impacted by the loss of their inheritance. They may have been forced to sell themselves as slaves in a foreign land.
2:11 prophet This rare Hebrew term for a prophet or preacher comes from the verb used here and in v. 6 for prophesying or preaching.
2:12 As is his custom, Micah follows his prophecy of judgment (1:1—2:11) with a prophecy of hope (see vv. 12–13; 3:1–12 and 4:1—5:15; 6:1—7:7 and 7:8–20).
2:12 all of you, Jacob Refers to the faithful remnant, those who have survived the time of judgment. See note on 1:5.
2:13 The One who breaks open The Messiah, the Ruler of Israel (see 5:2). The Messiah will act as a shepherd for the Israelites. The shepherd motif appears throughout the prophets (see Isa 40:11; Eze 34:5,8,12,23; Zec 11; compare Jn 10). **before them** The group described in Mic 2:12. **Their King** The Messiah, the Ruler of Israel (see 5:2).
3:1 Here, Jacob and Israel are used to refer to the entire nation, both the southern and northern kingdoms. See note on 1:5.

Should you not embrace justice,
2 you who hate good and love evil;
who tear the skin from my people
   and the flesh from their bones;
3 who eat my people's flesh,
   strip off their skin
   and break their bones in pieces;
who chop them up like meat for the pan,
   like flesh for the pot?"

4 Then they will cry out to the LORD,
   but he will not answer them.
At that time he will hide his face from them
   because of the evil they have done.

5 This is what the LORD says:

"As for the prophets
   who lead my people astray,
they proclaim 'peace'
   if they have something to eat,
but prepare to wage war against anyone
   who refuses to feed them.
6 Therefore night will come over you, without
      visions,
   and darkness, without divination.
The sun will set for the prophets,
   and the day will go dark for them.
7 The seers will be ashamed
   and the diviners disgraced.
They will all cover their faces
   because there is no answer from God."

8 But as for me, I am filled with power,
   with the Spirit of the LORD,
   and with justice and might,
to declare to Jacob his transgression,
   to Israel his sin.

9 Hear this, you leaders of Jacob,
   you rulers of Israel,
who despise justice
   and distort all that is right;
10 who build Zion with bloodshed,
   and Jerusalem with wickedness.
11 Her leaders judge for a bribe,
   her priests teach for a price,
   and her prophets tell fortunes for
      money.
Yet they look for the LORD's support and say,
   "Is not the LORD among us?
   No disaster will come upon us."
12 Therefore because of you,
   Zion will be plowed like a field,
Jerusalem will become a heap of rubble,
   the temple hill a mound overgrown with
      thickets.

The Mountain of the LORD

4:1-3pp — Isa 2:1-4

4 In the last days

the mountain of the LORD's temple will be
      established
   as the highest of the mountains;

3:1 justice The rulers of Israel were responsible for ensuring justice and equity for all people in the land. See note on Isa 1:17.

3:2 In Mic 3:2–3, the cruel oppression of the rulers against their own people is likened to cannibalism. The image is of a hunter cleaning his kill and making a pot of stew out of it.

3:5 the prophets These false prophets are not properly using their prophetic office. The prophetic office was formalized in Dt 18:15–22. This foundational passage revealed that God himself would raise up individuals who would speak his words to his people. The title "prophet" (Dt 18:15,18,20,22) denotes a spokesperson. A more complete definition is "one sent by God to announce his Word." **lead my people astray** The image is that of sheep, who naturally follow their shepherd. These prophets are to be contrasted with Yahweh who leads his people in Mic 2:13 (compare Eze 34:1–10 and note). **they proclaim 'peace'** For those who paid them, the false prophets prophesied peace and prosperity; for those who withheld support, they prophesied chaos and calamity. Compare Eze 13:10 and note.

3:6 without visions Numbers 12:6 confirms that God typically revealed himself to prophets through dreams and visions. Daniel, Amos and Zechariah are notable examples of prophets who were given a series of divine messages by means of visions.

3:7 seers A fuller definition of the Hebrew term here is "one who is given a message in a vision."

3:8 This verse sharply contrasts Micah, the true prophet, with the false prophets of Mic 3:5–7.

3:9 who despise justice Micah is filled with mighty justice (see v. 8) while the leaders of Israel abhor justice. **3:11 judge for a bribe** The OT condemns this practice (Ex 23:8; Dt 16:19). Making judgments based on money is the opposite of true justice (see Mic 3:1,9). **prophets tell fortunes for money** See note on v. 5. **No disaster will come upon us** The false prophets were saying that disaster would not come upon Israel because it was the home of Yahweh.

3:12 heap of rubble The fate of Jerusalem is the same as that of Samaria (see Mic 1:6). This prophecy was fulfilled with the destruction of Jerusalem in 586 BC at the hands of the Babylonians. **temple hill** Mount Zion, the site of the temple in Jerusalem (see 2Ch 33:15; Isa 2:2; Mic 4:1).

4:1–3 These verses are nearly identical to Isa 2:2–4. The similarity is likely the result of Micah's use of Isaiah's material, but it is possible that both Micah and Isaiah used a well-known prophetic tradition. See note on Isa 2:1–5.

4:1 the last days This phrase is used to designate a future time when the nation will repent and Yahweh will restore the prosperity of Israel (see Dt 4:30; Isa 2:2; Hos 3:5; Da 10:14; note on Isa 2:2). **mountain of the LORD's temple** Refers to Mount Zion, where the temple stood. **highest** Jerusalem will be the chief mountain in terms of authority and importance. **exalted above the hills** Jerusalem will

it will be exalted above the hills,
    and peoples will stream to it.

[2] Many nations will come and say,

"Come, let us go up to the mountain of the
    LORD,
to the temple of the God of Jacob.
He will teach us his ways,
    so that we may walk in his paths."
The law will go out from Zion,
    the word of the LORD from Jerusalem.
[3] He will judge between many peoples
    and will settle disputes for strong nations
        far and wide.
They will beat their swords into plowshares
    and their spears into pruning hooks.
Nation will not take up sword against nation,
    nor will they train for war anymore.
[4] Everyone will sit under their own vine
    and under their own fig tree,
and no one will make them afraid,
    for the LORD Almighty has spoken.
[5] All the nations may walk
    in the name of their gods,
but we will walk in the name of the LORD
    our God for ever and ever.

The LORD's Plan

[6] "In that day," declares the LORD,

"I will gather the lame;
I will assemble the exiles
    and those I have brought to grief.

[7] I will make the lame my remnant,
    those driven away a strong nation.
The LORD will rule over them in Mount Zion
    from that day and forever.
[8] As for you, watchtower of the flock,
    stronghold[a] of Daughter Zion,
the former dominion will be restored to you;
    kingship will come to Daughter
        Jerusalem."

[9] Why do you now cry aloud —
    have you no king[b]?
Has your ruler[c] perished,
    that pain seizes you like that of a woman
        in labor?
[10] Writhe in agony, Daughter Zion,
    like a woman in labor,
for now you must leave the city
    to camp in the open field.
You will go to Babylon;
    there you will be rescued.
There the LORD will redeem you
    out of the hand of your enemies.

[11] But now many nations
    are gathered against you.
They say, "Let her be defiled,
    let our eyes gloat over Zion!"
[12] But they do not know
    the thoughts of the LORD;
they do not understand his plan,
    that he has gathered them like sheaves to
        the threshing floor.

---

[a] 8 Or hill   [b] 9 Or King   [c] 9 Or Ruler

be elevated above all other kingdoms (compare Rev 21:2). **peoples will stream to it** There will be a steady stream of people coming to Jerusalem to worship Yahweh. Salvation will one day be available to all peoples.
4:3 beat their swords Swords will no longer be needed because there will be worldwide peace. This verse contrasts times of war, when plowshares are fashioned into swords and pruning hooks into spears (see Joel 3:10; note on Isa 2:4). **plowshares** A sharp iron blade attached to the beam of a plow. The blessings of the Messiah will include abundant harvests (see Joel 2:22–26). **into pruning hooks** A type of knife used for pruning and harvesting grapevines.
4:4 Everyone will sit under their own vine Meaning they shall sit in peace. **fig tree** This tree would provide abundant shade with its large palm-shaped leaves. Primarily because of this passage, it became customary in Israel to pray under fig trees for the coming of the Messiah (see Jn 1:48–50; note on Jer 24:1).
4:5 All the nations may walk in the name of their gods Foreign nations each worshiped their own gods. At the end of the age, all nations will worship Yahweh (see Mic 4:1–3).
4:7 remnant Those who will be gathered to the land of Israel (see 2:12; 4:6).
4:8 watchtower of the flock This verse refers to a watchtower that overlooks a flock of sheep. It is set in apposition to the hill (or stronghold) of the daughter of Zion (see 1:13 and note), meaning they both refer to the same thing—Jerusalem. The remnant is likened to a flock of sheep in 2:12. **the former dominion** Refers to a previous era in which Israel experienced great prosperity under a king (e.g., the period of David and Solomon).
4:9 have you no king Israel will soon experience a period during which the nation will have no king. Compare Jer 8:19. **your ruler** The Hebrew word used here is parallel to "king" and refers to wise, capable advisors. The title is used of the Messiah in Isa 9:6 (often translated as "counselor"). Elsewhere, it refers to the leaders that provide the skills necessary for government to function (Isa 3:3; 41:28; Pr 11:14). **that pain seizes you** The period during which Israel has no king will be a time of excruciating pain, similar to a woman experiencing labor pains.
4:10 camp in the open field The nation will live in exile. **You will go to Babylon** This prophecy is fulfilled in 586 BC when Jerusalem falls and many of the people are taken into exile. Babylon began its rise to prominence in approximately 1830 BC. The most significant ruler of this early period was Hammurabi (ca. 1728–1686 BC). The city achieved the height of its glory during the reign of Nebuchadnezzar (605–562 BC). Nebuchadnezzar beautified the city by constructing a series of magnificent gardens—a creation that became known as one of the seven wonders of the ancient world. He also built the Ishtar Gate and restored the temple of Marduk. **redeem** The Hebrew word used here is related to the term used for the guardian-redeemer (see note on Dt 19:6).
4:12 he has gathered them like sheaves A sheaf is harvested grain bound in a bundle. Sheaves are brought

¹³ "Rise and thresh, Daughter Zion,
　for I will give you horns of iron;
I will give you hooves of bronze,
　and you will break to pieces many
　　nations."
You will devote their ill-gotten gains to the
　Lord,
　their wealth to the Lord of all the earth.

A Promised Ruler From Bethlehem

5 ᵃ Marshal your troops now, city of troops,
　for a siege is laid against us.
They will strike Israel's ruler
　on the cheek with a rod.

² "But you, Bethlehem Ephrathah,
　though you are small among the clansᵇ
　　of Judah,
out of you will come for me
　one who will be ruler over Israel,
whose origins are from of old,
　from ancient times."

³ Therefore Israel will be abandoned
　until the time when she who is in labor
　　bears a son,
and the rest of his brothers return
　to join the Israelites.

⁴ He will stand and shepherd his flock
　in the strength of the Lord,
　in the majesty of the name of the Lord
　　his God.

And they will live securely, for then his
　greatness
　will reach to the ends of the earth.

⁵ And he will be our peace
　when the Assyrians invade our land
　and march through our fortresses.
We will raise against them seven shepherds,
　even eight commanders,
⁶ who will ruleᶜ the land of Assyria with the
　sword,
　the land of Nimrod with drawn sword.ᵈ
He will deliver us from the Assyrians
　when they invade our land
　and march across our borders.

⁷ The remnant of Jacob will be
　in the midst of many peoples
like dew from the Lord,
　like showers on the grass,
which do not wait for anyone
　or depend on man.
⁸ The remnant of Jacob will be among the
　nations,
　in the midst of many peoples,
like a lion among the beasts of the forest,
　like a young lion among flocks of sheep,
which mauls and mangles as it goes,
　and no one can rescue.

ᵃ In Hebrew texts 5:1 is numbered 4:14, and 5:2-15 is numbered
5:1-14.　ᵇ 2 Or *rulers*　ᶜ 6 Or *crush*　ᵈ 6 Or *Nimrod in its
gates*

---

to a threshing floor to have the grain dislodged from the stalk. **threshing floor** A site where harvested grain is brought to be threshed, either by the use of a flail or a threshing sledge. Threshing is a somewhat violent process, an apt illustration of Yahweh's judgment of his people. See the infographic "A Threshing Floor" on p. 497. **4:13 I will give you horns of iron** The strongest and hardest metal known in ancient times. **horns** An animal's horn was the symbol of its strength. See note on Eze 29:21. **you will break to pieces many nations** Those who had been threshed (i.e., Israelites) are now doing the threshing. **Lord of all the earth** Yahweh will rule over the entire earth (see Zec 14:9). **5:1 now, city of troops** The reference to troops indicates that Jerusalem has had a long history of warfare. **Israel's ruler** Probably King Zedekiah, who reigned from 597–586 BC. See the timeline "The Divided Kingdom" on p. 536. **on the cheek** A form of humiliation. **5:2 Bethlehem Ephrathah** Bethlehem was a very small village at the time of Micah, with a population of only a few hundred. **small** Bethlehem was located in the territory given to the tribe of Judah; however, it was not significant enough to be listed among the cities of Judah when the land was divided in the time of Joshua. **out of you will come** The Gospel of Matthew appeals to this verse regarding the birth of the Messiah in Bethlehem (see Mt 2:1–6). **from ancient times** The Messiah existed from the beginning of time (compare Jn 1:1). Micah claims this Messiah, who existed from old, will shepherd the people of Israel and judge between people and nations.

Micah 5:2

BETHLEHEM EPHRATHAH
Bethlehem ("house of bread") Ephrathah ("fruitful") is located five miles south of Jerusalem in the Judean hill country. The region is known as Ephrath, hence the secondary designation. Bethlehem Ephrathah was the birthplace of David and Jesus (1Sa 17:12; Mt 2:1).

5:3 she who is in labor bears a son Judah is in birth pains for a purpose: The Israelites, God's people, might be scattered around the world, but the Messiah will come forth from them. After a period of anguish, the Messiah will gather and lead God's people. The Gospel of Matthew draws on this passage to describe Jesus' birth, apparently to connect the birth pains of the nation and the difficulty of Mary's pregnancy (Mt 1–2). All of these struggles result in the joy and reign of Jesus. **return** The Hebrew word for returning is used here to indicate repentance as well as physical return. **5:4 shepherd** The idea of a king as the shepherd and leader of his people is a common motif in the ancient Near East (see note on Jer 2:8). The role of the ideal shepherd caring for the flock of Israel is taken on by Yahweh himself in prophetic depictions of divine restoration (Isa 40:11; Jer 23:3; 31:10; Eze 34:11–24). The Messiah also takes on the role of the ideal shepherd, representing Yahweh as the ideal Davidic ruler (Jer

9 Your hand will be lifted up in triumph over
    your enemies,
  and all your foes will be destroyed.

10 "In that day," declares the LORD,

"I will destroy your horses from among you
  and demolish your chariots.
11 I will destroy the cities of your land
  and tear down all your strongholds.
12 I will destroy your witchcraft
  and you will no longer cast spells.
13 I will destroy your idols
  and your sacred stones from among you;
 you will no longer bow down
  to the work of your hands.
14 I will uproot from among you your Asherah
    poles[a]
  when I demolish your cities.
15 I will take vengeance in anger and wrath
  on the nations that have not obeyed me."

The LORD's Case Against Israel

6 Listen to what the LORD says:

"Stand up, plead my case before the
    mountains;
  let the hills hear what you have to say.

2 "Hear, you mountains, the LORD's accusation;
  listen, you everlasting foundations of the
    earth.
 For the LORD has a case against his people;
  he is lodging a charge against Israel.

3 "My people, what have I done to you?
  How have I burdened you? Answer me.
4 I brought you up out of Egypt
  and redeemed you from the land of slavery.
 I sent Moses to lead you,
  also Aaron and Miriam.
5 My people, remember
  what Balak king of Moab plotted
  and what Balaam son of Beor answered.
 Remember your journey from Shittim to
    Gilgal,
  that you may know the righteous acts of
    the LORD."

6 With what shall I come before the LORD
  and bow down before the exalted God?
 Shall I come before him with burnt offerings,
  with calves a year old?
7 Will the LORD be pleased with thousands of
    rams,
  with ten thousand rivers of olive oil?

a 14 That is, wooden symbols of the goddess Asherah

23:4–5; Eze 34:23; see note on Mic 2:13.). Jesus uses this imagery to emphasize his perfect fusion of both God as Shepherd and Messiah as Shepherd (Jn 10:1–18). **reach to the ends of the earth** All the nations of the earth will submit to the Messiah's authority (see Zec 14:9; compare Mt 24:14).
5:5 Assyrians People from Assyria, which claims Nimrod as its founder (see Ge 10:11). **march** The Hebrew term here is the same word used of Yahweh treading on the high places of the earth in Mic 1:3. **seven shepherds, even eight commanders** An example of number parallelism, a common poetic literary device representing many (see Job 33:29; Ps 62:11; Pr 6:16; 30:15,18; Ecc 11:2; Am 1:3; 2:1).
5:6 Nimrod A famous warrior and hunter who founded several cities in northern Mesopotamia, including Nineveh and Calah (Ge 10:8–12). **He will deliver** That is, the ruler of Mic 5:2.
5:9 Your hand The Hebrew word for "hand" is used here as a symbol of authority. See Isa 41:10 and note.
5:10 In that day The day when the Messiah, the ruler described in Mic 5:2, rules over the land of Israel. See note on 2:4.
5:12 witchcraft Such activity would have fallen under the category of divination, which was prohibited in Israel (Dt 18:10–14).
5:13 your sacred stones Sacred objects representing deities. They were typically made out of stone or wood.
5:14 Asherah poles A wooden pole planted in honor of the Canaanite goddess Asherah. See note on Ex 34:13.
6:1–5 Throughout this chapter, the prophet uses legal language to picture a courtroom scene. In a sense, this chapter represents God's lawsuit against Israel (see Hos 4:1–19 and note).

6:1 Listen to what the LORD says Marks the beginning of the third major section of Micah. See note on Mic 1:2. **plead my case** The Hebrew terminology used here (and throughout this passage) has judicial significance. It often occurs in the Prophets to denote Yahweh's covenantal lawsuit against those guilty of breaking his laws (e.g., Isa 3:13; Jer 2:9; Hos 4:1). **let the hills hear what you have to say** The hills and mountains are called on to serve as a jury. They will hear the testimony provided by Yahweh, the prosecuting attorney.
6:2 LORD's accusation More judicial terminology. See note on Mic 6:1. **foundations of the earth** A relatively common title for mountains in the Bible (see Ps 82:5; Pr 8:29; Isa 24:18). See the infographic "Ancient Hebrew Conception of the Universe" on p. 5. **he is lodging a charge** The Hebrew word used here is a legal term meaning "to judge" or "render a decision" (compare Isa 2:4; Mic 4:3).
6:3 Answer The Hebrew word here is often used in the sense of giving testimony or bearing witness (see Ex 20:16; Pr 25:18; Hos 5:5; 7:10).
6:4 I brought you up out of Egypt The nation spent 430 years in Egypt between the time of Joseph and Moses.
6:5 Moab Moab was a nation to the east of the Dead Sea. The events of the first half of this verse are narrated in Nu 22–24. **Balaam son of Beor** Balaam was a highly successful and famous diviner who was hired by Balak to curse the nation of Israel. Yahweh turned Balaam's intended curse into a blessing (Ne 13:2). **Shittim** A place in Moab where Israel encamped prior to their entrance into the promised land (see Nu 25:1–9; Jos 3:1). **Gilgal** The first camp of Israel after crossing the Jordan River (see Jos 4:18–19). **that you may know** Yahweh reminds the people of their history to illustrate the many times he delivered Israel.

Shall I offer my firstborn for my transgression,
    the fruit of my body for the sin of my soul?
[8] He has shown you, O mortal, what is good.
    And what does the LORD require of you?
To act justly and to love mercy
    and to walk humbly[a] with your God.

Israel's Guilt and Punishment

[9] Listen! The LORD is calling to the city —
    and to fear your name is wisdom —
    "Heed the rod and the One who appointed
    it.[b]
[10] Am I still to forget your ill-gotten treasures,
    you wicked house,
    and the short ephah,[c] which is accursed?
[11] Shall I acquit someone with dishonest scales,
    with a bag of false weights?
[12] Your rich people are violent;
    your inhabitants are liars
    and their tongues speak deceitfully.
[13] Therefore, I have begun to destroy you,
    to ruin[d] you because of your sins.
[14] You will eat but not be satisfied;
    your stomach will still be empty.[e]

You will store up but save nothing,
    because what you save[f] I will give to the
    sword.
[15] You will plant but not harvest;
    you will press olives but not use the oil,
    you will crush grapes but not drink the
    wine.
[16] You have observed the statutes of Omri
    and all the practices of Ahab's house;
    you have followed their traditions.
Therefore I will give you over to ruin
    and your people to derision;
    you will bear the scorn of the nations.[g]"

Israel's Misery

7 What misery is mine!
    I am like one who gathers summer fruit
    at the gleaning of the vineyard;

[a] 8 Or *prudently*   [b] 9 The meaning of the Hebrew for this line
is uncertain.   [c] 10 An ephah was a dry measure.
[d] 13 Or *Therefore, I will make you ill and destroy you; / I will
ruin*   [e] 14 The meaning of the Hebrew for this word is
uncertain.   [f] 14 Or *You will press toward birth but not give
birth, / and what you bring to birth*   [g] 16 Septuagint; Hebrew
scorn due my people

Micah 6:5

MOABITES
Moabites were the descendants of Moab, the son of
an incestuous relationship between Lot and his elder
daughter (see Ge 19:30–38). The Moabites lived in the
Transjordan, the eastern side of the Jordan River and the
Dead Sea, just to the south of the Ammonites. Notable
Moabites include Balak, the king who hired Balaam to
curse the Israelites (Nu 22–24); Eglon, the king who was
assassinated by Ehud (Jdg 3:15–30); Ruth, the widow of
Mahlon and wife of Boaz (Ru 4:10,13); and Mesha, the
king who rebelled against King Jehoram of Israel (2Ki 3).

6:6 shall I come before the LORD Here, Micah puts
himself in the role of a worshiping Israelite. **burnt offerings, with calves a year old** One-year-old calves were
viewed as a premium sacrifice (Lev 9:2–3). Burnt offerings
represented a person's dedication to Yahweh. In a sense,
the person was dying (giving himself wholly to Yahweh);
however, the animal was put to death as a substitute.
6:7 with thousands of rams This and the other examples in this verse are hyperbolic. Even if a worshiper
could make such extreme sacrifices, they would not be
enough. This is not what God is asking for.
6:8 does the LORD require of you This verse gives the
answer to the question the prophet asked in Mic 6:6–7.
What God requires is heartfelt love and obedience. **To
act justly** A proper relationship with God also involves
a proper relationship with one's neighbor. See 3:1; Isa
5:7 and note. **mercy** The Hebrew word here often occurs
in reference to Yahweh's covenant with Israel (see Dt
7:9,12; 1Ki 8:23; Ne 1:5). **humbly** This Hebrew word
occurs only here in the Old Testament. It traditionally has
been understood as referring to humility, but it also can
indicate carefulness or thoughtfulness.

6:9 to fear your name See Pr 1:7. **Heed the rod** There
are two connotations to this phrase: "rod" or "tribe." The
meaning "rod" would indicate that Jerusalem must fear
Yahweh's correction. The meaning "tribe" refers to the
tribe of Judah, appointed by Yahweh to lead the nation
of Israel; they must listen to Yahweh and fear his name.
6:10 wicked house Probably a reference to the tribe
of Judah.
6:11 false weights The wealthy abused the poor through
the use of false scales and deceitful weights (see note
on Jer 32:10). These faulty measuring devices increased
the profits of merchants by cheating the poor. These
false scales were seen as accursed because Yahweh
demanded true and accurate scales (Dt 25:15).
6:14 but not be satisfied One of the curses Yahweh
promised to bring on his people if they disobeyed him
(Lev 26:26).
6:16 Omri and Ahab serve as representatives of the
long history of wickedness among Israelite kings. Ahab
was the son of Omri.

6:16 Omri Like Ahab in the next clause, Omri represents
corruption and evil. **Ahab** The wicked husband of the evil
queen Jezebel; he likewise represents corruption. See
the people diagram "King Ahab's Family Tree" on p. 546.

Micah 6:16

AHAB
Ahab (meaning "father is brother") reigned from
874–853 BC. He was the most wicked king to rule
over the northern kingdom, primarily because he married Jezebel, the daughter of Ethbaal, the Sidonian
king. Together, Ahab and Jezebel attempted to make
Baal worship the official religion of Israel.

there is no cluster of grapes to eat,
none of the early figs that I crave.
2 The faithful have been swept from the land;
not one upright person remains.
Everyone lies in wait to shed blood;
they hunt each other with nets.
3 Both hands are skilled in doing evil;
the ruler demands gifts,
the judge accepts bribes,
the powerful dictate what they desire —
they all conspire together.
4 The best of them is like a brier,
the most upright worse than a thorn
hedge.
The day God visits you has come,
the day your watchmen sound the alarm.
Now is the time of your confusion.
5 Do not trust a neighbor;
put no confidence in a friend.
Even with the woman who lies in your
embrace
guard the words of your lips.
6 For a son dishonors his father,
a daughter rises up against her mother,
a daughter-in-law against her mother-in-
law —
a man's enemies are the members of his
own household.

7 But as for me, I watch in hope for the LORD,
I wait for God my Savior;
my God will hear me.

Israel Will Rise

8 Do not gloat over me, my enemy!
Though I have fallen, I will rise.
Though I sit in darkness,
the LORD will be my light.

9 Because I have sinned against him,
I will bear the LORD's wrath,
until he pleads my case
and upholds my cause.
He will bring me out into the light;
I will see his righteousness.
10 Then my enemy will see it
and will be covered with shame,
she who said to me,
"Where is the LORD your God?"
My eyes will see her downfall;
even now she will be trampled underfoot
like mire in the streets.

11 The day for building your walls will come,
the day for extending your boundaries.
12 In that day people will come to you
from Assyria and the cities of Egypt,
even from Egypt to the Euphrates
and from sea to sea
and from mountain to mountain.
13 The earth will become desolate because
of its inhabitants,
as the result of their deeds.

Prayer and Praise

14 Shepherd your people with your staff,
the flock of your inheritance,
which lives by itself in a forest,
in fertile pasturelands.a
Let them feed in Bashan and Gilead
as in days long ago.

15 "As in the days when you came out of Egypt,
I will show them my wonders."

16 Nations will see and be ashamed,
deprived of all their power.

a 14 Or in the middle of Carmel

7:1–7 The first seven verses of this chapter are an individual lament psalm.

7:1 What misery is mine The only other occurrence of this phrase is found in Job 10:15. **one who gathers summer fruit** Micah compares his discouragement with the state of Israel to the disappointment experienced by the fruit pickers and grape gatherers at the end of a poor harvest (see Mic 6:15).
7:3 Both hands are skilled in doing evil May refer to the skill of the evildoers (i.e., ambidextrous) or to both princes and judges. **the ruler demands gifts, the judge accepts bribes** Forbidden by the Law (e.g., Ex 23:8).

7:8 The city of Zion speaks in vv. 8–10 as one who has been defeated by its enemies yet is confident of restoration. The city warns its enemies against premature celebration. Even though Jerusalem has fallen, it will be rebuilt.

7:11 walls The Hebrew term here refers to the hedges around vineyards (see Nu 22:24; Isa 5:5), not city walls, indicating that Jerusalem will not have walls (Zec 2:4).
7:12 that day The "Day of Yahweh," a day of divine judgment (see Joel 2:1; Am 5:18; Ob 15). **Assyria and**

the cities of Egypt On Assyria, see note on Isa 10:24.
the Euphrates The Euphrates River formed the border of Assyria on the southwest, the side closest to Israel. The river served as the northern border of Israel during the time of David (2Sa 8:3). The Euphrates is the longest river in western Asia, its headwaters originating in eastern Turkey and its terminus in the Persian Gulf.
7:14 staff The Hebrew term here has a wide range of meanings, including rod, staff, club, walking stick and scepter. The word occurs here with a dual meaning: that of a shepherd's staff and that of a king's scepter. Yahweh will serve as both shepherd and king for his people. **Bashan and Gilead** Regions of northeastern Israel noted for their lush vegetation (see Am 4:1 and note). **days long ago** Refers to the years prior to the rise of the Assyrians, who dominated the regions of Bashan and Gilead during the time of Micah.
7:15 days when you came out of Egypt The periods of the exodus, wilderness wanderings and conquest of the promised land were filled with a number of miracles performed by Yahweh on behalf of his people (e.g., plagues on Egypt, crossing of the Red Sea, manna and

They will put their hands over their mouths
and their ears will become deaf.
[17] They will lick dust like a snake,
like creatures that crawl on the ground.
They will come trembling out of their dens;
they will turn in fear to the LORD our God
and will be afraid of you.
[18] Who is a God like you,
who pardons sin and forgives the
transgression
of the remnant of his inheritance?

You do not stay angry forever
but delight to show mercy.
[19] You will again have compassion on us;
you will tread our sins underfoot
and hurl all our iniquities into the
depths of the sea.
[20] You will be faithful to Jacob,
and show love to Abraham,
as you pledged on oath to our
ancestors
in days long ago.

---

water in the wilderness, crossing of the Jordan River, walls of Jericho falling down, sun standing still, etc.).
7:18 Who is a God like you A pun on Micah's name, which means "Who is like Yahweh?" **his inheritance** A phrase that is used often in the OT to describe Israel (see Ps 28:9; 33:12; Isa 19:25; Joel 2:17). **mercy** See note on Mic 6:8.

7:19 You will again have compassion on us See Hos 2:1.
7:20 Abraham Both Abraham and Jacob were given covenantal promises by Yahweh (see Ge 12:2–3; 13:15; 15:18–21; 28:13–14; 35:10–12). He will honor his promises to their descendants.

NAHUM

INTRODUCTION TO NAHUM

The book of Nahum is a collection of prophetic oracles that proclaim the fall of Nineveh, a prominent city of the Assyrian Empire. Nahum poetically portrays Nineveh's demise at the hands of the Babylonians. To do so, he employs images that are common in the Prophetic Books, such as devouring lions (Nah 2:11–12), shameless prostitutes (3:4–6) and swarming locusts (3:14–17).

BACKGROUND

The book begins by describing its contents as an oracle concerning Nineveh—one that was received in a vision by Nahum of Elkosh (1:1). The name "Nahum" comes from the Hebrew verb meaning "comfort." Elkosh, Nahum's hometown, is not mentioned anywhere else in the Old Testament. However, Nahum was probably from Judah (1:15).

Nineveh was one of the most prominent cities of the Assyrian Empire, which was renowned in the ancient world for its cruelty. The Old Testament records the Assyrians destroying and displacing the northern kingdom of Israel (722 BC) and repeatedly threatening the southern kingdom of Judah (see 2Ki 18–19; 2Ch 33:10–13). The book of Jonah records an earlier time when the people of Nineveh expressed repentance (Jnh 3:5), though it appears that this attitude of contrition was long gone by Nahum's time.

The text of Nahum most likely was written soon after 663 BC, when the Egyptian city of Thebes fell to the Assyrian king Ashurbanipal. The prophet uses this event as an example of the destruction coming to Nineveh (Na 3:8–10). After Ashurbanipal's death in 627 BC, Assyria was weakened by a series of internal struggles. At the same time, Babylon grew stronger. In 612 BC Nineveh was conquered by a coalition of Babylonians and Medes. The weakened Assyrians then moved their capital to Harran. Eventually they allied with Egypt, and the Babylonians under Nebuchadnezzar defeated them again at the Battle of Carchemish in 605 BC (2Ch 35:20–24; Jer 46:1–2). After this final defeat, they faded from the world stage. Within this turbulent context, Nahum delivers a message of justice.

This map depicts many of the locations related to the book of Nahum; however, Nineveh and Jerusalem are the main focus of the book.

STRUCTURE

Nahum can be divided into three parts. In the first (Na 1:2–15), the prophet announces that

Yahweh will take vengeance on Nineveh. This section includes a partial acrostic poem (1:2–8). The second section (2:1–13) describes in poetic detail the fall of Nineveh at the hand of Yahweh. The final section (3:1–19) presents a mocking song (a dirge), which portrays celebration over the fall of Nineveh and its king rather than lamentation.

OUTLINE

- God's wrath against Nineveh (1:1–15)
- Depiction of Nineveh's fall (2:1–13)
- A mocking lament for Nineveh (3:1–19)

THEMES

Nahum shows us that God will bring justice. Oppressors will be punished when God takes vengeance on behalf of the oppressed. He brings judgment not only on his own people, but also on all the nations. In Nahum, we see God's anger toward evil and his desire to rid the world of it. He is the God not only of Israel, but of the whole world—he raises up and throws down nations.

Nahum's depiction of Nineveh contrasts with the city's portrayal in the book of Jonah, where the people repent and receive mercy. Even though Nahum's prophecies against Nineveh are grim, they come from a God who doesn't anger easily (1:3). Nineveh had been given opportunities to

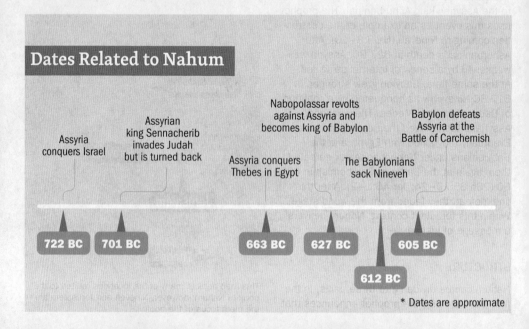

Dates Related to Nahum

| Assyria conquers Israel | Assyrian king Sennacherib invades Judah but is turned back | | Nabopolassar revolts against Assyria and becomes king of Babylon | | Babylon defeats Assyria at the Battle of Carchemish |
| | | Assyria conquers Thebes in Egypt | | The Babylonians sack Nineveh | |

722 BC **701 BC** **663 BC** **627 BC** **605 BC**

612 BC

* Dates are approximate

turn from wickedness, but now the time has come for judgment. This judgment amounts to good news for the people of Judah, whom God promises to protect and restore (1:15; 2:2). Judah and all the other nations that had been terrorized by the Assyrian armies cried out for justice, and God granted it. Nahum concludes his oracle with a message to the Assyrians: Everyone who hears of their downfall will applaud (3:19). As we seek justice, we should take comfort in knowing that oppression will not last forever. In the face of overwhelming injustice, God is still a refuge for those who trust in him (1:7). Yahweh hears, and he will deliver.

1
A prophecy concerning Nineveh. The book of the vision of Nahum the Elkoshite.

The Lord's Anger Against Nineveh

2 The Lord is a jealous and avenging God;
  the Lord takes vengeance and is filled
    with wrath.
The Lord takes vengeance on his foes
  and vents his wrath against his enemies.
3 The Lord is slow to anger but great
    in power;
  the Lord will not leave the guilty
    unpunished.
His way is in the whirlwind and
    the storm,
  and clouds are the dust of his feet.
4 He rebukes the sea and dries it up;
  he makes all the rivers run dry.
Bashan and Carmel wither
  and the blossoms of Lebanon fade.
5 The mountains quake before him
  and the hills melt away.

The earth trembles at his presence,
  the world and all who live in it.
6 Who can withstand his indignation?
  Who can endure his fierce anger?
His wrath is poured out like fire;
  the rocks are shattered before him.

7 The Lord is good,
  a refuge in times of trouble.
He cares for those who trust in him,
8   but with an overwhelming flood
he will make an end of Nineveh;
  he will pursue his foes into the realm
    of darkness.

9 Whatever they plot against the Lord
  he will bring[a] to an end;
  trouble will not come a second time.
10 They will be entangled among thorns
  and drunk from their wine;
  they will be consumed like dry stubble.[b]

a 9 Or *What do you foes plot against the Lord? / He will bring it*
b 10 The meaning of the Hebrew for this verse is uncertain.

1:1—3:19 The book of Nahum, about events in the seventh century BC, is structured with three sections, each corresponding to a chapter. The first section (1:1–14) announces judgment on Nineveh, emphasizing Yahweh's power and his anger toward those who oppose him. The second section (1:15—2:13) provides a vivid description of the destruction of Nineveh, the capital of the Assyrian Empire. The third section (3:1–19) defends Yahweh's decision to destroy Nineveh and includes a list of the sins committed by the wicked people in the city.

In the Septuagint (the Greek translation of the Old Testament), Nahum appears immediately after Jonah. This may be due to the belief that Nahum serves as its complement: Jonah's preaching produced temporary repentance in Nineveh, resulting in mercy from God; Nahum, however, is a judgment oracle against Nineveh. While judgment oracles usually appear in collections (e.g., Isa 13–35; Jer 46–51; Eze 25–32; Am 1–2), they also occur independently (e.g., Obadiah, Nahum). See the table "Oracles Against the Nations" on p. 1244; see the timeline "Approximate Dates of Old Testament Prophets" on p. 1070.

1:1 A prophecy The Hebrew term here refers to a form of speech and also means "burden" (e.g., Jer 23:33). The term is common in identifying a prophet's oracle (e.g., Isa 13:1; 15:1; 17:1; 19:1; Eze 12:10; Hab 1:1; Zec 9:1; 12:1; Mal 1:1). **Nineveh** A city located on the east bank of the Tigris River in northeastern Mesopotamia (in modern Iraq). At the time of Nahum, Nineveh was the capital of the Assyrian Empire, which dominated the ancient Near East. **book** This is the only occurrence where the heading of a prophetic book explicitly identifies the work as a written document using the Hebrew word *sepher*. This label may indicate the book of Nahum was intentionally crafted as literature. **vision** The Hebrew word used here appears in the opening of the books of Obadiah (Ob 1:1) and Isaiah (Isa 1:1). It is commonly used for prophetic messages (Hab 2:2; Mic 3:6; Eze 12:22). **Nahum** A prophet of God who announced the forthcoming destruction of Nineveh. **Elkoshite** Nahum is the only OT text to mention Elkosh. The location may be the same as Capernaum, meaning "city of nahum (comfort)."

NAHUM
Nahum means "comfort." Nahum ministered in the mid-seventh century BC, probably between the destruction of No-amon (Thebes) in Egypt in 663 BC (Na 3:8–10) and the destruction of Nineveh in 612 BC (1:8; 2:1,13).

1:2–15 This section (Na 1:2–15) is a poetic hymn centered on God's sovereignty. The first part (vv. 2–8) is similar to a praise psalm like Ps 145. Nahum describes Yahweh's power and character, emphasizing his ability to bring his enemies to a complete end (Na 1:9–11). The conclusion of the oracle reassures the people of Judah that their oppression by Assyria is coming to an end (vv. 12–15).

1:2 filled with wrath The Hebrew phrase used here, *ba'al chemah*, literally means "lord of anger." The first of these Hebrew words, *ba'al*, is also the name of the Canaanite god of storm and fertility. Nahum's phrasing is terse and pointed in these opening poetic lines. Literally, the text reads: "God is jealous, and Yahweh avenges, the master of wrath." There is wordplay with the repetition of "avenge" and through the use of *ba'al*, which may allude to a subtle polemic against the worship of the Canaanite deity.

1:3 slow to anger The wording echoes the common formulaic expression of Yahweh's attributes—balancing mercy and compassion with holiness and justice (compare Ex 34:6–7; Nu 14:18; Joel 2:13; Jnh 4:2; Ne 9:17; Ps 86:15; 103:8; 145:8). **in the whirlwind and the storm** As opposed to the impotent storm gods of the pagan fertility cults (e.g., Baal-Hadad), Yahweh is the omnipotent storm God. **clouds are the dust of his feet** A popular motif throughout the Bible (e.g., 2Sa 22:10; Ps 97:2; 104:3; Isa 19:1; Mt 24:30; Rev 1:7).

1:4 Bashan A region in northeastern Israel noted for its lush vegetation (see Am 4:1 and note). Isaiah 33:9

[11] From you, Nineveh, has one come forth
who plots evil against the LORD
and devises wicked plans.

[12] This is what the LORD says:

"Although they have allies and are
numerous,
they will be destroyed and pass away.
Although I have afflicted you, Judah,
I will afflict you no more.
[13] Now I will break their yoke from your neck
and tear your shackles away."

[14] The LORD has given a command concerning
you, Nineveh:
"You will have no descendants to bear
your name.
I will destroy the images and idols
that are in the temple of your gods.
I will prepare your grave,
for you are vile."

[15] Look, there on the mountains,
the feet of one who brings good news,
who proclaims peace!
Celebrate your festivals, Judah,
and fulfill your vows.
No more will the wicked invade you;
they will be completely destroyed.[a]

Nineveh to Fall

2 [b] An attacker advances against you,
Nineveh.
Guard the fortress,
watch the road,
brace yourselves,
marshal all your strength!

[2] The LORD will restore the splendor of Jacob
like the splendor of Israel,

[a] 15 In Hebrew texts this verse (1:15) is numbered 2:1.   [b] In Hebrew texts 2:1-13 is numbered 2:2-14.

---

also mentions these three locations (Bashan, Carmel, Lebanon) together. **Carmel** A ridgeline in northwestern Israel noted for its lush vegetation (Jer 46:18). **Lebanon** An extended coastal mountain range located northwest of Israel. Lebanon (or Phoenicia) is famous for its cedar trees, which were prized throughout the ancient Near East. The OT uses cedar trees from Lebanon as the epitome of the world's strength, surpassed only by Yahweh's power (e.g., Ps 29:5; Isa 2:13; Am 2:9; Zec 11:2). Israelites used cedars of Lebanon to build the temple in Jerusalem (see 1Ki 5:6).
1:5 mountains quake before him A common poetic motif in the OT (compare Jdg 5:4-5; Ps 114:4-7; Jer 4:24; Hab 3:10). Yahweh's arrival on earth is characterized by storm, fire and earthquakes.
1:7 He cares for those who trust in him The Hebrew term here denotes the sense of protection or providence.
1:8 an overwhelming flood Archaeological excavations have shown that Nineveh was partially destroyed by floodwaters from the Tigris River (compare the Babylonian Chronicles). See the infographic "The Babylonian Chronicles" on p. 605. **darkness** May be a reference to Sheol, the underworld and the land of darkness (see Job 14:13).
1:9 Whatever they plot against the LORD The Hebrew expression here could be a rhetorical question about Nineveh's schemes against Yahweh. It also could be a direct statement: "Whatever you plot against Yahweh." **a second time** The Assyrians rose up for the first time when they invaded the southern kingdom of Judah in 701 BC (see note on Na 1:11).
1:11 who plots evil against the LORD Likely refers to Sennacherib, the Assyrian king who reigned from 705–681 BC. In 701 BC, Sennacherib invaded Judah, destroying 46 cities before preparing a siege of Jerusalem. In response to King Hezekiah's prayer for deliverance (2Ki 19:19), the Angel of Yahweh struck down 185,000 Assyrians in a single night (2Ki 19:35). Sennacherib's Prism, a hexagonal baked-clay inscription of the annals of Sennacherib, attests to the events of this campaign. While it does not mention the loss of 185,000 warriors, it provides indirect verification of the Biblical account: "As to Hezekiah, the Jew, he did not submit to my yoke ... Himself I made a

prisoner in Jerusalem, his royal residence, like a bird in a cage," the inscription reads. See the infographic "Sennacherib's Prism" on p. 597. **wicked plans** The Hebrew term used here, *beliyya'al*, occurs throughout the Old Testament to identify the most reprehensible characters (e.g., Jdg 19:22; 1Sa 10:27; 1Ki 21:10).
1:13 yoke A wooden or iron frame placed on the backs of draft animals (such as oxen, horses or donkeys) so they could pull a cart or plow. A yoke usually consisted of a single crossbar with leather or rope nooses placed around the animals' necks. The yoke symbolizes submission to foreign oppression. Yahweh will break Assyria's power and end its dominance of Judah (compare Isa 10:27; Jer 28:2,10).
1:14 You will have no descendants to bear your name Nahum declares that the Assyrian race will be cut off. **images and idols** Describes idols, images or statues of a deity. Ancients most often carved idols out of wood or stone, but they also could fashion them from metal. **temple of your gods** Refers to the temple of Ishtar in Nineveh.
1:15 one who brings good news Refers to a herald who brings news of victory and announces the coming of Yahweh's deliverance for his people (compare Isa 40:9 and note). **festivals** Refers to the yearly feasts of the Jewish calendar: the Festival of Unleavened Bread, the Festival of Weeks and the Festival of Tabernacles (Lev 23). See the table "Israelite Festivals" on p. 200. **your vows** An offering promised to Yahweh (Lev 7:16; 22:18; 23:38).
2:1–13 This oracle describes a city under attack. In Na 2:8, the city is revealed to be Nineveh. The language is similar to prophetic descriptions of invaders approaching a city as in Isa 10:28–34. In Isaiah 10, Assyria is God's instrument of judgment, but Jerusalem is assured that Assyria's own day of judgment is coming (Isa 10:24–27). Nahum 2 depicts the foretold time when Yahweh's anger would be directed against Assyria (Isa 10:24–25). (Nahum 2:1–13 corresponds to vv. 2–14 in the Hebrew Bible.)
2:1 An attacker advances against you A reference to the combined army of Babylonians, Medes and Scythians

though destroyers have laid them waste
and have ruined their vines.

³ The shields of the soldiers are red;
the warriors are clad in scarlet.
The metal on the chariots flashes
on the day they are made ready;
the spears of juniper are brandished.ᵃ
⁴ The chariots storm through the streets,
rushing back and forth through the squares.
They look like flaming torches;
they dart about like lightning.

⁵ Nineveh summons her picked troops,
yet they stumble on their way.
They dash to the city wall;
the protective shield is put in place.
⁶ The river gates are thrown open
and the palace collapses.
⁷ It is decreedᵇ that Nineveh
be exiled and carried away.

Her female slaves moan like doves
and beat on their breasts.
⁸ Nineveh is like a pool
whose water is draining away.
"Stop! Stop!" they cry,
but no one turns back.
⁹ Plunder the silver!
Plunder the gold!
The supply is endless,
the wealth from all its treasures!
¹⁰ She is pillaged, plundered, stripped!
Hearts melt, knees give way,
bodies tremble, every face grows pale.

¹¹ Where now is the lions' den,
the place where they fed their young,
where the lion and lioness went,
and the cubs, with nothing to fear?

ᵃ 3 Hebrew; Septuagint and Syriac *ready; / the horsemen rush to and fro.*   ᵇ 7 The meaning of the Hebrew for this word is uncertain.

---

that eventually conquered Nineveh. The Babylonians routinely scattered (i.e., exiled) prisoners of war to all parts of their empire and transplanted foreigners into conquered territories. This practice prevented rebellions throughout Babylon's vast empire; the mixture of different cultures, languages and religions made a unified revolt nearly impossible. See the timeline "Dates Related to Isaiah and 2 Kings" on p. 1116. **Guard the fortress** The first of four commands for Nineveh to prepare for battle. The warnings are urgent and terse.

2:2 Lᴏʀᴅ will restore The prophets often use the language of restoration to signal the end of judgment and the imminence of Yahweh's salvation (see 1:15; Jer 29:14; 30:3,18; 33:7; Eze 39:25; Hos 6:11; Joel 3:1; Zep 2:7). **Jacob** A synonym for the people of Israel (see note on Mic 1:5). Israel's original name was Jacob (see Ge 32:28). **like the splendor of Israel** May be comparative ("like the majesty of Israel") or emphatic ("indeed, the majesty of Israel"). **their vines** Refers to Judah metaphorically as a cultivated vine damaged by invaders (compare Ps 80:8–13; Isa 5:1–7).

2:3–10 These verses describe a progression of attack: the offensive force assembles its troops (Na 2:3), advances toward the city (v. 4), launches an assault (vv. 5–6), takes prisoners (v. 7), and plunders the city (vv. 8–10).

2:3 shields of the soldiers are red The Babylonians' shields may have been painted red to strike fear in their enemies. Or, the shields may have gleamed red in the sunlight because of highly polished metal fittings. Alternatively, the prophet may be describing the aftermath of the attack, when shields (and clothing) are dyed red with blood. **the chariots** Vehicles of two wheels usually pulled by two horses. Chariots were powerful instruments of war that could dominate battles. In effect, they were the tanks of ancient warfare. **spears of juniper** Tall evergreens found throughout the Mediterranean. They often grow in conjunction with cedars and oaks. The polished spears would have a reddish appearance, especially in the sunlight.

2:5 summons The Hebrew word here is used in the sense of giving orders, a meaning found in the Akkadian cognate. **wall** When Sennacherib, king of Assyria, built

the massive walls of Nineveh, he named the outer wall "The Wall That Terrifies the Enemy" and the inner wall "The Wall Whose Splendor Overwhelms the Foe." **protective shield** The Hebrew word here likely refers to a screen designed to protect those assaulting the city wall from projectiles thrown down from above. Siege warfare consisted of surrounding a city until it surrendered or was captured. Those conducting a siege used many offensive weapons, including siege towers, battering rams, siege ramps and scaling ladders. The siege ramp was used to allow the battering rams access to the city walls or gates. Siege towers gave archers a higher vantage point to protect the soldiers building the siege mound or manning the battering rams.

2:6 river gates When ancients built city walls over rivers, they included gates that allowed water (and fish) to continue to flow through the city. **are thrown open** During the siege of Nineveh, a series of torrential downpours swelled the Tigris River and its channels. The city flooded, and the water caused portions of the walls to collapse. These breaches granted the Babylonians access into the city. **the palace** May refer to the south palace built by Sennacherib (who reigned 705–681 BC) or the north palace built by Ashurbanipal (the last great king of Assyria, 668–627 BC).

2:8 like a pool whose water is draining away Much of Nineveh lay under water when the city fell (see note on v. 6), but this image of a pool without water describes an empty artificial pool or reservoir. The city will be empty of people just like a reservoir that has been drained.

2:9 supply is endless The Babylonian Chronicles — which are tablets that record the history of Babylon — state that the amount of treasure in Nineveh was "a quantity beyond counting." The Assyrians had collected a massive amount of wealth from looting cities like Susa, Babylon, Damascus, Samaria, Memphis and Thebes. See the infographic "The Babylonian Chronicles" on p. 605.

2:11 Verses 11–12 are a taunt song, a derogatory proverbial chant against an object of scorn and ridicule (e.g., Dt 28:37; Isa 14:4; Jer 24:9; Mic 2:4; Hab 2:6). The taunt mocks Assyria: The once mighty predator of the ancient Near East is now the prey.

2:11 lions' These large, fast, powerful cats are found

¹²The lion killed enough for his cubs
  and strangled the prey for his mate,
filling his lairs with the kill
  and his dens with the prey.

¹³"I am against you,"
  declares the LORD Almighty.
"I will burn up your chariots in smoke,
  and the sword will devour your young lions.
I will leave you no prey on the earth.
The voices of your messengers
  will no longer be heard."

Woe to Nineveh

3 Woe to the city of blood,
  full of lies,
full of plunder,
  never without victims!
²The crack of whips,
  the clatter of wheels,
galloping horses
  and jolting chariots!
³Charging cavalry,
  flashing swords
  and glittering spears!

Many casualties,
  piles of dead,
bodies without number,
  people stumbling over the corpses —
⁴all because of the wanton lust of
    a prostitute,
  alluring, the mistress of sorceries,
who enslaved nations by her prostitution
  and peoples by her witchcraft.

⁵"I am against you," declares the LORD
    Almighty.
  "I will lift your skirts over your face.
I will show the nations your nakedness
  and the kingdoms your shame.
⁶I will pelt you with filth,
  I will treat you with contempt
  and make you a spectacle.
⁷All who see you will flee from you and say,
  'Nineveh is in ruins — who will mourn
      for her?'
  Where can I find anyone to comfort you?"

⁸Are you better than Thebes,
  situated on the Nile,
  with water around her?

---

throughout the ancient Near East. The lion motif is particularly fitting for Assyria; many reliefs discovered on walls and palaces depict Assyrian kings holding lions in their arms or engaging in lion hunts. This verse uses four different Hebrew words for lions.
2:13 I am against you A challenge formula (see note on Eze 35:3; compare Na 3:5). **LORD Almighty** The divine title here is used throughout the prophets (e.g., Isa 1:9; Jer 6:6; Mic 4:4; Hab 2:13; Zep 2:9; Hag 1:2; Zec 1:3; Mal 1:4). The title asserts Yahweh's role as commander-in-chief of the heavenly armies. **your young lions** A reference to Assyria's warriors — or perhaps, more specifically, its nobles and princes. **I will leave you no prey** Assyria will no longer conquer other nations. **messengers will no longer be heard** Fulfilled with the fall of Nineveh in 612 BC.

3:1–19 In this chapter, Yahweh addresses the people of Nineveh directly, condemning them for violence and bloodshed and announcing the inevitability of their downfall. The woe pronouncement of Na 3:1–7 has a chiastic structure: vv. 1 and 7 (at either end) are the accusation, vv. 2–3 and 5–6 are the threat and v. 4 (at the center) is the criticism. In vv. 4–7, the city is personified as a woman who will be punished for her infidelity (compare Eze 16; 23). The pronouncements in Na 3:8–19 emphasize the dire reality of the situation. Just as Assyria conquered Thebes, the great city of Egypt, so will Nineveh, the great city of Assyria, be conquered. The warnings to prepare for attack in v. 14 are reminiscent of similar commands in 2:1. Their preparations, however, will not be enough to avoid destruction. The oracle closes by reminding the Assyrians that their horrible treatment of other nations will mean that all will rejoice over their destruction.

3:1 Woe The prophet uses this term as a divine threat; he is introducing a woe pronouncement. **city of blood** The Assyrians were known for their numerous atrocities.

See Eze 24:6,9. **full of lies, full of plunder** The Assyrians were notorious for their use of treachery and deceit.
3:4 wanton lust of a prostitute A reference to the Assyrians' idolatry. Old Testament writers often use harlotry to figuratively refer to idolatry (e.g., Jer 3:6; Eze 23:3; Hos 4:12). **mistress of sorceries** God viewed idolatrous forms of divination as detestable (Dt 18:10–12). Common types of divination in the ancient Near East included astrology (study of the heavenly bodies), augury (study of birds), extispicy (examination of the entrails of a sacrificed sheep), kleromancy (casting of lots), necromancy (calling up the dead), oneiromancy (interpretation of dreams) and sorcery (witchcraft or communication with spirits).
3:5 LORD Almighty See note on Na 2:13. **I will lift your skirts** Nakedness and exposure to public shame and ridicule was a typical punishment for infidelity or prostitution (compare Jer 13:22,26; Isa 47:3).
3:7 Where can I find anyone to comfort you A play on Nahum's name (see note on Na 1:1).
3:8 Thebes This ancient city, which was associated with the foreign god Amon, is called both "No Amon" and "Thebes" (compare Eze 30:14–16, where the Hebrew refers to the city simply as "No").

THEBES
Thebes, the capital of southern Egypt (Memphis was the capital of northern Egypt), was the worship center of the god Amon, who was the southern counterpart to Memphis' Ra. The city was known for its magnificent temples (e.g., Luxor, Karnak) and the Valley of the Dead, where many pharaohs were buried. Thebes was situated on both sides of the Nile River, which gave the city an aura of invincibility. However, the Assyrian king Ashurbanipal conquered the city in 663 BC.

The river was her defense,
the waters her wall.
[9] Cush[a] and Egypt were her boundless
strength;
Put and Libya were among her allies.
[10] Yet she was taken captive
and went into exile.
Her infants were dashed to pieces
at every street corner.
Lots were cast for her nobles,
and all her great men were put in chains.
[11] You too will become drunk;
you will go into hiding
and seek refuge from the enemy.

[12] All your fortresses are like fig trees
with their first ripe fruit;
when they are shaken,
the figs fall into the mouth of the eater.
[13] Look at your troops —
they are all weaklings.
The gates of your land
are wide open to your enemies;
fire has consumed the bars of your gates.

[14] Draw water for the siege,
strengthen your defenses!
Work the clay,
tread the mortar,
repair the brickwork!

[15] There the fire will consume you;
the sword will cut you down —
they will devour you like a swarm of
locusts.
Multiply like grasshoppers,
multiply like locusts!
[16] You have increased the number of your
merchants
till they are more numerous than the stars
in the sky,
but like locusts they strip the land
and then fly away.
[17] Your guards are like locusts,
your officials like swarms of locusts
that settle in the walls on a cold day —
but when the sun appears they fly away,
and no one knows where.

[18] King of Assyria, your shepherds[b] slumber;
your nobles lie down to rest.
Your people are scattered on the mountains
with no one to gather them.
[19] Nothing can heal you;
your wound is fatal.
All who hear the news about you
clap their hands at your fall,
for who has not felt
your endless cruelty?

[a] 9 That is, the upper Nile region   [b] 18 That is, rulers

---

3:9 Cush A nation bordering Egypt on the south that was allied with Egypt during the Assyrian period. "Cush" is often translated as "Ethiopia," though it is not synonymous with modern Ethiopia. Biblical Cush was the northern part of modern-day Sudan. **Put** A nation bordering Egypt on the west that was allied with Egypt during the Assyrian period.

3:10 Her infants were dashed to pieces Other OT passages also attest to this barbaric practice (see 2Ki 8:12; Ps 137:9; Isa 13:16; Hos 13:16). **Lots were cast** A common practice in the ancient Near East (see e.g., Ne 11:1; Ps 22:18; Ob 11; Jnh 1:7). Here, people cast lots to determine which of Assyria's honored men would become slaves.

3:12 your fortresses May refer to the fortress cities surrounding Nineveh or the heavily fortified towers of the city itself. **fall into the mouth of the eater** The first figs produced by fig trees often fall to the ground before becoming fully ripe.

3:13 weaklings The Hebrew term used here plays on gender stereotypes to convey the idea of weakness or fright. **The gates of your land** May refer to the fortified

cities protecting Nineveh or the gates of Nineveh itself (understanding "land" as sections of the city).

3:14 Draw water for the siege Ancients prepared for siege by ensuring that they had an adequate supply of water. **your defenses** Heavily fortified areas of the city typically built with clay bricks. **the clay** Assyria's proximity to the Tigris River and its channels meant that the region had an abundance of clay.

3:15 There the fire will consume you The Babylonian Chronicles — containing the history of Babylon — state that a fire broke out in Nineveh in the midst of the city's fall. See the infographic "The Babylonian Chronicles" on p. 605.

3:16 merchants As a center of trade, Nineveh was filled with merchants trading their goods. **more numerous than the stars in the sky** A common OT idiom representing a great number (see also Ge 26:4; Dt 1:10; 1Ch 27:23; Ne 9:23).

3:18 King of Assyria Probably Sin-sar-iskun. **your shepherds** The portrayal of nobles as shepherds was a common motif in the ancient Near East.

3:19 clap their hands at your fall Everyone who learns of Nineveh's fall will celebrate.

HABAKKUK

INTRODUCTION TO HABAKKUK

The book of Habakkuk examines injustice from the experience of a righteous person crying out to God for a remedy. God responds to the prophet: Be patient, observant and steady in your faith, for my judgment will happen at the appointed time. God's response allows Habakkuk to rejoice in God's saving power—even while struggling with a question that every generation asks: Why is evil allowed to thrive? The answer is profound yet difficult: Trust God because he is both powerful and just.

BACKGROUND

The opening verse identifies the book as the oracle of the prophet Habakkuk. His name seems to come from the Hebrew word for "embrace." Habakkuk might have been a Levite and even a priest, since the end of the book contains musical instruction, typically associated with Levites (3:19). A dual role as prophet and priest was not necessarily uncommon: The prophets Jeremiah, Ezekiel and Zechariah also served as priests.

The book of Habakkuk was written during a time when the Chaldeans were gaining significant power. The Chaldeans were a Semitic people living in southeastern Babylonia (modern-day Iraq) after migrating from Aram (modern-day Syria). The Old Testament sometimes uses the term "Chaldeans" to refer to the Babylonians (e.g., Ge 11:28; Job 1:17; Eze 23:14). The Hebrew text of Habakkuk does the same; consequently, some English translations use the term "Babylonians."

Habakkuk probably was written in the late seventh century BC—when the Babylonians were beginning to overtake the Assyrians as the major power in the ancient Near East.

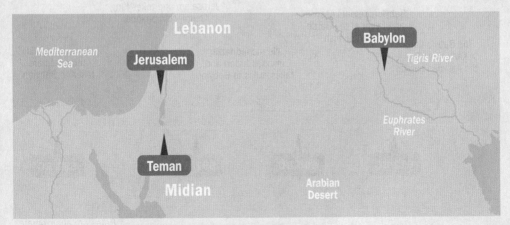

This map depicts some of the locations related to the book of Habakkuk.

STRUCTURE

The book includes an oracle (Hab 1:1—2:20) and a hymn-like prayer (3:1–19). Within the oracle, two sections follow a similar order of events—Habakkuk puts forth a complaint, to which Yahweh then offers an explanation. In Habakkuk's first complaint, he asks why the wicked go unpunished (1:1–4). God responds: The Babylonians (or Chaldeans) will be an instrument in his plan to judge Judah for its sin (1:5–11). Before Yahweh restores his relationship with his people, they must repent of the evil actions separating them from him. Yahweh intends to use a foreign power to cause his people to change.

In his second complaint, Habakkuk asks how God can use a wicked nation like Babylon to carry out his judgment on Judah (1:12—2:1). God responds that while Babylon will bring about his judgment on Judah, he will also judge Babylon (2:2–20). The implication is that God also disapproves of the Babylonians' wickedness, but in the short term he will use them to carry out his purposes. In the long term, Babylon also will be held accountable. In the book's closing prayer, Habakkuk declares his faith in Yahweh, even in the face of future calamity (3:1–19). He realizes that his perspective is more limited than God's and trusts that God's ways are good.

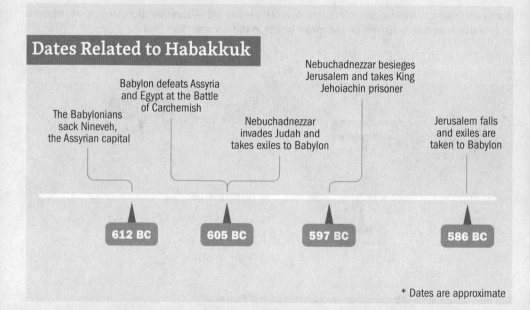

Dates Related to Habakkuk

The Babylonians sack Nineveh, the Assyrian capital — 612 BC

Babylon defeats Assyria and Egypt at the Battle of Carchemish — 605 BC

Nebuchadnezzar invades Judah and takes exiles to Babylon — 605 BC

Nebuchadnezzar besieges Jerusalem and takes King Jehoiachin prisoner — 597 BC

Jerusalem falls and exiles are taken to Babylon — 586 BC

* Dates are approximate

OUTLINE

- Habakkuk's first complaint (1:1–4)
- God's first answer (1:5–11)
- Habakkuk's second complaint (1:12—2:1)
- God's second answer (2:2–20)
- Habakkuk's prayer (3:1–19)

THEMES

Habakkuk contends with two main questions: why God permits evil to flourish (1:1–4), and how, if God is righteous, a wicked nation could function as the means of judgment (1:12—2:1). Habakkuk also protests that the righteous—himself included—are suffering punishment alongside those who deserve such judgment.

Yahweh answers by declaring that the righteous shall live by faith (2:4)—in other words, the prophet will have to trust that God knows what he is doing. Centuries later, New Testament writers like the Apostle Paul quote this verse to show that faith is the only path to righteousness (Ro 1:17; Gal 3:11; Heb 10:38). Within the book of Habakkuk, Yahweh clarifies why he is just in bringing calamity via the Babylonians (Hab 2:6–20). The end of the book signals that Habakkuk finds God's answer sufficient: In the closing verses, he praises God (3:1–19).

We still find ourselves in Habakkuk's predicament—we wrestle with God as we try to understand the presence of evil in the world. We are easily and quickly discouraged. Habakkuk reminds us to shift our questions from the evil surrounding us and instead focus on the ways of God. We might not always understand how God works, but if we truly seek him, we will learn the same thing Habakkuk did: God is just, faithful and worthy to be praised. We can always cry out to God, knowing that he is good. It takes patience to see Yahweh's plans come to fruition, but ultimately he will prevail.

1 The prophecy that Habakkuk the prophet received.

Habakkuk's Complaint

² How long, LORD, must I call for help,
    but you do not listen?
Or cry out to you, "Violence!"
    but you do not save?
³ Why do you make me look at injustice?
    Why do you tolerate wrongdoing?
Destruction and violence are before me;
    there is strife, and conflict abounds.
⁴ Therefore the law is paralyzed,
    and justice never prevails.
The wicked hem in the righteous,
    so that justice is perverted.

The LORD's Answer

⁵ "Look at the nations and watch —
    and be utterly amazed.
For I am going to do something in your days
    that you would not believe,
    even if you were told.

⁶ I am raising up the Babylonians,ᵃ
    that ruthless and impetuous people,
who sweep across the whole earth
    to seize dwellings not their own.
⁷ They are a feared and dreaded people;
    they are a law to themselves
    and promote their own honor.
⁸ Their horses are swifter than leopards,
    fiercer than wolves at dusk.
Their cavalry gallops headlong;
    their horsemen come from afar.
They fly like an eagle swooping to
        devour;
⁹   they all come intent on violence.
Their hordesᵇ advance like a desert wind
    and gather prisoners like sand.
¹⁰ They mock kings
    and scoff at rulers.
They laugh at all fortified cities;
    by building earthen ramps they capture
        them.

ᵃ 6 Or *Chaldeans*   ᵇ 9 The meaning of the Hebrew for this word is uncertain.

1:1 Habakkuk is set in the southern kingdom of Judah during the late seventh century BC—a few decades before the Babylonians destroyed Jerusalem and deported the people of Judah. The book begins with the prophet's complaint to Yahweh over the injustices in Judah that he seemingly permits (vv. 1–4). Yahweh sends his answer: the Babylonians (Chaldeans; see note on v. 6) will be his instrument of discipline (vv. 5–11). Habakkuk wonders how God can use a wicked nation to carry out his plans (1:12—2:1). Yahweh answers by chastising the prophet (2:2–3), declaring that the righteous will live by faith (2:4). God then announces the destruction of the Babylonians (Chaldeans) in the form of five woe pronouncements (2:6–20). Yahweh closes the section by demanding that the earth be silent before him (2:20). The prophet, moved to worship and praise God, concludes the book with a psalm of adoration and declaration of faith (3:1–19). See the timeline "Approximate Dates of Old Testament Prophets" on p. 1070.

1:1 prophecy See note on Na 1:1. **Habakkuk** A prophet of Judah who ministered prior to the exile. Habakkuk was a contemporary of Zephaniah and Jeremiah. Habakkuk's name seems to be derived from the Hebrew word *chavaq*, meaning "embrace," and may indicate that he wrestled with God.

1:2–4 Habakkuk complains that wicked leaders are oppressing the righteous remnant within Judah. According to the formula Yahweh established, the wicked are supposed to suffer while the righteous prosper (compare Lev 26; Dt 28). In Habakkuk's day, this formula seems to have been reversed.

1:2 you do not listen The prophet undoubtedly assumed that if Yahweh had heard his prayers, he would have answered. **Violence** Several other prophets bemoaned the presence of violence among the Israelites (see Jer 6:7; Eze 7:23; Am 3:10; Mic 6:12; Zep 1:9).

1:3 Why do you make me look at injustice Habakkuk was forced to witness violence and wickedness on a continual basis. These sins may have been committed by wicked leaders in Judah. It is possible that the reference here is to a foreign nation that is oppressing Judah. The first suggestion is the Assyrians, who tormented the Jews during Sennacherib's invasion in 701 BC. Another possibility is the Egyptians, who afflicted the Jews during the invasion of Pharaoh Necho in 609 BC. A final suggestion is the Babylonians, who eventually conquered Jerusalem in 586 BC, destroying the city and exiling its inhabitants. **strife** The Hebrew word used here, *riv*, refers to disputes and quarrels between people and is often used in the Prophets to denote Yahweh's covenantal lawsuit against those guilty of breaking his laws (see Isa 3:13; Jer 2:9; Hos 4:1).

1:4 law is paralyzed The Hebrew verb used here denotes that the Mosaic Law has grown numb. Here, it refers to the law being rendered powerless and ineffective. **justice never prevails** The rulers of Israel were responsible for ensuring justice for all people in the land (see Mic 3:1).

1:5–11 On this occasion, Yahweh chooses to answer Habakkuk's repeated prayer (compare Hab 1:2).

1:5 in your days The Babylonians likely first arrived in Jerusalem in 605 BC. However, the news of the rise of the Babylonians would have reached Israel shortly after their conquest of Nineveh in 612 BC. **you would not believe** The news of the rise of the Babylonians (Chaldeans) would have come as an absolute shock to the prophet. At the time of Habakkuk, Assyria dominated the ancient Near East.

1:6 I am raising up The idea that God would raise up foreign armies to punish the Jews for their sins is a common theme in prophetic literature. **the Babylonians** The OT writers often used "Chaldeans" and "Babylonians" synonymously (compare Isa 13:19; 47:1; 48:14; Job 1:17). The Babylonians were a Semitic people who lived in southeastern Babylonia.

1:8 fiercer than wolves at dusk See Zep 3:3.

1:10 by building earthen ramps A reference to a siege, perhaps specifically to trenches dug under or ramps built to approach city walls with battering rams.

¹¹ Then they sweep past like the wind and
  go on —
  guilty people, whose own strength is
  their god."

Habakkuk's Second Complaint

¹² Lord, are you not from everlasting?
  My God, my Holy One, youᵃ will never die.
  You, Lord, have appointed them to execute
  judgment;
  you, my Rock, have ordained them to
  punish.
¹³ Your eyes are too pure to look on evil;
  you cannot tolerate wrongdoing.
  Why then do you tolerate the treacherous?
  Why are you silent while the wicked
  swallow up those more righteous than
  themselves?
¹⁴ You have made people like the fish in the sea,
  like the sea creatures that have no ruler.
¹⁵ The wicked foe pulls all of them up with
  hooks,
  he catches them in his net,
  he gathers them up in his dragnet;
  and so he rejoices and is glad.
¹⁶ Therefore he sacrifices to his net
  and burns incense to his dragnet,
  for by his net he lives in luxury
  and enjoys the choicest food.

¹⁷ Is he to keep on emptying his net,
  destroying nations without mercy?

2 I will stand at my watch
  and station myself on the ramparts;
  I will look to see what he will say to me,
  and what answer I am to give to this
  complaint.ᵇ

The Lord's Answer

² Then the Lord replied:

"Write down the revelation
  and make it plain on tablets
  so that a heraldᶜ may run with it.
³ For the revelation awaits an appointed time;
  it speaks of the end
  and will not prove false.
  Though it linger, wait for it;
  itᵈ will certainly come
  and will not delay.

⁴ "See, the enemy is puffed up;
  his desires are not upright —
  but the righteous person will live by his
  faithfulnessᵉ —

ᵃ 12 An ancient Hebrew scribal tradition; Masoretic Text we
ᵇ 1 Or and what to answer when I am rebuked   ᶜ 2 Or so that whoever reads it   ᵈ 3 Or Though he linger, wait for him; / he   ᵉ 4 Or faith

1:11 their god Marduk (Bel), a storm god, was the patron god of Babylon and head of the Mesopotamian gods.

1:12—2:1 Habakkuk is appalled at Yahweh's answer to his initial complaint. The prophet questions how God could use such a wicked nation to carry out his plans. After all, the Babylonians themselves had already been marked for judgment (see Isa 13–14; Jer 51). For the prophet, Yahweh's use of the ungodly is incompatible with his holy nature (see Ps 5:4; 34:16).
  Part of his protest is that the righteous, including himself, are being punished along with the wicked according to Yahweh's plan. Having made what he believes is a sound argument, the prophet proudly announces his intention to wait for Yahweh's reply, eager to respond to whatever God might say.

1:12 my Holy One A common divine title (Job 6:10; Pr 9:10; Hos 11:9), similar to "Holy One of Israel" (2Ki 19:22; Ps 71:22; Isa 1:4; Jer 51:5). you will never die This phrase is to be understood as a question in light of the prophet's fear expressed in Hab 1:13. Rock A common divine title (see Dt 32:18; 1Sa 2:2; 2Sa 22:2; Ps 18:2).
1:13 while the wicked swallow up those more righteous Habakkuk questions why Yahweh permits the Babylonians to devour the kingdom of Judah The prophet suggests that Yahweh's holiness should have caused him to prevent the oppression of the people of Judah, especially since some of them remained faithful to him.
1:16 he sacrifices to his net The net represents military strength, which was provided by Marduk, the god of Babylon. See note on Hab 1:11. See the infographic "Furnishings of the Tabernacle" on p. 136.

2:1 my watch Watchmen were stationed at the highest part of a city wall to warn of impending danger (see Eze 33:2–6). As watchmen, prophets were to communicate the divine message to the people (see Jer 6:17; Eze 3:17–21; Hos 9:8).
2:2 Write down the revelation The vision might be a reference to the revelation concerning the imminent Chaldean invasion described in Hab 1:5–11. It is also possible the vision consists of the exhortation of 2:3–5, an appeal for patient endurance marked by faithfulness. A final possibility is the revelation of Yahweh's appearance in 3:3–15 (compare Na 1:1 and note). on tablets Clay tablets, though stone tablets are possible. These tablets would have been placed in public gathering spots. For a later example of this, see the deuterocanonical writing 1 Maccabees 14:25–49.
2:3 wait for it The fulfillment of the prophecy of Hab 1:5–11 would take at least 20 years, depending on the date of Habakkuk's ministry. Yahweh's encouragement is to wait in patience and faith.
2:4 the righteous person will live by his faithfulness Righteous people are commanded to live by faith; they must practice obedience and trust that Yahweh will remain faithful to his covenantal promises. The New Testament cites v. 4 three times. For the author of Hebrews, who seems to be drawing on an ancient Greek reading of the passage from the Septuagint, vv. 3–4 provides OT support for the call to patiently await the fulfillment of God's promise rather than sliding back in faith (see Heb 10:38). Paul twice cites Hab 2:4 in his letters to explain God's gift of righteousness on the basis of faith (Ro 1:17; Gal 3:11). Paul finds in Hab 2:4 a scriptural citation that justification is given by God in his faithfulness

⁵ indeed, wine betrays him;
    he is arrogant and never at rest.
Because he is as greedy as the grave
    and like death is never satisfied,
he gathers to himself all the nations
    and takes captive all the peoples.

⁶ "Will not all of them taunt him with ridicule
and scorn, saying,

"'Woe to him who piles up stolen goods
    and makes himself wealthy by extortion!
    How long must this go on?'
⁷ Will not your creditors suddenly arise?
    Will they not wake up and make you
        tremble?
    Then you will become their prey.
⁸ Because you have plundered many nations,
    the peoples who are left will plunder you.
For you have shed human blood;
    you have destroyed lands and cities and
        everyone in them.

⁹ "Woe to him who builds his house by unjust
        gain,
    setting his nest on high
    to escape the clutches of ruin!
¹⁰ You have plotted the ruin of many peoples,
    shaming your own house and forfeiting
        your life.
¹¹ The stones of the wall will cry out,
    and the beams of the woodwork will echo it.

¹² "Woe to him who builds a city with
        bloodshed
    and establishes a town by injustice!
¹³ Has not the LORD Almighty determined
    that the people's labor is only fuel for the
        fire,
    that the nations exhaust themselves for
        nothing?
¹⁴ For the earth will be filled with the
        knowledge of the glory of the LORD
    as the waters cover the sea.

¹⁵ "Woe to him who gives drink to his
        neighbors,
    pouring it from the wineskin till they are
        drunk,
    so that he can gaze on their naked bodies!
¹⁶ You will be filled with shame instead of
        glory.
    Now it is your turn! Drink and let your
        nakedness be exposedᵃ!
The cup from the LORD's right hand is coming
        around to you,
    and disgrace will cover your glory.
¹⁷ The violence you have done to Lebanon will
        overwhelm you,
    and your destruction of animals will
        terrify you.

ᵃ 16 Masoretic Text; Dead Sea Scrolls, Aquila, Vulgate and Syriac
(see also Septuagint) and stagger

to all people—both Jews and non-Jews—who place faith in his Son.

2:5 grave Used throughout the OT to identify the place of the dead (see Ge 37:35; Nu 16:33; 1Sa 2:6; 1Ki 2:6; Job 21:13; Ps 6:5; Pr 5:5; Isa 28:15; Eze 31:17; Hos 13:14).

2:6–20 The woe pronouncements of Hab 2:6–20 are neatly structured into five stanzas consisting of three verses each. Verses 6–8 denounce the imperialistic behavior of the Babylonians (Chaldeans); vv. 9–11 condemn the Babylonians' covetousness; vv. 12–14 criticize the Babylonians' violence; vv. 15–17 censure the Babylonians' treachery; and vv. 18–20 address the Babylonians' idolatry. While the first four woes deal with the Babylonians' sins against fellow humans, the fifth addresses the Babylonians' sin against God. The first and fourth woes end in a refrain, possibly a chorus sung by a congregation of people.

2:6 taunt The Hebrew word used here, *mashal*, is the common term for a proverb (see note on Pr 1:1). The taunt song was used as a derogatory proverbial chant against an object of scorn (see Dt 28:37; 1Sa 10:12; Isa 14:4; Jer 24:9; Mic 2:4). **Woe** The Hebrew word used here, *hoy,* denotes a divine threat. In this form, the prophetic oracle is called a "woe pronouncement." **makes himself wealthy by extortion** Pledges are items used as security in case of default on a loan. This practice could lead to the enslavement of the borrowers (see Ne 5:1–5) because the last pledge or surety they could offer would be themselves. The practice of usury was forbidden by the Mosaic Law (see Dt 24:10; compare Job 24:3,9–10).

2:7 you will become their prey A reversal of fortune reminiscent of Ob 15. The conquests of the Babylonians are amply documented. Their reputation as plunderers was well known even before they became a world power, and they built their empire with bloodshed and violence (see Hab 1:9; 2:12,17). Verse 8 explains that the nations that had been plundered by the Babylonians would have their revenge.

2:9 him who builds his house by unjust gain The Babylonian (Chaldean) empire's thirst for loot and spoil arose from their proud desire to build a great empire.

2:10 You have plotted the ruin of many peoples, shaming your own house Instead of achieving their goal of building an everlasting, indestructible empire, the Babylonians created a short-lived dynasty full of shame (v. 10) and violence (v. 12).

2:12 him who builds a city with bloodshed The cost of building their great empire had been exacted from the lives of the victims of their bloody wars (and through the extensive use of slavery in their building projects).

2:13 LORD Almighty A title that identifies God as the leader of the heavenly armies. See note on Na 2:13. **that the people's labor is only fuel for the fire** The great buildings of the Babylonians would end up being burned (see Jer 50:32).

2:14 the glory of the LORD A reference to the visible manifestation of Yahweh (see Ex 16:7; 40:34; 1Ki 8:11; Eze 10:4; 43:4).

2:16 You will be filled with shame instead of glory A reversal of fortune. See note on Hab 2:7. **The cup** The cup of Yahweh is often used to symbolize divine judgment (see Isa 51:17; Jer 25:15). **LORD's right hand** A reference to Yahweh's strength (see Ex 15:6; Ps 98:1; Isa 41:10).

For you have shed human blood;
　you have destroyed lands and cities and
　　everyone in them.

18 "Of what value is an idol carved by a
　　craftsman?
　Or an image that teaches lies?
For the one who makes it trusts in his own
　creation;
　he makes idols that cannot speak.
19 Woe to him who says to wood, 'Come to life!'
　Or to lifeless stone, 'Wake up!'
Can it give guidance?
　It is covered with gold and silver;
　　there is no breath in it."

20 The Lord is in his holy temple;
　let all the earth be silent before him.

Habakkuk's Prayer

3 A prayer of Habakkuk the prophet. On
　shigionoth.[a]

2 Lord, I have heard of your fame;
　I stand in awe of your deeds, Lord.
Repeat them in our day,
　in our time make them known;
　in wrath remember mercy.

3 God came from Teman,
　the Holy One from Mount Paran.[b]

His glory covered the heavens
　and his praise filled the earth.
4 His splendor was like the sunrise;
　rays flashed from his hand,
　where his power was hidden.
5 Plague went before him;
　pestilence followed his steps.
6 He stood, and shook the earth;
　he looked, and made the nations tremble.
The ancient mountains crumbled
　and the age-old hills collapsed —
　but he marches on forever.
7 I saw the tents of Cushan in distress,
　the dwellings of Midian in anguish.

8 Were you angry with the rivers, Lord?
　Was your wrath against the streams?
Did you rage against the sea
　when you rode your horses
　and your chariots to victory?
9 You uncovered your bow,
　you called for many arrows.
You split the earth with rivers;
10 　the mountains saw you and writhed.
Torrents of water swept by;
　the deep roared
　and lifted its waves on high.

---

[a] 1 Probably a literary or musical term　[b] 3 The Hebrew has
Selah (a word of uncertain meaning) here and at the middle of
verse 9 and at the end of verse 13.

2:17 The violence you have done to Lebanon The
Babylonians stripped the forests of cedar from Lebanon
and used them for their monumental building projects.

Habakkuk 2:17

LEBANON
The mountainous region of Lebanon, directly north of Israel, was famous for its magnificent cedar trees, which
were used to build the Jerusalem temple. The OT refers
to cedars from Lebanon to symbolize physical strength,
but a strength still easily surpassed by Yahweh's power
(see Ps 29:5; Isa 2:13; Am 2:9; Zec 11:2).

2:18 what value is an idol Like other pagan nations,
the Babylonians trusted in idols for guidance (see note
on Hab 1:11). Yahweh strongly condemned this practice
in the Ten Commandments (see Ex 20:4). The condemnation of idolatry is a central theme among the OT prophets
(see Isa 44:9–20; Jer 5:7; 44:1–8; Hos 8:4).

2:19–20 The final verses of the chapter highlight a stunning contrast between the lifeless wooden god and the
living God, enthroned in his holy temple. The living God
speaks with words of comfort for his faithful and words
of judgment for the pagan. Yahweh is on his throne in
heaven waiting to appear before the nations, at which
time he will inflict judgment on them.

2:20 his holy temple Either the temple in Jerusalem or
Yahweh's heavenly abode. The Hebrew phrase used here

occurs elsewhere only in Psalms (Ps 5:7; 11:4; 65:4;
79:1; 138:2), Jonah (Jnh 2:4,7) and Micah (Mic 1:2).

3:1–19 Habakkuk's prayer is in the form of a psalm
designed to be sung (see Hab 3:19). Yahweh's answer
filled the proud prophet with fear and awe (see 2:2–20).
Habakkuk humbly responded with prayer and praise.
The psalm here is filled with exodus imagery, as the
prophet vividly recounts the theophany on Mount Sinai,
the wilderness wanderings and the crossings of the Red
Sea and Jordan River.

3:1 On shigionoth The Hebrew word used here refers
to the musical setting of the psalm, either the melody or
style in which it was to be sung. See Ps 7 (title).

3:3 from Teman One of the principal cities of Edom. The
name comes from Teman, the grandson of Esau (see Ge
36:11). **Mount Paran** A wilderness region just to the
south of the border of Canaan. The Israelites camped
at Paran after leaving Mount Sinai. The spies were sent
into the promised land from Paran (see Nu 13–14).

3:6 The ancient mountains crumbled The mountains
quaking at the presence of Yahweh is a common motif in
the OT (see Jdg 5:4–5; Ps 114:4–7; Jer 4:24; Na 1:5).

3:8 with the rivers The Red Sea and Jordan River, both
of which the Israelites crossed on dry ground. **chariots**
Chariots were powerful instruments of war that could
dominate battles.

3:9 bow Archers were of such great significance in ancient battles that the Hebrew term for "bow" was often
used figuratively for warfare (see Isa 22:3).

3:10 Torrents of water A reference to the Jordan River,
which was at the flood stage when the Israelites crossed
into the promised land (see Jos 3:15).

¹¹ Sun and moon stood still in the heavens
    at the glint of your flying arrows,
    at the lightning of your flashing spear.
¹² In wrath you strode through the earth
    and in anger you threshed the nations.
¹³ You came out to deliver your people,
    to save your anointed one.
You crushed the leader of the land of
    wickedness,
    you stripped him from head to foot.
¹⁴ With his own spear you pierced his head
    when his warriors stormed out to
    scatter us,
    gloating as though about to devour
    the wretched who were in hiding.
¹⁵ You trampled the sea with your horses,
    churning the great waters.

¹⁶ I heard and my heart pounded,
    my lips quivered at the sound;

decay crept into my bones,
    and my legs trembled.
Yet I will wait patiently for the day of
    calamity
    to come on the nation invading us.
¹⁷ Though the fig tree does not bud
    and there are no grapes on the vines,
    though the olive crop fails
    and the fields produce no food,
    though there are no sheep in the pen
    and no cattle in the stalls,
¹⁸ yet I will rejoice in the LORD,
    I will be joyful in God my Savior.

¹⁹ The Sovereign LORD is my strength;
    he makes my feet like the feet of a deer,
    he enables me to tread on the heights.

For the director of music. On my stringed
    instruments.

3:11 Sun and moon stood still Possibly an allusion to
the sun standing still in Jos 10:12–13.
3:13 anointed The Hebrew term used here, *mashiach*
(meaning "anointed one"), is probably a reference to
Moses, although Joshua is another possibility. Throughout the OT, it is used to designate individuals specially
chosen by God to perform a divine service, including

David (2Sa 22:51), Saul (1Sa 24:6) and even the Persian
king, Cyrus (Isa 45:1).
3:14 With his own spear you pierced his head Perhaps a reference to the armies of Sihon and Og (see Nu
21:21–25,33–35).
3:17 olive crop In this verse, figs, grapes and olives
represent the entire agricultural system of Israel.

ZEPHANIAH

INTRODUCTION TO ZEPHANIAH

This book contains the prophecies that came to Zephaniah during a time of renewed devotion to Yahweh. The king was purging Judah of idols and improper worship practices, but the people's hearts also needed correcting. Zephaniah's message is that that anyone who combines worship of Yahweh with other gods—and who exercises deceit, violence and complacency—will be destroyed on the coming Day of Yahweh. However, people who are righteous and humble will be gathered together in peace. When evil is all around us, how do we guard our hearts so that we can live a holy life? Zephaniah's message assures us that in his time, Yahweh will make all things right.

BACKGROUND

The first line of Zephaniah indicates that the book contains the word of Yahweh that came to Zephaniah son of Cushi. The unusually long genealogy in Zephaniah 1:1 shows that Zephaniah was the great-great grandson of Hezekiah. This could refer to King Hezekiah of Judah, who ruled 715–697 BC, but this cannot be proven. In addition, the Babylonians executed a priest named Zephaniah when they captured Jerusalem in 586 BC (2Ki 25:18–21; Jer 52:24–27), but it remains uncertain whether this priest was the prophet of the same name.

Zephaniah son of Cushi prophesied during the reign of King Josiah (640–609 BC), who was the last godly king of Judah and who engaged in widespread religious reforms. Jeremiah, Nahum and Habakkuk also prophesied during this period.

Josiah's reforms began around 622 BC with the discovery of the Book of the Law in the temple (2Ch 34:1–7; 2Ki 22–23). He sought to end idolatry and do away with corrupt leadership, and to bring the people back to Yahweh. These themes are also present in Zephaniah and indicate

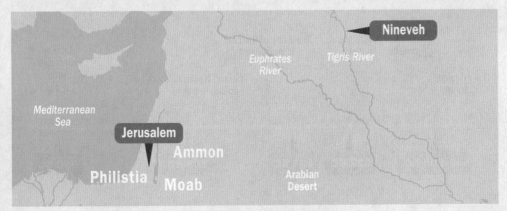

This map depicts some of the locations related to the book of Zephaniah. During the prophet's lifetime, the Assyrians were invading from the north; Nineveh was their capital.

that Zephaniah likely began his ministry shortly before Josiah's reforms or perhaps when they were just beginning (Zep 1:4–9; 3:1–4). After Josiah's death, Judah went back to its sinful ways. The next four kings did not follow Yahweh, and Babylon conquered God's disobedient people and deported them in 586 BC.

STRUCTURE

Zephaniah incorporates a variety of literary elements, including judgment speeches, calls for response, a hymn and salvation speeches. The book starts and ends with prophecies of worldwide judgment (1:2–3; 3:8). In between, the structure resembles that of Isaiah and Ezekiel—beginning with oracles against Judah, then shifting to oracles against other nations, and concluding with oracles about the future restoration of God's people. In the first section, Zephaniah warns of Yahweh's impending judgment on Jerusalem and Judah (1:2—2:3). Then he affirms Yahweh's sovereignty over all peoples, proclaiming that Yahweh will judge the nations (in addition to Judah) for their wickedness (2:4—3:8). Finally, Zephaniah promises that Yahweh's judgment will ultimately produce a small group of holy believers from Israel and the nations who will stand together under the kingship of Yahweh (3:9–20).

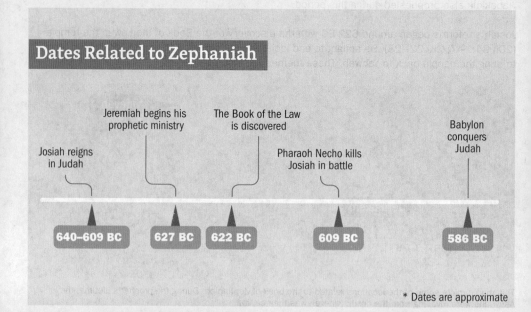

Dates Related to Zephaniah

Jeremiah begins his prophetic ministry

The Book of the Law is discovered

Babylon conquers Judah

Josiah reigns in Judah

Pharaoh Necho kills Josiah in battle

| 640–609 BC | 627 BC | 622 BC | 609 BC | 586 BC |

* Dates are approximate

OUTLINE

- Judgment against Judah (1:1—2:3)
- Judgment against the nations (2:4–15)
- The future of Jerusalem (3:1–20)

THEMES

The major theme of Zephaniah is the coming Day of Yahweh—similar to the message of Joel but with a stronger emphasis on the sins of the people. Zephaniah dramatically exposes the iniquities of Judah, accusing the nation of idolatry and moral corruption. In this respect, Zephaniah resembles Jeremiah, who prophesied around the same time. In fact, the ministries of Zephaniah and Jeremiah parallel those of Isaiah and Micah a century earlier.

Zephaniah's message is not entirely negative. Along with the warnings about the Day of Yahweh comes the hope of a holy remnant. In the midst of judgment, God will remain faithful. He will destroy evil, but he will advance his work among his people, setting apart a group of people for his purposes. This is the same message of redemption at the heart of the gospel of Christ—in the midst of a world still suffering from the effects of sin, we hold onto hope in God's faithfulness and his continual work among his people. God prompts us to change our ways—away from false religion and toward true faithfulness. God calls us to humbly love others and to live transparently as one people of God (2:3; 3:12–13).

1

The word of the LORD that came to Zephaniah son of Cushi, the son of Gedaliah, the son of Amariah, the son of Hezekiah, during the reign of Josiah son of Amon king of Judah:

Judgment on the Whole Earth in the Day of the LORD

2 "I will sweep away everything
  from the face of the earth,"
                declares the LORD.
3 "I will sweep away both man and beast;
  I will sweep away the birds in the sky
  and the fish in the sea —
  and the idols that cause the wicked to
    stumble."*a*

"When I destroy all mankind
  on the face of the earth,"
                declares the LORD,
4 "I will stretch out my hand against Judah
  and against all who live in Jerusalem.
I will destroy every remnant of Baal worship
  in this place,
  the very names of the idolatrous
    priests —
5 those who bow down on the roofs
  to worship the starry host,
  those who bow down and swear by the LORD
  and who also swear by Molek,*b*

---

a 3 The meaning of the Hebrew for this line is uncertain.
b 5 Hebrew *Malkam*

1:1–18 Like Joel, the major theme of Zephaniah is the Day of Yahweh. The Hebrew word for "day" occurs 20 times in this short book. However, while Joel never mentions the sins of the nation, Zephaniah dramatically exposes the iniquities of Judah, accusing the nation of idolatry and moral corruption. In this respect, Zephaniah, who prophesied during the late seventh century BC, resembles his contemporary, Jeremiah. The ministries of Zephaniah and Jeremiah parallel those of Isaiah and Micah from a century earlier.

The book of Zephaniah announces the Day of Yahweh to encourage Judah to repent and practice obedience. It incorporates a variety of literary techniques, including judgment speeches, calls for response, a hymn and salvation speeches. The book's structure resembles Isaiah and Ezekiel: It begins with a set of oracles against Judah, moves to a collection of oracles against foreign nations and concludes with a series of oracles concerning the future restoration of Israel. See the timeline "Approximate Dates of Old Testament Prophets" on p. 1070.

1:1 Zephaniah's genealogy is the longest of the writing prophets. The writer includes this lengthy genealogy to show that Zephaniah was the great-great-grandson of King Hezekiah. Zephaniah's royal lineage makes him a distant relative of King Josiah, during whose reign he prophesied. The prophet's position in the royal family provided him with an ideal opportunity to witness the apostasy of Judah's leaders firsthand (see vv. 8–12; 3:3–4).

1:1 The word of the LORD A standard introductory formula (see also Hos 1:1; Joel 1:1; Mic 1:1; Hag 1:1; Zec 1:1). **Zephaniah** A prophet of Judah who ministered during the reign of Josiah (640–609 BC). **Hezekiah** Hezekiah, who reigned from 715–697 BC, was a king who did right in the sight of Yahweh (2Ki 18:3). **Josiah** Josiah reigned from 640–609 BC, having gained the throne at only eight years of age. He initiated many reforms during his reign and would be known as the final "good" king of Judah.

ZEPHANIAH
Zephaniah means "Yahweh hides" (or "protects") or "Yahweh has hidden." The name may refer to God's protection of Zephaniah in his childhood during Manasseh's

wicked reign (2Ki 21:16). As a member of the royal family, Zephaniah would have lived in Jerusalem, which explains his familiarity with the capital city (e.g., Zep 1:10–11). Zephaniah's contemporaries include Habakkuk and Jeremiah.

1:2–6 The prophet begins this section with a general announcement of worldwide destruction (Zep 1:2–3) and then announces Judah's destruction specifically (vv. 4–6).

1:4 my hand An anthropomorphic figure attributing human characteristics to God that is commonly used to emphasize God's judgment (see Isa 5:25; Jer 21:5). **Judah** The southern kingdom of Israel. The territory is named for the tribe of Judah, the descendants of the fourth son of the patriarch Jacob and his wife Leah. **Jerusalem** The religious and political capital of Judah. **Baal** The Canaanite storm god. The prophets consistently condemned the worship of Baal (compare 1Ki 18:20–21; Jer 2:8,23; Hos 2:13; 11:2). See the table "Pagan Deities of the Old Testament" on p. 1287. **idolatrous priests** Refers to the priests who served foreign gods at the high places.

JERUSALEM
Means "city of peace"; located 14 miles west of the Dead Sea and 33 miles east of the Mediterranean Sea. The city is situated on a rocky plateau 2,550 feet above sea level. Its central position in Israel made it the ideal location for the capital. The Israelites had conquered the city of Jerusalem in the time of the judges (ca. 1210–1051 BC), but they did not occupy it during that time (Jdg 1:8). Jerusalem was made the political capital of the nation after King David (1011–971 BC) conquered it and built a palace there (2Sa 5:6–12). In 960 BC, when Solomon built the temple, Jerusalem became the religious capital of the nation as well. From this point forward, the city of Jerusalem occupied a place of prominence in the political and religious life of Israel.

1:5 those who bow down and swear by the LORD The Israelites had developed a syncretistic form of religion, blending the worship of Yahweh with the worship of pagan gods like the chief god of the Ammonites, known

⁶ those who turn back from following the LORD
and neither seek the LORD nor inquire
of him.”

⁷ Be silent before the Sovereign LORD,
for the day of the LORD is near.
The LORD has prepared a sacrifice;
he has consecrated those he has invited.

⁸ “On the day of the LORD’s sacrifice
I will punish the officials
and the king’s sons
and all those clad
in foreign clothes.
⁹ On that day I will punish
all who avoid stepping on the threshold,^a
who fill the temple of their gods
with violence and deceit.

¹⁰ “On that day,”
declares the LORD,
“a cry will go up from the Fish Gate,
wailing from the New Quarter,
and a loud crash from the hills.
¹¹ Wail, you who live in the market district ^b;
all your merchants will be wiped out,
all who trade with^c silver will be destroyed.
¹² At that time I will search Jerusalem with lamps
and punish those who are complacent,
who are like wine left on its dregs,

who think, ‘The LORD will do nothing,
either good or bad.’
¹³ Their wealth will be plundered,
their houses demolished.
Though they build houses,
they will not live in them;
though they plant vineyards,
they will not drink the wine.”

¹⁴ The great day of the LORD is near —
near and coming quickly.
The cry on the day of the LORD is bitter;
the Mighty Warrior shouts his
battle cry.
¹⁵ That day will be a day of wrath —
a day of distress and anguish,
a day of trouble and ruin,
a day of darkness and gloom,
a day of clouds and blackness —
¹⁶ a day of trumpet and battle cry
against the fortified cities
and against the corner towers.

¹⁷ “I will bring such distress on all people
that they will grope about like those who
are blind,
because they have sinned against the
LORD.

^a 9 See 1 Samuel 5:5.   ^b 11 Or the Mortar   ^c 11 Or in

as Molek (or Milcom, Milkom or Molech; 1Ki 11:5–7; 2Ki 23:10–13).

1:7 Be silent The Hebrew term used here is an onomatopoetic expression, much like the English term “Hush!” (Hab 2:20; Zec 2:13). **the day of the LORD** The prophets use this phrase to denote the time when God will intervene in human affairs and judge the wicked (see Isa 13:6,9; Eze 30:3; Joel 1:15; 2:1; Am 5:18; Ob 15; Mal 4:5). **prepared a sacrifice** Refers to a sacrificial feast to which guests are invited (Dt 12:17–18; 1Ki 1:9–10,24–25).

1:8 the officials The Hebrew term here is used to designate city officials (Jdg 8:6), provincial supervisors (1Ki 20:14), military leaders (2Ki 5:1) and religious leaders (Ezr 8:24). These officials were especially important during the early years of Josiah’s reign since the king was too young to govern the nation himself. **king’s sons** Refers to Josiah’s sons, the princes. This prophecy was fulfilled when Josiah’s sons became the victims of foreign invaders. Pharaoh Necho captured Jehoahaz in 609 BC and took him to Egypt. Jehoiakim was the vassal of the Babylonian king, Nebuchadnezzar, for three years before he rebelled; he was murdered in Jerusalem in 597 BC. Three months later (597 BC), Nebuchadnezzar captured Jehoiachin, Josiah’s grandson, and took him to Babylon. Finally, Zedekiah, the last son of Josiah to rule over Judah, rebelled against Babylon and was taken captive by Nebuchadnezzar in 586 BC. See 2Ki 23–25. See the timeline “Judah From the Fall of Samaria to the Exile” on p. 606; see the timeline “The Divided Kingdom” on p. 536. **those clad in foreign clothes** Though the prophet may refer figuratively to adopting pagan customs, the literal meaning is also possible.

1:9 violence and deceit Several other prophets also bemoan the presence of violence among the Israelites (see Jer 6:7; Am 3:10; Mic 6:12; Hab 1:2).

1:10–11 All three of the districts mentioned in Zep 1:10–11 are located on the northern side of Jerusalem, the section where Nebuchadnezzar broke through the walls of the city in 586 BC.

1:10 Fish Gate An entrance to Jerusalem located on the northern section of city walls. It was the site of a fish market (2Ch 33:14; Ne 3:3; 12:39). **New Quarter** A newer section of the city, probably located near the Tyropoeon Valley on the north side of the city. It was probably built after the construction of the temple to provide housing for those who worked in the temple and surrounding area. **from the hills** Refers to the western (Mount Zion), central (Mount Moriah) and eastern (Mount of Olives) hills of Jerusalem.

1:11 the market district The Hebrew term used here doesn’t appear anywhere else in the Bible. It may be a place name associated with a site in the northern Tyropoeon Valley. **your merchants** The Hebrew phrase used here is literally translated “people of Canaan,” but it usually denotes traders or merchants because the Canaanites were known as traders.

1:12 complacent The Hebrew phrase used here appears nowhere else in the OT. It describes the residents of Jerusalem, who do not believe that Yahweh will interfere in the affairs of the nation and are at ease.

1:15 distress and anguish The imagery of distress, disaster and darkness echoes similar language used to describe the Day of Yahweh by other OT prophets (e.g., Ob 12; Isa 13:9; Am 5:18; Eze 30:3; see note on Joel 2:2).

1:16 a day of trumpet and battle cry The trumpet

Their blood will be poured out like dust
and their entrails like dung.
18 Neither their silver nor their gold
will be able to save them
on the day of the LORD's wrath."

In the fire of his jealousy
the whole earth will be consumed,
for he will make a sudden end
of all who live on the earth.

Judah and Jerusalem Judged Along With the Nations

Judah Summoned to Repent

2 Gather together, gather yourselves together,
you shameful nation,
2 before the decree takes effect
and that day passes like windblown chaff,
before the LORD's fierce anger
comes upon you,
before the day of the LORD's wrath
comes upon you.
3 Seek the LORD, all you humble of the land,
you who do what he commands.
Seek righteousness, seek humility;
perhaps you will be sheltered
on the day of the LORD's anger.

Philistia

4 Gaza will be abandoned
and Ashkelon left in ruins.
At midday Ashdod will be emptied
and Ekron uprooted.

5 Woe to you who live by the sea,
you Kerethite people;
the word of the LORD is against you,
Canaan, land of the Philistines.
He says, "I will destroy you,
and none will be left."
6 The land by the sea will become pastures
having wells for shepherds
and pens for flocks.
7 That land will belong
to the remnant of the people of Judah;
there they will find pasture.
In the evening they will lie down
in the houses of Ashkelon.
The LORD their God will care for them;
he will restore their fortunes. ª

Moab and Ammon

8 "I have heard the insults of Moab
and the taunts of the Ammonites,
who insulted my people
and made threats against their land.
9 Therefore, as surely as I live,"
declares the LORD Almighty,
the God of Israel,
"surely Moab will become like Sodom,
the Ammonites like Gomorrah—
a place of weeds and salt pits,
a wasteland forever.
The remnant of my people will plunder them;
the survivors of my nation will inherit
their land."

ª 7 Or *will bring back their captives*

---

warned the people of coming danger. See Jer 4:5 and note.

2:1–15 In the opening of this section, Zephaniah declares that the only hope for the children of Israel is repentance (Zep 2:1–3). He calls the nation to gather together and seek Yahweh before the announced decree takes effect. Zephaniah begs the inhabitants of Judah to humble themselves, obey Yahweh's commands, and be filled with righteousness in the hope that they will then be hidden on the Day of Yahweh's anger (v. 3; compare Am 5:15). Having described the judgment of Judah (Zep 1:4–15), the prophet turns his attention to the nations surrounding Judah (2:4–15). The first nation he marks out for judgment is Philistia (vv. 4–7), located west of Judah. The second and third nations are Moab and Ammon (vv. 8–11), located east of Judah. The fourth nation is Cush (v. 12), located south of Judah and the fifth and final nation marked out for judgment is Assyria (vv. 13–15), located generally north of Judah. The pronouncements of doom recorded here resemble those found in other prophetic books (see Isa 13–23; Jer 46–51; Eze 25–32; Am 1–2).

2:3 you humble of the land Refers to those who are humble (Hab 2:4) and obedient to Yahweh or possibly to those who are afflicted and poor (see Ex 1:11; Ps 76:9; Isa 58:10; Am 8:4).

2:4 The four cities mentioned in this verse (Gaza, Ekron,

Ashkelon and Ashdod) were part of the "Philistine pentapolis" (see note on Jer 25:20). Each of these cities was governed by a lord (Jdg 3:3). Zephaniah doesn't mention the fifth city, Gath, suggesting that Gath had already been destroyed by the time of his ministry (2Ch 26:6; Am 1:6–8; Zec 9:5–7).

2:4 Gaza An important center of trade located on the Mediterranean shore about 40 miles south of Jaffa. Probably the oldest of the Philistine cities. Identified with the modern Tell Harube. **Ashkelon** A commercial seaport situated on the Mediterranean shore between Jaffa and Gaza. Identified with the modern Ashkelon. **Ashdod** A heavily fortified city located about two miles inland of the Mediterranean Sea and nine miles north of Ashkelon. Identified with the modern Ashdod. **Ekron** The northernmost Philistine city, located approximately 35 miles southwest of Jerusalem on the edge of the Shephelah. Identified with the modern Tell Miqne.

2:5 Kerethite people A title related to Crete, the native land of the Philistines.

2:8 Moab Neighbor of Israel located east of the Jordan River and the Dead Sea. See note on 2Ki 13:20. **Ammonites** Neighbors of the Israelites who lived east of the Jordan River, just north of the Moabites. See note on 1Ch 19:1.

2:9 like Gomorrah Sodom and Gomorrah were cities located near the Dead Sea during the time of Abraham (Ge 19). God judged the two cities for their wickedness.

¹⁰ This is what they will get in return for their
pride,
for insulting and mocking
the people of the LORD Almighty.
¹¹ The LORD will be awesome to them
when he destroys all the gods of
the earth.
Distant nations will bow down to him,
all of them in their own lands.

Cush

¹² "You Cushites,^a too,
will be slain by my sword."

Assyria

¹³ He will stretch out his hand against
the north
and destroy Assyria,
leaving Nineveh utterly desolate
and dry as the desert.
¹⁴ Flocks and herds will lie down there,
creatures of every kind.
The desert owl and the screech owl
will roost on her columns.
Their hooting will echo through the
windows,
rubble will fill the doorways,
the beams of cedar will be exposed.
¹⁵ This is the city of revelry
that lived in safety.
She said to herself,
"I am the one! And there is none
besides me."
What a ruin she has become,
a lair for wild beasts!
All who pass by her scoff
and shake their fists.

Jerusalem

3 Woe to the city of oppressors,
rebellious and defiled!
² She obeys no one,
she accepts no correction.
She does not trust in the LORD,
she does not draw near to her God.
³ Her officials within her
are roaring lions;
her rulers are evening wolves,
who leave nothing for the morning.
⁴ Her prophets are unprincipled;
they are treacherous people.
Her priests profane the sanctuary
and do violence to the law.
⁵ The LORD within her is righteous;
he does no wrong.
Morning by morning he dispenses his justice,
and every new day he does not fail,
yet the unrighteous know no shame.

Jerusalem Remains Unrepentant

⁶ "I have destroyed nations;
their strongholds are demolished.
I have left their streets deserted,
with no one passing through.
Their cities are laid waste;
they are deserted and empty.
⁷ Of Jerusalem I thought,
'Surely you will fear me
and accept correction!'
Then her place of refuge^b would not be
destroyed,
nor all my punishments come upon^c her.

^a 12 That is, people from the upper Nile region   ^b 7 Or *her
sanctuary*   ^c 7 Or *all those I appointed over*

2:12 Cushites The reference to Cushites (also rendered "Ethiopians") may be intended to include Egypt. The Cushites invaded and defeated Egypt in 716 BC. The Cushite dynasty in Egypt lasted until 663 BC, when the Assyrian king, Ashurbanipal, took the city of Thebes. On Egypt, see note on Mic 6:4.

2:13 Assyria The Assyrians migrated north from Babylon and settled in the region surrounding Nineveh (Ge 10:11; see note on Isa 10:24). The region was governed by a collection of powerful city-states, including Ashur, Calah and Nineveh. Ashur was located on the west bank of the Tigris River, about 60 miles south of Nineveh, which was situated on the east bank of the Tigris. Calah was located about 20 miles south of Nineveh and was also on the east bank of the Tigris.

2:15 that lived in safety Nineveh was believed to be impregnable because of its strategic location on the Tigris River (compare Zep 3:8). **I am the one! And there is none besides me** This and similar phrases are found in various passages to describe something as incomparable (see Isa 47:8,10). Nineveh is not claiming there are no other cities on earth; rather, she is claiming that no other cities can compare to her.

3:1–8 Having described the judgment of the surrounding

nations, Zephaniah returns to his denouncement of Jerusalem. The prophet's attack takes the form of a woe pronouncement (see Hab 2:6–20).

3:1 Woe to the city of oppressors, rebellious and defiled The prophet introduces another woe pronouncement. Compare Zep 2:5.

3:3 evening wolves As large, mostly nocturnal members of the canine family, wolves stalk their prey at night in large packs. When they make a kill, the pack ferociously fights over pieces of flesh (see Eze 22:27). Most Biblical references to wolves are symbolic, as here.

3:4 Her prophets are unprincipled; they are treacherous people These are false prophets. See Mic 3:5 and note; 3:11. **treacherous people** The prophets were treacherous primarily because they delivered false messages to the nation. They promised peace instead of warning the nation of impending judgment (e.g., Mic 3:5). **Her priests** The descendants of Aaron were responsible for teaching the Law throughout Israel. Instead, their ungodly conduct profaned the temple and brought shame to the practice of the Law.

3:5 LORD within her is righteous Contrasts Yahweh with the wicked leaders of Jerusalem.

But they were still eager
    to act corruptly in all they did.
⁸ Therefore wait for me,"
    declares the LORD,
    "for the day I will stand up to testify.ᵃ
I have decided to assemble the nations,
    to gather the kingdoms
and to pour out my wrath on them—
    all my fierce anger.
The whole world will be consumed
    by the fire of my jealous anger.

Restoration of Israel's Remnant

⁹ "Then I will purify the lips of the peoples,
    that all of them may call on the name of
        the LORD
    and serve him shoulder to shoulder.
¹⁰ From beyond the rivers of Cushᵇ
    my worshipers, my scattered people,
    will bring me offerings.
¹¹ On that day you, Jerusalem, will not be put to
    shame
for all the wrongs you have done to me,
because I will remove from you
    your arrogant boasters.
Never again will you be haughty
    on my holy hill.
¹² But I will leave within you
    the meek and humble.
The remnant of Israel
    will trust in the name of the LORD.
¹³ They will do no wrong;
    they will tell no lies.
A deceitful tongue
    will not be found in their mouths.
They will eat and lie down
    and no one will make them afraid."

¹⁴ Sing, Daughter Zion;
    shout aloud, Israel!
Be glad and rejoice with all your heart,
    Daughter Jerusalem!
¹⁵ The LORD has taken away your punishment,
    he has turned back your enemy.
The LORD, the King of Israel, is with you;
    never again will you fear any harm.
¹⁶ On that day
    they will say to Jerusalem,
"Do not fear, Zion;
    do not let your hands hang limp.
¹⁷ The LORD your God is with you,
    the Mighty Warrior who saves.
He will take great delight in you;
    in his love he will no longer rebuke you,
    but will rejoice over you with singing."

¹⁸ "I will remove from you
    all who mourn over the loss of your
        appointed festivals,
    which is a burden and reproach for you.
¹⁹ At that time I will deal
    with all who oppressed you.
I will rescue the lame;
    I will gather the exiles.
I will give them praise and honor
    in every land where they have suffered
        shame.
²⁰ At that time I will gather you;
    at that time I will bring you home.
I will give you honor and praise
    among all the peoples of the earth
when I restore your fortunesᶜ
    before your very eyes,"
                         says the LORD.

ᵃ 8 Septuagint and Syriac; Hebrew *will rise up to plunder*   ᵇ 10 That is, the upper Nile region   ᶜ 20 Or *I bring back your captives*

3:8 This verse forms an inclusio (indicating bracketing by repetition) with Zep 1:2–3. Both passages announce the coming of divine judgment on the entire earth.

3:9–20 Following the prophetic custom, Zephaniah concludes his book with a message of hope (e.g., Hos 14:1–9; Joel 3:18–21; Am 9:11–15). He begins by announcing the future restoration of the Gentile nations; then he communicates God's promise to restore the Israelites, his chosen people.

3:11 On that day The prophet emphasizes the blessings associated with the Day of Yahweh (Joel 3:16–21; Zec 14:8–9). **your arrogant boasters** This Hebrew phrase also occurs in Isa 13:3, where it describes God's victorious warriors. Here, the emphasis is on those who excitedly brag of their sinful deeds.

3:14–20 Zephaniah ends with salvation and consolation. The people of Jerusalem should rejoice since they no longer have anything to fear; Yahweh has taken away judgment and once again dwells among his people (Zep 3:15,17). Zephaniah's closing message takes up Yahweh's promises throughout the book about salvation and restoration, encouraging faith in the future fulfillment of those promises. The call to rejoice is a call to believe in God's faithfulness.

3:14 Daughter Zion Jerusalem. See note on Isa 1:8.
3:15 LORD, the King of Israel, is with you In the Day of Yahweh, Yahweh himself will reign over the entire earth from Jerusalem (see Joel 3:16–17; Zec 14:9). **harm** The Hebrew term used here, *ra'*, refers to calamity or disaster.
3:16 do not let your hands hang limp The inhabitants of Jerusalem should no longer live in fear (see Isa 13:7–8; Jer 6:24).

HAGGAI

INTRODUCTION TO HAGGAI

The Jews who returned to Jerusalem after the Babylonian exile began rebuilding the temple around 537 BC, but because of opposition they became discouraged and stopped. When Haggai's prophetic career began in 520 BC, he challenged their decision to stop building God's house while they continued building houses for themselves. Haggai aimed to convince the people and their leaders to finish the temple—to make sacrifices to obey God instead of focusing entirely on their own needs.

BACKGROUND

The opening verse attributes the book to the prophet Haggai, whose name is related to the Hebrew word for "festival." It also identifies the date as the second year of Darius I, the king of Persia (who reigned 522–486 BC). The precise dates provided in this book are between August and December 520 BC (Hag 1:1,15; 2:1,10,18,20).

Haggai's prophetic activity is situated during the events narrated in the historical book of Ezra. The first exiles had come to Jerusalem shortly after an earlier Persian king, Cyrus the Great, allowed them to return (538 BC). They had begun to rebuild the temple at that time but had stopped because they encountered opposition from other inhabitants of the land (Ezr 4:1–5,24; 5:16). Beginning in 520 BC, Haggai and another prophet, Zechariah, prophesied to the people (see Zec 1:1). They encouraged the people to begin the work again (Ezr 5:1; 6:14). Their preaching had the intended effect, and with the support of King Darius, the temple was finished around 516 BC (Ezr 6:6–15). Here, we see Yahweh using the power of persuasion and the leader of the international superpower of the time—the king of Persia—to rally support for his intended purposes.

STRUCTURE

The book of Haggai contains four dated messages. In the first message (Hag 1:1–11), the prophet declares that the time has come to honor Yahweh by rebuilding the temple. The governor Zerubbabel, the high priest Joshua, and the people of Judah respond positively to this message (1:12), and Yahweh reassures them of his presence (1:13). In the second message (2:1–9), Yahweh says that the restored temple will be greater than the previous temple that was destroyed. The third message (2:10–19) reveals that the people's uncleanness—meaning the impurity that resulted from their sin and failure to keep God's law—played a part in their difficulties. However, Yahweh will still bless them from that day forward: The return of Yahweh's people to him and the laying of the new temple's foundation represents a critical juncture, one that will result in his blessing. In the fourth and final message (2:20–23), Yahweh announces that he will overthrow existing powerful nations and use Zerubbabel as a signet ring—a sign of Yahweh's rule manifest through the servanthood of Zerubbabel.

OUTLINE

- First message: God's call to rebuild the temple (1:1–11)
- Response to first message (1:12–15)
- Second message: future glory of the temple (2:1–9)
- Third message: uncleanness and blessing (2:10–19)
- Fourth message: prophecy concerning Zerubbabel (2:20–23)

THEMES

Haggai is about people making God's priorities their priorities—a message that applies as much to our lives today as it did in the days of Zerubbabel and Joshua. The book affirms that, if the people of Yahweh devote themselves to his work, he will faithfully finish it.

A secondary theme in Haggai is the promised prosperity of God's people if they will make him their priority. But this promise is not about personal wealth; instead, it is an assurance that Yahweh will provide the necessary resources to accomplish his purposes. Yahweh's presence itself guarantees that his work will be completed, even from beginnings that do not seem favorable according to human standards.

Dates Related to Haggai

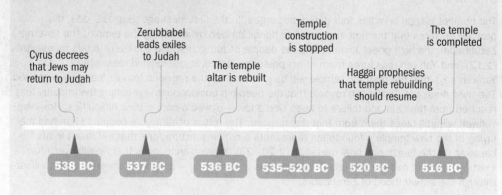

| 538 BC | 537 BC | 536 BC | 535–520 BC | 520 BC | 516 BC |

Cyrus decrees that Jews may return to Judah — Zerubbabel leads exiles to Judah — The temple altar is rebuilt — Temple construction is stopped — Haggai prophesies that temple rebuilding should resume — The temple is completed

* Dates are approximate

Haggai teaches us to make God the priority, to base our actions on faith and to seek Yahweh's presence (2:4–5,10–19). Yahweh reveals his desire to be among his people in the temple-building project. Further, the story of the temple's completion shows us that God is not concerned with the world's standards of honor and wealth (1:8); instead, he seeks our dedication and best efforts, exerted via his Spirit's outpouring.

Yahweh declares that he is with the returned exiles in Haggai (1:13; 2:4). And this is still true— God accompanies those who work for him. When we rely on Yahweh for all things, he will act powerfully among us.

A Call to Build the House of the LORD

1 In the second year of King Darius, on the first day of the sixth month, the word of the LORD came through the prophet Haggai to Zerubbabel son of Shealtiel, governor of Judah, and to Joshua son of Jozadak,[a] the high priest:

2 This is what the LORD Almighty says: "These people say, 'The time has not yet come to rebuild the LORD's house.'"

3 Then the word of the LORD came through the prophet Haggai: 4 "Is it a time for you yourselves to be living in your paneled houses, while this house remains a ruin?"

5 Now this is what the LORD Almighty says: "Give careful thought to your ways. 6 You have planted much, but harvested little. You eat, but never have enough. You drink, but never have your fill. You put on clothes, but are not warm. You earn wages, only to put them in a purse with holes in it."

7 This is what the LORD Almighty says: "Give careful thought to your ways. 8 Go up into the mountains and bring down timber and build my house, so that I may take pleasure in it and be honored," says the LORD. 9 "You expected much, but see, it turned out to be little. What you brought home, I blew away. Why?" declares the LORD Almighty. "Because of my house, which remains a ruin, while each of you is busy with your own house. 10 Therefore, because of you the heavens have withheld their dew and the earth its crops. 11 I called for a drought on the fields and the mountains, on the grain, the new wine, the olive oil and everything else the ground produces, on people and livestock, and on all the labor of your hands."

12 Then Zerubbabel son of Shealtiel, Joshua son of Jozadak, the high priest, and the whole remnant of the people obeyed the voice of the LORD their God and the message of the prophet

a 1 Hebrew *Jehozadak*, a variant of *Jozadak*; also in verses 12 and 14

1:1-11 The opening verse of Haggai establishes the time and place of Haggai's ministry. Haggai was a contemporary of the prophet Zechariah. Both prophets addressed the remnant in Jerusalem—those who had returned after the Babylonian exile of the Jewish people, around 520 BC—and encouraged the people to finish rebuilding the temple. The message in vv. 2–11 reflects the content Haggai preached in Ezr 5:1 that inspired the people to resume work on the temple (compare Hag 1:12; Ezr 5:2). See the timeline "Approximate Dates of Old Testament Prophets" on p. 1070.

1:1 second year of King Darius Refers to 520 BC. Darius I Hystaspes was ruler of the Persian Empire from 522–486 BC (see note on Ezr 4:5). **the word of the LORD** A common way for the prophets to identify their messages as coming from Yahweh. Compare Joel 1:1; Mic 1:1; Zep 1:1. **Haggai** Meaning "festival." This name suggests Haggai may have been born on a religious holiday. The details of his ancestry are missing—a noteworthy omission considering the emphasis on genealogies in texts from after the exile (e.g., 1Ch 1–9; Ezr 7:1–5; Zec 1:1) and the recording of the fathers' names (patronyms) of both Zerubbabel and Joshua (1:1). Haggai was a contemporary of Zechariah; the beginning of his ministry preceded that of Zechariah by about two months. Although chronological notations indicate that Haggai's ministry lasted less than four months, he probably served much longer. Haggai carefully dates each of his four prophecies. His ministry began with his first prophetic utterance on the first day of the sixth month (Elul) of the second year of the Persian King Darius (Hag 1:1). This date corresponds to August 29, 520 BC. The prophet's second discourse was delivered on the twenty-first day of the seventh month (Tishri; 2:1; October 17, 520 BC). Haggai's third and fourth messages were delivered on the twenty-fourth day of the ninth month (Chislev; 2:10,20; December 18, 520 BC). **Zerubbabel son of Shealtiel** A leader of the postexilic community. He was appointed governor of the Persian province of Judah (Yehud). See Ezr 2:2 and note. **Joshua** The first high priest of the remnant who reestablished worship of Yahweh in Jerusalem. See note on Zec 3:1.

1:2 LORD Almighty This divine title is used throughout the book of Haggai. It evokes the idea that Yahweh commands heavenly beings, including cherubim and seraphim (compare Jos 5:14; note on Isa 1:9). **These people** This phrase provides a sense of detachment between Haggai and the rest of the community. It indicates that the prophet has a different opinion. **The time has not yet come to rebuild** Initially, those who had returned from exile had started to rebuild the temple (see Ezr 3:1–13). However, the project was halted when the people became fearful of surrounding enemies—foreigners who opposed the efforts of the Jews (see Ezr 4:1–5). By Haggai's day, work on the temple had been suspended for 16 years.

1:4 your paneled houses Many of the Israelites' homes had been decorated with ornate paneling. The Hebrew word used here is the same word used in 1Ki 6:9 to describe the opulent interior of Solomon's temple. See the infographic "Solomon's Temple" on p. 520. **this house remains a ruin** The nation's priorities were misplaced; the people had focused on decorating their homes instead of rebuilding the temple.

1:6 You have planted much Throughout this verse, the prophet emphasizes how the people's efforts to improve their own lives have proved futile while they have ignored the important task of restoring Yahweh's house.

1:8 bring down timber The famous cedars of Lebanon. Following the example of Solomon (compare 2Ch 2:16), the people contracted the Phoenicians to bring timber from the region of Lebanon to the port city of Joppa when they began to rebuild the temple (Ezr 3:7).

1:11 drought Prolonged lack of water resulted in drought, which had a significant effect on an agrarian society. It was commonly viewed as divine judgment (compare 1Ki 8:35), and Yahweh explicitly takes credit for causing this hardship to punish the people for not diligently working on the temple.

1:12-15 Haggai's message inspires the correct response: Zerubbabel, Joshua and the rest of the people restart their work on the temple. The project resumes on the twenty-fourth day of the sixth month, several weeks after the oracle of Haggai 1:1–11 (dated to the first day of the sixth month).

Haggai, because the LORD their God had sent him. And the people feared the LORD.

[13] Then Haggai, the LORD's messenger, gave this message of the LORD to the people: "I am with you," declares the LORD. [14] So the LORD stirred up the spirit of Zerubbabel son of Shealtiel, governor of Judah, and the spirit of Joshua son of Jozadak, the high priest, and the spirit of the whole remnant of the people. They came and began to work on the house of the LORD Almighty, their God, [15] on the twenty-fourth day of the sixth month.

The Promised Glory of the New House

2 In the second year of King Darius, [1] on the twenty-first day of the seventh month, the word of the LORD came through the prophet Haggai: [2] "Speak to Zerubbabel son of Shealtiel, governor of Judah, to Joshua son of Jozadak,[a] the high priest, and to the remnant of the people. Ask them, [3] 'Who of you is left who saw this house in its former glory? How does it look to you now? Does it not seem to you like nothing? [4] But now be strong, Zerubbabel,' declares the LORD. 'Be strong, Joshua son of Jozadak, the high priest. Be strong, all you people of the land,' declares the LORD, 'and work. For I am with you,' declares the LORD Almighty. [5] 'This is what I covenanted with you when you came out of Egypt. And my Spirit remains among you. Do not fear.'

[6] "This is what the LORD Almighty says: 'In a little while I will once more shake the heavens and the earth, the sea and the dry land. [7] I will shake all nations, and what is desired by all nations will come, and I will fill this house with glory,' says the LORD Almighty. [8] 'The silver is mine and the gold is mine,' declares the LORD Almighty. [9] 'The glory of this present house will be greater than the glory of the former house,' says the LORD Almighty. 'And in this place I will grant peace,' declares the LORD Almighty."

[a] 2 Hebrew *Jehozadak*, a variant of *Jozadak*; also in verse 4

1:13 the LORD's messenger Here the Hebrew phrase *malakh yhwh* refers to the prophet as God's messenger, but the OT often uses the phrase to refer to the "angel of Yahweh" (e.g., Ge 22:11; Ex 3:2; Jdg 13:3; Zec 1:11). The word denoting "messenger" (*malakh*) is common for human messengers speaking on behalf of their masters (Ge 32:3,6; 1Ki 20:2; 2Ki 19:9), but it is rarely used to refer to the prophets as human messengers speaking for God (Isa 42:19; 44:26; Mal 2:7; 3:1). A prophet and a messenger had essentially the same role. Both spoke on behalf of one greater than themselves (compare 1Ki 20:2,5). **I am with you** One of the great divine promises in the Bible (compare Mt 28:20). Yahweh gives the same message to Isaac (Ge 26:24), Jacob (Ge 28:15), the Israelites (Isa 41:10; 43:5; Jer 30:11; 46:28) and Jeremiah (Jer 1:8,19; 15:20). Similar language is also used in Yahweh's promises to Moses (Ex 3:12), Joshua (Dt 31:23; Jos 1:5; 3:7) and Gideon (Jdg 6:16).
1:14 the spirit The Hebrew term used here is describing a person's volitional will. God gave them the desire and willingness to work on the temple. **house of the LORD Almighty** The community would continue to work on the temple for the next five years, finally completing the project on the third day of Adar (the twelfth month, roughly February—March) in the sixth year of Darius (March 12, 515 BC in the modern calendar; compare Ezr 6:15).

2:1–9 Haggai again addresses Zerubbabel and Joshua, reassuring them with a message promising Yahweh's presence (Hag 2:4; compare 1:13). Even though their temple appears inadequate in comparison to Solomon's, Yahweh assures them that his glory will be present there just as it was for the earlier temple (compare v. 7 and 1Ki 8:10–11).

2:1 on the twenty-first day of the seventh month The seventh month was Tishri (September—October). This day was the seventh day of the Festival of Tabernacles (compare Nu 29:32–34). The year is still the second year of Darius as noted in Hag 1:15 and repeated in v. 10. See the table "Israelite Calendar" on p. 763. **through the prophet Haggai** A shift from the typical prophetic formula (e.g., Hos 1:1; Zep 1:1). In Haggai, the word of

Yahweh comes literally "by the hand of" the prophet, perhaps emphasizing the prophet's role as Yahweh's agent. Compare Hag 1:1.
2:2 the remnant of the people These Jews returned to Judah from Babylon in 538 BC. See the timeline "Dates Related to Ezra, Nehemiah and Esther" on p. 716.
2:3 Who of you is left The Solomonic temple had been destroyed by the Babylonians in 586 BC. The date is now 520 BC. See the timeline "Approximate Dates of Old Testament Prophets" on p. 1070. **this house** The Solomonic temple was approximately 90 feet long, 30 feet wide, and 45 feet high. It was constructed on Mount Moriah (compare Ge 22:2) at the threshing floor of Araunah. Mount Moriah was located just north of the City of David. Like the tabernacle, the temple was divided into the most Holy Place (the Holy of Holies), the Holy Place and an outer courtyard. The most Holy Place was 30 feet long and the Holy Place was 60 feet long. The ark of the covenant, the most important piece of furniture in the temple, was placed in the most Holy Place. The temple was completed in 960 BC, seven years after the start of construction. See the infographic "Solomon's Temple" on p. 520; see the infographic "The Most Holy Place" on p. 525.
2:4 be strong, Zerubbabel These words resemble Yahweh's words to Joshua at the commencement of his ministry (see Jos 1:6,7,9).
2:5 my Spirit This may refer to the Holy Spirit; but the Hebrew term here could be used in the sense of power, inspiration or divine presence and providence (Ne 9:20), recalling Yahweh's presence with his people during the exodus (Ex 14:24; Nu 12:5).
2:6 shake the heavens and the earth The coming of Yahweh is figuratively described as an earthquake.
2:7 what is desired by all nations will come This phrase indicates a future period in which all nations will come to Jerusalem to worship (see note on Isa 60:5; compare Isa 60:5–7; 66:18–20). **I will fill this house with glory** The future temple will once again be filled with the glory of Yahweh (compare Eze 43:5; compare 1Ki 8:11).
2:9 And in this place I will grant peace The Hebrew word used here, *shalom*, meaning "peace," is a play

Blessings for a Defiled People

¹⁰On the twenty-fourth day of the ninth month, in the second year of Darius, the word of the LORD came to the prophet Haggai: ¹¹"This is what the LORD Almighty says: 'Ask the priests what the law says: ¹²If someone carries consecrated meat in the fold of their garment, and that fold touches some bread or stew, some wine, olive oil or other food, does it become consecrated?'"

The priests answered, "No."

¹³Then Haggai said, "If a person defiled by contact with a dead body touches one of these things, does it become defiled?"

"Yes," the priests replied, "it becomes defiled."

¹⁴Then Haggai said, "'So it is with this people and this nation in my sight,' declares the LORD. 'Whatever they do and whatever they offer there is defiled.

¹⁵"'Now give careful thought to this from this day onᵃ—consider how things were before one stone was laid on another in the LORD's tem-

ple. ¹⁶When anyone came to a heap of twenty measures, there were only ten. When anyone went to a wine vat to draw fifty measures, there were only twenty. ¹⁷I struck all the work of your hands with blight, mildew and hail, yet you did not return to me,' declares the LORD. ¹⁸'From this day on, from this twenty-fourth day of the ninth month, give careful thought to the day when the foundation of the LORD's temple was laid. Give careful thought: ¹⁹Is there yet any seed left in the barn? Until now, the vine and the fig tree, the pomegranate and the olive tree have not borne fruit.

"'From this day on I will bless you.'"

Zerubbabel the LORD's Signet Ring

²⁰The word of the LORD came to Haggai a second time on the twenty-fourth day of the month: ²¹"Tell Zerubbabel governor of Judah that I am

ᵃ 15 Or to the days past

---

on the name Jerusalem, which means "city of peace." Peace will be the result of the coming of the King (Zec 9:9–10). **this place** Jerusalem in general or, more specifically, the temple.

2:10–19 This oracle uses priestly regulations and agricultural imagery to communicate the point that the people's failure to complete the temple was a sin that had caused a general state of uncleanness. That unclean state affected everything because Yahweh was not blessing their efforts. Their earlier sacrifices were not accepted because of the uncleanness (Hag 2:14). They also suffered from crop failures and natural disasters as a result (v. 17). Now that the people have resumed work on the temple, they can be assured that they will receive Yahweh's blessings (v. 19). Since this oracle dates to a few months after the work resumed (1:14–15), Haggai could be drawing attention to an improvement in their agricultural production that season: The situation turned around when the people returned to work on the temple.

2:10 On the twenty-fourth day of the ninth month The people have now been working on the temple for almost three months. Zechariah began his ministry during this period (Zec 1:1). The ninth month was Chislev (November—December). The harvest for the season would have been complete by that time. See the timeline "Approximate Dates of Old Testament Prophets" on p. 1070.

2:12 consecrated meat Meat that had been offered as a sacrifice. Most likely the meat would be from a fellowship offering (see Lev 3:1–17). Anyone who was ritually clean could eat the meat from that sacrifice. For other sacrifices, only the priests could eat or handle the meat. **some bread or stew, some wine, olive oil** This is common food, not something that would be offered on the altar. The question is whether holiness can be transferred indirectly; it cannot.

2:13 a person defiled Dead bodies contaminated all who touched them (see Nu 19:11). While holiness cannot be transmitted indirectly, uncleanness can be.

2:14 So it is with this people Haggai applies the priests' answer to the people. The process of being

made clean or holy before Yahweh requires intentional effort. Becoming impure, on the other hand, requires no effort, only contact with the unclean. The lesson for the people was that they had not taken appropriate action to deal with their uncleanness. Their failure to rebuild the temple created a cloud of disobedience over all they did.

2:15 consider how things were before one stone was laid on another Refers to the time prior to restarting the temple project. Possibly Zerubbabel and Joshua held a ceremony to mark the day when work resumed, so this could be a reference to the formal placing of a symbolic stone to commemorate the event (compare Zec 3:8–10; 4:6–10).

2:16 a heap of twenty The Hebrew does not specify the measure used. Grain was usually measured in homers (see Hos 3:2) or ephahs (see 1Sa 17:17). Liquid was usually measured in baths or cors (see Eze 45:14). The point is that grain yield was half of what was expected and wine production was 40 percent of what was expected.

2:17 I struck Haggai's language closely echoes Am 4:9. The message of Am 4 is similar to Haggai's: Israel sinned and was suffering the consequences. Even though they were experiencing the fallout from their sinfulness, they still stubbornly refused to repent and return to Yahweh so that he might restore his blessing on the land. **blight** The Hebrew word used here refers to a condition caused by scorching winds from the eastern desert. Compare Am 4:9.

2:19 I will bless you The people can take comfort in the assurance that Yahweh will bless their obedience.

2:20–23 Haggai's closing verses emphasize the future hope of redemption represented by Yahweh's Messiah at the coming Day of Yahweh, when Yahweh will claim victory over all the kingdoms of the earth and establish his ideal kingdom.

2:21 shake the heavens and the earth Symbolizes the cosmic upheaval that accompanies the arrival of the Divine Warrior (compare note on Hag 2:6). Zerubbabel—like other anointed figures for Yahweh's ministry—foreshadows Christ, who personifies their calling in perfect form (see Heb 12:1–2; note on Zec 6:13). The imagery

going to shake the heavens and the earth. ²²I will overturn royal thrones and shatter the power of the foreign kingdoms. I will overthrow chariots and their drivers; horses and their riders will fall, each by the sword of his brother.

²³"'On that day,' declares the LORD Almighty, 'I will take you, my servant Zerubbabel son of Shealtiel,' declares the LORD, 'and I will make you like my signet ring, for I have chosen you,' declares the LORD Almighty."

---

of cosmic upheaval is also associated with the coming of the Son of Man (see Mt 24:29–35).
2:23 that day Refers to the day of Yahweh (see Joel 2:1; 1:15 and note; Am 5:18; Ob 15; Zep 1:7). **signet ring** A stamp seal. In this passage, Zerubbabel is identified as a signet ring, the symbol that the Davidic line was still in place, thus reversing the curse placed upon Jehoiachin (Coniah) in Jer 22:24. In patriarchal times, the stamp seal was worn on a cord around the neck; later, it was worn as a ring on a finger. The stamp was engraved by a jeweler with a unique symbol. Stamp seals were most often used to seal correspondence by imprinting the stamp on soft clay or wax placed over the crease of a letter, thus guaranteeing that the contents of the letter were authorized by the bearer of the signet ring. See the infographic "Royal Seals of Judah" on p. 593.

ZECHARIAH

INTRODUCTION TO ZECHARIAH

Zechariah's prophecies were delivered when God's people had returned to the promised land after their exile in Babylon. Although the messages address a specific situation, they also are timeless. Zechariah encouraged the leaders of Jerusalem and called the Jewish people to rebuild the temple—and he looked forward to the ultimate fulfillment of Yahweh's promise to restore and save.

BACKGROUND

Like the prophet Haggai, Zechariah appears in 520 BC as a prophet to the Jewish exiles who returned to the promised land. Zechariah's efforts are set against the backdrop of a trying time for God's people. The story of Zechariah really begins back in 586 BC, when the Babylonian king Nebuchadnezzar destroyed Jerusalem and took most of its people back to Babylon (2Ki 25:1–21). In 538 BC the Persian king Cyrus allowed these deported Jews to return to their land and to begin rebuilding the temple (2Ch 36:22–23; Ezr 1:1–4). The historical book of Nehemiah identifies Zechariah as part of a priestly family that returned to Jerusalem under the leadership of Zerubbabel the governor and the high priest Joshua (Ne 12:4,16).

Although the returning exiles were initially enthusiastic to rebuild the temple, they soon encountered opposition and persecution from other people living in Judah, and they ceased working. After Haggai and Zechariah urged the people to finish the project, they resumed rebuilding the temple in 520 BC (Ezr 4:24), and in 516 BC they finished its construction (Ezr 6:15).

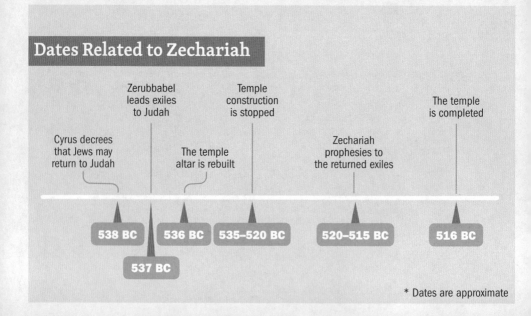

Dates Related to Zechariah

Cyrus decrees that Jews may return to Judah	Zerubbabel leads exiles to Judah	The temple altar is rebuilt	Temple construction is stopped	Zechariah prophesies to the returned exiles	The temple is completed
538 BC	537 BC	536 BC	535–520 BC	520–515 BC	516 BC

* Dates are approximate

STRUCTURE

The book of Zechariah has five sections. It begins with an introductory call to repentance (Zec 1:1–6). The second, and longest, section (1:7—6:15) describes Zechariah's eight visions, which he uses to challenge the people to rebuild the temple and affirm the leadership of Joshua and Zerubbabel. In the third section (7:1—8:23), four messages highlight the restoration of God's relationship with his people, as summed up in God's proclamation that they shall be his people and he will be their God (8:8).

The latter half of the book presents two oracles that use typical features of apocalyptic literature. The term "apocalyptic" comes from the Greek word meaning "revelation" or "uncovering," and apocalyptic texts often describe visions using symbolic language and angelic interpreters. Other examples of apocalyptic literature within the Bible include the second half of Daniel and the New Testament book of Revelation. The first of Zechariah's apocalyptic oracles (9:1—11:17) presents the coming messianic king as a warrior who will fight for Yahweh's people. In the second oracle (12:1—14:21), the Messiah's suffering leads to God's ultimate victory. The New Testament includes many references to this part of Zechariah.

OUTLINE

- A call to repentance (1:1–6)
- Eight night visions and Joshua's crowning (1:7—6:15)
- Four prophetic messages (7:1—8:23)
- Two apocalyptic oracles (9:1—14:21)

THEMES

Zechariah's message is one of encouragement: He tells the returned exiles that, in spite of humble appearances, God truly cares about Jerusalem and its temple. When Zechariah looked at the stalled rebuilding project, he saw God's vision for what it could be and sought to communicate that vision to the people. More important, he encouraged the people so that, just as God had returned to them, they would return to God and follow his ways.

Zechariah's vision of the future contained more than a rebuilt temple and a restored community. The later chapters in Zechariah look forward to the coming of a humble ruler from the house of David. The New Testament writers saw the fulfillment of this prophecy in Jesus (9:9–11; Mt 21:5; Jn 12:15).

It can be challenging to fully complete a task—especially when we struggle to see beyond our immediate circumstances or are opposed by outside forces. At these times, it can help to refocus and to try to see things from God's point of view. Zechariah reminds us that when we are discouraged, we must look to Yahweh for direction (Zec 4:10). Yahweh is the ultimate cosmic force—and he is victorious through Jesus.

A Call to Return to the Lord

1 In the eighth month of the second year of Darius, the word of the Lord came to the prophet Zechariah son of Berekiah, the son of Iddo:

² "The Lord was very angry with your ancestors. ³ Therefore tell the people: This is what the Lord Almighty says: 'Return to me,' declares the Lord Almighty, 'and I will return to you,' says the Lord Almighty. ⁴ Do not be like your ancestors, to whom the earlier prophets proclaimed: This is what the Lord Almighty says: 'Turn from your evil ways and your evil practices.' But they would not listen or pay attention to me, declares the Lord. ⁵ Where are your ancestors now? And the prophets, do they live forever? ⁶ But did not my words and my decrees, which I commanded my servants the prophets, overtake your ancestors?

"Then they repented and said, 'The Lord Almighty has done to us what our ways and practices deserve, just as he determined to do.'"

The Man Among the Myrtle Trees

⁷ On the twenty-fourth day of the eleventh month, the month of Shebat, in the second year of Darius, the word of the Lord came to the prophet Zechariah son of Berekiah, the son of Iddo.

⁸ During the night I had a vision, and there before me was a man mounted on a red horse. He was standing among the myrtle trees in a ravine. Behind him were red, brown and white horses.

1:1—8:23 Zechariah is set after the Jewish people had experienced exile in Babylon following the desolation and complete takeover of their land by foreign powers. Zechariah prophesied to a small community of Jews living among the ruins of Jerusalem after returning from exile in Babylon. This community had begun rebuilding the temple on their initial return around 537 BC (Ezr 3:10–12), but the work had stopped when the Jews faced opposition from their neighbors (Ezr 4:4–5). The prophets Haggai and Zechariah encouraged the community to begin rebuilding again (Ezr 5:1–2; Zec 4:9).

The book of Zechariah is commonly divided into two major sections—chs. 1–8 and chs. 9–14. This first section is dominated by a series of eight visions, culminating in the crowning of Joshua, the high priest (6:9–15). The section concludes with a series of four messages addressing proper worship, reflecting on Israel's past failures, and looking ahead to divine restoration (7:1–8:23). See the timeline "Approximate Dates of Old Testament Prophets" on p. 1070.

1:1 eighth month Corresponding to late October and early November. Zechariah's ministry began about a month before Haggai received his final vision (see Hag 2:10,20). See table "Israelite Calendar" on p. 763. **second year of Darius** 520 BC. Darius I Hystaspes ruled Persia from 522–486 BC (see note on Hag 1:1). The visions of Zec 1–6 date to the same period as the events in Ezr 4:24—6:13. **word of the Lord** A standard introductory formula used by the prophets to indicate that they were communicating God's words, not their own (e.g., Hos 1:1; Joel 1:1; Mic 1:1; Hag 1:1; Zep 1:1; see note on Isa 1:10). **Zechariah** A member of one of the priestly families of Judah. His name means "Yahweh remembers." His grandfather Iddo had returned from the exile with Zerubbabel (Ne 12:1–7). Zechariah eventually became the head of the priestly clan of Iddo (Ne 12:16). Although Zechariah was the son of Berekiah (also rendered "Berechiah") and the grandson of Iddo (Zec 1:1,7), the book of Ezra indicates he was a descendant of Iddo (Ezr 5:1; 6:14)—likely to indicate that he was a member of that priestly family. Zechariah probably was a young man when he began to prophesy; the Hebrew term used to identify him in Zec 2:4 typically means "boy" or "youth." Like Jeremiah and Ezekiel, Zechariah was both a prophet and a priest. The writing prophet (and priest) Zechariah must be distinguished from the priest Zechariah who was killed by King Joash around 800 BC (2Ch 24:20–22; compare note on Mt 23:35).

1:3 Lord Almighty The title emphasizes Yahweh's role as commander-in-chief of the heavenly armies, evoking the metaphor of Yahweh as a warrior (see 1Sa 17:45). **Return** The Hebrew term used here conveys the idea of repentance (e.g., Jer 25:5; 35:15; Mal 3:7). This command to repent, placed at the beginning of Zechariah, functions as a call to the people to turn to Yahweh and demonstrate their commitment to him by rebuilding the temple. See Jer 15:19 and note.
1:4 Turn from your evil ways Zechariah probably isn't referring to a specific prophet, but the call to return evokes the essence of Jeremiah's preaching (see Jer 15:19; 18:11; 25:5; 35:15).

1:7—6:8 This passage records eight visions that appear to be in a rough chronological sequence stretching from the time of writing to the coming of the Messiah. The overriding theme of the visions is the expectation of the coming Messiah. This first vision seems to parallel the eighth vision (Zec 6:1–8), as both feature four kinds of horses. The remaining visions also seem to be structured in parallel, in order to present the oracle about the Messianic Branch (3:8–10) as the central point of chs. 1–6. The first vision in 1:7–17 is a pronouncement of hope for the nation. Yahweh promised to put an end to Jerusalem's 70 years of misery and return the people to the city with comfort and compassion. Zechariah may have experienced all eight visions in a single night, but the text never explicitly indicates this. Since a date is given only at 1:7—and because the vision reports are presented in a continuous chain linked by the formula "I lifted my eyes and saw"—it can be inferred that Zechariah saw one vision after another in close succession.

1:7 the twenty-fourth day of the eleventh month The vision dates to January or February of 519 BC, a few months after the message delivered in vv. 1–6.
1:8 a man mounted on a red horse This figure is sometimes referred to as "man" (vv. 8,10) and other times explicitly identified as the angel of Yahweh (v. 11). Similar imagery is used in Rev 6:4. He appears to be distinct from the angelic messenger guiding Zechariah through the vision (Zec 1:9,13–14). **myrtle trees** A fragrant tree whose branches were often used in connection with the Festival of Tabernacles (Ne 8:15). Isaiah depicts myrtle replacing nettle (a desert plant) in the renewal of creation accompanying Yahweh's salvation of his people, often taken to refer to the establishment of the Messiah's reign (Isa 55:13).

⁹I asked, "What are these, my lord?"

The angel who was talking with me answered, "I will show you what they are."

¹⁰Then the man standing among the myrtle trees explained, "They are the ones the Lᴏʀᴅ has sent to go throughout the earth."

¹¹And they reported to the angel of the Lᴏʀᴅ who was standing among the myrtle trees, "We have gone throughout the earth and found the whole world at rest and in peace."

¹²Then the angel of the Lᴏʀᴅ said, "Lᴏʀᴅ Almighty, how long will you withhold mercy from Jerusalem and from the towns of Judah, which you have been angry with these seventy years?" ¹³So the Lᴏʀᴅ spoke kind and comforting words to the angel who talked with me.

¹⁴Then the angel who was speaking to me said, "Proclaim this word: This is what the Lᴏʀᴅ Almighty says: 'I am very jealous for Jerusalem and Zion, ¹⁵and I am very angry with the nations that feel secure. I was only a little angry, but they went too far with the punishment.'

¹⁶"Therefore this is what the Lᴏʀᴅ says: 'I will return to Jerusalem with mercy, and there my house will be rebuilt. And the measuring line will be stretched out over Jerusalem,' declares the Lᴏʀᴅ Almighty.

¹⁷"Proclaim further: This is what the Lᴏʀᴅ Almighty says: 'My towns will again overflow with prosperity, and the Lᴏʀᴅ will again comfort Zion and choose Jerusalem.'"

Four Horns and Four Craftsmen

¹⁸Then I looked up, and there before me were four horns. ¹⁹I asked the angel who was speaking to me, "What are these?"

He answered me, "These are the horns that scattered Judah, Israel and Jerusalem."

²⁰Then the Lᴏʀᴅ showed me four craftsmen. ²¹I asked, "What are these coming to do?"

He answered, "These are the horns that scattered Judah so that no one could raise their head, but the craftsmen have come to terrify them and throw down these horns of the nations who lifted up their horns against the land of Judah to scatter its people."ᵃ

A Man With a Measuring Line

2ᵇ Then I looked up, and there before me was a man with a measuring line in his hand. ²I asked, "Where are you going?"

ᵃ 21 In Hebrew texts 1:18-21 is numbered 2:1-4.   ᵇ In Hebrew texts 2:1-13 is numbered 2:5-17.

1:9 The angel An angelic messenger, probably distinct from the Angel of Yahweh in this instance.

Zechariah 1:9

MAL'AKH
The Hebrew term *mal'akh*, often translated "angel" or "messenger," is used more than 200 times throughout the OT to identify human messengers, angelic messengers and the divine Messenger (the Angel of Yahweh; see Ge 16:7; Ex 3:2; Jdg 13:21).

1:11 the angel of the Lᴏʀᴅ Identifies the man in Zec 1:8 and 1:10 as the Angel of Yahweh. **found the whole world at rest** Based on the angel's reaction in v. 12, the report that the earth is at rest is likely critical of the nations' selfish inactivity (compare Isa 30:7; Jer 48:11; Eze 16:49).

1:12 how long will you withhold mercy The angel's question alludes to earlier prophetic messages about the nature and extent of God's displeasure with his people (see Isa 6:11–13; Hos 1:6–7). **these seventy years** The nation had been afflicted for 70 years in fulfillment of the prophecies of Jeremiah (see Jer 25:11–12; 29:10). The angel's request indicates that the return of exiles from Babylon did not necessarily mark the fulfillment of the 70 years. See note on Ezr 1:1; note on Jer 25:11.

1:16 with mercy God's displeasure with his people was temporary. The language of restoration in vv. 13–17 fulfills promises such as Jer 31:20 (compare Isa 40:1–2; Hos 2:1). **my house** Refers to the temple. The fulfillment of Yahweh's promise for restoration lies in the rebuilding of the temple and the city. Compare 4:9; Ezr 6:14.

measuring line The measuring line was used in both construction and demolition, making the image useful as a metaphor for both judgment (e.g., 2Ki 21:13; Isa 34:11; La 2:8) and restoration (compare Isa 34:17; Eze 40:3).
1:17 comfort The Hebrew term used here is often used to describe Yahweh's post-judgment attitude toward his people. Compare Isa 12:1; 40:1; Jer 31:13.

Zechariah 1:17

NACHAM
The Hebrew word *nacham*, often translated "comfort," can describe regret, remorse, comfort, compassion or consolation. The theme of divine comfort and restoration of God's people following their punishment is prominent in prophetic salvation oracles (e.g., Isa 12:1–6; 40–66; Jer 31). The experience of judgment or suffering is often characterized by a lack of comfort (see La 1:2,9,16–17,21; Job 16:2; Ps 69:20).

1:18–21 Zechariah's second vision depicts God's judgment on the nations that were responsible for the dispersion of the Israelites.

1:18 four horns Animal horns are a common ancient Near Eastern symbol for political and military power.
1:19 the horns that scattered Represents the nations that used their power to scatter the Israelites across foreign lands.
1:21 throw down these horns of the nations Yahweh sends four craftsmen to destroy the four horns.

2:1–13 The third vision reveals the importance of Jerusalem in God's restoration program for Israel. Rebuilding

He answered me, "To measure Jerusalem, to find out how wide and how long it is."

³While the angel who was speaking to me was leaving, another angel came to meet him ⁴and said to him: "Run, tell that young man, 'Jerusalem will be a city without walls because of the great number of people and animals in it. ⁵And I myself will be a wall of fire around it,' declares the LORD, 'and I will be its glory within.'

⁶"Come! Come! Flee from the land of the north," declares the LORD, "for I have scattered you to the four winds of heaven," declares the LORD.

⁷"Come, Zion! Escape, you who live in Daughter Babylon!" ⁸For this is what the LORD Almighty says: "After the Glorious One has sent me against the nations that have plundered you — for whoever touches you touches the apple of his eye — ⁹I will surely raise my hand against them so that their slaves will plunder them.ᵃ Then you will know that the LORD Almighty has sent me.

¹⁰"Shout and be glad, Daughter Zion. For I am coming, and I will live among you," declares the LORD. ¹¹"Many nations will be joined with the LORD in that day and will become my people. I will live among you and you will know that the LORD Almighty has sent me to you. ¹²The LORD will inherit Judah as his portion in the holy land and will again choose Jerusalem. ¹³Be still before the LORD, all mankind, because he has roused himself from his holy dwelling."

Clean Garments for the High Priest

3 Then he showed me Joshua the high priest standing before the angel of the LORD, and Satanᵇ standing at his right side to accuse him. ²The LORD said to Satan, "The LORD rebuke you, Satan! The LORD, who has chosen Jerusalem, rebuke you! Is not this man a burning stick snatched from the fire?"

³Now Joshua was dressed in filthy clothes as he stood before the angel. ⁴The angel said to those who were standing before him, "Take off his filthy clothes."

ᵃ 8,9 Or *says after . . . eye:* ⁹"*I . . . plunder them.*"   ᵇ 1 Hebrew *satan* means *adversary.*

---

the city was a necessary part of the restoration, but this vision points ahead to the ultimate fulfillment of a city protected by Yahweh's presence (v. 5; compare Rev 21:1–4), not physical walls. The Babylonians' destruction of the city and temple was caused not by the failure of Jerusalem's physical defenses, but by the withdrawal of Yahweh's protective presence (compare Eze 10:18–19). Rebuilding the temple will make way for Yahweh's presence to return because Yahweh desires a Holy Place to dwell. The vision addresses the conflicting priorities of the returned exiles: rebuild the temple, or rebuild the city walls in order to protect the temple. Yahweh's messenger is informing them of the proper priority—rebuilding the temple.

2:1 a man with a measuring line This figure with a measuring line is likely in the background of Rev 11:1, which draws on imagery from Zechariah (see note on Zec 1:16) and Ezekiel (see Eze 40:3 and note).

2:4 without walls The population of Jerusalem will be so great that it cannot be contained by a walled city. An unwalled city also symbolized openness to all who would come (see Zec 8:20–22; compare Eze 38:11). The image points to a future fulfillment when all Israel and all the nations are gathered under Yahweh's rule, a prominent theme throughout the Prophets.

2:5 a wall of fire around it The message revealed to Zechariah is that Jerusalem does not need walls because Yahweh himself will protect it when his presence returns to the city (see note on Zec 2:1–13). **I will be its glory within** Refers to the glory of Yahweh that inhabited the tabernacle and temple (Ex 40:35; 1Ki 8:11). In Isaiah, God's glory among his people often symbolized salvation and restoration (see Isa 4:5; 24:23; 60:18–19).

2:6–13 The third vision is followed by prophetic oracles emphasizing themes from the earlier visions: the restoration of Israel and judgment on the nations. The oracle in Zec 2:6–9 calls for Jewish exiles still living among the nations to return to Zion before Yahweh judges those nations. The oracle in vv. 10–12 emphasizes Yahweh's intention to return to Zion and gather Israel and the nations to worship together. The section ends by affirming that Yahweh has set his plan in motion to fulfill the promises of salvation and restoration (v. 13).

2:6 land of the north May refer to Babylon, but this phrase probably is used figuratively for the foreign lands where Jewish exiles were scattered. Jeremiah refers to the north as the direction from which both invasion and returning exiles would come (Jer 3:18; 6:22; 10:22; 16:15; 31:8). **the four winds of heaven** See note on Zec 6:5.

2:10 Daughter Zion A metaphor for the inhabitants of Jerusalem. See note on Isa 1:8.

2:11 will become my people The Israelites were the original people of Yahweh, the nation he redeemed from Egypt (see Ex 3:7; 5:1; 6:7). This verse proclaims that foreigners have the same opportunity to become the people of God. See note on Jer 30:22; note on Eze 11:20; compare Zec 8:7–8.

2:12 will inherit The Hebrew verb used here commonly appears in legal texts of the OT in reference to a property acquisition or an inheritance. See note on Eze 36:12. **holy land** This is the only occurrence of the Hebrew phrase used here in the OT, but the same concept of sacred space appears elsewhere in the Hebrew text with designations such as "holy ground" (Ex 3:5) or "holy mountain" (Isa 11:9).

2:13 he has roused himself from his holy dwelling Yahweh is coming from the heavenly temple to make Jerusalem his home (Zec 1:16; 2:5).

3:1–7 Zechariah's fourth vision describes the nation's cleansing from sin and the reinstatement of its priestly office and functions (compare Ex 19:6). The vision reestablishes the authority of the Zadokite priesthood and addresses some of the criticisms toward it in the last part of Isaiah (which also seems to address the situation of the early postexilic community; compare Isa 57:1–10; 58:1–5). Zechariah's vision emphasizes the purification of the high priest, allowing him to properly represent the people before Yahweh.

Then he said to Joshua, "See, I have taken away your sin, and I will put fine garments on you."

⁵Then I said, "Put a clean turban on his head." So they put a clean turban on his head and clothed him, while the angel of the LORD stood by.

⁶The angel of the LORD gave this charge to Joshua: ⁷"This is what the LORD Almighty says: 'If you will walk in obedience to me and keep my requirements, then you will govern my house and have charge of my courts, and I will give you a place among these standing here.

⁸"'Listen, High Priest Joshua, you and your associates seated before you, who are men symbolic of things to come: I am going to bring my servant, the Branch. ⁹See, the stone I have set in front of Joshua! There are seven eyes*ᵃ* on that one stone, and I will engrave an inscription on it,' says the LORD Almighty, 'and I will remove the sin of this land in a single day.

¹⁰"'In that day each of you will invite your

ᵃ 9 Or *facets*

3:1 Joshua Refers to Joshua son of Jozadak (also rendered "Jehozadak"), the first high priest of the remnant that returned from exile. The Hebrew name for Joshua, *yehoshua'*, means "Yahweh is salvation" or "Yahweh saves." The name "Jesus" derives from this name. **angel of the LORD** Representing Yahweh himself in the vision (see note on Zec 1:11). Since the Angel of Yahweh can either be a representative of Yahweh or the embodiment of Yahweh on earth, the scene here could include either three or four figures: the Angel of Yahweh, Satan and the priest, or those three plus Yahweh himself. **Satan** Literally "the adversary." See note on Job 1:6.

Zechariah 3:1

JOSHUA SON OF JEHOZADAK
As the first high priest of the returned remnant, Joshua reestablished proper worship of Yahweh by building an altar and resuming sacrificial worship (ca. 537 BC; Ezr 3:1–6). He is identified elsewhere as the son of Jehozadak (or "Jozadak"; Hag 1:1; Ezr 3:2). His first name is sometimes spelled as "Jeshua" (e.g., Ezr 3:2 uses *yeshua* in Hebrew, not *yehoshua* as in Zec 3:1). His father was among the priests taken into exile after the fall of Jerusalem in 586 BC (1Ch 6:15). His grandfather, Seraiah, who had been high priest when Jerusalem fell, was put to death by Nebuchadnezzar (2Ki 25:18–21; 1Ch 6:14). Joshua plays an important role when the prophets Haggai and Zechariah remind the exiles of their need to finish rebuilding the temple (Ezr 5:1–2; Hag 1:1–15).

3:3 filthy clothes Describes garments stained with excrement, representing Joshua's sinfulness and ritual impurity.
3:4 those who were standing before him Probably refers to other angels, though human associates of the priest are possible.
3:7 you will govern Denotes the act of judging. The priests' duties also extended to deciding legal issues (Dt 17:9). Their decisions involved maintaining the ritual purity of the temple (compare Eze 44:23–24). **a place** The high priest was the only person authorized to enter the holiest part of the temple (here, "my house" and "my courts"). This access was permitted once a year on the Day of Atonement (Lev 16:29–33).
3:8–10 This oracle expands on the vision in Zec 3:1–7 by placing the leadership of Joshua (see note on Zec 3:1) within the context of Yahweh's full plan of restoration, culminating in the coming of the Messiah. The imagery in v. 8 connects the Messianic expectations of Isa 4:2–6 with the suffering servant figure from Isa 42–53.

3:8 your associates seated before you These friends are probably distinct from the standing ones of Zec 3:4,7. They likely are associates of the priest, perhaps even priests themselves. **symbolic** Joshua and those with him are symbols of the future fulfillment of the coming of the Messiah (compare Isa 8:18). **my servant** Probably refers to the Messiah based on the connection with "the Branch," but this phrase is sometimes understood as a reference to a leader such as Zerubbabel (see Zec 4:9; 6:11–14; note on Isa 53:2). A connection can be made between the prophecies of Isaiah related to the suffering servant (see Isa 53:2,10–12), Isaiah's mention of a Messianic figure affiliated with David's line (Isa 11:1–2) and the servant figure in Zechariah. Zechariah depicts the servant figure as being present with God's divine council and as playing an integral role in the transformation of the land of God (see note on Ps 82:1). In Luke's Gospel, Jesus might be drawing on a connection between this passage and other passages about the suffering servant when he remarks that the prophets foretold that he would suffer, die and rise again—all for the purpose of salvation (Lk 18:29–34). When Zechariah is conceptually linked with Isaiah, it becomes apparent that the servant will come from David's line and then suffer, die and rise for humanity—and thus in a single day remove the iniquity of the land and of God's people (Zec 3:9; Isa 53:10,12). **the Branch** The Hebrew word used here, *tsemach*, means "growth" or "branch," usually in reference to vegetation. However, the major significance of the term comes from its use as a metaphor for the Messiah (e.g., Isa 4:2; Jer 23:5; 33:15; Zec 6:12). The Messianic implications of *tsemach* were introduced in 2Sa 23:5, where David anticipates the fulfillment of the covenant that Yahweh had made with him by faithfully asserting that all of his promises will come to pass (or "grow"; *tsamach* in Hebrew). In Jeremiah, the word is modified with the adjective "righteous," possibly alluding to the Branch's divine nature (Jer 23:5; 33:15,16). The Branch also can be conceptually linked to the branch, the shoot and the young or tender plant of Isa 4:2; 11:1–14; and 53:2, respectively—all of which are surrounded with Messianic expectations.
3:9 the stone Probably a foundation stone for the temple. Compare Isa 28:16. **seven eyes** Since seven is often used in the Bible to denote totality, the idea here is probably that of divine omniscience—God's ability to see and know everything (compare Zec 4:10; 2Ch 16:9). **an inscription** In the ancient Near East, cornerstones often had inscriptions bearing the name of the builder and the purpose of the structure. This inscription announces that the sins of the nation will be removed. **single day** Both the land and humanity are completely transformed in a moment by the action of Yahweh and the servant he has appointed (compare Isa 53:12).
3:10 under your vine and fig tree An image of peace and safety (compare 1Ki 4:25; 2Ki 18:31; Mic 4:4).

neighbor to sit under your vine and fig tree,' declares the LORD Almighty."

The Gold Lampstand and the Two Olive Trees

4 Then the angel who talked with me returned and woke me up, like someone awakened from sleep. ²He asked me, "What do you see?"

I answered, "I see a solid gold lampstand with a bowl at the top and seven lamps on it, with seven channels to the lamps. ³Also there are two olive trees by it, one on the right of the bowl and the other on its left."

⁴I asked the angel who talked with me, "What are these, my lord?"

⁵He answered, "Do you not know what these are?"

"No, my lord," I replied.

⁶So he said to me, "This is the word of the LORD to Zerubbabel: 'Not by might nor by power, but by my Spirit,' says the LORD Almighty.

⁷"What are you, mighty mountain? Before Zerubbabel you will become level ground. Then he will bring out the capstone to shouts of 'God bless it! God bless it!'"

⁸Then the word of the LORD came to me: ⁹"The hands of Zerubbabel have laid the foundation of this temple; his hands will also complete it. Then you will know that the LORD Almighty has sent me to you.

¹⁰"Who dares despise the day of small things, since the seven eyes of the LORD that range throughout the earth will rejoice when they see the chosen capstone*a* in the hand of Zerubbabel?"

¹¹Then I asked the angel, "What are these two olive trees on the right and the left of the lampstand?"

¹²Again I asked him, "What are these two olive branches beside the two gold pipes that pour out golden oil?"

¹³He replied, "Do you not know what these are?"

"No, my lord," I said.

¹⁴So he said, "These are the two who are anointed to*b* serve the Lord of all the earth."

The Flying Scroll

5 I looked again, and there before me was a flying scroll.

²He asked me, "What do you see?"

I answered, "I see a flying scroll, twenty cubits long and ten cubits wide. *c*"

³And he said to me, "This is the curse that is going out over the whole land; for according to what

a 10 Or *the plumb line*   *b* 14 Or *two who bring oil and*
c 2 That is, about 30 feet long and 15 feet wide or about 9 meters long and 4.5 meters wide

---

Peace and renewal in the natural world also characterize the reign of the Messiah. See Isa 4:6; 11:6–9; note on Isa 11:6.

4:1–14 Zechariah's fifth vision is a symbolic picture of the Spirit of Yahweh as he gives power to the anointed ones currently in view—probably Zerubbabel and Joshua. This vision has some similarities to the fourth vision, including a reference to seven eyes, a reference to a stone for the temple and an emphasis on a historical person. The vision is presented almost as if it were a dream, with an angelic guide explaining the fantastic imagery (compare Da 8:18; 10:9–10). Zechariah is shown an unusual lampstand—one that is different from a typical menorah or temple lampstand. In the cryptic fashion typical of apocalyptic visions (compare Da 7:15–28), the angel's explanation offers little clarity, emphasizing simply that Yahweh has chosen Zerubbabel for this mission to rebuild the temple and that Yahweh himself will overcome the worldly obstacles to its reconstruction.

4:2 a solid gold lampstand Describes a column that supported one or more oil lamps. The lampstands mentioned in the OT were almost always made of gold and designed to be used in religious worship settings (compare 2Ki 4:10).

4:3 two olive trees The surprising thing about this lampstand was that it was fed with oil directly from the trees through the golden pipes (Zec 4:12).

4:6 Zerubbabel A descendant of King David (1Ch 3:17–19; Mt 1:12), as well as the governor of Judah (Hag 1:1) who oversaw the rebuilding of the temple (Ezr 3:2,8; 5:2; see note on Ezr 3:2). **my Spirit** Emphasizing that divine power—not human power—will enable them to overcome the opposition to rebuilding the temple. Throughout the OT, God's Spirit gives divine

empowerment to the individuals God selects (e.g., Ex 31:3; Nu 11:25–26; 24:2; Jdg 3:10; 6:34; 11:29; 1Sa 10:10; 16:13).

4:7 mighty mountain A metaphor for a difficult task. **God bless it! God bless it** Acknowledges that Yahweh's Spirit—not human might—was responsible for completing the temple project (v. 6).

4:10 the seven eyes of the LORD See note on Zec 3:9. **chosen capstone** The Hebrew term used here seems to refer to a string with a weight attached to the end. Ancients used tools like plumb lines to determine whether a wall was straight.

4:14 who are anointed The Hebrew text here reads "sons of fresh oil." The Israelites commonly used olive oil for anointing (Ex 29:7; 1Sa 16:12–13), which served to set an individual apart for a special purpose. The "anointed ones" here are probably Zerubbabel and Joshua, the representatives of David and Aaron in this renewed covenant community. Compare note on Zec 6:11.

5:1–4 Zechariah's sixth vision illustrates Yahweh's judgment or curse against all who have sinned by violating his commandments. Just as the fourth vision dealt with the cleansing of the priest's sin (see 3:1–5), this imagery is likely related to the need for all to be cleansed from their sins brought on by breaking Yahweh's covenant. The vision addresses the sins of social injustice and religious apostasy. Sin must be dealt with before Yahweh can return and dwell among his people (2:10).

5:1 flying scroll This scroll descends from God's presence in heaven. The written word plays an important role in prophetic and apocalyptic vision imagery (e.g., Eze 2:8—3:4; Hab 2:2; Isa 8:1; Da 5:7–25; Rev 5:1–5; compare note on Eze 2:9).

5:2 twenty cubits long Approximately 30–34 feet. **ten cubits wide** About 15–17 feet.

it says on one side, every thief will be banished, and according to what it says on the other, everyone who swears falsely will be banished. ⁴The LORD Almighty declares, 'I will send it out, and it will enter the house of the thief and the house of anyone who swears falsely by my name. It will remain in that house and destroy it completely, both its timbers and its stones.'"

The Woman in a Basket

⁵Then the angel who was speaking to me came forward and said to me, "Look up and see what is appearing."

⁶I asked, "What is it?"

He replied, "It is a basket." And he added, "This is the iniquity*a* of the people throughout the land."

⁷Then the cover of lead was raised, and there in the basket sat a woman! ⁸He said, "This is wickedness," and he pushed her back into the basket and pushed its lead cover down on it.

⁹Then I looked up — and there before me were two women, with the wind in their wings! They had wings like those of a stork, and they lifted up the basket between heaven and earth.

¹⁰"Where are they taking the basket?" I asked the angel who was speaking to me.

¹¹He replied, "To the country of Babylonia*b* to build a house for it. When the house is ready, the basket will be set there in its place."

Four Chariots

6 I looked up again, and there before me were four chariots coming out from between two mountains — mountains of bronze. ²The first chariot had red horses, the second black, ³the third white, and the fourth dappled — all of them powerful. ⁴I asked the angel who was speaking to me, "What are these, my lord?"

⁵The angel answered me, "These are the four spirits*c* of heaven, going out from standing in the presence of the Lord of the whole world. ⁶The one with the black horses is going toward the north country, the one with the white horses toward the west,*d* and the one with the dappled horses toward the south."

a 6 Or *appearance*   *b* 11 Hebrew *Shinar*   *c* 5 Or *winds*
d 6 Or *horses after them*

5:3 curse The Hebrew term used here alludes to the punishments associated with breaking the covenant (see Dt 29:10–29; Eze 16:59). **according to what it says on the other** A scroll with writing on both sides was uncommon (see note on 2:10). The two sides of the scroll reflect the two main types of sin: sin against a neighbor (or another person) and sin against God. The Ten Commandments (Ex 20:1–17) break down along two major categories: laws governing the people's relationship with Yahweh and laws governing their relationships with each other. One side of the scroll in Zechariah's vision contained a curse against misusing the name of God. The other side contained a curse against all who steal. Since each is the middle command (the third and eighth) of these two parts of the Ten Commandments, they are probably meant to represent the entire Law.

5:5–11 The seventh vision presents Zechariah with the strange sight of a woman imprisoned in a barrel or basket. The woman personifies wickedness and is about to be taken to the land of Babylon. The passage reveals that the land of Babylon will become a center of evil when the woman is established there as an idol for those who worship evil. The personification of evil or wickedness in female form has parallels with the image of the forbidden woman in Pr 7:5–27 and the great prostitute of Rev 17. The imagery focuses on evil as a power in and of itself—an external, objective force, not merely the sinful actions of people. God alone has supreme power over evil, directing his angels to remove it to distant Shinar (also known as Babylon or Babylonia), a location symbolic of rebellious opposition to Yahweh (Ge 11:2; compare Rev 14:8).

5:6 a basket The Hebrew word *ephah* used here is a technical term for a unit used to measure volume (both dry and liquid). It is possible that this passage does not indicate the unit of measure but relates to Mesopotamian religion. One proposal based on possible Semitic cognates is that *ephah* refers to the small room or shrine that sat on top of a ziggurat. The destination of the basket as described in v. 11 favors this possibility.

5:9 the wind The Hebrew term here may be used with the connotation of "spirit," indicating that God's Spirit was empowering these women (compare 4:6).

5:11 Babylonia This land was known variously as Babylon, Babylonia or Shinar (Ge 10:10; see note on Ezr 1:11). The Bible, at times, uses Babylon as a symbol for the center of humankind's wickedness (e.g., Ge 11:1–9; Isa 13–14; Jer 50–51). Babylon eventually will be depicted as the center of Satan's earthly kingdom (Rev 17–18).

6:1–8 The eighth and final vision illustrates the universal reign of Yahweh. This vision parallels the opening vision (Zec 1:7–17): Both feature the number four, horses of various colors, a valley—all with an emphasis on the entire earth. The two visions function as an inclusio, bracketing the sequence of visions in chs. 1–6.

6:1 four chariots Compare with the four horses of 1:8. **two mountains** The two bronze mountains function symbolically like the two bronze pillars framing the entrance to the temple (compare 1Ki 7:15–22). The symbolism of the two mountains also might parallel ancient Near Eastern imagery of a sun god rising between the mountains. There may be a connection to Zec 14:4, which describes how two mountains are created when Yahweh stands on the Mount of Olives and it splits in two.

6:5 the four spirits of heaven The Hebrew term *ruach* is likely used here to denote "spirit" rather than "wind" (see note on Eze 37:5; compare Eze 37:9). Some translations phrase this passage to imply the chariots are being sent out *to* the four winds—that is, in all four directions. The underlying Hebrew phrase, however, clearly equates the chariots with the winds. The number four represents the whole of the created order and often appears in depictions of divine judgment. The four chariots represent the four winds (or "spirits") of heaven, Yahweh's messengers of judgment (compare Jer 49:36; Da 7:2; Ps 104:4).

6:6 north country Symbolic of the location of Yahweh's

⁷When the powerful horses went out, they were straining to go throughout the earth. And he said, "Go throughout the earth!" So they went throughout the earth.

⁸Then he called to me, "Look, those going toward the north country have given my Spirit*a* rest in the land of the north."

A Crown for Joshua

⁹The word of the LORD came to me: ¹⁰"Take silver and gold from the exiles Heldai, Tobijah and Jedaiah, who have arrived from Babylon. Go the same day to the house of Josiah son of Zephaniah. ¹¹Take the silver and gold and make a crown, and set it on the head of the high priest, Joshua son of Jozadak.*b* ¹²Tell him this is what the LORD Almighty says: 'Here is the man whose name is the Branch, and he will branch out from his place and build the temple of the LORD. ¹³It is he who will build the temple of the LORD, and he will be clothed with majesty and will sit and rule on his throne. And he*c* will be a priest on his throne. And there will be harmony between the two.' ¹⁴The crown will be given to Heldai,*d* Tobijah, Jedaiah and Hen*e* son of Zephaniah as a memorial in the temple of the LORD. ¹⁵Those who are far away will

---

a 8 Or spirit   *b* 11 Hebrew Jehozadak, a variant of Jozadak   *c* 13 Or there   *d* 14 Syriac; Hebrew Helem   *e* 14 Or and the gracious one, the

---

enemies throughout much of the OT (compare Zec 2:6 and note). The greater importance of the north as symbolic of evil is indicated by the two chariots heading that direction; in comparison, only one heads south. Jeremiah describes divine judgment coming from the north (Jer 1:14 and note). Ezekiel also emphasizes the northern county as the home of Israel's eschatological enemy who will invade at the end of days (Eze 38:14–16). The imagery probably developed out of the reality that Israel was usually subject to catastrophic invasion from the north by different Mesopotamian powers (e.g., Babylon, Assyria). The Canaanite god Baal was also depicted living on a mountain in the north (see note on Isa 2:2). North also indicated the left side, based on the eastward orientation common to the ancient Near East (see Ge 14:15; Eze 16:46). In Semitic cultures, the left side is associated with calamity. These factors made the north country symbolic of all that was evil and sinister in the world. The end of the vision in Zec 6:8 indicates that these divine messengers subdued the evil power of the north, making the world ready for Yahweh's presence to return. **south** Possibly refers to Egypt. Israel's location, with the Mediterranean to the west and the desert to the east, meant that large-scale invasion only came from the south (Egypt) or the north. The most destructive invasions came from the north. The opposing powers of north and south play an important role in the vision of Da 11:2–45.

6:9–15 This oracle serves as a climax to the eight night visions and reiterates Yahweh's choice of Joshua as high priest (see note on 3:1–7). Zechariah is commanded to make a crown for Joshua out of silver and gold. This symbolic act establishes the priests as the divinely appointed leaders of the community. The emphasis on the temple and religious leadership reflects the realistic situation of the exiles, who had more freedom over religious matters than political affairs. The passage also serves to connect the visions of chs. 1–6 with the oracles of chs. 7–8. See the table "Symbolic Actions of the Prophets" on p. 1195.

6:11 set it on the head of the high priest, Joshua The identification of the Messianic Branch with a priest (v. 12) foreshadows the uniting of kingship and priesthood in the person of the Messiah (compare Ps 110:2,4). This passage probably inspired expectations of a priestly Messiah in Second Temple Judaism. The group responsible for the sectarian Dead Sea Scrolls expected a priestly messiah in addition to a prophet like Moses and a royal Davidic messiah (see the documents Rule of Community 9.11; Rule of the Congregation 2.12–22; and Melchize-

dek scroll). The author of Hebrews makes a similar connection when proclaiming Jesus' high priesthood (Heb 2:17–18; compare note on Jn 1:21). For more on Joshua, see note on 3:1.

6:12 the Branch See note on Zec 3:8. **build the temple of the LORD** Zechariah's vision in 4:1–14 had identified Zerubbabel as the one who would successfully complete the temple rebuilding project (see 4:9), but he is not directly in view in this prophecy. Instead, it is Joshua the high priest who is emphasized. The ultimate fulfillment of this imagery comes when Jesus, from the line of David, unites the roles of priest and king to truly establish Yahweh's kingdom on earth (Heb 3:3; Eph 2:20–22).

6:13 he who will build the temple of the LORD The repetition of this phrase from the end of Zec 6:12 emphasizes the role of the Branch and underscores the importance of rebuilding the temple. The word order in Hebrew could be highlighting the figure in v. 13 as ultimately distinct from either Joshua the high priest or Zerubbabel. Joshua also is involved in the prophecy of the servant figure in 3:8–9. The image of the Branch points to a future figure whose importance is greater than either of the contemporary leaders of the Jewish community (see 3:8 and note). Since the rebuilding of the temple is also in view here, there seems to be a further parallel to Jesus' connection of the temple with his body, which he proclaimed would be destroyed and raised three days later (Jn 2:19–22). **rule on his throne** Establishes the Branch as a royal authority figure. **a priest on his throne** This juxtaposition could suggest that both the Branch and the priest are distinct figures on the same throne. Alternatively, the offices of king and priest could be united in the Branch as a Messianic figure. In the historical context of Zechariah's day, the two figures would be Zerubbabel (Hag 2:21) and Joshua—the major leaders of the postexilic community (see note on Ezr 2:2). However, if the verse is understood as uniting the roles of priest and king, the plural address in the text also could be interpreted as pointing to the perfect harmony that would exist between Yahweh and his Messiah (a harmony that the author of Hebrews envisions; compare Heb 7:11–28).

6:15 Those who are far away May refer to Jews scattered throughout the world, but more likely indicates the future inclusion of the nations among the worshipers of Yahweh—a prominent theme in Isaiah. **build the temple of the LORD** Likely does not refer to Zerubbabel's temple project. Rather, the oracle looks ahead to the ultimate fulfillment through the Messiah and the inauguration of his earthly kingdom.

come and help to build the temple of the Lord, and you will know that the Lord Almighty has sent me to you. This will happen if you diligently obey the Lord your God."

Justice and Mercy, Not Fasting

7 In the fourth year of King Darius, the word of the Lord came to Zechariah on the fourth day of the ninth month, the month of Kislev. ²The people of Bethel had sent Sharezer and Regem-Melek, together with their men, to entreat the Lord ³by asking the priests of the house of the Lord Almighty and the prophets, "Should I mourn and fast in the fifth month, as I have done for so many years?"

⁴Then the word of the Lord Almighty came to me: ⁵"Ask all the people of the land and the priests, 'When you fasted and mourned in the fifth and seventh months for the past seventy years, was it really for me that you fasted? ⁶And when you were eating and drinking, were you not just feasting for yourselves? ⁷Are these not the words the Lord proclaimed through the earlier prophets when Jerusalem and its surrounding towns were at rest and prosperous, and the Negev and the western foothills were settled?'"

⁸And the word of the Lord came again to Zechariah: ⁹"This is what the Lord Almighty said: 'Administer true justice; show mercy and compassion to one another. ¹⁰Do not oppress the widow or the fatherless, the foreigner or the poor. Do not plot evil against each other.'

¹¹"But they refused to pay attention; stubbornly they turned their backs and covered their ears. ¹²They made their hearts as hard as flint and would not listen to the law or to the words that the Lord Almighty had sent by his Spirit through the earlier prophets. So the Lord Almighty was very angry.

¹³"'When I called, they did not listen; so when they called, I would not listen,' says the Lord Almighty. ¹⁴'I scattered them with a whirlwind among all the nations, where they were strangers. The land they left behind them was so desolate that no one traveled through it. This is how they made the pleasant land desolate.'"

The Lord Promises to Bless Jerusalem

8 The word of the Lord Almighty came to me. ²This is what the Lord Almighty says: "I am very jealous for Zion; I am burning with jealousy for her."

7:1–14 This passage addresses the practical implications of Judah's renewed faith in Yahweh. The occasion of the oracles in Zec 7:4–14 is the inquiry of a delegation from Bethel regarding the observance of fast days commemorating the siege and destruction of Jerusalem and the temple (vv. 1–3). Zechariah's first message criticizes these fasts as inappropriate to the new beginning symbolized by the reestablished Jewish community (vv. 4–7). The second message emphasizes the importance of ethical living over empty religious observances (vv. 8–14).

7:1 In the fourth year of King Darius Refers to 518 BC. This final chronological heading in Zechariah indicates that about two years had passed since he delivered his call to repentance (see 1:1 and note) and experienced the eight visions (see 1:7–6:8 and note).

7:2 Bethel A city about 10 miles north of Jerusalem, near the southern border of the former northern kingdom of Israel. **to entreat the Lord** This group from Bethel is sent to offer sacrifices at the temple in Jerusalem. The remnant had set up the altar immediately after returning (Ezr 3:1–3) following the decree of Cyrus (Ezr 1:2–4). At this time, they were rebuilding the temple (Ezr 3:10–13).

BETHEL
Bethel, which means "house of God," was an ancient sacred site (see Ge 28:10–22) that was associated with improper worship during the time of the northern kingdom (1Ki 12:28–33; Am 3:14; 4:4; 7:13). Jeroboam, the first king of the northern kingdom, had established Israelite religious centers at Bethel in the southern part of his kingdom and at Dan in the north

(1Ki 12:28–29). The purpose of the shrine was to discourage people from making a pilgrimage to Jerusalem for worship. Biblical writers routinely criticized the worship at Bethel as idolatry, lamenting that the kings of Israel continued this practice begun by Jeroboam (see 1Ki 16:25–26; Am 4:4; 7:7–13).

7:3 fast The Jews had imposed a religious observance commemorating Nebuchadnezzar's destruction of Jerusalem and the temple in 586 BC (2Ki 25:8–9); this involved fasting (see Zec 7:5). **the fifth month** The month of Ab, late July and early August.

7:5 seventh Tishri—late September and early October. This observance may have commemorated the murder of Gedaliah, the governor Nebuchadnezzar placed over Judah (2Ki 25:22–25). This event precipitated the remnant's flight to Egypt (2Ki 25:26). **seventy years** Referring to the time of exile. See note on Jer 25:11.

7:6 for yourselves They were observing the fast simply to draw attention to themselves instead of offering true repentance to Yahweh.

7:9 true justice The prophets continually emphasize that the ethical aspects of God's law are just as important as the ritual aspects (see Isa 1:17 and note; compare Mic 6:8; Mt 23:23). **mercy** The Hebrew term used here, *chesed*, is often used in reference to Yahweh's covenant with Israel (e.g., Dt 7:9,12; 1Ki 8:23; Ne 1:5). Here, it is used of people's treatment of their fellow Israelites.

7:12 hearts as hard as flint The Hebrew term used here indicates an unknown extremely hard substance—possibly corundum. The prophet describes the hardening of one's heart—an act of defiant stubbornness (compare Ex 8:15; Pr 28:14). **very angry** Referring to Yahweh's eventual decision to bring judgment instead of patiently awaiting their repentance. See v. 14 and note.

7:14 I scattered them with a whirlwind Describes the deportations of the northern kingdom to Assyria in

³This is what the LORD says: "I will return to Zion and dwell in Jerusalem. Then Jerusalem will be called the Faithful City, and the mountain of the LORD Almighty will be called the Holy Mountain."

⁴This is what the LORD Almighty says: "Once again men and women of ripe old age will sit in the streets of Jerusalem, each of them with cane in hand because of their age. ⁵The city streets will be filled with boys and girls playing there."

⁶This is what the LORD Almighty says: "It may seem marvelous to the remnant of this people at that time, but will it seem marvelous to me?" declares the LORD Almighty.

⁷This is what the LORD Almighty says: "I will save my people from the countries of the east and the west. ⁸I will bring them back to live in Jerusalem; they will be my people, and I will be faithful and righteous to them as their God."

⁹This is what the LORD Almighty says: "Now hear these words, 'Let your hands be strong so that the temple may be built.' This is also what the prophets said who were present when the foundation was laid for the house of the LORD Almighty. ¹⁰Before that time there were no wages for people or hire for animals. No one could go about their business safely because of their enemies, since I had turned everyone against their neighbor. ¹¹But now I will not deal with the remnant of this people as I did in the past," declares the LORD Almighty.

¹²"The seed will grow well, the vine will yield its fruit, the ground will produce its crops, and the heavens will drop their dew. I will give all these things as an inheritance to the remnant of this people. ¹³Just as you, Judah and Israel, have been a curse*a* among the nations, so I will save you, and you will be a blessing.*b* Do not be afraid, but let your hands be strong."

¹⁴This is what the LORD Almighty says: "Just as I had determined to bring disaster on you and showed no pity when your ancestors angered me," says the LORD Almighty, ¹⁵"so now I have determined to do good again to Jerusalem and Judah. Do not be afraid. ¹⁶These are the things you are to do: Speak the truth to each other, and render true and sound judgment in your courts; ¹⁷do not plot evil against each other, and do not love to swear falsely. I hate all this," declares the LORD.

¹⁸The word of the LORD Almighty came to me. ¹⁹This is what the LORD Almighty says: "The fasts of the fourth, fifth, seventh and tenth months will become joyful and glad occasions and happy festivals for Judah. Therefore love truth and peace."

²⁰This is what the LORD Almighty says: "Many peoples and the inhabitants of many cities will yet come, ²¹and the inhabitants of one city will go to another and say, 'Let us go at once to entreat the LORD and seek the LORD Almighty. I myself am going.' ²²And many peoples and powerful nations will come to Jerusalem to seek the LORD Almighty and to entreat him."

---

a 13 That is, your name has been used in cursing (see Jer. 29:22); or, you have been regarded as under a curse. *b* 13 Or *and your name will be used in blessings* (see Gen. 48:20); or *and you will be seen as blessed*

---

722 BC and the southern kingdom to Babylon in 586 BC. See note on Ezr 4:2.

8:1–23 This chapter contains Zechariah's final two explanatory messages (see note on Zec 7:1–14). Zechariah's third message is one of restoration (vv. 1–17). The fourth message is one of rejoicing (vv. 18–23).

8:1 LORD Almighty See note on Na 2:13.

8:2 Zion Another name for Jerusalem. See note on Isa 1:8.

8:3 dwell in Jerusalem A reference to the Messianic reign (Ps 2:6), when Yahweh himself will reign over the entire earth from Jerusalem (Joel 3:16–17; Zec 14:9; see note on Zep 1:4).

8:7 my people Refers to the Israelites, whom Yahweh redeemed from Egypt (Ex 3:7,10; 5:1; 6:7; 7:4,16; 8:1). **countries of the east and the west** Represents all nations on the earth.

8:8 they will be my people Compare Hos 2:23.

8:9 your hands This phrase forms an inclusio (a bracketing by repetition) with the end of Zec 8:13. **what the prophets said** Includes Haggai and Zechariah, who were instrumental in encouraging the Jewish people to restart the rebuilding of the temple in 520 BC (see Ezr 5:1–2). The Jewish people halted the rebuilding project shortly after rebuilding the altar in 536 BC because they feared their enemies (Ezr 4:1–5). See the timeline "Dates Related to Ezra, Nehemiah and Esther" on p. 716.

8:10 that time Refers to the days when the temple project was restarted. The rebuilding of the temple re-sumed in 520 BC after a period of inactivity (compare note on 8:9).

8:11 the past Refers to the days prior to the commencement of the rebuilding project when the temple lay in ruins.

8:12 seed will grow well Yahweh will allow the produce of the ground to grow without destroying it (see Hag 1:10–11).

8:14 your ancestors Refers to the pre-exilic generations and perhaps even the people of 536–520 BC.

8:15 to do good Contrasts with the disaster that God brought in judgment. After restoration, Yahweh desires to provide blessing, not judgment.

8:16 Speak the truth Yahweh desires righteous moral behavior over external ritual obedience (compare Mic 6:8; Hos 6:6 and note). Paul seems to allude to this passage in Eph 4:25.

8:19 The fasts of the fourth Commemorates Nebuchadnezzar's breach of Jerusalem's walls (586 BC; Jer 39:2). The fourth month, Tammuz, corresponds with June and July. **fifth** See note on Zec 7:3. **seventh** See note on 7:5. **tenth** Commemorates the beginning of Nebuchadnezzar's siege of Jerusalem (588 BC; 2Ki 25:1). The 10th month, Tebeth, corresponds with December and January. **joyful and glad occasions and happy festivals** Days of fasting will turn to days of feasting. Compare Isa 35:10.

8:20 Many peoples and the inhabitants of many cities will yet come A common theme in the prophets (e.g., Isa 2:3; Jer 3:17; Mic 4:1–3; Hag 2:7; Zec 14:16).

23This is what the LORD Almighty says: "In those days ten people from all languages and nations will take firm hold of one Jew by the hem of his robe and say, 'Let us go with you, because we have heard that God is with you.'"

Judgment on Israel's Enemies

9 A prophecy:

The word of the LORD is against the land of
    Hadrak
and will come to rest on Damascus —
for the eyes of all people and all the tribes
    of Israel
are on the LORD — [a]
2 and on Hamath too, which borders on it,
    and on Tyre and Sidon, though they are
        very skillful.
3 Tyre has built herself a stronghold;
    she has heaped up silver like dust,
    and gold like the dirt of the streets.
4 But the Lord will take away her
        possessions
    and destroy her power on the sea,
    and she will be consumed by fire.

5 Ashkelon will see it and fear;
    Gaza will writhe in agony,
    and Ekron too, for her hope will wither.
Gaza will lose her king
    and Ashkelon will be deserted.
6 A mongrel people will occupy Ashdod,
    and I will put an end to the pride of the
        Philistines.
7 I will take the blood from their mouths,
    the forbidden food from between their
        teeth.
Those who are left will belong to our God
    and become a clan in Judah,
    and Ekron will be like the Jebusites.
8 But I will encamp at my temple
    to guard it against marauding forces.
Never again will an oppressor overrun my
        people,
    for now I am keeping watch.

The Coming of Zion's King

9 Rejoice greatly, Daughter Zion!
    Shout, Daughter Jerusalem!

[a] 1 Or *Damascus. / For the eye of the* LORD *is on all people, / as well as on the tribes of Israel,*

8:23 ten people from all languages and nations This numerical expression is used here to represent many (Ge 31:7; 1Sa 1:8; Job 19:3; Am 6:9). **one Jew by the hem** Indicates that foreigners will grab the robe of a Jewish person (or people) in an attempt to journey to Jerusalem with them, because God is present with the Jewish people.

9:1–17 This oracle proclaims Yahweh's judgment against Israel's neighbors (Zec 9:1–8) and emphasizes his concern to protect his people (vv. 11–17). The list of cities in vv. 1–7 proceeds generally from north to south, and v. 8 depicts Yahweh's return to his temple in Jerusalem. The passage ends with Yahweh establishing complete peace and security (vv. 11–17). Two verses in the middle of the chapter announce the return of a king to Zion who takes his place to rule over a now-pacified world (vv. 9–10). This king's arrival brings the ultimate peace over all the earth that will follow Yahweh's total restoration of his rule (Isa 2:4; Hos 2:18). The entire oracle reflects the imagery of the Divine Warrior battling on behalf of his people.

9:1 A prophecy The Hebrew term used here (*massa*) can be used to refer to both a burden (e.g., Ex 23:5; Dt 1:12) and an oracle or prophecy (e.g., Eze 12:10; Isa 13:1; Hab 1:1). It is frequently used to identify prophetic oracles (Na 1:1; Isa 15:1; 17:1; 19:1). The prophets may use this word ironically, referring to the oracle as a burden that they must carry or implying that the message is a burden for the audience to bear (see Jer 23:33 and note). **Damascus** A city in southern Syria; the chief city of the Arameans.
9:2 Hamath A city in northern Syria that is located on the Orontes River about 130 miles north of Damascus. **Tyre** The most important Phoenician city. See note on Ne 13:16; note on Eze 26:2. **Sidon** A city in central Phoenicia (modern Lebanon). Located about 25 miles south of modern-day Beirut. **they are very skillful** Likely

mocking Tyre and Sidon for their confidence in their own abilities. Ezekiel similarly mocks the ruler of Tyre for his arrogant reliance on his own wisdom (see Eze 28:3–5).

9:5–6 The four cities mentioned here were part of the "Philistine pentapolis" (Gaza, Gath, Ekron, Ashkelon and Ashdod). See note on Zep 2:4

9:6 pride of the Philistines Refers to the wealth and power of the nation.
9:7 forbidden food The Hebrew word here is commonly used to refer to idols, associating them with something disgusting or abhorrent (see 1Ki 11:7; 2Ki 23:24). Here, it probably refers to meat sacrificed to idols.
9:8 encamp at my temple Refers to the temple in Jerusalem. Yahweh will return to dwell in Jerusalem and protect his people from oppression by foreign nations.

9:9–10 Zechariah draws on the language and imagery of a number of other OT passages in these two verses. His description of the Messianic king echoes passages from Isaiah and Micah (e.g., Isa 9:6–7; 11:1–5; Mic 5:2–4). The extent of the king's power and influence also contains echoes of Ps 72 (especially Ps 72:1–11). The nations' acceptance of Judah's rule and the references to a donkey and a donkey's colt are likely allusions to Ge 49:10–11.

9:9 your king Refers to the Messiah (compare Jer 23:5). **righteous and victorious** Yahweh has equipped the coming Messianic king with righteousness (Isa 9:7; 11:4–5; compare Ps 72:1). He will fulfill Yahweh's ideal for kingship (see note on Jer 22:3; compare Dt 10:18). **donkey** A donkey was a common mount for transportation in Biblical times (see Nu 22:21; Jdg 5:10; 2Sa 16:2). In this context, the reference to the donkey is likely meant to evoke the image of an ideal king who rules justly and accepts his rule with humility, not pomp and arrogance. This could also be an allusion to the expectations of a

See, your king comes to you,
  righteous and victorious,
lowly and riding on a donkey,
  on a colt, the foal of a donkey.
10 I will take away the chariots from
    Ephraim
and the warhorses from Jerusalem,
  and the battle bow will be broken.
He will proclaim peace to the nations.
  His rule will extend from sea to sea
and from the River[a] to the ends of the
    earth.
11 As for you, because of the blood of my
    covenant with you,
I will free your prisoners from the
    waterless pit.
12 Return to your fortress, you prisoners of
    hope;
even now I announce that I will restore
    twice as much to you.
13 I will bend Judah as I bend my bow
  and fill it with Ephraim.
I will rouse your sons, Zion,
  against your sons, Greece,
and make you like a warrior's sword.

The LORD Will Appear

14 Then the LORD will appear over them;
  his arrow will flash like lightning.

The Sovereign LORD will sound the trumpet;
  he will march in the storms of the south,
15 and the LORD Almighty will shield them.
They will destroy
  and overcome with slingstones.
They will drink and roar as with wine;
  they will be full like a bowl
used for sprinkling[b] the corners of the
    altar.
16 The LORD their God will save his people on
    that day
as a shepherd saves his flock.
  They will sparkle in his land
like jewels in a crown.
17 How attractive and beautiful they will be!
  Grain will make the young men thrive,
  and new wine the young women.

The LORD Will Care for Judah

10 Ask the LORD for rain in the springtime;
  it is the LORD who sends the
    thunderstorms.
He gives showers of rain to all people,
  and plants of the field to everyone.
2 The idols speak deceitfully,
  diviners see visions that lie;
they tell dreams that are false,
  they give comfort in vain.

a 10 That is, the Euphrates   *b* 15 Or *bowl, / like*

Davidic king (see note on 1Ki 1:33). When Jesus enters the city of Jerusalem on a donkey (see Mt 21:7 and note), the people shout praises and blessings (see Jn 12:13). The crowd interprets Jesus' action as a claim to royalty in light of Zec 9:9 (Jn 12:15), which envisions a righteous and humble king riding on a donkey. The Gospel of Matthew presents Jesus' triumphal entry as the fulfillment of this prophecy (Mt 21:5), though Matthew's quotation seems to also allude to Isa 62:11.

9:10 the warhorses from Jerusalem Under the rule of the Messiah, the most important elements of military power will no longer be needed. Jerusalem represents the territory of Judah. See note on Zep 1:4. **battle bow** Archers were of such great significance in ancient battles that the Hebrew term for bow was often used figuratively for warfare (e.g., Isa 22:3). **the River** The Euphrates, the longest and most important river of Mesopotamia. This statement about the extent of the Messiah's kingdom is likely an allusion to Ps 72:8.

9:11–17 This section returns to the theme of Yahweh's protection of his people from Zec 9:1–8. The focus is on how God will bring about the peaceful world that is the backdrop for the ideal king's return to Jerusalem (vv. 9–10). The first section emphasizes Yahweh reclaiming the land (vv. 1–8), while this section emphasizes Yahweh bringing back his people.

9:11 the blood Ancients often viewed blood as the sign of a covenant because they often ratified covenants with an animal sacrifice. **I will free your prisoners** The release of prisoners was a key part of the reign of Yahweh's ideal king (compare Isa 42:7; 49:9; 61:1). As in Isa 42:7, the exiles are depicted as prisoners who can

expect that Yahweh will set them free. The Messiah's coming deliverance should give them hope.

9:12 I will restore twice as much to you Perhaps as compensation for undeserved suffering brought on by the brutality of the nations (1:15). Alternately, the double restoration could symbolize Yahweh's commitment to bless his people and make them prosperous (1:17; compare Isa 61:7; Job 42:10).

9:14 LORD will appear Describes Yahweh arriving to fight on behalf of his people. Compare Isa 29:6 and note; 1Th 4:16. **the trumpet** The horn could be sounded to signal the start of an attack (Jdg 3:27), to summon the people for war (Jer 51:27; Hos 5:8), or to raise an alarm and warn the people of danger (Jer 4:5). In this verse, Yahweh is likely signaling his attack.

9:16 on that day Common prophetic language for referring to the future Day of Yahweh's ultimate victory—which involves judgment on his enemies and salvation for his people (e.g., Isa 2:11–12; 4:2; 11:10–11; Zec 2:11).

10:1 rain in the springtime The rains that commence in March or April are known as the spring rain or latter rain. The former rains are those of autumn that follow the harvest time. See Joel 2:23 and note.

10:2 idols The Hebrew term used here (*teraphim*) is also used for the household idols that Rachel steals from her father, Laban (see Ge 31:19 and note). These idols might have been used for ancestor worship. **diviners** Those who use a variety of techniques to determine messages from the gods. Such practices are prohibited in Biblical law (Dt 18:10–14). The prophets frequently condemn these methods of attempting to communicate with supernatural beings (see Eze 13:23; 21:21; Jer 27:9; Mic 3:6–7). **lack of a shepherd** Without godly

Therefore the people wander like sheep
  oppressed for lack of a shepherd.

³ "My anger burns against the shepherds,
  and I will punish the leaders;
for the LORD Almighty will care
  for his flock, the people of Judah,
  and make them like a proud horse in
    battle.
⁴ From Judah will come the cornerstone,
  from him the tent peg,
from him the battle bow,
  from him every ruler.
⁵ Together theyᵃ will be like warriors in battle
  trampling their enemy into the mud of the
    streets.
They will fight because the LORD is with
    them,
  and they will put the enemy horsemen to
    shame.

⁶ "I will strengthen Judah
  and save the tribes of Joseph.
I will restore them
  because I have compassion on them.
They will be as though
  I had not rejected them,
for I am the LORD their God
  and I will answer them.
⁷ The Ephraimites will become like warriors,
  and their hearts will be glad as with wine.
Their children will see it and be joyful;
  their hearts will rejoice in the LORD.

⁸ I will signal for them
  and gather them in.
Surely I will redeem them;
  they will be as numerous as before.
⁹ Though I scatter them among the peoples,
  yet in distant lands they will remember me.
They and their children will survive,
  and they will return.
¹⁰ I will bring them back from Egypt
  and gather them from Assyria.
I will bring them to Gilead and Lebanon,
  and there will not be room enough for them.
¹¹ They will pass through the sea of trouble;
  the surging sea will be subdued
  and all the depths of the Nile will dry up.
Assyria's pride will be brought down
  and Egypt's scepter will pass away.
¹² I will strengthen them in the LORD
  and in his name they will live securely,"
    declares the LORD.

11 Open your doors, Lebanon,
  so that fire may devour your cedars!
² Wail, you juniper, for the cedar has fallen;
  the stately trees are ruined!
Wail, oaks of Bashan;
  the dense forest has been cut down!
³ Listen to the wail of the shepherds;
  their rich pastures are destroyed!
Listen to the roar of the lions;
  the lush thicket of the Jordan is ruined!

ᵃ 4,5 Or ruler, all of them together. / ⁵They

---

leadership, the people go astray and suffer (compare Eze 34:5 and note). The leaders should be protecting the people as a shepherd would protect his flock, but they have failed (see 1Ki 22:17; Jer 2:8; note on Eze 34:1–10). In Ezekiel, Yahweh himself takes over for the failed shepherds (Eze 34:10–11; compare Ps 78:72), but he also assigns that role to his Messiah (Eze 34:23; 37:24; Mic 5:4).

10:6 save the tribes of Joseph The northern kingdom of Israel is sometimes referred to as Joseph or Ephraim, using the most powerful northern tribe as a representative of the entire kingdom (compare Ps 78:67).

10:7 Ephraimites Referring to the northern kingdom of Israel. See note on Hos 4:17.

10:9 Though I scatter them among the peoples A common image for Israel's punishment for breaking the covenant: They were taken captive and resettled in different lands. They were scattered, but Yahweh will bring them back (compare Isa 11:11–12; 27:13; Hos 11:11).

11:1–17 Zechariah 11 paints a gloomy picture of death and destruction. The narrative of the shepherd of the sheep for slaughter in vv. 4–16 is surrounded by two poetic oracles in vv. 1–3 and 11:17. The first describes the destruction of the natural beauty of the regions north of Israel—Lebanon, Bashan and the fertile Jordan Valley. The closing oracle pronounces woe on the shepherd who has failed in his duty to protect his flock. These three segments are unified by the continued use of shepherd imagery, introduced in 10:2–3. The basic message is one of judgment on the people and on their leaders for rejecting Yahweh. In the central narrative, Yahweh orders the prophet to become shepherd of the sheep for slaughter. His service appears to symbolize Yahweh's relationship with Israel through the prophets: They attempt to lead the people back to Yahweh, but the people persist in their obstinate rebellion until both prophet and Yahweh are frustrated.

11:1 Lebanon The mountainous region north of the Sea of Galilee, known for its cedar trees (see note on Isa 14:8).

11:2 juniper A type of evergreen fir tree known for its thick foliage. Only the cedar trees are destroyed; the junipers (or cypresses in some translations) and oaks are called to mourn the loss of the glorious cedar forests. **oaks of Bashan** Oaks, the other prized tree of the region, often were used as symbols of strength and power. The cedars of Lebanon and oaks of Bashan are similarly paired in Isa 2:13 and Eze 27:5–6. Amos 2:9 also uses cedar and oak to symbolize height and power, respectively.

11:3 the lush thicket of the Jordan The largest and most important river in Canaan. The vegetation along the banks of the Jordan River is extremely dense, creating a tropical environment that contrasts sharply with the surrounding barren terrain and provides a habitat for wildlife, including lions. Jeremiah uses similar language to describe the area (see Jer 12:5; 49:19; 50:44).

Two Shepherds

⁴This is what the LORD my God says: "Shepherd the flock marked for slaughter. ⁵Their buyers slaughter them and go unpunished. Those who sell them say, 'Praise the LORD, I am rich!' Their own shepherds do not spare them. ⁶For I will no longer have pity on the people of the land," declares the LORD. "I will give everyone into the hands of their neighbors and their king. They will devastate the land, and I will not rescue anyone from their hands."

⁷So I shepherded the flock marked for slaughter, particularly the oppressed of the flock. Then I took two staffs and called one Favor and the other Union, and I shepherded the flock. ⁸In one month I got rid of the three shepherds.

The flock detested me, and I grew weary of them ⁹and said, "I will not be your shepherd. Let the dying die, and the perishing perish. Let those who are left eat one another's flesh."

¹⁰Then I took my staff called Favor and broke it, revoking the covenant I had made with all the nations. ¹¹It was revoked on that day, and so the oppressed of the flock who were watching me knew it was the word of the LORD.

¹²I told them, "If you think it best, give me my pay; but if not, keep it." So they paid me thirty pieces of silver.

¹³And the LORD said to me, "Throw it to the potter"—the handsome price at which they valued me! So I took the thirty pieces of silver and threw them to the potter at the house of the LORD.

¹⁴Then I broke my second staff called Union, breaking the family bond between Judah and Israel.

¹⁵Then the LORD said to me, "Take again the equipment of a foolish shepherd. ¹⁶For I am going to raise up a shepherd over the land who will not care for the lost, or seek the young, or heal the injured, or feed the healthy, but will eat the meat of the choice sheep, tearing off their hooves.

¹⁷"Woe to the worthless shepherd,
who deserts the flock!
May the sword strike his arm and his right eye!
May his arm be completely withered,
his right eye totally blinded!"

Jerusalem's Enemies to Be Destroyed

12 A prophecy: The word of the LORD concerning Israel.

The LORD, who stretches out the heavens, who lays the foundation of the earth, and who forms the human spirit within a person, declares: ²"I am going to make Jerusalem a cup that sends all the surrounding peoples reeling. Judah will be besieged as well as Jerusalem. ³On that day, when all the nations of the earth are gathered against her, I will make Jerusalem an immovable rock for all the nations. All who try to move it will injure themselves. ⁴On that day I will strike every horse with panic and its rider with madness," declares the LORD. "I will keep a watchful eye over Judah, but I will blind all the horses of the nations. ⁵Then the clans of Judah will say in their hearts, 'The people of Jerusalem are strong, because the LORD Almighty is their God.'

⁶"On that day I will make the clans of Judah like a firepot in a woodpile, like a flaming torch among sheaves. They will consume all the surrounding peoples right and left, but Jerusalem will remain intact in her place.

⁷"The LORD will save the dwellings of Judah first, so that the honor of the house of David and

---

11:4 Shepherd The idea of a prophet (Zechariah) as the symbolic representation of his message is common in prophetic literature (e.g., Isaiah, Jeremiah, Ezekiel, Hosea, Jonah).

11:7 I shepherded Zechariah is now speaking. **called one Favor** The staffs are indicative of the shepherd's guiding principles. The name used here can denote beauty, favor or delight, symbolizing God's blessing on his people (Ps 90:17). **the other Union** The name can denote harmony, unity and bands or bonds. Harmony or agreement is the outcome of leadership guided by divine favor.

11:8 three shepherds The identity of these shepherds is unclear. Many possibilities have been suggested, such as the last three kings of Judah: Jehoiakim, Jehoiachin and Zedekiah.

11:9 Let those who are left eat one another's flesh A reference to the cannibalism that accompanied the siege of Jerusalem (see Dt 28:54–55; La 4:10).

11:12 give me my pay Having lost his sheep, the prophet asks the nation to provide his wages. **thirty pieces of silver** The afflicted nation determined that the service of the shepherd was worth 30 pieces of silver, the legal compensation for the loss of a slave (see Ex 21:32). The reference here is to the shekel, the basic unit of silver that weighed just over 11 grams. Matthew's Gospel likely alludes to this passage in recounting the 30 pieces of silver given to Judas Iscariot for betraying Jesus (Mt 26:15). Later, Matthew reports the fulfillment of this prophecy when the priests use the 30 pieces of silver discarded by Judas to buy a potter's field (Mt 27:3–10). See the infographic "A Silver Denarius" on p. 1578.

11:13 Throw it to the potter Refers to the potter's field, a place of debris where a potter would discard broken pottery. God instructs the prophet to throw his wages into the trash. Compare Mt 27:7–10.

12:1—14:21 The second revelatory oracle (Zec 12:1—14:21) focuses on the events surrounding Yahweh's second coming and his enthronement as the King of Israel. The consistent use of the phrase "on that day" demonstrates the future-oriented nature of the oracle.

12:2 a cup that sends all the surrounding peoples reeling The surrounding nations will become like a stumbling, drunken man. Isaiah 51:17,22 and Jeremiah 25:15–16 also use this metaphor (see note on Jer 25:15).

of Jerusalem's inhabitants may not be greater than that of Judah. ⁸On that day the LORD will shield those who live in Jerusalem, so that the feeblest among them will be like David, and the house of David will be like God, like the angel of the LORD going before them. ⁹On that day I will set out to destroy all the nations that attack Jerusalem.

Mourning for the One They Pierced

¹⁰"And I will pour out on the house of David and the inhabitants of Jerusalem a spirit*ᵃ* of grace and supplication. They will look on*ᵇ* me, the one they have pierced, and they will mourn for him as one mourns for an only child, and grieve bitterly for him as one grieves for a firstborn son. ¹¹On that day the weeping in Jerusalem will be as great as the weeping of Hadad Rimmon in the plain of Megiddo. ¹²The land will mourn, each clan by itself, with their wives by themselves: the clan of the house of David and their wives, the clan of the house of Nathan and their wives, ¹³the clan of the house of Levi and their wives, the clan of Shimei and their wives, ¹⁴and all the rest of the clans and their wives.

Cleansing From Sin

13 "On that day a fountain will be opened to the house of David and the inhabitants of Jerusalem, to cleanse them from sin and impurity.

²"On that day, I will banish the names of the idols from the land, and they will be remembered no more," declares the LORD Almighty. "I will remove both the prophets and the spirit of impurity from the land. ³And if anyone still prophesies,

their father and mother, to whom they were born, will say to them, 'You must die, because you have told lies in the LORD's name.' Then their own parents will stab the one who prophesies.

⁴"On that day every prophet will be ashamed of their prophetic vision. They will not put on a prophet's garment of hair in order to deceive. ⁵Each will say, 'I am not a prophet. I am a farmer; the land has been my livelihood since my youth.*ᶜ*' ⁶If someone asks, 'What are these wounds on your body*ᵈ*?' they will answer, 'The wounds I was given at the house of my friends.'

The Shepherd Struck, the Sheep Scattered

⁷"Awake, sword, against my shepherd,
    against the man who is close to me!"
        declares the LORD Almighty.
"Strike the shepherd,
    and the sheep will be scattered,
    and I will turn my hand against the little
        ones.
⁸In the whole land," declares the LORD,
    "two-thirds will be struck down and
        perish;
    yet one-third will be left in it.
⁹This third I will put into the fire;
    I will refine them like silver
    and test them like gold.
They will call on my name
    and I will answer them;
I will say, 'They are my people,'
    and they will say, 'The LORD is our God.'"

ᵃ 10 Or *the Spirit*   *ᵇ* 10 Or *to*   *ᶜ* 5 Or *farmer; a man sold me in my youth*   *ᵈ* 6 Or *wounds between your hands*

12:10 one they have pierced This phrase refers to the heartbreaking effect the nation's idolatry has on God (compare Zec 13:3). John's Gospel uses this phrase at the end of a sequence of OT allusions and quotations designed to show how the details of Jesus' crucifixion aligned with Biblical prophecy. In Jn 19:32–37, the soldiers pierce Jesus' side with a spear, and John identifies that action as the fulfillment of Zec 12:10 (see Jn 19:37).
12:12 house of Nathan The third son of David born in Jerusalem. Shortly after the exile, the royal line began to be traced through Nathan. (Zerubbabel was of the line of Nathan, not Solomon.)
12:13 Shimei The family of Shimei, the grandson of Levi (Nu 3:18,21). Here they represent the priestly line in Israel.
12:14 all the rest of the clans Everyone will mourn, from the least to the greatest.
13:1 that day The Day of Yahweh was a day of judgment (Zec 12:2–3) as well as a day of restoration. **cleanse them from sin and impurity** The people must be restored to a state of purity before God.
13:2 I will banish the names Refers to removing the idols completely so that not even the memory of them remains.
13:3 You must die Deuteronomy 13:1–11 commands the death penalty for those who engage in idolatry and

false prophecy. In this restored future, loyalty to Yahweh trumps loyalty to family.
13:5 I am not a prophet False prophets will go into hiding and masquerade as farmers. The false prophets' claim echoes Am 7:14, where Amos asserts that he is not a professional prophet—just a working man called by God.
13:6 these wounds on your body False prophets often cut themselves as part of their idolatrous rituals. The custom originated as a way to show one's devotion to the gods.
13:7 my shepherd Here the metaphor of the shepherd likely represents a royal leader, using the imagery in the sense of Ezekiel and Jeremiah (see Eze 34:1–10; Jer 23:1–6; compare 1Ki 22:17). The shepherd imagery of Zec 10–11 likely included religious leaders such as false prophets (see 11:16–17). **Strike the shepherd** The NT quotes this verse in relation to the arrest of Jesus (see Mt 26:31; Mk 14:27).
13:9 They are my people A covenant formula expressing the intimate relationship between Yahweh and Israel (see Ex 6:7; Lev 26:12). Hosea uses this formulaic language to describe breaking as well as restoring the relationship (Hos 1:9; 2:23). Variations on the formula appear a number of times in Jeremiah and Ezekiel (e.g., Jer 7:23; 11:4; 24:7; 31:33; Eze 36:28; 37:27).

The Lord Comes and Reigns

14 A day of the Lord is coming, Jerusalem, when your possessions will be plundered and divided up within your very walls.

²I will gather all the nations to Jerusalem to fight against it; the city will be captured, the houses ransacked, and the women raped. Half of the city will go into exile, but the rest of the people will not be taken from the city. ³Then the Lord will go out and fight against those nations, as he fights on a day of battle. ⁴On that day his feet will stand on the Mount of Olives, east of Jerusalem, and the Mount of Olives will be split in two from east to west, forming a great valley, with half of the mountain moving north and half moving south. ⁵You will flee by my mountain valley, for it will extend to Azel. You will flee as you fled from the earthquakeᵃ in the days of Uzziah king of Judah. Then the Lord my God will come, and all the holy ones with him.

⁶On that day there will be neither sunlight nor cold, frosty darkness. ⁷It will be a unique day — a day known only to the Lord — with no distinction between day and night. When evening comes, there will be light.

⁸On that day living water will flow out from Jerusalem, half of it east to the Dead Sea and half of it west to the Mediterranean Sea, in summer and in winter.

⁹The Lord will be king over the whole earth. On that day there will be one Lord, and his name the only name.

¹⁰The whole land, from Geba to Rimmon, south of Jerusalem, will become like the Arabah. But Jerusalem will be raised up high from the Benjamin Gate to the site of the First Gate, to the Corner Gate, and from the Tower of Hananel to the royal winepresses, and will remain in its place. ¹¹It will be inhabited; never again will it be destroyed. Jerusalem will be secure.

¹²This is the plague with which the Lord will strike all the nations that fought against Jerusalem: Their flesh will rot while they are still standing on their feet, their eyes will rot in their sockets, and their tongues will rot in their mouths. ¹³On that day people will be stricken by the Lord with great panic. They will seize each other by the hand and attack one another. ¹⁴Judah too will fight at Jerusalem. The wealth of all the surrounding nations will be collected — great quantities of gold and silver and clothing. ¹⁵A similar plague will strike the horses and mules, the camels and donkeys, and all the animals in those camps.

¹⁶Then the survivors from all the nations that have attacked Jerusalem will go up year after year to worship the King, the Lord Almighty, and to celebrate the Festival of Tabernacles. ¹⁷If any of the peoples of the earth do not go up to Jerusalem to worship the King, the Lord Almighty, they will have no rain. ¹⁸If the Egyptian people do not go up

---

ᵃ 5 Or ⁵My mountain valley will be blocked and will extend to Azel. It will be blocked as it was blocked because of the earthquake

---

14:1–2 The events described in Zec 14:1–2 correspond to Joel 2:1–11. Jeremiah refers to this period as a time of distress for Jacob (Jer 30:7), whereas Daniel refers to it as the most distressing time since the beginning of nations (Da 12:1). Each of these passages describes a period of great suffering for the nation of Israel.

14:1 A day of the Lord is coming A phrase used throughout the prophets to denote the day when God will intervene in human affairs and judge the wicked (Isa 13:6,9; Eze 30:3; Joel 1:15; 2:1; Am 5:18; Ob 15; Mal 4:5) or bless the righteous (Joel 3:16–21; Ob 17–21; Zep 3:9–20). **divided up within your very walls** Refers to a conquering army dividing the spoils of war.

14:2 I will gather all the nations Yahweh gathers the nations in order to purify his people (Zec 13:9) and judge their enemies (Joel 3:2; Zec 14:3).

14:4 Mount of Olives An extended ridgeline bordering Jerusalem to the east. The Mount of Olives is higher in elevation than Jerusalem; it is situated 230 feet above the Temple Mount. **a great valley** Refers to the Valley of Jehoshaphat—the valley of Yahweh's judgment (compare Joel 3:2). This great valley will allow the faithful remnant to escape the armies that have captured Jerusalem (Zec 14:5).

14:5 days of Uzziah king of Judah Also known as Azariah, meaning "Yahweh is my strength"; reigned ca. 792–742 BC. See the timeline "The Divided Kingdom" on p. 536.

14:8 living water Describes waters flowing rapidly with constant movement and a variety of twists and turns, so that they appear to be something alive. Ezekiel 47:1–12 also describes a river flowing from Jerusalem in the last days.

14:9 there will be one Lord An allusion drawing attention to the statement of Yahweh's essential unity in Dt 6:4 (sometimes referred to as the Shema).

14:10 from Geba A town given to the Levites located about six miles north of Jerusalem in the territory of Benjamin. The town is to be identified with the modern Jaba. **Rimmon, south of Jerusalem** A town originally given to the tribe of Simeon located about nine miles north of Beersheba. **like the Arabah** The rugged terrain south of Jerusalem that is filled with steep hills and deep valleys. It is commonly called the Judean Wilderness. **in its place** Each of the subsequent locations is within Jerusalem.

14:12 the plague Alludes to the plagues Yahweh brought against Egypt in Ex 7–11 (compare Zec 14:18).

14:14 The wealth of all the surrounding nations A reversal of the situation of v. 1, where Jerusalem was plundered.

14:16 survivors The prophets describe how all the nations will one day come to worship Yahweh (compare Isa 2:3; Mic 4:2; Zec 8:20). **Festival of Tabernacles** One of the three feasts during which every male Jew was required to be in Jerusalem (Dt 16:16). During this festival, the Jews commemorated the wilderness wanderings of the exodus generation by living in tents set up around Jerusalem. The dedication of Solomon's temple took place during this feast.

14:18 Egyptian people All the nations of the world, including Egypt, will worship Yahweh (see Isa 19:21

and take part, they will have no rain. The Lord[a] will bring on them the plague he inflicts on the nations that do not go up to celebrate the Festival of Tabernacles. ¹⁹This will be the punishment of Egypt and the punishment of all the nations that do not go up to celebrate the Festival of Tabernacles.

²⁰On that day HOLY TO THE LORD will be inscribed on the bells of the horses, and the cooking pots in the Lord's house will be like the sacred bowls in front of the altar. ²¹Every pot in Jerusalem and Judah will be holy to the Lord Almighty, and all who come to sacrifice will take some of the pots and cook in them. And on that day there will no longer be a Canaanite[b] in the house of the Lord Almighty.

a 18 Or *part, then the* Lord   *b* 21 Or *merchant*

and note). They will be subject to judgment for failing to observe Yahweh's laws, just as Israel is.

14:20 HOLY TO THE LORD will be inscribed on the bells of the horses The horse, originally an unclean animal (Lev 11:1–8), will now be viewed as a clean animal. This change in status will be announced by tinkling bells that describe the horse as "holy to Yahweh."

14:21 a Canaanite The expression here refers to the people of Canaan; in context, it represents all unbelievers and foreigners. There will no longer be any foreigners because all the nations now worship Yahweh and thus are one people under Yahweh's kingship (Zec 14:16–21; compare Isa 19:16–25 and note; Ac 2).

MALACHI

INTRODUCTION TO MALACHI

The book of Malachi addresses the situation in Judah sometime after the temple was rebuilt in 516 BC, following the return of Jewish exiles from Babylon. The message of the book is about the covenant—Israel's contract with God (compare Ex 24:1–8). The book records six legal disputes in which God either defends his own faithfulness or accuses the people and their leaders of forsaking their covenant. The book ends with a promise of the coming of Elijah and the Day of Yahweh. Malachi addresses how God is faithful to his covenant love, even when we doubt his faithfulness.

BACKGROUND

Based on the book's opening verse, the author is traditionally thought to be a prophet named Malachi. However, "Malachi" is the Hebrew word for "my messenger," and it might not be used here as a proper name. No date is given in the book, but the prophet's ministry seems to have occurred sometime between the rebuilding of the Jerusalem temple (516 BC) and the time of Nehemiah (ca. 444–432 BC). Although the temple had been rebuilt, Malachi shows that the reforms inspired by the prophets Haggai and Zechariah (starting in 520 BC) had little effect.

Malachi concludes the Old Testament canon of the Protestant Christian tradition. Thus, the Old Testament ends with Malachi's promise of God's messenger who is to come (Mal 4:5–6). When you turn the page to the New Testament, the Gospels show the fulfillment of this expectation. The Gospel writers show how John the Baptist, in the spirit of Elijah, prepares the way for Jesus (Mal 3:1–4; 4:5; Lk 1:16–17).

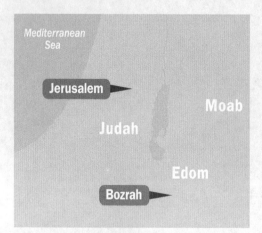

This map depicts some of the locations related to the book of Malachi.

STRUCTURE

Just as priests would help resolve legal conflicts (Dt 17:8–13), Malachi is mediating a court case between God and the people. The book contains a series of six disputes that have a similar pattern: God speaks, the people question him and God delivers a rebuttal. The theme of the first dispute (Mal 1:2–5) is that God loves Israel. When the people ask *how* he has loved them, he contrasts his unwarranted kindness toward them with his anger toward their neighbors, the Edomites. In the second dispute (1:6—2:9), God rebukes the priests for failing to honor him. In the third dispute (2:10–16), he criticizes his people for being unfaithful to him and to one another. The theme of the fourth dispute (2:17—3:5)

is that God is just, but the people have acted unjustly. In the fifth dispute (3:6–12), God speaks against the people for withholding tithes from him. In the sixth dispute (3:13—4:3), God draws a distinction between those who speak arrogantly and those who revere him. Those who revere God will be blessed on the Day of Yahweh, which is a promised day of judgment and restoration. The book ends with a reminder to uphold the law of Moses and a promise that God will send Elijah the prophet before the Day of Yahweh (4:4–6).

OUTLINE

- First dispute: against Edom (1:1–5)
- Second dispute: against the priests (1:6—2:9)
- Third dispute: God despises unfaithfulness (2:10–16)
- Fourth dispute: the messenger of Yahweh (2:17—3:5)
- Fifth dispute: withholding tithes (3:6–12)
- Sixth dispute: the Day of Yahweh (3:13—4:3)
- Summary and the prophecy of Elijah to come (4:4–6)

THEMES

Malachi addresses the motive behind people's worship. Merely going through the religious motions does not guarantee that God will bless a person or community. When religion is practiced for

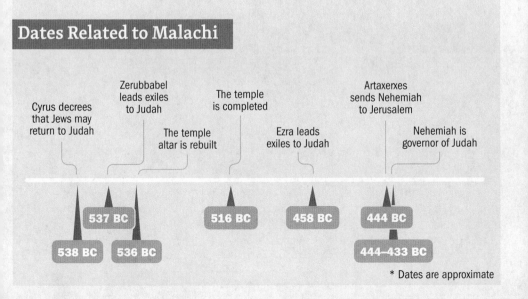

Dates Related to Malachi

Cyrus decrees that Jews may return to Judah

Zerubbabel leads exiles to Judah

The temple altar is rebuilt

The temple is completed

Ezra leads exiles to Judah

Artaxerxes sends Nehemiah to Jerusalem

Nehemiah is governor of Judah

537 BC

516 BC

458 BC

444 BC

538 BC   536 BC

444–433 BC

* Dates are approximate

personal gain, it can cause great harm. The people's accusations against God reveal their true motives: They were performing their religious duties and thought that God owed them for their obedience, even though their worship was halfhearted and hypocritical. Although the people had a temple in which to worship, the nature of their worship had not been changed by the exile: They were still living as if religion could save them. Instead, they must remember that they are God's cherished possession and that he loves them as a father loves a son, just as he loves us today (3:17–18).

The prophet calls for renewal, both in the temple and in the community as a whole. He calls out the people for failing to worship properly and failing to honor their covenant with Yahweh. The prophet also proclaims that while sin demands God's judgment, a faithful remnant of people will survive—with the help of a new Elijah (3:1–5; 4:5–6). These actions set the stage for the Messiah, the one who will bring justice and salvation to the world (Mk 8:28; 9:11–13). Malachi shows us that what we really need is a transformative relationship with Yahweh himself.

1 A prophecy: The word of the Lord to Israel through Malachi.[a]

Israel Doubts God's Love

[2]"I have loved you," says the Lord.

"But you ask, 'How have you loved us?'

"Was not Esau Jacob's brother?" declares the Lord. "Yet I have loved Jacob, [3]but Esau I have hated, and I have turned his hill country into a wasteland and left his inheritance to the desert jackals."

[4]Edom may say, "Though we have been crushed, we will rebuild the ruins."

But this is what the Lord Almighty says: "They may build, but I will demolish. They will be called the Wicked Land, a people always under the wrath of the Lord. [5]You will see it with your own eyes and say, 'Great is the Lord — even beyond the borders of Israel!'

Breaking Covenant Through Blemished Sacrifices

[6]"A son honors his father, and a slave his master. If I am a father, where is the honor due me? If I am a master, where is the respect due me?" says the Lord Almighty.

[a] 1 Malachi means my messenger.

1:1 This verse acts as a title or heading to the book of Malachi, which addresses the people of Judah sometime between the completion of the rebuilt temple (516 BC) and the period of Nehemiah (ca. 444–432 BC). The exiles had returned from Babylon, but the people's faithfulness to Yahweh and his covenant continued to waver. Malachi's messages appear to indicate that while the prophets Haggai and Zechariah had motivated the people to finish the temple and reinstitute the temple service, their efforts to renew the people's commitment to Yahweh had not resulted in long-term change (these efforts began in 520 BC; Ezr 5:1). It is for this reason that Ezra the priest's actions were required (beginning in 458 BC and continuing into the time of Nehemiah; Ezr 7–10). There are similarities between the message of Malachi and the reforms of Ezra and Nehemiah, which could indicate that Malachi is their contemporary (compare Mal 3:7–10 to Ne 10:37–39; also compare Mal 2:10–16 to Ne 13:23–29 and Ezr 9–10). See the timeline "Approximate Dates of Old Testament Prophets" on p. 1070.

1:1 A prophecy See note on Na 1:1. **to Israel** The remnant of people who returned from exile in Babylon. This title is used because Israel serves as another name for the people's forefather Jacob (Ge 35:10), whose election is described in the verses following his naming. In 538 BC, the Persian Empire—who had succeeded Babylon as the world's superpower—allowed for the Jewish people to return from their exile to their homeland. The words of Malachi were addressed to this group of people, who were now living in Jerusalem. **Malachi** Meaning "my messenger." Possibly a descriptive title of the author rather than a personal name. The argument that "malachi" is a title rather than a name is based on the following reasons: the name appears nowhere else in the OT; the name is highly unusual in that it ends with the possessive i (meaning "my"); the Greek translation (Septuagint) and the Aramaic translation (Targum) took the phrase to represent an office as opposed to a proper name; and the book contains no information regarding the prophet's parentage or hometown. In addition, there is no mention of Malachi in Ezra and Nehemiah, whereas the prophets Haggai and Zechariah are both mentioned in Ezr 5:1. See the table "Symbolic Names of People in Hebrew" on p. 1388.

1:2–5 Malachi is written in a disputation style, much like the record of a court case. The pattern is used to raise a point made by certain individuals, and then offer a contradiction in a point-counterpoint formula. There are six cycles of disputation in Malachi. Each cycle begins with Yahweh making a statement of truth concerning his character. A hypothetical audience then offers a rebuttal in the form of a question. Each cycle ends with Yahweh responding by presenting supporting evidence. Other examples of the disputation pattern include Isa 40:27–28; Jer 2:23–37; Eze 12:21–28; and Mic 2:6–11.

1:2 I have loved you This Hebrew term for "love" is a technical term in ancient Near Eastern treaty and covenant texts indicating choice or election to covenant relationship. **Esau** The son of Isaac and older brother of Jacob (see Ge 25:21–26). Esau's descendants were the inhabitants of Edom, the region to the southeast of Judah on the southeastern corner of the Dead Sea. **Jacob** The son of Isaac and younger brother of Esau (see Ge 25:21–26).

1:3 Esau I have hated The term for hate is an ancient Near Eastern covenant term. It is used here to denote rejection. Yahweh chose Jacob, not Esau, to continue the covenant relationship began with Abraham. This choice reflects a regular pattern in the OT where a younger son is favored (e.g., Abel in Ge 4, Isaac in Ge 21, Joseph in Ge 37 and David in 1Sa 16). This recurring theme reveals that Yahweh is not bound by the conventions of human society. **I have turned his hill country into a wasteland** The destruction described here is probably what resulted from the repeated invasions of Edom by the Babylonians between 605 and 540 BC. There is no evidence that Edom was invaded or destroyed during Nebuchadnezzar's campaign against Judah around 586 BC. However, Nabonidus, one of Nebuchadnezzar's later successors, claims to have destroyed a place that was probably the Edomite capital city of Bozrah around 552 BC. **desert jackals** A canine similar to but smaller than a wolf. These nocturnal scavengers howl with an eerie wail. See note on La 4:3.

1:4 I will demolish Yahweh will frustrate all of the Edomites' attempts to reassert themselves as a regional power. This detailed picture of Yahweh's attitude toward Edom appears to represent a counterexample to his attitude toward Judah. Although Edom was able to rebuild their empire after the Babylonian conquest, they quickly fell prey to the Nabateans (ca. 350 BC; compare Ob 7–9).

1:6—2:9 Yahweh rebukes the priests for their failure to maintain the temple service with proper honor and respect. The people should show honor toward God as a son would honor his father, but Israel shows dishonor through their indifference, carelessness and deception with regard to bringing sacrifices and offerings (Mal 1:6–9). No sacrifice at all would have been better than their polluted offerings (v. 10). The priests were allowing animals with physical defects to be offered as sacrifices

"It is you priests who show contempt for my name.

"But you ask, 'How have we shown contempt for your name?'

⁷"By offering defiled food on my altar.

"But you ask, 'How have we defiled you?'

"By saying that the LORD's table is contemptible. ⁸When you offer blind animals for sacrifice, is that not wrong? When you sacrifice lame or diseased animals, is that not wrong? Try offering them to your governor! Would he be pleased with you? Would he accept you?" says the LORD Almighty.

⁹"Now plead with God to be gracious to us. With such offerings from your hands, will he accept you? — says the LORD Almighty.

¹⁰"Oh, that one of you would shut the temple doors, so that you would not light useless fires on my altar! I am not pleased with you," says the LORD Almighty, "and I will accept no offering from your hands. ¹¹My name will be great among the nations, from where the sun rises to where it sets. In every place incense and pure offerings will be brought to me, because my name will be great among the nations," says the LORD Almighty.

¹²"But you profane it by saying, 'The Lord's table is defiled,' and, 'Its food is contemptible.' ¹³And you say, 'What a burden!' and you sniff at it contemptuously," says the LORD Almighty.

"When you bring injured, lame or diseased animals and offer them as sacrifices, should I accept them from your hands?" says the LORD. ¹⁴"Cursed is the cheat who has an acceptable male in his flock and vows to give it, but then sacrifices a blemished animal to the Lord. For I am a great king," says the LORD Almighty, "and my name is to be feared among the nations.

Additional Warning to the Priests

2 "And now, you priests, this warning is for you. ²If you do not listen, and if you do not resolve to honor my name," says the LORD Almighty, "I will send a curse on you, and I will curse your blessings. Yes, I have already cursed them, because you have not resolved to honor me.

³"Because of you I will rebuke your descendantsᵃ; I will smear on your faces the dung from

ᵃ 3 Or *will blight your grain*

---

even though Biblical law stipulated only unblemished animals were appropriate for sacrifice (see Lev 1:3 and note). The priests do not even appear to recognize the seriousness of this violation (Mal 1:13). The priests above all should realize their responsibility to carry out their duties in a way that brings honor to Yahweh. Their failure brings judgment, and they will be held to account for causing the people to stumble (2:1–9).

1:6 his master The Hebrew word used here, *adon*, is the root word of Adonai, a title for God meaning "my master." **LORD Almighty** This divine title is used throughout this section (see Mal 1:8,9,10,11,13,14; 2:2,4,7,8). **my name** See vv. 11,14; 2:2,5. The priests' disobedience was causing harm to Yahweh's reputation.

1:7 By offering defiled food The priests were responsible for offering sacrifices to Yahweh using animals of the highest quality. **the LORD's table** Refers to the sacrificial altar in the rebuilt temple (see Ezr 3:1–3)

1:8 lame or diseased animals The law prohibited the use of imperfect animals for offerings to Yahweh (see Dt 15:21). The priests are being reprimanded for their lax attention to proper sacrificial practices. **your governor** The political leader in Judah who was appointed by the Persian king. The Hebrew term appears most frequently in post-exilic books (Hag 2:21; Ezr 8:36; Ne 2:7; Est 3:12), often with reference to officials appointed by the Persians. **Would he accept you** Hebrew uses the idiom of lifting the face (*nasa panim*) to describe showing favor to someone. The idiom likely developed from the act of responding to someone bowing in humility or shame by raising their downcast face to look them in the eye.

1:10 would shut the temple doors It would be better to close the gates of the temple so that the priests could no longer offer unclean sacrifices.

1:11 incense One of the regular duties of the priests was keeping the incense altar burning continually in the Holy Place of the temple (Ex 30:1–8; 2Ch 13:11).

1:13 a burden The priests viewed the sacrificial system

as an oppressive burden, especially in light of the fact that the remnant—the small community of Jews who had returned from exile—was in a state of extreme poverty. **1:14 the cheat** Promising one thing and offering another amounts to cheating Yahweh out of what was rightfully his. **great king** This title is full of covenantal implications; it was commonly used in ancient Near Eastern treaty texts to identify the suzerain (or high king) that others pledge loyalty to (compare Ps 47:2). **my name is to be feared** Evokes the image of the Divine Warrior whose reputation should strike fear into all who hear of him (compare Jos 2:8–11; Ps 76:12).

2:2 listen This is the same Hebrew word used in Dt 6:4 (*shama*). There, however, the emphasis is on hearing with understanding, whereas here it indicates obedience. This parallels the allusion to Dt 6:4 in Mal 2:10 (see note on v. 10). Collectively, these allusions act as a reminder to the people of their commitments to Yahweh. **I will send a curse on you** Violating the covenant, like breaking a contract, invoked the negative consequences stipulated by the agreement, specifically curses as described in Lev 26 and Dt 28. **I have already cursed them** The promised blessings for God's people have not materialized and will not as long as the people continue in their disobedience. The community is already in a state of poverty because of their unfaithfulness (compare Hag 1:10–11).

2:3 Because of you I will rebuke your descendants Refers to judgment, but the Hebrew phrasing to rebuke (*go'er*) the offspring (*zera'*) is unusual. Possibly *zera'* is meant as seed for planting, making the rebuke about preventing a good harvest (Lev 26:20). However, a more serious curse directed at the priests would be the loss of family (Dt 28:18,41). Cutting off someone's offspring (*zera'*) refers to bringing their family line to an end (1Sa 24:21; Ps 37:28). **smear on your faces the dung from your festival sacrifices, and you will be carried off with it** The priests will be carried away outside the camp along with the refuse from the sacrifices that must be disposed of (Ex 29:14; Lev 4:11–12).

your festival sacrifices, and you will be carried off with it. ⁴And you will know that I have sent you this warning so that my covenant with Levi may continue," says the LORD Almighty. ⁵"My covenant was with him, a covenant of life and peace, and I gave them to him; this called for reverence and he revered me and stood in awe of my name. ⁶True instruction was in his mouth and nothing false was found on his lips. He walked with me in peace and uprightness, and turned many from sin.

⁷"For the lips of a priest ought to preserve knowledge, because he is the messenger of the LORD Almighty and people seek instruction from his mouth. ⁸But you have turned from the way and by your teaching have caused many to stumble; you have violated the covenant with Levi," says the LORD Almighty. ⁹"So I have caused you to be despised and humiliated before all the people, because you have not followed my ways but have shown partiality in matters of the law."

Breaking Covenant Through Divorce

¹⁰Do we not all have one Father[a]? Did not one God create us? Why do we profane the covenant of our ancestors by being unfaithful to one another?

¹¹Judah has been unfaithful. A detestable thing has been committed in Israel and in Jerusalem: Judah has desecrated the sanctuary the LORD loves by marrying women who worship a foreign god. ¹²As for the man who does this, whoever he may be, may the LORD remove him from the tents of Jacob[b] — even though he brings an offering to the LORD Almighty.

¹³Another thing you do: You flood the LORD's altar with tears. You weep and wail because he no longer looks with favor on your offerings or accepts them with pleasure from your hands. ¹⁴You ask, "Why?" It is because the LORD is the witness between you and the wife of your youth. You have been unfaithful to her, though she is your partner, the wife of your marriage covenant.

¹⁵Has not the one God made you? You belong to him in body and spirit. And what does the one God seek? Godly offspring.[c] So be on your guard, and do not be unfaithful to the wife of your youth.

---

a 10 Or *father*   *b* 12 Or *¹²May the* LORD *remove from the tents of Jacob anyone who gives testimony in behalf of the man who does this*   *c* 15 The meaning of the Hebrew for the first part of this verse is uncertain.

2:4 my covenant with Levi may continue Yahweh had made a special covenant with the tribe of Levi, commanding them to teach his laws to the rest of the nation (see Lev 10:11; Dt 31:11–13; 33:10). Yahweh's attitude toward this covenant is consistent; his rebuke is meant for correction and does not symbolize that he has abandoned his people (compare Pr 3:11–12).

2:6 True instruction was in his mouth The things taught by the priests were accurate, at least initially. "His mouth" refers collectively to the Levitical priesthood.

2:7 messenger The Hebrew word used here, *mal'akh*, is the common word for a messenger. Since Malachi's name means "my messenger," the use of the word here may be a play on the prophet's name. See note on 1:1.

2:8 from the way The image of following the appropriate way or path is used throughout Proverbs to designate the way of wisdom and righteousness (see Pr 2:8,20; 4:11; 6:23).

2:9 shown partiality in matters of the law The Hebrew uses the same idiom for showing favoritism or partiality as in Mal 1:8 (see note on 1:8). Lifting the face (*nasa panim*) is an idiom for showing favoritism. Here it is used with reference to the law, and amounts to an accusation that the priests are breaking God's repeated commands to deal fairly with everyone (Ex 23:3; Lev 19:15; Dt 16:19).

2:10–16 This is the third of six disputes in Malachi between God and his people (see note on Mal 1:2–5). Here, Malachi shifts from speaking on behalf of Yahweh to speaking as one of the people of Israel. In v. 11, Malachi critiques God's people as a whole. This indicates that the first two disputes proved that Yahweh was in the right, and adequately showed the people's guilt; now the people must respond by correcting their actions.

2:10 one Father Possibly an indirect reference (or allusion) to Isa 63:16. The idea of Israel as the offspring of Yahweh originally appears in Ex 4:22, where the nation is identified as Yahweh's firstborn (compare Jer 31:9).

one God An allusion to Dt 6:4. This is a reminder that the people should serve God with their entire being.

2:11 marrying women who worship a foreign god May refer to intermarriage with foreigners who did not worship Yahweh (Ex 34:16). The prophets regularly blend the imagery of marriage and idolatry (see Hos 2:1–23; Jer 3:2–7; Eze 16:8–21). Malachi may be echoing those earlier prophets, but in his day, the defiling of the sanctuary through inappropriate observance of Yahweh's commands was a more pressing problem than the active idol worship that Ezekiel witnessed (see Eze 8–10). Yahweh's command against foreign intermarriage appears in Dt 7:1–4. The command of Dt 7:1 is specifically addressed against the seven nations that occupied the land of Israel at that time. Ezra later broadens the scope of the original command to include other nations (Ezr 9:1–2), thus indicating that the original command applied to all foreign women. Nehemiah also considered intermarriage with other nations to pose a threat to God's people (Ne 13:23–29).

2:12 may the LORD remove him from the tents of Jacob Refers to excommunication (see Ex 12:15,19; compare Lev 19:8). Jacob is used here as a synonym for Israel. See note on Mal 2:3. **he brings an offering to the LORD Almighty** Any offering that was not handled properly and presented appropriately would not be accepted by God (Lev 26:31; compare Am 5:21–27). Even obedience to the letter of the law did not guarantee acceptance if people were not worshiping with the proper attitude (Mic 6:6–8).

2:13 weep and wail Cain likewise had a negative response when his offering was rejected (see Ge 4:5). However, these emotional displays may have been associated with how foreign idols were worshiped (compare 1Ki 18:26–30). Their offerings are rejected because they are practicing worship in a way that emulates idol worship.

2:14 the wife of your youth Since a Jewish marriage was religious and involved a covenant, God served as

16"The man who hates and divorces his wife," says the LORD, the God of Israel, "does violence to the one he should protect,"[a] says the LORD Almighty.

So be on your guard, and do not be unfaithful.

Breaking Covenant Through Injustice

17You have wearied the LORD with your words.

"How have we wearied him?" you ask.

By saying, "All who do evil are good in the eyes of the LORD, and he is pleased with them" or "Where is the God of justice?"

3 "I will send my messenger, who will prepare the way before me. Then suddenly the Lord you are seeking will come to his temple; the messenger of the covenant, whom you desire, will come," says the LORD Almighty.

2But who can endure the day of his coming? Who can stand when he appears? For he will be like a refiner's fire or a launderer's soap. 3He will sit as a refiner and purifier of silver; he will purify the Levites and refine them like gold and silver.

Then the LORD will have men who will bring offerings in righteousness, 4and the offerings of Judah and Jerusalem will be acceptable to the LORD, as in days gone by, as in former years.

5"So I will come to put you on trial. I will be quick to testify against sorcerers, adulterers and perjurers, against those who defraud laborers of their wages, who oppress the widows and the fatherless, and deprive the foreigners among you of justice, but do not fear me," says the LORD Almighty.

Breaking Covenant by Withholding Tithes

6"I the LORD do not change. So you, the descendants of Jacob, are not destroyed. 7Ever since the time of your ancestors you have turned away from my decrees and have not kept them. Return to me, and I will return to you," says the LORD Almighty.

a 16 Or "I hate divorce," says the LORD, the God of Israel, "because the man who divorces his wife covers his garment with violence,"

---

the witness (Mal 2:10). Thus, a Jewish man abandoning his Jewish wife was tantamount to abandoning a vow to God himself. **You have been unfaithful to her** The unfaithfulness results from divorcing her to marry a foreign woman. This divorce was viewed as an abomination (v. 11), a profaning action (vv. 10,11) and an act of treachery (vv. 10,11,14,15,16).

2:15 Godly offspring One of the main purposes of a marriage in the ancient Near East was to procreate, as doing so was necessary for the economic growth of both families and a nation. Malachi appropriates this idea, but through the lens of the commands in the law (e.g., Dt 6:7; 11:19), to argue that God desires more godly people and that his people having children is one way that goal is accomplished.

2:16 man who hates and divorces Divorce for selfish reasons is prohibited. God hates that the Hebrew people he is addressing divorced their original Jewish wives to marry foreign ones (see Mal 2:11). The foreign wives were leading the Hebrew males and their families to worship foreign gods instead of Yahweh (see note on Ezr 9:2; and note on Ezr 10:3).

2:17—3:5 Malachi's fourth dispute addresses the people's doubts about God's justice. They appear to be questioning the very rationale for covenant observance, implying that the framework of blessings for obedience and curses for disobedience has no effect in the real world. Evil people sometimes prosper and are not visibly cursed because of their sins (compare Hab 1:13). Malachi presents Yahweh's answer to that charge—judgment is coming, Yahweh's messenger is preparing the way, and when that day suddenly comes, the people will experience Yahweh's justice firsthand.

2:17 he is pleased with them Yahweh has seemingly blessed those who practice evil. **Where is the God of justice** The nation was questioning the existence of the "God of justice" (compare Isa 30:18) because it seemed that the wicked were being blessed instead of cursed (see Dt 28; Hab 1:2–4).

3:1 I will send my messenger An individual who prepares the way for the arrival of the Messiah (see Isa

40:3–5). Malachi later identifies this messenger as the prophet Elijah (Mal 4:5). This messenger is identified in the NT as John the Baptist (Mt 11:10; Mk 1:2), the forerunner of Jesus Christ. Mark quotes this verse juxtaposed with Isa 40:3; both passages are applied to John the Baptist. **the Lord you are seeking** The Jews eagerly anticipated the coming of the promised Messiah and the Day of Yahweh because they understood the coming primarily as a day of salvation for them and judgment on their enemies (compare Am 5:18–20). However, it would also be a day when they too would be judged for sin (Mal 3:5). **his temple** When the Messiah comes, he will enter the temple in fulfillment of prophecy (see Isa 66:6; Eze 46:12; Hag 2:9; Zec 6:12).

3:2 the day of his coming The Day of Yahweh. See Joel 1:15 and note; Am 5:18 and note. **refiner's fire** A refiner uses fire to melt metals such as gold and silver to remove impurities. Fire is both purifying and destructive. Compare Zec 13:9. **a launderer's soap** A launderer washes cloth to remove oil and grime so that it can be dyed. Both processes described in this verse—refining metal and cleaning clothes—involved separating what was of value from that which was of no value.

3:3 he will purify the Levites The sons of Levi were in need of purification because of their disobedience to Yahweh's covenant (see Mal 2:8).

3:4 will be acceptable Jeremiah 6:20 uses this Hebrew term together with a negative word to describe the unclean sacrifices of his day as not being pleasing to God.

3:5 quick to testify Yahweh will testify against those who are unrighteous. Lists explicitly detailing the people's offenses are common in the prophets (compare Isa 1:23; Jer 7:5–10; Eze 22:7–13; Zec 7:10). Certain practices are regularly singled out for criticism—mistreating marginal groups in society such as the poor, orphans, widows and foreigners; engaging in sexual immorality; and participating in idol worship.

3:6–12 This fifth disputation continues the focus on Israel's failure to observe Yahweh's laws as they had promised (Ex 24:1–8). The first verse asserting that Yahweh himself has not changed can also be read as another response to the people's doubts about God's

"But you ask, 'How are we to return?'

⁸"Will a mere mortal rob God? Yet you rob me.

"But you ask, 'How are we robbing you?'

"In tithes and offerings. ⁹You are under a curse — your whole nation — because you are robbing me. ¹⁰Bring the whole tithe into the storehouse, that there may be food in my house. Test me in this," says the Lord Almighty, "and see if I will not throw open the floodgates of heaven and pour out so much blessing that there will not be room enough to store it. ¹¹I will prevent pests from devouring your crops, and the vines in your fields will not drop their fruit before it is ripe," says the Lord Almighty. ¹²"Then all the nations will call you blessed, for yours will be a delightful land," says the Lord Almighty.

Israel Speaks Arrogantly Against God

¹³"You have spoken arrogantly against me," says the Lord.

"Yet you ask, 'What have we said against you?'

¹⁴"You have said, 'It is futile to serve God. What do we gain by carrying out his requirements and going about like mourners before the Lord Almighty? ¹⁵But now we call the arrogant blessed.

Certainly evildoers prosper, and even when they put God to the test, they get away with it.'"

The Faithful Remnant

¹⁶Then those who feared the Lord talked with each other, and the Lord listened and heard. A scroll of remembrance was written in his presence concerning those who feared the Lord and honored his name.

¹⁷"On the day when I act," says the Lord Almighty, "they will be my treasured possession. I will spare them, just as a father has compassion and spares his son who serves him. ¹⁸And you will again see the distinction between the righteous and the wicked, between those who serve God and those who do not.

Judgment and Covenant Renewal

4 ᵃ "Surely the day is coming; it will burn like a furnace. All the arrogant and every evildoer will be stubble, and the day that is coming will set them on fire," says the Lord Almighty. "Not a

ᵃ In Hebrew texts 4:1-6 is numbered 3:19-24.

---

justice (Mal 2:17), but it also emphasizes the call to repentance in v. 7. The people were the ones who changed and turned away from God, but they question whether it is even possible for them to turn back. Yahweh asserts that one way they could show renewed loyalty would be to stop robbing him of the tithes and offerings that are rightly his (vv. 8–10). Obedience in this matter would be a significant step in restoring their relationship with God (vv. 11–12).

3:6 I the Lord do not change The primary reason Israel has not been destroyed is because of Yahweh's faithfulness to his covenants with the nation. Yahweh will not change his mind concerning Israel.
3:7 Return to me The Hebrew word for returning or turning around appears here with the idea of repentance — one of its common uses.
3:8 tithes A tenth part of the produce of the ground and livestock. See Lev 27:30 and note. **offerings** Freewill offerings. See 1Ch 29:6.
3:10 the storehouse There were several storehouses located in the temple complex. **I will not throw open the floodgates of heaven** The point of this passage is not that Yahweh would bless the people based on their giving, but instead that he would honor his covenant with them, as told in the law (Lev 26:1–14; Dt 28:12). The people were currently experiencing only the negative side of the covenant, because they were not in proper relationship with Yahweh (Mal 3:6–7; see Dt 28:15–68). The act of giving was a step toward restoring the people's relationship with Yahweh. The tithe represents the people's obedience to their covenant with Yahweh. God is challenging Israel to keep their part of the covenant, so that he may show that he will keep his end of the covenant. Paul explains this concept further in 2Co 9:5, emphasizing that giving must be done with a cheerful spirit. The gift does not earn God's favor; instead, it is the natural response of a person in relationship with God.

3:11 pests An animal that feeds on agricultural produce, such as a locust.

3:13 — 4:3 This passage contains the sixth and final disputation and returns to topics raised in the fourth dispute (Mal 2:17 — 3:5), especially the perceived futility of obedience and the nature of the Day of Yahweh. However, the day of judgment described here emphasizes the positive experience for those who are faithful to Yahweh (4:1–3). In this dispute, the people give clear expression to the objection that serving Yahweh properly, as the prophet has urged, seems pointless, an objection implied by 2:17 (see note on 2:17 — 3:5). They repeat the charge that those who practice evil appear to escape judgment, so there is no incentive for them to obey (3:13–15). The section in vv. 16–18 answers the charge by emphasizing the existence of those who remained faithful to Yahweh and the reality of the distinction between the righteous and the wicked. The acknowledgment that there would be faithful followers of God likely explains why the discussion of the Day of Yahweh draws attention to the salvation of the righteous (4:1–3).

3:15 they get away with it Refers to the evildoers' escaping judgment. Compare 2:17.
3:16 those who feared the Lord The righteous; those who are obedient to Yahweh's commands. **A scroll of remembrance** This book, a metaphor of Yahweh's omniscient recall, first appears in Ex 32:32–33 in reference to the golden calf incident.
3:17 the day The Day of Yahweh. Compare Mal 3:2. Compare Joel 1:15 and note; Am 5:18 and note. **my treasured possession** This Hebrew term first appears in Ex 19:5 in the context of the offer of a covenant relationship by Yahweh to Israel.
4:1 the day The Day of Yahweh. Compare Mal 3:2. Compare Joel 1:15 and note; Am 5:18 and note. **a furnace** Refers to either an oven used to bake bread or a kiln used to harden pottery.

root or a branch will be left to them. [2]But for you who revere my name, the sun of righteousness will rise with healing in its rays. And you will go out and frolic like well-fed calves. [3]Then you will trample on the wicked; they will be ashes under the soles of your feet on the day when I act," says the LORD Almighty.

[4]"Remember the law of my servant Moses,

the decrees and laws I gave him at Horeb for all Israel.

[5]"See, I will send the prophet Elijah to you before that great and dreadful day of the LORD comes. [6]He will turn the hearts of the parents to their children, and the hearts of the children to their parents; or else I will come and strike the land with total destruction."

4:2 the sun of righteousness Although this may be a Messianic title, the expression more likely characterizes the day as one of blessing upon the righteous.

4:3 you will trample on the wicked As treading grapes in a winepress. See the infographic "A Winepress in Ancient Israel" on p. 1157.

4:4–6 These final verses of Malachi are generally understood as the conclusion to the entire book, but it may also function as the conclusion to the sixth disputation. These three verses summarize the essence of Malachi's message: the need for proper observance of God's law, the reality of future judgment and the importance of maintaining a proper society that remains aligned with God's instruction.

4:4 Remember The ancient Greek translation of the Bible (the Septuagint) places Mal 4:4 after v. 6, an arrangement designed to end the book on a positive note. It also serves to end the book with an explicit call to remain obedient to the Law of Moses.

4:5 prophet Elijah The messenger announced in 3:1

is now explicitly identified as the prophet Elijah (see note on 3:1). Second Temple Judaism developed many traditions around the Biblical character of Elijah. Since Elijah did not die but was supernaturally taken to heaven (2Ki 2:11–12), the expectation of his return played into Messianic speculation in the time of Christ. Additionally, it influenced later Jewish traditions that depicted Elijah as an intermediary between the rabbis and Yahweh (see Jn 1:21 and note). Elijah also appears in the NT at Jesus' transfiguration (Mt 17:3–4). In rabbinic literature, Elijah appears as a teacher and dialogue partner for the rabbis (as in the Babylonian Talmud tractate *Berakhot* 3a).

4:6 He will turn the hearts of the parents to their children The Hebrew word for turning or returning (compare Mal 3:7 and note) appears here with the idea of repentance. **with total destruction** The Hebrew word used here, *cherem*, is used throughout the first five books of the Bible (the Pentateuch) to refer to the complete destruction of something that has been put under a sacred ban, usually in reference to the Canaanites and their religion (see Ex 22:20 and note; Nu 21:2–3; Dt 7:2,26).

NEW
TESTAMENT

THE FORMATION OF
THE NEW TESTAMENT

W hat we today call the New Testament is composed of a 27-document collection that Christians view as bearing unique authority—along with the Old Testament—as the Word of God. But the reason that this particular collection of documents—from among other Christian writings of the first century—came to be received and accepted by the church as the New Testament Canon isn't immediately clear.

It is necessary to begin with the definition of the word "canon." A canon is a standard or norm, something against which other things are measured—and as such, it is used in reference to both the Old Testament and New Testament. When we hear the New Testament described as "Canon," it is an acknowledgment that this collection is limited and has authority for the church.[1]

The study of the formation of the New Testament Canon can be understood largely as an ever-narrowing definition of the term "Canon" in reference to Christian writings. Confusion has resulted because not all Canon historians understand the term in the same way. This can be seen in the three main answers to how the church came to accept only the New Testament documents from among other first-century Christian writings.

The first answer was given by Theodore Zahn in the late 19th century when he argued that the New Testament arose as a spontaneous occurrence. Zahn believed that once a New Testament document was cited by a church father, the document should be seen as canonical—citation proved canonicity. Thus, according to Zahn, by the end of the first century there was already a New Testament in existence that was not forced on the church but rather was a spontaneous creation that occurred in the life of the church.[2]

Zahn's position received an important qualification in the early 20th century from Adolf von Harnack, who developed answer number two. Harnack argued that citing a New Testament document as Scripture is very different from simply citing or alluding to New Testament documents; Harnack paid particular attention to the way a document was cited. Whether a citation was preceded by a formula referring to it as "Scripture" became the test for canonicity because doing so gave the document at the same status as the Old Testament. The effect of this qualification was to move the emergence of a New Testament Canon from the first century into the mid- to late second century, when documents attest to citations of New Testament documents as Scripture.[3]

The third answer to the question was offered by Albert C. Sundberg, Jr. Sundberg continued to narrow the definition of Canon in light of his reassessment of the Old Testament Canon in early Christianity.[4] Sundberg observed that the church fathers cited documents as Scripture that are not known to us as canonical Scripture.[5] He concluded that the church did not receive a closed

1 Bruce Metzger, *The Canon of the New Testament* (Oxford: Clarendon Press, 1997), 289–93. 2 Craig D. Allert, *A High View of Scripture?: The Authority of the Bible and the Formation of the New Testament Canon* (Grand Rapids: Baker Academic, 2007), 41–42. 3 Craig D. Allert, *A High View of Scripture?: The Authority of the Bible and the Formation of the New Testament Canon* (Grand Rapids: Baker Academic, 2007), 42–44. 4 A. C. Sundberg, Jr., "Towards a Revised History of the New Testament Canon," *Studia evangelica* 4, no. 1 (1968): 452–61; "The Making of the New Testament Canon," in *The Interpreter's One-Volume Commentary on the Bible*, ed. C. M. Laymon (Nashville: Abingdon Press, 1971), 1216–24; Craig D. Allert, *A High View of Scripture?: The Authority of the Bible and the Formation of the New Testament Canon* (Grand Rapids: Baker Academic, 2007), 45. 5 Craig D. Allert, *A High View of Scripture?: The Authority of the Bible and the Formation of the New Testament Canon* (Grand Rapids: Baker Academic, 2007), 177–85.

Old Testament Canon but rather they received Scripture moving in the direction of being considered a Canon. Because of this, Sundberg believed Harnack's answer was difficult to sustain. The church fathers cited documents not in the closed Old Testament Canon as Scripture. Thus, one cannot claim, as Harnack did, that citation of a document as Scripture proves canonicity. If the church did not receive a closed Old Testament from Judaism, but rather Scripture on the way to canonization, then the comparison of the citations of Christian literature with Old Testament citations cannot establish canonicity for Christian writings.

Sundberg's research has led some to agree that an essential distinction be made between the terms "Scripture" and "Canon."[6] Sundberg thus argued that "Scripture" should be understood as writings that are held in some sense as authoritative for religion. "Canon," on the other hand, should be understood as a defined collection that is to be held as exclusively authoritative with respect to all other documents. The issue here is one of anachronism: We should not refer to a document as "Canon" that would historically have been referred to as "Scripture." Thus, we cannot claim canonicity for a New Testament document that is cited with the same formula as an Old Testament document unless we are prepared to say that the church fathers had a larger Old Testament Canon than we currently have. Based on these conclusions, Sundberg argues that a New Testament Canon did not appear in Christianity until the latter half of the fourth century when lists of canonical books begin to appear.

The definition of the term "Canon"—which has become increasingly narrow—is influential in determining the date and therefore composition of the New Testament Canon. Zahn and Harnack understand "canonical" as referring to a writing that functions authoritatively. If we accept this definition, then a Canon emerges quite early (later first to the end of the second century). Sundberg, on the other hand, views "Canon" in a stricter sense—as a closed list of writings. If we accept this definition, a Canon emerges much later in the fourth century when such lists began to appear.

These three answers are often viewed as mutually exclusive. However, as John Barton points out, when we look at the actual arguments, each position makes some good points.[7] Zahn is correct that most New Testament documents did have authority in the late first and early second centuries; Harnack is correct that these books were discriminately added to in the second and third centuries; Sundberg is correct that it is only from the fourth century onward that authoritative rulings about the exact limits of the Canon appear.

However, we could also call each position overstated. Zahn asserted that the New Testament books would one day form a Canon, but it is an overstatement to claim that this was the intent of first-century Christians. Harnack does not give enough attention to the reality that, in the second century, there was still an openness to receive other books—that is, to add them to the "Canon." Sundberg states that the latter part of the fourth century is decisive because this is when strict canonical lists began to appear, but it is probable that these lists were documenting what were already accepted earlier lists.

The frequency with which a particular book was cited by church fathers appears to be a more helpful consideration. As Barton explains, "The picture that emerges is surprisingly clear. From the Apostolic Fathers onwards, the Synoptic Gospels (especially Matthew), the Fourth Gospel, and the major Pauline letters are cited much more often than one would predict, if one supposed that the whole of the New Testament we now have was equally 'canonical' or important. Correspondingly,

6 Harry Y. Gamble, *The New Testament Canon: Its Making and Meaning* (Minneapolis: Fortress Press, 1985); compare Christopher R. Seitz, *The Goodly Fellowship of the Prophets* (Grand Rapids: Baker Academic, 2009).   7 John Barton, *Holy Writings, Sacred Text: The Canon in Early Christianity* (Louisville: Westminster John Knox Press, 1997), 11–14.

the rest of the New Testament (including Acts) is manifestly less important. The third category, books scarcely cited at all, contains most of those which later decisions and decrees affirm to be noncanonical; even in the earliest period none of them is cited even so often as the books of the second class."[8]

By focusing on how often books are cited, we can understand the three answers outlined above as three phases of New Testament canonicity that correspond to the chronological positions given by Zahn, Harnack and Sundberg.[9] The history of the New Testament Canon framed in these phases focuses on the function of Scripture in the early church.

In the first phase, the core of the present New Testament was already beginning to be treated as the main Christian texts. The identification of these core texts was completed before the end of the first century. Technically speaking, it was not a fixed Canon, but it would be equally inappropriate to say there was no core collection of writings.

In the second phase, during the second and third centuries, certain other documents began to be cited more often, suggesting—but not explicitly acknowledging—their addition to the core collection. In studying this phase, one still cannot clearly distinguish between those documents in the New Testament and those outside it. Instead, the distinction is between documents cited often, documents cited little and books discouraged from use. While the core had ceased to grow, the thought of forming a fixed collection had still not appeared. (Thus, a canonical/noncanonical distinction is misguided at this point.)

In the third phase, during the fourth century, lists of canonical documents proliferated, giving very strong indication that the church was thinking about a closed Canon. But we must realize that to speak even here of a closed Canon is difficult because some documents that appear on some of the lists are not in the present Canon. Further, a few documents that are in our present Canon are absent from some lists.[10]

Rather than conceiving of a closed New Testament in the second century, to which the church appealed for its sole source of teaching, this three-phase paradigm forces us to consider how the church judged and appropriated the writings it included in the New Testament Canon. We can talk of an authoritative body of Christian Scripture in the first century, but we cannot claim that that collection of writings was closed even into the fifth century.

Consistent with this focus on the function of Scripture, New Testament Canon historians have employed a rubric called the criteria of canonicity—that is, the qualifications that documents needed to meet for inclusion in the Canon. This is not to say that there was an explicit list of criteria to which the early church referred and through which each document was screened before being included in or rejected from the Canon. The criteria are a retrospective means for us to attempt to understand why certain documents came to be valued above other documents in the early church. This rubric derives from examining the writings of the church fathers and their use of these documents. We must avoid the temptation to view these criteria as hard and fast rules, and it is difficult to rank them in importance because they were not invoked with great consistency or rigor. Rather, they operated interdependently or concurrently—not independently or sequentially. Further, some churches and leaders gave different weight to certain criteria, which explains why some documents took longer to gain universal acceptance in the church.

8 John Barton, *Holy Writings, Sacred Text: The Canon in Early Christianity* (Louisville: Westminster John Knox Press, 1997), 17.   9 John Barton, *Holy Writings, Sacred Text: The Canon in Early Christianity* (Louisville: Westminster John Knox Press, 1997), 18–24; A. C. Sundberg, Jr., "Towards a Revised History of the New Testament Canon," *Studia evangelica* 4, no. 1 (1968): 452–61.   10 Bruce Metzger, *The Canon of the New Testament* (Oxford: Clarendon Press, 1997), 305–15.

The first criterion is apostolicity. While this could mean that a document was written by an apostle, it was not necessarily essential. Some of our New Testament documents were received as written by an apostle (e.g., Paul's letters). But other documents gained wide acceptance because of a direct link to the apostles. Some documents experienced difficulty when it came to widespread acceptance by the church. The best-known example is the book of Hebrews—as Origen of Alexandria's (ca. AD 184–253) comments illustrate: "If I gave my opinion, I should say that the thoughts are those of the apostle, but the style and composition belong to someone who remembered the apostle's teachings and wrote down at his leisure what had been said by his teacher. Therefore, if any church holds that this Epistle is by Paul, let it be commended for this also. For it is not without reason that the men of old time have handed it down as Paul's. But who wrote the Epistle in truth, God knows."[11] Although Origen believed those who accept Hebrews as written by Paul to be mistaken, he did not dismiss Hebrews on that basis—rather, because it is apostolic in teaching, he accepted Hebrews.

The second criterion is orthodoxy. Orthodoxy indicates the congruity of a document with the apostolic faith. To see how this criterion functioned in the life of the church, it is helpful to see how Serapion of Antioch dealt with such a document in the early third century. Eusebius tells us that Serapion wrote a refutation of the *Gospel of Peter*, the content of which had led a parish in his jurisdiction astray.[12] The church at Rhossus was using the *Gospel of Peter* in their teaching and worship. Initially, this did not trouble Serapion; he believed that they held "the true faith" and could discern this gospel's doctrine. However, he soon came to learn that he was mistaken after securing a copy of the document. He found that it taught Docetism—which was viewed as a heresy by the orthodox church. Thus, the document denied "the true faith."

This illustrates orthodoxy being applied as a criterion for a document's acceptance. Serapion did not appeal to a New Testament Canon to see if the *Gospel of Peter* was included; his appeal was to "the true faith" to discern its teaching. Serapion's issue was not that the church was using a document outside of a Canon but that they did not discern the heterodoxy of the document. The "rule of faith" was used in this way in the early church as its standard of orthodoxy—something against which teaching and documents were measured. R. P. C Hanson calls it a "graph of the interpretation of the Bible by the church of the second and third centuries."[13] Even the Christian writings that were eventually included in the New Testament Canon were subjected to this rule of faith.[14]

The third criterion is catholicity (or universality) and traditional use. This criterion is best illustrated in Augustine (AD 354–430): "Now, in regard to the canonical Scriptures, he must follow the judgment of the greater number of catholic churches; and among these, of course, a high place must be given to such as have been thought worthy to be the seat of an apostle and to receive epistles. Accordingly, among the canonical Scriptures he will judge according to the following standard: to prefer those that are received by all the catholic churches to those which some do not receive. Among those, again, which are not received by all, he will prefer such as have the sanction of the greater number and those of greater authority, to such as are held by the smaller number and those of less authority. If, however, he shall find that some books are held by the greater number of churches, and others by the churches of greater authority (though this is not a very likely thing to happen), I think that in such a case the authority on the two sides is to be looked upon as equal."[15]

For Augustine, widespread use of a document carried considerable weight for its acceptance. Some churches—like Rome, Antioch, Alexandria and Constantinople—were given preference over

11 Origen, *Homilies on Hebrews*, in Eusebius, *Ecclesiastical History*, 6.25.11–14; quoted in Craig D. Allert, *A High View of Scripture?: The Authority of the Bible and the Formation of the New Testament Canon* (Grand Rapids: Baker Academic, 2007), 54. 12 Eusebius, *Ecclesiastical History*, 6.12.1–6. 13 R. P. C. Hanson, *Tradition in the Early Church* (London: SCM Press, 1962), 127. 14 Craig D. Allert, *A High View of Scripture?: The Authority of the Bible and the Formation of the New Testament Canon* (Grand Rapids: Baker Academic, 2007), 54–56, 78–84, 121–26. 15 Augustine, On *Christian Doctrine*, in Nicene and Post-Nicene Fathers 1.2: *St. Augustin's City of God and Christian Doctrine*, ed. Philip Schaff, trans. J. F. Shaw (Buffalo: The Christian Literature Company, 1887), 2.8.12.

other churches concerning the documents they used. In the case of a writing that was accepted by all compared to a writing that some did not accept, preference was given to the writing accepted by all. When dealing with those documents not accepted by all, one was to accept those with the greater representation among the churches (with greater weight given to the more important churches). Augustine also references the improbable possibility where the majority of the churches use one document while the most important churches employ another document; if this should happen, Augustine's counsel is to accept both.

Augustine reveals an important reality in the life of the early church: For a document to be received, it had to be accepted and valued as Scripture by a local church. Through gradual and more widespread recognition, that same document gained an even higher stature in the church catholic. But although the passage displays an explicit consideration of Canon issues, the variety of canonical lists in the fourth and fifth centuries shows that even then the issue was not settled for all churches.

Some have offered another criterion of canonicity: inspiration. Some claim this as the predominant criterion. Thus, R. Laird Harris states, "The test of canonicity is inspiration. The early church put into its Canon, and we receive, those books which were regarded as inspired, and no others."[16] Harris argues that the Christian documents that came to form the New Testament were the only documents that the early church viewed as inspired.

From one perspective, it is accurate to say that inspiration was a criterion for canonicity; all documents considered orthodox by the early church were, by implication, believed to be inspired. But from another perspective, it is inaccurate to say that inspiration functioned as a criterion of canonicity if we mean that inspiration was believed to belong only to the documents that later became part of the New Testament. This does not mean that the fathers did not regard these New Testament documents as unique—their elevation to canonical status clearly indicates otherwise. It does mean, however, that it was not inspiration that determined their uniqueness above all other Scriptures.

If the argument of writers like Harris is correct and everything in the Canon was considered inspired and everything outside it uninspired, one would expect this to be indicated somewhere by the leaders of the early church. But on the rare occasion when a father did declare a writing not to be inspired, he was not saying that it was not a canonical document, but rather that the document was heretical, that it lay outside the community of faith where the Spirit was at work. In other words, canonical versus noncanonical is not synonymous with inspired versus uninspired.

The assertion that the early church's criteria for the New Testament Canon included inspiration has one further problem—the church fathers' references to noncanonical books as inspired.[17] For example, Gregory of Nyssa (ca. AD 330–395) references his brother Basil's commentary on creation as "an inspired [theopneustos] exposition ... [admired] no less than the words composed by Moses himself."[18] In addition, the second-century bishop Abercius Marcellus of Hierapolis composed an inscription that was placed over his future tomb. The Life of Abercius, which was written about this bishop in the fourth century, contains a text of this inscription and describes it as an "inspired inscription."[19] A further example is seen in a letter issued by the Council of Ephesus (AD 431) describing its condemnation of Nestorius as "their inspired decision."[20]

16 R. Laird Harris, Inspiration and Canonicity of the Bible: An Historical and Exegetical Study (Grand Rapids: Zondervan, 1969), 200.
17 Craig D. Allert, A High View of Scripture?: The Authority of the Bible and the Formation of the New Testament Canon (Grand Rapids: Baker Academic, 2007), 60–65, 185–88.   18 Gregory of Nyssa, Apologia in Hexaemeron; quoted in Craig D. Allert, A High View of Scripture? (Grand Rapids: Baker Academic, 2007), 65.   19 Life of Abercius, 76; quoted in Craig D. Allert, A High View of Scripture?: The Authority of the Bible and the Formation of the New Testament Canon (Grand Rapids: Baker Academic, 2007), 65.   20 Edward Schwartz, ed., Acta Conciliorum Oecumenicorum (Berlin: Walter de Gruyter, 1923), 1.1.2:70; quoted in Craig D. Allert, A High View of Scripture?: The Authority of the Bible and the Formation of the New Testament Canon (Grand Rapids: Baker Academic, 2007), 65.

These three examples should give one pause when claiming that the early church reserved the term "inspired" for only the canonical documents—each example describes a noncanonical document as "inspired." This would be very high praise for these documents if inspiration was a designation for only canonical documents. Thus, inspiration did not guarantee inclusion; inspiration was not viewed as the unique possession of only the documents that would come to be canonical.

It is important not to force a 21st-century perspective back onto the sources of the early church. Christianity had a somewhat fluid body of literature that the church used as authoritative. While certain documents rose to preeminence in the life of the church, that rise, in some cases, was not immediate. This is not meant to deny the providence of God in the process but, rather, to say that there were very practical reasons why certain documents came to be valued (and eventually canonized) by the church, and it is on this very practical road to canonization that God providentially led his people by his Spirit.

Craig D. Allert

THE SYNOPTIC GOSPELS AND ACTS

The Gospels of Matthew, Mark, Luke and John have much in common, but because the first three share a particularly strong resemblance, they are called the "Synoptic Gospels" (literally, Gospels with a common vision). The differences between the Synoptic Gospels and the Gospel of John are as interesting as they are significant. For example, where the Synoptics have numerous parables focusing on the kingdom of God, the Fourth Gospel rarely includes parables, and the term "kingdom" is used sparingly (Jn 3:3,5; 18:36). Likewise, in the Synoptic Gospels Jesus is declared to be Messiah at Caesarea Philippi in the middle of the narrative (Mt 16:13–16; Mk 8:27–30; Lk 9:18–20); in John's account, Jesus' messiahship is announced at the beginning of the text (Jn 1:35,49).

The considerable overlap (in terms of plot, wording and substance) between the Synoptic Gospels suggests that the three texts are related—one or more of the evangelists used or was aware of the work of the others. According to the traditional view of the early church fathers, Matthew was the first Gospel written. Mark, who used Matthew as a reference, was written second, and Luke, who used both Matthew and Mark, was written last. Although this view prevailed for centuries, other solutions have been put forward to explain the relation between the Synoptic Gospels.

The most common theory today claims that Mark was the earliest Gospel, composed independently of another early—but lost—source. Both Mark and this hypothesized "lost source" supposedly provided the basis for Matthew and Luke, who worked independently of each other. This view eventually came to be called the "Two-Source Hypothesis." The hypothetical lost source is called "Q" for "Quelle," the German word for "source." A variation of this view argues that Mark was, in fact, the first Gospel, but that there was no "Q"—Matthew used Mark as a source, and Luke used both Matthew and Mark.

THE GOSPEL OF MARK

If the Gospel of Mark was indeed written first, its likely author was not the most illustrious among the evangelists. According to church tradition, John Mark (Ac 12:12,25; 15:37; 2Ti 4:11) authored the Gospel, and there is little reason to think otherwise. Church tradition also reports that he worked under the auspices of the apostle Peter. Exactly when the author of Mark's Gospel completed his work is less certain. Depending on a variety of considerations, scholars date this Gospel anywhere between the 40s and the 70s AD. A composition in the mid-60s or just after AD 70 are the most widely accepted options.

Mark's Gospel was most likely written in Rome, though Alexandria and Palestine are also possibilities. A Roman setting is suggested by the various Latinisms in the text and by the author's numerous attempts to translate events into Roman terms (Mk 12:42; 15:16). The church fathers Irenaeus and Clement of Alexandria affirm the likelihood of Rome as the place of composition.[1]

The author of the Gospel of Mark seems to have been particularly interested in issues of theodicy (the vindication of God and his ways)—more specifically, why the followers of a supposedly risen

[1] Irenaeus, *Against Heresies*, 3.1.1; for Clement of Alexandria, see Eusebius, *Ecclesiastical History*, 6.15.6–7.

and triumphant Messiah should experience suffering and rejection. Mark seems to suggest that the answer lies in the fact that Jesus has redefined the terms of messiahship altogether. In the first half of the Gospel, prior to the revelation of Caesarea Philippi (Mk 8:27–30), the evangelist seeks to establish Jesus as the promised Messiah. In the second half of the narrative, he conveys the surprising things that Messianic identity entails. The reason why so many do not accept the Messiah is because only some are "good soil" (Mk 4:1–20), receptive to the claims of Jesus. Mark's Gospel, with its twin focus on Christ's compelling character and suffering, serves as an unparalleled charter document for Christian discipleship.

THE GOSPEL OF MATTHEW

The Gospel of Matthew is often assigned a date much later than that of Mark. This is primarily a consequence not only of the Two-Source Hypothesis, but also of the sense that the author of Matthew's Gospel is addressing concerns relevant to the late first century AD (e.g., Christians' conflicts with the synagogue and issues of church order). Moreover, the twice-used phrase "to this day" (Mt 27:8; 28:15) seems to imply some historical distance between Matthew's recording of the events and the events themselves. These factors may suggest an authorship date in the late first-century AD, although other factors suggest an earlier date; the dating of Matthew remains open to discussion.

Antioch in Syria is the most probable place of origin for Matthew's Gospel. Other suggested locations include Caesarea Maritima, Alexandria and the territory east of the Jordan. The Gospel has an obvious concern for the Gentiles, and Syrian Antioch was a cosmopolitan mix of Jewish and Gentile cultures during the first century AD. The earliest attestations of Matthew's Gospel stemming from the church father Ignatius of Antioch also suggest a Syrian origin for the Gospel.[2]

The first Gospel seems to have been written with a Jewish audience foremost in mind. Matthew's modeling of Jesus on the figure of Moses, the polemic against institutional Judaism and the various "fulfillment citations" (referencing an Old Testament passage as being fulfilled in the NT, especially how Jesus personally fulfills Old Testament Scriptures; e.g., Mt 1:22–23; 2:15,17–18,23; 4:14–16) all seem to presuppose an attempt to legitimize a fledgling Christian movement within an established Jewish culture. Matthew shows Jesus as the true teacher of Torah, indeed as the embodiment of Torah itself, and as the culmination of the history of God's redeeming purposes through Israel.

THE GOSPEL OF LUKE AND BOOK OF ACTS

The Gospel of Luke, the latest of the Synoptic Gospels, has traditionally been credited to Luke, a Gentile physician and companion of the apostle Paul (Col 4:11,14; 2Ti 4:11; Phm 24). The book of Acts (or Acts of the Apostles) is also traditionally attributed to Luke since the prologue presents it as a sequel to the Gospel (Ac 1:1–2). There are also four "we passages" in Acts, which appear as if the author was present for the events being narrated (Ac 16:10–17; 20:5–15; 21:1–18; 27:1—28:16). This would make sense if Luke was indeed the author.

Assuming that Luke and Acts were written together as one piece (the two works show striking structural parallels that make it hard to believe otherwise), the dating of Luke-Acts is closely connected with prior judgments relating not only to the authorship of Mark (on whom Luke presumably depends) but also to the events narrated in Acts. The earliest that Luke–Acts could have been

2 E.g., Ignatius of Antioch, *To the Smyrnaeans*, 1.1; *To the Ephesians*, 19.1–3.

completed would have been just after Paul's Roman imprisonment (Ac 28:11–31) in the early 60s. Another view dates the writing of Luke–Acts to the 80s or 90s. This possibility rests mainly on the belief that its author was aware of the destruction of Jerusalem (AD 70). Moreover, Luke's Gospel appears to be an attempt to address early Christian anxieties over the so-called delay of the Parousia, or second coming of Christ (see Mt 24:27). On the assumption that such anxieties presented themselves (a debated issue), they must have done so measurably later than the writing of Mark or even Matthew.

Luke–Acts have their own distinctive style and offer their own unique contribution to the New Testament. The texts contain very polished Greek; their rich allusiveness (to both pagan and Jewish sources) and attention to historical detail (such as in the travelogue of Paul's journey to Rome in Ac 27–28) betray a well-educated author writing for a well-educated audience. Judging by the prologues (Lk 1:1–4; Ac 1:1–2), which are modeled on the prologues of other serious Greek historical works, it can be concluded that the author wished to be understood as an equally serious historian. Addressing both the Gospel and Acts to one Theophilus (Lk 1:3; Ac 1:1), Luke announces his intention of rooting the story of Jesus and the early church firmly within history. Thus, Luke–Acts as a whole not only carries out an apologetic function—confirming the factual validity of the church's proclamation—but also offers a founding account of the identity of an expanding and increasingly diversified movement. The outworking of that story is consistently tied back to the sovereign purposes of God, the reign of the risen Christ, the activity of the Holy Spirit, and the character and mission of the church. In addition to these themes, the author of Luke–Acts maintains a distinctive interest in prayer, hospitality, the poor and salvation (Lk 2:11; 4:21; 19:10; 23:43; Ac 1:14; 2:42–47; 4:12,32–35; 28:28).

THREE GOSPELS, ONE PORTRAIT

Together, the Synoptic Gospels offer a compelling and mutually enriching portrait of Jesus. Although readers have not always agreed on the meaning of the Gospels, all can agree that were it not for Matthew, Mark and Luke, we would know very little about the historical Jesus or his kingdom message. It is thus hardly by chance that the earliest compilers of the New Testament Canon chose to begin not with the earliest-written books but with those books that tell the lead story: the Synoptic Gospels.

Nicholas Perrin

MATTHEW

INTRODUCTION TO MATTHEW

Each of the four Gospels (Matthew, Mark, Luke and John) tells the story of Jesus from its own perspective. Matthew emphasizes that Jesus is the long-awaited Jewish Messiah and King, who fulfills God's promises in the Old Testament. Jesus is not just a wise teacher; he is the one God has chosen to usher in the kingdom of heaven. He has come to save and to restore humanity into right relationship with God—starting first with Israel and then moving to the wider world.

BACKGROUND

The text of Matthew doesn't identify its author, but ever since the second century AD, Christian tradition has ascribed this Gospel to Matthew the tax collector—called Levi in Mark and Luke's accounts—who became one of Jesus' 12 disciples (Mt 9:9; 10:3; Mk 2:14; Lk 5:27–29). Various features in Matthew reflect a writing style that is more Jewish than the other three Gospels, although John's Gospel is also steeped in Judaism. Matthew seems to have been intended for a community of Jewish people who believed that Jesus was the Messiah. Based on Matthew's focus on the negative elements of the Judaism of Jerusalem and Judaea, it seems that the Gospel's audience probably lived outside of the Israel region. It was probably written in the late first century, around AD 60–85.

STRUCTURE

One way to organize the Gospel of Matthew is by the five major blocks of Jesus' teaching. Each block ends with a phrase noting what happened when Jesus was finished speaking (for example, Mt 7:28). These five blocks are: the Sermon on the Mount (5:1—7:29); the missionary discourse (9:35—10:42); Jesus' parables (13:1–52); Jesus' teaching on discipleship (ch. 18); and Jesus' teaching about his return and the day of judgment (23:1—25:46). This five-part division could serve as an echo of the Pentateuch (the first five books of the Old Testament). Matthew is presenting Jesus as a new Moses. Like Moses, Jesus is leading God's people in an exodus—this new exodus involves breaking the bonds of sin. And just as Moses delivered God's law, Jesus fulfills it (5:17–20).

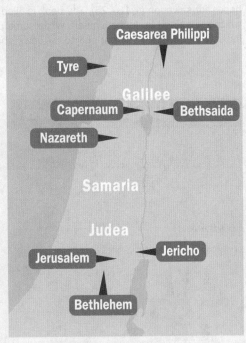

This map depicts many of the locations of Jesus' ministry according to Matthew's Gospel.

Another way to organize Matthew's Gospel is to structure it around significant turning points in Jesus' ministry. These turning points are marked by a transition in the aspect or location of Jesus' ministry (4:17; 16:21). The first section describes the time before Jesus' public ministry, including his family history and early childhood, his baptism and his temptation by the devil (1:1—4:16). The second section, which details Jesus' public ministry in Galilee, particularly focuses on his miracles, teachings and conflicts with religious leaders (4:17—16:20). The last section tells of the rejection and suffering of Jesus in Jerusalem and concludes with his crucifixion, resurrection and ascension (16:21—28:20).

OUTLINE

- Prelude to Jesus' ministry (1:1—4:16)
- Jesus' ministry in Galilee (4:17—16:20)
- Jesus in Jerusalem (16:21—28:20)

THEMES

One of Matthew's primary goals is to show that Jesus is the Messiah—the fulfillment of Jewish hopes for salvation (1:18–25). The book is filled with references to the Old Testament—most of which are quoted by Jesus himself. While some passages, such as 10:5–6 and 15:24, seem to indicate that Jesus was sent only to the Jews, the Gospel as a whole portrays him as the Savior

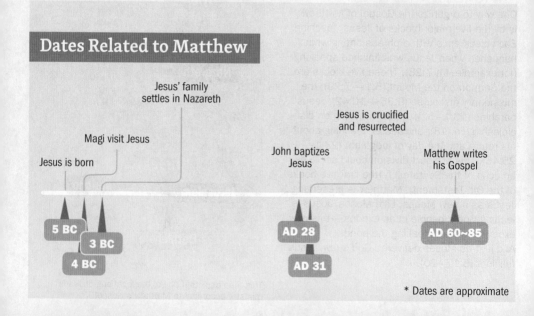

Dates Related to Matthew

Jesus' family
settles in Nazareth

Magi visit Jesus

Jesus is crucified
and resurrected

Jesus is born

John baptizes
Jesus

Matthew writes
his Gospel

5 BC

3 BC

4 BC

AD 28

AD 31

AD 60~85

* Dates are approximate

of the entire world (e.g., 8:5–13; 12:21). Matthew emphasizes that the kingdom of heaven has arrived with Jesus—but at the same time, the kingdom has not yet come in its fullness (compare 4:17; 26:29). That will happen with Jesus' return (24:3–31).

Matthew uses the designation Son of David to point to Jesus' human lineage from King David in the Old Testament, showing Jesus' legitimate right to the throne (1:1–17). In addition, Matthew emphasizes Jesus' identity as the divine Son of God (3:14–17), who has authority to control nature, heal disease and forgive sin. The theme of authority runs just below the surface of the entire Gospel—in the miracle stories, in Jesus' teachings and parables, and in his confrontations with the religious leaders. In everything he does, Jesus is acting in the name and power of God himself.

By the end of Matthew's Gospel, some of Jesus' disciples are worshiping him—and it is here that it becomes apparent that the people realize what we have also found to be true: Jesus is God himself (28:17). Today, we proclaim Jesus as our Jewish Messiah, who is also our King and God! He is all we ever hoped for and far more. And this savior, Jesus, inspires us to both praise him and take action—he motivates us to make disciples of all nations, a work that is far from done (28:18–20).

The Genealogy of Jesus the Messiah

1:1-17pp — Lk 3:23-38
1:3-6pp — Ru 4:18-22
1:7-11pp — 1Ch 3:10-17

1 This is the genealogy[a] of Jesus the Messiah[b] the son of David, the son of Abraham:

2 Abraham was the father of Isaac,
Isaac the father of Jacob,
Jacob the father of Judah and his brothers,
3 Judah the father of Perez and Zerah, whose mother was Tamar,
Perez the father of Hezron,
Hezron the father of Ram,
4 Ram the father of Amminadab,
Amminadab the father of Nahshon,
Nahshon the father of Salmon,
5 Salmon the father of Boaz, whose mother was Rahab,
Boaz the father of Obed, whose mother was Ruth,
Obed the father of Jesse,
6 and Jesse the father of King David.

David was the father of Solomon, whose mother had been Uriah's wife,
7 Solomon the father of Rehoboam,
Rehoboam the father of Abijah,
Abijah the father of Asa,
8 Asa the father of Jehoshaphat,
Jehoshaphat the father of Jehoram,
Jehoram the father of Uzziah,
9 Uzziah the father of Jotham,
Jotham the father of Ahaz,
Ahaz the father of Hezekiah,
10 Hezekiah the father of Manasseh,
Manasseh the father of Amon,
Amon the father of Josiah,
11 and Josiah the father of Jeconiah[c] and his brothers at the time of the exile to Babylon.

12 After the exile to Babylon:
Jeconiah was the father of Shealtiel,
Shealtiel the father of Zerubbabel,
13 Zerubbabel the father of Abihud,
Abihud the father of Eliakim,
Eliakim the father of Azor,
14 Azor the father of Zadok,
Zadok the father of Akim,
Akim the father of Elihud,
15 Elihud the father of Eleazar,
Eleazar the father of Matthan,
Matthan the father of Jacob,
16 and Jacob the father of Joseph, the husband of Mary, and Mary was the mother of Jesus who is called the Messiah.

17 Thus there were fourteen generations in all from Abraham to David, fourteen from David to

a 1 Or is an account of the origin   b 1 Or Jesus Christ. Messiah (Hebrew) and Christ (Greek) both mean Anointed One; also in verse 18.   c 11 That is, Jehoiachin; also in verse 12

1:1–17 The Gospel of Matthew probably was written sometime between AD 60–85 by the apostle Matthew, one of Jesus' twelve disciples (Mt 9:9; 10:3). The book begins with Jesus' genealogy, identifying him as a descendant of David and Abraham. These connections serve to establish Jesus' identity as a Jew (son of Abraham) and his right to rule (son of David). Additionally, both titles evoke Messianic expectations and recall God's promises in his covenants with Abraham and David.

Matthew arranges his material in three groups of roughly 14 generations each. Matthew traces Jesus' lineage back to Abraham, though the genealogy is not exhaustive. It gives priority to the theme of the royal Messiah rather than to strict chronology. See the event line "Jesus' Early Life and Ministry" on p. 1530; see people diagram "Jesus' Family Tree According to Matthew" on p. 1528.

1:1 the genealogy Family descent was very important to Matthew's original audience, who hoped in the promises that God had made to specific ancestors. The book of Matthew shows how Jesus fulfills these promises. **Messiah** The Greek word used here, *christos*, can be rendered as "Christ," "Messiah" or "anointed one." This term is used in the OT primarily to describe kings—although other figures, such as priests and prophets, are occasionally referred to as anointed. Matthew applies the term to Jesus and connects him with David, thereby emphasizing Jesus' kingly role. Jews in the first century had varied and multifaceted expectations of the Messiah. Many longed for a political leader like King David who would free them from Roman oppression and restore national independence. Others anticipated a priestly figure who would legitimize the temple worship, which the Hasmonean rulers had taken over. **son of David** The Jews expected the true Messiah to be from David's line (2Sa 7:11–16). For Matthew, Jesus' Davidic heritage is evidence of his Messiahship, stemming from passages such as Jer 23:5 and 33:15. By connecting Jesus with David, Matthew asserts that the Davidic covenant reaches its ultimate fulfillment in Jesus (see 2Sa 7:16 and note). **Abraham** The forefather of Israel. God had promised Abraham that he would be the source of blessing for all peoples (Ge 12:3; compare Ac 3:25; Gal 3:8). For Matthew, this promise ultimately is fulfilled in Jesus.

1:5 Ruth The great-grandmother of King David. See Ru 4:17 and note.

1:6 Uriah's wife Refers to Bathsheba—the woman David committed adultery with (see 2Sa 11).

1:8 Jehoram the father of Uzziah Matthew omits three intervening kings (Ahaziah, Joash and Amaziah; 1Ch 3:11–12), possibly in order to tidy up the structure of the genealogy (see note on Mt 1:1–17).

1:11 exile to Babylon Occurred when Nebuchadnezzar took the southern tribe of Judah into captivity in Babylon (2Ki 25:8–11).

1:16 Joseph, the husband of Mary The culture of this time considered adoption to be real sonship. Even though Jesus had no biological relation to Joseph, he continued Joseph's familial line.

the exile to Babylon, and fourteen from the exile to the Messiah.

Joseph Accepts Jesus as His Son

¹⁸This is how the birth of Jesus the Messiah came about[a]: His mother Mary was pledged to be married to Joseph, but before they came together, she was found to be pregnant through the Holy Spirit. ¹⁹Because Joseph her husband was faithful to the law, and yet[b] did not want to expose her to public disgrace, he had in mind to divorce her quietly.

²⁰But after he had considered this, an angel of the Lord appeared to him in a dream and said, "Jo-seph son of David, do not be afraid to take Mary home as your wife, because what is conceived in her is from the Holy Spirit. ²¹She will give birth to a son, and you are to give him the name Jesus,[c] because he will save his people from their sins."

²²All this took place to fulfill what the Lord had said through the prophet: ²³"The virgin will conceive and give birth to a son, and they will call him Immanuel"[d] (which means "God with us").

²⁴When Joseph woke up, he did what the angel of the Lord had commanded him and took Mary home as his wife. ²⁵But he did not consummate

---

[a] 18 Or *The origin of Jesus the Messiah was like this*
[b] 19 Or *was a righteous man and*   [c] 21 *Jesus* is the Greek form of *Joshua*, which means *the LORD saves.*   [d] 23 Isaiah 7:14

WOMEN IN JESUS' GENEALOGY				
Tamar	Rahab	Ruth	Uriah's Wife (Bathsheba)	Mary
Ge 38	Jos 2; 6:22–25	Ru 1–4	2Sa 11	Mt 1–2; Lk 1–2

1:18–25 The birth narrative in Matthew gives a different perspective from Luke's (see Lk 1–2). Matthew cites several passages from the OT that show Jesus to be Israel's long-awaited Messiah.

1:18 pledged to be married Refers to a permanent relationship nearly equivalent to marriage.

1:19 did not want to expose her to public disgrace The law demanded that an adulteress receive the death penalty (Dt 22:21). However, the Jewish community of this time often did not carry out the death penalty; instead, they punished adulteresses through public disgrace.

1:20 in a dream Angelic visitation and dreams are a common means of supernatural revelation in the sacred literature of this time.

1:21 you are to give him the name A father was responsible for naming his son at the time of his circumcision (eight days after birth). The angel's words implicitly command that Joseph accept his role as father of the child. In antiquity, names were often thought to be emblematic of the character or calling of the individual. **Jesus** From the Hebrew name *yeshua'*, which means "Yahweh saves." **he will save his people from their sins** Announces more than a royal or political Messiah. Jesus saves, even from sin (compare Is 53:12). This declaration—which reflects the meaning of Jesus' name—is programmatic for Matthew's Gospel. The remainder of the narrative justifies this statement, culminating in the sacrificial death of Jesus on the cross. The salvation of which the angel spoke differed vastly from Jewish expectations of the Messiah; Jesus brought forgiveness of sins, not expulsion of the occupying Roman army or political-religious restoration.

1:22 fulfill Matthew often interprets events in Jesus' life in terms of prophecies from the OT; this is the first instance of this type of interpretation. See the table "Jesus' Fulfillment of OT Prophecy" on p. 1573.

1:23 virgin The Greek word used here, *parthenos*, reflects the Septuagint (ancient Greek translation of the OT) version of Isa 7:14, which Matthew drew from when quoting the Hebrew Bible (or OT). Matthew appropriates this prophecy and applies it to the virgin birth of Jesus. In the Septuagint version of Isa 7:14, the Greek word

parthenos is used to translate the Hebrew word *almah*. The other six occurrences of *almah* in the OT refer to young women of marriageable age with no direct indication of whether they are virgins or not (Ge 24:43; Ex 2:8; Ps 68:25; Pr 30:19; SS 1:3; 6:8); in contrast, *parthenos* normally indicates a virgin, though not exclusively (in the Septuagint version of Ge 34:3 *parthenos* is used to describe Dinah following intercourse). However, women of marriageable age in ancient patriarchal culture like Matthew's were expected to be virgins. While the Hebrew word used most often to indicate a virgin is *bethulah* (Lev 21:3; Jdg 21:12; Dt 22:23,28; Ex 22:16), *almah* is used as a synonym for *bethulah* (Ge 24:16,43; compare Ge 24:14). In addition, SS 6:8 lists queens, concubines and *alamoth* (the plural form of *almah*)—this last group, the *alamoth*, seems to be a group of women who do not have a sexual relationship with the king. This same distinction between the queen, concubines and virgins occurs in the book of Esther (Est 2:3,8,14), but in Esther, the virgins are described as *na'arah bethulah* ("young virgins"). This parallel suggests SS 6:8 is using the same language as the book of Esther but using *alamoth* in place of *na'arah bethulah*—indicating that both terms can describe virgins. These connections explain Matthew's use of Isa 7:14 to reference the virgin birth (see Isa 7:14 and note). **they will call him Immanuel** Matthew presents Jesus as the fulfillment of Isa 7:14, which says that the child's name will be Immanuel (meaning "God with us"; compare Mt 28:20). While in the original context of Isaiah, this is a prophecy about a child born during the reign of King Ahaz of Judah (ca. 735–715 BC; Isa 7:16; compare Isa 8:8,10), Matthew sees this prophecy as finding its ultimate fulfillment in Jesus. The book of Isaiah as a whole connects Immanuel with the Messiah figure from David's line (Isa 11:10) and by extension the suffering servant (Isa 52:13—53:12). Like the Messiah in Isaiah's portrayal over 500 years earlier, Jesus comes from David's line as God's anointed one and then suffers and dies on behalf of humanity—to save people from their sins. He is also prophesied as being resurrected (Isa 53:10). See note on Isa 7:14; note on Isa 11:10; note on Isa 53:2; and note on Isa 53:10.

1:25 he did not consummate their marriage Matthew does not record any command for Joseph to refrain from marital relations with Mary, although abstinence was the rule of the time during the betrothal period. Matthew is careful to indicate that no human father had any role in Jesus' conception. **gave birth to a son** The date of Jesus' birth is approximately 5 BC, based on aligning it with the reign of Herod the Great (compare note on 2:1).

Jesus' Family Tree According to Matthew

(Mt 1:1–17)

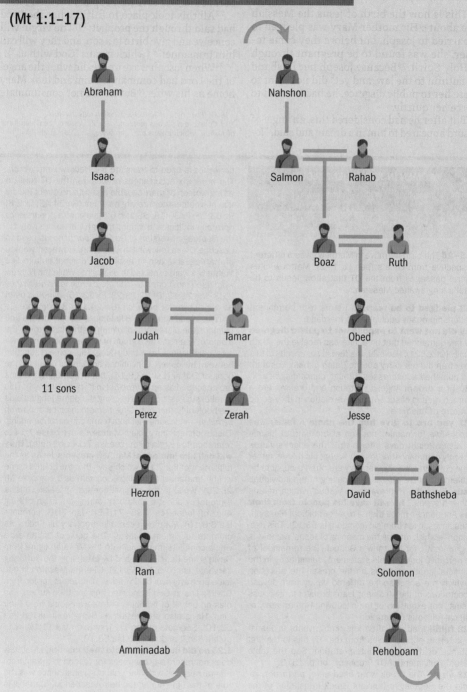

Abraham

Isaac

Jacob

11 sons

Judah — Tamar

Perez   Zerah

Hezron

Ram

Amminadab

Nahshon

Salmon — Rahab

Boaz — Ruth

Obed

Jesse

David — Bathsheba

Solomon

Rehoboam

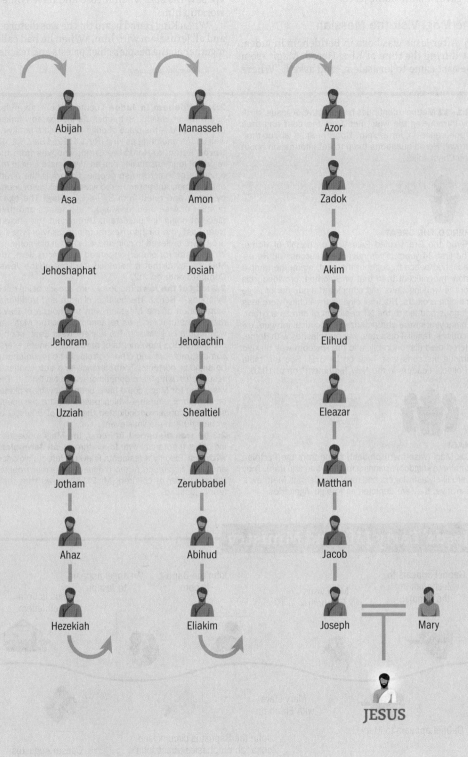

their marriage until she gave birth to a son. And he gave him the name Jesus.

The Magi Visit the Messiah

2 After Jesus was born in Bethlehem in Judea, during the time of King Herod, Magi[a] from the east came to Jerusalem ²and asked, "Where is the one who has been born king of the Jews? We saw his star when it rose and have come to worship him."

³When King Herod heard this he was disturbed, and all Jerusalem with him. ⁴When he had called together all the people's chief priests and teachers

a 1 Traditionally *wise men*

2:1–12 Matthew continues his narrative of Jesus' birth by introducing the wise men from the east and their appearance in Jerusalem. Upon hearing about their arrival, Herod questions them to get information about the Christ-child.

HEROD THE GREAT
Herod the Great ruled Palestine on behalf of Rome. The first 24 years of his reign were successful: He established peace throughout the land, made the temple more magnificent than that of Solomon, provided jobs for the working class and completed a number of large building projects. His final nine years as king were less glorious and led to the NT depiction of him as a tyrant. These years were characterized by political intrigue, executions, familial disputes, war and clashes with Rome. Herod died dishonorably, and his kingdom was divided among his sons (see note on Lk 3:1). See the table "Political Leaders in the New Testament" on p. 1916.

MAGI
The Magi (wise men) probably came from the Parthian Empire (a kingdom spanning modern Iraq and Iran). They were likely astrologers and royal courtiers. In Matthew's narrative, they are depicted as foreign dignitaries.

2:1 Bethlehem in Judea Located about six miles south of Jerusalem. Bethlehem is inseparably linked to King David—the place of origin for David's family as well as his anointing as king (Ru 1:1,19; 1Sa 16:1,4). **Herod** Refers to Herod the Great, who was from the region of Idumea, making him an illegitimate king in the opinions of many Jewish people. Following the death of his father, Antipater, Herod was made king of Judea by Rome and ruled from 37–4 BC. **Magi** The exact number of wise men (or Magi), their names and their place of origin are uncertain. Throughout the ancient Near East, the births of extraordinary, savior-type figures were believed to coincide with astral phenomena. When a star (or planet) appeared over Jerusalem, the Magi believed that it heralded the king of the Jews. Compare note on 2:2.
2:2 king of the Jews The Jews were already being ruled by a king—Herod. The political climate and traditional association of the Messiah with the house of David made it natural for Jews to assume that the Messiah would be a king. **star** In the ancient Near East, people considered the movements of particular planets, stars, comets, meteors and other astrological phenomena to be signs or portents. The reference to a star connects Jesus' birth with the prophetic oracle in Nu 24:17. The wise men (or Magi) could have been following a planet on a natural course—which based on the particular signs they observed indicated the birth of a king—or witnessed a miraculous event.
2:3 he was disturbed To Herod, the Magi's question indicates a potential rival to his throne. **all Jerusalem with him** The city's residents knew of Herod's violence and were frightened at the prospect of further trouble. His slaughter of children (Mt 2:16) shows that their fear is justified.

Jesus' Early Life and Ministry

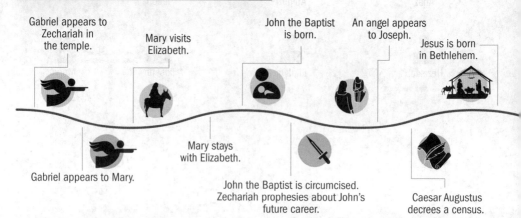

Gabriel appears to Zechariah in the temple.

Mary visits Elizabeth.

John the Baptist is born.

An angel appears to Joseph.

Jesus is born in Bethlehem.

Gabriel appears to Mary.

Mary stays with Elizabeth.

John the Baptist is circumcised. Zechariah prophesies about John's future career.

Caesar Augustus decrees a census.

of the law, he asked them where the Messiah was to be born. ⁵"In Bethlehem in Judea," they replied, "for this is what the prophet has written:

⁶"'But you, Bethlehem, in the land
    of Judah,
  are by no means least among the rulers
    of Judah;
for out of you will come a ruler
  who will shepherd my people Israel.'ᵃ

⁷Then Herod called the Magi secretly and found out from them the exact time the star had appeared. ⁸He sent them to Bethlehem and said, "Go and search carefully for the child. As soon as you find him, report to me, so that I too may go and worship him."

⁹After they had heard the king, they went on their way, and the star they had seen when it rose went ahead of them until it stopped over the place where the child was. ¹⁰When they saw the star, they were overjoyed. ¹¹On coming to the house, they saw the child with his mother Mary, and they bowed down and worshiped him. Then they opened their treasures and presented him with gifts of gold, frankincense and myrrh. ¹²And having been warned in a dream not to go back to Herod, they returned to their country by another route.

The Escape to Egypt

¹³When they had gone, an angel of the Lord appeared to Joseph in a dream. "Get up," he said, "take the child and his mother and escape to Egypt. Stay there until I tell you, for Herod is going to search for the child to kill him."

¹⁴So he got up, took the child and his mother during the night and left for Egypt, ¹⁵where he stayed until the death of Herod. And so was fulfilled what the Lord had said through the prophet: "Out of Egypt I called my son."ᵇ

ᵃ 6 Micah 5:2,4   ᵇ 15 Hosea 11:1

2:4 called together all the people's chief priests Herod is not demonstrating piety or respect for the priests in this instance; they functioned as his own cabinet and body of advisers. He requires their expertise to determine the Messiah's birthplace. **teachers of the law** Refers to trained interpreters of the Law of Moses. Their reply in vv. 5–6 reflects a tradition stemming from Isa 11:1–2; Isa 11:10; and Mic 5:2, where the Messiah is said to originate from the clan of Jesse (David's father) in Bethlehem.

2:6 no means least Matthew's reading of Mic 5:2 reflects neither the original Hebrew nor the Septuagint (Greek) translation. However, it is likely that multiple Greek translations were available at this time. Despite the variations in the text, the sense is the same: Bethlehem's importance comes from its connection to David and the Davidic Messiah. See the table "Jesus' Fulfillment of OT Prophecy" on p. 1573. **will shepherd** Ancient Near Eastern rulers often are portrayed as shepherds. The

same imagery is used throughout the OT (see Eze 34:23 and note; Jer 23:1–4; note on Jn 10:1–42).

2:7 the exact time the star had appeared Indicates that time had already passed since Jesus' birth. Compare note on 2:16.

2:8 As soon as you find him, report to me The Magi likely came to Herod expecting to find the child in his palace.

2:11 they bowed down and worshiped him This was a common custom in the ancient Near East for honoring kings, who were viewed as divine figures. **gold, frankincense and myrrh** These were costly luxury items suitable as gifts for the birth of an important or royal figure.

2:13–15 Joseph is warned in a dream to flee with his family to Egypt. They hide there until Herod dies, and then return home.

2:15 was fulfilled The ordinary expectations of the Messiah would not have included fleeing into Egypt, but

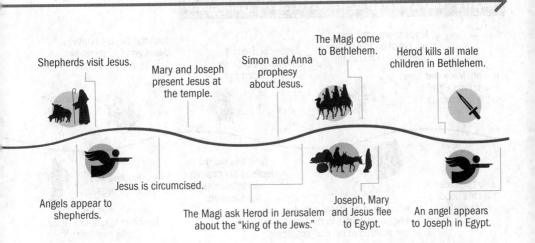

Shepherds visit Jesus.

Mary and Joseph present Jesus at the temple.

Simon and Anna prophesy about Jesus.

The Magi come to Bethlehem.

Herod kills all male children in Bethlehem.

Angels appear to shepherds.

Jesus is circumcised.

The Magi ask Herod in Jerusalem about the "king of the Jews."

Joseph, Mary and Jesus flee to Egypt.

An angel appears to Joseph in Egypt.

[16] When Herod realized that he had been outwitted by the Magi, he was furious, and he gave orders to kill all the boys in Bethlehem and its vicinity who were two years old and under, in accordance with the time he had learned from the Magi. [17] Then what was said through the prophet Jeremiah was fulfilled:

[18] "A voice is heard in Ramah,
    weeping and great mourning,
Rachel weeping for her children
    and refusing to be comforted,
    because they are no more."[a]

The Return to Nazareth

[19] After Herod died, an angel of the Lord appeared in a dream to Joseph in Egypt [20] and said, "Get up, take the child and his mother and go to the land of Israel, for those who were trying to take the child's life are dead."

[21] So he got up, took the child and his mother and went to the land of Israel. [22] But when he heard that Archelaus was reigning in Judea in place of his father Herod, he was afraid to go there. Having been warned in a dream, he withdrew to the district of Galilee, [23] and he went and lived in a town called Nazareth. So was fulfilled what was said through the prophets, that he would be called a Nazarene.

John the Baptist Prepares the Way

3:1-12pp — Mk 1:3-8; Lk 3:2-17

3 In those days John the Baptist came, preaching in the wilderness of Judea [2] and saying, "Repent, for the kingdom of heaven has come

[a] 18 Jer. 31:15

Matthew presents even this as fulfilling prophecy. He sees an analogy between Israel — the children of God (Ex 4:23) — and Jesus, the Son of God. Jesus emerged from Egypt just as Israel had during the exodus (Ex 9–14). In addition, the rulers in both narratives order the slaughter of infants (Ex 1:22; Mt 2:16). **Out of Egypt I called my son** Quoted from Hos 11:1, where it refers to the historic events of the exodus. Matthew uses typology in applying this this text — which originally referred to God's corporate people, Israel — to Jesus, God's Messiah.

2:16–18 In a desperate move, Herod slaughters all the male children in and around Bethlehem in hopes of exterminating the promised child.

2:16 he had been outwitted The Greek word used here, *empaizō*, usually means "to mock" or "to ridicule," indicating that the Magi's noncompliance was disgraceful to Herod. **two years old and under** This detail implies that the wise men (Magi) first saw the star long before they came to Jerusalem. It also suggests that Jesus was probably more than a year old at this time. Bethlehem was very small; perhaps about 20 children were killed.

2:18 A voice is heard in Ramah Matthew quotes Jer 31:15; the context of children being slaughtered and Jesus' family being uprooted parallels the context of Jeremiah's prophecy.

2:19–23 Upon Herod the Great's death (ca. 4 BC), Joseph, Mary and Jesus return from Egypt.

2:19 After Herod died After Herod's death, his kingdom was divided among his sons, Archelaus, Antipas and Philip. See note on Lk 3:1.

2:22 he was afraid to go there Joseph's fear is justified; Archelaus was as cruel as his father. See the table "Political Leaders in the New Testament" on p. 1916. **Having been warned in a dream** The Greek text here does not identify a specific messenger. There is no warning given against Antipas, Herod the Great's son, who ruled in Galilee; this region is portrayed as a safe place for Jesus throughout Matthew's Gospel.

2:23 he would be called a Nazarene The source of this quotation is unknown and it seems that Jewish people at the time did not expect the Messiah to come from Nazareth (see Mt 2:4–5; Jn 1:46). Matthew might have

---

Jesus' Early Life and Ministry (continued)

Jesus spends the rest of his childhood and early adulthood in Nazareth.

Joseph, Mary and Jesus return from Egypt to settle in Nazareth.

John the Baptist calls for repentance in the wilderness.

John the Baptist baptizes Jesus and proclaims him as the Messiah.

Jesus calls the first disciples.

Jesus spends his childhood in Nazareth.

When he is 12, Jesus speaks to religious teachers in the temple. They are amazed at his understanding.

John the Baptist declares his mission and tells about the Messiah.

Satan tempts Jesus in the wilderness.

Andrew brings his brother Simon to Jesus, and Jesus calls him Peter.

near." ³This is he who was spoken of through the prophet Isaiah:

"A voice of one calling in the wilderness,
'Prepare the way for the Lord,
    make straight paths for him.'"ᵃ

⁴John's clothes were made of camel's hair, and he had a leather belt around his waist. His food was locusts and wild honey. ⁵People went out to him from Jerusalem and all Judea and the whole region of the Jordan. ⁶Confessing their sins, they were baptized by him in the Jordan River.

⁷But when he saw many of the Pharisees and Sadducees coming to where he was baptizing, he

ᵃ 3 Isaiah 40:3

---

had the Hebrew word *netser* ("branch") in mind from Isa 11:1, where it is used to describe a Messianic figure descended from Jesse, the father of David.

3:1–12 Matthew introduces the life and preaching of John the Baptist. John served as a forerunner to Jesus, proclaiming the advent of the kingdom and the arrival of the Messiah. See the event line "Jesus' Early Life and Ministry" on p. 1530.

3:1 In those days This phrase serves to anchor Matthew's narrative in Scripture. The OT prophets often use this phrase to describe the time of fulfilled prophecy. **John the Baptist** A prophet who is both a fulfillment of OT prophecies and a model of the OT prophets themselves (see Mt 11:13–14; 16:14; 17:10–13; Mal 4:5). See note on Jn 1:6. **the wilderness of Judea** Robbers, displaced peasants and religious ascetics often sought refuge in the wilderness. John's way of life resembles that of wilderness ascetics. Concerned about self-denial, spiritual discipline and devotion to the law, ascetic men and women went to the wilderness in order to distance themselves from the evils of society (compare note on Mk 1:4). According to Josephus (a first-century Jewish historian), Herod Antipas thought that John might become a political threat because of John's many followers. The socioeconomic situation of Jesus' day was bleak. Consequently, there were reprisals by the peasant class against the wealthy elite and aristocracy. Political leaders considered fringe movements—of which John was considered to have been a part—with suspicion.

3:2 Repent A decision to turn away from sin and toward God's ways. **kingdom of heaven** Synonymous with "kingdom of God." Both expressions refer to the time when God's rule would be enacted on earth as it is in heaven. Biblical writers often used "heaven" as a way of referring to God and his abode without having to use the divine name (Yahweh). See note on Mk 1:15.

3:3 of one calling in the wilderness Matthew cites Isa 40:3 from the Septuagint (the Greek translation of the OT). **Prepare the way for the Lord** In Isa 40:3, this prophecy refers to the Lord's restoration of his people to their land following the exile. Later, it became part of Messianic expectations. Both uses involve restoration and reconciliation.

3:4 clothes were made of camel's hair Matthew has already shown how John fulfills Isa 40:3; this description portrays John as the new Elijah (compare 2Ki 1:8). Throughout his Gospel, Matthew draws parallels between the dress, diet and ministries of John and Elijah (compare Mt 17:9–13; Jn 1:21 and note). Both men were bold, prophetic figures whose calling ran counter to religious norms. **His food was locusts and wild honey** Locusts were common food in the Middle East. Leviticus 11:20–23 identifies four varieties that are clean and good to eat.

3:6 they were baptized Likely derived from the Jewish custom of ritual washings. Jewish baptisms were intended to signify spiritual cleansing; John's baptisms are depicted as preparations for the coming of the Messiah. **Jordan River** The Jordan was significant because it served as the border that Israel crossed to enter the promised land (e.g., Dt 9:1). It does not seem to have been important for ritual washings (except in the case of Naaman; 2Ki 5:10,12).

3:7 Pharisees and Sadducees These groups were opposed to each other but appear united in their opposition

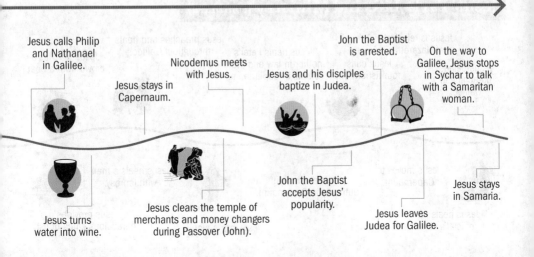

Jesus calls Philip and Nathanael in Galilee.

Jesus stays in Capernaum.

Nicodemus meets with Jesus.

John the Baptist is arrested.

Jesus and his disciples baptize in Judea.

On the way to Galilee, Jesus stops in Sychar to talk with a Samaritan woman.

Jesus turns water into wine.

Jesus clears the temple of merchants and money changers during Passover (John).

John the Baptist accepts Jesus' popularity.

Jesus leaves Judea for Galilee.

Jesus stays in Samaria.

said to them: "You brood of vipers! Who warned you to flee from the coming wrath? [8]Produce fruit in keeping with repentance. [9]And do not think you can say to yourselves, 'We have Abraham as our father.' I tell you that out of these stones God can raise up children for Abraham. [10]The ax is already at the root of the trees, and every tree that does not produce good fruit will be cut down and thrown into the fire.

[11]"I baptize you with[a] water for repentance. But after me comes one who is more powerful than I, whose sandals I am not worthy to carry. He will baptize you with[a] the Holy Spirit and fire. [12]His winnowing fork is in his hand, and he will clear his threshing floor, gathering his wheat into the barn and burning up the chaff with unquenchable fire."

The Baptism of Jesus

3:13-17pp — Mk 1:9-11; Lk 3:21,22; Jn 1:31-34

[13]Then Jesus came from Galilee to the Jordan to be baptized by John. [14]But John tried to deter him, saying, "I need to be baptized by you, and do you come to me?"

[15]Jesus replied, "Let it be so now; it is proper for us to do this to fulfill all righteousness." Then John consented.

[16]As soon as Jesus was baptized, he went up out of the water. At that moment heaven was opened, and he saw the Spirit of God descending like a dove and alighting on him. [17]And a voice from heaven said, "This is my Son, whom I love; with him I am well pleased."

Jesus Is Tested in the Wilderness

4:1-11pp — Mk 1:12,13; Lk 4:1-13

4 Then Jesus was led by the Spirit into the wilderness to be tempted[b] by the devil. [2]After fasting forty days and forty nights, he was hungry. [3]The tempter came to him and said, "If you are the Son of God, tell these stones to become bread."

---

a 11 Or in   b 1 The Greek for tempted can also mean tested.

---

to John. See note on Jn 1:24; note on Mk 12:18. See the table "Major Groups in Jesus' Time" on p. 1630. **brood of vipers** This phrase could be a generic insult; it also might allude to the Jewish leaders' cunning.
3:8 fruit in keeping with repentance Refers to deeds that show true contrition.
3:9 We have Abraham as our father See note on Lk 3:8.
3:10 The ax is already at the root of the trees An image of impending judgment (compare Mt 7:17–20). **fire** A symbol of divine wrath. See note on Lk 3:9.
3:11 sandals I am not worthy to carry See note on Lk 3:16. **baptize you with the Holy Spirit and fire** See note on Lk 3:16.
3:12 winnowing See note on Ru 3:2. This image shows that there is nothing arbitrary about judgment: The good, solid grain falls to the threshing floor, while the dry, empty chaff is blown away (see Isa 64:6; compare Jn 12:47–48). See the infographic "A Threshing Floor" on p. 497.

3:13–17 Jesus comes from Galilee to be baptized by John (compare 2:22). At first John refuses, but Jesus convinces him that it is necessary. After Jesus comes up out of the water, a voice from heaven and a manifestation of the Spirit signal that he is ready to begin his public ministry.
3:15 to fulfill all righteousness John's baptism for repentance was a means of identification with the kingdom of God. Although Jesus—the sinless Son of God—had nothing for which to repent, he publicly identified with God's kingdom through his baptism. **Then John consented** John, in his role as a prophet, has been accepting or rejecting people seeking baptism. Here the roles are reversed for the first time. John only dares to baptize Jesus because Jesus commands him to do so.
3:16 heaven was opened A standard prophetic image (e.g., Eze 1:1). **he saw** The referent of "he" is unclear. Here and in Mark, it seems to refer to Jesus.

Jesus' Early Life and Ministry (continued)

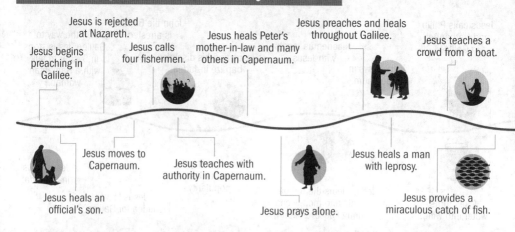

Jesus is rejected at Nazareth.

Jesus begins preaching in Galilee.

Jesus calls four fishermen.

Jesus heals Peter's mother-in-law and many others in Capernaum.

Jesus preaches and heals throughout Galilee.

Jesus teaches a crowd from a boat.

Jesus moves to Capernaum.

Jesus teaches with authority in Capernaum.

Jesus heals a man with leprosy.

Jesus heals an official's son.

Jesus prays alone.

Jesus provides a miraculous catch of fish.

⁴Jesus answered, "It is written: 'Man shall not live on bread alone, but on every word that comes from the mouth of God.'ᵃ"

⁵Then the devil took him to the holy city and had him stand on the highest point of the temple. ⁶"If you are the Son of God," he said, "throw yourself down. For it is written:

"'He will command his angels concerning you,
 and they will lift you up in their hands,
 so that you will not strike your foot against
   a stone.'ᵇ"

⁷Jesus answered him, "It is also written: 'Do not put the Lord your God to the test.'ᶜ"

⁸Again, the devil took him to a very high mountain and showed him all the kingdoms of the world and their splendor. ⁹"All this I will give you," he said, "if you will bow down and worship me."

¹⁰Jesus said to him, "Away from me, Satan! For it is written: 'Worship the Lord your God, and serve him only.'ᵈ"

ᵃ 4 Deut. 8:3   ᵇ 6 Psalm 91:11,12   ᶜ 7 Deut. 6:16
ᵈ 10 Deut. 6:13

Luke 3:21 may imply that the Holy Spirit was visible to everyone present, but Jn 1:32 indicates that John the Baptist witnessed the Spirit. **like a dove** Luke also uses dove imagery (Lk 3:22), but neither Matthew nor Luke describes the details of this event.

3:17 a voice from heaven It is unclear whether all or only some of those present heard this voice, or whether anyone recognized it (compare Jn 12:28–29). A voice speaks the same words at Jesus' transfiguration (Mt 17:5). **This is my Son, whom I love** Similar to Ps 2:7; see note on Mk 1:11. **with him I am well pleased** Similar to the description of the suffering servant in Isa 42:1, which Jesus quotes in Mt 12:18.

4:1–11 The temptations faced by Jesus follow the same pattern as the Israelites' disobedience in the desert. The Israelites demanded bread, doubted the Lord's presence and despaired of his help (compare Nu 11). Jesus reverses all of these acts of faithlessness.

4:1 was led by the Spirit into the wilderness God led his people through the desert for 40 years due to their unfaithfulness (see note on Lk 4:1). The Spirit leads Jesus into the wilderness for 40 days so that his fidelity might be set in contrast to the nation's infidelity. **devil** The Greek term used here, *diabolos*, refers to a spiritual figure who is adversarial to God and his purposes. In Mk 1:13 and Mt 4:10, this figure is referred to by the Greek term *satanas* (see note on Mk 1:13). **4:2 After fasting forty days and forty nights** Fasting during this time period meant eating nothing at all. The text does not seem to imply that Jesus was sustained

supernaturally during his fast; instead, it emphasizes that he experienced hunger. Jesus' 40-day fast recalls Moses' 40 days on the mountain (Ex 24:18), the Israelites' 40 years in the desert (Nu 14:33–34) and Elijah's 40 days at Mount Horeb (1Ki 19:1–8).

4:3 If you are the Son of God The devil uses this challenge twice in his temptations of Jesus. He turns the words of Mt 3:17 into a taunt. **tell these stones to become bread** Parallels the Israelites' failure in the desert. They complained that God did not provide enough food for them (Ex 16:3). The devil is tempting Jesus to break his fast, which the text implies would be equivalent to disobedience to God the Father.

4:4 It is written Jesus' reply comes from Dt 8:3.

4:5 holy city A common term for Jerusalem. **highest point** See note on Lk 4:9.

4:6 throw yourself down This test of God's providence is far more extreme than any test Israel underwent in the desert. **He will command his angels concerning you** See note on Mt 4:10.

4:7 Do not put the Lord your God to the test A quotation from Dt 6:16, which refers to the Israelites' testing Yahweh in Ex 17:2–7.

4:8 showed him all the kingdoms The apparent implication is that the devil simply points out the general direction of the kingdoms of the earth, naming them as he does so.

4:9 I will give See note on Lk 4:6. **worship me** The Greek word used here, *proskyneō*, does not necessarily refer to religious worship. It also can be used to describe the act of honoring an earthly king. Here the devil tempts Jesus to trust in him rather than God.

4:10 Away from me, Satan Jesus later rebukes Satan's

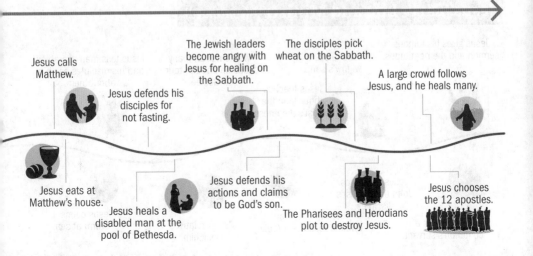

Jesus calls Matthew.

The Jewish leaders become angry with Jesus for healing on the Sabbath.

The disciples pick wheat on the Sabbath.

Jesus defends his disciples for not fasting.

A large crowd follows Jesus, and he heals many.

Jesus eats at Matthew's house.

Jesus heals a disabled man at the pool of Bethesda.

Jesus defends his actions and claims to be God's son.

The Pharisees and Herodians plot to destroy Jesus.

Jesus chooses the 12 apostles.

[11]Then the devil left him, and angels came and attended him.

Jesus Begins to Preach

[12]When Jesus heard that John had been put in prison, he withdrew to Galilee. [13]Leaving Nazareth, he went and lived in Capernaum, which was by the lake in the area of Zebulun and Naphtali— [14]to fulfill what was said through the prophet Isaiah:

[15] "Land of Zebulun and land of Naphtali,
 the Way of the Sea, beyond the Jordan,
 Galilee of the Gentiles—
[16] the people living in darkness
 have seen a great light;
 on those living in the land of the shadow
 of death
 a light has dawned."[a]

[17]From that time on Jesus began to preach, "Repent, for the kingdom of heaven has come near."

Jesus Calls His First Disciples

4:18-22pp — Mk 1:16-20; Lk 5:2-11; Jn 1:35-42

[18]As Jesus was walking beside the Sea of Galilee, he saw two brothers, Simon called Peter and his brother Andrew. They were casting a net into the lake, for they were fishermen. [19]"Come, follow me," Jesus said, "and I will send you out to fish for people." [20]At once they left their nets and followed him.

[21]Going on from there, he saw two other brothers, James son of Zebedee and his brother John. They were in a boat with their father Zebedee, preparing their nets. Jesus called them, [22]and

a 16 Isaiah 9:1,2

---

work through Peter using a similar remark (Mt 16:23). **it is written** Jesus quotes Dt 6:13, where the entire passage speaks against doubting Yahweh.

4:12–17 Following his temptation in the wilderness, Jesus returns to the region of Galilee and begins his ministry. This is approximately AD 28. Luke estimates that Jesus was around 30 when he began his public ministry (Lk 3:23).

4:13 Capernaum A fishing village on the Sea of Galilee (see note on Lk 4:31). See the infographic "The Synagogue at Capernaum" on p. 1656. **Zebulun and Naphtali** These tribes were allotted territory in what became known as Galilee, but the Jewish population was largely displaced during the Persian period (ca. 559–331 BC). The inhabitants of Jesus' day were mostly Gentiles (non-Jewish people) or descendants of Jews who had resettled in the region.

4:14 said through the prophet Isaiah Matthew quotes Isa 9:1–2, which emphasizes an ideal king from David's line (compare Isa 9:6 and note). By the time of Matthew's writing, the passage had become associated

with the Messiah. See the table "Jesus' Fulfillment of OT Prophecy" on p. 1573.

4:17 From that time on Indicates the start of Jesus' public ministry (compare Mt 16:21). **to preach** The Greek word used here, *kēryssō*, connotes a different sort of proclamation than the modern verb "preach" expresses. It often was used to describe official pronouncements of sovereigns, such as declarations of state visits or changes in taxation. **kingdom of heaven has come near** This concept communicated great urgency in John's proclamation. Several of Jesus' parables likewise emphasize impending judgment and that people should repent. See note on 3:2.

4:18–22 Matthew records Jesus' calling of two sets of brothers. Three of the four—Peter, James and John—became the inner circle of his disciples and rose to greater positions of leadership among the apostles and the early church.

4:18 two brothers Capernaum was small, and Jesus had been preaching the coming of the kingdom of heaven (compare 4:17). The two brothers, Peter and Andrew, had probably already heard of Jesus. John 1:40–42 also re-

---

Jesus' Early Life and Ministry (continued)

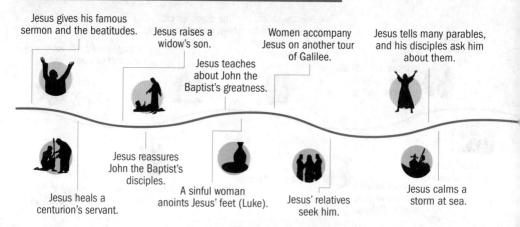

Jesus gives his famous sermon and the beatitudes.

Jesus raises a widow's son.

Jesus teaches about John the Baptist's greatness.

Women accompany Jesus on another tour of Galilee.

Jesus tells many parables, and his disciples ask him about them.

Jesus reassures John the Baptist's disciples.

Jesus heals a centurion's servant.

A sinful woman anoints Jesus' feet (Luke).

Jesus' relatives seek him.

Jesus calms a storm at sea.

immediately they left the boat and their father and followed him.

Jesus Heals the Sick

[23]Jesus went throughout Galilee, teaching in their synagogues, proclaiming the good news of the kingdom, and healing every disease and sickness among the people. [24]News about him spread all over Syria, and people brought to him all who were ill with various diseases, those suffering severe pain, the demon-possessed, those having seizures, and the paralyzed; and he healed them. [25]Large crowds from Galilee, the Decapolis,[a] Jerusalem, Judea and the region across the Jordan followed him.

Introduction to the Sermon on the Mount

5 Now when Jesus saw the crowds, he went up on a mountainside and sat down. His disciples came to him, [2]and he began to teach them.

[a] 25 That is, the Ten Cities

---

cords an early interaction of Peter and Andrew, noting that Andrew was one of John the Baptist's disciples (Jn 1:35) and that he originally brought Peter to meet Jesus. **a net** A small, circular net that a single person could handle. See the infographic "First-Century Galilean Fishing Boat" on p. 1560.

4:23 synagogues Usually refers to a building where a local community assembled. The synagogue was not a distinctively religious institution, as nonreligious activities also took place there. Synagogues provided Jews who lived far from the temple in Jerusalem a place to pray, teach and—most importantly—read Scripture. Rabbis could lecture there, interpreting the Scriptures, explaining the law and offering instructions. See the infographic "The Synagogue at Capernaum" on p. 1656; see the infographic "Ancient Home Synagogue" on p. 1971.

4:24 those suffering severe pain People during this time did not distinguish between physical diseases and the ill effects of unclean, evil spirits. Matthew makes no statement about these maladies in this verse beyond observing that Jesus cured them all, regardless of their cause. **Syria** A Roman province located north and east of Israel and Galilee. Syria was a large and influential region, and Matthew mentions it to show how far and how fast Jesus' reputation had spread.

4:25 The list of places in this verse represent the major areas inhabited by Jews, showing the extent of Jesus' influence.

4:25 Large crowds Might describe as many as a few thousand people. **Decapolis** This Greek name means "ten cities" and refers to a federation of Hellenized (highly Greek-influenced) cities and towns located east of the Sea of Galilee. It may have comprised more than ten cities.

5:1–12 Matthew 5–7 contains Jesus' Sermon on the Mount, which describes how members of the kingdom of heaven should live. Jesus' statements in vv. 3–12 are known as the Beatitudes. This is the first of five primary speeches by Jesus and sets the tone for the rest of Matthew's Gospel. See the event line "Jesus' Early Life and Ministry" on p. 1530.

5:1 he went up on a mountainside Jesus' giving new instruction on a mountain reflects Ex 19–24. His comparisons with various points of the law (Mt 5:21,27,31,33,38,43) allude to Moses. Mountains provide the setting for significant teachings and events in Matthew (e.g., 17:1; 24:3; 26:30; 28:16). **sat down** In Jesus' day, the most important person or persons in a group would sit while the rest stood. Rabbis sat while giving instruction. **His disciples came to him** The language of this verse reflects Moses' reception of the law at Mount Sinai. Moses went up Mount Sinai into the cloud; the disciples—like the Israelites in the desert—may have thought that they should wait below while he spoke with God. Matthew presents Jesus as the new Moses, but so much greater than Moses that

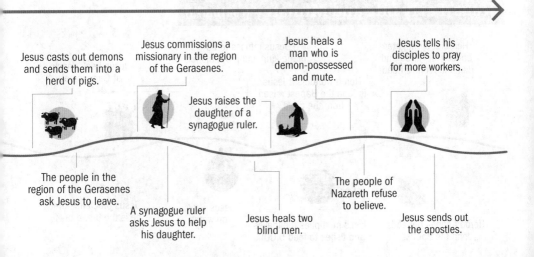

Jesus casts out demons and sends them into a herd of pigs.

Jesus commissions a missionary in the region of the Gerasenes.

Jesus raises the daughter of a synagogue ruler.

Jesus heals a man who is demon-possessed and mute.

Jesus tells his disciples to pray for more workers.

The people in the region of the Gerasenes ask Jesus to leave.

A synagogue ruler asks Jesus to help his daughter.

Jesus heals two blind men.

The people of Nazareth refuse to believe.

Jesus sends out the apostles.

The Beatitudes

5:3-12pp — Lk 6:20-23

He said:

3 "Blessed are the poor in spirit,
for theirs is the kingdom of
heaven.
4 Blessed are those who mourn,
for they will be comforted.
5 Blessed are the meek,
for they will inherit the earth.
6 Blessed are those who hunger and
thirst for righteousness,
for they will be filled.
7 Blessed are the merciful,
for they will be shown mercy.
8 Blessed are the pure in heart,
for they will see God.

9 Blessed are the peacemakers,
for they will be called children
of God.
10 Blessed are those who are persecuted because
of righteousness,
for theirs is the kingdom of heaven.

11 "Blessed are you when people insult you, persecute you and falsely say all kinds of evil against you because of me. 12 Rejoice and be glad, because great is your reward in heaven, for in the same way they persecuted the prophets who were before you.

Salt and Light

13 "You are the salt of the earth. But if the salt loses its saltiness, how can it be made salty again? It is no longer good for anything, except to be thrown out and trampled underfoot.

---

he does not have to consult with God before giving his new law — hinting at Jesus' divinity.

5:3 Blessed The Greek word used here, *makarios* (meaning "happy" or "fortunate"), often indicates someone who is favored by God. **poor in spirit** Refers to those in Jesus' day who recognize and bear their desperate plight, and who long for God's restoration through the Messiah. **kingdom of heaven** The crowd was already familiar with this terminology through John the Baptist's proclamation; they anticipated a time of restoration. See note on 3:2.

5:4 those who mourn Could refer to those who mourn for Israel and for their plight within its present conditions (e.g., Roman occupation, what seems like a lack of God's presence, impoverishment). Alternatively, it could refer to those who mourn over their personal sin or are currently enduring difficult times.

5:5 the meek Refers to someone who is humble or gentle. The meek do not seek gain for themselves; instead, they hope in the Lord. **they will inherit the earth** A reference to Ps 37:11, which foretells the destruction of evildoers (compare Rev 21), so that those who hope in Yahweh will live in peace.

5:6 who hunger and thirst for righteousness A metaphor for moral uprightness. This may be an allusion to Ps 37:12–17 (compare note on Mt 5:5), which speaks of a time when oppressors will be no more. This line expresses a deep desire both for personal righteousness and for a world characterized by God's righteousness (or justice). It implies that those who observe God's commandments should do so not out of resignation, but out of a fundamental desire. Due to widespread poverty, many of those listening to Jesus were probably hungry and thirsty in a literal sense.

5:7 Blessed are the merciful This beatitude has the same emphasis as the others: God's kingdom is breaking in upon the world. When it does, God will show mercy to those who have been merciful to others.

5:8 pure in heart Possibly an allusion to Ps 18:26. This beatitude uses the terminology of ritual purity and cleanness, which would have been common in Judaism. But Jesus' original audience likely would have made no distinction between having a heart pure from sin and being a person who is ritually pure according to the law. This parallels Jesus' emphasis on God being

---

Jesus' Early Life and Ministry *(continued)*

Herodias's daughter
dances for Herod and
demands John's head.

Herod wonders if Jesus
is John the Baptist raised
from the dead.

Jesus refuses to be
made king and prays alone.

Jesus heals many
at Gennesaret.

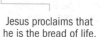

Herod Antipas beheads
John the Baptist.

Jesus multiplies the loaves
and fishes to feed 5,000.

Jesus walks
on water.

Jesus proclaims that
he is the bread of life.

¹⁴"You are the light of the world. A town built on a hill cannot be hidden. ¹⁵Neither do people light a lamp and put it under a bowl. Instead they put it on its stand, and it gives light to everyone in the house. ¹⁶In the same way, let your light shine before others, that they may see your good deeds and glorify your Father in heaven.

The Fulfillment of the Law

¹⁷"Do not think that I have come to abolish the Law or the Prophets; I have not come to abolish them but to fulfill them. ¹⁸For truly I tell you, until heaven and earth disappear, not the smallest letter, not the least stroke of a pen, will by any means disappear from the Law until everything is accomplished. ¹⁹Therefore anyone who sets aside one of the least of these commands and teaches others accordingly will be called least in the kingdom of heaven, but whoever practices and teaches these commands will be called great in the kingdom of heaven. ²⁰For I tell you that unless your righteousness surpasses that of the Pharisees and the teachers of the law, you will certainly not enter the kingdom of heaven.

concerned about the spiritual state of a person, not just their outward, religious purity (compare Mt 15:11). **they will see God** Likely an allusion to the temple entrance liturgy of Ps 24:3–4. The idea being that they will witness God's entrance.

5:9 Blessed are the peacemakers Jewish literature of the time valued those who worked for peace. **children of God** Those whose lives reflect the ethics of Jesus will be clearly identified as children of God (see Ro 8:14 and note).

5:10–12 These three verses address persecution and likely reflect the situation of those who first read Matthew's Gospel (which may explain why the theme receives such extensive treatment). Later in the narrative, Jesus encounters each form of persecution recorded here and suffers the same fate as many OT prophets (see Mt 23:29–37).

5:11 because of me Jesus is speaking to his disciples about a radical way of life that reflects the ideals of the kingdom of heaven. He seems to imply that persecution is a result of practicing his teaching and believing in him.

5:13–16 In what follows, Jesus shifts from pronouncements of blessing to instructions about the law. He compares his followers to salt and light, elements commonly used as metaphors in antiquity. His point is that disciples who fail to live a lifestyle that reflects the values of the kingdom of heaven are akin to something tasteless or devoid of light—undesirable and of no value.

5:13 salt of the earth Salt was valued for its many uses, such as flavoring (Job 6:6), preserving, healing (Eze 16:4) and destroying (Jdg 9:45). It also served a liturgical function (Lev 2:13; Eze 43:24) and was used in covenant making (Nu 18:19; 2Ch 13:5).

5:14 light of the world Recalls Israel's role as a light to the nations (Isa 42:6; 49:6).

5:16 Father Jesus commonly refers to God by this designation, which indicates their relationship of father and son. The concept of Yahweh as a father was common throughout Israel's history (e.g., 2Sa 7:14; 1Ch 22:9–10; Ps 2:7).

5:17 to fulfill The Greek word used here, *plēroō*, refers in this instance to carrying something out. Matthew is saying that Jesus performed or upheld that which was required by the law and met the expectations of the predictions about him in the writings of the prophets. In him, the Law and the Prophets reached their fullest expression (e.g., Mt 1:22; 2:15,17,23). See the table "Jesus' Fulfillment of OT Prophecy" on p. 1573.

5:18 will by any means disappear All of the law was important to Jesus (compare 5:17).

5:20 surpasses that of the Pharisees and the teachers of the law These groups were associated with a high degree of righteousness. This should not be considered an endorsement of the scribes (teachers of the law, see note on Mt 2:4) and Pharisees (see note on Jn 7:32). Instead, Jesus points out that not even their righteousness is enough to enter the kingdom of heaven.

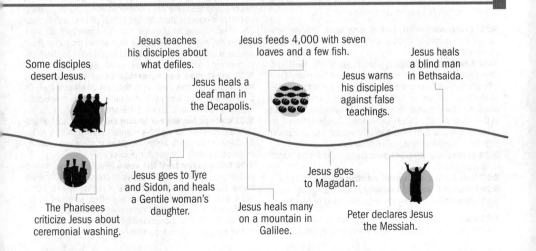

Some disciples desert Jesus.

Jesus teaches his disciples about what defiles.

Jesus heals a deaf man in the Decapolis.

Jesus feeds 4,000 with seven loaves and a few fish.

Jesus warns his disciples against false teachings.

Jesus heals a blind man in Bethsaida.

The Pharisees criticize Jesus about ceremonial washing.

Jesus goes to Tyre and Sidon, and heals a Gentile woman's daughter.

Jesus heals many on a mountain in Galilee.

Jesus goes to Magadan.

Peter declares Jesus the Messiah.

Murder

5:25,26pp — Lk 12:58,59

²¹"You have heard that it was said to the people long ago, 'You shall not murder,ᵃ and anyone who murders will be subject to judgment.' ²²But I tell you that anyone who is angry with a brother or sisterᵇ,ᶜ will be subject to judgment. Again, anyone who says to a brother or sister, 'Raca,'ᵈ is answerable to the court. And anyone who says, 'You fool!' will be in danger of the fire of hell.

²³"Therefore, if you are offering your gift at the altar and there remember that your brother or sister has something against you, ²⁴leave your gift there in front of the altar. First go and be reconciled to them; then come and offer your gift.

²⁵"Settle matters quickly with your adversary who is taking you to court. Do it while you are still together on the way, or your adversary may hand you over to the judge, and the judge may hand you over to the officer, and you may be thrown into prison. ²⁶Truly I tell you, you will not get out until you have paid the last penny.

Adultery

²⁷"You have heard that it was said, 'You shall not commit adultery.'ᵉ ²⁸But I tell you that anyone who looks at a woman lustfully has already committed adultery with her in his heart. ²⁹If your right eye causes you to stumble, gouge it out and throw it away. It is better for you to lose one part of your body than for your whole body to be thrown into hell. ³⁰And if your right hand causes

you to stumble, cut it off and throw it away. It is better for you to lose one part of your body than for your whole body to go into hell.

Divorce

³¹"It has been said, 'Anyone who divorces his wife must give her a certificate of divorce.'ᶠ ³²But I tell you that anyone who divorces his wife, except for sexual immorality, makes her the victim of adultery, and anyone who marries a divorced woman commits adultery.

Oaths

³³"Again, you have heard that it was said to the people long ago, 'Do not break your oath, but fulfill to the Lord the vows you have made.' ³⁴But I tell you, do not swear an oath at all: either by heaven, for it is God's throne; ³⁵or by the earth, for it is his footstool; or by Jerusalem, for it is the city of the Great King. ³⁶And do not swear by your head, for you cannot make even one hair white or black. ³⁷All you need to say is simply 'Yes' or 'No'; anything beyond this comes from the evil one.ᵍ

Eye for Eye

³⁸"You have heard that it was said, 'Eye for eye, and tooth for tooth.'ʰ ³⁹But I tell you, do not resist

ᵃ 21 Exodus 20:13   ᵇ 22 The Greek word for brother or sister (adelphos) refers here to a fellow disciple, whether man or woman; also in verse 23.   ᶜ 22 Some manuscripts brother or sister without cause   ᵈ 22 An Aramaic term of contempt
ᵉ 27 Exodus 20:14   ᶠ 31 Deut. 24:1   ᵍ 37 Or from evil
ʰ 38 Exodus 21:24; Lev. 24:20; Deut. 19:21

5:21–48 Jesus presents six antitheses—statements using opposites to make a point—to illustrate what it means to have a righteousness that surpasses that of the scribes (teachers of the law) and Pharisees. The righteousness required of Jesus' disciples goes beyond the observation of the written law. However, Jesus' teaching here does not overturn the existing Jewish law; it merely supplements or elaborates its teachings with principles for living the ethics of the kingdom of heaven (see note on v. 17).

5:21 You have heard that it was said This expression (or a variation) occurs six times in this passage. Compare Ex 20:13.

5:22 I tell you Highlights Jesus' authority. **hell** The Greek word used here is *geenna*, often transliterated into English as "Gehenna." The underlying reference is to the Hebrew name "Valley of Hinnom," which was a place near Jerusalem linked with idolatrous sacrifices in the OT (e.g., 2Ch 28:3). Over time, Gehenna came to represent a place of God's wrath, hence the affiliation with fire. Compare note on 1Pe 3:19.

5:23 something against you Likely refers to a legitimate complaint.

5:27 You shall not commit adultery See Ex 20:14.

5:28 looks at a woman lustfully Jesus wants his followers to deal with sin where it starts: the mind or emotions.

5:29–30 The two examples Jesus gives in Mt 5:29–30 call for extreme measures to prevent and eradicate sin.

However, they are not intended literally; they are hyperboles—deliberate exaggerations to make a point. Jesus is saying that people should be vigilant in avoiding sin, making every effort to remain pure.

5:29 hell See note on v. 22.

5:30 lose one part of your body Jesus uses this illustration to emphasize the way that sin stands between people and God. He also demonstrates the desperate need for a person, through the power of God, to rid their life of sin. Jesus is showing that for many people their desire for sin is so powerful that it keeps them from having relationship with God and thus leads to them experiencing God's judgment and wrath. See note on v. 22.

5:31 must give her a certificate of divorce Jesus later indicates that divorce in the Law of Moses (see Dt 24:1–4 and note) was permitted only because of people's hardness of heart (see Mt 19:8 and note).

5:32 except for sexual immorality Jesus addresses this issue again at various points in his ministry (e.g., 19:3–9). In this text, Jesus indicates that sexual infidelity is an acceptable reason for divorce.

5:33 fulfill to the Lord the vows People swore oaths to guarantee their truthfulness. Jesus calls on his followers to practice honesty without the use of oaths. See Nu 30:2.

5:38 Eye for eye This principle, often referred to as *lex talionis* or the "law of retaliation" (see Ex 21–24) contrasts with the unexpected generosity that a member of the kingdom of heaven should display.

an evil person. If anyone slaps you on the right cheek, turn to them the other cheek also. ⁴⁰And if anyone wants to sue you and take your shirt, hand over your coat as well. ⁴¹If anyone forces you to go one mile, go with them two miles. ⁴²Give to the one who asks you, and do not turn away from the one who wants to borrow from you.

Love for Enemies

⁴³"You have heard that it was said, 'Love your neighborᵃ and hate your enemy.' ⁴⁴But I tell you, love your enemies and pray for those who persecute you, ⁴⁵that you may be children of your Father in heaven. He causes his sun to rise on the evil and the good, and sends rain on the righteous and the unrighteous. ⁴⁶If you love those who love you, what reward will you get? Are not even the tax collectors doing that? ⁴⁷And if you greet only your own people, what are you doing more than others? Do not even pagans do that? ⁴⁸Be perfect, therefore, as your heavenly Father is perfect.

Giving to the Needy

6 "Be careful not to practice your righteousness in front of others to be seen by them. If you do, you will have no reward from your Father in heaven.

²"So when you give to the needy, do not announce it with trumpets, as the hypocrites do in the synagogues and on the streets, to be honored by others. Truly I tell you, they have received their reward in full. ³But when you give to the needy, do not let your left hand know what your right hand is doing, ⁴so that your giving may be in secret. Then your Father, who sees what is done in secret, will reward you.

Prayer

6:9-13pp — Lk 11:2-4

⁵"And when you pray, do not be like the hypocrites, for they love to pray standing in the synagogues and on the street corners to be seen by others. Truly I tell you, they have received their reward in full. ⁶But when you pray, go into your room, close the door and pray to your Father, who is unseen. Then your Father, who sees what is done in secret, will reward you. ⁷And when you pray, do not keep on babbling like pagans, for they think they will be heard because of their many words. ⁸Do not be like them, for your Father knows what you need before you ask him.

⁹"This, then, is how you should pray:

"'Our Father in heaven,
  hallowed be your name,
¹⁰ your kingdom come,
  your will be done,
    on earth as it is in heaven.

ᵃ 43 Lev. 19:18

5:39 do not resist an evil person Jesus is speaking of someone who does wrong to another person. He encourages his followers to return good when someone else intends evil.

5:41 If anyone forces you to go one mile The Roman military occupied Israel during this time, and soldiers could require bystanders to carry a load for a mile.

5:42 Give to the one who asks you Members of God's kingdom should be characterized by overwhelming generosity.

5:43 Love your neighbor Jesus is quoting Lev 19:18 here. **hate your enemy** This phrase does not appear in the law (or anywhere else in the Hebrew Bible), but it might allude to Dt 23:3–6 (compare Ps 137:7–9; 139:21–22). It could also be a colloquialism of the time.

5:44 love The focus of Jesus' ethical teaching (see Mt 22:34–40).

5:45 you may be children of your Father Just as God gives the good gifts of sun and rain to all people without distinction, members of the kingdom should act with love, kindness and generosity toward all. Jesus' followers should reflect God's character.

5:46 tax collectors These were some of the most hated people in Israel, due to the nature of their work and their association with the Roman government. Tax collectors generally obtained their posts from Roman authorities through a bidding system. They often made sizeable profits by levying higher taxes than Rome required. Consequently, Jews regarded Jewish tax collectors as traitors and as members of the lowest level of society. The mention of tax collectors alongside non-Jewish people (v. 47) reflects not only their poor reputation, but also the scope

of Jesus' ministry to redeem all of humanity, including the outcasts of society. Matthew, the likely author of this Gospel, was a tax collector, and Jews viewed his inclusion among Jesus' disciples as scandalous (9:9–13).

5:47 pagans The Greek text here refers to non-Jews — people who were not ethnically part of Israel.

5:48 Be perfect Those who demonstrate love in the manner attributed to God the Father will become perfect — complete or mature.

6:1–18 Jesus' examples in this passage involve personal piety and expand on his opening command in v. 1. Members of the kingdom of heaven should practice these disciplines so that the Father — not others — can witness their acts of devotion.

6:1 not to practice your righteousness in front of others This warning points back to 5:20. The examples that follow are noted abuses of the scribes (teachers of the law) and Pharisees (compare ch. 23). **reward** Refers to future blessing, not an immediate payoff.

6:2 received their reward This phrase also occurs in vv. 5 and 16. The hypocrites, having been rewarded with praise from other people, will receive no blessing from God.

6:5 when you pray This does not prohibit public prayer (as in corporate prayer); rather, it prohibits praying for the purpose of public recognition.

6:7 their many words In Greco-Roman religions, repetition was used to pester the gods so they would grant someone's request.

6:9 This, then, is how you should pray After describing how not to pray, Jesus gives a positive example.

¹¹Give us today our daily bread.
¹²And forgive us our debts,
 as we also have forgiven our debtors.
¹³And lead us not into temptation,ᵃ
 but deliver us from the evil one.ᵇ'

¹⁴For if you forgive other people when they sin against you, your heavenly Father will also forgive you. ¹⁵But if you do not forgive others their sins, your Father will not forgive your sins.

Fasting

¹⁶"When you fast, do not look somber as the hypocrites do, for they disfigure their faces to show others they are fasting. Truly I tell you, they have received their reward in full. ¹⁷But when you fast, put oil on your head and wash your face, ¹⁸so that it will not be obvious to others that you are fasting, but only to your Father, who is unseen; and your Father, who sees what is done in secret, will reward you.

Treasures in Heaven

6:22,23pp — Lk 11:34-36

¹⁹"Do not store up for yourselves treasures on earth, where moths and vermin destroy, and where thieves break in and steal. ²⁰But store up for yourselves treasures in heaven, where moths and vermin do not destroy, and where thieves do not break in and steal. ²¹For where your treasure is, there your heart will be also.

²²"The eye is the lamp of the body. If your eyes are healthy,ᶜ your whole body will be full of light.

²³But if your eyes are unhealthy,ᵈ your whole body will be full of darkness. If then the light within you is darkness, how great is that darkness!

²⁴"No one can serve two masters. Either you will hate the one and love the other, or you will be devoted to the one and despise the other. You cannot serve both God and money.

Do Not Worry

6:25-33pp — Lk 12:22-31

²⁵"Therefore I tell you, do not worry about your life, what you will eat or drink; or about your body, what you will wear. Is not life more than food, and the body more than clothes? ²⁶Look at the birds of the air; they do not sow or reap or store away in barns, and yet your heavenly Father feeds them. Are you not much more valuable than they? ²⁷Can any one of you by worrying add a single hour to your lifeᵉ?

²⁸"And why do you worry about clothes? See how the flowers of the field grow. They do not labor or spin. ²⁹Yet I tell you that not even Solomon in all his splendor was dressed like one of these. ³⁰If that is how God clothes the grass of the field, which is here today and tomorrow is thrown into the fire, will he not much more clothe you — you of little faith? ³¹So do not worry, saying, 'What

---

ᵃ 13 The Greek for *temptation* can also mean *testing*.
ᵇ 13 Or *from evil*; some late manuscripts *one, / for yours is the kingdom and the power and the glory forever. Amen.*
ᶜ 22 The Greek for *healthy* here implies *generous*.
ᵈ 23 The Greek for *unhealthy* here implies *stingy*.
ᵉ 27 Or *single cubit to your height*

Verses 9–13 and the parallel passage of Lk 11:1–4 provide a model for prayer. The Gospels make no explicit claims regarding Jesus' intentions for creating this prayer, but the context indicates that he is teaching people how to pray (compare Lk 11:1–4 and note).

6:10 your will be done Jesus prays similar words as he faces arrest and crucifixion (compare Mt 26:39,42).

6:11 Give us today our daily bread The people of rural Galilee were poor and oppressed, and resources such as food were scarce.

6:12 our debts The language used here for debt can reflect an Aramaic idiom referring to sin (compare note on Lk 11:4).

6:13 into temptation This refers to hardship in a general sense. **the evil one** The Greek term used here may indicate a specific entity (such as the devil; compare Eph 6:16) or evil in its many forms. Following this phrase, many ancient manuscripts add an affirmation that the kingdom, power and glory belong to God. Although this statement likely is not original, it appears to have been incorporated into Christian liturgy from the earliest days of the church. It probably comes from David's speech in 1Ch 29:11.

6:16 do not look somber as the hypocrites Fasting involves abstaining from food for the purpose of religious reflection and devotion. In order to be noticed by others, hypocrites who were fasting would display a disheveled appearance.

6:17 put oil on your head Refers to basic hygiene practices of the time.

6:19–24 Most of Jesus' audience probably was very poor, and with poverty comes a concern for the material aspects of life. Jesus addresses these earthly concerns in the next section (Mt 6:25–34); here, he calls people to devote themselves to the pursuit of heavenly blessings.

6:19 treasures on earth Detachment from worldly goods is a prominent theme in Matthew's Gospel (e.g., Mt 19:16–30).

6:21 there your heart will be Jews of the time typically perceived the heart as the seat of intelligence and will. Jesus' teaching reflects this view: People's choices and actions are shaped by the things they cherish most.

6:24 You cannot serve both God and money The problem that Jesus identifies is not money itself, but the divided loyalties that result from the pursuit of money (compare 1Ti 6:10). Being a disciple of Jesus requires complete devotion to God (compare Mt 8:18–22; 19:16–26).

6:25–34 This section covers the practical implications of the preceding discussion (vv. 19–24). People who serve God faithfully can trust him to meet their material needs.

6:29 not even Solomon in all his splendor See 1Ki 10.

6:30 into the fire Grass and weeds were used as fuel for fires. **you of little faith** Jesus uses this phrase when the disciples doubt God's ability to take care of them (Mt 8:26; 14:31; 16:8).

shall we eat?' or 'What shall we drink?' or 'What shall we wear?' [32]For the pagans run after all these things, and your heavenly Father knows that you need them. [33]But seek first his kingdom and his righteousness, and all these things will be given to you as well. [34]Therefore do not worry about tomorrow, for tomorrow will worry about itself. Each day has enough trouble of its own.

Judging Others

7:3-5pp — Lk 6:41,42

7 "Do not judge, or you too will be judged. [2]For in the same way you judge others, you will be judged, and with the measure you use, it will be measured to you.

[3]"Why do you look at the speck of sawdust in your brother's eye and pay no attention to the plank in your own eye? [4]How can you say to your brother, 'Let me take the speck out of your eye,' when all the time there is a plank in your own eye? [5]You hypocrite, first take the plank out of your own eye, and then you will see clearly to remove the speck from your brother's eye.

[6]"Do not give dogs what is sacred; do not throw your pearls to pigs. If you do, they may trample them under their feet, and turn and tear you to pieces.

Ask, Seek, Knock

7:7-11pp — Lk 11:9-13

[7]"Ask and it will be given to you; seek and you will find; knock and the door will be opened to you. [8]For everyone who asks receives; the one who seeks finds; and to the one who knocks, the door will be opened.

[9]"Which of you, if your son asks for bread, will give him a stone? [10]Or if he asks for a fish, will give him a snake? [11]If you, then, though you are evil, know how to give good gifts to your children, how much more will your Father in heaven give good gifts to those who ask him! [12]So in everything, do to others what you would have them do to you, for this sums up the Law and the Prophets.

The Narrow and Wide Gates

[13]"Enter through the narrow gate. For wide is the gate and broad is the road that leads to destruction, and many enter through it. [14]But small is the gate and narrow the road that leads to life, and only a few find it.

True and False Prophets

[15]"Watch out for false prophets. They come to you in sheep's clothing, but inwardly they are

---

6:33 seek first his kingdom and his righteousness When people make God's kingdom their primary object of desire, they find the ability to trust him to meet their needs.
6:34 tomorrow will worry about itself Jesus is not telling people to postpone their worrying for a day; he is instructing them to stop worrying altogether and to rely on God's gracious provision (compare Php 4:6).

7:1–12 As with the rest of the Sermon on the Mount, Jesus is describing how to live as members of the kingdom of heaven. He begins this section by explaining the dangers of a judgmental attitude (vv. 1–5). He also emphasizes God's goodness (vv. 7–11) and instructs his followers to replicate that goodness as they interact with others (v. 12).

7:2 you will be judged Jesus is saying that God will judge people according to the same standards they apply when judging others. Those who judge harshly, for example, will be judged harshly by God.
7:3 the speck Describes something so small it is almost irrelevant. **plank** Jesus uses an absurd contrast to make his point.
7:5 first take the plank Jesus commands his followers to address their own sins before they judge the sins of others. **see clearly to remove the speck** When people deal with sin and its distorting effects in their own lives, they have the discernment to help others repent from sin.
7:6 Do not give dogs what is sacred; do not throw your pearls to pigs These images characterize God's kingdom — and Jesus' teaching about it — as something valuable that should not be discarded. Dogs were considered unclean according to the Jewish law (Lev 11:27), as were swine (see Lev 11:7 and note).
7:7 Ask The first of three commands in this verse. **it will be given to you** In each of the three statements here,

Jesus' point is the same: When God's people pursue something — by asking, seeking, knocking — he responds in faithfulness and generosity. This verse emphasizes the need for an authentic relationship with God.
7:10 will give him a snake The rhetorical questions in Mt 7:9–10 set up the comparison in v. 11 between earthly fathers and the heavenly Father.
7:11 how much more Jesus argues from a lesser principle to a greater one. Human parents know how to give their children good things; by comparison, the heavenly Father can do abundantly more for his children.
7:12 do to others what you would have them do to you This command, often called the Golden Rule, epitomizes Jesus' ethical teaching and describes how people should interact with one another. Jesus' expression of this command reflects teachings from the Hebrew Bible (e.g., Lev 19:18) and other ancient Jewish texts (e.g., Sirach 31:15; Tobit 4:15). **for this sums up the Law and the Prophets** Jesus later says that the Law and the Prophets can be summarized by two commandments — to love God completely, and to love your neighbor as yourself (Mt 22:37–40).

7:13–14 Jesus explains that the way of God's kingdom is like a road less traveled. The concept of two ways — one leading to life and the other to destruction — appears in the Hebrew Bible, Greco-Roman literature and the Jewish writings from the Dead Sea Scrolls (ca. 250 BC–50 AD).

7:15–20 Jesus teaches that people — godly and ungodly — are distinguishable by their deeds (compare Eph 2:8–10).

7:15 false prophets Refers to those whose teaching contradicts Jesus' teaching. Beginning in Mt 5:17, Jesus has reinterpreted the established religious and social norms of his day. Here, he portrays those who

ferocious wolves. [16] By their fruit you will recognize them. Do people pick grapes from thornbushes, or figs from thistles? [17] Likewise, every good tree bears good fruit, but a bad tree bears bad fruit. [18] A good tree cannot bear bad fruit, and a bad tree cannot bear good fruit. [19] Every tree that does not bear good fruit is cut down and thrown into the fire. [20] Thus, by their fruit you will recognize them.

True and False Disciples

[21] "Not everyone who says to me, 'Lord, Lord,' will enter the kingdom of heaven, but only the one who does the will of my Father who is in heaven. [22] Many will say to me on that day, 'Lord, Lord, did we not prophesy in your name and in your name drive out demons and in your name perform many miracles?' [23] Then I will tell them plainly, 'I never knew you. Away from me, you evildoers!'

The Wise and Foolish Builders

7:24-27pp — Lk 6:47-49

[24] "Therefore everyone who hears these words of mine and puts them into practice is like a wise man who built his house on the rock. [25] The rain came down, the streams rose, and the winds blew and beat against that house; yet it did not fall, because it had its foundation on the rock. [26] But everyone who hears these words of mine and does not put them into practice is like a foolish man who built his house on sand. [27] The rain came down, the streams rose, and the winds blew and beat against that house, and it fell with a great crash."

[28] When Jesus had finished saying these things, the crowds were amazed at his teaching, [29] because he taught as one who had authority, and not as their teachers of the law.

Jesus Heals a Man With Leprosy

8:2-4pp — Mk 1:40-44; Lk 5:12-14

8 When Jesus came down from the mountainside, large crowds followed him. [2] A man with leprosy[a] came and knelt before him and said, "Lord, if you are willing, you can make me clean."

[3] Jesus reached out his hand and touched the man. "I am willing," he said. "Be clean!" Immedi-

---

[a] 2 The Greek word traditionally translated *leprosy* was used for various diseases affecting the skin.

---

contradict his instruction as false prophets—people who falsely claim to speak on God's behalf (compare 2Pe 2:1 and note). **sheep's clothing** Refers to disguises that portray innocence. **ferocious wolves** Describes those seeking to undermine Jesus' teaching for personal gain.
7:16 their fruit Refers to people's deeds—the natural outcomes of their choices and inclinations. **grapes from thornbushes, or figs from thistles** Images drawn from horticulture would have resonated with Jesus' audience, as first-century Palestine was primarily an agrarian society.
7:19 thrown into the fire See Mt 3:10 and note.

7:21–23 Jesus continues the theme of false prophets, emphasizing the need for obedience to his teaching.
7:21 Not everyone who says to me, 'Lord, Lord' Those who say this acknowledge Jesus as master. The affirmation that Jesus is Lord is meaningless if it is not backed by obedience to God's will. **my Father** See note on 5:16.
7:22 on that day Refers to the day of judgment (compare Isa 2:11,17; Zec 14:4–21; Rev 20:11–15). **did we not prophesy in your name** The three activities mentioned in this verse are associated with the prophetic office.
7:23 I never knew you Communicates disassociation or estrangement. **Away from me, you evildoers** A citation of Ps 6:8.

7:24–27 The Sermon on the Mount ends with this parable, which attests to the reliability of Jesus' teaching. Wise people hear his words and respond in obedience; foolish people disregard his words, fail to act according to his teachings and suffer destructive consequences.

7:24 these words of mine Refers to the entire Sermon on the Mount (Mt 5–7). **puts them into practice** Hearing and understanding Jesus' teaching is not sufficient; being his disciple requires action (compare Jas 1:22–25). **on the rock** The builder of this house used bedrock—as opposed to soil or sand—as the foundation.

7:25 streams rose Refers to flash floods. In dry climates like that of Palestine, the ground often could not absorb large amounts of rainwater, resulting in rapid flooding that could produce violent rivers.
7:27 it fell with a great crash Indicates complete destruction—the fate of those who do not heed Jesus' teaching. He may be referring to the day of judgment, since this seems to be the focus of Mt 7:21–23.
7:28–29 The crowds immediately recognize Jesus' authority. He does not interpret or teach based on the interpretation of earlier rabbis, as was the custom; rather, he speaks prophetically on behalf of God.

7:29 one who had authority See note on Lk 4:32. **teachers of the law** See note on Mt 2:4.

8:1–17 In the Sermon on the Mount (Mt 5–7), Jesus teaches about the kingdom of heaven; now he begins to demonstrate it through powerful deeds.

8:2 leprosy This refers to a variety of skin problems that rendered a person ritually unclean (Lev 13–14). People with this ailment lived apart from society and often banded together to form semi-quarantined colonies. When they encountered people, lepers were required to shout a warning so that others would not become contaminated. People suffering from leprosy rarely recovered. **Lord** Many of those who come to Jesus for healing call him "Lord" (*kyrios* in Greek). In Greco-Roman society, *kyrios* was an appropriate title for any superior (like "sir"), but it also could be used to address the emperor, who was considered divine. In the Septuagint (the Greek translation of the OT), *kyrios* occurs about 6,000 times to render the Hebrew text's *yhwh* (Yahweh), the divine name of God. Matthew frequently uses *kyrios* in reference to Jesus; the context determines whether the speaker is recognizing Jesus' divinity or simply showing respect.
8:3 touched the man Normally, touching a leper would

ately he was cleansed of his leprosy. ⁴Then Jesus said to him, "See that you don't tell anyone. But go, show yourself to the priest and offer the gift Moses commanded, as a testimony to them."

The Faith of the Centurion

8:5-13pp — Lk 7:1-10

⁵When Jesus had entered Capernaum, a centurion came to him, asking for help. ⁶"Lord," he said, "my servant lies at home paralyzed, suffering terribly."

⁷Jesus said to him, "Shall I come and heal him?"

⁸The centurion replied, "Lord, I do not deserve to have you come under my roof. But just say the word, and my servant will be healed. ⁹For I myself am a man under authority, with soldiers under me. I tell this one, 'Go,' and he goes; and that one, 'Come,' and he comes. I say to my servant, 'Do this,' and he does it."

¹⁰When Jesus heard this, he was amazed and said to those following him, "Truly I tell you, I have not found anyone in Israel with such great faith. ¹¹I say to you that many will come from the east and the west, and will take their places at the feast with Abraham, Isaac and Jacob in the kingdom of heaven. ¹²But the subjects of the kingdom will be thrown outside, into the darkness, where there will be weeping and gnashing of teeth."

¹³Then Jesus said to the centurion, "Go! Let it be done just as you believed it would." And his servant was healed at that moment.

Jesus Heals Many

8:14-16pp — Mk 1:29-34; Lk 4:38-41

¹⁴When Jesus came into Peter's house, he saw Peter's mother-in-law lying in bed with a fever. ¹⁵He touched her hand and the fever left her, and she got up and began to wait on him.

---

make a person unclean (Lev 5:3), but in this case Jesus' touch heals the leper. Jesus' response would have been as shocking as the leper's request. Physical contact apparently was unnecessary to effect healing, since Jesus later demonstrates the power to heal from a distance (Mt 8:5–13). By touching the leper, Jesus dramatically shows God's love for outcasts.

8:4 See that you don't tell anyone Jesus was strategic about displaying his power and revealing his identity as the Messiah. **show yourself to the priest** Priests at the temple examined people with leprosy to verify that their leprosy was completely gone. They would then carry out the purification ritual (Lev 14:1–32). **the gift Moses commanded** Two clean birds, used in the purification ritual (Lev 14:1–7).

8:5 Capernaum Town where Jesus based his ministry in Galilee (Mt 4:13). See note on Lk 4:31. **centurion** A Roman military officer who commanded about 80 men. These officers served their entire careers as soldiers and were highly experienced and esteemed. **asking for help** The Greek word used here, *parakaleō*, carries the sense of strongly urging or begging. Matthew's choice of words would have conveyed a shocking scene: A high-ranking Roman military official — part of the imperial forces currently occupying Palestine — begs for help from one of the subjugated people, even calling him "Lord" (Mt 8:8).

8:6 lies at home paralyzed, suffering terribly The servant is bedridden and in great pain; in Luke's parallel account (Lk 7:1–10), he is about to die. The Greek term used here, *paralytikos*, refers to being disabled or crippled. This healing backs up Matthew's earlier report about Jesus' power to heal paralysis, among other conditions (Mt 4:24).

8:8 Lord See note on v. 2. **I do not deserve** The centurion humbles himself before Jesus, who would have been perceived as a lowly Jewish rabbi. He also might be indicating an awareness that Jews could not acceptably enter the homes of Gentiles (see Ac 10:28; 11:3). **just say the word** A statement of faith. The centurion expresses belief not only in Jesus' authority over sickness and disease, but also over time and space (anticipating his ability to heal from a distance).

8:9 a man under authority The centurion served within a chain of command; his own authority was derived from those above him. He seems to recognize a similar situation with Jesus, whose authority comes from God (Mt 11:27;

28:18). Just as the centurion can command his soldiers or slaves and know that his orders will be accomplished, so too — he perceives — can Jesus. All Jesus has to do is say the word (v. 8), and it will be done (compare v. 32).

8:10 he was amazed Matthew frequently refers to the astonishment of Jesus' audience (e.g., 8:27; 9:33; 15:31; 22:22), but this is the only place in this Gospel where Jesus himself is astonished (compare Mk 6:6; Lk 7:9). **Truly I tell you** Jesus employs this statement throughout his ministry to emphasize the words that follow. **anyone in Israel with such great faith** Jesus makes the astounding statement that no Jew has as much faith as this Gentile (non-Jew). Jesus often describes his own followers as having very little faith (Mt 6:30; 8:26; 14:31; 16:8).

8:11 many will come from the east and the west Refers to many Gentiles, in addition to the centurion. Jesus is pointing to the time when people all over the world would become his followers. **will take their places at the feast** Refers to the Messianic banquet that will accompany the end of the age (compare Mt 22:1–14; Rev 19:6–10). The Old Testament predicts a gathering of Israel from all over the earth (e.g., Isa 43:5–6; Ps 107:3), as well as the Gentiles' worship of God (e.g., Isa 2; 60:3–4; Mic 4:1–2; Zec 8:20–23). **Abraham, Isaac and Jacob** The three patriarchs of the Jewish faith.

8:12 the subjects of the kingdom This may refer to some Jewish people (Mt 13:38), who expected to be heirs of God's future blessing (compare 8:10), but by extension it refers to people in general who claim belief in Jesus but don't actually practice his message (7:21–23; 25:31–46). **will be thrown outside** A consequence of their unbelief or lack of faith. **into the darkness** Elsewhere, darkness refers to distance from the light of God's gracious presence (4:16). The place of God's wrath is depicted as the gloom of darkness, probably signifying departure from his presence (2Pe 2:17; Jude 13). **weeping and gnashing of teeth** Reflects the unspeakable anguish of being separated from God (compare Mt 13:42,50; 22:13; 24:51; 25:30).

8:13 just as you believed Likely expresses the cause of the healing.

8:15 she got up and began to wait on him Probably refers to serving Jesus food and drink. He takes care of her physical needs (sickness), then she takes care of his (hunger and thirst).

¹⁶When evening came, many who were demon-possessed were brought to him, and he drove out the spirits with a word and healed all the sick. ¹⁷This was to fulfill what was spoken through the prophet Isaiah:

"He took up our infirmities
and bore our diseases."[a]

The Cost of Following Jesus

8:19-22pp — Lk 9:57-60

¹⁸When Jesus saw the crowd around him, he gave orders to cross to the other side of the lake. ¹⁹Then a teacher of the law came to him and said, "Teacher, I will follow you wherever you go."

²⁰Jesus replied, "Foxes have dens and birds have nests, but the Son of Man has no place to lay his head."

²¹Another disciple said to him, "Lord, first let me go and bury my father."

²²But Jesus told him, "Follow me, and let the dead bury their own dead."

Jesus Calms the Storm

8:23-27pp — Mk 4:36-41; Lk 8:22-25
8:23-27Ref — Mt 14:22-33

²³Then he got into the boat and his disciples followed him. ²⁴Suddenly a furious storm came up on the lake, so that the waves swept over the boat. But Jesus was sleeping. ²⁵The disciples went and woke him, saying, "Lord, save us! We're going to drown!"

²⁶He replied, "You of little faith, why are you so afraid?" Then he got up and rebuked the winds and the waves, and it was completely calm.

²⁷The men were amazed and asked, "What kind

---

[a] 17 Isaiah 53:4 (see Septuagint)

8:16 drove out the spirits with a word and healed all the sick Although ancient people often attributed sickness to demonic activity, Matthew appears to be describing the possessed and the sick as two distinct groups.
8:17 to fulfill See 1:22 and note. **He took up our infirmities** A quotation of Isa 53:4. Compare Mt 1:22 and note; see the table "Jesus' Fulfillment of OT Prophecy" on p. 1573.

8:18–22 This section functions as a transition from Jesus' time in Capernaum to his arrival in the country of the Gadarenes. Given the itinerant nature of Jesus' ministry and the size of the crowds that followed him, interactions like the ones described here were probably common.

8:18 to the other side Jesus crosses the Sea of Galilee. He leaves the northern shores of Capernaum for the southeastern banks of Gadara.
8:19 teacher of the law To this point in Matthew, the legal experts (see note on 2:4) have not been portrayed in a positive light (e.g., 5:20; 7:29). **Teacher** No one in Matthew who refers to Jesus as "Teacher" appears to be a true follower (12:38; 19:16; 22:16,24,36). **I will follow** As a disciple.
8:20 Son of Man Jesus uses this self-designation more than any other; it comes from the OT book of Daniel (see Da 7:13 and note). This title occurs 30 times in the Gospel of Matthew and often stresses the exaltation of Jesus. Here, however, it highlights his position as a homeless itinerant. Generally, the phrase "son of man" means "human one." However, in some contexts the phrase appears to point to the divine figure in Da 7:13 (see Mt 26:64). In Matthew, the title "Son of Man" has three primary senses. First, it focuses on Jesus' suffering and humility (11:19; 12:40; 17:12,22; 20:28; 26:64). Second, it stresses the power and authority Jesus had on earth (9:6; 12:8, 12:32; 13:37). Finally, it highlights his future coming as the exalted king, the "one like a son of man" portrayed in Da 7 (Mt 13:41; 16:27–28; 24:27,30,37,39; 25:31). Daniel uses the phrase "one like a son of man" to describe a figure who approaches the Ancient of Days and receives an everlasting kingdom. Contextually, the expression likely refers to a Messianic figure; as a result, it developed into a Messianic title, "Son of Man." In several applications of the title to himself,

Jesus communicates his status as Messiah and his role as the inaugurator and ruler of the kingdom of God. **no place to lay his head** Refers to Jesus' traveling ministry and lack of a permanent home.
8:21 Another disciple Matthew indicates that this man and the scribe before him are, in some sense, followers of Jesus; the meaning and extent of discipleship are determined by the context.
8:22 let the dead bury their own dead The exchange here is similar to one in Lk 9:59–62. In both passages, potential disciples hesitate in light of their earthly responsibilities. However, Jesus is concerned with discipleship, not familial obligations. The urgent matter of the kingdom of God, inaugurated by Jesus' presence, requires his followers' full attention. Jesus' statement here should be understood as hyperbole—a deliberate exaggeration for rhetorical effect. Since any man whose father had just died likely would not be out in public listening to Jesus, this man's request probably reflects an indefinite postponement of joining Jesus' disciples. The phrase "bury one's father" could be understood as an idiom for the man's familial responsibilities for the remainder of his father's life.

8:23—9:8 After displaying his authority over sickness and disease, Jesus now shows his power over nature, evil spiritual powers and sin. These acts confirm the demons' confession in Mt 8:29: Jesus is the Son of God.

8:23 his disciples Refers to the Twelve.

MIRACLES AT THE SEA OF GALILEE	
Jesus Calms a Storm	Mt 8:23–27; Mk 4:35–41; Lk 8:22–25
Jesus Walks on Water	Mt 14:22–33; Mk 6:45–52; Jn 6:16–21
The Miraculous Catch of Fish	Lk 5:4–11
A Second Miraculous Catch	Jn 21:1–14

8:26 You of little faith Jesus uses this phrase to respond to his disciples' doubt that God would take care of them (compare 14:31; 16:8). **rebuked the winds and the waves** Since in the ancient Near East the sea

of man is this? Even the winds and the waves obey him!"

Jesus Restores Two Demon-Possessed Men

8:28-34pp — Mk 5:1-17; Lk 8:26-37

28 When he arrived at the other side in the region of the Gadarenes,[a] two demon-possessed men coming from the tombs met him. They were so violent that no one could pass that way. 29 "What do you want with us, Son of God?" they shouted. "Have you come here to torture us before the appointed time?"

30 Some distance from them a large herd of pigs was feeding. 31 The demons begged Jesus, "If you drive us out, send us into the herd of pigs."

32 He said to them, "Go!" So they came out and went into the pigs, and the whole herd rushed down the steep bank into the lake and died in the water. 33 Those tending the pigs ran off, went into the town and reported all this, including what had happened to the demon-possessed men. 34 Then the whole town went out to meet Jesus. And when they saw him, they pleaded with him to leave their region.

Jesus Forgives and Heals a Paralyzed Man

9:2-8pp — Mk 2:3-12; Lk 5:18-26

9 Jesus stepped into a boat, crossed over and came to his own town. 2 Some men brought to him a paralyzed man, lying on a mat. When Jesus saw their faith, he said to the man, "Take heart, son; your sins are forgiven."

3 At this, some of the teachers of the law said to themselves, "This fellow is blaspheming!"

4 Knowing their thoughts, Jesus said, "Why do you entertain evil thoughts in your hearts? 5 Which is easier: to say, 'Your sins are forgiven,' or to say, 'Get up and walk'? 6 But I want you to know that the Son of Man has authority on earth to forgive sins." So he said to the paralyzed man, "Get up, take your mat and go home." 7 Then the man got up and went home. 8 When the crowd saw this, they were filled with awe; and they praised God, who had given such authority to man.

[a] 28 Some manuscripts *Gergesenes*; other manuscripts *Gerasenes*

---

represented chaotic forces controllable only by God, Jesus' command of the waves serves as a sign of his deity. See note on Ge 1:2.

8:28–34 Jesus briefly visits Gadara and heals two demon-possessed persons. His miracle there demonstrates his power over evil and the spiritual realm. It also creates such a stir that he is forced to leave.

8:28 from the tombs These men lived among tombs or in a graveyard. In Jesus' day, these places were considered to be the haunt of demons.

8:29 Son of God The demons ironically recognize Jesus for who he is; Satan did the same and tried to keep Jesus from acting on God's purposes (Mt 4:3,6). **before the appointed time** Refers to the day of judgment, when God will judge evil spiritual powers (compare Ro 16:20; Rev 20:7–10). Their question indicates an awareness of both Jesus' identity and their future judgment. It also reflects Matthew's understanding that God's kingdom is present but not yet finalized (or fully arrived).

8:31 send us into the herd of pigs The text does not indicate the reason for this particular request, but it is possible that Matthew means to suggest the suitability of unclean animals as dwelling places for unclean spirits (see Lev 11:7 and note).

8:32 died in the water This passage ultimately demonstrates Jesus' power over the spiritual realm. He expels the demons with one word, and they apparently are destroyed with the pigs.

8:33 Those tending These must have been Gentiles, since pigs were unclean to Jews.

8:34 to leave their region In contrast to the believing Gentile in Mt 8:5–13, these Gentiles (non-Jewish people) want nothing to do with Jesus. In addition to suffering economic loss, they might have feared his power.

9:1–8 Jesus continues to display his power, including his authority to forgive sins. The scribes (teachers of the law) begin to express discontent and accuse Jesus of blasphemy.

9:1 his own town Refers to Capernaum, on the northern

shore of the Sea of Galilee. See the infographic "The Synagogue at Capernaum" on p. 1656.

9:2 Some men brought to him a paralyzed man Parallel accounts appear in Mk 2:3–12 and Lk 5:18–26, both of which describe the man's friends lowering him through the roof due to the large crowd. **son** A term of endearment. Jesus exercises his authority with compassion. **your sins are forgiven** People in ancient Israel commonly saw a relationship between sin and sickness (or suffering; e.g., Jn 9). Although Matthew does not explicitly state this connection, it could explain why Jesus begins by announcing forgiveness for the paralytic.

9:3 This fellow is blaspheming This is the first time in Matthew the religious leaders accuse Jesus of blasphemy (compare Mt 9:34; 12:24,31–32). Their objection is that, in proclaiming forgiveness, Jesus is doing something that only God could do (compare Mk 2:7).

9:4 Knowing their thoughts The Greek idiom used here seems to emphasize Jesus' perceptive abilities — that he perceives the scribes' (teachers of the law) negative reaction — not necessarily that he is reading their minds.

9:5 Which is easier Because there was no way to determine whether the man's sins were forgiven, it was an easy claim to make (and dismiss). The command to rise and walk, however, was subject to immediate verification — putting the speaker's credibility on the line.

9:6 Son of Man See Mt 8:20 and note. **authority on earth to forgive sins** Jesus states that he is acting on God's authority.

9:7 the man got up and went home By showing his power to heal, Jesus demonstrates his authority to forgive. The healing also shows that Jesus truly is God's representative. See the table "Miracles of Jesus" on p. 1741.

9:8 authority A central theme throughout Matthew, especially as Jesus' authority is contrasted with established Jewish authorities such as the law, the temple and the religious readers (e.g., 5:17–20; 7:29; 12:6; 21:23–27; 23:1–36). See 28:18 and note.

The Calling of Matthew

9:9-13pp — Mk 2:14-17; Lk 5:27-32

⁹As Jesus went on from there, he saw a man named Matthew sitting at the tax collector's booth. "Follow me," he told him, and Matthew got up and followed him.

¹⁰While Jesus was having dinner at Matthew's house, many tax collectors and sinners came and ate with him and his disciples. ¹¹When the Pharisees saw this, they asked his disciples, "Why does your teacher eat with tax collectors and sinners?"

¹²On hearing this, Jesus said, "It is not the healthy who need a doctor, but the sick. ¹³But go and learn what this means: 'I desire mercy, not sacrifice.'ᵃ For I have not come to call the righteous, but sinners."

Jesus Questioned About Fasting

9:14-17pp — Mk 2:18-22; Lk 5:33-39

¹⁴Then John's disciples came and asked him, "How is it that we and the Pharisees fast often, but your disciples do not fast?"

¹⁵Jesus answered, "How can the guests of the bridegroom mourn while he is with them? The time will come when the bridegroom will be taken from them; then they will fast.

¹⁶"No one sews a patch of unshrunk cloth on an old garment, for the patch will pull away from the garment, making the tear worse. ¹⁷Neither do people pour new wine into old wineskins. If they do, the skins will burst; the wine will run out and the wineskins will be ruined. No, they pour new wine into new wineskins, and both are preserved."

Jesus Raises a Dead Girl and Heals a Sick Woman

9:18-26pp — Mk 5:22-43; Lk 8:41-56

¹⁸While he was saying this, a synagogue leader came and knelt before him and said, "My daughter has just died. But come and put your hand on her, and she will live." ¹⁹Jesus got up and went with him, and so did his disciples.

²⁰Just then a woman who had been subject to bleeding for twelve years came up behind him and touched the edge of his cloak. ²¹She said to herself, "If I only touch his cloak, I will be healed."

²²Jesus turned and saw her. "Take heart, daughter," he said, "your faith has healed you." And the woman was healed at that moment.

²³When Jesus entered the synagogue leader's

ᵃ 13 Hosea 6:6

9:9–17 Jesus calls Matthew to be his disciple and responds to questions about the validity of his ministry.

9:9 tax collector's booth See 5:46 and note. **Matthew** This Gospel is attributed to Matthew, who is called Levi in other Gospel accounts (Mk 2:14; Lk 5:27). It was not uncommon for first-century Jews to have more than one name.

9:11 Pharisees See note on Jn 1:24.

9:12 the healthy Jesus' answer might be a simple analogy. It also could reflect the cultural assumption that disease was associated with sin (compare Mt 8:16–17; 9:1–8).

9:13 go and learn A common formula used by rabbis to direct their followers toward a particular passage in the Scriptures. Jesus' use of this formula might be a subtle jab at the Pharisees, who are not his disciples and represent the learned of Jewish society. Because they have failed to properly understand the spirit of the law, Jesus treats these experts as beginners. **I desire mercy, not sacrifice** Jesus is quoting Hos 6:6, which critiques Israel for focusing on the letter of the law while ignoring its spirit. God desires his people's faithfulness and steadfast love more than their ritual observances. **the righteous** Refers to people who are perceived as being righteous. According to Jesus, true righteousness involves showing mercy toward outcasts.

9:14 John's disciples Refers to disciples of John the Baptist (Mt 3). **fast** John's disciples likely are referring to a voluntary practice of fasting twice a week as an act of religious piety (compare Lk 18:12). Jews fasted corporately on the Day of Atonement, and they fasted privately for various reasons. Jesus and his disciples likely would have participated in such fasting.

9:15 when the bridegroom will be taken Alludes to Jesus' crucifixion. The bridegroom in the metaphor is Jesus, and the guests are his disciples.

9:16 unshrunk cloth Refers to new cloth that has not been washed or treated.

9:17 new wine Unfermented wine. **wineskins** Leather pouches used for storing wine. Old wineskins have already been stretched to capacity by the fermentation process. If unfermented wine is placed in these skins, the gases produced by fermentation can cause them to explode. Conversely, new skins have not been stretched and are slightly elastic. During fermentation, new skins expand to accommodate the pressure from the gases and do not burst. See the infographic "A Winepress in Ancient Israel" on p. 1157.

9:18–26 Jesus has already displayed his authority over sickness, nature, evil spiritual powers and sin; now he demonstrates authority over death. All three Synoptic Gospels (Matthew, Mark, Luke) report this episode, and all three interrupt it with the report of Jesus healing a woman (compare Mk 5:21–43; Lk 8:40–56).

9:18 a synagogue leader Mark and Luke identify this man as Jairus, a synagogue official (Mk 5:22; Lk 8:41).

9:20 subject to bleeding for twelve years Depending on the nature of her ailment, the woman might have been ceremonially unclean during the entire 12-year span (see Lev 15:25–30). In this case, her condition was not only a physical problem, but a social and religious problem as well. Anyone who associated closely with her would have become unclean, too.

9:21 If I only touch his cloak She believed that even Jesus' clothes contained some of his miraculous powers.

9:22 daughter A term of endearment (compare Mt 9:2). **your faith has healed you** Jesus often cites a person's faith as the impetus for healing (compare 8:13; 9:29; 15:28).

9:23 When Jesus entered the synagogue leader's house The narrative shifts back to the situation of

house and saw the noisy crowd and people playing pipes, ²⁴he said, "Go away. The girl is not dead but asleep." But they laughed at him. ²⁵After the crowd had been put outside, he went in and took the girl by the hand, and she got up. ²⁶News of this spread through all that region.

Jesus Heals the Blind and the Mute

²⁷As Jesus went on from there, two blind men followed him, calling out, "Have mercy on us, Son of David!"

²⁸When he had gone indoors, the blind men came to him, and he asked them, "Do you believe that I am able to do this?"

"Yes, Lord," they replied.

²⁹Then he touched their eyes and said, "According to your faith let it be done to you"; ³⁰and their sight was restored. Jesus warned them sternly, "See that no one knows about this." ³¹But they went out and spread the news about him all over that region.

³²While they were going out, a man who was demon-possessed and could not talk was brought to Jesus. ³³And when the demon was driven out, the man who had been mute spoke. The crowd was amazed and said, "Nothing like this has ever been seen in Israel."

³⁴But the Pharisees said, "It is by the prince of demons that he drives out demons."

The Workers Are Few

³⁵Jesus went through all the towns and villages, teaching in their synagogues, proclaiming the good news of the kingdom and healing every disease and sickness. ³⁶When he saw the crowds, he had compassion on them, because they were harassed and helpless, like sheep without a shepherd. ³⁷Then he said to his disciples, "The harvest is plentiful but the workers are few. ³⁸Ask the Lord of the harvest, therefore, to send out workers into his harvest field."

Jesus Sends Out the Twelve

10:2-4pp — Mk 3:16-19; Lk 6:14-16; Ac 1:13
10:9-15pp — Mk 6:8-11; Lk 9:3-5; 10:4-12
10:19-22pp — Mk 13:11-13; Lk 21:12-17
10:26-33pp — Lk 12:2-9
10:34,35pp — Lk 12:51-53

10 Jesus called his twelve disciples to him and gave them authority to drive out impure spirits and to heal every disease and sickness.

²These are the names of the twelve apostles: first, Simon (who is called Peter) and his brother

---

vv. 18–19. the noisy crowd and people playing pipes Participants in a funeral. Burial in first-century Palestine took place soon after death, so the presence of these mourners indicates that the process is already underway.

9:24 asleep Jesus is not denying the fact of the girl's condition as much as the finality of it. Sleep is a euphemism for death elsewhere in the Bible (e.g., Da 12:2; Jn 11:11–12; Ac 7:60; 13:36; 1Co 15:6).

9:25 took the girl by the hand Touching a corpse rendered a person ceremonially unclean, but Jesus is not concerned with that (Nu 19:11; compare Mt 8:3 and note). **got up** The Greek verb used here, *egeirō*, is also used to describe Jesus' resurrection (28:6–7).

9:27–31 Jesus' ministry of healing continues with two blind men receiving their sight.

9:27 Son of David A Messianic title meaning "descendant of King David" (see note on 1:1; compare 12:23; 15:22; 20:30; 21:9,15; 22:42).

9:30 See that no one knows Despite Jesus' apparent desire to keep a low profile, his call for secrecy is not obeyed. Once these men experience the good news, they cannot keep it to themselves.

9:32–34 Jesus again asserts his authority over the spirit realm (compare 8:28–32) and causes all of Israel to marvel at his deeds.

9:34 It is by the prince of demons that he drives out demons Jesus later shows the absurdity of this statement (see 12:22–32).

9:35–38 These final verses summarize Jesus' ministry (compare 4:23). They also set up the next chapter, in which Jesus sends out his disciples.

9:36 like sheep without a shepherd Jesus' compassion for the people was intensified by the lack of leadership to help them (compare Jn 10:1–18; Eze 34). Without a shepherd, sheep are prone to wander and vulnerable to danger. The Old Testament often portrays Israel as God's flock and the nation's leaders as shepherds—who failed in their responsibility to look after for the sheep (e.g., Nu 27:17; 2Sa 5:2; Isa 56:11; Jer 10:21).

10:1–15 Matthew 9 ends with the need for laborers for God's harvest; ch. 10 begins with Jesus commissioning his disciples (compare Mk 6:7–13; Lk 9:1–6). Matthew records the names of Jesus' twelve primary disciples—later called apostles—as well as his instructions for spreading the message of the kingdom of heaven.

10:1 called his twelve disciples to him So far, Matthew has described the calling of only five disciples (Mt 4:18–22; 9:9). Jesus had many followers, but these were his leaders—those whom he commissioned to build his church.

10:2 the twelve apostles Matthew initially refers to this group as disciples. Here, he calls them "apostles"—those who are sent out with the authority of the sender (Jesus). No explicit reason is given here for the choice of twelve disciples, but it may have been in part to reflect the fact that there were twelve tribes of Israel. Matthew later presents the twelve disciples as Israel's new leaders (19:28). See the table "The Twelve Apostles" on p. 1550. **first** Rather than identifying Simon as the leader of the Twelve, this term simply designates the starting point of the list. **Simon (who is called Peter)** Simon is his Hebrew name, while Peter is his Greek name (see 4:18; 16:17–18). Elsewhere, Biblical writers refer to him by his Aramaic name, Cephas (e.g., Jn 1:42; 1Co 1:12; Gal 2:9). Simon and the next three disciples listed (Andrew, James and John) were mentioned earlier in Matthew (Mt 4:18,21). **Andrew** This is the last mention of Andrew

Andrew; James son of Zebedee, and his brother John; ³Philip and Bartholomew; Thomas and Matthew the tax collector; James son of Alphaeus, and Thaddaeus; ⁴Simon the Zealot and Judas Iscariot, who betrayed him.

⁵These twelve Jesus sent out with the following instructions: "Do not go among the Gentiles or enter any town of the Samaritans. ⁶Go rather to the lost sheep of Israel. ⁷As you go, proclaim this message: 'The kingdom of heaven has come near.' ⁸Heal the sick, raise the dead, cleanse those who have leprosy,ᵃ drive out demons. Freely you have received; freely give.

⁹"Do not get any gold or silver or copper to take with you in your belts — ¹⁰no bag for the journey or extra shirt or sandals or a staff, for the worker

---

ᵃ 8 The Greek word traditionally translated *leprosy* was used for various diseases affecting the skin.

---

by name in Matthew. **James son of Zebedee, and his brother John** James, John and Peter serve as Jesus' inner circle and often are privy to special circumstances (see 17:1; 26:37).
10:3 Philip Not mentioned anywhere else in Matthew (compare Jn 1:43–48; 6:5–7; 12:21–22; 14:8–9). This apostle is not the same as Philip the evangelist in the book of Acts (Ac 6:5; 8:1–8; 21:8). **Bartholomew** Traditionally thought to be Nathanael (see Jn 1:46); not mentioned anywhere else in Matthew. **Thomas** Not mentioned anywhere else in Matthew (compare Jn 11:16; 14:5; 20:24–28; 21:2). **Matthew the tax collector** See note on Mt 9:9. **James son of Alphaeus** A second James, differentiated by the name of his father. **Thaddaeus** He is mentioned here and in Mark's list, but the lists in Luke and Acts have "Judas, son of James." The other disciples appear on all four lists (with the exception of Judas Iscariot, who was dead by Ac 1). The identity of Thaddeus remains uncertain.
10:4 Simon the Zealot The Greek word used here to describe Simon, *kananaios*, translates an Aramaic word meaning "enthusiast." In the first century, the term could refer to a sect of Jewish anti-Roman activists or describe a person of religious zeal. This Simon is not mentioned anywhere else in Matthew. See the table "Major Groups in Jesus' Time" on p. 1630. **Judas Iscariot** Judas' placement at the end of the list

probably reflects his later betrayal of Jesus (see Mt 26:14–16,25,47–49; 27:3).
10:5 Gentiles Jesus first extends his announcement of the kingdom of heaven to the Jews, who were eagerly awaiting its arrival. Their eventual rejection of Jesus leads to the Gentile mission, which receives its clearest expression in the ministry of the apostle Paul (e.g., Ac 9:15). **Samaritans** Refers to people of mixed Israelite and foreign descent who lived in the region of Samaria (formerly the northern kingdom of Israel). See note on Jn 4:9.
10:6 the lost sheep of Israel Refers to Jews.
10:7 The kingdom of heaven has come near The disciples were to preach the same message that Jesus preached and that John the Baptist preached before him (compare Mt 3:2; 4:17). See note on 3:2.

10:8 The actions listed here authenticate the disciples' message. These actions also show the arrival of the kingdom of heaven (Lk 4:17–19).

10:8 Freely you have received; freely give Jesus calls on the disciples to share the blessings of the kingdom of heaven with no expectation of being compensated.
10:9 Do not get The disciples were to go without money or supplies. Their needs would be met through God's provision.

The Twelve Apostles

MATTHEW 10:2–4	MARK 3:16–19	LUKE 6:13–16	ACTS 1:13
Simon "Peter"	Simon "Peter"	Simon "Peter"	Peter
Andrew	James, son of Zebedee	Andrew	John
James, son of Zebedee	John	James	James
John	Andrew	John	Andrew
Philip	Philip	Philip	Philip
Bartholomew	Bartholomew	Bartholomew	Thomas
Thomas	Matthew	Matthew	Bartholomew
Matthew	Thomas	Thomas	Matthew
James, son of Alphaeus	James, son of Alphaeus	James, son of Alphaeus	James, son of Alphaeus
Thaddaeus	Thaddaeus	Simon the Zealot	Simon the Zealot
Simon the Zealot	Simon the Zealot	Judas, son of James	Judas, son of James
Judas Iscariot	Judas Iscariot	Judas Iscariot	—

is worth his keep. ¹¹Whatever town or village you enter, search there for some worthy person and stay at their house until you leave. ¹²As you enter the home, give it your greeting. ¹³If the home is deserving, let your peace rest on it; if it is not, let your peace return to you. ¹⁴If anyone will not welcome you or listen to your words, leave that home or town and shake the dust off your feet. ¹⁵Truly I tell you, it will be more bearable for Sodom and Gomorrah on the day of judgment than for that town.

¹⁶"I am sending you out like sheep among wolves. Therefore be as shrewd as snakes and as innocent as doves. ¹⁷Be on your guard; you will be handed over to the local councils and be flogged in the synagogues. ¹⁸On my account you will be brought before governors and kings as witnesses to them and to the Gentiles. ¹⁹But when they arrest you, do not worry about what to say or how to say it. At that time you will be given what to say, ²⁰for it will not be you speaking, but the Spirit of your Father speaking through you.

²¹"Brother will betray brother to death, and a father his child; children will rebel against their parents and have them put to death. ²²You will be hated by everyone because of me, but the one who stands firm to the end will be saved. ²³When you are persecuted in one place, flee to another. Truly I tell you, you will not finish going through the towns of Israel before the Son of Man comes.

²⁴"The student is not above the teacher, nor a servant above his master. ²⁵It is enough for students to be like their teachers, and servants like their masters. If the head of the house has been called Beelzebul, how much more the members of his household!

²⁶"So do not be afraid of them, for there is nothing concealed that will not be disclosed, or hidden that will not be made known. ²⁷What I tell you in the dark, speak in the daylight; what is whispered in your ear, proclaim from the roofs. ²⁸Do not be afraid of those who kill the body but cannot kill the soul. Rather, be afraid of the One who can destroy both soul and body in hell. ²⁹Are not two sparrows sold for a penny? Yet not one of them will fall to the ground outside your Father's care.ᵃ ³⁰And even the very hairs of your head are all numbered. ³¹So don't be afraid; you are worth more than many sparrows.

³²"Whoever acknowledges me before others, I will also acknowledge before my Father in heaven. ³³But whoever disowns me before others, I will disown before my Father in heaven.

³⁴"Do not suppose that I have come to bring peace to the earth. I did not come to bring peace, but a sword. ³⁵For I have come to turn

"'a man against his father,
    a daughter against her mother,

ᵃ 29 Or *will*; or *knowledge*

10:11 worthy person Refers to someone willing to welcome the disciples and show them hospitality. This also might indicate those who welcome the disciples' message.

10:13 your peace return to you The initial blessing or greeting would not take effect on the house or its inhabitants.

10:14 shake the dust off your feet This symbolic act was a renunciation and indicated a severed relationship (compare Ac 13:51).

10:15 Sodom and Gomorrah These cities are often used as examples of divine judgment (e.g., Mt 11:23–24; 2Pe 2:6; Jude 7; Rev 11:8). Those who reject the disciples and the message of the kingdom of heaven are left to inevitable judgment. See Ge 19:1–29. **the day of judgment** Refers to the time when God will take account of humanity (Rev 20:11–14).

10:16–25 Jesus himself will face persecution; so too will his disciples. Here, he warns them of their fate and assures them that the Spirit will give them the appropriate words in times of trial.

10:16 as shrewd as snakes In the Biblical world, serpents were associated with wisdom and cleverness (e.g., Ge 3:1; 2Co 11:3).

10:18 governors and kings The highest officials. Jesus is looking beyond his mission and predicting what would happen to his followers in the future.

10:21 Brother will betray brother to death Jesus predicts that his followers will face persecution and betrayal by those closest to them.

10:22 will be saved See note on Mt 24:13.

10:23 before the Son of Man comes There are at least

five plausible options for understanding this reference: Jesus' coming to his disciples upon their return from this particular mission (vv. 6–15), Jesus' resurrection, the coming of the Holy Spirit at Pentecost, the destruction of Jerusalem in AD 70, and the second coming of Jesus at the end of the age. The overall passage is difficult to interpret, but it seems to be looking ahead to final judgment. Jesus probably means that, at his second coming, there will still be people left in the towns of Israel who have not accepted him. See note on 8:20.

10:25 Beelzebul A deity in the ancient Near East. The name means "Baal the Prince" (see 2Ki 1:2–6). This figure is later identified with Satan and the demons.

10:26–33 Despite the hardships they will face, Jesus commands the disciples not to fear; rather, they should be bold witnesses to Jesus' message and faithfully carry out their tasks.

10:26 nothing concealed that will not be disclosed In connection with Mt 10:27, this may refer to Jesus' message of the arrival of the kingdom of heaven (4:17). It also might refer to the persecutors' hidden sins that will be revealed at the judgment.

10:28 be afraid of the One People should have a healthy fear of God—treating him with reverence.

10:31 So don't be afraid If God watches over sparrows, he surely cares for his people.

10:34–39 While some receive Jesus' message eagerly and with great joy, others reject it with hostility.

10:34 a sword Jesus' message inherently brings conflict. The context may indicate persecution and martyrdom, but interpersonal discord also results (vv. 21–22).

a daughter-in-law against her mother-
in-law—
36 a man's enemies will be the members of
his own household.'ᵃ

³⁷"Anyone who loves their father or mother
more than me is not worthy of me; anyone who
loves their son or daughter more than me is not
worthy of me. ³⁸Whoever does not take up their
cross and follow me is not worthy of me. ³⁹Who-
ever finds their life will lose it, and whoever loses
their life for my sake will find it.

⁴⁰"Anyone who welcomes you welcomes me, and
anyone who welcomes me welcomes the one who
sent me. ⁴¹Whoever welcomes a prophet as a prophet will receive a prophet's reward, and whoever
welcomes a righteous person as a righteous person
will receive a righteous person's reward. ⁴²And if
anyone gives even a cup of cold water to one of
these little ones who is my disciple, truly I tell you,
that person will certainly not lose their reward."

Jesus and John the Baptist
11:2-19pp—Lk 7:18-35

11 After Jesus had finished instructing his
twelve disciples, he went on from there to
teach and preach in the towns of Galilee.ᵇ

²When John, who was in prison, heard about
the deeds of the Messiah, he sent his disciples
³to ask him, "Are you the one who is to come, or
should we expect someone else?"

⁴Jesus replied, "Go back and report to John what
you hear and see: ⁵The blind receive sight, the
lame walk, those who have leprosyᶜ are cleansed,
the deaf hear, the dead are raised, and the good
news is proclaimed to the poor. ⁶Blessed is anyone
who does not stumble on account of me."

⁷As John's disciples were leaving, Jesus began to
speak to the crowd about John: "What did you go
out into the wilderness to see? A reed swayed by
the wind? ⁸If not, what did you go out to see? A man
dressed in fine clothes? No, those who wear fine
clothes are in kings' palaces. ⁹Then what did you go
out to see? A prophet? Yes, I tell you, and more than
a prophet. ¹⁰This is the one about whom it is written:

" 'I will send my messenger ahead of you,
who will prepare your way before you.'ᵈ

¹¹Truly I tell you, among those born of women
there has not risen anyone greater than John the
Baptist; yet whoever is least in the kingdom of
heaven is greater than he. ¹²From the days of John
the Baptist until now, the kingdom of heaven has
been subjected to violence,ᵉ and violent people

ᵃ 36 Micah 7:6   ᵇ 1 Greek *in their towns*   ᶜ 5 The Greek
word traditionally translated *leprosy* was used for various
diseases affecting the skin.   ᵈ 10 Mal. 3:1   ᵉ 12 Or *been
forcefully advancing*

10:37 loves their father or mother more than me
Devotion to family should not supersede allegiance to
Jesus (compare Dt 33:9).
10:38 take up their cross and follow me Jesus' words
here foreshadow his death and call on his followers to
identify themselves fully with him, to the point of being
willing to die as he did. Crucifixion—a Roman form of
capital punishment reserved for criminals, foreigners and
slaves—was a particularly undesirable way to die. The
condemned person had to carry his or her own cross (or
in certain instances, just the crossbeam).

10:40-42 Jesus will reward those who receive his disciples joyfully.

10:42 one of these little ones Likely indicates low
status (compare Mt 18:10,14).

11:1-19 Jesus continues his teaching and preaching
ministry, and disciples of John the Baptist approach him
with a question from the imprisoned John. Jesus uses
this as an opportunity to affirm his messiahship and to
praise John's life and ministry.

11:2 John Refers to John the Baptist, who had been
imprisoned by Herod Antipas (see 14:1-12).
11:3 the one who is to come Refers to the Messiah
(see 3:11). John knew who Jesus was, but he wants to
be sure he is the Messiah (compare 3:7-12).
11:4 what you hear and see Jesus' response in
11:5-6 underscores his fulfillment of prophetic expectations for the Messiah. His answer points to recent
events from his ministry (e.g., 4:23-24; 5:3; 8:2;
9:18-33) while alluding to passages in Isaiah (Isa
8:14-15; 26:19; 29:18; 35:5-6; 42:18; 61:1; compare

Lk 4:17-21). See the table "Jesus' Fulfillment of OT
Prophecy" on p. 1573.
11:5 those who have leprosy are cleansed There
is no clear OT prophecy about lepers being cleansed
(compare Mt 8:2; 10:8), but this probably alludes to the
general prophecy of the oppressed being set free in Isa
61:1-2, quoted in Lk 4:18.
**11:6 anyone who does not stumble on account of
me** Jesus likely is alluding to Isa 8:14-15. Compare
Mt 11:20-24.
11:8 A man dressed in fine clothes Such clothing was
more suitable for royalty than prophets in the wilderness.
John's clothing was made of camel's hair (Mt 3:4).
11:9 more than a prophet As the forerunner of the
Messiah, John was not merely a prophet. Compare
note on 11:14.
11:10 I will send my messenger This citation is from
Mal 3:1. John the Baptist played a critical role in salvation history by preparing the way for Jesus the Messiah
(see Mt 3:3; Isa 40:3).
11:11 among those born of women Jesus indicates
that John was the most important person who had lived
until that point. The last part of the verse provides
Jesus' reason for this statement: The lowliest member
of the kingdom of heaven—the most humble and God-
serving—is greater than the greatest man who ever
lived. Jesus is not making a moral distinction between
his disciples and John; he is contrasting heavenly and
earthly conceptions of greatness.
11:12 violent people have been raiding it The kingdom of heaven and its workers have suffered at the
hands of violent people who try to prevent or usurp
God's rule.

have been raiding it. ¹³For all the Prophets and the Law prophesied until John. ¹⁴And if you are willing to accept it, he is the Elijah who was to come. ¹⁵Whoever has ears, let them hear.

¹⁶"To what can I compare this generation? They are like children sitting in the marketplaces and calling out to others:

¹⁷"'We played the pipe for you,
    and you did not dance;
we sang a dirge,
    and you did not mourn.'

¹⁸For John came neither eating nor drinking, and they say, 'He has a demon.' ¹⁹The Son of Man came eating and drinking, and they say, 'Here is a glutton and a drunkard, a friend of tax collectors and sinners.' But wisdom is proved right by her deeds."

Woe on Unrepentant Towns

11:21-23pp — Lk 10:13-15

²⁰Then Jesus began to denounce the towns in which most of his miracles had been performed, because they did not repent. ²¹"Woe to you, Chorazin! Woe to you, Bethsaida! For if the miracles that were performed in you had been performed in Tyre and Sidon, they would have repented long ago in sackcloth and ashes. ²²But I tell you, it will be more bearable for Tyre and Sidon on the day of judgment than for you. ²³And you, Capernaum, will you be lifted to the heavens? No, you will go down to Hades.ᵃ For if the miracles that were performed in you had been performed in Sodom, it would have remained to this day. ²⁴But I tell you that it will be more bearable for Sodom on the day of judgment than for you."

The Father Revealed in the Son

11:25-27pp — Lk 10:21,22

²⁵At that time Jesus said, "I praise you, Father, Lord of heaven and earth, because you have hidden these things from the wise and learned, and revealed them to little children. ²⁶Yes, Father, for this is what you were pleased to do.

²⁷"All things have been committed to me by my Father. No one knows the Son except the Father, and no one knows the Father except the Son and those to whom the Son chooses to reveal him.

²⁸"Come to me, all you who are weary and burdened, and I will give you rest. ²⁹Take my yoke upon you and learn from me, for I am gentle and humble in heart, and you will find rest for your souls. ³⁰For my yoke is easy and my burden is light."

Jesus Is Lord of the Sabbath

12:1-8pp — Mk 2:23-28; Lk 6:1-5
12:9-14pp — Mk 3:1-6; Lk 6:6-11

12 At that time Jesus went through the grainfields on the Sabbath. His disciples were hungry and began to pick some heads of grain

---

ᵃ 23 That is, the realm of the dead

11:14 he is the Elijah The prophet Malachi had foretold the coming of a messenger—Elijah—who would prepare the way of the Messiah (Mal 3:1; 4:5); consequently, some Jews expected the return of Elijah himself (e.g., Jn 1:25). However, Jesus explains here that Malachi's prophecy was fulfilled by John the Baptist, who ministered in the spirit and power of Elijah (Lk 1:17, compare Mt 16:14).

11:17 We played the pipe for you In this illustration, children play music and sing, but their friends do not play along. Jesus makes the point that the Jews rejected John's message of judgment (expressed by not eating and drinking) and Jesus' message of joy and hope (expressed by eating and drinking) because John and Jesus did not fit their expectations of Elijah and the Messiah (compare note on 11:14).

11:18 neither eating nor drinking A reference to John's ascetic lifestyle.

11:19 wisdom is proved right by her deeds See note on Lk 7:35.

11:20–24 Continuing the themes of vv. 16–19, Jesus pronounces woes on those who failed to heed his preaching.

11:21 Chorazin A town near Capernaum. **Bethsaida** A town near Capernaum. **Tyre and Sidon** Powerful Gentile city-states in Phoenicia, northwest of Israel on the Mediterranean coast.

11:23 Capernaum Jesus' base of ministry. Most of his miracles are performed in the region of Chorazin, Bethsaida and Capernaum. **Hades** The realm of the dead. Compare note on Mt 16:18. **Sodom** The destruction of Sodom is described in Ge 19:1–29. See note on Mt 10:15.

11:25–30 After criticizing the unbelieving Jews, Jesus thanks the Father for his believing disciples (v. 25). He contrasts the burdensome teaching of the Pharisees by telling his disciples that his burden is light (v. 30), inviting them to full discipleship (vv. 28–29).

11:27 All things In light of v. 25, this could refer to all knowledge. It also could indicate complete authority, the totality of existence or everything needed to carry out the ministry of Jesus (compare 28:18; Da 7:14).

11:29 Take my yoke upon you Yokes were heavy, wooden crossbars used to connect two oxen together for more efficient plowing. Here, Jesus' yoke represents his teaching. Allegiance to him and his kingdom results in a sense of peace—it is not laborious, like keeping the requirements of the Jewish leaders of the time, but instead is joyful.

11:30 my burden is light In contrast to the burdens imposed by Israel's religious leaders (compare Mt 23:4).

12:1–8 Jesus asserts his authority over the Sabbath in an encounter with the Pharisees. He cites two examples to demonstrate that people's needs outweigh the observance of Sabbath law.

12:1 the Sabbath The traditional day of rest for the Jewish people as prescribed by the law (Ex 20:8–11; 34:21).

and eat them. ²When the Pharisees saw this, they said to him, "Look! Your disciples are doing what is unlawful on the Sabbath."

³He answered, "Haven't you read what David did when he and his companions were hungry? ⁴He entered the house of God, and he and his companions ate the consecrated bread — which was not lawful for them to do, but only for the priests. ⁵Or haven't you read in the Law that the priests on Sabbath duty in the temple desecrate the Sabbath and yet are innocent? ⁶I tell you that something greater than the temple is here. ⁷If you had known what these words mean, 'I desire mercy, not sacrifice,'ᵃ you would not have condemned the innocent. ⁸For the Son of Man is Lord of the Sabbath."

⁹Going on from that place, he went into their synagogue, ¹⁰and a man with a shriveled hand was there. Looking for a reason to bring charges against Jesus, they asked him, "Is it lawful to heal on the Sabbath?"

¹¹He said to them, "If any of you has a sheep and it falls into a pit on the Sabbath, will you not take hold of it and lift it out? ¹²How much more valuable is a person than a sheep! Therefore it is lawful to do good on the Sabbath."

¹³Then he said to the man, "Stretch out your hand." So he stretched it out and it was completely restored, just as sound as the other. ¹⁴But the Pharisees went out and plotted how they might kill Jesus.

God's Chosen Servant

¹⁵Aware of this, Jesus withdrew from that place. A large crowd followed him, and he healed all who were ill. ¹⁶He warned them not to tell others about him. ¹⁷This was to fulfill what was spoken through the prophet Isaiah:

¹⁸ "Here is my servant whom I have chosen,
    the one I love, in whom I delight;
  I will put my Spirit on him,
    and he will proclaim justice to
      the nations.
¹⁹ He will not quarrel or cry out;
    no one will hear his voice in the streets.
²⁰ A bruised reed he will not break,
    and a smoldering wick he will not
      snuff out,
  till he has brought justice through
    to victory.
²¹   In his name the nations will put their
      hope."ᵇ

Jesus and Beelzebul

12:25-29pp — Mk 3:23-27; Lk 11:17-22

²²Then they brought him a demon-possessed man who was blind and mute, and Jesus healed him, so that he could both talk and see. ²³All the people were astonished and said, "Could this be the Son of David?"

²⁴But when the Pharisees heard this, they said, "It is only by Beelzebul, the prince of demons, that this fellow drives out demons."

²⁵Jesus knew their thoughts and said to them, "Every kingdom divided against itself will be ruined, and every city or household divided against

ᵃ 7 Hosea 6:6 ᵇ 21 Isaiah 42:1-4

12:2 Pharisees These Jewish teachers consider the plucking of grain to be a violation of the Sabbath prohibition against work. See note on Mk 2:23.
12:3 what David did Refers to 1Sa 21:1–6.
12:4 consecrated bread Loaves of bread placed in the tabernacle sanctuary (Lev 24:5–9).
12:5 desecrate the Sabbath A reference to the duties of the priests, which technically violated the Sabbath but were permitted by God.
12:6 something greater than the temple is here Likely refers to Jesus and his authority (compare Jn 2:18–21), or perhaps to the kingdom of heaven itself.
12:7 I desire mercy, not sacrifice Jesus quotes Hos 6:6 for a second time (compare Mt 9:13 and note).
12:8 Son of Man See 8:20 and note. **Lord of the Sabbath** Jesus asserts his authority over the Sabbath.
12:9–14 In a second Sabbath controversy, Jesus heals a man with a withered hand, again demonstrating that people's needs trump ritual observances.
12:9 synagogue See note on 4:23; see the infographic "The Synagogue at Capernaum" on p. 1656.
12:10 to bring charges against Jesus If Jesus heals the man, the Pharisees can accuse him of working — thus breaking the Sabbath.
12:11 and lift it out Some rabbis taught that, in life and death circumstances, it was permissible to work on the Sabbath (see the rabbinic work, the Babylonian Talmud, Shabbat 148b). Others, such as those in

the Dead Sea Scrolls community, forbade anything that might be considered work, regardless of the circumstances. The Damascus Document — an early collection of Jewish laws found among the Dead Sea Scrolls — states that if an animal falls in a pit on the Sabbath, it must be left until after the Sabbath (Damascus Document A.10).

12:15–21 In this brief passage, Matthew identifies Jesus as the suffering servant, who was prophesied in the book of Isaiah.

12:18 The quotation in Mt 12:18–21 comes from Isa 42:1–4, which is a prophecy about the suffering servant. See the table "Jesus' Fulfillment of OT Prophecy" on p. 1573.

12:18 in whom I delight At Jesus' baptism and transfiguration, a voice from heaven speaks these words (Mt 3:17; 17:5).

12:22–32 In the following section, the Pharisees hear the crowds speaking of Jesus in Messianic terms, so they attempt to discredit his ministry. In return, Jesus accuses them of committing an unpardonable sin.

12:23 Son of David A Messianic title. See note on 1:1.
12:24 Beelzebul, the prince of demons The people have just wondered whether Jesus is the Messiah, and the Pharisees accuse him of being demonic. See 10:25 and note.

itself will not stand. ²⁶If Satan drives out Satan, he is divided against himself. How then can his kingdom stand? ²⁷And if I drive out demons by Beelzebul, by whom do your people drive them out? So then, they will be your judges. ²⁸But if it is by the Spirit of God that I drive out demons, then the kingdom of God has come upon you.

²⁹"Or again, how can anyone enter a strong man's house and carry off his possessions unless he first ties up the strong man? Then he can plunder his house.

³⁰"Whoever is not with me is against me, and whoever does not gather with me scatters. ³¹And so I tell you, every kind of sin and slander can be forgiven, but blasphemy against the Spirit will not be forgiven. ³²Anyone who speaks a word against the Son of Man will be forgiven, but anyone who speaks against the Holy Spirit will not be forgiven, either in this age or in the age to come.

³³"Make a tree good and its fruit will be good, or make a tree bad and its fruit will be bad, for a tree is recognized by its fruit. ³⁴You brood of vipers, how can you who are evil say anything good? For the mouth speaks what the heart is full of. ³⁵A good man brings good things out of the good stored up in him, and an evil man brings evil things out of the evil stored up in him. ³⁶But I tell you that everyone will have to give account on the day of judgment for every empty word they have spoken. ³⁷For by your words you will be acquitted, and by your words you will be condemned."

The Sign of Jonah

12:39-42pp — Lk 11:29-32
12:43-45pp — Lk 11:24-26

³⁸Then some of the Pharisees and teachers of the law said to him, "Teacher, we want to see a sign from you."

³⁹He answered, "A wicked and adulterous generation asks for a sign! But none will be given it except the sign of the prophet Jonah. ⁴⁰For as Jonah was three days and three nights in the belly of a huge fish, so the Son of Man will be three days and three nights in the heart of the earth. ⁴¹The men of Nineveh will stand up at the judgment with this generation and condemn it; for they repented at the preaching of Jonah, and now something greater than Jonah is here. ⁴²The Queen of the South will rise at the judgment with this generation and condemn it; for she came from the ends of the earth to listen to Solomon's wisdom, and now something greater than Solomon is here.

⁴³"When an impure spirit comes out of a person, it goes through arid places seeking rest and does not find it. ⁴⁴Then it says, 'I will return to the house I left.' When it arrives, it finds the house unoccupied, swept clean and put in order. ⁴⁵Then it goes and takes with it seven other spirits more wicked than itself, and they go in and live there. And the final condition of that person is worse than the first. That is how it will be with this wicked generation."

12:26 If Satan drives out Satan Jesus argues that, if Satan were facilitating exorcisms, he would be counteracting his own attempts to control the world, because he is the ruler of the demons (compare note on 10:25).
12:27 your people Refers to Jewish exorcists.
12:29 enter a strong man's house Jesus uses this illustration to assert that he already has defeated Satan (the strong man)—which is why he can expel demons (plunder the house). Jesus' analogy likely comes from Isa 22:15–25. Compare Mk 3:27 and note.
12:31 blasphemy against the Spirit Speaking with degradation against God's truth (compare 1Ti 1:20). In this case, it refers to the Pharisees' claim that Jesus' power comes from Satan, rather than the Spirit of God.
12:33–37 The Pharisees' assessment of Jesus' power reveals their true nature. As the fruit of a tree indicates the nature of a tree, so their actions indicate their evil intent.
12:34 You brood of vipers See note on Mt 3:7.
12:38–42 Some Pharisees wish to see a sign from Jesus to prove his authority. The only sign they will receive is Jesus' resurrection, which he refers to metaphorically. Compare 16:1–4.
12:38 Pharisees and teachers of the law Two groups of Jewish religious leaders. See note on 2:4; note on Jn 1:24.
12:39 adulterous generation Adultery is widely used in the Bible as a metaphor for sin and unfaithfulness

to God (e.g., Isa 57:3; Eze 16:32; Hos 1–3; Jas 4:4).
the sign of the prophet Jonah Jonah's rescue from the great fish was a sign that the prophet and his message were from God. Similarly, the ultimate sign validating Jesus would be his triumph over death (Mt 12:40). Although the Pharisees likely did not understand Jesus' statement, they might have recalled it after his resurrection.
12:40 three days and three nights See note on Lk 24:1. **Son of Man** See note on Mt 8:20 and note.
12:41 they repented at the preaching of Jonah In contrast to many of Jesus' contemporaries, the recipients of Jonah's message—who were Assyrians, the enemy of God's people—repented. See Jnh 3.
12:42 The Queen of the South Refers to the Queen of Sheba, who visited Solomon and marveled at his wisdom (1Ki 10:1–13; 2Ch 9:1–12). In contrast, the scribes (teachers of the law) and Pharisees refuse to accept the wisdom of one greater than Solomon.
12:43–45 Jesus describes the evil and adulterous generation in terms of a disembodied spirit who returns to its host with greater severity.
12:45 seven other spirits Seven is often used as a number of completeness or totality in the Bible; here, the possession by demons involves a complete takeover of the person. **this wicked generation** Despite his many miracles, Jesus' divine authority is called into question repeatedly. This parable warns against such stubborn disbelief. By rejecting Jesus, the generation will become

Jesus' Mother and Brothers

12:46-50pp — Mk 3:31-35; Lk 8:19-21

⁴⁶While Jesus was still talking to the crowd, his mother and brothers stood outside, wanting to speak to him. ⁴⁷Someone told him, "Your mother and brothers are standing outside, wanting to speak to you."

⁴⁸He replied to him, "Who is my mother, and who are my brothers?" ⁴⁹Pointing to his disciples, he said, "Here are my mother and my brothers. ⁵⁰For whoever does the will of my Father in heaven is my brother and sister and mother."

The Parable of the Sower

13:1-15pp — Mk 4:1-12; Lk 8:4-10
13:16,17pp — Lk 10:23,24
13:18-23pp — Mk 4:13-20; Lk 8:11-15

13 That same day Jesus went out of the house and sat by the lake. ²Such large crowds gathered around him that he got into a boat and sat in it, while all the people stood on the shore. ³Then he told them many things in parables, saying: "A farmer went out to sow his seed. ⁴As he was scattering the seed, some fell along the path, and the birds came and ate it up. ⁵Some fell on rocky places, where it did not have much soil. It sprang up quickly, because the soil was shallow. ⁶But when the sun came up, the plants were scorched, and they withered because they had no root. ⁷Other seed fell among thorns, which grew up and choked the plants. ⁸Still other seed fell on good soil, where it produced a crop—a hundred, sixty or thirty times what was sown. ⁹Whoever has ears, let them hear."

¹⁰The disciples came to him and asked, "Why do you speak to the people in parables?"

¹¹He replied, "Because the knowledge of the secrets of the kingdom of heaven has been given to you, but not to them. ¹²Whoever has will be given more, and they will have an abundance. Whoever does not have, even what they have will be taken from them. ¹³This is why I speak to them in parables:

"Though seeing, they do not see;
  though hearing, they do not hear or
   understand.

¹⁴In them is fulfilled the prophecy of Isaiah:

"'You will be ever hearing but never
   understanding;
  you will be ever seeing but never perceiving.
¹⁵For this people's heart has become calloused;
  they hardly hear with their ears,
  and they have closed their eyes.
Otherwise they might see with their eyes,
  hear with their ears,
  understand with their hearts
and turn, and I would heal them.'ᵃ

¹⁶But blessed are your eyes because they see, and your ears because they hear. ¹⁷For truly I tell you, many prophets and righteous people longed to see what you see but did not see it, and to hear what you hear but did not hear it.

ᵃ *15* Isaiah 6:9,10 (see Septuagint)

---

even more vulnerable to the forces of darkness. This could also refer to the fall of Jerusalem, which occurred 35–40 years after Jesus' ministry (AD 70).

12:46–50 Jesus' direct opposition to the religious establishment of his day drew the attention and concern of his family. Here, Jesus defines his extended family as those who do the will of his heavenly Father.

12:46 mother and brothers Jesus' earthly father, Joseph, is not mentioned in any of the Gospels after the trip to Jerusalem when Jesus was 12 (Lk 2:41–51). His absence might indicate that he had died.

12:50 my brother and sister and mother Jesus is not negating the importance of the natural family, but he is emphasizing the greater importance of the spiritual family. Commitment to Jesus and his cause is a higher loyalty than familial loyalty.

13:1–9 Matthew 13 consists of eight parables. The first—the parable of the sower—describes four different responses to the message of the kingdom of heaven that Jesus and his disciples preach. Jesus interprets the parable in vv. 18–23. See the table "Parables of Jesus" on p. 1584.

13:1 sat See note on 5:1. **by the lake** The Sea of Galilee.
13:2 got into a boat Jesus may have gone out on the water a short distance to improve people's ability to hear him—sound travels better over the water.
13:3 parables In his parables, Jesus compares the kingdom of heaven, or certain aspects of it, to common situations of his day (such as farming and fishing).

13:5 rocky places Not loose stones in the soil, but ground with a shelf of bedrock close to the surface. The soil above the bedrock warms quickly, so seeds readily sprout, but the shallow soil cannot sustain growth.

13:8 a hundred An extraordinary harvest. A tenfold harvest would have been considered a good crop.

13:10–17 The disciples ask Jesus why he speaks in parables. He responds by quoting the OT and drawing a comparison between his ministry and Isaiah's.

13:12 Whoever has Refers to those who have been given understanding regarding the kingdom of heaven and Jesus' message. **what they have will be taken** Those who do not have understanding about the kingdom of heaven have nothing of value because the kingdom of heaven is the only thing of lasting value (compare 13:45–46; 25:29).

13:13 I speak to them in parables Rabbis used parables for illustrative purposes and typically provided an explanation. Jesus, however, did not always offer an interpretation. His followers likely viewed some of his parables as riddles rather than illustrations. **seeing, they do not see** An allusion to Isa 6:9. Just as Israel rejected Isaiah's message then, so Israel rejects Jesus' message now.

13:14 prophecy of Isaiah Introduces Jesus' quotation of Isa 6:9–10 as it appears in the Septuagint (the Greek

¹⁸"Listen then to what the parable of the sower means: ¹⁹When anyone hears the message about the kingdom and does not understand it, the evil one comes and snatches away what was sown in their heart. This is the seed sown along the path. ²⁰The seed falling on rocky ground refers to someone who hears the word and at once receives it with joy. ²¹But since they have no root, they last only a short time. When trouble or persecution comes because of the word, they quickly fall away. ²²The seed falling among the thorns refers to someone who hears the word, but the worries of this life and the deceitfulness of wealth choke the word, making it unfruitful. ²³But the seed falling on good soil refers to someone who hears the word and understands it. This is the one who produces a crop, yielding a hundred, sixty or thirty times what was sown."

The Parable of the Weeds

²⁴Jesus told them another parable: "The kingdom of heaven is like a man who sowed good seed in his field. ²⁵But while everyone was sleeping, his enemy came and sowed weeds among the wheat, and went away. ²⁶When the wheat sprouted and formed heads, then the weeds also appeared.

²⁷"The owner's servants came to him and said, 'Sir, didn't you sow good seed in your field? Where then did the weeds come from?'

²⁸"'An enemy did this,' he replied.

"The servants asked him, 'Do you want us to go and pull them up?'

²⁹"'No,' he answered, 'because while you are pulling the weeds, you may uproot the wheat with them. ³⁰Let both grow together until the harvest. At that time I will tell the harvesters: First collect the weeds and tie them in bundles to be burned; then gather the wheat and bring it into my barn.'"

The Parables of the Mustard Seed and the Yeast

13:31,32pp — Mk 4:30-32
13:31-33pp — Lk 13:18-21

³¹He told them another parable: "The kingdom of heaven is like a mustard seed, which a man took and planted in his field. ³²Though it is the smallest of all seeds, yet when it grows, it is the largest of garden plants and becomes a tree, so that the birds come and perch in its branches."

³³He told them still another parable: "The kingdom of heaven is like yeast that a woman took and mixed into about sixty pounds^a of flour until it worked all through the dough."

³⁴Jesus spoke all these things to the crowd in parables; he did not say anything to them without using a parable. ³⁵So was fulfilled what was spoken through the prophet:

"I will open my mouth in parables,
    I will utter things hidden since the
        creation of the world."^b

The Parable of the Weeds Explained

³⁶Then he left the crowd and went into the house. His disciples came to him and said, "Explain to us the parable of the weeds in the field."

³⁷He answered, "The one who sowed the good seed is the Son of Man. ³⁸The field is the world, and the good seed stands for the people of the kingdom. The weeds are the people of the evil one, ³⁹and the enemy who sows them is the devil. The harvest is the end of the age, and the harvesters are angels.

---

a 33 Or about 27 kilograms   *b* 35 Psalm 78:2

---

translation of the OT). See the table "Jesus' Fulfillment of OT Prophecy" on p. 1573.

13:18–23 In a rare display, Jesus explains one of his parables—but only to his disciples (compare Mt 13:36–43).

13:19 message about the kingdom Represented by the seeds in Jesus' initial telling of the parable. The seed is always good; the variance is in where the seed lands.

13:24–30 Jesus returns to addressing the crowd (as opposed to his disciples in the boat) and offers them a second parable. Jesus later offers his disciples an explanation (vv. 36–43).

13:25 weeds The Greek word used here refers to a kind of weed that resembles wheat until both reach maturity.

13:31–33 The next two parables in ch. 13 stress the inevitable growth of the kingdom of heaven, despite the resistance it faces. The parable of the mustard seed contrasts the seemingly insignificant inception of the kingdom of heaven, in the world and in a person's life, with its momentous results.

13:31 mustard seed A tiny seed that grows into a ten-foot-high shrub. The shrub grew along the shores of the Sea of Galilee and may have been immediately in view of Jesus' hearers.

13:32 the smallest of all seeds Rabbis used the mustard seed as a proverbial object to denote the smallest possible amount or size of something. Compare 17:20.

13:33 yeast A substance that causes dough to ferment and rise. Normally, yeast or leaven has negative connotations in the Bible, symbolizing sin or impurity (e.g., 16:6; 1Co 5:6–7). Here, Jesus uses it positively to symbolize the kingdom of heaven's expansion.

13:34–35 Similar to Mt 13:10–17, this section reiterates Jesus' purpose in using parables.

13:35 fulfilled See note on 1:22. **the prophet** The quotation in this verse is from Ps 78:2. This psalm identifies its author as Asaph, who is described in 2 Chronicles as a seer (see note on Ps 73:title; note on Ps 78:2; 2Ch 29:30).

13:36–43 Jesus privately interprets the parable of the weeds (Mt 13:24–30) for his disciples.

13:37 the Son of Man See note on 8:20.

[40] "As the weeds are pulled up and burned in the fire, so it will be at the end of the age. [41]The Son of Man will send out his angels, and they will weed out of his kingdom everything that causes sin and all who do evil. [42]They will throw them into the blazing furnace, where there will be weeping and gnashing of teeth. [43]Then the righteous will shine like the sun in the kingdom of their Father. Whoever has ears, let them hear.

The Parables of the Hidden Treasure and the Pearl

[44] "The kingdom of heaven is like treasure hidden in a field. When a man found it, he hid it again, and then in his joy went and sold all he had and bought that field.

[45] "Again, the kingdom of heaven is like a merchant looking for fine pearls. [46]When he found one

13:42 blazing furnace Fire is a common symbol for divine judgment. See note on Lk 3:9. **weeping and gnashing of teeth** This refers to the day of final judgment (Rev 20:11–15). Once God's judgment comes, it will be unbearable for those who have not chosen to follow Jesus. See note on Mt 8:12.
13:43 the righteous will shine like the sun An allusion to Da 12:3.

13:44–46 These two parables describe the great value of the kingdom of heaven, as well as the extreme and urgent measures people should take because of it.

13:46 he went away and sold everything The point is not that the man purchased a place in the kingdom of heaven, but rather that entering the kingdom is worth giving up everything.

Temple Comparison

Herod the Great's expansion of the second temple in Jerusalem, begun around 20 BC, made the temple more than twice the size of Solomon's temple, finished in 960 BC. Herod the Great ruled Judea at Jesus' birth and attempted to kill him (Mt 2:1-20). Herod the Great's son, Herod Antipas, became tetrarch of Galilee and Perea in 4 BC. He is the Herod involved in John the Baptist's execution and Jesus' trial (Mt 14:1-12; Luke 9:7-9; 23:6-12).

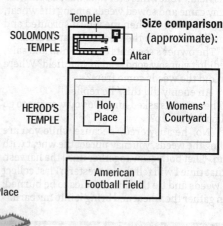

SOLOMON'S TEMPLE

Temple

Altar

HEROD'S TEMPLE

Holy Place

Womens' Courtyard

Size comparison (approximate):

American Football Field

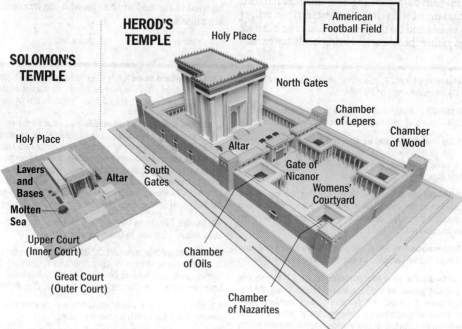

HEROD'S TEMPLE

Holy Place

North Gates

Chamber of Lepers

Chamber of Wood

Altar

Gate of Nicanor

Womens' Courtyard

SOLOMON'S TEMPLE

Holy Place

Lavers and Bases

Altar

South Gates

Molten Sea

Upper Court (Inner Court)

Great Court (Outer Court)

Chamber of Oils

Chamber of Nazarites

of great value, he went away and sold everything he had and bought it.

The Parable of the Net

47"Once again, the kingdom of heaven is like a net that was let down into the lake and caught all kinds of fish. 48When it was full, the fishermen pulled it up on the shore. Then they sat down and collected the good fish in baskets, but threw the bad away. 49This is how it will be at the end of the age. The angels will come and separate the wicked from the righteous 50and throw them into the blazing furnace, where there will be weeping and gnashing of teeth.

51"Have you understood all these things?" Jesus asked.

"Yes," they replied.

52He said to them, "Therefore every teacher of the law who has become a disciple in the kingdom of heaven is like the owner of a house who brings out of his storeroom new treasures as well as old."

A Prophet Without Honor

13:54-58pp — Mk 6:1-6

53When Jesus had finished these parables, he moved on from there. 54Coming to his hometown, he began teaching the people in their synagogue, and they were amazed. "Where did this man get this wisdom and these miraculous powers?" they asked. 55"Isn't this the carpenter's son? Isn't his mother's name Mary, and aren't his brothers James, Joseph, Simon and Judas? 56Aren't all his sisters with us? Where then did this man get all these things?" 57And they took offense at him.

But Jesus said to them, "A prophet is not without honor except in his own town and in his own home."

58And he did not do many miracles there because of their lack of faith.

John the Baptist Beheaded

14:1-12pp — Mk 6:14-29

14 At that time Herod the tetrarch heard the reports about Jesus, 2and he said to his attendants, "This is John the Baptist; he has risen from the dead! That is why miraculous powers are at work in him."

3Now Herod had arrested John and bound him and put him in prison because of Herodias, his brother Philip's wife, 4for John had been saying to him: "It is not lawful for you to have her." 5Herod wanted to kill John, but he was afraid of the people, because they considered John a prophet.

6On Herod's birthday the daughter of Herodias danced for the guests and pleased Herod so much 7that he promised with an oath to give her whatever she asked. 8Prompted by her mother, she said, "Give me here on a platter the head of John the Baptist." 9The king was distressed, but because of his oaths and his dinner guests, he ordered that her request be granted 10and had John beheaded in the prison. 11His head was brought in on a platter and given to the girl, who carried it to her mother. 12John's disciples came and took his body and buried it. Then they went and told Jesus.

Jesus Feeds the Five Thousand

14:13-21pp — Mk 6:32-44; Lk 9:10-17; Jn 6:1-13
14:13-21Ref — Mt 15:32-38

13When Jesus heard what had happened, he withdrew by boat privately to a solitary place. Hearing of this, the crowds followed him on foot from the towns. 14When Jesus landed and saw a large crowd, he had compassion on them and healed their sick.

13:47-52 Similar to the parable of the weeds (Mt 13:24-30), this parable describes the ingathering of the righteous and wicked and their subsequent fates. The kingdom of heaven will consist of those who follow Jesus.

13:47 a net A net with floats on one end and weights on the other. Fishermen cast the net into the sea and allowed the weighted end to sink to a sufficient depth. When they pulled it in, the net scooped up everything in its path.

13:50 weeping and gnashing of teeth See note on 13:42.

13:52 new treasures as well as old The disciples were beginning to understand the new things Jesus was teaching in conjunction with the traditions from the Scriptures they already knew.

13:53-58 Following his teaching in parables, Jesus travels to his hometown. Because of their familiarity with Jesus, the people of Nazareth reject him as a prophet.

13:54 his hometown Jesus' base of ministry was Capernaum, but he had grown up in Nazareth (2:23). **Where did this man get this wisdom** The people know that, unlike their rabbis, Jesus has no formal training; he was raised as a craftsman.

13:57 And they took offense at him Their offense comes from Jesus' claim to be something that they assume he is not.

13:58 because of their lack of faith Jesus does not need to prove his authenticity with signs; the people have already rejected his message.

14:1-12 Matthew begins this section by recounting the death of John the Baptist. Since Herod mistakenly identifies Jesus with John, Matthew provides the background to the story. See the event line "Jesus' Early Life and Ministry" on p. 1530.

14:1 Herod the tetrarch Refers to Herod Antipas; a tetrarch is one who rules over a fourth of the kingdom. See note on Lk 3:1. See the table "Political Leaders in the New Testament" on p. 1916.

14:6 the daughter of Herodias Identified as Salome by the first-century Jewish historian Josephus (Josephus, *Antiquities* 18.136).

14:9 was distressed Refers to Herod's fear of the crowd (Mt 14:5); he didn't want to incite a rebellion.

14:13-21 Matthew's Gospel records two mass feedings (compare 15:32-39). In addition to caring about his followers' spiritual needs, Jesus also evidences concern for their physical well-being.

¹⁵As evening approached, the disciples came to him and said, "This is a remote place, and it's already getting late. Send the crowds away, so they can go to the villages and buy themselves some food."

¹⁶Jesus replied, "They do not need to go away. You give them something to eat."

¹⁷"We have here only five loaves of bread and two fish," they answered.

¹⁸"Bring them here to me," he said. ¹⁹And he directed the people to sit down on the grass. Taking the five loaves and the two fish and looking up to heaven, he gave thanks and broke the loaves. Then he gave them to the disciples, and the disciples gave them to the people. ²⁰They all ate and were satisfied, and the disciples picked up twelve basketfuls of broken pieces that were left over. ²¹The number of those who ate was about five thousand men, besides women and children.

Jesus Walks on the Water

14:22-33pp — Mk 6:45-51; Jn 6:16-21
14:34-36pp — Mk 6:53-56

²²Immediately Jesus made the disciples get into the boat and go on ahead of him to the other side, while he dismissed the crowd. ²³After he had dismissed them, he went up on a mountainside by

14:17 five loaves of bread and two fish A meal that might feed two people. Bread and fish were the staples of a Galilean peasant diet.

14:20 twelve basketfuls One per disciple. In the OT, God fed his people with manna, but there were no edible leftovers (Ex 16:14–21).

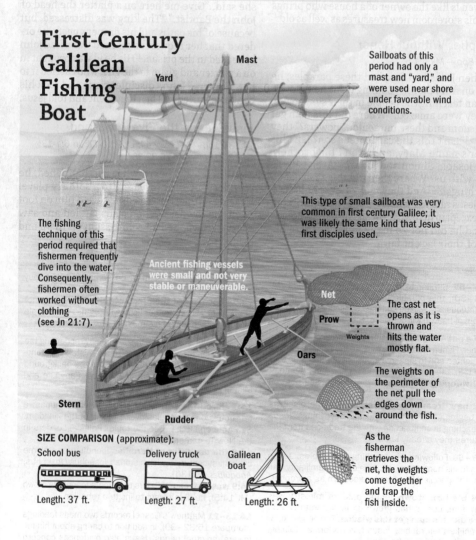

First-Century Galilean Fishing Boat

Mast

Yard

Sailboats of this period had only a mast and "yard," and were used near shore under favorable wind conditions.

The fishing technique of this period required that fishermen frequently dive into the water. Consequently, fishermen often worked without clothing (see Jn 21:7).

Ancient fishing vessels were small and not very stable or maneuverable.

This type of small sailboat was very common in first century Galilee; it was likely the same kind that Jesus' first disciples used.

Net

Prow

Weights

The cast net opens as it is thrown and hits the water mostly flat.

Oars

The weights on the perimeter of the net pull the edges down around the fish.

Stern

Rudder

As the fisherman retrieves the net, the weights come together and trap the fish inside.

SIZE COMPARISON (approximate):

School bus
Length: 37 ft.

Delivery truck
Length: 27 ft.

Galilean boat
Length: 26 ft.

himself to pray. Later that night, he was there alone, 24and the boat was already a considerable distance from land, buffeted by the waves because the wind was against it.

25Shortly before dawn Jesus went out to them, walking on the lake. 26When the disciples saw him walking on the lake, they were terrified. "It's a ghost," they said, and cried out in fear.

27But Jesus immediately said to them: "Take courage! It is I. Don't be afraid."

28"Lord, if it's you," Peter replied, "tell me to come to you on the water."

29"Come," he said.

Then Peter got down out of the boat, walked on the water and came toward Jesus. 30But when he saw the wind, he was afraid and, beginning to sink, cried out, "Lord, save me!"

31Immediately Jesus reached out his hand and caught him. "You of little faith," he said, "why did you doubt?"

32And when they climbed into the boat, the wind died down. 33Then those who were in the boat worshiped him, saying, "Truly you are the Son of God."

34When they had crossed over, they landed at Gennesaret. 35And when the men of that place recognized Jesus, they sent word to all the surrounding country. People brought all their sick to him 36and begged him to let the sick just touch the edge of his cloak, and all who touched it were healed.

That Which Defiles

15:1-20pp — Mk 7:1-23

15 Then some Pharisees and teachers of the law came to Jesus from Jerusalem and asked, 2"Why do your disciples break the tradition of the elders? They don't wash their hands before they eat!"

3Jesus replied, "And why do you break the command of God for the sake of your tradition? 4For God said, 'Honor your father and mother'*a* and 'Anyone who curses their father or mother is to be put to death.'*b* 5But you say that if anyone declares that what might have been used to help their father or mother is 'devoted to God,' 6they are not to 'honor their father or mother' with it. Thus you nullify the word of God for the sake of

a 4 Exodus 20:12; Deut. 5:16   *b* 4 Exodus 21:17; Lev. 20:9

14:21 besides women and children The women and children likely added 1,000–3,000 people.

14:22–33 Jesus sends his disciples to the other side of the Sea of Galilee while he goes away to pray. He then comes to them by walking on the surface of the water. For the first time in Matthew's Gospel, the disciples confess Jesus' true identity—which Satan and demons have already acknowledged (Mt 4:3,6; 8:29). The statement here foreshadows the great confession in 16:16. See the table "Miracles of Jesus" on p. 1741.

14:24 a considerable distance The Greek phrase used here, *stadious pollous*, does not give an exact distance but simply indicates "many stadia." A stadion is about 1/8 of a Roman mile, or roughly 600 feet (185 meters). This suggests that the boat was a significant distance from the shore. John's parallel account gives a more specific distance of 25–30 stadia (Jn 6:19).

14:25 Shortly before dawn Romans divided the 12-hour span between 6 p.m. and 6 a.m. into four watches of three hours each. The fourth watch (mentioned here in the Greek text of Matthew) was 3–6 a.m. **walking on the lake** This demonstration of power over the sea served as a sign of Jesus' deity. See note on Mt 8:26.

14:27 It is I Matthew may be employing this phrase in a colloquial manner ("it's me"). Alternatively, he could be intentionally using the Greek translation of the divine name (*egō eimi*) revealed in Ex 3:14. The miraculous nature of this event and the confession in Mt 14:33 seem to favor the interpretation that Jesus is equating himself with Yahweh. See the table "Jesus' 'I Am' Statements" on p. 1727.

14:28 Lord Peter respectfully and fearfully addresses Jesus; this address may indicate that Peter is addressing Jesus as Yahweh (see note on 8:2). **if it's you** The disciples did not recognize Jesus at this point.

14:33 Truly you are the Son of God The first apostolic confession of Jesus' divine messiahship. This answers the disciples' question from their previous incident out on the lake (8:27).

14:34–36 The people in this episode exercise great faith, believing that Jesus can heal them if they simply touch his clothes (compare 9:21).

14:34 Gennesaret A town on the northwest shore of the Sea of Galilee. See the map "Jesus' Ministry in Galilee" on p. 2260.

15:1–9 In Gennesaret, Pharisees from Jerusalem approach Jesus and accuse him of being lax toward their legal traditions. Jesus responds by pointing out their inconsistencies and condemns them by quoting the prophet Isaiah.

15:1 Pharisees and teachers of the law Two groups of Jewish religious leaders. See note on 2:4; note on Jn 1:24.

15:2 tradition of the elders Refers to the oral teachings of the Pharisees throughout the centuries. These teachings served to clarify and preserve the law. In Jesus' day, these traditions carried nearly equal authority with the Jewish law; they were intended to allow people to better apply the law to their daily lives. However, Jesus claims that they unnecessarily burden the people (Mt 23:2–4; compare 11:28,30). **They don't wash** The disciples' negligence makes them ritually unclean according to the tradition of the Pharisees. However, this point is not elucidated in the law, which required only priests to wash prior to service. The Pharisees applied this ceremonial purity to all Jews (compare Ex 30:17–21; Lev 15:11; Mk 7:3–4).

15:3 break the command of God Jesus turns the tables on his opponents. In the following verses, he highlights their guilt for a much greater offense than handwashing.

15:4 Honor your father and mother The fifth commandment. See Ex 20:12; Dt 5:16. **Anyone who curses their father or mother is to be put to death** See Ex 21:17; Lev 20:9.

15:5 what might have been used to help their father or mother is 'devoted to God' This apparently involves pledging to support the religious establishment with resources that otherwise might go to one's parents. The Pharisees seem to have allowed—or even encouraged—such a trade-off, which Jesus says elevates human tradition above God's commands.

your tradition. [7]You hypocrites! Isaiah was right when he prophesied about you:

[8]"'These people honor me with their lips,
   but their hearts are far from me.
[9]They worship me in vain;
   their teachings are merely human
      rules.' [a]"

[10]Jesus called the crowd to him and said, "Listen and understand. [11]What goes into someone's mouth does not defile them, but what comes out of their mouth, that is what defiles them."

[12]Then the disciples came to him and asked, "Do you know that the Pharisees were offended when they heard this?"

[13]He replied, "Every plant that my heavenly Father has not planted will be pulled up by the roots. [14]Leave them; they are blind guides.[b] If the blind lead the blind, both will fall into a pit."

[15]Peter said, "Explain the parable to us."

[16]"Are you still so dull?" Jesus asked them. [17]"Don't you see that whatever enters the mouth goes into the stomach and then out of the body? [18]But the things that come out of a person's mouth come from the heart, and these defile them. [19]For out of the heart come evil thoughts — murder, adultery, sexual immorality, theft, false testimony, slander. [20]These are what defile a person; but eating with unwashed hands does not defile them."

The Faith of a Canaanite Woman
15:21-28pp — Mk 7:24-30

[21]Leaving that place, Jesus withdrew to the region of Tyre and Sidon. [22]A Canaanite woman from that vicinity came to him, crying out, "Lord, Son of David, have mercy on me! My daughter is demon-possessed and suffering terribly."

[23]Jesus did not answer a word. So his disciples came to him and urged him, "Send her away, for she keeps crying out after us."

[24]He answered, "I was sent only to the lost sheep of Israel."

[25]The woman came and knelt before him. "Lord, help me!" she said.

[26]He replied, "It is not right to take the children's bread and toss it to the dogs."

[27]"Yes it is, Lord," she said. "Even the dogs eat the crumbs that fall from their master's table."

[28]Then Jesus said to her, "Woman, you have great faith! Your request is granted." And her daughter was healed at that moment.

Jesus Feeds the Four Thousand
15:29-31pp — Mk 7:31-37
15:32-39pp — Mk 8:1-10
15:32-39Ref — Mt 14:13-21

[29]Jesus left there and went along the Sea of Galilee. Then he went up on a mountainside and

[a] 9 Isaiah 29:13   [b] 14 Some manuscripts blind guides of the blind

---

15:7 Isaiah Jesus quotes Isa 29:13, which originally referred to the people of Jerusalem, and by extension God's people as a whole, and applies it to the Pharisees.

15:10–20 Jesus turns the confrontation with the Pharisees into a teaching opportunity for his disciples. He emphasizes the priority of the heart over external matters, such as handwashing and ritual purity.

15:11 defile Make ritually unclean.

15:13 Every plant Drawing from Isaiah, Jesus uses plant imagery to describe the people of God (see Isa 60:21). **will be pulled up by the roots** Jesus implies that the Pharisees, who oppose his message and burden the people with human-made laws, do not come from the Father (even though they are Jews) and therefore will be destroyed.

15:14 they are blind guides The Pharisees, who knew the law better than the rest of the Jews, should have been teaching and instructing the people in the ways of God. Instead, they became caught up in ritual concerns of the law, unnecessarily burdening the people with secondary matters.

15:18 come from the heart In the Hebrew conception of personhood, the heart represents intelligence and will.

15:20 These are what defile a person Jews believed that ritual purity protected them from incurring God's wrath; they would not approach God if they were unclean. Jesus teaches that matters of the heart—not external ceremonial regulations—render people unfit to enter God's presence.

15:21–28 Jesus seizes this opportunity to instruct his disciples about the value of faith and their Gentile (non-Jewish) neighbors.

15:21 Leaving that place Refers to Gennesaret (Mt 14:34). **Tyre and Sidon** Powerful Gentile city-states on the coast of the Mediterranean Sea, northwest of Gennesaret.

15:22 Canaanite woman The Canaanites, Israel's enemies in the Hebrew Scriptures (e.g., Dt 7:1), no longer existed as a distinct people. Mark uses the more historically accurate designation "Syrophoenician" (Mk 7:26). Matthew probably is employing "Canaanite" to emphasize the woman's outsider status as a Gentile (non-Jewish person). **Lord, Son of David** The title "lord" could simply be a sign of respect (see Mt 8:2 and note), but the title "Son of David" has Messianic overtones, indicating that the Canaanite woman had better insight into Jesus' identity than many Jews.

15:24 lost sheep of Israel Refers to the Jews. Eventually, the gospel will be preached among non-Jewish people (as recorded in the book of Acts), but Jesus focused on teaching and healing among the people of Israel. His interaction with the Canaanite woman represents an exception to his normal pattern of ministry (compare 8:5–13).

15:26 children's Refers to the Jews. **dogs** Refers to the Gentiles. Rather than conveying personal hostility toward non-Jewish people, Jesus' choice of words likely reflects a common Jewish sentiment, which he uses to evoke a response from her about Jewish and non-Jewish relations.

15:28 Your request is granted Jesus' response illustrates his point in vv. 10–20: The state of one's heart, shaped by faith, is the decisive factor.

15:29–31 Jesus leaves Tyre and Sidon and returns to Galilee. The summary statement of his healing ministry (v. 30) is reminiscent of 4:23–25; 9:35–36; 14:34–35. Wherever Jesus went, he brought physical and spiritual restoration.

sat down. [30]Great crowds came to him, bringing the lame, the blind, the crippled, the mute and many others, and laid them at his feet; and he healed them. [31]The people were amazed when they saw the mute speaking, the crippled made well, the lame walking and the blind seeing. And they praised the God of Israel.

[32]Jesus called his disciples to him and said, "I have compassion for these people; they have already been with me three days and have nothing to eat. I do not want to send them away hungry, or they may collapse on the way."

[33]His disciples answered, "Where could we get enough bread in this remote place to feed such a crowd?"

[34]"How many loaves do you have?" Jesus asked.

"Seven," they replied, "and a few small fish."

[35]He told the crowd to sit down on the ground. [36]Then he took the seven loaves and the fish, and when he had given thanks, he broke them and gave them to the disciples, and they in turn to the people. [37]They all ate and were satisfied. Afterward the disciples picked up seven basketfuls of broken pieces that were left over. [38]The number of those who ate was four thousand men, besides women and children. [39]After Jesus had sent the crowd away, he got into the boat and went to the vicinity of Magadan.

The Demand for a Sign

16:1-12pp — Mk 8:11-21

16 The Pharisees and Sadducees came to Jesus and tested him by asking him to show them a sign from heaven.

[2]He replied, "When evening comes, you say, 'It will be fair weather, for the sky is red,' [3]and in the morning, 'Today it will be stormy, for the sky is red and overcast.' You know how to interpret the appearance of the sky, but you cannot interpret the signs of the times.[a] [4]A wicked and adulterous generation looks for a sign, but none will be given it except the sign of Jonah." Jesus then left them and went away.

The Yeast of the Pharisees and Sadducees

[5]When they went across the lake, the disciples forgot to take bread. [6]"Be careful," Jesus said to them. "Be on your guard against the yeast of the Pharisees and Sadducees."

[7]They discussed this among themselves and said, "It is because we didn't bring any bread."

[8]Aware of their discussion, Jesus asked, "You of little faith, why are you talking among yourselves about having no bread? [9]Do you still not understand? Don't you remember the five loaves for the five thousand, and how many basketfuls you gathered? [10]Or the seven loaves for the four thousand, and how many basketfuls you gathered? [11]How is it you don't understand that I was not talking to you about bread? But be on your guard against the yeast of the Pharisees and Sadducees." [12]Then they understood that he was not telling them to guard against the yeast used in bread, but against the teaching of the Pharisees and Sadducees.

Peter Declares That Jesus Is the Messiah

16:13-16pp — Mk 8:27-29; Lk 9:18-20

[13]When Jesus came to the region of Caesarea Philippi, he asked his disciples, "Who do people say the Son of Man is?"

---

[a] *2,3* Some early manuscripts do not have *When evening comes . . . of the times.*

15:32–39 This passage presents the second mass feeding in Matthew's Gospel. This account, coupled with vv. 29–31, mirrors 14:13–21. See the table "Miracles of Jesus" on p. 1741.

15:37 seven basketfuls The number seven is frequently used to express totality or completeness. See 14:20.

15:39 the vicinity of Magadan The location is unknown, but it might be an alternate name for Magdala on the western shore of the Sea of Galilee.

16:1–4 The Pharisees and Sadducees—who were often opposed to each other—unite in order to test Jesus. They demand a sign to authenticate his credentials as Messiah. Having already performed many signs, he refuses their request, instead choosing to comment on their spiritual blindness.

16:1 Pharisees See note on Jn 1:24. **Sadducees** See note on Mk 12:18. **a sign from heaven** A means of authentication. Prophets who claimed to speak on God's behalf often had to prove their assertions (see Ex 4:1–9; 7:8–13). "Heaven" is likely a figurative reference to God, although the Jewish leaders may have wanted to see a celestial sign (e.g., Mt 24:27,30).

16:3 you cannot interpret the signs Jesus' point is that the Jews could predict the weather based on simple observations, but they could not discern the presence of the kingdom of heaven through his miracles ("the signs of the times"; compare 4:17).

16:4 sign of Jonah See note on 12:39.

16:5–12 Jesus warns his disciples about the misguided teachings of the Jewish leaders. He speaks metaphorically, and, as usual, the disciples misunderstand. Jesus then warns them plainly and reminds them that he can meet their needs.

16:5 across the lake Refers to the Sea of Galilee.

16:6 yeast Yeast or leaven typically symbolizes sin or impurity in the Bible, though Jesus used it earlier as a positive metaphor (13:33).

16:12 teaching of the Pharisees and Sadducees Likely a reference to their oral traditions (see 15:2 and note), as well as their opposition to Jesus.

16:13–20 Peter reaffirms Jesus' identity as Messiah (compare 14:33 and note). In response, Jesus promises to establish his church in an enduring way through Peter.

16:13 Caesarea Philippi City about 25 miles north of the Sea of Galilee, at the base of Mount Hermon and near the source of the Jordan River. In NT times, a cult

¹⁴They replied, "Some say John the Baptist; others say Elijah; and still others, Jeremiah or one of the prophets."

¹⁵"But what about you?" he asked. "Who do you say I am?"

¹⁶Simon Peter answered, "You are the Messiah, the Son of the living God."

¹⁷Jesus replied, "Blessed are you, Simon son of Jonah, for this was not revealed to you by flesh and blood, but by my Father in heaven. ¹⁸And I tell you that you are Peter,ᵃ and on this rock I will build my church, and the gates of Hadesᵇ will not overcome it. ¹⁹I will give you the keys of the kingdom of heaven; whatever you bind on earth will beᶜ bound in heaven, and whatever you loose on earth will beᶜ loosed in heaven." ²⁰Then he ordered his disciples not to tell anyone that he was the Messiah.

Jesus Predicts His Death

16:21-28pp — Mk 8:31 – 9:1; Lk 9:22-27

²¹From that time on Jesus began to explain to his disciples that he must go to Jerusalem and suffer many things at the hands of the elders, the chief priests and the teachers of the law, and that he must be killed and on the third day be raised to life.

²²Peter took him aside and began to rebuke him. "Never, Lord!" he said. "This shall never happen to you!"

²³Jesus turned and said to Peter, "Get behind me, Satan! You are a stumbling block to me; you do not have in mind the concerns of God, but merely human concerns."

²⁴Then Jesus said to his disciples, "Whoever wants to be my disciple must deny themselves and take up their cross and follow me. ²⁵For whoever wants to save their lifeᵈ will lose it, but whoever loses their life for me will find it. ²⁶What good will it be for someone to gain the whole world, yet forfeit their soul? Or what can anyone give in exchange for their soul? ²⁷For the Son of Man is going to come in his Father's glory with his angels, and then he will reward each person according to what they have done.

²⁸"Truly I tell you, some who are standing here will not taste death before they see the Son of Man coming in his kingdom."

ᵃ 18 The Greek word for *Peter* means *rock*. ᵇ 18 That is, the realm of the dead ᶜ 19 Or *will have been* ᵈ 25 The Greek word means either *life* or *soul*; also in verse 26.

---

center for the worship of Pan was carved into mountain rocks there, as well as a temple dedicated to Zeus, the chief god in the Greco-Roman pantheon. **the Son of Man** See 8:20 and note.

16:14 Some say John the Baptist Given the proximity and closely aligned message of Jesus and John the Baptist, this is a natural connection (see ch. 3; compare Mk 1:7–8,14–15). **Elijah** Jesus' ministry closely reflects Elijah's. According to Mal 4:5, the coming of Elijah would precede the great and terrible day of Yahweh (final judgment). The portrayal of John as Elijah signals that Mal 4:5 already has been fulfilled (see Mt 11:14). Therefore, the judgment is near, and the kingdom of heaven inaugurated by the Messiah will soon arrive in fullness (compare 4:17). **Jeremiah** A prophet of judgment and repentance who was strongly opposed by the religious leaders of his day.

16:16 You are the Messiah The Greek word used here, *christos*, meaning "Christ," "Messiah," or "anointed one," is equivalent to the Hebrew, *mashiach*, which primarily describes kings in the OT (see 1:1 and note).

16:17 Jonah Probably a reference to the name of Peter's father (compare Jn 1:42).

16:18 you are Peter There is a wordplay here, as the name Peter is associated with the word for "rock" in both Greek (the language of the NT text) and Aramaic (the language spoken by Jesus and the disciples). **on this rock** This may refer to Jesus, Peter as a leader (compare Mt 16:16), Peter as a representative of the leadership of the church, or the church in general. **the gates of Hades** In this instance, this likely refers to the realm of the dead in general (the underworld)—similar to the Hebrew word *she'ol*. Jesus and his disciples are at Caesarea Philippi, located at the base of Mount Hermon. This region is affiliated in ancient Near Eastern, Jewish and Greek literature with the gateway to the underworld, the gods and other spiritual beings. The OT also affiliates the region, called Bashan in the OT, with an evil giant

clan and idolatry (Dt 2:10–12; 3:1,10–11; Jos 12:1–5). Jesus seems to be saying that through his power, the church will overcome the powers of evil and death itself.

16:19 keys of the kingdom of heaven Refers either to the authoritative roles given to Peter and the apostles or to the church as the advocate for God's ways and spreader of the message of salvation. **whatever you bind** Binding and releasing may refer to what Peter and the church leaders prohibit (bind) or permit (release). This seems to indicate that the church and its leadership are given authority to carry out God's will and to oppose the powers of evil (compare Mt 12:29–32).

16:20 not to tell anyone As the next passage indicates, Jesus knows that his Messianic role will involve suffering and death, and he apparently recognizes a divine timetable for these events to unfold. Compare 8:4 and note.

16:21–23 For the first time in Matthew's Gospel, Jesus predicts his death. Peter does not comprehend the notion of a suffering Messiah (compare Isa 52:13–53:12); instead, he focuses on the power and authority described in Mt 16:18–19. Jesus rebukes Peter for failing to grasp the larger purposes of God's plan.

16:21 From that time on This marks the end of Jesus' Galilean ministry, as he turns toward Jerusalem and the events that must take place there. **chief priests** Prominent priests who were involved in Jewish religious government. **teachers of the law** See note on 2:4.

16:22 Peter took him aside In Peter's view, the Messiah should not have to endure the suffering that Jesus predicts.

16:23 Get behind me, Satan With a sharp rebuke, Jesus confronts Peter's misunderstanding of the Messiah's ultimate mission. Peter's implicit desires align better with Satan's aims (to convince Jesus to avoid suffering and death; 4:1–11) than with God's plan (the cross).

The Transfiguration

17:1-8pp — Lk 9:28-36
17:1-13pp — Mk 9:2-13

17 After six days Jesus took with him Peter, James and John the brother of James, and led them up a high mountain by themselves. ²There he was transfigured before them. His face shone like the sun, and his clothes became as white as the light. ³Just then there appeared before them Moses and Elijah, talking with Jesus.

⁴Peter said to Jesus, "Lord, it is good for us to be here. If you wish, I will put up three shelters — one for you, one for Moses and one for Elijah."

⁵While he was still speaking, a bright cloud covered them, and a voice from the cloud said, "This is my Son, whom I love; with him I am well pleased. Listen to him!"

⁶When the disciples heard this, they fell facedown to the ground, terrified. ⁷But Jesus came and touched them. "Get up," he said. "Don't be afraid." ⁸When they looked up, they saw no one except Jesus.

⁹As they were coming down the mountain, Jesus instructed them, "Don't tell anyone what you have seen, until the Son of Man has been raised from the dead."

¹⁰The disciples asked him, "Why then do the teachers of the law say that Elijah must come first?"

¹¹Jesus replied, "To be sure, Elijah comes and will restore all things. ¹²But I tell you, Elijah has already come, and they did not recognize him, but have done to him everything they wished. In the same way the Son of Man is going to suffer at their hands." ¹³Then the disciples understood that he was talking to them about John the Baptist.

Jesus Heals a Demon-Possessed Boy

17:14-19pp — Mk 9:14-28; Lk 9:37-42

¹⁴When they came to the crowd, a man approached Jesus and knelt before him. ¹⁵"Lord,

---

16:24–28 Jesus revisits his earlier remarks about taking up one's cross (10:38–39).

16:24 take up their cross See 10:38 and note.
16:25 whoever wants to save their life Compare 10:39.
16:27 the Son of Man is going to come Compare 13:37–43; see 8:20 and note.
16:28 the Son of Man coming in his kingdom The meaning here — and in the parallel statements at Mk 9:1 and Lk 9:27 — is difficult to determine. A reference to the transfiguration is unlikely, since it occurs only six days later (Mt 17:1). Options clearly corresponding to the disciples' lifetimes include: Jesus' resurrection; Jesus' ascension; the outpouring of the Holy Spirit at Pentecost; the powerful growth of Jesus' kingdom among non-Jewish people and divine judgment against Jerusalem and the temple, carried out by the Romans in AD 70. Various combinations of these options are possible as well.

17:1–13 Three disciples catch a glimpse of the intersection between heaven and earth, as they observe Jesus in his heavenly glory. See the event line "Jesus' Journey to Jerusalem" on p. 1616.

17:1 Peter, James and John the brother of James These men compose the inner circle of Jesus' disciples. They occasionally become privy to events that the rest of the group does not see. **a high mountain** There is no indication that Jesus and the disciples have moved away from Caesarea Philippi (16:13), located at the base of Mount Hermon. Another possibility is Mount Tabor, southwest of the Sea of Galilee.
17:2 he was transfigured Jesus' appearance changes in some way, apparently reflecting his heavenly glory. **His face shone like the sun** This description places Jesus within the prophetic tradition of Moses (see Ex 34:29,30,35; compare Da 12:3; Rev 1:16). **white as the light** Used elsewhere to describe heavenly garments (Mt 28:3; Mk 9:2–3; Rev 3:5).
17:3 Moses and Elijah The presence of these men might signify that both the Law (Moses) and the Prophets (Elijah) point to Jesus (see Mt 5:1 and note; 11:14 and note). Either directly or by allusion, Matthew often compares Jesus' ministry with those of Moses and Elijah

(4:8; 5:1; 8:1; 14:23; 15:29; 17:1,9; 28:16; compare Ex 34:1–9; 1Ki 19:1–18).
17:4 three shelters Describes temporary residences or tents.
17:5 bright cloud Reminiscent of Yahweh's presence appearing in a cloud in the OT (e.g., Ex 13:21; 16:10; 19:9; Nu 12:5). **a voice from the cloud said** A voice at Jesus' baptism speaks these same words, which reflect Ps 2:7 and Isa 42:1 (compare Mt 3:17; 12:18).
17:6 they fell facedown to the ground A typical response to a divine encounter (e.g., Eze 1:28; Da 10:9,15–19; Rev 1:17).
17:7 Don't be afraid A common divine greeting to mortals (e.g., Da 10:12; Ge 15:1; 21:17; Lk 1:13,30).
17:9 raised from the dead Jesus mentions his forthcoming resurrection for the second time (see Mt 16:21). **Son of Man** See 8:20 and note.
17:10 Elijah must come first Malachi had prophesied that Elijah would come before the Messiah (Mal 4:5). See note on Mt 11:14.
17:11 Elijah comes In vv. 11–12, Jesus could be referring to two Elijah-figures — one in the future and one in the past — or he might be restating the prophecy of Mal 4:5 and then speaking about its fulfillment in John the Baptist. If Jesus is speaking about two Elijah-figures, the identity of Elijah-to-come is unclear, although the reference to restoring all things suggests that it is Jesus at his second coming. Earlier in Matthew, Jesus identified Elijah-already-come as John the Baptist (Mt 11:14); this is confirmed again in v. 13.
17:12 done to him everything they wished Refers to John the Baptist's beheading (14:6–11).

17:14–20 Apparently back in Caesarea Philippi (16:13), Jesus encounters a demon-possessed person and demonstrates his power over evil. His disciples had tried to cast out the demon, but they failed due to their weak faith. At the end of this story, some ancient manuscripts have an extra verse (v. 21) in which Jesus gives a second reason for the disciples' failure: Casting out this kind of demon required prayer and fasting. This extra verse appears to have been added by a scribe, likely influenced by Mark's ending to this exorcism story (see Mk 9:29). See the table "Miracles of Jesus" on p. 1741.

have mercy on my son," he said. "He has seizures and is suffering greatly. He often falls into the fire or into the water. ¹⁶I brought him to your disciples, but they could not heal him."

¹⁷"You unbelieving and perverse generation," Jesus replied, "how long shall I stay with you? How long shall I put up with you? Bring the boy here to me." ¹⁸Jesus rebuked the demon, and it came out of the boy, and he was healed at that moment.

¹⁹Then the disciples came to Jesus in private and asked, "Why couldn't we drive it out?"

²⁰He replied, "Because you have so little faith. Truly I tell you, if you have faith as small as a mustard seed, you can say to this mountain, 'Move from here to there,' and it will move. Nothing will be impossible for you." [²¹]ᵃ

Jesus Predicts His Death a Second Time

²²When they came together in Galilee, he said to them, "The Son of Man is going to be delivered into the hands of men. ²³They will kill him, and on the third day he will be raised to life." And the disciples were filled with grief.

The Temple Tax

²⁴After Jesus and his disciples arrived in Capernaum, the collectors of the two-drachma temple tax came to Peter and asked, "Doesn't your teacher pay the temple tax?"

²⁵"Yes, he does," he replied.

When Peter came into the house, Jesus was the first to speak. "What do you think, Simon?" he asked. "From whom do the kings of the earth collect duty and taxes—from their own children or from others?"

²⁶"From others," Peter answered.

"Then the children are exempt," Jesus said to him. ²⁷"But so that we may not cause offense, go to the lake and throw out your line. Take the first fish you catch; open its mouth and you will find a four-drachma coin. Take it and give it to them for my tax and yours."

The Greatest in the Kingdom of Heaven

18:1-5pp — Mk 9:33-37; Lk 9:46-48

18 At that time the disciples came to Jesus and asked, "Who, then, is the greatest in the kingdom of heaven?"

²He called a little child to him, and placed the child among them. ³And he said: "Truly I tell you, unless you change and become like little children, you will never enter the kingdom of heaven. ⁴Therefore, whoever takes the lowly position of this child is the greatest in the kingdom of

ᵃ 21 Some manuscripts include here words similar to Mark 9:29.

17:17 perverse Jesus rebukes the people of his day for their weak faith and distorted perception (compare Dt 32:5,20). This criticism might be aimed at his disciples.

17:20 faith as small as a mustard seed A minuscule amount of faith can overcome overwhelming obstacles. See Mt 13:31 and note.

17:22–23 Jesus again predicts his death and resurrection (compare 16:21; 17:9,12).

17:24–27 Unique to Matthew's Gospel, this passage addresses whether Jewish followers of Jesus' day should continue to pay the temple tax. This was particularly relevant to Matthew's audience, since they were most likely Jews. Jesus' response not only communicates the continued sanctity of the temple, but also demonstrates the miraculous ways in which God provides for his people.

17:24 the two-drachma temple tax Every Jewish man 20 years and older was required to pay the temple tax, which was used for the general maintenance of the temple (Ex 30:13–14,16). Priests (Levites) were exempt, and by Jesus' time some rabbis were as well. This section is particularly significant if Matthew's Gospel was compiled and circulated after AD 70. After the Romans destroyed Jerusalem and its temple in AD 70, they continued to enforce the temple tax. However, rather than use the funds to maintain the Jewish religious centers, the Romans used them for the temple of Jupiter Capitolinus. In doing so, they punished the Jews for their revolt. Matthew could have included this passage for the sake of his Jewish audience, who probably struggled with the idea of paying taxes for a pagan temple. Matthew might be advising his readers to pay the tax out of respect for their overlords (Mt 17:27) instead of enlisting further

reprisals from Rome. See the infographic "Coins of the Gospels" on p. 1613.

17:26 the children Just as children of earthly kings are tax-exempt, so too the children of the heavenly King, Jesus, have no obligation to pay a tax for his temple. Jesus' followers are not required to pay the temple tax, but he makes a way for them to do so anyway (compare 22:15–22).

17:27 may not cause offense Jesus gives instructions that allow Peter to pay the tax voluntarily, to avoid offending the authorities. **a four-drachma coin** A miraculous provision—and exactly the amount needed for Jesus and Peter to pay the temple tax. See the infographic "A Silver Denarius" on p. 1578.

18:1–14 The disciples' question prompts another discourse from Jesus. He uses this opportunity to teach on humility, the value of children (spiritual children, as well as literal children) and the need for holy living. Jesus also discusses the health and unity of the local congregation.

18:1 the greatest in the kingdom of heaven In the parallel passages of Mark and Luke, this question arises out of an argument among the disciples (Mk 9:33–37; Lk 9:46–48).

18:2 a little child Illustrates humility and dependence. For Jesus' audience, a child represented someone completely reliant on others—perhaps even a burden. Children were without status in the ancient world and at the mercy of adults.

18:3 become like little children Describes a change in attitude. Jesus contrasts the disciples' pride with the humility of children. Unlike children, who had no status, the disciples were expecting to be honored in God's kingdom.

heaven. ⁵And whoever welcomes one such child in my name welcomes me.

Causing to Stumble

⁶"If anyone causes one of these little ones — those who believe in me — to stumble, it would be better for them to have a large millstone hung around their neck and to be drowned in the depths of the sea. ⁷Woe to the world because of the things that cause people to stumble! Such things must come, but woe to the person through whom they come! ⁸If your hand or your foot causes you to stumble, cut it off and throw it away. It is better for you to enter life maimed or crippled than to have two hands or two feet and be thrown into eternal fire. ⁹And if your eye causes you to stumble, gouge it out and throw it away. It is better for you to enter life with one eye than to have two eyes and be thrown into the fire of hell.

The Parable of the Wandering Sheep

18:12-14pp — Lk 15:4-7

¹⁰"See that you do not despise one of these little ones. For I tell you that their angels in heaven always see the face of my Father in heaven. [11]a

¹²"What do you think? If a man owns a hundred sheep, and one of them wanders away, will he not leave the ninety-nine on the hills and go to look for the one that wandered off? ¹³And if he finds it, truly I tell you, he is happier about that one sheep than about the ninety-nine that did not wander off. ¹⁴In the same way your Father in heaven is not willing that any of these little ones should perish.

Dealing With Sin in the Church

¹⁵"If your brother or sister^b sins,^c go and point out their fault, just between the two of you. If they listen to you, you have won them over. ¹⁶But if they will not listen, take one or two others along, so that 'every matter may be established by the testimony of two or three witnesses.'^d ¹⁷If they still refuse to listen, tell it to the church; and if they refuse to listen even to the church, treat them as you would a pagan or a tax collector.

¹⁸"Truly I tell you, whatever you bind on earth will be^e bound in heaven, and whatever you loose on earth will be^e loosed in heaven.

---

^a 11 Some manuscripts include here the words of Luke 19:10.
^b 15 The Greek word for *brother or sister* (*adelphos*) refers here to a fellow disciple, whether man or woman; also in verses 21 and 35.
^c 15 Some manuscripts *sins against you*   ^d 16 Deut. 19:15
^e 18 Or *will have been*

18:4 greatest in the kingdom of heaven Paradoxically, humility leads to greatness.

18:6–9 In these verses, Jesus uses hyperbole (deliberate exaggeration) to make a point about the seriousness of sin. In Mt 18:6, Jesus warns about the danger awaiting anyone who causes another to sin. In v. 7, he expresses grief over things that cause people to stumble into sin. In vv. 8–9, Jesus' extreme statements reveal that the causes for stumbling may come from within ourselves.

18:6 these little ones Refers to status, not age (compare 10:42). Rather than indicating actual children, this description likely points to new or immature believers, or perhaps humble or lowly disciples of Jesus. **large millstone** Donkeys turned millstones to grind grain.

18:8 cut it off and throw it away Another use of hyperbole for the sake of making a point, not advice that should be taken literally. **better for you to enter life** Refers to eternal life (compare Jn 3:16–17). **eternal fire** A common symbol for divine judgment. See note on Lk 3:9.

18:9 thrown into the fire of hell Refers to the experience of God's wrath and ultimately destruction. See note on Mt 5:30.

18:10–14 This section anticipates Jesus' instructions in 18:15–20 about seeking lost sheep. In Luke, the parable of the lost sheep (Lk 15:3–7) appears in the context of Jesus' association with tax collectors and sinners. See the table "Parables of Jesus" on p. 1584.

18:10 one of these little ones See note on Mt 18:6. **their angels** The concept of guardian angels for individuals as well as nations pervades Jewish writings of this period (e.g., Da 10:13; Ac 12:15). By connecting these little ones to guardian angels, Jesus communicates their infinite worth; they mean so much to the Father that his angels watch out for them. See Heb 1:14.

18:14 perish Indicates being lost and ultimately destroyed.

18:15–20 In this section, Jesus explains how to handle a sinning brother or sister in the community.

18:15 just between the two of you Approaching the offender in private would avoid bringing shame on that person. It also would minimize the opportunity for misunderstanding and gossip.

18:16 the testimony of two or three witnesses This emphasizes the importance of the issue and provides the benefit of others' wisdom. It is unclear if these additional witnesses are meant to verify the original charge, as people who witnessed the wrongdoing, or to witness that the person has been charged of a wrongdoing. Either way, they become witnesses of the efforts to resolve it. See Dt 19:15.

18:17 the church The Greek word used here, *ekklēsia*, means "assembly." It occurs in other NT writings in reference to the corporate body of all believers (the body of Christ; e.g., Ac 9:31; 1Co 15:9; Eph 5:23; Col 1:18) as well as to a local congregation (e.g., Ac 13:1; 14:23; Ro 16:1,4–5). The *ekklēsia* as the body of Christ became a reality only in the wake of Jesus' ascension and Pentecost (Ac 1–2). While this reference was probably to a general assembly of Jewish people, it can be understood in retrospect as a reference to a gathering of Christians. **If they still refuse to listen** Reconciliation is the goal of Jesus' instruction; the entire assembly must try to bring the straying brother or sister back to the fold. **as you would a pagan or a tax collector** In the narrative's Jewish context, Gentiles and tax collectors would be regarded as outsiders (see note on Mt 5:46; note on 5:47). This instruction to cut ties with the unrepentant sinner is intended to remove sin from the local group of believers.

18:18 whatever you bind on earth See 16:19 and note.

¹⁹"Again, truly I tell you that if two of you on earth agree about anything they ask for, it will be done for them by my Father in heaven. ²⁰For where two or three gather in my name, there am I with them."

The Parable of the Unmerciful Servant

²¹Then Peter came to Jesus and asked, "Lord, how many times shall I forgive my brother or sister who sins against me? Up to seven times?"

²²Jesus answered, "I tell you, not seven times, but seventy-seven times.ᵃ

²³"Therefore, the kingdom of heaven is like a king who wanted to settle accounts with his servants. ²⁴As he began the settlement, a man who owed him ten thousand bags of goldᵇ was brought to him. ²⁵Since he was not able to pay, the master ordered that he and his wife and his children and all that he had be sold to repay the debt.

²⁶"At this the servant fell on his knees before him. 'Be patient with me,' he begged, 'and I will pay back everything.' ²⁷The servant's master took pity on him, canceled the debt and let him go.

²⁸"But when that servant went out, he found one of his fellow servants who owed him a hundred silver coins.ᶜ He grabbed him and began to choke him. 'Pay back what you owe me!' he demanded.

²⁹"His fellow servant fell to his knees and begged him, 'Be patient with me, and I will pay it back.'

³⁰"But he refused. Instead, he went off and had the man thrown into prison until he could pay the debt. ³¹When the other servants saw what had happened, they were outraged and went and told their master everything that had happened.

³²"Then the master called the servant in. 'You wicked servant,' he said, 'I canceled all that debt of yours because you begged me to. ³³Shouldn't you have had mercy on your fellow servant just as I had on you?' ³⁴In anger his master handed him over to the jailers to be tortured, until he should pay back all he owed.

³⁵"This is how my heavenly Father will treat each of you unless you forgive your brother or sister from your heart."

Divorce

19:1-9pp — Mk 10:1-12

19 When Jesus had finished saying these things, he left Galilee and went into the region of Judea to the other side of the Jordan. ²Large crowds followed him, and he healed them there.

³Some Pharisees came to him to test him. They asked, "Is it lawful for a man to divorce his wife for any and every reason?"

⁴"Haven't you read," he replied, "that at the beginning the Creator 'made them male and female,'ᵈ ⁵and said, 'For this reason a man will leave his father and mother and be united to his wife, and the two will become one flesh'ᵉ? ⁶So they are no

---

ᵃ 22 Or *seventy times seven*   ᵇ 24 Greek *ten thousand talents*; a talent was worth about 20 years of a day laborer's wages.   ᶜ 28 Greek *a hundred denarii*; a denarius was the usual daily wage of a day laborer (see 20:2).   ᵈ 4 Gen. 1:27   ᵉ 5 Gen. 2:24

18:21-35 Apparently in response to Jesus' statement in v. 15, Peter asks about the limitations of forgiveness. Jesus replies that he should forgive lavishly. This prompts the parable of the unforgiving servant.

18:21 Up to seven times A generous offer, but not enough for Jesus (see v. 22). In Lk 17:4, Jesus suggests unlimited forgiveness by using the number seven, which often represents totality or completeness.
18:22 seventy-seven times Represents an unlimited amount. Jesus tells Peter and the rest of his disciples that they should forgive continuously and without limit, just as God forgives them.
18:24 ten thousand bags of gold The servant owes roughly 150,000 years' worth of wages—an absurdly insurmountable debt intended to shock Jesus' listeners and pale in comparison to the much smaller amount demanded by the servant in Mt 18:28. The Greek text's reference to 10,000 talents represents the largest number used in ancient calculations and the highest monetary unit at that time (one talent was equivalent to 15 years' worth of wages).
18:25 be sold Being forced into slavery to settle a debt was common in the ancient world (e.g., Ex 22:3; 2Ki 4:1; Ne 5:1-5).
18:26 I will pay back everything An impossible undertaking, given the absurd amount.
18:28 a hundred silver coins Equal to 100 days' wages—a paltry sum in comparison to the servant's debt.
18:34 until he should pay back all he owed The man's debt was insurmountable; once in jail, he would not be able to make restitution.

19:1-12 When the Pharisees test Jesus with a question about divorce, he turns the tables on them to stress the permanence of marriage and corrects their misunderstanding about acceptable grounds for divorce.

19:1 went into the region of Judea Jesus may have taken a path that goes around Samaria to reach Judea. Both Galilee and Judea were west of the Jordan, so it was possible to travel between the two regions without crossing the Jordan River. However, because Jews and Samaritans despised each other (see note on Jn 4:9), Jews traveling between Galilee and Jerusalem would go out of their way to avoid Samaria. The southbound journey from Galilee involved crossing the Jordan River into Perea, heading south around Samaria, and then crossing back over the Jordan at Jericho to enter Judea. From there, it was roughly ten miles to Jerusalem.
19:3 Pharisees See note on Jn 1:24. **to test him** Their real intention is to discredit Jesus by getting him to contradict what Moses taught about divorce (compare Mt 16:1; 22:18,35). **for a man to divorce his wife** The Pharisees themselves had different interpretations of the law on divorce. The school of Hillel interpreted Dt 24:1 loosely and taught that Moses permitted divorce for any reason. The school of Shammai followed a stricter interpretation that allowed divorce only in cases of adultery. Compare Dt 24:1-4 and note.
19:4 male and female Jesus refers to the creation account (Ge 1:27).
19:5 the two will become one flesh Jesus appeals to Ge 2:24 to teach that God intended marriage to be permanent.

longer two, but one flesh. Therefore what God has joined together, let no one separate."

[7]"Why then," they asked, "did Moses command that a man give his wife a certificate of divorce and send her away?"

[8]Jesus replied, "Moses permitted you to divorce your wives because your hearts were hard. But it was not this way from the beginning. [9]I tell you that anyone who divorces his wife, except for sexual immorality, and marries another woman commits adultery."

[10]The disciples said to him, "If this is the situation between a husband and wife, it is better not to marry."

[11]Jesus replied, "Not everyone can accept this word, but only those to whom it has been given. [12]For there are eunuchs who were born that way, and there are eunuchs who have been made eunuchs by others—and there are those who choose to live like eunuchs for the sake of the kingdom of heaven. The one who can accept this should accept it."

The Little Children and Jesus

19:13-15pp — Mk 10:13-16; Lk 18:15-17

[13]Then people brought little children to Jesus for him to place his hands on them and pray for them. But the disciples rebuked them.

[14]Jesus said, "Let the little children come to me, and do not hinder them, for the kingdom of heaven belongs to such as these." [15]When he had placed his hands on them, he went on from there.

The Rich and the Kingdom of God

19:16-29pp — Mk 10:17-30; Lk 18:18-30

[16]Just then a man came up to Jesus and asked, "Teacher, what good thing must I do to get eternal life?"

[17]"Why do you ask me about what is good?" Jesus replied. "There is only One who is good. If you want to enter life, keep the commandments."

[18]"Which ones?" he inquired.

Jesus replied, "'You shall not murder, you shall not commit adultery, you shall not steal, you shall not give false testimony, [19]honor your father and mother,'[a] and 'love your neighbor as yourself.'[b]"

[20]"All these I have kept," the young man said. "What do I still lack?"

[21]Jesus answered, "If you want to be perfect, go, sell your possessions and give to the poor, and you will have treasure in heaven. Then come, follow me."

[22]When the young man heard this, he went away sad, because he had great wealth.

[a] *19* Exodus 20:12-16; Deut. 5:16-20   [b] *19* Lev. 19:18

19:7 "Why then," they asked, "did Moses command" At first, Jesus seems to be prohibiting all divorce, so the Pharisees invoke Moses' law as justification for divorce. See Dt 24.

19:8 hearts were hard Jesus is saying that Moses made a concession due to the sinful attitude of their Jewish ancestors.

19:9 except for sexual immorality Jesus allows for divorce—the tearing of a union made by God (Mt 19:6)—when someone is sexually unfaithful. To Jesus, divorce is never desirable. However, Jesus (and Moses before him) recognized that human sinfulness can irrevocably damage a marriage. In the Greek text, Jesus speaks only about men because, in the patriarchal culture of ancient Israel, only men had this type of legal right. It seems that Jesus' overall intention is not to specify every possible exception for divorce, but rather to emphasize the importance of keeping marriages intact. **marries another** Jesus seems to be addressing Dt 24:1, which speaks of a wife losing favor in her husband's eyes and then being divorced. Men might have been misusing this passage in Jesus' lifetime, as the Pharisees' questions seem to imply (Mt 19:3,7). Thus, Jesus likely is speaking about divorces that are based on the wrong reasons—such as a man choosing to divorce his wife so that he can be with another woman without committing adultery. The purpose of Jesus' statement is to emphasize that divorce goes against God's intention for marriage. He likely means that divorce for sinful reasons is the equivalent of adultery.

19:12 eunuchs who were born that way Refers to men who cannot reproduce due to a physical defect. **who have been made eunuchs by others** Refers in this instance to castration, whether intentional or accidental. In the ancient Near East, some slaves or palace officials would be castrated so that they could not sleep with the master's wife (or wives) or women in his harem. See note on Est 1:10. **choose to live like eunuchs** Refers

metaphorically to a voluntary decision to remain single and sexually abstinent. Jesus is not prescribing mutilation of the genitalia, as that would involve destroying God's creation. Compare 1Co 7:8–9.

19:13–15 In this short scene, Jesus welcomes children and lays his hands on them in prayer as a sign of blessing.

19:14 kingdom of heaven belongs to such as these Compare Mt 18:3–4.

19:16–30 Jesus uses this encounter with a wealthy young man to teach his disciples about the dangers of wealth. He also gives a glimpse into what awaits those who have left everything to follow him.

19:16 eternal life Describes life in the kingdom of the Messiah, which starts now but extends forever (compare Jn 3:16–17).

19:17 Why do you ask me about what is good God already had defined what is good when he gave the Israelites the Ten Commandments. **One who is good** Refers to God, the giver of the commandments.

19:18 Which ones Jesus responds with a representative sampling of the Ten Commandments (see Ex 20:2–17), to which he adds the command about loving one's neighbor (Lev 19:18).

19:21 perfect Describes being complete or mature. **sell your possessions** Jesus sees the young man's attachment to his possessions as a hindrance to faith. He commands the man to rid himself of whatever prevents him from making a total commitment to the kingdom of heaven. Jesus' instructions suggest that the man has not truly kept the commandments, beginning with the first one—the command to have no other gods except Yahweh (Ex 20:3). The man's wealth is his god, and he is unwilling to part with it.

19:22 he went away sad The only instance of someone declining to follow Jesus after a direct invitation.

²³Then Jesus said to his disciples, "Truly I tell you, it is hard for someone who is rich to enter the kingdom of heaven. ²⁴Again I tell you, it is easier for a camel to go through the eye of a needle than for someone who is rich to enter the kingdom of God."

²⁵When the disciples heard this, they were greatly astonished and asked, "Who then can be saved?"

²⁶Jesus looked at them and said, "With man this is impossible, but with God all things are possible."

²⁷Peter answered him, "We have left everything to follow you! What then will there be for us?"

²⁸Jesus said to them, "Truly I tell you, at the renewal of all things, when the Son of Man sits on his glorious throne, you who have followed me will also sit on twelve thrones, judging the twelve tribes of Israel. ²⁹And everyone who has left houses or brothers or sisters or father or mother or wife[a] or children or fields for my sake will receive a hundred times as much and will inherit eternal life. ³⁰But many who are first will be last, and many who are last will be first.

The Parable of the Workers in the Vineyard

20 "For the kingdom of heaven is like a landowner who went out early in the morning to hire workers for his vineyard. ²He agreed to pay them a denarius[b] for the day and sent them into his vineyard.

³"About nine in the morning he went out and saw others standing in the marketplace doing nothing. ⁴He told them, 'You also go and work in my vineyard, and I will pay you whatever is right.' ⁵So they went.

"He went out again about noon and about three in the afternoon and did the same thing. ⁶About five in the afternoon he went out and found still others standing around. He asked them, 'Why have you been standing here all day long doing nothing?'

⁷"'Because no one has hired us,' they answered.

"He said to them, 'You also go and work in my vineyard.'

⁸"When evening came, the owner of the vineyard said to his foreman, 'Call the workers and pay them their wages, beginning with the last ones hired and going on to the first.'

⁹"The workers who were hired about five in the afternoon came and each received a denarius. ¹⁰So when those came who were hired first, they expected to receive more. But each one of them also received a denarius. ¹¹When they received it, they began to grumble against the landowner. ¹²'These who were hired last worked only one hour,' they said, 'and you have made them equal to us who have borne the burden of the work and the heat of the day.'

¹³"But he answered one of them, 'I am not being unfair to you, friend. Didn't you agree to work for a denarius? ¹⁴Take your pay and go. I want to give the one who was hired last the same as I gave you. ¹⁵Don't

---

[a] 29 Some manuscripts do not have *or wife.*   [b] 2 A denarius was the usual daily wage of a day laborer.

19:24 through the eye of a needle Jesus employs this ridiculous impossibility to capture his hearers' attention and emphasize the great sacrifice necessitated by the kingdom of heaven (Mt 19:21). See note on Mk 10:25.
19:25 they were greatly astonished Jesus' remarks in Mt 19:23–24 reverse the conventional wisdom of his day. It was commonly believed that if someone was blessed with riches, they had God's approval and were thereby assured of entrance into his kingdom of heaven.
19:28 at the renewal of all things The larger trajectory of Jesus' comment is the forthcoming new heaven and earth (Rev 21). The language of the Greek text, though, implies a process—one that began with Jesus coming to earth and continues through the gospel spreading around the world (compare Ro 8:19–22; Mk 1:15). The culmination of this process is the new creation. **sit on twelve thrones, judging the twelve tribes** Jesus states that the Twelve will share in the leadership responsibilities of his kingdom—which they begin doing shortly after Jesus' ascension, when they become ambassadors for the gospel (see Ac 2).
19:30 many who are first will be last, and many who are last will be first Jesus describes an end-times reversal of roles in the kingdom of heaven. This statement corresponds with the reversal of expectations in Mt 19:23–24 (see note on v. 25).
20:1–16 Bracketed by role-reversal statements in 19:30 and 20:16, the parable of the vineyard workers portrays God's gracious generosity. See the table "Parables of Jesus" on p. 1584.

20:1 workers Indicates day-laborers, not slaves. As a result of heavy taxation, high debt and scarce resources, peasants in Jesus' day were forced to hire themselves out on a daily basis.
20:2 denarius A day's wage. See the infographic "A Silver Denarius" on p. 1578.
20:3 nine in the morning The Greek text identifies the time as the "third hour." The day was counted from 6 a.m. (first hour) to 6 p.m. (twelfth hour).
20:4 I will pay you whatever is right These day laborers probably assumed that they would be paid less because of their late start.
20:6 five in the afternoon The fact that the owner recruited workers this late in the day might indicate the urgency of the harvest (compare 9:37–38). It also shows the desperation of these workers who have been waiting all day for someone to hire them.
20:8 pay them their wages According to the law, hired workers had to be paid at the end of the day (see Lev 19:13; Dt 24:15). **beginning with the last ones hired and going on to the first** This wording associates the workers in the parable with Jesus' statements in Mt 19:30 and 20:16.
20:9 each received a denarius These workers are paid a full day's wage—which would have shocked Jesus' audience. See the infographic "Coins of the Gospels" on p. 1613.
20:12 you have made them equal to us Jesus' audience probably agreed that the owner was being unfair: Those who worked more should be paid more.

I have the right to do what I want with my own money? Or are you envious because I am generous?'

¹⁶"So the last will be first, and the first will be last."

Jesus Predicts His Death a Third Time

20:17-19pp — Mk 10:32-34; Lk 18:31-33

¹⁷Now Jesus was going up to Jerusalem. On the way, he took the Twelve aside and said to them, ¹⁸"We are going up to Jerusalem, and the Son of Man will be delivered over to the chief priests and the teachers of the law. They will condemn him to death ¹⁹and will hand him over to the Gentiles to be mocked and flogged and crucified. On the third day he will be raised to life!"

A Mother's Request

20:20-28pp — Mk 10:35-45

²⁰Then the mother of Zebedee's sons came to Jesus with her sons and, kneeling down, asked a favor of him.

²¹"What is it you want?" he asked.

She said, "Grant that one of these two sons of mine may sit at your right and the other at your left in your kingdom."

²²"You don't know what you are asking," Jesus said to them. "Can you drink the cup I am going to drink?"

"We can," they answered.

²³Jesus said to them, "You will indeed drink from my cup, but to sit at my right or left is not for me to grant. These places belong to those for whom they have been prepared by my Father."

²⁴When the ten heard about this, they were indignant with the two brothers. ²⁵Jesus called them together and said, "You know that the rulers of the Gentiles lord it over them, and their high officials exercise authority over them. ²⁶Not so with you. Instead, whoever wants to become great among you must be your servant, ²⁷and whoever wants to be first must be your slave — ²⁸just as the Son of Man did not come to be served, but to serve, and to give his life as a ransom for many."

Two Blind Men Receive Sight

20:29-34pp — Mk 10:46-52; Lk 18:35-43

²⁹As Jesus and his disciples were leaving Jericho, a large crowd followed him. ³⁰Two blind men were sitting by the roadside, and when they heard that Jesus was going by, they shouted, "Lord, Son of David, have mercy on us!"

³¹The crowd rebuked them and told them to be quiet, but they shouted all the louder, "Lord, Son of David, have mercy on us!"

³²Jesus stopped and called them. "What do you want me to do for you?" he asked.

³³"Lord," they answered, "we want our sight."

³⁴Jesus had compassion on them and touched their eyes. Immediately they received their sight and followed him.

Jesus Comes to Jerusalem as King

21:1-9pp — Mk 11:1-10; Lk 19:29-38
21:4-9pp — Jn 12:12-15

21 As they approached Jerusalem and came to Bethphage on the Mount of Olives, Jesus

---

20:14 I want to give the one who was hired last By ignoring when the workers started, the owner demonstrates grace — giving some more than they deserve.

20:17–19 Matthew includes a reminder that Jesus is on his way to Jerusalem.

20:17 Jesus was going up to Jerusalem This journey apparently began in Galilee (see note on 19:1). Travelers on this route would start uphill at Jericho (see v. 29; compare note on Mk 10:32). From there, it was about a ten-mile ascent to Jerusalem. See the event line "Jesus' Journey to Jerusalem" on p. 1616.

20:18 Son of Man See Mt 8:20 and note. **chief priests** Prominent priests who were involved in Jewish religious government. **teachers of the law** See note on 2:4.

20:20–28 The mother of James and John boldly asks Jesus to give her sons positions of honor in his kingdom of heaven. Jesus uses this as an opportunity to teach about humility.

20:20 the mother of Zebedee's sons She apparently was traveling with Jesus and her sons (27:55–56).
20:21 at your right and the other at your left Refers to preeminent positions of authority and honor — the first and second in importance after Jesus himself.
20:22 the cup I am going to drink Refers to suffering (26:39; compare Jn 18:11; Ps 75:8; Isa 51:17; Zec 12:2). **We can** The disciples probably didn't understand exactly what Jesus was talking about.

20:23 You will indeed drink from my cup Both men ultimately suffer. James was executed as a martyr by Herod Agrippa (Ac 12:1–2). John was persecuted and banished to the island of Patmos (Rev 1:9), but it is not clear whether he was martyred. According to writers in the early church, John died as an old man in Ephesus (see note on Jn 21:23).
20:26 must be your servant Another paradoxical statement of role-reversal (compare Mt 19:30; 20:16). Rather than exercising authority, a godly leader willingly becomes a servant of others.
20:28 but to serve Jesus does not merely instruct his disciples about what they should do; he models it for them.

20:29–34 In the final episode before Jesus' arrival in Jerusalem, Jesus is again shown to be the Messiah from David's line. Jesus continues to show his concern for the castoffs of society and heals two blind men whom the crowds attempt to silence.

20:29 Jericho Northwest of the Dead Sea, about ten miles from Jerusalem.
20:30 Son of David A Messianic title. See note on 1:1.

21:1–11 At the height of Messianic fervor, Jesus enters the holy city amid great pomp and pageantry. See the event line "Jesus' Passion and Resurrection" on p. 1698.

21:1 Bethphage Likely located near Bethany on the

sent two disciples, ²saying to them, "Go to the village ahead of you, and at once you will find a donkey tied there, with her colt by her. Untie them and bring them to me. ³If anyone says anything to you, say that the Lord needs them, and he will send them right away."

⁴This took place to fulfill what was spoken through the prophet:

⁵ "Say to Daughter Zion,
  'See, your king comes to you,
  gentle and riding on a donkey,
    and on a colt, the foal of a donkey.'"ᵃ

⁶The disciples went and did as Jesus had instructed them. ⁷They brought the donkey and the colt and placed their cloaks on them for Jesus to sit on. ⁸A very large crowd spread their cloaks on the road, while others cut branches from the trees and spread them on the road. ⁹The crowds that went ahead of him and those that followed shouted,

"Hosannaᵇ to the Son of David!"

"Blessed is he who comes in the name of the Lord!"ᶜ

"Hosannaᵇ in the highest heaven!"

¹⁰When Jesus entered Jerusalem, the whole city was stirred and asked, "Who is this?"

¹¹The crowds answered, "This is Jesus, the prophet from Nazareth in Galilee."

Jesus at the Temple
21:12-16pp — Mk 11:15-18; Lk 19:45-47

¹²Jesus entered the temple courts and drove out all who were buying and selling there. He overturned the tables of the money changers and the benches of those selling doves. ¹³"It is written," he said to them, "'My house will be called a house of prayer,'ᵈ but you are making it 'a den of robbers.'ᵉ"

¹⁴The blind and the lame came to him at the temple, and he healed them. ¹⁵But when the chief priests and the teachers of the law saw the wonderful things he did and the children shouting in the temple courts, "Hosanna to the Son of David," they were indignant.

¹⁶"Do you hear what these children are saying?" they asked him.

"Yes," replied Jesus, "have you never read,

"'From the lips of children and infants
  you, Lord, have called forth your praise'ᶠ?"

¹⁷And he left them and went out of the city to Bethany, where he spent the night.

ᵃ 5 Zech. 9:9   ᵇ 9 A Hebrew expression meaning "Save!" which became an exclamation of praise; also in verse 15   ᶜ 9 Psalm 118:25,26   ᵈ 13 Isaiah 56:7   ᵉ 13 Jer. 7:11   ᶠ 16 Psalm 8:2 (see Septuagint)

---

eastern slope of the Mount of Olives. **Mount of Olives** East of Jerusalem across the Kidron Valley. It offers a panoramic view of Jerusalem and the temple.

21:2 the village ahead of you Refers to Bethphage or perhaps Bethany, which was nearby.

21:4 the prophet Refers to Zechariah. The quotation that follows is from Zec 9:9 (compare Isa 62:11).

21:5 Daughter Zion Refers to Jerusalem and its inhabitants. See the table "Jesus' Fulfillment of OT Prophecy" on p. 1573.

21:7 the donkey and the colt Matthew includes both animals; the other Gospels mention only a colt (Mk 11:1–7; Lk 19:30–35; Jn 12:14–15). See note on 1Ki 1:33. **to sit on** Another son of David, Solomon, rode in a similar royal procession (1Ki 1:38–40).

21:8 A very large crowd This crowd probably consists of peasants, most of whom seem to have accompanied Jesus from Galilee. Unlike the city dwellers who later call for Jesus' death (Mt 27:22–25), these peasants believe that he is the Messiah. **spread them on the road** Part of the crowd's acknowledgment that Jesus was King. Compare 2Ki 9:13 and note.

21:9 Hosanna This Hebrew expression, meaning "help" or "save us," developed into a liturgical expression of praise. **who comes in the name of the Lord** The crowd understood that Jesus was declaring himself to be the Messiah. Their shouts of praise reflect Ps 118:25–26. See the table "Messianic Psalms" on p. 847.

21:10 Jesus entered Jerusalem This procession symbolizes Jesus' messiahship. In Jesus' day, dignitaries would go on procession through a city in an act of triumph or celebration. City officials would welcome the dignitary outside the gates, and the group would parade victoriously to the city's temple. The people would offer a sacrifice to honor the dignitary and acclaim his gods, and a feast would be held.

21:11 the prophet This title came to have Messianic overtones (compare Dt 18:18).

21:12–17 In keeping with custom, Jesus' procession ends at the temple (see Mt 21:10 and note). He disrupts the merchants in righteous anger, replacing their commercial activity with healings. The crowds hail him as the Messianic Son of David, which angers the religious leaders (v. 15).

21:12 buying and selling Merchants were selling animals for sacrifices, and money changers converted the foreign currency of pilgrims into the temple's official currency. See note on Mk 11:15. **doves** The poor offered these in place of lambs (Lev 5:7–10).

21:13 a den of robbers Jesus' rebuke—which quotes Isa 56:7 and Jer 7:11—suggests that he is condemning corruption of the temple. This judgment might be aimed at commercial activity within the temple courts, or it might signal that oppressive (or unjust) practices were involved.

21:16 Do you hear The religious leaders are disturbed not only because the people hail Jesus as the Son of David, but also because he does not disavow this Messianic title. **From the lips of children** By quoting Ps 8:2, Jesus appears to confirm that the crowd's Messianic praises are appropriate.

21:17 Bethany A village roughly two miles from Jerusalem.

Jesus' Fulfillment of OT Prophecy

DESCRIPTION	NT REFERENCE	PROPHETIC PASSAGE(S) CITED/ FULFILLED
The virgin birth	Mt 1:22–23	Isa 7:14 (LXX)
The Messiah originating from Bethlehem	Mt 2:5–6	Combination of Mic 5:2 and 2Sa 5:2
The holy family escapes to Egypt	Mt 2:15	Hos 11:1
The massacre of the infants	Mt 2:17–18	Jer 31:15
The holy family settles in Nazareth	Mt 2:23	No clear OT referent; possibly alluding to Isa 11:1, or to the OT concept of a Nazirite (e.g., Jdg 13:5, 7; 16:17; 1Sa 2).
John the Baptist as precursor to Jesus	Mt 3:3; Mk 1:2–3; Lk 3:4–6	Combines elements of Mal 3:1; Isa 40:3; and Ex 23:20.
Jesus settles in Capernaum, in the territory of Zebulun and Naphtali	Mt 4:14–16	Isa 9:1–2
Jesus claims to fulfill the Law and the Prophets	Mt 5:17	No specific OT referent.
Jesus' ministry of healing and exorcism	Mt 8:17	Isa 53:4
Jesus appeals to Isaianic prophecy as proof that he is "the one who is to come"	Mt 11:4–6; compare Jn 6:14	Likely based on Isa 29:18–19; 35:5–6; 61:1–2.
John the Baptist prepares the way for Jesus	Mt 11:10; Lk 7:27	Based on Mal 3:1.
The secrecy of Jesus' ministry	Mt 12:17–21	Isa 42:1–4
Jesus offers the sign of Jonah	Mt 12:39–40; 16:4; Lk 11:29–30	Jesus here refers to the story of Jonah more broadly rather than to a specific prophetic quote.
The reason for Jesus' parabolic teaching	Mt 13:14–15; Mk 4:12; Lk 8:10	Isa 6:9–10
More prophetic support for Jesus' parabolic teaching	Mt 13:35	Ps 78:2
Jesus sitting on a donkey's colt	Mt 21:4–5; Jn 12:15	Zec 9:9; compare Isa 62:11.
"Blessed is he (or, the king) who comes in the name of the Lord"	Mk 11:9; Lk 19:38; Jn 12:13	Ps 118:26
The suffering death of the Son of Man at the hands of Gentiles, and the resurrection	Lk 18:31–33	"the prophets"
The betrayal of the Son of Man	Mt 26:24; Mk 14:21	No clear OT references.
The desertion by the disciples	Mt 26:31; Mk 14:27	Based on Zec 13:7; compare Isa 53:6
Jesus' violent arrest	Mt 26:56	"the scriptures of the prophets"
The chief priests use Judas' abandoned blood money to purchase a field.	Mt 27:9–10	Matthew attributes the quote to Jeremiah (possibly thinking of both Jer 18:1–3 and 32:6–15), though the text is a paraphrase of Zec 11:13.

Jesus' Fulfillment of OT Prophecy *(continued)*

DESCRIPTION	NT REFERENCE	PROPHETIC PASSAGE(S) CITED/ FULFILLED
The mistreatment of the Son of Man	Mk 9:12	No clear OT references. Perhaps based partly on Ps 22:7.
The rejection of Jesus	Mk 12:10–11; Ac 4:11; Eph 2:20; 1Pe 2:7	Ps 118:22–23
Jesus presents himself as the fulfillment of Isaiah's prophecies	Lk 4:18–21	Combines elements of Isa 61:1–2; 58:6.
Jesus counted as one of the criminals	Lk 22:37	Based on Isa 53:12
The resurrected Jesus interprets Scripture with reference to Himself	Lk 24:26–27	No clear OT reference.
"Everything must be fulfilled that is written about me."	Lk 24:44	the law of Moses and the prophets and psalms
Jesus, the one about whom Moses and the prophets wrote	Jn 1:45	No explicit OT reference.
The cleansing of the temple	Jn 2:17	Ps 69:9
Moses wrote about Jesus	Jn 5:39,40,46,47	No explicit OT reference.
Jesus is the prophet like Moses	Jn 6:14; Acts 3:22–23	Dt 18:15–20
The Messiah is descended from David, and from Bethlehem	Jn 7:42	Ps 89:4; Mic 5:2
Authorities deny that Scripture predicts a prophet from Galilee	Jn 7:52	No explicit OT reference.
The rejection of Jesus	Jn 12:38–40	Quotes from Isa 6:10; 53:1
Hatred of Jesus	Jn 15:25	Likely based on Ps 35:19; 69:4; 109:3.
Roman soldiers divide Jesus' clothes and cast lots for his tunic	Jn 19:24	Ps 22:18
The Messiah must rise from the dead	Jn 20:9	No explicit OT reference.
Christ's death took place according to God's plan	Ac 2:23	Here "plan" may allude to prophetic fulfillment, i.e., that God's plan concerning Christ is discernible in the OT.
Christ's resurrection was spoken of by David	Ac 2:25–28	Ps 16:8–11
The Messiah's resurrection	Ac 2:31; 13:32–33; 26:22–23	Ps 2:7; 16:10
God, through the prophets, foretold the suffering of the Messiah	Ac 3:18	Referring back to the proof-texts in Ac 2:23–31.
Gentile authorities stand against the Messiah	Ac 4:25–26	Ps 2:1–2
Philip teaches the Ethiopian eunuch that Isaianic prophecy refers to Jesus	Ac 8:32–35	Isa 53:7–8

Jesus Curses a Fig Tree

21:18-22pp — Mk 11:12-14,20-24

[18]Early in the morning, as Jesus was on his way back to the city, he was hungry. [19]Seeing a fig tree by the road, he went up to it but found nothing on it except leaves. Then he said to it, "May you never bear fruit again!" Immediately the tree withered.

[20]When the disciples saw this, they were amazed. "How did the fig tree wither so quickly?" they asked.

[21]Jesus replied, "Truly I tell you, if you have faith and do not doubt, not only can you do what was done to the fig tree, but also you can say to this mountain, 'Go, throw yourself into the sea,' and it will be done. [22]If you believe, you will receive whatever you ask for in prayer."

21:18–22 When Jesus reenters Jerusalem the next morning, he pronounces a curse on a barren fig tree as a symbolic act of judgment against the city and its leaders. In rejecting the Messiah, Jerusalem is failing to fulfill its purpose—just like the fig tree.

21:19 Immediately the tree withered The fig tree is a common OT metaphor for Israel, and fruitless fig trees represented judgment (e.g., Isa 34:4; Jer 24:1–10; Hos 2:12; Joel 1:7). Compare Mk 11:12–14,20–21.

Jesus' Fulfillment of OT Prophecy (continued)

DESCRIPTION	NT REFERENCE	PROPHETIC PASSAGE(S) CITED/FULFILLED
The prophets testify to Jesus and forgiveness of sins through his name	Ac 10:43	"the prophets"
Jesus the savior from the seed of David	Ac 13:22-23	No specific OT reference.
The death of the Messiah	Ac 13:29; 26:22-23; 1Pe 1:10-11	"the prophets and Moses" in Ac 26:22
The Messiah's resurrection and protection from corruption	Ac 13:34-35	Isa 55:3 (LXX); Ps 16:10
The gospel promised beforehand in the Scriptures	Ro 1:2	"through his prophets"
The righteousness of God through faith in Christ is attested by the Law and the Prophets	Ro 3:21-22	"the law and the prophets"
The Deliverer from Zion	Ro 11:26-27	Isa 59:20-21
"Christ did not please himself"	Ro 15:3	Ps 68:10
Christ became a servant of the Jews so that Gentiles would come to glorify God	Ro 15:8-12; Ac 26:22-23	Ps 18:49; Dt 32:43 (LXX); Ps 117:1; Isa 11:10 (LXX)
"Christ died for our sins according to the Scriptures"	1Co 15:3-4	No specific OT reference.
Christ became a "life-giving spirit" as a natural development from the fleshly Adam	1Co 15:45	Ge 2:7
Christ became a curse	Gal 3:13	See Ge 12:3; Dt 27:15-26; 28:15-68.
God's Son was temporarily made "a little lower than the angels"	Heb 2:7	Ps 8:4-6
The Messiah's death and resurrection	1Pe 1:10-11	"the prophets"

The Authority of Jesus Questioned

21:23-27pp — Mk 11:27-33; Lk 20:1-8

²³Jesus entered the temple courts, and, while he was teaching, the chief priests and the elders of the people came to him. "By what authority are you doing these things?" they asked. "And who gave you this authority?"

²⁴Jesus replied, "I will also ask you one question. If you answer me, I will tell you by what authority I am doing these things. ²⁵John's baptism — where did it come from? Was it from heaven, or of human origin?"

They discussed it among themselves and said, "If we say, 'From heaven,' he will ask, 'Then why didn't you believe him?' ²⁶But if we say, 'Of human origin' — we are afraid of the people, for they all hold that John was a prophet."

²⁷So they answered Jesus, "We don't know."

Then he said, "Neither will I tell you by what authority I am doing these things.

The Parable of the Two Sons

²⁸"What do you think? There was a man who had two sons. He went to the first and said, 'Son, go and work today in the vineyard.'

²⁹"'I will not,' he answered, but later he changed his mind and went.

³⁰"Then the father went to the other son and said the same thing. He answered, 'I will, sir,' but he did not go.

³¹"Which of the two did what his father wanted?"

"The first," they answered.

Jesus said to them, "Truly I tell you, the tax collectors and the prostitutes are entering the kingdom of God ahead of you. ³²For John came to you to show you the way of righteousness, and you did not believe him, but the tax collectors and the prostitutes did. And even after you saw this, you did not repent and believe him.

The Parable of the Tenants

21:33-46pp — Mk 12:1-12; Lk 20:9-19

³³"Listen to another parable: There was a landowner who planted a vineyard. He put a wall around it, dug a winepress in it and built a watchtower. Then he rented the vineyard to some farmers and moved to another place. ³⁴When the harvest time approached, he sent his servants to the tenants to collect his fruit.

³⁵"The tenants seized his servants; they beat one, killed another, and stoned a third. ³⁶Then he sent other servants to them, more than the first time, and the tenants treated them the same way. ³⁷Last of all, he sent his son to them. 'They will respect my son,' he said.

³⁸"But when the tenants saw the son, they said to each other, 'This is the heir. Come, let's kill him and take his inheritance.' ³⁹So they took him and threw him out of the vineyard and killed him.

⁴⁰"Therefore, when the owner of the vineyard comes, what will he do to those tenants?"

⁴¹"He will bring those wretches to a wretched end," they replied, "and he will rent the vineyard to other tenants, who will give him his share of the crop at harvest time."

⁴²Jesus said to them, "Have you never read in the Scriptures:

"'The stone the builders rejected
   has become the cornerstone;
the Lord has done this,
   and it is marvelous in our eyes'^a?

⁴³"Therefore I tell you that the kingdom of God

---

^a *42* Psalm 118:22,23

21:23–27 The Jewish leaders demand to know the source of Jesus' authority, but he declines to answer them. His miraculous deeds and the people's praises have already borne witness to his divine authority.

21:24 If you answer me The answer to his question would reveal the answer to theirs. That is, if the Jewish officials answered correctly about John's authority (that his baptism was from heaven), then they would have their answer about Jesus' authority (also from heaven). What was true of John was true of Jesus, since John served as his prophetic forerunner.

21:25 from heaven A way of referring to God without using his sacred name.

21:28—22:14 Jesus condemns the Jews' rejection of him through three parables. The first parable involves two sons (Mt 21:28–32); the second is about tenant farmers in a vineyard (vv. 33–46); the third is about a wedding feast (22:1–14). See the table "Parables of Jesus" on p. 1584.

21:28 the first Symbolizes repentant sinners (i.e., the tax collectors and prostitutes; v. 32).

21:30 the other Represents the religious leaders, who ultimately reject Jesus (vv. 45–46).

21:33 a vineyard Jesus draws on imagery from Isaiah's parable of the vineyard (Isa 5:1–7). In Isaiah, the problem is the lack of fruit, and the solution is the destruction of the vineyard. In Jesus' parable, the problem is the tenants, who refuse the owner his fruit. The solution is replacing the tenants. **to some farmers** Represents the religious leaders of Israel who rejected Jesus.

21:42 The stone A quotation of Ps 118:22–23; the rejected stone is Jesus, who comes from Yahweh.

21:43 will be taken away Together with the quotation in the previous verse, Jesus' declaration here confirms that the judgment predicted by the religious leaders will indeed come to pass (Mt 21:41). **to a people who will produce its fruit** Compare the barren fig tree (vv. 18–22 and note). This passage does not necessarily describe the church replacing Israel, but identifies those worthy of being the tenants of God's kingdom: people who recognize the identity of the Son (Jesus). Identity in the kingdom of heaven, as Jesus' followers, is demonstrated by acting according to God's will—which the religious leaders of Israel failed to do (see Mt 21:12–17; compare 21:28–32).

will be taken away from you and given to a people who will produce its fruit. [44] Anyone who falls on this stone will be broken to pieces; anyone on whom it falls will be crushed."[a]

[45] When the chief priests and the Pharisees heard Jesus' parables, they knew he was talking about them. [46] They looked for a way to arrest him, but they were afraid of the crowd because the people held that he was a prophet.

The Parable of the Wedding Banquet

22:2-14Ref — Lk 14:16-24

22 Jesus spoke to them again in parables, saying: [2] "The kingdom of heaven is like a king who prepared a wedding banquet for his son. [3] He sent his servants to those who had been invited to the banquet to tell them to come, but they refused to come.

[4] "Then he sent some more servants and said, 'Tell those who have been invited that I have prepared my dinner: My oxen and fattened cattle have been butchered, and everything is ready. Come to the wedding banquet.'

[5] "But they paid no attention and went off — one to his field, another to his business. [6] The rest seized his servants, mistreated them and killed them. [7] The king was enraged. He sent his army and destroyed those murderers and burned their city.

[8] "Then he said to his servants, 'The wedding banquet is ready, but those I invited did not deserve to come. [9] So go to the street corners and invite to the banquet anyone you find.' [10] So the servants went out into the streets and gathered all the people they could find, the bad as well as the good, and the wedding hall was filled with guests.

[11] "But when the king came in to see the guests, he noticed a man there who was not wearing wedding clothes. [12] He asked, 'How did you get in here without wedding clothes, friend?' The man was speechless.

[13] "Then the king told the attendants, 'Tie him hand and foot, and throw him outside, into the darkness, where there will be weeping and gnashing of teeth.'

[14] "For many are invited, but few are chosen."

Paying the Imperial Tax to Caesar

22:15-22pp — Mk 12:13-17; Lk 20:20-26

[15] Then the Pharisees went out and laid plans to trap him in his words. [16] They sent their disciples to him along with the Herodians. "Teacher," they said, "we know that you are a man of integrity and that you teach the way of God in accordance with the truth. You aren't swayed by others, because you pay no attention to who they are. [17] Tell us then, what is your opinion? Is it right to pay the imperial tax[b] to Caesar or not?"

[18] But Jesus, knowing their evil intent, said, "You hypocrites, why are you trying to trap me? [19] Show me the coin used for paying the tax." They brought him a denarius, [20] and he asked them, "Whose image is this? And whose inscription?"

[21] "Caesar's," they replied.

Then he said to them, "So give back to Caesar what is Caesar's, and to God what is God's."

[22] When they heard this, they were amazed. So they left him and went away.

---

[a] 44 Some manuscripts do not have verse 44.   [b] 17 A special tax levied on subject peoples, not on Roman citizens

---

21:44 on this stone Jesus likely is alluding to Isa 8:14; 28:16. Compare Da 2:34–35,44–45.
21:45 Pharisees See note on Jn 1:24.
22:2 The kingdom of heaven See note on Mt 3:2. **a wedding banquet** Festivities for such an event would have lasted several days. In this parable, Jesus alludes to the great end-times feast (compare 8:11 and note), when God's people will enjoy fellowship with the Messiah in his fully inaugurated kingdom (compare Rev 19:6–10).
22:3 they refused to come These invited guests represent those who respond to the message of the kingdom of heaven with indifference (v. 5) and hostility (v. 6).
22:7 burned their city Foreshadows the Romans' destruction of Jerusalem in AD 70.
22:11 who was not wearing wedding clothes This man accepted the king's invitation, but on his own terms — which the king found improper.
22:13 weeping and gnashing of teeth Reactions of great anguish. This signals that Jesus is talking about a time of judgment — likely upon his return (see note on Mt 8:12).
22:14 For many are invited, but few are chosen Summarizes the theme of the preceding parables (21:28 — 22:14). God invites many people into his kingdom, as seen in the parable Jesus has just told (22:1–13).

However, as the man thrown out of the wedding feast illustrates (vv. 11–13), not all who consider themselves part of God's kingdom are genuine members of it (compare 7:13–14,21–23). Those who hear and respond favorably to God's invitation are able to join him in celebration (compare 25:31–46).

22:15–22 Using a question about taxes, the Pharisees aim to get Jesus to speak against the emperor — which would support a charge of treason. This exchange is similar to 19:3–9, where their question about divorce sought to draw Jesus into contradicting the Jewish law.
22:16 Herodians Likely refers to Jews who supported Herod Antipas and, by extension, Roman rule. Although it was unusual for the Pharisees — who opposed Roman occupation — to work with Herodians, in this case it was practical: The presence of the Herodians ensures that any remarks against the empire would be reported to the proper authorities. **we know that you are a man of integrity** This flattery is intended to provoke Jesus into criticizing imperial taxes.
22:17 Is it right to pay the imperial tax to Caesar A clever query. Answering yes could discredit Jesus among the people for supporting the empire; but answering no would incriminate him for opposing it.
22:21 give back to Caesar what is Caesar's Jesus

Marriage at the Resurrection

22:23-33pp — Mk 12:18-27; Lk 20:27-40

²³That same day the Sadducees, who say there is no resurrection, came to him with a question. ²⁴"Teacher," they said, "Moses told us that if a man dies without having children, his brother must marry the widow and raise up offspring for him. ²⁵Now there were seven brothers among us. The first one married and died, and since he had no children, he left his wife to his brother. ²⁶The same thing happened to the second and third brother,

right on down to the seventh. ²⁷Finally, the woman died. ²⁸Now then, at the resurrection, whose wife will she be of the seven, since all of them were married to her?"

²⁹Jesus replied, "You are in error because you do not know the Scriptures or the power of God. ³⁰At the resurrection people will neither marry nor be given in marriage; they will be like the angels in heaven. ³¹But about the resurrection of the dead — have you not read what God said to you, ³²'I am the God of Abraham, the God of Isaac, and

brilliantly avoids the Pharisees' trap (compare note on v. 17). Since the coin bears Caesar's image, it belongs to him. However, God should likewise be given his due — the faithful obedience of humanity, which bears his image (Ge 1:27). See the infographic "A Silver Denarius" below; see the infographic "Coins of the Gospels" on p. 1613.

22:23–33 The Sadducees ask Jesus a question about the future resurrection of the dead (a belief they did not support).

22:23 Sadducees This Jewish group apparently based its doctrine on the Pentateuch alone (see note on Mk 12:18). **22:24 Moses told** The Sadducees appeal to Moses as the mediator of the law. Deuteronomy 25:5–10 provides the law on levirate marriage, which calls for a man to marry his deceased brother's widow and produce an heir. **22:31 God said to you** They appealed to Moses, but Jesus appeals to God himself, who spoke to Moses. **22:32 I am the God of Abraham** Jesus quotes Ex 3:6

SILVER DENARIUS

The denarius was considered a fair day's pay for a common laborer in the first century. Jesus asked to see this coin when asked if it were lawful to pay taxes to Caesar (Mt 22:17–21).

What one coin could buy:
15 lbs. of wheat (in a basket).

Translation of coin text: "Tiberius Caesar, son of the divine [Augustus], [himself now] Augustus"

A Silver Denarius

When the Pharisees asked Jesus if it was lawful to pay taxes to Caesar, Jesus asked to see a coin for the tax. They gave him a denarius like this. The motto on this coin proclaims Tiberius to be the son of the divine Caesar who preceded him. Jesus, the true Son of God, would have recognized the irony of Tiberius' claim (Mt 22:17–22; Mk 12:14–17; Lk 20:21–26).

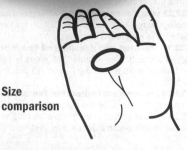

Size comparison

the God of Jacob'^{a}? He is not the God of the dead but of the living."

^{33}When the crowds heard this, they were astonished at his teaching.

The Greatest Commandment

22:34-40pp — Mk 12:28-31

^{34}Hearing that Jesus had silenced the Sadducees, the Pharisees got together. ^{35}One of them, an expert in the law, tested him with this question: ^{36}"Teacher, which is the greatest commandment in the Law?"

^{37}Jesus replied: "'Love the Lord your God with all your heart and with all your soul and with all your mind.'^{b} ^{38}This is the first and greatest commandment. ^{39}And the second is like it: 'Love your neighbor as yourself.'^{c} ^{40}All the Law and the Prophets hang on these two commandments."

Whose Son Is the Messiah?

22:41-46pp — Mk 12:35-37; Lk 20:41-44

^{41}While the Pharisees were gathered together, Jesus asked them, ^{42}"What do you think about the Messiah? Whose son is he?"

"The son of David," they replied.

^{43}He said to them, "How is it then that David, speaking by the Spirit, calls him 'Lord'? For he says,

^{44}"'The Lord said to my Lord:
    "Sit at my right hand
    until I put your enemies
        under your feet."'^{d}

^{45}If then David calls him 'Lord,' how can he be his son?" ^{46}No one could say a word in reply, and from that day on no one dared to ask him any more questions.

A Warning Against Hypocrisy

23:1-7pp — Mk 12:38,39; Lk 20:45,46
23:37-39pp — Lk 13:34,35

23 Then Jesus said to the crowds and to his disciples: ^{2}"The teachers of the law and the Pharisees sit in Moses' seat. ^{3}So you must be careful to do everything they tell you. But do not do what they do, for they do not practice what they preach. ^{4}They tie up heavy, cumbersome loads and put them on other people's shoulders, but they themselves are not willing to lift a finger to move them.

^{5}"Everything they do is done for people to see: They make their phylacteries^e wide and the tassels on their garments long; ^{6}they love the place of honor at banquets and the most important seats in the synagogues; ^{7}they love to be greeted with respect in the marketplaces and to be called 'Rabbi' by others.

^{8}"But you are not to be called 'Rabbi,' for you have one Teacher, and you are all brothers. ^{9}And do not call anyone on earth 'father,' for you have one Father, and he is in heaven. ^{10}Nor are you to be called instructors, for you have one Instructor, the Messiah. ^{11}The greatest among you will be your

---

^{a} 32 Exodus 3:6 ^{b} 37 Deut. 6:5 ^{c} 39 Lev. 19:18
^{d} 44 Psalm 110:1 ^{e} 5 That is, boxes containing Scripture verses, worn on forehead and arm

---

(which, as part of the Pentateuch, was authoritative for the Sadducees; see note on Mt 22:23). This verse reports God's self-revelation to Moses at the burning bush. By saying "I am" (rather than "I was"), God indicates that his relationship with the patriarchs is ongoing even after their deaths—which supports a future resurrection (compare Rev 20:4–6,11–15).

22:34–40 The Pharisees again attempt to discredit Jesus—this time with a legal question.

22:36 which is the greatest commandment Among ancient Jewish legal experts, there was an ongoing attempt to prioritize the commandments. Their debates considered which laws were "light" and which were "weighty." In this case, their goal was not to gain insight from Jesus but to induce him to say something they could use to discredit him. See the infographic "The Sanhedrin" on p. 1746.

22:37 Love the Lord your God A citation of Dt 6:5.

22:38 the first and greatest commandment Deuteronomy 6:5 also was one of the best-known commands, as it was part of the Shema—an ancient prayer recited by Jews twice every day.

22:39 Love your neighbor as yourself Jesus is referencing Lev 19:18 (compare Mt 7:12).

22:41–46 Jesus asks the Pharisees a textual question, which he expects they will easily answer as teachers of the Jewish scriptures (see note on 1:1).

22:44 The Lord said to my Lord "The Lord" refers to Yahweh; "my Lord" refers to the Messiah. See Ps 110:1. **your enemies under your feet** In the ancient Near East, warriors would stand on the necks of their defeated enemies as a sign of victory (e.g., Jos 10:24).

22:45 David calls him 'Lord,' how can he be his son Jesus' question hints at his Messianic identity, as the crowds had recently hailed him as the "Son of David" (Mt 21:9,15).

23:1–36 Chapter 23 presents the finale of Jesus' invective against Israel's religious leaders. He pronounces seven woes in response to their unbelief and hypocrisy. A parallel account appears in Lk 11:42–52.

23:2 teachers of the law See note on 2:4. **Pharisees** See note on Jn 1:24. **Moses' seat** Refers to the tradition and authority of Moses. The Pharisees believed that they alone interpreted the words of Moses properly.

23:4 They tie up heavy, cumbersome loads Refers to the traditions of the elders, not the law itself (see Mt 15:2 and note). This contrasts with the light, easy burden of Jesus (11:30).

23:5 phylacteries Likely refers to small boxes containing Scripture passages that Jews wore on their foreheads or arms. **tassels on their garments long** Refers to tassels on outer garments or prayer shawls (see Nu 15:37–39; Dt 22:12). Tassels reminded people to obey the commandments; the more visible the tassel, the more devout one appeared.

23:9 do not call anyone on earth 'father' The honorary

servant. [12] For those who exalt themselves will be humbled, and those who humble themselves will be exalted.

Seven Woes on the Teachers of the Law and the Pharisees

[13] "Woe to you, teachers of the law and Pharisees, you hypocrites! You shut the door of the kingdom of heaven in people's faces. You yourselves do not enter, nor will you let those enter who are trying to. [14] a

[15] "Woe to you, teachers of the law and Pharisees, you hypocrites! You travel over land and sea to win a single convert, and when you have succeeded, you make them twice as much a child of hell as you are.

[16] "Woe to you, blind guides! You say, 'If anyone swears by the temple, it means nothing; but anyone who swears by the gold of the temple is bound by that oath.' [17] You blind fools! Which is greater: the gold, or the temple that makes the gold sacred? [18] You also say, 'If anyone swears by the altar, it means nothing; but anyone who swears by the gift on the altar is bound by that oath.' [19] You blind men! Which is greater: the gift, or the altar that makes the gift sacred? [20] Therefore, anyone who swears by the altar swears by it and by everything on it. [21] And anyone who swears by the temple swears by it and by the one who dwells in it. [22] And anyone who swears by heaven swears by God's throne and by the one who sits on it.

[23] "Woe to you, teachers of the law and Pharisees, you hypocrites! You give a tenth of your spices — mint, dill and cumin. But you have neglected the more important matters of the law — justice, mercy and faithfulness. You should have practiced the latter, without neglecting the former. [24] You

blind guides! You strain out a gnat but swallow a camel.

[25] "Woe to you, teachers of the law and Pharisees, you hypocrites! You clean the outside of the cup and dish, but inside they are full of greed and self-indulgence. [26] Blind Pharisee! First clean the inside of the cup and dish, and then the outside also will be clean.

[27] "Woe to you, teachers of the law and Pharisees, you hypocrites! You are like whitewashed tombs, which look beautiful on the outside but on the inside are full of the bones of the dead and everything unclean. [28] In the same way, on the outside you appear to people as righteous but on the inside you are full of hypocrisy and wickedness.

[29] "Woe to you, teachers of the law and Pharisees, you hypocrites! You build tombs for the prophets and decorate the graves of the righteous. [30] And you say, 'If we had lived in the days of our ancestors, we would not have taken part with them in shedding the blood of the prophets.' [31] So you testify against yourselves that you are the descendants of those who murdered the prophets. [32] Go ahead, then, and complete what your ancestors started!

[33] "You snakes! You brood of vipers! How will you escape being condemned to hell? [34] Therefore I am sending you prophets and sages and teachers. Some of them you will kill and crucify; others you will flog in your synagogues and pursue from town to town. [35] And so upon you will come all the righteous blood that has been shed on earth, from the blood of righteous Abel to the blood of Zechariah son of Berekiah, whom you murdered between the temple and the altar. [36] Truly I tell you, all this will come on this generation.

a 14 Some manuscripts include here words similar to Mark 12:40 and Luke 20:47.

---

term "father" was commonly used for teachers (e.g., Ac 22:1).

23:13 Woe A prophetic indictment for behavior that will lead to disaster (e.g., Isa 5:8; Hab 2:6; Zec 11:17; compare Mt 11:21).

23:15 twice as much a child of hell An exaggerated expression that highlights the destructive nature of the teaching of the scribes (teachers of the law) and Pharisees. Compare note on 5:22.

23:16 blind guides See 15:14 and note. **If anyone swears by the temple** Refers to trivial distinctions about what made an oath binding. In the Sermon on the Mount, Jesus taught his followers to avoid swearing oaths (5:33–37).

23:23 you have neglected the more important matters of the law Jesus criticizes the religious leaders for paying meticulous attention to tiny details while disregarding the law's true heart.

23:27 whitewashed tombs Jews would paint their tombs white so that other Jews would not become unclean through inadvertent contact with a corpse (compare Nu 19:16; Lk 11:44).

23:29 You build tombs for the prophets Jesus denounces the scribes (teachers of the law) and Pharisees

for honoring the graves of prophets whom their ancestors killed.

23:32 complete what your ancestors started By instructing them to finish their fathers' murderous deeds, Jesus alludes to the scribes' (teachers of the law) and Pharisees' role in his impending death.

23:33 You brood of vipers See note on Mt 3:7. **being condemned to hell** Based on their current actions, the scribes (teachers of the law) and the Pharisees are on their way to experiencing God's judgment and wrath. Jesus' rhetorical language warns the Pharisees of the inevitability of their judgment unless they change course. See note on 5:22; note on 5:30.

23:35 the blood of righteous Abel The first person to be killed in the Bible (Ge 4:8,10). **Zechariah son of Berekiah** Jesus' statement about Abel and Zechariah likely is intended as a merism, a figure of speech that uses the ends of a range to indicate the whole (e.g., "from head to toe" refers to the entire body). The text appears to be pointing to the prophet Zechariah (Zec 1:1), whose death is not recorded. Alternatively, it could refer to the Zechariah of 2Ch 24:20–22, who was killed in the temple courtyard.

23:36 all this will come on this generation In light

³⁷"Jerusalem, Jerusalem, you who kill the prophets and stone those sent to you, how often I have longed to gather your children together, as a hen gathers her chicks under her wings, and you were not willing. ³⁸Look, your house is left to you desolate. ³⁹For I tell you, you will not see me again until you say, 'Blessed is he who comes in the name of the Lord.'ᵃ"

The Destruction of the Temple and Signs of the End Times

24:1-51pp — Mk 13:1-37; Lk 21:5-36

24 Jesus left the temple and was walking away when his disciples came up to him to call his attention to its buildings. ²"Do you see all these things?" he asked. "Truly I tell you, not one stone here will be left on another; every one will be thrown down."

³As Jesus was sitting on the Mount of Olives, the disciples came to him privately. "Tell us," they said, "when will this happen, and what will be the sign of your coming and of the end of the age?"

⁴Jesus answered: "Watch out that no one deceives you. ⁵For many will come in my name, claiming, 'I am the Messiah,' and will deceive many. ⁶You will hear of wars and rumors of wars, but see to it that you are not alarmed. Such things must happen, but the end is still to come. ⁷Nation will rise against nation, and kingdom against kingdom. There will be famines and earthquakes in various places. ⁸All these are the beginning of birth pains.

⁹"Then you will be handed over to be persecuted and put to death, and you will be hated by all nations because of me. ¹⁰At that time many will turn away from the faith and will betray and hate each other, ¹¹and many false prophets will appear and deceive many people. ¹²Because of the increase of wickedness, the love of most will grow cold, ¹³but the one who stands firm to the end will be saved. ¹⁴And this gospel of the kingdom will be preached in the whole world as a testimony to all nations, and then the end will come.

¹⁵"So when you see standing in the holy place 'the abomination that causes desolation,'ᵇ spoken of through the prophet Daniel — let the reader understand — ¹⁶then let those who are in Judea flee to the mountains. ¹⁷Let no one on the housetop go down to take anything out of the house. ¹⁸Let no one in the field go back to get their cloak. ¹⁹How dreadful it will be in those days for pregnant women and nursing mothers! ²⁰Pray that your flight will not take place in winter or on the Sabbath. ²¹For then there will be great distress, unequaled from the beginning of the world until now — and never to be equaled again.

²²"If those days had not been cut short, no one would survive, but for the sake of the elect those days will be shortened. ²³At that time if anyone says to you, 'Look, here is the Messiah!' or, 'There he is!' do not believe it. ²⁴For false messiahs and false prophets will appear and perform great signs and wonders to deceive, if possible, even the elect. ²⁵See, I have told you ahead of time.

²⁶"So if anyone tells you, 'There he is, out in the wilderness,' do not go out; or, 'Here he is, in the inner rooms,' do not believe it. ²⁷For as lightning that comes from the east is visible even in the

ᵃ 39 Psalm 118:26   ᵇ 15 Daniel 9:27; 11:31; 12:11

---

of Jesus' remarks in Mt 23:37—24:2, this may allude to the destruction of Jerusalem in AD 70.

23:37–39 Recalling the past rejection of God's prophets, Jesus laments his people's unwillingness to believe and repent.

23:37 gathers her chicks under her wings Compare Ps 17:8; 36:7; Isa 31:5.

23:39 until you say, 'Blessed is he who comes' Refers to Jesus' second coming.

24:1–2 Jesus' prediction that the temple will be destroyed sets up the next two chapters. See the event line "Jesus' Passion and Resurrection" on p. 1698.

24:3–44 The disciples ask Jesus about his prediction in Mt 24:2. He responds by discussing the troubling events that will signal his return and the end of the age. Jesus' teaching in 24:3—25:46 is commonly called the Olivet Discourse because it was his teaching on the Mount of Olives (v. 3).

24:3 Mount of Olives See 21:1 and note.

24:7 famines and earthquakes A common motif in apocalyptic writings (e.g., Rev 6:8,12; 16:18; 18:8).

24:8 birth pains This metaphor is used throughout the Bible in reference to suffering and judgment (e.g., Isa 26:17–18; Jer 22:23; 1Th 5:3).

24:13 will be saved Elsewhere, it is clear that salvation is dependent on Christ alone (compare Jn 3:16–17). It seems that here Jesus is contrasting those with true faith (compare Mt 13:18–23) — which proves itself through endurance, in the midst of persecution — with those who are willing to sacrifice their faith (24:10; compare 10:22). Faith requires action and perseverance (25:14–30).

24:14 will be preached Compare 28:19–20.

24:15 abomination that causes desolation This enigmatic term from Daniel describes an event of desecration and destruction (Da 8:13; 9:27; 11:31; 12:11). In Daniel, this term might refer to an altar to Zeus erected by Antiochus IV Epiphanes over the altar in the Jerusalem temple in 167 BC. In Matthew, the term may have had an idolatrous connotation; if so, it may be describing images of the Roman imperial eagle in and around the temple. Alternatively, the destruction of the temple itself might represent the abomination of desolation.

24:16 flee to the mountains Compare Zec 14:5.

24:20 in winter or on the Sabbath A winter flight would be difficult and dangerous. Traveling on the Sabbath was forbidden by the Law of Moses (Ex 16:29). A Sabbath flight also might limit opportunities to receive help along the way, due to restrictions on work.

24:27 as lightning Depicts the Son of Man's arrival as being sudden and unmistakable. **the coming** The Greek word used here, *parousia* (indicating "presence" or "arrival"), has developed into a technical term referring to Jesus' return in glory. **Son of Man** See Mt 8:20 and note.

west, so will be the coming of the Son of Man. [28] Wherever there is a carcass, there the vultures will gather.

[29] "Immediately after the distress of those days

"'the sun will be darkened,
  and the moon will not give its light;
the stars will fall from the sky,
  and the heavenly bodies will be shaken.'[a]

[30] "Then will appear the sign of the Son of Man in heaven. And then all the peoples of the earth[b] will mourn when they see the Son of Man coming on the clouds of heaven, with power and great glory.[c] [31] And he will send his angels with a loud trumpet call, and they will gather his elect from the four winds, from one end of the heavens to the other.

[32] "Now learn this lesson from the fig tree: As soon as its twigs get tender and its leaves come out, you know that summer is near. [33] Even so, when you see all these things, you know that it[d] is near, right at the door. [34] Truly I tell you, this generation will certainly not pass away until all these things have happened. [35] Heaven and earth will pass away, but my words will never pass away.

The Day and Hour Unknown

24:37-39pp — Lk 17:26,27
24:45-51pp — Lk 12:42-46

[36] "But about that day or hour no one knows, not even the angels in heaven, nor the Son,[e] but only the Father. [37] As it was in the days of Noah, so it will be at the coming of the Son of Man. [38] For in the days before the flood, people were eating and drinking, marrying and giving in marriage, up to the day Noah entered the ark; [39] and they knew nothing about what would hap-

pen until the flood came and took them all away. That is how it will be at the coming of the Son of Man. [40] Two men will be in the field; one will be taken and the other left. [41] Two women will be grinding with a hand mill; one will be taken and the other left.

[42] "Therefore keep watch, because you do not know on what day your Lord will come. [43] But understand this: If the owner of the house had known at what time of night the thief was coming, he would have kept watch and would not have let his house be broken into. [44] So you also must be ready, because the Son of Man will come at an hour when you do not expect him.

[45] "Who then is the faithful and wise servant, whom the master has put in charge of the servants in his household to give them their food at the proper time? [46] It will be good for that servant whose master finds him doing so when he returns. [47] Truly I tell you, he will put him in charge of all his possessions. [48] But suppose that servant is wicked and says to himself, 'My master is staying away a long time,' [49] and he then begins to beat his fellow servants and to eat and drink with drunkards. [50] The master of that servant will come on a day when he does not expect him and at an hour he is not aware of. [51] He will cut him to pieces and assign him a place with the hypocrites, where there will be weeping and gnashing of teeth.

The Parable of the Ten Virgins

25 "At that time the kingdom of heaven will be like ten virgins who took their lamps and went out to meet the bridegroom. [2] Five of

---

[a] 29 Isaiah 13:10; 34:4   [b] 30 Or *the tribes of the land*
[c] 30 See Daniel 7:13-14.   [d] 33 Or *he*   [e] 36 Some manuscripts do not have *nor the Son*.

24:28 the vultures will gather This expression may have been a proverb of Jesus' day. Just as vultures signal the presence of a corpse, these events will clearly signal the Son of Man's arrival.
24:29 the sun will be darkened Jesus quotes the Septuagint (the ancient Greek translation of the OT) versions of Isa 13:10; 34:4. These cosmic signs could be intended literally, figuratively, or both. In Exodus, the account of the ten plagues involves literal disturbances in the heavens (Ex 10:21–23). The OT prophets use similar language figuratively to prophesy God's judgment on Israel (e.g., Eze 32:7; Joel 2:10; Am 8:9).
24:30 sign of the Son of Man Probably refers to the Son of Man himself; he, Jesus, is the sign. **Son of Man coming on the clouds** Compare Da 7:13–14.
24:31 he will send his angels Compare Mt 13:41–43. **with a loud trumpet call** In the OT, trumpets typically accompany religious or military events (e.g., Jer 4:19; Joel 2:15; Zep 1:16). The sound of the trumpet is also a motif signaling the day of God's judgment (Isa 27:13; Zec 9:14; Zep 1:14–16; compare 1Co 15:52; 1Th 4:16 and note). **they will gather his elect** See note on Mt 24:40.
24:34 this generation See note on Mk 13:30.

24:40 one will be taken This phrase might describe the gathering of God's people to himself (Mt 24:31); if that is the case there is no indication here of what happens to the remaining people. The point of this parable is that believers need to be vigilant for Jesus' return, because it will be sudden and unexpected.

24:45–51 Jesus uses a parable to reiterate the need to be faithful.

24:51 weeping and gnashing of teeth Refers to great anguish—signaling that Jesus means that this type of person will experience God's judgment upon his return (see note on 8:12).

25:1–13 Continuing his discourse on the Mount of Olives (see note on 24:3–44), Jesus tells another parable that underscores his call to be prepared for the Son of Man's arrival (24:44). See the table "Parables of Jesus" on p. 1584.

25:1 virgins Refers to young women who are guests at a wedding, possibly as attendants to the bride. **to meet the bridegroom** To escort him to the wedding banquet (v. 10).

them were foolish and five were wise. ³The foolish ones took their lamps but did not take any oil with them. ⁴The wise ones, however, took oil in jars along with their lamps. ⁵The bridegroom was a long time in coming, and they all became drowsy and fell asleep.

⁶"At midnight the cry rang out: 'Here's the bridegroom! Come out to meet him!'

⁷"Then all the virgins woke up and trimmed their lamps. ⁸The foolish ones said to the wise, 'Give us some of your oil; our lamps are going out.'

⁹"'No,' they replied, 'there may not be enough for both us and you. Instead, go to those who sell oil and buy some for yourselves.'

¹⁰"But while they were on their way to buy the oil, the bridegroom arrived. The virgins who were ready went in with him to the wedding banquet. And the door was shut.

¹¹"Later the others also came. 'Lord, Lord,' they said, 'open the door for us!'

¹²"But he replied, 'Truly I tell you, I don't know you.'

¹³"Therefore keep watch, because you do not know the day or the hour.

The Parable of the Bags of Gold

25:14-30Ref — Lk 19:12-27

¹⁴"Again, it will be like a man going on a journey, who called his servants and entrusted his wealth to them. ¹⁵To one he gave five bags of gold, to another two bags, and to another one bag,ᵃ each according to his ability. Then he went on his journey. ¹⁶The man who had received five bags of gold went at once and put his money to work and gained five bags more. ¹⁷So also, the one with two bags of gold gained two more. ¹⁸But the man who had received one bag went off, dug a hole in the ground and hid his master's money.

¹⁹"After a long time the master of those servants returned and settled accounts with them. ²⁰The man who had received five bags of gold brought the other five. 'Master,' he said, 'you entrusted me with five bags of gold. See, I have gained five more.'

²¹"His master replied, 'Well done, good and faithful servant! You have been faithful with a few things; I will put you in charge of many things. Come and share your master's happiness!'

²²"The man with two bags of gold also came. 'Master,' he said, 'you entrusted me with two bags of gold; see, I have gained two more.'

²³"His master replied, 'Well done, good and faithful servant! You have been faithful with a few things; I will put you in charge of many things. Come and share your master's happiness!'

²⁴"Then the man who had received one bag of gold came. 'Master,' he said, 'I knew that you are a hard man, harvesting where you have not sown and gathering where you have not scattered seed. ²⁵So I was afraid and went out and hid your gold in the ground. See, here is what belongs to you.'

²⁶"His master replied, 'You wicked, lazy servant! So you knew that I harvest where I have not sown and gather where I have not scattered seed? ²⁷Well then, you should have put my money on deposit with the bankers, so that when I returned I would have received it back with interest.

²⁸"'So take the bag of gold from him and give it to the one who has ten bags. ²⁹For whoever has will be given more, and they will have an abundance. Whoever does not have, even what they have will be taken from them. ³⁰And throw that worthless servant outside, into the darkness, where there will be weeping and gnashing of teeth.'

The Sheep and the Goats

³¹"When the Son of Man comes in his glory, and all the angels with him, he will sit on his glorious throne. ³²All the nations will be gathered before him, and he will separate the people one from another as a shepherd separates the sheep from the goats. ³³He will put the sheep on his right and the goats on his left.

ᵃ 15 Greek *five talents . . . two talents . . . one talent*; also throughout this parable; a talent was worth about 20 years of a day laborer's wage.

25:4 The wise ones, however, took oil All ten women are expecting the bridegroom, but only five are fully prepared.
25:10 wedding banquet A possible allusion to the Messianic banquet at the end of the age (compare 8:11 and note). **door was shut** Compare Isa 22:22; Lk 13:25; Rev 3:7-8.

25:14-30 Like the illustration in Mt 24:45-51, this parable focuses on the theme of responsibility in the master's absence.

25:15 five bags of gold The Greek text indicates an amount equal to 75 years' wages (see note on 18:24).
25:24 harvesting where you have not sown Refers to the shrewdness of the master. The servant's statement shows that he should have known better than to simply give back the same amount that he received. He understood what the master wanted—a return on the investment—but he chose a different course of action.
25:29 For whoever has will be given more Faithfulness results in blessing and reward (see 13:12; Pr 9:9).
25:30 weeping and gnashing of teeth See note on Mt 8:12.

25:31-46 Jesus' final parable in Matthew looks ahead to a time of judgment. The scene he describes here seems to resume his earlier account of the Son of Man sending out the angels (24:31).

25:31 Son of Man See 8:20 and note.
25:32 a shepherd separates the sheep from the goats When shepherds brought in their flocks at the end of the day, they typically put the goats in a sheltered area while leaving the sheep in an open-air pen.

Parables of Jesus

PARABLE	MATTHEW	MARK	LUKE
Lamp Under a Bowl	Mt 5:15 – 16	Mk 4:21 – 22	Lk 8:16 – 17; 11:33 – 36
Wise and Foolish Builders	Mt 7:24 – 27	—	Lk 6:47 – 49
Unshrunk Cloth on an Old Garment	Mt 9:16	Mk 2:21	Lk 5:36
New Wine in Old Wineskins	Mt 9:17	Mk 2:22	Lk 5:37 – 38
The Sower and the Soils	Mt 13:3 – 9	Mk 4:3 – 9	Lk 8:5 – 8
The Weeds and the Wheat*	Mt 13:24 – 30	—	—
The Mustard Seed*	Mt 13:31 – 32	Mk 4:30 – 32	Lk 13:18 – 19
The Yeast*	Mt 13:33	—	Lk 13:20 – 21
The Hidden Treasure*	Mt 13:44	—	—
Fine Pearls*	Mt 13:45 – 46	—	—
The Net*	Mt 13:47 – 50	—	—
The Owner of a House	Mt 13:52	—	—
The Lost Sheep	Mt 18:12 – 14	—	Lk 15:4 – 7
The Unmerciful Servant*	Mt 18:23 – 35	—	—
The Workers in the Vineyard*	Mt 20:1 – 16	—	—
The Two Sons	Mt 21:28 – 32	—	—
The Tenants	Mt 21:33 – 45	Mk 12:1 – 12	Lk 20:9 – 19
The Wedding Banquet*	Mt 22:2 – 14	—	—
The Fig Tree	Mt 24:32 – 34	Mk 13:28 – 29	Lk 21:29 – 31
The Faithful and Wise Servant	Mt 24:45 – 51	—	Lk 12:42 – 48
The Ten Virgins*	Mt 25:1 – 13	—	—
The Bags of Gold/Minas	Mt 25:14 – 30	—	Lk 19:12 – 27
The Growing Seed*	—	Mk 4:26 – 29	—
The Absent Homeowner	—	Mk 13:34 – 37	—
The Two Debtors	—	—	Lk 7:41 – 43
The Good Samaritan	—	—	Lk 10:30 – 37
The Friend Who Asks	—	—	Lk 11:5 – 13
The Rich Fool	—	—	Lk 12:16 – 21
The Watchful Servants	—	—	Lk 12:35 – 40
The Barren Fig Tree	—	—	Lk 13:6 – 9
The Great Banquet	—	—	Lk 14:16 – 24
Counting the Cost	—	—	Lk 14:28 – 33

³⁴"Then the King will say to those on his right, 'Come, you who are blessed by my Father; take your inheritance, the kingdom prepared for you since the creation of the world. ³⁵For I was hungry and you gave me something to eat, I was thirsty and you gave me something to drink, I was a stranger and you invited me in, ³⁶I needed clothes and you clothed me, I was sick and you looked after me, I was in prison and you came to visit me.'

³⁷"Then the righteous will answer him, 'Lord, when did we see you hungry and feed you, or thirsty and give you something to drink? ³⁸When did we see you a stranger and invite you in, or needing clothes and clothe you? ³⁹When did we see you sick or in prison and go to visit you?'

⁴⁰"The King will reply, 'Truly I tell you, whatever you did for one of the least of these brothers and sisters of mine, you did for me.'

⁴¹"Then he will say to those on his left, 'Depart from me, you who are cursed, into the eternal fire prepared for the devil and his angels. ⁴²For I was hungry and you gave me nothing to eat, I was thirsty and you gave me nothing to drink, ⁴³I was a stranger and you did not invite me in, I needed clothes and you did not clothe me, I was sick and in prison and you did not look after me.'

⁴⁴"They also will answer, 'Lord, when did we see you hungry or thirsty or a stranger or needing clothes or sick or in prison, and did not help you?'

⁴⁵"He will reply, 'Truly I tell you, whatever you did not do for one of the least of these, you did not do for me.'

⁴⁶"Then they will go away to eternal punishment, but the righteous to eternal life."

The Plot Against Jesus

26:2-5pp — Mk 14:1,2; Lk 22:1,2

26 When Jesus had finished saying all these things, he said to his disciples, ²"As you know, the Passover is two days away — and the Son of Man will be handed over to be crucified."

³Then the chief priests and the elders of the people assembled in the palace of the high priest,

---

25:34 your inheritance, the kingdom prepared for you The Jewish worldview of Jesus' day envisioned the present age ending with a time of tribulation, followed by divine judgment. Then God's kingdom—the age to come—would be fully inaugurated. This schema also is reflected in the books of Daniel and Revelation.
25:35 For I was hungry The actions described here (and in the next verse) reflect obedience to the command to love one's neighbor—and thereby demonstrate love for God, as well (22:37–39).
25:40 the least of these Jesus' remarks here call for Christian care to reach all the way to the bottom of the social structure, thus inverting earthly values.
25:41 eternal fire Refers to divine wrath. See note on Lk 3:9.

26:1–5 At this point, Matthew's narrative shifts from Jesus' ministry and teaching to the events that lead to his death.
26:2 Passover An annual Jewish feast commemorating the Israelites' deliverance from slavery in Egypt (Ex 12–13; see note on Lk 2:41).
26:3 chief priests and the elders of the people Refers to members of the Sanhedrin, the Jewish ruling body in Jerusalem. **Caiaphas** The acting high priest. John's Gospel indicates that Caiaphas' predecessor and father-in-law, Annas, still held some authority at this time (Jn 18:12–13,19–24). See the table "Political Leaders in the New Testament" on p. 1916.

Parables of Jesus (continued)

PARABLE	MATTHEW	MARK	LUKE
The Lost Coin	—	—	Lk 15:8–10
The Lost Son	—	—	Lk 15:11–32
The Shrewd Manager	—	—	Lk 16:1–13
The Rich Man and Lazarus	—	—	Lk 16:19–31
Unworthy Servants	—	—	Lk 17:7–10
The Unjust Judge	—	—	Lk 18:1–8
The Pharisee and the Tax Collector	—	—	Lk 18:9–14

* Denotes a parable which Jesus introduces by saying, "The kingdom of heaven/God is like ..."

whose name was Caiaphas, ⁴and they schemed to arrest Jesus secretly and kill him. ⁵"But not during the festival," they said, "or there may be a riot among the people."

Jesus Anointed at Bethany

26:6-13pp — Mk 14:3-9
26:6-13Ref — Lk 7:37,38; Jn 12:1-8

⁶While Jesus was in Bethany in the home of Simon the Leper, ⁷a woman came to him with an alabaster jar of very expensive perfume, which she poured on his head as he was reclining at the table.

⁸When the disciples saw this, they were indignant. "Why this waste?" they asked. ⁹"This perfume could have been sold at a high price and the money given to the poor."

¹⁰Aware of this, Jesus said to them, "Why are you bothering this woman? She has done a beautiful thing to me. ¹¹The poor you will always have with you,^a but you will not always have me. ¹²When she poured this perfume on my body, she did it to prepare me for burial. ¹³Truly I tell you, wherever this gospel is preached throughout the world, what she has done will also be told, in memory of her."

Judas Agrees to Betray Jesus

26:14-16pp — Mk 14:10,11; Lk 22:3-6

¹⁴Then one of the Twelve — the one called Judas Iscariot — went to the chief priests ¹⁵and asked, "What are you willing to give me if I deliver him over to you?" So they counted out for him thirty pieces of silver. ¹⁶From then on Judas watched for an opportunity to hand him over.

The Last Supper

26:17-19pp — Mk 14:12-16; Lk 22:7-13
26:20-24pp — Mk 14:17-21
26:26-29pp — Mk 14:22-25; Lk 22:17-20; 1Co 11:23-25

¹⁷On the first day of the Festival of Unleavened Bread, the disciples came to Jesus and asked, "Where do you want us to make preparations for you to eat the Passover?"

¹⁸He replied, "Go into the city to a certain man and tell him, 'The Teacher says: My appointed time is near. I am going to celebrate the Passover with my disciples at your house.'" ¹⁹So the disciples did as Jesus had directed them and prepared the Passover.

²⁰When evening came, Jesus was reclining at the table with the Twelve. ²¹And while they were eating, he said, "Truly I tell you, one of you will betray me."

²²They were very sad and began to say to him one after the other, "Surely you don't mean me, Lord?"

²³Jesus replied, "The one who has dipped his hand into the bowl with me will betray me. ²⁴The Son of Man will go just as it is written about him. But woe to that man who betrays the Son of Man! It would be better for him if he had not been born."

²⁵Then Judas, the one who would betray him, said, "Surely you don't mean me, Rabbi?"

^a *11* See Deut. 15:11.

HIGH PRIESTS IN THE NT	
Annas (Lk 3:2; Jn 18:13,24; Ac 4:6)	AD 6–15
Caiaphas (Mt 26:3,57; Lk 3:2; Jn 11:49; 18:13,14,24,28; Ac 4:6)	AD 18–36
Ananias (Ac 23:2; 24:1)	AD 47–58

26:4 secretly The Greek word used here, *dolos*, carries a sense of underhandedness, cunning or treachery. Matthew might employ this term to portray the religious establishment as being guilty and wicked, in contrast to Jesus' innocence and righteousness.

26:5 a riot among the people Civil unrest was a constant threat during festival times, due to the influx of peasants into the city. The Romans often suppressed riots harshly.

26:6–13 As Jesus and his disciples eat at their host's home in Bethany, a woman enters the house and anoints Jesus' head with costly perfume.

26:6 Bethany See 21:17 and note. **Simon the Leper** Most likely, Simon had been cleansed from his skin disease; he would have been required to live in isolation had it not been healed (Lev 13:46). He might have been among those healed by Jesus. Luke's parallel account presents Simon as a Pharisee (Lk 7:36–40).

26:7 a woman John's parallel account identifies her as "Mary" — presumably the sister of Martha and Lazarus (Jn 12:3).

26:9 given to the poor The disciples' concern for the poor is in keeping with the heart of Jesus' ministry.

26:12 to prepare me for burial The woman likely intended to display her devotion, but Jesus reinterprets her act.

26:14–16 Judas seeks out the chief priests, who were involved in Jewish religious government, in order to betray Jesus. In John's Gospel, Judas seems to be motivated (at least in part) by his objection to the extravagant anointing that occurs in the previous scene (Jn 12:4–6).

26:15 thirty pieces of silver Approximately equal to four months' wages (see Mt 27:9 and note). See the infographic "A Silver Denarius" on p. 1578.

26:17–25 Jesus eats the Passover meal with his disciples and reveals that one of them will betray him.

26:17 On the first day of the Festival of Unleavened Bread The day of preparation for Passover.

26:20 reclining at the table The setting likely involved a low table, with guests leaning on cushions.

26:23 one who has dipped his hand into the bowl This statement probably is intended to emphasize the betrayer's breach of fellowship, not to single out a disciple (i.e., Judas) who had his hand in the bowl at the same moment as Jesus. Compare Jn 13:26–30.

Jesus answered, "You have said so."

²⁶While they were eating, Jesus took bread, and when he had given thanks, he broke it and gave it to his disciples, saying, "Take and eat; this is my body."

²⁷Then he took a cup, and when he had given thanks, he gave it to them, saying, "Drink from it, all of you. ²⁸This is my blood of the^a covenant, which is poured out for many for the forgiveness of sins. ²⁹I tell you, I will not drink from this fruit of the vine from now on until that day when I drink it new with you in my Father's kingdom."

³⁰When they had sung a hymn, they went out to the Mount of Olives.

Jesus Predicts Peter's Denial

26:31-35pp — Mk 14:27-31; Lk 22:31-34

³¹Then Jesus told them, "This very night you will all fall away on account of me, for it is written:

"'I will strike the shepherd,
    and the sheep of the flock will be scattered.'^b

³²But after I have risen, I will go ahead of you into Galilee."

³³Peter replied, "Even if all fall away on account of you, I never will."

³⁴"Truly I tell you," Jesus answered, "this very night, before the rooster crows, you will disown me three times."

³⁵But Peter declared, "Even if I have to die with you, I will never disown you." And all the other disciples said the same.

Gethsemane

26:36-46pp — Mk 14:32-42; Lk 22:40-46

³⁶Then Jesus went with his disciples to a place called Gethsemane, and he said to them, "Sit here while I go over there and pray." ³⁷He took Peter and the two sons of Zebedee along with him, and he began to be sorrowful and troubled. ³⁸Then he said to them, "My soul is overwhelmed with sorrow to the point of death. Stay here and keep watch with me."

³⁹Going a little farther, he fell with his face to the ground and prayed, "My Father, if it is possible, may this cup be taken from me. Yet not as I will, but as you will."

⁴⁰Then he returned to his disciples and found them sleeping. "Couldn't you men keep watch with me for one hour?" he asked Peter. ⁴¹"Watch and pray so that you will not fall into temptation. The spirit is willing, but the flesh is weak."

⁴²He went away a second time and prayed, "My Father, if it is not possible for this cup to be taken away unless I drink it, may your will be done."

⁴³When he came back, he again found them sleeping, because their eyes were heavy. ⁴⁴So he left them and went away once more and prayed the third time, saying the same thing.

⁴⁵Then he returned to the disciples and said to them, "Are you still sleeping and resting? Look, the hour has come, and the Son of Man is delivered into the hands of sinners. ⁴⁶Rise! Let us go! Here comes my betrayer!"

Jesus Arrested

26:47-56pp — Mk 14:43-50; Lk 22:47-53

⁴⁷While he was still speaking, Judas, one of the Twelve, arrived. With him was a large crowd armed with swords and clubs, sent from the chief priests and the elders of the people. ⁴⁸Now the betrayer had arranged a signal with them: "The one I kiss is the man; arrest him." ⁴⁹Going at once to Jesus, Judas said, "Greetings, Rabbi!" and kissed him.

^a 28 Some manuscripts *the new*   ^b 31 Zech. 13:7

26:25 Rabbi Judas' query differs from that of the other disciples (Mt 26:22). Throughout Matthew's Gospel, only those who show faith in Jesus call him "Lord."

26:26–30 As the meal continues, Jesus gives his disciples the bread and cup as sacraments signifying his atoning death.

26:26 Take and eat; this is my body Jesus' body was the final sacrifice that would atone for sins, just as the Passover lamb signified the atonement for the people's sins every year (Lev 16).

26:27 he took a cup The Passover meal includes four (sometimes five) cups of wine; this is likely the third, the cup of blessing.

26:28 my blood of the covenant In the ancient Near East, covenants often were ratified using blood (through sacrifice). At Sinai, Moses sprinkled the people with the blood of the covenant (Ex 24:8). The elements of the Lord's Supper serve as signs of the new covenant (Jer 31:31–34).

26:29 drink it new with you Likely a reference to the Messianic banquet (see Mt 8:11 and note).

26:30 When they had sung a hymn Refers to portions of Ps 113–118.

26:31–56 Jesus states that the disciples—even Peter—will abandon him. He takes them to a secluded place to pray, but the disciples, failing to grasp the urgency of his distress, fall asleep. A short time later, an armed mob led by Judas arrives to arrest Jesus. As predicted, the disciples flee.

26:31 I will strike the shepherd Jesus quotes Zec 13:7. See the table "Jesus' Fulfillment of OT Prophecy" on p. 1573.

26:36 Gethsemane See note on Mk 14:32.

26:37 Peter and the two sons of Zebedee Peter, James and John (see Mt 17:1 and note).

26:38 keep watch with me The Greek word used here, *grēgoreō* ("to be awake" or "watchful"), appears in Jesus' teachings in 24:42 and 25:13 to stress the importance of being ready for the Son of Man's arrival.

26:39 this cup Refers to suffering (compare 20:22–23).

26:48 The one I kiss A customary greeting.

⁵⁰Jesus replied, "Do what you came for, friend."ᵃ Then the men stepped forward, seized Jesus and arrested him. ⁵¹With that, one of Jesus' companions reached for his sword, drew it out and struck the servant of the high priest, cutting off his ear.

⁵²"Put your sword back in its place," Jesus said to him, "for all who draw the sword will die by the sword. ⁵³Do you think I cannot call on my Father, and he will at once put at my disposal more than twelve legions of angels? ⁵⁴But how then would the Scriptures be fulfilled that say it must happen in this way?"

⁵⁵In that hour Jesus said to the crowd, "Am I leading a rebellion, that you have come out with swords and clubs to capture me? Every day I sat in the temple courts teaching, and you did not arrest me. ⁵⁶But this has all taken place that the writings of the prophets might be fulfilled." Then all the disciples deserted him and fled.

Jesus Before the Sanhedrin

26:57-68pp — Mk 14:53-65; Jn 18:12,13,19-24

⁵⁷Those who had arrested Jesus took him to Caiaphas the high priest, where the teachers of the law and the elders had assembled. ⁵⁸But Peter followed him at a distance, right up to the courtyard of the high priest. He entered and sat down with the guards to see the outcome.

⁵⁹The chief priests and the whole Sanhedrin were looking for false evidence against Jesus so that they could put him to death. ⁶⁰But they did not find any, though many false witnesses came forward.

Finally two came forward ⁶¹and declared, "This fellow said, 'I am able to destroy the temple of God and rebuild it in three days.'"

⁶²Then the high priest stood up and said to Jesus, "Are you not going to answer? What is this testimony that these men are bringing against you?" ⁶³But Jesus remained silent.

The high priest said to him, "I charge you under oath by the living God: Tell us if you are the Messiah, the Son of God."

⁶⁴"You have said so," Jesus replied. "But I say to all of you: From now on you will see the Son of Man sitting at the right hand of the Mighty One and coming on the clouds of heaven."ᵇ

⁶⁵Then the high priest tore his clothes and said, "He has spoken blasphemy! Why do we need any more witnesses? Look, now you have heard the blasphemy. ⁶⁶What do you think?"

"He is worthy of death," they answered.

⁶⁷Then they spit in his face and struck him with their fists. Others slapped him ⁶⁸and said, "Prophesy to us, Messiah. Who hit you?"

Peter Disowns Jesus

26:69-75pp — Mk 14:66-72; Lk 22:55-62; Jn 18:16-18,25-27

⁶⁹Now Peter was sitting out in the courtyard, and a servant girl came to him. "You also were with Jesus of Galilee," she said.

⁷⁰But he denied it before them all. "I don't know what you're talking about," he said.

⁷¹Then he went out to the gateway, where another servant girl saw him and said to the people there, "This fellow was with Jesus of Nazareth."

⁷²He denied it again, with an oath: "I don't know the man!"

ᵃ 50 Or "Why have you come, friend?"   ᵇ 64 See Psalm 110:1; Daniel 7:13.

26:50 friend Compare 20:13; 22:12.
26:51 one of Jesus' companions Identified in Jn 18:10 as Peter. **cutting off his ear** In Luke's account, Jesus heals the man (Lk 22:51).
26:53 twelve legions of angels A Roman legion had about 5,000–6,000 soldiers, so this indicates at least 60,000 angels.

26:57–68 Jesus is tried before the Jewish religious leaders and condemned to death on a charge of blasphemy. See the infographic "The Sanhedrin" on p. 1746.

26:59 Sanhedrin See note on Lk 22:66.
26:61 rebuild it in three days This saying does not appear in Matthew. John 2:19 records Jesus making a similar statement, but the false witnesses clearly misunderstand the statement, which is about Jesus' death and resurrection. The intention of the testimony is entrapment.
26:63 Jesus remained silent Compare Isa 53:7.
26:64 You have said so Jesus answers indirectly but affirmatively. **the Son of Man** A Messianic title connected to royal authority. See Mt 8:20 and note. **sitting at the right hand of the Mighty One and coming on the clouds** With this phrase, Jesus clearly identifies himself as the Messiah. In Ps 110:1, Yahweh invites the Messiah

to sit at his right hand in authority (compare Mt 22:44). Thus, Jesus is saying that he will be in the position of ultimate authority over humanity, as the Messiah. In Da 7:13–14, a Messianic figure—depicted in the Hebrew text as being like a son of man—comes before Yahweh on the clouds of heaven and receives an eternal, worldwide kingdom (compare Mt 24:30). The language of coming on the clouds also is used for Yahweh, suggesting that Jesus is claiming to be Yahweh (Ps 68:4; Isa 19:1). The high priest seems to pick up on this implication in the next verse.
26:65 tore his clothes This gesture symbolizes extreme grief. **He has spoken blasphemy** Refers to claiming authority that belongs to God alone.
26:66 He is worthy of death The prescribed punishment for blasphemy (Lev 24:16).

26:69–75 When people recognize Peter as one of the disciples, he denies any association with Jesus—fulfilling Jesus' prophecy in Mt 26:34.

26:72 He denied it again, with an oath In his second denial, Peter swears an oath—a call for divine judgment if the oath-taker is lying. Jesus taught against oaths (5:33–37).

[73] After a little while, those standing there went up to Peter and said, "Surely you are one of them; your accent gives you away."

[74] Then he began to call down curses, and he swore to them, "I don't know the man!"

Immediately a rooster crowed. [75] Then Peter remembered the word Jesus had spoken: "Before the rooster crows, you will disown me three times." And he went outside and wept bitterly.

Judas Hangs Himself

27 Early in the morning, all the chief priests and the elders of the people made their plans how to have Jesus executed. [2] So they bound him, led him away and handed him over to Pilate the governor.

[3] When Judas, who had betrayed him, saw that Jesus was condemned, he was seized with remorse and returned the thirty pieces of silver to the chief priests and the elders. [4] "I have sinned," he said, "for I have betrayed innocent blood."

"What is that to us?" they replied. "That's your responsibility."

[5] So Judas threw the money into the temple and left. Then he went away and hanged himself.

[6] The chief priests picked up the coins and said, "It is against the law to put this into the treasury, since it is blood money." [7] So they decided to use the money to buy the potter's field as a burial place for foreigners. [8] That is why it has been called the Field of Blood to this day. [9] Then what was spoken by Jeremiah the prophet was fulfilled: "They took the thirty pieces of silver, the price set on him by the people of Israel, [10] and they used them to buy the potter's field, as the Lord commanded me." [a]

Jesus Before Pilate

27:11-26pp — Mk 15:2-15; Lk 23:2,3,18-25; Jn 18:29 – 19:16

[11] Meanwhile Jesus stood before the governor, and the governor asked him, "Are you the king of the Jews?"

"You have said so," Jesus replied.

[12] When he was accused by the chief priests and the elders, he gave no answer. [13] Then Pilate asked him, "Don't you hear the testimony they are bringing against you?" [14] But Jesus made no reply, not even to a single charge — to the great amazement of the governor.

[15] Now it was the governor's custom at the festival to release a prisoner chosen by the crowd. [16] At that time they had a well-known prisoner whose name was Jesus [b] Barabbas. [17] So when the crowd had gathered, Pilate asked them, "Which one do you want me to release to you: Jesus Barabbas, or Jesus who is called the Messiah?" [18] For he knew it was out of self-interest that they had handed Jesus over to him.

[19] While Pilate was sitting on the judge's seat, his wife sent him this message: "Don't have anything to do with that innocent man, for I have suffered a great deal today in a dream because of him."

[a] *10* See Zech. 11:12,13; Jer. 19:1-13; 32:6-9. [b] *16* Many manuscripts do not have *Jesus*; also in verse 17.

26:73 your accent gives you away Peter speaks as a Galilean.

26:74 to call down curses, and he swore Peter's third denial adds a curse to the oath. The meaning of this detail is not clear; it does not necessarily refer to using profanity.

27:1-2 As the day dawns, the religious leaders take Jesus to Pilate to be sentenced. See the event line "Jesus' Passion and Resurrection" on p. 1698.

27:2 handed him over to Pilate Roman governor of Judea. Only Roman authorities could impose the death penalty (Jn 18:31). See the infographic "Pontius Pilate's Inscription" on p. 1707.

PILATE
Little is known of this Roman governor of Judea, but his rule of the Jews is often depicted as turbulent. Philo, a first-century Hellenistic-Jewish philosopher, describes Pilate's reign as characterized by theft, dishonesty, violence and frequent executions of untried prisoners (Philo, *Gaium* 302; compare Lk 13:1 and note). See the table "Political Leaders in the New Testament" on p. 1916.

27:3-10 Recognizing his guilt in Jesus' death sentence, Judas hangs himself.

27:5 threw the money into the temple A parallel to Zec 11:13. **he went away and hanged himself** Compare Ac 1:18 and note.

27:7 a burial place for foreigners Gentiles could not be buried with Jews.

27:8 Field of Blood See Ac 1:19 and note.

27:9 spoken by Jeremiah the prophet The reference to the potter and 30 pieces of silver comes from Zec 11:12-13; the allusion to a business transaction appears to reflect Jer 32:6-9. Thirty pieces of silver is also the price someone owed if their ox killed a slave (Ex 21:32). See the table "Jesus' Fulfillment of OT Prophecy" on p. 1573.

27:11-26 The religious leaders hand Jesus over to Pilate. Apparently wanting to free Jesus, Pilate offers to release a prisoner, but the crowd calls for Barabbas instead of Jesus.

27:16 Jesus Barabbas The other Gospels identify Barabbas as a violent insurrectionist (Mk 15:7; Lk 23:19; Jn 18:40).

27:19 the judge's seat An elevated bench that allowed Pilate to be heard over the crowd. See the infographic "A Judgment Seat in Jerusalem" on p. 1761. **dream** In writings from this period, dreams were common means of supernatural revelation.

²⁰But the chief priests and the elders persuaded the crowd to ask for Barabbas and to have Jesus executed.

²¹"Which of the two do you want me to release to you?" asked the governor.

"Barabbas," they answered.

²²"What shall I do, then, with Jesus who is called the Messiah?" Pilate asked.

They all answered, "Crucify him!"

²³"Why? What crime has he committed?" asked Pilate.

But they shouted all the louder, "Crucify him!"

²⁴When Pilate saw that he was getting nowhere, but that instead an uproar was starting, he took water and washed his hands in front of the crowd. "I am innocent of this man's blood," he said. "It is your responsibility!"

²⁵All the people answered, "His blood is on us and on our children!"

²⁶Then he released Barabbas to them. But he had Jesus flogged, and handed him over to be crucified.

The Soldiers Mock Jesus

27:27-31pp — Mk 15:16-20

²⁷Then the governor's soldiers took Jesus into the Praetorium and gathered the whole company of soldiers around him. ²⁸They stripped him and put a scarlet robe on him, ²⁹and then twisted together a crown of thorns and set it on his head. They put a staff in his right hand. Then they knelt in front of him and mocked him. "Hail, king of the Jews!" they said. ³⁰They spit on him, and took the staff and struck him on the head again and again.

³¹After they had mocked him, they took off the robe and put his own clothes on him. Then they led him away to crucify him.

The Crucifixion of Jesus

27:33-44pp — Mk 15:22-32; Lk 23:33-43; Jn 19:17-24

³²As they were going out, they met a man from Cyrene, named Simon, and they forced him to carry the cross. ³³They came to a place called Golgotha (which means "the place of the skull"). ³⁴There they offered Jesus wine to drink, mixed with gall; but after tasting it, he refused to drink it. ³⁵When they had crucified him, they divided up his clothes by casting lots. ³⁶And sitting down, they kept watch over him there. ³⁷Above his head they placed the written charge against him: THIS IS JESUS, THE KING OF THE JEWS.

³⁸Two rebels were crucified with him, one on his right and one on his left. ³⁹Those who passed by hurled insults at him, shaking their heads ⁴⁰and saying, "You who are going to destroy the temple and build it in three days, save yourself! Come down from the cross, if you are the Son of God!" ⁴¹In the same way the chief priests, the teachers of the law and the elders mocked him. ⁴²"He saved others," they said, "but he can't save himself! He's the king of Israel! Let him come down now from the cross, and we will believe in him. ⁴³He trusts in God. Let God rescue him now if he wants him, for he said, 'I am the Son of God.'" ⁴⁴In the same way the rebels who were crucified with him also heaped insults on him.

27:20 persuaded the crowd Probably residents of Jerusalem, not the Galilean peasants who had hailed Jesus as Messiah (compare Mt 21:8–11).

27:24 that instead an uproar was starting See 26:5 and note. **took water and washed his hands** An act signifying absolution, although technically as governing authority, Pilate is still partly responsible.

27:25 on us and on our children The Jewish leaders who oppose Jesus are partly responsible for his death. Despite the crowd's rash statement in v. 25, this does not amount to culpability for an entire nation or people group. In addition, Isa 52:10, as well as Jesus' own words (Mt 16:21), indicate that Jesus' death was ultimately God's decision, for the salvation of humanity. Although the Jewish leaders and Pilate issue the order to execute Jesus, which is portrayed as an evil act, Jesus' death is ultimately God the Father's decision (compare Mk 14:36).

27:26 flogged Refers to being beaten with whips, which often contained bits of bone, rock and metal to flay the skin.

27:27–44 After beating and mocking Jesus, Roman soldiers take him outside the city and crucify him. While he is hanging on the cross, the Jewish leaders and others ridicule him.

27:28 scarlet The color of royalty.

27:29 crown A mock crown for one perceived to be a mock king; also likely a means of torture.

27:32 a man from Cyrene, named Simon Cyrene was on the Mediterranean Sea in North Africa. **they forced him to carry the cross** See note on Mk 15:21.

27:33 Golgotha An Aramaic word meaning "skull." **place of the skull** The Latin word for "skull" is *calvaria*, from which the English word Calvary derives.

27:34 wine to drink, mixed with gall Meant to mitigate the pain (see Ps 69:21).

27:35 crucified him This brutal method of capital punishment was not used on Roman citizens. The guilty party was fastened to intersecting beams of wood by nails (sometimes rope was used) driven through the hands (or wrists) and feet (usually one foot on top of the other, held in place by one nail). The person was left hanging—often naked—until dead. The prevalence of crucifixion in Jesus' day makes his command to take up a cross and follow him all the more vivid (see Mt 10:38; 16:24). **they divided up his clothes by casting lots** A parallel to Ps 22:18. Compare Isa 53:3 and note.

27:37 THIS IS JESUS, THE KING OF THE JEWS Ironically, this sign proclaims Jesus' true identity.

27:43 Let God rescue him Compare Ps 22:8. **I am the Son of God** The religious leaders assume that God would not let his Son be executed. Compare Isa 53:12 and note.

27:45–56 Jesus dies for the sin of the world. The significance of his death is conveyed through supernatural occurrences.

The Death of Jesus

27:45-56pp — Mk 15:33-41; Lk 23:44-49; Jn 19:29-30

⁴⁵From noon until three in the afternoon darkness came over all the land. ⁴⁶About three in the afternoon Jesus cried out in a loud voice, *"Eli, Eli,ᵃ lema sabachthani?"* (which means "My God, my God, why have you forsaken me?").ᵇ

⁴⁷When some of those standing there heard this, they said, "He's calling Elijah." ⁴⁸Immediately one of them ran and got a sponge. He filled it with wine vinegar, put it on a staff, and offered it to Jesus to drink. ⁴⁹The rest said, "Now leave him alone. Let's see if Elijah comes to save him."

⁵⁰And when Jesus had cried out again in a loud voice, he gave up his spirit.

⁵¹At that moment the curtain of the temple was torn in two from top to bottom. The earth shook, the rocks split ⁵²and the tombs broke open. The bodies of many holy people who had died were raised to life. ⁵³They came out of the tombs after Jesus' resurrection andᶜ went into the holy city and appeared to many people.

⁵⁴When the centurion and those with him who were guarding Jesus saw the earthquake and all that had happened, they were terrified, and exclaimed, "Surely he was the Son of God!"

⁵⁵Many women were there, watching from a distance. They had followed Jesus from Galilee to care for his needs. ⁵⁶Among them were Mary Magdalene, Mary the mother of James and Joseph,ᵈ and the mother of Zebedee's sons.

The Burial of Jesus

27:57-61pp — Mk 15:42-47; Lk 23:50-56; Jn 19:38-42

⁵⁷As evening approached, there came a rich man from Arimathea, named Joseph, who had himself become a disciple of Jesus. ⁵⁸Going to Pilate, he asked for Jesus' body, and Pilate ordered that it be given to him. ⁵⁹Joseph took the body, wrapped it in a clean linen cloth, ⁶⁰and placed it in his own new tomb that he had cut out of the rock. He rolled a big stone in front of the entrance to the tomb and went away. ⁶¹Mary Magdalene and the other Mary were sitting there opposite the tomb.

The Guard at the Tomb

⁶²The next day, the one after Preparation Day, the chief priests and the Pharisees went to Pilate. ⁶³"Sir," they said, "we remember that while he was still alive that deceiver said, 'After three days I will rise again.' ⁶⁴So give the order for the tomb to be made secure until the third day. Otherwise, his disciples may come and steal the body and tell the people that he has been raised from the dead. This last deception will be worse than the first."

⁶⁵"Take a guard," Pilate answered. "Go, make the tomb as secure as you know how." ⁶⁶So they went and made the tomb secure by putting a seal on the stone and posting the guard.

ᵃ 46 Some manuscripts *Eloi, Eloi*   ᵇ 46 Psalm 22:1
ᶜ 53 Or *tombs, and after Jesus' resurrection they*   ᵈ 56 Greek *Joses,* a variant of *Joseph*

27:45 darkness came over all the land Likely represents divine disfavor over the imminent death of the Messiah. The Greek text says the darkness lasted from the sixth hour to the ninth hour. The first hour of the day was 6 a.m., so the period of darkness was noon to 3 p.m. Isaiah and Joel speak of the sun being darkened, often in connection with the day of Yahweh — an association made by Jesus in his teaching about apocalyptic signs (see Mt 24:29 and note; Isa 13:10; 34:4; Joel 2:10).

27:46 My God, my God, why have you forsaken me Jesus quotes the opening line of Ps 22, which closely parallels the events of Jesus' suffering and death (see note on 22:1).

27:47 He's calling Elijah Jesus' cry (in Aramaic) sounds like the name of the prophet.

27:48 filled it with wine vinegar To dull the pain or quench the thirst (Ps 69:21).

27:50 gave up his spirit An idiom meaning "died."

27:51 curtain of the temple was torn Perhaps symbolizing unrestricted access to God — no longer mediated by the temple and its sacred space (see note on Mk 15:38; compare Ex 26:31–35; Heb 6:19–20; 10:20). **from top to bottom** The direction of the tear — along with the passive verb — implies an act of God.

27:52 the tombs broke open This detail is unique to Matthew. Although the tombs open at Jesus' death, the raised saints do not emerge until his resurrection (Mt 27:53). Matthew appears to be emphasizing the significance of Jesus' death and resurrection as the dawn of the final era of humanity, which is marked by

resurrection — God's power over death itself (see Rev 20:4–6; compare 20:11–14).

27:56 Mary Magdalene According to Luke, Mary was a follower of Jesus from whom he had cast out seven demons (Lk 8:2). **Mary the mother of James and Joseph** This could be Jesus' mother, his aunt or another Mary not mentioned elsewhere in the gospels (compare Mk 6:3; 15:40; Jn 19:25). **mother of Zebedee's sons** The mother of James and John, Jesus' disciples.

27:57–61 Joseph of Arimathea receives Jesus' body and provides a proper burial. The religious leaders place guards at the tomb to prevent Jesus' disciples from stealing his body.

27:57 rich man from Arimathea, named Joseph Arimathea was about 20 miles northwest of Jerusalem. Compare Isa 53:9 and note. **who had himself become a disciple of Jesus** The other Gospels identify Joseph as a member of the Jewish ruling council, the Sanhedrin (Mk 15:43; Lk 23:50; Jn 19:38).

27:58 asked for Jesus' body Without Joseph's intervention, Jesus likely would have been buried with executed criminals or discarded on a trash heap. Under Jewish law, the corpse needed to be buried the same day or the land would be defiled (Dt 21:22–23).

27:62 chief priests Prominent priests who were involved in Jewish religious government. **Pharisees** See note on Jn 1:24.

27:63 After three days I will rise See Mt 16:21; 17:23; 20:19.

27:66 by putting a seal on the stone Refers to pressing

Jesus Has Risen

28:1-8pp — Mk 16:1-8; Lk 24:1-10; Jn 20:1-8

28 After the Sabbath, at dawn on the first day of the week, Mary Magdalene and the other Mary went to look at the tomb.

²There was a violent earthquake, for an angel of the Lord came down from heaven and, going to the tomb, rolled back the stone and sat on it. ³His appearance was like lightning, and his clothes were white as snow. ⁴The guards were so afraid of him that they shook and became like dead men.

⁵The angel said to the women, "Do not be afraid, for I know that you are looking for Jesus, who was crucified. ⁶He is not here; he has risen, just as he said. Come and see the place where he lay. ⁷Then go quickly and tell his disciples: 'He has risen from the dead and is going ahead of you into Galilee. There you will see him.' Now I have told you."

⁸So the women hurried away from the tomb, afraid yet filled with joy, and ran to tell his disciples. ⁹Suddenly Jesus met them. "Greetings," he said. They came to him, clasped his feet and worshiped him. ¹⁰Then Jesus said to them, "Do not be afraid. Go and tell my brothers to go to Galilee; there they will see me."

The Guards' Report

¹¹While the women were on their way, some of the guards went into the city and reported to the chief priests everything that had happened. ¹²When the chief priests had met with the elders and devised a plan, they gave the soldiers a large sum of money, ¹³telling them, "You are to say, 'His disciples came during the night and stole him away while we were asleep.' ¹⁴If this report gets to the governor, we will satisfy him and keep you out of trouble." ¹⁵So the soldiers took the money and did as they were instructed. And this story has been widely circulated among the Jews to this very day.

The Great Commission

¹⁶Then the eleven disciples went to Galilee, to the mountain where Jesus had told them to go. ¹⁷When they saw him, they worshiped him; but some doubted. ¹⁸Then Jesus came to them and said, "All authority in heaven and on earth has been given to me. ¹⁹Therefore go and make disciples of all nations, baptizing them in the name of the Father and of the Son and of the Holy Spirit, ²⁰and teaching them to obey everything I have commanded you. And surely I am with you always, to the very end of the age."

---

wax or clay between the stone and the tomb entrance and then stamping it with an imperial insignia (see Da 6:17 and note.)

28:1–10 In fulfillment of his predictions, Jesus conquers the grave and rises to new life (compare Isa 53:10 and note; 53:12 and note).

28:1 After the Sabbath Jews calculated the Sabbath from sundown on Friday night to sundown on Saturday night. During that time, no one could do any work. **first day of the week** Refers to Sunday. See note on Lk 24:1.
28:4 became like dead men Describes a typical response to a divine encounter (compare Rev 1:17).
28:6 he has risen The Greek verb used here is passive, indicating an act of God. **just as he said** See Mt 16:21; 17:9,23; 20:19; 26:32.
28:9 Jesus met them. "Greetings," he said The women are the first to encounter the risen Christ. The Greek word Jesus speaks here is an expression of well-being or gladness. See the table "Resurrection Appearances of Jesus" on p. 1896.
28:10 my brothers Despite the disciples' earlier abandonment of him (26:56,69–75), Jesus addresses them with a term of utmost endearment.

28:11–15 The chief priests, who were involved in Jewish religious government, bribe the Roman soldiers to spread a false report about Jesus' disciples stealing his body.

28:14 keep you out of trouble The soldiers would have faced punishment—perhaps death—because they failed in their duty to secure the tomb.

28:16–20 Jesus commissions his disciples to spread the good news and make disciples throughout the whole earth.

28:16 the mountain where Jesus had told them Perhaps the mountain where Jesus was transfigured (see note on 17:1).
28:17 some doubted The Greek verb used here implies hesitation or indecision, rather than unbelief. The disciples are struggling to comprehend what they are witnessing.
28:18 All authority in heaven and on earth The resurrection is the ultimate validation of Jesus' divine authority (compare 12:38–40; Eph 1:20–23). He extends this authority to his disciples to continue the work of the kingdom of heaven. Matthew emphasizes this theme throughout his Gospel (e.g., Mt 7:29; 9:6; 21:23). Jesus has repeatedly demonstrated his authority over all things—the human body, demons, natural elements (such as wind and water), the Sabbath, sin and even death.
28:19 baptizing A public signal of identification with Jesus and his kingdom (compare 3:11–17).
28:20 to the very end of the age Marked by Jesus' second coming.

THE PARABLES OF JESUS
by Dean Deppe

P arables are stories drawn from everyday life that illustrate a religious truth. They compare familiar situations, persons or events to an unfamiliar or unrecognized truth. The hearers of parables often identify with a particular character and react to the parable's reversal of expectations. Parables act as both a window to the kingdom of God and a mirror that convicts listeners, trapping them through the element of surprise.

The beginning of the parable of the Workers in the Vineyard offers insight into the graciousness of the God of the kingdom (Mt 20:1–10), whereas its conclusion raises a mirror to the ungracious- ness of the first workers (Mt 20:11–16). Listeners who identify with the first workers get caught in the trap of Jesus' story—identifying this element of surprise is crucial to understanding the theme of the parable.

Parables are frequently organized according to their literary form. Parables that use simile pre- sent an explicit comparison using "like" or "as" (e.g., "I am sending you out like sheep among wolves," Mt 10:16). Parables that use metaphor equate two things in order to compare them (e.g., "You are the salt of the earth," Mt 5:13). Those using similitude link a common event with a spiritual lesson (e.g., the parable of the Lost Sheep, Lk 15:3–7). Parables often occur as exam- ple stories, where characters serve as examples for listeners, such as in the Good Samaritan (Lk 10:29–37). There are also parables that are allegories, which consist of a series of metaphors that together establish an extended comparison at a number of points, such as in the parable of the Sower (Mk 4:1–9).

THEMES THAT CAN BE SEEN IN THE PARABLES INCLUDE:

Responses to Jesus' teaching. These stories call listeners to respond faithfully to Jesus; examples include the parable of the Ten Virgins (Mt 25:1–13) or the Wise and Foolish Builders (Mt 7:24–27).

Warnings about an imminent judgment. These include the parable of the Rich Fool (Lk 12:16–21) and the Narrow Door (Lk 13:25–28).

Kingdom of God parables. These stories proclaim the coming of the kingdom of God and illustrate its characteristics. Examples of this theme include the parables of the Wedding Guests (Mt 22:1–14), and the Patch and Wineskins (Mk 2:19–22).

Growth of the kingdom parables. The parables of the Mustard Seed and Yeast (Lk 13:18–21) illustrate the special presence of God.

Parables of God's mercy. These stories show God as one who offers unconditional love; examples include the parables of the Lost Sheep, Lost Coin and Lost Son (Lk 15:1–32).

Displays of God's mercy by Jesus. Jesus showers the mercy of God upon marginalized people as in the Rich Man and Lazarus (Lk 16:19–31) and the Pharisee and Tax Collector (Lk 18:9–14).

Calls to deeper discipleship. These stories stress the importance of obedience (the Two Sons in Mt 21:28–32), placing the kingdom first (the Hidden Treasure and Costly Pearl in Mt 13:44–46), humility (Places at the Table in Lk 14:7–10) and prayer (the Persistent Widow in Lk 18:1–8).

Consequences of a lack of discipleship. The parable of the Wicked Tenants in Mk 12:1–9 and the Children Sitting in the Marketplace in Mt 11:16–17 illustrate how destructive a lack of discipleship is. The majority of Jesus' parables center on discipleship or a lack of discipleship.

The identifying marks of godly community. Stories like the Teacher of the Law (Mt 13:51–52) and the parable of the Weeds (Mt 13:24–30) illustrate the true community of believers.

The influence of Jesus' followers. These parables show the effect of Jesus' followers upon the world as in the parables of the Salt and Light (Mt 5:13–16).

Throughout the Gospels, Jesus employs memorable parables to depict life in the kingdom of God. The kingdom of God is like a festive wedding banquet (Mt 22:2; 25:10); everyone desires invitation to this jubilant celebration. For field laborers, the kingdom is like the unbelievable harvest—the kind every farmer plagued with drought and insects dreams about (Mt 13:8). For fisherman, the kingdom is like a net that unexpectedly catches a huge multitude of fish (Mt 13:47). And for everyone, the kingdom of God is like a hidden treasure one stumbles upon unexpectedly (Mt 13:44).

Jesus also uses parables to present a brilliantly painted image of God as a compassionate father overflowing with grace and mercy (Lk 15). God dresses himself to serve, as one who places our needs first (Lk 12:37). Imagine a debt that would take 164,000 years to repay—God forgives it entirely (Mt 18:24,27).

Parables also show God coming to the aid of the social outcasts, the marginalized, disenfranchised and underprivileged. Samaritans (Lk 10:29–37), tax collectors (Lk 18:9–14), beggars (Lk 16:19–26) and widows (Lk 18:1–8) become the heroes in parables.

Jesus uses parables to note how people can live his teachings on love and justice. The follower of Jesus must be like a tree that bears fruit (Mt 7:16–20; Lk 13:6–9); God's true children not only hear but do his will (Mt 7:21–23; 21:28–30). Jesus' disciples must be ready as they actively wait for his second coming (Mt 24:42—25:46).

Finally, Jesus' use of parables helps envision the type of difference a community of Christ followers can make in the world. It is the salt of the earth and the city set upon a hill (Mt 5:13–16).

MARK

INTRODUCTION TO MARK

The Gospel of Mark abruptly opens by proclaiming the Good News of Jesus the Messiah (Mk 1:1). The story depicts Jesus and the kingdom of God that he announces as advancing against both worldly powers and supernatural forces. While the disciples consistently struggle to understand his mission, Jesus proceeds unflinchingly toward the cross. Along the way, he calls those who would follow him to take up their own crosses (8:34–38).

BACKGROUND

The Gospel of Mark is attributed by early church fathers to John Mark, whose mother was a prominent member of the early church in Jerusalem (Ac 12:12). In the first century, it was not unusual for some Jews to have a Hebrew name ("John") as well as a Greek one ("Mark"). Mark joined his cousin Barnabas and the apostle Paul on their initial missionary journey (Ac 12:25; 13:5; Col 4:10). Somewhere along the way, he had a falling out with Paul, but they apparently reconciled in later years (Ac 15:37–40; 2Ti 4:11; Phm 24). Mark also is associated with the apostle Peter's ministry in Rome (1Pe 5:13, where "Babylon" is generally understood to be a metaphorical reference to Rome). According to early Christian tradition, Peter told Mark all about Jesus' earthly ministry, and Mark put these accounts in writing.

Among the four Gospels, Mark is likely the earliest. It might have been written even before Peter's execution in Rome in the mid–60s AD. Because of Mark's connection to Peter, the Gospel could have been addressed initially to the church in Rome. The Gospel may also have been written not long after the destruction of the Jerusalem temple in AD 70.

STRUCTURE

Mark is the shortest Gospel, and its repeated use of language such as "immediately" or "soon" gives the narrative a sense of urgent action. The fast-paced narrative is depicted in two major sections. Roughly the first half of this Gospel (Mk 1:1—8:26) details Jesus' ministry in Galilee. The rest of the book (8:27—16:8) focuses on Jesus' journey toward Jerusalem and the events of his final week before his death: His triumphal entry into Jerusalem, actions in the temple, the Last Supper with his disciples, arrest and death on the cross. This is followed by news

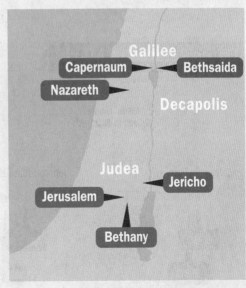

This map depicts many of the locations of Jesus' ministry according to Mark's Gospel.

of Jesus' resurrection (16:1–8). In both major sections, Mark emphasizes God's power, which becomes evident as the kingdom of God arrives through Jesus' presence. At the beginning of the second half of the book, Peter proclaims that Jesus is the Messiah (the Christ)—this is the thematic center of the book and what the entire book's message depends upon (compare 1:1).

OUTLINE

- Jesus' ministry in Galilee (1:1—8:26)
- Jesus' journey to Jerusalem (8:27—10:52)
- Jesus' actions in Jerusalem (11:1—13:37)
- The plot to kill Jesus (14:1—15:47)
- Jesus' victory (16:1–8)
- The longer ending of Mark (16:9–20)

THEMES

In Mark, the Good News of God's kingdom has come in the person of Jesus (1:15)—but this kingdom looks different from the one that most Jews were anticipating. Instead of coming as a conquering military hero, Jesus brings about the kingdom as he humbly serves others—going even to the point of dying for humanity. In light of this unexpected development, a major theme of Mark's Gospel is the so-called "Messianic secret." During the majority of his ministry, Jesus

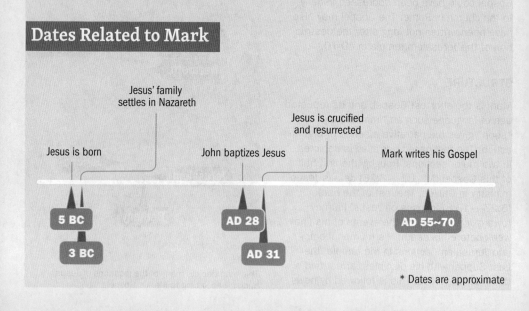

Dates Related to Mark

Jesus' family settles in Nazareth

Jesus is crucified and resurrected

Jesus is born

John baptizes Jesus

Mark writes his Gospel

5 BC

AD 28

AD 55~70

3 BC

AD 31

* Dates are approximate

alludes to his true identity as the Messiah, the Anointed One of Israel, all the while commanding his disciples and most people not to speak openly about his identity. Jesus also often teaches his disciples separately from the crowds. When he does address the masses, he speaks in parables (4:10–20). Only during his trial does Jesus make it clear publicly that he is the Messiah, the Savior that the Jews have been anticipating (14:61–62). Jesus seems to do this to wait for the appointed time—the right time—to tell the world of his identity.

The advancement of God's kingdom throughout Jesus' ministry leads him to clash with political and religious authorities who do not recognize what God is doing (4:11–12). This opposition leads to Jesus' crucifixion—but he is victorious through his resurrection (ch. 16).

Jesus teaches that the only way to follow him involves self-sacrifice (8:34–38). In order to live as members of the kingdom of God, we must humble ourselves, just as he did (10:42–45). Since this way of living is such a stark reversal of most people's values, Jesus' disciples have a hard time grasping it—just as we often do (8:17–21). But the way of the cross is the way of the kingdom of God, and it is open to those willing to listen to Jesus.

John the Baptist Prepares the Way

1:2-8pp — Mt 3:1-11; Lk 3:2-16

1 The beginning of the good news about Jesus the Messiah,[a] the Son of God,[b] 2 as it is written in Isaiah the prophet:

"I will send my messenger ahead of you,
 who will prepare your way"[c] —
3 "a voice of one calling in the wilderness,
 'Prepare the way for the Lord,
  make straight paths for him.'"[d]

4 And so John the Baptist appeared in the wilderness, preaching a baptism of repentance for the forgiveness of sins. 5 The whole Judean countryside and all the people of Jerusalem went out to him. Confessing their sins, they were baptized by him in the Jordan River. 6 John wore clothing made of camel's hair, with a leather belt around his waist, and he ate locusts and wild honey. 7 And this was his

[a] 1 Or *Jesus Christ. Messiah* (Hebrew) and *Christ* (Greek) both mean *Anointed One.* [b] 1 Some manuscripts do not have *the Son of God.* [c] 2 Mal. 3:1 [d] 3 Isaiah 40:3

1:1–8 Mark appears to be the earliest of the four Gospels. It could have been written before Peter's martyrdom in the mid-60s AD (roughly 30 years after Jesus' ministry) or shortly after the destruction of the temple in AD 70. The author is thought to be John Mark (Ac 12:12,25; 13:5), and church tradition considers Peter's testimony to be a source for the Gospel.

The book begins by describing the activities of John the Baptist, whose call for repentance receives an overwhelmingly positive response. Mark links John's ministry to Jesus' ministry by relating both to the content of Isaiah (Mk 1:2). See the event line "Jesus' Early Life and Ministry" on p. 1530.

1:1 the good news The Greek word used here, *euangelion* ("gospel" or "good news"), eventually came to describe the genre of the first four books of the NT; but Mark probably uses it to describe the content of the Christian message (compare 1Co 15:1). Mark 1:1 introduces the good news concerning the person, teaching and life of Jesus, God's Son (see vv. 14–15). The term *euangelion* ("good news") is used in an ancient inscription to announce Caesar Augustus' birth (Inscription Priene 105.40). This suggests that Mark could have been intentionally using *euangelion* in a subversive way—to say that the truly good news is Jesus and that he is owed the ultimate allegiance of humanity. **Jesus** The name *iēsous* (Jesus) is the Greek version of the Hebrew name Joshua (*yehoshua'* or *yeshua'*), a common Jewish name in the first century AD. **the Messiah** The Greek word used here, *christos*, translates the Hebrew title *mashiach*, meaning "anointed one." The term often functions as part of Jesus' name, though elsewhere it is used as a title (e.g., Mk 8:29; 12:35; 14:61). **1:2 it is written** A conventional formula used for introducing a biblical quotation. **Isaiah** Though only Isaiah is mentioned by name, Mark conflates Mal 3:1 and Isa 40:3 into one quotation—mixing traditions from various Scripture texts was common at the time (e.g., 2Co 6:14—7:1). Mark likely only mentions Isaiah because he is the earlier prophet and Mark primarily quotes from Isaiah. Both Mal 3:1 and Isa 40:3 are used in the Gospels to refer to John the Baptist's ministry as a forerunner to the Messiah (Mt 3:3; 11:10; Lk 3:4; Jn 1:23). Malachi 3:1 prophesies about God's messenger who will prepare the way for God himself. Malachi 3:1 also speaks of the Lord (or ruler)—whom the people seek—coming to God's temple as a messenger of Yahweh's covenant with his people. Mark depicts the first messenger of Mal 3:1 as John the Baptist and the Lord (or ruler) as Jesus. **who will prepare** In addition to resembling Mal 3:1, Mark's quotation echoes Ex 23:20, where an angel is described as protecting God's people during their wilderness journey and fighting on their behalf (Ex 23:21–23). The people are commanded to listen to this angel and not rebel

against him. Likewise, John the Baptist presents the very truths of God and acts as the advocate for God's ministry in Jesus. **1:3 wilderness** The Greek word used here, *erēmos*, describes an uncultivated or unpopulated region. In the Bible, the term often refers to the arid expanses south and east of Judah. See note on Mt 3:1. **way** The Greek word used here, *hodos*, often refers to a road or path. Mark uses it predominantly to describe a journey. Mark often describes Jesus' journey to Jerusalem as the "way" that he undertakes in obedience to God, fully aware it will lead to suffering and death (Mk 8:27; 9:33–34; 10:17,32,46,52). In Isa 40:3, which Mark is quoting, the "way" refers to God's path back to Jerusalem, following the exile of the Jewish people in Babylon (586–538 BC). This anticipates the temple being rebuilt and God's presence dwelling once again among his people in the promised land. It represents the restoration of God's people after their exile in Babylon. Mark presents John the Baptist as making the way for Yahweh's presence and the full restoration of Yahweh's people, as seen in Jesus. **make straight paths for him** The cry of a herald who runs in advance of a king announcing his imminent arrival—the king in Isa 40:3, being quoted here, is God himself. In Mark's Gospel, the herald is John the Baptist, who announces Jesus' arrival and the kingdom of God (Mk 1:4–8). It seems that for Mark the return of the Jewish people to Jerusalem only marked the beginning of God's plans for restoration; John the Baptist makes the way for the final fulfilment in Jesus (1:14–15). **1:4 John** See note on Jn 1:6. **baptism of repentance** In ancient Israel, water was often used as an instrument for purification (e.g., Lev 17:15; 22:4–6; Nu 19:11–12). As a result, baptism in Judaism often was about ritual cleansing and may have involved multiple and regular baptisms. By contrast, John's baptism stressed transformation—a turning from sin—and thus marked a turning point in a person's life. **for the forgiveness of sins** John points to Jesus' greater ministry, even calling him the Lamb of God who takes away the sin of the world (Jn 1:29–31). John's baptism was about forgiveness of sins in the sense that it pointed to Jesus, who was the means of providing that forgiveness. **1:5 Jordan River** After 40 years of wandering in the wilderness, the Israelites crossed the Jordan to take possession of the promised land (Jos 3). The river carried symbolic connotations of national renewal and the fulfillment of God's work among them. It is at this location that John the Baptist inaugurates the way for spiritual renewal. See note on Mk 3:6. **1:6 camel's hair, with a leather belt** John's ministry is associated with Elijah, one of Israel's greatest prophets (Mk 6:14–16; 9:11–14; Mt 11:14). Elijah is characteristically described as wearing garments of hair and a leather belt (2Ki 1:8). **ate locusts and wild honey** See note on Mt 3:4.

message: "After me comes the one more powerful than I, the straps of whose sandals I am not worthy to stoop down and untie. ⁸I baptize you with[a] water, but he will baptize you with[a] the Holy Spirit."

The Baptism and Testing of Jesus

1:9-11pp — Mt 3:13-17; Lk 3:21,22
1:12,13pp — Mt 4:1-11; Lk 4:1-13

⁹At that time Jesus came from Nazareth in Galilee and was baptized by John in the Jordan. ¹⁰Just as Jesus was coming up out of the water, he saw heaven being torn open and the Spirit descending on him like a dove. ¹¹And a voice came from heaven: "You are my Son, whom I love; with you I am well pleased."

¹²At once the Spirit sent him out into the wilderness, ¹³and he was in the wilderness forty days,

being tempted[b] by Satan. He was with the wild animals, and angels attended him.

Jesus Announces the Good News

1:16-20pp — Mt 4:18-22; Lk 5:2-11; Jn 1:35-42

¹⁴After John was put in prison, Jesus went into Galilee, proclaiming the good news of God. ¹⁵"The time has come," he said. "The kingdom of God has come near. Repent and believe the good news!"

Jesus Calls His First Disciples

¹⁶As Jesus walked beside the Sea of Galilee, he saw Simon and his brother Andrew casting a net into the lake, for they were fishermen. ¹⁷"Come,

[a] 8 Or in   [b] 13 The Greek for tempted can also mean tested.

1:7 one more powerful than I John understands himself to be the forerunner of the Messiah (compare Mk 1:2–3). **I am not worthy** Removing and carrying sandals was the work of slaves. John is stating that he is not worthy even to be a slave of the Messiah (the anointed one of God). **1:8 baptize you with water** John's baptism was in preparation for the Messiah, through whom God would pour out his Spirit on the people of Israel (Joel 2:28; Isa 32:15; 44:3; Eze 36:26; compare Isa 42:1). John anticipates that Jesus' appearance would directly precede the arrival of God's Spirit (compare Ac 2:1–13).

1:9–11 Jesus' baptism links his future ministry to John's program of national transformation and renewal. It also serves as a commissioning scene, identifying Jesus as the primary subject of the prophecy quoted in Mk 1:2–3.

1:9 from Nazareth A small town in Galilee. Jesus seems to have spent the majority of his childhood and youth years, and perhaps his early adulthood, in Nazareth (Mt 2:23; Lk 4:16). He does not begin his adult ministry until around age 30 (Lk 3:23). **Galilee** The northernmost region of Palestine. After the death of Herod the Great in 4 BC, his son, Antipas, administered Galilee (along with Perea, where John was baptizing). See note on Lk 3:1. **1:10 heaven being torn open** Evokes the language of Isa 64:1–2. Isaiah 64 is about the awesome arrival of God's presence and the need for sinful people to be saved; the passage has in view both the Jewish people and the nations (the entire world). In culmination of Isa 64, Jesus' baptism marks the arrival of God's presence (compare Mk 1:15). **Spirit** This connects Jesus to Isa 42:1, where God states that he will put his Spirit on his servant. It portrays Jesus as the anointed servant in Isaiah who is commissioned by God to establish justice on the earth (Isa 42:1,4). Mark only mentions Jesus seeing the heavens being torn open and the Spirit descending. John's Gospel states that John the Baptist also saw the Spirit descend on Jesus from heaven (compare Jn 1:32–34). This suggests that Jesus' identity is known to very few people at this point (see note on Mk 1:34). **1:11 You are my Son, whom I love** Drawn from Ps 2:7. Psalm 2 speaks about the role of the anointed one of Yahweh (the Messiah) and how the kings of the earth should fear Yahweh and his Son, for all nations will ultimately be his heritage (Ps 2:7,11–12; compare Isa 52:15; 53:12). This language also is reminiscent of Isa 42:1. This further articulates Jesus' role as the

suffering servant who will suffer, die and rise in order to restore people to right relationship with God, bearing their iniquities and carrying their sins (Isa 42:1–9; 49:1–12; 50:4–11; 52:13—53:12; compare 61:1–3). Jesus being called God's Son also seems to have a subversive, political dimension; on the silver denarius coin of the period, Roman Emperor Tiberius is called "son of the divine" (compare note on Mk 1:1). Jesus, not the emperor, is the son of God.

1:12–13 Having commissioned Jesus, the Spirit now exposes Jesus to a period of testing by Satan, preparing him for the task ahead.

1:12 into the wilderness See note on Lk 4:1.
1:13 forty days Suggests a deliberate parallel between Jesus' testing and Israel's 40 years of wandering in the wilderness, which also involved testing (Dt 2:7; 8:1–18). **being tempted by Satan** Satan is called the devil in the other gospel accounts of this event (Mt 4:1; Lk 4:2). In the OT, Satan is portrayed as an accuser and as a figure who is part of God's council operating in a limited role (see Job 1:6 and note; Zec 3:2). By the time of Mark's Gospel, Satan is understood as a renegade spiritual figure who is openly opposing God's will and has considerable evil power in the present age (2Co 4:4). The figure who tempts Eve in the Garden of Eden is never called Satan (see note on Ge 3:1); however, Revelation conceptually relates the serpent from Eden to Satan (Rev 12:9; 20:2). This same kind of conceptual connection seems to be at work in Mark—this is the primary adversary of God tempting Jesus. Jesus' 40-day testing in the wilderness seems to symbolically reenact the 40-year testing of Israel, although Jesus—as the representative of Israel—succeeds where Israel had failed. His resistance to Satan demonstrates his obedience as God's Son.

1:14–15 As soon as John the Baptist is arrested, Jesus emerges from the wilderness to declare the arrival of God's kingdom on earth.

1:15 time In this context, the Greek word used here, kairos, indicates a period of time predetermined by God. **kingdom** The Greek word used here, basileia, can denote a geographical territory or the reign of a particular monarch. The kingdom of God refers to God's reign over all of creation and humanity. Jesus' teaching in Mark reveals that members of the kingdom of God are marked by childlike humility (Mk 9:33–37;

follow me," Jesus said, "and I will send you out to fish for people." [18]At once they left their nets and followed him.

[19]When he had gone a little farther, he saw James son of Zebedee and his brother John in a boat, preparing their nets. [20]Without delay he called them, and they left their father Zebedee in the boat with the hired men and followed him.

Jesus Drives Out an Impure Spirit

1:21-28pp — Lk 4:31-37

[21]They went to Capernaum, and when the Sabbath came, Jesus went into the synagogue and began to teach. [22]The people were amazed at his teaching, because he taught them as one who had authority, not as the teachers of the law. [23]Just then a man in their synagogue who was possessed by an impure spirit cried out, [24]"What do you want with us, Jesus of Nazareth? Have you come to destroy us? I know who you are — the Holy One of God!"

[25]"Be quiet!" said Jesus sternly. "Come out of him!" [26]The impure spirit shook the man violently and came out of him with a shriek.

[27]The people were all so amazed that they asked each other, "What is this? A new teaching — and with authority! He even gives orders to impure spirits and they obey him." [28]News about him spread quickly over the whole region of Galilee.

10:13–16), concern for the poor (10:21–31), sacrificial service (10:42–45), and love for God and neighbor (12:28–34). The language Mark uses to describe God's rule demonstrates its dynamic character: The kingdom comes (v. 15; 9:1; compare 15:43), it grows like a seed (4:26,30), and people can enter it, but only by responding to God's will (9:47; 10:15,23–25; 12:34). The OT often speaks about God's everlasting and worldwide rule (e.g., Ps 9:7; 47:8; 145:11–13). Yahweh is described as enthroned in heaven and in his temple in Jerusalem (Ps 9:11; 11:4; Isa 24:23; Eze 20:33–40; 43:1–7; Mic 4:7–8; compare Isa 66:1–2). It is this reign that Mark's Gospel affiliates with Jesus. Jesus' ministry involves the cleansing of Yahweh's temple (the symbol of his earthly presence), and Jesus himself is the epitome of that presence: His body is described as God's temple (Mk 11:15–19; 14:58; compare Jn 2:19–22). The OT also affiliates God's reign with the Davidic dynasty (1Ch 28:5; 2Ch 13:8); in parallel, later in Mark's Gospel, a crowd proclaims that Jesus has inaugurated David's kingdom (Mk 11:10; compare 2Sa 7:13–16). **has come near** There are obvious examples in history before this time of Yahweh reigning on earth, such as when Israel was established in the promised land or when Yahweh's temple was built in Jerusalem. However, God's full reign — as seen in the Garden of Eden shortly after creation — had not existed since sin entered the world (Ge 2:4–9; 3; compare Rev 22:1–5). Jesus' proclamation suggests that the time of God's full reign on earth is near. God's presence on earth has arrived in the flesh in Jesus. Jesus is saying that since that has occurred, it is only a matter of time until the justice and order that mark God's reign are in place over all the earth (compare Isa 9; 66:15–24). The kingdom of God is described as near (present) but not fully arrived because its full arrival on earth takes place upon Jesus' second coming (compare 1Co 15:20–28). **believe the good news** Since Jesus announces the advent of a new kingdom, belief in the gospel entails allegiance to the new king, Jesus.

1:16–21 Jesus begins to call individual disciples.

1:16 Sea of Galilee A lake fed by the Jordan River; it forms the eastern boundary of the region of Galilee. Much of Jesus' ministry takes place along its western shores. **Simon** Jesus will rename him Peter (Mk 3:16). In addition to being Jesus' first disciple named in Mark, Simon will be the first person in Mark's Gospel to recognize Jesus as the Messiah (8:29).

1:17 Come, follow me Jesus as rabbi calls his first disciples using a phrase that evokes OT images of prophetic succession (1Ki 19:20; compare Mk 9:5; 11:21). Jesus' call also is a reminder that he is on a journey that has been prepared for him (vv. 2–3).

1:18 At once they left their nets and followed The immediacy of their response conveys the urgency of Jesus' message about the kingdom of God and the level of commitment that it requires (compare 10:28).

1:19 James son of Zebedee One of the first disciples and a member of Jesus' inner group of disciples; not to be confused with James the brother of Jesus. Along with his brother John, James was given the Aramaic title *boanērges*, which means "sons of thunder" (3:17). Despite his influential position as a disciple, he does not play an influential role in the early church. Jesus alludes to his martyrdom, which takes place in AD 44 under Herod Agrippa (10:38; Ac 12:2). **John** One of the first disciples and a member of Jesus' inner circle. John is likely the unnamed "beloved disciple" in the Gospel of John and is thought to have written the fourth Gospel (see note on Jn 13:23). He plays an important role in the early church (Gal 2:9) but often is portrayed simply as a silent companion of Peter (Ac 3:1–10; 4:1–22).

1:21–28 Jesus demonstrates the kingdom's presence in his amazing teaching and in his ability to perform an exorcism, which verifies his authority. See the table "Miracles of Jesus" on p. 1741.

1:21 Capernaum A village on the northern shore of the Sea of Galilee. **Sabbath** The traditional day of rest for the Jewish people as prescribed by the law (Ex 20:8–11; Dt 5:12–15). **synagogue** See note on Mt 4:23; see the infographic "The Synagogue at Capernaum" on p. 1656.

1:22 teachers of the law Refers to experts in the Law of Moses. They served a religious function alongside the priests and Pharisees.

1:23 an impure spirit The term used here links the idea of malevolent supernatural forces to the Jewish concern for purity and holiness. **cried out** Refers to the man with the unclean spirit. His next words, however, indicate that the unclean spirit is actually speaking through him, since a plural ("us") is used.

1:24 I know who you are So far in Mark's Gospel, only Jesus seems to know his true identity (v. 11). Mark emphasizes the demons' recognition of Jesus as the one God has set apart for a purpose. This highlights both human ignorance of who Jesus is and how fearful evil powers were of him.

1:25 Be quiet With this command, Jesus simultaneously neutralizes the spirit's attempt to oppose him and pre-

Jesus Heals Many

1:29-31pp — Mt 8:14,15; Lk 4:38,39
1:32-34pp — Mt 8:16,17; Lk 4:40,41

²⁹As soon as they left the synagogue, they went with James and John to the home of Simon and Andrew. ³⁰Simon's mother-in-law was in bed with a fever, and they immediately told Jesus about her. ³¹So he went to her, took her hand and helped her up. The fever left her and she began to wait on them. ³²That evening after sunset the people brought to Jesus all the sick and demon-possessed. ³³The whole town gathered at the door, ³⁴and Jesus healed many who had various diseases. He also drove out many demons, but he would not let the demons speak because they knew who he was.

Jesus Prays in a Solitary Place

1:35-38pp — Lk 4:42,43

³⁵Very early in the morning, while it was still dark, Jesus got up, left the house and went off to a solitary place, where he prayed. ³⁶Simon and his companions went to look for him, ³⁷and when they found him, they exclaimed: "Everyone is looking for you!"

³⁸Jesus replied, "Let us go somewhere else — to the nearby villages — so I can preach there also. That is why I have come." ³⁹So he traveled throughout Galilee, preaching in their synagogues and driving out demons.

Jesus Heals a Man With Leprosy

1:40-44pp — Mt 8:2-4; Lk 5:12-14

⁴⁰A man with leprosy*ᵃ* came to him and begged him on his knees, "If you are willing, you can make me clean."

⁴¹Jesus was indignant.*ᵇ* He reached out his hand and touched the man. "I am willing," he said. "Be clean!" ⁴²Immediately the leprosy left him and he was cleansed.

ᵃ 40 The Greek word traditionally translated *leprosy* was used for various diseases affecting the skin. *ᵇ 41* Many manuscripts *Jesus was filled with compassion*

---

vents his identity as the Messiah from becoming public knowledge (see v. 24 and note).

1:27 they obey him Exorcists were common in the ancient Near East. For example, among the Dead Sea Scrolls (ca. 250 BC–AD 50), a text containing an incantation formula designed to exorcise demons was discovered. Jesus distinguishes himself from other exorcists in that he did not rely on complex incantations. He could simply command the demons and they would leave their hosts.

1:28–34 Jesus' inaugural exorcism sets off a chain reaction, as those who hear the good news respond to it.

1:30 immediately The Greek word used here, *euthys*, occurs more than 40 times in Mark, giving Mark's Gospel an unrelenting pace.

1:31 helped her up The Greek term used here, *egeirō*, is used frequently throughout Mark to describe Jesus' healings (e.g., a paralytic in 2:9,11–12; a dead girl in 5:41; an epileptic in 9:27). Mark uses the same verb to describe the resurrection of the dead (6:14,16; 12:26; 14:28; 16:6). This overlap connects Jesus' resurrection with his ministry; his divine power and purpose enable both. **she began to wait on them** See Mt 8:15 and note.

1:32–34 These specific types of healing that had already taken place in Capernaum—the silencing and exorcism of the unclean spirit (Mk 1:21–28) and the healing of Simon Peter's mother-in-law (vv. 29–31)—now take place on a larger scale. The multiplication of these types of healing illustrates that God's rule is advancing. The text implies that after observers viewed Jesus' initial demonstrations of divine power, they told others. This leads Jesus to perform an increasing number of deeds.

1:32 after sunset Indicates the close of the Sabbath day, after which the prohibition against work ended (1:21). The townspeople, who observed the law, waited until this moment to bring the sick and demon-possessed people to Jesus (compare 3:1–6).

1:34 would not let the demons speak Jesus continues to veil his true identity (compare note on 1:24). Jesus'

true identity so challenged the religious leaders of the time that it led to his execution. Mark's Gospel notes that Jesus is aware that the unveiling of his true identity, as God's Son and the Messiah, will lead to his death (2:20; 8:31). Unlike the characters in the narrative, from the very first line of Mark's Gospel forward, the reader is aware of Jesus' identity (1:1). The secrecy of Jesus' identity is a common theme in Mark's Gospel. Jesus' identity is only revealed to everyone when it is time for Jesus to suffer, die and rise again (e.g., 1:44; 5:43; 8:26).

1:35–39 Having completed his work in Capernaum, Jesus expands his ministry to the whole of Galilee, but before doing so, he spends time alone in prayer. Instead of embracing the potential fame he could have in Capernaum (v. 38), Jesus moves on so that he may minister in other places.

1:40–45 This particular healing story shows the unhindered expansion of God's rule.

1:40 A man with leprosy The Greek word used here, *lepros*, identifies a person afflicted by a skin disease. Leviticus categorizes such individuals as ritually unclean and prohibits them from coming in contact with other Israelites during their illness (Lev 13:1–46). **If you are willing, you can** Jesus already demonstrated his ability to eliminate uncleanness when he expelled the demonic spirit at Capernaum (Mk 1:21–28). Now, a man with a different type of impurity seeks cleansing, and Jesus' success confirms that God's rule overcomes all obstacles to health and holiness.

1:41 Jesus was indignant In a few ancient manuscripts, the Greek word *splanchnizō*, which refers to being moved with pity, replaces the term *orgizō*, which indicates anger. However, the substitution likely reflects a later change by a copyist, to avoid the difficulty of this verse. Jesus affirms his desire to cleanse the man, indicating he is not upset by the leper's plea. He might be reacting in anger to the illness itself. The disease represents pain and suffering and also made a person unclean according to the law (Lev 13). Jesus also might

⁴³Jesus sent him away at once with a strong warning: ⁴⁴"See that you don't tell this to anyone. But go, show yourself to the priest and offer the sacrifices that Moses commanded for your cleansing, as a testimony to them." ⁴⁵Instead he went out and began to talk freely, spreading the news. As a result, Jesus could no longer enter a town openly but stayed outside in lonely places. Yet the people still came to him from everywhere.

Jesus Forgives and Heals a Paralyzed Man

2:3-12pp — Mt 9:2-8; Lk 5:18-26

2 A few days later, when Jesus again entered Capernaum, the people heard that he had come home. ²They gathered in such large numbers that there was no room left, not even outside the door, and he preached the word to them. ³Some men came, bringing to him a paralyzed man, carried by four of them. ⁴Since they could not get him to Jesus because of the crowd, they made an opening in the roof above Jesus by digging through it and then lowered the mat the man was lying on. ⁵When Jesus saw their faith, he said to the paralyzed man, "Son, your sins are forgiven."

⁶Now some teachers of the law were sitting there, thinking to themselves, ⁷"Why does this fellow talk like that? He's blaspheming! Who can forgive sins but God alone?"

⁸Immediately Jesus knew in his spirit that this was what they were thinking in their hearts, and he said to them, "Why are you thinking these things? ⁹Which is easier: to say to this paralyzed man, 'Your sins are forgiven,' or to say, 'Get up, take your mat and walk'? ¹⁰But I want you to know that the Son of Man has authority on earth to forgive sins." So he said to the man, ¹¹"I tell you, get up, take your mat and go home."

---

regard the man's condition as caused by a demonic spirit. **touched** Jesus' physical contact with the leper, followed by his immediate cleansing of him, emphasizes that Jesus' spirit of holiness is more powerful than the uncleanness generated by the skin disease (compare Lev 13–14). Rather than Jesus becoming unclean, he makes the leper clean.

1:44 that you don't tell this to anyone The first of many such requests that Jesus will make so people do not reveal his identity as the Messiah before the time intended by God (see Mk 5:43; 8:30; 9:9). Most of these requests achieve the opposite effect: Instead of staying silent, the people broadcast what he has done for them (7:36), forcing him to go elsewhere to minister. **that Moses commanded** Refers to a sequence of two sacrificial offerings God mandated to mark a diseased individual's healing and reintegration into the community (Lev 14:1–32). Jesus has already cleansed the man. Now, the priest must directly examine him to certify that the source of uncleanness has indeed gone.

1:45 could no longer enter a town openly Probably due to Jesus' increasing popularity, not opposition. The sequence of settings in Mk 1:21–45 suggests that Jesus' ministry was consistently expanding: He moves from teaching in Capernaum's synagogue to all of Capernaum, all Galilean towns, then the deserted places between them. In each case, the report about Jesus' action attracts larger crowds. See the infographic "The Synagogue at Capernaum" on p. 1656.

2:1–12 Jesus' return to Capernaum brings him into tension with rival teachers: the scribes (teachers of the law) and Pharisees.

2:1 home Might refer to Simon Peter and Andrew's house, where Jesus had previously stayed (1:29–34).
2:2 the word The Greek phrase used here, *ho logos*, refers in this instance to the gospel that Jesus has been proclaiming throughout Galilee (1:15,38–39; see note on 1:1).
2:4 they made an opening in the roof Most buildings in ancient Palestine had flat roofs made of a mixture of clay and brush, reinforced by wooden beams. See the infographic "First-Century Israelite House" on p. 1658.
2:5 Son Since the paralytic needs four people to lift him,

he likely is an adult. In a way similar to his statement here, Jesus later speaks of the children — Israel — as the intended recipients of his ministry (7:27; 10:24). **sins are forgiven** Jesus' words to the man suggest a connection between sin and illness, an assumption rooted in the OT understanding of disobedience to God's law resulting in various curses (Dt 28:15–46). The healing that follows authenticates Jesus' claim to forgive sins.

2:6 teachers of the law Introduced indirectly in Mk 1:22. The people's increasing recognition of Jesus' authority provokes conflict with these teachers. **thinking** In Mark, the Greek term used here, *dialogizomai*, is often used in contexts where a sense of disapproval or disagreement is involved (8:16–17; 9:33; 11:31).

2:7 Why Each episode of controversy in this chapter is provoked by a question about the behavior of Jesus or his disciples (vv. 16,18,24; compare 3:4). **He's blaspheming** The scribes (teachers of the law) accuse Jesus of blasphemy because he, a human being, claims to do something only God can. Blasphemy — a significant theme in Mark's Gospel — is the first and last charge Jesus' Jewish adversaries will bring against him (14:64). **God alone** In the OT, only God is able to forgive sins (e.g., Ps 32:5; Isa 43:25).

2:9 Which is easier For Jesus' opponents, his claim to forgive the man's sins — equivalent to claiming divinity — is easily dismissible since there is no proof of the success of his claim. Jesus' rhetorical question and following action are meant to stimulate his audience, and especially his accusers, to recognize that he had authority to act with God's power.

2:10 the Son of Man The phrase, which may be literally rendered "human one" (compare Eze 2:1), refers in Da 7:13–14 to a Messiah figure who comes to Yahweh (called the Ancient of Days), with the clouds surrounding him, to be given dominion over all of the world. Yahweh is also depicted as riding on the clouds (e.g., Isa 19:1), which means the Son of Man is depicted like Yahweh himself — indicating that the Son of Man figure is also divine. This is fitting as a description for Jesus' ministry, since he is divine and human, and is establishing the kingdom of God on earth (Mk 1:15). Compare note on Da 7:13; Mk 13:24–27; 14:62.

¹²He got up, took his mat and walked out in full view of them all. This amazed everyone and they praised God, saying, "We have never seen anything like this!"

Jesus Calls Levi and Eats With Sinners

2:14-17pp — Mt 9:9-13; Lk 5:27-32

¹³Once again Jesus went out beside the lake. A large crowd came to him, and he began to teach them. ¹⁴As he walked along, he saw Levi son of Alphaeus sitting at the tax collector's booth. "Follow me," Jesus told him, and Levi got up and followed him.

¹⁵While Jesus was having dinner at Levi's house, many tax collectors and sinners were eating with him and his disciples, for there were many who followed him. ¹⁶When the teachers of the law who were Pharisees saw him eating with the sinners and tax collectors, they asked his disciples: "Why does he eat with tax collectors and sinners?"

¹⁷On hearing this, Jesus said to them, "It is not the healthy who need a doctor, but the sick. I have not come to call the righteous, but sinners."

Jesus Questioned About Fasting

2:18-22pp — Mt 9:14-17; Lk 5:33-38

¹⁸Now John's disciples and the Pharisees were fasting. Some people came and asked Jesus, "How is it that John's disciples and the disciples of the Pharisees are fasting, but yours are not?"

¹⁹Jesus answered, "How can the guests of the bridegroom fast while he is with them? They cannot, so long as they have him with them. ²⁰But the time will come when the bridegroom will be taken from them, and on that day they will fast.

²¹"No one sews a patch of unshrunk cloth on an old garment. Otherwise, the new piece will pull away from the old, making the tear worse. ²²And no one pours new wine into old wineskins. Otherwise, the wine will burst the skins, and both the wine and the wineskins will be ruined. No, they pour new wine into new wineskins."

2:12 never seen anything like this Jesus acted with an unprecedented authority over physical maladies and demons.

2:13–17 Jesus' choice of a tax collector as disciple provokes controversy over the aim of his ministry, which seems to be incompatible with the Pharisees' vision for Israel.

2:13 the lake Refers to the Sea of Galilee; Capernaum was on its northern shore.

2:14 Levi son of Alphaeus Possibly the brother of James the son of Alphaeus (see 3:18), not to be confused with James the son of Zebedee (1:16–20) or James the brother of Jesus (6:3). Levi is called Matthew in Matthew's Gospel (Mt 9:9; compare Lk 5:27).

2:15 Levi's house The Greek text here, literally rendered as "his house," is ambiguous. Jesus may be eating at Levi's house or Simon Peter and Andrew's house in Capernaum, where Jesus stayed in the past (Mk 1:29–34; compare v. 1). If Levi is representative of the group eating with Jesus, the tax collectors who dined with Jesus would have been low-level functionaries who worked on behalf of more powerful government agents (e.g., 6:21). They were probably classified with sinners in this verse because their work exploited people (compare Lk 3:13–14; 19:8). See the infographic "First-Century Israelite House" on p. 1658. **sinners** In the Gospels, this term is generally used for people who are considered sinful by Jewish leaders. While certainly many of these people were involved in habits, lifestyles or occupations that led to unrighteous behavior, the label seems to be applied primarily to distinguish between those who were considered pious and those who were not. Jesus' ministry was often focused on outsiders, including this group of people (see Mk 2:17). **eating with him** In the ancient world, dining together was a primary expression of identity and belonging. For tax collectors and sinners to seek out table fellowship with Jesus implies they were interested in the kingdom of God that Jesus proclaimed (Mk 1:15).

2:16 teachers of the law who were Pharisees Some scribes (teachers of the law) in Jesus' day may have identified themselves with the agenda of the Pharisaic movement.

Mark 2:16

PHARISEES
One of the three Jewish schools of thought in Palestine at the time of Jesus, according to the Jewish historian Josephus. While the extent of their influence is unclear, the Pharisees apparently had some influence in political, religious and social spheres in Jewish Palestine. The Pharisees were known for their skill at interpreting the Law of Moses, and they held strict views on what was appropriate behavior for a righteous person. In Mark, Jesus criticizes the Pharisees for holding to traditions rather than obeying God's commands (Mk 7:6–13). In Mark 2, they condemn Jesus' choice to eat with those they viewed as unrighteous and unworthy, but Jesus is not interested in their rules about who is worthy of his attention.

2:17 to call the righteous With this statement, Jesus is neither affirming nor denying that the Pharisees are righteous. He is simply pointing out that the call to repentance and offering of forgiveness are for those who need it—sinners.

2:18–22 In this section, Jesus discusses fasting with a group of people—explaining why his disciples do not fast when others do. Fasting was a key element of Judaism in the first century AD, even though only one day of fasting was required by the law (Lev 16:29–30). Jesus in no way condemns fasting (compare Ac 13:2); instead, he explains why it was not necessary while he was bodily present with his disciples.

2:18 Pharisees Luke 18:11–12 indicates that fasting was characteristic of the Pharisees' piety. As a religious

Jesus Is Lord of the Sabbath

2:23-28pp — Mt 12:1-8; Lk 6:1-5
3:1-6pp — Mt 12:9-14; Lk 6:6-11

²³One Sabbath Jesus was going through the grainfields, and as his disciples walked along, they began to pick some heads of grain. ²⁴The Pharisees said to him, "Look, why are they doing what is unlawful on the Sabbath?"

²⁵He answered, "Have you never read what David did when he and his companions were hungry and in need? ²⁶In the days of Abiathar the high priest, he entered the house of God and ate the consecrated bread, which is lawful only for priests to eat. And he also gave some to his companions."

²⁷Then he said to them, "The Sabbath was made for man, not man for the Sabbath. ²⁸So the Son of Man is Lord even of the Sabbath."

Jesus Heals on the Sabbath

3 Another time Jesus went into the synagogue, and a man with a shriveled hand was there. ²Some of them were looking for a reason to ac-

cuse Jesus, so they watched him closely to see if he would heal him on the Sabbath. ³Jesus said to the man with the shriveled hand, "Stand up in front of everyone."

⁴Then Jesus asked them, "Which is lawful on the Sabbath: to do good or to do evil, to save life or to kill?" But they remained silent.

⁵He looked around at them in anger and, deeply distressed at their stubborn hearts, said to the man, "Stretch out your hand." He stretched it out, and his hand was completely restored. ⁶Then the Pharisees went out and began to plot with the Herodians how they might kill Jesus.

Crowds Follow Jesus

3:7-12pp — Mt 12:15,16; Lk 6:17-19

⁷Jesus withdrew with his disciples to the lake, and a large crowd from Galilee followed. ⁸When they heard about all he was doing, many people came to him from Judea, Jerusalem, Idumea, and the regions across the Jordan and around Tyre and Sidon. ⁹Because of the crowd he told

---

practice, fasting could express mourning, repentance or preparation for an event. It also could accompany petitionary prayer. **asked Jesus** In both Jewish and Greco-Roman culture, a teacher was held responsible for the behavior of his students (compare Mk 2:23–24). Previously, the Pharisees asked Jesus' disciples to explain Jesus' behavior (v. 16); now they ask Jesus to explain his disciples' behavior.

2:19 fast Mourning or penitential activity would be inappropriate at a joyous occasion such as a wedding.

2:20 will be taken from them Jesus' remark foreshadows his own future—his betrayal, arrest and execution.

2:21 the new piece will pull away from the old Jesus emphasizes the change brought about by the kingdom's arrival. While the previous analogy (vv. 19–20) contrasted present and future, this verse distinguishes between old and new. See note on Mt 9:16.

2:23–28 The contrast between the ways of the Pharisees and the ways of Jesus descends into hostile interrogation and rebuttal, climaxing in another declaration of Jesus' authority.

2:24 what is unlawful Jews at this time debated about when human need could legitimately override the command to observe the Sabbath, and many people had strict rules regarding the Sabbath, the Jewish day of rest (see note on Mt 12:11). The Pentateuch doesn't specifically prohibit plucking grain on the Sabbath, though it could be understood as discouraging the gathering and preparation of food on the Sabbath (Ex 16:11–30; 34:21). Jesus and his disciples are impoverished, which means that they may be practicing OT laws that allowed the poor to gather from a farmer's harvest (Lev 19:9–10; 23:22; Dt 24:19–22; compare Ru 2:2).

2:25–26 Jesus refers to 1Sa 21:1–6. When David was fleeing from King Saul, he persuaded a priest to give him consecrated bread by claiming that he was on his way to a secret meeting with other servants of the king.

2:26 which is lawful only for priests to eat Because David had need, his action was justified (compare Ex 25:30; Lev 24:5–9); the same is true for Jesus' disciples.

2:27 Sabbath was made for man This enigmatic statement likely means that the Sabbath was established in order to give people rest. The Pharisees' overzealous protection of the Sabbath has lost sight of its purpose and turned it into something burdensome.

2:28 Lord even of the Sabbath Jesus' ministry often takes place on the Sabbath (Mk 1:21–27; 3:1–5; 6:1–5). By asserting lordship over the Sabbath, he claims authority over its laws and limitations, and he claims the ability to heal on the Sabbath (3:1–5; compare note on 2:10).

3:1–6 Jesus demonstrates his lordship over the Sabbath by healing a man. This action provokes the Pharisees and their allies to plot against him.

3:2 for a reason to accuse Jesus Profaning the Sabbath was a capital offense (Ex 31:14–15; 35:2; Nu 15:32–36). **they watched him closely** Probably refers to the Pharisees (v. 6).

3:4 to save life or to kill Jesus' question about the Sabbath is provocative and was intended to question common viewpoints (compare note on Mk 2:24). Elsewhere Jesus teaches that love of neighbor not only fulfills the law but is central to the kingdom of God (12:29–34). Here, Jesus tangibly demonstrates that human traditions and moral codes should not conflict with love of neighbor.

3:5 their stubborn hearts This Biblical idiom, often rendered as "hardness of heart" (compare Ex 4:21 and note), indicates both stubbornness and opposition to God's workings (2:6–8).

3:6 Pharisees See note on 2:16. **the Herodians** A political party who generally supported Herod Antipas' regime. See the table "Major Groups in Jesus' Time" on p. 1630.

his disciples to have a small boat ready for him, to keep the people from crowding him. [10]For he had healed many, so that those with diseases were pushing forward to touch him. [11]Whenever the impure spirits saw him, they fell down before him and cried out, "You are the Son of God." [12]But he gave them strict orders not to tell others about him.

Jesus Appoints the Twelve

3:16-19pp — Mt 10:2-4; Lk 6:14-16; Ac 1:13

[13]Jesus went up on a mountainside and called to him those he wanted, and they came to him. [14]He appointed twelve[a] that they might be with him and that he might send them out to preach [15]and to have authority to drive out demons. [16]These are the twelve he appointed: Simon (to whom he gave the name Peter), [17]James son of Zebedee and his brother John (to them he gave the name Boanerges, which means "sons of thunder"), [18]Andrew, Philip, Bartholomew, Matthew, Thomas, James son of Alphaeus, Thaddaeus, Simon the Zealot [19]and Judas Iscariot, who betrayed him.

Jesus Accused by His Family and by Teachers of the Law

3:23-27pp — Mt 12:25-29; Lk 11:17-22
3:31-35pp — Mt 12:46-50; Lk 8:19-21

[20]Then Jesus entered a house, and again a crowd gathered, so that he and his disciples were not even able to eat. [21]When his family[b] heard about

---

[a] 14 Some manuscripts twelve—designating them apostles—
[b] 21 Or his associates

3:7–12 Mark briefly summarizes the first phase of Jesus' ministry by detailing the large region from which Jesus' followers had come and the amazing actions that had drawn them.

3:7 to the lake Jesus again follows a confrontation with the Pharisees by withdrawing to the sea, accompanied by crowds receptive to his ministry (compare 2:13).

3:8 Judea Roman province corresponding roughly to the OT kingdom of Judah, with Jerusalem as the capital. This list of places indicates that news of Jesus' deeds has reached beyond Galilee (compare 1:39,45). **Idumea** A territory southeast of Judea. The places mentioned here—Idumea, the region across the Jordan, Tyre and Sidon—were inhabited predominantly by non-Jewish people, which suggests that Jesus was attracting non-Jews as well as Jews. Idumea is far south of Galilee, and Tyre is far north; this indicates the broad geographic spread of Jesus' message. The reception of Jesus by Gentiles is a significant theme in Mark (5:1–20; 7:24–30,31–37). **regions across the Jordan** Also known as Perea.

3:10 touch him The motif of Jesus healing by touch will become more prominent in the narratives that follow (5:25–34; 6:56; 7:32–37; 8:22–26; compare 1:40–45).

3:11 You are the Son of God Resembles the behavior of the first unclean spirit Jesus encountered in Mark's Gospel—a cry, followed by recognition of Jesus' identity (see 1:23–24; compare 15:39).

3:12 not to tell others about him For first-century Jews, the Messiah was a political as well as a religious figure. Jesus' desire to conceal his identity may have been motivated by a desire to avoid violent repercussions early in his ministry (compare note on 1:11).

3:13–19 Having proclaimed and enacted the arrival of God's kingdom, Jesus now appoints others to multiply its effects. Echoing the twelve tribes of Israel, the twelve apostles likely serve as a symbolic reconstitution of the people of God around Jesus' mission and teaching.

3:13 went up Reflects Ex 24:1–11, where Moses summons Israel's tribal leaders to join him on Mount Sinai. In Mark's Gospel, Jesus ascends mountains at significant points involving the twelve apostles: He chooses them (Mk 3:13–19), he prays for them (6:46) and he reveals his identity to them (9:2–8).

3:15 authority to drive out demons A key sign of the presence of God's kingdom and Jesus' deliverance of humanity (1:21–28).

3:16 Peter The Greek word for Peter, petros, means "rock." Paul refers to Peter with the Aramaic form of this name, kephas (e.g., Gal 1:18), suggesting that Jesus originally gave him this name in Aramaic (the primary language of Jesus and his disciples).

3:17 Boanerges, which means "sons of thunder" Mark includes what is presumably the original Semitic form of James and John's new name. It is unclear why Jesus calls them this, but it may be because of their reputation as strong-willed people (compare Mt 20:20–28).

3:18 Matthew Since Levi the tax collector is not listed here, this seems to be a reference to him. Compare note on Mk 2:14. **James son of Alphaeus** Possibly the brother of Levi the tax collector (2:14). **the Zealot** This title serves to distinguish Simon from Simon Peter. While most translations have "Zealot" here, some follow a manuscript that reads "Canaanite." The two words are similar in Greek. Simon the Zealot is sometimes linked to the priest-led faction that occupied the Jerusalem temple during the first year of the First Jewish Revolt against Rome (AD 66–70). According to the first-century Jewish historian Josephus, this group called themselves Zealots (Josephus, Jewish War 4.160–61). However, no evidence indicates that this group existed before the revolt; rather, it seems to have formed as a result of the revolt. Alternatively, this title might show that Simon was particularly zealous for the Jewish law and traditions (compare Ac 21:20; Gal 1:14). See the table "Major Groups in Jesus' Time" on p. 1630.

3:19 Iscariot The meaning of this epithet is uncertain. It could be a version of the Hebrew phrase ish qeriyyoth, meaning "the man from Kerioth," referring to a town in Judea. Alternatively, it could be an Aramaic slur, ishqarya', meaning "the false one."

3:20–35 Despite Jesus' growing fame, he receives a mixed reception from the religious leaders and even his own family. Jesus confronts the accusation that his ministry is fueled by demonic power.

3:20 a house See note on Mk 2:1.

this, they went to take charge of him, for they said, "He is out of his mind."

²²And the teachers of the law who came down from Jerusalem said, "He is possessed by Beelzebul! By the prince of demons he is driving out demons."

²³So Jesus called them over to him and began to speak to them in parables: "How can Satan drive out Satan? ²⁴If a kingdom is divided against itself, that kingdom cannot stand. ²⁵If a house is divided against itself, that house cannot stand. ²⁶And if Satan opposes himself and is divided, he cannot stand; his end has come. ²⁷In fact, no one can enter a strong man's house without first tying him up. Then he can plunder the strong man's house. ²⁸Truly I tell you, people can be forgiven all their sins and every slander they utter, ²⁹but whoever blasphemes against the Holy Spirit will never be forgiven; they are guilty of an eternal sin."

³⁰He said this because they were saying, "He has an impure spirit."

³¹Then Jesus' mother and brothers arrived. Standing outside, they sent someone in to call him. ³²A crowd was sitting around him, and they told him, "Your mother and brothers are outside looking for you."

³³"Who are my mother and my brothers?" he asked.

³⁴Then he looked at those seated in a circle around him and said, "Here are my mother and my brothers! ³⁵Whoever does God's will is my brother and sister and mother."

The Parable of the Sower

4:1-12pp — Mt 13:1-15; Lk 8:4-10
4:13-20pp — Mt 13:18-23; Lk 8:11-15

4 Again Jesus began to teach by the lake. The crowd that gathered around him was so large that he got into a boat and sat in it out on the lake, while all the people were along the shore at the water's edge. ²He taught them many things by parables, and in his teaching said: ³"Listen! A farmer went out to sow his seed. ⁴As he was scattering the seed, some fell along the path, and the birds came and ate it up. ⁵Some fell on rocky places, where it did not have much soil. It sprang up quickly, because the soil was shallow. ⁶But when the sun came up, the plants were scorched, and they withered because they had no root. ⁷Other seed fell among thorns, which grew up and choked the plants, so that they did not bear grain. ⁸Still other seed fell on good soil. It came up, grew and produced a crop, some multiplying thirty, some sixty, some a hundred times."

⁹Then Jesus said, "Whoever has ears to hear, let them hear."

3:21 his family The Greek idiom used here, meaning "the ones from his side," can refer to anyone who is closely related to a person, whether by blood or voluntary association. **for they said** Jesus' family might have wanted to preserve their reputation. The political ramifications of Jesus' actions and teaching also could have caused his family to attempt to restrain him, for fear of reprisal from Roman authorities or local Jewish leaders. Alternatively, they might have not have believed that Jesus was the Messiah and so attempted to silence him to avoid being ostracized from the religious system (believing that it, too, would reject him). Since Jesus has been at the center of a crowd almost continuously since his first teaching in Capernaum, it is unclear why his family reacts now.
3:22 teachers of the law See note on 1:22. **came down from Jerusalem** This is the first time someone has come from beyond Galilee's borders to challenge Jesus. **Beelzebul** The context of this term suggests that these Jewish leaders understood this figure to be the ruler of the demons. See note on Mt 10:25.
3:23 in parables Jesus speaks in parables only three times in Mark's Gospel (Mk 3:20–30; 4:1–34; 12:1–12). Jesus' parables contained truths about the kingdom of God (4:10–12).
3:24 a kingdom is divided Jesus confronts the religious leaders with the possibility that, by opposing him, they might be aligning themselves with evil powers. The defining mark of a disciple of God's kingdom is allegiance to Jesus and his teaching (v. 35).
3:26 opposes himself Likewise, Jesus cannot be possessed by Beelzebul, as that would mean that the ruler of demons has risen up against himself by vanquishing demons.
3:27 tying him up Refers to Jesus triumphing over Satan during his temptation (1:12–13) and Jesus casting out

demons. These exorcisms indicate that Beelzebul (the strong man in the parable) was defeated through Jesus' resistance of temptation.
3:29 blasphemes against the Holy Spirit In this context, this refers to insistently and unapologetically misrepresenting the workings of the Holy Spirit as demonic.
3:31 Jesus' mother and brothers arrived Possibly indicates that they were not among the family members who sought to restrain Jesus in v. 21. These brothers could be Mary's sons or the sons of Joseph by a previous wife, if he was a widower prior to marrying Mary.
3:35 Whoever does God's will In first-century Greco-Roman and Jewish society, it was a person's family that primarily determined identity and social standing. Jesus' teaching radically modifies this custom by prioritizing participation in the kingdom of God.

4:1–34 The second of three sections in Mark in which Jesus teaches in parables (3:20–30; 4:1–34; 12:1–12). Although these parables teach about the kingdom of God, the disciples are confused about the meaning and purpose of the parables (vv. 10–12). He explains one parable to his disciples (vv. 13–20) but continues to give a number of other parables without explanation. See the table "Parables of Jesus" on p. 1584.

4:3 Listen Jesus' opening phrase here mirrors his closing formula (vv. 9,23). It also highlights the theme of listening in the interpretation of the parable that follows (vv. 15,16,18,20).
4:5 rocky places Indicates ground that could appear fertile but actually is a shallow layer of topsoil over rocks.
4:8 a hundred times See note on Mt 13:8.
4:9 Whoever has ears to hear Divides people into those who accept Jesus' message and those who do not. One of the purposes of Jesus' parables is to reveal and

Jerusalem

By 34 BC, under King Herod's rule, ancient Jerusalem went through major redevelopment, crowned with the rebuilding of the Second Temple and a bigger Temple Mount. In AD 66, the First Jewish Revolt challenged Roman rule over Jerusalem, resulting in the destruction of the temple and the fall of Jerusalem by AD 70.

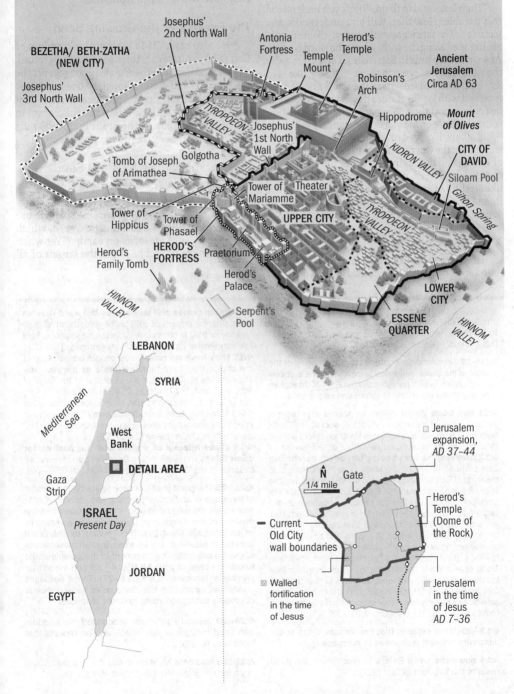

- Josephus' 2nd North Wall
- Antonia Fortress
- Temple Mount
- Herod's Temple
- **Ancient Jerusalem** Circa AD 63
- **BEZETHA/ BETH-ZATHA (NEW CITY)**
- Josephus' 3rd North Wall
- Robinson's Arch
- TYROPOEON VALLEY
- Josephus' 1st North Wall
- Hippodrome
- *Mount of Olives*
- KIDRON VALLEY
- **CITY OF DAVID**
- Tomb of Joseph of Arimathea
- Golgotha
- Siloam Pool
- Gihon Spring
- Tower of Mariamme
- Theater
- TYROPOEON VALLEY
- **UPPER CITY**
- Tower of Hippicus
- Tower of Phasael
- **HEROD'S FORTRESS**
- Praetorium
- Herod's Family Tomb
- Herod's Palace
- **LOWER CITY**
- HINNOM VALLEY
- Serpent's Pool
- **ESSENE QUARTER**
- HINNOM VALLEY

LEBANON

SYRIA

Mediterranean Sea

West Bank

☐ **DETAIL AREA**

Gaza Strip

ISRAEL *Present Day*

JORDAN

EGYPT

☐ Jerusalem expansion, *AD 37–44*

N

1/4 mile

Gate

Herod's Temple (Dome of the Rock)

━ Current Old City wall boundaries

☐ Walled fortification in the time of Jesus

☐ Jerusalem in the time of Jesus *AD 7–36*

[10]When he was alone, the Twelve and the others around him asked him about the parables. [11]He told them, "The secret of the kingdom of God has been given to you. But to those on the outside everything is said in parables [12]so that,

> "'they may be ever seeing but never perceiving,
>   and ever hearing but never understanding;
> otherwise they might turn and be forgiven!'[a]

[13]Then Jesus said to them, "Don't you understand this parable? How then will you understand any parable? [14]The farmer sows the word. [15]Some people are like seed along the path, where the word is sown. As soon as they hear it, Satan comes and takes away the word that was sown in them. [16]Others, like seed sown on rocky places, hear the word and at once receive it with joy. [17]But since they have no root, they last only a short time. When trouble or persecution comes because of the word, they quickly fall away. [18]Still others, like seed sown among thorns, hear the word; [19]but the worries of this life, the deceitfulness of wealth and the desires for other things come in and choke the word, making it unfruitful. [20]Others, like seed sown on good soil, hear the word, accept it, and produce a crop—some thirty, some sixty, some a hundred times what was sown."

A Lamp on a Stand

[21]He said to them, "Do you bring in a lamp to put it under a bowl or a bed? Instead, don't you put it on its stand? [22]For whatever is hidden is meant to be disclosed, and whatever is concealed is meant to be brought out into the open. [23]If anyone has ears to hear, let them hear."

[24]"Consider carefully what you hear," he continued. "With the measure you use, it will be measured to you—and even more. [25]Whoever has will be given more; whoever does not have, even what they have will be taken from them."

The Parable of the Growing Seed

[26]He also said, "This is what the kingdom of God is like. A man scatters seed on the ground. [27]Night and day, whether he sleeps or gets up, the seed sprouts and grows, though he does not know how. [28]All by itself the soil produces grain—first the stalk, then the head, then the full kernel in the head. [29]As soon as the grain is ripe, he puts the sickle to it, because the harvest has come."

The Parable of the Mustard Seed

4:30-32pp — Mt 13:31,32; Lk 13:18,19

[30]Again he said, "What shall we say the kingdom of God is like, or what parable shall we use to describe it? [31]It is like a mustard seed, which is the smallest of all seeds on earth. [32]Yet when planted, it grows and becomes the largest of all

---

[a] 12 Isaiah 6:9,10

---

accentuate this distinction (Mk 4:11–12,24–25). The emphasis on hearing and obeying Jesus' words alludes to Isaiah's depiction of sinful people as blind and deaf (Isa 6:9–10). See note on Mk 4:12.

4:10–12 The disciples, confused by the meaning of the parable of the sower, ask Jesus to explain why he is speaking in parables. Jesus paraphrases Isa 6:9–10 to explain that only those within the kingdom can understand.

4:11 has been given Refers to people who receive Jesus' message (see note on Mk 4:12). **secret** The Greek term used here, *mystērion*, in this instance refers primarily to the hidden or unexpected nature of God's work.

4:12 they may be ever seeing but never perceiving One purpose of Jesus' parables is to reveal the true meaning of God's kingdom only to those who receive it in faith. Jesus paraphrases Isa 6:9–10, in which God asks the prophet Isaiah to allow the people to continue on the path of disobedience they have previously selected. This fits with Jesus' overall message that he has come for the sinners who are willing to repent and that the self-proclaimed righteous may find themselves in opposition to God's purposes (Mk 2:17; compare note on 3:24). Jesus does not aim to convince the religious authorities to change their way—instead, as Jesus understands it, they should already know better. It is those who desire salvation or already feel desperation who understand his message (e.g., 2:15; compare 4:21–23).

4:13–20 Jesus explains that the parable of the sower describes different responses to his message.

4:14 sows the word Refers to proclaiming the good news of the kingdom of God (2:2).

4:15 Satan comes and takes away the word The idea being that the powers of evil, or the temptation for self-reliance (or trust in other powers), keeps these people from faithfully embracing Jesus' teachings (compare 1:12–13).

4:17 they have no root These people are not sure of the choice they have made. **trouble or persecution** These kinds of difficulties are depicted in the book of Acts (e.g., Ac 4; 5:17–42; 21:27–36). In addition, during Jesus' arrest, Jesus' disciples experienced persecution (Mk 14:26–50). **they quickly fall away** The Greek term used here also occurs when Jesus predicts the disciples' desertion at Gethsemane (14:27,29).

4:19 deceitfulness of wealth and the desires for other things There are examples of this type of response to Jesus in the Gospels (e.g., 10:17–31; Lk 9:57–62).

4:21–25 The parable of the lamp following the parable of the sower—and Jesus' teaching about who is able to receive his message and who is not—implies that the mystery of the kingdom of God is already revealed by Jesus (compare Mk 4:11). Those willing to embrace it are able to receive it. The idea conveyed in these verses is given more extensive treatment in the parable of the talents (or bags of gold; Mt 25:14–30) and the similar parable of ten minas (Lk 19:11–27). These passages clarify that embracing the kingdom of heaven means obediently acting according to God's purposes.

4:26–29 Jesus has already associated the kingdom with seed that grows (Mk 4:20), and he repeats that motif here (v. 28).

4:31 the smallest Mustard seeds are around 1/10th of an inch in diameter. See note on Mt 13:31.

garden plants, with such big branches that the birds can perch in its shade."

³³With many similar parables Jesus spoke the word to them, as much as they could understand. ³⁴He did not say anything to them without using a parable. But when he was alone with his own disciples, he explained everything.

Jesus Calms the Storm

4:35-41pp — Mt 8:18,23-27; Lk 8:22-25

³⁵That day when evening came, he said to his disciples, "Let us go over to the other side." ³⁶Leaving the crowd behind, they took him along, just as he was, in the boat. There were also other boats with him. ³⁷A furious squall came up, and the waves broke over the boat, so that it was nearly swamped. ³⁸Jesus was in the stern, sleeping on a cushion. The disciples woke him and said to him, "Teacher, don't you care if we drown?"

³⁹He got up, rebuked the wind and said to the waves, "Quiet! Be still!" Then the wind died down and it was completely calm.

⁴⁰He said to his disciples, "Why are you so afraid? Do you still have no faith?"

⁴¹They were terrified and asked each other, "Who is this? Even the wind and the waves obey him!"

Jesus Restores a Demon-Possessed Man

5:1-17pp — Mt 8:28-34; Lk 8:26-37
5:18-20pp — Lk 8:38,39

5 They went across the lake to the region of the Gerasenes.^a ²When Jesus got out of the boat, a man with an impure spirit came from the tombs

to meet him. ³This man lived in the tombs, and no one could bind him anymore, not even with a chain. ⁴For he had often been chained hand and foot, but he tore the chains apart and broke the irons on his feet. No one was strong enough to subdue him. ⁵Night and day among the tombs and in the hills he would cry out and cut himself with stones.

⁶When he saw Jesus from a distance, he ran and fell on his knees in front of him. ⁷He shouted at the top of his voice, "What do you want with me, Jesus, Son of the Most High God? In God's name don't torture me!" ⁸For Jesus had said to him, "Come out of this man, you impure spirit!"

⁹Then Jesus asked him, "What is your name?"

"My name is Legion," he replied, "for we are many." ¹⁰And he begged Jesus again and again not to send them out of the area.

¹¹A large herd of pigs was feeding on the nearby hillside. ¹²The demons begged Jesus, "Send us among the pigs; allow us to go into them." ¹³He gave them permission, and the impure spirits came out and went into the pigs. The herd, about two thousand in number, rushed down the steep bank into the lake and were drowned.

¹⁴Those tending the pigs ran off and reported this in the town and countryside, and the people went out to see what had happened. ¹⁵When they came to Jesus, they saw the man who had been possessed by the legion of demons, sitting there, dressed and in his right mind; and they

---

^a 1 Some manuscripts *Gadarenes*; other manuscripts *Gergesenes*

4:32 largest Mature mustard plants can grow to ten feet in height.

4:34 when he was alone with his own disciples, he explained Confirms Jesus' statement in Mk 4:11. But even with Jesus explaining the kingdom of God to his disciples, they sometimes fail to comprehend the full implications of Jesus' identity (e.g., 4:40; 8:14–21).

4:35 other side Refers to the Decapolis (5:20; 7:31), a federation of cities east of the Sea of Galilee. Although Jewish communities existed in these cities, Mark depicts this region as Gentile (non-Jewish) territory.

4:39 Quiet! Be still Jesus' words mirror his response to the unclean spirit at Capernaum (1:25). Jesus shows himself to have power over both spiritual and elemental forces, demonstrating his divinity. See note on Mt 8:26.

4:40 Do you still have no faith Jesus has made clear that he is God's chosen agent. He expects the disciples to recognize this and have faith in his ability to act with divine power.

4:41 Who is this Reflects the reaction of those who witnessed Jesus' first exorcism (Mk 1:27). **the wind and the waves obey him** Jesus' command of the raging sea demonstrates his unique authority and power. God alone is able to control the sea (e.g., Ex 15; Isa 51:9–11).

5:1–20 Upon his arrival in the primarily non-Jewish Decapolis, Jesus is met by a man possessed by many demons.

5:1 region of the Gerasenes The region southeast of the Sea of Galilee. See the map "Jesus' Ministry in Galilee" on p. 2260.

JESUS' MIRACLES IN GENTILE CITIES	
Gadarenes/Gerasenes	Mt 8:28–34; Mk 5:1–20; Lk 8:26–39
Tyre and Sidon	Mt 15:21–28; Mk 7:24–30
Caesarea Philippi	Mt 17:14–21; Mk 9:14–29; Lk 9:37–43
Decapolis	Mk 7:31–37

5:3 This man lived in the tombs Indicates that the man was socially ostracized because of his demonic possession. **5:6 fell on his knees in front of him** The Greek text here could be understood as the man submitting in the same way someone would to royalty or as the man worshiping Jesus (Mk 15:19).

5:7 Most High God In the OT, this phrase is used to indicate that Yahweh, Israel's God, is supreme—the chief God. This title is associated with God's ultimate dominion over non-Jewish nations and Yahweh's power over the gods those nations worshiped (e.g., Dt 32:8–9; Da 4:17).

5:9 Legion The Greek word used here, *legiōn*, comes from the Latin term *legio*, which designates a division of the Roman army (5,400 infantry and 120 cavalry). This man is possessed by a multitude of spirits (Mk 5:12–13); "Legion" is not the man's proper name (v. 15).

5:11 large herd of pigs Underscores that this region is not Jewish (the law classifies pigs as unclean; Lev 11:7–8).

5:13 He gave them permission Reinforces Jesus' ultimate authority over all powers.

were afraid. [16]Those who had seen it told the people what had happened to the demon-possessed man — and told about the pigs as well. [17]Then the people began to plead with Jesus to leave their region.

[18]As Jesus was getting into the boat, the man who had been demon-possessed begged to go with him. [19]Jesus did not let him, but said, "Go home to your own people and tell them how much the Lord has done for you, and how he has had mercy on you." [20]So the man went away and began to tell in the Decapolis[a] how much Jesus had done for him. And all the people were amazed.

Jesus Raises a Dead Girl and Heals a Sick Woman

5:22-43pp — Mt 9:18-26; Lk 8:41-56

[21]When Jesus had again crossed over by boat to the other side of the lake, a large crowd gathered around him while he was by the lake. [22]Then one of the synagogue leaders, named Jairus, came, and when he saw Jesus, he fell at his feet. [23]He pleaded earnestly with him, "My little daughter is dying. Please come and put your hands on her so that she will be healed and live." [24]So Jesus went with him.

A large crowd followed and pressed around him. [25]And a woman was there who had been subject to bleeding for twelve years. [26]She had suffered a great deal under the care of many doctors and had spent all she had, yet instead of getting better she grew worse. [27]When she heard about Jesus, she came up behind him in the crowd and touched his cloak, [28]because she thought, "If I just touch his clothes, I will be healed." [29]Immediately her bleeding stopped and she felt in her body that she was freed from her suffering.

[30]At once Jesus realized that power had gone out from him. He turned around in the crowd and asked, "Who touched my clothes?"

[31]"You see the people crowding against you," his disciples answered, "and yet you can ask, 'Who touched me?' "

[32]But Jesus kept looking around to see who had done it. [33]Then the woman, knowing what had happened to her, came and fell at his feet and, trembling with fear, told him the whole truth. [34]He said to her, "Daughter, your faith has healed you. Go in peace and be freed from your suffering."

[35]While Jesus was still speaking, some people came from the house of Jairus, the synagogue leader. "Your daughter is dead," they said. "Why bother the teacher anymore?"

[36]Overhearing[b] what they said, Jesus told him, "Don't be afraid; just believe."

[37]He did not let anyone follow him except Peter, James and John the brother of James. [38]When they came to the home of the synagogue leader, Jesus saw a commotion, with people crying and wailing loudly. [39]He went in and said to them, "Why all

---

[a] 20 That is, the Ten Cities   [b] 36 Or *Ignoring*

5:17 region The Greek term used here, *horion*, which may be literally rendered as "borders," is reserved by Mark for times when Jesus crosses political boundaries: the Gerasene territory, Tyrian territory (Mk 7:24) and the Judean territory (10:1). Each case seems to indicate that God's kingdom, through Jesus, is expanding.

5:19 tell them This is the only episode in Mark's Gospel in which Jesus does not attempt to conceal his identity, but he also does not tell the man to proclaim to his friends how much he, Jesus, has done for him. Instead, it seems that he is telling the man to share how much "the Lord" — likely a reference to the divine name Yahweh in this instance — has done for him.

5:21 the other side Refers to the western or northern shore of the Sea of Galilee.

5:23 she will be healed The Greek term used here, *sōzō*, can indicate salvation in a spiritual sense or from an ailment (a healing). In this case, it describes deliverance from a life-threatening illness (3:4; 5:28; 6:56; 10:26; 15:30-31).

5:25-43 The narrative about Jairus' daughter (vv. 21-43) frames the interrupting story of a hemorrhaging woman (vv. 25-34). Both stories show Jesus' incredible and surprising power.

5:25 who had been subject to bleeding Likely describing some kind of ongoing vaginal bleeding, which according to Lev 15:19-33 would have made the woman ceremonially unclean — preventing her from worshiping in the temple or joining her people in everyday activities.

5:27 up behind In contrast to others who approach Jesus directly, this woman is cautious and hesitant — perhaps because her condition makes her ritually impure. Alternatively, this might be the only way the woman could reach Jesus through the crowd.

5:29 suffering Since people of this time generally believed that illness was caused by supernatural forces, they often spoke of illness as a deliberate affliction or harassment.

5:30 power This story and the story of Jairus' daughter focus on the relationship between power and faith. Belief gives people access to Jesus' life-giving power; unbelief blocks it (e.g., 2:5; 9:19-24).

5:33 trembling with fear If she would admit to the healing, she would acknowledge that she had compromised the ritual purity of Jesus as well as members of the crowd (see v. 27 and note). The woman likely feared reprisal for violating religious law. She may also be afraid because she has just experienced divine power, and without permission, and is concerned about how Jesus will respond (v. 32).

5:36 Don't be afraid; just believe This parallels the story of the woman whom Jesus just healed (vv. 33-34).

5:37 except Peter, James and John the brother of James Jesus likely brings this select group of disciples along with him because he has already decided that he is going to heal Jairus' daughter — he does not want word about this to spread. Compare note on 5:43.

5:39 not dead but asleep Jesus seems to be drawing on Jewish apocalyptic imagery of death as sleep (e.g., Da 12:2). If the girl was in a coma, or actually asleep, her breathing likely would have been detectable. This narrative seems to involve resurrection. This narrative resembles stories from the lives of the prophets Elijah and Elisha (1Ki 17:17-24; 2Ki 4:18-37).

this commotion and wailing? The child is not dead but asleep." ⁴⁰But they laughed at him.

After he put them all out, he took the child's father and mother and the disciples who were with him, and went in where the child was. ⁴¹He took her by the hand and said to her, *"Talitha koum!"* (which means "Little girl, I say to you, get up!"). ⁴²Immediately the girl stood up and began to walk around (she was twelve years old). At this they were completely astonished. ⁴³He gave strict orders not to let anyone know about this, and told them to give her something to eat.

A Prophet Without Honor
6:1-6pp — Mt 13:54-58

6 Jesus left there and went to his hometown, accompanied by his disciples. ²When the Sabbath came, he began to teach in the synagogue, and many who heard him were amazed.

"Where did this man get these things?" they asked. "What's this wisdom that has been given him? What are these remarkable miracles he is performing? ³Isn't this the carpenter? Isn't this Mary's son and the brother of James, Joseph,ᵃ Judas and Simon? Aren't his sisters here with us?" And they took offense at him.

⁴Jesus said to them, "A prophet is not without honor except in his own town, among his relatives and in his own home." ⁵He could not do any miracles there, except lay his hands on a few sick people and heal them. ⁶He was amazed at their lack of faith.

Jesus Sends Out the Twelve
6:7-11pp — Mt 10:1,9-14; Lk 9:1,3-5

Then Jesus went around teaching from village to village. ⁷Calling the Twelve to him, he began to send them out two by two and gave them authority over impure spirits.

⁸These were his instructions: "Take nothing for the journey except a staff — no bread, no bag, no money in your belts. ⁹Wear sandals but not an extra shirt. ¹⁰Whenever you enter a house, stay there until you leave that town. ¹¹And if any place will not welcome you or listen to you, leave that place and shake the dust off your feet as a testimony against them."

¹²They went out and preached that people should repent. ¹³They drove out many demons and anointed many sick people with oil and healed them.

ᵃ 3 Greek *Joses*, a variant of *Joseph*

5:41 Talitha koum A transliteration of an Aramaic phrase meaning, "Girl, get up!" Jesus' native language was Aramaic.

5:43 not to let anyone know Jesus intends to continue to keep his identity secret until the appropriate time (compare Mk 8:31–38). If he revealed his identity at this stage, as the Son of God (1:10–11), it could result in him being prosecuted and executed immediately.

6:1–6 Jesus' hometown fails to receive him, citing the knowledge of his family and origins as the reason. Jesus rebukes them and does not perform miracles, since they are unable to receive him in faith.

6:1 his hometown Refers to Nazareth, a town in Galilee (Mk 1:9). See Mt 2:19–23.

6:2 Where did this man get these things Here and in Mk 1:27, onlookers relate Jesus' teaching to his acts of power. **been given him** Illustrates the Nazarenes' belief that Jesus' wisdom is not his own, but has come from some external, unknown source (vv. 14–16).

6:3 carpenter The Greek text here could refer to any specialized craftsperson, such as a woodworker or stonemason. **brother** Jesus' siblings mentioned in this verse may be Mary and Joseph's children or Joseph's children by another, deceased, wife (making him a widower prior to marrying Mary). **James** The NT letter of James is often attributed to this brother of Jesus. **Joseph** Referred to in the Greek text here as *Joses*, which is another form of the name Joseph; the spelling "Joseph" is used for the same brother in the parallel verse of Mt 13:55. However, Mk 15:40 and Mt 27:56 confuse this matter further because in those passages a woman named Mary is referred to as the mother of Joses (Joseph) and James (compare Lk 24:10). This could be a reference to Jesus' mother, Jesus' aunt or another woman named Mary. (Mary, Joseph and James were all very common names among Jews of the first century AD.) Outside of

these references, this brother is otherwise unknown. **Judas** The individual to whom the NT letter of Jude is often attributed. **Simon** Outside of the mention in a parallel passage in Mt 13:55, this brother of Jesus is also otherwise unknown (compare Jn 7:5; Ac 1:14). **sisters** Mark 3:35 may also allude to Jesus' sisters. **they took offense at him** This abrupt shift from amazement to offense is unexplained. Verse 4 seems to imply that no one respected Jesus in Nazareth after this point, suggesting that those who were amazed (v. 2) became convinced by certain naysayers. It may also be that some people believed but the majority of people agreed with the opinion of those who cited Jesus' background as evidence of why not to believe him.

6:4 not without honor Jesus declares that it is normal for a prophet's own people to reject the prophet. This statement reintroduces the issue of what true family is (see 3:31–35). **among his relatives and in his own home** See 3:20–34.

6:7–13 Jesus fulfills the purpose for which he chose the twelve apostles. Mark set up the initial choosing of the twelve apostles with a story of opposition (3:1–6) followed by a summary of how Jesus sent out his disciples (3:7–12). He now repeats that narrative sequence: opposition, ministry and the sending of the Twelve.

6:8 Take nothing Jesus sends the disciples out in a manner that requires them to both depend on God for their provision and to receive the hospitality of others. In the ancient Near East, it was common (and expected) for visiting travelers to be cared for — not doing so could result in the traveler's death, if they lacked provision. The decision for the disciples to go out in full awareness that they will be in need encourages them to enter the homes of people and share the message of the kingdom of God (see vv. 12–13).

6:11 shake the dust off See note on Mt 10:14.

John the Baptist Beheaded

6:14-29pp — Mt 14:1-12
6:14-16pp — Lk 9:7-9

[14] King Herod heard about this, for Jesus' name had become well known. Some were saying,[a] "John the Baptist has been raised from the dead, and that is why miraculous powers are at work in him."

[15] Others said, "He is Elijah."

And still others claimed, "He is a prophet, like one of the prophets of long ago."

[16] But when Herod heard this, he said, "John, whom I beheaded, has been raised from the dead!"

[17] For Herod himself had given orders to have John arrested, and he had him bound and put in prison. He did this because of Herodias, his brother Philip's wife, whom he had married. [18] For John had been saying to Herod, "It is not lawful for you to have your brother's wife." [19] So Herodias nursed a grudge against John and wanted to kill him. But she was not able to, [20] because Herod feared John and protected him, knowing him to be a righteous and holy man. When Herod heard John, he was greatly puzzled[b]; yet he liked to listen to him.

[21] Finally the opportune time came. On his birthday Herod gave a banquet for his high officials and military commanders and the leading men of Galilee. [22] When the daughter of[c] Herodias came in and danced, she pleased Herod and his dinner guests.

The king said to the girl, "Ask me for anything you want, and I'll give it to you." [23] And he promised her with an oath, "Whatever you ask I will give you, up to half my kingdom."

[24] She went out and said to her mother, "What shall I ask for?"

"The head of John the Baptist," she answered.

[25] At once the girl hurried in to the king with the request: "I want you to give me right now the head of John the Baptist on a platter."

[26] The king was greatly distressed, but because of his oaths and his dinner guests, he did not want to refuse her. [27] So he immediately sent an executioner with orders to bring John's head. The man went, beheaded John in the prison, [28] and brought back his head on a platter. He presented it to the girl, and she gave it to her mother. [29] On hearing of this, John's disciples came and took his body and laid it in a tomb.

Jesus Feeds the Five Thousand

6:32-44pp — Mt 14:13-21; Lk 9:10-17; Jn 6:5-13
6:32-44Ref — Mk 8:2-9

[30] The apostles gathered around Jesus and reported to him all they had done and taught. [31] Then, because so many people were coming and going that they did not even have a chance to eat, he said

---

[a] 14 Some early manuscripts *He was saying*   [b] 20 Some early manuscripts *he did many things*   [c] 22 Some early manuscripts *When his daughter*

6:13 The disciples emulate Jesus' ministry, which they have observed throughout the Gospel.

6:14–29 The narrative shifts to events surrounding John the Baptist, who was last mentioned in Mk 1:9–11; his disciples were mentioned in 2:18.

6:14 King Herod Refers to Herod Antipas, the Jewish ruler of Galilee and Perea (see note on Lk 3:1). See the table "Political Leaders in the New Testament" on p. 1916. **raised from the dead** Mark hasn't yet mentioned John's death; it is reported in Mk 6:17–29. Herod's fear suggests that he saw a link between John and Jesus and perceived both as political threats.

6:15 He is Elijah Second Kings 2:11 records that the prophet Elijah did not die, but was taken up into heaven alive. As a result of this and Malachi's prophecy many Jews believed he would return someday (Mal 4:5–6; compare Mk 9:11; 15:35–36).

6:17 Herodias, his brother Philip's wife According to the first-century Jewish historian Josephus, Herodias was a granddaughter of Herod the Great. Her first husband (Philip) and second husband (Antipas, who is called Herod in this text) were both sons of Herod the Great by different mothers, making them her uncles as well as her spouses (Josephus, *Antiquities* 18.109–10,136).

6:18 It is not lawful Herodias was initially married to Philip, the half-brother of Herod Antipas. Herod divorced his first wife in order to marry Herodias, taking her away from Philip (Josephus, *Antiquities* 18.109–10). John condemns this as unlawful because it violates Lev 18:16; 20:21.

6:19 Herodias nursed a grudge Given John the Baptist's influence, his disapproval of Herod and Herodias' marriage would threaten her position as queen.

6:20 feared John Herod may fear John in the sense that he is afraid of John's power from Yahweh and the wrath Yahweh may bring against him if he was to execute John. Herod may also fear the political ramifications of killing John: The Jewish people could rise against Herod because John's ministry was very popular (Mk 1:5). **was greatly puzzled** Similar to those who do not understand Jesus' message (see note on 4:12).

6:22 daughter of Herodias See note on Mt 14:6. **Ask me for anything you want** Kings in the ancient Near East commonly made absurd statements like this on monumental occasions in a show of power (Mk 6:21). Herod's expression is ironic since Herod Antipas is not a real king, but instead the tetrarch under the Roman Empire, with less jurisdiction than his father Herod the Great (compare note on Mt 2:19). Within Mark, this scene showing the absurdity and terribleness of the supposed king of the Jews stands in contrast to the real king of the Jews, Jesus (compare Mk 15:2,9,12).

6:23 up to half my kingdom An idiom, not a literal expression (compare Est 5:3,6).

6:30–44 Having described King Herod's despicable birthday banquet, Mark presents Jesus presiding over an even larger feast as the true leader of God's kingdom who truly provides for God's people.

6:30 The apostles gathered The departure and return of the twelve apostles frames the story of John's death (Mk 6:14–29), which interrupts the apostles' mission as a flashback.

to them, "Come with me by yourselves to a quiet place and get some rest."

³²So they went away by themselves in a boat to a solitary place. ³³But many who saw them leaving recognized them and ran on foot from all the towns and got there ahead of them. ³⁴When Jesus landed and saw a large crowd, he had compassion on them, because they were like sheep without a shepherd. So he began teaching them many things.

³⁵By this time it was late in the day, so his disciples came to him. "This is a remote place," they said, "and it's already very late. ³⁶Send the people away so that they can go to the surrounding countryside and villages and buy themselves something to eat."

³⁷But he answered, "You give them something to eat."

They said to him, "That would take more than

6:34 sheep without a shepherd A common OT expression used to describe Israel's inadequate or oppressive leadership (e.g., 1Ki 22:17; compare Eze 34).

6:35 This is a remote place The two feeding stories

that frame this section of Mark's Gospel take place in the wilderness (compare Mk 8:4). This barren setting contrasts with Herod's lavish banquet.

6:37 more than half a year's wages The Greek text

Coins of the Gospels

SILVER DENARIUS

The denarius was considered a fair day's pay for a common laborer in the first century. Jesus asked to see this coin when asked if it were lawful to pay taxes to Caesar (Mt 22:19).

What one coin could buy:
15 lbs. of wheat (in a basket).

SILVER HALF SHEKEL

The temple tax was one half-shekel per year.

Worth: 2 denarii

What one coin could buy:
A wooden bucket, 15 lbs. of wheat, and a clay oil lamp.

SILVER SHEKEL

Minted in Tyre, the shekel and half-shekel were the only coins accepted for the temple tax in Jesus' time because of the high purity of their silver.

Worth: 4 denarii

What one coin could buy:
A tunic, a liter of olive oil, two 1lb. loaves of bread, and a half-liter of cheap wine.

JUDAS' SILVER

The 30 pieces of silver that Judas took in exchange for betraying Jesus were silver shekels, the equivalent of 120 denarii.

Size comparison

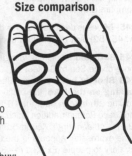

BRONZE PRUTAH

The bronze prutah was a common coin, worth only 1/64th of a denarius.

What one coin could buy:
1/3 lb. of bread.

BRONZE LEPTON

The widow in Mark 12 gave two lepta coins to the temple, each worth only half a prutah.

What one coin could buy:
A bath at the public bathhouse.

half a year's wages[a]! Are we to go and spend that much on bread and give it to them to eat?"

[38]"How many loaves do you have?" he asked. "Go and see."

When they found out, they said, "Five — and two fish."

[39]Then Jesus directed them to have all the people sit down in groups on the green grass. [40]So they sat down in groups of hundreds and fifties. [41]Taking the five loaves and the two fish and looking up to heaven, he gave thanks and broke the loaves. Then he gave them to his disciples to distribute to the people. He also divided the two fish among them all. [42]They all ate and were satisfied, [43]and the disciples picked up twelve basketfuls of broken pieces of bread and fish. [44]The number of the men who had eaten was five thousand.

Jesus Walks on the Water

6:45-51pp — Mt 14:22-32; Jn 6:15-21
6:53-56pp — Mt 14:34-36

[45]Immediately Jesus made his disciples get into the boat and go on ahead of him to Bethsaida, while he dismissed the crowd. [46]After leaving them, he went up on a mountainside to pray.

[47]Later that night, the boat was in the middle of the lake, and he was alone on land. [48]He saw the disciples straining at the oars, because the wind was against them. Shortly before dawn he went out to them, walking on the lake. He was about to pass by them, [49]but when they saw him walking on the lake, they thought he was a ghost. They cried out, [50]because they all saw him and were terrified.

Immediately he spoke to them and said, "Take courage! It is I. Don't be afraid." [51]Then he climbed into the boat with them, and the wind died down. They were completely amazed, [52]for they had not understood about the loaves; their hearts were hardened.

[53]When they had crossed over, they landed at Gennesaret and anchored there. [54]As soon as they got out of the boat, people recognized Jesus. [55]They ran throughout that whole region and carried the sick on mats to wherever they heard he was. [56]And wherever he went — into villages, towns or countryside — they placed the sick in the marketplaces. They begged him to let them touch even the edge of his cloak, and all who touched it were healed.

That Which Defiles

7:1-23pp — Mt 15:1-20

7 The Pharisees and some of the teachers of the law who had come from Jerusalem gathered around Jesus [2]and saw some of his disciples eating food with hands that were defiled, that is, unwashed. [3](The Pharisees and all the Jews do not eat unless they give their hands a ceremonial washing, holding to the tradition of the elders. [4]When

[a] 37 Greek *take two hundred denarii*

here, which refers to 200 denarii, references a silver coin roughly corresponding to the value of a day's labor. Two hundred denarii was a substantial sum of money, sufficient to feed 5,000 men and the other people present (v. 44). See the infographic "Coins of the Gospels" on p. 1613; see the infographic "A Silver Denarius" on p. 1578.

6:40 hundreds and fifties Israel camped in groups of hundreds and fifties during its flight from Egypt (Ex 18:25). Jesus' organization of the crowd in this way represents the symbolism of this meal: With the coming of God's rule, a new exodus is taking place (compare Mk 1:15).

6:41 gave them to his disciples This verse parallels Jesus' distribution of bread at the Passover meal in 14:22–23. In both passages, Jesus takes bread, gives thanks, breaks the bread and gives it to his disciples (compare 8:6).

6:45–56 Jesus demonstrates his divine power once again (vv. 45–52) over both nature and disease (vv. 53–56).

6:45 Bethsaida A fishing village on the northeastern shore of the Sea of Galilee.

6:48 Shortly before dawn See note on Mt 14:25. **walking on the lake** The ability to control the sea is a divine attribute in both the OT (e.g., Ps 18:15; 65:7) and Greco-Roman tradition (such as seen in Homer, *Iliad* 13.23–31 and Virgil, *Aeneid* 5.816–21). **pass by** The same expression appears in the OT when God displays his glory to people (Ex 33:17 — 34:8; 1Ki 19:11–13). **6:50 It is I** Jesus' words likely evoke God's self-identification to Moses at the burning bush (Ex 3:14).

6:52 they had not understood Jesus might have ex-

pected them to understand the significance of gathering 12 baskets of leftovers (Mk 8:17–21). Although Jesus gives the disciples special access to knowledge about the kingdom (4:11), there are points in Mark where the disciples are ignorant of the significance of Jesus' teaching (e.g., 7:17–18; 9:32) or actions (e.g., 8:21; 10:13). **hearts were hardened** Indicates stubbornness (see Ex 4:21 and note). Based on Jesus' later comment in Mk 8:17–21, it seems that it is the disciples' own will that keeps them from understanding the full meaning of Jesus' message.

6:53 Gennesaret Jesus had instructed the disciples to go to Bethsaida (6:45), at the northeastern end of the lake. Gennesaret, however, is the region on the lake's western shore. See the map "Jesus' Ministry in Galilee" on p. 2260.

7:1–13 The Pharisees challenge Jesus on points of ritual cleanliness—which much of the law was about (e.g., Lev 11–15). Jesus responds to their attack by pointing out how their traditions contradict God's commandments.

7:1 Pharisees See note on 2:16. **teachers of the law** See note on 1:22.

7:3 holding to Connotes chosen, regular observance.

7:4–5 The implication of these verses is not just that the Pharisees and scribes (or teachers of the law) washed their hands and objects in ways that showed observance of the law (e.g., Lev 11:32; 15:4–12; Nu 19:18), but that they observed these regulations in absurd ways.

7:4 unless they wash Probably to guard against de-

they come from the marketplace they do not eat unless they wash. And they observe many other traditions, such as the washing of cups, pitchers and kettles.ᵃ)

⁵So the Pharisees and teachers of the law asked Jesus, "Why don't your disciples live according to the tradition of the elders instead of eating their food with defiled hands?"

⁶He replied, "Isaiah was right when he prophesied about you hypocrites; as it is written:

"'These people honor me with their lips,
    but their hearts are far from me.
⁷They worship me in vain;
    their teachings are merely human rules.'ᵇ

⁸You have let go of the commands of God and are holding on to human traditions."

⁹And he continued, "You have a fine way of setting aside the commands of God in order to observeᶜ your own traditions! ¹⁰For Moses said, 'Honor your father and mother,'ᵈ and, 'Anyone who curses their father or mother is to be put to death.'ᵉ ¹¹But you say that if anyone declares that what might have been used to help their father or mother is Corban (that is, devoted to God) — ¹²then you no longer let them do anything for their father or mother. ¹³Thus you nullify the word of God by your tradition that you have handed down. And you do many things like that."

¹⁴Again Jesus called the crowd to him and said, "Listen to me, everyone, and understand this. ¹⁵Nothing outside a person can defile them by going into them. Rather, it is what comes out of a person that defiles them." [16]ᶠ

¹⁷After he had left the crowd and entered the house, his disciples asked him about this parable. ¹⁸"Are you so dull?" he asked. "Don't you see that nothing that enters a person from the outside can defile them? ¹⁹For it doesn't go into their heart but into their stomach, and then out of the body." (In saying this, Jesus declared all foods clean.)

²⁰He went on: "What comes out of a person is what defiles them. ²¹For it is from within, out of a person's heart, that evil thoughts come — sexual immorality, theft, murder, ²²adultery, greed, malice, deceit, lewdness, envy, slander, arrogance and folly. ²³All these evils come from inside and defile a person."

Jesus Honors a Syrophoenician Woman's Faith

7:24-30pp — Mt 15:21-28

²⁴Jesus left that place and went to the vicinity of Tyre.ᵍ He entered a house and did not want anyone to know it; yet he could not keep his presence secret. ²⁵In fact, as soon as she heard about him, a woman whose little daughter was possessed by an impure spirit came and fell at his feet. ²⁶The woman was a Greek, born in Syrian Phoenicia. She begged Jesus to drive the demon out of her daughter.

²⁷"First let the children eat all they want," he told her, "for it is not right to take the children's bread and toss it to the dogs."

ᵃ 4 Some early manuscripts *pitchers, kettles and dining couches*   ᵇ 6,7 Isaiah 29:13   ᶜ 9 Some manuscripts *set up*   ᵈ 10 Exodus 20:12; Deut. 5:16   ᵉ 10 Exodus 21:17; Lev. 20:9   ᶠ 16 Some manuscripts include here the words of 4:23.   ᵍ 24 Many early manuscripts *Tyre and Sidon*

---

filement by unintentional contact with ritually unclean objects or people.

7:6 it is written Jesus quotes Isa 29:13, which is part of an oracle condemning the people of Jerusalem, and by extension God's people in general, for failing to follow God's commandments.

7:9 You have a fine way of setting aside Jesus is accusing the Pharisees of favoring their own traditions over the Law of Moses—which is ironic, since they claimed to be leading interpreters and practitioners of Mosaic Law.

7:10 Jesus quotes Ex 20:12 and 21:17 respectively, applying these laws to situations when the parents of an adult are in need.

7:11 Corban The Greek text here uses the Hebrew term *qorban*, which commonly refers to sacrificial offerings.

7:12 anything for their father or mother The tradition probably held that if a person dedicated resources to God, they could no longer be used for another purpose. Thus, the promise in v. 11 would mean that no resources could be used to support one's parents, because those resources had been dedicated to God. The Mishnah, a text of Jewish traditional law from about AD 200, records a similar law concerning a case where a person dedicates to God any food they would eat with a particular other person (Nedarim 1:4).

7:13 your tradition In ancient Near Eastern culture, the expectation would have been that children help care for their older parents (compare note on Mk 7:10).

7:14–23 Jesus radically departs from the Pharisees' teaching that contact with ritually unclean things makes one impure. This suggests that Jesus viewed the purposes of the laws about uncleanness as rituals (e.g., Lev 7:19–21) meant to remind the people of Israel of their need to be holy (set apart) before God. Rather, he says, impurity comes from a person's sinful desires.

7:19 declared all foods clean These words are not part of the quotation, but are Mark's interpretation of Jesus' statement. They link this story and the account of the Syrophoenician woman that follows (Mk 7:24–30). Compare Ac 10:9–29.

7:24–30 Jesus heals the daughter of Syrophoenician woman. This is his second significant interaction with a non-Jewish person (see Mk 5:1–20), further developing the theme that God's kingdom is not exclusively for Jews.

7:24 Tyre A Phoenician port on the Mediterranean Sea, northwest of Galilee.

7:26 Syrian Phoenicia The Greek phrase used here is used by Roman authors to distinguish the Phoenicians of Syria from those of North Africa.

7:27 First let the children eat Jesus is noting that Israel was first chosen to benefit from God's rule, before

²⁸"Lord," she replied, "even the dogs under the table eat the children's crumbs."

²⁹Then he told her, "For such a reply, you may go; the demon has left your daughter."

³⁰She went home and found her child lying on the bed, and the demon gone.

Jesus Heals a Deaf and Mute Man

7:31-37pp — Mt 15:29-31

³¹Then Jesus left the vicinity of Tyre and went through Sidon, down to the Sea of Galilee and into the region of the Decapolis.ᵃ ³²There some people brought to him a man who was deaf and could hardly talk, and they begged Jesus to place his hand on him.

³³After he took him aside, away from the crowd, Jesus put his fingers into the man's ears. Then he spit and touched the man's tongue. ³⁴He looked up to heaven and with a deep sigh said to him,

"Ephphatha!" (which means "Be opened!"). ³⁵At this, the man's ears were opened, his tongue was loosened and he began to speak plainly.

³⁶Jesus commanded them not to tell anyone. But the more he did so, the more they kept talking about it. ³⁷People were overwhelmed with amazement. "He has done everything well," they said. "He even makes the deaf hear and the mute speak."

Jesus Feeds the Four Thousand

8:1-9pp — Mt 15:32-39
8:1-9Ref — Mk 6:32-44
8:11-21pp — Mt 16:1-12

8 During those days another large crowd gathered. Since they had nothing to eat, Jesus called his disciples to him and said, ²"I have compassion for these people; they have already been with me three days and have nothing to eat. ³If

---

ᵃ 31 That is, the Ten Cities

---

people from the rest of the world. Jesus is also affirming that his mission is first to the Jewish people, although he foreshadows the inclusion of non-Jewish people (see vv. 14–23). Paul makes similar remarks (e.g., Ro 1:16; compare Isa 49:6). **toss it to the dogs** Jesus is trying to evoke a response about Jewish-Gentile relations—he is likely using a common adage among Jewish people to do so (compare note on Mt 15:26).
7:28 Lord The Greek term used here, *kyrios*, means either "lord" or "sir"; it was a typical title for formally addressing a social superior and it seems that the woman is using the phrase in this way.
7:29 For such a reply, you may go This turning point inaugurates Jesus' mission to non-Jewish people (Mk 7:31–37).

7:31–37 Jesus returns from the Gentile (non-Jewish) region of Phoenicia to Galilee and continues into another Gentile region, the Decapolis. While there, he heals a disabled man. The feeding of the four thousand (8:1–10) also might take place in the Decapolis.

7:31 Sidon A Phoenician port on the Mediterranean Sea, about 20 miles north of Tyre. **Decapolis** A region of ten cities; the same region where the demon-possessed man had proclaimed what Jesus did for him (5:20).
7:34 Ephphatha A transliteration of the Aramaic term *eppathah*, meaning "be opened." The recordings of Jesus speaking in Aramaic (his native language) in the Gospel of Mark suggest its very early date.
7:36 commanded them Jesus probably gives this instruction to the man and the people who brought him, in order to conceal his identity until the proper time (v. 32). See note on 1:34.

8:1–10 The previous miracle occurred in the Gentile Decapolis (7:31); assuming that Jesus had not traveled someplace else, this setting would fit thematically with a series of accounts demonstrating the Gentiles' inclusion in the kingdom of God (see 7:14–37). This passage brings closure to Jesus' ministry in Galilee and leads into his journey to Jerusalem. This passage is similar to the feeding of the five thousand (6:30–44).

Jesus' Journey to Jerusalem

Jesus predicts his death for the first time.

The disciples ask about the coming of Elijah—Jesus says that he has already come.

Jesus predicts his death for the second time.

Jesus teaches that the least are the greatest.

Jesus teaches about forgiveness.

Jesus is transfigured on a mountain.

Jesus heals a demon-possessed boy that his disciples could not heal.

Jesus instructs Peter to find a coin for the temple tax in a fish's mouth.

The disciples try to stop someone working in Jesus' name.

I send them home hungry, they will collapse on the way, because some of them have come a long distance."

[4]His disciples answered, "But where in this remote place can anyone get enough bread to feed them?"

[5]"How many loaves do you have?" Jesus asked.

"Seven," they replied.

[6]He told the crowd to sit down on the ground. When he had taken the seven loaves and given thanks, he broke them and gave them to his disciples to distribute to the people, and they did so. [7]They had a few small fish as well; he gave thanks for them also and told the disciples to distribute them. [8]The people ate and were satisfied. Afterward the disciples picked up seven basketfuls of broken pieces that were left over. [9]About four thousand were present. After he had sent them away, [10]he got into the boat with his disciples and went to the region of Dalmanutha.

[11]The Pharisees came and began to question Jesus. To test him, they asked him for a sign from heaven. [12]He sighed deeply and said, "Why does this generation ask for a sign? Truly I tell you, no sign will be given to it." [13]Then he left them, got back into the boat and crossed to the other side.

The Yeast of the Pharisees and Herod

[14]The disciples had forgotten to bring bread, except for one loaf they had with them in the boat. [15]"Be careful," Jesus warned them. "Watch out for the yeast of the Pharisees and that of Herod."

[16]They discussed this with one another and said, "It is because we have no bread."

[17]Aware of their discussion, Jesus asked them: "Why are you talking about having no bread? Do you still not see or understand? Are your hearts hardened? [18]Do you have eyes but fail to see, and ears but fail to hear? And don't you remember? [19]When I broke the five loaves for the five thousand, how many basketfuls of pieces did you pick up?"

"Twelve," they replied.

[20]"And when I broke the seven loaves for the four thousand, how many basketfuls of pieces did you pick up?"

8:6 When he had taken the seven loaves and given thanks Jesus' words and actions here closely resemble those in the establishment of the Lord's Supper (14:22–23; see note on 6:41). This miraculous supply of bread in the wilderness is reminiscent of God's provision of manna for the Israelites during their desert wanderings. This suggests that Jesus is leading a new exodus from sin—for Gentiles (non-Jewish people), as well as Jews (compare 1:13–14).

8:10 Dalmanutha This location is unknown.

8:11 Pharisees See note on 2:16.

8:12 this generation This refers to those who are blind to Jesus' true identity and so want proof of their own choosing (compare v. 38; 9:19). For those who approach in faith, Jesus confirms their faith with powerful deeds.

8:14–21 Jesus speaks enigmatically about the Pharisees, Herod and the leftover bread. He questions the disciples when they don't understand.

8:14 bread The form of the Greek word used here, *artous*, refers to multiple loaves and anticipates Jesus' questions about the number of loaves broken in each feeding story (vv. 19–20).

8:15 Watch out Jesus is probably warning the disciples against the same lack of discernment that characterizes his opponents (vv. 17–18; compare 4:24–25). **yeast** In the context of the Passover, leaven symbolizes all that must be removed from Israel when the nation transfers its allegiance from Pharaoh to God (Ex 12:15–20; Dt 16:3–4). Here, the Pharisees and Herod are obstacles to the kingdom. Jesus might be warning the disciples against requesting a sign to bolster their faith, as the Pharisees had just done.

8:18 fail to see Jesus invokes a prophetic critique

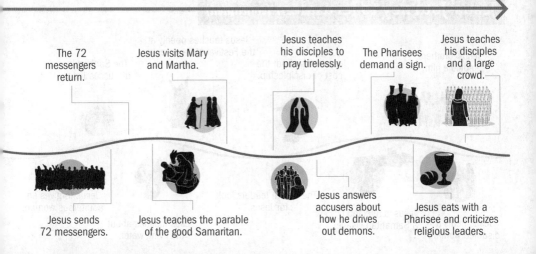

The 72 messengers return.

Jesus visits Mary and Martha.

Jesus teaches his disciples to pray tirelessly.

The Pharisees demand a sign.

Jesus teaches his disciples and a large crowd.

Jesus sends 72 messengers.

Jesus teaches the parable of the good Samaritan.

Jesus answers accusers about how he drives out demons.

Jesus eats with a Pharisee and criticizes religious leaders.

They answered, "Seven."

²¹He said to them, "Do you still not understand?"

Jesus Heals a Blind Man at Bethsaida

²²They came to Bethsaida, and some people brought a blind man and begged Jesus to touch him. ²³He took the blind man by the hand and led him outside the village. When he had spit on the man's eyes and put his hands on him, Jesus asked, "Do you see anything?"

²⁴He looked up and said, "I see people; they look like trees walking around."

²⁵Once more Jesus put his hands on the man's eyes. Then his eyes were opened, his sight was restored, and he saw everything clearly. ²⁶Jesus sent him home, saying, "Don't even go into[a] the village."

Peter Declares That Jesus Is the Messiah

8:27-29pp — Mt 16:13-16; Lk 9:18-20

²⁷Jesus and his disciples went on to the villages around Caesarea Philippi. On the way he asked them, "Who do people say I am?"

²⁸They replied, "Some say John the Baptist;

---

[a] 26 Some manuscripts *go and tell anyone in*

---

of rebellious Israel (Jer 5:21; Eze 12:2), similar to his earlier quotation of Isa 6:9–10. See note on Mk 4:12.
8:21 Do you still not understand Jesus sees the same kind of stubbornness that characterizes the Pharisees and Herodians in his own disciples. They are not understanding what his identity really means—that they do not need to be concerned about provisions (because he can take care of that; vv. 19–20) and that he is bringing the kingdom of God to the whole world, including non-Jewish people (compare note on 8:1–10).

8:22–26 This healing story in Bethsaida, along with a similar story in 10:46–52, frames Jesus' journey to Jerusalem, which is interrupted by incidents of the disciples misunderstanding or misrepresenting Jesus.

8:22 Bethsaida A village on the northeastern shore of the sea of Galilee. The hometown of Jesus' disciples Peter, Andrew and Philip (Jn 1:44).
8:24 like trees walking around Indicates that the man is not fully healed. Only here in Mark's Gospel does Jesus heal someone in two stages.
8:25 his eyes were opened, his sight was restored The apostles demonstrate the same distinction between partial and full vision: While they occasionally show some understanding about Jesus, they struggle to grasp the full implications (compare note on Mk 8:21).
8:26 Don't even go into the village With the exception of the demon-possessed man healed in the region

of the Gerasenes (5:1–17), Jesus has always been secretive about his individual healings. Yet this command is particularly emphatic, possibly because people likely would notice a previously blind man walking through town. See note on 1:34.

8:27–33 This is the structural center of the Gospel of Mark: Peter's proclamation of who Jesus is and Jesus' explanation of what his journey will entail. Jesus continues the dialogue of this scene in 8:34—9:1.

8:27 Caesarea Philippi The capital of the territory ruled by Philip, the brother of Herod Antipas. This region included the northeastern coast of the Sea of Galilee. See note on Mt 16:13. **On the way** The various stages of Jesus' journey from Caesarea Philippi to Jerusalem are marked in the Greek text by a version of this phrase (Mk 9:33–34; 10:17,32,46,52; compare note on 1:3). **Who do people say I am** The speculation around Jesus' identity suggests that some considered him a prophet—that is, an agent of God's power—but not the Messiah.

8:28 John the Baptist See 6:14. **Elijah** See note on 6:15. **one of the prophets** This could be a reference to one of the prophets that Jewish people of the time believed would return (see note on Rev 11:3) or to people thinking Jesus is a prophet in general.

Jesus' Journey to Jerusalem *(continued)*

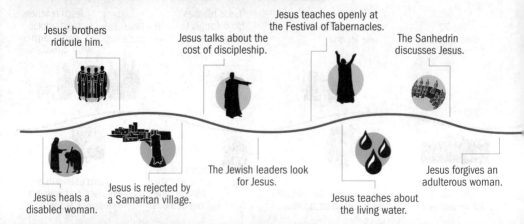

Jesus teaches openly at the Festival of Tabernacles.

Jesus' brothers ridicule him.

Jesus talks about the cost of discipleship.

The Sanhedrin discusses Jesus.

Jesus heals a disabled woman.

Jesus is rejected by a Samaritan village.

The Jewish leaders look for Jesus.

Jesus teaches about the living water.

Jesus forgives an adulterous woman.

others say Elijah; and still others, one of the prophets."

²⁹"But what about you?" he asked. "Who do you say I am?"

Peter answered, "You are the Messiah."

³⁰Jesus warned them not to tell anyone about him.

Jesus Predicts His Death

8:31 — 9:1pp — Mt 16:21-28; Lk 9:22-27

³¹He then began to teach them that the Son of Man must suffer many things and be rejected by the elders, the chief priests and the teachers of the law, and that he must be killed and after three days rise again. ³²He spoke plainly about this, and Peter took him aside and began to rebuke him.

³³But when Jesus turned and looked at his disciples, he rebuked Peter. "Get behind me, Satan!" he said. "You do not have in mind the concerns of God, but merely human concerns."

The Way of the Cross

³⁴Then he called the crowd to him along with his disciples and said: "Whoever wants to be my disciple must deny themselves and take up their cross and follow me. ³⁵For whoever wants to save

8:29 Who do you say I am By redirecting the question to his disciples, Jesus implies that he expects a different answer. **You are the Messiah** Peter's response is the first time that Jesus is identified as the anointed one by anyone in the narrative, but Mark told the reader the identity of Jesus at the beginning of the book (Mk 1:1). Nevertheless, the exchange that follows indicates that Peter still did not fully understand Jesus' mission (vv. 31–33).

8:30 not to tell anyone about him Many Jews at the time expected the Messiah to be a political figure. If they found out about Jesus' identity, they might attempt to make him king, misunderstanding his true mission to suffer and die on behalf of humanity (see vv. 31–38; 10:45). In contemporary Jewish thought, many thought that it was necessary for the Messiah to throw off oppressive foreign rule and reestablish Israel as an independent kingdom. Local Roman officials could violently cut short his ministry, even if they just heard that he claimed to be the Jewish Messiah. Although Jesus continues to teach that it is necessary for him to suffer, die and be raised, the events must occur according to God's will and timing.

8:31 He then began to teach them This, along with two other predictions by Jesus about his death, frame his journey to Jerusalem (9:30–32; 10:32–34). See the event line "Jesus' Journey to Jerusalem" on p. 1616. **Son of Man must suffer** When Jesus previously identified himself by the messianic title Son of Man (2:10,28), he did so against the backdrop of Da 7, which portrays the Son of Man as a figure of authority. The element

of suffering is without precedent in Jewish interpretations of Daniel from the time of Jesus, and probably is influenced by the depiction of the suffering servant of Isaiah—another prophesy related to the Messiah (Isa 52:13—53:12; see note on Mk 2:10). Jesus' mission as a suffering, dying Messiah contrasts the expectation of a militant, political Messiah. **chief priests** See note on 11:18. **teachers of the law** See note on 1:22.

8:32 began to rebuke Peter treats Jesus as though his revelation of the Son of Man's destiny has made him an obstacle to God's rule. Although Peter is the one to identify Jesus as the Messiah, he is yet to understand what being the Messiah means.

8:33 Satan See note on Mt 16:23.

8:34 — 9:1 Jesus begins to teach about the implications of his mission for his disciples.

8:34 take up their cross Those condemned to crucifixion were made to carry their own cross (or at least the crossbeam). Jesus' followers must be prepared to face martyrdom for their allegiance to him. Such a fate would have meant public shame and scorn (see note on Mt 10:38). Based on Peter's earlier response to Jesus (Mk 8:32) it seems that the disciples expected they would receive political power and favor in the Messianic kingdom that they believed Jesus would inaugurate (compare note on Mk 8:30; 10:35–45).

8:35 whoever wants to save their life Those who place themselves first, instead of the gospel, will be

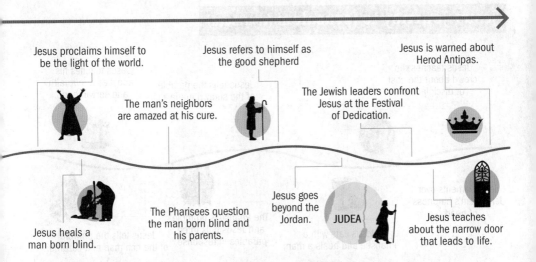

Jesus proclaims himself to be the light of the world.

Jesus refers to himself as the good shepherd

Jesus is warned about Herod Antipas.

The man's neighbors are amazed at his cure.

The Jewish leaders confront Jesus at the Festival of Dedication.

Jesus heals a man born blind.

The Pharisees question the man born blind and his parents.

Jesus goes beyond the Jordan.

JUDEA

Jesus teaches about the narrow door that leads to life.

their life[a] will lose it, but whoever loses their life for me and for the gospel will save it. 36 What good is it for someone to gain the whole world, yet forfeit their soul? 37 Or what can anyone give in exchange for their soul? 38 If anyone is ashamed of me and my words in this adulterous and sinful generation, the Son of Man will be ashamed of them when he comes in his Father's glory with the holy angels."

9 And he said to them, "Truly I tell you, some who are standing here will not taste death before they see that the kingdom of God has come with power."

The Transfiguration

9:2-8pp — Lk 9:28-36
9:2-13pp — Mt 17:1-13

2 After six days Jesus took Peter, James and John with him and led them up a high mountain, where they were all alone. There he was transfigured before them. 3 His clothes became dazzling white, whiter than anyone in the world could bleach them. 4 And there appeared before them Elijah and Moses, who were talking with Jesus.

5 Peter said to Jesus, "Rabbi, it is good for us to be here. Let us put up three shelters — one for you, one for Moses and one for Elijah." 6 (He did not know what to say, they were so frightened.)

7 Then a cloud appeared and covered them, and a voice came from the cloud: "This is my Son, whom I love. Listen to him!"

8 Suddenly, when they looked around, they no longer saw anyone with them except Jesus.

9 As they were coming down the mountain, Jesus gave them orders not to tell anyone what they had seen until the Son of Man had risen from the dead. 10 They kept the matter to themselves, discussing what "rising from the dead" meant.

[a] 35 The Greek word means either *life* or *soul*; also in verses 36 and 37.

---

unsuccessful in their self-preservation goals (v. 37). Jesus' message leads to eternal life (compare Jn 3:16–17) — anything else leads to standing in opposition to God, and ultimately to being on the wrong side of his judgment (Mk 8:38). **whoever loses their life** The Romans reserved crucifixion primarily for those who revolted against the empire's authority. Jesus is noting that allegiance to him may require the ultimate sacrifice.
8:37 can anyone give in exchange for their soul Echoes Ps 49:7–9. This background clarifies that Jesus is speaking of the eternal life of the kingdom of God (Mk 8:38; 10:17,30).
8:38 in his Father's glory The suffering and death that Jesus must undergo is not the end of his reign; instead it is part of him accomplishing his purposes on earth. It seems that Jesus is referencing here his second coming on the day of judgment (Rev 20:11–15), but he also could be referencing his ascension (Lk 24:50–52).
9:1 who are standing here will not taste death See note on Mt 16:28.

9:2–13 The transfiguration demonstrates that Jesus is divine. The words of blessing on Jesus recall God the Father's blessing at Jesus' baptism (Mk 1:11) and further establish that Jesus teaches with the authority of God. This event prefigures Jesus' resurrection — when his identity will no longer be veiled — as well as his return in power and glory (13:26; 16:6).
9:2 After six days Recalls Moses' six-day waiting period prior to ascending Mount Sinai to encounter God (Ex 24:16–18). **a high mountain** See note on Mt 17:1. **he was transfigured** The Greek term used here, *metamorphoō*, means his appearance was changed, suggesting that Jesus changed into the form of heavenly glory.
9:3 His clothes became dazzling white Echoes Moses' appearance when he descended from Mount Sinai (Ex 34:29).
9:4 there appeared before them Elijah and Moses Both men encountered God on mountains (Ex 19–34; 1Ki 19). In the context of Mark's Gospel, Moses may represent the law

---

Jesus' Journey to Jerusalem (continued)

Jesus teaches the crowd about the cost of discipleship.

Jesus tells the parable of the shrewd manager.

Jesus teaches his apostles about faith and servanthood.

Jesus laments over Jerusalem's hardness of heart.

Jesus eats with a Pharisee and heals a man.

The Pharisees grumble, and Jesus tells three parables in response.

Jesus tells the parable of the rich man and Lazarus.

¹¹And they asked him, "Why do the teachers of the law say that Elijah must come first?"

¹²Jesus replied, "To be sure, Elijah does come first, and restores all things. Why then is it written that the Son of Man must suffer much and be rejected? ¹³But I tell you, Elijah has come, and they have done to him everything they wished, just as it is written about him."

Jesus Heals a Boy Possessed by an Impure Spirit

9:14-28; 30-32pp — Mt 17:14-19; 22,23; Lk 9:37-45

¹⁴When they came to the other disciples, they saw a large crowd around them and the teachers of the law arguing with them. ¹⁵As soon as all the people saw Jesus, they were overwhelmed with wonder and ran to greet him.

¹⁶"What are you arguing with them about?" he asked.

¹⁷A man in the crowd answered, "Teacher, I brought you my son, who is possessed by a spirit that has robbed him of speech. ¹⁸Whenever it seizes him, it throws him to the ground. He foams at the mouth, gnashes his teeth and becomes rigid. I asked your disciples to drive out the spirit, but they could not."

¹⁹"You unbelieving generation," Jesus replied, "how long shall I stay with you? How long shall I put up with you? Bring the boy to me."

---

and Elijah the prophets (compare Mal 4:4–6). **who were talking with Jesus** This connects earlier stages of God's revelation—the Law and the Prophets—with the present revelation, the Son, as God the Father affirms (Mk 9:7).

9:5 three shelters Peter may be thinking of the Biblical festival of Sukkot (Tabernacles), when Israel lived in temporary booths to commemorate the exodus (Lev 23:42–43).

9:7 a voice came from the cloud Echoes Moses' encounter with God at Sinai (Ex 24:15–18) and Elijah's encounter at Horeb (1Ki 19:8–18). This heavenly declaration, recalling Jesus' baptism (Mk 1:11), reveals Jesus' identity to his closest confidants—this parallels Peter's earlier affirmation that Jesus is the Messiah (8:29).

9:9 risen from the dead Once again affirming that Jesus' death and resurrection is forthcoming (compare 8:31).

9:11 teachers of the law See note on 1:22. **Elijah must come first** Many Jews expected that Elijah would come before the Messiah, based on Mal 4:5 (see note on Mk 6:15).

9:12 Elijah does come first Jesus is referring to John the Baptist, who came in the spirit of Elijah (Mt 11:13–14). **restores all things** Jesus seems to be referencing the deuterocanonical text Sirach (also called Ben Sira), which speaks of Elijah coming again to restore the tribes of Jacob (Israel; Sirach 48:10). John the Baptist fulfills this role in convincing many Jewish people to repent from their sins, consequently preparing the way for Jesus (see Mk 1:1–8;

note on 1:4). He restores people to relationship with God the Father, so that they may receive the kingdom of God and the inaugurator of that kingdom, Jesus. **written that the Son of Man must suffer** Although no OT text explicitly says that the Son of Man must suffer, Jesus is making a connection between the messianic prophecy about the Son of Man in Da 7 and the messianic prophecy about the suffering servant of Isa 52:13—53:12. In Mk 10:45, Jesus makes this connection more directly. Jesus' connection between his own resurrection (v. 9) and the suffering servant suggests that he understood the suffering servant prophecy to tell about resurrection (see Isa 53:10 and note). See note on Mk 2:10. See the table "Jesus' Fulfillment of OT Prophecy" on p. 1573.

9:13 everything they wished An allusion to the execution of John the Baptist (6:14–29). **just as it is written about him** It is not clear which OT text Jesus has in mind here; any number of passages about suffering could be applied in this context, although none directly speak about Elijah's suffering or death.

9:14–29 Jesus heals a boy possessed by a demon that the disciples were unable to cast out.

9:17 I brought you The man is referring to bringing the boy to Jesus' disciples—he had expected to see Jesus but encountered the disciples first.

9:19 You unbelieving generation Jesus' remark

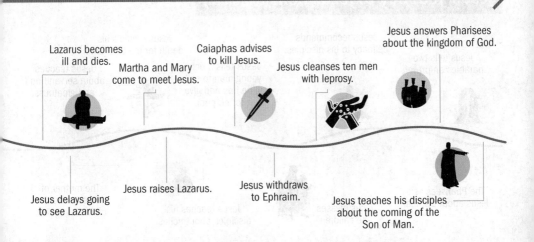

Lazarus becomes ill and dies.

Martha and Mary come to meet Jesus.

Caiaphas advises to kill Jesus.

Jesus cleanses ten men with leprosy.

Jesus answers Pharisees about the kingdom of God.

Jesus delays going to see Lazarus.

Jesus raises Lazarus.

Jesus withdraws to Ephraim.

Jesus teaches his disciples about the coming of the Son of Man.

²⁰So they brought him. When the spirit saw Jesus, it immediately threw the boy into a convulsion. He fell to the ground and rolled around, foaming at the mouth.

²¹Jesus asked the boy's father, "How long has he been like this?"

"From childhood," he answered. ²²"It has often thrown him into fire or water to kill him. But if you can do anything, take pity on us and help us."

²³"'If you can'?" said Jesus. "Everything is possible for one who believes."

²⁴Immediately the boy's father exclaimed, "I do believe; help me overcome my unbelief!"

²⁵When Jesus saw that a crowd was running to the scene, he rebuked the impure spirit. "You deaf and mute spirit," he said, "I command you, come out of him and never enter him again."

²⁶The spirit shrieked, convulsed him violently and came out. The boy looked so much like a corpse that many said, "He's dead." ²⁷But Jesus took him by the hand and lifted him to his feet, and he stood up.

²⁸After Jesus had gone indoors, his disciples asked him privately, "Why couldn't we drive it out?"

²⁹He replied, "This kind can come out only by prayer.ᵃ"

Jesus Predicts His Death a Second Time

9:33-37pp — Mt 18:1-5; Lk 9:46-48

³⁰They left that place and passed through Galilee. Jesus did not want anyone to know where they were, ³¹because he was teaching his disciples. He said to them, "The Son of Man is going to be delivered into the hands of men. They will kill him, and after three days he will rise." ³²But they did not understand what he meant and were afraid to ask him about it.

³³They came to Capernaum. When he was in the house, he asked them, "What were you arguing about on the road?" ³⁴But they kept quiet because on the way they had argued about who was the greatest.

³⁵Sitting down, Jesus called the Twelve and said, "Anyone who wants to be first must be the very last, and the servant of all."

³⁶He took a little child whom he placed among them. Taking the child in his arms, he said to them, ³⁷"Whoever welcomes one of these little children in my name welcomes me; and whoever welcomes me does not welcome me but the one who sent me."

ᵃ 29 Some manuscripts *prayer and fasting*

---

appears to be directed at the crowds and perhaps his disciples as well (compare 8:38).

9:20 it immediately threw the boy into a convulsion As in Jesus' previous encounters with unclean spirits, the demon causes a commotion within its host when Jesus appears (e.g., 5:6).

9:23 for one who believes Jesus' response redirects the conversation from the question of his ability to the need for faith.

9:29 only by prayer This seems to refer to the prayer of the petitioner—the father in this instance (v. 24) rather than the exorcist. Although it is possible that the disciples were attempting to exorcise the demon without praying—just using a command.

9:30–50 Jesus and his disciples leave the region of the Decapolis and head back to Galilee, making their way southeast toward Capernaum (v. 33). Jesus again predicts his death and resurrection (compare 8:31; 10:32–34). Although the disciples do not understand what Jesus means (v. 32), none of them openly disagrees with Jesus, as Peter did earlier (8:31–33). Their lack of understanding is further reflected in their discussion about who is greatest (vv. 33–37) and in their reaction to someone casting out demons in Jesus' name (vv. 38–41). Jesus then speaks about future judgment and the need to avoid sin at all costs (vv. 42–50).

9:34 who was the greatest The disciples' inability to

Jesus' Journey to Jerusalem (continued)

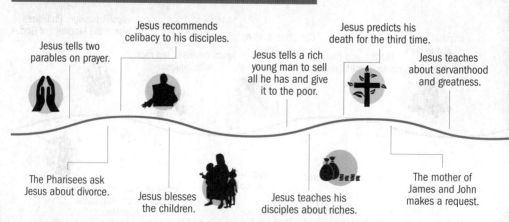

Jesus tells two parables on prayer.

Jesus recommends celibacy to his disciples.

Jesus tells a rich young man to sell all he has and give it to the poor.

Jesus predicts his death for the third time.

Jesus teaches about servanthood and greatness.

The Pharisees ask Jesus about divorce.

Jesus blesses the children.

Jesus teaches his disciples about riches.

The mother of James and John makes a request.

Whoever Is Not Against Us Is for Us

9:38-40pp — Lk 9:49,50

[38]"Teacher," said John, "we saw someone driving out demons in your name and we told him to stop, because he was not one of us."

[39]"Do not stop him," Jesus said. "For no one who does a miracle in my name can in the next moment say anything bad about me, [40]for whoever is not against us is for us. [41]Truly I tell you, anyone who gives you a cup of water in my name because you belong to the Messiah will certainly not lose their reward.

Causing to Stumble

[42]"If anyone causes one of these little ones — those who believe in me — to stumble, it would be better for them if a large millstone were hung around their neck and they were thrown into the sea. [43]If your hand causes you to stumble, cut it off. It is better for you to enter life maimed than with two hands to go into hell, where the fire never goes out. [44]a [45]And if your foot causes you to stumble, cut it off. It is better for you to enter life crippled than to have two feet and be thrown into hell. [46]a [47]And if your eye causes you to stumble, pluck it out. It is better for you to enter the kingdom of God with one eye than to have two eyes and be thrown into hell, [48]where

> "'the worms that eat them do not die,
>   and the fire is not quenched.'b

a 44,46 Some manuscripts include here the words of verse 48.
b 48 Isaiah 66:24

---

comprehend Jesus' destiny, or perhaps its significance, matches their distorted understanding of their own futures (v. 38; 10:35–37).

9:35 servant Echoes the words of Isa 52:13—53:12, which Jesus will fulfill (compare note on Mk 9:12). Jesus demonstrates this principle by sacrificing his own life.

9:38 he was not one of us The apostles apparently believe that they are the only authorized agents of Jesus.

9:41 will certainly not lose their reward Alludes to the day of final judgment and the expectations that Jesus' followers treat all people with love and kindness. This distinguishes them from those who do not follow Jesus (compare Mt 25:31–46).

9:42 these little ones In Jesus' analogy, this refers most directly to children (Mk 9:36–37), but the implication is that God will deal with those who mislead other people (compare 10:24).

9:43 cut it off Jesus' hyperbolic language here and in his similar descriptions in vv. 43–47, shows the drastic effects of sin—that it only produces death and destruction. **life** Refers to eternal life, continuing the theme of final judgment (v. 41). **hell** The Greek term used here, *geenna*, is a transliteration for the Hebrew phrase for the "Valley of Hinnom." This valley, located near Jerusalem,

was associated with idolatrous sacrifices in Israel's past (e.g., 2Ch 33:6). In Jesus' time it was used as a metaphor for God's wrath. **the fire never goes out** This and v. 48 could imply that those who perpetually and unrepentantly turn from Jesus will experience eternal punishment for their sin. It could also be an affirmation that God's decision to vanquish sin from the earth—and consequently eliminate unrepentant sinners—cannot be undone (see note on 2Pe 3:7; note on 2Pe 3:9). Either way, God must ultimately bring final judgment for there to be peace on earth, because sin is what causes disharmony with God's good purposes.

9:45 better for you It is unlikely that Jesus intends for his followers to cut off their appendages. Rather, he indicates the seriousness of sin and the exceeding worth of the life he offers.

9:47 enter the kingdom of God Focuses on the eternal aspects of God's kingdom. Jesus is referring here to entering God's presence after bodily death or final judgment.

9:48 where the worms that eat them do not die Jesus alludes to Isaiah's description of the ultimate fate of the unrepentant wicked (see Isa 66:24 and note). **fire is not quenched** See note on Mk 9:43; note on Isa 66:24.

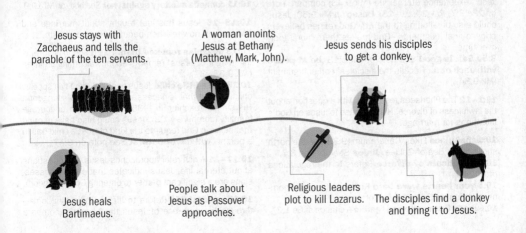

Jesus stays with Zacchaeus and tells the parable of the ten servants.

A woman anoints Jesus at Bethany (Matthew, Mark, John).

Jesus sends his disciples to get a donkey.

Jesus heals Bartimaeus.

People talk about Jesus as Passover approaches.

Religious leaders plot to kill Lazarus.

The disciples find a donkey and bring it to Jesus.

[49]Everyone will be salted with fire.

[50]"Salt is good, but if it loses its saltiness, how can you make it salty again? Have salt among yourselves, and be at peace with each other."

Divorce

10:1-12pp — Mt 19:1-9

10 Jesus then left that place and went into the region of Judea and across the Jordan. Again crowds of people came to him, and as was his custom, he taught them.

[2]Some Pharisees came and tested him by asking, "Is it lawful for a man to divorce his wife?"

[3]"What did Moses command you?" he replied.

[4]They said, "Moses permitted a man to write a certificate of divorce and send her away."

[5]"It was because your hearts were hard that Moses wrote you this law," Jesus replied. [6]"But at the beginning of creation God 'made them male and female.'[a] [7]'For this reason a man will leave his father and mother and be united to his wife,[b] [8]and the two will become one flesh.'[c] So they are no longer two, but one flesh. [9]Therefore what God has joined together, let no one separate."

[10]When they were in the house again, the disciples asked Jesus about this. [11]He answered, "Anyone who divorces his wife and marries another woman commits adultery against her. [12]And if she divorces her husband and marries another man, she commits adultery."

The Little Children and Jesus

10:13-16pp — Mt 19:13-15; Lk 18:15-17

[13]People were bringing little children to Jesus for him to place his hands on them, but the disciples rebuked them. [14]When Jesus saw this, he was indignant. He said to them, "Let the little children come to me, and do not hinder them, for the kingdom of God belongs to such as these. [15]Truly I tell you, anyone who will not receive the kingdom of God like a little child will never enter it." [16]And he took the children in his arms, placed his hands on them and blessed them.

The Rich and the Kingdom of God

10:17-31pp — Mt 19:16-30; Lk 18:18-30

[17]As Jesus started on his way, a man ran up to him and fell on his knees before him. "Good teacher," he asked, "what must I do to inherit eternal life?"

[18]"Why do you call me good?" Jesus answered. "No one is good — except God alone. [19]You know the commandments: 'You shall not murder, you shall not commit adultery, you shall not steal, you shall not give false testimony, you shall not defraud, honor your father and mother.'[d]"

[20]"Teacher," he declared, "all these I have kept since I was a boy."

[21]Jesus looked at him and loved him. "One thing you lack," he said. "Go, sell everything you have and give to the poor, and you will have treasure in heaven. Then come, follow me."

[22]At this the man's face fell. He went away sad, because he had great wealth.

[23]Jesus looked around and said to his disciples, "How hard it is for the rich to enter the kingdom of God!"

[24]The disciples were amazed at his words. But Jesus said again, "Children, how hard it is[e] to enter the kingdom of God! [25]It is easier for a camel to go through the eye of a needle than for someone who is rich to enter the kingdom of God."

---

[a] 6 Gen. 1:27   [b] 7 Some early manuscripts do not have *and be united to his wife.*   [c] 8 Gen. 2:24   [d] 19 Exodus 20:12-16; Deut. 5:16-20   [e] 24 Some manuscripts *is for those who trust in riches*

9:49 Everyone will be salted with fire In the previous verses, Jesus associates fire with judgment for unrepentant sinners, suggesting that here Jesus is referring to everyone being judged. Those who choose Jesus experience eternal life (Mk 9:43; compare note on 2Pe 3:7; Rev 20:11–15). Based on Mk 9:50, Jesus could also be alluding to the way God refines believers prior to final judgment—God makes them more godly over time.

9:50 Salt is good See note on Mt 5:13. **be at peace with each other** Recalls the disciples' earlier argument (Mk 9:34).

10:1–12 The Pharisees test Jesus with a question about the lawfulness of divorce. His response focuses on God's intentions for marriage.

10:1 that place Likely Capernaum (9:33), on the north shore of the Sea of Galilee. **Judea** See note on 3:7.
10:4 certificate of divorce Refers to the regulations of Dt 24:1–4.
10:5 your hearts were hard Refers to their stubbornness (compare Ex 4:21 and note).
10:6 made them male and female A citation of Ge 1:27.

10:7–8 Jesus cites Ge 2:24, explaining that a married couple becomes a unit—God's intentions are that it not be separated.

10:11 commits adultery against her See note on Mt 19:9.

10:13–16 Jesus has just taught about marriage and divorce and now teaches about children and faith.

10:13 disciples rebuked them This reaction is surprising in light of Jesus' remarks about welcoming children (Mk 9:33–37).
10:15 like a little child Jesus does not identify a specific childlike trait that is necessary to enter God's kingdom. His similar teaching in 9:35–36 seems to encourage humility (compare v. 23); Jesus could also have in mind that belief in God requires the kind of trust a child has in a parent. **will never enter it** See note on 9:47.

10:17–31 A rich ruler approaches Jesus with questions about eternal life. Jesus indicates that earthly possessions are a significant barrier to entering God's kingdom.

10:17 eternal life Refers to life in God's kingdom—through the embrace of Jesus the Messiah (compare

²⁶The disciples were even more amazed, and said to each other, "Who then can be saved?"

²⁷Jesus looked at them and said, "With man this is impossible, but not with God; all things are possible with God."

²⁸Then Peter spoke up, "We have left everything to follow you!"

²⁹"Truly I tell you," Jesus replied, "no one who has left home or brothers or sisters or mother or father or children or fields for me and the gospel ³⁰will fail to receive a hundred times as much in this present age: homes, brothers, sisters, mothers, children and fields — along with persecutions — and in the age to come eternal life. ³¹But many who are first will be last, and the last first."

Jesus Predicts His Death a Third Time

10:32-34pp — Mt 20:17-19; Lk 18:31-33

³²They were on their way up to Jerusalem, with Jesus leading the way, and the disciples were astonished, while those who followed were afraid. Again he took the Twelve aside and told them what was going to happen to him. ³³"We are going up to Jerusalem," he said, "and the Son of Man will be delivered over to the chief priests and the teachers of the law. They will condemn him to death and will hand him over to the Gentiles, ³⁴who will mock him and spit on him, flog him and kill him. Three days later he will rise."

The Request of James and John

10:35-45pp — Mt 20:20-28

³⁵Then James and John, the sons of Zebedee, came to him. "Teacher," they said, "we want you to do for us whatever we ask."

³⁶"What do you want me to do for you?" he asked.

³⁷They replied, "Let one of us sit at your right and the other at your left in your glory."

³⁸"You don't know what you are asking," Jesus said. "Can you drink the cup I drink or be baptized with the baptism I am baptized with?"

³⁹"We can," they answered.

Jesus said to them, "You will drink the cup I drink and be baptized with the baptism I am baptized with, ⁴⁰but to sit at my right or left is not for me to grant. These places belong to those for whom they have been prepared."

⁴¹When the ten heard about this, they became indignant with James and John. ⁴²Jesus called them together and said, "You know that those who are regarded as rulers of the Gentiles lord it over them, and their high officials exercise authority over them. ⁴³Not so with you. Instead, whoever wants to become great among you must be your servant, ⁴⁴and whoever wants to be first must be slave of all. ⁴⁵For even the Son of Man did not come to be served, but to serve, and to give his life as a ransom for many."

9:43–48). Although some Jews in Jesus' day denied the possibility of resurrection and eternal life, many others believed that they would be resurrected and granted entrance into the kingdom of God (compare Da 12:2).
10:19 You know the commandments See Ex 20:12–17; Dt 5:16–21.
10:21 Go, sell everything you have Compare Mk 8:34–38.
10:24 Children Jesus uses familial language to address his disciples and perhaps others who are present.
10:25 eye of a needle Describes an impossible scenario (compare v. 27). It is possible that the Greek word *kamilos* ("rope") was intended here, instead of *kamēlos* ("camel"). The image of a rope passing through a needle is less absurd, although still impossible. It also is possible that the phrase "eye of a needle" refers to a specific gate that was large enough for humans but not camels. Regardless of how Jesus' statement is interpreted, his point is clear: Entering God's kingdom necessitates great sacrifice. If wealth stands between a person and God, it is wealth that must be sacrificed. In v. 27, Jesus affirms that it is possible for God to change a person's heart, even when the situation seems impossible, like this one.

10:29–31 Jesus offers a similar teaching to 8:34—9:1 and 9:35–37—explaining once again that following him requires sacrifice, but that God recognizes the sacrifice.

10:32–45 This is the first reference in Mark to Jesus heading toward Jerusalem. Jesus' prediction of his death (vv. 32–34) is contrasted with James and John seeking places of honor (vv. 35–41). Jesus responds by revisiting his teaching about the least and the greatest (vv. 42–45; compare 9:35; 10:31).

10:32 up Because Jerusalem was at a high elevation relative to the rest of Israel, it was common to speak of going up to the holy city. This expression is associated with sacred pilgrimages, when most Jews in Israel would go up to Jerusalem (see Dt 16:16). Jesus and the disciples' journey might correspond with the Passover, which happens not long after their arrival.
10:33 will be delivered over Jesus said earlier that he would be handed over to human authorities (Mk 9:31), but this is the first time he explicitly identifies those who will arrest him. Using the same verb that Mark uses here, the Septuagint (ancient Greek translation of the OT) version of Isaiah states that the suffering servant was handed over to death for the sins of many (Isa 53:12).
chief priests See note on Mk 11:18. **teachers of the law** See note on 1:22.
10:37 one of us sit at your right and the other at your left James and John apparently think that Jesus is going to Jerusalem to set up the kingdom of God. Although Jesus has just predicted his death for the third time, they do not grasp the nature of his mission.
10:38 cup I drink Refers to Jesus' death. See note on 14:36.
10:39 You will drink the cup Jesus seems to be referring to suffering and perhaps dying for the sake of the gospel.
10:40 those for whom they have been prepared Jesus indicates that God the Father decides who has particular privileges or honor in the kingdom of God.
10:45 Son of Man See note on 2:10. **did not come to be served, but to serve** In Da 7:14, the Son of Man is given authority and glory. Jesus seems to identify the Son of Man with Isaiah's suffering servant, who bears people's iniquities and carries the sin of many (Isa

Blind Bartimaeus Receives His Sight

10:46-52pp — Mt 20:29-34; Lk 18:35-43

⁴⁶Then they came to Jericho. As Jesus and his disciples, together with a large crowd, were leaving the city, a blind man, Bartimaeus (which means "son of Timaeus"), was sitting by the roadside begging. ⁴⁷When he heard that it was Jesus of Nazareth, he began to shout, "Jesus, Son of David, have mercy on me!"

⁴⁸Many rebuked him and told him to be quiet, but he shouted all the more, "Son of David, have mercy on me!"

⁴⁹Jesus stopped and said, "Call him."

So they called to the blind man, "Cheer up! On your feet! He's calling you." ⁵⁰Throwing his cloak aside, he jumped to his feet and came to Jesus.

⁵¹"What do you want me to do for you?" Jesus asked him.

53:11–12). **ransom for many** In the Septuagint (the Greek translation of the OT), the term Greek term used here, *lytron*, often designates monetary compensation given to a wronged party in lieu of capital punishment for the perpetrator (e.g., Ex 21:29–30; 30:11–16; Nu 3:11–13). Jesus seems to be evoking the prophecy of Isa 53:10–12 that the suffering servant would bear people's iniquities as a guilt offering, so that they may become righteous before Yahweh (compare Isa 53:12).

10:46–52 On his way to Jerusalem, Jesus heals a blind beggar. This is the final healing miracle recorded in Mark. The blind man receives his sight by believing that Jesus

is the Messiah—unlike the blind generation who will reject Jesus shortly.

10:46 Jericho Located five miles west of a major crossing of the Jordan River. Jericho was the only large settlement that a traveler would pass through when going up from the Jordan Valley to Jerusalem. Jericho held a significant role in Israel's history (Jos 6).

10:47 Son of David The first time Jesus is called by this title in Mark. The OT prophesied that the Messiah would be a descendent of David (Isa 11:1–5; Jer 23:5–6; Eze 34:23–24; compare 2Sa 7:16). Although Bartimaeus' use

Herod's Temple

The Israelites' Courtyard, where sacrifices were made, was used only by male Jews who were worshiping. The Holy Place, which was the temple of Yahweh, was only used by priests. The Womens' Courtyard was accessible to all Jews. The Gentiles' Courtyard, which was outside on the Temple Mount, was open to the general public.

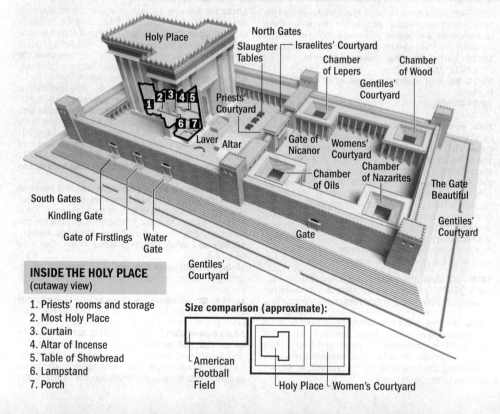

INSIDE THE HOLY PLACE (cutaway view)

1. Priests' rooms and storage
2. Most Holy Place
3. Curtain
4. Altar of Incense
5. Table of Showbread
6. Lampstand
7. Porch

Size comparison (approximate):

American Football Field

Holy Place — Women's Courtyard

The blind man said, "Rabbi, I want to see."
⁵²"Go," said Jesus, "your faith has healed you." Immediately he received his sight and followed Jesus along the road.

Jesus Comes to Jerusalem as King

11:1-10pp — Mt 21:1-9; Lk 19:29-38
11:7-10pp — Jn 12:12-15

11 As they approached Jerusalem and came to Bethphage and Bethany at the Mount of Olives, Jesus sent two of his disciples, ²saying to them, "Go to the village ahead of you, and just as you enter it, you will find a colt tied there, which no one has ever ridden. Untie it and bring it here. ³If anyone asks you, 'Why are you doing this?' say, 'The Lord needs it and will send it back here shortly.'"

⁴They went and found a colt outside in the street, tied at a doorway. As they untied it, ⁵some people standing there asked, "What are you doing, untying that colt?" ⁶They answered as Jesus had told them to, and the people let them go. ⁷When they brought the colt to Jesus and threw their cloaks over it, he sat on it. ⁸Many people spread their cloaks on the road, while others spread branches they had cut in the fields. ⁹Those who went ahead and those who followed shouted,

"Hosanna!ᵃ"

"Blessed is he who comes in the name of the Lord!"ᵇ

¹⁰"Blessed is the coming kingdom of our father David!"

"Hosanna in the highest heaven!"

¹¹Jesus entered Jerusalem and went into the temple courts. He looked around at everything, but since it was already late, he went out to Bethany with the Twelve.

Jesus Curses a Fig Tree and Clears the Temple Courts

11:12-14pp — Mt 21:18-22
11:15-18pp — Mt 21:12-16; Lk 19:45-47; Jn 2:13-16
11:20-24pp — Mt 21:19-22

¹²The next day as they were leaving Bethany, Jesus was hungry. ¹³Seeing in the distance a fig tree in leaf, he went to find out if it had any fruit. When he reached it, he found nothing but leaves, because it was not the season for figs. ¹⁴Then he said to the tree, "May no one ever eat fruit from you again." And his disciples heard him say it.

¹⁵On reaching Jerusalem, Jesus entered the temple courts and began driving out those who were buying and selling there. He overturned the tables of the money changers and the benches of those selling doves, ¹⁶and would not allow anyone to carry merchandise through the temple

---

ᵃ 9 A Hebrew expression meaning "Save!" which became an exclamation of praise; also in verse 10   ᵇ 9 Psalm 118:25,26

---

of this title has clear political implications, Jesus does nothing to silence him, suggesting that Jesus is now ready for his identity to be widely known (compare Mk 1:34 and note).
10:52 your faith has healed you The man's recognition that Jesus is the Messiah prompts Jesus to heal the man. See the table "Miracles of Jesus" on p. 1741.

11:1–11 As Jesus enters Jerusalem on a colt, many gather to bless him and hail the return of the Davidic kingdom (compare 2Sa 7; note on Mk 10:47). The scene is reminiscent of a triumphal, kingly procession, but Jesus does not proceed to act like an earthly king—he does not take military action against occupying Rome or Herod Antipas (compare 6:14). Neither the religious leaders nor the Romans seem to take note of Jesus' entry into Jerusalem until Jesus cleanses the temple (vv. 15–19).
11:1 Bethphage A village on the eastern outskirts of Jerusalem. **Bethany** One of Jerusalem's outlying settlements. **Mount of Olives** A two-mile-long ridge that forms Jerusalem's eastern border and rises about 300 feet above the city; a site of many olive groves.
11:2 colt Reflects the OT image and prophecy of Jerusalem's king riding on a donkey (see Zec 9:9 and note; compare 1Ki 1:38 and note).
11:3 Lord This instance of the Greek term, *kyrios*, is likely the common usage to refer to a social superior, meaning something akin to "teacher" or "sir."
11:8 Many people spread their cloaks on the road A public declaration of political allegiance (compare 2Ki 9:13). Jesus enters Jerusalem as its king, and the people accept him as such. **branches** A common element in festal processions (Lev 23:40).

11:9 shouted They shout an adaptation of Ps 118:25–26, which commemorates God's victory over foreign armies through his agent (presumably the Davidic king). **Hosanna** A transliteration of the Hebrew phrase *hoshi'ah na*, which means "save us!" Compare Ps 118:25. **Blessed is he who comes** A quotation of Ps 118:26. This announcement happens in response to a display of God's favor (Ps 118:27).
11:10 coming kingdom of our father David Reflects the expectation that the kingdom of David would be restored to Israel, involving someone from David's line sitting on the throne and the restoration of Israel (see note on Mk 10:47). **in the highest** Refers to the heavens and their inhabitants (compare Ps 148:1–4).
11:11 entered Jerusalem and went into the temple courts This reflects the prophecy of Mal 3:1 (compare Mk 1:2). See note on Mt 21:10. See the infographic "Herod's Temple on the Temple Mount" on p. 1722. **he went out to Bethany with the Twelve** An unexpected conclusion to the fanfare that accompanied Jesus' arrival.
11:12–14 Jesus curses a fig tree that bears no fruit, symbolizing the fruitlessness of Israel—especially its religious leaders—and the judgment his ministry brings.
11:13 fig tree Israel is frequently compared to a fruitless fig tree in OT prophetic literature (e.g., Jer 8:13; Mic 7:1).
11:15–19 Jesus' cleansing of the temple enacts his implied judgment on Israel's corrupt religious system (Mk 11:12–14). This act also is consistent with his Messianic mission of restoring true religion and right relationship to God.
11:15 who were buying and selling The vendors likely

courts. ¹⁷And as he taught them, he said, "Is it not written: 'My house will be called a house of prayer for all nations'ᵃ? But you have made it 'a den of robbers.'ᵇ"

¹⁸The chief priests and the teachers of the law heard this and began looking for a way to kill him, for they feared him, because the whole crowd was amazed at his teaching.

¹⁹When evening came, Jesus and his disciplesᶜ went out of the city.

²⁰In the morning, as they went along, they saw the fig tree withered from the roots. ²¹Peter remembered and said to Jesus, "Rabbi, look! The fig tree you cursed has withered!"

²²"Have faith in God," Jesus answered. ²³"Trulyᵈ I tell you, if anyone says to this mountain, 'Go, throw yourself into the sea,' and does not doubt in their heart but believes that what they say will happen, it will be done for them. ²⁴Therefore I tell you, whatever you ask for in prayer, believe that you have received it, and it will be yours. ²⁵And when you stand praying, if you hold anything against anyone, forgive them, so that your Father in heaven may forgive you your sins." [26]ᵉ

The Authority of Jesus Questioned

11:27-33pp — Mt 21:23-27; Lk 20:1-8

²⁷They arrived again in Jerusalem, and while Jesus was walking in the temple courts, the chief priests, the teachers of the law and the elders came to him. ²⁸"By what authority are you doing these things?" they asked. "And who gave you authority to do this?"

²⁹Jesus replied, "I will ask you one question. Answer me, and I will tell you by what authority I am doing these things. ³⁰John's baptism — was it from heaven, or of human origin? Tell me!"

³¹They discussed it among themselves and said, "If we say, 'From heaven,' he will ask, 'Then why didn't you believe him?' ³²But if we say, 'Of human origin' . . ." (They feared the people, for everyone held that John really was a prophet.)

³³So they answered Jesus, "We don't know."

Jesus said, "Neither will I tell you by what authority I am doing these things."

The Parable of the Tenants

12:1-12pp — Mt 21:33-46; Lk 20:9-19

12 Jesus then began to speak to them in parables: "A man planted a vineyard. He put a wall around it, dug a pit for the winepress and built a watchtower. Then he rented the vineyard to some farmers and moved to another place. ²At harvest time he sent a servant to the tenants to collect from them some of the fruit of the vineyard. ³But they seized him, beat him and sent him away empty-handed. ⁴Then he sent another servant to them; they struck this man on the head and treated him shamefully. ⁵He sent still another, and that one they killed. He sent many others; some of them they beat, others they killed.

⁶"He had one left to send, a son, whom he loved.

ᵃ 17 Isaiah 56:7   *ᵇ 17* Jer. 7:11   *ᶜ 19* Some early manuscripts *came, Jesus*   *ᵈ 22,23* Some early manuscripts *"If you have faith in God," Jesus answered, ²³"truly*   *ᵉ 26* Some manuscripts include here words similar to Matt. 6:15.

---

were selling animals designated for sacrifice. To be fit for sacrifice, an animal had to be free from illness and physical defect (e.g., Lev 1:3; Mal 1:8). Many people preferred to purchase the animal inside the temple courts—especially during pilgrimage festivals, when thousands of people were around. **tables of the money changers** Monetary exchange was necessary because all contributions made at the temple had to be rendered in a uniform currency (the Tyrian shekel). See the infographic "Coins of the Gospels" on p. 1613.

11:17 a house of prayer for all nations Jesus quotes Isa 56:7, part of a declaration about the importance of justice and covenant observance. **a den of robbers** Jesus quotes Jer 7:11, part of an indictment of the people of Judah for injustices they committed against God and neighbor.

11:18 chief priests Refers to the leading members of the priesthood, who were responsible for the operation of the Jerusalem temple. They also played an essential role in mediating Roman rule. **the teachers of the law** Depicted as associates of the chief priests in their plot to kill Jesus (e.g., Mk 14:1). See note on 1:22.

11:20-25 The fig tree that Jesus cursed (vv. 12–14) has now withered. The disciples ask him about it, and he responds by teaching about faith, prayer and forgiveness.

11:23 this mountain Jesus may be referring to a specific mountain visible to his disciples—likely the Mount of Olives or the Temple Mount.

11:27 the elders Represents the Jewish aristocracy of Jerusalem or a governing body.

11:28 By what authority Those who question Jesus are likely aware of Jesus' Davidic association; his triumphal entry into Jerusalem was a public assertion of authority. **these things** Probably refers to Jesus' actions in this temple.

11:30 John's baptism Although Jesus does not answer the question directly, his response alludes to the source of his authority: It is the same source that legitimized John's ministry.

12:1–12 This parable has an obvious and incriminating meaning for the religious leaders (v. 12). The vineyard is Israel, and the one who plants it is God. The religious leaders are to tend the vineyard, but they turn out to be unfaithful tenants. The servants that are sent and killed are the many martyred prophets. The final messenger is the vineyard owner's beloved son—Jesus himself. This identification implies that he is the Son of God. Jesus' clear message is that the religious leaders, due to their unfaithfulness, will no longer have responsibility over God's people.

12:1 A man planted a vineyard Recalls the imagery of Isa 5:1–2 (compare Isa 5:7). Jesus modifies this image by focusing on the role of the tenant farmers rather than the vineyard itself (compare Isa 5:12).

12:5 they killed In the OT, God condemns the people of Israel for rejecting his prophets (e.g., Jer 7:25–28; Zec 1:4–6).

He sent him last of all, saying, 'They will respect my son.'

⁷"But the tenants said to one another, 'This is the heir. Come, let's kill him, and the inheritance will be ours.' ⁸So they took him and killed him, and threw him out of the vineyard.

⁹"What then will the owner of the vineyard do? He will come and kill those tenants and give the vineyard to others. ¹⁰Haven't you read this passage of Scripture:

"'The stone the builders rejected
    has become the cornerstone;
¹¹ the Lord has done this,
    and it is marvelous in our eyes'ᵃ?"

¹²Then the chief priests, the teachers of the law and the elders looked for a way to arrest him because they knew he had spoken the parable against them. But they were afraid of the crowd; so they left him and went away.

Paying the Imperial Tax to Caesar

12:13-17pp — Mt 22:15-22; Lk 20:20-26

¹³Later they sent some of the Pharisees and Herodians to Jesus to catch him in his words. ¹⁴They came to him and said, "Teacher, we know that you are a man of integrity. You aren't swayed by others, because you pay no attention to who they are; but you teach the way of God in accordance with the truth. Is it right to pay the imperial taxᵇ to Caesar or not? ¹⁵Should we pay or shouldn't we?"

But Jesus knew their hypocrisy. "Why are you trying to trap me?" he asked. "Bring me a denari-

us and let me look at it." ¹⁶They brought the coin, and he asked them, "Whose image is this? And whose inscription?"

"Caesar's," they replied.

¹⁷Then Jesus said to them, "Give back to Caesar what is Caesar's and to God what is God's."

And they were amazed at him.

Marriage at the Resurrection

12:18-27pp — Mt 22:23-33; Lk 20:27-38

¹⁸Then the Sadducees, who say there is no resurrection, came to him with a question. ¹⁹"Teacher," they said, "Moses wrote for us that if a man's brother dies and leaves a wife but no children, the man must marry the widow and raise up offspring for his brother. ²⁰Now there were seven brothers. The first one married and died without leaving any children. ²¹The second one married the widow, but he also died, leaving no child. It was the same with the third. ²²In fact, none of the seven left any children. Last of all, the woman died too. ²³At the resurrectionᶜ whose wife will she be, since the seven were married to her?"

²⁴Jesus replied, "Are you not in error because you do not know the Scriptures or the power of God? ²⁵When the dead rise, they will neither marry nor be given in marriage; they will be like the angels in heaven. ²⁶Now about the dead rising — have you not read in the Book of Moses, in the account of the burning bush, how God said to

---

ᵃ *11* Psalm 118:22,23   ᵇ *14* A special tax levied on subject peoples, not on Roman citizens   ᶜ *23* Some manuscripts *resurrection, when people rise from the dead,*

12:10–11 Jesus cites Ps 118:22–23. The imagery of this psalm is associated with Yahweh's salvation from foreign enemies. Yahweh unexpectedly uses the stone rejected by a group of builders as the most important stone in his building project. Jesus concludes his parable with these lines to show the folly of the religious leaders of Jerusalem. They have rejected Jesus, but he will be used by God the Father as the most integral part of the plan of salvation. See the table "Jesus' Fulfillment of OT Prophecy" on p. 1573.

12:13 Pharisees See note on Mk 2:16. **Herodians** See note on 3:6; see the table "Major Groups in Jesus' Time" on p. 1630.
12:14 Caesar Refers to the office of the Roman emperor. During Jesus' ministry, the emperor was Tiberius (reigned AD 14–37).
12:15 denarius A silver coin worth roughly a day's wages. See the infographic "Coins of the Gospels" on p. 1613; see the infographic "A Silver Denarius" on p. 1578.
12:17 Give back to Caesar Jesus' teaching makes clear that his followers should be willing to be subject to political authorities (provided that it does not compromise their allegiance to him). However, just as denarii belong to Caesar because they bear his image, the whole of one's life belongs to God because people bear the image of God (Ge 1:26–27).

12:18–27 The Sadducees present a hypothetical

situation about bodily resurrection. Their intention is to propose a riddle based on an OT law in order to disagree with Jesus' view of resurrection. His response, however, condemns them for not understanding the Scripture and denying the power of God.

12:18 Sadducees A prominent Jewish sect.

Mark 12:18

SADDUCEES
The Sadducees were a Jewish religious group probably associated with the priests (Ac 5:17). They are known from the NT, the first-century Jewish historian Josephus and later rabbinic traditions. Josephus lists them as one of the three main schools of thought among the Jews in the first century AD. Sadducees did not believe in the resurrection of the dead—probably because there was no clear basis for such a doctrine in the Pentateuch (Genesis-Deuteronomy), which they seem to have held as their sole authoritative scripture (Ac 23:6–8). Mark does not indicate that the Sadducees conspire in the plot to eliminate Jesus. See the table "Major Groups in Jesus' Time" on p. 1630.

12:19 the man must marry the widow Refers to the law of levirate marriage found in Dt 25:5–10.

him, 'I am the God of Abraham, the God of Isaac, and the God of Jacob'[a]? [27]He is not the God of the dead, but of the living. You are badly mistaken!"

The Greatest Commandment

12:28-34pp — Mt 22:34-40

[28]One of the teachers of the law came and heard them debating. Noticing that Jesus had given them a good answer, he asked him, "Of all the commandments, which is the most important?"

[29]"The most important one," answered Jesus, "is this: 'Hear, O Israel: The Lord our God, the Lord is one.[b] [30]Love the Lord your God with all your heart and with all your soul and with all your mind and with all your strength.'[c] [31]The second is this: 'Love your neighbor as yourself.'[d] There is no commandment greater than these."

[32]"Well said, teacher," the man replied. "You are

---

[a] 26 Exodus 3:6   [b] 29 Or *The Lord our God is one Lord*
[c] 30 Deut. 6:4,5   [d] 31 Lev. 19:18

12:27 He is not the God of the dead Jesus argues that because God's statement is in the present tense ("I am"), he is not concerned with issues that result from a person dying, but instead with the resurrected life, which is decidedly different (Mk 12:25).

12:28–34 Jesus affirms that a person's highest obligation is to love God with his or her whole life (v. 30). This

also alludes to the things of God that must be given back to him, which he mentioned earlier (v. 17).

12:28 teachers of the law See note on 1:22.
12:29 The Lord our God, the Lord is one Jesus recites the Shema (Dt 6:4–5), the central confession of Israel's faith.
12:30 all your mind While the Hebrew text of Dt 6:5

Major Groups in Jesus' Time

GROUP	DESCRIPTION	IN THE BIBLE	IN JOSEPHUS
Essenes	A Jewish party characterized by strict asceticism.	—	*J.W.* 2.120–161; *Ant.* 13.172; 15.373–379; 18.18–22
Herodians	A Jewish political party who sympathized with the rulers in the Herodian dynasty.	Mt 22:16; Mk 3:6; 12:13	*J.W.* 1.319; *Ant.* 14.450
Pharisees	A lay Jewish party that exercised strict piety according to Mosaic and oral law.	Mt 15:1–20; 23:1–36; Mk 7:1–13; Lk 7:29–30; 11:37–44; 16:14; Ac 5:34–39; 23:6–10; 26:5	*J.W.* 2.162–163,411; *Ant.* 13.172,288–298; 17.41; 18.12–15; *Life* 1.12
Sadducees	A Jewish party that was part of the aristocracy and connected to the temple priesthood.	Mt 22:23; Mk 12:18; Lk 20:27; Ac 5:17; 23:6–10	*J.W.* 2.164–166; *Ant.* 13.173,297–298; 18.16–17; 20:199
Samaritans	A group who lived in the region of Samaria. They worshiped on Mount Gerizim instead of at the temple in Jerusalem.	Lk 10:33; 17:16–18; Jn 4:9, 20; 8:48	*Ant.* 9.288–291; 12.156,257–264; 13.74; 20.118–136
Zealots	A militant, anti-Roman Jewish political and religious group. There is debate about whether this group existed in an organized way before the First Jewish Revolt of AD 66–73.	Mt 10:4; Mk 3:18; Ac 1:13	*J.W.* 4.160–161; 7.267–274; Josephus may have called them the "Fourth Philosophy" in *Ant.* 18.23–25.

right in saying that God is one and there is no other but him. [33]To love him with all your heart, with all your understanding and with all your strength, and to love your neighbor as yourself is more important than all burnt offerings and sacrifices."

[34]When Jesus saw that he had answered wisely, he said to him, "You are not far from the kingdom of God." And from then on no one dared ask him any more questions.

Whose Son Is the Messiah?

12:35-37pp — Mt 22:41-46; Lk 20:41-44
12:38-40pp — Mt 23:1-7; Lk 20:45-47

[35]While Jesus was teaching in the temple courts, he asked, "Why do the teachers of the law say that the Messiah is the son of David? [36]David himself, speaking by the Holy Spirit, declared:

" 'The Lord said to my Lord:
   "Sit at my right hand
until I put your enemies
   under your feet." ' [a]

[37]David himself calls him 'Lord.' How then can he be his son?"

The large crowd listened to him with delight.

Warning Against the Teachers of the Law

[38]As he taught, Jesus said, "Watch out for the teachers of the law. They like to walk around in flowing robes and be greeted with respect in the marketplaces, [39]and have the most important seats in the synagogues and the places of honor at banquets. [40]They devour widows' houses and for a show make lengthy prayers. These men will be punished most severely."

The Widow's Offering

12:41-44pp — Lk 21:1-4

[41]Jesus sat down opposite the place where the offerings were put and watched the crowd putting their money into the temple treasury. Many rich people threw in large amounts. [42]But a poor widow came and put in two very small copper coins, worth only a few cents.

[43]Calling his disciples to him, Jesus said, "Truly I tell you, this poor widow has put more into the treasury than all the others. [44]They all gave out of their wealth; but she, out of her poverty, put in everything — all she had to live on."

The Destruction of the Temple and Signs of the End Times

13:1-37pp — Mt 24:1-51; Lk 21:5-36

13 As Jesus was leaving the temple, one of his disciples said to him, "Look, Teacher! What massive stones! What magnificent buildings!"

[2]"Do you see all these great buildings?" replied Jesus. "Not one stone here will be left on another; every one will be thrown down."

[3]As Jesus was sitting on the Mount of Olives opposite the temple, Peter, James, John and Andrew

[a] 36 Psalm 110:1

---

includes three aspects of loving God, Jesus lists four, including a reference to the "mind." In ancient Hebrew thought, the heart was the seat of human intelligence and will. When the scribe (teacher of the law) restates the command, he refers to "understanding" rather than "soul" and "mind" (Mk 12:33). Jesus then recognizes that the scribe has answered "wisely" or "with understanding" (v. 34). This cluster of words related to the mind and understanding reflects a larger theme of Jesus' ministry in Mark: The true character of Jesus and the kingdom is veiled and requires true understanding.
12:31 Love your neighbor as yourself Jesus quotes a portion of Lev 19:18.
12:36 The Lord said to my Lord A quotation from Ps 110:1. "The Lord" refers to Yahweh; "my Lord" identifies the Messiah—whose position at Yahweh's right hand indicates superiority over all the world, including David. This parallels Jesus' self-designated title "Son of Man" (see note on Mk 2:10).
12:37 How then can he be his son In antiquity, being the son or descendant of someone implies a hierarchy; the son is inferior to the older and more important forebear. David, as the most famous and celebrated king in Israel's history, naturally was held in high regard. However, the Messiah would be superior to David. The dilemma Jesus is presenting (by means of Ps 110:1) concerns how the Messiah could be both superior and inferior to David. Jesus is showing that the figure in Ps 110:1 cannot be David, because David in the psalm refers to two figures called "Lord," neither of which

are him. Thus, Ps 110:1 must be referring to another figure—Jesus implies that he is this second figure.
12:38 in flowing robes Worn by the learned as a sign of their status.
12:42 a poor widow Compare Mk 12:40. **a few cents** The Greek word used here refers to a small monetary denomination worth 1/64th of a denarius. A denarius was worth about a day's labor.
12:44 all she had to live on This links the widow's action to the greatest commandment (see note on v. 30) and to Jesus' explanation of what belongs to God (see note on v. 17).

13:1–36 Jesus' departure from the temple leads to his prediction of its destruction. This prompts questions from the disciples about when these events would happen (vv. 3–36). Jesus responds by discussing portents (or signs) of the arrival of God's kingdom and his own climactic return. His teachings have practical significance for his followers: They must remain alert and loyal while waiting for him (vv. 32–37).

13:1 What magnificent buildings The plural form used in the Greek text here suggests that the disciple probably is commenting on the courts (or buildings) surrounding the temple, not just the temple itself. See the infographic "Herod's Temple on the Temple Mount" on p. 1722.
13:2 Not one stone here will be left Jesus might be predicting the destruction of the temple, which happened in AD 70 at the hands of the Romans. He also refers to his own body as the temple (14:58; 15:29; Jn 2:19). See the table "Political Leaders in the New Testament" on p. 1916.

asked him privately, [4]"Tell us, when will these things happen? And what will be the sign that they are all about to be fulfilled?"

[5]Jesus said to them: "Watch out that no one deceives you. [6]Many will come in my name, claiming, 'I am he,' and will deceive many. [7]When you hear of wars and rumors of wars, do not be alarmed. Such things must happen, but the end is still to come. [8]Nation will rise against nation, and kingdom against kingdom. There will be earthquakes in various places, and famines. These are the beginning of birth pains.

[9]"You must be on your guard. You will be handed over to the local councils and flogged in the synagogues. On account of me you will stand before governors and kings as witnesses to them. [10]And the gospel must first be preached to all nations. [11]Whenever you are arrested and brought to trial, do not worry beforehand about what to say. Just say whatever is given you at the time, for it is not you speaking, but the Holy Spirit.

[12]"Brother will betray brother to death, and a father his child. Children will rebel against their parents and have them put to death. [13]Everyone will hate you because of me, but the one who stands firm to the end will be saved.

[14]"When you see 'the abomination that causes desolation'[a] standing where it[b] does not belong — let the reader understand — then let those who are in Judea flee to the mountains. [15]Let no one on the housetop go down or enter the house to take anything out. [16]Let no one in the field go back to get their cloak. [17]How dreadful it will be in those days for pregnant women and nursing mothers! [18]Pray that this will not take place in winter, [19]because those will be days of distress unequaled from the beginning, when God created the world, until now — and never to be equaled again.

[20]"If the Lord had not cut short those days, no one would survive. But for the sake of the elect, whom he has chosen, he has shortened them. [21]At that time if anyone says to you, 'Look, here is the Messiah!' or, 'Look, there he is!' do not believe it. [22]For false messiahs and false prophets will appear and perform signs and wonders to deceive, if possible, even the elect. [23]So be on your guard; I have told you everything ahead of time.

[24]"But in those days, following that distress,

> "'the sun will be darkened,
>   and the moon will not give its light;
> [25]the stars will fall from the sky,
>   and the heavenly bodies will be shaken.'[c]

[26]"At that time people will see the Son of Man coming in clouds with great power and glory. [27]And he will send his angels and gather his elect from the four winds, from the ends of the earth to the ends of the heavens.

[28]"Now learn this lesson from the fig tree: As soon as its twigs get tender and its leaves come out,

---

[a] 14 Daniel 9:27; 11:31; 12:11   [b] 14 Or he   [c] 25 Isaiah 13:10; 34:4

13:4 these things The disciples might be asking about the destruction predicted in Mk 13:2 or about other events related to God's coming kingdom.

13:6 Many will come in my name Indicates that other people will claim to be the Messiah.

13:7 the end Refers to the end of the present age (which is followed by the age to come). See note on 1:15.

13:8 birth pains This reference to pains experienced in labor is a common prophetic image for divine judgment (Isa 13:6–8; 66:7; Mic 4:9–10). In Jewish apocalyptic literature (e.g., 1 Enoch 62:4; 2 Baruch 22:7), imagery of birth pains came to refer to a final period of hardship preceding the full establishment of God's reign at the end times.

13:10 first be preached to all nations Jesus speaks explicitly about a Gentile (non-Jewish) mission, which his actions in the regions surrounding Galilee have anticipated (Mk 5:1–20; 7:24–37).

13:14–23 Using apocalyptic language, Jesus warns that before he returns an abomination of desolation will affect the entire world.

13:14 the abomination that causes desolation In this context, this phrase could refer to some worldwide or regional catastrophe (see vv. 19–20). It also could indicate the Romans' attack on Jerusalem and destruction of the temple in AD 70. In the OT, this expression appears only in Daniel, indicating a terrible event that was detestable to God (Da 9:27; 11:31; 12:11). The references in Daniel might be connected to the erecting of a pagan altar by Antiochus IV Epiphanes in the temple sanctuary in 167 BC and the sacrifice of a pig upon it (as depicted in the deuterocanonical books of 1 Mac-

cabees 6:7; 2 Maccabees 6:2). See Mt 24:15 and note.

flee to the mountains During the First Jewish Revolt (AD 66–70), many who lived in Jerusalem attempted to flee the city to avoid the violence between the Romans and the rebels.

13:20 Lord had not cut short those days To save his people, God will curtail the period of tribulation. The idea of the elect is rooted in the OT understanding of Israel's identity and vocation as chosen by God (Dt 7:6; 14:2). In Jesus' time, it also could be used to refer to a portion of Israel considered to have remained faithful to God's covenant amid the general disobedience of the nation (Isa 65:8–10; as seen in the Dead Sea Scrolls document, Rule of the Community 8.1–6).

13:22 false messiahs and false prophets A false messiah pretends to be God's agent of deliverance, and a false prophet pretends to be God's messenger.

13:24 the sun will be darkened Indicates that cosmic dysfunction of some sort will be a sign of the Son of Man's coming. Mark's imagery draws on a number of prophetic motifs (e.g., Joel 2:30–31; Eze 32:7–8).

13:26 the Son of Man coming in clouds Refers to Jesus' return. See note on 2:10.

13:27 gather his elect Presupposes a time when God's people are spread around the globe. The scene evokes a prophetic motif about the ingathering of Israel to the promised land (e.g., Jer 30–31).

13:28–31 Jesus again uses the fig tree as an example of judgment (Mk 11:12–14,20–25). The point of this parable is that the presence of leaves clearly indicates the changing season, just as the cosmological signs indicate the changing eras.

you know that summer is near. [29]Even so, when you see these things happening, you know that it[a] is near, right at the door. [30]Truly I tell you, this generation will certainly not pass away until all these things have happened. [31]Heaven and earth will pass away, but my words will never pass away.

The Day and Hour Unknown

[32]"But about that day or hour no one knows, not even the angels in heaven, nor the Son, but only the Father. [33]Be on guard! Be alert[b]! You do not know when that time will come. [34]It's like a man going away: He leaves his house and puts his servants in charge, each with their assigned task, and tells the one at the door to keep watch.

[35]"Therefore keep watch because you do not know when the owner of the house will come back — whether in the evening, or at midnight, or when the rooster crows, or at dawn. [36]If he comes suddenly, do not let him find you sleeping. [37]What I say to you, I say to everyone: 'Watch!'"

Jesus Anointed at Bethany

14:1-11pp — Mt 26:2-16
14:1,2,10,11pp — Lk 22:1-6
14:3-8Ref — Jn 12:1-8

14 Now the Passover and the Festival of Unleavened Bread were only two days away, and the chief priests and the teachers of the law were scheming to arrest Jesus secretly and kill him. [2]"But not during the festival," they said, "or the people may riot."

[3]While he was in Bethany, reclining at the table in the home of Simon the Leper, a woman came with an alabaster jar of very expensive perfume, made of pure nard. She broke the jar and poured the perfume on his head.

[4]Some of those present were saying indignantly to one another, "Why this waste of perfume? [5]It could have been sold for more than a year's wages[c] and the money given to the poor." And they rebuked her harshly.

[6]"Leave her alone," said Jesus. "Why are you bothering her? She has done a beautiful thing to me. [7]The poor you will always have with you,[d] and you can help them any time you want. But you will not always have me. [8]She did what she could. She poured perfume on my body beforehand to prepare for my burial. [9]Truly I tell you, wherever the gospel is preached throughout the world, what she has done will also be told, in memory of her."

[10]Then Judas Iscariot, one of the Twelve, went to the chief priests to betray Jesus to them. [11]They were delighted to hear this and promised to give him money. So he watched for an opportunity to hand him over.

The Last Supper

14:12-26pp — Mt 26:17-30; Lk 22:7-23
14:22-25pp — 1Co 11:23-25

[12]On the first day of the Festival of Unleavened Bread, when it was customary to sacrifice the

---

a 29 Or he   *b 33 Some manuscripts alert and pray*   *c 5 Greek than three hundred denarii*   *d 7 See Deut. 15:11.*

13:28 fig tree The fruitless fig tree in 11:14 symbolizes Israel's corrupt religious leaders as the object of judgment; here, a fruitful fig tree, which may refer to positive work coming from God's people, is a sign of the imminent coming of the kingdom of God.

13:30 this generation will certainly not pass away Jesus seems to be referring to the present age of humanity (before God's rule is fully established; compare note on 1:15; note on Gal 1:4). The context of Jesus' remarks is the final judgment (Mk 13:26–27), which will occur at a time known only to the Father (v. 32). This seems to rule out the possibility that Jesus is referring only to the generation of people in his day.

13:32–37 The above predictions and signs of the age to come are held in tension with Jesus' teaching that only the Father knows the day and hour. For Jesus' followers, the implication is that they must be alert and ready for the appearance of the Son of Man at any time (vv. 34–36). This means, primarily, that his followers should continue his mission of proclaiming the good news of the kingdom of God.

13:34 puts his servants in charge Compare 12:1–12.

13:35 keep watch When Jesus leaves, he tells his followers to proclaim the gospel in all the world (v. 10; compare Mt 28:16–20; Ac 1:6–9). Remaining alert requires expectant faithfulness to Jesus until he returns in glory. **whether in the evening** The time references here parallel four markers in the Passion Narrative that follows: the evening Passover meal (Mk 14:17), Jesus' nighttime arrest in Gethsemane (14:41), his arraignment before the temple leaders when

the rooster crows (14:68,72), and his appearance before Pilate when morning comes (15:1). See the event line "Jesus' Passion and Resurrection" on p. 1698.

13:37 everyone Jesus clarifies that his charge to remain alert is for all who follow him, not simply the four disciples who are present for this teaching (v. 3).

14:1 the Passover and the Festival of Unleavened Bread Feasts commemorating Israel's deliverance from slavery in Egypt. Passover memorializes the evening God spared Israel's houses while striking down the firstborn of the Egyptians (Ex 12:12–13,26–27). The Festival of Unleavened Bread recalls Israel's departure from Egypt the following morning (Ex 12:17,39; Dt 16:3). **chief priests** See note on Mk 11:18. **teachers of the law** See note on 1:22.

14:2 people may riot During the pilgrimage for the festivals, Jerusalem's population would grow considerably — likely including many of Jesus' supporters from Galilee. Arresting Jesus could lead quickly to a volatile situation.

14:3 Simon the Leper Presumably a follower of Jesus. See note on Mt 26:6. **nard** A costly, aromatic oil from an herb native to India (see Jn 12:3 and note).

14:5 a year's wages See Mk 6:37 and note.

14:7 you will not always have me Jesus speaks of a time after his resurrection when he will no longer be present with the disciples.

14:8 to prepare for my burial The woman likely intended to display her devotion, but Jesus interprets her act in light of his impending death.

14:11 he watched for Judas must be careful to avoid rioting among Jesus' supporters (see vv. 1–2). As one

Passover lamb, Jesus' disciples asked him, "Where do you want us to go and make preparations for you to eat the Passover?"

¹³So he sent two of his disciples, telling them, "Go into the city, and a man carrying a jar of water will meet you. Follow him. ¹⁴Say to the owner of the house he enters, 'The Teacher asks: Where is my guest room, where I may eat the Passover with my disciples?' ¹⁵He will show you a large room upstairs, furnished and ready. Make preparations for us there."

¹⁶The disciples left, went into the city and found things just as Jesus had told them. So they prepared the Passover.

¹⁷When evening came, Jesus arrived with the Twelve. ¹⁸While they were reclining at the table eating, he said, "Truly I tell you, one of you will betray me—one who is eating with me."

¹⁹They were saddened, and one by one they said to him, "Surely you don't mean me?"

²⁰"It is one of the Twelve," he replied, "one who dips bread into the bowl with me. ²¹The Son of Man will go just as it is written about him. But woe to that man who betrays the Son of Man! It would be better for him if he had not been born."

²²While they were eating, Jesus took bread, and when he had given thanks, he broke it and gave it to his disciples, saying, "Take it; this is my body."

²³Then he took a cup, and when he had given thanks, he gave it to them, and they all drank from it.

²⁴"This is my blood of the[a] covenant, which is poured out for many," he said to them. ²⁵"Truly I tell you, I will not drink again from the fruit of the vine until that day when I drink it new in the kingdom of God."

²⁶When they had sung a hymn, they went out to the Mount of Olives.

Jesus Predicts Peter's Denial

14:27-31pp — Mt 26:31-35

²⁷"You will all fall away," Jesus told them, "for it is written:

"'I will strike the shepherd,
    and the sheep will be scattered.'[b]

²⁸But after I have risen, I will go ahead of you into Galilee."

²⁹Peter declared, "Even if all fall away, I will not."

³⁰"Truly I tell you," Jesus answered, "today—yes, tonight—before the rooster crows twice[c] you yourself will disown me three times."

³¹But Peter insisted emphatically, "Even if I have to die with you, I will never disown you." And all the others said the same.

Gethsemane

14:32-42pp — Mt 26:36-46; Lk 22:40-46

³²They went to a place called Gethsemane, and Jesus said to his disciples, "Sit here while I pray." ³³He took Peter, James and John along with him, and he began to be deeply distressed and troubled. ³⁴"My soul is overwhelmed with sorrow to the point of death," he said to them. "Stay here and keep watch."

³⁵Going a little farther, he fell to the ground and prayed that if possible the hour might pass from him. ³⁶"Abba,[d] Father," he said, "everything is possible for you. Take this cup from me. Yet not what I will, but what you will."

³⁷Then he returned to his disciples and found them sleeping. "Simon," he said to Peter, "are you

---

a 24 Some manuscripts *the new*   *b 27* Zech. 13:7   *c 30* Some early manuscripts do not have *twice.*   *d 36* Aramaic for *father*

---

of Jesus' closest disciples, he would be able to advise the chief priests on Jesus' movements and choose an opportune moment.

14:12–26 Jesus observes the Passover celebration with his disciples. Mark's account of the meal itself contains two parts: Jesus' announcement that he will be betrayed (vv. 18–21) and his remarks about his body and blood (vv. 22–26).

14:13–15 Jesus' directions in these verses are similar to his directions for obtaining the colt (11:1–3).

14:19 Surely you don't mean me In the Greek text, the grammatical form of this question indicates that a negative answer is expected.

14:22 when he had given thanks, he broke it Recalls Jesus' miraculous feedings (6:41; 8:6). In the Passover, God had constituted Israel as a liberated nation through a meal. Here, Jesus reconstitutes the people of God with those who receive him and his ministry. **Take it; this is my body** By receiving the Lord's Supper, Jesus' followers accept Jesus as the Messiah who suffers and dies on their behalf.

14:23 they all drank from it Recalls James and John's

desire to share in Jesus' vocation (10:38–39). See note on v. 36.

14:24 blood of the covenant Recalls Moses' ratification of Israel's covenant with God at Mount Sinai (Ex 24:8; compare Jer 31:31–34). **poured out for many** Compare Mk 10:45 and note.

14:25 in the kingdom of God The only occasion in Mark's Gospel when Jesus speaks of being in the kingdom. This could be a reference to heaven following Jesus' ascension or to the arrival of the kingdom of God in a more powerful manner following Jesus' resurrection.

14:26 When they had sung a hymn Refers to the conclusion of the Passover celebration. Compare note on Mt 26:30. **Mount of Olives** See note on Mk 11:1;.

14:27 I will strike the shepherd A citation of Zec 13:7. Shepherds represent kings in Zechariah. Although Zec 13:7 originally referred to a worthless leader, here it is appropriated to refer to Jesus' arrest, indicating that Jesus acts as a substitute.

14:32–42 Likely well after dark, Jesus goes to Gethsemane with his disciples in order to pray. In contrast to Jesus' anguish, the disciples fall asleep. After two periods of distressed prayer, Judas arrives with a crowd to arrest Jesus.

asleep? Couldn't you keep watch for one hour? ³⁸Watch and pray so that you will not fall into temptation. The spirit is willing, but the flesh is weak."

³⁹Once more he went away and prayed the same thing. ⁴⁰When he came back, he again found them sleeping, because their eyes were heavy. They did not know what to say to him.

⁴¹Returning the third time, he said to them, "Are you still sleeping and resting? Enough! The hour has come. Look, the Son of Man is delivered into the hands of sinners. ⁴²Rise! Let us go! Here comes my betrayer!"

Jesus Arrested

14:43-50pp — Mt 26:47-56; Lk 22:47-50; Jn 18:3-11

⁴³Just as he was speaking, Judas, one of the Twelve, appeared. With him was a crowd armed with swords and clubs, sent from the chief priests, the teachers of the law, and the elders.

⁴⁴Now the betrayer had arranged a signal with them: "The one I kiss is the man; arrest him and lead him away under guard." ⁴⁵Going at once to Jesus, Judas said, "Rabbi!" and kissed him. ⁴⁶The men seized Jesus and arrested him. ⁴⁷Then one of those standing near drew his sword and struck the servant of the high priest, cutting off his ear.

⁴⁸"Am I leading a rebellion," said Jesus, "that you have come out with swords and clubs to capture me? ⁴⁹Every day I was with you, teaching in the temple courts, and you did not arrest me. But the Scriptures must be fulfilled." ⁵⁰Then everyone deserted him and fled.

⁵¹A young man, wearing nothing but a linen garment, was following Jesus. When they seized him, ⁵²he fled naked, leaving his garment behind.

Jesus Before the Sanhedrin

14:53-65pp — Mt 26:57-68; Jn 18:12,13,19-24
14:61-63pp — Lk 22:67-71

⁵³They took Jesus to the high priest, and all the chief priests, the elders and the teachers of the law came together. ⁵⁴Peter followed him at a distance, right into the courtyard of the high priest. There he sat with the guards and warmed himself at the fire.

⁵⁵The chief priests and the whole Sanhedrin were looking for evidence against Jesus so that they could put him to death, but they did not find any. ⁵⁶Many testified falsely against him, but their statements did not agree.

⁵⁷Then some stood up and gave this false testimony against him: ⁵⁸"We heard him say, 'I will destroy this temple made with human hands and in three days will build another, not made with hands.'" ⁵⁹Yet even then their testimony did not agree.

⁶⁰Then the high priest stood up before them and asked Jesus, "Are you not going to answer? What is this testimony that these men are bringing against you?" ⁶¹But Jesus remained silent and gave no answer.

Again the high priest asked him, "Are you the Messiah, the Son of the Blessed One?"

⁶²"I am," said Jesus. "And you will see the Son of Man sitting at the right hand of the Mighty One and coming on the clouds of heaven."

14:32 Gethsemane Likely a privately owned olive grove located at the foot of the Mount of Olives, directly across the Kidron Valley from the Temple Mount.

14:34 My soul is overwhelmed with sorrow Jesus echoes the psalmist's similar cry (e.g., Ps 42:5).

14:36 *Abba*, Father The Greek word used here is a transliteration of an Aramaic word that means "father." In the NT, the word appears only here and twice in Paul's letters (Ro 8:15; Gal 4:6). **Take this cup from me** Refers to Jesus' impending torture and death (compare Mk 10:38–39).

14:42 Let us go Rather than suggest that Jesus was about to make an attempt to flee, this means just the opposite. Jesus arises to meet his betrayer.

14:43 chief priests, the teachers of the law, and the elders Representative of the religious establishment in Jerusalem.

14:45 kissed him A kiss signaled affection and respect, in contrast to Judas' betrayal.

14:47 cutting off his ear In Luke's account, Jesus immediately heals the man's ear (Lk 22:51; compare Mt 26:51).

14:49 Scriptures must be fulfilled Jesus is likely referring to Isa 52:13—53:12 and Ps 22—both passages speak of the unjust suffering of an individual and are messianic in message.

14:51 A young man The youth's identity is unknown, but it might be Mark himself. This figure appears only in his Gospel.

14:53–65 Although the Jewish leaders attempt to bring false witnesses against Jesus, the conflicting testimonies prevent them. After remaining silent throughout the accusations, Jesus acknowledges that he is the Messiah and the Son of Man. He immediately is condemned, beaten and mocked.

14:54 the courtyard of the high priest Refers to part of the high priest's private residence.

14:55 Sanhedrin A council consisting of the most influential members of Jewish society. The Romans gave this body limited authority over internal Jewish matters. See the infographic "The Sanhedrin" on p. 1746. **evidence** According to OT law, at least two witnesses were required in order to condemn someone to death (e.g., Nu 35:30; Dt 19:15).

14:58 destroy this temple Jesus' statements to this effect are not recorded in Mark (compare Jn 2:18–19). **in three days will build another** Possibly an allusion to Jesus' resurrection (see Mk 8:31; 9:31; 10:34).

14:61 Blessed One A way of referring to Yahweh without saying the divine name.

14:62 I am Jesus' response is a clear affirmation that he is the Messiah, unveiling what he tried to keep secret through much of Mark's Gospel. It also reflects Yahweh's self-revelation in the OT. In the Greek translation of Ex 3, Yahweh reveals himself to Moses with the same words that Jesus uses here (Ex 3:6,14). It is these words that may provoke the charge of blasphemy (Mk 14:64). See the table "Jesus' 'I Am' Statements" on p. 1727. **Son of**

⁶³The high priest tore his clothes. "Why do we need any more witnesses?" he asked. ⁶⁴"You have heard the blasphemy. What do you think?"

They all condemned him as worthy of death. ⁶⁵Then some began to spit at him; they blindfolded him, struck him with their fists, and said, "Prophesy!" And the guards took him and beat him.

Peter Disowns Jesus

14:66-72pp — Mt 26:69-75; Lk 22:56-62;
Jn 18:16-18,25-27

⁶⁶While Peter was below in the courtyard, one of the servant girls of the high priest came by. ⁶⁷When she saw Peter warming himself, she looked closely at him.

"You also were with that Nazarene, Jesus," she said.

⁶⁸But he denied it. "I don't know or understand what you're talking about," he said, and went out into the entryway.ᵃ

⁶⁹When the servant girl saw him there, she said again to those standing around, "This fellow is one of them." ⁷⁰Again he denied it.

After a little while, those standing near said to Peter, "Surely you are one of them, for you are a Galilean."

⁷¹He began to call down curses, and he swore to them, "I don't know this man you're talking about."

⁷²Immediately the rooster crowed the second time.ᵇ Then Peter remembered the word Jesus had spoken to him: "Before the rooster crows twiceᶜ you will disown me three times." And he broke down and wept.

Jesus Before Pilate

15:2-15pp — Mt 27:11-26; Lk 23:2,3,18-25;
Jn 18:29 - 19:16

15 Very early in the morning, the chief priests, with the elders, the teachers of the law and the whole Sanhedrin, made their plans. So they bound Jesus, led him away and handed him over to Pilate.

²"Are you the king of the Jews?" asked Pilate.

"You have said so," Jesus replied.

³The chief priests accused him of many things. ⁴So again Pilate asked him, "Aren't you going to answer? See how many things they are accusing you of."

⁵But Jesus still made no reply, and Pilate was amazed.

⁶Now it was the custom at the festival to release a prisoner whom the people requested. ⁷A man called Barabbas was in prison with the insurrectionists who had committed murder in the uprising. ⁸The crowd came up and asked Pilate to do for them what he usually did.

⁹"Do you want me to release to you the king of the Jews?" asked Pilate, ¹⁰knowing it was out of self-interest that the chief priests had handed Jesus over to him. ¹¹But the chief priests stirred up the crowd to have Pilate release Barabbas instead.

¹²"What shall I do, then, with the one you call the king of the Jews?" Pilate asked them.

¹³"Crucify him!" they shouted.

¹⁴"Why? What crime has he committed?" asked Pilate.

ᵃ 68 Some early manuscripts *entryway and the rooster crowed*
ᵇ 72 Some early manuscripts do not have *the second time.*
ᶜ 72 Some early manuscripts do not have *twice.*

Man See note on 2:10. **the Mighty One** Refers to God, focusing on the divine attribute most pertinent to the Son of Man's coming (9:1; 13:26). **coming on the clouds of heaven** An allusion to Da 7:13. See note Mk 2:10.
14:63 The high priest tore his clothes In the OT, tearing one's clothes is a sign of grief (e.g., 2Ki 22:11; Est 4:1).
14:65 began to spit at him Evokes Isaiah's portrayal of the suffering servant (Isa 50:6).
14:66-72 During the trial, Peter is in a nearby courtyard, where he is recognized as a disciple of Jesus. Peter denies any knowledge of Jesus three times, fulfilling Jesus' prediction (Mk 14:30-31).
14:71 to call down curses Peter is willing to take a curse upon himself rather than be associated with Jesus. His curse probably took the common formula, "May such-and-such happen to me if I am speaking falsely."
15:1 chief priests See note on 11:18. **teachers of the law** See note on 1:22. **Pilate** Refers to Pontius Pilate, who governed Judea for the Roman Empire ca. AD 26–36. As the emperor Tiberius' prefect in the region, Pilate was responsible for resolving both civil and criminal cases, and he had authority to carry out capital punishments. See the infographic "Pontius Pilate's Inscription" on p. 1707; see the table "Political Leaders in the New Testament" on p. 1916.

15:2 Are you the king of the Jews The charge that the temple leaders had formulated in 14:55–65 was blasphemy. They probably translated Jesus' claim to be the Messiah into an idiom that Pilate would understand—and one that they hoped would prompt him to act (compare v. 32). The Romans had bestowed the title "king of the Jews" on Herod the Great in 40 BC. Caesar Augustus declined to extend this status to Herod's sons following the king's death in 4 BC. In that year, many Palestinian Jews rallied around popular claimants to kingship, which encouraged subsequent Roman administrators to move swiftly against any rumors of aspirations to the kingship among their subjects.
15:4 they are accusing you Other than the treason implied by the title "king of the Jews," Mark doesn't identify specific charges against Jesus (compare v. 26).
15:7 with the insurrectionists It is unclear from Mark's gospel whether Barabbas was a rebel himself or was merely imprisoned with the rebels (compare note on Mt 27:16).
15:10 out of self-interest Indicates that Pilate did not take seriously the trumped-up charges of treason.
15:14 What crime has he committed Though Pilate seems to be defending Jesus' innocence, his question is double-edged: If he doesn't condemn Jesus' claim to kingship, Rome could view him as endorsing that claim.

But they shouted all the louder, "Crucify him!" [15] Wanting to satisfy the crowd, Pilate released Barabbas to them. He had Jesus flogged, and handed him over to be crucified.

The Soldiers Mock Jesus

15:16-20pp — Mt 27:27-31

[16] The soldiers led Jesus away into the palace (that is, the Praetorium) and called together the whole company of soldiers. [17] They put a purple robe on him, then twisted together a crown of thorns and set it on him. [18] And they began to call out to him, "Hail, king of the Jews!" [19] Again and again they struck him on the head with a staff and spit on him. Falling on their knees, they paid homage to him. [20] And when they had mocked him, they took off the purple robe and put his own clothes on him. Then they led him out to crucify him.

The Crucifixion of Jesus

15:22-32pp — Mt 27:33-44; Lk 23:33-43; Jn 19:17-24

[21] A certain man from Cyrene, Simon, the father of Alexander and Rufus, was passing by on his way in from the country, and they forced him to carry the cross. [22] They brought Jesus to the place called Golgotha (which means "the place of the skull"). [23] Then they offered him wine mixed with myrrh, but he did not take it. [24] And they crucified him. Dividing up his clothes, they cast lots to see what each would get.

[25] It was nine in the morning when they crucified him. [26] The written notice of the charge against him read: THE KING OF THE JEWS.

[27] They crucified two rebels with him, one on his right and one on his left. [28][a] [29] Those who passed by hurled insults at him, shaking their heads and saying, "So! You who are going to destroy the temple and build it in three days, [30] come down from the cross and save yourself!" [31] In the same way the chief priests and the teachers of the law mocked him among themselves. "He saved others," they said, "but he can't save himself! [32] Let this Messiah, this king of Israel, come down now from the cross, that we may see and believe." Those crucified with him also heaped insults on him.

The Death of Jesus

15:33-41pp — Mt 27:45-56; Lk 23:44-49; Jn 19:29-30

[33] At noon, darkness came over the whole land until three in the afternoon. [34] And at three in the afternoon Jesus cried out in a loud voice, *"Eloi, Eloi, lema sabachthani?"* (which means "My God, my God, why have you forsaken me?").[b]

[35] When some of those standing near heard this, they said, "Listen, he's calling Elijah."

[36] Someone ran, filled a sponge with wine vinegar, put it on a staff, and offered it to Jesus to drink. "Now leave him alone. Let's see if Elijah comes to take him down," he said.

[37] With a loud cry, Jesus breathed his last.

[38] The curtain of the temple was torn in two from top to bottom. [39] And when the centurion, who stood there in front of Jesus, saw how he died,[c] he said, "Surely this man was the Son of God!"

---

[a] 28 Some manuscripts include here words similar to Luke 22:37.   [b] 34 Psalm 22:1   [c] 39 Some manuscripts *saw that he died with such a cry*

15:15 flogged A typical preliminary to crucifixion.

15:16 company of soldiers Refers to one-tenth of a Roman legion—equally approximately 600 to 1,000 men.

15:21 Cyrene A city in North Africa where Jews had lived since the third century BC. **father of Alexander and Rufus** It is unclear why Mark identifies Simon's sons. Mark's original audience may have been familiar with them. **carry the cross** The condemned normally had to carry the crossbeam to the place of execution (Mk 8:34). Simon's enlistment implies that Jesus already was too weak to do so.

15:22 Golgotha An Aramaic word meaning "skull." The precise location of this place is uncertain.

15:23 wine mixed with myrrh Meant to alleviate some of the pain of crucifixion. **he did not take** Compare 14:25.

15:24 Dividing up his clothes, they cast lots An allusion to Ps 22:18, which describes the psalmist's suffering at the hands of the wicked. This statement may indicate Jesus' nakedness or near nakedness. See the table "Messianic Psalms" on p. 847.

15:25 nine in the morning Jesus' experience of the Roman justice system is extremely fast-paced: The approximate time of the events are: the trial occurred at 6 a.m. (Mk 15:1), his crucifixion at 9 a.m., and his death at 3 p.m. (v. 34).

15:26 THE KING OF THE JEWS Confirms the Roman justification for Jesus' death (compare v. 2).

15:27 one on his right and one on his left Similar to the description in Isa 53:9 (compare Mk 10:37).

15:29 hurled insults at him, shaking their heads Similar to the description in Ps 22:7.

15:33 darkness came Parallels the cosmic signs that Jesus said would herald the Son of Man's return (Mk 13:24).

15:34 Eloi, Eloi, lema sabachthani Jesus cries out in Aramaic; Mark provides the Greek translation. **My God, my God, why have you forsaken me** The opening line of Ps 22, which Mark references elsewhere (Mk 15:24,29)—demonstrating that Jesus epitomizes suffering itself, and the desperation felt with it, in this moment. See Ps 22:1 and note.

15:35 Listen, he's calling Elijah The bystanders misunderstand Jesus' cry of "Eloi! Eloi!" as "Eli(jah)! Eli(jah)!" They do not realize that the figurative Elijah—John the Baptist—has already come and gone (compare Mk 9:12–13).

15:38 The curtain of the temple This could refer to the outer curtain, which shielded the entrance to the sanctuary. Heavenly imagery was embroidered on the outer curtain, forming an appropriate parallel to the heavens tearing open at Jesus' baptism (1:10). Alternatively, it could indicate the inner veil, which hid the divine presence in the Most Holy Place (Holy of Holies); this might parallel the Holy Spirit descending at Jesus' baptism.

15:39 Surely this man was the Son of God Jesus'

[40]Some women were watching from a distance. Among them were Mary Magdalene, Mary the mother of James the younger and of Joseph,[a] and Salome. [41]In Galilee these women had followed him and cared for his needs. Many other women who had come up with him to Jerusalem were also there.

The Burial of Jesus

15:42-47pp — Mt 27:57-61; Lk 23:50-56; Jn 19:38-42

[42]It was Preparation Day (that is, the day before the Sabbath). So as evening approached, [43]Joseph of Arimathea, a prominent member of the Council, who was himself waiting for the kingdom of God, went boldly to Pilate and asked for Jesus' body. [44]Pilate was surprised to hear that he was already dead. Summoning the centurion, he asked him if Jesus had already died. [45]When he learned from the centurion that it was so, he gave the body to Joseph. [46]So Joseph bought some linen cloth, took down the body, wrapped it in the linen, and placed it in a tomb cut out of rock. Then he rolled a stone against the entrance of the tomb. [47]Mary Magdalene and Mary the mother of Joseph saw where he was laid.

Jesus Has Risen

16:1-8pp — Mt 28:1-8; Lk 24:1-10

16 When the Sabbath was over, Mary Magdalene, Mary the mother of James, and Salome bought spices so that they might go to anoint Jesus' body. [2]Very early on the first day of the week, just after sunrise, they were on their way to the tomb [3]and they asked each other, "Who will roll the stone away from the entrance of the tomb?"

[4]But when they looked up, they saw that the stone, which was very large, had been rolled away. [5]As they entered the tomb, they saw a young man dressed in a white robe sitting on the right side, and they were alarmed.

[6]"Don't be alarmed," he said. "You are looking for Jesus the Nazarene, who was crucified. He has risen! He is not here. See the place where they laid him. [7]But go, tell his disciples and Peter, 'He is going ahead of you into Galilee. There you will see him, just as he told you.'"

[8]Trembling and bewildered, the women went out and fled from the tomb. They said nothing to anyone, because they were afraid.[b]

[The earliest manuscripts and some other ancient witnesses do not have verses 9–20.]

[9]*When Jesus rose early on the first day of the week, he appeared first to Mary Magdalene, out of whom he had driven seven demons. [10]She went and told those who had been with him and who were mourning and weeping. [11]When they heard that Jesus was alive and that she had seen him, they did not believe it.*

[12]*Afterward Jesus appeared in a different form to two of them while they were walking in the country. [13]These returned and reported it to the rest; but they did not believe them either.*

[14]*Later Jesus appeared to the Eleven as they were eating; he rebuked them for their lack of faith and their stubborn refusal to believe those who had seen him after he had risen.*

[a] 40 Greek *Joses*, a variant of *Joseph*; also in verse 47
[b] 8 Some manuscripts have the following ending between verses 8 and 9, and one manuscript has it after verse 8 (omitting verses 9-20): *Then they quickly reported all these instructions to those around Peter. After this, Jesus himself also sent out through them from east to west the sacred and imperishable proclamation of eternal salvation. Amen.*

---

identity is fully revealed upon his death (compare note on Isa 53:12). At three key events in Mark's Gospel — Jesus' baptism, transfiguration and crucifixion — a voice confirms that Jesus is God's Son. Here, it is no longer God the Father proclaiming Jesus' identity, but instead a non-Jewish person — confirming Jesus' ministry and mission to Gentiles (see note on Mk 13:10).
15:40 Magdalene This designation likely refers to a resident of the Galilean town of Magdala. **the mother of James the younger and of Joseph** Possibly refers to Jesus' mother, since the names of two of Jesus' brothers are mentioned (see 6:3 and note). But it may also refer to Jesus' aunt or another woman named Mary.
15:43 Arimathea A town of Judea, probably identical to Ramah in the OT. **the Council** Refers to the Sanhedrin (see note on 14:55), which heard the first trial of Jesus (14:55–65). See the infographic "The Sanhedrin" on p. 1746.
15:44 he was already dead Jesus died over the course of six hours (vv. 25,34). Under normal circumstances, crucifixion could extend over multiple days.
15:46 a tomb cut out of rock Tombs cut from rock were more expensive to excavate and maintain than graves in the ground. They generally were family tombs. This action parallels Isa 53:9.

16:1–8 Upon arriving at Jesus' tomb, several women find that the stone is no longer covering the entrance. A man — likely an angel — instructs them to tell the disciples that Jesus had risen from the grave and would meet them in Galilee.
16:2 the first day of the week Refers to Sunday.
16:5 young man Mark does not explicitly state that the man is an angel (compare Mt 28:3,5; Lk 24:23; Jn 20:12).
16:6 See the place where they laid him Compare Mk 15:47.
16:7 just as he told you Refers to Jesus' statement to his disciples on the night of his betrayal (14:28).
16:8 because they were afraid This likely is the original ending of Mark's Gospel. It cuts off abruptly, with the only witnesses to the resurrection afraid and saying nothing to anyone. This clearly is not the whole story — and (apart from other Gospel accounts) Mark's earliest readers probably were aware that the women did tell others and Jesus did appear to his disciples in Galilee. This startling ending invites Mark's readers to join the story of Jesus and become his witnesses. Those who read Mark and come to recognize Jesus as the Messiah can carry on his mission by bearing

15He said to them, "Go into all the world and preach the gospel to all creation. 16Whoever believes and is baptized will be saved, but whoever does not believe will be condemned. 17And these signs will accompany those who believe: In my name they will drive out demons; they will speak in new tongues; 18they will pick up snakes with their hands; and when they drink deadly poison, it will not hurt them at all;

they will place their hands on sick people, and they will get well."

19After the Lord Jesus had spoken to them, he was taken up into heaven and he sat at the right hand of God. 20Then the disciples went out and preached everywhere, and the Lord worked with them and confirmed his word by the signs that accompanied it.

---

witness to his true character, showing love toward God and neighbor, proclaiming forgiveness in Jesus' name and awaiting his return.

16:9–20 This passage, which has been designated the longer ending of Mark, summarizes the risen Jesus' dealings with his disciples as narrated in the other canonical Gospels. Based on manuscript evidence, it probably is a later addition intended to harmonize Mark's account with those of Matthew, Luke and John. Some manuscripts include a so-called shorter ending—several sentences typically placed immediately before vv. 9–20. It, too, is thought to have been added later.

THE KINGDOM OF GOD: ALREADY BUT NOT YET

by Mike Goldsworthy

The kingdom of God is a central theme of the Gospels as well as other New Testament books. It is the message that John the Baptist declared in preparation for Jesus (Mt 3:2), the Good News that Jesus preached (Mk 1:14–15), what Jesus taught the disciples in the 40 days between his resurrection and ascension (Ac 1:3), and what Paul is recorded as proclaiming at the conclusion of the book of Acts (Ac 28:31).

A kingdom is a place where someone has rule or governance. The same is true of the kingdom of God. Jesus said in his prayer: "Your kingdom come, your will be done, on earth as it is in heaven" (Mt 6:10). The kingdom of God is where God's will is carried out.

The Old Testament theme of Yahweh's rule and reign is another way of describing the kingdom of God. The psalmist speaks of Yahweh's kingdom as an everlasting realm that endures throughout all generations (Ps 145:13). Isaiah declares that Yahweh will save (Isa 33:22) and speaks of a time when God will reign (Isa 52:7). The Old Testament portrays great anticipation for the time when God will be worshiped in all the earth (Isa 2).

During the first century AD, many Jews believed that the Messiah would initiate this reign, which was based on passages like Malachi 3:1–5; Zechariah 9:9–10; Isaiah 9:1–7; and Isaiah 52:13—53:12. They also believed that the kingdom would be established through political or military means (compare Mt 26:51–53; Lk 22:47–53)—but Jesus ushered in the kingdom in a radically unexpected way. He announced that the kingdom had come upon those whom he freed from demons (Mt 12:28); he taught that the kingdom should be received like a child (Mk 10:15) and explained that it belongs to the impoverished (Lk 6:20). Jesus declared the kingdom of God as a present reality that could be experienced by those he taught and to whom he ministered.

Jesus' teaching also assumed the kingdom was a future reality. While his disciples expected the kingdom to appear immediately, Jesus changed their expectations by telling them a parable about a ruler who had to leave before he could return to his kingdom (Lk 19:11–27). He described what good and faithful servants could do in the meantime. Paul spoke of the kingdom as something that could be inherited (1Co 6:9–10) and that does not perish (1Co 15:50). These examples testify to the kingdom of God as a future reality.

To borrow the phrase made popular by George Eldon Ladd, the kingdom of God is "already/not yet." God's kingdom has a dual dimension. Jesus initiated the kingdom on earth, and wherever God's will is carried out, the kingdom is a reality. The kingdom, however, had not been fully manifested in Jesus' day—nor has it in ours. We do not yet live in a world where God's will is a complete reality. We feel the tension of experiencing God's kingdom in our lives and communities before it is fully realized. We still see unbelief, brokenness and sin, telling us God's will is not yet fully expressed.

Many believers neglect to focus on the kingdom as a present reality. Their concern centers on the future reality of getting to heaven—but this focus can easily sever the relationship between the Christian life and life here and now. When Jesus prayed, "Your kingdom come, your will be done, on earth as it is in heaven" (Mt 6:10), he asked that God would bring the experience of heaven to

earth. Through Jesus, God's reign, rule and power are available to us today, not just in the distant future. The present reality of the kingdom of God should prompt us to examine our lives and ask what areas we have not yet surrendered to God's rule.

On a larger level, the notion of God's kingdom should lead us to examine both our neighborhoods and the global community and ask what lies outside of God's desire. Where are people not being treated with the dignity and honor they deserve as God's image-bearers?

As we anticipate the time when all things will be made fully new (Rev 21:4–5), we can actively participate in the kingdom of God now (Mt 4:17). As we surrender to the reign of God, we will begin to experience the kingdom of God now—as God's will is done on earth as it is in heaven (Mt 6:9–15).

LUKE

INTRODUCTION TO LUKE

Luke proclaims Jesus as the Savior of the world. This Gospel presents Jesus as the climactic turning point in world history, and it sets the stage for Luke's second volume—the Acts of the Apostles. In both books, Luke focuses on the mission of Jesus, which continues and expands with the church, out from Jerusalem to the world (Lk 24:47). In Jesus, everyone—Jewish and non-Jewish alike—may come to salvation.

BACKGROUND

Early church tradition holds that both the Gospel of Luke and the book of Acts were written by Luke the physician, Paul's frequent companion during his missionary journeys (Col 4:14). Early church history also says Luke was a Gentile (non-Jewish) and came from Antioch—where Paul spent a great deal of time (Ac 11:25–26; 15:35). These biographical details fit with the Gospel's familiarity with Greco-Roman culture and its emphasis on Gentiles becoming followers of Christ. The Gospel also uses very sophisticated Greek, including technical terms for ailments, suggesting that a well-educated person (like a doctor) authored it.

Luke identifies his primary audience and purpose in the opening verses: He is writing to Theophilus, to give him confidence regarding the events of Jesus' life (Lk 1:3–4). The identity of Theophilus is unknown; since the name means "lover of God," it's possible that Luke uses it generically to address any believer. However, it's more likely that he is writing to an individual named Theophilus, who may be the sponsor of the work. In any case, features in the Gospel suggest that Luke assumed both Jews and Gentiles would read it. He seems to address people curious about Christianity and its relationship to Judaism, often utilizing Old Testament Scriptures and motifs.

Luke seems to rely on the Gospel of Mark as a source text, supplementing it with other material, which means Luke's Gospel was written after Mark. Luke also references his Gospel in the opening of Acts, indicating it was written before (Ac 1:1). In addition, Luke traveled with Paul and often speaks in the first person as he documents their travels in the book of Acts (e.g., Ac 16:10; 21:1,17). This suggests Luke's Gospel was likely composed during Paul's

Galilee
Capernaum — Bethsaida
Nazareth — Nain
Decapolis
Arimathea
Judea
Emmaus — Jericho
Bethlehem — Jerusalem

This map depicts many of the locations of Jesus' ministry according to Luke's Gospel.

ministry or soon after Paul's death, likely sometime between AD 60 and 85, with Luke finishing Acts not too long after.

STRUCTURE

After the prologue (Lk 1:1–4), the Gospel of Luke can be divided into two parts. The first part (1:5—9:50) deals with establishing Jesus' identity. It includes the birth narratives for John the Baptist and Jesus (1:5—2:52), as well as Jesus' baptism, temptation and genealogy (3:1—4:13). It then narrates Jesus' ministry in Galilee, including his declaration of his identity and purpose in Nazareth (4:14—9:50).

The second part of Luke (9:51—24:53) covers the weeks leading up to Jesus' crucifixion and resurrection. It includes a long section (9:51—19:44) in which Jesus and his followers travel to Jerusalem, and he teaches them extensively about what it means to be his disciples. The next section (19:45—23:56) deals with what happens once Jesus arrives in Jerusalem; it describes the escalating opposition he faced from the religious elite, along with his trials and death. The last chapter narrates events that followed Jesus' resurrection, including his appearance on the road to Emmaus (24:1–53).

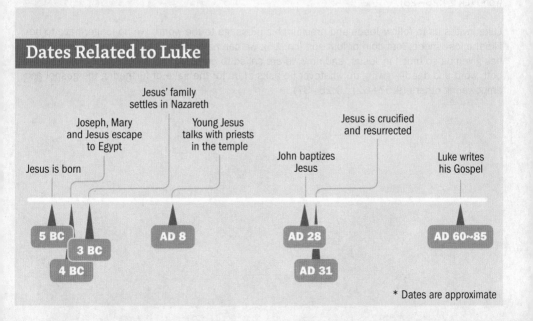

Dates Related to Luke

Jesus' family settles in Nazareth

Joseph, Mary and Jesus escape to Egypt

Young Jesus talks with priests in the temple

Jesus is crucified and resurrected

Jesus is born

John baptizes Jesus

Luke writes his Gospel

| 5 BC | AD 8 | AD 28 | AD 60~85 |

3 BC

4 BC

AD 31

* Dates are approximate

OUTLINE

- The births of John and Jesus (1:1—2:52)
- Preparation for Jesus' ministry (3:1—4:13)
- Jesus' ministry in Galilee (4:14—9:50)
- Jesus' journey to Jerusalem (9:51—19:44)
- Jesus in Jerusalem (19:45—23:56)
- Jesus' resurrection and ascension (24:1–53)

THEMES

Luke highlights Jesus' identity and mission as the suffering servant prophesied by Isaiah (4:17–19; compare 3:4–6), emphasizing that the Good News of Jesus is for the whole world (4:20–27). Jesus offers freedom, healing and liberty to the world's hurting and oppressed.

Luke shows the validity of Jesus' identity by recording his backstory. His is the only canonical Gospel to record the history of John the Baptist and an event from Jesus' childhood (1:5—2:52). While Matthew's Gospel traces Jesus' genealogy to Abraham (Mt 1:1–17), Luke follows Jesus' family tree to Adam (Lk 3:23–38), emphasizing that Jesus is not just the culmination of Israel's history but also the world's. Luke presents Jesus' death and resurrection as fulfillments of Old Testament prophecy (22:35–38; 24:25–27,36–49; compare Isa 53:10–12). Luke's Gospel concludes by urging Jesus' followers to proclaim the message of forgiveness of sin throughout the world (Lk 24:26–28).

Luke invites us to follow Jesus and proclaim his message to the world. We no longer have to be like the lost sheep, lost coin or lost son (ch. 15); we can have the salvation Jesus offers. God has given us so much in Jesus, and now we are called to proclaim that message to the world in both word and deed—giving up whatever he asks of us for the sake of furthering the gospel and empowering others (9:57–62; 10:25–37).

Introduction

1:1-4Ref—Ac 1:1

1 Many have undertaken to draw up an account of the things that have been fulfilled[a] among us, [2]just as they were handed down to us by those who from the first were eyewitnesses and servants of the word. [3]With this in mind, since I myself have carefully investigated everything from the beginning, I too decided to write an orderly account for you, most excellent Theophilus, [4]so that you may know the certainty of the things you have been taught.

The Birth of John the Baptist Foretold

[5]In the time of Herod king of Judea there was a priest named Zechariah, who belonged to the priestly division of Abijah; his wife Elizabeth was also a descendant of Aaron. [6]Both of them were righteous in the sight of God, observing all the Lord's commands and decrees blamelessly. [7]But they were childless because Elizabeth was not able to conceive, and they were both very old.

[8]Once when Zechariah's division was on duty and he was serving as priest before God, [9]he was chosen by lot, according to the custom of the priesthood, to go into the temple of the Lord and burn incense. [10]And when the time for the burning of incense came, all the assembled worshipers were praying outside.

[11]Then an angel of the Lord appeared to him, standing at the right side of the altar of incense. [12]When Zechariah saw him, he was startled and was gripped with fear. [13]But the angel said to him: "Do not be afraid, Zechariah; your prayer has been heard. Your wife Elizabeth will bear you a son, and you are to call him John. [14]He will be a joy and delight to you, and many will rejoice because of his birth, [15]for he will be great in the sight of the Lord. He is never to take wine or other fermented drink, and he will be filled with the Holy Spirit even before he is born. [16]He will bring back many of the people of Israel to the Lord their God. [17]And he will go on before the Lord, in the spirit and power of Elijah, to turn the hearts of the parents to their children and the disobedient to the wisdom of the righteous — to make ready a people prepared for the Lord."

---

[a] 1 Or *been surely believed*

1:1-4 The Gospel of Luke, along with the book of Acts, was attributed in early church history to Luke the physician, who traveled with Paul the apostle (Col 4:14; compare note on Ac 16:10; 21:1,17). Luke's Gospel was likely composed between AD 60 and 85, shortly before he finished Acts.

In a manner similar to Hellenistic Greek histories and Greco-Roman literature, Luke begins his Gospel with a prologue that identifies his audience and explains his reason for writing. See the event line "Jesus' Early Life and Ministry" on p. 1530.

1:1 Many have undertaken Indicates that Luke is familiar with other sources that discuss Jesus. Luke was familiar with Mark's Gospel and probably Matthew's as well. The unique content in Luke—material not found in the other Synoptic Gospels (Mark and Matthew)—is the result of his research (see Lk 1:3) and access to sources not available to Mark or Matthew.

1:2 from the first Refers to the start of Jesus' ministry.

1:3 Theophilus This Greek name means "friend of God." It might refer to a specific individual, or Luke could have been writing to the church at large—to all who consider themselves friends of God. Theophilus might have been Luke's patron, a wealthy person responsible for funding the writing, copying and distribution of Luke's Gospel and the book of Acts (see Ac 1:1).

1:4 the things you have been taught Luke likely is referring to teaching about Jesus' ministry, death and resurrection.

1:5-25 This section marks the beginning of the birth narratives in Luke's Gospel (continuing through ch. 2). Unlike Matthew, who records only Jesus' birth, Luke includes the announcement and birth of John the Baptist.

1:5 In the time of Herod king of Judea Herod the Great ruled 37-4 BC. See note on Mt 2:1. **Zechariah** Means "Yahweh has remembered," which is fitting for the circumstances of the narrative. **division of Abijah**

Zechariah belonged to the eighth priestly division, according to King David's arrangement (1Ch 24:1-10). **a descendant of Aaron** Indicates that Elizabeth (as well as Zechariah) came from the priestly class.

1:7 Elizabeth was not able to conceive Barrenness was common among the prominent women of the OT (see 1Sa 1:2 and note). By identifying Elizabeth with these women, Luke hints that God will provide her with a son. **they were both very old** Like Abraham and Sarah (Ge 17:17).

1:8 Zechariah's division was on duty Each division of priests served in the temple twice annually, with each session lasting one week.

1:9 burn incense A rare honor normally received once during a priest's lifetime.

1:10 were praying The Greek verb used here, *proseuchomai*, occurs more frequently in Luke and Acts than in Matthew or Mark. Luke emphasizes prayer more than the other Synoptic Gospels.

1:11 an angel of the Lord Identified later as Gabriel (see note on Lk 1:19). See the table "Angels in the Bible" on p. 2120.

1:13 Do not be afraid A common heavenly greeting and message of reassurance found throughout the Bible (e.g., v. 30; 2:10; Jdg 6:23; Da 10:12; Rev 1:17). **John** Means "Yahweh has shown favor," which aligns with John's vocation.

1:15 never to take wine or other fermented drink Like Samson and Samuel, John the Baptist was to be a Nazirite from birth (see Nu 6:1-4; Jdg 13:2-5; 1Sa 1:11). According to Nu 6, Nazirites were Israelites who were separated or consecrated for God's service. They were to abstain from wine and strong drink, vinegar products and anything produced from grapes. They also had to take care not to come into contact with dead bodies. They were not permitted to cut their hair until their vow was complete, at which time they were to offer sacrifices to Yahweh.

1:17 to turn the hearts Gabriel alludes to Mal 4:5-6

[18]Zechariah asked the angel, "How can I be sure of this? I am an old man and my wife is well along in years."

[19]The angel said to him, "I am Gabriel. I stand in the presence of God, and I have been sent to speak to you and to tell you this good news. [20]And now you will be silent and not able to speak until the day this happens, because you did not believe my words, which will come true at their appointed time."

[21]Meanwhile, the people were waiting for Zechariah and wondering why he stayed so long in the temple. [22]When he came out, he could not speak to them. They realized he had seen a vision in the temple, for he kept making signs to them but remained unable to speak.

[23]When his time of service was completed, he returned home. [24]After this his wife Elizabeth became pregnant and for five months remained in seclusion. [25]"The Lord has done this for me," she said. "In these days he has shown his favor and taken away my disgrace among the people."

The Birth of Jesus Foretold

[26]In the sixth month of Elizabeth's pregnancy, God sent the angel Gabriel to Nazareth, a town in Galilee, [27]to a virgin pledged to be married to a man named Joseph, a descendant of David. The virgin's name was Mary. [28]The angel went to her and said, "Greetings, you who are highly favored! The Lord is with you."

[29]Mary was greatly troubled at his words and wondered what kind of greeting this might be. [30]But the angel said to her, "Do not be afraid, Mary; you have found favor with God. [31]You will conceive and give birth to a son, and you are to call him Jesus. [32]He will be great and will be called the Son of the Most High. The Lord God will give him the throne of his father David, [33]and he will reign over Jacob's descendants forever; his kingdom will never end."

[34]"How will this be," Mary asked the angel, "since I am a virgin?"

[35]The angel answered, "The Holy Spirit will come on you, and the power of the Most High will overshadow you. So the holy one to be born will be called[a] the Son of God. [36]Even Elizabeth your relative is going to have a child in her old age, and she who was said to be unable to conceive is in her sixth month. [37]For no word from God will ever fail."

[a] 35 Or *So the child to be born will be called holy,*

---

to compare John the Baptist with the OT prophet Elijah. Jesus refers to John as a type of Elijah in Mt 11:14 (see note on Mt 16:14). **to make ready a people prepared for the Lord** Possibly an allusion to Mal 3:1, which Jesus quotes explicitly to refer to John the Baptist (Lk 7:27).
1:18 an old man and my wife is well along Recalls Abraham's disbelief (see v. 7 and note).
1:19 Gabriel One of only two named angels in the Bible (the other is Michael, mentioned in Da 12:1; Rev 12:7). Gabriel also appears to Daniel and explains his vision (Da 8:15–26).
1:20 you will be silent This is the sign Zechariah asked for in Lk 1:18. He regains his speech after confirming John's name (vv. 63–64).
1:21 the people were waiting for Zechariah Refers to the crowd that was praying (v. 10).
1:22 he could not speak to them It was customary for a priest to pronounce a blessing after coming out of the temple.
1:23 his time of service Refers to the one-week period (see v. 8 and note).
1:25 my disgrace Elizabeth declares that God has taken away her barrenness (v. 7).

1:26–38 After describing the announcement of John's birth, Luke reports Gabriel's announcement to Mary about Jesus.
1:26 In the sixth month Occurs six months after Elizabeth conceived (v. 24). **Nazareth, a town in Galilee** A small agricultural village to the southwest of the Sea of Galilee. Nazareth has been inhabited continuously since the third century BC. Nazareth was firmly within the territory allotted to Herod the Great's son Antipas (see note on 3:1). Jesus' later move to Capernaum placed him in a more neutral location on the border between Antipas' and Philip's territories (see note on 4:31). See the map "Jesus' Ministry in Galilee" on p. 2260.

1:27 a virgin Luke calls Mary a virgin twice in this verse to demonstrate that Jesus' conception was an act of God (see vv. 34–35; Mt 1:23 and note). Throughout his Gospel, Luke draws extensively from the book of Isaiah. By doing so, he portrays Jesus' life through Isaiah's theological lens. In this verse, Luke alludes to the Septuagint (ancient Greek translation) version of Isa 7:14, applying Isaiah's prophecy about the virgin (*parthenos* in Greek) being with child as a reference to Mary's miraculous conception. In this way, Luke portrays Jesus as God's promised Messiah. See note on Mt 1:23. **pledged to be married** At this time, betrothal represented a permanent relationship nearly equivalent to marriage; breaking off a betrothal required a decision akin to divorce. **a descendant of David** Luke alludes to Isa 11:1–2 to portray Jesus as the shoot and branch of Jesse (compare Lk 1:32 and note). This portrays Jesus as the Messiah, from King David's line. (David was Jesse's son.)
1:28 The Lord is with you Recalls "Immanuel" ("God with us") from Isa 7:14, which was already alluded to in Lk 1:27 (compare Mt 1:23).
1:31 Jesus From the Hebrew name Joshua, which means "Yahweh is help (or, salvation)" (see Mt 1:21).
1:32 Son of the Most High Highlights Jesus' divinity and royalty (compare Lk 1:35,76). **give him the throne of his father David** Gabriel implies that Jesus will fulfill the Davidic covenant (2Sa 7:12–13).
1:33 Jacob's descendants A common OT phrase referring to Israel (e.g., Ex 19:3; Isa 48:1). **his kingdom will never end** Gabriel again alludes to the Davidic covenant (compare note on Lk 1:32), but this allusion also evokes Messianic imagery from Daniel (see Da 7:13 and note; 7:14 and note).
1:35 Son of God This title reflects Jesus' miraculous conception and, consequently, his divinity (see note on Lk 1:27).

[38]"I am the Lord's servant," Mary answered. "May your word to me be fulfilled." Then the angel left her.

Mary Visits Elizabeth

[39]At that time Mary got ready and hurried to a town in the hill country of Judea, [40]where she entered Zechariah's home and greeted Elizabeth. [41]When Elizabeth heard Mary's greeting, the baby leaped in her womb, and Elizabeth was filled with the Holy Spirit. [42]In a loud voice she exclaimed: "Blessed are you among women, and blessed is the child you will bear! [43]But why am I so favored, that the mother of my Lord should come to me? [44]As soon as the sound of your greeting reached my ears, the baby in my womb leaped for joy. [45]Blessed is she who has believed that the Lord would fulfill his promises to her!"

Mary's Song

1:46-53pp — 1Sa 2:1-10

[46]And Mary said:

"My soul glorifies the Lord
[47]   and my spirit rejoices in God my Savior,
[48]for he has been mindful
    of the humble state of his servant.
From now on all generations will call me
    blessed,
[49]   for the Mighty One has done great things
    for me —
    holy is his name.

[50]His mercy extends to those who fear him,
    from generation to generation.
[51]He has performed mighty deeds with his arm;
    he has scattered those who are proud in
    their inmost thoughts.
[52]He has brought down rulers from their
    thrones
    but has lifted up the humble.
[53]He has filled the hungry with good things
    but has sent the rich away empty.
[54]He has helped his servant Israel,
    remembering to be merciful
[55]to Abraham and his descendants forever,
    just as he promised our ancestors."

[56]Mary stayed with Elizabeth for about three months and then returned home.

The Birth of John the Baptist

[57]When it was time for Elizabeth to have her baby, she gave birth to a son. [58]Her neighbors and relatives heard that the Lord had shown her great mercy, and they shared her joy.

[59]On the eighth day they came to circumcise the child, and they were going to name him after his father Zechariah, [60]but his mother spoke up and said, "No! He is to be called John."

[61]They said to her, "There is no one among your relatives who has that name."

[62]Then they made signs to his father, to find out what he would like to name the child. [63]He asked for a writing tablet, and to everyone's astonishment he wrote, "His name is John." [64]Immediately

---

1:38 the Lord's servant Mary indicates that she is willing to do whatever God requires of her.

1:39–45 Mary visits Elizabeth to assist her in the final months of her pregnancy. Given the immense social pressures and stigma that Mary was about to endure as an unwed mother, she likely sought solace in Elizabeth, who would believe the divine nature of her conception.

1:41 the baby leaped in her womb John leaps in Elizabeth's womb at the sound of Mary's voice because Mary is pregnant with Jesus.

1:42 Blessed are you among women Mary is blessed because she has the privilege of giving birth to the Messiah, the savior of the world.

1:43 my Lord Elizabeth calls the unborn Jesus her Lord, recognizing him as Messiah and perhaps also as Yahweh.

1:45 Blessed is she who has believed In contrast to Zechariah, Mary believed Gabriel's words (compare Lk 1:20).

1:46–56 Known as the Magnificat, Mary's song marks the first of four hymns in Luke's birth narratives. It is styled after Hannah's song of praise in 1Sa 2:1–10.

1:48 the humble state of his servant Mary highlights her modest condition in a similar fashion to Hannah in 1Sa 2:8 (compare 1Sa 1:11). The theme of God's care for the lowly is highlighted throughout Luke's Gospel.

1:52 but has lifted up the humble Both Mary's and Hannah's songs describe a reversal of fortunes: The lowly

are exalted, while the exalted (or haughty) are brought low (see 1Sa 2:4,7–8; compare Job 5:11).

1:53 He has filled the hungry with good things Expresses God's gracious provision for the lowly (compare Ps 107:9). In 1Sa 2:5, a similar phrase expresses Hannah's newfound joy associated with the birth of Samuel.

1:55 to Abraham and his descendants In fulfillment of Yahweh's proclamation to Abraham, Mary's son was to be a channel of blessing and salvation to the nation of Israel (Ge 12:1–3; 17:1–27).

1:56 about three months Mary stays until roughly the time of John's birth (compare Lk 1:26,36).

1:57–66 As Gabriel had predicted (v. 13), Zechariah and Elizabeth receive a son from God. While deciding the child's name, Zechariah writes the name John on a tablet and regains his ability to speak. Consequently, all who hear of this event wonder about the child's future, thereby igniting Messianic hopes in that region (compare 3:15).

1:57 she gave birth to a son Fulfills the proclamation of v. 13.

1:59 On the eighth day As prescribed by Yahweh and the law (Ge 17:12; Lev 12:3).

1:60 He is to be called John Demonstrates Elizabeth's faith in Gabriel's message (Lk 1:13).

1:62 what he would like to name the child In ancient Israel, fathers held the final naming rights.

1:64 Immediately his mouth was opened and his tongue set free Fulfills Gabriel's words in v. 20.

his mouth was opened and his tongue set free, and he began to speak, praising God. ⁶⁵All the neighbors were filled with awe, and throughout the hill country of Judea people were talking about all these things. ⁶⁶Everyone who heard this wondered about it, asking, "What then is this child going to be?" For the Lord's hand was with him.

Zechariah's Song

⁶⁷His father Zechariah was filled with the Holy Spirit and prophesied:

⁶⁸"Praise be to the Lord, the God of Israel,
　　because he has come to his people and
　　　redeemed them.
⁶⁹He has raised up a horn[a] of salvation for us
　　in the house of his servant David
⁷⁰(as he said through his holy prophets of
　　　long ago),
⁷¹salvation from our enemies
　　and from the hand of all who hate us—
⁷²to show mercy to our ancestors
　　and to remember his holy covenant,
⁷³　the oath he swore to our father Abraham:
⁷⁴to rescue us from the hand of our enemies,
　　and to enable us to serve him without fear
⁷⁵　in holiness and righteousness before him
　　all our days.

⁷⁶And you, my child, will be called a prophet
　　of the Most High;
　　for you will go on before the Lord to
　　　prepare the way for him,
⁷⁷to give his people the knowledge of salvation
　　through the forgiveness of their sins,
⁷⁸because of the tender mercy of our God,
　　by which the rising sun will come to us
　　　from heaven
⁷⁹to shine on those living in darkness
　　and in the shadow of death,
　　to guide our feet into the path of peace."

⁸⁰And the child grew and became strong in spirit[b]; and he lived in the wilderness until he appeared publicly to Israel.

The Birth of Jesus

2 In those days Caesar Augustus issued a decree that a census should be taken of the entire Roman world. ²(This was the first census that took place while[c] Quirinius was governor of Syria.) ³And everyone went to their own town to register.

⁴So Joseph also went up from the town of Nazareth in Galilee to Judea, to Bethlehem the town of David, because he belonged to the house and line

---

[a] 69 Horn here symbolizes a strong king.　[b] 80 Or *in the Spirit*
[c] 2 Or *This census took place before*

1:66 What then is this child going to be Hints at Messianic expectation (see note on Mt 1:1).

1:67–80 In the second of the four hymns in Luke's birth narratives, Zechariah praises God for his great redemption, provision and blessing. This song is known as the Benedictus due to its first word in the Latin Vulgate (an ancient Latin translation of the Bible; compare note on Lk 1:46–56).

1:67 was filled with the Holy Spirit Compare vv. 15,41.
1:69 a horn of salvation A metaphor for power (e.g., 2Sa 22:3; Ps 18:2; 148:14).
1:73 to our father Abraham Yahweh's covenant with Abraham is recorded in Ge 17:1–27.
1:76 a prophet of the Most High Refers to John the Baptist. **before the Lord to prepare the way for him** Compare Lk 3:4.
1:77 through the forgiveness of their sins Compare 3:3.
1:79 those living in darkness Perhaps an allusion to Isa 9:2 (compare Mt 4:16).
1:80 the child grew This verse summarizes approximately 30 years (compare Lk 3:23). **in the wilderness** This detail sets up the quotation of Isaiah's prophecy in 3:4–6 (compare Isa 40:3 and note). It also might be intended to evoke Israel's wilderness wanderings after the exodus. See note on Lk 4:1.

2:1–7 After narrating John's birth, Luke relates the birth of Jesus. In this section, he explains how Jesus came to be born in Bethlehem.

2:1 Caesar Augustus Ruler of the Roman Empire. See the table "Political Leaders in the New Testament" on p. 1916. **a census should be taken of the entire**

Roman world Known censuses in proximity to Caesar Augustus' reign (27 BC–AD 14) occurred around 28 BC, 8 BC, and AD 14. Given the size of the Roman Empire, the task of registering its people would have taken years; consequently, Luke could be pointing to the census of 8 BC. Based on the reference to Quirinius (see v. 2 and note), this would place Jesus' birth around 6–4 BC.

Luke 2:1

AUGUSTUS
Born Gaius Octavius in September of 63 BC, the Roman senate gave him the name "Augustus" in 27 BC to honor his defeat and annexation of Egypt. Formerly one of three co-rulers, Augustus gained sole control of the empire and reigned from 27 BC to AD 14. Although harsh and unrelenting, he was a master administrator who restored order to the empire after two decades of civil war. He was responsible for ushering in Rome's Golden Age—an era known as *Pax Romana* or *Pax Augusta* (meaning "Roman Peace" or "Augustus' Peace"), which lasted for roughly 250 years.

2:2 Quirinius was governor of Syria Quirinius was a legate or emissary of Augustus Caesar. He served in this capacity AD 6–9, and conducted a census in about AD 6 (see Ac 5:37). However, he may have served on two separate occasions. A possible term in 6–4 BC would align with a potential date for Jesus' birth (compare Lk 2:1 and note).
2:4 Nazareth See 1:26 and note. **to Bethlehem the town of David** Joseph must travel to his ancestral city for the census. Since he is a descendant of King

of David. ⁵He went there to register with Mary, who was pledged to be married to him and was expecting a child. ⁶While they were there, the time came for the baby to be born, ⁷and she gave birth to her firstborn, a son. She wrapped him in cloths and placed him in a manger, because there was no guest room available for them.

⁸And there were shepherds living out in the fields nearby, keeping watch over their flocks at night. ⁹An angel of the Lord appeared to them, and the glory of the Lord shone around them, and they were terrified. ¹⁰But the angel said to them, "Do not be afraid. I bring you good news that will cause great joy for all the people. ¹¹Today in the town of David a Savior has been born to you; he is the Messiah, the Lord. ¹²This will be a sign to you: You will find a baby wrapped in cloths and lying in a manger."

¹³Suddenly a great company of the heavenly host appeared with the angel, praising God and saying,

¹⁴"Glory to God in the highest heaven,
    and on earth peace to those on whom his
      favor rests."

¹⁵When the angels had left them and gone into heaven, the shepherds said to one another, "Let's go to Bethlehem and see this thing that has happened, which the Lord has told us about."

¹⁶So they hurried off and found Mary and Joseph, and the baby, who was lying in the manger. ¹⁷When they had seen him, they spread the word concerning what had been told them about this child, ¹⁸and all who heard it were amazed at what the shepherds said to them. ¹⁹But Mary treasured up all these things and pondered them in

---

David (1:27; 3:31), he travels to David's hometown of Bethlehem (1Sa 16:1,4; 17:12; compare Mt 2:5–6). A Roman census normally did not require people to travel to their ancestral town. Censuses served the purpose of registering people for military service or taxation, and it is possible that Joseph owned land in Bethlehem on which he paid taxes.

2:7 to her firstborn, a son Luke probably notes this detail here because Yahweh had consecrated Israel's firstborn children (Nu 3:13). **She wrapped him in cloths** Wrapping or swaddling provides warmth, comfort and security to newborn infants (and is still practiced today). **a manger** A trough out of which animals were fed. This may imply that they were in a barn of some sort, but a house is a stronger possibility; animals were often kept indoors at night in the house's lower level. See the infographic "First-Century Israelite House" on p. 1658. **available for them** The Greek text here (at the end of this verse) uses the term *katalyma* in reference to a guest room (compare Lk 22:11). In this context, a *katalyma* is best understood as a caravansary—a roadside lodging in which several groups of travelers could spend the night. This is the same word used to describe Hannah's accommodations in the Septuagint (ancient Greek OT) version of 1Sa 1:18; Luke alludes to Hannah's story throughout his opening chapters. The Greek word *pandocheion*, which refers more clearly to an inn, appears at Lk 10:34.

2:8–21 In this passage, angels announce the news of Jesus' birth to shepherds.

2:8 shepherds By noting that the announcement comes to lowly shepherds rather than to the religious elite, Luke continues the theme developed in 1:48–52 (compare 7:22).

2:10 Do not be afraid See note on 1:13. **good news** The Greek word used here, *euangelion*, commonly refers in Luke's Gospel to the saving message that the savior of humanity has come into the world. **great joy for all the people** Hints that the good news is not just for Jewish people, but also for non-Jewish people.

2:11 town of David Refers to Bethlehem (see v. 4 and note). **a Savior** In Mary's song of praise, this title refers to Yahweh (1:47); now it is aptly applied to Jesus. **Messiah, the Lord** The angels employ two titles: "Christ" or "Messiah" emphasizes Jesus' anointing as God's

promised Servant; "Lord" emphasizes his sovereign authority. Luke uses the title "Lord" (*kyrios* in Greek) interchangeably to refer to both Yahweh and Jesus (compare v. 9). This seems to indicate that Luke intended to refer to Jesus as Yahweh.

2:12 lying in a manger Mangers—though quite familiar to the shepherds—were unusual beds for babies (v. 7). This oddity would serve as a sign to the shepherds that they had found the Messiah.

2:13 a great company of the heavenly host Refers to a massive group of angels.

2:14 Glory to God This third hymn in Luke's birth narratives echoes the angelic song in Isa 6:3 (see Lk 1:27 and note; compare 1:46–55,68–79). **in the highest heaven** A reference to God's abode (compare 19:38). **on earth** The angels' reference to glory in the highest heaven is complemented by their message of peace of earth. **peace** The Greek word used here, *eirēnē*, is similar in meaning to the Hebrew word *shalom* (which means "peace," "wholeness" or "completeness"); it carries connotations of well-being, harmony and security. Peace is a major theme of Luke's Gospel (e.g., 1:79; 7:50; 10:5–6; 19:38; 24:36). At first, it seems that the idea of Messianic peace contradicts 12:51, where Jesus declares that he will bring division rather than peace. He is explaining that people will have to make a decision about him which may cause division. Ultimately, those who choose to follow him will receive peace. Jesus brings peace to the whole world upon his second coming (see Rev 21). Luke likely intends a contrast between the peace offered by God through his Messiah and that offered by Rome through the emperor. The idea that peace came from Caesar Augustus was prevalent throughout the Roman Empire at the time of Jesus' birth (see note on Mk 1:1). During his reign (27 BC–AD 14), Augustus ended the civil strife and widespread warfare that dominated the reigns of other emperors. Consequently, people erected shrines to him with inscriptions hailing him as savior of the whole world. For example, an inscription found in the city of Priene (located in modern-day Turkey) declares: "the birthday of the god Augustus was the beginning of the good news for the world that came through him." In contrast, Luke portrays Jesus as the true Savior of the world, the authentic bearer and proclaimer of good news (the gospel). Jesus' words divide people as they choose allegiances, but unlike Augustus, Jesus can offer true salvation.

her heart. ²⁰The shepherds returned, glorifying and praising God for all the things they had heard and seen, which were just as they had been told.

²¹On the eighth day, when it was time to circumcise the child, he was named Jesus, the name the angel had given him before he was conceived.

Jesus Presented in the Temple

²²When the time came for the purification rites required by the Law of Moses, Joseph and Mary took him to Jerusalem to present him to the Lord ²³(as it is written in the Law of the Lord, "Every firstborn male is to be consecrated to the Lord"ᵃ), ²⁴and to offer a sacrifice in keeping with what is said in the Law of the Lord: "a pair of doves or two young pigeons."ᵇ

²⁵Now there was a man in Jerusalem called Simeon, who was righteous and devout. He was waiting for the consolation of Israel, and the Holy Spirit was on him. ²⁶It had been revealed to him by the Holy Spirit that he would not die before he had seen the Lord's Messiah. ²⁷Moved by the Spirit, he went into the temple courts. When the parents brought in the child Jesus to do for him what the custom of the Law required, ²⁸Simeon took him in his arms and praised God, saying:

²⁹"Sovereign Lord, as you have promised,
  you may now dismissᶜ your servant in peace.
³⁰For my eyes have seen your salvation,
³¹ which you have prepared in the sight of all nations:
³²a light for revelation to the Gentiles,
  and the glory of your people Israel."

³³The child's father and mother marveled at what was said about him. ³⁴Then Simeon blessed them and said to Mary, his mother: "This child is destined to cause the falling and rising of many in Israel, and to be a sign that will be spoken against, ³⁵so that the thoughts of many hearts will be revealed. And a sword will pierce your own soul too."

³⁶There was also a prophet, Anna, the daughter of Penuel, of the tribe of Asher. She was very old; she had lived with her husband seven years after her marriage, ³⁷and then was a widow until she was eighty-four.ᵈ She never left the temple but worshiped night and day, fasting and praying. ³⁸Coming up to them at that very moment, she gave thanks to God and spoke about the child to all who were looking forward to the redemption of Jerusalem.

³⁹When Joseph and Mary had done everything

ᵃ 23 Exodus 13:2,12   ᵇ 24 Lev. 12:8   ᶜ 29 Or promised, / now dismiss   ᵈ 37 Or then had been a widow for eighty-four years.

2:21 named Jesus, the name the angel had given See Lk 1:31 and note.

2:22–24 In obedience to the law, Joseph and Mary offer a sacrifice to God in the temple.

2:22 the time came for the purification rites According to the law, Mary had to undergo a time of purification after giving birth (see Lev 12:1–4).

2:23 to be consecrated to the Lord In a separate ceremony from Mary's purification, Jesus is consecrated. See Ex 13:2,12; Nu 3:13.

2:24 a pair of doves or two young pigeons The offering of a poor woman. The law stipulated that a lamb be offered, but if the woman could not afford a lamb then she could offer two turtledoves or pigeons (Lev 12:8).

2:25–35 While they are at the temple, Joseph and his family are introduced to two prophetic figures. The first is Simeon—an elderly prophet to whom God made a promise (see Lk 2:26). Simeon longed to see the arrival of the Messiah; when he finally meets him, he delivers a message of hope and sorrow to Mary and Joseph.

2:25 the consolation of Israel This likely alludes to OT prophecies anticipating a time of redemption for Israel, which would be signified by an incredible sense of Yahweh's presence (e.g., Isa 40:1–2,10–11; 61:1–2; compare Lk 2:38). This time of restoration was expected to be accomplished through Yahweh's anointed representative, the Messiah (christos in Greek). This phrase has its roots in Isa 40–66, which begins with Yahweh announcing comfort for his people (see Isa 40:1 and note). The idea of Yahweh comforting his people by delivering them is found throughout this section of Isaiah (e.g., 49:13; 51:3; 66:13). **Holy Spirit was on him** A common theme in Luke's Gospel (see Lk 1:15,35,41,67).
2:26 the Lord's Messiah This phrase refers to Yahweh's anointed one.

2:29–32 This passage comprises the fourth hymn in Luke's birth narratives. It is known as the Nunc dimittis because of how the first few words are translated in the Latin Vulgate (the Latin translation of the Bible).

2:29 dismiss your servant in peace Simeon declares that he can die now that he has seen Yahweh's Messiah (see v. 26).

2:32 revelation to the Gentiles These references—coupled with the whole-world decree in Lk 2:1—speak to the worldwide significance of Jesus' arrival (compare v. 10 and note; v. 31). This line echoes Isa 42:6, which explains the vocation of Yahweh's suffering servant.

2:34 falling and rising In words taken from Isa 8:14, Simeon summarizes the divided response people will later have to Jesus' ministry (compare note on Lk 2:14).

2:35 a sword will pierce your own soul too Perhaps a reference to the grief that Jesus' premature death will bring Mary.

2:36–40 The second prophetic figure who encounters Jesus in the temple is the aged prophetess Anna. Upon seeing the child, she begins to praise God.

2:36 a prophet Female prophets appear in Acts as well (e.g., Ac 21:9), but they were rare in Israel's history. Anna's inclusion in Luke's narrative continues the theme that Jesus is the savior of all people (Lk 2:10): Jesus' identity was revealed to a man (Simeon) and now a woman. **Anna** The Greek version of the Hebrew name Hannah—another reference to 1Sa 1–2 (compare Lk 1:46–56 and note).

2:38 spoke about the child Refers to Jesus. Anna's message likely echoes Simeon's (vv. 30–32). **to the redemption of Jerusalem** See v. 25 and note.

2:39 everything required by the Law of the Lord See vv. 22–24. **Nazareth** See 1:26 and note.

required by the Law of the Lord, they returned to Galilee to their own town of Nazareth. ⁴⁰And the child grew and became strong; he was filled with wisdom, and the grace of God was on him.

The Boy Jesus at the Temple

⁴¹Every year Jesus' parents went to Jerusalem for the Festival of the Passover. ⁴²When he was twelve years old, they went up to the festival, according to the custom. ⁴³After the festival was over, while his parents were returning home, the boy Jesus stayed behind in Jerusalem, but they were unaware of it. ⁴⁴Thinking he was in their company, they traveled on for a day. Then they began looking for him among their relatives and friends. ⁴⁵When they did not find him, they went back to Jerusalem to look for him. ⁴⁶After three days they found him in the temple courts, sitting among the teachers, listening to them and asking them questions. ⁴⁷Everyone who heard him was amazed at his understanding and his answers. ⁴⁸When his parents saw him, they were aston-

ished. His mother said to him, "Son, why have you treated us like this? Your father and I have been anxiously searching for you."

⁴⁹"Why were you searching for me?" he asked. "Didn't you know I had to be in my Father's house?"ᵃ ⁵⁰But they did not understand what he was saying to them.

⁵¹Then he went down to Nazareth with them and was obedient to them. But his mother treasured all these things in her heart. ⁵²And Jesus grew in wisdom and stature, and in favor with God and man.

John the Baptist Prepares the Way

3:2-10pp — Mt 3:1-10; Mk 1:3-5
3:16,17pp — Mt 3:11,12; Mk 1:7,8

3 In the fifteenth year of the reign of Tiberius Caesar — when Pontius Pilate was governor of Judea, Herod tetrarch of Galilee, his brother Philip tetrarch of Iturea and Traconitis, and Lysanias

ᵃ 49 Or *be about my Father's business*

2:40 the child grew and became strong Compare 1:80; 2:52.

2:41-52 This story, which is unique to Luke's Gospel, shifts from the birth narratives to Jesus' early adolescence. It shows that Jesus was devout and understood his role from even the age of 12. When Jesus next appears in Luke's narrative, he is about 30 and beginning his public ministry (3:23). See the event line "Jesus' Early Life and Ministry" on p. 1530.

2:41 to Jerusalem for the Festival of the Passover Refers to the time that many Jewish people made pilgrimage to Jerusalem for the Jews' annual commemoration of the exodus — God's deliverance of their ancestors from bondage in Egypt (Ex 12–13; Dt 16:1–8). Passover is considered the most important feast of the Jewish calendar. To celebrate Passover, Jews were to travel to Jerusalem and offer a lamb as a sacrifice (Ex 12:21; Dt 16:2,5–6). The meal began at sunset — the time of Israel's departure from Egypt (Ex 12:29–32,42; Dt 16:6). This celebration also provides the setting for the story of Hannah (1Sa 1:3), which Luke reflects through the opening chapters of his Gospel (compare Lk 1:46–56 and note).

2:44 their company They were probably part of a caravan traveling from Nazareth to Jerusalem. At this time, traveling in groups was common because it offered protection from bandits and allowed people to distribute resources. Given the communal nature of rural first-century Palestine, Joseph and Mary were right to assume that their son was in the group; this passage is not intended to reflect poorly on them as parents.

2:47 was amazed Elsewhere, Luke uses the Greek verb here to indicate amazement at supernatural events, such as the reaction to Jesus raising a girl from the dead (8:56), the disciples speaking in tongues (Ac 2:7,12), Saul's conversion (Ac 9:21) and the Holy Spirit coming upon Gentiles (Ac 10:45).

2:49 in my Father's house In the previous verse, Mary mentions Joseph, Jesus' earthly father; in contrast, Jesus refers here to his heavenly Father.

2:51 his mother treasured all these things Compare Lk 1:66; 2:19.

2:52 in wisdom and stature, and in favor Compare 1:80; 2:40.

3:1-20 Having described John's birth, Luke now recounts John's teaching ministry (compare Mt 3:1–12). John proclaims that he is a forerunner of a more powerful figure — the Messiah — whose arrival is imminent (Lk 3:16).

3:1 fifteenth year of the reign of Tiberius Caesar Successor of Caesar Augustus; ruled ca. AD 14–37. This reference puts the start of John's ministry around AD 28. **Pontius Pilate** Ruled ca. AD 26–36. See note on Mt 27:2. **Herod tetrarch of Galilee** Refers to Herod Antipas. After the death of Herod the Great, his kingdom was divided among his sons. Antipas controlled Galilee and Perea; Archelaus ruled Samaria, Judea and Idumea; and Philip governed the smaller enclaves northeast of the Sea of Galilee, composed primarily of Syrians and Greeks. See the table "Political Leaders in the New Testament" on p. 1916.

Luke 3:1

HEROD ANTIPAS

Herod Antipas controlled Galilee and Perea from 4 BC to AD 39. The son of Herod the Great and Malthrace, he was raised in Rome. This background made him the logical choice to preside over "Galilee of the Gentiles" (Mt 4:15), given the region's large Gentile population and its proximity to the Decapolis (a federation of Hellenized cities). Like his father, Herod Antipas was a master builder, and, generally speaking, he respected Jewish religious customs. The Gospels mention him twice in connection with important events: the beheading of John the Baptist (Mt 14:1–12; Mk 6:14–29; Lk 3:19–20; 9:7–9) and the questioning of Jesus before the crucifixion (Lk 23:6–12).

tetrarch of Abilene — ²during the high-priesthood of Annas and Caiaphas, the word of God came to John son of Zechariah in the wilderness. ³He went into all the country around the Jordan, preaching a baptism of repentance for the forgiveness of sins. ⁴As it is written in the book of the words of Isaiah the prophet:

"A voice of one calling in the wilderness,
'Prepare the way for the Lord,
    make straight paths for him.
⁵ Every valley shall be filled in,
    every mountain and hill made low.
The crooked roads shall become straight,
    the rough ways smooth.
⁶ And all people will see God's salvation.'"ᵃ

⁷John said to the crowds coming out to be baptized by him, "You brood of vipers! Who warned you to flee from the coming wrath? ⁸Produce fruit in keeping with repentance. And do not begin to say to yourselves, 'We have Abraham as our father.' For I tell you that out of these stones God can raise up children for Abraham. ⁹The ax is already at the root of the trees, and every tree that does not produce good fruit will be cut down and thrown into the fire."

¹⁰"What should we do then?" the crowd asked.

¹¹John answered, "Anyone who has two shirts should share with the one who has none, and anyone who has food should do the same."

¹²Even tax collectors came to be baptized. "Teacher," they asked, "what should we do?"

¹³"Don't collect any more than you are required to," he told them.

¹⁴Then some soldiers asked him, "And what should we do?"

He replied, "Don't extort money and don't accuse people falsely — be content with your pay."

¹⁵The people were waiting expectantly and were all wondering in their hearts if John might possibly be the Messiah. ¹⁶John answered them all, "I baptize you withᵇ water. But one who is more powerful than I will come, the straps of whose sandals I am not worthy to untie. He will baptize you withᵇ the Holy Spirit and fire. ¹⁷His winnowing fork is in his hand to clear his threshing floor and to gather the wheat into his barn, but he will burn up the chaff with unquenchable fire." ¹⁸And with many other words John exhorted the people and proclaimed the good news to them.

¹⁹But when John rebuked Herod the tetrarch because of his marriage to Herodias, his brother's wife, and all the other evil things he had done, ²⁰Herod added this to them all: He locked John up in prison.

ᵃ 6 Isaiah 40:3-5   ᵇ 16 Or in

3:2 Annas High priest ca. AD 6–15. The title high priest seems to have been permanent even though the functions were temporary. In other words, ex-high priests bore the honorific title for life even after they were replaced by another high priest. **Caiaphas** Annas' son-in-law; served as high priest ca. AD 18–36. **John son of Zechariah** See Lk 1:13. **in the wilderness** See note on 4:1 (compare 1:80).

3:3 baptism of repentance for the forgiveness of sins Baptism demonstrated repentance and a commitment to a changed life in preparation for the coming Messiah. In this way John's baptism was related to forgiveness of sins.

3:4 the words of Isaiah the prophet Introduces the quotation of Isa 40:3–5. John's ministry was in preparation for the Messiah.

3:6 all people will see God's salvation See 2:32 and note.

3:7 said to the crowds Matthew 3:7 identifies the recipients of John's rebuke as the Pharisees and Sadducees.

3:8 fruit in keeping with repentance Anticipates the tree metaphor in the next verse. John is calling for obedience — behavior that is the natural result of a truly repentant heart. Compare Lk 6:43–44. **We have Abraham as our father** An authoritative appeal to Jewish ethnic identity as a means of deliverance from God's judgment. However, John argues that repentance — not legal observance or familial descent — is most important. Jesus addresses this issue in the Gospel of John (compare Jn 8:39 and note).

3:9 ax is already at the root An image of impending judgment. Compare Lk 13:6–9. **fire** A symbol of divine wrath. Fire also became an image for final punishment — especially connected with the Valley of Ben Hinnom (2Ch 33:6; Jer 7:31–32) on the west side of Jerusalem at Wadi er-Rababi. See note on Lk 12:5.

3:10–14 In this passage, John offers exhortations on how to treat others.

3:11 share The people of God demonstrate this quality (see note on Mt 5:1–12; compare Lk 6:29; Ac 2:42–47; 4:32–37).

3:12 tax collectors Associated with sinners throughout Luke's Gospel (e.g., Lk 5:30; 7:34; 15:1; 19:1–7). Jews in the first century despised tax collectors, who profited by charging people more than they owed. See note on Mt 5:46.

3:13 Don't collect any more than you are required to John advises the tax collectors to stop defrauding people. Zacchaeus exemplifies obedience to this exhortation in Lk 19:1–10.

3:14 don't accuse people falsely — be content John advises the soldiers to practice honesty and contentment.

3:15 The people were waiting expectantly Jews in the first century AD anticipated the coming of the Messiah (compare 1:66; 2:25–37).

3:16 more powerful John makes it clear that he is not the Messiah (compare Jn 1:20; note on Mk 1:7). **straps of whose sandals I am not worthy to untie** Refers to a task normally given to a slave. An alternate form of this saying appears in Jn 1:27. **baptize you with the Holy Spirit and fire** This likely signals the purifying function of Jesus' efforts, reflecting prophetic imagery (compare Isa 6:5–7). It also could anticipate the events of Pentecost (Ac 2). Another possibility draws on the symbolic association of fire with divine wrath (e.g., Lk 3:9,17; Mt 3:10,12) and envisions a twofold baptism: The repentant will receive baptism with the Holy Spirit, but the non-repentant will receive the baptism associated with judgment.

3:17 winnowing fork A symbol of judgment. See note on Mt 3:12. **unquenchable fire** A symbol of divine wrath (compare Rev 19:11—20:10).

The Baptism and Genealogy of Jesus

3:21,22pp — Mt 3:13-17; Mk 1:9-11
3:23-38pp — Mt 1:1-17

²¹When all the people were being baptized, Jesus was baptized too. And as he was praying, heaven was opened ²²and the Holy Spirit descended on him in bodily form like a dove. And a voice came from heaven: "You are my Son, whom I love; with you I am well pleased."

²³Now Jesus himself was about thirty years old when he began his ministry. He was the son, so it was thought, of Joseph,

the son of Heli, ²⁴the son of Matthat,
the son of Levi, the son of Melki,
the son of Jannai, the son of Joseph,
²⁵the son of Mattathias, the son of Amos,
the son of Nahum, the son of Esli,
the son of Naggai, ²⁶the son of Maath,
the son of Mattathias, the son of Semein,
the son of Josek, the son of Joda,
²⁷the son of Joanan, the son of Rhesa,
the son of Zerubbabel, the son of Shealtiel,
the son of Neri, ²⁸the son of Melki,
the son of Addi, the son of Cosam,
the son of Elmadam, the son of Er,
²⁹the son of Joshua, the son of Eliezer,
the son of Jorim, the son of Matthat,
the son of Levi, ³⁰the son of Simeon,
the son of Judah, the son of Joseph,
the son of Jonam, the son of Eliakim,

³¹the son of Melea, the son of Menna,
the son of Mattatha, the son of Nathan,
the son of David, ³²the son of Jesse,
the son of Obed, the son of Boaz,
the son of Salmon,ᵃ the son of Nahshon,
³³the son of Amminadab, the son of Ram,ᵇ
the son of Hezron, the son of Perez,
the son of Judah, ³⁴the son of Jacob,
the son of Isaac, the son of Abraham,
the son of Terah, the son of Nahor,
³⁵the son of Serug, the son of Reu,
the son of Peleg, the son of Eber,
the son of Shelah, ³⁶the son of Cainan,
the son of Arphaxad, the son of Shem,
the son of Noah, the son of Lamech,
³⁷the son of Methuselah, the son of Enoch,
the son of Jared, the son of Mahalalel,
the son of Kenan, ³⁸the son of Enosh,
the son of Seth, the son of Adam,
the son of God.

Jesus Is Tested in the Wilderness

4:1-13pp — Mt 4:1-11; Mk 1:12,13

4 Jesus, full of the Holy Spirit, left the Jordan and was led by the Spirit into the wilderness, ²where for forty days he was temptedᶜ by the devil. He ate nothing during those days, and at the end of them he was hungry.

ᵃ 32 Some early manuscripts *Sala*   ᵇ 33 Some manuscripts *Amminadab, the son of Admin, the son of Arni*; other manuscripts vary widely.   ᶜ 2 The Greek for *tempted* can also mean *tested*.

3:19 because of his marriage to Herodias, his brother's wife John had spoken out against Herod's marriage to Herodias. See Mt 14:3–12; Mk 6:14–29.

3:21–22 Luke offers a shorter treatment of Jesus' baptism than the account in Matthew's Gospel (compare Mt 3:13–17). However, Luke still includes the important elements of this episode: Jesus receives John's baptism, the Spirit descends as a dove, and a voice speaks from heaven.

3:21 Jesus was baptized See Mt 3:15 and note.
3:22 in bodily form Luke is the only Gospel to include this detail. See Mt 3:16 and note. **You are my Son, whom I love** See note on Mk 1:11. **with you I am well pleased** Possibly an allusion to Isaiah (see Isa 42:1 and note).

3:23–38 Luke presents a more fully developed genealogy than Matthew (compare Mt 1:1–17) alluding to various parts of the OT while detailing Jesus' genealogy (compare Ge 5:3–32; 11:10–26; Ru 4:18–22; 1Ch 1:1–4,24–28; 2:1–15). Due to the differences between the two genealogies, it has been suggested that Luke traces Jesus' line through Mary while Matthew traces it through Joseph. However, both genealogies actually follow Joseph's lineage. A second explanation is that Matthew is primarily interested in the line of royal descent from David, whereas Luke relates the biological descent. A third is that there were one or more levirate marriages along the line (see Dt 25:5–10).
　However the divergences are explained, it seems that

Luke and Matthew have different theological aims: Luke traces Jesus' genealogy all the way back to Adam, while Matthew begins with Abraham. In addition to showing Jesus' credentials as the Davidic Messiah (and thus the savior of Israel), Luke emphasizes that Jesus is the savior of all of humanity. For this reason, Luke traces Jesus' genealogy back to Adam, the first human (see Lk 3:38).

3:23 about thirty years old Luke uses the Greek preposition *hōsei* (meaning "like," "as" or "about") to approximate Jesus' age at the inception of his ministry (compare 1:80 and note). If Jesus was born sometime between 6 and 4 BC (see note on 2:1) and John's ministry began around AD 28 (see note on 3:1), then Jesus could have been around 33 years old when his public ministry began. However, this cannot be determined from the text, and Jesus' age should remain an approximation—just as Luke intended it. **so it was thought** Not everyone knew of Jesus' miraculous conception, and people would have assumed that Joseph was his biological father (e.g., 4:22). Nonetheless, Jesus is presented as Joseph's rightful heir.

4:1–13 Like Matthew, Luke records Jesus' wilderness temptation following his baptism. The temptation accounts in Luke and Matthew are nearly identical, with only a few minor variations (compare Mt 4:1–11; Mk 1:12–13). Luke's Gospel has a different ordering for the second and third temptations, placing the temptation of power before the temptation to test God. Luke also abbreviates the quotation from Dt 8:3 (Lk 4:4). In vv. 6–7,

³The devil said to him, "If you are the Son of God, tell this stone to become bread."

⁴Jesus answered, "It is written: 'Man shall not live on bread alone.'*a*"

⁵The devil led him up to a high place and showed him in an instant all the kingdoms of the world. ⁶And he said to him, "I will give you all their authority and splendor; it has been given to me, and I can give it to anyone I want to. ⁷If you worship me, it will all be yours."

⁸Jesus answered, "It is written: 'Worship the Lord your God and serve him only.'*b*"

⁹The devil led him to Jerusalem and had him stand on the highest point of the temple. "If you are the Son of God," he said, "throw yourself down from here. ¹⁰For it is written:

"'He will command his angels concerning you
 to guard you carefully;

¹¹they will lift you up in their hands,
 so that you will not strike your foot against
 a stone.'*c*"

¹²Jesus answered, "It is said: 'Do not put the Lord your God to the test.'*d*"

¹³When the devil had finished all this tempting, he left him until an opportune time.

Jesus Rejected at Nazareth

¹⁴Jesus returned to Galilee in the power of the Spirit, and news about him spread through the whole countryside. ¹⁵He was teaching in their synagogues, and everyone praised him.

¹⁶He went to Nazareth, where he had been brought up, and on the Sabbath day he went into the synagogue, as was his custom. He stood up to

a 4 Deut. 8:3   *b 8* Deut. 6:13   *c 11* Psalm 91:11,12
d 12 Deut. 6:16

Luke elaborates on the devil's dominion (compare Mt 4:9). In contrast to Matthew's account, which concludes with angels ministering to Jesus, Luke's temptation account concludes on an ominous note (Lk 4:13).

4:1 into the wilderness In the OT, the wilderness is the place where God meets with his appointed messengers, such as Moses at the burning bush (Ex 3) and on Mount Sinai (Ex 19). The wilderness also is where God tests the Israelites on their journey to the promised land (Dt 8:1–18). During their wilderness testing, the Israelites failed to trust God and consequently were punished with 40 years of wandering in the desert (Nu 14).

4:2 forty days Recalls Moses' 40 days on Mount Sinai, the Israelites' 40 years of wandering and Elijah's 40 days in the wilderness of Horeb. **the devil** The Greek word used here, *diabolos*, is used in the Septuagint (the ancient Greek translation of the OT) to render the Hebrew word *satan*, which means "the accuser" or "the adversary." This term appears infrequently in the OT. It is used for the accuser of Joshua the high priest (Zec 3:1–2), for the inciter of David to conduct a census (1Ch 21:1) and for the spiritual being in Job 1–2 (see Job 1:6 and note). Here *diabolos* refers to an evil, spiritual figure—synonymous with *satan* in Mark's synopsis of Jesus' temptation (see note on Mk 1:13). **He ate nothing** See note on Mt 4:2.

4:3 If you are the Son of God This identity is affirmed explicitly in Lk 3:38.

4:4 It is written Jesus refutes each of the devil's temptations by quoting Scripture. Here he quotes Dt 8:3.

4:5 in an instant The precise meaning here is uncertain. Some kind of visionary experience might be involved, but the text does not indicate this.

4:6 I will give The devil uses language reminiscent of the ancient Israelite belief that the nations were under the control of evil foreign powers (see Dt 32:8 and note).

4:7 worship me See Mt 4:9 and note.

4:8 Worship the Lord your God Jesus' reply comes from Dt 6:13.

4:9 highest point Probably refers to a high point on the front of the temple, rather than a point overlooking the Kidron Valley. If the devil is encouraging Jesus to make a public display, the side of the temple facing the city is a more likely setting. In Matthew's account, this is the second temptation (compare Mt 4:1–11). Luke may

have arranged the temptations to conclude in Jerusalem, in order to mirror the sequence of Jesus' ministry (see note on Lk 4:14).

4:10 He will command his angels concerning you In vv. 10–11, the devil quotes Ps 91:11–12, perhaps mocking Jesus' use of Scripture. Both lines are taken out of context; the psalm clearly is not about angels protecting people who jump off buildings. Rather, the sense is that Yahweh's protection is so near and careful that his angels could even stop people from hurting their feet while walking. By the time of Jesus, Ps 91 probably had acquired a Messianic interpretation. The devil likely is suggesting that if Jesus really is the Son of God, then these verses should apply to him. Alternatively, the devil could be suggesting that if a promise such as that in Ps 91:11–12 is given to ordinary humans, then it must apply even more to Jesus as the Son of God.

4:12 to the test Jesus quotes Dt 6:16, which refers back to the Israelites testing Yahweh in Ex 17:2–7.

4:13 until an opportune time Unlike Luke, Matthew's and Mark's temptation accounts report angels ministering to Jesus at this point (Mt 4:11; Mk 1:13). Luke adds that the devil will return. This might refer to Lk 22:3.

4:14–15 These verses imply that Jesus left his hometown of Nazareth and moved to Capernaum for a time (Mt 4:13 states this explicitly).

4:14 Galilee Jesus begins his mission in the most ethnically and culturally diverse portion of Israel. The rest of the Jewish people viewed Galilee as only moderately Jewish. Jesus begins where he is most needed—among the marginalized. Luke structures the ministry of Jesus geographically: in Galilee (Lk 4:14—9:50), en route to Jerusalem (9:51—19:28) and in Jerusalem (19:29—21:38). Compare Ac 1:8 and note.

4:15 synagogues See note on Mt 4:23.

4:16–30 In addition to John's arrest (see Mt 4:12), Jesus' rejection in his hometown might have influenced his move to Capernaum. The people in Nazareth knew him as the son of Joseph and Mary, not as the Messiah. Although they initially received Jesus' message favorably, the people of Nazareth eventually try to kill Jesus because he criticizes their unbelief. Compare Mt 13:53–58.

4:16 Nazareth See note on Lk 1:26.

read, [17]and the scroll of the prophet Isaiah was handed to him. Unrolling it, he found the place where it is written:

[18] "The Spirit of the Lord is on me,
  because he has anointed me
    to proclaim good news to the poor.
He has sent me to proclaim freedom for
      the prisoners
    and recovery of sight for the blind,
  to set the oppressed free,
[19]   to proclaim the year of the Lord's favor."[a]

[20]Then he rolled up the scroll, gave it back to the attendant and sat down. The eyes of everyone in the synagogue were fastened on him. [21]He began by saying to them, "Today this scripture is fulfilled in your hearing."

[22]All spoke well of him and were amazed at the gracious words that came from his lips. "Isn't this Joseph's son?" they asked.

[23]Jesus said to them, "Surely you will quote this proverb to me: 'Physician, heal yourself!' And you will tell me, 'Do here in your hometown what we have heard that you did in Capernaum.'"

[24]"Truly I tell you," he continued, "no prophet is accepted in his hometown. [25]I assure you that there were many widows in Israel in Elijah's time, when the sky was shut for three and a half years and there was a severe famine throughout the land. [26]Yet Elijah was not sent to any of them, but to a widow in Zarephath in the region of Sidon. [27]And there were many in Israel with leprosy[b] in the time of Elisha the prophet, yet not one of them was cleansed — only Naaman the Syrian."

[28]All the people in the synagogue were furious when they heard this. [29]They got up, drove him out of the town, and took him to the brow of the hill on which the town was built, in order to throw him off the cliff. [30]But he walked right through the crowd and went on his way.

Jesus Drives Out an Impure Spirit

4:31-37pp — Mk 1:21-28

[31]Then he went down to Capernaum, a town in Galilee, and on the Sabbath he taught the people.

---

[a] *19* Isaiah 61:1,2 (see Septuagint); Isaiah 58:6
[b] *27* The Greek word traditionally translated *leprosy* was used for various diseases affecting the skin.

4:17 the scroll of the prophet Isaiah The following quotation of Isa 61:1–2 and 58:6 is a proclamation by Jesus that he is the anointed one of Yahweh (see note on Lk 1:27; compare 3:22; 4:1,22). Within the context of Isaiah, this indicates that Jesus is claiming to be the Messiah (Isa 11; compare Isa 7:10–25; 9:1–7) and the suffering servant (Isa 42:1–9; 49:1–12; 50:4–11; and Isa 52:13—53:12). This section (Lk 4:17–21), which is unique to Luke, is a clear reflection of Isaiah's theology. In its original context, Isa 61:1–2 proclaimed comfort for God's oppressed people. Jesus uses it in a similar fashion here, proclaiming himself to be God's servant, the Messiah, arriving to deliver his suffering and oppressed people (see Lk 4:21 and note). Jesus identifies himself as the bearer of good news to the poor and evokes imagery reminiscent of the Year of Jubilee — an observance occurring every 50 years in which debt was forgiven and property restored (Lev 25). Jesus connects his ministry to not just salvation, but good news for all on the underside of power.

4:20 sat down Jesus assumes the usual position of a teacher; the reader stood while reading (v. 16) but sat to offer the explanation. **were fastened on him** They were waiting for him to interpret the passage he had just read.

4:21 Today this scripture is fulfilled Jesus explicitly declares that he is fulfilling the promise of consolation to Zion (Isa 61:1–2) in a new way (see Lk 2:25; 7:22). Through this declaration, he implies that he is Yahweh's Messiah.

4:22 All spoke well of him The people of Nazareth initially receive Jesus' Messianic claims favorably. **Isn't this Joseph's son** Questions about Jesus' identity are a recurring theme in Luke's account of Jesus' ministry in Galilee (see v. 34 and note; 5:21; 7:20; 8:25).

4:23 Physician, heal yourself The Greek text here could be understood as "heal your kin," as the rest of this verse indicates. The people of Nazareth want to experience Jesus' healing power.

4:24 no prophet is accepted in his hometown To illustrate this remark, Jesus proceeds to cite two stories in which OT prophets aided Gentiles (non-Jews) rather than Israelites (vv. 25–27). Jesus contrasts the faith of two Gentiles (the widow of Zarephath and Naaman the Syrian) with the unbelief of the Nazarenes. In response to the Gentiles' faith, God sent his prophets to meet their needs. The people of Nazareth, however, will not receive such provision because of their unbelief.

4:26 to a widow in Zarephath The story of Elijah and the widow of Zarephath appears in 1Ki 17:8–24. **Sidon** Located northwest of Israel. Its residents were Gentiles (non-Jews) who worshiped Baal, the Canaanite storm-god.

4:27 Naaman the Syrian Commander of the army of Syria (Aram), an enemy of Israel. The account of Naaman's healing appears in 2Ki 5:1–14.

4:28 people in the synagogue were furious The people are angry because Jesus spoke of Gentiles (non-Jews) receiving God's aid while Israel had to suffer.

4:31–44 Jesus returns to Capernaum, his new base of operations. Luke summarizes some of the teaching and miracles that occurred there.

4:31 Capernaum A village on the northern shore of the Sea of Galilee. See the infographic "The Synagogue at Capernaum" on p. 1656.

Luke 4:31

CAPERNAUM
A fishing town with both Jewish and Gentile (non-Jewish) inhabitants, Capernaum's position on a trade route made it more cosmopolitan and diverse than other towns of similar size. Jesus performed many of his signs in Capernaum and made a special example out of its residents' unbelief (Mt 11:23). Although much of Galilee was ruled by Herod Antipas (see note on Lk 3:1), it is possible that Capernaum was considered part of Philip's territory since it was close to the assumed border and since he ruled over the smaller enclaves northeast of the Sea of Galilee.

[32]They were amazed at his teaching, because his words had authority.

[33]In the synagogue there was a man possessed by a demon, an impure spirit. He cried out at the top of his voice, [34]"Go away! What do you want with us, Jesus of Nazareth? Have you come to destroy us? I know who you are — the Holy One of God!"

[35]"Be quiet!" Jesus said sternly. "Come out of him!" Then the demon threw the man down before them all and came out without injuring him.

[36]All the people were amazed and said to each other, "What words these are! With authority and power he gives orders to impure spirits and they come out!" [37]And the news about him spread throughout the surrounding area.

4:32 because his words had authority Jesus did not refer to the rabbis when he taught; he did not need any authority beyond his own. He expounded on the words and ideals of the Hebrew Scriptures without consulting others.

4:33 In the synagogue It is surprising that a demon-possessed person was in a synagogue. Luke might be subtly critiquing the spiritual state of Capernaum at the inception of Jesus' public ministry. Elsewhere, encounters with demons mark the inauguration of the kingdom of God (Mt 12:28; Lk 11:18–20). See the infographic "The Synagogue at Capernaum" below. **by a demon, an impure spirit** See note on Mk 1:23.

4:34 the Holy One of God The demon is aware of Jesus' identity and divine authority.

The Synagogue at Capernaum

Luke's Gospel says the synagogue in Capernaum was built by the centurion of whom Jesus later said, "I have not found such great faith even in Israel" (Lk 7:5-9). It was destroyed and rebuilt in the fourth century.

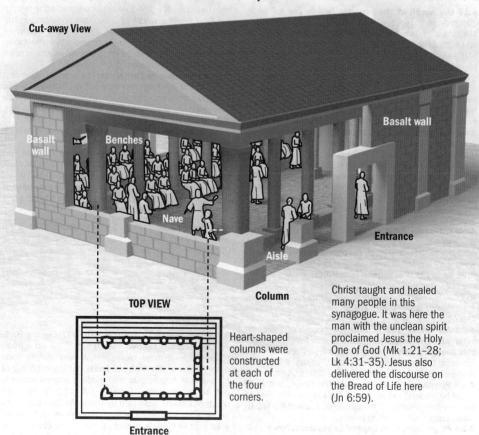

Cut-away View

Basalt wall

Benches

Basalt wall

Nave

Aisle

Entrance

Column

TOP VIEW

Entrance

Heart-shaped columns were constructed at each of the four corners.

Christ taught and healed many people in this synagogue. It was here the man with the unclean spirit proclaimed Jesus the Holy One of God (Mk 1:21–28; Lk 4:31–35). Jesus also delivered the discourse on the Bread of Life here (Jn 6:59).

Jesus Heals Many

4:38-41pp — Mt 8:14-17
4:38-43pp — Mk 1:29-38

³⁸Jesus left the synagogue and went to the home of Simon. Now Simon's mother-in-law was suffering from a high fever, and they asked Jesus to help her. ³⁹So he bent over her and rebuked the fever, and it left her. She got up at once and began to wait on them.

⁴⁰At sunset, the people brought to Jesus all who had various kinds of sickness, and laying his hands on each one, he healed them. ⁴¹Moreover, demons came out of many people, shouting, "You are the Son of God!" But he rebuked them and would not allow them to speak, because they knew he was the Messiah.

⁴²At daybreak, Jesus went out to a solitary place. The people were looking for him and when they came to where he was, they tried to keep him from leaving them. ⁴³But he said, "I must proclaim the good news of the kingdom of God to the other towns also, because that is why I was sent." ⁴⁴And he kept on preaching in the synagogues of Judea.

Jesus Calls His First Disciples

5:1-11pp — Mt 4:18-22; Mk 1:16-20; Jn 1:40-42

5 One day as Jesus was standing by the Lake of Gennesaret,ᵃ the people were crowding around him and listening to the word of God. ²He saw at the water's edge two boats, left there by the fishermen, who were washing their nets. ³He got into one of the boats, the one belonging to Simon, and asked him to put out a little from shore. Then he sat down and taught the people from the boat.

⁴When he had finished speaking, he said to Simon, "Put out into deep water, and let down the nets for a catch."

⁵Simon answered, "Master, we've worked hard all night and haven't caught anything. But because you say so, I will let down the nets."

⁶When they had done so, they caught such a large number of fish that their nets began to break. ⁷So they signaled their partners in the other boat to come and help them, and they came and filled both boats so full that they began to sink.

⁸When Simon Peter saw this, he fell at Jesus' knees and said, "Go away from me, Lord; I am a sinful man!" ⁹For he and all his companions were astonished at the catch of fish they had taken, ¹⁰and so were James and John, the sons of Zebedee, Simon's partners.

Then Jesus said to Simon, "Don't be afraid; from now on you will fish for people." ¹¹So they pulled their boats up on shore, left everything and followed him.

ᵃ 1 That is, the Sea of Galilee

4:36 What words these are People continue to wonder about the identity of Jesus (see note on Lk 4:22).

4:38 Simon's mother-in-law was suffering Parallel accounts of this healing occur in the other Synoptic Gospels (Mt 8:14–17; Mk 1:29–34).

4:43 kingdom of God Refers to God's sovereign rule and its effects. See note on Mk 1:15; note on Ac 1:3.

5:1–11 Like the other Gospel writers, Luke records the calling of Jesus' three most prominent disciples: Peter, James and John. These three form Jesus' inner circle, and they are privy to events that the others are not. The great catch of fish recorded here by Luke is unique to his Gospel. However, John has a similar episode occurring at Peter's recommissioning in Jn 21:4–7, after Jesus' resurrection. See the table "Miracles of Jesus" on p. 1741.

5:1 the Lake of Gennesaret Refers to the Sea of Galilee. Gennesaret (or Ginnesar) was a village located next to Capernaum, so Jesus was likely within its vicinity. See the map "Jesus' Ministry in Galilee" on p. 2260.

5:2 at the water's edge two boats Belonging to Simon Peter, James and John (see Lk 5:10).

5:3 he sat down and taught the people from the boat Compare Mt 13:2–3.

5:4 let down the nets for a catch Jesus seems to be responding to their lack of success the night before (Lk 5:5).

5:5 because you say so, I will let down the nets Luke portrays Peter (also called Simon) as pious and ready to obey Jesus (compare v. 8).

5:7 they signaled This group likely includes Andrew, Peter's brother, since they fished together; this may also be a parallel, expanded account of Jesus' calling of these disciples recorded in Matthew's Gospel (see Mt 4:18). Luke likely leaves Andrew unnamed because the purpose of this episode is to record the calling of Jesus' three most influential disciples (see note on Lk 8:51). **their partners in the other boat** James and John (Lk 5:10). **they began to sink** A massive amount of fish. This catch was clearly understood to be supernatural, as Peter's response indicates (5:8).

5:8 Go away from me, Lord; I am a sinful man Peter believed Jesus' Messianic claims, and this event confirmed his belief. He was aware of his sinfulness and considered himself unworthy to be near Yahweh's Messiah. Given the relatively small size of the villages on the northern shore of the Sea of Galilee (e.g., Capernaum, Gennesaret), their residents would have been aware of Jesus' ministry (4:37). In addition, John's Gospel records that Peter learned of Jesus from his brother Andrew, who was a disciple of John the Baptist (Jn 1:38–41). Peter was probably also familiar with the events recorded in Lk 4:31–36 and could have been present to observe the exorcism. He certainly knew of Jesus' power to heal, due to the miracle involving his mother-in-law (4:38–39). In addition to hearing Jesus' teaching, Peter has observed Jesus' Messianic power and was ready to obey his call to discipleship (v. 10).

5:10 you will fish for people A parallel account appears in Mt 4:18–22.

Jesus Heals a Man With Leprosy

5:12-14pp — Mt 8:2-4; Mk 1:40-44

[12]While Jesus was in one of the towns, a man came along who was covered with leprosy.[a] When he saw Jesus, he fell with his face to the ground and begged him, "Lord, if you are willing, you can make me clean."

[13]Jesus reached out his hand and touched the man. "I am willing," he said. "Be clean!" And immediately the leprosy left him.

[14]Then Jesus ordered him, "Don't tell anyone, but go, show yourself to the priest and offer the sacrifices that Moses commanded for your cleansing, as a testimony to them."

[15]Yet the news about him spread all the more, so that crowds of people came to hear him and to be healed of their sicknesses. [16]But Jesus often withdrew to lonely places and prayed.

a 12 The Greek word traditionally translated leprosy was used for various diseases affecting the skin.

5:12–16 The next four episodes have parallels in the other Synoptic Gospels (Matthew and Mark). Luke includes this miracle to further demonstrate Jesus' power over sickness and disease and to account for his widespread fame. See Mt 8:1–4; Mk 1:40–45.

5:12 leprosy The Greek word used here could refer to a variety of skin diseases, including leprosy itself. Leprosy damages the skin, nerves, limbs and eyes. It was thought to be highly contagious in this period and was greatly feared. **clean** Refers to ceremonial cleanness according to the law (Lev 13:2–3). The man's condition renders him unclean, and he asks Jesus to heal him (see Lev 13–14).

5:14 Don't tell anyone Jesus was strategic about revealing his identity as the Messiah. See note on Lk 8:56.

show yourself to the priest As a means of verification and validation (see Lev 14:1–32).

5:16 often withdrew to lonely places and prayed

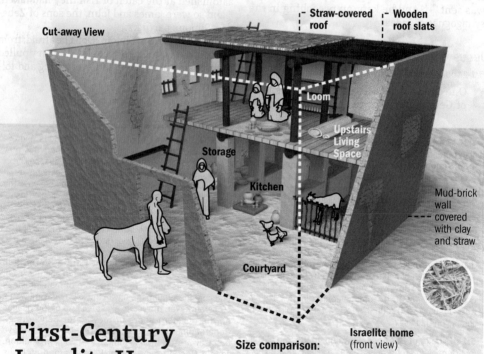

Cut-away View — Straw-covered roof — Wooden roof slats — Loom — Upstairs Living Space — Storage — Kitchen — Courtyard — Mud-brick wall covered with clay and straw

First-Century Israelite House

The homes of poor families were small and plain. They were built of rough stone (or mud-brick) walls and roofs of woven branches covered with clay. Living spaces were used for household work—cooking and weaving. At night, the family's domestic animals were housed in the lower level.

Size comparison:
First-century houses were smaller than modern double-wide trailers and accommodated an entire family.

Israelite home (front view)

Each floor 7' high
Door
Height 15'
Width 24', Length 24'

Double-wide mobile home (front view)

Width 24', Length 60'

Jesus Forgives and Heals a Paralyzed Man

5:18-26pp — Mt 9:2-8; Mk 2:3-12

¹⁷One day Jesus was teaching, and Pharisees and teachers of the law were sitting there. They had come from every village of Galilee and from Judea and Jerusalem. And the power of the Lord was with Jesus to heal the sick. ¹⁸Some men came carrying a paralyzed man on a mat and tried to take him into the house to lay him before Jesus. ¹⁹When they could not find a way to do this because of the crowd, they went up on the roof and lowered him on his mat through the tiles into the middle of the crowd, right in front of Jesus.

²⁰When Jesus saw their faith, he said, "Friend, your sins are forgiven."

²¹The Pharisees and the teachers of the law began thinking to themselves, "Who is this fellow who speaks blasphemy? Who can forgive sins but God alone?"

²²Jesus knew what they were thinking and asked, "Why are you thinking these things in your hearts? ²³Which is easier: to say, 'Your sins are forgiven,' or to say, 'Get up and walk'? ²⁴But I want you to know that the Son of Man has authority on earth to forgive sins." So he said to the paralyzed man, "I tell you, get up, take your mat and go home." ²⁵Immediately he stood up in front of them, took what he had been lying on and went home praising God. ²⁶Everyone was amazed and gave praise to God. They were filled with awe and said, "We have seen remarkable things today."

Jesus Calls Levi and Eats With Sinners

5:27-32pp — Mt 9:9-13; Mk 2:14-17

²⁷After this, Jesus went out and saw a tax collector by the name of Levi sitting at his tax booth. "Follow me," Jesus said to him, ²⁸and Levi got up, left everything and followed him.

²⁹Then Levi held a great banquet for Jesus at his house, and a large crowd of tax collectors and others were eating with them. ³⁰But the Pharisees and the teachers of the law who belonged to their sect complained to his disciples, "Why do you eat and drink with tax collectors and sinners?"

Rather than embracing his widespread fame, Jesus escapes to the wilderness to commune with his Father (compare Lk 4:42). Luke's inclusion of this detail highlights distinctive features of Jesus' ministry: prayer, reliance on God the Father and a determination to do his will.

5:17–26 Luke includes this incident to show Jesus' authority to forgive sins, as well as the growing opposition from the scribes (teachers of the law) and Pharisees. Their initial charge of blasphemy against Jesus builds throughout Luke's Gospel (compare Mt 9:2–8; Mk 2:1–12).

5:17 Pharisees and teachers of the law The Pharisees were Jewish religious authorities (not priests) who promoted strict adherence to the Law of Moses (see note on Jn 7:32). Luke's reference to teachers of the law probably is synonymous with the group mentioned in Lk 5:21 (see note on 5:21). **the power of the Lord** The details of this verse are not found in Matthew's or Mark's account of the paralytic's healing. The presence of the Pharisees and the teachers of the law—along with the description of Yahweh's healing power being present in Jesus—sets the stage for Jesus' miracle and his subsequent dispute with the religious authorities.

5:19 lowered him on his mat through the tiles Luke's telling of this miracle reflects Mark's tradition and includes many details that Matthew omits. This part of the story shows the great faith of the paralytic and his attendants; they are willing to do whatever is necessary in order to reach Jesus. Luke's version of the story reflects his Hellenistic (Greek-speaking and cultured) orientation. While Mark merely says that the paralytic's attendants dug through the roof, Luke adds the detail about the tiles—a common feature of Hellenistic homes. The roofs of Palestinian homes in the first century consisted of wooden beams overlaid with foliage and sticks, covered by mud and clay. Such a roof could easily be dug through. Luke's addition to Mark's description probably is intended to make the account more intelligible to Luke's audience, which likely consisted of many Hellenistic Jewish and Gentile (non-Jewish) Christians. See the infographic "First-Century Israelite House" on p. 1658.

5:20 When Jesus saw their faith Jesus often associates faith and healing (e.g., 7:9,50; 8:48; 17:19; 18:42).
5:21 teachers of the law Refers to trained interpreters of the Law of Moses. In Luke, they are sometimes linked with the Pharisees (e.g., 6:7; 11:53) and sometimes with the chief priests (e.g., 19:47; 20:19; 22:2). **blasphemy** Sacrilegious or irreverent speech about God. Such an act—depending on the context of the offense—was punishable by death under the law (Lev 24:16). Only God had the authority to forgive sins. Since Israel's religious leadership did not regard Jesus to be Yahweh's Messiah—who could speak with the authority of God—they considered his words blasphemous. In their minds, Jesus was usurping a role that belonged only to God.
5:23 Which is easier: to say The effects of forgiving sins could not be verified, but a miracle could be. In the verse that follows, Jesus takes the harder option and tells the man to stand up and walk. This exchange with the Pharisees sets up the healing to demonstrate Jesus' authority to forgive sins.
5:24 the Son of Man has authority The theme of this section. The title Son of Man can convey several meanings; Jesus uses it here with Messianic connotations (see Mt 8:20 and note).
5:27–32 Continuing a theme from the birth narratives, this account of Levi's calling as a disciple identifies Jesus with the marginalized (see note on Lk 2:8). Jesus' association with those on the fringes of Jewish society is part of his overall mission (see 4:17 and note; 7:22). Compare Mt 9:9–13; Mk 2:13–17.
5:27 tax collector A profession associated with corruption, greed and sin. See note on Lk 3:12. **Levi** Another name for Matthew (compare Mt 9:9), one of Jesus' twelve disciples and author of the Gospel of Matthew. **Follow me** An invitation to discipleship.
5:30 eat and drink with tax collectors and sinners The religious leaders frequently criticize Jesus over his fellowship with people viewed as unrighteous outcasts (e.g., Lk 15:2; 19:7).

³¹Jesus answered them, "It is not the healthy who need a doctor, but the sick. ³²I have not come to call the righteous, but sinners to repentance."

Jesus Questioned About Fasting
5:33-39pp — Mt 9:14-17; Mk 2:18-22

³³They said to him, "John's disciples often fast and pray, and so do the disciples of the Pharisees, but yours go on eating and drinking." ³⁴Jesus answered, "Can you make the friends of the bridegroom fast while he is with them? ³⁵But the time will come when the bridegroom will be taken from them; in those days they will fast."

³⁶He told them this parable: "No one tears a piece out of a new garment to patch an old one. Otherwise, they will have torn the new garment, and the patch from the new will not match the old. ³⁷And no one pours new wine into old wineskins. Otherwise, the new wine will burst the skins; the wine will run out and the wineskins will be ruined. ³⁸No, new wine must be poured into new wineskins. ³⁹And no one after drinking old wine wants the new, for they say, 'The old is better.'"

Jesus Is Lord of the Sabbath
6:1-11pp — Mt 12:1-14; Mk 2:23-3:6

6 One Sabbath Jesus was going through the grainfields, and his disciples began to pick some heads of grain, rub them in their hands and eat the kernels. ²Some of the Pharisees asked, "Why are you doing what is unlawful on the Sabbath?"

³Jesus answered them, "Have you never read what David did when he and his companions were hungry? ⁴He entered the house of God, and taking the consecrated bread, he ate what is lawful only for priests to eat. And he also gave some to his companions." ⁵Then Jesus said to them, "The Son of Man is Lord of the Sabbath."

⁶On another Sabbath he went into the synagogue and was teaching, and a man was there whose right hand was shriveled. ⁷The Pharisees and the teachers of the law were looking for a reason to accuse Jesus, so they watched him closely to see if he would heal on the Sabbath. ⁸But Jesus knew what they were thinking and said to the man with the shriveled hand, "Get up and stand in front of everyone." So he got up and stood there.

5:31 healthy Refers to the Pharisees and scribes (teachers of the law), who were spiritually well in their own eyes. **a doctor** A reference to Jesus and his healing, reconciling ministry. **sick** Alludes to tax collectors and sinners (v. 30).

5:32 I have not come to call Jesus is not interested in the self-righteousness of the Pharisees. Rather, he seeks to redeem the outcasts of society and calls them to discipleship. Compare 15:7 and note.

5:33-39 Here, Jesus speaks about his ministry and mission, which is fundamentally incompatible with the ways of the Pharisees. The dialogue in vv. 29-32 is between Jesus and the religious leaders who were present at Levi's banquet. Although the content of this account is basically the same in Matthew, the conversation in Mt 9:14-17 takes place between Jesus and the disciples of John the Baptist; in Mark's account it is unclear whether only John's disciples are present or whether some Pharisees are also present (Mk 2:18-21). In all three versions, the conversation contains Jesus' first hint that he will be taken away, a veiled reference to his death.

5:33 fast Abstention from food for religious purposes.
5:34 Jesus answered Jesus presents three brief metaphors. In the first, he uses the story of a bridegroom to show that his ministry is a reason to celebrate. Similar imagery occurs in Rev 19:6-9.
5:35 when the bridegroom will be taken Jesus alludes to his crucifixion.
5:36 a piece out of a new garment Removing a section of the new garment would ruin it while not sufficiently helping the old garment.
5:37 new wine into old wineskins New wineskins are slightly elastic, allowing them to accommodate the fermentation process without rupturing. See note on Mt 9:17.
5:39 The old is better This saying is found only in Luke. Jesus' point seems to be that those who are content with the current way of doing things tend to resist anything new—even when it involves God's work of salvation.

6:1-5 This is the first of two accounts in ch. 6 in which Jesus claims authority over the Sabbath. This section, and vv. 6-11, show the priority of human needs over religious observance (compare Mt 12:1-8; Mk 2:23-27).
6:2 Pharisees See note on Lk 5:17. **what is unlawful on the Sabbath** The law did not specifically prohibit plucking heads of grain. Rather, the Pharisees apparently viewed this activity as harvesting, which violated the command against working on the Sabbath (Ex 20:8-11; 34:21). See note on Jn 5:10.
6:3 what David did Refers to the events of 1Sa 21:1-6. In this passage David does something unlawful when he and his companions eat the bread of Presence (see Lev 24:5-9). Although this OT story did not take place on the Sabbath, Jesus uses it to show that it is permissible to carry out unlawful acts for the purpose of meeting human needs (compare Mk 2:27). Jesus also draws attention to David's authority in the narrative to demonstrate his own authority as the Son of Man (see note on Lk 6:5).
6:5 The Son of Man David possessed the authority to set aside the law to fulfill his mission, but Jesus' authority is even greater than David's. As the Son of Man, Jesus has unique authority to interpret matters of the law, such as keeping the Sabbath. See Mt 8:20 and note.

6:6-11 Jesus' healing of a man's withered hand serves as a second demonstration of his superiority over the Sabbath (compare Mt 12:9-14; Mk 3:1-6). Luke separates this incident from the previous one (Lk 6:1-5) by noting that it occurred on a different day, while Matthew more closely connects the events (Mt 12:9). Jesus' point remains the same as in Lk 6:1-5: People's needs trump legal observance. The scribes (teachers of the law) and Pharisees react with condemnation. While Luke's language in v. 11 about their response is somewhat ambiguous, Matthew reports clearly that the Pharisees plotted to kill Jesus (Mt 12:14).

6:7 teachers of the law See note on Lk 5:21. **heal on the Sabbath** The scribes (teachers of the law) and Pharisees show no interest in the man's condition; they

⁹Then Jesus said to them, "I ask you, which is lawful on the Sabbath: to do good or to do evil, to save life or to destroy it?"

¹⁰He looked around at them all, and then said to the man, "Stretch out your hand." He did so, and his hand was completely restored. ¹¹But the Pharisees and the teachers of the law were furious and began to discuss with one another what they might do to Jesus.

The Twelve Apostles

6:13-16pp — Mt 10:2-4; Mk 3:16-19; Ac 1:13

¹²One of those days Jesus went out to a mountainside to pray, and spent the night praying to God. ¹³When morning came, he called his disciples to him and chose twelve of them, whom he also designated apostles: ¹⁴Simon (whom he named Peter), his brother Andrew, James, John, Philip, Bartholomew, ¹⁵Matthew, Thomas, James son of Alphaeus, Simon who was called the Zealot, ¹⁶Judas son of James, and Judas Iscariot, who became a traitor.

Blessings and Woes

6:20-23pp — Mt 5:3-12

¹⁷He went down with them and stood on a level place. A large crowd of his disciples was there and a great number of people from all over Judea, from Jerusalem, and from the coastal region around Tyre and Sidon, ¹⁸who had come to hear him and to be healed of their diseases. Those troubled by impure spirits were cured, ¹⁹and the people all tried to touch him, because power was coming from him and healing them all.

²⁰Looking at his disciples, he said:

"Blessed are you who are poor,
    for yours is the kingdom of God.
²¹ Blessed are you who hunger now,
    for you will be satisfied.
Blessed are you who weep now,
    for you will laugh.
²² Blessed are you when people hate you,
    when they exclude you and insult you
    and reject your name as evil,
        because of the Son of Man.

²³"Rejoice in that day and leap for joy, because great is your reward in heaven. For that is how their ancestors treated the prophets.

²⁴"But woe to you who are rich,
    for you have already received your
        comfort.
²⁵ Woe to you who are well fed now,
    for you will go hungry.

---

are focused on whether Jesus will violate the Sabbath. In their view, the Sabbath is an inappropriate day to seek or perform healing—which they ostensibly regard as a form of work (compare Lk 13:14). See note on Jn 5:16.

6:12–16 This is the first of two lists in Luke's writings that give the names of the twelve apostles (compare Ac 1:13). Similar lists occur in Mt 10:1–4; Mk 3:16–19. Although the order of the twelve apostles varies across the lists in Matthew, Mark and Luke, all three give priority to Peter and mention Judas Iscariot last. See the table "The Twelve Apostles" on p. 1550.

6:12 spent the night praying Before choosing the apostles, Jesus seeks solitude and conversation with God the Father. Luke often describes Jesus praying before major events (e.g., Lk 3:21; 9:18; 22:39–46).
6:13 twelve Likely meant to reflect the 12 tribes of Israel. **apostles** The Greek word used here comes from a verb meaning "to send out" (compare Mk 3:14).
6:15 Matthew Earlier called "Levi" (see Lk 5:27 and note). **Simon who was called the Zealot** Matthew and Mark describe Simon with the Greek word *kananaios*, which comes from an Aramaic word meaning "an enthusiast" (Mt 10:4; Mk 3:18). Luke here uses the Greek term *zēlōtēs*, which has a similar meaning. This could describe Jewish anti-Roman activists, but they likely did not originate as a distinct political group until shortly before the Roman-Jewish War of AD 66–70.
6:16 Judas son of James Matthew, Mark and Luke agree on the names of the twelve disciples, with one exception: Luke includes Judas son of James, whereas Matthew and Mark list Thaddeus. "Judas" probably reflects the original name, which was changed to "Thaddeus" to avoid association and confusion with Judas Iscariot, who later betrays Jesus (Lk 22:3–6,47–48). Luke, then, likely reflects an earlier tradition than Matthew or Mark. **who became a traitor** See 22:3–6.

6:17–23 The rest of ch. 6 consists of the Sermon on the Plain, which seems to consist of excerpts of Jesus' most famous sermon, the Sermon on the Mount, recorded in Mt 5:1–7:28. Whereas Matthew describes Jesus delivering very similar teaching on a mountain (Mt 5:1), Luke refers to a level place (Lk 6:17). Luke could be reworking the account that occurs in Matthew for thematic reasons, highlighting the aspects of the sermon most applicable to his audience, and framing Jesus' words based on how they were applied to a broader audience. However, it remains possible that Luke is describing a different sermon than Matthew; given the itinerant nature of Jesus' ministry, he could have delivered the same teachings, with just slight changes, on different occasions. Luke also records some unique material (see 6:24–26 and note).

6:17 a great number of people from all over Judea Compare Mt 4:23—5:2; Mk 3:7–8.
6:19 power was coming from him Mark records a specific occurrence of this (Mk 5:30).
6:20 Blessed are you who are poor In Luke, these beatitudes focus on the socioeconomic conditions of first-century Palestine. In Matthew, they suggest a more spiritualized application (see Mt 5:3 and note).
6:21 Blessed are you who hunger Matthew refers to those who hunger and thirst for righteousness (see Mt 5:6 and note). **Blessed are you who weep** Refers to those who mourn over the brokenness of the present world and the suffering it causes. They will experience great joy when God's kingdom arrives in full, upon Jesus' second coming. See Mt 5:4 and note.
6:22 because of the Son of Man Jesus praises both those who suffer for the sake of doing what is right (see Mt 5:10; 5:11 and note), and also those who experience persecution because of their allegiance to Jesus himself.
6:23 great is your reward in heaven Throughout Luke's

Woe to you who laugh now,
  for you will mourn and weep.
26 Woe to you when everyone speaks well of you,
  for that is how their ancestors treated the
    false prophets.

Love for Enemies

6:29,30pp — Mt 5:39-42

27 "But to you who are listening I say: Love your enemies, do good to those who hate you, 28 bless those who curse you, pray for those who mistreat you. 29 If someone slaps you on one cheek, turn to them the other also. If someone takes your coat, do not withhold your shirt from them. 30 Give to everyone who asks you, and if anyone takes what belongs to you, do not demand it back. 31 Do to others as you would have them do to you.

32 "If you love those who love you, what credit is that to you? Even sinners love those who love them. 33 And if you do good to those who are good to you, what credit is that to you? Even sinners do

that. 34 And if you lend to those from whom you expect repayment, what credit is that to you? Even sinners lend to sinners, expecting to be repaid in full. 35 But love your enemies, do good to them, and lend to them without expecting to get anything back. Then your reward will be great, and you will be children of the Most High, because he is kind to the ungrateful and wicked. 36 Be merciful, just as your Father is merciful.

Judging Others

6:37-42pp — Mt 7:1-5

37 "Do not judge, and you will not be judged. Do not condemn, and you will not be condemned. Forgive, and you will be forgiven. 38 Give, and it will be given to you. A good measure, pressed down, shaken together and running over, will be poured into your lap. For with the measure you use, it will be measured to you."

39 He also told them this parable: "Can the blind lead the blind? Will they not both fall into a pit?

Gospel, Jesus contrasts earthly and heavenly rewards (e.g., Lk 12:21,33; 16:11; 18:22).

6:24–26 Unlike Matthew, Luke includes woes to accompany the Beatitudes — these are commonly called antitheses to the Beatitudes. Using a common apocalyptic motif, Jesus declares that the present circumstances of the rich and poor will be reversed in the future.

6:24 you have already received your comfort Refers to their comfortable lifestyles, in contrast to the conditions of Galilean peasants.

6:26 the false prophets In contrast to God's true prophets, who were mistreated and killed. Those most deserving of death — the false prophets — were allowed to live.

6:27–36 This section draws on the same material as Matthew (compare Mt 5:38–48; Mt 7:12 and note). Jesus emphasizes love, charity and goodness — traits that should characterize the people of God as residents of his kingdom. The version in Luke's Gospel reorganizes and slightly expands the material. The love command is moved to the front (Lk 6:27) and then it is elaborated on below (v. 35). The version in Luke also inserts the Golden Rule (v. 31), which Matthew records much later in the sermon (Mt 7:12). Luke's version concludes with a command to reflect God's mercy (Lk 6:36); in Matthew, Jesus calls for emulating God's perfection (see Mt 5:48 and note).

6:27 Love your enemies Jesus teaches his followers that they must love all people, including their enemies (compare Lev 19:18). This love involves more than tolerance; it expresses itself in doing good even to enemies who are hostile and full of hatred. See Mt 5:44 and note.

6:30 Give to everyone who asks you See Mt 5:42 and note.

6:31 Do to others This is known as the Golden Rule: treating others with respect regardless of their conduct. In comparison to similar expressions recorded in ancient writings, Jesus' version of this rule emphasizes its positive effect. He demands that his followers show love to all people — neighbors and enemies alike — regardless of their behavior toward them. See Mt 7:12 and note.

6:35 love your enemies, do good to them, and lend A summary statement for this section that is unique to Luke. **your reward will be great** Followers of Jesus who freely give away and share their material goods not only obey Jesus' teaching but demonstrate they are true followers of God by acting according to his ways. See note on Lk 6:23.

6:36 Be merciful, just as your Father is merciful God's character and actions are the ethical standards for his followers. Compare Lev 19:2; Dt 10:17–18; Mt 5:48; 1Pe 1:15.

6:37–42 This section parallels several traditions that also occur in Mark and Matthew — some of these occur in Matthew's Sermon on the Mount (compare note on Lk 6:17–23). As in the preceding section, Jesus is calling for righteous behavior and emphasizing love, forgiveness and generosity.

6:37 Do not judge, and you will not be judged See Mt 7:2 and note. **Forgive, and you will be forgiven** In response to God's forgiveness of them, Jesus' followers should offer forgiveness to those who have wronged them. As with his teaching in Lk 6:27–36, Jesus calls his followers to imitate God by displaying sacrificial love. See Mt 6:14–15.

6:38 good measure, pressed down, shaken together and running over, will be poured into your lap This statement has no parallel in Matthew. It describes the abundance that is given to the generous. This saying describes a generous (or good) measuring process. First, an ingredient — such as barley — is placed into a measuring jar or basket and compacted to maximize space. Next, the jar or basket is shaken, causing the ingredient to shift down into any open spaces. The measuring continues until the jar or basket is overflowing. Its contents are then dumped into the lap of the recipient, into the fold of the outer garment that was used to transport goods (e.g., Ru 3:15). Such generosity would come to those who themselves were generous. Jesus has already rebuked wealth for wealth's sake (Lk 6:24–26), which means he has a larger purpose in view here: those who give receive, because their generosity is recognized

⁴⁰The student is not above the teacher, but everyone who is fully trained will be like their teacher.

⁴¹"Why do you look at the speck of sawdust in your brother's eye and pay no attention to the plank in your own eye? ⁴²How can you say to your brother, 'Brother, let me take the speck out of your eye,' when you yourself fail to see the plank in your own eye? You hypocrite, first take the plank out of your eye, and then you will see clearly to remove the speck from your brother's eye.

A Tree and Its Fruit

6:43,44pp — Mt 7:16,18,20

⁴³"No good tree bears bad fruit, nor does a bad tree bear good fruit. ⁴⁴Each tree is recognized by its own fruit. People do not pick figs from thornbushes, or grapes from briers. ⁴⁵A good man brings good things out of the good stored up in his heart, and an evil man brings evil things out of the evil stored up in his heart. For the mouth speaks what the heart is full of.

The Wise and Foolish Builders

6:47-49pp — Mt 7:24-27

⁴⁶"Why do you call me, 'Lord, Lord,' and do not do what I say? ⁴⁷As for everyone who comes to me and hears my words and puts them into practice, I will show you what they are like. ⁴⁸They are like a man building a house, who dug down deep and laid the foundation on rock. When a flood came, the torrent struck that house but could not shake it, because it was well built. ⁴⁹But the one who hears my words and does not put them into practice is like a man who built a house on the ground without a foundation. The moment the torrent struck that house, it collapsed and its destruction was complete."

The Faith of the Centurion

7:1-10pp — Mt 8:5-13

7 When Jesus had finished saying all this to the people who were listening, he entered Capernaum. ²There a centurion's servant, whom his master valued highly, was sick and about to die. ³The centurion heard of Jesus and sent some elders of the Jews to him, asking him to come and heal his servant. ⁴When they came to Jesus, they pleaded earnestly with him, "This man deserves to have you do this, ⁵because he loves our nation and has built our synagogue." ⁶So Jesus went with them.

He was not far from the house when the centurion sent friends to say to him: "Lord, don't trouble yourself, for I do not deserve to have you come under my roof. ⁷That is why I did not even consider myself worthy to come to you. But say the word, and my servant will be healed. ⁸For I myself am a man under authority, with soldiers under me. I tell this one, 'Go,' and he goes; and that one, 'Come,' and he comes. I say to my servant, 'Do this,' and he does it."

(by God and others) and because they are the kind of people who will continue to give. **it will be measured** See Mt 7:2 and note.

6:39 parable A short, vivid story designed to teach an important truth. See the table "Parables of Jesus" on p. 1584. **Can the blind lead the blind** Jesus implies that unqualified (or still apprenticing) leaders are unfit to lead God's people since they cannot yet fully understand God's purposes. The reference to blindness likely refers to living out of self-interest rather than love for others (Lk 6:37–38). Those who lead God's people must embody and display his sacrificial love. Compare Mt 15:14 and note.

6:40 student is not above the teacher Compare Mt 10:24.

6:41 Why do you look at the speck of sawdust in your brother's eye In Lk 6:41–42, Jesus uses a ridiculous exaggeration to convey the importance of confronting one's own sinfulness before God. This teaching also appears in Mt 7:3–5.

6:43–49 Matthew's parallel passages — about the sources of righteous and evil behavior and the houses built on sand and rock — appear in Mt 7:15–27.

6:45 what the heart is full of The contents of a person's heart are made manifest through their speech.

6:46 Lord, Lord A confession of Jesus' authority. Jesus states that this confession is meaningless unless it is accompanied by obedience to his commands.

6:48 When a flood came See Mt 7:25 and note.

6:49 it collapsed and its destruction was complete People who choose to build their lives on something other than Jesus will ultimately experience anguish. See Mt 7:27 and note.

7:1–10 The report of Jesus healing the centurion's slave demonstrates that not just Jews, but also Gentiles (non-Jews), can have faith that is acceptable to Jesus (compare Mt 8:5–13). By including narratives like this one, Luke continues to support his central theme that Jesus is the Messiah for the whole world (see Lk 2:10 and note).

7:1 Capernaum See note on 4:31. This fishing village on the northern shore of the Sea of Galilee served as Jesus' base of operations during his public ministry.

7:2 centurion's A centurion was a Roman military officer in charge of roughly 80 soldiers.

7:3 sent some elders of the Jews Since he was a Gentile (non-Jew), the centurion sent Jewish leaders to vouch for him to Jesus, a Jewish teacher.

7:4 deserves The elders' opinion of the centurion is based on his generosity to the Jewish community. The centurion himself recognizes that he is not worthy (vv. 6–7).

7:6 I do not deserve Coming from a leader in the Roman occupying force, this would have been a shocking expression of reverence toward a Jewish teacher. The centurion probably was aware that a Jew who entered a Gentile's house became ritually unclean and thus doing so would have been a serious inconvenience for a Jewish person like Jesus (compare Ac 10:28 and note).

7:8 a man under authority The centurion recognizes that Jesus has considerable authority over sickness, similar to his own authority within the military chain of command.

⁹When Jesus heard this, he was amazed at him, and turning to the crowd following him, he said, "I tell you, I have not found such great faith even in Israel." ¹⁰Then the men who had been sent returned to the house and found the servant well.

Jesus Raises a Widow's Son

7:11-16Ref — 1Ki 17:17-24; 2Ki 4:32-37; Mk 5:21-24,35-43; Jn 11:1-44

¹¹Soon afterward, Jesus went to a town called Nain, and his disciples and a large crowd went along with him. ¹²As he approached the town gate, a dead person was being carried out — the only son of his mother, and she was a widow. And a large crowd from the town was with her. ¹³When the Lord saw her, his heart went out to her and he said, "Don't cry."

¹⁴Then he went up and touched the bier they were carrying him on, and the bearers stood still. He said, "Young man, I say to you, get up!" ¹⁵The dead man sat up and began to talk, and Jesus gave him back to his mother.

¹⁶They were all filled with awe and praised God. "A great prophet has appeared among us," they said. "God has come to help his people." ¹⁷This news about Jesus spread throughout Judea and the surrounding country.

Jesus and John the Baptist

7:18-35pp — Mt 11:2-19

¹⁸John's disciples told him about all these things. Calling two of them, ¹⁹he sent them to the Lord to ask, "Are you the one who is to come, or should we expect someone else?"

²⁰When the men came to Jesus, they said, "John the Baptist sent us to you to ask, 'Are you the one who is to come, or should we expect someone else?'"

²¹At that very time Jesus cured many who had diseases, sicknesses and evil spirits, and gave sight to many who were blind. ²²So he replied to the messengers, "Go back and report to John what you have seen and heard: The blind receive sight, the lame walk, those who have leprosy[a] are cleansed, the deaf hear, the dead are raised, and the good news is proclaimed to the poor. ²³Blessed is anyone who does not stumble on account of me."

²⁴After John's messengers left, Jesus began to speak to the crowd about John: "What did you go out into the wilderness to see? A reed swayed by the wind? ²⁵If not, what did you go out to see? A man dressed in fine clothes? No, those who wear expensive clothes and indulge in luxury are in palaces. ²⁶But what did you go out to see? A prophet? Yes, I tell you, and more than a prophet. ²⁷This is the one about whom it is written:

"'I will send my messenger ahead of you,
who will prepare your way before you.'[b]

²⁸I tell you, among those born of women there is no one greater than John; yet the one who is least in the kingdom of God is greater than he."

²⁹(All the people, even the tax collectors, when

---

[a] 22 The Greek word traditionally translated *leprosy* was used for various diseases affecting the skin.   [b] 27 Mal. 3:1

7:9 such great faith This statement, praising one of Israel's foreign rulers, would not have been well received by Jesus' Jewish listeners. Jesus frequently links faith and healing (compare Lk 5:20).

7:11–17 This is the first incident of Jesus raising someone from the dead in Luke's Gospel. The episode portrays Jesus like Israel's great prophets, as he restores life to a woman's son — a miracle also performed by Elijah and Elisha. See the table "Miracles of Jesus" on p. 1741.

7:11 Nain Approximately 20 miles southwest of Capernaum.
7:12 was being carried out Graveyards were typically located outside the city walls for the sake of ritual cleanliness (see Nu 5:1–4; 19:11–20). **she was a widow** With no husband or sons, the widow's means of provision were gone. She would be forced to rely on the charity of her neighbors and struggle for her livelihood.
7:13 his heart went out Jesus is moved to action due to her suffering and destitution. The Greek word used here, *splanchnizomai*, occurs in Luke two other times, both in parables: The father has compassion when his wayward son returns (Lk 15:20), and the Samaritan has compassion on the injured man (10:33).
7:16 A great prophet has appeared among us Accounts of Elijah and Elisha raising sons from the dead appear in 1Ki 17:17–24; 2Ki 4:32–37. The parallel between Jesus and Elijah is a prominent theme in Matthew (see Mt 16:14 and note).

7:18–35 In this section, John the Baptist sends his disciples to question Jesus about his Messianic identity (compare Mt 11:1–19). Jesus takes the opportunity to praise John to his listeners, rebuking those who failed to heed John's message.

7:18 all these things Refers to the events in Lk 7:11–17 and probably Jesus' other reported teachings and healings (e.g., those recorded in chs. 4–6).
7:19 Are you the one who is to come A legitimate question, since John is in prison at this time.
7:22 report to John what you have seen and heard Rather than answering John's question directly, Jesus points to his works that fulfill Isaiah's prophecies related to the Messiah (e.g., Isa 26:19; 29:18; 35:5–6; 42:18; 61:1). This is a further example of Luke portraying Jesus as the Messiah figure in Isaiah (see Lk 1:27 and note).
7:23 who does not stumble on account of me Jesus is aware that his message is difficult for some to accept; this is partly because Jesus did not fulfill the Messianic expectations of his day — people were hoping for a ruler who would overthrow Rome (see Mt 11:6 and note).
7:26 more than a prophet John was not only a prophet; he was the forerunner to the Messiah. See Mt 11:9 and note.
7:27 I will send my messenger ahead of you A quotation of the prophecy of Mal 3:1 (see Mt 3:3 and note).
7:28 no one greater Jesus emphasizes the superiority of God's kingdom, contrasting heavenly greatness with

they heard Jesus' words, acknowledged that God's way was right, because they had been baptized by John. ³⁰But the Pharisees and the experts in the law rejected God's purpose for themselves, because they had not been baptized by John.)

³¹Jesus went on to say, "To what, then, can I compare the people of this generation? What are they like? ³²They are like children sitting in the marketplace and calling out to each other:

"'We played the pipe for you,
    and you did not dance;
we sang a dirge,
    and you did not cry.'

³³For John the Baptist came neither eating bread nor drinking wine, and you say, 'He has a demon.' ³⁴The Son of Man came eating and drinking, and you say, 'Here is a glutton and a drunkard, a friend of tax collectors and sinners.' ³⁵But wisdom is proved right by all her children."

Jesus Anointed by a Sinful Woman

7:37-39Ref — Mt 26:6-13; Mk 14:3-9; Jn 12:1-8
7:41,42Ref — Mt 18:23-34

³⁶When one of the Pharisees invited Jesus to have dinner with him, he went to the Pharisee's house and reclined at the table. ³⁷A woman in that town who lived a sinful life learned that Jesus was eating at the Pharisee's house, so she came

there with an alabaster jar of perfume. ³⁸As she stood behind him at his feet weeping, she began to wet his feet with her tears. Then she wiped them with her hair, kissed them and poured perfume on them.

³⁹When the Pharisee who had invited him saw this, he said to himself, "If this man were a prophet, he would know who is touching him and what kind of woman she is — that she is a sinner."

⁴⁰Jesus answered him, "Simon, I have something to tell you."

"Tell me, teacher," he said.

⁴¹"Two people owed money to a certain moneylender. One owed him five hundred denarii,ᵃ and the other fifty. ⁴²Neither of them had the money to pay him back, so he forgave the debts of both. Now which of them will love him more?"

⁴³Simon replied, "I suppose the one who had the bigger debt forgiven."

"You have judged correctly," Jesus said.

⁴⁴Then he turned toward the woman and said to Simon, "Do you see this woman? I came into your house. You did not give me any water for my feet, but she wet my feet with her tears and wiped them with her hair. ⁴⁵You did not give me a kiss, but this woman, from the time I entered, has not stopped kissing my feet. ⁴⁶You did not

ᵃ 41 A denarius was the usual daily wage of a day laborer (see Matt. 20:2).

---

earthly greatness. John was great because he had prepared for the Messiah; now the Messiah and his kingdom are here, offering a far greater ministry of righteousness. Compare Mt 11:11.

7:30 Pharisees and the experts in the law See note on Lk 5:17. **rejected God's purpose for themselves** Refers to a rejection of God's plan for salvation. John's baptism had announced a new era in God's redemptive work — the coming of the Messiah and the inauguration of the kingdom of God.

7:32 We played the pipe for you Jesus may be quoting some common children's song of the time. Jesus' imagery here describes the refusal to participate in God's unfolding kingdom, which involves both celebration and judgment. Compare Mt 11:17 and note.

7:33 neither eating bread Possibly refers to fasting (see Lk 5:33). **nor drinking wine** This might refer to John's Nazirite vow (see Nu 6:1–4).

7:34 eating and drinking Jesus did not fast like the disciples of John (see Lk 5:33), and he was not under a Nazirite vow like John was. Furthermore, he was known for dining with tax collectors and sinners — those whom he clearly says he came to save (see 5:27–32). The Jewish religious leaders rejected the ministries of both John and Jesus.

7:35 wisdom is proved right by all her children This likely reflects a proverbial saying in Jesus' day — essentially meaning that a teaching is shown to be wise based on what it produces (compare 6:44). The OT personifies divine wisdom as addressing her children (e.g., Pr 8:1–36). Jesus seems to be saying that his and John's accomplishments ultimately will confirm God's wisdom in sending them to fulfill his plan for salvation.

Another possibility is that Jesus is portraying himself as the personification of divine wisdom (compare note on Jn 1:1).

7:36–50 Luke reports a woman anointing Jesus' feet and pairs this scene with a parable about forgiveness. Matthew places this event just before the Last Supper and portrays it as related to Judas' betrayal (Mt 26:6–13; compare Mk 14:3–9).

7:36 one of the Pharisees Although Jesus often rebuked the self-righteousness of Israel's religious leaders, they were not always antagonistic toward one another.

7:37 an alabaster jar of perfume A costly item. Mark and John both record its cost as 300 denarii (roughly a year's wages for a laborer; Mk 14:5; Jn 12:3).

7:39 what kind of woman The Pharisee's comment here might indicate that the woman was a prostitute.

7:40 Simon In Matthew's account, this refers to Simon the Leper, a Pharisee who might have been cured of leprosy by Jesus (see Mt 26:6 and note).

7:41 denarii The denarius was the usual daily wage for a laborer. A debt of 500 denarii was seemingly insurmountable. See the infographic "A Silver Denarius" on p. 1578.

7:42 which of them will love him more Rather than making the point himself, Jesus prompts Simon to give an answer that condemns his own attitude. Jesus uses this same tactic with the parable of the good Samaritan (Lk 10:36–37).

7:43 one who had the bigger debt forgiven The parable reflects the scene. The woman, who appeared to be in great need of forgiveness, expresses her love and appreciation more than the Pharisee, who likely thought that he needed little or no forgiveness (compare v. 47).

put oil on my head, but she has poured perfume on my feet. [47]Therefore, I tell you, her many sins have been forgiven—as her great love has shown. But whoever has been forgiven little loves little."

[48]Then Jesus said to her, "Your sins are forgiven."

[49]The other guests began to say among themselves, "Who is this who even forgives sins?"

[50]Jesus said to the woman, "Your faith has saved you; go in peace."

The Parable of the Sower

8:4-15pp — Mt 13:2-23; Mk 4:1-20

8 After this, Jesus traveled about from one town and village to another, proclaiming the good news of the kingdom of God. The Twelve were with him, [2]and also some women who had been cured of evil spirits and diseases: Mary (called Magdalene) from whom seven demons had come out; [3]Joanna the wife of Chuza, the manager of Herod's household; Susanna; and many others. These women were helping to support them out of their own means.

[4]While a large crowd was gathering and people were coming to Jesus from town after town,

he told this parable: [5]"A farmer went out to sow his seed. As he was scattering the seed, some fell along the path; it was trampled on, and the birds ate it up. [6]Some fell on rocky ground, and when it came up, the plants withered because they had no moisture. [7]Other seed fell among thorns, which grew up with it and choked the plants. [8]Still other seed fell on good soil. It came up and yielded a crop, a hundred times more than was sown."

When he said this, he called out, "Whoever has ears to hear, let them hear."

[9]His disciples asked him what this parable meant. [10]He said, "The knowledge of the secrets of the kingdom of God has been given to you, but to others I speak in parables, so that,

"'though seeing, they may not see;
  though hearing, they may not understand.'[a]

[11]"This is the meaning of the parable: The seed is the word of God. [12]Those along the path are the ones who hear, and then the devil comes and takes away the word from their hearts, so that they may not believe and be saved. [13]Those on the

---

[a] 10 Isaiah 6:9

7:49 Who is this who even forgives sins Forgiveness of sins could be granted by God alone. See 5:21 and note.
7:50 Your faith has saved you Jesus often recognizes faith as the catalyst for healing and salvation (see note on 5:20).
8:1–3 This chapter begins by noting Jesus' proclamation of the kingdom of God and summarizing several healings and exorcisms.
8:1 the kingdom of God Jesus signals that his life represents God's reign being established in a new way. See Mt 3:2 and note; note on Mk 1:15. **The Twelve** Refers to the apostles (see Lk 6:13–16).
8:2 some women In a patriarchal culture, such as Jesus', women were often mistreated and undervalued; in contrast, Jesus welcomes them among his followers. This seems to have been unusual for a rabbi; it seems rabbis mainly had male disciples. Throughout his Gospel, Luke highlights Jesus' concern for people on the fringes of Jewish society. So far, through the life of Jesus, God has shown his love to shepherds, a barren woman, a peasant girl, Gentiles, a tax collector, the ceremonially unclean and the sick and unwell, among others. In the immediately preceding passage (7:36–50), Luke recounts Jesus' forgiveness and acceptance of a woman who might have been a prostitute (see note on 7:39). Toward the end of Luke, Jesus' resurrection is announced first to a group of women (23:55—24:10). **Mary (called Magdalene)** Apparently from the town of Magdala on the western shore of the Sea of Galilee, not far from Capernaum. See the infographic "The Synagogue at Magdala" on p. 1681.
8:3 many others The Greek phrase used here appears in the feminine form, indicating that Luke is referring specifically to women. **helping to support them out of their own means** Refers to financial support, as well as food and lodging (compare Mt 27:55).

8:4–15 In one of his best-known parables, Jesus describes four responses to his preaching about the kingdom (Lk 8:4–8); he then explains the meaning (vv. 9–15). There are parallel accounts in the other Synoptic Gospels (compare Mt 13:1–23; Mk 4:1–20).
8:6 because they had no moisture Matthew states that the soil was shallow (see Mt 13:5 and note). Luke clarifies the statement, but the meaning is the same: The plants did not have sufficient root depth to absorb moisture.
8:8 let them hear With this closing phrase, Jesus is calling on his audience to do more than hear; he wants them to understand and apply his teaching. The Greek verb used here, meaning "to hear" (*akouō*), is closely related to the verb meaning "to obey" (*hypakouō*). In the Septuagint (the ancient Greek translation of the OT), *akouō* is used to translate Hebrew and Aramaic terms that call for obedience to God; this conceptual overlap between hearing and obeying is reflected in Luke's use of *akouō*. In Acts (also written by Luke), Peter and John state that they must listen (*akouō*) to God rather than the Jewish leaders (Ac 4:19). Compare Mk 9:7; Jn 10:8,16.
8:10 though seeing, they may not see In another quotation of Isaiah, Jesus compares his ministry with that of the OT prophets (see Isa 6:9–10; compare Jer 5:21; Eze 12:2). In the same way that Israel rejected Isaiah's message centuries earlier, many Jews reject Jesus' teaching. They are unable to see the truth about God's kingdom concealed within his parables.
8:11 word of God In the context of Jesus' ministry in the Gospels, "God's word" or "word of God" typically refers to Jesus' teaching about God's kingdom.
8:12 Those along the path The seed described in Lk 8:5. The enemy who devours the seed is the devil, who is successful in preventing some people who hear Jesus' proclamation from believing it.

rocky ground are the ones who receive the word with joy when they hear it, but they have no root. They believe for a while, but in the time of testing they fall away. [14] The seed that fell among thorns stands for those who hear, but as they go on their way they are choked by life's worries, riches and pleasures, and they do not mature. [15] But the seed on good soil stands for those with a noble and good heart, who hear the word, retain it, and by persevering produce a crop.

A Lamp on a Stand

[16] "No one lights a lamp and hides it in a clay jar or puts it under a bed. Instead, they put it on a stand, so that those who come in can see the light. [17] For there is nothing hidden that will not be disclosed, and nothing concealed that will not be known or brought out into the open. [18] Therefore consider carefully how you listen. Whoever has will be given more; whoever does not have, even what they think they have will be taken from them."

Jesus' Mother and Brothers

8:19-21pp — Mt 12:46-50; Mk 3:31-35

[19] Now Jesus' mother and brothers came to see him, but they were not able to get near him because of the crowd. [20] Someone told him, "Your mother and brothers are standing outside, wanting to see you."

[21] He replied, "My mother and brothers are those who hear God's word and put it into practice."

Jesus Calms the Storm

8:22-25pp — Mt 8:23-27; Mk 4:36-41
8:22-25Ref — Mk 6:47-52; Jn 6:16-21

[22] One day Jesus said to his disciples, "Let us go over to the other side of the lake." So they got into a boat and set out. [23] As they sailed, he fell asleep. A squall came down on the lake, so that the boat was being swamped, and they were in great danger.

[24] The disciples went and woke him, saying, "Master, Master, we're going to drown!"

He got up and rebuked the wind and the raging waters; the storm subsided, and all was calm. [25] "Where is your faith?" he asked his disciples.

In fear and amazement they asked one another, "Who is this? He commands even the winds and the water, and they obey him."

Jesus Restores a Demon-Possessed Man

8:26-37pp — Mt 8:28-34
8:26-39pp — Mk 5:1-20

[26] They sailed to the region of the Gerasenes,[a] which is across the lake from Galilee. [27] When Jesus stepped ashore, he was met by a demon-possessed man from the town. For a long time this man had not worn clothes or lived in a house, but had lived in the tombs. [28] When he saw Jesus, he cried out and fell at his feet, shouting at the top of his voice, "What do you want with me, Jesus, Son of the Most High God? I beg you, don't torture me!" [29] For Jesus had commanded the impure spirit to come

a 26 Some manuscripts Gadarenes; other manuscripts Gergesenes; also in verse 37

8:13 Those on the rocky ground The seed described in v. 6. They initially receive the kingdom message but quickly abandon it when testing comes.
8:14 fell among thorns The seed described in v. 7. For these people, the cares and pursuits of their culture prevent their growth and choke out their faith.
8:15 the seed on good soil The seed described in v. 8. These people receive Jesus' message and give evidence of it in their lives.

8:16-18 This short parable presents three of Jesus' sayings about the response to his proclamation of the kingdom of God.

8:16 No one lights a lamp In Mt 5:14-16 Jesus uses this analogy to encourage his disciples to show their belief through their actions. It may indicate something similar here, although the lamp also could represent the mysteries of God's kingdom (Lk 8:10) or the word of God (v. 11).
8:17 there is nothing hidden that will not be disclosed Likely refers to the mysteries of the kingdom of God (v. 10). Compare Mt 10:26 and note.
8:18 Whoever has will be given more Compare Mt 13:12 and note; 25:29 and note.

8:19-21 Continuing the theme of obedience, Jesus identifies his true family as those who hear the word of God and do it. Compare Mt 12:46-50; Mk 3:31-35.

8:21 who hear God's word The people in God's family are identified by their obedience to God's will (see Lk 2:49).

8:22-25 The first part of this chapter deals with responses to Jesus' teaching about the kingdom of God. In the second part, Luke provides three examples of Jesus' power and authority over every realm of existence. The first of these examples demonstrates Jesus' lordship over the forces of nature (compare Mt 8:23-27; Mk 4:35-41).

8:22 the lake Refers to the Sea of Galilee.
8:24 and all was calm In the ancient Near East, the sea represented the forces of chaos; Jews believed the sea could only be controlled by Yahweh. Jesus' command over the storm signals his divine authority.
8:25 Who is this Questions about Jesus' identity are a recurring theme in Luke (see Lk 4:22 and note).

8:26-39 Luke shows Jesus' power over the forces of the spiritual realm. There are parallel accounts of this exorcism in the other Synoptic Gospels (compare Mt 8:28-34; Mk 5:1-20).
8:26 the region of the Gerasenes Refers to Gadara, southeast of the Sea of Galilee.
8:28 Son of the Most High God In contrast to Jesus' disciples (v. 25), the demons are well aware of Jesus' divine identity and authority.

out of the man. Many times it had seized him, and though he was chained hand and foot and kept under guard, he had broken his chains and had been driven by the demon into solitary places.

30 Jesus asked him, "What is your name?"

"Legion," he replied, because many demons had gone into him. 31 And they begged Jesus repeatedly not to order them to go into the Abyss.

32 A large herd of pigs was feeding there on the hillside. The demons begged Jesus to let them go into the pigs, and he gave them permission. 33 When the demons came out of the man, they went into the pigs, and the herd rushed down the steep bank into the lake and was drowned.

34 When those tending the pigs saw what had happened, they ran off and reported this in the town and countryside, 35 and the people went out to see what had happened. When they came to Jesus, they found the man from whom the demons had gone out, sitting at Jesus' feet, dressed and in his right mind; and they were afraid. 36 Those who had seen it told the people how the demon-possessed man had been cured. 37 Then all the people of the region of the Gerasenes asked Jesus to leave them, because they were overcome with fear. So he got into the boat and left.

38 The man from whom the demons had gone out begged to go with him, but Jesus sent him away, saying, 39 "Return home and tell how much God has done for you." So the man went away and told all over town how much Jesus had done for him.

Jesus Raises a Dead Girl and Heals a Sick Woman

8:40-56pp — Mt 9:18-26; Mk 5:22-43

40 Now when Jesus returned, a crowd welcomed him, for they were all expecting him. 41 Then a man named Jairus, a synagogue leader, came and fell at Jesus' feet, pleading with him to come to his house 42 because his only daughter, a girl of about twelve, was dying.

As Jesus was on his way, the crowds almost crushed him. 43 And a woman was there who had been subject to bleeding for twelve years,[a] but no one could heal her. 44 She came up behind him and touched the edge of his cloak, and immediately her bleeding stopped.

45 "Who touched me?" Jesus asked.

When they all denied it, Peter said, "Master, the people are crowding and pressing against you."

46 But Jesus said, "Someone touched me; I know that power has gone out from me."

47 Then the woman, seeing that she could not go unnoticed, came trembling and fell at his feet. In the presence of all the people, she told why she had touched him and how she had been instantly healed. 48 Then he said to her, "Daughter, your faith has healed you. Go in peace."

49 While Jesus was still speaking, someone came from the house of Jairus, the synagogue leader. "Your daughter is dead," he said. "Don't bother the teacher anymore."

50 Hearing this, Jesus said to Jairus, "Don't be afraid; just believe, and she will be healed."

51 When he arrived at the house of Jairus, he did not let anyone go in with him except Peter, John and James, and the child's father and mother. 52 Meanwhile, all the people were wailing and mourning for her. "Stop wailing," Jesus said. "She is not dead but asleep."

53 They laughed at him, knowing that she was dead. 54 But he took her by the hand and said, "My child, get up!" 55 Her spirit returned, and at once she stood up. Then Jesus told them to give her something to eat. 56 Her parents were astonished, but he ordered them not to tell anyone what had happened.

---

a 43 Many manuscripts *years, and she had spent all she had on doctors*

8:30 "Legion," he replied, because many demons had gone into him A Roman legion consisted of 5,000–6,000 troops, thus indicating a massive horde of demons. Luke and Mark include this detail, but Matthew omits it.

8:31 Abyss By the end of the first century AD—when much of the NT probably reached its final form—the Abyss became known as the place where God confines demons (see Rev 9:1–2; 2Pe 2:4 and note; Jude 6 and note; compare Rev 11:7; 17:8; 20:1).

8:33 and was drowned The demons apparently meet their demise along with the pigs.

8:35 at Jesus' feet Luke describes the man taking the place and posture of a learning disciple.

8:37 they were overcome with fear Luke's narrative notes that the people are afraid (compare Mt 8:34). It is not clear whether they are afraid of Jesus or perhaps of further conflict with demons should he remain in the area.

8:39 how much Jesus had done for him The man spread the news about God's saving power and the arrival of the Messiah. Jesus tells the man to proclaim all that God had done for him; Luke states that the man proclaimed all that Jesus had done for him. Luke regularly associates Jesus with Yahweh (see note on Lk 2:11).

8:40–56 Luke's third demonstration of Jesus' messiahship in this chapter involves two miracles. The first testifies to his power over sickness and the human body; the second shows his power over death. Parallel accounts appear in the other Synoptic Gospels (Mt 9:18–26; Mk 5:21–43).

8:42 only daughter The Greek text implies that she was Jairus' only child and heir, not merely his only daughter.

8:43 subject to bleeding for twelve years The exact nature of the woman's condition is unknown, but it would have rendered her unclean according to the law (see Lev 15:25–31). Luke, a physician himself, notes that no doctors were able to heal her. An ongoing discharge and perpetual impurity would have made the woman an outcast.

8:48 your faith has healed you See note on Lk 5:20.

8:51 except Peter, John and James These three disciples are portrayed as Jesus' inner circle, with an up-close view of his power and authority (compare 9:28–29).

Jesus Sends Out the Twelve

9:3-5pp — Mt 10:9-15; Mk 6:8-11
9:7-9pp — Mt 14:1,2; Mk 6:14-16

9 When Jesus had called the Twelve together, he gave them power and authority to drive out all demons and to cure diseases, ²and he sent them out to proclaim the kingdom of God and to heal the sick. ³He told them: "Take nothing for the journey — no staff, no bag, no bread, no money, no extra shirt. ⁴Whatever house you enter, stay there until you leave that town. ⁵If people do not welcome you, leave their town and shake the dust off your feet as a testimony against them." ⁶So they set out and went from village to village, proclaiming the good news and healing people everywhere.

⁷Now Herod the tetrarch heard about all that was going on. And he was perplexed because some were saying that John had been raised from the dead, ⁸others that Elijah had appeared, and still others that one of the prophets of long ago had come back to life. ⁹But Herod said, "I beheaded John. Who, then, is this I hear such things about?" And he tried to see him.

Jesus Feeds the Five Thousand

9:10-17pp — Mt 14:13-21; Mk 6:32-44; Jn 6:5-13
9:13-17Ref — 2Ki 4:42-44

¹⁰When the apostles returned, they reported to Jesus what they had done. Then he took them with him and they withdrew by themselves to a town called Bethsaida, ¹¹but the crowds learned about it and followed him. He welcomed them and spoke to them about the kingdom of God, and healed those who needed healing.

¹²Late in the afternoon the Twelve came to him and said, "Send the crowd away so they can go to the surrounding villages and countryside and find food and lodging, because we are in a remote place here."

¹³He replied, "You give them something to eat."

They answered, "We have only five loaves of bread and two fish — unless we go and buy food for all this crowd." ¹⁴(About five thousand men were there.)

But he said to his disciples, "Have them sit down in groups of about fifty each." ¹⁵The disciples did so, and everyone sat down. ¹⁶Taking the five loaves and the two fish and looking up to heaven, he gave thanks and broke them. Then he gave them to the disciples to distribute to the people. ¹⁷They all ate and were satisfied, and the disciples picked up twelve basketfuls of broken pieces that were left over.

Peter Declares That Jesus Is the Messiah

9:18-20pp — Mt 16:13-16; Mk 8:27-29
9:22-27pp — Mt 16:21-28; Mk 8:31 - 9:1

¹⁸Once when Jesus was praying in private and his disciples were with him, he asked them, "Who do the crowds say I am?"

8:55 Her spirit returned This is the second person raised from the dead by Jesus in Luke's Gospel (compare 7:15).
8:56 he ordered them not to tell anyone The reason behind this instruction is not clear. Earlier in the chapter, after Jesus drove out the legion of demons, he gave the opposite advice, encouraging the man to tell everyone what God had done (v. 39). The different approaches might be due to the nature of the miracle (casting out demons as opposed to raising the dead), or it might be due to the location and audience (a non-Jewish region east of the Sea of Galilee versus the mostly Jewish area around Capernaum).

9:1-6 In 6:13-16, Luke describes Jesus' call of the Twelve to discipleship. Here, he records their commissioning as apostles — representatives sent out to proclaim the message that Jesus has inaugurated the kingdom of God. There are parallel accounts in the other Synoptic Gospels (compare Mt 10:1-14; Mk 6:6-13).
9:1 authority to drive out all demons and to cure diseases These powerful signs will show the validity of the disciples' proclamation of the kingdom of God.
9:3 Take nothing for the journey They were to rely on God for their provisions.
9:4 stay there until you leave that town The Twelve should not be concerned with procuring better accommodations, which would be offensive to their hosts.
9:5 shake the dust off your feet A sign of protest and a warning of impending judgment (compare Ac 13:51; 18:6).

9:7-9 Some people regarded Jesus as John the Baptist risen from the dead; others viewed him as the OT prophet Elijah, who was expected to return someday (Mal 4:5). Herod, who beheaded John (Mt 14:1-12), was anxious to learn about the true identity of Jesus.

9:8 Elijah had appeared See note on Lk 9:19.
9:9 he tried to see him Herod's curiosity is finally satisfied when Pilate sends Jesus to Herod (23:6-12).

9:10-17 This section describes the return of the Twelve and the feeding of the 5,000. Luke reports only one mass feeding, but Matthew and Mark include two — the 5,000 (Mt 14:13-21; Mk 6:30-44) and the 4,000 (Mt 15:32-39; Mk 8:1-9). See the event line "Jesus' Early Life and Ministry" on p. 1530.

9:10 When the apostles returned Luke resumes the narrative from Lk 9:6. **Bethsaida** A village near Capernaum and the hometown of Peter, Andrew and Philip (Jn 1:44).
9:13 You give them Jesus sets the stage for the miracle to follow. **only five loaves of bread and two fish** This response highlights that Jesus' instruction must have seemed absurd to the apostles.
9:14 About five thousand men This estimate does not include women and children (compare Mt 14:21).

9:18-20 In light of the earlier discussion about Jesus' identity (Lk 9:7-9), Jesus asks his disciples what they have heard people saying. Then he asks for their opinion, and Peter responds correctly: Jesus is Yahweh's Messiah (compare Mt 16:13-19; Mk 8:27-29).
9:18 Who do the crowds say I am In Matthew, Jesus refers to the Son of Man when he asks this question,

¹⁹They replied, "Some say John the Baptist; others say Elijah; and still others, that one of the prophets of long ago has come back to life."

²⁰"But what about you?" he asked. "Who do you say I am?"

Peter answered, "God's Messiah."

Jesus Predicts His Death

²¹Jesus strictly warned them not to tell this to anyone. ²²And he said, "The Son of Man must suffer many things and be rejected by the elders, the chief priests and the teachers of the law, and he must be killed and on the third day be raised to life."

²³Then he said to them all: "Whoever wants to be my disciple must deny themselves and take up their cross daily and follow me. ²⁴For whoever wants to save their life will lose it, but whoever loses their life for me will save it. ²⁵What good is it for someone to gain the whole world, and yet lose or forfeit their very self? ²⁶Whoever is ashamed of me and my words, the Son of Man will be ashamed of them when he comes in his glory and in the glory of the Father and of the holy angels.

²⁷"Truly I tell you, some who are standing here will not taste death before they see the kingdom of God."

The Transfiguration

9:28-36pp — Mt 17:1-8; Mk 9:2-8

²⁸About eight days after Jesus said this, he took Peter, John and James with him and went up onto a mountain to pray. ²⁹As he was praying, the appearance of his face changed, and his clothes became as bright as a flash of lightning. ³⁰Two men, Moses and Elijah, appeared in glorious splendor, talking with Jesus. ³¹They spoke about his departure,ᵃ which he was about to bring to fulfillment at Jerusalem. ³²Peter and his companions were very sleepy, but when they became fully awake, they saw his glory and the two men standing with him. ³³As the men were leaving Jesus, Peter said to him,

ᵃ 31 Greek exodos

---

associating this apocalyptic, messianic figure with himself (Mt 16:13; compare Mt 8:20 and note).

9:19 Elijah The OT prophet Malachi had foretold that the return of Elijah would precede the day of judgment (Mal 4:5). Although Jesus' ministry may be compared to Elijah's, who was prophesied by Malachi as preceding the day of judgment, John the Baptist was the primary fulfillment of that prophecy (compare Mt 16:14; 17:11 and note). In Lk 4:25–26, Jesus implies that his mission, like Elijah's, includes the Gentiles (non-Jews). In 7:11–17, Jesus travels to Nain to raise the widow's son, which resembles Elijah's raising of the widow's son in Zarephath (1Ki 17). Jesus' statement in Lk 9:62 is similar to Elijah's prophetic call to Elisha (1Ki 19:19–21). The story of Elijah also is reflected in Lk 9:54, when two of Jesus' disciples ask about calling down fire from heaven (compare 2Ki 1:10,12).

9:20 God's Messiah Peter, perhaps acting as the group's spokesman, identifies Jesus as God's anointed one (see Lk 4:17–21).

9:21–22 As in Matthew and Mark, Peter's confession is followed immediately by Jesus' first prediction of his death and resurrection (compare Mt 16:20–21; Mk 8:30–31).

9:21 not to tell this to anyone Following his resurrection, Jesus' disciples would be commissioned to make known explicitly what his signs and wonders revealed — Jesus' identity as God's Son and anointed one. Compare Lk 8:56 and note.

9:23–27 This is Jesus' first discussion in Luke about the cost of discipleship (compare Mt 16:24–28; Mk 8:34—9:1). Jesus teaches more fully about this theme in Lk 14:25–35.

9:23 must deny themselves Refers to setting aside one's interests for the sake of God's kingdom. **take up their cross daily** Jesus' disciples must be willing to follow him every day, no matter what the cost. See note on Mt 10:38.

9:24 will lose it By seeking to avoid the potential hardships associated with following Jesus, a person ends up losing his or her life. Although the timeframe is not specified here, Jesus likely is referring to final judgment (see Lk 10:14 and note; 11:31,32). Jesus also seems to be referring to people losing out on relationship with God in general — the true meaning of life. **will save it** Those who embrace Jesus' call to discipleship — including the difficulties it brings — will be saved (compare Jn 3:16–17).

9:27 before they see the kingdom The precise meaning of Jesus' statement here is difficult to determine. See note on Mt 16:28.

9:28–36 Jesus ascends a mountain to pray and is transformed into his heavenly glory. Parallel accounts appear in the other Synoptic Gospels (Mt 17:1–9; Mk 9:2–10). Although all three Synoptic Gospels describe Jesus' transfiguration, Luke includes two unique details. First, he notes that Moses and Elijah were talking with Jesus about his mission in Jerusalem (Lk 9:31). Second, Luke states that Peter, James and John were exhausted (v. 32), perhaps from their trek up the mountain.

9:28 Peter, John and James See note on 8:51. **a mountain** Luke's account offers few geographical clues, but Matthew appears to place the transfiguration near Caesarea Philippi, a city located at the base of Mount Hermon, roughly 25 miles north of the Sea of Galilee. Another possibility is Mount Tabor, southwest of the Sea of Galilee.

9:29 As he was praying, the appearance of his face changed Recalls Moses' change in appearance when he met with God (Ex 34:29–30).

9:30 Moses and Elijah Moses received the law; Elijah was one of Israel's great prophets. This scene portrays Jesus' ministry as fulfilling those traditions. It also clarifies Jesus' identity: He is not Elijah or another ancient prophet; he is the Messiah — he is God incarnate (compare Lk 1:29–38; 9:19–20).

9:31 They spoke about his departure This element advances Luke's portrayal of Jesus' divine Messiahship: Jesus knew what awaited him in Jerusalem and that he would soon return to God the Father.

9:33 three shelters The Greek term used here refers to tents or another form of temporary dwelling.

"Master, it is good for us to be here. Let us put up three shelters — one for you, one for Moses and one for Elijah." (He did not know what he was saying.) 34While he was speaking, a cloud appeared and covered them, and they were afraid as they entered the cloud. 35A voice came from the cloud, saying, "This is my Son, whom I have chosen; listen to him." 36When the voice had spoken, they found that Jesus was alone. The disciples kept this to themselves and did not tell anyone at that time what they had seen.

Jesus Heals a Demon-Possessed Boy

9:37-42,43-45pp — Mt 17:14-18,22,23;
  Mk 9:14-27,30-32

37The next day, when they came down from the mountain, a large crowd met him. 38A man in the crowd called out, "Teacher, I beg you to look at my son, for he is my only child. 39A spirit seizes him and he suddenly screams; it throws him into convulsions so that he foams at the mouth. It scarcely ever leaves him and is destroying him. 40I begged your disciples to drive it out, but they could not."

41"You unbelieving and perverse generation," Jesus replied, "how long shall I stay with you and put up with you? Bring your son here."

42Even while the boy was coming, the demon threw him to the ground in a convulsion. But Jesus rebuked the impure spirit, healed the boy and gave him back to his father. 43And they were all amazed at the greatness of God.

Jesus Predicts His Death a Second Time

While everyone was marveling at all that Jesus did, he said to his disciples, 44"Listen carefully to what I am about to tell you: The Son of Man is going to be delivered into the hands of men." 45But they did not understand what this meant. It was hidden from them, so that they did not grasp it, and they were afraid to ask him about it.

46An argument started among the disciples as to which of them would be the greatest. 47Jesus, knowing their thoughts, took a little child and had him stand beside him. 48Then he said to them, "Whoever welcomes this little child in my name welcomes me; and whoever welcomes me welcomes the one who sent me. For it is the one who is least among you all who is the greatest."

49"Master," said John, "we saw someone driving out demons in your name and we tried to stop him, because he is not one of us."

50"Do not stop him," Jesus said, "for whoever is not against you is for you."

Samaritan Opposition

51As the time approached for him to be taken up to heaven, Jesus resolutely set out for Jerusalem. 52And he sent messengers on ahead, who went into a Samaritan village to get things ready for him; 53but the people there did not welcome him,

---

9:34 cloud In the OT, God's presence is often indicated by the appearance of a cloud (e.g., Ex 13:21–22; 19:9,16; Eze 10:4).

9:35 This is my Son For the second time in Luke, God directly affirms Jesus as his Son—the first being at Jesus' baptism (Lk 3:22); Gabriel also proclaimed this to Mary (1:32). Here, the voice addresses the disciples rather than Jesus (compare 3:22).

9:37–43 After the disciples are unable to heal a demon-possessed boy, his father implores Jesus to intervene. After critiquing the present generation for its weak faith, Jesus casts out the evil spirit. Parallel passages occur in the other Synoptic Gospels (Mt 17:14–21; Mk 9:14–29).

9:40 they could not Despite the power and authority the disciples received from Jesus (Lk 9:1), they cannot cast out the demon. In Mark's account, Jesus explains their inability (Mk 9:28–29).

9:41 You unbelieving and perverse generation See Mt 17:17 and note.

9:44–45 In Lk 9:22, Jesus predicted his death and resurrection; now he predicts his betrayal. Compare Mt 17:22–23; Mk 9:30–32.

9:45 It was hidden from them This insight is not recorded by Matthew or Mark.

9:46–48 Jesus perceives the disciples arguing over which of them is the greatest. He explains that the least among them is the greatest in God's kingdom. Compare Mt 18:1–5; Mk 9:33–37.

9:47 a little child Greco-Roman society regarded children as insignificant. Jesus calls the child to illustrate the reversal of values in God's kingdom (compare Lk 13:30; 14:12–14; Mt 18:2 and note).

9:49–50 Jesus tells his disciples not to hinder the ministry of others who follow Jesus differently than them. Compare Mk 9:38–41.

9:50 not against you is for you The ministry of God's kingdom is not exclusive to the Twelve; it is the responsibility of all of Jesus' followers.

9:51–56 Departing Galilee for Jerusalem, Jesus attempts to take the direct route through Samaria. When the Samaritans refuse to welcome him, James and John ask if he would like them to call down fire from heaven. Jesus rebukes his disciples and moves on. Luke is the only Gospel writer to include this account during Jesus' journey to Jerusalem. See the event line "Jesus' Journey to Jerusalem" on p. 1616.

9:51 for him to be taken up The Greek text here uses a noun (analēmpsis) that appears only this one time in the NT, but the related verb (analambanō) often refers to Jesus' ascension to heaven (e.g., Ac 1:11; 1Ti 3:16). Other verbs connoting upward movement are used in reference to Jesus' crucifixion and resurrection (e.g., Lk 24:34; Jn 3:14; 12:32–33). **resolutely set out for Jerusalem** This marks a major turning point in Luke's Gospel, as Jesus' ministry shifts from Galilee and advances toward Jerusalem and the cross. The long section that starts here is sometimes called Luke's travel narrative (Lk 9:51—19:27).

9:52 he sent messengers on ahead Probably due to the size of the crowd traveling with him. **Samaritan** Jews

because he was heading for Jerusalem. [54]When the disciples James and John saw this, they asked, "Lord, do you want us to call fire down from heaven to destroy them[a]?" [55]But Jesus turned and rebuked them. [56]Then he and his disciples went to another village.

The Cost of Following Jesus

9:57-60pp — Mt 8:19-22

[57]As they were walking along the road, a man said to him, "I will follow you wherever you go."

[58]Jesus replied, "Foxes have dens and birds have nests, but the Son of Man has no place to lay his head."

[59]He said to another man, "Follow me."

But he replied, "Lord, first let me go and bury my father."

[60]Jesus said to him, "Let the dead bury their own dead, but you go and proclaim the kingdom of God."

[61]Still another said, "I will follow you, Lord; but first let me go back and say goodbye to my family."

[62]Jesus replied, "No one who puts a hand to the plow and looks back is fit for service in the kingdom of God."

Jesus Sends Out the Seventy-Two

10:4-12pp — Lk 9:3-5
10:13-15,21,22pp — Mt 11:21-23,25-27
10:23,24pp — Mt 13:16,17

10 After this the Lord appointed seventy-two[b] others and sent them two by two ahead of him to every town and place where he was about to go. [2]He told them, "The harvest is plentiful, but the workers are few. Ask the Lord of the harvest, therefore, to send out workers into his harvest field. [3]Go! I am sending you out like lambs among wolves. [4]Do not take a purse or bag or sandals; and do not greet anyone on the road.

[5]"When you enter a house, first say, 'Peace to this house.' [6]If someone who promotes peace is there, your peace will rest on them; if not, it will return to you. [7]Stay there, eating and drinking whatever they give you, for the worker deserves his wages. Do not move around from house to house.

[8]"When you enter a town and are welcomed, eat what is offered to you. [9]Heal the sick who are there and tell them, 'The kingdom of God has come near to you.' [10]But when you enter a town and are not welcomed, go into its streets and say, [11]'Even the dust of your town we wipe from our feet as a warning to you. Yet be sure of this: The kingdom of God has come near.' [12]I tell you, it will be more bearable on that day for Sodom than for that town.

[13]"Woe to you, Chorazin! Woe to you, Bethsaida! For if the miracles that were performed in you had been performed in Tyre and Sidon, they would have repented long ago, sitting in sackcloth and ashes. [14]But it will be more bearable for Tyre and Sidon at the judgment than for you. [15]And you, Capernaum, will you be lifted to the heavens? No, you will go down to Hades.[c]

[a] 54 Some manuscripts *them, just as Elijah did*   [b] 1 Some manuscripts *seventy*; also in verse 17   [c] 15 That is, the realm of the dead

---

and Samaritans typically had a mutual hostility, based on ethnic, religious and political barriers. See note on 10:33; note on Jn 4:9.

9:53 he was heading for Jerusalem Samaritans worshiped on Mount Gerizim (compare Jn 4:20 and note). They viewed Jerusalem as an illegitimate center of worship and deterred Jewish pilgrims heading there from Galilee. Matthew seems to indicate that Jesus took a circuitous route to Jerusalem, crossing the Jordan River in order to avoid Samaria (see note on Mt 19:1).

9:54 fire down from heaven Reminiscent of Elijah (2Ki 1:9–16).

9:57–62 This episode combines several short sayings of Jesus. As he travels toward Jerusalem, people respond in various ways to his call for discipleship. Jesus emphasizes that his followers must be willing to face hardships and make sacrifices. Compare Mt 8:18–22.

9:60 Let the dead bury their own dead The call to discipleship takes precedence over all other duties. See note on Mt 8:22.

9:62 to the plow and looks back Followers of Jesus must have a singular focus on the work of God's kingdom. This may be an allusion to 1Ki 19:19–21.

10:1–20 Luke is the only Gospel to record disciples being sent ahead of Jesus on his way to Jerusalem. The material in this passage appears in Matthew in the commissioning of the Twelve (compare Mt 9:37–38; 10:7–16). The section concludes with more material

unique to Luke's Gospel: The disciples return and report their success to Jesus, who comments on Satan's downfall and his followers' authority.

10:1 the Lord appointed seventy-two others Some manuscripts report 70 disciples; others have 72. Appointed in addition to the Twelve, these disciples serve as heralds of Jesus' proclamation of the kingdom of God.

10:2 The harvest is plentiful, but the workers are few Describes the large number of people ready to receive Jesus' kingdom message and the relatively few people available to share the message of the kingdom of God. **to send out workers** Sets the stage for the instructions that follow.

10:4 Do not take a purse Compare Lk 9:3 and note.

10:6 someone who promotes peace Refers to a believer. Peace is used throughout Luke in reference to God's blessing (e.g., 2:14; 7:50; 8:48). **it will return to you** The initial greeting or blessing would not take effect on the house or its inhabitants.

10:7 Do not move around from house to house See 9:4 and note.

10:11 we wipe from our feet as a warning to you See 9:5 and note.

10:12 on that day Refers to the day of judgment (see v. 14 and note). **Sodom** A city destroyed by Yahweh along with Gomorrah (Ge 19:24). These cities are mentioned in the NT to illustrate divine judgment (e.g., Mt 10:15; Ro 9:29; 2Pe 2:6; Jude 7).

10:13 Chorazin A town near Capernaum. Jesus pro-

[16]"Whoever listens to you listens to me; whoever rejects you rejects me; but whoever rejects me rejects him who sent me."

[17]The seventy-two returned with joy and said, "Lord, even the demons submit to us in your name."

[18]He replied, "I saw Satan fall like lightning from heaven. [19]I have given you authority to trample on snakes and scorpions and to overcome all the power of the enemy; nothing will harm you. [20]However, do not rejoice that the spirits submit to you, but rejoice that your names are written in heaven."

[21]At that time Jesus, full of joy through the Holy Spirit, said, "I praise you, Father, Lord of heaven and earth, because you have hidden these things from the wise and learned, and revealed them to little children. Yes, Father, for this is what you were pleased to do.

[22]"All things have been committed to me by my Father. No one knows who the Son is except the Father, and no one knows who the Father is except the Son and those to whom the Son chooses to reveal him."

[23]Then he turned to his disciples and said privately, "Blessed are the eyes that see what you see. [24]For I tell you that many prophets and kings wanted to see what you see but did not see it, and to hear what you hear but did not hear it."

The Parable of the Good Samaritan
10:25-28pp — Mt 22:34-40; Mk 12:28-31

[25]On one occasion an expert in the law stood up to test Jesus. "Teacher," he asked, "what must I do to inherit eternal life?"

[26]"What is written in the Law?" he replied. "How do you read it?"

[27]He answered, "'Love the Lord your God with all your heart and with all your soul and with all your strength and with all your mind'[a]; and, 'Love your neighbor as yourself.'[b]"

[28]"You have answered correctly," Jesus replied. "Do this and you will live."

[29]But he wanted to justify himself, so he asked Jesus, "And who is my neighbor?"

[a] 27 Deut. 6:5   [b] 27 Lev. 19:18

---

nounces judgment against the residents of Chorazin, Bethsaida and Capernaum—people who had a front-row seat to Jesus' ministry and yet failed to believe (compare Mt 11:20–24). **Bethsaida** A town near Capernaum.
10:14 Tyre and Sidon Gentile (non-Jewish) cities on the Mediterranean coast, northwest of Galilee. Jesus is saying that the Gentiles living in these cities will fare better at the final judgment than the Jews of Chorazin and Bethsaida, who witnessed Jesus' ministry but rejected him. **at the judgment** Refers to the final judgment, when God will take account of humanity and deliver his people; associated in the OT with the day of the Lord (or day of Yahweh; see Joel 1:15 and note).
10:15 Capernaum The home base of Jesus' public ministry (see note on Lk 4:31). **you will go down to Hades** Jesus' statement echoes Isa 14:13–15, which originally was a taunt against the king of Babylon. The Greek word used here, *hadēs*, is used in substitution for the Hebrew word *she'ol*—the realm of the dead—originally used by Isaiah. *Hadēs* is the Greek equivalent of the realm of the dead (the netherworld). This echo—and the overall theme of people rejecting Jesus, which evokes this judgment—recalls Luke's frequent allusions to Isaiah (see Lk 1:27 and note). These allusions culminate with Jesus' crucifixion and resurrection as the epitome of the call of the suffering servant (Isa 53:10–12).
10:17 The seventy-two returned with joy An unspecified amount of time has passed since the conclusion of Jesus' discourse in Lk 10:16.
10:18 I saw Satan fall like lightning from heaven Jesus could be referencing a vision he has had of the future and Satan's final defeat (compare Rev 20:1–10). It may also be that Jesus is referencing an event that has occurred in the past—such as Satan's actual fall from God's presence when he rebelled (compare Isa 14:12), or some defeat of Satan that occurred during Jesus' lifetime. If this is a reference to Satan being defeated in some way during Jesus' lifetime, it could reference Jesus overcoming Satan during his temptation in the wilderness (Lk 4:1–13) or the efforts of Jesus' disciples

being a direct affront on Satan's efforts (compare v. 17). See note on Lk 4:2.
10:20 your names are written in heaven See Da 7:10 and note; Rev 3:5 and note.

10:21–24 In this section, Jesus pronounces a blessing on his disciples (compare Mt 11:25–27; 13:16–17).
10:21 little children Likely refers to Jesus' disciples, indicating status rather than age. Compare Mt 10:42.
10:22 All things have been committed to me Compare Mt 28:18.
10:24 to see what you see For centuries, the righteous among God's people had desired to see the arrival of God's kingdom (compare Lk 2:25–26).

10:25–37 In this episode, an expert on the law tests Jesus about how to inherit eternal life. Jesus' first answer speaks of loving God, while his second calls for loving people. After the lawyer questions him further, Jesus illustrates the heart of his ministry through the parable of the Good Samaritan, which is unique to the Luke's Gospel.

10:25 an expert in the law One trained in the Law of Moses; likely a Pharisee (see Jn 7:32 and note). **to test Jesus** To entrap Jesus in argumentation for the purpose of discrediting him (see Mt 22:36 and note).
10:26 in the Law Since he is conversing with a legal expert, Jesus appeals to the law.
10:27 Love the Lord your God The lawyer's answer parallels Jesus' teaching in Matthew and Mark about the greatest commandments (Mt 22:35–40; Mk 12:28–31). Compare Lev 19:18; Dt 6:5; Jos 22:5.
10:28 Do this and you will live These commands reflect the heart of Jesus' proclamation of the kingdom of God: love of God and love of neighbor.
10:29 wanted to justify himself The legal expert seeks to support his claim to be righteous (perhaps only in his own mind) and presses Jesus to define the term "neighbor." **And who is my neighbor** The legal expert's question and his own answer in Lk 10:37 frame the parable of the Good Samaritan.

³⁰In reply Jesus said: "A man was going down from Jerusalem to Jericho, when he was attacked by robbers. They stripped him of his clothes, beat him and went away, leaving him half dead. ³¹A priest happened to be going down the same road, and when he saw the man, he passed by on the other side. ³²So too, a Levite, when he came to the place and saw him, passed by on the other side. ³³But a Samaritan, as he traveled, came where the man was; and when he saw him, he took pity on him. ³⁴He went to him and bandaged his wounds, pouring on oil and wine. Then he put the man on his own donkey, brought him to an inn and took care of him. ³⁵The next day he took out two denarii^a and gave them to the innkeeper. 'Look after him,' he said, 'and when I return, I will reimburse you for any extra expense you may have.'

³⁶"Which of these three do you think was a neighbor to the man who fell into the hands of robbers?"

³⁷The expert in the law replied, "The one who had mercy on him."

Jesus told him, "Go and do likewise."

At the Home of Martha and Mary

³⁸As Jesus and his disciples were on their way, he came to a village where a woman named Martha opened her home to him. ³⁹She had a sister called Mary, who sat at the Lord's feet listening to what he said. ⁴⁰But Martha was distracted by all the preparations that had to be made. She came to him and asked, "Lord, don't you care that my sister has left me to do the work by myself? Tell her to help me!"

⁴¹"Martha, Martha," the Lord answered, "you are worried and upset about many things, ⁴²but few things are needed — or indeed only one.^{b} Mary has chosen what is better, and it will not be taken away from her."

Jesus' Teaching on Prayer

11:2-4pp — Mt 6:9-13
11:9-13pp — Mt 7:7-11

11 One day Jesus was praying in a certain place. When he finished, one of his disciples said to him, "Lord, teach us to pray, just as John taught his disciples."

²He said to them, "When you pray, say:

"'Father,^{c}
hallowed be your name,
your kingdom come.^{d}

---

^{a} 35 A denarius was the usual daily wage of a day laborer (see Matt. 20:2). ^{b} 42 Some manuscripts *but only one thing is needed* ^{c} 2 Some manuscripts *Our Father in heaven* ^{d} 2 Some manuscripts *come. May your will be done on earth as it is in heaven.*

10:30 was going down The road from Jerusalem and Jericho dropped roughly 3,500 feet over about 10 miles.
10:31 A priest Refers to a religious leader of Israel. Priests performed sacrifices, maintained the temple and provided instruction. **he passed by on the other side** Demonstrating his lack of compassion for the injured man. Since the priest was leaving Jerusalem (and likely the temple), it is unlikely that he was concerned primarily with matters of ritual purity.
10:32 Levite Refers to a member of the tribe of Levi. The Levites served in various functions in the temple.
10:33 Samaritan Jews and Samaritans despised each other (see note on 9:52). For Jesus' audience, the idea of a good Samaritan would have been a contradiction. **he took pity on him** With a Samaritan playing the positive role — and a priest and Levite in negative roles — Jesus' parable would have been shocking. It shows the extreme universality of the term "neighbor" and demonstrates the depths of mercy that should be extended to all people.

SAMARITANS
The people of Samaria were of mixed Israelite and foreign descent, so the Jewish people did not accept them as part of the Jewish community (see note on Jn 4:9). The hostilities between Jews and Samaritans dated all the way back to the late sixth century BC. The Samaritans worshiped Yahweh and used a version of the Pentateuch as their Scripture, but they worshiped on Mount Gerizim, not in Jerusalem. Thus the Samaritans were despised by Jews for both ethnic and religious reasons; there was mutual hatred by the Samaritans toward Jews.

10:34 oil and wine To promote healing and prevent infection.
10:35 took out two denarii This amount of money would have paid for roughly two months in the inn, which might indicate the severity of the beaten man's condition.
10:37 The one who had mercy on him Jesus' parable prompts the lawyer to consider what it means to be a neighbor to someone rather than how to identify who is to be considered a neighbor. This exchange is similar to Jesus' earlier conversation with Simon the Pharisee (7:39–43). **Go and do likewise** Jesus' response implies that all people are to be treated as neighbors — with mercy and compassion.

10:38–42 Also unique to Luke, this account introduces Martha and Mary, two of Jesus' supporters and friends. The Gospel of John elaborates on Jesus' friendship with these women and their brother, Lazarus (e.g., Jn 11:1–44).

10:38 to a village Bethany, about half a mile east of Jerusalem (Jn 11:1).
10:39 sat at the Lord's feet The posture of a learning disciple.
10:40 by all the preparations Likely making provisions for Jesus and his followers.
10:41 Martha, Martha The double use of her name serves as a gentle rebuke.
10:42 few things are needed — or indeed only one While the work Martha is doing is important, it is not the most important thing — Jesus himself is. **what is better** Mary has chosen to listen and learn as a disciple — spending time in Jesus' presence. **will not be taken away from her** A relationship with Jesus cannot be stolen from a person. Jesus is pleased that Mary is learning from him and that her focus is on time with him. Jesus had made a similar point earlier about concerns that his disciples did not fast — there

³Give us each day our daily bread.
⁴Forgive us our sins,
    for we also forgive everyone who sins
        against us.ᵃ
And lead us not into temptation.ᵇ'"

⁵Then Jesus said to them, "Suppose you have a friend, and you go to him at midnight and say, 'Friend, lend me three loaves of bread; ⁶a friend of mine on a journey has come to me, and I have no food to offer him.' ⁷And suppose the one inside answers, 'Don't bother me. The door is already locked, and my children and I are in bed. I can't get up and give you anything.' ⁸I tell you, even though he will not get up and give you the bread because of friendship, yet because of your shameless audacityᶜ he will surely get up and give you as much as you need.

⁹"So I say to you: Ask and it will be given to you; seek and you will find; knock and the door will be opened to you. ¹⁰For everyone who asks receives; the one who seeks finds; and to the one who knocks, the door will be opened.

¹¹"Which of you fathers, if your son asks forᵈ a fish, will give him a snake instead? ¹²Or if he asks for an egg, will give him a scorpion? ¹³If you then, though you are evil, know how to give good gifts to your children, how much more will your Father in heaven give the Holy Spirit to those who ask him!"

Jesus and Beelzebul

11:14,15,17-22,24-26pp — Mt 12:22,24-29,43-45
11:17-22pp — Mk 3:23-27

¹⁴Jesus was driving out a demon that was mute. When the demon left, the man who had been mute spoke, and the crowd was amazed. ¹⁵But some of them said, "By Beelzebul, the prince of demons, he is driving out demons." ¹⁶Others tested him by asking for a sign from heaven.

¹⁷Jesus knew their thoughts and said to them: "Any kingdom divided against itself will be ruined, and a house divided against itself will fall. ¹⁸If Satan is divided against himself, how can his kingdom stand? I say this because you claim that I drive out demons by Beelzebul. ¹⁹Now if I drive out demons by Beelzebul, by whom do your followers drive them out? So then, they will be your judges. ²⁰But if I drive out demons by the finger of God, then the kingdom of God has come upon you.

²¹"When a strong man, fully armed, guards his own house, his possessions are safe. ²²But when someone stronger attacks and overpowers him, he takes away the armor in which the man trusted and divides up his plunder.

ᵃ 4 Greek *everyone who is indebted to us*   ᵇ 4 Some manuscripts *temptation, but deliver us from the evil one*   ᶜ 8 Or *yet to preserve his good name*   ᵈ 11 Some manuscripts *for bread, will give him a stone? Or if he asks for*

---

he noted that time celebrating with him is the focus of his disciples (Lk 5:34).

11:1–13 This section presents Jesus' discourse on prayer. A disciple asks him how to pray and Jesus responds. He assures the disciples that their heavenly Father will hear and respond accordingly. Jesus' teaching begins with Luke's version of the Lord's Prayer. Compare Mt 6:9–13; 7:7–11; Lk 18:1–5.

11:1 just as John taught his disciples Refers to John the Baptist.

11:4 Forgive us our sins Matthew's version of the Lord's Prayer speaks of forgiveness for debts; metaphorically, sin and debt are related — sin functions like a debt before God and others (Mt 6:12). Luke conveys this idea in the prayer's next line.

11:5 Suppose you have a friend Jesus employs a parable to instruct his disciples to pray with persistence and with faith.

11:6 I have no food In Israel's culture of hospitality, hosts were expected to feed their guests.

11:7 my children and I are in bed The image is one of a single-room house or a dwelling where the sleeping quarters were confined to one room — usually on an elevated platform above the main floor. To meet the friend's request would cause the entire family to be disturbed.

11:8 because of your shameless audacity Refers to the friend requesting bread. His persistence illustrates how Jesus' disciples should pray.

11:9 Ask With all three commands in this verse, Jesus encourages his followers to anticipate God's generosity and kindness.

11:11 Which of you fathers Jesus asks rhetorical questions to set up his closing remark about giving good gifts (Lk 11:13).

11:13 how much more Since sinful parents know how to provide for their children, God can be expected to do abundantly more — even pouring out his Spirit upon his children.

11:14–23 Jesus' healing of a demon-possessed man elicits mixed responses. Some people are amazed; some accuse him of using satanic power to perform his exorcisms. Compare Mt 12:22–30; Mk 3:22–27.

11:15 Beelzebul Refers to a Canaanite deity associated with Satan and demons (see note on Mt 10:25).

11:18 If Satan is divided against himself By explicitly linking Satan and Beelzebul (Lk 11:15), Jesus exposes a flaw in his accusers' logic: If Satan were enabling exorcisms, he would be weakening his own demonic forces.

11:19 by whom do your followers drive them out Jesus turns the tables on his accusers, asking them where Jewish exorcists get their power to drive out demons. Some Jews practiced incantations intended to ward off or remove evil spirits; for example, among the Dead Sea Scrolls (ca. 250 BC–AD 50), an incantation text commonly called Aramaic Exorcism was discovered.

11:20 the kingdom of God has come upon you Jesus' exorcisms are signs of his authority and the arrival of God's kingdom.

11:22 someone stronger Refers to Jesus, who defeats the strong man (Satan) and scatters his plunder. Jesus' victory over Satan offers people a life freed from the powerful grip of evil.

²³"Whoever is not with me is against me, and whoever does not gather with me scatters.

²⁴"When an impure spirit comes out of a person, it goes through arid places seeking rest and does not find it. Then it says, 'I will return to the house I left.' ²⁵When it arrives, it finds the house swept clean and put in order. ²⁶Then it goes and takes seven other spirits more wicked than itself, and they go in and live there. And the final condition of that person is worse than the first."

²⁷As Jesus was saying these things, a woman in the crowd called out, "Blessed is the mother who gave you birth and nursed you."

²⁸He replied, "Blessed rather are those who hear the word of God and obey it."

The Sign of Jonah

11:29-32pp — Mt 12:39-42

²⁹As the crowds increased, Jesus said, "This is a wicked generation. It asks for a sign, but none will be given it except the sign of Jonah. ³⁰For as Jonah was a sign to the Ninevites, so also will the Son of Man be to this generation. ³¹The Queen of the South will rise at the judgment with the people of this generation and condemn them, for she came from the ends of the earth to listen to Solomon's wisdom; and now something greater than Solomon is here. ³²The men of Nineveh will stand up at the judgment with this generation and condemn

it, for they repented at the preaching of Jonah; and now something greater than Jonah is here.

The Lamp of the Body

11:34,35pp — Mt 6:22,23

³³"No one lights a lamp and puts it in a place where it will be hidden, or under a bowl. Instead they put it on its stand, so that those who come in may see the light. ³⁴Your eye is the lamp of your body. When your eyes are healthy,ᵃ your whole body also is full of light. But when they are unhealthy,ᵇ your body also is full of darkness. ³⁵See to it, then, that the light within you is not darkness. ³⁶Therefore, if your whole body is full of light, and no part of it dark, it will be just as full of light as when a lamp shines its light on you."

Woes on the Pharisees and the Experts in the Law

³⁷When Jesus had finished speaking, a Pharisee invited him to eat with him; so he went in and reclined at the table. ³⁸But the Pharisee was surprised when he noticed that Jesus did not first wash before the meal.

³⁹Then the Lord said to him, "Now then, you Pharisees clean the outside of the cup and dish,

---

ᵃ 34 The Greek for *healthy* here implies *generous*.
ᵇ 34 The Greek for *unhealthy* here implies *stingy*.

11:24–28 Jesus tells of a disembodied spirit who returns to its host and causes even more trouble. In Matthew's parallel account (Mt 12:43–45), this passage serves as a parable of condemnation against the present generation for rejecting Jesus and his message of God's kingdom (see note on Mt 12:45). Luke, however, seems to take Jesus' remarks as a literal reference to demonic activity; this interpretation is supported by the passage's proximity to Jesus' defense of his exorcisms (Lk 11:14–23).

11:24 arid places Demons were thought in some parts of Judaism to reside in the desert, where God's life-giving blessings were considered to be scarce (compare Isa 13:21; 34:14). **house** Refers to the person whom the spirit previously inhabited.
11:26 worse than the first See note on Mt 12:45.
11:27 Blessed is the mother who gave you birth An echo of what Mary, the mother of Jesus, has already articulated about her own role (Lk 1:48). As Jesus is moving toward his death, he states the inverse of the woman's cry, pronouncing that someday those who are childless will be called blessed (23:29).
11:28 who hear the word of God and obey True blessedness, according to Jesus, is found in obedience to God's revelation (compare 8:21).

11:29–32 Jesus rebukes his generation for its lack of faith. Compare Mt 12:38–42; Mk 8:11–12.

11:29 a wicked generation The majority of people in Jesus' generation choose not to trust him, even though reports about him were surely circulating. **the sign of Jonah** In Matthew, this clearly alludes to Jesus' resurrection on the third day, which parallels the prophet Jonah's

deliverance after spending three days in the great fish (see Mt 12:39 and note; compare Lk 24:7; Jnh 1:17). Luke's account of this teaching is more ambiguous. Here, the sign of Jonah might reflect Matthew's understanding, or it could refer to Jonah's message of divine judgment and the Ninevites' repentance (Lk 11:30,32; Jnh 3:1–5). This would hint at Jesus delivering a simple message of repentance and mainly foreigners hearing it. This aligns with Luke's emphasis on non-Jewish people accepting Jesus and what occurs in the book of Acts.
11:31 The Queen of the South A reference to the Queen of Sheba (1Ki 10:1–13; 2Ch 9:1–12). **something greater** Refers to Jesus himself, the Messiah.
11:32 Nineveh An Assyrian city on the Tigris River. God commanded Jonah to preach judgment and repentance to the people of Nineveh (Jnh 1:2; 3:1–5).

11:33–36 Jesus uses imagery of light and darkness to teach about the kingdom of God (compare Mt 5:15; 6:22–23; Mk 4:21; see note on 1Jn 2:1–11).

11:33 No one lights a lamp See Lk 8:16 and note.
11:35 light within you is not darkness Light and darkness are often used as metaphors for the spiritual condition.

11:37–54 Reflecting the light and darkness imagery of the previous passage, Jesus' remarks here highlight the importance of sincere obedience over religious pretense. This section combines two episodes recounted in Matthew and Mark. The first involves the dispute over ceremonial washing before meals (Mt 15:1–9; Mk 7:1–8). The second is Jesus' condemnation of the scribes (teachers of the law) and Pharisees (Mt 23:1–36).

11:37 Pharisee See note on Lk 5:17.

but inside you are full of greed and wickedness. ⁴⁰You foolish people! Did not the one who made the outside make the inside also? ⁴¹But now as for what is inside you — be generous to the poor, and everything will be clean for you.

⁴²"Woe to you Pharisees, because you give God a tenth of your mint, rue and all other kinds of garden herbs, but you neglect justice and the love of God. You should have practiced the latter without leaving the former undone.

⁴³"Woe to you Pharisees, because you love the most important seats in the synagogues and respectful greetings in the marketplaces.

⁴⁴"Woe to you, because you are like unmarked graves, which people walk over without knowing it."

⁴⁵One of the experts in the law answered him, "Teacher, when you say these things, you insult us also."

⁴⁶Jesus replied, "And you experts in the law, woe to you, because you load people down with burdens they can hardly carry, and you yourselves will not lift one finger to help them.

⁴⁷"Woe to you, because you build tombs for the prophets, and it was your ancestors who killed them. ⁴⁸So you testify that you approve of what your ancestors did; they killed the prophets, and you build their tombs. ⁴⁹Because of this, God in his wisdom said, 'I will send them prophets and apostles, some of whom they will kill and others they will persecute.' ⁵⁰Therefore this generation will be held responsible for the blood of all the prophets that has been shed since the beginning of the world, ⁵¹from the blood of Abel to the blood of Zechariah, who was killed between the altar and the sanctuary. Yes, I tell you, this generation will be held responsible for it all.

⁵²"Woe to you experts in the law, because you have taken away the key to knowledge. You yourselves have not entered, and you have hindered those who were entering."

⁵³When Jesus went outside, the Pharisees and the teachers of the law began to oppose him fiercely and to besiege him with questions, ⁵⁴waiting to catch him in something he might say.

Warnings and Encouragements

12:2-9pp — Mt 10:26-33

12 Meanwhile, when a crowd of many thousands had gathered, so that they were trampling on one another, Jesus began to speak first to his disciples, saying: "Be^a on your guard against the yeast of the Pharisees, which is hypocrisy. ²There is nothing concealed that will not be disclosed, or hidden that will not be made known. ³What you have said in the dark will be heard in the daylight, and what you have whispered in the ear in the inner rooms will be proclaimed from the roofs.

⁴"I tell you, my friends, do not be afraid of those who kill the body and after that can do no more. ⁵But I will show you whom you should fear: Fear him who, after your body has been killed, has authority to throw you into hell. Yes, I tell you, fear

---

^a 1 Or *speak to his disciples, saying: "First of all, be*

11:38 did not first wash Washing one's hands before eating is not required in the Law of Moses, but was part of the Pharisees' tradition (see Mt 15:2).

11:39 clean the outside Jesus contrasts external purity (proper behavior) with internal cleansing (transformation of the heart).

11:42 your mint, rue and all other kinds of garden herbs These examples of tithing illustrate the Pharisees' meticulous attention to the smallest details of the Law of Moses. **justice and the love of God** Echoes the two greatest commandments (Lk 10:27–28), as well as the teaching of the prophets (e.g., Isa 1:17; Jer 22:3; Zec 7:9–10; Mic 6:8).

11:44 unmarked graves A metaphor for the Pharisees' pious appearances, which disguised their inner wickedness (compare Lk 11:39). When graves were not appropriately marked, people could walk over them and potentially become ritually unclean (see Nu 5:2; 19:11–13).

11:46 with burdens they can hardly carry Compare Mt 23:4; 15:2 and note.

11:47 you build tombs for the prophets See Mt 23:29–36.

11:51 blood of Abel to the blood of Zechariah Jesus seems to be referring to all of the righteous people of the OT who were killed unjustly. See note on Mt 23:35.

12:1–12 Jesus issues a series of warnings for his disciples. Following his condemnation of the Pharisees in Lk 11, Jesus now warns his disciples not to be led astray by their hypocrisy (compare Mt 16:5–6; Mk 8:14–15). He then tells them not to fear those who threaten violence, but rather to fear God, who will decide their eternal destiny (compare Mt 10:26–33). Jesus also teaches his disciples about making a proper confession and the peril of speaking against the Holy Spirit (compare Mt 10:19–20; 12:31–32; Mk 3:28–30; 13:11).

12:1 yeast The Greek word used here refers to fermented dough that was mixed in with new dough and used as a rising agent. The small amount used in baking would permeate the entire batch of new dough. Leaven serves as an apt metaphor to describe the widespread effects of the Pharisees' hypocritical teachings and actions. **Pharisees** See note on Lk 5:17.

12:2 concealed that will not be disclosed Jesus seems to be referring to the Pharisees' hidden sins, which will be exposed at the final judgment (compare Rev 20:11–15).

12:4 not be afraid of those who kill Perhaps a reference to Israel's religious leaders, who were plotting against Jesus (Lk 11:53–54).

12:5 him who, after your body has been killed, has authority Refers to God and final judgment. **hell** The Greek word used here, *gehenna*, may refer to a valley near Jerusalem associated with fiery judgment (see note on 3:9). Early in Israel's history, the Valley of Hinnom became synonymous with idolatry and child sacrifice due to the actions of kings Ahaz and Manasseh (2Ch 28:3; 33:6). Josiah attempted to

him. ⁶Are not five sparrows sold for two pennies? Yet not one of them is forgotten by God. ⁷Indeed, the very hairs of your head are all numbered. Don't be afraid; you are worth more than many sparrows.

⁸"I tell you, whoever publicly acknowledges me before others, the Son of Man will also acknowledge before the angels of God. ⁹But whoever disowns me before others will be disowned before the angels of God. ¹⁰And everyone who speaks a word against the Son of Man will be forgiven, but anyone who blasphemes against the Holy Spirit will not be forgiven.

¹¹"When you are brought before synagogues, rulers and authorities, do not worry about how you will defend yourselves or what you will say, ¹²for the Holy Spirit will teach you at that time what you should say."

The Parable of the Rich Fool

¹³Someone in the crowd said to him, "Teacher, tell my brother to divide the inheritance with me."

¹⁴Jesus replied, "Man, who appointed me a judge or an arbiter between you?" ¹⁵Then he said to them, "Watch out! Be on your guard against all kinds of greed; life does not consist in an abundance of possessions."

¹⁶And he told them this parable: "The ground of a certain rich man yielded an abundant harvest. ¹⁷He thought to himself, 'What shall I do? I have no place to store my crops.'

¹⁸"Then he said, 'This is what I'll do. I will tear down my barns and build bigger ones, and there I will store my surplus grain. ¹⁹And I'll say to myself, "You have plenty of grain laid up for many years. Take life easy; eat, drink and be merry."'

²⁰"But God said to him, 'You fool! This very night your life will be demanded from you. Then who will get what you have prepared for yourself?'

²¹"This is how it will be with whoever stores up things for themselves but is not rich toward God."

Do Not Worry

12:22-31pp — Mt 6:25-33

²²Then Jesus said to his disciples: "Therefore I tell you, do not worry about your life, what you will eat; or about your body, what you will wear. ²³For life is more than food, and the body more than clothes. ²⁴Consider the ravens: They do not sow or reap, they have no storeroom or barn; yet God feeds them. And how much more valuable you are than birds! ²⁵Who of you by worrying can add a single hour to your life*ᵃ*? ²⁶Since you cannot do this very little thing, why do you worry about the rest?

²⁷"Consider how the wild flowers grow. They do not labor or spin. Yet I tell you, not even Solomon in all his splendor was dressed like one of these. ²⁸If that is how God clothes the grass

---

ᵃ 25 Or single cubit to your height

---

reverse this trend (2Ki 23:10). However, Baal worship had been instituted again by the time of the prophet Jeremiah (Jer 2:23; 7:31–32). In the time of Jesus, Jews recognized this valley as the place that represented judgment on the enemies of God and Israel (Isa 30:29–33; 66:24; Joel 3:2,12,14). The valley is often designated *gehenna*, a Greek transliteration of its Hebrew name.

12:6 not one of them is forgotten Jesus' point here relates to suffering; the disciples must not fear their trials because God is watching over them.

12:9 before the angels of God A reference to the divine council present at the final judgment.

12:10 blasphemes against the Holy Spirit This likely refers to denying the Spirit's power, what God has revealed in Jesus, or perhaps claiming that the Spirit's power is somehow associated with evil forces. Compare Mt 12:31 and note.

12:12 what you should say The Spirit will give the disciples an appropriate response. This might not necessarily lead to their acquittal (all but one of the apostles reportedly died as martyrs), but it will bear faithful witness to the gospel.

12:13–21 In a parable unique to Luke's Gospel, Jesus teaches on the pitfalls of abundance and the evil of greed. See the table "Parables of Jesus" on p. 1584.

12:13 divide the inheritance with me This might refer to the double portion allotted to the firstborn son (Dt 21:17).

12:14 who appointed me a judge Jesus has no interest in settling material disputes.

12:15 life does not consist in an abundance of possessions For Jesus, life consists of hearing and obeying the word of God—a relationship with God himself (see Lk 8:21; 10:42 and note; 11:28 and note).

12:16 And he told them this parable The parable is meant to illustrate Jesus' statement in v. 15.

12:19 Take life easy; eat, drink and be merry Compare Ecc 8:15; Isa 22:13.

12:21 rich toward God The Greek phrase used here could mean "rich with God." Jesus' point is to show the futility and deception of acquiring wealth, which he sets in contrast to storing up treasure that matters to God. The application of this parable relates back to the initial demand of Lk 12:13.

12:22–34 Luke appropriately connects Jesus' parable about greed (vv. 13–21) with his teaching on anxiety over material provisions (vv. 22–34). The parable, it seems, is directed toward the rich, whereas this section addresses the impoverished. The point is that material possessions can overcome the faith of both those who have much and those who have little—both types of people need to seek God and trust him with the outcome. Compare Mt 6:19–21,25–34.

12:23 life is more than food Echoes Jesus' response to Satan's first temptation (Lk 4:4).

12:24 how much more valuable Jesus repeats a comparison he made earlier (v. 7). If God takes care of the birds, he surely will provide for his people.

12:25 can add a single hour An additional reason to not worry: Anxiety accomplishes nothing.

12:28 you of little faith Jesus uses this phrase in reference to the disciples when they doubt God's providence (see Mt 6:30; 8:26; 14:31; 16:8).

of the field, which is here today, and tomorrow is thrown into the fire, how much more will he clothe you — you of little faith! ²⁹And do not set your heart on what you will eat or drink; do not worry about it. ³⁰For the pagan world runs after all such things, and your Father knows that you need them. ³¹But seek his kingdom, and these things will be given to you as well.

³²"Do not be afraid, little flock, for your Father has been pleased to give you the kingdom. ³³Sell your possessions and give to the poor. Provide purses for yourselves that will not wear out, a treasure in heaven that will never fail, where no thief comes near and no moth destroys. ³⁴For where your treasure is, there your heart will be also.

Watchfulness

12:35,36pp — Mt 25:1-13; Mk 13:33-37
12:39,40; 42-46pp — Mt 24:43-51

³⁵"Be dressed ready for service and keep your lamps burning, ³⁶like servants waiting for their master to return from a wedding banquet, so that when he comes and knocks they can immediately open the door for him. ³⁷It will be good for those servants whose master finds them watching when he comes. Truly I tell you, he will dress himself to serve, will have them recline at the table and will come and wait on them. ³⁸It will be good for those servants whose master finds them ready, even if he comes in the middle of the night or toward daybreak. ³⁹But understand this: If the owner of the house had known at what hour the thief was coming, he would not have let his house be broken into. ⁴⁰You also must be ready, because the Son of Man will come at an hour when you do not expect him."

⁴¹Peter asked, "Lord, are you telling this parable to us, or to everyone?"

⁴²The Lord answered, "Who then is the faithful and wise manager, whom the master puts in charge of his servants to give them their food allowance at the proper time? ⁴³It will be good for that servant whom the master finds doing so when he returns. ⁴⁴Truly I tell you, he will put him in charge of all his possessions. ⁴⁵But suppose the servant says to himself, 'My master is taking a long time in coming,' and he then begins to beat the other servants, both men and women, and to eat and drink and get drunk. ⁴⁶The master of that servant will come on a day when he does not expect him and at an hour he is not aware of. He will cut him to pieces and assign him a place with the unbelievers.

⁴⁷"The servant who knows the master's will and does not get ready or does not do what the master wants will be beaten with many blows. ⁴⁸But the one who does not know and does things deserving punishment will be beaten with few blows. From everyone who has been given much, much will be demanded; and from the one who has been entrusted with much, much more will be asked.

Not Peace but Division

12:51-53pp — Mt 10:34-36

⁴⁹"I have come to bring fire on the earth, and how I wish it were already kindled! ⁵⁰But I have a baptism to undergo, and what constraint I am under until it is completed! ⁵¹Do you think I came to bring peace on earth? No, I tell you, but division.

12:31 seek his kingdom Echoes the Lord's prayer (Lk 11:2).

12:32 little flock Refers to believers who belong to God's kingdom and live under God's loving care (vv. 22–31). This image recalls the OT's depiction of God as a caring shepherd of his people (e.g., Ps 77:20; Jer 13:17; Mic 4:8). Elsewhere the NT presents Jesus as the fulfillment of the OT's promise of a true shepherd of God's people (see Mt 9:36; Mk 6:34; Jn 10:11–18; compare Isa 40:11; Eze 34:11–31; 34:23 and note).

12:33 treasure in heaven Refers to eternal riches, those not lost when a person dies. This idea corresponds with being rich toward God (see Lk 12:21).

12:34 there your heart will be A summary of Jesus' teaching that began in v. 13. Instead of focusing on accumulating earthly riches (vv. 16–21), Jesus' followers are to pursue heavenly rewards by seeking God's kingdom and giving generously to the impoverished (vv. 31–33). The focus of everyone, whether wealthy or not, should be the kingdom of God. Compare Mt 6:21 and note.

12:35–48 Jesus encourages his disciples to remain faithful to him and ready for his return. Compare Mt 24:42–51.

12:36 wedding banquet Possibly alludes to the great meal that was expected to accompany the start of the era

inaugurated by the Messiah (see Rev 19:6–9; compare Lk 14:15; 22:29–30; Isa 25:6–8; 55:1–2).

12:37 will come and wait on them Describes the master serving his slaves — an unusual role reversal (compare Lk 13:30; Jn 13:1–20).

12:40 the Son of Man will come A reference to Jesus' return (compare Lk 9:26). The title Son of Man is associated with divine judgment on the day of Yahweh (see note on Mt 8:20).

12:42 puts in charge Jesus responds to Peter's question with a parable hinting at the role the apostles will play after his ascension (compare Ac 1:8; 20:28).

12:45 taking a long time in coming Perhaps anticipating a lengthy interval before Jesus' return.

12:49–53 The proclamation of God's kingdom brings conflict because it forces those who hear to make a decision about Jesus. Compare Mt 10:34–36.

12:49 to bring fire Fire imagery is often used as a symbol of divine judgment (see note on Lk 3:9; compare 3:16). Jesus suggests that there are elements of judgment associated with his mission.

12:50 a baptism to undergo Refers to Jesus' impending death.

12:51 but division At face value, this statement seems to contradict the angels' announcement of peace at

⁵²From now on there will be five in one family divided against each other, three against two and two against three. ⁵³They will be divided, father against son and son against father, mother against daughter and daughter against mother, mother-in-law against daughter-in-law and daughter-in-law against mother-in-law."

Interpreting the Times

⁵⁴He said to the crowd: "When you see a cloud rising in the west, immediately you say, 'It's going to rain,' and it does. ⁵⁵And when the south wind blows, you say, 'It's going to be hot,' and it is. ⁵⁶Hypocrites! You know how to interpret the appearance of the earth and the sky. How is it that you don't know how to interpret this present time?

⁵⁷"Why don't you judge for yourselves what is right? ⁵⁸As you are going with your adversary to the magistrate, try hard to be reconciled on the way, or your adversary may drag you off to the judge, and the judge turn you over to the officer, and the officer throw you into prison. ⁵⁹I tell you, you will not get out until you have paid the last penny."

Repent or Perish

13 Now there were some present at that time who told Jesus about the Galileans whose blood Pilate had mixed with their sacrifices. ²Jesus answered, "Do you think that these Galileans were worse sinners than all the other Galileans because they suffered this way? ³I tell you, no! But unless you repent, you too will all perish. ⁴Or those eighteen who died when the tower in Siloam fell on them — do you think they were more guilty than all the others living in Jerusalem? ⁵I tell you, no! But unless you repent, you too will all perish."

⁶Then he told this parable: "A man had a fig tree growing in his vineyard, and he went to look for fruit on it but did not find any. ⁷So he said to the man who took care of the vineyard, 'For three years now I've been coming to look for fruit on this fig tree and haven't found any. Cut it down! Why should it use up the soil?'

⁸"'Sir,' the man replied, 'leave it alone for one more year, and I'll dig around it and fertilize it. ⁹If it bears fruit next year, fine! If not, then cut it down.'"

Jesus' birth (see 2:14 and note). However, Jesus is not denying the reality of Messianic peace; rather, he is affirming that his death and resurrection will force people to choose sides. Although the way of Jesus certainly leads to peace in God's kingdom, not everyone decides to follow him (compare 19:42).
12:53 father against son Jesus incorporates phrases from Mic 7:6 to describe the divisive nature of his message.

12:54–56 Jesus rebukes the crowd for heeding insignificant signs but neglecting more important ones that point to God's kingdom. As with the preceding sections, this one is oriented toward the final judgment. Compare Mt 16:2–3.

12:56 you don't know how to interpret this present time As Jesus indicates earlier, his works provide sufficient evidence that the Messianic age is beginning (Lk 7:22–23). Compare Mt 16:3 and note.

12:57–59 This section parallels Mt 5:25–26, part of Jesus' teaching about anger in the Sermon on the Mount. Here, Luke incorporates the same material into Jesus' teaching about final judgment.

13:1–5 Continuing the theme of judgment from Lk 12, Jesus uses two calamities that befell certain Jews to illustrate the fate that awaits those who do not repent. This material is unique to Luke's Gospel.

13:1 at that time Refers to the time of Jesus' discourse in ch. 12. **whose blood Pilate had mixed with their sacrifices** Refers to the killing of Galilean pilgrims as they were offering sacrifices in Jerusalem. Pontius Pilate, the Roman governor of Judea from AD 26 to 36, apparently ordered their deaths. No other details are known, as these verses give the only account of this incident.
13:2 these Galileans were worse sinners Jesus' rhetorical question reflects the belief—common among first-century Jews—that physical affliction was caused by sin (compare Jn 9:2). Jesus counters this assumption in the next verse.

13:3 no Jesus asserts that the Galileans' deaths were not the result of excessive sin. **unless you repent, you too will all perish** Jesus uses this incident (and that mentioned in Lk 13:4) to illustrate the necessity of repentance. Jesus' references to perishing (vv. 3,5) involve more than physical death; they look ahead to the final judgment, the context of his teachings in ch. 12. If his hearers did not repent, then they too would meet a catastrophic end.

13:4 the tower in Siloam Siloam was located in the southeastern corner of Jerusalem, and the tower may have been an original structure from the City of David, as described by the first-century AD Jewish historian Josephus (Josephus, *Jewish War* 5:145). Like the report in v. 1, this is the only account of this incident.

13:6–9 This parable is found only in Luke, but it resembles Jesus' rebuke of the fig tree in the other Synoptic Gospels (Mt 21:18–19; Mk 11:12–14). The primary point of the parable, expressed in Lk 13:8–9, continues the theme of judgment. See the table "Parables of Jesus" on p. 1584.

13:8 leave it alone for one more year Suggests a period of grace. The gardener advises the vineyard owner to give the fig tree more time; perhaps it can be nurtured, so that it will bear fruit. Earlier in Luke, both John the Baptist and Jesus referred to a fruit-bearing tree as a metaphor for obedience to God (compare 3:8–9; 6:43–44). Jesus could be indicating here that his call for repentance and obedience is accompanied by a period of grace, during which God's final judgment is delayed. It could also be that Jesus is referring to the period of time before he himself came to judge the religious leadership of Jerusalem, just as Jesus curses a fig tree in symbolism of his judgment against them.

Jesus Heals a Crippled Woman on the Sabbath

¹⁰On a Sabbath Jesus was teaching in one of the synagogues, ¹¹and a woman was there who had been crippled by a spirit for eighteen years. She was bent over and could not straighten up at all. ¹²When Jesus saw her, he called her forward and said to her, "Woman, you are set free from your infirmity." ¹³Then he put his hands on her, and immediately she straightened up and praised God.

¹⁴Indignant because Jesus had healed on the Sabbath, the synagogue leader said to the people, "There are six days for work. So come and be healed on those days, not on the Sabbath."

13:10–17 In another passage unique to Luke, Jesus again faces criticism after he performs a healing on the Sabbath (compare Lk 6:6–11).

13:11 crippled by a spirit The woman's distorted posture appears to be the result of demonic activity, as opposed to a defect suffered from birth.

13:14 come and be healed on those days The people were coming to Jesus for healing without regard for the day. Jesus was not bothered by this; indeed, his actions encouraged it. The religious leaders saw his healings as a violation of God's command to honor the Sabbath by refraining from work. See the table "Miracles of Jesus" on p. 1741.

The Synagogue at Magdala

The recently discovered synagogue at Magdala in Galilee provides a good example of a public synagogue within the area in which Jesus ministered.

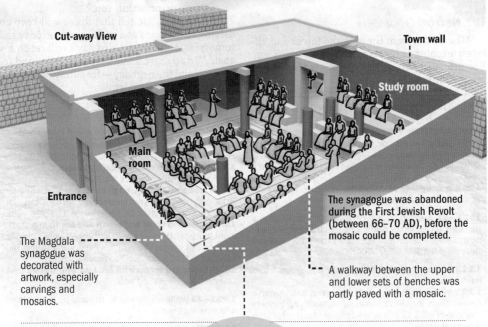

Cut-away View

Town wall

Study room

Main room

Entrance

The synagogue was abandoned during the First Jewish Revolt (between 66–70 AD), before the mosaic could be completed.

The Magdala synagogue was decorated with artwork, especially carvings and mosaics.

A walkway between the upper and lower sets of benches was partly paved with a mosaic.

STONE TABLE

The synagogue at Magdala contained a carved stone table, discovered in the synagogue's central open area. This stone carving depicts a representation of the Jerusalem temple, complete with a menorah and archway at the front, and a depiction of the Most Holy Place (holy of holies) at the back.

While the purpose of this stone carving is still uncertain, it may have served as a base for a stand used for reading Scripture. If so, this artifact speaks to the central importance of both the temple and Scripture reading for this synagogue community.

¹⁵The Lord answered him, "You hypocrites! Doesn't each of you on the Sabbath untie your ox or donkey from the stall and lead it out to give it water? ¹⁶Then should not this woman, a daughter of Abraham, whom Satan has kept bound for eighteen long years, be set free on the Sabbath day from what bound her?"

¹⁷When he said this, all his opponents were humiliated, but the people were delighted with all the wonderful things he was doing.

The Parables of the Mustard Seed and the Yeast

13:18,19pp — Mk 4:30-32
13:18-21pp — Mt 13:31-33

¹⁸Then Jesus asked, "What is the kingdom of God like? What shall I compare it to? ¹⁹It is like a mustard seed, which a man took and planted in his garden. It grew and became a tree, and the birds perched in its branches."

²⁰Again he asked, "What shall I compare the kingdom of God to? ²¹It is like yeast that a woman took and mixed into about sixty pounds[a] of flour until it worked all through the dough."

The Narrow Door

²²Then Jesus went through the towns and villages, teaching as he made his way to Jerusalem. ²³Someone asked him, "Lord, are only a few people going to be saved?"

He said to them, ²⁴"Make every effort to enter through the narrow door, because many, I tell you, will try to enter and will not be able to. ²⁵Once the owner of the house gets up and closes the door, you will stand outside knocking and pleading, 'Sir, open the door for us.'

"But he will answer, 'I don't know you or where you come from.'

²⁶"Then you will say, 'We ate and drank with you, and you taught in our streets.'

²⁷"But he will reply, 'I don't know you or where you come from. Away from me, all you evildoers!'

²⁸"There will be weeping there, and gnashing of teeth, when you see Abraham, Isaac and Jacob and all the prophets in the kingdom of God, but you yourselves thrown out. ²⁹People will come from east and west and north and south, and will take their places at the feast in the kingdom of God. ³⁰Indeed there are those who are last who will be first, and first who will be last."

Jesus' Sorrow for Jerusalem

13:34,35pp — Mt 23:37-39
13:34,35Ref — Lk 19:41

³¹At that time some Pharisees came to Jesus and said to him, "Leave this place and go somewhere else. Herod wants to kill you."

³²He replied, "Go tell that fox, 'I will keep on driving out demons and healing people today and tomorrow, and on the third day I will reach my goal.' ³³In any case, I must press on today and tomorrow and the next day — for surely no prophet can die outside Jerusalem!

---

a 21 Or about 27 kilograms

13:15 untie your ox or donkey Jesus calls attention to the religious leaders' willingness to make exceptions to the law to care for animals but not to care for God's people.
13:16 a daughter of Abraham Identifies the woman as a Jew.
13:18–21 Jesus tells two parables that illustrate the tremendous growth of God's kingdom from small beginnings. Parallel accounts appear in the other Synoptic Gospels (Mt 13:31–33; Mk 4:30–32).
13:19 a mustard seed A tiny seed that grows into a ten-foot-high shrub.
13:21 yeast Normally, yeast or leaven has negative connotations in Jewish literature, symbolizing impurity (compare Lk 12:1). Here, Jesus uses the metaphor in a positive sense.
13:22–30 Jesus elaborates on the nature of the salvation he offers.
13:22 to Jerusalem Luke reiterates that Jesus is on his way to Jerusalem, the site of his eventual suffering and death. Jesus began this journey in 9:51.
13:23 only a few The question concerns how many will be saved. Jesus does not answer directly, but indicates that many people who seek salvation will not find it (v. 24).
13:24 the narrow door Depicts a single, small entrance.
13:25 Sir, open the door for us Matthew uses similar language in the parable of the ten virgins, five of whom are shut out of the wedding celebration (Mt 25:10–12).
13:27 Away from me, all you evildoers Reflects the wording of Ps 6:8; compare Mt 7:23.
13:28 weeping there, and gnashing of teeth See Mt 8:12 and note. **but you yourselves thrown out** Not everyone who expects to be saved will be (Lk 13:25–28).
13:29 east and west and north and south In a statement that would have shocked his hearers, Jesus alludes to non-Jews coming from all over the world to join the banquet in God's kingdom (compare Mt 8:11).
13:30 there are those who are last who will be first Compare Mt 19:30 and note.
13:31–35 While on his way to Jerusalem, Jesus offers a lament for the city.
13:31 Pharisees came to Jesus and said to him Despite largely negative portrayals of the Pharisees, not all of them were hostile toward Jesus (see 7:36 and note). **Leave this place and go somewhere else** Galilee and Perea, the regions where Jesus has been traveling and ministering, were under the jurisdiction of Herod Antipas (see Lk 3:1 and note).
13:32 Go tell A rhetorical reply, not an instruction to report back to Herod. **fox** An unflattering metaphor that alludes to Herod's cunning. **I will reach my goal** Jesus speaks figuratively about his ministry, death and resurrection—that he will accomplish his purposes and work (compare 9:22; 18:33).

[34]"Jerusalem, Jerusalem, you who kill the prophets and stone those sent to you, how often I have longed to gather your children together, as a hen gathers her chicks under her wings, and you were not willing. [35]Look, your house is left to you desolate. I tell you, you will not see me again until you say, 'Blessed is he who comes in the name of the Lord.'[a]"

Jesus at a Pharisee's House

14:8-10Ref — Pr 25:6,7

14 One Sabbath, when Jesus went to eat in the house of a prominent Pharisee, he was being carefully watched. [2]There in front of him was a man suffering from abnormal swelling of his body. [3]Jesus asked the Pharisees and experts in the law, "Is it lawful to heal on the Sabbath or not?" [4]But they remained silent. So taking hold of the man, he healed him and sent him on his way.

[5]Then he asked them, "If one of you has a child[b] or an ox that falls into a well on the Sabbath day, will you not immediately pull it out?" [6]And they had nothing to say.

[7]When he noticed how the guests picked the places of honor at the table, he told them this parable: [8]"When someone invites you to a wedding feast, do not take the place of honor, for a person more dis- tinguished than you may have been invited. [9]If so, the host who invited both of you will come and say to you, 'Give this person your seat.' Then, humiliat- ed, you will have to take the least important place. [10]But when you are invited, take the lowest place, so that when your host comes, he will say to you, 'Friend, move up to a better place.' Then you will be honored in the presence of all the other guests. [11]For all those who exalt themselves will be humbled, and those who humble themselves will be exalted."

[12]Then Jesus said to his host, "When you give a luncheon or dinner, do not invite your friends, your brothers or sisters, your relatives, or your rich neighbors; if you do, they may invite you back and so you will be repaid. [13]But when you give a banquet, invite the poor, the crippled, the lame, the blind, [14]and you will be blessed. Although they cannot repay you, you will be repaid at the resurrection of the righteous."

The Parable of the Great Banquet

14:16-24Ref — Mt 22:2-14

[15]When one of those at the table with him heard this, he said to Jesus, "Blessed is the one who will eat at the feast in the kingdom of God."

[a] 35 Psalm 118:26   [b] 5 Some manuscripts *donkey*

13:33 prophet can die outside Jerusalem In this not-so-subtle indictment of the Jewish capital and its religious establishment, Jesus insinuates that prophets are killed only inside the holy city.
13:34 Jerusalem, Jerusalem Compare Mt 23:37–39. **who kill the prophets** See Lk 11:47–51. **under her wings** A common metaphor in the OT used to show God's protection (e.g., Ps 17:8; 57:1; 91:4; see note on Ru 2:12).
13:35 your house is left to you desolate Jesus might be referring to the temple, Jerusalem itself or the people of Jerusalem. **who comes in the name of the Lord** Jesus quotes from Ps 118:26, probably referring to his second coming. This same verse is quoted by Jesus' followers as he enters Jerusalem (Lk 19:38).
14:1–6 This passage deals with Jesus' authority to heal on the Sabbath (compare 13:10–17). See the table "Miracles of Jesus" on p. 1741.
14:1 a prominent Pharisee Jesus' third meal with a Pharisee in Luke's Gospel (compare 7:36; 11:37). **he was being carefully watched** Others at the dinner were looking for a way to publicly discredit Jesus (see Mt 19:3 and note).
14:2 suffering from abnormal swelling of his body Refers to a condition in which fluid accumulation in con- nective tissues or bodily cavities causes swelling and inhibits circulation.
14:3 it lawful to heal on the Sabbath Jesus previously healed at least two people on the Sabbath: a man with a withered hand (Lk 6:6–11) and a disabled woman (13:10–17).
14:5 a child or an ox that falls into a well Jesus' point is that the religious leaders will work to save that which is important to them, so he too should work in order to restore a life (compare 13:15).
14:6 they had nothing to say A similar reaction as the last time Jesus healed on the Sabbath (compare 13:17).

14:7–24 Jesus delivers three parables while at the Pharisee's house (v. 1). The first is directed toward the Pharisee's guests (vv. 7–11); the second addresses the Pharisee himself (vv. 12–14); and the third is told to the entire gathering (vv. 15–24). All three parables serve as a call to humility.
14:7 the places of honor The prominent seats where attendees were highly visible and likely close to the host or other distinguished guests.
14:10 Then you will be honored In contrast to the shame of having to move from the place of honor to a lower place, a guest who chooses a less distinguished seat will be honored when the host elevates him or her to a better position. Jesus' discussion has little to do with dinner etiquette. He is calling for his followers to show humility in every aspect of life — to put the needs of others first and act as a servant to all.
14:11 will be exalted Implies being exalted by God. Jesus consistently teaches a reversal of expectations (compare 9:48; 13:30; 18:14).
14:13 the poor, the crippled, the lame, the blind The people Jesus mentions would have been social outcasts. To their conditions, Jewish people often ascribed some sort of sinful behavior (Jn 9:2). Jesus' ministry is to these type of people (Lk 4:18–19).
14:14 they cannot repay you The truly humble person gives without hope of reciprocation. Jesus' statement in vv. 13–14 sums up the heart of his teaching, calling his followers to care for their neighbors out of love and to give no thought to self-interest. **the resurrection of the righteous** Refers to the resurrection of God's people at the time of judgment — an idea rooted in Da 12 (see Da 12:2 and note).
14:15 will eat at the feast in the kingdom of God Al- ludes to the great Messianic feast anticipated at the start of the era inaugurated by the Messiah, which involves

¹⁶Jesus replied: "A certain man was preparing a great banquet and invited many guests. ¹⁷At the time of the banquet he sent his servant to tell those who had been invited, 'Come, for everything is now ready.'

¹⁸"But they all alike began to make excuses. The first said, 'I have just bought a field, and I must go and see it. Please excuse me.'

¹⁹"Another said, 'I have just bought five yoke of oxen, and I'm on my way to try them out. Please excuse me.'

²⁰"Still another said, 'I just got married, so I can't come.'

²¹"The servant came back and reported this to his master. Then the owner of the house became angry and ordered his servant, 'Go out quickly into the streets and alleys of the town and bring in the poor, the crippled, the blind and the lame.'

²²"'Sir,' the servant said, 'what you ordered has been done, but there is still room.'

²³"Then the master told his servant, 'Go out to the roads and country lanes and compel them to come in, so that my house will be full. ²⁴I tell you, not one of those who were invited will get a taste of my banquet.'"

The Cost of Being a Disciple

²⁵Large crowds were traveling with Jesus, and turning to them he said: ²⁶"If anyone comes to me and does not hate father and mother, wife and children, brothers and sisters—yes, even their own life—such a person cannot be my disciple. ²⁷And whoever does not carry their cross and follow me cannot be my disciple.

²⁸"Suppose one of you wants to build a tower. Won't you first sit down and estimate the cost to see if you have enough money to complete it? ²⁹For if you lay the foundation and are not able to finish it, everyone who sees it will ridicule you, ³⁰saying, 'This person began to build and wasn't able to finish.'

³¹"Or suppose a king is about to go to war against another king. Won't he first sit down and consider whether he is able with ten thousand men to oppose the one coming against him with twenty thousand? ³²If he is not able, he will send a delegation while the other is still a long way off and will ask for terms of peace. ³³In the same way, those of you who do not give up everything you have cannot be my disciples.

³⁴"Salt is good, but if it loses its saltiness, how can it be made salty again? ³⁵It is fit neither for the soil nor for the manure pile; it is thrown out.

"Whoever has ears to hear, let them hear."

The Parable of the Lost Sheep

15:4-7pp — Mt 18:12-14

15 Now the tax collectors and sinners were all gathering around to hear Jesus. ²But the Pharisees and the teachers of the law muttered, "This man welcomes sinners and eats with them."

---

people from all nations (Isa 25:6; compare Lk 12:36 and note; Rev 19:6–10).

14:16 a great banquet Matthew records a similar banquet parable in Mt 22:1–14.

14:17 everything is now ready Suggests that the feast was prepared.

14:18 they all alike began to make excuses They refused to accept the invitation, citing what they believed to be more important obligations. Rules of hospitality were important in the ancient Near East—it would have been extremely rude to change one's mind at the last minute and decline a previously accepted invitation.

14:21 the poor, the crippled, the blind and the lame Corresponds with Jesus' recommended guest list in the previous parable (Lk 14:13 and note).

14:23 the roads and country lanes Likely refers to extending the invitation to travelers. This may represent the inclusion of Gentiles (non-Jews) in God's kingdom (compare 13:29 and note). **compel them to come in** Foreigners and marginalized people likely would be hesitant to accept an invitation to such a banquet.

14:24 not one of those who were invited Another role reversal; those originally invited were excluded and those who were originally excluded participated in the banquet.

14:25–35 Continuing his journey to Jerusalem (see 9:51 and note), Jesus teaches on the cost of being his follower (compare Mt 5:13; 10:37–38; Mk 8:34; 9:49–50).

14:26 and does not hate Jesus is using hyperbole—a figure of speech that relies on exaggeration to make a point. He is not encouraging his followers to turn against their family members; rather, he is explaining that even devotion to family does not supersede the call to disciple-

ship. Jesus and God's kingdom must come first in the life of a believer. Compare Mt 10:37 and note.

14:27 does not carry their cross With death awaiting him in Jerusalem, Jesus wants his disciples to understand that they may be subject to the same fate. See Mt 10:38 and note.

14:28 estimate the cost Jesus encourages his followers—as well as those in the crowd of pilgrims who had not yet become his disciples—to consider the great sacrifices involved in their decision. This section is unique to Luke's travel narrative.

14:33 who do not give up everything Jesus sees an abundance of possessions as a hindrance to faith. He instructs his followers to rid themselves of anything that prevents a total commitment to God's kingdom (see note on Mt 19:21). For many this meant selling everything they had for the betterment of the impoverished and for the sake of spreading the news about Jesus. This is seen in a tangible way in the lives of Jesus' earliest followers (e.g., Ac 2:42–47).

14:34 Salt Salt was used as a preservative and for flavoring (compare Mt 5:13 and note).

14:35 neither for the soil Even tasteless salt could be harmful to soil in large quantities.

15:1–7 Luke 15 presents three parables about recovering what is lost. All three appear to be prompted by the complaint of the scribes (teachers of the law) and Pharisees over Jesus' fellowship with tax collectors and sinners (v. 2). The first parable concerns a stray sheep (vv. 3–7).

15:1 the tax collectors See Mt 5:46 and note.

³Then Jesus told them this parable: ⁴"Suppose one of you has a hundred sheep and loses one of them. Doesn't he leave the ninety-nine in the open country and go after the lost sheep until he finds it? ⁵And when he finds it, he joyfully puts it on his shoulders ⁶and goes home. Then he calls his friends and neighbors together and says, 'Rejoice with me; I have found my lost sheep.' ⁷I tell you that in the same way there will be more rejoicing in heaven over one sinner who repents than over ninety-nine righteous persons who do not need to repent.

The Parable of the Lost Coin

⁸"Or suppose a woman has ten silver coinsᵃ and loses one. Doesn't she light a lamp, sweep the house and search carefully until she finds it? ⁹And when she finds it, she calls her friends and neighbors together and says, 'Rejoice with me; I have found my lost coin.' ¹⁰In the same way, I tell you, there is rejoicing in the presence of the angels of God over one sinner who repents."

The Parable of the Lost Son

¹¹Jesus continued: "There was a man who had two sons. ¹²The younger one said to his father, 'Father, give me my share of the estate.' So he divided his property between them.

¹³"Not long after that, the younger son got together all he had, set off for a distant country and there squandered his wealth in wild living. ¹⁴After he had spent everything, there was a severe famine in that whole country, and he began to be in need. ¹⁵So he went and hired himself out to a citizen of that country, who sent him to his fields to feed pigs. ¹⁶He longed to fill his stomach with the pods that the pigs were eating, but no one gave him anything.

¹⁷"When he came to his senses, he said, 'How many of my father's hired servants have food to spare, and here I am starving to death! ¹⁸I will set out and go back to my father and say to him: Father, I have sinned against heaven and against you. ¹⁹I

ᵃ 8 Greek *ten drachmas*, each worth about a day's wages

15:2 Pharisees and the teachers of the law See note on Lk 5:17. **welcomes sinners and eats with them** In response to the religious leaders' complaint, Jesus tells parables to explain his purpose in welcoming sinners and sharing table fellowship with them. He teaches that each repentant sinner prompts a heavenly celebration (15:7,10,32).

15:4 until he finds it When this detail is applied to Jesus' teaching about sinners, it conveys the divine initiative to recover those who are lost. The prophetic book of Ezekiel includes an extended metaphor in which the people of Israel are portrayed as a stray flock of sheep and Yahweh promises to raise up a shepherd for Israel—a proper leader whose focus is the will of Yahweh (Eze 34:1–24; compare Jn 10:1–21).

15:5 he joyfully puts it on his shoulders The shepherd carries the sheep to safety.

15:6 Rejoice with me There is shared joy over the recovery of the lost sheep (compare Lk 15:7,10).

15:7 rejoicing in heaven over one sinner This does not indicate that sinful people are valued more dearly than righteous people. Rather, the heavenly hosts are celebrating repentance—the return of one who was lost.

15:8–10 Jesus' second parable, about a lost coin, reiterates the point of the first: When the lost becomes found, heaven throws a party. This parable is unique to Luke.

15:11–32 Jesus again expresses his point about rejoicing over repentance, this time with a much longer parable about a wayward son. Although the basic pattern remains the same (the seeker recovers what is lost, leading to a celebration), the perspective changes. The primary character is not the seeker, but the lost—and unlike the sheep and the coin, the wayward son becomes found by his own choice. Consequently, this third parable—which is unique to Luke—provides a complete picture of repentance: The son rebels (vv. 12–16), returns (vv. 17–21), and is restored (vv. 22–24). This parable also has much to say about the behavior of those who view themselves as righteous, represented by the older son who refuses to join the celebration (vv. 25–30). Although Jesus explains the first two parables, the meaning of the third is summed up within the story by the rejoicing father (vv. 31–32).

15:11 a man who had two sons The parable's opening line sets up two parts, one for each son (vv. 12–24,25–32).

15:12 give me my share of the estate The younger son is demanding his share of the inheritance, which could be paid out at any time as permitted by his father. The older son would have received a double portion amounting to two-thirds of what belonged to his father (see Dt 21:17). Although the most natural time of bequeathing or transference occurred at the father's death (see Nu 27:8–11), this request does not amount to a wish that his father were dead. A man could give property to his heirs or distribute it on request while he was still alive (as in this parable). A warning against this practice in Sirach (a Jewish, deuterocanonical book from the second century BC) suggests that it was a common occurrence (Sirach 33:19–24). **So he divided his property between them** The older son did not necessarily receive his two-thirds share at this time. The division of assets was for the purpose of determining the one-third portion due to the younger son.

15:13 got together all According to parallels in Greek literature, the word *synagō* used here (meaning "gather together") suggests that the younger son converted his assets—perhaps livestock and property—to currency. **in wild living** The older brother later notes that this includes spending money on prostitutes (Lk 15:30).

15:15 pigs Since pigs were unclean animals according to the law (Lev 11:7; Dt 14:8), Jesus suggests that the younger son became a swine-herding slave to a Gentile (non-Jewish person)—a threefold dishonor. The scribes (teachers of the law) and Pharisees to whom Jesus is speaking (Lk 15:2) would have equated this existence to a cursed life.

15:16 pods The Greek word used here refers to seed pods similar to peapods but from the carob tree, which was common throughout the Mediterranean region. They were used as animal feed and have a sweet, chocolate-like flavor.

15:18 heaven A way of referring to God without uttering his name.

15:19 no longer worthy to be called your son Since he already had received (and spent) his inheritance,

am no longer worthy to be called your son; make me like one of your hired servants.' [20]So he got up and went to his father.

"But while he was still a long way off, his father saw him and was filled with compassion for him; he ran to his son, threw his arms around him and kissed him.

[21]"The son said to him, 'Father, I have sinned against heaven and against you. I am no longer worthy to be called your son.'

[22]"But the father said to his servants, 'Quick! Bring the best robe and put it on him. Put a ring on his finger and sandals on his feet. [23]Bring the fattened calf and kill it. Let's have a feast and celebrate. [24]For this son of mine was dead and is alive again; he was lost and is found.' So they began to celebrate.

[25]"Meanwhile, the older son was in the field. When he came near the house, he heard music and dancing. [26]So he called one of the servants and asked him what was going on. [27]'Your brother has come,' he replied, 'and your father has killed the fattened calf because he has him back safe and sound.'

[28]"The older brother became angry and refused to go in. So his father went out and pleaded with him. [29]But he answered his father, 'Look! All these years I've been slaving for you and never disobeyed your orders. Yet you never gave me even a young goat so I could celebrate with my friends. [30]But when this son of yours who has squandered your property with prostitutes comes home, you kill the fattened calf for him!'

[31]"'My son,' the father said, 'you are always with me, and everything I have is yours. [32]But we had to celebrate and be glad, because this brother of yours was dead and is alive again; he was lost and is found.'"

The Parable of the Shrewd Manager

16 Jesus told his disciples: "There was a rich man whose manager was accused of wasting his possessions. [2]So he called him in and asked him, 'What is this I hear about you? Give an account of your management, because you cannot be manager any longer.'

[3]"The manager said to himself, 'What shall I do now? My master is taking away my job. I'm not strong enough to dig, and I'm ashamed to beg— [4]I know what I'll do so that, when I lose my job here, people will welcome me into their houses.'

---

this statement must refer to more than the son's legal standing within the family. He regards his actions as being so reprehensible that he deserves to be cut off from his family in a relational sense.

15:20 ran The father's act of running toward his lost son alludes to the divine initiative to seek and welcome sinners (see v. 4 and note). Nothing in the text indicates that the father's act of running was somehow shameful. **kissed him** Suggestive of forgiveness (compare 2Sa 14:33 and note).

15:21 worthy to be called your son The father does not let him finish the speech he prepared (Lk 15:18–19).

15:22 Quick! Bring the best robe Probably reserved for honored guests. **Put a ring on his finger** Indicative of sonship and the ability to approve transactions on behalf of his father. **sandals on his feet** Being impoverished, the son was likely barefoot. All three gifts in this verse, coupled with the food in v. 23, are gracious provisions by his father.

15:23 the fattened calf Reserved for joyous, lavish celebrations.

15:24 he was lost and is found This phrase conveys the point of all three parables in ch. 15. Jesus is telling the scribes (teachers of the law) and Pharisees (vv. 2–3) that the Father rejoices over repentant sinners and embraces them as his children.

15:25 Meanwhile, the older son was in the field Indicates a shift to the second part of the parable (see note on v. 11).

15:28 became angry Instead of rejoicing that his lost brother was found, the older brother responds with resentment. This attitude reflects the scribes (teachers of the law) and Pharisees' complaint about Jesus' fellowship with sinners (v. 2). **refused to go in** The older brother refuses to join the celebration in the house.

15:29 never disobeyed your orders Possibly intended to reflect the thinking of the scribes (teachers of the law), Pharisees and perhaps other Jews who considered themselves righteous and were bothered by the warm welcome that Jesus gave to those they classified as sinners (vv. 1–2).

15:30 this son of yours The older brother avoids calling the younger son "my brother."

15:31 everything I have is yours Indicative of the older son's status as the firstborn.

15:32 we had to celebrate and be glad Compare v. 7 and note; v. 10. **he was lost and is found** The story concludes with the father repeating his joyful statement from v. 24. Through all three parables in this chapter, Jesus conveys God the Father's deep desire to embrace sinners and those that many in Israel treated as outcasts.

16:1–13 In the previous parable, the wayward son squanders his inheritance; now Jesus delivers a parable about the use of resources. The main character is a household manager who appears to win the respect of his master by acting dishonestly. Jesus explains the parable in vv. 10–13. This parable is unique to Luke's Gospel.

16:1 his disciples Jesus is no longer addressing the scribes (teachers of the law) and Pharisees as in the previous chapter (15:2–3). However, they apparently are still listening to him (15:14). **manager** Refers to someone who oversees his master's property and finances, often a slave born in the master's house. **wasting his possessions** Either foolishly mismanaging his master's money or spending it extravagantly; both would be grounds for termination. The Greek verb used here, *diaskorpizō*, often translated as "to squander," also appears in 15:13 to describe the activities of the lost son.

16:3 to dig Probably intended as a general reference: The manager considers himself unfit for manual labor of any kind.

16:4 people will welcome me into their houses The manager uses his current position not to help his current

5 "So he called in each one of his master's debtors. He asked the first, 'How much do you owe my master?'

6 "'Nine hundred gallons*a* of olive oil,' he replied.

"The manager told him, 'Take your bill, sit down quickly, and make it four hundred and fifty.'

7 "Then he asked the second, 'And how much do you owe?'

"'A thousand bushels*b* of wheat,' he replied.

"He told him, 'Take your bill and make it eight hundred.'

8 "The master commended the dishonest manager because he had acted shrewdly. For the people of this world are more shrewd in dealing with their own kind than are the people of the light. 9 I tell you, use worldly wealth to gain friends for yourselves, so that when it is gone, you will be welcomed into eternal dwellings.

10 "Whoever can be trusted with very little can also be trusted with much, and whoever is dishonest with very little will also be dishonest with much. 11 So if you have not been trustworthy in handling worldly wealth, who will trust you with true riches? 12 And if you have not been trustworthy with someone else's property, who will give you property of your own?

13 "No one can serve two masters. Either you will hate the one and love the other, or you will be devoted to the one and despise the other. You cannot serve both God and money."

14 The Pharisees, who loved money, heard all this and were sneering at Jesus. 15 He said to them, "You are the ones who justify yourselves in the eyes of others, but God knows your hearts. What people value highly is detestable in God's sight.

Additional Teachings

16 "The Law and the Prophets were proclaimed until John. Since that time, the good news of the kingdom of God is being preached, and everyone

a 6 Or about 3,000 liters   *b* 7 Or about 30 tons

---

master, but instead to position himself better for the future. Nonetheless, his cunning also helps him with his master, even though that does not seem to be his intent (v. 8).

16:6 make it four hundred and fifty Before he is officially dismissed, the manager acts quickly to reduce the debts owed to his master. It seems that in doing this favor for the debtors, he hopes to receive their kindness after he is dismissed—and maybe even gain a place in one of their households.

16:8 commended the dishonest manager Although the reduction of debts cost the master money in the long term, the master recognizes the manager's cleverness. The manager also brought funds in right away for his master, resulting in a temporary gain. Although the master had more receivables than the manager retrieved, the master apparently desired to have part of the receivables right away. This suggests that the master needed to have more funds on hand. The manager probably knew this and may have even caused this problem by his own laziness (v. 3). **he had acted shrewdly** The Greek word used here, *phronimōs*, can be translated as "shrewdly," "wisely" or "prudently." The term is morally ambiguous but the overall parable implies that Jesus does not endorse the actions of the manager. **are more shrewd** This is the point of Jesus' parable: There is a fundamental difference between the conduct of those who follow Jesus and those who seek after wealth. **the people of the light** Refers to those who belong to the light—God's ways (1Jn 1:5–10). Light and darkness are used frequently as metaphors for people's spiritual condition (Lk 11:33–36; Jn 12:36 and note). In Jewish writings found among the Dead Sea Scrolls, such as the Rule of the Community or the War Scroll, the phrase "sons of light" is used frequently to refer to those who hold to the values of the Dead Sea Scrolls community.

16:9 use worldly wealth Reflects the means the manager used to secure his future. Jesus seems to be speaking ironically here. People cannot offer salvation or usher others into eternity; only God can. Jesus makes this point earlier in Lk 12:4–7. Jesus also seems to be saying that wealth can be a means of helping others find the ways of God—a point he made with the parable of the Good Samaritan (10:34–37). The manager is capable of saving

his job and gaining friends, but that will not save him from his disreputable actions. The manager spends his energy on self-serving actions. In further irony, these actions are rewarded by the manager's master, because the master too seems to be a person interested in riches (v. 13). This is in juxtaposition to how Jesus' followers should use their resources (see note on v. 11; note on v. 12). **you will be welcomed into eternal dwellings** Refers to life with God.

16:11 true riches Refers to God's truth (compare v. 9). Jesus is calling his disciples to be faithful in everything God gives to them. Jesus' point is that people have a choice: to act like the manager and his master, or act as followers of Jesus—utilizing what they have been entrusted with for God's purposes. Compare 12:33.

16:12 with someone else's property Likely a reference to everything ultimately belonging to God. Jesus also seems to be emphasizing another point of his parable: His followers should be faithful when given any resources to steward. **who will give you property of your own** Probably refers to true riches—eternal relationship with God (v. 9; compare Mt 6:19–21).

16:13 serve two masters Compare Mt 6:24.

16:14–31 The Pharisees scoff at Jesus' teaching, and he rebukes their emphasis on human values and traditions (Lk 16:14–15). He also comments on the purpose and durability of the Scriptures and summarizes his teaching on divorce (vv. 16–18). This discussion leads into another parable that contrasts the fates of the unrepentant rich and faithful poor in the afterlife (vv. 19–31). This story corresponds with Jesus' teachings about the reversal of roles in God's kingdom (e.g., 9:48; 13:30; 14:11; 18:14). The parable's conclusion, however, shifts to a deeper meaning about people not listening to God's word, not even when it comes from Jesus (vv. 29–31).

16:14 Pharisees See note on 5:17.

16:15 What people value highly Probably a reference to coveting or desiring wealth.

16:16 The Law and the Prophets were proclaimed until John The Greek phrase used here has no verb, making it difficult to translate. Jesus could mean that the Law and Prophets were proclaimed until John the Baptist's ministry. He also could be indicating that the

is forcing their way into it. ¹⁷It is easier for heaven and earth to disappear than for the least stroke of a pen to drop out of the Law.

¹⁸"Anyone who divorces his wife and marries another woman commits adultery, and the man who marries a divorced woman commits adultery.

The Rich Man and Lazarus

¹⁹"There was a rich man who was dressed in purple and fine linen and lived in luxury every day. ²⁰At his gate was laid a beggar named Lazarus, covered with sores ²¹and longing to eat what fell from the rich man's table. Even the dogs came and licked his sores.

²²"The time came when the beggar died and the angels carried him to Abraham's side. The rich man also died and was buried. ²³In Hades, where he was in torment, he looked up and saw Abraham far away, with Lazarus by his side. ²⁴So he called to him, 'Father Abraham, have pity on me and send Lazarus to dip the tip of his finger in water and cool my tongue, because I am in agony in this fire.'

²⁵"But Abraham replied, 'Son, remember that in your lifetime you received your good things, while Lazarus received bad things, but now he is comforted here and you are in agony. ²⁶And besides all this, between us and you a great chasm has been set in place, so that those who want to go from here to you cannot, nor can anyone cross over from there to us.'

²⁷"He answered, 'Then I beg you, father, send Lazarus to my family, ²⁸for I have five brothers. Let him warn them, so that they will not also come to this place of torment.'

²⁹"Abraham replied, 'They have Moses and the Prophets; let them listen to them.'

³⁰"'No, father Abraham,' he said, 'but if someone from the dead goes to them, they will repent.'

³¹"He said to him, 'If they do not listen to Moses and the Prophets, they will not be convinced even if someone rises from the dead.'"

Sin, Faith, Duty

17 Jesus said to his disciples: "Things that cause people to stumble are bound to come, but woe to anyone through whom they come. ²It would be better for them to be thrown into the

---

Law and Prophets were the only guides for the people of Israel until John came. Given what Jesus says in the next verse, he does not mean that the Law and Prophets are no longer relevant. "The Law and the Prophets" seems to have been a common way of referring to two collections of the Jewish Scriptures. The Hebrew Bible (corresponding with the Protestant OT, but in a different order) is divided into three parts: the Law, the Prophets and the Writings. The Law (or Pentateuch) includes the first five books of the Bible; the Prophets includes the books of Joshua, Judges, 1–2 Samuel, 1–2 Kings, Isaiah, Jeremiah, Ezekiel and the Book of the Twelve (the Minor Prophets: Hosea to Malachi). The Writings includes Ruth, 1–2 Chronicles, Ezra, Nehemiah, Esther, Job, Psalms, Proverbs, Ecclesiastes, Song of Songs (Song of Solomon), Lamentations and Daniel.
16:17 for the least stroke of a pen to drop out of the Law Jesus affirms the enduring validity of the Scriptures. Compare Mt 5:18 and note.
16:18 Anyone who divorces his wife and marries another woman Jesus' teaching here seems to go beyond the instructions about divorce given by Moses (Dt 24:1–4). The differences are more apparent in Matthew's Gospel, which records Jesus' teaching on divorce in greater detail (Mt 19:1–12).
16:19 in purple and fine linen Indications of opulence.
16:20 Lazarus This is the only named character in Jesus' parables. Jesus probably uses the name due to its meaning, "God helps." This character is not to be confused with Martha and Mary's brother whom Jesus raised from the dead (Jn 11:1–44).
16:21 longing to eat A similar expression is used to describe the lost son (Lk 15:16). **Even the dogs came and licked his sores** Rather than Lazarus getting the dogs' food (the rich man's table scraps), his oozing wounds become food for the dogs.
16:22 to Abraham's side The presence of Abraham—Israel's patriarch (Ge 17:5–8)—implies a state of blessedness. Lazarus' proximity to Abraham also might indicate that he obtained an honorable position in the afterlife.

was buried This extra detail, not mentioned in relation to Lazarus, is appropriate for someone who is wealthy; the implication may be that Lazarus was so impoverished that he was not even buried properly.
16:23 In Hades The realm of the dead (see note on Lk 10:15).
16:24 I am in agony in this fire Fire is a symbol of divine wrath (see note on 3:9).
16:25 he is comforted here and you are in agony These words convey the reversal of fortunes that Jesus commonly associates with God's kingdom (e.g., 9:48; 13:30; 14:11; 18:14; Mt 20:26–27).
16:26 a great chasm has been set in place Indicates the permanence of the characters' eternal destinies.
16:28 will not also come to this place of torment The rich man wanted to help his family avoid his torturous fate.
16:29 let them listen to them Abraham asserts that the rich man's family must rely on the Scriptures.
16:30 someone from the dead Disagreeing with Abraham, the rich man contends that the Law and the Prophets are not enough to persuade his family to repent. They need to hear from someone like Lazarus who can bear witness about the afterlife.
16:31 if someone rises from the dead Abraham says the family members are too hardhearted to receive any call to repentance. This remark alludes to Jesus' resurrection—which gives him authority as a witness who has come from the dead. In the context of Jesus' response to the Pharisees (Lk 16:14–15), this closing comment serves to rebuke their unbelief: They will not heed the Law and the Prophets, nor will they heed Jesus' powerful revelation of God's truth—even when it comes in the form of his resurrection.

17:1–10 This section recounts some of Jesus' sayings from his journey to Jerusalem; he teaches about stumbling blocks, forgiveness, faith and service (compare Mt 17:19–21; 18:6–22; Mk 9:28–29,42).

sea with a millstone tied around their neck than to cause one of these little ones to stumble. ³So watch yourselves.

"If your brother or sister*ᵃ* sins against you, rebuke them; and if they repent, forgive them. ⁴Even if they sin against you seven times in a day and seven times come back to you saying 'I repent,' you must forgive them."

⁵The apostles said to the Lord, "Increase our faith!"

⁶He replied, "If you have faith as small as a mustard seed, you can say to this mulberry tree, 'Be uprooted and planted in the sea,' and it will obey you.

⁷"Suppose one of you has a servant plowing or looking after the sheep. Will he say to the servant when he comes in from the field, 'Come along now and sit down to eat'? ⁸Won't he rather say, 'Prepare my supper, get yourself ready and wait on me while I eat and drink; after that you may eat and drink'? ⁹Will he thank the servant because he did what he was told to do? ¹⁰So you also, when you have done everything you were told to do, should say, 'We are unworthy servants; we have only done our duty.'"

Jesus Heals Ten Men With Leprosy

¹¹Now on his way to Jerusalem, Jesus traveled along the border between Samaria and Galilee. ¹²As he was going into a village, ten men who had leprosy*ᵇ* met him. They stood at a distance ¹³and called out in a loud voice, "Jesus, Master, have pity on us!"

¹⁴When he saw them, he said, "Go, show yourselves to the priests." And as they went, they were cleansed.

¹⁵One of them, when he saw he was healed, came back, praising God in a loud voice. ¹⁶He threw himself at Jesus' feet and thanked him — and he was a Samaritan.

¹⁷Jesus asked, "Were not all ten cleansed? Where are the other nine? ¹⁸Has no one returned to give praise to God except this foreigner?" ¹⁹Then he said to him, "Rise and go; your faith has made you well."

The Coming of the Kingdom of God

17:26,27pp — Mt 24:37-39

²⁰Once, on being asked by the Pharisees when the kingdom of God would come, Jesus replied, "The coming of the kingdom of God is not something that can be observed, ²¹nor will people say, 'Here it is,' or 'There it is,' because the kingdom of God is in your midst."*ᶜ*

ᵃ 3 The Greek word for *brother or sister* (*adelphos*) refers here to a fellow disciple, whether man or woman.   *ᵇ 12* The Greek word traditionally translated *leprosy* was used for various diseases affecting the skin.   *ᶜ 21* Or *is within you*

17:2 millstone A large stone used to grind grain in a mill. **little ones** Likely refers to new or immature believers (compare Mt 18:1–6).

17:3 forgive Forgiving someone who repents is not just an option; it is commanded by Jesus.

17:4 seven times Suggests the need for abundant forgiveness (compare Mt 18:21–22). Jesus advocates for forgiving as a response to divine forgiveness. See note on Lk 6:37.

17:6 a mustard seed A tiny seed that grows into a ten-foot-high shrub (see note on Mt 17:20). **mulberry tree** The Greek word used here indicates a large tree that would be difficult to uproot. In a parallel saying from Matthew, Jesus refers to a mountain instead of a tree (Mt 17:20).

17:7–10 This final set of Jesus' sayings in this section (Lk 17:7–10) is unique to Luke's Gospel.

17:10 We are unworthy servants Jesus encourages his disciples to conduct themselves as humble slaves to God, in contrast to the self-aggrandizing Pharisees (16:14–15).

17:11–19 On his way to Jerusalem, Jesus encounters ten people with leprosy (or some other skin disease). He heals them and sends them to a priest to be examined, so their cleansing can be verified. One of them, a Samaritan, returns to thank Jesus and praise God. Here again, Luke highlights the faith of an outsider in contrast to the unbelief of the Jewish leaders. See the table "Miracles of Jesus" on p. 1741.

17:11 on his way to Jerusalem Luke reminds his readers that Jesus is still in the midst of his travels. **the border between Samaria and Galilee** Samaria was between Galilee and Judea, where Jerusalem was located.

17:12 who had leprosy This description could indicate a range of skin diseases (see note on 5:12). **They stood**

at a distance Due to the fear of contagion, people with skin diseases were required to withdraw from the community and alert anyone who was approaching. See Nu 5:2–3; Lev 13:45–46.

17:13 Jesus, Master, have pity on us Their prior knowledge of Jesus suggests that they are calling for him to heal them, not begging for alms.

17:14 Go, show yourselves to the priests According to the law, people with a skin disease had to be examined by a priest, who would determine whether they were clean or unclean (see Lev 13:1–59 and note; 14:1–32 and note). **they were cleansed** Healed of their leprosy and rendered ceremonially clean.

17:16 He threw himself at Jesus' feet Paying homage to Jesus as he praises God the Father. **he was a Samaritan** Luke withholds this detail until now for dramatic effect. Samaritans and Jews despised each other (see note on Lk 10:33).

17:18 except this foreigner Presumably, then, the other nine lepers were Jews. Jesus marvels at their lack of expressed gratitude.

17:19 your faith The faith of one of Israel's loathed neighbors — a Samaritan — is elevated above the faith of Jews. Jesus often associates faith and healing (e.g., 5:20; 7:9,50; 8:48; 18:42).

17:20–21 These remarks are found only in Luke. They lead into Jesus' teaching about his return.

17:20 when the kingdom of God would come The Pharisees (see note on 5:17) likely are envisioning a political and military kingdom that would be established by overthrowing Judea's Roman overlords. Compare note on Mk 1:15. **something that can be observed** Such as acts of worldly power.

17:21 the kingdom of God is in your midst Refers to Jesus' ministry (see Lk 11:20; Mt 12:28).

²²Then he said to his disciples, "The time is coming when you will long to see one of the days of the Son of Man, but you will not see it. ²³People will tell you, 'There he is!' or 'Here he is!' Do not go running off after them. ²⁴For the Son of Man in his day*a* will be like the lightning, which flashes and lights up the sky from one end to the other. ²⁵But first he must suffer many things and be rejected by this generation.

²⁶"Just as it was in the days of Noah, so also will it be in the days of the Son of Man. ²⁷People were eating, drinking, marrying and being given in marriage up to the day Noah entered the ark. Then the flood came and destroyed them all.

²⁸"It was the same in the days of Lot. People were eating and drinking, buying and selling, planting and building. ²⁹But the day Lot left Sodom, fire and sulfur rained down from heaven and destroyed them all.

³⁰"It will be just like this on the day the Son of Man is revealed. ³¹On that day no one who is on the housetop, with possessions inside, should go down to get them. Likewise, no one in the field should go back for anything. ³²Remember Lot's wife! ³³Whoever tries to keep their life will lose it, and whoever loses their life will preserve it. ³⁴I tell you, on that night two people will be in one bed; one will be taken and the other left. ³⁵Two

women will be grinding grain together; one will be taken and the other left." [36] *b*

³⁷"Where, Lord?" they asked.

He replied, "Where there is a dead body, there the vultures will gather."

The Parable of the Persistent Widow

18 Then Jesus told his disciples a parable to show them that they should always pray and not give up. ²He said: "In a certain town there was a judge who neither feared God nor cared what people thought. ³And there was a widow in that town who kept coming to him with the plea, 'Grant me justice against my adversary.'

⁴"For some time he refused. But finally he said to himself, 'Even though I don't fear God or care what people think, ⁵yet because this widow keeps bothering me, I will see that she gets justice, so that she won't eventually come and attack me!'"

⁶And the Lord said, "Listen to what the unjust judge says. ⁷And will not God bring about justice for his chosen ones, who cry out to him day and night? Will he keep putting them off? ⁸I tell you, he will see that they get justice, and quickly. How-

---

a 24 Some manuscripts do not have *in his day.*   *b 36* Some manuscripts include here words similar to Matt. 24:40.

17:22-37 Following the Pharisees' question, Jesus informs his disciples about what will happen when the Son of Man is revealed—referring to his second coming. Compare Mt 24:17–41; Mk 13:14–23.

17:22 one of the days Refers to the day of Jesus' appearing. Luke uses the plural form to correspond with the later references to the days of Noah and Lot (Lk 17:26,28). **the Son of Man** This title, used frequently by Jesus in reference to himself, comes from Da 7:13–14, where it describes an enigmatic figure associated with an everlasting kingdom (see note on Mt 8:20). **but you will not see** Jesus indicates that the disciples will not see his return at the time when they desire it. This is not necessarily referring to a postponement of Jesus' return, but likely is related to his statement about God's kingdom arriving in ways that cannot be observed (Lk 17:20).

17:24 like the lightning, which flashes Indicating that Jesus' coming will be sudden and apparent to everyone.

17:25 suffer many things Alludes to the fate that awaits Jesus in Jerusalem—his death on the cross.

17:26 the days of Noah A time of judgment, when humanity was destroyed by the flood due to its depravity (Ge 6:5–8). See note on Lk 17:30.

17:28 the days of Lot Another reference to divine judgment, when the cities of Sodom and Gomorrah were destroyed due to their wickedness (Ge 19:23–29). See note on Lk 17:30.

17:30 It will be just like Throughout the passage, Jesus is comparing his future return in glory to the divine judgment carried out in the days of Noah and Lot (vv. 26,28). The Son of Man's revealing will be characterized by destruction of evil and salvation of believers—factors that associate Jesus' return with

the day of Yahweh envisioned by OT prophets (see Joel 1:15 and note).

17:32 Remember Lot's wife Lot's wife was turned into a pillar of salt for disobeying the angel's command to not look back (Ge 19:17,26).

17:33 Whoever tries to keep their life Luke records Jesus making a similar statement during his ministry in Galilee (Lk 9:24).

17:37 there the vultures will gather Jesus' statement here might reflect a known proverb of his day. In the same way that circling birds signal the presence of a corpse, there will be discernible signs that point to impending divine judgment and Jesus' return in glory.

18:1-8 Reflecting the context of final judgment from the previous passage, Jesus tells a parable (which is unique to Luke) about a judge and a widow. The story has parallels with Jesus' teaching about prayer in 11:5–8.

18:1 that they should always pray and not give up In anticipation of the events outlined in 17:22–37.

18:2 neither feared God The judge was indifferent toward God's law.

18:3 Grant me justice against my adversary Moses declares that those who refuse justice for widows (among others) shall be opposed by God (Dt 27:19).

18:4 he refused The judge did not care about the widow's plight.

18:5 she won't eventually come and attack me The widow's persistence eventually provoked the judge to grant her request.

18:7 will not God bring about justice If the repeated petitions of a helpless widow are granted by a dishonest judge, Jesus' followers can expect that their righteous God in heaven will respond to their cries for justice.

18:8 will he find faith on the earth The widow's per-

ever, when the Son of Man comes, will he find faith on the earth?"

The Parable of the Pharisee and the Tax Collector

⁹To some who were confident of their own righteousness and looked down on everyone else, Jesus told this parable: ¹⁰"Two men went up to the temple to pray, one a Pharisee and the other a tax collector. ¹¹The Pharisee stood by himself and prayed: 'God, I thank you that I am not like other people — robbers, evildoers, adulterers — or even like this tax collector. ¹²I fast twice a week and give a tenth of all I get.'

¹³"But the tax collector stood at a distance. He would not even look up to heaven, but beat his breast and said, 'God, have mercy on me, a sinner.' ¹⁴"I tell you that this man, rather than the other, went home justified before God. For all those who exalt themselves will be humbled, and those who humble themselves will be exalted."

The Little Children and Jesus

18:15-17pp — Mt 19:13-15; Mk 10:13-16

¹⁵People were also bringing babies to Jesus for him to place his hands on them. When the disciples saw this, they rebuked them. ¹⁶But Jesus called the children to him and said, "Let the little children come to me, and do not hinder them, for the kingdom of God belongs to such as these. ¹⁷Truly I tell you, anyone who will not receive the kingdom of God like a little child will never enter it."

The Rich and the Kingdom of God

18:18-30pp — Mt 19:16-29; Mk 10:17-30

¹⁸A certain ruler asked him, "Good teacher, what must I do to inherit eternal life?"

¹⁹"Why do you call me good?" Jesus answered. "No one is good — except God alone. ²⁰You know the commandments: 'You shall not commit adultery, you shall not murder, you shall not steal, you

---

sistence reflected faith that her request would be granted someday. Jesus calls on his followers to demonstrate this same kind of faith as they wait for his return.

18:9–14 In Lk 17:22—18:8, Jesus addresses his disciples; now he directs a parable toward people who are self-righteous (v. 9). This parable is unique to the Gospel of Luke. Jesus is still working his way toward Jerusalem for Passover (a journey he began at 9:51). He could be speaking to Pharisees or other religious leaders who were making the same pilgrimage and were walking with Jesus' followers (compare 16:14). Jesus' parable reveals that humility is critical to obtaining true righteousness.

18:9 confident of their own righteousness This phrase suggests strict adherence to the law.
18:10 one a Pharisee Refers to a Jewish group that emphasized careful observance of the law. See note on Jn 7:32. **the other a tax collector** Many Jews likely regarded tax collectors as traitors because they worked for the Romans and often exploited their authority over fellow Jews to increase their own wealth (see note on Mt 5:46). Jesus frequently mentions marginalized people (such as Samaritans and lepers) in order to contrast the genuine faith of outsiders with the unbelief and self-righteousness of many Jewish insiders.
18:12 I fast twice a week Fasting twice a week goes beyond the requirements of the law (e.g., Lev 16:29–31; 23:27–32; Nu 29:7). **a tenth of all I get** Tithing a tenth of all income goes beyond what the law required; only certain items were tithed (see Dt 14:22–23).
18:13 stood at a distance Perhaps in the court of Israel or the court of Gentiles (where non-Jews were allowed to gather at the temple). The court of Gentiles might be more likely, since tax collectors typically were ostracized as collaborators with the Romans. See the infographic "Herod's Temple on the Temple Mount" on p. 1722. **even look up to heaven** A normal posture of prayer (see Ps 123:1). The avoidance of such a posture reflects shame from sin. **beat his breast** A sign of mourning and contrition. **God, have mercy on me, a sinner** His location, posture and speech reveal his humility and recognition of his sinfulness—a stunning contrast to the self-righteous Pharisee (Lk 18:11–12).

18:14 rather than the other, went home justified A shocking role reversal—especially since Jesus could be telling this parable to Pharisees (see note on vv. 9–14). The character who would have been perceived as righteous is rejected by God, while the character known for wickedness receives God's acceptance. This teaching no doubt enraged Jesus' audience. **all those who exalt themselves will be humbled** Compare 9:48; 13:30; 14:11.

18:15–17 This scene reflects Jesus' call to humility in the surrounding passages—the parable of vv. 9–14 and the conversation with the rich young ruler (vv. 18–25). Compare Mt 19:13–15; Mk 10:13–16.

18:15 for him to place his hands on them Describes a gesture commonly used when imparting a blessing (Lk 5:13; 6:19; compare Mt 19:13). **they rebuked them** The disciples prevented people from bringing their children to Jesus.
18:17 like a little child Jesus likely makes this comparison to illustrate humility. In the Greco-Roman world, children were viewed as having a low status (see note on Mt 18:2).

18:18–30 The rich young man who converses here with Jesus sets up a contrast with Zacchaeus in the next chapter (Lk 19:1–10). Parallel accounts of this conversation appear in the other Synoptic Gospels (Mt 19:16–30; Mk 10:17–31).

18:18 ruler The young man's exact position of authority is not identified. The Greek term used here can describe various offices (e.g., Lk 8:41; 12:58; 14:1; 23:35). Luke probably intends to highlight the young man's great wealth (v. 23). **what must I do to inherit** The young man seems to be asking sincerely. Earlier in Luke, a scribe used the same question in an attempt to trap Jesus (10:25). **eternal life** Describes life in God's eternal kingdom in contrast to experiencing the absence of God's presence, especially upon death.
18:20 You know the commandments In quoting five of the Ten Commandments, Jesus is essentially referring to all of them. See Ex 20:12–16; Dt 5:16–20.

shall not give false testimony, honor your father and mother.'*ᵃ*"

²¹"All these I have kept since I was a boy," he said.

²²When Jesus heard this, he said to him, "You still lack one thing. Sell everything you have and give to the poor, and you will have treasure in heaven. Then come, follow me."

²³When he heard this, he became very sad, because he was very wealthy. ²⁴Jesus looked at him and said, "How hard it is for the rich to enter the kingdom of God! ²⁵Indeed, it is easier for a camel to go through the eye of a needle than for someone who is rich to enter the kingdom of God."

²⁶Those who heard this asked, "Who then can be saved?"

²⁷Jesus replied, "What is impossible with man is possible with God."

²⁸Peter said to him, "We have left all we had to follow you!"

²⁹"Truly I tell you," Jesus said to them, "no one who has left home or wife or brothers or sisters or parents or children for the sake of the kingdom of God ³⁰will fail to receive many times as much in this age, and in the age to come eternal life."

Jesus Predicts His Death a Third Time
18:31-33pp — Mt 20:17-19; Mk 10:32-34

³¹Jesus took the Twelve aside and told them, "We are going up to Jerusalem, and everything that is written by the prophets about the Son of Man will be fulfilled. ³²He will be delivered over to the Gentiles. They will mock him, insult him and spit on him; ³³they will flog him and kill him. On the third day he will rise again."

³⁴The disciples did not understand any of this. Its meaning was hidden from them, and they did not know what he was talking about.

A Blind Beggar Receives His Sight
18:35-43pp — Mt 20:29-34; Mk 10:46-52

³⁵As Jesus approached Jericho, a blind man was sitting by the roadside begging. ³⁶When he heard the crowd going by, he asked what was happening. ³⁷They told him, "Jesus of Nazareth is passing by."

³⁸He called out, "Jesus, Son of David, have mercy on me!"

³⁹Those who led the way rebuked him and told him to be quiet, but he shouted all the more, "Son of David, have mercy on me!"

⁴⁰Jesus stopped and ordered the man to be brought to him. When he came near, Jesus asked him, ⁴¹"What do you want me to do for you?"

"Lord, I want to see," he replied.

⁴²Jesus said to him, "Receive your sight; your faith has healed you." ⁴³Immediately he received his sight and followed Jesus, praising God. When all the people saw it, they also praised God.

Zacchaeus the Tax Collector

19 Jesus entered Jericho and was passing through. ²A man was there by the name of Zacchaeus; he was a chief tax collector and was wealthy. ³He wanted to see who Jesus was, but because he was short he could not see over the crowd. ⁴So he ran ahead and climbed a sycamore-fig tree to see him, since Jesus was coming that way.

⁵When Jesus reached the spot, he looked up and

ᵃ 20 Exodus 20:12-16; Deut. 5:16-20

18:22 Sell everything you have Jesus knows that the young man's allegiance is to his possessions and the status they provide. Consequently, Jesus tells him to detach himself from all those things, which are preventing his full commitment to God's kingdom (see note on Mt 19:21). **treasure in heaven** Refers to the eternal life that the young man seeks (Lk 18:18).

18:23 he became very sad This response seems to indicate that the young man ultimately declines to follow Jesus (compare Mt 19:22). If so, he is the only person in the Gospels who refuses a direct, one-on-one invitation to become Jesus' disciple.

18:24 How hard Because their trust is in their wealth, not God.

18:25 the eye of a needle Jesus uses hyperbole (intentional exaggeration) to show how difficult it is for the rich to enter God's kingdom. See note on Mk 10:25.

18:26 Who then can be saved In ancient Israel, wealth was seen as a sign of God's blessing. It was assumed that those who were rich were in God's favor, since he had blessed them so much. Similarly, people who suffered were often thought to have sinned greatly (e.g., Lk 13:1–5; Jn 9:1–2). Jesus shows that while wealth may be a blessing it has a larger purpose—to be used to help others—and does not have any bearing on whether a person is a true believer or not.

18:28 We have left all we had Unlike the rich ruler, Peter and the other disciples left everything to follow Jesus (Lk 5:11).

18:31–34 As Jesus and his disciples approach Jerusalem, Jesus again predicts his death and resurrection (the first prediction is recorded in 9:21–22). The disciples still do not understand what Jesus is saying. Compare Mt 20:17–19; Mk 10:32–34.

18:31 by the prophets Passages such as Ps 22 and Isa 53 were understood by the early church as referring to the sufferings endured by Christ (compare Ac 3:18; 17:2–3; 26:22–23).

18:32 mock him, insult him and spit on him Fulfilled in Lk 22:63–65; Mt 26:67.

18:34 was hidden from them Compare Lk 9:45.

18:35–43 As Jesus approaches Jericho, he heals a blind man who responds by affirming Jesus' Messianic identity. Parallel accounts of this scene appear in Mt 20:29–34 (which reports two blind men); Mk 10:46–52.

18:38 Son of David A Messianic title (see note on Mt 1:1).

18:42 Receive your sight Recalls Jesus' proclamation at the start of his ministry, when he quoted Isaiah's prophecy about Yahweh restoring his people (Lk 4:18).

said to him, "Zacchaeus, come down immediately. I must stay at your house today." ⁶So he came down at once and welcomed him gladly.

⁷All the people saw this and began to mutter, "He has gone to be the guest of a sinner."

⁸But Zacchaeus stood up and said to the Lord, "Look, Lord! Here and now I give half of my possessions to the poor, and if I have cheated anybody out of anything, I will pay back four times the amount."

⁹Jesus said to him, "Today salvation has come to this house, because this man, too, is a son of Abraham. ¹⁰For the Son of Man came to seek and to save the lost."

The Parable of the Ten Minas

19:12-27Ref — Mt 25:14-30

¹¹While they were listening to this, he went on to tell them a parable, because he was near Jerusalem and the people thought that the kingdom of God was going to appear at once. ¹²He said: "A man of noble birth went to a distant country to have himself appointed king and then to return. ¹³So he called ten of his servants and gave them ten minas.ᵃ 'Put this money to work,' he said, 'until I come back.'

¹⁴"But his subjects hated him and sent a delegation after him to say, 'We don't want this man to be our king.'

¹⁵"He was made king, however, and returned home. Then he sent for the servants to whom he had given the money, in order to find out what they had gained with it.

¹⁶"The first one came and said, 'Sir, your mina has earned ten more.'

¹⁷"'Well done, my good servant!' his master replied. 'Because you have been trustworthy in a very small matter, take charge of ten cities.'

¹⁸"The second came and said, 'Sir, your mina has earned five more.'

¹⁹"His master answered, 'You take charge of five cities.'

²⁰"Then another servant came and said, 'Sir, here is your mina; I have kept it laid away in a piece of cloth. ²¹I was afraid of you, because you are a hard man. You take out what you did not put in and reap what you did not sow.'

ᵃ *13 A mina was about three months' wages.*

---

your faith has healed you Jesus again cites someone's faith in relation to healing (compare 5:20; 7:9,50; 8:48; 17:19).

19:1–10 In contrast to the rich young ruler in the preceding chapter (18:18–25), another wealthy Jew, Zacchaeus, responds rightly to Jesus. When Zacchaeus, the area's top tax collector, learns that Jesus is passing by, he climbs a tree to get a better view. Jesus bestows on Zacchaeus the blessing of hosting him, which provokes complaints from the local residents who know Zacchaeus' corrupt practices. Overcome with joy, Zacchaeus pledges to donate half of his possessions to the impoverished and to repay fourfold the money he has taken wrongfully. Jesus declares Zacchaeus' salvation and affirms his own mission to recover the lost. The story of Zacchaeus is only in Luke's Gospel.

19:1 Jericho An ancient city in the Jordan Valley, about ten miles northeast of Jerusalem; conquered by Joshua and the Israelites when the walls collapsed. Jericho is Jesus' last major stop before entering Jerusalem.

19:2 a chief tax collector Jews typically despised tax collectors as traitors, because they worked for the Roman Empire. **wealthy** Tax collectors often used their authority to take money for themselves (see note on Mt 5:46).

19:3 He wanted to see who Jesus was No doubt there was a great commotion as Jesus—a renowned rabbi—and the crowd traveling with him entered Jericho.

19:5 Zacchaeus, come down immediately Jesus calls Zacchaeus by name and bestows on him the honor of host—again reaching out to someone who is marginalized and despised (e.g., Lk 5:12–14; 7:36–50; 15:1–2).

19:8 I give half of my possessions to the poor As Jesus implies in v. 9, Zacchaeus' remarks in this verse signify his repentance. This is in stark contrast to the rich young ruler in 18:22–23 who denies Jesus' command to sell his possession and follow him. **I will pay back four times the amount** Zacchaeus' pledge goes well beyond the Law of Moses, which generally called for repaying 1.2 times the amount that was stolen or extorted (Lev 6:5; Nu 5:6–7). In the case of stolen livestock, more was required (Ex 22:1).

19:9 salvation Refers to deliverance from sin and restoration of right relationship with God. **because this man, too, is a son of Abraham** Jesus affirms Zacchaeus' identity as a faithful Jew, despite his detested role as a tax collector.

19:10 to seek and to save Recalls Isaiah's imagery of restoration (cited by Jesus in Lk 4:18–19), as well as the divine initiative to seek the lost (portrayed in the parables of ch. 15).

19:11–27 While at Zacchaeus' house, Jesus tells a parable about a nobleman who entrusts money to his servants. The parable explains that God expects for his people to properly steward the resources he gives. The parable also emphasizes the importance of obedience to God's commands. A parallel account appears in Mt 25:14–30.

19:11 was going to appear at once Jesus' proximity to Jerusalem heightened expectations about his Messianic kingdom. It seems that people were expecting Jesus to overthrow Rome's occupation of Judea, but instead Jesus tells a parable about being faithful while the master (Jesus) is gone. This is because God's kingdom is not fully inaugurated until Jesus' second coming.

19:12 a distant country Suggests a lengthy interval between the man's departure and return.

19:13 ten minas A mina was roughly equal to three months' wages for a day-laborer.

19:14 sent a delegation after him Presumably to the ruler bestowing authority on the nobleman. According to the next verse, this delegation was unsuccessful in blocking the appointment.

19:17 take charge of ten cities The nobleman rewards the slave by assigning him territory in the newly acquired kingdom.

²²"His master replied, 'I will judge you by your own words, you wicked servant! You knew, did you, that I am a hard man, taking out what I did not put in, and reaping what I did not sow? ²³Why then didn't you put my money on deposit, so that when I came back, I could have collected it with interest?'

²⁴"Then he said to those standing by, 'Take his mina away from him and give it to the one who has ten minas.'

²⁵"'Sir,' they said, 'he already has ten!'

²⁶"He replied, 'I tell you that to everyone who has, more will be given, but as for the one who has nothing, even what they have will be taken away. ²⁷But those enemies of mine who did not want me to be king over them — bring them here and kill them in front of me.'"

Jesus Comes to Jerusalem as King

19:29-38pp — Mt 21:1-9; Mk 11:1-10
19:35-38pp — Jn 12:12-15

²⁸After Jesus had said this, he went on ahead, going up to Jerusalem. ²⁹As he approached Bethphage and Bethany at the hill called the Mount of Olives, he sent two of his disciples, saying to them, ³⁰"Go to the village ahead of you, and as you enter it, you will find a colt tied there, which no one has ever ridden. Untie it and bring it here. ³¹If anyone asks you, 'Why are you untying it?' say, 'The Lord needs it.'"

³²Those who were sent ahead went and found it just as he had told them. ³³As they were untying the colt, its owners asked them, "Why are you untying the colt?"

³⁴They replied, "The Lord needs it."

³⁵They brought it to Jesus, threw their cloaks on the colt and put Jesus on it. ³⁶As he went along, people spread their cloaks on the road.

³⁷When he came near the place where the road goes down the Mount of Olives, the whole crowd of disciples began joyfully to praise God in loud voices for all the miracles they had seen:

³⁸ "Blessed is the king who comes in the name
of the Lord!"ᵃ

"Peace in heaven and glory in the highest!"

³⁹Some of the Pharisees in the crowd said to Jesus, "Teacher, rebuke your disciples!"

⁴⁰"I tell you," he replied, "if they keep quiet, the stones will cry out."

⁴¹As he approached Jerusalem and saw the city, he wept over it ⁴²and said, "If you, even you, had only known on this day what would bring you peace — but now it is hidden from your eyes. ⁴³The days will come upon you when your enemies will build an embankment against you and encircle you and hem you in on every side. ⁴⁴They will dash you to the ground, you and the children within your walls. They will not leave one stone on another, because you did not recognize the time of God's coming to you."

Jesus at the Temple

19:45,46pp — Mt 21:12-16; Mk 11:15-18; Jn 2:13-16

⁴⁵When Jesus entered the temple courts, he began to drive out those who were selling. ⁴⁶"It

ᵃ 38 Psalm 118:26

19:22 I will judge you The slave will be judged severely. He disobeyed the master's command to conduct business while he was away (Lk 19:13), opting instead to simply hide the mina (v. 20).

19:26 more will be given The new king indicates that faithful obedience leads to greater responsibility in managing the kingdom's resources. Jesus made this same point in the parable of the lamp (8:18; compare note on Mt 25:29).

19:28–40 Luke's travel narrative, which began at Lk 9:51, ends with this passage as Jesus enters Jerusalem (compare Mt 21:1–9; Mk 11:1–10; Jn 12:12–18). The remainder of Luke's Gospel recounts the events surrounding Jesus' death and resurrection.

19:28 going up to Jerusalem Refers to the final ascent to the holy city, which was located on a plateau in the Judean Mountains.

19:29 Bethphage and Bethany Villages on the outskirts of Jerusalem. **Mount of Olives** The location has prophetic connotations. In the book of Zechariah, the Mount of Olives (on the east side of Jerusalem) is identified as the place where God will take his stand in battle against those who attack his people (Zec 14:4).

19:32 just as he had told them Suggests divine arrangement.

19:35 put Jesus on it This scene reflects Zechariah's image of the king triumphantly returning to Jerusalem from battle (Zec 9:9). This act has Messianic connotations: Jesus is riding into Jerusalem as the king of the Jews, in David's line (see 1Ki 1:33 and note).

19:36 people Likely refers to the Galilean peasants who followed Jesus to Jerusalem, as opposed to residents of the city. **spread their cloaks** An act of homage. In 2Ki 9:13 the people performed this same action when announcing Jehu as the new king of Israel.

19:38 comes in the name of the Lord Quoted from Ps 118:26.

19:39 Pharisees See note on Lk 5:17. **rebuke your disciples** The Pharisees recognize the symbolism of Jesus' manner of arrival (see note on 19:35), as well as the Messianic overtones in the cries of the crowd. Also, they might have feared that shouts of praise to the king (v. 38) would incite a violent response from the Romans, as it could have been viewed as anti-imperial.

19:40 the stones will cry out Jesus alludes to Hab 2:11. His reply to the Pharisees accepts the people's praises as appropriate, implying that he truly is Israel's king who comes in the name of Yahweh.

19:41–44 As Jesus enters Jerusalem, he weeps and delivers a lament. Compare Lk 13:33–34; 23:27–31.

19:43 encircle you and hem you in Jesus probably is describing the Romans' destruction of Jerusalem that will occur in AD 70 (about 40 years later).

19:44 the children Jesus is addressing the city itself; the reference to children indicates Jerusalem's inhabitants, the Jews. The language is reminiscent of several OT passages (e.g., Ps 137:9; Hos 10:14; Na 3:10).

is written," he said to them, "'My house will be a house of prayer'ᵃ; but you have made it 'a den of robbers.'ᵇ"

⁴⁷Every day he was teaching at the temple. But the chief priests, the teachers of the law and the leaders among the people were trying to kill him. ⁴⁸Yet they could not find any way to do it, because all the people hung on his words.

The Authority of Jesus Questioned

20:1-8pp — Mt 21:23-27; Mk 11:27-33

20 One day as Jesus was teaching the people in the temple courts and proclaiming the good news, the chief priests and the teachers of the law, together with the elders, came up to him. ²"Tell us by what authority you are doing these things," they said. "Who gave you this authority?"

³He replied, "I will also ask you a question. Tell me: ⁴John's baptism — was it from heaven, or of human origin?"

⁵They discussed it among themselves and said, "If we say, 'From heaven,' he will ask, 'Why didn't you believe him?' ⁶But if we say, 'Of human origin,' all the people will stone us, because they are persuaded that John was a prophet."

⁷So they answered, "We don't know where it was from."

⁸Jesus said, "Neither will I tell you by what authority I am doing these things."

The Parable of the Tenants

20:9-19pp — Mt 21:33-46; Mk 12:1-12

⁹He went on to tell the people this parable: "A man planted a vineyard, rented it to some farmers and went away for a long time. ¹⁰At harvest time he sent a servant to the tenants so they would give him some of the fruit of the vineyard. But the tenants beat him and sent him away empty-handed. ¹¹He sent another servant, but that one also they beat and treated shamefully and sent away empty-handed. ¹²He sent still a third, and they wounded him and threw him out.

¹³"Then the owner of the vineyard said, 'What shall I do? I will send my son, whom I love; perhaps they will respect him.'

¹⁴"But when the tenants saw him, they talked the matter over. 'This is the heir,' they said. 'Let's kill him, and the inheritance will be ours.' ¹⁵So they threw him out of the vineyard and killed him.

"What then will the owner of the vineyard do to them? ¹⁶He will come and kill those tenants and give the vineyard to others."

When the people heard this, they said, "God forbid!"

¹⁷Jesus looked directly at them and asked, "Then what is the meaning of that which is written:

"'The stone the builders rejected
has become the cornerstone'ᶜ?

ᵃ 46 Isaiah 56:7   ᵇ 46 Jer. 7:11   ᶜ 17 Psalm 118:22

19:45–48 Jesus disrupts the business transactions taking place at the temple. Parallel accounts appear in the other three Gospels (Mt 21:12–13; Mk 11:15–17; Jn 2:13–17).

19:45 those who were selling Refers to the sale of animals for sacrifices. See note on Mk 11:15.

19:46 a house of prayer Jesus quotes from Isaiah (see Isa 56:7 and note). **a den of robbers** A phrase from Jeremiah (see Jer 7:11 and note).

19:47 teachers of the law See note on Lk 5:21. **were trying to kill him** Several factors likely contributed to the religious leaders' desire to kill Jesus: They viewed him as a Messianic pretender and a blasphemer, they lost control of the masses due to his popularity and they feared that civil unrest during the Passover festival would lead to violent reprisals from Rome. Josephus, a first-century Jewish historian, records a number of riots that occurred during festivals in Jerusalem. As peasants from outlying regions (like Galilee) filled the city for the religious holiday, they often protested their perceived mistreatment at the hands of wealthy urbanites. The Romans often responded by violently quelling these demonstrations, resulting in many deaths.

19:48 all the people Fearing the response of the crowd, the religious leaders took no immediate action against Jesus.

20:1–8 While Jesus is teaching in the temple, the religious leaders question his authority. This is the first of several instances in which they attempt to publicly discredit Jesus' ministry. Compare Mt 21:23–27; Mk 11:27–33.

20:3 I will also ask you a question Matthew's account frames Jesus' response as a condition: If the religious leaders answer Jesus' question, then he will answer theirs. Although this condition is unstated in Luke, it is reflected in Jesus' response in Lk 20:8.

20:4 John's baptism Described in ch. 3 as a baptism of repentance (3:3 and note).

20:6 stone us The Jewish law's penalty for blasphemy (see Lev 24:11–16; compare Jn 8:59; 10:31–33).

20:8 Neither will I tell you The religious leaders evade the dilemma that Jesus' question presented (Lk 20:5–6); in the same way, Jesus avoids their attempt to trap him in a statement that they could use against him.

20:9–19 In response to the questioning of his authority, Jesus tells a parable about tenant farmers who respond with violence to various messengers sent by the landowner—even killing his son. The parable foreshadows Jesus' rejection by the Jews and his crucifixion. Compare Mt 21:33–46; Mk 12:1–12.

20:10 fruit of the vineyard Recalls Jesus' parable of the sower, in which bearing fruit represents the appropriate response to hearing God's word (Lk 8:15).

20:14 Let's kill him Echoes Joseph's hostile brothers in Ge 37:19–20. Joseph, like Jesus, enjoyed the status of beloved son, though the connotations are very different—with Jesus' status also representing his divinity (Ge 37:3).

20:17 become the cornerstone A quote from Ps 118:22. Jesus implies that he is the rejected stone.

[18]Everyone who falls on that stone will be broken to pieces; anyone on whom it falls will be crushed." [19]The teachers of the law and the chief priests looked for a way to arrest him immediately, because they knew he had spoken this parable against them. But they were afraid of the people.

Paying Taxes to Caesar

20:20-26pp — Mt 22:15-22; Mk 12:13-17

[20]Keeping a close watch on him, they sent spies, who pretended to be sincere. They hoped to catch Jesus in something he said, so that they might hand him over to the power and authority of the governor. [21]So the spies questioned him: "Teacher, we know that you speak and teach what is right, and that you do not show partiality but teach the way of God in accordance with the truth. [22]Is it right for us to pay taxes to Caesar or not?"

[23]He saw through their duplicity and said to them, [24]"Show me a denarius. Whose image and inscription are on it?"

"Caesar's," they replied.

[25]He said to them, "Then give back to Caesar what is Caesar's, and to God what is God's."

[26]They were unable to trap him in what he had said there in public. And astonished by his answer, they became silent.

The Resurrection and Marriage

20:27-40pp — Mt 22:23-33; Mk 12:18-27

[27]Some of the Sadducees, who say there is no resurrection, came to Jesus with a question. [28]"Teacher," they said, "Moses wrote for us that if a man's brother dies and leaves a wife but no children, the man must marry the widow and raise up offspring for his brother. [29]Now there were seven brothers. The first one married a woman and died childless. [30]The second [31]and then the third married her, and in the same way the seven died, leaving no children. [32]Finally, the woman died too. [33]Now then, at the resurrection whose wife will she be, since the seven were married to her?"

[34]Jesus replied, "The people of this age marry and are given in marriage. [35]But those who are considered worthy of taking part in the age to come and in the resurrection from the dead will neither marry nor be given in marriage, [36]and they can no longer die; for they are like the angels. They are God's children, since they are children of the resurrection. [37]But in the account of the

---

20:18 broken to pieces Jesus seems to be using imagery from Isaiah or Daniel (see Isa 8:14–15; Da 2:45 and note). These passages seems to envision the final judgment of those who reject Jesus' place in God's plan. All of those who reject Jesus' place in God's plan are acting in opposition to God's purposes and will be judged accordingly. **20:19 teachers of the law** See note on Lk 5:21. **they were afraid of the people** See 19:47 and note.

20:20–26 The Jewish authorities attempt to implicate Jesus in rebellion against the Roman government—a charge that could lead to his arrest and, possibly, his death. However, Jesus is aware of their intentions and responds to their questions with wisdom. Parallel accounts appear in the other Synoptic Gospels (Mt 22:15–22; Mk 12:13–27).

20:20 authority of the governor If the religious leaders could produce witnesses of Jesus speaking against Caesar, then the Romans would arrest him and perhaps execute him as an enemy of the state.

20:21 you speak and teach what is right The spies flatter Jesus in an attempt to conceal their intention. **20:22 Is it right for us** Their question is carefully crafted: A positive answer would alienate Jesus from the Jews, who opposed Roman taxation; a negative answer would incriminate him against Rome. **pay taxes to Caesar** Since Jesus' central message was that the kingdom of God had arrived (e.g., Lk 4:43; 8:1), a question about paying taxes to another kingdom—the Roman Empire—was fully relevant. Judeans began paying taxes to Rome in AD 6 when Caesar Augustus terminated the rule of Archelaus (son of Herod the Great) and made his territory a Roman province. According to the first-century historian Josephus, a Galilean (or Gaulanite) named Judas provoked widespread opposition over this taxation, maintaining that it was inconsistent with God's sovereignty over Israel (Josephus, *Jewish War* 2.117–18; *Antiquities* 18.1–10). Taxation also was a motivating factor in the

Jews' revolt against Rome in AD 66, which ultimately led to the destruction of Jerusalem (Josephus, *Jewish War* 2.403–4; 6.422).

20:24 a denarius A coin representing about a day's wages. See the infographic "A Silver Denarius" on p. 1578. **Whose image and inscription** The denarius bore the image and title of Tiberius Caesar. **image** The Greek word used here, *eikōn*, is the same word used in the Septuagint (the Greek translation of the OT) to describe people being made in the image of God (Ge 1:26–27). **20:25 to God what is God's** The coin bore Caesar's image and thus belongs to him. By this same logic, that which bore the image of God—all of humanity—belongs to God. Jesus' response, then, challenges his questioners and anyone else listening to show allegiance to God by devoting their lives to him.

20:27–40 The Sadducees—a wealthy priestly group—ask Jesus a question about the resurrection from the dead (a doctrine that they did not support). His response rejects their view and foreshadows his own resurrection. Compare Mt 22:23–33; Mk 12:18–27. See the table "Major Groups in Jesus' Time" on p. 1630.

20:28 man must marry the widow A custom called levirate marriage (see Dt 25:5–10). The Sadducees' hypothetical question applies this law to an absurd situation, apparently seeking to ridicule belief in a future resurrection of the dead and perhaps to mock Jesus. **20:34 this age** The present age, before final judgment. **20:35 the age to come and in the resurrection** Refers to the age that will follow final judgment—when God's enemies are defeated and his kingdom is fully established (compare Rev 20–21). **20:36 they can no longer die** They will be immortal. Jesus suggests that marriage is appropriate only for the period leading up to resurrection and immortality. **20:37 in the account of the burning bush** Refers to God's appearance to Moses in the burning bush (Ex

burning bush, even Moses showed that the dead rise, for he calls the Lord 'the God of Abraham, and the God of Isaac, and the God of Jacob.'[a] [38]He is not the God of the dead, but of the living, for to him all are alive."

[39]Some of the teachers of the law responded, "Well said, teacher!" [40]And no one dared to ask him any more questions.

Whose Son Is the Messiah?
20:41-47pp — Mt 22:41-23:7; Mk 12:35-40

[41]Then Jesus said to them, "Why is it said that the Messiah is the son of David? [42]David himself declares in the Book of Psalms:

"'The Lord said to my Lord:
"Sit at my right hand
[43]until I make your enemies
a footstool for your feet."'[b]

[44]David calls him 'Lord.' How then can he be his son?"

Warning Against the Teachers of the Law

[45]While all the people were listening, Jesus said to his disciples, [46]"Beware of the teachers of the law.

They like to walk around in flowing robes and love to be greeted with respect in the marketplaces and have the most important seats in the synagogues and the places of honor at banquets. [47]They devour widows' houses and for a show make lengthy prayers. These men will be punished most severely."

The Widow's Offering
21:1-4pp — Mk 12:41-44

21 As Jesus looked up, he saw the rich putting their gifts into the temple treasury. [2]He also saw a poor widow put in two very small copper coins. [3]"Truly I tell you," he said, "this poor widow has put in more than all the others. [4]All these people gave their gifts out of their wealth; but she out of her poverty put in all she had to live on."

The Destruction of the Temple and Signs of the End Times
21:5-36pp — Mt 24; Mk 13
21:12-17pp — Mt 10:17-22

[5]Some of his disciples were remarking about how the temple was adorned with beautiful stones

a 37 Exodus 3:6   b 43 Psalm 110:1

3:1–6). even Moses showed Since the Sadducees appeal to Moses in Lk 20:28, Jesus does the same to correct their faulty understanding of resurrection.
20:38 He is not the God of the dead Jesus points out that, although Abraham, Isaac and Jacob are dead, God describes his relationship with them using the present tense (Ex 3:6). This ongoing relationship must mean that Abraham, Isaac and Jacob experience life with God after their death—thus proving the truth of resurrection.
20:39 Some of the teachers of the law Although these legal experts were among those plotting against Jesus (Lk 19:47—20:1), some who believed in resurrection found themselves impressed by his answer to the Sadducees.

20:41–44 Following the questions from the religious leaders, Jesus now asks them about the nature of the relationship of David to the Messiah. Unlike Matthew's version of this incident, Luke's account offers no response from the leaders (compare Mt 22:41–46; Mk 12:35–37).

20:41 Why is it said Jesus is raising an apparent paradox: The Messiah is described as David's son or descendant, but David also addresses him as a superior.
20:42 in the Book of Psalms Jesus quotes Ps 110:1. **The Lord said to my Lord** In the OT, this phrase is "a saying of Yahweh to my Lord (a ruler)" (*ne'um yhwh ladoni* in Hebrew). Yahweh is addressing either David or David's descendant. Since this is ascribed as a psalm of David, Jesus understands David as the speaker of the entire psalm, and thus is the person citing Yahweh himself. This means that the "my Lord" who Yahweh is addressing must be someone other than David. Luke's citation reflects how this verse is rendered in the Septuagint (the Greek translation of the OT).
20:44 How then can he be his son Jesus understands "my Lord" from Ps 110:1 as referring to David's offspring.

Unlike David, Jesus the Messiah sits at the right hand of Yahweh. While Jesus is the descendent of David, he is also David's Lord. The early church likewise understood Ps 110:1 as a reference to Jesus, the Davidic Messiah (e.g., Ac 2:34–36; 1Co 15:25–28; Heb 1:3,13).

20:45–47 Jesus warns the people about the hypocrisy of the scribes (teachers of the law). Matthew includes a much longer passage in which Jesus pronounces seven woes on the scribes and Pharisees (Mt 23:1–36; compare Mk 12:37–40).

20:46 teachers of the law See note on Lk 5:21. **the places of honor at banquets** Compare 14:7–10.
20:47 They devour widows' houses This phrase sets up Jesus' remarks about the widow's offering in 21:1–4.

21:1–4 Jesus' assessment of the widow's action is at once a commendation of her generosity and a word of judgment against greed. Compare Mk 12:41–44.
21:1 temple treasury The Greek word used here, *gazophylakion*, may refer to a room in the temple or to a box used to collect contributions.
21:2 two very small copper coins The coins described here had the least value of any currency in Jesus' time.
21:4 all she had to live on The Greek phrase used here means "all the livelihood" or "all the life," implying that her giving was so generous it could impede upon her survival. See note on Mk 12:44.

21:5–28 Jesus again predicts the forthcoming destruction of the temple, which leads into his second discourse about the difficulties that will come before his second coming, including the persecution of his followers (compare Lk 17:22–37). Parallel passages appear in the other Synoptic Gospels (Mt 24:1–31; Mk 13:1–27).

and with gifts dedicated to God. But Jesus said, ⁶"As for what you see here, the time will come when not one stone will be left on another; every one of them will be thrown down."

⁷"Teacher," they asked, "when will these things happen? And what will be the sign that they are about to take place?"

⁸He replied: "Watch out that you are not deceived. For many will come in my name, claiming, 'I am he,' and, 'The time is near.' Do not follow them. ⁹When you hear of wars and uprisings, do not be frightened. These things must happen first, but the end will not come right away."

¹⁰Then he said to them: "Nation will rise against nation, and kingdom against kingdom. ¹¹There will be great earthquakes, famines and pestilences in various places, and fearful events and great signs from heaven.

¹²"But before all this, they will seize you and persecute you. They will hand you over to synagogues and put you in prison, and you will be brought before kings and governors, and all on account of my name. ¹³And so you will bear testimony to me. ¹⁴But make up your mind not to worry beforehand how you will defend yourselves. ¹⁵For I will give you words and wisdom that none of your adversaries will be able to resist or contradict. ¹⁶You will be betrayed even by parents, brothers and sisters, relatives and friends, and they will put some of you to death. ¹⁷Everyone will hate you because of me. ¹⁸But not a hair of your head will perish. ¹⁹Stand firm, and you will win life.

²⁰"When you see Jerusalem being surrounded by armies, you will know that its desolation is near. ²¹Then let those who are in Judea flee to the mountains, let those in the city get out, and let those in the country not enter the city. ²²For this is the time of punishment in fulfillment of all that has been written. ²³How dreadful it will

---

21:6 not one stone will be left This likely describes the destruction of the temple—and most of Jerusalem—by the Romans in AD 70 (compare Lk 19:41–44).

21:8 many will come in my name Jesus might be referring to people claiming to be the Messiah or people falsely claiming to work under Jesus' authority.

21:10 Nation will rise against nation Language reminiscent of several OT passages (e.g., 2Ch 15:6; Isa 19:2).

21:11 great earthquakes, famines and pestilences Common motifs of divine judgment (e.g., Dt 32:24; Eze 6:11; Rev 6:12; 16:18).

21:12 and persecute you Jesus describes the suffering that his disciples will undergo. In Acts, Luke details some of this persecution (e.g., Ac 5:17–18; 7:54—8:3; 12:1–5).

21:13 testimony Persecution will give Jesus' followers opportunities to proclaim the gospel.

21:15 For I will give you words Earlier in Luke, this ability to testify about God's work is attributed to the Holy Spirit (see Lk 12:12 and note). Here, Jesus says that he himself will empower his followers to speak wisely and persuasively, showing a strong connection between Jesus and the Holy Spirit (see Jn 14:26 and note).

21:18 not a hair of your head will perish Likely refers to eternal life in the age to come (see Lk 20:35 and note). Verse 16 states that some of the disciples will be put to death, and church tradition holds that all but one (John) were martyred. Jesus is thus referencing the eternal fate of his followers.

21:20 When you see Jerusalem being surrounded by armies Jesus could be warning about the Roman attack of AD 70. He also might be referring to other tribulation prior to his second coming. **its desolation is near** Jesus could be alluding to an act that causes desolation in the OT book of Daniel, which is a reference to idolatry (see Da 8:13 and note; Mt 24:15 and note). This may also just be another reference to the destruction of Jerusalem by the Romans.

21:22 this is the time of punishment Jesus is likely referencing Hos 9:7, which describes Israel's impending destruction for rejecting God and his prophet (compare Isa 63:4; Jer 5:29). **all that has been written** Refers to other oracles of destruction against Jerusalem (e.g., Jer 6:1–8; 26:1–9; Mic 3:12).

Jesus' Passion and Resurrection

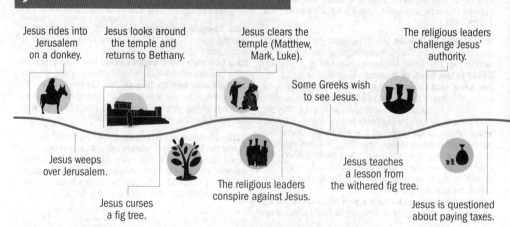

Jesus rides into Jerusalem on a donkey.

Jesus looks around the temple and returns to Bethany.

Jesus clears the temple (Matthew, Mark, Luke).

Some Greeks wish to see Jesus.

The religious leaders challenge Jesus' authority.

Jesus weeps over Jerusalem.

Jesus curses a fig tree.

The religious leaders conspire against Jesus.

Jesus teaches a lesson from the withered fig tree.

Jesus is questioned about paying taxes.

be in those days for pregnant women and nursing mothers! There will be great distress in the land and wrath against this people. [24] They will fall by the sword and will be taken as prisoners to all the nations. Jerusalem will be trampled on by the Gentiles until the times of the Gentiles are fulfilled.

[25] "There will be signs in the sun, moon and stars. On the earth, nations will be in anguish and perplexity at the roaring and tossing of the sea. [26] People will faint from terror, apprehensive of what is coming on the world, for the heavenly bodies will be shaken. [27] At that time they will see the Son of Man coming in a cloud with power and great glory. [28] When these things begin to take place, stand up and lift up your heads, because your redemption is drawing near."

[29] He told them this parable: "Look at the fig tree and all the trees. [30] When they sprout leaves, you can see for yourselves and know that summer is near. [31] Even so, when you see these things happening, you know that the kingdom of God is near.

[32] "Truly I tell you, this generation will certainly not pass away until all these things have happened. [33] Heaven and earth will pass away, but my words will never pass away.

[34] "Be careful, or your hearts will be weighed down with carousing, drunkenness and the anxieties of life, and that day will close on you suddenly like a trap. [35] For it will come on all those who live on the face of the whole earth. [36] Be always on the watch, and pray that you may be able to escape all that is about to happen, and that you may be able to stand before the Son of Man."

21:24 Jerusalem will be trampled on An allusion to the ancient Greek (Septuagint) translation of Zec 12:3, which describes Jerusalem as a stone trampled by the nations. This is part of Zechariah's oracle against the city for its unfaithfulness. Compare Da 8:13; Rev 11:2. **until the times of the Gentiles are fulfilled** Jesus could be referring to the end of Roman oppression or to the end of the present age, before God's reign is experienced in fullness (see Lk 20:35 and note).
21:25 There will be signs Jesus brings together various apocalyptic motifs associated with OT portrayals of the day of Yahweh. Jesus partly answers the disciples' question in Lk 21:7 regarding a sign, but he gives no clear time indicator. These signs appear to serve as the culmination of the suffering described in the preceding verses (vv. 10–12,20–24) and as a precursor to Jesus' second coming (v. 27).
21:27 Son of Man coming in a cloud The book of Daniel describes a Messianic figure like a son of man receiving an everlasting kingdom (see Da 7:13 and note). Jesus applies this tradition to himself—the risen Messiah at his glorious return (Mt 8:20 and note).
21:28 stand up and lift up your heads In contrast to the fearful response described in Lk 21:26, Jesus' followers can joyfully rise to welcome their deliverer.

21:29–33 Jesus delivers a parable about a fig tree, encouraging his disciples to discern the signs of the times. Compare Mt 24:32–36; Mk 13:28–32. See the table "Parables of Jesus" on p. 1584.
21:31 when you see these things happening Refers to the events Jesus describes in Lk 21:8–28—especially the final signs before his second coming (vv. 25–28). **the kingdom of God** The culmination of apocalyptic events is the arrival of the Son of Man—Jesus—in power and glory (v. 27) and the full establishment of God's reign.
21:32 this generation See note on Mk 13:30.
21:33 Heaven and earth will pass away Compare Rev 21:1–8.

21:34–38 Jesus tells his followers to remain alert for the events described in Lk 21:8–28. Compare Mt 24:43–51; 25:13; Mk 13:33–37.

21:34 the anxieties of life Reminiscent of the seed sown among the thorns in the parable of the sower (Lk 8:14).
21:35 it will come on all Indicates the universality of judgment.
21:36 to stand before the Son of Man Refers to being judged by him (see Rev 20:11–15).

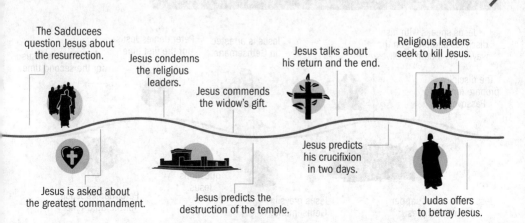

The Sadducees question Jesus about the resurrection.

Jesus condemns the religious leaders.

Jesus commends the widow's gift.

Jesus talks about his return and the end.

Religious leaders seek to kill Jesus.

Jesus is asked about the greatest commandment.

Jesus predicts the destruction of the temple.

Jesus predicts his crucifixion in two days.

Judas offers to betray Jesus.

37Each day Jesus was teaching at the temple, and each evening he went out to spend the night on the hill called the Mount of Olives, 38and all the people came early in the morning to hear him at the temple.

Judas Agrees to Betray Jesus

22:1,2pp — Mt 26:2-5; Mk 14:1,2,10,11

22 Now the Festival of Unleavened Bread, called the Passover, was approaching, 2and the chief priests and the teachers of the law were looking for some way to get rid of Jesus, for they were afraid of the people. 3Then Satan entered Judas, called Iscariot, one of the Twelve. 4And Judas went to the chief priests and the officers of the temple guard and discussed with them how he might betray Jesus. 5They were delighted and agreed to give him money. 6He consented, and watched for an opportunity to hand Jesus over to them when no crowd was present.

The Last Supper

22:7-13pp — Mt 26:17-19; Mk 14:12-16
22:17-20pp — Mt 26:26-29; Mk 14:22-25; 1Co 11:23-25
22:21-23pp — Mt 26:21-24; Mk 14:18-21; Jn 13:21-30
22:25-27pp — Mt 20:25-28; Mk 10:42-45
22:33,34pp — Mt 26:33-35; Mk 14:29-31; Jn 13:37,38

7Then came the day of Unleavened Bread on which the Passover lamb had to be sacrificed. 8Jesus sent Peter and John, saying, "Go and make preparations for us to eat the Passover."

9"Where do you want us to prepare for it?" they asked.

10He replied, "As you enter the city, a man carrying a jar of water will meet you. Follow him to the house that he enters, 11and say to the owner of the house, 'The Teacher asks: Where is the guest room, where I may eat the Passover with my disciples?' 12He will show you a large room upstairs, all furnished. Make preparations there."

13They left and found things just as Jesus had told them. So they prepared the Passover.

22:1–6 Luke records the Jewish leaders plotting to kill Jesus—and Judas conspiring with them. Parallel accounts occur in the other three Gospels (Mt 26:2–5,14–16; Mk 14:1–2,10–11; Jn 11:47–53,13:2).

22:1 Festival of Unleavened Bread A seven-day festival that began immediately after Passover (see note on Lev 23:6). Luke links both celebrations here and in Ac 12:3–4.

22:2 teachers of the law See note on Lk 5:21. **they were afraid of the people** The religious leaders are afraid that arresting Jesus would result in protests among his many supporters, possibly inviting persecution by the Romans and leading to their own power being diminished (see Lk 19:47–48; note on 19:47).

22:3 Satan entered Judas See Jn 13:27 and note.

22:7–23 Jesus and the apostles celebrate Passover. The details about preparing for the meal (Lk 22:7–13) might reflect prior arrangements made by Jesus or—

more in keeping with Luke's portrayal of him—Jesus' supernatural knowledge.

As Jesus leads the ritual meal, he instructs his disciples to remember him each time they eat it in the future (vv. 14–20). Jesus also predicts his betrayal by one of those present (vv. 21–23). Parallel accounts occur in the other three Gospels (Mt 26:17–29; Mk 14:12–25; Jn 13:21–30; compare Jn 6:51–58). See the event line "Jesus' Passion and Resurrection" on p. 1698.

22:7 the Passover lamb Jews celebrated Passover on the 14th day of the month of Nisan (March–April). Because they sacrificed the Passover lamb at twilight (Ex 12:6; Lev 23:5; Nu 9:3), they actually consumed it on the evening that began the 15th of Nisan, the first day of the feast of Unleavened Bread (Lev 23:6).

22:10 a man carrying a jar of water These details likely are meant to show Jesus' supernatural knowledge, which supports Luke's portrayal of him as the divine Messiah (compare Lk 2:11 and note).

Jesus' Passion and Resurrection *(continued)*

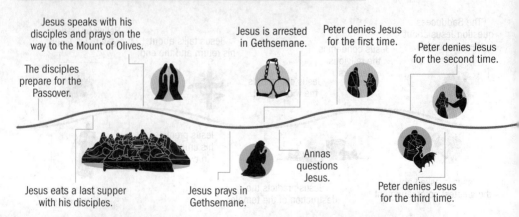

Jesus speaks with his disciples and prays on the way to the Mount of Olives.

Jesus is arrested in Gethsemane.

Peter denies Jesus for the first time.

Peter denies Jesus for the second time.

The disciples prepare for the Passover.

Jesus eats a last supper with his disciples.

Jesus prays in Gethsemane.

Annas questions Jesus.

Peter denies Jesus for the third time.

[14]When the hour came, Jesus and his apostles reclined at the table. [15]And he said to them, "I have eagerly desired to eat this Passover with you before I suffer. [16]For I tell you, I will not eat it again until it finds fulfillment in the kingdom of God."

[17]After taking the cup, he gave thanks and said, "Take this and divide it among you. [18]For I tell you I will not drink again from the fruit of the vine until the kingdom of God comes."

[19]And he took bread, gave thanks and broke it, and gave it to them, saying, "This is my body given for you; do this in remembrance of me."

[20]In the same way, after the supper he took the cup, saying, "This cup is the new covenant in my blood, which is poured out for you.[a] [21]But the hand of him who is going to betray me is with mine on the table. [22]The Son of Man will go as it has been decreed. But woe to that man who betrays him!"

[23]They began to question among themselves which of them it might be who would do this.

[24]A dispute also arose among them as to which of them was considered to be greatest. [25]Jesus said to them, "The kings of the Gentiles lord it over them; and those who exercise authority over them call themselves Benefactors. [26]But you are not to be like that. Instead, the greatest among you should be like the youngest, and the one who rules like the one who serves. [27]For who is greater, the one who is at the table or the one who serves? Is it not the one who is at the table? But I am among you as one who serves. [28]You are those who have stood by me in my trials. [29]And I confer on you a kingdom, just as my Father conferred one on me, [30]so that you may eat and drink at my table in my

[a] 19,20 Some manuscripts do not have *given for you . . . poured out for you.*

22:14 his apostles Specifically the twelve apostles named in 6:13–16.

22:16 until it finds fulfillment in the kingdom A reference to the Messianic banquet, which was expected to accompany the full arrival of God's kingdom (Isa 25:6–8; compare Lk 12:36; 14:15–24; Rev 19:6–9).

22:19 This is my body Jesus reinterprets the symbolism of the bread consumed to commemorate the Passover meal (Dt 16:1–8), applying it to his impending death. Compare Mk 14:22 and note. **given for you** Indicates the vicarious nature of Jesus' sacrificial death. **do this in remembrance of me** Jesus instructs his followers to commemorate his crucifixion and all the saving actions he accomplishes in his death. The early church continued this tradition.

22:20 This cup Perhaps meant to recall OT imagery of the cup of wrath and affliction (Jer 25:15–29). **the new covenant in my blood** Jesus is referencing Jer 31:31. Jesus states that his imminent death enacts the new covenant centered on forgiveness (see Jer 31:34; Mt 26:28 and note; Mk 14:24 and note). The blood of the covenant recalls Moses' ratification of Israel's covenant with Yahweh at Mount Sinai (Ex 24:8). This language also

appears in Zechariah's oracle concerning God's deliverance of Jerusalem during the end-times battle (Zec 9:11).

22:22 as it has been decreed Jesus acknowledges that Judas' betrayal will be used by God to accomplish his purpose of Jesus dying on behalf of humanity (compare Isa 53:10 and note). **woe to that man** Judas remains responsible for his actions. In the book of Acts, Luke portrays Judas' violent death to illustrate this point (see Ac 1:18 and note).

22:24–30 The disciples' argument about who is the greatest emerges from their puzzlement over who might betray Jesus (Lk 22:23). Jesus gently rebukes them, explaining their future role in his kingdom. Compare Mt 20:24–28; Mk 10:41–45.

22:26 like the one who serves Jesus provides a vivid example of humble service in John's account of the Last Supper (Jn 13:1–20; compare Mt 20:26 and note). **22:27 as one who serves** Descriptive of Jesus' life and ministry (see Mk 10:45 and note). **22:29 I confer on you a kingdom** Jesus' apostles share in God's kingdom. **22:30 sit on thrones, judging the twelve tribes**

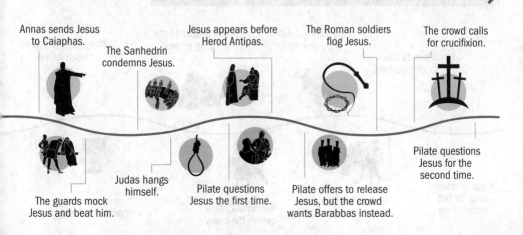

Annas sends Jesus to Caiaphas.

The Sanhedrin condemns Jesus.

Jesus appears before Herod Antipas.

The Roman soldiers flog Jesus.

The crowd calls for crucifixion.

The guards mock Jesus and beat him.

Judas hangs himself.

Pilate questions Jesus the first time.

Pilate offers to release Jesus, but the crowd wants Barabbas instead.

Pilate questions Jesus for the second time.

kingdom and sit on thrones, judging the twelve tribes of Israel.

³¹"Simon, Simon, Satan has asked to sift all of you as wheat. ³²But I have prayed for you, Simon, that your faith may not fail. And when you have turned back, strengthen your brothers."

³³But he replied, "Lord, I am ready to go with you to prison and to death."

³⁴Jesus answered, "I tell you, Peter, before the rooster crows today, you will deny three times that you know me."

³⁵Then Jesus asked them, "When I sent you without purse, bag or sandals, did you lack anything?"

"Nothing," they answered.

³⁶He said to them, "But now if you have a purse, take it, and also a bag; and if you don't have a sword, sell your cloak and buy one. ³⁷It is writ-

ten: 'And he was numbered with the transgressors'ᵃ; and I tell you that this must be fulfilled in me. Yes, what is written about me is reaching its fulfillment."

³⁸The disciples said, "See, Lord, here are two swords."

"That's enough!" he replied.

Jesus Prays on the Mount of Olives
22:40-46pp — Mt 26:36-46; Mk 14:32-42

³⁹Jesus went out as usual to the Mount of Olives, and his disciples followed him. ⁴⁰On reaching the place, he said to them, "Pray that you will not fall into temptation." ⁴¹He withdrew about a stone's throw beyond them, knelt down and prayed, ⁴²"Father, if you are willing, take this cup from me; yet

ᵃ 37 Isaiah 53:12

The disciples are to exercise their authority as humble servants, in a manner opposite their foreign oppressors (Lk 22:25–26).

22:31–34 Following the disciples' dispute over which of them is the greatest, Jesus turns to their spokesman, Peter—who might have been bragging the loudest—and predicts his failure. Compare Mt 26:31–35; Mk 14:27–31; Jn 13:36–38.

22:31 Satan has asked to sift all of you The Greek word translated "you" is plural here, referring to all of the disciples. This seems to be a reference to the testing of the faithfulness of Jesus' followers, not an indication that Jesus is handing them over to destruction (compare Job 1:6–12; 2:1–6).

22:32 But I have prayed for you Here, the Greek word for "you" is singular and refers to Peter.

22:33 to prison and to death While Peter seems overconfident here, his devotion to Jesus does eventually lead to both imprisonment (Ac 12:1–19) and martyrdom (as recorded in the early church letter 1 Clement 5:4).

22:34 before the rooster crows Indicates that Peter's denials will take place before dawn.

22:35–38 This section is unique to Luke's Gospel. It records Jesus preparing his disciples for his arrest.

22:35 Nothing During the disciples' earlier mission (Lk 9:1–6), God saw to it that their needs were met.

22:36 have a purse, take The change in Jesus' instructions indicates that a crisis is coming, as explained in v. 37. **sell your cloak and buy one** Jesus' instructions to buy a sword seems strange, especially in light of his condemnation of violence when Peter cuts off the guard's ear in vv. 50–51. Jesus could be endorsing the legitimacy of self-protection or be speaking in hyperbole, since Peter has just spoken about his willingness to face violence (v. 33).

22:37 And he was numbered with the transgressors Jesus quotes Isa 53:12 as a reference to his imminent crucifixion alongside two criminals (Lk 23:32). See the table "Jesus' Fulfillment of OT Prophecy" on p. 1573. **is reaching its fulfillment** This phrase likely refers to arrangements for Jesus' arrest. In John's Gospel, Jesus sends Judas away just prior to this point in the narrative (Jn 13:27).

22:38 That's enough Two swords certainly would not

Jesus' Passion and Resurrection (continued)

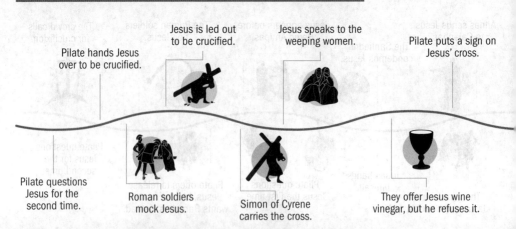

Pilate hands Jesus over to be crucified.

Jesus is led out to be crucified.

Jesus speaks to the weeping women.

Pilate puts a sign on Jesus' cross.

Pilate questions Jesus for the second time.

Roman soldiers mock Jesus.

Simon of Cyrene carries the cross.

They offer Jesus wine vinegar, but he refuses it.

not my will, but yours be done." [43]An angel from heaven appeared to him and strengthened him. [44]And being in anguish, he prayed more earnestly, and his sweat was like drops of blood falling to the ground.[a]

[45]When he rose from prayer and went back to the disciples, he found them asleep, exhausted from sorrow. [46]"Why are you sleeping?" he asked them. "Get up and pray so that you will not fall into temptation."

Jesus Arrested

22:47-53pp — Mt 26:47-56; Mk 14:43-50; Jn 18:3-11

[47]While he was still speaking a crowd came up, and the man who was called Judas, one of the Twelve, was leading them. He approached Jesus to kiss him, [48]but Jesus asked him, "Judas, are you betraying the Son of Man with a kiss?"

[49]When Jesus' followers saw what was going to happen, they said, "Lord, should we strike with our swords?" [50]And one of them struck the servant of the high priest, cutting off his right ear.

[51]But Jesus answered, "No more of this!" And he touched the man's ear and healed him.

[52]Then Jesus said to the chief priests, the officers of the temple guard, and the elders, who had come for him, "Am I leading a rebellion, that you have come with swords and clubs? [53]Every day I was with you in the temple courts, and you did not lay a hand on me. But this is your hour—when darkness reigns."

Peter Disowns Jesus

22:55-62pp — Mt 26:69-75; Mk 14:66-72;
   Jn 18:16-18,25-27

[54]Then seizing him, they led him away and took him into the house of the high priest. Peter followed at a distance. [55]And when some there had

[a] *43,44* Many early manuscripts do not have verses 43 and 44.

---

have been enough to establish Jesus as the earthly king in Jerusalem. See note on Lk 22:36.

22:39-46 Jesus leads his disciples to a secluded place to pray; he asks God the Father for strength to carry out his will (compare Isa 53:12). There are parallel accounts in the other three Gospels (Mt 26:36-46; Mk 14:32-42; Jn 18:1-2).

22:40 that you will not fall into temptation Echoes the Lord's Prayer (Lk 11:2-4).

22:42 this cup Refers to suffering and death (see v. 20 and note).

22:43 An angel from heaven appeared Verses 43-44 do not appear in several of the oldest manuscripts of Luke. They likely were added later to reflect the oral tradition of the early church.

22:47-53 As the mob arrives to arrest Jesus, his disciples ask whether they should attack. All four Gospels record that one disciple drew his sword and cut off the

ear of the high priest's slave; Luke is the only Gospel to report that Jesus reattached the man's ear (compare Mt 26:47-56; Mk 14:43-52; Jn 18:2-12).

22:47 one of the Twelve This description magnifies Judas' treachery: One of Jesus' closest disciples is betraying him.

22:48 Son of Man A title with Messianic overtones (see note on Mt 8:20).

22:50 one of them Identified in Jn 18:10 as Peter.

22:51 he touched the man's ear and healed him This shows that Jesus had compassion even on those who came to arrest him.

22:53 darkness reigns Likely a reference to satanic influence (compare Lk 4:13; 22:3).

22:54-65 This section records Peter's three denials of Jesus; it also describes the guards beating and mocking Jesus. Compare parallel accounts in Mt 26:67-75; 27:27-31; Mk 14:65-72; 15:16-20; Jn 18:12-27; 19:2-3.

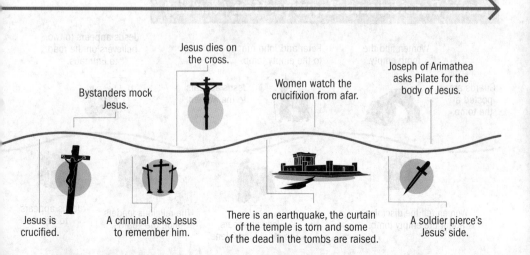

Bystanders mock Jesus.

Jesus dies on the cross.

Women watch the crucifixion from afar.

Joseph of Arimathea asks Pilate for the body of Jesus.

Jesus is crucified.

A criminal asks Jesus to remember him.

There is an earthquake, the curtain of the temple is torn and some of the dead in the tombs are raised.

A soldier pierce's Jesus' side.

kindled a fire in the middle of the courtyard and had sat down together, Peter sat down with them. [56] A servant girl saw him seated there in the firelight. She looked closely at him and said, "This man was with him."

[57] But he denied it. "Woman, I don't know him," he said.

[58] A little later someone else saw him and said, "You also are one of them."

"Man, I am not!" Peter replied.

[59] About an hour later another asserted, "Certainly this fellow was with him, for he is a Galilean."

[60] Peter replied, "Man, I don't know what you're talking about!" Just as he was speaking, the rooster crowed. [61] The Lord turned and looked straight at Peter. Then Peter remembered the word the Lord had spoken to him: "Before the rooster crows to-

day, you will disown me three times." [62] And he went outside and wept bitterly.

The Guards Mock Jesus

22:63-65pp — Mt 26:67,68; Mk 14:65; Jn 18:22,23

[63] The men who were guarding Jesus began mocking and beating him. [64] They blindfolded him and demanded, "Prophesy! Who hit you?" [65] And they said many other insulting things to him.

Jesus Before Pilate and Herod

22:67-71pp — Mt 26:63-66; Mk 14:61-63; Jn 18:19-21
23:2,3pp — Mt 27:11-14; Mk 15:2-5; Jn 18:29-37
23:18-25pp — Mt 27:15-26; Mk 15:6-15;
Jn 18:39 – 19:16

[66] At daybreak the council of the elders of the people, both the chief priests and the teachers of

---

22:57 But he denied it Peter's first denial of Jesus.
22:58 "Man, I am not!" Peter replied Peter's second denial of Jesus.
22:59 he is a Galilean This final charge includes evidence of Peter's association with Jesus: They are both from Galilee. Matthew notes that Peter's accent gave him away as a Galilean (Mt 26:73).
22:60 I don't know Peter's third denial of Jesus. **rooster crowed** Fulfilling Jesus' prediction in Lk 22:34.
22:61 looked straight at Peter Luke is the only Gospel writer to include this detail. Presumably, Jesus was somewhere in the courtyard at this point.
22:63 began mocking and beating him Fulfills Jesus' prediction in 18:32.
22:64 Prophesy! Who hit you The guards mockingly expect Jesus to have supernatural knowledge—similar to Simon the Pharisee, who dismissed Jesus when the sinful woman anointed his feet (7:39).

22:66 – 71 The chapter concludes with Jesus' trial before the Sanhedrin. He affirms that he is the Messiah, and the council condemns him to death. All three of the other Gospels include parallel accounts (Mt 26:59–65; Mk 14:55–63; Jn 18:12–14,19–23).

22:66 before them The Greek word used here, *synedrion*, refers to the council in charge of Jewish affairs in Roman Palestine.

Luke 22:66

SANHEDRIN
The Sanhedrin, the Jewish high council, consisted of the most influential members of Jewish society. The Romans gave this body limited authority over internal Jewish matters. Jewish tradition claims that the Sanhedrin had existed since the time of Moses (Nu 11:16); however, in existing sources, the earliest support for the council comes from the late second century BC. It remains possible that the Sanhedrin's origins date to the Persian period (ca. 559–331 BC), when the Jews enjoyed a degree of autonomy after the return from the Babylonian exile. The Sanhedrin was disbanded in the aftermath of the events of AD 70 when the Romans destroyed Jerusalem and removed the Jews' privilege of self-governance.

Jesus' Passion and Resurrection (continued)

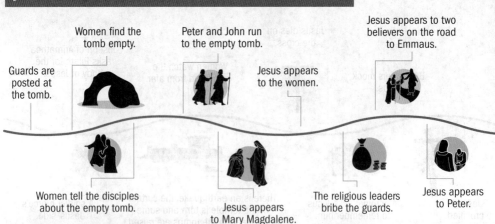

Guards are posted at the tomb.

Women find the tomb empty.

Peter and John run to the empty tomb.

Jesus appears to the women.

Jesus appears to two believers on the road to Emmaus.

Women tell the disciples about the empty tomb.

Jesus appears to Mary Magdalene.

The religious leaders bribe the guards.

Jesus appears to Peter.

the law, met together, and Jesus was led before them. ⁶⁷"If you are the Messiah," they said, "tell us."

Jesus answered, "If I tell you, you will not believe me, ⁶⁸and if I asked you, you would not answer. ⁶⁹But from now on, the Son of Man will be seated at the right hand of the mighty God."

⁷⁰They all asked, "Are you then the Son of God?"

He replied, "You say that I am."

⁷¹Then they said, "Why do we need any more testimony? We have heard it from his own lips."

23 Then the whole assembly rose and led him off to Pilate. ²And they began to accuse him, saying, "We have found this man subverting our nation. He opposes payment of taxes to Caesar and claims to be Messiah, a king."

³So Pilate asked Jesus, "Are you the king of the Jews?"

"You have said so," Jesus replied.

⁴Then Pilate announced to the chief priests and the crowd, "I find no basis for a charge against this man."

⁵But they insisted, "He stirs up the people all over Judea by his teaching. He started in Galilee and has come all the way here."

⁶On hearing this, Pilate asked if the man was a Galilean. ⁷When he learned that Jesus was under Herod's jurisdiction, he sent him to Herod, who was also in Jerusalem at that time.

⁸When Herod saw Jesus, he was greatly pleased, because for a long time he had been wanting to see him. From what he had heard about him, he hoped to see him perform a sign of some sort. ⁹He plied him with many questions, but Jesus gave him no answer. ¹⁰The chief priests and the teachers of the law were standing there, vehemently accusing him. ¹¹Then Herod and his soldiers ridiculed and

---

22:69 the Son of Man will be seated A Messianic reference, drawn from Da 7:13–14 (see Lk 21:27 and note; note on Mk 2:10). **at the right hand of the mighty God** A position of supreme honor and authority. According to Jesus' interpretation of Ps 110:1, Yahweh invites the Messiah to sit at his right hand (compare Lk 20:41–44).

22:70 You say that I am A terse affirmation similar to the English expression "you said it."

23:1–5 The Sanhedrin brings Jesus before Pilate, the Roman governor of Judea, because only imperial authorities could impose the death sentence. Despite the Jewish leaders' heated accusations, Pilate exonerates Jesus. Parallel accounts appear in the other three Gospels (Mt 27:11–14; Mk 15:1–5; Jn 18:28–38). See the infographic "The Sanhedrin" on p. 1746.

23:1 Pilate The governor of the Roman province of Judea from AD 26–36. He was responsible for maintaining order in the region, including resolving civil and criminal cases. See note on Mt 27:2.

23:2 he opposes payment of taxes An outright lie. Earlier in Luke, Jesus advises people to give Caesar the things that belong to Caesar—including taxes (Lk 20:20–26).

23:3 You have said so See 22:70 and note.
23:4 Then Pilate announced The dialogue that Luke includes here probably summarizes a much longer interrogation of Jesus.

23:6–12 Luke's Gospel is the only one to record Jesus' appearance before Herod. Although the ruler of Galilee is overjoyed to finally meet the miracle-worker he has heard so much about, he reacts scornfully when Jesus refuses to speak (vv. 8–9). After ridiculing Jesus, Herod sends him back to Pilate. See the table "Political Leaders in the New Testament" on p. 1916.

23:7 Herod's jurisdiction Refers to Herod Antipas, who ruled Galilee and Perea from 4 BC to AD 39. See note on 3:1. **in Jerusalem at that time** Rulers from outlying regions often came to the holy city during major festivals.
23:8 When Herod saw Jesus, he was greatly pleased Compare 9:7–9.
23:9 Jesus gave him no answer Likely an allusion to the prophecy about the suffering servant in Isaiah (see Isa 53:7 and note). Jesus' silence frustrates Herod's hope of seeing a miracle (Lk 23:8).
23:10 teachers of the law See note on 5:21.
23:11 elegant The Greek word used here, *lampros*, refers

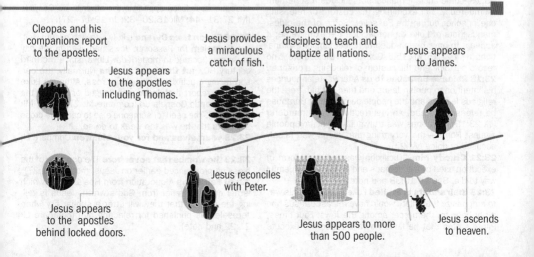

Cleopas and his companions report to the apostles.

Jesus appears to the apostles including Thomas.

Jesus provides a miraculous catch of fish.

Jesus commissions his disciples to teach and baptize all nations.

Jesus appears to James.

Jesus appears to the apostles behind locked doors.

Jesus reconciles with Peter.

Jesus appears to more than 500 people.

Jesus ascends to heaven.

mocked him. Dressing him in an elegant robe, they sent him back to Pilate. [12]That day Herod and Pilate became friends — before this they had been enemies.

[13]Pilate called together the chief priests, the rulers and the people, [14]and said to them, "You brought me this man as one who was inciting the people to rebellion. I have examined him in your presence and have found no basis for your charges against him. [15]Neither has Herod, for he sent him back to us; as you can see, he has done nothing to deserve death. [16]Therefore, I will punish him and then release him." [17]a

[18]But the whole crowd shouted, "Away with this man! Release Barabbas to us!" [19](Barabbas had been thrown into prison for an insurrection in the city, and for murder.)

[20]Wanting to release Jesus, Pilate appealed to them again. [21]But they kept shouting, "Crucify him! Crucify him!"

[22]For the third time he spoke to them: "Why? What crime has this man committed? I have found in him no grounds for the death penalty. Therefore I will have him punished and then release him."

[23]But with loud shouts they insistently demanded that he be crucified, and their shouts prevailed. [24]So Pilate decided to grant their demand. [25]He released the man who had been thrown into prison for insurrection and murder, the one they asked for, and surrendered Jesus to their will.

The Crucifixion of Jesus

23:33-43pp — Mt 27:33-44; Mk 15:22-32; Jn 19:17-24

[26]As the soldiers led him away, they seized Simon from Cyrene, who was on his way in from the country, and put the cross on him and made him carry it behind Jesus. [27]A large number of people followed him, including women who mourned and wailed for him. [28]Jesus turned and said to them, "Daughters of Jerusalem, do not weep for me; weep for yourselves and for your children. [29]For the time will come when you will say, 'Blessed are the childless women, the wombs that never bore and the breasts that never nursed!' [30]Then

"'they will say to the mountains, "Fall on us!"
  and to the hills, "Cover us!"'b

[31]For if people do these things when the tree is green, what will happen when it is dry?"

[32]Two other men, both criminals, were also led out with him to be executed. [33]When they came to the place called the Skull, they crucified him there, along with the criminals — one on his right, the other on his left. [34]Jesus said, "Father, forgive them, for they do not know what they are doing."c And they divided up his clothes by casting lots.

a 17 Some manuscripts include here words similar to Matt. 27:15 and Mark 15:6.   b 30 Hosea 10:8   c 34 Some early manuscripts do not have this sentence.

---

to something shiny or bright. In Jas 2:2, the same word refers to clothing worn by wealthy men. In Ac 10:30, it describes the clothing of a heavenly figure in a vision.

23:13–25 Pilate again finds no reason to execute Jesus and makes several attempts to release him, but the Jews demand that he be crucified (compare Mt 27:15–26; Mk 15:6–15; Jn 18:39–40; 19:12–16).

23:13 and the people The people now join the religious leaders in the dispute with Pilate over Jesus' fate.
23:16 I will punish him and then release Following Lk 23:16, some ancient manuscripts include a statement (numbered v. 17) explaining the custom of releasing one prisoner during the Passover. Some of the oldest manuscripts of Luke do not include the extra verse; it appears to have been added to reflect similar explanations in Mt 27:15; Mk 15:6. Outside the Bible, there is no record pertaining to the custom of releasing a prisoner.
23:18 Release Barabbas to us After Pilate announces his intention to punish Jesus and then set him free, the religious leaders and the people demand that Barabbas be released instead. An insurrectionist and murderer (Lk 23:19), Barabbas was truly guilty of inciting people against Rome — the very thing that Jesus was falsely accused of doing (vv. 2,5).
23:21 Crucify him Crucifixion was the main form of execution used by the Romans and an extremely painful way to die. See Mt 10:38 and note.
23:23 their shouts prevailed Luke goes out of his way to emphasize that Pilate would have released Jesus had it not been for the uproar among the Jews. Four times, Pilate states that he finds no valid reason to execute

Jesus (Lk 23:4,14,15,22); twice, Pilate resolves to set him free (vv. 16,22). Ultimately, Pilate's own will succumbs to the will of the mob (vv. 24–25).

23:26–43 The events of this section recall language and imagery used by Isaiah (compare 1:27 and note). Luke presents Jesus as Isaiah's suffering servant, with allusions to verses from the servant songs of Isaiah (Isa 42:1; 52:15; 53:5,6,9,10,12). Luke's entire Gospel builds toward this passage, in which Jesus suffers for the sin of humanity and fulfills his mission as Savior of the world (see Lk 1:31 and note; 1:69). Parallel accounts of Jesus' crucifixion appear in the other three Gospels (Mt 27:31–44; Mk 15:20–32; Jn 19:17–27).

23:26 Simon from Cyrene Likely a Jewish pilgrim visiting Jerusalem for Passover. Jews had lived in the city of Cyrene (located in modern-day Libya) since the third century BC. **put the cross on him** Normally, the person facing crucifixion carried the cross. Although Luke does not report that Jesus was flogged or beaten, the other Synoptic Gospels do (compare Mt 27:26,30; Mk 15:15,19). The need for someone else to carry the cross suggests that he was too weak to do so.
23:28 yourselves and for your children Compare Lk 19:44 and note.
23:29 the wombs that never bore The opposite of the blessing pronounced earlier on Jesus' mother (11:27).
23:30 Fall on us A quotation from Hos 10:8, in which Israel cries for relief from God's wrath. Jesus is telling the women that they will utter a similar cry when Jerusalem is punished for rejecting him (compare Lk 21:22 and note).

³⁵The people stood watching, and the rulers even sneered at him. They said, "He saved others; let him save himself if he is God's Messiah, the Chosen One."

³⁶The soldiers also came up and mocked him. They offered him wine vinegar ³⁷and said, "If you are the king of the Jews, save yourself."

³⁸There was a written notice above him, which read: THIS IS THE KING OF THE JEWS.

³⁹One of the criminals who hung there hurled insults at him: "Aren't you the Messiah? Save yourself and us!"

⁴⁰But the other criminal rebuked him. "Don't you fear God," he said, "since you are under the

---

23:31 when the tree is green Jesus' statement in this verse probably contrasts his own fate with the coming judgment against Jerusalem (19:41–44). The women are weeping now, at the death of an innocent man, but their sorrow will be much greater when great anguish will come upon Judea and its inhabitants.

23:32 Two other men, both criminals Luke does not specify their crimes. Matthew and Mark describe them as robbers or rebels.

23:33 the place called the Skull Luke does not mention the site's Aramaic name, "Golgotha" (see Mt 27:33 and note).

23:34 Father, forgive them, for they do not know what they are doing Several ancient manuscripts of

Luke do not include this quote from Jesus, suggesting that it may have been added later based on early church oral tradition. **they divided up his clothes by casting lots** A reference to Ps 22:18. Psalm 22 is a lament psalm closely associated with the suffering and death of Jesus (see note on Ps 22:title–31).

23:35 let him save himself This taunt from the rulers is full of irony. Had Jesus saved himself, he would not have fulfilled his mission to save humanity.

23:38 THIS IS THE KING OF THE JEWS In addition to stating the charges against Jesus (Lk 23:2–3), this inscription is meant to mock him. Ironically, it correctly identifies Jesus as Israel's Messiah.

Pontius Pilate's Inscription

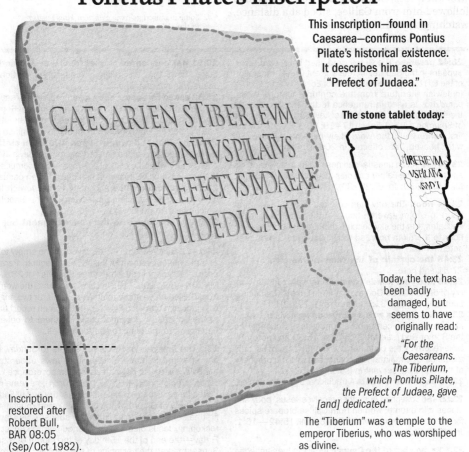

This inscription—found in Caesarea—confirms Pontius Pilate's historical existence. It describes him as "Prefect of Judaea."

CAESARIEN STIBERIEVM
PONTIVSPILATVS
PRAEFECTVSIVDAEAE
DIDITDEDICAVIT

The stone tablet today:

IBERIEVM
VSPILATVS
IVDT

Today, the text has been badly damaged, but seems to have originally read:

"For the Caesareans. The Tiberium, which Pontius Pilate, the Prefect of Judaea, gave [and] dedicated."

The "Tiberium" was a temple to the emperor Tiberius, who was worshiped as divine.

Inscription restored after Robert Bull, BAR 08:05 (Sep/Oct 1982).

same sentence? ⁴¹We are punished justly, for we are getting what our deeds deserve. But this man has done nothing wrong."

⁴²Then he said, "Jesus, remember me when you come into your kingdom.ᵃ"

⁴³Jesus answered him, "Truly I tell you, today you will be with me in paradise."

The Death of Jesus

23:44-49pp — Mt 27:45-56; Mk 15:33-41; Jn 19:29-30

⁴⁴It was now about noon, and darkness came over the whole land until three in the afternoon, ⁴⁵for the sun stopped shining. And the curtain of the temple was torn in two. ⁴⁶Jesus called out with a loud voice, "Father, into your hands I commit my spirit."ᵇ When he had said this, he breathed his last.

⁴⁷The centurion, seeing what had happened, praised God and said, "Surely this was a righteous man." ⁴⁸When all the people who had gathered to witness this sight saw what took place, they beat their breasts and went away. ⁴⁹But all those who knew him, including the women who had followed him from Galilee, stood at a distance, watching these things.

The Burial of Jesus

23:50-56pp — Mt 27:57-61; Mk 15:42-47; Jn 19:38-42

⁵⁰Now there was a man named Joseph, a member of the Council, a good and upright man, ⁵¹who had not consented to their decision and action. He came from the Judean town of Arimathea, and he himself was waiting for the kingdom of God. ⁵²Going to Pilate, he asked for Jesus' body. ⁵³Then he took it down, wrapped it in linen cloth and placed it in a tomb cut in the rock, one in which no one had yet been laid. ⁵⁴It was Preparation Day, and the Sabbath was about to begin.

⁵⁵The women who had come with Jesus from Galilee followed Joseph and saw the tomb and how his body was laid in it. ⁵⁶Then they went home and prepared spices and perfumes. But they rested on the Sabbath in obedience to the commandment.

Jesus Has Risen

24:1-10pp — Mt 28:1-8; Mk 16:1-8; Jn 20:1-8

24 On the first day of the week, very early in the morning, the women took the spices they had prepared and went to the tomb. ²They

---

ᵃ 42 Some manuscripts *come with your kingly power*
ᵇ 46 Psalm 31:5

23:43 paradise The Greek word used here, *paradeisos*, appears in the Septuagint (the ancient Greek translation of the OT) to describe the garden of Eden (Ge 2:9; 13:10). In Jewish literature from the centuries before Jesus, *paradeisos* is used in reference to the blissful place of the righteous dead (Testament of Levi 18:10–11; Psalms of Solomon 14:3; 1 Enoch 17–19; 60:8; 61:12). By the first century AD, the word likely became synonymous with "heaven," as reflected in 2Co 12:4 and Rev 2:7.

23:44–49 As an unusual darkness falls, Jesus yields his spirit to God the Father and dies (compare Mt 27:45–54; Mk 15:33–39; Jn 19:28–30).

23:44 noon The day was counted from 6 a.m. (first hour) to 6 p.m. (twelfth hour). In the Greek text, Luke indicates that the sky became dark from about the sixth hour to the ninth hour, so roughly noon to 3 p.m. (see note on Mt 27:45).

23:45 the curtain of the temple was torn See Mt 27:51 and note.

23:46 into your hands I commit my spirit Jesus' final cry of dedication to God the Father in Luke's Gospel is a quotation from Ps 31:5 (compare Lk 22:42).

23:47 Surely this was a righteous man Matthew and Mark record the centurion affirming Jesus' identity as the Son of God (see Mt 27:54; Mk 15:39 and note). By Luke recording the centurion commenting on Jesus' righteousness, he maintains a connection with the prophecy of the suffering servant in Isaiah (Isa 53:11).

23:48 beat their breasts A traditional sign of mourning.

23:50–56 Joseph of Arimathea receives Jesus' body and places it in a tomb; women from Galilee prepare spices for the burial (compare Mt 27:57–61; Mk 15:42—16:1; Jn 19:38–42).

23:50 a member of the Council Refers to the Sanhedrin (see Lk 22:66 and note).

23:51 not consented to their decision and action Luke shows that the religious leaders' opposition to Jesus was not unanimous.

23:52 asked for Jesus' body Joseph apparently sought to give Jesus a proper burial before the Sabbath. Roman law permitted the burial of condemned criminals. If no one claimed the body, it would be buried in a common pit.

23:53 he took it down, wrapped it in linen cloth A burial shroud, part of the funerary customs of Jews in the first century. After the body of a person had decomposed, the bones would be collected and placed in an ossuary.

23:54 Preparation Day According to the Jewish law, work had to be completed in advance of the Sabbath, which began at sundown.

23:56 in obedience to the commandment See Ex 20:8–11; compare note on Jn 5:10.

24:1–12 Luke recounts the discovery of the empty tomb and the announcement of Jesus' resurrection. Parallel passages appear in the other three Gospels (Mt 28:1–8; Mk 16:1–8; Jn 20:1–13). In Luke's account, the women from Galilee arrive at the tomb and encounter two angels who proclaim that Jesus is risen. The women report back to the apostles but cannot convince them to believe. Peter runs to the tomb to see for himself.

24:1 the first day of the week Refers to Sunday, the day after the Sabbath. First-century Jews understood the calendar day to begin at sunset. In accordance with Jesus' predictions (Mk 8:31; 9:31; 10:34), he remained buried for parts of three calendar days: the end of Friday, the entirety of Saturday (the Sabbath), and roughly the first half of Sunday (from sunset to sunrise). By Mark's reckoning, Jesus died and was buried before sunset on Friday—the end of the 15th day of the month of Nisan. Sunset marked the beginning of the Sabbath (Saturday, the 16th of Nisan). The following sunset was the start

found the stone rolled away from the tomb, ³but when they entered, they did not find the body of the Lord Jesus. ⁴While they were wondering about this, suddenly two men in clothes that gleamed like lightning stood beside them. ⁵In their fright the women bowed down with their faces to the ground, but the men said to them, "Why do you look for the living among the dead? ⁶He is not here; he has risen! Remember how he told you, while he was still with you in Galilee: ⁷'The Son of Man must be delivered over to the hands of sinners, be crucified and on the third day be raised again.' " ⁸Then they remembered his words.

⁹When they came back from the tomb, they told all these things to the Eleven and to all the others. ¹⁰It was Mary Magdalene, Joanna, Mary the mother of James, and the others with them who told this to the apostles. ¹¹But they did not believe the women, because their words seemed to them like nonsense. ¹²Peter, however, got up and ran to the tomb. Bending over, he saw the strips of linen lying by themselves, and he went away, wondering to himself what had happened.

On the Road to Emmaus

¹³Now that same day two of them were going to a village called Emmaus, about seven miles[a] from Jerusalem. ¹⁴They were talking with each other about everything that had happened. ¹⁵As they talked and discussed these things with each other, Jesus himself came up and walked along with them; ¹⁶but they were kept from recognizing him.

¹⁷He asked them, "What are you discussing together as you walk along?"

They stood still, their faces downcast. ¹⁸One of them, named Cleopas, asked him, "Are you the only one visiting Jerusalem who does not know the things that have happened there in these days?"

¹⁹"What things?" he asked.

"About Jesus of Nazareth," they replied. "He was a prophet, powerful in word and deed before God and all the people. ²⁰The chief priests and our rulers handed him over to be sentenced to death, and they crucified him; ²¹but we had hoped that he was the one who was going to redeem Israel. And what is more, it is the third day since all this took place. ²²In addition, some of our women amazed us. They went to the tomb early this morning ²³but didn't find his body. They came and told us that they had seen a vision of angels, who said he was alive. ²⁴Then some of our companions went to the tomb and found it just as the women had said, but they did not see Jesus."

²⁵He said to them, "How foolish you are, and how slow to believe all that the prophets have spoken! ²⁶Did not the Messiah have to suffer these things and then enter his glory?" ²⁷And beginning with Moses and all the Prophets, he explained to them what was said in all the Scriptures concerning himself.

²⁸As they approached the village to which they were going, Jesus continued on as if he were going farther. ²⁹But they urged him strongly, "Stay with us, for it is nearly evening; the day is almost over." So he went in to stay with them.

_a 13_ Or about 11 kilometers

---

of Sunday (the 17th of Nisan); later that day, as the sun was rising, the women visited the tomb. **went to the tomb** The women from Galilee return to anoint the body of Jesus (see Lk 23:55–56).

24:2 the stone rolled away All four Gospels include this detail (Mt 28:2; Mk 16:3–4; Jn 20:1).

24:4 two men in clothes that gleamed like lightning Luke's description of the clothing implies that these men were heavenly beings (compare Lk 24:23).

24:7 and on the third day be raised See 9:22; 18:32–33; compare note on 24:1.

24:9 to the Eleven No longer the Twelve, due to Judas' betrayal of Jesus. Luke records Judas' death in Ac 1:18–19 (compare Mt 27:3–5). Judas is later replaced by Matthias (Ac 1:21–26).

24:11 they did not believe the women In the Greco-Roman world of the first century, the testimony of women was considered unreliable and could not be used to settle legal disputes. For this reason, the mention of women being the first eyewitnesses of the empty tomb suggests that Luke is faithfully reporting the early church's recollection of this event. It also shows the vital role of women in Jesus' ministry.

24:12 Peter, however, got up and ran to the tomb Compare Jn 20:3–10.

24:13–35 Only Luke reports Jesus' appearance on the road to Emmaus. Two followers of Jesus set out from Jerusalem; as they walk toward the village of Emmaus,

they talk about Jesus' death. A third man joins them and asks about the events they are discussing, leading to an incredible revelation.

24:13 two of them Two previously unnamed followers of Jesus—one of which is named in 24:18 as Cleopas (not any of the 11 remaining apostles).

24:16 they were kept from recognizing him As far as the men could tell, he was just another traveler.

24:18 Cleopas Probably a different person from Clopas, mentioned in Jn 19:25.

24:21 the one who was going to redeem Israel See Lk 2:25 and note; 4:21 and note.

24:24 they did not see Jesus In light of their sadness (v. 17), these followers clearly did not believe that Jesus had risen from the dead. The empty tomb and the report of the angels' announcement were not enough to convince them.

24:25 all that the prophets have spoken Jesus explains that the OT prophets foretold of the Messiah's death. He implies that Cleopas and his companion should have been aware of this and believed.

24:27 beginning with Moses Refers to the Law (or Pentateuch)—the first five books of the OT, which traditionally are ascribed to Moses. **all the Prophets** This refers to a specific collection of Hebrew Scriptures and is likely synonymous with the section called the Prophets in Hebrew Bibles. This section includes the OT books of Joshua through 2 Kings (except Ruth) and Isaiah

³⁰When he was at the table with them, he took bread, gave thanks, broke it and began to give it to them. ³¹Then their eyes were opened and they recognized him, and he disappeared from their sight. ³²They asked each other, "Were not our hearts burning within us while he talked with us on the road and opened the Scriptures to us?"

³³They got up and returned at once to Jerusalem. There they found the Eleven and those with them, assembled together ³⁴and saying, "It is true! The Lord has risen and has appeared to Simon." ³⁵Then the two told what had happened on the way, and how Jesus was recognized by them when he broke the bread.

Jesus Appears to the Disciples

³⁶While they were still talking about this, Jesus himself stood among them and said to them, "Peace be with you."

³⁷They were startled and frightened, thinking they saw a ghost. ³⁸He said to them, "Why are you troubled, and why do doubts rise in your minds? ³⁹Look at my hands and my feet. It is I myself! Touch me and see; a ghost does not have flesh and bones, as you see I have."

⁴⁰When he had said this, he showed them his hands and feet. ⁴¹And while they still did not believe it because of joy and amazement, he asked them, "Do you have anything here to eat?" ⁴²They gave him a piece of broiled fish, ⁴³and he took it and ate it in their presence.

⁴⁴He said to them, "This is what I told you while I was still with you: Everything must be fulfilled that is written about me in the Law of Moses, the Prophets and the Psalms."

⁴⁵Then he opened their minds so they could understand the Scriptures. ⁴⁶He told them, "This is what is written: The Messiah will suffer and rise from the dead on the third day, ⁴⁷and repentance for the forgiveness of sins will be preached in his name to all nations, beginning at Jerusalem. ⁴⁸You are witnesses of these things. ⁴⁹I am going to send you what my Father has promised; but stay in the city until you have been clothed with power from on high."

The Ascension of Jesus

⁵⁰When he had led them out to the vicinity of Bethany, he lifted up his hands and blessed them. ⁵¹While he was blessing them, he left them and was taken up into heaven. ⁵²Then they worshiped him and returned to Jerusalem with great joy. ⁵³And they stayed continually at the temple, praising God.

---

through Malachi (except Lamentations and Daniel). **all the Scriptures** It is unclear precisely which OT books this entailed.

24:30 gave thanks Jesus' words and actions here might be intended as an allusion to the Last Supper (compare 22:19). The same language is used at the feeding of the 5,000 (Lk 9:16).

24:31 This verse describes a supernatural occurrence that unfolds in three quick stages: God opens the eyes of the two men—meaning they are given the ability to recognize Jesus for who he is (compare v. 16); they then recognize the risen Jesus; and Jesus vanishes.

24:32 Were not our hearts burning Reflects their excitement and renewed hope as Jesus explained the Scriptures to them.

24:33 They got up and returned at once to Jerusalem They walk seven miles back to Jerusalem despite the dangers of traveling at night.

24:34 has appeared to Simon When Cleopas and his companion arrive in Jerusalem, their experience is confirmed: The risen Jesus has also appeared to Simon Peter (although Luke does not describe this event). See the table "Resurrection Appearances of Jesus" on p. 1896.

24:35 recognized by them when he broke the bread This may be a subtle reference to the post-Easter institution of the Lord's Supper (see v. 30 and note). Luke could be affirming that the Christian community knows Jesus by remembering him via the celebration of the Lord's Supper (see 22:19).

24:36–43 Jesus appears to the entire gathering of his followers (compare Jn 20:19–31).

24:39 Look at my hands and my feet Jesus appeals to his crucifixion wounds as evidence of his humanity in resurrected form.

24:43 he took it and ate it in their presence Additional proof that Jesus is not merely a spirit, but is alive in full human form.

24:44–53 Luke closes his Gospel with Jesus commissioning his disciples and ascending into heaven. Luke adds additional details about Jesus' commands to his disciples before his ascension in his second book, the Acts of the Apostles (Ac 1:3–11).

24:45 he opened their minds so they could understand the Scriptures A supernatural enablement to comprehend the significance of Jesus' statement in Lk 24:46–47 (compare 24:31 and note). See the table "Jesus' Fulfillment of OT Prophecy" on p. 1573.

24:47 beginning at Jerusalem In the Acts of the Apostles, Luke reports that the ministry of Jesus' followers begins in Jerusalem (see Ac 1:12).

24:48 witnesses Luke's account of the Great Commission emphasizes that the disciples will act as Jesus' witnesses. This commission is repeated in Ac 1:8.

24:49 what my Father has promised A reference to the Holy Spirit (see Ac 1:4,8; 2:1–21; compare Joel 2:28–32; Jn 14:26).

24:51 taken up into heaven Jesus' ascension to heaven foreshadows his return (Ac 1:9–11).

24:52 with great joy The disciples' doubt, fear and sadness (compare Lk 24:11,17,37) is replaced with joy after seeing the risen Jesus.

THE GOSPEL OF JOHN AND
THE JOHANNINE LETTERS

The Gospel and letters of John together make up a significant portion of the New Testament. The Gospel presents an account of the life of Jesus, whereas the letters provide insights into the nature and challenges of the early church. Both continue to nourish and sustain the life of the church.

AUTHORSHIP

John's Gospel is most often attributed to the "Beloved Disciple." The Gospel suggests that this disciple knew Jesus well and was an eyewitness even to his death and the empty tomb (Jn 13:23; 19:35; 20:4–5). A circle around this disciple could have then affirmed and circulated his account (Jn 21:24).

Ancient tradition identifies this disciple as John, son of Zebedee. Fitting this identification, the sons of Zebedee were Jesus' most intimate disciples who were not individually named in the Gospel (though they appear once together in Jn 21:2). The Beloved Disciple holds a place of special honor in John 13:23, and options for who occupied this position appear limited (though some suggest Lazarus or Thomas). Besides John, Jesus' inner circle in the other first-century Gospels included only James, who was martyred early (Ac 12:2), and Peter, whom John's Gospel distinguishes from the Beloved Disciple (Jn 13:24; 20:4–6).

While the most common author suggested is John, more than one John serves as a candidate for authorship. The fourth-century church historian Eusebius suggests two potential authors: John the apostle (the son of Zebedee) and John the Elder. Differing significantly from the earlier Synoptic Gospels, the Gospel of John itself took time to gain wide acceptance, which may suggest John the Elder as its author. However, the son of Zebedee, by contrast, is clearly close to Jesus and this gives him probable status as the Beloved Disciple.

Even if the Beloved Disciple was not the author but merely the primary source, a school of disciples around the Beloved Disciple could have developed and finished the Gospel over time.

However, the Gospel as a whole most likely comes from the Beloved Disciple, an eyewitness. Although the author framed the Gospel in his own words—a common practice of the first-century—it reflects real information about Jesus. More important for the author is the Spirit's work of inspiration of true testimony for Jesus (Jn 15:26–27).

For the Johannine Letters (1–3 John), it seems that 1 John alludes to John's Gospel in its opening text and that the author of the Johannine Letters is also the author of the Gospel. The styles are very close, and the differences seem no more than what would be expected for documents addressing different settings. It could also be that a later editor of the Gospel authored one or more of the letters. It is also possible that the author or authors of the letters were familiar with, but did not necessarily write, the earlier Gospel. Until the 20th century, however, most readers assumed that the common style and content did indeed suggest the same author for the Gospel and letters.

TYPES OF WRITINGS

The Gospels can be classified as ancient biographies. At that time, most biographies about figures (within a generation or two of the author) included substantial historical information about the person. A range of biographies existed, some exhibiting greater flexibility in putting their material in their own words. Most interpreters agree that John used greater flexibility in this process than the other Gospel writers. However, this feature of his Gospel does not mean that he lacked historical information.

While John did not try to tell Jesus' story the same way the Synoptic Gospels of Matthew, Mark and Luke did, points of overlap show that John, like the authors of the Synoptics, depended on some prior information. Hence, while John often provides different information than the Synoptics, his narratives resemble them. The greatest differences appear in the speeches, which overlap with certain ideas in the Synoptics but offer a greater elaboration of Jesus' identity (compare Mt 11:27; Jn 5:19–30).

Although 2 John and 3 John resemble typical ancient letters, 1 John seems more like a homily (or brief sermon). If a letter, it may be what is sometimes called a letter essay, a letter addressing a particular topic.

CONTEXT AND BACKGROUND

Ancient tradition suggests that John wrote his Gospel in the final decade of the first century, when Domitian was emperor. Although the earliest form of John's Gospel (probably oral accounts in John's preaching) may have circulated in Judaea, very early tradition places the final form in Asia Minor (modern-day Turkey), around Ephesus.

Familiarity with the ancient Jewish setting of John's Gospel helps in understanding its themes and content. Contrasts between light and darkness and between God and the world throughout the Gospel resemble similar contrasts in the Dead Sea Scrolls. (John's circle, however, was not isolated like the wilderness community of the Scrolls.)

Because John undoubtedly sought to emphasize the points most significant to his audience, it is possible to compare his emphasis with our understanding of the first-century world. It could be that John wrote to encourage Jewish believers in Jesus who had been expelled from their synagogues (see Jn 9:22; 12:42; 16:2). Ancient rabbis and Christians both attest to this conflict, and it probably affected certain cities in Asia Minor (see Rev 2:9; 3:8–9). John wrote after the temple's destruction in AD 70, which may explain his special interest in worship in the Spirit that transcends earthly temples (Jn 4:20–24).

There are a variety of Jewish symbols and allusions in the Gospel. With these, John may be encouraging his audience that following Jesus affirms their heritage. Jesus fulfills traditional elements of Biblical festivals. On the last day of the Festival of Tabernacles, priests in Jerusalem read texts about rivers of water from Jerusalem (Eze 47:1–12; Zec 14:8). On the last day of that festival, Jesus promises rivers of living water (Jn 7:2,37–39). Jesus uses water from the Pool of Siloam, also used for a special ritual at that festival, to heal a man born blind (Jn 9:7).

If John's audience was expelled from their synagogues, their critics may have challenged their Jewish identity; John's Gospel affirms the identity of Jesus' followers as, like Israel, his "flock" or "sheep" (Eze 34:11–12; Jn 10:3–4). Critics may have challenged the faithfulness of Jesus' fol-

lowers to the Law, God's Word; John responds that Jesus himself is the Word, the embodiment of God's revelation. While God revealed his glory in giving the Law, no one could endure seeing the full revelation of his glory (Ex 33:19–20; 34:6); in Jesus, however, God fully reveals his grace and truth (Jn 1:14–18).

The Johannine Letters draw on much of the vocabulary of John's Gospel, but they address different issues. First John and 2 John address a situation in which certain people have turned away from recognizing Jesus as the Christ. While this may refer to believers who abandoned Christianity because of pressure from the synagogues, it could be that these separatists were followers of a false teaching that claimed Jesus was not fully human (1Jn 4:1–3; 2Jn 7). John emphasizes that the Spirit honors the real Jesus to whom he was bearing witness (Jn 14:26; 16:13–15; 1Jn 4:1–3). Third John probably addresses a power struggle in a local church.

THEOLOGICAL SIGNIFICANCE

Of John's many emphases, the most prominent surround Jesus's identity. John frames the prologue of his Gospel by emphasizing both Jesus' deity and his intimacy with the Father (Jn 1:1,18). John sees Jesus as God, yet distinct from the Father. Jesus is called the king of Israel and God's holy one—but Thomas offers the Gospel's climactic confession: "My Lord and my God!" (Jn 20:28; compare 1:29,49; 6:69). John immediately offers his climactic message: He writes so that his audience can have faith, even though they do not see as Thomas did. Jesus also reveals his identity in this Gospel with various "I am" statements. He calls himself the bread of life, the good shepherd and the vine (Jn 6:35,48; 10:11,14; 15:1). Ultimately, Jesus claims that before Abraham was born, "I am" (Jn 8:58). Here he echoes earlier Biblical language for God. This may also be implied in his claim, "It is I," when walking on the waves in John 6:20 (see Mk 6:50). Literally, Jesus says, "I am." This theme of Jesus' deity carries throughout the rest of the book, although not to the exclusion of his humanity (Jn 1:14). Jesus also becomes weary (Jn 4:6) and thirsty (Jn 19:28). He fully embraced our condition, even dying for us, to reveal God's love.

Another prominent theme in John is the Spirit, whom God sends through Jesus (Jn 3:34; 14:16,26; 15:26). The Spirit reveals Jesus so people can know him and be in relationship with him (Jn 16:13–15). "Knowing" God in this way is a major theme in Johannine literature (Jn 10:14–15; 17:3; 1Jn 4:7–8). The Spirit also comes to purify and transform, as Jesus says to Nicodemus (Jn 3:5). Using the motif of water, the Gospel highlights a living relationship with God over merely human traditions and rituals. Jesus' baptism in the Spirit is greater than John's baptism in water; Jesus is greater than ritual water, the water of Samaria's sacred well, a healing pool and the sacred water of Siloam (Jn 1:33; 2:6; 4:12–14; 5:7–9; 9:7). The true water of the Spirit effects what mere ritual water cannot (Jn 7:37–39). Jesus emphasizes that the Spirit comes to reveal and honor him (Jn 14:26; 16:13–15) so that subsequent generations of disciples may also know him personally. This Spirit will teach the real Jesus made known through John's witness. The Spirit works through Jesus' followers to continue making Jesus known (Jn 15:26–27; 16:7–11; 20:21–23).

Those who believe in Jesus have eternal life, also an important theme for John. In Jewish usage, "eternal life" meant the life of the world to come, but in Jesus, this life starts in the present (Jn 1:12–13; 3:3–6; compare Jn 8:44). John does not treat all faith equally; faith must persevere to the end to be saving faith (Jn 2:23–25; 8:30–32). Faith must also have the right object. When Thomas confesses Jesus as Lord and God, Jesus praises him for believing the truth, yet offers even higher praise for those who recognize this without seeing him (Jn 20:28–29).

The Gospel also teaches us a lot about love. Jesus' highest command is to love one another as he loved us (Jn 13:34–35). He loved by serving and, ultimately, by laying down his life for us. From the preaching of John the Baptist to the sending of the disciples, the theme of witness is also important. Jesus' followers are not the light; yet they have the privilege of bearing witness to the one who is the light (Jn 1:8–9).

First John develops several of these themes in the Fourth Gospel, referring back to Jesus' coming as the Word of life in our human nature (1Jn 1:1) and to the Spirit's anointing associated with that message (1Jn 4:2–6). It apparently addresses a situation in which false teachers have proclaimed a conflicting message about Jesus (1Jn 4:2–3). Some have abandoned the community of believers and stopped loving them; John seems to portray departure from adequate belief in Jesus and from loving fellow believers as a sin leading to death (1Jn 2:18–19; 5:16–17). By contrast, John reassures the believers who continue to follow Jesus and to love one another. Second John may address a similar issue, and 3 John addresses proper relationships among believers. The letters illustrate that whoever embraces God's love—of which the Fourth Gospel speaks so eloquently—must also love fellow believers, following Jesus' example of self-sacrifice (Jn 13:14–15,34–35; 1Jn 2:7–11).

Craig S. Keener

JOHN

INTRODUCTION TO JOHN

The Gospel of John illustrates what it looks like when God the Son comes to dwell among his people. John's Gospel profoundly shows how God's Son, Jesus, makes it possible for us to have an eternal relationship with God the Father (Jn 3:16–17).

BACKGROUND

The text of the Gospel of John identifies its author as a witness of Jesus' crucifixion (19:35) and as the disciple loved by Jesus (21:20,24). According to early church tradition, the author is the apostle John, the son of Zebedee (also called John the Evangelist)—whom the early church fathers also regarded as the author of 1 John. However, the Gospel of John was originally anonymous, and thus it is possible that another church leader, whom the early church called John the elder, is the author or final compiler. Some church fathers thought John the elder might have been the author of 2–3 John, but others ascribed 2–3 John to the apostle John (see the "Introduction to 2 John"). In addition, Revelation may be ascribed to the apostle John, John the Elder or another John (see the "Introduction to Revelation").

The Gospel was most likely written ca. AD 85–95, although if John the Elder is its author it could have been written in the early second century AD. The "Rylands Fragment," a tiny piece of papyrus (about the size of a credit card), contains parts of John 18 in Greek and dates to AD 125–150.

Although John's Gospel is associated by early church tradition with Ephesus, in modern-day Turkey, it contains details about Jewish customs that reflect firsthand knowledge of Judea. Based on this content, the original audience likely consisted of Jewish Christians who affirmed Jesus as the God of Israel. The Gospel may have been written to encourage them during a time of opposition (see 9:22; 12:42; 16:2). This may be why John's Gospel seems to emphasize Jesus' difficulties with "the Jews." Jesus himself and his earliest followers were Jewish, but struggled to find acceptance among their own people group, especially Jewish religious leaders. For this reason, John emphasizes all the ways Jesus fulfills the law (e.g., 12:38; 15:25; 19:24) and highlights the great command to love (13:34–35).

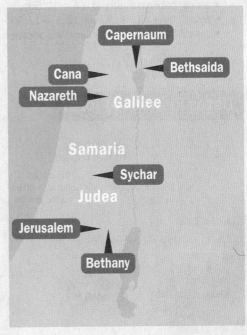

This map depicts many of the locations of Jesus' ministry according to John's Gospel.

STRUCTURE

The Gospel of John stands apart from the Synoptic Gospels (Matthew, Mark and Luke) in its content, order, wording and themes. John 1:1–18 serves as a prologue that identifies Jesus as the Word (*logos* in Greek). Jesus is described as pre-existent—already present at the beginning of the universe—and as being the one through whom creation happened. After the prologue, there is not another significant break until the end of ch. 12. This first major section (1:19—12:50) narrates Jesus' public ministry, with special emphasis on his activities during various Jewish festivals: Passover (chs. 2; 6; 11–12); an unnamed feast (5:1); Tabernacles (chs. 7–9); and Dedication (ch. 10).

The second major section begins with Jesus' last meal, prior to his death, with his disciples (ch. 13) and presents a detailed account of what is often called Jesus' farewell discourse (chs. 14–17). The final section of the Gospel records Jesus' arrest, trial, death and resurrection (chs. 18–20). The last chapter (ch. 21)—Jesus appearing to his disciples in Galilee—could function in part, or in entirety, as an appendix.

OUTLINE

- Prologue (1:1–18)
- Jesus' public ministry (1:19—12:50)
- Jesus' farewell discourse (13:1—17:26)
- Jesus' passion, resurrection and post-resurrection appearances (18:1—21:25)

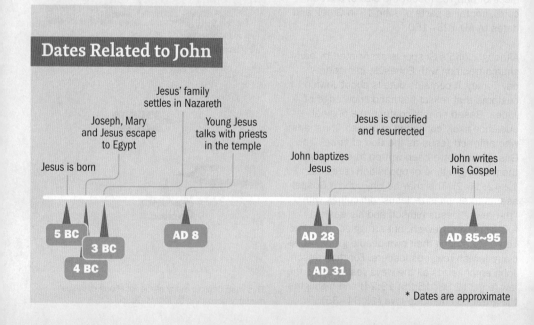

Dates Related to John

Jesus' family settles in Nazareth

Joseph, Mary and Jesus escape to Egypt

Young Jesus talks with priests in the temple

Jesus is crucified and resurrected

Jesus is born

John baptizes Jesus

John writes his Gospel

5 BC

3 BC

4 BC

AD 8

AD 28

AD 31

AD 85~95

* Dates are approximate

THEMES

From the beginning of the Gospel of John to the end, this book shows that Jesus is God in flesh (1:1–3,14). He has authority and thus is right to call people to abide in his love and share that love with others (e.g., 13:34–35; 15:9–17). Throughout John's Gospel, Jesus uses "I am" phrases, which equate him with Yahweh, the God of the Old Testament (e.g., 6:35; 8:24; 10:11,14; 13:19; 15:1; 18:5–9; compare Ex 3:14–16).

Unlike the Synoptic Gospels—which focus on the kingdom of God/heaven—the emphasis of John's Gospel is the unity of Jesus, God's Son, with God the Father (Jn 10:30; 14). On the basis of this, Jesus emphasizes that his followers should be unified with him and with one another. Jesus also says that the Holy Spirit will come to his followers—God's eternal presence is with his followers (ch. 15).

Thomas even calls Jesus his Lord—which may indicate that he is calling him Yahweh—and his God (20:28). John emphasizes that the only way to true and eternal relationship with God the Father is through Jesus' sacrificial death and resurrection (e.g., 3:16–17; 14:16–17; 17:3). And this is the message our world needs to hear today.

The Word Became Flesh

1 In the beginning was the Word, and the Word was with God, and the Word was God. ²He was with God in the beginning. ³Through him all things were made; without him nothing was made that has been made. ⁴In him was life, and that life was the light of all mankind. ⁵The light shines in the darkness, and the darkness has not overcome*ᵃ* it.

⁶There was a man sent from God whose name was John. ⁷He came as a witness to testify concerning that light, so that through him all might believe. ⁸He himself was not the light; he came only as a witness to the light.

⁹The true light that gives light to everyone was coming into the world. ¹⁰He was in the world, and though the world was made through him, the world did not recognize him. ¹¹He came to that which was his own, but his own did not receive him. ¹²Yet to all who did receive him, to those who believed in his name, he gave the right to become children of God — ¹³children born not of natural descent, nor of human decision or a husband's will, but born of God.

¹⁴The Word became flesh and made his dwelling

ᵃ 5 Or understood

1:1–18 The Gospel of John is a complex theological work, weaving events from the life of Jesus into a dramatic presentation of Jesus as Messiah and Son of God. The authority and person of Jesus as theological themes are much more important to the writer than historical chronology or his own authority. The writer only identifies himself as an eyewitness (Jn 19:35) and as the beloved disciple (21:24; see note on 1Jn 1:1); it is early church tradition that ascribes the work to the apostle John. The Gospel of John was probably written ca. AD 85–95.

John's Gospel opens with a prologue that is rich with allusions to OT themes and influenced by Jewish traditions on the exaltation of divine wisdom (see Pr 8:22–31; Job 28:12–28; compare the deuterocanonical works Sirach 24:1–34 and Wisdom of Solomon 7:22—8:1). This prologue also introduces the concept of Jesus as the divine "Word." In doing so, it establishes a claim to Jesus' divinity—connecting Jesus' identity with philosophical and Biblical concepts about creation and the organization of the universe.

1:1 In the beginning John begins by quoting the opening words of Genesis in Greek (Ge 1:1). He uses Ge 1:1–5 to establish the "Word" as a preexistent agent of creation present with Yahweh from the beginning. In making this connection, John states that Jesus existed prior to the first acts of creation. God's Son isn't an act of creation, but the means of it (compare Col 1:15–23; Heb 1:1–4). It is all the more dramatic, therefore, that the one through whom all of creation came to be has become part of the creation. **the Word** John uses the term "Word" as a title for Jesus throughout this prologue. He doesn't specify that "Word" refers to Jesus until Jn 1:17. The Greek term used here, *logos*, had a rich network of associations in the Hellenistic Judaism of the first century AD due to its ability to evoke both Biblical and philosophical concepts. The "word of Yahweh" evokes associations with creation, divine revelation, personified wisdom and the Law of Moses. The "word of Yahweh" and the law had already been closely related in prophetic poetry (see Isa 2:3). The "word" is the agent of creation in Ps 33:6, but divine wisdom is personified and depicted in that role in Pr 8:22–31. By choosing this language, John makes Jesus the very power and essence of God. **the Word was with God** This phrasing testifies to the distinction between God the Father and Jesus while emphasizing the intimate relationship between the Father and the Son. **the Word was God** The Word shares the same character, quality and essence of God. John's phrasing preserves the distinction between God the Father and God the Son while emphasizing their unity in all other regards.
1:3 Through him all things were made The concept of

creation through the divine Word reflects Yahweh's act of speaking the universe into existence in Ge 1:3–26. Jesus' preexistence and role as Creator and Sustainer of all things is also seen in Col 1:15–20.
1:4 In him was life The Word is the source of life, both physical through the creation of all things (looking back to Jn 1:3; compare Col 1:17) and spiritual (looking ahead to Jn 1:4; compare 6:35). **life** A key word for John; it is used 36 times in the Gospel. This Gospel and other NT writings associated with John account for more than 40 percent of the total occurrences of this word in the NT. For John, Jesus' ability to grant life to those who walked in "darkness" or "death" is the key issue at stake. Jesus has the ability and authority to do so because he was there in the beginning when God's creative works took place. John uses the words "life" or "eternal life" as technical terms much like the Synoptic Gospels (Matthew, Mark and Luke) use "kingdom of heaven" or "kingdom of God" (see note on Mt 3:2). "Life" denotes salvation, the state of reconciliation, and access to the presence of God. **was the light of all mankind** John alludes to the initial act of creation involving light (Ge 1:3) and invokes the association of light with divine glory (Isa 60:19). Light is often used in the OT as a metaphor for salvation and spiritual awakening (see note on Isa 51:4). "Light" is another key word for John (used 21 times). The light metaphor is connected to "the Word" motif (see note on Jn 1:1).
1:5 The light shines in the darkness The contrast between light and darkness is a prominent theme in John's Gospel (compare 1:8–10). This antithesis draws on Ge 1:1–5 (see note on Jn 1:1) as well as OT traditions of the advent of the Messiah as a light dawning over a world of physical and spiritual darkness (e.g., Isa 9:2; 60:1–2). Light and darkness dualism is also present in Jewish literature from this period. The War Scroll, a Dead Sea Scrolls' document, depicts a cosmic, end times battle between the "sons of light" and the "sons of darkness." John's analogy is similar, but emphasizes one, ultimate light for humanity, which is Jesus. Compare 1Jn 1:5 and note. **overcome** A variety of figurative senses are available for the Greek verb used here, *katalambanō*—which means "take hold of" or "seize"—making its meaning ambiguous. It typically is taken as a reference either to mental comprehension or to triumph over an enemy. The best English equivalent to capture a similar range of meaning is "apprehend."
1:6 whose name was John Introduces John the Baptist as the messenger sent by God to announce the coming of his salvation into the world through Jesus. John was the prophesied forerunner of the Messiah (see Mal 4:5–6; compare Mt 11:9). He is depicted as a prophet, modeled after OT prophets like Elijah, and he is of priestly descent like Jeremiah and Ezekiel (see note on Mk 1:4; compare Mt 11:14; Mk 11:32; Lk 1:5,17).

among us. We have seen his glory, the glory of the one and only Son, who came from the Father, full of grace and truth.

[15](John testified concerning him. He cried out, saying, "This is the one I spoke about when I said, 'He who comes after me has surpassed me because he was before me.'") [16]Out of his fullness we have all received grace in place of grace already given. [17]For the law was given through Moses; grace and truth came through Jesus Christ. [18]No one has ever seen God, but the one and only Son, who is himself God and[a] is in closest relationship with the Father, has made him known.

John the Baptist Denies Being the Messiah

[19]Now this was John's testimony when the Jewish leaders[b] in Jerusalem sent priests and Levites to ask him who he was. [20]He did not fail to confess, but confessed freely, "I am not the Messiah."

[21]They asked him, "Then who are you? Are you Elijah?"

[a] 18 Some manuscripts *but the only Son, who*   [b] 19 The Greek term traditionally translated *the Jews* (*hoi Ioudaioi*) refers here and elsewhere in John's Gospel to those Jewish leaders who opposed Jesus; also in 5:10, 15, 16; 7:1, 11, 13; 9:22; 18:14, 28, 36; 19:7, 12, 31, 38; 20:19.

John 1:6

JOHN THE BAPTIST
John's ministry began around AD 29 in the Judean wilderness along the Jordan River (Lk 3:1–3; Mt 3:1–2). His primary message was calling Israel to repentance in preparation for the coming of the Messianic age (Mt 3:2; Mk 1:4; Lk 3:3).

1:7 a witness John's mission is articulated in legal terms; he is a witness coming to testify. The motif of a trial with witnesses offering testimony is a key component structuring John's Gospel. The most concentrated development of this theme is in Jn 5:31–47. John presents numerous witnesses who testify to Jesus' identity as the Messiah. The world's failure to recognize Jesus as Messiah is a rejection of these witnesses and their testimony.
1:10 the world The Greek word used here, *kosmos*, occurs 78 times throughout John's Gospel. Sometimes it refers broadly to the whole created order (11:27; 21:25), but most of the time it refers specifically to humanity in rebellion against God and hostile to Christ (7:7; 12:31; 14:17; 15:18–19; 16:20; 17:14,25).
1:11 his own did not receive him Not only did the entire world not recognize its Creator (v. 10), but God's chosen people rejected their Messiah.
1:12 children of God Unlike the people who rejected him (v. 11), those who accepted Jesus as Messiah are the true "children of God" (compare Jn 3:3–8; 1Jn 5:1).
1:13 not of natural descent See John 3:3 and note.
1:14 The Word became flesh Continues the symbolism of v. 1 by describing how the *logos* took on human form (see note on v. 1). This depiction of the *logos* as a personal being in human flesh is a reversal of the philosophical concept of the *logos* as an impersonal principle or force. The emphasis on the "flesh" could be an attempt to correct misunderstandings about the humanity of Jesus present in the early church. One of the earliest Christological heresies from the second century AD was Docetism, which held that Jesus was fully divine and only appeared human and only appeared to die on the cross (see note on 1Jn 4:2). The idea that divine beings could appear in human form was common in the ancient world, so John seems to take extra care to emphasize that Jesus was human, not that he merely appeared in human form. **made his dwelling** The Greek verb used here literally means "to dwell in a tent" and likely alludes to the OT tabernacle as God's dwelling among his people (see Ex 33:7–11; note on Ex 27:21). Through

his Son, God is taking up a post among his people just as he had done for ancient Israel. **his glory** Alludes to the manifestations of divine glory in the OT. Yahweh's presence could be found in the tabernacle or temple (Ex 40:34–38; Nu 14:10; 1Ki 8:10–11; Isa 6:1).
1:17 the law was given through Moses John contrasts Moses with Jesus, emphasizing the superiority of the gospel of Christ to the Law of Moses. Throughout his Gospel, John presents Jesus as the fulfillment of OT expectations. Compare 5:46–47.
1:19—12:50 The first half of John's Gospel is sometimes referred to as the Book of Signs, as it centers on the miracles Jesus performs as proof that he is the Son of God (e.g., 2:11; 4:54). This section deals with the public ministry of Jesus, culminating in the triumphal entry of Jesus into Jerusalem a week before Passover (12:12–19). The remainder of the Gospel focuses on the last week of Jesus' life.
1:19–51 The preaching of John the Baptist and his baptism of Jesus marks the beginning of Jesus' public ministry, just as in the Synoptic Gospels (compare Mt 3; Mk 1; Lk 3). The first disciples also join Jesus during this time. Unlike the Synoptics, John has no account of Jesus' temptation in the wilderness (Mk 1:12–13).
1:19 the Jewish leaders Refers to the religious leaders in Jerusalem. John often uses this label to categorize those who are opposed to Jesus and his ministry (e.g., Jn 5:16). While the term can be used in a neutral or even a positive sense (e.g., Jn 2:6; 4:22), the prevailing connotation with the expression is "unbelieving Jews." John's usage is spiritual, not racial; indeed, John, Jesus, and the earliest Christians were themselves Jews. Yet, John never refers to the group of Christ followers as "Jews"; he prefers the term "Israel" or "Israelite" to describe those who believe in Jesus (v. 47). Later applications of John's rhetoric have had an unfortunate influence in promoting anti-Semitism in certain circles of Christianity. See 8:44 and note. **Jerusalem** The chief city of Judea, the site of the Jewish temple, and the ancient capital of Israel and Judah. See the infographic "Jerusalem" on p. 1607. **priests and Levites** The official religious leaders in charge of the temple in Jerusalem. See Dt 18:1 and note.
1:20 I am not the Messiah The Greek word used here, *christos* (meaning "anointed one"), is equivalent to the Hebrew term *mashiach*, meaning "Messiah."
1:21 Are you Elijah The prophet Elijah's miraculous ascent into heaven on a fiery divine chariot (2Ki 2:11) fueled the belief that he would return as a forerunner of the Messiah. The OT explicitly attests to this expectation

He said, "I am not."

"Are you the Prophet?"

He answered, "No."

²²Finally they said, "Who are you? Give us an answer to take back to those who sent us. What do you say about yourself?"

²³John replied in the words of Isaiah the prophet, "I am the voice of one calling in the wilderness, 'Make straight the way for the Lord.'"ᵃ

²⁴Now the Pharisees who had been sent ²⁵questioned him, "Why then do you baptize if you are not the Messiah, nor Elijah, nor the Prophet?"

²⁶"I baptize withᵇ water," John replied, "but among you stands one you do not know. ²⁷He is the one who comes after me, the straps of whose sandals I am not worthy to untie."

²⁸This all happened at Bethany on the other side of the Jordan, where John was baptizing.

John Testifies About Jesus

²⁹The next day John saw Jesus coming toward him and said, "Look, the Lamb of God, who takes away the sin of the world! ³⁰This is the one I meant when I said, 'A man who comes after me has surpassed me because he was before me.' ³¹I myself did not know him, but the reason I came baptizing with water was that he might be revealed to Israel."

³²Then John gave this testimony: "I saw the Spirit come down from heaven as a dove and remain on him. ³³And I myself did not know him, but the one who sent me to baptize with water told me, 'The man on whom you see the Spirit come down and remain is the one who will baptize with the Holy Spirit.' ³⁴I have seen and I testify that this is God's Chosen One."ᶜ

John's Disciples Follow Jesus

1:40-42pp — Mt 4:18-22; Mk 1:16-20; Lk 5:2-11

³⁵The next day John was there again with two of his disciples. ³⁶When he saw Jesus passing by, he said, "Look, the Lamb of God!"

³⁷When the two disciples heard him say this, they followed Jesus. ³⁸Turning around, Jesus saw them following and asked, "What do you want?"

They said, "Rabbi" (which means "Teacher"), "where are you staying?"

³⁹"Come," he replied, "and you will see."

So they went and saw where he was staying, and they spent that day with him. It was about four in the afternoon.

⁴⁰Andrew, Simon Peter's brother, was one of the two who heard what John had said and who had followed Jesus. ⁴¹The first thing Andrew did was to find his brother Simon and tell him, "We have found the Messiah" (that is, the Christ). ⁴²And he brought him to Jesus.

Jesus looked at him and said, "You are Simon

ᵃ 23 Isaiah 40:3   ᵇ 26 Or in; also in verses 31 and 33 (twice)
ᶜ 34 See Isaiah 42:1; many manuscripts is the Son of God.

---

in Mal 4:5. **Are you the Prophet** This line of questioning reflects the varying categories of Messianic expectation in the Second Temple period. Since John denied being the Messiah or his forerunner, Elijah, he is asked whether he is the prophet Moses predicted in Dt 18:15–18. John disclaims this role as well, showing complete humility in his calling. He understands that his office is to point to the Messiah and lead people to repent.

1:23 one calling John identifies himself by quoting Isa 40:3. All four Gospels apply this Scripture to John the Baptist, but John's Gospel is the only one that puts the quote on the lips of John the Baptist himself (compare Mt 3:3; Mk 1:3; Lk 3:4).

1:24 Pharisees A Jewish lay movement of experts in the interpretation of the law. See the table "Major Groups in Jesus' Time" on p. 1630.

1:25 Why then do you baptize They ask John by what authority he has taken it upon himself to baptize Jews. Washing with water was a common practice in Jewish ritual purification, but baptism was associated with the conversion of Gentiles. See note on Jn 7:32.

1:27 straps of whose sandals I am not worthy to untie In Jesus' time, untying someone's sandals was a menial job reserved for slaves. Jewish tradition taught that a disciple must serve his teacher in every task that a slave would perform except for removing his shoe—a task deemed too menial for a disciple.

1:28 Bethany on the other side of the Jordan The location of this Bethany is uncertain, but it is different from the Bethany near Jerusalem (11:18; 12:1).

1:29 Lamb of God, who takes away the sin An allusion to the symbolism of the Passover lamb (Ex 12:3). Compare Isa 53:7,11; Rev 5:6. See the table "Israelite Festivals" on p. 200.

1:32 the Spirit come down from heaven as a dove Jesus' baptism is depicted more fully in Mt 3:13–17 and Lk 3:21–22.

1:34 testify See note on Jn 1:7.

1:35–51 This account of the call of Jesus' disciples differs from that of the Synoptic Gospels (compare Mt 4:18–22; Mk 1:16–20; Lk 5:1–11). For example, John gives a more detailed account of the call of Philip and Nathanael.

1:37 the two disciples Jesus' first disciples were followers of John the Baptist. One of these disciples is identified as Andrew (Jn 1:40), but the other remains anonymous.

1:38 Rabbi A Hebrew title originally meaning "my master" but eventually taking on the sense of "authoritative religious teacher." Here, John transliterates the Hebrew title into Greek; in 20:16, he uses the Greek word didaskalos, meaning "teacher," which captures the sense. However, he normally simply transcribes the Hebrew title into Greek letters and refers to Jesus as "Rabbi."

1:39 four in the afternoon The Greek text identifies the time as the "tenth hour." The hours were typically counted from sunrise to sunset, generally 6 a.m. to 6 p.m. The tenth hour would be 4 p.m.

son of John. You will be called Cephas" (which, when translated, is Peter[a]).

Jesus Calls Philip and Nathanael

[43]The next day Jesus decided to leave for Galilee. Finding Philip, he said to him, "Follow me."

[44]Philip, like Andrew and Peter, was from the town of Bethsaida. [45]Philip found Nathanael and told him, "We have found the one Moses wrote about in the Law, and about whom the prophets also wrote — Jesus of Nazareth, the son of Joseph."

[46]"Nazareth! Can anything good come from there?" Nathanael asked.

"Come and see," said Philip.

[47]When Jesus saw Nathanael approaching, he said of him, "Here truly is an Israelite in whom there is no deceit."

[48]"How do you know me?" Nathanael asked.

Jesus answered, "I saw you while you were still under the fig tree before Philip called you."

[49]Then Nathanael declared, "Rabbi, you are the Son of God; you are the king of Israel."

[50]Jesus said, "You believe[b] because I told you I saw you under the fig tree. You will see greater things than that." [51]He then added, "Very truly I tell you,[c] you[c] will see 'heaven open, and the angels of God ascending and descending on'[d] the Son of Man."

Jesus Changes Water Into Wine

2 On the third day a wedding took place at Cana in Galilee. Jesus' mother was there, [2]and Jesus and his disciples had also been invited to the wedding. [3]When the wine was gone, Jesus' mother said to him, "They have no more wine."

[4]"Woman,[e] why do you involve me?" Jesus replied. "My hour has not yet come."

[5]His mother said to the servants, "Do whatever he tells you."

[6]Nearby stood six stone water jars, the kind used by the Jews for ceremonial washing, each holding from twenty to thirty gallons.[f]

---

[a] 42 Cephas (Aramaic) and Peter (Greek) both mean rock.
[b] 50 Or Do you believe . . . ?   [c] 51 The Greek is plural.
[d] 51 Gen. 28:12   [e] 4 The Greek for Woman does not denote any disrespect.   [f] 6 Or from about 75 to about 115 liters

---

1:40 Andrew, Simon Peter's brother See Mt 4:18–22 and note.

1:41 We have found the Messiah John is the only NT writer to use the word messias, transliterating the Hebrew word mashiach into Greek. See note on Jn 1:20.

1:42 Cephas Aramaic for "rock," translated to Greek as petros or Peter. This renaming of Simon takes place later in Jesus' ministry according to Matthew (Mt 16:16–18).

1:43 Galilee The northern region of Israel, along the Sea of Galilee. **Philip** The other Gospels mention Philip only in lists of the Twelve; John's Gospel gives Philip a greater role (Jn 6:5–7; 12:20–26; 14:8–9).

1:44 Bethsaida A fishing town on the northeastern shore of the Sea of Galilee.

1:45 Nathanael Not mentioned as one of the Twelve in the Synoptic Gospels, but usually identified with Bartholomew (whom John never mentions by name). **the Law, and about whom the prophets** This phrase was a common way of referring to the entire Hebrew Scriptures (compare Mt 5:17; 22:40). See the table "Jesus' Fulfillment of OT Prophecy" on p. 1573. **Jesus of Nazareth, the son of Joseph** Unlike Matthew and Luke, John does not provide an elaborate genealogy for Jesus (Mt 1:1–17; Lk 3:23–38). Here, he is identified in the traditional way with his earthly father's name and hometown. **Nazareth** A town in Galilee about 15 miles west of the Sea of Galilee.

1:49 you are the Son of God The first confession of Jesus' divine role as the Messiah by one of his disciples (compare Mt 14:33).

1:51 Very truly A common expression in the Gospels to introduce Jesus' teaching or a traditional saying. The phrase seems to function to emphasize the importance of what Jesus is about to say. **the angels of God ascending and descending** Alludes to Ge 28:12, representing Jesus as the embodiment of all earthly access to the divine realm. **the Son of Man** A Messianic title that Jesus often uses for himself (see note on Mt 8:20; note on Da 7:13). The title also can mean "human one" (see note on Eze 2:1). Here, Jesus may be acknowledging his humanity; this would parallel Jn 1:14.

2:1–12 Beginning in ch. 2, John presents a series of signs or miracles designed to prove Jesus' identity as the Messiah and Son of God. In this first sign, Jesus turns water into wine at a wedding in Cana attended by his family and disciples. See the table "Miracles of Jesus" on p. 1741.

2:1 the third day John is narrating the events of the first week of Jesus' ministry. This is two days after the call of Philip and Nathanael (1:43–51). **Cana in Galilee** A village in central Galilee, nine miles north of Nazareth. According to 21:2, Cana was Nathanael's hometown. See the map "Jesus' Ministry in Galilee" on p. 2260. **Jesus' mother** Mary (Mt 1:18). John never uses her name in his Gospel.

ISRAELITE FESTIVALS IN JOHN'S GOSPEL	
Passover (3 different years)	Jn 2:13,23; 6:4; 11:55; 12:1; 13:1; 18:28,39; 19:14
An unnamed festival	Jn 5:1
Festival of Tabernacles	Jn 7:2
Festival of Dedication (Hanukkah)	Jn 10:22

2:3 When the wine was gone The host was responsible for providing wine throughout the wedding feast, which typically lasted seven days. **the wine** An essential part of the diet in the ancient world. In the OT, wine was a symbol of covenantal blessing (Ge 27:28), which prophets associated with a time of future abundance (Hos 2:21–22; Joel 1:10; 3:18).

2:4 Woman This usage is not disrespectful, but a simple, informal form of address. **why do you involve me** Jesus is likely petitioning his mother to consider whether the request is really the type of thing he should be addressing with his power; he probably wants her to consider his purpose.

2:6 six stone water jars Large stone pots were used for storing water for ritual purification. Examples have been unearthed in Palestine from this period. The jars were cut from single blocks of stone; stone was used because it did not convey ritual impurity. **from twenty**

⁷Jesus said to the servants, "Fill the jars with water"; so they filled them to the brim.

⁸Then he told them, "Now draw some out and take it to the master of the banquet."

They did so, ⁹and the master of the banquet tasted the water that had been turned into wine. He did not realize where it had come from, though the servants who had drawn the water knew.

Then he called the bridegroom aside ¹⁰and said, "Everyone brings out the choice wine first and then the cheaper wine after the guests have had too much to drink; but you have saved the best till now."

¹¹What Jesus did here in Cana of Galilee was the first of the signs through which he revealed his glory; and his disciples believed in him.

---

to thirty gallons All six jars would have held 120–180 gallons. Large quantities of water were needed for ritual purification.

2:7 they filled them to the brim Making it impossible for the miracle to have been a deception.

2:8 master of the banquet This phrase denotes an honorary position, a person primarily tasked with regulating the distribution of the wine.

2:10 Everyone brings out the choice wine first Over the course of a feast, diluting wine with water was a common practice to make it go further.

2:11 the first of the signs The signs are designed to reveal Jesus' identity as the Messiah. John declares that

his purpose in writing the Gospel was to promote belief through the story of Jesus and the signs he performed (Jn 20:30–31). Only two of the signs are numbered, and both occur in Cana (compare 4:54). While John alludes to many signs (vv. 23; 20:30), there seems to be a sequence of seven signs culminating with the raising of Lazarus in 11:1–44. The seven major signs are: changing water into wine (vv. 1–11); healing the official's son (4:46–54); healing a lame man (5:1–15); feeding the 5,000 (6:1–15); walking on water (6:16–21); healing a blind man (9:1–41); and raising Lazarus from the dead (11:1–44).

Herod's Temple on the Temple Mount

King Herod the Great began renovations on the temple around 20 BC. The expansion of the temple and the temple mount was completed around AD 62-64, only to be destroyed by the Romans in AD 70.

1. Holy Place
2. Altar
3. Priests' Courtyard
4. Israelites' Courtyard
5. Chamber of Lepers
6. Chamber of Oils
7. Gate of Nicanor
8. Chamber of Nazarites
9. Women's Courtyard
10. Chamber of Wood
11. The Gate Beautiful

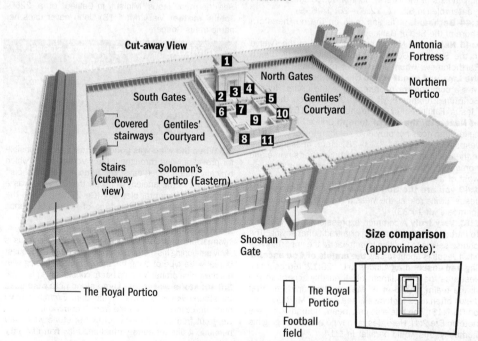

Cut-away View

Antonia Fortress

North Gates

Northern Portico

South Gates

Gentiles' Courtyard

Covered stairways

Gentiles' Courtyard

Stairs (cutaway view)

Solomon's Portico (Eastern)

Shoshan Gate

The Royal Portico

Size comparison (approximate):

The Royal Portico

Football field

¹²After this he went down to Capernaum with his mother and brothers and his disciples. There they stayed for a few days.

Jesus Clears the Temple Courts

2:14-16pp — Mt 21:12,13; Mk 11:15-17; Lk 19:45,46

¹³When it was almost time for the Jewish Passover, Jesus went up to Jerusalem. ¹⁴In the temple courts he found people selling cattle, sheep and doves, and others sitting at tables exchanging money. ¹⁵So he made a whip out of cords, and drove all from the temple courts, both sheep and cattle; he scattered the coins of the money changers and overturned their tables. ¹⁶To those who sold doves he said, "Get these out of here! Stop turning my Father's house into a market!" ¹⁷His disciples remembered that it is written: "Zeal for your house will consume me."ᵃ

¹⁸The Jews then responded to him, "What sign can you show us to prove your authority to do all this?" ¹⁹Jesus answered them, "Destroy this temple, and I will raise it again in three days." ²⁰They replied, "It has taken forty-six years to build this temple, and you are going to raise it in three days?" ²¹But the temple he had spoken of was his body. ²²After he was raised from the dead, his disciples recalled what he had said. Then they believed the scripture and the words that Jesus had spoken.

²³Now while he was in Jerusalem at the Passover Festival, many people saw the signs he was performing and believed in his name.ᵇ ²⁴But Jesus would not entrust himself to them, for he knew all people. ²⁵He did not need any testimony about mankind, for he knew what was in each person.

ᵃ 17 Psalm 69:9   ᵇ 23 Or *in him*

MIRACLES UNIQUE TO JOHN'S GOSPEL		
Water into Wine, 2:1–11	Official's Son Healed, 4:46–52	Paralytic Healed, 5:1–13
Blind Man Healed, 9:1–12	Lazarus Raised from the Dead, 11:38–44	Miraculous Catch of Fish, 21:1–14

2:12 Capernaum A town on the northwest shore of the Sea of Galilee where Jesus based his ministry (Mt 4:13; Mk 2:1). See the map "Jesus' Ministry in Galilee" on p. 2260; see the infographic "The Synagogue at Capernaum" on p. 1656.

2:13–25 Jesus and his disciples travel to Jerusalem to observe the Passover. While there, Jesus drives those conducting business for profit out of the temple courts for violating the sanctity of the site. He also performs more miracles while in Jerusalem.

2:13 the Jewish Passover One of the three pilgrimage festivals during which all Jews were to travel to Jerusalem to worship at the temple (Ex 12:1–28). See the table "Israelite Festivals" on p. 200.

2:14–22 All four Gospels contain an account of the cleansing of the temple (Mt 21:12–13; Mk 11:15–17; Lk 19:45–46), but John's is the most detailed. John mentions the trade in oxen and sheep as well as doves, and he adds the detail of Jesus fashioning the whip of cords used to drive out the animals. John also records a command not found in the other accounts (Jn 2:16). However, John does not allude to the two Scripture passages (Isa 56:7; Jer 7:11) used by Jesus to justify his actions in the Synoptic Gospels (Matthew, Mark and Luke). The disciples apply Ps 69:9 to Jesus' action in Jn 2:17.

One major difference with John's account of the temple clearing is timing. John presents this as one of the first public acts of Jesus' ministry. In the Synoptic Gospels, this scene comes toward the end of Jesus' ministry. Either Jesus cleared the temple twice or the various gospel authors took liberties with the precise placement of the story. The latter explanation is most likely. The Synoptics only record one visit to Jerusalem by Jesus and the disciples, so the event

would have to be placed then. John records multiple visits to Jerusalem to celebrate the Passover over Jesus' ministry. Based on John's preference for arranging chronology to suit his theological purpose and the likelihood that this event could have set off some of the opposition that led to Jesus' crucifixion, the later placement by the Synoptics is most historically probable.

2:14 temple courts The temple complex had been greatly expanded by Herod the Great in the late first century BC, and work continued into the mid-first century AD. Herod's temple complex included a huge outer courtyard known as the Gentiles' Courtyard. This large court surrounding the temple proper was probably where the business was conducted. Only Jews could enter the inner courts of the temple. See the infographic "Herod's Temple" on p. 1626. **cattle, sheep and doves** People who had traveled from a great distance for the festival could hardly have brought their sacrificial offerings with them; traders took advantage of that by selling animals for sacrifice in the outer courts. People likely paid exorbitant prices for the convenience of buying at the temple.

2:16 doves Pigeons or doves were the offerings of the poor (Lev 5:7). **Get these out of here!** This commandment is unique to John's Gospel. **turning my Father's house into a market** Turning the outer courts into a market effectively prevented worship for non-Jewish people.

2:17 Zeal for your house will consume me The disciples remembered Ps 69:9 and applied its image of the righteous sufferer to Jesus. See the table "Jesus' Fulfillment of OT Prophecy" on p. 1573.

2:19 I will raise it again in three days Foreshadows Jesus' death and resurrection.

2:20 forty-six years The renovations and expansion begun by Herod the Great were still underway. Compare note on Jn 2:14. See the infographic "Temple Comparison" on p. 1558.

2:21 temple he had spoken of was his body The use of misunderstanding is a prominent part of John's style. He regularly records Jesus' hearers misunderstanding his sayings, sometimes requiring further elaboration as in the case of Nicodemus (3:1–10).

Jesus Teaches Nicodemus

3 Now there was a Pharisee, a man named Nicodemus who was a member of the Jewish ruling council. [2]He came to Jesus at night and said, "Rabbi, we know that you are a teacher who has come from God. For no one could perform the signs you are doing if God were not with him."

[3]Jesus replied, "Very truly I tell you, no one can see the kingdom of God unless they are born again.[a]"

[4]"How can someone be born when they are old?" Nicodemus asked. "Surely they cannot enter a second time into their mother's womb to be born!"

[5]Jesus answered, "Very truly I tell you, no one can enter the kingdom of God unless they are born of water and the Spirit. [6]Flesh gives birth to flesh, but the Spirit[b] gives birth to spirit. [7]You should not be surprised at my saying, 'You[c] must be born again.' [8]The wind blows wherever it pleases. You hear its sound, but you cannot tell where it comes from or where it is going. So it is with everyone born of the Spirit."[d]

[9]"How can this be?" Nicodemus asked.

[10]"You are Israel's teacher," said Jesus, "and do you not understand these things? [11]Very truly I tell

[a] 3 The Greek for *again* also means *from above*; also in verse 7. [b] 6 Or *but spirit* [c] 7 The Greek is plural. [d] 8 The Greek for *Spirit* is the same as that for *wind*.

3:1–21 A Jewish leader named Nicodemus visits Jesus at night, confessing that he believes Jesus to have come from God. Jesus takes the opportunity to teach Nicodemus about his need for spiritual rebirth. John's narration of Jesus' life and ministry is structured around alternating blocks of signs and discourses. The signs are miracles attesting to Jesus' identity as Messiah and Son of God. The discourses are lengthy accounts of Jesus' teaching. John's discourses often appear to be modeled on sermons or homilies that interpret and explain traditional sayings of Jesus. Here, Jesus' saying about being born again (or from above) echoes the teaching in Mt 18:3 and Mk 10:15 and expands on the subject.

3:1 a Pharisee See note on Jn 7:32. **Nicodemus** Apparently a secret follower of Jesus (7:50–51; 19:38–39). **member of the Jewish ruling council** Indicates he was a member of the Sanhedrin (see note on Mk 14:55). See the infographic "The Sanhedrin" on p. 1746.
3:2 at night Indicates Nicodemus came to speak with Jesus privately and secretly. He may have feared being publicly associated with Jesus. **Rabbi** Nicodemus' use of the title indicates his respect for Jesus. See note on Jn 1:38.
3:3 kingdom of God A prominent theme of the Synoptic Gospels (e.g., Mt 3:2; see note on Mk 1:15). For Nicodemus, the phrase would have evoked the prophetic images of a future universal reign of Yahweh or the Messiah (Ob 21; Da 7:12–14; Eze 34:23–24), which were symbolic of Yahweh's future plan to redeem Israel. John uses the phrase only in this passage (Jn 3:3,5; see note on Ac 1:3). For Jesus, the idea of coming to God through his saving work is about transitioning from the earthly kingdom (as articulated in the temple scene in Jn 2:13–21) to God's kingdom as articulated in a transformed life lived out of love for God and other people. The prominence of the "kingdom of God" or "kingdom of heaven" language in the Synoptic Gospels compared to its relative absence in John's Gospel suggests that John's discourse here may be quoting and developing a saying from oral tradition. John prefers the terms "life" or "eternal life" (see note on 1:4) to denote a concept similar to "kingdom of God." **born again** Nicodemus' misunderstanding (v. 4) stems from the ambiguity of this phrase. The Greek adverb used here, *anōthen*, can mean "from above" (i.e., heaven), "from the beginning," "for a long time," or "again." That is, the term can indicate either timing or location. Jesus is using the word to point to a location (heaven, the source of the rebirth), but Nicodemus understands

it in reference to time or a repeated activity (that the birth must happen multiple times). Nicodemus also appears to take Jesus' answer to be much more literal (or physical) than he intends; Jesus is talking about a spiritual transformation.
3:4 be born when they are old Nicodemus misunderstands Jesus. Misunderstanding is a common motif in the narrative of John's Gospel (see note on 2:21). The misunderstanding gives Jesus a chance to elaborate. Nicodemus takes Jesus' statement literally, thinking he must be born anew. See note on v. 3.
3:5 born of water and the Spirit Jesus elaborates on the meaning of being born from above in v. 3, emphasizing the need for spiritual birth (see note on v. 3). The OT overtones of the Greek phrase used here, literally rendered as "born of water and spirit," are meant to make Nicodemus realize that Jesus is inaugurating the age of renewal anticipated by the OT prophets (Joel 2:28; Isa 32:15; 44:3; Eze 11:19–20; 36:25–27). Interpretations of this verse often attempt to connect Jesus' statement with some type of water baptism, understanding references to both physical and spiritual rebirth symbolized by baptism. The phrase "born of water and spirit" could refer to two births, since Jn 3:6 contrasts being born of the flesh with being born of the Spirit. However, a reference to the Christian sacrament of baptism is unlikely. The mention of water, though, may allude to John's baptism, which emphasizes repentance from sin. The danger with understanding "born of water" as a reference to water baptism is that it could be misconstrued as making baptism a requirement for salvation. Any secondary implications about water baptism should be understood as symbolic of spiritual rebirth, not as a necessary part of salvation.
3:6 flesh Refers to the physical body in contrast to what is spiritual. This becomes the fundamental change in living for God's kingdom versus a human kingdom (paralleled by light and darkness throughout John's Gospel): People are transformed by the work of the Holy Spirit.
3:7 You should not be surprised at my saying, 'You must be born again' In the Greek text of this verse, the first "you" is singular and the second is plural. The implication is that Jesus is speaking about God's kingdom in reference to all people, not just Nicodemus.
3:8 wind The Greek word used here, *pneuma*, can mean "wind," "breath" or "spirit." John uses the metaphor of the wind as a power that is felt but unseen to explain the power of the Spirit of God.
3:10 Israel's teacher With this title—the Greek equivalent of "rabbi"—Jesus places Nicodemus among the educated elite of Judaism. See note on 1:38.

you, we speak of what we know, and we testify to what we have seen, but still you people do not accept our testimony. [12]I have spoken to you of earthly things and you do not believe; how then will you believe if I speak of heavenly things? [13]No one has ever gone into heaven except the one who came from heaven—the Son of Man.[a] [14]Just as Moses lifted up the snake in the wilderness, so the Son of Man must be lifted up,[b] [15]that everyone who believes may have eternal life in him."[c]

[16]For God so loved the world that he gave his one and only Son, that whoever believes in him shall not perish but have eternal life. [17]For God did not send his Son into the world to condemn the world, but to save the world through him. [18]Whoever believes in him is not condemned, but whoever does not believe stands condemned already because they have not believed in the name of God's one and only Son. [19]This is the verdict: Light has come into the world, but people loved darkness instead of light because their deeds were evil. [20]Everyone who does evil hates the light, and will not come into the light for fear that their deeds will be exposed. [21]But whoever lives by the truth comes into the light, so that it may be seen plainly that what they have done has been done in the sight of God.

John Testifies Again About Jesus

[22]After this, Jesus and his disciples went out into the Judean countryside, where he spent some time with them, and baptized. [23]Now John also was baptizing at Aenon near Salim, because there was plenty of water, and people were coming and being baptized. [24](This was before John was put in prison.) [25]An argument developed between some of John's disciples and a certain Jew over

---

[a] 13 Some manuscripts Man, who is in heaven   [b] 14 The Greek for lifted up also means exalted.   [c] 15 Some interpreters end the quotation with verse 21.

3:11 our testimony Jesus can attest to both worldly and heavenly truths, but Nicodemus needs to be willing to accept his witness. See note on 1:7.

3:13 No one has ever gone into heaven See note on 1:51. Jesus is alluding to his heavenly origin. Since he comes from heaven, he is qualified to speak authoritatively about heavenly things. **the Son of Man** See note on 1:51.

3:14 Moses lifted up the snake in the wilderness Alludes to the events of Nu 21:9 and presents the Son of Man as superior to Moses. **the Son of Man must be lifted up** Alludes to both the crucifixion and the exaltation of Jesus in his death and resurrection. Compare Isa 52:13; Da 7:13–14.

3:16–21 The speaker in this section may be the narrator expanding on Jesus' teaching or Jesus still speaking with Nicodemus. The Greek manuscripts did not use punctuation that would have indicated a change of speaker. The content of this short discourse reflects themes typical to John such as the opposition of light and darkness (see note on Jn 1:5). For that reason, the speaker is most likely the narrator.

3:16 God so loved the world This verse presents a concise summary of the gospel message, tying the events of Jesus' death to God's love for the world he created. The statement is remarkable in its depiction of divine care for the entire world—not just his chosen people, Israel. **one and only Son** The Greek term used here is *monogenēs*, meaning "one of a kind." At one time, it was presumed that the term derived from the Greek words *monos* ("one" or "only") and *gennaō* ("to beget"). The translation "only begotten" is based on this assumption. Subsequent manuscript discoveries produced evidence that the term actually comes from *monos* and the noun *genos* ("kind" or "type"). The term *monogenēs* therefore refers to uniqueness and has no inherent reference to chronology or origin. Hebrews 11:17 reinforces this by referring to Isaac as the *monogenēs* of Abraham. Isaac was not Abraham's first child—chronologically, Ishmael came first. But Isaac was considered unique because of the supernatural intervention that aided in his birth and his role as the son through whom God's covenant with Abraham continued. Ancient critics of the doctrine of the Trinity used this term to claim a chronological beginning for Jesus. Conversely, the Nicene Creed used this term to assert Jesus' inherent relationship to the Father: that as the eternal Son he is "begotten [*gennēthenta*], not made" by the Father.

3:17 his Son John prefers to refer to Jesus as the "Son" and God as the "Father" (compare Jn 3:35; 6:40; 17:1). Jesus' reflection and representation of the Father is complete (14:9–10). As one sent by God, Jesus fully represented him on earth (compare 13:16,20).

3:18 whoever does not believe Rejection of Jesus results in condemnation. The NT ultimately roots all salvation in faith in Christ (e.g., Ro 4:1–24; Heb 11:13,26). There is no other way to achieve right standing with God.

3:19 evil In this context, "evil" refers to deeds that flow from unbelief.

3:22–36 This section recounts an overlapping period of ministry of both Jesus and John the Baptist in the Judean wilderness. In the Synoptic Gospels (Matthew, Mark and Luke), the account of Jesus' ministry begins after John's imprisonment (Mk 1:14). This account offers the additional detail that Jesus was also baptizing like John (although, technically, his disciples were doing the baptizing per Jn 4:2). This scene allows John the Baptist to emphasize that his ministry was simply preparing the way for Jesus. Like 1:19–28, the scene may be necessary to convince some that John the Baptist was not a Messianic figure himself.

3:22 Judean countryside Jesus' ministry begins in Galilee in the Synoptic Gospels (e.g., Mt 4:12–14). John is narrating a period of ministry activity in Judea prior to that described in the Synoptics (compare Jn 3:24 with Mt 4:12). **baptized** The other Gospels do not mention Jesus baptizing anyone, but John qualifies this in Jn 4:2, stating the disciples were actually baptizing.

3:23 John also was baptizing at Aenon near Salim Aenon is a name based on the Aramaic word for "spring." The exact location is uncertain, but tradition suggests the site is about six miles south of Beth-Shan or Scythopolis, just west of the Jordan River. The precise location of Salim also is unknown.

3:24 This was before John was put in prison See Mt 4:12 and note; compare Mk 6:17.

the matter of ceremonial washing. ²⁶They came to John and said to him, "Rabbi, that man who was with you on the other side of the Jordan — the one you testified about — look, he is baptizing, and everyone is going to him."

²⁷To this John replied, "A person can receive only what is given them from heaven. ²⁸You yourselves can testify that I said, 'I am not the Messiah but am sent ahead of him.' ²⁹The bride belongs to the bridegroom. The friend who attends the bridegroom waits and listens for him, and is full of joy when he hears the bridegroom's voice. That joy is mine, and it is now complete. ³⁰He must become greater; I must become less."ᵃ

³¹The one who comes from above is above all; the one who is from the earth belongs to the earth, and speaks as one from the earth. The one who comes from heaven is above all. ³²He testifies to what he has seen and heard, but no one accepts his testimony. ³³Whoever has accepted it has certified that God is truthful. ³⁴For the one whom God has sent speaks the words of God, for Godᵇ gives the Spirit without limit. ³⁵The Father loves the Son and has placed everything in his hands. ³⁶Whoever believes in the Son has eternal life, but whoever rejects the Son will not see life, for God's wrath remains on them.

Jesus Talks With a Samaritan Woman

4 Now Jesus learned that the Pharisees had heard that he was gaining and baptizing more disciples than John — ²although in fact it was not Jesus who baptized, but his disciples. ³So he left Judea and went back once more to Galilee.

⁴Now he had to go through Samaria. ⁵So he came to a town in Samaria called Sychar, near the plot of ground Jacob had given to his son Joseph. ⁶Jacob's well was there, and Jesus, tired as he was from the journey, sat down by the well. It was about noon.

⁷When a Samaritan woman came to draw water, Jesus said to her, "Will you give me a drink?" ⁸(His disciples had gone into the town to buy food.)

⁹The Samaritan woman said to him, "You are a Jew and I am a Samaritan woman. How can you ask me for a drink?" (For Jews do not associate with Samaritans.ᶜ)

ᵃ 30 Some interpreters end the quotation with verse 36.
ᵇ 34 Greek he   ᶜ 9 Or do not use dishes Samaritans have used

---

3:25 An argument developed Suggests there was a dispute between John's disciples and an unidentified Jew concerning the relationship between John's water baptism and washing for Jewish ritual purity (e.g., Lev 14:8–9). The precise nature of the disagreement is unknown. See Mk 1:4 and note.

3:26 Rabbi See note on Jn 1:38.

3:27 only what is given them from heaven John's disciples were concerned about the diminishing interest in his baptism compared to Jesus' rising popularity. John reassures them by again explicitly deferring to Jesus' superiority.

3:28 I am not the Messiah See 1:20 and note.

3:29 friend who attends the bridegroom John styles himself in the role of friend of the bridegroom, participating in the ceremony but not the center of attention. Compare Mt 25:1.

3:30 become less John the Baptist had accomplished his mission: to point the world to Jesus (Jn 1:6–9).

3:32 no one accepts his testimony Compare 1:10–11.

4:1–42 Jesus travels through Samaria on his journey from Judea to Galilee. His encounter with a Samaritan woman at the well outside of the city of Sychar leads many Samaritans to believe in Jesus as the Messiah.

4:1 Pharisees See note on 7:32.

4:2 in fact it was not Jesus who baptized See note on 3:22.

4:3 Judea The southern region of Palestine, essentially the territory of the tribe of Judah, where Jerusalem and Bethlehem were located. **Galilee** See note on 1:43.

4:4 Samaria The central region of Palestine between Judea and Galilee. This area had been the heart of the northern kingdom of Israel until the Assyrians deported many Israelites in 722 BC. See note on 1Ki 16:24.

4:5 Sychar This is the only Biblical reference to this location. It probably is to be identified with 'Askar at the foot of Mount Ebal, or perhaps as a corruption of the name "Shechem" (compare Ge 33:19). The reference

to land owned by Jacob suggests that the connection with Shechem is plausible.

4:6 Jacob's well Usually identified with a well at the foot of Mount Gerizim, not far from Shechem. **It was about noon** The Greek text identifies the time as "about the sixth hour." The hours were counted from sunrise to sunset (roughly 6 a.m. to 6 p.m.), so the "sixth hour" was around noon.

4:7 came to draw water The normal time to draw water was morning or evening during the cooler hours of the day. This woman is coming to draw water at a time when no one else would normally be at the well.

4:9 Samaritan An inhabitant of the region of Samaria who was of mixed Israelite and foreign descent. After Assyria conquered and deported the northern kingdom of Israel in 722 BC, Samaria was inhabited by a mixed population. This included Israelites left behind after the deportation and foreign peoples relocated to the region from other parts of the Assyrian Empire (see 2Ki 17:24–41). Those groups intermarried and lost a distinct Israelite identity. However, Samaritans worshiped Yahweh and used a version of the Pentateuch as their Scripture. Jews and Samaritans typically had a mutual hostility, based on ethnic, religious, and political barriers. **Jews do not associate with Samaritans** The woman was surprised that Jesus would speak to her, much less ask her for a drink. This parenthetical comment is added for the benefit of John's non-Jewish readers (see note on Jn 4:27).

John 4:9

SAMARITANS
After Assyria conquered the northern kingdom of Israel in 722 BC and deported most of its people, Samaria was inhabited by a mixed population. This included Israelites left behind after the deportation and foreign

[10]Jesus answered her, "If you knew the gift of God and who it is that asks you for a drink, you would have asked him and he would have given you living water."

[11]"Sir," the woman said, "you have nothing to draw with and the well is deep. Where can you get this living water? [12]Are you greater than our father Jacob, who gave us the well and drank from it himself, as did also his sons and his livestock?"

[13]Jesus answered, "Everyone who drinks this water will be thirsty again, [14]but whoever drinks the water I give them will never thirst. Indeed, the

---

peoples relocated to the region from other parts of the Assyrian Empire (2Ki 17:24–41). Those groups intermarried and thus a distinctly Israelite identity in Samaria was lost, forming the people group the Samaritans. However, like the Jews, Samaritans worshiped Yahweh and used a version of the Pentateuch as their Scripture. Jews and Samaritans typically had a mutual hostility based on ethnic, religious and political barriers. See the box on Lk 10:33; the table "Major Groups in Jesus' Time" on p. 1630.

4:10 living water A Semitic idiom for "spring water" or "fresh water" (Ge 26:19; Lev 14:6), though Jesus uses it as a metaphor for eternal life.

4:11 you have nothing to draw with The woman misunderstands Jesus as speaking of literal water; this is reasonable based on the use of "living water" as an idiom for spring water (see note on Jn 4:10). Misunderstanding often comes before spiritual insight in John's Gospel (see note on 2:21; note on 3:4).

4:12 Jacob The woman's identification of Jacob as her ancestor shows the Samaritans believed themselves to be the rightful descendants of Jacob and true Israelites.

4:14 eternal life See note on 1:4.

Jesus' "I Am" Statements

STATEMENT	REFERENCE
"Take courage! *It is I*! Don't be afraid!"	Mt 14:27; parallel in Mk 6:50; Jn 6:20
"*I am*," said Jesus. "And you will see the Son of Man sitting at the right hand of the Mighty One and coming on the clouds of heaven."	Mk 14:62
"I, the one speaking to you—I *am* he."	Jn 4:26
"*I am* the bread of life. Whoever comes to me will never go hungry, and whoever believes in me will never be thirsty."	Jn 6:35; repeated in Jn 6:48,51
"*I am* the light of the world. Whoever follows me will never walk in darkness, but will have the light of life."	Jn 8:12
"*I am* one who testifies for myself; my other witness is the Father, who sent me."	Jn 8:18
"Very truly I tell you, before Abraham was born, *I am*!"	Jn 8:58
"Very truly I tell you, *I am* the gate for the sheep."	Jn 10:7; also in Jn 10:9
"*I am* the good shepherd. The good shepherd lays down his life for the sheep."	Jn 10:11; also in Jn 10:14
"*I am* the resurrection and the life."	Jn 11:25
"I am telling you now before it happens, so that when it does happen you will believe that *I am* who I am."	Jn 13:19
"*I am* the way and the truth and the life."	Jn 14:6
"*I am* the true vine, and my Father is the gardener."	Jn 15:1; "I am the vine" in Jn 15:5
"Who is it you want?" "Jesus of Nazarene," they replied. "*I am* he," Jesus said.	Jn 18:4–5; also in Jn 18:6,8

water I give them will become in them a spring of water welling up to eternal life."

¹⁵The woman said to him, "Sir, give me this water so that I won't get thirsty and have to keep coming here to draw water."

¹⁶He told her, "Go, call your husband and come back."

¹⁷"I have no husband," she replied.

Jesus said to her, "You are right when you say you have no husband. ¹⁸The fact is, you have had five husbands, and the man you now have is not your husband. What you have just said is quite true."

¹⁹"Sir," the woman said, "I can see that you are a prophet. ²⁰Our ancestors worshiped on this mountain, but you Jews claim that the place where we must worship is in Jerusalem."

²¹"Woman," Jesus replied, "believe me, a time is coming when you will worship the Father neither on this mountain nor in Jerusalem. ²²You Samaritans worship what you do not know; we worship what we do know, for salvation is from the Jews. ²³Yet a time is coming and has now come when the true worshipers will worship the Father in the Spirit and in truth, for they are the kind of worshipers the Father seeks. ²⁴God is spirit, and his worshipers must worship in the Spirit and in truth."

²⁵The woman said, "I know that Messiah" (called Christ) "is coming. When he comes, he will explain everything to us."

²⁶Then Jesus declared, "I, the one speaking to you—I am he."

The Disciples Rejoin Jesus

²⁷Just then his disciples returned and were surprised to find him talking with a woman. But no one asked, "What do you want?" or "Why are you talking with her?"

²⁸Then, leaving her water jar, the woman went back to the town and said to the people, ²⁹"Come, see a man who told me everything I ever did. Could this be the Messiah?" ³⁰They came out of the town and made their way toward him.

³¹Meanwhile his disciples urged him, "Rabbi, eat something."

4:15 coming here to draw She still misunderstands Jesus, believing they are talking about literal water. See note on v. 11.

4:17 I have no husband The woman's answer seems intended to politely deflect further discussion of the subject.

4:18 five husbands This Greek word can mean "man" or "husband." If the woman had five previous husbands who either died or divorced her, she would have exceeded the traditional limit of three husbands in Jewish law (according to the rabbinic text Babylonian Talmud Yebamot 64b; Niddah 64a). However, the ambiguity of the word suggests the possibility that none of the five was a legal husband just as the current man is not her husband. This comment also reveals a reason why Jesus chose to speak with her about her place before God.

4:19 a prophet Jesus' exceptional knowledge of her affairs yields the concession that he must be a prophet.

4:20 this mountain Refers to Mount Gerizim, the holy mountain for the Samaritan community. The mountain was visible from the well where Jesus and the woman were speaking. The Samaritan temple on Mount Gerizim had been destroyed by the Jews in the late second century BC. Josephus records how the Jews and Samaritans disputed over whether Gerizim or Jerusalem was the proper site for the temple of Yahweh. He dates the construction of the Gerizim temple to the time of Alexander the Great, around 332 BC, but excavations suggest it was built about a century earlier. During the first century AD, the ruins of the temple probably were still visible. **you Jews claim** The woman moves quickly to change the subject from her immoral lifestyle to the ongoing religious controversy between the Jews and Samaritans over sacred space.

4:21 neither on this mountain nor in Jerusalem Jesus does not take up the debate over legitimate holy places. Rather, he points to a future time of salvation when worship will not be limited to any local sacred site, neither Mount Gerizim nor Jerusalem. How one worships is more important than where one worships.

4:22 salvation is from the Jews Jesus probably is alluding to the Jews' preservation of the entire OT Scrip-

tures that revealed God's plan for salvation. Also, the Messiah would be from the Jews, a son of David—not a Samaritan or Gentile.

4:23 a time is coming and has now come A unique expression in the Gospel of John that conveys both future expectation and present reality. Jesus' work in the present inaugurates a new phase in redemptive history. Jesus' phrasing also echoes the language of the OT prophets (Jer 31:31; 2Ki 20:17). **Spirit and in truth** Authentic worship involves an inward change of heart, not just outward observance.

4:25 Messiah The Samaritans expected a deliverer called the *taheb* or "Returning One" who fulfilled the promise of a prophet like Moses (Dt 18:15–18). Compare note on Jn 1:20 and note on 1:41.

4:26 I am he Jesus rarely confirms being the Messiah, probably due to expectations of political deliverance among Jews. The Samaritan concept of a Messiah was linked more to the restoration of proper worship of God. John depicts Jesus using the Greek phrase *egō eimi* ("I am") 23 times, and each use functions in some way to underscore Jesus' identity. The occurrences in 8:58 and 18:6 are particularly striking when the audience understands the phrase as Jesus identifying himself with Yahweh by alluding to Ex 3:14. See the table "Jesus' 'I Am' Statements" on p. 1727.

4:27 talking with a woman It would have been unusual for a rabbi (like Jesus) or any Jewish man to converse publicly with a woman. Jewish teaching warned against spending too much time talking with women because of temptation and the appearance of impropriety. Through this interaction, Jesus is showing care for the lowliest of people in the eyes of Jews.

4:28 water jar In her haste to tell the townspeople about Jesus, she abandons the original purpose of her trip to the well.

4:29 Could this be the Messiah The woman's question implies hesitation and doubt. The Greek text indicates that a negative response is expected: "This cannot be the Messiah, can it?"

4:31 Rabbi See note on Jn 1:38.

³²But he said to them, "I have food to eat that you know nothing about."

³³Then his disciples said to each other, "Could someone have brought him food?"

³⁴"My food," said Jesus, "is to do the will of him who sent me and to finish his work. ³⁵Don't you have a saying, 'It's still four months until harvest'? I tell you, open your eyes and look at the fields! They are ripe for harvest. ³⁶Even now the one who reaps draws a wage and harvests a crop for eternal life, so that the sower and the reaper may be glad together. ³⁷Thus the saying 'One sows and another reaps' is true. ³⁸I sent you to reap what you have not worked for. Others have done the hard work, and you have reaped the benefits of their labor."

Many Samaritans Believe

³⁹Many of the Samaritans from that town believed in him because of the woman's testimony, "He told me everything I ever did." ⁴⁰So when the Samaritans came to him, they urged him to stay with them, and he stayed two days. ⁴¹And because of his words many more became believers.

⁴²They said to the woman, "We no longer believe just because of what you said; now we have heard for ourselves, and we know that this man really is the Savior of the world."

Jesus Heals an Official's Son

⁴³After the two days he left for Galilee. ⁴⁴(Now Jesus himself had pointed out that a prophet has no honor in his own country.) ⁴⁵When he arrived in Galilee, the Galileans welcomed him. They had seen all that he had done in Jerusalem at the Passover Festival, for they also had been there.

⁴⁶Once more he visited Cana in Galilee, where he had turned the water into wine. And there was a certain royal official whose son lay sick at Capernaum. ⁴⁷When this man heard that Jesus had arrived in Galilee from Judea, he went to him and begged him to come and heal his son, who was close to death.

⁴⁸"Unless you people see signs and wonders," Jesus told him, "you will never believe."

⁴⁹The royal official said, "Sir, come down before my child dies."

⁵⁰"Go," Jesus replied, "your son will live."

The man took Jesus at his word and departed. ⁵¹While he was still on the way, his servants met him with the news that his boy was living. ⁵²When he inquired as to the time when his son got better, they said to him, "Yesterday, at one in the afternoon, the fever left him."

⁵³Then the father realized that this was the exact time at which Jesus had said to him, "Your son will live." So he and his whole household believed.

⁵⁴This was the second sign Jesus performed after coming from Judea to Galilee.

The Healing at the Pool

5 Some time later, Jesus went up to Jerusalem for one of the Jewish festivals. ²Now there is in Jerusalem near the Sheep Gate a pool, which in Aramaic is called Bethesda*a* and which is surrounded

a 2 Some manuscripts *Bethzatha*; other manuscripts *Bethsaida*

4:33 Could someone have brought him food Just like the woman at the well (v. 11) and Nicodemus (3:4), the disciples misunderstand Jesus.

4:34 will of him who sent me Jesus' mission is more important than his need to eat. Compare Mt 4:4.

4:35 still four months until harvest Harvest imagery has overtones of end-time abundance (compare Joel 2:18–27). Jesus draws on a common proverb about a lack of urgency to emphasize the immediacy of his work. Compare Mt 9:37–38.

4:37 One sows and another reaps The sowing was the expectation of the prophet laid out in Dt 18:18. The reaping will be the belief of the Samaritans. Jesus emphasizes that it's not always the one who first tells someone about salvation (as the prophets had done for the Samaritans) who brings them to belief, but often it's those who come later. No matter who reaps, God alone deserves the credit.

4:39 because of the woman's testimony The testimony of a woman had little weight, and this particular woman's reputation would have further weakened the credibility of her witness. That "many of the Samaritans believed" despite these obstacles underscores the divine work in preparing the harvest.

4:42 Savior of the world The salvation of a large group of Samaritans provides a glimpse of the universal nature of God's plan of salvation. Compare Ac 1:8, where the disciples are sent to Jerusalem, Judea, Samaria and the whole world.

4:43–45 Jesus stays with the Samaritans for two days before continuing on to Galilee.

4:44 no honor in his own country Compare Mt 13:57.

4:46–54 The second miraculous sign recorded by John is the healing of a government official's son in Cana (compare note on Jn 2:11). The first two signs take place in the same village. See the table "Miracles of Jesus" on p. 1741.

4:46 Cana in Galilee See note on 2:1. **where he had turned the water into wine** See 2:1–11. **royal official** The Greek term used here could denote a member of the royal family of Herod, but it more likely refers to a Roman official serving Herod Antipas as ruler of Galilee on behalf of Rome. **Capernaum** See note on 2:12.

4:50 The man took Jesus at his word The boy's healing is connected to the father's belief in Jesus' ability to heal. Compare Mt 8:5–13; 9:22.

5:1–18 Jesus returns to Jerusalem for another Jewish religious festival and heals a lame man on the Sabbath. The religious leaders are more concerned with the man carrying his mat on the Sabbath than with his miraculous healing. See the table "Miracles of Jesus" on p. 1741.

5:1 Some time later Refers to an indeterminate period of time. John shifts to a new scene in his narrative without giving specific chronological details (compare Jn 6:1; 21:1). **Jesus went up to Jerusalem** The Synoptic

by five covered colonnades. ³Here a great number of disabled people used to lie — the blind, the lame, the paralyzed. [4]ᵃ ⁵One who was there had been an invalid for thirty-eight years. ⁶When Jesus saw him lying there and learned that he had been in this condition for a long time, he asked him, "Do you want to get well?"

⁷"Sir," the invalid replied, "I have no one to help me into the pool when the water is stirred. While I am trying to get in, someone else goes down ahead of me."

⁸Then Jesus said to him, "Get up! Pick up your mat and walk." ⁹At once the man was cured; he picked up his mat and walked.

The day on which this took place was a Sabbath, ¹⁰and so the Jewish leaders said to the man who had been healed, "It is the Sabbath; the law forbids you to carry your mat."

¹¹But he replied, "The man who made me well said to me, 'Pick up your mat and walk.'"

¹²So they asked him, "Who is this fellow who told you to pick it up and walk?"

¹³The man who was healed had no idea who it was, for Jesus had slipped away into the crowd that was there.

¹⁴Later Jesus found him at the temple and said to him, "See, you are well again. Stop sinning or something worse may happen to you." ¹⁵The man went away and told the Jewish leaders that it was Jesus who had made him well.

The Authority of the Son

¹⁶So, because Jesus was doing these things on the Sabbath, the Jewish leaders began to persecute him. ¹⁷In his defense Jesus said to them, "My Father is always at his work to this very day, and I too am working." ¹⁸For this reason they tried all the more to kill him; not only was he breaking the Sabbath, but he was even calling God his own Father, making himself equal with God.

¹⁹Jesus gave them this answer: "Very truly I tell

ᵃ 3,4 Some manuscripts include here, wholly or in part, paralyzed — and they waited for the moving of the waters. ⁴From time to time an angel of the Lord would come down and stir up the waters. The first one into the pool after each such disturbance would be cured of whatever disease they had.

Gospels (Matthew, Mark and Luke) record only one trip to Jerusalem, but John has several. **one of the Jewish festivals** Most likely one of the other two pilgrimage festivals besides Passover, either the Festival of Weeks or the Festival of Tabernacles. See note on 2:13. See the table "Israelite Festivals" on p. 200.

5:2 Sheep Gate A gate on the northern end of the temple complex. See the map "New Testament Jerusalem" on p. 2259. **Aramaic** The Greek term used here, *hebraisti*, refers to the Hebrew and Aramaic languages. **Bethesda** Greek manuscripts show a variety of renderings for this place name: "Beth-zatha," "Bethesda" or "Bethsaida." The most common English rendering is "Bethesda." John is the only NT writer to mention this pool. **five covered colonnades** Evidence of a healing sanctuary and pool with five porticoes was found in Jerusalem just north of the Sheep Gate. Porticoes are covered walkways, with the roof supported by columns.

5:3 Some later manuscripts have an additional line in v. 3 and include v. 4, which explains that an angel would stir the waters of the pool and whoever entered the pool first would be healed. Some translations include this line, some omit it, and some mention it in a note or in brackets.

5:5 an invalid The Greek term used here, *astheneia*, refers to any kind of debilitating condition. Since the man is unable to move into the pool on his own (v. 7), it's assumed that he is either disabled or paralyzed. **thirty-eight years** The man's age is unknown, but he had been sick for longer than many people lived in antiquity. **5:7 when the water is stirred** The additional information provided in v. 4 explains this otherwise enigmatic statement as a divine stirring of the water that results in healing (compare note on v. 3). The pools at Bethesda probably were fed by springs that may have intermittently added fresh water to the pools. **5:8 Get up** Compare Mk 2:11. **5:9 At once** The Gospels regularly emphasize the immediate nature of Jesus' healings. Compare Mk 2:12.

Sabbath The seventh day of the week, when Jews were to abstain from work (compare note on Mt 12:1; note on Ex 20:10). **5:10 law forbids** Physical labor was forbidden on the Sabbath, but Biblical law did not explicitly define what qualified as work. Rabbinic legal tradition defined work according to 39 types of behavior that were forbidden on the Sabbath. Carrying anything out of the house was one of the forbidden activities. Compare Jer 17:22 and note. **5:12 Who is this fellow** The religious leaders want to find the person responsible for leading this man to sin by working on the Sabbath. **5:14 or something worse may happen to you** While NT teaching generally rejects the assumption that all suffering is a result of sin (compare Jn 9:1–3; Lk 13:2–3), Jesus seems to imply here that the man's affliction was related to sin. The worse fate that could happen is likely a reference to the eternal consequences of sin and failure to be reconciled with God. **5:16 doing these things on the Sabbath** The religious leaders regularly quarreled with Jesus over his apparent lack of respect for the Sabbath prohibitions (compare Lk 6:1–11; 13:10–17; 14:1–6). A local synagogue leader even entreated the people to seek out healing on the other six days of the week (Lk 13:14), but not on the Sabbath. Jesus rejects all attempts by the authorities to force him into their interpretation of Scripture, teaching instead that love and compassion trump legalism. **5:17 and I too am working** Because Jesus is "Lord of the Sabbath," he is not limited by their interpretations of what was not allowed (compare Lk 6:5). Jewish tradition held that God was constantly working (sustaining the universe), but that this did not constitute a violation of the Sabbath (according to the Jewish text Exodus Rabbah 30.9). Jesus' assertion puts him on the same plane as God the Father and was clearly understood as a claim to deity by his audience (Jn 5:18). John's explanation, however, focuses on the reference to God as "my Father." Jesus claims the divine prerogative to give and sustain life on the Sabbath.

you, the Son can do nothing by himself; he can do only what he sees his Father doing, because whatever the Father does the Son also does. ²⁰For the Father loves the Son and shows him all he does. Yes, and he will show him even greater works than these, so that you will be amazed. ²¹For just as the Father raises the dead and gives them life, even so the Son gives life to whom he is pleased to give it. ²²Moreover, the Father judges no one, but has entrusted all judgment to the Son, ²³that all may honor the Son just as they honor the Father. Whoever does not honor the Son does not honor the Father, who sent him.

²⁴"Very truly I tell you, whoever hears my word and believes him who sent me has eternal life and will not be judged but has crossed over from death to life. ²⁵Very truly I tell you, a time is coming and has now come when the dead will hear the voice of the Son of God and those who hear will live. ²⁶For as the Father has life in himself, so he has granted the Son also to have life in himself. ²⁷And he has given him authority to judge because he is the Son of Man.

²⁸"Do not be amazed at this, for a time is coming when all who are in their graves will hear his voice ²⁹and come out — those who have done what is good will rise to live, and those who have done what is evil will rise to be condemned. ³⁰By myself I can do nothing; I judge only as I hear,

and my judgment is just, for I seek not to please myself but him who sent me.

Testimonies About Jesus

³¹"If I testify about myself, my testimony is not true. ³²There is another who testifies in my favor, and I know that his testimony about me is true.

³³"You have sent to John and he has testified to the truth. ³⁴Not that I accept human testimony; but I mention it that you may be saved. ³⁵John was a lamp that burned and gave light, and you chose for a time to enjoy his light.

³⁶"I have testimony weightier than that of John. For the works that the Father has given me to finish — the very works that I am doing — testify that the Father has sent me. ³⁷And the Father who sent me has himself testified concerning me. You have never heard his voice nor seen his form, ³⁸nor does his word dwell in you, for you do not believe the one he sent. ³⁹You study*a* the Scriptures diligently because you think that in them you have eternal life. These are the very Scriptures that testify about me, ⁴⁰yet you refuse to come to me to have life.

⁴¹"I do not accept glory from human beings, ⁴²but I know you. I know that you do not have

a 39 Or ³⁹Study

5:19–47 This discourse focuses on the person and authority of Jesus. This passage is the clearest summary of Jesus' relationship with the Father, his position as judge of all things, and the witnesses to his mission as Messiah found in the NT.

5:19 the Son can do nothing by himself Jesus asserts his dependence on the Father and his distinct role subordinate to the Father's will and plan. It is impossible for Jesus to act in any way that would somehow place him in opposition to the Father.

5:21 the Son gives life to whom he is pleased Jesus claims delegated authority over life and death; this authority is given to him by the Father. See v. 17 and note.

5:22 judgment The OT depicts Yahweh as the judge of all peoples (Isa 41:1; 51:5; Jer 25:15–38) but sometimes foreshadows the transfer of that role to the Messiah (Isa 11:3; 16:5).

5:25 a time is coming See note on Jn 4:23. **Son of God** See note on 10:36.

5:29 will rise to live Refers to Jewish beliefs on the resurrection rooted in OT passages such as Isa 26:19; Eze 37:1–10; Hos 6:2; Da 12:2–3. Compare Jn 11:24; 1Co 15:52. The various Jewish sects in the first century AD had conflicting beliefs on the concept of resurrection (Mt 22:23; Ac 23:6–9).

5:31–47 In this section of the discourse, Jesus takes up the trial motif established in Jn 1:7 and discusses the witnesses who have been sent to testify to his identity. The witnesses listed here are John the Baptist (vv. 33–35), Jesus' signs (v. 36), God the Father (vv. 37–38) and the Scriptures (vv. 39,45–47). All four testify to God sending Jesus to bring eternal life to those who would believe.

5:31 testify See note on 1:7. **my testimony is not true** In the legal sense of "true" as evidence for trial. One

who testifies about himself needs supporting witnesses to validate his testimony. Biblical law requires two witnesses for testimony to be legally valid (Dt 17:6; 19:15).

5:32 another who testifies Refers to the testimony of God the Father (Jn 5:36–37). The initial appeal to John's testimony is simply a segue to the greater divine testimony.

5:33 John The testimony of John the Baptist is recorded in 1:29–35.

5:35 a lamp that burned and gave light The metaphor indicates John's ministry was a dim reflection of the true light (compare 1:6–9). The reference may also allude to Ps 132:17, where God says he is preparing "a lamp for my anointed."

5:36 works Refers to everything he says or does in public ministry. The signs Jesus has performed are only part of his earthly works that testify to his identity as Messiah and Son of God.

5:37 Father who sent me Compare Jn 3:2. All the miracles and teaching Jesus has done (his "works") are also part of the Father's witness since God the Father guided and empowered all of that activity. The Father's witness also includes the revelation through Scripture (vv. 45–47). **You have never heard his voice** The current generation of God's people knew God only through the tradition and teaching of their ancestors, not their own experience. Compare Dt 4:12. At Sinai, Israel heard from God but accepted the revelation through Moses as intermediary (Ex 20:19).

5:38 you do not believe The people are rejecting the testimony of God himself by rejecting Jesus.

5:39 You study the Scriptures diligently Studying sacred texts was a central part of ancient Judaism. Jewish scribes meticulously copied the Biblical text and developed detailed interpretations. See the table "Jesus' Fulfillment of OT Prophecy" on p. 1573.

the love of God in your hearts. ⁴³I have come in my Father's name, and you do not accept me; but if someone else comes in his own name, you will accept him. ⁴⁴How can you believe since you accept glory from one another but do not seek the glory that comes from the only God*ᵃ*?

⁴⁵"But do not think I will accuse you before the Father. Your accuser is Moses, on whom your hopes are set. ⁴⁶If you believed Moses, you would believe me, for he wrote about me. ⁴⁷But since you do not believe what he wrote, how are you going to believe what I say?"

Jesus Feeds the Five Thousand

6:1-13pp — Mt 14:13-21; Mk 6:32-44; Lk 9:10-17

6 Some time after this, Jesus crossed to the far shore of the Sea of Galilee (that is, the Sea of Tiberias), ²and a great crowd of people followed him because they saw the signs he had performed by healing the sick. ³Then Jesus went up on a mountainside and sat down with his disciples. ⁴The Jewish Passover Festival was near.

⁵When Jesus looked up and saw a great crowd coming toward him, he said to Philip, "Where shall we buy bread for these people to eat?" ⁶He asked this only to test him, for he already had in mind what he was going to do.

⁷Philip answered him, "It would take more than half a year's wages*ᵇ* to buy enough bread for each one to have a bite!"

⁸Another of his disciples, Andrew, Simon Peter's brother, spoke up, ⁹"Here is a boy with five small barley loaves and two small fish, but how far will they go among so many?"

¹⁰Jesus said, "Have the people sit down." There was plenty of grass in that place, and they sat down (about five thousand men were there). ¹¹Jesus then took the loaves, gave thanks, and distributed to those who were seated as much as they wanted. He did the same with the fish.

¹²When they had all had enough to eat, he said to his disciples, "Gather the pieces that are left over. Let nothing be wasted." ¹³So they gathered them and filled twelve baskets with the pieces of the five barley loaves left over by those who had eaten.

¹⁴After the people saw the sign Jesus performed, they began to say, "Surely this is the Prophet who is to come into the world." ¹⁵Jesus, knowing that they intended to come and make him king by force, withdrew again to a mountain by himself.

Jesus Walks on the Water

6:16-21pp — Mt 14:22-33; Mk 6:47-51

¹⁶When evening came, his disciples went down to the lake, ¹⁷where they got into a boat and set off across the lake for Capernaum. By now it was dark, and Jesus had not yet joined them. ¹⁸A strong wind was blowing and the waters grew rough. ¹⁹When they had rowed about three or four miles,*ᶜ* they saw Jesus approaching the boat, walking on the water; and they were frightened. ²⁰But he said to them, "It is I; don't be afraid." ²¹Then they were willing to take him into the boat, and immediately the boat reached the shore where they were heading.

²²The next day the crowd that had stayed on the opposite shore of the lake realized that only one boat had been there, and that Jesus had not

---

ᵃ 44 Some early manuscripts *the Only One*   *ᵇ 7* Greek *take two hundred denarii*   *ᶜ 19* Or about 5 or 6 kilometers

---

5:43 in his own name Alludes to Israel's tendency to accept false prophets who tell them what they want to hear (compare Jer 14:14; 29:25,31).

6:1–15 Jesus performs another miraculous sign: feeding a crowd of about 5,000 men (besides women and children) with five loaves and two fish. This event is recorded in all four Gospels (Mt 14:13–21; Mk 6:32–44; Lk 9:10–17). On the symbolism of Jesus' signs in John, see note on Jn 2:11. See the table "Miracles of Jesus" on p. 1741.

6:1 Some time after this See note on 5:1. **the Sea of Galilee** A large freshwater lake in northern Palestine, 13 miles long by 8 miles wide and up to 150 feet deep. Jesus is heading to the eastern shore. Most Jewish settlements are on the west and northern shores. **Tiberias** This alternative name for the Sea of Galilee also was the name of a city on its western shore. Tiberias was the largest and most important city in Galilee and was the regional capital for Herod Antipas.

6:4 Passover This is the second of three Passovers mentioned by John (compare note on 2:13).

6:6 He asked this only to test him The narrator clarifies that the purpose of Jesus' question is didactic. He is not seeking knowledge from Philip.

6:7 half a year's wages The amount referred to here, 200 denarii, was a substantial sum. A denarius was about a day's wage for a laborer. See Mt 20:2; note on Mk 6:37. See the infographic "A Silver Denarius" on p. 1578.

6:9 five small barley loaves and two small fish A relatively small amount of food, normally enough for one or two people (compare note on Mt 14:17).

6:10 about five thousand See note on Mt 14:21.

6:13 twelve baskets See note on Mt 14:20.

6:14 the Prophet See Jn 1:21 and note (compare 4:19 and note). See the table "Jesus' Fulfillment of OT Prophecy" on p. 1573.

6:15 make him king The people recognized Jesus as the Messiah but wrongly equated that idea with political revolution.

6:16–21 Three of the four Gospels record the disciples seeing Jesus walking across the Sea of Galilee. In all accounts, the scene directly follows the feeding of the 5,000. Compare Mt 14:22–33; Mk 6:45–51.

6:17 See the infographic "First-Century Galilean Fishing Boat" on p. 1560. **Capernaum** They were on the eastern shore of the sea; Capernaum was on the northwest shore (see note on Jn 2:12).

6:19 three or four miles They were roughly halfway

entered it with his disciples, but that they had gone away alone. ²³Then some boats from Tiberias landed near the place where the people had eaten the bread after the Lord had given thanks. ²⁴Once the crowd realized that neither Jesus nor his disciples were there, they got into the boats and went to Capernaum in search of Jesus.

Jesus the Bread of Life

²⁵When they found him on the other side of the lake, they asked him, "Rabbi, when did you get here?"

²⁶Jesus answered, "Very truly I tell you, you are looking for me, not because you saw the signs I performed but because you ate the loaves and had your fill. ²⁷Do not work for food that spoils, but for food that endures to eternal life, which the Son of Man will give you. For on him God the Father has placed his seal of approval."

²⁸Then they asked him, "What must we do to do the works God requires?"

²⁹Jesus answered, "The work of God is this: to believe in the one he has sent."

³⁰So they asked him, "What sign then will you give that we may see it and believe you? What will you do? ³¹Our ancestors ate the manna in the wilderness; as it is written: 'He gave them bread from heaven to eat.'ᵃ"

³²Jesus said to them, "Very truly I tell you, it is not Moses who has given you the bread from heaven, but it is my Father who gives you the true bread from heaven. ³³For the bread of God is the bread that comes down from heaven and gives life to the world."

³⁴"Sir," they said, "always give us this bread."

³⁵Then Jesus declared, "I am the bread of life. Whoever comes to me will never go hungry, and whoever believes in me will never be thirsty. ³⁶But as I told you, you have seen me and still you do not believe. ³⁷All those the Father gives me will come to me, and whoever comes to me I will never drive away. ³⁸For I have come down from heaven not to do my will but to do the will of him who sent me. ³⁹And this is the will of him who sent me, that I shall lose none of all those he has given me, but raise them up at the last day. ⁴⁰For my Father's will is that everyone who looks to the Son and

ᵃ *31* Exodus 16:4; Neh. 9:15; Psalm 78:24,25

---

across the sea. The distance from the eastern shore to Capernaum was six miles or more. **walking on the water** See Mk 6:48 and note.
6:20 It is I The Greek phrase used here, literally rendered as "I am," evokes the motif of Jesus' "I am" sayings (see Jn 4:26 and note; note on Mt 14:27).

6:22–58 This discussion about Jesus as the "bread of life" is often understood as John's treatment of the Lord's Supper (also called Holy Communion or Eucharist). The Synoptic Gospels record Jesus' instituting the observance during the Last Supper using the bread to symbolize his body and the wine to symbolize his blood (Mt 26:26–28; Mk 14:22–24; Lk 22:17–20). The apostle Paul also teaches about the Lord's Supper in 1Co 11:23–25. While the Eucharistic interpretation of these verses is common, it is not the only way to understand the passage. Some parts of Jesus' teaching here are inexplicable when read as references to the future observance of a Christian sacrament. For example, Jn 6:53 (under that interpretation) would imply that taking communion was a requirement for salvation. In addition, the benefits of gaining the "bread of life" in this passage are closely connected with what John describes as natural results of belief in Jesus as the Christ (vv. 35,40,47). The spiritual meaning of the image points to Jesus as the source of eternal life. Most likely the spiritual interpretation is the primary emphasis, but the sacramental interpretation has significance for a later Christian audience.

6:25 Rabbi See note on 1:38.
6:26 you ate the loaves Jesus accuses the crowd of following him in pursuit of material satisfaction, not out of genuine faith.
6:27 the Son of Man See note on 1:51. **placed his seal of approval** See note on Rev 5:1.
6:28 What must we do The people are asking what actions are required by God, missing the point that eternal life is something that will be given to them (Jn 6:27).

They may have understood Jesus' reference to food in the previous verse to be observance of the law rather than Jesus himself.
6:29 believe The only "work" necessary for salvation is faith in Jesus as the Messiah sent by God.
6:31 the manna Refers to the events of Ex 16:4–36 and Yahweh's miraculous provision of bread for his people in the wilderness. Jewish tradition looked for the Messiah to provide manna as Moses had (as depicted by the Jewish work Ecclesiastes Rabbah 1.9). **He gave them bread from heaven to eat** Quoting Ps 78:24. The people are still focused on their earthly, material needs.
6:32 not Moses who has given you the bread from heaven The manna in the wilderness was physical bread for their physical needs. The "true bread from heaven" is spiritual. **true bread from heaven** Jesus is emphasizing his role as the one sent from God in heaven to fulfill God's plan to sustain his people with eternal life. Jesus' entire discourse on the "bread of life" is essentially an extended interpretation of Ps 78:24 as quoted in Jn 6:31.
6:35 I am the bread of life Since the audience continues to miss the point that Jesus is referring to himself as the one sent by God, Jesus makes the point explicit. Jesus uses seven metaphorical "I am" statements to define his role as Savior and Messiah (see note on 4:26). These sayings also carry strong overtones of being claims to divinity. He identifies himself as the bread of life (vv. 35,48,51), the light of the world (8:12; 9:5), the gate for the sheep (10:7,9), the good shepherd (10:11,14), the resurrection and the life (11:25), the way and the truth and the life (14:6), and the true vine (15:1). See the table "Jesus' 'I Am' Statements" on p. 1727. **will never go hungry** Alludes to OT expectations of divine redemption (compare Isa 49:10; 55:1).

6:36–40 Jesus briefly sets aside the topic of the "bread of life" to expound on the issue of the Jews' persistent unbelief, reiterating his role as agent of the divine will and stressing that eternal life is gained through belief in him.

believes in him shall have eternal life, and I will raise them up at the last day."

⁴¹At this the Jews there began to grumble about him because he said, "I am the bread that came down from heaven." ⁴²They said, "Is this not Jesus, the son of Joseph, whose father and mother we know? How can he now say, 'I came down from heaven'?"

⁴³"Stop grumbling among yourselves," Jesus answered. ⁴⁴"No one can come to me unless the Father who sent me draws them, and I will raise them up at the last day. ⁴⁵It is written in the Prophets: 'They will all be taught by God.'ᵃ Everyone who has heard the Father and learned from him comes to me. ⁴⁶No one has seen the Father except the one who is from God; only he has seen the Father. ⁴⁷Very truly I tell you, the one who believes has eternal life. ⁴⁸I am the bread of life. ⁴⁹Your ancestors ate the manna in the wilderness, yet they died. ⁵⁰But here is the bread that comes down from heaven, which anyone may eat and not die. ⁵¹I am the living bread that came down from heaven. Whoever eats this bread will live forever. This bread is my flesh, which I will give for the life of the world."

⁵²Then the Jews began to argue sharply among themselves, "How can this man give us his flesh to eat?"

⁵³Jesus said to them, "Very truly I tell you, unless you eat the flesh of the Son of Man and drink his blood, you have no life in you. ⁵⁴Whoever eats my flesh and drinks my blood has eternal life, and I will raise them up at the last day. ⁵⁵For my flesh

is real food and my blood is real drink. ⁵⁶Whoever eats my flesh and drinks my blood remains in me, and I in them. ⁵⁷Just as the living Father sent me and I live because of the Father, so the one who feeds on me will live because of me. ⁵⁸This is the bread that came down from heaven. Your ancestors ate manna and died, but whoever feeds on this bread will live forever." ⁵⁹He said this while teaching in the synagogue in Capernaum.

Many Disciples Desert Jesus

⁶⁰On hearing it, many of his disciples said, "This is a hard teaching. Who can accept it?"

⁶¹Aware that his disciples were grumbling about this, Jesus said to them, "Does this offend you? ⁶²Then what if you see the Son of Man ascend to where he was before! ⁶³The Spirit gives life; the flesh counts for nothing. The words I have spoken to you—they are full of the Spiritᵇ and life. ⁶⁴Yet there are some of you who do not believe." For Jesus had known from the beginning which of them did not believe and who would betray him. ⁶⁵He went on to say, "This is why I told you that no one can come to me unless the Father has enabled them."

⁶⁶From this time many of his disciples turned back and no longer followed him.

⁶⁷"You do not want to leave too, do you?" Jesus asked the Twelve.

⁶⁸Simon Peter answered him, "Lord, to whom

ᵃ 45 Isaiah 54:13   ᵇ 63 Or are Spirit; or are spirit

6:40 will raise them up at the last day Alludes to the belief in bodily resurrection. See note on Jn 5:29.

6:41 the Jews In this context, "the Jews" seems to refer to those present and listening to Jesus' teaching in the synagogue at Capernaum (v. 59; compare note on 1:19). They are displeased by the implications of his teaching. See the infographic "The Synagogue at Capernaum" on p. 1656.

6:42 Jesus, the son of Joseph Knowledge of his earthly origin leads the people to reject his claim to heavenly origin (compare Mt 13:55).

6:45 They will all be taught by God Jesus quotes Is 54:13 in support of his assertion that true disciples will recognize him in the teachings of Scripture.

6:47–65 Jesus' teaching in this section repeats and reinforces the themes laid out in Jn 6:26–45. Belief in Jesus leads to eternal life. He repeats the metaphor that he is the "bread of life" (v. 48) and heightens the contrast between the manna that provided only physical nourishment and the bread from heaven that provides eternal life (vv. 49–51). His teaching is interrupted again by the misunderstanding of the audience (v. 52) and their willful rejection of a spiritual concept they cannot understand (vv. 60–61).

6:51 is my flesh Jesus' physical death is the price for the world's spiritual life. The reference to "flesh" likely points back to 1:14. See note on 3:6.

6:52 How can this man give us his flesh The audience remains unable to understand that Jesus' language

symbolically points to a spiritual reality, not a physical requirement.

6:53 eat the flesh As if to underscore the absurdity of their confusion, Jesus presses the metaphor further, using the literal imagery of eating and drinking that they had assumed as the context. Eating and drinking are metaphors for faith (see v. 35 and note). Jesus makes the point that faith in him—to the point of partaking of his role in the world (including his suffering)—is the way to God.

6:54 eats my flesh and drinks my blood In light of v. 35, this statement appears to refer metaphorically to believing in Jesus. This section of the discourse and especially Jesus' language here evokes the strongest connections to the Lord's Supper. See note on vv. 22–58.

6:59 the synagogue See note on Mk 1:21. See the infographic "The Synagogue at Capernaum" on p. 1656.

6:60 This is a hard teaching Even Jesus' own disciples were confused and put off by this teaching.

6:66–71 While other followers turned away from Jesus because of the difficulty of this teaching, the Twelve reaffirm their commitment to Jesus, and Simon Peter acknowledges their acceptance of him as Messiah.

6:68 Simon Peter Compare Peter's confession in Mt 16:16. The Synoptic Gospels (Matthew, Mark and Luke) depict Peter in the role of spokesman for the Twelve (see Mt 14:28). His prominence in the Synoptics and their account of the formation of the Twelve seem to be assumed here.

shall we go? You have the words of eternal life. [69]We have come to believe and to know that you are the Holy One of God."

[70]Then Jesus replied, "Have I not chosen you, the Twelve? Yet one of you is a devil!" [71](He meant Judas, the son of Simon Iscariot, who, though one of the Twelve, was later to betray him.)

Jesus Goes to the Festival of Tabernacles

7 After this, Jesus went around in Galilee. He did not want[a] to go about in Judea because the Jewish leaders there were looking for a way to kill him. [2]But when the Jewish Festival of Tabernacles was near, [3]Jesus' brothers said to him, "Leave Galilee and go to Judea, so that your disciples there may see the works you do. [4]No one who wants to become a public figure acts in secret. Since you are doing these things, show yourself to the world." [5]For even his own brothers did not believe in him.

[6]Therefore Jesus told them, "My time is not yet here; for you any time will do. [7]The world cannot hate you, but it hates me because I testify that its works are evil. [8]You go to the festival. I am not[b]

going up to this festival, because my time has not yet fully come." [9]After he had said this, he stayed in Galilee.

[10]However, after his brothers had left for the festival, he went also, not publicly, but in secret. [11]Now at the festival the Jewish leaders were watching for Jesus and asking, "Where is he?"

[12]Among the crowds there was widespread whispering about him. Some said, "He is a good man."

Others replied, "No, he deceives the people." [13]But no one would say anything publicly about him for fear of the leaders.

Jesus Teaches at the Festival

[14]Not until halfway through the festival did Jesus go up to the temple courts and begin to teach. [15]The Jews there were amazed and asked, "How did this man get such learning without having been taught?"

[16]Jesus answered, "My teaching is not my own. It comes from the one who sent me. [17]Anyone who chooses to do the will of God will find out whether

---

a 1 Some manuscripts *not have authority*   *b 8* Some manuscripts *not yet*

6:69 Holy One of God See Mk 1:24 and note.
6:71 Judas, the son of Simon Iscariot See note on Mk 3:19.

7:1–5 The doubt over Jesus' identity and teachings extended even to his own family, who apparently mistook him for a fame-seeking miracle worker (compare Jn 6:42,60–66).

7:1 After this The events of ch. 6 had taken place around Passover, a spring holiday. See note on 5:1. **Jewish leaders there were looking for a way to kill him** Jesus had upset the religious authorities by healing a man on the Sabbath (see v. 23; 5:16–18; compare note on 1:19).

7:2 Festival of Tabernacles One of the three pilgrimage festivals when Jews were to travel to Jerusalem if possible. See Lev 23:33–44 and note. See the table "Israelite Festivals" on p. 200.

7:3 Jesus' brothers The most straightforward interpretation is that these were other biological sons of Mary and Joseph, distinguished from the disciples. Based on John's side comment in Jn 7:5, the best explanation for the brothers' remarks is that they are mocking Jesus: If he truly is who he claims to be (which they doubt), then he should take his message to the world.

7:6–52 After declining his brothers' mocking invitation to attend the festival in Jerusalem, Jesus quietly travels there. His followers are noticeably absent from this narrative. Traveling alone would have allowed Jesus to more easily blend with the crowds, especially if the religious leaders were looking for him to have an entourage of disciples. This is the third time that Jesus travels to Judea (2:13; 5:1). He remains in Jerusalem for several months, and the events of chs. 7–10 are set there. The Messianic speculation surrounding Jesus builds throughout this section and centers on Jewish disputes about the origin of the Messiah.

7:6 My time is not yet here Refers to the time for Jesus' glorification through the crucifixion (12:23). John uses this motif numerous times to point ahead to the time for Jesus' death and to explain why he was not arrested or killed earlier (compare 2:4; 7:30; 8:20; 12:23; 13:1; 17:1).

7:8 I am not going up to this festival Jesus indicates that he will not go at that time or with his brothers. The Greek present tense can have the sense of "I am not going right now."

7:12 whispering The Greek noun used here refers to behind-the-scenes talk that can be either positive or negative depending on context. In private discussions, people were speculating about Jesus and had both positive and negative opinions about him. **he deceives the people** This accusation is intended to depict Jesus as one among the false teachers and Messianic pretenders of the day (compare Mt 27:63). On the basis of this accusation, later Jewish tradition condemned Jesus of sorcery and leading Israel astray (in the Babylonian Talmud Sanhedrin 43a; Sotah 47a).

7:14–24 In this short scene, Jesus appears openly in the temple complex and begins teaching. The content of his teaching is not important in the narrative, which focuses on the people's reaction to Jesus and Jesus' assertion of his authority to teach and to heal.

7:14 Not until halfway through the festival The feast was seven days long. This could refer to the actual midpoint (the fourth day) or to any time in the middle. The first and last days of the feast involved special Sabbath-like observances.

7:15 without having been taught While it was normal for Jewish men at this time to be able to read and have a rudimentary knowledge of Scripture, the type of sustained theological discourse characteristic of Jesus' teaching in the Gospels was considered the realm of the well-educated rabbis.

my teaching comes from God or whether I speak on my own. ¹⁸Whoever speaks on their own does so to gain personal glory, but he who seeks the glory of the one who sent him is a man of truth; there is nothing false about him. ¹⁹Has not Moses given you the law? Yet not one of you keeps the law. Why are you trying to kill me?"

²⁰"You are demon-possessed," the crowd answered. "Who is trying to kill you?"

²¹Jesus said to them, "I did one miracle, and you are all amazed. ²²Yet, because Moses gave you circumcision (though actually it did not come from Moses, but from the patriarchs), you circumcise a boy on the Sabbath. ²³Now if a boy can be circumcised on the Sabbath so that the law of Moses may not be broken, why are you angry with me for healing a man's whole body on the Sabbath? ²⁴Stop judging by mere appearances, but instead judge correctly."

Division Over Who Jesus Is

²⁵At that point some of the people of Jerusalem began to ask, "Isn't this the man they are trying to kill? ²⁶Here he is, speaking publicly, and they are not saying a word to him. Have the authorities really concluded that he is the Messiah? ²⁷But we know where this man is from; when the Messiah comes, no one will know where he is from."

²⁸Then Jesus, still teaching in the temple courts, cried out, "Yes, you know me, and you know where I am from. I am not here on my own authority, but he who sent me is true. You do not know him, ²⁹but I know him because I am from him and he sent me."

³⁰At this they tried to seize him, but no one laid a hand on him, because his hour had not yet come. ³¹Still, many in the crowd believed in him. They said, "When the Messiah comes, will he perform more signs than this man?"

³²The Pharisees heard the crowd whispering such things about him. Then the chief priests and the Pharisees sent temple guards to arrest him.

³³Jesus said, "I am with you for only a short time, and then I am going to the one who sent me. ³⁴You will look for me, but you will not find me; and where I am, you cannot come."

³⁵The Jews said to one another, "Where does this man intend to go that we cannot find him? Will he go where our people live scattered among the Greeks, and teach the Greeks? ³⁶What did he mean when he said, 'You will look for me, but you will not find me,' and 'Where I am, you cannot come'?"

³⁷On the last and greatest day of the festival, Jesus stood and said in a loud voice, "Let anyone who is thirsty come to me and drink. ³⁸Whoever believes in me, as Scripture has said, rivers of living water

---

7:19 Moses The Pharisees considered themselves disciples of Moses himself through their study of the law (Jn 9:28). Their care for the Scriptures should have led them to recognize Jesus as the Messiah (5:46; compare note on 1:45).

7:20 You are demon-possessed Essentially saying, "You're crazy!" to Jesus (compare 8:48; 10:20; Mt 11:18). Insane raving was one of the symptoms of demon possession (compare Mk 5:5; Lk 9:39). **Who is trying to kill you** The crowd listening as Jesus teaches is unaware of the behind-the-scenes plotting being done by the religious authorities.

7:21 one miracle Probably the healing on the Sabbath that had gotten him into trouble before. See Jn 5:6–9.

7:22 you circumcise a boy on the Sabbath Jesus is returning to the issue of healing on the Sabbath (see 5:16 and note), supporting his decision to heal on the Sabbath with an appeal to precedent in Jewish practice. Jewish practice required circumcising newborn boys on the eighth day, regardless of whether that day was a Sabbath. Jesus is arguing from the lesser to the greater, known in Jewish tradition as *qal wa-chomer* ("light to heavy") and in modern logic as *a fortiori*. If breaking the Sabbath was allowed for circumcision (involving part of the body), how much more should healing on the Sabbath be allowed when it involves the entire body?

7:25–52 The remainder of this chapter records both the crowds and the Jewish religious authorities disputing over whether Jesus is really the Messiah. When the authorities do not arrest Jesus, the crowds interpret it as a sign that perhaps they believe he is the Messiah. Then, when the authorities try to arrest him, Jesus slips away unharmed while more people begin to believe in him.

7:28 You do not know him While the people may have known Jesus' earthly origins, they had failed to recognize his heavenly origins.

7:32 the chief priests The official religious leaders in charge of the temple. See note on Mk 11:18.

John 7:32

PHARISEES
While the Sadducees derived their religious influence from official priestly circles, the Pharisees' influence stemmed primarily from their knowledge of Biblical law and their ability to interpret that law. As a lay association of legal experts, their Biblical interpretations had a direct effect on Jewish life and practice. The apostle Paul acknowledges being a Pharisee trained in Jewish legal tradition before his conversion (Php 3:5). See note on Mk 2:16.

7:35 scattered among the Greeks A reference to the settlements of Jews scattered throughout the Roman Empire and Mesopotamia. The Greek term *diaspora* is used for all Jewish communities outside of Palestine. "Greeks" is probably used in the sense of "non-Jews" or "Gentiles."

7:37 the last and greatest day of the festival Jewish tradition prescribes additional rituals for the final day of the festival—the culmination of their weeklong prayers for deliverance (according to the Babylonian Talmud Sukkah 53a). **Let anyone who is thirsty come** A subtle appeal to imagery of Messianic deliverance associated with the Festival of Tabernacles. Jesus

will flow from within them."*a* [39]By this he meant the Spirit, whom those who believed in him were later to receive. Up to that time the Spirit had not been given, since Jesus had not yet been glorified.

[40]On hearing his words, some of the people said, "Surely this man is the Prophet."

[41]Others said, "He is the Messiah."

Still others asked, "How can the Messiah come from Galilee? [42]Does not Scripture say that the Messiah will come from David's descendants and from Bethlehem, the town where David lived?" [43]Thus the people were divided because of Jesus. [44]Some wanted to seize him, but no one laid a hand on him.

Unbelief of the Jewish Leaders

[45]Finally the temple guards went back to the chief priests and the Pharisees, who asked them, "Why didn't you bring him in?"

[46]"No one ever spoke the way this man does," the guards replied.

[47]"You mean he has deceived you also?" the Pharisees retorted. [48]"Have any of the rulers or of the Pharisees believed in him? [49]No! But this

mob that knows nothing of the law — there is a curse on them."

[50]Nicodemus, who had gone to Jesus earlier and who was one of their own number, asked, [51]"Does our law condemn a man without first hearing him to find out what he has been doing?"

[52]They replied, "Are you from Galilee, too? Look into it, and you will find that a prophet does not come out of Galilee."

———

[The earliest manuscripts and many other ancient witnesses do not have John 7:53 — 8:11. A few manuscripts include these verses, wholly or in part, after John 7:36, John 21:25, Luke 21:38 or Luke 24:53.]

8 [53]Then they all went home, [1]but Jesus went to the Mount of Olives.

[2]At dawn he appeared again in the temple courts, where all the people gathered around him, and he sat down to teach them. [3]The teachers of the law and the Pharisees brought in a woman caught in adultery. They made her

a 37,38 Or me. And let anyone drink [38]who believes in me." As Scripture has said, "Out of him (or them) will flow rivers of living water."

makes the point that he is the source of life — a claim that only God could make. This would have provoked his opponents, but it brought comfort to his followers. A ritual of bringing water from the pool of Siloam and pouring it at the base of the altar was part of the daily festival celebration. This ritual memorialized the miracle of water from the rock in the wilderness (Nu 20:2–13) and became symbolic of hope for Messianic deliverance (Isa 12:3). The Festival of Tabernacles was associated with God providing rain (Zec 14:16–18), and Zec 14 was to be read on the first day of the feast (according to the rabbinic text Babylonian Talmud Megillah 31a). The seventh day of the festival, the last official day (Lev 23:34,41–42), had a special water-pouring ritual and lights ceremony (according to the rabbinic text Mishnah Sukkah 4.9–10; 5.2–4). The festival came to be a celebration of God's future restoration of Israel and the extension of salvation to the nations. Jesus' invitation draws on those expectations of future ideal reality under the rule of the Messiah.

7:38 rivers of living water will flow No specific verse from the OT matches Jesus' words here exactly. He may be paraphrasing Zec 14:8 since that chapter was read during Tabernacles (see note on Jn 7:37). Numerous OT passages represent salvation metaphorically as a life-giving source of water (Isa 12:3; 44:3; 58:11; Eze 47:1; Zec 14:8; Pr 18:4).

7:39 Spirit OT visions of God's future salvation for his people included the image of the Spirit being poured out on all believers (Isa 44:3; Eze 36:27; Joel 2:28).

7:40 Prophet As they had with John the Baptist, people are trying to identify Jesus with various strands of Messianic expectation (see note on Jn 1:21).

7:41 How can the Messiah come from Galilee Reflecting the expectation that the Messiah would come from Bethlehem in Judea (see Mic 5:2; compare Mt 2:1; Lk 2:1–7).

7:42 See the table "Jesus' Fulfillment of OT Prophecy" on p. 1573.

7:48 any of the rulers Nicodemus, one of the rulers, had in fact believed but had not publicly admitted it.

7:50 Nicodemus He was a member of the Jewish governing council (the Sanhedrin). See Jn 3:1–15. See the infographic "The Sanhedrin" on p. 1746.

7:51 Does our law condemn a man Nicodemus' appeal to the other rulers is based on their shared commitment to the law. He does not offer a direct defense of Jesus or confess his faith; he asks for fair consideration of Jesus' case under the law.

7:52 See the table "Jesus' Fulfillment of OT Prophecy" on p. 1573. **a prophet does not come out of Galilee** Likely referring to Messianic expectations, not the historical origin of any of Israel's past prophets. The prophets Jonah (2Ki 14:25) and Elijah (1Ki 17:1) were from the northern region of Israel.

7:53 — 8:11 The religious authorities bring Jesus a woman caught in the act of adultery and ask him to pass judgment. The scene is similar to many legal test cases or hypothetical scenarios that the Jewish religious leaders bring to Jesus (compare the two examples in Mt 22:15–23). Adultery was not a capital offense under Roman law. This story is missing from the earliest manuscripts of the NT. Some manuscripts place the story after Lk 21:38, where it fits the narrative context better. Also, the phrase "scribes (or teachers of the law) and Pharisees" in Jn 8:3 is otherwise not used by John, but it is in Matthew and Luke (Mt 12:38; 23:13; Lk 5:21; 6:7; 11:53). The story may be an accurate tradition about Jesus that was mistakenly added to John's Gospel even though it would fit better with the style and content of Matthew, Mark or Luke.

8:1 Mount of Olives A small ridge on Jerusalem's eastern border.

8:3 The teachers of the law and the Pharisees Refers to the religious authorities. **a woman caught in adultery** The Biblical law prescribed death for both partners involved in an adulterous relationship (Lev 20:10). The

stand before the group [4]and said to Jesus, "Teacher, this woman was caught in the act of adultery. [5]In the Law Moses commanded us to stone such women. Now what do you say?" [6]They were using this question as a trap, in order to have a basis for accusing him.

But Jesus bent down and started to write on the ground with his finger. [7]When they kept on questioning him, he straightened up and said to them, "Let any one of you who is without sin be the first to throw a stone at her." [8]Again he stooped down and wrote on the ground.

[9]At this, those who heard began to go away one at a time, the older ones first, until only Jesus was left, with the woman still standing there. [10]Jesus straightened up and asked her, "Woman, where are they? Has no one condemned you?"

[11]"No one, sir," she said.

"Then neither do I condemn you," Jesus declared. "Go now and leave your life of sin."

Dispute Over Jesus' Testimony

[12]When Jesus spoke again to the people, he said, "I am the light of the world. Whoever follows me will never walk in darkness, but will have the light of life."

[13]The Pharisees challenged him, "Here you are, appearing as your own witness; your testimony is not valid."

[14]Jesus answered, "Even if I testify on my own behalf, my testimony is valid, for I know where I came from and where I am going. But you have no idea where I come from or where I am going. [15]You judge by human standards; I pass judgment on no one. [16]But if I do judge, my decisions are true, because I am not alone. I stand with the Father,

who sent me. [17]In your own Law it is written that the testimony of two witnesses is true. [18]I am one who testifies for myself; my other witness is the Father, who sent me."

[19]Then they asked him, "Where is your father?"

"You do not know me or my Father," Jesus replied. "If you knew me, you would know my Father also." [20]He spoke these words while teaching in the temple courts near the place where the offerings were put. Yet no one seized him, because his hour had not yet come.

Dispute Over Who Jesus Is

[21]Once more Jesus said to them, "I am going away, and you will look for me, and you will die in your sin. Where I go, you cannot come."

[22]This made the Jews ask, "Will he kill himself? Is that why he says, 'Where I go, you cannot come'?"

[23]But he continued, "You are from below; I am from above. You are of this world; I am not of this world. [24]I told you that you would die in your sins; if you do not believe that I am he, you will indeed die in your sins."

[25]"Who are you?" they asked.

"Just what I have been telling you from the beginning," Jesus replied. [26]"I have much to say in judgment of you. But he who sent me is trustworthy, and what I have heard from him I tell the world."

[27]They did not understand that he was telling them about his Father. [28]So Jesus said, "When you

---

religious authorities' condemnation is unjustly selective since her partner has apparently been let off.

8:6 on the ground What Jesus writes is unknown. It appears to prompt the leaders' later conviction of conscience (Jn 8:9)—perhaps by reminding them of their own sinfulness or of the law's higher considerations (mercy and compassion). Compare Jer 17:13.

8:7 any one of you who is without sin Since Jesus has, throughout the Gospel of John, alluded to being God in flesh (see note on Jn 8:12), the implication is that he is the only one permitted to pass judgment in this scenario—yet he chooses to be gracious.

8:12–59 Jesus begins another round of teaching centered on his divine origin and relationship with God the Father. The passage reinforces thematic content and divine claims already presented in the discourses of chs. 5–6. This teaching expands on the light and darkness antithesis that John uses to contrast belief and unbelief (see note on 1:5).

8:12 I am the light of the world This is the second metaphorical "I am" statement used by Jesus. See 6:35 and note (compare 1:4 and note). See the table "Jesus' 'I Am' Statements" on p. 1727.

8:13 your testimony is not valid Jesus admitted as much himself (see 5:31 and note). As in 5:31–47, Jesus invokes the testimony of God the Father to validate his claims, but first he disputes the Pharisees' right to charge him with error.

8:14 I know where I came from No earthly witness is capable of testifying on his behalf because of his divine origin (compare 3:13 and note).

8:16 I am not alone After claiming that his testimony is actually exempt from their requirement because of his unique origin, Jesus demonstrates that he is in compliance with their legal procedure anyway. There are two witnesses: Jesus himself and God the Father.

8:17 the testimony of two witnesses is true In the sense of legally admissible or valid (Dt 19:15; see note on Jn 5:31).

8:19 Where is your father A typical example of John's motif of misunderstanding (see 2:21 and note; 3:4 and note). Other examples include 4:11; 6:52; 7:35. **You do not know me or my Father** A common charge in John (e.g., v. 55; 14:7; 16:3).

8:20 place where the offerings were put The site was probably next to the Court of the Women (compare Mk 12:41). **his hour had not yet come** See note on Jn 7:6.

8:22 Will he kill himself Another example of misunderstanding. See note on v. 19.

8:23 You are from below; I am from above Contrasts the divine realm with the human world (compare 3:13).

8:24 if you do not believe Jesus condemns the people for failing to believe in himself; possibly alluding to Isa 43:10 and thus may be a subtle claim to divinity. Jesus has offered them grace—and indeed has not come to condemn them but save them—but they choose not to believe in the salvation he offers (Jn 3:17).

have lifted up[a] the Son of Man, then you will know that I am he and that I do nothing on my own but speak just what the Father has taught me. [29]The one who sent me is with me; he has not left me alone, for I always do what pleases him." [30]Even as he spoke, many believed in him.

Dispute Over Whose Children Jesus' Opponents Are

[31]To the Jews who had believed him, Jesus said, "If you hold to my teaching, you are really my disciples. [32]Then you will know the truth, and the truth will set you free."

[33]They answered him, "We are Abraham's descendants and have never been slaves of anyone. How can you say that we shall be set free?"

[34]Jesus replied, "Very truly I tell you, everyone who sins is a slave to sin. [35]Now a slave has no permanent place in the family, but a son belongs to it forever. [36]So if the Son sets you free, you will be free indeed. [37]I know that you are Abraham's descendants. Yet you are looking for a way to kill me, because you have no room for my word. [38]I am telling you what I have seen in the Father's presence, and you are doing what you have heard from your father.[b]"

[39]"Abraham is our father," they answered.

"If you were Abraham's children," said Jesus, "then you would[c] do what Abraham did. [40]As it is, you are looking for a way to kill me, a man who has told you the truth that I heard from God.

Abraham did not do such things. [41]You are doing the works of your own father."

"We are not illegitimate children," they protested. "The only Father we have is God himself."

[42]Jesus said to them, "If God were your Father, you would love me, for I have come here from God. I have not come on my own; God sent me. [43]Why is my language not clear to you? Because you are unable to hear what I say. [44]You belong to your father, the devil, and you want to carry out your father's desires. He was a murderer from the beginning, not holding to the truth, for there is no truth in him. When he lies, he speaks his native language, for he is a liar and the father of lies. [45]Yet because I tell the truth, you do not believe me! [46]Can any of you prove me guilty of sin? If I am telling the truth, why don't you believe me? [47]Whoever belongs to God hears what God says. The reason you do not hear is that you do not belong to God."

Jesus' Claims About Himself

[48]The Jews answered him, "Aren't we right in saying that you are a Samaritan and demon-possessed?"

[49]"I am not possessed by a demon," said Jesus, "but I honor my Father and you dishonor me. [50]I am not seeking glory for myself; but there is one

---

[a] 28 The Greek for lifted up also means exalted.
[b] 38 Or presence. Therefore do what you have heard from the Father. [c] 39 Some early manuscripts "If you are Abraham's children," said Jesus, "then

---

8:28 you have lifted up Refers to the crucifixion; simultaneously symbolizes Jesus' atoning death and glorification (see note on 3:14). The imagery may also allude to Isa 52:13. **the Son of Man** See note on Jn 1:51. **then you will know** The act of crucifixion will bring awareness of Jesus' true identity.

8:31–59 Jesus debates his Jewish audience over the value of their ancestry in bringing them into right standing with God. Initially, the audience is depicted as Jews who had believed Jesus; by the end of the passage, they are prepared to stone him for blasphemy (which suggests that their faith was superficial).

8:31 If you hold to my teaching These disciples have agreed in principle with Jesus' teaching, but their perseverance in following his teaching will reveal whether they are genuine disciples.

8:32 the truth Likely invokes the OT concept of truth, referring to a dependable foundation for building a way of life (see note on Ps 26:3).

8:33 Abraham's descendants Refers to God's promises to Abraham concerning descendants (see Ge 12:2 and note). Their ancestry was a great source of pride (Isa 41:8; compare Mt 3:9 and note).

8:35 a son belongs to it forever Membership by birth was superior to membership by obligation. The "son" imagery here is likely a Messianic allusion to 1Ch 17:13–14.

8:39 Abraham's children Jesus concedes their physical descent from Abraham but disputes their automatic

inheritance of the promises to Abraham on that basis alone. Behavior, not bloodline, determines who are truly children of Abraham. **what Abraham did** Refers to Abraham's faith. The NT frequently credits Abraham with saving faith because of his trust in Yahweh (Ro 4:3; Gal 3:6; Jas 2:23; Heb 11:8; compare Ge 15:6).

8:41 only Father we have is God With Jesus questioning their parentage, they appeal to one greater than Abraham—God himself—as the founder of their faith and the one who established the behavior by which they claim to live.

8:42 If God were your Father Their rejection of Jesus reveals how distant they truly are from following God properly (compare 1Jn 5:1).

8:44 You belong to your father, the devil Their sinful behavior, exemplified by unbelief, puts them in opposition to God and Jesus. The accusation is an intentionally offensive counterclaim to their assertion that God was their father. This rhetoric from a discussion of spiritual legitimacy has had an unfortunate afterlife in the association of the Jews with Satan. This association was common in anti-Semitic language and imagery from the late Middle Ages in Christian Europe and has had an influence on modern anti-Semitism. While the NT is sometimes critical of the Jewish people for their failure to recognize and believe in Jesus as the Messiah, the earliest Christians and writers of the NT were themselves Jews and at no time advocated hatred or violence toward the Jews as a race.

8:48 The Jews Refers to the audience that initially was

who seeks it, and he is the judge. [51]Very truly I tell you, whoever obeys my word will never see death."

[52]At this they exclaimed, "Now we know that you are demon-possessed! Abraham died and so did the prophets, yet you say that whoever obeys your word will never taste death. [53]Are you greater than our father Abraham? He died, and so did the prophets. Who do you think you are?"

[54]Jesus replied, "If I glorify myself, my glory means nothing. My Father, whom you claim as your God, is the one who glorifies me. [55]Though you do not know him, I know him. If I said I did not, I would be a liar like you, but I do know him and obey his word. [56]Your father Abraham rejoiced at the thought of seeing my day; he saw it and was glad."

[57]"You are not yet fifty years old," they said to him, "and you have seen Abraham!"

[58]"Very truly I tell you," Jesus answered, "before Abraham was born, I am!" [59]At this, they picked up stones to stone him, but Jesus hid himself, slipping away from the temple grounds.

Jesus Heals a Man Born Blind

9 As he went along, he saw a man blind from birth. [2]His disciples asked him, "Rabbi, who sinned, this man or his parents, that he was born blind?"

[3]"Neither this man nor his parents sinned," said Jesus, "but this happened so that the works of God might be displayed in him. [4]As long as it is day, we must do the works of him who sent me. Night is coming, when no one can work. [5]While I am in the world, I am the light of the world."

[6]After saying this, he spit on the ground, made some mud with the saliva, and put it on the man's eyes. [7]"Go," he told him, "wash in the Pool of Siloam" (this word means "Sent"). So the man went and washed, and came home seeing.

[8]His neighbors and those who had formerly seen him begging asked, "Isn't this the same man who used to sit and beg?" [9]Some claimed that he was.

Others said, "No, he only looks like him."

But he himself insisted, "I am the man."

[10]"How then were your eyes opened?" they asked.

[11]He replied, "The man they call Jesus made some mud and put it on my eyes. He told me to go to Siloam and wash. So I went and washed, and then I could see."

[12]"Where is this man?" they asked him.

"I don't know," he said.

The Pharisees Investigate the Healing

[13]They brought to the Pharisees the man who had been blind. [14]Now the day on which Jesus had made the mud and opened the man's eyes was a Sabbath. [15]Therefore the Pharisees also asked him how he had received his sight. "He put mud

---

favorable toward Jesus' teaching (Jn 8:31). **a Samaritan** A derisive label meant to insult Jesus by classifying him as a non-Jew. See note on 4:7.

8:51 will never see death A promise of eternal life (compare 1:4 and note; 3:16).

8:52 Abraham died and so did the prophets Jesus' reply has only heightened their misunderstanding and reinforced their belief that he is demon-possessed because all the prominent figures from Israel's past have died. Jesus' promise of eternal life sounds irrational and ridiculous (compare Zec 1:5).

8:56 seeing my day In Jewish tradition, details about the final judgment of all people are revealed to Abraham before his death.

8:58 before Abraham was born, I am Jesus' claim combines both his preexistence and his divinity. This is the culmination of the earlier "I am" sayings in Jn 8:24,28. The statement was clearly understood as a claim to divinity (v. 59) and echoes Ex 3:14. See note on Jn 4:26. See the table "Jesus' 'I Am' Statements" on p. 1727.

8:59 they picked up stones Death by stoning was the prescribed punishment for blasphemy (Lev 24:16).

9:1–41 Jesus heals a man born blind. This public healing again has repercussions (as in Jn 5:1–18) because the healing takes place on the Sabbath. Much of the chapter is concerned with the reaction to the healing and the ensuing discussion over Jesus' authority, identity and origin. The Pharisees react indignantly, accusing Jesus of failing to observe the Sabbath, which means he cannot be from God. Others point out the difficulty of such a successful healing being performed by one who was not

from God. The testimony of the healed man is central to the depiction of his spiritual insight contrasted with the Pharisees' continued spiritual blindness. See the table "Miracles of Jesus" on p. 1741.

9:1 a man blind from birth That the man was born blind makes his healing that much more miraculous.

9:2 who sinned Reflects the belief that congenital disabilities were the result of sin on the part of the individual or his parents. This way of thinking derived from the desire to avoid making God responsible for afflicting suffering on the innocent. Wicked, sinful behavior led to suffering and punishment. The innocent should not suffer. Despite the popularity of these beliefs, the Bible does not teach a uniform cause-and-effect relationship between sin and suffering. For example, the main point of the OT book of Job is to demonstrate the theological possibility of righteous, innocent suffering. Elsewhere, Jesus also affirms that sin and disaster are not always directly related (Lk 13:2–3).

9:4 As long as it is day Jesus' enigmatic saying invokes the opposition of light and darkness.

9:5 I am the light of the world See Jn 8:12 and note.

9:6 he spit Compare Mk 8:23.

9:7 wash Compare Elisha's healing of Naaman the Syrian in 2Ki 5:10–13. **Pool of Siloam** Part of the water system of the City of David, in the older southeastern part of Jerusalem. Siloam likely had some mythological reputation surrounding it, suggesting that someone could be healed by entering the pool at particular times under certain conditions. See the infographic "Inscription From Hezekiah's Tunnel" on p. 599.

9:8 who used to sit and beg The man was a fixture in the area. People who are used to seeing him are

Miracles of Jesus

MIRACLE	MATTHEW	MARK	LUKE	JOHN
Jesus heals many people	Mt 4:23–25	Mk 1:32–34	–	–
Jesus cleanses a leper	Mt 8:1–4	Mk 1:40–45	Lk 5:12–16	–
Jesus heals a centurion's servant	Mt 8:5–13	–	Lk 7:1–10	–
Jesus heals Peter's mother-in-law and others	Mt 8:14–17	Mk 1:29–34	Lk 4:38–44	–
Jesus calms a storm	Mt 8:23–27	Mk 4:35–41	Lk 8:22–25	–
Jesus heals the demon-possessed	Mt 8:28–34	Mk 5:1–20	Lk 8:26–39	–
Jesus heals a paralytic	Mt 9:1–8	Mk 2:1–12	Lk 5:17–26	–
Jesus heals a woman with a hemorrhage	Mt 9:20–22	Mk 5:24–34	Lk 8:43–48	–
Jesus raises Jairus's daughter	Mt 9:18–19, 23–26	Mk 5:21–23, 35–43	Lk 8:40–42, 49–56	–
Jesus heals two blind men	Mt 9:27–31	–	–	–
Jesus heals a demon-possessed man	Mt 9:32–34	–	–	–
Jesus heals a man's withered hand	Mt 12:9–14	Mk 3:1–6	Lk 6:6–11	–
Jesus feeds 5,000 people	Mt 14:13–21	Mk 6:30–44	Lk 9:10–17	Jn 6:1–14
Jesus walks on water	Mt 14:22–33	Mk 6:45–52	–	Jn 6:16–21
Jesus heals the Syrophoenician's daughter	Mt 15:21–28	Mk 7:24–30	–	–
Jesus heals many people	Mt 15:29–31	–	–	–
Jesus feeds 4,000 people	Mt 15:32–39	Mk 8:1–10	–	–
Jesus heals an epileptic boy	Mt 17:14–21	Mk 9:14–29	Lk 9:37–43	–

Miracles of Jesus (continued)

MIRACLE	MATTHEW	MARK	LUKE	JOHN
Jesus heals two blind men at Jericho	Mt 20:29–34	–	–	–
Jesus heals a man with an unclean spirit	–	Mk 1:22–28	Lk 4:32–37	–
Jesus heals a deaf and speechless man	–	Mk 7:31–37	–	–
Jesus heals a blind man at Bethsaida	–	Mk 8:22–26	–	–
Jesus heals a blind man named Bartimaeus	–	Mk 10:46–52	Lk 18:35–43	–
Jesus causes a miraculous catch of fish	–	–	Lk 5:4–11	–
Jesus raises a widow's son	–	–	Lk 7:11–17	–
Jesus heals a disabled woman	–	–	Lk 13:10–17	–
Jesus heals a man with dropsy	–	–	Lk 14:1–6	–
Jesus heals ten lepers	–	–	Lk 17:11–19	–
Jesus heals Malchus' ear	–	–	Lk 22:50–53	–
Jesus turns water into wine	–	–	–	Jn 2:1–11
Jesus heals the official's son	–	–	–	Jn 4:46–52
Jesus heals a paralytic at Bethesda	–	–	–	Jn 5:1–13
Jesus heals a blind man	–	–	–	Jn 9:1–12
Jesus raises Lazarus	–	–	–	Jn 11:38–44
Jesus causes a miraculous catch of fish	–	–	–	Jn 21:1–14

on my eyes," the man replied, "and I washed, and now I see."

¹⁶Some of the Pharisees said, "This man is not from God, for he does not keep the Sabbath."

But others asked, "How can a sinner perform such signs?" So they were divided.

¹⁷Then they turned again to the blind man, "What have you to say about him? It was your eyes he opened."

The man replied, "He is a prophet."

¹⁸They still did not believe that he had been blind and had received his sight until they sent for the man's parents. ¹⁹"Is this your son?" they asked. "Is this the one you say was born blind? How is it that now he can see?"

²⁰"We know he is our son," the parents answered, "and we know he was born blind. ²¹But how he can see now, or who opened his eyes, we don't know. Ask him. He is of age; he will speak for himself." ²²His parents said this because they were afraid of the Jewish leaders, who already had decided that anyone who acknowledged that Jesus was the Messiah would be put out of the synagogue. ²³That was why his parents said, "He is of age; ask him."

²⁴A second time they summoned the man who had been blind. "Give glory to God by telling the truth," they said. "We know this man is a sinner."

²⁵He replied, "Whether he is a sinner or not, I don't know. One thing I do know. I was blind but now I see!"

²⁶Then they asked him, "What did he do to you? How did he open your eyes?"

²⁷He answered, "I have told you already and you did not listen. Why do you want to hear it again? Do you want to become his disciples too?"

²⁸Then they hurled insults at him and said, "You are this fellow's disciple! We are disciples of Moses! ²⁹We know that God spoke to Moses,

but as for this fellow, we don't even know where he comes from."

³⁰The man answered, "Now that is remarkable! You don't know where he comes from, yet he opened my eyes. ³¹We know that God does not listen to sinners. He listens to the godly person who does his will. ³²Nobody has ever heard of opening the eyes of a man born blind. ³³If this man were not from God, he could do nothing."

³⁴To this they replied, "You were steeped in sin at birth; how dare you lecture us!" And they threw him out.

Spiritual Blindness

³⁵Jesus heard that they had thrown him out, and when he found him, he said, "Do you believe in the Son of Man?"

³⁶"Who is he, sir?" the man asked. "Tell me so that I may believe in him."

³⁷Jesus said, "You have now seen him; in fact, he is the one speaking with you."

³⁸Then the man said, "Lord, I believe," and he worshiped him.

³⁹Jesus said,ᵃ "For judgment I have come into this world, so that the blind will see and those who see will become blind."

⁴⁰Some Pharisees who were with him heard him say this and asked, "What? Are we blind too?"

⁴¹Jesus said, "If you were blind, you would not be guilty of sin; but now that you claim you can see, your guilt remains.

The Good Shepherd and His Sheep

10 "Very truly I tell you Pharisees, anyone who does not enter the sheep pen by the gate, but climbs in by some other way, is a thief and

---

ᵃ 38,39 Some early manuscripts do not have *Then the man said . . . ³⁹Jesus said.*

---

astonished at his healing; some even deny that it can be the same man.

9:16 they were divided The healing is either a sin (because it was performed on the Sabbath) or a miraculous sign. The law cautioned people to be wary of teachers who might lead them astray by performing signs and wonders (Dt 13:1–5).

9:17 He is a prophet See Jn 4:19 and note.

9:18 sent for the man's parents To verify the identity of the man and corroborate that he had, in fact, been born blind.

9:21 he will speak for himself The parents are trying to excuse themselves from further inquiry by disclaiming legal responsibility for their son.

9:22 put out of the synagogue Tantamount to being excluded from the community. The synagogue was the community gathering place. See note on Mk 1:21.

9:24 We know this man is a sinner Because he had broken the Sabbath by healing a man (see Jn 9:16).

9:28 disciples of Moses The Pharisees took special pride in their study of Torah, the Law of Moses (see note on 7:19). Their appeal to Moses is ironic based

on Jesus' words in 5:45–47, where he pointed out that their knowledge of Moses' writings should have led them to recognize him as Messiah.

9:34 You were steeped in sin at birth See note on v. 2.

9:38 I believe The formerly blind man is the only one to respond appropriately to Jesus. His journey from physical blindness to sight also symbolized his transition from spiritual darkness to finding the Light of the World (v. 5).

9:39 blind will see Giving sight to the blind was one of the miraculous signs expected to accompany the coming of the Messiah. See Isa 42:7. **those who see will become blind** Compare Isa 6:9–10.

9:41 If you were blind, you would not be guilty of sin If the Pharisees were truly without knowledge of God and his requirements, then they would not be accountable for breaking that law (compare Ro 1:18–20; 3:20).

10:1–42 In his final public address, Jesus continues teaching and uses another "I am" saying with a metaphor (see note on Jn 6:35) to explain his identity as Messiah. Jesus uses the imagery of the good shepherd (v. 11), which should be understood in the light of OT passages

a robber. ²The one who enters by the gate is the shepherd of the sheep. ³The gatekeeper opens the gate for him, and the sheep listen to his voice. He calls his own sheep by name and leads them out. ⁴When he has brought out all his own, he goes on ahead of them, and his sheep follow him because they know his voice. ⁵But they will never follow a stranger; in fact, they will run away from him because they do not recognize a stranger's voice." ⁶Jesus used this figure of speech, but the Pharisees did not understand what he was telling them.

⁷Therefore Jesus said again, "Very truly I tell you, I am the gate for the sheep. ⁸All who have come before me are thieves and robbers, but the sheep have not listened to them. ⁹I am the gate; whoever enters through me will be saved.ᵃ They will come in and go out, and find pasture. ¹⁰The thief comes only to steal and kill and destroy; I have come that they may have life, and have it to the full.

¹¹"I am the good shepherd. The good shepherd lays down his life for the sheep. ¹²The hired hand is not the shepherd and does not own the sheep. So when he sees the wolf coming, he abandons the sheep and runs away. Then the wolf attacks the flock and scatters it. ¹³The man runs away because he is a hired hand and cares nothing for the sheep.

¹⁴"I am the good shepherd; I know my sheep and my sheep know me— ¹⁵just as the Father knows me and I know the Father—and I lay down my life for the sheep. ¹⁶I have other sheep that are not of this sheep pen. I must bring them also. They too

will listen to my voice, and there shall be one flock and one shepherd. ¹⁷The reason my Father loves me is that I lay down my life—only to take it up again. ¹⁸No one takes it from me, but I lay it down of my own accord. I have authority to lay it down and authority to take it up again. This command I received from my Father."

¹⁹The Jews who heard these words were again divided. ²⁰Many of them said, "He is demon-possessed and raving mad. Why listen to him?"

²¹But others said, "These are not the sayings of a man possessed by a demon. Can a demon open the eyes of the blind?"

Further Conflict Over Jesus' Claims

²²Then came the Festival of Dedicationᵇ at Jerusalem. It was winter, ²³and Jesus was in the temple courts walking in Solomon's Colonnade. ²⁴The Jews who were there gathered around him, saying, "How long will you keep us in suspense? If you are the Messiah, tell us plainly."

²⁵Jesus answered, "I did tell you, but you do not believe. The works I do in my Father's name testify about me, ²⁶but you do not believe because you are not my sheep. ²⁷My sheep listen to my voice; I know them, and they follow me. ²⁸I give them eternal life, and they shall never perish; no one will snatch them out of my hand. ²⁹My Father, who has given them to me, is greater than allᶜ;

ᵃ 9 Or kept safe   ᵇ 22 That is, Hanukkah   ᶜ 29 Many early manuscripts What my Father has given me is greater than all

---

that criticize Israel's shepherds (a metaphor for their kings) who have failed in their duty (Jer 23:1–8; Zec 11:4–17; Isa 56:11; Eze 34:1–31). The remedy for the failure of the shepherds in many OT passages is that God himself takes on the role of the shepherd of Israel (compare Ps 23:1; 80:1; Isa 40:10–11). At the same time, God promises to raise up another shepherd for Israel who will lead his people properly (Eze 34:23). Jesus depicts himself in that Messianic role of the ideal shepherd. He is both the shepherd who lays down his life for the sheep (Jn 10:11) and the gateway to eternal life (v. 7). See the event line "Jesus' Journey to Jerusalem" on p. 1616.

10:1 the sheep pen This was a courtyard surrounded by a stone wall. If it had a gate, there was usually a gatekeeper guarding it (v. 3) who would know which shepherds had legitimate business there. Several families might use the same sheep pen.

10:6 Pharisees did not understand The audience misses the symbolism of the parable. Just as sheep recognize their shepherd and follow him, so those who truly belong to Jesus will recognize him and follow him.

10:7 I am the gate for the sheep Jesus is the gateway for eternal life as well as the one who leads the sheep (compare note on 6:35). See the table "Jesus' 'I Am' Statements" on p. 1727.

10:8 thieves and robbers Highlights the misleading ministry of previous generations of Israel's leaders who had been leading them astray. See note on Eze 34:1–10.

10:10 they may have life, and have it to the full See Eze 34:25–31 and note (compare Eze 34:12–15).

10:11 I am the good shepherd Jesus fulfills the Messianic role of the shepherd. This role in Ezekiel is depicted as fulfilled by God; Jesus makes the claim that he (as God in flesh) is the one fulfilling it (see note on Eze 34:23). On the "I am" saying, see note on Jn 6:35. See the table "Jesus' 'I Am' Statements" on p. 1727.

10:16 I have other sheep Alluding to the Gentiles and the ultimate universal scope of salvation via Christ's atoning death. Compare Isa 56:8.

10:21 Can a demon It was believed that only God himself had the ability to overcome blindness. See Ps 146:8.

10:22 Festival of Dedication Refers to the feast of Hanukkah, celebrated to commemorate the rededication of the temple. Dedication was an eight-day festival, also called the Festival of Lights, which began on the 25th of Chislev (November—December). The festival celebrated the rededication of the temple in December 164 BC after the Seleucid king, Antiochus Epiphanes, had defiled it (1 Maccabees 1:59; Da 11:31). Lamps are lit for eight days to memorialize the miracle of the temple lamps burning for eight days with only a single day's supply of oil. See the table "Israelite Festivals" on p. 200.

10:23 Solomon's Colonnade A covered walkway on the eastern side of the Court of the Gentiles in the temple complex.

10:24 the Messiah See note on Jn 1:20.

no one can snatch them out of my Father's hand. ³⁰I and the Father are one."

³¹Again his Jewish opponents picked up stones to stone him, ³²but Jesus said to them, "I have shown you many good works from the Father. For which of these do you stone me?"

³³"We are not stoning you for any good work," they replied, "but for blasphemy, because you, a mere man, claim to be God."

³⁴Jesus answered them, "Is it not written in your Law, 'I have said you are "gods"'ᵃ? ³⁵If he called them 'gods,' to whom the word of God came—and Scripture cannot be set aside— ³⁶what about the one whom the Father set apart as his very own and sent into the world? Why then do you accuse me of blasphemy because I said, 'I am God's Son'? ³⁷Do not believe me unless I do the works of my Father. ³⁸But if I do them, even though you do not believe me, believe the works, that you may know and understand that the Father is in me, and I in the Father." ³⁹Again they tried to seize him, but he escaped their grasp.

⁴⁰Then Jesus went back across the Jordan to the place where John had been baptizing in the early days. There he stayed, ⁴¹and many people came to him. They said, "Though John never performed a sign, all that John said about this man was true." ⁴²And in that place many believed in Jesus.

The Death of Lazarus

11 Now a man named Lazarus was sick. He was from Bethany, the village of Mary and her sister Martha. ²(This Mary, whose brother Lazarus now lay sick, was the same one who poured perfume on the Lord and wiped his feet with her hair.) ³So the sisters sent word to Jesus, "Lord, the one you love is sick."

⁴When he heard this, Jesus said, "This sickness will not end in death. No, it is for God's glory so that God's Son may be glorified through it." ⁵Now Jesus loved Martha and her sister and Lazarus. ⁶So when he heard that Lazarus was sick, he stayed where he was two more days, ⁷and then he said to his disciples, "Let us go back to Judea."

⁸"But Rabbi," they said, "a short while ago the Jews there tried to stone you, and yet you are going back?"

⁹Jesus answered, "Are there not twelve hours of daylight? Anyone who walks in the daytime will not stumble, for they see by this world's light. ¹⁰It is when a person walks at night that they stumble, for they have no light."

¹¹After he had said this, he went on to tell them, "Our friend Lazarus has fallen asleep; but I am going there to wake him up."

¹²His disciples replied, "Lord, if he sleeps, he will get better." ¹³Jesus had been speaking of his death, but his disciples thought he meant natural sleep.

¹⁴So then he told them plainly, "Lazarus is dead, ¹⁵and for your sake I am glad I was not there, so that you may believe. But let us go to him."

¹⁶Then Thomas (also known as Didymusᵇ) said to the rest of the disciples, "Let us also go, that we may die with him."

Jesus Comforts the Sisters of Lazarus

¹⁷On his arrival, Jesus found that Lazarus had already been in the tomb for four days. ¹⁸Now Bethany was less than two milesᶜ from Jerusalem,

---

ᵃ *34* Psalm 82:6   ᵇ *16* *Thomas* (Aramaic) and *Didymus* (Greek) both mean *twin.*   ᶜ *18* Or about 3 kilometers

---

10:30 I and the Father are one Understood by the audience as an allusion to Dt 6:4 and a claim to divinity. See Jn 10:36 and note.

10:31 Again his Jewish opponents picked up stones Compare 8:59 and note.

10:34 your Law Here, Jesus refers collectively to the Hebrew Scriptures. **you are "gods"** A quotation of Ps 82:6, which refers either to the divine council or to human judges as God's representatives administering justice on earth.

10:36 I said, 'I am God's Son' In addition to subtle allusions to his divine nature, Jesus has explicitly identified himself as the Son of God (Jn 5:25). The sonship language used throughout John's Gospel emphasizes Jesus' divine origin. It also links his role as Son of God with the power and privileges associated with the Davidic Messiah by drawing a subtle allusion to the royal coronation imagery in Ps 2:7. Kingship and divine sonship were interrelated concepts in the ancient Near East. The king ruled as representative of the god and wielded the power and authority bestowed by the god. The threads of royal Davidic kingship, Messianic fulfillment, and divine origin are explicitly brought together by the apostle Paul and the writer of Hebrews (Ac 13:33; Heb 1:5; 5:5). John's presentation of Jesus as Messiah and Son of God blends the imagery to the point where belief

in Jesus as Messiah cannot be separated from belief in his status as Son of God.

11:1 Bethany Located roughly half a mile east of Jerusalem on the eastern slope of the Mount of Olives. **Mary** The sister of Lazarus. Mary sits at Jesus' feet to learn in Lk 10:39, a scene that occurs prior to this one. **Martha** Lazarus' other sister. Martha is depicted as being anxious to be hospitable to Jesus and his disciples in Lk 10:38–42. See note on Lk 10:41.

11:3 Lord See note on Jn 13:6. **one you love is sick** Lazarus is not yet dead when Jesus hears this report.

11:4 will not end in death Jesus predicts that Lazarus will not die in the sense that he will not be permanently dead. **may be glorified** This circumstance will demonstrate Jesus' greatness as well as God's.

11:9 this world's light Refers to Jesus. Light was a common metaphor in Judaism for God's providence and guidance. See Jn 8:12.

11:10 they have no light Jesus refers to God's power to guide a person's life through the Holy Spirit. In this setting, he is referring to himself as their guide (see 14:16).

11:11 has fallen asleep A common metaphor for death, yet once again, Jesus' disciples do not understand. This is likely because they thought Lazarus was still sick (v. 6).

11:16 we may die with him Thomas shows enthusiasm to follow Jesus, a point that later becomes ironic (20:27).

19and many Jews had come to Martha and Mary to comfort them in the loss of their brother. 20When Martha heard that Jesus was coming, she went out to meet him, but Mary stayed at home.

21"Lord," Martha said to Jesus, "if you had been here, my brother would not have died. 22But I know that even now God will give you whatever you ask."

23Jesus said to her, "Your brother will rise again."

24Martha answered, "I know he will rise again in the resurrection at the last day."

25Jesus said to her, "I am the resurrection and the life. The one who believes in me will live, even though they die; 26and whoever lives by believing in me will never die. Do you believe this?"

11:22 God will give you Martha is confident not just in Jesus' ability to heal, but also in his power to do whatever he asks God. Her response in v. 24 to Jesus' proclamation that he will raise Lazarus suggests she is not asking Jesus to raise Lazarus from the dead at this time—that would seem to be impossible.

11:23 rise again Resurrection is traditionally the first sign of the restoration of God's people (Eze 37:1–28; Isa 53:10–12; Da 12:1–13; see note on Ro 1:4). Elijah and Elisha—who were seen as two of the greatest

prophets of Israel—both raised people from the dead (1Ki 17:17–24; 2Ki 4:18–37). Like Jesus, both do so for women. John the Baptist acted in the spirit of Elijah. Here, John parallels Jesus with Elisha; he picks up part of the mantle of John the Baptist now that his ministry has ended, just like Elisha had done after Elijah (2Ki 2:8; Mt 14:10; Jn 10:41). As Elisha received a double portion of Elijah's spirit, so Jesus is far greater than John the Baptist, as John himself acknowledged (2Ki 2:9; Jn 1:27).

11:25 the resurrection and the life Jesus declares

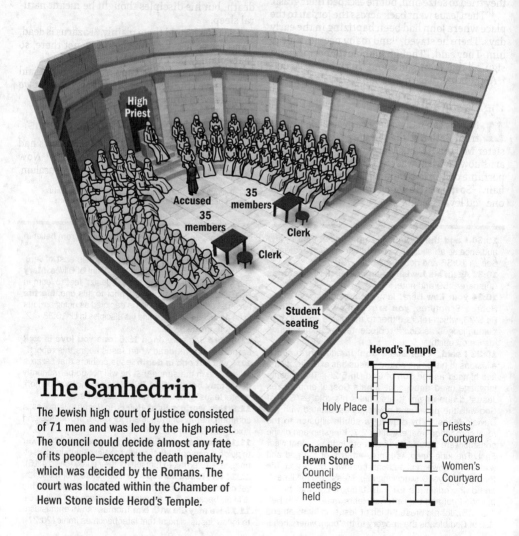

The Sanhedrin

The Jewish high court of justice consisted of 71 men and was led by the high priest. The council could decide almost any fate of its people—except the death penalty, which was decided by the Romans. The court was located within the Chamber of Hewn Stone inside Herod's Temple.

High Priest

Accused
35 members

35 members

Clerk

Clerk

Student seating

Herod's Temple

Holy Place

Chamber of Hewn Stone
Council meetings held

Priests' Courtyard

Women's Courtyard

²⁷"Yes, Lord," she replied, "I believe that you are the Messiah, the Son of God, who is to come into the world."

²⁸After she had said this, she went back and called her sister Mary aside. "The Teacher is here," she said, "and is asking for you." ²⁹When Mary heard this, she got up quickly and went to him. ³⁰Now Jesus had not yet entered the village, but was still at the place where Martha had met him. ³¹When the Jews who had been with Mary in the house, comforting her, noticed how quickly she got up and went out, they followed her, supposing she was going to the tomb to mourn there.

³²When Mary reached the place where Jesus was and saw him, she fell at his feet and said, "Lord, if you had been here, my brother would not have died."

³³When Jesus saw her weeping, and the Jews who had come along with her also weeping, he was deeply moved in spirit and troubled. ³⁴"Where have you laid him?" he asked.

"Come and see, Lord," they replied.

³⁵Jesus wept.

³⁶Then the Jews said, "See how he loved him!"

³⁷But some of them said, "Could not he who opened the eyes of the blind man have kept this man from dying?"

Jesus Raises Lazarus From the Dead

³⁸Jesus, once more deeply moved, came to the tomb. It was a cave with a stone laid across the entrance. ³⁹"Take away the stone," he said.

"But, Lord," said Martha, the sister of the dead man, "by this time there is a bad odor, for he has been there four days."

⁴⁰Then Jesus said, "Did I not tell you that if you believe, you will see the glory of God?"

⁴¹So they took away the stone. Then Jesus looked up and said, "Father, I thank you that you have heard me. ⁴²I knew that you always hear me, but I said this for the benefit of the people standing here, that they may believe that you sent me."

⁴³When he had said this, Jesus called in a loud voice, "Lazarus, come out!" ⁴⁴The dead man came out, his hands and feet wrapped with strips of linen, and a cloth around his face.

Jesus said to them, "Take off the grave clothes and let him go."

The Plot to Kill Jesus

⁴⁵Therefore many of the Jews who had come to visit Mary, and had seen what Jesus did, believed in him. ⁴⁶But some of them went to the Pharisees and told them what Jesus had done. ⁴⁷Then the chief priests and the Pharisees called a meeting of the Sanhedrin.

"What are we accomplishing?" they asked. "Here is this man performing many signs. ⁴⁸If we let him go on like this, everyone will believe in him, and then the Romans will come and take away both our temple and our nation."

⁴⁹Then one of them, named Caiaphas, who was high priest that year, spoke up, "You know nothing at all! ⁵⁰You do not realize that it is better for you that one man die for the people than that the whole nation perish."

⁵¹He did not say this on his own, but as high priest that year he prophesied that Jesus would die for the Jewish nation, ⁵²and not only for that nation but also for the scattered children of God,

---

that he is the source and power that will enable the resurrection of the dead on the day of judgment, when God's people will rise in glorified bodies to be one with him. This parallels the breath coming into the bodies in Eze 37:10.

11:33 troubled Although Jesus intended to use this situation as an example to glorify God, it still disturbs him (Jn 11:3). Jesus feels the pained emotions of one who has lost a friend, and he is sympathetic toward others who grieve.

11:37 opened the eyes of the blind In 9:1–6, Jesus declares that even blindness can be used for God's glory (similar to the situation with Lazarus' death) because it provides an opportunity for God's work through Jesus (compare v. 4). God did not cause Lazarus to die, nor did he cause the man's blindness in 9:1–6; rather, he allowed for these things to happen by their own natural courses and then used the situations for good.

11:41 looked up Jesus looks up not because God the Father is physically located above him but because it was common to look to the heavens (the skies) when praying. He wishes for those who witness this event to realize that God the Father is the source of the miracle he is about to perform. **I thank** Jesus does not begin his prayer by petitioning God to intervene; instead, he begins with thanks for what God has already done.

11:42 may believe that you sent me Jesus acknowledges that it isn't necessary for him to pray because he is already anointed with the power of God to give life. Instead, he prays to proclaim God's greatness in the moment, just as he had told his disciples prior to Lazarus' dying (v. 4).

11:47 many signs Jesus performs a series of signs throughout John's Gospel so that people may believe in him and have eternal life (see note on 2:11). Here, the Pharisees do the opposite: They seek to find a way to end Jesus' ministry because they fear losing their power over the Jewish people.

11:48 Romans The Pharisees and Sanhedrin are concerned about the empire's perception of a ruler rising up among them. See the infographic "The Sanhedrin" on p. 1746.

11:50 that the whole nation perish Caiaphas' prophecy is correct: Jesus will die for the nation (Isa 53:6,12). But his understanding of how the death will occur is incorrect. He is thinking in terms of other leaders, like Judas Maccabeus, and imagining Jesus as a martyred military leader.

11:52 to bring them together Evokes imagery of God's people returning from exile in foreign nations, as well as prophetic imagery of God restoring his people—not

to bring them together and make them one. [53]So from that day on they plotted to take his life.

[54]Therefore Jesus no longer moved about publicly among the people of Judea. Instead he withdrew to a region near the wilderness, to a village called Ephraim, where he stayed with his disciples.

[55]When it was almost time for the Jewish Passover, many went up from the country to Jerusalem for their ceremonial cleansing before the Passover. [56]They kept looking for Jesus, and as they stood in the temple courts they asked one another, "What do you think? Isn't he coming to the festival at all?" [57]But the chief priests and the Pharisees had given orders that anyone who found out where Jesus was should report it so that they might arrest him.

Jesus Anointed at Bethany

12:1-8Ref — Mt 26:6-13; Mk 14:3-9; Lk 7:37-39

12 Six days before the Passover, Jesus came to Bethany, where Lazarus lived, whom Jesus had raised from the dead. [2]Here a dinner was given in Jesus' honor. Martha served, while Lazarus was among those reclining at the table with him. [3]Then Mary took about a pint[a] of pure nard, an expensive perfume; she poured it on Jesus' feet and wiped his feet with her hair. And the house was filled with the fragrance of the perfume.

[4]But one of his disciples, Judas Iscariot, who was later to betray him, objected, [5]"Why wasn't this perfume sold and the money given to the poor? It was worth a year's wages.[b]" [6]He did not say this because he cared about the poor but because he was a thief; as keeper of the money bag, he used to help himself to what was put into it.

[7]"Leave her alone," Jesus replied. "It was intended that she should save this perfume for the day of my burial. [8]You will always have the poor among you,[c] but you will not always have me."

[9]Meanwhile a large crowd of Jews found out that Jesus was there and came, not only because of him but also to see Lazarus, whom he had raised from the dead. [10]So the chief priests made plans to kill Lazarus as well, [11]for on account of him many of the Jews were going over to Jesus and believing in him.

Jesus Comes to Jerusalem as King

12:12-15pp — Mt 21:4-9; Mk 11:7-10; Lk 19:35-38

[12]The next day the great crowd that had come for the festival heard that Jesus was on his way to Jerusalem. [13]They took palm branches and went out to meet him, shouting,

"Hosanna![d]"

"Blessed is he who comes in the name
    of the Lord!"[e]

"Blessed is the king of Israel!"

[14]Jesus found a young donkey and sat on it, as it is written:

[15]"Do not be afraid, Daughter Zion;
    see, your king is coming,
    seated on a donkey's colt."[f]

[16]At first his disciples did not understand all this. Only after Jesus was glorified did they realize that these things had been written about him and that these things had been done to him.

[17]Now the crowd that was with him when he called Lazarus from the tomb and raised him from the dead continued to spread the word. [18]Many

---

[a] 3 Or about 0.5 liter   [b] 5 Greek *three hundred denarii*
[c] 8 See Deut. 15:11.   [d] 13 A Hebrew expression meaning "Save!" which became an exclamation of praise
[e] 13 Psalm 118:25,26   [f] 15 Zech. 9:9

---

only to their land but to relationship with him (e.g., Ne 1:9; Joel 2:16; 3:2). Jesus is the facilitator of this work, though this gathering is spiritual, not physical.

11:54 Ephraim Near Jerusalem; the precise location is unknown.

11:55 Passover See note on Jn 2:13. **their ceremonial cleansing** It was customary for Jewish people to enter ritual pools prior to entering the temple or enjoying the Passover meal.

12:3 pure nard, an expensive perfume The pound of ointment would have cost about 300 denarii. Its high cost means it had likely been in Mary's family for quite some time and was used only in small portions as a perfume on special occasions. Nard was made from a root and likely was imported from Nepal, the nearest major source of the product at the time.

12:7 my burial Jesus seems to confirm that the nard was traditionally used in burial preparations of the time. He recognizes that he will die soon.

12:8 You will always have the poor among you Although Jesus had emphasized the need for his disciples to care for the poor, he explains that he should be their focus—especially in these days prior to his death.

12:9 also to see Lazarus The raising of Lazarus had become the pinnacle of Jesus' miraculous work (compare note on 11:23).

12:13 palm branches The people make a path for Jesus to enter the city as royalty. **Hosanna** This Hebrew expression, meaning "help us" or "save us," developed into a liturgical expression of praise. **name of the Lord** Jesus comes as a representation of the divine name—as "I am" or Yahweh (compare note on Ex 3:14). **king of Israel** The people recognize Jesus as their king, though they likely do not understand this vocation in the same way as he does. The people who are calling Jesus king likely think that he has come to save them from foreign oppressors by fighting on their behalf (like Judas Maccabeus); instead, God intends for his divine warrior to come to Jerusalem to suffer and die (compare note on Isa 53:1; and note on Isa 53:12).

12:15 Daughter Zion See note on Mt 21:5.

people, because they had heard that he had performed this sign, went out to meet him. ¹⁹So the Pharisees said to one another, "See, this is getting us nowhere. Look how the whole world has gone after him!"

Jesus Predicts His Death

²⁰Now there were some Greeks among those who went up to worship at the festival. ²¹They came to Philip, who was from Bethsaida in Galilee, with a request. "Sir," they said, "we would like to see Jesus." ²²Philip went to tell Andrew; Andrew and Philip in turn told Jesus.

²³Jesus replied, "The hour has come for the Son of Man to be glorified. ²⁴Very truly I tell you, unless a kernel of wheat falls to the ground and dies, it remains only a single seed. But if it dies, it produces many seeds. ²⁵Anyone who loves their life will lose it, while anyone who hates their life in this world will keep it for eternal life. ²⁶Whoever serves me must follow me; and where I am, my servant also will be. My Father will honor the one who serves me.

²⁷"Now my soul is troubled, and what shall I say? 'Father, save me from this hour'? No, it was for this very reason I came to this hour. ²⁸Father, glorify your name!"

Then a voice came from heaven, "I have glorified it, and will glorify it again." ²⁹The crowd that was there and heard it said it had thundered; others said an angel had spoken to him.

³⁰Jesus said, "This voice was for your benefit, not mine. ³¹Now is the time for judgment on this world; now the prince of this world will be driven out. ³²And I, when I am lifted up[a] from the earth, will draw all people to myself." ³³He said this to show the kind of death he was going to die.

³⁴The crowd spoke up, "We have heard from the Law that the Messiah will remain forever, so how can you say, 'The Son of Man must be lifted up'? Who is this 'Son of Man'?"

³⁵Then Jesus told them, "You are going to have the light just a little while longer. Walk while you have the light, before darkness overtakes you. Whoever walks in the dark does not know where they are going. ³⁶Believe in the light while you have the light, so that you may become children of light." When he had finished speaking, Jesus left and hid himself from them.

Belief and Unbelief Among the Jews

³⁷Even after Jesus had performed so many signs in their presence, they still would not believe in him. ³⁸This was to fulfill the word of Isaiah the prophet:

"Lord, who has believed our message
    and to whom has the arm of the Lord been
        revealed?"[b]

³⁹For this reason they could not believe, because, as Isaiah says elsewhere:

⁴⁰"He has blinded their eyes
    and hardened their hearts,
so they can neither see with their eyes,
    nor understand with their hearts,
    nor turn—and I would heal them."[c]

[a] 32 The Greek for *lifted up* also means *exalted.*
[b] 38 Isaiah 53:1   [c] 40 Isaiah 6:10

12:20 some Greeks Although they were not Jewish by heritage, these people believed in Yahweh. They did not always abide by all Jewish practices, but they followed enough to be allowed into one of the courts of the temple. See the infographic "Herod's Temple" on p. 1626.
12:23 Son of Man to be glorified See note on Jn 13:31.
12:24 it remains only a single seed A grain of wheat is not valuable unless it becomes something else. Jesus is willing to suffer for the cause God has set before him. He suggests that his value is substantially less if he is unwilling to follow through on God's will.
12:25 who loves their life will lose it If people decide that their lives are more important than God's will, then they will forfeit the type of life God wants to give them—a life of relationship with him now and in eternity. **while anyone who hates their life in this world** Jesus asks people to forfeit their usual wants and desires for the sake of God's will. **eternal life** Those who choose to believe in Jesus will receive life forever, in communion with God the Father, because of their relationship with Jesus. See note on 1:4.
12:27 save me from this hour The time of suffering foreshadowed earlier has finally come (see note on 7:6). Jesus wishes that he could forego suffering, but he knows that his death is necessary in order for him to fulfill the will of the Father and save people from their sins.

12:28 I have glorified Jesus glorified his Father's name by performing signs and following the Father's will even when doing so was painful or difficult (11:47; compare v. 33). **glorify it again** When Jesus suffers and dies on behalf of God's people.
12:31 prince of this world Jesus likely is referencing the devil. See note on 13:2.
12:32 lifted up Likely a reference to Jesus' death on a cross (see 3:14 and note; 8:28 and note; 18:32 and note). **all people to myself** Possibly a reference to the crowds gathered for his crucifixion, though more likely Jesus is referring to the resurrection of the dead (compare Isa 52:13). He also could be referring to the renown he will gain as the one God raised from the dead (see note on Ro 1:4; note on 1Co 15:13).
12:35 darkness Symbolizes the evil in the world. The opposition between light and darkness is a prominent motif in John. See Jn 1:5 and note.
12:36 you may become children of light They are united with Jesus in his cause and empowered by him.
12:38 arm of the Lord See note on Isa 53:1. See the table "Jesus' Fulfillment of OT Prophecy" on p. 1573.
12:40 blinded This quote from Isa 6:10 follows Isaiah's prophetic warnings. The people have already been warned, but they have ignored the prophet yet again, so God will no longer tell them his will (compare Jn 9:39; Isa 6:9–10 and note).

⁴¹Isaiah said this because he saw Jesus' glory and spoke about him.

⁴²Yet at the same time many even among the leaders believed in him. But because of the Pharisees they would not openly acknowledge their faith for fear they would be put out of the synagogue; ⁴³for they loved human praise more than praise from God.

⁴⁴Then Jesus cried out, "Whoever believes in me does not believe in me only, but in the one who sent me. ⁴⁵The one who looks at me is seeing the one who sent me. ⁴⁶I have come into the world as a light, so that no one who believes in me should stay in darkness.

⁴⁷"If anyone hears my words but does not keep them, I do not judge that person. For I did not come to judge the world, but to save the world. ⁴⁸There is a judge for the one who rejects me and does not accept my words; the very words I have spoken will condemn them at the last day. ⁴⁹For I did not speak on my own, but the Father who sent me commanded me to say all that I have spoken. ⁵⁰I know that his command leads to eternal life. So whatever I say is just what the Father has told me to say."

Jesus Washes His Disciples' Feet

13 It was just before the Passover Festival. Jesus knew that the hour had come for him to leave this world and go to the Father. Having loved his own who were in the world, he loved them to the end.

²The evening meal was in progress, and the devil had already prompted Judas, the son of Simon Iscariot, to betray Jesus. ³Jesus knew that the Father had put all things under his power, and that he had come from God and was returning to God; ⁴so he got up from the meal, took off his outer clothing, and wrapped a towel around his waist. ⁵After that, he poured water into a basin and began to wash his disciples' feet, drying them with the towel that was wrapped around him.

⁶He came to Simon Peter, who said to him, "Lord, are you going to wash my feet?"

⁷Jesus replied, "You do not realize now what I am doing, but later you will understand."

⁸"No," said Peter, "you shall never wash my feet."

Jesus answered, "Unless I wash you, you have no part with me."

⁹"Then, Lord," Simon Peter replied, "not just my feet but my hands and my head as well!"

¹⁰Jesus answered, "Those who have had a bath need only to wash their feet; their whole body is clean. And you are clean, though not every one of you." ¹¹For he knew who was going to betray him, and that was why he said not every one was clean.

¹²When he had finished washing their feet, he put on his clothes and returned to his place. "Do you understand what I have done for you?" he asked them. ¹³"You call me 'Teacher' and 'Lord,'

12:41 he saw Jesus' glory The quotation of Isa 53:1 establishes a parallel between the suffering servant and Jesus, and between the people who refused to believe God's prophet, Isaiah, and those who refuse to believe Jesus. The people will not be given another chance to accept God's message.

12:42 Pharisees See note on Jn 7:32. See the table "Major Groups in Jesus' Time" on p. 1630.

12:45 seeing the one who sent me Jesus equates himself with God the Father; they are one.

12:46 no one who believes in me should stay in darkness A believer in Jesus chooses to follow Jesus' will. The intellectual decision begins a relationship with Jesus, but entering into a relationship with him through that initial belief is only the beginning of the faith journey.

12:48 words I have spoken Although God the Father is the judge, Jesus' message is the same as that of God the Father (v. 50); his words against those who choose not to enter into a relationship with him are true and will be true on the day of judgment (see note on 11:25).

12:50 command leads to eternal life The commandment Jesus requires his disciples to keep is to believe in his ability to grant eternal life.

13:1–30 Jesus has a final meal with his disciples and washes their feet as a model of humble, compassionate service (vv. 1–17; compare Lk 22:27). Jesus also reveals his imminent betrayal by one of the disciples and alludes to his coming death (Jn 13:18–30). See the event line "Jesus' Passion and Resurrection" on p. 1698.

13:1 Passover See note on 2:13. **this world** Jesus'

work continues; his coming suffering and death is not the end, but the beginning. Although he is troubled by his coming death (12:27), he wants his disciples to have confidence in their knowledge that his death does not mark the end of his ministry.

13:2 devil Refers to the enemy of God's people, the tempter and oppressor (Mt 4:5; 13:39; Ac 10:38; see note on Heb 2:14; compare 1Ti 3:6–7). Jesus has known all along that Judas was (or would be) influenced by the devil to betray him (Jn 6:70).

13:3 had put all things Here, John tells the reader that Jesus is not acting as an ordinary person; he is acting as the Son of God—to whom the entire kingdom has been given. This makes his sacrifice all the more profound. **he had come from God** John is clear: Jesus came from God the Father and deserves to reign because all things have been given to him by the Creator (Ge 1:1; Jn 1:1). Jesus knows his identity in God, yet he will choose to die because of God's love for people (3:16).

13:5 to wash his disciples' feet This is an act that only slaves performed. When the master of a wealthy household returned from a journey or, at times, a day of labor, a slave would wash his feet. People wore open-toed sandals in the first century, which would have made this an unpleasant task.

13:6 Lord The Greek term used here, *kyrios*, means "ruler" or "master." In the Septuagint (the Greek version of the Hebrew Scriptures, commonly used by early Christians), *kyrios* is used in place of the divine name, Yahweh. If Peter is using *kyrios* in the sense of the divine name, then he is referring to Jesus as God. This seems to fit Jesus' "I am" remark in v. 13.

and rightly so, for that is what I am. [14]Now that I, your Lord and Teacher, have washed your feet, you also should wash one another's feet. [15]I have set you an example that you should do as I have done for you. [16]Very truly I tell you, no servant is greater than his master, nor is a messenger greater than the one who sent him. [17]Now that you know these things, you will be blessed if you do them.

Jesus Predicts His Betrayal

[18]"I am not referring to all of you; I know those I have chosen. But this is to fulfill this passage of Scripture: 'He who shared my bread has turned[a] against me.'[b]

[19]"I am telling you now before it happens, so that when it does happen you will believe that I am who I am. [20]Very truly I tell you, whoever accepts anyone I send accepts me; and whoever accepts me accepts the one who sent me."

[21]After he had said this, Jesus was troubled in spirit and testified, "Very truly I tell you, one of you is going to betray me."

[22]His disciples stared at one another, at a loss to know which of them he meant. [23]One of them, the disciple whom Jesus loved, was reclining next to him. [24]Simon Peter motioned to this disciple and said, "Ask him which one he means."

[25]Leaning back against Jesus, he asked him, "Lord, who is it?"

[26]Jesus answered, "It is the one to whom I will give this piece of bread when I have dipped it in the dish." Then, dipping the piece of bread, he gave it to Judas, the son of Simon Iscariot. [27]As soon as Judas took the bread, Satan entered into him.

So Jesus told him, "What you are about to do, do quickly." [28]But no one at the meal understood why Jesus said this to him. [29]Since Judas had charge of the money, some thought Jesus was telling him to buy what was needed for the festival, or to give something to the poor. [30]As soon as Judas had taken the bread, he went out. And it was night.

Jesus Predicts Peter's Denial

13:37,38pp — Mt 26:33-35; Mk 14:29-31; Lk 22:33,34

[31]When he was gone, Jesus said, "Now the Son of Man is glorified and God is glorified in him. [32]If God is glorified in him,[c] God will glorify the Son in himself, and will glorify him at once.

[33]"My children, I will be with you only a little longer. You will look for me, and just as I told the Jews, so I tell you now: Where I am going, you cannot come.

[a] 18 Greek *has lifted up his heel*　[b] 18 Psalm 41:9　[c] 32 Many early manuscripts do not have *If God is glorified in him.*

13:7 later Not until Jesus dies and is resurrected will his disciples fully understand his mission and role in the world.

13:10 their whole body is clean Cleansing rituals were part of everyday life for Jews of the first century. Jesus suggests that his work in the believer eliminates the need for repetitive cleansing. **though not every one of you** Jesus references Judas, who has chosen to reject him.

13:13 I am Jesus is likely evoking God's chosen way of identifying himself in the OT—saying that he is Yahweh, the God of Israel and ruler of the universe. This parallels what John says about Jesus in 1:1–4 and what Jesus knows of his own identity, revealed in v. 3. See note on 4:26.

13:16 servant Jesus is doing the work of a slave (see note on v. 5); he now suggests that his disciples do the same in service to others. Jesus is also likely evoking imagery from the prophecies about the suffering servant (Isa 52:13—53:12). He becomes a servant to God and to others to fulfill his role as the one who (through his death and resurrection) restores God's people into right relationship with him (Isa 53:10,12). He now calls his disciples to sacrifice themselves for the purposes of God. This is a vocation Paul clearly understood: He regularly called himself a slave of Christ (see note on Ro 1:1).

13:20 accepts the one who sent me Anyone who accepts and embraces the work of Jesus' disciples embraces the work of God the Father.

13:21 troubled in spirit Jesus feels the weight of his imminent suffering and death.

13:23 the disciple whom Jesus loved This is the first reference to this disciple (Jn 19:26–27; 20:2–9; 21:7,20–25), who could be the apostle John, Lazarus (based on 11:3,36), or another follower of Jesus. The reference in 21:24 suggests that the disciple Jesus loved is the author of this Gospel. Since church tradition and the vocabulary of 1–3 John and Revelation connect this Gospel to the apostle John, he likely is the disciple described here. He probably chose this ambiguous reference to downplay his own role in the story of Jesus. Jesus loved (and loves) all of his disciples and all people (Jn 3:16–17; 17:1–26). The phrase in this verse signals a personal friendship and likely emphasizes the disciple's familiarity with Jesus. The disciple saw himself in as much need of Jesus' love as anyone else.

13:25 Leaning back against Jesus Refers to the position of the disciple Jesus loved—he is sitting in the normal reclining position for this sort of meal setup, probably sharing the same couch with Jesus. This position of honor probably lets him speak to Jesus without the other disciples overhearing.

13:27 Satan entered into him The Greek term *satanas* is used here instead of the word *diabolos* ("devil"; v. 2).

13:31—16:33 Jesus' farewell discourse (13:31—16:33) is a block of teaching in which he instructs his disciples about the significance of his upcoming death, resurrection and exaltation, as well as the coming of the Holy Spirit.

13:31 Son of Man Jesus understands that he must suffer in order for his role as the Son of Man to be fulfilled and for God to glorify him. See note on Mt 8:20 (compare Jn 1:51 and note). **is glorified** Because Jesus allowed God's will to be done when presented with the option of stopping the person who would betray him, God makes Jesus great.

13:33 My children A common way for a teacher to address disciples. **Where I am going, you cannot come** Jesus refers to his death and resurrection.

³⁴"A new command I give you: Love one another. As I have loved you, so you must love one another. ³⁵By this everyone will know that you are my disciples, if you love one another."

³⁶Simon Peter asked him, "Lord, where are you going?"

Jesus replied, "Where I am going, you cannot follow now, but you will follow later."

³⁷Peter asked, "Lord, why can't I follow you now? I will lay down my life for you."

³⁸Then Jesus answered, "Will you really lay down your life for me? Very truly I tell you, before the rooster crows, you will disown me three times!

Jesus Comforts His Disciples

14 "Do not let your hearts be troubled. You believe in God^a; believe also in me. ²My Father's house has many rooms; if that were not so, would I have told you that I am going there to prepare a place for you? ³And if I go and prepare a place for you, I will come back and take you to be with me that you also may be where I am. ⁴You know the way to the place where I am going."

Jesus the Way to the Father

⁵Thomas said to him, "Lord, we don't know where you are going, so how can we know the way?"

⁶Jesus answered, "I am the way and the truth and the life. No one comes to the Father except through me. ⁷If you really know me, you will know^b my Father as well. From now on, you do know him and have seen him."

⁸Philip said, "Lord, show us the Father and that will be enough for us."

⁹Jesus answered: "Don't you know me, Philip, even after I have been among you such a long time? Anyone who has seen me has seen the Father. How can you say, 'Show us the Father'? ¹⁰Don't you believe that I am in the Father, and that the Father is in me? The words I say to you I do not speak on my own authority. Rather, it is the Father, living in me, who is doing his work. ¹¹Believe me when I say that I am in the Father and the Father is in me; or at least believe on the evidence of the works themselves. ¹²Very truly I tell you, whoever believes in me will do the works I have been doing, and they will do even greater things than these, because I am going to the Father. ¹³And I will do whatever you ask in my name, so that the Father may be glorified in the Son. ¹⁴You may ask me for anything in my name, and I will do it.

^{a} 1 Or *Believe in God* ^{b} 7 Some manuscripts *If you really knew me, you would know*

13:34 As I have loved you Jesus inserts this phrase into the commandment from Lev 19:18. The new part of the commandment is that Jesus' disciples are instructed to love other people the way Jesus loved them—serving them like a slave would, as he does in this scene, even to the point of laying down their lives for others.

13:36 will follow later Peter won't die with Jesus, but he will later die for his faith (according to church tradition). Jesus means that after Peter dies, he will follow Jesus into eternal life.

13:38 you will disown me three times Although Peter believes he is completely dedicated to following Jesus, he actually is not.

14:1–14 Jesus reiterates to his disciples that faith in him alone will bring salvation. He uses another metaphorical "I am" statement—this time that he is the way, the truth and the life (Jn 14:6). See note on 6:35.

14:2 Father's house Jesus is referring to the heavenly abode, where God the Father sits enthroned (Isa 6:1–6). Jesus had already declared God's symbolic earthly dwelling, the temple, to be insignificant in comparison to God's work through his new temple, Jesus (see Jn 2:19; compare note on 1:14). This and Jesus' condemnation of the conduct of the earthly keepers of his "Father's house" establish Jesus as a better, heavenly alternative (2:16). **rooms** There is room for many people in God's kingdom and his heavenly abode, where those who accept Jesus dwell eternally. Here, Jesus is likely drawing on imagery of God's people dwelling in the wilderness in his presence, after the exodus from Egypt (Ex 19:2). John 14:6 alludes to Jesus as the fulfillment of God dwelling among his people. See the infographic "The Israelite Encampment" on p. 215; see the table "Israelite Festivals" on p. 200. **14:3 I will come back** Jesus is describing an event that

will occur after his ascension to God's heavenly abode (v. 2). Consequently, this refers to his return to earth, not his resurrection. **you also may be** Refers to Jesus' followers living with him in God's heavenly dwelling place.

14:4 the way Meaning his betrayal, suffering, death and resurrection (12:27–34).

14:6 the way The person and work of Jesus serves as believers' pathway to God the Father. See the table "Jesus' 'I Am' Statements" on p. 1727. **the truth** Since there were divergent Jewish traditions, it was difficult for the Jewish person of the first century to know which tradition was Yahweh's will. See note on 1:14 (compare 1:17). **the life** Refers to Jesus as the source and power of believers' resurrection to eternal life. See note on 11:25. **except through me** Salvation does not come through the law, sacrifices, religious practices or the overthrow of foreign oppressors—all of which were beliefs held by Jews in the first century. Instead, Jesus himself is the channel through which people can have relationship with God the Father and spend eternity with him.

14:7 have seen him Jesus equates his presence with God's presence.

14:11 works Jesus' signs and actions demonstrate he is the Son of God and the Son of Man sent to suffer and die for God's people so they may have a restored relationship with God without sin standing in the way (see note on 11:47). Yet some don't believe even after seeing signs. Doing God's work is the way believers demonstrate their love for Jesus (v. 21).

14:12 greater This term refers to the amount of miracles (as described in v. 11). Believers will collectively (and perhaps individually) perform more miracles than Jesus. It is Jesus' intention to extend the work of the Spirit beyond himself to all believers, as he had already begun to do (Lk 9:1–6).

Jesus Promises the Holy Spirit

15 "If you love me, keep my commands. 16 And I will ask the Father, and he will give you another advocate to help you and be with you forever — 17 the Spirit of truth. The world cannot accept him, because it neither sees him nor knows him. But you know him, for he lives with you and will be*a* in you. 18 I will not leave you as orphans; I will come to you. 19 Before long, the world will not see me anymore, but you will see me. Because I live, you also will live. 20 On that day you will realize that I am in my Father, and you are in me, and I am in you. 21 Whoever has my commands and keeps them is the one who loves me. The one who loves me will be loved by my Father, and I too will love them and show myself to them."

22 Then Judas (not Judas Iscariot) said, "But, Lord, why do you intend to show yourself to us and not to the world?"

23 Jesus replied, "Anyone who loves me will obey my teaching. My Father will love them, and we will come to them and make our home with them. 24 Anyone who does not love me will not obey my teaching. These words you hear are not my own; they belong to the Father who sent me.

25 "All this I have spoken while still with you. 26 But the Advocate, the Holy Spirit, whom the Father will send in my name, will teach you all things and will remind you of everything I have said to you. 27 Peace I leave with you; my peace I give you. I do not give to you as the world gives. Do not let your hearts be troubled and do not be afraid.

28 "You heard me say, 'I am going away and I am coming back to you.' If you loved me, you would be glad that I am going to the Father, for the Father is greater than I. 29 I have told you now before it happens, so that when it does happen you will believe. 30 I will not say much more to you, for the prince of this world is coming. He has no hold over me, 31 but he comes so that the world may learn that I love the Father and do exactly what my Father has commanded me.

"Come now; let us leave."

The Vine and the Branches

15 "I am the true vine, and my Father is the gardener. 2 He cuts off every branch in me that bears no fruit, while every branch that does bear fruit he prunes*b* so that it will be even more fruitful. 3 You are already clean because of the word I have spoken to you. 4 Remain in me, as I also remain in you. No branch can bear fruit by itself; it must remain in the vine. Neither can you bear fruit unless you remain in me.

5 "I am the vine; you are the branches. If you

a 17 Some early manuscripts *and is* *b* 2 The Greek for *he prunes* also means *he cleans*.

14:13 whatever you ask in my name Refers to those occasions when he is given credit for the work, rather than the person performing the work, and when it is in his will. Jesus provides several examples for this (e.g., Jn 11:41–42). Miracles must be performed for the purpose of leading others to believe (11:15).

14:17 in you This refers to the Spirit dwelling in the believer—making them, when they choose to follow God's will, a testimony by which others can see and understand God (compare note on v. 2).

14:21 keeps them Refers to loving God and others, as Jesus has loved people. See note on v. 11.

14:26 Advocate The Greek term used here, *paraklētos*, refers to a legal assistant in a court who pleads someone's case before the judge (compare 1Jn 2:1). The judge is God, and people are judged based on whether they follow Jesus' command to believe that eternal life comes through his death and resurrection (Jn 12:48–50). When on earth, Jesus was the means for believers to interact with God the Father since their sin prevented them from doing so directly. The Spirit is sent to do the same work. This is one of his many tasks. **will teach** The Spirit, as God's means of communication on earth, instructs believers and leads them to follow God's will. The Spirit gives them access to God, his plans and his wisdom. He can do so because of Jesus' sacrifice for sins.

14:27 Peace Refers to wholeness in their relationship with God. They now have a way (the Spirit) to reach God—unencumbered by rituals, sacrifices or laws—and atonement for their sins (Jesus' death and resurrection), so that they are free to communicate with God and be in his presence.

14:28 I am coming back to you Refers to his resurrec-tion. Jesus wants his disciples to know that his coming suffering and death is not the end of his ministry; it is the beginning of his ministry's final purpose and the completion of God's will for Jesus' life. **going to the Father** Refers to his ascension. Jesus' disciples should have rejoiced and recognized this was essential for him to complete God's work and to unite them with God the Father.

14:30 He has no hold over me Jesus is empowered by God the Father (12:42,49). Since all authority ultimately finds its source in God the Father, the rulers of this world do not have authority over Jesus (19:11).

15:1–17 Jesus continues teaching the disciples with an extended metaphor in which he is the true vine and his followers are the branches (vv. 1,5). The imagery alludes to OT depictions of Israel as Yahweh's vineyard (Isa 5:1–7). Jesus replaces Israel as the central focus of Yahweh's plan of salvation, fulfilling the role of Israel as the true vine. This passage features the last of the seven metaphorical "I am" statements John uses to define Jesus' identity. See note on Jn 6:35.

15:1 the true vine Jesus is likely referring to a grape-vine. Jesus is the center of the Christian faith—he is the source of life and the way to eternal life (14:6). See the table "Jesus' 'I Am' Statements" on p. 1727.

15:2 he prunes Grapevines are more plentiful if pruned. The pruning may refer to hardship that (eventually) produces faithfulness and closer relationship with God, such as the disciples are about to experience (compare Ro 5:3–5; Jas 1:2–4). Jesus also could be referring to the pruning of dead branches, which would entail removing what is undesirable.

15:5 you can do nothing Jesus means that people

remain in me and I in you, you will bear much fruit; apart from me you can do nothing. ⁶If you do not remain in me, you are like a branch that is thrown away and withers; such branches are picked up, thrown into the fire and burned. ⁷If you remain in me and my words remain in you, ask whatever you wish, and it will be done for you. ⁸This is to my Father's glory, that you bear much fruit, showing yourselves to be my disciples.

⁹"As the Father has loved me, so have I loved you. Now remain in my love. ¹⁰If you keep my commands, you will remain in my love, just as I have kept my Father's commands and remain in his love. ¹¹I have told you this so that my joy may be in you and that your joy may be complete. ¹²My command is this: Love each other as I have loved you. ¹³Greater love has no one than this: to lay down one's life for one's friends. ¹⁴You are my friends if you do what I command. ¹⁵I no longer call you servants, because a servant does not know his master's business. Instead, I have called you friends, for everything that I learned from my Father I have made known to you. ¹⁶You did not choose me, but I chose you and appointed you so that you might go and bear fruit—fruit that will last—and so that whatever you ask in my name the Father will give you. ¹⁷This is my command: Love each other.

The World Hates the Disciples

¹⁸"If the world hates you, keep in mind that it hated me first. ¹⁹If you belonged to the world, it would love you as its own. As it is, you do not belong to the world, but I have chosen you out of the world. That is why the world hates you. ²⁰Remember what I told you: 'A servant is not greater than his master.'[a] If they persecuted me, they will persecute you also. If they obeyed my teaching, they will obey yours also. ²¹They will treat you this way because of my name, for they do not know the one who sent me. ²²If I had not come and spoken to them, they would not be guilty of sin; but now they have no excuse for their sin. ²³Whoever hates me hates my Father as well. ²⁴If I had not done among them the works no one else did, they would not be guilty of sin. As it is, they have seen, and yet they have hated both me and my Father. ²⁵But this is to fulfill what is written in their Law: 'They hated me without reason.'[b]

The Work of the Holy Spirit

²⁶"When the Advocate comes, whom I will send to you from the Father—the Spirit of truth who goes out from the Father—he will testify about me. ²⁷And you also must testify, for you have been with me from the beginning.

[a] 20 John 13:16   [b] 25 Psalms 35:19; 69:4

---

cannot access God without him, and consequently they cannot bear fruit. All life-giving things require access to the source of life, Jesus (Jn 14:6; 15:1).

15:6 into the fire Jesus is referring to those who choose not to accept him as Savior. The dead branches are people who are useless to God's work—people like Judas, who chose to reject Jesus when faced with the truth (13:2). The people who reject Jesus will be judged on the last day—fire refers to judgment (12:31). The judgment is based primarily on rejection of Jesus because acceptance of Jesus' ability to grant eternal life was his word and his command (12:50).

15:7 it will be done for you See note on 14:13.

15:8 showing yourselves to be my disciples Jesus wants the opposite of destruction for his disciples: He wants them to make God's greatness known. The way his disciples prove to be his is by loving others as he loved them and by believing and proclaiming God's gift of eternal life through Jesus' death and resurrection (12:50; 13:34).

15:9 in my love Indicates that they follow Jesus, who showed his love for them by being willing to sacrifice his life for them. The Spirit will be their guide in this process (14:26).

15:14 my friends The way that Jesus' disciples reciprocate the friendship he showed them is by doing what he asked of them (v. 10).

15:15 I have made known to you Jesus is referencing the subject matter at hand, not everything he knows. He means that he has told his disciples everything regarding salvation and what it means to follow God and obey his will. There is no secret way to receive salvation; it simply involves accepting Jesus as Savior. Compare note on 16:12.

15:16 bear fruit Involves keeping Jesus' commands (vv. 8,10) and being guided by his Spirit in the process of doing so (14:26). **that will last** Not only must the disciples follow Jesus, but their works should align with his purposes (14:11).

15:18–27 Jesus expands on the vine and branches imagery by explaining to his disciples how their connection with him, the true vine, will lead to their rejection and persecution by the world. The world will hate them because it opposes him.

15:19 out of the world The disciples will remain part of the world, but they will be spiritually united with Jesus. In this way, they will no longer be part of the world's purposes, but God's (14:12).

15:20 they will obey yours also The disciples become God's ambassadors and speakers on Jesus' behalf through the work of the Holy Spirit (14:26).

15:21 do not know the one In John's Gospel people often misunderstand God's role in sending Jesus into the world (e.g., Jn 7:28–29; 8:54–55).

15:22 they would not be guilty of sin People who have not encountered Jesus or his message—which can come through his disciples and believers (v. 20)—cannot make a choice to accept or deny him. They cannot sin against him because they do not know of him.

15:24 hated both me and my Father Even though the Jewish leaders who killed Jesus claimed to be following God's will, they neglected to acknowledge Jesus as part of his will and thus showed their love for their own positions over God's work (12:43; compare note on Isa 53:10).

15:26 Advocate See note on Jn 14:26.

16 "All this I have told you so that you will not fall away. [2] They will put you out of the synagogue; in fact, the time is coming when anyone who kills you will think they are offering a service to God. [3] They will do such things because they have not known the Father or me. [4] I have told you this, so that when their time comes you will remember that I warned you about them. I did not tell you this from the beginning because I was with you, [5] but now I am going to him who sent me. None of you asks me, 'Where are you going?' [6] Rather, you are filled with grief because I have said these things. [7] But very truly I tell you, it is for your good that I am going away. Unless I go away, the Advocate will not come to you; but if I go, I will send him to you. [8] When he comes, he will prove the world to be in the wrong about sin and righteousness and judgment: [9] about sin, because people do not believe in me; [10] about righteousness, because I am going to the Father, where you can see me no longer; [11] and about judgment, because the prince of this world now stands condemned.

[12] "I have much more to say to you, more than you can now bear. [13] But when he, the Spirit of truth, comes, he will guide you into all the truth. He will not speak on his own; he will speak only what he hears, and he will tell you what is yet to come. [14] He will glorify me because it is from me that he will receive what he will make known to you. [15] All that belongs to the Father is mine. That is why I said the Spirit will receive from me what he will make known to you."

The Disciples' Grief Will Turn to Joy

[16] Jesus went on to say, "In a little while you will see me no more, and then after a little while you will see me."

[17] At this, some of his disciples said to one another, "What does he mean by saying, 'In a little while you will see me no more, and then after a little while you will see me,' and 'Because I am going to the Father'?" [18] They kept asking, "What does he mean by 'a little while'? We don't understand what he is saying."

[19] Jesus saw that they wanted to ask him about this, so he said to them, "Are you asking one another what I meant when I said, 'In a little while you will see me no more, and then after a little while you will see me'? [20] Very truly I tell you, you will weep and mourn while the world rejoices. You will grieve, but your grief will turn to joy. [21] A woman giving birth to a child has pain because her time has come; but when her baby is born she forgets the anguish because of her joy that a child is born into the world. [22] So with you: Now is your time of grief, but I will see you again and you will rejoice, and no one will take away your joy. [23] In that day you will no longer ask me anything. Very truly I tell you, my Father will give you whatever you ask in my name. [24] Until now you have not asked for anything in my name. Ask and you will receive, and your joy will be complete.

[25] "Though I have been speaking figuratively, a time is coming when I will no longer use this kind of language but will tell you plainly about my Father. [26] In that day you will ask in my name. I am not saying that I will ask the Father on your behalf. [27] No, the Father himself loves you because you have loved me and have believed that I came from God. [28] I came from the Father and entered the world; now I am leaving the world and going back to the Father."

[29] Then Jesus' disciples said, "Now you are speaking clearly and without figures of speech. [30] Now we can see that you know all things and that you do not even need to have anyone ask you questions. This makes us believe that you came from God."

[31] "Do you now believe?" Jesus replied. [32] "A time

16:2 synagogue See note on Mt 4:23. See the infographic "Ancient Home Synagogue" on p. 1971.

16:7 I will send him to you Jesus is looking ahead to the time when his disciples will carry on his work. When Jesus has gone, the Spirit will become their advocate (see note on Jn 14:26).

16:8 prove the world to be in the wrong The Spirit reveals people's sins and teaches them the ways of God (14:26). Because Jesus' self-sacrifice atones for sins, people's sins do not result in death (13:15–17). **judgment** Refers to the way that God actually judges — he judges based on whether people accept Jesus. The Spirit's work in the world will be a reminder of Jesus' previous actions. He will work through believers to accomplish God's purposes and reveal his power over the powers of darkness and his power to convince people to believe (12:28–50).

16:11 prince of this world See note on 12:31.

16:12 more than you can now bear Jesus has told them information that would be difficult to accept — such as his coming suffering and death and the fact that he won't be physically present with them after his ascen-

sion. He also likely means that they are not yet ready to accept how difficult following him will be. He has spoken about these challenges in general, but the specifics may be too difficult to hear.

16:15 All that belongs to the Father is mine All of creation came to be through God's Son, so everything in it belongs to him (1:1–3). Jesus is also likely suggesting that God's heavenly abode belongs to him since he and the Father are one (14:2,11; 17:11).

16:20 will turn to joy This occurs when the disciples meet Jesus after his resurrection. See note on 14:28.

16:27 because you have loved me Loving Jesus is like loving the Father, because they are one (14:11; 17:11).

16:28 I came from the Father See note on 1:1 (compare 1:2–3,10).

16:30 you know all things Jesus' disciples finally answer the question that he has been asking throughout his discourse: whether they are willing to follow him based on the knowledge that he has shared with them about his death and resurrection (see note on v. 31).

16:31 Do you now believe The fundamental point in Jesus' message: People must choose to believe in

is coming and in fact has come when you will be scattered, each to your own home. You will leave me all alone. Yet I am not alone, for my Father is with me.

33"I have told you these things, so that in me you may have peace. In this world you will have trouble. But take heart! I have overcome the world."

Jesus Prays to Be Glorified

17 After Jesus said this, he looked toward heaven and prayed:

"Father, the hour has come. Glorify your Son, that your Son may glorify you. 2For you granted him authority over all people that he might give eternal life to all those you have given him. 3Now this is eternal life: that they know you, the only true God, and Jesus Christ, whom you have sent. 4I have brought you glory on earth by finishing the work you gave me to do. 5And now, Father, glorify me in your presence with the glory I had with you before the world began.

Jesus Prays for His Disciples

6"I have revealed you[a] to those whom you gave me out of the world. They were yours; you gave them to me and they have obeyed your word. 7Now they know that everything you have given me comes from you. 8For I gave them the words you gave me and they accepted them. They knew with certainty that I came from you, and they believed that you sent me. 9I pray for them. I am not praying for the world, but for those you have given me, for they are yours. 10All I have is yours, and all you have is mine. And glory has come to me through them. 11I will remain in the world no longer, but they are still in the world, and I am coming to you. Holy Father, protect them by the power of[b] your name, the name you gave me, so that they may be one as we are one. 12While I was with them, I protected them and kept them safe by[c] that

---

[a] 6 Greek *your name*   [b] 11 Or *Father, keep them faithful to*
[c] 12 Or *kept them faithful to*

---

him. Jesus repeats this point throughout John's Gospel, emphasizing it in his discourses in chs. 14–17 (compare 3:16–17; 11:40,42; 12:36,44–50).

16:32 scattered When Jesus is persecuted and suffers, they will not stick by him (compare Mt 26:31). Although some of his followers are there, they eventually all return home.

16:33 peace Jesus wants his disciples to understand that they can be at peace when he suffers and dies. It is the Spirit's ongoing work to grant peace to believers (see note on Jn 14:27). **overcome the world** Jesus has overcome the powers of darkness (1:5) through his death and resurrection. He proclaims this now because he has already healed people and driven out demons, proving he is able to overpower what people consider unmovable forces. Jesus makes this claim as though it has already happened because he is confident in his prophetic proclamation that he will rise again after suffering and dying for the sins of God's people.

17:1–26 Jesus' prayer in this chapter is intimately linked with the themes and language of his teaching in the Gospel of John to this point. The prayer also serves as a summary of the major themes and underlying message of the Gospel leading up to the final climactic event of the passion of the Christ. Throughout chs. 14–16, Jesus foreshadowed his imminent return to the Father through death and suffering. That time is now at hand. He continues to exemplify obedience to the Father, following the inevitable path to his glorification through crucifixion. See the event line "Jesus' Passion and Resurrection" on p. 1698.

17:1 Glorify your Son See note on 13:31.
17:2 authority over all people Jesus has performed miracles and exorcisms, and he even demonstrated his power to raise someone from the dead. God also created the world through him, which means that he is the ruler of it (1:1–3). Adam and Eve were supposed to have authority over the earth, acting as the heirs and stewards of God's work to bring order to chaos (see note on Ge 1:28). Since they failed by sinning, God needed to send his only Son to carry out this work. Only someone united with God—as

Adam and Eve were before their sin—has the ability to righteously rule over the earth as steward (Ge 3:8; Ro 5:12–21; 1Co 15:22,45). Since God's Son was the means of the creation work to begin with and is sinless, he is the only choice for this task. But in order to hand this authority back to humanity, Jesus must deal with the problem that kept them from carrying out this task: sin. In order for their sin to be removed, God's Son, who is the means of creation and the sinless one, must die. This creates a direct connection between humanity and God again, and they are able to bear God's image once more (see note on Ge 1:27; compare 1Co 15:49; Col 1:15; 3:10). **give eternal life** Occurs through his death and resurrection (compare note on Isa 53:10). See note on Jn 1:4.

17:4 the work Jesus taught the disciples God's plan for salvation, what it means to believe in him, God's plan for eternal life and how to proclaim the message of salvation. Jesus is also saying that none of his disciples have been lost outside of the one whom God knew from the beginning would be lost (Judas; see note on v. 12). Jesus may also be making a claim about his future suffering and death; he is so confident that this work will occur that he can proclaim it as being in the past, as finished (compare Isa 53:1,12).

17:5 glory I had with you Describes a position of power. Jesus is asking God the Father to raise him to the same position he had before entering the world (compare Jn 1:1–4; note on Isa 53:12). **before the world began** See note on Jn 1:1.

17:6 I have revealed you Throughout his ministry, Jesus has made the Father known (1:18; 5:43; 14:6–9; 17:26). **to those whom you gave me** Refers to those who came to Jesus to hear his message of salvation.

17:11 I will remain in the world no longer Jesus seems to be anticipating the state of affairs after his ascension, when the disciples are carrying on his earthly ministry. The term "world" could refer to those who oppose Jesus (see note on 16:20; compare note on 16:33). If this is the case, Jesus means that he will no longer dialogue with those who oppose him. From this point forward, Jesus' answers to his oppressors are minimal and straightforward; he speaks plainly (e.g.,

name you gave me. None has been lost except the one doomed to destruction so that Scripture would be fulfilled.

¹³"I am coming to you now, but I say these things while I am still in the world, so that they may have the full measure of my joy within them. ¹⁴I have given them your word and the world has hated them, for they are not of the world any more than I am of the world. ¹⁵My prayer is not that you take them out of the world but that you protect them from the evil one. ¹⁶They are not of the world, even as I am not of it. ¹⁷Sanctify them by[a] the truth; your word is truth. ¹⁸As you sent me into the world, I have sent them into the world. ¹⁹For them I sanctify myself, that they too may be truly sanctified.

Jesus Prays for All Believers

²⁰"My prayer is not for them alone. I pray also for those who will believe in me through their message, ²¹that all of them may be one, Father, just as you are in me and I am in you. May they also be in us so that the world may believe that you have sent me. ²²I have given them the glory that you gave me, that they may be one as we are one — ²³I in them and you in me — so that they may be brought to complete unity. Then the world will know that you sent me and have loved them even as you have loved me.

²⁴"Father, I want those you have given me to be with me where I am, and to see my glory, the glory you have given me because you loved me before the creation of the world. ²⁵"Righteous Father, though the world does not know you, I know you, and they know that you have sent me. ²⁶I have made you[b] known to them, and will continue to make you known in order that the love you have for me may be in them and that I myself may be in them."

Jesus Arrested

18:3-11pp — Mt 26:47-56; Mk 14:43-50; Lk 22:47-53

18 When he had finished praying, Jesus left with his disciples and crossed the Kidron Valley. On the other side there was a garden, and he and his disciples went into it.

²Now Judas, who betrayed him, knew the place, because Jesus had often met there with his disciples. ³So Judas came to the garden, guiding a detachment of soldiers and some officials from the chief priests and the Pharisees. They were carrying torches, lanterns and weapons.

⁴Jesus, knowing all that was going to happen to him, went out and asked them, "Who is it you want?"

⁵"Jesus of Nazareth," they replied.

"I am he," Jesus said. (And Judas the traitor was standing there with them.) ⁶When Jesus said, "I am he," they drew back and fell to the ground.

⁷Again he asked them, "Who is it you want?"

"Jesus of Nazareth," they said.

⁸Jesus answered, "I told you that I am he. If you are looking for me, then let these men go." ⁹This happened so that the words he had spoken would be fulfilled: "I have not lost one of those you gave me."[c]

¹⁰Then Simon Peter, who had a sword, drew it and struck the high priest's servant, cutting off his right ear. (The servant's name was Malchus.)

¹¹Jesus commanded Peter, "Put your sword away! Shall I not drink the cup the Father has given me?"

¹²Then the detachment of soldiers with its commander and the Jewish officials arrested Jesus. They bound him ¹³and brought him first to Annas, who was the father-in-law of Caiaphas, the high priest that year. ¹⁴Caiaphas was the one who had advised the Jewish leaders that it would be good if one man died for the people.

---

[a] 17 Or *them to live in accordance with*   [b] 26 Greek *your name*   [c] 9 John 6:39

16:25). He will go to his death in the same way as the suffering servant—silently (Isa 53:7). **I am coming to you** Jesus will come to God's heavenly abode through his ascension (see note on Jn 14:2). **your name** God has given his authority to Jesus. This fits with the "I am" sayings used throughout the Gospel of John (see note on 13:13). **they may be one as we are one** Since believers are one with Jesus, and Jesus is one with God the Father, believers are one with God the Father. However, proximity to God's holiness requires a sacrifice for believers' sins—which takes place in Jesus' death. **17:12 I protected them and kept them safe by that name** Indicates that Jesus kept his disciples secure in their faith through divine authority and power. **one doomed to destruction** Refers to Judas (see note on 13:2; note on 13:27).
17:15 evil one A general term referring to a malicious figure. In some contexts, it can refer to the devil specifically (see note on 13:2; note on 13:27).

17:17 Sanctify Refers to God's ongoing work to set his people apart for his purposes—to make them holy as he is holy (see note on 1Th 4:3). The Spirit is the one who prompts and tends to this work (see note on Jn 14:26).
17:24 before the creation of the world See note on 1:1 (compare note on Ge 7:19).
18:1 Kidron Jesus went through the valley that separated the walled city of Jerusalem from the Mount of Olives (see note on Mk 14:32).
18:3 detachment of soldiers and some officials The chief priests had their own military guard of Jewish males who acted as temple police. **chief priests** See note on Mk 11:18 (compare note on Mt 2:4). **Pharisees** See note on Jn 7:32.
18:9 I have not lost one See note on 17:4 and note on 17:6.
18:10 Simon Peter See note on Mt 10:2 and note on Jn 1:42.
18:13 Annas The former high priest. See note on Lk 3:2.

Peter's First Denial

18:16-18pp — Mt 26:69,70; Mk 14:66-68; Lk 22:55-57

¹⁵Simon Peter and another disciple were following Jesus. Because this disciple was known to the high priest, he went with Jesus into the high priest's courtyard, ¹⁶but Peter had to wait outside at the door. The other disciple, who was known to the high priest, came back, spoke to the servant girl on duty there and brought Peter in.

¹⁷"You aren't one of this man's disciples too, are you?" she asked Peter.

He replied, "I am not."

¹⁸It was cold, and the servants and officials stood around a fire they had made to keep warm. Peter also was standing with them, warming himself.

The High Priest Questions Jesus

18:19-24pp — Mt 26:59-68; Mk 14:55-65; Lk 22:63-71

¹⁹Meanwhile, the high priest questioned Jesus about his disciples and his teaching.

²⁰"I have spoken openly to the world," Jesus replied. "I always taught in synagogues or at the temple, where all the Jews come together. I said nothing in secret. ²¹Why question me? Ask those who heard me. Surely they know what I said."

²²When Jesus said this, one of the officials nearby slapped him in the face. "Is this the way you answer the high priest?" he demanded.

²³"If I said something wrong," Jesus replied, "testify as to what is wrong. But if I spoke the truth, why did you strike me?" ²⁴Then Annas sent him bound to Caiaphas the high priest.

Peter's Second and Third Denials

18:25-27pp — Mt 26:71-75; Mk 14:69-72; Lk 22:58-62

²⁵Meanwhile, Simon Peter was still standing there warming himself. So they asked him, "You aren't one of his disciples too, are you?"

He denied it, saying, "I am not."

²⁶One of the high priest's servants, a relative of the man whose ear Peter had cut off, challenged him, "Didn't I see you with him in the garden?" ²⁷Again Peter denied it, and at that moment a rooster began to crow.

Jesus Before Pilate

18:29-40pp — Mt 27:11-18,20-23; Mk 15:2-15; Lk 23:2,3,18-25

²⁸Then the Jewish leaders took Jesus from Caiaphas to the palace of the Roman governor. By now it was early morning, and to avoid ceremonial uncleanness they did not enter the palace, because they wanted to be able to eat the Passover. ²⁹So Pilate came out to them and asked, "What charges are you bringing against this man?"

³⁰"If he were not a criminal," they replied, "we would not have handed him over to you."

³¹Pilate said, "Take him yourselves and judge him by your own law."

"But we have no right to execute anyone," they objected. ³²This took place to fulfill what Jesus had said about the kind of death he was going to die.

³³Pilate then went back inside the palace, summoned Jesus and asked him, "Are you the king of the Jews?"

³⁴"Is that your own idea," Jesus asked, "or did others talk to you about me?"

Caiaphas The acting high priest in charge of the Jerusalem temple; leader of the Sadducees (see note on Mt 26:3; compare note on Jn 11:50). See the table "Political Leaders in the New Testament" on p. 1916.

18:19 the high priest questioned Jesus Rome largely permitted the Jewish people to hold trials according to their own laws.

18:20 synagogues See note on Mt 4:23.

18:28 took Jesus from Caiaphas The narrative does not report anything from Jesus' appearance before Caiaphas (perhaps because the author did not have access to anyone who witnessed it). **palace of the Roman governor** Probably the former palace of Herod the Great at the western edge of Jerusalem. Although Caesarea was the Roman Empire's regional base, the governor of Judea typically spent Jewish high feast days in Jerusalem because of the potential for civil unrest (compare Ac 23:33-35). **avoid ceremonial uncleanness** According to the Jewish law, being defiled would have prevented people from entering the temple to make the sacrifices required for the Passover meal. It also would have prevented them from celebrating the meal with other Jews, who would have been concerned about becoming defiled from being in their presence. Jews who followed the regulations of the Pharisees (and some Sadducees) believed that even being in the presence of a non-Jewish person could make them unclean, because Gentiles did not abide by their same regulations. The governor's residence may have been associated with defilement also because unclean food was prepared and consumed there. See note on Ac 21:24. **eat the Passover** According to the Synoptic Gospels, Jesus' last supper with his disciples was a Passover meal (Mt 26:17-19; Mk 14:12-16; Lk 22:7-13). This meal, then, would be another of the meals eaten during the Festival of Unleavened Bread (which also was called Passover; Lk 22:1).

18:29 Pilate Roman governor of Judea from AD 26 to 36.

18:31 no right Because the Romans did not allow the Jews to carry out executions, the Jewish leaders bring Jesus to Pilate (who did have such authority).

18:32 fulfill what Jesus had said Refers to Jesus' earlier statement alluding to his crucifixion (Jn 12:32-33; compare Mt 20:19). In seeking Jesus' death sentence from Pilate, the Jewish officials tacitly accept the Roman form of execution—leading to the fulfillment of Jesus' words.

18:33 king of the Jews The Jewish officials wished to execute Jesus primarily because he claimed to be the Son of God (Jn 10:36) and the Christ (or Messiah; 10:24)—titles that evoked ideas about King David and God's anointed deliverer. Jesus was making claims to the throne (see note on Mt 2:2).

³⁵"Am I a Jew?" Pilate replied. "Your own people and chief priests handed you over to me. What is it you have done?"

³⁶Jesus said, "My kingdom is not of this world. If it were, my servants would fight to prevent my arrest by the Jewish leaders. But now my kingdom is from another place."

³⁷"You are a king, then!" said Pilate.

Jesus answered, "You say that I am a king. In fact, the reason I was born and came into the world is to testify to the truth. Everyone on the side of truth listens to me."

³⁸"What is truth?" retorted Pilate. With this he went out again to the Jews gathered there and said, "I find no basis for a charge against him. ³⁹But it is your custom for me to release to you one prisoner at the time of the Passover. Do you want me to release 'the king of the Jews'?"

⁴⁰They shouted back, "No, not him! Give us Barabbas!" Now Barabbas had taken part in an uprising.

Jesus Sentenced to Be Crucified

19:1-16pp — Mt 27:27-31; Mk 15:16-20

19 Then Pilate took Jesus and had him flogged. ²The soldiers twisted together a crown of thorns and put it on his head. They clothed him in a purple robe ³and went up to him again and again, saying, "Hail, king of the Jews!" And they slapped him in the face.

⁴Once more Pilate came out and said to the Jews gathered there, "Look, I am bringing him out to you to let you know that I find no basis for a charge against him." ⁵When Jesus came out wearing the crown of thorns and the purple robe, Pilate said to them, "Here is the man!"

⁶As soon as the chief priests and their officials saw him, they shouted, "Crucify! Crucify!"

But Pilate answered, "You take him and crucify him. As for me, I find no basis for a charge against him."

⁷The Jewish leaders insisted, "We have a law, and according to that law he must die, because he claimed to be the Son of God."

⁸When Pilate heard this, he was even more afraid, ⁹and he went back inside the palace. "Where do you come from?" he asked Jesus, but Jesus gave him no answer. ¹⁰"Do you refuse to speak to me?" Pilate said. "Don't you realize I have power either to free you or to crucify you?"

¹¹Jesus answered, "You would have no power over me if it were not given to you from above. Therefore the one who handed me over to you is guilty of a greater sin."

¹²From then on, Pilate tried to set Jesus free, but the Jewish leaders kept shouting, "If you let this man go, you are no friend of Caesar. Anyone who claims to be a king opposes Caesar."

¹³When Pilate heard this, he brought Jesus out and sat down on the judge's seat at a place known

---

18:36 not of this world Rather than trying to rule the world as it is (Jn 1:1–4), Jesus is turning it into a new world; he is connecting the kingdom of God to earth. See note on Ac 1:3.
18:37 reason I was born Jesus acknowledges that his ultimate purpose in life is to die for the people's sins. This fulfills his role as suffering servant, which John acknowledges throughout the Gospel (see note on Jn 12:41).
18:39 your custom Pilate invokes this custom to emphasize that the decision belongs to the Jewish rulers and the other Jews present, not himself. The practice of releasing a prisoner for Passover must have been negotiated between Rome and the Jewish people. There is no OT law supporting it, and no ancient sources explicitly document it.
18:40 in an uprising Mark and Luke indicate that Barabbas had killed someone during a rebellion (Mk 15:7; Lk 23:19). See the table "Major Groups in Jesus' Time" on p. 1630.

19:1–16 Even though he is certain that Jesus is innocent, Pilate sentences him to be crucified at the insistence of the crowd, fearing an uprising if he does not. See the event line "Jesus' Passion and Resurrection" on p. 1698.
19:1 flogged See note on Mt 20:19. The Greek verbs used for the punishment may allude to the Septuagint of Isa 50:6, which refers to the physical punishment of the suffering servant. The Romans used three forms of flogging with increasing levels of severity: *fustigatio*, *flagellatio*, and *verberatio*. The first flogging prior to sentencing was likely the least severe form; it was usually reserved for small offenses and accompanied by a stern reprimand. The most severe flogging probably followed the sentenc-

ing in Jn 19:16. This third form (the *verberatio*) always accompanied more severe punishments, like crucifixion.
19:2 crown of thorns An instrument of mockery and, likely, torture. **purple robe** The soldiers use this symbol of royalty to mock Jesus, because the religious leaders asserted that he claimed to be "king of the Jews" (18:33).
19:5 Here is the man Pilate may be ironically pointing out the weakness of Jesus; he hardly appears to be a king at this moment. John's audience, however, knew the truth.
19:7 law Refers to Lev 24:16. In Jn 10:33, Jesus' Jewish opponents wanted to kill him because he made claims they regarded as blasphemous (compare 5:18). **Son of God** The Jews believed that Jesus, by professing to be the Son of God, was claiming to be God's chosen king, his representative on earth. Pilate would have understood this claim in relation to Caesar being called "son of god" — that is, as a claim to be king of the whole earth, to be god-like, and to have ultimate authority. See note on 10:36.
19:8 he was even more afraid Pilate's worst fear would have been a Jewish uprising against Roman rule — a potential result of a revolutionary claiming to be the rightful king.
19:11 given to you from above Jesus claims that all authority comes from God. Since Jesus is one with the Father, he also is claiming that Pilate's authority is from him (1:1–4; see note on 17:2).
19:12 no friend of Caesar The Jewish authorities knew that this accusation would prompt Pilate to sentence Jesus to death. Although the Jews oppose Jesus' release on grounds that he is trying to be king over Caesar, it is Barabbas who actually has fought against Rome's authority (see 18:40 and note).
19:13 the Stone Pavement The place from which Pilate issued public decrees. It likely was an elevated

as the Stone Pavement (which in Aramaic is Gabbatha). [14]It was the day of Preparation of the Passover; it was about noon.

"Here is your king," Pilate said to the Jews.

[15]But they shouted, "Take him away! Take him away! Crucify him!"

"Shall I crucify your king?" Pilate asked.

"We have no king but Caesar," the chief priests answered.

[16]Finally Pilate handed him over to them to be crucified.

The Crucifixion of Jesus

19:17-24pp — Mt 27:33-44; Mk 15:22-32; Lk 23:33-43

So the soldiers took charge of Jesus. [17]Carrying his own cross, he went out to the place of the Skull (which in Aramaic is called Golgotha). [18]There they crucified him, and with him two others — one on each side and Jesus in the middle.

[19]Pilate had a notice prepared and fastened to the cross. It read: JESUS OF NAZARETH, THE KING OF THE JEWS. [20]Many of the Jews read this sign, for the place where Jesus was crucified was near the city, and the sign was written in Aramaic, Latin and Greek. [21]The chief priests of the Jews protested to Pilate, "Do not write 'The King of the Jews,' but that this man claimed to be king of the Jews."

[22]Pilate answered, "What I have written, I have written."

[23]When the soldiers crucified Jesus, they took his clothes, dividing them into four shares, one for each of them, with the undergarment remaining. This garment was seamless, woven in one piece from top to bottom.

[24]"Let's not tear it," they said to one another. "Let's decide by lot who will get it."

This happened that the scripture might be fulfilled that said,

"They divided my clothes among them
    and cast lots for my garment."[a]

So this is what the soldiers did.

[25]Near the cross of Jesus stood his mother, his mother's sister, Mary the wife of Clopas, and Mary Magdalene. [26]When Jesus saw his mother there, and the disciple whom he loved standing nearby, he said to her, "Woman,[b] here is your son," [27]and to the disciple, "Here is your mother." From that time on, this disciple took her into his home.

The Death of Jesus

19:29,30pp — Mt 27:48,50; Mk 15:36,37; Lk 23:36

[28]Later, knowing that everything had now been finished, and so that Scripture would be fulfilled, Jesus said, "I am thirsty." [29]A jar of wine vinegar was there, so they soaked a sponge in it, put the sponge on a stalk of the hyssop plant, and lifted it to Jesus' lips. [30]When he had received the drink, Jesus said, "It is finished." With that, he bowed his head and gave up his spirit.

[31]Now it was the day of Preparation, and the next day was to be a special Sabbath. Because the Jewish leaders did not want the bodies left on the crosses during the Sabbath, they asked Pilate to have the legs broken and the bodies

a 24 Psalm 22:18   *b 26* The Greek for *Woman* does not denote any disrespect.

---

platform connected to the governor's residence. See the infographic "A Judgment Seat in Jerusalem" on p. 1761.
19:14 day of Preparation Friday, the day before the Sabbath of Passover week. **noon** According to Mark, Jesus was crucified at the third hour (9 a.m.; Mk 15:25,33).
19:17 place of the Skull See note on Mk 15:22 and note on Mt 27:33.
19:20 Aramaic The majority of Judeans would have understood this language. See note on Jn 5:2. **Latin** The official language across the Roman Empire. Government documents, well-educated people, and the Roman military and guard used Latin. **Greek** The common language of commerce and writing used in the eastern part of the Roman Empire.
19:25 Mary the wife of Clopas Nothing is known of this Mary outside of this passage. The Greek term translated "wife" allows for the interpretation that she is either Clopas' wife or mother. Nothing more is known of Clopas. **Mary Magdalene** Jesus exorcised seven demons from Mary (Lk 8:2). "Magdalene" likely derives from the name of the place she was from.
19:26 disciple whom he loved Likely refers to John. See note on Jn 13:23.
19:27 Here is your mother Suggests that Mary had been following her son during (at least) this portion of his ministry and was relying on him and his disciples for support. Because men usually married much younger

women (about 15 years younger, on average), Joseph probably had passed away already — especially since he is not present in any Gospel after the visit to Jerusalem when Jesus was 12 (Lk 2:41–51). Even if Joseph were alive, his age would have inhibited him from caring for Mary, which explains why Jesus asks John to take care of her. Women without husbands or male support were rendered impoverished because they could not earn enough wages to buy food and could not own property.
19:29 wine vinegar This indicates a cheap wine and might allude to Ps 69:21. Compare Mk 15:36. **on a stalk of the hyssop plant** Used by Jews to smear the blood of their Passover lamb over their doorposts. This would deter the angel of destruction from taking their firstborn (Ex 12:22). This is symbolic of Jesus' role as the Passover Lamb: God will pass over people's sins because Jesus' blood is present. As a sacrifice, he carried the weight of their sins in his death (fulfilling Isa 53:6–7,10–12).
19:30 It is finished Jesus knows that God's plan for him has reached its completion — he has done what he came to earth to do (compare Jn 17:4–5). This is likely a citation of Ps 22 (see note on Ps 22:31; note on Ps 22:30–31). Jesus is claiming that he is the ultimate sufferer for God's people.
19:31 day of Preparation See note on Jn 19:14. **Sabbath** The Jewish authorities are so calloused that they are more concerned with their religious day and their

taken down. ³²The soldiers therefore came and broke the legs of the first man who had been crucified with Jesus, and then those of the other. ³³But when they came to Jesus and found that he was already dead, they did not break his legs. ³⁴Instead, one of the soldiers pierced Jesus' side with a spear, bringing a sudden flow of blood and water. ³⁵The man who saw it has given testimony, and his testimony is true. He knows that he tells the truth, and he testifies so that you also may believe. ³⁶These things happened so that the scripture would be fulfilled: "Not one of his bones will be broken,"[a] ³⁷and, as another scripture says, "They will look on the one they have pierced."[b]

[a] 36 Exodus 12:46; Num. 9:12; Psalm 34:20   [b] 37 Zech. 12:10

place in the celebrations and remembrances than they are about Jesus' unwarranted death (see 12:42–43). **the legs broken** Crucifixion was an intentionally long and painful death. When people were crucified, their feet and hands would be nailed to the cross. With the rib cage and lungs stretched out, people would need to put weight on their legs to lift themselves up and make it easier to breathe. If someone stayed alive for what was deemed too long on a cross, executioners would break their legs. **19:33 did not break his legs** Like the Passover lamb, none of Jesus' bones are broken (Ex 12:46; see note on Jn 1:29; note on v. 29). **19:34 pierced Jesus' side with a spear** Fulfills the prophecy in Zec 12:10, which parallels Jesus' role as the suffering servant via the connection in Zec 3:8–9 (see Isa 11:1–12 and note; Zec 3:8–9 and note; Isa 53:1 and note; compare Jn 12:38). **bringing a sudden flow of blood and water** In including this detail, John may be emphasizing that Jesus was truly human (1:14) or that life and cleansing power come from the blood of Jesus (6:53–56; 7:38–39).

A Judgment Seat in Jerusalem

Pilate held Jesus' trial at a judgment seat, which John reports was located at Gabbatha, or "the Stone Pavement" (Jn 19:13; Mt 27:19). The judgment seat was likely part of the massive architectural base Herod the Great constructed as the foundation for his palace. During Roman control of Jerusalem, the Herodian palace was used as the Praetorium—where Pilate lived.

Paul, who stood before a judgment seat in Corinth (Ac 18:12-17), used the image of the judgment seat in his letters (Ro 14:10; 2Co 5:10).

The benches used by modern judges descend from the larger benches of the ancient world. In Jesus' day, judgment seats were elevated to allow the magistrate to be seen and heard. They were also defensive structures, keeping important officials above the crowd in case of riots.

The Burial of Jesus

19:38-42pp — Mt 27:57-61; Mk 15:42-47; Lk 23:50-56

³⁸Later, Joseph of Arimathea asked Pilate for the body of Jesus. Now Joseph was a disciple of Jesus, but secretly because he feared the Jewish leaders. With Pilate's permission, he came and took the body away. ³⁹He was accompanied by Nicodemus, the man who earlier had visited Jesus at night. Nicodemus brought a mixture of myrrh and aloes, about seventy-five pounds.ᵃ ⁴⁰Taking Jesus' body, the two of them wrapped it, with the spices, in strips of linen. This was in accordance with Jewish burial customs. ⁴¹At the place where Jesus was crucified, there was a garden, and in the garden a new tomb, in which no one had ever been laid. ⁴²Because it was the Jewish day of Preparation and since the tomb was nearby, they laid Jesus there.

The Empty Tomb

20:1-8pp — Mt 28:1-8; Mk 16:1-8; Lk 24:1-10

20 Early on the first day of the week, while it was still dark, Mary Magdalene went to the tomb and saw that the stone had been removed from the entrance. ²So she came running to Simon Peter and the other disciple, the one Jesus loved, and said, "They have taken the Lord out of the tomb, and we don't know where they have put him!"

³So Peter and the other disciple started for the tomb. ⁴Both were running, but the other disciple outran Peter and reached the tomb first. ⁵He bent over and looked in at the strips of linen lying there but did not go in. ⁶Then Simon Peter came along behind him and went straight into the tomb. He saw the strips of linen lying there, ⁷as well as the cloth that had been wrapped around Jesus' head. The cloth was still lying in its place, separate from the linen. ⁸Finally the other disciple, who had reached the tomb first, also went inside. He saw and believed. ⁹(They still did not understand from Scripture that Jesus had to rise from the dead.) ¹⁰Then the disciples went back to where they were staying.

Jesus Appears to Mary Magdalene

¹¹Now Mary stood outside the tomb crying. As she wept, she bent over to look into the tomb ¹²and saw two angels in white, seated where Jesus' body had been, one at the head and the other at the foot.

¹³They asked her, "Woman, why are you crying?"

"They have taken my Lord away," she said, "and I don't know where they have put him." ¹⁴At this, she turned around and saw Jesus standing there, but she did not realize that it was Jesus.

¹⁵He asked her, "Woman, why are you crying? Who is it you are looking for?"

Thinking he was the gardener, she said, "Sir, if you have carried him away, tell me where you have put him, and I will get him."

¹⁶Jesus said to her, "Mary."

She turned toward him and cried out in Aramaic, "Rabboni!" (which means "Teacher").

¹⁷Jesus said, "Do not hold on to me, for I have not yet ascended to the Father. Go instead to my brothers and tell them, 'I am ascending to my Father and your Father, to my God and your God.'"

¹⁸Mary Magdalene went to the disciples with the news: "I have seen the Lord!" And she told them that he had said these things to her.

Jesus Appears to His Disciples

¹⁹On the evening of that first day of the week, when the disciples were together, with the doors locked for fear of the Jewish leaders, Jesus came

---

ᵃ 39 Or about 34 kilograms

19:38 Joseph See note on Lk 23:50–56.

19:39 mixture of myrrh and aloes May have been used to embalm his body and linen shroud. The myrrh was likely imported from Arabia, and it may have been tapped from trees and used in a powdered form (see note on Mk 15:23; note on Pr 7:17). Matthew reports that the Magi brought myrrh as a gift for the infant Jesus, marking the beginning of his life (Mt 2:11); now, myrrh marks his death.

19:40 spices Spices were meant to reduce the smell of decay. This was an expensive burial ritual (compare note on Jn 12:3).

19:41 a new tomb This fulfills the prophecy that the suffering servant would be rich in his death (Isa 53:9). Only wealthy people had tombs, and only the very wealthiest people had new tombs.

20:1–31 This chapter reports Jesus' resurrection and his post-resurrection appearances to his followers. In general, John's account mirrors the major points of the resurrection narrative as described in Matthew, Mark and Luke.

RESURRECTION APPEARANCES IN JOHN'S GOSPEL	
Appearance to Mary Magdalene	Jn 20:11–18
Appearance to the disciples without Thomas	Jn 20:19–24
Appearance to the disciples including Thomas	Jn 20:26–29
Appearance at the Sea of Galilee	Jn 21:1–24

20:9 Scripture Refers to Ps 16:10 or Isa 53:10 or both. See the table "Jesus' Fulfillment of OT Prophecy" on p. 1573.

20:12 two angels in white Messengers of God. Angels in Scripture typically wear white, which symbolizes holiness (see note on Mk 16:5; note on Ac 1:10; note on Da 7:9). See the table "Angels in the Bible" on p. 2120.

20:14 she did not realize that it was Jesus Mary might not have recognized Jesus because his resurrected form was somehow different from his previous physical form (compare Lk 24:16; Jn 21:4). It also might have been too dark to see clearly (v. 1). See the table "Resurrection Appearances of Jesus" on p. 1896.

and stood among them and said, "Peace be with you!" 20After he said this, he showed them his hands and side. The disciples were overjoyed when they saw the Lord.

21Again Jesus said, "Peace be with you! As the Father has sent me, I am sending you." 22And with that he breathed on them and said, "Receive the Holy Spirit. 23If you forgive anyone's sins, their sins are forgiven; if you do not forgive them, they are not forgiven."

Jesus Appears to Thomas

24Now Thomas (also known as Didymus[a]), one of the Twelve, was not with the disciples when Jesus came. 25So the other disciples told him, "We have seen the Lord!"

But he said to them, "Unless I see the nail marks in his hands and put my finger where the nails were, and put my hand into his side, I will not believe."

26A week later his disciples were in the house again, and Thomas was with them. Though the doors were locked, Jesus came and stood among them and said, "Peace be with you!" 27Then he said to Thomas, "Put your finger here; see my hands. Reach out your hand and put it into my side. Stop doubting and believe."

28Thomas said to him, "My Lord and my God!"

29Then Jesus told him, "Because you have seen me, you have believed; blessed are those who have not seen and yet have believed."

The Purpose of John's Gospel

30Jesus performed many other signs in the presence of his disciples, which are not recorded in this book. 31But these are written that you may believe[b] that Jesus is the Messiah, the Son of God, and that by believing you may have life in his name.

Jesus and the Miraculous Catch of Fish

21 Afterward Jesus appeared again to his disciples, by the Sea of Galilee.[c] It happened this way: 2Simon Peter, Thomas (also known as Didymus[a]), Nathanael from Cana in Galilee, the sons of Zebedee, and two other disciples were together. 3"I'm going out to fish," Simon Peter told them, and they said, "We'll go with you." So they went out and got into the boat, but that night they caught nothing.

4Early in the morning, Jesus stood on the shore, but the disciples did not realize that it was Jesus.

5He called out to them, "Friends, haven't you any fish?"

"No," they answered.

6He said, "Throw your net on the right side of the boat and you will find some." When they did, they were unable to haul the net in because of the large number of fish.

7Then the disciple whom Jesus loved said to Peter, "It is the Lord!" As soon as Simon Peter heard him say, "It is the Lord," he wrapped his outer garment around him (for he had taken it off) and jumped into the water. 8The other disciples followed in the boat, towing the net full of fish, for they were not far from shore, about a hundred yards.[d] 9When they landed, they saw a fire of burning coals there with fish on it, and some bread.

10Jesus said to them, "Bring some of the fish you have just caught." 11So Simon Peter climbed back into the boat and dragged the net ashore. It was full of large fish, 153, but even with so many the net was not torn. 12Jesus said to them, "Come and have breakfast." None of the disciples dared ask him, "Who are you?" They knew it was the

---

a 24,2 Thomas (Aramaic) and Didymus (Greek) both mean twin.
b 31 Or may continue to believe   c 1 Greek Tiberias
d 8 Or about 90 meters

20:20 they saw the Lord In his farewell discourse, Jesus had taught his disciples that his resurrection was coming after his death (13:31—16:33).

20:22 he breathed After the disciples affirm that Jesus is God, he breathes on them, as God had breathed life into Adam (Ge 2:7). In both Hebrew and Greek, the word for "breath" also is the word for "spirit." **Receive the Holy Spirit** Jesus had promised this prior to his death (Jn 14:16,26).

20:23 their sins are forgiven A reference to the Holy Spirit's work within people. The Holy Spirit is the one who forgives and uses believers to deliver his words and message, carrying out God's will. This fits with the Spirit's role as an advocate for sinners (see note on 14:26).

20:28 my God Thomas affirms what Jesus has been alluding to throughout the Gospel: Jesus is more than a teacher and a master—he is God (see note on 12:13).

20:29 who have not seen and yet have believed Refers to people—like John's audience, and believers today—who have not seen the resurrected Jesus with their own eyes (see note on 2:11; note on 14:11; compare 9:38).

20:31 that you may believe Presents the theme and purpose of John's Gospel. On the basis of the book's testimony, John calls for people to believe in Jesus—the world's King and Savior, as well as God's Son—and receive the eternal life that comes through his death and resurrection (3:16–17).

21:1–25 John ends his Gospel with an epilogue in which Jesus appears again to his disciples in Galilee and offers encouragement to them, charging Peter to care for his followers. See the table "Resurrection Appearances of Jesus" on p. 1896.

21:3 I'm going out to fish Peter returns to his original occupation. As a leader of the group, he leads the others to do the same (Mk 1:16–20).

21:7 disciple whom Jesus loved Likely refers to John the evangelist (the apostle). See note on Jn 13:23. **his outer garment** Peter may have been nude, or he may have been wearing an undergarment to work in (the Greek of this verse can mean either). In any case, Peter takes his outer robe with him so that he can go ashore clothed.

Lord. ¹³Jesus came, took the bread and gave it to them, and did the same with the fish. ¹⁴This was now the third time Jesus appeared to his disciples after he was raised from the dead.

Jesus Reinstates Peter

¹⁵When they had finished eating, Jesus said to Simon Peter, "Simon son of John, do you love me more than these?"

"Yes, Lord," he said, "you know that I love you."

Jesus said, "Feed my lambs."

¹⁶Again Jesus said, "Simon son of John, do you love me?"

He answered, "Yes, Lord, you know that I love you."

Jesus said, "Take care of my sheep."

¹⁷The third time he said to him, "Simon son of John, do you love me?"

Peter was hurt because Jesus asked him the third time, "Do you love me?" He said, "Lord, you know all things; you know that I love you."

Jesus said, "Feed my sheep. ¹⁸Very truly I tell you, when you were younger you dressed yourself and went where you wanted; but when you are old you will stretch out your hands, and someone else will dress you and lead you where you do not want to go." ¹⁹Jesus said this to indicate the kind of death by which Peter would glorify God. Then he said to him, "Follow me!"

²⁰Peter turned and saw that the disciple whom Jesus loved was following them. (This was the one who had leaned back against Jesus at the supper and had said, "Lord, who is going to betray you?") ²¹When Peter saw him, he asked, "Lord, what about him?"

²²Jesus answered, "If I want him to remain alive until I return, what is that to you? You must follow me." ²³Because of this, the rumor spread among the believers that this disciple would not die. But Jesus did not say that he would not die; he only said, "If I want him to remain alive until I return, what is that to you?"

²⁴This is the disciple who testifies to these things and who wrote them down. We know that his testimony is true.

²⁵Jesus did many other things as well. If every one of them were written down, I suppose that even the whole world would not have room for the books that would be written.

21:14 third time John is probably referring to the first two appearances mentioned in his Gospel (20:19–23,26–29).

21:15–19 Jesus reaffirms Peter's calling following his denial (18:15–27). Since Peter had denied three times that he knew Jesus, Jesus asks three times whether Peter loves him. In the Greek text, Jesus and Peter use different words for "love." Jesus uses the term *agapaō* the first two times, while Peter responds with *phileō* each time, which Jesus adopts the third time. Rather than emphasizing a difference in the depth of love expressed by the two words, they should be understood as synonyms. Both are used interchangeably in the Gospel of John (3:35; 5:20; 11:5,36). The Septuagint (the ancient Greek translation of the OT) also uses the two terms interchangeably (Ge 37:3–4; Pr 8:17). John uses three other word pairs interchangeably in this passage with no discernible difference in emphasis: *boskō* and *poimainō* ("feed" or "take care of"), *arnion* and *probaton* ("lamb" and "sheep"), and *oida* and *ginōskō* ("know"). See the event line "Jesus' Passion and Resurrection" on p. 1698.

21:15 than these Jesus may be asking Peter whether he loves him more than the other disciples do—forcing him to acknowledge his shortcomings as one who had denied Jesus (Jn 18:15–18,25–27). Jesus also could be asking Peter whether he loves him more than he loves his fellow disciples.

21:16 Take care Jesus instructs Peter to guide his people (compare 10:11–15).

21:17 hurt Peter seems to understand that Jesus' three questions parallel his three denials. **you know all things** Peter affirms what he and the other disciples had articulated after Jesus explained God's plans for salvation to them (chs. 14–16; see note on 16:30).

21:18 will dress you and lead you Jesus is referring to Peter's death. According to church tradition, he was crucified upside down in Rome roughly 30 years after Jesus' ministry (see note on 1Pe 5:1).

21:19 Follow me Jesus' central command since the beginning of his ministry (Jn 1:43).

21:21 what about him Peter likely is inquiring about John (see note on 13:23).

21:22 what is that to you Jesus tells Peter that he should not be concerned with God's will for others.

21:23 that he would not die Apparently, Jesus' saying caused confusion. John emphasizes that Jesus' statement was not a prediction, but rather a hypothetical scenario intended to instruct Peter.

21:24 This is the disciple Refers to author of this Gospel. See note on 13:23. **We know that his testimony is true** An editor may have written this postscript based on the eyewitness accounts of John. Alternatively, the use of "we" might refer to all the disciples who were present with Jesus. John also could be intentionally including his audience in this statement, to emphasize that they are a part of the account that goes on through the Holy Spirit's work in their lives.

21:25 many other things John acknowledges that the Gospels don't record everything that Jesus did. What they include was recorded to encourage belief in Jesus (see 20:31 and note).

THE ETERNAL WORD IN JOHN'S GOSPEL
by Douglas Mangum

In the Gospel of John, Jesus is cast as the Word (the *logos* in Greek). John's use of the concept of the Word conveys the ideas that Jesus is preexistent (Jn 1:1–2) and divine—one with God the Father, yet a distinct person.

The Greek term *logos*, as used in the Gospel of John, draws on a wide range of Jewish and Greek concepts, evoking associations with the Old Testament, Hellenistic Jewish literature and Greek philosophy. Using the title "the Word" for Jesus simultaneously evoked and subverted the assumptions of John's Jewish and Greek audiences. His use of the term was a deliberate attempt to persuade them of the divinity of Jesus using categories of thought they would have found familiar.

For Jews, John's use of *logos* would have evoked the phrase "the word of Yahweh." This title was an important part of Biblical traditions about Yahweh and his effective power over the universe. The phrase was regularly used to refer to Scripture as divine law (Isa 2:3), written instruction (Ps 119:11) and prophetic revelation (Hos 4:1; Eze 6:1). More important, the "word of Yahweh" was depicted as an active force at work in the world to accomplish his will (Isa 55:11; Jer 23:29). This force was the agent through which Yahweh created the world (Ps 33:6,9; Ge 1:3,6,11).

A Jewish audience in the first century AD would also likely have accepted "the Word" as a divine title based on the regular substitution of *memra* (Aramaic for "the Word") for the divine name in Aramaic translations of the Old Testament, also called Targumim. The Aramaic translators used this title to avoid instances where Yahweh was described in human terms (i.e., with an arm or hand). This tradition connected "the Word" with creation even more: The Targum for Isaiah 48:13a reads, "By my word I have founded the earth" (replacing "my hand" in the Hebrew text with *memra*).

For Greeks, the idea of "the Word" as God's active agent on earth would have resonated with the Greek notion that the Logos was the stabilizing principle of the universe. In Greek, *logos* can mean reason or rational thought; in Greek philosophy, *logos* referred to the ordering principle behind the universe, the all-pervasive creative energy at the source of all things. The philosopher Heraclitus (sixth century BC) declared this principle always existed and was responsible for all things. The Logos was ultimate reality, the ever-present wisdom organizing the universe. The Stoic philosophers developed this idea further in the third century BC, envisioning the Logos as the rational principle of the universe that made everything understandable. The Logos was the impersonal power that originated, permeated and directed everything.

John's usage combines Jewish and Greek concepts about the universe and ultimate reality. His use of the term *logos* does not appear to be indebted solely to Greek philosophy; his presentation of the Logos as a personal creator involved in his creation and incarnated in the person of Jesus completely subverted the philosophical idea of the Logos as an impersonal force. A Greek audience would have recognized the concept as important, even if they did not fully understand John's use of the idea. In a similar way to John, the first-century AD Jewish philosopher Philo of Alexandria also explicitly combined these two worlds of thought, describing the Logos as the rationality of the mind of God and the template for the divine ordering of creation.

John's assignment of "the Word" to the role of the active agent in creation (Jn 1:3) connects with the Biblical picture of creation through the divine word (Ge 1:3; Ps 33:6) and through divine wisdom (Pr 3:19; 8:22–31). Proverbs 3:19 describes "wisdom" as Yahweh's agent in creation. Wisdom is regularly personified in Proverbs 1–9 and takes an active role in creation in Proverbs 8. Just like divine wisdom, "the Word" was also life-giving (compare Pr 3:18 and Jn 1:4).

Creation is the central concept of the message of John's Gospel. Both the Jewish and the Greek associations of "the Word" find their ultimate meaning in creation. The Greeks were searching for knowledge, for a way to understand the impersonal principle bringing order to the universe. John proclaims that the one who gives order to creation is personal and divine. For the Jews, the connection between "the Word" and creation was natural since the role of Creator inherently belongs to God. But neither the Jews nor the Greeks would have expected John's conclusion. He took a familiar concept, rich with meaning, and gave it a surprising twist. "The Word" was God, not an impersonal force, not just a tool God used to accomplish his purpose. "The Word" was personal. "The Word" was God, and God came in human form as Jesus (Jn 1:14).

John puts it all together: Jesus is none other than God's creative, life-giving, light-giving Word. Jesus, the *logos*, who has come to earth in the flesh, is the power of God that created the world and the reason of God that sustains the world.

ACTS

INTRODUCTION TO ACTS

The book of Acts (also called Acts of the Apostles) begins where the Gospel of Luke left off. Before ascending into heaven, Jesus commissions his disciples to be his witnesses from Jerusalem to the end of the Earth (Ac 1:8). In fulfillment of this command, and through the power of the Holy Spirit, the early church expands. Acts shows what it means to be part of Jesus' mission to the world. The apostles set the example of what it means to be fully devoted to Christ and enveloped by the Holy Spirit.

BACKGROUND

According to early church tradition, the author of Acts is Luke the physician, who traveled with the apostle Paul (Col 4:14; 2Ti 4:11; Phm 24). The Gospel of Luke is also ascribed to him; this makes Acts his second volume about the story of early Christianity (Ac 1:1; see the "Introduction to Luke"). Four passages in Acts seem to indicate that the narrator is a firsthand witness of particular events he describes (Ac 16:10–17; 20:5–15; 21:1–18; 27:1–28:16)—which is fitting with Luke being the author.

Like the Gospel of Luke, the book of Acts is addressed to Theophilus, who might have provided financial support for Luke to write both books (Lk 1:3; Ac 1:1). Luke's broader audience appears to

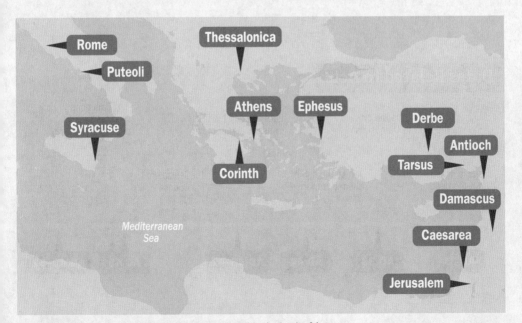

This map depicts many significant locations mentioned in the book of Acts.

have been people who were already Christians or at least were interested in Christianity (Lk 1:4). Since the narrative of Acts ends with Paul's captivity in Rome, it might have been written shortly after his arrival there, in the early to mid–60s AD. Another possibility is that Paul preaching the gospel in Rome provided a natural stopping point for the book because it showed that the church was fulfilling Jesus' command to be his witnesses to the ends of the earth—Jerusalem and Rome were on opposite sides of the empire (Ac 1:8). In this case, Acts could have been written later in the first century AD.

STRUCTURE

The structure of Acts follows the outward expansion of the gospel, which spreads from Jerusalem to Judaea, Samaria, to the ends of the earth—across the world (1:8). This geographical framework takes shape in the first section (1:1—8:3), which is set in Jerusalem. In Acts 2, Peter preaches to a crowd of Jews from all over the world (2:9–11); in Acts 6, Greek-speaking Jews become leaders in the church. The first major expansion comes in Acts 8:4—12:25, with the apostles taking the gospel to other parts of Judaea and to Samaria. In Acts 13, another expansion occurs as Paul launches his first missionary journey. The rest of the book follows his church-planting activity through Asia Minor and Greece until he finally makes his way to Rome, the capital of the empire, and a place representative of the entire known world of the time.

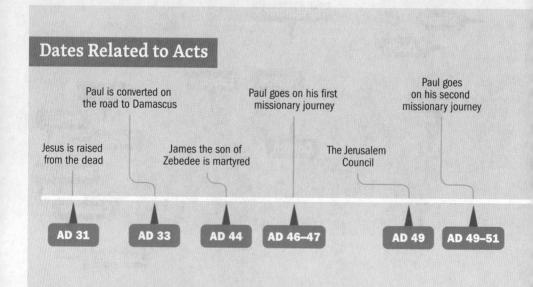

Dates Related to Acts

Jesus is raised from the dead	Paul is converted on the road to Damascus	James the son of Zebedee is martyred	Paul goes on his first missionary journey	The Jerusalem Council	Paul goes on his second missionary journey
AD 31	AD 33	AD 44	AD 46–47	AD 49	AD 49–51

Within this geographical framework, Acts also expands from the Jewish mission of the church to the Gentile mission. Peter, as head of the Jewish mission, figures prominently in the early chapters, but fades from view after Acts 12. Paul, the leader of the Gentile (non-Jewish) mission, becomes the focus in the remainder of the book.

OUTLINE

- The church in Jerusalem (1:1—8:3)
- The church in Judaea and Samaria (8:4—12:25)
- Paul's missions to the Gentiles (13:1—21:16)
- Paul in Jerusalem (21:17—26:32)
- Paul's journey to Rome (27:1—28:31)

THEMES

Acts repeatedly demonstrates that the gospel involves unexpected reversals. The scene at Pentecost (ch. 2)—with its depiction of people from various languages understanding the good news of Jesus in their own tongues—reverses the confusion of human language at Babel (Ge 11:7). And it is Saul the Pharisee, the leading persecutor of the church, who becomes known as the Apostle to the Gentiles. And it is the Gentiles who themselves are a surprise inclusion in God's people (Ac 10:45; 11:18). Salvation through Jesus is not just for Jews; it's for everyone.

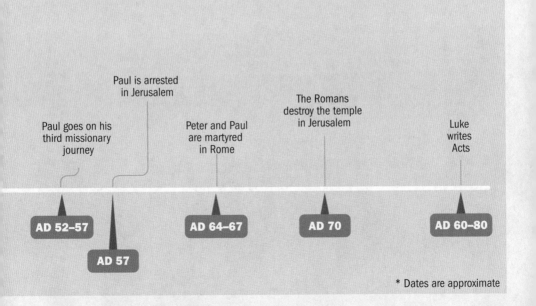

Paul is arrested in Jerusalem

Paul goes on his third missionary journey

The Romans destroy the temple in Jerusalem

Peter and Paul are martyred in Rome

Luke writes Acts

AD 52–57

AD 57

AD 64–67

AD 70

AD 60–80

* Dates are approximate

Acts broadly depicts the rapid outward movement of the gospel to people from an incredible array of races, languages, social ranks and religious backgrounds. In tandem with the depiction of Jesus in Luke's Gospel, Acts demonstrates that Jesus is the culmination of world history: He is what the world needs. Acts shows how Jesus continues his work in the world through his followers, by the power of the Holy Spirit in them.

Instead of providing a fully detailed account of the early church's expansion and leadership structure, Acts focuses on specific moments, showing in broad strokes the gospel's rapid expansion. Acts is meant to inspire us to be part of God's work in the world.

The work of bringing the gospel to the ends of the earth is far from finished—as God's people today we are called to continue the effort.

Jesus Taken Up Into Heaven

1 In my former book, Theophilus, I wrote about all that Jesus began to do and to teach ²until the day he was taken up to heaven, after giving instructions through the Holy Spirit to the apostles he had chosen. ³After his suffering, he presented himself to them and gave many convincing proofs that he was alive. He appeared to them over a period of forty days and spoke about the kingdom of God. ⁴On one occasion, while he was eating with them, he gave them this command: "Do not leave Jerusalem, but wait for the gift my Father promised, which you have heard me speak about. ⁵For John baptized with*a* water, but in a few days you will be baptized with*a* the Holy Spirit."

⁶Then they gathered around him and asked him, "Lord, are you at this time going to restore the kingdom to Israel?"

⁷He said to them: "It is not for you to know the times or dates the Father has set by his own authority. ⁸But you will receive power when the Holy

a 5 Or *in*

1:1–5 In this preface (Ac 1:1–5), Luke the physician—who traveled with the apostle Paul (Col 4:14)—introduces the book of Acts to Theophilus as a continuation of his Gospel. While the Gospel tells the story of the earthly ministry of Christ, Acts continues that story after his resurrection and ascension, focusing on his work accomplished through his apostles in the power of the Holy Spirit. It also includes a brief elaboration (Ac 1:6–11) on the end of the Gospel of Luke (Lk 24:36–52), speaking of an event that took place prior to Jesus' ascension.

At several points in Acts, Luke speaks of his firsthand involvement in the events involving the apostle Paul (Ac 16:10–17; 20:5–15; 21:1–18; 27:1—28:16). Acts ends with Paul's Roman imprisonment (28:16–31), which took place in the early to mid-60s AD. Luke could have written Acts shortly after Paul arrived in Rome or later in the first century AD—depending on whether Paul's arrival in Rome was merely the last event Luke knew of, or if it was a natural stopping point because it demonstrated that the gospel was spreading across the earth, as Jesus had commissioned (1:8). See the timeline "The Early Church to AD 100" on p. 1776.

1:1 In my former book The Gospel of Luke. See Lk 1:1–4. **Theophilus** This Greek name means "friend of God." Theophilus could have been a specific person (perhaps Luke's benefactor), or Luke could have intended this as a general description for all readers who considered themselves friends of God (compare Jn 15:15). **began** The ministry of Jesus recorded in the Gospel of Luke was not the end of Christ's work; Acts recounts the ongoing work of Jesus through the Holy Spirit and the early church. **1:2 until the day** The Gospel of Luke records Jesus' earthly ministry from his birth through his crucifixion and resurrection, ending with his ascension (Lk 24:50–53). **1:3 After his suffering** A reference to Jesus' crucifixion, which together with his resurrection forms the foundation of the apostles' preaching of repentance and forgiveness to all people (Lk 24:46–48). **proofs** Jesus' post-resurrection appearances to his disciples established beyond a doubt that he was physically alive, not merely present as a ghost or spiritual being. **alive** Luke emphasizes the reality of Jesus' physical, bodily resurrection (compare 1Co 15). His resurrection and its implications then become the heart of the apostles' message (e.g., Ac 2:24,32; 3:15; 17:31). **forty days** This time period may have theological significance for Luke (the narrator), who could be comparing the disciples' time learning from Jesus after his ascension to Moses' time learning from God on Mount Sinai (Ex 24:18). **kingdom of God** In the OT, the kingdom of God (Yahweh) refers to God's dominion (e.g., Ps 145:13; Isa 9:7; see 1Ch 17:14 and note). Ultimately, the OT looks forward to fulfillment of God's kingdom in the Messiah's reign in grace and righteousness over the whole earth (e.g., Ge 49:10–11; Isa 11:1–9; Da 2:44). Jesus is the King and

proclaims a kingdom that fulfills the OT promises, yet in a way unexpected by his contemporaries. His kingdom is not political or geographic in the sense that nations and kingdoms are thought of today (Mk 12:13–17). Instead, it exists wherever God's will is done (Mt 6:10). It is the effective reign of God expressed in and through the lives and actions of his people, extending throughout a world pained by the curse (Ge 3), growing and spreading as those who embrace it are welcomed as members of God's people (Mk 4:30–32). God's kingdom—via the Messiah, Jesus—also deals with sin, which is the world's fundamental problem (Dt 30:1–6; Isa 53:10—54:1); Jesus emphasizes this in his preaching (Mt 5:3–10; Lk 8:10). Compare note on Mk 1:15. **1:4 gift my Father promised** God promised to give a new spirit (or his Spirit) abundantly when he inaugurates the new covenant (Eze 36:26; Joel 2:28–32). Jesus had told his disciples that the Holy Spirit would empower them to be effective in their mission (Lk 12:11–12; Jn 14:26). **1:5 John baptized** John the Baptist's ministry occurred just prior to, and in the early days of, Jesus' ministry (compare Mk 1:8; Lk 3:16). **in a few days** If Jesus' instruction here occurs 40 days (Ac 1:3) after Passover when he was crucified (see Lk 2:41 and note), no more than 10 days remain before the Festival of Weeks, or Pentecost (since the two feasts were 50 days apart; Lev 23:16). Pentecost is when the apostles' baptism by the Holy Spirit took place (Ac 2:1).

1:6–11 While the Gospel of Luke concentrates on Jesus' ministry on earth, his ascension and heavenly rule define the book of Acts. With his earthly ministry accomplished, Christ returns to God the Father, but he sends the Holy Spirit to make the work he accomplished fruitful through the proclamation of the gospel to the ends of the earth.

1:6 asked him The OT affirms that the kingdom of God as inaugurated by the Messiah would be applicable to all people, marking the completion of God's purposes of blessing the entire world through Abraham's descendants (compare Ge 12:1–3; Isa 2:2–4; 53:12; Zec 14:9–21). The apostles may have expected a political fulfillment of this kingdom (compare Jn 6:15 and note; note on Ac 1:3). **1:7 not for you to know** Jesus deflects the apostles' question and tells them they should not be concerned with timing.

1:8 The locations mentioned in this verse represent a geographical broadening in scope of the apostles' mission, from Israel's capital, to the land of Israel and to the entire world. This also reflects the structure of the book of Acts: the church spreads in Jerusalem (chs. 1–7), in Judea and Samaria (ch. 8) and to the surrounding nations (chs. 9–28). Compare Isa 49:6.

1:8 power The Greek word used here, *dynamis*, can refer to power displayed in miracles (e.g., Ac 2:22; 4:7; 19:11), or (more generally) the ability of God or people

Spirit comes on you; and you will be my witnesses in Jerusalem, and in all Judea and Samaria, and to the ends of the earth."

⁹After he said this, he was taken up before their very eyes, and a cloud hid him from their sight.

¹⁰They were looking intently up into the sky as he was going, when suddenly two men dressed in white stood beside them. ¹¹"Men of Galilee," they said, "why do you stand here looking into the sky? This same Jesus, who has been taken from you into heaven, will come back in the same way you have seen him go into heaven."

Matthias Chosen to Replace Judas

¹²Then the apostles returned to Jerusalem from the hill called the Mount of Olives, a Sabbath day's walkᵃ from the city. ¹³When they arrived, they went upstairs to the room where they were staying. Those present were Peter, John, James and Andrew; Philip and Thomas, Bartholomew and Matthew; James son of Alphaeus and Simon the Zealot, and Judas son of James. ¹⁴They all joined together constantly in prayer, along with the women and Mary the mother of Jesus, and with his brothers.

¹⁵In those days Peter stood up among the believers (a group numbering about a hundred and twen-

ty) ¹⁶and said, "Brothers and sisters,ᵇ the Scripture had to be fulfilled in which the Holy Spirit spoke long ago through David concerning Judas, who served as guide for those who arrested Jesus. ¹⁷He was one of our number and shared in our ministry."

¹⁸(With the payment he received for his wickedness, Judas bought a field; there he fell headlong, his body burst open and all his intestines spilled out. ¹⁹Everyone in Jerusalem heard about this, so they called that field in their language Akeldama, that is, Field of Blood.)

²⁰"For," said Peter, "it is written in the Book of Psalms:

"'May his place be deserted;
let there be no one to dwell in it,'ᶜ

and,

"'May another take his place of leadership.'ᵈ

²¹Therefore it is necessary to choose one of the men who have been with us the whole time the Lord Jesus was living among us, ²²beginning from

---

ᵃ 12 That is, about 5/8 mile or about 1 kilometer   ᵇ 16 The Greek word for *brothers and sisters* (*adelphoi*) refers here to believers, both men and women, as part of God's family; also in 6:3; 11:29; 12:17; 16:40; 18:18, 27; 21:7, 17; 28:14, 15.   ᶜ 20 Psalm 69:25   ᵈ 20 Psalm 109:8

---

to carry out their purposes (e.g., 3:12; 4:33). God will enable the apostles to accomplish his work, wherever and whatever it is. **my witnesses** The apostles are called to testify about Christ—to proclaim the reality of his death and resurrection as well as his kingdom and lordship (compare v. 3 and note).
1:10 two men dressed in white The dress of these figures suggests they are angels (compare Lk 24:4). See the table "Angels in the Bible" on p. 2120.
1:11 will come back The angels attest to Jesus' future bodily return. Since Jesus ascended from the Mount of Olives (Ac 1:12), the angels may be alluding to the prophet Zechariah's vision of the day of Yahweh, when Yahweh will come to stand upon the Mount of Olives, defeat his people's enemies and establish his rule over the earth (Zec 14).
1:12–26 This section marks the beginning of the apostles' work in Jerusalem.
1:12 Mount of Olives The Mount of Olives is a ridge east of Jerusalem. **a Sabbath day's walk** The later rabbinic work, the Mishnah, sets this at about three-fifths of a mile, the longest distance Jews were allowed to walk without breaking the Sabbath (Mishnah Eruvin 4.8).
1:13 Luke, the narrator, lists the remaining eleven of the twelve original apostles. The names are the same as those listed in Lk 6:14–16, although some occur in a different order. James and John appear before Andrew in Acts but not in Luke, perhaps indicating the importance of James and John (along with Peter) as the most influential leaders in the young church (compare Ac 3:1; 15:13).
1:14 prayer Luke often shows how God uses prayer to work in and through his church (e.g., 4:24–30; 16:25; 21:5). **the women and Mary the mother of Jesus** The mention of women in Luke's account (9:36; 16:14; 21:9) reflects his theological emphasis that all people

(Jew and Gentile, rich and poor, men and women) are included in the community and mission of the church.
1:15 Peter stood up Peter is portrayed throughout Luke and Acts as one of the primary leaders among the apostles—although that does not mean he possessed sole authority (15:6,22–23) or was beyond rebuke (see Gal 2:11–14 and note; compare note on Ac 1:13). James the brother of Jesus was also very influential, as the leader of the Jerusalem church (e.g., 15:13; 21:18).
1:16 had to be fulfilled Peter's speech continues its emphasis on the fulfillment of Scripture. In v. 20, Peter explains that he has in mind two psalms of David being fulfilled via Judas' actions. Peter interprets Judas' betrayal of Jesus as, though evil, ultimately used by God for his purposes of saving sinners, since it led to Jesus' sacrificial death (compare Lk 22:21–22; Mt 26:23–25; Jn 13:18–30). The Gospel of Luke's depiction of Jesus shows how Jesus' entire mission aligns with what was prophesied about him (e.g., Lk 4:16–21).
1:18 Judas bought a field Acts records that Judas purchased the property himself with the 30 pieces of silver the Jewish religious leaders had paid him for betraying Jesus (Mt 26:14–15) and died in a gruesome manner, falling and bursting open in the field. Matthew records that these religious leaders bought the field with Judas' money after Judas had hung himself (Mt 27:3–8). The two accounts could provide different aspects of the same episode: Judas hung himself, and his body fell and burst open on the ground; the religious leaders then bought the property in his name following his suicide.
1:19 in their language Aramaic, the primary language spoken by Jews in the first century AD. **Akeldama** The exact location of this field is uncertain. It may be on the southeast side of the Hinnom Valley, which is on the southwest side of Jerusalem.
1:20 it is written in the Book of Psalms Peter claims two psalms foretell God's judgment upon Judas (citing Ps 69:25) and the need for his replacement (Ps 109:8).

John's baptism to the time when Jesus was taken up from us. For one of these must become a witness with us of his resurrection."

²³So they nominated two men: Joseph called Barsabbas (also known as Justus) and Matthias. ²⁴Then they prayed, "Lord, you know everyone's heart. Show us which of these two you have chosen ²⁵to take over this apostolic ministry, which Judas left to go where he belongs." ²⁶Then they cast lots, and the lot fell to Matthias; so he was added to the eleven apostles.

The Holy Spirit Comes at Pentecost

2 When the day of Pentecost came, they were all together in one place. ²Suddenly a sound like the blowing of a violent wind came from heaven and filled the whole house where they were sitting.

³They saw what seemed to be tongues of fire that separated and came to rest on each of them. ⁴All of them were filled with the Holy Spirit and began to speak in other tongues[a] as the Spirit enabled them.

⁵Now there were staying in Jerusalem God-fearing Jews from every nation under heaven. ⁶When they heard this sound, a crowd came together in bewilderment, because each one heard their own language being spoken. ⁷Utterly amazed, they asked: "Aren't all these who are speaking Galileans? ⁸Then how is it that each of us hears them in our native language? ⁹Parthians, Medes and Elamites; residents of Mesopotamia, Judea and Cappadocia, Pontus and Asia,[b] ¹⁰Phrygia and Pamphylia, Egypt and the parts of Libya near Cyrene;

---

[a] 4 Or languages; also in verse 11   [b] 9 That is, the Roman province by that name

---

These are psalms of David (compare Ac 1:16). Just as God judged David's betrayers, so he has judged and punished Judas, the one who betrayed the Son of David (Jesus). **1:21 whole time** The new apostle must have been a companion of Jesus and his disciples from the beginning of his earthly ministry to the end, especially the defining moments—John the Baptist's time, seeing the resurrected Jesus, and witnessing Jesus' ascension. These moments pointed the disciples toward a true understanding of who Jesus is and what he came to accomplish. The apostle who replaces Judas must be able to bear witness to all that occurred in Jesus' ministry and have been the beneficiary of the whole of Jesus' ministry. **living** Judas' replacement had to have personally interacted with Jesus during his earthly ministry. This is so that the new apostle can be a legitimate and effective eyewitness alongside the other apostles, as Jesus had specified (see 1:8). **1:23 Joseph called Barsabbas (also known as Justus) and Matthias** Neither of these figures appears elsewhere in the NT. Although the narrative of Acts does not provide details about Joseph (Justus) and Matthias, it implies that both men were worthy candidates to replace Judas among the disciples. **1:24 know everyone's heart** This description of God also occurs in 15:8. The disciples acknowledge that God perceives their needs and their motives and will guide them in the way that is best. **you have chosen** Just as the Lord Jesus had chosen the original twelve apostles, so he will choose Judas' replacement as well. The Greek word used here for choosing also appears in v. 2. **1:25 where he belongs** This could refer either to Judas abandoning his role as Jesus' apostle to take up his role as Jesus' traitor, or to Judas departing this life in condemnation and taking his place in death or hell. **1:26 cast lots** The practice of casting lots is known from the OT. The OT depicts certain types of lot casting not as a matter of chance but as an opportunity for God to make his will known in an unmistakable way (e.g., Lev 16:8; Jos 18:6,8). **added** The Greek word used here, synkatapsēphizomai, denotes an official enrollment into the ranks of the apostles: Matthias becomes one of the twelve apostles. The number twelve here is likely representative of the twelve tribes of Israel. The apostles will minister to both Jewish and non-Jewish people alike. Although the amount of apostles will expand when Paul is added to their ranks (Ac 9:1–31; Ro 1:1)—and likely others later on—the original eleven apostles plus Mat-

thias represent those who personally knew Jesus during his time on earth and act as eyewitnesses to his ministry (see Mt 19:28 and note; compare note on Ac 1:21).

2:1–13 The coming of the Holy Spirit at Pentecost marks the official inauguration of the new covenant and serves as a witness to the nation of Israel. The church's reception of the Holy Spirit, preaching and sudden growth testify to the reality of Christ's resurrection and his ongoing reign.

2:1 day of Pentecost One of three festivals or feasts that required all Jewish men to come to Jerusalem (Ex 23:14–17; Lev 23:1–44; Dt 12:5–6). Pentecost occurs 50 days after Passover, around May or June, and celebrates the gathering of the firstfruits of the harvest (Ex 23:16). See the table "Israelite Festivals" on p. 200. **2:2 wind** The Greek word used here, pnoē, sounds like the word for Spirit (pneuma). The intensity of the sound and its origin from heaven announce its divine origin (compare Eze 1:4). **2:3 what seemed to be tongues of fire** Fire is often used to describe God's holy presence and his ability to purify (e.g., Ex 3:2; 13:21; Mk 9:49; 1Pe 1:7). The reference to tongues or languages indicates that this is a reversal of the Tower of Babel, where God confused the languages of those who rebelled against him (Ge 11:7; see note on Ac 2:6). **came to rest** May imply the permanence and intimacy of the Spirit's ministry. **2:4 other tongues** These languages were not heavenly utterances, but human speech understood by a wide variety of people groups present in Jerusalem for the feast (v. 5). In Acts, tongues are an outward manifestation of the power of the Holy Spirit. Speaking in tongues occurs three major times in the book (v. 4; 10:46; 19:6). Each instance pertains to the acceptance of a new people group into the body of Christ. **2:6 in bewilderment** The wording used here, together with the reference to tongues or languages in v. 4 and to the many nations in v. 5, recalls the OT account of the Tower of Babel (Ge 11:1–9). There, Yahweh came down to thwart ill-founded human ambition and pride by confusing their languages. In Acts, the Spirit of the Lord comes down to proclaim salvation in Christ by making the gospel intelligible in all languages. See the infographic "The Tower of Babel" on p. 29. **2:7 Galileans** It seems that Galileans were generally considered by cosmopolitan Jews in Jerusalem, and Jews in wider Judea, to be uneducated and culturally

Miracles in Acts

MIRACLE	REFERENCE
Everyone is awestruck by the miracles done by the apostles	Ac 2:43
Peter heals a man lame from birth; the authorities are forced to recognize that a "sign" has been performed	Ac 3:2 – 10; 4:16,22
The apostles perform many signs and wonders, healings and exorcisms; Peter's mere shadow has healing power	Ac 5:12 – 16
An angel rescues the apostles from prison	Ac 5:18 – 20
Stephen performs signs and wonders	Ac 6:8
Philip performs signs, healings and exorcisms in Samaria	Ac 8:6 – 7
Philip's signs and miracles amaze Simon the Magician	Ac 8:13
The spirit of the Lord snatches Philip from the road to Gaza and places him in Azotus	Ac 8:39 – 40
Saul's conversion, blindness and healing at the hands of Ananias	Ac 9:1 – 18; 22:6 – 13; 26:12 – 18
Peter heals Aeneas in Lydda	Ac 9:33 – 34
Peter raises Tabitha/Dorcas	Ac 9:36 – 41
An angel rescues Peter from prison	Ac 12:6 – 11
Paul strikes Bar-Jesus/Elymas blind	Ac 13:6 – 11
Paul and Barnabas perform signs and wonders in Phrygian Iconium	Ac 14:3
Paul heals a man lame from birth	Ac 14:8 – 10
Paul and Barnabas recount the signs and wonders performed among non-Jews	Ac 15:12
Paul casts out a spirit of divination	Ac 16:16 – 18
Paul and Silas are freed from prison by an earthquake	Ac 16:26
God works "extraordinary miracles" through Paul; garments that have merely touched him have healing power	Ac 19:11 – 12
Paul raises Eutychus after he falls from a third-story window	Ac 20:9 – 10
Paul survives a viper's bite	Ac 28:3 – 6
Paul heals the father of Publius and others	Ac 28:8 – 9

visitors from Rome [11](both Jews and converts to Judaism); Cretans and Arabs — we hear them declaring the wonders of God in our own tongues!" [12]Amazed and perplexed, they asked one another, "What does this mean?"

[13]Some, however, made fun of them and said, "They have had too much wine."

Peter Addresses the Crowd

[14]Then Peter stood up with the Eleven, raised his voice and addressed the crowd: "Fellow Jews and all of you who live in Jerusalem, let me explain this to you; listen carefully to what I say. [15]These people are not drunk, as you suppose. It's only nine in the morning! [16]No, this is what was spoken by the prophet Joel:

[17]"'In the last days, God says,
  I will pour out my Spirit on all people.
Your sons and daughters will prophesy,
  your young men will see visions,
  your old men will dream dreams.
[18]Even on my servants, both men and
    women,
  I will pour out my Spirit in those days,
    and they will prophesy.

[19]I will show wonders in the heavens above
    and signs on the earth below,
    blood and fire and billows of smoke.
[20]The sun will be turned to darkness
    and the moon to blood
    before the coming of the great and glorious
      day of the Lord.
[21]And everyone who calls
    on the name of the Lord will be saved.'[a]

[22]"Fellow Israelites, listen to this: Jesus of Nazareth was a man accredited by God to you by miracles, wonders and signs, which God did among you through him, as you yourselves know. [23]This man was handed over to you by God's deliberate plan and foreknowledge; and you, with the help of wicked men,[b] put him to death by nailing him to the cross. [24]But God raised him from the dead, freeing him from the agony of death, because it was impossible for death to keep its hold on him. [25]David said about him:

"'I saw the Lord always before me.
  Because he is at my right hand,
  I will not be shaken.

---

[a] 21 Joel 2:28-32   [b] 23 Or of those not having the law (that is, Gentiles)

---

backward (compare Mt 26:73). The cosmopolitan Jews in Jerusalem were astounded that such men could speak other languages so fluently.

2:9–10 This list of regions moves generally from east to west and north to south. Luke (the narrator) demonstrates that the kingdom of God is destined to reach the entire world.

2:14–36 Peter explains the significance of each person being able to understand the apostles in their own language (Ac 2:6) and proclaims the gospel. Peter emphasizes that he and others are witnesses to Jesus' saving death and resurrection. He argues that the pouring out of the Holy Spirit testifies that the last days have arrived, leading up to a time of judgment. In line with the early church's mission as articulated in the book of Acts, Peter preaches the good news of Jesus as the true king who fulfills God's OT promises and that Jesus is the hope of Israel and all nations.

2:14 Peter By the power of the Spirit, the man who had denied Jesus three times (Lk 22:54–62) now preaches boldly before the crowd (compare Jn 21:15–19).
2:16 spoken by the prophet Joel Peter quotes Joel 2:28–32 to explain the events of Pentecost.
2:17 the last days This phrase evokes OT language associated with the final time before God's purposes of making all things right on earth are fulfilled—which includes the Messiah's victory and impending ultimate judgment of all, demanding that everyone repent (Nu 24:14–17; Dt 4:30; Joel 2:28–29; Dan 7). It marks the time when God will establish his kingdom over the earth and end oppression (Isa 2:2; Joel 2:28–29; Da 2:28). The events of Pentecost demonstrate to the Jewish audience that the promises made to them are fulfilled in Jesus, who is the true Messiah, and that the time of the last days has begun. **pour out my Spirit** In Joel, God's

full and final restoration of his people involves inner transformation by his Spirit (Joel 2:28–29).
2:18 servants The Spirit's ministry and the gifts he bestows are not restricted by social position or status (compare 1Co 3:16–23; 12:1–26).
2:19 I will show wonders in the heavens above In the original context, Joel's language reflects the plagues of Egypt (compare Ex 7:3; 9:23–29). The fire mentioned here might also recall Ac 2:3.
2:20 sun will be turned to darkness Though these descriptions originally referred to the exodus plagues, this language was also used by the prophets to describe signs of God's coming judgment (Ex 10:22; Joel 3:15; Am 5:18).
2:22 Jesus of Nazareth Peter describes Jesus in a similar way elsewhere in Acts (e.g., Ac 3:6; 4:10; 6:14). He emphasizes that Jesus' character and his works were often openly demonstrated and widely known to his audience.
2:23 God's deliberate plan and foreknowledge Although the Jews and Romans violently rejected Jesus and his claims, Peter asserts that God's saving purposes in Jesus' crucifixion were planned and could not be overthrown (compare Isa 53:12; Lk 22:22; 1Pe 1:20–21). See the table "Jesus' Fulfillment of OT Prophecy" on p. 1573.
2:24 God raised him from the dead Peter shows the triumph of God, who raised Jesus from the dead—demonstrating how the evil intended by the Jewish mob was used by God for the ultimate good (compare Lk 23:18–25). **impossible for death to keep its hold on him** Since he is life (Jn 14:6) and the only righteous one who did not deserve the wages of sin (Ro 6:23), Jesus could not be defeated by death.
2:25 David said Peter cites Ps 16:8–11, a psalm of David, stating that the reference to the Holy One in Ps 16: 10 speaks of the Messiah's resurrection (compare

²⁶ Therefore my heart is glad and my tongue
  rejoices;
 my body also will rest in hope,
²⁷ because you will not abandon me to the
  realm of the dead,
 you will not let your holy one see decay.
²⁸ You have made known to me the paths
  of life;
 you will fill me with joy in your presence.'^a

²⁹ "Fellow Israelites, I can tell you confidently

that the patriarch David died and was buried, and
his tomb is here to this day. ³⁰ But he was a prophet and knew that God had promised him on oath
that he would place one of his descendants on
his throne. ³¹ Seeing what was to come, he spoke
of the resurrection of the Messiah, that he was
not abandoned to the realm of the dead, nor did
his body see decay. ³² God has raised this Jesus to
life, and we are all witnesses of it. ³³ Exalted to

^a 28 Psalm 16:8-11 (see Septuagint)

Ac 2:31). Peter understands David's trust in Yahweh to
be rooted in his belief that God will ultimately overcome
death through the Messiah.
2:26 my body also will rest in hope The psalm shows
that David had confidence in his ultimate safety in Yahweh. For Peter, this hints at a confidence in the resurrection of Jesus.
2:27 abandon me to the realm of the dead In the
original context, this psalm could emphasize David's
belief that Yahweh would not allow him to die at that
particular moment, or that God would not allow him to
experience permanent death (represented by Hades or
Sheol). The idea of a resurrection from death is where
Peter finds the ultimate significance of David's words.
your holy one Elsewhere Jesus is given a similar title by

the apostles (Jn 6:69) and even called that by demons
when they recognize his true identity (Lk 4:34).
2:29 died and was buried Peter reasons that since
David died and remains in the grave, his words in Ps 16
cannot refer primarily or exclusively to himself.
2:30 he was a prophet David was inspired by the Spirit
to write what he wrote (Ac 4:25). **God had promised
him** Peter reminds his audience of the Davidic covenant,
in which God promised that one of David's descendants
would reign forever (2Sa 7:14–15). God kept this promise
in Jesus, David's descendant, whose reign would not
end (Lk 1:32–33).
2:32 we are all witnesses of it See Ac 1:8.
2:33 Exalted to the right hand of God In his ascension, the resurrected Jesus is glorified by God the Father

---

The Early Church to AD 100

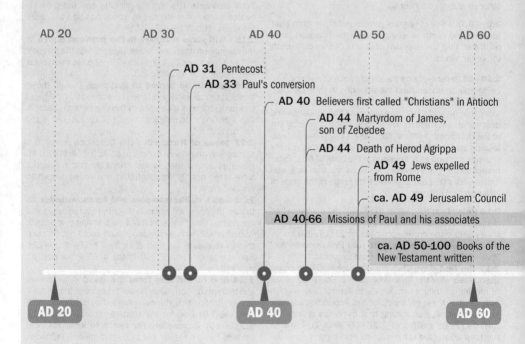

| AD 20 | AD 30 | AD 40 | AD 50 | AD 60 |

AD 31 Pentecost
AD 33 Paul's conversion
AD 40 Believers first called "Christians" in Antioch
AD 44 Martyrdom of James, son of Zebedee
AD 44 Death of Herod Agrippa
AD 49 Jews expelled from Rome
ca. AD 49 Jerusalem Council
AD 40-66 Missions of Paul and his associates
ca. AD 50-100 Books of the New Testament written

AD 20   AD 40   AD 60

All dates are approximate

the right hand of God, he has received from the Father the promised Holy Spirit and has poured out what you now see and hear. ³⁴For David did not ascend to heaven, and yet he said,

"'The Lord said to my Lord:
    "Sit at my right hand
³⁵until I make your enemies
    a footstool for your feet."'ᵃ

³⁶"Therefore let all Israel be assured of this: God has made this Jesus, whom you crucified, both Lord and Messiah."

³⁷When the people heard this, they were cut to the heart and said to Peter and the other apostles, "Brothers, what shall we do?"

³⁸Peter replied, "Repent and be baptized, every

to a position of authority over all things (compare Da 7:13–14). **he has received from the Father the promised Holy Spirit** As Jesus promised earlier in Acts (Ac 1:5,8; compare Jn 14:15–31; Gal 3:14). In claiming that Jesus does the work of sending God's Spirit, Peter implies Jesus' unity with God the Father in purpose and power (compare Isa 44:3; 61:1; Jn 14:26).
2:34 The Lord said to my Lord Peter cites Ps 110:1 to assert that this psalm of David shows that David was aware that someone far greater than himself would fulfill God's promises to him of an everlasting kingdom, someone who was simultaneously distinct from Yahweh and yet also David's Lord. David did not ascend into heaven or claim all authority, but Jesus did. Compare note on Lk 20:42. See the table "Messianic Psalms" on p. 847.
2:35 enemies a footstool According to Peter's interpretation, this psalm of David envisions a time when the Messiah

would reign, but would still await the time when all his enemies would be conquered. This echoes how the kingdom of God is understood in the Gospels—that it is both present yet in many ways coming (see note on Mk 1:15).
2:36 both Lord and Messiah The Jewish mob who had killed Jesus had grossly misunderstood him. God still used their actions to authenticate him as both Israel's king and the fulfillment of the promises about the Messiah (compare Isa 52:13—53:12).

2:37–41 Many in the crowd respond to Peter's sermon in repentance and faith, are baptized and receive the gift of the Holy Spirit.

2:38 Repent The Greek word used here, *metanoeō*, denotes a change of mind, will or actions. Peter calls the people to believe that Jesus is the Messiah promised in the OT. Peter's exhortation involves two actions:

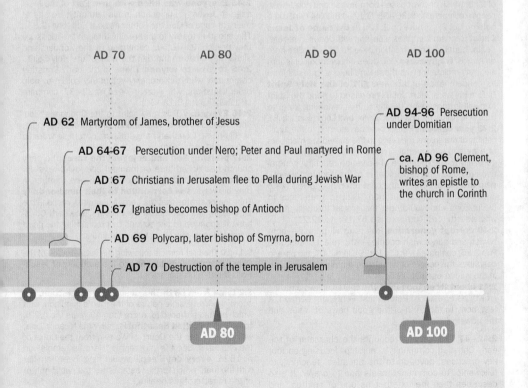

AD 70   AD 80   AD 90   AD 100

AD 62 Martyrdom of James, brother of Jesus

AD 64-67 Persecution under Nero; Peter and Paul martyred in Rome

AD 67 Christians in Jerusalem flee to Pella during Jewish War

AD 67 Ignatius becomes bishop of Antioch

AD 69 Polycarp, later bishop of Smyrna, born

AD 70 Destruction of the temple in Jerusalem

AD 94-96 Persecution under Domitian

ca. AD 96 Clement, bishop of Rome, writes an epistle to the church in Corinth

AD 80

AD 100

one of you, in the name of Jesus Christ for the forgiveness of your sins. And you will receive the gift of the Holy Spirit. ³⁹The promise is for you and your children and for all who are far off — for all whom the Lord our God will call."

⁴⁰With many other words he warned them; and he pleaded with them, "Save yourselves from this corrupt generation." ⁴¹Those who accepted his message were baptized, and about three thousand were added to their number that day.

The Fellowship of the Believers

⁴²They devoted themselves to the apostles' teaching and to fellowship, to the breaking of bread and to prayer. ⁴³Everyone was filled with awe at the many wonders and signs performed by the apostles. ⁴⁴All the believers were together and had everything in common. ⁴⁵They sold property and possessions to give to anyone who had need. ⁴⁶Every day they continued to meet together in the temple courts. They broke bread in their homes and ate together with glad and sincere hearts, ⁴⁷praising God and enjoying the favor of all the people. And the Lord added to their number daily those who were being saved.

Peter Heals a Lame Beggar

3 One day Peter and John were going up to the temple at the time of prayer — at three in the afternoon. ²Now a man who was lame from birth was being carried to the temple gate called Beautiful, where he was put every day to beg from those going into the temple courts. ³When he saw Peter and John about to enter, he asked them for money.

---

repentance and baptism. These are connected with two promises: forgiveness of sins and the gift of the Holy Spirit. In Acts, Luke presents saving faith, repentance, forgiveness, baptism and the gift of the Spirit as inter-related aspects of embracing Jesus and coming to belong to the people of God in Christ. **be baptized** Just as circumcision served as a visible external marker of inclusion in the covenant community of Israel, so baptism serves as the public sign and seal of a person's solidarity with Christ and participation in the new covenant community of faith, which encompasses both Jewish and non-Jewish people (compare Ac 8:36–38; 9:17–18; 10:47–48; see note on Col 2:11; note on 2:12). **in the name of Jesus Christ** Baptism identifies a person with Jesus in his life, death, burial and resurrection (see Ro 6:3–4). See note on Ac 3:6. **forgiveness** God does not overlook or ignore sin, but graciously frees those who belong to Jesus from its condemnation and power. **gift of the Holy Spirit** Before his ascension, Jesus promised to send the Spirit to dwell in those who belong to him, enabling them to trust and follow him as their Savior and Lord (see 1:5,8). **2:39 your children** Peter could be referring to the applicability of the gospel message to the immediate members of a person's household (compare 16:15,33) or more generally to the message of salvation reaching generations to come (the descendants of the people present). **who are far off** This could be a reference to Jews who lived in distant lands, but more likely is a reference to the nations who would hear the gospel throughout the whole earth (1:8; compare Isa 57:19; Ac 22:21). **2:40 corrupt generation** Refers to all people — both Jewish and non-Jewish people — who reject Jesus (see Php 2:15; compare Lk 9:41; 11:29). In the OT, the phrase describes the people of Israel who rebelled against God in the wilderness (Dt 32:5). **2:41 about three thousand** The church enjoys amazing growth as a result of Peter's first Pentecost sermon, a testimony to the truth of the good news of Jesus and the power of his Spirit.

2:42–47 This section recounts the character of the early Christian community's worship, focusing on four key practices: devotion to the apostles' teaching, to fellowship, to communal meals and to prayer. It also describes their life together as one of spiritual and material sharing among all.

2:42 to the apostles' teaching The gathered community listened to and followed the preaching and teaching of the twelve apostles from — and based on — the Scriptures (compare Ac 2:14–41; Lk 24:27). **breaking of bread** This could refer to participation in the Lord's Supper, or to sharing in other meals together, as in Ac 2:46 — the same language is used for each practice (e.g., Lk 22:19; Ac 20:7; 27:35; 1Co 10:16). It is highly likely that both are in view. **to prayer** In Acts, prayer indicates dependence on God, hope in the future and desire for the advancement of God's work (e.g., Ac 1:24; 12:5; 14:23).

2:43 Everyone was filled with awe Part of the message of Jesus' resurrection is his authority: He sits at the right hand of God the Father as Lord and King (2:33). The apostles testify to that reality through the message they preach. Its truth is confirmed by the wonders and signs they perform through the work of the Holy Spirit. **2:45 to give to anyone** Those in the early Christian community who had property voluntarily sold it to help other Christians who were in need (4:32–37; compare Lk 12:32–34; 18:18–30). **2:46 Every day** This may point to the Christians' continued observance of Jewish daily prayers in the temple. At this point, Christians are still part of temple worship services in Jerusalem. **2:47 praising God and enjoying the favor** The early church had an attitude of thankful and joyful worship, and demonstrated the love of God to one another in tangible ways. **the Lord added to their number daily** This demonstrates that the Lord is ultimately responsible for building his community of believers. The early Christians responded to his actions by proclaiming the good news of Jesus and living with love and joy.

3:1–10 The first miracle following the inauguration of the Christian community testifies to the authority of Jesus' word through his apostles.

3:2 lame from birth This description underscores the seemingly irreversible nature of the man's condition, with which he had suffered for more than 40 years (Ac 4:22). **temple gate called Beautiful** Possibly the Nicanor Gate, which separates the Court of Women from the Court of the Israelites. See the infographic "Herod's Temple" on p. 1626. **every day** People would have been familiar with the man, which further establishes the public nature of the miracle of his healing. **3:3 for money** Having no prior relationship with the disciples, the lame man treats them like everyone else (compare v. 2).

⁴Peter looked straight at him, as did John. Then Peter said, "Look at us!" ⁵So the man gave them his attention, expecting to get something from them.

⁶Then Peter said, "Silver or gold I do not have, but what I do have I give you. In the name of Jesus Christ of Nazareth, walk." ⁷Taking him by the right hand, he helped him up, and instantly the man's feet and ankles became strong. ⁸He jumped to his feet and began to walk. Then he went with them into the temple courts, walking and jumping, and praising God. ⁹When all the people saw him walking and praising God, ¹⁰they recognized him as the same man who used to sit begging at the temple gate called Beautiful, and they were filled with wonder and amazement at what had happened to him.

Peter Speaks to the Onlookers

¹¹While the man held on to Peter and John, all the people were astonished and came running to them in the place called Solomon's Colonnade. ¹²When Peter saw this, he said to them: "Fellow Israelites, why does this surprise you? Why do you stare at us as if by our own power or godliness we had made this man walk? ¹³The God of Abraham, Isaac and Jacob, the God of our fathers, has glorified his servant Jesus. You handed him over to be killed, and you disowned him before Pilate, though he had decided to let him go. ¹⁴You disowned the Holy and Righteous One and asked that a murderer be released to you. ¹⁵You killed the author of life, but God raised him from the dead. We are witnesses of this. ¹⁶By faith in the name of Jesus, this man whom you see and know was made strong. It is Jesus' name and the faith that comes through him that has completely healed him, as you can all see.

¹⁷"Now, fellow Israelites, I know that you acted in ignorance, as did your leaders. ¹⁸But this is how God fulfilled what he had foretold through all the prophets, saying that his Messiah would suffer.

3:4 At this point in Acts, Luke's account includes seemingly unnecessary details, which slows the pace of the narrative. This points to the importance of what follows.

3:6 In the name Peter is careful to note that his miracle is truly done by Jesus; in doing so, he expresses Jesus' nature, character and power. The apostle has already called on the Jews in Jerusalem to believe in Jesus' name for salvation (2:21) and to be baptized in his name (2:38). References to Jesus' name appear frequently in the early chapters of Acts (e.g., 3:16; 4:10,30; 5:40). **Jesus Christ of Nazareth** See note on 2:22.

3:7 man's feet and ankles Luke, who is a physician, observes the specific way Jesus' power works instantly to overcome the man's lifelong disability.

3:8 praising God The man attributes his healing to God, testifying to the divine power of Jesus.

3:10 they recognized Luke (the narrator) has already established the familiarity of local people with the once lame, but now healed, man. The people in the temple clearly grasped that a miracle had taken place; there was no doubt about its authenticity. **amazement** Although the crowd knew God had acted to heal this man, they were unsure of the significance of the event. Their curiosity and questions facilitate Peter's sermon (vv. 11–26).

3:11–26 Peter explains the meaning of the miracle to the crowd: It provides proof of the church's message that God raised Jesus from the dead as Lord and King, the true Messiah of Israel.

3:11 place called Solomon's Colonnade A shaded area along the eastern wall of the Court of the Gentiles. It was used for commerce, teaching and conversation. Acts later records that Christians sometimes gathered there (5:12).

3:12 by our own power or godliness Peter focuses on the power and authority of Jesus, not on any supernatural abilities that may be attributed to the apostles.

3:13 The God of Abraham The phrase recalls God's covenant promises to Abraham and faithfulness to Israel, including making Israel a great nation, and blessing the entire world (Ge 12:1–3; Ex 3:6; 1Ki 18:36). **servant** The Greek word used here, *pais*, may allude to the suffering

servant mentioned in Isa 52:13. **You handed him over to be killed, and you disowned him** Peter recalls the betrayals that occurred during Christ's trial and execution—and his audience's implication in them—not many days earlier in Jerusalem (Mt 20:19; Lk 23:1).

3:14 the Holy and Righteous One Isaiah frequently describes God as the Holy One to show God's distinctive character as well as Israel's guilt in being unfaithful to him (e.g., Isa 1:4; 5:24; 10:17). By giving to Jesus the title Isaiah uses for God, Peter implies the Messiah's divine character and status. Isaiah also speaks of the works of the suffering servant that make him righteous (or just) and the perfect sacrifice, giving him the grounds to bring both Jewish and non-Jewish people into a right relationship with God the Father (Isa 53:5–11).

3:15 author The Greek term used here, *archēgos*, can mean "leader," "prince" or "source" (compare Ac 5:31). Jesus is not only the servant of God, but the master of life from whom everyone receives their meaning and to whom all owe allegiance. **raised** Although in their rebellion the people had crucified the only one who could give them life, Jesus' resurrection proclaims that God's grace has the final word. Just as Jesus' resurrection results in indestructible life for him, so he becomes the one who gives that life to others who put their trust in him (compare Jn 3:16–17). **witnesses** The apostles and the broader Christian community are commissioned by Jesus to testify continually to his resurrection and its implications. Compare Ac 1:8; Isa 43:10.

3:16 faith that comes through him This could mean either that the man understood what Peter's words meant and placed his faith in Jesus, or that he placed his hope in the promise inherent in Peter's words and was given faith through Jesus (compare Mt 17:20).

3:17 you acted in ignorance Peter acknowledges that his fellow Jews did not have complete knowledge of their actions in crucifying Jesus—while he does not excuse their sin, he does desire to show them God's mercy by offering them pardon in Jesus and calling them to repentance and faith (compare Lk 23:34). **your leaders** Peter's claim that the leaders were wrong and in need of repentance will later draw their anger (Ac 4:1–2).

3:18 fulfilled Isaiah 53:12 speaks of the suffering and

[19]Repent, then, and turn to God, so that your sins may be wiped out, that times of refreshing may come from the Lord, [20]and that he may send the Messiah, who has been appointed for you — even Jesus. [21]Heaven must receive him until the time comes for God to restore everything, as he promised long ago through his holy prophets. [22]For Moses said, 'The Lord your God will raise up for you a prophet like me from among your own people; you must listen to everything he tells you. [23]Anyone who does not listen to him will be completely cut off from their people.'[a]

[24]"Indeed, beginning with Samuel, all the prophets who have spoken have foretold these days. [25]And you are heirs of the prophets and of the covenant God made with your fathers. He said to Abraham, 'Through your offspring all peoples on earth will be blessed.'[b] [26]When God raised up his servant, he sent him first to you to bless you by turning each of you from your wicked ways."

Peter and John Before the Sanhedrin

4 The priests and the captain of the temple guard and the Sadducees came up to Peter and John while they were speaking to the people. [2]They were greatly disturbed because the apostles were teaching the people, proclaiming in Jesus the resurrection of the dead. [3]They seized Peter and John and, because it was evening, they put them in jail until the next day. [4]But many who heard the message believed; so the number of men who believed grew to about five thousand.

[5]The next day the rulers, the elders and the teachers of the law met in Jerusalem. [6]Annas the

[a] 23 Deut. 18:15,18,19   [b] 25 Gen. 22:18; 26:4

death of the Messiah (the suffering servant) being in Yahweh's will. Peter is likely drawing on this passage, since he is still elaborating on his point in Ac 3:17 that the crucifixion of Jesus was ultimately in God's will—and that in Jesus even those who wrongly killed him may find salvation. **the prophets** Peter speaks broadly of the OT attesting to the Messiah's suffering (compare 2:30). He has alluded primarily to Isaiah throughout his sermon (see v. 14 and note; compare Ps 22).

3:19 Repent The call to repentance is always included in the gospel message. Acts emphasizes the essential place of repentance in embracing the salvation Christ offers. See 2:38. **refreshing** The Greek word used here, *anapsyxis*, refers to rejuvenation, recalling OT promises of the restoration of all creation in the days when God's kingdom comes (e.g., Ge 49:10–11; Isa 11:1–10; Joel 3:17–21; Mic 4:1–8). Those who repent will take part in God's renewal of the world (compare Ro 8:22; Rev 21).

3:21 Heaven Jesus reigns at the right hand of God the Father (Ac 2:33–34; compare Ps 110:1) while awaiting the time when he will return to judge the world and restore all things (Ac 1:6–7,11; compare Mt 24).

3:22 The Lord your God will raise up Peter quotes from Dt 18:15, where Moses establishes the nature of the prophetic office: The prophet is the one through whom Yahweh speaks to his people with authority and effectiveness.

3:23 will be completely cut off Moses stresses the people's accountability to hear and obey the prophet as one who speaks on behalf of Yahweh himself.

3:24 beginning with Samuel, all the prophets who have spoken Peter affirms what Jesus had told his disciples after his resurrection: that the OT Scriptures testify to him (Lk 24:25–27,44–47). **these days** Peter notes that the prophets spoke of the Messiah, Jesus, and the time he is currently living in—when the Holy Spirit would be poured out and the day of final judgment for all of humanity would be imminent (Joel 2:28–31).

3:25 heirs Stresses the privileged position of Israel to receive the word of God and to inherit the benefits of God's gracious covenant promises to Abraham (Ge 12:1–3; 15; 17:1–21). **offspring** The Greek word used here, *sperma*, often translated "seed" or "offspring," can refer to a singular descendant or to someone's descendants as a collective whole. Peter's language here

recalls the promise to Abraham that in his offspring all the nations of the earth would be blessed (Ge 22:18).

3:26 his servant A reference to the suffering servant prophesied by Isaiah (Isa 42:1–9; 49:1–12; 50:4–10; 52:13—53:12). See note on Ac 3:13. **he sent him first to you** Peter shows the responsibility that his fellow Jews have because they received Yahweh's covenant and the Messiah came to them.

4:1–4 In response to the apostles' proclamation of Jesus as resurrected Lord, the religious leaders attempt to show their own authority by arresting Peter and John. The power of the message of Jesus Christ makes their efforts futile.

4:1 were speaking Peter and John are explaining the significance of the miracle the crowd has witnessed (3:1–10), but the religious leaders try to silence their message.

4:2 apostles were teaching the people The religious leaders were not only disturbed at the apostles' teaching, but likely offended that they were instructing the people in the first place. The priests and Sadducees, along with the Pharisees, typically occupied the role of teachers, and the apostles have usurped that status—with great success. **proclaiming in Jesus the resurrection** The preaching of resurrection in Jesus threatens the religious leaders because it asserts his unique authority for determining the truth and God's will, and condemns them for rejecting him. The Sadducees, as well, did not believe in a real, physical resurrection (Lk 20:27). They objected to the apostles' teaching that Jesus rose bodily from the grave and its implication that his death and resurrection are the firstfruits of a resurrection to everlasting life for all who believe in him (compare 1Co 15; Da 12:1–4).

4:4 about five thousand This builds on previous statements of the church's extraordinary growth (Ac 1:15; 2:41).

4:5–22 Peter's third speech in Acts—which is a response to the persecution of local religious leaders—emphasizes a consequence of the reality of Jesus' resurrection as Lord and King: There is no other ultimate authority on earth (v. 12). The miracle and the apostles' unexplainable understanding and eloquence reinforce the truth of their claims.

4:5 elders In Judea in the first century AD, elders were trusted older men who functioned as important rulers

high priest was there, and so were Caiaphas, John, Alexander and others of the high priest's family. [7]They had Peter and John brought before them and began to question them: "By what power or what name did you do this?"

[8]Then Peter, filled with the Holy Spirit, said to them: "Rulers and elders of the people! [9]If we are being called to account today for an act of kindness shown to a man who was lame and are being asked how he was healed, [10]then know this, you and all the people of Israel: It is by the name of Jesus Christ of Nazareth, whom you crucified but whom God raised from the dead, that this man stands before you healed. [11]Jesus is

"'the stone you builders rejected,
    which has become the cornerstone.'[a]

[12]Salvation is found in no one else, for there is no other name under heaven given to mankind by which we must be saved."

[13]When they saw the courage of Peter and John and realized that they were unschooled, ordinary men, they were astonished and they took note that these men had been with Jesus. [14]But since they could see the man who had been healed standing there with them, there was nothing they could say. [15]So they ordered them to withdraw from the Sanhedrin and then conferred together. [16]"What are we going to do with these men?" they asked. "Everyone living in Jerusalem knows they have performed a notable sign, and we cannot deny it. [17]But to stop this thing from spreading any further among the people, we must warn them to speak no longer to anyone in this name."

[18]Then they called them in again and commanded them not to speak or teach at all in the name of Jesus. [19]But Peter and John replied, "Which is right in God's eyes: to listen to you, or to him? You be

[a] 11 Psalm 118:22

in the synagogues, helping to govern the community's affairs. **teachers of the law** These individuals had varying functions in the ancient world; Luke (the narrator) portrays them as experts in the law who possessed significant authority over its interpretation and teaching (compare Lk 11:37–54; Ac 6:12–14; 23:9).

4:6 Annas the high priest Annas was the former high priest, who served AD 6–15 (see Lk 3:2 and note). He was the father-in-law of the current high priest, Caiaphas. The title high priest seems to have been used even after someone left office; it seems that Annas was still very influential at this time.

4:7 By what power The council questions Peter and John (the son of Zebedee) about how they were able to perform the miracle (Ac 3:1–10). The religious leaders are trying to understand the nature of the apostles' mission and message, whether it is allowed by the law (Dt 18:20), and whether it operates within their rules.

4:8 filled In Acts, this term seems to denote a special empowering by the Holy Spirit that is in addition to his work of enabling believers to trust God and to live faithfully (e.g., Ac 2:4; 4:31; 9:17; 13:9). This empowering of the Spirit reflects Jesus' promise of power (1:8) that will allow the apostles to speak in a way that amazes their audience and confirms the truth of their message (see v. 13). It also denotes the miracle-working power seen in the ministry of the apostles. **people** Peter addresses the rulers as those who have been given authority over the Jewish people.

4:9 being called to account The Greek word used here, *anakrinō*, can denote an official judicial proceeding. **an act of kindness** Peter points out that trials are convened for crimes, not for acts of mercy and love. He implies that the religious leaders' are corrupt (compare note on 4:2).

4:10 all the people Peter uses the opportunity of the proceedings to publicly proclaim the gospel. **name** Referring to a person's name was shorthand for their character and reputation. See 3:6 and note. **whom you crucified** Peter turns the trial back on his judges, accusing them of the real crime (compare Lk 22:52; 23). **whom God raised from the dead** God, the ultimate authority, raised the one whom the council rejected—Jesus. The religious leaders have dramatically misunderstood both the true identity and mission of Jesus and their true standing before God.

4:11 the stone Peter quotes from Ps 118:22. This metaphor is picked up again by Peter (1Pe 2:4) and Paul (Ro 9:32–33; Eph 2:20). **you builders** Just as the builders did not perceive the stone's value in Ps 118:22, so Israel's religious leaders did not recognize their Messiah. **rejected** From the perspective of the Jewish leaders Peter addresses, Jesus' crucifixion is like a stumbling block (see 1Co 1:23), because anyone who hung on a tree (or a cross, in their view) was viewed as cursed by God (Dt 21:22–23).

4:12 Salvation is found in no one else Salvation refers to deliverance from God's wrath and to enjoyment of his favor. This is only given through faith in Jesus, who grants new life to all who follow him and embrace the message of his death and resurrection for the forgiveness of their sins (Ac 3:19–21).

4:13 courage of Peter and John The apostles had unshakeable confidence in speaking the truth, despite the undoubtedly intimidating circumstances. **unschooled** This does not imply that Peter and John were ignorant, but that they lacked formal training in the Law of Moses. **had been with Jesus** This is the only explanation for the apostles' unexpected eloquence and effective speech.

4:14 there was nothing they could say The religious leaders could not deny the reality of the man standing—for the first day in his life—right in front of them (3:1–10). They would, however, continue to deny the meaning of the miracle.

4:16 What are we going to do The religious leaders are uncertain what to do in the face of the evident power of the apostles' words and deeds; this emphasizes the emptiness of the religious leaders' claim to have authority over them.

4:17 stop this thing from spreading Although the religious leaders cannot deny the miracle, they still refuse to accept the message about Jesus to which it bore witness. Their chief concern is to keep the message's reach and influence from growing.

4:18 in the name of Jesus See note on 3:6.

4:19 right The Greek word used here, *dikaios*, refers in this instance to conformity to a certain standard; in a legal context, it describes whether the accused is, in the court's opinion, innocent of the charge and may in fact be considered in the right regarding the law's requirements. Here Peter again appeals to the court's authority

the judges! ²⁰As for us, we cannot help speaking about what we have seen and heard."

²¹After further threats they let them go. They could not decide how to punish them, because all the people were praising God for what had happened. ²²For the man who was miraculously healed was over forty years old.

The Believers Pray

²³On their release, Peter and John went back to their own people and reported all that the chief priests and the elders had said to them. ²⁴When they heard this, they raised their voices together in prayer to God. "Sovereign Lord," they said, "you made the heavens and the earth and the sea, and everything in them. ²⁵You spoke by the Holy Spirit through the mouth of your servant, our father David:

"'Why do the nations rage
    and the peoples plot in vain?
²⁶The kings of the earth rise up
    and the rulers band together
against the Lord
    and against his anointed one.^{a'b}

²⁷Indeed Herod and Pontius Pilate met together with the Gentiles and the people of Israel in this city to conspire against your holy servant Jesus, whom you anointed. ²⁸They did what your power and will had decided beforehand should happen. ²⁹Now, Lord, consider their threats and enable your servants to speak your word with great boldness. ³⁰Stretch out your hand to heal and perform signs and wonders through the name of your holy servant Jesus."

³¹After they prayed, the place where they were meeting was shaken. And they were all filled with the Holy Spirit and spoke the word of God boldly.

The Believers Share Their Possessions

³²All the believers were one in heart and mind. No one claimed that any of their possessions was their own, but they shared everything they had. ³³With great power the apostles continued to testify to the resurrection of the Lord Jesus. And God's grace was so powerfully at work in them all

^a 26 That is, Messiah or Christ   ^b 26 Psalm 2:1,2

---

to call them to a higher standard. This response echoes his earlier charge that the proceedings themselves are against the law (see v. 9).

4:20 we have seen and heard The apostles, as eyewitnesses to Jesus, must act as faithful witnesses according to Jesus' command (1:8).

4:21 They could not decide how to punish them The apostles have violated no law, and the religious leaders have no legal grounds for disciplining them. **all the people were praising** The contrast between the crowd worshiping God and the leaders focused on threatening the apostles shows the leaders' spiritual backwardness and rebellion against God.

4:22 over forty See note on 3:7.

4:23–31 In reaction to the opposition to the gospel they experienced, the apostles gather to pray. Like previous prayers, this one points to the church's dependence on God's strength. Their prayer once again asks for the name of Jesus to be exalted through the word of God and the power of the Spirit (vv. 30–31).

4:24 together in prayer to God The Christians were unified not only in their prayer, but in their mindset, desires and mission. **Sovereign Lord** This way of addressing God is suitable in light of the recently failed challenges to Jesus' lordship by the religious leaders. **made the heavens and the earth** Because God reigns over all creation, he is the only one able to answer his people's prayers and preserve them in the midst of danger. Compare Ge 1:1; 2Ki 19:15; Ne 9:6; Ps 146:6.

4:25–26 The early church quotes from Ps 2:1–2, which they ascribe to David, in their prayer. The early church saw this psalm as pointing to Jesus' sonship and role as the Messiah (Ac 13:33; Heb 1:5; 5:5) as well as foretelling opposition to him (Ac 4:25).

4:25 rage The Greek word used here may imply arrogance as well. Those in authority who set themselves against

Jesus and his church feel their power threatened and respond in fierce opposition.

4:26 his anointed one The psalmist envisioned the political entities of the world uniting against Yahweh and his anointed one (the Messiah), who bears his name and inherits his kingdom.

4:27 Herod and Pontius Pilate Psalm 2 envisions all types of earthly authorities opposing Jesus. Both Herod and Pilate belong to the governmental structure ruling over Israel. See the table "Political Leaders in the New Testament" on p. 1916. **with the Gentiles** In sad irony, in opposing Yahweh and his Messiah, the religious leaders of Israel have taken their stand with the Gentiles (non-Jewish people)—those who had oppressed God's people. See Ac 4:25. **anointed** The Greek verb used here, chriō, is related to the word christos, meaning Christ or Messiah. Just as God anointed David to rule Israel (1Sa 16:12), Jesus is anointed to fulfill God's plan and serve as the ultimate, eternal king of God's people.

4:29 servants The Greek word used here, doulos, is a frequent NT designation for disciples of Christ, alluding to Christians' status as freed people purchased by another—Jesus—and submitted to the authority of Christ and his will (e.g., 1Co 7:22–23). Luke (the narrator) uses a different word when speaking of Jesus (Ac 3:13,26; 4:27,30) and of David (v. 25).

4:30 your hand In the OT, this phrase refers to his strength and ability to accomplish his purposes—especially to save (Dt 4:34; 5:15; Ps 44:3; Isa 62:8). The early church expresses confidence that God will continue to uphold them and bless them as they carry out the mission he has given them. **signs and wonders** Alludes to the miracle in Ac 3:1–10.

4:31 was shaken The OT frequently describes shaking or earthquakes as a sign of God's presence (e.g., Ex 19:18; Ps 114:1–7; Isa 6:4). **they were all filled** See note on Ac 4:8.

³⁴that there were no needy persons among them. For from time to time those who owned land or houses sold them, brought the money from the sales ³⁵and put it at the apostles' feet, and it was distributed to anyone who had need.

³⁶Joseph, a Levite from Cyprus, whom the apostles called Barnabas (which means "son of encouragement"), ³⁷sold a field he owned and brought the money and put it at the apostles' feet.

Ananias and Sapphira

5 Now a man named Ananias, together with his wife Sapphira, also sold a piece of property. ²With his wife's full knowledge he kept back part of the money for himself, but brought the rest and put it at the apostles' feet.

³Then Peter said, "Ananias, how is it that Satan has so filled your heart that you have lied to the Holy Spirit and have kept for yourself some of the money you received for the land? ⁴Didn't it belong to you before it was sold? And after it was sold, wasn't the money at your disposal? What made you think of doing such a thing? You have not lied just to human beings but to God."

⁵When Ananias heard this, he fell down and died. And great fear seized all who heard what had happened. ⁶Then some young men came forward, wrapped up his body, and carried him out and buried him.

⁷About three hours later his wife came in, not knowing what had happened. ⁸Peter asked her, "Tell me, is this the price you and Ananias got for the land?"

"Yes," she said, "that is the price."

⁹Peter said to her, "How could you conspire to

4:32–37 This summary of the church's growth and activities resembles that in 2:42–47. This section also serves as context for the deception and perverse testimony of Ananias and Sapphira in 5:1–11.

4:32 their possessions This emphasizes that Jesus is Lord and master over the early Christians' entire lives. They belong to him (see v. 29 and note). Accordingly, the church's view of possessions testifies to Jesus' kingship. The members of the early church did not treat their possessions as their own, but freely gave them away (compare 2:45 and note). **shared** This reiterates the theme of the Christian community's unity. See 2:42–46.

4:33 great power This may be referring to the boldness and effectiveness of the apostles' preaching, or to the miraculous signs they performed that bolstered the truth of the message, or both. **grace was so powerfully at work** The Greek text here likely means that God's favor was present with the early believers in an especially powerful way. It could also mean that the church continued to be held in high esteem by people in and around Jerusalem (as in 2:47).

4:34 needy The Greek word used here probably refers to those who require assistance in order to meet their daily necessities.

4:35 it was distributed See note on 2:45.

4:36 Cyprus The ancient Jewish writer Philo mentions Jewish colonies on the Mediterranean island of Cyprus. Barnabas and Paul will visit Cyprus on their first missionary journey (13:4), and Barnabas will later return with John Mark (15:39). **Barnabas** Barnabas will play a larger role later in the book, especially with regard to extending the mission of the church to the Gentiles (see 9:27; 11:28–30; 13:2; 15:2–12). **son of encouragement** This title is characteristic of how God uses Barnabas in Acts to build others up and support them in their work for the kingdom (compare Ac 13).

4:37 brought the money The language in this verse is similar to that in 4:34–35. The narrative portrays Barnabas as an individual Christian who puts the needs of the community first, without regard to himself. Luke (the narrator) will present Ananias and Sapphira as the antithesis to Barnabas (5:1–11).

5:1–11 The account of Ananias and Sapphira is full of ironic and sad twists. The story demonstrates how seriously people should take their commitments before God.

5:2 With his wife's full knowledge This establishes that Sapphira was complicit in this sin and no less guilty than Ananias. **kept back** Ananias and Sapphira's sin was not in failing to give the entire sum of money (see v. 4 and note); they sinned in pretending to honor Christ with the whole amount while withholding some of it for themselves. They lied in order to keep some of the money, certainly, but perhaps more significantly, they desired to be honored for their perceived generosity.

5:3 Satan This was no small matter; this sin was a betrayal of Jesus and harmed the integrity of the entire community. Ananias' act was equivalent to giving into the will of Satan, the primary spiritual enemy of Jesus and his church (see note on Mk 1:13; compare Eph 6:11; 1Pe 5:8). **the Holy Spirit** Ananias did not merely lie to the apostles and fellow believers in the church; his deceit is an affront to God himself.

5:4 Didn't it belong to you Peter's rhetorical questions point out that Ananias was not obligated to sell his property or give the proceeds away. In addition, it was his choice to give all or part of the proceeds of the sale. Deception was not necessary to retain part of the money, so the only reason to lie was in order to claim greater honor and status within the church. **You have not lied just to human beings but to God** In Ac 5:3, and again in v. 9, the sin is described as lying to the Holy Spirit; here, it is lying to God. This language seems to implicitly assume the Holy Spirit's identity as a divine person.

5:5 heard this Speaking in the power of the Spirit, Peter's words are effective in bringing about the judgment that God pronounces upon Ananias. **great fear** The community realizes with renewed gravity that Jesus' lordship and the holiness of the community must be taken seriously.

5:7 three hours The irony of the story continues in this picture of the wife going about her day's business knowing of her husband's planned deceit yet ignorant of his unexpected death.

5:9 test Sapphira's actions challenged God's holy reputation within the church and outside it, and her continued adherence to the lie when she was given a chance to tell the truth was a defiant act (v. 8). In making this decision, she placed herself not only in opposition to God but essentially claimed to be beyond his power and ability to hold her accountable for her actions.

test the Spirit of the Lord? Listen! The feet of the men who buried your husband are at the door, and they will carry you out also."

¹⁰At that moment she fell down at his feet and died. Then the young men came in and, finding her dead, carried her out and buried her beside her husband. ¹¹Great fear seized the whole church and all who heard about these events.

The Apostles Heal Many

¹²The apostles performed many signs and wonders among the people. And all the believers used to meet together in Solomon's Colonnade. ¹³No one else dared join them, even though they were highly regarded by the people. ¹⁴Nevertheless, more and more men and women believed in the Lord and were added to their number. ¹⁵As a result, people brought the sick into the streets and laid them on beds and mats so that at least Peter's shadow might fall on some of them as he passed by. ¹⁶Crowds gathered also from the towns around Jerusalem, bringing their sick and those tormented by impure spirits, and all of them were healed.

The Apostles Persecuted

¹⁷Then the high priest and all his associates, who were members of the party of the Sadducees, were filled with jealousy. ¹⁸They arrested the apostles and put them in the public jail. ¹⁹But during the night an angel of the Lord opened the doors of the jail and brought them out. ²⁰"Go, stand in the temple courts," he said, "and tell the people all about this new life."

²¹At daybreak they entered the temple courts, as they had been told, and began to teach the people.

When the high priest and his associates arrived, they called together the Sanhedrin—the full assembly of the elders of Israel—and sent to the jail for the apostles. ²²But on arriving at the jail, the officers did not find them there. So they went back and reported, ²³"We found the jail securely locked, with the guards standing at the doors; but when we opened them, we found no one inside." ²⁴On hearing this report, the captain of the temple guard and the chief priests were at a loss, wondering what this might lead to.

²⁵Then someone came and said, "Look! The men you put in jail are standing in the temple courts teaching the people." ²⁶At that, the captain went with his officers and brought the apostles. They did not use force, because they feared that the people would stone them.

²⁷The apostles were brought in and made to appear before the Sanhedrin to be questioned by the high priest. ²⁸"We gave you strict orders not to

---

5:11 the whole church The reputation of the power and seriousness of the Holy Spirit's work now extends not only to those within the church but also to anyone who heard, regardless of whether they followed Jesus or not. The Christian community learns that God will protect the purity of the early church.

5:12–16 After the deaths of Ananias and Sapphira, the church continues its effort. Those outside the church seem to understand the nature of its power more than before. The church's witness spreads beyond Jerusalem, eventually leading to increased opposition (vv. 17–26). This account is very similar to 2:42–47 and 4:32–37. While the passages may seem to repeat one another, Luke (the narrator) shows how God continues to deepen and extend the witness of the church.

5:12 signs and wonders A common marker in Acts, attesting to both Christ's power and the apostles' authority to carry the message of his kingdom (e.g., 2:43; 4:30). See the table "Miracles in Acts" on p. 1774. **all the believers used to meet together** This repeats Luke's emphasis on the unity of the early church (e.g., 1:14; 2:46; 4:24) and their sense of single-mindedness in faith and purpose. **Solomon's Colonnade** See note on 3:11. **5:13 No one else dared** Refers to people who were intrigued by the Christian message or respected the Christian community but were afraid to join—probably in light of the deaths of Ananias and Sapphira (5:1–11).

5:14 more and more Compare note on 2:47.

5:15 shadow The narrative does not confirm the truth or falsity of the people's belief; the belief itself testifies to the reality of the apostles' power and authority demonstrated among them.

5:16 the towns around Jerusalem Until this point the church's witness focused on Jerusalem. Its influence is spreading as people recognize the truth of the gospel and embrace the lordship of Christ (compare 1:8).

5:17–26 The church's increasing visibility ignites another conflict between the apostles and the religious leaders. The religious leaders' lack of ability to stop the actions of the church demonstrates Peter's earlier assertion that Christ is the only Lord with ultimate authority (4:12).

5:17 filled In Acts, the Greek word used here, *pimplēmi*, most often refers to a special enabling of God's Spirit (e.g., 2:4; 4:8,31). In what may be an ironic use of the word, the religious leaders being full of jealousy testifies to their failure to spiritually lead Israel to the true Messiah or to recognize their own need for forgiveness in Jesus' name.

5:18 put them in the public jail The religious leaders assert their power by attempting to humiliate and discredit the apostles (and thus their message).

5:19 an angel Frequently in Acts, God rescues the apostles from danger or furthers the mission of the church through angelic intermediaries (e.g., 8:26; 12:7; 27:23).

5:20 stand in the temple courts The apostles must stand as public proof that God's purposes cannot be overturned and that Christ's lordship is the true power in this spiritual struggle. **this new life** Jesus' resurrection proves that he grants to believers new life that cannot be overcome by death (1:3; 3:15; compare Ro 6:8–10; Jn 14:6).

5:21–26 The religious leaders of Jerusalem demonstrate their inability to thwart the proclamation of the gospel (Ac 5:21). They also demonstrate their ineptitude when the soldiers cannot find the apostles, adding a note of comedy to the drama (vv. 23–24). Finally, news comes that the apostles are free, and the religious leaders fear them (vv. 25–26).

teach in this name," he said. "Yet you have filled Jerusalem with your teaching and are determined to make us guilty of this man's blood."

²⁹Peter and the other apostles replied: "We must obey God rather than human beings! ³⁰The God of our ancestors raised Jesus from the dead—whom you killed by hanging him on a cross. ³¹God exalted him to his own right hand as Prince and Savior that he might bring Israel to repentance and forgive their sins. ³²We are witnesses of these things, and so is the Holy Spirit, whom God has given to those who obey him."

³³When they heard this, they were furious and wanted to put them to death. ³⁴But a Pharisee named Gamaliel, a teacher of the law, who was honored by all the people, stood up in the Sanhedrin and ordered that the men be put outside for a little while. ³⁵Then he addressed the Sanhedrin: "Men of Israel, consider carefully what you intend to do to these men. ³⁶Some time ago Theudas appeared, claiming to be somebody, and about four hundred men rallied to him. He was killed, all his followers were dispersed, and it all came to nothing. ³⁷After him, Judas the Galilean appeared in the days of the census and led a band of people in revolt. He too was killed, and all his followers were scattered. ³⁸Therefore, in the present case I advise you: Leave these men alone! Let them go! For if their purpose or activity is of human origin, it will fail. ³⁹But if it is from God, you will not be able to stop these men; you will only find yourselves fighting against God."

⁴⁰His speech persuaded them. They called the apostles in and had them flogged. Then they ordered them not to speak in the name of Jesus, and let them go.

⁴¹The apostles left the Sanhedrin, rejoicing because they had been counted worthy of suffering disgrace for the Name. ⁴²Day after day, in the temple courts and from house to house, they never stopped teaching and proclaiming the good news that Jesus is the Messiah.

5:21 Sanhedrin The supreme council in charge of many Jewish affairs in the land of Israel has convened to deal with the threat of the apostles and their quickly spreading message about the risen Jesus. See the infographic "The Sanhedrin" on p. 1746.

5:27–42 In Peter's earlier speech in Solomon's Portico (or Colonnade),he acknowledged that the people and their rulers had acted against Jesus in ignorance (3:17). Events have since escalated, and now Peter stresses that the leaders are pronouncing judgments contrary to God and his Word.

5:28 We gave you strict orders The leaders assert their authority once more, insisting the apostles should have been loyal to them instead of to Jesus (see 4:18). **to make us guilty** Peter had testified that Jesus was crucified with the approval of the council (4:10), indicting them as accomplices in his murder.

5:29 obey God rather than human beings Peter pits the council's motives and judgments directly against the will of God.

5:30 by hanging him on a cross The high priest had protested in v. 28 that the apostles' preaching implied that the religious leaders were responsible for Jesus' death. Peter now directly charges them with crucifying Jesus. His language alludes to Dt 21:22–23.

5:31 Savior Jesus rescues all who trust in him from sin and its consequences. He is given this title at his birth (Lk 2:11). **that he might bring Israel to repentance** The OT asserts that God must intervene in the life of Israel for them to have new spiritual life (Dt 30:1–6; Jer 31:31–34). This power to intervene in the life of people, and offer salvation, is attributed to Jesus. **forgive** Israel's hope is based on God's gracious forgiveness of the sins of those who believe in Jesus (compare Isa 53:10—54:3; Zec 3:8–10; 12:10—13:1).

5:32 witnesses See Ac 1:8. **Holy Spirit** The work of the Holy Spirit to make the proclamation of the gospel effective and to perform miracles in the church testifies to the reality of Jesus' resurrection and salvation in him.

5:33 they were furious The religious leaders' rage contrasts sharply with the enthusiastic response to Peter's first sermon (2:37).

5:34 Gamaliel A prominent rabbi and leader of the Pharisees during the NT period. Paul was his pupil (22:3). **that the men be put outside** God intervenes through Gamaliel's reasonableness in order to preserve the apostles' lives.

5:36 Theudas The first-century Jewish historian Josephus mentions a Theudas who led a revolt around AD 44–46 (Josephus, *Antiquities* 20.97–98). This places Theudas' revolt about a decade after the events in ch. 5. It may be that there was another rebel leader named Theudas (a relatively common name) since Gamaliel is referring to events that took place before the time Josephus mentions.

5:37 Judas the Galilean The Jewish historian Josephus mentions this well-known figure led a revolt against Rome around AD 6 (Josephus, *Antiquities* 18.23; compare note on Ac 5:36). **the census** A census under Quirinius, the governor of Syria, in AD 6, later than the one taken around the time of Jesus' birth (Lk 2:2).

5:38 Leave these men alone In light of the pattern set by earlier failed revolutionary movements, Gamaliel advises the leaders not to intervene. That is their safest route, in his opinion, regardless of God's position toward the new Christian movement.

5:40 flogged The Greek word used here, *derō*, probably refers to flogging with no more than 40 lashes (see Dt 25:3). The person being punished was often whipped with leather strips, sometimes embedded with sharp objects to tear the skin. This is a much harsher action than the warning they issued previously (Ac 4:18). **name of Jesus** The council again focuses on suppressing the apostles' proclamation of the good news about Jesus, his resurrection and the forgiveness and new life God grants to those who trust in Jesus (compare 4:7,18).

5:41 rejoicing Intimidation and physical violence do not deter the apostles. Instead, they find joy in being found worthy to suffer for Christ's sake (compare 1Pe 4:12–16).

5:42 they never stopped The apostles do not falter in pursuing the mission Jesus has given them despite increasing danger from the religious leaders.

The Choosing of the Seven

6 In those days when the number of disciples was increasing, the Hellenistic Jews[a] among them complained against the Hebraic Jews because their widows were being overlooked in the daily distribution of food. [2]So the Twelve gathered all the disciples together and said, "It would not be right for us to neglect the ministry of the word of God in order to wait on tables. [3]Brothers and sisters, choose seven men from among you who are known to be full of the Spirit and wisdom. We will turn this responsibility over to them [4]and will give our attention to prayer and the ministry of the word."

[5]This proposal pleased the whole group. They chose Stephen, a man full of faith and of the Holy Spirit; also Philip, Procorus, Nicanor, Timon, Parmenas, and Nicolas from Antioch, a convert to Judaism. [6]They presented these men to the apostles, who prayed and laid their hands on them.

[7]So the word of God spread. The number of disciples in Jerusalem increased rapidly, and a large number of priests became obedient to the faith.

Stephen Seized

[8]Now Stephen, a man full of God's grace and power, performed great wonders and signs among the people. [9]Opposition arose, however, from members of the Synagogue of the Freedmen (as it was called) — Jews of Cyrene and Alexandria as well as the provinces of Cilicia and Asia — who began to argue with Stephen. [10]But they could not stand up against the wisdom the Spirit gave him as he spoke.

[11]Then they secretly persuaded some men to say, "We have heard Stephen speak blasphemous words against Moses and against God."

[12]So they stirred up the people and the elders and the teachers of the law. They seized Stephen and brought him before the Sanhedrin. [13]They produced false witnesses, who testified, "This fellow never stops speaking against this holy place and against the law. [14]For we have heard him say that this Jesus of Nazareth will destroy

a 1 That is, Jews who had adopted the Greek language and culture

---

6:1–7 The church continues to grow in number. As conflict arises between two cultures represented in the church (see note on Ac 6:1). Stephen, a Greek-speaking Jew, becomes a key figure.

6:1 the Hellenistic Jews Refers to ethnic Jews who practiced Judaism and largely adopted Greek language and culture. They may have lived most of their lives outside of Judea. **the Hebraic Jews** Refers to Jews who have not widely adopted Greek language or culture. This group primarily spoke Aramaic or Hebrew, and although they may have spoken Greek too, they remained fundamentally Jewish in their lifestyle. The antagonism between these two groups is likely rooted in the Hebraic Jews viewing other Jews with suspicion — seeing them as not purely Jewish or as compromisers of their identity. This antagonism represents an obstacle to the early church's goal of becoming a new expression of humanity, united in Christ rather than divided along ethnic or social lines (compare 1Co 12:13; Gal 3:28). **widows** In the ancient Near East, widows often could not survive unless immediate family members provided for them (compare 1Ti 5:9–16). Overlooking fellow believers who were in such need because of a cultural difference betrays a serious and highly problematic tension within the Jerusalem church. **daily distribution of food** This was for those in need. Compare Ac 4:32,34.

6:2 to neglect the ministry of the word of God The disciples remind the other believers of their true responsibility to teach the message of God and witness to Christ — the main priority of the church (compare Ac 1:8). **in order to wait on tables** The apostles do not denigrate the practice of meeting the practical needs of other believers, but delegate responsibilities based on calling and suitability. The Greek word used here, *diakoneō*, is related to the Greek term *diakonos* (commonly translated as "deacon"). There seems to be overlap between the roles of those chosen in this chapter and the description of the office later given in 1Ti 3:8–13.

6:3 who are known To protect the holiness of the community and to safeguard impartiality in the distribution

of goods, the community must choose people who have shown themselves godly and wise. The qualifications for these leaders is similar to the more elaborate list given for the office of deacon in 1Ti 3:8–13.

6:5 All of the men listed in this verse have Greek names. The community acts to ensure care for those outside its original social and cultural bounds — those who were previously marginalized — by appointing to leadership people who are from the same background.

6:5 the whole group It is significant that the narrative records the church's single-mindedness in this matter in light of the previous disunity between cultural factions.
6:6 laid their hands on Compare 1Ti 4:14; 2Ti 1:6.
6:7 increased rapidly The story of the community's struggle to overcome internal divisions begins and ends with the growth of the church (see Ac 6:1). **a large number of priests** The gospel message begins to win over even religious leaders, despite ongoing opposition by the local Jewish religious leadership.
6:8 wonders and signs Stephen's gifts and empowerment by the Spirit are similar to that of the apostles.
6:9 Synagogue of the Freedmen Men who belonged to a Greek-speaking synagogue, perhaps founded by or attended by freed slaves. See note on Mt 4:23. **Cyrene** From the region around Cyrene, a city in northern Africa. **Alexandria** From the region around Alexandria, a city in Egypt. **Cilicia and Asia** Referring to Asia Minor (modern Turkey).
6:10 they could not stand up against Stephen's opponents try but fail to overcome him in theological debate (compare Lk 21:15).
6:11 they secretly persuaded Since Stephen's opponents cannot counter the wisdom he has been given by the Spirit, they resort to deceit and slander.
6:13 false witnesses These witnesses and their accusations are reminiscent of those brought forward in Jesus' trial (Mk 14:56–58). The temple served as the center of Israel's worship and the symbol of authority for the Sadducees, the priests and the system of worship in Israel. The Jews allege that Stephen is undoing what God has established.

this place and change the customs Moses handed down to us."

¹⁵All who were sitting in the Sanhedrin looked intently at Stephen, and they saw that his face was like the face of an angel.

Stephen's Speech to the Sanhedrin

7 Then the high priest asked Stephen, "Are these charges true?"

²To this he replied: "Brothers and fathers, listen to me! The God of glory appeared to our father Abraham while he was still in Mesopotamia, before he lived in Harran. ³'Leave your country and your people,' God said, 'and go to the land I will show you.'ᵃ

⁴"So he left the land of the Chaldeans and settled in Harran. After the death of his father, God sent him to this land where you are now living. ⁵He gave him no inheritance here, not even enough ground to set his foot on. But God promised him that he and his descendants after him would possess the land, even though at that time Abraham had no child. ⁶God spoke to him in this way: 'For four hundred years your descendants will be strangers in a country not their own, and they will be enslaved and mistreated. ⁷But I will punish the nation they serve as slaves,' God said, 'and afterward they will come out of that country and worship me in this place.'ᵇ ⁸Then he gave Abra-

ham the covenant of circumcision. And Abraham became the father of Isaac and circumcised him eight days after his birth. Later Isaac became the father of Jacob, and Jacob became the father of the twelve patriarchs.

⁹"Because the patriarchs were jealous of Joseph, they sold him as a slave into Egypt. But God was with him ¹⁰and rescued him from all his troubles. He gave Joseph wisdom and enabled him to gain the goodwill of Pharaoh king of Egypt. So Pharaoh made him ruler over Egypt and all his palace.

¹¹"Then a famine struck all Egypt and Canaan, bringing great suffering, and our ancestors could not find food. ¹²When Jacob heard that there was grain in Egypt, he sent our forefathers on their first visit. ¹³On their second visit, Joseph told his brothers who he was, and Pharaoh learned about Joseph's family. ¹⁴After this, Joseph sent for his father Jacob and his whole family, seventy-five in all. ¹⁵Then Jacob went down to Egypt, where he and our ancestors died. ¹⁶Their bodies were brought back to Shechem and placed in the tomb that Abraham had bought from the sons of Hamor at Shechem for a certain sum of money.

¹⁷"As the time drew near for God to fulfill his promise to Abraham, the number of our people in Egypt had greatly increased. ¹⁸Then 'a new king, to whom Joseph meant nothing, came to power

ᵃ 3 Gen. 12:1   ᵇ 7 Gen. 15:13,14

6:14 will destroy The witnesses twist Stephen's words about Jesus and his work. Jesus never claimed he would destroy the temple (compare Jn 2:19–21); he did, however, predict its destruction (Mk 13:1–2), which took place in AD 70. He also did not claim to overturn the law, but to fulfill it (Mt 5:17).
6:15 the face of an angel Compare Ex 34:29–35.

7:1–53 In his speech, Stephen defends himself and condemns the Jewish leaders. He recounts Israel's history and shows how the current generation aligns with their rebellious ancestors. Stephen becomes the church's first martyr (someone put to death because of their faith).

7:1 these charges The high priest refers to the accusations concerning the temple and the law (see Ac 6:14 and note).
7:2 The God of glory Stephen begins recounting Israel's history in a way similar to OT prophets, reminding the Israelites of the nature of their covenant responsibilities to Yahweh (compare Dt 1–3; Ps 78; Da 9; Ne 9). This often occurred in the context of Israel's failure to be faithful to God (e.g., Jer 2:1–19; Hos 11:1–7). **before he lived in Harran** Genesis 11:31—12:1 seems to indicate Abram reached Harran before God spoke to him. The Genesis account, however, does not seem to require a strict chronological ordering between Ge 11 and Ge 12. Genesis 11 may serve as an overview or background to the events in Ge 12.
7:5 his descendants after him Instead of granting the land to Abram to possess personally, God fulfills the promise in his descendants (Ge 12:7; 13:14–15; 17:8; compare Ac 3:25–26).

7:6 four hundred years A round number indicating many generations (compare Ge 15:13; Ac 13:20). **a country not their own** Stephen references Ge 15:13–14, a passage which foreshadowed Israel's sojourn in Egypt before the Exodus.
7:7 God said Stephen is not quoting any specific OT passage (compare Ex 3:12; Jer 25:12; 30:20).
7:8 the covenant of circumcision In the OT, circumcision was the sign that Abraham's descendants were God's chosen nation. It demonstrated God's commitment to keep his promises to Abraham's family (Ge 17:1–14). See the people diagram "Family Tree of the Patriarchs" on p. 52. **twelve patriarchs** The original heads of the twelve tribes of Israel, who were primarily Jacob's sons (see Ge 49).
7:9 jealous of Joseph Stephen is likely suggesting a parallel between Joseph's brothers' rejection of him (Ge 37:11) and the religious leaders' rejection of Jesus and his followers (compare Ac 5:17–18). He is also implying that God is with the church—just as he was with Joseph—rather than the religious leaders.
7:10 rescued him See Ge 41:37–45.
7:11 famine See Ge 41:54–55; 42:5.
7:12 Jacob heard See Ge 42:1–3.
7:13 their second visit See Ge 43:2–15; 45:1–4,16.
7:14 seventy-five in all This number is likely approximate (compare Ge 46:26,27; Ex 1:5; Dt 10:22).
7:15 Jacob went down to Egypt Compare Ac 7:6.
7:16 tomb that Abraham had bought Stephen's reference recalls Ge 33:19 (compare Jos 24:32), and possibly Ge 23:16–18.
7:17 Acts 7:17–19 summarizes Ex 1:7–22.

in Egypt.'ᵃ ¹⁹He dealt treacherously with our people and oppressed our ancestors by forcing them to throw out their newborn babies so that they would die.

²⁰"At that time Moses was born, and he was no ordinary child.ᵇ For three months he was cared for by his family. ²¹When he was placed outside, Pharaoh's daughter took him and brought him up as her own son. ²²Moses was educated in all the wisdom of the Egyptians and was powerful in speech and action.

²³"When Moses was forty years old, he decided to visit his own people, the Israelites. ²⁴He saw one of them being mistreated by an Egyptian, so he went to his defense and avenged him by killing the Egyptian. ²⁵Moses thought that his own people would realize that God was using him to rescue them, but they did not. ²⁶The next day Moses came upon two Israelites who were fighting. He tried to reconcile them by saying,

'Men, you are brothers; why do you want to hurt each other?'

²⁷"But the man who was mistreating the other pushed Moses aside and said, 'Who made you ruler and judge over us? ²⁸Are you thinking of killing me as you killed the Egyptian yesterday?'ᶜ ²⁹When Moses heard this, he fled to Midian, where he settled as a foreigner and had two sons.

³⁰"After forty years had passed, an angel appeared to Moses in the flames of a burning bush in the desert near Mount Sinai. ³¹When he saw this, he was amazed at the sight. As he went over to get a closer look, he heard the Lord say: ³²'I am the God of your fathers, the God of Abraham, Isaac and Jacob.'ᵈ Moses trembled with fear and did not dare to look.

³³"Then the Lord said to him, 'Take off your sandals, for the place where you are standing is

ᵃ 18 Exodus 1:8   ᵇ 20 Or was fair in the sight of God
ᶜ 28 Exodus 2:14   ᵈ 32 Exodus 3:6

7:20 he was no ordinary child God chose Moses and set him apart to lead his people out of Egypt.

7:21 placed outside See Ex 2:3–10.

7:22 wisdom of the Egyptians There is no description of Moses' education in the OT, but an adopted son of Pharaoh's daughter would have been well educated in Egyptian thought. Compare 1Ki 4:30. **powerful in speech and action** The Greek text applies the same description to Jesus in Lk 24:19.

7:23–29 Acts 7:23–29 summarizes and interprets Ex 2:11–15.

7:23 forty years old While the OT does not specify Moses' age, Stephen is likely referring to the point at which Moses reached adult maturity (see Ex 2:11). Stephen implies that at age forty Moses was ready to act on behalf of and lead the Israelites.

7:25 thought Stephen interprets Moses' reasoning in light of Moses' call from Yahweh (Ex 3:7–12).

7:29 Moses heard this, he fled According to Ex 2:14–15, Moses was afraid because others had discovered he was the one who murdered an Egyptian, and Pharaoh was seeking to kill him. **Midian** A region in the Arabian Peninsula east of the Red Sea. **two sons** Gershom and Eliezer (see Ex 18:3–4).

7:30–34 Acts 7:30–34 is a summary and interpretation of Ex 3:1–12.

7:32 God of your fathers This language ties Moses' calling to the promise to Abraham with which Stephen began his speech (Ac 7:2; compare Ex 3:6).

Pagan Deities in the New Testament

DEITY	REFERENCE	NOTE
Molek	Ac 7:43	Quotation of Amos 5:25–27 (LXX)
Rephan	Ac 7:43	Quotation of Amos 5:25–27 (LXX)
The "Great Power of God"	Ac 8:10	—
Herod Agrippa I declared a god	Ac 12:22	—
Zeus	Ac 14:11–13	The people of Lystra mistook Barnabas for Zeus
Hermes	Ac 14:11–13	The people of Lystra mistook Paul for Hermes
"An Unknown God"	Ac 17:23	Paul asserted this is the God of Israel
Artemis	Ac 19:23, 27, 28, 34, 35	There was a large temple dedicated to Artemis in Ephesus

holy ground. [34]I have indeed seen the oppression of my people in Egypt. I have heard their groaning and have come down to set them free. Now come, I will send you back to Egypt.'[a]

[35]"This is the same Moses they had rejected with the words, 'Who made you ruler and judge?' He was sent to be their ruler and deliverer by God himself, through the angel who appeared to him in the bush. [36]He led them out of Egypt and performed wonders and signs in Egypt, at the Red Sea and for forty years in the wilderness.

[37]"This is the Moses who told the Israelites, 'God will raise up for you a prophet like me from your own people.'[b] [38]He was in the assembly in the wilderness, with the angel who spoke to him on Mount Sinai, and with our ancestors; and he received living words to pass on to us.

[39]"But our ancestors refused to obey him. Instead, they rejected him and in their hearts turned back to Egypt. [40]They told Aaron, 'Make us gods who will go before us. As for this fellow Moses who led us out of Egypt — we don't know what has happened to him!'[c] [41]That was the time they made an idol in the form of a calf. They brought sacrifices to it and reveled in what their own hands had made. [42]But God turned away from them and gave them over to the worship of the sun, moon and stars. This agrees with what is written in the book of the prophets:

"'Did you bring me sacrifices and offerings
    forty years in the wilderness, people of
    Israel?
[43]You have taken up the tabernacle of Molek
    and the star of your god Rephan,
    the idols you made to worship.
Therefore I will send you into exile'[d] beyond
    Babylon.

[44]"Our ancestors had the tabernacle of the covenant law with them in the wilderness. It had been made as God directed Moses, according to the pattern he had seen. [45]After receiving the tabernacle, our ancestors under Joshua brought it with them when they took the land from the nations God drove out before them. It remained in the land until the time of David, [46]who enjoyed God's favor and asked that he might provide a dwelling place for the God of Jacob.[e] [47]But it was Solomon who built a house for him.

<hr>

[a] 34 Exodus 3:5,7,8,10   [b] 37 Deut. 18:15   [c] 40 Exodus 32:1
[d] 43 Amos 5:25-27 (see Septuagint)   [e] 46 Some early manuscripts *the house of Jacob*

<hr>

7:35 This is the same Moses The language here echoes Peter's speech about Jesus (compare Ac 2:32,36). Stephen imitates Peter's logic. Israel has consistently misjudged and rejected Yahweh's chosen leaders; in doing so, they fought against Yahweh. Rejecting Jesus as Messiah is the ultimate example of this pattern.

7:36 wonders and signs The apostles' works by the Spirit parallel Moses' miracles (compare 5:12).

7:37 your own people Yahweh continued to fulfill the promise of offspring to Abraham (see note on v. 5), which has culminated in Jesus, who is heir to both Abraham's covenant promises and Moses' prophetic office.

7:38 in the wilderness See Ex 19–31. **living words** Moses' unique position as mediator between God and the Israelites is seen in God's direct revelation of his will to Moses at Sinai (Ex 20–31; compare 1Co 10:2; Gal 3:19).

7:39–41 Acts 7:39–41 is a summary of Ex 32.

7:39 to Egypt The nature of the people's rebellious hearts was seen in their repeated tendency, when things became difficult in the wilderness, to desire to return to their previous enslavement (e.g., Ex 16:3; 17:3; Nu 11:5; 14:2–3).

7:42 God turned away Yahweh allowed the people to continue the path they chose for themselves, giving them over to their idolatry. **the sun, moon and stars** God had warned the people through Moses that they must not turn away from exclusive devotion to him and begin worshiping or trusting in heavenly bodies and false deities like all the other nations did (Dt 4:19). The history of the nation proves that they frequently failed to heed his warning (e.g., 2Ki 17:16; 21:3; Jer 19:13). **in the book of the prophets** This is a reference to the twelve minor prophets (Hosea to Malachi) being transmitted on one scroll, as seen among the Dead Sea Scrolls (ca. 250 BC–AD 50). In its original context, Stephen's

quote from Am 5:25–27 falls in the midst of a legal argument God has brought against his people for their unfaithfulness to the covenant. Stephen implies that he has a similar case against the religious leaders. They have disobeyed the covenant and followed their ancestors' rebellious ways.

7:43 tabernacle The religious leaders had accused Stephen—and Jesus—of threatening the temple (Ac 6:13), which was the permanent successor to the tabernacle (or tent) Yahweh had instructed them to build to accompany them in the wilderness (Ex 26; compare Ac 7:44). Stephen reminds them that, by turning to the tabernacles of other gods, Israel has consistently failed to respond in faith to the one true God present in their midst. **Molek** A deity whose worship likely originated in Canaan and involved child sacrifice (Lev 18:21; 20:2–5). See the table "Pagan Deities in the New Testament" on p. 1788. **beyond Babylon** Amos 5:27, which Stephen is quoting here, originally read "beyond Damascus," referring to the Assyrian deportation of the northern kingdom of Israel. In an interpretive move, Stephen refers to an exile "beyond Babylon," referring to the later deportation of Judah to Babylon. The reference to the exile of Judah may have been more relevant for Stephen's Jerusalem audience. Both events were brought about by disloyalty to Yahweh.

7:45 when they took the land See Jos 6–12. **of David** Stephen has described how Yahweh has accomplished his purposes and kept his promises—despite Israel's failings—through Abraham, Joseph and Moses. Stephen now introduces David's role in the history of Israel.

7:46 a dwelling place Instead of allowing David to build him a house (the temple), Yahweh told David that he will build David a house, or dynasty. See 2Sa 7.

7:47 a house Solomon built the temple as a permanent tabernacle where Yahweh's presence would dwell in a special way among his people (1Ki 6; see Ac 7:43 and note).

⁴⁸"However, the Most High does not live in houses made by human hands. As the prophet says:

⁴⁹"'Heaven is my throne,
and the earth is my footstool.
What kind of house will you build for me?
says the Lord.
Or where will my resting place be?
⁵⁰ Has not my hand made all these things?'ᵃ

⁵¹"You stiff-necked people! Your hearts and ears are still uncircumcised. You are just like your ancestors: You always resist the Holy Spirit! ⁵²Was there ever a prophet your ancestors did not persecute? They even killed those who predicted the coming of the Righteous One. And now you have betrayed and murdered him— ⁵³you who have received the law that was given through angels but have not obeyed it."

The Stoning of Stephen

⁵⁴When the members of the Sanhedrin heard this, they were furious and gnashed their teeth at him. ⁵⁵But Stephen, full of the Holy Spirit, looked up to heaven and saw the glory of God, and Jesus standing at the right hand of God. ⁵⁶"Look," he said, "I see heaven open and the Son of Man standing at the right hand of God."

⁵⁷At this they covered their ears and, yelling at the top of their voices, they all rushed at him, ⁵⁸dragged him out of the city and began to stone him. Meanwhile, the witnesses laid their coats at the feet of a young man named Saul.

⁵⁹While they were stoning him, Stephen prayed, "Lord Jesus, receive my spirit." ⁶⁰Then he fell on his knees and cried out, "Lord, do not hold this sin against them." When he had said this, he fell asleep.

8 And Saul approved of their killing him.

The Church Persecuted and Scattered

On that day a great persecution broke out against the church in Jerusalem, and all except the apostles were scattered throughout Judea and Samaria. ²Godly men buried Stephen and mourned deeply for him. ³But Saul began to destroy the church. Going from house to house, he dragged off both men and women and put them in prison.

Philip in Samaria

⁴Those who had been scattered preached the word wherever they went. ⁵Philip went down to a city in Samaria and proclaimed the Messiah there.

ᵃ 50 Isaiah 66:1,2

7:48 the Most High By placing so much emphasis on the temple as Yahweh's exclusive dwelling place, Israel disrespects Solomon who built it—he recognized that no physical building could contain Yahweh, the Lord of heaven and earth (1Ki 8:27; 2Ch 6:2). The implication is that the religious leaders are the ones who have misunderstood the true nature of the temple (compare Jer 7:1–15).

7:49–50 Stephen quotes Isa 66:1–2.

7:51 stiff-necked people By using Yahweh's words against the wilderness generation (Ex 32:9; 33:3) against his accusers, Stephen turns the full force of the implications of Israel's history against his opponents. **uncircumcised** Yahweh sometimes used this term against Israel to expose their unfaithfulness to his covenant (compare Dt 10:16; Jer 9:26). It is meant to be a derogatory term equating them with their neighboring nations who worshiped other gods and often oppressed them.

7:52 Was there ever a prophet During his earthly ministry Jesus frequently made this point in order to demonstrate the religious leaders' spiritual blindness and hypocrisy (e.g., Mt 5:12; 21:35; 23:29–31,37). **Righteous One** See Ac 3:14.

7:53 that was given through angels Compare Gal 3:19.

7:54 furious Compare Ac 5:33.

7:55 Jesus standing at the right hand of God Stephen witnesses the risen Jesus at the right hand of the Father. The scene may allude to Da 7:9–14, where the divine figure of the Son of Man receives the kingdom from Yahweh (compare Lk 22:69; Ac 2:33–34).

7:57 yelling In response to what the religious leaders see as the height of blasphemy—exalting Jesus alongside God—the trial becomes a mob scene.

7:58 began to stone Death by stoning was the legal penalty for blaspheming the name of God (Lev 24:16).

Saul Luke (the narrator) introduces the man who will eventually lead the church's mission to the Gentiles (non-Jewish people)—he is later called Paul (Ac 9; 13:9). In the meantime, he stands in approving witness of Stephen's stoning.

7:59 receive my spirit This echoes Jesus' words on the cross recorded by Luke (Lk 23:46).

7:60 he fell asleep A euphemism often used in the NT to describe the death of the faithful (e.g., Ac 13:36; 1Co 15:6,51; 1Th 4:13–15).

8:1–3 Luke has just set up his account of the church's witness beyond Jerusalem with two men who are (at this point) opposites: Saul, a zealous enemy of the church (Ac 7:58), and Stephen, the Christian who has just laid down his life as a witness to Jesus (v. 60). In very different ways both men motivate the church's growth, as God continues to build his church in spite of persecution. The story of Saul and the events following Stephen's death act as a backdrop for the church's efforts and Saul's later, changed life (ch. 9).

8:1 killing him Saul's support for the council's vicious treatment of Stephen anticipates his passionate hatred for the church (8:3,9:1–2; Gal 1:13–14). **except the apostles** Since at this point the church is centered in Jerusalem and the persecution is so intense there, the apostles remain there to continue to lead and support the Christian community. **Judea and Samaria** The persecution scatters believers beyond Jerusalem. God uses this moment to spread the gospel of the salvation Jesus offers and his lordship (Ac 1:8).

8:3 from house to house The early Christian community gathered for worship and meals in homes, likely the large residences of wealthy converts (compare 2:46; 5:42; 20:20). **both men and women** Saul pursued Christians without mercy or discretion.

⁶When the crowds heard Philip and saw the signs he performed, they all paid close attention to what he said. ⁷For with shrieks, impure spirits came out of many, and many who were paralyzed or lame were healed. ⁸So there was great joy in that city.

Simon the Sorcerer

⁹Now for some time a man named Simon had practiced sorcery in the city and amazed all the people of Samaria. He boasted that he was someone great, ¹⁰and all the people, both high and low, gave him their attention and exclaimed, "This man is rightly called the Great Power of God." ¹¹They followed him because he had amazed them for a long time with his sorcery. ¹²But when they believed Philip as he proclaimed the good news of the kingdom of God and the name of Jesus Christ, they were baptized, both men and women. ¹³Simon himself believed and was baptized. And he followed Philip everywhere, astonished by the great signs and miracles he saw.

¹⁴When the apostles in Jerusalem heard that Samaria had accepted the word of God, they sent Peter and John to Samaria. ¹⁵When they arrived, they prayed for the new believers there that they might receive the Holy Spirit, ¹⁶because the Holy Spirit had not yet come on any of them; they had simply been baptized in the name of the Lord Jesus. ¹⁷Then Peter and John placed their hands on them, and they received the Holy Spirit.

¹⁸When Simon saw that the Spirit was given at the laying on of the apostles' hands, he offered them money ¹⁹and said, "Give me also this ability so that everyone on whom I lay my hands may receive the Holy Spirit."

²⁰Peter answered: "May your money perish with you, because you thought you could buy the gift of God with money! ²¹You have no part or share in this ministry, because your heart is not right before God. ²²Repent of this wickedness and pray to the Lord in the hope that he may forgive you for having such a thought in your heart. ²³For I see that you are full of bitterness and captive to sin."

8:4–8 The gospel spreads to Samaria, as Jesus promised (1:8). In Jerusalem the Christian community has witnessed to fellow Jews, proclaiming the kingdom of God's arrival in the risen Jesus and the outpouring of his Spirit, fulfilling the promises of the OT. In Samaria, they will reach Samaritans also.

8:4 who had been scattered Gamaliel had predicted that those who were against God would be scattered (5:37); the church scatters, but instead of dying out like the religious leaders expect, it grows all the more. **8:5 Philip** One of the seven Hellenistic (Greek-speaking and cultured) Jews elected to meet the material needs of the community. See 6:3–5; compare 21:8. **city in Samaria** The spread of the gospel to the Samaritans represents an important advance in preaching the gospel to the ends of the earth (1:8). The gospel has already crossed cultural and language barriers among Jews (2:1–13; 6:1–7), now it spreads to those who share some Jewish beliefs but were—on the basis of race, religion and general history—generally viewed by Jews with derision (compare Jn 4; see note on 4:9). See the table "Major Groups in Jesus' Time" on p. 1630. **8:6 signs he performed** As with Peter and Stephen, Philip's message was accompanied by miracles attesting its validity and authority (compare Ac 2:43; 6:8).

8:7–8 Luke (the narrator) lists the specific types of signs Philip performed. These signs demonstrate that Jesus has power not only over the physical realm (as in Peter's healing of the lame man; 3:6–10), but also over the supernatural realm.

8:9–11 Verses 9–11 present Simon as a direct challenger to, and counterfeit of, Jesus' claims. Simon practiced magic, drew praise and perhaps even worship from the people, and claimed to be great (v. 9). **8:10 gave him their attention** The Greek term used here, *prosechō*, also occurs with reference to Philip in (8:6) and later to Lydia (16:14). In each case it describes attentive listening that leads to acceptance of the message of the gospel. **the Great Power of God** The people of

Samaria gave Simon this title because they believed his sorcery was somehow associated with God's own power. **8:12 they believed** The truth of the gospel of Jesus and the power of his Spirit overcome the Samaritans' enchantment with Simon and his sorcery. **kingdom of God** See note on 1:3. **name of Jesus Christ** See note on 3:6. **they were baptized** The Samaritans publicly identify themselves with Jesus and his church. See note on 2:38; compare Jn 4:21–24. **8:13 Simon** Even Simon is convinced by the power of Philip's message and miracles—although he will prove to be ignorant of its true significance (compare Ac 8:20–23). **8:14 Peter and John** The church sends Peter and John to confirm the acceptance of the Samaritan believers into the Christian community. **8:15 Holy Spirit** The Spirit himself affirms that the Samaritan believers belong fully to the community of believers. See 2:38. **8:17 placed their hands on them** The distinct separation in time between new Christians' baptism and the Holy Spirit coming to indwell them through the apostles laying hands on them (v. 18) only occurs here in Acts (although something similar occurs with a group of John the Baptist's disciples; 19:1–6). This may be so that the apostles have an opportunity to officially endorse the Samaritan believers as fully continuous with the ministry and mission of the church in Jerusalem, according to Jesus' promise (1:8). **8:18 he offered them money** Simon grossly misunderstands the Spirit's power, the apostles' ministry and the character of Jesus and his kingdom. **8:19 Give me also this ability** Simon shows he has not genuinely understood or submitted to the lordship of Jesus Christ. He is interested in possessing the apostles' power rather than embracing their message. **8:20 gift of God** Meaning the Holy Spirit (see 2:38; 10:45). **8:21 no part or share** Peter excludes Simon from the church and its ministry. **your heart is not right** Peter discerns Simon's true motives through Simon's actions. **8:22 Repent** Even as Peter condemns Simon, he still

²⁴Then Simon answered, "Pray to the Lord for me so that nothing you have said may happen to me."

²⁵After they had further proclaimed the word of the Lord and testified about Jesus, Peter and John returned to Jerusalem, preaching the gospel in many Samaritan villages.

Philip and the Ethiopian

²⁶Now an angel of the Lord said to Philip, "Go south to the road—the desert road—that goes down from Jerusalem to Gaza." ²⁷So he started out, and on his way he met an Ethiopianᵃ eunuch, an important official in charge of all the treasury of the Kandake (which means "queen of the Ethiopians"). This man had gone to Jerusalem to worship, ²⁸and on his way home was sitting in his chariot reading the Book of Isaiah the prophet. ²⁹The Spirit told Philip, "Go to that chariot and stay near it."

³⁰Then Philip ran up to the chariot and heard the man reading Isaiah the prophet. "Do you understand what you are reading?" Philip asked.

³¹"How can I," he said, "unless someone explains it to me?" So he invited Philip to come up and sit with him.

³²This is the passage of Scripture the eunuch was reading:

"He was led like a sheep to the slaughter,
    and as a lamb before its shearer is silent,
    so he did not open his mouth.
³³ In his humiliation he was deprived of justice.
    Who can speak of his descendants?
    For his life was taken from the earth."ᵇ

³⁴The eunuch asked Philip, "Tell me, please, who is the prophet talking about, himself or someone else?" ³⁵Then Philip began with that very passage of Scripture and told him the good news about Jesus.

³⁶As they traveled along the road, they came to some water and the eunuch said, "Look, here is water. What can stand in the way of my being baptized?" [37]ᶜ ³⁸And he gave orders to stop the chariot. Then both Philip and the eunuch went down into the water and Philip baptized him. ³⁹When they came up out of the water, the Spirit of the Lord suddenly took Philip away, and the

---

ᵃ 27 That is, from the southern Nile region   ᵇ 33 Isaiah 53:7,8 (see Septuagint)   ᶜ 37 Some manuscripts include here *Philip said, "If you believe with all your heart, you may." The eunuch answered, "I believe that Jesus Christ is the Son of God."*

---

holds out hope to him if he will genuinely turn from his sin and ask the Lord for forgiveness.
8:24 Pray to the Lord Simon understands the gravity of Peter's words, but Luke does not report whether Simon ever truly repented. Simon's statement could be understood as him seeking to avoid the Holy Spirit being against him, not necessarily him seeking Christ.
8:25 in many Samaritan villages Compare 1:8; 8:4–5.

8:26–40 God continues to show that his mission is to all people by accepting an Ethiopian eunuch as a Christian. This man's identity—both ethnically distant from Israel and possibly sociologically distinct and marginalized as a eunuch (see Dt 23:1)—shows God's concern for all people.

8:26 angel See note on Ac 5:19. **road** This desert road was a major trade highway connecting Israel and the key Mediterranean ports of the area (including Caesarea, Joppa and Gaza).
8:27 an Ethiopian eunuch An official employed by the queen of a kingdom in Africa south of Egypt (not necessarily in modern-day Ethiopia). Eunuchs often served in royal courts (compare Est 2:3). **to Jerusalem to worship** This suggests that the eunuch is a convert to Judaism.
8:28 Isaiah the prophet See Ac 8:32.
8:31 explains it to me His humbleness and willingness to seek answers creates an opportunity for Philip to guide him into the knowledge of Jesus' identity as the promised Messiah.

8:32–33 The eunuch was reading Isa 53:7–8 in the Septuagint (the ancient Greek translation of the OT). This passage is about Yahweh's suffering servant; it is one of the key Messianic passages in the OT.

8:32 like a sheep This passage about the suffering servant relates his death to Israel's sacrificial system (compare Isa 53:7 and note). The voluntary submission

of the suffering servant to death would atone for sin and vindicate his innocence (compare Isa 53:12 and note).
8:33 he was deprived of justice Isaiah proclaims that the Messiah was grossly mistreated, and his death was unjust. Through this injustice, the one without guilt would bear the punishment for his guilty people (compare Isa 53:10 and note). **Who can speak of his descendants** In the original Hebrew text, this describes the suffering servant symbolically taking on the role of the exiled Israelites. In the ancient Greek version being quoted here this idea is framed as a rhetorical question that hints at that destitute state of the servant—he will have nothing, not even descendants, in his death (compare Isa 53:10).

8:35 good news Philip used the fourth suffering servant song (Isa 52:13—53:12) to explain the gospel of Jesus' sacrificial death, victorious resurrection and the significance of Jesus' actions for all people (compare note on Isa 53:10). In answer to the eunuch's question (Ac 8:34), Philip would have explained that the prophet is speaking about an individual suffering servant, who takes on the sin of all of humanity (Isa 53:12). He would have then connected the suffering servant prophecy (Isa 52:13—53:12) to Jesus. Not long after this passage in Isaiah is the proclamation that eunuchs will be able to join God's people (Isa 56:3–5). Isaiah reverses Dt 23:1, which excludes eunuchs from gathering with the assembly of Israel. Philip may have also made this connection.
8:36 some water After Philip's message, the necessary element (water) is presented for the eunuch to demonstrate his allegiance to Christ. **What can stand in the way** The eunuch, who is not Jewish, wonders if any barrier remains to prevent his identification with Jesus and reception of the blessings of his work.
8:38 into the water The Greek phrasing used here may be meant to emphasize Philip's spiritual solidarity with

eunuch did not see him again, but went on his way rejoicing. [40]Philip, however, appeared at Azotus and traveled about, preaching the gospel in all the towns until he reached Caesarea.

Saul's Conversion

9:1-19pp — Ac 22:3-16; 26:9-18

9 Meanwhile, Saul was still breathing out murderous threats against the Lord's disciples. He went to the high priest [2]and asked him for letters to the synagogues in Damascus, so that if he found any there who belonged to the Way, whether men or women, he might take them as prisoners to Jerusalem. [3]As he neared Damascus on his journey, suddenly a light from heaven flashed around him. [4]He fell to the ground and heard a voice say to him, "Saul, Saul, why do you persecute me?"

[5]"Who are you, Lord?" Saul asked.

"I am Jesus, whom you are persecuting," he replied. [6]"Now get up and go into the city, and you will be told what you must do."

[7]The men traveling with Saul stood there speechless; they heard the sound but did not see anyone. [8]Saul got up from the ground, but when he opened his eyes he could see nothing. So they led him by the hand into Damascus. [9]For three days he was blind, and did not eat or drink anything.

[10]In Damascus there was a disciple named Ananias. The Lord called to him in a vision, "Ananias!"

"Yes, Lord," he answered.

[11]The Lord told him, "Go to the house of Judas on Straight Street and ask for a man from Tarsus named Saul, for he is praying. [12]In a vision he has seen a man named Ananias come and place his hands on him to restore his sight."

[13]"Lord," Ananias answered, "I have heard many reports about this man and all the harm he has done to your holy people in Jerusalem. [14]And he has come here with authority from the chief priests to arrest all who call on your name."

[15]But the Lord said to Ananias, "Go! This man is my chosen instrument to proclaim my name to the Gentiles and their kings and to the people of Israel. [16]I will show him how much he must suffer for my name."

the eunuch: both of the men enter the water together, and both come up out of it together (Ac 8:39).

8:39 suddenly took Philip away Compare 1Ki 18:12; 2Ki 2:16. **rejoicing** The eunuch's journey from confusion to joy displays the Spirit's transforming power. Both the Gospel of Luke and Acts often emphasize this characteristic in the lives of believers (e.g., Lk 1:14; 24:52; Ac 5:41).

8:40 appeared at Azotus The city of Ashdod, which is along the coast of the Mediterranean Sea. **he reached Caesarea** Philip moves on to proclaim the gospel up the Mediterranean coast. Caesarea had been a key city for Herod the Great, with a substantial Gentile population and a major port. God is preparing the church to reach beyond Jews and those affiliated with the Jews to the other Gentiles and their territories. Philip comes into the story of Acts again much later, having settled in Caesarea (21:8).

9:1–9 The gospel witness has extended from Jerusalem to Judea and Samaria. Now, God begins to build the church to reach the farthest parts of the earth (1:8). The conversion of Saul (who is also called Paul) will launch a full-fledged mission to the Gentiles.

9:1 murderous threats Saul may not have been the actual executioner, but his arrests led to the imprisonment and deaths of many in the church. See 22:4; 26:10; and Gal 1:13.

9:2 Damascus A city in modern-day Syria, northeast of Jerusalem. It was an important commercial center and a key stop along the trade route between Egypt and Mesopotamia. **the Way** An early name for the community of those who confessed Jesus as Messiah (compare Jn 14:6; Ac 19:9; 24:14).

9:3 flashed around Light suddenly and overwhelmingly enveloped Saul.

9:4 fell to the ground This experience of Jesus' glory is so overwhelming that it forces Saul to the ground (compare Eze 1:28; Da 10:9; Rev 1:17). **Saul, Saul** Jesus' repetition of Saul's name may suggest a sense of urgency or of compassion (compare Lk 10:41; 22:31). A

repetition of a name occurs at several key points in the OT when God directly calls someone to a special office or role (e.g., Ge 22:11; Ex 3:4; 1Sa 3:10). Jesus both confronts Saul's sin and commissions him for apostolic ministry. **why do you persecute me** In persecuting the church, Saul persecutes Jesus himself.

9:5 Who are you, Lord Saul's question, as well as Jesus' response with the words "I am" (*egō eimi* in Greek), may be an allusion to Moses' encounter with Yahweh in the burning bush (Ex 3:14). Like Moses, Saul is here being called by Yahweh to rescue a people (in Saul's case, the Gentiles). See the table "Resurrection Appearances of Jesus" on p. 1896.

9:7 did not see anyone Compare Da 10:7.

9:8 he could see nothing Saul's physical blindness may be the result of the intense glory of Jesus' appearance, or it may be an outward manifestation of his own spiritual blindness that he (ironically) has just begun to see for the first time. It could also be Jesus' way of humbling Saul.

9:9 did not eat or drink anything Jesus had just turned Saul's understanding of God, Scripture and his own identity and values upside down (compare Ro 10:1–4; Gal 1:11–17; Php 3:3–11). Saul's fast may be a response to this.

9:10–19 Through Jesus' words to Ananias, the significance of Paul's experience on the road to Damascus is revealed.

9:11 Straight Street A major road in Damascus.

9:13 I have heard Ananias is concerned; the Lord is sending him to a vicious persecutor of the church.

9:15 chosen instrument There is irony surrounding the name of Jesus in his dialog with Ananias about Saul. Ananias objects that Saul has persecuted those who call on Jesus' name (Ac 9:14); Jesus reveals that he has chosen and transformed Saul precisely so that he will carry that name to the Gentiles—and even suffer for it (v. 16).

9:16 suffer Compare 2Co 11:16–33.

[17]Then Ananias went to the house and entered it. Placing his hands on Saul, he said, "Brother Saul, the Lord — Jesus, who appeared to you on the road as you were coming here — has sent me so that you may see again and be filled with the Holy Spirit." [18]Immediately, something like scales fell from Saul's eyes, and he could see again. He got up and was baptized, [19]and after taking some food, he regained his strength.

Saul in Damascus and Jerusalem

Saul spent several days with the disciples in Damascus. [20]At once he began to preach in the synagogues that Jesus is the Son of God. [21]All those who heard him were astonished and asked, "Isn't he the man who raised havoc in Jerusalem among those who call on this name? And hasn't he come here to take them as prisoners to the chief priests?" [22]Yet Saul grew more and more powerful and baffled the Jews living in Damascus by proving that Jesus is the Messiah.

[23]After many days had gone by, there was a conspiracy among the Jews to kill him, [24]but Saul learned of their plan. Day and night they kept close watch on the city gates in order to kill him. [25]But his followers took him by night and lowered him in a basket through an opening in the wall.

[26]When he came to Jerusalem, he tried to join the disciples, but they were all afraid of him, not believing that he really was a disciple. [27]But Barnabas took him and brought him to the apostles. He told them how Saul on his journey had seen the Lord and that the Lord had spoken to him, and how in Damascus he had preached fearlessly in the name of Jesus. [28]So Saul stayed with them and moved about freely in Jerusalem, speaking boldly in the name of the Lord. [29]He talked and debated with the Hellenistic Jews,[a] but they tried to kill him. [30]When the believers learned of this, they took him down to Caesarea and sent him off to Tarsus.

[31]Then the church throughout Judea, Galilee and Samaria enjoyed a time of peace and was strengthened. Living in the fear of the Lord and encouraged by the Holy Spirit, it increased in numbers.

Aeneas and Dorcas

[32]As Peter traveled about the country, he went to visit the Lord's people who lived in Lydda. [33]There he found a man named Aeneas, who was paralyzed and had been bedridden for eight years. [34]"Aeneas," Peter said to him, "Jesus Christ heals you. Get up and roll up your mat." Immediately Aeneas got up. [35]All those who lived in Lydda and Sharon saw him and turned to the Lord.

[a] 29 That is, Jews who had adopted the Greek language and culture

---

9:17 Brother In welcoming Saul in this way, Ananias displays both his obedience to Jesus' call and Saul's full inclusion in the fellowship of the church. **filled with the Holy Spirit** Saul now receives the empowering of the Holy Spirit for his mission to the Gentiles (compare Ac 2:4). This is an anointing to fulfill a specific calling and mission placed on Saul by God. Saul will also have a role spreading the gospel before kings (e.g., 26:1–23) and his fellow Israelites (9:15; compare 22:1–21).
9:18 scales This could be a figure of speech meant to depict the sense of suddenly regaining sight.

9:20–25 This section shows the suddenness and genuineness of Saul's conversion, and begins to fulfill Jesus' promise about how he will use Saul (v. 15).

9:20 At once Saul has been radically transformed; he now uses his extensive training and zeal to build up and defend the gospel rather than to attack it (v. 22; 18:28). **Son of God** In the OT, being a son of God usually belongs either to Israel in general (Ex 4:22) or to the Davidic line in particular (2Sa 7:14–15). The ultimate Israelite and descendant of David, the Messiah, is identified as God's Son (Ps 2:7). Compare Gal 1:16; 2:20.
9:23 many days This may allude to the time Paul sojourned in Arabia and returned again to Damascus before going to Jerusalem (Gal 1:17–18). **to kill him** The Jews in Damascus could not argue against Saul's powerful preaching and reasoning from the Scriptures, so they sought to kill him.
9:24 Day and night Initially one of the greatest threats to the church, Saul's witness is now an equally serious threat to the church's enemies.
9:25 in a basket Compare 2Co 11:32–33.

9:26–31 The church in Jerusalem becomes convinced of Saul's conversion, and the apostles affirm him and his ministry.

9:27 Barnabas Barnabas, who was already well known and respected (Ac 4:36–37; 11:22–24), had listened to Saul's story and gives Saul credibility with the church and its leadership.
9:28 moved about freely Similar language is used to describe Jesus' life and ministry among the disciples (1:21).
9:29 Hellenistic Jews Refers to Greek-speaking and cultured Jews. Stephen's initial dispute was with a similar group in 6:9–10. See note on 6:1.
9:30 Tarsus The birth city of Paul (see 22:3).

9:31 Luke (the narrator) highlights the successful beginnings of Christ's promise to the apostles about the spread of the gospel (1:8).

9:31 peace This could refer primarily to the church's contentment in the face of persecution, or to their internal unity and camaraderie. **strengthened** Despite persecution, the church was growing both in number and in maturity (compare 4:4).

9:32–35 Like Philip (8:40), Peter proclaims the good news along the Mediterranean coast.

9:32 Lydda Located about ten miles inland from Joppa.
9:33 Aeneas A Greek name; Aeneas is likely a Hellenistic Jew (compare 9:29 and note).
9:35 who lived in Lydda and Sharon Refers to the area of the coastal plain. At first the church interacts with those who have been influenced by non-Jewish people

³⁶In Joppa there was a disciple named Tabitha (in Greek her name is Dorcas); she was always doing good and helping the poor. ³⁷About that time she became sick and died, and her body was washed and placed in an upstairs room. ³⁸Lydda was near Joppa; so when the disciples heard that Peter was in Lydda, they sent two men to him and urged him, "Please come at once!"

³⁹Peter went with them, and when he arrived he was taken upstairs to the room. All the widows stood around him, crying and showing him the robes and other clothing that Dorcas had made while she was still with them.

⁴⁰Peter sent them all out of the room; then he got down on his knees and prayed. Turning toward the dead woman, he said, "Tabitha, get up." She opened her eyes, and seeing Peter she sat up. ⁴¹He took her by the hand and helped her to her feet. Then he called for the believers, especially the widows, and presented her to them alive. ⁴²This became known all over Joppa, and many people believed in the Lord. ⁴³Peter stayed in Joppa for some time with a tanner named Simon.

Cornelius Calls for Peter

10 At Caesarea there was a man named Cornelius, a centurion in what was known as the Italian Regiment. ²He and all his family were devout and God-fearing; he gave generously to those in need and prayed to God regularly. ³One day at about three in the afternoon he had a vision. He distinctly saw an angel of God, who came to him and said, "Cornelius!"

⁴Cornelius stared at him in fear. "What is it, Lord?" he asked.

The angel answered, "Your prayers and gifts to the poor have come up as a memorial offering before God. ⁵Now send men to Joppa to bring back a man named Simon who is called Peter. ⁶He is staying with Simon the tanner, whose house is by the sea."

⁷When the angel who spoke to him had gone, Cornelius called two of his servants and a devout soldier who was one of his attendants. ⁸He told them everything that had happened and sent them to Joppa.

Peter's Vision

10:9-32Ref — Ac 11:5-14

⁹About noon the following day as they were on their journey and approaching the city, Peter went up on the roof to pray. ¹⁰He became hungry and wanted something to eat, and while the meal was being prepared, he fell into a trance. ¹¹He saw heaven opened and something like a large sheet being let down to earth by its four corners. ¹²It contained all kinds of four-footed animals, as well as reptiles and birds. ¹³Then a voice told him, "Get up, Peter. Kill and eat."

(the Gentiles)—the Samaritans and Greek-speaking Jews. Now God moves Peter closer to the Gentiles.

9:36–43 Dorcas' resurrection shows Jesus' power over life and death. The event also calls Peter to Joppa, marking the next step in the church's mission to the Gentiles.

9:36 Joppa An important Roman-controlled port city. **Tabitha** Based on her name, she was likely a Jewish believer who also had a Greek version of her name.

9:37 upstairs room This location creates an echo with the miracles of two of Israel's great prophets (Elijah and Elisha) and Jesus' miracles (1Ki 17:19; 2Ki 4:10; Lk 4:25–27; 8:49–56).

9:39 All the widows Dorcas' ministry among widows is testimony not only to her godliness and compassion, but to her importance for the community (compare note on Ac 9:36).

9:40 Tabitha, get up This scene especially evokes Jesus' raising of Jairus' daughter (Lk 8:54).

9:43 tanner Simon worked with dead animal carcasses, a job inherently unclean by Jewish standards (Lev 5:2; 11:24). Peter has moved to a region requiring him to interact with, and even stay with, Jews who are more influenced by non-Jewish culture and traditions.

10:1–8 This chapter marks a breakthrough in the church's mission to the Gentiles (non-Jewish people). The conversion of Cornelius, a Roman centurion, indicates to the church that God fully accepts Gentiles into God's people without the necessity of conforming to Jewish law. Luke's Gospel anticipates the mission to the Gentiles recorded in Luke's second work, Acts, by emphasizing the place of the Gentiles in God's plan (e.g., Lk 2:32; 3:6; 24:47) and favorably describing several Gentiles (e.g., Lk 7:1–10; 8:26–39; 23:47).

10:1 Caesarea See note on Ac 8:40. **Italian Regiment** This group may have been an auxiliary Roman force in Palestine consisting of Italian volunteers rather than local mercenaries or draftees.

10:2 devout and God-fearing This is Luke's designation for Gentiles (non-Jewish people) who worshiped the God of Israel (e.g., v. 22; 13:26; 18:7). Cornelius was not Jewish and may not have been a full convert—in the sense of abiding by Jewish food practices and circumcision (compare 10:28–29,45)—but he was a worshiper of Yahweh.

10:3 a vision The Greek word used here always refers in Acts to experiencing something supernatural (e.g., 9:10; 12:9; 16:9; 18:9). **an angel** See note on 5:19.

10:4 memorial offering This suggests either that Cornelius' prayers are a remembrance of God's goodness toward him, or more likely, that in response to Cornelius' prayers God is about to remember him—that is, to act on his behalf (compare Ps 141:2).

10:7 devout This term implies the soldier also worshiped the true God, Yahweh (see note on Ac 10:2).

10:8 Joppa See note on 9:36.

10:9–24 God gives Peter a vision that prepares him for the arrival of the messengers from Cornelius (vv. 7–8). The vision's meaning and OT allusions reinforce the universal cultural scope of the church's message and mission.

10:9 About noon At this time Peter would have been hungry and waiting for his midday meal to be ready (v. 10), an appropriate time for a vision involving food.

10:11 heaven opened Compare Eze 1:1; Rev 19:11.

10:12 animals Luke, the narrator, probably intends to convey that virtually every sort of creature was present.

Life of Paul

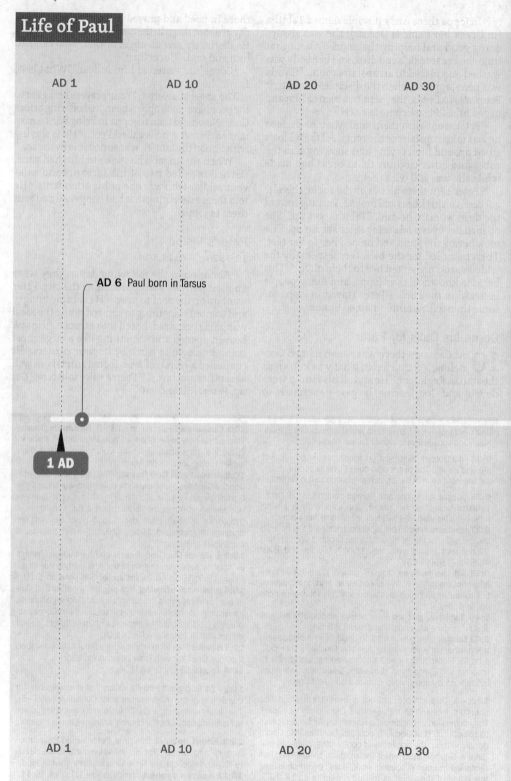

AD 1   AD 10   AD 20   AD 30

AD 6 Paul born in Tarsus

1 AD

AD 1   AD 10   AD 20   AD 30

All dates are approximate

AD 40　　　　　　AD 50　　　　　　AD 60　　　　　　AD 70

AD 33 Paul's conversion (Acts 9:1-19)

AD 35 Paul's first visit to Jerusalem (Acts 9:26-29; Gal 1:18-20)

AD 40 Barnabas brings Paul to Antioch (Acts 11:25-26)

AD 49 or 51 Jerusalem Council
(Acts 15:1-21; Gal 2:1-10)

AD 51 Paul appears before Gallio in Corinth
(Acts 18:12-17)

AD 57 Paul's arrest in Jerusalem
(Acts 21:27-34)

AD 60 Paul travels to Rome
(Acts 27:1-28:14)

AD 66
Martyrdom
in Rome

AD 70

AD 61-63 Paul in Rome
(Acts 28:30-31)

AD 57-59 Paul imprisoned in
Caesarea (Acts 23:23-26:32)

AD 52-57 Paul's third missionary journey
(Acts 18:23-21:26)

AD 49-51 Paul's second missionary journey
(Acts 15:40-18:22)

AD 46-47 Paul's first missionary journey (Acts 13:1-14:28)

AD 35-48 Paul in Syria and Cilicia (Gal 1:21-2:1)

AD 33-35 Paul in Arabia (Gal 1:16-17)

AD 40　　　　　　AD 50　　　　　　AD 60　　　　　　AD 70

¹⁴"Surely not, Lord!" Peter replied. "I have never eaten anything impure or unclean."

¹⁵The voice spoke to him a second time, "Do not call anything impure that God has made clean."

¹⁶This happened three times, and immediately the sheet was taken back to heaven.

¹⁷While Peter was wondering about the meaning of the vision, the men sent by Cornelius found out where Simon's house was and stopped at the gate. ¹⁸They called out, asking if Simon who was known as Peter was staying there.

¹⁹While Peter was still thinking about the vision, the Spirit said to him, "Simon, three*ᵃ* men are looking for you. ²⁰So get up and go downstairs. Do not hesitate to go with them, for I have sent them."

²¹Peter went down and said to the men, "I'm the one you're looking for. Why have you come?"

²²The men replied, "We have come from Cornelius the centurion. He is a righteous and God-fearing man, who is respected by all the Jewish people. A holy angel told him to ask you to come to his house so that he could hear what you have to say." ²³Then Peter invited the men into the house to be his guests.

Peter at Cornelius's House

The next day Peter started out with them, and some of the believers from Joppa went along. ²⁴The following day he arrived in Caesarea. Cornelius was expecting them and had called together his relatives and close friends. ²⁵As Peter entered the house, Cornelius met him and fell at his feet in reverence. ²⁶But Peter made him get up. "Stand up," he said, "I am only a man myself."

²⁷While talking with him, Peter went inside and found a large gathering of people. ²⁸He said to them: "You are well aware that it is against our law for a Jew to associate with or visit a Gentile. But God has shown me that I should not call anyone impure or unclean. ²⁹So when I was sent for, I came without raising any objection. May I ask why you sent for me?"

³⁰Cornelius answered: "Three days ago I was in my house praying at this hour, at three in the afternoon. Suddenly a man in shining clothes stood before me ³¹and said, 'Cornelius, God has heard your prayer and remembered your gifts to the poor. ³²Send to Joppa for Simon who is called Peter. He is a guest in the home of Simon the tanner, who lives by the sea.' ³³So I sent for you immediately, and it was good of you to come. Now we are all here in the presence of God to listen to everything the Lord has commanded you to tell us."

³⁴Then Peter began to speak: "I now realize how true it is that God does not show favoritism ³⁵but accepts from every nation the one who fears him and does what is right. ³⁶You know the message God sent to the people of Israel, announcing the good news of peace through Jesus Christ, who is Lord of all. ³⁷You know what has happened throughout the province of Judea,

---

ᵃ 19 One early manuscript *two*; other manuscripts do not have the number.

10:14 impure or unclean Some of the creatures the Lord tells Peter to eat would have been forbidden for a Jew to eat, and others would have been acceptable. Peter's strong reaction against God's command likely stemmed from the fact that he would have considered even the otherwise clean animals to be contaminated by being mingled with the unclean, on the basis of OT law (see Lev 11).

10:15 made clean Compare 15:9.

10:16 three times Just as Peter had denied Jesus three times (Lk 22:34), here he refuses to obey three times.

10:19 the Spirit The Spirit helps Peter to understand the vision by acting on it instead of merely continuing to contemplate it.

10:20 Do not hesitate See note on Ac 11:12. **I have sent them** The Spirit has not only sent the apostles to the Gentiles, but he has sent the Gentiles to the apostles.

10:23 invited the men into the house to be his guests Peter abides by the vision's message. Ancient Near Eastern hospitality would have required that Peter offer food to his guests.

10:25–43 This passage describes the culmination of Cornelius' and Peter's visions, leading to the full incorporation of a large group of non-Jewish people (Gentiles) into the Christian community.

10:25 in reverence Cornelius' actions—kneeling to the ground and paying homage—demonstrate his respect for Peter.

10:26 only a man Describes Peter's refusal to be considered superior to Cornelius (compare 14:15).

10:28 against our law While no specific OT law forbade interaction with non-Jewish people (Gentiles), the purity laws often meant Jews limited interaction with Gentiles in order to remain ritually pure. **impure or unclean** Peter's presence in Cornelius' home with the many Gentiles gathered there shows that he finally realizes the full implication of his vision (see note on 10:14).

10:34 favoritism Peter realizes that God does not exclude people from joining his people (compare Isa 2:1–5). Salvation in Jesus is not based on ethnicity or culture but is an offer to all.

10:35 accepts Peter acknowledges that faith and a transformed life, not ethnicity or keeping the OT laws, authenticates a person as one of God's own. Peter is about to explain how salvation in Jesus makes this possible (Ac 10:36–43).

10:36 Lord of all Peter emphasizes certain details of the gospel message that specifically relate to God's plans for non-Jewish people. Foremost is the theology that Jesus' lordship extends over all; he is not a cultural or national king, but the true king for everyone in the world.

10:37 You know Peter assumes those present are familiar with Jesus' earthly ministry, perhaps because the broad outlines of the events were widely known (compare 2:22), or because Cornelius and his family believed in Yahweh and would keep informed of Jewish religious developments (see 10:2 and note).

beginning in Galilee after the baptism that John preached — [38]how God anointed Jesus of Nazareth with the Holy Spirit and power, and how he went around doing good and healing all who were under the power of the devil, because God was with him.

[39]"We are witnesses of everything he did in the country of the Jews and in Jerusalem. They killed him by hanging him on a cross, [40]but God raised him from the dead on the third day and caused him to be seen. [41]He was not seen by all the people, but by witnesses whom God had already chosen — by us who ate and drank with him after he rose from the dead. [42]He commanded us to preach to the people and to testify that he is the one whom God appointed as judge of the living and the dead. [43]All the prophets testify about him that everyone who believes in him receives forgiveness of sins through his name."

[44]While Peter was still speaking these words, the Holy Spirit came on all who heard the message. [45]The circumcised believers who had come with Peter were astonished that the gift of the Holy Spirit had been poured out even on Gentiles. [46]For they heard them speaking in tongues[a] and praising God.

Then Peter said, [47]"Surely no one can stand in the way of their being baptized with water. They have received the Holy Spirit just as we have." [48]So he ordered that they be baptized in the name of Jesus Christ. Then they asked Peter to stay with them for a few days.

Peter Explains His Actions

11 The apostles and the believers throughout Judea heard that the Gentiles also had received the word of God. [2]So when Peter went up to Jerusalem, the circumcised believers criticized him [3]and said, "You went into the house of uncircumcised men and ate with them."

[4]Starting from the beginning, Peter told them the whole story: [5]"I was in the city of Joppa praying, and in a trance I saw a vision. I saw something like a large sheet being let down from heaven by its four corners, and it came down to where I was. [6]I looked into it and saw four-footed animals of the earth, wild beasts, reptiles and birds. [7]Then I heard a voice telling me, 'Get up, Peter. Kill and eat.'

[8]"I replied, 'Surely not, Lord! Nothing impure or unclean has ever entered my mouth.'

[9]"The voice spoke from heaven a second time, 'Do not call anything impure that God has made clean.' [10]This happened three times, and then it was all pulled up to heaven again.

[11]"Right then three men who had been sent to me from Caesarea stopped at the house where I was staying. [12]The Spirit told me to have no hesitation about going with them. These six brothers also went with me, and we entered the man's house. [13]He told us how he had seen an angel appear in his house and say, 'Send to Joppa for Simon who is called Peter. [14]He will bring you a message through which you and all your household will be saved.'

a 46 Or other languages

10:38–40 Peter's summary here of Jesus' identity, ministry, crucifixion and resurrection is similar to the one he provides in his Pentecost sermon (2:22–24).

10:39 by hanging him on a cross The Greek text here seems to allude to Dt 21:22–23, which says that anyone who is executed by hanging on a tree is cursed by God. The implication is that, by taking on himself God's curse on the cross, Jesus satisfied the penalty of the law on behalf of all who will put their faith in him (see Gal 3:13–14; compare Isa 53:5; Zec 12:10).

10:41 ate and drank Peter stresses the bodily nature of Jesus' resurrection (compare Jn 21:1–19).

10:42 judge of the living and the dead Jesus is the one to whom all will give account on the day of judgment (see Ac 17:31; 2Ti 4:1; 1Pe 4:5; Rev 20).

10:43 All the prophets Peter argues that his brief synopsis of Christ's ministry and its implications are based on the OT (compare Ps 22:1–31; Isa 52:13—53:12; Zec 11:4–14). See the table "Jesus' Fulfillment of OT Prophecy" on p. 1573. **through his name** See note on Ac 3:6.

10:44–48 The Holy Spirit's dramatic induction of Cornelius' Gentile household into the Christian community echoes Pentecost and emphasizes that non-Jews are full citizens of the kingdom of God by faith.

10:46 speaking in tongues This expression of the Spirit's indwelling and power echoes the initial events of Pentecost (2:3–4). However, the expression here

seems more likely related to worship (see note on 1Co 13:1), since there is no need for Cornelius and those with him to speak a human language that would have been otherwise unknown to them (see 1Co 14:1–25).

10:47 being baptized The baptism of these believers before representatives of the Jewish Christian community signifies not only their identification with Christ but their full incorporation into the church without being required to adopt the regulations of Judaism.

11:1–18 While much of this narrative mirrors Ac 10, it focuses on God's intervention on behalf of the Gentiles (non-Jewish people), showing that Peter has not just accepted the Gentiles as Christians but has become their advocate.

11:2 circumcised believers Likely refers to those in the Christian community who wanted to require Gentiles to first become Jews — including requiring the men to be circumcised — in order to be considered true Christians (compare Gal 2:3 and note).

11:12 to have no hesitation The phrasing here could suggest either that Peter should not delay in going with the men to see Cornelius, or that Peter should go without discriminating against them (since they were Gentiles).

11:14 household Compare Ac 2:39 and note. **will be saved** It appears Cornelius had not communicated to Peter this part of the angel's message before Peter began speaking to those gathered at his house (10:33).

¹⁵"As I began to speak, the Holy Spirit came on them as he had come on us at the beginning. ¹⁶Then I remembered what the Lord had said: 'John baptized with*ᵃ* water, but you will be baptized with*ᵃ* the Holy Spirit.' ¹⁷So if God gave them the same gift he gave us who believed in the Lord Jesus Christ, who was I to think that I could stand in God's way?"

¹⁸When they heard this, they had no further objections and praised God, saying, "So then, even to Gentiles God has granted repentance that leads to life."

The Church in Antioch

¹⁹Now those who had been scattered by the persecution that broke out when Stephen was killed traveled as far as Phoenicia, Cyprus and Antioch, spreading the word only among Jews. ²⁰Some of them, however, men from Cyprus and Cyrene, went to Antioch and began to speak to Greeks also, telling them the good news about the Lord Jesus. ²¹The Lord's hand was with them, and a great number of people believed and turned to the Lord.

²²News of this reached the church in Jerusalem, and they sent Barnabas to Antioch. ²³When he arrived and saw what the grace of God had done, he was glad and encouraged them all to remain true to the Lord with all their hearts. ²⁴He was a good man, full of the Holy Spirit and faith, and a great number of people were brought to the Lord.

²⁵Then Barnabas went to Tarsus to look for Saul, ²⁶and when he found him, he brought him to Antioch. So for a whole year Barnabas and Saul met with the church and taught great numbers of people. The disciples were called Christians first at Antioch.

²⁷During this time some prophets came down from Jerusalem to Antioch. ²⁸One of them, named Agabus, stood up and through the Spirit predicted that a severe famine would spread over the entire Roman world. (This happened during the reign of Claudius.) ²⁹The disciples, as each one was able, decided to provide help for the brothers and sisters living in Judea. ³⁰This they did, sending their gift to the elders by Barnabas and Saul.

Peter's Miraculous Escape From Prison

12 It was about this time that King Herod arrested some who belonged to the church, intending to persecute them. ²He had James, the

---

ᵃ 16 Or in

11:15 at the beginning Peter refers to the events at Pentecost (2:2–4).
11:16 what the Lord had said See 1:5.
11:17 who was I to think that I could stand in God's way Peter's language and reasoning here seem to echo Gamaliel's argument to the Sanhedrin that if God is indeed behind the church's message and mission, then no one will be able to stop it (5:38–39).

11:19–30 The early church's mission continues to the Gentiles, as demonstrated in Antioch and the reintroduction of Saul to the Acts narrative.
11:19 as far as Phoenicia The mission of the early church extends into the region of Phoenicia—in modern-day Lebanon, north of Israel along the Mediterranean coast—beyond Caesarea (8:40) and to areas besides Damascus (9:1–2). **Cyprus** A large Mediterranean island that figures prominently in Acts (e.g., 4:36; 15:39; 21:3; 27:4). **Antioch** The Roman military and administrative capital of its region in southern Asia Minor (modern-day Turkey). **only among Jews** Luke (the narrator) underlines the culturally limited scope of the church's witness beyond Jerusalem prior to this point. See 8:4.
11:20 Cyrene A city in northern Africa (modern-day Libya) settled by Greeks, which in the first century had a large Jewish population. **Greeks** Referring to Greek-speaking non-Jews, as opposed to traditional Jewish people and Greek-speaking Jews, to whom Christians had primarily been spreading the gospel message. Compare note on 6:1.
11:21 a great number of people believed In Acts, a large number of converts often accompanies the gospel reaching new regions (e.g., 2:41; 5:14; 6:7).
11:26 Christians The Greek term used here, *christianos*, which may be literally rendered "of Christ" or "belonging to Christ," refers to "Christ followers." The community

began to be known as a distinct movement from Judaism that was loyal to Jesus as Messiah (or Christ) and Lord (compare 2:36 and note; 10:36). See the timeline "The Early Church to AD 100" on p. 1776.
11:28 Agabus This prophet appears again in 21:10. **during the reign of Claudius** Claudius was emperor of Rome from AD 41–54. The famine may have begun in AD 40, but reached its pinnacle in AD 44–48, as reported by the first-century Jewish historian Josephus (Josephus, *Antiquities* 3.320; 20.101).
11:29 decided to provide help The new Gentile believers in Antioch desired to show the same grace that they had been shown, by helping to relieve the suffering of their Jewish Christian brothers and sisters.
11:30 Barnabas and Saul Two of the most vital people in the church's call to establish the Gentile mission and move it forward. Compare Ro 15:25–27; 2Co 8–9.

12:1–19 Luke (the narrator) tells the story of James' death and Peter's imprisonment at the hands of Herod Agrippa I, a grandson of Herod the Great. In doing so, Luke illustrates that, in spite of opposition, no earthly king can succeed for long in hindering the kingdom of Jesus.

12:1 Herod This is not the same Herod as in Jesus' day (Herod the Great; Mt 2:3,19). This is Herod Agrippa I, a grandson of Herod the Great. In AD 37 he was given the territory of Philip the tetrarch (see Lk 3:1). He added Galilee and Perea in AD 39 and the rest of Judea two years later, reigning over all of them for just three years. Later in Acts, Paul encounters his son Agrippa II (Ac 25:13—26:32). See the table "Political Leaders in the New Testament" on p. 1916; see the people diagram "Herod the Great's Family Tree" on p. 1826.
12:2 James The brother of John and son of Zebedee (Mk 3:17; Ac 1:13), not the brother of Jesus (see v. 17). **sword** This type of execution may signify that Agrippa I considered the growth and mission of the Christian

brother of John, put to death with the sword. ³When he saw that this met with approval among the Jews, he proceeded to seize Peter also. This happened during the Festival of Unleavened Bread. ⁴After arresting him, he put him in prison, handing him over to be guarded by four squads of four soldiers each. Herod intended to bring him out for public trial after the Passover.

⁵So Peter was kept in prison, but the church was earnestly praying to God for him.

⁶The night before Herod was to bring him to trial, Peter was sleeping between two soldiers, bound with two chains, and sentries stood guard at the entrance. ⁷Suddenly an angel of the Lord appeared and a light shone in the cell. He struck Peter on the side and woke him up. "Quick, get up!" he said, and the chains fell off Peter's wrists.

⁸Then the angel said to him, "Put on your clothes and sandals." And Peter did so. "Wrap your cloak around you and follow me," the angel told him. ⁹Peter followed him out of the prison, but he had no idea that what the angel was doing was really happening; he thought he was seeing a vision. ¹⁰They passed the first and second guards and came to the iron gate leading to the city. It opened for them by itself, and they went through it. When they had walked the length of one street, suddenly the angel left him.

¹¹Then Peter came to himself and said, "Now I know without a doubt that the Lord has sent his angel and rescued me from Herod's clutches and from everything the Jewish people were hoping would happen."

¹²When this had dawned on him, he went to the house of Mary the mother of John, also called Mark, where many people had gathered and were praying. ¹³Peter knocked at the outer entrance, and a servant named Rhoda came to answer the door. ¹⁴When she recognized Peter's voice, she was so overjoyed she ran back without opening it and exclaimed, "Peter is at the door!"

¹⁵"You're out of your mind," they told her. When she kept insisting that it was so, they said, "It must be his angel."

¹⁶But Peter kept on knocking, and when they opened the door and saw him, they were astonished. ¹⁷Peter motioned with his hand for them to be quiet and described how the Lord had brought him out of prison. "Tell James and the other brothers and sisters about this," he said, and then he left for another place.

¹⁸In the morning, there was no small commotion among the soldiers as to what had become of Peter. ¹⁹After Herod had a thorough search made for him and did not find him, he cross-examined the guards and ordered that they be executed.

---

community to be not just a religious but a political threat. The Jewish people were not allowed to issue the death penalty (see Jn 18:31 and note). The earlier execution of Stephen could have been construed by the Jewish people as an action of the mob (see Ac 7:57 and note), but Agrippa I would have had to conceal the death of James.

12:3 this met with approval among the Jews According to the first-century Jewish historian Josephus, Agrippa I enjoyed a good relationship with the Jewish people (Josephus, *Antiquities* 19.328–31). Agrippa I may have seen persecution of Christians as an opportunity to further improve his relationship with the Jewish people (compare Ac 9:1).

during the Festival of Unleavened Bread This Jewish feast took place for seven days every spring in conjunction with Passover (Ex 12:14–20; 23:15; compare Lk 22:1).

12:4 prison Compare Ac 5:18.

12:6 between two soldiers Two of the soldiers in the squad are chained to Peter while the other two keep watch. This choice to guard him this closely is probably due to him being freed miraculously earlier (5:17–26).

12:7 angel See note on 5:19. **struck Peter on the side** The Greek word used here suggests a forceful blow (compare Lk 22:49–50; Ac 7:24)—which, ironically, an angel will deal to Agrippa I as well (v. 23)—although in Peter's case, it is for his deliverance. See the table "Angels in the Bible" on p. 2120. **Quick, get up** The detailed series of instructions the angel must give Peter may anticipate the information revealed afterward that Peter was in some sort of daze (see vv. 8–11).

12:11 came to himself Peter finally realized that his dream was real (compare note on v. 7). **the Jewish people** This is not a reference primarily to Jews as opposed to Gentiles (non-Jewish people), but to Jews who have rejected Jesus as Messiah and are opposed to the Christian community and its mission.

12:12 Mark Also known as John Mark. A missionary companion to Paul and Barnabas (v. 25; 15:37), who seems to have been Barnabas' cousin (Col 4:10) to whom the early church ascribed the authorship of the Gospel of Mark.

12:13 servant The Greek word used here, *paidiskē*, always refers to slaves in the NT (e.g., Lk 22:56; Ac 16:16). This means Rhoda was a household slave.

12:14 overjoyed Humorously, Rhoda is so overjoyed to realize Peter is alive and has escaped that she forgets to let him in. Since Rhoda responds with joy at Peter's arrival, she is likely a Christian.

12:15 You're out of your mind The church had been praying fervently for Peter's release (vv. 5,12). They were not anticipating their prayers to be answered in such a remarkable way. **angel** The Greek word used here is not *phantasma*, the typical Greek word for ghost used elsewhere in the NT (Mt 14:26; Mk 6:49) and in other ancient Greek literature. Instead the Greek word used is *angelos*, which is used to describe a heavenly being sent from Yahweh or a messenger. The church's reaction likely testifies to an ancient belief that one's angel was a kind of celestial entity that accompanied a person for his or her welfare (compare Mt 18:10; Heb 1:14).

12:17 James This James is the brother of Jesus, and the early church ascribed the authorship of the book of James to him. He seems to have been prominent in the Jerusalem church leadership (compare Ac 15:13).

12:18 no small commotion The Greek phrase used here is known as a litotes—a figure of speech that states facts conservatively for effect. The point is that there was a great commotion.

12:19 that they be executed Allowing a prisoner to escape was a crime punishable by death.

Herod's Death

Then Herod went from Judea to Caesarea and stayed there. [20]He had been quarreling with the people of Tyre and Sidon; they now joined together and sought an audience with him. After securing the support of Blastus, a trusted personal servant of the king, they asked for peace, because they depended on the king's country for their food supply.

[21]On the appointed day Herod, wearing his royal robes, sat on his throne and delivered a public address to the people. [22]They shouted, "This is the voice of a god, not of a man." [23]Immediately, because Herod did not give praise to God, an angel of the Lord struck him down, and he was eaten by worms and died.

[24]But the word of God continued to spread and flourish.

Barnabas and Saul Sent Off

[25]When Barnabas and Saul had finished their mission, they returned from[a] Jerusalem, taking

13 with them John, also called Mark. [1]Now in the church at Antioch there were prophets and teachers: Barnabas, Simeon called Niger, Lu-

cius of Cyrene, Manaen (who had been brought up with Herod the tetrarch) and Saul. [2]While they were worshiping the Lord and fasting, the Holy Spirit said, "Set apart for me Barnabas and Saul for the work to which I have called them." [3]So after they had fasted and prayed, they placed their hands on them and sent them off.

On Cyprus

[4]The two of them, sent on their way by the Holy Spirit, went down to Seleucia and sailed from there to Cyprus. [5]When they arrived at Salamis, they proclaimed the word of God in the Jewish synagogues. John was with them as their helper.

[6]They traveled through the whole island until they came to Paphos. There they met a Jewish sorcerer and false prophet named Bar-Jesus, [7]who was an attendant of the proconsul, Sergius Paulus. The proconsul, an intelligent man, sent for Barnabas and Saul because he wanted to hear the word of God. [8]But Elymas the sorcerer (for that is what his name means) opposed them and tried to turn the proconsul from the faith. [9]Then

---

[a] 25 Some manuscripts *to*

12:20–25 The narration of the work of the early church is interrupted by a narrative about Herod Agrippa I (see note on 12:1). This is for the purpose of showing how the persecution of Agrippa I subsided.

12:20 Tyre and Sidon Important cities in Phoenicia on the Mediterranean coast. It may be that Herod (Agrippa I) was in some sort of economic struggle with the cities and had applied sanctions against them, affecting their food supply.

12:21 on his throne The official bench where a ruler would evaluate a judicial case or examine and reward an athlete. The reference suggests Herod may have been in the hippodrome of Caesarea.

12:22 voice of a god Perhaps to regain Herod's favor, the people flatter him.

12:23 Immediately God, who will not share his glory with any other (e.g., Isa 42:8; Eze 28:2,6), acts without delay to judge Herod for accepting divine honor and praise for himself. Compare note on Ac 12:7. **was eaten by worms** The nature of this disease is uncertain, but its effect is to judge Herod (Agrippa I) for his pride and to prove that he was certainly no god.

12:24 word of God In contrast to the speech of Herod that brought on his destruction, the word of the true God—that is, the proclamation of Jesus' death and resurrection for the forgiveness of sins and new life in the Spirit—continues to grow and spread.

12:25 finished their mission Paul and Barnabas had been sent from Antioch to Jerusalem to bring a famine relief offering (11:29–30), and now returned to Antioch with John Mark (see 12:12 and note). See the infographic "Jerusalem" on p. 1607.

13:1–3 Luke now transitions away from the church in Jerusalem to focus on Saul's missionary activity. The Holy Spirit commissions Barnabas and Saul at Antioch, initiating his first missionary journey. Saul will later be called Paul—the same Paul who wrote the NT letters.

13:1 prophets and teachers Refers to distinct offices that support the ministry of the church (compare note on 1Co 12:28).

13:2–3 The church at Antioch with its various Gentile believers may have felt a great need for God to send the gospel to Gentiles around the world. It seems that they were fasting and praying to discern how to go about this mission—or at least God's will for their church.

13:4–12 Saul (Paul) and Barnabas begin their first missionary journey by visiting the island of Cyprus.

13:4 Seleucia A port 16 miles from Antioch. **Cyprus** Barnabas grew up in Cyprus (4:36), which had a significant Gentile (non-Jewish) population (see note on 11:19).

13:5 Salamis A major commercial city on Cyprus, with a large Jewish population. **in the Jewish synagogues** Saul (Paul) routinely preaches in Jewish synagogues when he arrives in a new area (v. 14; 14:1; 17:1,10). **John** Also known as Mark (see note on 12:12). He travels with Barnabas and Saul for much of this first missionary journey.

13:6 Paphos This city was Cyprus' political center and an important harbor (compare v. 13). **sorcerer** Both Simon (ch. 8) and Bar-Jesus are magicians. There are several significant parallels between them, which Luke (the narrator) shows. **Bar-Jesus** This name means "son of Jesus." Fitting to his name, he is an imitator who is attempting to compete with Jesus Christ. Paul calls him not a son of Jesus but a son of the devil (v. 10).

13:7 proconsul A type of governor appointed by the Roman Empire.

13:8 Elymas Another name for Bar-Jesus. See note on 13:6.

13:9 Paul Saul's Roman name. While Paul begins to use his Roman name for the sake of spreading the gospel, Elymas (or Bar-Jesus) betrays his own heritage by going against the principles of Judaism (see Lev 19:31).

Saul, who was also called Paul, filled with the Holy Spirit, looked straight at Elymas and said, [10]"You are a child of the devil and an enemy of everything that is right! You are full of all kinds of deceit and trickery. Will you never stop perverting the right ways of the Lord? [11]Now the hand of the Lord is against you. You are going to be blind for a time, not even able to see the light of the sun."

Immediately mist and darkness came over him, and he groped about, seeking someone to lead him by the hand. [12]When the proconsul saw what had happened, he believed, for he was amazed at the teaching about the Lord.

In Pisidian Antioch

[13]From Paphos, Paul and his companions sailed to Perga in Pamphylia, where John left them to return to Jerusalem. [14]From Perga they went on to Pisidian Antioch. On the Sabbath they entered the synagogue and sat down. [15]After the reading from the Law and the Prophets, the leaders of the synagogue sent word to them, saying, "Brothers, if you have a word of exhortation for the people, please speak."

[16]Standing up, Paul motioned with his hand and said: "Fellow Israelites and you Gentiles who worship God, listen to me! [17]The God of the people of Israel chose our ancestors; he made the people prosper during their stay in Egypt; with mighty power he led them out of that country; [18]for about forty years he endured their conduct[a] in the wilderness; [19]and he overthrew seven nations in Canaan, giving their land to his people as their inheritance. [20]All this took about 450 years.

"After this, God gave them judges until the time of Samuel the prophet. [21]Then the people asked for a king, and he gave them Saul son of Kish, of the tribe of Benjamin, who ruled forty years. [22]After removing Saul, he made David their king. God testified concerning him: 'I have found David son of Jesse, a man after my own heart; he will do everything I want him to do.'

[23]"From this man's descendants God has brought to Israel the Savior Jesus, as he promised. [24]Before the coming of Jesus, John preached repentance and baptism to all the people of Israel. [25]As John was completing his work, he said: 'Who do you suppose I am? I am not the one you are looking for. But there is one coming after me whose sandals I am not worthy to untie.'

[26]"Fellow children of Abraham and you God-fearing Gentiles, it is to us that this message of salvation has been sent. [27]The people of Jerusalem and their rulers did not recognize Jesus, yet in condemning him they fulfilled the words of the prophets that are read every Sabbath. [28]Though they found no proper ground for a death sentence, they asked Pilate to have him executed. [29]When they had carried out all that was written about him, they took him down from the cross and laid him in a tomb. [30]But God raised him from the dead, [31]and for many days he was seen by those who had traveled with him from Galilee to Jerusalem. They are now his witnesses to our people.

[32]"We tell you the good news: What God promised our ancestors [33]he has fulfilled for us, their

_____

[a] 18 Some manuscripts *he cared for them*

13:13–41 Paul and Barnabas continue their ministry farther from Jewish territories, moving into Asia Minor for the first time. Most of this section consists of Paul's sermon in Pisidian Antioch (Ac 13:16–41), which presents Jesus' death and resurrection as the fulfillment of the story of Israel and concludes with an invitation to accept the message of the gospel.

13:13 Pamphylia This region was on the southern coast of what is now Turkey. **John** Also called Mark or John Mark (compare note on 12:12). The reason for his departure is not given, but it later becomes a source of contention between Barnabas and Paul (15:37–38).

13:14 Pisidian Antioch Located about 100 miles north of Perga across the Taurus Mountains. It was located in the region of Phrygia, on the border with Pisidia. It had a large Jewish population.

13:16 you Gentiles who worship God Paul addresses Jews as well as non-Jewish people who worshiped Yahweh; this likely meant attending synagogue and perhaps going to the temple in Jerusalem (see 10:2 and note; vv. 44–48).

13:17 God of the people of Israel Paul wants his hearers to know that his message is not something completely new, but is connected to God's dealings with Israel throughout history.

13:20 about 450 years This number appears to be a combination of the years Israel spent in Egypt (400 years; see 7:6 and note), the wilderness wanderings (40 years) and the conquest (10 years).

13:22 after my own heart Paul here sets up the distinction between apparent physical conformity and true spiritual conformity to God's will and purposes.

13:23 descendants The Greek word used here, *sperma*, not only refers to the offspring of David, but relates to the Davidic covenant (2Sa 7:12), and Yahweh's promises to Abraham (Ge 22:18–19). By using the word in this context, Paul proclaims that God has fulfilled his promises through Jesus.

13:27 fulfilled The Jerusalem religious leaders' ignorance of who Jesus was fulfills Scripture (Ac 3:18).

13:29 from the cross Paul does not use the typical Greek word for a cross here; instead, he refers to a tree. This alludes to Dt 21:22–23, which proclaims God's curse against anyone who was executed in such a way (Gal 3:13). Compare Ac 5:30; 10:39.

13:31 witnesses Acts stresses the role of witnesses to Jesus' resurrection (e.g., 2:32; 3:15; 10:40–41).

13:33 second psalm Paul quotes Ps 2:7. **my son** This title alludes to the Davidic covenant, where God states that David's offspring will have a unique relationship with God and that this will be seen in his relationship with David's descendants (2Sa 7:14–15; compare Heb 1:5). **today I have become your father** Psalm 2 does not

children, by raising up Jesus. As it is written in the second Psalm:

"'You are my son;
today I have become your father.'[a]

[34] God raised him from the dead so that he will never be subject to decay. As God has said,

"'I will give you the holy and sure blessings promised to David.'[b]

[35] So it is also stated elsewhere:

"'You will not let your holy one see decay.'[c]

[36] "Now when David had served God's purpose in his own generation, he fell asleep; he was buried with his ancestors and his body decayed. [37] But the one whom God raised from the dead did not see decay.

[38] "Therefore, my friends, I want you to know that through Jesus the forgiveness of sins is proclaimed to you. [39] Through him everyone who believes is set free from every sin, a justification you were not able to obtain under the law of Moses. [40] Take care that what the prophets have said does not happen to you:

[41] "'Look, you scoffers,
wonder and perish,
for I am going to do something in your days
that you would never believe,
even if someone told you.'[d]"

[42] As Paul and Barnabas were leaving the synagogue, the people invited them to speak further about these things on the next Sabbath. [43] When the congregation was dismissed, many of the Jews and devout converts to Judaism followed Paul and Barnabas, who talked with them and urged them to continue in the grace of God.

[44] On the next Sabbath almost the whole city gathered to hear the word of the Lord. [45] When the Jews saw the crowds, they were filled with jealousy. They began to contradict what Paul was saying and heaped abuse on him.

[46] Then Paul and Barnabas answered them boldly: "We had to speak the word of God to you first. Since you reject it and do not consider yourselves worthy of eternal life, we now turn to the Gentiles. [47] For this is what the Lord has commanded us:

"'I have made you[e] a light for the Gentiles,
that you[e] may bring salvation to the ends
of the earth.'[f]"

[48] When the Gentiles heard this, they were glad and honored the word of the Lord; and all who were appointed for eternal life believed.

[49] The word of the Lord spread through the whole region. [50] But the Jewish leaders incited the God-fearing women of high standing and the leading men of the city. They stirred up persecution against Paul and Barnabas, and expelled them from their region. [51] So they shook the dust off their feet as a warning to them and went to Iconium. [52] And the disciples were filled with joy and with the Holy Spirit.

In Iconium

14 At Iconium Paul and Barnabas went as usual into the Jewish synagogue. There they spoke so effectively that a great number of Jews and Greeks

---

[a] 33 Psalm 2:7   [b] 34 Isaiah 55:3   [c] 35 Psalm 16:10 (see Septuagint)   [d] 41 Hab. 1:5   [e] 47 The Greek is singular.
[f] 47 Isaiah 49:6

---

teach that God gives birth to a son—rather its language is Messianic in tone. When this language is applied to Jesus it describes his inauguration as King.

13:34 I will give you the holy and sure blessings promised to David Paul implies that the promises to David (see 2Sa 7) are fulfilled in the death and resurrection of Christ. To make this point, Paul quotes from Isa 55:3, which was originally addressed to God's people as a group.

13:35 You will not let your holy one see decay Paul quotes Ps 16:10 from the Septuagint (the ancient Greek translation of the OT); Peter also applied this verse to Jesus (see Ac 2:27 and note).

13:36 God's purpose Compare 2:29–30.

13:39 justification This is a legal declaration that someone is innocent and in good standing—right before God. Paul is arguing that justification is based on the work of Christ. Human effort—even when directed at keeping the Law of Moses (as primarily seen in the laws of Exodus, Leviticus, Numbers and Deuteronomy)—could never attain God's standard.

13:41 Paul concludes with a quote from Hab 1:5. This passage originally warned Israel about God's impending judgment coming in the form of their exile to Babylon. Here, Paul warns that the rejection of the Messiah would also result in judgment.

13:46 had to Paul acknowledges that because the Jews were chosen by Yahweh and had unique promises from him, they had to be presented the gospel first.

13:47 Paul quotes from Isaiah, which speaks of the suffering servant's mission to the entire world (see Isa 49:6 and note). Paul applies this prophecy to the mission of Jesus' followers and more specifically to the efforts of himself and Barnabas. Paul is essentially making a connection between the prophecy of the suffering servant and Jesus, and then proclaiming that the mission of Jesus is seen in the actions of his followers (who follow his example).

13:48 appointed for eternal life Luke (the narrator) could mean that the individuals whom God intended to believe did, or this could be a broad reference that, according to God's plan, the gospel reached the Gentiles in this region (compare Eph 1:5 and note). Either way, Luke is stating that despite opposition, God's intended purposes are accomplished.

13:51 shook the dust off their feet Jesus commanded the disciples to shake the dust off their feet when they left any place that rejected them (Mt 10:14; Mk 6:11; Lk 9:5). This signaled that the people in a location were now responsible for their own fate.

believed. [2]But the Jews who refused to believe stirred up the other Gentiles and poisoned their minds against the brothers. [3]So Paul and Barnabas spent considerable time there, speaking boldly for the Lord, who confirmed the message of his grace by enabling them to perform signs and wonders. [4]The people of the city were divided; some sided with the Jews, others with the apostles. [5]There was a plot afoot among both Gentiles and Jews, together with their leaders, to mistreat them and stone them. [6]But they found out about it and fled to the Lycaonian cities of Lystra and Derbe and to the surrounding country, [7]where they continued to preach the gospel.

In Lystra and Derbe

[8]In Lystra there sat a man who was lame. He had been that way from birth and had never walked. [9]He listened to Paul as he was speaking. Paul looked directly at him, saw that he had faith to be healed [10]and called out, "Stand up on your feet!" At that, the man jumped up and began to walk.

[11]When the crowd saw what Paul had done, they shouted in the Lycaonian language, "The gods have come down to us in human form!" [12]Barnabas they called Zeus, and Paul they called Hermes because he was the chief speaker. [13]The priest of Zeus, whose temple was just outside the city, brought bulls and wreaths to the city gates because he and the crowd wanted to offer sacrifices to them.

[14]But when the apostles Barnabas and Paul heard of this, they tore their clothes and rushed out into the crowd, shouting: [15]"Friends, why are you doing this? We too are only human, like you. We are bringing you good news, telling you to turn from these worthless things to the living God, who made the heavens and the earth and the sea and everything in them. [16]In the past, he let all nations go their own way. [17]Yet he has not left himself without testimony: He has shown kindness by giving you rain from heaven and crops in their seasons; he provides you with plenty of food and fills your hearts with joy." [18]Even with these words, they had difficulty keeping the crowd from sacrificing to them.

[19]Then some Jews came from Antioch and Iconium and won the crowd over. They stoned Paul and dragged him outside the city, thinking he was dead. [20]But after the disciples had gathered around him, he got up and went back into the city. The next day he and Barnabas left for Derbe.

The Return to Antioch in Syria

[21]They preached the gospel in that city and won a large number of disciples. Then they returned to Lystra, Iconium and Antioch, [22]strengthening the disciples and encouraging them to remain true to the faith. "We must go through many hardships to enter the kingdom of God," they said. [23]Paul and Barnabas appointed elders[a] for them in each church and, with prayer and fasting, committed them to the Lord, in whom they had put their trust. [24]After going through Pisidia, they came into Pamphylia, [25]and when they had preached the word in Perga, they went down to Attalia.

[26]From Attalia they sailed back to Antioch, where they had been committed to the grace of God for the work they had now completed. [27]On arriving there, they gathered the church together

[a] 23 Or Barnabas ordained elders; or Barnabas had elders elected

---

14:1–7 Paul and Barnabas continue further into Gentile (non-Jewish) territories, where the pattern seen in Pisidian Antioch repeats itself in Iconium (compare Ac 13:13–51). They are initially received well in the Jewish synagogue, but later experience opposition from both Jews and Gentiles.

14:1 Iconium Located in the central region of modern Turkey, about 90 miles southeast of Pisidian Antioch. See the map "Paul's First and Second Missionary Journey" on p. 2262.

14:4 apostles Normally this word in Acts refers to the twelve apostles (1:12–26), but here and in 14:14 it refers to Paul and Barnabas. See note on Ro 1:1.

14:6 Lycaonian cities of Lystra and Derbe These cities were, respectively, 18 miles south and 55 miles southwest of Iconium (Ac 14:1).

14:8–20 Even when Paul and Barnabas are accepted after healing a lame man, they find that the non-Jewish people in Lystra misunderstand their message.

14:10 Stand up on your feet A similar miracle occurred in 3:1–7. See the table "Miracles in Acts" on p. 1774.
14:12 Zeus The head god of the pantheon in Greek mythology. The crowd perceived that Barnabas was the group's leader. See the table "Pagan Deities in the New Testament" on p. 1788. **Hermes** The Greek deity in charge of delivering messages. Since Paul was the spokesman, the people thought he was Hermes.

14:13 priest Even the highest religious officials misunderstand the apostles' identities.

14:14 tore their clothes A sign of severe distress in ancient Near Eastern cultures (compare Ge 37:29; Jos 7:6; Mk 14:63–64).

14:15 living God By using this description, Paul and Barnabas distinguish Israel's God, Yahweh, from any other deity.

14:16 he let Yahweh did not intervene to directly instruct nations other than Israel about himself. He allowed them to follow their own desires. Paul explains this point further in Romans (Ro 1:18–32).

14:19 stoned Paul Paul refers to this event in 2Co 11:25 and more generally in 2Ti 3:11.

14:21–28 After a brief stop in Derbe, Paul and Barnabas conclude the first missionary journey (ca. AD 46–47) by retracing their steps to strengthen the newly founded churches (Ac 11:19—14:19).

14:23 elders One aspect of strengthening the churches was installing proper leadership to care for the community (see 1Ti 3:1–12; Titus 1:5–8).

14:27 he had opened The apostles' report confirms

and reported all that God had done through them and how he had opened a door of faith to the Gentiles. ²⁸And they stayed there a long time with the disciples.

The Council at Jerusalem

15 Certain people came down from Judea to Antioch and were teaching the believers: "Unless you are circumcised, according to the custom taught by Moses, you cannot be saved." ²This brought Paul and Barnabas into sharp dispute and debate with them. So Paul and Barnabas were appointed, along with some other believers, to go up to Jerusalem to see the apostles and elders about this question. ³The church sent them on their way, and as they traveled through Phoenicia and Samaria, they told how the Gentiles had been converted. This news made all the believers very glad. ⁴When they came to Jerusalem, they were welcomed by the church and the apostles and elders, to whom they reported everything God had done through them.

⁵Then some of the believers who belonged to the party of the Pharisees stood up and said, "The Gentiles must be circumcised and required to keep the law of Moses."

⁶The apostles and elders met to consider this question. ⁷After much discussion, Peter got up and addressed them: "Brothers, you know that some time ago God made a choice among you that the Gentiles might hear from my lips the message of the gospel and believe. ⁸God, who knows the heart, showed that he accepted them by giving the Holy Spirit to them, just as he did to us. ⁹He did not discriminate between us and them, for he purified their hearts by faith. ¹⁰Now then, why do you try to test God by putting on the necks of Gentiles a yoke that neither we nor our ancestors have been able to bear? ¹¹No! We believe it is through the grace of our Lord Jesus that we are saved, just as they are."

¹²The whole assembly became silent as they listened to Barnabas and Paul telling about the signs and wonders God had done among the Gentiles through them. ¹³When they finished, James spoke up. "Brothers," he said, "listen to me. ¹⁴Simon[a] has described to us how God first intervened to choose a people for his name from the Gentiles. ¹⁵The words of the prophets are in agreement with this, as it is written:

¹⁶ "'After this I will return
    and rebuild David's fallen tent.
Its ruins I will rebuild,
    and I will restore it,
¹⁷ that the rest of mankind may seek
        the Lord,
    even all the Gentiles who bear my
        name,
says the Lord, who does these things'[b] —
¹⁸   things known from long ago.[c]

¹⁹"It is my judgment, therefore, that we should not make it difficult for the Gentiles who are turning to God. ²⁰Instead we should write to them, telling them to abstain from food polluted by idols, from sexual immorality, from the meat of strangled animals and from blood. ²¹For the law of Moses has been preached in every city from the earliest times and is read in the synagogues on every Sabbath."

---

[a] 14 Greek *Simeon*, a variant of *Simon*; that is, Peter   [b] 17 Amos 9:11,12 (see Septuagint)   [c] 17,18 Some manuscripts things' — / ¹⁸the Lord's work is known to him from long ago

---

God's blessing of the Gentile (non-Jewish) mission. The church was to take the good news to the ends of the earth (Ac 1:8).

15:1–21 As the mission to Gentiles (non-Jewish people) continues forward, the early church is faced with the challenge of understanding theologically how the Gentiles have been accepted into God's people. The meeting recorded here, regularly called the Jerusalem Council, took place ca. AD 49. See the timeline "The Early Church to AD 100" on p. 1776.

15:1 Unless you are circumcised The Jews practiced circumcision on the eighth day as established by Ge 17:9–14. The Jews here are arguing that a person enters God's people by becoming part of Israel first.

15:4 everything God had done God's work clearly demonstrates he has opened the door to the Gentiles (see Ac 14:27).

15:5 the party of the Pharisees Apparently several Pharisees had converted to Christianity. Paul, also a Pharisee (23:6; Php 3:5), will not agree with their sentiments. See note on Jn 7:32.

15:6 The apostles and elders Luke (the narrator) stresses that the ruling of the Jerusalem Council will represent the church's official verdict on the matter.

15:7 some time ago Peter cites his own experience with the Gentile Cornelius and his vision about clean and pure food, which he has already explained to the church leadership in Jerusalem (Ac 10:1—11:18).

15:10 why do you try to test God Peter reasons that since God is working among both Jews and Gentiles that to demand that the Gentiles become Jews is to doubt what God has declared. This point seems to be based on Peter's vision about clean and pure food (10:9–23).

have been able Peter reminds the audience that no Jew was able to satisfy the law.

15:13 James The half-brother of Jesus and, according to the early church fathers, the author of the book of James (see Mt 13:55; Mk 6:3; Jas 1:1 and note).

15:15–18 James quotes from Am 9:11–12.

15:16 David's fallen tent This refers to the humbled Davidic dynasty (see note on Am 9:11). God promised to restore the dynasty to fulfill his promises about the royal line (2Sa 7).

15:20 Each of the four practices mentioned in this verse took place regularly in Gentile culture and worship and were condemned by Jews as unclean.

The Council's Letter to Gentile Believers

²²Then the apostles and elders, with the whole church, decided to choose some of their own men and send them to Antioch with Paul and Barnabas. They chose Judas (called Barsabbas) and Silas, men who were leaders among the believers. ²³With them they sent the following letter:

The apostles and elders, your brothers,

To the Gentile believers in Antioch, Syria and Cilicia:

Greetings.

²⁴We have heard that some went out from us without our authorization and disturbed you, troubling your minds by what they said. ²⁵So we all agreed to choose some men and send them to you with our dear friends Barnabas and Paul— ²⁶men who have risked their lives for the name of our Lord Jesus Christ. ²⁷Therefore we are sending Judas and Silas to confirm by word of mouth what we are writing. ²⁸It seemed good to the Holy Spirit and to us not to burden you with anything beyond the following requirements: ²⁹You are to abstain from food sacrificed to idols, from blood, from the meat of strangled animals and from sexual immorality. You will do well to avoid these things.

Farewell.

³⁰So the men were sent off and went down to Antioch, where they gathered the church together and delivered the letter. ³¹The people read it and were glad for its encouraging message. ³²Judas and Silas, who themselves were prophets, said much to encourage and strengthen the believers. ³³After spending some time there, they were sent off by the believers with the blessing of peace to return to those who had sent them. [34]ᵃ ³⁵But Paul and Barnabas remained in Antioch, where they and many others taught and preached the word of the Lord.

Disagreement Between Paul and Barnabas

³⁶Some time later Paul said to Barnabas, "Let us go back and visit the believers in all the towns where we preached the word of the Lord and see how they are doing." ³⁷Barnabas wanted to take John, also called Mark, with them, ³⁸but Paul did not think it wise to take him, because he had deserted them in Pamphylia and had not continued with them in the work. ³⁹They had such a sharp disagreement that they parted company. Barnabas took Mark and sailed for Cyprus, ⁴⁰but Paul chose Silas and left, commended by the believers to the grace of the Lord. ⁴¹He went through Syria and Cilicia, strengthening the churches.

Timothy Joins Paul and Silas

16 Paul came to Derbe and then to Lystra, where a disciple named Timothy lived, whose mother was Jewish and a believer but whose father was a Greek. ²The believers at Lystra and Iconium spoke well of him. ³Paul wanted to take him along on the journey, so he circumcised him because of the Jews who lived in that area, for they all knew that his father was a Greek. ⁴As they traveled from town to

---

ᵃ 34 Some manuscripts include here *But Silas decided to remain there.*

15:22–29 The letter from the Jerusalem Council codifies its conclusions. It aims to make theological unity within the church a practical reality.

15:22 Silas Silas is mentioned here for the first time; he will accompany Paul on his later travels (Ac 15:40; 2Co 1:19; 1Th 1:1; 2Th 1:1).

15:29 See note on Ac 15:20.

15:30–35 The church of Antioch rejoices after reading the letter, which has encouraged their unity and love for each other.

15:34 This verse is not found in the oldest and most reliable manuscripts. Only two of the major manuscripts attest to the presence of v. 34, and they differ.

15:36–41 As Paul's second missionary journey (ca. AD 49–51) begins, he and Barnabas disagree on whether to keep John Mark with them.

15:37 Mark Barnabas' cousin (see Col 4:10). See note on Ac 12:12.
15:38 had deserted Because of the timing of his departure, it may be that John Mark left because of uneasiness with going further into Gentile regions. See 13:13.
15:41 Syria and Cilicia Two neighboring provinces in modern-day Turkey. While Barnabas serves the church in Cyprus, Paul journeys through these areas toward Derbe and Lystra.

16:1–5 Paul gathers additional missionaries to continue the work among the Gentiles (non-Jewish people) and the Jews. The composition of the team indicates Paul's philosophy of ministry and his commitment to the Jerusalem Council's conclusions.

16:1 Derbe and then to Lystra Paul visited these places on his first missionary journey and was looking to strengthen the churches there (14:6). See the map "Paul's First and Second Missionary Journeys" on p. 2262. **a disciple named Timothy** This is the same Timothy to whom the letters 1 Timothy and 2 Timothy are addressed. **mother** Named Eunice (see 2Ti 1:5). **Greek** Timothy's mixed ethnic origin meant that he was familiar with both the Jewish and Gentile cultures.

16:3 circumcised Timothy had not been circumcised since his father was Greek. Paul circumcises Timothy for the sake of the church's mission, in order not to unnecessarily offend the Jews—Timothy would be entering into Jewish synagogues and homes.
16:4 the decisions reached Refers to the decisions of the Jerusalem Council. See Ac 15:22–29.

town, they delivered the decisions reached by the apostles and elders in Jerusalem for the people to obey. [5]So the churches were strengthened in the faith and grew daily in numbers.

Paul's Vision of the Man of Macedonia

[6]Paul and his companions traveled throughout the region of Phrygia and Galatia, having been kept by the Holy Spirit from preaching the word in the province of Asia. [7]When they came to the border of Mysia, they tried to enter Bithynia, but the Spirit of Jesus would not allow them to. [8]So they passed by Mysia and went down to Troas. [9]During the night Paul had a vision of a man of Macedonia standing and begging him, "Come over to Macedonia and help us." [10]After Paul had seen the vision, we got ready at once to leave for Macedonia, concluding that God had called us to preach the gospel to them.

Lydia's Conversion in Philippi

[11]From Troas we put out to sea and sailed straight for Samothrace, and the next day we went on to Neapolis. [12]From there we traveled to Philippi, a Roman colony and the leading city of that district[a] of Macedonia. And we stayed there several days.

[13]On the Sabbath we went outside the city gate to the river, where we expected to find a place of prayer. We sat down and began to speak to the women who had gathered there. [14]One of those listening was a woman from the city of Thyatira named Lydia, a dealer in purple cloth. She was a worshiper of God. The Lord opened her heart to respond to Paul's message. [15]When she and the members of her household were baptized, she invited us to her home. "If you consider me a believer in the Lord," she said, "come and stay at my house." And she persuaded us.

Paul and Silas in Prison

[16]Once when we were going to the place of prayer, we were met by a female slave who had a spirit by which she predicted the future. She earned a great deal of money for her owners by fortune-telling. [17]She followed Paul and the rest of us, shouting, "These men are servants of the Most High God, who are telling you the way to be saved." [18]She kept this up for many days. Finally Paul became so annoyed that he turned around and said to the spirit, "In the name of Jesus Christ I command you to come out of her!" At that moment the spirit left her.

[19]When her owners realized that their hope of making money was gone, they seized Paul and Silas and dragged them into the marketplace to face the authorities. [20]They brought them before the magistrates and said, "These men are

---

[a] 12 The text and meaning of the Greek for *the leading city of that district* are uncertain.

16:6–10 Paul's second missionary journey (ca. AD 49–51) takes him further into areas that were primarily Gentile (non-Jewish). This passage narrates how Paul's dependence on the Holy Spirit takes him and his companions to Macedonia.

16:6 region of Phrygia and Galatia This region included both Jewish and Gentile populations. **having been kept by the Holy Spirit** The narrative provides no reasoning for this—outside of showing that God had other plans (16:8–9)—nor does it explain how this occurred. This shows, though, that Paul and his companions listen to the Holy Spirit's leading and do as the Spirit directs. **Asia** Refers to the Roman province of Asia, which was on the west coast of Asia Minor (modern-day Turkey) and was home to Ephesus.

16:7 Bithynia By prohibiting Paul from going to this area, the Spirit directs them westward. **Spirit of Jesus** Another name for the Holy Spirit (Php 1:19). **would not allow them to** See note on Ac 16:6.

16:8 Troas A major port city along the Aegean Sea.

16:9 Macedonia A Roman province in the north of Greece situated approximately 150 miles across the Aegean Sea from Paul's current location in Troas.

16:10 we This is the first time in Acts where Luke (the narrator) includes himself in the story (vv. 10–17). This implies that Luke has joined Paul on the journey.

16:11–15 The first city Paul visits in Macedonia is Philippi. The conversion of Lydia signals God's affirmation for Paul to travel to new territory in sharing the gospel with non-Jewish people.

16:12 Philippi This city held colonial status and privilege in the Roman Empire.

16:13 a place of prayer Since they did not meet in an official synagogue, it appears the Jewish population was very small. A synagogue required ten Jewish men. See the infographic "Ancient Home Synagogue" on p. 1971.

16:14 Thyatira A city in the province of Asia, where Paul wanted to minister but was prevented by the Holy Spirit (v. 6). **a dealer in purple cloth** A very valuable good, which only people of great financial means could afford. Lydia, the first convert in the region, has the financial means to become a key supporter of the early church.

16:15 come and stay at my house Jews generally avoided staying with non-Jewish people (see 10:28 and note). By staying at her home, Paul seems to be embodying the message given to Peter in his vision and, as such, the conclusions of the Jerusalem Council (10:9–16; 15:22–29).

16:16–24 Paul and Silas are jailed for exorcising a demon from a slave girl.

16:17 servants of the Most High God The lack of Jewish influence in Philippi means that the crowd surrounding Paul would likely assume that the girl was speaking about Zeus as the chief god of the Greek pantheon.

16:20 Jews The apostles' ethnicity becomes part of the rhetoric used to stir up the leadership against them. Jews were uncommon in this region and were disliked by non-Jewish people due to their differences in lifestyle and insistence on one true God.

Jews, and are throwing our city into an uproar ²¹by advocating customs unlawful for us Romans to accept or practice."

²²The crowd joined in the attack against Paul and Silas, and the magistrates ordered them to be stripped and beaten with rods. ²³After they had been severely flogged, they were thrown into prison, and the jailer was commanded to guard them carefully. ²⁴When he received these orders, he put them in the inner cell and fastened their feet in the stocks.

²⁵About midnight Paul and Silas were praying and singing hymns to God, and the other prisoners were listening to them. ²⁶Suddenly there was such a violent earthquake that the foundations of the prison were shaken. At once all the prison doors flew open, and everyone's chains came loose. ²⁷The jailer woke up, and when he saw the prison doors open, he drew his sword and was about to kill himself because he thought the prisoners had escaped. ²⁸But Paul shouted, "Don't harm yourself! We are all here!"

²⁹The jailer called for lights, rushed in and fell trembling before Paul and Silas. ³⁰He then brought them out and asked, "Sirs, what must I do to be saved?"

³¹They replied, "Believe in the Lord Jesus, and you will be saved — you and your household." ³²Then they spoke the word of the Lord to him and to all the others in his house. ³³At that hour of the night the jailer took them and washed their wounds; then immediately he and all his household were baptized. ³⁴The jailer brought them into his house and set a meal before them; he was filled with joy because he had come to believe in God — he and his whole household.

³⁵When it was daylight, the magistrates sent their officers to the jailer with the order: "Release those men." ³⁶The jailer told Paul, "The magistrates have ordered that you and Silas be released. Now you can leave. Go in peace."

³⁷But Paul said to the officers: "They beat us publicly without a trial, even though we are Roman citizens, and threw us into prison. And now do they want to get rid of us quietly? No! Let them come themselves and escort us out."

³⁸The officers reported this to the magistrates, and when they heard that Paul and Silas were Roman citizens, they were alarmed. ³⁹They came to appease them and escorted them from the prison, requesting them to leave the city. ⁴⁰After Paul and Silas came out of the prison, they went to Lydia's house, where they met with the brothers and sisters and encouraged them. Then they left.

In Thessalonica

17 When Paul and his companions had passed through Amphipolis and Apollonia, they came to Thessalonica, where there was a Jewish synagogue. ²As was his custom, Paul went into the synagogue, and on three Sabbath days he reasoned with them from the Scriptures, ³explaining and proving that the Messiah had to suffer and rise from the dead. "This Jesus I am proclaiming to you is the Messiah," he said. ⁴Some of the Jews were persuaded and joined Paul and Silas, as did a large number of God-fearing Greeks and quite a few prominent women.

⁵But other Jews were jealous; so they rounded

16:21 Romans The opponents argue that Paul and Silas seek to persuade people to follow religious practices that are a threat to the Roman way of life.

16:25–34 People have opposed the gospel in Philippi (vv. 16–24), but Paul and Silas are miraculously released from prison. Rather than fleeing, they take this opportunity to preach to their jailer.

16:26 a violent earthquake Earthquakes are relatively common throughout this region. Luke shows that the timing of this earthquake coincides with Paul and Silas' worship.

16:30 what must I do The jailer asks about the way of salvation Paul and Silas preached. In the jailer's mind, two miracles have taken place since there was an earthquake and the prisoners did not flee. The deliverance and power the jailer experienced point to the truth of the power and deliverance found in the gospel preached by Paul and Silas.

16:31 you and your household This could mean that both the jailer and his family should believe in the gospel or that it is rather certain that those in the jailer's family will also believe in the gospel if he does.

16:34 his house By his hospitality the jailer demonstrates that his life has been radically changed by the gospel.

16:35–40 The apology of the Philippian officials demonstrates their confusion about Paul's message and whether he was advocating sedition against the empire. Paul and Silas use this moment as an opportunity to strengthen the new Philippian church.

16:37 Roman citizens It was illegal to beat a Roman citizen without a full hearing (v. 22). **Let them come themselves and escort us out** Paul requests a public display of his innocence. This would provide official affirmation that the church had done nothing illegal and would further strengthen the church and the position of the new believers in the community.

17:1–9 Paul travels to Thessalonica, the capital of the province of Macedonia. His stay there is cut short by persecution, and his letters to the church there (1–2 Thessalonians) display his care for them and desire that they remain faithful in the midst of opposition.

17:1 Thessalonica A major city in the Roman province of Macedonia, Thessalonica was about 95 miles west of Philippi along the Egnatian Way. It served as a port with close ties with Rome. **a Jewish synagogue** Compare 16:13 and note.

17:2 from the Scriptures There are earlier examples of Paul preaching this type of message (e.g., 13:13–41).

17:3 had to suffer and rise from the dead Paul's preaching centers on the death and resurrection of Jesus. He could have supported this viewpoint with Isa 53:10–12 (see note on Isa 53:10).

17:5 jealous As happened earlier in Pisidian Antioch

up some bad characters from the marketplace, formed a mob and started a riot in the city. They rushed to Jason's house in search of Paul and Silas in order to bring them out to the crowd.[a] 6But when they did not find them, they dragged Jason and some other believers before the city officials, shouting: "These men who have caused trouble all over the world have now come here, 7and Jason has welcomed them into his house. They are all defying Caesar's decrees, saying that there is another king, one called Jesus." 8When they heard this, the crowd and the city officials were thrown into turmoil. 9Then they made Jason and the others post bond and let them go.

In Berea

10As soon as it was night, the believers sent Paul and Silas away to Berea. On arriving there, they went to the Jewish synagogue. 11Now the Berean Jews were of more noble character than those in Thessalonica, for they received the message with great eagerness and examined the Scriptures every day to see if what Paul said was true. 12As a result, many of them believed, as did also a number of prominent Greek women and many Greek men.

13But when the Jews in Thessalonica learned that Paul was preaching the word of God at Berea, some of them went there too, agitating the crowds and stirring them up. 14The believers immediately sent Paul to the coast, but Silas and Timothy stayed at Berea. 15Those who escorted Paul brought him to Athens and then left with instructions for Silas and Timothy to join him as soon as possible.

In Athens

16While Paul was waiting for them in Athens, he was greatly distressed to see that the city was full of idols. 17So he reasoned in the synagogue with both Jews and God-fearing Greeks, as well as in the marketplace day by day with those who happened to be there. 18A group of Epicurean and Stoic philosophers began to debate with him. Some of them asked, "What is this babbler trying to say?" Others remarked, "He seems to be advocating foreign gods." They said this because Paul was preaching the good news about Jesus and the resurrection. 19Then they took him and brought him to a meeting of the Areopagus, where they said to him, "May

[a] 5 Or the assembly of the people

(Ac 13:45), Iconium (14:2), and Lystra (14:19), the jealousy of particular local Jews compels them to oppose Paul and the movement of the early church.
17:7 all defying Caesar's decrees To press their case, the opposition accuses the church of promoting sedition.
another king, one called Jesus The church's promotion of Jesus as the true king makes its opponents see it as a threat to Caesar (compare Lk 23:2–3).

17:10–15 Having been driven out of Thessalonica, Paul moves on to Berea. In contrast to those in Thessalonica, the Jews in Berea are much more honorable and open-minded.

17:10 Berea Located approximately 45 miles west of Thessalonica, about a three-day journey by foot. It was another major city in the Roman province of Macedonia.
17:11 noble character Originally, the Greek term used here denoted noble birth. It later came to refer to anyone who had royal bearing—people who were more refined.
examined In nonjudicial contexts, the Greek term used here, *anakrinō*, often deals with questioning and discernment (compare 1Co 2:15; 10:25).
17:12 women and many Greek men Compare Ac 17:4.
17:14 sent Paul It appears the main opposition was against Paul. Since Silas and Timothy do not leave, the ministry continues despite the opponents' best efforts.
17:15 Athens Paul heads south to Athens, the center of Greek culture.

17:16–34 Paul's ministry in Athens shows how he altered his approach in carrying out his mission to the Gentiles. His earlier speech at Pisidian Antioch depicts his message to Jews and God-fearing Gentiles (13:16–41), but his speech in Athens (17:22–34) shows how he approached Gentiles who had no knowledge of or commitment to the God of Israel. See the infographic "The Areopagus (Mars Hill) in Athens" on p. 1811.

17:18 Epicurean Epicureanism was a system of thought that asserted there was no connection between people and the divine. This belief was expressed in a desire to seek contentment and satisfaction and to avoid pain and discomfort. **Stoic** Stoicism was an essentially pantheistic system of thought that prioritized logic over all other faculties. **the resurrection** Resurrection was contradictory both to the Epicurean idea that death ended all existence and the Stoic idea of uniting with the divine and disengaging from the material.

Acts 17:18

STOICS
Stoicism was founded by Zeno in the third century BC. Contrary to Epicureanism, Stoicism contended that the physical universe is empowered by a reasoning force known as *logos*, which connects the divine with the material. Ethically, stoics attempted to live in accordance with the natural laws they observed and systematized.

Acts 17:18

EPICUREANS
Epicureanism began with Epicurus (341–270 BC), who argued that the world was made of atoms and that the world was purely material. Epicureans attempted to free people from the idea of the gods, the afterlife and the fear of death. The only value that remained was the physical reality of the individual, and thus the individual was freed from fear to pursue what truly gave pleasure; Epicurus stressed that contentment and nobility produced the best, most enjoyable life.

we know what this new teaching is that you are presenting? [20]You are bringing some strange ideas to our ears, and we would like to know what they mean." [21](All the Athenians and the foreigners who lived there spent their time doing nothing but talking about and listening to the latest ideas.)

[22]Paul then stood up in the meeting of the Areopagus and said: "People of Athens! I see that in every way you are very religious. [23]For as I walked around and looked carefully at your objects of worship, I even found an altar with this inscription: TO AN UNKNOWN GOD. So you are ignorant of the very thing you worship — and this is what I am going to proclaim to you.

[24]"The God who made the world and everything in it is the Lord of heaven and earth and does not live in temples built by human hands. [25]And he is not served by human hands, as if he needed anything. Rather, he himself gives everyone life and breath and everything else. [26]From one man he made all the nations, that they should inhabit the whole earth; and he marked out their appointed times in history and the boundaries of their lands. [27]God did this so that they would seek him and

---

17:19 Areopagus Meaning the "hill of Aries." Aries was the god of war in Greek mythology, who is called Mars in Latin. This was the name of a location and also of the civil and religious council that met there. The Greek phrasing used here is unclear whether Paul was standing on the hill or in a meeting of the council.

17:21 This description of the regular activity at the Areopagus (Mars Hill) helps establish the irony of Paul's discourse. While the Athenians put Paul and Christianity on trial, Paul puts their philosophies on trial. Thus, what looks to the Athenians like confused thinking actually points to the incoherence in their philosophies.

17:23 TO AN UNKNOWN GOD This unknown god demonstrates the lack of clarity and certainty in Athenian philosophy.

They freely admit there could be a deity they are unaware of. See the table "Pagan Deities in the New Testament" on p. 1788. **proclaim** Paul claims he will clarify the mysteries of the Athenians' own philosophies.

17:24 built by human hands Since God transcends creation, he does not need a place to live — including the shrines on the nearby Acropolis.

17:26 From one man Paul mentions Adam as the individual from whom all people are descended. While the Stoics believed in divine creation, they also believed in pantheism, in which God was to be identified with the universe. Paul instead argues that God is distinct from creation and humanity.

17:27 would seek him People have a desire to seek God, but their sin confuses their understanding. **reach**

Mars' Hill
Height: Reaches 377 ft.

Stairway cut into the rock (still in use today).

Paul

The Areopagus (Mars' Hill) in Athens

At Mars' Hill, also known as the Areopagus, Paul used an inscription to an "unknown god" as a starting point for proclaiming the Good News of Christ to the Greeks. He confronted widespread idol worship by declaring the true identity of the Creator. Appealing to Greek ideas and worship practices, Paul articulated God's demand for repentance and his provision of salvation. Paul states that the "unknown god" is known through Jesus and his resurrection (Ac 17:22–31).

GREECE Aegean Sea
Athens TURKEY

Mediterranean Sea RHODES

CRETE

perhaps reach out for him and find him, though he is not far from any one of us. ²⁸'For in him we live and move and have our being.'ᵃ As some of your own poets have said, 'We are his offspring.'ᵇ

²⁹"Therefore since we are God's offspring, we should not think that the divine being is like gold or silver or stone — an image made by human design and skill. ³⁰In the past God overlooked such ignorance, but now he commands all people everywhere to repent. ³¹For he has set a day when he will judge the world with justice by the man he has appointed. He has given proof of this to everyone by raising him from the dead."

³²When they heard about the resurrection of the dead, some of them sneered, but others said, "We want to hear you again on this subject." ³³At that, Paul left the Council. ³⁴Some of the people became followers of Paul and believed. Among them was Dionysius, a member of the Areopagus, also a woman named Damaris, and a number of others.

In Corinth

18 After this, Paul left Athens and went to Corinth. ²There he met a Jew named Aquila, a native of Pontus, who had recently come from Italy with his wife Priscilla, because Claudius had ordered all Jews to leave Rome. Paul went to see them, ³and because he was a tentmaker as they were, he stayed and worked with them. ⁴Every Sabbath he reasoned in the synagogue, trying to persuade Jews and Greeks.

⁵When Silas and Timothy came from Macedonia, Paul devoted himself exclusively to preaching, testifying to the Jews that Jesus was the Messiah. ⁶But when they opposed Paul and became abusive, he shook out his clothes in protest and said to them, "Your blood be on your own heads! I am innocent of it. From now on I will go to the Gentiles."

⁷Then Paul left the synagogue and went next door to the house of Titius Justus, a worshiper of God. ⁸Crispus, the synagogue leader, and his entire household believed in the Lord; and many of the Corinthians who heard Paul believed and were baptized.

⁹One night the Lord spoke to Paul in a vision: "Do not be afraid; keep on speaking, do not be silent. ¹⁰For I am with you, and no one is going to attack and harm you, because I have many people in this city." ¹¹So Paul stayed in Corinth for a year and a half, teaching them the word of God.

¹²While Gallio was proconsul of Achaia, the Jews of Corinth made a united attack on Paul and brought him to the place of judgment. ¹³"This man," they charged, "is persuading the people to worship God in ways contrary to the law."

ᵃ 28 From the Cretan philosopher Epimenides   ᵇ 28 From the Cilician Stoic philosopher Aratus

---

out for The Greek verb used here denotes attempting to touch or handle something. In Greek literature, it refers to a blind person walking in the dark. **he is not far** This clashes both with the Epicurean belief of the divine as separate from the world, and Stoic notions of God's presence in creation itself—that parts of creation were divine or divinely embodied.

17:28 For in him we live and move and have our being Paul may be quoting the poet Epimenedes of Crete (compare Titus 1:12). Alternatively, he may simply be using a common statement in Greek thought. **We are his offspring** This is a quotation from one of the ancient poet-philosophers, probably the Stoic poet Aratus.

17:29 God's offspring Paul builds on the previous statement. The fact that people are God's offspring shows that the living God is grander than idols.

17:31 judge Paul has established God as Creator. As such, God has the right to judge the world.

17:32 the resurrection See note on Ac 17:18.

17:34 Dionysius, a member of the Areopagus While it is unclear whether Paul was appearing before an official meeting of the Areopagus (see note on v. 19), at least one member of the council was present and came to faith.

18:1–11 Paul moves on from Athens and spends 18 months in Corinth (v. 11), another prominent city in the province of Achaia.

18:1 Corinth Located about 40 miles west of Athens, Corinth was the capital of the Roman province Achaia and a major seaport. Its strategic location on an isthmus between the mainland of Greece and the Peloponnesian peninsula brought economic prosperity and a diverse set of cultures and practices. Even among the Gentiles (non-Jewish people), Corinth was known for its immorality.

18:2 Pontus A region of northern Asia Minor (modern-day Turkey) near the Black Sea. **Priscilla** Also known as Prisca (see 1Co 16:19; Ro 16:3–5; 2Ti 4:19). **Claudius had ordered** Claudius' expulsion of Jews from Rome occurred in AD 49, about two years before Paul arrived in Corinth. See the timeline "The Early Church to AD 100" on p. 1776.

18:3 a tentmaker This is the only reference to Paul's trade as a tentmaker, though he writes in his letters about working with his hands in some places rather than accepting financial assistance (e.g., 1Co 4:12; 1Th 2:9; 2Th 3:7–8).

18:6 shook out his clothes This may allude to Ne 5:13 as well as Jesus' words concerning those who reject God (Mt 10:14; Mk 6:11; Lk 10:11). Compare note on Lk 9:5. **Gentiles** Paul does not mean that he is completely giving up on his mission to the Jews (compare Ac 18:19; 19:8; 28:17–22). Rather, he indicates that he will focus the rest of his time in Corinth elsewhere.

18:8 Crispus Mentioned in 1Co 1:14.

18:9 vision Jesus appears to Paul to encourage him. He exhorts Paul to not fear and reveals that, unlike his experiences in previous cities, Paul would be able to remain in Corinth to preach the gospel and not be driven away by opposition.

18:12–17 Paul's opponents, unable to hinder his successful mission in Corinth, try to forcibly stop him by taking him before the proconsul, the head of government in a Roman province. The proconsul decides that Paul's activity is no crime and allows him to continue.

18:12 Gallio Proconsul of Achaia (the province where Corinth was located) ca. AD 51–52. **place of judgment** Refers to the location of trials held before the proconsul (see note on Ac 13:7).

¹⁴Just as Paul was about to speak, Gallio said to them, "If you Jews were making a complaint about some misdemeanor or serious crime, it would be reasonable for me to listen to you. ¹⁵But since it involves questions about words and names and your own law — settle the matter yourselves. I will not be a judge of such things." ¹⁶So he drove them off. ¹⁷Then the crowd there turned on Sosthenes the synagogue leader and beat him in front of the proconsul; and Gallio showed no concern whatever.

Priscilla, Aquila and Apollos

¹⁸Paul stayed on in Corinth for some time. Then he left the brothers and sisters and sailed for Syria, accompanied by Priscilla and Aquila. Before he sailed, he had his hair cut off at Cenchreae because of a vow he had taken. ¹⁹They arrived at Ephesus, where Paul left Priscilla and Aquila. He himself went into the synagogue and reasoned with the Jews. ²⁰When they asked him to spend more time with them, he declined. ²¹But as he left, he promised, "I will come back if it is God's will." Then he set sail from Ephesus. ²²When he landed at Caesarea, he went up to Jerusalem and greeted the church and then went down to Antioch.

²³After spending some time in Antioch, Paul set out from there and traveled from place to place throughout the region of Galatia and Phrygia, strengthening all the disciples.

²⁴Meanwhile a Jew named Apollos, a native of Alexandria, came to Ephesus. He was a learned man, with a thorough knowledge of the Scriptures. ²⁵He had been instructed in the way of the Lord, and he spoke with great fervor[a] and taught about Jesus accurately, though he knew only the baptism of John. ²⁶He began to speak boldly in the synagogue. When Priscilla and Aquila heard him, they invited him to their home and explained to him the way of God more adequately.

²⁷When Apollos wanted to go to Achaia, the brothers and sisters encouraged him and wrote to the disciples there to welcome him. When he arrived, he was a great help to those who by grace had believed. ²⁸For he vigorously refuted his Jewish opponents in public debate, proving from the Scriptures that Jesus was the Messiah.

Paul in Ephesus

19 While Apollos was at Corinth, Paul took the road through the interior and arrived at Ephesus. There he found some disciples ²and asked them, "Did you receive the Holy Spirit when[b] you believed?"

They answered, "No, we have not even heard that there is a Holy Spirit."

³So Paul asked, "Then what baptism did you receive?"

"John's baptism," they replied.

⁴Paul said, "John's baptism was a baptism of repentance. He told the people to believe in the one coming after him, that is, in Jesus." ⁵On hearing this, they were baptized in the name of the Lord Jesus. ⁶When Paul placed his hands on them, the Holy Spirit came on them, and they spoke

---

a 25 Or with fervor in the Spirit   b 2 Or after

18:15 I will not be a judge Gallio recognizes that Christianity has emerged from Judaism and so any decisions about it should be made on the basis of their own Scriptures.
18:17 Sosthenes Possibly the same Sosthenes mentioned in 1Co 1:1. If this is the case, he may have become a Christian after this incident.

18:18–23 Paul travels east across the Aegean Sea to Ephesus. Paul then concludes his second missionary journey (ca. AD 49–51) by returning to Antioch.
18:18 stayed on in Corinth for some time Paul later wrote at least three letters to the Corinthians, including the letters known today as 1 Corinthians and 2 Corinthians. Compare Ac 20:3. **Syria** Paul is returning to Antioch in Syria, from which he launched his first missionary journey (13:1–3). **a vow** Paul may have taken a temporary Nazirite vow (see Nu 6:1–21). Such a vow was usually completed with a sacrifice in Jerusalem, which Acts does not explicitly record.
18:19 Ephesus An important port city on the west coast of Asia Minor (modern-day Turkey). See the infographic "Ephesus in Paul's Day" on p. 1939.
18:22 Caesarea Paul has returned to Israel after ministering to Gentiles (non-Jewish people) and Jews. See note on Ac 8:40. **went up** A typical descriptor of visiting Jerusalem due to the physical elevation of the city as well as its elevated status as home of the temple.

18:24–28 Luke (the narrator) provides a glimpse of the occurrences in Ephesus in Paul's absence. The account introduces Apollos, a skilled speaker who was also well versed in the Scriptures. It also shows the Spirit's continued work in Ephesus. Paul later wrote a letter to the Ephesians.

18:24 a native of Alexandria Although he was Jewish, Apollos was probably knowledgeable in other customs since he came from a major Roman city where Jews were more influenced by Greco-Roman culture than they were in Judea and the nearby regions.
18:27 Achaia This Roman province, across the Aegean Sea from Ephesus, includes Corinth and Athens.

19:1–10 During Paul's third missionary journey (ca. AD 52–57; 18:23; 19:1—21:26), he returns to Ephesus, where he stopped briefly on his second missionary journey (ca. 49–51; 18:19–21). This time, he stays in the city for about three years (19:10; 20:31).
19:1 While Apollos was at Corinth Compare 1Co 1:12–13; 3:4–6. **disciples** While this term usually refers to followers of Jesus, these people were likely originally followers of John the Baptist, since they had received his baptism (Ac 19:3).
19:6 they spoke in tongues This is likely a reference to an act related to worship (see note on 10:46), not miraculously speaking in another person's native language (compare 2:4–6). In Acts, speaking in tongues

in tongues*a* and prophesied. ⁷There were about twelve men in all.

⁸Paul entered the synagogue and spoke boldly there for three months, arguing persuasively about the kingdom of God. ⁹But some of them became obstinate; they refused to believe and publicly maligned the Way. So Paul left them. He took the disciples with him and had discussions daily in the lecture hall of Tyrannus. ¹⁰This went on for two years, so that all the Jews and Greeks who lived in the province of Asia heard the word of the Lord.

a 6 Or other languages

---

is related to the Holy Spirit indwelling and empowering believers (2:4–6; 10:45–46).

19:7 about twelve Refers to John's disciples. This may parallel the twelve apostles.

19:8 kingdom of God See note on 1:3.

19:10 for two years Paul's lengthy stay in Ephesus allowed him to use the city as his base of ministry operations for his third missionary journey (compare 18:11). **who lived in the province of Asia** Because Ephesus is a key city for travel and business, it allowed

---

In Greek mythology, Artemis was known as the virgin archer-huntress, Apollo's sister, and one of the 12 Olympians. When Paul wrote to the Ephesians, he would have been concerned with the issues accompanying Artemis worship and submitting to religious practices associated with her.

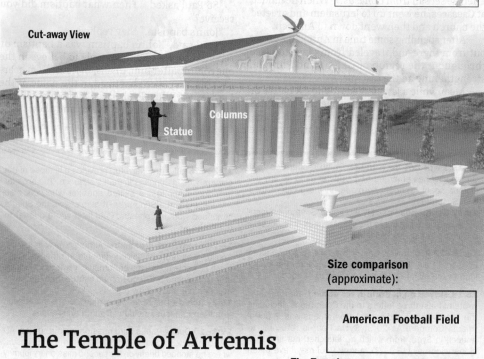

Cut-away View

Columns

Statue

Size comparison (approximate):

American Football Field

The Temple of Artemis

This temple, called Artemision, was one of the Seven Wonders of the Ancient World. Construction began in the mid-sixth century BC; more than a century later, it was the largest building in Rome, Greece or Asia. Roughly four times the size of the Parthenon in Athens, it featured 127 columns, each measuring 60 ft. in height. It made Ephesus the center of Artemis worship.

The Temple Columns Statue

[11]God did extraordinary miracles through Paul, [12]so that even handkerchiefs and aprons that had touched him were taken to the sick, and their illnesses were cured and the evil spirits left them.

[13]Some Jews who went around driving out evil spirits tried to invoke the name of the Lord Jesus over those who were demon-possessed. They would say, "In the name of the Jesus whom Paul preaches, I command you to come out." [14]Seven sons of Sceva, a Jewish chief priest, were doing this. [15]One day the evil spirit answered them, "Jesus I know, and Paul I know about, but who are you?" [16]Then the man who had the evil spirit jumped on them and overpowered them all. He gave them such a beating that they ran out of the house naked and bleeding.

[17]When this became known to the Jews and Greeks living in Ephesus, they were all seized with fear, and the name of the Lord Jesus was held in high honor. [18]Many of those who believed now came and openly confessed what they had done. [19]A number who had practiced sorcery brought their scrolls together and burned them publicly. When they calculated the value of the scrolls, the total came to fifty thousand drachmas.[a] [20]In this way the word of the Lord spread widely and grew in power.

[21]After all this had happened, Paul decided[b] to go to Jerusalem, passing through Macedonia and Achaia. "After I have been there," he said, "I must visit Rome also." [22]He sent two of his helpers, Timothy and Erastus, to Macedonia, while he stayed in the province of Asia a little longer.

The Riot in Ephesus

[23]About that time there arose a great disturbance about the Way. [24]A silversmith named Demetrius, who made silver shrines of Artemis,

[a] 19 A drachma was a silver coin worth about a day's wages.
[b] 21 Or decided in the Spirit

Paul's testimony of Jesus to spread throughout the Roman province of Asia (a region on the west coast of modern-day Turkey; see 16:6 and note). People visiting Ephesus had the opportunity to hear Paul preach the gospel, and those who believed would have then spread the message to the various places they visited and lived. See the infographic "Ephesus in Paul's Day" on p. 1939.

19:11–20 Paul continues his work in Ephesus to establish it as a base location for his missionary work. This narrative is primarily concerned with Jesus' true power versus the counterfeit authority of other exorcists. See the table "Miracles in Acts" on p. 1774.

19:12 handkerchiefs and aprons that had touched him This evokes the story of a woman being healed by merely touching Jesus (see Lk 8:43–48), showing that the power of the Holy Spirit continues the work of Jesus in the life of Paul.

19:13 Jews who went around driving out evil spirits Exorcising, or driving out evil spirits, seems to have been widely practiced by Jews in the first century AD. For example, among the Dead Sea Scrolls (ca. 250 BC–AD 50) was discovered a work—commonly called Aramaic Exorcism—that includes an incantation intended to remove evil spirits (or demons). Against this practice, Paul simply commanded demons in Jesus' name. **name of the Lord Jesus** Within parts of Greco-Roman culture and Judaism in the first century AD, it was believed that evoking a particular incantation or name granted special power to the person evoking it. In this case, the exorcists attempted to copy Paul's use of the name of Jesus to drive out evil spirits.

19:14 Sceva, a Jewish chief priest The book of Acts is the only source to mention this person.

19:15 I know The man (or the demons that possessed him) demonstrates awareness of both Jesus and Paul. **who are you** Even the evil spirit recognizes the unique authority of Jesus' name. Because the sons of Sceva were not servants of the true God, the evil spirit essentially proclaims that they are illegitimately using Jesus' name.

19:16 overpowered them all The possessed man is able to overpower the sons of Sceva; they were not able to use the name of Jesus because they lacked genuine faith in him. Compare Mt 7:22–23. **naked and**

bleeding The fraudulent claims of the sons of Sceva leave them humiliated. Instead of casting out the evil spirit from the man, the sons of Sceva are driven out of the house.

19:18–19 It is unclear whether the people described here were formerly mixing Christianity with pagan religion or if they had only chosen to believe in Jesus following the event with the sons of Sceva.

19:19 fifty thousand drachmas The Greek text here could refer to drachmas or to denarii, two different kinds of silver coins. They were both a worker's daily wage, so this amount would equal approximately 135 years' worth of wages. See the infographic "Coins of the Gospels" on p. 1613.

19:20 grew Through their dramatic actions, the believers demonstrate the gospel's influence in every area of their lives. Their actions testify to their joyful submission to Jesus and to the power of Jesus over evil powers.

19:21–41 Paul's time in Ephesus ends with a riot, which ironically displays the dramatic impact of God's work through the gospel in the city. See the infographic "Ephesus in Paul's Day" on p. 1939.

19:21 Jerusalem The completion of Paul's work in Ephesus shows how Christ has established the essential framework to minister to both Jews and Gentiles (non-Jewish people) from Jerusalem to the ends of the earth (Ac 1:8). **Rome** Paul's aim is to journey to the center of the Roman Empire to testify to the good news of Jesus and demonstrate that the gospel cannot be hindered. See the infographic "Rome in Paul's Day" on p. 1844.

19:22 Timothy See 16:1; 1Ti 1:2 and note. **Erastus** The name Erastus occurs two other times in the NT (Ro 16:23; 2Ti 4:20). Because Erastus was a common name at the time, it is difficult to determine if the person mentioned here should be identified with the other references to Erastus.

19:24 Artemis Refers to a local representation of the Greek goddess of the moon, who was called Diana by the Romans. Artemis was the patron deity of Ephesus. There were numerous shrines to her in the city, and the temple devoted to her was considered one of the seven wonders of the ancient world.

brought in a lot of business for the craftsmen there. ²⁵He called them together, along with the workers in related trades, and said: "You know, my friends, that we receive a good income from this business. ²⁶And you see and hear how this fellow Paul has convinced and led astray large numbers of people here in Ephesus and in practically the whole province of Asia. He says that gods made by

human hands are no gods at all. ²⁷There is danger not only that our trade will lose its good name, but also that the temple of the great goddess Artemis will be discredited; and the goddess herself, who is worshiped throughout the province of Asia and the world, will be robbed of her divine majesty."

²⁸When they heard this, they were furious and began shouting: "Great is Artemis of the Ephe-

19:25 this business Demetrius appeals to the livelihood of the Ephesian artisans to incite them against Paul. See the infographic "The Temple of Artemis" on p. 1814.
19:26 gods Paul has established the folly of worshiping created objects, since the only true God is the Creator, Yahweh (Ac 17:16–34), and gods created by people are false. Compare 1Co 8:4–6.

19:27 temple of the great goddess The city took great pride in the temple. For it to be discredited would be an enormous insult to the city and to its economic detriment. Compare note on Ac 19:24. See the infographic "The Temple of Artemis" on p. 1814.
19:28 began shouting Having heard that their city could fall into disrepute, the people are rallying to protect the

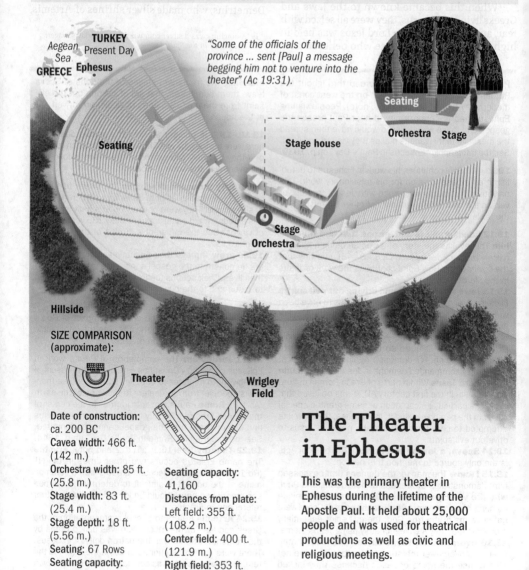

"Some of the officials of the province ... sent [Paul] a message begging him not to venture into the theater" (Ac 19:31).

Aegean Sea · GREECE · **TURKEY** Present Day · Ephesus

Seating

Stage house

Seating

Orchestra · Stage

Seating

Stage
Orchestra

Hillside

SIZE COMPARISON (approximate):

Theater · **Wrigley Field**

Date of construction: ca. 200 BC
Cavea width: 466 ft. (142 m.)
Orchestra width: 85 ft. (25.8 m.)
Stage width: 83 ft. (25.4 m.)
Stage depth: 18 ft. (5.56 m.)
Seating: 67 Rows
Seating capacity: 17,000–25,000

Seating capacity: 41,160
Distances from plate:
Left field: 355 ft. (108.2 m.)
Center field: 400 ft. (121.9 m.)
Right field: 353 ft. (107.6 m.)

The Theater in Ephesus

This was the primary theater in Ephesus during the lifetime of the Apostle Paul. It held about 25,000 people and was used for theatrical productions as well as civic and religious meetings.

sians!" ²⁹Soon the whole city was in an uproar. The people seized Gaius and Aristarchus, Paul's traveling companions from Macedonia, and all of them rushed into the theater together. ³⁰Paul wanted to appear before the crowd, but the disciples would not let him. ³¹Even some of the officials of the province, friends of Paul, sent him a message begging him not to venture into the theater.

³²The assembly was in confusion: Some were shouting one thing, some another. Most of the people did not even know why they were there. ³³The Jews in the crowd pushed Alexander to the front, and they shouted instructions to him. He motioned for silence in order to make a defense before the people. ³⁴But when they realized he was a Jew, they all shouted in unison for about two hours: "Great is Artemis of the Ephesians!"

³⁵The city clerk quieted the crowd and said: "Fellow Ephesians, doesn't all the world know that the city of Ephesus is the guardian of the temple of the great Artemis and of her image, which fell from heaven? ³⁶Therefore, since these facts are undeniable, you ought to calm down and not do anything rash. ³⁷You have brought these men here, though they have neither robbed temples nor blasphemed our goddess. ³⁸If, then, Demetrius and his fellow craftsmen have a grievance against anybody, the courts are open and there are proconsuls. They can press charges. ³⁹If there is anything further you want to bring up, it must be settled in a legal assembly. ⁴⁰As it is, we are in danger of being charged with rioting because of what happened today. In that case we would not be able to account for this commotion, since there is no reason for it." ⁴¹After he had said this, he dismissed the assembly.

Through Macedonia and Greece

20 When the uproar had ended, Paul sent for the disciples and, after encouraging them, said goodbye and set out for Macedonia. ²He traveled through that area, speaking many words of encouragement to the people, and finally arrived in Greece, ³where he stayed three months. Because some Jews had plotted against him just as he was about to sail for Syria, he decided to go back through Macedonia. ⁴He was accompanied by Sopater son of Pyrrhus from Berea, Aristarchus and Secundus from Thessalonica, Gaius from Derbe, Timothy also, and Tychicus and Trophimus from the province of Asia. ⁵These men went on ahead and waited for us at Troas. ⁶But we sailed from Philippi after the Festival of Unleavened Bread, and five days later joined the others at Troas, where we stayed seven days.

---

honor of the city and attack those who oppose it. **Artemis of the Ephesians** While Artemis was worshiped all over the Greco-Roman world, the Ephesians took pride in the temple dedicated to her in their city. Artemis was the patron god of the city.
19:29 Gaius A travel companion of Paul. He is most likely not the same Gaius mentioned in 20:4 since Luke describes the two men as coming from two different places. **Aristarchus** A travel companion of Paul who was from Thessalonica (20:4). Paul seems to refer to this same Aristarchus in his letters (Col 4:10; Phm 24). **the theater** This structure was cut into the side of Mount Pion and faced west, toward the harbor. The preserved remains indicate that it could seat around 24,000. Since it was expanded over the course of the first century, the capacity may have been somewhat smaller in Paul's day. See the infographic "The Theater in Ephesus" on p. 1816.
19:31 the officials of the province The upper-class civic rulers who were in charge of the administration of Ephesus. Their insight and reaction into the circumstances demonstrate the serious nature of the riot caused by Demetrius. **friends** Paul's message affected every tier of society.
19:33 Alexander A Jew who is otherwise unmentioned in the NT. Acts does not mention whether Alexander was a Christian.
19:34 a Jew The crowd, already confused, would have reacted strongly to Alexander's ethnicity. Jews would have refused to worship Artemis on account of their exclusive worship of Yahweh.
19:35-40 The city clerk (or secretary) speaks in a rhetorical pattern commonly used in Greco-Roman society of the first century AD. He begins with a review, which he follows with his thesis (Ac 19:35,36). He then presents an argument to support his main idea before ending with an appeal to the audience to act appropriately (vv. 37–39,40).

19:35 her image, which fell from heaven Refers to the Greek mythology that Artemis' stone fell from the sky. This image likely refers to a meteorite fallen from the sky and is intended to highlight Artemis' divine origin. The reference shows the Ephesians' great reverence for Artemis. It also counters Paul's claim that their gods were not real because they were made with human hands (v. 26).
19:36 to calm down The main point of the clerk (or secretary) is that if the audience acts consistently with their beliefs, they would maintain the civic peace. If Artemis worship is so strong and powerful, then she has no need for the crowd to act on her behalf.
19:40 rioting Roman officials would consider rioting an act of rebellion and would take military steps to resolve the situation, resulting in violence and loss of life; in addition, they would likely strip Ephesus of certain privileges and rights, especially of self-governance.

20:1–6 Paul's third missionary journey (ca. AD 52–57) focuses on his efforts to strengthen churches. Paul's mission pioneered into regions far from Jerusalem, and the apostle now works to ensure that the churches he established or helped will remain faithful. See the map "Paul's Third Missionary Journey" on p. 2263.
20:1 Macedonia In chs. 16–17, Paul ministered in Macedonia. He now retraces his steps.
20:3 three months Paul spends some time in Greece, likely in Corinth, as he did before (18:11; see 1Co 16:6).
back through Macedonia This journey would take him past more churches he had established or strengthened.
20:5 Troas A major port city along the Aegean Sea in the Roman province of Asia and modern Turkey, northwest of Ephesus.
20:6 we sailed Luke, the narrator, includes himself again in the narrative here. See 16:10 and note. **Philippi** The city itself is located about nine miles from the Aegean

Eutychus Raised From the Dead at Troas

[7] On the first day of the week we came together to break bread. Paul spoke to the people and, because he intended to leave the next day, kept on talking until midnight. [8] There were many lamps in the upstairs room where we were meeting. [9] Seated in a window was a young man named Eutychus, who was sinking into a deep sleep as Paul talked on and on. When he was sound asleep, he fell to the ground from the third story and was picked up dead. [10] Paul went down, threw himself on the young man and put his arms around him. "Don't be alarmed," he said. "He's alive!" [11] Then he went upstairs again and broke bread and ate. After talking until daylight, he left. [12] The people took the young man home alive and were greatly comforted.

Paul's Farewell to the Ephesian Elders

[13] We went on ahead to the ship and sailed for Assos, where we were going to take Paul aboard. He had made this arrangement because he was going there on foot. [14] When he met us at Assos, we took him aboard and went on to Mitylene. [15] The next day we set sail from there and arrived off Chios. The day after that we crossed over to Samos, and on the following day arrived at Miletus. [16] Paul had decided to sail past Ephesus to avoid spending time in the province of Asia, for he was in a hurry to reach Jerusalem, if possible, by the day of Pentecost.

[17] From Miletus, Paul sent to Ephesus for the elders of the church. [18] When they arrived, he said to them: "You know how I lived the whole time I was with you, from the first day I came into the province of Asia. [19] I served the Lord with great humility and with tears and in the midst of severe testing by the plots of my Jewish opponents. [20] You know that I have not hesitated to preach anything that would be helpful to you but have taught you publicly and from house to house. [21] I have declared to both Jews and Greeks that they must turn to God in repentance and have faith in our Lord Jesus.

[22] "And now, compelled by the Spirit, I am going to Jerusalem, not knowing what will happen to me there. [23] I only know that in every city the Holy Spirit warns me that prison and hardships are facing me. [24] However, I consider my life worth nothing to me; my only aim is to finish the race and complete the task the Lord Jesus has given me — the task of testifying to the good news of God's grace.

[25] "Now I know that none of you among whom I have gone about preaching the kingdom will ever

---

coast and the port is about 150 miles northwest of Troas by sea. Compare 16:12–40; note on 16:12. **Unleavened Bread** The festival of Passover (Ex 12). See the table "Israelite Festivals" on p. 200.

20:7–12 Luke transitions from an overview of Paul's travel and draws attention to his miracle involving Eutychus. The mighty deed performed by Paul depicts the power that drives the church: the resurrection of Jesus (Ac 1:2–3; 2:24).

20:7 first day Refers to Sunday. **to break bread** Possibly referring to the Lord's Supper, which often accompanied a fellowship meal (e.g., 1Co 11:17–34). This may also refer to simply the sharing of a meal with fellow Christians.

20:10 threw himself on the young man Paul's actions recall the act of Elisha, who did a similar action for the Shunammite woman's son (2Ki 4:34). When Elisha did this, the dead boy was revived. **He's alive** Eutychus was dead (Ac 20:9), but because of Paul's actions, he is raised from the dead. Paul makes this statement either because he is confident of Eutychus' resurrection or because at this point Eutychus has already been resurrected. Compare 9:36–42.

20:13–16 Paul's mission transitions from strengthening churches to his return to Jerusalem.

20:13 We went on ahead Referring to Luke (the narrator) and those traveling with Paul (16:10). **Assos** A port city. Located along the coast of the Roman province of Asia, which is in modern Turkey—approximately 20 miles south of Troas (20:6).
20:14 Mitylene A port on the island of Lesbos.
20:16 day of Pentecost Paul's arrival at Pentecost

to announce the completion of his third journey would testify to the tremendous work Christ has done to build his church. Compare ch. 2.

20:17–38 Paul's speech describes his desire for the church in Ephesus to grow strong and play a leading role among the churches in the region.

20:17 sent to Ephesus for the elders While Paul intends to hurry through this region, he makes an effort to have one last moment with those from Ephesus (compare ch. 19). Paul does not want to travel to Ephesus itself because he wants to ensure the efficiency of his journey to Jerusalem (20:16).
20:18 first day Paul bases his argument on his actions that have consistently supported his character.
20:19 I served Paul has been faithful to God's calling and has served Jesus sacrificially. **severe testing** Demonstrates the struggle in Paul's work. The apostle served God through great sacrifice in the trials brought about by his fellow Jews and others. Here he may be specifically referring to the difficulties the church has experienced in Ephesus (see 19:23–41).
20:20 to preach The proclamation of the gospel was central to Paul's calling as an apostle to the non-Jewish people (see 1Co 9:16).
20:21 repentance Acknowledging sin and turning from it to follow Christ (Ac 2:38).
20:23 the Holy Spirit warns Compare 16:6.
20:24 good news of God's grace Refers to the message of Jesus' sacrificial death and resurrection, which allows people to be made right before God the Father.
20:25 the kingdom Refers to the kingdom of God, which was inaugurated by Jesus. See note on 1:3; note on Mk 1:15.

see me again. ²⁶Therefore, I declare to you today that I am innocent of the blood of any of you. ²⁷For I have not hesitated to proclaim to you the whole will of God. ²⁸Keep watch over yourselves and all the flock of which the Holy Spirit has made you overseers. Be shepherds of the church of God,ᵃ which he bought with his own blood.ᵇ ²⁹I know that after I leave, savage wolves will come in among you and will not spare the flock. ³⁰Even from your own number men will arise and distort the truth in order to draw away disciples after them. ³¹So be on your guard! Remember that for three years I never stopped warning each of you night and day with tears.

³²"Now I commit you to God and to the word of his grace, which can build you up and give you an inheritance among all those who are sanctified. ³³I have not coveted anyone's silver or gold or clothing. ³⁴You yourselves know that these hands of mine have supplied my own needs and the needs of my companions. ³⁵In everything I did, I showed you that by this kind of hard work we must help the weak, remembering the words the Lord Jesus himself said: 'It is more blessed to give than to receive.' "

³⁶When Paul had finished speaking, he knelt down with all of them and prayed. ³⁷They all wept as they embraced him and kissed him. ³⁸What grieved them most was his statement that they would never see his face again. Then they accompanied him to the ship.

On to Jerusalem

21 After we had torn ourselves away from them, we put out to sea and sailed straight to Kos. The next day we went to Rhodes and from there to Patara. ²We found a ship crossing over to Phoenicia, went on board and set sail. ³After sighting Cyprus and passing to the south of it, we sailed on to Syria. We landed at Tyre, where our ship was to unload its cargo. ⁴We sought out the disciples there and stayed with them seven days. Through the Spirit they urged Paul not to go on to Jerusalem. ⁵When it was time to leave, we left and continued on our way. All of them, including wives and children, accompanied us out of the city, and there on the beach we knelt to pray. ⁶After saying goodbye to each other, we went aboard the ship, and they returned home.

⁷We continued our voyage from Tyre and landed at Ptolemais, where we greeted the brothers and sisters and stayed with them for a day. ⁸Leaving the next day, we reached Caesarea and stayed at the house of Philip the evangelist, one of the Seven. ⁹He had four unmarried daughters who prophesied.

ᵃ 28 Many manuscripts *of the Lord*   ᵇ 28 Or *with the blood of his own Son.*

20:26–28 Paul states that he has completed his responsibilities to the Ephesian believers. Paul can make this statement because he has shared the complete message of the gospel to those in Ephesus and because he now will pass his responsibilities to the elders (or overseers) of Ephesus. The language borrows from 1Sa 12:2–5, where Samuel declares his innocence and holds the audience accountable.

20:27 the whole will of God Paul's preaching has covered all the core principles God has revealed to him about his purposes. Here he seems to be specifically referring to the message of salvation in Jesus, but he could also more broadly be speaking of passing along the necessary knowledge for the Ephesian elders to continue the work of the gospel.

20:28 overseers The Greek word used here, *episkopos*, refers to those with leadership responsibility over the church. These leaders are likely collectively responsible for multiple churches. Luke usually uses a different term for these same leaders in Ac 20:17, *presbyteros*. This parallel use of "overseer" and "elder" implies they are the same office but may stress two aspects of the same role. The continuation of Paul's plan for the Ephesian leadership, and the specific instructions regarding the appointment of these individuals, is seen in 1 Timothy (see 1Ti 1:3; 3:1–7). See note on 1Ti 3:1.

20:29 wolves Since Paul has called the church a flock and the elders its shepherd, he extends the metaphor to label false teachers as wolves.

20:32 sanctified This term usually refers to the process of God transforming a person's life to make them holy (set apart) for him. Here it seems to refer to believers in Jesus in general who have been made holy because of Christ's sacrifice on their behalf.

20:35 It is more blessed to give than to receive This phrase is not recorded in the Gospels, though Jesus did more than is recorded there (compare Jn 21:25).

21:1–16 Paul's journey back to Jerusalem demonstrates the balance of his ministry. While recent chapters emphasized his work among Gentiles, his ministry in a location regularly began with his fellow Jewish people and now he desires to return to Jerusalem to report on his work (Ac 20:16). His priority is to unite Jew and Gentile in their faith in Christ.

21:2 crossing over to Phoenicia A journey of more than 400 miles. Such a voyage would have taken three to five days.

21:3 Cyprus Paul has ministered in Cyprus before. Compare 11:19 and note.

21:4 Through the Spirit they urged Paul Paul has already been commanded by the Holy Spirit to go to Jerusalem (20:22). Rather than the Spirit giving contradictory messages, it may be that the believers know through the Spirit what will happen to Paul in Jerusalem, and they then worry about the dangers facing Paul there. Paul is ready to suffer for the gospel, but they do not want him to.

21:7 at Ptolemais A city on the southern Phoenician coast. In the OT the city was known as Akko (Jdg 1:31).

21:8 Caesarea A major seaport for Israel, constructed by Herod the Great. **one of the Seven** Philip was one of those whom God used initially to advance the gospel beyond the Jews to the Gentiles (Ac 6:1–7). He ministered to the Ethiopian eunuch (8:26–40).

21:9 daughters Joel 2:28–32 proclaims the coming of the Holy Spirit on both men and women, and Peter cites this prophecy in Ac 2:17–18. Paul's first letter to the

¹⁰After we had been there a number of days, a prophet named Agabus came down from Judea. ¹¹Coming over to us, he took Paul's belt, tied his own hands and feet with it and said, "The Holy Spirit says, 'In this way the Jewish leaders in Jerusalem will bind the owner of this belt and will hand him over to the Gentiles.'"

¹²When we heard this, we and the people there pleaded with Paul not to go up to Jerusalem. ¹³Then Paul answered, "Why are you weeping and breaking my heart? I am ready not only to be bound, but also to die in Jerusalem for the name of the Lord Jesus." ¹⁴When he would not be dissuaded, we gave up and said, "The Lord's will be done."

¹⁵After this, we started on our way up to Jerusalem. ¹⁶Some of the disciples from Caesarea accompanied us and brought us to the home of Mnason, where we were to stay. He was a man from Cyprus and one of the early disciples.

Paul's Arrival at Jerusalem

¹⁷When we arrived at Jerusalem, the brothers and sisters received us warmly. ¹⁸The next day Paul and the rest of us went to see James, and all the elders were present. ¹⁹Paul greeted them and reported in detail what God had done among the Gentiles through his ministry.

²⁰When they heard this, they praised God. Then they said to Paul: "You see, brother, how many thousands of Jews have believed, and all of them are zealous for the law. ²¹They have been informed that you teach all the Jews who live among the Gentiles to turn away from Moses, telling them not to circumcise their children or live according to our customs. ²²What shall we do? They will certainly hear that you have come, ²³so do what we tell you. There are four men with us who have made a vow. ²⁴Take these men, join in their purification rites and pay their expenses, so that they can have their heads shaved. Then everyone will know there is no truth in these reports about you, but that you yourself are living in obedience to the law. ²⁵As for the Gentile believers, we have written to them our decision that they should abstain from food sacrificed to idols, from blood, from the meat of strangled animals and from sexual immorality."

²⁶The next day Paul took the men and purified himself along with them. Then he went to the temple to give notice of the date when the days of purification would end and the offering would be made for each of them.

Paul Arrested

²⁷When the seven days were nearly over, some Jews from the province of Asia saw Paul at the temple. They stirred up the whole crowd and seized him, ²⁸shouting, "Fellow Israelites, help us! This is the man who teaches everyone everywhere against

---

Corinthian church indicates that at least some women there prophesied (1Co 11:5).
21:10 Agabus See Ac 11:28.

21:11 Agabus' proclamation of a capture by the Jews and arrest by the Gentile authorities indicates a more serious situation than Paul has experienced thus far. The Jewish leadership has far greater power in Jerusalem, and the Gentile (non-Jewish) authorities are more likely to listen to their accusations there.

21:16 the disciples from Caesarea These probably included some Jews but also Hellenists or Gentiles. **Mnason** Being from a predominantly Gentile area, Mnason was likely someone who would be understanding of the predominately non-Jewish group accompanying Paul.

21:17—28:31 While it is not usually counted among Paul's missionary journeys, the remainder of the book of Acts narrates how Paul is enabled to take the gospel to Rome. First he is arrested in Jerusalem (21:17—23:35). Then he is transferred to Caesarea where, after a period of imprisonment, he appeals for his case to be heard by Caesar (24:1—26:32). Finally, he makes the difficult journey by ship to the center of the empire and is able to preach there (27:1—28:31).

21:17-26 Paul and his colleagues visit Jerusalem to report on their work among the predominately Gentile (non-Jewish) regions.

21:17 we arrived at Jerusalem Luke (the narrator) includes himself in his narrative. See note on 16:10.
21:18 James Brother of Jesus and leader of the church in Jerusalem (15:13).
21:21 to turn away from Moses Some Jewish people

in Jerusalem believed incorrectly that Paul was discouraging Jews from keeping the law. This was not true, since Paul himself continued to observe Jewish customs (see 16:3; 18:18; 1Co 7:18–19).
21:23 a vow Likely a Nazirite vow (Nu 6:1–21).
21:24 purification rites A Nazirite vow was connected with becoming pure or holy before Yahweh for a set period of time (Nu 6:5,8). James may be suggesting that Paul join in the Nazirite vow himself—which he may have already voluntarily done at one point (see Ac 18:18 and note)—or that Paul undergo a different kind of purification rite (e.g., Nu 19:12). By doing this, Paul will show that he is still sensitive to Jewish culture, which James believes will overturn their fellow Jews' concerns about Paul. This action demonstrates that Paul is not encouraging Jews to abandon their traditions, cultural identity or religious identity.

21:25 James affirms the decision of the Jerusalem Council (Ac 15:19). Paul's actions are purely social, showing respect for Israelite customs.

21:27–36 Paul is falsely accused of bringing Gentiles (non-Jewish people) into the parts of the temple they were not allowed in. Gentiles were allowed in the court of the Gentiles but not beyond that. Roman soldiers rescue him from an angry mob and take him into custody, fulfilling Agabus' prophecy (v. 11).

21:27 the seven days Purification rites affiliated with the Nazirite vow took about seven days to complete (see Nu 6:9; compare note on Ac 21:24). **from the province of Asia** The Jews from this province—which is roughly equivalent to modern Turkey and northern Greece—recognize Paul from his missionary journeys. They stir up the crowd to oppose him.
21:28 teaches The Greek text here implies habitual or

our people and our law and this place. And besides, he has brought Greeks into the temple and defiled this holy place." ²⁹(They had previously seen Trophimus the Ephesian in the city with Paul and assumed that Paul had brought him into the temple.)

³⁰The whole city was aroused, and the people came running from all directions. Seizing Paul, they dragged him from the temple, and immediately the gates were shut. ³¹While they were trying to kill him, news reached the commander of the Roman troops that the whole city of Jerusalem was in an uproar. ³²He at once took some officers and soldiers and ran down to the crowd. When the rioters saw the commander and his soldiers, they stopped beating Paul.

³³The commander came up and arrested him and ordered him to be bound with two chains. Then he asked who he was and what he had done. ³⁴Some in the crowd shouted one thing and some another, and since the commander could not get at the truth because of the uproar, he ordered that Paul be taken into the barracks. ³⁵When Paul reached the steps, the violence of the mob was so great he had to be carried by the soldiers. ³⁶The crowd that followed kept shouting, "Get rid of him!"

Paul Speaks to the Crowd

22:3-16pp — Ac 9:1-22; 26:9-18

³⁷As the soldiers were about to take Paul into the barracks, he asked the commander, "May I say something to you?"

"Do you speak Greek?" he replied. ³⁸"Aren't you the Egyptian who started a revolt and led four thousand terrorists out into the wilderness some time ago?"

³⁹Paul answered, "I am a Jew, from Tarsus in Cilicia, a citizen of no ordinary city. Please let me speak to the people."

⁴⁰After receiving the commander's permission, Paul stood on the steps and motioned to the crowd. When they were all silent, he said to them **22** in Aramaic*ᵃ*: ¹"Brothers and fathers, listen now to my defense."

²When they heard him speak to them in Aramaic, they became very quiet.

Then Paul said: ³"I am a Jew, born in Tarsus of Cilicia, but brought up in this city. I studied under Gamaliel and was thoroughly trained in the law of our ancestors. I was just as zealous for God as any of you are today. ⁴I persecuted the followers of this Way to their death, arresting both men and women and throwing them into prison, ⁵as the high priest and all the Council can themselves testify. I even obtained letters from them to their associates in Damascus, and went there to bring these people as prisoners to Jerusalem to be punished.

⁶"About noon as I came near Damascus, suddenly a bright light from heaven flashed around me. ⁷I fell to the ground and heard a voice say to me, 'Saul! Saul! Why do you persecute me?'

ᵃ 40 Or possibly Hebrew; also in 22:2

continual practice. The leaders are making an accusation about Paul's ministry in general. **Greeks** The Jews cite further supposed evidence of Paul's apostasy. This action would have violated the sanctity of the temple and thus likely would have been understood as carrying the death penalty.

21:29 Trophimus Trophimus is a Gentile from Ephesus (in modern Turkey) and like the accusers of Paul, he is from the Roman province of Asia (Ac 20:4; compare 21:27 and note). Compare 2Ti 4:20.

21:30 The whole city Paul is perceived to have violated the sanctity of the temple, and the Jews are determined to kill him.

21:31 of the Roman troops The Greek text here uses terminology that indicates that the Roman commander is over about 1,000 soldiers. See the infographic "Jerusalem" on p. 1607. **in an uproar** Such unrest could actually be a crime in the eyes of Roman officials (compare Ac 19:32–40). The soldiers were forced to act to keep the peace.

21:32 the commander This officer's presence saves Paul's life. His name is given later as Claudius Lysias (23:26).

21:34 the crowd shouted The violent outcries of the crowd show potential for a riot (compare 19:32).

21:37 — 22:5 Paul takes advantage of his Roman citizenship to testify to the crowd.

21:37 Do you speak Greek Paul's knowledge of Greek would indicate he was well educated.

21:38 the Egyptian The officer confuses Paul with some-

one else. **terrorists** The Greek word used here, *sicarios*, refers to a violent anti-Roman Jewish revolutionary group. See the table "Major Groups in Jesus' Time" on p. 1630.

21:39 no ordinary city Paul uses this rhetoric to emphasize that Tarsus was a city known for scholarship and culture. Paul's citizenship and the identity of his hometown show that he is not a rebel as the officer in charge may have thought.

21:40 in Aramaic The Greek term used here, *hebrais*, can refer in the NT to either Hebrew or Aramaic. Aramaic is probably meant here, since it was the more common spoken language at the time. Paul's use of it demonstrates to those present that he is a Jew and respects their culture.

22:1–21 In speaking to a hostile Jewish audience, Paul uses OT imagery as he seeks to show that his message is not an abandonment of his Jewish heritage. He explains his message via his own encounter with Jesus. Compare Ac 9:1–19.

22:3 a Jew Paul proudly proclaims he is a Jew. This emphasizes to the audience that the allegations against him are false. **born in Tarsus of Cilicia** See note on 21:39. **brought up in this city** Paul had evidently moved to Jerusalem as a young man and studied under Gamaliel. See 5:34 and note.

22:5 high priest Paul was well known among the nation's elite.

22:7 I fell to the ground Paul's reaction matches the reactions of those in the OT who have divine encounters (e.g., Eze 1:28; Da 10:9). **Saul! Saul!** See note on Ac 9:4.

8 "'Who are you, Lord?' I asked.

"'I am Jesus of Nazareth, whom you are persecuting,' he replied. 9 My companions saw the light, but they did not understand the voice of him who was speaking to me.

10 "'What shall I do, Lord?' I asked.

"'Get up,' the Lord said, 'and go into Damascus. There you will be told all that you have been assigned to do.' 11 My companions led me by the hand into Damascus, because the brilliance of the light had blinded me.

12 "A man named Ananias came to see me. He was a devout observer of the law and highly respected by all the Jews living there. 13 He stood beside me and said, 'Brother Saul, receive your sight!' And at that very moment I was able to see him.

14 "Then he said: 'The God of our ancestors has chosen you to know his will and to see the Righteous One and to hear words from his mouth. 15 You will be his witness to all people of what you have seen and heard. 16 And now what are you waiting for? Get up, be baptized and wash your sins away, calling on his name.'

17 "When I returned to Jerusalem and was praying at the temple, I fell into a trance 18 and saw the Lord speaking to me. 'Quick!' he said. 'Leave Jerusalem immediately, because the people here will not accept your testimony about me.'

19 "'Lord,' I replied, 'these people know that I went from one synagogue to another to imprison and beat those who believe in you. 20 And when the blood of your martyr[a] Stephen was shed, I stood there giving my approval and guarding the clothes of those who were killing him.'

21 "Then the Lord said to me, 'Go; I will send you far away to the Gentiles.'"

Paul the Roman Citizen

22 The crowd listened to Paul until he said this. Then they raised their voices and shouted, "Rid the earth of him! He's not fit to live!"

23 As they were shouting and throwing off their cloaks and flinging dust into the air, 24 the commander ordered that Paul be taken into the barracks. He directed that he be flogged and interrogated in order to find out why the people were shouting at him like this. 25 As they stretched him out to flog him, Paul said to the centurion standing there, "Is it legal for you to flog a Roman citizen who hasn't even been found guilty?"

26 When the centurion heard this, he went to the commander and reported it. "What are you going to do?" he asked. "This man is a Roman citizen."

27 The commander went to Paul and asked, "Tell me, are you a Roman citizen?"

"Yes, I am," he answered.

28 Then the commander said, "I had to pay a lot of money for my citizenship."

"But I was born a citizen," Paul replied.

29 Those who were about to interrogate him withdrew immediately. The commander himself was alarmed when he realized that he had put Paul, a Roman citizen, in chains.

Paul Before the Sanhedrin

30 The commander wanted to find out exactly why Paul was being accused by the Jews. So the next day he released him and ordered the chief priests and all the members of the Sanhedrin to assemble. Then he brought Paul and had him stand before them.

23 Paul looked straight at the Sanhedrin and said, "My brothers, I have fulfilled my duty to God in all good conscience to this day." 2 At this the high priest Ananias ordered those standing near Paul to strike him on the mouth. 3 Then Paul said to him, "God will strike you, you whitewashed wall! You sit there to judge me according to the law, yet you yourself violate the law by commanding that I be struck!"

a 20 Or witness

22:8 of Nazareth Earlier, Acts records a shorter statement, leaving out this phrase (9:5), which was one way Jesus was identified (e.g., 2:22; 3:6; 4:10; 6:14).

22:9 they did not understand Paul's description echoes Da 10:7, where people around the prophet could not understand the entire event but knew the vision was terrifying. Compare Ac 9:7.

22:12 observer of the law Since Ananias, an upstanding Jew, approved of Paul, then other Jews should not object.

22:14 God of our ancestors Reinforces that the God who commissioned Paul is the God of Israel, Yahweh. This phrase is used in the OT to refer to Yahweh and to his promises (compare Dt 1:11; 26:7). **the Righteous One** This title is used in the prophecy of the suffering servant in Isa 53:11, to refer to how the suffering servant makes others right before Yahweh via his death and resurrection (compare note on Isa 53:10). See Ac 3:14 and note.

22:15 witness This matches Jesus' original commission at the beginning of Acts (see 1:8). Compare 9:15–16.

22:22–29 Paul's audience reacts violently to his speech, and the Roman commander seeks to learn why the Jewish people are so upset with Paul by using torture. Paul escapes flogging by calling attention to his Roman citizenship (see 16:37).

22:23 cloaks Paul's Jewish opponents may be actually tearing their garments because they believe he is committing blasphemy (see 14:14 and note) or taking them off in order to kill Paul by stoning him (7:58).

22:25 a Roman citizen Paul appeals to his Roman citizenship and his judicial standing. Roman law forbade the punishment of a citizen without a trial.

22:28 a lot of money Paul's citizenship is by birth, due to him being from Tarsus—a municipality of the Roman Empire that automatically granted citizenship. The commander as a member of the military would have been a citizen of military order. From his military position, he then likely purchased his higher rank, which would move him to the upper (ruling) class order of citizens.

22:30 released him Paul's use of his Roman citizenship

⁴Those who were standing near Paul said, "How dare you insult God's high priest!"

⁵Paul replied, "Brothers, I did not realize that he was the high priest; for it is written: 'Do not speak evil about the ruler of your people.'ᵃ"

⁶Then Paul, knowing that some of them were Sadducees and the others Pharisees, called out in the Sanhedrin, "My brothers, I am a Pharisee, descended from Pharisees. I stand on trial because of the hope of the resurrection of the dead." ⁷When he said this, a dispute broke out between the Pharisees and the Sadducees, and the assembly was divided. ⁸(The Sadducees say that there is no resurrection, and that there are neither angels nor spirits, but the Pharisees believe all these things.)

⁹There was a great uproar, and some of the teachers of the law who were Pharisees stood up and argued vigorously. "We find nothing wrong with this man," they said. "What if a spirit or an angel has spoken to him?" ¹⁰The dispute became so violent that the commander was afraid Paul would be torn to pieces by them. He ordered the troops to go down and take him away from them by force and bring him into the barracks.

¹¹The following night the Lord stood near Paul and said, "Take courage! As you have testified about me in Jerusalem, so you must also testify in Rome."

The Plot to Kill Paul

¹²The next morning some Jews formed a conspiracy and bound themselves with an oath not to eat or drink until they had killed Paul. ¹³More than forty men were involved in this plot. ¹⁴They went to the chief priests and the elders and said, "We have taken a solemn oath not to eat anything until we have killed Paul. ¹⁵Now then, you and the Sanhedrin petition the commander to bring him before you on the pretext of wanting more accurate information about his case. We are ready to kill him before he gets here."

¹⁶But when the son of Paul's sister heard of this plot, he went into the barracks and told Paul.

¹⁷Then Paul called one of the centurions and said, "Take this young man to the commander; he has something to tell him." ¹⁸So he took him to the commander.

The centurion said, "Paul, the prisoner, sent for me and asked me to bring this young man to you because he has something to tell you."

¹⁹The commander took the young man by the hand, drew him aside and asked, "What is it you want to tell me?"

²⁰He said: "Some Jews have agreed to ask you to bring Paul before the Sanhedrin tomorrow on the pretext of wanting more accurate information about him. ²¹Don't give in to them, because more than forty of them are waiting in ambush for him. They have taken an oath not to eat or drink until they have killed him. They are ready now, waiting for your consent to their request."

²²The commander dismissed the young man with this warning: "Don't tell anyone that you have reported this to me."

Paul Transferred to Caesarea

²³Then he called two of his centurions and ordered them, "Get ready a detachment of two hundred soldiers, seventy horsemen and two hundred spearmenᵇ to go to Caesarea at nine tonight.

ᵃ 5 Exodus 22:28   ᵇ 23 The meaning of the Greek for this word is uncertain.

---

prevents him from being imprisoned immediately. Instead, he must go through a major Roman judicial process.

23:1–11 Paul testifies before the Sanhedrin.

23:1 Sanhedrin The governing Jewish body in Jerusalem over religious matters. The group consisted of both Pharisees and Sadducees who held many opposing viewpoints. See the infographic "The Sanhedrin" on p. 1746.

23:2 Ananias A corrupt high priest who ruled around AD 47–58. First-century Jewish historian Josephus records that he was quick-tempered (Josephus, *Antiquities* 20.197–99).

23:3 strike you Paul proclaims that God's justice against the high priest will match his disregard for the law. **you yourself violate the law** Paul accuses Ananias of failing to uphold the law by presuming Paul's guilt and punishing him before Paul could make his case. See Lev 19:15.

23:5 I did not realize It is possible Paul had never seen Ananias and was not aware he was the high priest. It is also possible that Paul was speaking sarcastically: He did not recognize Ananias because Ananias was not acting the way the high priest was supposed to act. **Do not speak evil about the ruler of your people** Paul quotes Ex 22:28.

23:6 Sadducees The Sadducees were the ruling religious class in Judea in the first century AD. See Mk 12:18 and note. **Pharisees** The Pharisees were devoted to the practice and teaching of the law. See note on Jn 7:32. **the resurrection** The Sadducees rejected the notion of a resurrection of the dead; the Pharisees believed in it (see note on Ac 24:15).

23:9 a spirit or an angel The Pharisees support Paul and condemn the Sadducees at the same time.

23:11 the Lord This likely refers to Jesus. It seems that Paul saw Jesus in a vision again, as he had earlier (18:9).

23:12–35 The Jews' conspiracy to kill Paul is discovered by Paul's nephew. For his protection, the Romans transfer Paul to Caesarea, the seat of the Roman government in Judea.

23:13 More than forty men By showing the strength of the plot against Paul, Luke (the narrator) illustrates God's power and involvement to overturn such a plot. Since these men go to the governing authorities of the temple and request that the governing authorities appeal to the Sanhedrin, it seems that they were ordinary Jewish men who held the same beliefs as the Sadducees.

23:16 son of Paul's sister It is unclear how Paul's nephew is in a position to hear of the plot.

²⁴Provide horses for Paul so that he may be taken safely to Governor Felix."

²⁵He wrote a letter as follows:

²⁶Claudius Lysias,

To His Excellency, Governor Felix:

Greetings.

²⁷This man was seized by the Jews and they were about to kill him, but I came with my troops and rescued him, for I had learned that he is a Roman citizen. ²⁸I wanted to know why they were accusing him, so I brought him to their Sanhedrin. ²⁹I found that the accusation had to do with questions about their law, but there was no charge against him that deserved death or imprisonment. ³⁰When I was informed of a plot to be carried out against the man, I sent him to you at once. I also ordered his accusers to present to you their case against him.

³¹So the soldiers, carrying out their orders, took Paul with them during the night and brought him as far as Antipatris. ³²The next day they let the cavalry go on with him, while they returned to the barracks. ³³When the cavalry arrived in Caesarea, they delivered the letter to the governor and handed Paul over to him. ³⁴The governor read the letter and asked what province he was from. Learning that he was from Cilicia, ³⁵he said, "I will hear your case when your accusers get here." Then he ordered that Paul be kept under guard in Herod's palace.

Paul's Trial Before Felix

24 Five days later the high priest Ananias went down to Caesarea with some of the elders and a lawyer named Tertullus, and they brought their charges against Paul before the governor. ²When Paul was called in, Tertullus presented his case before Felix: "We have enjoyed a long period of peace under you, and your foresight has brought about reforms in this nation. ³Everywhere and in every way, most excellent Felix, we acknowledge this with profound gratitude. ⁴But in order not to weary you further, I would request that you be kind enough to hear us briefly.

⁵"We have found this man to be a troublemaker, stirring up riots among the Jews all over the world. He is a ringleader of the Nazarene sect ⁶and even tried to desecrate the temple; so we seized him. ⁷a ⁸By examining him yourself you will be able to learn the truth about all these charges we are bringing against him."

⁹The other Jews joined in the accusation, asserting that these things were true.

¹⁰When the governor motioned for him to speak, Paul replied: "I know that for a number of years you have been a judge over this nation; so I gladly make my defense. ¹¹You can easily verify that no more than twelve days ago I went up to Jerusalem to worship. ¹²My accusers did not find me arguing with anyone at the temple, or stirring up a crowd in the synagogues or anywhere else in the city. ¹³And they cannot prove to you the charges they are now making against me. ¹⁴However, I admit that I worship the God of our ancestors as a follower of the Way, which they call a sect. I believe everything that is in accordance with the Law and that is written in the Prophets, ¹⁵and I have the same hope in God as these men themselves have, that there will be a resurrection of both the righteous and the wicked. ¹⁶So I strive always to keep my conscience clear before God and man.

---

a 6-8 Some manuscripts include here *him, and we would have judged him in accordance with our law.* ⁷*But the commander Lysias came and took him from us with much violence,* ⁸*ordering his accusers to come before you.*

23:24 Governor Felix Marcus Antonius Felix was the Roman governor of Judea from AD 52–60. According to first-century Jewish historian Josephus, Felix was appointed by the emperor Claudius (Josephus, *Antiquities* 20.137–38). See the table "Political Leaders in the New Testament" on p. 1916.

23:26 Claudius Lysias The Roman commander's name is mentioned for the first time.

23:27 he is a Roman citizen The charge against Paul is a Jewish issue irrelevant to the Romans, but they must take interest because he is a Roman citizen. Claudius is giving himself more credit than he deserves; he did not know Paul was a Roman citizen until after he was in custody and about to be flogged (Ac 21:31–36; 22:24–29).

23:31 Antipatris Halfway between Jerusalem and Caesarea, and the site of a significant Roman garrison that could protect Paul overnight.

23:34 Cilicia Paul's hometown of Tarsus was in the larger Roman province of Syria-Cilicia at this time (see Gal 1:21), and so was under the jurisdiction of Felix's superior, the legate of Syria. Felix decides to try Paul instead of handing him off to his superior.

24:1–21 As Paul makes his defense to the Roman governor Felix, he first argues for the legitimacy of the church within the Roman Empire. The Romans may wonder if this new movement is rebellious or illegal; Luke (the narrator) has repeatedly shown it is not (e.g., Ac 18:15; 19:36–40).

24:1 Tertullus The Jewish leadership hires an attorney to persuade Felix that Paul had committed a crime against the empire.

24:2 peace Tertullus praises Felix for bringing peace to the nation, a rhetorical ploy to gain the sympathy and goodwill of the governor. This may be empty flattery.

24:5 riots Riots were illegal and viewed by the Roman Empire as equivalent to rebellion (19:40). **Nazarene** Tertullus associates followers of Jesus with his hometown. This was not what Christians called themselves (v. 14); it may have been a dismissive term meant to evoke the insignificance of Nazareth (compare Jn 1:46).

24:10–21 Paul defends himself against his accusers, showing the falsehood of the accusations against him and how his beliefs actually align with the OT Scriptures.

¹⁷"After an absence of several years, I came to Jerusalem to bring my people gifts for the poor and to present offerings. ¹⁸I was ceremonially clean when they found me in the temple courts doing this. There was no crowd with me, nor was I involved in any disturbance. ¹⁹But there are some Jews from the province of Asia, who ought to be here before you and bring charges if they have anything against me. ²⁰Or these who are here should state what crime they found in me when I stood before the Sanhedrin— ²¹unless it was this one thing I shouted as I stood in their presence: 'It is concerning the resurrection of the dead that I am on trial before you today.'"

²²Then Felix, who was well acquainted with the Way, adjourned the proceedings. "When Lysias the commander comes," he said, "I will decide your case." ²³He ordered the centurion to keep Paul under guard but to give him some freedom and permit his friends to take care of his needs.

²⁴Several days later Felix came with his wife Drusilla, who was Jewish. He sent for Paul and listened to him as he spoke about faith in Christ Jesus. ²⁵As Paul talked about righteousness, self-control and the judgment to come, Felix was afraid and said, "That's enough for now! You may leave. When I find it convenient, I will send for you."

²⁶At the same time he was hoping that Paul would offer him a bribe, so he sent for him frequently and talked with him.

²⁷When two years had passed, Felix was succeeded by Porcius Festus, but because Felix wanted to grant a favor to the Jews, he left Paul in prison.

Paul's Trial Before Festus

25 Three days after arriving in the province, Festus went up from Caesarea to Jerusalem, ²where the chief priests and the Jewish leaders appeared before him and presented the charges against Paul. ³They requested Festus, as a favor to them, to have Paul transferred to Jerusalem, for they were preparing an ambush to kill him along the way. ⁴Festus answered, "Paul is being held at Caesarea, and I myself am going there soon. ⁵Let some of your leaders come with me, and if the man has done anything wrong, they can press charges against him there."

⁶After spending eight or ten days with them, Festus went down to Caesarea. The next day he convened the court and ordered that Paul be brought before him. ⁷When Paul came in, the Jews who had come down from Jerusalem stood around

---

24:10 for a number of years Unlike Tertullus, who uses flattery (Ac 24:1), Paul uses a simple introduction.

24:14 I admit Paul has denied Tertullus' accusation that he started riots, but he does admit to being a Jewish Christian.

24:15 hope in God Paul centers the disagreement on theological matters, knowing that Roman officials generally stayed out of internal religious disputes. **resurrection of both the righteous and the wicked** This belief, which was shared by the Pharisees but not by the Sadducees, was based on passages like Da 12:1–4 (compare Mt 22:31–32; Rev 20).

24:17 gifts for the poor Paul collected money from Gentile (non-Jewish) churches to help those in Jerusalem who were suffering from a famine (e.g., Ro 15:26; 1Co 16:1–4).

24:18 I was ceremonially clean Contrary to Tertullus' accusation (Ac 24:6), Paul's submission to purity rites supports his claim that he has caused no disturbance and did not defile the temple (see 21:24 and note).

24:19 Jews from the province of Asia Those who brought the charges against Paul actually caused the near riot (21:27–28).

24:21 concerning the resurrection of the dead Paul quotes what he said earlier (23:6).

24:22–23 Paul believes his message offers hope for Jewish people (v. 15). Felix's reaction confirms that the Gentiles (non-Jewish people) understand Paul's presentation, and he allows Paul limited freedom (v. 23).

24:22 Lysias Referring to Claudius Lysias, the Roman commander Paul had encountered earlier (23:26–27). **I will decide** Felix never makes a decision, outside of to leave Paul in prison (v. 27). Lysias is not even recorded as being summoned.

24:24–27 Paul proclaims the gospel message to Felix and his wife.

24:24 Drusilla Felix's third wife, the daughter of Herod Agrippa I. She disobeyed Jewish law by divorcing her husband and marrying Felix.

24:26 offer him a bribe Apparently bribes were so common in cases such as Paul's that Felix expected it. The bribe Felix expected might have been to ensure Paul received a hearing, not necessarily to free him.

24:27 Felix was succeeded According to first-century Jewish historian Josephus, Felix was removed from office two years after Paul's hearing because he was unable to keep the peace between Jews and Gentiles in Caesarea (Josephus, *Antiquities* 20.182). **a favor** Since the situation with the Jews is volatile, Felix leaves Paul in prison to appease them.

25:1–12 Festus, the new Roman provincial governor, faces the Jewish leaders, who hope to assassinate Paul (vv. 1–3). Paul defends himself by stating that he has not broken any law, either Jewish or Roman (vv. 6–9). Finally, he exercises his rights as a Roman citizen by appealing to Caesar, which required that he be tried in a court in Rome (vv. 10–12).

25:1 Three days after Festus quickly attempts to put himself on good terms with the potentially troublesome religious leaders. **Caesarea** Located about 75 miles from Jerusalem.

25:3 ambush The earlier trial under Felix has already proven that Paul is not guilty by Roman law. The Jews ask to put Paul on trial in their own courts as a ploy to assassinate him instead.

25:6 court The Greek word used here, *bēma*, indicates the place where a ruler would make civic decisions including criminal proceedings. When the ruler sat in judgment, his voice was the final authority.

him. They brought many serious charges against him, but they could not prove them.

⁸Then Paul made his defense: "I have done nothing wrong against the Jewish law or against the temple or against Caesar."

⁹Festus, wishing to do the Jews a favor, said to Paul, "Are you willing to go up to Jerusalem and stand trial before me there on these charges?"

¹⁰Paul answered: "I am now standing before Caesar's court, where I ought to be tried. I have not done any wrong to the Jews, as you yourself know very well. ¹¹If, however, I am guilty of doing anything deserving death, I do not refuse to die. But if the charges brought against me by these Jews are not true, no one has the right to hand me over to them. I appeal to Caesar!"

¹²After Festus had conferred with his council, he declared: "You have appealed to Caesar. To Caesar you will go!"

Festus Consults King Agrippa

¹³A few days later King Agrippa and Bernice arrived at Caesarea to pay their respects to Festus.

25:8 I have done nothing wrong Judging by Paul's response, the Jewish leaders had apparently repeated their earlier false accusations that Paul had incited sedition and desecrated the temple (24:5–6). See the infographic "Herod's Temple" on p. 1626.

25:9 to Jerusalem Festus acquiesces to the Jews' wish for Paul to be tried in Jerusalem, but he offers to preside at the trial. Paul's response indicates that he

suspects Festus is really intending to hand him over to the Jewish authorities.

25:10 Caesar's court Festus is acting as Caesar's representative when he makes judicial decisions. Paul is saying that, since he has discredited the Jewish accusations that he violated the Mosaic Law, a Roman court is the only place where he should be tried.

25:11 I appeal to Caesar As a Roman citizen (see

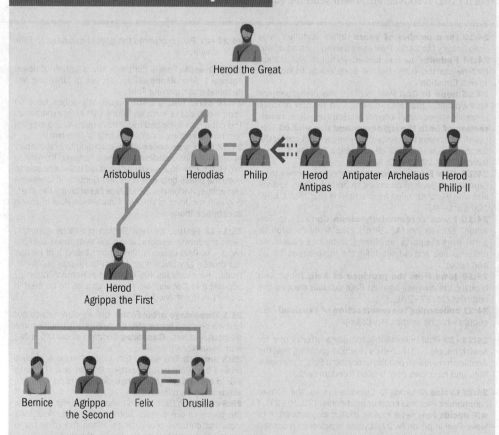

Herod the Great's Family Tree

Herod the Great

Aristobulus — Herodias = Philip ⟸ Herod Antipas — Antipater — Archelaus — Herod Philip II

Herod Agrippa the First

Bernice — Agrippa the Second — Felix = Drusilla

¹⁴Since they were spending many days there, Festus discussed Paul's case with the king. He said: "There is a man here whom Felix left as a prisoner. ¹⁵When I went to Jerusalem, the chief priests and the elders of the Jews brought charges against him and asked that he be condemned.

¹⁶"I told them that it is not the Roman custom to hand over anyone before they have faced their accusers and have had an opportunity to defend themselves against the charges. ¹⁷When they came here with me, I did not delay the case, but convened the court the next day and ordered the man to be brought in. ¹⁸When his accusers got up to speak, they did not charge him with any of the crimes I had expected. ¹⁹Instead, they had some points of dispute with him about their own religion and about a dead man named Jesus who Paul claimed was alive. ²⁰I was at a loss how to investigate such matters; so I asked if he would be willing to go to Jerusalem and stand trial there on these charges. ²¹But when Paul made his appeal to be held over for the Emperor's decision, I ordered him held until I could send him to Caesar."

²²Then Agrippa said to Festus, "I would like to hear this man myself."

He replied, "Tomorrow you will hear him."

Paul Before Agrippa

26:12-18pp — Ac 9:3-8; 22:6-11

²³The next day Agrippa and Bernice came with great pomp and entered the audience room with the high-ranking military officers and the prominent men of the city. At the command of Festus, Paul was brought in. ²⁴Festus said: "King Agrippa, and all who are present with us, you see this man! The whole Jewish community has petitioned me about him in Jerusalem and here in Caesarea, shouting that he ought not to live any longer. ²⁵I found he had done nothing deserving of death, but because he made his appeal to the Emperor I decided to send him to Rome. ²⁶But I have nothing definite to write to His Majesty about him. Therefore I have brought him before all of you, and especially before you, King Agrippa, so that as a result of this investigation I may have something to write. ²⁷For I think it is unreasonable to send a prisoner on to Rome without specifying the charges against him."

26 Then Agrippa said to Paul, "You have permission to speak for yourself."

So Paul motioned with his hand and began his defense: ²"King Agrippa, I consider myself fortunate to stand before you today as I make my defense against all the accusations of the Jews, ³and especially so because you are well acquainted with all the Jewish customs and controversies. Therefore, I beg you to listen to me patiently.

⁴"The Jewish people all know the way I have lived ever since I was a child, from the beginning of my life in my own country, and also in Jerusalem. ⁵They have known me for a long time and can testify, if they are willing, that I conformed to the strictest sect of our religion, living as a Pharisee. ⁶And now it is because of my hope in

---

22:25), Paul could appeal to Caesar for an official trial. The appeal to Caesar may have served to protect Roman citizens against corrupt or weak local rulers. The emperor at this time was Nero (AD 54–68). See the table "Political Leaders in the New Testament" on p. 1916.
25:12 council This group may be made up of both Roman and Jewish legal experts.

25:13–22 Festus will send Paul to Caesar but must state the precise charges against him. He uses a visit by King Agrippa as an opportunity to ask for advice about the situation since Agrippa would have been very familiar with matters pertaining to Judaism. Intrigued, Agrippa asks to see Paul for himself.

25:13 King Agrippa Agrippa II, the son of Herod Agrippa I whose death is recorded in 12:23. He initially ruled over the northern part of Israel, under the authority of Rome, but eventually received more territory in the northeast (ca. AD 56). **Bernice** Agrippa's sister. She was later a mistress to two Roman emperors, Vespasian and Titus.
25:14 Felix Festus blames Felix for creating the problem by leaving Paul in prison.
25:16 the Roman custom Festus appeals to the practice and procedure of Roman law as the basis for his denial of the Jews' request; this comment by Festus is not recorded in the earlier account of his interactions with the Jewish leaders (25:3–5).
25:19 religion Festus rightly concludes that the primary cause of contention over Paul's message is of a theological nature.

25:23 — 26:32 Paul is tried before King Agrippa so that Festus may determine what Paul should be charged with when he is sent to Rome, to be tried before Caesar (25:20–21).
25:24 whole Jewish community Festus presents Paul's case as a serious matter based on the amount of unrest he has caused.
25:26 definite Festus explains that although the Jews have reacted violently to Paul, he cannot communicate anything of certainty or substance to Caesar. He asks Agrippa to help determine why this matter is so serious and why it warrants Caesar's attention.

26:1–23 As he had previously done in 22:1–21 and 24:10–21, Paul now gives an account of himself and his beliefs in response to Agrippa's invitation. He describes himself as an exemplary Jew (26:4–5) and presents the gospel as a fulfillment of his Jewish hope (vv. 6–8). While he persecuted the church at first (vv. 9–11), through his miraculous conversion he was commissioned to become an apostle and missionary to both Jews and Gentiles (vv. 12–23). Compare 9:1–19; 22:1–21.

26:1 motioned with his hand Paul takes on the posture of an orator, which implies he had training in classical rhetoric and was well educated.
26:5 Pharisee See note on Jn 7:32.
26:6 my hope Paul is on trial for claiming that the hope of Israel is fulfilled in Jesus. Paul proclaims that the promises made to the Jewish people have now been

what God has promised our ancestors that I am on trial today. ⁷This is the promise our twelve tribes are hoping to see fulfilled as they earnestly serve God day and night. King Agrippa, it is because of this hope that these Jews are accusing me. ⁸Why should any of you consider it incredible that God raises the dead?

⁹"I too was convinced that I ought to do all that was possible to oppose the name of Jesus of Nazareth. ¹⁰And that is just what I did in Jerusalem. On the authority of the chief priests I put many of the Lord's people in prison, and when they were put to death, I cast my vote against them. ¹¹Many a time I went from one synagogue to another to have them punished, and I tried to force them to blaspheme. I was so obsessed with persecuting them that I even hunted them down in foreign cities.

¹²"On one of these journeys I was going to Damascus with the authority and commission of the chief priests. ¹³About noon, King Agrippa, as I was on the road, I saw a light from heaven, brighter than the sun, blazing around me and my companions. ¹⁴We all fell to the ground, and I heard a voice saying to me in Aramaic,ᵃ 'Saul, Saul, why do you persecute me? It is hard for you to kick against the goads.'

¹⁵"Then I asked, 'Who are you, Lord?'

"'I am Jesus, whom you are persecuting,' the Lord replied. ¹⁶'Now get up and stand on your feet. I have appeared to you to appoint you as a servant and as a witness of what you have seen and will see of me. ¹⁷I will rescue you from your own people and from the Gentiles. I am sending you to them ¹⁸to open their eyes and turn them

from darkness to light, and from the power of Satan to God, so that they may receive forgiveness of sins and a place among those who are sanctified by faith in me.'

¹⁹"So then, King Agrippa, I was not disobedient to the vision from heaven. ²⁰First to those in Damascus, then to those in Jerusalem and in all Judea, and then to the Gentiles, I preached that they should repent and turn to God and demonstrate their repentance by their deeds. ²¹That is why some Jews seized me in the temple courts and tried to kill me. ²²But God has helped me to this very day; so I stand here and testify to small and great alike. I am saying nothing beyond what the prophets and Moses said would happen — ²³that the Messiah would suffer and, as the first to rise from the dead, would bring the message of light to his own people and to the Gentiles."

²⁴At this point Festus interrupted Paul's defense. "You are out of your mind, Paul!" he shouted. "Your great learning is driving you insane."

²⁵"I am not insane, most excellent Festus," Paul replied. "What I am saying is true and reasonable. ²⁶The king is familiar with these things, and I can speak freely to him. I am convinced that none of this has escaped his notice, because it was not done in a corner. ²⁷King Agrippa, do you believe the prophets? I know you do."

²⁸Then Agrippa said to Paul, "Do you think that in such a short time you can persuade me to be a Christian?"

²⁹Paul replied, "Short time or long — I pray to God that not only you but all who are listening

ᵃ 14 Or Hebrew

---

fulfilled. Paul is also referencing his belief in the resurrection of the dead, which he has mentioned during his previous trials (Ac 23:6; see note on 24:15; compare 26:8 and note).

26:7 our twelve tribes Paul claims that his hope is shared by every Jew, including himself as a Jew.

26:8 God raises the dead The source of controversy is Jesus' death and resurrection (see v. 23). Paul understands it as the fulfillment of what Jews hoped for (see Da 12:1–4; Eze 37; Isa 53:10 and note).

26:10 cast my vote This reference to vote-casting may be literal, perhaps indicating that Paul was a member of the Sanhedrin, or it may simply be a way of saying that he endorsed the execution of Christians. See Ac 7:58–59.

26:14 kick against the goads Like a stubborn animal attempting to fight the sticks used as prods, Paul cannot succeed in fighting against God.

26:16–18 Paul records what Jesus said to him on the road to Damascus, elaborating both on the earlier account in Acts and what he has previously articulated during his former trials (compare 9:1–19; 22:1–21).

26:16 witness Compare 1:8.

26:18 from the power of Satan to God Articulates the idea that those who do not belong to Christ are in many ways influenced by evil and as such opposed to God's purposes (compare note on 2Co 6:15). **sanctified by faith in me** See note on Ac 20:32.

26:21 That is why Paul is being persecuted for following Jesus' command to spread the gospel. This ministry, particularly to the Gentiles (non-Jewish people), has caused many of his fellow Jews to oppose him. Paul proclaims that both Gentiles and Jews receive forgiveness of sins and can be part of the people of God.

26:22 the prophets and Moses Throughout Acts, the good news about Jesus is presented as the fulfillment of promises made by God in the OT Scriptures (e.g., 2:24–36; 3:22–26; 13:32–39; compare Lk 24:25–27). See the table "Jesus' Fulfillment of OT Prophecy" on p. 1573.

26:23 Messiah would suffer Paul could be referencing a variety of OT passages (e.g., Isa 52:13—53:12; Ps 22). Paul has explained this message in his earlier speeches in Acts and used a variety of passages to do so (see Ac 13:26–41). **as the first to rise** Jesus was not raised from the dead temporarily, as other people were (e.g., Mk 5:42; Lk 7:11–17; Jn 11:43–44). He was the first who absolutely conquered death and was the guarantee that others would as well (Ac 2:24; 1Co 15:20; Col 1:18; Rev 1:5).

26:24 out of your mind To Festus, Paul's reasoning seemed foolish (compare 1Co 1:23).

26:27 I know you do Paul makes it personal: He knew that Agrippa knew the OT Scriptures, so he should believe the fulfillment of OT promises.

26:28 Christian See note on Ac 11:26.

to me today may become what I am, except for these chains."

³⁰The king rose, and with him the governor and Bernice and those sitting with them. ³¹After they left the room, they began saying to one another, "This man is not doing anything that deserves death or imprisonment."

³²Agrippa said to Festus, "This man could have been set free if he had not appealed to Caesar."

Paul Sails for Rome

27 When it was decided that we would sail for Italy, Paul and some other prisoners were handed over to a centurion named Julius, who belonged to the Imperial Regiment. ²We boarded a ship from Adramyttium about to sail for ports along the coast of the province of Asia, and we put out to sea. Aristarchus, a Macedonian from Thessalonica, was with us.

³The next day we landed at Sidon; and Julius, in kindness to Paul, allowed him to go to his friends so they might provide for his needs. ⁴From there we put out to sea again and passed to the lee of Cyprus because the winds were against us. ⁵When we had sailed across the open sea off the coast of Cilicia and Pamphylia, we landed at Myra in Lycia. ⁶There the centurion found an Alexandrian ship sailing for Italy and put us on board. ⁷We made slow headway for many days and had difficulty arriving off Cnidus. When the wind did not allow us to hold our course, we sailed to the lee of Crete, opposite Salmone. ⁸We moved along the coast with difficulty and came to a place called Fair Havens, near the town of Lasea.

⁹Much time had been lost, and sailing had already become dangerous because by now it was after the Day of Atonement.ᵃ So Paul warned them, ¹⁰"Men, I can see that our voyage is going to be disastrous and bring great loss to ship and cargo, and to our own lives also." ¹¹But the centurion, instead of listening to what Paul said, followed the advice of the pilot and of the owner of the ship. ¹²Since the harbor was unsuitable to winter in, the majority decided that we should sail on, hoping to reach Phoenix and winter there. This was a harbor in Crete, facing both southwest and northwest.

The Storm

¹³When a gentle south wind began to blow, they saw their opportunity; so they weighed anchor and sailed along the shore of Crete. ¹⁴Before very long, a wind of hurricane force, called the Northeaster, swept down from the island. ¹⁵The ship was caught by the storm and could not head into the wind; so we gave way to it and were driven along. ¹⁶As we passed to the lee of a small island called Cauda, we were hardly able to make the lifeboat secure, ¹⁷so the men hoisted it aboard. Then they passed ropes under the ship itself to hold it together. Because they were afraid they would run aground on the sandbars of Syrtis, they lowered the sea anchorᵇ and let the ship be driven along. ¹⁸We took such a violent battering from the storm that the next day they began to throw the cargo overboard. ¹⁹On the third day, they threw the ship's tackle overboard with their own hands. ²⁰When neither sun nor stars appeared for many

---

ᵃ 9 That is, Yom Kippur   ᵇ 17 Or the sails

26:32 if he had not appealed Roman citizens had the right to appeal to Caesar for judgment. Apparently this appeal could not be overturned or ignored by local governors, likely so that citizens could be tried in official courts for their own protection. Compare 25:11 and note.

27:1–44 This section contains a detailed account of Paul's sea voyage to Rome. By narrating the successful navigation of the perils along the way, Luke stresses to his readers that God is providing secure transportation so Paul can preach the gospel in Rome, as the Lord has proclaimed he will do (23:11).

27:1 we Luke (the narrator) includes himself in this portion of the story, as he has also done earlier (see note on 16:10). **to the Imperial Regiment** Probably refers to the Cohors Augusta I, which is known from various ancient inscriptions to have been stationed in Syria during the first century.

27:2 Aristarchus One of Paul's friends (19:29; 20:4; Col 4:10; Phm 24) travels with him for support. **from Thessalonica** Although some Jews in Thessalonica opposed Paul's work (Ac 17:5–8), Aristarchus' presence here shows the support Paul received from the church he founded there.

27:3 Sidon About 70 miles north of Caesarea. Jesus had visited this area during his ministry (Mt 15:21–28).

27:6 Alexandrian ship Alexandria, an important Egyptian city, exported grain and other goods to Rome.

27:8 Fair Havens The typical route would have taken the ship north of Crete. They were diverted from the original itinerary because of the unfavorable winds.

27:9 the Day of Atonement The Greek text here refers to a fast that would have occurred on the Day of Atonement (Lev 16:29), which falls in September or October. This would be near the end of the usual shipping season, when travel on the Mediterranean became too hazardous to attempt.

27:12 Phoenix The location of this harbor is unknown, but is possibly the modern Phineka Bay.

27:13–38 The ship continues its voyage against Paul's advice, and he is soon proven correct. The ship's crew gives up hope, but Paul receives a vision that nobody will die. God has ordained that Paul will testify in Rome and shows favor to all aboard the ship because of Paul.

27:14 Northeaster The Greek word used here, *eurakylōn*, refers to a cold Mediterranean wind from the northeast, known today as the *gregale*.

27:16 Cauda An island 23 miles south of Crete, known today as Gozzo.

27:17 Syrtis An area of sandbars off the North African coast where a ship could be stranded.

27:19 ship's tackle While throwing the cargo overboard

days and the storm continued raging, we finally gave up all hope of being saved.

21 After they had gone a long time without food, Paul stood up before them and said: "Men, you should have taken my advice not to sail from Crete; then you would have spared yourselves this damage and loss. 22 But now I urge you to keep up your courage, because not one of you will be lost; only the ship will be destroyed. 23 Last night an angel of the God to whom I belong and whom I serve stood beside me 24 and said, 'Do not be afraid, Paul. You must stand trial before Caesar; and God has graciously given you the lives of all who sail with you.' 25 So keep up your courage, men, for I have faith in God that it will happen just as he told me. 26 Nevertheless, we must run aground on some island."

The Shipwreck

27 On the fourteenth night we were still being driven across the Adriatic[a] Sea, when about midnight the sailors sensed they were approaching land. 28 They took soundings and found that the water was a hundred and twenty feet[b] deep. A short time later they took soundings again and found it was ninety feet[c] deep. 29 Fearing that we would be dashed against the rocks, they dropped four anchors from the stern and prayed for daylight. 30 In an attempt to escape from the ship, the sailors let the lifeboat down into the sea, pretending they were going to lower some anchors from the bow. 31 Then Paul said to the centurion and the soldiers, "Unless these men stay with the ship, you cannot be saved." 32 So the soldiers cut the ropes that held the lifeboat and let it drift away.

33 Just before dawn Paul urged them all to eat. "For the last fourteen days," he said, "you have been in constant suspense and have gone without food—you haven't eaten anything. 34 Now I urge you to take some food. You need it to survive. Not one of you will lose a single hair from his head." 35 After he said this, he took some bread and gave thanks to God in front of them all. Then he broke it and began to eat. 36 They were all encouraged and ate some food themselves. 37 Altogether there were 276 of us on board. 38 When they had eaten as much as they wanted, they lightened the ship by throwing the grain into the sea.

39 When daylight came, they did not recognize the land, but they saw a bay with a sandy beach, where they decided to run the ship aground if they could. 40 Cutting loose the anchors, they left them in the sea and at the same time untied the ropes that held the rudders. Then they hoisted the foresail to the wind and made for the beach. 41 But the ship struck a sandbar and ran aground. The bow stuck fast and would not move, and the stern was broken to pieces by the pounding of the surf.

42 The soldiers planned to kill the prisoners to prevent any of them from swimming away and escaping. 43 But the centurion wanted to spare Paul's life and kept them from carrying out their plan. He ordered those who could swim to jump overboard first and get to land. 44 The rest were to get there on planks or on other pieces of the ship. In this way everyone reached land safely.

Paul Ashore on Malta

28 Once safely on shore, we found out that the island was called Malta. 2 The islanders showed us unusual kindness. They built a fire and welcomed us all because it was raining and cold. 3 Paul gathered a pile of brushwood

---

a 27 In ancient times the name referred to an area extending well south of Italy.   b 28 Or about 37 meters   c 28 Or about 27 meters

---

would eliminate immediate profits, throwing this gear overboard would eliminate the longevity of the ship's business. This shows the desperation those onboard are feeling.

27:22 not one of you will be lost Paul had said the conditions could result in the loss of life (Ac 27:10), but God has now revealed to him that no one will die.

27:28 it was ninety feet deep The drop in depth shows that they were quickly approaching land and the ship would soon run aground.

27:32 the soldiers While the soldiers did not listen to Paul before (v. 11), now they follow his advice.

27:35 took some bread Paul sets an example by thanking God for providing both food and safety. Giving thanks before breaking bread was a common practice among Jews and early Christians (e.g., Mt 14:19; Lk 24:30; Ac 2:42,46). It is unlikely that the Lord's Supper is intended here, especially since there is no mention of the cup and nonbelievers are present.

27:38 they lightened Lightening the ship allowed it to float higher. It would run aground in shallower waters, closer to dry land.

27:39–44 The ship runs aground and everyone makes it safely to shore, as Paul had earlier proclaimed would happen. The centurion also ensures that the prisoners are not executed—confirming Paul's prediction that nobody would die.

27:42 kill The soldiers wanted to kill the prisoners to prevent them from escaping, likely because they would be executed themselves if they let the prisoners get away (compare 12:19).

27:43 to spare Paul's life The centurion who originally disbelieved Paul now saves his life (v. 11).

28:1–10 Now shipwrecked on Malta, Paul is unharmed when bitten by a venomous snake (vv. 1–6) and heals the sick on the island (vv. 7–10). Luke makes it clear that, even though he is a prisoner, Paul continues to display God's powerful work.

28:1 Malta Located 58 miles south of modern Sicily.

28:2 islanders The Greek word used here, barbaros, implies the local inhabitants were considered foreign by

and, as he put it on the fire, a viper, driven out by the heat, fastened itself on his hand. ⁴When the islanders saw the snake hanging from his hand, they said to each other, "This man must be a murderer; for though he escaped from the sea, the goddess Justice has not allowed him to live." ⁵But Paul shook the snake off into the fire and suffered no ill effects. ⁶The people expected him to swell up or suddenly fall dead; but after waiting a long time and seeing nothing unusual happen to him, they changed their minds and said he was a god.

⁷There was an estate nearby that belonged to Publius, the chief official of the island. He welcomed us to his home and showed us generous hospitality for three days. ⁸His father was sick in bed, suffering from fever and dysentery. Paul went in to see him and, after prayer, placed his hands on him and healed him. ⁹When this had happened, the rest of the sick on the island came and were cured. ¹⁰They honored us in many ways; and when we were ready to sail, they furnished us with the supplies we needed.

Paul's Arrival at Rome

¹¹After three months we put out to sea in a ship that had wintered in the island — it was an Alexandrian ship with the figurehead of the twin gods Castor and Pollux. ¹²We put in at Syracuse and stayed there three days. ¹³From there we set sail and arrived at Rhegium. The next day the south wind came up, and on the following day we reached Puteoli. ¹⁴There we found some brothers and sisters who invited us to spend a week with them. And so we came to Rome. ¹⁵The brothers and sisters there had heard that we were coming, and they traveled as far as the Forum of Appius and the Three Taverns to meet us. At the sight of these people Paul thanked God and was encouraged. ¹⁶When we got to Rome, Paul was allowed to live by himself, with a soldier to guard him.

Paul Preaches at Rome Under Guard

¹⁷Three days later he called together the local Jewish leaders. When they had assembled, Paul said to them: "My brothers, although I have done nothing against our people or against the customs of our ancestors, I was arrested in Jerusalem and handed over to the Romans. ¹⁸They examined me and wanted to release me, because I was not guilty of any crime deserving death. ¹⁹The Jews objected, so I was compelled to make an appeal to Caesar. I certainly did not intend to bring any charge against my own people. ²⁰For this reason I have asked to see you and talk with you. It is because of the hope of Israel that I am bound with this chain."

²¹They replied, "We have not received any letters from Judea concerning you, and none of our people who have come from there has reported or said anything bad about you. ²²But we want to hear what your views are, for we know that people everywhere are talking against this sect."

²³They arranged to meet Paul on a certain day, and came in even larger numbers to the place where he was staying. He witnessed to them from morning till evening, explaining about the kingdom of God, and from the Law of Moses and from the Prophets he tried to persuade them about Jesus. ²⁴Some were convinced by what he said,

---

the Roman Empire and did not speak the languages or share the customs of either Greeks or Romans.

28:4 This man must be a murderer This comment is based on the belief prevalent in Greek mythology that the fates align against people who commit evil. **Justice** In Greek mythology, Justice was a goddess. The daughter of Zeus and Themis, she was believed to work circumstantially in establishing people's fate.

28:6 said he was a god The circumstances were obviously miraculous, leading the people to believe that if such a miraculous event could occur that Paul must be a deity of some sort.

28:7 chief official Evidence of the use of this title has been confirmed by inscriptions found on Malta.

28:11–16 This section narrates the final leg of Paul's journey to Rome and his initial reception there.

28:12 Syracuse The capital of Sicily, on the southeast coast of the island.

28:13 Rhegium A city at the southern tip of Italy, about 75 miles from Syracuse. **Puteoli** This city (modern Pozzuoli), about 130 miles south of the capital, was Rome's major port at the time.

28:15 The brothers and sisters While this is his first visit to Rome, Paul had connections there. He greets many of the Roman believers by name in his letter to the Roman church, which was written before this visit (Ro 16:3–15). This shows that despite Paul traveling for his trial under arrest that he had quite a bit of freedom at this point.

28:17–31 Luke concludes his narrative with Paul arriving in Rome and preaching the gospel there. Paul reaching Rome with the gospel shows that the church is fulfilling its commission by Jesus (Ac 1:8). Rome is both on the western side of the Roman Empire from Jerusalem, where the work of the church began, and is the political and economic center of the Roman Empire. Although the gospel itself has already reached Rome prior to this point (as Paul's letter to the Romans attests), it is fitting for the narrative itself to end with the church's most prominent missionary reaching Rome.

28:17 the local Jewish leaders Paul goes to the Jews first upon his arrival, as he usually does in Acts (e.g., 13:14; 14:1; 17:10; 19:8).

28:23 the kingdom of God At the beginning of Acts, Jesus describes the values of his kingdom (1:3–8). Luke (the narrator) concludes the book similarly to how it began (compare Lk 1:33; 4:43). See note on Ac 1:3; Mk 1:15.

28:24 would not believe This divided response is typical of many groups of Jews to whom Paul has preached (e.g., Ac 13:42–45; 14:1–2; 17:4–5).

but others would not believe. [25]They disagreed among themselves and began to leave after Paul had made this final statement: "The Holy Spirit spoke the truth to your ancestors when he said through Isaiah the prophet:

[26] "'Go to this people and say,
    "You will be ever hearing but never
        understanding;
    you will be ever seeing but never
        perceiving."
[27] For this people's heart has become
        calloused;
    they hardly hear with their ears,
    and they have closed their eyes.

Otherwise they might see with their eyes,
    hear with their ears,
    understand with their hearts
and turn, and I would heal them.'[a]

[28] "Therefore I want you to know that God's salvation has been sent to the Gentiles, and they will listen!" [29][b]

[30] For two whole years Paul stayed there in his own rented house and welcomed all who came to see him. [31] He proclaimed the kingdom of God and taught about the Lord Jesus Christ — with all boldness and without hindrance!

---

[a] 27 Isaiah 6:9,10 (see Septuagint)   [b] 29 Some manuscripts include here *After he said this, the Jews left, arguing vigorously among themselves.*

28:26–27 Paul quotes Isa 6:9–10. Jesus quotes this passage when noting the unbelief of many of his fellow Jews (Mt 13:14–15; Mk 4:12; Lk 8:10). Paul expounds on the same theme in Ro 11:8–10. In parallel, in Luke's Gospel Jesus' ministry is often framed in terms of what the book of Isaiah proclaimed about him (e.g., Lk 4:17–21).

28:28 sent to the Gentiles Paul's statement here reflects Jesus' words at the beginning of Acts: The gospel must go from Jerusalem outward to the ends of the earth. This is a prominent OT theme as well (e.g., Isa 49:6; 66:18; Zec 2:11). Luke's Gospel also anticipates this (see note on Ac 10:1–8).

28:30 two whole years About AD 60–62. According to the early church fathers, Paul was released from his Roman imprisonment, continued to travel for a few more years — during which he would have written the Pastoral Letters (1 Timothy, 2 Timothy and Titus) — and was eventually martyred in Rome under Nero (ca. AD 66). Compare note on Ac 1:1–5.

28:31 without hindrance No one stopped Paul's ministry, and even though he was essentially under house arrest he continued his ministry with complete freedom. Luke (the narrator) concludes by reasserting a major theme of Acts: The progress of the gospel cannot be stopped.

SPREADING THE GOOD NEWS OF JESUS

SPREADING THE GOOD NEWS OF JESUS
by Ed Stetzer

Mission is the reason the church exists and the church joins Jesus on his mission. And, this mission is from everywhere to everywhere.

Christians are to be both engaged in missions—the international pursuit to preach the gospel to all corners of the earth—and be missional each and every day. Being missional conveys the idea of living on a purposeful, Biblical mission.

THE GREAT COMMISSION POINTS US TO MISSIONS IN THE NATIONS

Many Christians embrace one particular commission of Jesus without considering the context of Jesus' original audience or his other commissions. It's helpful to understand the Great Commission (Mt 28:16–20) in light of the context in which the commission was given.

For example, many of us are familiar with what has traditionally been termed the Pauline approach to missions: go out and plant churches. It's derived from the life of Paul, building upon Jesus' command to be witnesses in "Jerusalem, and in all Judea and Samaria, and to the ends of the earth" (Ac 1:8). But it is also closely related to Matthew 28 and Jesus' command to "Go and make disciples of all nations." In a sense, Paul personified the Great Commission in his ministry. Jesus' original hearers understood that, in giving the Great Commission, Jesus was making a paradigm shift in regard to missions.

The Old Testament depicts a clear God-given vision—that the nations would come to Jerusalem to worship with the one, true God. It was a very centripetal mission—from the edges (the nations) to the center (the temple in Jerusalem; e.g., Isa 2:1–5). Jesus is explaining that now his people need to go out and that he will go with them (compare Jn 14:15–31).

Jesus' earliest followers understood that the Great Commission meant more than simply telling their neighbor about Christ because they went far beyond next door. The Great Commission includes your neighbor, but the context was much more than your neighbor.

Acts 1:8 is literally lived out in the book of Acts. It points out that something has changed—the mission is no longer centripetal but centrifugal. So, rather than bringing the nations up to Jerusalem, the people went out from Jerusalem. They went out from Jerusalem to Judaea, Samaria and the ends of their earth.

The Great Commission is the backbone of the missions movement and expresses God's expressed desire to be praised by everyone, all over the world. But God still desires us to reach our neighbor.

THE JOHANNINE COMMISSION POINTS US TO MISSION TO OUR NEIGHBOR

When the church's focus is solely on international missions, it becomes easy to think of ways to reach remote areas of the world but not engage our own neighborhood. This is where Jesus' commission in John 20:21 comes into play and a subsequent Johannine approach to mission:

It points to living in a missional way wherever you are. Jesus speaks to his disciples, explaining that he is sending them as his Father has sent him. Thus, the Bible teaches everyone is sent to continue Jesus' mission (Jn 20:21) and that everyone is called to the ministry (1Pe 4:10). The only questions are to where, among whom and doing what.

Embracing the John 20:21 commission has ignited a revival for churches to embrace mission locally. For example, many American churches are now able to see North America as a mission field, which it is.

MISSION AND MISSIONS

Mission and being missional need to be integrated into our lives. Missional churches—those focused on living in a missional way wherever we are—must remember that Jesus called us to reach people where the gospel is not. We need to be missional, living as agents of God's mission in context, but we can't take John 20:21 in isolation without also remembering Matthew 28:18–20 and Acts 1:8. Likewise, churches focused on international missions must also remember their mission to their neighborhood and own country. We need missional churches and to be engaged in global missions because both are clearly articulated in the teachings of Jesus and the actions of the disciples.

(This article is adapted in part from Ed Stetzer's "Missions vs. Missional," originally published on his blog, The Exchange.)

PAUL'S LETTERS

The collection of Paul's letters is the literal center of the New Testament, bracketed by the Gospels and Acts on one side and the General Letters and Revelation on the other. The Pauline letters make up roughly 24 percent of the New Testament and historically have constituted the main source for Christian theological instruction and exhortation to discipleship. All Christian theology, preaching and practice must engage deeply with Paul's letters.

These documents are not treatises or sermons; they are letters, and they represent pastoral correspondence between the apostle and several young churches in the eastern Mediterranean. They are rooted in the local situation of the churches they address and in the particular context of Paul's mission to the Gentiles. Reading these letters is a bit like listening to one side of a conversation or like reading someone else's mail.

AUTHORSHIP

Authorship of some of the 13 letters attributed to Paul is debated among modern scholars. Today, the letters usually are categorized as the undisputed letters (Romans, 1–2 Corinthians, Galatians, 1 Thessalonians, Philippians, Philemon), disputed letters (2 Thessalonians, Colossians, Ephesians), and pseudonymous letters (1–2 Timothy, Titus). Doubts about Pauline authorship of some of these letters are based on differences in vocabulary, theological themes and alleged post-Pauline settings for the letters. Yet these arguments are not decisive, especially if Paul used co-authors or secretaries in many of his letters, and if he was broader in his literary and theological repertoire than ordinarily recognized. Although there is current debate, the early church received all 13 letters as authentically Pauline and circulated them as such; some in the early church also attributed Hebrews to Paul, but this is improbable.

CONTEXT AND BACKGROUND

Paul's ministry takes place within the three-decade span between his conversion around AD 33 and his execution in Rome around AD 64. During this time, Paul engaged in three distinct missionary journeys to Asia Minor and Greece. He contended with opposition from local Jewish groups and civic officials, as well as from a faction of Jewish Christian proselytizers who wanted to bring his Gentile converts in line with Judaism by forcing them to be circumcised. Key events that occurred during Paul's time and shaped his ministry include the reigns of Claudius, Caligula and Nero as Roman Emperors; the rise of anti-Roman zealotry in Judaea (AD 40s–50s); the beginning of the Christian mission to non-Jews launched from Antioch (late AD 40s); the Jerusalem council (AD 50); missionary journeys across the Aegean Sea (AD 50–57); his return to Jerusalem with a collection of funds for famine relief, along with his subsequent arrest (AD 58); his journey to Rome (AD 59–60); and his imprisonment, release, second imprisonment and execution in Rome (AD 60–64).

It is also significant for understanding Paul and his letters that he lived in three cultural worlds. He was a native Jew—a Pharisee by training—and thus enmeshed in the Jewish way of life. Yet Paul grew up in Tarsus, a Greek-speaking university town, and was well acquainted with Greek language and culture. Finally, as a Roman citizen, Paul was familiar with the politics and power of the

Roman Empire. In many ways, Paul was the ideal figure to take the message of the Jewish Messiah to Greeks and Romans in the eastern Mediterranean, preaching and teaching in language, terms and images they understood.

BASIC THEOLOGICAL THEMES

Romans
Romans is the great letter about the "righteousness of God," the saving and transforming power of God revealed in the gospel. What is more, in Romans, Paul declares that his goal is to bring the Gentiles to the obedience of faith, as faithful followers of Jesus the Messiah and Lord.

1–2 Corinthians
Corinth was Paul's problem church, racked by divisions, immorality and even hostility toward him. In the Corinthian letters, Paul urges the believers to lead faithful lives in a pagan world, and he holds up Christ's sacrifice on the cross as the example and authenticator of genuine Christian service.

Galatians
Paul defends the gospel against Jewish Christian intruders in Galatia who asserted that the Galatians must first become Jews in order to become Christians. Paul in turn responds by defending justification by faith and life in the Spirit, proving that God accepts Gentiles on the basis of faith in the Messiah.

Ephesians
This letter is likely a circular letter meant to be shared among the churches in Asia Minor (modern-day Turkey), Ephesus chief among them. Paul provides an extended meditation on God's glory to enrich believers in their knowledge of God's grace. The lavish grace that believers have received should propel them to live in obedience to the one who called them.

Philippians
This letter of friendship reinforces the bonds of fellowship between Paul and the Philippians. Here Paul commends the virtues of faithfulness, generosity and humility, especially in the majestic Christ-hymn (Php 2:6–11), which shows that Christ is the paragon of self-giving love.

Colossians
Written to a church Paul did not plant, Colossians reminds the church of the sufficiency and supremacy of Jesus Christ and urges them on in faithfulness to him.

1–2 Thessalonians
In these letters, Paul writes to the Thessalonians to encourage them in the face of hardship, to encourage them to be enthusiastic about the Lord's return (1 Thessalonians), and to clarify any misunderstandings or misrepresentations about the Lord's return (2 Thessalonians).

1–2 Timothy and Titus
Commonly known as the Pastoral Letters, these three letters encourage Paul's co-workers Timothy and Titus in their respective ministries in Ephesus and Crete. They were written at the end of Paul's life during a Roman imprisonment. These letters are perhaps best described as faithful sayings for faithful friends, and they set out key Christian doctrines to be defended and describe the main qualifications for those in Christian leadership.

Philemon

This letter was written to a slave owner named Philemon, who was part of the church in Colossae. Philemon was converted under Paul's ministry, and Philemon's slave, Onesimus, either ran away or absconded to Paul, and was converted also. Paul writes to Philemon to receive Onesimus back as a brother in the Lord and tacitly asks Philemon to release Onesimus to Paul's care. The letter provides wonderful remarks on fellowship, love and brotherhood.

RELATIONSHIP TO THE LARGER BIBLICAL NARRATIVE AND THEMES

Paul's letters emphasize many major Biblical-theological themes; some of the most important are Adam and Christ, Abraham and Covenant, Israel and Law, Jesus the Messiah, and church and Mission.

Adam and Christ

The story of Adam's creation and fall lurks behind the scenes (or comes into the spotlight) in several of Paul's letters, especially in Romans 5:12–21; 7:6–25; 1 Corinthians 15:22,45; Philippians 2:5–11. Paul tells of a world gone wrong in Adam and put right in Jesus. The coming of Jesus, the New Adam, undoes the condemnation, corruption and death of the first Adam by bringing righteousness, renewal and life to believers.

Abraham and Covenant

Paul belabors the point—especially in Galatians and Romans—that the promises made to Abraham were not short circuited by the introduction of the covenant at Sinai, the Law of Moses, and Israel's subsequent rebellion and exile. No, God still has one plan to bring the nations into the family of Abraham through his offspring, Jesus the Messiah. Abraham is not the exemplary proselyte who is circumcised and saved; rather, he is the model Christian who believes in the life-giving power of God, and he is made right by faith alone, not by works of the law.

Israel and the Law

If salvation is by faith and not by observing the Law, if salvation is for all nations and not just for Israel, then many of Paul's hearers had some big questions. What was the point of the Law? How do you stop pagans from immoral idol-worship? Has God washed his hands of Israel? Paul's answer to these questions, worked out across his letters, is that the Law was a temporary marker pointing to the salvation to come, not the terminal expression of that salvation. The Law remains good and holy, but it is no longer the constitution or primary charter for God's people; these things have been replaced by the life and teaching of Jesus and new life in the Spirit. Ethnic Israel is not written off; God's election of the nation is irrevocable, but "Israel" is a calling—a vocation inherited by all those who belong to Christ. Christ became a servant to Israel so that the promises made to the patriarchs, and ultimately all the nations, would become a reality.

Jesus the Messiah

Paul the Pharisee believed Jesus was a Messianic pretender and a false prophet. But after his Damascus road experience, Paul came to believe that Jesus is the Messiah and Lord, who died and rose, and that he had been given a commission to proclaim this Jesus to the nations. For Paul, Jesus is the risen and exalted Son of God—an integral part of the very identity of the God of Israel. Paul knew that those crucified were, as Deuteronomy says, cursed (Dt 21:22–23). But if Christ was cursed, then God must have cursed him to take the curse of our disobedience upon himself. Jesus' death is his atonement for sin.

Church and Mission

For Paul, the churches of Jesus Christ are linked by sharing one Lord, one gospel, one baptism, one faith, and fellowship in one mission. The church in essence is just what Israel was always meant to become: the worshiping and Spirit-led community of the new covenant and the foretaste of the new creation. The church is to be empowered by the Spirit; made up of people from all ethnicities; focused on Jesus' death and resurrection; devoted to remembering Jesus' teachings and imitating his life; united around baptism and the Lord's Supper; and committed to God's mission by witnessing to—and being invested in—the world, without being a reflection of the world.

Michael F. Bird

ROMANS

INTRODUCTION TO ROMANS

In his letter to the Roman church, Paul lays out his argument for unifying Jews and non-Jews in Christ—and in the process, instructs his readers on how to restore their relationship with God. As Paul explains, we only find unity with God and with one another through God's Son, Jesus. Christ represents the fulfillment of God's covenant promises, going all the way back to Abraham. Paul proclaims that Christ is the very righteousness of God and the means for us sinners to become righteous—to be saved.

BACKGROUND

The book of Romans dates to the end of Paul's third missionary journey; he most likely wrote this letter from the Greek city of Corinth in the mid–50s AD (Ac 19:21; 20:3). Gaius, whom Paul mentions is his host (Ro 16:23), is likely the same Gaius mentioned as a resident of Corinth in another of Paul's letters (1Co 1:14).

Paul had not met the Christians at Rome (Ro 1:13), but the circumstances he mentions in the letter provide clues about his reasons for writing. Paul wanted to take the gospel to Spain, and he thought that Rome might make a good launching point for a westward mission (15:22–24)—

This map depicts the location of Rome in relation to some of the other places that Paul traveled to during his missionary journeys.

much like Antioch had been his home base in the east. In addition, Paul deeply desired to promote unity between believers in Jesus who were Jewish and those who were not Jewish (called "Gentiles" or "Greeks"; see, for example, 1:16). The Roman church probably was a mix of Jews and Gentiles. Paul wanted to communicate to these Christians that the gospel includes everyone.

STRUCTURE

Romans is structured as an ancient letter, with an opening (1:1–17), a body (1:18—15:13) and a closing (15:14—16:27). The two main parts of the letter's body include a section focusing on what God has done in Christ (1:18—11:36) and a section instructing Christians how to live the truths set forth in the first part (12:1—15:13).

In the first section, Paul's discussion focuses on four major points. First, everyone—including Jews *and* Gentiles—is under God's judgment (1:18—3:20). Second, Christ has become the living revelation of God's righteousness, so that everyone who believes—both Jews and Gentiles—can be made right and brought into God's family (3:21—5:21). Third, God's righteousness gives us hope in our battle against sin (6:1—8:39). Finally, despite many Jews' rejection of Christ, the people of Israel nevertheless have a role to play in God's redemption of the world (9:1—11:36).

In the section on Christian ethics, Paul aims to help the Roman believers put their faith into practice, particularly when it comes to living together as the diverse yet unified church (12:1—15:13).

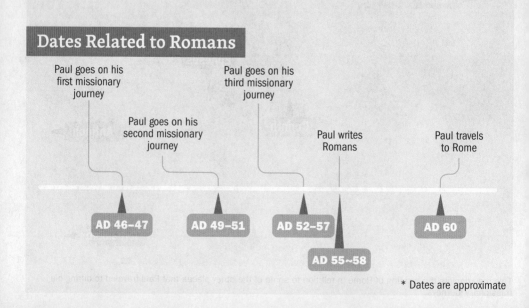

Dates Related to Romans

Paul goes on his first missionary journey

Paul goes on his second missionary journey

Paul goes on his third missionary journey

Paul writes Romans

Paul travels to Rome

AD 46–47

AD 49–51

AD 52–57

AD 55~58

AD 60

* Dates are approximate

For Paul, Christians ought to have their entire lives—in terms of both belief and action—centered first and foremost on Christ. The Good News of Jesus' saving act is meant to be transformative, and this Good News should be unapologetically proclaimed.

OUTLINE

- The gospel and God's righteous judgment (1:1—3:20)
- The gift of God's righteousness (3:21—5:21)
- The power of God's righteousness (6:1—8:39)
- God's righteousness toward Israel (9:1—11:36)
- Righteousness in relationships (12:1—15:13)
- Paul's ministry and personal greetings (15:14—16:27)

THEMES

Romans' major themes—righteousness and salvation—ring forth most clearly in Romans 1:16–17, Paul's declaration of the power of the gospel. Here, Paul proclaims that the Good News of Jesus opens God's salvation to Jews and Gentiles alike. Further, this salvation fulfills the Old Testament promises God made to the people of Israel—showing God's faithfulness to his covenant. Paul shows us that in Jesus we clearly see God's power to save all who believe. In Christ, our righteous God unites Jews and Gentiles alike into one people of God. All cultures, races and people can come to God for salvation. Christ's righteousness is enough for any and all of us to be saved.

Paul explains that all have all sinned and face the consequence of death (3:23; 5:12; 6:23). But God has provided the salvation we need through the death and resurrection of his Son (6:5–11; 8:1–4), and nothing can separate us from his love (8:38–39). Despite our wrongdoings against God and other people, Jesus saves each of us who believe. While our sin previously stood in the way, Jesus makes a way for us to have a relationship with God again. Jesus makes a way for us to be unified in his name. We are empowered to collectively and boldly proclaim—and live—the Good News of Jesus.

1 Paul, a servant of Christ Jesus, called to be an apostle and set apart for the gospel of God— ²the gospel he promised beforehand through his prophets in the Holy Scriptures ³regarding his Son, who as to his earthly life*ª* was a descendant of David, ⁴and who through the Spirit of holiness was appointed the Son of God in power*ᵇ* by his resurrection from the dead: Jesus Christ our Lord. ⁵Through him we received grace and apostleship to call all the Gentiles to the obedience that comes from*ᶜ* faith for his name's sake. ⁶And you also are among those Gentiles who are called to belong to Jesus Christ.

⁷To all in Rome who are loved by God and called to be his holy people:

Grace and peace to you from God our Father and from the Lord Jesus Christ.

Paul's Longing to Visit Rome

⁸First, I thank my God through Jesus Christ for all of you, because your faith is being reported all over the world. ⁹God, whom I serve in my spirit in preaching the gospel of his Son, is my witness how constantly I remember you ¹⁰in my prayers at all times; and I pray that now at last by God's will the way may be opened for me to come to you.

¹¹I long to see you so that I may impart to you some

ª 3 Or *who according to the flesh*   *ᵇ* 4 Or *was declared with power to be the Son of God*   *ᶜ* 5 Or *that is*

1:1–7 Paul wrote Romans toward the end of his third missionary journey (mid–50s AD), probably from Corinth (Ac 19:21; 20:3). Though he does not explicitly mention his purpose for writing this letter, he describes his circumstances: He plans to deliver financial relief to the believers in Jerusalem to promote unity among the Jewish and Gentile churches (Ro 15:25–27). Unity in Christ is a major theme of Romans.

Paul begins all of his letters with a greeting in which he identifies himself and the letter's recipient(s). The greeting in Rom 1:1–7 is the longest of any of his letters, as Paul emphasizes his apostolic authority and God's work of salvation through Jesus Christ.

1:1 Paul Formerly known as Saul of Tarsus (Ac 7:58; 9:11). **a servant of Christ Jesus** Paul uses this language metaphorically to indicate that his life and ministry exhibit humility and submissiveness—characteristics associated with slavery and servitude during the first century. The Greek phrase used here, *doulos christou iēsou*, might allude to the OT phrase "servant of Yahweh" (Dt 34:5). In the OT, the designation "servant" describes the nation of Israel (Isa 43:10), the prophets (2Ki 17:23), and the suffering servant (Isa 52:13—53:12). Paul, however, replaces the name "Yahweh" with "Christ Jesus," identifying Jesus with the God of the OT. In his letters, Paul uses "Christ Jesus" 80 times and "Jesus Christ" 25 times, reflecting his emphasis on Jesus' role as Messiah. See the table "Pauline Self-Designations" on p. 1904. **apostle** A person designated and sent to speak and act with special authority. Paul regularly introduces himself as an apostle in his letters (e.g., 1Co 1:1; Eph 1:1; 1Ti 1:1). Paul's use of the title "apostle" highlights that his authority was equal to that of the twelve apostles and that his commission was from Christ (compare 1Co 15:7–9; Gal 1:1). **set apart** The Greek word used here, *aphorizō*, describes setting something or someone apart for a particular function or task. God set Paul apart to proclaim the gospel message about Jesus Christ. Like the prophet Jeremiah, Paul considered himself set apart before he was born (compare Gal 1:15; Jer 1:5). **the gospel of God** Refers to the good news of Jesus coming to save humanity. In this context, the Greek word for the gospel (or good news), *euangelion*, refers to a message—the good news about the life, death and resurrection of Jesus Christ. It also might refer to the events that brought about salvation. When these two ideas are taken together, the gospel is the revelation of God's righteous deeds that put people in right relationship with himself.

PAUL
Paul's expertise in Jewish law and thorough understanding of Greek and Roman culture made him ideally suited to proclaim the gospel among the Gentiles (non-Jews). Born a Roman citizen (Ac 22:28), Paul grew up in Tarsus, one of the largest cities in the Roman Empire (located in the southeastern region of modern-day Turkey). In Tarsus, he was exposed to Greco-Roman customs, religions and philosophies, and he apparently became fluent in Greek. Paul's quotations of thinkers like Aratus (Ac 17:28), Menander (1Co 15:33) and Epimenides (Titus 1:12) are evidence of his knowledge of Greek philosophy.

1:2 prophets Refers to people who are designated by God to speak on his behalf and critique their society— telling about present problems and, at times, future events (see note on Ge 20:7). Here Paul mentions the prophets to emphasize continuity between the promises that God delivered through the prophets in the OT and the fulfillment of those promises in the gospel. See the table "Jesus' Fulfillment of OT Prophecy" on p. 1573. **Holy Scriptures** Israel's sacred writings. Paul's audience likely understood the Septuagint (the Greek translation of the OT) to be on par with the Hebrew version of the Scriptures.

1:3 his Son Shorthand for "Son of God," a reference to Jesus Christ—the focus of the gospel message. This designation expresses the unique, intimate relationship between Jesus Christ and God. It also might express that Jesus is the Messiah and the appointed King—like David, who also is given this title. God promised David that from David's line would come an eternal kingdom (2Sa 7:12–16). This promise became the source of Jewish expectations about a coming Messiah (see Isa 11:1,10; Jer 23:5–6). For example, Peter's quotation of the OT scriptures to Jews at Pentecost demonstrates that Jewish people expected a descendant of David to restore the kingdom to Israel (Ac 2:30–32; compare 13:32–39). By referring to Jesus as a descendant of David, Paul identifies him as the coming Messiah of whom the promise speaks.

1:4 Spirit of holiness The Holy Spirit demonstrated power through the resurrection of Jesus Christ. **resurrection** Paul describes resurrection as the foundation of Christian

spiritual gift to make you strong— ¹²that is, that you and I may be mutually encouraged by each other's faith. ¹³I do not want you to be unaware, brothers and sisters,ᵃ that I planned many times to come to you (but have been prevented from doing so until now) in order that I might have a harvest among you, just as I have had among the other Gentiles.

¹⁴I am obligated both to Greeks and non-Greeks, both to the wise and the foolish. ¹⁵That is why I am so eager to preach the gospel also to you who are in Rome.

¹⁶For I am not ashamed of the gospel, because it is the power of God that brings salvation to everyone who believes: first to the Jew, then to the Gentile. ¹⁷For in the gospel the righteousness of God is revealed— a righteousness that is by faith from first to last,ᵇ just as it is written: "The righteous will live by faith."ᶜ

ᵃ 13 The Greek word for *brothers and sisters* (*adelphoi*) refers here to believers, both men and women, as part of God's family; also in 7:1, 4; 8:12, 29; 10:1; 11:25; 12:1; 15:14, 30; 16:14, 17.   ᵇ 17 Or *is from faith to faith*   ᶜ 17 Hab. 2:4

---

hope (compare 1Co 15:15–19). Paul's view is based on connections among OT prophecies about resurrection. Isaiah 11:1–2 prophesies that a future king will come from David's line to unite God's people (the Jews) and all nations (the Gentiles) to himself—ultimately fulfilling Israel's role as a nation (compare Isa 26:19 and note). This is why Paul connects resurrection with David. In Isa 53:10, the suffering servant—who is connected to the Messianic figure in Isa 11:1–2 (both contextually and in Zec 3:8–9)—is resurrected. Ezekiel 37:1–27 and Da 12:2 both discuss a future resurrection of the dead. The vocabulary of Da 12:2 and its connections to Isa 53:10 suggest that God's first servant, Israel, will be resurrected when the individual servant of Isa 53:10 comes. This is Paul's understanding throughout his letters: Followers of Christ are spiritually resurrected upon belief and will be physically resurrected on the day of the Lord (the context of the Da 12:2 prophecy).

1:5 Gentiles Jesus chose Paul for the purpose of telling Gentiles (non-Jewish people) about the gospel (see Ac 9:15 and note). Paul understood that God included the Gentiles in his plan of salvation, and he therefore made the Gentiles the focus of his missionary efforts (see Ac 13:46; 18:6; compare Gal 3:14; Ge 12:3). The apostles in Jerusalem likewise recognized Paul's appointment by God as the apostle to the Gentiles (see Gal 2:9; Ro 11:13). **obedience that comes from faith** The Greek phrase used here might refer to obedience that is brought about by faith. Alternatively, it could mean "obedience, which is faith." The expression also could simply describe the inseparable nature of obedience and faith. **name's** The Greek word used here for "name," *onoma*, refers to a person's character and reputation. Paul's missionary efforts among the Gentiles are for the benefit of Christ's name, not his own. See note on 2:24.

1:7 Rome The capital city of the Roman Empire. Paul wanted to visit Rome on his way to Spain (Ac 19:21; Ro 15:24,29). See the infographic "Rome in Paul's Day" on p. 1844. **holy people** The Greek term used here, *hagioi*, refers to those who have been set apart as God's people. **Grace and peace to you** Paul's typical greeting throughout his letters (compare Gal 1:3; Eph 1:2; Php 1:2). It summarizes his gospel message: God's work through Christ (grace) brings people into a harmonious relationship with God and one another (peace). **God our Father** The word "our" indicates that Jews and Gentiles (non-Jewish people) are equal and united before God because of Christ. False teachers may have claimed that the Gentiles were not equal because they did not participate in circumcision (Col 2:11; Ro 3:1; Gal 6:12), Sabbath observance (Col 2:16; Gal 4:10–11; Ro 14:6) or dietary restrictions (Gal 2:12; Ro 14:20)—distinctly Jewish practices. Such teachings would have brought division to the church.

1:8 I thank Paul usually opened his letters with an expression of gratitude to God for his audience (e.g., 1Co 1:4; Eph 1:16; Php 1:3; 1Th 1:3; compare Gal 1:6–10 and note). He believed their positive response to the gospel affirmed his calling as an apostle to the Gentiles (Ro 11:13; Gal 2:8; 1Ti 2:7). See the table "Prayers in Paul's Letters" on p. 1925. **faith** The Greek word used here, *pistis*, refers to trust and reliance.

1:11 spiritual gift This may refer to spiritual gifts (Ro 12:6; 1Co 12:1) or some spiritual understanding of Paul's mission and message. Ultimately, it will benefit the believers.

1:13 have been prevented from doing so until now Paul apparently wanted to complete his ministry in the eastern part of the Roman Empire before heading west (compare Ro 15:22). **harvest** Refers to the positive outcome of Paul's ministry among non-Jewish people.

1:14 to Greeks and non-Greeks Because of his appointment as an apostle (v. 1), Paul felt a duty to preach the gospel to all people, regardless of ethnicity. The Greek text's reference to barbarians (sometimes translated as "non-Greeks") likely refers to native tribes that had not assimilated into Greco-Roman culture.

1:16 power The Greek word used here, *dynamis*, often refers to miraculous works (e.g., Mt 7:22; 11:20; Mk 6:2). Here, it refers to God's ability to deliver his people from sin and future judgment (compare Ex 9:16; Ro 8:2–3; 1Co 1:18; note on 2Ti 3:5). God's power also relates to the power of the Holy Spirit (see Ro 1:4). **salvation** The Greek word used here, *sōtēria*, refers to deliverance from the final judgment. It also might refer to deliverance from sin and the results of sin: death and alienation from God. **first to the Jew, then to the Gentile** Paul uses references to both Jews and Greeks (or Gentiles) to encompass all of humanity. Although the gospel message applies to all people, Paul describes it as being directed first toward the Jew because God gave the Jews the covenants and promises to which the gospel refers (Ro 9:4).

1:17 righteousness of God This is one of the key phrases in Romans and Paul's other letters (e.g., 3:5,21,22,25,26; 10:3; see 2Co 5:21). It could refer to righteousness that comes from God—that is, the righteous status or right standing that God grants to those who have faith in Jesus Christ. Alternatively, it may refer to God's own righteousness and his saving work. It's also possible to combine these possibilities: Righteousness is an attribute of God that is manifested in his provision of salvation. As a result, those who believe are granted righteous status before God, who is himself righteous. God reveals his righteousness in the life, death and resurrection of Jesus Christ (Ro 3:21). This good news about Jesus Christ—the gospel message—also might be the way that the righteousness of God is made known.

God's Wrath Against Sinful Humanity

[18]The wrath of God is being revealed from heaven against all the godlessness and wickedness of people, who suppress the truth by their wickedness, [19]since what may be known about God is plain to them, because God has made it plain to them. [20]For since the creation of the world God's invisible qualities — his eternal power and divine nature — have been clearly seen, being understood from what has been made, so that people are without excuse.

[21]For although they knew God, they neither glorified him as God nor gave thanks to him, but their thinking became futile and their foolish hearts were darkened. [22]Although they claimed to be wise, they became fools [23]and exchanged the glory of the immortal God for images made to look like a mortal human being and birds and animals and reptiles.

The righteous will live by faith Paul quotes Hab 2:4 to support his position that righteousness before God is only by faith (see note on Gal 3:11). **will live** Probably refers both to a life of trust in God and to the eternal life which God grants believers.

1:18 The wrath of God Refers to God's righteous judgment upon evil. In this context, the evil in view is immorality and the suppression of the truth about God.

God reveals his wrath by giving people over to their sin, thereby allowing them to morally decline even further (Ro 1:24–28). This foreshadows his final judgment (see 2Th 2:9–12). **truth** Elsewhere, the Greek word used here, *alētheia*, usually refers to the gospel (Col 1:5; 1Ti 2:4); here, however, it refers more generally to the truth about God (Ro 1:25). Those who suppress the truth deny what is made obvious about God through

---

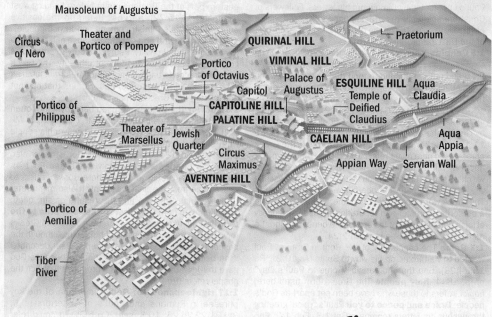

When Paul arrived in Rome, Nero was emperor. Rising tensions between Nero and the discontented upper classes—and an accusation that he started the great fire of AD 64—led Nero to blame the Christians and name them public enemies. Paul was in prison in Rome during the fire and was likely executed around the time Nero began to persecute Christians.

Mausoleum of Augustus

Circus of Nero

Theater and Portico of Pompey

QUIRINAL HILL

Praetorium

Portico of Octavius

VIMINAL HILL

Portico of Philippus

Capitol

Palace of Augustus

ESQUILINE HILL

Aqua Claudia

Temple of Deified Claudius

CAPITOLINE HILL

PALATINE HILL

Theater of Marsellus

Jewish Quarter

CAELIAN HILL

Aqua Appia

Circus Maximus

AVENTINE HILL

Appian Way

Servian Wall

Portico of Aemilia

Tiber River

ITALY

Adriatic Sea

Rome Sea

Tyrrhenian Sea

GREECE

SICILY Ionian Sea

Rome in Paul's Day

In Paul's day, Rome was not yet at the height of its splendor. The Coliseum would not be built for another decade, the great temple of Claudius was only partially constructed, and most of the elaborate baths and palaces were still more than a century away. Nonetheless, Rome was the greatest city in the known world and the center of power for all of Europe and the ancient Near East.

²⁴Therefore God gave them over in the sinful desires of their hearts to sexual impurity for the degrading of their bodies with one another. ²⁵They exchanged the truth about God for a lie, and worshiped and served created things rather than the Creator — who is forever praised. Amen.

²⁶Because of this, God gave them over to shameful lusts. Even their women exchanged natural sexual relations for unnatural ones. ²⁷In the same way the men also abandoned natural relations with women and were inflamed with lust for one another. Men committed shameful acts with other men, and received in themselves the due penalty for their error.

²⁸Furthermore, just as they did not think it worthwhile to retain the knowledge of God, so God gave them over to a depraved mind, so that they do what ought not to be done. ²⁹They have become filled with every kind of wickedness, evil, greed and depravity. They are full of envy, murder, strife, deceit and malice. They are gossips, ³⁰slanderers, God-haters, insolent, arrogant and boastful; they invent ways of doing evil; they disobey their parents; ³¹they have no understanding, no fidelity, no love, no mercy. ³²Although they know God's righteous decree that those who do such things deserve death, they not only continue to do these very things but also approve of those who practice them.

God's Righteous Judgment

2 You, therefore, have no excuse, you who pass judgment on someone else, for at whatever point you judge another, you are condemning yourself, because you who pass judgment do the same things. ²Now we know that God's judgment against those who do such things is based on truth.

---

creation (vv. 19–20) and do not acknowledge God as sovereign Creator.

1:20 divine nature The Greek word used here, *theiotēs*, is found only here in the NT. It is used to summarize God's divine attributes, especially those that can be observed through creation. Since God made such attributes discernable, people have no excuse for rejecting him. **without excuse** The universal revelation of God's power and deity in creation means that no one can claim ignorance for failing to honor God as God (vv. 21–23). God's wrath is therefore just (v. 18).

1:22 Although they claimed to be wise, they became fools A fool is not merely someone who is ignorant or lacks intelligence. The term has moral connotations that include a rejection of God (Ps 14:1; Jer 10:14). By refusing to acknowledge God, people reveal their foolishness.

1:23 glory In this context, the Greek term used here, *doxa*, indicates God's honor and majesty. **images made to look like** The Greek phrase used here refers to idolatry in general. Paul probably alludes to Ps 106:20, which speaks of Israel's worship of the golden calf (see Dt 4:16–18). In the OT and the ancient world, civilizations made physical representations of their gods (e.g., Ge 31:19,34; Nu 33:52; Dt 29:17).

DOXA
The Greek word *doxa*, often translated as "glory," refers to the splendor of God's manifested presence. This glory expresses the greatness of God, probably with reference to his attributes revealed in creation (Ro 1:20). Humans exchanged the glory of God for idols. They directed to idols what belongs to God: honor and thanksgiving (1:21).

1:24 God gave them over God allowed for people to do as they desired, even when it meant opposing his will for their lives. This is part of the judgment related to God's wrath (see note on Ro 1:18). Paul uses the Greek word *paradidōmi* (often translated "gave over" or "gave up") three times in this passage (vv. 24,26,28) to emphasize God's deliberate response to humanity's wicked ways: He allows people to continue to live a life of increasing sin. **sexual impurity** The Greek word used

here, *akatharsia*, refers to illicit sexual activity (2Co 12:21; Gal 5:19; Eph 5:3).

1:25 truth about God Refers to the truth that God revealed through his creation (see note on Ro 1:18). **who is forever praised** A doxology meaning that God is worthy of limitless adoration and worship. It also is an example of the kind of honor and thanksgiving that people should give to him (compare v. 21).

1:26 unnatural ones Refers to homosexual activity, which does not reflect God's original created order (see Ge 1:27; 2:18–25). Paul's view on homosexuality likely reflects Jewish attitudes in his day, which were based on the OT.

1:28 a depraved mind A mind that is incapable of moral or ethical discernment.

1:29–31 Paul lists vices that characterize those who reject God. Lists like this are common in Paul's writing. Sometimes he gives them to instruct the righteous on how to live (Ro 13:13; Gal 5:19–21; Col 3:5). Other times, as he does here, Paul uses these lists to describe the ungodly (1Co 6:9–10; 1Ti 1:9–10).

1:32 God's righteous decree This might refer to the sense of right and wrong that is present even in those who do not know God's law. **death** The penalty for all sin; possibly refers to eternal separation from God (Ro 6:23).

2:1–16 In this chapter, Paul shifts his focus from the guilt of the Gentiles to the guilt of the Jews. After describing God's judgment on Gentiles (non-Jewish people) who had rejected God and refused to acknowledge him (1:18–32), Paul now describes God's judgment on Jews or those who have the law (vv. 12–16). He makes the point that having the law does not justify people (v. 13). God will judge both Jews and Gentiles according to their works (v. 6).

2:1 You The referent of "you" is somewhat ambiguous at this point. In v. 17, it becomes clear that Paul is referring specifically to Jews. The use of "you" and the question-and-answer style suggest that Paul is using a rhetorical device called a diatribe, a hypothetical conversation that provides instruction. Paul regularly uses this method in Romans to address possible objections from his audience (see 3:5; 4:1; 6:1; 7:7; 9:14). **pass judgment** The Greek word used here, *krinō*, refers to condemning someone. **the same things** Refers to the sins listed in 1:28–31.

2:2 based on truth Paul affirms that God's judgment is just and true (see 1:18 and note).

³So when you, a mere human being, pass judgment on them and yet do the same things, do you think you will escape God's judgment? ⁴Or do you show contempt for the riches of his kindness, forbearance and patience, not realizing that God's kindness is intended to lead you to repentance?

⁵But because of your stubbornness and your unrepentant heart, you are storing up wrath against yourself for the day of God's wrath, when his righteous judgment will be revealed. ⁶God "will repay each person according to what they have done."^a ⁷To those who by persistence in doing good seek glory, honor and immortality, he will give eternal life. ⁸But for those who are self-seeking and who reject the truth and follow evil, there will be wrath and anger. ⁹There will be trouble and distress for every human being who does evil: first for the Jew, then for the Gentile; ¹⁰but glory, honor and peace for everyone who does good: first for the Jew, then for the Gentile. ¹¹For God does not show favoritism.

¹²All who sin apart from the law will also perish apart from the law, and all who sin under the law will be judged by the law. ¹³For it is not those who hear the law who are righteous in God's sight, but it is those who obey the law who will be declared righteous. ¹⁴(Indeed, when Gentiles, who do not have the law, do by nature things required by the law, they are a law for themselves, even though they do not have the law. ¹⁵They show that the requirements of the law are written on their hearts, their consciences also bearing witness, and their thoughts sometimes accusing them and at other times even defending them.) ¹⁶This will take place on the day when God judges people's secrets through Jesus Christ, as my gospel declares.

^a 6 Psalm 62:12; Prov. 24:12

2:4 forbearance and patience Describes God's patience in delaying judgment and punishment of people who sin and break the law. **repentance** The Greek word used here, *metanoia*, describes a change in mindset about sin and God. The purpose behind God's display of kindness, forbearance, and patience is not assurance, but repentance.

2:5 wrath The idea of storing up wrath is an ironic twist on the usual metaphor of storing up blessings or treasures (compare Ge 41:49; 1Ti 6:19). See note on 1:18. **day of God's wrath** An OT expression synonymous with the day of Yahweh (e.g., Isa 13:6–9; Joel 2:1–11). In the NT, it is also referred to as the day of Christ (1Co 1:8; Php 1:6)—the second coming of Jesus. On this day of final judgment, God will pour out his wrath against the wicked and deliver his people from evil (1Th 5:2 and note).

2:6 according to what they have done Paul emphasizes that God judges fairly and righteously (Ro 2:2). Similar statements are found throughout the OT (see Ps 62:12 and note; Job 34:11; Pr 24:12; Jer 17:10). Paul wants his fellow Jews to understand that they must not elevate their ethnicity over good works.

2:7–11 Paul emphasizes that God is a fair and just judge (Ro 2:6). Those who do good will receive glory, honor and eternal life (vv. 7,10). In contrast, those who do evil will receive wrath and affliction (vv. 8–9). This applies to both Jews and Gentiles (non-Jewish people), since God does not show partiality (v. 11).

2:7 doing good Refers to the collective sum of good deeds. These deeds are expressed especially in kindness toward others; therefore, they reflect God's character and belief in him (see v. 4; note on v. 13). **glory** In this context, the Greek word used here, *doxa*, probably refers to a future blessing that involves sharing in God's glory (see 5:2; 6:4; note on 1:23). **immortality** Life without end or not subject to decay. The notion of immortality was popular in Greek thought and literature (as reflected in the Deuterocanonical work Wisdom of Solomon 8:13,17). For Paul, immortality is an aspect of eternal life reserved for believers when God raises the dead to the resurrected life (see 1Co 15:42–54; 2Ti 1:10). **eternal life** Refers to life in the coming age or world. "Eternal" expresses not only the duration of life, but the quality of life (i.e., entering into God's life; see note on Ro 6:22). In the OT, life in the coming age commences with the resurrection of the dead (see Da 12:2 and note). Since Christ was raised from the dead, the life of the coming age has invaded the current age (see note on Gal 1:4). Believers now share in God's life through faith in Jesus Christ (Jn 3:16). At the resurrection, the glorious nature of the eternal life will be fully realized.

2:8 truth Probably refers to the gospel message or the truth about God (see Ro 1:18 and note). **evil** Refers to the sins that Paul listed in 1:28–31.

2:9 first for the Jew, then for the Gentile See 1:16 and note.

2:10 peace The Greek word used here, *eirēnē*, refers to perfect well-being that comes from God's righteous work through Christ.

2:12 All who sin apart from the law Refers to the Gentiles. They are not sinless merely because they do not know the requirements of God's law. Later, Paul argues that all have sinned (3:23) and that sin existed before the law defined it (5:13). **law** Refers to the Law of Moses—the commandments that God gave to Moses at Mount Sinai (Ex 20–22). **perish** The Greek word used here, *apollymi*, refers to suffering the wrath of God and therefore experiencing eternal separation from God. **all who sin under the law** Refers to Jews who know the requirements of the law and orient their lives around it.

2:13 declared righteous In this context, the Greek word used here, *dikaioō*, refers to God issuing a verdict by which he considers a person to be right or just in his eyes on the day of judgment. Paul's point here is to clarify who is righteous. For Paul, the hearers of the law—that is, those who possessed the law, the Jews—did not have a favored status before God. Instead, the impartial God will justify only those who meet God's requirements (see Ro 2:6–7). This leads to Paul's larger point of why there is an absolute need for the saving work of Jesus (v. 10; 3:20–26).

2:14 are a law for themselves Although God did not give the law to the Gentiles, some of them do what God requires in the law. This suggests that people have a natural moral sense or conscience.

2:15 written on their hearts Paul borrows the language of Jer 31:33 to assert that Gentiles have a sense of right and wrong.

2:16 my gospel Paul does not mean an interpretation of the gospel that is unique to him. His point is that the gospel he preaches upholds the law by insisting that all humanity will be judged according to obedience to the law.

The Jews and the Law

[17]Now you, if you call yourself a Jew; if you rely on the law and boast in God; [18]if you know his will and approve of what is superior because you are instructed by the law; [19]if you are convinced that you are a guide for the blind, a light for those who are in the dark, [20]an instructor of the foolish, a teacher of little children, because you have in the law the embodiment of knowledge and truth — [21]you, then, who teach others, do you not teach yourself? You who preach against stealing, do you steal? [22]You who say that people should not commit adultery, do you commit adultery? You who abhor idols, do you rob temples? [23]You who boast in the law, do you dishonor God by breaking the law? [24]As it is written: "God's name is blasphemed among the Gentiles because of you."[a]

[25]Circumcision has value if you observe the law, but if you break the law, you have become as though you had not been circumcised. [26]So then, if those who are not circumcised keep the law's requirements, will they not be regarded as though they were circumcised? [27]The one who is not circumcised physically and yet obeys the law will condemn you who, even though you have the[b] written code and circumcision, are a lawbreaker.

[28]A person is not a Jew who is one only outwardly, nor is circumcision merely outward and physical. [29]No, a person is a Jew who is one inwardly; and circumcision is circumcision of the heart, by the Spirit, not by the written code. Such a person's praise is not from other people, but from God.

God's Faithfulness

3 What advantage, then, is there in being a Jew, or what value is there in circumcision? [2]Much in every way! First of all, the Jews have been entrusted with the very words of God.

[3]What if some were unfaithful? Will their unfaithfulness nullify God's faithfulness? [4]Not at all! Let God be true, and every human being a liar. As it is written:

"So that you may be proved right when you speak
    and prevail when you judge."[c]

[5]But if our unrighteousness brings out God's righteousness more clearly, what shall we say? That God is unjust in bringing his wrath on us? (I am using a human argument.) [6]Certainly not! If that

---

[a] 24 Isaiah 52:5 (see Septuagint); Ezek. 36:20,22   [b] 27 Or who, by means of a   [c] 4 Psalm 51:4

2:17–29 Paul continues to show that Jews are not justified by having the law. He points out their hypocrisy as he describes them teaching others but not themselves and breaking the very law that they boast in (Ro 2:21–23). Using circumcision as an example, Paul argues that being Jewish is of value only if one keeps the law; obedience and action are more important than ethnicity (vv. 25–29).

2:17 you call yourself a Jew Paul clarifies that the "you" he has been speaking of refers to Jews (see note on v. 1). **rely on the law** Describes depending on the law for exemption from final judgment (see v. 5).
2:19 a guide for the blind In the OT, God describes himself using similar language (Isa 42:16). Paul is most likely mocking an attitude of moral superiority.
2:21 do you not teach yourself A central point of Paul's critique is that Jews, who possess the law, fail to faithfully heed its commands—thereby undermining the law's purpose.
2:23 by breaking the law Paul concludes that Jews do the very thing that the ungodly do: dishonor God (see Ro 1:21). The law doesn't exempt Jews from judgment.
2:24 God's name is blasphemed Paul quotes the ancient Greek translation (Septuagint) of Isa 52:5 to describe the negative outcome of breaking the law. God elected Israel as bearers of his promise to bless the nations, so that the Gentiles might call upon his name (see Ro 9:4–6; Ge 12:1–2; Ro 10:12–14). Instead, the Gentiles blaspheme God's name.
2:25 Circumcision This practice was closely connected to the covenant and to Jewish identity (see Ac 15:1 and note). Paul argues that circumcision loses its value for those who disobey the rest of the law. Circumcision proves that a person did not act out of ignorance when they transgressed; they knew the requirements of the law and still broke it.
2:26 those who are not circumcised Refers to a Gentile.
2:27 written code Refers to the law.

2:29 circumcision is circumcision of the heart Emphasizes genuine loyalty to God, becoming obedient with mind as well as body. Paul alludes to the prophecy of Jeremiah, who warned the people of Judah to circumcise their hearts (see Jer 4:4 and note; compare Jer 9:25–26). Christ is the one who does this work (Col 2:11; Eph 2:11; Php 3:3). **by the Spirit, not by the written code** This might represent a contrast between the new covenant (the Spirit) and the old covenant (the written code or letter). In Ro 7–8, Paul describes the transfer from life under the law to life under the Spirit.

3:1–8 Paul anticipates the response of his Jewish dialogue partner (see note on 2:1). He has argued that circumcision of the heart is what matters (2:28–29) and now addresses the question of the value of physical circumcision. Paul makes the point that Jews have the advantage of being given the promises of God (v. 2). However, this advantage does not prevent God from judging them for faithlessness (vv. 5–6).

3:2 with the very words of God Refers to the OT Scriptures, specifically the words spoken by the prophets. It especially refers to promises and covenants (2Sa 7:14–15; Ro 9:4–5). Jews had knowledge of God's purposes for humanity through their Scriptures. In this sense, they were bearers of God's promises.
3:3 God's faithfulness Paul raises the question about God's faithfulness in light of his people's unfaithfulness. Despite the failure of God's people to maintain the obligations associated with God's covenants with them, God was committed to being faithful to his promises.
3:4 Not at all Expresses an emphatic rejection (v. 31; 6:2; 7:7). **prevail when you judge** Paul quotes the Septuagint of Ps 51:4 to show that God's judgment is justified and does not nullify his faithfulness.
3:5 our unrighteousness brings out God's

were so, how could God judge the world? ⁷Someone might argue, "If my falsehood enhances God's truthfulness and so increases his glory, why am I still condemned as a sinner?" ⁸Why not say — as some slanderously claim that we say — "Let us do evil that good may result"? Their condemnation is just!

No One Is Righteous

⁹What shall we conclude then? Do we have any advantage? Not at all! For we have already made the charge that Jews and Gentiles alike are all under the power of sin. ¹⁰As it is written:

"There is no one righteous, not even one;
¹¹ there is no one who understands;
    there is no one who seeks God.
¹² All have turned away,
    they have together become worthless;
there is no one who does good,
    not even one."ᵃ
¹³ "Their throats are open graves;
    their tongues practice deceit."ᵇ
"The poison of vipers is on their lips."ᶜ
¹⁴ "Their mouths are full of cursing and
    bitterness."ᵈ

¹⁵ "Their feet are swift to shed blood;
¹⁶   ruin and misery mark their ways,
¹⁷ and the way of peace they do not know."ᵉ
¹⁸   "There is no fear of God before their eyes."ᶠ

¹⁹Now we know that whatever the law says, it says to those who are under the law, so that every mouth may be silenced and the whole world held accountable to God. ²⁰Therefore no one will be declared righteous in God's sight by the works of the law; rather, through the law we become conscious of our sin.

Righteousness Through Faith

²¹But now apart from the law the righteousness of God has been made known, to which the Law and the Prophets testify. ²²This righteousness is given through faith inᵍ Jesus Christ to all who believe. There is no difference between Jew and Gentile, ²³for all have sinned and fall short of the glory of God, ²⁴and all are justified freely

ᵃ 12 Psalms 14:1-3; 53:1-3; Eccles. 7:20   ᵇ 13 Psalm 5:9
ᶜ 13 Psalm 140:3   ᵈ 14 Psalm 10:7 (see Septuagint)
ᵉ 17 Isaiah 59:7,8   ᶠ 18 Psalm 36:1   ᵍ 22 Or through the faithfulness of

---

righteousness more clearly Paul reasons that human unrighteousness provides God—who judges sin—with an opportunity to demonstrate his righteousness through judgment. Compare Ro 1:17. **I am using a human argument** Paul does not actually mean that God is unjust; he only makes this assertion for the sake of his argument.
3:8 some slanderously claim that we say Likely refers to a distortion of Paul's gospel that misunderstands his devaluation of the law as a license to sin. He declares that whoever acts in such a way is worthy of condemnation.

3:9–20 By citing OT verses, Paul emphasizes that both Jews and non-Jewish people (Gentiles) are under sin (vv. 10–18). He concludes that because of humanity's universal sinfulness, the law does not lead to justification. Instead, it leads to the knowledge of sin (v. 20). This sets up Paul's next point—that God has provided a means to justification through faith in Jesus Christ (vv. 21–31).

3:9 Do we have any advantage Paul refers to himself and his fellow Jews (see v. 1). He acknowledges that they did have an advantage in having the law and God's covenants (v. 1; 9:4–5). But this advantage does not exempt them from God's judgment. **we have already made the charge** In 1:18—2:29, Paul argues that sin is universal. Therefore, both Jews and Gentiles are guilty before God, who shows no partiality (see 2:11 and note). **Jews and Gentiles** Encompasses all people. See note on 1:16.
3:10 There is no one righteous Paul quotes Ps 14:1–3 to support his argument that sin is common to both Jews and Greeks (Ro 3:10–12).
3:13 their tongues practice deceit Paul quotes Ps 5:9 to illustrate the potentially harmful effects of words. **poison of vipers is on their lips** Paul quotes Ps 140:3.
3:14 full of cursing and bitterness Paul quotes Ps 10:7.
3:15 swift to shed blood A quotation of Isa 59:7–8. Sinful people not only speak harmful words, but also act on those words (Ro 3:13–14).
3:18 There is no fear of God before their eyes A quotation of Ps 36:1.

3:19 those who are under the law Refers to Jews.
3:20 will be declared righteous The Greek word used here, *dikaioō*, describes being in right relationship with God. See note on Ro 1:17; compare 2:13 and note; 4:3 and note. **works of the law** This phrase could refer to all the requirements in the law. Alternatively, it might emphasize practices that distinguish Jews from Gentiles, such as observing the Sabbath, food laws and circumcision. **we become conscious of our sin** The law defines sin through its commands and prohibitions, thereby imparting knowledge about sin. But knowledge of sin is also experiential. When people break the law, they become aware of the presence and power of sin within them. See 7:7–25.

3:21–31 Having made the point that both Jews and Gentiles are under sin (v. 9), Paul explains that the righteousness of God is available to all people equally through faith in Jesus Christ (v. 22).

3:21 But now Expresses a significant transition in salvation history that began with the death and resurrection of Jesus (see 5:9; 8:1; 13:11). This also marks a shift in the argument in the letter. **the righteousness of God** See note on 1:17. **the Law and the Prophets** Paul does not want his Jewish audience to misunderstand the phrase "apart from the law" to mean "apart from the promises of the OT," as though the gospel was foreign to the Scriptures. He affirms that the Law and the Prophets (two sections of the Jewish canon of Scripture) testify about the revelation of God's righteousness apart from the requirements of the Jewish law. See the table "Jesus' Fulfillment of OT Prophecy" on p. 1573.
3:22 faith in Jesus Christ The Greek phrase here could mean "faith in Jesus Christ" or "the faithfulness of Jesus Christ." Paul could have had both meanings in mind. **all who believe** Emphasizes the inclusive nature of the gospel message.
3:23 all have sinned Both Jews and Gentiles have failed to live up to God's standard; sin is universal. **glory of**

by his grace through the redemption that came by Christ Jesus. [25]God presented Christ as a sacrifice of atonement,[a] through the shedding of his blood—to be received by faith. He did this to demonstrate his righteousness, because in his forbearance he had left the sins committed beforehand unpunished— [26]he did it to demonstrate his righteousness at the present time, so as to be just and the one who justifies those who have faith in Jesus.

[27]Where, then, is boasting? It is excluded. Because of what law? The law that requires works? No, because of the law that requires faith. [28]For we maintain that a person is justified by faith apart from the works of the law. [29]Or is God the God of Jews only? Is he not the God of Gentiles too? Yes, of Gentiles too, [30]since there is only one

God, who will justify the circumcised by faith and the uncircumcised through that same faith. [31]Do we, then, nullify the law by this faith? Not at all! Rather, we uphold the law.

Abraham Justified by Faith

4 What then shall we say that Abraham, our forefather according to the flesh, discovered in this matter? [2]If, in fact, Abraham was justified by works, he had something to boast about—but not before God. [3]What does Scripture say? "Abraham believed God, and it was credited to him as righteousness."[b]

[a] 25 The Greek for *sacrifice of atonement* refers to the atonement cover on the ark of the covenant (see Lev. 16:15,16).
[b] 3 Gen. 15:6; also in verse 22

God In Jewish tradition, God created humanity in his likeness to reflect his glory (see note on 1:23). But when Adam sinned, humanity lost the reflection of God's image. Alternatively, this phrase could refer to God's standard.
3:24 all are justified To be justified means to be set right or declared righteous (see v. 20 and note). Justification stands in contrast to condemnation (see v. 7). **redemption** The Greek word used here, *apolytrōsis*, refers to the act of freeing a slave or prisoner by payment. Paul's understanding of redemption probably was shaped by two paradigmatic acts of redemption in Israel's history—the exodus and the return from the Babylonian exile (e.g., Dt 7:8; Isa 51:11; 62:12).
3:25 sacrifice of atonement The Greek word used here, *hilastērion*, refers to the lid of the ark of the covenant (see Lev 16:15–16; Heb 9:5). Once a year, on the Day of Atonement, the Jewish high priest would apply animal's blood to this lid (Lev 16:14). Paul's description suggests that Christ functions as the locus of atonement in the new covenant. **through the shedding of his blood** Identifies Jesus' blood as the means for dealing with sin (see previous note). Elsewhere, references to the blood of Jesus signify his violent and sacrificial death (see Ro 5:9; Eph 1:7; Rev 1:5; compare Isa 52:15 and note). **demonstrate his righteousness** Through the crucifixion of Christ, God showed himself righteous. He judged sin but also provided righteousness for those who have faith in Christ (compare Isa 53:11). **his forbearance** Refers to the patience God displayed when delaying punishment for sin. **he had left the sins committed beforehand unpunished** God had left the sins of previous generations unpunished. This demonstrates his kindness toward humanity, not indifference toward sin.
3:26 just In Romans 3:5–6, Paul's hypothetical conversation partner raised a question about the legitimacy of God's character in relation to human sin. Paul argued that sin is universal and God's condemnation is therefore just (vv. 9–18). The apostle now explains that Christ's death showed that God was not indifferent to sin. He is just. If God is just, then he is the only one who can justify.
3:27 boasting The Greek word used here, *kauchēsis*, refers to pride toward human accomplishment. Some Jews boasted of their possession of the law and covenantal status as God's chosen people, but all people are prone to boasting. Paul rejects such pride. If all have sinned (v. 23), no one has any basis to boast—especially in relation to the law. Faith excludes boasting because people are saved not by their works, but by the work of Jesus on the cross and by God's raising him from the dead.

3:28 apart from the works of the law Since God justifies people regardless of whether they meet the requirements of the law, he can put the Gentiles—who were not under the law—in right relationship with himself.
3:31 Do we, then, nullify the law Paul's hypothetical conversation partner raises a concern about justification apart from the law. Paul does not mean that Jews should dismiss the law completely; rather, they should not consider it the means to a right relationship with God. The law remains useful for moral instruction; it also details God's promises and his purposes in the world.

4:1–25 Paul continues his discussion of justification by faith alone with an appeal to Abraham, the founding father of Israel and traditional model of Jewish piety. Paul has established that no one can be justified by the law and that justification occurs only by faith (see 3:20,28). To support this claim, Paul asserts that Abraham was justified by faith, not works.

4:1 Abraham The first OT patriarch. **our forefather** Paul speaks to those who are ethnically Jewish.

Romans 4:1

ABRAHAM
God promised Abraham that he would become a great nation and an instrument of blessing to all nations (Ge 12:2–3). However, Abraham didn't have the essential components for nationhood—land and descendants. God called Abraham to the land of Canaan and promised him a son through his barren wife, Sarah (Ge 17:19). Although neither promise seemed possible, Abraham believed God. For this reason, Paul regards Abraham's faith as exemplary for all believers (Gal 3:6; compare Heb 11:8,17).

4:2 was justified The Greek word used here, *edikaiōthē*, can be translated "was justified" or "was declared righteous"; it refers to being put in right relation with someone else. **works** May refer to Abraham's efforts—his good works. Alternatively, it may refer to works of the law. See note on 3:20.
4:3 it was credited to him as righteousness Through this quotation from Ge 15:6, Paul demonstrates that Abraham received righteousness through faith, not works.

⁴Now to the one who works, wages are not credited as a gift but as an obligation. ⁵However, to the one who does not work but trusts God who justifies the ungodly, their faith is credited as righteousness. ⁶David says the same thing when he speaks of the blessedness of the one to whom God credits righteousness apart from works:

⁷"Blessed are those
  whose transgressions are forgiven,
  whose sins are covered.
⁸Blessed is the one
  whose sin the Lord will never count
    against them."[a]

⁹Is this blessedness only for the circumcised, or also for the uncircumcised? We have been saying that Abraham's faith was credited to him as righteousness. ¹⁰Under what circumstances was it credited? Was it after he was circumcised, or before? It was not after, but before! ¹¹And he received circumcision as a sign, a seal of the righteousness that he had by faith while he was still uncircumcised. So then, he is the father of all who believe but have not been circumcised, in order that righteousness might be credited to them. ¹²And he is then also the father of the circumcised who not only are circumcised but who also follow in the footsteps of the faith that our father Abraham had before he was circumcised.

¹³It was not through the law that Abraham and his offspring received the promise that he would be heir of the world, but through the righteousness that comes by faith. ¹⁴For if those who depend on the law are heirs, faith means nothing and the promise is worthless, ¹⁵because the law brings wrath. And where there is no law there is no transgression.

¹⁶Therefore, the promise comes by faith, so that it may be by grace and may be guaranteed to all Abraham's offspring — not only to those who are of the law but also to those who have the faith of Abraham. He is the father of us all. ¹⁷As it is written: "I have made you a father of many nations."[b] He is our father in the sight of God, in whom he believed — the God who gives life to the dead and calls into being things that were not.

¹⁸Against all hope, Abraham in hope believed and so became the father of many nations, just as it had been said to him, "So shall your offspring be."[c] ¹⁹Without weakening in his faith, he faced the fact that his body was as good as dead — since he was about a hundred years old — and that Sarah's womb was also dead. ²⁰Yet he did not waver through unbelief regarding the promise of God, but was strengthened in his faith and gave glory to God, ²¹being fully persuaded that God had power to do what he had promised. ²²This is why

[a] 8 Psalm 32:1,2   [b] 17 Gen. 17:5   [c] 18 Gen. 15:5

4:5 ungodly In this context, "ungodly" also includes Abraham (Ro 4:1), who was similar to the Gentiles in that he was uncircumcised and not under the law when God called him. **their faith is credited as righteousness** God's interaction with Abraham establishes a pattern for interactions between him and people. God initiates and provides; people trust and receive.

4:6 David Considered Israel's greatest king. Paul mentions David to counter the possible objection that God's provision of righteousness for Abraham was an exception. **God credits righteousness apart from works** Paul includes this interpretative summary of Ps 32:1–2 to draw a connection between Abraham and David, both of whom experienced God's provision of righteousness.

4:7 transgressions are forgiven Paul quotes Ps 32:1 to support his argument that God credits righteousness apart from works. Although righteousness is not explicitly mentioned in Ps 32:1 (compare Ro 4:6), the psalm identifies lawless deeds and sin as problems that require God's provision of righteousness.

4:10 circumcised, or before Refers to Abraham being in the same position as most Gentiles (see note on v. 5). Paul argues that faith came first, then the covenant of circumcision. For this reason, faith is the means of right relationship with God.

4:11 circumcision as a sign An expression from Ge 17:11. In Jewish culture, circumcision identified a Jewish male as being under law. Paul's view departs from this tradition; he argues that, in the case of Abraham, circumcision signified Abraham's faith, not his place under the law. **in order that righteousness might be credited to them** Paul explains that God declared Abraham righteous while he was uncircumcised so that he could credit righteousness to uncircumcised Gentiles (non-Jewish people).

4:12 who also follow in the footsteps Describes Abraham as a model for both Jews and Gentiles (see note on Ro 4:3).

4:13 heir of the world God had promised that Abraham and his descendants would inherit the land of Canaan and be an instrument of blessing for all the nations of the earth (e.g., Ge 12:3; 13:16; 17:8; 22:18).

4:15 law brings wrath Because it directly identifies sin as a transgression against God.

4:16 faith of Abraham Jewish people regarded themselves as natural descendants of Abraham (Ro 4:1); Paul metaphorically extends this association to all people who exhibit Abraham's faith.

4:17 a father of many nations A quotation of Ge 17:5 from the Septuagint (the Greek translation of the OT). The plural of the Greek word used here, *ethnos* ("nation"), also (at times) refers to Gentiles in general. Paul uses this different meaning to assert that Abraham is father not only of Jews but also of Gentiles. **who gives life to the dead** Could refer to Jesus' resurrection. Abraham also is said to be as good as dead when God brought life (a child) from him and Sarah (Ro 4:19; Ge 17:17).

4:18 Against all hope Abraham trusted in the hope of God's ability to fulfill what he had promised. **So shall your offspring be** A quotation from Ge 15:5. When Abraham complained to God about not having an heir, God reassured him that his descendants would be as numerous as the stars in the sky.

4:19 Without weakening in his faith In this context, weakness involves lacking trust in God or wavering in unbelief (see Ro 4:20).

4:22 it was credited to him as righteousness See v. 3 and note.

"it was credited to him as righteousness." [23]The words "it was credited to him" were written not for him alone, [24]but also for us, to whom God will credit righteousness — for us who believe in him who raised Jesus our Lord from the dead. [25]He was delivered over to death for our sins and was raised to life for our justification.

Peace and Hope

5 Therefore, since we have been justified through faith, we[a] have peace with God through our Lord Jesus Christ, [2]through whom we have gained access by faith into this grace in which we now stand. And we[b] boast in the hope of the glory of God. [3]Not only so, but we[b] also glory in our sufferings, because we know that suffering produces perseverance; [4]perseverance, character; and character, hope. [5]And hope does not put us to shame, because God's love has been poured out into our hearts through the Holy Spirit, who has been given to us.

[6]You see, at just the right time, when we were still powerless, Christ died for the ungodly. [7]Very rarely will anyone die for a righteous person, though for a good person someone might possibly dare to die. [8]But God demonstrates his own love for us in this: While we were still sinners, Christ died for us.

[9]Since we have now been justified by his blood, how much more shall we be saved from God's wrath through him! [10]For if, while we were God's enemies, we were reconciled to him through the death of his Son, how much more, having been reconciled, shall we be saved through his life! [11]Not only is this so, but we also boast in God through our Lord Jesus Christ, through whom we have now received reconciliation.

Death Through Adam, Life Through Christ

[12]Therefore, just as sin entered the world through one man, and death through sin, and in this way death came to all people, because all sinned —

a 1 Many manuscripts *let us*   *b* 2,3 Or *let us*

4:24 who raised The resurrection is evidence of God's power and presence.
4:25 was delivered over Refers to Jesus' arrest, trials and execution (see Mt 20:19; Mk 15:1; Lk 22:6; Jn 19:16; compare Ro 1:24–28). **for our sins** Paul points out the vicarious nature of Jesus' arrest and, consequently, his death. Humanity's sins were the reason that Christ was handed over to die. **raised to life for our justification** Parallel to the previous clause, this statement indicates that the purpose of Christ's resurrection can be understood as justification, vindication or acquittal for sinners (compare Isa 53:10 and note).

5:1–21 Paul turns from his discussion of justification by faith to address the reconciliation with God that results from such justification. He emphasizes God's love for sinners, the atoning power of Christ's death and how Christ's death ultimately leads to the restoration of the relationship that existed at creation between God, Adam and the world.

5:1 since we have been justified through faith Paul has argued extensively that salvation comes only through faith (see note on Ro 3:22). He assumes that conclusion here, using it as the starting point to expound on the implications of being declared righteous by God. **peace** Paul uses this word similarly to how it is used throughout the OT: to describe well-being, prosperity, safety from harm and deliverance from enemies. This peace is more than just the absence of conflict; it is the result of having been declared righteous by faith (see Eph 2:14–17; Col 1:20).
5:2 this grace in which we now stand Indicates not only a past event, but also a present reality made possible by the work of Christ on the cross. **we boast** Refers to expressing trust in God to do what he promised. Paul uses a similar phrase to describe Abraham's response of faith to God's promise (Ro 4:20).
5:3 our sufferings Refers to suffering on account of persecution (e.g., 1Th 1:6; 2Th 1:4).
5:5 put us to shame The Greek word used here,

kataischynō, comes from the ancient Greek translation of the OT (the Septuagint), where it means "to suffer shame [when judged]" (e.g., Ps 22:5; Isa 28:16; Ro 9:33).
5:6 the right time Refers to the time that God appointed it should happen (compare Mk 1:15; Gal 4:4). **the ungodly** This term encompasses those who do not have the law (Gentiles) and those who transgress the law (Jews).
5:7 Very rarely Paul asserts a general truth to highlight the extraordinary nature of Christ's death on behalf of the ungodly.
5:8 Christ died for us The proof and revelation of God's love for his people.
5:9 we have now been justified See note on Ro 4:3. **by his blood** Refers to Christ's death, which put the ungodly in right relationship with God. Atonement through sacrifice required blood (compare Heb 9:22; note on Isa 52:15). **shall we be saved** In this context, the Greek verb used here, *sōzō*, probably refers to deliverance from final judgment. **from God's wrath** See note on Ro 1:18.
5:10 enemies Paul probably has in mind both humanity's sinful rebellion against God's ways and God's wrathful response to their sinful ways (see 1:18—2:11; 5:9; 8:7). **we were reconciled** The Greek word used here, *katallassō*, describes bringing two hostile parties into friendly relations. **through his life** Refers to the resurrection life of the risen Christ.
5:11 reconciliation Indicates that Jesus has repaired the relationship between God and humankind (see 2Co 5:18 and note).

5:12–21 Paul describes what is true on a small scale to establish truth on a larger scale. This rhetorical device is called an argument *a minori ad maius* (Latin for "from the lesser to the greater") or *qal wa-chomer* (Hebrew for "light to heavy").

5:12 one man Refers to Adam (Ge 2:7; Ro 5:14). Paul identifies Adam as a representative of humanity whose actions affected all of humanity, bringing mortality and death to all humankind. Paul is the only Biblical writer to use Adam to explain the origin of death and sin. **death**

[13]To be sure, sin was in the world before the law was given, but sin is not charged against anyone's account where there is no law. [14]Nevertheless, death reigned from the time of Adam to the time of Moses, even over those who did not sin by breaking a command, as did Adam, who is a pattern of the one to come.

[15]But the gift is not like the trespass. For if the many died by the trespass of the one man, how much more did God's grace and the gift that came by the grace of the one man, Jesus Christ, overflow to the many! [16]Nor can the gift of God be compared with the result of one man's sin: The judgment followed one sin and brought condemnation, but the gift followed many trespasses and brought justification. [17]For if, by the trespass of the one man, death reigned through that one man, how much more will those who receive God's abundant provision of grace and of the gift of righteousness reign in life through the one man, Jesus Christ!

[18]Consequently, just as one trespass resulted in condemnation for all people, so also one righteous act resulted in justification and life for all people. [19]For just as through the disobedience of the one man the many were made sinners, so also through the obedience of the one man the many will be made righteous.

[20]The law was brought in so that the trespass might increase. But where sin increased, grace increased all the more, [21]so that, just as sin reigned in death, so also grace might reign through righteousness to bring eternal life through Jesus Christ our Lord.

Dead to Sin, Alive in Christ

6 What shall we say, then? Shall we go on sinning so that grace may increase? [2]By no means! We are those who have died to sin; how can we live in it any longer? [3]Or don't you know that all of us who were baptized into Christ Jesus were baptized into his death? [4]We were therefore buried with him through baptism into death in order that, just as Christ was raised from the dead through the glory of the Father, we too may live a new life.

[5]For if we have been united with him in a death like his, we will certainly also be united with him in a resurrection like his. [6]For we know that our old self was crucified with him so that the body

---

Refers to the loss of immortality, which includes physical and spiritual death (Ge 3:22–24). Adam did not immediately die when he ate from the tree of the knowledge of good and evil (Ge 3:6–7); rather, his sin introduced mortality. This mortality, in Paul's view, spread to the entire human race (see 1Co 15:21–22). According to Paul, death will be the final enemy defeated by God (1Co 15:26). **because all sinned** Although Paul describes Adam as a representative of humanity, he states that people's own sin condemns them (Ro 3:23).
5:13 before the law Paul states that the law did not introduce sin into the world; rather, it identified the sin that Adam had introduced. In the same way that Abraham demonstrated faith apart from law, Adam demonstrates the existence of sin apart from law. See 7:7–25.
5:14 a pattern The Greek word used here, *typos*, refers to Adam's role as a representative for humanity. This sets a pattern for the one who is to come—Jesus Christ. Typology, using a person or event to represent an entire idea, was common in Greco-Roman rhetoric and interpretation.

5:15–21 In this section, Paul compares Adam's sin with God's gift. In doing so, he praises God's gift, which reverses the devastating effect of Adam's sin.

5:15 the gift Refers to the work of Christ—his sacrificial death, which puts believers in right relationship with God. **the trespass** Refers to Adam's disobedience, which resulted in death (see v. 12 and note; Ge 3:7). **many died by the trespass of the one man** Many died in the sense that they experienced the results of sin (death; see note on v. 12). For Paul, Adam and Christ serve as representative heads over two groups of people. Paul emphasizes that Adam's trespass brought death to all who belong to him. By contrast, those who belong to Christ receive the free gift of grace.
5:16 justification See note on 3:24.
5:18 one righteous act Refers to Jesus' death on the cross.
5:19 the many will be made righteous Although

Christ's obedience has implications for the justification of all people, it does not result in justification apart from their acceptance of the free gift (see v. 17).
5:20 The law Refers to the Law of Moses. **trespass might increase** Probably refers both to knowledge of trespasses through the law and sinful rebellion against the law's requirements (see 7:7–8).
5:21 eternal life See note on 2:7.

6:1–11 In vv. 1–11, Paul argues that believers have been transferred from the era of sin and death under Adam to the new era of righteousness and life under the second Adam, Christ. Paul returns to a question-and-answer style to teach the Roman believers about the implications of God's grace (compare 3:8).

6:1 that grace may increase Paul answers a potential objection to his teachings on grace—namely, that if the law caused sin to increase, which led to more grace, then continuing in sin would lead to even greater outpourings of grace. Paul rejects this on the basis that the reign of sin in the believer's life has definitively ended.
6:2 By no means See note on 3:4. **died to sin** Indicates that believers are no longer under the power and control of sin; therefore, they must not live as though they are still under it.
6:3 baptized into Christ Jesus Possibly shorthand for "baptized into the name of Christ Jesus," indicating being baptized into union with Christ Jesus. **were baptized into his death** Baptism is the practice through which believers identify with the second Adam, Christ (compare ch. 5). Paul uses water baptism by immersion as a metaphor for the believer's new life in Christ—identifying with Christ through his death, burial and resurrection (vv. 3–8; compare Mk 10:38–39). See note on Ac 2:38.
6:4 We were therefore buried See Col 2:12 and note. **glory** See note on Ro 1:23.
6:5 in a death like his Believers participate in Christ's death, through which they experience freedom and separation from the power of sin. **we will certainly also be**

ruled by sin might be done away with,[a] that we should no longer be slaves to sin — [7]because anyone who has died has been set free from sin.

[8]Now if we died with Christ, we believe that we will also live with him. [9]For we know that since Christ was raised from the dead, he cannot die again; death no longer has mastery over him. [10]The death he died, he died to sin once for all; but the life he lives, he lives to God.

[11]In the same way, count yourselves dead to sin but alive to God in Christ Jesus. [12]Therefore do not let sin reign in your mortal body so that you obey its evil desires. [13]Do not offer any part of yourself to sin as an instrument of wickedness, but rather offer yourselves to God as those who have been brought from death to life; and offer every part of yourself to him as an instrument of righteousness. [14]For sin shall no longer be your master, because you are not under the law, but under grace.

Slaves to Righteousness

[15]What then? Shall we sin because we are not under the law but under grace? By no means!

[16]Don't you know that when you offer yourselves to someone as obedient slaves, you are slaves of the one you obey — whether you are slaves to sin, which leads to death, or to obedience, which leads to righteousness? [17]But thanks be to God that, though you used to be slaves to sin, you have come to obey from your heart the pattern of teaching that has now claimed your allegiance. [18]You have been set free from sin and have become slaves to righteousness.

[19]I am using an example from everyday life because of your human limitations. Just as you used to offer yourselves as slaves to impurity and to ever-increasing wickedness, so now offer yourselves as slaves to righteousness leading to holiness. [20]When you were slaves to sin, you were free from the control of righteousness. [21]What benefit did you reap at that time from the things you are now ashamed of? Those things result in death! [22]But now that you have been set free from sin and have become slaves of God, the benefit you reap leads to holiness, and the result is eternal life.

[a] 6 Or be rendered powerless

Believers experience the spiritual effects of the resurrection now, but they won't be resurrected physically until Christ returns to earth. See note on 1:4.

6:6 our old self Might refer to the previous era of humanity under the effects of Adam's sin. Alternatively, it could refer to unregenerate or fallen human nature. **was crucified with him** Occurred either at the time of Christ's crucifixion or at the time of the believer's baptism. **body ruled by sin** The Greek phrase used here, *sōma tēs hamartias*, refers to a person's physical body or the whole person (*sōma*), which is still subject to sin (*hamartias*; compare 8:23). **no longer be slaves to sin** Paul does not mean that believers no longer sin, but that Christ's death and resurrection have freed them from the rule of sin (see v. 7).

6:7 has been set free The Greek verb used here, *dedikaiōtai*, can be translated in this instance as "justified" or "freed" (4:3). Believers are justified or acquitted from the consequences of sin.

6:8 we will also live with him The Greek verb used here, *syzēsomen*, is in the future tense; it may refer to an experience associated with the end times.

6:9 death no longer has mastery over him When God raised Jesus from the dead, he transformed his earthly body into a glorified human body that is no longer susceptible to death and decay. In this state, Christ represents the immortal life that awaits those who have faith in him.

6:10 he died to sin The power and influence of sin manifested itself in death. Ironically, by submitting to death, Christ died to the power and influence of sin.

6:11 alive to God Like Christ, believers live for God and are empowered to do his will.

6:12 mortal The Greek word used here, *thnētos*, refers to people's regular, non-resurrected bodies, which are susceptible to death. Compare note on v. 5.

6:13 any part The Greek word used here, *melos*, refers to a person's natural faculties. Since believers have died to sin (v. 2), Paul urges them not to offer their abilities to the power and control of sin.

6:14 you are not under the law, but under grace Paul presents another reason why sin will not exercise control over believers. "Law" refers to the set of regulations God gave to Moses that identified sin but did not help overcome it. Grace, on the other hand, refers to the unmerited favor of God and his empowering presence to overcome sin.

6:15–23 Paul continues to discuss whether sin results in more grace (see v. 1). Here Paul reformulates the discussion in terms of the law and grace. Believers are called to use their freedom to bring righteousness, since sin can only result in death.

6:16 slaves Paul uses the term "slave" to describe a person under the complete control of someone or something. Prior to faith in Christ and baptism, believers were enslaved to sin and suffered its effects. Paul presents salvation as deliverance from spiritual bondage. He illustrates it as a transfer from one master to another—from sin to God. **sin** In this context, the Greek word used here, *hamartia*, refers to the destructive power of sin. **death** The Greek word used here, *thanatos*, refers not only to spiritual or physical mortality, but to separation from God. **righteousness** The Greek word *dikaiosynē* is used here in an ethical sense to describe doing what is right (compare 4:3).

6:17 pattern of teaching Refers to the gospel message and its ethical implications. Paul emphasizes obedience because it functions as the only tangible expression of faith.

6:19 your human limitations Probably refers to people's limited capacity to understand God's truth because of their fallen nature. **ever-increasing** Submission to immorality and lawlessness results in further lawlessness (see 1:24). **yourselves** See note on v. 13. **slaves to righteousness** See note on v. 16. **holiness** The Greek word used here, *hagiasmos*, often translated as "sanctification," can refer to the process of becoming holy or the state of being holy. Ultimately, sanctification means that the believer's life reflects God's character.

6:20 slaves to sin See note on v. 16.

6:21 What benefit Refers to the negative outcome of a person's conduct apart from Christ.

6:22 eternal life Refers to the life of the age to come,

²³For the wages of sin is death, but the gift of God is eternal life in^a Christ Jesus our Lord.

Released From the Law, Bound to Christ

7 Do you not know, brothers and sisters — for I am speaking to those who know the law — that the law has authority over someone only as long as that person lives? ²For example, by law a married woman is bound to her husband as long as he is alive, but if her husband dies, she is released from the law that binds her to him. ³So then, if she has sexual relations with another man while her husband is still alive, she is called an adulteress. But if her husband dies, she is released from that law and is not an adulteress if she marries another man.

⁴So, my brothers and sisters, you also died to the law through the body of Christ, that you might belong to another, to him who was raised from the dead, in order that we might bear fruit for God. ⁵For when we were in the realm of the flesh,^b the sinful passions aroused by the law were at work in us, so that we bore fruit for death. ⁶But now, by dying to what once bound us, we have been released from the law so that we serve in the new way of the Spirit, and not in the old way of the written code.

The Law and Sin

⁷What shall we say, then? Is the law sinful? Certainly not! Nevertheless, I would not have known what sin was had it not been for the law. For I would not have known what coveting really was if the law had not said, "You shall not covet."^c ⁸But sin, seizing the opportunity afforded by the commandment, produced in me every kind of coveting. For apart from the law, sin was dead. ⁹Once I was alive apart from the law; but when the commandment came, sin sprang to life and I died. ¹⁰I found that the very commandment that was intended to bring life actually brought death. ¹¹For sin, seizing the opportunity afforded by the commandment, de-

---

^a 23 Or *through*   ^b 5 In contexts like this, the Greek word for *flesh* (*sarx*) refers to the sinful state of human beings, often presented as a power in opposition to the Spirit.
^c 7 Exodus 20:17; Deut. 5:21

---

which involves union with God under his reign. Paul describes eternal life as a result of sanctification and submission to God not because he denies it occurring in the present, but because he is focusing on the life that will begin at Christ's return. Eternal life contrasts with death in v. 21 (see v. 16 and note; compare Da 12:1–2 and note). Many Greeks believed that only the gods were immortal. For this reason, some Greeks were attracted to mystery cults, which promised union with a god and immortality through the completion of secret rituals. Paul affirmed the immortal nature of God alone (Ro 1:23) — and by extension Christ and the Holy Spirit — and the mortality of people (5:12). In contrast to secret rituals, the gospel announces that faith in Christ Jesus brings union with God and eternal life.

6:23 wages of sin is death Paul asserts that death is the wage paid to the person who serves sin. See note on v. 16. **gift of God is eternal life** In contrast to the "wages" earned through sin (which lead to death), no person can earn eternal life. It is a gift freely given according to God's prerogative. See 5:15–16.

7:1–25 In ch. 6, Paul asserts that believers are no longer under law, but under grace. In this chapter, Paul clarifies that statement with an analogy from marriage. He praises the law for its intended purpose — to identify sin — but also dismisses it as a solution for sin.

7:1 those who know the law Refers primarily to Jewish Christians, but also might include Gentile Christians who knew the Law of Moses from the synagogue. **only as long as that person lives** Here Paul introduces the key concept to his argument in vv. 1–6: Only death can terminate the bond between a person and the law. In vv. 2–3, Paul illustrates this principle using a marriage analogy.
7:4 died to the law Those who have participated in the death of Christ experience freedom from the law (6:4). **we might bear fruit for God** Refers to good deeds that come from union with Christ (6:22).
7:5 in the realm of the flesh Refers to existence apart from Christ, under the control of sin. Paul uses the Greek

word *sarx*, often translated "flesh," to refer to mortal human existence; Paul often contrasts it with the spiritual freedom found in Christ. **aroused by the law** The law identified sin and established boundaries for moral conduct — which ironically, because of people's propensity to sin, resulted in more transgressions. **we bore fruit for death** Refers to sinful deeds that result in death.
7:6 the written code Refers to the Law of Moses.

7:7–12 Anticipating an objection to his argument in vv. 1–6, Paul clarifies the relationship between the law and sin. Paul maintains that the law itself is not sinful, nor is it the source of sin. Instead, the law played a positive role by introducing knowledge of sin.

7:7 I would not have known There are several interpretations of Paul's first-person language in vv. 7–25. Many throughout church history have read the passage straightforwardly as an autobiographical account of Paul's struggles with the law and sin, while others think the passage refers to Adam, Israel or the deep human struggle with sinful nature. Additionally, Paul might be describing the struggle of either a non-believer attempting to keep the law or a believer who is freed from the law but continues to contend with sin. See vv. 13–25 and note. **had it not been for the law** The law sets moral boundaries that otherwise would be unknown.
7:9 Once I was alive apart from the law Paul describes a figurative existence in which a person is unaware of sin and undisturbed by condemnation from the law. This might refer to Paul's own experience before becoming a Christian or to the experience of Israel before receiving the law at Mount Sinai. **I died** Once the law identified sin, the person recognized sin — as well as the guilt and condemnation that it brings.
7:10 intended to bring life Paul does not blame the law for death; it was intended to bring life by revealing God's will for humanity. However, sin took advantage of human weakness through the law.
7:11 deceived Sin turned God's commandments, which should have been an occasion for good, into an occasion for death.

ceived me, and through the commandment put me to death. ¹²So then, the law is holy, and the commandment is holy, righteous and good.

¹³Did that which is good, then, become death to me? By no means! Nevertheless, in order that sin might be recognized as sin, it used what is good to bring about my death, so that through the commandment sin might become utterly sinful. ¹⁴We know that the law is spiritual; but I am unspiritual, sold as a slave to sin. ¹⁵I do not understand what I do. For what I want to do I do not do, but what I hate I do. ¹⁶And if I do what I do not want to do, I agree that the law is good. ¹⁷As it is, it is no longer I myself who do it, but it is sin living in me. ¹⁸For I know that good itself does not dwell in me, that is, in my sinful nature.ᵃ For I have the desire to do what is good, but I cannot carry it out. ¹⁹For I do not do the good I want to do, but the evil I do not want to do — this I keep on doing. ²⁰Now if I do what I do not want to do, it is no longer I who do it, but it is sin living in me that does it.

²¹So I find this law at work: Although I want to do good, evil is right there with me. ²²For in my inner being I delight in God's law; ²³but I see another law at work in me, waging war against the law of my mind and making me a prisoner of the law of sin at work within me. ²⁴What a wretched man I am! Who will rescue me from this body that is subject to death? ²⁵Thanks be to God, who delivers me through Jesus Christ our Lord!

So then, I myself in my mind am a slave to God's law, but in my sinful natureᵇ a slave to the law of sin.

Life Through the Spirit

8 Therefore, there is now no condemnation for those who are in Christ Jesus, ²because through Christ Jesus the law of the Spirit who gives life has set youᶜ free from the law of sin and death. ³For what the law was powerless to do because it was weakened by the flesh,ᵈ God did by sending his own Son in the likeness of sinful flesh to be a sin offering.ᵉ And so he condemned sin in the flesh, ⁴in order that the righteous requirement of the law might be fully met in us, who do not live according to the flesh but according to the Spirit.

⁵Those who live according to the flesh have their minds set on what the flesh desires; but those who live in accordance with the Spirit have

ᵃ 18 Or my flesh   ᵇ 25 Or in the flesh   ᶜ 2 The Greek is singular; some manuscripts me   ᵈ 3 In contexts like this, the Greek word for flesh (sarx) refers to the sinful state of human beings, often presented as a power in opposition to the Spirit; also in verses 4-13.   ᵉ 3 Or flesh, for sin

7:12 law is holy Paul praises the law as a good and holy gift from God, since it requires what is right for humanity. He rejects any argument that blames the law as the cause of human sin.

7:13–25 The focus of this passage is the law and human weakness, which magnified the problem of sin. Paul describes either a non-Christian who is under the law or a Christian struggling with sin. If the passage concerns an unbeliever, then it reflects the struggle to do what is good while living under the power of sin and without God's Spirit (vv. 18–19). If it concerns a believer, then it depicts the Christian who, despite the Spirit's indwelling presence, struggles to live according to righteousness because of the powers of sin and death (vv. 24–25; 8:10–11).

7:13 sin might become utterly sinful The commandment exposed sin as rebellion against God.
7:14 spiritual The Greek word used here, pneumatikos, is probably meant to indicate that the law came from God and reveals his character. **unspiritual** The Greek word used here, sarkinos, refers to the weakness that all people share: They are susceptible to sin and death. **sold as a slave to sin** See note on 6:16.
7:16 I agree that the law is good While the inability to do what is righteous and holy highlights humanity's fallen nature, it also demonstrates the goodness of the law in contrast to the power of sin.
7:17 no longer I myself who do it Reflects sin's power to enslave and control people (v. 14). **sin living in me** Paul does not deny personal responsibility for sinful behavior, but he recognizes that sin is an indwelling power. In ch. 8, Paul declares that believers are filled with God's Spirit — the antidote for sin.
7:21 law The Greek word used here, nomos, could refer to the fundamental pattern of sin's oppressive influence. Normally, this word refers to the Jewish law.

7:22 God's law Refers to the Law of Moses.
7:23 another law Compare v. 21.
7:25 Thanks be to God Paul expresses gratitude for the provision of Jesus Christ.

8:1–17 In this chapter, Paul presents God's solution to humanity's enslavement to sin — the Holy Spirit, who empowers believers to overcome the limitations of the flesh and live in righteousness.

8:1 condemnation Refers to the penalty for sin, which is separation from God. Paul's assertion that there is no condemnation for believers summarizes the primary message of this chapter: Christ has brought life to those who deserved death and freedom to those who were guilty under the law.
8:2 law of the Spirit who gives life Refers to the authority of the Holy Spirit, who gives life and empowers believers to do what is right.
8:3 what the law was powerless to do The law could not help a person overcome sin or escape the penalty for sin (see 3:20; 7:8,11). **in the likeness of sinful flesh** Jesus became human and experienced the weakness and vulnerability of human nature to sin, yet he did not sin. On the Greek term sarx (often translated "flesh"), see note on 7:5. **And so he condemned sin** Through Christ's sacrificial death, God carried out his judgment upon sin, thereby breaking its power to control (Gal 1:4; 1Pe 3:18). **in the flesh** Refers to Jesus' physical body.
8:4 might be fully met Through the death of Christ, believers receive righteousness; through the Spirit, they are empowered to obey the essence of the law — to love (Ro 5:8; 13:8–10). **who do not live according to the flesh but according to the Spirit** Throughout this section, Paul contrasts two ways of living: The flesh leads people to oppose God, so they are unable to obey him; the Spirit dwells within believers and empowers them to do God's will.

their minds set on what the Spirit desires. [6]The mind governed by the flesh is death, but the mind governed by the Spirit is life and peace. [7]The mind governed by the flesh is hostile to God; it does not submit to God's law, nor can it do so. [8]Those who are in the realm of the flesh cannot please God.

[9]You, however, are not in the realm of the flesh but are in the realm of the Spirit, if indeed the Spirit of God lives in you. And if anyone does not have the Spirit of Christ, they do not belong to Christ. [10]But if Christ is in you, then even though your body is subject to death because of sin, the Spirit gives life[a] because of righteousness. [11]And if the Spirit of him who raised Jesus from the dead is living in you, he who raised Christ from the dead will also give life to your mortal bodies because of[b] his Spirit who lives in you.

[12]Therefore, brothers and sisters, we have an obligation — but it is not to the flesh, to live according to it. [13]For if you live according to the flesh, you will die; but if by the Spirit you put to death the misdeeds of the body, you will live.

[14]For those who are led by the Spirit of God are the children of God. [15]The Spirit you received does not make you slaves, so that you live in fear again; rather, the Spirit you received brought about your adoption to sonship.[c] And by him we cry, "Abba,[d] Father." [16]The Spirit himself testifies with our spirit that we are God's children. [17]Now if we are children, then we are heirs — heirs of God and co-heirs with Christ, if indeed we share in his sufferings in order that we may also share in his glory.

Present Suffering and Future Glory

[18]I consider that our present sufferings are not worth comparing with the glory that will be revealed in us. [19]For the creation waits in eager expectation for the children of God to be revealed. [20]For the creation was subjected to frustration, not by its own choice, but by the will of the one who subjected it, in hope [21]that[e] the creation itself will be liberated from its bondage to decay and brought into the freedom and glory of the children of God.

[22]We know that the whole creation has been groaning as in the pains of childbirth right up to the present time. [23]Not only so, but we ourselves, who have the firstfruits of the Spirit, groan inwardly as we wait eagerly for our adoption to sonship, the redemption of our bodies. [24]For in this hope we were saved. But hope that is seen is no hope at all. Who hopes for what they already have? [25]But if we hope for what we do not yet have, we wait for it patiently.

[26]In the same way, the Spirit helps us in our weakness. We do not know what we ought to pray for, but the Spirit himself intercedes for us through wordless groans. [27]And he who searches our hearts knows the mind of the Spirit, because the Spirit intercedes for God's people in accordance with the will of God.

[a] 10 Or you, your body is dead because of sin, yet your spirit is alive   [b] 11 Some manuscripts bodies through
[c] 15 The Greek word for adoption to sonship is a term referring to the full legal standing of an adopted male heir in Roman culture; also in verse 23.   [d] 15 Aramaic for father
[e] 20,21 Or subjected it in hope. [21]For

8:6 death Refers to estrangement from God. **peace** Refers to reconciliation with God (compare 5:1).

8:7 submit to God's law This could refer to the Law of Moses or to God's will in general.

8:9 the Spirit of Christ Paul is talking about the same Spirit, but he changes his language here to identify Jesus with the Spirit of God (compare Php 1:19; Gal 4:6; 1Pe 1:11).

8:10 righteousness See note on Ro 1:17.

8:11 will also give life Refers to the bodily resurrection. See 1:4 and note.

8:12 an obligation — but it is not to the flesh Because of the indwelling Spirit, Paul declares that believers are no longer subject to the control of the flesh. They have been transferred from the realm of the flesh to the realm of the Spirit.

8:14 children of God The Greek text associates OT ideas of divine sonship with the church. Believers become part of God's family by adoption (v. 15), both on earth and upon glorification in the coming age.

8:15 does not make you slaves Alludes to enslavement to sin (compare Ro 6:6,16–22). **Abba, Father** The Aramaic word abba means "father." Both here and in Gal 4:6 Paul presents the phrase as an expression enabled by the Spirit to affirm the believer's place in the family of God. Paul and other Christians likely used the phrase because it reflected Jesus' own way of talking to God (see Mk 14:36 and note).

8:17 co-heirs with Christ Indicates that believers share in the same privileges as Christ. **if indeed we share in**

his sufferings Probably refers to persecution, but may include general hardship.

8:18–30 In this passage, Paul addresses the tension between present suffering and the hope of future glory, explaining why the redemption of the children of God and creation itself is only partially fulfilled.

8:18 glory The Greek word used here, doxa, points to the transformation of the body through resurrection (see 1Co 15:42–44; Col 3:4).

8:19 for the children of God to be revealed Refers to the final unveiling of God's family of glorified humanity — those glorified through faith in Christ.

8:20 subjected to frustration Sin affected more than humanity's relationship to God; creation itself was spoiled and suffered decay (Ro 8:21). **the one who subjected it** Usually identified as God, acting in response to the sin of Adam and Eve (compare Ge 3:17–19).

8:22 been groaning as in the pains of childbirth The created order is in turmoil. Like God's people, it is longing for Christ's return, when he will liberate the world from death and decay (see Rev 21:1 and note). This restoration is a prominent theme of the OT prophets (compare Isa 35:1–10).

8:23 firstfruits An OT expression referring to the first part of the harvest, which God designated for himself and his priests (Lev 23:10; Dt 18:4; see note on Lev 2:12). Here, its usage refers to God's initial transformative work in his people, which will result in resurrection glory.

8:24 in this hope In the NT, hope is not wishful think-

[28] And we know that in all things God works for the good of those who love him, who[a] have been called according to his purpose. [29] For those God foreknew he also predestined to be conformed to the image of his Son, that he might be the firstborn among many brothers and sisters. [30] And those he predestined, he also called; those he called, he also justified; those he justified, he also glorified.

More Than Conquerors

[31] What, then, shall we say in response to these things? If God is for us, who can be against us? [32] He who did not spare his own Son, but gave him up for us all—how will he not also, along with him, graciously give us all things? [33] Who will bring any charge against those whom God has chosen? It is God who justifies. [34] Who then is the one who condemns? No one. Christ Jesus who died—more than that, who was raised to life—is at the right hand of God and is also interceding for us. [35] Who shall separate us from the love of Christ? Shall trouble or hardship or persecution or famine or nakedness or danger or sword? [36] As it is written:

"For your sake we face death all day long;
    we are considered as sheep to be
        slaughtered."[b]

[37] No, in all these things we are more than conquerors through him who loved us. [38] For I am convinced that neither death nor life, neither angels nor demons,[c] neither the present nor the future, nor any powers, [39] neither height nor depth, nor anything else in all creation, will be able to separate us from the love of God that is in Christ Jesus our Lord.

Paul's Anguish Over Israel

9 I speak the truth in Christ—I am not lying, my conscience confirms it through the Holy Spirit— [2] I have great sorrow and unceasing anguish in my heart. [3] For I could wish that I myself were cursed and cut off from Christ for the sake of my people, those of my own race, [4] the people of Israel. Theirs is the adoption to sonship; theirs the divine glory, the covenants, the receiving of the law, the temple worship and the promises. [5] Theirs are the patriarchs, and from them is traced the human ancestry of the Messiah, who is God over all, forever praised![d] Amen.

---

[a] 28 Or *that all things work together for good to those who love God, who; or that in all things God works together with those who love him to bring about what is good—with those who love him to bring about what is good—with those who*
[b] 36 Psalm 44:22   [c] 38 Or *nor heavenly rulers*
[d] 5 Or *Messiah, who is over all. God be forever praised! Or Messiah. God who is over all be forever praised!*

---

ing; it is a confident expectation in the fulfillment of God's promises.

8:27 he who searches our hearts An expression of God's omniscience (see Ac 1:24; 2:23; 15:8). Paul tells the believers that God continues to work on their behalf, especially when they do not know what to pray for.

8:28 in all things God works for the good Paul has been discussing the perceived tension between human experience and divine promise. He assures believers that God is working for the ultimate good. Despite the Greek text's passive phrasing, the agent of the action must be God himself.

8:29 foreknew Paul is most likely drawing on OT language that describes Yahweh's choice of Israel as his covenant people. In Ge 18:19, Yahweh uses the Hebrew word for "know" to indicate his choice of Abraham (compare Am 3:2; Jer 1:5). **predestined** The Greek verb used here, *proorizō*, refers to choosing or deciding beforehand. Salvation ultimately depends on God's choice. Compare note on Ro 9:11. **conformed to the image of his Son** Refers to sanctification, the process by which a believer grows to be more like Christ.

8:30 justified Refers to being set right or declared righteous by God (3:20,24). **glorified** Paul's chain of verbs culminates in glorification, tying this section back to its starting point in v. 18 and emphasizing that the hoped for future glory is just as certain as the already evident work of calling and justification.

8:31–39 Paul ends this chapter by emphasizing how believers can look forward to Christ's ultimate victory over earthly suffering and supernatural oppression.

8:32 will he not also, along with him, graciously give us all things Underscores the future inheritance of believers as children of God and co-heirs with Christ (v. 17).

8:33 who justifies In legal contexts, the Greek word used here, *dikaioō*, refers to acquitting or vindicating.

8:34 who condemns Believers are not subject to condemnation (v. 1). **right hand of God** A position of honor and authority.

8:36 we are considered as sheep to be slaughtered Paul quotes Ps 44:22 to point out that God's people have always encountered opposition.

8:38 angels nor demons Both of the Greek terms used here (*angelos, archē*) commonly refer to unseen divine beings. **powers** The Greek word used here, *dynamis*, can describe supernatural forces (Heb 6:5; 1Pe 3:22).

9:1–13 Paul addresses the implications of God's fulfillment of his promises among non-Jewish people (the Gentiles) and Israel's unbelief. Paul rejects the possibility that Israel's denial of the gospel means that God's promises have failed and that God is therefore unjust (Ro 9:6–11).

9:2 anguish in my heart Despite his role as apostle to the Gentiles (11:13), Paul is still grieved that his fellow Jews, God's chosen people through his promises to Abraham, have not widely accepted Jesus as their Messiah.

9:3 I could wish that I myself were cursed and cut off Paul echoes Moses' prayer in Ex 32:32, showing solidarity with his people by wishing to share in their punishment or take the punishment for them.

9:4 people of Israel Paul describes six benefits or privileges that rightfully belonged to Israel as God's chosen people: joining God's family (adoption), experiencing his presence (glory), entering into relationship with him (covenants), receiving his revelation (law), worshiping at his temple (service) and inheriting his blessings (promises).

9:5 patriarchs Refers to Abraham, Isaac and Jacob.

God's Sovereign Choice

⁶It is not as though God's word had failed. For not all who are descended from Israel are Israel. ⁷Nor because they are his descendants are they all Abraham's children. On the contrary, "It is through Isaac that your offspring will be reckoned."ᵃ ⁸In other words, it is not the children by physical descent who are God's children, but it is the children of the promise who are regarded as Abraham's offspring. ⁹For this was how the promise was stated: "At the appointed time I will return, and Sarah will have a son."ᵇ

¹⁰Not only that, but Rebekah's children were conceived at the same time by our father Isaac. ¹¹Yet, before the twins were born or had done anything good or bad—in order that God's purpose in election might stand: ¹²not by works but by him who calls—she was told, "The older will serve the younger."ᶜ ¹³Just as it is written: "Jacob I loved, but Esau I hated."ᵈ

¹⁴What then shall we say? Is God unjust? Not at all! ¹⁵For he says to Moses,

"I will have mercy on whom I have mercy,
  and I will have compassion on whom I have
    compassion."ᵉ

¹⁶It does not, therefore, depend on human desire or effort, but on God's mercy. ¹⁷For Scripture says to Pharaoh: "I raised you up for this very purpose, that I might display my power in you and that my name might be proclaimed in all the earth."ᶠ ¹⁸Therefore God has mercy on whom he wants to have mercy, and he hardens whom he wants to harden.

¹⁹One of you will say to me: "Then why does God still blame us? For who is able to resist his will?" ²⁰But who are you, a human being, to talk back to God? "Shall what is formed say to the one who formed it, 'Why did you make me like this?'"ᵍ ²¹Does not the potter have the right to make out of the same lump of clay some pottery for special purposes and some for common use?

²²What if God, although choosing to show his wrath and make his power known, bore with great patience the objects of his wrath—prepared for destruction? ²³What if he did this to make the riches of his glory known to the objects of his mercy, whom he prepared in advance for glory— ²⁴even us, whom he also called, not only from the Jews but also from the Gentiles? ²⁵As he says in Hosea:

ᵃ 7 Gen. 21:12   ᵇ 9 Gen. 18:10,14   ᶜ 12 Gen. 25:23
ᵈ 13 Mal. 1:2,3   ᵉ 15 Exodus 33:19   ᶠ 17 Exodus 9:16
ᵍ 20 Isaiah 29:16; 45:9

9:6 God's word Refers to the promises God made to the patriarchs and Israel (see Ro 4:13–21). Paul addresses the implication that God's plan as revealed through Scripture had failed because ethnic Israel responded negatively to the fulfillment of his promises through Christ.
not all who are descended from Israel are Israel Many Jews appealed to their descent from Abraham as a symbol of their ongoing special relationship with God (compare Mt 3:9; Jn 8:39). Paul asserts that true membership in God's chosen people is based on faith, not physical ancestry.
9:7 Abraham's children Paul points out that God's choice of Israel followed the line of one chosen son, Isaac, instead of applying generally to all of Abraham's descendants. To underscore the point, he quotes Ge 21:12. **through Isaac** The son of promise born to Abraham through his wife, Sarah (Ge 21:1–7).
9:8 children of the promise Emphasizes that being included among the children of God depends on God's faithfulness to his promise, not a person's physical descent from Abraham.

9:10–13 Here, Paul continues to oppose the implication from Ro 9:6 that God had failed in his promises to Israel. Paul's primary defense comes from differentiating between an Israel based on ethnicity and an Israel based on God's choice. Both Jacob and Esau were natural descendants of Abraham through Isaac, but only Jacob was chosen by God to bear the promise of nationhood (see Ge 15:4–6). This event from Israel's national history serves as an explanation for the present situation.

9:11 before the twins were born Illustrates that God's selection of Jacob over Esau was not based on anything Jacob had done. **election** The Greek word used here, *eklogē*, refers to a choice or selection. Paul is referring to God's choice to have Jacob and his descendants bear the promise he had made to Abraham (Ge 12:1–2; 15:4–6).

Paul is emphasizing God's sovereign right as Creator to act free from any constraints imposed by human actions.
9:13 Jacob I loved, but Esau I hated Paul cites Mal 1:2–3 to summarize how God selected Jacob over Esau, even though both were sons of Isaac. See note on Ro 9:10–13.

9:14–33 Paul now discusses a potential objection to his previous point about Yahweh's election of Israel (vv. 10–13): He addresses whether God's seemingly arbitrary choice of Jacob over Esau, and now the Gentiles as his people, makes him unjust. In his explanation, Paul focuses on God's sovereignty and invokes several OT passages emphasizing Yahweh's authority over his creation.

9:15 I will have mercy on whom I have mercy Paul quotes Ex 33:19. In Exodus, both Israel and Pharaoh rebelled against God; consequently, they were subject to God's judgment. God would have been right to punish both parties, but he showed mercy to Israel.
9:17 I raised you up This quotation from Ex 9:16 demonstrates God's sovereignty for his redemptive purposes.
9:18 he hardens Refers to the hardening of Pharaoh's heart. See Ex 4:21 and note.
9:19 who is able to resist his will The objection expressed here highlights the central tension between divine sovereignty and human responsibility. There is tension between mercy and judgment being entirely dependent on God's will (Ro 9:18) and God holding people responsible for their sins (3:23). Paul addresses this difficulty in vv. 20–24, although he never attempts to resolve the fundamental tension. Instead, he maintains it, affirming both divine sovereignty (vv. 14–23) and human responsibility (9:30—10:21).
9:20 who are you, a human being Paul responds to the objection in v. 19 by emphasizing humanity's subordinate status in relation to God, the Creator.
9:21 potter The background of Paul's analogy in vv. 20–23 is found in the potter and clay metaphor

"I will call them 'my people' who are not my
people;
and I will call her 'my loved one' who is not
my loved one,"[a]

[26]and,

"In the very place where it was said to them,
'You are not my people,'
there they will be called 'children of the
living God.'"[b]

[27]Isaiah cries out concerning Israel:

"Though the number of the Israelites be like
the sand by the sea,
only the remnant will be saved.
[28]For the Lord will carry out
his sentence on earth with speed and
finality."[c]

[29]It is just as Isaiah said previously:

"Unless the Lord Almighty
had left us descendants,
we would have become like Sodom,
we would have been like Gomorrah."[d]

Israel's Unbelief

[30]What then shall we say? That the Gentiles,
who did not pursue righteousness, have obtained
it, a righteousness that is by faith; [31]but the people of Israel, who pursued the law as the way of
righteousness, have not attained their goal. [32]Why
not? Because they pursued it not by faith but as if
it were by works. They stumbled over the stumbling stone. [33]As it is written:

"See, I lay in Zion a stone that causes people
to stumble
and a rock that makes them fall,
and the one who believes in him will never
be put to shame."[e]

10 Brothers and sisters, my heart's desire and
prayer to God for the Israelites is that they
may be saved. [2]For I can testify about them that
they are zealous for God, but their zeal is not based
on knowledge. [3]Since they did not know the righteousness of God and sought to establish their
own, they did not submit to God's righteousness.
[4]Christ is the culmination of the law so that there
may be righteousness for everyone who believes.
[5]Moses writes this about the righteousness that
is by the law: "The person who does these things
will live by them."[f] [6]But the righteousness that is
by faith says: "Do not say in your heart, 'Who will

[a] 25 Hosea 2:23   [b] 26 Hosea 1:10   [c] 28 Isaiah 10:22,23 (see
Septuagint)   [d] 29 Isaiah 1:9   [e] 33 Isaiah 8:14; 28:16
[f] 5 Lev. 18:5

used by the prophets Isaiah and Jeremiah (e.g., Isa
45:9; 64:8; Jer 18:4–6).
9:22 objects of his wrath Paul pushes the boundaries
of his metaphor to make a rhetorical point. While it is
unlikely that a potter would make a pot just to destroy
it, the potter still has the right to do so if he wishes.
9:23 objects of his mercy In the previous verse, Paul
explains that God uses some vessels to demonstrate
his wrath, depending solely on his sovereign choice. In
the same way, God's choice of vessels of mercy rests
only on his decision to show mercy to them.
9:25 not my people Refers to the Gentiles. Paul cites
Hos 2:23 here. In the book of Hosea the people of Israel
had broken their covenant with God through idolatrous
practices; nevertheless, God showed them mercy and
promised to restore them as his people. Paul applies this
text to the Gentiles (non-Jewish people) because they, like
Israel, were separated from God's promises, but he still
showed them mercy and brought them into his people.
9:26 children of the living God A quotation of Hos
1:10. Compare Ro 8:14.
9:27 remnant will be saved Paul cites Isa
10:22–23. His point is that those who are Jewish should
not rely upon their race; it did not save those in Isaiah's
day, and it will not save them now. Only a remnant of
elect Israel would be saved.
9:29 become like Sodom Paul quotes Isa 1:9 in recognition of God's grace. Israel's idolatry required judgment,
but God did not annihilate them as he did Sodom and
Gomorrah (compare Ge 18:16—19:29).
9:30 obtained it Paul explains that non-Jewish people
attained righteousness even though they did not pursue
right standing before God—because righteousness
comes by faith, not works or the law.

9:33 Zion Refers to Jerusalem (see note on Isa 1:8). **a
stone that causes people to stumble** Paul's quotation
combines Isa 28:16 with 8:14. Drawing on OT imagery,
the stone or rock refers to Christ, whom most Jews rejected as the Messiah (Ps 118:22; compare 1Pe 2:4–8).

10:1–21 Paul's argument in this chapter builds directly
on his previous statements in Ro 9:30–33, expanding on
how Israel (meaning the Jewish people) failed to attain
righteousness (vv. 18,21).
10:1 they may be saved Paul desires that his fellow
Jews would put their faith in Christ.
10:2 zealous The Greek word used here, *zēlos*, refers
to an intense desire for something. In this context, Paul
suggests that his fellow Jews misdirected their zeal
because they did not recognize God's work.
10:3 righteousness of God Revealed in Jesus' life,
death and resurrection. See note on 1:17. **sought to
establish their own** Paul accuses his fellow Jews of pursuing right relationship with God through keeping the law.
10:4 the culmination The Greek word used here, *telos*,
often translated "end," could refer to a goal, result or
termination. Thus, Christ can be understood as the law's
fulfillment, in the sense that his death and resurrection
achieved God's purpose for the law.
10:5 person who does these things will live by them
Paul quotes Lev 18:5 to explain the relationship between
righteousness and the law. Righteousness that comes
from obeying the law requires a person to continue living by
the law. This orientation to the law excludes faith. Jews,
who sought righteousness from the law, would naturally
reason that those without the law (Gentiles) could not
obtain right relationship with God.
10:6 Who will ascend into heaven Paul quotes Dt 30:12

ascend into heaven?'"[a] (that is, to bring Christ down) [7]"or 'Who will descend into the deep?'"[b] (that is, to bring Christ up from the dead). [8]But what does it say? "The word is near you; it is in your mouth and in your heart,"[c] that is, the message concerning faith that we proclaim: [9]If you declare with your mouth, "Jesus is Lord," and believe in your heart that God raised him from the dead, you will be saved. [10]For it is with your heart that you believe and are justified, and it is with your mouth that you profess your faith and are saved. [11]As Scripture says, "Anyone who believes in him will never be put to shame."[d] [12]For there is no difference between Jew and Gentile — the same Lord is Lord of all and richly blesses all who call on him, [13]for, "Everyone who calls on the name of the Lord will be saved."[e]

[14]How, then, can they call on the one they have not believed in? And how can they believe in the one of whom they have not heard? And how can they hear without someone preaching to them? [15]And how can anyone preach unless they are sent? As it is written: "How beautiful are the feet of those who bring good news!"[f]

[16]But not all the Israelites accepted the good news. For Isaiah says, "Lord, who has believed our message?"[g] [17]Consequently, faith comes from hearing the message, and the message is heard through the word about Christ. [18]But I ask: Did they not hear? Of course they did:

"Their voice has gone out into all the earth,
their words to the ends of the world."[h]

[19]Again I ask: Did Israel not understand? First, Moses says,

"I will make you envious by those who are
not a nation;
I will make you angry by a nation that has
no understanding."[i]

[20]And Isaiah boldly says,

"I was found by those who did not seek me;
I revealed myself to those who did not ask
for me."[j]

[21]But concerning Israel he says,

"All day long I have held out my hands
to a disobedient and obstinate people."[k]

The Remnant of Israel

11 I ask then: Did God reject his people? By no means! I am an Israelite myself, a descendant of Abraham, from the tribe of Benjamin. [2]God did not reject his people, whom he foreknew. Don't you know what Scripture says in the passage about Elijah — how he appealed to God against Israel: [3]"Lord, they have killed your prophets and torn down your altars; I am the only one left, and they are trying to kill me"[l]? [4]And what was God's answer to him? "I have reserved for myself seven thousand who have not bowed the knee to Baal."[m]

---

[a] 6 Deut. 30:12   [b] 7 Deut. 30:13   [c] 8 Deut. 30:14
[d] 11 Isaiah 28:16 (see Septuagint)   [e] 13 Joel 2:32
[f] 15 Isaiah 52:7   [g] 16 Isaiah 53:1   [h] 18 Psalm 19:4
[i] 19 Deut. 32:21   [j] 20 Isaiah 65:1   [k] 21 Isaiah 65:2
[l] 3 1 Kings 19:10,14   [m] 4 1 Kings 19:18

---

to warn his audience about being ignorant regarding the nature of righteousness (compare Ro 10:2–3).
10:7 deep Refers to the place of the dead, the underworld.
10:8 The word is near you Paul cites Dt 30:14 to affirm the accessibility of the word of faith. This word is especially near because the Spirit wrote it upon the hearts and minds of believers (Jer 31:33; 2Co 3:3).
10:9 you declare with your mouth, "Jesus is Lord" Describes an outward expression of inward trust. Paul does not regard believing in the heart and confessing with the mouth as separate activities, but as parts of a singular expression of faith in Jesus' lordship.
10:10 justified Here the term is close in meaning to salvation. See note on Ro 1:17.
10:11 Anyone who believes in him Paul again quotes from Isa 28:16, adding the Greek word *pas*, meaning "everyone" or "all," to demonstrate that this promise applies to both Jewish and non-Jewish people (compare Ro 9:33).
10:13 Everyone who calls on Paul quotes Joel 2:32.
10:15 those who bring good news Paul quotes Isa 52:7 to emphasize the importance of spreading the gospel.
10:16 who has believed our message A quotation from Isa 53:1, where the report is about the suffering servant.
10:17 faith comes from hearing Righteousness comes by faith, and faith comes by hearing the gospel message. At the same time for Paul, faith demands obedience to the gospel (Ro 10:16).

10:18 Their voice has gone out Paul quotes Ps 19:4.
10:19 not a nation Although the Israelites rejected the gospel message, God turned their disobedience into a blessing for non-Israelites (compare Ac 13:46–47). In doing so, he provoked the rest of unbelieving Israel to jealousy so that they might turn to Christ.

10:20–21 In these verses, Paul quotes Isa 65:1–2 to describe the paradoxical nature of salvation. Non-Jewish people did not seek God, yet they found him; the Jews were God's chosen people, yet they rejected him.

11:1–12 Here, Paul acknowledges that Israel's rejection of Christ was part of God's sovereign plan to extend salvation to the Gentiles (non-Jewish people), but he insists that God is not yet finished with Israel as his chosen people.

11:1 Did God reject his people Despite present appearances, Israel still plays a role in God's plan of salvation, and his promises to Israel have not been invalidated.
from the tribe of Benjamin Paul emphasizes his own Jewish lineage as proof that at least some within ethnic Israel will be saved (compare Ro 9:27).
11:2 foreknew Compare Ro 8:29.
11:3 I am the only one left Paul quotes Elijah (from 1Ki 19:10,14), who thought he was Yahweh's last faithful servant.
11:4 I have reserved for myself Paul quotes 1Ki 19:18, God's reply to Elijah indicating the presence of a faithful remnant. **Baal** The Canaanite storm-god.

⁵So too, at the present time there is a remnant chosen by grace. ⁶And if by grace, then it cannot be based on works; if it were, grace would no longer be grace.

⁷What then? What the people of Israel sought so earnestly they did not obtain. The elect among them did, but the others were hardened, ⁸as it is written:

"God gave them a spirit of stupor,
  eyes that could not see
  and ears that could not hear,
to this very day."ᵃ

⁹And David says:

"May their table become a snare and a trap,
  a stumbling block and a retribution for them.
¹⁰ May their eyes be darkened so they cannot see,
  and their backs be bent forever."ᵇ

Ingrafted Branches

¹¹Again I ask: Did they stumble so as to fall beyond recovery? Not at all! Rather, because of their transgression, salvation has come to the Gentiles to make Israel envious. ¹²But if their transgression means riches for the world, and their loss means riches for the Gentiles, how much greater riches will their full inclusion bring!

¹³I am talking to you Gentiles. Inasmuch as I am the apostle to the Gentiles, I take pride in my ministry ¹⁴in the hope that I may somehow arouse my own people to envy and save some of them. ¹⁵For if their rejection brought reconciliation to the world, what will their acceptance be but life from the dead? ¹⁶If the part of the dough offered as firstfruits is holy, then the whole batch is holy; if the root is holy, so are the branches.

¹⁷If some of the branches have been broken off, and you, though a wild olive shoot, have been grafted in among the others and now share in the nourishing sap from the olive root, ¹⁸do not consider yourself to be superior to those other branches. If you do, consider this: You do not support the root, but the root supports you. ¹⁹You will say then, "Branches were broken off so that I could be grafted in." ²⁰Granted. But they were broken off because of unbelief, and you stand by faith. Do not be arrogant, but tremble. ²¹For if God did not spare the natural branches, he will not spare you either.

²²Consider therefore the kindness and sternness of God: sternness to those who fell, but kindness to you, provided that you continue in his kindness. Otherwise, you also will be cut off. ²³And if they do not persist in unbelief, they will be grafted in, for God is able to graft them in again.

ᵃ 8 Deut. 29:4; Isaiah 29:10   ᵇ 10 Psalm 69:22,23

11:5 a remnant Refers to a small number of people who remain faithful to God despite the unfaithfulness of others around them. In Romans, the remnant is composed of Jews who have put their faith in Christ.

11:7 elect Identifies those who are part of God's people due to his sovereign choice. Compare Ro 9:10–13.

11:8 God gave them a spirit of stupor Paul combines three partial quotations (Dt 29:4; Isa 29:10; 6:9). Each one comments on the Israelites' failure to recognize God's work among them.

11:9 a stumbling block In Ro 11:9–10, Paul quotes Ps 69:22–23, implying that the Jews stumbled over Christ and failed to recognize him as the Messiah (compare Ro 9:33).

11:11 Did they stumble so as to fall beyond recovery Israel is not past the point of redemption. **because of their transgression** Refers to Israel's rejection of Christ.

11:12 their full inclusion The Greek word used here, *plērōma*, might refer to the full number of Jews who turn to Christ. Alternatively, it could indicate the fullness of blessing that Jews and Gentiles experience together as one people of God.

11:13–24 Paul argues that Israel's rejection of Jesus as Messiah ultimately leads to reconciliation between God and the entire world. The passage uses the metaphor of an olive tree to explain how the Gentiles (non-Jewish people) have been included in God's plan of salvation.

11:14 I may somehow arouse my own people to envy Paul hopes that the work of salvation among the Gentiles might inspire the Jews to accept Jesus as Messiah.

11:15 reconciliation Compare 5:10 and note; 5:11 and note. **the world** Refers to Gentiles. **life from the dead** Probably refers to the final resurrection of believers.

11:16 firstfruits See note on 8:23. Here, the metaphor could refer to Israel's patriarchs (Abraham, Isaac, Jacob) or to the early church (both Gentiles and believing Jews). **whole batch** This might symbolize all Israel or all who will be saved. **root** Most likely represents Abraham—the foundational figure in God's plan of salvation (Ge 12:3). **branches** Refers to all who become children of God, both the natural descendants of Abraham and the Gentiles adopted by faith.

11:17 the branches have been broken off Refers to ethnic Jews who did not accept Jesus. **a wild olive shoot** Refers to Gentile believers. Paul's metaphor echoes Jesus' teaching about the true vine and the branches (see Jn 15:1–17 and note). In Jn 15, the branches that did not produce fruit were pruned to make way for abundant branches. According to Paul's metaphor, the olive tree's natural (but unfruitful) branches are broken off and replaced with wild branches. The symbolism of depicting Israel as an olive tree planted by God likely draws from Jer 11:16 or Hos 14:6. **have been grafted in among the others** Gentiles who put faith in Christ became part of God's people along with Jewish Christians.

11:18 do not consider yourself to be superior The Gentile Christians should not claim superiority over the Jewish origins of their faith. **branches** Refers in this case to all Jews, regardless of whether they have faith in Christ.

11:21 natural branches Refers to ethnic Israel. **he will not spare you either** A warning to Gentile believers to remain faithful and humble in light of God's grace.

11:23 God is able to graft them in again Although many ethnic Jews were cut off due to their unbelief, God still could reincorporate them.

²⁴After all, if you were cut out of an olive tree that is wild by nature, and contrary to nature were grafted into a cultivated olive tree, how much more readily will these, the natural branches, be grafted into their own olive tree!

All Israel Will Be Saved

²⁵I do not want you to be ignorant of this mystery, brothers and sisters, so that you may not be conceited: Israel has experienced a hardening in part until the full number of the Gentiles has come in, ²⁶and in this way*ᵃ* all Israel will be saved. As it is written:

"The deliverer will come from Zion;
    he will turn godlessness away from Jacob.
²⁷ And this is*ᵇ* my covenant with them
    when I take away their sins."*ᶜ*

²⁸As far as the gospel is concerned, they are enemies for your sake; but as far as election is concerned, they are loved on account of the patriarchs, ²⁹for God's gifts and his call are irrevocable. ³⁰Just as you who were at one time disobedient to God have now received mercy as a result of their disobedience, ³¹so they too have now become disobedient in order that they too may now*ᵈ* receive

mercy as a result of God's mercy to you. ³²For God has bound everyone over to disobedience so that he may have mercy on them all.

Doxology

³³Oh, the depth of the riches of the wisdom
        and*ᵉ* knowledge of God!
    How unsearchable his judgments,
        and his paths beyond tracing out!
³⁴ "Who has known the mind of the Lord?
        Or who has been his counselor?"*ᶠ*
³⁵ "Who has ever given to God,
        that God should repay them?"*ᵍ*
³⁶ For from him and through him and for him
        are all things.
    To him be the glory forever! Amen.

A Living Sacrifice

12 Therefore, I urge you, brothers and sisters, in view of God's mercy, to offer your bodies as a living sacrifice, holy and pleasing to

ᵃ 26 Or and so   ᵇ 27 Or will be   ᶜ 27 Isaiah 59:20,21; 27:9 (see Septuagint); Jer. 31:33,34   ᵈ 31 Some manuscripts do not have now.   ᵉ 33 Or riches and the wisdom and the   ᶠ 34 Isaiah 40:13   ᵍ 35 Job 41:11

11:25–32 Paul ends his discussion of Israel's place within God's redemptive plan by looking ahead to the future restoration of all Israel (Ro 11:26). Earlier, Paul alluded to the salvation of a remnant of Israel (9:27; 11:5) and a hardening of the rest (v. 7). Here, he explains that Israel's hardening is only partial and will endure only until the full number of Gentiles are saved (v. 25).

11:25 mystery In this context, this term probably refers to three difficult issues that Paul discusses in the passage: Israel's partial hardening, the inclusion of the Gentiles as part of God's people, and Israel's future role in God's plan of salvation. Paul hopes that the Gentile Christians will not become proud or boastful of their inclusion into the people of God. **full number of the Gentiles** Likely alludes to predictions that one day all nations will worship Yahweh (e.g., Isa 2:2–4; Zec 14:16–17; Mt 28:19–20). This also could refer to the completion of the mission to reach all people with the gospel. Paul viewed his ministry to the Gentiles (non-Jewish people) as integral to the fulfillment of this plan (Ro 15:24,28). **11:26 all Israel** This may refer to the nation of Israel proper—whether all of Abraham's natural descendants, or only the elect individuals within ethnic Israel. Alternatively, it could refer to Israel as symbolic of God's elect—all who are now part of God's people (both Jews and Gentiles). Paul's meaning here is widely disputed. "All Israel" may include all who had faith like Abraham prior to Jesus' coming, or Paul could be looking ahead to a future conversion when the entire nation of Israel accepts Jesus as Messiah. "All Israel" also could be understood as a symbolic group (of Jews and Gentiles), since Paul envisions all of God's elect as part of a single tree (v. 17). **deliverer will come** A quotation from Isa 59:20. While this passage originally refers to Yahweh, Paul seems to apply it to Christ (compare 1Th 1:10). See the table "Jesus' Fulfillment of OT Prophecy" on

p. 1573. **Zion** Refers to Jerusalem. Here, it might point to the heavenly Jerusalem from where Christ will return as deliverer (compare 1Th 1:10). **Jacob** Refers to Israel.
11:27 this is my covenant A quotation from Isa 59:21 (compare Isa 27:9). In the larger context of Isaiah, the covenant is mediated by the suffering servant (Isa 52:13—53:12). Jesus is the fulfillment of this prophecy, acting as the intercessor between God and humanity.
11:28 election See note on Ro 9:11. **on account of the patriarchs** A reference to the patriarchs, whom God chose to bear his promises. See 9:1–13.
11:29 God's gifts and his call Refers to privileges granted to Israel (9:4).
11:30 as a result of their disobedience Refers to Israel's rejection of Jesus.
11:32 God has bound everyone God allowed unfaithfulness—to which he responds in mercy (compare 3:23–25).

11:33–36 Paul presents a doxology about God's wisdom using two quotations from the OT (Isa 40:13; Job 41:11). Both quotations celebrate God's exalted status and wisdom over his creatures.

12:1–21 Romans 12 begins a section of practical teaching that brings the body of the letter to a close (12:1—15:13). Paul's letters often follow this pattern of doctrinal teaching followed by practical instruction aimed at helping believers live out their faith in Christ.
    In this passage, Paul discusses the individual's responsibility for worship and personal transformation (vv. 1–2), the variety of spiritual gifts endowed to the church (vv. 3–8) and the primacy of unconditional love over all other action (vv. 9–21).

12:1 Therefore Indicates a key transition in the letter. What follows appears in light of the preceding content of 1:18—11:36. **God's mercy** Refers to the undeserved

God—this is your true and proper worship. [2]Do not conform to the pattern of this world, but be transformed by the renewing of your mind. Then you will be able to test and approve what God's will is—his good, pleasing and perfect will.

Humble Service in the Body of Christ

[3]For by the grace given me I say to every one of you: Do not think of yourself more highly than you ought, but rather think of yourself with sober judgment, in accordance with the faith God has distributed to each of you. [4]For just as each of us has one body with many members, and these members do not all have the same function, [5]so in Christ we, though many, form one body, and each member belongs to all the others. [6]We have different gifts, according to the grace given to each of us. If your gift is prophesying, then prophesy in accordance with your[a] faith; [7]if it is serving, then serve; if it is teaching, then teach; [8]if it is to encourage, then give encouragement; if it is giving, then give generously; if it is to lead,[b] do it diligently; if it is to show mercy, do it cheerfully.

Love in Action

[9]Love must be sincere. Hate what is evil; cling to what is good. [10]Be devoted to one another in love. Honor one another above yourselves. [11]Never be lacking in zeal, but keep your spiritual fervor, serving the Lord. [12]Be joyful in hope, patient in affliction, faithful in prayer. [13]Share with the Lord's people who are in need. Practice hospitality.

[14]Bless those who persecute you; bless and do not curse. [15]Rejoice with those who rejoice; mourn with those who mourn. [16]Live in harmony with one another. Do not be proud, but be willing to associate with people of low position.[c] Do not be conceited.

[17]Do not repay anyone evil for evil. Be careful to do what is right in the eyes of everyone. [18]If it is possible, as far as it depends on you, live at peace with everyone. [19]Do not take revenge, my dear friends, but leave room for God's wrath, for it is written: "It is mine to avenge; I will repay,"[d] says the Lord. [20]On the contrary:

"If your enemy is hungry, feed him;
    if he is thirsty, give him something to drink.
In doing this, you will heap burning coals on
    his head."[e]

[21]Do not be overcome by evil, but overcome evil with good.

---

[a] 6 Or the   [b] 8 Or to provide for others   [c] 16 Or willing to do menial work   [d] 19 Deut. 32:35   [e] 20 Prov. 25:21,22

---

kindness God shows toward sinners—one of Paul's main themes so far in the letter. **bodies** The Greek word used here, *sōma*, refers to the entire person. **living sacrifice** This expression might indicate that believers are to continually offer themselves in service to God. It also could describe believers as dead to sin yet alive to God (6:11). **holy** Indicates that the sacrifice is set apart for God. **true and proper** The Greek word used here, *logikos*, can mean "spiritual," suggesting worship that involves the heart and mind in contrast to physical offerings and sacrifices. Alternatively, *logikos* could be translated as "reasonable" or "proper," indicating worship that reflects a correct understanding of the gospel message and a rational response to it. It also might mean "true," implying that worship is appropriate for those with a renewed mind (v. 2). **worship** The Greek word used here, *latreia*, commonly refers to priestly duties in the temple (Heb 9:1,6). Believers do not operate in a physical temple but are themselves God's temple (1Co 6:19).

12:2 this world Refers to the present evil age (see note on Gal 1:4), the time prior to Christ's return. **renewing of your mind** Refers to mental conformity to the truth of God.

12:3 faith God has distributed Likely refers to the amount of faith that a person exercises (compare Ro 12:6). It also could indicate that faith is the standard by which believers should measure themselves.

12:6 gifts The Greek word used here, *charismata*, refers to the abilities listed in vv. 6–8. God bestows these gifts as products of his grace intended for use in ministry. See Eph 4:12 and note. **prophesying** See note on 1Co 12:10. **in accordance with your faith** Paul says that prophets should prophesy in accordance with their faith in Christ. This also could refer to early Christian teaching as the standard for acceptable prophecy (compare Ro 12:3).

12:8 give encouragement In this instance, the Greek word used here, *paraklēsis*, refers to encouraging people to live as Jesus taught and in accordance with the gospel (1:5; 10:16). It also can refer to bringing general comfort. **giving** Probably refers to people who share their wealth, including possessions and food. For Paul, the use of this gift is to be characterized by generosity (2Co 8:21; 9:11,13). **show mercy** Refers to demonstrating kindness to those in need, such as the sick, poor and elderly. Although this is expected of all followers of Christ, some people are particularly gifted by the Spirit to show mercy.

12:13 hospitality In Paul's time, teachers and philosophers—and Christian missionaries—traveled from town to town, relying on local residents for food and lodging. Paul also relied on such hospitality during his missionary journeys (e.g., Ac 16:15; 18:3; 21:16).

12:15 mourn with those who mourn Christians are called to share in both the joy and suffering of fellow believers, since they are members of one body of Christ (Ro 12:4–5; 1Co 12:25–26).

12:16 Live in harmony Describes having the same mindset (Ro 15:5–6).

12:20 burning coals on his head Paul cites Pr 25:21–22 to encourage believers to show their enemies undeserved kindness, which might elicit a response of shame and perhaps repentance. This approach leaves room God to render punishment if he chooses (Ro 12:19).

12:21 overcome evil with good Describes the consequence of the Christian ethics in vv. 14–20. Good will prevail over evil when Christians respond to their enemies with love and blessings instead of revenge and curses.

Submission to Governing Authorities

13 Let everyone be subject to the governing authorities, for there is no authority except that which God has established. The authorities that exist have been established by God. [2]Consequently, whoever rebels against the authority is rebelling against what God has instituted, and those who do so will bring judgment on themselves. [3]For rulers hold no terror for those who do right, but for those who do wrong. Do you want to be free from fear of the one in authority? Then do what is right and you will be commended. [4]For the one in authority is God's servant for your good. But if you do wrong, be afraid, for rulers do not bear the sword for no reason. They are God's servants, agents of wrath to bring punishment on the wrongdoer. [5]Therefore, it is necessary to submit to the authorities, not only because of possible punishment but also as a matter of conscience.

[6]This is also why you pay taxes, for the authorities are God's servants, who give their full time to governing. [7]Give to everyone what you owe them: If you owe taxes, pay taxes; if revenue, then revenue; if respect, then respect; if honor, then honor.

Love Fulfills the Law

[8]Let no debt remain outstanding, except the continuing debt to love one another, for whoever loves others has fulfilled the law. [9]The commandments, "You shall not commit adultery," "You shall not murder," "You shall not steal," "You shall not covet,"[a] and whatever other command there may be, are summed up in this one command: "Love your neighbor as yourself."[b] [10]Love does no harm to a neighbor. Therefore love is the fulfillment of the law.

The Day Is Near

[11]And do this, understanding the present time: The hour has already come for you to wake up from your slumber, because our salvation is nearer now than when we first believed. [12]The night is nearly over; the day is almost here. So let us put aside the deeds of darkness and put on the armor of light. [13]Let us behave decently, as in the daytime, not in carousing and drunkenness, not in sexual immorality and debauchery, not in dissension and jealousy. [14]Rather, clothe yourselves with the Lord Jesus Christ, and do not think about how to gratify the desires of the flesh.[c]

The Weak and the Strong

14 Accept the one whose faith is weak, without quarreling over disputable matters. [2]One person's faith allows them to eat anything, but another, whose faith is weak, eats only vegetables. [3]The one who eats everything must not treat

---

[a] 9 Exodus 20:13-15,17; Deut. 5:17-19,21   [b] 9 Lev. 19:18
[c] 14 In contexts like this, the Greek word for *flesh* (*sarx*) refers to the sinful state of human beings, often presented as a power in opposition to the Spirit.

13:1–7 Paul consistently teaches that believers must submit to established authority in the contexts of the household and the government, since these institutions are ordained by God (see Eph 5:21 and note; compare Col 3:18; Titus 3:1). Paul's teaching here parallels that of Peter in 1Pe 2:13–14. Jesus also teaches about respecting authority (Mt 22:15–22).

13:1 be subject Paul wants to ensure that Christians act as good citizens and avoid civic conflicts. This does not mean blind obedience, however. The Bible sometimes depicts people acting against public authorities in order to obey God (e.g., Ex 1:17; Da 3:10–12; Ac 5:29). **authority** The Greek word used here, *exousia*, refers not to an abstract concept, but to the authority exercised by government officials. The OT consistently views God as the ultimate authority over human government (Da 4:17).
13:2 judgment In this context, Paul probably is referring to punishment from government authorities.
13:4 servant The Greek word used here, *diakonos*, is the basis for the English word "deacon"; it often refers to Christians who serve God in ministry (e.g., 2Co 6:4; Eph 3:7; Col 1:7). Here, however, Paul applies *diakonos* to the government's authority, which is ordained by God to serve his good purposes. **sword** Refers to the government's authority to punish rebels, even by death.

13:8–14 Here, Paul cites the OT law to underscore how acting in love fulfills the true intent of the law (Ro 13:10). His comments reflect Jesus' teaching about love (Mt 22:37–40; Jn 13:34–35).

13:8 has fulfilled the law Paul suggests that love of neighbor is the essence of the law (compare Gal 5:14; 6:2).

13:9 commandments Paul lists several of the Ten Commandments (see Ex 20:13–17; Dt 5:17–21; compare Lk 18:19–21). **Love your neighbor** A quotation from Lev 19:18.
13:11 wake up from your slumber Indicates awareness of God and sensitivity to his concerns (compare 1Th 5:6–7). **salvation** Refers to the day of the Lord. Paul asserts that Christ's return is closer than before.
13:12 armor of light Compare Eph 6:13–17.
13:14 clothe yourselves with the Lord A metaphor indicating that believers must appropriate Jesus' virtues and imitate his love (compare Gal 3:27; Col 3:9–10). **gratify the desires** Refers to providing an opportunity for sin.

14:1–23 In this passage Paul addresses the tension between two groups within the Christian community—the strong, who are able to regard all food and drink as ritually clean with a clear conscience, and the weak, who are unable to give up their commitment to the dietary laws and observance of the Sabbath. Paul's message urges the Roman Christians to withhold judgment of their fellow believers (Ro 14:1–12) and to avoid behaving in a manner that causes others to stumble in their faith (vv. 13–23).

14:1 whose faith is weak Likely refers to Christians who remained committed to observing certain parts of the law, such as food laws and the Sabbath (vv. 2–3). The immediate context probably refers to Jewish Christians, though other practices concerning food and observing certain days (v. 6) were issues for non-Jewish people as well (see Gal 4:1–11). The Law of Moses designated certain animals as ritually unclean, and it therefore prohibited Jews from eating them (see Lev 11:1–47). Many

with contempt the one who does not, and the one who does not eat everything must not judge the one who does, for God has accepted them. [4]Who are you to judge someone else's servant? To their own master, servants stand or fall. And they will stand, for the Lord is able to make them stand.

[5]One person considers one day more sacred than another; another considers every day alike. Each of them should be fully convinced in their own mind. [6]Whoever regards one day as special does so to the Lord. Whoever eats meat does so to the Lord, for they give thanks to God; and whoever abstains does so to the Lord and gives thanks to God. [7]For none of us lives for ourselves alone, and none of us dies for ourselves alone. [8]If we live, we live for the Lord; and if we die, we die for the Lord. So, whether we live or die, we belong to the Lord. [9]For this very reason, Christ died and returned to life so that he might be the Lord of both the dead and the living.

[10]You, then, why do you judge your brother or sister[a]? Or why do you treat them with contempt? For we will all stand before God's judgment seat. [11]It is written:

"'As surely as I live,' says the Lord,
'every knee will bow before me;
    every tongue will acknowledge God.'"[b]

[12]So then, each of us will give an account of ourselves to God.

[13]Therefore let us stop passing judgment on one another. Instead, make up your mind not to put any stumbling block or obstacle in the way of a brother or sister. [14]I am convinced, being fully persuaded in the Lord Jesus, that nothing is unclean in itself. But if anyone regards something as unclean, then for that person it is unclean. [15]If your brother or sister is distressed because of what you eat, you are no longer acting in love. Do not by your eating destroy someone for whom Christ died. [16]Therefore do not let what you know is good be spoken of as evil. [17]For the kingdom of God is not a matter of eating and drinking, but of righteousness, peace and joy in the Holy Spirit, [18]because anyone who serves Christ in this way is pleasing to God and receives human approval.

[19]Let us therefore make every effort to do what leads to peace and to mutual edification. [20]Do not destroy the work of God for the sake of food. All food is clean, but it is wrong for a person to eat anything that causes someone else to stumble. [21]It is better not to eat meat or drink wine or to do anything else that will cause your brother or sister to fall.

[22]So whatever you believe about these things keep between yourself and God. Blessed is the one who does not condemn himself by what he approves. [23]But whoever has doubts is condemned if they eat, because their eating is not from faith; and everything that does not come from faith is sin.[c]

15 We who are strong ought to bear with the failings of the weak and not to please ourselves. [2]Each of us should please our neighbors for

---

[a] 10 The Greek word for *brother or sister* (*adelphos*) refers here to a believer, whether man or woman, as part of God's family; also in verses 13, 15 and 21.   [b] 11 Isaiah 45:23   [c] 23 Some manuscripts place 16:25-27 here; others after 15:33.

Jews adhered to strict food regulations in accordance with the law even after they turned to faith in Christ (Ac 10:9–16). Some also avoided fellowship with those who did not adhere to such food laws (Ac 11:2–3).

14:2 faith allows them to eat anything Refers to the strong believers who were able to eat and drink all things with a clear conscience. Jesus clarifies that is it not what a person eats that defiles, but actions toward others (Mk 7:14–23). Also, the Lord revealed to Peter that he made all meat ritually clean (Ac 10:9–16). By this revelation, God also indicated that Peter should no longer regard Gentiles (non-Jewish people) as ritually unclean and outside the realm of his salvation.

14:4 servant Paul uses an analogy to indicate that believers answer to God.

14:5 considers one day more sacred than another The law required Jews to observe special days, such as the Sabbath, Jewish festivals and the new moon. Here, Paul refers to Christians who honor these observances (see Gal 4:10; Col 2:16). **should be fully convinced in their own mind** Paul emphasizes that each person must operate with a clear conscience, regardless of his or her practice.

14:7 none of us dies for ourselves Emphasizes dependence on God and unity among believers.

14:11 As surely as I live This oath formula expresses the certainty of God's declaration. Here it begins a quotation from Isa 45:23.

14:13 put any stumbling block Describes causing someone to do something against his or her conscience or moral principles.

14:14 nothing is unclean in itself Paul celebrates believers' freedom from the requirements of the law. However, he qualifies this statement by reminding the strong that some things might be considered unclean by the weak, whose faith is challenged by such freedom.

14:15 Do not by your eating destroy Paul warns the strong that, in some circumstances, their freedom might cause distress for the weak.

14:17 the kingdom of God This verse refers to the kingdom of God as a present reality (see 1Co 4:20; compare Gal 5:21; Eph 5:5). Because the values of the kingdom are righteousness, peace and joy in the Spirit, human relationships are more important than rules about food.

14:20 work of God Refers to a believer whose faith is weak (Ro 14:1). Paul urges the strong to avoid influencing the weak to act against their consciences.

14:22 believe The Greek word used here, *pistis*, refers to personal conviction in this context.

15:1 We who are strong Refers to believers who confidently trust that they no longer have to adhere to the religious rules they practiced before coming to Christ. Freedom in Christ clears their conscience (see 14:1). **bear** Paul encourages more than just tolerance; he wants the strong to be sympathetic toward the weak, even willing to restrict their freedom to prevent the weak from acting against their consciences. This is an opportunity for the strong to demonstrate the love of Christ and the unity of the Spirit. **the weak** Refers to those who are unconfident about what they can or cannot eat. See note on 14:1.

15:2 neighbors An allusion to Lev 19:18, the second

their good, to build them up. ³For even Christ did not please himself but, as it is written: "The insults of those who insult you have fallen on me."ᵃ ⁴For everything that was written in the past was written to teach us, so that through the endurance taught in the Scriptures and the encouragement they provide we might have hope.

⁵May the God who gives endurance and encouragement give you the same attitude of mind toward each other that Christ Jesus had, ⁶so that with one mind and one voice you may glorify the God and Father of our Lord Jesus Christ.

⁷Accept one another, then, just as Christ accepted you, in order to bring praise to God. ⁸For I tell you that Christ has become a servant of the Jewsᵇ on behalf of God's truth, so that the promises made to the patriarchs might be confirmed ⁹and, moreover, that the Gentiles might glorify God for his mercy. As it is written:

"Therefore I will praise you among the
     Gentiles;
   I will sing the praises of your name."ᶜ

¹⁰Again, it says,

"Rejoice, you Gentiles, with his people."ᵈ

¹¹And again,

"Praise the Lord, all you Gentiles;
   let all the peoples extol him."ᵉ

¹²And again, Isaiah says,

"The Root of Jesse will spring up,
   one who will arise to rule over the nations;
   in him the Gentiles will hope."ᶠ

¹³May the God of hope fill you with all joy and peace as you trust in him, so that you may overflow with hope by the power of the Holy Spirit.

Paul the Minister to the Gentiles

¹⁴I myself am convinced, my brothers and sisters, that you yourselves are full of goodness, filled with knowledge and competent to instruct one another. ¹⁵Yet I have written you quite boldly on some points to remind you of them again, because of the grace God gave me ¹⁶to be a minister of Christ Jesus to the Gentiles. He gave me the priestly duty of proclaiming the gospel of God, so that the Gentiles might become an offering acceptable to God, sanctified by the Holy Spirit.

¹⁷Therefore I glory in Christ Jesus in my service to God. ¹⁸I will not venture to speak of anything except what Christ has accomplished through me in leading the Gentiles to obey God by what I have said and done — ¹⁹by the power of signs and wonders, through the power of the Spirit of God. So from Jerusalem all the way around to Illyricum, I have fully proclaimed the gospel of Christ. ²⁰It has always been my ambition to preach the gospel where Christ was not known, so that I would not be building on someone else's foundation. ²¹Rather, as it is written:

"Those who were not told about him will see,
   and those who have not heard will
     understand."ᵍ

²²This is why I have often been hindered from coming to you.

ᵃ 3 Psalm 69:9   ᵇ 8 Greek circumcision   ᶜ 9 2 Samuel 22:50;
Psalm 18:49   ᵈ 10 Deut. 32:43   ᵉ 11 Psalm 117:1
ᶠ 12 Isaiah 11:10 (see Septuagint)   ᵍ 21 Isaiah 52:15 (see
Septuagint)

---

greatest commandment (compare Ro 13:8–9). **build them up** Refers to growth in faith and maturity in Christ.
15:3 The insults of those who insult you Paul quotes Ps 69:9 as an example of the attitude that Roman believers should imitate. Christ was willing to endure shame for the benefit of his Father and consequently for those who would put their trust in him. Christ didn't misuse his freedom to take advantage of people; rather, he used it to serve others. See the table "Messianic Psalms" on p. 847.
15:4 everything that was written in the past Refers to all of the OT Scriptures.
15:6 with one mind and one voice Refers to unity among the believers.
15:7 Accept one another In Ro 15:1, Paul specifically asked the strong to bear with the weak; now he urges both groups to accept one another.
15:8 of the Jews The Greek text here references circumcision; this is a way of referring to Jews. See note on 2:25.
promises made to the patriarchs See note on 9:4.
15:9 praise you among the Gentiles A quotation from Ps 18:49. **Gentiles** Non-Jewish people. See note on Ro 1:5.
15:10 Rejoice, you Gentiles A quotation from Dt 32:43.
his people Refers to Jews.
15:12 The Root of Jesse In the original context of this quotation from Isa 11:10, the Root of Jesse refers to

an individual ruler from the Davidic line. Paul's quotation comes from the Septuagint (the ancient Greek translation of the OT), which emphasizes that the Root of Jesse will rule the nations and provide them with hope. For Paul, Jesus is the Root of Jesse — the Messiah from David's line — who rules over both Jewish and non-Jewish people (Jews and Gentiles).

15:14–33 In this passage Paul changes topics and addresses his upcoming visit to Rome, as well as his plans to preach the gospel in Spain (see Ro 1:11–15).

15:16 priestly duty Paul relates his apostolic duties to those of the OT priests. He considers believers' obedience to be a type of offering to God (12:1).
15:19 signs and wonders Refers to Paul's performance of miracles and experience of miraculous events during his ministry (e.g., Ac 13:9–12; 16:25–34; 28:3–6). **to Illyricum** The region northwest of Greece on the Adriatic Sea. Paul probably intends for this phrase to encompass the boundaries of his ministry. See note on Ro 15:23.
15:20 where Christ was not known Paul apparently regarded his ministry strategy as a fulfillment of Isa 52:15, which he cites in Ro 15:21.
15:22 I have often been hindered Paul's visit to Rome was delayed by his commitment to completing his missionary work in the east.

Paul's Plan to Visit Rome

[23]But now that there is no more place for me to work in these regions, and since I have been longing for many years to visit you, [24]I plan to do so when I go to Spain. I hope to see you while passing through and to have you assist me on my journey there, after I have enjoyed your company for a while. [25]Now, however, I am on my way to Jerusalem in the service of the Lord's people there. [26]For Macedonia and Achaia were pleased to make a contribution for the poor among the Lord's people in Jerusalem. [27]They were pleased to do it, and indeed they owe it to them. For if the Gentiles have shared in the Jews' spiritual blessings, they owe it to the Jews to share with them their material blessings. [28]So after I have completed this task and have made sure that they have received this contribution, I will go to Spain and visit you on the way. [29]I know that when I come to you, I will come in the full measure of the blessing of Christ.

[30]I urge you, brothers and sisters, by our Lord Jesus Christ and by the love of the Spirit, to join me in my struggle by praying to God for me. [31]Pray that I may be kept safe from the unbelievers in Judea and that the contribution I take to Jerusalem may be favorably received by the Lord's people there, [32]so that I may come to you with joy, by God's will, and in your company be refreshed. [33]The God of peace be with you all. Amen.

Personal Greetings

16 I commend to you our sister Phoebe, a deacon[a],[b] of the church in Cenchreae. [2]I ask you to receive her in the Lord in a way worthy of his people and to give her any help she may need from you, for she has been the benefactor of many people, including me.

[3]Greet Priscilla[c] and Aquila, my co-workers in Christ Jesus. [4]They risked their lives for me. Not only I but all the churches of the Gentiles are grateful to them.
[5]Greet also the church that meets at their house.
Greet my dear friend Epenetus, who was the first convert to Christ in the province of Asia.
[6]Greet Mary, who worked very hard for you.
[7]Greet Andronicus and Junia, my fellow Jews who have been in prison with me. They are outstanding among[d] the apostles, and they were in Christ before I was.
[8]Greet Ampliatus, my dear friend in the Lord.

[a] 1 Or *servant*   [b] 1 The word *deacon* refers here to a Christian designated to serve with the overseers/elders of the church in a variety of ways; similarly in Phil. 1:1 and 1 Tim. 3:8,12.
[c] 3 Greek *Prisca*, a variant of *Priscilla*   [d] 7 Or *are esteemed by*

15:23 there is no more place Paul seems to have believed that he had completed his divinely appointed task of preaching the gospel throughout the eastern Roman Empire.
15:24 Spain Refers to the Iberian Peninsula, which includes modern-day Spain and Portugal. Rome would have been a strategic base for launching a missionary journey to Spain, which by the first century AD was part of the Roman Empire. It is unknown whether Paul reached Spain, though it is possible that he traveled there after his house arrest in Rome (Ac 28:16–31). **to have you assist me on my journey** Paul likely hoped for the Roman believers to support him in his Spanish mission.
15:26 Macedonia and Achaia Roman provinces located in modern-day Greece. Macedonia would have included the churches at Philippi and Thessalonica; Achaia would have included Corinth. **contribution** Paul uses the Greek word, *koinōnia*, here; this word is literally rendered as "fellowship" and in this instance refers to joining others via financial support. The Macedonian and Achaian churches offered financial support for the disadvantaged believers in Jerusalem. Paul hoped that through the collection, Gentile believers could show their generosity and love for their Jewish brothers and sisters. He also hoped that it would promote unity among the believers. See 2Co 8–9.
15:28 after I have completed this task Refers to delivering the collection to Jerusalem.
15:31 unbelievers in Judea Refers to potential opponents of Paul. See Ac 21:27–36.
15:33 God of peace See note on Ro 5:1.

16:1–16 In this final chapter, Paul sends greetings to various acquaintances and fellow missionaries who live in Rome. Paul encourages them to welcome Phoebe, who likely delivered Paul's letter to the Romans.

16:1 Phoebe Possibly a wealthy Gentile Christian who delivered Paul's letter to the Romans. **a deacon** Paul uses the Greek word *diakonos* here, suggesting that Phoebe may have held the office of deaconess in the church at Cenchreae. In its most basic sense, *diakonos* refers to a table waiter (see Jn 2:5), but it also could indicate anyone who offers personal help. The Jerusalem apostles appointed seven deacons to oversee the distribution of food among the widows (Ac 6:2). If Phoebe was a deaconess, she probably maintained the same focus as those original seven—ministering to the poor and needy. See note on 1Ti 3:8.
16:2 his people See note on Ro 1:7.
16:3 Priscilla and Aquila A wife and husband who assisted Paul in his missionary work (see Ac 18:2–3). They helped establish the church in Ephesus (Ac 18:18; 1Co 16:19). At the time they met Paul, they had left Rome because the emperor, Claudius, had expelled all the Jews (Ac 18:2). It is unknown when they returned to Rome or what type of ministry they had there.
16:4 for me Indicates that Prisca and Aquila put their lives in danger for Paul's sake, possibly during the riot in Ephesus (Ac 19; compare Ro 5:8). See the infographic "Ancient Home Synagogue" on p. 1971.
16:7 Andronicus and Junia "Junia" is most likely a woman's name, so this probably refers to another husband and wife ministry team. **apostles** This designation likely is used in a generic sense to refer to missionaries who are sent out (compare 2Co 8:23).

⁹Greet Urbanus, our co-worker in Christ, and my dear friend Stachys.
¹⁰Greet Apelles, whose fidelity to Christ has stood the test.

Greet those who belong to the household of Aristobulus.
¹¹Greet Herodion, my fellow Jew.

Greet those in the household of Narcissus who are in the Lord.
¹²Greet Tryphena and Tryphosa, those women who work hard in the Lord.

Greet my dear friend Persis, another woman who has worked very hard in the Lord.
¹³Greet Rufus, chosen in the Lord, and his mother, who has been a mother to me, too.
¹⁴Greet Asyncritus, Phlegon, Hermes, Patrobas, Hermas and the other brothers and sisters with them.
¹⁵Greet Philologus, Julia, Nereus and his sister, and Olympas and all the Lord's people who are with them.
¹⁶Greet one another with a holy kiss.

All the churches of Christ send greetings.

¹⁷I urge you, brothers and sisters, to watch out for those who cause divisions and put obstacles in your way that are contrary to the teaching you have learned. Keep away from them. ¹⁸For such people are not serving our Lord Christ, but their own appetites. By smooth talk and flattery they deceive the minds of naive people. ¹⁹Everyone has heard about your obedience, so I rejoice because of you; but I want you to be wise about what is good, and innocent about what is evil.

²⁰The God of peace will soon crush Satan under your feet.

The grace of our Lord Jesus be with you.

²¹Timothy, my co-worker, sends his greetings to you, as do Lucius, Jason and Sosipater, my fellow Jews.

²²I, Tertius, who wrote down this letter, greet you in the Lord.

²³Gaius, whose hospitality I and the whole church here enjoy, sends you his greetings.

Erastus, who is the city's director of public works, and our brother Quartus send you their greetings. [24]a

²⁵Now to him who is able to establish you in accordance with my gospel, the message I proclaim about Jesus Christ, in keeping with the revelation of the mystery hidden for long ages past, ²⁶but now revealed and made known through the prophetic writings by the command of the eternal God, so that all the Gentiles might come to the obedience that comes fromᵇ faith — ²⁷to the only wise God be glory forever through Jesus Christ! Amen.

ᵃ 24 Some manuscripts include here *May the grace of our Lord Jesus Christ be with all of you. Amen.*   ᵇ 26 Or *that is*

16:13 Rufus Possibly the son of Simon of Cyrene (Mk 15:21).
16:16 with a holy kiss A customary greeting that signified fellowship and unity within the body of Christ.

16:17–20 Paul adopts a surprisingly harsh tone to urge the Roman believers to be vigilant against false teachers who might cause dissension.

16:18 their own appetites This might describe false teachers who emphasized Jewish dietary laws (see Ro 14:2 and note; Php 3:19 and note) or sought to serve their selfish desires (see Ro 13:14).
16:19 your obedience Compare 6:17.
16:20 God of peace Refers to the God who brings peace (see note on 5:1), in contrast to the discord caused by false teachers (v. 17). **Satan** The enemy of God's people who, like the false teachers, tries to disrupt the unity of believers (compare 2Co 2:5–11; 11:13–15). **under your feet** Paul draws on the OT scriptures (Ps 110:1) to comfort his audience with a message of hope: God will soon defeat Satan and their enemies. The NT frequently quotes Ps 110:1 to depict all things being placed under the feet of Christ (e.g., Lk 20:43; Ac 2:35; Heb 10:13). Here Paul refers to all things being placed under the feet of believers, to emphasize their participation in God's victory.

16:21 Timothy See note on 1Ti 1:1. **Lucius** Possibly a prophet from the church at Antioch in Syria (Ac 13:1). **Jason** Possibly the same individual who provided Paul with refuge during a riot in Thessalonica (Ac 17:5–9).
16:22 Tertius Probably a professional scribe who took Paul's dictation.
16:23 Gaius This could refer to one of several people: a man from Derbe who accompanied Paul on a missionary journey (Ac 20:4), a Corinthian whom Paul baptized (1Co 1:14) or a leader of a church in Asia Minor (3Jn 1). **Erastus** Possibly the man whom Paul sent to Macedonia (Ac 19:21–22).

16:25–27 Some ancient manuscripts place Ro 16:25–27 after 14:23 or 15:33, while others omit the verses entirely. These verses contain a doxology—a hymn to God—using several of the key themes of the letter (e.g., mystery, Gentiles and obedience).

THE GLORY OF GOD IN PAUL'S LETTERS
by N. T. Wright

The great underlying subject at the heart of much of Paul's theology is God himself. Paul most fully celebrates the glory of God when he presents his gospel, which is not simply a message of how individuals get saved from sin and death but how God has brought heaven and earth together in the Messiah (Eph 1:10). For Paul, the coming together of Jews and the Gentile nations into one body is a sign of this. Romans 15:1–13 states this great aim: that both Jew and Gentile "with one mind ... may glorify the God and Father of our Lord Jesus Christ" (Ro 15:6). Mutual welcome is indispensable within the body of Christ—Christians coming together across the boundaries of race, class, gender and culture. Paul states that what was predicted in the Old Testament has now been accomplished, as people from across the world place their hope in Jesus Christ, the root of Jesse who rises to rule the nations (Ro 15:12). In Philippians 2:11 Paul rejoices that every tongue shall confess that Jesus Christ is Lord, "to the glory of God the Father."

Paul sees God glorified when people become truly themselves through the grace and power of the gospel (Col 3:10–11). God created us to bear his image in the world, and when that image is restored through the very image of God—Jesus Christ (Col 1:15)—and through the work of the Spirit, the living God is glorified as he is reflected into the world.

The primal sin of humanity is idolatry, worshipping and trusting that which is not God and so losing the glory of God. This stands in stark contrast to what happened when Abraham believed God and trusted that he could do what he had promised (Ro 1:18–25; 3:23; 4:18–21). That is part of the larger logic of Romans 1–4 as a whole. The reversal of the fall of humanity and the renewal of the whole cosmos is the theme of God's overall plan of salvation. Within this scope, the saving plan for humanity is one vital part; we are justified in order to be justice-bringers, saved to be the agents of salvation for the world. God's plan always was to rescue the world through Israel: This has been accomplished through Jesus, Israel's representative Messiah.

God called Abraham so that through his family he might undo the sin of Adam. This is what the covenant with Israel was all about, and why—as Moses correctly saw—God's own glory was at stake when the covenant appeared to have failed. After the Israelites forged the golden calf while Moses was on Mount Sinai, he asked God, in effect, "If you let us die in the wilderness, the Egyptians will hear of it, and then what will you do for your great name?" (Ex 32:11–13). God's glory was at stake, then and throughout the story of Israel.

Here we arrive at one of the great truths of the gospel: The accomplishment of Jesus Christ is accounted to all those who are "in him." Paul's view of God's covenant plan focuses on Jesus as the Messiah in whom God's people are summed up, and through whom, in their unity, they give glory and praise to the Creator. He will demonstrate it finally when he gives resurrection life to his people and through their "glory"—that is, their new, risen "rule" (compare Ps 8)—rescues the whole cosmos from bondage and decay (Ro 8:21).

In 1 Corinthians 15:20–28, as in Romans 8, Paul allows the argument to mount higher and higher, with Jesus already reigning as Messiah and Lord until he has put all his enemies under his feet, in fulfillment of Psalms 8 and 110. When the task is complete, and death itself is destroyed, he hands over the kingdom to the Father, so that God may be all in all. For Paul, the sole glory

of God is intimately bound up with the healing and restoration of the whole of creation, and with the rescue of human beings from sin and death so that they may be restored as God's image-bearers. "We boast in the hope of the glory of God," Paul says in Romans 5:2, and by the end of Romans 8 we know what he means. *Soli Deo gloria!* ("Glory to God alone!") is the cry that arises from fully understanding what Paul is saying in terms of creation and covenant.

(This article was adapted in part from a transcript of N. T. Wright's lecture "Paul in Different Perspectives," delivered on January 3, 2005.)

1 CORINTHIANS

INTRODUCTION TO 1 CORINTHIANS

First Corinthians is all about living like followers of Christ. A couple of years after Paul established a group of believers in Corinth, he received word that they were losing their way. In 1 Corinthians, Paul gives them practical advice on how to live as Christians in the midst of a culture that pressures them to compromise.

BACKGROUND

Paul founded the church in Corinth around AD 51 (Ac 18:1–11). As he moved on with his missionary activity, he spent three years in Ephesus (Ac 20:31). While he was there (1Co 16:8), he heard that things were not going well in Corinth—believers were quarrelling (1:11; 5:1). Paul wrote at least one letter to try to straighten things out (5:9), but it did not solve the problem—so he wrote what we call 1 Corinthians and sent it with his associate Timothy (4:17). The letter probably was written toward the end of Paul's stay in Ephesus, around AD 54–55.

Corinth was in Greece, but during Paul's time the city was part of the Roman Empire. It was a major commercial center, had a bustling port, and as the third largest city in the Roman Empire, was a cosmopolitan city; it also was known for its sexual permissiveness. Many of the problems Paul addresses come from the Corinthian Christians' tendency to reflect the values of their city rather than those of the body of Christ (6:15).

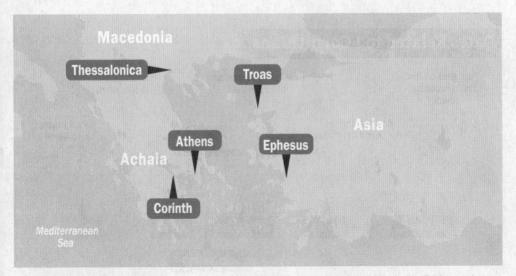

This map depicts many of the locations Paul visited on his second missionary journey, including Ephesus, where he wrote 1 Corinthians.

STRUCTURE

Like a typical Greco-Roman letter, 1 Corinthians has an opening (1:1–9), a body (1:10—15:58) and a closing (16:1–24). Paul begins the letter by greeting the Corinthians as saints—people made holy by Jesus—and giving thanks for them. In the first part of the letter's body (1:10— 6:20), Paul responds to things that he has heard in Ephesus about the Corinthians. They didn't report these things themselves. They have acted divisively, assessing their leaders based on their own definition of what it means to be wise and spiritual. Paul responds that their views don't fit with the gospel he preached to them (1:10—4:21). Then he addresses other issues he has heard about: incest, lawsuits and sexual immorality (5:1—6:20).

The second part of the letter's body (7:1—15:58) discusses issues raised in the Corinthians' letter to Paul. He responds to them about marriage (7:1–40), food sacrificed to idols (8:1—11:1), conduct in worship (11:2–34), the practice of spiritual gifts (12:1—14:40) and resurrection (15:1–58). Paul concludes the letter by going over some personal items, including his travel plans and the offering he was collecting for the impoverished church in Jerusalem (16:1–24).

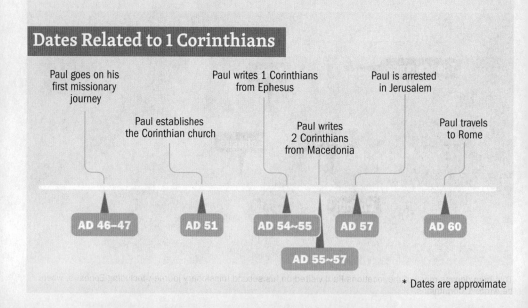

Dates Related to 1 Corinthians

Paul goes on his first missionary journey

Paul writes 1 Corinthians from Ephesus

Paul is arrested in Jerusalem

Paul establishes the Corinthian church

Paul writes 2 Corinthians from Macedonia

Paul travels to Rome

AD 46–47

AD 51

AD 54~55

AD 57

AD 60

AD 55~57

* Dates are approximate

OUTLINE

- Introduction (1:1–9)
- Paul responds to reports of the Corinthians' conduct (1:10—6:20)
- Paul responds to the Corinthians' letter (7:1—15:58)
- Concluding matters (16:1–24)

THEMES

In 1 Corinthians, Paul emphasizes how to live as a Christian community, which differs from the values of secular culture. The Corinthians had heard the story of Jesus and embraced it with enthusiasm, but over time it had been twisted. Their culture's stories were distorting their views about following Jesus.

Paul strongly criticizes the believers' misguided attempts to live according to Christian values, pointing them instead to life in the Spirit of God, based on the work of the Lord Jesus Christ (6:11). The Corinthians think they know what wisdom is, but their wisdom looks no different from their culture's. They think they know what being spiritual means, but their spirituality leads them to be divisive, immoral and selfish. By contrast, truly living in the Spirit leads to unity, to putting others first and to living a holy life. Paul tells the believers to see themselves as a community, and as individuals, as God's temple—as members of Christ's body (3:16; 6:15).

Like the Corinthians, we live in a world filled with ideas and practices that are at odds with the gospel. Every day, we hear stories about what it means to be wise and spiritual based on our secular culture, and these often cause us to misunderstand our place in the world or distort the gospel for our own purposes (compare chs. 8; 10). Paul challenges our desires to be sophisticated and powerful and shows them to be empty counterfeits. We are challenged to walk away from immorality and live as God's people, empowered by the Holy Spirit (chs. 5; 12–14). We are to embrace the power of the resurrection and work for the Lord (1:2,9; 7:17; 15).

1 Paul, called to be an apostle of Christ Jesus by the will of God, and our brother Sosthenes,

²To the church of God in Corinth, to those sanctified in Christ Jesus and called to be his holy people, together with all those everywhere who call on the name of our Lord Jesus Christ—their Lord and ours:

³Grace and peace to you from God our Father and the Lord Jesus Christ.

Thanksgiving

⁴I always thank my God for you because of his grace given you in Christ Jesus. ⁵For in him you have been enriched in every way—with all kinds of speech and with all knowledge— ⁶God thus confirming our testimony about Christ among you. ⁷Therefore you do not lack any spiritual gift as you eagerly wait for our Lord Jesus Christ to be revealed. ⁸He will also keep you firm to the end, so that you will be blameless on the day of our Lord Jesus Christ. ⁹God is faithful, who has called you into fellowship with his Son, Jesus Christ our Lord.

A Church Divided Over Leaders

¹⁰I appeal to you, brothers and sisters,ᵃ in the name of our Lord Jesus Christ, that all of you agree with one another in what you say and that there be no divisions among you, but that you be perfectly united in mind and thought. ¹¹My brothers and sisters, some from Chloe's household have informed me that there are quarrels among you. ¹²What I mean is this: One of you says, "I follow Paul"; another, "I follow Apollos"; another, "I follow Cephasᵇ"; still another, "I follow Christ."

ᵃ 10 The Greek word for *brothers and sisters* (*adelphoi*) refers here to believers, both men and women, as part of God's family; also in verses 11 and 26; and in 2:1; 3:1; 4:6; 6:8; 7:24, 29; 10:1; 11:33; 12:1; 14:6, 20, 26, 39; 15:1, 6, 50, 58; 16:15, 20.   ᵇ 12 That is, Peter

---

1:1–9 Paul founded the church at Corinth during his second missionary journey (probably around AD 51). Paul likely wrote the letter known as 1 Corinthians in AD 54–55 after he had received a report concerning the Corinthian believers quarreling (see note on v. 11) and a letter from them that raised questions about spiritual gifts, collections and marriage. The work now called 1 Corinthians is actually (at least) Paul's second letter to the Corinthians; there is not a known copy of the letter mentioned in 5:9.

Paul begins 1 Corinthians according to the letter-writing conventions of his day. He identifies himself and his co-sender, Sosthenes, and greets the Corinthians with grace and peace (1Co 1:3). He then gives thanks to God, anticipating many of the main themes of the letter (vv. 4–9).

1:1 Paul The apostle formerly known as Saul of Tarsus. **an apostle** See note on Ro 1:1. See the table "Pauline Self-Designations" on p. 1904. **by the will of God** Paul's appointment to the office of apostle was God's decision, not a person's or group's. Paul doesn't need the affirmation of the Corinthians because God chose him. **Sosthenes** He may be the synagogue leader Sosthenes, who was beaten in front of the judgment seat while Paul was in Corinth (Ac 18:17).

1:2 church The Greek word used here, *ekklēsia,* refers to a gathering of people, not a building; here, it references the gathering of Christ followers in Corinth. **Corinth** Located on the coast of Greece, Corinth was a major metropolis in Paul's day. **sanctified** The process of a believer becoming more like Christ in thought and action. Since the Spirit is working in the Corinthian believers to make them more like Christ (sanctified), they should be unified in their purpose and behavior (1Co 12:12–20). But the opposite is happening: They are divided based on the teachers they're claiming to follow—Paul, Peter and Apollos (vv. 12–17). **holy people** See note on Ro 1:7. **Lord** Paul uses the Greek word *kyrios* here to show Jesus' rightful reign and authority over all things and people. In the Septuagint (the ancient Greek translation of the OT), *kyrios* is the word used to translate God's holy name, Yahweh.

CORINTH

Corinth was a metropolitan city on the Mediterranean Sea with a population consisting of between 150,000 and 300,000 Roman citizens and approximately 460,000 slaves. In the first century AD, when Paul wrote his letter, Corinth was known for its banking industry and incredible wealth. Shrines to deities of Greek, Roman and even Egyptian gods have been discovered, and cult prostitution was common.

1:3 Grace and peace to you See note on Ro 1:7.
1:4 I always thank Statements of thanksgiving are a common feature in ancient letters. See the table "Prayers in Paul's Letters" on p. 1925. **his grace** Refers either to the undeserved gifts the believers have received from God—speech, knowledge and spiritual gifts (1Co 1:5–7; 12–14; 2Co 8:7)—or to their receiving salvation. **in Christ Jesus** Emphasizes that spiritual gifts and salvation do not come from people but from Christ.
1:5 in him you have been enriched Since there was a very large wealth gap in Corinth, Paul emphasizes that riches are found in a life of following Christ; Christ's gifts are what matter. Paul is modeling a life that doesn't revolve around economy but on a relationship with God and others. His life is focused on love as God is focused on love (1Co 13:1–3). **speech** The Greek word used here, *logos,* refers to that which is spoken (in this instance). The Corinthians highly esteemed both speech and knowledge for their cultural value (compare 12:8; 13:1–2; 2Co 8:7). **knowledge** The Greek word used here, *gnōsis,* may refer to an understanding of Christian teaching (compare 1Co 12:8; 13:8), but based on Paul's subsequent reference to the testimony of Christ among believers in v. 6, it likely refers to remembrance of how Christ has worked in people's lives.
1:6 testimony Paul is referring to the work that he told the Corinthians that Christ would do in them; it's now happening and is providing a witness for Christ in the world.
1:7 spiritual gift Literally "spiritual things"—refers to the

[13] Is Christ divided? Was Paul crucified for you? Were you baptized in the name of Paul? [14] I thank God that I did not baptize any of you except Crispus and Gaius, [15] so no one can say that you were baptized in my name. [16] (Yes, I also baptized the household of Stephanas; beyond that, I don't remember if I baptized anyone else.) [17] For Christ did not send me to baptize, but to preach the gospel — not with wisdom and eloquence, lest the cross of Christ be emptied of its power.

Christ Crucified Is God's Power and Wisdom

[18] For the message of the cross is foolishness to those who are perishing, but to us who are being saved it is the power of God. [19] For it is written:

"I will destroy the wisdom of
the wise;
the intelligence of the intelligent I will
frustrate."[a]

[20] Where is the wise person? Where is the teacher of the law? Where is the philosopher of this age? Has not God made foolish the wisdom of the world? [21] For since in the wisdom of God the world through its wisdom did not know him, God was pleased through the foolishness of what was preached to save those who believe. [22] Jews demand signs and Greeks look for wisdom, [23] but we preach Christ crucified: a stumbling block to Jews and foolishness to Gentiles, [24] but to those whom God has called, both Jews and Greeks, Christ the power

[a] 19 Isaiah 29:14

---

gifts described in chs. 12–14. **revealed** The Greek word used here, *apokalypsis,* often rendered as "revelation," can either refer to the second coming of Christ (compare 2Th 1:7; 1Pe 1:13) or to God revealing something directly to a believer through the gift of tongues, prophecy or a vision (e.g., 1Co 14:6, 14:26; Rev 1:1). The second coming of Christ interpretation best fits the context here. Paul also uses the Greek word *apokalypsis* in reference to spiritual gifts later in 1 Corinthians (e.g., 1Co 14:6,26) and in reference to visions in 2Co 12:1,7.
1:8 blameless Meaning being free from accusation (compare Col 1:22; 1Ti 3:10; Titus 1:6–7). **day of our Lord** Refers to the day when Christ will fully inaugurate justice in the world by delivering his followers and purging the world of evil (see note on 1Th 4:16; compare note on 1Th 5:2).
1:9 fellowship Paul uses the Greek word *koinōnia* here — meaning "to fellowship" or "join together." God intended for the Corinthian believers to join together because of Christ; instead, they focused on leaders and teachers, which (among many other things) caused division within their church (see 1Co 1:11–12).

1:10–17 Paul responds to reports he received concerning the Corinthian church dividing itself over different leaders.

1:10 all of you agree with one another in what you say Paul means that the Corinthian believers should all agree on how the Spirit works among them and the type of values that Christ would have them to hold — both of these things Paul clarifies within this letter (see note on v. 2).
1:11 some from Chloe's household In Ephesus, people from Chloe's household informed Paul of the quarreling in the Corinthian church (compare 1Co 16:19). **quarrels among you** The divisions among the Corinthian believers were likely based on personalities rather than theological disputes.
1:12 Apollos A Jew from Alexandria who was an eloquent speaker and knowledgeable in the Scriptures. Apollos ministered in Corinth after Paul left (Ac 18:27–19:1). Some Corinthian believers may have preferred his teaching style (and even teachings) over Paul's (see note on 1Co 1:5). **Cephas** The apostle Simon Peter (Jn 1:42; Gal 2:9). It is unknown whether he traveled to Corinth.
1:13 Is Christ divided Paul's rhetorical question challenges the Corinthians regarding the divisions within their congregation. Since Christ is one with his body, the Corinthian church (which Paul calls "the body"; 1Co 12:27) should be united. He also may be critiquing them for ranking Christ among other church leaders, when

Christ actually serves as head over the entire body (compare Eph 1:22; 5:23–24).
1:14 Crispus Probably the synagogue ruler in Corinth. He was likely the first person to accept Christ in Corinth during Paul's second missionary journey (Ac 18:8). **Gaius** Possibly the same Gaius who hosted Paul in Corinth while he wrote his letter to the Romans (Ro 16:23).
1:16 household of Stephanas Paul described Stephanas and his household as the first converts in the province of Achaia (1Co 16:15). In first-century AD Greco-Roman society, it was customary for the rest of the household to follow the pattern set by the head of the household (Ac 11:14; 16:31–34).
1:17 to preach the gospel Although Paul baptized people as part of his ministry, he believed his primary calling was to preach the gospel (e.g., Ro 15:20; 2Co 10:16; Gal 1:8).

1:18 — 2:5 In this passage Paul explains the true nature of God's wisdom and the meaning of the cross. The Corinthians failed to grasp both of these issues. This explanation serves as the basis of Paul's appeal for church unity (1Co 1:10), which he revisits in 3:1 — 4:21.

1:18 foolishness God's provision of salvation through the crucifixion of a messiah appeared to be foolishness according to the wisdom of the world. The Romans used the cross as a humiliating form of execution reserved for the worst criminals — insurrectionists. The Greeks believed that the gods operated above the limitations of people and would not have allowed themselves to be treated as Jesus was. Jews regarded the cross as a shameful punishment and even a curse from God (see Dt 21:23). **who are being saved** Although Paul believed that people were made right with God when they entered into a relationship with Jesus, he also viewed God's work of making people more like him as an ongoing process.
1:19 I will destroy Paul quotes Isa 29:14 to further highlight the contrast between divine wisdom and human wisdom. **I will frustrate** In Christ's death and resurrection, those who have understanding (wisdom) according to people's standards — those who deem Christ's resurrection as foolishness — are shown to actually be ignorant.
1:20 wise person Refers to a Greek philosopher. Such people were highly regarded for their analytical skills and persuasive speech. **teacher of the law** An expert in the Mosaic Law (compare Mt 5:20). **the philosopher** A person trained as a skilled rhetorician or public speaker.
1:22 Jews demand signs In Jewish tradition, miraculous deeds functioned as a sign of authority and legitimacy

of God and the wisdom of God. ²⁵For the foolishness of God is wiser than human wisdom, and the weakness of God is stronger than human strength.

²⁶Brothers and sisters, think of what you were when you were called. Not many of you were wise by human standards; not many were influential; not many were of noble birth. ²⁷But God chose the foolish things of the world to shame the wise; God chose the weak things of the world to shame the strong. ²⁸God chose the lowly things of this world and the despised things — and the things that are not — to nullify the things that are, ²⁹so that no one may boast before him. ³⁰It is because of him that you are in Christ Jesus, who has become for

us wisdom from God — that is, our righteousness, holiness and redemption. ³¹Therefore, as it is written: "Let the one who boasts boast in the Lord."ᵃ

2 And so it was with me, brothers and sisters. When I came to you, I did not come with eloquence or human wisdom as I proclaimed to you the testimony about God.ᵇ ²For I resolved to know nothing while I was with you except Jesus Christ and him crucified. ³I came to you in weakness with great fear and trembling. ⁴My message and my preaching were not with wise and persuasive words, but with a demonstration of the Spirit's

ᵃ 31 Jer. 9:24   ᵇ 1 Some manuscripts *proclaimed to you God's mystery*

---

from God (see Mk 8:11–12; Jn 2:18–20). **Greeks look for wisdom** Greeks were renowned for their love of new ideas (see Ac 17:20–21).

1:23 a stumbling block The message about a crucified Messiah would have offended Jewish people. According to Jewish tradition, a person hung on a tree (e.g., a cross) was considered to be cursed (Dt 21:23). Jews would not have expected God's chosen Messiah to experience such a horrific execution.

1:24 the power of God Jesus' death on the cross reveals God's power to save people from sin and death, and thus his power to redeem seemingly irredeemable situations (like the problems at Corinth). The description of Christ as the power of God also challenges the Roman Empire's use of crucifixion as a symbol of its own power. Since Jesus' resurrection is at the center of the Christian faith, everything Christians do is under the reign of God's power. **the wisdom of God** Christ can be described as the wisdom of God because his death and resurrection uniquely express God's mysterious plan of salvation (2:7; 4:1). Paul's description of Jesus as the wisdom of God also recalls the OT concept of personified Wisdom as God's agent of creation (Pr 8:22–31; compare note on Jn 1:1).

1:26 when you were called Refers to God's call to be saved by accepting his work through Christ and entering into a relationship with him.

1:27 the strong Paul is likely referencing the upper-class Corinthians who considered themselves superior (compare 1Co 11:17–34). Those who live by common wisdom rather than God's revelation in Christ are choosing to depend on their own strength over God's. Professional rhetoricians (sophists) of the first century mocked those of low status, considering them foolish and weak because they had not succeeded in gaining wealth and power. Paul argues against this view, suggesting that those who consider themselves better than people of low social standing are unwise and will be subject to public humiliation.

1:28 lowly things of this world Paul is likely referencing God's choice to bring salvation by sending his Son in the way he did — as a poor man from an unimportant region in the frailty of human form — rather than in the triumphant image of a god. This emphasizes that God does not value people based on status or wealth; all people are given the opportunity to be saved and have the right to be at God's table and be cared for (compare 11:21–22,33–34). Jesus' parables emphasize mercy and compassion for the weak rather than the status and accomplishments of the strong (e.g., Mt 20:1–16; Mk 2:15–17; Lk 11:45–53).

1:29 boast Some Corinthians may have placed their confidence in their rhetorical skills or spiritual gifts (compare ch. 14). Paul challenges them to depend on God's work in the cross rather than their self-sufficiency.

1:30 wisdom See note on v. 24. **righteousness** See note on Ro 1:17. **holiness** See note on 1Th 4:3; compare note on Ro 6:19. **redemption** Jesus paid the price for sin: death (Ro 6:23). This evokes the OT understanding of "redeemer" or *go'el* (see note on Ru 2:20 and note on Job 19:25).

1:31 the one who boasts Paul paraphrases Jer 9:24. In Jer 8:3—9:26, the prophet issues several oracles of God's judgment on those who lie, oppress people and commit idolatry. Those people who are wise in their own eyes will be put to shame (Jer 8:9; compare 1Co 1:21). God's people must not put their trust in their own wisdom, ability or wealth. The only safeguard is to boast in what God has done — in his accomplishments.

2:1–5 Paul describes the nature of his ministry to the Corinthians. He reminds them that when he came to Corinth he preached "foolishness"—that is, the message of Christ crucified—rather than relying on persuasive speech or worldly wisdom.

2:1 When I came to you Refers to Paul's missionary work in Corinth (Ac 18:1–18). **testimony about God** The Greek phrase used here, *martyrion tou theou*, refers to the news about God's redemptive work through the crucifixion of Jesus Christ.

2:2 to know nothing while I was with you Due to the influence of Greek culture, the Corinthians valued knowledge and rhetoric. Here, Paul uses hyperbole to explain why he made Christ's actions on behalf of humanity the primary focus of his teaching instead of delivering a speech in the style of secular rhetoric and knowledge. **except Jesus Christ and him crucified** For Paul, Jesus' death is central to the gospel message; he bore the sins of humanity through his death. Because the Corinthians seemed to have considered crucifixion to be foolishness, Paul emphasizes the humility of Jesus' death on the cross (see note on 1Co 1:18). This sets up Paul to describe the humble nature of his ministry in vv. 3–5.

2:3 great fear and trembling Paul draws a contrast between himself and professional public speakers who used eloquence and wisdom to gather an audience. The apostle was a skillful speaker, but his delivery may have been unimpressive by Corinthian standards (2Co 10:10).

2:4 not with wise and persuasive words Paul is not interested in seeing people come to Christ because of his persuasiveness; instead, he wants to see the Spirit working among them (see note on 1Co 1:28).

power, [5]so that your faith might not rest on human wisdom, but on God's power.

God's Wisdom Revealed by the Spirit

[6]We do, however, speak a message of wisdom among the mature, but not the wisdom of this age or of the rulers of this age, who are coming to nothing. [7]No, we declare God's wisdom, a mystery that has been hidden and that God destined for our glory before time began. [8]None of the rulers of this age understood it, for if they had, they would not have crucified the Lord of glory. [9]However, as it is written:

"What no eye has seen,
    what no ear has heard,
and what no human mind has conceived"[a] —
    the things God has prepared for those who
    love him —

[10]these are the things God has revealed to us by his Spirit.
    The Spirit searches all things, even the deep things of God. [11]For who knows a person's thoughts except their own spirit within them? In the same way no one knows the thoughts of God except the Spirit of God. [12]What we have received is not the spirit of the world, but the Spirit who is from God, so that we may understand what God has freely given us. [13]This is what we speak, not in words taught us by human wisdom but in words taught by the Spirit, explaining spiritual realities with Spirit-taught words.[b] [14]The person without the Spirit does not accept the things that come from the Spirit of God but considers them foolishness, and cannot understand them because they are discerned only through the Spirit. [15]The person with the Spirit makes judgments about all things, but such a person is not subject to merely human judgments, [16]for,

"Who has known the mind of the Lord
    so as to instruct him?"[c]

But we have the mind of Christ.

[a] 9 Isaiah 64:4   [b] 13 Or *Spirit, interpreting spiritual truths to those who are spiritual*   [c] 16 Isaiah 40:13

---

demonstration The Greek word used here, *apodeixis*, conveys the certainty of the Spirit's work among the Corinthian believers. While they value wisdom and logic, they cannot deny their experience of the Spirit's power, which is demonstrated in their own conversion (see 1:18,24; compare note on v. 3).
2:5 God's power See note on 1:24.

2:6–16 Paul argues that the Spirit is necessary to understand God's wisdom, since it cannot be perceived through human nature. Paul wants the Corinthians to recognize their need for true wisdom from God's Spirit before he resumes his appeal for unity beginning in 3:1 (see 1:10).

2:6 the mature The Greek word used here, *teleios*, refers to those who understand and conform to the message of Jesus Christ. Paul also may be applying the term ironically to the Corinthian believers, who considered themselves to be highly spiritual when in fact they were immature in the faith (compare 3:1–2). **not the wisdom of this age** God's wisdom—which is revealed in Christ's death, resurrection and the saving of humanity—is not bound by time; it is eternal. The particular age that Paul refers to is the time between Christ's ascension and his return—the time that people are living in now (compare 2Co 4:4; Gal 1:4). **rulers** The Greek word used here, *archōn*, can refer either to humans or to divine beings. This term may refer to the Jewish and Roman officials who were involved in the crucifixion of Christ. It also could refer to evil spiritual entities (compare Jn 12:31; 14:30).
2:8 Lord of glory Refers to Jesus Christ. This designation echoes the OT names of Yahweh: "King of glory" (Ps 24:7–10) and "God of glory" (Ps 29:3; Ac 7:2).
2:9 no eye has seen Paul uses Isa 64:4 to assert that people cannot understand the things of God through human faculties (compare Isa 52:15; 65:17); they must rely on the Spirit graciously given to believers by God (1Co 2:10). **for those who love him** Emphasizes that God grants insight regarding his work to those who follow him and do his will.
2:10 God has revealed to us God has shown the hidden wisdom of God to those who follow Christ (v. 7).

2:11 their own spirit Paul uses this phrase to draw a contrast with the Spirit of God. Just as people know their own minds, so the Spirit (*pneuma* in Greek) knows the things of God.
2:12 spirit of the world God's Spirit is not like the spirit of people or anything that can be comprehended, computed or reasoned in this world (compare 1:20; 2:6). While God's work is eternal, everything of this world is temporal—including current rulers and evil spiritual beings. **freely given** Refers to God's gracious gift of salvation, which believers can comprehend because of the Spirit (compare Ro 6:23). It therefore describes the content of God's revealed wisdom and thus refers to Christ himself (see note on 1Co 1:24).
2:13 by human wisdom Without God's help through the Spirit (v. 12), people lack the ability to understand his plans or work (i.e., God's plan of salvation; compare note on 1:24). **in words taught by the Spirit** Paul is likely referring to the gift of prophecy, which involves speaking on behalf of God (see note on 12:3; and note on 12:10; compare 14:1).
2:14 person without the Spirit Refers to a person who cannot grasp the things of God. **foolishness** See note on 1:18.
2:15 makes judgments about Paul again stresses that a true understanding of spiritual things occurs only with the aid of God's Spirit. Additionally, Paul might be referring to the spiritual gift of distinguishing between spirits (see note on 12:10), or the gift of wisdom (see note on 12:8). **such a person is not subject to merely human judgments** Those who belong to the Spirit do not need to subject themselves to human condemnation or approval; they recognize that God is their only judge (4:3).
2:16 so as to instruct him Paul draws from Isa 40:13 to emphasize the gift of the Spirit. Since Christ has no need of an advisor, this quotation suggests that God's wisdom is incomprehensible—yet he has enabled believers to understand the wisdom of his salvation through the crucified Messiah, Jesus. **the mind of Christ** Probably refers to God's gift of the Holy Spirit to his people. The presence of the Spirit grants believers the ability to discern God's will and works within them to make them more like Christ.

The Church and Its Leaders

3 Brothers and sisters, I could not address you as people who live by the Spirit but as people who are still worldly — mere infants in Christ. ²I gave you milk, not solid food, for you were not yet ready for it. Indeed, you are still not ready. ³You are still worldly. For since there is jealousy and quarreling among you, are you not worldly? Are you not acting like mere humans? ⁴For when one says, "I follow Paul," and another, "I follow Apollos," are you not mere human beings?

⁵What, after all, is Apollos? And what is Paul? Only servants, through whom you came to believe — as the Lord has assigned to each his task. ⁶I planted the seed, Apollos watered it, but God has been making it grow. ⁷So neither the one who plants nor the one who waters is anything, but only God, who makes things grow. ⁸The one who plants and the one who waters have one purpose, and they will each be rewarded according to their own labor. ⁹For we are co-workers in God's service; you are God's field, God's building.

¹⁰By the grace God has given me, I laid a foundation as a wise builder, and someone else is building on it. But each one should build with care. ¹¹For no one can lay any foundation other than the one already laid, which is Jesus Christ. ¹²If anyone builds on this foundation using gold, silver, costly stones, wood, hay or straw, ¹³their work will be shown for what it is, because the Day will bring it to light. It will be revealed with fire, and the fire will test the quality of each person's work. ¹⁴If what has been built survives, the builder will receive a reward. ¹⁵If it is burned up, the builder will suffer loss but yet will be saved — even though only as one escaping through the flames.

3:1–23 Paul warns the Corinthians against judging their leaders according to human wisdom instead of God's wisdom. He also reminds them that it is God who feeds and grows the church, not human leaders (1Co 3:4–9). Paul reminds the church that there is no room for rivalries. All leaders build on a single foundation — Jesus Christ — to help build up God's temple — his people (vv. 16–17).

3:1 Brothers and sisters The Greek word used here, *adelphoi*, collectively refers to both male and female believers. **as people who live by the Spirit** Paul's inability to address the Corinthian believers as spiritual people does not mean they do not have the Spirit; rather, they are conducting themselves like people who do not have the Spirit. **infants** Implies immaturity. The Corinthian believers demonstrated their immaturity through divisiveness and failure to grasp the significance of Jesus' death on the cross.

3:2 milk Probably refers to the original gospel message that the Corinthian believers accepted (2:6–16) — God's salvation revealed through the crucified Messiah, Jesus. **solid food** Involves the same basic content as "milk" (i.e., the gospel message), but with a more full and descriptive treatment (2:6–13).

3:3 worldly Emphasizes the Corinthian believers' immoral behavior, first mentioned in 1:11. The Greek word used here, *sarkikos*, refers to what is physical or earthly in contrast to what is spiritual; here, it refers specifically to the Corinthians' behavior.

3:4 I follow Paul See note on 1:12.

3:5 Apollos See note on 1:12. **through whom you came to believe** The Corinthian believers heard and received the gospel message from both Paul and Apollos (see Ac 18:11,27–28).

3:6 I planted Paul uses an agricultural metaphor to explain that different leaders have different roles in the growth of the church. Paul was responsible for founding the Corinthian church (2Co 10:14). Since these ministries are interdependent, each one is important. **watered** Refers to the instruction of the church community (Ac 18:27–28). **God has been making it grow** Identifies God as the source of maturity in the faith. The OT prophets often described God as a planter or builder (e.g., Jer 18:7–9; Eze 36:9–10).

3:8 rewarded God will reward Paul and Apollos for strengthening the faith of the church community. Their reward may include sharing in the joy of their master or receiving praise from God (Mt 25:21; 1Co 4:5).

3:9 field Represents the people of God, among whom his servants labor (compare 2Co 10:13–16). **God's building** Presents a unified picture of the church community. In 1Co 3:16–17, Paul describes the Corinthian believers as the temple of God.

3:10 the grace God has given Refers to God enabling the apostle Paul to plant new churches, especially the one in Corinth. **a foundation** Figuratively refers to Jesus Christ (2:2; 3:11), who is essential to the stability of the church community.

3:12 gold, silver, costly stones, wood, hay or straw The six items listed here collectively represent building materials that are compatible with the foundation of the building — Jesus Christ. The OT lists gold, silver, and precious stones as building materials of the temple, which Paul mentions in vv. 16–17 (e.g., 1Ch 22:14–16; 29:2; 2Ch 3:6).

3:13 Day See note on 1Co 1:8; note on 1Th 5:2. **with fire** Symbolizes testing and judgment. This judgment does not refer to a person's salvation, but to the quality of work done by those who labor on the foundation of Jesus Christ.

3:14 receive a reward Although Paul does not specify the reward here, it may include greater responsibility (Mt 25:21), praise from God (1Co 4:5), and the satisfaction of having one's work endure testing by fire.

3:15 builder will suffer loss Implies that the builders (leaders or teachers) will not receive payment because their work was consumed. These builders didn't use sound instruction. Instead, they used their own wisdom, which resulted in the weakening of believers rather than their strengthening and growth (compare v. 12 and note).

even though only as one escaping through the flames As in v. 13, the nature of this fire is evaluative, not punitive. Here, Paul completes the building metaphor from vv. 9–10. He claims that Jesus is the foundation of a building (the church), and that the teachers of Corinth are building a structure on top of that foundation (the Corinthian church). The function of this metaphor is both practical and cautionary: The Corinthians can evaluate the message of their teachers against received apostolic teaching, and they are warned against overestimating the worth of any individual teacher (1:12–17; 3:4–9).

16Don't you know that you yourselves are God's temple and that God's Spirit dwells in your midst? 17If anyone destroys God's temple, God will destroy that person; for God's temple is sacred, and you together are that temple.

18Do not deceive yourselves. If any of you think you are wise by the standards of this age, you should become "fools" so that you may become wise. 19For the wisdom of this world is foolishness in God's sight. As it is written: "He catches the wise in their craftiness"[a]; 20and again, "The Lord knows that the thoughts of the wise are futile."[b] 21So then, no more boasting about human leaders! All things are yours, 22whether Paul or Apollos or Cephas[c] or the world or life or death or the present or the future — all are yours, 23and you are of Christ, and Christ is of God.

The Nature of True Apostleship

4 This, then, is how you ought to regard us: as servants of Christ and as those entrusted with the mysteries God has revealed. 2Now it is required that those who have been given a trust must prove faithful. 3I care very little if I am judged by you or by any human court; indeed, I do not even judge myself. 4My conscience is clear, but that does not make me innocent. It is the Lord who judges me. 5Therefore judge nothing before the appointed time; wait until the Lord comes. He will bring to light what is hidden in darkness and will expose the motives of the heart. At that time each will receive their praise from God.

6Now, brothers and sisters, I have applied these things to myself and Apollos for your benefit, so that you may learn from us the meaning of the saying, "Do not go beyond what is written." Then you will not be puffed up in being a follower of one of us over against the other. 7For who makes you different from anyone else? What do you have that you did not receive? And if you did receive it, why do you boast as though you did not?

8Already you have all you want! Already you have become rich! You have begun to reign — and that without us! How I wish that you really had begun to reign so that we also might reign with you! 9For it seems to me that God has put us apostles on display at the end of the procession, like

a 19 Job 5:13   b 20 Psalm 94:11   c 22 That is, Peter

3:16 God's temple Extending his metaphor from v. 9, Paul now calls the Corinthian congregation "God's temple"—the location of his presence in the Spirit in that city. Elsewhere, this language is applied to individual believers (see 6:19; compare Ro 8:9). Here, however, the notion applies to the entire congregation. Just as the Jerusalem temple served to unify Israel, the corporate temple concept in Paul's writings serves to unify the church. The Corinthians represent a unified body wherein God dwells; there can be no divisions among them. **in your midst** Paul uses the plural form of a Greek term to emphasize that the entire church community is God's temple (his dwelling place on earth), not just select individuals.
3:17 destroys A result of disputes and poor teaching. **God will destroy that person** God's wrath will come upon those who attempt to destroy his metaphorical temple—the Corinthian church. Specifically, Paul is likely thinking of those who caused divisions within the congregation (1Co 1:11–13; 3:4).
3:19 catches Paul is asserting that the "wise" are really without understanding, a point he makes similarly in 2:8. Compare Job 5:13.
3:20 futile Paul quotes Ps 94:11 to disparage human wisdom.
3:21 no more boasting Paul's instruction echoes Jer 9:24 (see note on 1Co 1:31). The Corinthian believers must no longer identify themselves by the ministers they prefer, because it is causing rivalry and strife in the community. **All things are yours** Paul reminds them that the ministers actually belong to the people being taught, not the other way around (v. 22). Paul subverts the Corinthians' allegiance to individual leaders (being "of" a particular leader) by reminding them that they are all "of Christ" (v. 23).
3:22 Paul or Apollos or Cephas See note on 1:12.

4:1–13 In this passage, Paul discusses the nature of genuine Christian leadership. He argues that the standard for Christian leaders is set by God alone (vv. 1–5) and that suffering is a hallmark of Christian ministry (vv. 6–13).

4:1 This, then, is how you ought to regard us Refers to the ministers Paul, Apollos and Cephas (3:22). **servants** The Greek word used here, *hypēretas*, is plural, emphasizing that Paul is one of many who ministered among the believers in Corinth. **mysteries God has revealed** Refers to the truth of the gospel message which the Spirit reveals apart from the wisdom of people (see 1:24 and note).
4:4 that does not make me innocent He does not rely on his conscience, but on God to judge his faithfulness; this does not mean that he is acquitted of unfaithfulness. Because Paul does not evaluate himself, he is not aware of any charge of unfaithfulness against him (v. 2).
4:6 not go beyond what is written The difficult Greek phrase used here, *to mē hyper ha gegraptai*, likely reflects a common slogan among the Corinthian believers. They may have used it in response to teachers who supplemented received apostolic teaching with worldly wisdom or divisiveness, thereby causing divisions within the congregation (see v. 7; compare 3:15 and note). By using this phrase, Paul is saying that he and Apollos adhered to the accepted standard (preaching the gospel) and did not elevate one teacher over another (compare 1:10–17; 3:4–9). It is also possible that the phrase refers to Scripture in a general sense or, more specifically, to scriptures already cited in the letter (e.g., 1:19,31; 2:9,16; 3:19–20).
4:8 You have begun to reign The statements in this verse are ironic. Paul contrasts himself with the believers in Corinth to expose the absurdity of their attitude. They cannot credit themselves for their wisdom, wealth or status.
4:9 apostles Includes not only the Twelve (Mt 10:2–4), but others sent out to proclaim the gospel message, such as Paul and Barnabas (Ac 14:14), Andronicus and Junia (Ro 16:7), and James (Gal 1:19). **like those condemned to die** Refers to subjection to humiliation as well as execution.

those condemned to die in the arena. We have been made a spectacle to the whole universe, to angels as well as to human beings. [10]We are fools for Christ, but you are so wise in Christ! We are weak, but you are strong! You are honored, we are dishonored! [11]To this very hour we go hungry and thirsty, we are in rags, we are brutally treated, we are homeless. [12]We work hard with our own hands. When we are cursed, we bless; when we are persecuted, we endure it; [13]when we are slandered, we answer kindly. We have become the scum of the earth, the garbage of the world — right up to this moment.

Paul's Appeal and Warning

[14]I am writing this not to shame you but to warn you as my dear children. [15]Even if you had ten thousand guardians in Christ, you do not have many fathers, for in Christ Jesus I became your father through the gospel. [16]Therefore I urge you to imitate me. [17]For this reason I have sent to you Timothy, my son whom I love, who is faithful in the Lord. He will remind you of my way of life

in Christ Jesus, which agrees with what I teach everywhere in every church.

[18]Some of you have become arrogant, as if I were not coming to you. [19]But I will come to you very soon, if the Lord is willing, and then I will find out not only how these arrogant people are talking, but what power they have. [20]For the kingdom of God is not a matter of talk but of power. [21]What do you prefer? Shall I come to you with a rod of discipline, or shall I come in love and with a gentle spirit?

Dealing With a Case of Incest

5 It is actually reported that there is sexual immorality among you, and of a kind that even pagans do not tolerate: A man is sleeping with his father's wife. [2]And you are proud! Shouldn't you rather have gone into mourning and have put out of your fellowship the man who has been doing this? [3]For my part, even though I am not physically present, I am with you in spirit. As one who is present with you in this way, I have already passed judgment in the name of our Lord

---

4:10 fools The Corinthian believers assume they have wisdom, but in reality they have acted like fools (1Co 4:7). In contrast, the apostles endure humiliation for the sake of Christ and the church, yet the Corinthians consider them foolish.

4:11 homeless Paul was an itinerant minister—he moved from place to place without a settled residence. This contrasts the Corinthians, whom Paul sarcastically describes as rich and satiated (v. 8). This line also relates Paul's work to the ministry and life of Jesus Christ (see Lk 9:58).

4:12 our own hands Paul worked as a tentmaker when he arrived in Corinth (Ac 18:1–4). **when we are persecuted, we endure** The three statements in 1Co 4:12–13 articulate some of the opposition Paul encountered during his evangelistic efforts. Like Christ, he persevered for the sake of the gospel. Some of Jesus' sayings may lie behind Paul's statements here (see Mt 5:44; Lk 6:28).

4:13 the scum Paul is using degrading terms to convey the world's contemptuous evaluation of the apostles. Those who faithfully serve Christ by preaching the message of the cross will always appear to be worthless according to the world's wisdom.

4:14–21 Paul appeals to the Corinthians as the person who first preached the gospel to them and founded their church. Drawing on his unique relationship with the church, Paul urges the Corinthians to trust his character and imitate him as a worthy Christ follower.

4:14 to shame you People in Greco-Roman society sought to avoid losing public honor. Paul does not want to provoke or discourage the Corinthians with his letter; rather, he wants to warn them about the disastrous consequences of pride and division. **my dear children** See 2Co 6:13 and note.

4:15 guardians Typically refers to a person who accompanied a child to school and was responsible for their safety. Here Paul probably applies the term to other Christian ministers who served the Corinthians but did not instruct them. **I became your father** Paul

was responsible for the initial conversions in the city of Corinth (Ac 18:4,8,11; compare 2Co 10:14).

4:16 to imitate me Paul encourages the Corinthians to practice his life model since he is imitating Jesus (1Co 4:9–13), whom he met personally (Ac 9:1–9). Paul made this appeal to other churches in Macedonia and Achaia (1Th 2:14; 2Th 3:9; Php 4:9).

4:17 I have sent Paul had sent Timothy to Corinth before he wrote this letter (see Ac 19:22). **my son whom I love, who is faithful** Paul refers to Timothy as his spiritual son (see note on Php 1:1; 1Ti 1:2).

4:20 kingdom of God Refers to the reign of God expressed in the lives of his people. While the kingdom of God is a present reality, it is not yet fully here. Here Paul urges the Corinthian believers to live according to the value system of God's kingdom, which prizes powerful deeds more than persuasive speech.

4:21 a rod An instrument used for punishment or discipline. **with a gentle spirit** Compare Gal 6:1.

5:1–13 Paul addresses an instance of appalling sexual immorality within the church. In this passage, Paul aims to correct not only the behavior of the sexually immoral man, but also the church's boastful tolerance of sin.

5:1 sexual immorality The Greek word used here, *porneia*, can refer to a number of illicit sexual behaviors. Here it refers to a specific instance of sexual immorality that jeopardized the health of the Corinthian church. **his father's wife** This phrase likely refers to a stepmother, not a biological mother.

5:2 you are proud Members of Greco-Roman and Jewish society considered this an abhorrent act, yet some within the church community mistakenly tolerated it because of a distorted understanding of grace (compare Ro 6:1,15).

5:3 I am with you in spirit Paul either means that he is present with the Corinthians through the presence of the Holy Spirit or his own spirit (compare 1Co 5:4). **in the name of our Lord Jesus** Expresses the authoritative nature of Paul's instruction to expel the man practicing sexual immorality (1Co 5:1).

Jesus on the one who has been doing this. ⁴So when you are assembled and I am with you in spirit, and the power of our Lord Jesus is present, ⁵hand this man over to Satan for the destruction of the flesh,ᵃ,ᵇ so that his spirit may be saved on the day of the Lord.

⁶Your boasting is not good. Don't you know that a little yeast leavens the whole batch of dough? ⁷Get rid of the old yeast, so that you may be a new unleavened batch — as you really are. For Christ, our Passover lamb, has been sacrificed. ⁸Therefore let us keep the Festival, not with the old bread leavened with malice and wickedness, but with the unleavened bread of sincerity and truth.

⁹I wrote to you in my letter not to associate with sexually immoral people — ¹⁰not at all meaning the people of this world who are immoral, or the greedy and swindlers, or idolaters. In that case you would have to leave this world. ¹¹But now I am writing to you that you must not associate with anyone who claims to be a brother or sisterᶜ but is sexually immoral or greedy, an idolater or

slanderer, a drunkard or swindler. Do not even eat with such people.

¹²What business is it of mine to judge those outside the church? Are you not to judge those inside? ¹³God will judge those outside. "Expel the wicked person from among you."ᵈ

Lawsuits Among Believers

6 If any of you has a dispute with another, do you dare to take it before the ungodly for judgment instead of before the Lord's people? ²Or do you not know that the Lord's people will judge the world? And if you are to judge the world, are you not competent to judge trivial cases? ³Do you not know that we will judge angels? How much more the things of this life! ⁴Therefore, if you have disputes about

ᵃ 5 In contexts like this, the Greek word for *flesh* (*sarx*) refers to the sinful state of human beings, often presented as a power in opposition to the Spirit.   ᵇ 5 Or *of his body*   ᶜ 11 The Greek word for *brother or sister* (*adelphos*) refers here to a believer, whether man or woman, as part of God's family; also in 8:11, 13.   ᵈ 13 Deut. 13:5; 17:7; 19:19; 21:21; 22:21,24; 24:7

5:5 hand this man over Refers to expulsion from the church community — probably including their worship gatherings, their meals and the Lord's Supper (compare 1Ti 1:20). **to Satan** Paul is likely suggesting that those outside the community of believers belong to the realm of Satan (see 2Co 4:4 and note; Eph 2:2). In that scenario, Paul would be suggesting that the sinner was handed over to the realm of sin ruled by the evil one (Satan). **for the destruction of the flesh** Paul is not referring to physical death for this person since the goal is repentance and eventual restoration. Immediate physical death accompanied divine judgment for sin (Ac 5:1–11; 1Co 11:30–32), but this is probably not the case here. The purpose of this discipline is to break the pattern of sin (compare Gal 5:24). **day of the Lord** See note on 1Co 1:8.

5:6 a little yeast In this context, the leaven (yeast) represents the man's sexual immorality (v. 1) as well as the community's prideful tolerance of his sin.

5:7 Get rid of the old yeast Paul urges believers to stop tolerating immoral behavior. God commanded the Israelites to celebrate Passover with unleavened bread (Ex 12:14–15). In preparation for the feast, Jews cleaned their homes of all leaven (yeast). Likewise, the Corinthian believers must expel the sexually immoral man from among them (1Co 5:1,13). **Christ, our Passover lamb** Refers to Christ's sacrificial death on the cross. Just as lambs were slaughtered during the Passover feast to atone for sin (see Ex 12), Christ died for the same purpose; his was the final payment for sin.

5:9 in my letter Probably refers to a previous letter that Paul wrote to the Corinthians. **not to associate with sexually immoral people** As he explains in 1Co 5:10–11, Paul is not referring to the sexually immoral people of the world (his mission field), but to those who call themselves Christians and participate in sexual immorality. He views such people as dangerous to the overall health of the congregation since they may entice others to follow them in sin.

5:11 Do not even eat Paul may be referring either to meals in the church community or to all meals in general, even those between individuals. In Paul's time, sharing a

meal communicated that the participants shared values. Paul does not want shared meals to implicitly express approval for the man's immorality (v. 1).

5:13 Expel the wicked person Paul intends for the immoral believer to be expelled so that he may repent and then be restored back to the community (see v. 5 and note). He uses OT language to make this point (see note on v. 9; compare Dt 13:5; 19:19; 21:21).

6:1–11 Paul counsels the Corinthian church regarding lawsuits between its members. He urges them to resolve matters internally rather than appeal to authorities outside the church.

6:1 a dispute Refers to a dispute that leads to a trial in court. The context is more comparable to civil litigation rather than a criminal case. **the ungodly** In this context, the word used here is closely related to "unbeliever" in 1Co 6:6. **Lord's people** See note on Ro 1:7.

6:2 Lord's people will judge the world Refers to a future judgment, probably on the day of the Lord (1Co 1:8; 5:5) when Jesus Christ returns to judge the world. Paul asserts that believers will participate in this event in some way. For this reason, he considers it inappropriate for them to take their disagreements before those whom they will judge.

6:3 judge angels Paul's suggestion that believers would rule over angels builds on his language in v. 2 alluding to the role of believers in the administration of the kingdom of God, as members of his family (compare Jn 1:12; Ro 8:18–25; Heb 2:10–13; 2Pe 1:4; 1Jn 3:1–3). The Jewish tradition of judging the angels was developed based on interpretations of texts such as Da 7 and 1 Enoch 1:10–12 (a Jewish, extrabiblical work). It is unclear whether Paul is referring to the judgment of all angels or just evil ones.

6:4 whose way of life is scorned in the church Probably refers to the unrighteous judges (see note on 1Co 6:1). These judges held a high social status, but Paul suggests that their status means nothing in the church community (*ekklēsia* in Greek). Alternatively, Paul could be referring ironically to believers who had low status within the Christian community.

such matters, do you ask for a ruling from those whose way of life is scorned in the church? [5]I say this to shame you. Is it possible that there is nobody among you wise enough to judge a dispute between believers? [6]But instead, one brother takes another to court — and this in front of unbelievers!

[7]The very fact that you have lawsuits among you means you have been completely defeated already. Why not rather be wronged? Why not rather be cheated? [8]Instead, you yourselves cheat and do wrong, and you do this to your brothers and sisters. [9]Or do you not know that wrongdoers will not inherit the kingdom of God? Do not be deceived: Neither the sexually immoral nor idolaters nor adulterers nor men who have sex with men[a] [10]nor thieves nor the greedy nor drunkards nor slanderers nor swindlers will inherit the kingdom of God. [11]And that is what some of you were. But you were washed, you were sanctified, you were justified in the name of the Lord Jesus Christ and by the Spirit of our God.

Sexual Immorality

[12]"I have the right to do anything," you say — but not everything is beneficial. "I have the right to do anything" — but I will not be mastered by anything. [13]You say, "Food for the stomach and the stomach for food, and God will destroy them both." The body, however, is not meant for sexual immorality but for the Lord, and the Lord for the body. [14]By his power God raised the Lord from the dead, and he will raise us also. [15]Do you not know that your bodies are members of Christ himself? Shall I then take the members of Christ and unite them with a prostitute? Never! [16]Do you not know that he who unites himself with a prostitute is one with her in body? For it is said, "The two will become one flesh."[b] [17]But whoever is united with the Lord is one with him in spirit.[c]

[18]Flee from sexual immorality. All other sins a person commits are outside the body, but whoever sins sexually, sins against their own body. [19]Do you not know that your bodies are temples of the Holy Spirit, who is in you, whom you have received from God? You are not your own; [20]you were bought at a price. Therefore honor God with your bodies.

---

[a] 9 The words *men who have sex with men* translate two Greek words that refer to the passive and active participants in homosexual acts.　[b] 16 Gen. 2:24　[c] 17 Or *in the Spirit*

6:5 to judge a dispute Although the Corinthians claimed to be wise (3:18; 4:10), no one among them was wise enough to resolve disputes between believers. Paul uses sarcasm to expose the absurdity of this situation.

6:7 you have lawsuits among you These believers have presented fellow Christians to the authorities, hurting the social standing of the church in Corinth. Paul insists that they must handle such matters within the church community, not the public courts.

6:8 you yourselves cheat and do wrong Paul addresses the defendants in the dispute, urging them not to defraud other believers and provoke a legal dispute.

6:9 will not inherit Paul further clarifies why believers should attempt to settle disputes among themselves: Those outside the faith community will not be part of God's kingdom. The description of unbelievers in vv. 9–10 reveals their unrighteous character; such persons are not qualified to judge God's holy people. **the kingdom of God** See note on 4:20. **idolaters** See 1Th 1:9 and note; compare Ex 20:3–6. **men who have sex with men** The two related Greek words used at the end of 1Co 6:9 are *malakos* and *arsenokoitēs*. Translated literally, *malakos* can mean "soft" or "effeminate." The term was used to describe a person—often a young boy—in a passive role in same-sex relations. The precise meaning of the second word, *arsenokoitēs*, is less clear, but it could be used to refer to the dominant role in same-sex intercourse. If these basic definitions are correct, then the two terms function together as a condemnation of same-sex relations (compare Ro 1:26–27).

6:11 you were sanctified See note on 1Co 1:2. **were justified** God acquitted them of their wrongdoing and accepted them as righteous in his sight (compare 4:4).

6:12–20 Paul continues to address the conduct of the Corinthian believers. Here he denounces them for using a distorted understanding of freedom in Christ to validate their visitations of prostitutes.

6:12 I have the right to do anything The Corinthians likely used this slogan as an excuse to mistreat and abuse the physical body (e.g., through sexual immorality; v. 19). Paul cites it negatively in 10:23.

6:13 the stomach for food Describes a person's sexual appetite using a well-known euphemism from the ancient world. The logic of the metaphor is that just as the stomach's appetite is meant to be satisfied with food, so the body is meant to be satisfied through sexual activity. **sexual immorality** See 5:1.

6:14 he will raise us Believers should not misuse their bodies for sexual immorality because God cares about their bodies that will be resurrected; rather, they must recognize that their bodies belong to the Lord, who will resurrect them (15:35–41).

6:15 members of Christ The individual members of the church comprise the body of Christ (the church as a unit). If a believer visits a prostitute, the person not only joins their entire self to a prostitute, but the whole body of Christ.

6:16 The two will become one flesh Paul quotes the Septuagint (Greek translation of the OT) version of Ge 2:24 to support his prohibition of sexual relations with prostitutes. Sexual intercourse creates a unique bond between two people. Because Paul addresses various Greco-Roman customs throughout this book (see 1Co 8), he is likely referring to temple prostitution, which was practiced in Corinth.

6:17 united with the Lord Paul draws from the OT, which describes the union between God and his people (Jer 50:5; Zec 2:11). When people enter into covenant with God, they become united with him in spirit by the Spirit. This union, like a marriage, restricts them from engaging in other unions that would defile their covenant relationship with God.

6:18 sexual immorality See note on 1Co 5:1. **outside the body** The Corinthians may have assumed that their physical bodies were not subject to moral instruction (see note on v. 13); thus, they believed that everything is permissible. Paul counters their assumption; he argues that those who sin sexually also sin against their own bodies.

6:19 temples In this context, Paul focuses on individual

Concerning Married Life

7 Now for the matters you wrote about: "It is good for a man not to have sexual relations with a woman." ²But since sexual immorality is occurring, each man should have sexual relations with his own wife, and each woman with her own husband. ³The husband should fulfill his marital duty to his wife, and likewise the wife to her husband. ⁴The wife does not have authority over her own body but yields it to her husband. In the same way, the husband does not have authority over his own body but yields it to his wife. ⁵Do not deprive each other except perhaps by mutual consent and for a time, so that you may devote yourselves to prayer. Then come together again so that Satan will not tempt you because of your lack of self-control. ⁶I say this as a concession, not as a command. ⁷I wish that all of you were as I am. But each of you has your own gift from God; one has this gift, another has that.

⁸Now to the unmarried[a] and the widows I say: It is good for them to stay unmarried, as I do. ⁹But if they cannot control themselves, they should marry, for it is better to marry than to burn with passion.

¹⁰To the married I give this command (not I, but the Lord): A wife must not separate from her husband. ¹¹But if she does, she must remain unmarried or else be reconciled to her husband. And a husband must not divorce his wife.

¹²To the rest I say this (I, not the Lord): If any brother has a wife who is not a believer and she is willing to live with him, he must not divorce her. ¹³And if a woman has a husband who is not a believer and he is willing to live with her, she must not divorce him. ¹⁴For the unbelieving husband has been sanctified through his wife, and the unbelieving wife has been sanctified through her believing husband. Otherwise your children would be unclean, but as it is, they are holy.

[a] 8 Or *widowers*

---

believers instead of the entire church community. See note on 3:16; compare 2Co 6:16 and note.

6:20 you were bought at a price In Paul's time, masters purchased slaves from other masters, thereby issuing a change in ownership for a slave. Paul reminds the Corinthians that God purchased them from slavery to sin and death through the sacrificial death of Christ. Therefore, they belong to God, not to themselves (1Co 6:13; compare Gal 2:19–20).

7:1–24 Paul now turns to answer questions from the Corinthian church. The Corinthian believers wrote to him about several issues in the church community, including marriage (1Co 7:1), virgins (v. 25), food sacrificed to idols (8:1), spiritual gifts (12:1), and the money he was collecting for Jerusalem Christians (16:1). Paul spends a majority of the rest of the letter responding to these inquiries.

7:1 the matters you wrote about The precise nature of the Corinthians' first question is unknown. Paul's response suggests that the inquiry was broadly related to matters of marriage and sexual relations. **to have sexual relations with a woman** The Greek text here uses an idiom to refer to having sexual intercourse with a woman; it may not imply marriage. This is most likely a quote from the Corinthians' previous letter to Paul and not the position of the apostle himself. Some married believers in Corinth deprived their spouses of sexual relations on the basis of this slogan.

7:4 The wife does not have authority In Paul's view, married men and women have pledged their bodies to their spouses and thus do not have authority to deny their spouses sexual relations. Paul's perspective assumes a framework in which a godly, loving husband does not take advantage of his wife (see note on Eph 5:23; note on Eph 5:25).

7:5 Do not deprive each other Paul advises married Corinthian believers not to deprive each other of sexual relations (see note on 1Co 7:1); doing so could lead them into temptation. **devote yourselves to prayer** Paul advises the Corinthians to practice abstinence within marriage only for the express purpose of a limited season of focused prayer. See the table "Prayers in Paul's Letters" on p. 1925. **Satan** This type of sexual deprivation within marriage provides an easy means for Satan to tempt people.

7:7 your own gift from God Paul implies that married believers should remain married and continue to fulfill their marital obligations (see v. 4), but those unmarried believers who don't have trouble with sexual desires should remain single.

7:8 unmarried The Greek work used here, *agamos*, occurs only four times in the NT, all in this passage (compare vv. 11,32,34). The word refers to someone who has no spouse, a state that may result from various circumstances: death of one's spouse, desertion by a spouse (see v. 15), divorce or remaining single. **good for them** Paul describes the advantages of remaining single in vv. 32–34, but he recognizes that not everyone has this "gift" (v. 7); some people should get married (v. 9; compare v. 39).

7:9 to burn with passion Refers to intense sexual desire. Some believers could not refrain from illicitly satisfying their sexual desire. He advises such people to marry and enjoy sexual relations within an exclusive relationship.

7:10 not I, but the Lord Refers to Jesus, who provided his own commands about divorce (e.g., Mt 5:32; 19:9; Mk 10:11; Lk 16:18). While Roman law and some Jewish teachers permitted divorce, Jesus did not permit divorce except in cases of marital unfaithfulness.

7:11 she must remain unmarried or else be reconciled to her husband Paul is not categorically prohibiting all remarriage after divorce; instead, he is encouraging people to be free in Christ just as he is, rather than seeking another spouse. There may have been a problem in Corinth with believers divorcing unbelievers for the sake of marrying a believer (compare note on 1Co 7:14).

7:12 he must not divorce her Paul applies the same instruction from vv. 10–11 to believers who are married to unbelievers. In this instance, if an unbeliever chooses to remain married to a believer, the couple should not seek divorce.

7:14 has been sanctified Some believing spouses in Corinth may have been concerned that sexual relations with their unbelieving spouse would cause defilement.

¹⁵But if the unbeliever leaves, let it be so. The brother or the sister is not bound in such circumstances; God has called us to live in peace. ¹⁶How do you know, wife, whether you will save your husband? Or, how do you know, husband, whether you will save your wife?

Concerning Change of Status

¹⁷Nevertheless, each person should live as a believer in whatever situation the Lord has assigned to them, just as God has called them. This is the rule I lay down in all the churches. ¹⁸Was a man already circumcised when he was called? He should not become uncircumcised. Was a man uncircumcised when he was called? He should not be circumcised. ¹⁹Circumcision is nothing and uncircumcision is nothing. Keeping God's commands is what counts. ²⁰Each person should remain in the situation they were in when God called them.

²¹Were you a slave when you were called? Don't let it trouble you — although if you can gain your freedom, do so. ²²For the one who was a slave when called to faith in the Lord is the Lord's freed person; similarly, the one who was free when called is Christ's slave. ²³You were bought at a price; do not become slaves of human beings. ²⁴Brothers and sisters, each person, as responsible to God, should remain in the situation they were in when God called them.

Concerning the Unmarried

²⁵Now about virgins: I have no command from the Lord, but I give a judgment as one who by the Lord's mercy is trustworthy. ²⁶Because of the present crisis, I think that it is good for a man to remain as he is. ²⁷Are you pledged to a woman? Do not seek to be released. Are you free from such a commitment? Do not look for a wife. ²⁸But if you do marry, you have not sinned; and if a virgin marries, she has not sinned. But those who marry will face many troubles in this life, and I want to spare you this.

²⁹What I mean, brothers and sisters, is that the time is short. From now on those who have wives should live as if they do not; ³⁰those who mourn, as if they did not; those who are happy, as if they were not; those who buy something, as if it were not theirs to keep; ³¹those who use the things of the world, as if not engrossed in them. For this world in its present form is passing away.

³²I would like you to be free from concern. An unmarried man is concerned about the Lord's affairs — how he can please the Lord. ³³But a married man is concerned about the affairs of this world — how he can please his wife — ³⁴and his interests are divided. An unmarried woman or virgin is concerned about the Lord's affairs: Her aim is to be devoted to the Lord in both body and spirit. But a married woman is concerned about the affairs of this world — how she can please her husband. ³⁵I am saying this for your own good, not

Paul explains to these believers that they are not defiled; instead, it is their unbelieving spouses who are sanctified through the process of knowing a believer (compare v. 16). **holy** Just as it is acceptable for a believing wife to have sexual relations with an unbelieving husband, it is also acceptable for her to have children by her husband.

7:16 you will save The believing spouse may have the opportunity to participate in the conversion of the unbelieving spouse. In this way, the believer becomes an instrument that helps the unbeliever turn toward God (9:20–22).

7:17 God has called them Paul encourages the Corinthian believers to maintain whatever marital situation they were in when they first heard God's call.

7:19 Circumcision A sign of the covenant that God made with Abraham (Ge 17:11). Jews valued circumcision as a sign that they were part of God's covenant people. But Paul suggests the Spirit replaced circumcision as that sign; therefore, it no longer has any value (Ro 2:29; compare Gal 6:15).

7:21 Don't let it trouble Some believing slaves in Corinth may have been concerned that their social status inhibited them from living for God. Paul argues that if their status did not inhibit God's call to salvation, it will not inhibit them now that they have the Spirit.

7:22 Christ's slave Paul asserts that those who were not slaves should regard Christ as their spiritual master. Since they no longer belong to themselves, they must seek to obey Jesus Christ.

7:23 You were bought at a price See note on 1Co 6:20. **slaves of human beings** Paul urges the believers not to become enslaved to human wisdom or troubled

by the traditions of marriage, slavery and circumcision; Paul wants them to focus on Christ and what he has done for them.

7:25–40 Paul addresses the unmarried believers in the Corinthian congregation.

7:25 virgins The Greek word used here, *parthenos*, can refer to a young woman who is engaged to be married. **7:26 present crisis** May refer to food shortages in Corinth. Alternatively, the phrase may refer to a period of intense difficulties prior to the return of Christ.

7:27 Do not look for a wife Paul notes that for some believers it is preferable that they remain unmarried (vv. 6–8,26), but he tells them in the next verse that if they do marry, it is not a sin.

7:28 if a virgin marries, she has not sinned The Corinthians may have assumed that marriage was somehow sinful, possibly based upon Paul's example or suggestion that they remain celibate when possible.

7:29 should live as if they do not Paul urges the Corinthians not to become consumed by temporal matters or worldly concerns.

7:30 those who mourn, as if they did not Paul alludes to Ecc 3:1–8.

7:31 this world in its present form Refers to the world's system rather than the physical appearance of the world.

7:34 unmarried woman or virgin Refers to two different groups of women in the church community (see note on 1Co 7:25).

7:35 not to restrict Paul hoped that his instruction would free the Corinthians from anxiety—not cause them more of it.

to restrict you, but that you may live in a right way in undivided devotion to the Lord.

³⁶If anyone is worried that he might not be acting honorably toward the virgin he is engaged to, and if his passions are too strong[a] and he feels he ought to marry, he should do as he wants. He is not sinning. They should get married. ³⁷But the man who has settled the matter in his own mind, who is under no compulsion but has control over his own will, and who has made up his mind not to marry the virgin — this man also does the right thing. ³⁸So then, he who marries the virgin does right, but he who does not marry her does better.[b]

³⁹A woman is bound to her husband as long as he lives. But if her husband dies, she is free to marry anyone she wishes, but he must belong to the Lord. ⁴⁰In my judgment, she is happier if she stays as she is — and I think that I too have the Spirit of God.

Concerning Food Sacrificed to Idols

8 Now about food sacrificed to idols: We know that "We all possess knowledge." But knowledge puffs up while love builds up. ²Those who think they know something do not yet know as they ought to know. ³But whoever loves God is known by God.[c]

⁴So then, about eating food sacrificed to idols: We know that "An idol is nothing at all in the world" and that "There is no God but one." ⁵For even if there are so-called gods, whether in heaven or on earth (as indeed there are many "gods" and many "lords"), ⁶yet for us there is but one God, the Father, from whom all things came and for whom we live; and there is but one Lord, Jesus Christ, through whom all things came and through whom we live.

⁷But not everyone possesses this knowledge. Some people are still so accustomed to idols that when they eat sacrificial food they think of it as having been sacrificed to a god, and since their conscience is weak, it is defiled. ⁸But food does not bring us near to God; we are no worse if we do not eat, and no better if we do.

⁹Be careful, however, that the exercise of your rights does not become a stumbling block to the weak. ¹⁰For if someone with a weak conscience sees you, with all your knowledge, eating in an idol's temple, won't that person be emboldened

---

[a] 36 Or *if she is getting beyond the usual age for marriage*
[b] 36-38 Or *³⁶If anyone thinks he is not treating his daughter properly, and if she is getting along in years (or if her passions are too strong), and he feels she ought to marry, he should do as he wants. He is not sinning. He should let her get married. ³⁷But the man who has settled the matter in his own mind, who is under no compulsion but has control over his own will, and who has made up his mind to keep the virgin unmarried — this man also does the right thing. ³⁸So then, he who gives his virgin in marriage does right, but he who does not give her in marriage does better.*
[c] 2,3 An early manuscript and another ancient witness *think they have knowledge do not yet know as they ought to know. ³But whoever loves truly knows.*

7:39 free to marry anyone she wishes Paul addresses the widows within the church community: they may remarry, but only to another believer.

7:40 I think that I too have the Spirit of God Some Corinthian believers claimed to be spiritual (2:15–16) yet offered troubling counsel to other believers in the church community. Paul describes himself as filled with the Spirit and therefore able to provide authoritative and wise instruction.

8:1–13 Paul takes up the next issue raised by the Corinthians: the question of whether believers should purchase and consume meat that was previously sacrificed to idols. Paul encourages the Corinthians to act out of love for their fellow believers rather than out of their allegedly superior knowledge.

8:1 about food sacrificed to idols When meat was sacrificed to idols, the priest or worshiper burned it at the altar and then ate some of it. Merchants often sold another portion of this meat for private use. **We all possess knowledge** Likely another slogan used by the Corinthians (compare 6:12; 7:1). This knowledge may refer to general knowledge about idols or to knowledge given by the Spirit.

8:2 Those who think they know something Some Corinthian believers assumed that knowledge was the true sign of spirituality. They did not understand that knowledge without love indicates a lack of knowledge.

8:3 loves Paul identifies love as the true basis of knowledge.

8:4 An idol is nothing at all in the world Some Corinthian believers correctly discerned that an idol was an inanimate object with no real divine power. **no God but one** Possibly an allusion to the Shema (see note on Dt 6:4). See 1Co 8:6.

8:5 there are many "gods" and many "lords" Paul acknowledges that people worshiped other divine beings as gods and lords (Gal 4:8; 1Co 10:20). It seems that Jews in the ancient Near East affirmed the existence of other gods (Dt 32:17; Ps 82:1) but considered them inherently inferior to the God of Israel, who created everything and is greater than all false gods (compare Ps 86:8; 95:3; 96:4; 135:5).

8:6 one Lord, Jesus Christ In a stunning turn of phrase, Paul boldly includes Jesus in his restatement of the great Jewish monotheistic prayer, the Shema. He then draws on this proclamation of the uniqueness of God the Father — and now the Lord Jesus Christ, as well — to deny the legitimacy of the so-called gods and lords of the pagan world.

8:7 having been sacrificed to a god In the Greco-Roman world eating food sacrificed to idols was sometimes considered a means of communion with the gods. **since their conscience is weak** Describes believers who could not understand that idols are not actual divine powers (1Co 8:4). To their consciences, consuming meat sacrificed to idols seemed like idolatry.

8:9 exercise of your rights The Corinthians who considered themselves more spiritual assumed that they had the right to do whatever they wanted without considering the effects of their actions upon other believers (see v. 12).

8:10 an idol's temple Some Corinthian believers not only ate meat sacrificed to idols but ate within the idol's temple. These meals caused some weak believers to

to eat what is sacrificed to idols? [11]So this weak brother or sister, for whom Christ died, is destroyed by your knowledge. [12]When you sin against them in this way and wound their weak conscience, you sin against Christ. [13]Therefore, if what I eat causes my brother or sister to fall into sin, I will never eat meat again, so that I will not cause them to fall.

Paul's Rights as an Apostle

9 Am I not free? Am I not an apostle? Have I not seen Jesus our Lord? Are you not the result of my work in the Lord? [2]Even though I may not be an apostle to others, surely I am to you! For you are the seal of my apostleship in the Lord.

[3]This is my defense to those who sit in judgment on me. [4]Don't we have the right to food and drink? [5]Don't we have the right to take a believing wife along with us, as do the other apostles and the Lord's brothers and Cephas[a]? [6]Or is it only I and Barnabas who lack the right to not work for a living?

[7]Who serves as a soldier at his own expense? Who plants a vineyard and does not eat its grapes? Who tends a flock and does not drink the milk? [8]Do I say this merely on human authority? Doesn't the Law say the same thing? [9]For it is written in the Law of Moses: "Do not muzzle an ox while it is treading out the grain."[b] Is it about oxen that God is concerned? [10]Surely he says this for us, doesn't he? Yes, this was written for us, because whoever plows and threshes should be able to do so in the hope of sharing in the harvest. [11]If we have sown spiritual seed among you, is it too much if we reap a material harvest from you? [12]If others have this right of support from you, shouldn't we have it all the more?

But we did not use this right. On the contrary, we put up with anything rather than hinder the gospel of Christ.

[13]Don't you know that those who serve in the temple get their food from the temple, and that those who serve at the altar share in what is offered on the altar? [14]In the same way, the Lord has commanded that those who preach the gospel should receive their living from the gospel.

[15]But I have not used any of these rights. And I am not writing this in the hope that you will do such things for me, for I would rather die than allow anyone to deprive me of this boast. [16]For when I preach the gospel, I cannot boast, since

---

[a] 5 That is, Peter   [b] 9 Deut. 25:4

---

return to their idolatrous practices. Paul advises these believers to choose a private venue to eat their meals.
8:11 is destroyed Refers to hurting a believer whose conscience was weak. Paul considers it sinful behavior for a believer to exercise their rights in a way that harms a fellow member of the church (see v. 12).
8:12 against Christ Implies that Christ counts what is done to his people as being done to him (Mt 25:40; Ac 9:4). The Corinthians must realize that their actions affect the entire community of believers.
8:13 I will never eat meat Although Paul knows that it is theoretically acceptable to consume meat sacrificed to idols, he does not act on such knowledge or appeal to his right to freedom (compare 1Co 8:1,9). Instead, he bases his decisions concerning ethically neutral matters on his love for believers in Christ.

9:1–27 Paul defends his work in Corinth by clarifying the nature of true apostleship and his right as an apostle to deny their financial support. Paul's comments in this passage frequently draw on his discussion of Christian freedom and rights in 8:1–13. He argues that he has a right not only to earn financial payment for his work in the Lord, but also to refuse it (vv. 15–18). Paul explains that he uses his freedom in Christ not for personal gain, but to become a slave to all in hopes they will know Christ (vv. 19–27).

9:1 Am I not an apostle Implies that the Corinthian believers questioned Paul's apostolic status and authority. **Have I not seen Jesus our Lord** Paul refers to his encounter with the risen Christ on the road to Damascus (see Ac 9:1–6; compare 1Co 15:3–9). **my work in the Lord** Paul founded the church in Corinth (see note on 1:1–9; compare Ac 18:1–11).
9:2 you are the seal of my apostleship If the Corinthian believers deny Paul's apostleship, then they would also have to deny their own legitimacy as a church

community. Their response to the gospel message and their maturity in the faith validate Paul's apostleship.
9:3 to those who sit in judgment on me Some of the Corinthians seem to have questioned Paul's apostolic credentials and authority because he did not accept financial support from them. In the first century, itinerant speakers regularly collected money to continue their services.
9:6 to not work Paul worked as a tentmaker in Corinth (Ac 18:3). Some Corinthians may have considered this kind of work to be unfit for an apostle. Paul's labor also alleviated his need for financial support for his ministry from the Corinthian church.
9:8 the Law Refers to the Pentateuch.
9:9 Do not muzzle an ox A quotation from Dt 25:4, which prohibited farmers from muzzling or closing their animal's mouth while it worked. Since the ox performed the threshing, Deuteronomy indicates that it should be allowed to eat grain and derive some benefit from its labor. Paul uses this as an analogy for ministers of the gospel who, he argues, are entitled to material benefits for their service.
9:12 we did not use this right Paul did not want anyone to question his motives for preaching the gospel, so he did not accept financial support. He also did not want to become socially indebted to potential benefactors because of their financial support.
9:13 those who serve in the temple May refer to the Levites who performed priestly duties in the Jewish temple (Dt 18:3–4; Nu 18:20). Gentiles were familiar with such practices from their religious ceremonies.
9:14 should receive their living from the gospel A divine mandate for ministry as vocation.
9:15 this boast Refers to Paul's refusal to accept any payment for his gospel ministry in Corinth. He can boast because he did not jeopardize the integrity of the gospel message (1Co 9:12).

I am compelled to preach. Woe to me if I do not preach the gospel! [17]If I preach voluntarily, I have a reward; if not voluntarily, I am simply discharging the trust committed to me. [18]What then is my reward? Just this: that in preaching the gospel I may offer it free of charge, and so not make full use of my rights as a preacher of the gospel.

Paul's Use of His Freedom

[19]Though I am free and belong to no one, I have made myself a slave to everyone, to win as many as possible. [20]To the Jews I became like a Jew, to win the Jews. To those under the law I became like one under the law (though I myself am not under the law), so as to win those under the law. [21]To those not having the law I became like one not having the law (though I am not free from God's law but am under Christ's law), so as to win those not having the law. [22]To the weak I became weak, to win the weak. I have become all things to all people so that by all possible means I might save some. [23]I do all this for the sake of the gospel, that I may share in its blessings.

The Need for Self-Discipline

[24]Do you not know that in a race all the runners run, but only one gets the prize? Run in such a way as to get the prize. [25]Everyone who competes in the games goes into strict training. They do it to get a crown that will not last, but we do it to get a crown that will last forever. [26]Therefore I do not run like someone running aimlessly; I do not fight like a boxer beating the air. [27]No, I strike a blow to my body and make it my slave so that after I have preached to others, I myself will not be disqualified for the prize.

Warnings From Israel's History

10 For I do not want you to be ignorant of the fact, brothers and sisters, that our ancestors were all under the cloud and that they all passed through the sea. [2]They were all baptized into Moses in the cloud and in the sea. [3]They all ate the same spiritual food [4]and drank the same spiritual drink; for they drank from the spiritual rock that accompanied them, and that rock was Christ. [5]Nevertheless, God was not pleased with most of them; their bodies were scattered in the wilderness.

[6]Now these things occurred as examples to keep us from setting our hearts on evil things as they did. [7]Do not be idolaters, as some of them were; as it is written: "The people sat down to eat and drink and got up to indulge in revelry."[a] [8]We should

[a] 7 Exodus 32:6

9:16 Woe to me Paul draws on language from the prophet Jeremiah to express the serious nature of his calling (Jer 10:19; 20:9; 45:3).

9:19 I have made myself a slave to everyone Paul put himself at the service of others in order that God may use him to bring people to Jesus (compare Php 2:5–8; Gal 4:4–5).

9:20 To the Jews I became like a Jew Paul lived according to Jewish customs not to be saved, but to appeal to those who also lived according to the law (Ac 16:3; 21:23–24; 1Co 8:8). **to win those under the law** Paul was not obligated to live under the law; rather, he used his freedom in Christ to relate to those under the law (Jews).

9:21 under Christ's law Paul did not think it necessary to observe the ceremonial commands of the law in relation to food (see his instructions in 10:27), but he did maintain the law of Christ (see Gal 6:2).

9:22 the weak See 1Co 8:7 and note; Ro 14:1. **all things to all people** Paul is not advocating syncretism or compromise of the gospel message. Rather, he is promoting a considerate evangelistic approach—one that accounts for different social circumstances, ethnicities and religious convictions.

9:24 the prize Refers to life in the age to come, especially the resurrection of the dead and the presence of Christ (compare 1Co 15:51–55; Php 3:12–14).

9:25 goes into strict training This series of extended athletic metaphors is intended to communicate the discipline necessary for ministers of the gospel. **but we do it to get a crown that will last forever** Contrasts the perishable crown of celery leaves that athletes won in the Isthmian games. Paul sought an imperishable crown, which here serves as a metaphor for the reward: eternal life and the glory of sharing in Christ's work.

9:27 I strike a blow to my body Paul is not referring to asceticism or self-abuse. He exercised self-discipline to provide for himself and to endure the hardship associated with his ministry (1Co 4:11–13).

10:1–13 Paul appeals to examples from Israel's history to warn the Corinthian church of the dangers of idolatry.

10:1 our ancestors Refers to the exodus generation that came out of Egypt (see Ex 12:33–42). **cloud** Represented God's presence among the Israelites (Ex 13:21; 14:19–20; compare 40:34). **they all passed through the sea** See Ex 14:21–31.

10:2 baptized into Moses Just as Christian salvation is symbolized by being baptized into Christ (see Gal 3:27), Israel's salvation from Egypt was symbolized through its figurehead and prophet, Moses.

10:4 drank During the wilderness wanderings, the Israelites drank water from the rock in Rephidim (Ex 17:1–6) and Kadesh (Nu 20:1–11). **that rock was Christ** Paul identifies Christ as the rock in a figurative sense, based on his reading of the descriptions of the rock in Ex 17 and Nu 21:16–20. Despite Christ's accompaniment and provision of water in the desert, the people still complained about God's provision and rebelled against his leadership. Paul urges the Corinthians not to follow the Israelites' example of complaining about provisions given by the rock (Christ).

10:5 their bodies were scattered in the wilderness See Nu 14:28–30; Ps 78:30–31.

10:7 idolaters See Ex 32:4,6, where the Israelites fashioned a golden calf and worshiped it.

10:8 as some of them did Refers to the events in Nu 25:1–9, when Israelite men engaged in sexual relations with Midianite female religious prostitutes. In judgment, God sent a plague.

not commit sexual immorality, as some of them did—and in one day twenty-three thousand of them died. [9]We should not test Christ,[a] as some of them did—and were killed by snakes. [10]And do not grumble, as some of them did—and were killed by the destroying angel.

[11]These things happened to them as examples and were written down as warnings for us, on whom the culmination of the ages has come. [12]So, if you think you are standing firm, be careful that you don't fall! [13]No temptation[b] has overtaken you except what is common to mankind. And God is faithful; he will not let you be tempted[b] beyond what you can bear. But when you are tempted,[b] he will also provide a way out so that you can endure it.

Idol Feasts and the Lord's Supper

[14]Therefore, my dear friends, flee from idolatry. [15]I speak to sensible people; judge for yourselves what I say. [16]Is not the cup of thanksgiving for which we give thanks a participation in the blood of Christ? And is not the bread that we break a participation in the body of Christ? [17]Because there is one loaf, we, who are many, are one body, for we all share the one loaf.

[18]Consider the people of Israel: Do not those who eat the sacrifices participate in the altar? [19]Do I mean then that food sacrificed to an idol is anything, or that an idol is anything? [20]No, but the sacrifices of pagans are offered to demons, not to God, and I do not want you to be participants with demons. [21]You cannot drink the cup of the Lord and the cup of demons too; you cannot have a part in both the Lord's table and the table of demons. [22]Are we trying to arouse the Lord's jealousy? Are we stronger than he?

The Believer's Freedom

[23]"I have the right to do anything," you say— but not everything is beneficial. "I have the right to do anything"—but not everything is constructive. [24]No one should seek their own good, but the good of others.

[25]Eat anything sold in the meat market without raising questions of conscience, [26]for, "The earth is the Lord's, and everything in it."[c]

[27]If an unbeliever invites you to a meal and you want to go, eat whatever is put before you without raising questions of conscience. [28]But if someone says to you, "This has been offered in sacrifice," then do not eat it, both for the sake of the one who told you and for the sake of conscience. [29]I am referring to the other person's conscience, not yours. For why is my freedom being judged by another's conscience? [30]If I take part in the meal with thankfulness, why am I denounced because of something I thank God for?

[31]So whether you eat or drink or whatever you

---

[a] 9 Some manuscripts *test the Lord*   [b] 13 The Greek for *temptation* and *tempted* can also mean *testing* and *tested*.
[c] 26 Psalm 24:1

10:9 We should not test Christ Paul is referring to committing evil to see whether God will respond in judgment. **killed by snakes** See Nu 21:4–9.

10:10 grumble Refers to Korah's rebellion and the Israelites' grumbling against Moses and Aaron (see Nu 16:1—17:13). **the destroying angel** Paul seems to be implying that God's judgment in Nu 16:41–50 was carried out by an angel figure (see Ex 12:23; 2Sa 24:16; Ps 78:49).

10:13 temptation Scripture depicts God testing the faith of his followers (Ge 22:1) or allowing other heavenly beings to tempt people (Job 1:6–12). Testing can build faith and character (compare Jas 1:2–4). The limits placed on temptation in this context indicate that God can use temptation as a tool to strengthen believers.

10:14–22 Paul applies Israel's examples from the past to the Corinthian church. Specifically, he addresses the Corinthians' idolatrous practices during the Lord's Supper.

10:16 cup of thanksgiving A reference to the cup in the Lord's Supper, symbolic of the blood that Jesus shed (see Mt 26:27–28). **participation in the blood of Christ** By partaking of the cup's contents in the Lord's Supper (see previous note), believers identify themselves as members of the new covenant (see Mt 26:28). **participation in the body of Christ** The other part of the Lord's Supper, the bread as Christ's body (see Mt 26:26). By partaking of the bread, believers testify to their union with Christ—not just his death, but also the achievements brought about by his resurrection.

10:19 food sacrificed to an idol is anything Paul's warning about food sacrificed to idols is based on his teaching from 8:1–13, where he conceded that for the sake of appearance, it would be better to avoid this food. While the food sacrificed to idols carries no true spiritual significance, avoiding it would save the conscience of weaker believers (see 8:7 and note).

10:20 to demons, not to God Paul knew that physical idols were nothing in and of themselves (compare Isa 46:1–11). He claims that worship offered to such idols is really offered to demons. **you to be participants with demons** See Dt 32:17.

10:21 cup of the Lord Refers to the cup the Lords' Supper (see 1Co 10:16) and signifies fellowship with the Lord and his church. **the table of demons** A reference to pagan altars.

10:23 I have the right to do anything See 1Co 6:12 and note.

10:25 sold in the meat market The market separated the meat from the context of the idol's temple and the sacrificial ritual (8:10; compare note on 8:1).

10:27 invites you to a meal Refers to eating at a private home or public venue, not a pagan temple.

10:28 This has been offered in sacrifice Meat offered in a pagan temple and sold in the marketplace, as opposed to meals at the temples themselves (8:10; see note on 8:1; compare note on 8:7).

10:29 the other person's The other person in this hypothetical scenario could be a nonbeliever at the meal who expects the Christian to avoid meat offered to idols,

do, do it all for the glory of God. [32]Do not cause anyone to stumble, whether Jews, Greeks or the church of God — [33]even as I try to please everyone in every way. For I am not seeking my own good but the good of many, so that they may be saved. [1]Follow my example, as I follow the example of Christ.

11

On Covering the Head in Worship

[2]I praise you for remembering me in everything and for holding to the traditions just as I passed them on to you. [3]But I want you to realize that the head of every man is Christ, and the head of the woman is man,[a] and the head of Christ is God. [4]Every man who prays or prophesies with his head covered dishonors his head. [5]But every woman who prays or prophesies with her head uncovered dishonors her head — it is the same as having her head shaved. [6]For if a woman does not cover her head, she might as well have her hair cut off; but if it is a disgrace for a woman to have her hair cut off or her head shaved, then she should cover her head.

[7]A man ought not to cover his head,[b] since he is the image and glory of God; but woman is the glory of man. [8]For man did not come from woman, but woman from man; [9]neither was man created for woman, but woman for man. [10]It is for this reason that a woman ought to have authority over her own[c] head, because of the angels. [11]Nevertheless, in the Lord woman is not independent of man, nor is man independent of woman. [12]For as woman came from man, so also man is born of woman. But everything comes from God.

[13]Judge for yourselves: Is it proper for a woman to pray to God with her head uncovered? [14]Does not the very nature of things teach you that if a man has long hair, it is a disgrace to him, [15]but that if a woman has long hair, it is her glory? For long hair is given to her as a covering. [16]If anyone wants to be contentious about this, we have no other practice — nor do the churches of God.

a 3 Or of the wife is her husband   *b 4-7 Or ⁴Every man who prays or prophesies with long hair dishonors his head. ⁵But every woman who prays or prophesies with no covering of hair dishonors her head — she is just like one of the "shorn women." ⁶If a woman has no covering, let her be for now with short hair; but since it is a disgrace for a woman to have her hair shorn or shaved, she should grow it again. ⁷A man ought not to have long hair*   *c 10 Or have a sign of authority on her*

---

or a weaker believer whose own conscience leads him to avoid the meat.

11:2–16 Paul turns to the topic of worship practices within the churches, a subject that dominates the remainder of his letter (11:2–14:40). Some of the specific issues Paul raises seem intended for particular areas of abuse within the Corinthian church: women failing to wear head coverings in worship (vv. 2–16), improper observance of the Lord's Supper (vv. 17–34) and misuse of spiritual gifts (12:1–14:40).

11:3 of every man Refers only to believers. **head** The Greek word used here, *kephalē*, may imply authority or source. The term could have either meaning in ancient Greek literature. Alternatively, the word may denote preeminence or a combination of these meanings. If *kephalē* means "head," Paul would assert that men have authority over women in the church community (see note on 1Ti 2:11–12). Under this interpretation, the creation of Adam prior to Eve sets a precedent for male and female relationships within the community. However, if *kephalē* means "source," then man is the source of woman — God created Eve from Adam (Ge 2:21–22). Hierarchy or authority may not be implied in this case.

11:4 with his head covered Paul may be referring to a head covering used in Roman religious practice. Socially elite believers may have continued to wear such head coverings when gathering for worship. If so, they brought attention to themselves and may have ostracized those who felt socially inferior, causing division in the church community.

11:5 prophesies Refers to inspired speech to edify and encourage the church community. See note on 1Co 12:10. **with her head uncovered** Paul's comment assumes the cultural practice of covering a women's hair and head during times of worship. Paul discouraged women from uncovering their heads in such contexts. **dishonors her head** Indicates that a woman dishonors a man when she takes on the appearance of a man.

11:6 to have her hair cut off or her head shaved In Paul's day, a woman with an uncovered head may have been considered sexually revealing and thus a distraction to men in the context of worship. Paul therefore recommends that women should wear head coverings to avoid such issues.

11:7 image and glory of God See note on Ge 1:27.

11:8 woman from man See note on Ge 2:18–23.

11:9 woman for man Paul is referencing the order of creation (Ge 2:18). He is not suggesting that women are created for the purpose of pleasing men; rather, he is focusing on the created order and Eve's role as a partner in maintaining God's creation.

11:11 independent of man Both men and women are created by God and are equally valued in the created order.

11:12 man is born of woman Refers to Ge 2:21–23 and reinforces the idea that woman and man are mutually dependent. Although Eve was created from Adam's rib, this does not make her inferior to him because by the same logic — according to Paul — men are derived from women because they are born from women.

11:13 pray to God with her head uncovered Head coverings may have signified that a woman participated in public worship through prayer.

11:14 nature The Greek text here may refer to a general opinion about what is appropriate for men and women. **disgrace to him** Men are able to grow their hair as long as women, but to do so would have been against social norms and thus problematic to the gospel message in Corinth.

11:15 her glory Paul is saying that it is permissible for a woman to have long hair. The sexual desire of men should not hinder this (see note on 1Co 11:6).

11:16 contentious Paul means that if his opinion will not be accepted by some in the community, then he lacks an alternative practice to offer them. The Corinthians need to decide on a resolution that will maintain unity within the church (see chs. 12–13).

Correcting an Abuse of the Lord's Supper

11:23-25pp — Mt 26:26-28; Mk 14:22-24; Lk 22:17-20

[17]In the following directives I have no praise for you, for your meetings do more harm than good. [18]In the first place, I hear that when you come together as a church, there are divisions among you, and to some extent I believe it. [19]No doubt there have to be differences among you to show which of you have God's approval. [20]So then, when you come together, it is not the Lord's Supper you eat, [21]for when you are eating, some of you go ahead with your own private suppers. As a result, one person remains hungry and another gets drunk. [22]Don't you have homes to eat and drink in? Or do you despise the church of God by humiliating those who have nothing? What shall I say to you? Shall I praise you? Certainly not in this matter!

[23]For I received from the Lord what I also passed on to you: The Lord Jesus, on the night he was betrayed, took bread, [24]and when he had given thanks, he broke it and said, "This is my body, which is for you; do this in remembrance of me." [25]In the same way, after supper he took the cup, saying, "This cup is the new covenant in my blood; do this, whenever you drink it, in remembrance of me." [26]For whenever you eat this bread and drink this cup, you proclaim the Lord's death until he comes.

[27]So then, whoever eats the bread or drinks the cup of the Lord in an unworthy manner will be guilty of sinning against the body and blood of the Lord. [28]Everyone ought to examine themselves before they eat of the bread and drink from the cup. [29]For those who eat and drink without discerning the body of Christ eat and drink judgment on themselves. [30]That is why many among you are weak and sick, and a number of you have fallen asleep. [31]But if we were more discerning with regard to ourselves, we would not come under such judgment. [32]Nevertheless, when we are judged in this way by the Lord, we are being disciplined so that we will not be finally condemned with the world.

[33]So then, my brothers and sisters, when you gather to eat, you should all eat together. [34]Anyone who is hungry should eat something at home, so that when you meet together it may not result in judgment.

And when I come I will give further directions.

Concerning Spiritual Gifts

12 Now about the gifts of the Spirit, brothers and sisters, I do not want you to be uninformed. [2]You know that when you were pagans, somehow or other you were influenced and led astray to mute idols. [3]Therefore I want you to know that no one who is speaking by the Spirit

---

11:17–34 Paul gives instructions about the proper observance of the Lord's Supper. Apparently, the church was divided on socioeconomic grounds, with the wealthier members abusing their position and status by inhibiting fellowship with the poorer members of the church. Paul hinted at the solution to this division earlier by emphasizing the unity of the body of Christ (10:17). The abuse of the Lord's Supper within the Corinthian church was causing them to lose sight of its purpose: fellowship between believers and identification with Christ and his sacrifice.

11:17 your meetings Refers to worship gatherings.
11:18 there are divisions among you Refers to divisions between social classes. In the Corinthian church, the wealthy believers held a worship gathering and a meal in their homes. The less wealthy believers worked long days and typically arrived late at the worship gathering and meal. Apparently, the wealthy believers did not wait for them; instead, they ate without them, getting drunk and leaving no food for them. This caused division between the wealthy and poor believers. See the infographic "Ancient Home Synagogue" on p. 1971.
11:20 the Lord's Supper Refers to the meal that Jesus instituted, symbolizing his death (Lk 22:14–23). The Corinthians, however, did not eat the Lord's Supper together; the division between the rich and poor altered their practice.
11:21 with your own private suppers Some of the wealthy believers may have had their own meals and did not share with (or invite) poor believers.
11:22 do you despise the church of God The actions of wealthy believers showed that they did not value poor believers in their church community (*ekklēsia* in Greek). Thus, they damaged the unity and fellowship of the church.
11:23 I received from the Lord May imply that Paul received this instruction by direct revelation, but most likely recognizes Jesus as the source of the instruction (compare 1Co 15:3).
11:25 cup Refers to the cup of blessing used in the

Passover meal, which symbolized the blood of the covenant (Ex 24:8; Lk 22:20). **new covenant** Refers to the covenant that fulfilled and replaced the Mosaic covenant (see Jer 31:31–34; 32:40; compare Ex 24; 2Co 3:7–18). Through this covenant of Christ's death, God offers forgiveness, eternal life and the Holy Spirit that empowers believers to live God's commandments. Compare Lk 22:20. **in my blood** Refers to Christ's violent and sacrificial death. Blood functioned to seal a covenant (see Ex 24:8; compare Zec 9:11; Heb 9:18–20; 13:20).
11:26 until he comes Refers to the second coming of Christ.
11:27 in an unworthy manner Paul is referring to the Corinthian believers' misuse of the Lord's Supper (1Co 11:18)—they were missing the point of the meal, hindering their relationships with other believers and thus hindering the spread of the gospel (especially among the poor). **will be guilty of sinning against the body** People who sin in this way are like those who originally crucified the Lord Jesus. They are not honoring Christ's death but are instead making a mockery of it.
11:28 examine Refers to testing or proving to be genuine.
11:30 That is why many among you are weak Represents God's judgment for their failure to recognize all believers as the body of Christ.
11:32 we will not be finally condemned Refers to the final judgment at his second coming (see v. 26; Ro 2:5 and note).
11:33 you should all eat together See note on 1Co 11:18.

12:1–11 Paul turns to a new topic here, contrasting the church's former life of idolatry with its new life empowered by the Holy Spirit. In his discussion of spiritual gifts, Paul emphasizes the diversity of the gifts and proper use of them for the mutual benefit of all believers.

12:1 gifts of the Spirit The Greek phrase used here, *tōn pneumatikōn*, could refer generically to "spiritual things" or to "spiritual people." Based on the reference

of God says, "Jesus be cursed," and no one can say, "Jesus is Lord," except by the Holy Spirit.

⁴There are different kinds of gifts, but the same Spirit distributes them. ⁵There are different kinds of service, but the same Lord. ⁶There are different kinds of working, but in all of them and in everyone it is the same God at work.

⁷Now to each one the manifestation of the Spirit is given for the common good. ⁸To one there is given through the Spirit a message of wisdom, to another a message of knowledge by means of the same Spirit, ⁹to another faith by the same Spirit, to another gifts of healing by that one Spirit, ¹⁰to another miraculous powers, to another prophecy,

---

to gifts in v. 4, the term is most likely referring to the gifts of the Spirit.

12:2 mute idols Jews considered idols to be senseless objects (see Ps 115:4–8; Hab 2:18–19; compare Isa 41:1–29; 46:1–13). See the infographic "The Temple of Artemis" on p. 1814.

12:3 speaking by the Spirit of God This may allude to an overemphasis on speaking in tongues among the Corinthians. Paul asserts that when a person speaks by the Spirit, the content is edifying, not blasphemous; it affirms that Jesus is Lord. **Jesus be cursed** Refers to the utterance of a curse against Jesus. The exact meaning and use of the phrase is uncertain. Paul may be presenting the statement as a hypothetical contrast with the true confession of faith, "Jesus is Lord" (e.g., Ro 10:9,12).

12:4–11 Paul mentions several gifts in this passage, but his list is representative, not exhaustive. His point is that all the gifts of the Spirit benefit the body of Christ in some way.

12:4 different kinds of gifts The Corinthian believers overemphasized the gift of tongues in worship (1Co 14:18–19). Paul reminds them that there are various kinds of spiritual gifts—all of which come from the Holy Spirit.

12:7 manifestation of the Spirit God reveals the Spirit through the various gifts provided to believers.

12:8 a message of wisdom The Greek phrase used here, *logos sophias*, likely alludes to Paul's discussion from 1:17—2:16 and should be understood in light of his teaching about wisdom from the Spirit in 2:6–16. The emphasis is not on wisdom itself but on the word or message produced by that wisdom. **a message of knowledge** This gift appears to specifically address the Corinthian overemphasis on knowledge while highlighting the pride that characterizes their knowledge (e.g., 8:1–7). It likely has to do with enriching others, particularly in light of the testimony of Christ working among people (1:4–6).

12:9–11 Paul now lists several more manifestations of the Spirit—faith, healing, miracles, prophecy, discerning spirits, tongues and interpretation of tongues. One view is that these miraculous spiritual gifts ceased after the age of the apostles because their purpose was to serve as signs validating the gospel message: Once the NT was complete (late first century or early second century AD), these gifts were no longer necessary. However, records of supernatural occurrences following the apostolic age present problems for this view. Another view is that these manifestations of the Spirit continue today and bear witness to the continuing presence of the Holy Spirit among believers. As such, the NT promotes the proper use of spiritual gifts because they are meant to be present among believers and empower them to do God's work, under the guidance of the Holy Spirit.

12:9 faith Since Paul groups this with other supernatural gifts, he likely means the kind of faith that can accomplish extraordinary achievements. See 13:2; compare Mt 17:20. **healing** This gift is given to the person whom God uses to restore someone. The Greek term used here,

iama, can be used to refer to both physical healing and spiritual restoration. Acts narrates Paul's use of the gift of healing in his ministry (Ac 14:8–10).

12:10 miraculous powers The Greek phrase used here, which may be literally rendered as "activities of power," refers to extraordinary activities like exorcizing demons and raising the dead (Ac 19:11–12; 9:36–42). Compare 2Co 12:12; Gal 3:5. **prophecy** Refers to utterances inspired by the Holy Spirit. Like the OT prophets, this role involves social critique, calling people to repentance, and revealing God's future plans for both judgment and salvation. Such utterances may include predictions of the future (e.g., Ac 11:28; 21:10–11), but they are intended to encourage believers, not confuse them (1Co 14:4–5). Paul's discussion in 14:6–40 contrasts the benefits of the gift of prophecy with those of the gift of tongues. **distinguishing between spirits** This gift allows an individual to recognize whether an utterance comes from God or an evil spirit (e.g., Ac 13:8–10). Alternatively, it may involve the ability to distinguish between good and evil spirits—whether the spiritual activity being encountered comes from God or demons. Paul may have intended both ideas. Compare 1Co 14:29; 1Jn 4:1. **kinds of tongues** The discussion in 1Co 14 indicates that the use of this gift was controversial, even in the days of the early church. The Greek word here, *glōssa*, is used both for the literal, physical tongue and metaphorically for language or speech. Paul discusses two types of tongues: those of people and those of angels (13:1). When someone speaks in the tongues of angels, they are speaking to God (14:2)—no one else understands them and thus they need an interpreter (14:28). When someone speaks in the tongues of people, they are miraculously speaking to someone in their own language, without training (Ac 2:3–4,11). Compare 1Co 13:8; 14:4–33. **interpretation of tongues** The person with this gift translates the utterance spoken in a tongue into the native language of the believers gathered.

GLŌSSA

The Greek word *glōssa* is literally the word for the tongue—the organ found on the floor of the mouth in humans and many animals. Due to the tongue's association with speech, words designating the tongue have metaphorically come to indicate language or speech in numerous languages, including Hebrew (*lashon*) and Greek (*glōssa*). In discussions of spiritual gifts, the argument is often made that *glōssa* only refers to real human languages that are unknown to the speaker—and thus, according to this argument, those Christians who engage in ecstatic utterances misrepresent the gift. However, the Greek usage also applies to the ecstatic speech of practitioners of Hellenistic mystery religions and angelic languages. In fact, NT examples also suggest the phrase "speaking in tongues" could refer to unintelligible ecstatic utterance (1Co 14:5; Ac 19:6). Paul also speaks of the tongues "of angels" (see 1Co 13:1 and note; compare 14:2 and note).

to another distinguishing between spirits, to another speaking in different kinds of tongues,[a] and to still another the interpretation of tongues.[a] [11]All these are the work of one and the same Spirit, and he distributes them to each one, just as he determines.

Unity and Diversity in the Body

[12]Just as a body, though one, has many parts, but all its many parts form one body, so it is with Christ. [13]For we were all baptized by[b] one Spirit so as to form one body — whether Jews or Gentiles, slave or free — and we were all given the one Spirit to drink. [14]Even so the body is not made up of one part but of many.

[15]Now if the foot should say, "Because I am not a hand, I do not belong to the body," it would not for that reason stop being part of the body. [16]And if the ear should say, "Because I am not an eye, I do not belong to the body," it would not for that reason stop being part of the body. [17]If the whole body were an eye, where would the sense of hearing be? If the whole body were an ear, where would the sense of smell be? [18]But in fact God has placed the parts in the body, every one of them, just as he wanted them to be. [19]If they were all one part,

where would the body be? [20]As it is, there are many parts, but one body.

[21]The eye cannot say to the hand, "I don't need you!" And the head cannot say to the feet, "I don't need you!" [22]On the contrary, those parts of the body that seem to be weaker are indispensable, [23]and the parts that we think are less honorable we treat with special honor. And the parts that are unpresentable are treated with special modesty, [24]while our presentable parts need no special treatment. But God has put the body together, giving greater honor to the parts that lacked it, [25]so that there should be no division in the body, but that its parts should have equal concern for each other. [26]If one part suffers, every part suffers with it; if one part is honored, every part rejoices with it.

[27]Now you are the body of Christ, and each one of you is a part of it. [28]And God has placed in the church first of all apostles, second prophets, third teachers, then miracles, then gifts of healing, of helping, of guidance, and of different kinds of tongues. [29]Are all apostles? Are all prophets? Are all teachers? Do all work miracles? [30]Do all have gifts of healing? Do all speak in

---

[a] 10 Or *languages*; also in verse 28   [b] 13 Or *with*; or *in*

12:11 the work of one and the same Spirit Paul summarizes the content of vv. 4–10. The Corinthian believers may have assumed that diversity in gifts meant diversity in access to the Spirit.

12:13 baptized Probably refers to the baptism of the Spirit that empowers a believer for new life in Christ (compare Mk 1:8; Jn 1:33; Ac 1:5; 11:16). Paul asserts that the presence of the Holy Spirit unifies believers because he makes all other social categories irrelevant.

12:14 the body is not made up of one part but of many Summarizes Paul's entire argument about the nature of church community. The diversity within the church does not mean that there should be diversity in purpose or mindset (1Co 1:10).

12:18 just as he wanted Because God assigns functions within the community of believers, no believers have a right to boast about their assignment as though they earned it.

12:19 If they were all one part Paul exposes the absurdity of the Corinthian believers' mindset. A body composed of a single part is not a body and could not function as a body; it is the same thing for believers, with each playing his or her own role.

12:20 one body Paul wants the Corinthians to focus on unity instead of their diverse gifts.

12:21 I don't need you Paul warns the Corinthians not to regard other believers, namely the poorer believers (see 11:17–34), as unhelpful or unnecessary within the church community.

12:24 presentable parts May refer to body parts such as the face or head. Paul is likely referencing the leaders in the Corinthian community that are visible to people outside the community. **parts that lacked** Represents the poorer believers in Corinth, to whom God gave an honored place within the church (see Jas 2:5 and note).

12:27–31 Paul first outlines offices within the church — the people who dictate and maintain the vision of the church. He then discusses particular gifts (as indicated by the shift in 1Co 12:28). The people with church offices may have the gifts he discusses, but having a gift does not indicate a church office — a governing position as a steward of God's vision for a particular community — but a role. Paul considers each of the gifts he lists in the second half of v. 28 and in vv. 29–30 as higher gifts. The point of these gifts is to unify believers around a common purpose, each with individual parts to play. The church offices are for the purpose of leading the community in spreading the gospel and growing in faith.

12:28 first The priority implied by this phrase refers either to the rank of the roles mentioned or to their importance for church growth. **apostles** See note on Ro 1:1. In the first century, the "apostles" included the Twelve (Mt 10:2–4; 1Co 15:5), but also others like James, Barnabas and Paul (Ac 14:4; Gal 1:19). The term "apostle" may also be applied to "sent ones" — the literal translation of the word — or those sent by God for the purpose of leading his people (e.g., 2Co 8:23). **prophets** See note on 1Co 12:10. **teachers** People who explain and impart truth to God's people (compare the roles of elders and overseers in 1Ti 3:2; 5:17). **miracles** Performing a miracle and healing someone are not synonymous; Paul uses two different terms. For miracles, see note on 1Co 12:10; compare note on v. 9 for healing. **then gifts** Paul now returns to discussing spiritual gifts. **helping** The Greek word used here, *antilēmpsis*, refers to assisting people in need (see Ac 20:35), but it also entails the idea of calling upon God in a time of turmoil so that he may act in the situation with his full power and force. The Greek word *antilēmpsis* is used in the Septuagint to translate Hebrew words meaning "shield" (Ps 89:18), "helmet"

tongues^a? Do all interpret? ³¹Now eagerly desire the greater gifts.

Love Is Indispensable

13 And yet I will show you the most excellent way. If I speak in the tongues^b of men or of angels, but do not have love, I am only a resounding gong or a clanging cymbal. ²If I have the gift of prophecy and can fathom all mysteries and all knowledge, and if I have a faith that can move mountains, but do not have love, I am nothing. ³If I give all I possess to the poor and give over my body to hardship that I may boast,^c but do not have love, I gain nothing.

⁴Love is patient, love is kind. It does not envy, it does not boast, it is not proud. ⁵It does not dishonor others, it is not self-seeking, it is not easily angered, it keeps no record of wrongs. ⁶Love does not delight in evil but rejoices with the truth. ⁷It always protects, always trusts, always hopes, always perseveres.

⁸Love never fails. But where there are prophecies, they will cease; where there are tongues, they will be stilled; where there is knowledge, it will pass away. ⁹For we know in part and we prophesy in part, ¹⁰but when completeness comes, what is in part disappears. ¹¹When I was a child, I talked like a child, I thought like a child, I reasoned like a child. When I became a man, I put the ways of childhood behind me. ¹²For now we see only a reflection as in a mirror; then we shall see face to face. Now I know in part; then I shall know fully, even as I am fully known.

¹³And now these three remain: faith, hope and love. But the greatest of these is love.

Intelligibility in Worship

14 Follow the way of love and eagerly desire gifts of the Spirit, especially prophecy. ²For anyone who speaks in a tongue^d does not speak to people but to God. Indeed, no one understands

---

^a 30 Or *other languages*   ^b 1 Or *languages*   ^c 3 Some manuscripts *body to the flames*   ^d 2 Or *in another language*; also in verses 4, 13, 14, 19, 26 and 27

(Ps 108:8), and "strength" (Ps 84:5). Each of these is used in the context of war. The gift of healing involves restoration, while the gift of helping (or helps) probably refers to assisting or helping believers in need. **guidance** Paul is likely referring to those who have the gift of providing guidance or direction to the church community. **12:31 greater gifts** Refers to gifts that benefit the entire church community (e.g., 1Co 14:4–5; see note on 12:27–31); there are other spiritual gifts as well. The Corinthian believers focused on the gift of tongues (v. 10), but without interpretation. Paul argues that without interpretation, the gift does not benefit anyone (14:1–25).

13:1–13 Paul explains the more excellent way that he mentioned in 12:31. Paul's goal is to show the Corinthians that the only proper use for gifts is through love.

13:1 tongues of men See note on 12:10. **of angels** The reference to tongues "of angels" probably indicates the belief that one type of "gift of tongues" involved speaking in the language of angels. This belief was not uncommon in the Greco-Roman world. Paul does not necessarily affirm this belief; he points out that even the language of angels is meaningless without love. Alternatively, the phrase "tongues of angels" may be an expression meaning "heavenly language." **love** A genuine and selfless concern for the well-being of others. Paul identifies it as the greatest of the three Christian virtues (v. 13). **a clanging cymbal** Paul mentions the crashing cymbal to suggest that spiritual gifts without love make the Corinthians' worship no different from the pagans'.

13:2 can move mountains See note on Mk 11:23; compare Zec 4:7.

13:3 I give all I possess to the poor Echoes Jesus' command to the rich young man (Mt 19:21; Lk 18:22).

13:6 truth Love rejoices in this truth because the gospel demonstrates God's love (Ro 5:8).

13:7 It always protects Involves enduring difficulties, and even taking on (spiritually) the difficulty of others (being compassionate; see 1Co 9:12). **always hopes** Exhibiting confidence in God and his promises. See note on Eph 1:18.

13:8 Love never fails The Corinthian believers emphasized the gift of tongues as a sign (perhaps even a required sign) of Christ dwelling with someone. Paul reveals that the gifts will one day be no longer necessary, but love will always be (1Co 13:13). Therefore, love is the true sign of someone who follows Christ (Jn 13:35). **tongues, they will be stilled** Paul refers to three spiritual gifts that will no longer be necessary in the age to come — prophecy, tongues and knowledge.

13:10 when completeness comes The Greek word used here, *teleios*, refers to the fullness of God's salvation that will come at the second coming of Jesus Christ (see note on Php 1:6). When Christ appears, believers will no longer need the gifts — Christ himself will be showing who he is and what he is doing in person (not just through others, but directly to all people).

13:12 as in a mirror In the Greco-Roman world, a mirror consisted of a polished metal disc with a handle. The reflection visible in the polished silver or bronze was a much more imperfect and indirect representation than modern mirrors. Alternatively, Paul may be referring to the idea of a mirror as an instrument of self-reflection (e.g., Jas 1:23–24).

13:13 the greatest of these is love Love is the greatest because it is eternal and reflects God's fundamental character (e.g., Ro 5:8). Love is also greater than the gifts because it remains while they cease (1Co 13:8).

14:1–25 In the previous chapter, Paul focuses entirely on love. He now returns to his previous instruction to pursue the greater gifts (12:31).

14:2 does not speak to people but to God A prayer language between a believer and God does not encourage the faith of those who cannot understand what is said; when used in public, an interpreter should be present. Paul distinguishes between two different manifestations of the gift of tongues: speaking in unknown human languages and using spiritual or angelic languages (see 13:1 and note). The purpose of Paul's argument here and in 13:1 is that any use of tongues is meaningless if it doesn't serve to encourage or build up others. **no one**

them; they utter mysteries by the Spirit. ³But the one who prophesies speaks to people for their strengthening, encouraging and comfort. ⁴Anyone who speaks in a tongue edifies themselves, but the one who prophesies edifies the church. ⁵I would like every one of you to speak in tongues,ᵃ but I would rather have you prophesy. The one who prophesies is greater than the one who speaks in tongues,ᵃ unless someone interprets, so that the church may be edified.

⁶Now, brothers and sisters, if I come to you and speak in tongues, what good will I be to you, unless I bring you some revelation or knowledge or prophecy or word of instruction? ⁷Even in the case of lifeless things that make sounds, such as the pipe or harp, how will anyone know what tune is being played unless there is a distinction in the notes? ⁸Again, if the trumpet does not sound a clear call, who will get ready for battle? ⁹So it is with you. Unless you speak intelligible words with your tongue, how will anyone know what you are saying? You will just be speaking into the air. ¹⁰Undoubtedly there are all sorts of languages in the world, yet none of them is without meaning. ¹¹If then I do not grasp the meaning of what someone is saying, I am a foreigner to the speaker, and the speaker is a foreigner to me. ¹²So it is with you. Since you are eager for gifts of the Spirit, try to excel in those that build up the church.

¹³For this reason the one who speaks in a tongue should pray that they may interpret what they say. ¹⁴For if I pray in a tongue, my spirit prays, but my mind is unfruitful. ¹⁵So what shall I do? I will pray with my spirit, but I will also pray with my understanding; I will sing with my spirit, but I will also sing with my understanding. ¹⁶Otherwise when you are praising God in the Spirit, how can someone else, who is now put in the position of an inquirer,ᵇ say "Amen" to your thanksgiving, since they do not know what you are saying? ¹⁷You are giving thanks well enough, but no one else is edified.

¹⁸I thank God that I speak in tongues more than all of you. ¹⁹But in the church I would rather speak five intelligible words to instruct others than ten thousand words in a tongue.

²⁰Brothers and sisters, stop thinking like children. In regard to evil be infants, but in your thinking be adults. ²¹In the Law it is written:

"With other tongues
    and through the lips of foreigners
I will speak to this people,
    but even then they will not listen to me,
        says the Lord."ᶜ

²²Tongues, then, are a sign, not for believers but for unbelievers; prophecy, however, is not for unbelievers but for believers. ²³So if the whole church comes together and everyone speaks in tongues, and inquirers or unbelievers come in, will they not say that you are out of your mind? ²⁴But if an unbeliever or an inquirer comes in while everyone is prophesying, they are convicted of sin and are brought under judgment by all, ²⁵as the

---

ᵃ 5 Or *in other languages*; also in verses 6, 18, 22, 23 and 39
ᵇ 16 The Greek word for *inquirer* is a technical term for someone not fully initiated into a religion; also in verses 23 and 24.
ᶜ 21 Isaiah 28:11,12

---

understands May suggest that the language requires an interpreter, or it may suggest that neither the speaker nor anyone else may understand it.

14:4 Anyone who speaks in a tongue Speaking in a tongue refers to a language between a person and God that is unintelligible to others. For this reason, Paul promotes prophecy over tongues for the Corinthian church. See note on 12:10.

14:5 I would like every one of you to speak in tongues Paul did not have a problem with the gift of tongues; he simply disapproved of the Corinthians' use of the gift without an interpreter. **The one who prophesies is greater** In this context, the gift of prophecy is greater than the gift of tongues because it can benefit the entire church community (see note on 12:31). The Corinthian believers preferred to speak in tongues over prophesying. Ecstatic speeches were common in mystery religions in Corinth, and thus the Corinthian believers probably thought speaking in tongues would attract new people to the faith.

14:6 revelation Refers to mysteries about the gospel message (how God wishes to use it in a particular community) that the Spirit reveals (Gal 2:2; see 2Co 12:1 and note).

14:9 into the air Implies that such speech is useless or ineffective.

14:11 a foreigner The Greek term used here, *barbaros*, originally referred to a person who speaks nonsense—

that is, someone who did not speak Greek. Here it's likely a reference to the people groups that the Greeks could not conquer and the Romans had minimal success ruling.

14:12 gifts of the Spirit Paul may be referring to the gift of tongues here instead of the spiritual gifts collectively. Compare note on 1Co 12:7.

14:14 my mind is unfruitful Without an interpretation, the speaker does not benefit intellectually, and neither does anyone else.

14:16 an inquirer Refers to someone who does not understand those speaking in tongues—probably a nonbeliever visiting the community (see vv. 23–24).

14:20 children Symbolizes immaturity.

14:21 it is written Paul draws on a passage from Isaiah to emphasize the use of tongues as a sign to unbelievers (Isa 28:11–12).

14:22 a sign Indicates that tongues are intended to function as a sign of God's activity. When rightly practiced, tongues have the power to draw people to God (1Co 14:23–24).

14:24 brought under judgment by all Implies that the Holy Spirit will convict the unbeliever of sin, so that he or she will turn to God in repentance.

14:25 secrets of their hearts Prophecy can reveal what is hidden to people, even the secret things within the heart (2:11). **they will fall down and worship God** Describes the conversion of the unbeliever to the Christian faith.

secrets of their hearts are laid bare. So they will fall down and worship God, exclaiming, "God is really among you!"

Good Order in Worship

²⁶What then shall we say, brothers and sisters? When you come together, each of you has a hymn, or a word of instruction, a revelation, a tongue or an interpretation. Everything must be done so that the church may be built up. ²⁷If anyone speaks in a tongue, two — or at the most three — should speak, one at a time, and someone must interpret. ²⁸If there is no interpreter, the speaker should keep quiet in the church and speak to himself and to God.

²⁹Two or three prophets should speak, and the others should weigh carefully what is said. ³⁰And if a revelation comes to someone who is sitting down, the first speaker should stop. ³¹For you can all prophesy in turn so that everyone may be instructed and encouraged. ³²The spirits of prophets are subject to the control of prophets. ³³For God is not a God of disorder but of peace — as in all the congregations of the Lord's people.

³⁴Women*ᵃ* should remain silent in the churches. They are not allowed to speak, but must be in submission, as the law says. ³⁵If they want to inquire about something, they should ask their own husbands at home; for it is disgraceful for a woman to speak in the church.*ᵇ*

³⁶Or did the word of God originate with you? Or are you the only people it has reached? ³⁷If anyone thinks they are a prophet or otherwise gifted by the Spirit, let them acknowledge that what I am writing to you is the Lord's command. ³⁸But if anyone ignores this, they will themselves be ignored.*ᶜ*

³⁹Therefore, my brothers and sisters, be eager to prophesy, and do not forbid speaking in tongues. ⁴⁰But everything should be done in a fitting and orderly way.

The Resurrection of Christ

15 Now, brothers and sisters, I want to remind you of the gospel I preached to you, which you received and on which you have taken your stand. ²By this gospel you are saved, if you hold firmly to the word I preached to you. Otherwise, you have believed in vain.

³For what I received I passed on to you as of first importance*ᵈ*: that Christ died for our sins according to the Scriptures, ⁴that he was buried,

---

ᵃ 33,34 Or peace. As in all the congregations of the Lord's people, ³⁴women   ᵇ 34,35 In a few manuscripts these verses come after verse 40.   ᶜ 38 Some manuscripts But anyone who is ignorant of this will be ignorant   ᵈ 3 Or you at the first

---

14:26 you come together Refers to the assembly of believers for worship. **so that the church may be built up** Indicates the purpose of the worship gathering. **14:28 should keep quiet in the church** When God's message is spoken through tongues in the context of the church (*ekklēsia* in Greek), it must be interpreted. **14:32 spirits** Paul uses the Greek word *pneuma* here, making this particular phrase ambiguous in Greek. It may refer to the prophet's spirit (indwelled by the Holy Spirit), the Holy Spirit himself, or the spiritual gift of prophecy (compare vv. 12,14–15). **14:33 as in all the congregations of the Lord's people** If this phrase begins v. 34 rather than ending Paul's previous argument, then he is prohibiting women from speaking in all churches. However, this phrase may instead function as the conclusion to Paul's specific instructions begun in vv. 26–33, as he uses it this way elsewhere (e.g., 4:17; 11:16). **14:34 Women should remain silent** If this functions as a rule for all churches in Paul's time (see note on v. 33), then Paul is forbidding women from speaking in church, especially during worship and is likely doing so for reasons specific to his first-century Greco-Roman context. However, Paul may be addressing a particular problem among the Corinthian congregation (or possibly all churches in the first century AD). In this case, Paul's prohibition may apply specifically to women who were speaking in tongues or uttering prophesies in an inappropriate manner. Alternatively, he may be addressing women who were disrupting worship services with questions and thereby challenging the authority of their husbands. Ultimately, Paul's goal in the passage is to reestablish order in worship, not to demean the honor of women or devalue their worship of God. **must be in submission** Paul is likely making this statement

either because some of the women in the congregation were causing strife, or perhaps because women were the center of local folk religion (often called mystery cults) and thus following Jesus was being confused with other religions. See note on Eph 5:21. **as the law says** While Paul refers to the Law and quotes it elsewhere (see 1Co 9:8; 14:21), this is not a quotation nor does it match the content of any OT law. It may refer to Ge 2:18–24, in which God created Adam first and Eve second. It is also possible that this refers to Ge 3:16, where God pronounces that the woman shall desire her husband. **14:35 disgraceful for a woman to speak in the church** Paul may be referring to women who caused disorder at the worship assembly (compare note on 1Co 14:34). **14:37 If anyone thinks** The Corinthian believers regarded themselves as spiritual, yet they were not convinced by Paul's views — instead they were employing syncretism with other religions and demoting the poor to a lower standing within the church.

15:1–58 After addressing problems regarding their worship practices (11:2—14:40), Paul continues by addressing reports about the Corinthians' beliefs. In this chapter, he focuses on the issue of resurrection. He begins by affirming the resurrection of Christ and then discusses the future hope of bodily resurrection and glorification for all followers of Christ.

15:1 gospel In the following verses, Paul gives a brief sketch of the gospel he preached. **15:3 what I received** Refers to the content of vv. 3–5. Paul emphasizes the continuity of his message with the early church's teaching. See the table "Jesus' Fulfillment of OT Prophecy" on p. 1573.

that he was raised on the third day according to the Scriptures, [5]and that he appeared to Cephas,[a] and then to the Twelve. [6]After that, he appeared to more than five hundred of the brothers and sisters at the same time, most of whom are still living, though some have fallen asleep. [7]Then he appeared to James, then to all the apostles, [8]and last of all he appeared to me also, as to one abnormally born.

[9]For I am the least of the apostles and do not even deserve to be called an apostle, because I persecuted the church of God. [10]But by the grace of God I am what I am, and his grace to me was not without effect. No, I worked harder than all of them — yet not I, but the grace of God that was

[a] 5 That is, Peter

15:5 he appeared Refers to a physical sighting of Christ with his eyes — not merely a vision. See the table "Resurrection Appearances of Jesus" below.
15:6 more than five hundred of the brothers and sisters This appearance is unknown outside of this passage, though it recalls the gathering of believers in Ac 2. some have fallen asleep A common metaphor for death (e.g., 1Ki 11:43; Jn 11:11).
15:7 apostles Likely a reference to the 11 apostles present at Christ's resurrection (and still living at this

Resurrection Appearances of Jesus

WITNESSES	SITE	TIME	REFERENCE
Mary Magdalene	Unspecified	The first day of the week	Mk 16:9-11; Jn 20:11-18
Mary Magdalene and the "other Mary"	On the way back from the tomb to where the disciples were staying	The first day of the week	Mt 28:9-10
Peter	Unspecified	The first day of the week	Lk 24:34; 1Co 15:5
Cleopas and an unnamed disciple	The road to Emmaus	The first day of the week	Mk 16:12-13; Lk 24:1-35
"The Eleven and those with them" (Lk 24:33), plus Cleopas and the other disciple. Thomas was not present.	Jerusalem	Evening on the first day of the week	Mk 16:14; Lk 24:36-43; Jn 20:19-23
The Eleven, including Thomas	Jerusalem; the same house as Jn 20:19-23	Eight days after the resurrection	Jn 20:24-29; 1Co 15:5
Simon Peter, Thomas, Nathanael, James, John and two unnamed disciples	The Sea of Galilee	Unspecified, though it is described as the third appearance to the disciples	Jn 21:1-24
The Eleven	Galilee, on the mountain to which Jesus had directed them	Unspecified	Mt 28:16-20; Mk 16:15-18
More than 500 brothers and sisters	Unspecified	Unspecified	1Co 15:6
James	Unspecified	Unspecified	1Co 15:7
The Eleven	Bethany	40 days after the resurrection	Mk 16:19-20; Lk 24:44-52; Ac 1:3-12; 1Co 15:7
Paul	Damascus	Unspecified, though in 1Co 15:8, Paul claims he was last of all	Ac 9:1-6; 22:6-10; 26:12-18; 1Co 15:8; Gal 1:12,16

with me. [11]Whether, then, it is I or they, this is what we preach, and this is what you believed.

The Resurrection of the Dead

[12]But if it is preached that Christ has been raised from the dead, how can some of you say that there is no resurrection of the dead? [13]If there is no resurrection of the dead, then not even Christ has been raised. [14]And if Christ has not been raised, our preaching is useless and so is your faith. [15]More than that, we are then found to be false witnesses about God, for we have testified about God that he raised Christ from the dead. But he did not raise him if in fact the dead are not raised. [16]For if the dead are not raised, then Christ has not been raised either. [17]And if Christ has not been raised, your faith is futile; you are still in your sins. [18]Then those also who have fallen asleep in Christ are lost. [19]If only for this life we have hope in Christ, we are of all people most to be pitied.

[20]But Christ has indeed been raised from the dead, the firstfruits of those who have fallen asleep. [21]For since death came through a man, the resurrection of the dead comes also through a man. [22]For as in Adam all die, so in Christ all will be made alive. [23]But each in turn: Christ, the firstfruits; then, when he comes, those who belong to him. [24]Then the end will come, when he hands over the kingdom to God the Father after he has destroyed all dominion, authority and power. [25]For he must reign until he has put all his enemies under his feet. [26]The last enemy to be destroyed is death. [27]For he "has put everything under his feet."[a] Now when it says that "everything" has been put under him, it is clear that this does not include God himself, who put everything under Christ. [28]When he has done this, then the Son himself will be made subject to him who put everything under him, so that God may be all in all.

[29]Now if there is no resurrection, what will those do who are baptized for the dead? If the dead are not raised at all, why are people baptized for them? [30]And as for us, why do we endanger ourselves every hour? [31]I face death every day — yes, just as surely as I boast about you in Christ Jesus our Lord. [32]If I fought wild beasts in Ephesus with no more than human hopes, what have I gained? If the dead are not raised,

"Let us eat and drink,
    for tomorrow we die."[b]

[a] 27 Psalm 8:6   [b] 32 Isaiah 22:13

---

time). May also refer to the 72 mentioned in Luke (see Lk 10:1 and note), and perhaps others; all of these people saw the risen Christ. See the table "Resurrection Appearances of Jesus" on p. 1896.

15:8 one abnormally born Refers to the abnormal manner in which Paul became an apostle. The Greek word used by Paul here, *ektrōma*, sometimes translated as "abortion," suggests that Paul considered himself different than the other apostles.

15:9 church Paul uses the Greek word *ekklēsia* here to refer to all Christians, especially those in Jerusalem (Ac 8:3; 9:1–2; compare Gal 1:13,22).

15:10 I worked harder than all of them Paul may mean that he planted churches and preached the gospel message in new areas (see 2Co 10:13–17).

15:12 how can some of you say The Corinthians were questioning the resurrection of the dead, despite claiming to believe in Christ's resurrection (1Co 15:1,11). Most Greeks believed that only the soul was immortal (see Ac 17:32 and note). Compare note on Ro 6:22.

15:17 your faith is futile In other words, denying the resurrection involves denying Christ's redemptive work in individuals and creation. **still in your sins** The core teaching of the early church presented Christ's death and resurrection as the solution to sin (1Co 15:3). If the resurrection of Christ is denied, then a person not only has an empty faith but remains under condemnation for their sins (compare Ro 3:23).

15:18 fallen asleep in Christ A metaphor for the death of believers (see 1Th 4:13). **are lost** Refers to a state of condemnation and judgment, still under the guilt and power of sin.

15:20 the firstfruits An allusion to the Jewish Festival of Firstfruits (see Lev 23:10). See note on Ac 26:23; compare note on Ro 8:23. Paul uses this metaphor to present Christ's resurrection as an example of the greatness of the future resurrection of believers (1Co 15:35–57).

15:21 death came through a man Refers to Adam as the representative of sinful humanity (see note on Ro 5:12). **resurrection of the dead comes also through a man** Refers to Jesus Christ as the representative of those who will overcome death and receive eternal life (see note on Ro 5:14).

15:22 in Christ all will be made alive While the unbelieving dead are raised to life for judgment (Rev 20:12–15), God will only raise those who are "in Christ"—that is, believers—to eternal life with him (compare Mt 25:46; 2Th 1:9; Php 3:19).

15:24 the end Refers to the end of the present age and the completion of the believers' salvation in Christ—their union with him (see Mk 13:7; Mt 24:6,14). **all dominion, authority and power** Refers to the evil entities that are opposed to God and oppress his people (e.g., Ro 8:38; Col 2:15; Eph 2:2).

15:25 his enemies under his feet In fulfillment of Ps 8:6 and 110:1. Paul's language suggests that Christ is presently reigning in his kingdom, but the kingdom is also still in the future.

15:28 the Son himself Just as Christ suffered and died for humanity in submission to the Father's will (compare Mk 14:36), at the end of the present age Christ will submit all things entrusted to him to God the Father. **that God may be all in all** Expresses the supremacy of God and his will in all things.

15:29 baptized for the dead Possibly a reference to washing the bodies of the dead. The idea may mean that believers were being baptized in honor of unbaptized deceased believers.

15:30 do we endanger Paul wants the Corinthians to know that he would not have risked his life if he did not believe that the bodily resurrection was true. See the infographic "The Tullianum: A Prison in Rome" on p. 2008.

[33]Do not be misled: "Bad company corrupts good character."[a] [34]Come back to your senses as you ought, and stop sinning; for there are some who are ignorant of God — I say this to your shame.

The Resurrection Body

[35]But someone will ask, "How are the dead raised? With what kind of body will they come?" [36]How foolish! What you sow does not come to life unless it dies. [37]When you sow, you do not plant the body that will be, but just a seed, perhaps of wheat or of something else. [38]But God gives it a body as he has determined, and to each kind of seed he gives its own body. [39]Not all flesh is the same: People have one kind of flesh, animals have another, birds another and fish another. [40]There are also heavenly bodies and there are earthly bodies; but the splendor of the heavenly bodies is one kind, and the splendor of the earthly bodies is another. [41]The sun has one kind of splendor, the moon another and the stars another; and star differs from star in splendor.

[42]So will it be with the resurrection of the dead. The body that is sown is perishable, it is raised imperishable; [43]it is sown in dishonor, it is raised in glory; it is sown in weakness, it is raised in power; [44]it is sown a natural body, it is raised a spiritual body.

If there is a natural body, there is also a spiritual body. [45]So it is written: "The first man Adam became a living being"[b]; the last Adam, a life-giving spirit. [46]The spiritual did not come first, but the natural, and after that the spiritual. [47]The first man was of the dust of the earth; the second man is of heaven. [48]As was the earthly man, so are those who are of the earth; and as is the heavenly man, so also are those who are of heaven. [49]And just as we have borne the image of the earthly man, so shall we[c] bear the image of the heavenly man.

[50]I declare to you, brothers and sisters, that flesh and blood cannot inherit the kingdom of God, nor does the perishable inherit the imperishable. [51]Listen, I tell you a mystery: We will not all sleep, but we will all be changed — [52]in a flash, in the twinkling of an eye, at the last trumpet. For the trumpet will sound, the dead will be raised imperishable, and we will be changed. [53]For the perishable must clothe itself with the imperishable, and the mortal with immortality. [54]When the perishable has been clothed with the imperishable, and the mortal with immortality, then the saying that is written will come true: "Death has been swallowed up in victory."[d]

[55]"Where, O death, is your victory?
　　Where, O death, is your sting?"[e]

[a] 33 From the Greek poet Menander   [b] 45 Gen. 2:7   [c] 49 Some early manuscripts so let us   [d] 54 Isaiah 25:8   [e] 55 Hosea 13:14

15:34 Come back to your senses as you ought, and stop sinning Paul chastised the Corinthians for their arrogance; in this context, their sin is the denial of the resurrection.

15:35 How are the dead raised Paul anticipates this question from the Corinthians who doubt the truth of the bodily resurrection. The question also implies that some Corinthians thought the resurrection was foolish (1Co 1:18–25).

15:36 What you sow does not come to life unless it dies Paul takes an example from nature to show the Corinthians that life can come from death.

15:37 wheat or of something else The wheat seed, though it dies, comes to life as a plant. In the same way, physical bodies perish, but God raises and transforms them into glorified spiritual bodies.

15:40 heavenly bodies Paul contrasts heavenly bodies with earthly bodies to emphasize that the body of resurrected believers will be distinctly different; earthly bodies rot and decay while heavenly ones do not (v. 42). **splendor** The Greek word used here, *doxa*, refers to the radiance or light of the heavenly bodies.

15:42 So it will be with the resurrection of the dead The Corinthians expressed skepticism about the transformation of a dead body through resurrection. Paul uses an example from nature to show that such transformation already takes place within creation. **that is sown is perishable** The corruption of the seed corresponds to the mortal bodies of people.

15:43 it is raised in glory When God raises the dead in Christ, they will receive glorified spiritual bodies (see Php 3:21). Thus, the bodies will become honorable before the Lord.

15:44 natural body Refers to life in the limited mortal body that is subject to the things of this present age: hunger, thirst and death. **spiritual body** Refers to a body fashioned and controlled by the Holy Spirit. The body belongs to the new age under the reign of God (compare 1:8 and note).

15:45 a life-giving spirit Refers to Jesus becoming a life-giving spirit as a result of his resurrection. Compare Ge 2:7.

15:47 second man is of heaven May refer to Christ's origin (heaven) or to his resurrected and glorified status in heaven.

15:49 bear the image of the heavenly man Paul informs the Corinthians that they will resemble Christ in his glorified spiritual body and his character (compare 1Jn 3:2).

15:50 flesh and blood cannot inherit the kingdom Eternal life with Christ and the inheritance of God's kingdom will require a heavenly spiritual body like Christ's (1Co 15:49). The perishable body of human existence will be replaced.

15:51 We will not all sleep Implies that not all believers will die before Jesus returns. Compare 1Th 4:15.

15:52 last trumpet This trumpet signals the day of redemption, when God brings to completion the salvation of his people (uniting them fully with him).

15:53 mortal with immortality Christ reverses the condition of mortality and grants to people the immortality God created them to enjoy.

15:54 Death has been swallowed up in victory Echoes Isa 25:8 as a sign of the new age. In the age to come, the effects of humanity's sin will be removed (1Co 15:21–22; Ro 5:17; compare Rev 21:4).

15:55 Where, O death, is your victory Paul quotes Hos 13:14 to taunt death on account of Christ's victory.

[56]The sting of death is sin, and the power of sin is the law. [57]But thanks be to God! He gives us the victory through our Lord Jesus Christ.

[58]Therefore, my dear brothers and sisters, stand firm. Let nothing move you. Always give yourselves fully to the work of the Lord, because you know that your labor in the Lord is not in vain.

The Collection for the Lord's People

16 Now about the collection for the Lord's people: Do what I told the Galatian churches to do. [2]On the first day of every week, each one of you should set aside a sum of money in keeping with your income, saving it up, so that when I come no collections will have to be made. [3]Then, when I arrive, I will give letters of introduction to the men you approve and send them with your gift to Jerusalem. [4]If it seems advisable for me to go also, they will accompany me.

Personal Requests

[5]After I go through Macedonia, I will come to you—for I will be going through Macedonia. [6]Perhaps I will stay with you for a while, or even spend the winter, so that you can help me on my journey, wherever I go. [7]For I do not want to see you now and make only a passing visit; I hope to spend some time with you, if the Lord permits. [8]But I will stay on at Ephesus until Pentecost, [9]because a great door for effective work has opened to me, and there are many who oppose me.

[10]When Timothy comes, see to it that he has nothing to fear while he is with you, for he is carrying on the work of the Lord, just as I am. [11]No one, then, should treat him with contempt. Send him on his way in peace so that he may return to me. I am expecting him along with the brothers.

[12]Now about our brother Apollos: I strongly urged him to go to you with the brothers. He was quite unwilling to go now, but he will go when he has the opportunity.

[13]Be on your guard; stand firm in the faith; be courageous; be strong. [14]Do everything in love.

[15]You know that the household of Stephanas were the first converts in Achaia, and they have devoted themselves to the service of the Lord's people. I urge you, brothers and sisters, [16]to submit to such people and to everyone who joins in the work and labors at it. [17]I was glad when Stephanas, Fortunatus and Achaicus arrived, because they have supplied what was lacking from you. [18]For they refreshed my spirit and yours also. Such men deserve recognition.

Final Greetings

[19]The churches in the province of Asia send you greetings. Aquila and Priscilla[a] greet you warmly in the Lord, and so does the church that meets at their house. [20]All the brothers and sisters here send you greetings. Greet one another with a holy kiss.

[21]I, Paul, write this greeting in my own hand.

[22]If anyone does not love the Lord, let that person be cursed! Come, Lord[b]!

[23]The grace of the Lord Jesus be with you.

[24]My love to all of you in Christ Jesus. Amen.[c]

a 19 Greek *Prisca*, a variant of *Priscilla*   *b 22* The Greek for *Come, Lord* reproduces an Aramaic expression (*Marana tha*) used by early Christians.   *c 24* Some manuscripts do not have *Amen*.

15:56 the power of sin is the law Compare Ro 5:12–14; 7:9–13.

16:1–24 As with many of his letters, Paul closes with minor instructions, personal news, encouragement, closing greetings and personal acknowledgments (compare Ro 15:22—16:24; Eph 6:21–24).

16:1 the collection Funds Paul was collecting to relieve the Jerusalem church (see 2Co 9; Ro 15:25–26). **Galatian churches** Refers to congregations located throughout the Roman province in Asia. See the timeline "Life of Paul" on p. 1796.

16:2 first day of every week Paul's reference to the first day of the week is evidence that early believers met on Sunday to celebrate Christ's resurrection.

16:8 Ephesus A harbor city located in Asia Minor. See note on Eph 1:1. **Pentecost** A Jewish festival celebrating the first fruits of the harvest. See the table "Israelite Festivals" on p. 200.

16:9 a great door for effective work Represents a special opportunity—probably to preach the gospel (compare 2Co 2:12; Col 4:3).

16:10 Timothy Timothy assisted Paul in Corinth (see Ac 18:1–5) and will return to Corinth as Paul's representa-

tive (see 1Co 4:17–21; Ac 19:22). Because of the tension between Paul and some of the Corinthian believers, Paul urges them to treat Timothy well.

16:12 Apollos See note on 1Co 1:12. **brothers** Refers to Stephanas, Fortunatus and Achaicus (v. 17).

16:15 Achaia The Roman province in the region of central and southern Greece. Corinth was the capital city of Achaia.

16:16 submit Paul encourages the believers in Corinth to voluntarily yield to the family of Stephanas in love (see Eph 5:21).

16:17 Stephanas, Fortunatus and Achaicus Three believers who visited Paul as representatives of the church in Corinth.

16:19 Aquila and Priscilla See note on Ro 16:3.

16:20 All the brothers and sisters Refers to Paul's missionary companions; may also include the believers in Ephesus.

16:21 this greeting in my own hand Implies that Paul dictated this letter to a scribe but wrote the last few verses himself.

16:22 cursed Compare 1Co 12:3; Gal 1:8,9. **Come, Lord** An appeal for the Lord to return.

2 CORINTHIANS

INTRODUCTION TO 2 CORINTHIANS

More than any of Paul's other letters, 2 Corinthians conveys the words of a pastor. Paul has had a rocky relationship with the Corinthian believers, but he continues to patiently love them like a father (2Co 12:14–15). Now, as some question his authority, Paul preaches a gospel of reconciliation, characterized by making important but hard decisions.

BACKGROUND

Paul had founded the church of Corinth around AD 51, during his second missionary journey. After staying about 18 months and some unspecified additional period (Ac 18:11–17), he continued with other missionary work. Occasionally, he would receive troubling reports about the Corinthians, prompting him to write them letters. Paul sent at least four letters to Corinth: an initial letter that is now lost (1Co 5:9); the letter we know as 1 Corinthians; another lost letter, described as Paul's severe letter to Corinth (2Co 2:3–4,9; compare 7:8,12); and the letter we know as 2 Corinthians.

Sometime after writing 1 Corinthians, Paul likely sent Timothy to Corinth (1Co 16:10–11). Paul was on his third missionary journey at the time and had originally intended to travel from Ephesus to Macedonia and then head south to Corinth (1Co 16:5–8). Instead he made a short visit directly to Corinth, only to have a sorrowful visit there (2Co 2:1; 12:21; 13:2). This painful visit prompted him to write his severe letter (2:3–4). From Corinth, he went to Macedonia, where he wrote 2 Corinthians (2:13; 7:5; 9:2)—likely sometime during AD 55–57. In Macedonia, Paul had received a

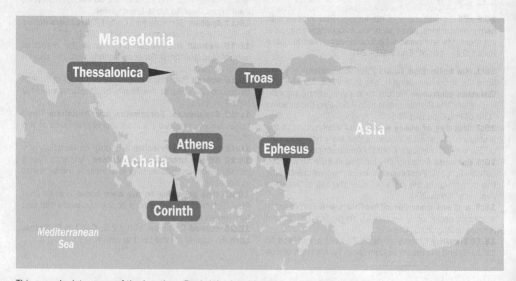

This map depicts many of the locations Paul visited on his second missionary journey.

positive report from his associate Titus about the Corinthians—his severe letter had essentially worked (7:6–10). However, 2 Corinthians shows that Paul's attempts to persuade the Corinthians to follow Jesus' ways, instead of the ways of their culture, were still very much in progress (see the "Introduction to 1 Corinthians").

Later in Paul's life he returned to Greece for three months—likely to Corinth (Ac 20:2–3); it is during this time that Paul probably wrote Romans (Ac 20:3—21:16).

STRUCTURE

Second Corinthians reflects the standard form of a Greco-Roman letter, with an introduction (2Co 1:1–11), a body (1:12—13:10) and a conclusion (13:11–14). The first part of the body (1:12—2:11) contains Paul's defense of his conduct toward the Corinthians—specifically, his reason for having not visited them again after his painful visit. Paul then explains the nature of his ministry (2:12—7:16). He also brings up the issue of his collection for the impoverished Jerusalem church (8:1—9:15): In light of God's generosity toward the Corinthians, Paul wants them to exercise generosity in supporting their fellow believers financially. Finally, Paul defends his authority as an apostle against people in Corinth who were questioning it (10:1—13:10).

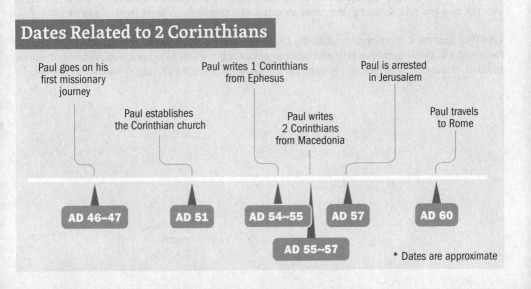

Dates Related to 2 Corinthians

Paul goes on his first missionary journey

Paul establishes the Corinthian church

Paul writes 1 Corinthians from Ephesus

Paul writes 2 Corinthians from Macedonia

Paul is arrested in Jerusalem

Paul travels to Rome

AD 46–47

AD 51

AD 54~55

AD 57

AD 60

AD 55~57

* Dates are approximate

OUTLINE

- Introduction and benediction (1:1–11)
- Paul's personal defense (1:12—2:11)
- Paul's defense of his ministry (2:12—7:16)
- The collection for the Jerusalem church (8:1—9:15)
- Preparation for Paul's visit (10:1—13:13)

THEMES

Second Corinthians is about reconciliation, making difficult choices about toxic relationships and separating from sinful behavior. Paul had a strained relationship with the Corinthians, and some church members had questioned his motives and authority, saying that a true apostle would act more boldly (ch. 10). These people were being divisive, but Paul was still hoping for reconciliation with the church—a possibility that existed because Jesus had reconciled these believers to God (5:17–21). But it seems that this reconciliation meant the Corinthians separating from the so-called super-apostles—and it meant separating from sinful behavior in general (6:14—7:1; 11:1–9).

Paul does not respond to his critics by talking about his importance or influence; instead, he points to his meekness and suffering—the very things that his opponents were criticizing—as signs that he was faithfully preaching the message about Jesus (11:16–33). Paul bares his heart to the Corinthians, hoping that they will recognize his sincere concern for them (6:11–13). Paul's interest in the collection for Jerusalem church also is about reconciliation. If God's people everywhere are brought together in Christ as the people of God, then they should care about each other. If one group is suffering, the other should make sacrifices to meet their needs (8:14).

Like Paul and the Corinthians, modern-day Christians are no strangers to conflict. We often can be deceived into thinking that worldly wisdom and power are the way to accomplish anything of value. Instead, Paul tells us to look to the example of Jesus, who is light shining in darkness (4:1–6).

1 Paul, an apostle of Christ Jesus by the will of God, and Timothy our brother,

To the church of God in Corinth, together with all his holy people throughout Achaia:

²Grace and peace to you from God our Father and the Lord Jesus Christ.

Praise to the God of All Comfort

³Praise be to the God and Father of our Lord Jesus Christ, the Father of compassion and the God of all comfort, ⁴who comforts us in all our troubles, so that we can comfort those in any trouble with the comfort we ourselves receive from God. ⁵For just as we share abundantly in the sufferings of Christ, so also our comfort abounds through Christ. ⁶If we are distressed, it is for your comfort and salvation; if we are comforted, it is for your comfort, which produces in you patient endurance of the same sufferings we suffer. ⁷And our

hope for you is firm, because we know that just as you share in our sufferings, so also you share in our comfort.

⁸We do not want you to be uninformed, brothers and sisters,ᵃ about the troubles we experienced in the province of Asia. We were under great pressure, far beyond our ability to endure, so that we despaired of life itself. ⁹Indeed, we felt we had received the sentence of death. But this happened that we might not rely on ourselves but on God, who raises the dead. ¹⁰He has delivered us from such a deadly peril, and he will deliver us again. On him we have set our hope that he will continue to deliver us, ¹¹as you help us by your prayers. Then many will give thanks on our behalf for the gracious favor granted us in answer to the prayers of many.

ᵃ 8 The Greek word for *brothers and sisters* (*adelphoi*) refers here to believers, both men and women, as part of God's family; also in 8:1; 13:11.

1:1–2 Paul founded the church in Corinth around AD 51 during his second missionary journey (Ac 18). After 18 months in Corinth, he departed the city to continue his missionary work. Paul planned to visit Corinth again via Macedonia (1Co 16:5–9; 2Co 1:16), but instead traveled straight from Ephesus to Corinth. This visit turned out to be a painful experience, so Paul departed and wrote a severe letter to the Corinthian church (2:1–5; 7:12). When Paul heard about the Corinthians' largely positive response to the letter (7:6–7), he wrote 2 Corinthians to commend the church, to prepare them for the collection for the Jerusalem poor (chs. 8–9), and to warn them of false apostles in their midst (chs. 10–13). But Paul is still experiencing great struggles with the Corinthian church; he addresses these issues throughout the letter. The events described in 2 Corinthians took place during Paul's third missionary journey, with him writing 2 Corinthians ca. AD 55–57 from Macedonia (2Co 2:13; 7:5; 9:2).

Second Corinthians begins with a greeting typical of Paul's letters. He identifies himself as an apostle and mentions Timothy, his cosender.

1:1 apostle Refers to Paul's role as a commissioned minister of the gospel. See the table "Pauline Self-Designations" on p. 1904. **by the will of God** Paul emphasizes that his apostleship comes from God's authority and not his own. He repeats this theme throughout the letter as a defense of his apostolic authority (v. 21; 2:17; 3:5–6; 10:8; 13:10). **Timothy** The Corinthians knew Timothy because he accompanied Paul during his ministry in Corinth (Ac 18:1,5). See note on Php 1:1; note on 1Ti 1:2. **church of God** By referring to the Corinthian church this way Paul emphasizes that the community belongs to God. **Corinth** See note on 1Co 1:2. **holy people** See note on Ro 1:7. **Achaia** The southern region of Greece; Corinth was the capital.

1:2 Grace and peace to you See note on Ro 1:7.

1:3–11 Paul begins his letter with a benediction to God rather than his typical thanksgiving address (compare 1Co 1:4–9; Php 1:3–11; 1Th 1:2–10). In this section, he discusses the comfort God provides during suffering.

1:3 Praise be Paul alludes to a Jewish expression of praise called the *barakhah*, the Hebrew word for "blessing" (Ps 66:20; 72:18; Eph 1:3; 1Pe 1:3). Paul praises God for his provision of comfort during hardship. **comfort** The Greek word Paul uses here, *paraklēsis* (and the corresponding verb *parakaleō*), occurs ten times in 2Co 1:3–7. It typically refers to encouragement or consolation given to someone who is suffering or in mourning (Mt 5:4). In the Septuagint (the ancient Greek version of the OT) of Isa 40–55, God's comfort (*parakaleō*) comes as he restores his people from captivity. Paul draws on Isa 40–55 to show that God—who brought his people back from captivity and restored them to himself—now restores his people to himself through Christ (2Co 5:18–20).

1:5 sufferings of Christ Refers primarily to the events Jesus underwent from his arrest to his death (Mt 26–27; Mk 14–15; Lk 22–23; Jn 18–19).

1:6 we are distressed Certain opponents in Corinth may have assumed that Paul's sufferings delegitimized his apostleship, as they regarded suffering as a sign of weakness. Paul reminds the believers that his sufferings brought about the spread of the gospel by displaying God's power (2Co 4:7–9). **your comfort** See note on v. 3. **salvation** See note on Ro 1:16.

1:7 hope The Greek word used here, *elpis,* refers to a confident expectation of deliverance. It indicates a firm trust that God will fulfill his promises (Ro 4:13–25; see 5:5 and note).

1:8 province of Asia Paul is probably referring to his hardships in Ephesus here (Ac 19:23–41; 1Co 15:31–32).

1:9 sentence of death The severity of Paul's persecution leads him to claim that he felt like a judge had condemned him to die (Ac 14:19–20). He juxtaposes death and life throughout this letter (2Co 2:16; 4:7–14; 5:1–10; 13:4).

1:10 our hope Paul confidently expects God to deliver him from persecution. He recognizes that God's deliverance will not be for his own sake, but for the sake of believers and those who have not yet heard the gospel message (see Php 1:21–26; 2Ti 4:17).

Paul's Change of Plans

¹²Now this is our boast: Our conscience testifies that we have conducted ourselves in the world, and especially in our relations with you, with integrity[a] and godly sincerity. We have done so, relying not on worldly wisdom but on God's grace. ¹³For we do not write you anything you cannot read or understand. And I hope that, ¹⁴as you have understood us in part, you will come to understand fully that you can boast of us just as we will boast of you in the day of the Lord Jesus.

¹⁵Because I was confident of this, I wanted to visit you first so that you might benefit twice. ¹⁶I wanted to visit you on my way to Macedonia and to come back to you from Macedonia, and then to have you send me on my way to Judea. ¹⁷Was I fickle when I intended to do this? Or do I make my plans in a worldly manner so that in the same breath I say both "Yes, yes" and "No, no"?

¹⁸But as surely as God is faithful, our message to you is not "Yes" and "No." ¹⁹For the Son of God, Jesus Christ, who was preached among you by us — by me and Silas[b] and Timothy — was not

a 12 Many manuscripts holiness   b 19 Greek Silvanus, a variant of Silas

1:12–14 After his opening greeting (2Co 1:1–2) and benediction (vv. 3–11), Paul begins to defend himself against the criticisms he faces. In this passage, he makes a general defense of his integrity and ministry.

1:12 boast See note on 1Co 1:29. **integrity and godly sincerity** Paul sought to maintain integrity in ministry to prevent the gospel from losing credibility. He was especially sensitive to the issue of financial support in the regions of Macedonia and Achaia; he did not want others to perceive him as a peddler or ordinary philosopher (2Co 2:17; 1Co 9:1–12; Php 4:14–17; 1Th 2:9). **worldly wisdom** See note on 1Co 1:24.
1:13 anything you cannot read The opponents in Corinth accused Paul of being insincere and deceitful (2Co 10:10), but Paul made his intentions and expectations clear in this letter.
1:14 day of the Lord Jesus Refers to the OT expression "day of Yahweh" (Isa 13:9; Joel 1:15; Mal 4:5). The NT writers equated this day with the day of Christ—the time when Christ returns to judge the wicked and deliver his people (see 1Th 5:2 and note).

1:15—2:4 Paul moves from a general defense of his ministry and integrity (2Co 1:12–14) to a specific defense of why he did not visit the Corinthians as he had planned (1Co 16:5–7). After a brief statement about God's faithfulness (2Co 1:18–22), Paul explains that he did not visit in order to spare them and give them an opportunity to repent (see v. 23 and note).

1:15 benefit twice This probably indicates that Paul intended to visit Corinth twice: once on his way to Macedonia and then again on his way back to Judea.
1:16 Macedonia The Roman province north of Corinth, also located in modern Greece.
1:17 "No, no" Some Corinthian believers accused Paul of being indecisive or inconsistent about his return to Corinth (compare vv. 15,17), when in fact he chose not to visit because he did not want to cause them grief (v. 22—2:4). Instead he wrote them a painful letter so they would repent (7:8–9).
1:18 as surely as God is faithful Paul may be using an oath formula similar to the expression "as surely as God lives ..." (see Job 27:2 and note). If so, he uses it

Pauline Self-Designations

LETTER	SELF-DESIGNATION IN LETTER OPENINGS
Romans	servant of Christ Jesus, apostle (Ro 1:1)
1 Corinthians	apostle of Christ Jesus (1Co 1:1)
2 Corinthians	apostle of Christ Jesus (2Co 1:1)
Galatians	apostle sent not from men nor by a man (Gal 1:1)
Ephesians	apostle of Christ Jesus (Eph 1:1)
Philippians	servant of Christ Jesus (Php 1:1)
Colossians	apostle of Christ Jesus (Col 1:1)
1 Thessalonians	none (1Th 1:1)
2 Thessalonians	none (2Th 1:1)
1 Timothy	apostle of Christ Jesus (1Ti 1:1)
2 Timothy	apostle of Christ Jesus (2Ti 1:1)
Titus	servant of God, apostle of Jesus Christ (Titus 1:1)
Philemon	a prisoner of Christ Jesus (Phm 1)

"Yes" and "No," but in him it has always been "Yes." [20] For no matter how many promises God has made, they are "Yes" in Christ. And so through him the "Amen" is spoken by us to the glory of God. [21] Now it is God who makes both us and you stand firm in Christ. He anointed us, [22] set his seal of ownership on us, and put his Spirit in our hearts as a deposit, guaranteeing what is to come.

[23] I call God as my witness — and I stake my life on it — that it was in order to spare you that I did not return to Corinth. [24] Not that we lord it over your faith, but we work with you for your joy, because it is by faith you stand firm. [1] So I made up my mind that I would not make another painful visit to you. [2] For if I grieve you, who is left to make me glad but you whom I have grieved? [3] I wrote as I did, so that when I came I would not be distressed by those who should have made me rejoice. I had confidence in all of you, that you would all share my joy. [4] For I wrote you out of great distress and anguish of heart and with many tears, not to grieve you but to let you know the depth of my love for you.

Forgiveness for the Offender

[5] If anyone has caused grief, he has not so much grieved me as he has grieved all of you to some extent — not to put it too severely. [6] The punishment inflicted on him by the majority is sufficient. [7] Now instead, you ought to forgive and comfort him, so that he will not be overwhelmed by excessive sorrow. [8] I urge you, therefore, to reaffirm your love for him. [9] Another reason I wrote you was to see if you would stand the test and be obedient in everything. [10] Anyone you forgive, I also forgive. And what I have forgiven — if there was anything to forgive — I have forgiven in the sight of Christ for your sake, [11] in order that Satan might not outwit us. For we are not unaware of his schemes.

Ministers of the New Covenant

[12] Now when I went to Troas to preach the gospel of Christ and found that the Lord had opened a door for me, [13] I still had no peace of mind, because I did not find my brother Titus there. So I said goodbye to them and went on to Macedonia.

---

to stress that his words are true (compare 2Co 1:23). **our message** Refers to Paul's communication to the Corinthians — the gospel message as well as his travel plans (1Co 1:23; 16:5–7).

1:19 Silas and Timothy Two missionary companions who ministered with Paul in Corinth (see Ac 18:5–6). Paul includes both Silvanus — referred to as Silas in Acts (e.g., Ac 15:22) — and Timothy as cosenders of the letters to the Thessalonians (1Th 1:1; 2Th 1:1). **"Yes" and "No"** Describes contradictory messages. Paul affirms that his message was consistent with the teaching of Christ.

1:20 promises God has made Refers to all of God's promises in the OT. Paul also mentions God's promises in 2Co 7:1, where he cites a series of OT quotations that highlight God's adoption of his people (see 6:16–18 and notes). **"Yes" in Christ** Indicates that God's promises are true, trustworthy and fulfilled in Christ.

1:21 He anointed Refers to an OT custom of marking a person for service to God.

1:23 to spare you Paul probably chose to delay his visit because he wanted to give the Corinthians the opportunity to repent and prove their obedience. He may have also wanted to avoid taking disciplinary measures — which would cause discouragement — against them.

2:1 that I would not make another painful visit to you Compare 2Co 1:23 and note; 7:8–9.

2:3 I wrote While Paul may be referring to 1 Corinthians here, he is probably referring to another letter written between 1 and 2 Corinthians.

2:4 let you know the depth of my love Paul emphasizes that he did not write the painful letter to hurt the Corinthian church; rather, he wrote out of love to rebuke the Corinthians toward repentance (7:8–12).

2:5–11 Apparently the Corinthians responded to Paul's letter (see note on v. 3) by disciplining the person most responsible for Paul's rebuke. Here, Paul encourages them to forgive and comfort the offender (vv. 7–8).

2:5 If anyone has caused grief Paul may be referring

to the incestuous person described in 1Co 5:1–5. He more likely refers, however, to the person who was the focus of Paul's rebuke in the painful letter (see note on 2Co 2:3).

2:6 punishment It is unclear what kind of punishment the church carried out; it may have been a public rebuke or expulsion from the church community.

2:7 and comfort him See note on 1:3.

2:8 I urge you The Greek word Paul uses here is *parakaleō* (see note on 1:3). **to reaffirm** The Greek word used here, *kyroō*, is a legal term meaning "to affirm" or "to ratify" (see Gal 3:15 and note). In forgiving the offender, the Corinthian church will validate their love (*agape* in Greek) as a community.

2:9 see if you would stand the test Paul reveals another reason for writing his painful letter (2Co 2:3–4): He wanted to see if they would obey him and discipline the individual requiring rebuke. In disciplining the offender, the Corinthian church demonstrated respect for Paul's apostolic authority.

2:11 Satan The Corinthians' forgiveness of the individual will restore unity in the church and ensure that Satan cannot take advantage of any division. Paul mentions Satan's activity several times in the Corinthian letters (1Co 5:5; 7:5; 2Co 4:4; 6:15; 11:14; 12:7).

2:12–13 Paul resumes the explanation of why he did not visit Corinth as he had previously planned (see 1:15—2:4 and note). These verses also lead into the defense of his apostolic ministry (2:14—7:4) by highlighting the reason for his travel — for the gospel of Christ — and God's active intervention in Paul's life.

2:12 Troas A city located on the coast of the Aegean Sea in modern Turkey. While Paul was in Troas, he received a vision and concluded that he should preach the gospel in Macedonia (Ac 16:8–10). **Lord** Paul defends his change of travel plans by emphasizing God's active intervention in his life.

2:13 Titus A Gentile missionary companion of the apostle Paul (Gal 2:1,3; 2Ti 4:10). Paul sent Titus to Corinth

¹⁴But thanks be to God, who always leads us as captives in Christ's triumphal procession and uses us to spread the aroma of the knowledge of him everywhere. ¹⁵For we are to God the pleasing aroma of Christ among those who are being saved and those who are perishing. ¹⁶To the one we are an aroma that brings death; to the other, an aroma that brings life. And who is equal to such a task? ¹⁷Unlike so many, we do not peddle the word of God for profit. On the contrary, in Christ we speak before God with sincerity, as those sent from God.

3 Are we beginning to commend ourselves again? Or do we need, like some people, letters of recommendation to you or from you? ²You yourselves are our letter, written on our hearts, known and read by everyone. ³You show that you are a letter from Christ, the result of our ministry, written not with ink but with the Spirit of the living God, not on tablets of stone but on tablets of human hearts.

⁴Such confidence we have through Christ be-fore God. ⁵Not that we are competent in ourselves to claim anything for ourselves, but our competence comes from God. ⁶He has made us competent as ministers of a new covenant — not of the letter but of the Spirit; for the letter kills, but the Spirit gives life.

The Greater Glory of the New Covenant

⁷Now if the ministry that brought death, which was engraved in letters on stone, came with glory, so that the Israelites could not look steadily at the face of Moses because of its glory, transitory though it was, ⁸will not the ministry of the Spirit be even more glorious? ⁹If the ministry that brought condemnation was glorious, how much more glorious is the ministry that brings righteousness! ¹⁰For what was glorious has no glory now in comparison with the surpassing glory. ¹¹And if what was transitory came with glory, how much greater is the glory of that which lasts!

---

with his earlier distressed letter (2Co 2:3–4; 7:13–15; 12:18) and again with 2 Corinthians (8:16–17). See note on Titus 1:4. **Macedonia** See note on 2Co 1:16.

PAUL'S THIRD MISSIONARY JOURNEY (AD 52–57)

Paul visits Galatia and Phrygia

Paul stays at Ephesus and writes 1 Corinthians

Paul visits Macedonia and writes 2 Corinthians

2:14–17 Paul here begins a defense of his apostolic ministry that makes up much of his letter (2:14—7:4). He gives thanks to God for leading him in victory (2:14). He also defends his motives as pure and describes himself as speaking before God (v. 17).

2:14 leads us as captives in Christ's triumphal procession May refer to a procession in which the ark of the covenant would be brought into Jerusalem (e.g., Ps 68), but most likely refers to a Roman victory parade. After a victorious battle, Roman generals led their captives in a procession to the capital. Here Paul likely alludes to his role as a suffering slave in God's victorious procession to validate the affliction he experienced—a perceived weakness to his opponents—as a result of his ministry (compare 2Co 4:7–12).

2:17 peddle the word of God for profit In contrast to the false apostles mentioned in 11:1–14, Paul did not accept any payment from the Corinthian church (11:7,9; 12:13–16).

3:1–18 Continuing the defense of his apostolic ministry, Paul states that he doesn't need letters of recommendation to validate his ministry (vv. 1–3); rather, God validates his ministry (vv. 4–6). Paul then transitions into a discussion of the new covenant aspect of his ministry, comparing Moses' ministry of the law (or old covenant) with his ministry of the new covenant (vv. 7–18).

3:1 beginning to commend ourselves again In 2:17, Paul reminded the Corinthians about the sincerity of his ministry. He does not, however, want them to misinterpret this reminder as self-commendation—boasting about his achievements to impress others and establish credibility.

letters of recommendation In Paul's time, itinerant ministers used letters of recommendation to establish their legitimacy and authority. Paul includes a letter of recommendation for Titus and two other unnamed men who deliver this letter to the Corinthian church (see note on 8:16–24).

3:2 You yourselves are our letter The Corinthians should realize their existence as a church is the result of Paul's apostolic ministry. In this sense, they serve as Paul's letter of recommendation, testifying to the legitimacy of his apostleship (compare 1Co 9:1–2).

3:3 a letter from Christ The Spirit's transforming work and indwelling presence among the Corinthians function as a recommendation from Christ. **tablets of human hearts** Paul contrasts the stone tablets, a reference to the Law of Moses (Ex 24:12) with the new covenant promised by Jeremiah and Ezekiel (Jer 31:33; Eze 11:20).

3:6 the letter kills This is a reference to the Law of Moses (compare Ro 2:27; 7:6). The law does not justify people; it only identifies sin and condemns (see Ro 3:20; 8:2). Instead, people are justified by faith (see Ro 3:28 and note).

3:7 ministry that brought death Paul contrasts his ministry with the ministry of Moses. The law, as given by Moses, only brings death and condemnation (compare note on 2Co 3:6). In contrast to God's Spirit, the law was not capable of giving life (Ro 8:3; Gal 3:21). **glory** The Greek word used here, *doxa*, refers to the splendor of God's manifest presence.

3:8 ministry of the Spirit Refers to the ministry that imparts the Holy Spirit (*pneuma* in Greek) and stands in contrast to the ministry of death described in 2Co 3:7. The glory of this ministry is greater and longer lasting because of the Spirit's presence within the believer (1Co 3:16; 6:19).

3:9 ministry that brings righteousness This ministry provides right standing before God. It not only removes the guilt of sin, it also empowers the believer to do what is right (compare 2Co 3:7 and note).

3:10 what was glorious Refers to the Law of Moses or the old covenant (Ex 34:29). Although God's splendor shone on the face of Moses, it cannot compare to the splendor of the new covenant.

¹²Therefore, since we have such a hope, we are very bold. ¹³We are not like Moses, who would put a veil over his face to prevent the Israelites from seeing the end of what was passing away. ¹⁴But their minds were made dull, for to this day the same veil remains when the old covenant is read. It has not been removed, because only in Christ is it taken away. ¹⁵Even to this day when Moses is read, a veil covers their hearts. ¹⁶But whenever anyone turns to the Lord, the veil is taken away. ¹⁷Now the Lord is the Spirit, and where the Spirit of the Lord is, there is freedom. ¹⁸And we all, who with unveiled faces contemplate[a] the Lord's glory, are being transformed into his image with ever-increasing glory, which comes from the Lord, who is the Spirit.

Present Weakness and Resurrection Life

4 Therefore, since through God's mercy we have this ministry, we do not lose heart. ²Rather, we have renounced secret and shameful ways;

we do not use deception, nor do we distort the word of God. On the contrary, by setting forth the truth plainly we commend ourselves to everyone's conscience in the sight of God. ³And even if our gospel is veiled, it is veiled to those who are perishing. ⁴The god of this age has blinded the minds of unbelievers, so that they cannot see the light of the gospel that displays the glory of Christ, who is the image of God. ⁵For what we preach is not ourselves, but Jesus Christ as Lord, and ourselves as your servants for Jesus' sake. ⁶For God, who said, "Let light shine out of darkness,"[b] made his light shine in our hearts to give us the light of the knowledge of God's glory displayed in the face of Christ.

⁷But we have this treasure in jars of clay to show that this all-surpassing power is from God and not from us. ⁸We are hard pressed on every side, but not crushed; perplexed, but not in despair; ⁹persecuted, but not abandoned; struck down, but not destroyed. ¹⁰We always carry around in our

---

ᵃ 18 Or *reflect*   ᵇ 6 Gen. 1:3

3:13 who would put a veil over his face Refers to Ex 34:33–35. The veil covered the radiance of the glory, but it also concealed its fading quality. The transitory nature of the glory corresponds to the transitory nature of the old covenant.

3:14 their minds were made dull Represents God's judgment. He hardens the minds and hearts of those who suppress his truth and revelation (Ex 32:9; 33:3; 34:9; compare Ro 1:28). **to this day** Many Israelites rejected God's word in the law and the prophets (e.g., Isa 6:9–10; Jer 5:21–24; compare Ro 11:7–8,25). **old covenant is read** Jews typically heard the Law read every week in the local synagogue (see Lk 4:16–17; Ac 13:27; 15:21; 17:2–3).

3:15 Moses is read Refers to the law that God gave to Moses (Ex 24:12). **a veil** Moses covered his face with a veil because of the radiance of God's glory (Ex 34:33–34). This veil represents the Jews' hardened hearts and their inability to grasp the gospel message and refusal to obey God.

3:16 anyone turns to the Lord Refers to conversion and the reception of the Spirit. **veil is taken away** Signifies that nothing stands between believers and God.

3:17 the Lord is the Spirit Paul may be identifying Christ with the Spirit—particularly in terms of their roles—while also distinguishing between them. Jesus and the Spirit are elsewhere identified with each other (e.g., Ro 8:9; Php 1:19; 1Pe 1:10–11). It also is possible that 2Co 3:17 clarifies v. 16, where "the Lord" refers to God the Father. In this case, Paul's point is that the Lord of the OT narrative mentioned in v. 16 (Ex 34:34) is the Spirit of God (2Co 3:3,6,8). Either way, the Spirit's role in lifting the veil is central to Paul's message. **freedom** The ministry of the Spirit (v. 8) brings freedom from the power of sin and death—those things that the law could not free people from.

3:18 his image Refers to the image of Christ that believers bear (Col 3:10; compare Ge 1:26–27). **with ever-increasing glory** Paul suggests that believers will progress through ever-greater degrees of glory (*doxa* in Greek). Alternatively, this progress may begin with the indwelling presence of the Holy Spirit and culminate in the transformation of the physical body into a glorious one (1Co 15:50–54).

4:1–6 Paul continues the defense of his ministry (2Co 2:17—7:4). In the previous section, Paul focused on the glory of the new covenant—especially when compared to the old covenant (3:7–18). Here, he claims he has openly proclaimed God's truth (vv. 1–2) and explains that if his message is hidden, it is because Satan has blinded unbelievers (vv. 3–4). Paul affirms that he is not promoting himself but proclaiming Christ Jesus as Lord (v. 5).

4:1 this ministry Refers to the ministry of the Spirit and the ministry of righteousness referenced in 3:8–9. **we do not lose heart** Despite his hardships and opposition (11:23–29), Paul remains encouraged in his proclamation of the message of reconciliation (5:18).

4:3 veiled Paul acknowledges that some did not accept the gospel message—not because he obscured or hid anything from them (see 3:12–14), but because they were blinded by the work of evil forces and false teachers (see v. 4).

4:4 The god of this age Refers to Satan (compare Jn 12:31; 14:30; Eph 2:2). Satan further blinds those who refuse to obey the gospel. **image of God** Jesus is described as the image of God here and in Col 1:15. Compare Php 2:6 and note. Elsewhere, Paul teaches that believers are to conform to the image of Christ just as Christ bears the image of God (Ro 8:29).

4:6 Let light shine out of darkness Paul alludes to the creation account (see Ge 1:3 and note). Just as God created the world, he now makes believers a new creation (2Co 5:17). Paul's language also recalls Isaiah's prophecy in Isa 9:2. See the infographic "The Days of Creation" on p. 6.

4:7–18 Having extolled the glory of the new covenant, which he preached (2Co 3:7—4:6), Paul now explains his suffering (see 1:6 and note). While believers share in the knowledge of the glory of God (4:6) and are being transformed into the image of Christ (3:18), they do so in their frail, mortal bodies. Because of this, Paul suffers and faces hardship, but he perseveres (vv. 8–10). Moreover, believers can endure suffering because of the hope provided by the resurrection of Jesus (vv. 14–15).

4:7 this treasure Refers to the knowledge of God's

body the death of Jesus, so that the life of Jesus may also be revealed in our body. [11]For we who are alive are always being given over to death for Jesus' sake, so that his life may also be revealed in our mortal body. [12]So then, death is at work in us, but life is at work in you.

[13]It is written: "I believed; therefore I have spoken."[a] Since we have that same spirit of[b] faith, we also believe and therefore speak, [14]because we know that the one who raised the Lord Jesus from the dead will also raise us with Jesus and present us with you to himself. [15]All this is for your benefit, so that the grace that is reaching more and more people may cause thanksgiving to overflow to the glory of God.

[16]Therefore we do not lose heart. Though outwardly we are wasting away, yet inwardly we are being renewed day by day. [17]For our light and momentary troubles are achieving for us an eternal glory that far outweighs them all. [18]So we fix our eyes not on what is seen, but on what is unseen, since what is seen is temporary, but what is unseen is eternal.

Awaiting the New Body

5 For we know that if the earthly tent we live in is destroyed, we have a building from God, an eternal house in heaven, not built by human hands. [2]Meanwhile we groan, longing to be clothed instead with our heavenly dwelling, [3]because when we are clothed, we will not be found naked. [4]For while we are in this tent, we groan and are burdened, because we do not wish to be unclothed but to be clothed instead with our heavenly dwelling, so that what is mortal may be swallowed up by life. [5]Now the one who has fashioned us for this very purpose is God, who has given us the Spirit as a deposit, guaranteeing what is to come.

[6]Therefore we are always confident and know that as long as we are at home in the body we are away from the Lord. [7]For we live by faith, not by sight. [8]We are confident, I say, and would prefer to be away from the body and at home with the Lord. [9]So we make it our goal to please him, whether we are at home in the body or away from it. [10]For we must all appear before the judgment seat of Christ, so that each of us may receive what is due us for the things done while in the body, whether good or bad.

The Ministry of Reconciliation

[11]Since, then, we know what it is to fear the Lord, we try to persuade others. What we are is plain to God, and I hope it is also plain to your conscience. [12]We are not trying to commend ourselves

a 13 Psalm 116:10 (see Septuagint)   *b* 13 Or *Spirit-given*

---

glory (v. 6) and may include the proclamation of this knowledge to the world. **jars of clay** Represents human frailty (Ps 31:12; Isa 30:14).
4:10 death of Jesus Represents the life-threatening situations Paul experienced because of his ministry (Ac 9:16; 14:22; 21:10–14). Paul's sufferings not only display God's power (2Co 4:7), but also bear witness to the death of Jesus and his resurrected life. This phrase also may include the sufferings of Christ as part of the content of Paul's gospel message.
4:11 his life Refers to the resurrected life of Christ.
4:13 I believed; therefore I have spoken Paul quotes Ps 116:10. Just like the psalmist, his faith enables him to proclaim God's Word.
4:14 who raised the Lord Jesus from the dead will also raise us The resurrection of the dead is Paul's hope and motivation for enduring hardship.
4:16 being renewed day by day Believers should continue to grow in the knowledge of God and be transformed into Christ's image in preparation for his return (see note on Php 1:6); the Holy Spirit does this work in believers.
4:18 we fix our eyes on what is not seen Paul does not focus on his afflictions. Instead, he reflects on God's promises and the hope of resurrection in Christ (2Co 1:20; 4:14).

5:1–10 Having just discussed human frailty (4:7), Paul talks about believers' future hope of an eternal heavenly dwelling. He contrasts the earthly house—which groans and is burdened—with the heavenly dwelling with the Lord.

5:1 earthly tent we live in The body, which is susceptible to death and decay (compare 4:7). **an eternal house in heaven, not built by human hands** Either refers to the resurrected body believers receive when Christ returns (1Co 15:50–54), the corporate body of Christ, the new Jerusalem or the temple in the city (Rev 21:10,22).
5:4 but to be clothed Paul describes this transformation in 1Co 15:50–54. **life** Refers to eternal life.
5:5 the Spirit as a deposit God provides believers with the Holy Spirit as a guarantee that they will receive resurrected spiritual bodies when Christ returns (see 2Co 1:22; compare note on Eph 1:14).
5:6 in the body Refers to life in the physical human body, not the church as the body of Christ. **we are away** The Greek word used here, *ekdidōmi*, often translated as "absent" or "away," can also mean "exiled." Paul may be drawing on the background of Isa 40–55, where God promises to restore his exiled people (see note on 2Co 1:3).
5:7 by faith, not by sight Believers have not seen proof of resurrection and glorification with their own eyes. Paul encourages them to live by faith and to confidently expect God to do what he promised in Christ (compare 1Pe 1:18).
5:8 away from the body Likely alludes to an intermediate period between a believer's death and the final resurrection of all people (compare Rev 20:11–15). When believers die, they leave the physical body and enter the presence of Christ (compare Php 1:23; 1Th 4:13–18).
5:10 we must all appear God will judge all individuals—including believers—not only in terms of salvation, but also with respect to eternal rewards for deeds performed while on earth (Ro 2:6–10; 1Co 4:5; compare 2Co 11:15). **judgment seat** In Romans, Paul uses the judgment seat of God to show that believers should not judge others (see Ro 14:10). Here, Paul uses it to encourage the Corinthian believers to live lives that are acceptable or pleasing to God (2Co 5:9). See the infographic "A Judgment Seat in Jerusalem" on p. 1761.

to you again, but are giving you an opportunity to take pride in us, so that you can answer those who take pride in what is seen rather than in what is in the heart. ¹³If we are "out of our mind," as some say, it is for God; if we are in our right mind, it is for you. ¹⁴For Christ's love compels us, because we are convinced that one died for all, and therefore all died. ¹⁵And he died for all, that those who live should no longer live for themselves but for him who died for them and was raised again.

¹⁶So from now on we regard no one from a worldly point of view. Though we once regarded Christ in this way, we do so no longer. ¹⁷Therefore, if anyone is in Christ, the new creation has come:[a] The old has gone, the new is here! ¹⁸All this is from God, who reconciled us to himself through Christ and gave us the ministry of reconciliation: ¹⁹that God was reconciling the world to himself in Christ, not counting people's sins against them. And he has committed to us the message of reconciliation. ²⁰We are therefore Christ's ambassadors, as though God were making his appeal through

us. We implore you on Christ's behalf: Be reconciled to God. ²¹God made him who had no sin to be sin[b] for us, so that in him we might become the righteousness of God.

6 As God's co-workers we urge you not to receive God's grace in vain. ²For he says,

"In the time of my favor I heard you,
  and in the day of salvation I helped you."[c]

I tell you, now is the time of God's favor, now is the day of salvation.

Paul's Hardships

³We put no stumbling block in anyone's path, so that our ministry will not be discredited. ⁴Rather, as servants of God we commend ourselves in every way: in great endurance; in troubles, hardships and distresses; ⁵in beatings, imprisonments and riots; in hard work, sleepless nights and hunger;

[a] 17 Or *Christ, that person is a new creation.*   [b] 21 Or *be a sin offering*   [c] 2 Isaiah 49:8

5:11–21 Paul explains the purpose of his ministry: reconciliation. He first notes that he is not commending himself; instead, he is being controlled by the love of Christ (vv. 12–14). Paul emphasizes that Christ's death was for all people (vv. 15–17). Through Christ, God provided reconciliation for all people, making all those who are in Christ a new creation. Paul presents this as the purpose of his ministry as he urges the Corinthians to be reconciled to God (vv. 18–21).

5:12 We are not trying to commend ourselves See note on 3:1. **those who take pride in what is seen** Paul's opponents may have boasted in their rhetorical skill (see 11:6 and note) or status as Jews (11:22). He instead boasts in his weakness because that is where Christ's power is displayed more clearly (see 12:9–10).
5:13 out of our mind Some of the individuals in the Corinthian church may have regarded Paul as crazy or foolish. Alternatively, Paul could be alluding to the painful letter he sent to the Corinthians (see 2:4), which may have negatively shaped their view of him.
5:14 Christ's love The Greek text here could refer to the love that Christ has for people or the love they have for him. Jesus demonstrated God's sacrificial love by dying for all (Ro 5:8).
5:15 he died for all Probably means that Christ died for all people without distinction (e.g., gender, social status). However, not all receive the benefits of his atoning death; only those who believe the gospel and live for Christ do.
5:16 from a worldly point of view Indicates assessing someone according to the common person's values and standards. **we once regarded Christ in this way** Before choosing to follow Jesus, Paul and his other Jewish companions evaluated Jesus and his Messianic claim according to their own standards.
5:17 in Christ Refers to being in union with Christ through the Holy Spirit; those who believe in Christ participate in his death and resurrection. **new creation** Believers are transformed in Christ as part of God's renewal of all creation (Ro 8:19–20; compare Isa 65:17–25). As a new creation, believers grow into the likeness of Christ (2Co 3:18; 4:4; compare Col 3:10).
5:18 reconciled us Christ's death provided the means

of reconciliation. His suffering made peace between God and humanity possible (see Isa 53:5 and note; compare note on 2Co 1:3). **ministry of reconciliation** Paul presented Christ's sacrifice as the basis of reconciliation and the source of his apostolic vocation (vv. 14–18).
5:19 not counting people's sins against them Compare Ro 4:7–8.
5:21 who had no sin Paul affirms that Christ did not sin, though he was tempted (Mt 4:1–11; Mk 1:12–13; Lk 4:1–13; Heb 4:15). **to be sin** This describes how God regarded Christ as sin for the sake of undeserving sinners (compare Gal 3:13). More specifically, Paul may be presenting Christ as a substitute for sinful humanity or he could be referring to Christ's identification with sin through his union with sinful humanity. Another possibility is that Paul is interpreting Christ's sacrifice in light of OT sacrificial concepts (e.g., Lev 4:24; 5:12; Isa 53:10). **the righteousness of God** Here Paul refers to the idea of Christians becoming the righteousness of God. He may mean that believers, as a result of God's justification, receive a right standing before God while Christ takes on their sins (Ro 5:8). Alternatively, Paul could be describing God's righteous character, which believers receive and should live out in their lives.

6:1–13 Having discussed his ministry of reconciliation (2Co 5:11–21), Paul now encourages the Corinthians to be reconciled to him by opening their hearts (6:11–13). He defends himself by explaining how he and his companions responded to adversity. The apostle lists these afflictions as evidence of the sincerity of his ministry; only those who are genuine would endure such hardship.

6:1 grace The Greek word used here, *charis*, refers in this instance to the unmerited favor God demonstrated in the sacrificial death of Christ (5:14–19).
6:2 day of salvation I helped you Paul quotes Isa 49:8 to appeal to the Corinthians and emphasize God's readiness to receive them when they turn to him. Just as God restored Israel from exile, he now reconciles people to himself through Christ (see note on 2Co 1:3). The day of salvation refers to the present period of time (between Christ's first and second comings) in which reconciliation with God is available to all people.

[6]in purity, understanding, patience and kindness; in the Holy Spirit and in sincere love; [7]in truthful speech and in the power of God; with weapons of righteousness in the right hand and in the left; [8]through glory and dishonor, bad report and good report; genuine, yet regarded as impostors; [9]known, yet regarded as unknown; dying, and yet we live on; beaten, and yet not killed; [10]sorrowful, yet always rejoicing; poor, yet making many rich; having nothing, and yet possessing everything.

[11]We have spoken freely to you, Corinthians, and opened wide our hearts to you. [12]We are not withholding our affection from you, but you are withholding yours from us. [13]As a fair exchange—I speak as to my children—open wide your hearts also.

Warning Against Idolatry

[14]Do not be yoked together with unbelievers. For what do righteousness and wickedness have in common? Or what fellowship can light have with darkness? [15]What harmony is there between Christ and Belial[a]? Or what does a believer have in common with an unbeliever? [16]What agreement is there between the temple of God and idols? For we are the temple of the living God. As God has said:

> "I will live with them
> and walk among them,
> and I will be their God,
> and they will be my people."[b]

[17]Therefore,

> "Come out from them
> and be separate,
> says the Lord.
> Touch no unclean thing,
> and I will receive you."[c]

[18]And,

> "I will be a Father to you,
> and you will be my sons and daughters,
> says the Lord Almighty."[d]

---

[a] 15 Greek *Beliar*, a variant of *Belial*   [b] 16 Lev. 26:12; Jer. 32:38; Ezek. 37:27   [c] 17 Isaiah 52:11; Ezek. 20:34,41
[d] 18 2 Samuel 7:14; 7:8

6:4–7 In several letters, Paul details the hardships he faced in his ministry (e.g., Ro 8:35; 1Co 4:9–13; 2Co 4:8–9; 11:23–29). Hellenistic writers in Paul's day used such lists to promote their own virtue. Paul, by contrast, boasted of his struggles because they highlight God's power working through his weakness (4:7; 12:9–10). The virtues listed in vv. 6–7 recall similar lists in the NT (e.g., Gal 5:22–23; Php 4:8; 1Pe 3:8; 2Pe 1:5–7).

6:7 weapons of righteousness Refers to weapons that equip believers to live righteously and resist the work of evil forces. Compare Ro 6:13; 2Co 10:4; Eph 6:10–20; 1Th 5:8.

6:8–10 The contrasting description of Paul's ministry highlights its true nature against the outward appearance of his conduct (2Co 4:16–18). The negative descriptions in these verses probably reflect accusations of misconduct by Paul's opponents, who sought to discredit his apostleship.

6:11 opened wide our hearts Paul pleads with the Corinthians to return the affection that he and his missionary companions have demonstrated to them.

6:13 I speak as to my children Since Paul founded the church in Corinth, he regards the believers as his spiritual children (1Co 4:14; compare Gal 4:19). **open wide** Paul will repeat this appeal (2Co 7:2) as he closes his defense of his apostolic ministry (2:17–7:4).

6:14—7:1 After encouraging the Corinthians to be reconciled to God, Paul exhorts them to separate themselves from anything unclean in Corinth. This would include idolatry (v. 16) as well as false apostles who undermine Paul's authority (11:1–15). Paul cites several OT passages that speak of God's adoption of his people (vv. 16–18). The promises in these passages—fulfilled in God's work of reconciliation through Christ (5:17–19)—are the reason the Corinthian believers should separate from evil and be holy (7:1).

6:14 yoked together with unbelievers Paul is not addressing the issue of marriage between believers and unbelievers here (compare 1Co 7:12–16); rather, he is urging the Corinthians to avoid aligning themselves with those who view him (and others) according to false standards (2Co 5:16). In instructing the Corinthian community to not be unevenly yoked, Paul suggests that when believers begin abiding by the principles of unbelievers or false teachers, they have compromised the gospel message and the work of Christ through them (see 1Co 5:11–13). Thus, by extension, Paul's words could be applied to a marriage situation—suggesting that believes should not marry unbelievers—but that is not Paul's main point.

6:15 Belial The Greek term used here, *beliar*, comes from a similar Hebrew word, *beliyya'al*, that literally means "worthless." The OT used this term to describe people who were wicked or lawless (Dt 13:13; 1Sa 2:12; 1Ki 21:10; Pr 6:12). In later Jewish literature, it was used as a proper noun to refer to Satan (see Testament of Levi 19:1, which contrasts "light" with "darkness" and "the law of the Lord" with "the works of beliar").

6:16 the temple of God and idols Paul reminds the Corinthians that they are God's temple—individually and collectively (see note on 1Co 3:16; 6:19). Therefore, they must not engage in idolatry, whether inside or outside a pagan temple. **they will be my people** Paul quotes the covenant formula found several places in the OT (e.g., Ex 6:7; Lev 26:12; Jer 31:33; Eze 11:20). These passages emphasize that God keeps his covenant (Ex 6:8; Lev 26:9; Jer 31:31).

6:17 Come out from them Paul quotes Isa 52:11 to urge the believers in Corinth to separate themselves from the harmful influence of unbelievers. **I will receive you** Paul is most likely quoting Eze 20:34 (compare Eze 20:41; Zep 3:20), where God promises exiled Israel that he will gather and restore them to his covenant (Eze 20:37–38).

6:18 I will be a Father to you Paul combines 2Sa 7:14 with Isa 43:6 to apply God's promise of adoption to all his people (compare Ro 8:14–15; Gal 3:26).

7 Therefore, since we have these promises, dear friends, let us purify ourselves from everything that contaminates body and spirit, perfecting holiness out of reverence for God.

Paul's Joy Over the Church's Repentance

²Make room for us in your hearts. We have wronged no one, we have corrupted no one, we have exploited no one. ³I do not say this to condemn you; I have said before that you have such a place in our hearts that we would live or die with you. ⁴I have spoken to you with great frankness; I take great pride in you. I am greatly encouraged; in all our troubles my joy knows no bounds.

⁵For when we came into Macedonia, we had no rest, but we were harassed at every turn — conflicts on the outside, fears within. ⁶But God, who comforts the downcast, comforted us by the coming of Titus, ⁷and not only by his coming but also by the comfort you had given him. He told us about your longing for me, your deep sorrow, your ardent concern for me, so that my joy was greater than ever.

⁸Even if I caused you sorrow by my letter, I do not regret it. Though I did regret it — I see that my letter hurt you, but only for a little while — ⁹yet now I am happy, not because you were made sorry, but because your sorrow led you to repentance. For you became sorrowful as God intended and so

were not harmed in any way by us. ¹⁰Godly sorrow brings repentance that leads to salvation and leaves no regret, but worldly sorrow brings death. ¹¹See what this godly sorrow has produced in you: what earnestness, what eagerness to clear yourselves, what indignation, what alarm, what longing, what concern, what readiness to see justice done. At every point you have proved yourselves to be innocent in this matter. ¹²So even though I wrote to you, it was neither on account of the one who did the wrong nor on account of the injured party, but rather that before God you could see for yourselves how devoted to us you are. ¹³By all this we are encouraged.

In addition to our own encouragement, we were especially delighted to see how happy Titus was, because his spirit has been refreshed by all of you. ¹⁴I had boasted to him about you, and you have not embarrassed me. But just as everything we said to you was true, so our boasting about you to Titus has proved to be true as well. ¹⁵And his affection for you is all the greater when he remembers that you were all obedient, receiving him with fear and trembling. ¹⁶I am glad I can have complete confidence in you.

The Collection for the Lord's People

8 And now, brothers and sisters, we want you to know about the grace that God has given the Macedonian churches. ²In the midst of a

---

7:1 since we have these promises Refers to the OT quotations in 2Co 6:16–18.

7:2–4 Paul concludes the lengthy defense of his ministry (2:14—7:4) by repeating his desire for the Corinthians to open their hearts to him (v. 2; 6:13). He defends his behavior (v. 2) and motivation (v. 3), characterizing both as pure. Finally, he expresses his confidence in the Corinthians (v. 4).

7:4 I am greatly encouraged Paul exhibits confidence because of the report of Titus, his missionary companion who visited Corinth on his behalf (v. 7).

7:5–16 Paul returns to his travel details after a long defense and explanation of the nature of his apostleship under the new covenant (2:14—7:4). He picks up where he left off in 2:13 with his arrival in Macedonia (7:5). He then expresses the comfort and encouragement he felt when hearing about the Corinthians' repentance and obedience from Titus (vv. 6–15).

7:6 Titus See note on Titus 1:4.

7:7 your deep sorrow Titus confirmed that the Corinthians responded to Paul's previous letter with repentance (2Co 7:8).

7:8 my letter See 2:3 and note. It is uncertain what specific issues Paul addressed in his letter, but there may have been some hostility toward him and his apostleship. While his letter caused them grief, his intention was to prompt them to turn from their sin and return to God (v. 9).

7:10 that leads to salvation Paul contrasts godly grief with worldly grief: Godly grief leads to salvation, whereas worldly grief leads to death. This is because godly grief brings repentance or a desire to change. In v. 11, Paul

points to the ways godly grief benefited the Corinthian believers.

7:12 the one who did the wrong Probably refers to the person who opposed Paul and questioned his apostolic authority (see 2:5–8). **how devoted** Refers to the Corinthians' effort to be reconciled with Paul.

7:13 refreshed by all of you Since some Corinthians expressed hostility toward Paul, he may have felt concern about how believers would receive Titus, his representative; Paul was relieved to know that they provided adequate hospitality for his coworker.

7:14 I had boasted Paul complimented the Corinthian believers when speaking to Titus about them. They experienced a powerful demonstration of the Spirit when Paul ministered in Corinth (1Co 2:4).

7:16 I can have complete confidence Paul rejoices because his confidence in the Corinthian church has not been in vain (see 2Co 7:13 and note). Here, his rejoicing serves as a transition to the next section (8:1—9:15), where Paul asks the Corinthians to donate to the collection for the church in Jerusalem, confident that they will willingly help (9:1–2).

8:1–15 Paul introduces the topic of the collection for the church in Jerusalem (8:1—9:15). He uses the example of the Macedonian churches' generosity to encourage the Corinthians to also give generously (8:1–6). Paul emphasizes that he is not commanding the Corinthians to give; rather, he is giving them an opportunity to follow Jesus' example by showing grace to the poorer believers in Jerusalem (vv. 7–15).

8:1 the grace that God has given Refers to God's kindness and grace as expressed in the generosity of the Macedonian churches.

8:2 rich generosity The Macedonian churches

very severe trial, their overflowing joy and their extreme poverty welled up in rich generosity. [3]For I testify that they gave as much as they were able, and even beyond their ability. Entirely on their own, [4]they urgently pleaded with us for the privilege of sharing in this service to the Lord's people. [5]And they exceeded our expectations: They gave themselves first of all to the Lord, and then by the will of God also to us. [6]So we urged Titus, just as he had earlier made a beginning, to bring also to completion this act of grace on your part. [7]But since you excel in everything — in faith, in speech, in knowledge, in complete earnestness and in the love we have kindled in you[a] — see that you also excel in this grace of giving.

[8]I am not commanding you, but I want to test the sincerity of your love by comparing it with the earnestness of others. [9]For you know the grace of our Lord Jesus Christ, that though he was rich, yet for your sake he became poor, so that you through his poverty might become rich.

[10]And here is my judgment about what is best for you in this matter. Last year you were the first not only to give but also to have the desire to do so. [11]Now finish the work, so that your eager willingness to do it may be matched by your completion of it, according to your means. [12]For if the willingness is there, the gift is acceptable according to what one has, not according to what one does not have.

[13]Our desire is not that others might be relieved while you are hard pressed, but that there might be equality. [14]At the present time your plenty will supply what they need, so that in turn their plenty will supply what you need. The goal is equality, [15]as it is written: "The one who gathered much did not have too much, and the one who gathered little did not have too little."[b]

Titus Sent to Receive the Collection

[16]Thanks be to God, who put into the heart of Titus the same concern I have for you. [17]For Titus not only welcomed our appeal, but he is coming to you with much enthusiasm and on his own initiative. [18]And we are sending along with him the brother who is praised by all the churches for his service to the gospel. [19]What is more, he was chosen by the churches to accompany us as we carry the offering, which we administer in order to honor the Lord himself and to show our eagerness to help. [20]We want to avoid any

---

[a] 7 Some manuscripts and in your love for us
[b] 15 Exodus 16:18

---

experienced adversity through hardships, yet they displayed generosity for the sake of others.

8:4 Lord's people Refers to the poor Jewish believers in the church at Jerusalem. Paul is gathering financial relief from the various Gentile churches for the Jewish Christians as a gesture of solidarity. The financial collection and presentation by the Gentiles relate to the Jerusalem apostles' commissioning of Paul. They affirmed his calling as apostle to Gentiles, and they asked that he continue to remember the poor (Gal 2:9–10). This project fulfills both aspects of their commission.

8:5 by the will of God Paul uses this same phrase to defend his apostolic authority as coming from God (see 2Co 1:1 and note).

8:6 Titus Paul sent Titus, his missionary companion, to complete the collection of financial relief to benefit the church in Jerusalem (vv. 17–24; 9:3–5).

8:7 everything Refers to the spiritual gifts of the Corinthian believers (see 1Co 1:4 and note; 1:5 and note). **this grace** The Greek word used here, *charis*, refers to an expression of generosity, and specifically in this instance to the collection, and the church in Jerusalem. See note on 2Co 8:4.

8:8 earnestness of others The generosity of the Macedonian churches sets an example for the Corinthian believers (compare note on v. 2). Paul also used those churches as a standard to test the sincerity of the Corinthians' love for other believers.

8:9 grace of our Lord Jesus Christ Refers to Jesus' generosity expressed in his incarnation and death. Christ offered himself willingly and sacrificially — an example for all believers (Jn 10:18; 1Jn 3:16). **though he was rich** Refers to Jesus' preexistence as the Son of God. He enjoyed the presence of the Father and shared in his glory (Jn 17:5). **he became poor** Refers to the incarnation of

Jesus and his social standing while on earth (Lk 9:58). Paul probably has in mind Jesus' earthly poverty, as well as his suffering and death (e.g., Php 2:6–8). Paul uses Jesus' choice to become poor as the basis of his appeal for the Jerusalem collection. **might become rich** Refers to the gift of salvation and its blessings — namely, the inheritance of God's kingdom, the righteousness of God and glorification (1Co 15:50; 2Co 5:21).

8:10 Last year you were the first Paul had originally laid the groundwork for this collection in 1 Corinthians (1Co 16:1–4).

8:12 according to what one has Echoes Jesus' teaching on giving and generosity (see Mk 12:41–44).

8:14 their plenty Paul envisions a time when the Corinthian church may need financial assistance.

8:15 as it is written Paul quotes Ex 16:18, a verse showing how God sufficiently supplied the needs of the Israelites in the wilderness by providing bread and quail (Ex 16:1–36).

8:16–24 Paul includes a brief aside to give a letter of recommendation for Titus and two other unnamed men who will deliver his letter to the Corinthian church. He encourages the Corinthians to show these three men proof of their love and thereby validate Paul's boasts (2Co 8:24).

8:18 brother The identity of this brother in Christ is unknown. The fact that Paul does not mention his name probably indicates that the church already knew him.

8:19 offering Refers to the collection of financial relief for the saints in Jerusalem (v. 4).

8:20 avoid any criticism Paul planned to have several men accompany him to deliver the financial relief collection to Jerusalem (1Co 16:3–4). These men ensured that all the money arrived safely and allowed Paul to avoid any accusations that he mishandled the money.

criticism of the way we administer this liberal gift. ²¹For we are taking pains to do what is right, not only in the eyes of the Lord but also in the eyes of man.

²²In addition, we are sending with them our brother who has often proved to us in many ways that he is zealous, and now even more so because of his great confidence in you. ²³As for Titus, he is my partner and co-worker among you; as for our brothers, they are representatives of the churches and an honor to Christ. ²⁴Therefore show these men the proof of your love and the reason for our pride in you, so that the churches can see it.

9 There is no need for me to write to you about this service to the Lord's people. ²For I know your eagerness to help, and I have been boasting about it to the Macedonians, telling them that since last year you in Achaia were ready to give; and your enthusiasm has stirred most of them to action. ³But I am sending the brothers in order that our boasting about you in this matter should not prove hollow, but that you may be ready, as I said you would be. ⁴For if any Macedonians come with me and find you unprepared, we — not to say anything about you — would be ashamed of having been so confident. ⁵So I thought it necessary to urge the brothers to visit you in advance and finish the arrangements for the generous gift you had promised. Then it will be ready as a generous gift, not as one grudgingly given.

Generosity Encouraged

⁶Remember this: Whoever sows sparingly will also reap sparingly, and whoever sows generously will also reap generously. ⁷Each of you should give what you have decided in your heart to give, not reluctantly or under compulsion, for God loves a cheerful giver. ⁸And God is able to bless you abundantly, so that in all things at all times, having all that you need, you will abound in every good work. ⁹As it is written:

"They have freely scattered their gifts
    to the poor;
        their righteousness endures forever."[a]

¹⁰Now he who supplies seed to the sower and bread for food will also supply and increase your store of seed and will enlarge the harvest of your righteousness. ¹¹You will be enriched in every way so that you can be generous on every occasion, and through us your generosity will result in thanksgiving to God.

¹²This service that you perform is not only supplying the needs of the Lord's people but is also overflowing in many expressions of thanks to God. ¹³Because of the service by which you have proved yourselves, others will praise God for the obedience that accompanies your confession of the gospel of Christ, and for your generosity in sharing with them and with everyone else. ¹⁴And

[a] 9 Psalm 112:9

8:21 but also in the eyes of man Paul echoes Pr 3:4 to explain the motivation for having a team accompany him and the collection to Jerusalem; he wants handling of this gift to be above criticism.

8:23 representatives The Greek word used here, *apostoloi*, often translated as "messengers," literally means "apostles" (see note on 1Co 12:28). Paul concludes by endorsing all three men as representatives of the churches who are working for the glory of Christ (2Co 4:4–6).

8:24 proof of your love In the first century, hospitality was the practical demonstration of love for visitors (Jn 13:20; Heb 13:2). Paul encourages the Corinthian believers to receive these three men with love and validate his boasting about them (see 2Co 7:16 and note).

9:1–15 Having endorsed Titus and two other men (8:16–24), Paul returns to the subject of the collection for the church in Jerusalem. Paul explains that he is sending Titus and the others so that the Corinthians' contribution can be ready when he visits. He points out that he has boasted about their willingness to help, and that he, along with the Corinthians themselves, would be embarrassed if he arrived with the Macedonians and found them unprepared (vv. 1–5). Paul encourages the Corinthians to give generously by arguing that God loves a cheerful giver (vv. 6–11). Their generosity would not only supply the needs of those in Jerusalem, it would also serve as an expression of thanksgiving to God and unite Jewish and Gentile believers (vv. 12–15).

9:1 service to the Lord's people See note on 8:4.
9:2 since last year you in Achaia were ready Paul advised the Corinthians to set aside money for this collection last year (1Co 16:1–3).

9:3 sending the brothers A team of believers would have collected the offering the Corinthian believers set aside for this project (1Co 16:1–3; 2Co 8:16–24).

9:4 would be ashamed Paul risked his reputation by commending the Corinthians' eagerness and generosity to the Macedonians. He presents their example as motivation to have their gift ready when Titus and the others arrive.

9:5 generous gift Paul wants to ensure that they give their generous gift with the right attitude and motivation; he sends some believers to help organize the gift to remove any sense of compulsion.

9:7 cheerful giver Paul echoes Pr 22:9 and other OT passages to emphasize God's delight in those who give with the right attitude (compare Ex 25:2; 35:5; Dt 15:10). Proverbs encourages generous giving several times (Pr 11:24; 22:9; 28:27) and equates generosity to the poor with generosity to God (Pr 19:17). It does this because the impoverished—like the rich—are likewise created by God (Pr 22:2).

9:8 God is able to bless you abundantly Paul affirms that God can provide everything they need, just as he is doing for the church in Jerusalem.

9:9 their righteousness endures forever Paul quotes Ps 112:9 to suggest that giving alms and being generous are expressions of God's righteousness.

9:10 supplies seed Paul alludes to Isa 55:10—a song of joy celebrating Israel's promised restoration (see note on 2Co 1:3)—as further support that God provides for his creation.

9:12 This service that you perform Paul points out that the Corinthians' generosity would not only benefit

in their prayers for you their hearts will go out to you, because of the surpassing grace God has given you. [15] Thanks be to God for his indescribable gift!

Paul's Defense of His Ministry

10 By the humility and gentleness of Christ, I appeal to you — I, Paul, who am "timid" when face to face with you, but "bold" toward you when away! [2] I beg you that when I come I may not have to be as bold as I expect to be toward some people who think that we live by the standards of this world. [3] For though we live in the world, we do not wage war as the world does. [4] The weapons we fight with are not the weapons of the world. On the contrary, they have divine power to demolish strongholds. [5] We demolish arguments and every pretension that sets itself up against the knowledge of God, and we take captive every thought to make it obedient to Christ. [6] And we will be ready to punish every act of disobedience, once your obedience is complete.

[7] You are judging by appearances.[a] If anyone is confident that they belong to Christ, they should consider again that we belong to Christ just as much as they do. [8] So even if I boast somewhat freely about the authority the Lord gave us for building you up rather than tearing you down, I will not be ashamed of it. [9] I do not want to seem to be trying to frighten you with my letters. [10] For some say, "His letters are weighty and forceful, but in person he is unimpressive and his speaking amounts to nothing." [11] Such people should realize that what we are in our letters when we are absent, we will be in our actions when we are present.

[12] We do not dare to classify or compare ourselves with some who commend themselves. When they measure themselves by themselves and compare themselves with themselves, they are not wise. [13] We, however, will not boast beyond proper limits, but will confine our boasting to the sphere of service God himself has assigned to us, a sphere that also includes you. [14] We are not going too far in our boasting, as would be the case if we had not come to you, for we did get as far as you with the gospel of Christ. [15] Neither do we go beyond our limits by boasting of work done by others. Our hope is that,

[a] 7 Or *Look at the obvious facts*

---

the church in Jerusalem, it would also be a gift of thanksgiving to God (see note on v. 7).

9:15 his indescribable gift Refers to Christ, who brought about salvation through his life, death and resurrection. It may also refer to his generosity: He became poor so that those who believe in him might become rich (8:9). Paul appropriately closes his appeal for the Corinthian church to give generously by thanking God for his generous gift.

10:1–18 Paul changes topics here to address his opponents in Corinth (chs. 10–13), offering an impassioned defense of his apostleship. The abrupt change in tone may suggest that chs. 10–13 were another letter entirely. It is possible that these chapters are the painful letter Paul refers to in 2:1–4.

10:1 gentleness of Christ While Paul seeks to defend himself, he does not want to do so in an angry or indignant manner; rather, he seeks to emulate the humility and gentleness shown by Christ (8:9; Mt 11:29; Lk 18:14; see Gal 6:1 and note). **"bold" toward you when away** Paul is probably referring to how some of the Corinthians perceived him (compare 2Co 10:10).

10:2 that we live by the standards of this world Some in the church community called Paul's character into question (compare 2:17).

10:3 we do not wage war as the world Paul uses spiritual weapons — such as the gospel, faith, truth and prayer — to wage battle against his opposition (compare 6:6–7; Eph 6:10–17).

10:4 strongholds This term is intended to refer to people's standard ways of thinking, especially about Paul and the nature of his apostleship.

10:5 we take captive every thought to make it obedient to Christ Implies believers must submit their thoughts to Christ and bring them into conformity with his will.

10:6 every act of disobedience Refers to opposition to Paul's apostolic authority. Compare 2Co 2:9.

10:7 by appearances Some Corinthians continued to judge Paul and his ministry according to the standards of the time; they evaluated him according to his rhetoric, logic and manner of reception by various communities.

10:8 authority the Lord gave See 1:1 and note. **building you up** Some Corinthians may have perceived that Paul used his authority to oppress or take advantage of them (12:17).

10:9 I do not want to seem Paul's wording here suggests that his opponents were accusing him of trying to frighten or intimidate the Corinthian believers with his letters. While Paul wrote things that grieved the Corinthians, he did not do so cruelly. Instead, he wrote out of love to encourage them toward repentance (see 2:4; compare 7:8–9).

10:10 his speaking amounts to nothing Paul may not have used any rhetorical techniques when he presented the gospel to the Corinthians; God's power, not Paul's speech, gave the message credibility.

10:12 to classify or compare ourselves with The opponents in Corinth compared their skill and gifts to Paul's as a means to devalue his authority within the church community. Paul asserts that such comparisons merely derive from people's perspectives and are useless; his apostolic authority comes from God (Ac 9:15; 2Co 10:18).

10:13 God himself has assigned Paul considered the Corinthian church to be his God-given ministry assignment ever since he first founded the community (v. 14). He did not get involved in churches that other missionaries had planted (e.g., Ro 15:18–20); thus, he expected his fellow workers in the gospel to respect his missionary field (see 2Co 10:16). This leads Paul to cast his opponents as false apostles, since they attempted to supplant his apostolic role in Corinth (see 11:13).

10:14 as far as you with the gospel Paul ministered in Corinth and established the church there during his second missionary journey (see Ac 18:1–16).

as your faith continues to grow, our sphere of activity among you will greatly expand, [16]so that we can preach the gospel in the regions beyond you. For we do not want to boast about work already done in someone else's territory. [17]But, "Let the one who boasts boast in the Lord."[a] [18]For it is not the one who commends himself who is approved, but the one whom the Lord commends.

Paul and the False Apostles

11 I hope you will put up with me in a little foolishness. Yes, please put up with me! [2]I am jealous for you with a godly jealousy. I promised you to one husband, to Christ, so that I might present you as a pure virgin to him. [3]But I am afraid that just as Eve was deceived by the serpent's cunning, your minds may somehow be led astray from your sincere and pure devotion to Christ. [4]For if someone comes to you and preaches a Jesus other than the Jesus we preached, or if you receive a different spirit from the Spirit you received, or a different gospel from the one you accepted, you put up with it easily enough.

[5]I do not think I am in the least inferior to those "super-apostles."[b] [6]I may indeed be untrained as a speaker, but I do have knowledge. We have made this perfectly clear to you in every way. [7]Was it a sin for me to lower myself in order to elevate you by preaching the gospel of God to you free of charge? [8]I robbed other churches by receiving support from them so as to serve you. [9]And when I was with you and needed something, I was not a burden to anyone, for the brothers who came from Macedonia supplied what I needed. I have kept myself from being a burden to you in any way, and will continue to do so. [10]As surely as the truth of Christ is in me, nobody in the regions of Achaia will stop this boasting of mine. [11]Why? Because I do not love you? God knows I do!

---

[a] 17 Jer. 9:24   [b] 5 Or to the most eminent apostles

10:16 someone else's territory Refers to those who opposed Paul; these people likely boasted about the church community in Corinth as though they planted it and cared for it.

10:17 Let the one who boasts boast in the Lord A quotation of Jer 9:24 (compare 1Co 1:31).

11:1–15 In this section, Paul defends himself against his opponents, whom he sarcastically calls super-apostles (see 2Co 11:5 and note). Paul defends his ministry by pointing out that he did not accept payment while in Corinth (vv. 7–9); his motive for ministry is the expansion of Christ's kingdom, not payment or respect (see 12:14).

11:1 a little foolishness Paul is being sarcastic: the super-apostles (v. 5) considered Paul's message and methods to be absurd. See note on 1Co 1:18.

11:2 with a godly jealousy Not resentment or envy, but intense devotion—like the devotion God had for his own people (Ex 20:5). Paul planted the church in Corinth, but they rebelled against him; Paul considers it his responsibility to bring them back to genuine faith through his godly jealousy (*zeloō* in Greek). **I promised you** According to Jewish tradition, fathers were to present their daughters as virgins. Paul feels that the church at Corinth has been defiled by following false teachers and presents this analogy to make his point. Although Paul's argument here focuses on the idea of betrothal, he often uses marriage as a metaphor to describe the relationship between Christ and the church (see Eph 5:27 and note; compare Col 1:22 and note; Rev 19:6–9).

11:3 was deceived by the serpent's cunning Refers to the events of Ge 3:1–13. Eve believed the lie of the serpent, which convinced her to eat from the tree that God had forbidden.

11:4 a Jesus other than the Jesus we preached Paul's opponents may have downplayed the importance of Jesus' crucifixion, since Greeks considered crucifixion to be a sign of weakness (see 1Co 1:18 and note). By contrast, Paul presented the crucifixion of Christ as the heart of his gospel (1Co 2:2; 2Co 13:4; Gal 3:1). **different spirit** The so-called super-apostles either proclaimed that Christ wasn't crucified or that his crucifixion degraded him as Savior (compare note on 2Co 11:5; note on 11:1). In doing so, they preached the opposite message of Paul, who only wanted to proclaim Christ crucified (13:4; 1Co 1:18). Paul was interested in their relationship with Jesus (compare 2Co 11:2), but his opponents were interested in their own gain (compare 1Co 4:6–13; 2Co 12:11–13). In this regard, the spirit of their teaching was one of arrogance. Paul's description here also has a spiritual component, emphasizing not only the arrogance of the false teachers but also the evil spiritual powers behind their false teaching (compare 1Ti 4:1). **different gospel** Paul is likely referring to his opponents' culturally motivated attempts to undermine the importance of Jesus' sacrificial death as the pivotal component of the gospel (see note on 1Co 2:2). These false teachers may have been attempting to elevate themselves as leaders in their community by removing the difficult parts of the gospel.

11:5 super-apostles A sarcastic reference to Paul's opponents in Corinth, who were trying to turn the church community against him. These people may have also boasted about the Corinthian church as if they had planted it (2Co 10:12–15; compare 1Co 4:6–13).

11:6 untrained as a speaker Paul's speaking abilities did not meet the standards of some in Corinth. Many people in the region were trained in professional rhetoric, which was highly valued in Greek culture. This does not suggest that Paul was an unskilled minister, only that the Corinthians thought he lacked proper training in Greek rhetoric. The false teachers in Corinth may have had training, and even knowledge, but Paul possesses the empowerment of the Spirit. See note on 1Co 1:5; compare note on 2:2.

11:8 I robbed Paul uses hyperbole to emphasize that the super-apostles' view of him is absurd (compare note on 2Co 11:5). He actually raised support from the impoverished Macedonian churches so he could minister in Corinth (see 8:2; Php 4:15), and he now requests that Corinth provide for churches with less wealth than them (see 2Co 8:4 and note).

11:9 I was not a burden to anyone While in Corinth, Paul provided for his own needs through manual labor and support from other churches (compare note on v. 7). **Macedonia** See note on 1:16.

11:10 regions of Achaia See note on 1:1.

11:11 Because I do not love you The so-called super-apostles may have suggested that Paul did not have genuine affection for the Corinthians since he did not

¹²And I will keep on doing what I am doing in order to cut the ground from under those who want an opportunity to be considered equal with us in the things they boast about. ¹³For such people are false apostles, deceitful workers, masquerading as apostles of Christ. ¹⁴And no wonder, for Satan himself masquerades as an angel of light. ¹⁵It is not surprising, then, if his servants also masquerade as servants of righteousness. Their end will be what their actions deserve.

---

allow them to share in his ministry financially (compare note on v. 5). Paul dismisses any charge that he lacks affection for the church in Corinth.
11:13 false apostles Refers to those who exploited the Corinthian church for self-gain (compare note on 10:13).

This group is likely synonymous with, or at least similar to, those Paul sarcastically refers to as super-apostles (see note on v. 5).
11:14 Satan See note on 1Co 5:5; note on Mk 1:13; compare note on 1Th 2:18. **angel of light** May refer to

Political Leaders in the New Testament

GROUP	NAME	PERIOD OF OFFICE	SCRIPTURAL REFERENCES
The Herods	Herod the Great	37 – 4 BC	Mt 2:1 – 22; Lk 1:5
	Archelaus	4 BC – AD 6	Mt 2:22
	Antipas	4 BC – AD 39	Mt 14:1 – 11; Mk 6:14 – 28; 8:15; Lk 3:1,19 – 20; 8:3; 9:7 – 9; 13:31 – 33; 23:5 – 16; Ac 4:27; 13:1
	Philip	4 BC – AD 33/4	Mt 14:3; Mk 6:17 – 18; Lk 3:1
	Agrippa I	AD 37 – 44	Ac 12:1 – 23
	Agrippa II	AD 53 – 93	Ac 25:13 – 26:32
High Priests	Annas	AD 6 – 15	Lk 3:2; Jn 18:13, 24; Ac 4:6
	Caiaphas	AD 18 – 36	Mt 26:3, 57; Lk 3:2; Jn 11:49; 18:13, 14, 24, 28; Ac 4:6
	Ananias	AD 47 – 58	Ac 23:2; 24:1
Kings of the Nabateans	Aretas IV	9 BC – AD 40	2Co 11:32
Roman Emperors	Augustus	27 BC – AD 14	Lk 2:1
	Tiberius	AD 14 – 37	Lk 3:1
	Claudius	AD 41 – 54	Ac 11:28; 18:2
	Nero	AD 54 – 68	Ac 25:10; 28:19 (called "Caesar")
Roman Proconsuls of Achaia	Gallio	AD 51 – 52	Ac 18:12 – 17
Roman Procurators of the Province of Judaea	Pontius Pilate	AD 26 – 36	Mt 27:11 – 31; Lk 3:1; 23:1; Mk 15:1 – 5; Jn 18:28 – 19:16
	M. Antonius Felix	AD 52 – 60	Ac 23:24 – 26; 24:1 – 27
	Porcius Festus	AD 60 – 62	Ac 24:27

Paul Boasts About His Sufferings

[16]I repeat: Let no one take me for a fool. But if you do, then tolerate me just as you would a fool, so that I may do a little boasting. [17]In this self-confident boasting I am not talking as the Lord would, but as a fool. [18]Since many are boasting in the way the world does, I too will boast. [19]You gladly put up with fools since you are so wise! [20]In fact, you even put up with anyone who enslaves you or exploits you or takes advantage of you or puts on airs or slaps you in the face. [21]To my shame I admit that we were too weak for that!

Whatever anyone else dares to boast about—I am speaking as a fool—I also dare to boast about. [22]Are they Hebrews? So am I. Are they Israelites? So am I. Are they Abraham's descendants? So am I. [23]Are they servants of Christ? (I am out of my mind to talk like this.) I am more. I have worked much harder, been in prison more frequently, been flogged more severely, and been exposed to death again and again. [24]Five times I received from the Jews the forty lashes minus one. [25]Three times I was beaten with rods, once I was pelted with stones, three times I was shipwrecked, I spent a night and a day in the open sea, [26]I have been constantly on the move. I have been in danger from rivers, in danger from bandits, in danger from my fellow Jews, in danger from Gentiles; in danger in the city, in danger in the country, in danger at sea; and in danger from false believers. [27]I have labored and toiled and have often gone without sleep; I have known hunger and thirst and have often gone without food; I have been cold and naked. [28]Besides everything else, I face daily the pressure of my concern for all the churches. [29]Who is weak, and I do not feel weak? Who is led into sin, and I do not inwardly burn?

[30]If I must boast, I will boast of the things that show my weakness. [31]The God and Father of the Lord Jesus, who is to be praised forever, knows that I am not lying. [32]In Damascus the governor under King Aretas had the city of the Damascenes guarded in order to arrest me. [33]But I was lowered in a basket from a window in the wall and slipped through his hands.

the kind of angel who ministers to believers (Heb 1:14) or simply to a good spiritual being aligned with God's purposes (compare note on Jn 1:4). This comparison suggests that the false apostles came across as genuine while inwardly desiring to destroy the church for their own benefit (see 2Co 10:8; 12:19; 13:10; compare note on 11:13; note on 11:5). The idea of Satan disguising himself as an angel of light recalls similar descriptions of Satan's activity in various ancient Jewish writings, though Paul does not seem directly dependent on them (e.g., Life of Adam and Eve 9:1; Apocalypse of Moses 17:1; Testament of Job 6:4; 17:2; 23:1).

11:15 his servants Suggests these servants, who may be the false apostles, actually serve Satan and stand as a threat to the church (compare v. 13).

11:16–21 The false apostles probably claimed that Paul's hardships invalidated his apostleship and made him look foolish (compare v. 13). Paul turns their accusations against them: He assumes the role of a fool to make them look foolish. His discussion of his hardships exposes the false apostles as people who are self-centered; they could never demonstrate Paul and his companions' endurance for the sake of bringing people to Christ and leading a church in Jesus' way and teachings.

11:17 a fool Paul may be juxtaposing the common Greek idea of the foolish person versus the wise person (a dichotomy that also appears in Proverbs; e.g., Pr 1:7). People who consider themselves wise may actually end up looking foolish if their view is based on false assumptions or self-glorification.

11:18 in the way the world does Unlike the false teachers, Paul is interested in Christ's work and his measurement of success. Even so, Paul can prove himself by their own standards (see 2Co 11:22–33 and note). Christ's measurement of success focuses on whether someone follows God's will in life, using the gifts given to them to do so.

11:19 since you are so wise Paul sarcastically points out how foolish the Corinthians were to believe the false apostles (v. 13; compare v. 5). This is made more ironic

by the fact that the Corinthians considered themselves to be wise (compare note on 1Co 1:20).

11:20 exploits The so-called super-apostles are merely using the Corinthian believers for their own benefit (compare note on 2Co 11:5). **slaps you in the face** Paul uses this metaphor to express his disbelief that the Corinthian believers cannot recognize the falsity of the super-apostles' teaching and work (see note on v. 4; compare note on v. 5).

11:22–33 In this section, Paul outlines his most important achievements according to people's standards: his ethnicity (v. 22), vocation (v. 23) and hardships (vv. 23–29). Paul does not actually place a high value on such things; he uses them to attest that even by the standards of the so-called super-apostles, he is greater, and yet he suffers for the sake of Christ and his church (12:11; compare note on 11:5). Compare Php 3:4–7.

11:24 forty lashes minus one Thirty-nine lashes were believed to be the maximum number a person could endure before dying from such a beating. Receiving this number of lashings served as a public warning that suggested that, "if you do this again, you will die for it next time" (compare note on Mt 27:26). The Jews flogged people because they weren't permitted by Roman law to execute individuals without the permission of a Roman prefect (see Jn 18:31).

11:25 Three times I was beaten with rods May reference and include Ac 16:22.

11:28 my concern for all the churches False doctrine and division threatened the churches that Paul planted (Ac 20:30). He also wrote letters to several of these churches to combat the negative influence of other teachers (Gal 1:6–8; Eph 4:14; Php 3:1–2; 1Ti 1:6–7). The pressure Paul faced as a minister to these churches caused him to worry constantly about their well-being.

11:30 my weakness Refers to the hardships Paul suffered for the sake of believers (2Co 11:23–29). Paul boasts about his hardships because they evidence his devotion to Christ and his work for the church.

11:32 Damascus See note on Ac 9:2. **King Aretas**

Paul's Vision and His Thorn

12 I must go on boasting. Although there is nothing to be gained, I will go on to visions and revelations from the Lord. ²I know a man in Christ who fourteen years ago was caught up to the third heaven. Whether it was in the body or out of the body I do not know — God knows. ³And I know that this man — whether in the body or apart from the body I do not know, but God knows — ⁴was caught up to paradise and heard inexpressible things, things that no one is permitted to tell.

⁵I will boast about a man like that, but I will not boast about myself, except about my weaknesses. ⁶Even if I should choose to boast, I would not be a fool, because I would be speaking the truth. But I refrain, so no one will think more of me than is warranted by what I do or say, ⁷or because of these surpassingly great revelations. Therefore, in order to keep me from becoming conceited, I was given a thorn in my flesh, a messenger of Satan, to torment me. ⁸Three times I pleaded with the Lord to take it away from me. ⁹But he said to me, "My grace is sufficient for you, for my power is

---

Specifically King Aretas IV, one of the Nabatean kings (9 BC – AD 40). Even though he had the title of king, Aretas was actually a governor. See the table "Political Leaders in the New Testament" on p. 1916. **in order to arrest me** See Ac 9:23–24.

12:1–10 In this section Paul talks about visions and revelations. He tells about a man who was taken up to paradise (2Co 12:2–4). Paul is probably referring to himself in the third person here (v. 6). He then discusses his thorn in the flesh (see v. 7 and note). He asked God to remove it, but God did not so that Christ's power would be made evident in Paul's weakness (vv. 8–10).

12:1 visions Via a vision (*optasia* in Greek), prophets could see God's plan for the future. These visions also revealed what was happening (or would happen) in the spiritual world. Here, Paul is uncertain whether he had a bodily or only a spiritual experience (v. 3). **revelations** The Greek word used here, *apokalypsis*, refers to God's unveiling information that was often previously unknown or concealed. In this instance, *apokalypsis* refers to God supplying Paul with information about his particular calling. At other times, it is used more broadly (see note on 1Co 14:6; compare note on Gal 2:2).

12:2 I know a man It appears that Paul is using the third-person voice to describe his own experience (2Co 12:6–10). He may have done this to avoid boasting; this may have also been typical of prophetic literature. **in Christ** To be in union with Christ, to have a relationship with him. In this scenario, Paul indicates that the man, who is likely him, was in Christ's presence while having his vision. See the timeline "Life of Paul" on p. 1796. **third heaven** Refers to the highest heaven (1Ki 8:27; 2Ch 2:6; Ps 148:4). Paul's reference is probably intentionally vague, and it may simply serve to contrast the place where God and heavenly beings dwell against the place where people dwell (earth). If Paul does have a precise place in mind, then he probably is thinking of the third heaven as the highest heaven and the place of God's presence. The idea that God's dwelling was above the firmament or sky (Ge 1:2) and had various levels was common in ancient Judaism and Greco-Roman thought. Ancient Jewish literature contains numerous accounts describing heavenly journeys such as this (compare Ge 5:21–24; 2Ki 2:11–12). See the infographic "Ancient Hebrew Conception of the Universe" on p. 5.

12:3 in the body or apart from the body Paul expresses uncertainty about whether the man was in his physical body during this experience. The man, who is likely Paul, may have been literally taken into heaven and then returned to earth, or he may have simply undergone a spiritual or mental experience.

12:4 caught This is typical prophetic language for the

work of the Holy Spirit temporarily taking over someone's life to give him or her a vision or revelation. The prophet Ezekiel used similar language (Eze 2:2; 3:14; 8:3). **paradise** Probably refers to the highest heaven (see notes on 2Co 12:2).

12:5 a man like that If Paul is referring to himself, he makes the switch back to the first person here; in doing so, he emphasizes that his authority came from God, not from his own decisions or persuasiveness. Paul can boast on behalf of what God did for him in Christ, not in who he is. **my weaknesses** Refers to Paul's hardships in ministry (2Co 11:23–29) and his forthcoming reference in v. 7. Ultimately, Paul has authority because God chose him, not because of his abilities. The Corinthian super-apostles were emphasizing their abilities; for Paul, this does not represent a rightful claim to authority (see note on 11:5).

12:6 say If the events described in vv. 1–5 happened to Paul, then here he reveals his motivation for not speaking about this experience directly in the first person: He does not want others to view him as special or elite.

12:7 because of these surpassingly great revelations Probably refers to the exceptional number or quality of revelations that caused Paul to become prideful. **was given** The use of the passive verb indicates that Paul considered God to be responsible for the thorn because it was ultimately used for good. **a thorn** May refer to Paul's inner emotional turmoil about the churches (2:4), an ongoing sin, his opponents (like the so called super-apostles; 11:1–5), a physical ailment (such as poor eyesight), his speaking ability (10:10), or demonic opposition (both in general or specific to him, as in 1Th 2:18). All of these options seem possible considering circumstances in Paul's life. **a messenger** Since the Greek word used here is *angelos*, which may be translated as "angel," this may be a reference to an evil being. It also is possible that *angelos* references a human opponent who caused him great pain (compare 2Co 2:5). **of Satan** While it is unclear whether Paul associated the thorn with a human messenger or a spiritual being, he explicitly identifies it with the figure of Satan. Satan's involvement suggests that Paul may have considered the figure to function as an unwitting agent of God's discipline. Satan intends to harm Paul, but God ultimately prevails in Paul's life by displaying his power when Paul submits to the sufficiency of God's grace.

12:8 Three times Paul emphasizes that he has pled his case before God and that God has chosen to allow this experience to continue.

12:9 grace In this context, the Greek word used here, *charis*, refers to Christ's power to help Paul endure hardship, be strengthened when struggling (physically, mentally or spiritually) or experience forgiveness. God's

made perfect in weakness." Therefore I will boast all the more gladly about my weaknesses, so that Christ's power may rest on me. [10]That is why, for Christ's sake, I delight in weaknesses, in insults, in hardships, in persecutions, in difficulties. For when I am weak, then I am strong.

Paul's Concern for the Corinthians

[11]I have made a fool of myself, but you drove me to it. I ought to have been commended by you, for I am not in the least inferior to the "super-apostles,"[a] even though I am nothing. [12]I persevered in demonstrating among you the marks of a true apostle, including signs, wonders and miracles. [13]How were you inferior to the other churches, except that I was never a burden to you? Forgive me this wrong!

[14]Now I am ready to visit you for the third time, and I will not be a burden to you, because what I want is not your possessions but you. After all, children should not have to save up for their parents, but parents for their children. [15]So I will very gladly spend for you everything I have and expend myself as well. If I love you more, will you love me less? [16]Be that as it may, I have not been a burden to you. Yet, crafty fellow that I am, I caught you by trickery! [17]Did

I exploit you through any of the men I sent to you? [18]I urged Titus to go to you and I sent our brother with him. Titus did not exploit you, did he? Did we not walk in the same footsteps by the same Spirit?

[19]Have you been thinking all along that we have been defending ourselves to you? We have been speaking in the sight of God as those in Christ; and everything we do, dear friends, is for your strengthening. [20]For I am afraid that when I come I may not find you as I want you to be, and you may not find me as you want me to be. I fear that there may be discord, jealousy, fits of rage, selfish ambition, slander, gossip, arrogance and disorder. [21]I am afraid that when I come again my God will humble me before you, and I will be grieved over many who have sinned earlier and have not repented of the impurity, sexual sin and debauchery in which they have indulged.

Final Warnings

13 This will be my third visit to you. "Every matter must be established by the testimony of two or three witnesses."[b] [2]I already gave

---

[a] 11 Or *the most eminent apostles*   [b] 1 Deut. 19:15

---

grace enables Paul to participate in Christ's sufferings for the gospel and the church and to still demonstrate God's power despite his weaknesses. Paul acknowledges this to set up a contrast between his ministry and that of the so-called super-apostles. Paul does his work because God chose to empower him. The super-apostles emphasize self-sufficiency (see note on 11:5). **power is made perfect in weakness** Weakness provides the opportunity for God to show his power. For this reason, Paul can boast about his weaknesses even though others may mock him (see 10:10).
12:10 when I am weak, then I am strong Paul restates the paradoxical nature of his life and ministry. When he is helpless and vulnerable, Christ empowers him to endure and fulfill his vocation.

12:11–21 Paul concludes his defense against the so-called super-apostles. He asserts that he has performed the signs of an apostle and reiterates that he was not a burden to the Corinthian church (vv. 12–13). He continues to emphasize that he will not receive payment from them as he prepares to visit them a third time (vv. 14–16). He claims that neither he nor his companions took advantage of them but preached Christ in order to build up the believers at Corinth (vv. 17–19).

12:11 to the "super-apostles" See note on 11:5.
12:12 persevered in Refers to the ability to endure hardships and persecutions in ministry (compare 6:4).
marks of a true apostle The phrasing suggests that an apostle could be recognized as such by the God-given ability to perform certain miraculous signs. These signs affirm Paul's identity in contrast with the false apostles who are causing problems at Corinth (11:13). **signs, wonders and miracles** Refers to mighty deeds performed as part of God's work of salvation. The signs and wonders that accompanied Paul's ministry demonstrated that he was in continuity with God's work to redeem humanity

(Ex 3:20; 10:1–2; Dt 4:34; Ps 105:27–36; Ac 7:36). See 1Co 12:9–11 and note.
12:13 never a burden to you See note on 2Co 11:9.
Forgive me this wrong Paul is either being sarcastic or merely asking for forgiveness for the sake of making peace. He did not wrong the Corinthians; he founded the church, and taught them the gospel as Jesus taught it.
12:14 for the third time Paul first visited Corinth during his second missionary journey (Ac 18:1–18). He refers to his second visit there as the painful visit (2Co 2:1). See the map "Paul's First and Second Missionary Journeys" on p. 2262; see the map "Paul's Third Missionary Journey" on p. 2263. **what I want is not your possessions** The wealthy believers in Corinth wanted to become Paul's patrons—supplying financial support to him (see v. 13). See note on 1:12; compare 1Co 4:15, where Paul reminds them that their relationship to him is like children to their father—the father provides for them, not the opposite.
12:18 Titus See note on 2Co 2:13. **brother** Perhaps the same individual mentioned earlier; see note on 8:18.
12:19 your strengthening Unlike the false apostles who mistreated the Corinthian believers (11:13–15), Paul and his associates strengthen their faith and endure hardship for their sake.
12:20 gossip, arrogance and disorder The sins Paul lists echo the works of the flesh he listed in Gal 5:19–21. Such vices are sins against the community and create division among believers.
12:21 sexual sin Compare 1Co 5:1–13.

13:1–10 Paul concludes his letter by encouraging the Corinthians to examine themselves (2Co 13:5). He warns them that he will not spare anyone when he visits again (v. 2) but hopes that he will not have to act severely (v. 10).

13:1 two or three witnesses Paul quotes Dt 19:5 to

you a warning when I was with you the second time. I now repeat it while absent: On my return I will not spare those who sinned earlier or any of the others, ³since you are demanding proof that Christ is speaking through me. He is not weak in dealing with you, but is powerful among you. ⁴For to be sure, he was crucified in weakness, yet he lives by God's power. Likewise, we are weak in him, yet by God's power we will live with him in our dealing with you.

⁵Examine yourselves to see whether you are in the faith; test yourselves. Do you not realize that Christ Jesus is in you — unless, of course, you fail the test? ⁶And I trust that you will discover that we have not failed the test. ⁷Now we pray to God that you will not do anything wrong — not so that people will see that we have stood the test but so that you will do what is right even though we may seem to have failed. ⁸For we cannot do anything against the truth, but only for the truth. ⁹We are glad whenever we are weak but you are strong; and our prayer is that you may be fully restored. ¹⁰This is why I write these things when I am absent, that when I come I may not have to be harsh in my use of authority — the authority the Lord gave me for building you up, not for tearing you down.

Final Greetings

¹¹Finally, brothers and sisters, rejoice! Strive for full restoration, encourage one another, be of one mind, live in peace. And the God of love and peace will be with you.

¹²Greet one another with a holy kiss. ¹³All God's people here send their greetings.

¹⁴May the grace of the Lord Jesus Christ, and the love of God, and the fellowship of the Holy Spirit be with you all.

---

establish a process for dealing with his opponents' accusations against him. Multiple witnesses were required to prevent false witnesses (see note on Dt 17:6). Jesus also applied this model for use in church discipline (Mt 18:16; see 1Ti 5:19 and note).

13:3 that Christ is speaking through me In the OT, a prophet functioned as a messenger for God. Paul describes himself as one through whom Christ speaks.

13:4 he was crucified in weakness Paul returns to the themes of life and death (2Co 2:16; 4:7–14; 5:1–10). The cross exhibited the weakness of Christ in his humanity, revealing that he was susceptible to death even as the Son of God. **weak in him** Paul acknowledges the Corinthians' perception that he is weak, stating that he patterns his life after Christ. Just as Christ was weak (by people's standards), so Paul is willing to be weak (1Co 2:3); just as Christ is strong (by God's standards), so Paul is strong.

13:5 test yourselves While Paul's opponents wish to test him, he urges them to examine themselves. If they reject his apostolic authority and instruction, they also reject Christ.

13:8 truth The Greek word used here, *alētheias*, likely refers to the gospel message. Earlier, Paul affirmed that he openly proclaimed the truth (2Co 4:2). This is in contrast to Paul's opponents, who distorted God's Word and proclaimed a different gospel (see 11:4 and note).

13:9 we are weak but you are strong Paul reminds the Corinthians about the paradoxical nature of his ministry: His vocation as an apostle requires that he endure hardship for the sake of other believers and so that more people can come to Christ (Ac 9:15–16; 2Co 11:23–29).

13:10 the Lord gave me Paul did not appoint himself as an apostle; Jesus Christ gave him authority and called him to apostleship.

13:11–14 As he closes his letter, Paul expresses his desire for the Corinthian believers to be united. He encourages them to seek restoration, comfort one another and live in peace. He concludes with a benediction.

13:11 be of one mind Paul urges the believers to have the same mindset and purpose. This does not mean that they will agree on everything, but they must live in harmony with each other (see 1Co 1:10; Php 4:2).

13:12 holy kiss Paul often concludes his letters with this greeting (Ro 16:16; 1Co 16:20). See note on 1Th 5:26.

13:14 The terms Paul uses — "grace," "love," and "fellowship" — emphasize his concern for reconciliation with God (5:20) and unity among believers (8:4).

GALATIANS

INTRODUCTION TO GALATIANS

In his letter to the Galatians, Paul discusses what it means to be God's people. Although many groups have special conditions for membership, the family of God is open to everyone. As Paul explains, there is incredible freedom in Christ—yet, at the same, his followers are called to live like him through the power of the Holy Spirit. Jesus has set us free, and we are to use our freedom to love others (Gal 5:1).

BACKGROUND

The opening verses of Galatians identify Paul and several of his traveling companions as the authors of the letter, although Paul was probably the main writer (1:1–2). The letter's recipients are described as the churches of Galatia—which were planted by Paul during his missionary journeys—but these churches' locations are debated.

Galatia was a region in central Asia Minor (modern-day Turkey). According to one theory, the Galatians Paul addressed were in the southern part of Galatia, primarily in the cities Acts 13–14 records him visiting: Antioch in Pisidia, Lystra, Iconium and Derbe (Ac 13–14). Paul would have written to these churches during AD 48–57—either before or shortly after the Jerusalem Council, held ca. AD 49 (or 51).

Galatia was a region in central Asia Minor (modern-day Turkey).

Another theory places the Galatian churches in the northern part of the region, corresponding to the mentions of Paul visiting Galatia in Acts 16:6 and 18:23. In this case, Paul's letter would have been written during his second or third missionary journeys (ca. AD 49–57), but likely before he wrote Romans (mid–50s AD).

Regardless of their location, the Galatian churches consisted mostly of non-Jewish (Gentile) believers. Paul taught them that they were free in Christ and that they did not need to start following Jewish law once they became Christians. However, after Paul left the area, some outsiders arrived and disputed his teaching (Gal 1:6–7). According to them, it simply wasn't possible to be God's people without observing the Jewish laws. Much of Galatians is Paul's response to this claim.

The debate about the letter's recipients and date arises partly because of a connection to the Jerusalem Council (Ac 15). At this critical meeting, church leaders settled the issue that dominates Galatians: deciding that non-Jewish Christians should not be required to keep Old Testament laws and regulations (outside of a few; Ac 15:22–29). In Galatians, Paul may be articulating the council's decision. Paul could also be offering the same viewpoint, prior to the council; this would mean that Paul's description of his time in Jerusalem and Antioch in Galatians 2:1–14 likely correlates with Paul's time in Antioch (Ac 11:19–30), but not the events of Acts 15. (If this is the case, Paul visited Jerusalem an additional time not recorded in Acts.)

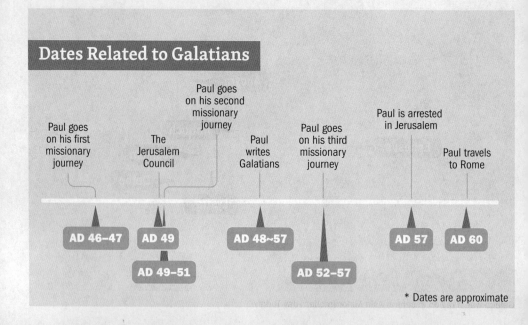

Dates Related to Galatians

Paul goes on his first missionary journey — AD 46–47

The Jerusalem Council — AD 49

AD 49–51

Paul goes on his second missionary journey

Paul writes Galatians — AD 48~57

Paul goes on his third missionary journey — AD 52–57

Paul is arrested in Jerusalem — AD 57

Paul travels to Rome — AD 60

* Dates are approximate

STRUCTURE

After a customary greeting (Gal 1:1–5), Paul challenges the Galatians' movement away from the gospel he preached (1:6–10), and he defends his apostleship (1:11—2:21). Paul argues that those in favor of non-Jewish people practicing Jewish law have a flawed understanding of the gospel.

In the next major section (3:1—5:12), Paul aims to correct the misunderstanding by contrasting his gospel and the false teaching. Relying on the law to secure a place among God's people is foolish, he says; that approach leads only to slavery. In the final part of the letter (5:13—6:18), Paul outlines the practical implications of his gospel. Believers are to live by the Spirit in freedom. If they do this, then sin and divisions will cease.

OUTLINE

- Paul's defense of his apostleship (1:1—2:21)
- Paul's defense of his gospel (3:1—5:12)
- Application of his viewpoint (5:13—6:18)

THEMES

In Galatians, Paul explains what holds the church together as God's people: accepting God's grace and living in step with his Spirit. The Good News Paul preaches is that Christ Jesus has reconciled us to God and thus freed us from having to keep Old Testament law (2:19–21).

Paul says that Christians have to choose between the law and faith (3:10–14). A person who relies on keeping the law has thrown away the need for Jesus. Being right with God doesn't have anything to do with our actions; salvation is all about Jesus—his sacrificial death for our sins and new life taking hold in us (2:19–21; 5:16–24).

The law did have a purpose, though. It guarded God's people until faith was revealed in Christ (3:24–25). But now, God's people have the Spirit. We are full heirs of the promise of salvation and true children of God, having inherited what was promised to Abraham (3:23–29; Ge 12:1–3). Now, by the power of the Holy Spirit, we are called to be there for one another and to do good for others (Gal 5:25—6:10).

1 Paul, an apostle — sent not from men nor by a man, but by Jesus Christ and God the Father, who raised him from the dead — ²and all the brothers and sisters[a] with me,

To the churches in Galatia:

³Grace and peace to you from God our Father and the Lord Jesus Christ, ⁴who gave himself for our sins to rescue us from the present evil age, according to the will of our God and Father, ⁵to whom be glory for ever and ever. Amen.

No Other Gospel

⁶I am astonished that you are so quickly deserting the one who called you to live in the grace of Christ and are turning to a different gospel — ⁷which is really no gospel at all. Evidently some people are throwing you into confusion and are trying to pervert the gospel of Christ. ⁸But even if we or an angel from heaven should preach a gospel other than the one we preached to you, let them be under God's curse! ⁹As we have already said, so now I say again: If anybody is preaching to you a gospel other than what you accepted, let them be under God's curse!

¹⁰Am I now trying to win the approval of human beings, or of God? Or am I trying to please people? If I were still trying to please people, I would not be a servant of Christ.

---

a 2 The Greek word for *brothers and sisters* (*adelphoi*) refers here to believers, both men and women, as part of God's family; also in verse 11; and in 3:15; 4:12, 28, 31; 5:11, 13; 6:1, 18.

1:1–5 The letter to the Galatians was written around AD 48–57 by the apostle Paul, perhaps with contributions from some of his fellow missionaries (Gal 1:1–2). Of Paul's 13 letters, Galatians features one of the most elaborate openings (compare 1Th 1:1; Col 1:1–2). Here, Paul introduces the themes addressed throughout the letter: the divine origin of his calling as an apostle, which he affirms in Gal 1:1, and the gospel message, which he summarizes in v. 4. He then addresses the legitimacy of his apostleship, the gospel, and its implications (respectively discussed in chs. 1–2; 3–4; 5–6).

1:1 Paul Formerly known as Saul of Tarsus (Ac 7:58; 9:11), Paul became an apostle of Jesus Christ and was a prominent figure in the growth of the early church (see note on Ro 1:1). **an apostle** See note on Ro 1:1. **not from men nor by a man** False teachers were accusing Paul of commissioning himself as an apostle; an illegitimate apostleship would discredit his preaching of the gospel and his missionary efforts (compare Gal 2:2). Paul distinguishes himself from the false teachers by emphasizing that God and Christ — not humans — sent him as an apostle. See the table "Pauline Self-Designations" on p. 1904.

1:2 brothers and sisters with me Paul often mentions his coworkers at the beginning of his letters (e.g., 1Co 1:1; 2Co 1:1; Php 1:1; Col 1:1; 1Th 1:1; Phm 1). Here Paul refers to several believers without naming specific individuals, perhaps to highlight the strong support he had from the community of believers. **Galatia** A region in central Asia Minor (modern-day Turkey). See the map "Paul's First and Second Missionary Journeys" on p. 2262.

GALATIA

Paul visited several cities in the region of Galatia during his missionary journeys. While the number of churches Paul addresses in Galatians is unknown, the letter suggests they were predominantly Gentiles — that is, non-Jews (Gal 2:8,14; 4:8–9; 6:13). The exact location of Galatia remains uncertain. It might refer to the territory in north-central Asia Minor inhabited by the Gauls beginning in the third century BC, or the southern area of Asia Minor that Paul visited during his first missionary journey.

1:3 Grace and peace to you This brief greeting summarizes Paul's gospel message. It is God's work, through Christ on our behalf, that brings us into a harmonious relationship with God and one another.

1:4 gave himself for our sins Refers to Jesus' sacrificial death on the cross. **present evil age** Jewish people divided history into two major sections: the present age, in which God's rule is not fully established (and evil persists), and the coming age, when God will complete his rule as King. For Christians, the sacrificial death of Christ enables believers to live under God's rule in the present age. For this reason (and others), the deeds Paul affiliates with the flesh (sinful acts) are inappropriate for the people of God (Gal 5:19–21). While this is the only occurrence of "present evil age" in Paul's letters, its meaning is similar to "this age" (1Co 3:18; 2Co 4:4) and "the world" (1Jn 2:15).

1:5 glory for ever and ever. Amen Expresses the conviction that God is worthy of our unending adoration and worship. The word "amen," meaning "so be it," is used to show agreement or endorsement of what is said about God.

1:6–10 At this point in his letters, Paul typically offers a prayer of thanksgiving for his audience (Ro 1:8; 1Co 1:4; Php 1:3). But with the Galatians, there is no cause for thanksgiving; they have turned to a different gospel. See the table "Prayers in Paul's Letters" on p. 1925.

1:6 the one who called you Refers to God, not Paul (Gal 5:8).

1:7 some people are throwing you into confusion The false teachers in Galatia probably presented their message as the true understanding of the gospel. According to Paul, these teachers have done more harm than good. All of Paul's descriptions of them are negative (v. 7; 5:10,12). They probably are Judaizers (see note on 2:14).

1:8 even if we or an angel Paul probably writes hypothetically here; neither he nor an angel from heaven would ever proclaim a different gospel. **under God's curse** The Greek word used here, *anathema*, refers to putting someone under God's judgment. Since the gospel is the message of God's salvation, God will punish those who distort it.

1:10 trying to please Paul was being accused of easing the requirements of obedience to the law for Gentile believers (non-Jewish people who believed in Jesus). For example, while circumcision was a sign of God's covenant with Abraham (Ge 17), Paul did not require that Gentile

Paul Called by God

[11]I want you to know, brothers and sisters, that the gospel I preached is not of human origin. [12]I did not receive it from any man, nor was I taught it; rather, I received it by revelation from Jesus Christ.

[13]For you have heard of my previous way of life in Judaism, how intensely I persecuted the church of God and tried to destroy it. [14]I was advancing in Judaism beyond many of my own age among my people and was extremely zealous for the traditions of my fathers. [15]But when God, who set me apart from my mother's womb and called me by his grace, was pleased [16]to reveal his Son in me so that I might preach him among the Gentiles, my immediate response was not to consult any

---

believers be circumcised. This made his message more appealing to Gentiles while opening him to the charge of seeking to appease people.

1:11–24 Paul's accusers probably claimed that his independence from the leaders at Jerusalem made him a rogue minister. In this section, Paul challenges this assessment. He says that, despite his independence, the leaders at Jerusalem supported his call and gospel, confirming the legitimacy of his ministry.

1:11 not of human origin Paul began the letter with a defense of his apostleship—it came from God, not people. His argument here is similar, but this time it is not about himself, but his gospel.

1:13 my previous way of life Before his encounter with

the risen Christ on the road to Damascus, Paul was a strict Jew and zealous opponent of Christianity (Ac 7–9; 22:2–11; Php 3:1–15).

1:14 traditions of my fathers Refers to Pharisaic traditions that likely include the Jewish law as well as oral traditions concerning its interpretation (compare Mk 7:5; Ac 22:3).

1:15 set me apart The OT prophets Jeremiah and Isaiah described their callings in similar ways (Jer 1:5; Isa 49:1). This phrase signals that Paul's ministry is a continuation of God's work and voice in the world.

1:16 to reveal his Son in me The end of this phrase is often translated "to me," but it is better understood as "in me." Paul emphasizes that God chose him as an instrument to take the gospel to the Gentiles.

Prayers in Paul's Letters

PRAYER	PASSAGE
Thanksgiving for the recipients of his letters	Ro 1:8–9; 1Co 1:3–8; Eph 1:15–16; Php 1:3–5; Col 1:3–8; 1Th 1:2–3; 2:13; 2Th 1:3–4; 2:13–14; 2Ti 1:3; Phm 4–6
Other prayers of thanksgiving	Ro 6:17–18; 7:25; 1Co 1:14; 14:18; 15:57; 2Co 1:3–4; 2:14; 8:16; 9:15; Eph 1:3–14; Col 1:12; 1Ti 1:12–14
"At last by God's will the way may be opened for me to come to you."	Ro 1:10
"they may be saved"	Ro 10:1
"Come, Lord!"	1Co 16:22
"that you will not do anything wrong..."	2Co 13:7–9
"that... God... may give you the Spirit of wisdom and revelation..."	Eph 1:16–23
"strengthen you with power through his Spirit..."	Eph 3:14–21
"that your love may abound..."	Php 1:9–11
"to fill you with the knowledge..."	Col 1:9–14
"that we may see you again..."	1Th 3:9–13
"that our God may make you worthy of his calling..."	2Th 1:11–12
Paul requests prayer	Ro 15:30–32; 2Co 1:11; Eph 6:19–20; Php 1:19 Col 4:3–4; 1Th 5:25; 2Th 3:1; Phm 22
Paul exhorts his recipients to pray	Ro 12:12; 1Co 7:5; Eph 5:4; 6:18; Php 4:6; Col 4:2; 1Th 5:17; 1Ti 2:1–2; 5:5

human being. ¹⁷I did not go up to Jerusalem to see those who were apostles before I was, but I went into Arabia. Later I returned to Damascus.

¹⁸Then after three years, I went up to Jerusalem to get acquainted with Cephas[a] and stayed with him fifteen days. ¹⁹I saw none of the other apostles — only James, the Lord's brother. ²⁰I assure you before God that what I am writing you is no lie.

²¹Then I went to Syria and Cilicia. ²²I was personally unknown to the churches of Judea that are in Christ. ²³They only heard the report: "The man who formerly persecuted us is now preaching the faith he once tried to destroy." ²⁴And they praised God because of me.

Paul Accepted by the Apostles

2 Then after fourteen years, I went up again to Jerusalem, this time with Barnabas. I took Titus along also. ²I went in response to a revelation and, meeting privately with those esteemed as leaders, I presented to them the gospel that I preach among the Gentiles. I wanted to be sure I was not running and had not been running my race in vain. ³Yet not even Titus, who was with me, was compelled to be circumcised, even though he was a Greek. ⁴This matter arose because some false believers had infiltrated our ranks to spy on the freedom we have in Christ Jesus and to make us slaves. ⁵We did not give in to them for a moment, so that the truth of the gospel might be preserved for you.

⁶As for those who were held in high esteem — whatever they were makes no difference to me; God does not show favoritism — they added nothing to my message. ⁷On the contrary, they recognized that I had been entrusted with the task of preaching the gospel to the uncircumcised,[b] just as Peter had been to the circumcised.[c] ⁸For God, who was at work in Peter as an apostle to the circumcised, was also at work in me as an apostle to the

a 18 That is, Peter   *b 7* That is, Gentiles   *c 7* That is, Jews; also in verses 8 and 9

---

among the Gentiles Paul directed his ministry primarily to the non-Jewish people (Ac 9:15; 22:21). He considers his missionary work a fulfillment of what God spoke through the prophet Isaiah about being a light to the Gentiles (Ac 13:46–47; Isa 49:6).

1:17 Arabia In this context, the reference is most likely to the southeast area of Damascus called Nabatea. However, in Greco-Roman sources of this era, the term "Arabia" was used broadly, referring to southern Canaan (Israel), the northern Sinai and Midian. See Gal 4:25.

1:18 after three years By specifying the length of time, Paul is offering support for his claim that the apostles did not teach him the gospel in Jerusalem; rather, his revelation of the gospel came directly from Jesus Christ. **Cephas** Refers to Simon Peter, an apostle of Jesus and one of the key leaders of the church at Jerusalem. Paul acknowledges that he met Cephas, but he emphasizes that he did not learn the gospel from him. Jesus changed Simon's name to Peter (Mk 3:16), which is the Greek word for "rock." Cephas, the Aramaic equivalent of Peter, also means "rock" (Jn 1:42).

1:19 James The brother of Jesus who became the leader of the church at Jerusalem.

1:21 Syria and Cilicia Syria lies directly north of Galilee and includes the cities of Antioch (Ac 11:19–30), Damascus (Ac 9:1–19) and Caesarea Maritima. Cilicia is the region west of Syria, and includes Paul's home city of Tarsus.

EVENT	APPROXIMATE DATE
Paul's conversion	AD 33
Paul in Arabia	AD 33–35
Paul's visit to Jerusalem	AD 35
Paul in Syria and Cilicia	AD 35–48

1:22 I was personally unknown During the persecution in Jerusalem recorded in Acts, many believers fled to Judaea and Samaria (Ac 8:1). Since Paul participated in the persecution, his victims would have warned other believers about him.

2:1–10 In Gal 1, Paul establishes that his apostleship and gospel came from God, not people. Here, Paul demonstrates that both were validated by the leaders of the church in Jerusalem. He presents this to ease the minds of the Galatians regarding the legitimacy of his apostleship and gospel message. The meeting that Paul describes in this passage likely corresponds with the Jerusalem Council (Ac 15:1–21).

2:1 after fourteen years It is unclear whether these 14 years are in addition to the three years Paul mentions in 1:18, or whether they include them. See the timeline "Life of Paul" on p. 1796. **Barnabas** Paul's mentor and companion during his first and second missionary journeys. During both journeys, they traveled through Galatia together (Ac 13–14). Paul mentions Barnabas to add credibility to his story: Barnabas witnessed the approval of Paul's gospel message by the apostles in Jerusalem. **Titus** Titus was a Greek Gentile and companion of Paul.

2:2 in response to a revelation Attests to Paul's motivation for traveling to Jerusalem. He was responding to God's direction, not human invitation. **with those esteemed** Peter, James and John (Gal 2:9). **running** This imagery is about faithfully living the gospel message (Php 2:16; 3:12–14; 2Ti 4:7). In this case, Paul hoped that the Jerusalem leaders would prove him to be faithful by approving of his law-free gospel.

2:3 Yet not even Titus Since Titus was Greek, he would not have been circumcised. His presence at this meeting supports Paul's claim that he fully disclosed his gospel message to the apostles (Gal 2:2). The question about whether non-Jewish believers needed to be circumcised (for salvation or acceptance into the Christian community) already had been resolved; hence, the apostles would not have compelled Titus to be circumcised.

2:4 false believers These individuals likely were suspicious of Paul because of his law-free gospel. **make us slaves** Indicates why the false brothers spied on the meeting between Paul and the leaders. In mentioning slavery, Paul anticipates the central theme of the following section (3:23—4:11). In contrast to the efforts of the false brothers, Paul's gospel brings freedom from legalism (5:1).

2:5 We did not give in to them Paul intends for his

Gentiles. ⁹James, Cephas*ᵃ* and John, those esteemed as pillars, gave me and Barnabas the right hand of fellowship when they recognized the grace given to me. They agreed that we should go to the Gentiles, and they to the circumcised. ¹⁰All they asked was that we should continue to remember the poor, the very thing I had been eager to do all along.

Paul Opposes Cephas

¹¹When Cephas came to Antioch, I opposed him to his face, because he stood condemned. ¹²For before certain men came from James, he used to eat with the Gentiles. But when they arrived, he began to draw back and separate himself from the Gentiles because he was afraid of those who belonged to the circumcision group. ¹³The other Jews joined him in his hypocrisy, so that by their hypocrisy even Barnabas was led astray.

¹⁴When I saw that they were not acting in line with the truth of the gospel, I said to Cephas in front of them all, "You are a Jew, yet you live like a Gentile and not like a Jew. How is it, then, that you force Gentiles to follow Jewish customs?

¹⁵"We who are Jews by birth and not sinful Gentiles ¹⁶know that a person is not justified by the works of the law, but by faith in Jesus Christ. So we, too, have put our faith in Christ Jesus that we may be justified by faith in*ᵇ* Christ and not by the

---

ᵃ 9 That is, Peter; also in verses 11 and 14   ᵇ 16 Or *but through the faithfulness of . . . justified on the basis of the faithfulness of*

---

response to the false brothers to serve as a model for the Galatians in their present situation. **truth of the gospel** This phrase refers to the integrity of the message of the gospel and its implications for Christian living (v. 14). In particular, Paul seems to have in mind the truth that the gospel frees believers from the law and its requirements, including dietary laws and circumcision (vv. 1–10; 5:2–6). For Paul, the truth of the gospel is more than an abstract concept; it is a new life of faith and love in Christ (5:6).

2:6 those who were held in high esteem Refers to the leaders of the Jerusalem church. **added nothing** Paul insists that the Jerusalem leaders approved of the gospel he preached to the Gentiles (non-Jewish people) without any objections. This statement is confirmed by the fact that they did not require Titus, a Gentile, to be circumcised (v. 3 and note).

2:7 just as Peter had been to the circumcised Peter was recognized as the apostle to the Jews. The leaders of the church in Jerusalem recognized that Paul's ministry to the Gentiles was just as valid as Peter's ministry to the Jews.

2:9 Cephas See note on 1:18. **pillars** This metaphor indicates the supportive and integral roles that James, Peter and John fulfilled as apostles in the early church (compare Mt 16:18). **the right hand of fellowship** This act indicates the acceptance of Paul's apostleship and gospel message by the apostles in Jerusalem, as well as the recognition of their partnership as ministers.

2:10 we should continue to remember the poor The leaders likely encouraged Paul to help the economically impoverished believers in Jerusalem. **very thing I had been eager to do** Paul frequently mentions in his letters his effort to raise funds among the Gentiles to support the poor Jewish believers in Jerusalem (Ro 15:25–28; 1Co 16:1–4; 2Co 8:1–6).

2:11–14 Paul's accusers likely claimed that he altered the gospel message to develop a version that would appeal to non-Jewish people (Gentiles). To counteract this view, Paul uses this section to argue that he defended the truth of the gospel when Peter failed to uphold its message. Paul strategically presents an exchange he had with Peter to address both the agitators and the Galatians. In allowing the Galatians to eavesdrop on his rebuke of Peter—a leader of greater rank than either the agitators or the Galatians—Paul shows that the relationship between Gentile believers and the law has been dealt with before.

2:11 Antioch Located in Syria, nearly 300 miles north of Jerusalem. Several Gentile believers lived in Antioch, and many missionaries went from Antioch to other Gentile regions (Ac 13:1–3). Peter's visit to Antioch is not recorded in Acts.

2:12 certain men Unlike the false brothers (false believers) mentioned in Gal 2:4, these people came to Antioch with authority from James the apostle. However, Paul does not specify the reason James sent them. **eat with the Gentiles** Since Gentiles did not observe Jewish food laws, the groups did not eat together. At first, Peter shared meals with Gentiles as an act of unity in Christ, but his later separation from them reinforced a divisive atmosphere in the Antioch church. **he was afraid** Paul does not mention that the people from James tried to persuade Peter, only that their presence intimidated Peter and caused him to act against the truth of the gospel—that God's cleansing mercy makes both Jew and Gentile one people of God (Ac 10:34–35,45,47).

2:13 other Jews joined him in his hypocrisy Peter's actions influenced the rest of the Jewish believers in Antioch, who previously had made it their custom to eat with Gentile believers. Paul calls their actions hypocritical because they were hiding their true beliefs and practices in order to be viewed favorably by the people from James.

2:14 Gentiles to follow Jewish customs Expresses the aim of Judaizers to force non-Jewish believers to observe certain aspects of the law.

Galatians 2:14

JUDAIZERS

Judaizers insisted that Gentile Christians be circumcised, obey food laws and observe calendar cycles in accordance with the law. In Gal 2:14, Paul accuses Peter (Cephas) of trying to "judaize" the Gentiles, using a Greek verb meaning "live in a Jewish way." Josephus uses the word to describe how a Roman soldier captured by the Jews during the revolt (AD 66–70) avoided execution by promising to be circumcised and live as a Jew. Paul believed Gentile followers of Jesus were not required to become Jewish in that sense because the gospel transcended ethnic and social boundaries.

2:15 not sinful Gentiles Captures the attitude of most Jewish people of the time toward Gentiles. From the Jewish point of view, a sinner is a person who does not live by the law. Because the Gentiles were not given the law, they are sinners by default (compare Ro 2:17–29).

2:16 justified Paul's notion of justification can be interpreted as an ethical transformation that makes a person righteous or as a forensic transaction by which a person is declared righteous and acquitted. Paul likely

works of the law, because by the works of the law no one will be justified.

[17]"But if, in seeking to be justified in Christ, we Jews find ourselves also among the sinners, doesn't that mean that Christ promotes sin? Absolutely not! [18]If I rebuild what I destroyed, then I really would be a lawbreaker.

[19]"For through the law I died to the law so that I might live for God. [20]I have been crucified with Christ and I no longer live, but Christ lives in me. The life I now live in the body, I live by faith in the Son of God, who loved me and gave himself for me. [21]I do not set aside the grace of God, for if righteousness could be gained through the law, Christ died for nothing!"[a]

Faith or Works of the Law

3 You foolish Galatians! Who has bewitched you? Before your very eyes Jesus Christ was clearly portrayed as crucified. [2]I would like to learn just

one thing from you: Did you receive the Spirit by the works of the law, or by believing what you heard? [3]Are you so foolish? After beginning by means of the Spirit, are you now trying to finish by means of the flesh?[b] [4]Have you experienced[c] so much in vain — if it really was in vain? [5]So again I ask, does God give you his Spirit and work miracles among you by the works of the law, or by your believing what you heard? [6]So also Abraham "believed God, and it was credited to him as righteousness."[d]

[7]Understand, then, that those who have faith are children of Abraham. [8]Scripture foresaw that God would justify the Gentiles by faith, and announced the gospel in advance to Abraham: "All nations will be blessed through you."[e] [9]So those

a 21 Some interpreters end the quotation after verse 14.   *b 3* In contexts like this, the Greek word for *flesh* (*sarx*) refers to the sinful state of human beings, often presented as a power in opposition to the Spirit.   *c 4* Or *suffered*   *d 6* Gen. 15:6   *e 8* Gen. 12:3; 18:18; 22:18

has both aspects in mind: Those who place saving trust in Christ are declared righteous by God and become righteous. **works of the law** Refers primarily to requirements of the law that Jews observed to preserve their ethnic identity and honor their covenantal obligations (dietary laws, circumcision, etc.). The phrase also might describe legalistic observance of these requirements to gain favor before God. Paul recognized the significance of these works for those under the law, but insists they have no value when it comes to justification (compare Gal 5:6). **faith in Jesus Christ** Refers to the believer's saving trust in what God has done through Christ or, possibly, to the faithfulness of Christ. Paul contrasts faith in Christ with the works of law that are described in chs. 3–4.
2:17 Christ promotes sin From the Jewish perspective, being without the law means being a sinner. According to this view, if Paul teaches that justification in Christ requires that one abandon the law—and thus become a sinner—then Christ must be a promoter of sin. Paul addresses this quandary in the following verse.
2:18 I really would be a lawbreaker Paul preached a law-free gospel that did not require non-Jewish people to observe the law. If his words or actions suggested that law observance was necessary for salvation, he would be contradicting that gospel.
2:19 through the law I died to the law Christ's death and resurrection frees believers from the law and its curse (3:10–14; 4:4–5).
2:20 I have been crucified with Christ Paul does not refer here to physical death, but to the death of his former self (see Eph 4:22). **Christ lives in me** Refers to new life in Christ as well as the presence of God's Spirit, which empowers obedience to the gospel (Gal 3:2; 4:6; 5:16–18,22–25). **gave himself for me** Paul describes the sacrificial love of Christ in personal terms.
2:21 the grace of God This suggests that Paul's opponents had accused him of using God's grace to justify unrighteous living. See v. 17 and note.

3:1–5 Paul presents a series of rhetorical questions, essentially asking the Galatians whether they have traded the ministry of God's Spirit for works of the law. He invites them to consider how they came to experience the Spirit—whether it was through the law or through faith.

3:1 You foolish Galatians Paul is referring not to mental incompetence, but to a lack of wisdom. **Who has bewitched you** Paul asks this question rhetorically of his audience. He isn't seeking the identities of the agitators; rather, he is commenting on the Galatians' rejection of freedom in Christ. It's as though someone has cast a spell on them. **Christ was clearly portrayed as crucified** Refers to the gospel, which Paul himself had presented to the Galatians (1:8). Elsewhere in his letters, Paul uses the crucifixion as shorthand for the gospel message (1Co 1:23; 2:2).
3:3 trying to finish by means of the flesh The agitators might have told the Galatians that keeping the law would make them legitimate or mature believers.
3:4 Have you experienced Refers to the Galatians' spiritual experiences (Gal 3:5) or possibly to social ostracism experienced because of the gospel. Paul rhetorically asks the Galatians whether they forgot these experiences in favor of observing the law.
3:5 by the works of the law, or by your believing what you heard Paul's question sets up a contrast between law and faith that will be addressed further in chs. 3–4 (compare 2:16).

3:6–29 In this passage Paul presents the model of true saving faith—Abraham. In doing so, Paul demonstrates that God has always justified people by faith, not works. Paul then clarifies the role of the law in God's plan: It was intended to serve as a guardian until the time of Christ.

3:6 believed God Refers to trusting that God will fulfill his promises (Ge 15:6). God had promised Abraham an heir and countless descendants (Ge 15:4–5).
3:7 children of Abraham Refers to those who express faith like Abraham—not Abraham's biological sons. Abraham represents the model of faith for all believers, both Jews and non-Jewish people (Gentiles).
3:8 Scripture In this context, this refers to what is now called the OT. Paul was fluent in Greek. His quotations of Scripture typically draw from the Greek translation of the Hebrew OT (Genesis–Malachi) called the Septuagint. This translation of the Bible was used by many Jews who lived in regions outside of Israel and did not speak or read Hebrew. Paul's use of the Septuagint indicates that he quoted Scripture in a language the

who rely on faith are blessed along with Abraham, the man of faith.

[10] For all who rely on the works of the law are under a curse, as it is written: "Cursed is everyone who does not continue to do everything written in the Book of the Law."[a] [11] Clearly no one who relies on the law is justified before God, because "the righteous will live by faith."[b] [12] The law is not based on faith; on the contrary, it says, "The person who does these things will live by them."[c] [13] Christ redeemed us from the curse of the law by becoming a curse for us, for it is written: "Cursed is everyone who is hung on a pole."[d] [14] He redeemed us in order that the blessing given to Abraham might come to the Gentiles through Christ Jesus, so that by faith we might receive the promise of the Spirit.

The Law and the Promise

[15] Brothers and sisters, let me take an example from everyday life. Just as no one can set aside or add to a human covenant that has been duly established, so it is in this case. [16] The promises were spoken to Abraham and to his seed. Scripture does not say "and to seeds," meaning many people, but "and to your seed,"[e] meaning one person, who is Christ. [17] What I mean is this: The law, introduced 430 years later, does not set aside the covenant previously established by God and thus do away with the promise. [18] For if the inheritance depends on the law, then it no longer depends on the promise; but God in his grace gave it to Abraham through a promise.

[19] Why, then, was the law given at all? It was added because of transgressions until the Seed to whom the promise referred had come. The law was given through angels and entrusted to a mediator. [20] A mediator, however, implies more than one party; but God is one.

[21] Is the law, therefore, opposed to the promises

a 10 Deut. 27:26   *b* 11 Hab. 2:4   *c* 12 Lev. 18:5
d 13 Deut. 21:23   *e* 16 Gen. 12:7; 13:15; 24:7

Galatians would have understood. **God would justify the Gentiles by faith** Paul argues here that his gospel message—the justification of Gentiles through faith apart from the law—was always part of God's plan. Elsewhere, Paul refers to this as a mystery (Ro 16:25; Eph 1:9; 3:9). Inclusion in the people of God would occur by faith in Christ, the promised seed of Abraham (Gal 3:7–8). **All nations will be blessed through you** This quotation comes from Ge 12:3. In the context of Galatians, this blessing is the Spirit and the gift of justification by faith.

3:9 those who rely on faith are blessed along with Abraham Paul emphasizes that faith, not ethnicity, is the determining factor—which means that Gentile believers like the Galatians can share in Abraham's blessing.

3:10 law are under a curse Paul draws on Dt 27:26 and 28:58 to show that every person—whether Jew or Gentile—who relies on works of the law is under the curse of the law. That curse stands in direct contrast to the blessing of Abraham that comes to those who trust God—including Gentiles (Gal 3:6–9). **as it is written** A standard formula used to introduce a quotation from Scripture. **does not continue to do everything written** Paul quotes Dt 27:26 to inform the Galatians that they must obey the entire law, not just portions of it. Failure to do so results in curse, not blessing.

3:11 on the law See Gal 2:16 and note. **righteous will live by faith** Paul's quotation from Hab 2:4 provides evidence that justification by faith was always part of God's plan of salvation. Also important to Paul's argument is that Hab 2:4 does not distinguish between Gentiles and Jews in reference to righteousness. Faith is what matters to God—not a person's ethnicity.

3:12 The law is not based on faith This phrase means that the law is based on doing, not trusting. Paul's point here is not that the law fails to justify those who do its works, but that God did not intend for the law to make people righteous. Paul cites Lev 18:5 in this verse to show that Scripture itself teaches that the law's function is to provide a way to live obediently under God's rule (see Ro 10:5; compare Lk 10:27–28).

3:13 Christ redeemed us from the curse God's provision through Christ's death on the cross enables believers to no longer live under the threat of condemnation. **Cursed is everyone who is hung on a pole** This quotation is from Dt 21:23. When Christ became a curse for us through his loving sacrifice on the cross, he accomplished redemption and atonement for those who believe. See the table "Jesus' Fulfillment of OT Prophecy" on p. 1573.

3:14 by faith we might receive the promise of the Spirit Paul began this section with rhetorical questions implying that the Galatians had received the Spirit through faith (Gal 3:2–5). Given this, the Galatians had already experienced the fulfillment of God's promise to Abraham.

3:15 to a human covenant that has been duly established In Paul's example, the covenant refers to the promise that God made to Abraham (before God instructed Abraham to be circumcised; Ge 17). This covenant was ratified not by circumcision, but by God himself (Ge 15:9–21).

3:16 and to your seed The promise of blessing and the Spirit is given to Christ through Abraham. This narrow application of the promise then expands to all who believe, leading to one people of faith descended from Abraham (including Jews and Gentiles).

3:17 430 years Refers to the Israelites' period of slavery in Egypt. **thus do away with the promise** Paul's point is that the law does not alter anything about God's earlier covenant with Abraham (Ge 15:12–21).

3:18 no longer depends on the promise The law is not, and never was intended to be, the means by which believers experience their inheritance as God's children.

3:19 It was added because of transgressions Paul's point is that the law was added subsequent to the covenant that God had made with Abraham. Paul's statement here can be interpreted to mean that the law's purpose was to define sin (Ro 4:15) or to increase sin (Ro 5:20). **until the Seed to whom the promise referred had come** Christ is the descendant (Gal 3:16). **given through angels and entrusted to a mediator** The tradition of angels' participation in the giving of the law is based on Dt 33:2 (compare Ac 7:38,53). The mediator Paul envisions here most likely is Moses.

3:20 A mediator, however, implies more than one party; but God is one This verse is notoriously difficult to

of God? Absolutely not! For if a law had been given that could impart life, then righteousness would certainly have come by the law. ²²But Scripture has locked up everything under the control of sin, so that what was promised, being given through faith in Jesus Christ, might be given to those who believe.

Children of God

²³Before the coming of this faith,ᵃ we were held in custody under the law, locked up until the faith that was to come would be revealed. ²⁴So the law was our guardian until Christ came that we might be justified by faith. ²⁵Now that this faith has come, we are no longer under a guardian.

²⁶So in Christ Jesus you are all children of God through faith, ²⁷for all of you who were baptized into Christ have clothed yourselves with Christ. ²⁸There is neither Jew nor Gentile, neither slave nor free, nor is there male and female, for you are all one in Christ Jesus. ²⁹If you belong to Christ, then you are Abraham's seed, and heirs according to the promise.

4 What I am saying is that as long as an heir is underage, he is no different from a slave, although he owns the whole estate. ²The heir is subject to guardians and trustees until the time set by his father. ³So also, when we were underage, we were in slavery under the elemental spiritual forcesᵇ of the world. ⁴But when the set time had fully come, God sent his Son, born of a woman, born under the law, ⁵to redeem those under the law, that we might receive adoption to sonship.ᶜ ⁶Because you are his sons, God sent the Spirit of his Son into our hearts, the Spirit who calls out, "Abba,ᵈ Father." ⁷So you are no longer a slave, but God's child; and since you are his child, God has made you also an heir.

Paul's Concern for the Galatians

⁸Formerly, when you did not know God, you were slaves to those who by nature are not gods. ⁹But now that you know God — or rather are known by God — how is it that you are turning back to those weak and miserable forcesᵉ? Do you wish to be enslaved by them all over again? ¹⁰You are observing special days and months and seasons and years! ¹¹I fear for you, that somehow I have wasted my efforts on you.

¹²I plead with you, brothers and sisters, become like me, for I became like you. You did me no

---

ᵃ 22,23 Or through the faithfulness of Jesus . . . ²³Before faith came   ᵇ 3 Or under the basic principles   ᶜ 5 The Greek word for adoption to sonship is a legal term referring to the full legal standing of an adopted male heir in Roman culture.   ᵈ 6 Aramaic for Father   ᵉ 9 Or principles

---

interpret. Regardless of the precise meaning, Paul seems to be emphasizing unity. In Gal 3:16, he contrasted the many with the one to show that Christ fulfills the promise given to Abraham. Similarly here, the law mediated by Moses leads to divisions (i.e., Jews and Gentiles), rather than to one family of faith worshiping the one true God. See v. 28 and note.

3:21 the law, therefore, opposed Although the law cannot give life, it does not counteract God's covenant promises.

3:22 Scripture has locked up everything under the control of sin Paul is further explaining the purpose of the law—to make all people aware of their need for deliverance from sin.

3:24 guardian The law had a temporary and protective role. It kept people mindful of their condition and guided them toward maturity in God's ways. The Greek word used here, *paidagōgos*—which may be rendered "guardian" or "tutor"—refers to someone who was responsible for protecting a child from harm, administering discipline and instilling virtue.

3:26 children of God Although they are Gentiles and thus not Jewish, the Galatians are eligible for adoption into God's family through faith in Christ.

3:28 neither Jew nor Gentile Paul emphasizes that the standard categories that often divide people—race, social status, gender—do not apply to those who are in Christ. It is not that such criteria cease to exist; rather, these distinctions are not grounds for exclusion from the life that God offers to all people in Christ. Because God is one (v. 20), he seeks to establish through Christ a single, unified family.

3:29 Abraham's seed Paul sees the work of Christ as the fulfillment of God's covenant with Abraham (vv. 7–9; Ge 12:1–3).

4:1–7 In this section of the text, Paul draws a contrast between sons and slaves. In doing so, he aims to help the Galatians understand that reliance on the law is a sign not of maturity, but of immaturity. In contrast to the law, faith in Christ produces children who become heirs of God's promises.

4:1 as long as an heir is underage In Paul's time, children received their inheritance when they came of age. Until then, they had neither decision-making rights nor freedom. **no different from a slave** Under Roman law, underage children could not exercise legal power over their inheritance; their status was almost identical to that of a slave.

4:3 under the elemental spiritual forces Paul's language here could refer to basic religious teachings that contradict the gospel; the material parts of the universe, such as water, earth, and fire; or spiritual powers, such as evil spirits and demonic entities. Ultimately, Paul makes it clear that these entities are negative influences (Gal 4:8–9).

4:4 when the set time had fully come With this phrase, Paul brings together the idea of coming of age and the coming of Jesus. Paul stresses that the life, death and resurrection of Christ occurred according to the plan of God (v. 2). **born under the law** Refers to Jesus' identity as a Jew. He was born into the people who lived according to God's law.

4:5 redeem The Greek word used here, *exagorazō*, is a legal term meaning "buy out." The idea is that Christ's death has bought freedom for those who are enslaved to the law. **adoption** A well-known legal procedure in the Roman Empire. The OT portrays God as adopting Israel when he delivered the Hebrew people from slavery in Egypt (Ex 4:22–23; Hos 11:1).

4:6 sent the Spirit of his Son The indwelling pres-

wrong. [13] As you know, it was because of an illness that I first preached the gospel to you, [14] and even though my illness was a trial to you, you did not treat me with contempt or scorn. Instead, you welcomed me as if I were an angel of God, as if I were Christ Jesus himself. [15] Where, then, is your blessing of me now? I can testify that, if you could have done so, you would have torn out your eyes and given them to me. [16] Have I now become your enemy by telling you the truth?

[17] Those people are zealous to win you over, but for no good. What they want is to alienate you from us, so that you may have zeal for them. [18] It is fine to be zealous, provided the purpose is good, and to be so always, not just when I am with you. [19] My dear children, for whom I am again in the pains of childbirth until Christ is formed in you, [20] how I wish I could be with you now and change my tone, because I am perplexed about you!

Hagar and Sarah

[21] Tell me, you who want to be under the law, are you not aware of what the law says? [22] For it is written that Abraham had two sons, one by the slave woman and the other by the free woman. [23] His son by the slave woman was born according to the flesh, but his son by the free woman was born as the result of a divine promise.

[24] These things are being taken figuratively: The women represent two covenants. One covenant is from Mount Sinai and bears children who are to be slaves: This is Hagar. [25] Now Hagar stands for Mount Sinai in Arabia and corresponds to the present city of Jerusalem, because she is in slavery with her children. [26] But the Jerusalem that is above is free, and she is our mother. [27] For it is written:

"Be glad, barren woman,
    you who never bore a child;
shout for joy and cry aloud,
    you who were never in labor;
because more are the children of the
        desolate woman
    than of her who has a husband."[a]

[28] Now you, brothers and sisters, like Isaac, are children of promise. [29] At that time the son born

[a] 27 Isaiah 54:1

---

ence of the Spirit legitimizes the Galatians' identity as children of God. **who calls out, "Abba, Father"** See note on Ro 8:15.

4:8 you did not know God A common way for Paul to describe Gentiles—people of non-Jewish origin (1Th 4:5; 2Th 1:8; Titus 1:16). Estrangement from the living God means being subject to other forces and powers.

4:9 weak and miserable forces Here, Paul may be referring to the law, spiritual beings, or astral deities (see Gal 4:3 and note).

4:10 days and months and seasons and years The law commanded special observances at various times (e.g., Lev 23:5,16,28; 25:4). The agitators likely convinced the Galatian believers that keeping the law was compatible with the gospel. See the table "Israelite Festivals" on p. 200.

4:11 I have wasted my efforts on you Paul often expresses his fear that his apostolic work would be ruined by the failure of his churches (e.g., Php 2:16; 1Th 3:5). The Galatians' predicament threatens the effectiveness of his ministry efforts.

4:12 become like me Paul regularly charged his disciples to imitate him (1Co 4:16; 11:1; Php 3:17).

4:13 an illness The nature of this situation is unknown. Paul might have had trouble with his eyesight that prompted aid from the Galatians (Gal 4:14–15).

4:17 Those people are zealous to win you In Paul's view, the agitators are motivated by self-centered divisiveness. They are not truly interested in the well-being of the Galatians—unlike Paul, who regards them as his children in the Lord (v. 19).

4:19 for whom I am again in the pains of childbirth Paul employs an evocative metaphor to depict the strained status of his relationship with the Galatians.

4:21–31 Paul again draws from the story of Abraham, this time to show that the law was never intended to bring freedom.

4:21 are you not aware of what the law says Paul

already stated that God sent his Son to redeem those under the law, the Jewish people (v. 5). The implication is that by putting themselves under the law through circumcision, food laws and calendar observance, the Galatians would be rejecting God's gift and missing the purpose of the law altogether.

4:22 Abraham had two sons Paul is referencing Ge 16–17,21. The two sons are Ishmael (Abraham's son with Hagar, an Egyptian slave) and Isaac (the son of Abraham and his wife, Sarah).

4:23 as the result of a divine promise Isaac's birth fulfilled the promise to Abraham; it was the work of God.

4:24 being taken figuratively In Paul's interpretation (which runs through Gal 4:31), the true sons of Abraham are the children of promise, not law.

4:25 Hagar stands for Mount Sinai in Arabia Paul links Hagar, a slave, with the idea of enslavement to the law (represented by Mount Sinai, where Yahweh gave his law to the Israelites; Ex 20). The term "Arabia" could refer to a wide range of geographical areas. The reference to Jerusalem associates Hagar with the Jewish people—those who live under the law.

4:26 the Jerusalem that is above Refers to God's heavenly dwelling place, which Paul associates with Sarah, the free woman (Gal 4:23,31).

4:27 Be glad, barren woman This quotation comes from Isa 54:1. In reference to the Babylonian exile, Isa 54:1–8 depicts Jerusalem as a woman whose husband has been taken away. Despite her loss, God promises that she will have many children. Paul brings the promise of this great reversal, originally given to Sarah and the city of Jerusalem, to the Galatians. The original condition of the Gentiles—being outsiders to God's covenant with the Jews—has been reversed. Through God's grace, justification and freedom are now available to them by faith.

4:28 like Isaac, are children of promise This phrase expresses the great reversal brought about by Christ: Gentiles (non-Jewish people) are part of God's family, like Jews.

4:29 persecuted the son born by the power of the

according to the flesh persecuted the son born by the power of the Spirit. It is the same now. ³⁰But what does Scripture say? "Get rid of the slave woman and her son, for the slave woman's son will never share in the inheritance with the free woman's son."ᵃ ³¹Therefore, brothers and sisters, we are not children of the slave woman, but of the free woman.

Freedom in Christ

5 It is for freedom that Christ has set us free. Stand firm, then, and do not let yourselves be burdened again by a yoke of slavery.

²Mark my words! I, Paul, tell you that if you let yourselves be circumcised, Christ will be of no value to you at all. ³Again I declare to every man who lets himself be circumcised that he is obligated to obey the whole law. ⁴You who are trying to be justified by the law have been alienated

from Christ; you have fallen away from grace. ⁵For through the Spirit we eagerly await by faith the righteousness for which we hope. ⁶For in Christ Jesus neither circumcision nor uncircumcision has any value. The only thing that counts is faith expressing itself through love.

⁷You were running a good race. Who cut in on you to keep you from obeying the truth? ⁸That kind of persuasion does not come from the one who calls you. ⁹"A little yeast works through the whole batch of dough." ¹⁰I am confident in the Lord that you will take no other view. The one who is throwing you into confusion, whoever that may be, will have to pay the penalty. ¹¹Brothers and sisters, if I am still preaching circumcision, why am I still being persecuted? In that case the offense of the cross has been abolished. ¹²As for

ᵃ 30 Gen. 21:10

Spirit Refers to Ge 21:9–10 where Ishmael ridicules Isaac, prompting Sarah to drive out Ishmael and Hagar.
4:30 Get rid of the slave woman and her son This quotation is from Ge 21:10. Ishmael, representing the law, cannot share the inheritance of Isaac, the child of promise.
4:31 not children of the slave woman This verse summarizes Paul's argument in this section, based on his allegorical reading of Ge 16–17,21. Through faith, Christians are children of promise, like Isaac. They inherit God's blessing to Abraham apart from the law.
5:1 for freedom that Christ has set us free This statement summarizes Paul's arguments in Gal 3 and 4. The freedom given by Christ liberates believers from the law. **yoke of slavery** In Jewish tradition, the image of the yoke was often used to describe the law's role of guiding people in righteousness (as is seen in the rabbinic work *Mishnah Abot* 3:5; compare Mt 11:29–30). Paul redirects this imagery to clarify the law's effect now that Christ has come: It does not lead or teach people anymore, but instead enslaves them (Gal 4:3,8).
5:2 if you let yourselves be circumcised If the Galatians allowed themselves to be circumcised, they would nullify Christ's work on their behalf, since his death had already redeemed them from the law (4:4–5). **will be of no value to you** Paul does not mean that (circumcised) Jews cannot become believers or that Christ's value can be diminished by the law. His point is that anyone who insists on living under the law fails to trust in Christ. For Paul, Christ's work is completely sufficient in the life of the believer. Therefore, to trust in the value of circumcision is to diminish the worth of Christ.
5:4 you have fallen away from grace If someone depends on the law for justification, they have effectively rejected God's gift of grace in Christ. There is considerable debate about whether this verse means that a Christian can lose his or her salvation. Paul's remarks do not resolve this issue. He certainly is concerned for the Galatians, but he also is confident in God who gave the Spirit to them in the first place.
5:5 we eagerly await by faith the righteousness for which we hope The Greek word used here for "hope," *elpis*, does not refer to something uncertain. Rather, it refers to the believer's anticipation of God's future deliverance of his people, whom he has made righteous.
5:6 neither circumcision nor uncircumcision has

any value God's gift of the Holy Spirit confirms believers' status as his children (compare Ro 8:14–16) and empowers them to obey God. God's people are no longer defined by their keeping of the law; rather, their status before God depends exclusively on their faith in Christ (Gal 2:16,20; 3:11–12,23–25). Paul therefore asserts that it no longer matters whether people are circumcised—that is, whether they are Jews or Gentiles. Because of the new creation begun by the work of Christ (compare 6:15), all who trust in God's gift of grace and receive his Spirit belong to the family of God (compare 3:28; Col 3:11). Paul is not betraying his Jewish heritage or the law with his comment on circumcision. The OT prophets rebuked the people of Israel for giving more value to the outward sign of circumcision than to the inward change of the heart (Jer 9:25–26). Like the prophets before him, Paul puts obedience to the law in the proper perspective.
faith expressing itself through love The goal of the Christian life is to express faith in Christ through love, not to live under the requirements of law. Believers are called to demonstrate their faith through sacrificial love for others because their faith is placed in the one who first demonstrated such love (Gal 2:20). Paul describes the fruit of sacrificial love in vv. 22–23.
5:7 You were running a good race In this context, the imagery of running illustrates exercising faith in Christ and his promises. **obeying the truth** Here, Paul equates obeying the truth with obeying his gospel message: There is no means of justification before God except faith in Christ.
5:8 not come from the one who calls you God is not the source of the Galatians' interest in the law.
5:9 A little yeast Refers to a few agitators having broad influence among the Galatians. Jesus refers figuratively to yeast or leaven to speak negatively about the Pharisees and their hypocrisy (Mt 16:6; Mk 8:15; Lk 12:1).
5:10 The one who is throwing you into confusion Earlier in the letter, Paul stated that those who distort the gospel and lead others astray are worthy of a curse (Gal 1:8–9). Here he anticipates God's final judgment of them for corrupting God's people.
5:11 why am I still being persecuted The agitators might have claimed that Paul advocated circumcision.
5:12 emasculate Paul expresses his frustration with the agitators in terms of a punishment that condemns their actions: Since they advocate circumcision, Paul wishes

those agitators, I wish they would go the whole way and emasculate themselves!

Life by the Spirit

[13]You, my brothers and sisters, were called to be free. But do not use your freedom to indulge the flesh[a]; rather, serve one another humbly in love. [14]For the entire law is fulfilled in keeping this one command: "Love your neighbor as yourself."[b] [15]If you bite and devour each other, watch out or you will be destroyed by each other.

[16]So I say, walk by the Spirit, and you will not gratify the desires of the flesh. [17]For the flesh desires what is contrary to the Spirit, and the Spirit what is contrary to the flesh. They are in conflict with each other, so that you are not to do whatever[c] you want. [18]But if you are led by the Spirit, you are not under the law.

[19]The acts of the flesh are obvious: sexual immorality, impurity and debauchery; [20]idolatry and witchcraft; hatred, discord, jealousy, fits of rage, selfish ambition, dissensions, factions [21]and envy; drunkenness, orgies, and the like. I warn you, as I did before, that those who live like this will not inherit the kingdom of God.

[22]But the fruit of the Spirit is love, joy, peace, forbearance, kindness, goodness, faithfulness, [23]gentleness and self-control. Against such things there is no law. [24]Those who belong to Christ Jesus have crucified the flesh with its passions and desires. [25]Since we live by the Spirit, let us keep in step with the Spirit. [26]Let us not become conceited, provoking and envying each other.

Doing Good to All

6 Brothers and sisters, if someone is caught in a sin, you who live by the Spirit should restore that person gently. But watch yourselves, or you also may be tempted. [2]Carry each other's burdens, and in this way you will fulfill the law of Christ. [3]If anyone thinks they are something when they are not, they deceive themselves. [4]Each one should test their own actions. Then they can take pride in themselves alone, without comparing themselves to someone else, [5]for each one should carry their own load. [6]Nevertheless, the one who receives instruction in the word should share all good things with their instructor.

[a] 13 In contexts like this, the Greek word for *flesh* (*sarx*) refers to the sinful state of human beings, often presented as a power in opposition to the Spirit; also in verses 16, 17, 19 and 24; and in 6:8.   [b] 14 Lev. 19:18   [c] 17 Or *you do not do what*

---

that they would instead castrate themselves. Essentially, Paul is saying that he wishes these men would cut themselves off from the Christian community rather than drive believers back into slavery under the law (compare v. 4).

5:13 You, my brothers and sisters, were called to be free Paul urges the Galatians to use their freedom from the law's requirements to fulfill the law's essence: love of neighbor. According to Paul, God frees believers from slavery under the law so that they choose to serve one another.

5:14 keeping this one command: "Love your neighbor as yourself" By quoting Lev 19:18, Paul shows that the law itself upholds love as the main goal of law keeping. In the context of the letter, Paul uses this quote as a springboard to present a series of instructions (Gal 5:16—6:10) that promote a healthy, godly church community in Galatia.

5:15 If you bite and devour each other Paul uses vivid imagery—wild animals in a deadly fight—to warn the Galatians that attacking one another ultimately will destroy their community.

5:16 walk by the Spirit Refers to being under the Spirit's direction and empowerment.

5:18 if you are led by the Spirit The Spirit and the law represent mutually exclusive ways of living. The law can define and identify sin, but it cannot provide the power to resist sin. Nor does the law instill within people the concerns, desires and character of God. However, believers are not left on their own. They have been given the Spirit of the living God to empower them against sin and to transform their hearts and minds.

5:19-21 More than half of the works of the flesh listed here denote forms of possible conflict among people. While this list is not exhaustive, it adequately represents life apart from the Spirit.

5:21 kingdom of God Refers to the domain in which God is king. In the Bible, believers extend God's reign through obedience, loyalty and love. Those who orient their lives

toward the flesh will not inherit the kingdom of God because they have established a kingdom of their own.

5:22 the fruit of the Spirit This list (vv. 22–23), which contrasts with the works of the flesh (vv. 19–21), is not exhaustive but representative. These traits describe the desires and characteristics that God cultivates in believers through his living presence.

5:25 let us keep in step with the Spirit It is not enough to claim to have new life in Christ by the power of the Spirit (compare 3:3); believers must continually follow after the Spirit in the way they live while also resisting the flesh.

5:26 provoking and envying each other Such actions represent a failure to live by the Spirit (compare v. 22).

6:1 gently Those who live by the Spirit should restore those who sin with gentleness and humility.

6:2 the law of Christ Paul likely uses this phrase to challenge the misguided understanding of the law held by his opponents. Instead of adhering to the agitators' view of the law, believers should keep the law of Christ—which probably represents Jesus' interpretation of the Mosaic Law. Even if Paul does not have Jesus' teaching in mind, the phrase certainly involves love of neighbor (5:13–14; compare Mt 19:19; Jn 13:34).

6:4 Each one should test their own actions Earlier in the letter, Paul discusses works of the law, which do not lead to righteousness (e.g., Gal 2:16). Here he addresses the work of the gospel, which every believer is called to pursue.

6:5 each one should carry their own load Although this verse seems to contradict v. 2, the context is different. Here Paul addresses individual accountability for doing the work of the gospel; each believer needs to do his or her part. Verse 2 is about mutual support within the body of Christ; believers should persevere together through hardships.

6:6 should share all good things Paul instructs the

⁷Do not be deceived: God cannot be mocked. A man reaps what he sows. ⁸Whoever sows to please their flesh, from the flesh will reap destruction; whoever sows to please the Spirit, from the Spirit will reap eternal life. ⁹Let us not become weary in doing good, for at the proper time we will reap a harvest if we do not give up. ¹⁰Therefore, as we have opportunity, let us do good to all people, especially to those who belong to the family of believers.

Not Circumcision but the New Creation

¹¹See what large letters I use as I write to you with my own hand! ¹²Those who want to impress people by means of the flesh are trying to compel you to be circumcised. The only reason they do this is to avoid being persecuted for the cross of Christ. ¹³Not even those who are circumcised keep the law, yet they want you to be circumcised that they may boast about your circumcision in the flesh. ¹⁴May I never boast except in the cross of our Lord Jesus Christ, through which*a* the world has been crucified to me, and I to the world. ¹⁵Neither circumcision nor uncircumcision means anything; what counts is the new creation. ¹⁶Peace and mercy to all who follow this rule — to*b* the Israel of God.

¹⁷From now on, let no one cause me trouble, for I bear on my body the marks of Jesus.

¹⁸The grace of our Lord Jesus Christ be with your spirit, brothers and sisters. Amen.

a 14 Or whom   *b* 16 Or rule and to

6:7 reaps Paul uses an agricultural metaphor to encourage the Galatians to live by the Spirit. A person cannot engage in works of the flesh (5:19) and expect to experience God's life.

6:8 eternal life This is not limited to life after death but begins in the present, as the believer is transformed by God's Spirit (5:22–23; Ro 8:2,10–11).

6:10 those who belong to the family of believers While believers should do good to all people, they should particularly assist those who belong to the community of believers.

6:11 what large letters I use as I write This detail suggests that Paul relieved his scribe and wrote the rest of the letter himself. It is possible that Paul uses this phrase to draw attention to the passage that immediately follows, in which he summarizes several of the letter's themes. In Paul's time, letters commonly were dictated to a professional writer, called an amanuensis. Paul's letter to the Romans, for example, was dictated by Paul to Tertius (Ro 16:22).

6:12 who want to impress people Paul seems to be indicating that the agitators are concerned about their own reputations as law-keepers. It is possible that, by

Galatians to regard their teachers as ministry partners and help meet their needs.

promoting the practice of circumcision, they are seeking to identify publicly as Jews and thereby avoid persecution. In Greco-Roman society, Jews tended to be accepted more readily than Christians.

6:14 world has been crucified to me Paul states that he has died to the values of the world: selfishness, ambition and pride.

6:15 Neither circumcision nor uncircumcision means anything Here, Paul puts circumcision in its proper place: It cannot define the status of the believer, nor can it transform the believer. What matters for Paul is the new-creation work of God, through Christ's death and resurrection and the indwelling power of his Spirit.

6:16 Israel of God There are several ways of understanding this phrase. It could indicate those who come to faith in Christ and follow the rule described in Gal 6:15. It also could refer specifically to believing Jews.

6:17 the marks of Jesus Paul refers to the persecution he endured for preaching the gospel message (e.g., Ac 14:19; 21:30–32). Paul interprets his suffering on behalf of the gospel in terms of Jesus' crucifixion, because he shares in it (Gal 2:19–20; 6:14).

6:18 grace of our Lord Paul closes most of his letters with a reference to grace (e.g., Ro 16:20; 1Co 16:23; Php 4:23).

EPHESIANS

INTRODUCTION TO EPHESIANS

Ephesians gives a cosmic view of God's plans for the world, explaining the mystery of the gospel. Because of Jesus' death, all people can receive the gift of forgiveness for their trespasses against God and others (Eph 1:3–10; 2:1–8). Through the sacrifice of Christ, God has brought believers in Jesus—Jews and non-Jews alike—together as one new humanity (2:11–18). God shows no partiality (6:9).

BACKGROUND

The letter identifies Paul as the author (1:1; 3:1), and sources from the early church unanimously affirm that he wrote Ephesians. However, there is some modern debate about its authorship. This debate centers around the letter lacking personal greetings at the end (as Paul's letters usually do), the difference in writing style and emphasis from his other letters (outside of Colossians), and the suggestion that someone may have imitated Colossians when composing Ephesians. However, the arguments against Paul's authorship are far from conclusive and could be explained by Paul dictating to a different scribe and other factors.

The oldest copies of Ephesians do not name the city of Ephesus in the opening verse. Paul apparently spent a lot of time there (Ac 19:8–10; 20:31), but some statements in the letter suggest that he might not know the recipients (Eph 1:15; 3:2). Along with the unusual style and emphasis, these statements could indicate that Ephesians was a circular letter, sent to multiple churches in Asia Minor. In this view, the letter eventually came to be associated with Ephesus because it was the most prominent city in the area.

This map depicts the location of Ephesus and the surrounding region.

Paul wrote Ephesians from prison (3:1; 6:20), perhaps in Rome, Caesarea or even Ephesus itself (if it was a circular letter). If written from Ephesus, the letter likely was composed around AD 54–57. If writing from Caesarea or Rome, Paul likely wrote the letter ca. AD 58–63. It seems that his audience consisted mainly of non-Jewish Christians (2:11–22; 3:1,6; 4:17–24). Paul emphasizes Christ's exaltation above all powers (1:20–23; 2:2) and instructs believers to stay strong in Christ against the schemes of the devil (6:10–20). These believers may have been tempted by the notion that other authorities could have some claim on them.

STRUCTURE

Unlike Paul's other writings, Ephesians reads more like a sermon—a style that supports it being intended to circulate among multiple churches. Nonetheless, Ephesians does include some standard features of a letter, including an opening salutation (1:1–2) and a conclusion and benediction (6:21–24). The body of the letter includes two broad sections: an opening theological section (1:3—3:21) and a second section that builds on that theology (4:1—6:20). Paul begins the first section by praising God for blessings in Christ (1:3–14) and praying that readers might know God's hope, glory and power (1:15–23). He emphasizes that they have been made alive in Christ (2:1–10) and that Jews and non-Jews (Gentiles) are united into a new humanity (2:11–22). Then Paul speaks about his own mission to proclaim this gospel (3:1–13), and he prays that believers will know the fullness of Christ's love (3:14–21).

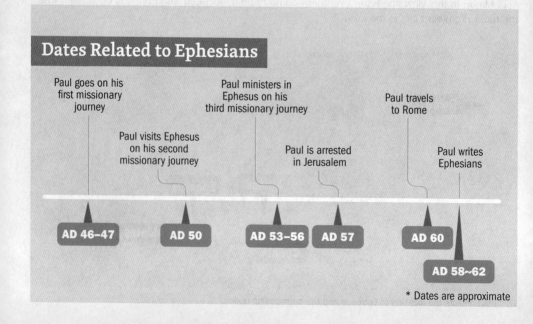

Dates Related to Ephesians

Paul goes on his first missionary journey

Paul visits Ephesus on his second missionary journey

Paul ministers in Ephesus on his third missionary journey

Paul is arrested in Jerusalem

Paul travels to Rome

Paul writes Ephesians

AD 46–47   AD 50   AD 53–56   AD 57   AD 60

AD 58~62

* Dates are approximate

In the second section, Paul urges his readers to live in light of these truths. They should seek unity (4:1–6) and use their gifts for ministry (4:7–16). They should put away their old life and embrace a new one characterized by wisdom and the Spirit (4:17—5:20). Then Paul provides instructions for each member of the typical Greco-Roman household (5:21—6:9). Finally, he tells readers to put on the armor of God to withstand evil powers (6:10–20).

OUTLINE

- Salutation (1:1–2)
- God's work of reconciliation in Christ (1:3—3:21)
- Living in response to God's work in Christ (4:1—6:20)
- Conclusion and benediction (6:21–24)

THEMES

The main theme of Ephesians is unity in Christ. All things are held together in Christ (1:10), and Christians need to consciously resist forces that seek to divide them. They are to live as people who have been saved by Jesus and who speak the truth and avoid evil; they are to seek unity with one another but avoid deceptive people (4:17—5:20).

In the church, God has created one unified people out of groups that previously were hostile toward each other. Every relationship is redefined, including those between Jews and non-Jews, and those within each household (5:21—6:9). The church itself is the household of God, built on Jesus as the cornerstone (2:19–22). Origin, race or status should not be a source of division.

Yet the powers of evil seek to divide people against one another and against God (6:12), but Jesus enables believers to overcome evil and remain united. Unity and peace among God's people are signs of Christ's supremacy: He can do what no one else can. The peace that Christ gives and his incorruptible love is the answer to our conflicts and difficulties and must be boldly proclaimed (6:19–20,23–24).

1 Paul, an apostle of Christ Jesus by the will of God,

To God's holy people in Ephesus,[a] the faithful in Christ Jesus:

[2]Grace and peace to you from God our Father and the Lord Jesus Christ.

Praise for Spiritual Blessings in Christ

[3]Praise be to the God and Father of our Lord Jesus Christ, who has blessed us in the heavenly realms with every spiritual blessing in Christ. [4]For he chose us in him before the creation of the world to be holy and blameless in his sight. In love [5]he[b] predestined us for adoption to sonship[c] through Jesus Christ, in accordance with his pleasure and will — [6]to the praise of his glorious grace, which he has freely given us in the One he loves. [7]In him we have redemption through his blood, the forgiveness of sins, in accordance with the riches of God's grace [8]that he lavished on us. With all wisdom and understanding, [9]he[d] made

[a] 1 Some early manuscripts do not have *in Ephesus.*
[b] 4,5 Or *sight in love.* [5]He   [c] 5 The Greek word for *adoption to sonship* is a legal term referring to the full legal standing of an adopted male heir in Roman culture.   [d] 8,9 Or *us with all wisdom and understanding.* [9]And he

---

1:1–2 The oldest copies of this letter do not include the Greek phrase *en epheso* ("in Ephesus") in Eph 1:1, which may indicate that Ephesus was not the original destination. Ephesians might have been a circular letter—one that was intentionally written for a wide audience and sent to multiple places. If so, it could be the letter mentioned in Col 4:16 as being sent to the church at Laodicea. The reference to Ephesus might have been inserted later, perhaps to reflect the letter's first destination. Since Paul had spent several years in Ephesus (Ac 19:10), several statements in the text implying that Paul was unfamiliar with his audience (Eph 1:15; 3:2) lend support to the circular-letter theory.

It is possible that Paul was even imprisoned in Ephesus when he wrote this letter; if so, it likely was composed around AD 54–57. Paul also could have written it from Caesarea (AD 58–60) or Rome (early 60s AD; see note on Php 1:7).

Paul begins this letter in the customary fashion for Greco-Roman letters: He identifies himself and his audience and offers his typical greeting of grace and peace (see Ro 1:7; 1Co 1:3; 2Co 1:2).

1:1 Paul, an apostle See note on Ro 1:1. See the table "Pauline Self-Designations" on p. 1904. **God's holy people** The Greek word used here, *hagioi,* refers to those who are set apart or who belong to God, not to the moral quality of being without sin. In the OT, this designation is reserved for angels or members of the covenant community (see Dt 7:6; Ps 89:5,7). Here, Paul applies the term to Gentile believers who—he will argue later—are now incorporated into the people of God (Eph 2:11–20; 3:6). **Ephesus** A harbor city located in southwest Asia Minor (modern-day Turkey); capital of the Roman province of Asia. See the infographic "Ephesus in Paul's Day" on p. 1939.

1:2 Grace and peace to you See note on Ro 1:7.

1:3–14 In the Greek text of Ephesians, Paul uses one long sentence stretching from Eph 1:3 to v. 14. He praises God for his blessings, which are mediated through Christ, and introduces the letter's major themes, including God's plan of salvation (vv. 5,9) and the work of the Spirit (v. 14).

1:3 Praise be This expression of praise in known in Hebrew as the *berakhah,* which means blessing (compare Ps 66:20; 1Pe 1:3). Paul praises God for what he has done through Christ and reminds believers of their status and privileges in Christ. Paul's blessing highlights the roles of the Father (Eph 1:3–4), Christ (vv. 5–7) and the Spirit (vv. 13–14). **Father** Paul's preferred designation for God in his letters (e.g., Ro 1:7; 1Co 8:6; Php 2:11). **heav-**

enly realms See Eph 1:20 and note. **every spiritual blessing** Refers to the range of blessings in vv. 3–14 made available in Christ. The blessings listed in this passage should be understood in their entirety, rather than as individual blessings. Together, these blessings express the full scope of God's redemptive activity. **in Christ** Refers to the believer's union and identification with Christ. Paul repeats this phrase throughout the letter to emphasize the work of Christ and the blessings that believers obtain through him.

1:4 he chose Here Paul applies to believers a concept that formerly applied to Israel alone (see Dt 7:6–8; compare Ro 9:11 and note; 2Th 2:13 and note). Just as God chose Israel as his treasured possession, he now elects believers to receive the blessings mediated through Christ. **holy** Refers to being dedicated to or set apart for God.

1:5 predestined The Greek word used here, *proorizo,* means "to choose" or "to decide beforehand." Paul uses the verb *proorizo* five times in his letters (Ro 8:29–30; 1Co 2:7; Eph 1:5,11). In every instance, God is the one who predestines; salvation as an overall plan depends on his will and authority. In Paul's time, many people believed that various supernatural forces controlled human destiny, and some used magic, believing they could manipulate these forces to escape harm and secure good fortune (e.g., Ac 8:9–25; 19:11–20). In this letter, Paul addresses the need for people to stand firm in the Lord against all other forces (Eph 6:10–20). Paul wants believers to understand that salvation is the result of God's purposes, which is independent of time, hostile forces and personal achievement. Believers should not worry about spiritual powers and authorities, nor should they take credit for being chosen by God; rather, they should recognize God's mercy and give him praise. **adoption** Paul uses this metaphor to illustrate believers' privileges in Christ. As children of God, they now have a heavenly inheritance (1:11–14). Compare Gal 4:5 and note.

1:6 the One he loves A reference to Jesus. In the OT, the Israelites (or specific tribes) are sometimes referred to as beloved to emphasize their status as God's chosen people (e.g., Dt 33:12; Isa 5:1; Jer 12:7). The Gospels use similar language to refer to Jesus as God's beloved son (e.g., Mt 3:17; Mk 9:7; Lk 3:22; compare 2Pe 1:17), and Paul describes Jesus similarly elsewhere (Col 1:13). Paul often applies similar terminology to believers (e.g., Eph 5:1; 1Th 1:4; Ro 9:25).

1:7 redemption The Greek word used here, *apolytrosis,* refers to the act of paying to free a slave. See also Col 1:14 and note. **through his blood** Refers to Jesus' sacrificial death on the cross (Ro 3:24; Rev 5:9).

1:9 mystery In Paul's writings, the Greek word used

known to us the mystery of his will according to his good pleasure, which he purposed in Christ, ¹⁰to be put into effect when the times reach their fulfillment — to bring unity to all things in heaven and on earth under Christ.

¹¹In him we were also chosen,ᵃ having been predestined according to the plan of him who works out everything in conformity with the purpose of his will, ¹²in order that we, who were the first to put our hope in Christ, might be for the praise of his glory. ¹³And you also were included in Christ when you heard the message of

ᵃ 11 Or were made heirs

here, *mystērion*, refers to God's plan of salvation, which was formerly kept secret but is now revealed in Christ. This plan includes the unification of Jews and Gentiles into one new people of God (Eph 3:3,5–6,9).
1:10 effect The Greek word used here, *oikonomia*, can refer to God's plan of salvation or to the sphere of Jesus' authority during his earthly life. **times reach their fulfillment** God's previously hidden plan has now been revealed to believers through Christ, the focal point of God's redemptive activity (compare 3:1–9). **to bring unity to** The Greek verb used here, *anakephalaioō*, means "to sum up" or "head up." Later in Ephesians, Paul describes Christ as the "head" (*kephalē*) of the church (1:22–23; 4:15; 5:23). **heaven and on earth**

God's work in Christ extends over all creation, including the heavens (see 1:20 and note).
1:11 we Reflecting Paul's own ethnicity, "we" likely refers to Jews — God's chosen people (in the OT) and those from whom the Messiah came (see Mt 10:5 and note, 10:6; 15:24 and note; Ac 1:8 and note; Ro 1:16 and note). This means that "you" often refers to Gentiles (non-Jews), including most of the believers in Ephesus and the surrounding areas (see Eph 2:11; 3:1). Compare note on 2:17.
1:12 glory Denotes honor and majesty. See note on Ro 1:23.
1:13 you Paul stresses that the same inheritance (Eph 1:14) God gave to Jews is also made available

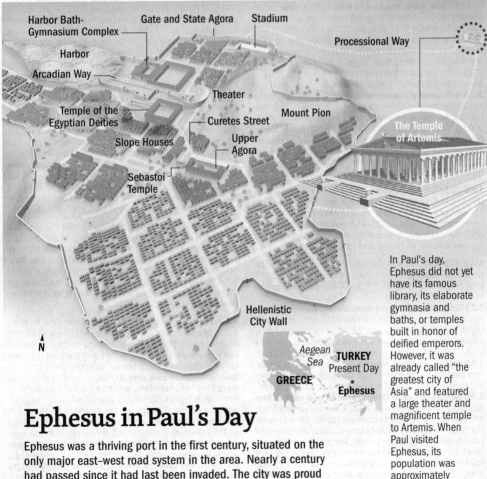

Harbor Bath-Gymnasium Complex

Gate and State Agora

Stadium

Processional Way

Harbor

Arcadian Way

Theater

Temple of the Egyptian Deities

Curetes Street

Mount Pion

The Temple of Artemis

Slope Houses

Upper Agora

Sebastoi Temple

Hellenistic City Wall

N

Aegean Sea

TURKEY Present Day

GREECE

Ephesus

In Paul's day, Ephesus did not yet have its famous library, its elaborate gymnasia and baths, or temples built in honor of deified emperors. However, it was already called "the greatest city of Asia" and featured a large theater and magnificent temple to Artemis. When Paul visited Ephesus, its population was approximately 250,000 people.

Ephesus in Paul's Day

Ephesus was a thriving port in the first century, situated on the only major east–west road system in the area. Nearly a century had passed since it had last been invaded. The city was proud and prosperous, and a strong Jewish community thrived there.

truth, the gospel of your salvation. When you believed, you were marked in him with a seal, the promised Holy Spirit, [14]who is a deposit guaranteeing our inheritance until the redemption of those who are God's possession — to the praise of his glory.

Thanksgiving and Prayer

[15]For this reason, ever since I heard about your faith in the Lord Jesus and your love for all God's people, [16]I have not stopped giving thanks for you, remembering you in my prayers. [17]I keep asking that the God of our Lord Jesus Christ, the glorious Father, may give you the Spirit[a] of wisdom and revelation, so that you may know him better. [18]I pray that the eyes of your heart may be enlightened in order that you may know the hope to which he has called you, the riches of his glorious inheritance in his holy people, [19]and his incomparably great power for us who believe.

That power is the same as the mighty strength [20]he exerted when he raised Christ from the dead and seated him at his right hand in the heavenly realms, [21]far above all rule and authority, power and dominion, and every name that is invoked, not only in the present age but also in the one to come. [22]And God placed all things under his feet and appointed him to be head over everything for the church, [23]which is his body, the fullness of him who fills everything in every way.

Made Alive in Christ

2 As for you, you were dead in your transgressions and sins, [2]in which you used to live when you followed the ways of this world and of the ruler of the kingdom of the air, the spirit who is now at work in those who are disobedient. [3]All of us also lived among them at one time, gratifying

[a] 17 Or a spirit

---

to non-Jews according to God's revealed mystery (v. 9; 3:3–9). **you were marked in him with a seal** In the ancient world, a seal indicated ownership and protection (compare Da 6:17 and note; 2Co 1:22). The notion of sealing in this context is related to the day of judgment: Sealed believers will be kept for their ultimate inheritance — redemption at the end of the age (Eph 1:14) — by the gift of the promised Spirit (Eze 36:26–27; Joel 2:28–30), which is given to Jews and Gentiles alike. **1:14 a deposit guaranteeing** The gift of the Holy Spirit not only empowers believers to live holy lives (Eph 3:16), but also serves as a guarantee and reminder that God will one day fully complete his work in believers. **inheritance** Refers to the complete experience of the salvation that God promises to his people but which they have yet to receive in full. This experience culminates in their redemption upon Jesus' return.

1:15–23 After elaborately praising God for his blessings (vv. 3–14), Paul expresses thankfulness for the believers. The prayer in vv. 15–23 is the first of two prayers in the letter (compare 3:14–21) that, together, enclose Paul's discussions on God's work of reconciliation (2:1–22) and his own role within God's plan (3:1–13).

1:15 For this reason Connects Paul's prayer to the preceding blessing section. Paul's thanksgiving for God's plan of salvation in Christ in 1:3–14 overflows into prayer in vv. 15–23.

1:17 Spirit of wisdom and revelation The Greek text here may refer to an attitude or disposition that the Holy Spirit brings to a person's life: one willing to receive and communicate the things of God. Alternatively, the text may refer to the Holy Spirit and attributes that characterize the Spirit. **1:18 hope** The Greek word used here, *elpis*, refers in this context to the fullness of salvation that believers will experience at Christ's return (see v. 14 and note). **1:20 he raised Christ from the dead and seated him** Jesus' resurrection displayed God's power over death and his approval of his Son (compare Isa 53:10 and note; Isa 53:12 and note). Crucifixion was the most shameful punishment in the ancient world. For many Jews, Jesus' death on the cross would have indicated that he was not the Messiah, God's anointed deliverer (see Gal 3:13 and note). Jesus' resurrection, however, demonstrated his triumph over death and affirmed his Messianic role and

authority. For this reason, the resurrection became the focus of Paul's preaching (e.g., Ac 2:32; 4:10; 5:30). **right hand** Implies that Christ holds a position of honor and authority with God the Father. This idea comes from Ps 110:1, which early Christians frequently cited to affirm their belief that God had raised Christ to a position of divine power over evil powers (e.g., Ac 2:34–35; see Ps 110:1 and note). **heavenly realms** A reference to the spiritual world to which believers now have access through Christ. In this realm believers experience spiritual blessings and share in Christ's authority over evil forces (compare Eph 1:3; 2:6; 3:10).

1:21 rule and authority, power and dominion This phrase seems to refer to angelic or evil forces of power in the heavenly places (see 1:20 and note). Paul argues that Christ has ultimate dominion over all things. **also in the one to come** Within Judaism time was generally divided into two ages — the current one, when God's rule is not fully manifest, and the coming one, when God will reveal his sovereign rule as king (see Mt 12:32; Mk 10:30).

2:1–10 Paul's prayer (Eph 1:15–23) refers to Gentiles (non-Jews) becoming part of God's family. In this chapter, Paul discusses how that happens: Christ's victory over evil powers makes reconciliation with God possible. Paul begins by reminding his readers that they lived in alienation from God (2:1–3). He then describes the blessings that believers receive as a result of being reconciled to God through Christ (vv. 4–10).

2:1 you Paul is referring here to non-Jews (see note on 1:11). **dead** Refers to being separated from God and under the rule of the evil one (see 2:2 and note). Paul's use of the metaphor of death is significant, as it allows for no middle ground; a person is either dead or alive. **transgressions and sins** The Greek words used here, *paraptōma* and *hamartia*, describe the evil that controls and characterizes human life apart from God. They are both the cause of death and the evidence of death. **2:2 ways** The Greek word used here, *aiōn*, may refer to the mindset, customs and practices of those who are estranged from God. Alternatively, it could indicate a hostile force in opposition to God and his people (i.e., the devil). **the ruler of the kingdom of the air** Refers to the devil (compare Jn 14:30; 2Co 4:4) or the evil one (Eph 6:16). Many people in the ancient Near East

the cravings of our flesh[a] and following its desires and thoughts. Like the rest, we were by nature deserving of wrath. [4]But because of his great love for us, God, who is rich in mercy, [5]made us alive with Christ even when we were dead in transgressions — it is by grace you have been saved. [6]And God raised us up with Christ and seated us with him in the heavenly realms in Christ Jesus, [7]in order that in the coming ages he might show the incomparable riches of his grace, expressed in his kindness to us in Christ Jesus. [8]For it is by grace you have been saved, through faith — and this is not from yourselves, it is the gift of God — [9]not by works, so that no one can boast. [10]For we are God's handiwork, created in Christ Jesus to do good works, which God prepared in advance for us to do.

Jew and Gentile Reconciled Through Christ

[11]Therefore, remember that formerly you who are Gentiles by birth and called "uncircumcised" by those who call themselves "the circumcision" (which is done in the body by human hands) — [12]remember that at that time you were separate from Christ, excluded from citizenship in Israel and foreigners to the covenants of the promise, without hope and without God in the world. [13]But now in Christ Jesus you who once were far away have been brought near by the blood of Christ.

[14]For he himself is our peace, who has made the two groups one and has destroyed the barrier, the dividing wall of hostility, [15]by setting aside in his flesh the law with its commands and regulations. His purpose was to create in himself one new humanity out of the two, thus making peace, [16]and in one body to reconcile both of them to God through the cross, by which he put to death their hostility. [17]He came and preached peace to you who were far away and peace to those who were

---

[a] 3 In contexts like this, the Greek word for *flesh* (*sarx*) refers to the sinful state of human beings, often presented as a power in opposition to the Spirit.

---

believed that the air (*aēr*) — the sphere between heaven and earth — was the residence of evil spirits. Before the Ephesian believers were in Christ, they lived under the influence of the world and the evil one. Paul uses many titles to refer to the devil — most commonly the Greek term *satanas* ("Satan"), probably intended as a proper name (see Ro 16:20; 1Co 5:5; 7:5; 2Co 2:11; 11:14; 12:7; 1Th 2:18; 2Th 2:9; 1Ti 1:20; 5:15). Paul sees Satan as an apocalyptic figure who, along with all evil forces, is destined for defeat (Ro 16:20). However, until that final judgment comes, Satan remains powerful in the world.
2:3 wrath Refers to God's righteous judgment upon evil.
2:5 made us alive with Christ Through union with Christ, believers receive new life that reverses the effects of death (see note on 2:1; compare Ro 6:4–11; Jn 3:16–17). **it is by grace** The basis of salvation is grace — God's undeserved generosity toward people. **you have been saved** In this context, the Greek word used here, *sōzō*, refers to God delivering people from death and giving them life.
2:6 raised us up with Christ Because believers are identified with Christ's resurrection, they also share in life that is no longer subject to death. **seated us with him** Believers share Christ's position of authority at the right hand of God by virtue of their union with Christ. See Eph 1:20 and note. **heavenly realms** See note on v. 20.
2:8 gift of God People cannot accomplish salvation through their own effort.
2:9 works In this context, the Greek word used here, *ergon*, may refer to the Jewish law or to specific components of the law that are related to Jewish ethnic identity (i.e., circumcision, food laws, Sabbath observance). The idea of works also might include any actions motivated by a desire to earn favor or right standing with God.
2:10 good works Different from the works of 2:9. Here Paul is talking about acts of faithfulness and service to God. Compare Col 1:10.

2:11–22 In this passage, which continues the discussion of Eph 2:1–10, Paul presents the broader scope of God's reconciliation — one new humanity saved in Christ, composed of both Jews and non-Jews alike.

2:11 uncircumcised A derogatory term emphasizing that non-Jewish people are outsiders in relation to God's covenant with Israel. This category includes most members of the churches planted or empowered by Paul. **who call themselves "the circumcision"** Refers to Jewish people. **by human hands** The Greek word used here, *cheiropoiētos*, portrays circumcision as a human rite. In the Septuagint (the ancient Greek translation of the OT), this word is used to refer to idols (e.g., Lev 26:1; Isa 2:18; 10:11; Da 5:4).
2:12 the covenants of the promise Refers to the covenants between God and his people in the OT. Paul probably is referring to the covenants God made with Abraham (Ge 15:7–21; 17:1–21), Isaac (Ge 26:2–5), Jacob (Ge 28:13–15), Moses (Ex 24:1–8) and David (2Sa 7:14–16). Each of these covenants involved a promise from God.
2:14 peace Paul echoes Isaiah's description of God's Messiah as the Prince of Peace (see Isa 9:6). Isaiah prophesied that the Messiah would end hostility and establish an era of well-being. Christ produces this peace; he is the essence of it. He brings harmony and wholeness to people's relationship with God and one another, a theme that fits with Paul's purpose of unifying Jews and Gentiles. **made the two groups one** The external distinctions between Jews and Gentiles are no longer grounds for hostility and division (compare Eph 3:6). This is the core message of the letter. **barrier, the dividing wall** Probably a figurative reference to the law (see 2:15). Alternatively (or perhaps additionally), this phrase might refer to the wall in the Jerusalem temple that divided the Court of the Gentiles from the Jewish areas. See the infographic "Herod's Temple" on p. 1626. **of hostility** Refers to hostility between Jews and Gentiles.
2:15 in his flesh Here, Paul refers to Jesus' physical body that was crucified. **the law** Christ's death on the cross fulfills the Law of Moses (primarily seen in the books of Exodus, Leviticus, Numbers and Deuteronomy) and removes the necessity of the regulations that once divided Jews from Gentiles (compare Ro 10:4; Gal 3:23–25). **one new humanity** Refers to Jews and Gentiles (non-Jewish people) being united in Christ.
2:16 in one body Refers to the church, comprised of Jews and Gentiles. **reconcile** Christ's death makes it possible for the hostility that often existed between Jews and Gentiles to be destroyed and for them to be restored together to God.
2:17 you who were far away Refers to Gentiles

near. [18]For through him we both have access to the Father by one Spirit.

[19]Consequently, you are no longer foreigners and strangers, but fellow citizens with God's people and also members of his household, [20]built on the foundation of the apostles and prophets, with Christ Jesus himself as the chief cornerstone. [21]In him the whole building is joined together and rises to become a holy temple in the Lord. [22]And in him you too are being built together to become a dwelling in which God lives by his Spirit.

God's Marvelous Plan for the Gentiles

3 For this reason I, Paul, the prisoner of Christ Jesus for the sake of you Gentiles —

[2]Surely you have heard about the administration of God's grace that was given to me for you, [3]that is, the mystery made known to me by revelation, as I have already written briefly. [4]In reading this, then, you will be able to understand my insight into the mystery of Christ, [5]which was not made known to people in other generations as it has now been revealed by the Spirit to God's holy apostles and prophets. [6]This mystery is that through the gospel the Gentiles are heirs together with Israel, members together of one body, and sharers together in the promise in Christ Jesus.

[7]I became a servant of this gospel by the gift of God's grace given me through the working of his power. [8]Although I am less than the least of all the Lord's people, this grace was given me: to preach to the Gentiles the boundless riches of Christ, [9]and to make plain to everyone the administration of this mystery, which for ages past was kept hidden in God, who created all things. [10]His intent was that

---

(non-Jewish people). **those who were near** Refers to Jews. Paul's use of the terminology near and far echoes the words of the prophet Isaiah. Isaiah 52:7 speaks of preaching good news of peace, and in Isa 57:19 Yahweh speaks peace to those near and far. Paul likely regarded Christ's preaching to those near (Jews) and far (Gentiles) as a fulfillment of Isaiah's hope of salvation — not just for Jews, but for all humanity (Isa 49:6; 56:6–8).

2:18 have access The Greek expression used here refers to the privilege to address one's superior. In the OT Scriptures, God provided specific instructions for building the tabernacle (Ex 26). He designated it as his dwelling, the place of worship and sacrifice. God gave the priesthood access to this tent to perform various duties, but he restricted other Israelites from it. Because of Christ's sacrificial death and the indwelling presence of the Spirit, believers — individually and corporately — have become the temple of God (Eph 2:21). See the infographic "The Tabernacle" on p. 138.

2:19 members of his household Although Gentiles used to be outsiders, they now belong to God's family. God has adopted Jew and Gentile alike through his Son, Jesus Christ (1:5).

2:20 apostles and prophets Refers to the early leaders of the church who imparted God's message to the people. The apostles include the twelve apostles who knew Jesus during his earthly ministry (with Matthias replacing Judas Iscariot; see Ac 1:15–26) as well as Paul, and perhaps others (see Ac 14:14). The prophets may include other influential leaders who were outside of the circle of apostles (compare Ac 13:1; 1Co 12:28; Eph 3:5; 4:11). Alternatively, the prophets may refer to people with the gift of prophecy (Ro 12:6; 1Co 12:10), or Paul could be pointing to the role of the OT prophets in laying the foundation for God's work through Christ. **cornerstone** Refers to the first and most important stone laid in a new building. Proper placement of a cornerstone ensured a straight and level foundation. Applied to Christ, this metaphor shows Christ's central role in the church. See Ac 4:11 and note; compare note on Mt 21:42; note on Ps 118:22.

2:21 holy temple The temple in Jerusalem had an outer area called the Court of the Gentiles. Gentiles could not enter the temple courtyard; they were segregated from the Jews. Through Christ's work of reconciliation, Gentiles are brought together with Jews (see Eph 2:14 and note). See the infographic "Herod's Temple" on p. 1626.

2:22 a dwelling in which God lives The temple in Jerusalem was destroyed by the Romans in AD 70, but it was still standing when Paul wrote the letter to the Ephesians. He boldly suggests that believers have become the location of God's presence on earth — the place where he is glorified on earth.

3:1–13 After discussing God's cosmic work of reconciliation (2:1–22), Paul now explains his role within the mystery of the gospel (3:2–12). He also urges his readers not to worry about the sufferings caused by his imprisonment (v. 13).

3:1 prisoner of Christ Jesus Ephesians is one of four letters that Paul wrote from prison (along with Philippians, Colossians and Philemon). The location and time of this imprisonment are unclear (see note on Php 1:7).

3:2 administration of God's grace that was given to me for you Refers to Paul's calling as apostle to the Gentiles — one of God's chosen agents to preach the gospel to non-Jewish people (compare Ro 1:5; 15:15–16; Gal 2:9). See note on Gal 1:16.

3:3 mystery The Greek word used here, *mystērion*, refers in this context to God's plan of salvation through Christ (see note on Eph 3:4). **by revelation** Paul affirms that he received God's plan of salvation directly from God (Ac 9:1–7; Gal 1:11–12). **as I have already written briefly** Possibly refers to 1:9–10 or 2:11–22, or to an earlier letter (unknown today).

3:4 the mystery of Christ Paul explains this phrase in v. 6: Through Christ's death and resurrection, God has invited Gentiles (non-Jews) to join his people — expanding the scope of his salvation to include the entire world, not just Israel (compare Isa 49:6; Gal 3:8). This stunning revelation is the heart of Paul's gospel and missionary work. Compare Ro 11:13–16.

3:5 apostles and prophets See note on Eph 2:20.

3:6 heirs together As God's chosen people, the Jews were heirs of the blessings promised to Abraham (Ge 17:4–8; Ro 9:4–5). Through Christ, non-Jews also become heirs of God's promise (see note on Eph 3:4; Gal 3:29).

3:7 servant The Greek word used here, *diakonos*, is the basis of the English word "deacon." Paul often uses this

now, through the church, the manifold wisdom of God should be made known to the rulers and authorities in the heavenly realms, [11]according to his eternal purpose that he accomplished in Christ Jesus our Lord. [12]In him and through faith in him we may approach God with freedom and confidence. [13]I ask you, therefore, not to be discouraged because of my sufferings for you, which are your glory.

A Prayer for the Ephesians

[14]For this reason I kneel before the Father, [15]from whom every family[a] in heaven and on earth derives its name. [16]I pray that out of his glorious riches he may strengthen you with power through his Spirit in your inner being, [17]so that Christ may dwell in your hearts through faith. And I pray that you, being rooted and established in love, [18]may have power, together with all the Lord's holy people, to grasp how wide and long and high and deep is the love of Christ, [19]and to know this love that surpasses knowledge — that you may be filled to the measure of all the fullness of God.

[20]Now to him who is able to do immeasurably more than all we ask or imagine, according to his power that is at work within us, [21]to him be glory in the church and in Christ Jesus throughout all generations, for ever and ever! Amen.

Unity and Maturity in the Body of Christ

4 As a prisoner for the Lord, then, I urge you to live a life worthy of the calling you have received. [2]Be completely humble and gentle; be patient, bearing with one another in love. [3]Make every effort to keep the unity of the Spirit through the bond of peace. [4]There is one body and one Spirit, just as you were called to one hope when you were called; [5]one Lord, one faith, one baptism; [6]one God and Father of all, who is over all and through all and in all.

[a] 15 The Greek for *family* (*patria*) is derived from the Greek for *father* (*pater*).

---

term to describe himself and his coworkers as servants or ministers (e.g., 1Co 3:5; Col 1:25; 4:7).
3:8 least of all the Lord's people Paul considered himself the least because he had persecuted the church prior to becoming a Christ-follower (1Co 15:9; compare Ac 9:4; 1Ti 1:15–16). **boundless riches of Christ** Refers to the blessings made available through Christ (Eph 1:3–8).
3:9 this mystery, which for ages past was kept hidden See vv. 3–6; note on v. 4. Paul means that the fullness of God's plan, and how it all would come together, was not known.
3:10 manifold wisdom Refers to God's plan of salvation through the death and resurrection of Jesus (compare 1Co 1:21–31; 2:6–8). **rulers and authorities** Refers to spiritual enemies of God (see Eph 1:21 and note). These forces were kept ignorant of Christ's role — that his death and resurrection would be the catalyst for redeeming Gentile people groups.
3:11 his eternal purpose Relates to God's plan of salvation (compare note on 2:5).
3:12 approach God with freedom Through Christ, believers are reconciled to God.
3:13 my sufferings Refers to Paul's imprisonment (v. 1). See the infographic "The Tullianum: A Prison in Rome" on p. 2008. **which are your glory** Indicates that Paul's hardships have contributed to the believers' life with Christ in the age to come — when Jesus returns and makes all things right.

3:14–21 Paul resumes the prayer he began in v. 1. It includes an introduction (vv. 14–15), a multifaceted request (vv. 16–19) and a blessing (vv. 20–21).

3:15 derives its name In the ancient Near East, naming something amounted to bringing it into existence, giving it identity and exercising authority over it. Since all creation derives its name from the Father, he is both its source and its ruler (compare Ge 1:1–5; Ps 147:4; Isa 40:26).
3:16 he may strengthen you with power The prayer's central appeal. The statements that follow branch off from this main request. **your inner being** God empowers believers through his indwelling presence in their lives.

3:17 Paul restates the prayer's central appeal, identifying the presence of Christ with the empowerment of the Spirit (Eph 3:16). Just as the church is becoming a holy temple for God (2:21–22), so the individual believer receives the presence of Christ (compare Gal 2:20).

3:17 may dwell The Greek word used here, *katoikeō*, carries the sense of residing permanently. **in your hearts** The heart in ancient Greek and Jewish thought represents the essential aspects of existence and identity: the inner being, will and intelligence. **in love** Refers to God's love (Eph 2:4).
3:18 wide and long and high and deep Evokes the boundless nature of Christ's love.
3:19 surpasses knowledge The love of Christ is beyond human comprehension. **fullness of God** This could refer to the blessings of God (1:3–8) or to his perfection and completeness. Compare note on Col 1:19.

4:1–3 In Eph 1–3, Paul affirms that Gentiles (non-Jews) have been reconciled to God and brought into his people. That discussion provides the starting point for chs. 4–6, where Paul explains how believers should live in the unity and peace accomplished through Christ (2:11–22). Paul begins by emphasizing the oneness of God's people (4:1–6). The material in vv. 4–6 might reflect an early Christian confession of faith (compare 1Co 8:6).

4:1 prisoner for the Lord See note on Eph 3:1.
4:2 humble and gentle; be patient Compare Gal 5:22–23. **bearing with one another** Compare Php 2:1–5.
4:3 unity of the Spirit Refers to unity that can only exist because of the work of the Holy Spirit. **bond of peace** Earlier, Paul portrays Christ as the personification of peace (Eph 2:14). The work of Christ leads to peace between God and humanity and between Jews and Gentiles (2:15).
4:4 one body and one Spirit Compare 1Co 12:12–14.

[7]But to each one of us grace has been given as Christ apportioned it. [8]This is why it[a] says:

"When he ascended on high,
    he took many captives
    and gave gifts to his people."[b]

[9](What does "he ascended" mean except that he also descended to the lower, earthly regions[c]? [10]He who descended is the very one who ascended higher than all the heavens, in order to fill the whole universe.) [11]So Christ himself gave the apostles, the prophets, the evangelists, the pastors and teachers, [12]to equip his people for works of service, so that the body of Christ may be built up [13]until we all reach unity in the faith and in the knowledge of the Son of God and become mature, attaining to the whole measure of the fullness of Christ.

[14]Then we will no longer be infants, tossed back and forth by the waves, and blown here and there by every wind of teaching and by the cunning and craftiness of people in their deceitful scheming. [15]Instead, speaking the truth in love, we will grow to become in every respect the mature body of him who is the head, that is, Christ. [16]From him the whole body, joined and held together by every supporting ligament, grows and builds itself up in love, as each part does its work.

Instructions for Christian Living

[17]So I tell you this, and insist on it in the Lord, that you must no longer live as the Gentiles do, in the futility of their thinking. [18]They are darkened in their understanding and separated from the life of God because of the ignorance that is in them due to the hardening of their hearts. [19]Having lost all sensitivity, they have given themselves over to sensuality so as to indulge in every kind of impurity, and they are full of greed.

[20]That, however, is not the way of life you learned [21]when you heard about Christ and were taught in him in accordance with the truth that is in Jesus. [22]You were taught, with regard to your former way of life, to put off your old self, which is being corrupted by its deceitful desires; [23]to be made new in the attitude of your minds; [24]and to put on the new self, created to be like God in true righteousness and holiness.

[25]Therefore each of you must put off falsehood and speak truthfully to your neighbor, for we are

[a] 8 Or God   [b] 8 Psalm 68:18   [c] 9 Or the depths of the earth

---

4:7–16 In this passage, Paul focuses on God's gifts that build up the body of Christ (the church).

4:7 grace In this context, the Greek word used here, *charis*, likely refers to a believer's God-given calling and ability to serve in ministry. Paul associated God's grace with his vocation as apostle to the Gentiles (Eph 3:2).

4:8 Paul quotes Ps 68:18 in reference to Christ's ascension (Ac 1:9). Psalm 68:15–18 describes God defeating evil at Mount Bashan, which represented the gateway to the underworld in Israelite and Canaanite thought. Paul quotes the psalm to express Christ's victory over evil powers (Eph 1:19–22; compare Col 2:15).

4:8 gave gifts to his people The psalm Paul quotes (Ps 68:18) describes God receiving gifts of plunder or tribute from a defeated foe. Paul adapts the wording to describe God giving spiritual gifts to the church.

4:9 he also descended to the lower, earthly regions The descent described in Eph 4:9–10 could be interpreted as Christ's descent into the underworld after his death (compare 1Pe 3:18–22; note on 1Pe 3:19). Alternatively, the descent could refer to Pentecost, when the Holy Spirit empowered the apostles (Ac 2:4; compare 16:6), or to Jesus' incarnation, when the Word (Jesus) descended from heaven to earth (Jn 1:1–5,14).

4:11 Paul's description here of particular roles (or offices) in the Church resembles his description in 1Co 12:28, but includes additional roles and does not include others (see note on 1Co 12:28). These roles are for advancing God's work in the world through the Church.

4:11 apostles Refers to those who are sent out by Christ to speak and act with special authority. See note on Eph 2:20; note on 1Co 12:28. **prophets** Refers to those who are designated by God to speak on his behalf. See note on Eph 2:20; note on 1Co 12:10. **evangelists** Refers

to those who proclaim the truth of the gospel and call others to live by Jesus' standards (compare Ac 21:8; 2Ti 4:5). **pastors** Refers to those who care for, or protect, the church. Since the Greek word used here, *poimēn*, literally means "shepherd" and is often translated as such, this role corresponds with the NT portrayal of the church as God's flock (1Pe 5:2; Ac 20:28). **teachers** Indicates those who faithfully pass on the teachings of Christ and the apostles, especially through explaining or applying Scripture (compare Titus 2:1).

4:13 Son of God See note on Ro 1:3.

4:14 infants Figuratively describes those who are immature in the faith.

4:16 whole body The church is one unified group directed by Christ to accomplish his purposes—yet there are many parts to it. Paul uses this metaphor to explain how many people with different roles and gifts can work together in unity (compare 1Co 12:12–20).

4:17–32 Continuing his emphasis on unity, Paul urges believers to abandon former ways of living that have nothing to do with Christ. As members of Christ's body, believers are called to show integrity, kindness and grace.

4:17 futility of their thinking When they lived apart from God, the Gentiles' entire way of thinking was ineffectual, distorted by the powers of sin (Eph 2:1–3).

4:19 given themselves over Refers to rejecting God and his ways (compare Ro 1:24–32).

4:21 when The Greek expression used here, *ei ge*, is sometimes translated using a conditional statement ("if"), but it actually implies confidence. Paul's point is that his audience does know and follow Christ. The same expression begins Eph 3:2.

4:24 to put on the new self As in v. 22, Paul uses the imagery of changing one's clothes to describe believers' responsibility to actively participate in Christ's transformative work in their lives (compare Col 3:9–10; 2Co 5:17).

all members of one body. 26"In your anger do not sin"[a]: Do not let the sun go down while you are still angry, 27and do not give the devil a foothold. 28Anyone who has been stealing must steal no longer, but must work, doing something useful with their own hands, that they may have something to share with those in need.

29Do not let any unwholesome talk come out of your mouths, but only what is helpful for building others up according to their needs, that it may benefit those who listen. 30And do not grieve the Holy Spirit of God, with whom you were sealed for the day of redemption. 31Get rid of all bitterness, rage and anger, brawling and slander, along with every form of malice. 32Be kind and compassionate to one another, forgiving each other, just as in Christ God forgave you. 1Follow God's example, therefore, as dearly loved children 2and walk in the way of love, just as Christ loved us and gave himself up for us as a fragrant offering and sacrifice to God.

3But among you there must not be even a hint of sexual immorality, or of any kind of impurity, or of greed, because these are improper for God's holy people. 4Nor should there be obscenity, foolish talk or coarse joking, which are out of place, but rather thanksgiving. 5For of this you can be sure: No immoral, impure or greedy person — such a person is an idolater — has any inheritance in the kingdom of Christ and of God.[b] 6Let no one

deceive you with empty words, for because of such things God's wrath comes on those who are disobedient. 7Therefore do not be partners with them.

8For you were once darkness, but now you are light in the Lord. Live as children of light 9(for the fruit of the light consists in all goodness, righteousness and truth) 10and find out what pleases the Lord. 11Have nothing to do with the fruitless deeds of darkness, but rather expose them. 12It is shameful even to mention what the disobedient do in secret. 13But everything exposed by the light becomes visible — and everything that is illuminated becomes a light. 14This is why it is said:

"Wake up, sleeper,
    rise from the dead,
    and Christ will shine on you."

15Be very careful, then, how you live — not as unwise but as wise, 16making the most of every opportunity, because the days are evil. 17Therefore do not be foolish, but understand what the Lord's will is. 18Do not get drunk on wine, which leads to debauchery. Instead, be filled with the Spirit, 19speaking to one another with psalms, hymns, and songs from the Spirit. Sing and make music from your heart to the Lord, 20always giving thanks to God the Father for everything, in the name of our Lord Jesus Christ.

a 26 Psalm 4:4 (see Septuagint)   b 5 Or kingdom of the Messiah and God

---

4:26 In your anger do not sin Paul quotes Ps 4:4 from the Septuagint (the ancient Greek translation of the OT). Paul seems to acknowledge that anger can be unavoidable, but he also recognizes that it can quickly develop into an occasion for sin.

4:28 with their own hands Paul calls believers to work for the sake of others (compare Eph 2:10).

4:30 do not grieve the Holy Spirit Paul seems to be indicating that poor treatment of others can constrain the work of the Spirit—essentially denying or resisting God's indwelling presence (compare Isa 63:10). **day of redemption** Refers to the day of the Lord, when Christ will return (see note on 1Th 5:2).

5:1–21 Paul continues to instruct his readers to live in ways that please God, reflecting his light into the world.

5:1 dearly loved children Alludes to believers' adoption into God's family (Eph 1:5; Gal 4:6–7).

5:2 fragrant In the OT, sacrifices are described as having an aroma pleasing to God (e.g., Ex 29:25; Lev 1:9). **offering and sacrifice** This description of Christ's death draws on language from the sacrificial system in the OT.

5:3 sexual immorality The Greek word used here, porneia, refers to any kind of sexual immorality. **God's holy people** See note on Eph 1:1.

5:5 kingdom of Christ and of God Refers to the domain in which Christ reigns as King. In acknowledgment of Christ's rule, believers are called to exhibit obedience, loyalty and love. Those who continue to participate in illicit behavior essentially are resisting Christ's reign and acting as though they reject an inheritance in his kingdom. In the Gospels, the kingdom of God (or kingdom

of heaven) is a central theme of Jesus' teaching (e.g., Mt 4:17; 13:10–52; see note on Mk 1:15).

5:6 with empty words Likely refers to attempts to trivialize or justify illicit behavior. **wrath** Refers to God's righteous judgment upon those who do evil. **those who are disobedient** Refers to those who oppose God.

5:8 darkness Symbolizes the realm dominated by sin and death (compare Eph 6:12; Col 1:13). Darkness also can refer to lack of understanding (e.g., Ps 82:5; Ro 2:19). **light** Represents righteousness and life (compare 2Co 6:14; Job 33:30); also refers to understanding (Ps 119:105,130). See note on 1Jn 1:5. **children of light** A common label (particularly among sectarian groups) for those who are in right relationship with God.

5:9 fruit Refers to natural results. Rooted in Christ, the believer's life should produce Christlike virtues.

5:14 Wake up, sleeper, rise from the dead This is not a direct quote from any OT passage. Paul might be alluding to Job 14:12 or Isa 26:19; he also might be borrowing from an early Christian hymn or traditions related to baptism.

5:15 but as wise The Bible closely associates wisdom with honoring and obeying God (e.g., Pr 1:7).

5:16 days are evil Refers to the current times, as opposed to the coming time when Jesus will return and vanquish evil. The current time (or present age) is characterized by disobedience and the corrupting influence of Satan. Compare 2Co 2:2; Gal 1:4; 2Co 4:4.

5:17 Lord's will God's will is to bring all of creation under the authority of Christ (Eph 1:9–10).

5:18 be filled with the Spirit In the Greek text of Ephesians, this command provides the basis for Paul's

Instructions for Christian Households

5:22 – 6:9pp — Col 3:18 – 4:1

21Submit to one another out of reverence for Christ.

22Wives, submit yourselves to your own husbands as you do to the Lord. 23For the husband is the head of the wife as Christ is the head of the church, his body, of which he is the Savior. 24Now as the church submits to Christ, so also wives should submit to their husbands in everything.

25Husbands, love your wives, just as Christ loved the church and gave himself up for her 26to make her holy, cleansing[a] her by the washing with water through the word, 27and to present her to himself as a radiant church, without stain or wrinkle or any other blemish, but holy and blameless. 28In this same way, husbands ought to love their wives as their own bodies. He who loves his wife loves himself. 29After all, no one ever hated their own body, but they feed and care for their body, just as Christ does the church — 30for we are members of his body. 31"For this reason a man will leave his father and mother and be united to his wife, and the two will become one flesh."[b] 32This is a profound mystery — but I am talking about Christ and the church. 33However, each one of you also must love his wife as he loves himself, and the wife must respect her husband.

6 Children, obey your parents in the Lord, for this is right. 2"Honor your father and mother" — which is the first commandment with a promise — 3"so that it may go well with you and that you may enjoy long life on the earth."[c]

a 26 Or having cleansed   b 31 Gen. 2:24   c 3 Deut. 5:16

---

statements in vv. 19 – 21, all of which describe the outworking of being filled with the Spirit.

5:21 Submit to one another Paul calls on believers to honor Christ by honoring, loving and helping one another.

5:22 — 6:9 Building on the principle of mutual submission in 5:21 (which itself stems from being filled with the Spirit in v. 18), Paul presents examples of how believers should be subject to one another in household relationships. In the first-century Greco-Roman world, it was standard for every household member to be subject in daily affairs to the patriarch. This viewpoint was central to Greco-Roman society. Paul works within this framework to suggest a model that makes Christ the ultimate authority — his viewpoint is based on mutual love.

In these sections of Ephesians, Paul addresses wives and husbands, children and parents, and servants and masters. As he does so, he follows a similar pattern: He first calls on the subordinate — according to Greco-Roman values — to submit to authority, and then reminds the superior to exercise authority considerately, in ways that honor Christ. Compare Col 3:18 — 4:1.

5:22 Wives While the cultural model for marriage in the Greco-Roman world emphasized male patriarchal leadership, Paul's model is based on mutual love and respect (v. 5:28,33) and grounded in the OT creation story (v. 31 cites Ge 2:24).

5:23 Christ is the head of the church Paul uses the relationship between Christ and the church as an analogy for the relationship between husband and wife. The wife's submission, which was expected by Greco-Roman values, is placed in the context of spiritual submission to Christ (see note on Eph 5:22 — 6:9). Likewise, husbands, as the heads of households in Greco-Roman society, are instructed by Paul to show their wives respect (compare 5:25 and note). Paul contextualizes Greco-Roman values within the larger perspective of Christ's self-sacrificial love.

5:25 Husbands, love your wives Paul is referring primarily to sacrificial actions for the benefit of the wife. The model for this kind of love is Christ's death on the cross. Paul's exhortation to husbands (5:25 – 33) is the longest single section in this teaching on households (5:22 — 6:9). Paul takes great care to set his command that wives submit to their husbands (5:22 – 24) within its proper context, emphasizing the husband's responsibilities in greater detail.

5:26 by the washing with water Possibly an allusion to the imagery of baptism. This image is applied to Christ's care for his church. Alternatively, Paul could be referring to an inward cleansing accomplished by the power of the gospel to free believers from sin. **word** The Greek word used here, *rhēma*, refers in this context to the gospel — the proclamation of Christ's sacrificial love (v. 25).

5:27 without stain or wrinkle Paul alludes to bridal garments as symbols of purity before God (compare Zec 3:3 – 5; Rev 7:13 – 14). Other NT writers figuratively portray Christ as a bridegroom and the renewed church as his bride (Mt 25:1 – 13; Rev 21:2,9). **holy and blameless** The glorious state of the church that was the purpose of Christ's sacrificial death.

5:31 two will become one flesh This quotation of Ge 2:24 supports Paul's statement in Eph 5:29: A husband is to love his wife as himself because, in the context of marriage, they have become one body.

5:32 a profound mystery Refers to the union that believers have with Christ as members of his church. Elsewhere in Ephesians, the Greek word used here, *mystērion*, refers to God's plan of reconciling all things in Christ (1:9; 3:3 – 6). Here Paul uses *mystērion* to describe the union of Christ and the church. These concepts overlap; God's cosmic reconciliation of all things, the center of theology in Ephesians, is most fully expressed in the joining together of sinful people to the one who died for their sins, Christ.

In vv. 31 – 32 Paul places Christian marriage within the context of God's cosmic redemption to show that marriage concerns more than just two people; it is a sign to the world of the powerful reconciliation made possible through the gospel. The union of male and female in marriage is meant to point beyond itself to God's work of redemption and unification.

6:2 Honor your father and mother Reflects the fifth commandment (Ex 20:12; Dt 5:16). In first-century Greco-Roman society, children were required by law to submit to the authority of their parents. Paul's instruction, however, is based on the principle of mutual submission (see note on Eph 5:22 — 6:9). Paul likewise expects that children be treated with respect by their parents (see 6:4).

⁴Fathers,ᵃ do not exasperate your children; instead, bring them up in the training and instruction of the Lord.

⁵Slaves, obey your earthly masters with respect and fear, and with sincerity of heart, just as you would obey Christ. ⁶Obey them not only to win their favor when their eye is on you, but as slaves of Christ, doing the will of God from your heart. ⁷Serve wholeheartedly, as if you were serving the Lord, not people, ⁸because you know that the Lord will reward each one for whatever good they do, whether they are slave or free.

⁹And masters, treat your slaves in the same way. Do not threaten them, since you know that he who is both their Master and yours is in heaven, and there is no favoritism with him.

The Armor of God

¹⁰Finally, be strong in the Lord and in his mighty power. ¹¹Put on the full armor of God, so that you can take your stand against the devil's schemes. ¹²For our struggle is not against flesh and blood, but against the rulers, against the authorities, against the powers of this dark world and against the spiritual forces of evil in the heavenly realms. ¹³Therefore put on the full armor of God, so that when the day of evil comes, you may be able to stand your ground, and after you have done everything, to stand. ¹⁴Stand firm then, with the belt of truth buckled around your waist, with the breastplate of righteousness in place, ¹⁵and with your feet fitted with the readiness that comes from the gospel of peace. ¹⁶In addition to all this, take up the shield of faith, with which you can extinguish all the flaming arrows of the evil one. ¹⁷Take the helmet of salvation and the sword of the Spirit, which is the word of God.

¹⁸And pray in the Spirit on all occasions with all kinds of prayers and requests. With this in mind, be alert and always keep on praying for all the Lord's people. ¹⁹Pray also for me, that whenever I speak, words may be given me so that I

ᵃ 4 Or Parents

6:4 do not exasperate your children In first-century Greco-Roman society, fathers—as the head of the household—had complete authority within the household to administer discipline. Paul advises them to avoid exercising that authority in ways that might cause their children to harbor resentment. Paul is advocating for fathers treating their children with kindness, which would have been unexpected for Greco-Roman society; he is arguing that parents treat their children as Christ would.

6:5 Slaves Often considered members of the household in Greco-Roman culture. See note on 5:22—6:9. **obey your earthly masters** Being under Christ's authority does not mean that believers are free of all civil or social authority. Paul maintains that slaves should serve their human masters as though they were obeying Christ. Greco-Roman slavery in the first century AD was very different from that of the colonial period (see note on Phm 10). Even though some slaves became part of the masters' household in the first century, they still were considered the legal property of their masters. Through Christ, slaves received a new identity: They became children of God, brothers and sisters of fellow believers (Eph 1:5). This meant that Christian slaves were united with their Christian masters in God's family (Gal 3:28; Col 3:11). Some slaves might have used this common bond to disregard their masters' authority. Paul warns against such a response and instructs slaves to do the will of their masters with a sincere heart, in the same way they do God's will. Compare Col 3:22—4:1; see note on Phm 10.

6:8 Lord will reward God takes account of the kindness and generosity people display to one another.

6:9 Do not threaten In Greco-Roman society, masters had the right to treat slaves as they saw fit. Paul commands masters to set aside their rights and to instead treat their slaves with kindness as people who are equal before Christ (compare note on Eph 6:5).

6:10–20 In the letter's final teaching section, Paul instructs believers to stand against the evil forces at work in the world. This discussion has three parts: a description of the nature of the battle (Eph 6:10–13), a call to resist the powers by putting on the armor of God (vv. 14–17) and a reminder to pray and be alert (vv. 18–20).

6:10 be strong in the Lord God gave the Israelites a similar charge before they engaged in battle with the inhabitants of the promised land (Dt 31:23; Jos 1:6).

6:11 full armor of God The book of Isaiah contains imagery similar to Paul's (Isa 11:4–5; 52:7; 59:17). **can take your stand** A military expression that refers to a posture of opposition toward an enemy. **devil's schemes** Refers to the devil's efforts to disrupt the church.

6:12 spiritual forces of evil Refers to hostile supernatural entities. Because of Christ's victory over the evil powers, believers have courage and strength to resist them (Eph 1:19–21; 3:10; Col 2:15).

6:14 with the belt of truth buckled around your waist The belt around a soldier's waist held the breastplate in place and provided an attachment for the sword. **breastplate of righteousness** See note on 1Th 5.

6:16 shield of faith The shield was the soldier's primary defense in battle. In the same way, the believer's trust in God provides protection against the devil and his schemes.

6:17 helmet of salvation The assurance of God's salvation protects the believer just as a helmet protects a soldier in battle. See note on 1Th 5:8. **sword of the Spirit** This weapon helps believers proclaim the gospel message, act on God's behalf and combat attacks from the devil (compare Eph 6:11–12). **word** Paul's use of the Greek word *rhēma* here primarily refers to the proclamation of the gospel and its ongoing work in the life of the believer (see 5:26 and note; compare Ro 10:17).

6:19 mystery of the gospel This might refer generally to the good news about Christ, or it could point specifically to the inclusion of Gentiles (non-Jews) into

will fearlessly make known the mystery of the gospel, ²⁰for which I am an ambassador in chains. Pray that I may declare it fearlessly, as I should.

Final Greetings

²¹Tychicus, the dear brother and faithful servant in the Lord, will tell you everything, so that you also may know how I am and what I am doing. ²²I am sending him to you for this very purpose,

that you may know how we are, and that he may encourage you.

²³Peace to the brothers and sisters,ᵃ and love with faith from God the Father and the Lord Jesus Christ. ²⁴Grace to all who love our Lord Jesus Christ with an undying love.ᵇ

ᵃ 23 The Greek word for *brothers and sisters* (*adelphoi*) refers here to believers, both men and women, as part of God's family.
ᵇ 24 Or *Grace and immortality to all who love our Lord Jesus Christ.*

---

the people of God (Eph 3:4–6; see note on 3:4; compare 2:11–22).

6:20 ambassador in chains Paul was compelled to proclaim the gospel even during his imprisonment (see 3:1 and note).

6:21–24 Paul gives concluding remarks (vv. 21–22) and a benediction (vv. 23–24).

6:21 Tychicus A companion of Paul during his ministry; courier for this letter, as well as Colossians and likely Philemon (Col 4:7–9). Paul's remarks about Tychicus in Eph 6:21–22 parallel Col 4:7–8 almost word for word.

Ephesians 6:21

TYCHICUS
A Gentile (non-Jewish) believer from the Roman province of Asia, Tychichus is mentioned throughout the NT as one of Paul's ministry partners (Ac 20:4; Eph 6:21; Col 4:7; 2Ti 4:12; Titus 3:12). According to Acts, Tychicus accompanied Paul during his third missionary journey through Asia Minor, Macedonia and Achaia (Ac 20:4).

6:23 Peace See Eph 2:14 and note.

ELECTION
by William W. Klein

C hristian teaching on election has drawn from a number of related Biblical themes pertaining to God's choice in salvation. Fundamentally, then, election is about selection (the English word "election" comes from the Greek verb to choose). Election is key for understanding the Bible's grand narrative—the account of God's plan to redeem and restore, through Christ, a holy people who had been lost in Adam. Unfortunately, election has also been at the center of considerable disagreement in Biblical interpretation and theology.

ELECTION TO SALVATION IS CORPORATE AND INDIVIDUAL

The Bible describes election as both corporate and individual. Following the account of God's good and glorious creation, the Bible presents the story of human rebellion and alienation from their Creator (Ge 3). By Genesis 12, we see God's strategy for redemption taking shape: God chooses Abram (Abraham) and promises that through him all the nations will be blessed (Ge 12:2–3). In doing so, God essentially embraces all of Abraham's offspring (Ge 13:16); Abraham will be the father of the Israelites and, eventually, of all who trust in God as Abraham did. Numerous Old Testament references reiterate God's gracious choice of Israel to be his people, such as: "You only have I chosen of all the families of the earth" (Am 3:2). Another example comes from Deuteronomy: "The LORD did not set his affection on you and choose you because you were more numerous than other peoples, for you were the fewest of all peoples. But it was because the LORD loved you and kept the oath he swore to your ancestors" (Dt 7:7–8).

Yet God's election of Israel as his chosen people did not equate to the personal salvation of every Israelite. That required a heart commitment to God (Isa 29:13). Why might some ethnic Jews forfeit the salvation obtained by Abraham? In Paul's words, "Because they pursued it not by faith but as if it were by works. They stumbled over the stumbling stone" (Ro 9:32).

The New Testament's teaching on election stands in continuity with the Old Testament, but with a crucial shift—one that was anticipated by the Old Testament prophets: God's chosen are no longer identified by ethnic or national markers, but spiritually by faith. See how Paul defines a "spiritual Jew": "A person is not a Jew who is one only outwardly, nor is circumcision merely outward and physical. No, a person is a Jew who is one inwardly; and circumcision is circumcision of the heart, by the Spirit, not by the written code. Such a person's praise is not from other people, but from God" (Ro 2:28–29). Both Jews and Gentiles—non-Jews—who believe in Jesus are the true children of Abraham (Jn 8:38–40,56–59; Ro 4:16–17).

Peter, for example, speaks of the election of the church in terms equally applicable to Old Testament Israel. He says, "But you are a chosen people, a royal priesthood, a holy nation, God's special possession, that you may declare the praises of him who called you out of darkness into his wonderful light. Once you were not a people, but now you are the people of God; once you had not received mercy, but now you have received mercy" (1Pe 2:9–10; compare 1Pe 1:1; 5:13).

DIFFERING INTERPRETATIONS OF INDIVIDUAL ELECTION

Historically, nearly all Christian interpreters have agreed that God's electing choice flows entirely from his grace, that human beings are moral agents responsible for our actions, and that personal participation in the community of the elect is by faith. But interpreters fall into two major approaches to the question of how God's electing purpose comes to expression in the salvation of individuals: what might be called election unto faith versus election in view of faith. Are people believers because they are elect, or are they elect because they believe?

Many interpreters (like Augustine and Calvin) have understood the Biblical data on election to mean that God has chosen to save an unknown number of specific individuals from the deserved consequences of all humanity's sin—a choice based solely on God's undeserved mercy. Because people are dead in sin if left to themselves, they cannot and will not embrace God's gift of salvation apart from God's own enabling power (Ro 3:9–19; Jn 10:26–29). God supplies his elect with a gracious and undeserved capacity to believe; election is unto faith, since faith is a gift of God (Eph 2:4–9).

Many other interpreters (like Arminius and Wesley) have understood the Biblical data differently, taking it to mean that God does not elect unto faith, but desires to give all people equally the ability to receive his offer of salvation (1Ti 2:4; 2Pe 3:9). Everyone who believes is (therefore) included among the chosen.

More recently, some interpreters (like N. T. Wright) have sought to refocus this traditional emphasis on the basis of the election of individuals toward the purpose of the election of the community: The people of God are called to be holy and to participate in his mission of reconciling the world to himself (Eph 1:4; 2:10; 2Co 5:17–20).

Whichever approach is taken, the Biblical theme of election should lead all believers to praise God, like Paul does, for graciously choosing—even before the foundation of the world—to love us and save us in Christ (Eph 1:4–5; 2:14–22).

PHILIPPIANS

INTRODUCTION TO PHILIPPIANS

In Paul's Letter to the Philippians, his writing overflows with joy and thankfulness, even though he is writing from prison. Unlike his interaction with other churches, Paul had very little to correct in the Philippian congregation. He was encouraged by the believers' concern for him and their faithfulness in living out the gospel. Paul teaches that the joy of the gospel should rule our lives, regardless of circumstances.

BACKGROUND

The opening verse identifies Paul and Timothy as the authors. Paul planted the church in Philippi (in modern-day northeastern Greece) on his second missionary journey, around AD 49–51 (Ac 16:12). Years later, Paul writes to these Christians from prison (Php 1:12–14; 4:22)—probably in Rome (early 60s AD), or perhaps in Caesarea (ca. AD 58–60) or Ephesus (ca. AD 54–55). While there is no record of Paul being imprisoned in Ephesus, he did encounter serious conflict there during his third missionary journey and could have been imprisoned there (Ac 19; compare 2Co 11:23).

Paul had a close relationship with the Philippian congregation. In the letter's opening, Paul doesn't need to declare his apostleship, as he often does when there is a conflict or doubts about his authority (Php 1:1; compare 2Co 1:1; Gal 1:1; 1Ti 1:1). The Philippians had supported Paul financially even when he was not in Philippi (Php 4:15–16; compare 2Co 8:1–4; 11:9), and it appears that they recently had sent Epaphroditus to deliver gifts to Paul in prison (Php 2:25; 4:18). However, Epaphroditus became sick during the journey (2:30), and Paul writes to tell the Philippians that their friend is recovering. He also thanks the believers for their ongoing support and gives an update on his situation.

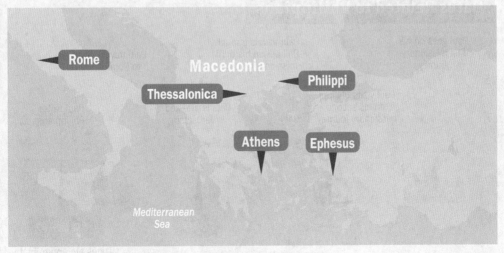

This map depicts the location of Philippi and the surrounding region.

Philippi had a strongly Roman character. Before Paul's time, during the first century BC, Philippi had become a Roman colony, and many of the empire's retired soldiers settled there. The importance of Roman citizenship—deeply valued by those who had it and coveted by those who did not—might be why Paul emphasizes that Christians are citizens of heaven (3:20). In contrast to Roman citizens, who by law could not be crucified, Paul urges the Philippians to imitate the humility and obedience of Christ, who willingly died on a cross (2:5–8).

STRUCTURE

Paul opens Philippians like many of his other letters—with a greeting (1:1–2), a thanksgiving (1:3–8) and a prayer (1:9–11). Then he reports about his circumstances (1:12–26), telling the believers not to worry about him. Even though he is in prison, he sees it as an opportunity to give thanks. In the next major section (1:27—2:30), Paul instructs the Philippians to remain united and humble. In a short hymn-like section, Paul praises the humility shown by Jesus (2:5–11). Timothy and Epaphroditus also reflect humble service to the gospel (2:19–30).

In the next section (3:1–21), Paul warns against false teachers who apparently were telling the believers to seek righteousness through Jewish practices, like circumcision. Paul tells the Philippians that he went this route in his earlier days, and he knows it doesn't work—it actually hindered him from knowing Christ. The closing section begins by addressing a specific situation: Two women in the church seem to be feuding, and Paul wants them to reconcile (4:1–3). He urges the

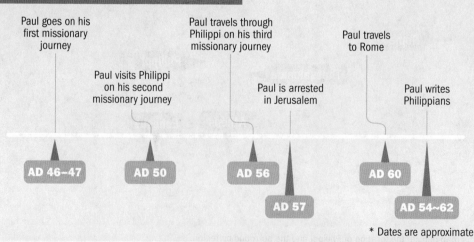

Dates Related to Philippians

Paul goes on his first missionary journey — AD 46–47

Paul visits Philippi on his second missionary journey — AD 50

Paul travels through Philippi on his third missionary journey — AD 56

Paul is arrested in Jerusalem — AD 57

Paul travels to Rome — AD 60

Paul writes Philippians — AD 54~62

* Dates are approximate

Philippians to rejoice in faith (4:4–9), and he thanks them for their generous gifts (4:10–20). The letter ends with a final greeting and benediction (4:21–23).

OUTLINE

- Introduction and Paul's report (1:1–26)
- Call to unity (1:27 — 2:30)
- Warnings against false teachers (3:1–21)
- Further instructions and thanksgiving (4:1–23)

THEMES

Philippians is about remaining steadfast in the faith and joy of the gospel. This is clear from Paul's own response to his hardships: His imprisonment could have led him to despair, but instead he chose to give thanks, to be content and to rely on God's strength (1:12–19; 4:10–13). Paul advises the Philippians to take this same approach, urging them to stand firm together for the gospel (1:27–28).

Throughout the letter, Paul uses personal examples—Christ, Timothy, Epaphroditus and himself—to show that faithfulness involves humility and often suffering. In several places, he encourages believers to be of one purpose (2:2; 3:15; 4:2)—serving Christ, who himself provides the pattern to live by (2:5–8). Humbling ourselves enables us to find unity with fellow believers in Christ, to stand together in the midst of suffering and to rejoice no matter the circumstances. Even when we are afflicted, God's power—the same power that resurrected Jesus from the dead (3:10–11)—is at work in us, transforming us (3:12–21). And there is nothing more valuable than Jesus (3:8–9).

1 Paul and Timothy, servants of Christ Jesus,

To all God's holy people in Christ Jesus at Philippi, together with the overseers and deacons [a]:

²Grace and peace to you from God our Father and the Lord Jesus Christ.

Thanksgiving and Prayer

³I thank my God every time I remember you. ⁴In all my prayers for all of you, I always pray with joy ⁵because of your partnership in the gospel from the first day until now, ⁶being confident of this, that he who began a good work in you will carry it on to completion until the day of Christ Jesus.

⁷It is right for me to feel this way about all of you, since I have you in my heart and, whether I am in chains or defending and confirming the gospel, all of you share in God's grace with me.

[a] 1 The word *deacons* refers here to Christians designated to serve with the overseers/elders of the church in a variety of ways; similarly in Romans 16:1 and 1 Tim. 3:8,12.

1:1–2 Paul begins his letter to the Philippians with a customary greeting identifying himself and the letter's cosender, Timothy. Paul is writing from prison, perhaps in Ephesus (AD 54–57), Caesarea (AD 58–60) or Rome (early 60s AD). See note on Php 1:7.

1:1 Paul See note on Gal 1:1. **Timothy** Paul's frequent companion during his missionary journeys. Timothy was a half-Jewish believer who met Paul in Lystra (Ac 16:1) and worked closely with him in ministry (Ac 16:3; 20:4–5; 2Co 1:19; 1Ti 1:3). As a result, Timothy became like a son to Paul (1Ti 1:2). **servants of Christ Jesus** This description sets up Paul's later remarks encouraging the Philippians to show humility—an attitude that Jesus himself demonstrated (Php 2:3–8). See the table "Pauline Self-Designations" on p. 1904. **To all God's holy people** See note on Eph 1:1. **Philippi** A city in Macedonia (northeast Greece, today); named after Alexander the Great's father, King Philip II. Based on Philippi's likely demographics, the church there would have been almost entirely non-Jewish, non-Roman and impoverished—perhaps joined by a few middle-class merchants. The believers probably faced severe persecution and economic hardships (see note on Php 1:29). This scenario corresponds with Paul's main themes in the letter: suffering and unity (see note on vv. 27–30). **overseers** The Greek word used here, *episkopos*, refers to those appointed to watch over, guide and protect the believers (Ac 20:28). Paul discusses church leadership more fully in his letters to Timothy and Titus (see 1Ti 3:1–13; Titus 1:5–9). **deacons** The Greek word used here, *diakonos*, describes helpers—anyone who carries out ministry work. The early church's first deacons were selected by the apostles to help distribute food to widows (Ac 6:1–6). See note on 1Ti 3:8.

PHILIPPI
Located about nine miles inland from the northern shore of the Aegean Sea, Philippi became a colony of the Roman Empire in 31 BC, and Roman military veterans were granted land there. Due to the influx of retired soldiers and other colonists, the Macedonian natives and Greek immigrants living at Philippi probably saw a sharp decline in their social and economic status. By the time Paul arrived to preach the gospel (around AD 50), the city's culture and institutions would have been decidedly Roman, with civic power concentrated in the hands of a relatively small number of elites who owned property in the surrounding countryside. These estates and farms would have been served by a large underclass that lived mainly in the city—non-Roman laborers, tradesmen and service workers. Unlike many cities that Paul visited (e.g., Pisidian Antioch, Iconium, Thessalonica, Ephesus), Philippi does not seem to have had a synagogue. Neither the text of Ac 16 nor the book of Philippians indicate a Jewish community (aside from several God-fearing women meeting for prayer outside the city; Ac 16:13).

1:2 Grace and peace to you from God our Father See note on Ro 1:7. **Lord** The title of "Lord" (*kyrios* in Greek) is especially significant in this letter. As a Roman colony, Philippi would have had a prominent cult dedicated to worshiping the emperor. It would have been common for residents—Roman citizens or not—to participate in the imperial religion, even if they worshiped other pagan gods. From public statues to household shrines, the environment of Philippi called for honoring Caesar above all. However, by affirming that Jesus is Lord, Paul challenges the Philippian Christians to redirect their allegiance. Compare Php 2:11.

1:3–11 It was common for Greco-Roman letters to include a thanksgiving section, but Paul's language here goes beyond the customary expression of gratitude. Ever since Paul first preached the gospel at Philippi (Ac 16:11–40), the believers there had been among his strongest supporters (Php 1:5). He thinks of them with warmth and affection (vv. 7–8) and prays that their love and wisdom will grow (v. 9). See the table "Prayers in Paul's Letters" on p. 1925.

1:5 partnership The Philippians provided financial support that helped Paul spread the gospel message (4:15,18). In Paul's time, friendship meant that two parties of equal standing—in this instance, Paul and the Philippians—would participate (*koinōnia* in Greek) in an ongoing exchange of gestures for mutual benefit. **from the first day** Paul first met the Philippian believers during a missionary journey through Macedonia (Ac 16:11–40). When he departed, the Philippians continued to support him financially (Php 4:15–16). The Christians at Philippi seem to have aligned themselves strongly with Paul's missionary endeavors.

1:6 who began Refers to God. Paul is certain that the Philippians will progress in faith because God is committed to transforming them. **day of Christ Jesus** Refers to the second coming of Jesus Christ (see note on 1Th 5:2). In Paul's letters, the "day of Christ" is synonymous with the OT phrase "day of the Lord" (see note on Lk 17:22).

1:7 I am in chains Romans did not use prisons for punishment, but only to detain those awaiting trial or execution. Like Ephesians, Colossians and Philemon, Philippians was written while Paul was in prison. However, due to Paul's frequent incarcerations (2Co 6:5; 11:23),

[8]God can testify how I long for all of you with the affection of Christ Jesus.

[9]And this is my prayer: that your love may abound more and more in knowledge and depth of insight, [10]so that you may be able to discern what is best and may be pure and blameless for the day of Christ, [11]filled with the fruit of righteousness that comes through Jesus Christ — to the glory and praise of God.

Paul's Chains Advance the Gospel

[12]Now I want you to know, brothers and sisters,[a] that what has happened to me has actually served to advance the gospel. [13]As a result, it has become clear throughout the whole palace guard[b] and to everyone else that I am in chains for Christ. [14]And because of my chains, most of the brothers and sisters have become confident in the Lord and dare all the more to proclaim the gospel without fear.

[15]It is true that some preach Christ out of envy and rivalry, but others out of goodwill. [16]The latter do so out of love, knowing that I am put here for the defense of the gospel. [17]The former preach Christ out of selfish ambition, not sincerely, supposing that they can stir up trouble for me while I am in chains. [18]But what does it matter? The important thing is that in every way, whether from false motives or true, Christ is preached. And because of this I rejoice.

Yes, and I will continue to rejoice, [19]for I know that through your prayers and God's provision of the Spirit of Jesus Christ what has happened to me will turn out for my deliverance.[c] [20]I eagerly expect and hope that I will in no way be ashamed, but will have sufficient courage so that now as always Christ will be exalted in my body, whether by life or by death. [21]For to me, to live is Christ and to die is gain. [22]If I am to go on living in the body, this will mean fruitful labor for me. Yet what shall I choose? I do not know! [23]I am torn between the

---

[a] 12 The Greek word for *brothers and sisters* (*adelphoi*) refers here to believers, both men and women, as part of God's family; also in verse 14; and in 3:1, 13, 17; 4:1, 8, 21. [b] 13 Or *whole palace* [c] 19 Or *vindication*; or *salvation*

---

it is difficult to determine the exact time and place of the imprisonment he refers to here. The events of Ac 23:33 — 26:32 take place in Caesarea (on the eastern shore of the Mediterranean Sea), where Paul was imprisoned for at least two years (Ac 24:27). Paul later is confined under some kind of house arrest in Rome (Ac 28:14 – 31) — also for at least two years (Ac 28:30). The main difficulty with the hypothesis that Paul wrote Philippians from these locations is their distance from Paul's main area of missionary work around the Aegean Sea (Philippi to Caesarea is roughly 1,200 miles; Philippi to Rome is about 800 miles). The Prison Letters mention various people traveling to and from Paul, and both Caesarea and Rome would have been at least a month's journey from Philippi. A more geographically probable location is Ephesus — about 300 miles southwest of Philippi, across the Aegean. Paul spent more than two years at Ephesus (Ac 19:10,22), but Acts records no imprisonment there. It does report that Paul's preaching led to a riot at Ephesus (Ac 19:23 – 40) and that he later avoided the city and met with the Ephesian elders elsewhere (Ac 20:16 – 17). These factors might reflect legal trouble in Ephesus that could have included imprisonment (compare 2Co 1:8 – 10). See the infographic "The Tullianum: A Prison in Rome" on p. 2008. **defending and confirming the gospel** See note on Php 1:16. **share in God's grace** Probably alludes to the Philippians' financial support, which aided Paul while in prison and funded his missionary work (compare 4:14 – 18). **1:10 pure and blameless** Refers to being without fault. **1:11 fruit of righteousness** Refers to the natural results of belonging to Christ, whose death and resurrection bring righteousness to all who believe (compare 3:9).

1:12 – 26 Paul provides an update on his circumstances. First, he describes how his imprisonment has provided opportunities for ministry (vv. 12 – 18); he then looks ahead to his possible release from prison and to the advance of the gospel — whether he lives or dies (vv. 19 – 26).

1:12 brothers and sisters The Greek term used here, *adelphoi*, collectively refers to both male and female believers. **advance the gospel** Paul's imprisonment did not mean that the gospel was held captive. On the contrary, those around Paul were captive to hearing his good news about Jesus.

1:13 whole palace guard Refers to a unit of elite Roman soldiers, some of whom functioned as the emperor's bodyguards; others were stationed throughout the empire. Alternatively, it could refer to a provincial governor's residence (e.g., Mt 27:27; Mk 15:16; Jn 18:28; Ac 23:35).

1:14 brothers and sisters In this case, Paul is referring to fellow missionaries (compare 1:12 and note).

1:15 preach Christ out of envy and rivalry Describes missionaries who, in Paul's estimation, saw themselves as his rivals.

1:16 I am put here for the defense of the gospel Paul was constantly taking criticism for his view of the gospel — specifically, for not requiring non-Jewish Christians to adopt the Jewish law. In these verses, Paul is contrasting fellow missionaries of goodwill, who recognized his authority and accepted his gospel, and those of envy and ambition, who opposed him (requiring him to defend his approach).

1:18 whether from false motives or true Ultimately, Paul rejoices in all efforts to spread the gospel — even the ministries of his detractors.

1:19 the Spirit of Jesus Christ This phrase parallels the common OT and NT phrase "Spirit of God" (e.g., Jn 7:39; 1Pe 4:14; Job 33:4) and links Jesus to God the Father.

deliverance The Greek word used here, *sōtēria*, means rescue from danger (compare Mt 14:30; Mk 15:31) and often is translated as "salvation" (Ac 4:12; Ro 10:10).

1:21 to live is Christ and to die is gain As long as he is alive, Paul will be consumed with Christ's concerns, values and mission. And if Paul dies, he will be relieved of his suffering and dwell with Christ (Php 1:23).

1:22 body The Greek word used here, *sarx*, refers in this context to the physical body, but Paul often uses *sarx* in other ways. See note on 3:3.

1:23 to depart and be with Christ Refers to dying. Christ's resurrection gives Paul hope in death (3:10 – 11,20 – 21; compare note on Ro 1:4).

two: I desire to depart and be with Christ, which is better by far; [24]but it is more necessary for you that I remain in the body. [25]Convinced of this, I know that I will remain, and I will continue with all of you for your progress and joy in the faith, [26]so that through my being with you again your boasting in Christ Jesus will abound on account of me.

Life Worthy of the Gospel

[27]Whatever happens, conduct yourselves in a manner worthy of the gospel of Christ. Then, whether I come and see you or only hear about you in my absence, I will know that you stand firm in the one Spirit,[a] striving together as one for the faith of the gospel [28]without being frightened in any way by those who oppose you. This is a sign to them that they will be destroyed, but that you will be saved — and that by God. [29]For it has been granted to you on behalf of Christ not only to believe in him, but also to suffer for him, [30]since you are going through the same struggle you saw I had, and now hear that I still have.

Imitating Christ's Humility

2 Therefore if you have any encouragement from being united with Christ, if any comfort from his love, if any common sharing in the Spirit, if any tenderness and compassion, [2]then make my joy complete by being like-minded, having the same love, being one in spirit and of one mind. [3]Do nothing out of selfish ambition or vain conceit. Rather, in humility value others above yourselves, [4]not looking to your own interests but each of you to the interests of the others.

[5]In your relationships with one another, have the same mindset as Christ Jesus:

[6]Who, being in very nature[b] God,
　did not consider equality with God
　　something to be used to his own
　　advantage;
[7]rather, he made himself nothing
　by taking the very nature[c] of a servant,
　being made in human likeness.

[a] 27 Or in one spirit　　[b] 6 Or in the form of　　[c] 7 Or the form

---

1:24 that I remain in the body Refers to remaining alive, which Paul knows would be better for his churches.

1:27–30 These verses convey Paul's main reason for writing to the Philippians—to urge them to stand together for the gospel in the face of persecution and suffering.

1:27 striving together as one The believers need to band together as they struggle against hardship and persecution (compare note on Php 1:29). Christian unity is one of Paul's major concerns throughout the letter (e.g., 2:2–4; 4:1–2).

1:28 without being frightened Standing firm together will strengthen the believers and give them confidence.
a sign to them that they will be destroyed Refers to God's final judgment on the day of Christ (v. 6 and note). The Philippians' fearlessness is evidence that God will rule against their adversaries. **you will be saved** Refers to the day of Christ and God's ultimate act of deliverance for those who put faith in him.

1:29 to suffer for him People in the Greco-Roman world who became Christians would have faced all kinds of persecution. The problem people had with Christians was not so much that they were following Christ, but that they were failing to properly worship the community's gods—especially the emperor. Dishonoring the gods was thought to invite disaster upon the community, and those who abandoned pagan and imperial worship practices would have been treated with suspicion. In a strongly Roman city like Philippi (see note on v. 1), the decision to follow Christ could have brought severe social, economic and legal consequences. Family and friends might cut ties with believers, employers might fire them and clients might take their business elsewhere. Personal conflicts could easily end up in court, with Christians facing harsh punishment as troublemakers or traitors. The precarious situation likely confronting the church at Philippi shapes much of what Paul says in this letter.

1:30 same struggle Likely refers to the opposition that Paul encountered in Philippi (Ac 16:20–24).

2:1–11 Paul encourages the Philippians to continue practicing love and humility among one another (Php 2:1–4). This topic leads into the hymn of vv. 5–11, which praises Jesus as the ultimate example of self-emptying love. This hymn might have been composed by Paul, or it could be from an early Christian liturgy.

2:1 if you have any Paul is not questioning whether the Philippians have these things; he is using a rhetorical expression to say that, since the believers do in fact have these things, they should complete his joy by demonstrating unity.
2:2 being one in spirit The Greek word used here, *sympsychos*, describes sharing the same attitude or mindset—namely, the mindset of Jesus Christ (vv. 5–8). This points back to the letter's main purpose of encouraging the Philippians to stand firm together (1:27).
2:3 vain conceit Refers to arrogance, pride or an inflated ego.
2:4 each of you to the interests of the others This attitude is reflected throughout the chapter in the examples of Christ (vv. 6–8), Timothy (vv. 19–20) and Epaphroditus (v. 26).
2:6 in very nature God Refers to Jesus' preexistence and divine characteristics. **something to be used to his own advantage** The Greek word used here, *harpagmos*, is difficult to interpret because it appears only here in the Bible. It seems to mean "robbery" or "something to be seized by force." Paul may be saying that Christ did not consider equality with God, which he already possessed, something to be exploited for selfish gain. Alternatively, Paul could be saying that Christ did not consider the state of being equal to God to consist in acts of grasping and taking. Either way, Paul's emphasis is on Christ's humble attitude and refusal to act selfishly despite his equality with God.
2:7 he made himself nothing The Greek verb used here, *kenoō*, refers to Jesus pouring himself out. In light of v. 6 and 8, this seems to imply that Jesus laid aside his rights as God in order to become the world's servant. During his earthly ministry, Jesus encouraged his disciples to follow this example (Mk 10:45). Paul urges

8 And being found in appearance as a man,
   he humbled himself
     by becoming obedient to death —
       even death on a cross!

9 Therefore God exalted him to the highest place
   and gave him the name that is above every
     name,
10 that at the name of Jesus every knee should
     bow,
   in heaven and on earth and under the earth,
11 and every tongue acknowledge that Jesus
     Christ is Lord,
   to the glory of God the Father.

Do Everything Without Grumbling

12 Therefore, my dear friends, as you have always obeyed — not only in my presence, but now much more in my absence — continue to work out your salvation with fear and trembling, 13 for it is God who works in you to will and to act in order to fulfill his good purpose.

14 Do everything without grumbling or arguing, 15 so that you may become blameless and pure, "children of God without fault in a warped and crooked generation."[a] Then you will shine among them like stars in the sky 16 as you hold firmly to the word of life. And then I will be able to boast on the day of Christ that I did not run or labor in vain. 17 But even if I am being poured out like a drink offering on the sacrifice and service coming from your faith, I am glad and rejoice with all of you. 18 So you too should be glad and rejoice with me.

Timothy and Epaphroditus

19 I hope in the Lord Jesus to send Timothy to you soon, that I also may be cheered when I receive news about you. 20 I have no one else like him, who will show genuine concern for your welfare. 21 For everyone looks out for their own interests, not those of Jesus Christ. 22 But you know that Timothy has proved himself, because as a son with his

a 15 Deut. 32:5

---

the Philippians to do the same. **being made in human likeness** Refers to Jesus' incarnation.
2:8 cross Refers to Jesus' crucifixion (Mt 27:35–37). Paul portrays Jesus' willingness to endure suffering as a model of love for the Philippians. In Jewish tradition, being hung on (or from) a tree—and later the cross, because it was made of wood—was a sign of God's disapproval (Dt 21:23; Jos 8:29; Gal 3:13). In the Roman Empire, the cross served as a symbol of Roman power and authority; a person who was crucified was considered a threat to the empire. Christ's death turned the cross—a symbol of judgment and rebellion—into an instrument of God's power to liberate (1Co 1:18).
2:9 name that is above every name Because of Jesus' obedient, self-emptying death on the cross, God exalted him to the highest place of honor (compare Ac 2:36). Paul is likely referring to Jesus being called "Lord" (*kyrios* in Greek)—the Septuagint (ancient Greek translation of the OT) term used for Yahweh (e.g., Isa 42:8). In this case, the name signifies Jesus' exalted status and unique relationship with God the Father. Another possibility is that the name God gives is "Jesus" (*iēsous* in Greek); Paul explicitly mentions this name in Php 2:10. This implies that God instilled the name "Jesus" with the highest honor when he exalted Christ. It also is possible that Paul is referring not to a personal name but to a title. In this view, this new title denotes Jesus' exalted status alongside God.
2:10 every knee should bow Paul alludes to Isa 45:23 to describe the entire universe worshiping Jesus and submitting to his sovereignty.
2:11 every tongue acknowledge An allusion to Isa 45:23. **Lord** See note on Php 1:2.

2:12–18 Paul encourages the Philippians to continue pursuing God's transformative work in their lives.

2:12 you have always obeyed Obedience is evidence of faith in God. Paul appeals to the entire community to continue to obey, which means adopting the attitude of Christ in their relationships with one another. **work out** Emphasizes that obedience is intentional and purposeful. Paul's point is that salvation, once received, must be put into practice through obedience. **fear and**

trembling Refers to reverence and awe before God (compare 1Co 2:3; 2Co 7:15; Eph 6:5). Paul's imagery is derived from similar language used in the OT (e.g., Ex 15:16; Isa 19:16).
2:13 who works in you God's transforming presence empowers believers to live in faithful obedience to his will. Compare Php 1:6.
2:15 blameless and pure Paul creates a contrast in this verse between the humility, kindness and purity of God's children and the sinful ways of the world. **a warped and crooked generation** Paul echoes Dt 32:5. **you will shine among them like stars** Alludes to Da 12:2–3, in which the wise shine like stars. By reflecting God's character through their conduct, believers stand out against the darkness of the world and reveal the transformative power of the gospel (compare Php 1:27).
2:16 word of life Refers to the message that brings life—the gospel. **I will be able to boast** The Philippian believers—mostly non-Jews—represent the fulfillment of Paul's calling as apostle to the Gentiles (Ac 9:15; Gal 2:9; Ro 11:13). Their faithful response to the gospel proves that his ministry has not been futile.
2:17 drink offering In the ancient world, a drink could be poured out as an offering to a god (e.g., Ge 35:14; Hos 9:4). In the present verse (and in 2Ti 4:6) Paul uses this imagery to describe his sufferings for the Philippians—including his present imprisonment—as an offering to God. He might be referring figuratively to the possibility of his death (compare Php 1:20–24). **I am glad** Following the example of Jesus, Paul is not only willing but glad to suffer for the gospel.

2:19–30 Paul follows up the Christ-hymn with two further examples of servants who demonstrate humble obedience to God—Timothy (vv. 19–24) and Epaphroditus (vv. 25–30).

2:21 everyone looks out for their own interests In contrast to these others, Timothy is presented as an example of someone who puts Christ and others ahead of himself. Compare v. 4 and note.
2:22 you know that Timothy has proved himself Timothy apparently was no stranger to the Philippians. Although he does not appear in Ac 16:11–40, the

father he has served with me in the work of the gospel. ²³I hope, therefore, to send him as soon as I see how things go with me. ²⁴And I am confident in the Lord that I myself will come soon.

²⁵But I think it is necessary to send back to you Epaphroditus, my brother, co-worker and fellow soldier, who is also your messenger, whom you sent to take care of my needs. ²⁶For he longs for all of you and is distressed because you heard he was ill. ²⁷Indeed he was ill, and almost died. But God had mercy on him, and not on him only but also on me, to spare me sorrow upon sorrow. ²⁸Therefore I am all the more eager to send him, so that when you see him again you may be glad and I may have less anxiety. ²⁹So then, welcome him in the Lord with great joy, and honor people like him, ³⁰because he almost died for the work of Christ. He risked his life to make up for the help you yourselves could not give me.

No Confidence in the Flesh

3 Further, my brothers and sisters, rejoice in the Lord! It is no trouble for me to write the same things to you again, and it is a safeguard for you. ²Watch out for those dogs, those evildoers, those mutilators of the flesh. ³For it is we who are the circumcision, we who serve God by his Spirit, who boast in Christ Jesus, and who put no confidence in the flesh— ⁴though I myself have reasons for such confidence.

If someone else thinks they have reasons to put confidence in the flesh, I have more: ⁵circumcised on the eighth day, of the people of Israel, of the

---

surrounding passages suggest that he was with Paul and Silas when they first visited Philippi (see Ac 16:1–3; 17:14–15). Through serving the gospel with Paul, Timothy came to share Paul's concerns and values.
2:24 I myself will come soon Paul expresses hope that he will be released from prison.
2:25 Epaphroditus The Philippians had sent Epaphroditus to deliver gifts for Paul and look after him in prison. Now, due to the Philippians' alarm over news that Epaphroditus had taken ill, Paul is sending him back to Philippi (with this letter).
2:27 sorrow upon sorrow Paul already was confronting the grief of imprisonment. If Epaphroditus had died, Paul's grief would have been compounded—especially because Epaphroditus put his life on the line to care for Paul.
2:29 honor Believers who take risks and endure suffering for the sake of others and for the gospel are worthy of great respect. Just as Christ serves as a model of loving sacrifice, so does Epaphroditus.
2:30 help you yourselves could not give me This could refer to the distance that separated the Philippians and Paul. In addition, Paul hints at a gap in their support (Php 4:10).

3:1–3 Shifting his tone and message from chs. 1–2, Paul warns against false teachers in Philippi.
3:1 my brothers and sisters See note on 1:12. **to write the same things to you again** Paul probably is referring to the warning and teaching that follows, which he might have delivered to the Philippians in person or in an earlier letter. Repeating this teaching is for their own good.
3:2 Watch out for All three warnings in this verse point to one group—most likely to people who taught that all Christians had to follow the Jewish law. The role of the law was a divisive topic in the early church, especially when it came to non-Jewish believers. Acts 15 records a meeting of the apostles (often called the Jerusalem council) to determine whether non-Jewish Christians should be required to observe the Jewish law. One major issue was the rite of circumcision, held to be the defining marker of God's people ever since the covenant with Abraham (Ge 17:9–14). Paul taught that non-Jewish believers did not need to observe the law or become circumcised, but others promoted the opposite view. According to Paul, these opponents had severely disfigured the gospel message by trying to supplement Jesus' sacrifice on the cross. **dogs** The Greek word used here was commonly used in a derogatory manner. **mutilators** It seems that Paul uses the Greek word *katatomē* here, which may be rendered "mutilation," to say that non-Jews who undergo circumcision for conversion purposes are essentially mutilating themselves, because the work of Christ has rendered circumcision unnecessary for membership in God's covenant people.
3:3 circumcision In Jewish tradition, circumcision was the sign of being in covenant with God (see note on Ro 2:25). Paul asserts that the sign of being God's people—the true circumcision—is worshiping by the Spirit and boasting in the work of Christ. **boast in Christ Jesus** Refers to trusting in Christ as the defining marker of God's people. **confidence in the flesh** Refers to relying on circumcision and the law to confirm one's place in God's people. Paul uses the Greek word *sarx* (usually translated "flesh") with remarkable flexibility. In this passage, it refers to the mark of circumcision, signifying Jewish identity through observance of the law; it also might point to religious practices in general. Elsewhere, Paul associates *sarx* with human corruptibility (e.g., Ro 8:3–8), the human race (e.g., 1Co 1:29) and the human body (e.g., Gal 4:13).
3:4–21 To demonstrate the emptiness of the false teachers' message, Paul presents himself as an example for the believers to follow—much like he portrayed Christ, Timothy and Epaphroditus as models in Php 2. Paul begins by highlighting his Jewish credentials (vv. 4–6), showing that he more than anyone stands to gain if Jewish identity is the essential criteria that designates God's people. However, because the Messiah has come, Paul's perspective has been transformed, so that he now regards his Jewish identity and everything else as worthless compared to Christ (vv. 7–8). The only thing that matters now is knowing, trusting and following the Messiah (vv. 9–11). Like Jesus' disciples, who gave up everything to follow him (Mt 19:27), Paul forgets his past and presses ahead toward his future—life with Christ in the age to come (Php 3:12–14). He encourages the Philippians to take this same approach (vv. 15–17), declaring that their salvation and resurrection are assured (vv. 20–21).
3:4 I have more If anyone has impeccable credentials under the Jewish law, it's Paul.
3:5 on the eighth day According to the law, male children had to be circumcised eight days after birth (Lev 12:3). This practice traces back to God's covenant

tribe of Benjamin, a Hebrew of Hebrews; in regard to the law, a Pharisee; [6]as for zeal, persecuting the church; as for righteousness based on the law, faultless.

[7]But whatever were gains to me I now consider loss for the sake of Christ. [8]What is more, I consider everything a loss because of the surpassing worth of knowing Christ Jesus my Lord, for whose sake I have lost all things. I consider them garbage, that I may gain Christ [9]and be found in him, not having a righteousness of my own that comes from the law, but that which is through faith in[a] Christ — the righteousness that comes from God on the basis of faith. [10]I want to know Christ — yes, to know the power of his resurrection and participation in his sufferings, becoming like him in his death, [11]and so, somehow, attaining to the resurrection from the dead.

[12]Not that I have already obtained all this, or have already arrived at my goal, but I press on to take hold of that for which Christ Jesus took hold of me. [13]Brothers and sisters, I do not consider myself yet to have taken hold of it. But one thing I do: Forgetting what is behind and straining toward what is ahead, [14]I press on toward the goal to win the prize for which God has called me heavenward in Christ Jesus.

Following Paul's Example

[15]All of us, then, who are mature should take such a view of things. And if on some point you think differently, that too God will make clear to you. [16]Only let us live up to what we have already attained.

[17]Join together in following my example, brothers and sisters, and just as you have us as a model, keep your eyes on those who live as we do. [18]For, as I have often told you before and now tell you again even with tears, many live as enemies of the cross of Christ. [19]Their destiny is destruction, their god is their stomach, and their glory is in their shame. Their mind is set on earthly

[a] 9 Or *through the faithfulness of*

---

with Abraham (Ge 17:9–14). **people of Israel** Although Paul was born outside the land of Israel (Ac 22:3), his parents were Jewish — making him ethnically a member of Israel, God's chosen people. **tribe of Benjamin** The only tribe that aligned with Judah and remained faithful to the dynasty of King David (2Ch 11:1). **a Hebrew of Hebrews** This could refer to Paul's pure bloodline (fully Jewish, not mixed) or to his family's loyalty to ancestral traditions. **Pharisee** The Pharisees had a reputation for interpreting and practicing the Jewish law with great care. See the table "Major Groups in Jesus' Time" on p. 1630.

3:6 zeal Jews considered passionate devotion to God to be a virtue (e.g., Nu 25:10–13; Gal 1:14). Before Paul followed Christ, he expressed his zeal for God by persecuting Christians (Ac 8:1), who were considered blasphemers for proclaiming Jesus as the Messiah. Christians claimed that the same Jesus who had been crucified was now alive and worthy of worship. But to Jews, the idea of a crucified Messiah would have been unthinkable. Most Jews expected that God's Messiah would triumph over Israel's enemies, not be executed at their hands. **righteousness based on the law** This statement sums up Paul's commitment to the covenant between Israel and Yahweh. Compare note on Php 3:9.

3:7 loss In relation to Christ, Paul's Jewish credentials and status meant nothing — and even worked against him by blinding him to God's plan of salvation in Christ (compare Ro 10:2–4).

3:8 everything a loss Paul intensifies his previous statement: Not just his Jewish identity, but everything is a disadvantage compared to knowing the Messiah.

3:9 righteousness The Greek word used here, *dikaiosynē*, can be associated with a range of meanings, including ethical uprightness, right legal standing before God, right relationship with God, covenant faithfulness, vindication, and deliverance. Regardless of how the term is understood, Paul's usage here concerns the function of *dikaiosynē* to designate God's people — the righteous. Those who put confidence in the flesh rely on the law for their righteousness; in contrast, Paul has come to rely on Christ (compare Php 3:3 and note; Ro 10:2–4; Gal

3:21–22). **faith in Christ** The Greek phrase here has only two words — *pisteōs christou* — leaving it to the reader to supply the connection between "faith/faithfulness" and "Christ." The traditional reading is "faith in Christ"; another option is "faithfulness of Christ," referring to his obedient death on the cross (Php 2:8). Compare Ro 3:22; Gal 2:16.

3:10 power of his resurrection See note on Ro 1:4. **participation in his sufferings** Paul seems to recognize that suffering — especially for the gospel — brings deeper fellowship with Christ. Paul sees his ministry as an extension of Jesus' ministry, portrayed in Isa 53's account of the suffering servant. **becoming like him in his death** Paul desires to emulate the self-emptying love that Jesus displayed on the cross.

3:11 attaining to the resurrection Paul anticipates that being conformed to Christ's death will lead to new life in the power of Christ's resurrection (compare Ro 6:4–11; Gal 2:19–20; Col 2:12–13).

3:12 already arrived at my goal Paul has not yet arrived at his goal. The Greek verb used here, *teleioō*, can refer to being perfected, being completed or reaching a goal.

3:14 the goal For Paul, the ultimate goal is knowing Christ's resurrection power and dwelling with him in the age to come (Php 3:10–11,21).

3:15 who are mature The Greek adjective used here, *teleios*, is related to the verb in v. 12. In this case, Paul probably is calling on mature believers to adopt the mindset he has just described (vv. 7–14).

3:17 in following my example Paul regularly presents himself as a model for believers to follow (compare 1Co 4:16; 11:1; Gal 4:12). In Philippians, he also praises others who are worthy of imitation — Christ, Timothy and Epaphroditus (Php 2:5,22,25,29).

3:18 enemies of the cross of Christ These enemies seem to be different from the group that was promoting circumcision for non-Jewish believers (3:2–3). Paul associates them with sensual pleasures and shameful behavior (v. 19), suggesting they are libertines rather than keepers of the law.

3:19 Their destiny is destruction Paul assures the Philippians that such people will face divine judgment.

things. ²⁰But our citizenship is in heaven. And we eagerly await a Savior from there, the Lord Jesus Christ, ²¹who, by the power that enables him to bring everything under his control, will transform our lowly bodies so that they will be like his glorious body.

Closing Appeal for Steadfastness and Unity

4 Therefore, my brothers and sisters, you whom I love and long for, my joy and crown, stand firm in the Lord in this way, dear friends!

²I plead with Euodia and I plead with Syntyche to be of the same mind in the Lord. ³Yes, and I ask you, my true companion, help these women since they have contended at my side in the cause of the gospel, along with Clement and the rest of my co-workers, whose names are in the book of life.

Final Exhortations

⁴Rejoice in the Lord always. I will say it again: Rejoice! ⁵Let your gentleness be evident to all. The Lord is near. ⁶Do not be anxious about anything, but in every situation, by prayer and petition, with thanksgiving, present your requests to God. ⁷And the peace of God, which transcends all understanding, will guard your hearts and your minds in Christ Jesus.

⁸Finally, brothers and sisters, whatever is true, whatever is noble, whatever is right, whatever is pure, whatever is lovely, whatever is admirable — if anything is excellent or praiseworthy — think about such things. ⁹Whatever you have learned or received or heard from me, or seen in me — put it into practice. And the God of peace will be with you.

Thanks for Their Gifts

¹⁰I rejoiced greatly in the Lord that at last you renewed your concern for me. Indeed, you were concerned, but you had no opportunity to show it. ¹¹I am not saying this because I am in need, for I have learned to be content whatever the circumstances. ¹²I know what it is to be in need, and I know what it is to have plenty. I have learned the secret of being content in any and every situation, whether well fed or hungry, whether living in plenty or in want. ¹³I can do all this through him who gives me strength.

¹⁴Yet it was good of you to share in my troubles. ¹⁵Moreover, as you Philippians know, in the early days of your acquaintance with the gospel, when I set out from Macedonia, not one church shared

---

3:20 our citizenship is in heaven Roman citizenship was highly prized, but Paul encourages believers to embrace a far better identity as citizens of God's kingdom. Most residents of Philippi probably lacked Roman citizenship (see note on 1:1). For any believers who did hold Roman citizenship, Paul's statement here presents a challenge to look beyond their earthly status and show highest allegiance to Christ. **a Savior from there, the Lord Jesus Christ** In the Roman Empire, the emperor was known as the savior and lord. By applying these titles to Jesus, Paul is calling the Philippians to live under the authority and reign of the universe's true Savior and Lord, Jesus Christ. It was likely this kind of message that landed Paul and Silas in jail in Philippi (Ac 16:21).

3:21 will transform our lowly bodies Those who believe in Christ will be raised and their bodies will be transformed (Ro 8:11; 1Co 15:20–22,51–54). This explains why Paul writes that distinctive markers, such as circumcision, do not hold value in Christ (Gal 6:15). Temporary signs pale in comparison to the glorious transformation that awaits believers.

4:1–3 Paul repeats his call for Christian unity, the letter's dominant theme (compare Php 1:27–30; 2:2–4; 3:15–17).

4:1 stand firm See note on 1:27.
4:2 I plead with Euodia and I plead with Syntyche Paul names two women who had worked with him (v. 3) and apparently were at odds.
4:3 true companion, help these women Paul calls for a church member to guide the women toward reconciliation. **book of life** Refers to God's record of his faithful people (Ex 32:32–33; Ps 69:28; Rev 3:5 and note; 21:27).

4:4–9 Paul provides closing instructions for the church.

4:4 Rejoice The motif of maintaining joy in the midst of suffering is common in Paul's writings (Col 1:24; 2:5; 1Th 1:6; 2Co 8:2).
4:5 gentleness Refers to showing consideration for one another (compare Php 2:3–4). By displaying gentleness toward all people — believers and unbelievers alike — Christians reveal the gospel's power to transform and reconcile. **The Lord is near** Paul again references the day of Christ as motivation to live in a godly manner (see 1:6 and note; 1:10; 2:16).
4:6 Do not be anxious about anything Paul probably was aware of hardships facing the Philippians (see note on 1:29). See the table "Prayers in Paul's Letters" on p. 1925.
4:7 peace The Greek word used here, *eirēnē*, conveys a range of meanings, including well-being, prosperity, freedom from anxiety, safety from harm and deliverance from enemies. **guard your hearts and your minds** Paul envisions God's peace as a soldier who protects the hearts and minds of believers from anxiety, fear and doubt.

4:10–20 Paul thanks the Philippian church for their generous support. Paul's gratitude toward this church gives way to praise of God in v. 20.

4:13 I can do all this Paul testifies to the sufficiency of Christ's strength. He is prepared to endure any circumstance in life because Christ empowers him to do so.
4:15 Macedonia Roman province on the Balkan Peninsula where Philippi was located. Paul traveled through this area during his second and third missionary journeys. See the map "Paul's First and Second Missionary Journeys" on p. 2262; see the map "Paul's Third Missionary Journey" on p. 2263.

with me in the matter of giving and receiving, except you only; [16]for even when I was in Thessalonica, you sent me aid more than once when I was in need. [17]Not that I desire your gifts; what I desire is that more be credited to your account. [18]I have received full payment and have more than enough. I am amply supplied, now that I have received from Epaphroditus the gifts you sent. They are a fragrant offering, an acceptable sacrifice, pleasing to God. [19]And my God will meet all your needs according to the riches of his glory in Christ Jesus.

[20]To our God and Father be glory for ever and ever. Amen.

Final Greetings

[21]Greet all God's people in Christ Jesus. The brothers and sisters who are with me send greetings. [22]All God's people here send you greetings, especially those who belong to Caesar's household. [23]The grace of the Lord Jesus Christ be with your spirit. Amen.[a]

[a] 23 Some manuscripts do not have *Amen*.

4:16 Thessalonica Macedonian port city on the Aegean Sea; Paul's next stop after Philippi during his second missionary journey (Ac 16:40—17:1).

PAUL'S SECOND MISSIONARY JOURNEY (AD 49–51)

Paul and Silas visit Lystra and Derbe

Paul and Silas visit Philippi

Paul and Silas visit Thessalonica

Paul visits Athens

Paul visits Corinth

Paul writes letters from Corinth to the Thessalonian church

4:17 be credited to your account Paul clarifies his previous comments (Php 4:10–16). By commending the Philippians' gift, he is not indirectly seeking another. Rather, he is celebrating their generosity as a sign of their growing faith.

4:18 Epaphroditus See 2:25–30; note on 2:25. His visit was a tangible expression of the Philippians' concern for Paul and his needs.

4:19 all your needs Paul's needs were met through the Philippians' generous financial gift. In the tradition of mutual exchange common to ancient friendship, Paul trusts God to meet the needs of the church at Philippi (see note on 1:5).

4:20 glory The Greek term used here, *doxa*, refers to God's majesty and honor. See note on Ro 1:23.

4:21–23 Paul ends the letter with closing greetings and a blessing.

4:22 Caesar's household Refers to believers in Caesar's family or among those who work for the emperor.

4:23 grace of the Lord Jesus Christ Paul's typical way of closing his letters (e.g., Gal 6:18; 1Th 5:28).

COLOSSIANS

INTRODUCTION TO COLOSSIANS

The letter to the Colossians proclaims the supreme power, authority and sufficiency of Christ. While Paul was in prison, he heard a report about false teaching in the city of Colossae. People apparently were saying that Jesus was a good start, but that other beliefs and practices had to be added. Paul responds by affirming that nothing needs to be added to the work of Christ. As Lord of all creation, he is more than enough for every believer.

BACKGROUND

The letter names Paul and Timothy as the authors (Col 1:1). While the differences in style between this letter and Paul's other letters have led to some modern debate about its authorship— including the suggestion that it was written by someone else—the differences can be accounted for by noting that here Paul is addressing a different set of issues. In addition, Colossians was unanimously accepted by the early church fathers as by Paul.

Paul wrote Colossians from prison (4:3,10,18), probably in Rome (early 60s AD; Ac 28:30). It is also possible that he wrote it during his imprisonment in Caesarea (ca. AD 58–60; Ac 23:23— 26:32) or during an otherwise unrecorded imprisonment in Ephesus (ca. AD 54–55; Ac 19).

The recipients of the letter were part of a church in Colossae, a town in southwest Asia Minor. It seems that Paul did not plant this church and did not know (at least) some of the believers in Colossae (Col 1:4; 2:1). Epaphras, a leader of the church, likely visited Paul in Rome and told him about what was going on in the church (1:7; 4:12). Both Colossians and Ephesians mentions Tychicus as the carrier of the letters; this and parallels in the language between the two letters suggest they were written around the same time (see the "Introduction to Ephesians"; Col 4:7; Eph 6:21). There is also a connection between Colossians and Paul's Letter to Philemon (see the "Introduction to Philemon").

The issue in the Colossian church was that some false teachers had begun emphasizing what they claimed was superior wisdom and its accompanying regulations (Col 2:6–23). This heresy seems to have involved asceticism (2:23), an emphasis on special knowledge (2:4), and some Jewish elements: Circumcision, dietary laws and festival observances are mentioned (2:11,16; compare 3:11). Paul responds that the real wisdom of God has been

This map depicts the location of Colossae and the surrounding region. Paul wrote Colossians from prison, possibly in Rome.

revealed in Christ, and people don't need to follow special rules or have secret knowledge to have access to him (2:2–4). Paul also suggests that the letter to the Colossians be read in the church at Laodicea, indicating that he intended its message for more than just the Colossians (4:16).

STRUCTURE

Colossians is structured similarly to Paul's other letters, with an opening that consists of a greeting, thanksgiving and prayer (1:1–14), a body (1:15—4:6), and closing remarks and a benediction (4:7–18). In Paul's greeting, he picks up on the faith and love of the Colossians (1:4). The body begins with a hymn to Christ, emphasizing that Jesus is the full expression of the image of God (1:15–23). Paul then speaks about his own sufferings (1:24—2:5) and presents an argument against the false teachers (2:6–23). Nothing else is needed but Christ, who reorganizes the way people live life (3:1–17). He then details how the people in a typical Greco-Roman household should treat one another (3:18—4:1). He ends the body of the letter with final advice on prayer and wise living (4:2–6).

OUTLINE

- Salutation and prayer (1:1–14)
- The Christ hymn and reconciliation (1:15–23)
- Paul, the Colossians and empty philosophy (1:24—2:23)
- Living according to the cross (3:1—4:6)
- Final exhortations and greetings (4:7–18)

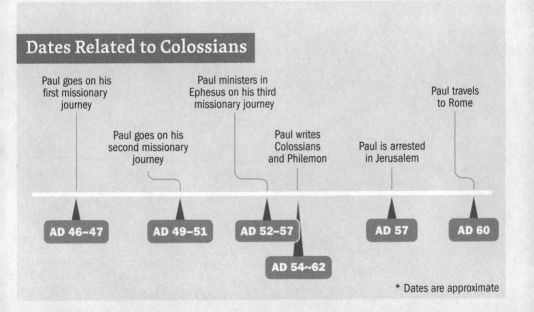

Dates Related to Colossians

Paul goes on his first missionary journey — AD 46–47

Paul goes on his second missionary journey — AD 49–51

Paul ministers in Ephesus on his third missionary journey — AD 52–57

Paul writes Colossians and Philemon — AD 54~62

Paul is arrested in Jerusalem — AD 57

Paul travels to Rome — AD 60

* Dates are approximate

THEMES

The main theme of Colossians is that Christ is Lord over all, and nothing else is needed to supplement the salvation found in him. False teachers suggested that more than Christ was needed—special knowledge and particular practices. Paul teaches against this philosophy because it promises much but ultimately does not deliver (2:20–23). In the end, only Christ delivers, and he should be the focus (3:1–4). Christians have been made alive with Christ (2:13), and their lives are already hidden with Christ in God (3:3). Nothing needs to be added to that.

The marker of true Christian spirituality is love (3:14). Believers are empowered by Christ to walk away from evil and embrace the ways of God (3:5–17). We are to wisely use our time, declaring—as Paul did while imprisoned—the wonderful mystery of Christ, each time a door is opened for us to do so.

1 Paul, an apostle of Christ Jesus by the will of God, and Timothy our brother,

²To God's holy people in Colossae, the faithful brothers and sisters*a* in Christ:

Grace and peace to you from God our Father.*b*

Thanksgiving and Prayer

³We always thank God, the Father of our Lord Jesus Christ, when we pray for you, ⁴because we have heard of your faith in Christ Jesus and of the love you have for all God's people — ⁵the faith and love that spring from the hope stored up for you in heaven and about which you have already heard in the true message of the gospel ⁶that has come to you. In the same way, the gospel is bearing fruit and growing throughout the whole world — just as it has been doing among you since the day you heard it and truly understood God's grace. ⁷You

---

a 2 The Greek word for *brothers and sisters* (*adelphoi*) refers here to believers, both men and women, as part of God's family; also in 4:15.   *b* 2 Some manuscripts *Father and the Lord Jesus Christ*

1:1–2 From prison, Paul writes to the Christians at Colossae (Col 4:3,10)—whom he may have never met (compare 1:4)—to encourage their progress in the faith (vv. 9–10). His location at this time is uncertain. If he was in Ephesus, roughly 120 miles west of Colossae, then he wrote the letter around AD 54–55; he also could have written it during imprisonments in Caesarea (AD 58–60) or Rome (early 60s AD; see note on Php 1:7). See the infographic "The Tullianum: A Prison in Rome" on p. 2008.

1:1 Paul Formerly known as Saul, he persecuted the early Christians until a dramatic encounter with the risen Christ led to him becoming Christianity's most prolific missionary (Ac 8:1–3; 9:1–22; see note on Ro 1:1). He preached the gospel and planted churches throughout Asia Minor, Macedonia and Greece, but there is no record that he ever visited Colossae. See the timeline "Life of Paul" on p. 1796. **apostle** A person designated by God to speak and act with special authority. Paul did not always refer to himself as an apostle (Php 1:1), but does so here to establish his credentials among the Colossians, most of whom he had never met (Col 2:1). In the Gospels, the apostles exercise their office by proclaiming the good news of the kingdom of God, casting out demons, and performing healings—actions that express and extend Christ's ministry (e.g., Mt 10:1–4; Lk 9:1–6). In the book of Acts, Jesus commissions the apostles to be his witnesses to the end of the earth (Ac 1:7–8). The apostles express this witness through their ministry of teaching, miraculous deeds (Ac 2:42–43), and church planting (1Co 3:6). See the table "Pauline Self-Designations" on p. 1904. **Timothy** Served with Paul in the region west of Colossae and might have been known by the believers there.

TIMOTHY
A disciple and companion of Paul. Timothy met Paul in Lystra (Ac 16:1) and assisted in his missionary efforts (v. 3; 20:4–5; 2Co 1:19; 1Ti 1:3), becoming like a son to Paul (1Ti 1:2). Paul also names Timothy as a co-sender in the opening of several other letters (Php 1:1; 1Th 1:1; 2Th 1:1).

1:2 God's holy people The Greek word used here, *hagioi*, often translated "saints" or "holy ones," refers to those who are set apart or who belong to God. **Colossae** A city located in southwest Asia Minor (modern-day Turkey). In the first century AD, Colossae was a small

agricultural community in Phrygia, a region known for an obsession with magic and the occult. The church at Colossae apparently was planted by a man named Epaphras (see Col 1:7 and note), who also ministered in the nearby cities of Laodicea and Hierapolis (4:12–13). **Grace and peace to you** See note on Ro 1:7. **God our Father** See note on Ro 1:7.

1:3–23 Paul expresses gratitude for the Colossian believers and a desire that their witness to Christ's lordship will mature and grow. Embedded within this passage is a hymn to Christ that affirms his authority over all things (Col 1:15–20). The importance of this theme becomes evident later in the letter, as Paul confronts false teachings that apparently were gaining a foothold in the Colossian church (2:4,8,16–23; see note on 2:8). In ch. 1, Paul's references to false teaching are subtle; he is preparing his audience for the more direct discussion in ch. 2.

1:3 We always thank See note on Ro 1:8.
1:4 faith The Greek word used here, *pistis*, refers to trust and reliance. **love** The greatest of the three Christian virtues (1Co 13:13), the others being faith and hope. The natural result of faith in Christ is love (*agapē* in Greek) for God and others.

AGAPĒ
The Greek word *agapē*, often translated "love," is a general word for affection and warm regard. The NT uses the word to describe compassion for other people, love for God or Christ, and the love God and Christ have for humanity and for each other. The gospel message makes the love denoted by *agapē* more of a mindset than a feeling. It involves putting the needs and interests of others before your own—even enduring suffering and hardship for the sake of others.

1:5 hope stored up for you The Greek word used in this phrase, *elpis*, often rendered as "hope," refers to confident expectation, not wishful thinking. The Colossians have hope because of their union with Christ (Col 1:27). This means they are free from corruption and death and are qualified to participate in Christ's life, resurrection and glory. Paul reminds them that their hope of a glorious future does not come from a religious philosophy (2:8), but from God. Therefore, they do not need to accept the demands of false teachers. **true message** Paul wants the Colossians to know that the gospel message they received is God's true revelation. See note on v. 9. **1:7 Epaphras** A believer who shared the gospel message with the Colossians. Paul later describes him as a

learned it from Epaphras, our dear fellow servant,[a] who is a faithful minister of Christ on our[b] behalf, [8] and who also told us of your love in the Spirit.

[9] For this reason, since the day we heard about you, we have not stopped praying for you. We continually ask God to fill you with the knowledge of his will through all the wisdom and understanding that the Spirit gives,[c] [10] so that you may live a life worthy of the Lord and please him in every way: bearing fruit in every good work, growing in the knowledge of God, [11] being strengthened with all power according to his glorious might so that you may have great endurance and patience, [12] and giving joyful thanks to the Father, who has qualified you[d] to share in the inheritance of his holy people in the kingdom of light. [13] For he has rescued us from the dominion of darkness and brought us into the kingdom of the Son he loves, [14] in whom we have redemption, the forgiveness of sins.

The Supremacy of the Son of God

[15] The Son is the image of the invisible God, the firstborn over all creation. [16] For in him all things were created: things in heaven and on earth, visible and invisible, whether thrones or powers or rulers or authorities; all things have been created through him and for him. [17] He is before all things, and in him all things hold together. [18] And he is the

[a] 7 Or slave   [b] 7 Some manuscripts your   [c] 9 Or all spiritual wisdom and understanding   [d] 12 Some manuscripts us

servant-hearted leader who works hard on behalf of Christians in Colossae, Laodicea and Hierapolis (4:12–13). **fellow servant** This description of Epaphras does not mean that he was literally a servant or slave. Rather, Paul is using figurative language to characterize Epaphras as a humble servant of God.

1:9 knowledge of his will Refers to the believers' awareness of Christ's desires for how they ought to conduct themselves (see vv. 10–12). False teachers might have described God's will as unknowable—or knowable only through secret rituals. Paul rejects this idea: Followers of Christ, filled with the knowledge of his will, can live in a manner pleasing to God because they know what matters to him. Mystery cults considered knowledge to be secretive or hidden; only insiders who adhered to secret rituals could obtain true knowledge. In contrast, Paul prays that the Colossians will be filled with knowledge. This is the purpose of his ministry (2:1–2), which is possible only because Christ himself is the source of all wisdom and knowledge (2:3). **wisdom** The Biblical conception of wisdom is oriented around God as the source of all wisdom; a wise person is a godly person (Hos 14:9; Col 4:5; Ro 16:19). **understanding that the Spirit gives** Refers to insight that comes from the Spirit. This stands in contrast to the mystery religions, which promoted insight through secret rituals.

1:10 knowledge of God Refers to experiential knowledge, not just intellectual understanding. As believers trust and obey God's will, they become more acquainted with God's ways—and with God himself.

1:12 qualified you to share in the inheritance As non-Jews (Gentiles), the Colossians would have been considered outsiders to God's blessings, which were reserved for the people of Israel. However, the central truth of the gospel for Paul was that Christ's death and resurrection brought salvation for all who believed, Jews and Gentiles alike. Throughout his letters, Paul conveys this central truth using different kinds of imagery. Here, he affirms believers as God's heirs; in the next verse, he shifts to language of deliverance.

1:13 dominion of darkness Refers to the realm dominated by sin and death (compare Eph 6:12). **kingdom** The realm in which Christ reigns as king, where his sovereign rule is carried out. The transfer from one realm to the other is accomplished by God: In his love and grace, he brings believers out of the domain of sin and death and moves them into the kingdom of his Son. The kingdom of God (or kingdom of heaven) is one of the most dominant themes in Jesus' teaching ministry

(e.g., Mt 4:17; 5:3–20; 13:10–52). In this verse, Paul indicates that God's kingdom is not just about the future; in some sense, it must already be present, because God has delivered believers from darkness and transferred them into his kingdom.

1:14 redemption Refers to the act of freeing someone who is enslaved. Just as Israel was enslaved in Egypt before being rescued by Yahweh, so the Colossian believers had been enslaved to the domain of sin and death before they responded in faith to God's act of salvation in Christ (Ex 6:6; 14:30; compare Ro 6:16–17). **forgiveness** God's forgiveness removes sin (Col 2:14) and provides reconciliation (1:22). Forgiveness is an expression of God's grace and love.

1:15–20 Paul proclaims the supremacy and sovereignty of Christ, who was present and active in the creation of the universe and who remains active in sustaining and reconciling all things. Whether Paul himself wrote this hymn is debated; he could have borrowed material used in early Christian worship. Regardless of authorship, the hymn is a central component of the letter, providing the basis for Paul's key points in chs. 2–3 about the sufficiency of Christ and the futility of false teachings. Because God's fullness dwells in Christ (v. 19), he is all that believers need.

1:15 image of the invisible God Jesus Christ makes the Father and the Spirit visible to people. Paul later draws on the notion of resembling God when writing about how people should treat one another (3:10). **firstborn** In this context, the Greek word used here, *prōtotokos*, affirms Christ's supremacy and sovereignty over all things (see vv. 17–18). In its OT context, *prōtotokos* refers primarily to preeminent status, as the Israelites recognized the firstborn son to have special privileges. In some cases, the special status of the firstborn was applied to a son who was not born first. For example, Isaac was not Abraham's first son, yet he inherited blessings that indicate that he was treated as the firstborn (Ge 16–17; 21:1–21).

1:16 visible and invisible These terms refer to earthly creatures and spiritual beings. **all things have been created through him** There is nothing outside the scope of Christ's sovereignty. Since all things—natural and supernatural—were created through him, they are subject to his authority.

1:18 head Indicates Christ's leadership of the church. His authority and empowerment enable the body of Christ to grow and mature. **church** The Greek word used here,

head of the body, the church; he is the beginning and the firstborn from among the dead, so that in everything he might have the supremacy. ¹⁹For God was pleased to have all his fullness dwell in him, ²⁰and through him to reconcile to himself all things, whether things on earth or things in heaven, by making peace through his blood, shed on the cross.

²¹Once you were alienated from God and were enemies in your minds because of*a* your evil behavior. ²²But now he has reconciled you by Christ's physical body through death to present you holy in his sight, without blemish and free from accusation — ²³if you continue in your faith, established and firm, and do not move from the hope held out in the gospel. This is the gospel that you heard and that has been proclaimed to every creature under heaven, and of which I, Paul, have become a servant.

Paul's Labor for the Church

²⁴Now I rejoice in what I am suffering for you, and I fill up in my flesh what is still lacking in regard to Christ's afflictions, for the sake of his body, which is the church. ²⁵I have become its servant by the commission God gave me to present to you the word of God in its fullness — ²⁶the mystery that has been kept hidden for ages and generations, but is now disclosed to the Lord's people. ²⁷To them God has chosen to make known among the Gentiles the glorious riches of this mystery, which is Christ in you, the hope of glory.

²⁸He is the one we proclaim, admonishing and teaching everyone with all wisdom, so that we may present everyone fully mature in Christ. ²⁹To this

a 21 Or minds, as shown by

---

ekklēsia, refers to an assembly of people. In Christian contexts, it describes the people who assemble in the name of Christ. See the infographic "Ancient Home Synagogue" on p. 1971. **the firstborn from among the dead** Refers to Jesus' resurrection, which Paul regards as a template for the resurrection of all believers (e.g., 1Co 15:20–23; 1Th 4:14). Compare Col 1:15 and note. **1:19 to have all his fullness dwell in him** Refers to God being fully present in Christ, parallel with Paul's statement in 2:9. Consequently, Christ is sufficient for the Colossians' salvation. This phrase echoes the glory of God filling the tabernacle (Ex 40:34). The Gospel of John describes Christ as the tabernacle or the dwelling of God (Jn 1:14) — an allusion that demonstrates the continuity between God's presence among the Israelites and his presence in the person of Christ. **1:20 reconcile** The Greek word used here, *apokatallassō*, refers to the act of restoring a relationship to harmony. The purpose of Christ's death on the cross was to bring all things created by Christ and for Christ (Col 1:16) into harmonious relationship. **1:22 Christ's physical body** Christ was not an angel or a nonphysical being; he had a body, and he endured suffering and death in this body. By emphasizing Christ's physical body, Paul may be combatting early Gnostic-like influences that could have been at work in Colossae. Gnostics emphasized spiritual, nonmaterial reality over the material world, prompting some people to deny that Christ had a physical body. Gnostics wrongly considered material reality to be evil and sought to escape it through abstaining from worldly comforts and pleasures. While fully developed Gnosticism postdates the NT, the beliefs Paul seems to be addressing here resemble later Gnostic thought. **holy** Describes belonging to or being set apart for God. The Colossians cannot claim responsibility for their status before God; no human tradition or rule made them holy. Rather, Christ's work of reconciliation brought them into relationship with God, making them holy. Since believers belong to God, they bear his image (3:10), which enables them to live out God's command to holiness. **1:23 if you continue in your faith** Paul seems to be acknowledging that the Colossians are at a crossroads. He charges them to continue trusting in Christ and living out the gospel message. However, they must refuse to observe the rules and traditions of false teachings, which

threaten to lead them in a different direction. **hope held out in the gospel** Refers to living in union with Christ and sharing in Christ's resurrection (compare v. 27).

1:24–29 The center of this passage is God's plan of salvation, revealed in Christ and expanded to include Gentiles (non-Jews) as well as Jews.

1:24 I rejoice in what I am suffering Paul refers to his imprisonment (4:3), which he considers part of his calling — not a cause for shame. His attitude serves as a model for the Colossians of how to endure hardship for the sake of others. See the infographic "The Tullianum: A Prison in Rome" on p. 2008. **what is still lacking in regard to Christ's afflictions** This difficult phrase might refer to the hardships traditionally expected to befall the Messiah's people in advance of his return (sometimes called the "Messianic woes"). The idea behind this tradition was that a certain amount of suffering was necessary before God's people would be vindicated. Paul seems to be referring here to this remainder of afflictions that the church must endure. He considers his own sufferings to represent some portion of this remainder; in this way, he is suffering on behalf of the church (compare 2Co 1:5; 4:10; Php 3:10). **1:26 mystery** Refers to God's plan of salvation revealed through the death and resurrection of Christ. This specifically involves Christ's ministry of reconciliation, which unites Gentiles (non-Jews, such as the Colossians) with Jews and creates one people of God (e.g., Eph 3:6–9). **to the Lord's people** See note on Col 1:2. **1:27 among the Gentiles** The Colossians' non-Jewish ethnicity did not exclude them or disqualify them from God's promises and plan. On the contrary, the work of Christ makes them eligible to share in the inheritance of God's people (v. 12). The inclusion of Gentiles into the people of God was always part of God's plan of salvation (Ge 12:3; Isa 49:6; Gal 3:8). **Christ in you** Refers to union with Christ. **1:28 everyone** Paul wants the Colossians to understand that the truth and wisdom of the gospel is available to everyone in their congregation; all believers are called to full maturity in Christ. **1:29 I strenuously contend** Paul explains that he, too, is on the path to Christian maturity. Like all believers, he is pursuing the hard work of discipleship in cooperation with Christ's indwelling presence.

end I strenuously contend with all the energy Christ so powerfully works in me.

2 I want you to know how hard I am contending for you and for those at Laodicea, and for all who have not met me personally. ²My goal is that they may be encouraged in heart and united in love, so that they may have the full riches of complete understanding, in order that they may know the mystery of God, namely, Christ, ³in whom are hidden all the treasures of wisdom and knowledge. ⁴I tell you this so that no one may deceive you by fine-sounding arguments. ⁵For though I am absent from you in body, I am present with you in spirit and delight to see how disciplined you are and how firm your faith in Christ is.

Spiritual Fullness in Christ

⁶So then, just as you received Christ Jesus as Lord, continue to live your lives in him, ⁷rooted and built up in him, strengthened in the faith as you were taught, and overflowing with thankfulness.

⁸See to it that no one takes you captive through hollow and deceptive philosophy, which depends on human tradition and the elemental spiritual forces[a] of this world rather than on Christ.

⁹For in Christ all the fullness of the Deity lives in bodily form, ¹⁰and in Christ you have been brought to fullness. He is the head over every power and authority. ¹¹In him you were also circumcised with a circumcision not performed by human hands. Your whole self ruled by the flesh[b] was put off when you were circumcised by[c] Christ, ¹²having been buried with him in baptism, in which you were also raised with him through your faith in the working of God, who raised him from the dead.

---

[a] 8 Or *the basic principles*; also in verse 20   [b] 11 In contexts like this, the Greek word for *flesh* (*sarx*) refers to the sinful state of human beings, often presented as a power in opposition to the Spirit; also in verse 13.   [c] 11 Or *put off in the circumcision of*

2:1–5 Paul begins this chapter by assuring the Colossians that Christ reveals the full truth of God.

2:1 contending This seems to refer to Paul's deep concern for the believers. He also might be referring to his intense effort in prayer. **Laodicea** A city about 11 miles from Colossae.

2:2 mystery of God Paul uses the term "mystery" to refer to Christ, who reveals and fulfills God's plan of salvation. See note on Col 1:26.

2:3 wisdom and knowledge Jewish traditions prized wisdom, and mystery cults valued knowledge. Paul affirms Christ as the true source of both. Since the believers of Colossae have Christ (1:27), they have no need for the wisdom and knowledge offered by false teachers.

2:4 fine-sounding arguments Ancient philosophers used lofty arguments to persuade their audiences. Paul warns the Colossians that such teachings may appear logical, but their conclusions are false.

2:6–15 This passage builds on Paul's remarks in vv. 2–3. Because Christ represents the full revelation of God (vv. 3,9), and because believers are united with Christ (vv. 6,10), the Colossians can be confident of their salvation and the defeat of worldly powers (vv. 7,13–15).

2:6 you received The Greek word used here, *paralambanō*, can refer to the reception of a tradition — in this case, the message of the gospel handed down from the apostles (Ac 2:42; 2Th 3:6).

2:7 rooted and built up Indicates the stability that the Colossians have in Christ. Old Testament writers used similar imagery to describe those who are faithful to God (Ps 1:3; Isa 61:3).

2:8 hollow and deceptive philosophy The false teaching that Paul opposes in this letter is sometimes called "the Colossian heresy." This philosophy cannot be identified precisely; it could reflect the influences of several ancient traditions, including Judaism, mysticism, asceticism, mystery cults and Gnosticism (see note on Col 1:22). Regardless of the specific teachings, the fundamental problem Paul identifies is that human rules and traditions are being recommended as necessary supplements to Christ. However, it is also possible that Paul is not correcting a particular false teaching. Instead, Paul could be concerned with the immaturity

and ignorance of the Colossian believers. The Greek word for philosophy, *philosophia*, literally means "love of wisdom." Philosophy originated in Greece during the sixth century BC as the systematic and logical investigation of a subject. By the first century, "philosophy" broadly referred to any moral or religious belief system. See the table "Major Groups in Jesus' Time" on p. 1630. **human tradition** Refers to teaching that has its origin in human beings. In contrast, the gospel message has its origin in God (Gal 1:11). **elemental spiritual forces** The Greek phrase used here could refer to several concepts: the basic religious teachings of Jews and Gentiles; the material parts of the universe (such as water, earth and fire); or spiritual powers (such as evil spirits or demonic entities). In this context, the first and third options are most likely. Paul makes clear that these teachings or forces are negative influences.

2:9 fullness of the Deity The very nature of God is fully present in Christ. False teachers may have asserted that Christ was one of many divine beings or that God's fullness was distributed throughout supernatural beings, not just Christ — claims that Paul rejects.

2:11 circumcision Although the physical act of circumcision was a sign of Jewish identity within the covenant, God continually expresses concern for circumcision of the heart (Dt 10:16; Jer 4:4; Ro 2:29). Here, Paul affirms that the Colossians already have received Christ's spiritual circumcision through their union with him in baptism; therefore, they do not need the sign of physical circumcision to legitimize their identity as God's people.

2:12 baptism The sacrament of washing with water as a sign of Christian commitment. Through baptism, believers identify with Christ's crucifixion and burial, symbolizing death to sin. **you were also raised with him** Paul often speaks of being raised with Christ as a future event (e.g., Ro 6:5; 1Th 4:16–17). In this verse, however, the Greek verb indicates a past event: The Colossians already have been raised with Christ in some sense. Paul likely intends to counter any uncertainty about salvation that the false teaching might have generated. By stating that believers have been raised with Christ, Paul affirms that they share in his resurrection life and are alive to God, empowered to live in ways that please God. This anticipates the future resurrection: When Christ returns, every believer will be raised from the dead and

¹³When you were dead in your sins and in the uncircumcision of your flesh, God made you[a] alive with Christ. He forgave us all our sins, ¹⁴having canceled the charge of our legal indebtedness, which stood against us and condemned us; he has taken it away, nailing it to the cross. ¹⁵And having disarmed the powers and authorities, he made a public spectacle of them, triumphing over them by the cross.[b]

Freedom From Human Rules

¹⁶Therefore do not let anyone judge you by what you eat or drink, or with regard to a religious festival, a New Moon celebration or a Sabbath day. ¹⁷These are a shadow of the things that were to come; the reality, however, is found in Christ. ¹⁸Do not let anyone who delights in false humility and the worship of angels disqualify you. Such a person also goes into great detail about what they have seen; they are puffed up with idle notions by their unspiritual mind. ¹⁹They have lost connection with the head, from whom the whole body, supported and held together by its ligaments and sinews, grows as God causes it to grow.

²⁰Since you died with Christ to the elemental spiritual forces of this world, why, as though you still belonged to the world, do you submit to its rules: ²¹"Do not handle! Do not taste! Do not touch!"? ²²These rules, which have to do with things that are all destined to perish with use, are based on merely human commands and teachings. ²³Such regulations indeed have an appearance of wisdom, with their self-imposed worship, their false humility and their harsh treatment of the body, but they lack any value in restraining sensual indulgence.

Living as Those Made Alive in Christ

3 Since, then, you have been raised with Christ, set your hearts on things above, where Christ is, seated at the right hand of God. ²Set your minds on things above, not on earthly things. ³For you died, and your life is now hidden with Christ in God. ⁴When Christ, who is your[c] life, appears, then you also will appear with him in glory.

a 13 Some manuscripts *us*　*b* 15 Or *them in him*　*c* 4 Some manuscripts *our*

will receive a glorified human body, incorruptible and immortal (1Co 15:51–53).

2:13 dead Paul refers to the Colossians' situation prior to faith and baptism, when they lived apart from Christ.

2:14 charge The Greek term used here means "handwriting," but it denotes a written record of indebtedness. The initial image is one of tearing up or burning a debt record, although later in the verse this document is nailed to the cross. Paul is confirming the significance of the crucifixion: Through his sacrificial death, Jesus both embodies the debt of human sin and wipes it out (compare Ro 8:3; 2Co 5:21). It is also possible that the expression refers to the regulations of the Mosaic Law, which Paul also discusses in Col 2:20–23. In this case, the law functions like a record book of humanity's sins (compare Ro 4:15; Gal 3:19–22).

2:15 having disarmed the powers and authorities This verse describes Christ exposing, defeating and subjugating the hostile spiritual powers (compare Lk 10:18; Jn 12:31; 1Pe 3:22).

2:16–23 Because God's presence, salvation and victory are revealed fully in Christ (Col 2:9–15), he is sufficient for the Colossians' salvation. There is no need to pursue additional teachings or practices.

2:16 judge The Greek word used here, *krinō*, can mean "to condemn"; it also can refer to assessing value. **what you eat or drink** The criteria listed in this verse correspond with Jewish practices like food laws and calendar observances.

2:17 a shadow of the things that were to come Although Israelites were required to observe food laws and certain days, Paul asserts that the law ultimately points to Christ (compare Ro 10:4; Gal 3:24).

2:18 delights in false humility Likely refers to ascetic practices (see note on Col 2:21). **worship of angels** The Greek phrase used here could indicate people worshiping angels or being led in worship by angels. The latter might refer to the heavenly worship liturgy mentioned in several ancient Jewish traditions. **what they have seen** Probably refers to visionary experiences.

2:19 head Paul emphasizes the need for believers (the body) to be connected to Christ (the head). See note on 1:18.

2:20 elemental spiritual forces Since Christ has defeated the powers and authorities (v. 15), those in union with Christ must not subject themselves to other forces (see note on v. 8; compare Gal 4:8–9).

2:21 Do not handle! Do not taste! Do not touch! These appear to represent regulations set by the false teachers, who were promoting ascetic practices (abstaining from worldly comforts and pleasures) as the means to holiness and salvation.

2:23 an appearance of wisdom The false teaching might have sounded convincing, but it ultimately was futile because it did not address the root of the problem: sin. In Christ, however, the worldly powers of sin have been defeated. Believers have been raised to new life and therefore have no need for man-made rules (Col 2:12–15,20).

3:1—4:1 Earlier, Paul affirmed that the Colossians have been raised to new life in Christ (2:12–13). Now he presents the implications of that life. This teaching section of the letter has its own short introduction (vv. 1–4), a contrast between the old and new ways of living (vv. 5–11), guidelines for the Christian community (vv. 12–17) and instructions for family relationships (3:18—4:1).

3:1 you have been raised with Christ See note on 2:12. **things above** Paul's remarks here echo Jesus' instruction to seek first the kingdom of heaven (Mt 6:33). **seated at the right hand of God** A position of favor, honor and authority (Ps 110:1; Eph 1:20). In the OT, God's right hand symbolizes strength and salvation (Ex 15:6; Ps 20:6).

3:2 earthly things Paul probably has in mind the empty human traditions and worldly elemental forces he spoke against throughout ch. 2.

3:3 you died Refers to believers sharing in Christ's death through baptism.

3:4 Christ, who is your life Paul underscores the significance of Christ for the believer: Jesus is not peripheral to

⁵Put to death, therefore, whatever belongs to your earthly nature: sexual immorality, impurity, lust, evil desires and greed, which is idolatry. ⁶Because of these, the wrath of God is coming.ᵃ ⁷You used to walk in these ways, in the life you once lived. ⁸But now you must also rid yourselves of all such things as these: anger, rage, malice, slander, and filthy language from your lips. ⁹Do not lie to each other, since you have taken off your old self with its practices ¹⁰and have put on the new self, which is being renewed in knowledge in the image of its Creator. ¹¹Here there is no Gentile or Jew, circumcised or uncircumcised, barbarian, Scythian, slave or free, but Christ is all, and is in all.

¹²Therefore, as God's chosen people, holy and dearly loved, clothe yourselves with compassion, kindness, humility, gentleness and patience. ¹³Bear with each other and forgive one another if any of you has a grievance against someone. Forgive as the Lord forgave you. ¹⁴And over all these virtues put on love, which binds them all together in perfect unity.

¹⁵Let the peace of Christ rule in your hearts, since as members of one body you were called to peace. And be thankful. ¹⁶Let the message of Christ dwell among you richly as you teach and admonish one another with all wisdom through psalms, hymns, and songs from the Spirit, singing to God with gratitude in your hearts. ¹⁷And whatever you do, whether in word or deed, do it all in the name of the Lord Jesus, giving thanks to God the Father through him.

Instructions for Christian Households

3:18 – 4:1pp — Eph 5:22 – 6:9

¹⁸Wives, submit yourselves to your husbands, as is fitting in the Lord.

¹⁹Husbands, love your wives and do not be harsh with them.

²⁰Children, obey your parents in everything, for this pleases the Lord.

²¹Fathers,ᵇ do not embitter your children, or they will become discouraged.

²²Slaves, obey your earthly masters in everything; and do it, not only when their eye is on you and to curry their favor, but with sincerity of heart and reverence for the Lord. ²³Whatever you do, work at it with all your heart, as working

---

ᵃ 6 Some early manuscripts *coming on those who are disobedient*
ᵇ 21 Or *Parents*

---

life; he is life. He imparts God's life, and he is the center around which life should be oriented. **will appear with him** The believer's life is hidden in God, and the world does not recognize it. Here, Paul reminds the Colossians that they will share in Christ's glory when he returns.
3:5 Put to death, therefore, whatever belongs to your earthly nature The list of sinful actions in this verse echoes the deeds of the flesh in Gal 5:19 – 21. **idolatry** Paul associates idolatry with the consuming desire to possess more than others, regardless of actual need.
3:6 wrath of God Refers to divine judgment against evil. See note on Ro 1:18.
3:10 put on Here the Greek text of Colossians uses the imagery of changing one's clothes to illustrate Christ's transformative work in believers' lives (compare Ro 13:14; Gal 3:27). **being renewed** The Greek word used here, *anakainoō*, refers to the process of becoming new, which is ongoing for the believer. **knowledge** True knowledge reflects the image of the Creator. Compare the opening of the Christ-hymn in ch. 1, which identifies Christ as both the image of God and the agent of creation (Col 1:15 – 16). Paul also states that divine wisdom and knowledge are hidden in Christ (2:3).
3:11 Gentile The Greek word used here, *hellēn*, is an ethnic term denoting the people of Greece. Paul sometimes uses this term as a synonym for "Gentiles" (non-Jews). **circumcised or uncircumcised** Another way of referring to Jews (those who are circumcised according to the law) and Gentiles (those who are not). **barbarian** A person considered uncultured according to Greco-Roman standards — i.e., those who did not speak Greek or Latin and who practiced foreign customs or traditions. **Scythian** Like barbarians, Scythians were typically regarded as uncivilized people. **Christ is all** The standard categories of race and social status that normally divide people do not apply to those who are in Christ (compare Gal 3:28) — there is equality. This does not mean that Christians cease to have ethnic and social identities; rather, it means that people are not excluded from new life in Christ because of such distinctions. Moreover, these distinctions must not cause divisions in the community of believers.
3:12 God's chosen people Originally, God chose the nation of Israel to be his people (Dt 14:2; Ro 9:4 – 5). However, because such distinctions are rendered irrelevant in Christ (Col 3:11), Paul affirms the Colossian believers as being among God's chosen people (compare 1:12,21 – 22).
3:15 peace The Greek word used here, *eirēnē*, refers to wholeness or the absence of conflict in a relationship.
3:16 message of Christ Refers either to the gospel message about Christ or to Christ's teaching (as opposed to human philosophies or traditions; 2:8).
3:18 submit Paul is not saying that a wife ought to respond to her husband with mindless obedience; being subject to one's spouse should be voluntary and conscious. Submission in marriage is not demeaning; it is informed by God's relationship to the church (see Eph 5:22 – 23; note on 5:22).
3:19 love In this context, to love (*agapaō*) means to put the needs and interests of others before your own. In his letter to the Ephesians, Paul presents Christ's sacrificial death on behalf of the church as the model of love that husbands should have for their wives (see Eph 5:25 and note).
3:20 obey your parents This reflects the fifth commandment (Ex 20:12).
3:21 do not embitter In Paul's time, fathers had considerable authority within the household. He urges fathers to use that authority in a way that avoids causing resentment.
3:22 Slaves Paul includes slaves in his discussion of the family because they were considered members of the Greco-Roman household. Compare note on 4:1.

for the Lord, not for human masters, ²⁴since you know that you will receive an inheritance from the Lord as a reward. It is the Lord Christ you are serving. ²⁵Anyone who does wrong will be repaid for their wrongs, and there is no favoritism.

4 Masters, provide your slaves with what is right and fair, because you know that you also have a Master in heaven.

Further Instructions

²Devote yourselves to prayer, being watchful and thankful. ³And pray for us, too, that God may open a door for our message, so that we may proclaim the mystery of Christ, for which I am in chains. ⁴Pray that I may proclaim it clearly, as I should. ⁵Be wise in the way you act toward outsiders; make the most of every opportunity.

4:1 Masters In Greco-Roman society, masters assumed complete authority over their slaves and could freely mistreat them. Paul urges masters who are believers to use their authority with integrity; in God's kingdom, they too are slaves, and God is their master (compare Eph 6:5–9). Unlike slavery of the pre-Civil War era in North America, slavery in the Greco-Roman world often functioned like a credit system. To pay debts, people sometimes sold themselves into slavery (compare note on Phm 10; note on 1Pe 2:18). Slaves could hold positions of authority and even own property, and many gained their freedom. Nonetheless, Paul never commends slavery and he shows how both slaves and masters are equal before Christ—making a radical statement for his culture and time (Col 3:11). Paul exhorts believers to approach the institution in light of their relationship with Christ. Through the gos-

pel, slaves and masters became brothers and sisters in Christ—demanding that all parties exhibit God's values of justice, mercy and love (compare Phm 16 and note).

4:2–18 Paul concludes the letter with final instructions and greetings.

4:3 mystery of Christ Refers to God's plan of redemption for creation and humanity (compare Col 1:26–27; 2:2; see note on 1:26). This mystery has been revealed through Jesus Christ and the teaching of his apostles. **I am in chains** Paul wants the Colossians to understand that his imprisonment is a result of his gospel work, and that it demonstrates his love for them (1:24). See the infographic "The Tullianum: A Prison in Rome" on p. 2008. **4:5 wise** Paul refers to practical and transformational wisdom, not intellectual insight (compare 1Co 1:21,27).

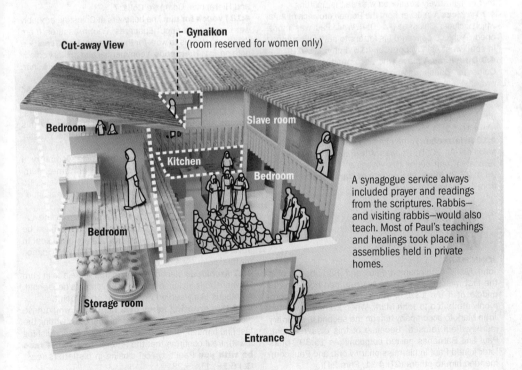

Cut-away View

Gynaikon (room reserved for women only)

Bedroom

Slave room

Kitchen

Bedroom

Bedroom

Storage room

Entrance

A synagogue service always included prayer and readings from the scriptures. Rabbis—and visiting rabbis—would also teach. Most of Paul's teachings and healings took place in assemblies held in private homes.

Ancient Home Synagogue

The term "synagogue" refers generally to a Jewish assembly for prayer. During the first-century AD, the term referred primarily to buildings designed to house such assemblies. Jews living in Greek towns usually assembled for prayer in private homes—and if an assembly member was wealthy, the synagogue might have been held in a home like this one.

⁶Let your conversation be always full of grace, seasoned with salt, so that you may know how to answer everyone.

Final Greetings

⁷Tychicus will tell you all the news about me. He is a dear brother, a faithful minister and fellow servant[a] in the Lord. ⁸I am sending him to you for the express purpose that you may know about our[b] circumstances and that he may encourage your hearts. ⁹He is coming with Onesimus, our faithful and dear brother, who is one of you. They will tell you everything that is happening here.

¹⁰My fellow prisoner Aristarchus sends you his greetings, as does Mark, the cousin of Barnabas. (You have received instructions about him; if he comes to you, welcome him.) ¹¹Jesus, who is called Justus, also sends greetings. These are the only Jews[c] among my co-workers for the kingdom of God, and they have proved a comfort to me. ¹²Epaphras, who is one of you and a servant of Christ Jesus, sends greetings. He is always wrestling in prayer for you, that you may stand firm in all the will of God, mature and fully assured. ¹³I vouch for him that he is working hard for you and for those at Laodicea and Hierapolis. ¹⁴Our dear friend Luke, the doctor, and Demas send greetings. ¹⁵Give my greetings to the brothers and sisters at Laodicea, and to Nympha and the church in her house.

¹⁶After this letter has been read to you, see that it is also read in the church of the Laodiceans and that you in turn read the letter from Laodicea.

¹⁷Tell Archippus: "See to it that you complete the ministry you have received in the Lord."

¹⁸I, Paul, write this greeting in my own hand. Remember my chains. Grace be with you.

---

a 7 Or *slave*; also in verse 12   *b* 8 Some manuscripts *that he may know about your*   *c* 11 Greek *only ones of the circumcision group*

Those who apply such wisdom can reflect God's values and character.

4:6 seasoned with salt In the ancient world, salt was used to preserve food and enhance flavor. Conversation that is figuratively seasoned with salt is uplifting.

4:7 Tychicus A believer from the Roman province of Asia, which included Colossae (Ac 20:4). While Paul was imprisoned, Tychicus delivered his letters to several churches in southwest Asia Minor (Col 4:16; Eph 6:21–22).

4:9 Onesimus A slave who accompanied Tychicus to Colossae. Onesimus apparently had run away from his owner, Philemon, who might have hosted the Colossian church in his home (Phm 2). Paul seems to have met Onesimus while in prison and now was sending him back to Colossae to be reconciled to Philemon (Phm 10,12).

4:10 Aristarchus A missionary companion from Thessalonica (Ac 20:4). He was with Paul in Ephesus and Jerusalem and during his voyage to Rome (Ac 19:29; 20:4; 27:2). **Mark, the cousin of Barnabas** John Mark from Jerusalem (Ac 12:12).

Colossians 4:10

JOHN MARK
John Mark accompanied Paul and Barnabas during the first missionary journey, but returned home in the middle of it (Ac 13:13). The Gospel of Mark is commonly attributed to John Mark. When Barnabas wanted John Mark to accompany him on the second missionary journey, Paul refused. Because of this disagreement, Paul and Barnabas parted company (Ac 15:39). Mark later joined Paul in his missionary work, and Paul commended him to others (2Ti 4:11; Phm 24).

4:11 Jesus, who is called Justus Nothing is known of this man.

4:12 Epaphras A believer who likely planted the church at Colossae and perhaps also the churches at Laodicea and Hierapolis. Compare Col 1:7.

4:13 I vouch for him The believers at Colossae probably were concerned about Epaphras. Paul reassures them that he continues to work for their benefit. **Laodicea** See note on 2:1. **Hierapolis** A commercial and military colony near Colossae and Laodicea in southwest Asia Minor. Hierapolis was known for its mystery cults.

4:14 Luke A missionary companion of Paul (see Ac 16:10 and note; 2 Ti 4:11); traditionally identified as the author of the Gospel of Luke and the book of Acts. **Demas** Although he was with Paul at the time of this letter, Demas later deserts Paul and goes to Thessalonica (2Ti 4:10).

4:15 Nympha Probably a wealthy single woman or a widow, since she hosted a church in her home. Members of the early church typically met in homes (e.g., Ro 16:5). See the infographic "Ancient Home Synagogue" on p. 1971.

4:16 letter from Laodicea Paul's letter to the Laodiceans is unknown. One proposal is that it might be the letter to the Ephesians (which Paul may have sent to several churches), but there is no conclusive evidence for this claim. See note on Eph 1:1.

4:17 Archippus Mentioned only in this verse and in Phm 2, where he is included as part of Philemon's household. Archippus likely served with Paul at some point.

4:18 this greeting in my own hand Paul would have dictated his letter to a professional scribe. By writing the last line himself (and perhaps including a distinguishing mark), Paul confirms that the letter is from him. **Grace be with you** Paul's typical closing in his letters (e.g., Gal 6:18; 1Th 5:28).

1 THESSALONIANS

INTRODUCTION TO 1 THESSALONIANS

Paul writes to the church at Thessalonica to encourage believers. He is enthusiastic—both about the Thessalonians' faith and about the way in which they have shared the Good News of Jesus in their region (1Th 1:7–8). But Paul also addresses two pressing issues. First, he offers an explanation and a defense of his work among them. Second, he assures them that all fellow believers who have already died will be resurrected to life with Jesus (4:15–18). This letter charges the Thessalonians—and us—to place our confidence in Christ.

BACKGROUND

The opening verse lists Paul as the primary author, along with Silvanus (Silas) and Timothy. Paul wrote the letter from Corinth during his 18-month plus stay there in AD 50–51 (Ac 18:11). This can be dated precisely because of an archeological inscription found at Delphi that mentions Gallio, the proconsul who heard charges against Paul in Corinth (Ac 18:12–17; compare 1Th 3:4).

Before writing this letter, Paul had visited the city of Thessalonica on his second missionary journey (ca. AD 49–51). He started his ministry in Thessalonica by preaching in the local synagogue, leading several people to follow Jesus (Ac 17:2–4). However, a riot instigated by other Jews compelled him to leave the city (Ac 17:5–10). After Paul went south to Athens, he sent Timothy back to Thessalonica to check on the believers there (1Th 3:1–2). Later, Timothy joined Paul in Corinth and gave him an update on the Thessalonians, and Paul decided to write to them (Ac 18:5; 1Th 3:6).

Thessalonica was the capital of Macedonia (northern Greece), a Roman province. It was one of the major commercial centers in the area and a strategic city for Paul's ministry. First Thessalonians and Acts suggest that most of the church there consisted of non-Jewish people (1Th 1:9; 2:14; Ac 17:4). During Paul's visit and after his departure, the believers in Thessalonica experienced persecution (1Th 1:6; 2:14; 3:3–4). Roman emperor worship—which was popular in the city—made the residents suspicious of Christians, who claimed that Jesus was a king (Ac 17:7). In response to this persecution, Paul encourages the Thessalonians to continue in the faith and to put their hope in the resurrected Christ, who suffered and died for them and who will come again (1Th 4:13–18).

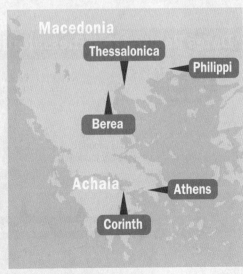

This map depicts the location of Thessalonica and the surrounding region.

STRUCTURE

Like a typical Greco-Roman letter, 1 Thessalonians has a greeting (1:1), a body (1:2—5:22) and a conclusion (5:23–28). The body of the letter can be divided into two sections: The first section (1:2—3:13) looks backward to Paul's time with the Thessalonians; the second section (4:1—5:22) addresses issues and concerns in the church. Immediately after the greeting, Paul gives thanks for the Thessalonians' conversion (1:2–10). Paul then defends his conduct when he was with them (2:1–12), expresses thanks for their response (2:13–16), states his desire to visit them (2:17–20) and describes Timothy's visit and return (3:1–13).

In the second section of the letter body, Paul offers guidance on a variety of practical issues. First he addresses sexual conduct (4:1–8), then brotherly love (4:9–12). Then he answers questions about Christians who have died (4:13–18) and Christ's return (5:1–11). He gives several quick instructions (5:12–22) before concluding the letter.

OUTLINE

- Paul and the Thessalonian church (1:1—3:13)
- Practical instructions and Christ's return (4:1—5:22)
- Prayer and conclusion (5:23–28)

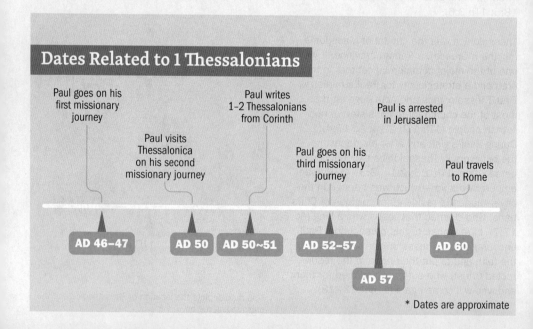

Dates Related to 1 Thessalonians

Paul goes on his first missionary journey

Paul visits Thessalonica on his second missionary journey

Paul writes 1–2 Thessalonians from Corinth

Paul goes on his third missionary journey

Paul is arrested in Jerusalem

Paul travels to Rome

AD 46–47

AD 50

AD 50~51

AD 52–57

AD 57

AD 60

* Dates are approximate

THEMES

In the midst of great difficulties, Paul encourages the Thessalonians—noting that the message he preached, and the gospel they received, is authentic (2:13–16). The Good News of Jesus could have come only from God, and they can trust it to sustain them until the very end (5:1–11). They have proven that they can endure persecution and turn away from idols (1:6,9), and now they must continue to faithfully follow Jesus (4:1–12; 5:12–22).

Paul's message in 1 Thessalonians is that we can trust the character of God and the truth of the gospel (1:10; 2:19–20; 5:1–11). Paul reassures believers who have died that they have not missed anything; both the living and the dead will participate in Christ's return (4:13–18). This would have encouraged the Thessalonians to endure persecution, even to the point of death.

Since Christ will surely come again, we must live faithfully in light of this reality. Like the Thessalonians, we still grieve for those who have died. But we do not grieve like those who have no hope. Because Jesus has been raised, our resurrection is certain—and we can face any hardship with the confidence that God is with us.

1

Paul, Silas[a] and Timothy,

To the church of the Thessalonians in God the Father and the Lord Jesus Christ:

Grace and peace to you.

Thanksgiving for the Thessalonians' Faith

[2] We always thank God for all of you and continually mention you in our prayers. [3] We remember before our God and Father your work produced by faith, your labor prompted by love, and your endurance inspired by hope in our Lord Jesus Christ. [4] For we know, brothers and sisters[b] loved by God,

that he has chosen you, [5] because our gospel came to you not simply with words but also with power, with the Holy Spirit and deep conviction. You know how we lived among you for your sake. [6] You became imitators of us and of the Lord, for you welcomed the message in the midst of severe suffering with the joy given by the Holy Spirit. [7] And so you became a model to all the believers in Macedonia and Achaia. [8] The Lord's message rang out from you not only in Macedonia and Achaia—your faith in God has become known everywhere. Therefore we do not

---

[a] 1 Greek *Silvanus*, a variant of *Silas*   [b] 4 The Greek word for *brothers and sisters* (*adelphoi*) refers here to believers, both men and women, as part of God's family; also in 2:1, 9, 14, 17; 3:7; 4:1, 10, 13; 5:1, 4, 12, 14, 25, 27.

1:1–10 Paul visited Thessalonica during his second missionary journey (ca. AD 49–51; Ac 17:1–9). Preaching in the local synagogue, Paul converted many Thessalonians—both Jew and Gentile—to Christianity (Ac 17:2–4). Some Jews, however, became jealous and caused a disturbance in the city (Ac 17:5). They accused Paul of claiming there was another king, named Jesus (Ac 17:7)—an act of treason against the Roman emperor. Before they could arrest him, Paul was sent away, leaving behind a community of new believers.

Concerned they might not withstand the threat of persecution, Paul sent Timothy to encourage the Thessalonians (1Th 3:2). Timothy reported back that they endured the persecution but now had concerns about the Lord's return. In addition, some believers continued to engage in sexual immorality, while others refused to work for a living. Paul wrote this letter in response to Timothy's report. He likely wrote the letter from Corinth between AD 50–51 (compare Ac 18:1), making it one of the earliest books of the NT.

First Thessalonians opens with a typical greeting that indicates that Paul, along with Silas and Timothy, sent this letter to the Thessalonian church. Paul then offers a thanksgiving prayer to God on behalf of the Thessalonian believers that recalls the power of their conversion (1Th 1:4–7) and their effective witness among other believers in the region (vv. 8–10).

1:1 Paul See note on Ro 1:1. See the timeline "Life of Paul" on p. 1796. **Silas** Silas, also known as Silvanus, was a well-respected leader from the Jerusalem church who accompanied Paul on his second missionary journey (Ac 15:22,40; 16:16–40). Paul likely includes Silas as a cosender of this letter because he also ministered to the Thessalonians (Ac 17:4,14). **Timothy** Half-Gentile, half-Jewish disciple and companion of Paul. Paul includes Timothy as a cosender because, like Silvanus, the Thessalonians knew him (Ac 17:14). Timothy met Paul in Lystra (Ac 16:1) and assisted him in his missionary efforts (e.g., Ac 20:4–5; 2Co 1:19; 1Ti 1:3), becoming like a son to Paul (1Ti 1: 2). **Thessalonians** The city of Thessalonica was located in the Roman province of Macedonia (modern-day Greece). Its harbor and proximity to a major highway (Via Egnatia) made it a strategic location for Paul's ministry in Macedonia. The Romans captured Thessalonica in 168 BC. They later made it a free city because of its support of the Roman emperor, Augustus Caesar. As a free city, Thessalonica was allowed to retain its Greek culture and language, despite Roman control (e.g., they could

mint their own coins). In response, the Thessalonians established a cult for the emperor. A variety of gods were also worshiped in Thessalonica: Cabirus, Dionysus, Serapis and Isis. **Grace and peace to you** Paul's typical greeting throughout his letters (e.g., Ro 1:7; Php 1:2). It summarizes his gospel message: God's work through Christ ("grace") brings people into a harmonious relationship with God and one another ("peace"). The Greek word used here *charis*, usually translated as "grace," is an alteration of the standard term *chairein* (from *chairō*, meaning "to rejoice"). The other Greek term used here, *eirēnē*, is equivalent to the Hebrew term *shalom* ("peace"), which carries the idea of wholeness.

1:2 We always thank Paul's letters often follow conventions for ancient letter-writing by including a prayer for the recipients. Here Paul thanks God for the Thessalonians' faith, which continued to grow despite his absence (1Th 2:17—3:5). See the table "Prayers in Paul's Letters" on p. 1925.

1:3 work produced by faith, your labor prompted by love, and your endurance inspired by hope Faith, love and hope are the three core Christian virtues (1Co 13:13; 1Th 5:8). They serve as evidence of the Thessalonians' salvation and the effectiveness of missionary efforts among them.

1:5 how we lived among you Paul and his companions worked while they lived among the Thessalonians (2:9). Later he reminds the Thessalonians that he and his coworkers served among them with gentleness and loving care (vv. 7–8).

1:6 imitators In joyfully enduring persecution, the Thessalonians imitated Paul, his companions and the Lord Jesus (compare Mt 5:11–12; Ac 5:41). In the ancient world, students imitated their teachers as part of their education. In the Christian faith, disciples imitate God's character (Eph 5:1)—and in doing so, live lives worthy of imitation (1Co 11:1; Php 3:17). **suffering** Refers to the opposition and persecution experienced by the believers in Thessalonica (1Th 3:3–4,7; 2Th 1:4,6–7).

1:7 Macedonia A Roman province on the Balkan Peninsula. Thessalonica was located in Macedonia. Paul visited Macedonia because of a vision (Ac 16:9–12). Despite opposition (2Co 7:5; 1Th 2:2), he planted several churches there (Ac 17:10–12). **Achaia** A Roman province south of Macedonia (modern-day Greece). The cities of Athens and Corinth were located in Achaia.

need to say anything about it, [9]for they themselves report what kind of reception you gave us. They tell how you turned to God from idols to serve the living and true God, [10]and to wait for his Son from heaven, whom he raised from the dead — Jesus, who rescues us from the coming wrath.

Paul's Ministry in Thessalonica

2 You know, brothers and sisters, that our visit to you was not without results. [2]We had previously suffered and been treated outrageously in Philippi, as you know, but with the help of our God we dared to tell you his gospel in the face of strong opposition. [3]For the appeal we make does not spring from error or impure motives, nor are we trying to trick you. [4]On the contrary, we speak as those approved by God to be entrusted with the gospel. We are not trying to please people but God, who tests our hearts. [5]You know we never used flattery, nor did we put on a mask to cover up greed — God is our witness. [6]We were not looking for praise from people, not from you or anyone else, even though as apostles of Christ we could have asserted our authority. [7]Instead, we were like young children[a] among you.

Just as a nursing mother cares for her children, [8]so we cared for you. Because we loved you so much, we were delighted to share with you not only the gospel of God but our lives as well. [9]Surely you remember, brothers and sisters, our toil and hardship; we worked night and day in order not to be a burden to anyone while we preached the gospel of God to you. [10]You are witnesses, and so is God, of how holy, righteous and blameless we were among you who believed. [11]For you know that we dealt with each of you as a father deals with his own children, [12]encouraging, comforting and urging you to live lives worthy of God, who calls you into his kingdom and glory.

[a] 7 Some manuscripts *were gentle*

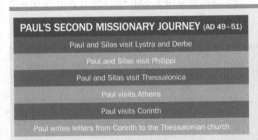

PAUL'S SECOND MISSIONARY JOURNEY (AD 49–51)

Paul and Silas visit Lystra and Derbe

Paul and Silas visit Philippi

Paul and Silas visit Thessalonica

Paul visits Athens

Paul visits Corinth

Paul writes letters from Corinth to the Thessalonian church

1:8 Lord's message Refers to the gospel message (compare Ac 8:25; 15:35–36; 2Th 3:1).

1:9 idols In Greco-Roman society, polytheism — the belief in or worship of more than one god — was the norm. The social, political and religious life of the Thessalonians was intertwined with idolatrous beliefs and practices. Idolatry was not just a personal matter; it was a corporate one.

1:10 to wait for his Son from heaven Refers to Christ's visible and personal return to earth at the end of the present age. Paul says that Jesus will return from heaven because it is the place where he reigns with God (compare Eph 1:20–21). The Thessalonians apparently were discouraged at the delay of Christ's return because some believers had already died. Paul addresses their concern in this letter (1Th 4:13–18). **raised from the dead** Christ's resurrection from the dead is the foundation of Christian hope (compare 1Co 15:17–22; 2Ti 2:11). It is also the reason believers await his return. Even death cannot hinder union with Christ (1Th 5:10). **wrath** The Greek word used here, *orgē*, refers in this context to God's judgment upon the wicked. The believers of Thessalonica are encouraged to not mistake affliction and persecution (*thlipsis*) for God's final judgment on the wicked (*orgē*).

2:1–12 Paul reminds the Thessalonians how he and his fellow workers conducted themselves while in Thessalonica. He first contrasts himself with contemporary philosophers to show that they were not motivated by greed or self-indulgence (vv. 2–6). He then reminds the Thessalonians that he and his fellow missionaries ministered to them with gentleness and love (vv. 7–12). He concludes this section with another thanksgiving prayer.

2:2 been treated outrageously in Philippi See Ac 16:19–39.

2:3 from error or impure motives, nor are we trying to trick Paul reassures the Thessalonians about the integrity of his teaching, motives and methods. See note on 1Th 1:5.

2:5 greed The Greek word used here, *pleonexia*, refers to the desire to possess more than others, regardless of actual need. Paul and his companions were not greedy, nor did not they use any pretext to disguise greediness — a common practice among traveling philosophers. **God is our witness** Compare v. 10; Ro 1:9; 2Co 1:23.

2:6 apostles of Christ An apostle is a person designated by God to speak and act with special authority.

2:7 young children The Greek word used here varies in ancient manuscripts. If Paul intended to use the term *nēpios*, then he is saying that he and his coworkers behaved like infants among the Thessalonians. In other words, they were guileless and undemanding. Most manuscripts support this variation. If Paul meant to use the word *ēpios*, then he is saying that they were gentle among the Thessalonians. **nursing** Paul is likely using the image of a nursing mother or a wet nurse here. In the Greco-Roman world, wet nurses were commonly used for feeding infants. Such nurses were highly esteemed for their work and were used by both the upper and lower classes of society. Paul presents this metaphor to characterize the love and care that he and his coworkers showed to the Thessalonians.

2:9 our toil and hardship Greeks considered manual labor the duty of slaves. But Paul and his companions worked in order to set an example for the Thessalonians and relieve them of having to provide financial support (compare 1Th 5:13). Paul's goal was to support himself through his long hours of labor so that he would not become a burden to his churches (compare 1Co 9:3–14).

2:11 as a father Paul considered himself to be a spiritual father to those he led to Christ (e.g., 1Co 4:15; Phm 10). Drawing on this image, Paul describes how he played the role of a father by helping his children mature in the faith after their conversion.

2:12 live lives worthy In doing so, the Thessalonians will please God and win the respect of outsiders (1Th 4:1,12).

¹³And we also thank God continually because, when you received the word of God, which you heard from us, you accepted it not as a human word, but as it actually is, the word of God, which is indeed at work in you who believe. ¹⁴For you, brothers and sisters, became imitators of God's churches in Judea, which are in Christ Jesus: You suffered from your own people the same things those churches suffered from the Jews ¹⁵who killed the Lord Jesus and the prophets and also drove us out. They displease God and are hostile to everyone ¹⁶in their effort to keep us from speaking to the Gentiles so that they may be saved. In this way they always heap up their sins to the limit. The wrath of God has come upon them at last.ᵃ

Paul's Longing to See the Thessalonians

¹⁷But, brothers and sisters, when we were orphaned by being separated from you for a short time (in person, not in thought), out of our intense longing we made every effort to see you. ¹⁸For we wanted to come to you—certainly I, Paul, did, again and again—but Satan blocked our way. ¹⁹For what is our hope, our joy, or the crown in which we will glory in the presence of our Lord Jesus when he comes? Is it not you? ²⁰Indeed, you are our glory and joy.

3 So when we could stand it no longer, we thought it best to be left by ourselves in Athens. ²We sent Timothy, who is our brother and co-worker in God's service in spreading the gospel of Christ, to strengthen and encourage you in your faith, ³so that no one would be unsettled by these trials. For you know quite well that we are destined for them. ⁴In fact, when we were with you, we kept telling you that we would be persecuted. And it turned out that way, as you well know. ⁵For this reason, when I could stand it no longer, I sent to find out about your faith. I was afraid that in some way the tempter had tempted you and that our labors might have been in vain.

Timothy's Encouraging Report

⁶But Timothy has just now come to us from you and has brought good news about your faith and

ᵃ 16 Or *them fully*

In Paul's time, ethics—the study of morality—was not the subject of religion, but philosophy. According to Paul, the Gentiles lacked standards regarding sexual immorality (4:5). **kingdom** The Greek word used here, *basilea*, refers in this context to the domain God rules as King. Believers must live in accordance with his commands as subjects within his kingdom. When Paul proclaimed the arrival of another king in Thessalonica, the people took offense because of their allegiance to the Roman emperor (Ac 17:7).

2:14 imitators See note on 1Th 1:6. **Judea** The Greek and Roman designation for Judah—the territory in Israel including the cities of Jerusalem, Caesarea and Capernaum. The churches in this region experienced early persecution (compare Ac 8:1). **suffered** Refers to the suffering caused by persecution. When the believers in Thessalonica turned to God and abandoned their idols, they also abandoned their civic obligations—even their allegiance to Caesar. For this reason, the Thessalonian believers likely suffered persecution that consisted of social exclusion and religious shame. Paul informs the Thessalonians that persecution is the expectation, not the exception. Jesus, Paul and the prophets all experienced suffering at the hand of their own people (compare Mk 10:33–34; Ac 13:45; Mt 5:12).

2:16 Gentiles Non-Jewish people. God included the Gentiles in his redemptive plan (compare Isa 49:6). **always heap up their sins to the limit** Depicts a period of recurring sin that eventually reaches a breaking point and induces God's judgment. This expectation was common to Jewish theology (e.g., Ge 15:16; Da 8:23). Although Paul seems to focus only on the judgment of Jews here, elsewhere he stresses that God's judgment will come upon all unrepentant people regardless of their ethnicity (e.g., Ro 2:9–10). **wrath** Those persecuting the believers at Thessalonica were the objects of God's anger. Such people sinned against God by opposing Paul's missionary work to the Gentiles. See note on 1Th 1:10.

2:17—3:13 Paul narrates his sudden departure from the Thessalonians to allay their fear that he abandoned them. He recounts his repeated but failed attempts to return to Thessalonica (vv. 17–20) and his decision to send Timothy to check on them when he could not return in person (3:1–10). After expressing his relief in response to Timothy's positive report (vv. 6–10), Paul prays that his desire to return to Thessalonica will be fulfilled (vv. 11–13).

2:17 when we were orphaned by being separated The Greek term used here, *aporphanizō*, describes separation between people. It was often used in the context of parent-child relationships in which it could describe either children who had been orphaned by their parents or parents who had lost their children. Here Paul depicts himself as a father cut off from his children—the Thessalonian believers (compare 2:11).

2:18 Satan blocked our way Satan is the enemy of God who opposes Paul and his apostolic ministry (e.g., 3:5; 2Co 2:11; 11:13–15; 12:7). Some of the Thessalonians likely worried that Paul abandoned them when he abruptly left the city and did not return (see note on 1Th 1:1–10). Paul assures the believers at Thessalonica that his separation from them was not his choice—Satan hindered him. The Greek verb used here, *enkoptō*, literally means "to cut up." It could be used to describe an army destroying an enemy's road, consequently hindering their travel. The exact nature of the hindrance is unknown.

3:1 Athens A city in the Roman province of Achaia (modern-day Greece). Paul visited Athens during his second missionary journey (Ac 17:10–34).

3:2 Timothy Since Paul encountered trouble in Thessalonica (see Ac 17:5–10), he sent Timothy on his behalf to help the new believers. See note on 1Th 1:1–10.

3:3 we are destined Paul reminds the new believers that persecution is not a sign of God's wrath; rather, faith and suffering are both part of the Christian life (Php 1:29).

3:5 tempter Refers to Satan (compare Mt 4:3; 1Co 7:5). Paul likely considered the Thessalonians to be especially vulnerable to temptation because they had converted to

love. He has told us that you always have pleasant memories of us and that you long to see us, just as we also long to see you. [7]Therefore, brothers and sisters, in all our distress and persecution we were encouraged about you because of your faith. [8]For now we really live, since you are standing firm in the Lord. [9]How can we thank God enough for you in return for all the joy we have in the presence of our God because of you? [10]Night and day we pray most earnestly that we may see you again and supply what is lacking in your faith.

[11]Now may our God and Father himself and our Lord Jesus clear the way for us to come to you. [12]May the Lord make your love increase and overflow for each other and for everyone else, just as ours does for you. [13]May he strengthen your hearts so that you will be blameless and holy in the presence of our God and Father when our Lord Jesus comes with all his holy ones.

Living to Please God

4 As for other matters, brothers and sisters, we instructed you how to live in order to please God, as in fact you are living. Now we ask you and urge you in the Lord Jesus to do this more and more. [2]For you know what instructions we gave you by the authority of the Lord Jesus.

[3]It is God's will that you should be sanctified: that you should avoid sexual immorality; [4]that each of you should learn to control your own body[a] in a way that is holy and honorable, [5]not in passionate lust like the pagans, who do not know God; [6]and that in this matter no one should wrong or take advantage of a brother or sister.[b] The Lord will punish all those who commit such sins, as we told you and warned you before. [7]For God did not call us to be impure, but to live a holy life. [8]Therefore, anyone who rejects this instruction does not reject a human being but God, the very God who gives you his Holy Spirit.

[9]Now about your love for one another we do not need to write to you, for you yourselves have been taught by God to love each other. [10]And in fact, you do love all of God's family throughout Macedonia. Yet we urge you, brothers and sisters, to do so more and more, [11]and to make it your

---

[a] 4 Or *learn to live with your own wife*; or *learn to acquire a wife*
[b] 6 The Greek word for *brother or sister* (*adelphos*) refers here to a believer, whether man or woman, as part of God's family.

---

faith in Christ only recently. The NT frequently describes Satan's attempts to take advantage of people who are either young in the faith or in a weakened state (e.g., 1Co 7:5; 1Ti 3:6–7). **labors might have been in vain** If the Thessalonians give into temptation and abandon their faith, his missionary efforts among them would be in vain—a recurring concern for Paul (e.g., Gal 4:11; Php 2:16).

3:6 you always have pleasant memories of us Paul was concerned about the Thessalonians' perception of him (see 1Th 2:3 and note).

3:9 How can we thank God enough for you in return Paul knows he cannot take credit for the believers' perseverance through suffering—he was not there with them. He gives thanks that God strengthened them to endure the persecution.

3:10 supply what is lacking in your faith Paul is relieved and grateful for the believers' perseverance but recognizes that they still have needs. This phrase refers to the Thessalonians' need for further instruction, not to a failure to have genuine faith in Christ. Since Paul cannot be there in person, he writes this letter to strengthen their faith in Christ.

3:11 clear the way for us to come to you Satan hindered Paul's plan to return to Thessalonica (2:18). But God ultimately directs Paul's missionary efforts, and he will make a path for his return to Thessalonica—it seems that Paul later returned to Thessalonica (see Ac 20:4–5).

3:13 our Lord Jesus comes See note on 1Th 1:10.

4:1–12 Paul exhorts the Thessalonians, who were relatively young believers, to continue to grow in the faith. His instructions focus on issues related to sexual immorality, holiness and manual labor.

4:3 God's will God makes his desires known to his people so they will display his character to the world. **should be sanctified** The Greek word used here, *hagiasmos*, refers to the process of becoming holy. In this context, Paul's primary concern is for the Thes-

salonians to avoid sexual immorality. Paul urges the believers to serve God and distinguish themselves from those around them—a key feature of holiness. Christ has already set them apart; now they must cooperate with God's Holy Spirit to live holy lives (v. 8). Through the Spirit, God imparts his desires, values and concerns to believers so that they share in his likeness and image. **sexual immorality** The Greek word used here, *porneia*, refers to all sexual immorality, not just premarital sex or prostitution. The apostles advised Gentile (non-Jewish) believers to abstain from such activity (Ac 15:20).

4:4 your own body The Greek word used here, *skeuos*, can refer to various objects or things (compare 2Co 4:7; Heb 9:21). Here it probably functions as a metaphorical reference to the human body. Believers must use their bodies in a manner pleasing to God and abstain from sexual immorality.

4:6 take advantage The Greek word used here, *pleonekteō*, refers to taking advantage of someone, especially for financial or material gain. It is possible that Paul is concerned with believers taking advantage of one another in terms of finances. However, the context of the passages suggests that Paul is still addressing the issue of sexual immorality (1Th 4:2–5). In this case, he is urging believers to avoid taking advantage of each other in sexual matters. Such behavior not only would represent a moral failure, but also would damage the community of believers and its reputation within society.

4:8 God Paul's instructions about holiness are based not on human philosophy or tradition, but on God's holy character as the standard for behavior.

4:9 your love for one another The Greek word here, *philadelphia*, originally referred to affection among blood relatives. Christians adopted this word because they considered themselves the family of God.

4:10 Macedonia See note on 1:7.

4:11 to lead a quiet life By discarding their idols (1:9), the Thessalonians abandoned many of their social, religious and civic obligations. Since their response to

ambition to lead a quiet life: You should mind your own business and work with your hands, just as we told you, ¹²so that your daily life may win the respect of outsiders and so that you will not be dependent on anybody.

Believers Who Have Died

¹³Brothers and sisters, we do not want you to be uninformed about those who sleep in death, so that you do not grieve like the rest of mankind, who have no hope. ¹⁴For we believe that Jesus died and rose again, and so we believe that God will bring with Jesus those who have fallen asleep in him. ¹⁵According to the Lord's word, we tell you that we who are still alive, who are left until the coming of the Lord, will certainly not precede those who have fallen asleep. ¹⁶For the Lord himself will come down from heaven, with a loud command, with the voice of the archangel and with the trumpet call of God, and the dead in Christ will rise first. ¹⁷After that, we who are still alive and are left will be caught up together with them in the clouds to meet the Lord in the air. And so we will be with the Lord forever. ¹⁸Therefore encourage one another with these words.

the gospel already disrupted the city, Paul urges them not to make the matter worse. **work with your hands** It is possible that some of the believers may have used Christ's future return as an excuse to stop working. However, the most likely case is that some of the poor believers had stopped being responsible to support themselves. Paul urges them to earn their own living instead of taking advantage of other believers' wealth.

4:13–18 The Thessalonians likely expressed concern that their deceased brothers and sisters in the Lord—and those who may die before his return—will miss out on Christ's return and the glorious future of the age to come (see v. 14 and note). Paul writes to reassure them that deceased believers will be raised to enjoy Christ's appearing. Christ will even give deceased believers priority (see v. 16).

4:13 those who sleep in death In both the OT and NT, as well as in wider Jewish and Greco-Roman literature, "sleep" serves as a euphemism for death (e.g., Ge 47:30; Ps 13:3; Jn 11:11–13; Ac 13:36; compare 2 Maccabees 12:45; Homer, *Iliad* 11.241). Paul uses "sleep" metaphorically to refer to those who will die before the return of Christ, including deceased Thessalonian Christians. **hope** The Greek word used here, *elpis*, does not refer to wishful thinking; it is the confident expectation that God will fulfill what he has promised. Paul does not include the material of 1Th 4:13–18 in order to develop an end-time chronology; rather, he aims to instill hope in the Thessalonians (see especially v. 18).

4:14 For we believe May indicate that this verse was a creedal statement of the early church (compare 1Co 15:3–4). **will bring with Jesus those who have fallen asleep** The Thessalonians were troubled about the state of believers who died before the Lord's return. Paul assures them that these believers are not lost, nor will they miss out on his return; rather, they will be with the Lord and reunited with other believers (1Th 5:10). Based on the Greek in this verse, it is unclear whether Paul implies that Jesus will return from heaven to earth with an entourage of departed saints (including deceased Thessalonian believers) or if he will raise them prior to the reunion in the air. However, the mention of Christ's resurrection in the preceding clause coupled with the use of *anastēsontai* ("will rise") in v. 16 suggests that the departed saints will be resurrected before meeting the Lord in the air—they will not accompany him from heaven.

4:15 Lord's word Paul assures the Thessalonians that the hope of Christ's return and the resurrection of believers are based on God's promises. These words are intended to console (v. 18). **coming of the Lord** See note on 1:10.

4:16 the Lord himself The Greek expression used here emphasizes that this is a personal visitation by the Lord Jesus, not just his angelic messengers. **the voice of the**

archangel Probably refers to the archangel Michael (see Jude 9). See the table "Angels in the Bible" on p. 2120. **trumpet call of God** Announcing the Lord's arrival. Paul's language describes a visible and audible event. Paul likely draws on the day of the Lord traditions from the Hebrew Bible and Second Temple literature. In them, God's arrival is signaled by the blowing of a trumpet (see Isa 27:13; Joel 2:1; Zec 9:14; compare 1Co 15:52). In antiquity, great announcements preceded the arrival of foreign dignitaries, who were welcomed with great pomp and pageantry. **dead in Christ will rise first** The Thessalonians were concerned that the "dead in Christ" (i.e., believers who died before the Lord's return) would be excluded from Christ's return and the blessings of the age to come. However, Paul informs them that those believers will not be lost; in fact, they will precede living believers to resurrection glory. Paul appropriated material about the end times and the notion of those who are asleep being awakened to resurrection from the book of Daniel (see Da 12:2 and note). This tradition is further developed in other Jewish literature written close to Paul's era (compare Testament of Judah 25; Testament of Issachar 7:9; 2 Maccabees 12:44–45; 1 Enoch 91:10). Far from being excluded from the return of Christ, the deceased Thessalonian believers will be blessed because they will meet the Lord first.

4:17 will be caught up The Greek term used here, *harpazō*, means "to seize with force" (e.g., Ac 8:39); the emphasis is on reunion with Jesus, not necessarily removal from earth. Believers who are alive during Christ's return will be forcibly united with him, no matter what type of interference evil brings. Paul could be suggesting that believers will literally be united with Christ in the air (the rapture view), or simply that believers will be united with Christ in bringing God's presence, which is in heaven (the "clouds"), fully to earth. The event when believers are "seize[d] with force" is described by some as the rapture. This view is that believers are removed from earth; in other words, the "seiz[ing]" involves going to heaven with Christ forever. Alternatively, it may be that believers join Christ "in the air" and then continue their work with him on earth; they're not taken away but are forever united with him (compare Rev 21:1–4). If a rapture view is adopted, then there are different possibilities of when this event takes place in relation to the great tribulation mentioned in Revelation. Whichever view is preferred, Paul's ultimate point is that all believers, dead and alive, will one day be united with Christ. **clouds** In the OT, clouds represent theophany—a visible manifestation of God's presence (e.g., Ex 13:21; 19:16; 24:15–18; 40:34; Nu 12:5; Da 7:13). Cloud imagery in the OT also signifies the saving and avenging activities of God on behalf of his people. See Dt 33:26; 2Sa 22:11; Ps 18:11; 68:33–34; 104:3; Isa 19:1; Hab 3:8. By Daniel's time, cloud imagery is linked to Messianic expectations (see Da 7:13). Just as

The Day of the Lord

5 Now, brothers and sisters, about times and dates we do not need to write to you, ²for you know very well that the day of the Lord will come like a thief in the night. ³While people are saying, "Peace and safety," destruction will come on them suddenly, as labor pains on a pregnant woman, and they will not escape.

⁴But you, brothers and sisters, are not in darkness so that this day should surprise you like a thief. ⁵You are all children of the light and children of the day. We do not belong to the night or to the darkness. ⁶So then, let us not be like others, who are asleep, but let us be awake and sober. ⁷For those who sleep, sleep at night, and those who get drunk, get drunk at night. ⁸But since we belong to the day, let us be sober, putting on faith and love as a breastplate, and the hope of salvation as a helmet. ⁹For God did not appoint us to suffer wrath but to receive salvation through our Lord Jesus Christ. ¹⁰He died for us so that, whether we are awake or asleep, we may live together with him. ¹¹Therefore encourage one another and build each other up, just as in fact you are doing.

Final Instructions

¹²Now we ask you, brothers and sisters, to acknowledge those who work hard among you, who

---

God fights for his people, the Messiah rides to rescue God's people and rid the land of its enemies. Jesus uses this language for himself, and NT authors describe Jesus similarly (see Mt 24:30; Lk 9:34–35; Ac 1:9; Rev 1:7 and note). Paul urges the Thessalonian believers to take comfort in the fact that Jesus will return, resurrect their departed brothers and sisters, and vanquish evil. **meet** The Greek term used here, *apantēsis*, could be used to describe the meeting between a visiting dignitary and the citizens of a city. **Lord in the air** Paul does not say whether believers will return to the earth with Christ or ascend to heaven with him. He simply states that believers will be with the Lord forever following their reunion with him in the sky. **we will be with the Lord** Addresses the believers' primary concern: separation from Christ and other fellow believers. This point is reiterated in 1Th 4:18.

1 Thessalonians 4:17

APANTĒSIS
The Greek word *apantēsis* refers to meeting an arriving visitor, especially the act of honoring an important person, such as a dignitary or newly appointed official, by meeting them on arrival. According to Greco-Roman customs, citizens went out to meet the dignitary and escort them back to their city amid great celebration. Paul may have drawn on this socio-political image because the Thessalonians would have been familiar with the custom. Its use also may imply that believers will escort the Lord back to earth, where he will judge the wicked and establish his kingdom.

4:18 encourage one another with these words Paul's brief message about Christ's return is meant to comfort the Thessalonian church with regard to their departed loved ones and reassure them that they will not miss out on the day of the Lord.

5:1–11 Paul continues his discussion of the Lord's return but now turns to another question that the Thessalonians had raised—the timing. Paul dismisses the need for speculation. Instead, he urges believers to be alert and self-controlled as they live in expectation of the day of the Lord.

5:1 times and dates This phrase refers to a single idea—the events that would allow a person to predict the "day of the Lord." But Paul does not need to write the Thessalonians about such things. Knowing how to live in preparation for the Lord's return is more important than knowing the timing of his return (Ac 1:6–7).

5:2 day of the Lord Refers to the time when God judges his enemies and delivers his people, establishing his reign (Joel 2:1–2,31–32). The apostles applied this same expression to Christ's return (e.g., 1Co 1:8; Php 1:6; 2Pe 3:10). **thief in the night** Jesus described his return this same way (Mt 24:43; Rev 3:3; 16:15). His return will surprise some people, but believers must be ready.

5:3 Peace and safety The Roman Empire used the phrase "peace and safety" in its propaganda to promote the idea of Roman Peace (*Pax Romana*). In the OT, the prophet Jeremiah rebuked those who ignored the threat of God's judgment (e.g., Jer 6:14).

5:5 children of the light The Greek phrase used here, *huioi phōtos*, refers to people characterized by light. In this context, light symbolizes God's favor toward those who will be spared from his judgment.

5:6 not be like others, who are asleep Earlier in this letter, Paul used a Greek word for "sleep," *koimaō*, metaphorically to describe those who have died (1Th 4:13). In this verse, he uses a different Greek word, *katheudō*, also translated "sleep," to refer to being unaware of God, his workings and his return.

5:8 faith and love as a breastplate Breastplates protected the chest area—the place of the body's most vital organs. As a form of protective armor, the breastplate serves as a metaphor for the Christian virtues of faith and love (compare 1:3). Like armor, these virtues protect believers from being unprepared for the day of the Lord. God himself wears similar armor as the Divine Warrior (Isa 59:17). He supplies believers with armor so that they may engage in spiritual battle against the enemy (compare Eph 6:10–20). **hope of salvation as a helmet** Armor that covers the head and cheek bones. The helmet is described as the "hope of salvation." This expression refers to a confident expectation of God's saving work. This work was put into effect by Christ and will come to completion on the day of the Lord. Therefore, the "hope of salvation" reminds believers to be prepared for that day.

5:9 God did not appoint us to suffer wrath See note on 1Th 1:10.

5:10 awake or asleep Physically alive or dead. **we may live together with him** Neither life nor death can separate believers from Christ (compare Ro 8:35–39).

5:12–28 Paul offers the Thessalonians numerous pieces of practical advice focusing on issues related to the Christian community. Two of the key subjects are leadership in the church (1Th 5:12–13) and the importance of prophecy (vv. 19–21). Paul concludes the letter with a benediction that anticipates the Lord's return (vv. 23–24).

5:12 to acknowledge those who work hard among you Paul seems to be urging the Thessalonians to

care for you in the Lord and who admonish you. [13]Hold them in the highest regard in love because of their work. Live in peace with each other. [14]And we urge you, brothers and sisters, warn those who are idle and disruptive, encourage the disheartened, help the weak, be patient with everyone. [15]Make sure that nobody pays back wrong for wrong, but always strive to do what is good for each other and for everyone else.

[16]Rejoice always, [17]pray continually, [18]give thanks in all circumstances; for this is God's will for you in Christ Jesus.

[19]Do not quench the Spirit. [20]Do not treat prophecies with contempt [21]but test them all; hold on to what is good, [22]reject every kind of evil.

[23]May God himself, the God of peace, sanctify you through and through. May your whole spirit, soul and body be kept blameless at the coming of our Lord Jesus Christ. [24]The one who calls you is faithful, and he will do it.

[25]Brothers and sisters, pray for us. [26]Greet all God's people with a holy kiss. [27]I charge you before the Lord to have this letter read to all the brothers and sisters.

[28]The grace of our Lord Jesus Christ be with you.

---

respect those who labored and supported the church. These people likely held positions of leadership within the church (compare 1Co 16:15–18).

5:14 those who are idle and disruptive Refers to believers in Thessalonica who refused to work and support themselves.

5:15 nobody pays back wrong for wrong Believers must extend to others (i.e., believers and unbelievers) the same goodness the Lord has shown them.

5:18 God's will See note on 1Th 4:3.

5:19 Do not quench the Spirit Paul uses the image of quenching to describe the idea of resisting the Spirit's work in and among believers. In this context, the notion of quenching the Spirit likely refers to a prohibition on prophetic activity within the Thessalonian church (vv. 20–21).

5:20 prophecies The Greek word used here, *prophēteia*, refers in this context to an utterance inspired by the Holy Spirit for the edification of the church community (1Co 14:4). Some believers at Thessalonica may have felt uncomfortable with the spiritual gift of prophecy because of their past experience with idolatry (1Th 1:9).

5:21 test them all Probably refers to testing the legitimacy of the prophetic activity mentioned in vv. 19–20. In 1 Corinthians, Paul mentions the need for discernment within the church (1Co 12:10; 14:29).

5:23 God of peace Compare Ro 15:33; 16:20. **sanctify** See note on 1Th 4:3. **coming of our Lord Jesus Christ** See note on 1:10.

5:24 faithful The new believers at Thessalonica endured persecution even without the presence of Paul and his companions (see 3:9 and note), demonstrating God's faithfulness.

5:26 holy kiss A kiss was a common greeting in the ancient world. A kiss exchanged upon greeting could also symbolize reconciliation (Ge 45:15; Lk 15:20). In the Christian context, it expresses unity (Ro 16:16; 2Co 13:12).

2 THESSALONIANS

INTRODUCTION TO 2 THESSALONIANS

Paul's second letter to the Christians at Thessalonica urges them to faithfully continue the work of the gospel. Paul revisits some of the same issues that he addressed in his first letter to this church. He commends the believers for standing firm in the face of persecution; he also explains more about the day of the Lord and tells idlers in the community to get back to work. A true understanding of the gospel will inspire hope for the future, as well as diligence for the here and now.

BACKGROUND

Like 1 Thessalonians, Paul, Silvanus (Silas) and Timothy are identified as the authors of 2 Thessalonians (2Th 1:1; 3:17; 1Th 1:1), but there is some modern debate about its authorship. This debate centers around the style and vocabulary differences with Paul's other letters, the suggestion that its theology is more developed than this period of early Christianity, and the close parallels with 1 Thessalonians. This leads to the theory that an author other than Paul drew upon the material of 1 Thessalonians to compose 2 Thessalonians. However, it could be that Paul felt like he needed to emphasize the same matters twice, had a large vocabulary, used a different scribe and that early Christian theology was more developed than is often theorized. In addition, 2 Thessalonians was unanimously accepted by the early church fathers as by Paul.

The recipients of 2 Thessalonians were Christians in Thessalonica, a city in Macedonia (northern Greece) where Paul and his companions had planted a church (Ac 17:1–9; see the "Introduction to 1 Thessalonians"). This letter does not provide as many clues about the date and place of its writing as 1 Thessalonians (which was sent from Corinth around AD 50–51). Since the two letters cover many of the same issues, 2 Thessalonians was likely written soon after 1 Thessalonians (2Th 2:15) near the end of Paul's second missionary journey (ca. AD 49–51).

In the time since Paul wrote 1 Thessalonians, it seems that several factors he addressed in that letter had intensified: persecution, uncertainty about Christ's return and idleness in the church. The persecution and suffering mentioned in the first letter were still continuing (2Th 1:5–6; 1Th 1:6; 2:14; 3:3–4). Despite Paul's teaching, some people in the community were apparently saying that the day of the Lord had already come (2Th 2:1–2; compare 1Th 5:1–11). In addition, some of

This map depicts the location of Thessalonica and the surrounding region.

the Thessalonian Christians apparently had decided that they did not need to work for a living (2Th 3:10–12; compare 1Th 4:11–12; 5:14).

STRUCTURE

Like many of Paul's other letters, 2 Thessalonians has a greeting (2Th 1:1–2) which flows immediately into a thanksgiving section (1:3–12) that introduces the letter's main concerns. In this case, Paul's primary intention is to comfort and exhort the Thessalonian believers as they are facing persecution. In the next major section (2:1–17), Paul reassures the Thessalonians that the return of Christ has not taken place already, because the events before that day had not taken place. Paul had already taught them about these matters when he was with them (2:5).

Next, Paul addresses the issue of people in the community who had stopped working (3:1–15). This behavior might be connected to assumptions about Christ's return: If it had already come or is coming soon, people have thought there was no point in working. In rebuke, Paul tells the Thessalonians to follow his example: When with them, he did everything he could to avoid being a burden (3:7–9). The letter closes with a benediction emphasizing the peace of God, which is especially important given the persecution and uncertainty that was troubling the Thessalonian church (3:16–18).

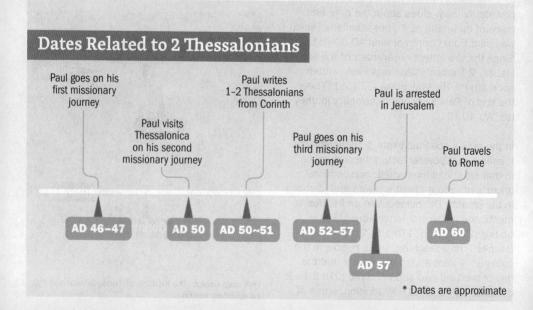

Dates Related to 2 Thessalonians

Paul goes on his first missionary journey

Paul visits Thessalonica on his second missionary journey

Paul writes 1–2 Thessalonians from Corinth

Paul goes on his third missionary journey

Paul is arrested in Jerusalem

Paul travels to Rome

AD 46–47   AD 50   AD 50~51   AD 52–57   AD 57   AD 60

* Dates are approximate

OUTLINE

- Thanksgiving and prayer (1:1–12)
- Misunderstanding regarding the day of the Lord (2:1–17)
- Exhortations to avoid idleness, benediction and closing (3:1–18)

THEMES

Second Thessalonians' central point is that God is just and faithful—which means that our present and future are safe in his hands. Because God is just, the Thessalonians can trust him in the midst of their current troubles (1:5–6), knowing that he will preserve them and judge those who persecute them (1:7–10). Because God is faithful, they can entrust their future to him (3:3).

Paul encourages the Thessalonians, and us, to stay faithful in all we do; we are to work hard—ultimately for his purposes (2:13–17; 3:6–9). We also have to exhort others to do the same; this will, at times, result in us making difficult decisions in regards to our relationships (3:10–15). But since we know that God is just and faithful, we can put our whole lives, present and future, in his hands.

1 Paul, Silas[a] and Timothy,

To the church of the Thessalonians in God our Father and the Lord Jesus Christ:

[2] Grace and peace to you from God the Father and the Lord Jesus Christ.

Thanksgiving and Prayer

[3] We ought always to thank God for you, brothers and sisters,[b] and rightly so, because your faith is growing more and more, and the love all of you have for one another is increasing. [4] Therefore, among God's churches we boast about your perseverance and faith in all the persecutions and trials you are enduring. [5] All this is evidence that God's judgment is right, and as a result you will be counted worthy of the kingdom of God, for which you are suffering. [6] God is just: He will pay back trouble to those who trouble you [7] and give relief to you who are troubled, and to us as well. This will happen when the Lord Jesus is revealed from heaven in blazing fire with his powerful angels. [8] He will punish those who do not know God and do not obey the gospel of our Lord Jesus. [9] They will be punished with everlasting destruction and shut out from the presence of the Lord and from the glory of his might [10] on the day he comes to be glorified in his holy people and to be marveled at among all those who have believed. This includes you, because you believed our testimony to you.

a 1 Greek *Silvanus,* a variant of *Silas   b 3* The Greek word for *brothers and sisters (adelphoi)* refers here to believers, both men and women, as part of God's family; also in 2:1, 13, 15; 3:1, 6, 13.

1:1–2 Among the shorter letters written by Paul, 2 Thessalonians opens with a greeting typical of Greco-Roman letters. As he does in 1 Thessalonians, Paul includes Silas and Timothy as cosenders of the letter (see note on 1Th 1:1–10).

Paul previously wrote a letter to comfort the persecuted church in Thessalonica. Sometime later he learned that matters had become worse: The persecution of the Thessalonian believers had intensified, a forged letter in Paul's name claiming that the second coming of Christ already happened may have been circulated (2:2), and certain believers were using Christ's return as an excuse to quit working. Paul addresses each of these issues in this letter, which he probably wrote shortly after 1 Thessalonians, near the end of his second missionary journey (ca. AD 49–51). See the timeline "Life of Paul" on p. 1796.

1:1 Paul See note on Ro 1:1. **Silas** See note on 1Th 1:1. **Timothy** His report to Paul prompted the first letter to the Thessalonians (1Th 3:6–7).

1:3–12 Paul offers a prayer of thanksgiving on behalf of the Thessalonian believers. He begins by praising their faith in God and love for one another (2Th 1:3). He then commends their endurance in the face of persecution, which he claims serves as proof of God's righteous judgment (vv. 4–5). Paul then offers a warning of the harsh punishment awaiting those who oppose God's people (vv. 6–10). The section ends with an intercessory prayer for the Thessalonians' faith (vv. 11–12).

1:3 your faith is growing more and more The Thessalonian believers' trust in God continued to grow despite persecution by nonbelievers. For this reason, Paul gives thanks to God. **for one another is increasing** An answer to Paul's prayer (see 1Th 3:12).

1:4 persecutions and trials Paul encourages the Thessalonians by reminding them that their situation is only temporary. Christ will return and reward them for their faithfulness while judging those who persecute them. See note on 1Th 2:14.

1:5 God's judgment is right The persecution endured by the Thessalonians is not the result of God's condemnation; rather, their endurance will result in God's counting them worthy of his kingdom. **kingdom of God** The domain God rules as King. The believers suffer persecution because they have declared allegiance to

Jesus, a king other than Caesar (see note on 1Th 2:12; compare Ac 17:6–7). Paul encourages them that their response to this persecution—increased faith in God and love for others (1Th 1:3)—is proof that they are worthy of God's kingdom.

1:6 trouble to those who trouble you Believers need not avenge themselves because God—the righteous judge (Dt 32:35)—will avenge them at his second coming (see Ro 12:19; note on 1Th 5:15).

1:7 Lord Jesus is revealed Refers to the second coming of Jesus Christ. The Thessalonians were discouraged because some claimed that the day of the Lord already happened. Paul assures them that day has yet to come (2Th 2:1–3). When the day comes, Christ will unleash his righteous judgment upon persecutors while granting rest to the persecuted. Until this time, the Thessalonians must remain faithful. **blazing fire** Symbolizes God's visitation (Ex 3:2; 19:18) and judgment (Isa 66:15–16; Jer 15:14). This phrase is an allusion to Isa 66:15. There, Yahweh comes in flaming fire to judge the disobedient. Paul applies this imagery to Christ, identifying him with Yahweh of the OT. Whereas obedience was directed to Yahweh in Isaiah, it is now directed to the Lord Jesus Christ. **angels** Supernatural beings in service to God who deliver messages on his behalf and provide help to his people (Heb 1:13–14). Jesus will be accompanied by angels at his second coming. This detail echoes what is written about the day of the Lord in the OT—Yahweh will come with all his holy ones—his holy army (Zec 14:5; compare 1Th 3:13). See the table "Angels in the Bible" on p. 2120.

1:8 those who do not know God Knowing God is not just mental assent to facts about God, but personal loyalty to Jesus as Lord and God (see Mt 7:21–22; Lk 6:46). **gospel** The good news of Jesus Christ whose life, death and resurrection make relationship with God possible. Those who oppose the gospel (in Greek, *euangelion*) will face God's wrath (see 1Th 2:14–16).

1:9 with everlasting destruction Those who reject Jesus Christ will be separated from God's presence and glory. This punishment will be everlasting (compare 2Th 2:16). Paul's language recalls similar descriptions of God's final judgment in the NT (e.g., Mt 25:46; Jude 7).

1:10 on the day Refers to the day of the Lord (or the day of Yahweh; see 1Th 5:2 and note). In the OT, it is the day in which Yahweh grants his people salvation and punishes his enemies with everlasting destruction (e.g., Isa 11:10–11; Joel 2:1–12,31–32).

[11]With this in mind, we constantly pray for you, that our God may make you worthy of his calling, and that by his power he may bring to fruition your every desire for goodness and your every deed prompted by faith. [12]We pray this so that the name of our Lord Jesus may be glorified in you, and you in him, according to the grace of our God and the Lord Jesus Christ.[a]

The Man of Lawlessness

2 Concerning the coming of our Lord Jesus Christ and our being gathered to him, we ask you, brothers and sisters, [2]not to become easily unsettled or alarmed by the teaching allegedly from us — whether by a prophecy or by word of mouth or by letter — asserting that the day of the Lord has already come. [3]Don't let anyone deceive you in any way, for that day will not come until the rebellion occurs and the man of lawlessness[b] is revealed, the man doomed to destruction. [4]He will oppose and will exalt himself over everything that is called God or is worshiped, so that he sets himself up in God's temple, proclaiming himself to be God.

[5]Don't you remember that when I was with you I used to tell you these things? [6]And now you know what is holding him back, so that he may be revealed at the proper time. [7]For the secret power of lawlessness is already at work; but the one who now holds it back will continue to do so till he is taken out of the way. [8]And then the lawless one

---

[a] 12 Or God and Lord, Jesus Christ   [b] 3 Some manuscripts sin

---

2:1–12 In 1Th 5:1–11, Paul urged the Thessalonians not to worry about the timing of the day of the Lord, but instead to focus on how they should live in anticipation of Christ's return. Apparently, some of the Thessalonians did not heed the message; they worried that the day had already come and they had missed it (2Th 2:2). In this passage, Paul refutes this suggestion by describing two future events that will take place before the day of the Lord: the great rebellion against God and the coming of the man of lawlessness (vv. 3–12).

2:1 coming of our Lord Jesus Christ See note on 1Th 1:10. **our being gathered to him** When the day of the Lord comes, believers will be united with Christ. Paul wrote about this in his previous letter to the Thessalonians (see note on 1Th 4:17).

2:2 unsettled Some of the Thessalonian believers apparently were disturbed by rumors that the day of the Lord had happened already. Paul does not seem to know the source of this rumor. **allegedly from us** Someone may have forged a letter in Paul's name, claiming the day of the Lord had already come. For this reason, Paul signs this letter with a distinguishing mark (see 2Th 3:17 and note). **day of the Lord** In his first letter, Paul addressed confusion about the timing of the "day of the Lord" (1Th 5:2). He addresses this again because the Thessalonians had been persuaded that day had already come — news that caused them great distress. Their ability to endure persecution depended on the promise that God would return to judge their persecutors and deliver them from suffering.

2:3 the rebellion occurs In this context, the Greek word used here, *apostasia*, likely refers to an intentional and hostile rejection of Christ by unbelievers. It is also possible that the term refers to spiritual apostasy by believers (suggesting the "delusion" of 2Th 2:11 refers to divine judgment). This event will happen before the day of the Lord — the second coming of Christ. **man of lawlessness** A person in hostile opposition to God and his law. The expression "man of" is a Hebraism that characterizes this person by lawlessness. The identity of this figure is unknown. It is possible that he is the same figure as the "antichrist" (e.g., 1Jn 2:18,22; 2Jn 7). The OT alludes to various anti-God figures (e.g., Ps 89:22; Isa 57:3–4; Da 12:9–10); Paul's thought may have been influenced by these texts. Paul also could be thinking of a future political figure reminiscent of foreign rulers who oppressed God's people. **man doomed to**

destruction Refers to the "man of lawlessness." The phrase here means he causes destruction, but he is also doomed to destruction. Paul wants the Thessalonian believers to understand that as terrifying as he may be, his destruction is certain. Both the "man of lawlessness" and the "son of destruction" could be literary or symbolic representations of evil people, not one person per se.

2:4 will exalt himself The "man of lawlessness" exalts himself but is eventually humbled by God (2Th 2:8). **everything that is called God or is worshiped** The "man of lawlessness" not only opposes God, he opposes everything that is worshiped. Paul uses the language of Da 11:36 and Eze 28:2 to describe this destructive person (see note on Eze 28:2). **he sets himself up** The imagery used here suggests enthronement as a king (compare Mt 19:28; Ac 12:21). This individual appoints himself to a position of authority (compare Eze 28:2). **God's temple** This phrase most likely refers to the physical temple in Jerusalem (destroyed in AD 70) or to the church as the community of believers (1Co 3:16).

2:5 when I was with you Paul ministered in Thessalonica during his second missionary journey (Ac 17:1–9). In his previous letter, he taught extensively about the second coming of Christ (1Th 4:13—5:2), repeatedly urging the Thessalonians to remember what he taught them (1Th 2:9; 4:1; 2Th 3:10). See the map "Paul's First and Second Missionary Journeys" on p. 2262.

2:6 what is holding him back The identity of this restraining person or power remains unknown. Paul does not provide additional details since he already discussed the matter with the Thessalonian believers (v. 5). Paul describes this restraining power as both impersonal (v. 6) and personal (v. 7). This combination may refer to the Roman Empire and the emperor, the power of evil and Satan, or Roman law or government and political leaders. Alternatively, Paul could be referring to a thing or person that plays a positive role in God's plans, such as the Holy Spirit, the church or the preaching of the gospel. Either way, Paul reassures the Thessalonians that God is using this restrainer until the proper time comes for Christ's destruction of the man of lawlessness (vv. 7–8).

2:7 secret power Probably refers to the hidden activity of lawlessness or merely deception. The Greek word used here, *mystērion* (meaning "mystery"), may also refer to the initiation ritual used in mystery cults since the "man of lawlessness" is a pseudo-religious figure (see v. 4).

2:8 will overthrow with the breath of his mouth

will be revealed, whom the Lord Jesus will overthrow with the breath of his mouth and destroy by the splendor of his coming. ⁹The coming of the lawless one will be in accordance with how Satan works. He will use all sorts of displays of power through signs and wonders that serve the lie, ¹⁰and all the ways that wickedness deceives those who are perishing. They perish because they refused to love the truth and so be saved. ¹¹For this reason God sends them a powerful delusion so that they will believe the lie ¹²and so that all will be condemned who have not believed the truth but have delighted in wickedness.

Stand Firm

¹³But we ought always to thank God for you, brothers and sisters loved by the Lord, because God chose you as firstfruits*a* to be saved through the sanctifying work of the Spirit and through belief in the truth. ¹⁴He called you to this through our gospel, that you might share in the glory of our Lord Jesus Christ.

¹⁵So then, brothers and sisters, stand firm and hold fast to the teachings*b* we passed on to you, whether by word of mouth or by letter.

¹⁶May our Lord Jesus Christ himself and God our Father, who loved us and by his grace gave us eternal encouragement and good hope, ¹⁷encourage your hearts and strengthen you in every good deed and word.

Request for Prayer

3 As for other matters, brothers and sisters, pray for us that the message of the Lord may spread rapidly and be honored, just as it was with you. ²And pray that we may be delivered from wicked and evil people, for not everyone has faith. ³But the Lord is faithful, and he will strengthen you and protect you from the evil one. ⁴We have confidence in the Lord that you are doing and will continue to do the things we command. ⁵May the Lord direct your hearts into God's love and Christ's perseverance.

Warning Against Idleness

⁶In the name of the Lord Jesus Christ, we command you, brothers and sisters, to keep away from every believer who is idle and disruptive and does not live according to the teaching*c* you received

---

a 13 Some manuscripts *because from the beginning God chose you*   *b* 15 Or *traditions*   *c* 6 Or *tradition*

Believers should not fear the "man of lawlessness" because the Lord will easily destroy him at his second coming.
2:9 Satan The enemy of God. See note on 1Th 2:18. **power through signs and wonders that serve the lie** Power, signs and wonders were features of the ministry of Jesus and Paul (Ac 2:22; Ro 15:19). Paul's description of the "man of lawlessness" echoes Jesus' prediction in the Gospels (Mk 13:22; Mt 24:24).
2:10 the truth The Greek word used here, *alētheia*, stands in contrast to the deception of the "man of lawlessness" and probably refers to the gospel message.
2:11 God sends them a powerful delusion This is part of God's judgment: He gives his enemies over to their own sin. They already regarded his truth as a delusion; now they will become even more convinced of it (Ro 1:28; 11:8; 2Ti 4:4). Paul's language recalls OT passages that also mention divine retribution for sin (e.g., Dt 29:4; Isa 6:9–10).
2:12 delighted in wickedness This includes those who persecute the Thessalonian believers (see note on 2Th 1:6).

2:13–17 Paul prays again for the Thessalonians while also exhorting them to endure in the face of affliction. His prayer reassures the believers of their position before God and the Spirit's work of sanctification.

2:13 always to thank God See note on 1Th 1:2. **God chose** Paul emphasizes that salvation came through God's initiative for the Thessalonian believers. See Ro 9:11 and note. **the sanctifying work of the Spirit** The process by which the Spirit makes believers holy. Paul addresses matters of holiness in his previous letter (see note on 1Th 4:3) and in this letter (2Th 3:6). **through belief in the truth** Trust in the gospel message.
2:14 gospel See note on 1:8. **glory** The Greek term used here, *doxa*, refers to the honor and splendor of Jesus Christ. Jesus suffered a humiliating death on the cross

in order to put God's redemptive plan into effect. God exalted him as a result (Php 2:6–8). The Thessalonian believers also suffered humiliation and shame because of persecution by nonbelievers. Paul encourages them that they will share in the greatest of honors: the glory of the Lord Jesus Christ.
2:15 stand firm Paul's favorite expression for remaining faithful to the gospel message (Gal 5:1; Php 4:1; 1Th 3:8). **by letter** Refers to Paul's first letter to the Thessalonians.

3:1–5 Having offered prayers on behalf of the Thessalonian church earlier in the letter, Paul now requests the believers to pray for him.

3:1 pray for us Even when asking for prayer, Paul considers the interests of Jesus Christ—that his message would rapidly spread and be honored. See the table "Prayers in Paul's Letters" on p. 1925. **message of the Lord** Refers to the gospel message (1Th 1:8; Ac 8:25; 15:35–36).
3:2 wicked and evil people Those who opposed Paul and his companions during their missionary efforts—both Jew and Gentile (see Ac 18:12–13). Paul's language echoes the prophet Isaiah. He may have been alluding to the Septuagint (the ancient Greek translation of the OT) of Isa 25:4, which includes the phrase "you will deliver them from wicked men."
3:3 the evil one Refers to Satan, the enemy of God (see Mt 6:13; Eph 6:16). The promise that believers will be protected from Satan by the Lord may be an allusion to the Lord's Prayer. See note on 1Th 2:18.
3:5 direct your hearts An expression from the OT (e.g., Pr 23:19; 2Ch 20:33). Paul asks God to guide the hearts of the Thessalonians—the center of desire and purpose. See 1Th 3:13. **Christ's perseverance** The patient endurance displayed by Christ in his own suffering. His example helps believers endure persecution.

from us. [7]For you yourselves know how you ought to follow our example. We were not idle when we were with you, [8]nor did we eat anyone's food without paying for it. On the contrary, we worked night and day, laboring and toiling so that we would not be a burden to any of you. [9]We did this, not because we do not have the right to such help, but in order to offer ourselves as a model for you to imitate. [10]For even when we were with you, we gave you this rule: "The one who is unwilling to work shall not eat."

[11]We hear that some among you are idle and disruptive. They are not busy; they are busybodies. [12]Such people we command and urge in the Lord Jesus Christ to settle down and earn the food they eat. [13]And as for you, brothers and sisters, never tire of doing what is good.

[14]Take special note of anyone who does not obey our instruction in this letter. Do not associate with them, in order that they may feel ashamed. [15]Yet do not regard them as an enemy, but warn them as you would a fellow believer.

Final Greetings

[16]Now may the Lord of peace himself give you peace at all times and in every way. The Lord be with all of you.

[17]I, Paul, write this greeting in my own hand, which is the distinguishing mark in all my letters. This is how I write.

[18]The grace of our Lord Jesus Christ be with you all.

3:6–15 Paul returns to another subject he addressed in his first letter to the Thessalonians: believers who refused to work and instead relied on financial support from other believers (1Th 5:14). Because these people ignored Paul's previous instruction, he commands the rest of the church to avoid them (2Th 3:6,14–15). He then appeals to the work ethic that he and his coworkers had demonstrated when they were visiting Thessalonica (vv. 7–10). Paul also directly addresses those refusing to work; he exhorts them to support themselves and not to damage the church's reputation in society (v. 12).

3:6 who is idle and disruptive Those who do not work, but take advantage of the charity of others (1Th 5:14). **the teaching** Paul's gospel message communicated in word and deed (see 1Th 2:8).

3:7 to follow our example See note on 1Th 1:6. **We were not idle when we were with you** Paul and his companions worked to provide for their own needs while living with the Thessalonians, setting an example for them to follow. See 1 Th2:9 and note.

3:8 without paying Paul and his companions could have taken advantage of the hospitality of the Thessalonians. Instead, they left them with an example of self-sacrifice. Paul did not want to burden his churches with financial responsibility for his ministry. Compare 1Co 9:1–18. **laboring and toiling** Paul did not see his work as a distraction from ministry, but as part of the ministry itself. **we would not be a burden** The socioeconomic status of believers in Thessalonica may have also motivated Paul to provide for himself.

3:9 because we do not have the right Paul did not use his status as an apostle to take advantage of people. He set aside his rights in order to teach the Thessalonians about hard work and sacrifice (compare 1Co 9:12,15). **to imitate** Paul lived in such a way that he could call others to imitate him (1Co 4:16; 11:1; Php 4:9).

3:10 even when we were with you Paul and his companions visited Thessalonica during his second missionary journey (Ac 17:1–9). See the map "Paul's First and Second Missionary Journeys" on p. 2262. **unwilling to work** Believers may have stopped working out of expectations of the Lord's imminent return or their own laziness. The early church had a lot of charity (compare Ac 6:1–7); some believers may have taken advantage of this.

3:11 busybodies Those who meddle in matters that don't concern them.

3:12 we command and urge Paul is not offering advice. The health and witness of the church in Thessalonica is at stake.

3:14 letter Paul's letters carried just as much authority as his personal presence with the believers. See 2Co 10:9–11. **in order that they may feel ashamed** In Greco-Roman culture, shame was a powerful tool for motivating a person to realign his or her behavior with the community's values. The believers in Thessalonica were already ostracized from the rest of the city's population because they turned from idols to the living God (1Th 1:9). Those who were shunned because of their disobedience were even further removed from community.

3:15 warn Paul regards this as the responsibility of the community. Likewise, Paul provides a model of church discipline that aims toward the restoration of the person, not condemnation.

3:16–18 Paul closes the letter with a benediction (2Th 3:16) and a note regarding his signature (v. 17).

3:16 Lord of peace Compare note on 1Th 5:3.

3:17 this greeting in my own hand The need for a signature of authenticity may reflect an awareness of letters forged in Paul's name (compare 2Th 2:2; 1Co 16:21; Col 4:18).

3:18 The grace of our Lord Jesus Christ Paul's typical closing in his letters (Gal 6:18; Php 4:23).

1 TIMOTHY

INTRODUCTION TO 1 TIMOTHY

First Timothy shows what it looks like when a church goes astray and how to get it back on track. Prior to writing 1 Timothy, Paul had left his apprentice Timothy in Ephesus to instill sound teaching and practices. The church leaders in Ephesus were focused, not on proclaiming Jesus, but on promoting and protecting their own privileges. Paul was always concerned with removing hindrances to the Christian mission, and he wanted to resolve the problems in Ephesus so there would be no obstacles for the gospel.

BACKGROUND

First Timothy's opening verse names Paul as its author. He would have written 1 Timothy and the two other Pastoral Letters (2 Timothy and Titus) toward the end of his life during the mid–60s AD, sometime after his captivity in Rome (ca. AD 61–63). However, there is modern debate about the authorship of the Pastoral Letters. The theory often proposed is that after Paul's death—in the late first or early second century AD—the Pastoral Letters were written by one of Paul's close associates in tribute to him, to record ideas developed from his teachings.

This theory of pseudonymous authorship is based on supposed inconsistencies between the Pastoral Letters and Paul's other letters in vocabulary, writing style and the treatment of particular church matters such as leadership. It is difficult to align the events and tactics described in the Pastoral Letters with Acts and Paul's other letters. Also, the false teachings opposed in the Pastoral Letters align better with known problems of the second century than the 60s AD.

However, the Pastoral Letters could reflect different circumstances: Paul was writing to an individual rather than a congregation, addressing very specific situations, and possibly dictating to a different scribe (compare Ro 16:22). In addition, Paul's other letters and Acts may not record the full church leadership structure, and Paul's views could have progressed as a response to the false teachers and his imminent death. Either way, early on in church history, all 13 of the New Testament letters ascribed to Paul were received as an authentic and authoritative collection.

Paul sent Timothy as his representative on several important missions—to Thessalonica (1Th 3:1–6), Corinth (1Co 4:17; 16:10), Philippi (Php 2:19–24) and now Ephesus (see the "Introduction to 2 Timothy").

Macedonia

Philippi

Thessalonica

Asia

Achaia

Ephesus

This map depicts Ephesus, the primary location of Timothy's ministry at the time of this letter, and the surrounding region.

The problem in the Ephesian church was false teaching. Paul needed to leave for Macedonia (1Ti 1:3), so he left Timothy behind to handle this issue. The false teaching apparently was coming from the church's leaders (3:1–16; 5:17–25), which is why Paul had to write to Timothy. Although the letter has Timothy's name on it, Paul also is speaking through him to the congregation.

The false teachers wrongly placed too much value on genealogies and myths (1:4) and special rules about food and marriage (4:3). They also were conceited (6:3–5) and motivated by greed (6:6–10)—and they loved to argue about theology (1:5–7).

STRUCTURE

First Timothy is structured like a typical Greco-Roman letter—it contains a greeting, main body and conclusion. After a brief greeting (1:1–2), Paul charges Timothy with rooting out false teaching (1:3–20). The body of the letter begins with Paul's instructions for proper Christian conduct (2:1—3:16). He then applies this to men and women in the Ephesian church (2:1–15) and to general leadership (3:1–13). The next section (3:14—4:16) begins with Paul's reason for emphasizing conduct: The church provides a foundation for the truth (3:14–16). He then contrasts false teaching (4:1–5) with the sound teaching that Timothy needs to provide (4:6–16).

In the final major section (5:1—6:19), Paul offers instructions for particular groups of people in the church. He discusses the behavior of widows (5:3–16), elders (5:17–25), and slaves

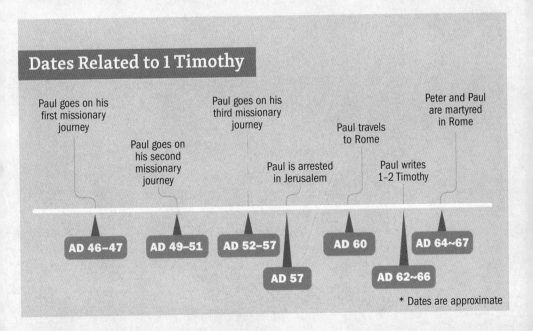

Dates Related to 1 Timothy

Paul goes on his first missionary journey

Paul goes on his second missionary journey

Paul goes on his third missionary journey

Paul is arrested in Jerusalem

Paul travels to Rome

Paul writes 1-2 Timothy

Peter and Paul are martyred in Rome

AD 46–47

AD 49–51

AD 52–57

AD 57

AD 60

AD 62~66

AD 64~67

* Dates are approximate

(6:1–2). Then he comments on the greed of the false teachers (6:2–10), contrasting them with the attitude that Timothy ought to model (6:11–19). Paul closes the letter with a blessing (6:20–21), encouraging Timothy to not deviate from the truth.

OUTLINE

- Greeting and instructions on dealing with false teaching (1:1–20)
- Instructions on conduct (2:1—3:13)
- Contrasting sound teaching with false teaching (3:14—4:16)
- Instructions about particular groups and closing exhortation to Timothy (5:1—6:21)

THEMES

First Timothy shows the power of, and need for, Christ-focused teaching. It leads to godly conduct, peace and the advancement of God's mission in the world. False teaching leads to conflict within the church and a bad reputation in the wider community.

Paul instructs believers to counteract the bad example of others by being a good example. We have the assurance that only our relationship with God, through Christ, can truly transform a person (1:12–16; 4:12).

1 Paul, an apostle of Christ Jesus by the command of God our Savior and of Christ Jesus our hope,

² To Timothy my true son in the faith:

Grace, mercy and peace from God the Father and Christ Jesus our Lord.

Timothy Charged to Oppose False Teachers

³ As I urged you when I went into Macedonia, stay there in Ephesus so that you may command certain people not to teach false doctrines any longer ⁴ or to devote themselves to myths and endless genealogies. Such things promote controversial speculations rather than advancing God's work — which is by faith. ⁵ The goal of this command is love, which comes from a pure heart and a good conscience and a sincere faith. ⁶ Some have departed from these and have turned to meaningless talk. ⁷ They want to be teachers of the law, but they do not know what they are talking about or what they so confidently affirm.

⁸ We know that the law is good if one uses it properly. ⁹ We also know that the law is made not for the righteous but for lawbreakers and rebels,

---

1:1–2 Sometime after his captivity in Rome (ca. AD 61–63), Paul would have written the Pastoral Letters — 1 Timothy, 2 Timothy and Titus. This would have occurred toward the end of his life sometime in the mid-60s AD.

Of all 13 NT letters attributed to Paul, modern scholarship has challenged Paul's authorship of 1 Timothy and the other Pastoral Letters (2 Timothy and Titus) the most. The reasons for questioning whether Paul really wrote these letters involve differences in vocabulary and style (compared to other letters such as Romans), perceived inconsistencies in teaching about church leadership, and historical difficulties aligning the Pastorals with Paul's circumstances (as known from Acts and other letters). However, this debate is still ongoing and all 13 of Paul's letters were received as an authentic and authoritative collection early on in church history.

Although 1 Timothy is addressed primarily to Timothy (who is in Ephesus), its instructions regarding godliness and the qualifications of leadership in the church apply not only to him, but to all the believers. First Timothy opens with a greeting typical of Greco-Roman letters.

1:1 Paul A missionary to the Gentiles and the writer of 13 NT letters. Paul's ministry is the focus of Ac 13–28. See note on Ro 1:1. See the timeline "Life of Paul" on p. 1796. **apostle** One commissioned for a particular task and given the authority to carry out the task. Having appointed Timothy as leader of the churches in Ephesus, Paul refers to himself as an apostle to remind those under Timothy's leadership of his authority. See the table "Pauline Self-Designations" on p. 1904. **the command** Jesus commissioned Paul as an apostle (Ac 9:3–6). Paul often appeals to his appointment from God to demonstrate his apostolic credentials (e.g., Ro 1:1; 1Co 1:1; Gal 1:15–16). **God our Savior** In the Pastoral Letters, salvation is presented as the work of God and Jesus Christ. Paul designates both as Savior, equating the Lord Jesus with Yahweh of the OT (2Ti 2:8–10). Jesus' second coming brings together the themes of salvation and hope mentioned here in 1 Timothy (see Titus 2:11–14). **hope** Describes a confident expectation of God's promises, not a wishful expectation. Paul refers to Christ Jesus as the believers' hope because his resurrection means believers also share in his life (see 1Co 15:13–19).

1:2 Timothy A traveling companion and coworker of Paul who aided in the spread of the gospel to the Gentiles. **true son** This description likely reflects Paul's high regard for Timothy as a trustworthy disciple (1Co 4:17; Php 2:22; Titus 1:4). The reference may also reflect Paul's discipleship of Timothy; Paul considered himself to be a spiritual father to those he brought to faith or nurtured in Christ (1Co 4:15; Gal 4:19). **Grace, mercy**

and peace This greeting captures the essence of the gospel message — God's grace through the sacrifice of Jesus Christ brings peace with God. Here Paul adds "mercy" to his typical greeting (compare Ro 1:7; Gal 1:3; Col 1:2).

1 Timothy 1:2

TIMOTHY
A half-Gentile, half-Jewish disciple Paul met in Lystra (Ac 16:1; see box on Php 1:1). Timothy's mother, Eunice, was Jewish (2Ti 1:5), but his father was Greek (Ac 16:1–3). Timothy joined Paul on his second missionary journey and traveled with him in Asia Minor (modern-day Turkey). Paul appointed Timothy as a leader of the church in Ephesus. Paul's letters frequently mention Timothy, indicating that he was a trusted member of Paul's inner circle (2Co 1:1,19; Php 1:1; Col 1:1; 1Th 1:1; 2Th 1:1; Phm 1; compare Ac 20:4–5).

1:3–11 After the greeting, Paul immediately addresses the problem that Timothy is facing at Ephesus — false teachers who are spreading errant teaching and conducting themselves in a manner unworthy of the gospel. Paul stresses the importance of upholding the sound teaching of the gospel and instructs Timothy to ensure that others are not teaching things contrary to God's plan. The subject of combating false teaching is prominent in the beginning and end of 1 Timothy (1Ti 6:3–10). The nature of the false teaching is unclear, but Paul's references to myths, genealogies and teachers of the law may indicate that Timothy is facing a movement interested in spiritual speculation, mystical knowledge and the Mosaic Law.

1:3 Macedonia A Roman province on the Balkan Peninsula; its territory roughly corresponds with the northern portion of modern Greece. Thessalonica and Philippi were located in Macedonia. The event that Paul mentions in this verse is not recorded in Acts. Paul was inspired to visit Macedonia through a vision (Ac 16:9–12). Though he encountered opposition (2Co 7:5; 1Th 2:2), he planted several churches there (Ac 17:10–12). **Ephesus** A harbor city located in Asia Minor (modern Turkey). Ephesus was one of the largest cities in the Roman Empire. Paul went to Ephesus on his second missionary journey (Ac 19:1) and spent three years there. In a farewell speech, he warned the Ephesian elders about the threat of false teachers (Ac 20:29–31). **to teach false doctrines** Refers to teaching that does not align with the understanding of the gospel that Paul and other apostles proclaimed. Paul's command assumes that Timothy is in a position

the ungodly and sinful, the unholy and irreligious, for those who kill their fathers or mothers, for murderers, ¹⁰for the sexually immoral, for those practicing homosexuality, for slave traders and liars and perjurers — and for whatever else is contrary to the sound doctrine ¹¹that conforms to the gospel concerning the glory of the blessed God, which he entrusted to me.

The Lord's Grace to Paul

¹²I thank Christ Jesus our Lord, who has given me strength, that he considered me trustworthy, appointing me to his service. ¹³Even though I was once a blasphemer and a persecutor and a violent man, I was shown mercy because I acted in ignorance and unbelief. ¹⁴The grace of our Lord was poured out on me abundantly, along with the faith and love that are in Christ Jesus.

¹⁵Here is a trustworthy saying that deserves full acceptance: Christ Jesus came into the world to save sinners — of whom I am the worst. ¹⁶But for that very reason I was shown mercy so that in me, the worst of sinners, Christ Jesus might display his immense patience as an example for those who would believe in him and receive eternal life. ¹⁷Now to the King eternal, immortal, invisible, the only God, be honor and glory for ever and ever. Amen.

The Charge to Timothy Renewed

¹⁸Timothy, my son, I am giving you this command in keeping with the prophecies once made about you, so that by recalling them you may fight the battle well, ¹⁹holding on to faith and a good conscience, which some have rejected and so have suffered shipwreck with regard to the faith. ²⁰Among them are Hymenaeus and Alexander,

---

to instruct these people, so it is likely that the false teaching arose within the church, possibly even among the elders. If that is the case, Timothy is being charged to correct their misunderstandings and misrepresentations of the gospel (compare 2Th 2:15; 2Pe 3:15–16). **1:4 myths** The Greek term used here, *mythos*, refers to legendary stories about the gods. It also could be used to describe stories generally understood to be false. Such tales distracted believers from the truth (i.e., the gospel message) and sound doctrine, resulting in ungodly behavior. The wording here should not be taken as a complete rejection of all Jewish religious writings outside the Biblical canon, since elsewhere the NT writers draw on such material to articulate their points (e.g., see 2Pe 2:4 and note; Jude 9 and note). **genealogies** A list of descendants (e.g., Ge 10; 1Ch 1–9; Mt 1:1–17). Genealogies were used to legitimize the inclusion of an individual into a group or the succession of an individual into a role. Some believers in Ephesus may have used genealogies to exclude others from fellowship or ministry. Paul argues that no one should be excluded; rather, prayer should be made for all because God wants all people to be saved (1Ti 2:1,4). Believers must not make genealogies the subject of pointless speculation. **work** The Greek term here, *oikonomia*, can be used to refer to God's administration or management of the cosmos or specifically to God's plan of salvation (e.g., Eph 1:10; 3:9). Paul also uses *oikonomia* to refer to his mission to spread the gospel (e.g., 1Co 9:17; Eph 3:2; Col 1:25), so the phrase here could be contrasting proper gospel-oriented ministry with the doctrinal mismanagement of the false teachers. **1:5 conscience** The virtue of conscience along with love and faith were cardinal virtues for Jews, Greeks and Christians in the Greco-Roman world. Here Paul seems to be using these virtues to emphasize to Timothy that his instruction and condemnation of false teaching is being done in good faith, motivated by a moral responsibility to correct error and restore the faith of those led astray. **1:7 teachers of the law** Likely refers to teachers focused on interpretation of the Mosaic Law. The people described here are not actually teachers of the law — they just want to be. **1:8 the law is good** Refers to the Mosaic Law. Paul emphasizes that the legitimate use of the law is ethical, setting a standard for moral behavior. See Ro 7:13–25 and note. **1:9 for lawbreakers and rebels** Paul stresses that the purpose of the law was to set a standard, not for the

righteous but for the lawless (in Greek, *anomos*). The law identifies what behaviors should be condemned as sin, outlined in the vice list in 1Ti 1:9–10. The list echoes the interpersonal ethics of the Ten Commandments in Ex 20:12–17. **1:10 sound doctrine** Refers to instruction that is consistent with the gospel message and teaching of the apostles — a theme of the Pastoral Letters (1Ti 6:3; 2Ti 1:13; Titus 1:9). In contrast to foolish controversies, sound teaching stirs God's people to good works. **1:11 the gospel** The good news (in Greek, *euangelion*) about God's victory over sin and death on behalf of a sinful humanity. See Ro 1:1 and note.

1:12–17 After referring to the gospel God entrusted to him in 1Ti 1:11, Paul expresses his gratitude for the grace and mercy of Christ that he has benefited from even though he had violently persecuted the church before his conversion. Paul uses the extreme example of his own experience to prove that Christ's plan to save sinners applies to all, even people like him who had sinned directly against Christ by persecuting his followers.

1:13 blasphemer A person who speaks disrespectfully about God in order to damage his reputation. **persecutor** Before his conversion, Paul sought to persecute followers of Christ by arresting and imprisoning them (Ac 9:1–2; 22:5). **a violent man** Paul not only sought to arrest followers of Christ, he also approved the murder of Stephen (Ac 8:1). **1:14 faith and love** Two of the three core Christian virtues: faith, love and hope (see 1Co 13:13; 1Th 1:3). **1:15 trustworthy saying that deserves full acceptance** Variations of this formulaic expression occur five times throughout the Pastoral Letters (1Ti 1:15; 3:1; 4:9; 2Ti 2:11; Titus 3:8). This phrase serves to introduce or conclude a quotation of established teaching and to emphasize the truth of what is being said. **1:16 I was shown mercy** Paul recognized that his violent actions against the followers of Christ deserved punishment (1Ti 1:12). **1:17 Amen** Expresses agreement or endorsement of what is said about God (e.g., Ps 72:19; 89:52).

1:18–20 This section concludes Paul's opening instruction to Timothy regarding his ministry and his obligation to combat false teachers. Paul gives two examples of people who have not heeded his teaching and have gone astray from the faith — Hymenaeus and Alexander.

whom I have handed over to Satan to be taught not to blaspheme.

Instructions on Worship

2 I urge, then, first of all, that petitions, prayers, intercession and thanksgiving be made for all people — ²for kings and all those in authority, that we may live peaceful and quiet lives in all godliness and holiness. ³This is good, and pleases God our Savior, ⁴who wants all people to be saved and to come to a knowledge of the truth. ⁵For there is one God and one mediator between God and mankind, the man Christ Jesus, ⁶who gave himself as a ransom for all people. This has now been witnessed to at the proper time. ⁷And for this purpose I was appointed a herald and an apostle — I am telling the truth, I am not lying — and a true and faithful teacher of the Gentiles.

⁸Therefore I want the men everywhere to pray, lifting up holy hands without anger or disputing.

1:18 prophecies Pronouncements inspired by God. These prophecies provide Timothy with direction for ministry and motivation to serve faithfully (i.e., to fight the good fight; compare 1Ti 6:12). In difficult circumstances, he must remember that the Spirit of God is ultimately behind his appointment to leadership in Ephesus (see v. 3).

1:20 Hymenaeus A believer who turned from the faith and opposed Paul. Hymenaeus damaged the faith of other believers by claiming the resurrection had already taken place (2Ti 2:17–18). **Alexander** A believer who also deviated from the faith. He may be the same Alexander who did Paul much harm (2Ti 4:14–15). **whom I have handed over to Satan** Paul most likely means that he expelled Hymenaeus and Alexander from the community of believers and placed them into the realm of God's enemy, Satan (see 1Co 5:5). The purpose of such discipline is restoration, not condemnation. As the church came to be understood as the people of God (as Israel had been), being expelled from the church was viewed as forcible removal from divine protection to the realm of darkness (compare 2Co 4:4; Eph 2:2). **to blaspheme** Refers to speaking irreverently about God and his truth (compare 1Ti 1:13). In this context, the blasphemy committed by Hymenaeus and Alexander involves their rejection of a godly conscience, which resulted in the erosion of their faith (v. 19).

2:1–7 Paul instructs Timothy on prayer. In particular, he urges him to pray for all people since there is only one God who is over all people. The exhortation to prayer leads into Paul's discussion of the proper role for women in the context of prayer and worship (vv. 8–15).

2:1 petitions The Greek word used here, *deēsis*, refers to requests made on the basis of urgency or need. Sometimes these requests are made on behalf of others as an act of intercession (see Lk 22:32; Ac 8:24). See the table "Prayers in Paul's Letters" on p. 1925. **all people** Regardless of race, social status or gender. God does not discriminate between persons; neither should the believers in Ephesus (compare Ro 2:10–11; Gal 3:26–29). The prayers offered on behalf of all people become an expression of faith in God and love for others (1Ti 1:14). In this chapter, Paul could be repeating the word "all" several times to counter the elitist rhetoric of certain people in Ephesus.

2:2 quiet lives In this context, this phrase is describing a life free from the turmoil of persecution (1Th 4:11–12). Without the threat of persecution, believers could openly demonstrate their faith through word and deed. **godliness** The Greek word used here, *eusebeia*, refers to living according to religious standards and values. In the Pastoral Letters, godly people uphold and conform to sound doctrine. As a result, they treat others with love and respect.

2:3 God our Savior See note on 1Ti 1:1.

2:4 who wants all people to be saved In contrast to the elitist rhetoric of false teachers within the community—who may have attempted to exclude certain people from the gospel (see note on 1Ti 1:4)—Paul emphasizes that God wishes for all people to be saved. **knowledge of the truth** Refers to hearing and understanding the gospel message. Knowledge does not replace faith as a response to the gospel message, but it does play a crucial role in combatting false teaching. Compare 1Ti 4:3; Titus 1:1.

2:5 one God Alludes to the Jewish prayer called the Shema (see Dt 6:4 and note; compare 1Co 8:6 and note). Paul draws on this prayer to highlight God's universal reign; because there is only one God, he is the God of all people (1Ti 2:3–4). **mediator** A person who negotiates reconciliation between two parties in conflict. The need for a mediator testifies to the sinfulness of humanity, while the provision of a mediator demonstrates the kindness of God. **the man Christ Jesus** Paul refers to Jesus as a "man" here to stress his full identification with humanity. Because he was fully human, Christ was able to mediate on behalf of humanity and offer himself as a ransom for humanity. Jesus' role in this passage recalls Paul's description of Jesus as a second Adam (e.g., Ro 5:12–21; 1Co 15:45–49).

2:6 who gave himself as a ransom for all people Refers to the sacrificial death of Jesus. Echoes Jesus' words regarding his sacrificial death. Paul reminds believers that Jesus' life was the price paid to free people from sin (see Mk 10:45 and note; compare Isa 53:12).

2:7 was appointed Paul did not appoint himself; God appointed him. While in leadership at Ephesus, Timothy experienced opposition from other believers. Paul asserts his own authority as an apostle in support of Timothy's leadership to bring correction to wayward believers. **herald** The Greek word used here, *keryx*, refers to a person with authority to preach the gospel message. **I am telling the truth** Emphasizes the validity of Paul's statement (see Ro 9:1; Gal 1:20). **a true and faithful teacher of the Gentiles** Although Paul preached the gospel to all people, his primary calling was to bring the gospel to Gentiles (non-Jews). See Ro 11:13–16; 15:18–21.

2:8–15 Paul's teachings here addressed to women may allude to a trend in Roman society that undermined Greco-Roman views on family and thus caused widespread concern in secular Greek and Roman society. Greek and Roman sources from the first century AD reveal an emerging movement in society where wealthy and influential women openly flouted Greco-Roman values related to dress and sexual propriety. Greco-Roman writers strongly criticized the trend, which had disrupted the status quo so much that imperial legislation was issued to address it. Paul begins this section addressing the issue of appropriate clothing, perhaps because the style of public dress and adornment was an obvious symbol of this particular movement, and he did not want anything to hinder the gospel.

2:8 lifting up holy hands A common posture in prayer (e.g., Ex 9:29; 1Ki 8:22; Ps 28:2). "Holy hands" symbolize living according to God's standards.

⁹I also want the women to dress modestly, with decency and propriety, adorning themselves, not with elaborate hairstyles or gold or pearls or expensive clothes, ¹⁰but with good deeds, appropriate for women who profess to worship God.

¹¹A woman*a* should learn in quietness and full submission. ¹²I do not permit a woman to teach or to assume authority over a man;*b* she must be quiet. ¹³For Adam was formed first, then Eve. ¹⁴And Adam was not the one deceived; it was the woman who was deceived and became a sinner.

¹⁵But women*c* will be saved through childbearing — if they continue in faith, love and holiness with propriety.

Qualifications for Overseers and Deacons

3 Here is a trustworthy saying: Whoever aspires to be an overseer desires a noble task. ²Now the overseer is to be above reproach, faithful to

a 11 Or *wife*; also in verse 12   *b* 12 Or *over her husband*
c 15 Greek *she*

2:9 to dress modestly Because clothing in the ancient world could reflect internal values, Paul called Christian women to dress in a manner that identified them as followers of Christ. In a particular, Paul discouraged women from adornment with particular hairstyles, jewelry and expensive clothing due to the connotations within that cultural context (compare note on 1Ti 2:8–15).

2:10 with good deeds Refers to the characteristics that women should be known by. Paul does not specify any particular works he has in view, though later he mentions good works in his discussions of young widows and wealthy believers (1Ti 5:10; 6:18; compare Titus 2:7–8; 3:8,14). Ultimately, Paul's point is that genuine faith in God should display itself in holiness. **for women who profess to worship God** Refers to women who claim to live according to God's standards and values. By implication, the manner in which some Christian women dressed identified them with secular women who did not profess faith in God (compare note on 1Ti 2:8–15).

2:11–15 Paul's instructions about women and teaching authority should be understood within the larger context of self-control introduced in 1Ti 2:9–10. Within that context, Paul's main concern seems to be the public (non-Christian) perception of the church. Even so, Paul's strong statements on women's submission can be taken in different directions. One option takes Paul's instruction about women as historically and culturally conditioned — Paul may have simply addressed a particular situation at Ephesus.

A reconstruction of the historical situation in Ephesus suggests that some Ephesian women, under the influence of false teachers, tried to usurp the authority of male leaders in their teaching ministry. As a result, the men became angry and dissension spread throughout the community. To remedy the situation, Paul prohibited women (see note on v. 11) from teaching with the intention of taking advantage or usurping someone else, particularly someone already in authority. According to this view, Paul's instructions address a specific situation and thus do not directly apply to believers outside of these circumstances.

Another interpretation is that Paul's instruction about women was intended to establish guidelines for Christian worship applicable to all believers at all times, not address an isolated instance of disobedience. This would mean that women could not teach or exercise authority in church communities over men, regardless of time and culture.

2:11 A woman Paul uses the singular Greek word, *gynē* ("a woman"), in vv. 11–12. This is a switch from the plural form used in vv. 9–10. It is possible that this subtle change in wording indicates that Paul's instructions are generic and intended for all women in the church instead of just the wealthy women criticized in

vv. 9–10, although Paul could be making this subtle change for rhetorical reasons (to strengthen his tone). **should learn in quietness and full submission** The meaning of the Greek term used here, *hēsychia* (meaning "silence" or "quiet"), can range from complete silence to a state of respectful quietness. If Paul is addressing a specific historical situation at Ephesus, it is possible that particular women were interrupting the worship of others by usurping or undermining the teachings of the church's previously established male authority figures. To outsiders, this gave the appearance of complete disregard for cultural norms and hindered the church's ability to effectively present the gospel in the community. Alternatively, Paul's instructions could reflect the emerging cultural trend of Roman women speaking at secular gatherings held in homes. Paul could be providing this command to ensure that the Christian community does not seem like other trends, especially since these trends were often perceived negatively (compare note on 2:8–15). Compare 1Co 14:34 and note.

2:12 to teach or to assume authority over a man The closest parallel to this instruction appears in 1Co 14:34–35. The context there is the church's public gatherings. The teaching role in public settings was traditionally assigned to males in Jewish and Greco-Roman culture. This statement may be read as two prohibitions: A woman cannot teach or exercise authority over a man. If so, Paul presents two independent but related commands. Alternatively, the statement can be read as a single prohibition (i.e., not to teach) followed by an explanation (i.e., not to exercise authority). This interpretation, based partially on a particular reading of the Greek syntax and combination of specific verbs, suggests that Paul prohibits women from teaching men because it inverted the accepted authority structure in Greco-Roman society. Either way, Paul's main concern was the church's ability to minister effectively without appearing to disregard cultural traditions, which would alienate the general population. At the same time, it is possible that the intent of Paul's prohibition is to prevent women from perpetuating false teaching within the church. One of Paul's main points of emphasis in the letter is the need for true doctrine to combat false teaching (e.g., 1Ti 1:3; 2:7; 4:11–16; compare 1:3; 6:3). In this case, Paul may have issued this command because some of the women in the church had been led astray by the false teachers.

2:13 For Adam was formed first, then Eve Paul appeals to the OT to support his argument (vv. 8–12). He asserts that the order of creation in Ge 2:7–25 sets a precedent for the situation in Ephesus. Paul does not mean that women are more inclined than men to sin; elsewhere he emphasizes the responsibility of all people (Ro 3:22–23) and even refers to Adam as the representative of sinful humanity (Ro 5:12–21; 1Co 15:22).

his wife, temperate, self-controlled, respectable, hospitable, able to teach, ³not given to drunkenness, not violent but gentle, not quarrelsome, not a lover of money. ⁴He must manage his own family well and see that his children obey him, and he must do so in a manner worthy of full*a* respect. ⁵(If anyone does not know how to manage his own family, how can he take care of God's church?) ⁶He must not be a recent convert, or he may become conceited and fall under the same

judgment as the devil. ⁷He must also have a good reputation with outsiders, so that he will not fall into disgrace and into the devil's trap.

⁸In the same way, deacons*b* are to be worthy of respect, sincere, not indulging in much wine, and not pursuing dishonest gain. ⁹They must keep hold of

a 4 Or *him with proper*   *b* 8 The word *deacons* refers here to Christians designated to serve with the overseers/elders of the church in a variety of ways; similarly in verse 12; and in Romans 16:1 and Phil. 1:1.

Rather, Paul cites the Genesis narrative to draw attention to Eve's deception by the serpent (compare 2Co 11:3). **2:15 will be saved through childbearing** The exact meaning of this statement is uncertain. Paul may mean that women will be saved because Jesus, the savior of the world, was born of a woman (see Gal 4:4). Alternatively, he may be arguing that women will be saved because a woman helped bring about the defeat of the devil (see Ge 3:15). Or, he may be saying that women will be saved from doing evil things by bearing children. Some of the Ephesian women may have been behaving in a manner that led them to neglect what was commonly viewed at the time as their household responsibilities. These women may have been influenced by new cultural trends about women and the false teachers' negative views on marriage (1Ti 4:3; compare 5:14; note on 2:8–15; note on 2:11–15). If these factors are in view, Paul's reference to childbirth may represent a woman's acceptance of what was considered her proper role within the household unit. **propriety** Describes moderate and sensible behavior (compare v. 9). In the Pastoral Letters (1 Timothy, 2 Timothy and Titus), those with self-control resist ungodliness (Titus 2:12) in proper anticipation of Christ's return (1Pe 4:7). Paul lists self-control as a required characteristic of overseers (1Ti 3:2; Titus 1:8), older men (Titus 2:2), younger men (Titus 2:6), and women (Titus 2:5).

3:1–7 Paul provides a list of qualifications for the individual desiring to serve the church as an overseer or elder. These qualifications emphasize the character of the leader, not the duties to be performed. Paul's emphasis on the untarnished reputation of the potential leader suggests a concern for the public perception of the church; he exhorts communities of faith to avoid appointing a leader whose respectability in the community is (or could be) questioned.

3:1 a trustworthy saying See note on 1Ti 1:15.
3:2 overseer The Greek word used here, *episkopos*, refers to those appointed to watch over and protect the local church community (see Ac 20:28; 1Pe 5:2). Paul provides a list of qualifications for overseers to help Timothy and Titus appoint church leaders in their communities. The qualifications for an overseer (*episkopos*) and an elder (*presbyteros*) are nearly identical, suggesting that at this point in church history the two roles were functionally equivalent (compare 1Ti 3:1–7; Titus 1:5–9; see note on Ac 20:28). **above reproach** The Greek word used here, *anepilēmptos*, means to be above criticism. Paul requires that leaders maintain a positive reputation inside and outside the community of believers. If not, their actions may become the subject of criticism and discredit the gospel message (compare 1Ti 3:2–7). Paul also used this word with respect to the conduct of widows (5:7) and Timothy (6:14). **faithful to his wife** The Greek text here, which rendered literally is

"the man of one woman," may mean that an overseer must be either a married man, abstain from polygamy and sexual immorality, avoid remarriage or be faithful to his wife. Since polygamy was already considered immoral in Greco-Roman society, it is unlikely that Paul specifically prohibits it here. Also, Paul elsewhere promotes remaining single (1Co 7:1) and supports remarriage (1Co 7:39). Therefore, it is most likely that Paul is promoting fidelity in the marriage relationship. **self-controlled** See note on 1Ti 2:15. **able to teach** Overseers who meet this qualification can refute false teachers and protect the church community from unsound doctrine.
3:3 not given to drunkenness Drunkenness leads to recklessness—the opposite of self-control. While Paul does not prohibit the use of wine (5:23), he prohibits being under its control. **not a lover of money** See note on 6:10.
3:4 his own family The basic unit of social structure in Greco-Roman society was the household. Paul reasons that if elders cannot manage their own households, they cannot manage the household of God (i.e., the community of believers). The Greco-Roman household—the immediate family, household slaves, laborers and other tenants—was a place of relationship and social interaction. It provided Christians with an environment to demonstrate the transformative power of the gospel. It also functioned as a microcosm of the larger society; if the gospel could take root in a household, then it could also take root in society.
3:6 not be a recent convert Refers to a person who is relatively new to the faith. Such people are particularly prone to becoming prideful, just as the false teachers were full of pride (6:4). **the same judgment as the devil** This could refer to the punishment reserved for the devil because of his pride (compare Jude 9) or to the devil's temptation of prideful believers. Either way, Paul's point is to caution the church regarding the suitability of recent converts for ministry. Because recent converts have not yet matured in the faith, they are particularly susceptible to pride and temptation.
3:7 a good reputation Paul provided a list of qualifications so that the church would maintain a good reputation among unbelievers. The church's good standing in society helps believers to maintain healthy relationships and preach the gospel. **the devil's trap** Compare note on 1Ti 3:6.

3:8–13 The list of qualifications for deacons also emphasizes personal character. The qualities of character required for both overseers and deacons are essentially the same. A unique aspect of the discussion of deacons is that qualifications for women participating in the ministry appear in v. 11.

3:8 deacons The Greek word used here, *diakonos*, generally means "servant." It is first used in the NT to

the deep truths of the faith with a clear conscience. ¹⁰They must first be tested; and then if there is nothing against them, let them serve as deacons.

¹¹In the same way, the womenᵃ are to be worthy of respect, not malicious talkers but temperate and trustworthy in everything.

¹²A deacon must be faithful to his wife and must manage his children and his household well. ¹³Those who have served well gain an excellent standing and great assurance in their faith in Christ Jesus.

Reasons for Paul's Instructions

¹⁴Although I hope to come to you soon, I am writing you these instructions so that, ¹⁵if I am delayed, you will know how people ought to conduct themselves in God's household, which is the church of the living God, the pillar and foundation

of the truth. ¹⁶Beyond all question, the mystery from which true godliness springs is great:

> He appeared in the flesh,
>   was vindicated by the Spirit,ᵇ
> was seen by angels,
>   was preached among the nations,
> was believed on in the world,
>   was taken up in glory.

4 The Spirit clearly says that in later times some will abandon the faith and follow deceiving spirits and things taught by demons. ²Such teachings come through hypocritical liars, whose consciences have been seared as with a hot iron. ³They forbid people to marry and order them to abstain from certain foods, which God created

ᵃ 11 Possibly deacons' wives or women who are deacons
ᵇ 16 Or vindicated in spirit

---

refer to those who helped with the distribution of food to widows (Ac 6:1–2). As the church grew, deacons assumed more responsibilities. Here, Paul did not focus on responsibilities, but qualifications. "Deacon" may refer to an official role in a church or more generally to a type of activity. For example, the term *diakonos* can be applied to Jesus since his ministry to the circumcised (the Jews) can be described in terms of service language (Ro 15:8; compare Mk 9:35; 10:43). In the same way, Paul's missionary endeavors make him a servant of the gospel (see Col 1:23–25). This usage of "deacon" is usually rendered as "servant." However, in Paul's letters, the term seems to be used in a more technical sense. This may indicate that Christians had begun to use *diakonos* as a title for a church office (see Ro 16:1 and note; Php 1:1; 1Ti 4:6).

3:9 the deep truths of the faith Refers to the gospel message about Jesus Christ as received by the apostles. In other passages, Paul uses similar language to refer to Christ's work of bringing both Jews and Gentiles into one people of God (e.g., Eph 3:6–9).

3:10 must first be tested The exact nature of the test or examination is uncertain; at the very least, it probably involves an evaluation of the candidate's qualifications based on the list in 1Ti 3:8–12.

3:11 the women Refers to either the office of the deaconess or the wife of a deacon. The Greek word used here, the plural form of *gynē*, could be understood generically as "women" or more specifically as "wives," referring to the wives of those serving as deacons. Paul's teachings elsewhere on the role of women in ministry should not be construed as prohibiting them from serving in this capacity, since the deacon's areas of responsibility are service oriented and not related to teaching (see note on 2:12). In Romans, Paul's application of the Greek term *diakonos* to a wealthy gentile woman named Phoebe may indicate that he knew of women serving as deaconesses (see Ro 16:1 and note).

3:12 faithful to his wife See note on 1Ti 3:2.

3:14–16 Paul clarifies the purpose of his letter to Timothy: to provide instructions on proper conduct in the church.

3:16 the mystery from which true godliness springs Probably refers to the hymn-like declaration in the rest of this verse. **He appeared in the flesh** Refers to the

incarnation of Jesus Christ (see note on Jn 1:14). **was vindicated by the Spirit** Through the resurrection, the Spirit confirmed Jesus as the Son of God and Lord (Ro 1:3–4; 8:11). **was seen by angels** The Greek word used here, *angelos*, can refer to a human messenger (Lk 7:24). In this context, it refers to supernatural beings in service to God. These angels saw Jesus, possibly during his resurrection appearances (e.g., Lk 24:31; Ac 13:31). Another possibility is that it refers to worship Jesus received from angels in heaven after his ascension. **was preached among the nations** God included the Gentiles (non-Jewish people) in his redemptive plan (Ge 22:17–18; Gal 3:8), and the apostle made them a focus of his missionary efforts (Ac 13:46; Gal 2:7–9). **was taken up in glory** Refers to Christ's ascension to heaven (Ac 1:9–11; Lk 9:51). The Greek word used here for "glory," *doxa*, probably refers to God's presence and the location of Christ's exultation (Php 2:9–11; Eph 1:20–23).

4:1–5 Paul returns to the subject of false teaching (compare 1Ti 1:3–11). Here Paul is concerned not with the content of the false teachers' doctrine, but with its source. Paul claims that false teaching comes from deceptive spirits and demons.

4:1 The Spirit clearly says Refers to a prophetic message known to Paul. The passage never reveals how Paul heard the message, though the Spirit is identified as its source. **later times** This particular Greek phrase only occurs here in the NT, but is synonymous with the last days (see note on 2Ti 3:1). Though the apostle describes these events as occurring in the future, they also describe Timothy's circumstances in the present age. **demons** Supernatural beings hostile to God and his people (e.g., Mk 9:38; 1Co 10:20). Demons and deceitful spirits probably refer to the same group of evil figures. Paul's point is to demonstrate the errant doctrine of the false teachers

4:2 hypocritical liars Refers to the false teachers. The following two verses likely describe key objections to their teaching.

4:3 They forbid people to marry Those who forbade marriage promoted a type of asceticism that seems to have promoted celibacy for anyone seeking a holy life. Paul reminds them that God created marriage and food, both of which are occasions for thanksgiving (1Ti 4:4).

to be received with thanksgiving by those who believe and who know the truth. ⁴For everything God created is good, and nothing is to be rejected if it is received with thanksgiving, ⁵because it is consecrated by the word of God and prayer.

⁶If you point these things out to the brothers and sisters,ᵃ you will be a good minister of Christ Jesus, nourished on the truths of the faith and of the good teaching that you have followed. ⁷Have nothing to do with godless myths and old wives' tales; rather, train yourself to be godly. ⁸For physical training is of some value, but godliness has value for all things, holding promise for both the present life and the life to come. ⁹This is a trustworthy saying that deserves full acceptance. ¹⁰That is why we labor and strive, because we have put our hope in the living God, who is the Savior of all people, and especially of those who believe.

¹¹Command and teach these things. ¹²Don't let anyone look down on you because you are young, but set an example for the believers in speech, in conduct, in love, in faith and in purity. ¹³Until I come, devote yourself to the public reading of Scripture, to preaching and to teaching. ¹⁴Do not neglect your gift, which was given you through prophecy when the body of elders laid their hands on you.

¹⁵Be diligent in these matters; give yourself wholly to them, so that everyone may see your progress. ¹⁶Watch your life and doctrine closely. Persevere in them, because if you do, you will save both yourself and your hearers.

Widows, Elders and Slaves

5 Do not rebuke an older man harshly, but exhort him as if he were your father. Treat younger men as brothers, ²older women as mothers, and younger women as sisters, with absolute purity.

ᵃ 6 The Greek word for *brothers and sisters* (*adelphoi*) refers here to believers, both men and women, as part of God's family.

Paul's teaching on marriage in the letter suggests that some of the believers had adopted the false teachers' seemingly negative view on the subject (e.g., 3:2,12; 5:9–16). **abstain from certain foods** It is unknown which kinds of food are in view here. There was some debate in the early church period about whether Christians should avoid meat sacrificed to idols or observe Jewish dietary laws (see Ro 14:1–23; 1Co 8:1—10:33; Col 2:16–23). The false teachers may have pressured believers in Ephesus to abstain from foods because of these issues. Paul condemns their teaching on theological grounds. He argues that believers who give thanks to God are free to eat any kind of food since they acknowledge God as the creator and provider of every good thing (see Ge 1:29; 9:3; Ps 24:1). **the truth** The gospel message. **4:4 everything God created** Paul's affirmation of the goodness of creation echoes the language of the creation narrative in Genesis (e.g., Ge 1:4,10). The false teachers apparently denied the inherent value of some created things (e.g., some kinds of food). **4:5 it is consecrated** Meaning acceptable for use or good for consumption. Because God has declared that creation is good, all things created by God are good. Believers are called to receive God's gifts with gratitude and in prayer. **4:6–16** Paul commends Timothy for his faithful service in the gospel. The description of Timothy in this passage provides a positive example for believers in contrast to the negative depiction of the false teachers in the letter (1Ti 1:3–11; 4:1–6).

4:6 a good minister The Greek word used here, *diakonos*, refers generically in this instance to a "minister" or "servant" (e.g., Col 1:7; 2Co 11:23). Compare note on 1Ti 3:8. **4:7 myths** See note on 1:4. **be godly** See note on 2:2. **4:8 physical training** The Greek word used here, *gymnasia*, refers to physical exercise or training. Paul uses the term here to describe training in godliness, in preparation for ministry and for combating the false teachers. Compare Heb 12:11. **4:9 a trustworthy saying** See note on 1Ti 1:15. **4:10 the Savior** See note on 1:1. **4:12 because you are young** It is difficult to determine an approximate age for Timothy since the Greek term used here does not denote a specific range. However, the implication of the passage is that Timothy was younger than Paul and, most likely, younger than some of the elders and the false teachers. Paul urges him not to allow others to make his age a point of criticism. His gifting validates his authority, not his age (v. 14). **4:13 public reading** Public reading of Scripture was a regular feature in early Christian worship and a tradition in religious education (e.g., Ac 13:15). In 1 Thessalonians, Paul advises the believers to read his letter aloud for the benefit of the church community (1Th 5:27). **to preaching** The Greek word used here, *paraklesis*, often refers to encouragement that helps a person take the right course of action. It can also refer to encouragement in the sense of comforting or lifting someone's spirits (2Co 1:4). **4:14 prophecy** See note on 1Ti 1:18. **laid their hands on** A gesture used to symbolize the impartation of power. Paul does not regard this as a special power (compare Ac 8:18–20); rather, he recognizes that God empowers and equips believers for ministry (Ac 1:8; Eph 4:11–12). In the OT, the laying on of hands was a ritual gesture used for consecration and identification. Moses laid his hands on Joshua to consecrate him as the leader of the people of Israel (Nu 27:18; Dt 34:9). Those who offered an animal sacrifice laid a hand upon the animal before the slaughter to identify it as their own (see Lev 1:4 and note). In the NT, laying on of hands was used for healing (Ac 28:8), blessing (Mk 10:16), imparting (or acknowledging) spiritual gifts (Ac 8:19) and ordination (Ac 6:6). **4:16 you will save** Timothy's proper response to his calling as a minister of the gospel is to persevere in the face of opposition and difficult seasons. By demonstrating proper conduct and teaching true doctrine, Timothy will confirm God's gift of salvation to him and other believers.

5:1–16 In 1Ti 5:1—6:2 Paul writes about several groups within the church under Timothy's charge. He begins by providing instructions regarding different age groups (vv. 1–2). He then turns to address widows. Paul aims to resolve difficulties with widows in the Ephesian church by defining the qualifications for "true" widows (vv. 3–10) and addressing young widows who were straying from the faith (vv. 11–16).

³Give proper recognition to those widows who are really in need. ⁴But if a widow has children or grandchildren, these should learn first of all to put their religion into practice by caring for their own family and so repaying their parents and grandparents, for this is pleasing to God. ⁵The widow who is really in need and left all alone puts her hope in God and continues night and day to pray and to ask God for help. ⁶But the widow who lives for pleasure is dead even while she lives. ⁷Give the people these instructions, so that no one may be open to blame. ⁸Anyone who does not provide for their relatives, and especially for their own household, has denied the faith and is worse than an unbeliever.

⁹No widow may be put on the list of widows unless she is over sixty, has been faithful to her husband, ¹⁰and is well known for her good deeds, such as bringing up children, showing hospitality, washing the feet of the Lord's people, helping those in trouble and devoting herself to all kinds of good deeds.

¹¹As for younger widows, do not put them on such a list. For when their sensual desires overcome their dedication to Christ, they want to marry. ¹²Thus they bring judgment on themselves, because they have broken their first pledge. ¹³Besides, they get into the habit of being idle and going about from house to house. And not only do they become idlers, but also busybodies who talk nonsense, saying things they ought not to. ¹⁴So I counsel younger widows to marry, to have children, to manage their homes and to give the enemy no opportunity for slander. ¹⁵Some have in fact already turned away to follow Satan.

¹⁶If any woman who is a believer has widows in her care, she should continue to help them and not let the church be burdened with them, so that the church can help those widows who are really in need.

¹⁷The elders who direct the affairs of the church well are worthy of double honor, especially those whose work is preaching and teach-

---

5:3 Give proper recognition In this context, the Greek word used here, *timaō*, describes showing respect with financial support. **widows** A woman whose husband has died and who has no male relative (e.g., a father or son) to support her. In the ancient world, widows were susceptible to injustice and poverty. Typically, wealth and land passed from father to son, leaving a widow without financial support. Old Testament laws provided widows with a means of financial security through a kinsman (Dt 25:5–10), and protected widows in the absence of an available kinsman (Dt 10:18; 24:17). The early church showed great care toward widows (e.g., Ac 6:1–6; 9:41; Jas 1:27).

5:4 so repaying their parents and grandparents To provide elderly parents with the support they once provided for their children. Paul encourages such good works because they please God.

5:5 widow These widows depend on God (compare Lk 2:36–38), and their persistence in prayer provides an example for believers (compare Lk 18:1–8). **to ask God for help** See note on 1Ti 2:1.

5:7 no one may be open to blame See note on 3:2.

5:8 household See note on 3:4. **is worse than an unbeliever** Paul's statement here suggests that even unbelievers—those without faith in Christ and the Spirit of God—support those in their household.

5:9 the list Probably a record of the needy widows supported by the church. This list may imply that widows held an office in the early church and, possibly, the existence of an order of widows. The notion of enrolling widows to a list and the established qualifications for widows supports this view. Alternatively, it is possible that the list's purpose was not to enroll widows to an office in the church, but to distinguish real widows (v. 3) from younger widows who are discussed in vv. 11–16.

5:10 good deeds Not the means to salvation, but evidence of it (see 2:10 and note; 5:25). **hospitality** The Greek word used here, *xenodocheō*, refers to the extension of friendship to a stranger or visitor. **washing the feet of the Lord's people** An act of humility and service among believers. Servants washed the dusty feet of guests upon their arrival (e.g., 1Sa 25:41; Lk 7:44).

Jesus washed his disciples' feet as an example of humility and service (Jn 13:3–5,14). **the Lord's people** The Greek word used here, *hagioi*, refers to those who are set apart or who belong to God.

5:11 younger widows Refers to widows younger than age 60 and still eligible for remarriage (compare 1Ti 5:9). **their sensual desires overcome their dedication to Christ** See v. 14 and note; compare 1Co 7:34 and note.

5:12 first pledge May refer to either a vow of chastity or, more likely, commitment to the Christian faith.

5:13 they get into the habit of being idle These widows neglected the responsibilities of real widows (1Ti 5:3–10). They have ceased to carry out their work in the household (which was a key value for Greco-Roman society), disrupted other house churches and spread gossip. Paul is trying to stop any behavior that could become a hindrance to the gospel, in terms of the church's reputation or function.

5:14 to marry Several verses earlier (v. 11), Paul takes issue with the young widows' desire to remarry—apparently because it exceeded the devotion they showed to Christ. As a result, these women were not qualified to be enrolled as real widows and therefore supported by the church (vv. 7–8,16; compare note on 5:9). Since they could not be counted among the real widows, Paul urges them to fulfill their desire to remarry in hopes that it will restore their devotion to Christ, as well as the reputation of the church. **to have children** See note on 2:15. **to manage their homes** See note on 3:4.

5:15 Satan Paul regards evil forces as the source of false teaching (4:1), which also manifests itself in false conduct. Here, to follow Satan means to abandon Christian values and responsibilities—especially those given to widows—because of the influence of false teaching.

5:17–25 Paul writes to Timothy regarding elders in the church. These instructions have two main concerns—financial payments for elders (vv. 17–18) and the high standard of godliness for elders (vv. 19–22).

5:17 elders Refers to mature believers responsible for managing and teaching in the church. Paul appointed elders in the local church and advised Titus do the same

ing. [18]For Scripture says, "Do not muzzle an ox while it is treading out the grain,"[a] and "The worker deserves his wages."[b] [19]Do not entertain an accusation against an elder unless it is brought by two or three witnesses. [20]But those elders who are sinning you are to reprove before everyone, so that the others may take warning. [21]I charge you, in the sight of God and Christ Jesus and the elect angels, to keep these instructions without partiality, and to do nothing out of favoritism.

[22]Do not be hasty in the laying on of hands, and do not share in the sins of others. Keep yourself pure.

[23]Stop drinking only water, and use a little wine because of your stomach and your frequent illnesses.

[24]The sins of some are obvious, reaching the place of judgment ahead of them; the sins of others trail behind them. [25]In the same way, good deeds are obvious, and even those that are not obvious cannot remain hidden forever.

6 All who are under the yoke of slavery should consider their masters worthy of full respect, so that God's name and our teaching may not be slandered. [2]Those who have believing masters should not show them disrespect just because they are fellow believers. Instead, they should serve them even better because their masters are dear to them as fellow believers and are devoted to the welfare[c] of their slaves.

False Teachers and the Love of Money

These are the things you are to teach and insist on. [3]If anyone teaches otherwise and does not agree to the sound instruction of our Lord Jesus Christ and to godly teaching, [4]they are conceited and understand nothing. They have an unhealthy interest in controversies and quarrels about words that result in envy, strife, malicious talk, evil suspicions [5]and constant friction between people of corrupt mind, who have been robbed of the truth and who think that godliness is a means to financial gain.

[6]But godliness with contentment is great gain. [7]For we brought nothing into the world, and we can take nothing out of it. [8]But if we have food and clothing, we will be content with that. [9]Those who want to get rich fall into temptation and a trap and into many foolish and harmful desires that plunge people into ruin and destruction. [10]For the love of money is a root of all kinds of evil. Some people, eager for money, have

<hr>

a 18 Deut. 25:4   *b* 18 Luke 10:7   *c* 2 Or *and benefit from the service*

<hr>

(Ac 14:23; Titus 1:5). Like overseers, elders nourish and protect the believers in the church community (see Ac 20:28 and note; 1Ti 3:2 and note). **double honor** This refers to an adequate compensation for the work of the ministry. In the context of 1Ti 5:3, this honor included financial support from the community.

5:18 Do not muzzle an ox while it is treading out the grain A quotation from Dt 25:4, also used in 1Co 9:9. The ox must be allowed to eat from the place where it works. Likewise, the elder must be allowed to receive financial support from the people to whom he ministers. **The worker deserves his wages** A quotation from Lk 10:7. Here Paul cites Jesus' words alongside Scripture.

5:19 by two or three witnesses A partial quotation from Dt 19:15. This practice protected people from false accusations. Like Jesus, Paul applies this practice to church discipline (Mt 18:16; 2Co 13:1).

5:20 who are sinning Refers to elders who fail to live by the standards detailed by Paul (1Ti 3:1–7; Titus 1:6–9). **before everyone** Paul advises Timothy to rebuke such an elder in the presence of the entire church community. The public nature of the rebuke coincides with the public nature of the elder's ministry.

5:21 elect angels Refers to angels who are faithful to God. Paul probably includes the elect angels as witnesses as a way of emphasizing the serious nature of his charge to Timothy. See the table "Angels in the Bible" on p. 2120.

5:22 laying on of hands See note on 1Ti 4:14.

5:23 wine Paul's advice may be indirectly aimed at the false teachers' promotion of abstinence from some food and drink (4:3; see note on 3:3).

6:1–2 Paul instructs Timothy regarding the attitude of Christian slaves. This is the final group of believers he writes about in the letter (see 5:1–25).

6:1 slavery Slavery was part of the Greco-Roman socioeconomic structure in the first century (see note on Phm 10). Paul is urging believers to demonstrate God's love and kindness even within this particular structure (e.g., 1Co 7:21–24; Eph 6:5–8; Phm 10–17). Here Paul urges slaves to remain respectful to their masters for the sake of the church's reputation—so that the work of the gospel may not be hindered.

6:3–10 In this passage, Paul condemns the greedy motivation of the false teachers. Paul claims that these people have erred in their understanding of doctrine, as well as in their conduct.

6:3 teaches otherwise See note on 1Ti 1:3.

6:4 envy, strife These two vices affect not only individuals, but the entire community of believers, causing disruption and dysfunction (compare Gal 5:19–21).

6:7 we can take nothing out Paul cautions the believers in Ephesus against prioritizing material wealth over godliness (see 1Ti 6:17; compare Job 1:21).

6:9 ruin and destruction This is not a pronouncement of judgment on all wealthy people. Paul's point is that the pursuit of riches is spiritually hazardous and does not contribute to contentment and godliness (compare 1Ti 6:6–7).

6:10 the love of money Love of money (not money itself) is the root of all kinds of evil. Paul here describes a deep desire and commitment to possess money over and against loyalty and love for God. Like the young widows who put their desire to remarry before Christ (see 5:11 and note), those who love money allow their allegiance to Christ to be compromised because of selfish desires. Jesus also spoke on the idolatrous pursuit of riches (Mt 6:24).

wandered from the faith and pierced themselves with many griefs.

Final Charge to Timothy

[11]But you, man of God, flee from all this, and pursue righteousness, godliness, faith, love, endurance and gentleness. [12]Fight the good fight of the faith. Take hold of the eternal life to which you were called when you made your good confession in the presence of many witnesses. [13]In the sight of God, who gives life to everything, and of Christ Jesus, who while testifying before Pontius Pilate made the good confession, I charge you [14]to keep this command without spot or blame until the appearing of our Lord Jesus Christ, [15]which God will bring about in his own time — God, the blessed and only Ruler, the King of kings and Lord of lords, [16]who alone is immortal and who lives in unapproachable light, whom no one has seen or can see. To him be honor and might forever. Amen.

[17]Command those who are rich in this present world not to be arrogant nor to put their hope in wealth, which is so uncertain, but to put their hope in God, who richly provides us with everything for our enjoyment. [18]Command them to do good, to be rich in good deeds, and to be generous and willing to share. [19]In this way they will lay up treasure for themselves as a firm foundation for the coming age, so that they may take hold of the life that is truly life.

[20]Timothy, guard what has been entrusted to your care. Turn away from godless chatter and the opposing ideas of what is falsely called knowledge, [21]which some have professed and in so doing have departed from the faith.

Grace be with you all.

6:11–21 Following his critique of the false teachers (1Ti 6:3–10), Paul commends Timothy for his exemplary character and faithful ministry of the gospel. Paul then adds a final warning to the rich (vv. 17–19) and a last charge to Timothy (vv. 20–21).

6:11 man of God This OT expression referred to prophets (i.e., a man who speaks on behalf of God), such as Moses (Dt 33:1), David (Ne 12:24) and the other prophets (1Sa 9:6). Timothy serves in a similar capacity because he preaches the word of God (2Ti 3:17). **godliness** See note on 1Ti 2:2.
6:12 Fight the good fight of the faith Timothy must remain faithful to God and his gospel message, despite opposition (compare 2Ti 4:7). **good confession** May refer to the confession of faith in Christ made at baptism.
6:13 Pontius Pilate The Roman governor of Judea who presided over Jesus' trial and authorized his execution.

See the infographic "Pontius Pilate's Inscription" on p. 1707.
6:16 immortal Not subject to death (compare note on 2Ti 1:10). Believers are blessed to share in Christ's immortality (1Co 15:22,54). **Amen** See note on 1Ti 1:17.
6:17 in this present world Refers to the present time, with a negative connotation (2Ti 4:10; Titus 2:12). **for our enjoyment** Some false teachers promoted an ascetic lifestyle, denying good things for the sake of what they claimed was holiness (or piety). Paul argues that true godliness leads to gratitude and generosity toward others, not asceticism.
6:18 good deeds The rich must seek to be rich not only in wealth, but in good deeds that benefit others (see note on 1Ti 5:10).
6:20 godless chatter Paul identified this as a common practice of false teachers (see 1:6). He urges Timothy to avoid any such chatter, which is empty and not beneficial (see 4:7).

2 TIMOTHY

INTRODUCTION TO 2 TIMOTHY

In his second letter to Timothy, Paul encourages his apprentice Timothy to persevere in the truth. Paul voices some of the same concerns that he expressed in his first letter to Timothy, like the importance of correct teaching and the keys to effective church leadership. This time, though, Paul's situation has changed. He is now in prison, perhaps for the last time, and he wants to make sure that Timothy will be able to complete the mission after he is gone. But Paul is not just concerned about his own legacy; his primary concern, as always, is advancing the gospel.

BACKGROUND

Like the other two Pastoral Letters (1 Timothy and Titus), 2 Timothy identifies Paul as its author (2Ti 1:1), but there is some modern debate about the authorship of the Pastoral Letters (see the "Introduction to 1 Timothy"). Paul would have written 2 Timothy from prison—likely in Rome (2Ti 1:8,16–17; 2:9). Considering that 1 Timothy indicates that Paul was able to visit Ephesus and leave Timothy there (1Ti 1:3), this imprisonment seems to be different from the one narrated in Acts (ca. AD 61–63; Ac 28:16–31). Paul must have been freed, at least for a time, allowing for him to take an additional journey not recorded in Acts. According to early church tradition, Paul was martyred in Rome during the mid–60s AD, so the imprisonment mentioned in 2 Timothy—and thus the writing of the letter—could have immediately preceded his death. Paul seems to anticipate this (2Ti 4:6–8).

Timothy, the recipient of 1–2 Timothy, is mentioned frequently throughout Paul's letters and the book of Acts as a close associate of Paul. During Paul's second missionary journey (ca.

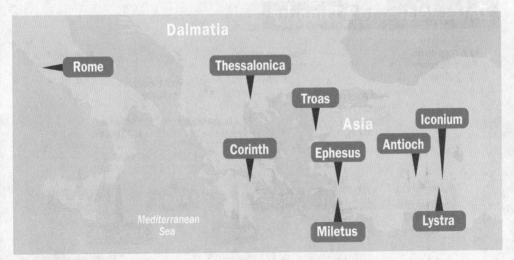

This map depicts many of the locations related to the book of 2 Timothy.

AD 49–51), the two met in Timothy's hometown, Lystra, which is a city in southern Asia Minor (modern-day Turkey). Timothy's mother was Jewish and his father was non-Jewish (Gentile); both his mother and grandmother were Christians (1:5).

Second Timothy does not mention Timothy's location, but given the similarity between the situations in 1–2 Timothy (compare 1Ti 1:20; 2Ti 2:17), he probably is still in Ephesus. Other clues are Paul's request that Timothy greet Priscilla (Prisca) and Aquila (who were living in Ephesus; 2Ti 4:19; compare Ac 18:18–19), and the mention of Troas (a city near Ephesus; 2Ti 4:13).

STRUCTURE

Paul begins 2 Timothy with a standard greeting (1:1–2) and gives thanks to God for Timothy's spiritual heritage (1:3–5). Then he charges Timothy to be bold and unashamed in his ministry, following Paul's own example of being willing to suffer for the gospel (1:6–18). In the next section (2:1–13), Paul encourages Timothy to be a passionate preacher of the gospel. Paul then discusses the false teaching that Timothy is encountering and the proper response (2:14—3:9). In Paul's charge to Timothy (3:10—4:8), he urges him to expect persecution, to continue relying on the Scriptures and to persevere in teaching. Toward the end of the letter, Paul gives details about his situation and final instructions for Timothy (4:9–18); he closes with greetings and a benediction (4:19–22).

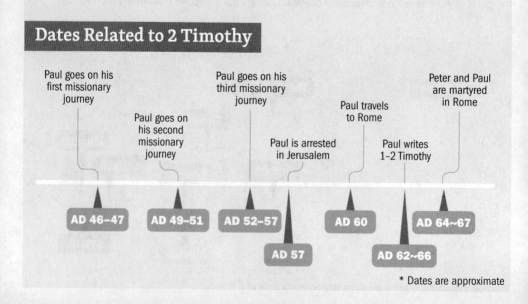

Dates Related to 2 Timothy

Paul goes on his first missionary journey

Paul goes on his second missionary journey

Paul goes on his third missionary journey

Paul is arrested in Jerusalem

Paul travels to Rome

Paul writes 1–2 Timothy

Peter and Paul are martyred in Rome

AD 46–47

AD 49–51

AD 52–57

AD 57

AD 60

AD 62~66

AD 64~67

* Dates are approximate

OUTLINE

- Greeting, thanksgiving and encouragement (1:1–18)
- Aspects of effective ministry (2:1–13)
- Opposing false teaching (2:14—3:9)
- Paul's charge to Timothy and closing remarks (3:10—4:22)

THEMES

Both Paul and Timothy were experiencing opposition. Paul had been thrown in prison for preaching the gospel of Jesus and was nearly alone—his situation was dire (1:15–18; 4:11). Meanwhile Timothy was struggling against false teachers in the church (3:1–9).

In the face of this opposition, Paul urges Timothy to view his mission in the way that a soldier, athlete or farmer would (2:3–6). It involves steady endurance—the gospel is his occupation. In juxtaposition, the false teachers Timothy faces are greedy and self-centered; they like to argue and engage in pointless chatter. Paul tells Timothy to avoid these people and their foolish controversies and stand firm in the truth (2:14—3:9).

The work of the gospel is not easy; some friends might turn away or even become enemies (4:10,16). But there is a reward at the end, and Paul has it in sight (4:7–8). It is always worth it to stay the course.

Paul insists that we look to Christ as our foundation and walk away from evil (2:19). We are called to be ready in and out of season to proclaim the gospel, and this means passionately advocating for the truth (4:1–4). A worker for the gospel does not look back—they press forward.

1 Paul, an apostle of Christ Jesus by the will of God, in keeping with the promise of life that is in Christ Jesus,

[2]To Timothy, my dear son:

Grace, mercy and peace from God the Father and Christ Jesus our Lord.

Thanksgiving

[3]I thank God, whom I serve, as my ancestors did, with a clear conscience, as night and day I constantly remember you in my prayers. [4]Recalling your tears, I long to see you, so that I may be filled with joy. [5]I am reminded of your sincere faith, which first lived in your grandmother Lois and in your mother Eunice and, I am persuaded, now lives in you also.

Appeal for Loyalty to Paul and the Gospel

[6]For this reason I remind you to fan into flame the gift of God, which is in you through the laying on of my hands. [7]For the Spirit God gave us does not make us timid, but gives us power, love and self-discipline. [8]So do not be ashamed of the testimony about our Lord or of me his prisoner. Rather, join with me in suffering for the gospel, by the power of God. [9]He has saved us and called us to a holy life — not because of anything we have done but because of his own purpose and grace. This grace was given us in Christ Jesus before the beginning of time, [10]but it has now been revealed through the appearing of our Savior, Christ Jesus, who has destroyed death and has brought life and immortality to light through the gospel. [11]And of this gospel I was appointed a herald and an apostle and a teacher. [12]That is why I am suffering as I am. Yet this is no cause for shame, because I know whom I have believed, and am convinced that he is able to guard what I have entrusted to him until that day.

[13]What you heard from me, keep as the pattern of sound teaching, with faith and love in Christ Jesus. [14]Guard the good deposit that was entrusted to you — guard it with the help of the Holy Spirit who lives in us.

Examples of Disloyalty and Loyalty

[15]You know that everyone in the province of Asia has deserted me, including Phygelus and Hermogenes.

[16]May the Lord show mercy to the household of

1:1–2 The greeting of 2 Timothy resembles that of 1 Timothy and follows the letter-writing conventions of the time. Paul would have written this letter from prison — likely in Rome — as he awaited his trial and execution in the mid-60s AD (2Ti 1:16–17; 2:9). This would have been his last letter (see note on 1Ti 1:1–2).

1:1 Paul A key apostle and missionary in the early church (see note on Ro 1:1). Timothy met Paul during Paul's second missionary journey (ca. AD 49–51) and served with him in various cities (Ac 16:1–5). **an apostle** See 1Ti 1:1 and note. See the table "Pauline Self-Designations" on p. 1904.
1:2 To Timothy, my dear son See note on 1Ti 1:2.

1:3–7 Paul begins the main part of the letter with a thanksgiving prayer. He praises God for Timothy's faithfulness and encourages Timothy to use his gifts well.

1:3 I serve The Greek word used here, *latreuō*, was used to describe the service of the priests in the Septuagint (the ancient Greek version of the OT). **as my ancestors** Paul asserts that his service to God stands in continuity with his Jewish ancestors (compare Ac 24:14).
1:4 Recalling your tears This tearful farewell may refer to Paul's departure for Macedonia when he left Timothy in Ephesus (1Ti 1:3).
1:5 sincere faith Because others have deserted Paul, he appreciates Timothy's faith even more (2Ti 4:10). **your mother Eunice** Traditionally, Jewish boys were instructed in the law by their fathers; however, since Timothy's father was Greek (Ac 16:1), his Jewish mother and grandmother served as examples of faith.
1:6 laying on of my hands See note on 1Ti 4:14.
1:7 timid The Greek word used here, *deilia*, refers to cowardice that results from a lack of moral strength. Timothy may have been fearful to fulfill his duties because of a timid personality and the intense opposition

he faced from false teachers. Paul reminds Timothy that such fear does not come from God's Spirit (compare Ro 8:15–16). **power** In this context, power refers to courage to fulfill his ministerial duties, namely, the proclamation of the gospel (compare Ac 1:8; 1Co 2:4; Eph 3:16).

1:8–18 Paul continues his instructions to Timothy. Paul's message aims to encourage Timothy in his ministerial duties, since he seems to have become somewhat ashamed of Paul's imprisonment and the message of the cross (2Ti 1:8,12). Paul exhorts Timothy to remain true to the teaching that he passed on to him (vv. 13–14).

1:8 his prisoner Paul was imprisoned in Rome. See the infographic "The Tullianum: A Prison in Rome" on p. 2008.
1:9 anything we have done Refers to righteous or good deeds. Such deeds do not earn or merit God's salvation (see Ro 4:5; Gal 2:16; Titus 3:4–5).
1:10 appearing Refers to the incarnation of Jesus Christ and probably the subsequent events of his life (e.g., his earthly ministry, death and resurrection). **death** Compare Heb 2:14. **immortality** The Greek word used here, *aphtharsia* — which may be literally rendered as "not subject to decay" — describes a quality of life (i.e., immortal life). Christ manifested this through his resurrection. Compare 1Co 15:50–54.
1:11 was appointed See note on 1Ti 2:7. **apostle** A person designated and sent by God to speak and act with special authority.
1:12 I am suffering as I am Refers to Paul's imprisonment in Rome. **until that day** Not the day of Paul's death but the day of the Lord (2Th 2:2; Isa 11:10–11; Joel 3:18) — the second coming of Christ.
1:14 Guard The Greek word used here, *phylassō*, means "to protect from loss or damage." Timothy must protect the church from false teachers and their instruction. Paul reminds Timothy that the Holy Spirit will help him

Onesiphorus, because he often refreshed me and was not ashamed of my chains. [17]On the contrary, when he was in Rome, he searched hard for me until he found me. [18]May the Lord grant that he will find mercy from the Lord on that day! You know very well in how many ways he helped me in Ephesus.

The Appeal Renewed

2 You then, my son, be strong in the grace that is in Christ Jesus. [2]And the things you have heard me say in the presence of many witnesses entrust to reliable people who will also be qualified to teach others. [3]Join with me in suffering, like a good soldier of Christ Jesus. [4]No one serving as a soldier gets entangled in civilian affairs, but rather tries to please his commanding officer. [5]Similarly, anyone who competes as an athlete does not receive the victor's crown except by competing according to the rules. [6]The hardworking farmer should be the first to receive a share of the crops. [7]Reflect on what I am saying, for the Lord will give you insight into all this.

[8]Remember Jesus Christ, raised from the dead, descended from David. This is my gospel, [9]for which I am suffering even to the point of being chained like a criminal. But God's word is not chained. [10]Therefore I endure everything for the sake of the elect, that they too may obtain the salvation that is in Christ Jesus, with eternal glory.
[11]Here is a trustworthy saying:

If we died with him,
  we will also live with him;
[12]if we endure,
  we will also reign with him.
If we disown him,
  he will also disown us;
[13]if we are faithless,
  he remains faithful,
  for he cannot disown himself.

Dealing With False Teachers

[14]Keep reminding God's people of these things. Warn them before God against quarreling about

---

fulfill his ministry duties. **good deposit** Refers to the gospel message.
1:15 Phygelus and Hermogenes These two men deserted Paul when he was imprisoned—probably because of the shame associated with imprisonment (compare 2Ti 1:8).
1:16 household In Greco-Roman society, the household included not only the immediate family but also slaves, laborers, and tenants. **Onesiphorus** A Christian from Ephesus who searched for Paul in Rome and brought him relief while he was imprisoned. Unlike Phygelus and Hermogenes, who deserted Paul, Onesiphorus was not ashamed of Paul's imprisonment.
1:18 Ephesus Paul traveled to Ephesus on his second and third missionary journeys (Ac 18:19; 19:1). See note on 1Ti 1:3.

EVENT	APPROXIMATE DATE
Paul's first missionary journey (Ac 13:1—14:28)	AD 46–47
Paul's second missionary journey (Ac 15:40—18:22)	AD 49–51
Paul's third missionary journey (Ac 19:1—21:26)	AD 52–57

2:1–7 Paul provides Timothy with further instructions for effective ministry (compare 2Ti 1:8–14).

2:1 my son Timothy's loyalty contrasts with those who deserted Paul in Asia (2Ti 1:15). Paul sometimes refers to those he brought to Christ as his spiritual children (see note on 1Ti 1:2). **grace** While the Greek word used here, *charis*, often refers to God's unmerited favor (Eph 2:8), in this context it denotes God's empowerment of believers to live the Christian life (see 2Co 9:8; Titus 2:11–14).
2:2 things you have heard me Timothy learned from Paul as he assisted him on his missionary efforts (Ac 19:22; 1Co 4:17; 1Th 3:2), learning firsthand about the hardship that Paul endured for the gospel (2Ti 3:10–11). **entrust** Paul entrusted the gospel to Timothy; now Timothy must entrust it to others. The apostles intended for teaching and traditions to be passed on to others (Ac 2:42; 2Th 2:15).

2:3 soldier Roman soldiers recognized the authority of their commanders (Lk 7:8). Paul exhorts Timothy to be single-minded in his devotion to the interests and concerns of Jesus Christ (2Ti 2:4; Php 2:20–22).
2:7 Reflect on what I am saying But Paul encourages Timothy to rely on God to give him insight into his sayings.

2:8–13 Paul explains his reason for enduring hardship. Despite the apparent ineffective situation of his imprisonment, Paul recognizes that he can still minister to believers and that God's word continues to spread.

2:8 raised from the dead Paul summarizes his gospel using similar language in Ro 1:1–4. **descended from David** Isaiah 11:1 describes the Messiah as the branch (i.e., a descendant) of Jesse, the father of King David—which is connected to the prophecies about the servant of the Lord who would suffer on behalf of God's people (e.g., Isa 11:1–12; 53:2,12). In their genealogies, Matthew and Luke trace Jesus' lineage to David (Mt 1:6; Lk 3:31), and even refer to Joseph as a "son of David" (Mt 1:20).
2:9 like a criminal Emphasizes the humiliating nature of Paul's imprisonment in Rome. See the infographic "The Tullianum: A Prison in Rome" on p. 2008. **not chained** During his previous imprisonment in Rome, Paul shared the gospel with the emperor's elite body guard (Php 1:12–14). Even the members of Caesar's household became believers (Php 4:22).
2:11 a trustworthy saying See note on 1Ti 1:15. **If we died with him** Believers unite with Christ in his death and his resurrection (Ro 6:5; Gal 2:19–20). In this context, death may imply martyrdom since it represented a genuine possibility for persecuted believers (Mk 14:31).
2:12 If we disown him, he will also disown us Echoes Jesus' teaching about enduring persecution (Mt 10:33; Lk 12:9).

2:14–26 Paul urges Timothy to expose the improper conduct and erring doctrine of the false teachers and to disassociate with those who follow such teaching.

2:14 quarreling about words A characteristic of false teachers (1Ti 6:4–5; Titus 3:9).

words; it is of no value, and only ruins those who listen. ¹⁵Do your best to present yourself to God as one approved, a worker who does not need to be ashamed and who correctly handles the word of truth. ¹⁶Avoid godless chatter, because those who indulge in it will become more and more ungodly. ¹⁷Their teaching will spread like gangrene. Among them are Hymenaeus and Philetus, ¹⁸who have departed from the truth. They say that the resurrection has already taken place, and they destroy the faith of some. ¹⁹Nevertheless, God's solid foundation stands firm, sealed with this inscription: "The Lord knows those who are his," and, "Everyone who confesses the name of the Lord must turn away from wickedness."

²⁰In a large house there are articles not only of gold and silver, but also of wood and clay; some are for special purposes and some for common use. ²¹Those who cleanse themselves from the latter will be instruments for special purposes, made holy, useful to the Master and prepared to do any good work.

²²Flee the evil desires of youth and pursue righ-

2:15 approved Meaning to consider genuine by testing (1Co 11:19). **who does not need to be ashamed** In contrast to those false teachers who deserve shame.
2:17 Hymenaeus and Philetus Two believers who became false teachers because they claimed the resurrection of believers already happened (see 1Ti 1:20 and note).
2:18 the resurrection Christians believed that the resurrection would bring the blessings of the age to come and deliverance from suffering; false rumors that it already occurred would have disturbed their faith (see 2Th 2:1–2).
2:19 sealed with this inscription Signifies God's ownership. The seal and its two inscriptions emphasize God's sovereignty and believers' perseverance despite the threat of false teachers.
2:22 who call on the Lord An OT expression here applied to Christians (e.g., Ge 26:25; 1Sa 12:17; Ps 86:5; compare Ac 9:14; Ro 10:12–14).

The Tullianum: A Prison in Rome

The Romans did not consider imprisonment itself a form of punishment—prisons were used to hold those awaiting trial or the death penalty and often served as places of execution. Prisons were filthy and crowded, and prisoners were treated as little better than dead. According to tradition, Peter and Paul were both imprisoned here.

Cut-away View

Prisoners were lowered into the prison through a hole in the floor.

This door led to an underground sewer.

The Tullianum, like many prisons in the ancient world, was dark, damp and cold. It was built originally as a cistern.

teousness, faith, love and peace, along with those who call on the Lord out of a pure heart. ²³Don't have anything to do with foolish and stupid arguments, because you know they produce quarrels. ²⁴And the Lord's servant must not be quarrelsome but must be kind to everyone, able to teach, not resentful. ²⁵Opponents must be gently instructed, in the hope that God will grant them repentance leading them to a knowledge of the truth, ²⁶and that they will come to their senses and escape from the trap of the devil, who has taken them captive to do his will.

3 But mark this: There will be terrible times in the last days. ²People will be lovers of themselves, lovers of money, boastful, proud, abusive, disobedient to their parents, ungrateful, unholy, ³without love, unforgiving, slanderous, without self-control, brutal, not lovers of the good, ⁴treacherous, rash, conceited, lovers of pleasure rather than lovers of God— ⁵having a form of godliness but denying its power. Have nothing to do with such people.

⁶They are the kind who worm their way into homes and gain control over gullible women, who are loaded down with sins and are swayed by all kinds of evil desires, ⁷always learning but never able to come to a knowledge of the truth. ⁸Just as Jannes and Jambres opposed Moses, so also these teachers oppose the truth. They are men of depraved minds, who, as far as the faith is concerned, are rejected. ⁹But they will not get very far because, as in the case of those men, their folly will be clear to everyone.

A Final Charge to Timothy

¹⁰You, however, know all about my teaching, my way of life, my purpose, faith, patience, love, endurance, ¹¹persecutions, sufferings — what kinds of things happened to me in Antioch, Iconium and Lystra, the persecutions I endured. Yet the Lord rescued me from all of them. ¹²In fact, everyone who wants to live a godly life in Christ Jesus will be persecuted, ¹³while evildoers and impostors will go from bad to worse, deceiving and being deceived. ¹⁴But as for you, continue in what you have learned and have become convinced of, because you know those from

---

2:23 foolish and stupid arguments Talking about foolish controversies leads to more conflict, not resolution. See 1Ti 1:4 and note.
2:24 not resentful The Greek word used here, *anexikakos*, describes tolerating difficulties without resentment. Such a leader must extend patience and kindness to those who oppose him or her.
2:25 a knowledge of the truth See note on 1Ti 2:4.
2:26 trap of the devil The idea of being captured by the devil to do his will most likely refers to accepting and living according to the doctrine of the false teachers (compare 1Ti 3:6; 4:1).

3:1–9 These verses contain further warnings about the false teachers. The list of vices in 2Ti 3:2–4 serves to contrast the selfish and corrosive behavior of false teachers with the conduct expected of God's people.

3:1 last days Refers to the period of time before Christ returns to establish his kingdom. Christians in the NT period believed they were already living in the last days (e.g., 1Co 10:11; 1Pe 1:20; Heb 1:2). The concept of the last days derives from the OT. The phrase and its variations (e.g., "latter days," "day to come," "that day") were used to refer to a period of time in the future (e.g., Nu 24:14; Dt 31:29), or to a period before the end of history (e.g., Hos 3:5; Mic 4:1). The last days were characterized by wickedness and unfaithfulness to God, and consequently, judgment (Jer 7:1–15); however, they were also characterized by restoration (Eze 11:14–21; Zec 10:6–12). The NT writers applied the phrase "last days" and its variations to the second coming of Christ.
3:5 form of godliness Someone who is godly only in outward appearance (see note on 1Ti 2:2). Such people look righteous but are only religious, not actually living according to God's standards.
3:6 gullible women Refers to women—probably including some of the younger widows (1Ti 5:11–16)—who apparently were overwhelmed by guilt from their past sins and overly eager to hear teaching of any substance. False teachers take advantage of these women because

of their desire for religious education. These women likely paid the teachers for their religious education (compare 1Ti 6:3–10).
3:7 always learning These women learn from false teachers whose instruction cannot yield a knowledge of the gospel or lead to godly living. **knowledge of the truth** See note on 1Ti 2:4.
3:8 Jannes and Jambres According to Jewish legend, Jannes and Jambres were the names of the magicians (unnamed in the OT Biblical narrative) who opposed Moses and imitated the miraculous signs of Aaron before Pharaoh (Ex 7:8–22). Versions of this legend occur in the Jewish text commonly called Jannes and Jambres and the text Targum Pseudo-Jonathan. Paul references these men to warn Timothy about the threat of false teachers. Such people will oppose Timothy and even imitate godliness (i.e., have an outward appearance of godliness), but they will not have knowledge of the gospel or possess any power that transforms lives.
3:9 their folly Paul assures Timothy that these religious peddlers will be shamed for their lack of understanding, like the Egyptian magicians who opposed Moses (Ex 8:18–19; 9:11).

3:10–17 Paul presents his conduct as an example of faithful service to God (2Ti 3:10–13). He then encourages Timothy to remain strong in the faith, using God's gift of Scripture to minister effectively (vv. 14–17).

3:10 teaching Refers to the instruction Paul passed down to Timothy (2:2). Paul connects his instruction and his lifestyle, listing the virtues that define true godliness, not just a form of it (see v. 5; 1Ti 4:12).
3:11 in Antioch, Iconium and Lystra Paul visited these cities during his first missionary journey (Ac 14:1–28).
3:12 will be persecuted Those who are godly (i.e., true Christians, as opposed to false teachers) should expect persecution (Ac 14:2; 1Th 3:4; Php 1:29).
3:14 from whom you learned Probably refers to Timothy's grandmother, mother and Paul. Their way of life and

whom you learned it, [15]and how from infancy you have known the Holy Scriptures, which are able to make you wise for salvation through faith in Christ Jesus. [16]All Scripture is God-breathed and is useful for teaching, rebuking, correcting and training in righteousness, [17]so that the servant of God[a] may be thoroughly equipped for every good work.

4 In the presence of God and of Christ Jesus, who will judge the living and the dead, and in view of his appearing and his kingdom, I give you this charge: [2]Preach the word; be prepared in season and out of season; correct, rebuke and encourage — with great patience and careful instruction. [3]For the time will come when people will not put up with sound doctrine. Instead, to suit their own desires, they will gather around them a great number of teachers to say what their itching ears want to hear. [4]They will turn their ears away from the truth and turn aside to myths. [5]But you, keep your head in all situations, endure hardship, do the work of an evangelist, discharge all the duties of your ministry.

[6]For I am already being poured out like a drink offering, and the time for my departure is near. [7]I have fought the good fight, I have finished the race, I have kept the faith. [8]Now there is in store for me the crown of righteousness, which the Lord, the righteous Judge, will award to me on that day — and not only to me, but also to all who have longed for his appearing.

Personal Remarks

[9]Do your best to come to me quickly, [10]for Demas, because he loved this world, has deserted me and has gone to Thessalonica. Crescens has gone to Galatia, and Titus to Dalmatia. [11]Only Luke is with me. Get Mark and bring him with you, because he is helpful to me in my ministry. [12]I sent Tychicus to Ephesus. [13]When you come, bring

[a] 17 Or that you, a man of God.

---

their source of teaching (i.e., the Scriptures) motivates Timothy to remain faithful.

3:15 Holy Scriptures The Greek phrase used here, *hiera grammata*, refers to the OT. **wise for salvation** Throughout the Pastoral Letters, Paul relates knowledge of the truth with salvation (see 1Ti 2:4 and note).

3:16 All Scripture The Greek phrase used here, *pasa graphē*, may refer to the totality of Scripture or to every passage of Scripture. **God-breathed** Paul uses the Greek term *theopneustos* here (meaning "God-breathed") to assure Timothy that Scripture is, in fact, from God. Although God used people to produce the Scriptures (2Pe 1:20–21), their ultimate origin is God. By contrast, the false teaching that Timothy opposed comes from evil forces who spread their doctrine through errant teachers (1Ti 1:3–7; 4:1). **useful** Scripture is valuable because it corrects false teaching while building up believers to live godly lives. **teaching** Timothy's primary task in Ephesus (1Ti 4:6,13). **rebuking** To rebuke false teachers and admonish those who believe their teaching (e.g., 1Ti 6:3–10). **correcting** To help believers grow in godly behavior. **training in righteousness** Describes training in doing what is right or what is in accordance with godliness.

3:17 equipped for every good work Paul reminds Timothy that Scripture helps believers fulfill the work of the ministry (2Ti 4:1–5). It is therefore a gift to his people. God has not left Timothy or the believers in Ephesus to do good works on their own; he has provided them with Scripture and each other, all for doing good works in Christ Jesus (Eph 2:10; 2Ti 2:21; Titus 3:1).

4:1–8 Paul offers additional encouragement to Timothy. He urges him to be prepared to teach sound doctrine at all times, since false teaching continues to deceive people in Ephesus.

4:1 his appearing and his kingdom Refers to the second coming of Jesus Christ, when he returns to establish his kingdom. Paul uses the certainty of Christ's return to motivate Timothy to fulfill his ministerial tasks, even in the face of opposition (2Ti 4:3–4; compare 3:1 and note).

4:2 in season and out of season Timothy must be ready whether it is convenient or inconvenient for him.

4:3 sound doctrine The Greek word used here refers to healthy teaching (see note on 1Ti 1:10; 2Ti 1:13).

4:4 myths These false stories promote useless speculation rather than knowledge of the truth (see note on 1Ti 1:4).

4:5 evangelist The Greek word used here, *euangelistēs*, refers to a person who proclaims or announces the gospel message as part of their particular church office or role. This term appears only three times in the NT. In Ac 21:8, Luke uses the title for Philip—one of the seven deacons (Ac 6:5) and a missionary to Samaria (Ac 8:5). Paul includes the term "evangelist" as a ministry office after "apostles" and "prophets" (Eph 4:11). In the present passage, Paul describes the need for Timothy to be ready to correct, rebuke and encourage, as needed and required—suggesting that all of these things are part of the work of an evangelist.

4:6 drink offering A sacrificial offering of wine poured out upon the altar (Nu 15:5–10). Paul references this drink because it symbolizes his devotion and sacrifice (see Php 2:17 and note). **departure** A euphemism for death.

4:7 I have fought the good fight Paul remained faithful to God and the gospel message, despite opposition. He also encouraged Timothy to follow his example and fight the good fight throughout 1 and 2 Timothy (1Ti 1:18; 6:12). **I have finished the race** Paul's use of athletic imagery seems to suggest that he expects to die soon.

4:8 crown of righteousness The reward for finishing the race (2Ti 4:7). In Greek games, victorious athletes were awarded a crown of laurel branches. Here the term likely refers to a crown awarded to the righteous person who faithfully perseveres for the sake of Christ.

4:9–22 Paul closes the letter with personal instructions to Timothy (vv. 9–18) and a final greeting (vv. 19–22).

4:10 Demas A missionary companion of Paul during his first imprisonment (Phm 24; Col 4:14). **this world** Refers to the present time with a negative connotation (see Gal 1:4; 2Co 4:4). Paul warned believers about the lure of temporary wealth in the present age (1Ti 6:17). See the map "Paul's First and Second Missionary Journeys" on p. 2262. **Titus** See note on Titus 1:1. **Dalmatia** A Roman province along the eastern shore of the Adriatic Sea, Dalmatia is mentioned only here in the NT.

4:11 Luke A physician and missionary companion of Paul who accompanied Paul to Macedonia (Ac 16:10–17)

the cloak that I left with Carpus at Troas, and my scrolls, especially the parchments.

[14]Alexander the metalworker did me a great deal of harm. The Lord will repay him for what he has done. [15]You too should be on your guard against him, because he strongly opposed our message.

[16]At my first defense, no one came to my support, but everyone deserted me. May it not be held against them. [17]But the Lord stood at my side and gave me strength, so that through me the message might be fully proclaimed and all the Gentiles might hear it. And I was delivered from the lion's mouth. [18]The Lord will rescue me from every evil attack and will bring me safely to his heavenly kingdom. To him be glory for ever and ever. Amen.

Final Greetings

[19]Greet Priscilla[a] and Aquila and the household of Onesiphorus. [20]Erastus stayed in Corinth, and I left Trophimus sick in Miletus. [21]Do your best to get here before winter. Eubulus greets you, and so do Pudens, Linus, Claudia and all the brothers and sisters.[b]

[22]The Lord be with your spirit. Grace be with you all.

[a] 19 Greek *Prisca*, a variant of *Priscilla* [b] 21 The Greek word for *brothers and sisters* (*adelphoi*) refers here to believers, both men and women, as part of God's family.

---

and Troas (Ac 20:5—21:18). He also accompanied Paul during a shipwrecked voyage to Rome for Paul's first imprisonment (Ac 27–28). Paul honored Luke for his loyalty when others deserted him (2Ti 1:15; 4:16). **Mark** See note on Col 4:10.

4:14 Alexander the metalworker This could refer to the Alexander whom Paul expelled from the Christian community (1Ti 1:19–20), Alexander the Ephesian Jew mentioned in Ac 19:33–34 (who could also be the same Alexander referred to in 1 Timothy), or another person named Alexander.

4:16 At my first defense Likely refers to a preliminary public hearing before the trial for Paul's present imprisonment (Ac 23:1–11). Sadly, no one came forward (or was available) to make a formal defense on Paul's behalf. Paul also could mean that none of his coworkers came to provide him moral support.

4:19 Priscilla and Aquila A husband and wife team who ministered with Paul in Corinth and later moved to Ephesus (Ac 18:1–3,18–19). **household of Onesiphorus** See note on 2Ti 1:16.

4:20 Trophimus A missionary companion of Paul who accompanied him to Jerusalem (Ac 20:4). **Miletus** A port city in southwestern Asia Minor. Paul said farewell to the elders of the church in Ephesus at Miletus (Ac 20:15–38).

4:21 winter The season from November to March when travel was most dangerous.

TITUS

INTRODUCTION TO TITUS

As Titus struggles to help the church on the island of Crete, his experienced mentor, Paul, writes to give him advice. Paul had left Titus in Crete to appoint church leaders and to oppose false teachers (Titus 1:5,10,16). In this letter, Paul shows the connection between right belief and right action, emphasizing that God's graciousness should prompt us to be godly people (2:11–15).

BACKGROUND

The letter names Paul as its writer (1:1), but as with the other Pastoral Letters (1–2 Timothy), there is some modern debate about its authorship (see the "Introduction to 1 Timothy"). Paul would have written his letter to Titus in the mid–60s AD, sometime after his initial confinement in Rome (Ac 28:16–31; ca. AD 61–63) and the later imprisonment that led to his death in the mid–60s (see the "Introduction to 2 Timothy"). Although his precise location when writing is unknown, Paul appears to be on a missionary journey, as he mentions his desire to spend the winter in Nicopolis, a city on the west coast of Greece (Titus 3:12).

Titus, the recipient of the letter, was a longstanding associate of Paul's. Before his assignment to bring order to the church on Crete, Titus acted as Paul's representative to the Corinthian church; he also went with Paul to Jerusalem to meet with leaders there (2Co 8:23; Gal 2:1–3; 2Ti 4:10). Unlike many early church leaders, Titus was not Jewish, yet he was not required to be circumcised by the Jewish leadership of the Jerusalem church (Gal 2:3). For Paul, this further proved his belief that Old Testament law was a placeholder and that believers in Jesus, whether Jewish or Gentile, were no longer under the law. In addition, they were now one people of God under Christ (Gal 3:23–29).

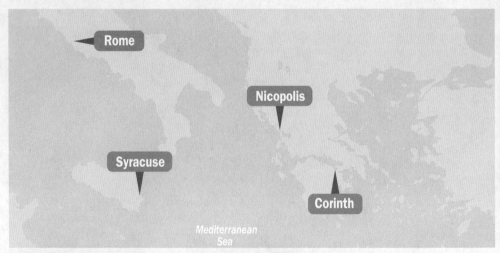

This map depicts many of the locations related to the book of Titus.

Like the Galatian situation, it seems that some among the church in Crete were arguing that non-Jewish men who converted to Christianity should be circumcised (Titus 1:10; compare Gal 5:2–15) and that they should keep Old Testament laws (Titus 1:14–15; 3:9; compare Gal 2:11–21). It seems that some people were also engaging in useless controversy, obsessing over genealogies, and causing dissension (Titus 3:9–11). Meanwhile these same people were proving the falsehood of their beliefs by their actions; they were acting against God's purposes (1:16). Paul tells Titus to have nothing to do with these individuals (3:10). Although Paul speaks to Titus about these matters, he is also speaking through him to the entire church (3:14–15).

STRUCTURE

Like a typical Greco-Roman letter, Titus has a greeting (1:1–4), a body (1:5—3:11) and a conclusion (3:12–15). In the greeting, Paul draws attention to the need to have a knowledge of the truth and to be godly, as he does throughout the rest of the letter. In the first major section of the body (1:5—2:15), Paul presents qualifications for the elders (high-level leaders) in the church (1:5–9), setting them in opposition to the false teachers (1:10–16). Paul then offers guidance for the behavior of several groups of people: older men, older women, younger men, younger women and slaves (2:1–15). In the second major section of the body (3:1–11), Paul explains that God's merciful salvation should motivate believers to devote themselves to good works. Paul argues that when we were hostile toward God, he showed us kindness, so we ought

Dates Related to Titus

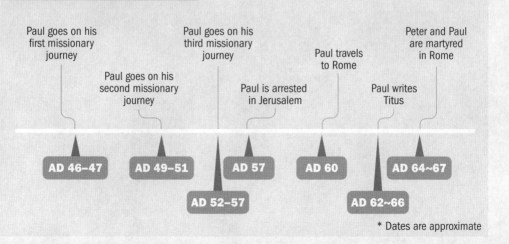

Paul goes on his first missionary journey

Paul goes on his second missionary journey

Paul goes on his third missionary journey

Paul is arrested in Jerusalem

Paul travels to Rome

Paul writes Titus

Peter and Paul are martyred in Rome

AD 46–47

AD 49–51

AD 52–57

AD 57

AD 60

AD 62~66

AD 64~67

* Dates are approximate

to show kindness to others and avoid divisive behavior. Paul concludes the letter with some final instructions for Titus and another reminder to engage in good works before offering his final benediction (3:12–15).

OUTLINE

- Introduction and instructions about elders, truth and various groups (1:1—2:15)
- Instructions for Christian living (3:1–11)
- Closing instructions and remarks (3:12–15)

THEMES

The letter to Titus is about the integration of right belief and right action. Paul makes this clear from the opening verse, where he connects truth and godliness (1:1). In contrast to the culture of Crete, which accepted dishonesty as a fact of life (1:12), followers of Christ are to have continuity between their beliefs and actions. Paul argues that Christians should strive to teach right beliefs to others in order to counteract false teachings (1:10–11; 3:9–11). He further shows that church leaders should model this (1:5–9).

Throughout this letter Paul emphasizes that the motivation to do good emerges from a true understanding of God and what he has done for us in Christ and through the Holy Spirit. God's grace—as seen in the person and actions of Jesus—saves us, changes us and gives us hope for eternity with him (3:4–7). This leads us to do what is good, declaring by word and deed God's grace to others (2:11–14).

1 Paul, a servant of God and an apostle of Jesus Christ to further the faith of God's elect and their knowledge of the truth that leads to godliness — [2]in the hope of eternal life, which God, who does not lie, promised before the beginning of time, [3]and which now at his appointed season he has brought to light through the preaching entrusted to me by the command of God our Savior,

[4]To Titus, my true son in our common faith:

Grace and peace from God the Father and Christ Jesus our Savior.

Appointing Elders Who Love What Is Good

1:6-8Ref — 1Ti 3:2-4

[5]The reason I left you in Crete was that you might put in order what was left unfinished and appoint[a] elders in every town, as I directed you. [6]An elder must be blameless, faithful to his wife, a man whose children believe[b] and are not open to the charge of being wild and disobedient. [7]Since an overseer manages God's household, he must be blameless — not overbearing, not quick-tempered, not given to drunkenness, not violent, not pursuing dishonest gain. [8]Rather, he must be hospitable, one who loves what is good, who is self-controlled, upright, holy and disciplined. [9]He must hold firmly to the trustworthy message as it has been taught, so that he can encourage others by sound doctrine and refute those who oppose it.

Rebuking Those Who Fail to Do Good

[10]For there are many rebellious people, full of meaningless talk and deception, especially those of the circumcision group. [11]They must be silenced, because they are disrupting whole households by teaching things they ought not to teach — and that for the sake of dishonest gain. [12]One of Crete's own prophets has said it: "Cretans are always liars, evil brutes, lazy gluttons."[c] [13]This saying is true. Therefore rebuke them sharply, so that they will be sound in the faith [14]and will pay no attention to Jewish myths or to the merely human commands of those who reject the truth.

a 5 Or ordain   b 6 Or children are trustworthy   c 12 From the Cretan philosopher Epimenides

---

1:1–4 This letter addresses Paul's colleague Titus, urging him to bring order to the church on the island of Crete, oppose false teachers and appoint leaders (Titus 1:5). Paul would have written this letter sometime in the mid-60s AD, between his first and second Roman imprisonments (see note on 1Ti 1:1–2). Paul notes that he plans to send Artemas and Tychicus to Crete, so that Titus can visit him in Nicopolis before winter (Titus 3:12). This suggests that Paul is on a missionary journey; he may even already be in Nicopolis.

The letter to Titus opens with a greeting resembling letter-writing conventions of the time — similar to those of 1 and 2 Timothy. Unlike the other Pastoral Letters (1 Timothy and 2 Timothy), the greeting includes a lengthy treatment of Paul's apostleship that indicates the letter may have been intended for a congregation and not merely an individual.

1:1 Paul Like many of Paul's letters, the greeting begins with Paul identifying himself by name. See Ro 1:1 and note. See the timeline "Life of Paul" on p. 1796. **a servant** Used timeline to indicate that Paul exhibits the same humility and submission of a slave (compare Ro 1:1). See the table "Pauline Self-Designations" on p. 1904. **apostle** A person designated by God to speak and act with special authority. See note on Ro 1:1. **knowledge of the truth** See note on 1Ti 2:4. **godliness** See note on 1Ti 2:2.
1:2 eternal life See note on Ro 2:7. **before the beginning of time** Conveying the purposeful nature of God's decision — God determined it before time began (compare 1Co 2:7; Eph 1:4).
1:3 God our Savior See note on 1Ti 1:1.
1:4 Titus A non-Jewish missionary companion of Paul. Titus is mentioned only in the apostle's letters (e.g., 2Co 2:13; Gal 2:3; 2Ti 4:10). **common faith** The faith common to Jews and Gentiles (non-Jewish people) in Christ.

TITUS
Titus accompanied Paul to Jerusalem, where the apostles Peter, James and John affirmed Paul's ministry to the Gentiles (Gal 2:1–10). Titus also served as Paul's representative to the church in Corinth, where he helped collect relief funds for the poor believers in Jerusalem (2Co 8:6–7). Because of his character and dedication, the apostle Paul and the churches held Titus in high regard (2Co 8:18–19).

1:5–16 Following the opening greeting (Titus 1:1–4), Paul outlines the qualifications for serving as an elder (vv. 5–9; compare 1Ti 5:17–22). This list closely reflects the qualifications set forth for overseers and deacons in 1Ti 3:1–13. Paul then describes the conduct and doctrine of the false teachers (Titus 1:10–16).

1:5 Crete The fourth-largest island in the Mediterranean, located southwest of Asia Minor (modern Turkey). On his way to Rome as a prisoner, Paul sailed past Crete and docked in the city of Fair Havens (Ac 27:8). Although the book of Acts does not provide details about Paul's work in Crete, Titus' presence on the island suggests that Paul or his coworkers had recently planted a church there. **you might put in order what was left unfinished** Implies that the Cretan churches were still relatively young. Titus' task is to continue the work started by Paul (or his coworkers) so that the churches will receive proper guidance. **appoint elders in every town** Paul also charged Timothy with appointing elders (*presbyteros*), which explains why Paul's first letter to Timothy and this letter to Titus overlap in content — especially regarding qualifications of leadership (compare 1Ti 3:1–7 and Titus 1:5–9). See note on 1Ti 3:1–7.

¹⁵To the pure, all things are pure, but to those who are corrupted and do not believe, nothing is pure. In fact, both their minds and consciences are corrupted. ¹⁶They claim to know God, but by their actions they deny him. They are detestable, disobedient and unfit for doing anything good.

Doing Good for the Sake of the Gospel

2 You, however, must teach what is appropriate to sound doctrine. ²Teach the older men to be temperate, worthy of respect, self-controlled, and sound in faith, in love and in endurance.

³Likewise, teach the older women to be reverent in the way they live, not to be slanderers or addicted to much wine, but to teach what is good. ⁴Then they can urge the younger women to love their husbands and children, ⁵to be self-controlled and pure, to be busy at home, to be kind, and to be subject to their husbands, so that no one will malign the word of God.

⁶Similarly, encourage the young men to be self-controlled. ⁷In everything set them an example by doing what is good. In your teaching show integrity, seriousness ⁸and soundness of speech that cannot be condemned, so that those who oppose you may be ashamed because they have nothing bad to say about us.

⁹Teach slaves to be subject to their masters in everything, to try to please them, not to talk back to them, ¹⁰and not to steal from them, but to show that they can be fully trusted, so that in every way they will make the teaching about God our Savior attractive.

¹¹For the grace of God has appeared that offers salvation to all people. ¹²It teaches us to say "No" to ungodliness and worldly passions, and to live self-controlled, upright and godly lives in this pres-

---

1:6 faithful to his wife Paul promotes fidelity in marriage as an example of how the leaders are to be above reproach in all areas of their lives. See note on 1Ti 3:2.
1:7 overseer Refers to one appointed to leadership over the local church (Ac 20:28). See note on 1Ti 3:2. **not given to drunkenness** All the positive qualities listed in Titus 1:8 would be undermined by the reckless and inappropriate behavior often associated with drunkenness. See note on 1Ti 3:3.
1:9 sound doctrine Church leaders must promote ideas that are consistent with the gospel. See note on 1Ti 1:10.
1:10 full of meaningless talk Compare 1Ti 1:6; Titus 3:9. **those of the circumcision group** Refers to Jewish converts to Christianity (e.g., Gal 2:12).
1:12 Cretans are always liars, evil brutes, lazy gluttons A quotation attributed to the Cretan poet Epimenides (ca. 600 BC). The Cretans gained a notorious reputation for their lack of moral integrity. Ancient writers popularized the verb "to Cretanize" as slang for lying and cheating. Here Paul applies this well-known saying to the false teachers, using it rhetorically to make a point—not necessarily because he agrees with it being applied to all Cretans.
1:14 Jewish myths A fascination with speculative stories was a hallmark of the false teachings that Paul addresses in 1–2 Timothy and Titus. See note on 1Ti 1:4.
1:15 To the pure, all things are pure Implies that all things from God are acceptable and pure for those whom God has accepted. This saying draws on the Jewish categories of clean and unclean in the context of temple worship and purity laws. Under that system, a person was required to observe dietary laws to be considered clean. For Paul, believers are considered pure solely on the basis of their faith. As a result, all things are clean and permissible for them (see 1Ti 4:4–5; compare Ro 14:20). It seems that the false teachers in Crete prohibited certain foods by requiring observance of Jewish dietary laws (Titus 1:14; compare 1Ti 4:3). Here, Paul responds in accordance with Jesus' teachings about purity and impurity (Mk 7). What goes into a person does not make him or her unclean; rather, what comes out of the heart makes a person unclean (Mk 7:18–20; compare Ac 10:14). **to those who are corrupted** Those who do not have genuine faith—like the false teachers—are not considered clean before God. Their lack of purity makes all things impure to them.

2:1–15 In this passage, Paul counsels Titus on how he should minister to various people groups within the church community—older men (Titus 2:2), older women (v. 3), younger women (vv. 4–5), younger men (v. 6), and slaves (vv. 9–10). The overarching concern in these instructions is the need for believers to live with self-control and godliness in the household and the church.
2:1 to sound doctrine See note on 1Ti 1:10.
2:2 older men In Paul's first-century AD context, this refers to men over age 50. The Greek word used here, *presbytēs,* should not be mistaken for *presbyteros,* often translated "elder" (i.e., church leader; see 1Ti 5:1,17,19).
2:3 older women This refers to women over age 50 (compare note on Titus 2:2). Their obedience to Paul's instruction allows them to disciple the next generation of young women. **slanderers** The Greek word used here, *diabolos,* describes a person who uses speech that damages the reputation of another, usually through false accusations. Paul instructs the believers about proper conduct so that the word of God will have a good reputation among outsiders (compare v. 5). **or addicted to much wine** See note on 1Ti 3:3.
2:4 younger women Likely refers to women 20–30 years of age, but primarily describes women younger than the group referred to in Titus 2:3 (compare note on v. 2).
2:5 busy at home Paul requests that young women be concerned with the matters of their households (compare 1Ti 5:13; 2Th 3:11). In Greek culture, young women were expected to occupy themselves with domestic matters. A violation of such basic social customs could weaken the credibility of the gospel message among outsiders.
2:6 young men Refers to men ages 20–30 (compare note on Titus 2:2).
2:8 soundness of speech See note on 1Ti 1:10.
2:9 slaves Refers to those in voluntary submission to another person due to debt or those in forced subjection to another person. Slavery was a central component to the economic system of first-century Greco-Roman society. It differs drastically from colonial and modern examples of human slavery (see note on Phm 10). Since status no longer represented grounds for discrimination in Christ, the gospel message restored the dignity of slaves (Gal 3:28). However, slaves were not to use their new status as a license for wrongdoing. Here, Paul urges

ent age, [13]while we wait for the blessed hope — the appearing of the glory of our great God and Savior, Jesus Christ, [14]who gave himself for us to redeem us from all wickedness and to purify for himself a people that are his very own, eager to do what is good.

[15]These, then, are the things you should teach. Encourage and rebuke with all authority. Do not let anyone despise you.

Saved in Order to Do Good

3 Remind the people to be subject to rulers and authorities, to be obedient, to be ready to do whatever is good, [2]to slander no one, to be peaceable and considerate, and always to be gentle toward everyone.

[3]At one time we too were foolish, disobedient, deceived and enslaved by all kinds of passions and pleasures. We lived in malice and envy, being hated and hating one another. [4]But when the kindness and love of God our Savior appeared, [5]he saved us, not because of righteous things we had done, but because of his mercy. He saved us through the washing of rebirth and renewal by the Holy Spirit, [6]whom he poured out on us generously through Jesus Christ our Savior, [7]so that, having been justified by his grace, we might become heirs having the hope of eternal life. [8]This is a trustworthy saying. And I want you to stress these things, so that those who have trusted in God may be careful to devote themselves to doing what is good. These things are excellent and profitable for everyone.

[9]But avoid foolish controversies and genealogies and arguments and quarrels about the law, because these are unprofitable and useless.

---

slaves to serve with integrity to preserve the integrity of the teaching of God—for the sake of the gospel reaching more people (Titus 2:10).

2:11 grace of God A reference to Christ's appearance on earth—including his life, death and resurrection—which manifested God's grace and made possible salvation.

2:12 present age Describes the present time, with a negative connotation (1Ti 6:17; 2Ti 4:10; compare Gal 1:4).

2:13 blessed hope Refers to the anticipation of the return of Jesus Christ. **appearing** Refers to the second coming of Christ (compare Titus 2:11). **our great God and Savior, Jesus Christ** This designation identifies Jesus with God.

2:14 who gave himself for us Refers to Christ's violent and sacrificial death (compare Gal 1:4; Eph 5:2; 1Ti 2:6). **redeem** The Greek word used here, *lytroō*, means "to release" or "set free," especially from slavery (compare Titus 2:9 and note; 1Pe 1:18). **a people that are his very own** Paul echoes the description of God's people in the OT (see Ex 19:5; Dt 7:6; 32:9 and note; compare Isa 53:12; note on Titus 3:7). **to do what is good** Refers to deeds done for the benefit of others (see 1Ti 5:10,25; 6:18). Good deeds are not a means to salvation; rather, they are the appropriate response to God's redemptive work in Christ (Titus 2:11–14). Compare 2Co 9:8; Eph 2:10.

3:1–7 After addressing specific groups within the church in Titus 2:1–15, Paul offers Titus instructions regarding the entire congregation. Paul first presents his instructions for believers (vv. 1–2), then presents a theological basis for his teaching—the appearance of God's grace in the world (Christ), resulting in new life for believers (vv. 3–7).

3:1 rulers and authorities Refers to government officials (compare Lk 12:11; 20:20). Paul is arguing that believers' new status in Christ (see Titus 3:7) must not become an excuse for civil unrest and disobedience. It seems that Paul is concerned about the gospel spreading effectively; believers opposing rulers and authorities would have hindered this effort. Compare Ro 13:1,5; 1Pe 2:13. **do whatever is good** Compare 1Ti 5:10; Titus 2:7,14; 3:8,14.

3:2 slander The Greek word used here, *blasphēmeō*, describes speaking against someone with the purpose of harming his or her reputation. **toward everyone** Paul

asserts that believers must show kindness to all people, not only to one another. Such commands (vv. 1–3; 1Ti 2:1–4) guard the Cretan believers against exclusivity. See note on 1Ti 2:1.

3:3 we too Those now saved must not forget the means of their salvation: the mercy of God.

3:4 appeared God's kindness and love appeared in the incarnation of Jesus Christ. In his saving work, Christ models the kindness and love that believers must show all people (see Titus 3:2).

3:5 because of his mercy See 2Ti 1:9 and note. **rebirth** Refers to the transformation of the corrupt human nature by the Holy Spirit. Jesus described salvation in similar terms, emphasizing God's radical work within a person (Jn 3:3,5,8). Through the work of the Holy Spirit, believers experience a rebirth from a state of spiritual death (compare Eph 2:1–6; Col 2:13). The presence of the Spirit enables them to live in a manner that pleases God (compare Ro 8:6–8). The washing here denotes an inner, spiritual cleansing (compare Eph 5:26); it probably does not refer to baptism.

3:7 justified Describes being declared righteous in God's sight—not by human merit, but by his grace. Justification represents God's pardoning and acceptance of sinners who express faith in Jesus Christ (and God's faithfulness shown through him). Christ's death and resurrection are central to justification because they demonstrate God's justice and mercy. **heirs** Refers to those who receive an inheritance. In this case, believers inherit eternal life. Believers are co-heirs with Christ and possess full rights as sons (Ro 8:17; Gal 4:1–7). Their inheritance includes salvation (Heb 1:14), eternal life (Titus 3:7; 1Pe 1:3–4,7), the earth (Mt 5:5), the kingdom of God (Mt 25:34) and all things (1Co 3:21–22; Rev 21:7). **eternal life** See note on Ro 2:7.

3:8–15 Paul issues a final warning about the dangers that false teachers pose to the church. He calls on Titus to avoid the interests of false teachers and to dissociate with those who reject church discipline (Titus 3:8–11). Paul closes the letter with brief instructions regarding some of his coworkers and a benediction (vv. 12–15).

3:8 a trustworthy saying See note on 1Ti 1:15. **to devote themselves to doing what is good** The believers in Crete will have an opportunity to do good to Zenas and Apollos (see v. 13). See note on Titus 2:14.

3:9 foolish controversies This seems to primarily

[10]Warn a divisive person once, and then warn them a second time. After that, have nothing to do with them. [11]You may be sure that such people are warped and sinful; they are self-condemned.

Final Remarks

[12]As soon as I send Artemas or Tychicus to you, do your best to come to me at Nicopolis, because I have decided to winter there. [13]Do everything you can to help Zenas the lawyer and Apollos on their way and see that they have everything they need. [14]Our people must learn to devote themselves to doing what is good, in order to provide for urgent needs and not live unproductive lives.

[15]Everyone with me sends you greetings. Greet those who love us in the faith.

Grace be with you all.

---

reference the problems the false teachers were causing. Titus is instructed to oppose these false teachers but should not allow for their controversies to dictate his agenda. This also seems to be a broad reference to controversies that are unprofitable in terms of the gospel reaching more people (compare note on 1Ti 6:4). **genealogies** See note on 1Ti 1:4.

3:11 self-condemned Paul asserts that they condemn themselves because they reject the warnings of leadership (Titus 3:10).

3:12 Artemas A believer who assisted Paul, Artemas is only mentioned here in the NT. **Tychicus** A believer from Asia Minor who accompanied Paul on his third missionary journey (Ac 20:4). Tychicus served as Paul's messenger to Ephesus (Eph 6:21; 2Ti 4:12), Colossae (Col 4:7) and Crete (Titus 3:12). **Nicopolis** Several cities in the Greco-Roman world were named Nicopolis. Paul most likely refers to Nicopolis in Achaia near Corinth. Following his first imprisonment, Paul intended to meet Titus in Nicopolis and continue his missionary efforts. Instead, he was arrested again and taken to Rome for his second imprisonment. There, he wrote his second letter to Timothy.

3:13 Apollos A Jewish Christian from Alexandria in Egypt (Ac 18:24).

3:15 Grace be with you all Paul's typical closing in his letters (Gal 6:18; 1Th 5:28).

PHILEMON

INTRODUCTION TO PHILEMON

When Paul was in prison, he shared the gospel with a runaway slave named Onesimus. Sometime after Onesimus had become a Christian and a friend, Paul sent him back to his master, Philemon, asking that Philemon welcome him back as a brother in Christ. This letter illustrates how the Good News about Jesus breaks down barriers, transforms relationships and unites all believers into the family of God.

BACKGROUND

The letter to Philemon is closely associated with Colossians. Paul's associate Tychicus, who apparently carried the letters of Colossians and Ephesians, probably delivered the letter to Philemon as well (Col 4:7–8; Eph 6:21–22). In addition, many of the same people are mentioned in both Colossians and Philemon (Phm 2,10,23–24; Col 4:9–17). Since Paul sent Onesimus back to the city of Colossae (Col 4:9), it seems that this is where Philemon was hosting a local congregation in his home (Phm 2).

Although the text of Philemon names both Paul and Timothy as authors (Phm 1), Paul uses the singular voice, which fits the letter's personal nature. Paul is writing to Philemon from prison (vv. 1,23). If this refers to Paul's confinement in Rome, the letter would have been composed in the early 60s AD (Ac 28:30). However, Paul could be composing during his imprisonment in Caesarea (ca. AD 58–59) or a possible imprisonment in Ephesus (ca. AD 54–57). Ephesus is far closer to Colossae than Rome or Caesarea—it is only about 100 miles away—which means it would be a far less extensive journey for Onesimus, the runaway slave.

Paul is sending Onesimus back to his master in accordance with Roman law. This is risky for Onesimus; slaveowners had the right to punish or even execute runaway slaves. However, since both Philemon and Onesimus came to faith through Paul's ministry (Phm 10,16,19), there is hope that Philemon will respond favorably to Paul's request and set aside his rights as a slaveowner.

Slavery in the Greco-Roman world differs greatly from colonial slavery. Volunteer slavery was often used as a type of credit system, and it seems Onesimus was this type of slave (v. 18). Paul advocates for equality while respecting Philemon's rights, telling Philemon to receive Onesimus not as a slave but as a brother (vv. 14–16; compare Col 4:1; Gal 3:28). Paul had become a spiritual father to Onesimus and cares deeply about him (Phm 10).

STRUCTURE

Philemon follows the typical outline of a Greco-Roman letter, beginning with a traditional greeting (vv. 1–3) and a thanksgiving section (vv. 4–7). The body of the letter (vv. 8–22) consists of Paul's appeal on behalf of Onesimus. Paul concludes with greetings from his fellow ministry workers and a benediction (vv. 23–25).

OUTLINE

- Greeting (vv. 1–3)
- Thanksgiving (vv. 4–7)
- Appeal on behalf of Onesimus (vv. 8–22)
- Conclusion (vv. 23–25)

THEMES

The main theme of Philemon is the gospel's power to transform people and relationships. Onesimus' name means "useful," but before becoming a Christian he had been useless to Philemon (v. 11). Onesimus was changed by his encounter with Jesus and had become so useful that Paul did not want to let him go (vv. 11–13). Another transformation occurred in the relationship between Onesimus and Philemon. Because of the gospel, the primary factor that defined them was not their identities as slave and master. Rather, they were primarily brothers in Christ (v. 16). Self-giving love, not socioeconomic position, was now the basis of their relationship. For this reason, Philemon is encouraged to welcome back his slave Onesimus just as he would welcome his friend and partner Paul (v. 17).

Even though Paul does not explicitly ask Philemon to set Onesimus free, Paul was subverting the social norms of his day. He knew that Philemon had certain rights as a slaveowner, but he asked

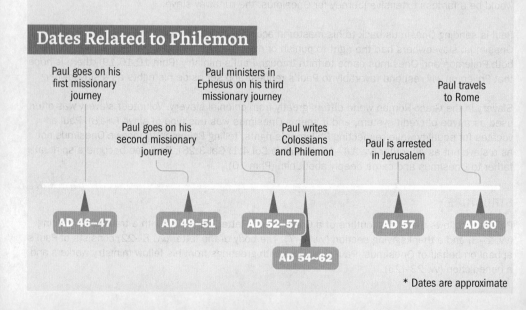

Dates Related to Philemon

Paul goes on his first missionary journey

Paul goes on his second missionary journey

Paul ministers in Ephesus on his third missionary journey

Paul writes Colossians and Philemon

Paul is arrested in Jerusalem

Paul travels to Rome

AD 46–47　　AD 49–51　　AD 52–57　　AD 57　　AD 60

AD 54~62

* Dates are approximate

Philemon to set aside those rights on the basis of what Christ had done for him. Philemon and Onesimus had the same standing before Jesus: They were forgiven and loved. This mindset would lead them to interact as equals.

This short letter challenges us to let the gospel reshape our approach to relationships. When we witness divisive or dehumanizing behavior, we should challenge it. If we are in a position of power, we should use that power in the service of love, restoration and equality. And if we are on the underside of power, we should still love generously and embrace our status as equals before Christ. The world we live in remains broken in many ways, with social and economic disparities driving people apart. But the love of Christ bids us to bring people together.

¹Paul, a prisoner of Christ Jesus, and Timothy our brother,

To Philemon our dear friend and fellow worker — ²also to Apphia our sister and Archippus our fellow soldier — and to the church that meets in your home:

³Grace and peace to you*a* from God our Father and the Lord Jesus Christ.

Thanksgiving and Prayer

⁴I always thank my God as I remember you in my prayers, ⁵because I hear about your love for all his holy people and your faith in the Lord Jesus. ⁶I pray that your partnership with us in the faith may be effective in deepening your understanding of every good thing we share for the sake of Christ. ⁷Your love has given me great joy and encouragement, because you, brother, have refreshed the hearts of the Lord's people.

Paul's Plea for Onesimus

⁸Therefore, although in Christ I could be bold and order you to do what you ought to do, ⁹yet I prefer to appeal to you on the basis of love. It is as none other than Paul — an old man and now also a prisoner of Christ Jesus — ¹⁰that I appeal to you for my son Onesimus,*b* who became my son while I was in chains. ¹¹Formerly he was useless to you, but now he has become useful both to you and to me.

a 3 The Greek is plural; also in verses 22 and 25; elsewhere in this letter "you" is singular.   *b* 10 *Onesimus* means *useful.*

1–7 In the letter to Philemon, Paul writes to persuade Philemon to receive back his runaway slave, Onesimus, as a brother in Christ. Paul is writing to Philemon from prison, although the place and time of this imprisonment is not certain. The most likely options include Ephesus (AD 54–55), Caesarea (AD 58–60), and Rome (early 60s AD). Paul sent this letter along with two others—one to the Colossians, and another (now lost) to the church at Laodicea (Col 4:7–9,16).

After a typical Greco-Roman greeting (Phm 1–3), Paul expresses gratitude for Philemon's faith and love (vv. 4–7).

1 Paul See note on Ro 1:1. **prisoner** Although Paul is imprisoned at this time, he does not regard himself as a prisoner of the state; rather, he is a prisoner of Christ, confined due to his efforts to spread the gospel. Compare note on Eph 3:1. See the table "Pauline Self-Designations" on p. 1904; see the infographic "The Tullianum: A Prison in Rome" on p. 2008. **Timothy** Paul names his associate Timothy as a cosender, although the personal nature of this letter suggests that its content comes primarily from Paul. **Philemon** The owner of the slave Onesimus and host of the church at Colossae (Phm 2). Philemon apparently became a believer through Paul's ministry (v. 19). Although Paul refers to Philemon as a fellow worker, the nature of Philemon's service is not clear; it does not seem that Paul visited Colossae (Col 2:1), so the two men must have met elsewhere (perhaps Ephesus). Although this letter does not mention the town of Colossae, Paul's letter to the Colossians conveys details indicating that Philemon lived there (Col 4:7–9). Colossae was a farming town in southwest Asia Minor (modern-day Turkey), roughly 120 miles east of Ephesus.
2 Apphia our sister Some manuscripts describe Apphia as "our sister," identifying her as a believer; other manuscripts read "the beloved." She might be Philemon's wife, in which case Paul is addressing her because wives often managed household slaves in Greco-Roman society (compare note on Phm 10). Paul is calling on her—as well as Philemon—to receive Onesimus as a brother in Christ. **Archippus** Probably another member of Philemon's household—perhaps his son. Archippus seems to have held some kind of ministry role at Colossae (Col 4:17 and note). **to the church that meets in your home** Paul addresses the church because the reconciliation he seeks between Philemon and Onesimus will involve the entire community. See the infographic "Ancient Home Synagogue" on p. 1971.

8–21 The body of this short letter conveys Paul's request for Philemon to welcome back Onesimus as a brother in Christ. Paul bases this appeal partly on his relationship with Onesimus (Phm 19–20), but the primary emphasis is on the bond that Philemon and Onesimus share as believers (vv. 15–16).

8 order As an apostle, Paul had the authority to command Philemon to receive Onesimus as a brother in the Lord, but he does not take this approach. Paul hopes that Philemon will be motivated by love, not duty (v. 9).
10 my son Paul considers Onesimus' to be his spiritual son, suggesting that Paul led him to faith in Christ. **Onesimus** Philemon's runaway slave (see note on v. 16). While he was on the run, Onesimus met Paul and became a believer (the details of their meeting are not mentioned). Slavery in the ancient Greco-Roman world was different from the form of slavery practiced by Europeans and Americans in the fifteenth to nineteenth centuries (compare note on 1Pe 2:18). People in the first century often sold themselves as slaves to pay debts or climb the social ladder—essentially using slavery as a credit system. Although slavery was not desirable, slaves in the Greco-Roman world could hold positions of authority and even own property. Not all slavery was a permanent situation, and many slaves gained their freedom. Paul consistently tells believers to view slavery within the framework of the gospel: Slaves are to work as if they were serving Christ; masters are to keep in mind that they, too, serve a master—God—and therefore should treat their slaves fairly (Eph 6:5–9; Col 3:22—4:1). In Colossians, which was likely sent with this letter, Paul proclaims that before Christ all people are equal—this would have served as further reason for Philemon to forgive Onesimus' debt (Col 3:11). A slave's status did not prevent them from having full dignity in Christ.
11 useful In this verse, Paul makes several wordplays suggesting that Onesimus—essentially useless without Christ—became truly useful to Paul and Philemon with Christ. The name Onesimus means "useful" or "profitable"; the Greek word for "useful," *euchrēstos,* sounds like the Greek word for "Christ," *christos;* and the Greek word for "useless," *achrēstos,* sounds like the Greek word *achristos,* meaning "without Christ."

¹²I am sending him—who is my very heart—back to you. ¹³I would have liked to keep him with me so that he could take your place in helping me while I am in chains for the gospel. ¹⁴But I did not want to do anything without your consent, so that any favor you do would not seem forced but would be voluntary. ¹⁵Perhaps the reason he was separated from you for a little while was that you might have him back forever— ¹⁶no longer as a slave, but better than a slave, as a dear brother. He is very dear to me but even dearer to you, both as a fellow man and as a brother in the Lord.

¹⁷So if you consider me a partner, welcome him as you would welcome me. ¹⁸If he has done you any wrong or owes you anything, charge it to me.

¹⁹I, Paul, am writing this with my own hand. I will pay it back—not to mention that you owe me your very self. ²⁰I do wish, brother, that I may have some benefit from you in the Lord; refresh my heart in Christ. ²¹Confident of your obedience, I write to you, knowing that you will do even more than I ask.

²²And one thing more: Prepare a guest room for me, because I hope to be restored to you in answer to your prayers.

²³Epaphras, my fellow prisoner in Christ Jesus, sends you greetings. ²⁴And so do Mark, Aristarchus, Demas and Luke, my fellow workers.

²⁵The grace of the Lord Jesus Christ be with your spirit.

---

12 I am sending him Paul takes a risk in sending Onesimus back to Philemon. According to Roman law, an owner could severely punish—even execute—a runaway slave (compare note on Phm 10); anyone who harbored a runaway slave could face charges, as well. Even so, Paul sends Onesimus back to Colossae with Tychicus and this letter (compare Col 4:7–9).

13 he could take your place Paul wants Philemon to know that Onesimus has helped him and his ministry. In the Greek text of Philemon, Paul's remark here is worded as if Philemon had sent Onesimus to assist Paul.

14 without your consent Paul recognizes that Onesimus' fate ultimately belongs in Philemon's hands. For this reason, Paul refrains from keeping Onesimus with him. **would not seem forced** Again, Paul indicates that he wants Philemon's decision regarding Onesimus to be made freely, not out of obligation (see Phm 8–9; note on v. 8).

16 better than a slave, as a dear brother This verse expresses the heart of Paul's request, which is based on his conviction that the gospel of Christ transforms human relationships. Because Philemon and Onesimus have been united with Christ, they both belong to the one family of God; Onesimus the slave has become Philemon's brother. By embracing Onesimus, Philemon can bear witness to the gospel's power to transform and reconcile. **brother** The Greek word used here, *adelphos*, often refers in the NT to those who have faith in Jesus Christ; it emphasizes unity and equality over division. In addition to using *adelphos* here to describe the transformation of Onesimus, Paul uses it twice in reference to Philemon (vv. 7,20), putting slave and master on equal terms in accord with the gospel.

17 partner The Greek word used here, *koinōnos*, indicates that Philemon shares in Paul's ministry. This partnership is the basis for Paul's reiteration of his request: Welcome Onesimus as you would welcome me.

18 charge it to me Acknowledging that Onesimus likely owes a debt to Philemon, Paul takes this obligation upon himself.

19 owe me your very self Paul has just volunteered to take over Onesimus' debt to Philemon; now Paul reminds Philemon of his own indebtedness to Paul. This likely refers to Philemon coming to faith in Christ through Paul's ministry. Even though Philemon cannot repay this debt, he can refresh Paul's heart by forgiving Onesimus and, perhaps, sending him back to Paul (see v. 20 and note).

20 benefit The Greek word used here, *oninēmi*, sounds like "Onesimus." Through this wordplay, Paul might be asking Philemon to send Onesimus back to him.

23–25 Paul concludes the letter with customary greetings.

23 Epaphras See note on Col 1:7.
24 Mark, Aristarchus See note on Col 4:10. **Demas and Luke** See note on Col 4:14.
25 The grace of the Lord Jesus Christ Paul's typical closing in his letters (e.g., Gal 6:18; 1Th 5:28).

HEBREWS AND THE GENERAL LETTERS

B
etween Paul's letters and Revelation are eight letters. Six of these letters are called by the designation General Letters because of the viewpoint that they are addressed to a broad group of people, rather than a specific church (Hebrews, James, 1–2 Peter, 1 John and Jude); 2–3 John are grouped with this collection because of their affiliation with 1 John. These letters are sometimes called the Catholic Letters after the Greek term *katholikç*, meaning "universal."

In the early church period, Hebrews was grouped with Paul's Letters. However, virtually all modern scholars do not believe Paul wrote it, and there was also some dispute about its authorship among early church fathers. Thus, even though it is one-of-a-kind in terms of style and genre, it is often grouped with the General Letters in contemporary literature.

AUTHORSHIP

Hebrews
While it is now commonly believed that Paul did not write Hebrews, it is clear that Hebrews comes from someone in the Pauline circle, because it refers to Timothy in the letter ending (Heb 13:23). On the other hand, the style is un-Pauline; its topics are not those Paul was known to address; its audience is not one that Paul wrote to; and its philosophical affinities do not align with his. Various people have been proposed as author, from Apollos to Aquila and Priscilla, but the author is unknown.

General Letters
Broadly speaking, early church tradition assigns six of the General Letters to the three "pillar apostles"—James, Peter and John—with Jude being ascribed to the brother of Jesus. While James does not call himself an apostle, Paul refers to James (the brother of Jesus) as an apostle (Gal 1:19) and groups him with Peter and John as a "pillar" (Gal 2:9). However, there was dispute among the early church fathers about the authorship of 2 Peter, 2 John and 3 John—a debate that continues today. Authorship of 2 Peter is questioned on the basis of stylistic differences compared to 1 Peter. The debate regarding 2 John and 3 John centers around the author's references to himself as "the elder," which could indicate that these letters were written by another church leader named John (2Jn 1; 3Jn 1). This has also led to modern debate about the authorship of 1 John (see the "The Gospel of John and Johannine Letters" on p. 1711).

In the early church period, 1 John, 1 Peter and James were attributed to the apostles John, Peter and James; likewise, the letter of Jude was attributed to Jesus' brother Jude. However, in modern scholarship there is some debate about the authorship of 1 Peter, James and Jude primarily on the basis of writing style. To some interpreters, these letters seem to reflect a higher level of education than the purported authors would have had. If this is the case, then the attribution signifies that they are written in the tradition of these church leaders, not necessarily by them.

CONTEXT AND STYLE

Hebrews
Hebrews is named Hebrews because it appears to address Jews who had become Christians and were under pressure to renounce Jesus and return to more traditional Judaism. The work as a

whole is more of a sermon or homily than a letter, but it does have a letter ending. That makes it something of a hybrid.

Hebrews is written in very educated Greek style, comparable to the style of Luke, using involved sentences and wide vocabulary. It uses the Greek version of the Old Testament (the Septuagint), so the author and addressees were probably outside Palestine. It shows the influence of Neoplatonism or what might be called Alexandrian Judaism. It is rhetorically elegant, which is another mark of education.

General Letters

The idea that these letters are "general," or addressed to Christians rather than specific churches or individuals, is partially true. First John does not name any addressees, but it envisions specific circumstances in a church or group of churches by addressing issues affiliated with a group that has left the church (1Jn 2:19). The books of 2 and 3 John name very specific addressees (2Jn 1; 3Jn 1). Only James is truly general in that it represents a diaspora letter, a letter on various subjects that Jewish authorities in Jerusalem sent out to Jews scattered outside of Palestine. First Peter is a circular letter, a letter sent to churches throughout five Roman provinces, arranged in the order that a letter-carrier would have visited them. Second Peter and Jude address specific situations in a church or group of churches, although the churches are not named.

In terms of style and use of the Old Testament, the General Letters are diverse. First Peter resembles the style of Paul's letters, although with distinct theological emphases. First Peter does not address the relationship of Gentile and Jewish believers, whereas the Pauline Letters lack 1 Peter's focus on the alienation of believers from society. James' style of composition is such that it does not contain a connected argument all the way through. The style of 2 Peter resembles Jude rather than 1 Peter, lacking 1 Peter's long sentences. James and 1 Peter quote the ancient Greek translation of the Old Testament (the Septuagint), whereas 2 Peter and Jude do not; Jude also refers directly to the extra-Biblical, Jewish work 1 Enoch.

BASIC THEOLOGICAL THEMES

Hebrews

Hebrews has some of the highest Christology in the New Testament. Its starting point is that God's Son became fully incarnate and thus is the highest revelation of God, as well as the greatest high priest and Lawgiver.

Hebrews also stresses the continuity of belief in Jesus with Old Testament revelation, but that continuity is one of "better than" rather than merely "more of the same." Thus the revelation by the Son is better than the revelation mediated through angels to Moses, the sacrifice of the Son is better than that of the Levitical priests, and the whole series of Old Testament saints points to and culminates in Jesus and his Church. There is no denigrating of the Torah (law) or Judaism, but rather a declaration that the vastly better has arrived.

Hebrews is concerned with the danger of apostasy (people abandoning their beliefs). Positively, the author outlines the basics of the faith—what was preached in the gospel—in Hebrews 6. Negatively, there is a series of warning passages starting in chapter two. The author is convinced that the addressees have not yet apostatized, but he warns them not to go too near to that edge; they are to draw nearer to Jesus instead.

Finally, Hebrews calls followers of Jesus to follow him in suffering. They are to be willing to suffer as the heroes of Hebrews 11 often suffered, and to identify with their great high priest.

James

James focuses primarily on the social-political climate of the early church, particularly how the wealthy believers were treating their poorer brothers and sisters. Like the Johannine Letters (1–3 John), James addresses a threat of division between rich and poor. In James' setting, Christians began to favor the rich at the expense of the needy; for James, this represented a moral abandonment of faith—a friendship with the world's values that made one an enemy of God (Jas 4:4). However, James maintains that the way of repentance remains open for his audience. His letter emphasizes wise, practical living—personally, communally and spiritually.

First Peter

Instead of threats of division within the early church, Peter addresses the place of believers within the Greco-Roman world around them. Beginning with the idea of new birth, Peter tells his audience that their fundamental identity is no longer as citizens of the empire; rather, as God's chosen people, his new temple and royal priesthood, they are resident aliens. First Peter, then, addresses how believers should live in a cultural atmosphere hostile to Christianity.

Peter tells his readers not to make concessions with Rome to ease their persecution, but to live honorably and stand firm in the tradition they received. The persecution experienced by these believers includes slander, economic disadvantages, and perhaps for some (such as slaves), beatings. However, Peter may have sensed an intensification in suffering in Rome and throughout the empire. His letter, then, is a call for endurance. Peter tells Christians that they must persevere through the trials they encounter and exhibit righteous conduct as they do so. They are to accept their trials as God's will, while waiting patiently for their ultimate vindication when Christ returns to judge the nations (1Pe 4:17,19).

Second Peter

Second Peter draws from Jude but addresses a slightly different situation: Teachers within the community who taught that Jesus would not return and that there was neither a resurrection nor final judgment. Second Peter does not express any hope for these false teachers (2Pe 2:1). As an alternative to the false message, 2 Peter argues vigorously for Jesus' return to rule and judge, and admonishes believers to live in the light of this expectation.

The Johannine Letters (1–3 John)

The Johannine Letters address the reality of division within the Christian community regarding how to understand the nature of Christ. Continuing the theology of the Fourth Gospel with its emphasis on love and unity, the letters of 1–2 John also emphasize Jesus' full humanity (see the "The Gospel of John and the Johannine Letters" on page 1711). The letters of 1–2 John address the issue of false teachers who deny the Christian teaching that Jesus had truly come in the flesh (1Jn 4:2; 2Jn 7). John urges the community to avoid the faction of false teachers and their followers who have departed from their community (e.g., 1Jn 2:19). The letter of 3 John addresses personal rivalries and hospitality.

Jude

Jude addresses the issues affiliated with a group that has fallen away from true faith and obedi-ence but has snuck into a believing community. Perhaps because they have Greco-Roman rather than Jewish mores, they violate the early church's ethics on both greed and sexuality. Jude roundly condemns the opponents but also ends his letter by instructing the faithful to help others walk away from falsehood (Jude 23), although the faithful should use caution as they do so. Thus, like James, Jude holds open the hope of repentance and restoration.

Each of the General Letters addresses a particular situation faced by the early church. Yet each one similarly emphasizes Christian conduct, either within a particular community or in response to outside persecution. In addition, they all possess an eschatological outlook—that is, they view themselves and those who persecute them in light of the return of Christ, who will judge all things with justice and vindicate his faithful servants.

Peter H. Davids

HEBREWS

INTRODUCTION TO HEBREWS

The first-century audience of Hebrews was experiencing opposition to their faith in Jesus and facing pressure to give up. The writer reassures them that everything they seek can be found in Christ. Hope in Christ is so much better than what society has to offer. Once their entire lives are transformed in Christ, the believers can withstand any persecution the world throws their way.

BACKGROUND

The author of Hebrews is unknown, and the audience is not clearly identified. Some early Christians grouped this letter among Paul's writings; others suggested authors in the early church, including Barnabas, Luke and Clement of Rome.

The author appears to have known the recipients, but nothing else about them is clear. Because the book was written in Greek but is filled with Jewish imagery, the recipients probably were Greek-oriented Jewish Christians. These believers seem to have wavered in their faith when they faced suffering and adversity because of the gospel. They also questioned whether Christ's sacrifice really dealt with their sins. As a result, it had become increasingly tempting to abandon Christ and return to their former life of Judaism.

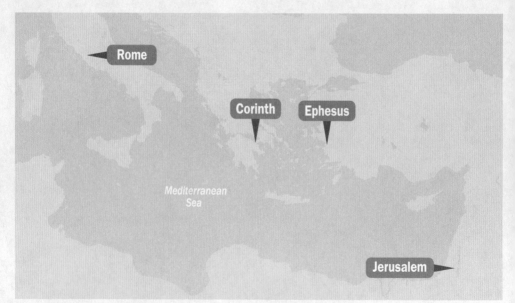

This map depicts Rome in relation to the locations of other major Christian churches. Hebrews may have been addressed to Christians in Italy.

The Christians who first received Hebrews were probably the target of social rejection from Jews and increasing pressure from those of other religions. The recipients may have lived in Rome or the surrounding area, as indicated by the greetings sent by people from Italy (Heb 13:24).

Hebrews likely was written before the mid–90s AD, since its material is used in an early church letter (1 Clement) that dates to the late first century. Since Hebrews is not structured like a typical letter, it may have originally been a sermon that circulated among churches in the Roman Empire.

STRUCTURE

There are three main parts to Hebrews. The first two focus on portraying Christ as the ultimate expression of God: He is superior to angels, Moses and Joshua (Heb 1:1—4:13), and he is also the great high priest, whose ministry transcends the work of all other priests, including the sacrifices made under the old covenant (4:14—10:18). This reason, among others, is why the author tells the believers to hold true to Christ, who was crucified for them and now intercedes in heaven on their behalf.

The third part of Hebrews describes the effects of Christ's superiority, particularly in believers' lives (10:19—13:17). This section includes a call to faithfulness (10:19–25), a warning against unfaithfulness (10:26–39), historical examples of faith in action (11:1–40), a call for endurance in suffering (12:1–11), a warning against refusing God (12:12–29) and exhortations to specific

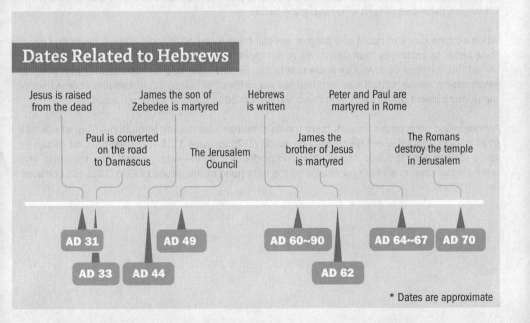

Dates Related to Hebrews

Jesus is raised from the dead

Paul is converted on the road to Damascus

James the son of Zebedee is martyred

The Jerusalem Council

Hebrews is written

James the brother of Jesus is martyred

Peter and Paul are martyred in Rome

The Romans destroy the temple in Jerusalem

AD 31

AD 33   AD 44

AD 49

AD 60~90

AD 62

AD 64~67   AD 70

* Dates are approximate

ethical actions (13:1–19). Christ's superiority has ramifications for all of life, particularly when it comes to standing firm against persecution and hardship.

OUTLINE

- The preeminence of Christ (1:1—4:13)
- The great high priest (4:14—10:18)
- Exhortations to faithfulness (10:19—13:25)

THEMES

The central theme of Hebrews is that Jesus is the ultimate revelation of God. All the things that came before—angels, Moses, Joshua, the Levitical priesthood, sacrifices, the tabernacle—point to Jesus and find in him their true fulfillment. The author essentially asks: Since Jesus is the supreme reality that everything else anticipates, why leave him and return to a pale imitation?

For the recipients of Hebrews, following Jesus was creating tension with the surrounding world, and they were unsure of which way to go. The author of Hebrews was concerned that they were close to abandoning their faith in Jesus—and it seems that some from the community had already done so. He writes to remind these wavering believers that Christ is superior to everything else. He challenges them to remain committed to their confession and to bear suffering with patient endurance. Rather than becoming discouraged by looking around them, they should look to Christ and to heroes of faith who have gone before.

When we face times of doubt and fatigue, we still have a source of hope: We will never find anything better to anchor us than Christ. He is worthy of our full devotion; he is the human incarnation of the image of God. And we know that in him we have one who can sympathize with our weaknesses, for he himself was tempted but was without sin (4:15). Our hardships should not be the primary object of our focus—instead, we are called to turn our focus on Jesus.

Although God once spoke through mere mortals, he has now spoken through his Son, who is heir of all things, through whom he created the world (1:2; compare 11:1–3). Therefore, let us set aside sin and cling to Jesus, the founder and perfecter of faith—who himself bore the cross and unwarranted shame, and is now seated at the right hand of the throne of God (12:1–2; compare Isa 53:10–12).

God's Final Word: His Son

1 In the past God spoke to our ancestors through the prophets at many times and in various ways, [2]but in these last days he has spoken to us by his Son, whom he appointed heir of all things, and through whom also he made the universe. [3]The Son is the radiance of God's glory and the exact representation of his being, sustaining all things by his powerful word. After he had provided purification for sins, he sat down at the right hand of the Majesty in heaven. [4]So he became as much superior to the angels as the name he has inherited is superior to theirs.

The Son Superior to Angels

[5]For to which of the angels did God ever say,

"You are my Son;
today I have become your Father"[a]?

Or again,

"I will be his Father,
and he will be my Son"[b]?

[6]And again, when God brings his firstborn into the world, he says,

"Let all God's angels worship him."[c]

[7]In speaking of the angels he says,

"He makes his angels spirits,
and his servants flames of fire."[d]

[8]But about the Son he says,

"Your throne, O God, will last for ever and ever;
a scepter of justice will be the scepter of
your kingdom.

---

[a] 5 Psalm 2:7   [b] 5 2 Samuel 7:14; 1 Chron. 17:13
[c] 6 Deut. 32:43 (see Dead Sea Scrolls and Septuagint)
[d] 7 Psalm 104:4

1:1–4 The letter to the Hebrews has many characteristics of a sermon. Early church writers suggest it could be by Paul, Luke, Barnabas (Ac 15) or the early church leader Clement of Rome. It was likely composed before the mid-90s AD as content from Hebrews appears in the early church letter of 1 Clement.

Hebrews focuses on the role of God's Son, Jesus, as the ultimate expression of God's work among humanity. Jesus' priestly service, now complete, brings about the purification of sins (Heb 1:3), and he sits with honor and authority at God's right hand.

1:1 In the past God spoke Primarily refers to the OT (vv. 5–13; 5:5–6; 7:17,21). The book of Hebrews emphasizes divine speech (e.g., vv. 1–6). **the prophets** This designation is not limited to the Biblical books of the Prophets; it describes all through whom God spoke. **1:2 in these last days** The phrase echoes the OT (e.g., Nu 24:14; Jer 23:20; 49:39). The new age has dawned because of Jesus' death and resurrection (Heb 1:3). **his Son** Refers to Jesus (4:14). **heir of all things** The Son is heir of all things because all things belong to God, his Father. **through whom also he made** The Son is described as the divine agent of creation. **1:3 the radiance** The Greek term used here is usually rendered as "reflection" or "radiance." Because of the connection between glory and light (e.g., Isa 60:1; 2Co 4:4–6; Rev 21:23), this is best understood as the Son radiating God's glory (e.g., Jn 1:9; 8:12; 1Jn 1:5,7). **glory** Describes God's divine presence and splendor. **his being** The Son accurately represents the very being of the Father. **by his powerful word** As God the Father brought the world into being through speech (Ge 1:1–2; compare Heb 11:3), so the Son sustains all things by means of his speech. **purification** In the NT, the Greek term used here, *katharismos*, often rendered as "purification," is primarily religious (Jn 3:25; Mk 1:44; Lk 5:14). In the Septuagint (the ancient Greek translation of the OT), it describes the removal of that which defiles the altar (Ex 29:36; 30:10) or the people (Lev 14:32; 15:13). The purpose of the sacrifices outlined in Lev 4 was purification; the blood was used to cleanse the sanctuary and the altar. The sacrifices temporarily restored people's relationship with God by repairing the damage caused by sin and guilt. **he sat down** The first of many allusions to Ps 110 in Hebrews. Instead of having to continually offer

sacrifice (Heb 10:1), the Son is able to sit down—his work is complete. **at the right hand** A position of favor and authority.
1:4 the angels This refers to messengers from the spiritual realm who dispense information and revelation on God's behalf.
1:5–14 Verses 5–14 provides proof for the statements about the Son in vv. 2–4 by demonstrating his superiority over angels. Appealing to the OT, this passage establishes the Son's worthiness of worship (v. 6) by emphasizing his relationship with God the Father (Heb 1:5; Ps 2:7; 2Sa 7:14), kingly rule (Heb 1:8–9; Ps 45:6–7), role in creation (Heb 1:10–12; Ps 102:25–27), authority, and victory (Heb 1:13; Ps 110:1).
1:5 You are my Son A quotation from Ps 2:7, which is viewed as a prophecy fulfilled by the Son, demonstrating his supremacy over angels. This same psalm is used in reference to Jesus' priestly work (Heb 5:5) and resurrection (Ac 13:33). **and he will be my Son** Like the citation from Ps 2:7, this quotation from 2Sa 7:14 reinforces the relationship between the Father and the Son. In 2Sa 7:12–16, Yahweh speaks of King David's future heir. Jewish interpreters during the Second Temple period (516 BC–AD 70) understood this passage as Messianic (Jn 7:42; compare the deuterocanonical work Sirach 47:11,22). The claim that God would establish an everlasting kingdom through David's descendant finds its fulfillment in Jesus.
1:6 his firstborn In Ex 4:22, God declared that Israel was his firstborn. Additionally, this might allude to the Greek Septuagint's reading of Ps 89:27, which says that God will appoint David as his firstborn. Both associations clarify that this description refers to preeminent status, not preexistence. **Let all God's angels worship him** Probably cited from the ancient Greek OT (Septuagint) translation of Dt 32:43. As angels worship God, they must worship God's Son, who is above them in status (Heb 1:3).
1:7 He makes his angels spirits Cited from Ps 104:4. The evanescent nature of the angels cannot compare to the glorious Son, described in the subsequent verses.

1:8–9 This citation from Ps 45:6–7 emphasizes the Son's exaltation and reign as king (compare 2Sa 7:14). Like other psalms quoted in this opening section of Hebrews (Ps 2:7; 110:1), this psalm addresses the enthronement of a king whose favorable position and exaltation can come only from Yahweh.

⁹ You have loved righteousness and hated
   wickedness;
   therefore God, your God, has set you above
       your companions
   by anointing you with the oil of joy."ᵃ

¹⁰ He also says,

   "In the beginning, Lord, you laid the
       foundations of the earth,
   and the heavens are the work of your hands.
¹¹ They will perish, but you remain;
   they will all wear out like a garment.
¹² You will roll them up like a robe;
   like a garment they will be changed.
   But you remain the same,
   and your years will never end."ᵇ

¹³ To which of the angels did God ever say,

   "Sit at my right hand
   until I make your enemies
       a footstool for your feet"ᶜ?

¹⁴ Are not all angels ministering spirits sent to
serve those who will inherit salvation?

Warning to Pay Attention

2 We must pay the most careful attention, therefore, to what we have heard, so that we do not
drift away. ²For since the message spoken through
angels was binding, and every violation and disobedience received its just punishment, ³how
shall we escape if we ignore so great a salvation?
This salvation, which was first announced by the
Lord, was confirmed to us by those who heard
him. ⁴God also testified to it by signs, wonders and
various miracles, and by gifts of the Holy Spirit
distributed according to his will.

Jesus Made Fully Human

⁵It is not to angels that he has subjected the
world to come, about which we are speaking. ⁶But
there is a place where someone has testified:

   "What is mankind that you are mindful
       of them,
   a son of man that you care for him?

ᵃ 9 Psalm 45:6,7   ᵇ 12 Psalm 102:25-27   ᶜ 13 Psalm 110:1

1:8 scepter The Greek word used here refers to a staff used by a ruler; it serves as a symbol of leadership and authority.

1:9 anointing In ancient Israel, oil was placed on a king at his coronation.

1:10–12 These verses, quoted from Ps 102:25–27, emphasize Yahweh's—and thus the Son's—role in creation (Heb 1:2). They also contrast the finitude of creation with the eternal nature of the Son. See the table "Messianic Psalms" on p. 847.

1:13 a footstool This citation from Ps 110:1 echoes Heb 1:3. The imagery likely refers to hieroglyphics on the footstools of Egyptian kings that depicted foreign enemies—symbolizing their subjugation. Compare also Jos 10:24, where Israelite leaders put their feet on the necks of defeated enemy leaders. Here in Hebrews, the scene is a divine throne room where the Son reigns as victor over all principalities and powers.

1:14 those who will inherit salvation Refers to be-lievers in the Son. The theme of inheritance appears throughout Hebrews (Heb 6:12; 9:15; 11:8; 12:17). Greek terminology for salvation generally indicates heal-ing, wholeness, deliverance from danger and victory over enemies. References in the NT usually refer to being saved from sin and death.

2:1–4 This section presents the first of five warning passages (vv. 1–4; 3:12–13; 6:4–8; 10:26–31; 12:25–29). This first warning instructs listeners to re-member what they have previously heard (v. 1) and not neglect the salvation that the Son offers (v. 3).

2:1 We The author includes himself in this warning. **to what we have heard** Likely refers to the message the apostles delivered—probably including the statements about the Son in 1:1–4.

2:2 message spoken through angels Refers to God giving the law at Sinai. Although Ex 19–20 does not include angels during the giving of the law, later Biblical texts (Dt 33:2; Ps 68:17) refer to the presence of angels.

every violation and disobedience The Greek terms used here describe sinful disregard for God's law: one of the terms, *parabasis*, expresses deviation from a bound-ary; the other term, *parakoē*, describes refusal to obey.

2:3 announced by the Lord In contrast to the law spoken through angels (Heb 2:2). **by those who heard** Likely refers to the apostles.

2:4 by signs, wonders A standard way of referring to the miraculous actions that God performed in Egypt (e.g., Ex 7:9; Dt 6:22; 34:11; Ps 135:9; Isa 20:3; Jer 32:20; Ac 7:36). In the NT, the phrase also refers to actions that Jesus and his followers performed (e.g., Mk 13:22; Ac 2:22,43; 4:30; 5:12; 2Co 12:12).

2:5–18 Following the warning to pay attention (Heb 2:1), the author continues to compare the divine Son with angels (vv. 5–9; see 1:5). The theme of Jesus' role as high priest begins to develop here (v. 17). The passage focuses heavily on the incarnate Son, whose subjection to suffering results in exaltation (v. 6) and qualifies him to act on behalf of humanity (vv. 14–17; compare Isa 53:10–12). The passage also focuses on Jesus' solidarity with humanity—especially his suffering and temptation (Heb 2:18).

2:5 not to angels that he has subjected Resumes the line of thought from 1:5–14 and sets up a comparison between the angels and the Son. **the world to come** The expectation of a future, ideal world closely parallels references to the Israelites expecting a heavenly country (11:14–16) and something better (11:40). Christ's work inaugurates the presence of the world to come (2Co 5:17).

2:6 there is a place where someone has testified This vague expression suggests that the author con-sidered the source of the testimony unimportant; only God—the one who speaks (Heb 1:1–2)—is important. **What is mankind** The citation that begins here is from Ps 8:4–6, which speaks of all of humanity as a collective individual, stating that God placed humanity a little lower than the angels—a place of honor. In the Greek text of

[7] You made them a little[a] lower than the angels;
   you crowned them with glory and honor
[8]   and put everything under their feet."[b,c]

In putting everything under them,[d] God left nothing that is not subject to them.[d] Yet at present we do not see everything subject to them.[d] [9] But we do see Jesus, who was made lower than the angels for a little while, now crowned with glory and honor because he suffered death, so that by the grace of God he might taste death for everyone.

[10] In bringing many sons and daughters to glory, it was fitting that God, for whom and through whom everything exists, should make the pioneer of their salvation perfect through what he suffered. [11] Both the one who makes people holy and those who are made holy are of the same family. So Jesus is not ashamed to call them brothers and sisters.[e] [12] He says,

"I will declare your name to my brothers
      and sisters;
   in the assembly I will sing your praises."[f]

[13] And again,

"I will put my trust in him."[g]

And again he says,

"Here am I, and the children God has
      given me."[h]

[14] Since the children have flesh and blood, he too shared in their humanity so that by his death he might break the power of him who holds the power of death—that is, the devil— [15] and free those who all their lives were held in slavery by their fear of death. [16] For surely it is not angels he helps, but Abraham's descendants. [17] For this reason he had to be made like them,[i] fully human in every way, in order that he might become a merciful and faithful high priest in service to God, and that he might make atonement for the sins of the people. [18] Because he himself suffered when he was tempted, he is able to help those who are being tempted.

Jesus Greater Than Moses

3 Therefore, holy brothers and sisters, who share in the heavenly calling, fix your thoughts on Jesus, whom we acknowledge as our apostle and high priest. [2] He was faithful to the one who appointed him, just as Moses was faithful in

---

[a] 7 Or *them for a little while*   [b] 6-8 Psalm 8:4-6
[c] 7,8 Or *[7]You made him a little lower than the angels;/ you crowned him with glory and honor/ [8]and put everything under his feet."*   [d] 8 Or *him*   [e] 11 The Greek word for *brothers and sisters* (adelphoi) refers here to believers, both men and women, as part of God's family; also in verse 12; and in 3:1, 12; 10:19; 13:22.   [f] 12 Psalm 22:22   [g] 13 Isaiah 8:17
[h] 13 Isaiah 8:18   [i] 17 Or *like his brothers*

Heb 2:8–9 the author applies this psalm to Christ (who represents all of humanity in his life and death), seeing within it references to his incarnation and exaltation (compare Php 2:5–11). Psalm 8 contains descriptions of humanity that probably represent interpretations of Ge 1:26–28, where God creates his image-bearers and entrusts them with stewardship of creation. **son of man** See Eze 2:1 and note and Da 7:13 and note.
2:8 Yet The Greek text here indicates that the Son's authority will be fully expressed in the future (Heb 2:5; compare note on 2:6).
2:9 he suffered death The teaching that the Son of God suffered and died appears in the earliest Christian confessions (1Co 15:3–8; compare Heb 5:7–8).
2:10 In bringing many sons and daughters to glory Enacted by Jesus' exaltation (compare Isa 53:12 and note). **make the pioneer of their salvation perfect** The idea here is that Jesus was made whole (or complete) through his suffering and death; he already was sinless (Heb 4:15; compare Isa 53:12 and note).
2:11 who makes people holy Refers to the work Christ does to remove sin from believers' lives. **the same family** Indicates the unity of Jesus and believers. The Greek text does not supply a referent, so some English translations insert "family" or "Father." The author could be referring to Jesus sharing in humanity (Heb 2:14).
2:12 I will declare The author cites Ps 22:22 to show Jesus' solidarity with the people he redeems. In this psalm, the writer of Hebrews sees a reference to the exalted Lord who proclaims God's name among his people. **in the assembly** Refers to God's assembly or council (Ps 82:1; 89:5–6). This points to the inclusion of human believers in God's heavenly family and their participation in Christ's rule (Heb 1:14; 2:5).

2:13 And again Both citations in this verse come from Isa 8:17–18, which refers to the faith that the prophet Isaiah had in Yahweh. The writer of Hebrews applies both texts to Christ, who trusts in God and stands in solidarity with God's people.
2:14 flesh and blood Refers to the common humanity of God's children. Jesus shares in that humanity in order to save them. **devil** The Greek term used here, *diabolos*, refers elsewhere in the NT to the one who tempts (Mt 4:1–11), lies (Jn 8:44; Rev 12:9), and oppresses (Ac 10:38). God has prepared destruction for the devil (Mt 25:41; Rev 20:10).
2:16 Abraham's descendants Refers to the people of Israel and perhaps all humanity, in contrast to the angels.
2:17 high priest High priests interceded for God's people by offering sacrifices, such as on the Day of Atonement, and performing other rituals (see Lev 23:26–32; note on Heb 9:7). **make atonement for the sins** This sacrificial language aligns with other phrases that speak of Christ as making purification (1:3), removing sin (9:26), and bearing the sins of many (9:28).
2:18 when he was tempted The temptation of Jesus is described in Mt 4:1–11; Mk 1:12–13; and Lk 4:1–12.

3:1–6 Because of his humiliation, exaltation and priestly work (Heb 2:5–18), Jesus has greater glory than Moses. Both were faithful to God; however, Moses was faithful as a servant of God, whereas Jesus is faithful as God's Son. Jesus' superiority does not negate the value and legitimacy of Moses and the law.

3:1 whom we acknowledge as Refers to a declaration or profession of belief in Jesus. The earliest Christian confessions include that Jesus is the Christ (Ac 5:42; 9:22), that he is Lord (1Co 12:3; 2Co 4:5), and that he

all God's house. ³Jesus has been found worthy of greater honor than Moses, just as the builder of a house has greater honor than the house itself. ⁴For every house is built by someone, but God is the builder of everything. ⁵"Moses was faithful as a servant in all God's house,"ᵃ bearing witness to what would be spoken by God in the future. ⁶But Christ is faithful as the Son over God's house. And we are his house, if indeed we hold firmly to our confidence and the hope in which we glory.

Warning Against Unbelief

⁷So, as the Holy Spirit says:

"Today, if you hear his voice,
8   do not harden your hearts
as you did in the rebellion,
      during the time of testing in the wilderness,
⁹ where your ancestors tested and tried me,
      though for forty years they saw what I did.
¹⁰ That is why I was angry with that generation;
      I said, 'Their hearts are always going astray,
      and they have not known my ways.'
¹¹ So I declared on oath in my anger,
      'They shall never enter my rest.'"ᵇ

¹²See to it, brothers and sisters, that none of you

has a sinful, unbelieving heart that turns away from the living God. ¹³But encourage one another daily, as long as it is called "Today," so that none of you may be hardened by sin's deceitfulness. ¹⁴We have come to share in Christ, if indeed we hold our original conviction firmly to the very end. ¹⁵As has just been said:

"Today, if you hear his voice,
      do not harden your hearts
      as you did in the rebellion."ᶜ

¹⁶Who were they who heard and rebelled? Were they not all those Moses led out of Egypt? ¹⁷And with whom was he angry for forty years? Was it not with those who sinned, whose bodies perished in the wilderness? ¹⁸And to whom did God swear that they would never enter his rest if not to those who disobeyed? ¹⁹So we see that they were not able to enter, because of their unbelief.

A Sabbath-Rest for the People of God

4 Therefore, since the promise of entering his rest still stands, let us be careful that none of you be found to have fallen short of it. ²For we also

ᵃ 5 Num. 12:7   ᵇ 11 Psalm 95:7-11   ᶜ 15 Psalm 95:7,8

---

is the Son of God (Ac 9:20; Ro 1:3–4). These assertions summarize early Christian teachings. The author later exhorts his audience to hold fast, which is likely part of the confession he references (Heb 4:14; 10:23). **apostle** The Greek term used here, *apostolos*, refers to someone who has been sent. **high priest** Jesus makes atonement for sin (2:17–18).

3:2 Moses Described as a faithful servant of God's household (Nu 12:7).

3:3 been found worthy of greater honor Jesus is held in higher esteem because he is the divine Son. It seems that the audience of Hebrews struggled with accepting Christ's superiority over the law and angels.

3:5 servant Someone who serves with devotion, particularly in a religious setting. The Greek term used here, *therapōn*, does not occur elsewhere in the NT; the word also appears in the Greek translation of the OT (the Septuagint) to describe Moses as God's servant (e.g., Nu 12:7).

3:6 Christ The Greek word used here, *christos*, is a Greek translation of the Hebrew word *mashiach*, meaning "anointed one." The letter to the Hebrews presents a progression of titles: "Son" (Heb 1:2), then "Jesus" (2:9), then "Christ." The author is revealing the identity of the one who is superior to all others except God the Father. For Jewish Christians in the letter's original audience, the term *christos* would have brought to mind Messianic expectations. **we are his house** Like the Israelites (e.g., Hos 8:1), Christians are described as God's house (compare 1Ti 3:15).

3:7–19 Recalling Israel's unfaithfulness in the wilderness, the author urges his audience to live faithfully, lest they fail to enter into God's rest (Heb 3:18). The passage includes quotes from Ps 95:7–11, followed by a warning against unfaithfulness (Heb 3:12–13—the letter's second such warning).

3:7 Holy Spirit says The author identifies the Holy Spirit as the speaker in the quotation that follows. Elsewhere, he identifies the Holy Spirit as a source of divine communication and Scripture (9:8; 10:15).

3:8 the rebellion Refers to Massah and Meribah (Ps 95:8), where the Israelites argued with Moses over God's provision for them (Ex 17:1–7; Nu 20:2–13).

3:9 what I did Refers to the acts God performed to save his people, miraculously sustaining them with manna, quail and water during their 40 years in the wilderness (Ex 16:11–15; 17:1–7). It also refers to God's righteous judgment on those who rebel against him (Dt 11:1–7).

3:11 my anger This phrase refers to divine judgment against evil, not an emotional disposition or outburst. **my rest** God promised the Israelites rest—safety, peace and freedom from slavery and wandering (Dt 12:9–10; 25:19)—if they would trust him and follow his will.

3:12 living God Even though God is merciful and loving, he is the living God who judges the sins of his people (Nu 14:17–32).

3:14 to the very end In this context, the Greek term used here, *telos*, could refer to death (perhaps martyrdom) or to Christ's return at the end of the age (e.g., Heb 6:11; 10:25).

3:17 perished in the wilderness The Israelites complained that they rather would have died in Egypt or the wilderness than be killed fighting for the promised land (Nu 14:2). God vowed that the unfaithful generation would die in the wilderness (Nu 14:29–33).

4:1–13 Israel's disobedience serves as a warning to fear God (Heb 4:1), lest the present generation also fail to enter God's rest. The writer explains that fearing God means being obedient to his word (v. 12).

4:1 promise The promise is rest and wholeness with God. See note on Heb 3:11. **let us be careful** Relates

have had the good news proclaimed to us, just as they did; but the message they heard was of no value to them, because they did not share the faith of those who obeyed.*ᵃ* ³Now we who have believed enter that rest, just as God has said,

"So I declared on oath in my anger,
'They shall never enter my rest.'"ᵇ

And yet his works have been finished since the creation of the world. ⁴For somewhere he has spoken about the seventh day in these words: "On the seventh day God rested from all his works."ᶜ ⁵And again in the passage above he says, "They shall never enter my rest."

⁶Therefore since it still remains for some to enter that rest, and since those who formerly had the good news proclaimed to them did not go in because of their disobedience, ⁷God again set a certain day, calling it "Today." This he did when a long time later he spoke through David, as in the passage already quoted:

"Today, if you hear his voice,
do not harden your hearts."ᵈ

⁸For if Joshua had given them rest, God would not have spoken later about another day. ⁹There remains, then, a Sabbath-rest for the people of God; ¹⁰for anyone who enters God's rest also rests

from their works,ᵉ just as God did from his. ¹¹Let us, therefore, make every effort to enter that rest, so that no one will perish by following their example of disobedience.

¹²For the word of God is alive and active. Sharper than any double-edged sword, it penetrates even to dividing soul and spirit, joints and marrow; it judges the thoughts and attitudes of the heart. ¹³Nothing in all creation is hidden from God's sight. Everything is uncovered and laid bare before the eyes of him to whom we must give account.

Jesus the Great High Priest

¹⁴Therefore, since we have a great high priest who has ascended into heaven,ᶠ Jesus the Son of God, let us hold firmly to the faith we profess. ¹⁵For we do not have a high priest who is unable to empathize with our weaknesses, but we have one who has been tempted in every way, just as we are—yet he did not sin. ¹⁶Let us then approach God's throne of grace with confidence, so that we may receive mercy and find grace to help us in our time of need.

ᵃ 2 Some manuscripts *because those who heard did not combine it with faith*   ᵇ 3 Psalm 95:11; also in verse 5   ᶜ 4 Gen. 2:2   ᵈ 7 Psalm 95:7,8   ᵉ 10 Or *labor*   ᶠ 14 Greek *has gone through the heavens*

---

to a disposition toward God and his word, similar to "the fear of Yahweh" (e.g., Job 28:28; Ps 34:11; 111:10).
4:2 faith The word used here, *pistis*, entails believing in the promises of God. People who do not trust God's promises, who reject that which they have not yet experienced, are excluded from the benefits of those promises. **those who obeyed** Refers to Caleb and Joshua (Nu 14:24,30).
4:4 from all his works This citation is from Ge 2:2. The promised rest reflects God's own rest after creating the world.
4:6 disobedience Refers to the Israelites (see Heb 3:17 and note).
4:7 Today Drawing again from Ps 95, the author announces a new opportunity to respond obediently to God's voice. **spoke through David** Both the Holy Spirit and David are presented as speaking the psalm (compare Heb 3:7).
4:8 Joshua Became the Israelites' leader after Moses died (Jos 1:1–2). Joshua led the conquest of the promised land, which represented rest for God's people (Jos 1:13). **had given them rest** Suggests that the Israelites' rest after settling in the promised land was not ultimate or final.
4:9 a Sabbath-rest The Greek word used here, *sabbatismos*, stresses the celebratory nature of rest. This image likely corresponds with the description of the festal gathering (Heb 12:22).
4:11 example of disobedience Refers to the behavior of the wilderness generation. If the present generation falls into similar patterns, they will turn away from the living God (3:12).
4:12 word of God Refers to God's speech, his word(s)—specifically those referred to in the previous context (Ps 95:7–11).
4:13 uncovered The idea here is that all things are open to examination by God. Exposure to the word of

God means exposure to God himself. **laid bare** The rare Greek expression used here could be synonymous with the previous term, or it might have the complementary sense of being helpless.

4:14–16 Sounding a theme that continues throughout the rest of Hebrews, this passage portrays Jesus as the great high priest who identifies with sinful humanity yet remains without sin (Heb 4:15).

4:14 who has ascended into heaven Refers to Jesus' exaltation (see Php 2:9–11). Because Jesus already has ascended into heaven and entered into God's rest, believers can be confident that they, too, will have a share in God's rest.
4:15 who is unable to empathize Because Jesus established his role as high priest by becoming like us (Heb 2:17–18), he can understand human struggles. **one who has been tempted in every way** Jesus faced the same temptations as people (Mt 4:3,6). Suffering believers can look to Jesus, who not only pioneered their faith but endured the cross—the cost of obedience to God (Heb 12:2; compare Isa 53:9). **he did not sin** Jesus remained faithful to the one who appointed him (Heb 3:2). Unlike other priests, Jesus didn't need to offer sacrifices for his own sins; instead, he offered himself unblemished to God (7:27; 9:14).
4:16 Let us then approach In the Jerusalem temple, only the high priest could enter the Most Holy Place—and only once per year on the Day of Atonement (Lev 16; Heb 9:7). By offering himself once for all, Jesus made a way for believers to draw near to God (compare Isa 53:10 and note). **throne of grace** The place of God's presence, from which grace emanates to his people. God's throne sits in the heavenly temple—the counterpart of the earthly temple (Heb 8:1; Isa 6:1; 66:1; Ex 25:17–22; compare Heb 9:5 and note).

5 Every high priest is selected from among the people and is appointed to represent the people in matters related to God, to offer gifts and sacrifices for sins. ²He is able to deal gently with those who are ignorant and are going astray, since he himself is subject to weakness. ³This is why he has to offer sacrifices for his own sins, as well as for the sins of the people. ⁴And no one takes this honor on himself, but he receives it when called by God, just as Aaron was.

⁵In the same way, Christ did not take on himself the glory of becoming a high priest. But God said to him,

"You are my Son;
today I have become your Father."ᵃ

⁶And he says in another place,

"You are a priest forever,
in the order of Melchizedek."ᵇ

⁷During the days of Jesus' life on earth, he offered up prayers and petitions with fervent cries and tears to the one who could save him from death, and he was heard because of his reverent submission. ⁸Son though he was, he learned obedience from what he suffered ⁹and, once made perfect, he became the source of eternal salvation for all who obey him ¹⁰and was designated by God to be high priest in the order of Melchizedek.

Warning Against Falling Away

6:4-6Ref — Heb 10:26-31

¹¹We have much to say about this, but it is hard to make it clear to you because you no longer try to understand. ¹²In fact, though by this time you ought to be teachers, you need someone to teach you the elementary truths of God's word all over

ᵃ 5 Psalm 2:7   ᵇ 6 Psalm 110:4

5:1–10 In this passage, the author explains Jesus' role as high priest. Just like Aaron and his sons, Jesus was appointed by God; however, he was appointed in the order of Melchizedek (vv. 4–6,10). This discussion prepares for the later exposition of the priesthood of Jesus (7:1 — 10:18).

5:1 appointed to represent God appointed priests to mediate between himself and the Israelites (Lev 8:2; Nu 8:6). While the OT emphasized that the priestly line was to be Levite and male (Ex 29:9,44; Nu 18:1–7), this passage emphasizes the common humanity between the priest and those he represents. **gifts and sacrifices** Likely refers to sin (or purification) offerings and burnt offerings (see Lev 4:4; 9:7; 16:16; compare Eze 45:15–17).

5:2 ignorant and are going astray Refers to unintentional sins, as opposed to intentional sins (see Heb 9:7; Lev 4:2,21–22; Nu 15:30–31).

5:3 he has to offer sacrifices The law required that priests offer an unblemished bull for their own sins before performing their priestly service on behalf of the people (Lev 4:3–12; 9:7). After this offering, they could offer sacrifices for the people of God (Lev 16:6,11,15–17). The Mishnah, a third-century AD Jewish work containing traditions of the rabbis, details the priestly sacrificial offerings that likely were used when this letter was written. It indicates that priests offered up prayers of confession two times, first while laying hands on the sacrificial animal just prior to its slaughter (Mishnah Yoma 4.2–3). The priest also made elaborate preparation of an animal within the temple infrastructure, culminating in the priest entering the Holy Place and sprinkling the animal's blood (Mishnah Yoma 4.3 — 5.3).

5:4 no one takes this honor on himself As the deuterocanonical work 1 Maccabees records, kings negotiated and granted the offices of the priesthood, meaning that the office of priest was hijacked by those vying for power (1 Maccabees 7:9; 10:20; 11:27). **called by God** God appointed Aaron and his sons to serve as priests within Israel (Ex 28:1).

5:5 today I have become your Father This quotation from Ps 2:7 emphasizes that God—who called Jesus his "Son"—appointed Christ as high priest.

5:6 Melchizedek A mysterious figure who appears in the Bible only in Ge 14:18, Ps 110:4 and several places in Hebrews (e.g., Heb 7).

Hebrew 5:6

MELCHIZEDEK

In the OT, Melchizedek is described as the king of Salem and a priest (Ge 14:18). In Ps 110:4, Melchizedek is evoked as an ideal priest-king; the psalm suggests that another Melchizedek will come from David's lineage. As a place, Salem is often identified with Jerusalem because of the similarity of names and because the meeting between Abraham and Melchizedek occurred within the King's Valley, which is associated with Jerusalem (Ge 14:17).

5:7 life on earth The Greek word used here, *sarx*, reinforces Jesus' humanity (2:14). His incarnation is essential to his experience of human life, which culminated in his suffering and death. **prayers and petitions** Likely refers to Jesus' prayers in the Garden of Gethsemane (Mt 26:36–40; Mk 14:32–42; Lk 22:40–46; Jn 12:27–28).

5:8 learned obedience Jesus fully enacted and conformed to God's will.

5:9 once made perfect The Greek word used here might refer to Jesus' perfect life of obedience, but the term appears elsewhere within Hebrews in reference to his suffering, death and exaltation (Heb 2:10; 7:28; 10:14).

5:11–14 The author emphasizes the importance of understanding the basic truths that undergird Christian faith. The letter's recipients apparently were making slow progress on the path to spiritual maturity (v. 12).

5:12 God's word The Greek term used here probably refers to the OT Scriptures in general or prophecy in particular (e.g., Ac 7:38; Ro 3:2; 1Pe 4:11). **milk, not solid food** A common metaphor for levels of teaching or instruction (e.g., 1Co 3:1–4)—the author calls his audience to Christian maturity.

again. You need milk, not solid food! ¹³Anyone who lives on milk, being still an infant, is not acquainted with the teaching about righteousness. ¹⁴But solid food is for the mature, who by constant use have trained themselves to distinguish good from evil.

6 Therefore let us move beyond the elementary teachings about Christ and be taken forward to maturity, not laying again the foundation of repentance from acts that lead to death,ᵃ and of faith in God, ²instruction about cleansing rites,ᵇ the laying on of hands, the resurrection of the dead, and eternal judgment. ³And God permitting, we will do so.

⁴It is impossible for those who have once been enlightened, who have tasted the heavenly gift, who have shared in the Holy Spirit, ⁵who have tasted the goodness of the word of God and the powers of the coming age ⁶and who have fallenᶜ away, to be brought back to repentance. To their loss they are crucifying the Son of God all over again and subjecting him to public disgrace. ⁷Land that drinks in the rain often falling on it and that produces a crop useful to those for whom it is farmed receives the blessing of God. ⁸But land that produces thorns and thistles is worthless and is in danger of being cursed. In the end it will be burned.

⁹Even though we speak like this, dear friends, we are convinced of better things in your case—the things that have to do with salvation. ¹⁰God is not unjust; he will not forget your work and

ᵃ 1 Or *from useless rituals*   ᵇ 2 Or *about baptisms*
ᶜ 6 Or *age*, ⁶*if they fall*

5:13 with the teaching about righteousness This expression could refer to sound ethical teaching, general Christian teachings, the doctrine of righteousness through Christ, or Israel's Scriptures.

6:1–3 These verses detail the aspects of elementary teachings. In Heb 5:12, the author equated such teachings with milk, not solid food.

6:1 foundation This image refers to the basic teachings of Christian faith. The metaphor suggests that Christians should not replace this foundation, but instead build upon it.

6:2 about cleansing rites Probably refers to ceremonial Jewish washings (see 9:10), not Christian baptism. **laying on of hands** Elsewhere in the NT, this gesture accompanies prayers of healing and blessing (Mk 5:23; Mt 19:13; Lk 13:13; Ac 28:8), designation to an office or task (Ac 6:6; 13:3; 1Ti 4:14; 2Ti 1:6), and the coming of the Holy Spirit (Ac 8:17–19). **resurrection of the dead** The Greek terminology here is plural, suggesting that this refers to the future resurrection of the many (see Da 12:2 and note). Christ's resurrection points ahead to the general resurrection (1Co 15:20). **eternal judgment** God is the judge of all things (Isa 33:22).

6:4–8 This passage—the third warning about apostasy and unbelief (Heb 2:1–4; 3:12–13; 10:26–31; 12:25–29)—is highly debated. In the Gospel of John, Jesus says that no one who truly believes will fall away (Jn 6:39–40). However, the warning at Heb 6:4–8 seems to imply that it was, indeed, possible for people to have been truly saved and later reject that salvation. Other warnings in the NT seem to acknowledge the possibility that some people who appear to be saved actually might not be (Mt 7:21–23; 25:1–13; Lk 13:22–30). Only God knows who is truly saved (2Ti 2:19). Saving faith is characterized by active involvement (Php 2:12; Jude 1:21), and those who have been truly transformed by the gospel will grow to reject sin as they become more like Christ (1Jn 3:9). Warnings such as this one in Hebrews are aimed at people who persist in a life of sin while claiming to have faith in Christ. Such people can expect to hear Jesus' statement from Mt 7:23 that he never knew them. Just like the Israelites in the wilderness, they have witnessed God's power and received his commands, but they have not responded in faith and obedience.

6:4 been enlightened Evokes the exodus narrative, when the pillar of fire enlightened the way for the Israelites

(Ne 9:12,19; Ps 105:39). This entails experiencing God's power, but not necessarily believing. Not all the wilderness generation believed; some later rebelled (e.g., Ex 16). **tasted** Implies knowledge from experience. Jesus tasted death—he experienced it fully (Heb 2:9). Even after experiencing all that God has to offer, some people still choose to not follow Christ. **heavenly gift** Recalls the bread from heaven received by the exodus generation (Ex 16:4,15; Ne 9:15; Ps 78:24). **who have shared in the Holy Spirit** God's Spirit guided the Israelites in the wilderness (Nu 11:17,25; Ne 9:20; Isa 63:11). Experiencing the Holy Spirit does not always lead to saving faith. In Ac 2:13, some of the people who witnessed the Spirit's power among the apostles still chose to mock them.

6:5 goodness of the word of God Refers to the gospel message—which someone can hear without accepting it (e.g., Mk 4:1–20; Ac 15:7). **powers of the coming age** Includes signs and wonders that accompany the outpouring of God's Spirit (Heb 2:4). The coming age has burst into the present one, beginning with Jesus' life, death and resurrection (2Co 5:14–19). Many people who witnessed Jesus' power didn't follow him; the same type of situation is likely in view here.

6:6 who have fallen away The Greek verb used here, *parapiptō*, refers in this context to a strong stance against God epitomized by sinful behavior. **brought back to repentance** It is impossible for humans to restore someone to a state of repentance, but God can still do so. **they are crucifying the Son of God all over again** Those who reject Christ become like those in the Gospel accounts who publicly dishonored him and put him to death. Such people have rejected God's truth—and thus are acting in league with forces that oppose him. (A similar sentiment is expressed in Heb 10:29.)

6:7 blessing of God People who have experienced God's goodness and shared in the Holy Spirit are transformed in ways that lead to good, godly works. Subsequently, they receive a blessing from God—both at present and in the future.

6:8 in the end it will be burned In Hebrews, fire is associated with judgment—referring to the peril of God's enemies (v. 2; 10:27; 12:29).

6:9–20 Throughout the rest of this chapter, the discussion focuses on the reliability of God's promise, which he made to Abraham by swearing an oath on the basis of his own reputation (vv. 13–14).

the love you have shown him as you have helped his people and continue to help them. [11]We want each of you to show this same diligence to the very end, so that what you hope for may be fully realized. [12]We do not want you to become lazy, but to imitate those who through faith and patience inherit what has been promised.

The Certainty of God's Promise

[13]When God made his promise to Abraham, since there was no one greater for him to swear by, he swore by himself, [14]saying, "I will surely bless you and give you many descendants."[a] [15]And so after waiting patiently, Abraham received what was promised.

[16]People swear by someone greater than themselves, and the oath confirms what is said and puts an end to all argument. [17]Because God wanted to make the unchanging nature of his purpose very clear to the heirs of what was promised, he confirmed it with an oath. [18]God did this so that, by two unchangeable things in which it is impossible for God to lie, we who have fled to take hold of the hope set before us may be greatly encouraged. [19]We have this hope as an anchor for the soul, firm and secure. It enters the inner sanctuary behind the curtain, [20]where our forerunner, Jesus, has entered on our behalf. He has become a high priest forever, in the order of Melchizedek.

Melchizedek the Priest

7 This Melchizedek was king of Salem and priest of God Most High. He met Abraham returning from the defeat of the kings and blessed him, [2]and Abraham gave him a tenth of everything. First, the name Melchizedek means "king of righteousness"; then also, "king of Salem" means "king of peace." [3]Without father or mother, without genealogy, without beginning of days or end of life, resembling the Son of God, he remains a priest forever.

[4]Just think how great he was: Even the patriarch Abraham gave him a tenth of the plunder! [5]Now the law requires the descendants of Levi who

[a] 14 Gen. 22:17

6:11 to the very end See note on Heb 3:14. **what you hope for may be fully realized** The Greek text here refers to complete confidence—in this case, confidence regarding God's promises (Ro 4:21).

6:12 imitate Chapter 11 provides a list of Biblical exemplars that culminates in the call to focus on Jesus, the pioneer of faith (12:2). **those who through faith and patience inherit what has been promised** Refers primarily to Abraham (v. 13) and the company of the faithful in ch. 11.

6:13 When God made his promise Refers specifically to Ge 22:16–17, as the citation in Heb 6:14 clarifies. **swore by himself** At several points in the OT (in addition to Ge 22:16), God swears by himself (Ex 32:13; Isa 45:23; Jer 22:5; 49:13). According to Heb 6:17–18, God's intention is to affirm the reliability of his promises.

6:14 give you many descendants This citation is from Ge 22:17.

6:15 after waiting patiently Abraham fathered Isaac—the fulfillment of this promise—at an old age (Ge 21:5). Isaac's birth represents trust in God to overcome all obstacles (Ge 15:2–6; 17:16–19).

6:16 oath Oaths served a legal function and involved calling upon someone to confirm the truthfulness of an assertion. In the OT, people take oaths in God's name (Ge 31:53; Dt 6:13; 10:20). In the Greco-Roman world, people swore oaths with reference to deities, kings and emperors (as depicted in Cicero, *Topica* 20.77).

6:17 unchanging nature of his purpose In contrast to the fickle gods of pagan religions, God's character is depicted as unchangeable (Nu 23:19; 1Sa 15:29; Isa 40:8). **he confirmed** See note on Heb 6:13.

6:18 two unchangeable things Refers to God's promise and the oath that guarantees it. **we who have fled** Refers to both author and audience—and by extension to all believers. The Greek verb used here, *katapheugō*, entails the idea of fleeing, especially from enemies (Ac 14:6; Ps 143:9; Isa 10:3). In this case, followers of Christ have fled from the powers of sin and the devil.

6:19 inner sanctuary behind the curtain Refers to the inner veil before the Holy of Holies (Most Holy Place). See note on Heb 9:3.

6:20 our forerunner, Jesus, has entered on our behalf Jesus does first what others will do after him (2:10; 12:2). His priestly actions allow believers to confidently draw near to God. **in the order of Melchizedek** See 7:1–10 and note.

7:1–10 This passage establishes Melchizedek's superiority over the priesthood of Israel (vv. 1–10).

7:1 king of Salem Genesis 14:18 identifies Melchizedek (*malki-tsedeq* in Hebrew) as the king of Salem (*melekh shalem* in Hebrew). The Hebrew term *tsedeq* means "righteousness," and the Hebrew term *shalem* can refer to "peace" or "Salem" (the place). The author of Hebrews understands the name Melchizedek to mean "king of righteousness" and the title king of Salem to mean "king of peace" (Heb 7:2). The combination of the terms "righteousness" and "peace" has Messianic implications within the OT—a factor that contributes to Melchizedek's prominent role in Hebrews (see Isa 9:6–7; Jer 23:5; Zec 9:9–10; compare Heb 1:8–9). As a place, Salem is often identified with Jerusalem because of the similarity of names and because the meeting between Abraham and Melchizedek occurred within the King's Valley, which is associated with Jerusalem (Ge 14:17). **priest of God Most High** Melchizedek is the first person identified as a priest in the OT. He served the God of Abraham (Ge 14:22). **defeat of the kings** Abraham defeated a group of kings to rescue his nephew Lot (Ge 14:1–16).

7:2 gave him a tenth Abraham gave Melchizedek one tenth of his spoils (Ge 14:20), likely because of Melchizedek's status as a priest (Ge 14:18). **means** See note on Heb 7:1.

7:3 without genealogy The Bible does not provide genealogical data for Melchizedek, who is mentioned only briefly in Ge 14:18–20 and Ps 110. The descriptions of Melchizedek as without father and without mother resemble descriptions of divine or semidivine beings in ancient literature (see the philosopher Philo's work *On the Creation* 100 and the Jewish pseudepigraphal work *Apocalypse of Abraham* 17:8–10). Because of this association, Melchizedek's lack of genealogy actually makes him more legitimate as a priest than the Levitical priests

become priests to collect a tenth from the people — that is, from their fellow Israelites — even though they also are descended from Abraham. ⁶This man, however, did not trace his descent from Levi, yet he collected a tenth from Abraham and blessed him who had the promises. ⁷And without doubt the lesser is blessed by the greater. ⁸In the one case, the tenth is collected by people who die; but in the other case, by him who is declared to be living. ⁹One might even say that Levi, who collects the tenth, paid the tenth through Abraham, ¹⁰because when Melchizedek met Abraham, Levi was still in the body of his ancestor.

Jesus Like Melchizedek

¹¹If perfection could have been attained through the Levitical priesthood — and indeed the law given to the people established that priesthood — why was there still need for another priest to come, one in the order of Melchizedek, not in the order of Aaron? ¹²For when the priesthood is changed, the law must be changed also. ¹³He of whom these things are said belonged to a different tribe, and no one from that tribe has ever served at the altar.

¹⁴For it is clear that our Lord descended from Judah, and in regard to that tribe Moses said nothing about priests. ¹⁵And what we have said is even more clear if another priest like Melchizedek appears, ¹⁶one who has become a priest not on the basis of a regulation as to his ancestry but on the basis of the power of an indestructible life. ¹⁷For it is declared:

"You are a priest forever,
  in the order of Melchizedek."ᵃ

¹⁸The former regulation is set aside because it was weak and useless ¹⁹(for the law made nothing perfect), and a better hope is introduced, by which we draw near to God.

²⁰And it was not without an oath! Others became priests without any oath, ²¹but he became a priest with an oath when God said to him:

"The Lord has sworn
  and will not change his mind:
  'You are a priest forever.'"ᵃ

²²Because of this oath, Jesus has become the guarantor of a better covenant.

ᵃ 17,21 Psalm 110:4

---

who had to prove their lineage (Nu 3:10,15–16; Ezr 2:61–63). Jesus also does not have a priestly lineage (Heb 7:14), but God appointed him as high priest (5:5). **resembling the Son of God** Melchizedek resembles Jesus because of his unique priesthood and the manner by which he obtained it. Just as the Son of God received his priesthood according to the power of an indestructible life (v. 16), the unrestricted quality of Melchizedek's life qualified him to serve as priest. **forever** The Greek phrase used here, *eis to diēnekes*, differs from the expressions used to affirm that Jesus is a priest forever (*eis ton aiōna* in Greek; e.g., 5:6; 7:17). Melchizedek serves without interruption, whereas Jesus serves for eternity.
7:5 law This could refer to specific commandments or to the entire Pentateuch (the first five books of the Bible). **descendants of Levi** Israel's priesthood was connected to the sons of Levi, Abraham's great-grandson (Ge 29:34; Nu 3:5–10).
7:6 did not trace his descent Refers to Melchizedek, who was not a Levite.
7:7 lesser is blessed by the greater Abraham was blessed by Melchizedek, demonstrating that Melchizedek's priesthood was superior to the priesthood of Abraham and his descendants (including the Levites).
7:8 by people who die Refers to the Levites. **by him who is declared to be living** The author of Hebrews assumes that Melchizedek never died.
7:10 still in the body Illustrates the ancient idea that descendants were contained within their ancestors (see Ge 25:23; Ro 5:12). Because Levi was still within Abraham, the Levitical priesthood—which by extension tithed to Melchizedek—is inferior to Melchizedek's priesthood.

7:11–28 Having demonstrated Melchizedek's superiority over the Levitical priests (Heb 7:1–10), the author establishes that Jesus' priesthood is superior to Melchizedek's. The theme of perfection frames the entire section; the author stresses the imperfection of the Levitical priests and the perfection of the Son of God (vv. 11,28).

7:11 perfection The Greek word used here, *teleiōsis*, refers to the qualifications required to draw near to God. The author of Hebrews denies the Levitical system's ability to produce perfection (see v. 19; 8:9; 10:4,10). God established it as a means for his people to maintain relationship with him (see Ex 40:15; Nu 18:19; 25:13). **another priest** Refers to Jesus, who like Melchizedek did not belong to the lineage of Levi and Aaron (Heb 7:13–14).
7:12 law must be changed Since the law was maintained by the Levitical priesthood, it must change now that a superior priest (Jesus) has arrived.
7:13 ever served at the altar That is, served as a priest. The altar was located in the courtyard of the tabernacle (Ex 27:9) and was used for sacrifices (Ex 40:29). See the infographic "Ancient Altars" on p. 127.
7:14 descended from Judah See Mt 1:3; Lk 3:33.
7:16 a regulation as to his ancestry Refers to the biological descent of the Levitical priesthood. **power of an indestructible life** Jesus defeated death through his resurrection (1Co 15:55; Col 2:12). His priesthood, like Melchizedek's, endures forever (Heb 7:17).
7:17 You are a priest forever Quotes Ps 110:4.
7:18 former regulation Refers to ordinances about the Levitical priesthood. The priestly functions of the OT are no longer necessary because of Jesus' priestly work (Heb 10:1–4). However, Hebrews does not claim that the OT no longer has relevance for God's people (compare Ro 15:4 and note). **set aside** The author of Hebrews reasons that God has the right to annul what he has instituted.
7:20 oath Refers to the opening line of Ps 110:4, quoted in Heb 7:21.
7:22 guarantor The Greek word used here, *engyos*, was a legal term within the Greco-Roman world, referring to someone who assumed an obligation in place of another. This expression parallels 8:6, which describes Jesus as the mediator of a better covenant. **better covenant** See 8:8–12; 9:11–14,23–26.

²³Now there have been many of those priests, since death prevented them from continuing in office; ²⁴but because Jesus lives forever, he has a permanent priesthood. ²⁵Therefore he is able to save completely[a] those who come to God through him, because he always lives to intercede for them.

²⁶Such a high priest truly meets our need—one who is holy, blameless, pure, set apart from sinners, exalted above the heavens. ²⁷Unlike the other high priests, he does not need to offer sacrifices day after day, first for his own sins, and then for the sins of the people. He sacrificed for their sins once for all when he offered himself. ²⁸For the law appoints as high priests men in all their weakness; but the oath, which came after the law, appointed the Son, who has been made perfect forever.

The High Priest of a New Covenant

8 Now the main point of what we are saying is this: We do have such a high priest, who sat down at the right hand of the throne of the Majesty in heaven, ²and who serves in the sanctuary, the true tabernacle set up by the Lord, not by a mere human being.

³Every high priest is appointed to offer both gifts and sacrifices, and so it was necessary for this one also to have something to offer. ⁴If he were on earth, he would not be a priest, for there are already priests who offer the gifts prescribed by the law. ⁵They serve at a sanctuary that is a copy and shadow of what is in heaven. This is why Moses was warned when he was about to build the tabernacle: "See to it that you make everything according to the pattern shown you on the mountain."[b] ⁶But in fact the ministry Jesus has received is as superior to theirs as the covenant of which he is mediator is superior to the old one, since the new covenant is established on better promises.

⁷For if there had been nothing wrong with that first covenant, no place would have been sought for another. ⁸But God found fault with the people and said[c]:

"The days are coming, declares the Lord,
    when I will make a new covenant
with the people of Israel
    and with the people of Judah.
⁹It will not be like the covenant
    I made with their ancestors
when I took them by the hand
    to lead them out of Egypt,
because they did not remain faithful to my
    covenant,
    and I turned away from them,
            declares the Lord.

---

a 25 Or *forever*   *b 5* Exodus 25:40   *c 8* Some manuscripts may be translated *fault and said to the people.*

7:24 Jesus lives forever See 1:8,11–12.

7:25 completely The Greek terminology here can refer either to the time or extent of salvation. Both senses are possible: Jesus offered himself once for all (v. 27), and believers will be made perfect in conformity with Jesus (5:9; 12:23). **because he always lives to intercede** Christ intercedes at the right hand of God (1:3; Ro 8:33–34; compare Isa 53:12).

7:26 holy, blameless, pure The qualities listed here enable Jesus to administer a better sacrifice (Heb 9:23). He is without sin (4:15; compare Isa 52:15; 53:6)—in contrast to the Levitical priests, who had to follow strict procedures to maintain ritual purity (Lev 21:11,17). **exalted above the heavens** See Heb 4:14; 8:1.

7:27 once for all Refers not only to the singular occasion of Jesus' sacrifice, but also to its unrepeatable nature (6:6). He was able to make an ultimate sacrifice, in the sense that no further sacrifices are necessary. **when he offered himself** Jesus did not need to make sacrifice in order to absolve his own sin (because he is without sin; 4:15; 7:26). Rather, he gave *himself* for the sake of the world (compare Isa 53:10 and note).

8:1–7 The author continues his discussion of Jesus as the great high priest, connecting this role to the heavenly tabernacle (Heb 8:2,5) and the new covenant (vv. 6–7,13). He explains that this new covenant is better than the old one, enacted on better promises (v. 6).

8:1 sat down at the right hand Symbolizes a place of favor and authority.
8:2 true tabernacle The earthly tabernacle represented the heavenly one. Thus, Jesus' high priestly work occurred in the true tabernacle—the one built by God (v. 5). Moses built the tabernacle according to the pattern God showed him (Ex 25:40; 27:8; Heb 8:5).

8:3 something to offer Refers to Jesus himself; he is both priest and sacrifice. See 7:27; 9:11–14.

8:4 If he were on earth Jesus' priestly work occurred in the heavenly sanctuary.

8:5 a copy The earthly tabernacle is a sketch (*hypodeigma* in Greek) of the true tabernacle (v. 2 and note). Elsewhere in the NT, the same Greek term is used to indicate human behavior that should be emulated or avoided (Jn 13:15; Heb 4:11; Jas 5:10; 2Pe 2:6). The word also appears in reference to the shape or pattern of the temple (Heb 9:23; compare the Septuagint reading of Eze 42:15). **make everything according to the pattern** This citation from Ex 25:40 reinforces the idea that the earthly tabernacle reflects the heavenly tabernacle.

8:6 mediator Moses was the mediator of the Sinai covenant; likewise, Jesus is the mediator between God and humanity (1Ti 2:5). **covenant of which he is mediator is superior** See Heb 8:8–13 and note; 9:11–14,23–26. **better promises** See note on vv. 8–13.

8:8–13 The author describes the better covenant and its promises (8:6) in terms of the blessings envisioned by the prophet Jeremiah (quoting Jer 31:31–34). This citation lays the foundation for Heb 9:1—10:18, which discusses the superiority of Jesus' sacrifice.

8:8 days are coming A stock phrase from Jeremiah that refers to the day of Yahweh, a time of future judgment (e.g., Jer 7:32; 9:25; 19:6; 51:52) or blessing (e.g., Jer 16:14; 23:5,7). This phrase recalls the opening of Hebrews (Heb 1:2). The latter days—those referred to within Jeremiah—arrived when Jesus was resurrected. **8:9 did not remain faithful to my covenant** Em-

¹⁰ This is the covenant I will establish with the
    people of Israel
  after that time, declares the Lord.
I will put my laws in their minds
  and write them on their hearts.
I will be their God,
  and they will be my people.
¹¹ No longer will they teach their neighbor,
    or say to one another, 'Know the Lord,'
because they will all know me,
  from the least of them to the greatest.
¹² For I will forgive their wickedness
  and will remember their sins no more."ᵃ

¹³ By calling this covenant "new," he has made
the first one obsolete; and what is obsolete and
outdated will soon disappear.

Worship in the Earthly Tabernacle

9 Now the first covenant had regulations for worship and also an earthly sanctuary. ² A tabernacle was set up. In its first room were the lampstand
and the table with its consecrated bread; this was
called the Holy Place. ³ Behind the second curtain
was a room called the Most Holy Place, ⁴ which had

ᵃ *12* Jer. 31:31-34

---

phasizes Israel's unfaithfulness. After the exodus, the
Israelites complained about wanting to return to Egypt
(e.g., Ex 15:24; 16:2,7–8; 17:3; Nu 14:2,27).
8:10 write them on their hearts God had instructed
the Israelites to recite and discuss his commands (Dt
6:6–9). However, sin was written on their hearts (Jer
17:1). Thus, God declares that he will rewrite what is on
their hearts (Jer 31:33). In this sense, the new covenant
is a renewed covenant.
8:12 forgive their wickedness Because of Moses'
intercession, God responded mercifully when his people
sinned (Nu 14:13–20). They were punished for their
unfaithfulness—banned from entering the promised
land—but they were not destroyed. **will remember
their sins no more** The old covenant included an annual reminder of sins (Heb 10:3 and note; on the Day of
Atonement, see note on 9:7; and note on 9:12).
8:13 obsolete The Greek term used here describes
something that is old or worn out.

9:1–10 In this section, the author focuses on provisions
within the tabernacle. The infrequency of access to God
under the old covenant serves to demonstrate that such
an arrangement could function only provisionally (Heb
9:7–8). Furthermore, the sacrifices' failure to properly
cleanse indicates the need for a more effective sacrifice
(vv. 9–10).

9:1 regulations for worship Refers broadly to the
design, contents and actions associated with Israel's
tabernacle. **earthly sanctuary** This description of the
sanctuary refers more to its composition than location,
and it contrasts the true tabernacle (8:2) that consists of
heavenly things (8:5). Israel's tabernacle, not the temple,
provides the primary imagery within the book of Hebrews.
The emphasis on the Sinai covenant makes sense of
this association, as does the reference to building the
tabernacle according to a pattern (8:5; Ex 25:9,40). This
also fits with the comparisons of the present generation
to the wilderness generation (Heb 3:7—4:13; 6:4–6).
9:2 lampstand God had commanded Aaron and his
sons to burn oil in this lamp perpetually (Ex 27:20–21;
Lev 24:2–3).
9:3 second curtain There were three curtains or veils
in the tabernacle complex (Ex 26:31–35; 27:16). The
one indicated here separated the Holy Place (where
priests performed their regular ministry) from the Most
Holy Place. Only the high priest was allowed beyond this
curtain, and only once a year on the Day of Atonement
(Lev 16:2). The curtain was made of fine blue linen and
had two cherubim embroidered on it (Ex 26:31). This
image of the cherubim served as a warning for people
to keep out, due to their depiction in the OT as super-

natural guardians who protect sacred space (Ge 3:24).
The reality of God's presence required a physical barrier,
to keep priests from inadvertently crossing into it. The
Gospel of Matthew depicts Jesus' death as an event
that tears the temple veil in two (Mt 27:51). The author
of Hebrews develops the idea of Jesus as a priest by
stating that he entered the inner sanctuary (Heb 6:20;
9:12). Moreover, believers themselves may confidently
enter into the sanctuary of God's presence because of
the new and living way opened by Jesus (10:19–22).
Most Holy Place The place of God's presence. The
Greek expression is superlative, emphasizing that this
inner sanctuary was the most holy of all holy places.
See the infographic "The Most Holy Place" on p. 525.
9:4 golden altar of incense On the Day of Atonement,
priests sprinkled blood from the sin offering upon the
horns of this incense altar and upon the mercy seat (Ex
30:10; Lev 16:15; compare Isa 52:15 and note). The OT
references to the incense altar generally place it in the
Holy Place (not the Most Holy Place), in the tabernacle
(Ex 30:6; 40:26; Lev 4:6). If it was in the Most Holy
Place, then it could have been accessed only once a
year, but procedures for two of the purification offerings
incorporate the incense altar, suggesting that it was in
front of the veil, not behind it (Lev 4:1–21). The copyist
of Codex Vaticanus—a Greek Bible containing much of
the OT and NT—recognized this problem and omitted
reference to the altar within Heb 9:4. However, in the
accounts of Israel's temple (as opposed to the tabernacle), the golden altar appears to be located within the
inner sanctuary (1Ki 6:20,22). This suggests that the
author of Hebrews is incorporating the possible setup of
Solomon's and Herod's temples into his description of
the tabernacle. See the infographic "The Tabernacle" on
p. 138. **ark of the covenant** The ark mediated God's
presence to the people (Ex 25:22). The Israelites carried
the ark using two long poles, so that no one would touch
the ark itself and die. See the infographic "The Ark of
the Covenant" on p. 412. **gold jar** Moses instructed
Aaron to collect some manna—the bread God gave the
Israelites in the wilderness—and place it in a jar before
the Lord (Ex 16:33–34). **Aaron's staff** Refers to Aaron's
staff that miraculously blossomed, demonstrating that
God called Aaron and his sons to the ministry of the
priesthood (Nu 17:1–11). The placement of the manna
jar and Aaron's rod in the ark is not attested anywhere
else (compare 1Ki 8:9). According to the OT, these
objects were placed outside the ark (Ex 16:32–34; Nu
17:10–11). Later Jewish texts, however—such as the
first-century AD work Lives of the Prophets 2.11—refer
to the ark of the covenant and the things in it, perhaps
suggesting that other items were placed in it. **tablets**

the golden altar of incense and the gold-covered ark of the covenant. This ark contained the gold jar of manna, Aaron's staff that had budded, and the stone tablets of the covenant. [5]Above the ark were the cherubim of the Glory, overshadowing the atonement cover. But we cannot discuss these things in detail now.

[6]When everything had been arranged like this, the priests entered regularly into the outer room to carry on their ministry. [7]But only the high priest entered the inner room, and that only once a year, and never without blood, which he offered for himself and for the sins the people had committed in ignorance. [8]The Holy Spirit was showing by this that the way into the Most Holy Place had not yet been disclosed as long as the first tabernacle was still functioning. [9]This is an illustration for the present time, indicating that the gifts and sacrifices being offered were not able to clear the conscience of the worshiper. [10]They are only a matter of food and drink and various ceremonial washings — external regulations applying until the time of the new order.

The Blood of Christ

[11]But when Christ came as high priest of the good things that are now already here,[a] he went through the greater and more perfect tabernacle that is not made with human hands, that is to say, is not a part of this creation. [12]He did not enter by means of the blood of goats and calves; but he entered the Most Holy Place once for all by his own blood, thus obtaining[b] eternal redemption. [13]The blood of goats and bulls and the ashes of a heifer sprinkled on those who are ceremonially unclean sanctify them so that they are outwardly clean. [14]How much more, then, will the blood of Christ, who through the eternal Spirit offered himself unblemished to God, cleanse our con-

[a] 11 Some early manuscripts *are to come*   [b] 12 Or *blood, having obtained*

Moses received the stone tablets with God's law written on them (Dt 9:9–10).

9:5 cherubim of the Glory Refers to two winged, angelic creatures made of gold (Ex 25:18–22). From either side of the ark, the cherubim overshadowed the mercy seat, where God was enthroned (1Sa 4:4; 2Sa 6:2; Isa 37:16). **atonement cover** The Greek term used here, *hilastērion*, refers to the golden lid of the ark. This lid was considered the earthly counterpart to the throne of grace (Heb 4:16). On the Day of Atonement, the divine presence appeared in a cloud over the lid (Lev 16:13–17). Moses (and later the priesthood) met with God there (Ex 25:22; Nu 7:89). See the infographic "Furnishings of the Tabernacle" on p. 136.

9:6 regularly into the outer room The detail that the priests could enter continually (*dia pantos* in Greek) highlights the perpetual and ongoing nature of the sacrifices.

9:7 inner room, and that only once In contrast to the constant service of the priests in the first tent (Heb 9:6), the high priest was permitted to enter the second tent only once a year, on the Day of Atonement. **never without blood** The high priest could not enter the Holy of Holies (Most Holy Place) without offering a blood sacrifice — a bull offered on behalf of himself and his household (Lev 16:11). After slaughtering the animal outside, the blood would be brought inside and sprinkled upon the mercy seat, the lid of the ark (Lev 16:14). The significance of blood for sacrificial purposes is emphasized in the remainder of Hebrews. Neither the Mosaic covenant (what the author of Hebrews refers to as the first covenant) or the new covenant was enacted without blood (Heb 9:18). The mention of blood here prepares for the discussion of Jesus' priestly ministry, wherein he entered the Most Holy Place by his own blood (v. 12).

9:8 Holy Spirit was showing by this The Holy Spirit provides special revelation for understanding the true purpose and provision of the sacrificial system.

9:9 an illustration The author describes the first tent — not the entire tabernacle infrastructure — as a symbol that points beyond itself. **to clear the conscience of the worshiper** See 7:11 and note. Defilement caused by sin extends to the conscience. The first covenant

was unable to produce true sanctification and peace (7:18–19; 10:1–4) because guilt offerings and offerings for unknown sins had to be made continually. The new covenant purifies the conscience (9:14; 10:22) and provides assurance to believers; Jesus' offering is once for all (7:27).

9:10 food and drink Refers to OT practices regarding clean and unclean foods (see Lev 11; Dt 14:1–21). **various ceremonial washings** Priests were required to cleanse themselves (Ex 29:4; Lev 8:6; 16:4). **time of the new order** Refers to the era of the new covenant (Heb 9:26).

9:11–28 In this section, the author focuses on Christ's death (which secures redemption; vv. 11–14), Christ's mediation of the new covenant (vv. 15–22), and the perfection of Christ's sacrifice (vv. 23–28).

9:11 the good things that are now already here Refers to the aspects of redemption available through the new covenant.

9:12 blood of goats and calves The author of Hebrews relies on the OT for the religious metaphors used to illustrate Jesus' sacrificial death. Three sacrifices were associated with the offering on the Day of Atonement: a bull and two goats. The priest offered the bull on behalf of himself and his family (Lev 16:6,11). One goat was presented alive as the scapegoat. The Israelites would then release the scapegoat into the wilderness in order to take away sins from Israel (Lev 16:10). The second goat would be slaughtered for a sin offering (Lev 16:15). **his own blood** Refers to Jesus' blood in the sacrificial sense — his life poured out in death.

9:13 ashes of a heifer Refers to the red heifer (see note on Nu 19:1–22). Although this sacrifice is not associated with the Day of Atonement, it is related to the idea of external ritual purity.

9:14 eternal Spirit The Greek phrase used here, *pneumatos aiōniou*, most likely refers to the Holy Spirit, as do most other references to "spirit" (*pneuma* in Greek) in the singular in Hebrews (e.g., Heb 2:4; 6:4; 9:8,14). The phrase also could refer to Jesus' spirit or divinity. **acts that lead to death** Describes acts that defile a person and create separation from God (6:1).

sciences from acts that lead to death,[a] so that we may serve the living God!

[15]For this reason Christ is the mediator of a new covenant, that those who are called may receive the promised eternal inheritance — now that he has died as a ransom to set them free from the sins committed under the first covenant.

[16]In the case of a will,[b] it is necessary to prove the death of the one who made it, [17]because a will is in force only when somebody has died; it never takes effect while the one who made it is living. [18]This is why even the first covenant was not put into effect without blood. [19]When Moses had proclaimed every command of the law to all the people, he took the blood of calves, together with water, scarlet wool and branches of hyssop, and sprinkled the scroll and all the people. [20]He said, "This is the blood of the covenant, which God has commanded you to keep."[c] [21]In the same way, he sprinkled with the blood both the tabernacle and everything used in its ceremonies. [22]In fact, the law requires that nearly everything be cleansed with blood, and without the shedding of blood there is no forgiveness.

[23]It was necessary, then, for the copies of the heavenly things to be purified with these sacrifices, but the heavenly things themselves with better sacrifices than these. [24]For Christ did not enter a sanctuary made with human hands that was only a copy of the true one; he entered heaven itself, now to appear for us in God's presence. [25]Nor did he enter heaven to offer himself again and again, the way the high priest enters the Most Holy Place every year with blood that is not his own. [26]Otherwise Christ would have had to suffer many times since the creation of the world. But he has appeared once for all at the culmination of the ages to do away with sin by the sacrifice of himself. [27]Just as people are destined to die once, and after that to face judgment, [28]so Christ was sacrificed once to take away the sins of many; and he will appear a second time, not to bear sin, but to bring salvation to those who are waiting for him.

Christ's Sacrifice Once for All

10 The law is only a shadow of the good things that are coming — not the realities themselves. For this reason it can never, by the same sacrifices repeated endlessly year after year, make perfect those who draw near to worship. [2]Otherwise, would they not have stopped being offered? For the worshipers would have been cleansed once for all, and would no longer have felt guilty for their sins. [3]But those sacrifices are an annual

[a] 14 Or *from useless rituals*   [b] 16 Same Greek word as *covenant*; also in verse 17   [c] 20 Exodus 24:8

9:15 those who are called The Greek terminology here refers to Christians, who share in a heavenly calling (3:1). Jesus mediates on our behalf so that we may receive an eternal inheritance.

9:16 a will The Greek term used here, *diathēkē*, was a general word for various kinds of legal contracts. The author uses this same word throughout vv. 15–20 but invokes the sense of *diathēkē* as a last will and testament in vv. 16–17. Ultimately, the author is alluding to the broken Sinai covenant, which brought a curse of death on those who did not keep it (2:2; 10:28). The analogy with a last will and testament explains how Christ's death brought this new covenant into effect. **the death** Connects two concepts of the Greek word *diathēkē* (legal contract versus last will and testament). Just as a will goes into effect when a person dies, the procedures for making a legally binding contract sometimes involved the representative death of a sacrificial animal (Jer 34:18).

9:18–21 This passage summarizes the enactment of the first covenant at Sinai (Ex 24:3–8), with an emphasis on the relationship between the covenant and blood.

9:19 water, scarlet wool and branches of hyssop These details do not appear in the Ex 24 account, but they do appear in other passages about sacrifices (Ex 12:22; Lev 14:4–7; Nu 19:6,18). **sprinkled** The sprinkling of blood enacted ritual purity (Ex 24:8). **the scroll** The act of sprinkling blood on the scroll is not attested elsewhere in the Bible.

9:21 In the same way This Greek terminology might be indicating that the verse describes another event (see Ex 29:12; Lev 8:15,23–24). Exodus 24 does not include the details provided here.

9:22 be cleansed with blood In accordance with the OT, blood was required for purification; it was understood to remove defilement.

9:23 copies of the heavenly things See Heb 8:2 and note. **heavenly things** The earthly tabernacle required sacrifices, so the true tent required a better sacrifice — the blood of Jesus. This term might refer to believers, since they are described as God's temple and dwelling place (e.g., 1Co 3:16–17; Eph 2:21). If this is the case, the act of cleansing purified the worshipers, providing them with access to God. Alternatively, the term could refer to heaven or the heavenly sanctuary.

9:24 a sanctuary made with human hands Refers to the tabernacle or temple built by God's servants. See note on Heb 9:1.

9:26 culmination of the ages Paul speaks of the end of the ages coming upon those who lived during his time (in contrast to the exodus generation; 1Co 10:6–13). Paul also speaks of the inauguration of the fullness of time following Jesus' incarnation (Gal 4:4–5). **to do away with sin** Refers to Jesus' death as an atoning sacrifice (Heb 2:17).

9:28 take away the sins of many Refers to Jesus' life and death on behalf of believers, referencing Isa 53:12. **he will appear a second time** When Christ returns, he will fully establish the kingdom of God — a work that has already begun — and dethrone the authorities and powers of this world (1Co 15:23–26).

10:1–18 Arguing from Ps 40:6–8, the author shows that the OT anticipates the demise of the first covenant and the sacrifices associated with it (Heb 10:5–7; see 8:8–12). The passage also affirms that Christ's sacrifice effectively sanctifies believers in accordance with the divine will (10:7,9–10).

10:1 law Likely referring collectively to the OT law found in the Pentateuch.

10:3 reminder of sins Refers to the Day of Atonement. See Lev 16:34; Heb 8:12; note on 9:7.

reminder of sins. ⁴It is impossible for the blood of bulls and goats to take away sins.

⁵Therefore, when Christ came into the world, he said:

> "Sacrifice and offering you did not desire,
>   but a body you prepared for me;
> ⁶with burnt offerings and sin offerings
>   you were not pleased.
> ⁷Then I said, 'Here I am — it is written about me in the scroll —
>   I have come to do your will, my God.'"ᵃ

⁸First he said, "Sacrifices and offerings, burnt offerings and sin offerings you did not desire, nor were you pleased with them" — though they were offered in accordance with the law. ⁹Then he said, "Here I am, I have come to do your will." He sets aside the first to establish the second. ¹⁰And by that will, we have been made holy through the sacrifice of the body of Jesus Christ once for all.

¹¹Day after day every priest stands and performs his religious duties; again and again he offers the same sacrifices, which can never take away sins. ¹²But when this priest had offered for all time one sacrifice for sins, he sat down at the right hand of God, ¹³and since that time he waits for his enemies to be made his footstool. ¹⁴For by

one sacrifice he has made perfect forever those who are being made holy.

¹⁵The Holy Spirit also testifies to us about this. First he says:

> ¹⁶"This is the covenant I will make with them after that time, says the Lord.
> I will put my laws in their hearts,
>   and I will write them on their minds."ᵇ

¹⁷Then he adds:

> "Their sins and lawless acts
>   I will remember no more."ᶜ

¹⁸And where these have been forgiven, sacrifice for sin is no longer necessary.

A Call to Persevere in Faith

¹⁹Therefore, brothers and sisters, since we have confidence to enter the Most Holy Place by the blood of Jesus, ²⁰by a new and living way opened for us through the curtain, that is, his body, ²¹and since we have a great priest over the house of God, ²²let us draw near to God with a sincere heart and with the full assurance that faith brings, having

---

ᵃ 7 Psalm 40:6-8 (see Septuagint)   ᵇ 16 Jer. 31:33
ᶜ 17 Jer. 31:34

10:4 impossible for the blood of bulls and goats An animal sacrifice cannot take away sins in an eternal way; only the sacrifice of Christ can accomplish that (see vv. 12–14). In the OT, animal sacrifices signified forgiveness of sin (Lev 4:20,26,31; 5:10,13,16). The Hebrew terms used in these contexts refer to the cleansing of the impurity caused by sin and God's pardoning of the sinner following that cleansing (see note on Lev 4:20; compare Ex 34:9; Nu 14:19–20).

10:5–7 In its original context, the psalm cited here (Ps 40:6–8) is associated with David, who understands right living to be better than right rituals. The author of Hebrews presents Christ as the speaker of this psalm (compare Mk 15:24,30–32,36; Jn 2:17; Ro 15:3,9; Heb 2:10–12).

10:5 body you prepared Likely refers to Jesus' body (sōma in Greek). Verse 10 speaks of believers being sanctified by the offering of the body (sōma) of Jesus.

10:6 with burnt offerings Such a sacrifice could be practiced for ritual cleansing (Lev 1:4; 5:7,10), vows (Nu 15:3,8), and festival offerings (Nu 10:10; 28:10). See Lev 1:3–17 and note. **sin offerings** Refers to the offering undertaken for unintentional sins (see Lev 4:1—5:13 and note). The requirements for this offering differed depending on who sinned. For example, the high priest's sin required a more costly sacrifice than that of a common Israelite.

10:7 scroll Since Ps 40:8 mentions the law, this might refer to a scroll of the Law of Moses (Heb 9:19).

10:9 the first to establish the second This contrast could refer to the two parts of the citation from Ps 40 (Heb 10:5–6,8 and 10:7,9) or the first and second covenants (8:7,13; 9:1,18).

10:10 once for all See 7:27; 9:12.

10:12 sat down at the right hand Alludes to Ps 110:1

and depicts Jesus' completed priestly action (see Heb 1:13). The author uses similar language at 1:3; 8:1.

10:13 he waits for his enemies At the end of the ages, Christ's enemies will be subjected to him completely (2:14–15). See note on 1:13.

10:14 he has made perfect forever Being made perfect does not necessarily imply no longer sinning. The author of Hebrews has emphasized the danger of falling into patterns of disobedience like the exodus generation (3:7–14; 6:4–6). Instead, believers are made whole (or complete) in their relationship with God.

10:15–17 The author quotes from Jer 31:33–34 again, forming an inclusio (that is, bracketing by repetition; see Heb 8:8–12). The citation shows that, because the new covenant has been inaugurated, God no longer remembers the sins of his people. God puts his laws in the hearts and minds of his people (v. 16), who consequently are empowered to obey him and conform to his holy character (3:1; 12:2).

10:15 Holy Spirit The author sets up the quotation from Jeremiah as an utterance of the Spirit.

10:16 in their hearts See note on 8:10.

10:19–25 Summarizing 8:1—10:19, the author offers three exhortations in light of Jesus' high priestly work.

10:19 blood of Jesus The basis for confidence is Jesus' atoning sacrifice (9:12,14; 10:19,29; 12:24; 13:12,20).

10:20 new and living way Refers to the entrance into God's life-giving presence that Jesus made possible. See 4:14; 5:9; 9:8,12. **curtain** See note on 6:19; note on 9:3. See the infographic "Herod's Temple" on p. 1626. **his body** Refers to Jesus' death (see Mt 27:51).

10:22 having our hearts sprinkled Recalls Moses sprinkling the people with blood to enact ritual purity (Heb 9:18–22; Ex 24:8). Whereas the OT sacrifices could

our hearts sprinkled to cleanse us from a guilty conscience and having our bodies washed with pure water. ²³Let us hold unswervingly to the hope we profess, for he who promised is faithful. ²⁴And let us consider how we may spur one another on toward love and good deeds, ²⁵not giving up meeting together, as some are in the habit of doing, but encouraging one another — and all the more as you see the Day approaching.

²⁶If we deliberately keep on sinning after we have received the knowledge of the truth, no sacrifice for sins is left, ²⁷but only a fearful expectation of judgment and of raging fire that will consume the enemies of God. ²⁸Anyone who rejected the law of Moses died without mercy on the testimony of two or three witnesses. ²⁹How much more severely do you think someone deserves to be punished who has trampled the Son of God underfoot, who has treated as an unholy thing the blood of the covenant that sanctified them, and who has insulted the Spirit of grace? ³⁰For we know him who said, "It is mine to avenge; I will repay,"ᵃ and again, "The Lord will judge his people."ᵇ ³¹It is a dreadful thing to fall into the hands of the living God.

³²Remember those earlier days after you had received the light, when you endured in a great conflict full of suffering. ³³Sometimes you were publicly exposed to insult and persecution; at other times you stood side by side with those who were so treated. ³⁴You suffered along with those in prison and joyfully accepted the confiscation of your property, because you knew that you yourselves had better and lasting possessions. ³⁵So do not throw away your confidence; it will be richly rewarded.

³⁶You need to persevere so that when you have done the will of God, you will receive what he has promised. ³⁷For,

"In just a little while,
    he who is coming will come
    and will not delay."ᶜ

³⁸And,

"But my righteousᵈ one will live by faith.
    And I take no pleasure
    in the one who shrinks back."ᵉ

³⁹But we do not belong to those who shrink back and are destroyed, but to those who have faith and are saved.

ᵃ 30 Deut. 32:35   ᵇ 30 Deut. 32:36; Psalm 135:14
ᶜ 37 Isaiah 26:20; Hab. 2:3   ᵈ 38 Some early manuscripts But the righteous   ᵉ 38 Hab. 2:4 (see Septuagint)

---

purify only the flesh, Jesus cleanses people's hearts and consciences (Heb 9:13–14). **bodies washed** An outward symbol of inward cleansing.
10:25 meeting together Early Christians typically gathered for worship in the home of a wealthy patron (Ac 2:46; 16:40; Phm 2). Paul describes the tradition of sharing a ceremonial meal, in which the sacrificial death of Jesus was remembered (1Co 10:16–17; 11:20–29). See the infographic "Ancient Home Synagogue" on p. 1971. **Day approaching** Refers to the coming day of the Lord, when Christ will return to free his people and condemn evil (Ro 2:16; 1Co 3:13).
10:26–39 This section contains the fourth warning (compare Heb 2:1–4; 3:12–13; 6:4–8), which focuses on the rejection of the truth of Christ's work (10:26–31). The author then shifts to a message of encouragement (vv. 32–39).
10:26 no sacrifice for sins is left Those who choose to reject Jesus' sacrifice continue to bear their own sin.
10:27 raging fire An allusion to Isa 26:11, which contrasts the righteous with the wicked. Regarding the wicked, Isaiah states that fire will consume them. The Bible and other ancient Jewish texts associate judgment with fire (e.g., Nu 16:35; 26:10). Within the OT, Yahweh not only comes in fire to judge (Isa 66:15), he also judges with it (Isa 66:16,24). The NT anticipates Jesus appearing with fire to enact vengeance on God's enemies (2Th 1:7–8; Rev 11:5; 20:14).
10:28 rejected the law of Moses Deliberately transgressed the law. **died without mercy** Perhaps drawing from Dt 17:2–7, this passage refers to the death that awaits those who reject God's covenant and serve other gods. Deuteronomy demands that idolaters be put to death without mercy (Dt 13:8) because they would naturally lead others to follow false gods. The testimony of two or three witnesses was sufficient evidence to carry out the death penalty (Dt 17:6).

10:30 him who said The verse quotes Dt 32:35–36, emphasizing that God will severely judge those who reject his covenant. This applies also to the new covenant inaugurated by Christ.
10:31 a dreadful thing Refers to God's judgment (Heb 10:27). **living God** See 3:12; 9:14; 12:22. In the context of this stern warning, this expression emphasizes that God lives, whereas idols do not. Turning to idolatry results in judgment or being cut off (v. 28; Dt 17:2–5).
10:32 conflict The Greek word used here, *athlēsis*, typically describes the struggle to win a contest in a sports arena.
10:33 you were publicly exposed to insult and persecution This persecution involved verbal abuse and acts of violence. Through this persecution, these believers participated in the sufferings of Christ (Heb 11:26; 13:13).
10:34 confiscation of your property In the first-century AD Roman Empire, authorities sometimes seized the property of accused criminals, and people sometimes looted homes after homeowners were imprisoned (according to first-century AD writer Philo, *Against Flaccus* 10, 56). **better and lasting possessions** Refers to believers' eternal salvation (Heb 5:9) and inheritance (9:15).
10:36 what he has promised Refers to the salvation inaugurated by Christ (4:1,8; 6:12,17; 8:6).
10:37 he who is coming The author cites Hab 2:3 to emphasize Christ's return. The author of Hebrews demonstrates that he is probably reading Hab 2:3–4 from a Christological perspective. Christ is referred to as the one who is coming (*ho erchomenos* in Greek) several places in the NT (e.g., Mt 11:3; Lk 7:19; Jn 1:27; Rev 1:4).
10:38 my righteous one The author cites the ancient Greek (Septuagint) translation of Hab 2:4, probably in reference to believers. The author of Hebrews applies this phrase to those who must keep faith during the challenge of trials.

Faith in Action

11 Now faith is confidence in what we hope for and assurance about what we do not see. ²This is what the ancients were commended for.

³By faith we understand that the universe was formed at God's command, so that what is seen was not made out of what was visible.

⁴By faith Abel brought God a better offering than Cain did. By faith he was commended as righteous, when God spoke well of his offerings. And by faith Abel still speaks, even though he is dead.

⁵By faith Enoch was taken from this life, so that he did not experience death: "He could not be found, because God had taken him away."ᵃ For before he was taken, he was commended as one who pleased God. ⁶And without faith it is impossible to please God, because anyone who comes to him must believe that he exists and that he rewards those who earnestly seek him.

⁷By faith Noah, when warned about things not yet seen, in holy fear built an ark to save his family. By his faith he condemned the world and became heir of the righteousness that is in keeping with faith.

⁸By faith Abraham, when called to go to a place he would later receive as his inheritance, obeyed and went, even though he did not know where he was going. ⁹By faith he made his home in the promised land like a stranger in a foreign country; he lived in tents, as did Isaac and Jacob, who were heirs with him of the same promise. ¹⁰For he was looking forward to the city with foundations, whose architect and builder is God. ¹¹And by faith even Sarah, who was past childbearing age, was enabled to bear children because sheᵇ considered him faithful who had made the promise. ¹²And so from this one man, and he as good as dead, came descendants as numerous as the stars in the sky and as countless as the sand on the seashore.

¹³All these people were still living by faith when they died. They did not receive the things promised; they only saw them and welcomed them from a distance, admitting that they were foreigners and strangers on earth. ¹⁴People who say such things show that they are looking for a country of their own. ¹⁵If they had been thinking of the country they had left, they would have had opportunity to return. ¹⁶Instead, they were longing for a better country — a heavenly one. Therefore God is not ashamed to be called their God, for he has prepared a city for them.

¹⁷By faith Abraham, when God tested him, of-

ᵃ 5 Gen. 5:24   ᵇ 11 Or *By faith Abraham, even though he was too old to have children — and Sarah herself was not able to conceive — was enabled to become a father because he*

11:1–38 Having introduced the theme of faithfulness in Heb 10:38–39, the author celebrates the character of faith throughout ch. 11 (compare 6:12–15). The author draws examples from the OT and applies them to the present generation.

11:2 commended for Refers to making a public witness in order to gain approval. In this case, God commends these OT figures through Scripture.

11:3 the universe was formed The theological concept of *creatio ex nihilo* ("creation out of nothing") could be implied by this verse's claim that the material world was not made from visible things. However, the context is set up by the definition of faith in 11:1 about trust in things unseen. The emphasis is on the universe's response to God's command, rather than God's work with physical materials. The author might also be indicating that God used a heavenly pattern to create the earth, as with the heavenly tabernacle (9:11). See the infographic "The Days of Creation" on p. 6.

11:4 Abel The second son of Adam, a shepherd (Ge 4:2). **brought God a better offering** See Ge 4:4 and note. **Cain** The first son of Adam, a farmer (Ge 4:2). **he was commended** God approved Abel as righteous because of his faith. The OT does not directly describe Abel as being righteous. The connection of faith with righteousness comes from Hab 2:4 (see Heb 10:38 and note). **Abel still speaks** Abel continues to speak through Scripture as an example of faithfulness.

11:5 Enoch Listed among the descendants of Adam (Ge 5:1–31). **God had taken him away** See Ge 5:24.

11:7 Noah See Ge 6–10. **heir of the righteousness that is in keeping with faith** The OT asserts that Noah was a righteous man (Ge 6:9; 7:1; Eze 14:14,20). The author of Hebrews again uses Hab 2:4 to draw a connection between faith and righteousness.

11:8 Abraham See Ge 12:1–4. Other NT writers also emphasize Abraham's righteousness. However, they usually point to his response to God's promise in Ge 15:6, not his faithful response to God's initial call in Ge 12 (see Ro 4:3,9,22; Gal 3:6; Jas 2:23).

11:9 heirs with him As Abraham's son and grandson, Isaac and Jacob inherited God's promise.

11:10 to the city with foundations Anticipates the description of God's unshakeable city (or kingdom) in Heb 12:28; 13:14.

11:11 Sarah The wife of Abraham; one of several women in Genesis who were barren (Ge 11:30; 25:21; 29:31).

11:12 as the stars in the sky See Ge 15:5; 22:17.

11:13 living by faith when they died Refers to Abraham, Sarah, Isaac and Jacob. **strangers on earth** Abraham and his offspring were nomads both literally (Heb 11:8–9) and figuratively (in the sense that they were awaiting a heavenly dwelling).

11:15 they had left Refers to ancient Mesopotamia. According to Ge 11:27–31, Abram's family was from Ur of the Chaldeans. They moved from there to Haran in northwest Mesopotamia. Abraham's Ur might have been the large city in southern Mesopotamia or a smaller city in northwest Mesopotamia, closer to Haran. See note on Ge 11:28. **opportunity to return** Abraham's unsettled existence within Canaan would have given him the option of returning to Ur or Haran, but Abraham resists that urge (Ge 24:6; 31:3).

11:17 one and only son The Greek term used here, *monogenēs*, has the sense of "unique" or "special" (see Jn 1:18; 3:16). Abraham fathered both Ishmael (Ge 16:15) and Isaac (Ge 21:2–3), but only Isaac is the child of promise (Ge 17:16; 21:1). The near-sacrifice of Isaac is recorded in Ge 22. James also identifies this event as a demonstration of Abraham's faith in God (Jas 2:21–24).

fered Isaac as a sacrifice. He who had embraced the promises was about to sacrifice his one and only son, [18]even though God had said to him, "It is through Isaac that your offspring will be reckoned."[a] [19]Abraham reasoned that God could even raise the dead, and so in a manner of speaking he did receive Isaac back from death.

[20]By faith Isaac blessed Jacob and Esau in regard to their future.

[21]By faith Jacob, when he was dying, blessed each of Joseph's sons, and worshiped as he leaned on the top of his staff.

[22]By faith Joseph, when his end was near, spoke about the exodus of the Israelites from Egypt and gave instructions concerning the burial of his bones.

[23]By faith Moses' parents hid him for three months after he was born, because they saw he was no ordinary child, and they were not afraid of the king's edict.

[24]By faith Moses, when he had grown up, refused to be known as the son of Pharaoh's daughter. [25]He chose to be mistreated along with the people of God rather than to enjoy the fleeting pleasures of sin. [26]He regarded disgrace for the sake of Christ as of greater value than the treasures of Egypt, because he was looking ahead to his reward. [27]By faith he left Egypt, not fearing the king's anger; he persevered because he saw him who is invisible. [28]By faith he kept the Passover and the application of blood, so that the destroyer of the firstborn would not touch the firstborn of Israel.

[29]By faith the people passed through the Red Sea as on dry land; but when the Egyptians tried to do so, they were drowned.

[30]By faith the walls of Jericho fell, after the army had marched around them for seven days.

[31]By faith the prostitute Rahab, because she welcomed the spies, was not killed with those who were disobedient.[b]

[32]And what more shall I say? I do not have time to tell about Gideon, Barak, Samson and Jephthah, about David and Samuel and the prophets, [33]who through faith conquered kingdoms, administered justice, and gained what was promised; who shut the mouths of lions, [34]quenched the fury of the flames, and escaped the edge of the sword; whose weakness was turned to strength; and who became powerful in battle and routed

[a] 18 Gen. 21:12   [b] 31 Or unbelieving

11:19 in a manner of speaking Because Abraham already had relinquished Isaac to the fate of death, receiving him back amounted to a resurrection (figuratively speaking)—and restored life to the promise that God had made to Abraham.

11:20 Jacob and Esau See Ge 27; 28:1–4.

11:21 Jacob See Ge 48:1–22. **worshiped as he leaned on the top of his staff** This detail comes from the Greek OT (Septuagint) of Ge 47:31. In contrast, the Hebrew text of Ge 47:31 describes Israel bowing himself upon the head of his bed—the posture of an old man nearing death.

11:22 exodus of the Israelites Refers to Joseph's words to his brothers in Ge 50:24. **gave instructions concerning the burial of his bones** Moses carried out these instructions (Ge 50:25; Ex 13:19); the Israelites eventually buried Joseph's bones at Shechem (Jos 24:32).

11:23 hid him See Ex 2:2. **the king's edict** Recalls Ex 1:22, where Pharaoh commands that every Hebrew boy be thrown into the Nile.

11:24 refused to be known as the son Moses protected a fellow Hebrew from an Egyptian master, demonstrating his true allegiance (Ex 2:11–15; compare Ac 7:23–25).

11:25 to enjoy the fleeting pleasures of sin Might refer to the comforts of Pharaoh's house. The Exodus account does not mention this detail.

11:26 disgrace for the sake of Christ By identifying with the people of God and sharing in their hardship, Moses ultimately served the cause of Christ.

11:27 he left Egypt Likely refers to Moses fleeing from Egypt after killing an Egyptian (Ex 2:15), though it could refer to the exodus event. **him who is invisible** Refers to God (Ex 33:18–23; Dt 4:12; Ps 97:2; Ro 1:20; Col 1:15; 1Ti 1:17). In Hebrews, the phrase primarily describes God's miraculous appearance to Moses at the burning bush (Ex 3:2–3).

11:28 Passover See Ex 12:1–30. **application of blood** God instructed Moses and the Hebrew people to sprinkle blood on their doorposts (Ex 12:22–23). This reflects the significance of blood in God's covenantal relationship with his people (e.g., Heb 9:12–22; 10:4,19,29; 12:24). **destroyer of the firstborn** See Ex 12:23 and note; Ex 12:29.

11:29 people passed through the Red Sea See Ex 14:15–22. The exodus from Egypt provides a framework for understanding later events in Scripture (1Sa 15:6; Isa 11:16; Mic 7:15). Matthew's Gospel portrays Jesus as Israel, God's Son, whom he brought out of Egypt (Mt 2:15; quoting Hos 11:1).

11:30 walls of Jericho See Jos 6. See the infographic "Ancient Jericho" on p. 330.

11:31 prostitute Rahab The letter of James also attests to Rahab's faithfulness (Jas 2:25). She expressed faith in God's plan to deliver Jericho to Israel (Jos 2:9–11) and played an integral role in accomplishing it (Jos 2:15–16). **the spies** Joshua sent spies to gather intelligence prior to the conquest of Canaan (Jos 2:1–15). Rahab kept the spies safe from the king of Jericho, so Joshua promised to deal kindly and faithfully with her (Jos 2:14). **those who were disobedient** Refers to the residents of Jericho, who perished when Israel plundered it (Jos 6:17,21).

11:32 Gideon, Barak, Samson and Jephthah Judges whom God appointed over Israel to deliver his justice and mercy to his people (Jdg 4–8,10–16). **David** Remembered as Israel's greatest king (1Sa 16–31; 2Sa 1–24; 1Ch 10–29; compare Ac 16:32). **Samuel** A prophet who anointed Israel's first two kings, Saul and David (1Sa 3–16).

11:33 mouths of lions An allusion to Daniel, who disobeyed the king's orders by worshiping God and was put into the lion's den. Daniel 6:23 records that he was unharmed because he had trusted God.

11:34 quenched the fury of the flames Refers to Shadrach, Meshach and Abednego—Daniel's friends

foreign armies. ³⁵Women received back their dead, raised to life again. There were others who were tortured, refusing to be released so that they might gain an even better resurrection. ³⁶Some faced jeers and flogging, and even chains and imprisonment. ³⁷They were put to death by stoning;ᵃ they were sawed in two; they were killed by the sword. They went about in sheepskins and goatskins, destitute, persecuted and mistreated — ³⁸the world was not worthy of them. They wandered in deserts and mountains, living in caves and in holes in the ground.

³⁹These were all commended for their faith, yet none of them received what had been promised, ⁴⁰since God had planned something better for us so that only together with us would they be made perfect.

12 Therefore, since we are surrounded by such a great cloud of witnesses, let us throw off everything that hinders and the sin that so easily entangles. And let us run with perseverance the race marked out for us, ²fixing our eyes on Jesus, the pioneer and perfecter of faith. For the joy set before him he endured the cross, scorning its shame, and sat down at the right hand of the throne of God. ³Consider him who endured such opposition from sinners, so that you will not grow weary and lose heart.

God Disciplines His Children

⁴In your struggle against sin, you have not yet resisted to the point of shedding your blood. ⁵And have you completely forgotten this word of encouragement that addresses you as a father addresses his son? It says,

"My son, do not make light of the Lord's
discipline,
and do not lose heart when he rebukes you,
⁶because the Lord disciplines the one
he loves,
and he chastens everyone he accepts as
his son."ᵇ

⁷Endure hardship as discipline; God is treating you as his children. For what children are not disciplined by their father? ⁸If you are not disciplined — and everyone undergoes discipline — then you are not legitimate, not true sons and daughters at all. ⁹Moreover, we have all had human fathers who disciplined us and we respected them for it. How much more should we submit to the Father of spirits and live! ¹⁰They disciplined us for a little while as they thought best; but God disciplines us for our good, in order that we may share in his holiness. ¹¹No discipline seems pleasant at the time, but painful. Later on, however, it produces a harvest of righteousness and peace for those who have been trained by it.

¹²Therefore, strengthen your feeble arms and weak knees. ¹³"Make level paths for your feet,"ᶜ so that the lame may not be disabled, but rather healed.

ᵃ 37 Some early manuscripts *stoning; they were put to the test;*
ᵇ 5,6 Prov. 3:11,12 (see Septuagint)   ᶜ 13 Prov. 4:26

---

who believed that God was able to deliver them from the fiery furnace (Da 3:17–18).
11:35 received back their dead, raised to life Elijah raised the son of the widow of Zarephath (1Ki 17:17–24). Likewise, Elisha raised the son of a wealthy Shunammite woman (2Ki 4:18–37).
11:37 sawed in two Likely an allusion to traditions surrounding the prophet Isaiah. First- to second-century works influenced by Judaism record that Isaiah died during Manasseh's reign by being sawn in two (Lives of the Prophets 1.1; compare Martyrdom of Isaiah 5.1–4,11–14). **They went about in sheepskins and goatskins** This description calls to mind Elijah and Elisha, who dressed in animal skins (Nu 31:20; 2Ki 1:8). The hairy cloak later became standard prophetic garb (Zec 13:4; Mt 3:4; 7:15).

11:39–40 These two verses summarize Heb 11:1–38 and provide a transition to the theme of endurance in ch. 12.
11:39 what had been promised The OT figures mentioned in ch. 11 did not experience the salvation of Christ's new covenant during their lifetimes (9:15). Rather, they saw the promise from afar and eagerly awaited its fulfillment (vv. 13,16).
11:40 only together with us would they be made perfect The chapter's closing statement suggests that all who trust in God, living and dead, will be transformed together.

12:1–11 The chapter's opening appeal (vv. 1–3) is based on the prior exposition of faithfulness among the people of God. The author exhorts his listeners by citing Pr 3:11–12 (Heb 12:5–6). He then goes on to illustrate the significance of fatherly discipline (vv. 7–11).

12:1 cloud A common way in Greek literature of metaphorically referring to a group of people. The models of faith in ch. 11 are included in this group (11:2,39).
12:2 fixing our eyes on Jesus In light of the footrace metaphor, the idea here might be that Jesus, who pioneered the course of the faith, awaits believers at the finish line. **the joy set before him** Prizes often were set before athletes to provide motivation (according to first-century Jewish historian Josephus, *Antiquities* 8:302). **cross** Jesus' endurance of the cross provides the paradigm for believers (12:1–7), who also will endure suffering and shame (10:32; 12:3).
12:4 struggle against sin While the author previously depicted sin as an entanglement to be cast off (v. 1), here he depicts it as an opponent to be resisted.
12:5 My son, do not make light Citing the Septuagint (the Greek OT) of Pr 3:11–12 (not the Hebrew text, which differs slightly), the author emphasizes that sonship and discipline go together. This provides OT support for the earlier teaching in Hebrews that suffering helped to bring many sons to glory (Heb 2:10).
12:9 the Father of spirits Reflects similar language used in the OT. In Numbers, the phrase emphasizes God's transcendence and authority (e.g., Nu 16:22; 27:16).

Warning and Encouragement

[14]Make every effort to live in peace with everyone and to be holy; without holiness no one will see the Lord. [15]See to it that no one falls short of the grace of God and that no bitter root grows up to cause trouble and defile many. [16]See that no one is sexually immoral, or is godless like Esau, who for a single meal sold his inheritance rights as the oldest son. [17]Afterward, as you know, when he wanted to inherit this blessing, he was rejected. Even though he sought the blessing with tears, he could not change what he had done.

The Mountain of Fear and the Mountain of Joy

[18]You have not come to a mountain that can be touched and that is burning with fire; to darkness, gloom and storm; [19]to a trumpet blast or to such a voice speaking words that those who heard it begged that no further word be spoken to them, [20]because they could not bear what was commanded: "If even an animal touches the mountain, it must be stoned to death."[a] [21]The sight was so terrifying that Moses said, "I am trembling with fear."[b]

[22]But you have come to Mount Zion, to the city of the living God, the heavenly Jerusalem. You have come to thousands upon thousands of angels in joyful assembly, [23]to the church of the firstborn, whose names are written in heaven. You have come to God, the Judge of all, to the spirits of the righteous made perfect, [24]to Jesus the mediator of a new covenant, and to the sprinkled blood that speaks a better word than the blood of Abel.

[25]See to it that you do not refuse him who speaks. If they did not escape when they refused him who warned them on earth, how much less will we, if we turn away from him who warns us from heaven? [26]At that time his voice shook the earth, but now he has promised, "Once more I will shake not only the earth but also the heavens."[c] [27]The words "once more" indicate the removing of what can be shaken—that is, created things—so that what cannot be shaken may remain.

[28]Therefore, since we are receiving a kingdom that cannot be shaken, let us be thankful, and so

a 20 Exodus 19:12,13   *b 21* See Deut. 9:19.   *c 26* Haggai 2:6

12:11 a harvest of righteousness and peace Although discipline is painful, it produces positive results.

12:12–17 Here, the author urges believers to live in peace and holiness. The OT figure of Esau serves as a negative example, showing how not to respond to God's grace (Heb 12:16–17).

12:12 feeble arms and weak knees This imagery draws on Isa 35:3–8, which describes the renewal of creation and the return of Jewish exiles to Jerusalem.

12:13 level paths for your feet Many Scriptures use similar language (e.g., Pr 3:6; 4:26; Isa 26:7; Jer 31:9; 2Pe 2:15).

12:15 bitter root Refers to someone who is idolatrous. This agricultural metaphor recalls the description of useless land in Heb 6:8.

12:16 Esau Refers to the brother of Jacob, son of Isaac (Ge 25:24–26). He took foreign wives, which was viewed negatively by his parents (Ge 26:34–35; 27:46) and in later passages Israelite men marrying foreign women is condemned because it could lead to idolatry (see note on Ezra 9:1—10:44). In addition, this negative portrayal of Esau could be drawing from Jewish sources that describe his wives as being involved in illicit behavior (e.g., the second-century BC Jewish work Jubilees 25.1,7–8). Also, the first-century AD Jewish writer Philo speaks of Esau being sexually immoral, even describing him as a man of wickedness (Philo, *Allegorical Interpretation* 3.2; *On the Virtues* 208). **inheritance rights as the oldest son** The heir apparently would receive a double portion of inheritance (Ge 43:33; Dt 21:17). In the case of Esau and Jacob, the elder son also would receive from Isaac the divine blessings that God had given to Abraham (Ge 12:1–3; 15:18–20). The remark that Esau despised this birthright (Ge 25:34)—which holds foundational significance for Israel—contributes to the negative assessment of him. See Ge 25:29–34.

12:17 sought the blessing with tears Refers to Ge 27:38.

12:18–29 This section contains the final warning of Hebrews (see Heb 2:1–4; 3:12–13; 6:4–8; 10:26–31). Imagery from Israel's encounter with God at Mount Sinai (Ex 19–24) forms the backdrop for a comparison between the consuming presence of God (Heb 12:29) and his presence in the heavenly Jerusalem (v. 22).

12:18 that can be touched Refers to Mount Sinai (Ex 19:16–22; 20:18–21; Dt 4:11–12; 5:23–27). The people of Israel were commanded to avoid touching the mountain, which was God's dwelling place (Ex 19:12–13). **that is burning with fire** Recalls Israel's experience at Sinai (Ex 19:18; Dt 4:11–12).

12:19 to a trumpet blast The trumpet blast at Sinai caused the exodus generation to shake in fear (Ex 19:16,19; 20:18). **a voice speaking words** God's voice from the fire on the mountainside spoke the Ten Commandments (called "words" in the Hebrew text; Ex 19:19; 20:1; Dt 4:11–13).

12:22 Mount Zion After David captured the hilltop fortress in Jerusalem, he resided there himself (2Sa 5:6–9) and placed the ark within a tent on Zion (2Sa 6:17). **in joyful assembly** Typically refers to a celebratory festival in the Greek Septuagint (Hos 2:11; 9:5; Am 5:21; Eze 46:11).

12:23 written in heaven See Rev 3:5 and note.

12:24 mediator See Heb 8:6 and note. **sprinkled blood** See 10:22 and note. **that speaks a better word than the blood of Abel** Unlike Jesus' redemptive blood, Abel's blood signals only condemnation (Ge 4:10–11).

12:25 they did not escape Refers primarily to the exodus generation who did not listen to God's voice (Heb 3:7–19).

12:26 shook the earth When God spoke at Mount Sinai, the mountain trembled and shook (Ex 19:18). The writer then quotes Hag 2:6 to remind his audience that God has promised a future time when he will again shake the heavens and the earth on the day of judgment.

12:27 what cannot be shaken Within the OT, the new

worship God acceptably with reverence and awe, ²⁹for our "God is a consuming fire."^a

Concluding Exhortations

13 Keep on loving one another as brothers and sisters. ²Do not forget to show hospitality to strangers, for by so doing some people have shown hospitality to angels without knowing it. ³Continue to remember those in prison as if you were together with them in prison, and those who are mistreated as if you yourselves were suffering.

⁴Marriage should be honored by all, and the marriage bed kept pure, for God will judge the adulterer and all the sexually immoral. ⁵Keep your lives free from the love of money and be content with what you have, because God has said,

"Never will I leave you;
never will I forsake you."^b

⁶So we say with confidence,

"The Lord is my helper; I will not be afraid.
What can mere mortals do to me?"^c

⁷Remember your leaders, who spoke the word of God to you. Consider the outcome of their way of life and imitate their faith. ⁸Jesus Christ is the same yesterday and today and forever.

⁹Do not be carried away by all kinds of strange teachings. It is good for our hearts to be strengthened by grace, not by eating ceremonial foods, which is of no benefit to those who do so. ¹⁰We have an altar from which those who minister at the tabernacle have no right to eat.

¹¹The high priest carries the blood of animals into the Most Holy Place as a sin offering, but the bodies are burned outside the camp. ¹²And so Jesus also suffered outside the city gate to make the people holy through his own blood. ¹³Let us, then, go to him outside the camp, bearing the disgrace he bore. ¹⁴For here we do not have an enduring city, but we are looking for the city that is to come.

¹⁵Through Jesus, therefore, let us continually offer to God a sacrifice of praise — the fruit of lips that openly profess his name. ¹⁶And do not forget

^a 29 Deut. 4:24   ^b 5 Deut. 31:6   ^c 6 Psalm 118:6,7

---

heavens and new earth are things that will remain (Isa 66:22). Similarly, those who share in God's holiness (Heb 12:10) will endure.

12:29 consuming fire Yahweh's glory on top of Mount Sinai appeared like a consuming fire (Ex 24:17; compare Dt 4:24; 9:3; Isa 33:14). This imagery depicts holiness and judgment.

13:1–19 Hebrews 13 contains instructions for believers. Similar to the discussion of religious objects and worship in ch. 9, this chapter relates the OT sacrificial altar to Jesus' death. Because Jesus has sacrificed himself for all (7:27; 9:12), believers are called to offer ongoing praise to God (v. 15).

13:2 hospitality Typically involved providing room and board to travelers (Ac 10:23; 21:16; 28:7). **shown hospitality to angels** Refers to Abraham, who received three visitors with generous hospitality (Ge 18:1–8).

13:5 will I forsake you An imprecise citation of Ge 28:15; Dt 31:6,8; or Jos 1:5. Each of these OT contexts provide hope in the face of uncertainty. This message is particularly relevant to the initial recipients of Hebrews, who were facing adversity and persecution (Heb 10:31–35; 13:1–3).

13:6 The Lord is my helper This citation from Ps 118:6 deals with confidence in the face of persecution, based on trust in God's character.

13:10–13 This passage alludes to the OT procedures surrounding the purification offering (often translated as "sin offering"; see note on Lev 4:1—5:13). This offering signified the removal of impurity from the community (Lev 4:1–21) and from individuals (Lev 4:22–35). The purification offerings of the community could not be eaten by the priests; instead, they had to be taken outside the camp and burned (Lev 4:11–12,20–21; 6:30; 16:27). The blood from those offerings was brought into the tabernacle and sprinkled before the veil that separated the Holy Place from the Most Holy Place—the Holy of Holies (Lev 4:5–7). The purification offerings required for the Day of Atonement followed similar procedures,

except that the high priest brought the blood all the way into the Holy of Holies (Lev 16:11–16).

13:10 altar Refers to Christ's death as sacrifice. This symbolic altar fulfills the purpose of the OT sacrificial altar. **those who minister** Refers to the priests. The priests who officiated over various sacrifices were entitled to eat the portion of that sacrifice designated for the priests (Lev 6:14–30). However, an offering presented for guilt that affected the whole community could not be eaten (Lev 6:30).

13:11 animals Refers to animals sacrificed for certain offerings (which the priests were not allowed to eat; Lev 6:30). **carries the blood of animals into the Most Holy Place** For the offerings described in Lev 4:1–21, some of the blood had to be sprinkled before God and placed on the horns of the incense altar inside the tabernacle (Lev 4:5–7). Those offerings had a higher level of sanctity and could not be eaten. See note on Heb 9:7. **burned outside the camp** Rather than eat them, the priests took the animal remains outside the camp and burned them (Lev 4:11–12,20–21; 16:27; Ex 29:14).

13:12 Jesus also suffered Refers to Jesus' crucifixion, which occurred just outside Jerusalem (see Jn 19:17–20).

13:13 Let us, then, go to him outside the camp Refers to Jesus enduring the shameful death of a criminal (Heb 12:2). To maintain the community's ritual purity, criminals were taken outside the camp or city for execution (e.g., Lev 24:14,23; Nu 15:35–36; Dt 22:24). In addition, dead bodies had to be taken outside the camp (e.g., Lev 10:4–5).

13:14 an enduring city Although Jerusalem was the center of Jewish religious life, Jesus' sacrifice outside the city detracts from Jerusalem's significance. **city that is to come** Refers to the heavenly Jerusalem (Heb 11:10,14,16) and expresses the theme of heavenly pilgrimage, prevalent throughout Hebrews (11:8–10,13–16; 12:18–24).

13:15 sacrifice of praise Refers to the verbal worship

to do good and to share with others, for with such sacrifices God is pleased.

[17]Have confidence in your leaders and submit to their authority, because they keep watch over you as those who must give an account. Do this so that their work will be a joy, not a burden, for that would be of no benefit to you.

[18]Pray for us. We are sure that we have a clear conscience and desire to live honorably in every way. [19]I particularly urge you to pray so that I may be restored to you soon.

Benediction and Final Greetings

[20]Now may the God of peace, who through the blood of the eternal covenant brought back from the dead our Lord Jesus, that great Shepherd of the sheep, [21]equip you with everything good for doing his will, and may he work in us what is pleasing to him, through Jesus Christ, to whom be glory for ever and ever. Amen.

[22]Brothers and sisters, I urge you to bear with my word of exhortation, for in fact I have written to you quite briefly.

[23]I want you to know that our brother Timothy has been released. If he arrives soon, I will come with him to see you.

[24]Greet all your leaders and all the Lord's people. Those from Italy send you their greetings. [25]Grace be with you all.

---

of God. Similar expressions occur in the Septuagint, the ancient Greek translation, of Lev 7:13,15; Ps 50:14,23; 107:22; and 116:17.

13:19 may be restored The author previously was part of the community he addresses (Heb 2:3–4; 6:9–12; 10:32–34). It is unclear why he is separated from them.

13:20–21 The author offers a closing prayer on the theme of God raising Jesus from the dead (v. 20) and equipping believers to accomplish his will (v. 21). Such prayers often appear toward the end of NT letters (1Th 5:23; 2Th 3:16).

13:20 that great Shepherd of the sheep Metaphors describing leaders as shepherds are common in the OT (2Sa 5:1–3; Isa 63:11). The Messiah is depicted as a shepherd (Isa 40:11; Eze 34:1–31; Jn 10:11,14; 1Pe 5:4).

13:22–25 Hebrews concludes with typical elements of an NT letter: greetings (Heb 13:22–24) and a benediction (v. 25; compare Ro 15:15—16:23; Phm 22–25). However, the author describes his writing as his word of exhortation, suggesting that the letter might actually be a sermon.

13:22 I have written to you quite briefly Brevity was an admirable trait in the ancient world, and mentioning it was a literary convention of politeness (e.g., 1Pe 5:12).

13:23 Timothy Possibly refers to the same Timothy that Paul mentions in his letters (Ro 16:21; 1Co 4:17; 2Co 1:1), but this was a common name in antiquity.

13:24 all the Lord's people Refers to those who have been made holy by Jesus (Heb 10:10) and who belong to the congregation of God (Ro 1:7; 1Co 1:2; 2Co 8:4). **Italy** This might suggest that Hebrews was written from Italy, or it could refer to a group of Italians who are sending a message home to Italy.

JAMES

INTRODUCTION TO JAMES

The letter of James is a practical and pastoral book. James' down-to-earth advice instructs believers on how to live wisely and with integrity. James tells Christians to endure whatever difficulties might come their way, with the knowledge that God will use their struggles to help them mature as Christians.

BACKGROUND

From the early church period forward, the James of this letter was often associated with James the brother of Jesus (Mk 6:3; Mt 13:55). This James is not one of the twelve disciples in the Gospels, yet according to Paul, the resurrected Jesus did appear to him (1Co 15:7). Paul indicates that James was identified with the apostles (Gal 1:19; 2:9; compare Ac 15:13; 21:18). James became a prominent leader among the Christians in Jerusalem, and the early church writer Hegesippus even describes him as the head of the Jerusalem church.

However, there is some modern discussion of whether this letter was, indeed, written by James the brother of Jesus. It's possible that it was written in James' name after his death—perhaps with material that originated with James and was reworked later by an editor. If James wrote the letter, it probably dates to the late 40s, around the time of the Jerusalem Council (described in Acts 15). The latest it could have been written would be AD 62, when James was martyred in Jerusalem.

The letter of James is addressed to the dispersed twelve tribes of Israel (Jas 1:1). This could be a way of describing the global church or Jewish Christians living outside Palestine (compare 1Pe 1:1). James might have been writing to Jewish Christians who had been scattered by the persecution that broke out in Jerusalem after the stoning of Stephen (Ac 8:1). It seems the letter has two main concerns: the attitude of Christians in response to adversity and living with true wisdom "from above," especially in manners concerning speech and wealth.

STRUCTURE

James is difficult to organize into an outline because the author frequently shifts from one set of issues to another. The letter bears some similarities to Proverbs and other Wisdom Literature. Although the letter has an opening (Jas 1:1) and a body (1:2—5:20), it lacks the standard closing (such as in Paul's letters, for example).

The body of the letter begins with a call for the readers to remain faithful in the trials they are experiencing (1:2–18). Then James offers them practical guidance for living out their faith (1:19—3:12). In particular, he is concerned about believers neglecting to care for the impoverished (2:1–13), failing to take action (2:14–26), and speaking carelessly (3:1–12). The next large section of the letter (3:13—5:6) deals with wisdom in action. The wise are not arrogant, boastful and ambitious, but rather pure, humble and peaceful. Finally, James counsels his readers to be patient in their suffering and to rely on God and each other (5:7–20).

OUTLINE

- Faithfulness in trials (1:1–18)
- Faith and works (1:19—3:12)
- Acting wisely and unwisely (3:13—5:6)
- Endurance and prayer (5:7–20)

THEMES

James is all about faith and wisdom coming to life through action. Trust in God can't be confined to one compartment of life; it has implications for everything. It affects how we speak and how we spend money. James says that if you can control your tongue, you can control your other actions as well. Wise speech leads to wise actions, including the wise use of time and resources (1:19—2:13; 5:1–6). We now live according to the leadership of Christ, whose words and message have become our new law of liberty (1:22–25).

James also sees a close relationship between wisdom and testing (5:7–18). We grow through perseverance in the face of hardship—responding to our struggles with prayer and trust in God. In this way, suffering produces wisdom in us.

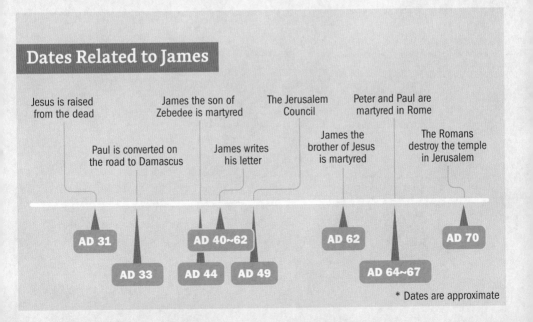

Dates Related to James

Jesus is raised from the dead

Paul is converted on the road to Damascus

James the son of Zebedee is martyred

James writes his letter

The Jerusalem Council

James the brother of Jesus is martyred

Peter and Paul are martyred in Rome

The Romans destroy the temple in Jerusalem

AD 31

AD 33

AD 40~62

AD 44

AD 49

AD 62

AD 64~67

AD 70

* Dates are approximate

The teachings of Jesus are echoed throughout the book of James, as he shows believers how to live a life that truly represents the good news of Christ (for example, compare 4:10 with Mt 23:12). Genuine faith produces a life that looks like Christ—and faith without works is dead (Jas 2:14–26). James' driving concern is for believers to live in total allegiance to God. The letter proclaims that our lives should be marked by love for God and others. We should show Jesus to every person around us, in every word we speak and every action we take.

1

James, a servant of God and of the Lord Jesus Christ,

To the twelve tribes scattered among the nations:

Greetings.

Trials and Temptations

[2] Consider it pure joy, my brothers and sisters,[a] whenever you face trials of many kinds, [3] because you know that the testing of your faith produces perseverance. [4] Let perseverance finish its work so that you may be mature and complete, not lacking anything. [5] If any of you lacks wisdom, you should ask God, who gives generously to all without finding fault, and it will be given to you. [6] But when you ask, you must believe and not doubt, because the one who doubts is like a wave of the sea, blown and tossed by the wind. [7] That person should not expect to receive anything from the Lord. [8] Such a person is double-minded and unstable in all they do.

[9] Believers in humble circumstances ought to take pride in their high position. [10] But the rich should take pride in their humiliation — since they will pass away like a wild flower. [11] For the sun rises with scorching heat and withers the plant; its blossom falls and its beauty is destroyed. In the same way, the rich will fade away even while they go about their business.

[12] Blessed is the one who perseveres under trial because, having stood the test, that person will

---

[a] 2 The Greek word for brothers and sisters (adelphoi) refers here to believers, both men and women, as part of God's family; also in verses 16 and 19; and in 2:1, 5, 14; 3:10, 12; 4:11; 5:7, 9, 10, 12, 19.

1:1 The date and audience of the letter of James depends on its composition history. Early church tradition affiliated this letter with James the brother of Jesus (Mk 6:3; Mt 13:55). If James is personally responsible for the letter, it likely dates to the late 40s AD, around the time of the Jerusalem Council (Ac 15), and no later than AD 62, when James was martyred in Jerusalem. However, it is possible that it was compiled from material that originated with James, which was finalized by a later editor.

The letter of James is like a series of loosely connected wisdom sayings or excurses on practical advice related to speech and money. This may indicate that the letter was originally a series of short sermons. The first verse functions as the opening to these sayings.

James may have been among Jesus' family who at first opposed him (Mk 3:20–21,31–35), but he became a leader of the church after Jesus' ascension (see Gal 1:15—2:12; Ac 12:17).

1:1 a servant By calling himself a slave or servant of Christ, James acknowledges his humble willingness to be at the Lord's disposal and live according to his principles. See note on Ro 1:1. The OT often labels individuals in positions of authority, such as Moses (e.g., 1Ki 8:53) or the prophets (e.g., Jer 7:25), as slaves or servants. These individuals demonstrate loyalty and submit to his will. **twelve tribes** Although the 12 tribal divisions ceased to function as geopolitical units in 722 BC, Biblical writers continued to use this designation for Israel. The prophets used this term to refer to the future restored people of God (e.g., Eze 47:13,22; Isa 49:6; Zec 9:1). **scattered among the nations** Usually refers to Jews living in or scattered outside of Israel, possibly suggesting that James wrote to Jewish believers in these areas. The 12 tribes could have a symbolic sense, representing all God's people under the new covenant who are scattered from their true homeland until God's promises come to fruition (Jas 5:7–8).

1:2–18 In this section, James calls his audience to persevere through the various difficulties they are experiencing, for it will result in their spiritual maturity.

1:2 pure joy Or "nothing but joy," or "supreme joy." James refers to an extended state of well-being rather than an immediate feeling of happiness or pleasure. **brothers and sisters** James speaks as one among peers; he is addressing his fellow Christians. **you face** The plural Greek verb here, peripesēte, indicates that James is speaking to the entire church rather than individual believers. He encourages a community of believers undergoing trials for their faith, not just individuals experiencing personal difficulties (e.g., 1:16–17; 2:15–16; 4:3–6). **trials of many kinds** The Greek word here, peirasmos, refers to an unwelcome or unexpected experience. James may be referring to trials in general, or to specific hardships such as persecution (2:6,7; 4:3,13), sickness (5:14), and poverty (1:9–11; 2:1–7; 5:1–6).

1:3 perseverance Expresses a growing determination in the face of adversity, based on hope. Those who suffer can express joy (v. 2) during times of trial because of their confidence in the day in which Christ will vindicate them (1Pe 4:13).

1:4 mature and complete Those who are suffering should have joy (Jas 1:2) because trials serve as a path to Christian maturity. Complete and mature individuals show integrity and single-minded devotion to God; they are characterized by godliness.

1:5 wisdom Refers to the knowledge of God's plans and purposes and the ability to live accordingly. Wise people can identify the nature and purpose of their trials and understand how to overcome them. **you should ask God** James describes God as the giver of wisdom (see note on Pr 2:6), which aids sufferers in their trials. **generously to all without finding fault** Indicates that God gives regardless of a person's previous record (Lk 6:35).

1:6 believe James describes faith that manifests itself in action. The wording used here does not imply that people must have a certain degree or standard of faith for God to hear their prayers. **a wave of the sea** James describes a life of instability and uncertainty—characteristics of one who doubts—as a continual succession of waves.

1:8 double-minded Describes someone who tries to live two contradictory lifestyles (see Pr 11:3).

1:9 Believers in humble circumstances The community that James addresses might have been facing conditions of poverty (see Jas 2:1–7). **take pride** Conveys the sense of being glad or joyful (rather than the familiar sense of arrogant boasting).

1:10 the rich should take pride in their humiliation It is unclear whether the rich person is a member of the church or a person outside the church. **like a wild flower** This imagery comes from Isa 40:6–7 (compare Ps 37:2; Job 15:30–33).

1:12 Blessed is the one who perseveres under trial In this context, "blessed" describes an attitude of determined courage that is unaffected by external circumstances. See Job 5:17; Ps 1:1 and note; Ps 32:2; Pr 8:32,34.

receive the crown of life that the Lord has promised to those who love him.

¹³When tempted, no one should say, "God is tempting me." For God cannot be tempted by evil, nor does he tempt anyone; ¹⁴but each person is tempted when they are dragged away by their own evil desire and enticed. ¹⁵Then, after desire has conceived, it gives birth to sin; and sin, when it is full-grown, gives birth to death.

¹⁶Don't be deceived, my dear brothers and sisters. ¹⁷Every good and perfect gift is from above, coming down from the Father of the heavenly lights, who does not change like shifting shadows. ¹⁸He chose to give us birth through the word of truth, that we might be a kind of firstfruits of all he created.

Listening and Doing

¹⁹My dear brothers and sisters, take note of this: Everyone should be quick to listen, slow to speak and slow to become angry, ²⁰because human anger does not produce the righteousness that God desires. ²¹Therefore, get rid of all moral filth and the evil that is so prevalent and humbly accept the word planted in you, which can save you.

²²Do not merely listen to the word, and so deceive yourselves. Do what it says. ²³Anyone who listens to the word but does not do what it says is like someone who looks at his face in a mirror ²⁴and, after looking at himself, goes away and immediately forgets what he looks like. ²⁵But whoever looks intently into the perfect law that gives freedom, and continues in it — not forgetting what they have heard, but doing it — they will be blessed in what they do.

²⁶Those who consider themselves religious and yet do not keep a tight rein on their tongues deceive themselves, and their religion is worthless. ²⁷Religion that God our Father accepts as pure and faultless is this: to look after orphans and widows in their distress and to keep oneself from being polluted by the world.

Favoritism Forbidden

2 My brothers and sisters, believers in our glorious Lord Jesus Christ must not show favoritism. ²Suppose a man comes into your meeting wearing a gold ring and fine clothes, and a poor man in filthy old clothes also comes in. ³If you show special attention to the man wearing fine clothes and say, "Here's a good seat for you," but say to the poor man, "You stand there" or "Sit on the floor by my feet," ⁴have you not discriminated among yourselves and become judges with evil thoughts?

⁵Listen, my dear brothers and sisters: Has not God chosen those who are poor in the eyes of the world to be rich in faith and to inherit the king-

---

1:13 When tempted, no one should say James cautions Christians against interpreting temptations of their sinful desires as a test from God. As James makes clear in the following verses, humans alone are responsible for choosing to sin.

1:15 gives birth to sin James uses the analogy of human conception and birth to describe sin. Desire is conceived when a person yields to temptation, which results in the "birth" of sin. As sin matures, this ultimately leads to God's judgment of death. All sin ultimately originates in individuals, not in any other source. According to James, desire (the negative, destructive kind) is the source of temptation, which explains the presence of sin and death in the world (compare Ro 7:17–23; Gal 5:16–21; Eph 2:3).

1:17 Every good and perfect gift James already has described one of these gifts as wisdom (Jas 1:5). **Father of the heavenly lights** Recalling the creation account, James refers to God's power over the sun, moon, and stars (Ge 1:14–18; Ps 136:7; Jer 31:35). See the infographic "The Days of Creation" on p. 6. **not change like shifting shadows** The fluctuation in light given off by the heavenly bodies contrasts with God's constant nature.

1:18 He chose to give us birth James probably refers to the new birth of Christians here (Jn 3:3–8; 1Pe 1:23), as this interpretation best contrasts the imagery of sin giving birth to death. See Jas 1:15 and note. **firstfruits** This term may refer to Israel, the first product of God's self-revelation to Abraham (Jer 2:3), or to Christians (1Co 15:20,23).

1:19—3:12 In this section, James shifts from instructions about life's difficulties to pragmatic thoughts on the full implications of faith in Jesus. He addresses issues like poverty (Jas 2:1–13), the need to take action for Jesus (2:14–26), and the reason why believers should be careful about what they say (3:1–12).

1:20 the righteousness that God desires The Greek phrase used here may describe the righteous character of God or the righteousness that comes from God — his gift of salvation. It may also refer to the righteousness that God expects from his people.

1:25 the perfect law that gives freedom Although James may be referring to the Law of Moses (Ps 19:7; 119:32,45–46,96), he more likely refers to the Law of Moses as now perceived through Jesus' interpretation and supplementation (Mt 5:17). Here, "law" is equivalent to "the word" in Jas 1:18,21,22. Biblical writers often speak of obedience in terms of practicing the law (Dt 28:58). Within the boundaries of the law, people have liberty to choose how they act (Jn 8:36). The Greek word used here for "perfect," *teleios*, is used to speak of completeness — meaning the law accomplishes its purposes.

2:4 discriminated among yourselves The OT prohibits people from discriminating between the rich and the poor (Lev 19:15); the practice also goes against God's character (Dt 10:17; Job 34:19). James may be addressing any expression of discrimination, whether based on race, socio-economic status, education, or gender.

2:5 poor in the eyes of the world James does not mean that the rich are at a disadvantage when it comes to believing, but that the poor are more apt to rely on God and subsequently come to faith because of their immediate physical needs. People without physical needs only feel spiritual needs (and at times the things they think are needs are actually desires), whereas people

dom he promised those who love him? ⁶But you have dishonored the poor. Is it not the rich who are exploiting you? Are they not the ones who are dragging you into court? ⁷Are they not the ones who are blaspheming the noble name of him to whom you belong?

⁸If you really keep the royal law found in Scripture, "Love your neighbor as yourself,"ᵃ you are doing right. ⁹But if you show favoritism, you sin and are convicted by the law as lawbreakers. ¹⁰For whoever keeps the whole law and yet stumbles at just one point is guilty of breaking all of it. ¹¹For he who said, "You shall not commit adultery,"ᵇ also said, "You shall not murder."ᶜ If you do not commit adultery but do commit murder, you have become a lawbreaker.

¹²Speak and act as those who are going to be judged by the law that gives freedom, ¹³because judgment without mercy will be shown to anyone who has not been merciful. Mercy triumphs over judgment.

Faith and Deeds

¹⁴What good is it, my brothers and sisters, if someone claims to have faith but has no deeds? Can such faith save them? ¹⁵Suppose a brother or a sister is without clothes and daily food. ¹⁶If one of you says to them, "Go in peace; keep warm and well fed," but does nothing about their physical needs, what good is it? ¹⁷In the same way, faith by itself, if it is not accompanied by action, is dead.

¹⁸But someone will say, "You have faith; I have deeds."

Show me your faith without deeds, and I will show you my faith by my deeds. ¹⁹You believe that there is one God. Good! Even the demons believe that — and shudder.

²⁰You foolish person, do you want evidence that faith without deeds is uselessᵈ? ²¹Was not our father Abraham considered righteous for what he did when he offered his son Isaac on the altar? ²²You see that his faith and his actions were working together, and his faith was made complete by what he did. ²³And the scripture was fulfilled that says, "Abraham believed God, and it was credited to him as righteousness,"ᵉ and he was called God's friend. ²⁴You see that a person

ᵃ 8 Lev. 19:18   ᵇ 11 Exodus 20:14; Deut. 5:18
ᶜ 11 Exodus 20:13; Deut. 5:17   ᵈ 20 Some early manuscripts dead   ᵉ 23 Gen. 15:6

with physical needs feel them and spiritual needs. In first-century Israel, society was divided between a small, wealthy class and a large, poor class of peasants or artisans. Jesus expressed a special interest in the impoverished throughout his ministry (Mt 11:5; Lk 4:18). Also, in the OT, God gave many of his promises specifically to the poor (1Sa 2:8; Ps 140:12; Isa 11:4). **to be rich in faith** James indicates that the poor are wealthy in terms of their salvation and its associated blessings, not in terms of material goods. From God's perspective, the impoverished are destined to possess the spiritual wealth that accompanies faith. **the kingdom** Refers to the full rule of God—a state of blessing in which God's will and reign are absolutely established. Being an heir of the kingdom means possessing eternal life (Mk 10:17–23; Lk 18:29–30) and salvation (Lk 18:18–26). See Mt 3:2 and note, as well as Mt 4:17 and note.

2:7 blaspheming the noble name James accuses the wealthy of insulting or slandering the name of Christ. See note on 2:6.

2:8 royal law James may use this term because he associates the law with the kingdom of God. See note on Jas 1:25. **Love your neighbor as yourself** James quotes Lev 19:18. Jesus cites this in Mt 22:39 as the second-greatest commandment (see Mt 7:12 and note).

2:10 is guilty of breaking all Reflects the belief that the OT law was to be kept in its entirety (Gal 5:3).

2:11 he who said Refers to God, who spoke these commands (Ex 20:13–14).

2:12 by the law that gives freedom See note on Jas 1:25.

2:13 to anyone who has not been merciful James might be drawing on ideas from Zec 7:9–10, where mercy is closely related to concern for the poor.

2:14 Can such faith save them James asserts that genuine faith affects the believer's behavior; faith that does not affect behavior is superficial and cannot save.

2:17 if it is not accompanied by action A living faith is expressed by deeds of Christian love (see note on Jas 2:8), such as looking after widows and orphans in their distress (1:27).

2:18 someone will say James now introduces a third person into the discussion to defend his position (for rhetorical purposes). **faith without deeds** James implies that faith cannot be demonstrated apart from action.

2:19 You believe that there is one God James continues to respond to the rhetorical opponent introduced in v. 18 (Dt 6:4; Mk 12:29; Ro 3:30). James may be referencing monotheism or Yahwism (belief in the superiority of Israel's God, Yahweh) here, but it seems more likely that his goal is to establish that God cannot disagree with himself. Thus, it's impossible to argue that God once wanted people to do good works and now wants them to do nothing. Instead, salvation is a gift—resulting in people no longer having to live by OT laws—and the natural output of believing in that salvation is doing good works, which is in line with God's ways. He is "one" in his mindset. **Even the demons believe that—and shudder** Demons expressed belief in the divine (Mk 1:24; 5:7; Ac 16:16–17). They also demonstrated fear before Christ (Mk 1:23,24; 5:7). Here, James emphasizes that acceptance of a creed is not enough to save a person.

2:20 foolish person The Greek term used here, *kenos*, refers to intellectual deficiency. In this context, it indicates a person who lacks understanding of spiritual truth.

2:21 our father See note on Jas 1:1. **when he offered his son Isaac on the altar** Abraham didn't actually sacrifice Isaac, but he bound and placed him on an altar in obedience to God's command. Thus, God found him faithful through his actions. See Ge 22:1–19.

2:23 it was credited to him as righteousness This phrase implies that the cooperation of Abraham's faith and deeds was acceptable in God's sight. **God's friend** See Isa 41:8.

2:24 considered righteous Here, the Greek term *dikaioō* means "to vindicate" or "to prove or demonstrate something to be true or just" (see Jas 2:21). Paul's use of

is considered righteous by what they do and not by faith alone.

²⁵In the same way, was not even Rahab the prostitute considered righteous for what she did when she gave lodging to the spies and sent them off in a different direction? ²⁶As the body without the spirit is dead, so faith without deeds is dead.

Taming the Tongue

3 Not many of you should become teachers, my fellow believers, because you know that we who teach will be judged more strictly. ²We all stumble in many ways. Anyone who is never at fault in what they say is perfect, able to keep their whole body in check.

³When we put bits into the mouths of horses to make them obey us, we can turn the whole animal. ⁴Or take ships as an example. Although they are so large and are driven by strong winds, they are steered by a very small rudder wherever the pilot wants to go. ⁵Likewise, the tongue is a small part of the body, but it makes great boasts. Consider what a great forest is set on fire by a small spark. ⁶The tongue also is a fire, a world of evil among the parts of the body. It corrupts the whole body, sets the whole course of one's life on fire, and is itself set on fire by hell.

⁷All kinds of animals, birds, reptiles and sea creatures are being tamed and have been tamed by mankind, ⁸but no human being can tame the tongue. It is a restless evil, full of deadly poison.

⁹With the tongue we praise our Lord and Father, and with it we curse human beings, who have been made in God's likeness. ¹⁰Out of the same mouth come praise and cursing. My brothers and sisters, this should not be. ¹¹Can both fresh water and salt water flow from the same spring? ¹²My brothers and sisters, can a fig tree bear olives, or a grapevine bear figs? Neither can a salt spring produce fresh water.

---

dikaioō in Ro 4 and Gal 2–3 has a different connotation (see note on Ro 4:2). There, he uses the term to speak of God's declaration of righteousness or innocence that a sinner achieves only through faith. The context there is being in front of God as judge, whereas the context here is how other people judge. **by what they do and not by faith alone** James is not saying that people must perform works in order for God to accept them. Rather, he is asserting that an individual's true conversion will be justified by deeds of Christian love; deeds are the proof of conversion to other people, and they are the natural result of being faithful to God. Deeds demonstrate the validity of a person's profession of faith. In the context of Romans and Galatians, "works" (*erga*) means being obedient to the Jewish law (Ro 3:20,28; Gal 2:16; 3:10–12). In the context of James, *erga* refers to showing one's faith through doing good deeds. Paul fights the idea that works are the way to be saved, arguing that no one can be saved by works, because all fall short. James is addressing the opposite problem: faith is being used as an excuse not to do any works (not to care for those on the underside of power). Paul also mentions this same problem, agreeing with James that salvation does not mean that Christians stop acting according to God's standards and doing good by others (Ro 6:15–23). The OT law is not the way Christians come to salvation—salvation comes through belief in God's faithfulness shown through Christ's death and resurrection—but it does help Christians understand how to best treat other people.

2:25 was not even Rahab the prostitute considered righteous See Jos 2:1–21 and Heb 11:31 and note.
3:1 Not many of you should become teachers James asserts that the judgment of teachers will be especially strict because greater responsibility rests on them: They teach God's word to others (Mt 12:36; 18:6). Unqualified teachers appears to have been a critical issue in the early church (1Jn 3:7; 2Pe 2:1; 1Ti 6:3; 2Ti 4:3).

3:2–12 These verses can be taken in three ways: as addressing topics related to teachers in the Christian community, as instruction generally applicable to all believers, or as instruction applicable to both groups in some sense. In these verses, James addresses issues related to the dangers of speech. Teachers were particularly vulnerable to errors of speech.

3:3–6 Here, James utilizes three images to illustrate that a small thing, like the tongue, can have far-reaching effects. He uses a horse's bit (Jas 3:3) and a ship's rudder (v. 4) to convey that those who have control over their tongues have control over themselves. He also uses the image of fire to convey that the tongue has great potential for destruction and harm (see note on v. 6).

3:5 it makes great boasts Some NT passages portray boasting positively as something to be encouraged (1Co 1:28–31), while others portray it negatively as something to be avoided (Jas 4:16).
3:6 tongue also is a fire The metaphor of fire would have resonated with James' first-century audience. Ancients relied on wood or charcoal braziers to cook and heat their homes, and the draft from open windows increased the danger of fire spreading rapidly. Furthermore, ancients possessed few effective means for extinguishing fires. James' writing style often reflects the Wisdom Literature of the OT, which also discussed the dangers of the tongue and speech (e.g., Pr 11:12–13; 15:1; 16:27–28). **world of evil** Could mean that the tongue is an example of the worldly evil opposed to God, or that the tongue, as a fire, exposes evil within a person (Mk 7:15). **It corrupts the whole body** Careless speech can render a person unclean before God. **itself set on fire by hell** See note on Jas 1:13.

3:9 In this verse, James describes the tongue as double-minded; see note on 1:8.

3:9 we curse human beings The Greek term here, *kataraomai*, often translated "to curse," refers to causing injury or harm to someone through a statement. Ancients believed such statements had supernatural power (Mk 11:12–14,21–22). **been made in God's likeness** Alludes to Ge 1:26–27. James asserts that it is logically inconsistent to curse humanity, the image-bearer, while blessing God, the one who is imaged.
3:11 fresh water and salt water A tongue that dishonors God is not compatible with speech that honors him.
3:12 can a fig tree It is against a tree's nature to produce two kinds of fruit. Similarly, a believer's mouth is not intended for both evil and good speech.

Two Kinds of Wisdom

[13]Who is wise and understanding among you? Let them show it by their good life, by deeds done in the humility that comes from wisdom. [14]But if you harbor bitter envy and selfish ambition in your hearts, do not boast about it or deny the truth. [15]Such "wisdom" does not come down from heaven but is earthly, unspiritual, demonic. [16]For where you have envy and selfish ambition, there you find disorder and every evil practice.

[17]But the wisdom that comes from heaven is first of all pure; then peace-loving, considerate, submissive, full of mercy and good fruit, impartial and sincere. [18]Peacemakers who sow in peace reap a harvest of righteousness.

Submit Yourselves to God

4 What causes fights and quarrels among you? Don't they come from your desires that battle within you? [2]You desire but do not have, so you kill. You covet but you cannot get what you want, so you quarrel and fight. You do not have because you do not ask God. [3]When you ask, you do not receive, because you ask with wrong motives, that you may spend what you get on your pleasures.

[4]You adulterous people,[a] don't you know that friendship with the world means enmity against God? Therefore, anyone who chooses to be a friend of the world becomes an enemy of God. [5]Or do you think Scripture says without reason that he jealously longs for the spirit he has caused to dwell in us[b]? [6]But he gives us more grace. That is why Scripture says:

"God opposes the proud
but shows favor to the humble."[c]

[7]Submit yourselves, then, to God. Resist the devil, and he will flee from you. [8]Come near to God and he will come near to you. Wash your hands, you sinners, and purify your hearts, you double-minded. [9]Grieve, mourn and wail. Change your laughter to mourning and your joy to gloom.

---

[a] 4 An allusion to covenant unfaithfulness; see Hosea 3:1.
[b] 5 Or that the spirit he caused to dwell in us envies intensely; or that the Spirit he caused to dwell in us longs jealously
[c] 6 Prov. 3:34

3:13—5:6 James turns from his pragmatic advice (Jas 1:19—3:2) to offer guidance on what Christian wisdom looks like in action.

3:13 wise and understanding The Septuagint, an ancient Greek translation of the OT, often employs this combination of words to describe a person who lives in accordance with the insight given by God (Dt 1:13,15; 4:6).
3:14 do not boast about it or deny the truth James likely is admonishing his audience to refrain from sinning against the truth by boasting of their wisdom.
3:15 earthly Refers to wisdom that is inferior to wisdom from God. **unspiritual** The Greek adjective *psychikos* refers to what is, by nature, human—things not inspired by the Holy Spirit. **demonic** Describes the ultimate origin of earthly wisdom (compare to Jas 3:6).
3:16 disorder and every evil practice James describes the evil consequences of false wisdom. Earthly wisdom leads to jealousy and selfish ambition, which can culminate in a troubling situation for Christian communities.
3:17 peace-loving, considerate, submissive In the Greek text, it is clear that James arranged this list of virtues using assonance, first with *e*, then with *a*: *eirēnikos, epieikēs, eupeithēs, eleos, karpos agathos, adiakritos, anypokritos*. Since ancients primarily learned through hearing, writers utilized sound to enhance the sense of the text and aid in memorization. Biblical writers composed lists of virtues and vices to inspire changes in behavior (e.g., Ps 15; Pr 6:17–19; Hos 4:1–2; 1Co 6:9–10; Gal 5:19–24; Eph 5:3–5).
3:18 Peacemakers True peace is found only in the character of God (Isa 9:6; 2Jn 3; 1Th 5:23; Php 4:7,9). **a harvest of righteousness** Righteousness and peace appear together often in the Bible (e.g., Ps 72:7; 85:10; Isa 32:17; Heb 12:11). This statement could have the sense of "fruit growing out of righteousness." Alternatively, it could be intended as a phrase defining the fruit, thus "fruit that consists of righteousness."
4:1 among you Refers to conflicts among church members.
4:2 so you kill James may be referring metaphorically to extreme anger or hatred (Mt 5:21–22; 1Jn 3:15). The Greek term used here could reflect a person's tendency toward anger; such a person is on the verge of murder. **You covet** Unsatisfied envy leads to fighting and quarreling.
4:4 You adulterous people Biblical writers often expressed Israel's unfaithfulness to God in terms of adultery (e.g., Hos 1:2; 9:1). In Pr 30:20, the adulterous woman feels no remorse for her unfaithfulness. James might have wanted to characterize his audience in this manner. In addition to being unfaithful to God, they were unwilling to acknowledge any wrongdoing.
4:5 spirit he has caused to dwell This statement is not found in the OT, suggesting that James could be summarizing several OT passages (compare Mt 2:23; Jn 7:38; Eph 5:14). This reference to a spirit could be pointing to the human spirit that God placed in humanity at creation (Ge 2:7). If so, the passage would indicate that God longs jealously for the loyalty and devotion of the human spirit. Alternatively, the passage could be referring to a human spirit that is prone to jealousy and sinful desires—the spirit representing the evil impulse in a person (Ge 6:5; 8:21) that leads to the conflicts discussed in Jas 4:1–2. However, this interpretation portrays the dwelling of the evil spirit to be an act of God. Another possibility is that James is describing the Holy Spirit; this interpretation is unlikely, however, as it would be the only reference to the Holy Spirit in the entire letter.
4:6 he gives us more grace God's grace is greater than the human inclination to sin. **God opposes the proud** James quotes Pr 3:34, highlighting God's opposition toward the proud who disregard him and despise others.
4:8 Come near to God Because the church was fractured and needed healing, James calls the community to collectively approach God. Here, James draws on OT language of sacrifice (Lev 10:3; 21:21–23), as the Septuagint (the ancient Greek OT) uses the term *engizō* ("to draw near") to describe the priest offering sacrifices in the temple. **Wash your hands** The Greek term used here, *cheir*, figuratively represents a person's deeds (compare Ps 24:4; Isa 1:15–16). The command to cleanse them indicates that they were defiled with sin and required purification (2Co 7:1). **double-minded** See note on Jas 1:8.
4:9 Grieve, mourn and wail James encourages Christians to embrace an attitude of humility and repentance.

¹⁰Humble yourselves before the Lord, and he will lift you up.

¹¹Brothers and sisters, do not slander one another. Anyone who speaks against a brother or sister[a] or judges them speaks against the law and judges it. When you judge the law, you are not keeping it, but sitting in judgment on it. ¹²There is only one Lawgiver and Judge, the one who is able to save and destroy. But you—who are you to judge your neighbor?

Boasting About Tomorrow

¹³Now listen, you who say, "Today or tomorrow we will go to this or that city, spend a year there, carry on business and make money." ¹⁴Why, you do not even know what will happen tomorrow. What is your life? You are a mist that appears for a little while and then vanishes. ¹⁵Instead, you ought to say, "If it is the Lord's will, we will live and do this or that." ¹⁶As it is, you boast in your arrogant schemes. All such boasting is evil. ¹⁷If anyone, then, knows the good they ought to do and doesn't do it, it is sin for them.

Warning to Rich Oppressors

5 Now listen, you rich people, weep and wail because of the misery that is coming on you. ²Your wealth has rotted, and moths have eaten your clothes. ³Your gold and silver are corroded. Their corrosion will testify against you and eat your flesh like fire. You have hoarded wealth in the last days. ⁴Look! The wages you failed to pay the workers who mowed your fields are crying out against you. The cries of the harvesters have reached the ears of the Lord Almighty. ⁵You have lived on earth in luxury and self-indulgence. You have fattened yourselves in the day of slaughter.[b] ⁶You have condemned and murdered the innocent one, who was not opposing you.

Patience in Suffering

⁷Be patient, then, brothers and sisters, until the Lord's coming. See how the farmer waits for the land to yield its valuable crop, patiently waiting for the autumn and spring rains. ⁸You too, be patient and stand firm, because the Lord's coming is near. ⁹Don't grumble against one another, brothers and sisters, or you will be judged. The Judge is standing at the door!

¹⁰Brothers and sisters, as an example of patience in the face of suffering, take the prophets who spoke in the name of the Lord. ¹¹As you know, we count as blessed those who have persevered. You have heard of Job's perseverance and have

---

[a] 11 The Greek word for *brother or sister* (*adelphos*) refers here to a believer, whether man or woman, as part of God's family.
[b] 5 Or *yourselves as in a day of feasting*

---

your laughter The OT often associates laughter with a person who has no fear of God (Pr 29:9; Ecc 7:6).

4:11 who speaks against a brother or sister or judges them The law requires that people love their brothers and sisters in Christ. To speak evil against them violates the kingdom command to love (see note on Jas 2:8).

4:12 who are you to judge your neighbor Those who judge others adopt a role that belongs to God alone (Ge 18:25; Ps 82:1,8; Ro 3:6; Heb 12:23).

4:13 Now listen The Greek phrase used here aims to gain the audience's attention heading into a serious discussion.

4:14 what will happen tomorrow James condemns rich business owners for their arrogant self-confidence; he accuses them of acting as though they alone determine the course of their lives, apart from God (Pr 27:1; Lk 12:16–20).

5:1 you rich people It is unclear whether these rich people are inside or outside the church. Only those inside the congregation would have had an opportunity to hear James' message. However, unlike in other passages, James does not call the rich to repent or refer to them as "brothers" (e.g., Jas 1:2,16,19; 2:1,5,14), possibly implying that he is addressing outsiders. **wail** The Septuagint (the Greek OT) employs this terminology to describe the reaction of the wicked to divine judgment (Isa 13:6; Eze 21:12; Am 8:3).

5:3 eat your flesh like fire The Bible often uses consuming fire to illustrate the judgment of God (e.g., Isa 10:16–17; 30:27; Jer 5:14; Mt 13:42; Mk 9:47–48). **You have hoarded wealth** This phrase may mean that the rich have stored up treasures in the form of God's wrath (Ro 2:5). James also could be asserting that the wealth of the rich is worthless; the rich should instead accumulate treasure in heaven (Mt 6:20).

5:4 wages you failed to pay the workers The law forbade Israelites from withholding wages from workers (Lev 19:13; Dt 24:15; Mal 3:5). **crying out** Possibly an allusion to Abel's blood crying out to God for justice (Ge 4:10) or to the Israelites groaning under Egyptian oppression (Ex 2:23)—both of which were protests voiced against injustice. James' comparison of the oppression of the poor to these former incidents highlights the severity of the offense and conveys God's care for the exploited. **Lord Almighty** Literally "Lord of armies"; conveys an image of God as a commander of a great army of angels going to war against the rich oppressors.

5:5 You have fattened yourselves James describes the rich oppressors as animals. In the OT, the time of God's judgment was spoken of as a day of slaughter (Isa 34:6; Eze 21:15).

5:6 You have condemned The rich may have been taking the poor to court, where they were being declared guilty and possibly condemned to death even though they were innocent. **murdered** An employer who withheld a person's wages, resulting in their starvation, may actually have been guilty of murder. See note on 5:4.

5:7–20 After offering his thoughts on practicing the virtues of wisdom (Jas 3:13—5:6), James turns to instructions about how to endure suffering, develop a reliance on God, and work with another.

5:7 until the Lord's coming Anticipates an end to all exploitation and suffering (Lk 4:16–21; Rev 21:1–4).

5:8 the Lord's coming is near First-century believers

seen what the Lord finally brought about. The Lord is full of compassion and mercy.

¹²Above all, my brothers and sisters, do not swear — not by heaven or by earth or by anything else. All you need to say is a simple "Yes" or "No." Otherwise you will be condemned.

The Prayer of Faith

¹³Is anyone among you in trouble? Let them pray. Is anyone happy? Let them sing songs of praise. ¹⁴Is anyone among you sick? Let them call the elders of the church to pray over them and anoint them with oil in the name of the Lord. ¹⁵And the prayer offered in faith will make the sick person well; the Lord will raise them up. If they have sinned, they will be forgiven. ¹⁶Therefore confess your sins to each other and pray for each other so that you may be healed. The prayer of a righteous person is powerful and effective.

¹⁷Elijah was a human being, even as we are. He prayed earnestly that it would not rain, and it did not rain on the land for three and a half years. ¹⁸Again he prayed, and the heavens gave rain, and the earth produced its crops.

¹⁹My brothers and sisters, if one of you should wander from the truth and someone should bring that person back, ²⁰remember this: Whoever turns a sinner from the error of their way will save them from death and cover over a multitude of sins.

---

expected Christ to return in their lifetime (Lk 21:28; Ro 13:11–12).

5:11 what the Lord finally brought about God eventually restored Job's family and fortune (Job 42:10–17).

5:12 swear The law required a person to be true to an oath they had taken (Lev 19:12).

5:14 Let them call the elders of the church By visiting sick individuals, the elders reestablish the person's fellowship with the community of faith. Elders made visits as representatives of the whole assembly. Their role involved nurturing life with God in the covenant community (1Th 2:11–12). The individual who called on an elder followed the authority structure within the body. **anoint them with oil** The exact nature and role of the anointing is debated. It may have been symbolic of God's special focus and consecration; all healing is of God. Oil seems to have been used medicinally as an ointment for injury and not sickness. For example, ancients used oil for bruises, welts and raw wounds (Isa 1:6); the good Samaritan in Jesus' parable used oil on the injuries of the injured person (Lk 10:34); ancients applied oil to their sheep's scratches and bruises (Ps 23:5). **in the name of the Lord** This phrase indicates that the elders were acting as representatives of God and calling on his power (compare Ac 2:38; 1Co 1:15;

5:4; 2Th 3:6; Jas 2:7). It serves as a powerful corporate confession of Christ as the one who is sovereign over disease and over the church.

5:15 the Lord will raise them up It is unclear whether James asserts that the Lord will raise the sick person to health during his earthy life, or raise the person to life in the age to come. **they will be forgiven** James acknowledges that there are occasions when illness is tied to sin. He informs the congregation that the sick will experience spiritual restoration because of the plea, if sin is involved in the sickness. While people suffer as a result of Adam's sin (Ro 5:19), the Bible sometimes directly correlates a person's suffering with sin. Texts such as Jn 5:14 and 1Co 11:29–30 reflect this idea.

5:16 confess your sins to each other While James instructs his audience to confess their sins to each other, few NT texts attest to a standard practice of public confession. James probably is referring to the act of confessing to the offended party, which would fit with the letter's emphasis on fellowship in the congregation (see Mt 5:23–24). **so that you may be healed** This could refer to physical healing or the restoration of the congregation's spiritual health. **a righteous person** Refers to a person who is committed to doing the will of God and to cultivating right relationship with him.

TRUE DISCIPLESHIP
by Charles Stanley

There are some people who have trusted in Jesus Christ as their Savior but do little to act on their belief (Jas 1:27; 2:14–26). Others actively follow Christ: They live as true disciples, passionately pursuing the Lord's will in all things. These are the ones who take their relationship with Christ seriously.

Ask yourself: Are you merely a believer or actually a follower of Jesus? Trusting in Jesus Christ is fundamental, but it's only the first step. Your primary purpose is to take a lifelong journey following in the Lord's footsteps—honoring him with your actions and speech and increasing in Biblical wisdom.

A Christ follower's life is summed up in the phrase, "Complete obedience." In fact, Jesus defined true Christians as those who prove their love for him by obeying his teaching (Jn 14:23). When it comes to obeying God, our only response is I will or I won't. It's tempting to say, "I will, but ..." as some of Jesus' would-be disciples did, but that's a roundabout way of saying no (Lk 9:57–62). Followers remain faithful to the Lord's plan whether doing so is easy or hard. Not only that, but they proclaim him in both blessing and calamity, and they follow him even when they are uncertain where he is leading.

Followers pursue the Lord because they know that the reward is a deeper, more passionate relationship with him. They are not just waiting to spend eternity with God in heaven; eternity begins now, as they accompany him on the righteous path he has set before them.

Matthew 22:14 says, "For many are invited, but few are chosen." The call has gone out, and it is still going out. Whatever your background, you are being called to Christ—away from sin, to him. Some take the call seriously. They are the ones who take the time to hear from God. They are the ones who actually do something. The call has gone out, and some will allow following Jesus Christ to shape their entire lives.

Jesus made it clear that being called as one of his disciples has a price. He said, "Whoever wants to be my disciple must deny themselves and take up their cross daily and follow me" (Lk 9:23). To the original disciples, crosses represented torture, physical abuse and death. Jesus' reference to "take up the cross" must have sent waves of fear through the ordinary people whom Jesus had called into extraordinary lives.

The conversation that followed could have gone something like this: "First you asked me to leave my business and my family to follow and learn from you, and now you're telling me that you're going to die and that I have to deny myself and follow in your steps! Don't you think that's asking a bit much?"

But Jesus responds: "Whoever finds their life will lose it, and whoever loses their life for my sake will find it" (Mt 10:39). It was only as his disciples acted on Christ's call that the true significance of his words became a reality for them. In time, confusion would disappear, and they would experience the exhilaration of giving their lives totally for the cause of Christ.

So, the question remains: Are you a believer in Christ or are you follower? Remember, being called to Christ means being called away from sin. That requires repentance. Realize you have sinned—repent and place your faith and trust in Jesus Christ. Then study God's Word and be obedient to it. Listen for God's direction in his Word and do it. Expect exciting days ahead as you live your calling.

(This article was adapted in part from Charles Stanley's article, "Understanding Your Call," originally published by In Touch Ministries.)

1 PETER

INTRODUCTION TO 1 PETER

First Peter is about maintaining hope in the midst of suffering. Because Jesus himself suffered, and because God can be trusted to put all things right, Peter counsels believers to maintain their faith in Jesus. Believers should do so even when they are being persecuted, mocked and misunderstood; they should also imitate Jesus by enduring unjust suffering with grace. Hardships are bound to come in this life, but they do not have the last word.

BACKGROUND

The author of 1 Peter identifies himself as the apostle Peter and a witness of the sufferings and resurrection of Christ (1Pe 1:1; 5:1). The early church widely accepted this view. However, there is some modern discussion about whether the letter's content reflects a later period; this would indicate that one of Peter's associates compiled the letter based on his teachings.

The recipients of 1 Peter are identified as God's people scattered throughout Pontus, Galatia, Cappadocia, Asia and Bithynia (1:1)—all regions of Asia Minor (modern-day Turkey). The letter seems to have been written to encourage Christians in these regions as they faced localized ostracism and persecution in reaction to their distinctively Christian perspective on social relationships and ethics.

The letter probably was written from Rome. First Peter 5:13 conveys a greeting from Babylon—a metaphorical reference to the capital city of the Roman Empire (see Rev 17:5,9). If Peter was the author, the letter must have been written sometime before the mid–60s AD. According to tradition, Peter was martyred in Rome around that time, during the persecution of Christians under the emperor Nero.

Peter addresses his letter to Christian communities in Pontus, Galatia, Cappadocia, Asia and Bithynia. "Babylon" in 1 Peter 5:13 is a reference to Rome.

STRUCTURE

Like other ancient letters, 1 Peter includes a formal greeting (1Pe 1:1–2) and closing (5:12–14) that frame the main message. Immediately after the greeting, Peter thanks God for the salvation and hope that he has provided (1:3–12). Peter then urges readers to be holy in everything they do (1:13—2:10).

The next section gives practical advice about living as Christians, particularly when it comes to navigating authority (2:11—3:12). Peter also addresses the hardships of his readers, saying that they are to follow Christ's example in endurance of suffering (3:13—4:19). The main part of the letter concludes by encouraging believers' conduct to model humble obedience to Christ (5:1–11). This is followed by some closing remarks.

OUTLINE

- Salutation and thanksgiving (1:1–12)
- Exhortation to holiness (1:13—2:10)
- Living as Christians in the world (2:11—3:12)
- Living with persecution (3:13—4:19)
- Appeal to elders and final greetings (5:1–14)

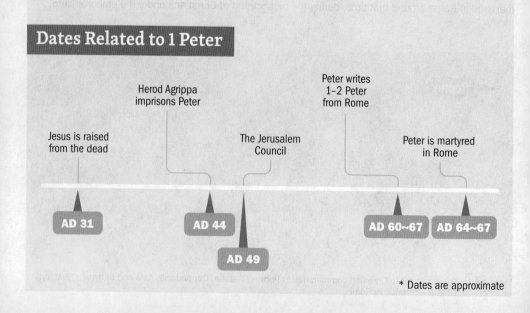

Dates Related to 1 Peter

Jesus is raised from the dead
AD 31

Herod Agrippa imprisons Peter
AD 44

The Jerusalem Council
AD 49

Peter writes 1–2 Peter from Rome
AD 60~67

Peter is martyred in Rome
AD 64~67

* Dates are approximate

THEMES

The thanksgiving section of 1 Peter (1:3–12) sets a tone of encouragement that runs throughout the letter. The readers are meant to see their difficult circumstances through a lens of hope, looking to Christ for strength. Peter knows that those who choose to follow Christ are no longer completely at home in this world. They are foreigners—not yet out of this world, but not fully part of it any longer (2:11). They are set apart as God's holy priesthood, part of the temple that has been built on Christ the cornerstone (2:4–5). As such, they should not be surprised if the world does not understand them—or in some circumstances even persecutes them.

But Peter's solution is not for Christians to remove themselves from the world. Instead, they are to follow Jesus' example by enduring persecution without protesting (2:19–21). Not only that, but the patient endurance of opposition and mocking might cause the persecutors to see Christian faith in a new light (2:12,15). The believers are to show faithfulness and courage by remaining within the world that doesn't understand them, not by seeking to resolve that tension by running away.

Christians can place their faith in God, who will restore them in the end (5:10). Just as Jesus suffered and then triumphed, so Christians are to persevere, knowing that they have a living hope that will be made visible when Jesus returns (1:3–7). Followers of Jesus should expect to feel like strangers on this earth—and precisely within their hostile environment, they are called to embrace every opportunity to speak and act in honor of Christ, the one who, by his suffering, reconciled all people to God.

1

Peter, an apostle of Jesus Christ,

To God's elect, exiles scattered throughout the provinces of Pontus, Galatia, Cappadocia, Asia and Bithynia, ²who have been chosen according to the foreknowledge of God the Father, through the sanctifying work of the Spirit, to be obedient to Jesus Christ and sprinkled with his blood:

Grace and peace be yours in abundance.

Praise to God for a Living Hope

³Praise be to the God and Father of our Lord Jesus Christ! In his great mercy he has given us new birth into a living hope through the resurrection of Jesus Christ from the dead, ⁴and into an inheritance that can never perish, spoil or fade. This inheritance is kept in heaven for you, ⁵who through faith are shielded by God's power until the coming of the salvation that is ready to be revealed in the last time. ⁶In all this you greatly rejoice, though now for a little while you may have had to suffer grief in all kinds of trials. ⁷These have come so that the proven genuineness of your faith — of greater worth than gold, which perishes even though refined by fire — may result in praise, glory and honor when Jesus Christ is revealed. ⁸Though you have not seen him, you love him; and

---

1:1–2 Peter's first letter follows the conventions of ancient letter writing. He begins with a greeting (1Pe 1:1–2) followed by thanksgiving (1:3–12). He then proceeds into the body of the letter, in which he discusses his main points (1:13–5:11). The letter concludes with a benediction (5:12–14). In the greeting, Peter identifies himself as the author. He also identifies the letter's authoritative status, its recipients, and the common bond that unites author and audience — the new covenant ratified by Jesus' shed blood.

The audience of 1 Peter is difficult to determine with precision and depends on the question of authorship. If Peter — the disciple of Jesus and early church leader — wrote the letter, then it probably dates to the period prior to Peter's death in the mid-60s AD. In this case, the letter addresses localized social pressure experienced by Peter's audience. However, if one of Peter's coworkers or disciples compiled the letter after his death based on his teachings, then it was probably written sometime before the 90s AD when persecution intensified under Emperor Domitian. Either way, the letter addresses the turbulent social environment believers faced while living among hostile nonbelievers.

1:1 Peter One of the disciples Jesus called, which made him an apostle (Mt 4:18–22). **To God's elect** In the Hebrew Bible, the nation of Israel is designated as God's chosen or elect people (see Dt 4:37; Isa 45:4). In the NT, this term is expanded to include the church, which consists of both Jews and Gentiles. **scattered throughout** The Greek term *diaspora* — used in the ancient Greek OT called the Septuagint — originally described Jews or Jewish communities scattered throughout the world outside of Israel (see Isa 49:6; Ps 147:2; Jn 7:35 and note). Here it is used figuratively to describe the Christian sojourn in this age before arriving in the coming age. Believers temporarily reside as exiles outside their true homeland, which is in heaven where their Lord reigns (see 1Pe 1:4; 3:22). Peter may also be describing the experience of Christians who were expelled from Rome and forced to resettle in other places in the world (see 2:11).

PETER
Peter denied Jesus three times during Jesus' trial, but after Jesus' resurrection, Jesus confirmed Peter's love for him three times, calling Peter to care for Jesus' people even to the point of Peter's death

(Jn 18:15–18,25–27; 21:15–19). Following Christ's ascension, Peter became a key figure in the early church and a missionary (see Gal 2:9 and note; Acts 2; 10–11). Both the Gospels and church tradition identify Simon Peter as a leader of the twelve disciples (see Mt 14:28 and note; Mt 15:15 and note; Mt 16:16 and note; and note on Mt 16:13–20).

1:2 the foreknowledge Conceptually related to those chosen by God in v. 1; this term refers to God's selection of his people, for a relationship with him. **to Jesus Christ and sprinkled with his blood** Refers to Christ's sacrificial and atoning work on the cross. In the OT God made a covenant with his people by instructing Moses to throw the blood of a sacrificial animal on them (see Ex 24:3–8). In a similar manner, Peter considers Christ's blood as the means of establishing a new covenant with God's redeemed people (see 1Pe 1:19 and note; compare Isa 52:15 and note).

1:3–12 Here, Peter expresses gratitude to God for his salvation through the person and work of God's Son, Jesus.

1:3 given us new birth Refers to the believer's new life that is only possible because of the death and resurrection of Christ. First Peter's use of new-birth language to describe salvation reflects Jesus' teaching (1Pe 1:23; 2:2; see Jn 3:3,7). **through the resurrection of Jesus Christ** This rebirth is accomplished by Jesus' resurrection from the dead and serves as the Christian reason for hope: certainty of future salvation. Once dead in their sins, Christians now live with assured hope of their own resurrection.

1:5 salvation Refers to God's deliverance of his people from physical and spiritual captivity. **ready to be revealed in the last time** For Peter, salvation is both a present reality experienced through the believer's new birth in Christ and a promise of final deliverance in the future.

1:6 for a little while Although Christians will receive their inheritance with joy when Christ is revealed (1Pe 1:7), they may face suffering and trials during the relatively brief present time. **in all kinds of trials** Peter exhorts the churches in Asia Minor to stand firm in the midst of persecution, which likely includes state-sponsored reprisals for refusing to pay tribute to Caesar as well as general persecution against Christians, who were viewed as a maligned offshoot of Judaism.

1:7 even though refined by fire Possibly refers to imperial persecution under the reign of Nero, but most likely describes the role trials play in the growth of Chris-

even though you do not see him now, you believe in him and are filled with an inexpressible and glorious joy, [9]for you are receiving the end result of your faith, the salvation of your souls.

[10]Concerning this salvation, the prophets, who spoke of the grace that was to come to you, searched intently and with the greatest care, [11]trying to find out the time and circumstances to which the Spirit of Christ in them was pointing when he predicted the sufferings of the Messiah and the glories that would follow. [12]It was revealed to them that they were not serving themselves but you, when they spoke of the things that have now been told you by those who have preached the gospel to you by the Holy Spirit sent from heaven. Even angels long to look into these things.

Be Holy

[13]Therefore, with minds that are alert and fully sober, set your hope on the grace to be brought to you when Jesus Christ is revealed at his coming. [14]As obedient children, do not conform to the evil desires you had when you lived in ignorance. [15]But just as he who called you is holy, so be holy in all you do; [16]for it is written: "Be holy, because I am holy."[a]

[17]Since you call on a Father who judges each person's work impartially, live out your time as foreigners here in reverent fear. [18]For you know that it was not with perishable things such as silver or gold that you were redeemed from the empty way of life handed down to you from your ancestors, [19]but with the precious blood of Christ, a lamb without blemish or defect. [20]He was chosen before the creation of the world, but was revealed in these last times for your sake. [21]Through him you believe in God, who raised him from the dead and glorified him, and so your faith and hope are in God.

[22]Now that you have purified yourselves by obeying the truth so that you have sincere love for each other, love one another deeply, from the heart.[b] [23]For you have been born again, not of perishable seed, but of imperishable, through the living and enduring word of God. [24]For,

"All people are like grass,
  and all their glory is like the flowers
    of the field;
the grass withers and the flowers fall,
25 but the word of the Lord endures forever."[c]

---

[a] 16 Lev. 11:44,45; 19:2   [b] 22 Some early manuscripts *from a pure heart*   [c] 25 Isaiah 40:6-8 (see Septuagint)

---

tian faith. **Jesus Christ is revealed** Refers to Jesus' second coming.

1:10–12 In this section, Peter suggests that the OT prophets received revelation from the Spirit about the Messiah, but they did not fully comprehend it. They researched who the Messiah would be and when he would arrive, but they were told that the prophecies were for a future time and people.

1:11 Spirit of Christ Refers to the Holy Spirit, although this designation is uncommon in the NT (see Ro 8:9; Php 1:19). Peter stresses the continuity of the Spirit's role in revealing God's plan: The same Spirit of Christ that spoke to the prophets about Christ helped reveal the gospel to believers (1Pe 1:12).

1:12 angels long to look into these things Peter seems to indicate that angels are curious about matters of grace (v. 10) and the gospel. This claim highlights the privilege of Christians who have matters of salvation revealed to them. Jewish tradition often depicted angelic beings as interested in human affairs (see Lk 15:10).

1:13–25 Peter encourages his audience to live holy, God-honoring lives in light of the dawning of the last time (see 1Pe 1:5 and note) and the salvation attained by Christ. This section marks the transition from the letter's introduction to the main body of 1 Peter.

1:14 to the evil desires you had Likely refers to the unethical behavior of Christians before their conversion. Due to its emphasis on separation from previous behavior, the phrase may indicate that Peter wrote the letter to churches composed primarily of Gentile believers who did not abide by the Jewish law (see v. 18; 2:9–10; 4:3–4).

1:16 Be holy, because I am holy Holiness can refer to being blameless and without sin, but it also describes a person set apart for service to God. Here Peter cites the Septuagint version of Lev 19:2 to exhort Christians

to lead holy lives. However, for Peter true holiness does not consist of keeping the law, but instead obeying the Father (1Pe 1:17).

1:17 live out your time as foreigners here in reverent fear Peter commands Christians to fear God, not those who persecute them (see 2:23). **your time as foreigners** See 1:1 and note.

1:19 precious blood of Christ Refers to the sacrifice of Christ on the cross (see v. 2 and note). **a lamb without blemish or defect** This may refer to a lamb qualified for sacrifice. Here Peter likens Christ's sacrifice to that of a lamb offered according to the OT sacrificial system (see Lev 22:21; 23:12; Ex 12:5; Nu 6:14) or, more likely, the Passover lamb in the exodus narrative. In the NT, Christ is depicted as the perfect Passover lamb whose sacrifice redeems believers from the slavery of sin (see Jn 1:29,36; 1Co 5:7 and note; compare Heb 9:14; Isa 53:10 and note).

1:20 before the creation of the world God's redemption of sinners through the precious blood of his Son was always part of the divine plan of salvation (compare Jn 1:1 and note).

1:22 you have purified yourselves The soul of a Christian is purified through acceptance of God's truth, as manifest in Jesus, and rejecting their former way of life (see 1Pe 1:18).

1:23 not of perishable seed, but of imperishable Contrasts temporary earthly life with eternal life. The new birth is completely distinct from human birth and life; it involves supernatural birth and is secure because God handles the process.

1:24–25 In these two verses, Peter quotes Isa 40:6–8 to contrast the assured and lasting nature of God's message of redemption with the temporary suffering of his people.

1:25 word that was preached to you The Greek word

And this is the word that was preached to you.

2 Therefore, rid yourselves of all malice and all deceit, hypocrisy, envy, and slander of every kind. [2]Like newborn babies, crave pure spiritual milk, so that by it you may grow up in your salvation, [3]now that you have tasted that the Lord is good.

The Living Stone and a Chosen People

[4]As you come to him, the living Stone — rejected by humans but chosen by God and precious to him — [5]you also, like living stones, are being built into a spiritual house[a] to be a holy priesthood, offering spiritual sacrifices acceptable to God through Jesus Christ. [6]For in Scripture it says:

"See, I lay a stone in Zion,
    a chosen and precious cornerstone,
and the one who trusts in him
    will never be put to shame."[b]

[7]Now to you who believe, this stone is precious. But to those who do not believe,

"The stone the builders rejected
    has become the cornerstone,"[c]

[8]and,

"A stone that causes people to stumble
    and a rock that makes them fall."[d]

They stumble because they disobey the message — which is also what they were destined for.

[9]But you are a chosen people, a royal priesthood, a holy nation, God's special possession, that you may declare the praises of him who called you out of darkness into his wonderful light. [10]Once you were not a people, but now you are the people of God; once you had not received mercy, but now you have received mercy.

Living Godly Lives in a Pagan Society

[11]Dear friends, I urge you, as foreigners and exiles, to abstain from sinful desires, which wage

---

a 5 Or *into a temple of the Spirit*   *b 6* Isaiah 28:16   *c 7* Psalm 118:22   *d 8* Isaiah 8:14

---

used here, *euangelizō*, describes the proclamation of good news and often references the gospel in the NT. Peter may have equated the word of the Lord from Isa 40:8 with the gospel (compare Lk 4:16–30).

2:1–12 Using many OT quotations and allusions, Peter continues to encourage his readers in their Christian conduct. Christians should respond to God's saving act in Jesus with behavior that honors him—they should act like they are indeed his people and representatives.

2:1 rid yourselves of all malice New Testament writers often utilize lists of vices to denounce certain types of behavior and activities (e.g., Mt 15:19; Ro 1:29–31; 1Co 6:9–10; Gal 5:19–21).

2:2 Like newborn babies Peter's point here does not concern new believers, but all believers as they mature in Christ. Peter urges believers to desire and depend on Christ as a newborn needs and thirsts for milk. **pure spiritual milk** May refer to the Scriptures (or the Word of God) as the source of Christian growth (see 1Pe 1:24–25); this may also refer to Christ as the "milk" that Christians drink to mature in the faith (see 2:3). By drinking this milk, which Peter describes literally as "unadulterated" or "pure" (*adolos*), Christians learn to follow Christ's example and put away their former sins such as malice and deceit (*dolos*; compare v. 22; 3:10).

2:3 you have tasted that the Lord is good Here Peter draws on Ps 34:8 and its surrounding context to encourage Christians to set aside the immoral behavior of their former lives (see Ps 34:13–14) and instead to place their hope in God (see Ps 34:9–10).

2:4 living Stone—rejected by humans The reference to the Lord in 1Pe 1:3 prompts Peter to discuss the relationship between Christ and the people of God. He draws on two OT passages to emphasize Christ's worth in God's eyes despite the world's rejection of him (Ps 118:22; Isa 28:16; compare Mt 21:42; Ac 4:11).

2:5 living stones Describes the status of Christians in relation to Christ, the cornerstone of the temple in this metaphor (compare Mt 21:42–44; 1Co 3:10–15). Believers function as building blocks in the spiritual house

of God (the temple); they do this by virtue of their new life in Christ (see 1Pe 1:3). **a holy priesthood** Peter explains the transfer of priesthood language from Israel to the church in a later verse (see v. 9 and note). Here Peter reminds his audience of the priesthood's ultimate purpose: to offer God praise and thanksgiving.

2:6 I lay a stone in Zion Here Peter cites Isa 28:16, to which he alluded in 1Pe 2:4, to emphasize the precious nature of Christ as the cornerstone of the spiritual temple.

2:7 cornerstone Peter cites in full Ps 118:22, which he already alluded to in 1Pe 2:4 (compare Mt 21:42).

2:8 A stone that causes people to stumble and a rock that makes them fall Here Peter cites Isa 8:14–15 to offer an explanation for the world's rejection of Christ. **they were destined** The Greek word used here, *tithēmi*, is also used in 1Pe 2:6, and thus may be literally rendered as "set," as in the setting of the stone in v. 6. This reveals that Peter's point is not that some people are preordained to destruction, but that some will stumble over the "cornerstone," Jesus. The cornerstone is set firmly in place, so for those who do not acknowledge it, it is a stumbling block and thus offensive—it is viewed as being in the way of their perceived path. Peter is not saying that people are destined to disobey; rather, people are destined to stumble since the gospel message is hard to accept and live by, as it requires complete self-sacrifice.

2:9 a royal priesthood, a holy nation Describes the people of God—those who place their trust in Christ—using language formerly used of Israel. In the OT, beginning with the exodus narrative, the people of Israel are often described as a nation chosen by God to serve as a priesthood (see Ex 19:5–6; Dt 4:20; 7:6; 14:2; Isa 43:20–21). This language is now applied to believers in Jesus since they are connected to the cornerstone, Christ, and belong to the chosen people of God (1Pe 2:9–10). As a royal priesthood, all believers are set apart as ministers of the new covenant to the world. Thus, Peter reminds his audience that their time living in exile serves as an opportunity to mediate God's blessing to the foreigners around them (see 1:1 and note). **you**

war against your soul. [12]Live such good lives among the pagans that, though they accuse you of doing wrong, they may see your good deeds and glorify God on the day he visits us.

[13]Submit yourselves for the Lord's sake to every human authority: whether to the emperor, as the supreme authority, [14]or to governors, who are sent by him to punish those who do wrong and to commend those who do right. [15]For it is God's will that by doing good you should silence the ignorant talk of foolish people. [16]Live as free people, but do not use your freedom as a cover-up for evil; live as God's slaves. [17]Show proper respect to everyone, love the family of believers, fear God, honor the emperor.

[18]Slaves, in reverent fear of God submit yourselves to your masters, not only to those who are good and considerate, but also to those who are harsh. [19]For it is commendable if someone bears up under the pain of unjust suffering because they are conscious of God. [20]But how is it to your credit if you receive a beating for doing wrong and endure it? But if you suffer for doing good and you endure it, this is commendable before God. [21]To this you were called, because Christ suffered for you, leaving you an example, that you should follow in his steps.

[22]"He committed no sin,
and no deceit was found in his mouth."[a]

[23]When they hurled their insults at him, he did not retaliate; when he suffered, he made no threats. Instead, he entrusted himself to him who judges

[a] 22 Isaiah 53:9

---

may declare the praises Christians are not only called to bless the world, but to make known the mighty acts of God they have witnessed (compare Ge 12:1–3). Here Peter probably has in mind the resurrection of Christ and the conversion of the believers to whom he writes (compare Ac 2:22–24). Peter is likely drawing on the language and imagery of Isa 43:21.

2:10 but now you are the people of God Peter appeals to the prophet Hosea to remind Christians that their new status as the people of God depends solely on his mercy and divine election (Hos 1:9–10; 2:23; compare Ro 9:25–26).

2:11 foreigners and exiles Believers, as those who have received eternal life, temporarily live in this world until either their death or Jesus' return. Thus, for a believer, life in this world is equivalent to how a foreigner or refugee feels. This parallels how the Greek text of Jn 1:14 describes God's Son taking on flesh (see note on Jn 1:14).

2:12 Live such good lives among the pagans Peter encourages his readers to maintain good conduct so that they can positively testify to others—in this case, the Gentiles—of God's grace. **the day he visits** A common metaphor for God's final judgment.

2:13–25 In this section, Peter appeals to Christ's submission to proper authorities (both God the Father and human institutions) to encourage his readers to do the same. By submitting to authority, they will maintain an honorable reputation, which will keep them from being a hindrance to people coming to Jesus (1Pe 2:12). Peter is not suggesting that they acquiesce to the injustice of a ruler or nation, but instead, when it does not compromise faith or the principles of Jesus, to obey a country's laws and its leaders. This is passive resistance, akin to Jesus' actions while on trial (Mt 26:57–68; Jn 19:1–16; compare Isa 53:7).

2:13 for the Lord's sake A proper Christian response to authority reflects positively on Jesus. **to the emperor, as the supreme authority** Peter's readers should submit to the emperor's rule, but they must not worship him (compare Mt 22:21).

2:14 governors Local officials who rule on behalf of the Roman emperor and represent Roman imperial power in the region.

2:17 fear God Respecting God is the hallmark of wisdom (Pr 1:7; 8:13; 9:10; 10:27; 19:23; Ecc 8:12; 12:13).

honor the emperor Although the emperor may cause them to suffer, believers must respect his position. Like Christ, believers are to be respectful even in the face of insult and hardship, for this gives them the opportunity to show the true character of Jesus.

2:18 Slaves Peter's use of the Greek word *oiketēs* here for a specific kind of slave indicates that he has household slaves in mind, although his comments are applicable also to slaves serving in other capacities. Greco-Roman literature did not often address slaves. The early Christian writings regard slaves as full members of the household unit; they too have rights and moral obligations to the members of their household (see Eph 5:21—6:9; Col 3:18—4:1). Slavery in the modern Western world is not equivalent to Greco-Roman slavery in the first century AD; the vast majority of slaves in the Greco-Roman world were agricultural workers earning a living, not forced into service. Slavery was a key socio-economic institution in Greco-Roman society. Abuse and slavery did not go hand in hand, although some slaves did live under harsh conditions. Early Christianity did not oppose slavery outright; instead, slaves were often encouraged to submit to their masters as an expression of obedience to the Lord (see Col 3:22). Outright opposition of the institution of slavery at this infancy stage of Christianity would have been detrimental to the gospel spreading around the world. However, the early Christians do critique the institution of slavery by challenging its unilateral authority structure and affording slaves a greater place within the household (see Eph 6:9; Col 4:1). Slaves were also taught in Christian circles that while they lack the freedom of freepersons, they possess the ultimate sense of liberty—freedom before the Lord (1Co 7:21–24).

2:19 unjust suffering Like the persecuted church at large, slaves must patiently endure (see note on Col 3:22; note on Col 4:1). God is aware of their suffering (compare Ex 2:23–25).

2:22–25 In this passage Peter draws extensively on the language and theology of the fourth servant song in Isaiah (Isa 52:13—53:12).

2:22 He committed no sin Here Peter interprets the significance of Jesus' unjust suffering through the lens of the suffering servant in Isa 53:9.

2:23 entrusted himself Peter uses Isa 53:7 to highlight Jesus' exemplary behavior in the face of threats and physical suffering. **to him who judges justly** Peter likely

justly. ²⁴"He himself bore our sins" in his body on the cross, so that we might die to sins and live for righteousness; "by his wounds you have been healed." ²⁵For "you were like sheep going astray,"ᵃ but now you have returned to the Shepherd and Overseer of your souls.

3 Wives, in the same way submit yourselves to your own husbands so that, if any of them do not believe the word, they may be won over without words by the behavior of their wives, ²when they see the purity and reverence of your lives. ³Your beauty should not come from outward adornment, such as elaborate hairstyles and the wearing of gold jewelry or fine clothes. ⁴Rather, it should be that of your inner self, the unfading beauty of a gentle and quiet spirit, which is of great worth in God's sight. ⁵For this is the way the holy women of the past who put their hope in God used to adorn themselves. They submitted themselves to their own husbands, ⁶like Sarah, who obeyed Abraham and called him her lord. You are her daughters if you do what is right and do not give way to fear.

⁷Husbands, in the same way be considerate as you live with your wives, and treat them with respect as the weaker partner and as heirs with you of the gracious gift of life, so that nothing will hinder your prayers.

ᵃ 24,25 Isaiah 53:4,5,6 (see Septuagint)

---

draws this from Isa 53:10, which notes that the suffering servant's anguish pleases Yahweh because of its results. God, who observes that the righteous are suffering, will ultimately reward their endurance and punish those who are afflicting them (see Rev 6:9 and note).

2:24 "He himself bore our sins" in his body Peter employs Isa 53:3–4 and 53:12 to identify Jesus' death and resurrection as the ultimate fulfillment of the suffering servant's vicarious sacrifice. On the cross, Christ bore our sins in his body (compare Dt 21:23) even though he was innocent and therefore undeserving of the suffering (see 1Pe 2:23; compare Isa 53:10). **we might die to sins and live for righteousness** This seems to evoke Isa 53:11's remark that it is because of the suffering servant's righteousness, even unto death—as the guilt offering for all of humanity—that people can be declared righteous before God (see Isa 53:10 and note; compare 2Pe 1:1 and note). **by his wounds you have been healed** This phrase also comes from Isaiah's fourth servant song (see Isa 53:5 and note). In its original context the bruises of the suffering servant bring healing to transgressors—those who are sinful and rebel against Yahweh (Isa 53:6; compare Isa 6:10; 61:1–11; Lk 4:16–20).

2:25 you were like sheep going astray Here Peter draws on Isa 53:6 but updates the language to apply it to his own audience—indicating, as the fourth servant song from Isaiah had, that all people have turned away from God and are in need of the savior Jesus. **Shepherd and Overseer of your souls** Jesus is the shepherd in view here (compare Jn 10:1–14; Heb 13:20–21). Jesus can protect the souls of believers because of his death and resurrection, which the fourth servant song of Isaiah foretold (see Isa 53:10 and note).

3:1–7 Having commented on the Christian's proper relationship to God and the empire, as well as how slaves can live godly lives even when oppressed by their masters, Peter now addresses familial relationships.

3:1 submit yourselves The Greek verb used here, *hypotassō*, is also used in Eph 5:21 and 5:24 for the submission of believers to one another and wives to husbands; husbands are encouraged to truly love their wives. See note on 1Co 14:34; see also note on 1Ti 2:11. Compare Eph 5:21 and note. First Peter 3:8 contextualizes all of Peter's commands within a larger framework of Christian humility and love. Peter's words are meant to be practiced by those who understand that their larger purpose is to live as people who reflect Christ's character. **they may be won over** Peter doesn't encour-

age wives to adopt submissive attitudes so that their husbands can rule over them; rather, he hopes they will exemplify Christ's character and serve as witnesses to Christ himself. Their example could lead their unbelieving husbands to faith in Christ. At the time 1 Peter was written, Christians were likely viewed as challenging social norms—and this may have been one of the main reasons why they were persecuted. To ensure the message of Jesus was not hindered, Peter may have offered his thoughts on various relationships. Peter seems to be advocating throughout 2:13–3:22 that although social norms should be challenged, the message of the gospel should not be hindered in the process—he encourages patient suffering, as Jesus suffered, even in the face of injustice and inequality.

3:3 Your beauty should not come from outward adornment The women in Peter's audience are urged not to depend on outward aids for beauty. Peter selects three ways of displaying wealth or sexuality to argue that external displays are not what matters; instead, inward beauty is what truly matters, as displayed by a life lived for Christ. It may be that the women Peter addresses were displaying their hair in a way that was intentionally sexually enticing or intended to indicate wealth. Their clothing choices may have had the same effect, and in the process showed a focus on vanity and perhaps a lack of Christian charity.

3:6 lord Here Peter uses the word *kyrios*, which often serves as a polite form of address, like "sir" (compare Ge 18:12). Peter seems to be respecting the culture of the ancient world, in which the husband of the home was usually proprietor (business owner)—as someone over servants, property, and livestock—and in charge of the family.

3:7 in the same way Husbands should also be people who reflect Christ's character (see 1Pe 3:1 and note). Peter emphasizes that they should practice consideration and love. See Eph 5:25 and note. Jesus had a high view of women during his ministry, setting an example for the men of his time to follow (see note on Lk 8:1–3). Ancient Near Eastern cultures, as well as the cultures of the first century, were dominated and controlled by men. Men often treated women disrespectfully, viewing them only as property. Jesus boldly aimed to reverse this trend; Peter encourages the same here. **weaker partner** The phrase likely refers to physical build and strength. Such a contrast was obvious in a labor-intensive culture. The context does not suggest any spiritual, intellectual or moral inferiority since both males and females were created in the image of God (Ge 1:26–27).

Suffering for Doing Good

[8] Finally, all of you, be like-minded, be sympathetic, love one another, be compassionate and humble. [9] Do not repay evil with evil or insult with insult. On the contrary, repay evil with blessing, because to this you were called so that you may inherit a blessing. [10] For,

"Whoever would love life
  and see good days
must keep their tongue from evil
  and their lips from deceitful speech.
[11] They must turn from evil and do good;
  they must seek peace and pursue it.
[12] For the eyes of the Lord are on the
    righteous
  and his ears are attentive to their
    prayer,
but the face of the Lord is against those who
  do evil."[a]

[13] Who is going to harm you if you are eager to do good? [14] But even if you should suffer for what is right, you are blessed. "Do not fear their threats[b]; do not be frightened."[c] [15] But in your hearts revere Christ as Lord. Always be prepared to give an answer to everyone who asks you to give the reason for the hope that you have. But do this with gentleness and respect, [16] keeping a clear conscience, so that those who speak maliciously against your good behavior in Christ may be ashamed of their slander. [17] For it is better, if it is God's will, to suffer for doing good than for doing evil. [18] For Christ also suffered once for sins, the righteous for the unrighteous, to bring you to God. He was put to death in the body but made alive in the Spirit. [19] After being made alive,[d] he went and made proclamation to the imprisoned spirits — [20] to those who were disobedient long ago when God waited patiently in the days of Noah while the ark was being built. In it only a few people, eight in all, were saved through water, [21] and this water symbolizes baptism that now saves you also — not the removal of dirt from the body but the pledge of a clear conscience toward God.[e] It saves you by the resurrection of Jesus Christ, [22] who has gone into heaven and is at God's right hand — with angels, authorities and powers in submission to him.

[a] 12 Psalm 34:12-16   [b] 14 Or fear what they fear
[c] 14 Isaiah 8:12   [d] 18,19 Or but made alive in the spirit, [19] in which also   [e] 21 Or but an appeal to God for a clear conscience

---

3:8–12 Peter calls his readers to inherit a blessing through unity, love, and upright conduct, and to repay evil with good (compare Lk 6:28; Ro 12:14).

3:10–12 Here, Peter quotes Ps 34:12–16 to emphasize his point that believers are called to be a blessing to the world. The larger context seems to indicate that believers are meant to live the words of this psalm through their long-suffering, so that the evil of the world may be gradually changed. Injustice can be endured in a way that upholds the values of justice, not through compromise or acquiescence to the ways of a culture, but rather through endurance. Underlying all this is the idea of trusting God for ultimate justice.

3:13–22 Peter reiterates a point made in 1Pe 2:20–21, stressing that those who persevere through unjust suffering are blessed by God.

3:15 Always be prepared to give an answer Peter asserts that Christians should be prepared at all times to defend their faith and explain the source of their hope (compare Mt 10:19 and note).

3:18–22 While this passage clearly functions as support for Peter's teaching that believers might suffer for doing good (1Pe 3:13–17), the precise meaning of several details is debated.

3:18 but made alive in the Spirit Jesus died a real, physical death and was raised to a new life.

3:19 he went and made proclamation to the imprisoned spirits This short phrase raises several difficult issues for the interpreter: the identity of the spirits in prison (v. 19), the reasons for their imprisonment, the location of the prison where Christ went to preach, the content of Christ's proclamation, the relationship of preaching to the "spirits" (v. 19) with preaching to those who are dead (4:6), and the possible allusions to Biblical (Ge 6–9; Jude) and extra-Biblical traditions (such as the Jewish work called 1 Enoch). A variety of interpretations have been put forward regarding these issues. Christ may have descended into the underworld (Tartarus, Hades, hell or Sheol) in connection with his death on the cross and preached to the deceased human souls imprisoned in the underworld. Alternatively, the pre-incarnate Christ could have visited the generation of Noah in their lifetime, preaching repentance from sin. Finally, the text may be an allusion to fallen angels (i.e., the "sons of God" from Ge 6:1–4). See Jude 6 and note; 2Pe 2:4 and note.

3:20 to those who were disobedient long ago The interpretation is closely connected to how the imprisoned spirits from 1Pe 3:19 are identified. See note on v. 19; compare Ge 6:1–4 and note on Ge 6:2. **in the days of Noah** See Ge 6–9. **people, eight in all** Refers to Noah, his wife, their three sons (Shem, Ham, and Japheth), and their wives (see Ge 7:1,6–7; compare note on 2Pe 2:5). See the infographic "Inside Noah's Ark" on p. 19.

3:21 baptism that now saves you Noah and his family were not saved by means of water, which served as God's agent to cleanse the earth of its evil (Ge 6:5–7). The ark was God's means of preserving life and starting anew. Baptism thus reflects the belief that Jesus is Lord, signifying the judgment of sin and subsequent salvation through the new life provided by the resurrection of Christ. Just as Noah and his family came through the flood waters to a new life, so do believers through baptism. It is not the baptism itself that saves, but the action of God that it signifies. See note on Ac 2:38. **pledge of a clear conscience toward God** Describes a pledge of loyalty to God.

3:22 with angels, authorities and powers An all-encompassing statement implying that all things, spiritual and physical, are ultimately under the authority of Jesus (compare note on 2Pe 3:10; Col 1:16 and note).

Living for God

4 Therefore, since Christ suffered in his body, arm yourselves also with the same attitude, because whoever suffers in the body is done with sin. [2] As a result, they do not live the rest of their earthly lives for evil human desires, but rather for the will of God. [3] For you have spent enough time in the past doing what pagans choose to do — living in debauchery, lust, drunkenness, orgies, carousing and detestable idolatry. [4] They are surprised that you do not join them in their reckless, wild living, and they heap abuse on you. [5] But they will have to give account to him who is ready to judge the living and the dead. [6] For this is the reason the gospel was preached even to those who are now dead, so that they might be judged according to human standards in regard to the body, but live according to God in regard to the spirit.

[7] The end of all things is near. Therefore be alert and of sober mind so that you may pray. [8] Above all, love each other deeply, because love covers over a multitude of sins. [9] Offer hospitality to one another without grumbling. [10] Each of you should use whatever gift you have received to serve others, as faithful stewards of God's grace in its various forms. [11] If anyone speaks, they should do so as one who speaks the very words of God. If anyone serves, they should do so with the strength God provides, so that in all things God may be praised through Jesus Christ. To him be the glory and the power for ever and ever. Amen.

Suffering for Being a Christian

[12] Dear friends, do not be surprised at the fiery ordeal that has come on you to test you, as though something strange were happening to you. [13] But rejoice inasmuch as you participate in the sufferings of Christ, so that you may be overjoyed when his glory is revealed. [14] If you are insulted because of the name of Christ, you are blessed, for the Spirit of glory and of God rests on you.

4:1–6 Peter again exhorts his audience to live holy lives in light of Christ's imminent return and God's final judgment. He calls believers to walk away from sin and follow Christ's pattern by enduring suffering faithfully.

4:1 suffers in the body is done with sin The suffering person in view here is likely a believer. If this is the case, Peter either means that when believers suffer for Christ, they overcome the power of sin, or that when people become believers and join Christ in his baptism, they prevail over the enslaving power of sin (see 1Pe 3:21 and note; compare Ro 6:1–12; 1Jn 5:18). This phrase could also refer to Christ and his suffering on the cross. If so, Peter's point is that Christ has conquered sin through his suffering in the flesh.

4:3 what pagans choose Peter metaphorically uses the Greek term for Gentiles to refer to nonbelievers and the various types of immoral behavior associated with them. **living** Peter includes a second vice list (see 1Pe 2:1 and note) to remind his audience that sinful behavior is unfit for Christians—who have been set apart for God (as holy people; 1:2,15; 2:9).

4:4 they heap abuse Nonbelievers do not understand the transforming power of Christ's atonement and the response that comes with it—a desire to live a godly life.

4:5 who is ready to judge Refers to God the Father.

4:6 to those who are now dead May refer to those who are spiritually dead (that is, nonbelievers), but more likely refers to those who are physically dead, as the use of the same Greek term (*nekros*) in v. 5 suggests. Peter's argument is that those who have died will not escape the judgment of God. One day, God will impartially judge all the works of all people.

4:7–11 Adding to his previous comments about the need for believers to live upright lives (vv. 1–6), Peter emphasizes Jesus' return to encourage his audience to actively do right by others.

4:7 end of all things is near Peter is certain of Jesus' return (see 1:5,7). Believers are called to live in confidence and anticipation of the consummation of God's work in Christ (this is referred to as eschatological hope).

4:8 because love covers over a multitude of sins Peter draws on Pr 10:12 to affirm the power of Christian love; it can result in forgiveness and reconciliation when people have been harmed or wronged (Jas 5:20). In this way, love overcomes sin.

4:10 gift This is the only use of the Greek word *charisma* in the NT outside of Paul's writings (see Ro 12:6; 1Co 12:28–31). Elsewhere, Paul discusses spiritual gifts in detail (see 1Co 12:4–11 and note), emphasizing their purpose to serve and build up the body of Christ (Eph 4:11–12). Peter's exhortation reflects the same concern here, though he may also have in mind God's gift of salvation (see Ro 5:15–16; 6:23).

4:11 speaks May refer to the gift of prophecy (see note on 1Co 12:10) or to any type of speaking about God and the truth of the gospel. However the next line seems to imply that Peter is referring to speaking and serving gifts in a broad sense, not to specific gifts (compare 1Co 12:1–11). **serves** This verse likely addresses the manner in which believers offer service to each other, since the same Greek word is used in 1Pe 4:10 to speak of serving others in a general sense. This verse may also refer to the office of the "deacon" or "servant" since the Greek verb *diakoneō* used here is related to the Greek noun *diakonos*, which is applied to the church office of "deacon" or "servant" (see 1Ti 3:8 and note).

4:12–19 Peter elaborates on what it means to share in the sufferings of Christ—picking up on his thoughts from 1Pe 3:12–22—and to trust God's judgment, believing that God is good and that he can use even suffering for his purposes.

4:12 fiery ordeal A reference to suffering and the refinement it brings to a believer's life (compare 1:6–7).

4:13 you participate in the sufferings of Christ Believers demonstrate their faith by sharing in Jesus' sufferings; they learn what it means to be like him in their anguish. They can have joy because they honor God through their suffering and know that God will vindicate their faithfulness one day (vv. 18–19). **his glory is revealed** Refers to Jesus' second coming.

4:14 insulted because of the name of Christ Christians living throughout the Greco-Roman world in the first

[15] If you suffer, it should not be as a murderer or thief or any other kind of criminal, or even as a meddler. [16] However, if you suffer as a Christian, do not be ashamed, but praise God that you bear that name. [17] For it is time for judgment to begin with God's household; and if it begins with us, what will the outcome be for those who do not obey the gospel of God? [18] And,

> "If it is hard for the righteous to be saved,
>   what will become of the ungodly and the
>   sinner?"[a]

[19] So then, those who suffer according to God's will should commit themselves to their faithful Creator and continue to do good.

To the Elders and the Flock

5 To the elders among you, I appeal as a fellow elder and a witness of Christ's sufferings who also will share in the glory to be revealed: [2] Be shepherds of God's flock that is under your care, watching over them — not because you must, but because you are willing, as God wants you to be; not pursuing dishonest gain, but eager to serve; [3] not lording it over those entrusted to you, but being examples to the flock. [4] And when the Chief Shepherd appears, you will receive the crown of glory that will never fade away.

[5] In the same way, you who are younger, submit yourselves to your elders. All of you, clothe yourselves with humility toward one another, because,

> "God opposes the proud
>   but shows favor to the humble."[b]

[6] Humble yourselves, therefore, under God's mighty hand, that he may lift you up in due time. [7] Cast all your anxiety on him because he cares for you.

a 18 Prov. 11:31 (see Septuagint)   *b 5* Prov. 3:34

---

century likely experienced discrimination and varying degrees of ostracism because of their faith.

4:16 as a Christian The Greek term used here rarely occurs in the NT despite its later popularity as a designation for people who follow Jesus and trust in his saving work (see Ac 11:26). Here Peter probably uses the term to affirm believers' identification with Christ and his sufferings (see 1Pe 4:13).

4:17 time for judgment to begin with This phrase likely refers to future judgment at Jesus' return rather than present sufferings. Those who suffer for Christ's sake can be confident that God's judgment will validate their hardship. Peter lives in the era between Jesus' resurrection and return—thus, relatively speaking, the judgment is imminent and has in many ways begun, since the time to choose Jesus is now (compare 2Pe 3:8 and note). **God's household** This evokes the building metaphor from 1Pe 2:4–5 and refers to the family of believers in Jesus. Peter maintains that God will judge all people impartially, but also stresses that he will begin with his own people. All people will be held accountable for their actions, even though God will grant mercy to those who chose the path of faith in Jesus (compare note on Jude 21).

4:18 Peter draws on the Septuagint (ancient Greek OT) version of Pr 11:31 to remind his audience of the high cost of following Jesus in a world that condones sinful behavior and reviles the name of Christ.

4:18 If it is hard for the righteous to be saved Just as Jesus faced suffering—being mocked, beaten, and crucified—to make the gift of salvation possible, believers must faithfully follow their Lord until the end of their lives or Jesus' return. This is not because their salvation depends on it—Jesus alone saves them (1Pe 1:3–12)—but because others may come to Jesus due to their model of faithfulness. **ungodly and the sinner** Those who do not walk the path of faith will experience the full ramifications of their sin when God judges all of humanity.

4:19 who suffer according to God's will They suffer according to God's will by suffering as Jesus would.

5:1–11 In this section, Peter gives parting instructions to the elders of the churches.

5:1 elder The Greek word here, *presbyteros*, designates a church leader or administrator (see 1Ti 3:1–7 and note; 3:2 and note). **a witness of Christ's sufferings** While Peter observed Jesus' ministry and could have drawn from these experiences, he likely is referring to his present role as a witness to the sufferings of Christ as seen in believers' responses to physical and social persecution. As with the rest of the letter, here Peter interprets the sufferings of believers as participation in the sufferings of Christ (see 1Pe 4:13). See the timeline "The Early Church to AD 100" on p. 1776.

5:2–4 Just as Christ serves as the ultimate model of faithful suffering (see 2:21 and note), Peter exhorts elders to be an example for other believers in their behavior and attitude—even in the midst of the suffering their community is experiencing (4:12–19)

5:2 Be shepherds of God's flock that is under your care Peter encourages the elders to exercise pastoral care and concern for the people in their communities.

5:4 when the Chief Shepherd appears Peter uses the metaphor of a shepherd to refer to Jesus at his return (see 1:7 and note; compare Jn 10:11–18; note on 1Sa 9:3). **crown of glory that will never fade away** In their faithful service as leaders, elders exude the glory of Jesus (the king who rightfully rules the universe); this will be recognized upon Christ's return.

5:5 you who are younger Most likely refers to youthful members of the church, although—if familial language is used metaphorically here—the expression may refer to offices of the church that are lower in rank than elder (e.g., deacon), or to all members of the church who do not hold official offices. **shows favor to the humble** Speaking now to all believers, Peter draws on the Septuagint (ancient Greek OT) version of Pr 3:34 to stress the importance of humility in the Christian community.

5:7 Cast all your anxiety on him Likely drawing on Ps 55:22, this line provides comfort to believers in the face of persecution and suffering. God not only will deliver believers from their troubles in the future, but he demonstrates his loving care in the present by hearing their prayers.

[8]Be alert and of sober mind. Your enemy the devil prowls around like a roaring lion looking for someone to devour. [9]Resist him, standing firm in the faith, because you know that the family of believers throughout the world is undergoing the same kind of sufferings.

[10]And the God of all grace, who called you to his eternal glory in Christ, after you have suffered a little while, will himself restore you and make you strong, firm and steadfast. [11]To him be the power for ever and ever. Amen.

Final Greetings

[12]With the help of Silas,[a] whom I regard as a faithful brother, I have written to you briefly, encouraging you and testifying that this is the true grace of God. Stand fast in it.

[13]She who is in Babylon, chosen together with you, sends you her greetings, and so does my son Mark. [14]Greet one another with a kiss of love.

Peace to all of you who are in Christ.

[a] 12 Greek *Silvanus*, a variant of *Silas*

5:8 Your enemy the devil The NT uses both "Satan" and "devil" as terms for the chief figure of evil in the Bible. The Hebrew term *satan* used in the OT means "adversary" (e.g., Job 1:6,12; 2:1; Zec 3:1–2). **a roaring lion looking for someone to devour** Peter alerts his audience to the devil's constant threat to the people of God (compare 2Co 2:11). Within the wider context of the passage, Peter's use of animal imagery depicts God's people as vulnerable sheep in desperate need of their shepherd's protection from all sorts of threats, including persecution and preying animals like the devil.
5:9 family of believers throughout the world Believ-

ers throughout the Roman empire were suffering both localized persecution as well as opposition from the devil (see 1Pe 5:8 and note).

5:12–14 Peter concludes by including greetings and offering a benediction.

5:12 Silas Peter's secretary (or amanuensis) and an associate of Paul.
5:13 Babylon Refers metaphorically to Rome (see Rev 14:8 and note). See the infographic "Rome in Paul's Day" on p. 1844. **Mark** An associate of Paul who was also an associate of Peter (see Ac 12:12,25; 15:37,39; Phm 24). Peter views himself as Mark's spiritual father.

2 PETER

INTRODUCTION TO 2 PETER

As the Christian movement gained steam, churches began to encounter more false teachers in their midst. Second Peter was written to warn about one of these groups—people who were essentially saying that Jesus would not return, so they could live any way they liked. Against this view, 2 Peter argues that the day of the Lord is surely coming, and that believers should live in light of this truth.

BACKGROUND

Second Peter is attributed to Simon Peter, an apostle of Jesus (2Pe 1:1; for more on Peter, see the "Introduction to 1 Peter"). He speaks of having witnessed Jesus' transfiguration (2Pe 1:16–18) and is familiar with Paul and his letters (3:15–16). However, 2 Peter seems very different from 1 Peter, and consequently there was some debate in the early church about 2 Peter's authorship. The attribution to Peter does not necessarily mean it was compiled or finalized by him; it could indicate the letter is based on Peter's eyewitness account of Jesus and Peter's teachings (likely just prior to his death). However, the differences between 1 Peter and 2 Peter could be due to Peter using different secretaries for the two letters—which is what the church father Jerome suggests (compare 1Pe 5:12, which names Silvanus, also known as Silas, as Peter's secretary for 1 Peter). The act of faithfully compiling a letter based on a teacher's words, and thus carrying forward the teacher's tradition, was a great compliment in the ancient world. When a teacher's authority was correctly evoked, it was done on the basis of a disciple succeeding the teacher or extending the teacher's reach.

If Peter authored 2 Peter, it must have been composed by the mid–60s AD, when he was martyred in Rome. If one of Peter's disciples wrote the letter in his name, then 2 Peter would have been written no later than the early second century AD (it is quoted before the mid-second century AD).

Second Peter identifies its recipients as people who have faith through the righteousness of God and Jesus (2Pe 1:1), and the author mentions that it is his second letter to them (3:1). If the earlier letter was 1 Peter, then both letters were written to the same audience. The recipients of 2 Peter apparently were struggling with false teachers who denied that Jesus would come again, causing some believers to lose faith. The false teachers also appear to have been encouraging immoral behavior in response to the allegedly strict ethics taught by Peter.

STRUCTURE

After the greeting, Peter reminds his audience of their Christian identity—as those saved from their sins by Jesus—and calls them to be godly people who live as if Jesus' return is a reality (1:3–21). Peter then warns about false teachers who are motivated by greed and lust rather than by love for God (2:1–22). Much of this section and the start of the next section have strong similarities with the letter of Jude (compare 2Pe 2:1–18; 3:1–3 with Jude 4–18). There are several

explanations for these overlaps: 2 Peter relies on Jude, Jude relies on 2 Peter, or both Jude and 2 Peter rely on a common source (perhaps oral tradition).

Peter then offers an additional argument against false teaching, assuring his readers that Christ will surely come again (2Pe 3:1–13). The letter closes with a final instruction for the believers to depend on what they know to be true, refusing to be led astray by the false teachers (3:14–18).

OUTLINE

- Greeting (1:1–2)
- Call to develop Christian character (1:3–21)
- The danger of false teaching (2:1–22)
- Hope in the Lord's return (3:1–13)
- Closing commands (3:14–18)

THEMES

As an antidote against false teachers, 2 Peter urges believers to remember who they are in Christ and trust in the promise of Jesus' coming. The fact that Christ has not returned yet is actually an act of grace, offering more people the opportunity to receive salvation—before evil itself is purged from the world and God's justice is restored over heaven and earth (3:9,13). This changes everything.

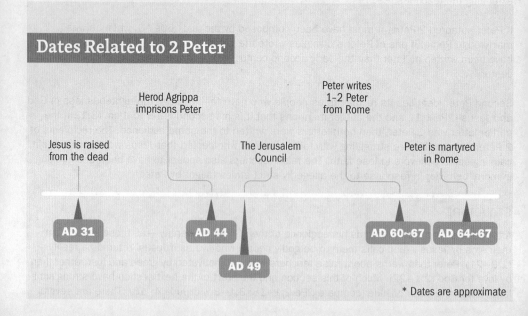

Dates Related to 2 Peter

Herod Agrippa
imprisons Peter

Peter writes
1–2 Peter
from Rome

Jesus is raised
from the dead

The Jerusalem
Council

Peter is martyred
in Rome

AD 31

AD 44

AD 60~67   **AD 64~67**

AD 49

* Dates are approximate

We should recognize that although some people celebrate the freedom to do whatever they want, they end up becoming slaves to their appetites (2:19). Some even do this in the name of God. We can recognize these false teachers by their greedy and lustful actions; they seek their own benefit and live for that purpose instead of the betterment of others (1:4–7). We should combat false teachings by both speaking against these heretics and living in the freedom of Jesus, as those saved. We should live for the eternal purposes of God, as if Jesus could return tomorrow, for he could (3:10,13).

1 Simon Peter, a servant and apostle of Jesus Christ,

To those who through the righteousness of our God and Savior Jesus Christ have received a faith as precious as ours:

²Grace and peace be yours in abundance through the knowledge of God and of Jesus our Lord.

Confirming One's Calling and Election

³His divine power has given us everything we need for a godly life through our knowledge of him who called us by his own glory and goodness. ⁴Through these he has given us his very great and precious promises, so that through them you may participate in the divine nature, having escaped the corruption in the world caused by evil desires.

⁵For this very reason, make every effort to add to your faith goodness; and to goodness, knowledge; ⁶and to knowledge, self-control; and to self-control, perseverance; and to perseverance, godliness; ⁷and to godliness, mutual affection; and to mutual affection, love. ⁸For if you possess these qualities in increasing measure, they will keep you from being ineffective and unproductive in your knowledge of our Lord Jesus Christ. ⁹But whoever does not have them is nearsighted and blind, forgetting that they have been cleansed from their past sins.

¹⁰Therefore, my brothers and sisters,ᵃ make every effort to confirm your calling and election. For if you do these things, you will never stumble, ¹¹and you will receive a rich welcome into the eternal kingdom of our Lord and Savior Jesus Christ.

ᵃ 10 The Greek word for *brothers and sisters* (*adelphoi*) refers here to believers, both men and women, as part of God's family.

1:1–7 Second Peter begins like 1 Peter, but skips the traditional thanksgiving (see note on 1Pe 1:1–2). Instead, the letter launches immediately into a word of instruction—perhaps indicating the urgency of its message.

The precise audience of the letter depends on the question of authorship, which was a matter of debate in the early church. If the attribution to Peter indicates he personally wrote the letter, then the audience should be understood as the same group who received 1 Peter. This would have happened sometime before the mid–60s AD (prior to Peter's martyrdom). If Peter's disciples compiled the letter after Peter's death, then the audience would be a community of Christians who lived sometime before the early second century AD.

1:1 Simon Peter A usage of both Peter's Hebrew name and Greek name, respectively. See 1Pe 1:1 and note; Mt 16:18 and note. **a servant** Peter uses the Greek term *doulos* to describe his total devotion to Jesus (see 1Co 6:19; compare Ro 1:1 and note). **apostle of Jesus Christ** Peter understands himself as one sent by Jesus to proclaim the salvation Jesus offers to the world (see note on 1Pe 1:1). **through the righteousness** Describes the right standing (or justice) of God, which believers are given. People are described here as obtaining faith not because of any action on their part; the only part believers play is their decision to stand in the righteousness God offers. **God and Savior Jesus Christ** Jesus is explicitly identified as God (compare Titus 2:13; Jn 1:1 and note). **a faith as precious as ours** While Peter knows that he has special authority as an apostle, he also knows that all people are equal in the eyes of God and that faith itself shows that to be the case.

1:2 knowledge of God Believers are encouraged to experience completeness through their growing knowledge of God himself. At its most basic level, this is the knowledge of the salvation that people can receive in Jesus. But there are radical implications of that message, including a transformed life; these implications will be described throughout the letter. **Lord** The ancient Greek OT (Septuagint) substitutes the same term, *kyrios*, for the divine name, Yahweh.

1:3 for a godly life Peter asserts that Christians are fully equipped to live a life pleasing to God, to overcome any obstacle they face, and to persevere under trial. In summary, God is sufficient—a concept that Peter will come back to later in this letter (see 2Pe 3). **goodness** It is solely because of who God is that believers have an opportunity to be in relationship with him. Yahweh regularly proclaims that he is righteous for the sake of his own reputation and simply because of who he is—one who makes things right, even when his creation (humanity) repeatedly acts unjustly (e.g., Eze 20:9; Isa 48:9).

1:4 very great and precious promises The reality described in 2Pe 1:3 and Jesus' second coming (see ch. 3). **participate in the divine nature** Here, Peter may be contrasting the Christian belief that believers participate in the divine nature with the Greek belief that humans could become gods. Christian theology distinguishes sharing in divinity (the glorification of believers by virtue of being in the body of Christ, God's family) from transformation to deity in the spiritual world. See Ro 8:29; 2Co 3:18; Php 3:21; 1Jn 3:1–3.

1:5–7 Here Peter uses a literary device called sorites, in which each virtue leads to the next one in a stair-step structure. Virtue lists, like vice lists (see 1Pe 2:1 and note), were common devices in Greco-Roman rhetoric.

1:5 goodness The idea of knowing about God is preceded by the principle of living a life of integrity, making the point that the disciplines of a faithful life lead to further understanding of God.

1:6 self-control Faith is not just a matter of obtaining salvation; it is a matter of life transformation—overcoming sin demonstrates the power of Jesus in a person's life. A person who lacks the disciplines of the Christian faith has failed to understand one of the primary purposes of salvation—the freedom to live apart from the bondage of sin (2Pe 2:19; compare Heb 6:4–6). **perseverance** Against daily opposition, believers were forced to explain their choice to serve the Lord Jesus Christ. Living as part of society without synchronizing their beliefs with those of the Roman Empire would have required incredible endurance.

1:8–15 Knowing that his death is quickly approaching (2Pe 1:14), Peter exhorts his audience to examine their faith continually so that they will remain established in the truth and truly be part of Christ's kingdom.

1:10 to confirm your calling and election Peter does not mean that people earn salvation through embodying virtues; Peter has already indicated that salvation depends

Prophecy of Scripture

¹²So I will always remind you of these things, even though you know them and are firmly established in the truth you now have. ¹³I think it is right to refresh your memory as long as I live in the tent of this body, ¹⁴because I know that I will soon put it aside, as our Lord Jesus Christ has made clear to me. ¹⁵And I will make every effort to see that after my departure you will always be able to remember these things.

¹⁶For we did not follow cleverly devised stories when we told you about the coming of our Lord Jesus Christ in power, but we were eyewitnesses of his majesty. ¹⁷He received honor and glory from God the Father when the voice came to him from the Majestic Glory, saying, "This is my Son, whom I love; with him I am well pleased."ᵃ ¹⁸We ourselves heard this voice that came from heaven when we were with him on the sacred mountain.

¹⁹We also have the prophetic message as something completely reliable, and you will do well to pay attention to it, as to a light shining in a dark place, until the day dawns and the morning star rises in your hearts. ²⁰Above all, you must understand that no prophecy of Scripture came about by the prophet's own interpretation of things. ²¹For prophecy never had its origin in the human will, but prophets, though human, spoke from God as they were carried along by the Holy Spirit.

False Teachers and Their Destruction

2 But there were also false prophets among the people, just as there will be false teachers among you. They will secretly introduce destructive heresies, even denying the sovereign Lord who bought them — bringing swift destruction

ᵃ 17 Matt. 17:5; Mark 9:7; Luke 9:35

on Jesus alone (see 1Pe 1:1 and note; compare Jn 3:16–17; Ro 8:28–30; 1Th 1:4). Peter is indicating that believers confirm the power of Jesus' work by their choices. **you will never stumble** People who are so focused on living a virtuous life, through the power of Jesus' work in them, do not have room for sinful behavior; instead, they honor God in all they do. By extension, Peter may also be referring to avoiding the compromising influences of the false teachers; those who embody the virtues will be able to discern truth from falsehood (2Pe 1:5–7; see 2:1 and note). Christ did not die just to cleanse us from our sins; he died so that we may be free from sin itself. **1:11 you will receive a rich welcome** Those who live the virtues Peter has listed are welcomed into God's eternal kingdom with honor, as those who have faithfully served him (compare Mt 25:14–30). **1:14 put it aside** Refers to Peter's death (compare 1Pe 5:1). **Christ has made clear to me** This may indicate that Jesus had revealed to Peter the approximate timing of his death or that Peter simply understood his life to be short in comparison to the eternal kingdom, and thus he viewed each day as if it could be his last.

1:16–21 Peter assures his audience that, in contrast to the lies of false teachers that he will discuss later in the letter, the teaching about Jesus' return he has passed on is authentic and reliable. Peter's preaching is not based on something he made up, but on both his firsthand experience of Jesus and the truth of Scripture. Therefore, his readers can be confident of its accuracy.

1:16 cleverly devised stories Peter is defending the truth of what he has preached about Jesus' return (2Pe 3). The myths here referenced may refer to false prophecies conjured up by Peter's opponents or Greco-Roman religious beliefs, such as prophetic utterances from mystery religions, being synchronized with Christianity. A combination of the two could also be in view. **eyewitnesses** Peter and the apostles testified about events they witnessed firsthand, particularly Jesus' transfiguration. **1:17 with him I am well pleased** Similar commendations from God the Father occurred at both Jesus' baptism and his transfiguration, but Peter particularly has in view Jesus' transfiguration, as v. 18 shows (Mt 3:17; 17:1–8; Mk 1:11; 9:2–8; Lk 3:22; 9:28–36). **1:18 on the sacred mountain** Peter asserts that he

was present at Jesus' transfiguration, which the Gospels confirm (see 2Pe 1:17 and note). Jesus' appearance in glory at that event looks forward to his future appearance in glory, which Peter is defending (see ch. 3). **1:19 prophetic message as something completely reliable** Scripture — particularly the words of the prophets — and Peter's own experience confirm the truth of his teachings. **the day dawns** Refers to the day of the Lord, a frequent subject of prophetic passages in the OT that the early church applied to the day of Jesus' return and judgment. **morning star** A metaphor for the return of Christ, with a particular focus on his glory (see Rev 2:28 and note; Rev 22:16 and note). **1:20 by the prophet's own interpretation** Peter asserts that true prophecy does not come from human ability but divine enablement (compare Isa 6:1–13). **1:21 spoke from God** Because God spoke through the prophets, their messages were true. Peter contrasts true prophets with the false teachers of 2Pe 2:1. **carried along** In this verse, the Greek verb used refers to guidance by the unseen hand of the Holy Spirit, both in the moment of writing and in the numerous circumstances of the writer's life — culminating in the production of Scripture.

2:1–22 Peter explicitly denounces the false teachers who had crept into the community. The harsh language of this chapter indicates the severity of the problems he combats. In 2:1–18 and 3:1–3, Peter incorporates much of the same material used in the letter of Jude, adapting it to the situation he is addressing. The similarities between 2 Peter and Jude may indicate that 2 Peter uses material from Jude, that Jude used material from 2 Peter, or that they shared a common (perhaps oral) tradition.

2:1–3 Peter appeals to the OT to explain how to deal with false teachers. He makes four of the same claims as Jude (employing four of the same terms; see Jude 4–5) to emphasize that destructive heretics will perish like the heretics of the wilderness wanderings (see Nu 14:26–38; 16:1–35). In doing so, Peter creates a rubric for identifying heretical leaders. Peter says that false teachers act in secret, deny God (and by extension, Christ) and behave immorally.

2:1 there will be false teachers among you Peter

on themselves. ²Many will follow their depraved conduct and will bring the way of truth into disrepute. ³In their greed these teachers will exploit you with fabricated stories. Their condemnation has long been hanging over them, and their destruction has not been sleeping.

⁴For if God did not spare angels when they sinned, but sent them to hell,ᵃ putting them in chains of darknessᵇ to be held for judgment; ⁵if he did not spare the ancient world when he brought the flood on its ungodly people, but protected Noah, a preacher of righteousness, and seven others; ⁶if he condemned the cities of Sodom and Gomorrah by burning them to ashes, and made them an example of what is going to happen to the

ungodly; ⁷and if he rescued Lot, a righteous man, who was distressed by the depraved conduct of the lawless ⁸(for that righteous man, living among them day after day, was tormented in his righteous soul by the lawless deeds he saw and heard) — ⁹if this is so, then the Lord knows how to rescue the godly from trials and to hold the unrighteous for punishment on the day of judgment. ¹⁰This is especially true of those who follow the corrupt desire of the fleshᶜ and despise authority.

Bold and arrogant, they are not afraid to heap

ᵃ 4 Greek *Tartarus*   ᵇ 4 Some manuscripts *in gloomy dungeons*
ᶜ 10 In contexts like this, the Greek word for *flesh* (*sarx*) refers to the sinful state of human beings, often presented as a power in opposition to the Spirit; also in verse 18.

identifies the current false teachers with the false prophets of the OT era. **destructive heresies** In the first century, a heresy (Greek *hairesis*) referred to a faction or a school of thought (compare Ac 26:5; 1Co 11:19). Therefore, Peter has to specify that these are not just any teachings, but destructive ones (compare 2Pe 3:7,16). Peter's primary concern with the false teachers is their denial of the return of Christ and God's judgment that will come with it (see 3:4–10). In addition, these teachers not only tolerated, but promoted immorality (2:2–3,13–14,18–19). Syncretism with other religions of the Greco-Roman world, particularly those that promoted prophecies and ritualistic sexual indulgences — like Greek mystery religions — could also be in view. **denying the sovereign Lord who bought them** Probably indicates that they distorted what the apostles taught about Jesus Christ (see note on 3:2; compare 1Jn 2:22–23; Titus 1:16). This may also refer to their blatant immorality (compare Jude 4; 1Co 6:20; 7:23).
2:2 depraved conduct Likely based on a false characterization of the freedom and grace Jesus offers, the heretics taught a form of liberty that promoted Christians enjoying sexual debauchery (see Jude 4 and note). **will bring the way of truth into disrepute** The presence of immoral false teachers in the church might give outsiders an excuse to dismiss all Christians as immoral.
2:3 condemnation has long been hanging over them Refers to the sure punishment that would come for their sin (Jude 4; Mt 7:15–19). There is no sign that these false leaders intend to repent, so Peter is certain that their end in destruction is inevitable.

2:4–9 Like Jude, Peter announces that God will bring judgment upon those who seek out sin and lead others to do the same. To do so, he uses the analogy of the rebellious spiritual beings (Ge 6:1–4; compare Jude 6–7) and Sodom and Gomorrah (Ge 19); Peter also includes the example of the flood during Noah's lifetime (Ge 7–9).

2:4 God did not spare angels when they sinned According to the Jewish tradition represented in the books 1 Enoch and Jubilees, these angels are the spiritual beings from Ge 6:1–4 who sinned by taking human wives (see Ge 6:1–4; compare 1 Enoch 6–11; Jubilees 4–5). **sent them to hell** The Greek here refers to Tartarus, a place of torment in Greek mythology where the Titans were imprisoned (see Hesiod's *Theogony*, which has conceptual parallels with Ge 6:1–4). **chains of darkness** The reference to the offending angels as being kept in darkness fits with Jewish tradition (reflected in 1 Enoch) that the offending angels of Ge 6:1–4 were imprisoned under the earth. **held for judgment** Now in

bondage in the underworld, these angels await God's final judgment, which will come on the day of the Lord (see note on 2Pe 3:7).
2:5 did not spare the ancient world God desires justice so much that he was willing to destroy his own good creation with a flood in order to vanquish corruption and violence (Ge 6:11–13; compare Ge 1:10). **protected Noah** Peter's addition of the Noah story fits well in this context because the story of the rebellious spiritual beings in Ge 6 can be read as a precursor to the flood event (see Ge 6:4 and note). The incident of spiritual beings having intercourse with women from earth and creating a subspecies could have been one of the reasons for the flood. **a preacher of righteousness** Noah represented the hope of humanity acting rightly, even though Noah ultimately failed to live righteously himself (Ge 6:9; 9:18–29). Noah also acted righteously by acting in faith, following God's instructions (Ge 6:22; compare Ge 3:6).
2:6 cities of Sodom and Gomorrah Two ancient cities that God destroyed because of their incredible wickedness (Ge 18:16—19:29; compare Jude 7 and note).
2:7 Lot Abraham's nephew who was rescued from Sodom. See Ge 19:16,29. **depraved** The Greek term used here, meaning "lack of restraint," occurs elsewhere in NT listings of sexual sin (e.g., Ro 13:13; 2Co 12:21; Gal 5:19; 1Pe 4:3).
2:8 righteous man Lot's disturbance at the sin of Sodom is seen in Ge 19:7–9. Lot is also depicted as a man so hospitable to foreign visitors that he ends up entertaining angels (Ge 19:1–3; compare Heb 13:2).
2:9 the Lord knows how to rescue the godly Peter's rebuke asserts that when God's full judgment upon the earth is unleashed, he will surely look out for his people, just like he spared Noah and Lot. **to hold the unrighteous for punishment** Peter draws on the fact that spiritual beings are reserved for judgment (2Pe 2:4) to argue that God surely has judgment planned for those who intentionally live unjust and wicked lives without repenting, especially those who should know better (2:9; compare note on 2:21).

2:10–12 Peter asserts that even spiritual beings do not claim to have the type of authority and insight that the false teachers in his audience claim to have (compare Jude 8–10). These false teachers were claiming authority and understanding of things they could not possibly comprehend — particularly regarding when and whether Christ would return.

2:10 to heap abuse on celestial beings Probably refers to high-ranking, powerful beings in the spiritual

abuse on celestial beings; [11]yet even angels, although they are stronger and more powerful, do not heap abuse on such beings when bringing judgment on them from[a] the Lord. [12]But these people blaspheme in matters they do not understand. They are like unreasoning animals, creatures of instinct, born only to be caught and destroyed, and like animals they too will perish.

[13]They will be paid back with harm for the harm they have done. Their idea of pleasure is to carouse in broad daylight. They are blots and blemishes, reveling in their pleasures while they feast with you.[b] [14]With eyes full of adultery, they never stop sinning; they seduce the unstable; they are experts in greed — an accursed brood! [15]They have left the straight way and wandered off to follow the way of Balaam son of Bezer,[c] who loved the wages of wickedness. [16]But he was rebuked for his wrongdoing by a donkey — an animal without speech — who spoke with a human voice and restrained the prophet's madness.

[17]These people are springs without water and mists driven by a storm. Blackest darkness is reserved for them. [18]For they mouth empty, boastful words and, by appealing to the lustful desires of the flesh, they entice people who are just escaping from those who live in error. [19]They promise them freedom, while they themselves are slaves of depravity — for "people are slaves to whatever has mastered them." [20]If they have escaped the corruption of the world by knowing our Lord and Savior Jesus Christ and are again entangled in it and are overcome, they are worse off at the end than they were at the beginning. [21]It would have been better for them not to have known the way of righteousness, than to have known it and then to turn their backs on the sacred command that was passed on to them. [22]Of them the proverbs are true: "A dog returns to its

a 11 Many manuscripts *being in the presence of* *b 13* Some manuscripts *in their love feasts* *c 15* Greek *Bosor*

realm. The same Greek phrase used here is found in Jude 8. The phrase in Jude and 2 Peter emphasizes that unlike angels, who sensibly refrain from speaking against higher-ranking beings, false teachers presumptuously slander the words or authority of spiritual beings. They assume authority they do not have.

2:12 blaspheme They have spoken against the truth and in the process of doing so spoken against spiritual powers themselves (2Pe 2:2,10; compare Jude 10; Jas 3:3–12).

2:13–15 In this passage, Peter uses the example of Balaam's error to describe the character of the false teachers (Nu 22–24; see Jude 11). In using this story, he presents another rubric for identifying false teachers (see note on 2Pe 2:1–3). Rather than also using the examples of Cain and Korah (as Jude does), Peter probably chose to focus on Balaam because the false teachers among his audience were using prophecy to legitimize their claims of authority (see 2Pe 2:20–21). The case of Balaam demonstrates that prophecy can be exploited and that it is truth and right action that truly matters.

2:13 paid back with harm for the harm they have done Unrepentant false prophets will receive their due judgment, which will be their destruction (compare note on 2:9; note on 3:7). **blots** Peter uses a similar word to Jude (Jude 12) to describe the false teachers' scandalous presence at community feasts. **while they feast with you** Refers to meals eaten in connection with worship services or the Lord's Supper. These "*agapē* meals" were meant to enrich Christian fellowship and strengthen the believers' sense of union with Christ.

2:15 the way of Balaam son of Bezer Balaam believed he could curse what God had blessed; his later teaching led the Israelites to idolatry and immorality (Nu 31:16; Rev 2:14). The false teachers likewise compromise God's truth by immorality and likely idolatry; they will perish like Balaam (Nu 31:8). Compare Jude 11.

2:16 by a donkey — an animal without speech See Nu 22:28–30.

2:17–22 Unlike other uses and expansions of the material 2 Peter shares with Jude, this portion of 2 Peter succinctly summarizes the storm imagery Jude uses (2Pe

2:17; see Jude 12–13). Second Peter then breaks from the material it shares with Jude to articulate warnings about the dangers of false teachers and their presence within the Christian community (2Pe 2:18–21). Peter concludes the section by quoting a proverb.

2:17 Blackest darkness is reserved Likely refers to the place of punishment for the spiritual beings who have been reserved for judgment (compare note on 2:4; note on 2:9).

2:18 they mouth empty, boastful words The church is being led astray by the charisma of the false leaders and how enticing their message sounds.

2:19 slaves of depravity The false teachers cast off sexual restraint in the name of freedom, but they are actually enslaved to their sin without realizing it (compare Ro 6:16 and note).

2:20 they are worse off at the end Having known the truth and denied it, their current spiritual situation is worse than before: Evil has gained a stronger footing in their lives because it is now using them to lead others astray (compare Lk 11:24–26). In addition, these false teachers will experience an especially harsh judgment from God; they will not only bear their own punishment, but also the punishment for those they led astray (Lk 17:1–2).

2:21 It would have been better Peter's comment here reflects the severity of the situation. The false teachers have experienced Christ's work enough to understand the basic principles of following him, but they resist coming to repentance (see note on 2Pe 3:9). **to turn their backs** Rather than turning to God, the false teachers have turned back to their own ways. The idea here is that the original knowledge of Jesus gave these leaders an opportunity to repent, but instead they exploited it to lead others astray. **the sacred command** It seems that Peter views the entire scope of the saving work of Jesus as a commandment, specifically as it is described in 2Pe 2:3–11 (compare Jude 3). Peter's description of Jesus' actions on humanity's behalf, and the godliness expected as a result, is in direct juxtaposition to the actions of the false teachers (2Pe 2:9).

2:22 A dog returns to its vomit A quotation of Pr 26:11 (compare 2Pe 2:12). This quotation emphasizes that false teachers will never change and any attempt to reform them is pointless.

vomit,"[a] and, "A sow that is washed returns to her wallowing in the mud."

The Day of the Lord

3 Dear friends, this is now my second letter to you. I have written both of them as reminders to stimulate you to wholesome thinking. [2]I want you to recall the words spoken in the past by the holy prophets and the command given by our Lord and Savior through your apostles.

[3]Above all, you must understand that in the last days scoffers will come, scoffing and following their own evil desires. [4]They will say, "Where is this 'coming' he promised? Ever since our ancestors died, everything goes on as it has since the beginning of creation." [5]But they deliberately forget that long ago by God's word the heavens came into being and the earth was formed out of water and by water. [6]By these waters also the world of that time was deluged and destroyed. [7]By the same word the present heavens and earth are reserved for fire, being kept for the day of judgment and destruction of the ungodly.

[8]But do not forget this one thing, dear friends: With the Lord a day is like a thousand years, and a thousand years are like a day. [9]The Lord is not slow in keeping his promise, as some understand slowness. Instead he is patient with you, not wanting anyone to perish, but everyone to come to repentance.

[10]But the day of the Lord will come like a thief. The heavens will disappear with a roar; the elements will be destroyed by fire, and the earth and everything done in it will be laid bare.[b]

[11]Since everything will be destroyed in this way,

---

[a] 22 Prov. 26:11   [b] 10 Some manuscripts be burned up

3:1–3 After a brief excursus about the purpose of the letter (2Pe 3:1), 2 Peter continues to parallel the letter of Jude in vv. 2–3 (see Jude 17–18; note on 2Pe 2:1–22). Here, Peter describes the coming of the day of the Lord, the destruction of the world with fire, and the hope of a new heaven and earth.

3:1 second letter The first letter is likely 1 Peter. This may indicate that the audience is the same for both letters, unless this refers to correspondence that is now lost.

3:2 the words spoken in the past As in 2Pe 1:16–21, Peter is appealing to his readers to remember what they were taught by him and by Scripture (particularly the OT prophets) regarding the second coming of Christ. **command given by our Lord** Peter may have in mind the entire message about Jesus' saving work, which necessitates action (see note on 2:21). Considering the context of this remark, Peter may also specifically have in mind Jesus' words about his second coming.

3:3 last days This phrase describes the time between Jesus' ascension to heaven (shortly after his resurrection) and the time when Jesus will return again (see Ac 2:17; Heb 1:2). **scoffers** Refers to people disputing the truth of Jesus' return (his second coming); this may be a reference to the false teachers or to a larger group (perhaps the false teachers and those who followed them).

3:4–12 Second Peter departs here from the material it shares with the letter of Jude to elaborate on the false teachers' comments about Christ's return. Peter also explains Christ's purpose in waiting for a later day to return.

3:4 Where is this 'coming' he promised The scoffers (or mockers) point to the fact that Christ has not yet returned as evidence for their understanding of the world. In the scoffers' view, God is not going to intervene and judge (compare Jer 17:15 and note; Mal 2:17 and note). **our ancestors died** This may refer to the patriarchs of Genesis, though the first generation of church leaders is another option.

3:5 the earth was formed out of water A reference to Ge 1:9–10, where dry land emerges from the waters, which in the ancient worldview, now surround the land (with water above the sky, below the land, and beside the land). This description reflects common cosmological beliefs in the ancient world (see note on Ge 1:6).

See the infographic "Ancient Hebrew Conception of the Universe" on p. 5.

3:6 destroyed Peter uses the example of God sending the flood (in response to humanity's great wickedness) to show that contrary to the scoffers' beliefs, things have indeed changed since creation (Ge 9–11).

3:7 heavens In this context, this refers to the area above the earth (the sky). **reserved for fire** After the flood, God promised that he would never again judge the world by water (Ge 9:11). Many passages speak of a coming judgment using fire imagery (e.g., Dt 32:22; Isa 66:15–16,24; Zep 1:18; Mal 4:1; 2Th 1:7–8). **destruction of the ungodly** As with the judgment of the flood, the focus of the future judgment is not creation itself; it is human sin. Also like the flood, in the future judgment the ungodly will be destroyed while those deemed godly will be spared (see 2Pe 2:5,9).

3:8 is like a thousand years People, as finite beings, cannot expect to understand God's timing, so they should not expect Christ to return according to their timetable. This is an allusion to Ps 90:4.

3:9 he is patient with you God delays the second coming so that more people can be redeemed. The day Christ returns, his entire kingdom will be inaugurated and evil will be purged from the world. For there to be justice in the world, evil must be purged. Since evil lives within people, evil people will have to be removed from the world as well—otherwise, evil will continue to perpetuate itself and the world will continue to be a place of injustice. **not wanting anyone to perish** God wishes for all people to come to faith and be saved. Within the context of 2Pe 3:9, this phrase indicates that Jesus has not returned yet because God desires that none be lost (or perish). **come to repentance** Refers to turning toward God and away from sin.

3:10 the day of the Lord This is an OT concept that describes Yahweh's full judgment of and reconciliation with the world. See Am 5:18–20; Joel 2. **like a thief** Jesus' return will be an unexpected event. **The heavens will disappear** Jesus also refers to the passing away of the heavens (or the sky), contrasting it with the permanence of his words (Mt 24:35; Mk 13:31; Lk 21:33). The same image is used toward the end of Revelation (Rev 21:1; compare Rev 6:14). **elements will be destroyed by fire** The Greek word stoicheia can refer to the physical elements (earth, air, fire, water), the heavenly

what kind of people ought you to be? You ought to live holy and godly lives [12]as you look forward to the day of God and speed its coming.[a] That day will bring about the destruction of the heavens by fire, and the elements will melt in the heat. [13]But in keeping with his promise we are looking forward to a new heaven and a new earth, where righteousness dwells.

[14]So then, dear friends, since you are looking forward to this, make every effort to be found spotless, blameless and at peace with him. [15]Bear in mind that our Lord's patience means salvation, just as our dear brother Paul also wrote you with the wisdom that God gave him. [16]He writes the same way in all his letters, speaking in them of these matters. His letters contain some things that are hard to understand, which ignorant and unstable people distort, as they do the other Scriptures, to their own destruction.

[17]Therefore, dear friends, since you have been forewarned, be on your guard so that you may not be carried away by the error of the lawless and fall from your secure position. [18]But grow in the grace and knowledge of our Lord and Savior Jesus Christ. To him be glory both now and forever! Amen.

---

[a] 12 Or as you wait eagerly for the day of God to come

---

bodies (sun, moon, stars), or spiritual powers (see Gal 4:9; Col 2:8,20). **will be laid bare** While some Greek manuscripts read *katakaēsetai* (often translated "burned up") here, the more likely original reading is *heurethēsetai* (often translated "found" or "laid bare"). The implication is that on the day of judgment all of the deeds done on earth will be brought to light.

3:13 in keeping with his promise Peter has now refuted the viewpoints of the scoffers (2Pe 3:4), so his audience can be confident in God's promise to bring justice on the day of the Lord (the day of Jesus' return). **a new heaven and a new earth** The terminology of a new heavens and new earth is found in Isaiah (Isa 65:17; 66:22) and is picked up in the NT here and in Revelation (Rev 21:1). While some of the language in 2Pe 3:10,12 might seem to indicate a destruction of the present heavens and earth, other passages make the future of creation look more like a renewal or purification (Mt 19:28; Ro 8:18–23; Rev 21:5). In light of Peter's close association between the past judgment by flood and the future judgment by fire in 2Pe 3:5–7, it seems likely that while Peter has a drastic change in view, he is not so much talking about complete destruction as he is renewal.

3:14–18 Having reassured his readers of the faithfulness of God and illustrated what they have to look forward to, Peter concludes by encouraging them to resist the allure of the false teachers and grow in the knowledge and grace of the Lord.

3:14 to this Refers to the coming of the day of the Lord and the new heavens and new earth. Since only the righteous will be at home in the new heavens and new earth, Peter's audience should take an interest in righteousness in the present. **spotless, blameless** Believers are to be morally pure (living ethically before God), in contrast with the false teachers (see 2:13; compare 1Pe 1:19).

3:15 our Lord's patience means salvation The scoffers regarded the delay in the Jesus' return as evidence that he would not come after all. Believers should take the delay in Jesus' return as evidence of his patient desire to save. **our dear brother Paul also wrote you** Paul expressed a similar view as Peter on the delay of Christ's return (see Ro 2:4; 9:22–24).

3:16 ignorant and unstable people distort The comments about Paul's writings suggest that their misuse was one of the problems underlying the heretical teachings. Based on the context, the false teachers were likely either exploiting one of Paul's teachings on the return of Jesus or using Paul's theology of salvation to argue that people could now do whatever they wished (compare Ro 6). **the other Scriptures** Peter expresses a high regard for Paul's writings, classifying them as part of the sacred writings of the early church.

3:17 fall from your secure position The false teachers have moved from Christ to destructive heresy (2Pe 2:20–22). Peter aims to caution his audience against this (see note on 1:10).

3:18 Here, at the conclusion of the letter, it seems that 2 Peter returns to the material shared with Jude (see Jude 24–25). Although Peter offers a shortened version of the hymn in Jude, the same terminology to describe God's work is deployed—calling Jesus "Lord" and "Savior" and proclaiming his glory for all time. Like Jude, Peter then ends with "Amen."

3:18 grow in the grace and knowledge Peter asserts that the best way to resist incorrect teachings is to grow in understanding of Christ and his work. **forever** This is a fitting closing in light of Peter's emphasis in this letter on the day of the Lord. Glory is given to Jesus both now and on the day when he returns in glory.

1 JOHN

INTRODUCTION TO 1 JOHN

In this letter, John speaks against false teachers who questioned Jesus' divine and human nature. His response is loud and clear: Jesus is fully God and fully man. This is not some obscure theological debate; John knows that if his readers get this teaching wrong, everything else falls apart. Because Jesus became human, he was a true sacrifice for sins. Because God is light, believers can walk in the light. Because God is love, believers know what love looks like and can respond in love.

BACKGROUND

The author of 1 John is not identified in the letter. However, the early church regarded the apostle John as the author of both the Gospel of John and 1 John. Because these texts share a similar writing style, it is common for them to be ascribed to the same author—whether this is understood to be the apostle John or someone else. The letters of 2–3 John, as well as Revelation, may also be the work of the apostle John, but this possibility was more disputed in the early church (see the "Introduction to 2 John" and "Introduction to Revelation").

The author of 1 John knew the recipients of his letter and likely had a close relationship with them. If the apostle John was the author, this community probably lived somewhere in western Asia Minor (modern-day Turkey). According to tradition, John spent his later years in Ephesus, a major city in that region. Considering that 1 John seems to build on the Gospel of John, 1 John was likely written after the Gospel, toward the end of the first century (AD 85–95).

In both 1 John and 2 John, a primary issue is the presence of false teachers. In 1 John, they appear to have started in the church and gone out (1Jn 2:19). These teachers were denying that Jesus was God in the flesh (4:1–3) and that Jesus' death atoned for sins (4:10; 5:6–8). They apparently also claimed to possess special knowledge of God and that they did not sin (e.g., 1:8,10; 2:3,11; 3:24; 4:2,6–7). Because of their denial of Jesus' incarnation, they might have minimized the importance of physical existence and elevated the spiritual life.

No geographical details are given in 1 John. However, according to tradition, John settled in Ephesus in the late first century.

STRUCTURE

First John is a difficult book to outline because the author shifts frequently between teaching doctrine and giving practical advice. One way to outline the letter recognizes five broad movements. In the introduction

(1:1–4), John establishes his trustworthiness by asserting that he was an eyewitness to Jesus' earthly life. The second major section (1:5—2:17) builds on the claim of 1 John 1:5 that God is light. God's forgiveness through Jesus is offered to those who know God (2:1–2). People who know God also strive to confess their sins and live like Jesus.

In the third major section (2:18—3:10), John speaks more explicitly about the false teachers. They denied Jesus, which means they denied the Father as well (2:23)—and those who deny the Father cannot be called his righteous children (3:1–10). The fourth section (3:11—5:12) focuses on love as the primary characteristic of God's children. God is love—so those who know God will love others, and those who don't know God will lack love. The sign of genuine love is obedience to God's commandments (5:3). In the fifth major section (5:13–21), John closes the letter by affirming that eternal life will be given to those who believe in Jesus as the Son of God. They can have confidence that God will protect them and answer their prayers.

OUTLINE

- Prologue: Jesus came in the flesh (1:1–4)
- God is light (1:5—2:17)
- God is righteous (2:18—3:10)
- God is love (3:11—5:12)
- Epilogue: concluding appeal (5:13–21)

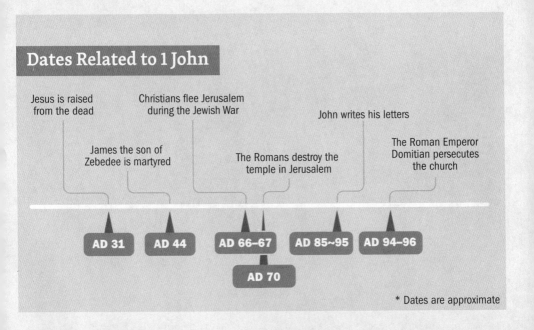

Dates Related to 1 John

Jesus is raised from the dead

Christians flee Jerusalem during the Jewish War

John writes his letters

James the son of Zebedee is martyred

The Romans destroy the temple in Jerusalem

The Roman Emperor Domitian persecutes the church

AD 31   AD 44   AD 66–67   AD 85~95   AD 94–96

AD 70

* Dates are approximate

THEMES

First John takes a strong stand against false teachers who denied that Jesus was God's Son in the flesh—yet the letter's strategy is grounded in love. John lovingly shows that a distorted view of Jesus has dangerous consequences: a life of disobedience, injustice and apathy.

John teaches his audience how to discern falsehood from truth: People who claim to know God yet are unloving show by their actions that they really don't know God (4:7–8). As people know God more, they live in a more selfless way—offering kindness to other people and showing compassion to those in need. Christians respond to God's love with gratitude, offering the same forgiveness and love to others. As believers, we are called to flee from the darkness that is evil and instead walk in the light of God. We are called to live as people who are truly saved by Jesus—loving with everything we have.

The Incarnation of the Word of Life

1 That which was from the beginning, which we have heard, which we have seen with our eyes, which we have looked at and our hands have touched — this we proclaim concerning the Word of life. ²The life appeared; we have seen it and testify to it, and we proclaim to you the eternal life, which was with the Father and has appeared to us. ³We proclaim to you what we have seen and heard, so that you also may have fellowship with us. And our fellowship is with the Father and with his Son, Jesus Christ. ⁴We write this to make ourᵃ joy complete.

Light and Darkness, Sin and Forgiveness

⁵This is the message we have heard from him and declare to you: God is light; in him there is no dark-ness at all. ⁶If we claim to have fellowship with him and yet walk in the darkness, we lie and do not live out the truth. ⁷But if we walk in the light, as he is in the light, we have fellowship with one another, and the blood of Jesus, his Son, purifies us from allᵇ sin.

⁸If we claim to be without sin, we deceive ourselves and the truth is not in us. ⁹If we confess our sins, he is faithful and just and will forgive us our sins and purify us from all unrighteousness. ¹⁰If we claim we have not sinned, we make him out to be a liar and his word is not in us.

2 My dear children, I write this to you so that you will not sin. But if anybody does sin, we have an advocate with the Father — Jesus Christ, the Righteous One. ²He is the atoning sacrifice

---

ᵃ 4 Some manuscripts *your*   ᵇ 7 Or *every*

1:1–4 First John is concerned with false teaching that denied Jesus' incarnation and the atoning significance of his death and resurrection.

First John's opening does not include the author's name, though early church tradition attributes this letter and the Gospel of John to John the apostle (compare Jn 13:23 and note). It also is possible that the author of 1 John is responsible for 2 John, 3 John, and Revelation, though this affiliation was less certain in the early church period. If the apostle is responsible for 1 John, it most likely was written toward the end of the first century AD to believers in Asia Minor (where John spent his later years).

In 1 John, John addresses a community divided in its beliefs about Jesus' identity. John begins his sermon-like letter by stating his view: Jesus is the incarnation of the preexistent Word, possessing true humanity and divinity (see Jn 1:1–2 and note).

1:1 That which was from the beginning As in John's Gospel, John begins this letter with the Word — the embodiment of God's revelation in the person of Jesus (Jn 1:1; compare Ge 1:1). John immediately states his thesis: Not only was Jesus from the beginning (eternal), he also was able to be heard, seen, and touched (he was human). This belief separates the community John addresses from those who withdrew from them (see 1Jn 2:19 and note). **we** John is referring either to himself only, or to himself and other eyewitnesses to Jesus' ministry. **the Word of life** Refers to Jesus, who is eternal life to those who believe in him (Jn 3:16–17; 14:6).

JOHN
John the apostle, also called the evangelist, was a fisherman. He was mending nets with his brother James when Jesus called them to follow him (Mk 1:19–21). If John is the disciple "whom Jesus loved" in John's Gospel, then he was one of the few people who stayed with Jesus at his crucifixion. In addition, this would make John the one who began caring for Jesus' mother, Mary (Jn 19:25–27).

1:2 The life appeared This echoes Jn 1:14, where the Word — who was with God and was God — becomes flesh and dwells with humanity as Jesus.
1:3 may have fellowship with us John is writing to address a division in the community of believers. This community might have been located in Ephesus, where the apostle John resided near the end of his life. These believers encountered false beliefs about the identity of Jesus from secessionists — literally those who "went out from us" (see 1Jn 2:19 and note). This group had separated from the church and was now negatively influencing those who remained in the church community. John aims to prevent further division.
1:4 make our joy complete It will be complete by ensuring the health of this Christian community that John loves.

1:5–10 After his opening remarks (vv. 1–4), John exhorts his audience to exhibit the attributes of God, honoring Jesus' ministry.

1:5 God is light A common metaphor in the OT and Jewish literature for God's perfection (e.g., Ps 4:6; Isa 60:1–2). God's light serves as a beacon for the righteous and leads others to him (see Ps 27:1). **darkness** Serves as a metaphor for sin, unrighteousness, and wickedness (see 1Jn 2:8–11; compare 2Cor 6:14—7:1).
1:7 purifies us from all sin Jesus' death is sacrificial and clears away the sin of those who believe in him, which makes relationship with God possible. The concept of atonement, which is derived from the OT (see Lev 16:30), is a common theme throughout the letter (see 1Jn 2:2; 4:10).
1:8 be without sin Every person should admit to themselves and God that they are sinful (compare Ro 3:23). John's opponents apparently claimed that they did not sin and therefore did not need to be cleansed. For John, the position of his opponents is the ultimate form of self-deception, since it prevents a person from accepting the truth of their sinful nature (see 1Jn 2:10–14).
1:9 confess our sins Confession of sin opens a person to the work of God within them, relinquishing the power of sin over their life through the power of Jesus (2:1; compare 3:8). John is not suggesting that the act of confession is required for salvation. God does the saving work; people cannot save themselves (2:12; Jn 3:16–17). Instead, confession opens a person to the work of the Holy Spirit, leading to the removal of sinful behaviors and desires (1Jn 3:24). **just** God demonstrates this attribute by carrying out his promise of bringing people into relationship with him through Christ's sacrificial death (compare Isa 53:10–12).
1:10 we make him out to be a liar When someone claims to have not sinned, they also are, in essence, rejecting God's statements about sinfulness and denying the need for Jesus' sacrifice.

for our sins, and not only for ours but also for the sins of the whole world.

Love and Hatred for Fellow Believers

[3] We know that we have come to know him if we keep his commands. [4] Whoever says, "I know him," but does not do what he commands is a liar, and the truth is not in that person. [5] But if anyone obeys his word, love for God[a] is truly made complete in them. This is how we know we are in him: [6] Whoever claims to live in him must live as Jesus did.

[7] Dear friends, I am not writing you a new command but an old one, which you have had since the beginning. This old command is the message you have heard. [8] Yet I am writing you a new command; its truth is seen in him and in you, because the darkness is passing and the true light is already shining.

[9] Anyone who claims to be in the light but hates a brother or sister[b] is still in the darkness. [10] Anyone who loves their brother and sister[c] lives in the light, and there is nothing in them to make them stumble. [11] But anyone who hates a brother or sister is in the darkness and walks around in the darkness. They do not know where they are going, because the darkness has blinded them.

Reasons for Writing

[12] I am writing to you, dear children,
because your sins have been forgiven on
account of his name.

[13] I am writing to you, fathers,
because you know him who is from
the beginning.
I am writing to you, young men,
because you have overcome
the evil one.

[14] I write to you, dear children,
because you know the Father.
I write to you, fathers,
because you know him who is from
the beginning.
I write to you, young men,
because you are strong,
and the word of God lives in you,
and you have overcome the evil one.

On Not Loving the World

[15] Do not love the world or anything in the world. If anyone loves the world, love for the Father[d] is not in them. [16] For everything in the world — the lust of the flesh, the lust of the eyes, and the pride of life — comes not from the Father but from the world. [17] The world and its desires pass away, but whoever does the will of God lives forever.

[a] 5 Or word, God's love   [b] 9 The Greek word for brother or sister (adelphos) refers here to a believer, whether man or woman, as part of God's family; also in verse 11; and in 3:15, 17; 4:20; 5:16.   [c] 10 The Greek word for brother and sister (adelphos) refers here to a believer, whether man or woman, as part of God's family; also in 3:10; 4:20, 21.   [d] 15 Or world, the Father's love

2:1–11 John reminds his audience of Jesus' saving work and exhorts them to love one another — which will show that they are true believers in Jesus. By contrast, those with hateful dispositions are clearly not followers of Jesus. Jewish literature of this period regularly understood the world in dichotomous terms such as light and darkness. For example, documents like the War Scroll and Book of War, from the Dead Sea Scrolls community, depict enemies as sons of darkness and the faithful as sons of light (see War Scroll 1:1–17; Book of War 3:13–4:26). John similarly sees himself as living near the end times and his followers as children of the light, founded by the righteous one, Jesus (1Jn 2:29; 4:4–6; 5:2–4).

2:1 My dear children John likely means that his audience is his spiritual children, in the sense that he was the instigator of their relationship with Jesus. **an advocate** John creates the image of a person pleading for or defending believers — a judicial advocate in the heavenly courtroom (compare Heb 4:14—5:6; 1Jn 1:8 and note; note on Jn 14:26).

2:2 the atoning sacrifice for our sins Refers to Jesus' sacrificial death for the sins of humanity (compare Ro 3:25; Heb 9:5). **whole world** This does not imply that everyone will be saved, but that Christ's death results in forgiveness for all those who enter into relationship with him.

2:8 a new command The commandment is old in that it has been proclaimed to John's audience since they first heard the gospel — and since it was given to Moses as part of the law (Lev 19:18; Mt 22:36–40). It is new in that it is now integral to the message of Jesus; it is

viewed in a new light. The commandment is not just to love one another, but to love as Christ loved — even to the point of being willing to lay down one's life (see Jn 13:34–35; 15:13; compare Ro 5:7–8). **true light is already shining** A reference to God's work in the world through Jesus, which is in the process of overcoming evil in the world (1Jn 1:5; Jn 8:12).

2:10 to make them stumble Refers to a person causing someone else to sin.

2:12–14 John reminds his audience that — unlike those who walk in darkness (1Jn 2:11) — they have overcome evil. The designations of children, fathers, and young men could be synonyms used for rhetorical purposes; they might represent different age groups or be labels for varying stages of spiritual maturity, or perhaps time in the Christian community.

2:13 you have overcome the evil one Believers share in Christ's victory on the cross, which defeated Satan (compare Col 2:14–15; Heb 2:14).

2:15–17 In these verses, John exhorts believers to oppose the values of the evil one. He also reminds his audience that those who love and obey God have the gift of eternal life.

2:15 Do not love the world The values of human societies should not define believers.

2:16 flesh John is not suggesting that being human is a negative thing; rather, he is referring to worldly values that are unacceptable to God.

2:17 The world and its desires pass away An allusion to the end of the present age, which is characterized by evil

Warnings Against Denying the Son

[18]Dear children, this is the last hour; and as you have heard that the antichrist is coming, even now many antichrists have come. This is how we know it is the last hour. [19]They went out from us, but they did not really belong to us. For if they had belonged to us, they would have remained with us; but their going showed that none of them belonged to us. [20]But you have an anointing from the Holy One, and all of you know the truth.[a] [21]I do not write to you because you do not know the truth, but because you do know it and because no lie comes from the truth. [22]Who is the liar? It is whoever denies that Jesus is the Christ. Such a person is the antichrist — denying the Father and the Son. [23]No one who denies the Son has the Father; whoever acknowledges the Son has the Father also.

[24]As for you, see that what you have heard from the beginning remains in you. If it does, you also will remain in the Son and in the Father. [25]And this is what he promised us — eternal life.

[26]I am writing these things to you about those who are trying to lead you astray. [27]As for you, the anointing you received from him remains in you, and you do not need anyone to teach you. But as his anointing teaches you about all things and as

that anointing is real, not counterfeit — just as it has taught you, remain in him.

God's Children and Sin

[28]And now, dear children, continue in him, so that when he appears we may be confident and unashamed before him at his coming.

[29]If you know that he is righteous, you know that everyone who does what is right has been born of him.

3 See what great love the Father has lavished on us, that we should be called children of God! And that is what we are! The reason the world does not know us is that it did not know him. [2]Dear friends, now we are children of God, and what we will be has not yet been made known. But we know that when Christ appears,[b] we shall be like him, for we shall see him as he is. [3]All who have this hope in him purify themselves, just as he is pure.

[4]Everyone who sins breaks the law; in fact, sin is lawlessness. [5]But you know that he appeared so that he might take away our sins. And in him is no sin. [6]No one who lives in him keeps on sinning. No one who continues to sin has either seen him or known him.

---

[a] 20 Some manuscripts *and you know all things*   [b] 2 *Or when it is made known*

(compare Gal 1:4; 2Co 4:4); John declares that the oppressive systems of human societies are coming to an end.

2:18–27 John now identifies the problem that needs addressing. He reassures his audience that the view of Christ that John passed along to them is correct, while the view of those who have left their Christian community is false (see 1Jn 2:26).

2:18 this is the last hour Refers to the time preceding Jesus' second coming (technically referred to as the *Parousia*; see v. 28). **antichrist is coming** John may have inherited this language about the false messiah from Jesus' discussion of the end times. Jesus had noted that those who falsely claim authority — as anointed (Messianic) leaders — would come (see Mk 13:21–22; Mt 24:4–5,24). The singular term "antichrist" (as opposed to "antichrists") might refer to the evil figures described in 2Th 2:3–10 and Rev 13:1–10. It also could refer to the general movement of people falsely representing Jesus (compare 1Jn 2:22; 4:3). **many antichrists** Refers to those who have withdrawn from the community John is addressing. He identifies them in this way because they spread false teaching about Jesus. By extension, the term could refer to anyone who is opposed to Jesus. **2:19 They went out from us** For John, the origin of a viewpoint (or someone's ministry) does not validate it. Rather, people must remain within Christ — within the church community and the guidance of the Holy Spirit. **showed** Because the antichrists withdrew from the Christian community, they could not receive correction. Their decision to depart from the church revealed their true character. **2:20 anointing from the Holy One** The Holy Spirit has come upon the believing community; God has chosen them for a specific purpose. **2:22 denies** The antichrists in the community denied that

Jesus was the anointed one of God, the Messiah, who suffered and died as a human (compare 4:2 and note). **2:24 heard from the beginning** A reference to the message of Jesus' saving work and, by extension, to the commandment to love as he loved (see v. 8 and note). **2:25 eternal life** See Jn 3:16 and note.

2:28 — 3:10 John characterizes God's children — those who remain in authentic relationship with him — as those who obey him and refrain from sin. He contrasts them with those who left the congregation.

2:28 when he appears John desires for the believers to be found doing Jesus' work at Christ's second coming. **2:29 been born of him** Believers in Jesus are adopted into God's family (compare note on Eph 1:5). **3:1 children of God** Refers to membership in God's spiritual family (compare Jn 1:12). **3:2 when Christ appears, we shall be like him** John likely is drawing on the imagery of new creation, as well as the idea that God's image is restored in a person through the saving work of Jesus (Rev 21; 2Co 3:18; 5:17; compare Ro 8:29 and note). **3:3 purify themselves** John is referring to the active role that a Christian plays in the effort to overcome sin, but his statement also points to ultimate reliance on Christ, the Pure One, to accomplish this effort. **3:4 breaks the law** John seems to be describing those who oppose Christ and the work of his church — which, in the letter's context, indicates the secessionists (or antichrists; 1Jn 2:18–19) and their followers. **3:6 No one who lives in him keeps on sinning** John likely is stating that those who are in Christ are free from a life of perpetual sin. John seems to be arguing against those who use God's grace as an excuse for sinful behavior (compare Ro 6:1–11).

⁷Dear children, do not let anyone lead you astray. The one who does what is right is righteous, just as he is righteous. ⁸The one who does what is sinful is of the devil, because the devil has been sinning from the beginning. The reason the Son of God appeared was to destroy the devil's work. ⁹No one who is born of God will continue to sin, because God's seed remains in them; they cannot go on sinning, because they have been born of God. ¹⁰This is how we know who the children of God are and who the children of the devil are: Anyone who does not do what is right is not God's child, nor is anyone who does not love their brother and sister.

More on Love and Hatred

¹¹For this is the message you heard from the beginning: We should love one another. ¹²Do not be like Cain, who belonged to the evil one and murdered his brother. And why did he murder him? Because his own actions were evil and his brother's were righteous. ¹³Do not be surprised, my brothers and sisters,ᵃ if the world hates you. ¹⁴We know that we have passed from death to life, because we love each other. Anyone who does not love remains in death. ¹⁵Anyone who hates a brother or sister is a murderer, and you know that no murderer has eternal life residing in him.

¹⁶This is how we know what love is: Jesus Christ laid down his life for us. And we ought to lay down our lives for our brothers and sisters. ¹⁷If anyone has material possessions and sees a brother or sister in need but has no pity on them, how can the love of God be in that person? ¹⁸Dear children, let us not love with words or speech but with actions and in truth.

¹⁹This is how we know that we belong to the truth and how we set our hearts at rest in his presence: ²⁰If our hearts condemn us, we know that God is greater than our hearts, and he knows everything. ²¹Dear friends, if our hearts do not condemn us, we have confidence before God ²²and receive from him anything we ask, because we keep his commands and do what pleases him. ²³And this is his command: to believe in the name of his Son, Jesus Christ, and to love one another as he commanded us. ²⁴The one who keeps God's commands lives in him, and he in them. And this is how we know that he lives in us: We know it by the Spirit he gave us.

On Denying the Incarnation

4 Dear friends, do not believe every spirit, but test the spirits to see whether they are from God, because many false prophets have gone out into the world. ²This is how you can recognize the Spirit of God: Every spirit that acknowledges that Jesus Christ has come in the flesh is from God, ³but every spirit that does not acknowledge Jesus is

---

ᵃ 13 The Greek word for *brothers and sisters* (*adelphoi*) refers here to believers, both men and women, as part of God's family; also in verse 16.

3:7 righteous Refers to living by right principles—the values of Jesus, such as caring for the needs of other people (1Jn 3:14,17).

3:8 is of the devil John is not suggesting that the devil possesses people when they sin; rather, he means that opposition to God gives evil room to operate.

3:9 God's seed remains Probably refers to God's Spirit working in believers.

3:10 children of the devil In John's worldview, people are either with God or against him. Opposing God results in affiliation with the devil's work—since all other work belongs to the devil (see note on 2:19; note on v. 8; compare note on Jn 14:6). John is not suggesting that believers should break all ties with unbelievers; rather, he is issuing a stern warning against the teachings of those who have left the community (see 1Jn 2:18–27).

3:11–24 Obedience and love serve as evidence of a genuine relationship with Jesus and other believers (see 2:3–6). It means loving other people, even at personal cost (2:7–11). Here John develops that argument more fully.

3:12 Cain Refers to the son of Adam and Eve who killed his brother, Abel (Ge 4:1–16). **who belonged to the evil one** Cain's story shows where sin leads—to works of evil, such as jealousy and murder.

3:13 the world hates you John's audience lived in a culture that often opposed the values of Christianity.

3:15 who hates a brother or sister is a murderer John applies the example of Cain murdering his biological brother to hatred between siblings in the Lord (other believers). Hatred comes from the same emotional place as murder—a point that Jesus also made (Mt 5:21–24; compare 1Jn 3:17).

3:16 lay down our lives John sees this act as being practiced primarily in everyday acts of compassion.

4:1–6 John continues to discuss the role of the Spirit in the life of the believer. He encourages the community to evaluate teachings to determine if they are from God or from those who have separated from the community (the antichrists; 1Jn 2:18–19).

4:1 spirit Refers to the spiritual source of a teaching or doctrine. According to John, every teaching about Christ originates from a spiritual source. A teaching is either true and from the Spirit of God, or false and from the spirit of deceit (v. 6). **test the spirits** Believers derive their ability to test truth and falsehood from their anointing by God, their knowledge of the teachings of Jesus, and the work of the Holy Spirit in them (2:20,27; 3:24). They can determine a spirit's origin by examining whether its teaching reflects the love of Christ. **because many false prophets** John likely is drawing on the descriptions in Dt 13:1–5 about the testing of prophets (see note on Dt 13:1; note on Dt 13:3; compare note on Mt 7:15), as well as the spiritual gift of discerning between spirits (see note on 1Co 12:10; compare Php 1:9–10).

4:2 Spirit of God Refers to the source of true teaching about Christ. **acknowledges that Jesus Christ has come in the flesh** A true spirit from God will confess

not from God. This is the spirit of the antichrist, which you have heard is coming and even now is already in the world.

[4]You, dear children, are from God and have overcome them, because the one who is in you is greater than the one who is in the world. [5]They are from the world and therefore speak from the viewpoint of the world, and the world listens to them. [6]We are from God, and whoever knows God listens to us; but whoever is not from God does not listen to us. This is how we recognize the Spirit[a] of truth and the spirit of falsehood.

God's Love and Ours

[7]Dear friends, let us love one another, for love comes from God. Everyone who loves has been born of God and knows God. [8]Whoever does not love does not know God, because God is love. [9]This is how God showed his love among us: He sent his one and only Son into the world that we might live through him. [10]This is love: not that we loved God, but that he loved us and sent his Son as an atoning sacrifice for our sins. [11]Dear friends, since God so loved us, we also ought to love one another. [12]No one has ever seen God; but if we love one another, God lives in us and his love is made complete in us.

[13]This is how we know that we live in him and he in us: He has given us of his Spirit. [14]And we have seen and testify that the Father has sent his Son to be the Savior of the world. [15]If anyone ac-knowledges that Jesus is the Son of God, God lives in them and they in God. [16]And so we know and rely on the love God has for us.

God is love. Whoever lives in love lives in God, and God in them. [17]This is how love is made complete among us so that we will have confidence on the day of judgment: In this world we are like Jesus. [18]There is no fear in love. But perfect love drives out fear, because fear has to do with punishment. The one who fears is not made perfect in love.

[19]We love because he first loved us. [20]Whoever claims to love God yet hates a brother or sister is a liar. For whoever does not love their brother and sister, whom they have seen, cannot love God, whom they have not seen. [21]And he has given us this command: Anyone who loves God must also love their brother and sister.

Faith in the Incarnate Son of God

5 Everyone who believes that Jesus is the Christ is born of God, and everyone who loves the father loves his child as well. [2]This is how we know that we love the children of God: by loving God and carrying out his commands. [3]In fact, this is love for God: to keep his commands. And his commands are not burdensome, [4]for everyone born of God overcomes the world. This is the victory that has overcome the world,

[a] 6 Or *spirit*

Jesus' true humanity. The later heretical teaching known as Docetism held that Jesus appeared to be human, but that his humanity was nothing more than an illusion. The secessionists in 1 John seem to have shared views similar to Docetism.

4:3 does not acknowledge Jesus Refers to denying Jesus' humanity (compare 1Jn 2:18 and note). John is opposing a group of people who hold this view, which goes against Jesus' true identity.

4:4 overcome them As believers face false teachings, they can have assurance in Jesus' victory over evil.

4:5 from the world Their values are derived from human society.

4:6 does not listen to us John is speaking about those who have left the recipients' congregation and rejected God's truth.

4:7—5:4 John explains that God's true children will reflect his character. John also emphasizes another central teaching denied by the false teachers—Christ's saving work on the cross.

4:7 been born of God Those whom God has fathered spiritually (believers in Christ) enjoy a relationship with him (1:3; 3:1,10); they have been adopted as God's children. As Father, God provides his children with guidance through the Spirit. John's use of this language reflects God's act of making people one with him and restoring the image that God intended for humanity in the beginning (compare note on Ge 1:27).

4:8 God is love John's point is that God can be known only through his demonstration of his love, most pro-foundly seen in sending his Son in the flesh as a sacrifice for humanity.

4:10 as an atoning sacrifice Refers to the reconciliatory significance of Christ's death and resurrection. See 1Jn 1:7 and note; compare 2:2.

4:12 No one has ever seen God John doesn't consider OT characters to have seen the fullness of God (e.g., Ex 33:20; compare note on Ex 24:10; note on Ex 24:16).

4:14 Savior of the world Describes the purpose of Christ's incarnation—to rescue humanity from sin (1Jn 1:7; 2:2; 4:10).

4:17 made complete among us God's love is made perfect, or complete, among believers when they reflect God's loving character in their lives (see 1:5–7; 2:1–6,28; 3:16–20). Love is not an abstract concept for John; it concerns the outworking of the believers' faith in ordinary interactions with people. **we will have confidence on the day of judgment** Believers can be confident on the basis of God's love toward them; they do not have to fear his judgment.

4:21 must also love their brother and sister The believer's responsibility to show Christ-like sacrificial love to other Christians is not optional; it is commanded by God as a way of displaying his love to the world (2:3–4,7–8; 3:22–24; 5:2–3).

5:1 born of God See note on 4:7. **father loves his child as well** Believers should love one another because they are now spiritual siblings, adopted into the same family by God the Father (4:21; 5:2; Jn 14:9–20).

5:2 carrying out his commands John is referring to the commandments of Jesus, not the Jewish law (1Jn 2:7–8).

even our faith. ⁵Who is it that overcomes the world? Only the one who believes that Jesus is the Son of God.

⁶This is the one who came by water and blood—Jesus Christ. He did not come by water only, but by water and blood. And it is the Spirit who testifies, because the Spirit is the truth. ⁷For there are three that testify: ⁸the*a* Spirit, the water and the blood; and the three are in agreement. ⁹We accept human testimony, but God's testimony is greater because it is the testimony of God, which he has given about his Son. ¹⁰Whoever believes in the Son of God accepts this testimony. Whoever does not believe God has made him out to be a liar, because they have not believed the testimony God has given about his Son. ¹¹And this is the testimony: God has given us eternal life, and this life is in his Son. ¹²Whoever has the Son has life; whoever does not have the Son of God does not have life.

Concluding Affirmations

¹³I write these things to you who believe in the name of the Son of God so that you may know that you have eternal life. ¹⁴This is the confidence we have in approaching God: that if we ask anything according to his will, he hears us. ¹⁵And if we know that he hears us—whatever we ask—we know that we have what we asked of him.

¹⁶If you see any brother or sister commit a sin that does not lead to death, you should pray and God will give them life. I refer to those whose sin does not lead to death. There is a sin that leads to death. I am not saying that you should pray about that. ¹⁷All wrongdoing is sin, and there is sin that does not lead to death.

¹⁸We know that anyone born of God does not

---

a 7,8 Late manuscripts of the Vulgate *testify in heaven: the Father, the Word and the Holy Spirit, and these three are one.* *⁸And there are three that testify on earth: the* (not found in any Greek manuscript before the fourteenth century)

5:5–12 John expands on his discussion of Jesus' true humanity, a topic he introduced in ch. 4 (see 4:2 and note). He also discusses the eternal life that Jesus' atoning death makes available to believers.

5:6 water and blood The reference to water possibly is meant to allude to Jesus' baptism, or perhaps to the anointing of God's Spirit (Mt 3:13–17; Jn 1:32–34). The mention of blood might allude to Jesus' death (Jn 19:28–34). The purpose of John's symbolism here is debated, but most likely he wanted to assert that Jesus was genuinely human—not human in appearance only. Taken together, the references to water and blood encapsulate the ministry of Jesus, from its beginning at his baptism to his sacrificial death on the cross. For John, confessing that Jesus is the Son of God meant confessing him as the anointed one of God—the Christ, who truly suffered and died on the cross.

5:7 three that testify Refers to testifying about the true humanity of Christ and his crucifixion. The three witnesses affirm the significance of Christ's atoning death, which the secessionists apparently denied. In the Bible, two or three witnesses are required to validate testimony (e.g., Dt 17:6; 19:15; Mt 18:16; 2Co 13:1; Heb 10:28). According to John, the Spirit of God—along with the water and the blood (likely referring to Christ's baptism and death)—bear witness to Christ's incarnation, which led to his sacrifice for sinful humanity.

5:8 Spirit, the water Throughout this letter, John identifies the Spirit as a testifier that confirms the truth (see 1Jn 3:24; 4:2,13). Some Bible translations, such as the King James Version, insert an additional clause between v. 7 and 8 (indicated by italics): "For there are three who bear witness *in heaven, the Father, the Word and the Holy Spirit; and these three are one. And there are three who bear witness in earth,* the spirit and the water and the blood; and these three are one." This clause emphasizes the oneness of God, as Father, Word (Jesus), and Spirit. This Trinitarian formula, called the Johannine Comma, is evident elsewhere in the NT, but it is stated explicitly in this addition. It is included in only four Greek manuscripts dating between the 14th and 18th centuries; it also is noted in the margin of five additional manuscripts, added in each case by a much later editorial hand. This means

that it does not appear until the second millennium in any Greek manuscripts.

5:10 made him out to be a liar The burden of proof stands against those who deny that Jesus came in the flesh. They are disputing with God, who speaks only truth.

5:11 eternal life Describes the gracious gift of life that Jesus offers believers, when the punishment for their sin should be death (compare 2:12; 3:15; Jn 3:16–17; Ro 6:23). This life begins now and is available only through relationship with God's Son, Jesus (Jn 14:6).

5:13–21 John insists that assurance of eternal life comes through belief in the Son of God, whom he has taken great care to properly identify throughout the letter. He also returns to the topics of sinful living and the identity of God's children.

5:14 according to his will This is an assurance that God hears all prayers; however, God answers prayers according to his will, which doesn't always align with human desires.

5:16 a sin that does not lead to death Refers to general sin, from which Christians should repent. Although the ultimate concern is the person committing sin, John's focus here is the Christian's responsibility to demonstrate love toward a fellow believer by intervening to curtail sinful behavior. **There is a sin that leads to death** John identifies a type of sin that cannot result in forgiveness and eternal life because it flatly rejects God's grace. This kind of sin likely includes denying that Jesus is the Son of God and God's anointed one (the Christ). It also might involve denying Jesus' humanity. John is not saying that people who commit such a sin cannot receive God's grace. Instead, he is explaining that those who continue to hold this belief are on the path to death; their disposition toward God makes it impossible for them to have relationship with him. **I am not saying** While John encourages Christians to pray for fellow believers who are committing sins that do not lead to death, they are not obligated to pray for those who intentionally oppose the grace of God. Such people are destructive to the Christian community and thus, by definition, antichrists (1Jn 2:18). The congregation is no longer responsible for them.

5:18 does not continue to sin John does not mean people automatically cease all sinful behavior after

continue to sin; the One who was born of God keeps them safe, and the evil one cannot harm them. ¹⁹We know that we are children of God, and that the whole world is under the control of the evil one. ²⁰We know also that the Son of God has come and has given us understanding, so that we may know him who is true. And we are in him who is true by being in his Son Jesus Christ. He is the true God and eternal life.

²¹Dear children, keep yourselves from idols.

---

they become believers (see 3:6 and note). Instead, he means that they do not deliberately continue sinful patterns, because they trust Christ's work on the cross that defeated sin's power.

5:19 evil one In contrast to believers who belong to the true family of God, people who merely abide by the values of human societies live under the power of the evil one—that is, the devil (2:13–14).

5:20 He is the true God and eternal life John affirms God and his Son, who are one (1:1–2). Believers in Jesus embrace the idea of God as Son in the flesh and live according to his commands.

5:21 idols Refers to anything that stands between people and God, whether physical or spiritual. All the falsehoods that John has opposed in the letter are forms of idolatry.

2 JOHN

INTRODUCTION TO 2 JOHN

Like 1 John, the brief letter of 2 John combats false teaching in the church. Christians are characterized by their love for one another, and this love embraces truth and resists evil. Instead of offering hospitality to false teachers, John's readers are not to share in their evil deeds in any fashion (2Jn 10–11).

BACKGROUND

The letters of both 2 and 3 John identify the author only as "the elder" (2Jn 1; 3Jn 1). Traditionally, this person has been understood to be the apostle John. However, in the early church there was some dispute about whether the apostle wrote 2–3 John, with some church fathers saying that these letters might have been written by a church leader whom they called "John the elder."

Second John is addressed to a woman and her children (2Jn 1). This could refer to a literal woman, but it could also be a metaphorical reference to the church. This would make the "children" members of a local congregation or a house church within the larger Christian community. The geographical location of this Christian community is unclear from the text. However, the apostle John spent his later years in Ephesus, so if he is the author, the letter might have been sent to one of the churches in the surrounding area of western Asia Minor.

The letters of 2–3 John were likely written sometime between AD 85 and the early second century. The dating of the letters depends on their relationship to 1 John and when the events they address took place.

The issue behind 2 John (as with 1 John) is that false teachers were trying to gain influence among the believers. It is not clear whether these are the same false teachers mentioned in 1 John, but it seems likely based on their denial of Jesus as God's Son in the flesh (compare 2Jn 7; 1Jn 4:2–3). The false teachers were apparently trying to pass themselves off as itinerant preachers to additional congregations (2Jn 10–11). Christians welcoming these preachers into their homes would have unwittingly helped them spread their false message. John tells his readers not to have fellowship or to speak with these false teachers. Christians should not support teaching that does not affirm the incarnation of Christ—such a refusal is a defense of the truth of God's Son.

STRUCTURE

The 13 verses of 2 John, which could have fit on one sheet of ancient paper (papyrus), follow the basic structure of a Greco-Roman letter, with a greeting (vv. 1–3), a body (vv. 4–11), and a conclusion (vv. 12–13). The letter's body begins with the command to love one another (vv. 4–6; compare Jn 13:34–35; 1Jn 3:23). The rest of the body of the letter focuses on how to identify and respond to false teaching (2Jn 7–11). The letter of 2 John concludes with John's hope to visit the letter's recipients (v. 12).

OUTLINE

- Greeting (vv. 1–3)
- The love commandment (vv. 4–6)
- Warning against false teachers (vv. 7–11)
- Conclusion (vv. 12–13)

THEMES

To confront the false teachers, 2 John emphasizes both love and truth. Love does not involve only positive feelings and acts of service; it requires true obedience to God—a real and authentic response (v. 6). Living according to God's commands means making difficult decisions. In this particular case, it means refusing to show hospitality to people who are circulating lies about Jesus. In discernment and love, followers of Christ must keep false teachers out of the Christian community in order to limit their influence and to protect those who might be led astray.

Love requires us to call out lies for what they are. The false teachers John writes about did not remain in Jesus' teaching (v. 9) and denied his incarnation (v. 7). Faith must be focused on the real personhood of Jesus. Even now, it is popular to claim to know God yet willfully ignore what the Bible says about him. When confronted with such teachings, John says, we should respond in love but also with the truth.

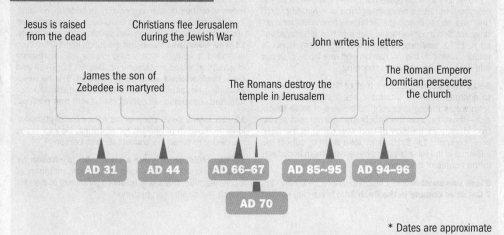

Dates Related to 2 John

Jesus is raised from the dead

Christians flee Jerusalem during the Jewish War

John writes his letters

James the son of Zebedee is martyred

The Romans destroy the temple in Jerusalem

The Roman Emperor Domitian persecutes the church

AD 31   AD 44   AD 66–67   AD 85–95   AD 94–96

AD 70

* Dates are approximate

¹The elder,

To the lady chosen by God and to her children, whom I love in the truth — and not I only, but also all who know the truth — ²because of the truth, which lives in us and will be with us forever:

³Grace, mercy and peace from God the Father and from Jesus Christ, the Father's Son, will be with us in truth and love.

⁴It has given me great joy to find some of your children walking in the truth, just as the Father commanded us. ⁵And now, dear lady, I am not writing you a new command but one we have had from the beginning. I ask that we love one another. ⁶And this is love: that we walk in obedience to his commands. As you have heard from the beginning, his command is that you walk in love.

⁷I say this because many deceivers, who do not acknowledge Jesus Christ as coming in the flesh, have gone out into the world. Any such person is the deceiver and the antichrist. ⁸Watch out that you do not lose what we[a] have worked for, but that you may be rewarded fully. ⁹Anyone who runs ahead and does not continue in the teaching of Christ does not have God; whoever continues in the teaching has both the Father and the Son. ¹⁰If anyone comes to you and does not bring this teaching, do not take them into your house or welcome them. ¹¹Anyone who welcomes them shares in their wicked work.

¹²I have much to write to you, but I do not want to use paper and ink. Instead, I hope to visit you and talk with you face to face, so that our joy may be complete.

¹³The children of your sister, who is chosen by God, send their greetings.

[a] 8 Some manuscripts *you*

1–4 Second John follows the conventions of ancient letter writing. It begins with a greeting and blessing followed by the body of the letter, and closes with a benediction. The author, who calls himself "the elder," greets the elect lady and expresses joy over her children, who walk in the truth. This is an official letter from an elder to a church likely in the midst of attempted deception by false teachers (see 2Jn 10 and note).

The date of 2 John depends on when the events the letter addresses took place and the relationship between 1 John and 2 John. The letter was likely written sometime between AD 85 and the early second century.

1 The elder The identity of the elder is unknown. It may be John the apostle, to whom church tradition ascribes the authorship of 1 John and the Gospel of John, or another early church leader named John, who is referred to in early church writings as "John the elder." **To the lady chosen by God and to her children** Although John may be addressing a literal woman (compare Rev 2:20,23), he is likely addressing a congregation within a community of believers in Ephesus (see 1Jn 1:3 and note).
4 some of your children If the reference to the lady in 2Jn 1 refers to a congregation, then this refers to the members of the same congregation or a house church that was part of the larger Christian community John addresses. See the infographic "Ancient Home Synagogue" on p. 1971. **walking in the truth** John metaphorically refers to living by the instruction and revelation of Jesus and the received apostolic teaching.

5–11 This warning echoes that of 1 John and seems to address a similar situation (see 2Jn 10 and note). John warns the congregation to beware of false teachers—those he calls the antichrists who contest Jesus' true identity as the Son of God who came in the flesh (v. 7; compare 1Jn 2:18–19). John aims to cut off the influence of the false teachers by denying them hospitality in the homes of believers.

5 love one another See 1Jn 2:8 and note; Jn 13:34–35.
7 Christ as coming in the flesh John is warning against the false belief that Jesus did not take on a physical body but only appeared to have a bodily existence. **the antichrist** Someone who denies the fully human and fully divine nature of Jesus and instead teaches a false Jesus. John has multiple people in mind, not just one individual.
8 rewarded fully Refers to the authentic work of the Christian community, especially as seen in the eternal life that Christ has granted them. John is not suggesting that people achieve their own salvation—only Jesus' work can offer that—but instead that they should witness the work of salvation within their community (1Jn 5:4–12; compare note on 5:18).
9 does not continue in the teaching of Christ This represents the main point of John's letter: Those who have bought into the false teachers' distorted view of Jesus no longer remain in the teaching of Christ.
10 do not take them into your house John encourages the Christian community to avoid those he calls the antichrists and their infectious heresy at all costs. The house here probably refers to the house church and thus John's audience may be welcoming these antichrists in as teachers, when they should be refuted and rejected. John realizes that the false teachers (the antichrists) will not be able to economically sustain their efforts if they are not received by the Christian community. In addition, hospitality in the ancient world would have been perceived as an endorsement and thus confused people in the community.
11 who welcomes them The greetings in mind involved extended hospitality that would create the impression of acceptance and endorsement. See Mt 10:9–14 and note. **their wicked work** John indicates that he views extending hospitality to an antichrist or false teacher from the community as collaboration with that person.

12–13 John's description of his future travel plans follows the custom of ancient letter writing. He expresses his desire to finish his conversation in person.

13 The children of your sister, who is chosen by God If the children referenced in 2Jn 4 are members of a congregation, this likely refers to members of a sister church—a nearby congregation.

3 JOHN

INTRODUCTION TO 3 JOHN

A major concern of 3 John, like 2 John, is hospitality. This time, instead of discouraging hospitality to false teachers (2Jn 10), John wants to encourage hospitality for traveling missionaries who speak the truth (3Jn 8). John contrasts one man's inhospitable actions with another's faithfulness — and in the process, John demonstrates the need for godly leadership like his own.

BACKGROUND

Third John, the shortest letter in the New Testament, concerns four individuals: John, Gaius, Diotrephes and Demetrius. The author introduces himself as John and is likely the same person responsible for 2 John. (For a discussion of authorship and dating, see the "Introduction to 2 John.") Third John is written to a man named Gaius to encourage him to continue in faithfulness. There are multiple people named Gaius in the New Testament (Ac 19:29; 1Co 1:14), but it was a common name, and the Gaius of 3 John cannot clearly be identified with any of them. If the apostle John wrote the letter, it is likely that Gaius was part of a church community in Asia Minor, where John lived in his later life.

Unlike 1–2 John, it is not clear that the primary issue behind this letter is false teachers. Instead, there seems to be some kind of power struggle in the church. A man named Diotrephes has tried to take control, while others such as Gaius are walking in the truth (3Jn 4). John, who clearly has some kind of authority over this community, is attempting to straighten out the issue from afar. John also rebukes Diotrephes for refusing to acknowledge his authority or to welcome his fellow ministers (vv. 9–10). In response to this situation, John has sent a man named Demetrius to represent him (v. 12), but the letter says that he might come himself (v. 10).

STRUCTURE

Third John follows the standard format of a Greco-Roman letter: introduction (vv. 1–4), body (vv. 5–12), and conclusion (vv. 13–14). The body includes John's instructions for Gaius to welcome missionaries visiting the community (vv. 5–8); John's criticism of Diotrephes, whose selfishness and desire for control implicate him in evil (vv. 9–11); and John's recommendation of Demetrius, who probably was the letter's carrier (v. 12). John closes by expressing his hope that he and Gaius can soon speak face to face (vv. 13–14).

OUTLINE

- Greeting (vv. 1–4)
- Gaius is instructed (vv. 5–8)
- Diotrephes is criticized (vv. 9–11)
- Demetrius is recommended (v. 12)
- Conclusion (vv. 13–14)

THEMES

Third John—like 1–2 John—highlights love and hospitality: Gaius is encouraged to give a warm welcome to the missionaries, who are strangers to him but who are doing good work. His actions should be the opposite of Diotrephes, who not only refuses to help the travelers, but also slanders and opposes those who disagree with him, including John.

Another theme of 3 John is the nature of church leadership. Diotrephes wants to be in control. He rejects others' authority and spreads lies about them. People like Diotrephes, who want to do battle with anyone who might challenge them, do not exhibit the self-sacrificial love that church leadership requires. John, on the other hand, provides a better model. He encourages Gaius to exercise hospitality and warns him to steer clear of Diotrephes and his arrogant ways. He clearly loves Gaius and gains joy from hearing that he is living out the truth (v. 4).

Like 1–2 John, 3 John connects intimacy with God to right actions. When people do evil, their claims about knowing God lose all merit. A genuine relationship with God always bears the fruit of right actions: loving others (1Jn 4:7), remaining in Christ's teachings (2Jn 9) and doing good (3Jn 11). This means getting out of our comfort zone for the sake of God's work. As John encourages us, we should embrace the blessing of welcoming missionaries into our lives and homes; we must then empower them to continue their efforts elsewhere (vv. 5–8). We confirm that we know God by our deeds: love, hospitality and walking in the truth.

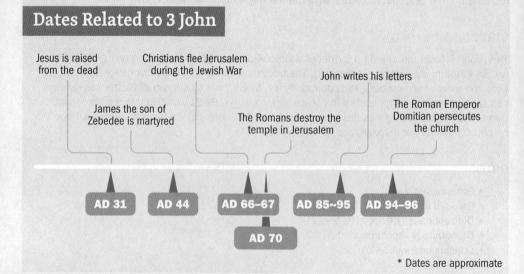

Dates Related to 3 John

Jesus is raised from the dead

Christians flee Jerusalem during the Jewish War

John writes his letters

James the son of Zebedee is martyred

The Romans destroy the temple in Jerusalem

The Roman Emperor Domitian persecutes the church

AD 31   **AD 44**   **AD 66–67**   **AD 85~95**   **AD 94–96**

AD 70

* Dates are approximate

¹The elder,

To my dear friend Gaius, whom I love in the truth.

²Dear friend, I pray that you may enjoy good health and that all may go well with you, even as your soul is getting along well. ³It gave me great joy when some believers came and testified about your faithfulness to the truth, telling how you continue to walk in it. ⁴I have no greater joy than to hear that my children are walking in the truth.

⁵Dear friend, you are faithful in what you are doing for the brothers and sisters,ᵃ even though they are strangers to you. ⁶They have told the church about your love. Please send them on their way in a manner that honors God. ⁷It was for the sake of the Name that they went out, receiving no help from the pagans. ⁸We ought therefore to show hospitality to such people so that we may work together for the truth.

⁹I wrote to the church, but Diotrephes, who loves to be first, will not welcome us. ¹⁰So when I come, I will call attention to what he is doing, spreading malicious nonsense about us. Not satisfied with that, he even refuses to welcome other believers. He also stops those who want to do so and puts them out of the church.

¹¹Dear friend, do not imitate what is evil but what is good. Anyone who does what is good is from God. Anyone who does what is evil has not seen God. ¹²Demetrius is well spoken of by everyone—and even by the truth itself. We also speak well of him, and you know that our testimony is true.

¹³I have much to write you, but I do not want to do so with pen and ink. ¹⁴I hope to see you soon, and we will talk face to face.

Peace to you. The friends here send their greetings. Greet the friends there by name.

ᵃ 5 The Greek word for *brothers and sisters* (*adelphoi*) refers here to believers, both men and women, as part of God's family.

1–4 Like 2 John, 3 John follows the conventions of ancient letter writing. John is writing to the same community, but in 3 John he addresses matters of hospitality rather than false teaching (compare note on 2Jn 1–4). John greets and blesses Gaius, whom he petitions for hospitality on behalf of fellow laborers for the gospel.

Like 2 John, the date of 3 John depends on when the events addressed in the letter took place and its relationship to 1 John. The letters may have been composed anytime between AD 85 and the early second century.

1 The elder See note on 2Jn 1. **To my dear friend Gaius** This title of admiration indicates that Gaius was a reputable member of the community. Based on the context of the rest of the letter, it seems that he was known for his hospitality and support of the apostolic mission (3Jn 3).
2 that you may enjoy good health and that all may go well The personal nature of this greeting and blessing may suggest that 3 John was only intended to be correspondence between associates, not a letter read aloud to the church (compare 2Jn 1–4).
4 my children A reference to John's spiritual children, the members of the churches (or the congregations themselves) that he is addressing. See 1Jn 2:1 and note.

5–8 In this section, John elicits support from Gaius for missionaries traveling to him—encouraging Gaius to help further the mission of Jesus' gospel.

5 brothers and sisters Refers to missionaries associated with or familiar to John.
6 They have told the church about your love Before appealing to Gaius for support, John praises the reputation that Gaius has made for himself by being hospitable and showing good will to traveling missionaries. **send them on their way** Refers to giving missionaries support and meeting their needs, possibly including lodging, sustenance and monetary support. Hospitality was central to the missionary endeavor in the first century (see Mt 10:9–14; 2Jn 10 and note; 2Jn 11 and note). Local believers would welcome traveling believers into their homes and meet their needs. This was viewed as paying the missionaries for their local ministry efforts while in an area, as well as a furthering of the gospel effort in general. In addition to ministering, the traveling

missionaries would impart a blessing on their hosts for showing them kindness (see Mt 10:12–14).
7 for the sake of the Name Refers to the name of Christ (1Jn 2:12; 3:23; 5:13). **receiving no help from the pagans** The first-century believers desired for missionary efforts to be funded solely by the Christian community, so that missionaries did not have to request support from the unreached people they were sharing the gospel with.
8 we may work together By assisting traveling missionaries, believers become part of the larger effort of the gospel reaching the world. Jesus introduced the idea of sharing in the evangelistic mission by offering hospitality (see Mt 10:40–42).

9–12 In this section, John notes Diotrephes' refusal to help missionaries on an earlier visit. John also promises to deal with Diotrephes when he comes to the community.

9 loves to be first Diotrephes was apparently a usurper of authority. John may also be describing Diotrephes' concern for his own needs—he did not want to share his resources with others.
10 puts them out of the church Diotrephes may have been using John's words against false teachers in 2 John against the missionaries and John himself (see 2Jn 10 and note; 2Jn 11 and note).
11 who does what is evil has not seen God The warning concerns unrighteous patterns of life rather than single, sporadic sins. Those who oppose the message of Jesus, especially while claiming otherwise (like Diotrephes has) show themselves to be people who do not know God at all.
12 well spoken of by everyone Contrasts the description of Diotrephes. Demetrius may have been the leader of the missionaries coming to Gaius, or he may have been the one who carried this letter (3 John) to Gaius.

13–14 In this closing section, John mentions his travel plans and offers a benediction (see 2Jn 12–13 and note).

14 The friends here send their greetings In the Gospel of John, Jesus says that the greatest display of love is for a person to lay down their life for their friends (Jn 15:13; compare 1Jn 3:16). John's language may be related to Jesus' description of his followers as friends (Jn 15:14–15). **Greet the friends there by name** Refers to members of Gaius' community.

JUDE

INTRODUCTION TO JUDE

Jude writes to a community that needs to take a stand for the truth. A group of false teachers has entered the church. Through false revelations, they are prompting believers to use the grace of God as license for immorality, especially of the sexual kind. Jude warns against compromising with evil. He points out that the false teachers, in their selfish actions, have rejected the authentic Jesus. Jude challenges Christians to remain firm in the faith that leads to eternal life. He encourages Christians to live as people empowered by the Holy Spirit, standing in the love of God (Jude 17–21).

BACKGROUND

The letter identifies Jude as a servant of Jesus Christ and brother of James (v. 1). In the early church, the most well-known James was the brother of Jesus (Gal 1:19)—so Jude (also called Judas) often has been understood to be another of Jesus' brothers, even though the letter does not state this (compare Mt 13:55; Mk 6:3).

It is not possible to know for certain when Jude was written. If the author was indeed a brother of Jesus, the letter probably was in circulation before the end of the first century. Jude has a literary relationship to 2 Peter, which could be used to help date Jude more accurately, but the date of 2 Peter also is unknown.

Jude warns against a heresy that in some ways resembles what later became Gnosticism, a philosophy that regarded physical matter as evil and spirit as good. This way of understanding the world often encouraged people to do whatever they wished with their physical body. In addition, the false teachers whom Jude addresses apparently were guilty of rebellion against authority, presumptuous speech, and sexual immorality. Jude rebukes them for deceiving unstable believers and corrupting the Lord's Supper. Although the date and author of Jude is uncertain, the social situation is obvious: A group of false teachers are wreaking havoc in the congregation, and this must be stopped.

STRUCTURE

The book of Jude is one chapter in modern Bibles. After the introduction and greeting (Jude 1–2), the author begins by explaining his reason for writing (vv. 3–4): He wants his readers to contend for the faith in its true form because false teachers are distorting it. The bulk of the letter (vv. 5–16) is devoted to describing and denouncing these opponents of the faith. The language that Jude uses in this section is similar to remarks in 2 Peter (with 2 Peter perhaps drawing on Jude's words). Jude characterizes the false teachers with examples from the Old Testament (vv. 5–7,11), from nature (vv. 12–13) and from ancient writings outside the Bible (vv. 9,14–15).

Jude advises believers to build themselves up in faith, prayer and love, and to help those whom the false teachers have led astray (vv. 17–23). The letter ends with a powerful statement called a doxology that praises the only God, our savior, through Jesus Christ our Lord (vv. 24–25).

OUTLINE

- Greeting (vv. 1–2)
- Purpose for writing (vv. 3–4)
- Judgment on false teachers (vv. 5–16)
- Exhortation to persevere (vv. 17–23)
- Doxology (vv. 24–25)

THEMES

The primary purpose of the letter of Jude is to warn against false teachers. Jude felt a pastoral responsibility to this community to keep them from straying into dangerous territory. In doing so, Jude shows that false teaching is nothing new: It has happened before in the community of God's people, and it even happens in the spiritual realm. The church always needs to be on guard against distortions of the truth.

Jude shows us that we are all vulnerable to mistaking our own desires for God's will. Although a false teaching might seem plausible at first—and a false teacher might appear authentic—it ends up pointing away from God and toward destruction. To avoid being led astray, we need to rely on the Spirit's guidance and invite other believers to help hold us accountable (vv. 17–23). We should take advantage of these safeguards—staying on the path and assisting others who are struggling. Jude encourages us to uncover falseness by contending boldly for the faith, with full assurance that God's power will keep us from stumbling (v. 24).

Dates Related to Jude

Jesus is raised from the dead	James the son of Zebedee is martyred	Jude writes his letter	Peter and Paul are martyred in Rome
Paul is converted on the road to Damascus	The Jerusalem Council	James the brother of Jesus is martyred	The Romans destroy the temple in Jerusalem
AD 31	AD 49	AD 60~80	AD 64~67
AD 33	AD 44	AD 62	AD 70

* Dates are approximate

¹Jude, a servant of Jesus Christ and a brother of James,

To those who have been called, who are loved in God the Father and kept for*ᵃ* Jesus Christ:

²Mercy, peace and love be yours in abundance.

The Sin and Doom of Ungodly People

³Dear friends, although I was very eager to write to you about the salvation we share, I felt compelled to write and urge you to contend for the faith that was once for all entrusted to God's holy people. ⁴For certain individuals whose condem-nation was written about*ᵇ* long ago have secretly slipped in among you. They are ungodly people, who pervert the grace of our God into a license for immorality and deny Jesus Christ our only Sovereign and Lord.

⁵Though you already know all this, I want to remind you that the Lord*ᶜ* at one time delivered his people out of Egypt, but later destroyed those who did not believe. ⁶And the angels who did not keep their positions of authority but abandoned their proper dwelling — these he has kept in darkness, bound with everlasting chains for judgment on the

---

ᵃ 1 Or *by*; or *in*   *ᵇ 4* Or *individuals who were marked out for condemnation*   *ᶜ 5* Some early manuscripts *Jesus*

1–2 Jude begins his letter by identifying himself, describing his relationship to Jesus and James, and defining his audience as believers in Jesus. If the author of the letter is the brother of Jesus (Mt 13:55; Mk 6:3), then the letter would have been written before the end of the first century AD. Based on its specific nature, the letter of Jude was probably originally addressed to an individual congregation, although which congregation is unknown.

After some introductory remarks about himself and his audience, Jude offers his audience a blessing; this blessing of mercy, peace and love corresponds closely to Paul's "grace, mercy and peace" (2Ti 1:2). These virtues would help Jude's audience withstand the influence of false teachers, whom he calls ungodly people and scoffers (Jude 4,18; see note on v. 4). Jude shares material with 2 Peter. However, the precise relationship between Jude and 2 Peter is a matter of debate (see note on 2Pe 1:1–7). Jude 4–13 parallels 2 Peter 2:1–17, although they use the same material differently. In addition, Jude 17–18 parallels 2Pe 3:2–3, and Jude 24–25 may be compared to 2Pe 3:18.

1 Jude The Greek name *Ioudas* derives from the Hebrew name Judah and was a popular name among Jewish men. The name Judah recalls the tribal founder and the patriarch Jacob. **a servant** Describes Jude's complete devotion to Jesus (see note on 2Pe 1:1). **brother of James** Jude is the only NT writer to introduce himself by identifying his family connections. The James here is likely Jesus' brother (Mt 13:55), but it could be another James. If Jude is the brother of the former James, then he is also Jesus' brother. James and Jude may be Mary and Joseph's children or just Joseph's (if Joseph was a widower prior to his marriage with Mary; compare Mk 15:40 and note). **kept for Jesus Christ** Indicates that Jesus is the one who is able to give believers the strength to persevere through all difficulties, either until their death or Jesus' return.

3–4 Jude notes that while he intended to write about salvation, he felt compelled to address the danger confronting his audience — false teachers.

3 salvation we share This salvation consists of freedom (Jude 5), the gift of the Spirit (v. 20) and the ability to live a pure life — all of which are offered freely because of Jesus' death and resurrection (Jude 24; compare Jn 3:16–17). **for the faith that was once for all entrusted** Refers to the work accomplished by Jesus' death and resurrection (compare Gal 1:23). **once for all** This faith has been delivered to believers as the one and only message of God's salvation (compare Heb 1:1–2; Jn 14:6–7). **to God's holy people** Refers to those who have been set apart for God's work. See note on Ro 1:7.

4 condemnation Since the false teachers mentioned here are intentionally and unrepentantly leading others astray, Jude is sure of their fate (compare note on 2Pe 2:3; Mt 7:15; Mk 13:22; Ac 20:29–30). **have secretly slipped in** This probably refers to traveling teachers who proclaimed falsehoods; itinerant preachers were common in the first-century church (Ac 13:15; 2Jn 7–11; compare the early Christian work *Didache* 11.1–12; 13.1–7). False teachers could also have arisen within the community, established themselves as trustworthy, and then brought in destructive teachings from the outside (compare 2Pe 2:1; Gal 2:4; Ac 20:29–30; Ro 16:17–18). Either way, it appears these people were acting as leaders and in the process were leading others astray. **ungodly people** The NT employs the Greek term, *asebēs*, to describe "ungodly" conduct (e.g., 2Pe 2:5–6; 1Ti 1:9). Jude uses the word here to describe the shameless deeds and illicit desires of the false teachers (Jude 15,18). Jude goes on to describe the specific activities that exemplify their ungodly actions. **a license for immorality** Implies sexual debauchery, which the false teachers were engaging in (see note on 2Pe 2:7). **deny Jesus Christ our only Sovereign and Lord** The misrepresentation of the gospel of Jesus by these false teachers was tantamount to denial of Jesus himself. See note on 2Pe 2:1.

5–7 In this section, Jude recalls three examples from the OT. Each of these examples highlights a particular aspect of the false teachers' errors: They practiced the sin of unbelief (Jude 5), they sought authority they did not deserve (v. 6) and they engaged in immoral behavior (v. 7).

5 Though you already know all this Jude's audience is fully informed about the message of Jesus and the events, derived primarily from the OT, Jude is about to cite (compare 2Pe 1:12–15). **Lord** While some manuscripts read "the Lord," the earliest manuscript evidence favors an original reading of "Jesus." If this is the case, Jude specifies that the preexistent Jesus was present throughout the exodus deliverance (see 1Co 10:4), perhaps as the Angel of Yahweh (see note on Ex 23:20). **destroyed those who did not believe** The Israelites did not believe that Yahweh would give them the promised land. As a result, Yahweh declared that the generation he first brought out of Egypt would die in the wilderness without entering the promised land (see Nu 14:20–35; compare Heb 3:16–19; 1Co 10:1–11).

6 Jude describes the fall of the rebellious angels, who sinned by abandoning their assigned domain. Because of their rebellion, God judged them and confined them to darkness. Jude likely draws this viewpoint from the "sons of God" narrative in Ge 6:1–4 and Jewish tradition

great Day. [7]In a similar way, Sodom and Gomorrah and the surrounding towns gave themselves up to sexual immorality and perversion. They serve as an example of those who suffer the punishment of eternal fire.

[8]In the very same way, on the strength of their dreams these ungodly people pollute their own bodies, reject authority and heap abuse on celestial beings. [9]But even the archangel Michael, when he was disputing with the devil about the body of Moses, did not himself dare to condemn him for slander but said, "The Lord rebuke you!"[a] [10]Yet these people slander whatever they do not understand, and the very things they do understand by instinct — as irrational animals do — will destroy them.

[11]Woe to them! They have taken the way of Cain; they have rushed for profit into Balaam's error; they have been destroyed in Korah's rebellion. [12]These people are blemishes at your love feasts, eating with you without the slightest qualm — shepherds who feed only themselves. They are clouds without rain, blown along by the wind; autumn trees, without fruit and uprooted — twice dead. [13]They are wild waves of the sea, foaming up their shame; wandering stars, for whom blackest darkness has been reserved forever.

[14]Enoch, the seventh from Adam, prophesied about them: "See, the Lord is coming with

[a] 9 Jude is alluding to the Jewish *Testament of Moses* (approximately the first century A.D.).

about that story, such as the extra-Biblical book 1 Enoch 6–19. See note on 2Pe 2:4.

6 who did not keep their positions of authority In Ge 6:1–4, the "sons of God" sin by leaving the spiritual realm and having intercourse with human women (see note on Ge 6:4). **darkness, bound with everlasting chains** Now in bondage, these fallen angels await God's judgment on the day Jesus returns to earth. See note on 2Pe 2:4. **darkness** Refers to some sort of underworld (Tartarus, Hades, hell, or Sheol; see note on 2Pe 2:4; compare note on 1Pe 3:19).
7 Sodom and Gomorrah and the surrounding towns Genesis 19 mentions only Sodom and Gomorrah by name, but Ge 19:25 states that other cities in the valley were also destroyed. **the punishment of eternal fire** Yahweh, whose judgment is eternally true, destroyed Sodom and Gomorrah with sulfur and fire (Ge 19:24).

8–9 In this section, Jude equates his three examples of sinful actions (Jude 5–7) with the preposterous actions of the false teachers, who he notes even dishonor spiritual powers.

8 dreams Likely indicates that the false teachers were relying on dreams (or visions) that they claimed were prophetic. They used these dreams to excuse their immoral behavior. **heap abuse on celestial beings** The false teachers act in a way that slanders the words or authority of powerful, spiritual beings. See note on 2Pe 2:10.
9 Michael One of two archangels mentioned in the Bible (the other is Gabriel; see Da 8:16; 9:21; Lk 1:19; Rev 12:7). Others, such as Raphael and Phanuel, are mentioned in early Jewish texts (see 1 Enoch 40:9; 71:8–9). Daniel 12:1 portrays Michael as a special guardian to Israel. See the table "Angels in the Bible" on p. 2120. **he was disputing with the devil about the body of Moses** The reason for their argument over Moses' body is unknown. This event does not appear in the OT (see Dt 34:5–6 for the death of Moses, and Zec 3:1–5 for a similar dispute). Jude may have derived this information from oral tradition or a pseudepigraphal work called *The Assumption of Moses*. It is unclear whether Jude regarded this event as historical; he may have merely been relying on it as a well-known story by way of illustration. **did not himself dare to condemn** While Michael showed restraint — even in dealing with the devil — the false teachers exhibited no reverence for authority.

10–13 After citing a contrasting example (Jude 9), Jude

shifts again to criticizing the false teachers for their words and actions. To illustrate his point, Jude presents figures from the past who resemble the false teachers. He discusses three OT figures — Cain, Balaam and Korah (v. 11). Jude then uses several metaphors from nature to condemn the false teachers. He compares them to clouds swept in the wind, fruitless trees, untamable waves, and stars (or planets) (vv. 12–13).

11 way of Cain See Ge 4:5–8; compare 1Jn 3:12.
Balaam's error A false prophet who spoke against God's people (Nu 22–24; compare note on 2Pe 2:15).
in Korah's rebellion Korah perished after rebelling against God's appointed leaders, Moses and Aaron (Nu 16:1–35).
12 love feasts In the ancient world, shared meals were significant social events; feasts were held for various celebrations and helped bring people together for a common purpose. In Christian circles, this included celebrating the Lord's Supper. **autumn** When fruit is gathered; implies that the false teachers are not offering anything productive (compare Mk 11:12–25). **twice dead** Trees bearing no fruit would first be declared dead and then uprooted, making them only useful as firewood (compare Jn 15:2–6).
13 wild waves of the sea The lives of the ungodly resemble raging tides that litter the shore with refuse or seas that are so tumultuous that they are impossible to navigate (compare Isa 57:20). **wandering stars** The Greek word used here may be literally rendered as "wanderer." It could refer to planets, which in the ancient mindset disappeared into blackness for no apparent reason. It may also reference shooting stars, which appear for just a moment and then vanish. Likewise the false teachers briefly provide light, only to move into darkness — leading others astray. They mix truth (light) with falsehood (darkness).

14–16 In Jude 14–15, Jude supports his arguments by quoting from the extra-Biblical work of 1 Enoch 1:9 (see v. 6 and note). Jude connects the judgment of 1 Enoch 1:9 to the false teachers, emphasizing the false teachers' arrogance and selfish desires (v. 16; see note on 2Pe 3:3). The fact that Jude quotes from 1 Enoch does not necessarily mean he regarded it as being at the same authoritative level as the OT; he could be using it as supplemental teaching.

14 thousands upon thousands of his holy ones Spiritual beings (likely angels) join in the judgment of

thousands upon thousands of his holy ones [15]to judge everyone, and to convict all of them of all the ungodly acts they have committed in their ungodliness, and of all the defiant words ungodly sinners have spoken against him."[a] [16]These people are grumblers and faultfinders; they follow their own evil desires; they boast about themselves and flatter others for their own advantage.

A Call to Persevere

[17]But, dear friends, remember what the apostles of our Lord Jesus Christ foretold. [18]They said to you, "In the last times there will be scoffers who will follow their own ungodly desires." [19]These are the people who divide you, who follow mere natural instincts and do not have the Spirit. [20]But you, dear friends, by building yourselves up in your most holy faith and praying in the Holy Spirit, [21]keep yourselves in God's love as you wait for the mercy of our Lord Jesus Christ to bring you to eternal life.

[22]Be merciful to those who doubt; [23]save others by snatching them from the fire; to others show mercy, mixed with fear—hating even the clothing stained by corrupted flesh.[b]

Doxology

[24]To him who is able to keep you from stumbling and to present you before his glorious presence without fault and with great joy— [25]to the only God our Savior be glory, majesty, power and authority, through Jesus Christ our Lord, before all ages, now and forevermore! Amen.

[a] 14,15 From the Jewish *First Book of Enoch* (approximately the first century B.C.) [b] 22,23 The Greek manuscripts of these verses vary at several points.

---

humanity. This group of spiritual beings seems to be identified by Mt 16:27 and 25:31 as angels (compare 2Th 1:7).

15 ungodly sinners Although Jude is specifically targeting unrepentant, false teachers (see Jude 16), an overall judgment of humanity is in view. For this reason Jude emphasizes the need for his audience to accept the love of God, as shown in the mercy that Jesus offers through his death and resurrection. Jesus offers payment for the sins of the ungodly, so that they may have eternal life (vv. 20–21).

17–23 In this section, Jude tells his audience that the apostles predicted scoffers, and that these people will attempt to create division in the church (vv. 17–19). Christians should be concerned with their personal spiritual condition, so that they can adequately face the dangers of false teaching. After noting that obedience to God finds its power in future hope (vv. 20–21; compare 1Jn 3:3), Jude asks believers to be concerned for those in danger of succumbing to false teachings (Jude 22–23).

17 the apostles This seems to be a reference to the eleven apostles whom Jesus called (Mt 10:2–4), plus Matthias (who replaced Judas; Ac 1:12–26).
18 They said to you This exact apostolic teaching is not recorded elsewhere. Jude may be summarizing the general sense of the apostles' teachings rather than the direct words. **the last times** Describes the time beginning with the resurrection and extending until Jesus' return. After this time, God's judgment will come (Heb 1:1–2; 1Ti 4:1; 2Ti 3:1). **scoffers** Likely a reference to the false teachers (compare Jude 8–10,19). These people dispute the truths of the gospel. **ungodly desires** The nature of these sins is detailed in v. 4.
19 who divide you, who follow mere natural instincts The scoffers are dividing the church, seeking the values of society rather than God.
20 by building yourselves up Believers are to focus on the truths of the Christian faith, as seen in the OT Scriptures (vv. 5–7) and the teachings of the apostles (v. 18).
21 keep yourselves in God's love Believers should make God's love for them the center of their lives (com-

pare Php 2:12–13). It is not that God's love is dependent on their actions, but that their actions are a result of experiencing God's love enveloping their lives. **as you wait for the mercy of our Lord** Refers to Jesus' return to earth (his second coming), which provides an eternal hope for believers (compare Heb 11:1–2).
22 Be merciful False teaching can cause those who are uncertain about what they believe (or those with less discernment) to be misled, even to the point of doubting Jesus' return (compare note on 2Pe 3:4). Rather than decide that they are lost, believers should lovingly convince doubters to return to true faith in Jesus.
23 by snatching False teachers are on the path to experiencing God's wrath (Jude 4). Those being misled by false teachings could suffer the same fate (see note on 2Pe 2:13; compare Zec 3:1–5). Christians are thus to take an active role in drawing doubters away from false teachings and toward truth. **fire** An instrument of God's judgment when Jesus returns (compare Am 4:11). **with fear** May refer to the need for caution when engaging with those who have succumbed to false teachings, lest the doubters mislead the person attempting to help them. It could also be that the fear of God, who will bring judgment, is in view. **the clothing stained by corrupted flesh** Jude evokes the metaphor of a long garment, worn close to the skin, being tainted by its use. Christians are to loathe how sinfulness, brought on by listening to false teachings, has ruined the lives of those who did not resist.

24–25 Jude concludes with a doxology expressing praise and blessing to God.

24 without fault This word recalls the description of sacrificial animals in the OT (see 1Pe 1:19 and note; compare Ro 12:1–2; Jas 1:27). Believers are able to be blameless before God because of Jesus' sacrificial death; he functions as the sacrifice on their behalf (Jude 3; 2Pe 1:1; Heb 7:26–28; compare Isa 53:10).
25 to the only God our Savior...through Jesus Christ Reflects the oneness of God, as well as the view that Jesus is a direct manifestation of God through whom people have a relationship with God. It is through Jesus that the saving act of God has come to humanity.

CONTENDING FOR THE FAITH — APOLOGETICS
by Lee Strobel

The word "apologetics" comes from the Greek word *apologia*, meaning "to offer a defense." Peter says, "But in your hearts revere Christ as Lord. Always be prepared to give an answer to everyone who asks you to give the reason for the hope that you have. But do this with gentleness and respect" (1Pe 3:15). The Greek word for "answer" or "defense" is *apologia*—so, in a broad sense, the Bible is saying all Christians are called to be apologists.

WHY APOLOGETICS?

Jude 3 says to "contend for the faith that was once for all entrusted to God's holy people" and 2 Corinthians 10:5 says, "We demolish arguments and every pretension that sets itself up against the knowledge of God, and we take captive every thought to make it obedient to Christ." Paul says in Philippians 1:7 that he was active in "defending and confirming the gospel." Acts 28:23 describes him in his last days in Rome as working from morning until evening, "explaining about the kingdom of God, and from the Law of Moses and from the Prophets he tried to persuade them about Jesus."

Learning about the intellectual basis for Christianity bolsters the faith of Christians—especially those who may be experiencing doubts—and prepares believers to share Christ with others. Offering evidence and presenting arguments for Christianity can be an effective way of sharing the gospel with nonbelievers, as doing so may help resolve questions they have about God. Pascal said that people "despise religion ... They hate it and are afraid it may be true. The cure for this is first to show that religion is not contrary to reason, but worthy of reverence and respect."[1]

The use of apologetics has become increasingly important in recent years. Interest in apologetics has risen among young Christians; they often face new doubts when starting college. The shrinking world has increased contact with those who adhere to other faiths, providing Christians with opportunities to defend the uniqueness of Christ.

APOLOGETICS AND MY STORY

God used an investigation of the evidence for Christianity to bring me to faith. As a law-trained journalist and atheist, I was hostile to the myths, legends and wishful thinking that I assumed were at the heart of Christianity. I thought that the Bible was full of contradictions, that churches were brimming with hypocrites, and that science had effectively disproven the supernatural. After my wife's conversion to Christianity, though, I decided to use my background to systematically explore whether there was any substance to the faith. I was surprised to find that modern science—from cosmology to physics to biochemistry to genetics—actually points toward the existence of a Creator. And the compelling evidence in the history of Jesus' resurrection authenticates his identity as the unique Son of God.

Apologetics unmasked my faulty assumptions and led me to the cross, where I received Christ as my Lord and Savior and became a child of God (Jn 1:12). I'm hardly unique—history is full

---

1 Blaise Pascal, *Pensées*, trans. A. J. Krailsheimer (New York: Penguin Books, 1995), 12.

of examples of one-time skeptics who became convinced that Christianity is objectively true. Among them is British author C. S. Lewis, who said, "Nearly everyone I know who has embraced Christianity in adult life has been influenced by what seemed to him to be at least a probable argument for Theism."[2] I've seen thousands of spiritually confused people become followers of Jesus once they've been exposed to the evidence that backs up Christianity.

THE IMPORTANCE OF GOOD APOLOGETICS

Two things are essential for a solid apology: establishment of the facts and defense against challenges. Evangelist Mark Mittelberg likens apologetics to a battery, which has positive and negative poles. He stresses the importance of presenting both the affirmative evidence for the credibility of Christianity while also giving convincing answers to the questions and criticisms that prevent people from believing.

"People rightly refuse to believe without evidence," said apologist Norman Geisler. "Since God creates humans as rational beings, he expects them to live rationally, to look before they leap. This does not mean there is no room for faith. But God wants us to take a step of faith in the light of evidence, rather than to leap in the dark."[3]

2 C. S. Lewis, "The Pains of Animals," in *God in the Dock: Essays on Theology and Ethics*, ed. Walter Hooper (New York: HarperOne, 2014), 173. 3 Norman Geisler, "Apologetics, Need for," in *Baker Encyclopedia of Christian Apologetics*, Baker Reference Library (Grand Rapids: Baker Books, 1999), 38.

APOCALYPTIC LITERATURE

pocalyptic literature takes its name from the Apocalypse, or Revelation, of John in the New Testament. The word "apocalypse" derives from the Greek word for revelation (*apokalypsis*), although it is reserved for revelations of a decidedly supernatural character—they often take the form of visions, which are then explained to the visionary by an angel. The visions concern heavenly mysteries, such as God's throne in heaven or the climax of history.

Because the end of history is accompanied by great upheavals, "apocalypse" has come to mean "catastrophe" in modern vernacular. The Biblical apocalypses, however, entail a good deal more than destruction. Especially important is the belief in a coming judgment leading to eternal reward or damnation.

THE BOOK OF DANIEL

The book of Daniel is the only full-fledged apocalyptic writing in the Old Testament. It contains a series of visions (Da 7–12) that may have been recorded at the time of the Maccabean revolt against the Seleucid Empire in the years 167–164 BC. In Daniel 7, Daniel sees four great beasts coming up out of the sea. These are explained to be the four kingdoms to which the Jews had been subjected, but the book draws its symbols from ancient myths and suggests the beasts are embodiments of primeval chaos. Daniel then sees the Most High depicted as an ancient figure seated on an amazing throne and surrounded by thousands of holy ones or angels. He presides over a judgment, and the fourth kingdom (representing the Greeks or perhaps Rome) is condemned to burn in the fire. Then the kingdom is given to one like a son of man who comes on the clouds—an identification used elsewhere in the Old Testament for Yahweh (e.g., Isa 19:1).

The symbolism and function of Daniel's visions become more specific in Daniel 10–12. The angel Gabriel appears to Daniel, telling him that he is engaged in a struggle in heaven against the "princes" of Persia and Greece, and that there is no one to help him but "Michael, your prince" (Da 10:21). He proceeds to tell Daniel what is written in the Book of Truth—the whole course of history in the Hellenistic period (ca. 330–168 BC) through the persecution of the Jews by King Antiochus IV Epiphanes of Syria. (The book was likely completed before the death of Antiochus Epiphanes in 164 BC.)

The revelation of Daniel concludes by looking beyond history to the resurrection of the dead. Some will rise to eternal life, some to shame and contempt. The "wise" who died for their faith in the time of persecution will shine like the brightness of the heavens, or the firmament; they will become companions to the stars or the host of heaven (Da 12:1–4). This is a clear reference to resurrection in the Hebrew Bible. In Israelite religion up to this point, salvation primarily meant living long in the promised land and seeing one's children's children. After the time of Daniel's writing—at least in the apocalyptic tradition—salvation meant to live forever with the angels in heaven. Belief in resurrection was especially powerful in times of persecution when people were being killed for keeping their faith.

OTHER JEWISH APOCALYPTIC LITERATURE

Some of Daniel's imagery parallels ancient Near Eastern mythology (beasts rising from the sea, the figure riding on the clouds, etc.) and some parallels earlier passages in the Hebrew Bible, especially in the later prophetic passages. A good example is Isaiah 24–27, which says that God will punish Leviathan, the twisting serpent, and will slay the dragon that is in the sea (Isa 27:1). There is no particular story in the Old Testament about Leviathan or the dragon—they are only mentioned in passing or as a general force against Yahweh's work—but they are featured in Canaanite myths from the second millennium BC.

In addition to Daniel, the cluster of extra-Biblical writings known collectively as 1 Enoch also illustrates individual judgment and afterlife. In Genesis, Enoch is among the seventh generation after Adam, before the flood. He was said to walk with God, and Genesis 5:24 says God "took" Enoch, likely meaning that Enoch ascended to heaven while still alive. He was, then, uniquely placed to reveal the mysteries of heaven. Dated from the second century BC, the collective writings known as 1 Enoch describe both the mysteries of the universe and the whole course of history, from creation to the final judgment.

Jewish apocalyptic writings can be divided broadly into two types: first, historical apocalypses, typified by Daniel, which are concerned with the course of history and its final resolution. Then there are otherworldly journeys, mainly heavenly ascents, in which the visionary passes through the heavens and sees the abodes of the dead. The Book of the Watchers (1 Enoch 1–36) is a prime example of this type of apocalypse.

Another cluster of apocalypses (e.g., the extra-Biblical books 2 Esdras and 2 Baruch) appeared in the period immediately after the destruction of Jerusalem by the Romans. In these revelations, consolation comes from the hope that Rome will eventually be overthrown, Jerusalem restored, and the righteous freed to enjoy eternal life in heaven. Most of these apocalypses were not preserved in the Jewish tradition, but they survived in Greek, Latin, Syriac or Ethiopic translations. Many more Jewish apocalypses likely existed that were not translated and did not survive. Fragments of the books of Enoch in Aramaic were found in the Dead Sea Scrolls, as were fragments of several other apocalyptic writings that were previously unknown. Moreover, the Dead Sea Scrolls show that apocalyptic ideas—such as the expectation of a war between the good and evil—were widespread even if they were not expressed in writings formally recognized as apocalypses.

EARLY CHRISTIANITY, REVELATION AND THE GOSPELS

To a great degree, these apocalyptic writings provide context for the writings and beliefs of early Christianity. Belief in the resurrection of Jesus Christ, for instance, was crucial for the development of Christianity. Yet, as Paul makes clear, "If there is no resurrection of the dead, then not even Christ has been raised" (1Co 15:13). The belief that Jesus was resurrected builds on the apocalyptic view of the end of history. Christ was the firstfruit of the resurrection, the beginning of the general resurrection. Paul expected that when Christ returned, those who were left alive would be caught up to meet him in the air (1Th 4:17).

By far the most elaborate apocalyptic writing in the New Testament is the book of Revelation, which includes a series of revelations received by John of Patmos. Some of the imagery derives from Daniel. John sees a beast rising from the sea (Rev 13:1) and another from the earth. For John, the beasts represent the Roman Empire, which is also symbolized by the great prostitute

Babylon, riding on a beast, in Revelation 17. In Revelation 19, however, Christ appears from heaven, riding a white horse and wielding a sword from his mouth (Rev 19:11–15). Satan is imprisoned for 1,000 years (Rev 20:2), and the righteous dead are raised to reign on earth for the same period (Rev 20:4–5). At the end of this period, Satan is released temporarily (Rev 20:7)—before his end in the lake of fire (Rev 20:10)—and all the dead are raised for judgment (Rev 20:12). Death and Hades, the underworld, are thrown into a lake of fire (Rev 20:14), and a new heaven and a new earth appear (Rev 21:1).

The Gospels suggest that Jesus, like John, was thoroughly apocalyptic. Mark 13 is often called "the little apocalypse." There, Jesus predicts great upheavals at the end of the age, after which the Son of Man will appear on the clouds. In addition to its appearance in Daniel 7, the motif of the Son of Man sitting on the throne of glory also appears in the Similitudes of Enoch (1 Enoch 37–71), a Jewish apocalypse from the first half of the first century AD. In apocalyptic language, Matthew 16 describes a judgment scene in which Jesus, as the Son of Man, comes again in the glory of God the Father with his angels and offers mercy to those who chose to follow him (Mt 16:24–28).

John J. Collins

REVELATION

INTRODUCTION TO REVELATION

Revelation draws back the curtain on the unseen realities of life for God's people. There is a spiritual battle going on, and the risen Jesus reveals these visions to John so that God's church will be aware of what is happening now and in the future. While the strange imagery might seem frightening, the ultimate message of Revelation is a hopeful one: Although evil appears to triumph, God remains on the throne.

BACKGROUND

The title of Revelation comes from the opening verse, which identifies this book as the revelation of Jesus Christ (Rev 1:1). The recipient is identified as "John" (1:4). In the early church period, this was often understood to be the apostle John, who spent the latter part of his life in Ephesus, a major city in Asia Minor (modern-day Turkey). However, some in the early church thought Revelation was not written by John the apostle but by another early church leader with the same name. Regardless, the author appears to be a church leader in Asia Minor who was fluent in the Jewish Scriptures.

The initial audience of Revelation is seven churches in Asia (1:4,11); "Asia" refers to the Roman province of Asia, which was located at the western end of Asia Minor. John writes to them from Patmos, a small island in the Aegean Sea, where he had been exiled (1:9). He wants to strengthen them in the face of cultural pressure and outright persecution.

There are two major options for dating Revelation: during the reign of the Roman emperor Nero (AD 54–68) and during the reign of Domitian (AD 81–96), when there was intense localized

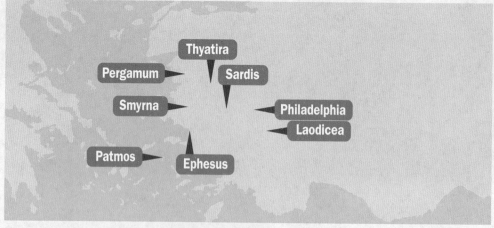

This map depicts the seven churches that received Revelation. It also shows Patmos, the location from which John wrote down his vision.

persecution by the Roman Empire. Irenaeus, a church father during the second century, connects Revelation with Domitian (*Against Heresies* 5.30.3), and many modern interpreters hold this view.

Revelation is written in an apocalyptic, prophetic style. This kind of writing often featured an angel or otherworldly being who revealed heavenly mysteries to a human recipient. These mysteries are delivered in the form of visions that use graphic imagery to symbolize cosmic realities. The cryptic language may have helped Revelation be easily circulated around the Roman Empire during a time of Christian persecution—the language, couched in Old Testament imagery, would have been difficult to understand for anyone without such knowledge. At the same time, Revelation echoes the concern of Old Testament prophecy for the status of God's people in the present day. The book uses apocalyptic imagery to anticipate the final realization of God's reign but ultimately functions as a prophetic message for the people of God in their current situation and trials.

STRUCTURE

Revelation opens with an introduction (1:1–20) that includes a vision of the Son of Man, a figure that also appears in the Old Testament prophecy of Daniel (Da 7:13). This figure, Jesus, then dictates to John seven letters—one for each of the seven churches (Rev 2:1—3:22; compare Mk 2:10; 8:31). The majority of Revelation (Rev 4:1—22:5) consists of a series of visions disclosing unseen realities concerning the future yet with implications for the present time. These visions unfold as three sets of seven—seals, trumpets and bowls. Each time a seal is broken, a trumpet

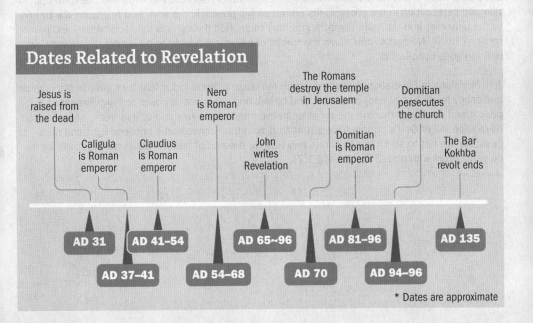

Dates Related to Revelation

Jesus is raised from the dead

Caligula is Roman emperor

Claudius is Roman emperor

Nero is Roman emperor

John writes Revelation

The Romans destroy the temple in Jerusalem

Domitian is Roman emperor

Domitian persecutes the church

The Bar Kokhba revolt ends

AD 31

AD 37–41

AD 41–54

AD 54–68

AD 65~96

AD 70

AD 81–96

AD 94–96

AD 135

* Dates are approximate

is sounded or a bowl is poured out, John witnesses a new scene of apocalyptic imagery. After the seventh bowl unleashes cataclysmic destruction, John has visions depicting the fall of "Babylon," the defeat of Satan and the renewal of heaven and earth (17:1—22:5). In the closing scene, Jesus assures John that he is coming soon, a promise that confirms the urgency of John's message (22:6–21).

OUTLINE

- Prologue and vision of Christ (1:1–20)
- Messages to the seven churches (2:1—3:22)
- Vision of heaven and the seven seals (4:1—8:5)
- The seven trumpets (8:6—11:19)
- The powers of evil attack the church (12:1—14:20)
- The seven bowls (15:1—16:21)
- The fall of Babylon (17:1—19:10)
- The final victory and the new Jerusalem (19:11—22:5)
- Epilogue (22:6–21)

THEMES

Revelation conveys the reality of evil using images that can be disconcerting and even terrifying, but that is not the book's ultimate message. Jesus wants his church to know that, despite opposition and persecution in the present, his purposes will prevail in the end. God reigns on the throne of the universe, and the slain Lamb, Jesus, has triumphed through his sacrificial death and resurrection (5:6,9). No matter how much the forces of evil might appear to be victorious, their defeat is a foregone conclusion.

John's visions in Revelation deliver the same message of hope today that they gave to his original audience. Jesus has already prevailed, and he will one day come in power to fully vindicate his people and dwell with them in the renewed heaven and earth. Assured of this truth, believers can have hope. All of God's people have a part to play in the cosmic battle between light and darkness; we are not to sit on the sidelines and wait for the end of history. Jesus himself calls us to be conquerors with him (2:7; 17:14; 21:7).

Prologue

1 The revelation from Jesus Christ, which God gave him to show his servants what must soon take place. He made it known by sending his angel to his servant John, ²who testifies to everything he saw — that is, the word of God and the testimony of Jesus Christ. ³Blessed is the one who reads aloud the words of this prophecy, and blessed are those who hear it and take to heart what is written in it, because the time is near.

Greetings and Doxology

⁴John,

To the seven churches in the province of Asia:

Grace and peace to you from him who is, and who was, and who is to come, and from the seven spirits^a before his throne, ⁵and from Jesus Christ, who is the faithful witness, the firstborn from the dead, and the ruler of the kings of the earth.

To him who loves us and has freed us from our sins by his blood, ⁶and has made us to be a kingdom and priests to serve his God and Father — to him be glory and power for ever and ever! Amen.

⁷"Look, he is coming with the clouds,"^b
  and "every eye will see him,
even those who pierced him";
  and all peoples on earth "will mourn
    because of him."^c
          So shall it be! Amen.

⁸"I am the Alpha and the Omega," says the Lord God, "who is, and who was, and who is to come, the Almighty."

John's Vision of Christ

⁹I, John, your brother and companion in the suffering and kingdom and patient endurance that are ours in Jesus, was on the island of Patmos

^a 4 That is, the sevenfold Spirit   ^b 7 Daniel 7:13
^c 7 Zech. 12:10

1:1–8 In the prologue, the book of Revelation is introduced as three types of literature blended into one: an apocalypse (or revelation; v. 1), a prophecy (v. 3) and a letter (vv. 4–5). Here, the author formally identifies his audience, introduces himself as John, and highlights the one who receives glory and dominion—Jesus Christ. Revelation may have been composed in the late 60s AD (during the religious difficulties of the Roman emperor Nero's reign) or in the 90s AD (during the reign of the emperor Domitian).

1:1 The revelation from Jesus Christ This revelation may be understood as being "of" Jesus or "from" Jesus. This phrase may mean that Jesus is the content of the revelation or that he is the revealer of the hidden realities being disclosed in this book. The title "Jesus Christ"— or "Jesus the Messiah"—occurs only in the first five verses, but nowhere else in the book. **soon take place** The events of the book are spoken of as imminent (v. 3; 22:10). New Testament writers often speak of end-time events as beginning in their own days (e.g., Ro 16:20; Heb 1:2; 1Pe 4:7). God's final victory over evil and the establishment of his kingdom will be completed in the future, but they have also been brought into the present through the death and resurrection of Jesus.

1:3 Blessed The first of seven beatitudes in Revelation (Rev 14:13; 16:15; 19:9; 20:6; 22:7,14), reminiscent of Jesus' Sermon on the Mount (Mt 5:3–11). **those who hear** Many people in the first century were illiterate and received instruction by having it read to them. **take to heart** The blessing is brought about through obedience and adherence to the revelation.

1:4 To the seven churches in the province of Asia While these seven churches were not the only ones in Asia (a western region of modern-day Turkey), they were influential and located on a well-known circular route. The number seven often denotes fullness or completion in the Old Testament (e.g., Ge 2:2; Lev 26:18; Jos 6:4). John uses the number in this way throughout Revelation—most notably in the judgment sequences (seven bowls, seven trumpets). The seven churches would have been understood as representing all the churches of

Asia, and perhaps the entire worldwide church. **seven spirits** Possibly alludes to the sevenfold spirit of God in Isa 11:2. The number seven indicates the fullness of the Holy Spirit's work (compare Rev 3:1; 4:5; 5:6).

1:5 faithful witness Refers to Jesus, who testified faithfully unto death (compare Jn 1:18; 18:37; 1Ti 6:13).

1:6 a kingdom and priests In Christ, God has done for the church what he had earlier done for Israel (compare Rev 5:10; 1Pe 2:9; Ex 19:5–6). **Amen** The Greek word used here, meaning "let it be so," served to strongly affirm something just stated. It expressed an indication of trust in God's ability to bring about a desired result.

1:7 he is coming with the clouds John applies the imagery of the son of man from Da 7:13–14 to Jesus. Cloud imagery also recalls the manner in which Jesus left the earth (Ac 1:9). **those who pierced him** An allusion to Zec 12:10.

1:8 the Alpha and the Omega The first and last letters of the Greek alphabet. The expression is a merism—a figure of speech that distinguishes opposites in order to accentuate the whole. God is the beginning and the end and everything in between.

1:9–20 John describes here the circumstances of his receiving the revelation, drawing on imagery from the book of Daniel to describe the glorified Christ. John then receives the commission to write to the seven churches.

1:9 the suffering and kingdom The language suggests that the believers to whom John is writing are suffering persecution (or tribulation) and that the kingdom is, through the power of the Spirit's work in their lives and the world, already present with the church. **Patmos** A small, rocky island in the Aegean Sea. Patmos may have been used as a Roman penal colony. **word of God** Church tradition indicates that John was banished to Patmos to hinder the growth of the church. Although Revelation is addressed to the seven churches in Asia, its contents served to instill hope in the lives of all persecuted believers. John intended for believers to recognize that their maltreatment was only for a time and that Christ will judge their oppressors and fully establish his kingdom on earth.

because of the word of God and the testimony of Jesus. [10]On the Lord's Day I was in the Spirit, and I heard behind me a loud voice like a trumpet, [11]which said: "Write on a scroll what you see and send it to the seven churches: to Ephesus, Smyrna, Pergamum, Thyatira, Sardis, Philadelphia and Laodicea."

[12]I turned around to see the voice that was speaking to me. And when I turned I saw seven golden lampstands, [13]and among the lampstands was someone like a son of man,[a] dressed in a robe reaching down to his feet and with a golden sash around his chest. [14]The hair on his head was white like wool, as white as snow, and his eyes were like blazing fire. [15]His feet were like bronze glowing in a furnace, and his voice was like the sound of rushing waters. [16]In his right hand he held seven stars, and coming out of his mouth was a sharp, double-edged sword. His face was like the sun shining in all its brilliance.

[17]When I saw him, I fell at his feet as though dead. Then he placed his right hand on me and said: "Do not be afraid. I am the First and the Last.

[18]I am the Living One; I was dead, and now look, I am alive for ever and ever! And I hold the keys of death and Hades.

[19]"Write, therefore, what you have seen, what is now and what will take place later. [20]The mystery of the seven stars that you saw in my right hand and of the seven golden lampstands is this: The seven stars are the angels[b] of the seven churches, and the seven lampstands are the seven churches.

To the Church in Ephesus

2 "To the angel[c] of the church in Ephesus write:

These are the words of him who holds the seven stars in his right hand and walks among the seven golden lampstands. [2]I know your deeds, your hard work and your perseverance. I know that you cannot tolerate wicked people, that you have tested those who claim to be apostles but are not, and have

---

[a] 13 See Daniel 7:13.   [b] 20 Or messengers
[c] 1 Or messenger; also in verses 8, 12 and 18

1:10 the Lord's Day Sunday, on which believers celebrate Christ's resurrection from the dead. **in the Spirit** Probably describes a visionary state (compare Ac 10:10; 2Co 12:2–4). John's visions are framed by his four experiences in the Spirit (Rev 1:10; 4:2; 17:3; 21:10).
1:11 seven churches See v. 4.
1:12 I turned around to see the voice John received the command to write and looked around to see who issued it. **seven golden lampstands** Golden lampstands stood in the Holy Place of the tabernacle and the temple (Ex 25:31–37; 1Ki 7:49). Zechariah also had a vision of a golden lampstand (Zec 4:2). The significance of these lampstands is explained in Rev 1:20.
1:13 among the lampstands Christ is present among his church. **like a son of man** John draws on the vision of the Ancient of Days in Da 7 and the vision of the angelic figure in Da 10 in the following verses (see Da 7:9; 10:5). During his ministry, Jesus used Daniel's son of man terminology in reference to himself (e.g., Mt 9:6; 10:23; 11:19).
1:14 white like wool In Da 7:9, the Ancient of Days' clothing is white like snow and the hair of his head is compared to pure wool. John combines the two descriptions to describe the head and hair of Christ. **his eyes were like blazing fire** In Da 10:6, the eyes of the angelic figure are compared to flaming torches. In Da 7:9, the throne of the Ancient of Days is compared to fire.
1:15 like the sound of rushing waters This is similar to Da 10:6, where the angelic voice is likened to the sound of a multitude (compare Eze 1:24; 43:2). Revelation 1:10 ascribes trumpet-like characteristics to Christ's voice. The emphasis is on the force and authority with which he speaks.
1:16 sharp, double-edged sword May indicate the power of his words—the words of the Word of God (see Jn 1:1–5; compare Rev 2:16; 19:15,21).
1:17 as though dead Falling to the ground from reverence and fear is a common reaction to encounters with the divine. **Do not be afraid** A common heavenly greeting to people (e.g., Ge 15:1; Da 10:12; Lk 1:30).
1:18 keys of death and Hades Keys represent author-

ity. Christ has the authority both to confine and release from death (see Jn 5:25–29; compare Mt 16:19). See note on Rev 6:8.
1:19 Write This verse is often viewed as an outline of the book: It contains what John saw (ch. 1), what is (chs. 2–3) and what will take place later (chs. 4–22). However, since there are elements of past, present and future mixed throughout the book, it is best to take this verse as a directive to John to write down the entire contents of his vision—both present and future (compare ch. 12). Disagreements about the timing and nature of the events depicted in John's vision have given rise to four typical approaches to interpreting Revelation: The preterist viewpoint understands the events of Revelation to have been fulfilled in the first century AD. The historicist view regards the book as a panorama of church history, probably without specific referents. The idealist approach sees in the book a constant, universal struggle between good and evil, not actual historical or future events. The futurist approach understands much of the book (chs. 4–22) to detail future events. See the table "Four Views of Revelation" on p. 2124.
1:20 the angels of the seven churches Could refer to angelic beings or human leaders. Since the Greek word for "angel" used here (angelos) can also describe human messengers (Mt 11:10; Lk 7:24; 9:52; Jas 2:25), it may represent the leaders or pastors of the seven churches in this instance. However, the term is never used with regard to church leadership. Alternatively, these angeloi (plural) may be angelic representatives of the churches. Still another alternative is that this is a metaphorical way of speaking about the spirit of each church, since each letter is addressed to the angel of that church. See the table "Angels in the Bible" on p. 2120.
2:1 Ephesus Ephesus, the largest city in Asia Minor, was situated where the Cayster River meets the Aegean Sea. Ephesus was both a major port city and the site of many temples, including a large one dedicated to goddess Artemis (see Ac 19:27 and note). **the seven stars in his right hand** Christ is identified as the speaker at

found them false. [3] You have persevered and have endured hardships for my name, and have not grown weary.

[4] Yet I hold this against you: You have forsaken the love you had at first. [5] Consider how far you have fallen! Repent and do the things you did at first. If you do not repent, I will come to you and remove your lampstand from its place. [6] But you have this in your favor: You hate the practices of the Nicolaitans, which I also hate.

[7] Whoever has ears, let them hear what the Spirit says to the churches. To the one who is victorious, I will give the right to eat from the tree of life, which is in the paradise of God.

To the Church in Smyrna

[8] "To the angel of the church in Smyrna write:

These are the words of him who is the First and the Last, who died and came to life again. [9] I know your afflictions and your poverty — yet you are rich! I know about the slander of those who say they are Jews and are not, but are a synagogue of Satan. [10] Do not be afraid of what you are about to suffer. I tell you, the devil will put some of you in prison to test you, and you will suffer persecution for ten days. Be faithful, even to the point of death, and I will give you life as your victor's crown.

[11] Whoever has ears, let them hear what the Spirit says to the churches. The one who is victorious will not be hurt at all by the second death.

To the Church in Pergamum

[12] "To the angel of the church in Pergamum write:

These are the words of him who has the sharp, double-edged sword. [13] I know where you live — where Satan has his throne. Yet you remain true to my name. You did not renounce your faith in me, not even in the days of Antipas, my faithful witness, who was put to death in your city — where Satan lives.

[14] Nevertheless, I have a few things against

---

the beginning of each of the addresses to the churches in Rev 2–3; this reflects aspects of John's introduction in 1:9–20.

2:3 persevered The church was probably encountering opposition, which may have resulted in persecution. Their refusal to conform would have also caused social and political backlash, causing tension in commercial and familial relationships.

2:4 I hold this against you Christ's commendation now turns to condemnation. **You have forsaken the love you had at first** The church was initially zealous and motivated by love, but that love diminished as time passed. This love could be directed at God or brothers and sisters in the Lord. Their love for unbelievers in the city may have also waned under the heavy hand of persecution.

2:5 Repent Condemnation is followed by an exhortation to repentance: abandon sin and return to serving God. **If you do not** Christ moves from exhortation to warning. **remove** Failure to repent would result in the church's removal from that place. If a church fails to fulfill its function, it will not continue to exist.

2:6 you have this Christ commends the church for zealously opposing that which is unjust in favor of righteousness. **practices of the Nicolaitans** Little is known of this group; they are probably not connected to the Nicolas of Ac 6:5. Given John's disdain for the religious practices of the Roman Empire, the Nicolaitans may have compromised by allowing pagan religious practices into the church, thereby avoiding persecution and social tension (compare Rev 2:14–15).

2:7 Whoever has ears Recalls Jesus' exhortation throughout the Gospels (e.g., Mt 13:9,43): Hear, understand and respond accordingly. This is reflected in the closing of each message to the seven churches (Rev 2:11,17,29; 3:6,13,22). **who is victorious** The first letter concludes with a promise reflecting the ultimate promise of the book in 21:7. Believers' endurance and victory results in two blessings in the book of Revelation: eternal life as glorified, adopted members of God's family (vv. 7,11,17; 3:5,12), and rule with Christ in the new earth's kingdom as members of his ruling administration

(v. 26; 3:21). **tree of life** See note on Ge 2:9; compare Rev 22:2; Ge 3:24. **the paradise of God** Paradise represents the ultimate place of rest and refuge with God. The new earth and arrival of the final kingdom of God is later cast in language like that used to describe Eden (Rev 22:1–2; compare Ge 2:8,10).

2:8 Smyrna Smyrna, an important exporting city known for its beauty, was located on a protected harbor of the Aegean Sea next to a major road system. It was the home of a temple to the Roman emperor Tiberius and was a center of the Roman imperial religion. Smyrna is the first of two churches (Philadelphia is the other) that receive no critique from the risen Christ. **the First and the Last** The phrases identifying Christ here reflect Rev 1:17–18.

2:9 I know your afflictions and your poverty The believers in Smyrna likely faced harsh treatment and scarcity of employment. When cities had large concentrations of artisans and craftsmen, trade guilds or unions were established. These guilds often required their members to participate in certain pagan activities. The believers' unwillingness to participate in these activities resulted in exclusion from the guilds and financial hardship. **slander of those who say they are Jews** This church not only faced pressure from the pagan world but also found themselves in conflict with the synagogues. **a synagogue of Satan** As opposed to being involved in the activities of God, they were doing the work of his adversary.

2:11 the second death See note on 20:14.

2:12 Pergamum Pergamum was famous for its civilization and learning. It was home to the pagan cults of Zeus, Athena, Dionysus and Asclepius. **who has the sharp, double-edged sword** The phrase identifying Christ here reflects 1:16.

2:13 Satan has his throne Probably a reference to the altar to Zeus, located at the top of Pergamum's acropolis, and which hailed him as savior. **Antipas, my faithful witness** Though little is known about this martyr, Antipas is heralded by Christ himself. See the timeline "The Early Church to AD 100" on p. 1776.

2:14 teaching of Balaam The prototypical unethical teacher whose compromise proved fatal to Israel

you: There are some among you who hold to the teaching of Balaam, who taught Balak to entice the Israelites to sin so that they ate food sacrificed to idols and committed sexual immorality. [15]Likewise, you also have those who hold to the teaching of the Nicolaitans. [16]Repent therefore! Otherwise, I will soon come to you and will fight against them with the sword of my mouth.

[17]Whoever has ears, let them hear what the Spirit says to the churches. To the one who is victorious, I will give some of the hidden manna. I will also give that person a white stone with a new name written on it, known only to the one who receives it.

To the Church in Thyatira

[18]"To the angel of the church in Thyatira write:

These are the words of the Son of God, whose eyes are like blazing fire and whose feet are like burnished bronze. [19]I know your deeds, your love and faith, your service and perseverance, and that you are now doing more than you did at first.

[20]Nevertheless, I have this against you: You tolerate that woman Jezebel, who calls herself a prophet. By her teaching she misleads my servants into sexual immorality and the eating of food sacrificed to idols. [21]I have given her time to repent of her immorality, but she is unwilling. [22]So I will cast her on a bed of suffering, and I will make those who commit adultery with her suffer intensely, unless they repent of her ways. [23]I will strike her children dead. Then all the churches will know that I am he who searches hearts and minds, and I will repay each of you according to your deeds.

[24]Now I say to the rest of you in Thyatira, to you who do not hold to her teaching and have not learned Satan's so-called deep secrets, 'I will not impose any other burden on you, [25]except to hold on to what you have until I come.'

[26]To the one who is victorious and does my will to the end, I will give authority over the nations— [27]that one 'will rule them with an iron scepter and will dash them to pieces like pottery'[a]—just as I have received authority from my Father. [28]I will also give that one the morning star. [29]Whoever has ears, let them hear what the Spirit says to the churches.

To the Church in Sardis

3 "To the angel[b] of the church in Sardis write:

These are the words of him who holds the seven spirits[c] of God and the seven stars.

[a] 27 Psalm 2:9   [b] 1 Or messenger; also in verses 7 and 14
[c] 1 That is, the sevenfold Spirit

(see Nu 25:1–2; 31:16). Some in Pergamum adopted a stance of religious compromise and encouraged others to do so. By being sexually immoral and participating in pagan activities, the individual would avoid being ostracized.
2:15 the teaching of the Nicolaitans In conjunction with Rev 2:14, this may indicate the Nicolaitans' teaching: compromise with pagan religious practices (see v. 6 and note).
2:16 will fight Although not everyone compromised, the church as a whole was guilty of indifference to those who had. Christ himself would wage war against them, proving the deadly nature of Balaam's teaching. **the sword of my mouth** See 1:16 and note; v. 12.
2:17 hidden manna Heavenly nourishment, in contrast to the food sacrificed to idols in v. 14 (compare Ex 16:32–34; Jn 6:31–35). **a new name written on it** Possibly refers to an invitation to partake in the banquet of the Lamb (Rev 19:9). This would contrast the pagan ceremonies of v. 14; believers had greater festivities awaiting them and did not need to compromise. See v. 7.
2:18 Thyatira This was probably the least significant city of chs. 2–3, but its letter is the longest. Thyatira was a center of manufacturing and trade, and the city's commerce was linked to an assortment of religious practices—posing a threat to the Christians who resided there (see v. 9 and note). **Son of God** Occurs only here in Revelation. The other phrases identifying Christ in this verse reflect 1:14–15.
2:19 now doing more than you did at first Their love for God and one another increased, in contrast to the church in Ephesus (vv. 4–5).

2:20 Jezebel The name of the murderous wife of King Ahab (e.g., 1Ki 18:4). Like Balaam, Jezebel is one of the villains of the Bible. Her indictment is probably similar to the one against the Balaamites in Rev 2:14. **sexual immorality and the eating of food sacrificed to idols** Refers to practices of religious compromise. See v. 14 and note.
2:23 her children Refers to those who follow in her teaching.
2:24 Satan's so-called deep secrets Jezebel claims secret knowledge, but her teaching comes from Satan and results in death and destruction.
2:26 I will give authority over the nations Joint rulership with the Messiah was a common feature of Jewish and early Christian teaching (see 20:6; 1Co 6:3; 2Ti 2:11; compare Ps 2:8–9).
2:28 the morning star In Rev 22:16, this refers to Jesus. It is probably an allusion to Nu 24:17, where it is associated with the tribe of Judah and Messianic rule. The act of giving the morning star to believers refers to them sharing in the duty of ruling the kingdom with Jesus (compare Da 7:27).
3:1 Sardis A military stronghold in antiquity, Sardis had a reputation for being impregnable, though in fact it had been conquered twice in its history. Archaeologists have uncovered a massive temple there dedicated to Artemis. See the infographic "The Temple of Artemis" on p. 1814. **him who holds** The phrases identifying the glorified Christ here reflect Rev 1:4,16,20. **you are dead** Although they appear alive, they are spiritually dead. This church receives the harshest censure among the seven.

I know your deeds; you have a reputation of being alive, but you are dead. ²Wake up! Strengthen what remains and is about to die, for I have found your deeds unfinished in the sight of my God. ³Remember, therefore, what you have received and heard; hold it fast, and repent. But if you do not wake up, I will come like a thief, and you will not know at what time I will come to you.

⁴Yet you have a few people in Sardis who have not soiled their clothes. They will walk with me, dressed in white, for they are worthy. ⁵The one who is victorious will, like them, be dressed in white. I will never blot out the name of that person from the book of life, but will acknowledge that name before my Father and his angels. ⁶Whoever has ears, let them hear what the Spirit says to the churches.

To the Church in Philadelphia

⁷"To the angel of the church in Philadelphia write:

These are the words of him who is holy and true, who holds the key of David. What he opens no one can shut, and what he shuts no one can open. ⁸I know your deeds. See, I have placed before you an open door that no one can shut. I know that you have little strength, yet you have kept my word and have not denied my name. ⁹I will make those who

are of the synagogue of Satan, who claim to be Jews though they are not, but are liars — I will make them come and fall down at your feet and acknowledge that I have loved you. ¹⁰Since you have kept my command to endure patiently, I will also keep you from the hour of trial that is going to come on the whole world to test the inhabitants of the earth.

¹¹I am coming soon. Hold on to what you have, so that no one will take your crown. ¹²The one who is victorious I will make a pillar in the temple of my God. Never again will they leave it. I will write on them the name of my God and the name of the city of my God, the new Jerusalem, which is coming down out of heaven from my God; and I will also write on them my new name. ¹³Whoever has ears, let them hear what the Spirit says to the churches.

To the Church in Laodicea

¹⁴"To the angel of the church in Laodicea write:

These are the words of the Amen, the faithful and true witness, the ruler of God's creation. ¹⁵I know your deeds, that you are neither cold nor hot. I wish you were either one or the other! ¹⁶So, because you are lukewarm — neither hot nor cold — I am about to spit you out of my mouth. ¹⁷You say, 'I am

---

3:2 about to die Because the believers in Sardis were complacent and lacked spiritual vigilance, they were close to death.

3:3 repent See 2:5 and note.

3:4 who have not soiled their clothes Christ offers encouragement to those few in Sardis who had not compromised with the surrounding culture. The use of clothing imagery may allude to Sardis' prominent garment industry. **They will walk with me, dressed in white** This is language of purity. It also symbolizes victory: Citizens would wear white clothing in a Roman triumphal procession.

3:5 the book of life The record of those who will inherit eternal life (20:12; Ex 32:32–34; Da 12:1). Eternal life is given to believers in Jesus (Jn 3:16–17).

3:7 Philadelphia Like the church in Smyrna, the Philadelphian church receives praise from the Lord. The city was known for its commercial and agricultural importance, particularly its grape crops. Its patron deity was Dionysus, god of wine. **holds the key of David** Describes the right to rule (compare Isa 22:22). Unlike the previous descriptions of the glorified Christ, this one does not draw on Rev 1:12–20. **What he opens no one can shut** Indicates Christ's authority to admit or exclude. In light of v. 8 and 3:12, this may refer to the new Jerusalem (ch. 21).

3:8 little strength The congregation was probably small and of little importance in the city, yet they remained faithful.

3:9 synagogue of Satan See 2:9 and note. **I will make them come and fall down** The church would be vindicated before nonbelieving Jews in the city (compare Isa 60:14).

3:10 the hour of trial Refers to the outpouring of God's

wrath on the world (beginning in Rev 6:1). Believers will be spiritually protected from various demonic attacks and plagues (see 9:4; 11:1 and note), and those who persevere will obtain eternal life (see 14:12–16) and admittance to the new Jerusalem (see chs. 21–22).

3:11 I am coming soon While Christ uses this phrase with some of the other churches to indicate judgment, here it refers to deliverance.

3:12 a pillar The temple was the dwelling place of God. Paul refers to believers, both individually and corporately, as the temple of God (1Co 3:16–17). The language here describes the believer's permanent residence in the abode and presence of God. **I will write on them** As a means of identification and belonging (compare Isa 62:2; Eze 48:35). The rewards for endurance and perseverance throughout Revelation all point to an abiding presence and relationship with God and Christ (see Rev 21:3–5). **the new Jerusalem** See 21:2.

3:14 Laodicea Located in the Lycus River valley not far from Colossae and Hierapolis, Laodicea was known for its banking, medical and clothing industries. **the ruler of God's creation** The Greek word used here to describe Christ can mean "ruler" or "originator." Compare Jn 1:1–5; Col 1:15–18.

3:15 you are neither cold nor hot This imagery may allude to the water system at Laodicea. The city had no water supply of its own; it had cold water piped in from Colossae or hot water piped in from the springs at Hierapolis. When the water arrived in the city, it had become lukewarm. Like the water, the church at Laodicea was neither refreshing (like cold water) nor healing (like hot spring water).

3:17 I am rich Thanks to its banking industry, Laodicea

rich; I have acquired wealth and do not need a thing.' But you do not realize that you are wretched, pitiful, poor, blind and naked. [18]I counsel you to buy from me gold refined in the fire, so you can become rich; and white clothes to wear, so you can cover your shameful nakedness; and salve to put on your eyes, so you can see.

[19]Those whom I love I rebuke and discipline. So be earnest and repent. [20]Here I am! I stand at the door and knock. If anyone hears my voice and opens the door, I will come in and eat with that person, and they with me.

[21]To the one who is victorious, I will give the right to sit with me on my throne, just as I was victorious and sat down with my Father on his throne. [22]Whoever has ears, let them hear what the Spirit says to the churches."

The Throne in Heaven

4 After this I looked, and there before me was a door standing open in heaven. And the voice I had first heard speaking to me like a trumpet said, "Come up here, and I will show you what must take place after this." [2]At once I was in the Spirit, and there before me was a throne in heav-

en with someone sitting on it. [3]And the one who sat there had the appearance of jasper and ruby. A rainbow that shone like an emerald encircled the throne. [4]Surrounding the throne were twenty-four other thrones, and seated on them were twenty-four elders. They were dressed in white and had crowns of gold on their heads. [5]From the throne came flashes of lightning, rumblings and peals of thunder. In front of the throne, seven lamps were blazing. These are the seven spirits[a] of God. [6]Also in front of the throne there was what looked like a sea of glass, clear as crystal.

In the center, around the throne, were four living creatures, and they were covered with eyes, in front and in back. [7]The first living creature was like a lion, the second was like an ox, the third had a face like a man, the fourth was like a flying eagle. [8]Each of the four living creatures had six wings and was covered with eyes all around, even under its wings. Day and night they never stop saying:

> "'Holy, holy, holy
> is the Lord God Almighty,'[b]
> who was, and is, and is to come."

a 5 That is, the sevenfold Spirit   *b 8* Isaiah 6:3

---

was a wealthy city. Like the city, the church there had convinced itself that it was self-sufficient—but was deceived about its true spiritual state.
3:18 gold refined in the fire Describes true wealth, as opposed to the money the Laodiceans made from commercial pursuits. This is a metaphor for removing sin (e.g., Job 23:10; Pr 27:21). **salve** The Laodicean medical school was known for producing eye salve. Christ prescribes his salve as the cure for spiritual blindness.
3:20 I stand at the door and knock Describes a request for a renewal of fellowship (e.g., SS 5:2). In their self-sufficiency, the church in Laodicea had locked Christ out. He wants them to repent and, ultimately, take part in the coming Messianic banquet (Rev 19:9).
3:21 who is victorious The one who endures in faith and following Christ. See note on 2:7.

4:1–11 Verses 1–11 introduce the throne-room vision of chs. 4 and 5. These chapters form one scene in which John is invited to behold future events (v. 1). He depends heavily on Moses, Ezekiel and Daniel to describe the wonders he witnessed. The vision in these chapters includes the introduction of the Lamb and leads to the seal judgments in ch. 6.
4:1 After this Refers to the reception of the letters to the seven churches. The phrase used here indicates that John received this vision after the previous one. **voice I had first heard** Belonging to the glorified Christ (1:10). **Come up here** A summons to behold the visions (compare Eze 3:12; 11:1). **what must take place after this** See Rev 1:19 and note.
4:2 At once I was in the Spirit This phrase occurs again in 17:3 and 21:10; it functions as a reminder that John is experiencing a prolonged vision. See note on 1:10. **a throne in heaven** Suggests sovereignty and power. Various aspects of the vision in this chapter reflect as-

pects of Ezekiel's and Isaiah's visions of God (Eze 1; Isa 6). **with someone sitting on it** God (see Rev 4:8,11).
4:3 jasper and ruby Ezekiel describes Yahweh in a similar way (Eze 1:26–27). In Ex 24:10, Moses also describes the divine presence of Yahweh using precious stones. Like Ezekiel and Isaiah, John does not attempt to give a precise description of God. Instead, he describes the overall effect of his glorious presence.
4:4 twenty-four elders May symbolize the twelve tribes of Israel and the twelve apostles, together representing the whole people of God. If true, this would fit with the context of Rev 2–3 of shared rulership for believers (see note on 2:7).
4:5 These are the seven spirits of God See 1:4.
4:6 sea of glass In Revelation, the sea likely symbolizes forces of chaos (see 13:1 and note; 21:1 and note). A calm sea points to God's ability to subdue chaos and bring order. **four living creatures** Possibly an allusion to the cherubim described in Eze 1 and 10 (see note on Eze 1:5), or the seraphim of Isa 6:2–3. The number four often represents the entire created order (e.g., Rev 7:1; Jer 49:36). Thus, these creatures may represent all living things worshiping God. **they were covered with eyes, in front and in back** The multiplicity of eyes symbolically suggests unceasing vigilance or great wisdom (compare Eze 1:18).
4:7 living creature was like a lion While John and Ezekiel both describe four living creatures in their visions, the descriptions vary. In Eze 1, all four creatures are identical. In Revelation, each has only one face and resembles a different creature: a lion, an ox, a human and a flying eagle. Ezekiel's creatures have four wings, but John's have six, like the seraphim in Isa 6:2. John's creatures are full of eyes, but the eyes in Ezekiel are on the wheels that move the creatures.
4:8 Holy, holy, holy This echoes the song of the seraphim in Isa 6:2–3.

[9]Whenever the living creatures give glory, honor and thanks to him who sits on the throne and who lives for ever and ever, [10]the twenty-four elders fall down before him who sits on the throne and worship him who lives for ever and ever. They lay their crowns before the throne and say:

[11]"You are worthy, our Lord and God,
   to receive glory and honor and power,
for you created all things,
   and by your will they were created
   and have their being."

The Scroll and the Lamb

5 Then I saw in the right hand of him who sat on the throne a scroll with writing on both sides and sealed with seven seals. [2]And I saw a mighty angel proclaiming in a loud voice, "Who is worthy to break the seals and open the scroll?" [3]But no one in heaven or on earth or under the earth could open the scroll or even look inside it. [4]I wept and wept because no one was found who was worthy to open the scroll or look inside. [5]Then one of the elders said to me, "Do not weep! See, the Lion of the tribe of Judah, the Root of David, has triumphed. He is able to open the scroll and its seven seals."

[6]Then I saw a Lamb, looking as if it had been slain, standing at the center of the throne, encircled by the four living creatures and the elders. The Lamb had seven horns and seven eyes, which are the seven spirits[a] of God sent out into all the earth. [7]He went and took the scroll from the right hand of him who sat on the throne. [8]And when he had taken it, the four living creatures and the twenty-four elders fell down before the Lamb. Each one had a harp and they were holding golden bowls full of incense, which are the prayers of God's people. [9]And they sang a new song, saying:

"You are worthy to take the scroll
   and to open its seals,
because you were slain,
   and with your blood you purchased for God
   persons from every tribe and language and
      people and nation.
[10]You have made them to be a kingdom and
      priests to serve our God,
   and they will reign[b] on the earth."

[11]Then I looked and heard the voice of many angels, numbering thousands upon thousands, and

---

[a] 6 That is, the sevenfold Spirit   [b] 10 Some manuscripts *they reign*

4:10 They lay The phrase describes submission: the 24 elders, though wearing crowns, realize the ultimate source of their power—God himself, the Great King.

4:11 our Lord and God Domitian (who ruled from AD 81–96), who may have been the Roman emperor during John's exile on Patmos, demanded that his subjects call him "our lord and god." John sets up a clear contrast between the true king and the one whose rule will eventually be done away with. See the timeline "The Early Church to AD 100" on p. 1776.

5:1–14 This continues the throne-room vision initiated in Rev 4. Here, the glorified Christ is reintroduced as the slain Lamb, and he takes the seven-sealed scroll in preparation for judgment. Verse 2 asks who is worthy to open the scroll and break its seals; the remainder of the chapter answers that question.

5:1 a scroll The scroll contains God's plan for history, spelled out in the events that are about to come upon the world (see ch. 6). **sealed with seven seals** The number seven indicates completion; the contents were completely inaccessible (see 22:10; compare Isa 29:11; Da 12:4). Seals have been used throughout history as indicators of authority, identity and approval. In ancient times, seals were impressed upon wet clay or hot wax. The images on each seal were unique to their owners and served to identify property, safeguard against fraudulent transactions and ratify official documents and rulings.

SEAL
Seals have been used throughout history as indicators of authority, identity and approval. The earliest known

seals date from the fourth millennium BC. They often took the form of necklaces or rings and were closely guarded. The seals were impressed upon wet clay or hot wax. The images on each seal were unique to their owners and served to safeguard against fraudulent transactions, identify property and ratify official documents and rulings.

5:4 I wept and wept If the scroll could not be opened, John would not be able to see the events that were to come (see Rev 4:1).

5:5 the tribe of Judah The royal tribe, or the tribe from which Israel's rulers would come (Ge 49:9–10). **the Root of David** An allusion to the prophecy of Isa 11:1,10 (see Rev 22:16).

5:6 a Lamb, looking as if it had been slain John hears about a lion, but turns to see a lamb. Lamb imagery relates to Jesus' death on the cross. The tradition of viewing his death as a sacrifice—like the sheep sacrificed in the OT—arises out of Isa 53 (see Isa 53:4–8,10–12). The early church applied the title "Lamb of God" to Jesus, understanding his death to substitute for their sin (e.g., Jn 1:29,36; 1Pe 1:19). The victory spoken of in Rev 5:5, then, was brought about through sacrifice. This concept would have instilled hope in those being persecuted; victory for them would likewise come through sacrifice. **seven horns and seven eyes** Horns symbolized power and eyes symbolized wisdom. Christ is completely powerful and wise. **the seven spirits of God** See 1:4 and note.

5:8 golden bowls full of incense Here and elsewhere, incense symbolizes the prayers of God's people (e.g., 8:3–5; Ps 141:2).

5:10 a kingdom and priests See Rev 1:6 and note.

5:11 numbering Rather than taking this as a precise number, this was probably John's way of saying they were innumerable (compare Da 7:10).

Angels in the Bible

APPEARS TO	NAME OF ANGEL(S)	REFERENCE
Hagar	Angel of Yahweh	Ge 16:1–16
Lot (and family)	The (two) angels	Ge 19:1–22
Abraham	Yahweh; "three men"	Ge 18:1–33
Abraham	Angel of Yahweh	Ge 22:1–22
Jacob (dream)	Angels of God	Ge 28:11–12
Jacob	Angel of God; "a man"	Ge 31:11–13; 32:22–32
Moses	Angel of Yahweh	Ex 3:2
All Israel	Angel of God	Ex 14:19
Balaam and Donkey	Angel of Yahweh	Nu 22:22–35
Joshua	Commander of the army of Yahweh	Jos 5:13–15
All Israel	Angel of Yahweh	Jdg 2:1–4
Gideon	Angel of Yahweh	Jdg 6:11–23
Manoah and Wife	Angel of Yahweh	Jdg 13:1–25
David	Angel of Yahweh	2Sa 24:15–17; 1Ch 21:16–18
Elijah	Angel of Yahweh	1Ki 19:1–8
Daniel	"God sent his angel"	Da 6:22
Daniel	Gabriel	Da 8:15–17
Zechariah (vision)	two angels	Zec 2:1–5
Zechariah	Gabriel	Lk 1:5–25,57–64
Mary	Gabriel	Lk 1:26–38
Joseph (dream)	An angel of the Lord	Mt 2:13
Shepherds	An angel of the Lord; "great company of the heavenly host"	Lk 2:8–15
Women at Jesus' Tomb	An angel of the Lord; "a young man"; "two men in clothes that gleamed like lightning"	Mt 28:2–7; Mk 16:5–7; Lk 24:4–7
Mary Magdalene	Two angels in white	Jn 20:11–13
Jesus' followers	Two men dressed in white	Ac 1:10–11
The Apostles	An angel of the Lord	Ac 5:17–21
Philip	An angel of the Lord	Ac 8:26–39
Cornelius (vision)	An angel of God	Ac 10:1–8
Peter	An angel of the Lord	Ac 12:1–19
Paul	An angel of God	Ac 27:21–25
N/A	Michael the Archangel	Jude 9
John (vision)	Angels of the seven churches	Rev 1:20
John (vision)	A mighty angel	Rev 5:2
John (vision)	Many angels around the throne	Rev 5:11; 7:11

ten thousand times ten thousand. They encircled the throne and the living creatures and the elders. [12]In a loud voice they were saying:

"Worthy is the Lamb, who was slain,
  to receive power and wealth and wisdom
    and strength
  and honor and glory and praise!"

[13]Then I heard every creature in heaven and on earth and under the earth and on the sea, and all that is in them, saying:

"To him who sits on the throne and to the Lamb
  be praise and honor and glory and power,
    for ever and ever!"

[14]The four living creatures said, "Amen," and the elders fell down and worshiped.

The Seals

6 I watched as the Lamb opened the first of the seven seals. Then I heard one of the four living creatures say in a voice like thunder, "Come!" [2]I

6:1–17 The opening of the first seal in Rev 6:1 unleashes a barrage of judgments that last through ch. 20. In the first series of these judgments (the opening of the seals in v. 1—8:1), John introduces the four horsemen of the apocalypse, the martyrs and the awesome, destructive power of the Lamb. Rather than bringing about total destruction, these judgments serve to call people to repentance.

6:1 one of the four living creatures Each of the four living creatures summons one of the riders as the first four seals are broken.
6:2 white horse Christ himself rides a white horse in 19:11–13, and it is sometimes argued that he is also referred to here. However, it is more likely that this rider represents evil in its pale imitation of Christ. In Mk 13:5–6, Jesus speaks of those who falsely come in his name, and the forces of evil in the NT are sometimes

Angels in the Bible (continued)

APPEARS TO	NAME OF ANGEL(S)	REFERENCE
John (vision)	Four angels at the four corners of the earth	Rev 7:1
John (vision)	An angel ascending from the east	Rev 7:2
John (vision)	Seven angels with seven trumpets	Rev 8:2; 8:6–9:14; 11:15
John (vision)	An angel with a golden censer	Rev 8:3
John (vision)	Four angels who kill a third of humanity	Rev 9:14–15
John (vision)	An angel holding a little scroll	Rev 10:1–11
John (vision)	Michael and his angels	Rev 12:7
John (vision)	Three angels with three messages	Rev 14:6–12
John (vision)	An angel that comes out of the temple	Rev 14:15
John (vision)	An angel that comes out of the temple with a sickle	Rev 14:17–20
John (vision)	Seven angels with seven plagues (one of whom speaks to John)	Rev 15:1; 16:1–21; 17:1; 21:9,15; 22:6–11
John (vision)	An angel announcing the fall of Babylon	Rev 18:1–2
John (vision)	An angel who throws a boulder the size of a millstone into the sea	Rev 18:21
John (vision)	An angel standing in the sun	Rev 19:17
John (vision)	An angel holding a key and a chain	Rev 20:1
John (vision)	Twelve angels at the gates of the New Jerusalem	Rev 21:12

looked, and there before me was a white horse! Its rider held a bow, and he was given a crown, and he rode out as a conqueror bent on conquest.

³When the Lamb opened the second seal, I heard the second living creature say, "Come!" ⁴Then another horse came out, a fiery red one. Its rider was given power to take peace from the earth and to make people kill each other. To him was given a large sword.

⁵When the Lamb opened the third seal, I heard the third living creature say, "Come!" I looked, and there before me was a black horse! Its rider was holding a pair of scales in his hand. ⁶Then I heard what sounded like a voice among the four living creatures, saying, "Two pounds*ª* of wheat for a day's wages,*ᵇ* and six pounds*ᶜ* of barley for a day's wages,*ᵇ* and do not damage the oil and the wine!"

⁷When the Lamb opened the fourth seal, I heard the voice of the fourth living creature say, "Come!" ⁸I looked, and there before me was a pale horse! Its rider was named Death, and Hades was following close behind him. They were given power over a fourth of the earth to kill by sword, famine and plague, and by the wild beasts of the earth.

⁹When he opened the fifth seal, I saw under the altar the souls of those who had been slain because of the word of God and the testimony they had maintained. ¹⁰They called out in a loud voice, "How long, Sovereign Lord, holy and true, until you judge the inhabitants of the earth and avenge our blood?" ¹¹Then each of them was given a white robe, and they were told to wait a little

longer, until the full number of their fellow servants, their brothers and sisters,*ᵈ* were killed just as they had been.

¹²I watched as he opened the sixth seal. There was a great earthquake. The sun turned black like sackcloth made of goat hair, the whole moon turned blood red, ¹³and the stars in the sky fell to earth, as figs drop from a fig tree when shaken by a strong wind. ¹⁴The heavens receded like a scroll being rolled up, and every mountain and island was removed from its place.

¹⁵Then the kings of the earth, the princes, the generals, the rich, the mighty, and everyone else, both slave and free, hid in caves and among the rocks of the mountains. ¹⁶They called to the mountains and the rocks, "Fall on us and hide us*ᵉ* from the face of him who sits on the throne and from the wrath of the Lamb! ¹⁷For the great day of their*ᶠ* wrath has come, and who can withstand it?"

144,000 Sealed

7 After this I saw four angels standing at the four corners of the earth, holding back the four winds of the earth to prevent any wind from blowing on the land or on the sea or on any tree. ²Then I saw another angel coming up from the east, having the seal of the living God. He called

---

ª 6 About 1 kilogram   *ᵇ 6* Greek *a denarius*   *ᶜ 6* Or about 3 kilograms   *ᵈ 11* The Greek word for *brothers and sisters* (*adelphoi*) refers here to believers, both men and women, as part of God's family; also in 12:10; 19:10.   *ᵉ 16* See Hosea 10:8.   *ᶠ 17* Some manuscripts *his*

---

depicted as imitating Christ (compare Rev 13:1 with 19:12; and 5:6 with 13:3). **given a crown** This rider is given a crown (a symbol of political power) by God to execute his judgments.

6:4 fiery red May suggest warfare and bloodshed (compare Mk 13:7–8).

6:5 black horse Represents famine, a common consequence of war (compare Rev 6:6; Mk 13:8).

6:6 Two pounds of wheat for a day's wages Suggestive of someone rationing out supplies in a government food line and selling them at inflated prices (compare 2Ki 6:24–25). A denarius, the coin mentioned here in the Greek text, was a day's wage earned by a common laborer. Such rations could feed only one person, so a worker would not have been able to afford to feed his family. The result would have been widespread hunger and starvation. See the infographic "A Silver Denarius" on p. 1578. **the oil and the wine** The necessities (wheat and barley) are sold for exorbitant prices, but luxury items (oil and wine) are unaffected. This may point to the role greed can play in intensifying the effects of a famine.

6:8 a pale horse May indicate pestilence and death, as its rider signifies. **named Death** This personification of death is in direct contrast to the life offered by the Lamb, Jesus (Rev 7:14). **Hades was following close behind** Physical, bodily death is connected to the netherworld of Greek mythology—the place where people go after their bodily death. This personification, along with the personification of death, is likely meant to evoke the idea that these two evil powers are at work in the

world—physical death and the spiritual death that can follow it (compare Hos 13:14).

6:9 fifth seal While the martyrs make an appeal for vengeance, God forestalls his wrath. More must be added to their number before he strikes back. **the souls of those who had been slain** The martyrs are under the altar: They were sacrificed because of their faith in Christ (see Rev 20:4).

6:10 How long This prayer often shows up in the midst of persecution (e.g., Zec 1:12; Ps 13:1–2; Isa 6:11). It is answered later in the book (Rev 10:6 and note; 19).

6:11 white robe See 3:4 and note; 7:14 and note. **fellow servants, their brothers and sisters** Believers appear to be going through the judgments as well.

6:12 great earthquake Language of natural phenomena, as in 6:12–14, is typical when referring to God's judgment. It normally refers to the end of the age (e.g., Isa 13:10; Eze 32:7–8; Joel 2:10; Mk 13:8).

6:15 everyone All kinds of people—rich and poor, powerful and weak, slave and free—will seek refuge from the wrath of the Lamb.

6:16 Fall on us Compare Hos 10:8; Lk 23:30.

6:17 the great day of their wrath The wrath is of God and the Lamb. This day is the final outpouring of judgment on the world. Those who have been bought by the Lamb are safe from this judgment (Rev 5:9). They are able to stand (compare Joel 2:11).

7:1–17 Following the judgments of the first six seals, an interlude takes place (just prior to the seventh) that

out in a loud voice to the four angels who had been given power to harm the land and the sea: [3]"Do not harm the land or the sea or the trees until we put a seal on the foreheads of the servants of our God." [4]Then I heard the number of those who were sealed: 144,000 from all the tribes of Israel.

[5] From the tribe of Judah 12,000 were sealed,
   from the tribe of Reuben 12,000,
   from the tribe of Gad 12,000,
[6] from the tribe of Asher 12,000,
   from the tribe of Naphtali 12,000,
   from the tribe of Manasseh 12,000,
[7] from the tribe of Simeon 12,000,
   from the tribe of Levi 12,000,
   from the tribe of Issachar 12,000,
[8] from the tribe of Zebulun 12,000,
   from the tribe of Joseph 12,000,
   from the tribe of Benjamin 12,000.

The Great Multitude in White Robes

[9]After this I looked, and there before me was a great multitude that no one could count, from every nation, tribe, people and language, standing before the throne and before the Lamb. They were wearing white robes and were holding palm branches in their hands. [10]And they cried out in a loud voice:

"Salvation belongs to our God,
   who sits on the throne,
   and to the Lamb."

[11]All the angels were standing around the throne and around the elders and the four living creatures. They fell down on their faces before the throne and worshiped God, [12]saying:

"Amen!
Praise and glory
and wisdom and thanks and honor
and power and strength
be to our God for ever and ever.
Amen!"

[13]Then one of the elders asked me, "These in white robes — who are they, and where did they come from?"

[14]I answered, "Sir, you know."

And he said, "These are they who have come out of the great tribulation; they have washed their robes and made them white in the blood of the Lamb. [15]Therefore,

"they are before the throne of God
   and serve him day and night in his temple;
and he who sits on the throne
   will shelter them with his presence.
[16]'Never again will they hunger;
   never again will they thirst.

---

allows for the sealing of the 144,000 (Rev 7:1–8) and John's vision of an innumerable crowd of the redeemed (vv. 9–17). Opinions differ on the identity of the two groups in this chapter. Some believe the 144,000 to be ethnic Jews who come to faith in Jesus during a future tribulation. Others believe the two sections of this chapter to be two different ways of speaking about the entirety of God's people. In any case, ch. 7 answers the question presented in 6:17 of who is able to stand before God and the Lamb, Jesus. The answer immediately follows: the whole host of the redeemed.

7:1 four corners of the earth The whole world is represented by the four points of the compass (see 4:6 and note). **four winds** Since the horsemen of Zechariah are called "winds" (or "spirits") in Zec 6:5, this image may refer to the four horsemen from Rev 6:1–8. **blowing** Whether this is natural wind or the activities of the four horsemen, destruction and judgment are implied.

7:2 the seal In contrast to the mark of the beast (13:16–17), the seal serves to authenticate and identify the people of God. See 5:1 and note.

7:3 on the foreheads Reminiscent of Eze 9:4. **the servants** The angel and his helpers mark those who are already servants of God.

7:4 144,000 There are differing views about the identity of the 144,000: They may be ethnic Jews who will become Christians and be kept from martyrdom during the seven-year tribulation period — a view usually taken by futurist readings of the book (see note on Rev 1:19). Alternatively, the number may figuratively represent the complete number of the redeemed — 12 multiplied by 12 multiplied by 1,000. This calculation derives from multiplying the tribes of Israel (21:12) by the apostles

(21:14) by the number of completeness or perfection (20:4). **from all the tribes of Israel** In the list that follows, Dan has been omitted and replaced by Manasseh. Ephraim is also excluded. These tribes may have been omitted due to their propensity toward idolatry (e.g., Jdg 17–18; Hos 4:17–19).

7:9 After this I looked John hears the number in Rev 7:4, whereas he sees the multitude in v. 9. He may be attempting to portray the surprising fulfillment of God's redemptive plan, just as he heard about a lion and saw a lamb in 5:5–6. **palm branches** Indicative of victory in royal and military processions, as demonstrated by its connection with white robes and salvation or victory in 7:10. Compare Jesus' entry into Jerusalem (e.g., Mk 11:8).

7:11 All the angels The angels participate in the same activity and posture as the 24 elders in 4:10 and 5:14.

7:12 Amen The angels affirm the statement of the great multitude in v. 10.

7:14 the great tribulation May refer generally to a time of intense persecution, a final period of persecution that will immediately precede the end of the age, or the total amount of persecution between Christ's ascension and return. **white in the blood of the Lamb** Christ's blood cleanses from sin, hence the paradox of red (blood) making white (pure or victorious). Compare 1:5; 22:14; Jn 1:29; 1Jn 1:7.

7:15 before the throne of God This indicates being in God's presence — the great hope to which all of Revelation points (see Rev 21:3–5). The themes in 7:16–17 are repeated in 21:3–5.

7:16 Never again will they hunger Hunger, thirst and exposure to the elements were common plights of the oppressed in antiquity (e.g., Ps 121:6; Isa 49:10).

Four Views of Revelation

	HISTORICIST	PRETERIST	FUTURIST	IDEALIST
Interpretation*	Records events which span from the apostolic period to end of the age	Records events which happened in the past from our vantage point	Records events which have yet to be fulfilled	Records events which are symbolic of the spiritual warfare between good and evil
Timing of Events	In process and are fulfilled over the course of history	Fulfilled during the age of the Roman Empire, shortly after John wrote Revelation	Will take place at the end of the age	May represent various historical periods rather than one specific event
Seven churches (Rev 2–3)	Seven periods of church history	Seven churches located in Roman province of Asia during the first century AD	(Possibly any one of the other views)	Any church which shares the same characteristics of the seven churches
Twenty-four elders (Rev 4:4,10; 5:8)	The church—those redeemed by Christ and triumphant	God's heavenly court, but not any specific group	Angelic beings or saints from the New Testament era	Angelic representatives of the old covenant (12 tribes) and the new covenant (12 apostles)
Sealed Scroll (Rev 5:1–9)	God's purpose and design for the world and the Church	God's sentence or judgment upon those who persecuted the saints	The title deed to the earth	God's redemptive plan for the world
Unsealing of the scroll (Rev 6:1,3,5,7, 9,12; 8:1)	The demise of the Roman empire, from the death of Domitian (AD 96) to the invasion of the Vandals (fifth century AD)	The execution of God's judgment upon Jerusalem	The rapture and the beginning of the Great Tribulation	The outworkings of God's redemptive plan throughout history, including wars, persecutions and judgments
144,000 (Rev 7:4–8)	The church	Symbolic number of Jewish Christians to escape the destruction of Jerusalem in 70 AD	The remnant of Jewish people or the last generation of Christians alive when the Tribulation takes place	A symbolic number of old covenant Israel and new covenant Israel (i.e., spiritual Israel)
Seven Trumpets (Rev 8:7,8, 10–11,12–13; 9:1–21; 11:14–19)	A series of invasions of the Roman empire by various groups (e.g., Vandals and Turks)	A series of Roman military actions against the Jews during the Jewish War	A series of disasters which will come upon the unrepentant during the seven-year Tribulation	A series of disasters which echo the plagues against Egypt (Rev 7:14–11:10). They express God's judgment upon the unrepentant.

Four Views of Revelation (continued)

	HISTORICIST	PRETERIST	FUTURIST	IDEALIST
Two witnesses (Rev 11:3–6)	People who rejected the authority of the Papacy prior to the Reformation (e.g., Waldenses and Albigenses)	Prophets who prophesied about the destruction of Jerusalem and the end of Jewish religious and political authority	Two prophets (possibly Elijah and Enoch or Moses)	The church throughout the church era
The woman (Rev 12:1–2, 5–6)	The church which endured persecution by Rome in the fourth century AD	Faithful Israel in the first century AD	Israel or the church which will be persecuted by the antichrist	The church through the church era
Red dragon (Rev 12:3)	Imperial Rome as a representative of Satan	A combination of the beasts in Daniel 7 which represent world empires	Satan	Satan
Male child (Rev 12:4–5)	The church or the Roman emperor Constantine	The church of the first century AD	Christ	Christ who ascended to heaven
Woman's escape into the wilderness (Rev 12:6)	The church which escaped the persecution of Rome or the Papacy	Judean Christians who escaped Edomite and Roman attacks during the Jewish War	Escape of Israel or the church from the coming persecution	The church which witnesses about Christ
1,260 days (Rev 12:6)	1,260 years of the authority of the Papacy in Rome	The period of the Jewish War (AD 66–70) or emperor Nero's persecution of the church	The final 1,260 days (3-1/2 years) before the return of Christ	Symbolizes the era of the church
Beast out of the sea (Rev 13:1–4)	The Papacy	Rome, specifically emperor Nero	Symbolic of Gentile nations, namely, a revived Roman Empire	Government or political system which opposes God
Beast out of the earth (Rev 13:11–15)	The Papacy	The Roman emperor cult or a false prophet	The religious version of the first beast	False religion associated with the political system
666 (Rev 13:16–18)	The Papacy	Roman emperor Nero	Represents a form of currency in an economic system	Represents the name of the anti-Christian government system
Babylon (Rev 17:5)	The religious system and authority of the Papacy	Rome or Jerusalem	A false religion. Possibly the reestablishment of Babylon or Rome.	A system (possibly economic) which entices believers to turn away from God
Rider on the white horse (Rev 19:11–21)	Christ's conquests and judgments upon his enemies	Christ's victory over the pagan nations by his Word	Christ's visible return to earth	Christ's ongoing conquest of the anti-Christian system through the gospel

*See Steve Gregg's *Revelation, Four Views: A Parallel Commentary* (Nashville, TN: Thomas Nelson Publishers, 1997).

The sun will not beat down on them,'ᵃ
nor any scorching heat.
¹⁷For the Lamb at the center of the throne
will be their shepherd;
'he will lead them to springs of living water.'ᵃ
'And God will wipe away every tear from
their eyes.'ᵇ"

The Seventh Seal and the Golden Censer

8 When he opened the seventh seal, there was silence in heaven for about half an hour.

²And I saw the seven angels who stand before God, and seven trumpets were given to them. ³Another angel, who had a golden censer, came and stood at the altar. He was given much incense to offer, with the prayers of all God's people, on the golden altar in front of the throne. ⁴The smoke of the incense, together with the prayers of God's people, went up before God from the angel's hand. ⁵Then the angel took the censer, filled it with fire from the altar, and hurled it on the earth; and there came peals of thunder, rumblings, flashes of lightning and an earthquake.

The Trumpets

⁶Then the seven angels who had the seven trumpets prepared to sound them.

⁷The first angel sounded his trumpet, and there came hail and fire mixed with blood, and it was hurled down on the earth. A third of the earth was burned up, a third of the trees were burned up, and all the green grass was burned up.

⁸The second angel sounded his trumpet, and something like a huge mountain, all ablaze, was thrown into the sea. A third of the sea turned into blood, ⁹a third of the living creatures in the sea died, and a third of the ships were destroyed.

¹⁰The third angel sounded his trumpet, and a great star, blazing like a torch, fell from the sky on a third of the rivers and on the springs of water — ¹¹the name of the star is Wormwood.ᶜ A third of the waters turned bitter, and many people died from the waters that had become bitter.

¹²The fourth angel sounded his trumpet, and a third of the sun was struck, a third of the moon, and a third of the stars, so that a third of them turned dark. A third of the day was without light, and also a third of the night.

¹³As I watched, I heard an eagle that was flying in midair call out in a loud voice: "Woe! Woe! Woe to the inhabitants of the earth, because of the trumpet blasts about to be sounded by the other three angels!"

9 The fifth angel sounded his trumpet, and I saw a star that had fallen from the sky to the earth. The star was given the key to the shaft of

ᵃ 16,17 Isaiah 49:10   ᵇ 17 Isaiah 25:8   ᶜ 11 Wormwood is a bitter substance.

7:17 the Lamb In what seems paradoxical, the Lamb will be the shepherd. Religious and political leaders are often portrayed as either good or bad shepherds in the Bible (e.g., 2Sa 5:2; Jn 10:11–18; see 1Sa 9:3 and note).

8:1–5 After the interlude of Rev 7, the seventh seal is opened and seven angels receive seven trumpets that signal a further round of judgments when blown (vv. 1–2). But first, another angel takes a censer, symbolizing the prayers of God's people, and hurls it to the earth (vv. 3–5).

8:1 he opened the seventh seal The Lamb resumes his activity from ch. 6.

8:2 seven angels These may be the seven archangels spoken of in Jewish tradition (see Tobit 12:15; 1 Enoch 20). Of these, only Michael is mentioned by name in Revelation (Rev 12:7). **seven trumpets** Instruments of battle (e.g., Jos 6:5). When blown by the angels, these trumpets initiate the next seven judgments.

8:3 incense Incense is also identified with prayers in Rev 5:8.

8:5 hurled it on the earth Initiates judgment in response to the prayers of the saints — probably those recorded in 6:10. **peals of thunder, rumblings, flashes of lightning and an earthquake** This formula, first mentioned in 4:5, is used again in 11:19 and 16:18. The latter three usages follow a set of judgments (the seals, trumpets and bowls).

8:6–13 The next wave of judgments begins; four of the seven trumpets are blown in this section. The attacks, which come against nature and the cosmos, are intended to lead sinful humanity to repentance, not totally destroy them.

8:6 to sound Describes the commencement of judgment. John's imagery recalls several of the plagues from the book of Exodus.

8:7 hail and fire mixed with blood Corresponds to Ex 9:22–25. John adds blood to the hail and fire of the exodus narrative.

8:8 like a huge mountain, all ablaze John may be speaking of a volcano or meteors. Jews viewed the unexpected eruption of Mount Vesuvius (AD 79) as divine punishment on Rome for the events of AD 70 — when Titus entered Jerusalem, sacked the city, destroyed the temple and killed many people. **A third of the sea turned into blood** Corresponds to Ex 7:20–25. The water may have become blood red due to the fiery mountain.

8:10 a great star, blazing like a torch Perhaps a meteor. **rivers and on the springs of water** Corresponds to Ex 7:20–25. Whereas the previous judgment was against salt water, this judgment is against fresh water.

8:11 Wormwood A leafy plant that causes water to become bitter.

8:12 a third of the sun The fourth trumpet corresponds to Ex 10:21–23 (compare Joel 3:15; Am 8:9).

8:13 Woe! Woe! Woe The threefold use of "woe" corresponds to the three remaining trumpet judgments. It communicates distress, pain, suffering and displeasure. **to the inhabitants of the earth** In Revelation this phrase refers to unbelievers, not all earth's inhabitants (compare Rev 3:10; 6:10; 11:10; 13:8). Whereas the first four trumpets affected everyone (or at least those in one-third of the earth), the final three are only for unbelievers. The seal mentioned in 7:3 protects the remaining believers from the demonic oppression of the final three trumpets (see 9:4).

the Abyss. [2]When he opened the Abyss, smoke rose from it like the smoke from a gigantic furnace. The sun and sky were darkened by the smoke from the Abyss. [3]And out of the smoke locusts came down on the earth and were given power like that of scorpions of the earth. [4]They were told not to harm the grass of the earth or any plant or tree, but only those people who did not have the seal of God on their foreheads. [5]They were not allowed to kill them but only to torture them for five months. And the agony they suffered was like that of the sting of a scorpion when it strikes. [6]During those days people will seek death but will not find it; they will long to die, but death will elude them.

[7]The locusts looked like horses prepared for battle. On their heads they wore something like crowns of gold, and their faces resembled human faces. [8]Their hair was like women's hair, and their teeth were like lions' teeth. [9]They had breastplates like breastplates of iron, and the sound of their wings was like the thundering of many horses and chariots rushing into battle. [10]They had tails with stingers, like scorpions, and in their tails they had power to torment people for five months. [11]They had as king over them the angel of the Abyss, whose name in Hebrew is Abaddon and in Greek is Apollyon (that is, Destroyer).

[12]The first woe is past; two other woes are yet to come.

[13]The sixth angel sounded his trumpet, and I heard a voice coming from the four horns of the golden altar that is before God. [14]It said to the sixth angel who had the trumpet, "Release the four angels who are bound at the great river Euphrates." [15]And the four angels who had been kept ready for this very hour and day and month and year were released to kill a third of mankind. [16]The number of the mounted troops was twice ten thousand times ten thousand. I heard their number.

[17]The horses and riders I saw in my vision looked like this: Their breastplates were fiery red, dark blue, and yellow as sulfur. The heads of the horses resembled the heads of lions, and out of their mouths came fire, smoke and sulfur. [18]A third of mankind was killed by the three plagues of fire, smoke and sulfur that came out of their mouths. [19]The power of the horses was in their mouths and in their tails; for their tails were like snakes, having heads with which they inflict injury.

[20]The rest of mankind who were not killed by these plagues still did not repent of the work of their hands; they did not stop worshiping demons, and idols of gold, silver, bronze, stone and

---

9:1–12 The blowing of the fifth trumpet, also called the first woe (v. 12), is recorded in vv. 1–12. John describes terrifying locusts unleashed upon the unrepentant oppressors for five months. As with the horses in the latter half of the chapter, the descriptions are meant to terrify and alarm the unrepentant.

9:1 that had fallen from the sky to the earth Stars are sometimes associated with angels (1:20). This figure may be the angel in v. 11 who is given charge over the abyss. The concept of a fallen star may suggest that the figure is Satan or one of his fallen angels (compare Lk 10:18; Rev 12:9). **the Abyss** Where demons and fallen angels were thought to be kept—the underworld (see 2Pe 2:4 and note; Jude 6; compare the ancient Jewish work of 1 Enoch 90:22–27).
9:2 smoke rose from it May reflect the notion of the underworld as a place of burning and judgment (e.g., Mk 9:47–48). Smoke could also be figurative, describing the appearance of the locusts hurrying out of the abyss.
9:3 locusts Echoes Ex 10:12–15. The imagery of locusts is used in the OT for invading armies (e.g., Jer 51:27; Na 3:15).
9:4 the seal of God on their foreheads See Rev 7:2 and note.
9:5 They were not allowed The passive voice indicates that their authority to act comes from someone else (God). **five months** The lifespan of locusts, which hatch in the springtime and die near the end of summer.
9:6 people will seek death Repeated in the following clause for emphasis. The pain will be so great that they will prefer death, but the stings will not be fatal (v. 5). Compare Jer 8:3.
9:11 angel of the Abyss See Rev 9:1 and note. **Abaddon** A Hebrew name for the place of the dead (meaning "destruction"). This place is sometimes mentioned in

the Hebrew text in parallel to Sheol (e.g., Job 26:6; Pr 15:11; 27:20). **Apollyon** Means "destroyer." This may indicate a connection to the Greek god Apollo, for whom the locust was often used as a symbol. Domitian—who may have been the emperor at the time Revelation was written—thought of himself as Apollo incarnate. Thus, this may be John's way of presenting worship of the emperor as evil and demonic.

9:13–21 The sixth trumpet releases another four angels tasked with killing a third of the remaining population. They bring an army of 200 million to assist in the slaughter. The outlook is bleak for those who oppressed the people of God (see Rev 6:2 and note; 6:9–10).

9:13 a voice Perhaps one of the martyrs under the altar or the angel with the censer (see 6:9–11; 8:3–5). In either case, the sixth trumpet is presented as a response to the prayers of the saints.
9:14 four angels Not the same four angels as those mentioned in 6:2–8 or 7:1. Many angels appear throughout the book, often in the same quantity (four, seven, etc.). **Euphrates** The easternmost border of the Roman Empire. The Euphrates protected the Romans from their eastern enemy, the Parthians.
9:15 kill a third of mankind This portion is in addition to the one-fourth already killed by Death and Hades in 6:8. The effects of the judgments are intensifying.
9:17 horses and riders The description of the demonic horde recalls the description of the locusts in vv. 7–9.
9:18 by the three plagues The fire, smoke and sulfur had a plague-like effect, killing the one-third mentioned in v. 15.
9:20 did not repent Despite clear demonstrations of God's power, prolonged anguish (five months) and otherworldly attacks, they still would not turn to God, give him glory and repent of their idolatry. **demons,**

wood — idols that cannot see or hear or walk. ²¹Nor did they repent of their murders, their magic arts, their sexual immorality or their thefts.

The Angel and the Little Scroll

10 Then I saw another mighty angel coming down from heaven. He was robed in a cloud, with a rainbow above his head; his face was like the sun, and his legs were like fiery pillars. ²He was holding a little scroll, which lay open in his hand. He planted his right foot on the sea and his left foot on the land, ³and he gave a loud shout like the roar of a lion. When he shouted, the voices of the seven thunders spoke. ⁴And when the seven thunders spoke, I was about to write; but I heard a voice from heaven say, "Seal up what the seven thunders have said and do not write it down."

⁵Then the angel I had seen standing on the sea and on the land raised his right hand to heaven. ⁶And he swore by him who lives for ever and ever, who created the heavens and all that is in them, the earth and all that is in it, and the sea and all that is in it, and said, "There will be no more delay! ⁷But in the days when the seventh angel is about to sound his trumpet, the mystery of God will be accomplished, just as he announced to his servants the prophets."

⁸Then the voice that I had heard from heaven spoke to me once more: "Go, take the scroll that lies open in the hand of the angel who is standing on the sea and on the land."

⁹So I went to the angel and asked him to give me the little scroll. He said to me, "Take it and eat it. It will turn your stomach sour, but 'in your mouth it will be as sweet as honey.'ᵃ" ¹⁰I took the little scroll from the angel's hand and ate it. It tasted as sweet as honey in my mouth, but when I had eaten it, my stomach turned sour. ¹¹Then I was told, "You must prophesy again about many peoples, nations, languages and kings."

The Two Witnesses

11 I was given a reed like a measuring rod and was told, "Go and measure the temple of God and the altar, with its worshipers. ²But exclude the outer court; do not measure it, because it has been given to the Gentiles. They will trample on the holy city for 42 months. ³And I will appoint my two witnesses, and they will prophesy for 1,260

ᵃ 9 Ezek. 3:3

---

and idols of gold John equates idol worship to demon worship. Compare 1Co 10:20–22.

10:1–11 Following the sixth trumpet judgment, John sees another mighty angel holding a little scroll. The angel announces a forthcoming fulfillment of the mystery of God, which will follow the next trumpet blast. John hears seven thunders after the angel speaks, but he is told not to communicate what they say. He is then given the little scroll to eat and is told he must prophesy again. Following a time of intense judgment, this chapter presents a message of hope to the people of God. This is the first of two interludes before the seventh trumpet is blown in Rev 11:15.

10:1 He was robed in a cloud Recalls the Son of Man imagery from Da 7:13 and Rev 1 as well as the ascension scene from Ac 1:9. This angel shares similarities with the glorified Christ from Rev 1; he may serve in close proximity to the Lamb. John identifies this being as an angel. **rainbow** Recalls God's covenant with humankind in Ge 9:8–17. Following the seven seals and six trumpets, this angel is a harbinger of mercy.

10:2 a little scroll The diminutive term is suggestive of size, not importance. It was small enough to be consumed.

10:3 seven thunders These may be heavenly voices or God's voice (compare Jn 12:28–29). The following verse, which indicates John was going to write down what they said, suggests that the thunder was more than just noise.

10:4 Seal up A seal would prevent disclosure. The little scroll and the message of the mighty angel are the focus of the chapter. They — not the words of the thunder — are important for humanity to hear.

10:6 There will be no more delay The heavenly reply to the martyrs' question about the timing of God's vengeance on their murderers (Rev 6:10).

10:7 the mystery of God The connection of the mystery with the seventh trumpet may indicate that the mystery is

the full establishment of God's kingdom (see 11:15–18; compare note on Mk 1:15).

10:8 take the scroll that lies open Unlike the scroll in ch. 5 (which could only be opened by the Lamb), this scroll is already open, and John is allowed to take it.

10:9 Take it and eat it By eating the scroll, John can speak the very words of God (v. 11). In Ezekiel, the prophet is also told to consume a scroll (the words of God) in order to make them known (compare Eze 2:9—3:4).

10:11 prophesy again Refers to the latter part of Revelation (Rev 12–22).

11:1–14 These verses comprise the second interlude between the sixth and seventh trumpet judgments. Similar to ch. 7 during the seal judgments, ch. 10 and this episode in ch. 11 disrupt the sequence of events. John introduces the concept of measuring the temple to connote God's protection and preservation of his people. He also presents two witnesses as God's prophetic harbingers of impending wrath.

11:1 measure This suggests God's protection of the people located within the measured area (compare Zec 2:1–5; Rev 21:15–17). Their preservation from spiritual harm recalls the sealing activity of ch. 7, where the 144,000 are protected prior to the opening of the seventh seal, the unleashing of the trumpet judgments and the unleashing of the demonic forces of ch. 9 (see 9:4). **temple of God** The Jerusalem temple could have been destroyed by the time John wrote his apocalypse. This temple may refer to a future rebuilt temple, the heavenly temple mentioned elsewhere in Revelation or the church as God's temple, either throughout history or in a final tribulation period (see note on 1:19; compare 11:19; 1Co 3:16).

11:2 the outer court Refers to the court of the Gentiles, the designated space for non-Jews visiting the temple. Gentiles who ventured beyond its confines into the Holy Place risked death if caught. **Gentiles** Contrasted with

days, clothed in sackcloth." [4]They are "the two olive trees" and the two lampstands, and "they stand before the Lord of the earth."[a] [5]If anyone tries to harm them, fire comes from their mouths and devours their enemies. This is how anyone who wants to harm them must die. [6]They have power to shut up the heavens so that it will not rain during the time they are prophesying; and they have power to turn the waters into blood and to strike the earth with every kind of plague as often as they want.

[7]Now when they have finished their testimony, the beast that comes up from the Abyss will attack them, and overpower and kill them. [8]Their bodies will lie in the public square of the great city — which is figuratively called Sodom and Egypt — where also their Lord was crucified. [9]For three and a half days some from every people, tribe, language and nation will gaze on their bodies and refuse them burial. [10]The inhabitants of the earth will gloat over them and will celebrate by sending each other gifts, because these two prophets had tormented those who live on the earth.

[11]But after the three and a half days the breath[b] of life from God entered them, and they stood on their feet, and terror struck those who saw them. [12]Then they heard a loud voice from heaven saying to them, "Come up here." And they went up to heaven in a cloud, while their enemies looked on.

[13]At that very hour there was a severe earthquake and a tenth of the city collapsed. Seven thousand people were killed in the earthquake, and the survivors were terrified and gave glory to the God of heaven.

[14]The second woe has passed; the third woe is coming soon.

The Seventh Trumpet

[15]The seventh angel sounded his trumpet, and there were loud voices in heaven, which said:

[a] 4 See Zech. 4:3,11,14.   [b] 11 Or Spirit (see Ezek. 37:5,14).

---

those who worship in the sanctuary, the Gentiles here represent unbelievers, upon whom judgment is coming (compare Rev 11:1). **42 months** Restated in v. 3 as 1,260 days (compare 12:6; 13:5). Both figures define, according to traditions from Daniel, the length of the persecution of God's people (e.g., Da 7:25; 12:11–12). This could refer literally to a future tribulation or symbolically to the whole amount of time between Jesus' first and second comings, when God's people are under pressure from the nations (compare Rev 7:14). **11:3 my two witnesses** The identity of these two figures is unknown. They may be symbolic of the overall witness of the church during tribulation. Alternatively, these two witnesses may be actual prophets who come to earth and proclaim God's message. Some Jewish people of the Second Temple period (516 BC–AD 70) believed that prophets would return at the end of the age—particularly figures like Elijah who never died but was taken to heaven (Mal 4:5; compare Mk 9:10–13; Lk 9:19). For example, the Deuterocanonical work of 2 Esdras 2:18 mentions Isaiah, Jeremiah and Daniel being sent to help Ezra. The description of the two witnesses in Rev 11:6 is particularly reminiscent of Moses and Elijah. **1,260 days** See note on v. 2. **clothed in sackcloth** Suggesting their somber ministry and their calling of the nations to repentance. **11:4 the two olive trees** This echoes the reference in Zechariah to two anointed ones (Zec 4:11–14). These may be identified with the postexilic high priest Joshua and the Davidic descendant Zerubbabel, both of whom were instrumental in the temple restoration efforts (see Zec 4:1–14). John seems to be appropriating this tradition of priestly and kingly figures and reapplying it to his two witnesses. **the two lampstands** Earlier in Revelation, lampstands are identified with the churches (Rev 1:12,20). Only two of these churches (Smyrna and Philadelphia) were entirely faithful and received no rebuke. The two witnesses thus may be a symbol of the church bearing faithful witness. **11:6 to shut up the heavens** Describes the ability to bring about drought-like conditions, similar to Elijah (see 1Ki 17:1). **to turn the waters** Reminiscent of Moses (see Ex 7:17–21). **with every kind of plague** Recalls the exodus (see Rev 8:6 and note).

11:7 the beast See 13:1–10. **the Abyss** Where demons and fallen angels resided. See 9:1 and note. **11:8 Sodom and Egypt** Used metaphorically to highlight spiritual corruption. In Biblical literature Egypt is vilified for its oppression and idolatry, and Sodom for its wickedness and immorality. **where also their Lord was crucified** Refers to Jerusalem. However, since references to a great city are used throughout Revelation to describe Rome (figuratively called Babylon; see chs. 16–18), this phrase may also refer to Rome, since crucifixion was a distinctly Roman form of execution. It may even be that John has in mind all cities that oppose the work of God in the world. **11:9 three and a half days** Related to the 42 months of v. 2 and the 1,260 days of v. 3—both of which signify a three-and-a-half-year period. **11:10 by sending each other gifts** Their deaths will be commemorated by a holiday. **11:11 the breath of life** John refers to resurrection, whether the two witnesses are interpreted as two individuals or the entire church. John likely borrows this phraseology from Eze 37:5,9–10. **11:12 Come up here** Reminiscent of Enoch and Elijah being taken up to heaven (see Rev 11:3 and note; Ge 5:24; 2Ki 2:11; compare Rev 4:1 and note). **in a cloud** See 10:1 and note; compare 1Th 4:17 and note. **11:13 gave glory to the God of heaven** The intended goal of the judgments throughout the book (compare Rev 9:20–21). Elsewhere in the Bible, this phrase sometimes refers to conversion (e.g., Mt 5:16; Lk 18:43); other times it serves as an expression of unbelievers forced to acknowledge the sovereignty of Israel's God (e.g., Jos 7:19; 1Sa 6:5). **11:14 The second woe has passed** The sixth trumpet judgment (see Rev 8:13 and note).

11:15–19 At the sounding of the seventh trumpet, another violent outpouring of God's wrath is expected. Instead, voices from heaven announce the arrival of God's kingdom. A message of doom for the nations of the world is implied by this proclamation, but this is not initially accompanied by destruction. The result of the arrival of God's kingdom is that he will once again dwell with his creation.

"The kingdom of the world has become
the kingdom of our Lord and of his Messiah,
and he will reign for ever and ever."

[16] And the twenty-four elders, who were seated on their thrones before God, fell on their faces and worshiped God, [17] saying:

"We give thanks to you, Lord God Almighty,
the One who is and who was,
because you have taken your great power
and have begun to reign.
[18] The nations were angry,
and your wrath has come.
The time has come for judging the dead,
and for rewarding your servants the
prophets
and your people who revere your name,
both great and small —
and for destroying those who destroy
the earth."

[19] Then God's temple in heaven was opened, and within his temple was seen the ark of his covenant. And there came flashes of lightning, rumblings, peals of thunder, an earthquake and a severe hailstorm.

The Woman and the Dragon

12 A great sign appeared in heaven: a woman clothed with the sun, with the moon under her feet and a crown of twelve stars on her head. [2] She was pregnant and cried out in pain as she was about to give birth. [3] Then another sign appeared in heaven: an enormous red dragon with seven heads and ten horns and seven crowns on its heads. [4] Its tail swept a third of the stars out of the sky and flung them to the earth. The dragon stood in front of the woman who was about to give birth, so that it might devour her child the moment he was born. [5] She gave birth to a son, a male child, who "will rule all the nations with an iron scepter."[a] And her child was snatched up to God and to his throne. [6] The woman fled into the wilderness to a place prepared for her by God, where she might be taken care of for 1,260 days.

[7] Then war broke out in heaven. Michael and his angels fought against the dragon, and the dragon and his angels fought back. [8] But he was not strong enough, and they lost their place in heaven. [9] The great dragon was hurled down — that ancient

[a] 5 Psalm 2:9

11:15 seventh angel sounded his trumpet This completes the cycle of seven trumpets. There is no woe explicitly stated in relation to this trumpet (see 8:13 and note). **of our Lord and of his Messiah** The kingdom of God and his Messiah has arrived. This was Daniel's great hope, the prophets' fervent desire, the focal point of Christ's preaching and the apostles' goal.
11:17 have begun to reign God has always been sovereign over his creation; however, in John's visions of the time of the end, God takes charge of the kingdoms of the world by setting his Messiah over them as king. This means the end of suffering for the people of God, the end of the kingdoms of the world and the arrival of justice.
11:19 God's temple in heaven was opened Similar to 11:17, God dwells among his people, and they have unrestricted access to him (compare Mk 15:38 and note). **the ark of his covenant** While the ark of the covenant is presumed to have been destroyed during Nebuchadnezzar's final siege of Jerusalem (586 BC), its fate is unknown. The ark was the locus of God's presence with his people and the symbol of his covenant with them, and here it carries the same significance (compare Rev 21:3). See the infographic "The Ark of the Covenant" on p. 412. **And there came flashes of lightning** See 8:5 and note.

12:1–17 After the cycle of trumpet judgments (8:2—11:19) and before the bowl judgments (15:1—16:21), John sees a series of visions that involve the powers of evil attacking the church (12:1—14:20). Revelation 12 explicitly casts the dragon as the great accuser of God's people. The kingdom of God was inaugurated by Jesus' ministry, bringing the body of Christ, the church, into existence (vv. 1–6). The dragon's role as the accuser is completely undermined because there is no condemnation for those in Christ (Ro 8:1). The dragon thus seeks vengeance against the church (Rev 12:17).

12:1 a woman The woman is unnamed and unidentified. Her association with the sun, moon and 12 stars recalls

Joseph's dream in Ge 37:9. In Revelation, the number 12 is associated with the 12 tribes of Israel and also the 12 apostles as the church's foundation (see Rev 21:14). Thus the woman could symbolically represent the faithful people of God—the Messiah is born from God's people, Israel, and his work continues with God's people, the church.
12:3 another sign The first sign is the woman, the second is the dragon. **an enormous red dragon with seven heads and ten horns** Identified in v. 9 as Satan, the archenemy of God. The horns recall the imagery of Da 7:7 (where they referred to ten kings).
12:4 swept a third of the stars out of the sky Since Greco-Roman people in John's day often equated stars with gods, and Jews thought of them as angels, this may be a reference to the dragon defeating some of the angelic host (compare Jewish literature 2 Enoch 4:1; 2 Baruch 51:10). John is probably drawing a parallel between the activities of this dragon-like kingly pretender and Antiochus in Da 8:10. Both usurpers harmed the stars.
12:5 with an iron scepter Originally applied to Israel's king, Ps 2 developed strong Messianic connections in the Second Temple period (516 BC–AD 70). An iron rod in the hands of the Messiah connotes an unyieldingly just reign; he will not deviate from his righteous standards or tolerate wickedness or sedition. See Ps 2:9; compare Rev 2:27; 19:15. **her child was snatched up to God** This phrase, coupled with the birth described earlier in the verse, likely represents Christ's ministry from his birth to his death, resurrection and ascension in summary fashion. Such abbreviated overviews are common in the NT (e.g., Jn 16:28; 1Ti 3:16).
12:6 wilderness Throughout the Bible, the wilderness is viewed as a safe haven where the afflicted hide (e.g., 1Sa 23:14; 1Kg 19:1–4). God often provides safety and sustenance in these circumstances (e.g., Dt 29:5; 1Ki 17:1–6). The concept of fleeing into the wilderness to a place prepared by God (spiritual protection or divine

serpent called the devil, or Satan, who leads the whole world astray. He was hurled to the earth, and his angels with him.

¹⁰Then I heard a loud voice in heaven say:

"Now have come the salvation and
    the power
and the kingdom of our God,
    and the authority of his Messiah.
For the accuser of our brothers and sisters,
    who accuses them before our God day
        and night,
    has been hurled down.
¹¹They triumphed over him
    by the blood of the Lamb
    and by the word of their testimony;
they did not love their lives so much
    as to shrink from death.
¹²Therefore rejoice, you heavens
    and you who dwell in them!
But woe to the earth and the sea,
    because the devil has gone down
        to you!
He is filled with fury,
    because he knows that his time is short."

¹³When the dragon saw that he had been hurled to the earth, he pursued the woman who had given birth to the male child. ¹⁴The woman was given the two wings of a great eagle, so that she might fly to the place prepared for her in the wilderness, where she would be taken care of for a time, times and half a time, out of the serpent's reach. ¹⁵Then from his mouth the serpent spewed water like a river, to overtake the woman and sweep her away with the torrent. ¹⁶But the earth helped the woman by opening its mouth and swallowing the river that the dragon had spewed out of his mouth. ¹⁷Then the dragon was enraged at the woman and went off to wage war against the rest of her offspring — those who keep God's commands and hold fast their testimony about Jesus.

The Beast out of the Sea

13 The dragon[a] stood on the shore of the sea. And I saw a beast coming out of the sea. It had ten horns and seven heads, with ten crowns on its horns, and on each head a blasphemous name. ²The beast I saw resembled a leopard, but had feet like those of a bear and a mouth like that of a lion. The dragon gave the beast his power and his throne and great authority. ³One of the heads of the beast seemed to have had a fatal wound, but the fatal wound had been healed. The whole world was filled with wonder and followed the

---

[a] 1 Some manuscripts *And I*

---

intervention) is similar to the measuring of the sanctuary in Rev 11 and the sealing of the 144,000 in ch. 7. See note on 11:2.

12:7 Michael An archangel; the protector of God's people (see Da 10:13 and note; 12:1 and note; compare Jude 9). See the table "Angels in the Bible" on p. 2120.

12:9 ancient serpent See Ge 3; Isa 27:1. **the devil, or Satan** The Greek terminology used here—*diablos* (meaning "slanderer") and *satan* (meaning "accuser")— appropriately coincide with the description of the dragon's activities in Rev 12:10.

12:11 triumphed over The knowledge that Satan could be defeated by faith, witness and perseverance would have been a tremendous encouragement to the members of the seven churches and others being pressured to compromise spiritually. **they did not love their lives so much as to shrink from death** They were willing to be martyred for the sake of remaining faithful to Christ.

12:12 because he knows that his time is short Satan has been banished from the heavenly assembly (Rev 12:9–10). Satan knows about the arrival of God's kingdom and seeks to disrupt it.

12:14 the two wings of a great eagle John again alludes to the imagery of the exodus event to describe the deliverance and protection of God's people (see Ex 19:4).

12:15–16 These verses describe the futile efforts of Satan to destroy the woman. These two verses should probably be understood as a metaphor for an attempted destruction of God's people (compare note on Rev 12:1).

12:17 the rest of her offspring John's concern for the persecuted church suggests this is a reference to the church. They will be attacked by the enemy, but they will be spiritually protected (see v. 6 and note).

13:1–10 Chapter 12 introduced readers of this vision to the dragon; this chapter introduces two beasts who act in concert with the dragon. The first half of the chapter (vv. 1–10) describes the first beast who aids the dragon in his destructive efforts.

13:1 sea Represents turmoil and chaos and connects this account with the account of ch. 12 (see Da 7:2 and note; compare Rev 12:12). **a beast** The description of the beast is reminiscent of Da 7:1–7. John's beast appears to be a combination of the first three beasts of Da 7. Daniel's fourth beast was essentially nondescript in terms of physical features; only its destructive character is mentioned. Since the beasts of Daniel's vision represent kingdoms, the beast here is most likely identified as Rome. Or, more generally, it may refer to a political leader or power that claims divine authority and sets itself in opposition to God. **ten horns and seven heads** This description is the same as the dragon (see Rev 12:3). Daniel's fourth beast had ten horns (Da 7:7,24). The ten horns and seven heads are later identified as ten kings and seven hills (Rev 17:9,12). **ten crowns** In contrast to the dragon, his crowns are on his horns rather than his heads.

13:2 great authority The beast is a vassal who acts on behalf of and with the destructive force of the dragon. Since the dragon bestows his power on the beast, the beast shares many of the dragon's characteristics.

13:3 to have had a fatal wound The beast's wound is a parody of the Lamb's wound in 5:6. **fatal wound had been healed** The exact nature of his wound is unknown. Presumably it was such that any recovery would be deemed miraculous. It is also possible that he would die and be brought back to life by the dragon or false prophet. This description might be a reference to a first-century myth that the dead emperor Nero (reigned AD 54–68)

beast. ⁴People worshiped the dragon because he had given authority to the beast, and they also worshiped the beast and asked, "Who is like the beast? Who can wage war against it?"

⁵The beast was given a mouth to utter proud words and blasphemies and to exercise its authority for forty-two months. ⁶It opened its mouth to blaspheme God, and to slander his name and his dwelling place and those who live in heaven. ⁷It was given power to wage war against God's holy people and to conquer them. And it was given authority over every tribe, people, language and nation. ⁸All inhabitants of the earth will worship the beast — all whose names have not been written in the Lamb's book of life, the Lamb who was slain from the creation of the world.ᵃ

⁹Whoever has ears, let them hear.

¹⁰ "If anyone is to go into captivity,
　　into captivity they will go.
If anyone is to be killedᵇ with the sword,
　　with the sword they will be killed."ᶜ

This calls for patient endurance and faithfulness on the part of God's people.

The Beast out of the Earth

¹¹Then I saw a second beast, coming out of the earth. It had two horns like a lamb, but it spoke like a dragon. ¹²It exercised all the authority of the first beast on its behalf, and made the earth and its inhabitants worship the first beast, whose fatal wound had been healed. ¹³And it performed great signs, even causing fire to come down from heaven to the earth in full view of the people. ¹⁴Because of the signs it was given power to perform on behalf of the first beast, it deceived the inhabitants of the earth. It ordered them to set up an image in honor of the beast who was wounded by the sword and yet lived. ¹⁵The second beast was given power to give breath to the image of the first beast, so that the image could speak and cause all who refused to worship the image to be killed. ¹⁶It also forced all people, great and small, rich and poor, free and slave, to receive a mark on their right hands or on their foreheads, ¹⁷so that they could not buy or sell unless they had the mark, which is the name of the beast or the number of its name.

¹⁸This calls for wisdom. Let the person who

ᵃ 8 Or *written from the creation of the world in the book of life belonging to the Lamb who was slain*　　ᵇ 10 Some manuscripts *anyone kills*　　ᶜ 10 Jer. 15:2

---

would be brought back to life and march against Rome (the Nero *redivivus* myth).

13:4 People worshiped the dragon By worshiping the beast, people are actually worshiping Satan—the force behind the beast's power (compare note on 12:9). **Who is like the beast** This is a parody of Israel's praises of Yahweh's uniqueness in the OT (e.g., Ex 15:11; Ps 35:10; Isa 40:25).

13:5 to utter proud words and blasphemies A further allusion to Da 7 (compare Da 7:8,11,20). **forty-two months** This defined period of time would have been a comfort to Christians; they knew the beast's reign of terror would not last forever. See Rev 11:2 and note.

13:8 from the creation of the world This may refer to the time when the names were entered in the book of life—suggesting that these people can have confidence in God's work. But the Greek phrase used here, *apo kataboles kosmou*, follows and may modify *tou esphagemenou* ("who was slain"). In this regard, it may be translated as: "those whose name has not been written in the book of life of the Lamb, who was slaughtered from the foundation (or founding) of the world." This translation could mean that Christ's saving death was always part of God's plan of salvation (compare 1Pe 1:19–20).

13:9 let them hear Repeats the exhortation from chs. 2 and 3 (see 2:7 and note).

13:10 patient endurance and faithfulness on the part of God's people John calls his readers to endure in the same manner as Christ. They are urged not to compromise their faith or fight back when encountering opposition.

13:11–18 In the following section, John introduces a second beast who is later described as the false prophet (see 16:13; 19:20). The second beast is a religious counterpart that encourages worship of the political, first beast. For John's original readers, this could have meant that Satan was behind the rise of the imperial religion, while the emperor sanctioned it and the second beast promoted it throughout the empire.

13:11 coming out of the earth This may be a parody on the Lamb, who rose from the earth at the resurrection. **it spoke like a dragon** Distinguishes him from the Lamb. Perhaps "like a dragon" refers to *the* dragon from which he receives authority.

13:12 whose fatal wound had been healed The text does not say how the first beast is healed, but the signs mentioned in the next verse suggest that this false prophet (the second beast) may have been responsible for healing the first beast (compare note on 13:3).

13:13 causing fire to come down from heaven As Elijah did in 1Ki 18:38 and 2Ki 1:10–12. This second beast may be imitating the miracles of God's prophets in an attempt to demonstrate his superiority over them and to identify the first beast as divine.

13:14 to set up an image in honor of the beast In John's day, images, busts and statues were set up throughout the empire in tribute to the deified emperor.

13:15 killed Illustrates the situation John's audience faced in Asia Minor.

13:16 a mark In the ancient world religious branding was a common way to display devotion to a particular deity. **right hands or on their foreheads** This may be a parody of the seal that Christians had (Rev 7:3; 14:1) or of the Israelites' bearing God's law. Jews often wore boxes (called phylacteries) containing portions of the law on their foreheads or hands (see Ex 13:9 and note; Dt 6:8).

13:17 could not buy or sell There would be economic depression and poverty for those who would not bear the mark. The church in Smyrna may have already been feeling these effects (see note on Rev 2:9).

13:18 That number is 666 John may be employing *gematria*—the practice of assigning numbers to letters of the alphabet. The number may allude to Roman oppression, since one spelling of emperor Nero's name, transliterated from Greek into Hebrew, adds up to 666 by this method. An alternative is to see a contrast between this

has insight calculate the number of the beast, for it is the number of a man.[a] That number is 666.

The Lamb and the 144,000

14 Then I looked, and there before me was the Lamb, standing on Mount Zion, and with him 144,000 who had his name and his Father's name written on their foreheads. [2]And I heard a sound from heaven like the roar of rushing waters and like a loud peal of thunder. The sound I heard was like that of harpists playing their harps. [3]And they sang a new song before the throne and before the four living creatures and the elders. No one could learn the song except the 144,000 who had been redeemed from the earth. [4]These are those who did not defile themselves with women, for they remained virgins. They follow the Lamb wherever he goes. They were purchased from among mankind and offered as firstfruits to God and the Lamb. [5]No lie was found in their mouths; they are blameless.

The Three Angels

[6]Then I saw another angel flying in midair, and he had the eternal gospel to proclaim to those who live on the earth — to every nation, tribe, language and people. [7]He said in a loud voice, "Fear God and give him glory, because the hour of his judgment has come. Worship him who made the heavens, the earth, the sea and the springs of water."

[8]A second angel followed and said, "'Fallen! Fallen is Babylon the Great,'[b] which made all the nations drink the maddening wine of her adulteries."

[9]A third angel followed them and said in a loud voice: "If anyone worships the beast and its image and receives its mark on their forehead or on their hand, [10]they, too, will drink the wine of God's fury, which has been poured full strength into the cup of his wrath. They will be tormented with burning sulfur in the presence of the holy angels and of the Lamb. [11]And the smoke of their torment will rise for ever and ever. There will be no rest day or night for those who worship the beast and its image, or for anyone who receives the mark of its name." [12]This calls for patient endurance on the part of the people of God who keep his commands and remain faithful to Jesus.

[13]Then I heard a voice from heaven say, "Write this: Blessed are the dead who die in the Lord from now on."

a 18 Or is humanity's number   *b* 8 Isaiah 21:9

---

number and seven, the number of completion. Three sixes might indicate that the beast falls short of completion.

14:1–5 In vv. 1–5, the Lamb is pictured standing with his 144,000 troops (see 7:4 and note) on Mount Zion. This passage answers the question of what happens to those who refuse the mark of the beast (13:16): They are marked with the name of the Lamb and his Father, and they are victorious.

14:1 Mount Zion Zion originally referred to the Jebusite stronghold captured by David (2Sa 5:6–7). It later came to symbolize the city of God, from which he exercises his reign (Isa 24:23; Heb 12:22). **144,000** See Rev 7:4 and note.
14:2 a sound The Greek word used here can mean "sound" or "voice." It refers to the song of the 144,000 (v. 3). **that of harpists playing their harps** Harps in Revelation often connote victory. It is later prophesied that Rome will no longer hear the sound of harps (18:22).
14:3 No one could learn the song It is likely a song praising God and the Lamb for redemption.
14:4 who did not defile themselves with women This is holy war imagery; it indicates those who are ritually clean according to the Mosaic laws governing holy war (Dt 23:9–10; see 1Sa 21:5 and note; note on Jos 6:16; note on Jos 6:17). **for they remained virgins** Indicates that they have remained loyal to Christ and have not defiled themselves by compromising with the world (compare Rev 19:7–9; 2Co 11:2).

14:6–13 Three angels arrive bearing announcements of impending judgment and a warning against religious compromise. There is a final exhortation to remain steadfast and an explanation of the consequences for those who do not.

14:6 flying in midair The last time this phrase was used (Rev 8:13), a threefold woe was announced—similar to what occurs here.

14:7 Fear God and give him glory The goal of judgment (see 9:20 and note). **Worship** The angel calls his audience to worship the true God as opposed to the beast. **heavens, the earth, the sea and the springs** All areas that God has judged so far.
14:8 Fallen! Fallen Repeated for emphasis and to communicate the complete devastation that would befall Rome (see 18:2; compare Isa 21:9). John foresees the eventual demise of the city as judgment from God; it did not occur in his day. **Babylon the Great** Rome. Babylon, the site of the tower of Babel and the destroyers of the Jerusalem temple (in 586 BC), was the symbol of human pride, idolatry and immorality (e.g., Ge 11:9; Da 4:30). Rome was guilty of the same sins that brought destruction on ancient Babylon (compare 1Pe 5:13). **her adulteries** Probably refers to idolatry, often described as adultery in the OT, but sexual sins may be in view as well (compare Rev 2:14 and note; Rev 18:3; Jer 51:7).
14:10 poured full strength into the cup of his wrath It was unmixed—not weakened by diluting with water. For the cup of wrath imagery, see Jer 25:15–29. **with burning sulfur** Foreshadows the events of Rev 19:20; 20:10,14–15. Sulfur is a foul-smelling element that burns extremely hot.
14:11 for ever and ever Unlike the torture of 9:5, which lasts five months, this final torture is permanent and will not be relieved.
14:12 patient endurance on the part of the people of God Refers to their perseverance in the pursuit of righteousness and faith. Like 13:10, this is an encouragement for believers but with a view toward eternal destiny: Those who persist in faith and do not take part in the worship of the beast will avoid the second death and receive divine blessing (see v. 13; 20:12–15).
14:13 Blessed A second beatitude (see 1:3 and note). **for their deeds will follow them** Describes a record

"Yes," says the Spirit, "they will rest from their labor, for their deeds will follow them."

Harvesting the Earth and Trampling the Winepress

[14]I looked, and there before me was a white cloud, and seated on the cloud was one like a son of man[a] with a crown of gold on his head and a sharp sickle in his hand. [15]Then another angel came out of the temple and called in a loud voice to him who was sitting on the cloud, "Take your sickle and reap, because the time to reap has come, for the harvest of the earth is ripe." [16]So he who was seated on the cloud swung his sickle over the earth, and the earth was harvested.

[17]Another angel came out of the temple in heaven, and he too had a sharp sickle. [18]Still another angel, who had charge of the fire, came from the altar and called in a loud voice to him who had the sharp sickle, "Take your sharp sickle and gather the clusters of grapes from the earth's vine, because its grapes are ripe." [19]The angel swung his sickle on the earth, gathered its grapes and threw them into the great winepress of God's wrath. [20]They were trampled in the winepress outside the city, and blood flowed out of the press, rising as high as the horses' bridles for a distance of 1,600 stadia.[b]

Seven Angels With Seven Plagues

15 I saw in heaven another great and marvelous sign: seven angels with the seven last plagues — last, because with them God's wrath is completed. [2]And I saw what looked like a sea of glass glowing with fire and, standing beside the sea, those who had been victorious over the beast and its image and over the number of its name. They held harps given them by God [3]and sang the song of God's servant Moses and of the Lamb:

[a] 14 See Daniel 7:13.   [b] 20 That is, about 180 miles or about 300 kilometers

---

of their service and faithfulness to Christ. This section (vv. 6–13) is an exhortation to believers to avoid compromise with the world and the beast and to persevere until death. In the end, their deeds will testify to their faith.

14:14–20 This section narrates two harvests: a grain harvest and a grape harvest. The first harvest is performed by the Son of Man, the second by an angel. It is not entirely clear whether these harvests indicate salvation or judgment. The first harvest appears to be a harvest of salvation, and the second harvest appears to be a harvest of judgment.

14:14 a son of man See 1:13 and note. **a crown of gold** Testifies to Jesus' kingship (compare 4:10). **sickle** A tool with a curved blade and handle used for reaping grain.
14:15 the harvest of the earth is ripe The imagery in this section may echo Joel 3:12–13 or Jesus' words about the end-time harvest (Mt 9:37–38; 13:36–43). If the Joel passage is in view, this may be a judgment on the wicked. If Jesus' words are in view, this first harvest consists of collecting those who will be with him.
14:18 charge of the fire While this could be suggestive of judgment, like the angels who control the water and wind, it most likely refers to the fire of the altar (Rev 8:3–5; compare 7:1; 14:10; 16:5). **from the altar** The altar is in the temple (vv. 15,17). The mention of the altar might suggest the atonement God requires (5:12). See the infographic "Ancient Altars" on p. 127.
14:19 the great winepress of God's wrath This reaping involves not just harvesting, but crushing in a winepress (compare Isa 63:3; Rev 19:15). See the infographic "A Winepress in Ancient Israel" on p. 1157.

Revelation 14:19

WINEPRESS
A winepress extracts juice from grapes. It was a large, enclosed stone structure into which baskets of grapes were poured. Workers stood inside the winepress and trampled the grapes as they were added. The juice from the clusters flowed out of the winepress through a channel cut into the wall and into a vat or bucket placed beneath the structure. John uses this image to vividly portray the fate of unbelievers: They will be trampled underfoot like grapes in a winepress, and their blood will flow profusely.

14:20 outside the city Criminals and the wicked were customarily executed outside the city. This may echo how Christ was executed outside the city (e.g., Mt 27:32; Heb 13:12). While this overall scene (14:14–20) may be about Jesus' judgment on evil, this line suggests it could also be about Christ's sacrificial death. Under this interpretation, this is still a harvest of judgment, but the judgment falls on Christ (see Isa 53:10–12). The blood that flows would thus not be the blood of the wicked but the blood of Christ.

15:1—16:21 Revelation 15—16 narrate the pouring out of seven bowls of God's wrath, described as the last plagues (15:1). These build on and consummate the earlier judgments of the seven seals (6:1—8:1) and trumpets (8:6—11:19). Whereas the seals destroyed a quarter of the earth (6:8) and the trumpets destroyed a third of the earth (8:7), the destruction of the bowls is comprehensive.

15:1–8 In this section, the reader is introduced to the seven angels who will carry out God's final earthly judgment (vv. 1,5–8). Those who conquered the beast vindicate God through song for his forthcoming judgment (vv. 2–4).

15:1 another great and marvelous sign A third sign (see 12:1,3). **last** The final set of seven judgments upon the earth following the seals and the trumpets.
15:2 a sea of glass glowing with fire The addition of fire here may be a reference to judgment. See 4:6 and note. **who had been victorious over the beast** Includes martyrs and survivors who did not succumb to pressure and persecution. The beast's conquest of them is short-lived (11:7); those who are killed by the beast enjoy divine blessing and eternal life (14:12–13). **harps given them by God** Signifying victory (see 14:2 and note).

"Great and marvelous are your deeds,
    Lord God Almighty.
Just and true are your ways,
    King of the nations.[a]
[4] Who will not fear you, Lord,
    and bring glory to your name?
For you alone are holy.
All nations will come
    and worship before you,
for your righteous acts have been revealed."[b]

[5] After this I looked, and I saw in heaven the temple—that is, the tabernacle of the covenant law—and it was opened. [6] Out of the temple came the seven angels with the seven plagues. They were dressed in clean, shining linen and wore golden sashes around their chests. [7] Then one of the four living creatures gave to the seven angels seven golden bowls filled with the wrath of God, who lives for ever and ever. [8] And the temple was filled with smoke from the glory of God and from his power, and no one could enter the temple until the seven plagues of the seven angels were completed.

The Seven Bowls of God's Wrath

16 Then I heard a loud voice from the temple saying to the seven angels, "Go, pour out the seven bowls of God's wrath on the earth."

[2] The first angel went and poured out his bowl on the land, and ugly, festering sores broke out on the people who had the mark of the beast and worshiped its image.

[3] The second angel poured out his bowl on the sea, and it turned into blood like that of a dead person, and every living thing in the sea died.

[4] The third angel poured out his bowl on the rivers and springs of water, and they became blood. [5] Then I heard the angel in charge of the waters say:

"You are just in these judgments, O Holy One,
    you who are and who were;
[6] for they have shed the blood of your holy
        people and your prophets,
    and you have given them blood to drink as
        they deserve."

[7] And I heard the altar respond:

"Yes, Lord God Almighty,
    true and just are your judgments."

[8] The fourth angel poured out his bowl on the sun, and the sun was allowed to scorch people with fire. [9] They were seared by the intense heat and they cursed the name of God, who had control over these plagues, but they refused to repent and glorify him.

[10] The fifth angel poured out his bowl on the throne of the beast, and its kingdom was plunged into darkness. People gnawed their tongues in

---

[a] 3 Some manuscripts *ages*   [b] 3,4 Phrases in this song are drawn from Psalm 111:2,3; Deut. 32:4; Jer. 10:7; Psalms 86:9; 98:2.

15:3 the song of God's servant Moses In Exodus, the song of Moses marveled at God's wonders, character and majesty, similar to the song in 15:3–4 (see Ex 15:1–21; Dt 32). **of the Lamb** There are not two songs, but one. It describes deliverance for God's people and judgment for their enemies (compare Rev 5:9–13; 7:10–17).

15:5 the temple—that is, the tabernacle of the covenant law This description emphasizes the tabernacle as the site of God's covenant testimony (compare Nu 17:7). **was opened** Similar to Rev 11:19. The opening of temple doors or gates could signal judgment, such as in the Deuterocanonical work 3 Maccabees 6:16–21.

15:6 the seven angels See Rev 15:1. **wore golden sashes** These angels resemble the figure from Da 10:5 and the glorified Christ in Rev 1:13.

15:7 one of the four living creatures See 4:6–8.

15:8 smoke Alludes to the theophany at Sinai (see Ex 19:18). Smoke or cloud often accompanies a visible manifestation of God's presence (1Ki 8:10–11; Isa 6:4).

16:1–21 The angels carrying the seven bowls of God's wrath pour them out upon the world. The bowls are God's final judgment prior to the great white throne judgment in ch. 20. These judgments are similar to the plagues on Egypt and the trumpet judgments earlier in the book (compare Ex 7–12).

16:1 loud voice While generally anonymous in Revelation, this likely refers to God's voice; no one could enter the temple because his presence was there. **seven angels** See Rev 15:1,6.

16:2 ugly, festering sores Describes oozing, open wounds or ulcers, corresponding to Ex 9:8–12. **mark of the beast** See note on Rev 13:16. **worshiped its image** See 13:14–15.

16:3 blood like that of a dead person This judgment and the one that follows mirror Ex 7:17–24. **every living thing** In contrast to the one-third that perished as a result of the second trumpet judgment (see Rev 8:8).

16:4 they became blood Compare 8:10–11, where the rivers and streams are made bitter.

16:6 they have shed the blood Those who delighted in shedding blood now are forced to drink blood as a fitting form of punishment.

16:7 I heard the altar respond Refers to those that dwell beneath the altar—the martyrs. This is the ultimate vindication in response to their query in 6:10. **just** God has avenged the blood of the martyrs. The murderers received righteous retribution.

16:8 was allowed Passive verbs in Revelation often connote divine permission (e.g., 6:4; 9:5 and note; 13:5,7,15). Here, the sun is an instrument of divine wrath.

16:9 they refused to repent and glorify him They did not glorify him or acknowledge his power, but they will be forced to do so. Compare 2:5 and note; 9:20 and note.

16:10 The fifth angel The first four bowls were directed toward the natural world. This is a frontal assault on evil. **throne of the beast** The symbol of the beast's power (see 13:2). In John's day, this was Rome and its divine pretensions, which were ultimately satanic (see 2:13 and note). **darkness** Corresponds to Ex 10:21–23, where the darkness is centralized in Egypt (compare Rev 8:12).

agony [11]and cursed the God of heaven because of their pains and their sores, but they refused to repent of what they had done.

[12]The sixth angel poured out his bowl on the great river Euphrates, and its water was dried up to prepare the way for the kings from the East. [13]Then I saw three impure spirits that looked like frogs; they came out of the mouth of the dragon, out of the mouth of the beast and out of the mouth of the false prophet. [14]They are demonic spirits that perform signs, and they go out to the kings of the whole world, to gather them for the battle on the great day of God Almighty.

[15]"Look, I come like a thief! Blessed is the one who stays awake and remains clothed, so as not to go naked and be shamefully exposed."

[16]Then they gathered the kings together to the place that in Hebrew is called Armageddon.

[17]The seventh angel poured out his bowl into the air, and out of the temple came a loud voice from the throne, saying, "It is done!" [18]Then there came flashes of lightning, rumblings, peals of thunder and a severe earthquake. No earthquake like it has ever occurred since mankind has been on earth, so tremendous was the quake. [19]The great city split into three parts, and the cities of the nations collapsed. God remembered Babylon the Great and gave her the cup filled with the wine of the fury of his wrath. [20]Every island fled away and the mountains could not be found. [21]From the sky huge hailstones, each weighing about a hundred pounds,[a] fell on people. And they cursed God on account of the plague of hail, because the plague was so terrible.

Babylon, the Prostitute on the Beast

17 One of the seven angels who had the seven bowls came and said to me, "Come, I will show you the punishment of the great prostitute, who sits by many waters. [2]With her the kings of the earth committed adultery, and the inhabitants of the earth were intoxicated with the wine of her adulteries."

[a] 21 Or about 45 kilograms

16:11 cursed the God of heaven The people's typical response (compare 16:9).

16:12 Euphrates The Euphrates River served as Rome's eastern border and protected Rome from invasion by the Parthian Empire. If the Euphrates were to dry up, Rome would be threatened.

16:13 three impure spirits that looked like frogs Corresponds to Ex 8:1–15. Evil spirits, not literal frogs, are in view here. The unholy trinity (the dragon, the beast and the false prophet) responds for the first time in Rev 16. Their realm comes under direct attack as a result of the fifth and sixth bowls. In reply, each unleashes a frog-like demon from his mouth to summon the kings of the earth for battle against God (v. 14). **the dragon** See 12:3,9. **the beast** The first beast (see 13:1 and note). **the false prophet** The second beast (see 13:11 and note).

16:14 that perform signs These demons summon people to battle and authenticate their message with signs. Ironically, though they were commissioned by the unholy trinity, they unknowingly work for the Holy Trinity by gathering the nations together in one place for judgment.

16:15 like a thief After mentioning the day of Yahweh (the Lord) in the previous verse, John inserts a parenthetical statement describing Christ's return in judgment (compare Mt 24:43–44; 1Th 5:2; 2Pe 3:10). **Blessed** The third beatitude in Revelation (see Rev 1:3 and note). **be shamefully exposed** In the ancient Near East, conquering armies often paraded prisoners of war naked to expose them to as much shame as possible (compare Eze 23:24–29).

16:16 Armageddon The Greek word used here, *harmageddōn*, could be a reference to Megiddo in the Esdraelon plain, but this is not definitive since Megiddo is a plain, not a mountain (the first part of the Greek word, *har*, is Hebrew for "mountain"). In the OT, Megiddo was the site of significant conflicts (e.g., Jdg 5:19; 2Ki 9:27; 2Ch 35:22). John may be drawing on a well-known battle site to indicate symbolically the final conflict between God and the dragon, as he has elsewhere drawn on the symbolism associated with Babylon (see Rev 14:8 and note) and Mount Zion (see 14:1 and note).

16:17 The seventh angel poured out his bowl In contrast with the seal and trumpet judgments, no interlude takes place between the sixth and seventh bowls—the time allotted for repentance has passed.

16:19 The great city Probably refers to Rome (see 17:18 and note; 18:10–24); Jerusalem is also possible (see 11:8). See the infographic "Rome in Paul's Day" on p. 1844. **Babylon the Great** Refers to Rome (see 14:8 and note).

16:20 Every island fled away Because of the quake in 16:18, the earth appeared to be running away. This type of language is used to describe divine punishment in the OT (e.g., Na 1:3–5).

16:21 about a hundred pounds Hailstones of this size would bring total destruction. Such a storm would level cities, obliterate forests, and leave few survivors among people or animals. This final bowl judgment brings wholesale devastation upon the earth.

17:1—19:5 This section contains a graphic portrayal of the great prostitute, Babylon—identified as Rome—and the beast she rides on, the larger Roman Empire (Rev 17:1–18). This is followed by an account of her fall (18:1–24) and a hymn of praise (19:1–5) over her destruction. John writes this section as though he is looking back—as if the judgment has already occurred (though it was future to his time of writing). It serves as a contrast to the new Jerusalem, described in chs. 21–22.

17:1 One of the seven angels Introduced in 15:1; 16:1. **the great prostitute** Identified in 17:18 as a major city (probably Rome). The prophets often depict cities using female imagery such as a bride, wife or prostitute (e.g., Isa 1:21; 23:17; Eze 23:2–4). The image of a prostitute is used to illustrate Rome's spiritual bankruptcy and moral degradation. **many waters** Identified in Rev 17:15 as the people of many nations.

17:2 the wine of her adulteries Sexual immorality may refer to religious infidelity, the sexual indiscretion involved in pagan ritual, or both (see 2:21 and note). Chapter 18 suggests that this immorality also represents the commercial and political dealings of Rome with the kings and merchants of the earth. All of Rome's relationships are corrupt. See 14:8; compare Jer 51:7.

³Then the angel carried me away in the Spirit into a wilderness. There I saw a woman sitting on a scarlet beast that was covered with blasphemous names and had seven heads and ten horns. ⁴The woman was dressed in purple and scarlet, and was glittering with gold, precious stones and pearls. She held a golden cup in her hand, filled with abominable things and the filth of her adulteries. ⁵The name written on her forehead was a mystery:

BABYLON THE GREAT
THE MOTHER OF PROSTITUTES
AND OF THE ABOMINATIONS OF THE EARTH.

⁶I saw that the woman was drunk with the blood of God's holy people, the blood of those who bore testimony to Jesus.

When I saw her, I was greatly astonished. ⁷Then the angel said to me: "Why are you astonished? I will explain to you the mystery of the woman and of the beast she rides, which has the seven heads and ten horns. ⁸The beast, which you saw, once was, now is not, and yet will come up out of the Abyss and go to its destruction. The inhabitants of the earth whose names have not been written in the book of life from the creation of the world will be astonished when they see the beast, because it once was, now is not, and yet will come.

⁹"This calls for a mind with wisdom. The seven heads are seven hills on which the woman sits. ¹⁰They are also seven kings. Five have fallen, one is, the other has not yet come; but when he does come, he must remain for only a little while. ¹¹The beast who once was, and now is not, is an eighth king. He belongs to the seven and is going to his destruction.

¹²"The ten horns you saw are ten kings who have not yet received a kingdom, but who for one hour will receive authority as kings along with the beast. ¹³They have one purpose and will give their power and authority to the beast. ¹⁴They will wage war against the Lamb, but the Lamb will triumph over them because he is Lord of lords and King of kings — and with him will be his called, chosen and faithful followers."

¹⁵Then the angel said to me, "The waters you saw, where the prostitute sits, are peoples, multitudes, nations and languages. ¹⁶The beast and the ten horns you saw will hate the prostitute. They will bring her to ruin and leave her naked; they will eat her flesh and burn her with fire. ¹⁷For God has put it into their hearts to accomplish his purpose by agreeing to hand over to the beast their royal authority, until God's words are fulfilled. ¹⁸The woman you saw is the great city that rules over the kings of the earth."

Lament Over Fallen Babylon

18 After this I saw another angel coming down from heaven. He had great authority, and the earth was illuminated by his splendor. ²With a mighty voice he shouted:

17:3 in the Spirit John's third such experience (see Rev 1:10 and note; compare 21:10). **scarlet beast** Since every description of this beast mirrors the first beast in 13:1–8, the two should be equated (see note on 13:1; note on 13:3). **blasphemous names** May describe a divine title ascribed to the emperor (see 13:1 and note). **had seven heads and ten horns** v. These are variously identified in 17:9–10,12. See 13:1.
17:4 purple and scarlet Connotes luxury and royalty (compare 18:16–17).
17:5 a mystery Indicates a mysterious name—one with a hidden meaning that requires interpretation.
17:7 the angel Angels often interpret key events in apocalyptic literature (e.g., Da 7:16; 8:15–16).
17:8 once was, now is not, and yet will come up A parody on the divine name (see Rev 1:4 and note). **the book of life** See 3:5 and note.
17:9 seven hills on which the woman sits The city of Rome was well-known for being built upon seven hills.
17:10 They are also seven kings The seven heads of the beast also represent seven kings (kingdoms may also be intended). If they are kings, they might refer to a succession of Roman emperors. If they are kingdoms, they might refer to a succession of empires. Alternatively, since seven is used symbolically to indicate fullness throughout Revelation, the number could reflect the fullness of the beastly kind of power that human empires wield. **one** Could refer to a particular Roman emperor (such as Domitian) or Rome itself, depending on how the seven kings are interpreted. **the other has not yet come** Refers to a future king or kingdom of the seven. **remain**

for only a little while The succession of beastly rulers will continue, but not for much longer.
17:11 an eighth king. He belongs to the seven The beast is referred to as an eighth who is of the seven. Perhaps what is meant here is that the beast is of the same kind as the seven; he is the power behind these seven kings or kingdoms.
17:12 who have not yet received a kingdom Refers to future rulers who will unite with the beast (see 17:16). These could be ten particular rulers, or ten may be a symbolic number representing all of the kings of the earth (compare 18:3; 19:19).
17:14 his called, chosen and faithful followers Refers to the whole people of God (see 14:1–5).
17:15 The waters you saw, where the prostitute sits Perhaps indicating an oppressive, heavy-handed style of leadership fitting with the reaction in 17:16–17. In the ancient Near East, water was a symbol of chaos and represented severe difficulty.
17:16 will hate the prostitute Babylon's former allies turn against her. As often happens, evil forces are not unified; they fight among themselves.
17:18 the great city Refers to Rome, which served as the embodiment of greed, idolatry and immorality for those who first read Revelation (see 18:16,19).

18:1–24 While the final verses of ch. 17 warn of Rome's impending demise, ch. 18 details its destruction (see vv. 3,24). Kings, merchants and seafarers offer a dirge for the once-great city.

18:1 the earth was illuminated by his splendor

"'Fallen! Fallen is Babylon the Great!'[a]
She has become a dwelling for demons
and a haunt for every impure spirit,
  a haunt for every unclean bird,
  a haunt for every unclean and detestable
    animal.
[3] For all the nations have drunk
  the maddening wine of her adulteries.
The kings of the earth committed adultery
    with her,
  and the merchants of the earth grew rich
    from her excessive luxuries."

Warning to Escape Babylon's Judgment

[4] Then I heard another voice from heaven say:

"'Come out of her, my people,'[b]
  so that you will not share in her sins,
  so that you will not receive any of her
    plagues;
[5] for her sins are piled up to heaven,
  and God has remembered her crimes.
[6] Give back to her as she has given;
  pay her back double for what she has done.
  Pour her a double portion from her own cup.
[7] Give her as much torment and grief
  as the glory and luxury she gave herself.
In her heart she boasts,
  'I sit enthroned as queen.
I am not a widow;[c]
  I will never mourn.'
[8] Therefore in one day her plagues will
    overtake her:
  death, mourning and famine.
She will be consumed by fire,
  for mighty is the Lord God who judges her.

Threefold Woe Over Babylon's Fall

[9] "When the kings of the earth who committed adultery with her and shared her luxury see

the smoke of her burning, they will weep and
mourn over her. [10] Terrified at her torment, they
will stand far off and cry:

"'Woe! Woe to you, great city,
  you mighty city of Babylon!
In one hour your doom has come!'

[11] "The merchants of the earth will weep and
mourn over her because no one buys their cargoes anymore — [12] cargoes of gold, silver, precious stones and pearls; fine linen, purple, silk
and scarlet cloth; every sort of citron wood, and
articles of every kind made of ivory, costly wood,
bronze, iron and marble; [13] cargoes of cinnamon
and spice, of incense, myrrh and frankincense, of
wine and olive oil, of fine flour and wheat; cattle
and sheep; horses and carriages; and human beings sold as slaves.

[14] "They will say, 'The fruit you longed for is
gone from you. All your luxury and splendor have
vanished, never to be recovered.' [15] The merchants
who sold these things and gained their wealth
from her will stand far off, terrified at her torment. They will weep and mourn [16] and cry out:

"'Woe! Woe to you, great city,
  dressed in fine linen, purple and scarlet,
  and glittering with gold, precious stones
    and pearls!
[17] In one hour such great wealth has been
    brought to ruin!'

"Every sea captain, and all who travel by ship,
the sailors, and all who earn their living from
the sea, will stand far off. [18] When they see the
smoke of her burning, they will exclaim, 'Was
there ever a city like this great city?' [19] They will
throw dust on their heads, and with weeping and
mourning cry out:

---

[a] 2 Isaiah 21:9   [b] 4 Jer. 51:45   [c] 7 See Isaiah 47:7,8.

Recalls the judgment motif of Eze 43:2–3. The light
emanating from the angel lit up the whole world and
identified him as God's messenger.
18:2 Fallen! Fallen is Babylon the Great See Rev 14:8
and note. **for every impure spirit** Rome was controlled
by and overrun with demonic powers (compare 9:20;
16:13–14). Following the judgments of chs. 16 and 17,
only demons inhabited the city.
18:3 kings of the earth See 17:2 and note. **merchants
of the earth** These traders grew rich from Rome's
idolatry, extravagance and lust.
18:4 Come out of her, my people A common OT in-
junction against sinful and deadly associations (e.g., Isa
52:11; Jer 50:8). Christians are told to abandon Rome's
idolatrous ways of operating. These areas are often linked
to religious life (see note on Rev 2:9). **you will not
receive any of her plagues** See 9:18; 15:1; ch. 16.
18:6 pay her back double Echoes the prophetic cen-
sures in the OT (compare Jer 16:18; 17:18).
18:7 I sit enthroned as queen Echoes the boastful
claims of OT Babylon (Isa 47:7–9).

18:8 in one day Describes a very short time (compare
Isa 47:9). **the Lord God who judges her** God himself
condemns Rome in response to its wickedness and
oppression (see Rev 18:3,24).
18:9 committed adultery See 17:2 and note.
18:10 they will stand far off The kings will watch from a
distance so as not to be included in Rome's punishment.
18:11 merchants of the earth See 18:3 and note.
18:12 cargoes The goods in vv. 12–13 are luxury
items, indicating the opulence and indulgence of the
city (compare Eze 27:2–24).
18:13 human beings The Greek phrase used here also
appears in the Septuagint (the Greek translation of the OT)
to represent prisoners of war and slaves (Nu 31:32–35;
1Ch 5:21; Eze 27:13). Approximately one-third to one-half
of the Roman Empire's population consisted of slaves.
18:16 dressed The same description as the prostitute
in Rev 17:4—identifying her with the city of Rome.
18:17 Every sea captain This list represents trades
that are engaged in maritime commerce.
18:18 Was there ever a city like this great city The

"'Woe! Woe to you, great city,
　　where all who had ships on the sea
　　became rich through her wealth!
In one hour she has been brought to ruin!'

20 "Rejoice over her, you heavens!
　　Rejoice, you people of God!
　　Rejoice, apostles and prophets!
For God has judged her
　　with the judgment she imposed on you."

The Finality of Babylon's Doom

21 Then a mighty angel picked up a boulder the size of a large millstone and threw it into the sea, and said:

"With such violence
　　the great city of Babylon will be thrown
　　　down,
　　never to be found again.
22 The music of harpists and musicians, pipers
　　　and trumpeters,
　　will never be heard in you again.
No worker of any trade
　　will ever be found in you again.
The sound of a millstone
　　will never be heard in you again.
23 The light of a lamp
　　will never shine in you again.
The voice of bridegroom and bride
　　will never be heard in you again.
Your merchants were the world's important
　　　people.
By your magic spell all the nations were led
　　astray.

24 In her was found the blood of prophets and
　　of God's holy people,
　　of all who have been slaughtered on
　　　the earth."

Threefold Hallelujah Over Babylon's Fall

19 After this I heard what sounded like the roar of a great multitude in heaven shouting:

"Hallelujah!
Salvation and glory and power belong to
　　our God,
2　for true and just are his judgments.
He has condemned the great prostitute
　　who corrupted the earth by her adulteries.
He has avenged on her the blood of his
　　servants."

3 And again they shouted:

"Hallelujah!
The smoke from her goes up for ever and ever."

4 The twenty-four elders and the four living creatures fell down and worshiped God, who was seated on the throne. And they cried:

"Amen, Hallelujah!"

5 Then a voice came from the throne, saying:

"Praise our God,
　　all you his servants,
you who fear him,
　　both great and small!"

6 Then I heard what sounded like a great

---

same question was asked of the first beast (see 13:4 and note).
18:19 They will throw dust on their heads A traditional sign of mourning and grief.
18:20 Rejoice over her In contrast to the mourning of the world's political and economic systems, those who have been oppressed by the great city rejoice over its demise (compare Jer 51:48).
18:21 threw it into the sea Symbolizes total destruction (compare Jer 51:63–64; Lk 17:2).
18:22 will never be heard in you again The joyous sounds of feasts, festival, celebrations and even of commerce in economically good times will disappear completely.
18:23 bridegroom and bride Recalls the language used to describe the loss of joy in Jer 7:34; 16:9; and 25:10.
18:24 In her was found the blood The angel blames Rome for the deaths of all the earth's slaughtered people. Here, John likely identifies Rome with the countless oppressive cities that preceded her. Because of them, untold numbers of people were slaughtered to spread false religion, sexual immorality and materialism.

19:1–5 This section shows the heavenly response to the command to rejoice in Rev 18:20 and concludes God's judgment on the city of Rome.

19:1 Hallelujah This is a Hebrew command meaning "Praise Yah." "Yah" is a shortened version of Yahweh.

Verses 1–3 are akin to the *Hallel* psalms (Ps 104–106; 111–118; 120–136; 146–150; from the Hebrew word *halel*, "to praise"). The *Hallel* psalms commemorate God's deliverance via the exodus event, a theme echoed many times in Revelation. **Salvation and glory and power** This grouping of three is meant to contrast with the dragon, the beast and the false prophet—who are undeserving and powerless before God.
19:2 true and just are his judgments See Rev 16:7 and note.
19:3 smoke from her goes up for ever and ever A perpetual testimony of her destruction and God's power (compare 14:11 and note; Isa 34:10).
19:5 a voice Since the voice says "our God," it probably does not belong to God. It may be the voice of one of the four living creatures (see Rev 4:6–8). **Praise our God** A Greek way of saying the Hebrew expression "Hallelujah" (see 19:1 and note).

19:6–10 This section contains four contrasts: God is praised for his reign, the bride of the Lamb is juxtaposed with the prostitute (who was destroyed in ch. 17), the new Jerusalem replaces fallen Babylon (Rome), and the marriage supper of the Lamb contrasts the judgment feast in 19:17–18. All these simultaneously highlight God's salvation of his people and his justification for destroying those who oppose him.

19:6 the roar of rushing waters Compare 1:15 and note; 14:2.

multitude, like the roar of rushing waters and like loud peals of thunder, shouting:

"Hallelujah!
For our Lord God Almighty reigns.
⁷Let us rejoice and be glad
and give him glory!
For the wedding of the Lamb has come,
and his bride has made herself ready.
⁸Fine linen, bright and clean,
was given her to wear."

(Fine linen stands for the righteous acts of God's holy people.)

⁹Then the angel said to me, "Write this: Blessed are those who are invited to the wedding supper of the Lamb!" And he added, "These are the true words of God."

¹⁰At this I fell at his feet to worship him. But he said to me, "Don't do that! I am a fellow servant with you and with your brothers and sisters who hold to the testimony of Jesus. Worship God! For it is the Spirit of prophecy who bears testimony to Jesus."

The Heavenly Warrior Defeats the Beast

¹¹I saw heaven standing open and there before me was a white horse, whose rider is called Faithful and True. With justice he judges and wages war. ¹²His eyes are like blazing fire, and on his head are many crowns. He has a name written on him that no one knows but he himself. ¹³He is dressed in a robe dipped in blood, and his name is the Word of God. ¹⁴The armies of heaven were following him, riding on white horses and dressed in fine linen, white and clean. ¹⁵Coming out of his mouth is a sharp sword with which to strike down the nations. "He will rule them with an iron scepter."ᵃ He treads the winepress of the fury of the wrath of God Almighty. ¹⁶On his robe and on his thigh he has this name written:

KING OF KINGS AND LORD OF LORDS.

¹⁷And I saw an angel standing in the sun, who cried in a loud voice to all the birds flying in midair, "Come, gather together for the great supper of God, ¹⁸so that you may eat the flesh of kings, generals, and the mighty, of horses and their riders, and the flesh of all people, free and slave, great and small."

¹⁹Then I saw the beast and the kings of the earth and their armies gathered together to wage war against the rider on the horse and his army. ²⁰But the beast was captured, and with it the false prophet who had performed the signs on its behalf. With these signs he had deluded those who had received the mark of the beast and worshiped its image. The two of them were thrown alive into the fiery lake of burning sulfur. ²¹The rest were

ᵃ 15 Psalm 2:9

19:7 his bride Identified as the new Jerusalem in 21:2,9. Here the bride of Christ is likely to be understood as the church (see 2Co 11:2; Eph 5:25–27,32; compare Isa 54:5–7).

19:8 the righteous acts of God's holy people May refer to their victory and refusal to compromise their faith (compare Rev 2–3). Throughout Revelation, white clothing represents victory (see 3:4 and note).

19:9 Blessed The fourth beatitude in Revelation (see 1:3 and note).

19:10 Don't do that The angel rebukes John's attempt to worship him. Revelation consistently affirms that God alone is worthy of worship (11:16; 14:7; compare 13:4–8). **the testimony of Jesus** May refer to the testimony about or concerning Jesus or the testimony that Jesus himself gave—the gospel (see 1:2; 12:17). Though both are true, the gospel that Jesus gave is likely in view here. **it is the Spirit of prophecy** Probably refers to the empowering force behind prophetic pronunciation.

19:11–21 The remainder of ch. 19 narrates the arrival of Christ on a white horse and the defeat of the beast and his minions. Coupled with ch. 20, this section presents the end of evil and the final judgments of God and the Lamb prior to the arrival of the new Jerusalem.

19:11 white horse White symbolizes victory (see 3:4 and note). **Faithful and True** These titles identify the rider as Jesus (see 3:14). **With justice he judges and wages war** See Isa 11:3–5.

19:12 His eyes are like blazing fire Matches the description of Christ in Rev 1. See 1:14; 2:18. **many crowns** Jesus' royal authority dwarfs that of the dragon

and the beast (see 12:3; 13:1). **that no one knows but he himself** See 2:17 and note; 3:12.

19:13 in a robe dipped in blood This may refer to Christ's own atoning blood or the blood of his enemies (compare Isa 63:1–6). **his name is the Word of God** This is not the name that no one else knows (in Rev 19:12). Rather, it is a name that emphasizes his status as the ultimate revelation of God's character (compare Jn 1:1–5).

19:14 The armies of heaven Composed of the whole people of God.

19:15 Coming out of his mouth is a sharp sword Matches the description of Christ in Rev 1. See 1:16 and note; 2:12,16. **will rule them with an iron scepter** Describes an unyieldingly just reign (see Ps 2:9; Rev 12:5 and note). **winepress** See Rev 14:17–20.

19:16 this name written A fourth name—in addition to Faithful and True (v. 11), the unknown name (v. 12) and the Word of God (v. 13). **KING OF KINGS AND LORD OF LORDS** This title emphasizes the absolute power of Christ as the divine warrior (compare 17:14; 1Ti 6:15; Dt 10:17).

19:17 in midair See Rev 8:13; 14:6. **great supper of God** In contrast to the marriage supper of the Lamb (see 19:7–9). Here, the carrion fowl feast upon the flesh of God's enemies (compare Eze 39:17–20).

19:18 the flesh of kings See Rev 16:14,16.

19:20 the beast See 13:1–10. **the false prophet** See 13:11–18; 16:13. **the fiery lake of burning sulfur** Here, the beast and false prophet are thrown into the lake of fire, while their followers are killed with the sword from Christ's mouth. See 14:10 and note; 20:14–15; 21:8.

19:21 killed with the sword coming out of the mouth

killed with the sword coming out of the mouth of the rider on the horse, and all the birds gorged themselves on their flesh.

The Thousand Years

20 And I saw an angel coming down out of heaven, having the key to the Abyss and holding in his hand a great chain. ²He seized the dragon, that ancient serpent, who is the devil, or Satan, and bound him for a thousand years. ³He threw him into the Abyss, and locked and sealed it over him, to keep him from deceiving the nations anymore until the thousand years were ended. After that, he must be set free for a short time.

⁴I saw thrones on which were seated those who had been given authority to judge. And I saw the souls of those who had been beheaded because of their testimony about Jesus and because of the word of God. They[a] had not worshiped the beast or its image and had not received its mark on their foreheads or their hands. They came to life and reigned with Christ a thousand years. ⁵(The rest of the dead did not come to life until the thousand years were ended.) This is the first resurrection. ⁶Blessed and holy are those who share in the first resurrection. The second death has no power over them, but they will be priests of God and of Christ and will reign with him for a thousand years.

The Judgment of Satan

⁷When the thousand years are over, Satan will be released from his prison ⁸and will go out to deceive the nations in the four corners of the earth — Gog and Magog — and to gather them for battle. In number they are like the sand on the seashore. ⁹They marched across the breadth of the earth and surrounded the camp of God's people, the city he loves. But fire came down from heaven and devoured them. ¹⁰And the devil, who deceived them, was thrown into the lake of burning sulfur, where the beast and the false prophet had been thrown. They will be tormented day and night for ever and ever.

a 4 Or God; I also saw those who

---

of the rider on the horse Apparently, only Christ will fight in the battle.

20:1–6 With his two emissaries gone and the arrival of the kingdom of God at hand, the dragon is chained in order to ensure a period of peace. Those who refused to worship the beast or his image are resurrected and made vicegerents with Christ.

20:1 key The fourth mention of a key in the book (see 1:18; 3:7; 9:1). Keys signify access and authority. **Abyss** Where demons and fallen angels resided. See 9:1 and note.

20:2 the dragon See 12:3 and note. **bound him** The angel binds Satan to prevent him from deceiving the nations, accusing believers and propagating evil (see 12:9–10). **a thousand years** Concurrent with the length of Christ's kingdom (see v. 4 and note).

20:3 locked and sealed it over him In vv. 2–3, John repeatedly describes Satan's binding to emphasize that the threat and influence of Satan has been thwarted by Christ during this period. **be set free for a short time** A final rebellion and judgment pave the way for the new heavens, new earth and new Jerusalem (see v. 7–10 and note).

20:4 those who had been beheaded Beheading was a common method of capital punishment exacted on citizens and prisoners of the Roman Empire. This group may represent martyrs only, or it may include all who remained faithful in the face of pressure to worship the beast. **a thousand years** This period is characterized by righteousness and unprecedented blessing. The 1,000-year duration may symbolize a perfect reign, or it may in fact last for 1,000 years. There are currently three major views concerning this 1,000-year period (the millennium) as it relates to the second coming of Christ. Premillennialism holds that Christ will return after a period of divine wrath and establish a kingdom on earth (i.e., that he will return before the millennium). Postmillennialism states that Christ will return after the millennium, which is defined as a period of unprecedented success in the preaching of the gospel, massive conversion, resolution of social evils and prosperity. Amillennialism argues that there is no literal 1,000-year reign. Under this view, humanity is currently living in the final period of history between Christ's ascension and second coming, during which Christ reigns in the heavens. Compare Da 7:14 and note; Da 7:22 and note. See the table "Views of the Millennium" on p. 2142.

20:5 The rest of the dead If those who came to life in the previous verse are only the martyrs, then these are Christians who were not martyred. Alternatively, this may refer to the wicked only, who will be raised for judgment. Either way all the dead are ultimately described as being judged (Rev 20:12–15; compare Da 12:1–4). **This is the first resurrection** Premillennialists take this to be a physical resurrection before the millennium. A second resurrection, narrated in vv. 11–15, would then occur after the millennium. Amillennialists and some postmillennialists generally take this to refer to the saints' reigning either in heaven or on earth before Christ's return (compare Eph 2:6).

20:6 Blessed John's fifth beatitude (see Rev 1:3 and note). **The second death** See note on 20:14.

20:7–10 Satan is briefly released after the millennium (see v. 2). He attempts one final assault against the people of God but receives final judgment before doing any harm. Amillennialists see this as the same battle (Armageddon) narrated in 16:13–16 and 19:17–21. Premillennialists see it as a separate battle (see note on v. 4).

20:8 Gog and Magog An allusion to Eze 38–39. Here, Gog and Magog probably represent the resurgence of evil nations, perhaps having been deceived by Satan to rebel against the Lamb's rule (see Rev 20:10).

20:9 the city he loves Perhaps referring to Jerusalem, though that city is portrayed negatively elsewhere in the book (see 11:8). This may not be a physical location but a reference to God's people (3:12; 21:2). Regardless, this beloved city is where the saints are.

20:10 lake of burning sulfur See 19:20 and note.

Views of the Millennium

AMILLENNIALISM	DISPENSATIONAL PREMILLENNIALISM	HISTORICAL PREMILLENNIALISM	POSTMILLENNIALISM
Is the millennium a literal thousand years?			
No. The number of years is symbolic, and not meant to be taken literally.	Yes.	Yes and no. Historical premillennialists disagree about whether it is a literal thousand years.	Yes and no. Postmillennialists disagree about whether it is a literal thousand years.
Is the millennium before or after the second coming?			
Before. The millennium was inaugurated with Christ's resurrection, and represents the total amount of time until his return.	After. Christ comes after the tribulation and before the millennium.	After. Christ comes after the tribulation and before the millennium.	Before. The millennium will be brought about through the working of the gospel in the world through the Church.
Is Satan currently bound?			
Yes. Satan was bound by Jesus.	No. It will happen after Christ returns and before the millennium.	No. It will happen after Christ returns and before the millennium.	Yes and no. Some postmillennialists believe that Satan was bound by Jesus, while others believe it is a future event.
How many judgments?			
One. Believers and unbelievers will be judged at the same time.	Two. Believers will be judged before the millennium and unbelievers after.	Two. Believers will be judged before the millennium and unbelievers after.	One, after the millennium.
Will there be a rapture separate from the second coming?			
No.	Yes. Dispensationalists disagree on whether the rapture will happen before, during or after a seven-year tribulation.	No. There will just be the second coming, after a time of tribulation.	No.
What is the role of Israel?			
The Church is spiritual Israel.	The Church and Israel are separate peoples of God.	The Church is spiritual Israel.	The Church is spiritual Israel.
Proponents			
Augustine, Louis Berkhof, John Calvin, Anthony Hoekema, Martin Luther, Geerhardus Vos	Lewis S. Chafer, John N. Darby, Tim LaHaye, Hal Lindsey, Charles Ryrie, C. I. Scofield, John Walvoord	Henry Alford, Wayne Grudem, Robert Gundry, Irenaeus, George Eldon Ladd, Ben Witherington III	Greg L. Bahnsen, Loraine Boettner, Jonathan Edwards, Rousas J. Rushdoony, B.B. Warfield

The Judgment of the Dead

[11]Then I saw a great white throne and him who was seated on it. The earth and the heavens fled from his presence, and there was no place for them. [12]And I saw the dead, great and small, standing before the throne, and books were opened. Another book was opened, which is the book of life. The dead were judged according to what they had done as recorded in the books. [13]The sea gave up the dead that were in it, and death and Hades gave up the dead that were in them, and each person was judged according to what they had done. [14]Then death and Hades were thrown into the lake of fire. The lake of fire is the second death. [15]Anyone whose name was not found written in the book of life was thrown into the lake of fire.

A New Heaven and a New Earth

21 Then I saw "a new heaven and a new earth,"[a] for the first heaven and the first earth had passed away, and there was no longer any sea. [2]I saw the Holy City, the new Jerusalem, coming down out of heaven from God, prepared as a bride beautifully dressed for her husband. [3]And I heard a loud voice from the throne saying, "Look! God's dwelling place is now among the people, and he will dwell with them. They will be his people, and God himself will be with them and be their God. [4]'He will wipe every tear from their eyes. There will be no more death'[b] or mourning or crying or pain, for the old order of things has passed away.'"

[5]He who was seated on the throne said, "I am making everything new!" Then he said, "Write this down, for these words are trustworthy and true."

[6]He said to me: "It is done. I am the Alpha and the Omega, the Beginning and the End. To the thirsty I will give water without cost from the spring of the water of life. [7]Those who are victorious will inherit all this, and I will be their God and they will be my children. [8]But the cowardly, the unbelieving, the vile, the murderers, the sexually immoral, those who practice magic arts, the idolaters and all liars — they will be consigned to the fiery lake of burning sulfur. This is the second death."

The New Jerusalem, the Bride of the Lamb

[9]One of the seven angels who had the seven bowls full of the seven last plagues came and said

---

[a] 1 Isaiah 65:17   [b] 4 Isaiah 25:8

20:11–15 John here narrates the final judgment, in which all the dead stand before God's throne and receive his justice.

20:11 great white throne White connotes victory throughout Revelation. See 4:2.
20:12 the dead Includes believers and unbelievers (see Da 12:2; Jn 5:28–29; Ac 24:15). Both will have their lives evaluated by the perfect judge. **books were opened** Contains the record of their deeds (see Da 7:10 and note). **the book of life** See Rev 3:5; 13:8; 17:8. **recorded in the books** Refers to their deeds. Believers have the finished work of the Lamb on their behalf to atone for their sins and rectify their shortcomings.
20:14 death and Hades Both death itself and the place of the dead (the netherworld) are destroyed (compare 1:8; 6:8). **the lake of fire** This final death is permanent and inescapable (see 2:11; 20:6 and note; 21:8). **the second death** This event, which is described here as occurring at the final judgment, is experienced by personified death and Hades and people who have not accepted Jesus (v. 15). It is called a second death because those who have already died bodily now die spiritually (vv. 12–13; compare Da 12:1–4).
20:15 book of life See note on 3:5.

21:1–8 Following the ultimate triumph over evil, God makes all things new and ushers in a period in which he dwells with his people, resulting in rest and blessedness. The new heavens and earth will be eternal.

21:1 new heaven and a new earth John seems to envision the relationship between the new heavens and earth to the old order similarly to how Paul understands the resurrected body as a transformation of the physical body (see 1Co 15:42–44; compare Isa 65:17). See note on 2Pe 3:13. **there was no longer any sea** Probably refers to the origin of evil and chaos (see Rev 13:1 and note; compare Ge 1:2).

21:2 a bride See Rev 19:6–9; note on 19:7.
21:3 he will dwell with them Describes the great hope in the book of Revelation and the whole Bible (e.g., Ex 25:8; Lev 26:11–12; Eze 37:26–27; Zec 2:10). Believers can be confident that in the end, they will be united with God.
21:4 He will wipe every tear from their eyes God will extinguish all sorrow and grief (see Rev 7:17). **There will be no more death** Christ conquered death on the cross; death was eradicated in 20:14. The saints will live eternally with God.
21:5 I am making everything new John's vision anticipates the restoration of an Eden-like state that also includes a reversal of the effects of humanity's sin as described in Ge 3.
21:6 It is done The Greek term used here refers to completion — probably in reference to the words in Rev 21:5 and the overall actions of 21:1–4. **the Alpha and the Omega, the Beginning and the End** Echoes the introduction of Christ in ch. 1 (see 1:8 and note; 1:17).
21:7 Those who are victorious Refers to those who remained faithful to Christ (compare 12:11; 15:2). **they will be my children** In these passages, the paternal relationship is used describing God as Father and the king as his son (compare e.g., 2Sa 7:14; Ps 2:7).
21:8 cowardly This verse issues a reminder to John's audience. The seven churches were pressured to compromise their allegiance to Christ. Here, in the midst of describing the wonders of God's new creation, John reminds them of the consequences of compromising with the present order.

21:9–27 A restored Jerusalem was at the center of Messianic expectations in the first century AD. God's people had longed for this ever since their return from exile (538 BC). In this vision, John describes what it will be like when God finally brings these hopes to fruition.

21:9 seven angels From Rev 15:1; 16:1; 17:1.

to me, "Come, I will show you the bride, the wife of the Lamb." [10]And he carried me away in the Spirit to a mountain great and high, and showed me the Holy City, Jerusalem, coming down out of heaven from God. [11]It shone with the glory of God, and its brilliance was like that of a very precious jewel, like a jasper, clear as crystal. [12]It had a great, high wall with twelve gates, and with twelve angels at the gates. On the gates were written the names of the twelve tribes of Israel. [13]There were three gates on the east, three on the north, three on the south and three on the west. [14]The wall of the city had twelve foundations, and on them were the names of the twelve apostles of the Lamb.

[15]The angel who talked with me had a measuring rod of gold to measure the city, its gates and its walls. [16]The city was laid out like a square, as long as it was wide. He measured the city with the rod and found it to be 12,000 stadia[a] in length, and as wide and high as it is long. [17]The angel measured the wall using human measurement, and it was 144 cubits[b] thick.[c] [18]The wall was made of jasper, and the city of pure gold, as pure as glass. [19]The foundations of the city walls were decorated with every kind of precious stone. The first foundation was jasper, the second sapphire, the third agate, the fourth emerald, [20]the fifth onyx, the sixth ruby, the seventh chrysolite, the eighth beryl, the ninth topaz, the tenth turquoise, the eleventh jacinth, and the twelfth amethyst.[d] [21]The twelve gates were twelve pearls, each gate made of a single pearl. The great street of the city was of gold, as pure as transparent glass.

[22]I did not see a temple in the city, because the Lord God Almighty and the Lamb are its temple. [23]The city does not need the sun or the moon to shine on it, for the glory of God gives it light, and the Lamb is its lamp. [24]The nations will walk by its light, and the kings of the earth will bring their splendor into it. [25]On no day will its gates ever be shut, for there will be no night there. [26]The glory and honor of the nations will be brought into it. [27]Nothing impure will ever enter it, nor will anyone who does what is shameful or deceitful, but only those whose names are written in the Lamb's book of life.

Eden Restored

22 Then the angel showed me the river of the water of life, as clear as crystal, flowing from the throne of God and of the Lamb [2]down the middle of the great street of the city. On each side of the river stood the tree of life, bearing twelve crops of fruit, yielding its fruit every month. And the leaves of the tree are for the healing of the nations. [3]No longer will there be any curse. The throne of God and of the Lamb will be in the city, and his servants will serve him. [4]They will see his face, and his name will be on their foreheads. [5]There will be no more night. They will not need the light of a lamp or the light of the sun, for the

[a] 16 That is, about 1,400 miles or about 2,200 kilometers
[b] 17 That is, about 200 feet or about 65 meters   [c] 17 Or high
[d] 20 The precise identification of some of these precious stones is uncertain.

21:10 in the Spirit John's fourth and final experience in the spirit (see 1:10 and note). **coming down out of heaven from God** The new Jerusalem descends to earth as a dwelling place for the saints. It comes from heaven, God's dwelling place: Heaven and earth are now united.
21:13 on the east The order of east, north, south and west reflects Eze 42:16–19.
21:14 the twelve apostles of the Lamb Refers to Jesus' main group of disciples who served as the church's foundation (compare Eph 2:20). Both the twelve tribes (Rev 21:12) and the twelve apostles are represented, emphasizing the continuity of the people of God.
21:16 as wide and high as it is long The city is depicted as a cube of gold (v. 18). This is perhaps an allusion to the Holy of Holies (Most Holy Place), the focus of God's holy presence throughout the OT (see 1Ki 6:20).
21:17 144 cubits Probably refers to the height of the wall, though it could refer to its thickness. Like the dimensions of the city itself, this is a multiple of 12 (a significant number in Revelation; see Rev 7:4 and note).
21:19 every kind of precious stone These stones recall those that were set into the high priest's breastplate (see Ex 28:17–20).
21:21 each gate made of a single pearl Describes 12 massive pearls—each pearl is its own gate.
21:22 I did not see a temple in the city Because God and the Lamb will be present, there will be no need for a temple.
21:24 The nations Fulfills the OT hope that the nations and foreign kings would come to Jerusalem to worship God (see Isa 2:1–3).

21:25 there will be no night there Because of the omnipresence and illumination of God and the Lamb (Rev 21:23).
21:27 the Lamb's book of life See 20:12 and note.
22:1–5 During his final vision, John presents the new Jerusalem as a restored Eden, including the tree of life, the rivers that flowed from the garden and the intimate relationship the first people enjoyed with God.
22:1 the river of the water of life This language recalls Eden (Ge 2:10), as well as the prophecies of Eze 47:1 and Zec 14:8 (compare Rev 7:17; 22:17).
22:2 the tree of life This fulfills the promise of 2:7 (see Ge 2:9; 3:24). The presence of the tree on both sides of the river is an allusion to Eze 47:12.
22:3 any curse There will be nothing that falls under the curse of God's judgment (see Zec 14:11). This includes the curse humanity brought upon itself because of its first sin against God (see Ge 3). **will serve** The Greek word used here can mean "to serve" or "to render religious service." Here it probably refers to offering worship as priests.
22:4 They will see his face This previously resulted in death (e.g., Ex 33:20; compare Isa 6:5). Now, it is described as a life-giving blessing for God's people. **his name will be on their foreheads** May allude to the plate on the high priest's forehead (Ex 28:36–38; compare Rev 3:12 and note; 14:1).
22:5 they will reign for ever and ever See 20:4 and note.

Lord God will give them light. And they will reign for ever and ever.

John and the Angel

[6]The angel said to me, "These words are trustworthy and true. The Lord, the God who inspires the prophets, sent his angel to show his servants the things that must soon take place."

[7]"Look, I am coming soon! Blessed is the one who keeps the words of the prophecy written in this scroll."

[8]I, John, am the one who heard and saw these things. And when I had heard and seen them, I fell down to worship at the feet of the angel who had been showing them to me. [9]But he said to me, "Don't do that! I am a fellow servant with you and with your fellow prophets and with all who keep the words of this scroll. Worship God!"

[10]Then he told me, "Do not seal up the words of the prophecy of this scroll, because the time is near. [11]Let the one who does wrong continue to do wrong; let the vile person continue to be vile; let the one who does right continue to do right; and let the holy person continue to be holy."

Epilogue: Invitation and Warning

[12]"Look, I am coming soon! My reward is with me, and I will give to each person according to what they have done. [13]I am the Alpha and the Omega, the First and the Last, the Beginning and the End.

[14]"Blessed are those who wash their robes, that they may have the right to the tree of life and may go through the gates into the city. [15]Outside are the dogs, those who practice magic arts, the sexually immoral, the murderers, the idolaters and everyone who loves and practices falsehood.

[16]"I, Jesus, have sent my angel to give you[a] this testimony for the churches. I am the Root and the Offspring of David, and the bright Morning Star."

[17]The Spirit and the bride say, "Come!" And let the one who hears say, "Come!" Let the one who is thirsty come; and let the one who wishes take the free gift of the water of life.

[18]I warn everyone who hears the words of the prophecy of this scroll: If anyone adds anything to them, God will add to that person the plagues described in this scroll. [19]And if anyone takes words away from this scroll of prophecy, God will take away from that person any share in the tree of life and in the Holy City, which are described in this scroll.

[20]He who testifies to these things says, "Yes, I am coming soon."

Amen. Come, Lord Jesus.

[21]The grace of the Lord Jesus be with God's people. Amen.

[a] 16 The Greek is plural.

22:6–16 Typical of apocalyptic literature, John emphasizes the imminent nature of the events described in the book and the need for perseverance. Christians need not compromise their faith in Christ or fear reprisals; they need only to endure and overcome.

22:6 God who inspires the prophets An authentication of John's message and visions. God himself inspires his prophets' spirits or inspires them to prophesy.

22:7 Blessed The sixth beatitude (see 1:3 and note), identical to the second half of the first beatitude.

22:9 Don't do that See 19:10 and note.

22:10 Do not seal up the words Opposite from the standard instructions of apocalyptic literature (e.g., Da 12:4,9). Revelation's words are not intended for a future, undisclosed audience; they are written to comfort and encourage God's people in John's day and in all periods of history.

22:11 the vile person Those who are morally or spiritually corrupt. **let the one who does right continue to do right** Describes persevering and remaining faithful in the face of persecution. **let the holy person continue to be holy** Describes being completely dedicated to God, belonging exclusively to him.

22:14 Blessed The seventh and final beatitude (see Rev 1:3 and note). **who wash their robes** See 7:14 and note.

22:16 the bright Morning Star Likely dependent on a Messianic interpretation of Nu 24:17.

22:17 the bride See Rev 19:6–9; 21:9.

22:18–21 Revelation closes with a warning about interpreting the message spoken through John. No one is to add to or subtract from what John has written. He speaks prophetically, and the message he delivers to the seven churches cannot be altered.

22:18 described in this scroll Refers to the message of Revelation (see 1:11). John warns those who hear the words of his prophecy against changing its message.

22:19 if anyone takes words away from Those who take away from John's words will be judged (see Dt 4:2; 12:32). Altering the apocalypse is equal to altering God's message; doing so leads to death.

22:20 He who testifies to these things Refers to Jesus. **Yes, I am coming soon** The third affirmation of this statement (see Rev 22:7,12). This threefold formula highlights the truth and certainty of Christ's claim. **Come, Lord Jesus** The Greek phrase used here is the equivalent to the Aramaic expression *Marana tha* (meaning "Our Lord, come!"; see 1Co 16:22). This became the cry of the early church, particularly as it began facing persecution under the Roman Empire.

22:21 grace of the Lord Jesus be with God's people A typical benediction, especially in Paul's letters (e.g., Ro 16:20; 1Co 16:23; Gal 6:18).

Table of Weights and Measures

	BIBLICAL UNIT	APPROXIMATE AMERICAN EQUIVALENT		APPROXIMATE METRIC EQUIVALENT	
WEIGHTS	talent (60 minas)	75	pounds	34	kilograms
	mina (50 shekels)	1 1/4	pounds	560	grams
	shekel (2 bekas)	2/5	ounce	11.5	grams
	pim (2/3 shekel)	1/4	ounce	7.8	grams
	beka (10 gerahs)	1/5	ounce	5.7	grams
	gerah	1/50	ounce	0.6	gram
	daric	1/3	ounce	8.4	grams
LENGTH	cubit	18	inches	45	centimeters
	span	9	inches	23	centimeters
	handbreadth	3	inches	7.5	centimeters
	stadion (pl. stadia)	600	feet	183	meters
CAPACITY *Dry Measure*	cor [homer] (10 ephahs)	6	bushels	220	liters
	lethek (5 ephahs)	3	bushels	110	liters
	ephah (10 omers)	3/5	bushel	22	liters
	seah (1/3 ephah)	7	quarts	7.5	liters
	omer (1/10 ephah)	2	quarts	2	liters
	cab (1/18 ephah)	1	quart	1	liter
Liquid Measure	bath (1 ephah)	6	gallons	22	liters
	hin (1/6 bath)	1	gallon	3.8	liters
	log (1/72 bath)	1/3	quart	0.3	liter

The figures of the table are calculated on the basis of a shekel equaling 11.5 grams, a cubit equaling 18 inches and an ephah equaling 22 liters. The quart referred to is either a dry quart (slightly larger than a liter) or a liquid quart (slightly smaller than a liter), whichever is applicable. The ton referred to in the footnotes is the American ton of 2,000 pounds. These weights are calculated relative to the particular commodity involved. Accordingly, the same measure of capacity in the text may be converted into different weights in the footnotes.

This table is based upon the best available information, but it is not intended to be mathematically precise; like the measurement equivalents in the footnotes, it merely gives approximate amounts and distances. Weights and measures differed somewhat at various times and places in the ancient world. There is uncertainty particularly about the ephah and the bath; further discoveries may shed more light on these units of capacity.

Concordance

INTRODUCTION TO THE NIV CONCORDANCE

The NIV Concordance, created by John R. Kohlenberger III, has been developed specifically for use with the New International Version (NIV). Like all concordances, it is a special index that contains an alphabetical listing of words used in the Bible text.

This concordance contains 2,474 word entries, with more than 10,000 Scripture references. Each word entry is followed by significant Scripture references in which that particular word is found, as well as by a brief excerpt from the surrounding context. In the context, the entry word is abbreviated by its first letter in bold print. Other forms of the entry word and related words indexed in this concordance are in parentheses.

This concordance also contains 155 biographical entries for significant people in the Bible. The descriptive phrases replace the brief context surrounding each occurrence of the name. In those instances where more than one Bible character has the same name, that name is placed under one block entry, and each person is given a number (1), (2), etc.

Two entries are marked with an asterisk (*). LORD* and LORD'S* list occurrences of the proper name of God, Yahweh, spelled "LORD" and "LORD's" in the NIV. These entries are distinguished from LORD and LORD's, which list occurrences of the title "Lord" and "Lord's."

This concordance is a valuable tool for Bible study. While one of its key purposes is to help the reader find forgotten references to familiar verses, it can also be used to do word studies and to locate and trace biblical themes. Whenever you find a significant context, be sure to read at least the whole verse in the NIV to discover its fuller meaning in its larger context.

AARON
Priesthood of (Ex 28:1; Nu 17; Heb 5:1-4; 7), garments (Ex 28; 39), consecration (Ex 29), ordination (Lev 8).
Spokesman for Moses (Ex 4:14-16, 27-31; 7:1-2). Supported Moses' hands in battle (Ex 17:8-13). Built golden calf (Ex 32; Dt 9:20). Talked against Moses (Nu 12). Priesthood opposed (Nu 16); staff budded (Nu 17). Forbidden to enter land (Nu 20:1-12). Death (Nu 20:22-29; 33:38-39).

ABANDON
Dt   4: 31   he will not **a** or destroy you
1Ti   4: 1   in later times some will **a** the faith

ABBA
Ro   8: 15   And by him we cry, "**A**, Father."
Gal   4: 6   the Spirit who calls out, "**A**,

ABEL
Second son of Adam (Ge 4:2). Offered proper sacrifice (Ge 4:4; Heb 11:4). Murdered by Cain (Ge 4:8; Mt 23:35; Lk 11:51; 1Jn 3:12).

ABIGAIL
Wife of Nabal (1Sa 25:30); pled for his life with David (1Sa 25:14-35). Became David's wife (1Sa 25:36-42).

ABIJAH
Son of Rehoboam; king of Judah (1Ki 14:31—15:8; 2Ch 12:16—14:1).

ABILITY (ABLE)
Ezr   2: 69   According to their **a** they gave
2Co   1: 8   far beyond our **a** to endure,
        8: 3   were able, and even beyond their **a**.

ABIMELEK
1. King of Gerar who took Abraham's wife Sarah, believing her to be his sister (Ge 20). Later made a covenant with Abraham (Ge 21:22-33).
2. King of Gerar who took Isaac's wife Rebekah, believing her to be his sister (Ge 26:1-11). Later made a covenant with Isaac (Ge 26:12-31).

ABLE (ABILITY ENABLE ENABLED ENABLES)
Eze   7: 19   gold will not be **a** to deliver them
Da   3: 17   the God we serve is **a** to deliver us
Ro   8: 39   will be **a** to separate us
    14: 4   the Lord is **a** to make them stand.
    16: 25   to him who is **a** to establish you
2Co   9: 8   God is **a** to bless you abundantly,

Eph 3: 20 him who is **a** to do immeasurably
2Ti 1: 12 that he is **a** to guard what I have
3: 15 which are **a** to make you wise
Heb 7: 25 he is **a** to save completely
Jude : 24 To him who is **a** to keep you
Rev 5: 5 He is **a** to open the scroll and its

ABOLISH
Mt 5: 17 think that I have come to **a** the Law

ABOMINATION
Da 11: 31 set up the **a** that causes desolation.

ABOUND (ABOUNDING ABOUNDS)
2Co 9: 8 you will **a** in every good work.
Php 1: 9 your love may **a** more and more

ABOUNDING (ABOUND)
Ex 34: 6 to anger, **a** in love and faithfulness,
Ps 86: 5 **a** in love to all who call to you.

ABOUNDS (ABOUND)
2Co 1: 5 also our comfort **a** through Christ.

ABRAHAM
Covenant relation with the LORD (Ge 12:1-3; 13:14-17; 15; 17; 22:15-18; Ex 2:24; Ne 9:8; Ps 105; Mic 7:20; Lk 1:68-75; Ro 4; Heb 6:13-15).
Called from Ur, via Harran, to Canaan (Ge 12:1; Ac 7:2-4; Heb 11:8-10). Moved to Egypt, nearly lost Sarah to Pharaoh (Ge 12:10-20). Divided the land with Lot (Ge 13). Saved Lot from four kings (Ge 14:1-16); blessed by Melchizedek (Ge 14:17-20; Heb 7:1-20). Declared righteous by faith (Ge 15:6; Ro 4:3; Gal 3:6-9). Fathered Ishmael by Hagar (Ge 16).
Name changed from Abram (Ge 17:5; Ne 9:7). Circumcised (Ge 17; Ro 4:9-12). Entertained three visitors (Ge 18); promised a son by Sarah (Ge 18:9-15; 17:16). Moved to Gerar; nearly lost Sarah to Abimelek (Ge 20). Fathered Isaac by Sarah (Ge 21:1-7; Ac 7:8; Heb 11:11-12); sent away Hagar and Ishmael (Ge 21:8-21; Gal 4:22-30). Tested by offering Isaac (Ge 22; Heb 11:17-19; Jas 2:21-24). Sarah died; bought field of Ephron for burial (Ge 23). Secured wife for Isaac (Ge 24). Death (Ge 25:7-11).

ABSALOM
Son of David by Maakah (2Sa 3:3; 1Ch 3:2). Killed Amnon for rape of his sister Tamar; banished by David (2Sa 13). Returned to Jerusalem; received by David (2Sa 14). Rebelled against David; seized kingdom (2Sa 15-17). Killed (2Sa 18).

ABSTAIN (ABSTAINS)
1Pe 2: 11 and exiles, to **a** from sinful desires,

ABSTAINS (ABSTAIN)
Ro 14: 6 and whoever **a** does so to the Lord

ABUNDANCE (ABUNDANT)
Lk 12: 15 not consist in an **a** of possessions."
Jude : 2 peace and love be yours in **a**.

ABUNDANT (ABUNDANCE)
Dt 28: 11 will grant you **a** prosperity—
Ps 145: 7 They celebrate your **a** goodness
Pr 28: 19 work their land will have **a** food,
Ro 5: 17 who receive God's **a** provision

ABUSE
2Pe 2: 11 do not heap **a** on such beings

ACCEPT (ACCEPTED ACCEPTS)
Ex 23: 8 "Do not **a** a bribe, for a bribe
Pr 10: 8 The wise in heart **a** commands,
19: 20 Listen to advice and **a** discipline,
Ro 15: 7 **A** one another, then, just as Christ
Jas 1: 21 humbly **a** the word planted in you,

ACCEPTED (ACCEPT)
Lk 4: 24 "no prophet is **a** in his hometown.

ACCEPTS (ACCEPT)
Ps 6: 9 the LORD **a** my prayer.
Jn 13: 20 whoever **a** anyone I send **a** me;

ACCOMPANY
Mk 16: 17 *these signs will **a** those who believe:*

ACCOMPLISH
Isa 55: 11 but will **a** what I desire and achieve

ACCORD
Nu 24: 13 not do anything of my own **a**,
Jn 10: 18 me, but I lay it down of my own **a**.

ACCOUNT (ACCOUNTABLE)
Mt 12: 36 will have to give **a** on the day
Ro 14: 12 of us will give an **a** of ourselves
Heb 4: 13 of him to whom we must give **a**.

ACCOUNTABLE (ACCOUNT)
Eze 33: 6 I will hold the watchman **a** for
Ro 3: 19 and the whole world held **a** to God.

ACCUSATION (ACCUSE)
1Ti 5: 19 not entertain an **a** against an elder

ACCUSE (ACCUSATION)
Pr 3: 30 Do not **a** anyone for no reason—
Lk 3: 14 money and don't **a** people falsely—

ACHAN
Sin at Jericho caused defeat at Ai; stoned (Jos 7; 22:20; 1Ch 2:7).

ACHE
Pr 14: 13 Even in laughter the heart may **a**,

ACKNOWLEDGE
Mt 10: 32 also **a** before my Father in heaven.
1Th 5: 12 **a** those who work hard among you,
Php 2: 11 every tongue **a** that Jesus Christ is
1Jn 4: 3 spirit that does not **a** Jesus is not

ACQUIT
Ex 23: 7 to death, for I will not **a** the guilty.

ACTION (ACTIONS ACTIVE ACTS)
Jas 2: 17 if it is not accompanied by **a**,

ACTIONS (ACTION)
Gal 6: 4 Each one should test their own **a**.
Titus 1: 16 God, but by their **a** they deny him.

ACTIVE (ACTION)
Heb 4: 12 For the word of God is alive and **a**.

ACTS (ACTION)
Ps 145: 12 people may know of your mighty **a**
150: 2 Praise him for his **a** of power;
Isa 64: 6 all our righteous **a** are like filthy

ADAM
First man (Ge 1:26—2:25; Ro 5:14; 1Ti 2:13). Sin of (Ge 3; Hos 6:7; Ro 5:12-21). Children of (Ge 4:1—5:5). Death of (Ge 5:5; Ro 5:12-21; 1Co 15:22).

ADD
Dt 12: 32 do not **a** to it or take away from it.
Pr 30: 6 Do not **a** to his words, or he will
Lk 12: 25 by worrying can **a** a single hour
Rev 22: 18 them, God will **a** to that person

ADMIRABLE
Php 4: 8 whatever is lovely, whatever is **a**—

ADMONISH
Col 3: 16 and **a** one another with all wisdom

ADOPTION
Ro 8: 23 wait eagerly for our **a** to sonship,
Eph 1: 5 he predestined us for **a** to sonship

ADORE
SS 1: 4 How right they are to **a** you!

ADORNMENT (ADORNS)
1Pe 3: 3 should not come from outward **a**,

ADORNS (ADORNMENT)
Ps 93: 5 holiness **a** your house for endless

ADULTERY
Ex 20: 14 "You shall not commit **a**.
Mt 5: 27 was said, 'You shall not commit **a**.'
     5: 28 lustfully has already committed **a**
     5: 32 a divorced woman commits **a**.
    15: 19 murder, **a**, sexual immorality, theft,

ADULTS
1Co 14: 20 but in your thinking be **a**.

ADVANCED
Job 32: 7 **a** years should teach wisdom.'

ADVANTAGE
Ex 22: 22 "Do not take **a** of the widow
Dt 24: 14 Do not take **a** of a hired worker
1Th 4: 6 should wrong or take **a** of a brother

ADVERSITY
Pr 17: 17 a brother is born for a time of **a**.

ADVICE
1Ki 12: 8 Rehoboam rejected the **a** the elders
    12: 14 he followed the **a** of the young men
Pr 12: 5 but the **a** of the wicked is deceitful.
    12: 15 to them, but the wise listen to **a**.
    19: 20 Listen to **a** and accept discipline,
    20: 18 Plans are established by seeking **a**;

ADVOCATE
Jn 14: 16 he will give you another **a** to help
    14: 26 But the **A**, the Holy Spirit,
1Jn 2: 1 sin, we have an **a** with the Father—

AFFECTION
2Pe 1: 7 and to godliness, mutual **a**; and to
        mutual **a**, love.

AFFLICTION
Ro 12: 12 patient in **a**, faithful in prayer.

AFRAID (FEAR)
Ge 26: 24 Do not be **a**, for I am with you;
Ex 3: 6 because he was **a** to look at God.
Ps 27: 1 of my life—of whom shall I be **a**?
    56: 3 When I am **a**, I put my trust in
Pr 3: 24 you lie down, you will not be **a**;
Jer 1: 8 Do not be **a** of them, for I am
Mt 8: 26 of little faith, why are you so **a**?"
    10: 28 Do not be **a** of those who kill
    10: 31 So don't be **a**; you are worth more
Mk 5: 36 said, Jesus told him, "Don't be **a**;
Jn 14: 27 hearts be troubled and do not be **a**.
Heb 13: 6 Lord is my helper; I will not be **a**.

AGED
Job 12: 12 Is not wisdom found among the **a**?
Pr 17: 6 children are a crown to the **a**,

AGREE
Mt 18: 19 earth **a** about anything they ask for,
Ro 7: 16 want to do, I **a** that the law is good.

AHAB
Son of Omri; king of Israel (1Ki 16:28—22:40), husband of Jezebel (1Ki 16:31). Promoted Baal worship (1Ki 16:31-33); opposed by Elijah (1Ki 17:1; 18; 21), a prophet (1Ki 20:35-43), Micaiah (1Ki 22:1-28). Defeated Ben-Hadad (1Ki 20). Killed for failing to kill Ben-Hadad and for murder of Naboth (1Ki 20:35—21:40).

AHAZ
Son of Jotham; king of Judah, (2Ki 16; 2Ch 28; Isa 7).

AHAZIAH
1. Son of Ahab; king of Israel (1Ki 22:51-2Ki 1:18; 2Ch 20:35-37).
2. Son of Jehoram; king of Judah (2Ki 8:25-29; 9:14-29), also called Jehoahaz (2Ch 21:17—22:9; 25:23).

AIM
1Co 7: 34 Her **a** is to be devoted to the Lord

AIR
1Co 9: 26 not fight like a boxer beating the **a**.
Eph 2: 2 the ruler of the kingdom of the **a**,
1Th 4: 17 clouds to meet the Lord in the **a**.

ALABASTER
Mt 26: 7 him with an **a** jar of very expensive

ALERT
Jos 8: 4 far from it. All of you be on the **a**.
Mk 13: 33 Be **a**! You do not know
Eph 6: 18 be **a** and always keep on praying
1Pe 1: 13 with minds that are **a** and fully

ALIENATED
Gal 5: 4 the law have been **a** from Christ;

ALIVE (LIVE)
Ac 1: 3 convincing proofs that he was **a**.
Ro 6: 11 to sin but **a** to God in Christ Jesus.
1Co 15: 22 die, so in Christ all will be made **a**.
Heb 4: 12 the word of God is **a** and active.

ALMIGHTY (MIGHT)
Ge 17: 1 to him and said, "I am God **A**;
Job 11: 7 Can you probe the limits of the **A**?
    33: 4 the breath of the **A** gives me life.
Ps 91: 1 will rest in the shadow of the **A**.
Isa 6: 3 "Holy, holy, holy is the Lᴏʀᴅ **A**;

ALTAR
Ge 22: 9 Abraham built an **a** there
Ex 27: 1 "Build an **a** of acacia wood,
1Ki 18: 30 he repaired the **a** of the Lᴏʀᴅ,
2Ch 4: 1 a bronze **a** twenty cubits long,
     4: 19 the golden **a**; the tables

ALWAYS
Ps 16: 8 I keep my eyes **a** on the Lᴏʀᴅ.
    26: 3 for I have **a** been mindful of your
    51: 3 and my sin is **a** before me.
Mt 26: 11 The poor you will **a** have with you,
    28: 20 And surely I am with you **a**,
1Co 13: 7 It **a** protects, **a** trusts, **a** hopes,
Php 4: 4 Rejoice in the Lord **a**. I will say it
1Pe 3: 15 **A** be prepared to give an answer

AMAZIAH
Son of Joash; king of Judah (2Ki 14; 2Ch 25).

AMBASSADORS
2Co 5: 20 We are therefore Christ's **a**,

AMBITION
Ro 15: 20 It has always been my **a** to preach
1Th 4: 11 make it your **a** to lead a quiet life:

AMON
Son of Manasseh; king of Judah (2Ki 21:18-26; 1Ch 3:14; 2Ch 33:21-25).

ANANIAS
1. Husband of Sapphira; died for lying to God (Ac 5:1-11).
2. Disciple who baptized Saul (Ac 9:10-19).
3. High priest at Paul's arrest (Ac 22:30—24:1).

ANCESTORS
Heb 1: 1 spoke to our **a** through the prophets

ANCHOR
Heb 6: 19 We have this hope as an **a**

ANCIENT
Da 7: 9 and the **A** of Days took his seat.

ANDREW
Apostle; brother of Simon Peter (Mt 4:18; 10:2; Mk 1:16–18, 29; 3:18; 13:3; Lk 6:14; Jn 1:35–44; 6:8–9; 12:22; Ac 1:13).

ANGEL (ANGELS ARCHANGEL)
Ps 34: 7 The **a** of the LORD encamps
Ac 6: 15 his face was like the face of an **a**.
2Co 11: 14 Satan himself masquerades as an **a**
Gal 1: 8 or an **a** from heaven should preach

ANGELS (ANGEL)
Ps 8: 5 a little lower than the **a**
91: 11 command his **a** concerning you
Mt 18: 10 that their **a** in heaven always see
25: 41 fire prepared for the devil and his **a**.
Lk 20: 36 for they are like the **a**.
1Co 6: 3 you not know that we will judge **a**?
Heb 1: 4 the **a** as the name he has inherited
1: 14 Are not all **a** ministering spirits
2: 7 them a little lower than the **a**;
13: 2 hospitality to **a** without knowing it.
1Pe 1: 12 Even **a** long to look into these
2Pe 2: 4 if God did not spare **a** when they

ANGER (ANGERED ANGRY)
Ex 32: 10 that my **a** may burn against them
34: 6 slow to **a**, abounding in love
Dt 29: 28 In furious **a** and in great wrath
2Ki 22: 13 Great is the LORD's **a** that burns
Ps 30: 5 For his **a** lasts only a moment,
Pr 15: 1 wrath, but a harsh word stirs up **a**.

ANGERED (ANGER)
Pr 22: 24 do not associate with one easily **a**,
1Co 13: 5 it is not easily **a**, it keeps no record

ANGRY (ANGER)
Ps 2: 12 he will be **a** and your way will lead
Pr 29: 22 An **a** person stirs up conflict,
Jas 1: 19 to speak and slow to become **a**,

ANOINT
Ps 23: 5 You **a** my head with oil;
Jas 5: 14 **a** them with oil in the name

ANOTHER
1Pe 3: 8 love one **a**, be compassionate

ANT
Pr 6: 6 Go to the **a**, you sluggard;

ANTICHRIST
1Jn 2: 18 have heard that the **a** is coming,
2Jn : 7 person is the deceiver and the **a**.

ANTIOCH
Ac 11: 26 were called Christians first at **A**.

ANXIETY (ANXIOUS)
Pr 12: 25 **A** weighs down the heart,
1Pe 5: 7 Cast all your **a** on him because he

ANXIOUS (ANXIETY)
Php 4: 6 Do not be **a** about anything,

APOLLOS
Christian from Alexandria, learned in the Scriptures; instructed by Aquila and Priscilla (Ac 18:24–28). Ministered at Corinth (Ac 19:1; 1Co 1:12; 3; Titus 3:13).

APOSTLES
See also Andrew, Bartholomew, James, John, Judas, Matthew, Nathanael, Paul, Peter, Philip, Simon, Thaddaeus, Thomas.
Ac 1: 26 so he was added to the eleven **a**.
2: 43 and signs performed by the **a**.
1Co 12: 28 placed in the church first of all **a**,
15: 9 For I am the least of the **a** and do
2Co 11: 13 For such people are false **a**,
Eph 2: 20 built on the foundation of the **a**

APPEAR (APPEARANCE APPEARING)
Mk 13: 22 false prophets will **a** and perform
2Co 5: 10 we must all **a** before the judgment
Col 3: 4 you also will **a** with him in glory.
Heb 9: 24 now to **a** for us in God's presence.
9: 28 and he will **a** a second time,

APPEARANCE (APPEAR)
1Sa 16: 7 People look at the outward **a**,

APPEARING (APPEAR)
2Ti 4: 8 to all who have longed for his **a**.
Titus 2: 13 the **a** of the glory of our great God

APPLY
Pr 22: 17 **a** your heart to what I teach,
23: 12 **A** your heart to instruction and

APPROACH
Eph 3: 12 we may **a** God with freedom
Heb 4: 16 then **a** God's throne of grace

APPROVED
2Ti 2: 15 to present yourself to God as one **a**,

AQUILA
Husband of Priscilla; co-worker with Paul, instructor of Apollos (Ac 18; Ro 16:3; 1Co 16:19; 2Ti 4:19).

ARARAT
Ge 8: 4 to rest on the mountains of **A**.

ARCHANGEL (ANGEL)
1Th 4: 16 with the voice of the **a**
Jude : 9 But even the **a** Michael, when he

ARCHITECT
Heb 11: 10 whose **a** and builder is God.

ARGUING
Php 2: 14 everything without grumbling or **a**,

ARK
Ge 6: 14 So make yourself an **a** of cypress
Dt 10: 5 put the tablets in the **a** I had made,
2Ch 35: 3 "Put the sacred **a** in the temple
Heb 9: 4 This **a** contained the gold jar

ARM (ARMY)
Nu 11: 23 "Is the LORD's **a** too short?
1Pe 4: 1 **a** yourselves also with the same

ARMAGEDDON
Rev 16: 16 place that in Hebrew is called **A**.

ARMOR (ARMY)
1Ki 20: 11 his **a** should not boast like one who
Eph 6: 11 Put on the full **a** of God, so that
6: 13 Therefore put on the full **a** of God,

ARMS (ARMY)
Dt 33: 27 underneath are the everlasting **a**.
Ps 18: 32 It is God who **a** me with strength
Pr 31: 20 She opens her **a** to the poor
Isa 40: 11 He gathers the lambs in his **a**
Mk 10: 16 And he took the children in his **a**,

ARMY (ARM ARMOR ARMS)
Ps 33: 16 king is saved by the size of his **a**;
Rev 19: 19 the rider on the horse and his **a**.

AROMA
2Co 2: 15 the pleasing **a** of Christ among
     2: 16 one we are an **a** that brings death;
     2: 16 to the other, an **a** that brings life.

ARRAYED
Ps 110: 3 **A** in holy splendor, your young
Isa 61: 10 **a** me in a robe of his righteousness,

ARROGANT
Ro 11: 20 Do not be **a**, but tremble.

ARROWS
Eph 6: 16 can extinguish all the flaming **a**

ASA
   King of Judah (1Ki 15:8–24; 1Ch 3:10; 2Ch 14–16).

ASCENDED
Eph 4: 8 "When he **a** on high, he took many

ASCRIBE
1Ch 16: 28 **A** to the LORD, all you families
     16: 28 **a** to the LORD glory and strength.
Job 36: 3 I will **a** justice to my Maker.
Ps 29: 2 **A** to the LORD the glory due his

ASHAMED (SHAME)
Lk 9: 26 Whoever is **a** of me and my words, the
               Son of Man will be **a** of them
Ro 1: 16 For I am not **a** of the gospel,
2Ti 1: 8 So do not be **a** of the testimony
    2: 15 worker who does not need to be **a**

ASSIGNED
Mk 13: 34 each with their **a** task, and tells
1Co 3: 5 as the Lord has **a** to each his task.
    7: 17 whatever situation the Lord has **a**

ASSOCIATE
Pr 22: 24 do not **a** with one easily angered,
Ro 12: 16 be willing to **a** with people of low
1Co 5: 11 you must not **a** with anyone who
2Th 3: 14 Do not **a** with them, in order

ASSURANCE
Heb 10: 22 and with the full **a** that faith brings,

ASTRAY
Pr 10: 17 ignores correction leads others **a**.
Isa 53: 6 have gone **a**, each of us has turned
Jer 50: 6 their shepherds have led them **a**
1Pe 2: 25 For "you were like sheep going **a**,"
1Jn 3: 7 do not let anyone lead you **a**.

ATHALIAH
   Evil queen of Judah (2Ki 11; 2Ch 23).

ATHLETE
2Ti 2: 5 competes as an **a** does not receive

ATONEMENT
Ex 25: 17 "Make an **a** cover of pure gold—
    30: 10 Once a year Aaron shall make **a**
Lev 17: 11 blood that makes **a** for one's life.
    23: 27 this seventh month is the Day of **A.**
Nu 25: 13 God and made **a** for the Israelites."
Ro 3: 25 presented Christ as a sacrifice of **a,**
Heb 2: 17 that he might make **a** for the sins

ATTENTION
Pr 4: 1 pay **a** and gain understanding.
    5: 1 My son, pay **a** to my wisdom,
    22: 17 Pay **a** and turn your ear
Titus 1: 14 and will pay no **a** to Jewish myths

ATTITUDE (ATTITUDES)
Eph 4: 23 made new in the **a** of your minds;
1Pe 4: 1 yourselves also with the same **a,**

ATTITUDES (ATTITUDE)
Heb 4: 12 the thoughts and **a** of the heart.

ATTRACTIVE
Titus 2: 10 teaching about God our Savior **a.**

AUTHORITIES (AUTHORITY)
Ro 13: 5 it is necessary to submit to the **a,**
    13: 6 for the **a** are God's servants,
Titus 3: 1 to be subject to rulers and **a,**
1Pe 3: 22 **a** and powers in submission to him.

AUTHORITY (AUTHORITIES)
Mt 7: 29 he taught as one who had **a,**
    9: 6 the Son of Man has **a** on earth
    28: 18 "All **a** in heaven and on earth has
Ro 13: 1 for there is no **a** except
    13: 2 rebels against the **a** is rebelling
1Co 11: 10 ought to have **a** over her own head,
1Ti 2: 2 for kings and all those in **a,** that we
    2: 12 to teach or to assume **a** over a man;
Heb 13: 17 your leaders and submit to their **a,**

AVENGE (VENGEANCE)
Dt 32: 35 It is mine to **a**; I will repay.

AVOID
Pr 20: 3 It is to one's honor to **a** strife,
    20: 19 so **a** anyone who talks too much.
1Th 4: 3 you should **a** sexual immorality;
2Ti 2: 16 **A** godless chatter, because those
Titus 3: 9 But **a** foolish controversies

AWAKE
Ps 17: 15 when I **a**, I will be satisfied
1Th 5: 6 asleep, but let us be **a** and sober.

AWE (AWESOME)
Job 25: 2 "Dominion and **a** belong to God;
Ps 119:120 of you; I stand in **a** of your laws.
Isa 29: 23 will stand in **a** of the God of Israel.
Jer 33: 9 they will be in **a** and will tremble
Hab 3: 2 I stand in **a** of your deeds, LORD.
Mal 2: 5 me and stood in **a** of my name.
Mt 9: 8 saw this, they were filled with **a**;
Lk 7: 16 They were all filled with **a**
Ac 2: 43 Everyone was filled with **a**
Heb 12: 28 acceptably with reverence and **a,**

AWESOME (AWE)
Ge 28: 17 and said, "How **a** is this place!
Ex 15: 11 majestic in holiness, **a** in glory,
Dt 7: 21 is among you, is a great and **a** God.
    10: 17 God, mighty and **a**, who shows no
    28: 58 revere this glorious and **a** name—
Jdg 13: 6 looked like an angel of God, very **a.**
Ne 1: 5 the great and **a** God, who keeps his
    9: 32 God, mighty and **a**, who keeps his
Job 10: 16 again display your **a** power against
    37: 22 God comes in **a** majesty.
Ps 45: 4 your right hand achieve **a** deeds.
    47: 2 For the LORD Most High is **a,**
    66: 5 has done, his **a** deeds for mankind!
    68: 35 You, God, are **a** in your sanctuary;
    89: 7 he is more **a** than all who surround
    99: 3 praise your great and **a** name—
    111: 9 holy and **a** is his name.
    145: 6 tell of the power of your **a** works—
Da 9: 4 the great and **a** God, who keeps his

BAAL
1Ki 18: 25 Elijah said to the prophets of **B,**

BAASHA
   King of Israel (1Ki 15:16—16:7; 2Ch 16:1-6).

BABIES (BABY)
Lk   18: 15   bringing **b** to Jesus for him to place
1Pe   2: 2   Like newborn **b**, crave pure

BABY (BABIES)
Isa   49: 15   "Can a mother forget the **b** at her
Lk   1: 44   the **b** in my womb leaped for joy.
      2: 12   You will find a **b** wrapped in cloths
Jn   16: 21   **b** is born she forgets the anguish

BABYLON
Ps   137: 1   By the rivers of **B** we sat and wept

BACKSLIDING
Jer   3: 22   I will cure you of **b**."
Eze   37: 23   save them from all their sinful **b**,

BAGS
Mt   25: 15   To one he gave five **b** of gold, to another
                two **b**, and to another one

BALAAM
   Prophet who attempted to curse Israel (Nu 22–24;
Dt 23:4–5; 2Pe 2:15; Jude 11). Killed (Nu 31:8; Jos 13:22).

BALM
Jer   8: 22   Is there no **b** in Gilead? Is there no

BANISH
Jer   25: 10   will **b** from them the sounds of joy

BANQUET
SS   2: 4   Let him lead me to the **b** hall,
Lk   14: 13   But when you give a **b**,

BAPTIZE (BAPTIZED)
Mt   3: 11   "I **b** you with water for repentance.
      3: 11   He will **b** you with the Holy Spirit
Mk   1: 8   I **b** you with water, but he will **b**
1Co   1: 17   For Christ did not send me to **b**,

BAPTIZED (BAPTIZE)
Mt   3: 6   they were **b** by him in the Jordan.
Mk   1: 9   and was **b** by John in the Jordan.
     10: 38   be **b** with the baptism I am **b** with?"
     16: 16   *believes and is **b** will be saved,*
Jn   4: 2   in fact it was not Jesus who **b**,
Ac   1: 5   For John **b** with water, but in a few

BARABBAS
Mt   27: 17   release to you: Jesus **B**, or Jesus

BARBS
Nu   33: 55   remain will become **b** in your eyes

BARE
Heb   4: 13   and laid **b** before the eyes of him

BARNABAS
   Disciple, originally Joseph (Ac 4:36), prophet (Ac
13:1), apostle (Ac 14:14). Brought Paul to apostles (Ac
9:27), Antioch (Ac 11:22–29; Gal 2:1–13), on the first
missionary journey (Ac 13–14). Together at Jerusalem
Council, they separated over John Mark (Ac 15). Later
co-workers (1Co 9:6; Col 4:10).

BARTHOLOMEW
   Apostle (Mt 10:3; Mk 3:18; Lk 6:14; Ac 1:13). Possibly
also known as Nathanael (Jn 1:45–49; 21:2).

BATH
Jn   13: 10   who have had a **b** need only

BATHSHEBA
   Wife of Uriah who committed adultery with and
became wife of David (2Sa 11), mother of Solomon (2Sa
12:24; 1Ki 1–2; 1Ch 3:5).

BATTLE
2Ch 20: 15   For the **b** is not yours, but God's.
Ps   24: 8   mighty, the LORD mighty in **b**.
Ecc   9: 11   to the swift or the **b** to the strong,

BEAR (BEARING BIRTH BIRTHRIGHT BORE BORN
   FIRSTBORN NEWBORN)
Ge   4: 13   punishment is more than I can **b**.
Ps   38: 4   me like a burden too heavy to **b**.
Isa   53: 11   many, and he will **b** their iniquities.
Da   7: 5   beast, which looked like a **b**.
Mt   7: 18   A good tree cannot **b** bad fruit,
Jn   15: 2   branch that does **b** fruit he prunes
     15: 16   so that you might go and **b** fruit—
Ro   15: 1   We who are strong ought to **b**
1Co 10: 13   tempted beyond what you can **b**.
Col   3: 13   **B** with each other and forgive one

BEARING (BEAR)
Eph   4: 2   patient, **b** with one another in love.
Col   1: 10   **b** fruit in every good work,

BEAST
Rev 13: 18   calculate the number of the **b**, for it

BEAT (BEATING)
Isa   2: 4   They will **b** their swords
Joel 3: 10   **B** your plowshares into swords

BEATING (BEAT)
1Co   9: 26   I do not fight like a boxer **b** the air.
1Pe   2: 20   if you receive a **b** for doing wrong

BEAUTIFUL (BEAUTY)
Ge   6: 2   the daughters of humans were **b**,
     12: 11   "I know what a **b** woman you are.
     12: 14   saw that Sarai was a very **b** woman.
     24: 16   The woman was very **b**, a virgin;
     26: 7   of Rebekah, because she is **b**."
     29: 17   had a lovely figure and was **b**.
Pr   11: 22   snout is a **b** woman who shows no
Ecc   3: 11   He has made everything **b** in its
Isa   4: 2   the Branch of the LORD will be **b**
     52: 7   How **b** on the mountains are the
Eze 20: 6   and honey, the most **b** of all lands.
Zec   9: 17   How attractive and **b** they will be!
Mt   23: 27   which look **b** on the outside
     26: 10   She has done a **b** thing to me.
Ro   10: 15   "How **b** are the feet of those who

BEAUTY (BEAUTIFUL)
Ps   27: 4   to gaze on the **b** of the LORD
     45: 11   the king be enthralled by your **b**;
Pr   31: 30   is deceptive, and **b** is fleeting;
Isa 33: 17   Your eyes will see the king in his **b**
     53: 2   He had no **b** or majesty to attract
     61: 3   them a crown of **b** instead of ashes,
Eze 28: 12   full of wisdom and perfect in **b**.
1Pe   3: 4   unfading **b** of a gentle and quiet

BED
Heb 13: 4   and the marriage **b** kept pure,

BEELZEBUL
Lk   11: 15   said, "By **B**, the prince of demons,

BEER
Pr   20: 1   Wine is a mocker and **b** a brawler;

BEERSHEBA
Jdg 20: 1   all Israel from Dan to **B**

BEGINNING
Ge   1: 1   In the **b** God created the heavens
Ps 102: 25   In the **b** you laid the foundations
    111: 10   of the LORD is the **b** of wisdom;
Pr   1: 7   the LORD is the **b** of knowledge,
      4: 7   The **b** of wisdom is this:
Jn   1: 1   In the **b** was the Word,
1Jn   1: 1   That which was from the **b**,
Rev 21: 6   and the Omega, the **B** and the End.

BEHAVE (BEHAVIOR)
Ro 13: 13 us **b** decently, as in the daytime,

BEHAVIOR (BEHAVE)
Pr 1: 3 receiving instruction in prudent **b**,

BELIEVE (BELIEVED BELIEVER BELIEVERS
    BELIEVES BELIEVING)
Pr 14: 15 The simple **b** anything,
Mt 18: 6 those who **b** in me—
   21: 22 If you **b**, you will receive whatever
Mk 1: 15 Repent and **b** the good news!"
    9: 24 the boy's father exclaimed, "I do **b**;
   16: 17 *accompany those who **b**:*
Lk 8: 50 just **b**, and she will be healed."
   24: 25 how slow to **b** all that the prophets
Jn 1: 7 so that through him all might **b**.
    3: 18 does not **b** stands condemned
    6: 29 to **b** in the one he has sent."
   10: 38 even though you do not **b** me,
   11: 27 "I **b** that you are the Messiah,
   14: 1 You **b** in God; **b** also in me.
   14: 11 **B** me when I say that I am
   16: 30 This makes us **b** that you came
   16: 31 "Do you now **b**?" Jesus replied.
   17: 21 the world may **b** that you have sent
   20: 27 into my side. Stop doubting and **b**."
   20: 31 may **b** that Jesus is the Messiah,
Ac 16: 31 They replied, "**B** in the Lord Jesus,
   24: 14 I **b** everything that is in accordance
Ro 3: 22 faith in Jesus Christ to all who **b**.
    4: 11 he is the father of all who **b**
   10: 9 **b** in your heart that God raised
   10: 14 how can they **b** in the one of whom
1Th 4: 14 For we **b** that Jesus died and rose
2Th 2: 11 delusion so that they will **b** the lie
1Ti 4: 10 and especially of those who **b**.
Titus 1: 6 a man whose children **b** and are
Heb 11: 6 comes to him must **b** that he exists
Jas 2: 19 You **b** that there is one God. Good! Even
    the demons **b** that—
1Jn 4: 1 Dear friends, do not **b** every spirit,

BELIEVED (BELIEVE)
Ge 15: 6 Abram **b** the Lord, and he
Jnh 3: 5 The Ninevites **b** God. A fast was
Jn 1: 12 to those who **b** in his name,
    2: 22 Then they **b** the scripture
    3: 18 already because they have not **b**
   20: 8 also went inside. He saw and **b**.
   20: 29 who have not seen and yet have **b**."
Ac 13: 48 were appointed for eternal life **b**.
Ro 4: 3 "Abraham **b** God, and it was
   10: 14 call on the one they have not **b** in?
1Co 15: 2 Otherwise, you have **b** in vain.
Gal 3: 6 So also Abraham "**b** God, and it
2Ti 1: 12 because I know whom I have **b**,
Jas 2: 23 that says, "Abraham **b** God, and it

BELIEVER (BELIEVE)
1Co 7: 12 brother has a wife who is not a **b**
2Co 6: 15 what does a **b** have in common

BELIEVERS (BELIEVE)
Ac 4: 32 All the **b** were one in heart
    5: 12 all the **b** used to meet together
1Co 6: 5 to judge a dispute between **b**?
1Ti 4: 12 set an example for the **b** in speech,
1Pe 2: 17 love the family of **b**, fear God,

BELIEVES (BELIEVE)
Mk 9: 23 is possible for one who **b**."
   11: 23 **b** that what they say will happen,
   16: 16 *Whoever **b** and is baptized*

Jn 3: 16 whoever **b** in him shall not perish
    3: 36 Whoever **b** in the Son has eternal
    5: 24 **b** him who sent me has eternal life
    6: 35 and whoever **b** in me will never be
    6: 40 and **b** in him shall have eternal life,
    6: 47 you, the one who **b** has eternal life.
    7: 38 Whoever **b** in me, as Scripture has
Ro 1: 16 salvation to everyone who **b**:
    9: 33 the one who **b** in him will never be
   10: 4 righteousness for everyone who **b**.
1Jn 5: 1 Everyone who **b** that Jesus is
    5: 5 Only the one who **b** that Jesus is

BELIEVING (BELIEVE)
Jn 11: 26 whoever lives by **b** in me will never
   20: 31 by **b** you may have life in his name.

BELONG (BELONGS)
Dt 29: 29 The secret things **b** to the Lord
Job 25: 2 "Dominion and awe **b** to God;
Ps 47: 9 for the kings of the earth **b** to God;
   95: 4 and the mountain peaks **b** to him.
Jn 8: 44 You **b** to your father, the devil,
   15: 19 As it is, you do not **b** to the world,
Ro 1: 6 those Gentiles who are called to **b**
    7: 4 that you might **b** to another, to him
   14: 8 we live or die, we **b** to the Lord.
Gal 5: 24 Those who **b** to Christ Jesus have
1Th 5: 8 But since we **b** to the day, let us be

BELONGS (BELONG)
Job 41: 11 Everything under heaven **b** to me.
Ps 111: 10 To him **b** eternal praise.
Eze 18: 4 For everyone **b** to me, the parent as
Jn 8: 47 Whoever **b** to God hears what God
Ro 12: 5 each member **b** to all the others.

BELOVED (LOVE)
Dt 33: 12 "Let the **b** of the Lord rest
SS 2: 16 My **b** is mine and I am his;
    7: 10 I belong to my **b**, and his desire is

BELT
Isa 11: 5 Righteousness will be his **b**
Eph 6: 14 the **b** of truth buckled around your

BENEFICIAL (BENEFIT)
1Co 10: 23 but not everything is **b**.

BENEFIT (BENEFICIAL BENEFITS)
Ro 6: 22 the **b** you reap leads to holiness,
2Co 4: 15 All this is for your **b**,

BENEFITS (BENEFIT)
Ps 103: 2 my soul, and forget not all his **b**—
Jn 4: 38 and you have reaped the **b** of their

BENJAMIN
    Twelfth son of Jacob by Rachel (Ge 35:16–24; 46:19–21;
1Ch 2:2). Jacob refused to send him to Egypt, but relented (Ge 42–45).

BEREAN
Ac 17: 11 the **B** Jews were of more noble

BESTOWS
Ps 84: 11 the Lord **b** favor and honor;

BETHLEHEM
Mt 2: 1 After Jesus was born in **B** in Judea,

BETRAY
Pr 25: 9 do not **b** another's confidence,

BIND (BINDS)
Dt 6: 8 and **b** them on your foreheads.
Pr 6: 21 **B** them always on your heart;
Isa 61: 1 He has sent me to **b**
Mt 16: 19 whatever you **b** on earth will be

BINDS (BIND)
Ps 147: 3 and **b** up their wounds.
Isa 30: 26 when the LORD **b** up the bruises

BIRDS
Mt 8: 20 "Foxes have dens and **b** have nests,

BIRTH (BEAR)
Ps 58: 3 Even from **b** the wicked go astray;
Mt 1: 18 This is how the **b** of Jesus
1Pe 1: 3 great mercy he has given us new **b**

BIRTHRIGHT (BEAR)
Ge 25: 34 up and left. So Esau despised his **b**.

BLAMELESS
Ge 17: 1 walk before me faithfully and be **b**.
Job 1: 1 This man was **b** and upright;
Ps 84: 11 from those whose walk is **b**.
119: 1 are those whose ways are **b**,
Pr 19: 1 poor whose walk is **b** than a fool
1Co 1: 8 so that you will be **b** on the day
Eph 5: 27 any other blemish, but holy and **b**.
Php 2: 15 that you may become **b** and pure,
1Th 3: 13 your hearts so that you will be **b**
5: 23 body be kept **b** at the coming of
Titus 1: 6 An elder must be **b**, faithful to his
Heb 7: 26 one who is holy, **b**, pure, set apart
2Pe 3: 14 spotless, **b** and at peace with him.

BLASPHEMES
Mk 3: 29 whoever **b** against the Holy Spirit

BLEMISH
1Pe 1: 19 Christ, a lamb without **b** or defect.

BLESS (BLESSED BLESSING BLESSINGS)
Ge 12: 3 I will **b** those who **b** you,
Ro 12: 14 **B** those who persecute you;

BLESSED (BLESS)
Ge 1: 22 God **b** them and said, "Be fruitful
2: 3 Then God **b** the seventh day
22: 18 all nations on earth will be **b**,
Ps 1: 1 **B** is the one who does not walk
2: 12 **B** are all who take refuge in him.
33: 12 **B** is the nation whose God is
41: 1 **B** are those who have regard
84: 5 **B** are those whose strength is
106: 3 **B** are those who act justly,
112: 1 **B** are those who fear the LORD,
118: 26 **B** is he who comes in the name
Pr 29: 18 **b** is the one who heeds wisdom's
31: 28 Her children arise and call her **b**;
Mt 5: 3 "**B** are the poor in spirit, for theirs
5: 4 **B** are those who mourn, for they
5: 5 **B** are the meek, for they will
5: 6 **B** are those who hunger and thirst
5: 7 **B** are the merciful, for they will
5: 8 **B** are the pure in heart, for they
5: 9 **B** are the peacemakers, for they
5: 10 **B** are those who are persecuted
5: 11 "**B** are you when people insult you,
Lk 1: 48 on all generations will call me **b**,
Jn 12: 13 "**B** is he who comes in the name
Ac 20: 35 'It is more **b** to give than
Titus 2: 13 while we wait for the **b** hope—
Jas 1: 12 **B** is the one who perseveres under
Rev 1: 3 **B** is the one who reads aloud
22: 14 "**B** are those who wash their robes,

BLESSING (BLESS)
Eze 34: 26 there will be showers of **b**.

BLESSINGS (BLESS)
Pr 10: 6 **B** crown the head of the righteous,

BLIND
Mt 15: 14 If the **b** lead the **b**, both will fall
23: 16 "Woe to you, **b** guides! You say,
Jn 9: 25 I do know. I was **b** but now I see!"

BLOOD
Ge 9: 6 "Whoever sheds human **b**, by humans
shall their **b** be shed;
Ex 12: 13 The **b** will be a sign for you
24: 8 "This is the **b** of the covenant
Lev 17: 11 For the life of a creature is in the **b**,
17: 11 it is the **b** that makes atonement
Ps 72: 14 for precious is their **b** in his sight.
Pr 6: 17 hands that shed innocent **b**,
Mt 26: 28 This is my **b** of the covenant,
Ro 3: 25 through the shedding of his **b**—
5: 9 have now been justified by his **b**,
1Co 11: 25 cup is the new covenant in my **b**;
Eph 1: 7 we have redemption through his **b**,
2: 13 brought near by the **b** of Christ.
Col 1: 20 by making peace through his **b**,
Heb 9: 12 once for all by his own **b**,
9: 22 everything be cleansed with **b**,
1Pe 1: 19 but with the precious **b** of Christ,
1Jn 1: 7 and the **b** of Jesus, his Son,
Rev 1: 5 has freed us from our sins by his **b**,
5: 9 with your **b** you purchased for God
7: 14 them white in the **b** of the Lamb.
12: 11 over him by the **b** of the Lamb

BLOT (BLOTS)
Ex 32: 32 **b** me out of the book you have
Ps 51: 1 to your great compassion **b** out my
Rev 3: 5 I will never **b** out the name

BLOTS (BLOT)
Isa 43: 25 "I, even I, am he who **b** out your

BLOWN
Eph 4: 14 and **b** here and there by every wind
Jas 1: 6 the sea, **b** and tossed by the wind.

BOAST
1Ki 20: 11 his armor should not **b** like one
Ps 44: 8 In God we make our **b** all day long,
Pr 27: 1 Do not **b** about tomorrow, for you
1Co 1: 31 "Let the one who boasts **b**
Gal 6: 14 May I never **b** except in the cross
Eph 2: 9 not by works, so that no one can **b**.

BOAZ
Wealthy Bethlehemite who showed favor to Ruth (Ru 2), married her (Ru 4). Ancestor of David (Ru 4:18–22; 1Ch 2:12–15), Jesus (Mt 1:5–16; Lk 3:23–32).

BODIES (BODY)
Ro 12: 1 to offer your **b** as a living sacrifice,
1Co 6: 15 not know that your **b** are members
6: 19 not know that your **b** are temples
Eph 5: 28 to love their wives as their own **b**.

BODY (BODIES)
Zec 13: 6 are these wounds on your **b**?'
Mt 10: 28 can destroy both soul and **b** in hell.
10: 28 be afraid of those who kill the **b**
26: 26 "Take and eat; this is my **b**."
Jn 13: 10 their whole **b** is clean.
1Co 11: 24 "This is my **b**, which is for you;
12: 12 Just as a **b**, though one, has many
Eph 5: 30 for we are members of his **b**.

BOLD (BOLDNESS)
Pr 21: 29 The wicked put up a **b** front,
28: 1 but the righteous are as **b** as a lion.

BOLDNESS (BOLD)
Ac 4: 29 to speak your word with great **b**.

BONDAGE
Ezr 9: 9 God has not forsaken us in our **b**.

BOOK (BOOKS)
Jos 1: 8 Keep this **B** of the Law always
Ne 8: 8 They read from the **B** of the Law
Jn 20: 30 which are not recorded in this **b**.
Php 4: 3 whose names are in the **b** of life.
Rev 21: 27 are written in the Lamb's **b** of life.

BOOKS (BOOK)
Ecc 12: 12 Of making many **b** there is no end,

BORE (BEAR)
Isa 53: 4 up our pain and **b** our suffering,

BORN (BEAR)
Isa 9: 6 For to us a child is **b**, to us a son is
Jn 3: 7 my saying, 'You must be **b** again.'
1Pe 1: 23 For you have been **b** again,
1Jn 4: 7 Everyone who loves has been **b**
5: 1 that Jesus is the Christ is **b** of God,

BORROWER
Pr 22: 7 and the **b** is slave to the lender.

BOUGHT
Ac 20: 28 which he **b** with his own blood.
1Co 6: 20 you were **b** at a price.
7: 23 You were **b** at a price;
2Pe 2: 1 the sovereign Lord who **b** them—

BOUNDLESS
Eph 3: 8 the Gentiles the **b** riches of Christ,

BOW
Ps 95: 6 Come, let us **b** down in worship,
Isa 45: 23 Before me every knee will **b**;
Ro 14: 11 Lord, 'every knee will **b** before me;
Php 2: 10 name of Jesus every knee should **b**,

BRANCH (BRANCHES)
Isa 4: 2 that day the **B** of the LORD will be
Jer 33: 15 I will make a righteous **B** sprout

BRANCHES (BRANCH)
Jn 15: 5 "I am the vine; you are the **b**.

BRAVE
2Sa 2: 7 then, be strong and **b**, for Saul your

BREAD
Dt 8: 3 that man does not live on **b** alone
Pr 30: 8 riches, but give me only my daily **b**.
Isa 55: 2 spend money on what is not **b**,
Mt 4: 4 'Man shall not live on **b** alone,
6: 11 Give us today our daily **b**.
Jn 6: 35 Jesus declared, "I am the **b** of life.
21: 13 took the **b** and gave it to them,
1Co 11: 23 the night he was betrayed, took **b**,

BREAK (BREAKING BROKEN)
Nu 30: 2 he must not **b** his word but must
Jdg 2: 1 'I will never **b** my covenant
Ps 2: 9 You will **b** them with a rod of iron;
Isa 42: 3 A bruised reed he will not **b**,
Mt 12: 20 A bruised reed he will not **b**,

BREAKING (BREAK)
Jas 2: 10 just one point is guilty of **b** all of it.

BREASTPIECE (BREASTPLATE)
Ex 28: 15 "Fashion a **b** for making decisions

BREASTPLATE (BREASTPIECE)
Isa 59: 17 He put on righteousness as his **b**,

Eph 6: 14 the **b** of righteousness in place,
1Th 5: 8 putting on faith and love as a **b**,

BREATHED (GOD-BREATHED)
Ge 2: 7 **b** into his nostrils the breath of life,
Jn 20: 22 with that he **b** on them and said,

BRIBE
Ex 23: 8 "Do not accept a **b**, for a **b** blinds
Pr 6: 35 he will refuse a **b**, however great it

BRIDE
Rev 19: 7 and his **b** has made herself ready.

BRIGHTER (BRIGHTNESS)
Pr 4: 18 shining ever **b** till the full light

BRIGHTNESS (BRIGHTER)
2Sa 22: 13 Out of the **b** of his presence bolts
Da 12: 3 who are wise will shine like the **b**

BROAD
Mt 7: 13 gate and **b** is the road that leads

BROKEN (BREAK)
Ps 51: 17 My sacrifice, O God, is a **b** spirit;
Ecc 4: 12 of three strands is not quickly **b**.

BROKENHEARTED (HEART)
Ps 34: 18 The LORD is close to the **b**
109: 16 the poor and the needy and the **b**.
147: 3 He heals the **b** and binds up their
Isa 61: 1 He has sent me to bind up the **b**,

BROTHER (BROTHER'S BROTHERS)
Pr 17: 17 a **b** is born for a time of adversity.
18: 24 a friend who sticks closer than a **b**.
Mt 18: 15 "If your **b** or sister sins,
Mk 3: 35 Whoever does God's will is my **b**
Lk 17: 3 "If your **b** or sister sins against you,
1Co 8: 13 if what I eat causes my **b** or sister
1Jn 2: 10 who loves their **b** and sister

BROTHER'S (BROTHER)
Ge 4: 9 "Am I my **b** keeper?"

BROTHERS (BROTHER)
Mt 25: 40 did for one of the least of these **b**
Mk 10: 29 "no one who has left home or **b**
Heb 13: 1 Keep on loving one another as **b**

BUILD (BUILDING BUILDS BUILT)
Mt 16: 18 on this rock I will **b** my church,
Ac 20: 32 which can **b** you up and give you
1Co 3: 10 But each one should **b** with care.
14: 12 excel in those that **b** up the church.
1Th 5: 11 one another and **b** each other up,

BUILDING (BUILD)
1Co 3: 9 you are God's field, God's **b**.
2Co 10: 8 authority the Lord gave us for **b**
Eph 4: 29 only what is helpful for **b** others

BUILDS (BUILD)
Ps 127: 1 Unless the LORD **b** the house,
1Co 8: 1 puffs up while love **b** up.

BUILT (BUILD)
Mt 7: 24 is like a wise man who **b** his house
1Co 14: 26 so that the church may be **b** up.
Eph 2: 20 on the foundation of the apostles
4: 12 that the body of Christ may be **b**

BURDEN (BURDENED BURDENS)
Ps 38: 4 overwhelmed me like a **b** too heavy
Mt 11: 30 my yoke is easy and my **b** is light."

BURDENED (BURDEN)
Gal 5: 1 do not let yourselves be **b** again

BURDENS (BURDEN)
Ps 68: 19 our Savior, who daily bears our **b**.
Gal 6: 2 Carry each other's **b**, and in this

BURIED
Ro 6: 4 We were therefore **b** with him
1Co 15: 4 that he was **b**, that he was raised

BURNING
Lev 6: 9 the fire must be kept **b** on the altar.
Ro 12: 20 you will heap **b** coals on his head."

BUSINESS
Da 8: 27 got up and went about the king's **b**.
1Th 4: 11 You should mind your own **b**

BUSY
1Ki 20: 40 While your servant was **b** here
2Th 3: 11 are not **b**; they are busybodies.
Titus 2: 5 pure, to be **b** at home, to be kind,

CAESAR
Mt 22: 21 give back to **C** what is Caesar's,

CAIN
Firstborn of Adam (Ge 4:1), murdered brother Abel (Ge 4:1-16; 1Jn 3:12).

CALEB
Judahite who spied out Canaan (Nu 13:6); allowed to enter land because of faith (Nu 13:30—14:38; Dt 1:36). Possessed Hebron (Jos 14:6—15:19).

CALF
Ex 32: 4 into an idol cast in the shape of a **c**,
Lk 15: 23 Bring the fattened **c** and kill it.

CALL (CALLED CALLING CALLS)
Ps 145: 18 LORD is near to all who **c** on him,
Pr 31: 28 children arise and **c** her blessed;
Isa 5: 20 Woe to those who **c** evil good
55: 6 **c** on him while he is near.
65: 24 Before they **c** I will answer;
Jer 33: 3 '**C** to me and I will answer you
Mt 9: 13 I have not come to **c** the righteous,
Ro 10: 12 richly blesses all who **c** on him,
11: 29 gifts and his **c** are irrevocable.
1Th 4: 7 For God did not **c** us to be impure,

CALLED (CALL)
1Sa 3: 5 and said, "Here I am; you **c** me."
2Ch 7: 14 my people, who are **c** by my name,
Ps 34: 6 This poor man **c**, and the LORD
Mt 21: 13 "'My house will be **c** a house
Ro 8: 30 And those he predestined, he also **c**;
those he **c**, he also justified;
1Co 7: 15 God has **c** us to live in peace.
Gal 5: 13 and sisters, were **c** to be free.
1Pe 2: 9 the praises of him who **c** you

CALLING (CALL)
Jn 1: 23 voice of one **c** in the wilderness,
Ac 22: 16 your sins away, **c** on his name.'
Eph 4: 1 worthy of the **c** you have received.
2Pe 1: 10 every effort to confirm your **c**

CALLS (CALL)
Joel 2: 32 everyone who **c** on the name
Jn 10: 3 He **c** his own sheep by name
Ro 10: 13 "Everyone who **c** on the name

CALM
Pr 29: 11 but the wise bring **c** in the end.

CAMEL
Mt 19: 24 easier for a **c** to go through the eye
23: 24 strain out a gnat but swallow a **c**.

CANAAN
1Ch 16: 18 **C** as the portion you will inherit."

CANCELED
Col 2: 14 having **c** the charge of our legal

CAPITAL
Dt 21: 22 someone guilty of a **c** offense is put

CARE (CAREFUL CAREFULLY CARES CARING)
Ps 8: 4 human beings that you **c** for them?
Pr 29: 7 The righteous **c** about justice
Lk 10: 34 him to an inn and took **c** of him.
Jn 21: 16 Jesus said, "Take **c** of my sheep."
1Co 3: 10 But each one should build with **c**.
Eph 5: 29 but they feed and **c** for their body,
Heb 2: 6 a son of man that you **c** for him?
1Pe 5: 2 of God's flock that is under your **c**,

CAREFUL (CARE)
Ex 23: 13 "Be **c** to do everything I have said
Dt 6: 3 be **c** to obey so that it may go well
Jos 23: 6 be **c** to obey all that is written
23: 11 So be very **c** to love the LORD
Pr 13: 24 one who loves their children is **c**
Mt 6: 1 "Be **c** not to practice your
Ro 12: 17 Be **c** to do what is right in the eyes
1Co 8: 9 Be **c**, however, that the exercise of
Eph 5: 15 Be very **c**, then, how you live—

CAREFULLY (CARE)
Pr 12: 26 righteous choose their friends **c**,

CARES (CARE)
Ps 55: 22 Cast your **c** on the LORD and he
Na 1: 7 He **c** for those who trust in him,
1Th 2: 7 Just as a nursing mother **c** for her
1Pe 5: 7 on him because he **c** for you.

CARING (CARE)
1Ti 5: 4 practice by **c** for their own family

CARRIED (CARRY)
Ex 19: 4 and how I **c** you on eagles' wings
Heb 13: 9 Do not be **c** away by all kinds
2Pe 1: 21 God as they were **c** along

CARRIES (CARRY)
Dt 32: 11 to catch them and **c** them aloft.
Isa 40: 11 arms and **c** them close to his heart;

CARRY (CARRIED CARRIES)
Lk 14: 27 whoever does not **c** their cross
Gal 6: 2 **C** each other's burdens, and in this
6: 5 each one should **c** their own load.

CAST
Ps 22: 18 them and **c** lots for my garment.
55: 22 **C** your cares on the LORD and he
Jn 19: 24 them and **c** lots for my garment."
1Pe 5: 7 **C** all your anxiety on him because

CATTLE
Ps 50: 10 and the **c** on a thousand hills.

CAUGHT
1Th 4: 17 are left will be **c** up together

CAUSE (CAUSES)
Pr 24: 28 against your neighbor without **c**—
Ecc 8: 3 Do not stand up for a bad **c**, for he
Mt 18: 7 the things that **c** people to stumble!
Ro 14: 21 that will **c** your brother or sister
1Co 10: 32 Do not **c** anyone to stumble,

CAUSES (CAUSE)
Isa 8: 14 he will be a stone that **c** people
Mt 18: 6 "If anyone **c** one of these little

CEASE
Ps 46: 9 He makes wars **c** to the ends

CELEBRATE
Ps 2: 11 fear and **c** his rule with trembling.

CENSER
Lev 16: 12 is to take a **c** full of burning coals

CENTURION
Mt 8: 5 Capernaum, a **c** came to him,

CERTAINTY
Lk 1: 4 you may know the **c** of the things
Jn 17: 8 They knew with **c** that I came

CHAFF
Ps 1: 4 They are like **c** that the wind blows

CHAINED
2Ti 2: 9 But God's word is not **c**.

CHAMPION
Ps 19: 5 like a **c** rejoicing to run his course.

CHANGE (CHANGED)
1Sa 15: 29 does not lie or **c** his mind;
Ps 110: 4 has sworn and will not **c** his mind:
Jer 7: 5 If you really **c** your ways and your
Mal 3: 6 "I the LORD do not **c**. So you,
Mt 18: 3 unless you **c** and become like little
Heb 7: 21 has sworn and will not **c** his mind:
Jas 1: 17 lights, who does not **c** like shifting

CHANGED (CHANGE)
1Co 15: 51 not all sleep, but we will all be **c**—

CHARACTER
Ru 3: 11 that you are a woman of noble **c**.
Pr 31: 10 A wife of noble **c** who can find?
Ro 5: 4 perseverance, **c**; and **c**, hope.
1Co 15: 33 "Bad company corrupts good **c**."

CHARGE
Ro 8: 33 will bring any **c** against those
2Co 11: 7 the gospel of God to you free of **c**?
2Ti 4: 1 and his kingdom, I give you this **c**:

CHARIOTS
2Ki 6: 17 and **c** of fire all around Elisha.
Ps 20: 7 Some trust in **c** and some in horses

CHARM
Pr 31: 30 **C** is deceptive, and beauty is

CHASE
Pr 12: 11 who **c** fantasies have no sense.

CHATTER (CHATTERING)
1Ti 6: 20 Turn away from godless **c**
2Ti 2: 16 Avoid godless **c**, because those who

CHATTERING (CHATTER)
Pr 10: 8 but a **c** fool comes to ruin.
10: 10 grief, and a **c** fool comes to ruin.

CHEAT (CHEATED)
Mal 1: 14 "Cursed is the **c** who has
1Co 6: 8 you yourselves **c** and do wrong,

CHEATED (CHEAT)
Lk 19: 8 if I have **c** anybody out of anything,
1Co 6: 7 Why not rather be **c**?

CHEEK
Mt 5: 39 turn to them the other **c** also.

CHEERFUL (CHEERS)
Pr 15: 13 A happy heart makes the face **c**,
15: 15 the **c** heart has a continual feast.
17: 22 A **c** heart is good medicine,
2Co 9: 7 for God loves a **c** giver.

CHEERS (CHEERFUL)
Pr 12: 25 the heart, but a kind word **c** it up.

CHILD (CHILDHOOD CHILDLESS CHILDREN)
Pr 22: 15 Folly is bound up in the heart of a **c**,

Pr 23: 13 not withhold discipline from a **c**;
29: 15 but a **c** left undisciplined disgraces
Isa 9: 6 For to us a **c** is born, to us a son is
11: 6 and a little **c** will lead them.
66: 13 As a mother comforts her **c**, so will
Mt 18: 2 He called a little **c** to him,
Lk 1: 42 and blessed is the **c** you will bear!
1: 80 And the **c** grew and became strong
1Co 13: 11 When I was a **c**, I talked like a **c**,
1Jn 5: 1 loves the father loves his **c** as well.

CHILDHOOD (CHILD)
1Co 13: 11 I put the ways of **c** behind me.

CHILDLESS (CHILD)
Ps 113: 9 settles the **c** woman in her home

CHILDREN (CHILD)
Dt 4: 9 Teach them to your **c** and to their **c**
11: 19 Teach them to your **c**,
Ps 8: 2 Through the praise of **c** and infants
Pr 13: 24 spares the rod hates their **c**,
17: 6 parents are the pride of their **c**.
20: 11 Even small **c** are known by their
22: 6 Start **c** off on the way they should
29: 17 Discipline your **c**, and they will
31: 28 Her **c** arise and call her blessed;
Mt 7: 11 how to give good gifts to your **c**,
11: 25 and revealed them to little **c**.
18: 3 change and become like little **c**,
19: 14 said, "Let the little **c** come to me,
21: 16 "'From the lips of **c** and infants
Mk 9: 37 these little **c** in my name welcomes
10: 14 them, "Let the little **c** come to me,
10: 16 And he took the **c** in his arms,
13: 12 **C** will rebel against their parents
Lk 10: 21 and revealed them to little **c**.
18: 16 said, "Let the little **c** come to me,
Jn 12: 36 so that you may become **c** of light."
Ro 8: 16 with our spirit that we are God's **c**.
2Co 12: 14 **c** should not have to save for
Eph 6: 1 **C**, obey your parents in the Lord,
6: 4 Fathers, do not exasperate your **c**;
Col 3: 20 **C**, obey your parents in everything,
3: 21 do not embitter your **c**, or they will
1Ti 3: 4 well and see that his **c** obey him,
3: 12 and must manage his **c** and his
5: 10 such as bringing up **c**,
Heb 12: 7 God is treating you as his **c**.
1Jn 3: 1 that we should be called **c** of God!

CHOOSE (CHOOSES CHOSE CHOSEN)
Dt 30: 19 Now **c** life, so that you and your
Jos 24: 15 **c** for yourselves this day whom you
Pr 8: 10 **C** my instruction instead of silver,
Jn 15: 16 You did not **c** me, but I chose you
Ac 15: 14 God first intervened to **c** a people

CHOOSES (CHOOSE)
Jn 7: 17 who **c** to do the will of God

CHOSE (CHOOSE)
Ge 13: 11 Lot **c** for himself the whole plain
Ps 33: 12 the people he **c** for his inheritance.
Jn 15: 16 but I **c** you and appointed you so
1Co 1: 27 But God **c** the foolish things
Eph 1: 4 For he **c** us in him before
2Th 2: 13 because God **c** you as firstfruits

CHOSEN (CHOOSE)
Isa 41: 8 whom I have **c**, you descendants
Mt 22: 14 many are invited, but few are **c**."
Lk 10: 42 Mary has **c** what is better, and it
23: 35 if he is God's Messiah, the **C** One."
Jn 15: 19 but I have **c** you out of the world.

1Pe 1: 20 He was **c** before the creation
2: 9 But you are a **c** people, a royal

CHRIST (CHRIST'S CHRISTIAN MESSIAH)
Jn 1: 41 found the Messiah" (that is, the **C**).
Ro 3: 22 faith in Jesus **C** to all who believe.
5: 6 powerless, **C** died for the ungodly.
5: 8 we were still sinners, **C** died for us.
5: 17 life through the one man, Jesus **C**!
6: 4 just as **C** was raised from the dead
8: 1 for those who are in **C** Jesus,
8: 9 does not have the Spirit of **C**, they do not belong to **C**.
8: 35 separate us from the love of **C**?
10: 4 **C** is the culmination of the law so
14: 9 **C** died and returned to life so that
15: 3 even **C** did not please himself but,
1Co 1: 23 but we preach **C** crucified:
2: 2 while I was with you except Jesus **C**
3: 11 one already laid, which is Jesus **C**.
5: 7 For **C**, our Passover lamb, has been
8: 6 Jesus **C**, through whom all things
10: 4 them, and that rock was **C**.
10: 9 We should not test **C**, as some
11: 1 as I follow the example of **C**.
11: 3 that the head of every man is **C**,
11: 3 and the head of **C** is God.
12: 27 Now you are the body of **C**,
15: 3 that **C** died for our sins according
15: 14 And if **C** has not been raised,
15: 22 die, so in **C** all will be made alive.
15: 57 victory through our Lord Jesus **C**.
2Co 3: 3 show that you are a letter from **C**,
4: 5 but Jesus **C** as Lord, and ourselves
5: 10 before the judgment seat of **C**,
5: 17 if anyone is in **C**, the new creation
11: 2 to **C**, so that I might present you as
Gal 2: 20 I have been crucified with **C**
3: 13 **C** redeemed us from the curse
6: 14 in the cross of our Lord Jesus **C**,
Eph 1: 3 and Father of our Lord Jesus **C**,
3: 8 Gentiles the boundless riches of **C**,
4: 13 whole measure of the fullness of **C**.
5: 2 just as **C** loved us and gave himself
5: 23 head of the wife as **C** is the head
5: 25 just as **C** loved the church and gave
Php 1: 21 to live is **C** and to die is gain.
1: 27 manner worthy of the gospel of **C**.
4: 19 to the riches of his glory in **C** Jesus.
Col 1: 27 which is **C** in you, the hope
1: 28 present everyone mature in **C**.
2: 6 as you received **C** Jesus as Lord,
2: 17 the reality, however, is found in **C**.
3: 15 Let the peace of **C** rule in your
2Th 2: 1 the coming of our Lord Jesus **C**
1Ti 1: 15 **C** Jesus came into the world to save
2: 5 and mankind, the man **C** Jesus,
2Ti 2: 3 like a good soldier of **C** Jesus.
3: 15 salvation through faith in **C** Jesus.
Titus 2: 13 our great God and Savior, Jesus **C**,
Heb 3: 14 We have come to share in **C**,
9: 14 will the blood of **C**, who through
9: 15 For this reason **C** is the mediator
9: 28 so **C** was sacrificed once to take
10: 10 of the body of Jesus **C** once for all.
13: 8 Jesus **C** is the same yesterday
1Pe 1: 19 but with the precious blood of **C**,
2: 21 called, because **C** suffered for you,
3: 18 For **C** also suffered once for sins,

4: 14 insulted because of the name of **C**,
1Jn 2: 22 whoever denies that Jesus is the **C**.
3: 16 Jesus **C** laid down his life for us.
5: 1 who believes that Jesus is the **C**
Rev 20: 4 reigned with **C** a thousand years.

CHRISTIAN (CHRIST)
1Pe 4: 16 if you suffer as a **C**, do not be

CHRIST'S (CHRIST)
2Co 5: 14 For **C** love compels us, because we
5: 20 We are therefore **C** ambassadors,
12: 9 so that **C** power may rest on me.

CHURCH
Mt 16: 18 and on this rock I will build my **c**,
18: 17 if they refuse to listen even to the **c**,
Ac 20: 28 Be shepherds of the **c** of God,
1Co 5: 12 mine to judge those outside the **c**?
14: 4 one who prophesies edifies the **c**.
14: 12 excel in those that build up the **c**.
14: 26 done so that the **c** may be built up.
Eph 5: 23 wife as Christ is the head of the **c**,
Col 1: 24 the sake of his body, which is the **c**.

CIRCUMCISED
Ge 17: 10 Every male among you shall be **c**.
Gal 2: 8 in Peter as an apostle to the **c**,

CIRCUMSTANCES
Php 4: 11 to be content whatever the **c**.
1Th 5: 18 give thanks in all **c**; for this is God's

CITIZENS (CITIZENSHIP)
Eph 2: 19 but fellow **c** with God's people

CITIZENSHIP (CITIZENS)
Php 3: 20 But our **c** is in heaven.

CITY
Heb 13: 14 here we do not have an enduring **c**,

CIVILIAN
2Ti 2: 4 a soldier gets entangled in **c** affairs,

CLAIM (CLAIMS)
Pr 25: 6 do not **c** a place among his great
1Jn 1: 6 If we **c** to have fellowship with him
1: 8 If we **c** to be without sin,
1: 10 If we **c** we have not sinned,

CLAIMS (CLAIM)
Jas 2: 14 if someone **c** to have faith but has
1Jn 2: 6 Whoever **c** to live in him must live
2: 9 Anyone who **c** to be in the light

CLAP
Ps 47: 1 **C** your hands, all you nations;
Isa 55: 12 trees of the field will **c** their hands.

CLAY
Isa 45: 9 Does the **c** say to the potter,
64: 8 We are the **c**, you are the potter,
Jer 18: 6 "Like **c** in the hand of the potter,
La 4: 2 are now considered as pots of **c**,
Da 2: 33 of iron and partly of baked **c**.
Ro 9: 21 the same lump of **c** some pottery
2Co 4: 7 this treasure in jars of **c** to show
2Ti 2: 20 and silver, but also of wood and **c**;

CLEAN
Lev 16: 30 you will be **c** from all your sins.
Ps 24: 4 one who has **c** hands and a pure
Mt 12: 44 swept **c** and put in order.
23: 25 You **c** the outside of the cup
Mk 7: 19 this, Jesus declared all foods **c**.)
Jn 13: 10 you are **c**, though not every one
15: 3 You are already **c** because
Ac 10: 15 impure that God has made **c**."
Ro 14: 20 All food is **c**, but it is wrong

CLING
Ps 63: 8 I **c** to you; your right hand upholds
Ro 12: 9 Hate what is evil; **c** to what is good.

CLOAK
2Ki 4: 29 "Tuck your **c** into your belt,

CLOSE (CLOSER)
Ps 34: 18 The LORD is **c**
Isa 40: 11 and carries them **c** to his heart;
Jer 30: 21 near and he will come **c** to me—

CLOSER (CLOSE)
Ex 3: 5 "Do not come any **c**," God said.
Pr 18: 24 friend who sticks **c** than a brother.

CLOTHE (CLOTHED CLOTHES CLOTHING)
Ps 45: 3 **c** yourself with splendor
Isa 52: 1 Zion, **c** yourself with strength!
Ro 13: 14 **c** yourselves with the Lord Jesus
Col 3: 12 **c** yourselves with compassion,
1Pe 5: 5 **c** yourselves with humility toward

CLOTHED (CLOTHE)
Ps 30: 11 my sackcloth and **c** me with joy,
Pr 31: 25 She is **c** with strength and dignity;
Lk 24: 49 the city until you have been **c**

CLOTHES (CLOTHE)
Mt 6: 25 food, and the body more than **c**?
6: 28 "And why do you worry about **c**?
Jn 11: 44 "Take off the grave **c** and let him

CLOTHING (CLOTHE)
Dt 22: 5 nor a man wear women's **c**,
Mt 7: 15 They come to you in sheep's **c**,

CLOUD (CLOUDS)
Ex 13: 21 them in a pillar of **c** to guide them
Isa 19: 1 the LORD rides on a swift **c** and is
Lk 21: 27 of Man coming in a **c** with power
Heb 12: 1 by such a great **c** of witnesses,

CLOUDS (CLOUD)
Ps 104: 3 He makes the **c** his chariot and
Da 7: 13 man, coming with the **c** of heaven.
Mk 13: 26 Man coming in **c** with great power
1Th 4: 17 them in the **c** to meet the Lord

CO-HEIRS (INHERIT)
Ro 8: 17 heirs of God and **c** with Christ,

COALS
Pr 25: 22 will heap burning **c** on his head,
Ro 12: 20 this, you will heap burning **c** on his

COAT
Lk 6: 29 If someone takes your **c**, do not

COLD
Pr 25: 25 Like **c** water to a weary soul is
Mt 10: 42 anyone gives even a cup of **c** water
24: 12 the love of most will grow **c**,

COMFORT (COMFORTED COMFORTS)
Ps 23: 4 your rod and your staff, they **c** me.
119: 52 ancient laws, and I find **c** in them.
119: 76 May your unfailing love be my **c**,
Zec 1: 17 the LORD will again **c** Zion
1Co 14: 3 strengthening, encouraging and **c**.
2Co 1: 4 that we can **c** those in any trouble
2: 7 you ought to forgive and **c** him,

COMFORTED (COMFORT)
Mt 5: 4 who mourn, for they will be **c**.

COMFORTS (COMFORT)
Job 29: 25 I was like one who **c** mourners.
Isa 49: 13 For the LORD **c** his people
51: 12 "I, even I, am he who **c** you.

COMMAND (COMMANDED COMMANDING COMMANDMENT COMMANDMENTS COMMANDS)
Ex 7: 2 You are to say everything I **c** you,
Nu 24: 13 to go beyond the **c** of the LORD—
Dt 4: 2 Do not add to what I **c** you and do
30: 16 For I **c** you today to love
32: 46 so that you may **c** your children
Ps 91: 11 he will **c** his angels concerning you
148: 5 for at his **c** they were created,
Pr 6: 23 For this **c** is a lamp, this teaching is
13: 13 whoever respects a **c** is rewarded.
Ecc 8: 2 Obey the king's **c**, I say,
Joel 2: 11 mighty is the army that obeys his **c**.
Jn 13: 34 "A new **c** I give you:
15: 12 My **c** is this: Love each other as I
1Co 14: 37 I am writing to you is the Lord's **c**.
Gal 5: 14 is fulfilled in keeping this one **c**:
1Ti 1: 5 The goal of this **c** is love,
Heb 11: 3 the universe was formed at God's **c**,
1Jn 3: 23 And this is his **c**: to believe
2Jn : 6 his **c** is that you walk in love.

COMMANDED (COMMAND)
Ps 33: 9 came to be; he **c**, and it stood firm.
Mt 28: 20 to obey everything I have **c** you.
1Co 9: 14 way, the Lord has **c** that those who
1Jn 3: 23 and to love one another as he **c** us.

COMMANDING (COMMAND)
2Ti 2: 4 rather tries to please his **c** officer.

COMMANDMENT (COMMAND)
Jos 22: 5 be very careful to keep the **c**
Mt 22: 38 This is the first and greatest **c**.
Ro 7: 12 and the **c** is holy,
Eph 6: 2 is the first **c** with a promise—

COMMANDMENTS (COMMAND)
Ex 20: 6 those who love me and keep my **c**.
34: 28 words of the covenant—the Ten **C**.
Dt 7: 9 those who love him and keep his **c**.
Ecc 12: 13 Fear God and keep his **c**, for this is
Da 9: 4 those who love him and keep his **c**,
Mt 22: 40 the Prophets hang on these two **c**."

COMMANDS (COMMAND)
Dt 11: 27 you obey the **c** of the LORD your
Ps 112: 1 who find great delight in his **c**.
119: 47 in your **c** because I love them.
119: 86 All your **c** are trustworthy;
119: 98 Your **c** are always with me
119:127 I love your **c** more than gold,
119:143 me, but your **c** give me delight.
119:172 word, for all your **c** are righteous.
Pr 3: 1 but keep my **c** in your heart,
10: 8 The wise in heart accept **c**,
Mt 5: 19 teaches these **c** will be called great
Jn 14: 15 "If you love me, keep my **c**.
14: 21 Whoever has my **c** and keeps them
Ac 17: 30 now he **c** all people everywhere
1Co 7: 19 Keeping God's **c** is what counts.
1Jn 5: 3 this is love for God: to keep his **c**. And
his **c** are not burdensome,

COMMEND (COMMENDED COMMENDS)
Ecc 8: 15 So I **c** the enjoyment of life,
1Pe 2: 14 wrong and to **c** those who do right.

COMMENDED (COMMEND)
Ro 13: 3 do what is right and you will be **c**.
Heb 11: 39 These were all **c** for their faith,

COMMENDED (COMMEND)
Isa 66: 13 As a mother **c** her child, so will I
2Co 1: 4 who **c** us in all our troubles,
7: 6 But God, who **c** the downcast,

COMMENDS (COMMEND)
2Co 10: 18 but the one whom the Lord **c**.

COMMIT (COMMITS COMMITTED)
Ex 20: 14 "You shall not **c** adultery.
Ps 37: 5 **C** your way to the LORD;
Mt   5: 27 was said, 'You shall not **c** adultery.'
Lk 23: 46 into your hands I **c** my spirit."
Ac 20: 32 "Now I **c** you to God
1Co 10: 8 We should not **c** sexual immorality,
1Pe 4: 19 to God's will should **c** themselves

COMMITS (COMMIT)
Pr   6: 32 a man who **c** adultery has no sense;
    29: 22 hot-tempered person **c** many sins.
Mt 19: 9 marries another woman **c** adultery."

COMMITTED (COMMIT)
Nu   5: 7 must confess the sin they have **c**.
1Ki 8: 61 may your hearts be fully **c**
2Ch 16: 9 those whose hearts are fully **c**
Mt   5: 28 lustfully has already **c** adultery
2Co 5: 19 And he has **c** to us the message
1Pe 2: 22 "He **c** no sin, and no deceit was

COMMON
Pr 22: 2 Rich and poor have this in **c**:
1Co 10: 13 has overtaken you except what is **c**
2Co 6: 14 and wickedness have in **c**?

COMPANION
Pr 13: 20 for a **c** of fools suffers harm.
    28: 7 a **c** of gluttons disgraces his father.
    29: 3 but a **c** of prostitutes squanders his

COMPANY
Pr 24: 1 the wicked, do not desire their **c**;
Jer 15: 17 I never sat in the **c** of revelers,
1Co 15: 33 "Bad **c** corrupts good character."

COMPARED (COMPARING)
Eze 31: 2 "'Who can be **c** with you

COMPARING (COMPARED)
Ro   8: 18 present sufferings are not worth **c**
2Co 8: 8 of your love by **c** it
Gal 6: 4 without **c** themselves to someone

COMPASSION (COMPASSIONATE COMPASSIONS)
Ex 33: 19 I will have **c** on whom I will have **c**.
Ne   9: 19 your great **c** you did not abandon
     9: 28 in your **c** you delivered them time
Ps 51: 1 to your great **c** blot out my
   103: 4 pit and crowns you with love and **c**,
   103: 13 As a father has **c** on his children,
   145: 9 he has **c** on all he has made.
Isa 49: 13 will have **c** on his afflicted ones.
    49: 15 and have no **c** on the child she has
Hos 2: 19 and justice, in love and **c**.
    11: 8 all my **c** is aroused.
Jnh 3: 9 with **c** turn from his fierce anger so
Mt   9: 36 saw the crowds, he had **c** on them,
Mk   8: 2 "I have **c** for these people;
Ro   9: 15 I will have **c** on whom I have **c**."
Col 3: 12 clothe yourselves with **c**, kindness,
Jas 5: 11 The Lord is full of **c** and mercy.

COMPASSIONATE (COMPASSION)
Ne   9: 17 gracious and **c**, slow to anger
Ps 103: 8 The LORD is **c** and gracious,
   112: 4 for those who are gracious and **c**
Eph 4: 32 Be kind and **c** to one another,
1Pe 3: 8 love one another, be **c** and humble.

COMPASSIONS (COMPASSION)
La   3: 22 not consumed, for his **c** never fail.

COMPEL (COMPELLED COMPELS)
Lk 14: 23 lanes and **c** them to come in,

COMPELLED (COMPEL)
Ac 20: 22 "And now, **c** by the Spirit, I am
1Co 9: 16 boast, since I am **c** to preach.

COMPELS (COMPEL)
2Co 5: 14 For Christ's love **c** us, because we

COMPETENCE (COMPETENT)
2Co 3: 5 but our **c** comes from God.

COMPETENT (COMPETENCE)
Ro 15: 14 and **c** to instruct one another.
1Co 6: 2 are you not **c** to judge trivial cases?
2Co 3: 5 Not that we are **c** in ourselves
     3: 6 He has made us **c** as ministers

COMPETES
1Co 9: 25 Everyone who **c** in the games goes
2Ti 2: 5 anyone who **c** as an athlete does

COMPLACENT
Am   6: 1 Woe to you who are **c** in Zion,

COMPLETE
Jn 15: 11 in you and that your joy may be **c**.
    16: 24 will receive, and your joy will be **c**.
    17: 23 they may be brought to **c** unity.
Ac 20: 24 **c** the task the Lord Jesus has given
Php 2: 2 then make my joy **c** by being
Col 4: 17 it that you **c** the ministry you have
Jas 1: 4 so that you may be mature and **c**,
     2: 22 faith was made **c** by what he did.

CONCEAL (CONCEALED CONCEALS)
Ps 40: 10 I do not **c** your love and your
Pr 25: 2 It is the glory of God to **c** a matter;

CONCEALED (CONCEAL)
Jer 16: 17 me, nor is their sin **c** from my eyes.
Mt 10: 26 for there is nothing **c** that will not
Mk   4: 22 whatever is **c** is meant to be

CONCEALS (CONCEAL)
Pr 28: 13 Whoever **c** their sins does not

CONCEITED
Gal 5: 26 Let us not become **c**,
1Ti 6: 4 they are **c** and understand nothing.

CONCEIVE (CONCEIVED)
Isa 7: 14 The virgin will **c** and give birth
Mt   1: 23 "The virgin will **c** and give birth

CONCEIVED (CONCEIVE)
Mt   1: 20 because what is **c** in her is
1Co 2: 9 and what no human mind has **c**"—

CONCERN (CONCERNED)
Eze 36: 21 I had **c** for my holy name,
1Co 7: 32 I would like you to be free from **c**.
    12: 25 that its parts should have equal **c**
2Co 11: 28 of my **c** for all the churches.

CONCERNED (CONCERN)
Jnh 4: 10 "You have been **c** about this plant,
1Co 7: 32 An unmarried man is **c**

CONDEMN (CONDEMNATION CONDEMNED CONDEMNING CONDEMNS)
Job 40: 8 you **c** me to justify yourself?
Isa 50: 9 Who will **c** me? They will all wear
Lk   6: 37 Do not **c**, and you will not be
Jn   3: 17 Son into the world to **c** the world,
    12: 48 words I have spoken will **c** them
Ro   2: 27 yet obeys the law will **c** you who,
1Jn 3: 20 If our hearts **c** us, we know that

CONDEMNATION (CONDEMN)
Ro   5: 18   just as one trespass resulted in **c**
      8: 1   there is now no **c** for those who are
2Co   3: 9   that brought **c** was glorious,

CONDEMNED (CONDEMN)
Ps   34: 22   who takes refuge in him will be **c**.
Mt   12: 37   and by your words you will be **c**."
      23: 33   How will you escape being **c**
Jn   3: 18   Whoever believes in him is not **c**,
      16: 11   prince of this world now stands **c**.
Ro   14: 23   whoever has doubts is **c** if they eat,
1Co   11: 32   that we will not be finally **c**
Heb   11: 7   By his faith he **c** the world

CONDEMNING (CONDEMN)
Pr   17: 15   the guilty and **c** the innocent—
Ro   2: 1   you are **c** yourself, because you

CONDEMNS (CONDEMN)
Pr   14: 34   exalts a nation, but sin **c** any people
Ro   8: 34   Who then is the one who **c**?

CONDUCT
Pr   20: 11   is their **c** really pure and upright?
      21: 8   but the **c** of the innocent is upright.
Ecc   6: 8   how to **c** themselves before others?
Jer   4: 18   "Your own **c** and actions have
      17: 10   each person according to their **c**,
Eze   7: 3   I will judge you according to your **c**
1Ti   3: 15   how people ought to **c** themselves

CONFESS (CONFESSION)
Lev   16: 21   and **c** over it all the wickedness
      26: 40   if they will **c** their sins and the sins
Nu   5: 7   **c** the sin they have committed.
Ps   38: 18   I **c** my iniquity; I am troubled by
Jas   5: 16   Therefore **c** your sins to each other
1Jn   1: 9   If we **c** our sins, he is faithful

CONFESSION (CONFESS)
2Co   9: 13   accompanies your **c** of the gospel

CONFIDENCE
Ps   71: 5   Lord, my **c** since my youth.
Pr   11: 13   A gossip betrays a **c**,
      25: 9   to court, do not betray another's **c**,
      31: 11   Her husband has full **c** in her
Isa   32: 17   will be quietness and **c** forever.
Jer   17: 7   in the Lord, whose **c** is in him.
Php   3: 3   and who put no **c** in the flesh—
Heb   4: 16   God's throne of grace with **c**,
      10: 19   since we have **c** to enter the Most
      10: 35   So do not throw away your **c**;
      11: 1   Now faith is **c** in what we hope
      13: 17   Have **c** in your leaders and submit
1Jn   5: 14   This is the **c** we have

CONFIRM
2Pe   1: 10   make every effort to **c** your calling

CONFLICT
Pr   6: 14   his heart—he always stirs up **c**.
      6: 19   a person who stirs up **c**
      10: 12   Hatred stirs up **c**, but love covers
      15: 18   A hot-tempered person stirs up **c**,
      16: 28   A perverse person stirs up **c**,
      28: 25   The greedy stir up **c**,
      29: 22   An angry person stirs up **c**,

CONFORM (CONFORMED)
Ro   12: 2   not **c** to the pattern of this world,
1Pe   1: 14   do not **c** to the evil desires you had

CONFORMED (CONFORM)
Ro   8: 29   predestined to be **c** to the image

CONQUERORS
Ro   8: 37   are more than **c** through him who

CONSCIENCE (CONSCIENCES)
Ro   13: 5   but also as a matter of **c**.
1Co   8: 7   a god, and since their **c** is weak,
      8: 12   this way and wound their weak **c**,
      10: 25   without raising questions of **c**,
      10: 29   being judged by another's **c**?
Heb   10: 22   to cleanse us from a guilty **c**
1Pe   3: 16   keeping a clear **c**, so that those who

CONSCIENCES (CONSCIENCE)
Ro   2: 15   hearts, their **c** also bearing witness,
1Ti   4: 2   whose **c** have been seared as
Titus   1: 15   their minds and **c** are corrupted.
Heb   9: 14   cleanse our **c** from acts that lead

CONSCIOUS
Ro   3: 20   through the law we become **c** of
1Pe   2: 19   unjust suffering because they are **c**

CONSECRATE (CONSECRATED)
Ex   13: 2   "**C** to me every firstborn male.
Lev   20: 7   "'**C** yourselves and be holy,

CONSECRATED (CONSECRATE)
Ex   29: 43   and the place will be **c** by my glory.
1Ti   4: 5   because it is **c** by the word of God

CONSIDER (CONSIDERATE CONSIDERED CONSIDERS)
1Sa   12: 24   **c** what great things he has done
Job   37: 14   stop and **c** God's wonders.
Ps   8: 3   When I **c** your heavens, the work
      143: 5   and **c** what your hands have done.
Lk   12: 24   **C** the ravens: They do not sow
      12: 27   "**C** how the wild flowers grow.
Php   3: 8   I **c** everything a loss because
Heb   10: 24   And let us **c** how we may spur one
Jas   1: 2   **C** it pure joy, my brothers
      1: 26   Those who **c** themselves religious

CONSIDERATE (CONSIDER)
Titus   3: 2   to be peaceable and **c**, and always
Jas   3: 17   then peace-loving, **c**, submissive,
1Pe   2: 18   only to those who are good and **c**,
      3: 7   the same way be **c** as you live

CONSIDERED (CONSIDER)
Job   1: 8   "Have you **c** my servant Job?
      2: 3   "Have you **c** my servant Job?
Ps   44: 22   we are **c** as sheep to be slaughtered.
Isa   53: 4   yet we **c** him punished by God,
Ro   8: 36   all day long; we are **c** as sheep to be

CONSIDERS (CONSIDER)
Pr   31: 16   She **c** a field and buys it; out of her
Ro   14: 5   One person **c** one day more sacred

CONSIST
Lk   12: 15   life does not **c** in an abundance

CONSOLATION
Ps   94: 19   within me, your **c** brought me joy.

CONSTRUCTIVE
1Co   10: 23   but not everything is **c**.

CONSUME (CONSUMING)
Jn   2: 17   "Zeal for your house will **c** me."

CONSUMING (CONSUME)
Dt   4: 24   For the Lord your God is a **c** fire,
Heb   12: 29   for our "God is a **c** fire."

CONTAIN
1Ki   8: 27   the highest heaven, cannot **c** you.
2Pe   3: 16   His letters **c** some things that are

CONTAMINATES
2Co 7: 1 from everything that **c** body

CONTEMPLATE
2Co 3: 18 unveiled faces **c** the Lord's glory,

CONTEMPT
Pr 14: 31 oppresses the poor shows **c** for
    17: 5 Whoever mocks the poor shows **c**
    18: 3 so does **c**, and with shame comes
Da 12: 2 others to shame and everlasting **c**.
Ro 2: 4 do you show **c** for the riches of his
Gal 4: 14 did not treat me with **c** or scorn.
1Th 5: 20 Do not treat prophecies with **c**

CONTEND
Jude : 3 urge you to **c** for the faith that was

CONTENT (CONTENTMENT)
Pr 13: 25 The righteous eat to their hearts' **c**,
Php 4: 11 to be **c** whatever the circumstances.
    4: 12 learned the secret of being **c** in any
1Ti 6: 8 clothing, we will be **c** with that.
Heb 13: 5 and be **c** with what you have,

CONTENTMENT (CONTENT)
1Ti 6: 6 But godliness with **c** is great gain.

CONTINUAL (CONTINUE)
Pr 15: 15 but the cheerful heart has a **c** feast.

CONTINUE (CONTINUAL)
Php 2: 12 **c** to work out your salvation
2Ti 3: 14 **c** in what you have learned and
1Jn 5: 18 born of God does not **c** to sin;
Rev 22: 11 let the one who does right **c** to do
    22: 11 let the holy person **c** to be holy."

CONTRITE
Ps 51: 17 a broken and **c** heart you, God,
Isa 57: 15 and to revive the heart of the **c**.
    66: 2 who are humble and **c** in spirit,

CONTROL (CONTROLLED SELF-CONTROL SELF-CONTROLLED)
1Co 7: 9 But if they cannot **c** themselves,
    7: 37 but has **c** over his own will,
1Th 4: 4 should learn to **c** your own body

CONTROLLED (CONTROL)
Ps 32: 9 understanding but must be **c** by bit

CONTROVERSIES
Titus 3: 9 But avoid foolish **c** and genealogies

CONVERSATION
Col 4: 6 Let your **c** be always full of grace,

CONVERT
1Ti 3: 6 He must not be a recent **c**, or he

CONVICTION
Heb 3: 14 we hold our original **c** firmly

CONVINCED (CONVINCING)
Ro 8: 38 I am **c** that neither death nor life,
2Ti 1: 12 am **c** that he is able to guard what I
    3: 14 have learned and have become **c** of,

CONVINCING (CONVINCED)
Ac 1: 3 and gave many **c** proofs that he was

CORNELIUS
Roman to whom Peter preached; first Gentile Christian (Ac 10).

CORNERSTONE (STONE)
Ps 118: 22 builders rejected has become the **c**;
Isa 28: 16 a precious **c** for a sure foundation;
Eph 2: 20 Christ Jesus himself as the chief **c**.
1Pe 2: 6 a chosen and precious **c**,
    2: 7 rejected has become the **c**,"

CORRECT (CORRECTING CORRECTION CORRECTS)
2Ti 4: 2 **c**, rebuke and encourage—

CORRECTING (CORRECT)
2Ti 3: 16 **c** and training in righteousness,

CORRECTION (CORRECT)
Pr 10: 17 but whoever ignores **c** leads others
    12: 1 but whoever hates **c** is stupid.
    15: 5 whoever heeds **c** shows prudence.
    15: 10 the one who hates **c** will die.

CORRECTS (CORRECT)
Job 5: 17 "Blessed is the one whom God **c**;
Pr 9: 7 Whoever **c** a mocker invites insults

CORRUPT (CORRUPTS)
Ge 6: 11 Now the earth was **c** in God's sight

CORRUPTS (CORRUPT)
Ecc 7: 7 into a fool, and a bribe **c** the heart.
1Co 15: 33 "Bad company **c** good character."
Jas 3: 6 It **c** the whole body, sets the whole

COST
Pr 4: 7 Though it **c** all you have,
Isa 55: 1 milk without money and without **c**.
Rev 21: 6 thirsty I will give water without **c**

COUNSEL (COUNSELOR)
1Ki 22: 5 "First seek the **c** of the LORD."
Pr 15: 22 Plans fail for lack of **c**,
Rev 3: 18 I **c** you to buy from me gold

COUNSELOR (COUNSEL)
Isa 9: 6 And he will be called Wonderful **C**,

COUNT (COUNTING COUNTS)
Ro 4: 8 Lord will never **c** against them."
    6: 11 **c** yourselves dead to sin but alive

COUNTING (COUNT)
2Co 5: 19 not **c** people's sins against them.

COUNTRY
Jn 4: 44 prophet has no honor in his own **c**.

COUNTS (COUNT)
Jn 6: 63 the flesh **c** for nothing.
1Co 7: 19 God's commands is what **c**.
Gal 5: 6 **c** is faith expressing itself through

COURAGE (COURAGEOUS)
Ac 23: 11 stood near Paul and said, "Take **c**!

COURAGEOUS (COURAGE)
Dt 31: 6 Be strong and **c**. Do not be afraid
Jos 1: 6 Be strong and **c**, because you will
1Co 16: 13 firm in the faith; be **c**; be strong.

COURSE
Ps 19: 5 a champion rejoicing to run his **c**.
Pr 15: 21 understanding keeps a straight **c**.

COURTS
Ps 84: 10 your **c** than a thousand elsewhere;
    100: 4 thanksgiving and his **c** with praise;

COVENANT (COVENANTS)
Ge 9: 9 "I now establish my **c** with you
Ex 19: 5 if you obey me fully and keep my **c**,
1Ch 16: 15 He remembers his **c** forever,
Job 31: 1 "I made a **c** with my eyes not
Jer 31: 31 I will make a new **c** with the people
1Co 11: 25 "This cup is the new **c** in my blood;
Gal 4: 24 One **c** is from Mount Sinai
Heb 9: 15 Christ is the mediator of a new **c**,

COVENANTS (COVENANT)
Ro 9: 4 the **c**, the receiving of the law,
Gal 4: 24 The women represent two **c**.

COVER (COVER-UP COVERED COVERS)
Ps 91: 4 He will **c** you with his feathers,
Jas 5: 20 and **c** over a multitude of sins.

COVERED (COVER)
Ps 32: 1 are forgiven, whose sins are **c**.
Isa 6: 2 With two wings they **c** their faces,
Ro 4: 7 are forgiven, whose sins are **c**.
1Co 11: 4 with his head **c** dishonors his head.

COVERS (COVER)
Pr 10: 12 conflict, but love **c** over all wrongs.
1Pe 4: 8 because love **c** over a multitude

COVER-UP (COVER)
1Pe 2: 16 do not use your freedom as a **c**

COVET
Ex 20: 17 "You shall not **c** your neighbor's
Ro 13: 9 "You shall not **c**," and whatever

COWARDLY
Rev 21: 8 But the **c**, the unbelieving, the vile,

CRAFTINESS (CRAFTY)
1Co 3: 19 "He catches the wise in their **c**";

CRAFTY (CRAFTINESS)
Ge 3: 1 the serpent was more **c** than any
2Co 12: 16 Yet, **c** fellow that I am, I caught you

CRAVE
Pr 23: 3 Do not **c** his delicacies, for that
1Pe 2: 2 babies, **c** pure spiritual milk,

CREATE (CREATED CREATION CREATOR)
Ps 51: 10 **C** in me a pure heart, O God,
Isa 45: 18 he did not **c** it to be empty,

CREATED (CREATE)
Ge 1: 1 In the beginning God **c** the heavens
1: 21 So God **c** the great creatures
1: 27 So God **c** mankind in his own
1: 27 male and female he **c** them.
Ps 148: 5 for at his command they were **c**,
Ro 1: 25 and served **c** things rather than
1Co 11: 9 neither was man **c** for woman,
Col 1: 16 For in him all things were **c**:
1Ti 4: 4 For everything God **c** is good,
Rev 10: 6 who **c** the heavens and all that is

CREATION (CREATE)
Mk 16: 15 *preach the gospel to all* **c**.
Jn 17: 24 because you loved me before the **c**
Ro 8: 19 For the **c** waits in eager expectation
8: 39 nor anything else in all **c**, will be
2Co 5: 17 is in Christ, the new **c** has come:
Col 1: 15 God, the firstborn over all **c**.
1Pe 1: 20 He was chosen before the **c**
Rev 13: 8 was slain from the **c** of the world.

CREATOR (CREATE)
Ge 14: 22 Most High, **C** of heaven and earth,
Isa 42: 5 LORD says—the **C** of the heavens,
Ro 1: 25 created things rather than the **C**—

CREATURE (CREATURES)
Lev 17: 11 For the life of a **c** is in the blood,

CREATURES (CREATURE)
Ge 6: 19 into the ark two of all living **c**,
Ps 104: 24 the earth is full of your **c**.

CREDIT (CREDITED)
Ro 4: 24 whom God will **c** righteousness—
1Pe 2: 20 it to your **c** if you receive a beating

CREDITED (CREDIT)
Ge 15: 6 and he **c** it to him as righteousness.
Ro 4: 5 their faith is **c** as righteousness.

Gal 3: 6 it was **c** to him as righteousness."
Jas 2: 23 it was **c** to him as righteousness,"

CRIED (CRY)
Ps 18: 6 I **c** to my God for help.

CRIMSON
Isa 1: 18 though they are red as **c**, they shall

CRIPPLED
Mk 9: 45 to enter life **c** than to have two feet

CRITICISM
2Co 8: 20 want to avoid any **c** of the way we

CROOKED
Pr 10: 9 whoever takes **c** paths will be
Php 2: 15 fault in a warped and **c** generation."

CROSS
Mt 10: 38 Whoever does not take up their **c**
Lk 9: 23 take up their **c** daily and follow me.
Ac 2: 23 to death by nailing him to the **c**.
1Co 1: 17 lest the **c** of Christ be emptied of
Gal 6: 14 in the **c** of our Lord Jesus Christ,
Php 2: 8 even death on a **c**!
Col 1: 20 through his blood, shed on the **c**.
2: 14 taken it away, nailing it to the **c**.
2: 15 triumphing over them by the **c**.
Heb 12: 2 joy set before him he endured the **c**,

CROWD
Ex 23: 2 pervert justice by siding with the **c**,

CROWN (CROWNED CROWNS)
Pr 4: 9 and present you with a glorious **c**."
10: 6 Blessings **c** the head
12: 4 noble character is her husband's **c**,
17: 6 Children's children are a **c**
Isa 61: 3 on them a **c** of beauty instead
Zec 9: 16 in his land like jewels in a **c**.
Mt 27: 29 then twisted together a **c** of thorns
1Co 9: 25 to get a **c** that will last forever.
2Ti 4: 8 store for me the **c** of righteousness,
Rev 2: 10 will give you life as your victor's **c**.

CROWNED (CROWN)
Ps 8: 5 the angels and **c** them with glory
Pr 14: 18 the prudent are **c** with knowledge.
Heb 2: 7 you **c** them with glory and honor

CROWNS (CROWN)
Rev 4: 10 They lay their **c** before the throne
19: 12 fire, and on his head are many **c**.

CRUCIFIED (CRUCIFY)
Mt 20: 19 to be mocked and flogged and **c**.
27: 38 Two rebels were **c** with him,
Lk 24: 7 be **c** and on the third day be raised
Jn 19: 18 they **c** him, and with him two
Ac 2: 36 Jesus, whom you **c**, both Lord
Ro 6: 6 that our old self was **c** with him so
1Co 1: 23 but we preach Christ **c**:
2: 2 you except Jesus Christ and him **c**.
Gal 2: 20 I have been **c** with Christ and I no
5: 24 Christ Jesus have **c** the flesh with

CRUCIFY (CRUCIFIED CRUCIFYING)
Mt 27: 22 They all answered, "**C** him!"
27: 31 Then they led him away to **c** him.

CRUCIFYING (CRUCIFY)
Heb 6: 6 their loss they are **c** the Son of God

CRUSH (CRUSHED)
Ge 3: 15 he will **c** your head, and you will
Isa 53: 10 it was the LORD's will to **c** him
Ro 16: 20 peace will soon **c** Satan under your

CRUSHED (CRUSH)
Ps 34: 18 and saves those who are **c** in spirit.

Isa 53: 5 he was **c** for our iniquities;
2Co 4: 8 pressed on every side, but not **c**;

CRY (CRIED)

Ps 34: 15 and his ears are attentive to their **c**;
40: 1 he turned to me and heard my **c**.
130: 1 Out of the depths I **c** to you,

CULMINATION

Ro 10: 4 Christ is the **c** of the law so

CUP

Ps 23: 5 my head with oil; my **c** overflows.
Mt 10: 42 anyone gives even a **c** of cold water
23: 25 You clean the outside of the **c**
26: 39 may this **c** be taken from me.
1Co 11: 25 "This **c** is the new covenant in my

CURSE (CURSED)

Dt 11: 26 you today a blessing and a **c**—
21: 23 is hung on a pole is under God's **c**.
Lk 6: 28 bless those who **c** you,
Gal 1: 8 to you, let them be under God's **c**!
3: 13 redeemed us from the **c** of the law by becoming a **c** for us,
Rev 22: 3 No longer will there be any **c**.

CURSED (CURSE)

Ge 3: 17 "**C** is the ground because of you;
Dt 27: 15 "**C** is anyone who makes an idol—
27: 16 "**C** is anyone who dishonors their
27: 17 "**C** is anyone who moves their
27: 18 "**C** is anyone who leads the blind
27: 19 "**C** is anyone who withholds justice
27: 20 "**C** is anyone who sleeps with his
27: 21 "**C** is anyone who has sexual
27: 22 "**C** is anyone who sleeps with his
27: 23 "**C** is anyone who sleeps with his
27: 24 "**C** is anyone who kills their
27: 25 "**C** is anyone who accepts a bribe
27: 26 "**C** is anyone who does not uphold
Ro 9: 3 I could wish that I myself were **c**
Gal 3: 10 "**C** is everyone who does not

CURTAIN

Ex 26: 33 Hang the **c** from the clasps
26: 33 The **c** will separate the Holy Place
Lk 23: 45 the **c** of the temple was torn in two.
Heb 10: 20 way opened for us through the **c**,

CYMBAL

1Co 13: 1 a resounding gong or a clanging **c**.

DANCE (DANCING)

Ecc 3: 4 a time to mourn and a time to **d**,
Mt 11: 17 the pipe for you, and you did not **d**;

DANCING (DANCE)

Ps 30: 11 You turned my wailing into **d**;
149: 3 Let them praise his name with **d**

DANGER

Pr 27: 12 The prudent see **d** and take refuge,
Ro 8: 35 or nakedness or **d** or sword?

DANIEL

Hebrew exile to Babylon, name changed to Belteshazzar (Da 1:6–7). Refused to eat unclean food (Da 1:8–21). Interpreted Nebuchadnezzar's dreams (Da 2; 4), writing on the wall (Da 5). Thrown into lions' den (Da 6). Visions of (Da 7–12).

DARK (DARKEST DARKNESS)

Ro 2: 19 a light for those who are in the **d**,
2Pe 1: 19 it, as to a light shining in a **d** place,

DARKEST (DARK)

Ps 23: 4 though I walk through the **d** valley,

DARKNESS (DARK)

Ge 1: 4 he separated the light from the **d**.
2Sa 22: 29 the Lord turns my **d** into light.
Job 34: 22 utter **d**, where evildoers can hide.
Jn 3: 19 but people loved **d** instead of light
2Co 6: 14 fellowship can light have with **d**?
Eph 5: 8 For you were once **d**, but now you
1Pe 2: 9 out of **d** into his wonderful light.
1Jn 1: 5 in him there is no **d** at all.
2: 9 a brother or sister is still in the **d**.

DAUGHTERS

Joel 2: 28 Your sons and **d** will prophesy,

DAVID

Son of Jesse (Ru 4:17–22; 1Ch 2:13–15), ancestor of Jesus (Mt 1:1–17; Lk 3:31).

Anointed king by Samuel (1Sa 16:1–13). Musician to Saul (1Sa 16:14–23; 18:10). Killed Goliath (1Sa 17). Relation with Jonathan (1Sa 18:1–4; 19–20; 23:16–18; 2Sa 1). Disfavor of Saul (1Sa 18:6—23:29). Spared Saul's life (1Sa 24; 26). Among Philistines (1Sa 21:10–14; 27–30). Lament for Saul and Jonathan (2Sa 1).

Anointed king of Judah (2Sa 2:1–11); of Israel (2Sa 5:1–4; 1Ch 11:1–3). Promised eternal dynasty (2Sa 7; 1Ch 17; Ps 132). Adultery with Bathsheba (2Sa 11–12). Absalom's revolt (2Sa 14–18). Last words (2Sa 23:1–7). Death (1Ki 2:10–12; 1Ch 29:28).

DAWN

Ps 37: 6 righteous reward shine like the **d**,

DAY (DAYS)

Ge 1: 5 God called the light "**d**,"
Ex 20: 8 "Remember the Sabbath **d**
Lev 23: 28 because it is the **D** of Atonement,
Nu 14: 14 them in a pillar of cloud by **d**
Jos 1: 8 meditate on it **d** and night,
Ps 84: 10 Better is one **d** in your courts than
96: 2 proclaim his salvation **d** after **d**.
118: 24 The Lord has done it this very **d**;
Pr 27: 1 do not know what a **d** may bring.
Joel 2: 31 great and dreadful **d** of the Lord.
Ob : 15 "The **d** of the Lord is near for all
Lk 11: 3 Give us each **d** our daily bread.
Ac 17: 11 examined the Scriptures every **d**
2Co 4: 16 we are being renewed **d** by **d**.
1Th 5: 2 the **d** of the Lord will come like
2Pe 3: 8 With the Lord a **d** is like a thousand

DAYS (DAY)

Dt 17: 19 he is to read it all the **d** of his life so
Ps 23: 6 love will follow me all the **d** of my
90: 10 Our **d** may come to seventy years,
Ecc 12: 1 Creator in the **d** of your youth,
Joel 2: 29 I will pour out my Spirit in those **d**.
Mic 4: 1 In the last **d** the mountain
Heb 1: 2 in these last **d** he has spoken to us
2Pe 3: 3 that in the last **d** scoffers will come,

DEACONS

1Ti 3: 8 way, **d** are to be worthy of respect,

DEAD (DIE)

Dt 18: 11 or spiritist or who consults the **d**.
Mt 28: 7 'He has risen from the **d** and is
Ro 6: 11 count yourselves **d** to sin but alive
Eph 2: 1 you were **d** in your transgressions
1Th 4: 16 and the **d** in Christ will rise first.
Jas 2: 17 is not accompanied by action, is **d**.
2: 26 so faith without deeds is **d**.

DEATH (DIE)

Nu 35: 16 the murderer is to be put to **d**.
Ps 116: 15 of the Lord is the **d** of his faithful

Pr   8: 36 all who hate me love **d**."
     14: 12 right, but in the end it leads to **d**.
Ecc   7: 2 for **d** is the destiny of everyone;
Isa 25: 8 he will swallow up **d** forever.
     53: 12 he poured out his life unto **d**,
Jn   5: 24 but has crossed over from **d** to life.
Ro   5: 12 **d** through sin, and in this way **d**
      6: 23 For the wages of sin is **d**,
      8: 13 Spirit you put to **d** the misdeeds
1Co 15: 21 For since **d** came through a man,
     15: 31 I face **d** every day—yes, just as
     15: 55 "Where, O **d**, is your victory?
1Pe   3: 18 He was put to **d** in the body
Rev   1: 18 I hold the keys of **d** and Hades.
     20: 6 The second **d** has no power over
     20: 14 The lake of fire is the second **d**.
     21: 4 There will be no more **d**'

DEBAUCHERY
Ro   13: 13 not in sexual immorality and **d**,
Eph   5: 18 drunk on wine, which leads to **d**.

DEBORAH
Prophetess who led Israel to victory over Canaanites (Jdg 4–5).

DEBT (DEBTORS DEBTS)
Ro   13: 8 except the continuing **d** to love

DEBTORS (DEBT)
Mt   6: 12 as we also have forgiven our **d**.

DEBTS (DEBT)
Dt   15: 1 seven years you must cancel **d**.
Mt   6: 12 And forgive us our **d**, as we

DECAY
Ps   16: 10 will you let your faithful one see **d**.
Ac   2: 27 will not let your holy one see **d**.

DECEIT (DECEIVE)
Mk   7: 22 greed, malice, **d**, lewdness, envy,
1Pe   2: 1 yourselves of all malice and all **d**,
      2: 22 and no **d** was found in his mouth."

DECEITFUL (DECEIVE)
Jer 17: 9 The heart is **d** above all things
2Co 11: 13 are false apostles, **d** workers,

DECEITFULNESS (DECEIVE)
Mk   4: 19 the **d** of wealth and the desires
Heb   3: 13 of you may be hardened by sin's **d**.

DECEIVE (DECEIT DECEITFUL DECEITFULNESS DECEIVED DECEPTIVE)
Lev 19: 11 "'Do not **d** one another.
Pr   14: 5 An honest witness does not **d**,
Mt   24: 5 am the Messiah,' and will **d** many.
Ro   16: 18 flattery they **d** the minds of naive
1Co   3: 18 Do not **d** yourselves. If any of you
Gal   6: 3 they are not, they **d** themselves.
Eph   5: 6 no one **d** you with empty words,
Jas   1: 22 to the word, and so **d** yourselves.
Jas   1: 26 rein on their tongues **d** themselves,
1Jn   1: 8 we **d** ourselves and the truth is not

DECEIVED (DECEIVE)
Ge   3: 13 said, "The serpent **d** me, and I ate."
Gal   6: 7 Do not be **d**: God cannot be
1Ti   2: 14 And Adam was not the one **d**; it was the woman who was **d**
2Ti   3: 13 to worse, deceiving and being **d**.
Jas   1: 16 Don't be **d**, my dear brothers

DECENCY
1Ti   2: 9 modestly, with **d** and propriety,

DECEPTIVE (DECEIVE)
Pr   31: 30 Charm is **d**, and beauty is fleeting;
Col   2: 8 through hollow and **d** philosophy,

DECLARE (DECLARED DECLARING)
1Ch 16: 24 **D** his glory among the nations,
Ps   19: 1 The heavens **d** the glory of God;
     96: 3 **D** his glory among the nations,
Isa 42: 9 taken place, and new things I **d**;
Ro   10: 9 If you **d** with your mouth, "Jesus is

DECLARED (DECLARE)
Mk   7: 19 saying this, Jesus **d** all foods clean.)
Ro   2: 13 the law who will be **d** righteous.
      3: 20 no one will be **d** righteous

DECLARING (DECLARE)
Ps   71: 8 **d** your splendor all day long.
Ac   2: 11 hear them **d** the wonders of God

DECREED (DECREES)
La   3: 37 it happen if the Lord has not **d** it?
Lk   22: 22 Son of Man will go as it has been **d**.

DECREES (DECREED)
Lev 10: 11 Israelites all the **d** the LORD has
Ps 119:112 on keeping your **d** to the very end.

DEDICATE (DEDICATION)
Pr   20: 25 It is a trap to **d** something rashly

DEDICATION (DEDICATE)
1Ti   5: 11 sensual desires overcome their **d**

DEED (DEEDS)
Col   3: 17 whether in word or **d**, do it all

DEEDS (DEED)
1Sa   2: 3 knows, and by him **d** are weighed.
Ps   65: 5 us with awesome and righteous **d**,
     66: 3 to God, "How awesome are your **d**!
     78: 4 next generation the praiseworthy **d**
     86: 10 you are great and do marvelous **d**;
     92: 4 For you make me glad by your **d**,
    111: 3 Glorious and majestic are his **d**,
Hab   3: 2 I stand in awe of your **d**, LORD.
Mt   5: 16 that they may see your good **d**
     11: 19 wisdom is proved right by her **d**."
Ac   26: 20 their repentance by their **d**.
Jas   2: 14 claims to have faith but has no **d**?
      2: 20 that faith without **d** is useless?
1Pe   2: 12 they may see your good **d**

DEEP (DEPTH)
1Co   2: 10 things, even the **d** things of God.
1Ti   3: 9 must keep hold of the **d** truths

DEER
Ps   42: 1 As the **d** pants for streams of water,

DEFEND (DEFENSE)
Ps   74: 22 Rise up, O God, and **d** your cause;
Pr   31: 9 **d** the rights of the poor and needy.
Jer 50: 34 He will vigorously **d** their cause so

DEFENSE (DEFEND)
Ps   35: 23 Awake, and rise to my **d**!
Php   1: 16 put here for the **d** of the gospel.

DEFERRED
Pr   13: 12 Hope **d** makes the heart sick,

DEFILE (DEFILED)
Da   1: 8 Daniel resolved not to **d** himself

DEFILED (DEFILE)
Isa 24: 5 The earth is **d** by its people;

DEFRAUD
Lev 19: 13 "'Do not **d** or rob your neighbor.

DEITY
Col   2: 9 Christ all the fullness of the **D** lives

DELIGHT (DELIGHTS)
1Sa 15: 22 "Does the LORD **d** in burnt

Ps   1: 2 but whose **d** is in the law
     16: 3 noble ones in whom is all my **d**."
     35: 9 the LORD and **d** in his salvation.
     37: 4 Take **d** in the LORD, and he will
     43: 4 of God, to God, my joy and my **d**.
     51: 16 You do not **d** in sacrifice,
    119: 77 I may live, for your law is my **d**.
Isa 42: 1 my chosen one in whom I **d**;
     55: 2 you will **d** in the richest of fare.
     61: 10 I **d** greatly in the LORD;
Jer   9: 24 earth, for in these I **d**,"
     15: 16 they were my joy and my heart's **d**,
Mic   7: 18 angry forever but **d** to show mercy.
Zep   3: 17 He will take great **d** in you;
Mt   12: 18 the one I love, in whom I **d**;
1Co 13: 6 Love does not **d** in evil but rejoices
2Co 12: 10 for Christ's sake, I **d** in weaknesses,

DELIGHTS (DELIGHT)
Ps   22: 8 deliver him, since he **d** in him."
     35: 27 who **d** in the well-being of his
     36: 8 them drink from your river of **d**.
Pr   3: 12 he loves, as a father the son he **d** in.
     12: 22 **d** in people who are trustworthy.
     29: 17 will bring you the **d** you desire.

DELILAH
    Woman who betrayed Samson (Jdg 16:4–22).

DELIVER (DELIVERANCE DELIVERED DELIVERER
    DELIVERS)
Ps   72: 12 he will **d** the needy who cry out,
     79: 9 **d** us and forgive our sins for your
Da   3: 17 the God we serve is able to **d** us
Mt   6: 13 but **d** us from the evil one.'
2Co   1: 10 that he will continue to **d** us,

DELIVERANCE (DELIVER)
Ps   3: 8 From the LORD comes **d**.
     32: 7 and surround me with songs of **d**.
     33: 17 A horse is a vain hope for **d**;

DELIVERED (DELIVER)
Ps   34: 4 he **d** me from all my fears.
Ro   4: 25 He was **d** over to death for our sins

DELIVERER (DELIVER)
Ps   18: 2 is my rock, my fortress and my **d**;
     40: 17 You are my help and my **d**;
    140: 7 my strong **d**, you shield my head
    144: 2 stronghold and my **d**, my shield,

DELIVERS (DELIVER)
Ps   34: 17 he **d** them from all their troubles.
     34: 19 the LORD **d** him from them all;
     37: 40 The LORD helps them and **d** them;

DEMANDED
Lk   12: 20 This very night your life will be **d**
     12: 48 been given much, much will be **d**;

DEMONS
Mt   12: 27 And if I drive out **d** by Beelzebul,
Mk   5: 15 been possessed by the legion of **d**,
Ro   8: 38 life, neither angels nor **d**,
Jas   2: 19 Good! Even the **d** believe that—

DEMONSTRATE (DEMONSTRATES)
Ac   26: 20 **d** their repentance by their deeds.
Ro   3: 26 he did it to **d** his righteousness

DEMONSTRATES (DEMONSTRATE)
Ro   5: 8 God **d** his own love for us in this:

DEN
Da   6: 16 and threw him into the lions' **d**.
Mt   21: 13 but you are making it 'a **d**

DENARIUS
Mk   12: 15 "Bring me a **d** and let me look

DENIED (DENY)
1Ti   5: 8 has **d** the faith and is worse than

DENIES (DENY)
1Jn   2: 23 No one who **d** the Son has

DENY (DENIED DENIES DENYING)
Ex   23: 6 "Do not **d** justice to your poor
Job 27: 5 till I die, I will not **d** my integrity.
La   3: 35 **d** people their rights before the
Lk   9: 23 be my disciple must **d** themselves
Titus 1: 16 but by their actions they **d** him.

DENYING (DENY)
Eze 22: 29 the foreigner, **d** them justice.
2Ti   3: 5 a form of godliness but **d** its power.
2Pe   2: 1 even **d** the sovereign Lord who

DEPART (DEPARTED)
Ge   49: 10 The scepter will not **d** from Judah,
Job   1: 21 mother's womb, and naked I will **d**.
Mt   25: 41 to those on his left, '**D** from me,
Php   1: 23 I desire to **d** and be with Christ,

DEPARTED (DEPART)
1Sa   4: 21 "The Glory has **d** from Israel"—
Ps 119:102 I have not **d** from your laws,

DEPOSIT
2Co   1: 22 put his Spirit in our hearts as a **d**,
      5: 5 who has given us the Spirit as a **d**,
Eph   1: 14 who is a **d** guaranteeing our
2Ti   1: 14 Guard the good **d** that was entrusted

DEPRAVED (DEPRAVITY)
Ro   1: 28 God gave them over to a **d** mind,
2Pe   2: 7 was distressed by the **d** conduct

DEPRAVITY (DEPRAVED)
Ro   1: 29 of wickedness, evil, greed and **d**.

DEPRIVE
Dt   24: 17 Do not **d** the foreigner
Pr   18: 5 and so **d** the innocent of justice.
Isa 10: 2 to **d** the poor of their rights
     29: 21 with false testimony **d** the innocent
1Co   7: 5 Do not **d** each other except

DEPTH (DEEP)
Ro   8: 39 neither height nor **d**, nor anything
     11: 33 the **d** of the riches of the wisdom

DESERTED (DESERTS)
Mt   26: 56 all the disciples **d** him and fled.
2Ti   1: 15 in the province of Asia has **d** me,

DESERTING (DESERTS)
Gal   1: 6 you are so quickly **d** the one who

DESERTS (DESERTED DESERTING)
Zec 11: 17 shepherd, who **d** the flock!

DESERVE (DESERVES)
Ps 103: 10 he does not treat us as our sins **d**
Jer 21: 14 I will punish you as your deeds **d**,
Mt   22: 8 those I invited did not **d** to come.
Ro   1: 32 those who do such things **d** death,

DESERVES (DESERVE)
Lk   10: 7 for the worker **d** his wages.
1Ti   5: 18 and "The worker **d** his wages."

DESIRABLE (DESIRE)
Pr   22: 1 name is more **d** than great riches;

DESIRE (DESIRABLE DESIRES)
Ge   3: 16   Your **d** will be for your husband,
Dt   5: 21   You shall not set your **d** on your
Ps 40: 6   and offering you did not **d**—
     40: 8   I **d** to do your will, my God;
    73: 25   earth has nothing I **d** besides you.
Pr   3: 15   nothing you **d** can compare
   10: 24   what the righteous **d** will be
   11: 23   The **d** of the righteous ends only
   19: 2   **D** without knowledge is not good
Isa 26: 8   and renown are the **d** of our hearts.
   53: 2   appearance that we should **d** him.
   55: 11   but will accomplish what I **d**
Hos 6: 6   For I **d** mercy, not sacrifice,
Mt   9: 13   'I **d** mercy, not sacrifice.'
Ro   7: 18   For I have the **d** to do what is good,
1Co 12: 31   Now eagerly **d** the greater gifts.
   14: 1   and eagerly **d** gifts of the Spirit,
Php 1: 23   I **d** to depart and be with Christ,
Heb 13: 18   **d** to live honorably in every way.
Jas   1: 15   after **d** has conceived, it gives birth

DESIRES (DESIRE)
Ge   4: 7   it **d** to have you, but you must rule
1Ch 29: 18   keep these **d** and thoughts
Ps 34: 12   life and **d** to see many good days,
   37: 4   will give you the **d** of your heart.
  103: 5   who satisfies your **d** with good
  145: 19   He fulfills the **d** of those who fear
Pr 11: 6   the unfaithful are trapped by evil **d**.
  19: 22   What a person **d** is unfailing love;
Mk   4: 19   and the **d** for other things come
Ro   8: 5   minds set on what the Spirit **d**.
  13: 14   how to gratify the **d** of the flesh.
Gal   5: 16   and you will not gratify the **d**
   5: 17   For the flesh **d** what is contrary
1Ti   3: 1   to be an overseer **d** a noble task.
   6: 9   harmful **d** that plunge people
2Ti   2: 22   Flee the evil **d** of youth and pursue
Jas   1: 20   the righteousness that God **d**.
   4: 1   from your **d** that battle within you?
1Pe   2: 11   to abstain from sinful **d**,
1Jn   2: 17   The world and its **d** pass away,

DESOLATE
Isa 54: 1   the children of the **d** woman than

DESPAIR
Isa 61: 3   of praise instead of a spirit of **d**.
2Co   4: 8   perplexed, but not in **d**;

DESPISE (DESPISED DESPISES)
Job 42: 6   Therefore I **d** myself and repent
Pr   1: 7   fools **d** wisdom and instruction.
   3: 11   do not **d** the LORD's discipline,
  14: 21   It is a sin to **d** one's neighbor,
  15: 32   disregard discipline **d** themselves,
  23: 22   do not **d** your mother when she is
Zec   4: 10   "Who dares **d** the day of small
Lk 16: 13   devoted to the one and **d** the other.
Titus 2: 15   Do not let anyone **d** you.

DESPISED (DESPISE)
Ge 25: 34   and left. So Esau **d** his birthright.
Isa 53: 3   He was **d** and rejected by mankind,
1Co   1: 28   of this world and the **d** things—

DESPISES (DESPISE)
Pr 15: 20   but a foolish man **d** his mother.

DESTINED (DESTINY)
Lk   2: 34   "This child is **d** to cause the falling

DESTINY (DESTINED PREDESTINED)
Ps 73: 17   then I understood their final **d**.
Ecc   7: 2   for death is the **d** of everyone;

DESTITUTE
Pr 31: 8   for the rights of all who are **d**.
Heb 11: 37   in sheepskins and goatskins, **d**,

DESTROY (DESTROYED DESTROYS DESTRUCTION)
Pr   1: 32   complacency of fools will **d** them;
  11: 9   the godless **d** their neighbors,
Mt 10: 28   of the One who can **d** both soul

DESTROYED (DESTROY)
Job 19: 26   And after my skin has been **d**,
1Co   8: 11   is **d** by your knowledge.
  15: 26   The last enemy to be **d** is death.
2Co   5: 1   if the earthly tent we live in is **d**,
Heb 10: 39   those who shrink back and are **d**,
2Pe   3: 10   the elements will be **d** by fire,

DESTROYS (DESTROY)
Pr   6: 32   whoever does so **d** himself.
  18: 9   his work is brother to one who **d**.
  28: 24   wrong," is partner to one who **d**.
Ecc   9: 18   but one sinner **d** much good.
1Co   3: 17   If anyone **d** God's temple, God will

DESTRUCTION (DESTROY)
Ps   1: 6   the way of the wicked leads to **d**.
Pr 16: 18   Pride goes before **d**, a haughty
Hos 13: 14   Where, O grave, is your **d**?
Mt   7: 13   broad is the road that leads to **d**,
Gal   6: 8   flesh, from the flesh will reap **d**;
2Th   1: 9   will be punished with everlasting **d**
1Ti   6: 9   that plunge people into ruin and **d**.
2Pe   2: 1   bringing swift **d** on themselves.
   3: 16   other Scriptures, to their own **d**.

DETERMINED (DETERMINES)
Job 14: 5   A person's days are **d**;
Isa 14: 26   This is the plan **d** for the whole
Da 11: 36   what has been **d** must take place.

DETERMINES (DETERMINED)
Ps 147: 4   He **d** the number of the stars
1Co 12: 11   them to each one, just as he **d**.

DETESTABLE (DETESTS)
Pr 21: 27   The sacrifice of the wicked is **d**—
  28: 9   even their prayers are **d**.
Isa   1: 13   Your incense is **d** to me.
Lk 16: 15   What people value highly is **d**
Titus 1: 16   They are **d**, disobedient and unfit

DETESTS (DETESTABLE)
Dt 22: 5   the LORD your God **d** anyone who
  23: 18   the LORD your God **d** them both.
  25: 16   the LORD your God **d** anyone who
Pr 11: 1   The LORD **d** dishonest scales,
  12: 22   The LORD **d** lying lips, but he
  15: 8   The LORD **d** the sacrifice
  15: 9   The LORD **d** the way
  15: 26   The LORD **d** the thoughts
  16: 5   The LORD **d** all the proud
  17: 15   The LORD **d** them both.
  20: 23   The LORD **d** differing weights,

DEVIL (DEVIL'S)
Mt 13: 39   the enemy who sows them is the **d**.
  25: 41   the eternal fire prepared for the **d**
Lk   4: 2   forty days he was tempted by the **d**
   8: 12   then the **d** comes and takes away
Eph 4: 27   and do not give the **d** a foothold.
2Ti   2: 26   and escape from the trap of the **d**,
Jas   4: 7   Resist the **d**, and he will flee

1Pe	5: 8	Your enemy the **d** prowls around
1Jn	3: 8	who does what is sinful is of the **d**,
Rev	12: 9	that ancient serpent called the **d**,

DEVIL'S (DEVIL)
Eph	6: 11	your stand against the **d** schemes.
1Ti	3: 7	into disgrace and into the **d** trap.
1Jn	3: 8	was to destroy the **d** work.

DEVISED
2Pe	1: 16	we did not follow cleverly **d** stories

DEVOTE (DEVOTED DEVOTING DEVOTION DEVOUT)
Job	11: 13	"Yet if you **d** your heart to him
Jer	30: 21	who is he who will **d** himself to be
Col	4: 2	**D** yourselves to prayer,
1Ti	4: 13	**d** yourself to the public reading
Titus	3: 8	may be careful to **d** themselves

DEVOTED (DEVOTE)
Ezr	7: 10	For Ezra had **d** himself to the study
Ac	2: 42	They **d** themselves to the apostles'
Ro	12: 10	Be **d** to one another in love.
1Co	7: 34	Her aim is to be **d** to the Lord

DEVOTING (DEVOTE)
1Ti	5: 10	**d** herself to all kinds of good deeds.

DEVOTION (DEVOTE)
1Ch	28: 9	serve him with wholehearted **d**
1Co	7: 35	way in undivided **d** to the Lord.
2Co	11: 3	your sincere and pure **d** to Christ.

DEVOUR
2Sa	2: 26	to Joab, "Must the sword **d** forever?
Mk	12: 40	They **d** widows' houses
1Pe	5: 8	lion looking for someone to **d**.

DEVOUT (DEVOTE)
Lk	2: 25	Simeon, who was righteous and **d**.

DIE (DEAD DEATH DIED DIES)
Ge	2: 17	eat from it you will certainly **d**."
Ex	11: 5	Every firstborn son in Egypt will **d**,
Ru	1: 17	Where you **d** I will **d**, and there I
2Ki	14: 6	each will **d** for their own sin."
Pr	5: 23	For lack of discipline they will **d**,
	10: 21	many, but fools **d** for lack of sense.
	11: 7	placed in mortals **d** with them;
	15: 10	one who hates correction will **d**.
	23: 13	them with the rod, they will not **d**.
Ecc	3: 2	a time to be born and a time to **d**,
Isa	66: 24	the worms that eat them will not **d**,
Eze	3: 18	wicked person will **d** for their sin,
	18: 4	one who sins is the one who will **d**.
	33: 8	wicked person will **d** for their sin,
Mt	26: 52	all who draw the sword will **d**
Jn	11: 25	in me will live, even though they **d**;
	11: 26	by believing in me will never **d**.
Ro	5: 7	Very rarely will anyone **d**
	14: 8	and if we **d**, we **d** for the Lord.
1Co	15: 22	For as in Adam all **d**, so in Christ
Php	1: 21	to live is Christ and to **d** is gain.
Heb	9: 27	as people are destined to **d** once,
Rev	14: 13	Blessed are the dead who **d**

DIED (DIE)
Ro	5: 6	Christ **d** for the ungodly.
	6: 2	We are those who have **d** to sin;
	6: 8	Now if we **d** with Christ, we believe
	14: 15	someone for whom Christ **d**.
1Co	8: 11	for whom Christ **d**, is destroyed
	15: 3	that Christ **d** for our sins according
2Co	5: 14	one **d** for all, and therefore all **d**.
Col	3: 3	For you **d**, and your life is now

1Th	5: 10	He **d** for us so that, whether we are
2Ti	2: 11	If we **d** with him, we will also live
Heb	9: 15	that he has **d** as a ransom to set
Rev	2: 8	Last, who **d** and came to life again.

DIES (DIE)
Job	14: 14	If someone **d**, will they live again?
1Co	15: 36	does not come to life unless it **d**.

DIFFERENCE (DIFFERENT)
Ro	10: 12	For there is no **d** between Jew

DIFFERENT (DIFFERENCE)
1Co	12: 4	There are **d** kinds of gifts,
2Co	11: 4	or a **d** gospel from the one you

DIGNITY
Pr	31: 25	She is clothed with strength and **d**;

DIGS
Pr	26: 27	Whoever **d** a pit will fall into it;

DILIGENCE (DILIGENT)
Heb	6: 11	show this same **d** to the very end,

DILIGENT (DILIGENCE)
Pr	21: 5	The plans of the **d** lead to profit as
1Ti	4: 15	Be **d** in these matters;

DIRECT (DIRECTS)
Ps	119: 35	**D** me in the path of your
	119:133	**D** my footsteps according to your
Jer	10: 23	it is not for them to **d** their steps.
2Th	3: 5	May the Lord **d** your hearts

DIRECTS (DIRECT)
Ps	42: 8	By day the LORD **d** his love,
Isa	48: 17	who **d** you in the way you should

DIRGE
Mt	11: 17	we sang a **d**, and you did not

DISAPPEAR
Mt	5: 18	until heaven and earth **d**,
Lk	16: 17	earth to **d** than for the least stroke

DISASTER
Ps	57: 1	your wings until the **d** has passed.
Pr	3: 25	Have no fear of sudden **d**
	17: 5	whoever gloats over **d** will not go
Isa	45: 7	I bring prosperity and create **d**;
Eze	7: 5	Unheard-of **d**! See, it comes!

DISCERN (DISCERNING)
Ps	19: 12	But who can **d** their own errors?
	139: 3	You **d** my going out and my lying
Php	1: 10	you may be able to **d** what is best

DISCERNING (DISCERN)
Pr	14: 6	knowledge comes easily to the **d**.
	15: 14	The **d** heart seeks knowledge,
	17: 10	A rebuke impresses a **d** person
	17: 24	A **d** person keeps wisdom in view,
	17: 28	and **d** if they hold their tongues.
	19: 25	rebuke the **d**, and they will gain
	28: 11	and **d** sees how deluded they are.

DISCIPLE (DISCIPLES)
Mt	10: 42	of these little ones who is my **d**,
Lk	14: 27	and follow me cannot be my **d**.

DISCIPLES (DISCIPLE)
Mt	28: 19	go and make **d** of all nations,
Jn	8: 31	my teaching, you are really my **d**.
	13: 35	will know that you are my **d**, if you
Ac	11: 26	The **d** were called Christians first

DISCIPLINE (DISCIPLINED DISCIPLINES)
Ps	38: 1	your anger or **d** me in your wrath.
	39: 11	rebuke and **d** anyone for their sin,
	94: 12	Blessed is the one you **d**, LORD,

Pr   3: 11 do not despise the LORD's **d**,
     5: 12 You will say, "How I hated **d**!
     5: 23 For lack of **d** they will die,
   10: 17 Whoever heeds **d** shows the way
   12: 1 Whoever loves **d** loves knowledge,
   13: 18 Whoever disregards **d** comes
   13: 24 their children is careful to **d** them.
   15: 5 A fool spurns a parent's **d**,
   15: 32 disregard **d** despise themselves,
   19: 18 **D** your children, for in that there is
   19: 20 Listen to advice and accept **d**,
   22: 15 the rod of **d** will drive it far away.
   23: 13 Do not withhold **d** from a child;
   29: 17 **D** your children, and they will give
Heb 12: 5 do not make light of the Lord's **d**,
   12: 7 Endure hardship as **d**;
   12: 11 No **d** seems pleasant at the time,
Rev 3: 19 Those whom I love I rebuke and **d**.

DISCIPLINED (DISCIPLINE)
Jer 31: 18 'You **d** me like an unruly calf,
1Co 11: 32 we are being **d** so that we will not
Col 2: 5 delight to see how **d** you are
Titus 1: 8 upright, holy and **d**.
Heb 12: 7 For what children are not **d** by

DISCIPLINES (DISCIPLINE)
Dt   8: 5 so the LORD your God **d** you.
Pr   3: 12 because the LORD **d** those he
Heb 12: 6 the Lord **d** the one he loves,
   12: 10 but God **d** us for our good,

DISCLOSED
Lk   8: 17 nothing hidden that will not be **d**,

DISCOURAGED
Jos 1: 9 do not be **d**, for the LORD your
   10: 25 "Do not be afraid; do not be **d**.
1Ch 28: 20 Do not be afraid or **d**,
Isa 42: 4 or be **d** till he establishes justice
Col 3: 21 children, or they will become **d**.

DISCREDITED
2Co 6: 3 so that our ministry will not be **d**.

DISCRETION
1Ch 22: 12 May the LORD give you **d**
Pr   1: 4 knowledge and **d** to the young—
     2: 11 **D** will protect you,
     5: 2 that you may maintain **d** and your
     8: 12 I possess knowledge and **d**.
   11: 22 beautiful woman who shows no **d**.

DISCRIMINATED
Jas 2: 4 have you not **d** among yourselves

DISFIGURED
Isa 52: 14 his appearance was so **d** beyond

DISGRACE (DISGRACEFUL DISGRACES)
Pr 11: 2 then comes **d**, but with humility
   19: 26 is a child who brings shame and **d**.
Ac   5: 41 worthy of suffering **d** for the Name.
Heb 13: 13 the camp, bearing the **d** he bore.

DISGRACEFUL (DISGRACE)
Pr 10: 5 sleeps during harvest is a **d** son.
   17: 2 servant will rule over a **d** son

DISGRACES (DISGRACE)
Pr 28: 7 companion of gluttons **d** his father.
   29: 15 left undisciplined **d** its mother.

DISGUISE
Pr 26: 24 Enemies **d** themselves with their

DISHONEST
Pr 11: 1 The LORD detests **d** scales,
   29: 27 The righteous detest the **d**;

Lk 16: 10 whoever is **d** with very little will
1Ti 3: 8 wine, and not pursuing **d** gain.

DISHONOR (DISHONORS)
Lev 18: 7 "'Do not **d** your father by having
Pr 30: 9 and so **d** the name of my God.
1Co 13: 5 It does not **d** others, it is not
   15: 43 it is sown in **d**, it is raised in glory;

DISHONORS (DISHONOR)
Dt 27: 16 is anyone who **d** their father

DISMAYED
Isa 41: 10 do not be **d**, for I am your God.

DISOBEDIENCE (DISOBEY)
Ro 5: 19 as through the **d** of the one man
   11: 32 has bound everyone over to **d** so
Heb 2: 2 and **d** received its just punishment,
    4: 6 did not go in because of their **d**,
    4: 11 by following their example of **d**.

DISOBEDIENT (DISOBEY)
2Ti 3: 2 proud, abusive, **d** to their parents,
Titus 1: 6 to the charge of being wild and **d**.
    1: 16 **d** and unfit for doing anything

DISOBEY (DISOBEDIENCE DISOBEDIENT)
Dt 11: 28 the curse if you **d** the commands
2Ch 24: 20 'Why do you **d** the LORD's
Ro 1: 30 of doing evil; they **d** their parents;

DISORDER
1Co 14: 33 For God is not a God of **d**
2Co 12: 20 slander, gossip, arrogance and **d**.
Jas 3: 16 there you find **d** and every evil

DISOWN
Pr 30: 9 I may have too much and **d** you
Mt 10: 33 will **d** before my Father in heaven.
   26: 35 to die with you, I will never **d** you."
2Ti 2: 12 If we **d** him, he will also **d** us;

DISPLAY (DISPLAYS)
Eze 39: 21 "I will **d** my glory among
1Ti 1: 16 Christ Jesus might **d** his immense

DISPLAYS (DISPLAY)
Isa 44: 23 Jacob, he **d** his glory in Israel.

DISPUTE (DISPUTES)
Pr 17: 14 the matter before a **d** breaks out.
1Co 6: 1 If any of you has a **d** with another,

DISPUTES (DISPUTE)
Pr 18: 18 Casting the lot settles **d** and keeps

DISQUALIFIED
1Co 9: 27 I myself will not be **d** for the prize.

DISREGARD
Pr 15: 32 Those who **d** discipline despise

DISREPUTE
2Pe 2: 2 will bring the way of truth into **d**.

DISSENSION
Ro 13: 13 debauchery, not in **d** and jealousy.

DISTINGUISH
1Ki 3: 9 and to **d** between right and wrong.
Heb 5: 14 have trained themselves to **d** good

DISTORT
2Co 4: 2 nor do we **d** the word of God.
2Pe 3: 16 ignorant and unstable people **d**,

DISTRESS (DISTRESSED)
Ps 18: 6 In my **d** I called to the LORD;
Jnh 2: 2 "In my **d** I called to the LORD,
Jas 1: 27 and widows in their **d** and to keep

DISTRESSED (DISTRESS)
Ro 14: 15 sister is **d** because of what you eat,

DIVIDED (DIVISION)
Mt 12: 25 "Every kingdom **d** against itself
Lk 23: 34 **d** up his clothes by casting lots.
1Co 1: 13 Is Christ **d**? Was Paul crucified

DIVINATION
Lev 19: 26 "'Do not practice **d** or seek

DIVINE
Ro 1: 20 his eternal power and **d** nature—
2Co 10: 4 they have **d** power to demolish
2Pe 1: 4 may participate in the **d** nature,

DIVISION (DIVIDED DIVISIONS DIVISIVE)
Lk 12: 51 peace on earth? No, I tell you, but **d**.
1Co 12: 25 there should be no **d** in the body,

DIVISIONS (DIVISION)
Ro 16: 17 to watch out for those who cause **d**
1Co 1: 10 and that there be no **d** among you,
     11: 18 as a church, there are **d** among you,

DIVISIVE (DIVISION)
Titus 3: 10 Warn a **d** person once,

DIVORCE (DIVORCES)
Mt 19: 3 for a man to **d** his wife for any
1Co 7: 11 a husband must not **d** his wife.

DIVORCES (DIVORCE)
Mal 2: 16 man who hates and **d** his wife,"

DOCTOR
Mt 9: 12 "It is not the healthy who need a **d**,

DOCTRINE
1Ti 4: 16 Watch your life and **d** closely.
Titus 2: 1 what is appropriate to sound **d**.

DOMINION
Ps 22: 28 for **d** belongs to the LORD and he

DOOR
Ps 141: 3 keep watch over the **d** of my lips.
Mt 6: 6 close the **d** and pray to your Father,
     7: 7 and the **d** will be opened to you.
Rev 3: 20 I stand at the **d** and knock.

DOORKEEPER
Ps 84: 10 I would rather be a **d** in the house

DOUBLE-EDGED
Heb 4: 12 Sharper than any **d** sword.
Rev 1: 16 of his mouth was a sharp, **d** sword.
     2: 12 of him who has the sharp, **d** sword.

DOUBLE-MINDED (MIND)
Ps 119:113 I hate **d** people, but I love your law.
Jas 1: 8 Such a person is **d** and unstable

DOUBT
Mt 14: 31 faith," he said, "why did you **d**?"
     21: 21 if you have faith and do not **d**,
Mk 11: 23 and does not **d** in their heart
Jas 1: 6 you must believe and not **d**,
Jude   : 22 Be merciful to those who **d**;

DOWNCAST
Ps 42: 5 Why, my soul, are you **d**?
2Co 7: 6 who comforts the **d**, comforted us

DRAW (DRAWING DRAWS)
Mt 26: 52 "for all who **d** the sword will die
Jn 12: 32 earth, will **d** all people to myself."
Heb 10: 22 let us **d** near to God with a sincere

DRAWING (DRAW)
Lk 21: 28 your redemption is **d** near."

DRAWS (DRAW)
Jn 6: 44 the Father who sent me **d** them,

DREADFUL
Heb 10: 31 It is a **d** thing to fall into the hands

DRESS
1Ti 2: 9 want the women to **d** modestly,

DRINK (DRUNK DRUNKARDS DRUNKENNESS)
Pr 5: 15 **D** water from your own cistern,
Lk 12: 19 eat, **d** and be merry.'"
Jn 7: 37 who is thirsty come to me and **d**.
1Co 12: 13 were all given the one Spirit to **d**.

DRIVES
1Jn 4: 18 But perfect love **d** out fear,

DROP
Pr 17: 14 so **d** the matter before a dispute
Isa 40: 15 Surely the nations are like a **d**

DRUNK (DRINK)
Eph 5: 18 Do not get **d** on wine, which leads

DRUNKARDS (DRINK)
Pr 23: 21 for **d** and gluttons become poor,
1Co 6: 10 the greedy nor **d** nor slanderers

DRUNKENNESS (DRINK)
Lk 21: 34 **d** and the anxieties of life,
Ro 13: 13 not in carousing and **d**,
Gal 5: 21 and envy; **d**, orgies, and the like.
1Pe 4: 3 living in debauchery, lust, **d**, orgies,

DRY
Isa 53: 2 and like a root out of **d** ground.
Eze 37: 4 bones and say to them, '**D** bones,

DUST
Ge 2: 7 a man from the **d** of the ground
Ps 103: 14 he remembers that we are **d**.
Ecc 3: 20 come from **d**, and to **d** all return.

DUTY
Ecc 12: 13 for this is the **d** of all mankind.
Ac 23: 1 I have fulfilled my **d** to God in all
1Co 7: 3 husband should fulfill his marital **d**

DWELL (DWELLING DWELLS)
1Ki 8: 27 "But will God really **d** on earth?
Ps 23: 6 I will **d** in the house of the LORD
Isa 43: 18 do not **d** on the past.
Eph 3: 17 Christ may **d** in your hearts
Col 1: 19 to have all his fullness **d** in him,
     3: 16 of Christ **d** among you richly

DWELLING (DWELL)
Eph 2: 22 built together to become a **d**

DWELLS (DWELL)
1Co 3: 16 that God's Spirit **d** in your midst?

EAGER
Pr 31: 13 and flax and works with **e** hands.
1Pe 5: 2 dishonest gain, but **e** to serve;

EAGLE'S (EAGLES)
Ps 103: 5 your youth is renewed like the **e**.

EAGLES (EAGLE'S)
Isa 40: 31 They will soar on wings like **e**;

EAR (EARS)
1Co 2: 9 eye has seen, what no **e** has heard,
     12: 16 And if the **e** should say, "Because I

EARS (EAR)
Job 42: 5 My **e** had heard of you but now my
Ps 34: 15 and his **e** are attentive to their cry;
Pr 21: 13 Whoever shuts their **e** to the cry
2Ti 4: 3 to say what their itching **e** want

EARTH (EARTHLY)
Ge 1: 1 God created the heavens and the **e**.
Ps 24: 1 The **e** is the LORD's,
     108: 5 let your glory be over all the **e**.

Isa   6: 3 the whole **e** is full of his glory."
     51: 6 the **e** will wear out like a garment
     55: 9 the heavens are higher than the **e**,
     66: 1 throne, and the **e** is my footstool.
Jer 23: 24 "Do not I fill heaven and **e**?"
Hab 2: 20 let all the **e** be silent before him.
Mt   6: 10 will be done, on **e** as it is in heaven.
     16: 19 you bind on **e** will be bound
     24: 35 Heaven and **e** will pass away,
     28: 18 and on **e** has been given to me.
Lk   2: 14 on **e** peace to those on whom his
1Co 10: 26 for, "The **e** is the Lord's,
Php 2: 10 heaven and on **e** and under the **e**,
2Pe 3: 13 to a new heaven and a new **e**,

EARTHLY (EARTH)
Php 3: 19 Their mind is set on **e** things.
Col   3: 2 on things above, not on **e** things.

EAST
Ps 103: 12 as far as the **e** is from the west,

EASY
Mt 11: 30 For my yoke is **e** and my burden is

EAT (EATING)
Ge   2: 17 you must not **e** from the tree
Isa 55: 1 have no money, come, buy and **e**!
     65: 25 the lion will **e** straw like the ox,
Mt 26: 26 his disciples, saying, "Take and **e**;
Ro 14: 2 faith allows them to **e** anything,
1Co 8: 13 if what I **e** causes my brother
    10: 31 So whether you **e** or drink
2Th 3: 10 is unwilling to work shall not **e**."

EATING (EAT)
Ro 14: 17 kingdom of God is not a matter of **e**

EDICT
Heb 11: 23 they were not afraid of the king's **e**.

EDIFIES
1Co 14: 4 speaks in a tongue **e** themselves,

EFFECT
Isa 32: 17 its **e** will be quietness
Heb 9: 18 was not put into **e** without blood.

EFFORT
Lk 13: 24 "Make every **e** to enter through
Ro   9: 16 depend on human desire or **e**,
    14: 19 Let us therefore make every **e** to do
Eph 4: 3 Make every **e** to keep the unity
Heb 4: 11 make every **e** to enter that rest,
    12: 14 Make every **e** to live in peace
2Pe 1: 5 make every **e** to add to your faith
     3: 14 make every **e** to be found spotless,

ELAH
Son of Baasha; king of Israel (1Ki 16:6–14).

ELDERLY (ELDERS)
Lev 19: 32 show respect for the **e** and revere

ELDERS (ELDERLY)
1Ti 5: 17 The **e** who direct the affairs

ELECTION
Ro   9: 11 God's purpose in **e** might stand:
2Pe 1: 10 to confirm your calling and **e**.

ELI
High priest in youth of Samuel (1Sa 1–4). Blessed Hannah (1Sa 1:12–18); raised Samuel (1Sa 2:11–26).

ELIJAH
Prophet; predicted famine in Israel (1Ki 17:1; Jas 5:17). Fed by ravens (1Ki 17:2–6). Raised Sidonian widow's son (1Ki 17:7–24). Defeated prophets of Baal at Carmel (1Ki 18:16–46). Ran from Jezebel (1Ki 19:1–9). Prophesied death of Azariah (2Ki 1). Succeeded by Elisha (1Ki 19:19–21; 2Ki 2:1–18). Taken to heaven in whirlwind (2Ki 2:11–12).

Return prophesied (Mal 4:5–6); equated with John the Baptist (Mt 17:9–13; Mk 9:9–13; Lk 1:17). Appeared with Moses in transfiguration of Jesus (Mt 17:1–8; Mk 9:1–8).

ELISHA
Prophet; successor of Elijah (1Ki 19:16–21); inherited his cloak (2Ki 2:1–18). Miracles of (2Ki 2–6).

ELIZABETH
Mother of John the Baptist, relative of Mary (Lk 1:5–58).

EMBITTER
Col   3: 21 Fathers, do not **e** your children,

EMPEROR
1Pe 2: 17 of believers, fear God, honor the **e**.

EMPTY
Mt 12: 36 for every **e** word they have spoken.
Eph 5: 6 no one deceive you with **e** words,
1Pe 1: 18 you were redeemed from the **e** way

ENABLE (ABLE)
Lk   1: 74 to **e** us to serve him without fear
Ac   4: 29 **e** your servants to speak your word

ENABLED (ABLE)
Lev 26: 13 **e** you to walk with heads held high.
Jn   6: 65 me unless the Father has **e** them."

ENABLES (ABLE)
Php 3: 21 by the power that **e** him to bring

ENCAMPS
Ps 34: 7 the Lord **e** around those who fear

ENCOURAGE (ENCOURAGEMENT ENCOURAGING)
Ps 10: 17 you **e** them, and you listen to their
Ac 15: 32 said much to **e** and strengthen
Ro 12: 8 if it is to **e**, then give
1Th 4: 18 Therefore **e** one another with these
2Ti 4: 2 correct, rebuke and **e**—
Titus 2: 6 Similarly, **e** the young men to be
Heb 3: 13 But **e** one another daily, as long as

ENCOURAGEMENT (ENCOURAGE)
Ac   4: 36 (which means "son of **e**"),
Ro 15: 4 the **e** they provide we might have
    15: 5 **e** give you the same attitude of
Heb 12: 5 completely forgotten this word of **e**

ENCOURAGING (ENCOURAGE)
1Co 14: 3 their strengthening, **e** and comfort.
Heb 10: 25 habit of doing, but **e** one another—

END
Ps 119: 33 that I may follow it to the **e**.
Pr 14: 12 right, but in the **e** it leads to death.
    19: 20 the **e** you will be counted among
    23: 32 In the **e** it bites like a snake
Ecc 12: 12 making many books there is no **e**,
Mt 10: 22 stands firm to the **e** will be saved.
Lk 21: 9 but the **e** will not come right away."
1Co 15: 24 Then the **e** will come, when he

ENDURANCE (ENDURE)
Ro 15: 4 so that through the **e** taught
    15: 5 May the God who gives **e**
2Co 1: 6 you patient **e** of the same sufferings
Col   1: 11 might so that you may have great **e**
1Ti 6: 11 faith, love, **e** and gentleness.
Titus 2: 2 and sound in faith, in love and in **e**.

ENDURE (ENDURANCE ENDURES)
Ps 72: 17 May his name **e** forever;

Pr 12: 19 Truthful lips **e** forever, but a lying
    27: 24 for riches do not **e** forever,
Ecc 3: 14 everything God does will **e** forever;
Mal 3: 2 who can **e** the day of his coming?
2Ti 2: 12 if we **e**, we will also reign with him.
Heb 12: 7 **E** hardship as discipline;
Rev 3: 10 kept my command to **e** patiently,

ENDURES (ENDURE)
Ps 112: 9 poor, their righteousness **e** forever;
    136: 1 *His love e forever.*
Da 9: 15 yourself a name that **e** to this day,
1Pe 1: 25 but the word of the Lord **e** forever."

ENEMIES (ENEMY)
Ps 23: 5 before me in the presence of my **e**.
Mic 7: 6 a man's **e** are the members of his
Mt 5: 44 love your **e** and pray for those who
Lk 20: 43 until I make your **e** a footstool

ENEMY (ENEMIES ENMITY)
Pr 24: 17 Do not gloat when your **e** falls;
    25: 21 If your **e** is hungry, give him food
    27: 6 trusted, but an **e** multiplies kisses.
1Co 15: 26 The last **e** to be destroyed is death.
1Ti 5: 14 and to give the **e** no opportunity
Jas 4: 4 of the world becomes an **e** of God.

ENJOY (JOY)
Dt 6: 2 and so that you may **e** long life.
Eph 6: 3 and that you may **e** long life
Heb 11: 25 than to **e** the fleeting pleasures

ENJOYMENT (JOY)
Ecc 4: 8 why am I depriving myself of **e**?"
1Ti 6: 17 us with everything for our **e**.

ENLIGHTENED (LIGHT)
Eph 1: 18 eyes of your heart may be **e** in
Heb 6: 4 for those who have once been **e**,

ENMITY (ENEMY)
Ge 3: 15 I will put **e** between you

ENOCH
Walked with God and taken by him (Ge 5:18–24; Heb 11:5). Prophet (Jude 14).

ENTANGLED (ENTANGLES)
2Ti 2: 4 soldier gets **e** in civilian affairs,
2Pe 2: 20 Jesus Christ and are again **e** in it

ENTANGLES (ENTANGLED)
Heb 12: 1 hinders and the sin that so easily **e**.

ENTER (ENTERED ENTERS)
Ps 100: 4 **E** his gates with thanksgiving
Mt 5: 20 will certainly not **e** the kingdom
    7: 13 "**E** through the narrow gate.
    18: 8 It is better for you to **e** life maimed
Mk 10: 15 like a little child will never **e** it."
    10: 23 the rich to **e** the kingdom of God!"

ENTERED (ENTER)
Ro 5: 12 just as sin **e** the world through one
Heb 9: 12 he **e** the Most Holy Place once

ENTERS (ENTER)
Mk 7: 18 that nothing that **e** a person
Jn 10: 2 The one who **e** by the gate is

ENTERTAIN
1Ti 5: 19 Do not **e** an accusation against

ENTHRALLED
Ps 45: 11 Let the king be **e** by your beauty;

ENTHRONED (THRONE)
1Sa 4: 4 who is **e** between the cherubim.
Ps 2: 4 The One **e** in heaven laughs;

102: 12 But you, LORD, sit **e** forever;
Isa 40: 22 He sits **e** above the circle

ENTICE
Pr 1: 10 if sinful men **e** you, do not give
2Pe 2: 18 they **e** people who are just escaping

ENTIRE
Gal 5: 14 For the **e** law is fulfilled in keeping

ENTRUSTED (TRUST)
1Ti 6: 20 guard what has been **e** to your care.
2Ti 1: 12 to guard what I have **e** to him until
    1: 14 good deposit that was **e** to you—
Jude : 3 once for all **e** to God's holy people.

ENVY
Pr 3: 31 Do not **e** the violent or choose any
    14: 30 to the body, but **e** rots the bones.
1Co 13: 4 It does not **e**, it does not boast,

EPHRAIM
1. Second son of Joseph (Ge 41:52; 46:20). Blessed as firstborn by Jacob (Ge 48).
2. Synonymous with Northern Kingdom (Isa 7:17; Hos 5).

EQUAL
Isa 40: 25 Or who is my **e**?" says the Holy
Jn 5: 18 Father, making himself **e** with God.
1Co 12: 25 its parts should have **e** concern

EQUIP (EQUIPPED)
Eph 4: 12 to **e** his people for works of service,
Heb 13: 21 **e** you with everything good

EQUIPPED (EQUIP)
2Ti 3: 17 God may be thoroughly **e** for every

ERROR
Jas 5: 20 the **e** of their way will save them

ESAU
Firstborn of Isaac, twin of Jacob (Ge 25:21–26). Also called Edom (Ge 25:30). Sold Jacob his birthright (Ge 25:29–34); lost blessing (Ge 27). Reconciled to Jacob (Gen 33).

ESCAPE (ESCAPING)
Ro 2: 3 think you will **e** God's judgment?
Heb 2: 3 how shall we **e** if we ignore so great

ESCAPING (ESCAPE)
1Co 3: 15 only as one **e** through the flames.

ESTABLISH (ESTABLISHED ESTABLISHES)
Ge 6: 18 But I will **e** my covenant with you,
1Ch 28: 7 I will **e** his kingdom forever if he is
Ro 10: 3 of God and sought to **e** their own,

ESTABLISHED (ESTABLISH)
Ps 8: 2 infants you have **e** a stronghold

ESTABLISHES (ESTABLISH)
Pr 16: 9 course, but the LORD **e** their steps.

ESTEEM (ESTEEMED)
Isa 53: 3 and we held him in low **e**.

ESTEEMED (ESTEEM)
Pr 22: 1 to be **e** is better than silver or gold.

ESTHER
Jewess who lived in Persia; cousin of Mordecai (Est 2:7). Chosen queen of Xerxes (Est 2:8–18). Foiled Haman's plan to exterminate the Jews (Est 3–4; 7–9).

ETERNAL (ETERNITY)
Ps 16: 11 with **e** pleasures at your right hand.
    111: 10 To him belongs **e** praise.
    119: 89 Your word, LORD, is **e**;
Isa 26: 4 the LORD himself, is the Rock **e**.

Mt 19: 16 good thing must I do to get **e** life?"
    25: 41 the **e** fire prepared for the devil
    25: 46 but the righteous to **e** life."
Jn   3: 15 who believes may have **e** life
     3: 16 him shall not perish but have **e** life.
     3: 36 believes in the Son has **e** life,
     4: 14 of water welling up to **e** life."
     5: 24 believes him who sent me has **e** life
     6: 47 the one who believes has **e** life.
     6: 68 You have the words of **e** life.
    10: 28 I give them **e** life, and they shall
    17: 3 Now this is **e** life: that they know
Ro   1: 20 his **e** power and divine nature—
     6: 23 of God is **e** life in Christ Jesus our
2Co 4: 17 for us an **e** glory that far outweighs
     4: 18 temporary, but what is unseen is **e**.
1Ti 1: 16 believe in him and receive **e** life.
     1: 17 Now to the King **e**, immortal,
Heb 9: 12 thus obtaining **e** redemption.
1Jn 5: 11 God has given us **e** life, and this life
     5: 13 you may know that you have **e** life.

ETERNITY (ETERNAL)
Ps 93: 2 you are from all **e**.
Ecc 3: 11 has also set **e** in the human heart;

ETHIOPIAN
Jer 13: 23 Can an **E** change his skin

EUNUCHS
Mt 19: 12 choose to live like **e** for the sake

EVANGELIST (EVANGELISTS)
2Ti 4: 5 do the work of an **e**, discharge all

EVANGELISTS (EVANGELIST)
Eph 4: 11 the **e**, the pastors and teachers,

EVE
2Co 11: 3 afraid that just as **E** was deceived
1Ti 2: 13 For Adam was formed first, then **E**.

EVEN-TEMPERED
Pr 17: 27 whoever has understanding is **e**.

EVER (EVERLASTING FOREVER)
Ex 15: 18 "The LORD reigns for **e** and **e**."
Dt   8: 19 you **e** forget the LORD your God
Ps   5: 11 you be glad; let them **e** sing for joy.
    10: 16 The LORD is King for **e** and **e**;
    25: 3 one who hopes in you will **e** be put
    45: 6 throne, O God, will last for **e** and **e**;
    52: 8 I trust in God's unfailing love for **e**
    89: 33 nor will I **e** betray my faithfulness.
   145: 1 I will praise your name for **e** and **e**.
Pr   4: 18 shining **e** brighter till the full light
     5: 19 may you **e** be intoxicated with her
Isa 66: 8 Who has **e** heard of such things?
Jer 31: 36 "will Israel **e** cease being a nation
Da   7: 18 possess it forever—yes, for **e** and **e**.'
    12: 3 like the stars for **e** and **e**.
Mk   4: 12 "'they may be **e** seeing but never
Jn   1: 18 No one has **e** seen God, but
Rev 1: 18 now look, I am alive for **e** and **e**!
    22: 5 And they will reign for **e** and **e**.

EVER-INCREASING (INCREASE)
Ro   6: 19 to impurity and to **e** wickedness,
2Co 3: 18 into his image with **e** glory,

EVERLASTING (EVER)
Dt 33: 27 and underneath are the **e** arms.
Ne   9: 5 your God, who is from **e** to **e**."
Ps 90: 2 world, from **e** to **e** you are God.
   139: 24 in me, and lead me in the way **e**.
Isa 9: 6 Mighty God, **E** Father,
    33: 14 of us can dwell with **e** burning?"

Isa 35: 10 **e** joy will crown their heads.
    45: 17 by the LORD with an **e** salvation;
    54: 8 **e** kindness I will have compassion
    55: 3 I will make an **e** covenant with you,
    63: 12 them, to gain for himself **e** renown,
Jer 31: 3 "I have loved you with an **e** love;
Da   9: 24 to bring in **e** righteousness, to seal
    12: 2 some to **e** life, others to shame and **e**
            contempt.
2Th 1: 9 will be punished with **e** destruction
Jude : 6 bound with **e** chains for judgment

EVER-PRESENT
Ps 46: 1 and strength, an **e** help in trouble.

EVIDENCE (EVIDENT)
Jn 14: 11 on the **e** of the works themselves.

EVIDENT (EVIDENCE)
Php 4: 5 Let your gentleness be **e** to all.

EVIL (EVILDOER EVILDOERS)
Ge   2: 9 of the knowledge of good and **e**.
Job 1: 1 he feared God and shunned **e**.
     1: 8 a man who fears God and shuns **e**."
    34: 10 Far be it from God to do **e**,
Ps 23: 4 will fear no **e**, for you are with me;
    34: 14 Turn from **e** and do good;
    51: 4 and done what is **e** in your sight;
    97: 10 those who love the LORD hate **e**,
   101: 4 have nothing to do with what is **e**.
Pr   8: 13 To fear the LORD is to hate **e**;
    11: 27 **e** comes to one who searches for it.
Isa 5: 20 who call **e** good and good **e**,
    13: 11 I will punish the world for its **e**,
Hab 1: 13 Your eyes are too pure to look on **e**;
Mt   5: 45 He causes his sun to rise on the **e**
     6: 13 but deliver us from the **e** one.'
     7: 11 you are **e**, know how to give
    12: 35 an **e** man brings **e** things out of the **e**
Jn 17: 15 you protect them from the **e** one.
Ro   2: 9 for every human being who does **e**:
    12: 9 Hate what is **e**; cling to what is
    12: 17 Do not repay anyone **e** for **e**.
    16: 19 and innocent about what is **e**.
1Co 13: 6 Love does not delight in **e**
    14: 20 In regard to **e** be infants, but in
Eph 6: 16 all the flaming arrows of the **e** one.
1Th 5: 22 reject every kind of **e**.
1Ti 6: 10 of money is a root of all kinds of **e**.
2Ti 2: 22 Flee the **e** desires of youth
Jas 1: 13 For God cannot be tempted by **e**,
1Pe 2: 16 your freedom as a cover-up for **e**;
     3: 9 Do not repay **e** with **e** or insult
     3: 9 the contrary, repay **e** with blessing,

EVILDOER (EVIL)
Pr 24: 20 for the **e** has no future hope,

EVILDOERS (EVIL)
Pr 24: 19 Do not fret because of **e** or be

EXACT
Heb 1: 3 the **e** representation of his being,

EXALT (EXALTED EXALTS)
Ps 30: 1 I will **e** you, LORD, for you lifted
    34: 3 let us **e** his name together.
   118: 28 you are my God, and I will **e** you.
Isa 24: 15 **e** the name of the LORD, the God
Mt 23: 12 For those who **e** themselves will be

EXALTED (EXALT)
2Sa 22: 47 **E** be my God, the Rock, my Savior!
1Ch 29: 11 you are **e** as head over all.
Ne   9: 5 and may it be **e** above all blessing

Ps   21: 13 Be **e** in your strength, Lord;
    46: 10 I will be **e** among the nations,
    57: 5 Be **e**, O God, above the heavens;
    97: 9 you are **e** far above all gods.
    99: 2 he is **e** over all the nations.
  108: 5 Be **e**, O God, above the heavens;
  148: 13 the Lord, for his name alone is **e**;
Isa   6: 1 high and **e**, seated on a throne;
    12: 4 and proclaim that his name is **e**.
    33: 5 The Lord is **e**, for he dwells
Eze 21: 26 The lowly will be **e** and the **e** will
Mt 23: 12 who humble themselves will be **e**.
Php 1: 20 now as always Christ will be **e**
    2: 9 Therefore God **e** him to the highest

EXALTS (EXALT)
Ps 75: 7 He brings one down, he **e** another.
Pr 14: 34 Righteousness **e** a nation, but sin

EXAMINE (EXAMINED)
Ps 26: 2 try me, **e** my heart and my mind;
Jer 17: 10 search the heart and **e** the mind,
La   3: 40 Let us **e** our ways and test them,
1Co 11: 28 to **e** themselves before they eat
2Co 13: 5 **E** yourselves to see whether you

EXAMINED (EXAMINE)
Ac 17: 11 **e** the Scriptures every day to see

EXAMPLE (EXAMPLES)
Jn 13: 15 I have set you an **e** that you should
1Co 11: 1 Follow my **e**, as I follow the **e**
1Ti   4: 12 set an **e** for the believers in speech,
Titus 2: 7 everything set them an **e** by doing
1Pe 2: 21 leaving you an **e**, that you should

EXAMPLES (EXAMPLE)
1Co 10: 6 Now these things occurred as **e**
    10: 11 things happened to them as **e**
1Pe   5: 3 to you, but being **e** to the flock.

EXASPERATE
Eph 6: 4 Fathers, do not **e** your children;

EXCEL (EXCELLENT)
1Co 14: 12 try to **e** in those that build
2Co 8: 7 you also **e** in this grace of giving.

EXCELLENT (EXCEL)
1Co 12: 31 yet I will show you the most **e** way.
Php 4: 8 if anything is **e** or praiseworthy—
1Ti   3: 13 have served well gain an **e** standing
Titus 3: 8 These things are **e** and profitable

EXCHANGED
Ro   1: 23 **e** the glory of the immortal God
    1: 25 **e** the truth about God for a lie,

EXCUSE (EXCUSES)
Jn 15: 22 now they have no **e** for their sin.
Ro   1: 20 made, so that people are without **e**.

EXCUSES (EXCUSE)
Lk 14: 18 "But they all alike began to make **e**.

EXISTS
Heb 2: 10 and through whom everything **e**,
    11: 6 to him must believe that he **e**

EXPECT (EXPECTATION)
Mt 24: 44 at an hour when you do not **e** him.

EXPECTATION (EXPECT)
Ro   8: 19 waits in eager **e** for the children
Heb 10: 27 but only a fearful **e** of judgment

EXPEL
1Co 5: 13 "**E** the wicked person from among

EXPENSIVE
1Ti   2: 9 or gold or pearls or **e** clothes,

EXPLOIT
Pr 22: 22 Do not **e** the poor because they are
2Co 12: 17 I **e** you through any of the men

EXPOSE
1Co 4: 5 and will **e** the motives of the heart.
Eph 5: 11 of darkness, but rather **e** them.

EXTENDS
Pr 31: 20 poor and **e** her hands to the needy.
Lk   1: 50 His mercy **e** to those who fear him,

EXTINGUISHED
2Sa 21: 17 the lamp of Israel will not be **e**."

EXTOL
Job 36: 24 Remember to **e** his work,
Ps 34: 1 I will **e** the Lord at all times;
    68: 4 **e** him who rides on the clouds;
    95: 2 thanksgiving and **e** him with music
  109: 30 mouth I will greatly **e** the Lord;
  111: 1 I will **e** the Lord with all my
  115: 18 it is we who **e** the Lord,
  117: 1 **e** him, all you peoples.
  145: 2 and **e** your name for ever
  145: 10 your faithful people **e** you.
  147: 12 **E** the Lord, Jerusalem;

EXTORT
Lk   3: 14 "Don't **e** money and don't accuse

EYE (EYES)
Ex 21: 24 **e** for **e**, tooth for tooth,
Ps 94: 9 Does he who formed the **e** not see?
Mt   5: 29 If your right **e** causes you
    5: 38 have heard that it was said, '**E** for **e**,
    7: 3 speck of sawdust in your brother's **e**
1Co 2: 9 "What no **e** has seen, what no ear
Col   3: 22 not only when their **e** is on you
Rev 1: 7 and "every **e** will see him,

EYES (EYE)
Nu 33: 55 remain will become barbs in your **e**
Jos 23: 13 your backs and thorns in your **e**,
2Ch 16: 9 For the Lord range
Job 31: 1 "I made a covenant with my **e** not
    36: 7 not take his **e** off the righteous;
Ps 119: 18 Open my **e** that I may see
  121: 1 I lift up my **e** to the mountains—
  141: 8 But my **e** are fixed on you,
Pr   3: 7 Do not be wise in your own **e**;
    4: 25 Let your **e** look straight ahead;
    15: 3 The **e** of the Lord are
Isa   6: 5 and my **e** have seen the King,
Hab 1: 13 Your **e** are too pure to look on evil;
Jn   4: 35 open your **e** and look at the fields!
2Co 4: 18 So we fix our **e** not on what is seen,
Heb 12: 2 fixing our **e** on Jesus, the pioneer
Jas   2: 5 who are poor in the **e** of the world
1Pe 3: 12 For the **e** of the Lord are
Rev 7: 17 away every tear from their **e**.'"
    21: 4 will wipe every tear from their **e**.

EZEKIEL
Priest called to be prophet to the exiles (Eze 1–3).

EZRA
Priest and teacher of the Law who led a return of exiles to Israel to reestablish temple and worship (Ezr 7–8). Corrected intermarriage of priests (Ezr 9–10). Read Law at celebration of Feast of Tabernacles (Neh 8).

FACE (FACES)
Ge 32: 30 "It is because I saw God **f** to **f**,
Ex 34: 29 that his **f** was radiant because he
Nu   6: 25 the Lord make his **f** shine on you
1Ch 16: 11 and his strength; seek his **f** always.

2Ch	7: 14	and seek my **f** and turn from their
Ps	4: 6	Let the light of your **f** shine on us.
	27: 8	My heart says of you, "Seek his **f**!"
	31: 16	Let your **f** shine on your servant;
	105: 4	and his strength; seek his **f** always.
	119:135	Make your **f** shine on your servant
Isa	50: 7	Therefore have I set my **f** like flint,
Mt	17: 2	His **f** shone like the sun, and his
1Co	13: 12	in a mirror; then we shall see **f** to **f**.
2Co	4: 6	glory displayed in the **f** of Christ.
1Pe	3: 12	the **f** of the Lord is against those
Rev	1: 16	His **f** was like the sun shining in all

FACES (FACE)

2Co	3: 18	unveiled **f** contemplate the Lord's

FACTIONS

Gal	5: 20	rage, selfish ambition, dissensions,

FADE

1Pe	5: 4	of glory that will never **f** away.

FAIL (FAILING FAILINGS FAILS)

1Ch	28: 20	He will not **f** you or forsake you
2Ch	34: 33	they did not **f** to follow the Lord,
Ps	89: 28	my covenant with him will never **f**.
Pr	15: 22	Plans **f** for lack of counsel,
Isa	51: 6	my righteousness will never **f**.
La	3: 22	for his compassions never **f**.
2Co	13: 5	unless, of course, you **f** the test?

FAILING (FAIL)

1Sa	12: 23	I should sin against the Lord by **f**

FAILINGS (FAIL)

Ro	15: 1	to bear with the **f** of the weak

FAILS (FAIL)

1Co	13: 8	Love never **f**. But where there are

FAINT

Isa	40: 31	weary, they will walk and not be **f**.

FAIR

Pr	1: 3	doing what is right and just and **f**;
Col	4: 1	your slaves with what is right and **f**,

FAITH (FAITHFUL FAITHFULLY FAITHFULNESS FAITHLESS)

2Ch	20: 20	Have **f** in the Lord your God
	20: 20	have **f** in his prophets
Mt	9: 29	"According to your **f** let it be done
	17: 20	if you have **f** as small as a mustard
	24: 10	many will turn away from the **f**
Mk	11: 22	"Have **f** in God," Jesus answered.
Lk	7: 9	I have not found such great **f** even
	12: 28	will he clothe you—you of little **f**!
	17: 5	said to the Lord, "Increase our **f**!"
	18: 8	comes, will he find **f** on the earth?"
Ac	14: 9	him, saw that he had **f** to be healed
	14: 27	how he had opened a door of **f**
Ro	1: 12	encouraged by each other's **f**.
	1: 17	"The righteous will live by **f**."
	1: 17	righteousness that is by **f** from first
	3: 22	righteousness is given through **f**
	3: 25	of his blood—to be received by **f**.
	4: 5	their **f** is credited as righteousness.
	5: 1	we have been justified through **f**,
	10: 17	**f** comes from hearing the message,
	14: 1	Accept the one whose **f** is weak,
	14: 23	that does not come from **f** is sin.
	16: 26	the obedience that comes from **f**—
1Co	13: 2	have a **f** that can move mountains,
	13: 13	three remain: **f**, hope and love.
	16: 13	stand firm in the **f**; be courageous;
2Co	5: 7	For we live by **f**, not by sight.
	13: 5	to see whether you are in the **f**;

Gal	2: 16	we may be justified by **f** in Christ
	2: 20	body, I live by **f** in the Son of God,
	3: 11	"the righteous will live by **f**."
	3: 24	that we might be justified by **f**.
Eph	2: 8	you have been saved, through **f**—
	4: 5	one Lord, one **f**, one baptism;
	6: 16	take up the shield of **f**,
Col	1: 23	if you continue in your **f**,
1Th	5: 8	be sober, putting on **f** and love as
1Ti	2: 15	if they continue in **f**,
	4: 1	later times some will abandon the **f**
	5: 8	has denied the **f** and is worse than
	6: 12	Fight the good fight of the **f**.
2Ti	3: 15	salvation through **f** in Christ Jesus.
	4: 7	finished the race, I have kept the **f**.
Phm	: 6	with us in the **f** may be effective
Heb	10: 38	my righteous one will live by **f**.
	11: 1	Now **f** is confidence in what we
	11: 3	By **f** we understand that the
	11: 5	By **f** Enoch was taken from this
	11: 6	without **f** it is impossible to please
	11: 7	By **f** Noah, when warned
	11: 7	By his **f** he condemned the world
	11: 8	By **f** Abraham, when called to go
	11: 17	By **f** Abraham, when God tested
	11: 20	By **f** Isaac blessed Jacob and Esau
	11: 21	By **f** Jacob, when he was dying,
	11: 22	By **f** Joseph, when his end was
	11: 24	By **f** Moses, when he had grown
	11: 31	By **f** the prostitute Rahab,
	12: 2	Jesus, the pioneer and perfecter of **f**.
Jas	2: 14	Can such **f** save them?
	2: 17	In the same way, **f** by itself, if it is
	2: 26	is dead, so **f** without deeds is dead.
2Pe	1: 5	effort to add to your **f** goodness;
1Jn	5: 4	overcome the world, even our **f**.
Jude	: 3	contend for the **f** that was once

FAITHFUL (FAITH)

Nu	12: 7	he is **f** in all my house.
Dt	7: 9	he is the **f** God, keeping his
	32: 4	**f** God who does no wrong,
2Sa	22: 26	"To the **f** you show yourself **f**,
Ps	16: 10	will you let your **f** one see decay.
	25: 10	and **f** toward those who keep
	31: 23	Love the Lord, all his **f** people!
	33: 4	right and true; he is **f** in all he does.
	37: 28	just and will not forsake his **f** ones.
	97: 10	for he guards the lives of his **f** ones
	116: 15	is the death of his **f** servants.
	145: 13	all he promises and **f** in all he does.
	145: 17	in all his ways and **f** in all he does.
	146: 6	he remains **f** forever.
Pr	31: 26	and **f** instruction is on her tongue.
Mt	25: 21	'Well done, good and **f** servant!
	25: 21	You have been **f** with a few things;
Ro	12: 12	patient in affliction, **f** in prayer.
1Co	4: 2	been given a trust must prove **f**.
	10: 13	And God is **f**; he will not let you be
1Th	5: 24	The one who calls you is **f**, and he
1Ti	3: 2	to be above reproach, **f** to his wife,
2Ti	2: 13	he remains **f**, for he cannot disown
Heb	3: 6	Christ is **f** as the Son over God's
	10: 23	profess, for he who promised is **f**.
1Pe	4: 10	as **f** stewards of God's grace in its
	4: 19	themselves to their **f** Creator
1Jn	1: 9	he is **f** and just and will forgive us
Rev	1: 5	who is the **f** witness, the firstborn
	2: 10	Be **f**, even to the point of death,
	19: 11	whose rider is called **F** and True.

FAITHFULLY (FAITH)

Dt	11: 13	So if you **f** obey the commands

1Sa 12: 24 and serve him **f** with all your heart;
1Ki 2: 4 if they walk **f** before me with all

FAITHFULNESS (FAITH)
Ps 51: 6 you desired **f** even in the womb;
57: 10 your **f** reaches to the skies.
85: 10 Love and **f** meet together;
86: 15 to anger, abounding in love and **f**.
89: 1 make your **f** known through all
89: 14 love and **f** go before you.
91: 4 his **f** will be your shield
117: 2 the **f** of the LORD endures forever.
119: 75 and that in **f** you have afflicted me.
Pr 3: 3 Let love and **f** never leave you;
Isa 11: 5 and **f** the sash around his waist.
La 3: 23 new every morning; great is your **f**.
Hab 2: 4 righteous person will live by his **f**—
Ro 3: 3 their unfaithfulness nullify God's **f**?
Gal 5: 22 forbearance, kindness, goodness, **f**,

FAITHLESS (FAITH)
Ps 119:158 I look on the **f** with loathing,
Jer 3: 22 "Return, **f** people; I will cure you
2Ti 2: 13 if we are **f**, he remains faithful,

FALL (FALLEN FALLS)
Ps 37: 24 he will not **f**, for the LORD
69: 9 of those who insult you **f** on me.
Pr 11: 28 who trust in their riches will **f**,
Lk 11: 17 a house divided against itself will **f**.
Jn 16: 1 you so that you will not **f** away.
Ro 3: 23 and **f** short of the glory of God,
14: 4 own master, servants stand or **f**.

FALLEN (FALL)
2Sa 1: 19 How the mighty have **f**!
Isa 14: 12 How you have **f** from heaven,
1Co 15: 20 of those who have **f** asleep.
Gal 5: 4 you have **f** away from grace.
1Th 4: 15 precede those who have **f** asleep.
Heb 6: 6 and who have **f** away, to be brought

FALLS (FALL)
Pr 24: 17 Do not gloat when your enemy **f**;
Jn 12: 24 a kernel of wheat **f** to the ground

FALSE (FALSEHOOD FALSELY)
Ex 20: 16 shall not give **f** testimony against
23: 1 "Do not spread **f** reports.
Pr 13: 5 The righteous hate what is **f**,
19: 5 A **f** witness will not go unpunished,
Mt 7: 15 "Watch out for **f** prophets.
19: 18 steal, you shall not give **f** testimony,
24: 11 and many **f** prophets will appear
Php 1: 18 whether from **f** motives or true,
1Ti 1: 3 not to teach **f** doctrines any longer
2Pe 2: 1 there will be **f** teachers among you.

FALSEHOOD (FALSE)
Ps 119:163 and detest **f** but I love your law.
Pr 30: 8 Keep **f** and lies far from me;
Eph 4: 25 each of you must put off **f**

FALSELY (FALSE)
Lev 19: 12 "'Do not swear **f** by my name
Lk 3: 14 money and don't accuse people **f**—
1Ti 6: 20 ideas of what is **f** called knowledge,

FALTER
Pr 24: 10 If you **f** in a time of trouble,
Isa 42: 4 he will not **f** or be discouraged till

FAMILIES (FAMILY)
Ps 68: 6 God sets the lonely in **f**, he leads

FAMILY (FAMILIES)
Pr 31: 15 she provides food for her **f**

Lk 9: 61 go back and say goodbye to my **f**."
12: 52 in one **f** divided against each other,
1Ti 3: 4 He must manage his own **f** well
3: 5 know how to manage his own **f**,
5: 4 practice by caring for their own **f**

FAMINE
Ge 41: 30 seven years of **f** will follow them.
Am 8: 11 I will send a **f** through the land—
Ro 8: 35 or persecution or **f** or nakedness

FAN
2Ti 1: 6 this reason I remind you to **f**

FAST
Dt 13: 4 serve him and hold **f** to him.
Jos 22: 5 to hold **f** to him and to serve him
23: 8 to hold **f** to the LORD your God,
Ps 119: 31 I hold **f** to your statutes, LORD;
139: 10 me, your right hand will hold me **f**.
Mt 6: 16 "When you **f**, do not look somber
1Pe 5: 12 the true grace of God. Stand **f** in it.

FATHER (FATHER'S FATHERLESS FATHERS)
Ge 2: 24 That is why a man leaves his **f**
17: 4 You will be the **f** of many nations.
Ex 20: 12 "Honor your **f** and your mother,
21: 15 "Anyone who attacks their **f**
21: 17 "Anyone who curses their **f**
Lev 18: 7 "'Do not dishonor your **f**
19: 3 must respect your mother and **f**,
Dt 5: 16 "Honor your **f** and your mother,
21: 18 son who does not obey his **f**
Ps 27: 10 Though my **f** and mother forsake
68: 5 A **f** to the fatherless, a defender
Pr 10: 1 A wise son brings joy to his **f**,
23: 22 Listen to your **f**, who gave you life,
23: 24 The **f** of a righteous child has great
28: 7 of gluttons disgraces his **f**.
29: 3 loves wisdom brings joy to his **f**,
Isa 9: 6 Everlasting **F**, Prince of Peace.
Mt 6: 9 "'Our **F** in heaven, hallowed be
10: 37 "Anyone who loves their **f**
15: 4 said, 'Honor your **f** and mother'
19: 5 this reason a man will leave his **f**
Lk 12: 53 **f** against son and son against **f**,
23: 34 Jesus said, "**F**, forgive them,
Jn 6: 44 unless the **F** who sent me draws
6: 46 from God; only he has seen the **F**.
8: 44 You belong to your **f**, the devil,
10: 30 I and the **F** are one."
14: 6 comes to the **F** except through me.
14: 9 who has seen me has seen the **F**.
Ro 4: 11 he is the **f** of all who believe
2Co 6: 18 And, "I will be a **F** to you, and you
Eph 6: 2 "Honor your **f** and mother"—
Heb 12: 7 are not disciplined by their **f**?

FATHER'S (FATHER)
Pr 13: 1 wise son heeds his **f** instruction,
19: 13 A foolish child is a **f** ruin,
Lk 2: 49 know I had to be in my **F** house?"
Jn 2: 16 Stop turning my **F** house
10: 29 can snatch them out of my **F** hand.
14: 2 My **F** house has many rooms;

FATHERLESS (FATHER)
Dt 10: 18 He defends the cause of the **f**
24: 17 the foreigner or the **f** of justice,
24: 19 the foreigner, the **f** and the widow,
Ps 68: 5 A father to the **f**, a defender
Pr 23: 10 or encroach on the fields of the **f**,

FATHERS (FATHER)
Lk 11: 11 "Which of you **f**, if your son asks

Eph 6: 4 **F**, do not exasperate your children;
Col 3: 21 **F**, do not embitter your children,

FATHOM
Job 11: 7 "Can you **f** the mysteries of God?
Ps 145: 3 his greatness no one can **f**.
Ecc 3: 11 no one can **f** what God has done
Isa 40: 28 his understanding no one can **f**.
1Co 13: 2 of prophecy and can **f** all mysteries

FAULT (FAULTS)
Mt 18: 15 sins, go and point out their **f**,
Php 2: 15 of God without **f** in a warped
Jas 1: 5 generously to all without finding **f**,
Jude : 24 his glorious presence without **f**

FAULTFINDERS
Jude : 16 These people are grumblers and **f**;

FAULTS (FAULT)
Ps 19: 12 Forgive my hidden **f**.

FAVORITISM
Ex 23: 3 do not show **f** to a poor person
Lev 19: 15 to the poor or **f** to the great,
Ac 10: 34 true it is that God does not show **f**
Ro 2: 11 For God does not show **f**.
Gal 2: 6 God does not show **f**—
Eph 6: 9 heaven, and there is no **f** with him.
Col 3: 25 for their wrongs, and there is no **f**.
1Ti 5: 21 and to do nothing out of **f**.
Jas 2: 1 Lord Jesus Christ must not show **f**.
2: 9 But if you show **f**, you sin and are

FEAR (AFRAID FEARS)
Dt 6: 13 **F** the LORD your God, serve him
10: 12 you but to **f** the LORD your God,
31: 12 learn to **f** the LORD your God
Ps 19: 9 The **f** of the LORD is pure,
23: 4 the darkest valley, I will **f** no evil,
27: 1 and my salvation—whom shall I **f**?
91: 5 You will not **f** the terror of night,
111: 10 The **f** of the LORD is
Pr 8: 13 To **f** the LORD is to hate evil;
9: 10 The **f** of the LORD is
10: 27 The **f** of the LORD adds length
14: 27 The **f** of the LORD is a fountain
15: 33 instruction is to **f** the LORD,
16: 6 through the **f** of the LORD evil is
19: 23 The **f** of the LORD leads to life;
29: 25 **F** of man will prove to be a snare,
Ecc 5: 7 Therefore **f** God.
Isa 11: 3 will delight in the **f** of the LORD.
41: 10 So do not **f**, for I am with you;
Lk 12: 5 will show you whom you should **f**:
Php 2: 12 to work out your salvation with **f**
1Jn 4: 18 There is no **f** in love. But perfect love
drives out **f**,

FEARS (FEAR)
Job 1: 8 a man who **f** God and shuns evil."
Ps 34: 4 he delivered me from all my **f**.
Pr 31: 30 a woman who **f** the LORD is to be
1Jn 4: 18 The one who **f** is not made perfect

FEED
Jn 21: 15 Jesus said, "**F** my lambs."
21: 17 Jesus said, "**F** my sheep.
Ro 12: 20 "If your enemy is hungry, **f** him;
Jude : 12 shepherds who **f** only themselves.

FEET (FOOT)
Ps 8: 6 you put everything under their **f**:
22: 16 they pierce my hands and my **f**.
40: 2 he set my **f** on a rock and gave me
110: 1 enemies a footstool for your **f**."
119:105 Your word is a lamp to my **f**

Ro 10: 15 "How beautiful are the **f** of those
1Co 12: 21 And the head cannot say to the **f**,
15: 25 has put all his enemies under his **f**.
Heb 12: 13 "Make level paths for your **f**,"

FELLOWSHIP
2Co 6: 14 **f** can light have with darkness?
13: 14 the **f** of the Holy Spirit be with you
1Jn 1: 6 If we claim to have **f** with him
1: 7 light, we have **f** with one another,

FEMALE
Ge 1: 27 male and **f** he created them.
Gal 3: 28 nor is there male and **f**, for you are

FERVOR
Ro 12: 11 but keep your spiritual **f**,

FIDELITY
Ro 1: 31 no understanding, no **f**, no love,

FIELD (FIELDS)
Mt 6: 28 See how the flowers of the **f** grow.
13: 38 The **f** is the world, and the good
1Co 3: 9 you are God's **f**, God's building.

FIELDS (FIELD)
Lk 2: 8 shepherds living out in the **f**
Jn 4: 35 open your eyes and look at the **f**!

FIERY (FIRE)
1Pe 4: 12 do not be surprised at the **f** ordeal

FIG (FIGS)
Ge 3: 7 so they sewed **f** leaves together

FIGHT (FOUGHT)
Ex 14: 14 The LORD will **f** for you;
Dt 1: 30 is going before you, will **f** for you,
3: 22 the LORD your God himself will **f**
Ne 4: 20 Our God will **f** for us!"
Ps 35: 1 **f** against those who **f** against me.
Jn 18: 36 my servants would **f** to prevent my
1Co 9: 26 I do not **f** like a boxer beating
2Co 10: 4 The weapons we **f** with are not
1Ti 1: 18 them you may **f** the battle well,
6: 12 **F** the good **f** of the faith.
2Ti 4: 7 I have fought the good **f**, I have

FIGS (FIG)
Lk 6: 44 People do not pick **f**

FILL (FILLED FILLS FULL FULLNESS FULLY)
Ge 1: 28 **f** the earth and subdue it.
Ps 16: 11 you will **f** me with joy in your
81: 10 wide your mouth and I will **f** it.
Pr 28: 19 chase fantasies will have their **f**
Hag 2: 7 and I will **f** this house with glory,'
Jn 6: 26 you ate the loaves and had your **f**.
Ac 2: 28 you will **f** me with joy in your
Ro 15: 13 May the God of hope **f** you with all

FILLED (FILL)
Ps 72: 19 may the whole earth be **f** with his
119: 64 The earth is **f** with your love,
Isa 11: 9 for the earth will be **f**
Eze 43: 5 glory of the LORD **f** the temple.
Hab 2: 14 For the earth will be **f**
Lk 1: 15 he will be **f** with the Holy Spirit
1: 41 Elizabeth was **f** with the Holy Spirit.
Jn 12: 3 the house was **f** with the fragrance
Ac 2: 4 of them were **f** with the Holy Spirit
4: 8 Then Peter, **f** with the Holy Spirit,
9: 17 and be **f** with the Holy Spirit."
13: 9 called Paul, **f** with the Holy Spirit,
Eph 5: 18 Instead, be **f** with the Spirit,
Php 1: 11 **f** with the fruit of righteousness

FILLS (FILL)
Nu 14: 21 of the LORD *f* the whole earth,
Ps 107: 9 and *f* the hungry with good things.
Eph 1: 23 him who *f* everything in every way.

FILTHY
Isa 64: 6 all our righteous acts are like *f* rags;
Col 3: 8 and *f* language from your lips.

FIND (FINDS FOUND)
Nu 32: 23 be sure that your sin will *f* you out.
Dt 4: 29 you will *f* him if you seek him
1Sa 23: 16 and helped him *f* strength in God.
Ps 91: 4 under his wings you will *f* refuge;
112: 1 LORD, who *f* great delight in his
Pr 14: 22 those who plan what is good *f* love
31: 10 wife of noble character who can *f*?
Jer 6: 16 and you will *f* rest for your souls.
Mt 7: 7 seek and you will *f*;
11: 29 and you will *f* rest for your souls.
16: 25 loses their life for me will *f* it.
Lk 18: 8 will he *f* faith on the earth?"
Jn 10: 9 come in and go out, and *f* pasture.

FINDS (FIND)
Ps 62: 1 Truly my soul *f* rest in God;
119:162 promise like one who *f* great spoil.
Pr 18: 22 He who *f* a wife *f* what is good
Mt 7: 8 the one who seeks *f*; and to the one
10: 39 Whoever *f* their life will lose it,
Lk 12: 37 whose master *f* them watching
15: 4 go after the lost sheep until he *f* it?

FINISH (FINISHED)
Jn 4: 34 him who sent me and to *f* his work.
5: 36 that the Father has given me to *f*—
Ac 20: 24 my only aim is to *f* the race
2Co 8: 11 Now *f* the work, so that your eager
Gal 3: 3 are you now trying to *f* by means
Jas 1: 4 Let perseverance *f* its work so

FINISHED (FINISH)
Ge 2: 2 seventh day God had *f* the work he
Jn 19: 30 the drink, Jesus said, "It is *f*."
2Ti 4: 7 the good fight, I have *f* the race,

FIRE (FIERY)
Ex 13: 21 in a pillar of *f* to give them light,
Lev 6: 12 The *f* on the altar must be kept
Isa 30: 27 and his tongue is a consuming *f*.
Jer 23: 29 "Is not my word like *f*,"
Mt 3: 11 you with the Holy Spirit and *f*.
5: 22 will be in danger of the *f* of hell.
25: 41 the eternal *f* prepared for the devil
Mk 9: 43 hell, where the *f* never goes out.
Ac 2: 3 to be tongues of *f* that separated
1Co 3: 13 It will be revealed with *f*, and the *f*
Heb 12: 29 for our "God is a consuming *f*."
Jas 3: 5 what a great forest is set on *f*
2Pe 3: 10 the elements will be destroyed by *f*,
Jude : 23 by snatching them from the *f*;
Rev 20: 14 *f*. The lake of *f* is the second death.

FIRM
Ex 14: 13 Stand *f* and you will see
2Ch 20: 17 stand *f* and see the deliverance
Ps 33: 11 plans of the LORD stand *f* forever,
37: 23 The LORD makes *f* the steps
40: 2 and gave me a *f* place to stand.
89: 2 that your love stands *f* forever,
119: 89 it stands *f* in the heavens.
Zec 8: 23 nations will take *f* hold of one Jew
Mk 13: 13 the one who stands *f* to the end
1Co 16: 13 on your guard; stand *f* in the faith;

2Co 1: 24 because it is by faith you stand *f*.
Eph 6: 14 Stand *f* then, with the belt of truth
Col 4: 12 that you may stand *f* in all the will
2Th 2: 15 stand *f* and hold fast to the teachings
2Ti 2: 19 God's solid foundation stands *f*,
Heb 6: 19 anchor for the soul, *f* and secure.
1Pe 5: 9 Resist him, standing *f* in the faith,

FIRST
Isa 44: 6 I am the *f* and I am the last;
48: 12 I am the *f* and I am the last.
Mt 5: 24 *F* go and be reconciled to them;
6: 33 But seek *f* his kingdom and his
7: 5 *f* take the plank out of your own
20: 27 wants to be *f* must be your slave—
22: 38 This is the *f* and greatest
23: 26 *F* clean the inside of the cup
Mk 13: 10 the gospel must *f* be preached to all
Ac 11: 26 disciples were called Christians *f*
Ro 1: 16 *f* to the Jew, then to the Gentile.
1Co 12: 28 in the church *f* of all apostles,
2Co 8: 5 They gave themselves *f* of all
1Ti 2: 13 For Adam was formed *f*, then Eve.
Jas 3: 17 comes from heaven is *f* of all pure;
1Jn 4: 19 We love because he *f* loved us.
3Jn : 9 who loves to be *f*, will not welcome
Rev 1: 17 I am the *F* and the Last.
2: 4 have forsaken the love you had at *f*.

FIRSTBORN (BEAR)
Ex 11: 5 Every *f* son in Egypt will die,

FIRSTFRUITS
Ex 23: 19 "Bring the best of the *f* of your soil

FISH
Mk 1: 17 I will send you out to *f* for people."
Lk 5: 10 from now on you will *f* for people."

FITTING
Ps 33: 1 it is *f* for the upright to praise him.
147: 1 how pleasant and *f* to praise him!
Pr 19: 10 It is not *f* for a fool to live
26: 1 in harvest, honor is not *f* for a fool.
1Co 14: 40 everything should be done in a *f*
Col 3: 18 your husbands, as is *f* in the Lord.
Heb 2: 10 to glory, it was *f* that God,

FIX (FIXING)
Dt 11: 18 *F* these words of mine in your
Pr 4: 25 *f* your gaze directly before you.
2Co 4: 18 So we *f* our eyes not on what is
Heb 3: 1 calling, *f* your thoughts on Jesus,

FIXING (FIX)
Heb 12: 2 *f* our eyes on Jesus, the pioneer

FLAME (FLAMES FLAMING)
2Ti 1: 6 you to fan into *f* the gift of God,

FLAMES (FLAME)
1Co 3: 15 only as one escaping through the *f*.

FLAMING (FLAME)
Eph 6: 16 you can extinguish all the *f* arrows

FLASH
1Co 15: 52 in a *f*, in the twinkling of an eye,

FLATTER (FLATTERING FLATTERY)
Ps 12: 2 they *f* with their lips but harbor
Job 32: 21 no partiality, nor will I *f* anyone;
Jude : 16 *f* others for their own advantage.

FLATTERING (FLATTER)
Ps 12: 3 May the LORD silence all *f* lips
Pr 26: 28 it hurts, and a *f* mouth works ruin.

FLATTERY (FLATTER)
Ro 16: 18 *f* they deceive the minds of naive
1Th 2: 5 You know we never used *f*, nor did

FLAWLESS
2Sa 22: 31 The Lord's word is **f**;
Job 11: 4 'My beliefs are **f** and I am pure
Ps 12: 6 And the words of the Lord are **f**,
18: 30 The Lord's word is **f**;
Pr 30: 5 "Every word of God is **f**; he is
SS 5: 2 my darling, my dove, my **f** one.

FLEE
Ps 139: 7 Where can I **f** from your presence?
1Co 6: 18 **F** from sexual immorality.
10: 14 my dear friends, **f** from idolatry.
1Ti 6: 11 man of God, **f** from all this,
2Ti 2: 22 **F** the evil desires of youth
Jas 4: 7 the devil, and he will **f** from you.

FLEETING
Ps 89: 47 Remember how **f** is my life.
Pr 31: 30 is deceptive, and beauty is **f**;

FLESH
Ge 2: 23 bone of my bones and **f** of my **f**;
2: 24 to his wife, and they become one **f**.
Job 19: 26 yet in my **f** I will see God;
Eze 11: 19 of stone and give them a heart of **f**.
36: 26 of stone and give you a heart of **f**.
Mt 26: 41 spirit is willing, but the **f** is weak."
Mk 10: 8 and the two will become one **f**.'
Jn 1: 14 The Word became **f** and made his
6: 51 bread is my **f**, which I will give
Ro 8: 4 do not live according to the **f** but
8: 8 realm of the **f** cannot please God.
1Co 6: 16 said, "The two will become one **f**."
Gal 3: 3 trying to finish by means of the **f**?
5: 19 The acts of the **f** are obvious:
5: 24 crucified the **f** with its passions
Eph 5: 31 and the two will become one **f**."
6: 12 For our struggle is not against **f**

FLOCK (FLOCKS)
Isa 40: 11 He tends his **f** like a shepherd:
Eze 34: 2 not shepherds take care of the **f**?
Zec 11: 17 shepherd, who deserts the **f**!
Mt 26: 31 the sheep of the **f** will be scattered.'
Ac 20: 28 all the **f** of which the Holy Spirit
1Pe 5: 2 of God's **f** that is under your care,

FLOCKS (FLOCK)
Lk 2: 8 keeping watch over their **f** at night.

FLOG
Ac 22: 25 **f** a Roman citizen who hasn't even

FLOODGATES
Mal 3: 10 will not throw open the **f** of heaven

FLOURISHING
Ps 52: 8 am like an olive tree **f** in the house

FLOW (FLOWING)
Nu 13: 27 and it does **f** with milk and honey!
Jn 7: 38 of living water will **f** from within

FLOWERS
Isa 40: 7 The grass withers and the **f** fall,
Lk 12: 27 "Consider how the wild **f** grow.

FLOWING (FLOW)
Ex 3: 8 a land **f** with milk and honey—

FOLDING
Pr 6: 10 a little **f** of the hands to rest—

FOLLOW (FOLLOWS)
Ex 23: 2 "Do not **f** the crowd in doing
Lev 18: 4 laws and be careful to **f** my decrees.
Dt 5: 1 Learn them and be sure to **f** them.

Ps 23: 6 love will **f** me all the days of my
Mt 16: 24 and take up their cross and **f** me.
Jn 10: 4 his sheep **f** him because they know
1Co 14: 1 **F** the way of love and eagerly desire
Eph 5: 1 **F** God's example, therefore,
Rev 14: 4 They **f** the Lamb wherever he goes.

FOLLOWS (FOLLOW)
Jn 8: 12 Whoever **f** me will never walk

FOOD (FOODS)
Pr 20: 13 awake and you will have **f** to spare.
22: 9 for they share their **f** with the poor.
25: 21 enemy is hungry, give him **f** to eat;
31: 15 she provides **f** for her family
Da 1: 8 to defile himself with the royal **f**
Jn 6: 27 Do not work for **f** that spoils, but for **f**
that endures to eternal life,
1Co 8: 8 **f** does not bring us near to God;
1Ti 6: 8 But if we have **f** and clothing,
Jas 2: 15 sister is without clothes and daily **f**.

FOODS (FOOD)
Mk 7: 19 this, Jesus declared all **f** clean.)

FOOL (FOOLISH FOOLISHNESS FOOLS)
Ps 14: 1 The **f** says in his heart, "There
Pr 15: 5 A **f** spurns a parent's discipline,
26: 5 Answer a **f** according to his folly,
Mt 5: 22 And anyone who says, 'You **f**!'

FOOLISH (FOOL)
Pr 10: 1 a **f** son brings grief to his mother.
17: 25 A **f** son brings grief to his father
Mt 7: 26 practice is like a **f** man who built
25: 2 Five of them were **f** and five were
1Co 1: 27 God chose the **f** things of the world

FOOLISHNESS (FOOL)
1Co 1: 18 of the cross is **f** to those who are
1: 25 the **f** of God is wiser than human
2: 14 Spirit of God but considers them **f**,
3: 19 of this world is **f** in God's sight.

FOOLS (FOOL)
Pr 14: 9 **F** mock at making amends for sin,
17: 28 Even **f** are thought wise if they
18: 2 **F** find no pleasure in understanding
28: 26 who trust in themselves are **f**,
1Co 4: 10 We are **f** for Christ, but you are so

FOOT (FEET FOOTHOLD)
Jos 1: 3 every place where you set your **f**,
Isa 1: 6 the sole of your **f** to the top of your
1Co 12: 15 Now if the **f** should say, "Because I

FOOTHOLD (FOOT)
Eph 4: 27 and do not give the devil a **f**.

FORBEARANCE
Ro 3: 25 his **f** he had left the sins committed
Gal 5: 22 love, joy, peace, **f**, kindness,

FORBID
1Co 14: 39 and do not **f** speaking in tongues.

FOREIGNER (FOREIGNERS)
Ex 22: 21 "Do not mistreat or oppress a **f**,

FOREIGNERS (FOREIGNER)
1Pe 2: 11 urge you, as **f** and exiles, to abstain

FOREKNEW (KNOW)
Ro 8: 29 those God **f** he also predestined
11: 2 not reject his people, whom he **f**.

FOREVER (EVER)
1Ch 16: 15 He remembers his covenant **f**,
16: 34 for he is good; his love endures **f**.

Ps   9: 7   The LORD reigns **f**;
    23: 6   dwell in the house of the LORD **f**.
    33: 11   plans of the LORD stand firm **f**,
    86: 12   I will glorify your name **f**.
    92: 8   But you, LORD, are **f** exalted.
  110: 4   "You are a priest **f**, in the order
  119: 111   Your statutes are my heritage **f**;
Jn   6: 51   Whoever eats this bread will live **f**.
    14: 16   to help you and be with you **f**—
1Co   9: 25   do it to get a crown that will last **f**.
1Th   4: 17   And so we will be with the Lord **f**.
Heb 13: 8   the same yesterday and today and **f**.
1Pe   1: 25   the word of the Lord endures **f**."
1Jn   2: 17   does the will of God lives **f**.

FORFEIT
Lk   9: 25   and yet lose or **f** their very self?

FORGAVE (FORGIVE)
Ps 32: 5   And you **f** the guilt of my sin.
Lk   7: 42   him back, so he **f** the debts of both.
Eph   4: 32   other, just as in Christ God **f** you.
Col   2: 13   He **f** us all our sins,
    3: 13   Forgive as the Lord **f** you.

FORGET (FORGETS FORGETTING)
Dt   6: 12   that you do not **f** the LORD,
Ps 103: 2   my soul, and **f** not all his benefits—
  137: 5   If I **f** you, Jerusalem, may my right
Isa 49: 15   Though she may **f**, I will not **f** you!
Heb   6: 10   will not **f** your work and the love

FORGETS (FORGET)
Jn 16: 21   is born she **f** the anguish because
Jas   1: 24   immediately **f** what he looks like.

FORGETTING (FORGET)
Php   3: 13   **F** what is behind and straining

FORGIVE (FORGAVE FORGIVENESS FORGIVING)
2Ch   7: 14   and I will **f** their sin and will heal
Ps 19: 12   **F** my hidden faults.
Mt   6: 12   And **f** us our debts, as we also have
    6: 14   if you **f** other people when they sin
  18: 21   many times shall I **f** my brother
Mk 11: 25   anything against anyone, **f** them,
Lk 11: 4   **F** us our sins, for we also **f** everyone
  23: 34   "Father, **f** them, for they do not
Col   3: 13   **F** as the Lord forgave you.
1Jn   1: 9   and will **f** us our sins and purify

FORGIVENESS (FORGIVE)
Ps 130: 4   But with you there is **f**, so that we
Ac 10: 43   in him receives **f** of sins through
Eph   1: 7   through his blood, the **f** of sins,
Col   1: 14   we have redemption, the **f** of sins.
Heb   9: 22   the shedding of blood there is no **f**.

FORGIVING (FORGIVE)
Ne   9: 17   But you are a **f** God,
Eph   4: 32   to one another, **f** each other, just as

FORMED
Ge   2: 7   the LORD God **f** a man
Ps 103: 14   for he knows how we are **f**,
Isa 45: 18   be empty, but **f** it to be inhabited—
Ro   9: 20   what is **f** say to the one who **f** it,
1Ti   2: 13   For Adam was **f** first, then Eve.
Heb 11: 3   that the universe was **f** at God's

FORSAKE (FORSAKEN)
Jos   1: 5   I will never leave you nor **f** you.
  24: 16   us to **f** the LORD to serve other
2Ch 15: 2   you, but if you **f** him, he will **f** you.
Ps 27: 10   Though my father and mother **f** me,

Isa 55: 7   Let the wicked **f** their ways
Heb 13: 5   will I leave you; never will I **f** you."

FORSAKEN (FORSAKE)
Ezr   9: 9   God has not **f** us in our bondage.
Ps 22: 1   God, my God, why have you **f** me?
  37: 25   I have never seen the righteous **f**
Mt 27: 46   my God, why have you **f** me?").
Rev   2: 4   You have **f** the love you had at first.

FORTIFIED
Pr 18: 10   name of the LORD is a **f** tower;

FORTRESS
Ps 18: 2   is my rock, my **f** and my deliverer;
  71: 3   me, for you are my rock and my **f**.

FOUGHT (FIGHT)
2Ti   4: 7   I have **f** the good fight, I have

FOUND (FIND)
1Ch 28: 9   If you seek him, he will be **f** by you;
Isa 55: 6   Seek the LORD while he may be **f**;
Da   5: 27   on the scales and **f** wanting.
Lk 15: 6   I have **f** my lost sheep.'
  15: 9   I have **f** my lost coin.'
Ac   4: 12   Salvation is **f** in no one else,

FOUNDATION
Isa 28: 16   a precious cornerstone for a sure **f**;
1Co   3: 11   can lay any **f** other than the one
Eph   2: 20   built on the **f** of the apostles
2Ti   2: 19   God's solid **f** stands firm,

FOXES
Mt   8: 20   "**F** have dens and birds have nests,

FRANKINCENSE
Mt   2: 11   him with gifts of gold, **f** and myrrh.

FREE (FREED FREEDOM FREELY)
Ps 146: 7   The LORD sets prisoners **f**,
Jn   8: 32   truth, and the truth will set you **f**."
Ro   6: 18   You have been set **f** from sin
Gal   3: 28   neither slave nor **f**, nor is there
1Pe   2: 16   Live as **f** people, but do not use

FREED (FREE)
Rev   1: 5   has **f** us from our sins by his blood,

FREEDOM (FREE)
Ro   8: 21   brought into the **f** and glory
2Co   3: 17   the Spirit of the Lord is, there is **f**.
Gal   5: 13   But do not use your **f** to indulge
1Pe   2: 16   do not use your **f** as

FREELY (FREE)
Isa 55: 7   to our God, for he will **f** pardon.
Mt 10: 8   **F** you have received; **f** give.
Ro   3: 24   and all are justified **f** by his grace
Eph   1: 6   which he has **f** given us in the One

FRIEND (FRIENDS)
Ex 33: 11   face to face, as one speaks to a **f**.
Pr 17: 17   A **f** loves at all times, and a brother
  18: 24   there is a **f** who sticks closer than
  27: 6   Wounds from a **f** can be trusted,
  27: 10   Do not forsake your **f** or a **f** of your
Jas   4: 4   to be a **f** of the world becomes

FRIENDS (FRIEND)
Pr 16: 28   and a gossip separates close **f**.
  18: 24   who has unreliable **f** soon comes
Zec 13: 6   I was given at the house of my **f**.'
Jn 15: 13   to lay down one's life for one's **f**.

FRUIT (FRUITFUL)
Ps   1: 3   which yields its **f** in season
Pr 11: 30   The **f** of the righteous is a tree
Mt   7: 16   By their **f** you will recognize them.

Jn 15: 2 branch that does bear **f** he prunes
Gal 5: 22 But the **f** of the Spirit is love, joy,
Rev 22: 2 bearing twelve crops of **f**, yielding its **f** every month.

FRUITFUL (FRUIT)
Ge   1: 22 "Be **f** and increase in number
Ps 128: 3 wife will be like a **f** vine within
Jn 15: 2 so that it will be even more **f**.

FULFILL (FULFILLED FULFILLMENT)
Ps 116: 14 I will **f** my vows to the LORD
Mt   5: 17 to abolish them but to **f** them.
1Co 7: 3 The husband should **f** his marital

FULFILLED (FULFILL)
Pr 13: 19 A longing **f** is sweet to the soul,
Mk 14: 49 But the Scriptures must be **f**."
Ro 13: 8 whoever loves others has **f** the law.

FULFILLMENT (FULFILL)
Ro 13: 10 Therefore love is the **f** of the law.

FULL (FILL)
Ps 127: 5 Blessed is the man whose quiver is **f**
Pr 31: 11 Her husband has **f** confidence in her
Isa 6: 3 the whole earth is **f** of his glory."
Lk   6: 45 speaks what the heart is **f** of.
Jn 10: 10 may have life, and have it to the **f**.
Ac   6: 3 who are known to be **f** of the Spirit

FULLNESS (FILL)
Col 1: 19 to have all his **f** dwell in him,
      2: 9 in Christ all the **f** of the Deity lives

FULLY (FILL)
1Ki 8: 61 may your hearts be **f** committed
2Ch 16: 9 whose hearts are **f** committed
Ps 119: 4 precepts that are to be **f** obeyed.
    119:138 righteous; they are **f** trustworthy.
1Co 15: 58 Always give yourselves **f**

FUTURE
Ps 37: 37 a **f** awaits those who seek peace.
Pr 23: 18 There is surely a **f** hope for you,
Ro   8: 38 neither the present nor the **f**,

GABRIEL
   Angel who interpreted Daniel's visions (Da 8:16–26; 9:20–27); announced births of John (Lk 1:11–20), Jesus (Lk 1:26–38).

GAIN (GAINED)
Ps 60: 12 With God we will **g** the victory,
Mk   8: 36 for someone to **g** the whole world,
1Co 13: 3 but do not have love, I **g** nothing.
Php 1: 21 me, to live is Christ and to die is **g**.
      3: 8 them garbage, that I may **g** Christ
1Ti 6: 6 with contentment is great **g**.
1Pe 5: 2 not pursuing dishonest **g**, but eager

GAINED (GAIN)
Ro   5: 2 through whom we have **g** access

GALILEE
Isa 9: 1 in the future he will honor **G**

GALL
Mt 27: 34 Jesus wine to drink, mixed with **g**;

GAP
Eze 22: 30 stand before me in the **g** on behalf

GARBAGE
Php 3: 8 I consider them **g**, that I may gain

GARDENER
Jn 15: 1 true vine, and my Father is the **g**.

GARMENT (GARMENTS)
Ps 102: 26 they will all wear out like a **g**.

Mt   9: 16 the patch will pull away from the **g**,
Jn 19: 23 This **g** was seamless, woven in one
     19: 24 them and cast lots for my **g**."

GARMENTS (GARMENT)
Ge   3: 21 The LORD God made **g** of skin
Isa 61: 10 For he has clothed me with **g**
     63: 1 with his **g** stained crimson?

GATE (GATES)
Mt   7: 13 "Enter through the narrow **g**.
Jn 10: 9 I am the **g**; whoever enters through

GATES (GATE)
Ps 100: 4 Enter his **g** with thanksgiving
Mt 16: 18 the **g** of Hades will not overcome

GATHER (GATHERS)
Zec 14: 2 I will **g** all the nations to Jerusalem
Mt 12: 30 and whoever does not **g** with me
     23: 37 longed to **g** your children together,

GATHERS (GATHER)
Isa 40: 11 He **g** the lambs in his arms
Mt 23: 37 as a hen **g** her chicks under her

GAVE (GIVE)
Ezr 2: 69 their ability they **g** to the treasury
Job 1: 21 The LORD **g** and the LORD has
Jn   3: 16 so loved the world that he **g** his
2Co 8: 5 They **g** themselves first of all
Gal 2: 20 loved me and **g** himself for me.
1Ti 2: 6 who **g** himself as a ransom for all

GAZE
Ps 27: 4 to **g** on the beauty of the LORD
Pr   4: 25 fix your **g** directly before you.

GENEALOGIES
1Ti 1: 4 themselves to myths and endless **g**.

GENERATIONS
Ps 22: 30 **g** will be told about the Lord.
    102: 12 renown endures through all **g**.
    145: 13 dominion endures through all **g**.
Lk   1: 48 now on all **g** will call me blessed,
Eph 3: 5 other **g** as it has now been revealed

GENEROUS
Ps 112: 5 Good will come to those who are **g**
Pr 22: 9 The **g** will themselves be blessed,
2Co 9: 5 Then it will be ready as a **g** gift,
1Ti 6: 18 and to be **g** and willing to share.

GENTILE (GENTILES)
Ro   1: 16 first to the Jew, then to the **G**.
     10: 12 no difference between Jew and **G**—

GENTILES (GENTILE)
Isa 42: 6 for the people and a light for the **G**,
Ro   3: 9 **G** alike are all under the power
     11: 13 as I am the apostle to the **G**, I take
1Co 1: 23 block to Jews and foolishness to **G**,

GENTLE (GENTLENESS)
Pr 15: 1 A **g** answer turns away wrath,
Mt 11: 29 for I am **g** and humble in heart,
     21: 5 to you, **g** and riding on a donkey,
1Co 4: 21 I come in love and with a **g** spirit?
1Pe 3: 4 unfading beauty of a **g** and quiet

GENTLENESS (GENTLE)
2Co 10: 1 By the humility and **g** of Christ,
Gal 5: 23 **g** and self-control.
Php 4: 5 Let your **g** be evident to all.
Col 3: 12 kindness, humility, **g** and patience.
1Ti 6: 11 faith, love, endurance and **g**.
1Pe 3: 15 But do this with **g** and respect,

GETHSEMANE
Mt 26: 36 his disciples to a place called **G**,

GIDEON

Judge, also called Jerub-Baal; freed Israel from Midianites (Jdg 6-8; Heb 11:32). Given sign of fleece (Jdg 6:36-40).

GIFT (GIFTS)

Pr	21: 14	A **g** given in secret soothes anger,
Mt	5: 23	you are offering your **g** at the altar
Ac	2: 38	you will receive the **g** of the Holy
Ro	6: 23	the **g** of God is eternal life in Christ
1Co	7: 7	of you has your own **g** from God;
2Co	8: 12	the **g** is acceptable according
	9: 15	be to God for his indescribable **g**!
Eph	2: 8	yourselves, it is the **g** of God—
1Ti	4: 14	Do not neglect your **g**, which was
2Ti	1: 6	you to fan into flame the **g** of God,
Jas	1: 17	good and perfect **g** is from above,
1Pe	4: 10	should use whatever **g** you have

GIFTS (GIFT)

Ro	11: 29	for God's **g** and his call are
	12: 6	We have different **g**,
1Co	12: 4	There are different kinds of **g**,
	12: 31	Now eagerly desire the greater **g**.
	14: 1	and eagerly desire **g** of the Spirit,
	14: 12	Since you are eager for **g**

GILEAD

Jer	8: 22	Is there no balm in **G**? Is there no

GIVE (GAVE GIVEN GIVER GIVES GIVING)

Nu	6: 26	toward you and **g** you peace."
1Sa	1: 11	forget your servant but **g** her a son,
	1: 11	I will **g** him to the LORD for all
2Ch	15: 7	be strong and do not **g** up, for your
Pr	21: 26	the righteous **g** without sparing,
	23: 26	**g** me your heart and let your eyes
	28: 27	Those who **g** to the poor will lack
	30: 8	but **g** me only my daily bread.
Eze	36: 26	I will **g** you a new heart and put
Mt	6: 11	**G** us today our daily bread.
	10: 8	Freely you have received; freely **g**.
	22: 21	them, "So **g** back to Caesar what is
Mk	8: 37	what can anyone **g** in exchange
Lk	6: 38	**G**, and it will be given to you.
	11: 13	Father in heaven **g** the Holy Spirit
Jn	10: 28	I **g** them eternal life, and they shall
	13: 34	"A new command I **g** you:
Ac	20: 35	'It is more blessed to **g** than
Ro	12: 8	encourage, then **g** encouragement;
	12: 8	if it is giving, then **g** generously;
	13: 7	**G** to everyone what you owe them:
	14: 12	then, each of us will **g** an account
2Co	9: 7	should **g** what you have decided
Rev	14: 7	voice, "Fear God and **g** him glory,

GIVEN (GIVE)

Nu	8: 16	Israelites who are to be **g** wholly
Ps	115: 16	but the earth he has **g** to mankind.
Isa	9: 6	a son is **g**, and the government
Mt	6: 33	all these things will be **g** to you as
	7: 7	"Ask and it will be **g** to you;
Lk	22: 19	saying, "This is my body **g** for you;
Jn	3: 27	can receive only what is **g** them
Ro	5: 5	Holy Spirit, who has been **g** to us.
1Co	4: 2	those who have been **g** a trust must
	12: 13	and we were all **g** the one Spirit
Eph	4: 7	of us grace has been **g** as Christ

GIVER (GIVE)

Pr	18: 16	ushers the **g** into the presence
2Co	9: 7	for God loves a cheerful **g**.

GIVES (GIVE)

Ps	119:130	unfolding of your words **g** light;

Pr	14: 30	A heart at peace **g** life to the body,
	15: 30	good news **g** health to the bones.
Isa	40: 29	He **g** strength to the weary
Mt	10: 42	anyone **g** even a cup of cold water
Jn	6: 63	The Spirit **g** life; the flesh counts
1Co	15: 57	He **g** us the victory through our
2Co	3: 6	the letter kills, but the Spirit **g** life.

GIVING (GIVE)

Ne	8: 8	**g** the meaning so that the people
Ps	19: 8	LORD are right, **g** joy to the heart.
Mt	6: 4	so that your **g** may be in secret.
2Co	8: 7	you also excel in this grace of **g**.

GLAD (GLADNESS)

Ps	31: 7	I will be **g** and rejoice in your love,
	46: 4	whose streams make **g** the city
	97: 1	LORD reigns, let the earth be **g**;
	118: 24	let us rejoice today and be **g**.
Zec	2: 10	"Shout and be **g**, Daughter Zion.
Mt	5: 12	Rejoice and be **g**, because great is

GLADNESS (GLAD)

Ps	45: 15	Led in with joy and **g**, they enter
	51: 8	Let me hear joy and **g**;
	100: 2	Worship the LORD with **g**;
Jer	31: 13	I will turn their mourning into **g**;

GLORIFIED (GLORY)

Jn	13: 31	"Now the Son of Man is **g** and God is **g** in him.
Ro	8: 30	those he justified, he also **g**.
2Th	1: 10	he comes to be **g** in his holy people

GLORIFY (GLORY)

Ps	34: 3	**G** the LORD with me; let us exalt
	86: 12	I will **g** your name forever.
Mt	5: 16	deeds and **g** your Father in heaven.
Jn	13: 32	God will **g** the Son in himself,
	17: 1	**G** your Son, that your Son may **g**

GLORIOUS (GLORY)

Ps	45: 13	All **g** is the princess within her
	111: 3	**G** and majestic are his deeds,
	145: 5	They speak of the **g** splendor
Isa	4: 2	the LORD will be beautiful and **g**,
	12: 5	LORD, for he has done **g** things;
	42: 21	to make his law great and **g**.
	63: 15	from your lofty throne, holy and **g**.
Mt	19: 28	Son of Man sits on his **g** throne,
Lk	9: 30	and Elijah, appeared in **g** splendor,
Ac	2: 20	of the great and **g** day of the Lord.
2Co	3: 8	of the Spirit be even more **g**?
Php	3: 21	so that they will be like his **g** body.
Jude	: 24	you before his **g** presence without

GLORY (GLORIFIED GLORIFY GLORIOUS)

Ex	15: 11	awesome in **g**, working wonders?
	33: 18	said, "Now show me your **g**."
1Sa	4: 21	"The **G** has departed from Israel"
1Ch	16: 24	Declare his **g** among the nations,
	16: 28	ascribe to the LORD **g**
	29: 11	power and the **g** and the majesty
Ps	8: 5	crowned them with **g** and honor.
	19: 1	The heavens declare the **g** of God;
	24: 7	that the King of **g** may come in.
	29: 1	beings, ascribe to the LORD **g**
	34: 2	I will **g** in the LORD;
	72: 19	the whole earth be filled with his **g**
	96: 3	Declare his **g** among the nations,
Pr	19: 11	is to one's **g** to overlook an offense.
	25: 2	It is the **g** of God to conceal
	25: 2	a matter is the **g** of kings.
Isa	6: 3	the whole earth is full of his **g**."

Isa	42: 8	I will not yield my **g** to another
	48: 11	I will not yield my **g** to another.
Eze	43: 2	and I saw the **g** of the God of Israel
Mt	24: 30	of heaven, with power and great **g**.
	25: 31	the Son of Man comes in his **g**,
Mk	8: 38	in his Father's **g** with the holy
	13: 26	in clouds with great power and **g**.
Lk	2: 9	and the **g** of the Lord shone around
	2: 14	"**G** to God in the highest heaven,
Jn	1: 14	have seen his **g**, the **g** of the one
	17: 5	your presence with the **g** I had
	17: 24	and to see my **g**, the **g** you have
Ac	7: 2	God of **g** appeared to our father
Ro	1: 23	exchanged the **g** of the immortal
	3: 23	and fall short of the **g** of God,
	8: 18	with the **g** that will be revealed
	9: 4	theirs the divine **g**, the covenants,
1Co	10: 31	you do, do it all for the **g** of God.
	11: 7	since he is the image and **g** of God;
	11: 7	but woman is the **g** of man.
	15: 43	sown in dishonor, it is raised in **g**;
2Co	3: 10	what was glorious has no **g** now
	3: 18	faces contemplate the Lord's **g**,
	4: 17	us an eternal **g** that far outweighs
Php	4: 19	the riches of his **g** in Christ Jesus.
Col	1: 27	is Christ in you, the hope of **g**.
	3: 4	you also will appear with him in **g**.
1Ti	3: 16	on in the world, was taken up in **g**.
Titus	2: 13	appearing of the **g** of our great God
Heb	1: 3	The Son is the radiance of God's **g**
	2: 7	crowned them with **g** and honor
1Pe	1: 24	all their **g** is like the flowers
Rev	4: 11	to receive **g** and honor and power,
	21: 23	for the **g** of God gives it light,

GLUTTONS

Titus	1: 12	always liars, evil brutes, lazy **g**."

GNASHING

Mt	8: 12	will be weeping and **g** of teeth."

GNAT

Mt	23: 24	You strain out a **g** but swallow

GOAL

2Co	5: 9	So we make it our **g** to please him,
Php	3: 14	on toward the **g** to win the prize

GOAT (GOATS SCAPEGOAT)

Isa	11: 6	leopard will lie down with the **g**,

GOATS (GOAT)

Nu	7: 17	five male **g** and five male lambs

GOD (GOD'S GODLINESS GODLY GODS)

Ge	1: 1	beginning **G** created the heavens
	1: 2	of **G** was hovering over the waters.
	1: 26	Then **G** said, "Let us make
	1: 27	So **G** created mankind in his own
	1: 31	**G** saw all that he had made, and it
	2: 3	Then **G** blessed the seventh day
	2: 22	the Lord **G** made a woman
	3: 21	The Lord **G** made garments
	3: 23	So the Lord **G** banished him
	5: 22	walked faithfully with **G** 300 years
	6: 2	sons of **G** saw that the daughters
	9: 16	everlasting covenant between **G**
	17: 1	to him and said, "I am **G** Almighty;
	21: 33	name of the Lord, the Eternal **G**.
	22: 8	"**G** himself will provide the lamb
	28: 12	the angels of **G** were ascending
	32: 28	because you have struggled with **G**
	32: 30	"It is because I saw **G** face to face,
	35: 10	**G** said to him, "Your name is
	41: 51	said, "It is because **G** has made me

Ge	50: 20	me, but **G** intended it for good
Ex	2: 24	**G** heard their groaning and he
	3: 6	he said, "I am the **G** of your father,
	3: 6	because he was afraid to look at **G**.
	6: 7	know that I am the Lord your **G**,
	8: 10	is no one like the Lord our **G**.
	13: 18	So **G** led the people around
	15: 2	He is my **G**, and I will praise him,
	17: 9	with the staff of **G** in my hands."
	19: 3	Then Moses went up to **G**,
	20: 2	"I am the Lord your **G**,
	20: 5	the Lord your **G**, am a jealous **G**,
	20: 19	But do not have **G** speak to us
	22: 28	"Do not blaspheme **G** or curse
	31: 18	stone inscribed by the finger of **G**.
	34: 6	the compassionate and gracious **G**,
	34: 14	name is Jealous, is a jealous **G**.
Lev	18: 21	not profane the name of your **G**.
	19: 2	I, the Lord your **G**, am holy.
	26: 12	walk among you and be your **G**,
Nu	22: 38	I must speak only what **G** puts
	23: 19	**G** is not human, that he should lie,
Dt	1: 17	anyone, for judgment belongs to **G**.
	3: 22	the Lord your **G** himself will
	3: 24	For what **g** is there in heaven
	4: 24	**G** is a consuming fire, a jealous **G**.
	4: 31	the Lord your **G** is a merciful **G**;
	4: 39	day that the Lord is **G** in heaven
	5: 11	the name of the Lord your **G**,
	5: 14	is a sabbath to the Lord your **G**.
	5: 26	voice of the living **G** speaking
	6: 4	The Lord our **G**, the Lord is
	6: 5	Love the Lord your **G** with all
	6: 13	Fear the Lord your **G**, serve him
	6: 16	Do not put the Lord your **G**
	7: 9	is **G**; he is the faithful **G**,
	7: 12	the Lord your **G** will keep his
	7: 21	is a great and awesome **G**.
	8: 5	the Lord your **G** disciplines you.
	10: 12	what does the Lord your **G** ask you but
		to fear the Lord your **G**,
	10: 14	To the Lord your **G** belong
	10: 17	For the Lord your **G** is **G** of gods
	11: 13	to love the Lord your **G**
	13: 3	The Lord your **G** is testing you
	13: 4	It is the Lord your **G** you must
	15: 6	the Lord your **G** will bless you
	19: 9	to love the Lord your **G**
	25: 16	the Lord your **G** detests anyone
	29: 29	things belong to the Lord our **G**,
	30: 2	return to the Lord your **G**
	30: 16	today to love the Lord your **G**,
	30: 20	you may love the Lord your **G**,
	31: 6	the Lord your **G** goes with you;
	32: 3	Oh, praise the greatness of our **G**!
	32: 4	A faithful **G** who does no wrong,
	33: 27	The eternal **G** is your refuge,
Jos	1: 9	the Lord your **G** will be with you
	14: 8	the Lord my **G** wholeheartedly.
	22: 5	to love the Lord your **G**, to walk
	22: 34	that the Lord is **G**.
	23: 11	careful to love the Lord your **G**.
	23: 14	the Lord your **G** gave you has
Jdg	16: 28	Please, **G**, strengthen me just once
Ru	1: 16	be my people and your **G** my **G**.
1Sa	2: 2	there is no Rock like our **G**.
	2: 3	for the Lord is a **G** who knows,
	2: 25	**G** may mediate for the offender;
	10: 26	men whose hearts **G** had touched.
	12: 12	the Lord your **G** was your king.

1Sa	17: 26	defy the armies of the living **G**?"
	17: 46	know that there is a **G** in Israel.
	30: 6	found strength in the LORD his **G**.
2Sa	14: 14	But that is not what **G** desires;
	22: 3	my **G** is my rock, in whom I take
	22: 31	"As for **G**, his way is perfect:
1Ki	4: 29	**G** gave Solomon wisdom and very
	8: 23	there is no **G** like you in heaven
	8: 27	"But will **G** really dwell on earth?
	8: 61	committed to the LORD our **G**,
	18: 21	If the LORD is **G**, follow him;
	18: 37	are **G**, and that you are turning
	20: 28	think the LORD is a **g** the hills
2Ki	19: 15	you alone are **G** over all
1Ch	16: 35	Cry out, "Save us, **G** our Savior,
	28: 2	for the footstool of our **G**, and I
	28: 9	acknowledge the **G** of your father,
	29: 10	LORD, the **G** of our father Israel,
	29: 17	my **G**, that you test the heart and
2Ch	2: 4	for the Name of the LORD my **G**
	5: 14	the LORD filled the temple of **G**.
	6: 18	will **G** really dwell on earth
	18: 13	can tell him only what my **G** says."
	20: 6	you not the **G** who is in heaven?
	25: 8	for **G** has the power to help
	30: 9	for the LORD your **G** is gracious
	33: 12	the favor of the LORD his **G**
Ezr	8: 22	"The gracious hand of our **G** is
	9: 6	my **G**, to lift up my face to you,
	9: 13	our **G**, you have punished us less
Ne	1: 5	the great and awesome **G**,
	8: 8	from the Book of the Law of **G**,
	9: 17	But you are a forgiving **G**,
	9: 32	"Now therefore, our **G**, the great **G**,
Job	1: 1	he feared **G** and shunned evil.
	2: 10	Shall we accept good from **G**,
	4: 17	mortal be more righteous than **G**?
	5: 17	is the one whom **G** corrects;
	11: 7	you fathom the mysteries of **G**?
	19: 26	yet in my flesh I will see **G**;
	22: 13	Yet you say, 'What does **G** know?
	25: 4	a mortal be righteous before **G**?
	33: 14	For **G** does speak—now one way,
	34: 12	unthinkable that **G** would do wrong,
	36: 26	How great is **G**—
	37: 22	**G** comes in awesome majesty.
Ps	18: 2	my **G** is my rock, in whom I take
	18: 28	my **G** turns my darkness into light.
	19: 1	The heavens declare the glory of **G**;
	22: 1	My **G**, my **G**, why have you
	29: 3	the **G** of glory thunders, the LORD
	31: 14	I say, "You are my **G**."
	40: 3	mouth, a hymn of praise to our **G**.
	40: 8	I desire to do your will, my **G**;
	42: 2	My soul thirsts for **G**, for the living
	42: 2	When can I go and meet with **G**?
	42: 11	Put your hope in **G**, for I will yet
	45: 6	O **G**, will last for ever and ever;
	46: 1	**G** is our refuge and strength,
	46: 10	"Be still, and know that I am **G**;
	47: 7	For **G** is the King of all the earth;
	50: 3	Our **G** comes and will not be silent
	51: 1	O **G**, according to your unfailing
	51: 10	O **G**, and renew a steadfast spirit
	51: 17	sacrifice, O **G**, is a broken spirit;
	62: 7	and my honor depend on **G**;
	65: 5	and righteous deeds, **G** our Savior,
	66: 1	Shout for joy to **G**, all the earth!
	66: 16	Come and hear, all you who fear **G**;
	68: 6	**G** sets the lonely in families,
	71: 17	my youth, **G**, you have taught
	71: 19	Who is like you, **G**?
	71: 22	harp for your faithfulness, my **G**;
	73: 26	but **G** is the strength of my heart
	77: 13	What **g** is as great as our **G**?
	78: 19	They spoke against **G**,
	81: 1	Sing for joy to **G** our strength;
	84: 2	my flesh cry out for the living **G**.
	84: 10	the house of my **G** than dwell
	86: 12	you, Lord my **G**, with all my heart;
	89: 7	of the holy ones **G** is greatly feared;
	90: 2	to everlasting you are **G**.
	91: 2	fortress, my **G**, in whom I trust."
	95: 7	for he is our **G** and we are
	100: 3	Know that the LORD is **G**. It is he
	108: 1	My heart, O **G**, is steadfast;
	113: 5	Who is like the LORD our **G**,
	139: 23	Search me, **G**, and know my heart;
Pr	3: 4	a good name in the sight of **G**
	25: 2	It is the glory of **G** to conceal
	30: 5	"Every word of **G** is flawless;
Ecc	3: 11	can fathom what **G** has done
	11: 5	cannot understand the work of **G**,
	12: 13	of the matter: Fear **G** and keep his
Isa	9: 6	Mighty **G**, Everlasting Father,
	37: 16	you alone are **G** over all
	40: 3	in the desert a highway for our **G**.
	40: 8	the word of our **G** endures forever."
	40: 28	The LORD is the everlasting **G**,
	41: 10	not be dismayed, for I am your **G**.
	44: 6	apart from me there is no **G**.
	52: 7	who say to Zion, "Your **G** reigns!"
	55: 7	and to our **G**, for he will freely
	57: 21	says my **G**, "for the wicked."
	59: 2	have separated you from your **G**;
	61: 10	my soul rejoices in my **G**.
	62: 5	so will your **G** rejoice over you.
Jer	23: 23	"Am I only a **G** nearby,
	31: 33	I will be their **G**, and they will be
	32: 27	the LORD, the **G** of all mankind.
Eze	28: 13	You were in Eden, the garden of **G**;
Da	3: 17	the **G** we serve is able to deliver us
	9: 4	the great and awesome **G**,
Hos	12: 6	But you must return to your **G**;
Joel	2: 13	Return to the LORD your **G**, for he
Am	4: 12	Israel, prepare to meet your **G**."
Mic	6: 8	and to walk humbly with your **G**.
Na	1: 2	is a jealous and avenging **G**;
Zec	14: 5	Then the LORD my **G** will come,
Mal	3: 8	"Will a mere mortal rob **G**?
Mt	1: 23	(which means "**G** with us").
	5: 8	pure in heart, for they will see **G**.
	6: 24	You cannot serve both **G**
	19: 6	Therefore what **G** has joined
	19: 26	but with **G** all things are possible."
	22: 21	Caesar's, and to **G** what is God's."
	22: 37	"'Love the Lord your **G** with all
	27: 46	(which means "My **G**, my **G**,
Mk	12: 29	The Lord our **G**, the Lord is one.
	16: 19	*at the right hand of* **G**.
Lk	1: 37	For no word from **G** will ever fail."
	1: 47	my spirit rejoices in **G** my Savior,
	10: 9	'The kingdom of **G** has come near
	10: 27	"'Love the Lord your **G** with all
	18: 19	"No one is good—except **G** alone.
Jn	1: 1	and the Word was with **G**, and the Word was **G**.
	1: 18	No one has ever seen **G**, but
	1: 18	who is himself **G** and is in closest
	3: 16	For **G** so loved the world that he

Jn 4: 24 **G** is spirit, and his worshipers must
7: 17 to do the will of **G** will find
14: 1 You believe in **G**;
20: 28 said to him, "My Lord and my **G!**"
Ac 2: 24 But **G** raised him from the dead,
5: 4 lied just to human beings but to **G.**"
5: 29 "We must obey **G** rather than
7: 55 to heaven and saw the glory of **G,**
17: 23 inscription: TO AN UNKNOWN **G.**
20: 27 to you the whole will of **G.**
20: 32 "Now I commit you to **G**
Ro 1: 17 righteousness of **G** is revealed—
2: 11 For **G** does not show favoritism.
3: 4 Let **G** be true, and every human
3: 23 and fall short of the glory of **G,**
4: 24 **G** will credit righteousness—
5: 8 **G** demonstrates his own love for us
6: 23 the gift of **G** is eternal life in Christ
8: 28 in all things **G** works for the good
11: 22 the kindness and sternness of **G:**
14: 12 give an account of ourselves to **G.**
1Co 1: 20 not **G** made foolish the wisdom
2: 9 the things **G** has prepared for those
3: 6 it, but **G** has been making it grow.
6: 20 Therefore honor **G** with your
7: 24 they were in when **G** called them.
8: 8 food does not bring us near to **G;**
10: 13 **G** is faithful; he will not let you
10: 31 you do, do it all for the glory of **G.**
14: 33 For **G** is not a **G** of disorder
15: 28 him, so that **G** may be all in all.
2Co 1: 9 not rely on ourselves but on **G,**
2: 14 But thanks be to **G,** who always
3: 5 our competence comes from **G.**
4: 7 this all-surpassing power is from **G**
5: 19 that **G** was reconciling the world
5: 21 become the righteousness of **G.**
6: 16 we are the temple of the living **G.**
9: 7 for **G** loves a cheerful giver.
9: 8 **G** is able to bless you abundantly,
Gal 2: 6 **G** does not show favoritism—
6: 7 **G** cannot be mocked.
Eph 2: 10 **G** prepared in advance for us
4: 6 one **G** and Father of all, who is
Php 2: 6 being in very nature **G,** did not consider
equality with **G**
4: 19 And my **G** will meet all your needs
1Th 2: 4 not trying to please people but **G,**
4: 7 For **G** did not call us to be impure,
4: 9 yourselves have been taught by **G**
5: 9 For **G** did not appoint us to suffer
1Ti 2: 5 there is one **G** and one mediator
4: 4 For everything **G** created is good,
5: 4 for this is pleasing to **G.**
Titus 2: 13 of the glory of our great **G**
Heb 1: 1 the past **G** spoke to our ancestors
4: 12 For the word of **G** is alive
6: 10 **G** is not unjust; he will not forget
10: 31 fall into the hands of the living **G.**
11: 6 faith it is impossible to please **G,**
12: 10 but **G** disciplines us for our good,
12: 29 for our "**G** is a consuming fire."
13: 15 us continually offer to **G** a sacrifice
Jas 1: 13 For **G** cannot be tempted by evil,
2: 19 You believe that there is one **G.**
2: 23 "Abraham believed **G,** and it was
4: 4 the world becomes an enemy of **G.**
4: 8 Come near to **G** and he will come
1Pe 4: 11 who speaks the very words of **G.**
2Pe 1: 21 from **G** as they were carried along

1Jn 1: 5 him and declare to you: **G** is light;
2: 5 love for **G** is truly made complete
3: 20 that **G** is greater than our hearts,
4: 7 another, for love comes from **G.**
4: 7 has been born of **G** and knows **G.**
4: 9 This is how **G** showed his love
4: 11 Dear friends, since **G** so loved us,
4: 12 No one has ever seen **G**; but if we
4: 16 Whoever lives in love lives in **G,**
Rev 4: 8 holy is the Lord **G** Almighty,'
7: 17 **G** will wipe away every tear
19: 6 For our Lord **G** Almighty reigns.

GOD-BREATHED (BREATHED)
2Ti 3: 16 All Scripture is **G** and is useful

GODLINESS (GOD)
1Ti 2: 2 quiet lives in all **g** and holiness.
4: 8 value, but **g** has value for all things,
6: 6 **g** with contentment is great gain.
6: 11 and pursue righteousness, **g,** faith,

GODLY (GOD)
2Co 7: 10 **G** sorrow brings repentance
11: 2 jealous for you with a **g** jealousy.
2Ti 3: 12 live a **g** life in Christ Jesus will be
2Pe 3: 11 You ought to live holy and **g** lives

GOD'S (GOD)
2Ch 20: 15 For the battle is not yours, but **G.**
Job 37: 14 stop and consider **G** wonders.
Ps 52: 8 I trust in **G** unfailing love for ever
69: 30 I will praise **G** name in song
Mk 3: 35 Whoever does **G** will is my brother
Jn 10: 36 because I said, 'I am **G** Son'?
Ro 2: 3 think you will escape **G** judgment?
2: 4 that **G** kindness is intended
3: 3 nullify **G** faithfulness?
7: 22 my inner being I delight in **G** law;
9: 16 desire or effort, but on **G** mercy.
11: 29 for **G** gifts and his call are
12: 2 test and approve what **G** will is—
13: 6 for the authorities are **G** servants,
1Co 7: 19 Keeping **G** commands is what
2Co 6: 2 now is the time of **G** favor, now is
Eph 1: 7 with the riches of **G** grace
5: 1 Follow **G** example, therefore,
1Th 4: 3 It is **G** will that you should be
5: 18 for this is **G** will for you in Christ
1Ti 6: 1 so that **G** name and our teaching
2Ti 2: 19 **G** solid foundation stands firm,
Titus 1: 7 an overseer manages **G** household,
Heb 1: 3 The Son is the radiance of **G** glory
9: 24 to appear for us in **G** presence.
11: 3 was formed at **G** command,
1Pe 2: 15 For it is **G** will that by doing good
3: 4 which is of great worth in **G** sight.

GODS (GOD)
Ex 20: 3 shall have no other **g** before me.
Ac 19: 26 by human hands are no **g** at all.

GOLD
Job 23: 10 tested me, I will come forth as **g.**
Ps 19: 10 precious than **g,** than much pure **g;**
119:127 love your commands more than **g,**
Pr 22: 1 esteemed is better than silver or **g.**

GOLGOTHA
Jn 19: 17 (which in Aramaic is called **G**).

GOLIATH
Philistine giant killed by David (1Sa 17; 21:9).

GOOD
Ge 1: 4 God saw that the light was **g,**

Ge	1: 31	he had made, and it was very **g**.
	2: 18	"It is not **g** for the man to be alone.
	50: 20	God intended it for **g**
Job	2: 10	Shall we accept **g** from God,
Ps	14: 1	there is no one who does **g**.
	34: 8	Taste and see that the LORD is **g**;
	37: 3	Trust in the LORD and do **g**;
	84: 11	no **g** thing does he withhold
	86: 5	are forgiving and **g**,
	103: 5	your desires with **g** things so
	119: 68	You are **g**, and what you do is **g**;
	133: 1	How **g** and pleasant it is
	147: 1	How **g** it is to sing praises to our
Pr	3: 4	and a **g** name in the sight of God
	11: 27	Whoever seeks **g** finds favor,
	13: 21	are rewarded with **g** things.
	17: 22	A cheerful heart is **g** medicine,
	18: 22	He who finds a wife finds what is **g**
	22: 1	A **g** name is more desirable than
	31: 12	She brings him **g**, not harm,
Isa	5: 20	Woe to those who call evil **g** and **g**
	52: 7	the feet of those who bring **g** news,
Jer	6: 16	ask where the **g** way is, and walk
Mic	6: 8	shown you, O mortal, what is **g**.
Mt	5: 45	sun to rise on the evil and the **g**,
	7: 17	Likewise, every **g** tree bears **g** fruit,
	12: 35	A **g** man brings **g** things out of the **g**
	19: 17	"There is only One who is **g**.
	25: 21	'Well done, **g** and faithful servant!
Mk	3: 4	to do **g** or to do evil, to save life
	8: 36	What **g** is it for someone to gain
Lk	6: 27	do **g** to those who hate you,
Jn	10: 11	"I am the **g** shepherd. The **g**
Ro	8: 28	for the **g** of those who love him,
	10: 15	feet of those who bring **g** news!"
	12: 9	Hate what is evil; cling to what is **g**.
1Co	10: 24	their own **g**, but the **g** of others.
	15: 33	company corrupts **g** character."
2Co	9: 8	you will abound in every **g** work.
Gal	6: 9	us not become weary in doing **g**,
	6: 10	let us do **g** to all people,
Eph	2: 10	in Christ Jesus to do **g** works,
Php	1: 6	he who began a **g** work in you will
1Th	5: 21	test them all; hold on to what is **g**,
2Th	3: 13	never tire of doing what is **g**.
1Ti	3: 7	have a **g** reputation with outsiders,
	4: 4	For everything God created is **g**,
	6: 12	Fight the **g** fight of the faith.
	6: 18	do **g**, to be rich in **g** deeds,
2Ti	3: 17	equipped for every **g** work.
	4: 7	I have fought the **g** fight, I have
Heb	12: 10	but God disciplines us for our **g**,
1Pe	2: 3	you have tasted that the Lord is **g**.
	2: 12	Live such **g** lives among the pagans

GOSPEL

Ro	1: 16	For I am not ashamed of the **g**,
	15: 16	duty of proclaiming the **g** of God,
1Co	1: 17	to baptize, but to preach the **g**—
	9: 16	Woe to me if I do not preach the **g**!
	15: 1	to remind you of the **g** I preached
Gal	1: 7	trying to pervert the **g** of Christ.
Php	1: 27	a manner worthy of the **g** of Christ.
	1: 27	as one for the faith of the **g**

GOSSIP

Pr	11: 13	A **g** betrays a confidence,
	16: 28	and a **g** separates close friends.
	18: 8	of a **g** are like choice morsels;
	26: 20	without a **g** a quarrel dies down.
2Co	12: 20	slander, **g**, arrogance and disorder.

GOVERNED

Ro	8: 6	the mind **g** by the Spirit is life

GRACE (GRACIOUS)

Ps	45: 2	lips have been anointed with **g**,
Jn	1: 17	**g** and truth came through Jesus
Ac	20: 32	to God and to the word of his **g**,
Ro	3: 24	by his **g** through the redemption
	5: 15	that came by the **g** of the one man,
	5: 17	God's abundant provision of **g**
	5: 20	increased, **g** increased all the more,
	6: 14	are not under the law, but under **g**.
	11: 6	if it were, **g** would no longer be **g**.
2Co	6: 1	you not to receive God's **g** in vain.
	8: 9	you know the **g** of our Lord Jesus
	12: 9	to me, "My **g** is sufficient for you,
Gal	2: 21	I do not set aside the **g** of God,
	5: 4	you have fallen away from **g**.
Eph	1: 7	with the riches of God's **g**
	2: 5	it is by **g** you have been saved.
	2: 7	the incomparable riches of his **g**,
	2: 8	For it is by **g** you have been saved,
Php	1: 7	all of you share in God's **g** with me.
Col	4: 6	conversation be always full of **g**,
2Th	2: 16	**g** gave us eternal encouragement
2Ti	2: 1	be strong in the **g** that is in Christ
Titus	2: 11	For the **g** of God has appeared
	3: 7	having been justified by his **g**,
Heb	2: 9	the **g** of God he might taste death
	4: 16	approach God's throne of **g**
	4: 16	**g** to help us in our time of need.
Jas	4: 6	But he gives us more **g**. That is why
2Pe	3: 18	grow in the **g** and knowledge of

GRACIOUS (GRACE)

Nu	6: 25	face shine on you and be **g** to you;
Isa	30: 18	the LORD longs to be **g** to you;

GRAIN

Ecc	11: 1	Ship your **g** across the sea;
1Co	9: 9	an ox while it is treading out the **g**."

GRANTED

Php	1: 29	For it has been **g** to you on behalf

GRASS

Ps	103: 15	The life of mortals is like **g**,
1Pe	1: 24	the **g** withers and the flowers fall,

GRAVE (GRAVES)

Pr	7: 27	Her house is a highway to the **g**,
Hos	13: 14	Where, O **g**, is your destruction?

GRAVES (GRAVE)

Jn	5: 28	are in their **g** will hear his voice
Ro	3: 13	"Their throats are open **g**;

GREAT (GREATER GREATEST GREATNESS)

Ge	12: 2	"I will make you into a **g** nation,
Dt	10: 17	gods and Lord of lords, the **g** God,
2Sa	7: 36	your help has made me **g**.
Ps	19: 11	in keeping them there is **g** reward.
	89: 1	sing of the LORD's **g** love forever;
	103: 11	so **g** is his love for those who fear
	108: 4	For **g** is your love, higher than
	119:165	**G** peace have those who love your
	145: 3	**G** is the LORD and most worthy
Pr	23: 24	father of a righteous child has **g** joy
Isa	42: 21	his righteousness to make his law **g**
La	3: 23	**g** is your faithfulness.
Mk	10: 43	become **g** among you must be your
Lk	21: 27	in a cloud with power and **g** glory.
1Ti	6: 6	with contentment is **g** gain.
Titus	2: 13	appearing of the glory of our **g** God
Heb	2: 3	if we ignore so **g** a salvation?
1Jn	3: 1	See what **g** love the Father has

GREATER (GREAT)
Mk 12: 31 is no commandment **g** than these."
Jn 1: 50 You will see **g** things than that."
    15: 13 **G** love has no one than this:
1Co 12: 31 Now eagerly desire the **g** gifts.
Heb 11: 26 as of **g** value than the treasures
1Jn 3: 20 that God is **g** than our hearts,
    4: 4 is in you is **g** than the one who is

GREATEST (GREAT)
Mt 22: 38 is the first and **g** commandment.
Lk 9: 48 least among you all who is the **g**."
1Co 13: 13 But the **g** of these is love.

GREATNESS (GREAT)
Ps 145: 3 his **g** no one can fathom.
    150: 2 praise him for his surpassing **g**.
Isa 9: 7 the **g** of his government and peace
    63: 1 forward in the **g** of his strength?

GREED (GREEDY)
Lk 12: 15 guard against all kinds of **g**;
Ro 1: 29 wickedness, evil, **g** and depravity.
Eph 5: 3 or of **g**, because these are improper
Col 3: 5 desires and **g**, which is idolatry.
2Pe 2: 14 they are experts in **g**—

GREEDY (GREED)
Pr 15: 27 The **g** bring ruin to their
1Co 6: 10 thieves nor the **g** nor drunkards
Eph 5: 5 No immoral, impure or **g** person—

GREEN
Ps 23: 2 makes me lie down in **g** pastures,

GREW (GROW)
Lk 2: 52 And Jesus **g** in wisdom and stature,
Ac 16: 5 in the faith and **g** daily in numbers.

GRIEF (GRIEVE)
Ps 10: 14 you consider their **g** and take it
Pr 14: 13 ache, and rejoicing may end in **g**.
La 3: 32 Though he brings **g**, he will show
Jn 16: 20 grieve, but your **g** will turn to joy.
1Pe 1: 6 have had to suffer **g** in all kinds

GRIEVE (GRIEF)
Eph 4: 30 do not **g** the Holy Spirit of God,
1Th 4: 13 so that you do not **g** like the rest

GROUND
Ge 3: 17 it,' "Cursed is the **g** because of you;
Ex 3: 5 where you are standing is holy **g**."
Eph 6: 13 you may be able to stand your **g**,

GROW (GREW)
Pr 13: 11 money little by little makes it **g**.
1Co 3: 6 it, but God has been making it **g**.
2Pe 3: 18 But **g** in the grace and knowledge

GRUMBLE (GRUMBLING)
1Co 10: 10 do not **g**, as some of them did—
Jas 5: 9 Don't **g** against one another,

GRUMBLING (GRUMBLE)
Jn 6: 43 "Stop **g** among yourselves,"
1Pe 4: 9 hospitality to one another without **g**.

GUARANTEEING (GUARANTOR)
2Co 1: 22 as a deposit, **g** what is to come.
Eph 1: 14 is a deposit **g** our inheritance until

GUARANTOR (GUARANTEEING)
Heb 7: 22 Jesus has become the **g** of a better

GUARD (GUARDIAN, GUARDIAN-REDEEMER)
Ps 141: 3 Set a **g** over my mouth, LORD;
Pr 4: 23 Above all else, **g** your heart,
    13: 3 Those who **g** their lips preserve
    21: 23 Those who **g** their mouths and

Isa 52: 12 God of Israel will be your rear **g**.
Mk 13: 33 Be on **g**! Be alert! You do not know
1Co 16: 13 Be on your **g**; stand firm
Php 4: 7 will **g** your hearts and your minds
1Ti 6: 20 **g** what has been entrusted to your

GUARDIAN (GUARD)
Gal 3: 25 come, we are no longer under a **g**.

GUARDIAN-REDEEMER (GUARD)
Ru 3: 9 since you are a **g** of our family."

GUIDE
Ex 13: 21 of cloud to **g** them on their way
    15: 13 In your strength you will **g** them
Ne 9: 19 cloud did not fail to **g** them on
Ps 25: 5 **G** me in your truth and teach me,
    48: 14 he will be our **g** even to the end.
    67: 4 and **g** the nations of the earth.
    73: 24 You **g** me with your counsel,
    139: 10 even there your hand will **g** me,
Pr 6: 22 When you walk, they will **g** you;
Isa 58: 11 The LORD will **g** you always;
Jn 16: 13 he will **g** you into all the truth.

GUILTY
Ex 34: 7 does not leave the **g** unpunished;
Jn 8: 46 Can any of you prove me **g** of sin?
Heb 10: 22 to cleanse us from a **g** conscience
Jas 2: 10 at just one point is **g** of breaking all

HADES
Mt 16: 18 the gates of **H** will not overcome it.
Lk 16: 23 In **H**, where he was in torment,

HAGAR
Servant of Sarah, wife of Abraham, mother of Ishmael (Ge 16:1–6; 25:12). Driven away by Sarah while pregnant (Ge 16:5–16); after birth of Isaac (Ge 21:9–21; Gal 4:21–31).

HAGGAI
Post-exilic prophet who encouraged rebuilding of the temple (Ezr 5:1; 6:14; Hag 1–2).

HAIR (HAIRS)
Lk 21: 18 not a **h** of your head will perish.
1Co 11: 6 for a woman to have her **h** cut off

HAIRS (HAIR)
Mt 10: 30 even the very **h** of your head are all

HALLELUJAH
Rev 19: 1, multitude in heaven shouting: "**H**!

HALLOWED (HOLY)
Mt 6: 9 Father in heaven, **h** be your name,

HAND (HANDIWORK HANDS)
Ps 16: 8 With him at my right **h**, I will not
    37: 24 the LORD upholds him with his **h**.
    139: 10 even there your **h** will guide me,
Ecc 9: 10 Whatever your **h** finds to do, do it
Mt 6: 3 not let your left **h** know what your
    right **h** is doing,
Jn 10: 28 one will snatch them out of my **h**.
1Co 12: 15 say, "Because I am not a **h**, I do not

HANDIWORK (HAND WORK)
Eph 2: 10 For we are God's **h**,

HANDS (HAND)
Ps 22: 16 they pierce my **h** and my feet.
    24: 4 one who has clean **h** and a pure
    31: 5 Into your **h** I commit my spirit;
    31: 15 My times are in your **h**;
Pr 10: 4 but diligent **h** bring wealth.
    31: 20 and extends her **h** to the needy.
Isa 55: 12 trees of the field will clap their **h**.
    65: 2 out my **h** to an obstinate people,

Lk 23: 46 into your **h** I commit my spirit."
1Th 4: 11 business and work with your **h**,
1Ti 2: 8 lifting up holy **h** without anger
5: 22 not be hasty in the laying on of **h**,

HANNAH
Wife of Elkanah, mother of Samuel (1Sa 1). Prayer at dedication of Samuel (1Sa 2:1-10). Blessed (1Sa 2:18-21).

HAPPY
Ps 68: 3 may they be **h** and joyful.
Pr 15: 13 A **h** heart makes the face cheerful,
Ecc 3: 12 better for people than to be **h**
Jas 5: 13 Is anyone **h**? Let them sing songs

HARD (HARDEN HARDSHIP)
Ge 18: 14 Is anything too **h** for the LORD?
Ps 118: 5 When **h** pressed, I cried
Mt 19: 23 it is **h** for someone who is rich
1Co 4: 12 We work **h** with our own hands.
1Th 5: 12 those who work **h** among you,

HARDEN (HARD)
Ro 9: 18 he hardens whom he wants to **h**.
Heb 3: 8 do not **h** your hearts as you did

HARDHEARTED (HEART)
Dt 15: 7 do not be **h** or tightfisted toward

HARDSHIP (HARD)
Ro 8: 35 Shall trouble or **h** or persecution
2Ti 4: 5 endure **h**, do the work
Heb 12: 7 Endure **h** as discipline;

HARM
Ps 121: 6 the sun will not **h** you by day,
Pr 3: 29 not plot **h** against your neighbor,
31: 12 good, not **h**, all the days of her life.
Ro 13: 10 Love does no **h** to a neighbor.
1Jn 5: 18 and the evil one cannot **h** them.

HARMONY
Ro 12: 16 Live in **h** with one another.
2Co 6: 15 What **h** is there between Christ

HARVEST
Mt 9: 37 "The **h** is plentiful but the workers
Jn 4: 35 at the fields! They are ripe for **h**.
Gal 6: 9 at the proper time we will reap a **h**
Heb 12: 11 it produces a **h** of righteousness

HASTE (HASTY)
Pr 21: 5 lead to profit as surely as **h** leads
29: 20 you see someone who speaks in **h**?

HASTY (HASTE)
Pr 19: 2 how much more will **h** feet miss
Ecc 5: 2 do not be **h** in your heart to utter
1Ti 5: 22 Do not be **h** in the laying

HATE (HATED HATES HATRED)
Lev 19: 17 "'Do not **h** a fellow Israelite
Ps 5: 5 You **h** all who do wrong;
45: 7 righteousness and **h** wickedness;
97: 10 those who love the LORD **h** evil,
139: 21 Do I not **h** those who **h** you,
Pr 8: 13 To fear the LORD is to **h** evil; I **h**
Am 5: 15 **H** evil, love good;
Mt 5: 43 your neighbor and **h** your enemy.'
Lk 6: 27 do good to those who **h** you,
Ro 12: 9 **H** what is evil; cling to what is

HATED (HATE)
Mt 10: 22 be **h** by everyone because of me,
Ro 9: 13 "Jacob I loved, but Esau I **h**."
Eph 5: 29 all, no one ever **h** their own body,
Heb 1: 9 righteousness and **h** wickedness;

HATES (HATE)
Pr 6: 16 There are six things the LORD **h**,
13: 24 spares the rod **h** their children,
Mal 2: 16 "The man who **h** and divorces his
Jn 3: 20 Everyone who does evil **h** the light,
1Jn 2: 9 to be in the light but **h** a brother

HATRED (HATE)
Pr 10: 12 **H** stirs up conflict, but love covers

HAUGHTY
Pr 16: 18 destruction, a **h** spirit before a fall.

HAY
1Co 3: 12 costly stones, wood, **h** or straw,

HEAD (HEADS HOTHEADED)
Ge 3: 15 he will crush your **h**, and you will
Ps 23: 5 You anoint my **h** with oil;
Pr 25: 22 will heap burning coals on his **h**,
Isa 59: 17 the helmet of salvation on his **h**;
Mt 8: 20 of Man has no place to lay his **h**."
Ro 12: 20 will heap burning coals on his **h**."
1Co 11: 3 the **h** of every man is Christ, and the **h** of the woman is man, and the **h** of Christ is God.
12: 21 And the **h** cannot say to the feet,
Eph 5: 23 the husband is the **h** of the wife as Christ is the **h**
2Ti 4: 5 keep your **h** in all situations,
Rev 19: 12 fire, and on his **h** are many crowns.

HEADS (HEAD)
Lev 26: 13 you to walk with **h** held high.
Isa 35: 10 everlasting joy will crown their **h**.

HEAL (HEALED HEALING HEALS)
2Ch 7: 14 their sin and will **h** their land.
Ps 41: 4 **h** me, for I have sinned against
Mt 10: 8 **H** the sick, raise the dead,
Lk 4: 23 'Physician, **h** yourself!'
5: 17 Lord was with Jesus to **h** the sick.

HEALED (HEAL)
Isa 53: 5 him, and by his wounds we are **h**.
Mt 9: 22 he said, "your faith has **h** you."
14: 36 and all who touched it were **h**.
Ac 4: 10 that this man stands before you **h**.
14: 9 saw that he had faith to be **h**
Jas 5: 16 each other so that you may be **h**.
1Pe 2: 24 "by his wounds you have been **h**."

HEALING (HEAL)
Eze 47: 12 for food and their leaves for **h**."
Mal 4: 2 righteousness will rise with **h** in its
1Co 12: 9 to another gifts of **h** by that one
12: 30 Do all have gifts of **h**? Do all speak
Rev 22: 2 the tree are for the **h** of the nations.

HEALS (HEAL)
Ex 15: 26 for I am the LORD, who **h** you."
Ps 103: 3 your sins and **h** all your diseases,
147: 3 He **h** the brokenhearted and binds

HEALTH (HEALTHY)
Pr 3: 8 This will bring **h** to your body
15: 30 good news gives **h** to the bones.

HEALTHY (HEALTH)
Mk 2: 17 "It is not the **h** who need a doctor,

HEAR (HEARD HEARING HEARS)
Dt 6: 4 **H**, O Israel: The LORD our God,
31: 13 law, must **h** it and learn to fear
2Ch 7: 14 then I will **h** from heaven,
Ps 94: 9 he who fashioned the ear not **h**?
Isa 29: 18 day the deaf will **h** the words
65: 24 they are still speaking I will **h**.

Mt	11: 15	Whoever has ears, let them **h**.
Jn	8: 47	The reason you do not **h** is that
2Ti	4: 3	what their itching ears want to **h**.

HEARD (HEAR)

Job	42: 5	My ears had **h** of you but now my
Isa	66: 8	Who has ever **h** of such things?
Mt	5: 21	"You have **h** that it was said
	5: 27	"You have **h** that it was said,
	5: 33	you have **h** that it was said
	5: 38	"You have **h** that it was said,
	5: 43	"You have **h** that it was said,
1Co	2: 9	what no ear has **h**, and what no
1Th	2: 13	which you **h** from us, you accepted
2Ti	1: 13	What you **h** from me, keep as
Jas	1: 25	not forgetting what they have **h**,

HEARING (HEAR)

Ro	10: 17	faith comes from **h** the message,

HEARS (HEAR)

Jn	5: 24	whoever **h** my word and believes
1Jn	5: 14	according to his will, he **h** us.
Rev	3: 20	If anyone **h** my voice and opens

HEART (BROKENHEARTED HARDHEARTED
HEARTS WHOLEHEARTEDLY)

Ex	25: 2	everyone whose **h** prompts them
Lev	19: 17	not hate a fellow Israelite in your **h**.
Dt	4: 29	him if you seek him with all your **h**
	6: 5	LORD your God with all your **h**
	10: 12	LORD your God with all your **h**
	15: 10	and do so without a grudging **h**;
	30: 6	you may love him with all your **h**
	30: 10	LORD your God with all your **h**
Jos	22: 5	and to serve him with all your **h**
1Sa	13: 14	sought out a man after his own **h**
	16: 7	but the LORD looks at the **h**."
2Ki	23: 3	and decrees with all his **h** and
1Ch	28: 9	for the LORD searches every **h**
2Ch	7: 16	eyes and my **h** will always be there.
Job	22: 22	and lay up his words in your **h**.
	37: 1	"At this my **h** pounds and leaps
Ps	14: 1	says in his **h**, "There is no God."
	19: 14	this meditation of my **h** be pleasing
	37: 4	will give you the desires of your **h**.
	45: 1	My **h** is stirred by a noble theme as
	51: 10	Create in me a pure **h**, O God,
	51: 17	a broken and contrite **h** you, God,
	66: 18	If I had cherished sin in my **h**,
	86: 11	give me an undivided **h**, that I may
	119: 11	in my **h** that I might not sin against
	139: 23	Search me, God, and know my **h**;
Pr	3: 5	Trust in the LORD with all your **h**
	4: 21	sight, keep them within your **h**;
	4: 23	guard your **h**, for everything you
	7: 3	write them on the tablet of your **h**.
	13: 12	Hope deferred makes the **h** sick,
	14: 13	Even in laughter the **h** may ache,
	15: 30	eyes brings joy to the **h**, and good
	17: 22	A cheerful **h** is good medicine,
	24: 17	stumble, do not let your **h** rejoice,
	27: 19	the face, so one's life reflects the **h**.
Ecc	3: 11	also set eternity in the human **h**;
	8: 5	the wise **h** will know the proper
SS	4: 9	You have stolen my **h**, my sister,
Isa	40: 11	and carries them close to his **h**;
	57: 15	and to revive the **h** of the contrite.
Jer	17: 9	The **h** is deceitful above all things
	29: 13	when you seek me with all your **h**.
Eze	36: 26	I will give you a new **h** and put
Mt	5: 8	Blessed are the pure in **h**, for they
	6: 21	treasure is, there your **h** will be

	12: 34	mouth speaks what the **h** is full of.
	22: 37	the Lord your God with all your **h**
Lk	6: 45	mouth speaks what the **h** is full of.
Ro	2: 29	is circumcision of the **h**,
	10: 10	it is with your **h** that you believe
Eph	5: 19	music from your **h** to the Lord,
	6: 6	doing the will of God from your **h**.
Col	3: 23	you do, work at it with all your **h**,
1Pe	1: 22	one another deeply, from the **h**.

HEARTS (HEART)

Dt	11: 18	Fix these words of mine in your **h**
1Ki	8: 39	do, since you know their **h** (for you
	8: 61	may your **h** be fully committed
Ps	62: 8	pour out your **h** to him, for God is
Jer	31: 33	their minds and write it on their **h**.
Lk	16: 15	of others, but God knows your **h**.
	24: 32	"Were not our **h** burning within us
Jn	14: 1	"Do not let your **h** be troubled.
Ac	15: 9	for he purified their **h** by faith.
Ro	2: 15	of the law are written on their **h**,
1Co	14: 25	the secrets of their **h** are laid bare.
2Co	3: 2	written on our **h**, known and read
	3: 3	of stone but on tablets of human **h**.
	4: 6	shine in our **h** to give us the light
Eph	3: 17	may dwell in your **h** through faith.
Col	3: 1	Christ, set your **h** on things above,
Heb	3: 8	do not harden your **h** as you did
	10: 16	I will put my laws in their **h**, and I
1Jn	3: 20	that God is greater than our **h**,

HEAT

2Pe	3: 12	and the elements will melt in the **h**.

HEAVEN (HEAVENLY HEAVENS)

Ge	14: 19	Most High, Creator of **h** and earth.
1Ki	8: 27	even the highest **h**, cannot contain
2Ki	2: 1	take Elijah up to **h** in a whirlwind,
2Ch	7: 14	then I will hear from **h**, and I will
Isa	14: 12	How you have fallen from **h**,
	66: 1	"**H** is my throne, and the earth is
Da	7: 13	man, coming with the clouds of **h**,
Mt	6: 9	"'Our Father in **h**, hallowed be
	6: 20	up for yourselves treasures in **h**,
	16: 19	you the keys of the kingdom of **h**;
	16: 19	bind on earth will be bound in **h**,
	19: 23	is rich to enter the kingdom of **h**.
	24: 35	**H** and earth will pass away, but my
	26: 64	and coming on the clouds of **h**."
	28: 18	"All authority in **h** and on earth has
Mk	16: 19	*was taken up into **h***
Lk	15: 7	**h** over one sinner who repents
	18: 22	and you will have treasure in **h**.
Ro	10: 6	heart, 'Who will ascend into **h**?'"
2Co	5: 1	an eternal house in **h**, not built
	12: 2	ago was caught up to the third **h**.
Php	2: 10	in **h** and on earth and under
	3: 20	But our citizenship is in **h**.
1Th	1: 10	and to wait for his Son from **h**,
Heb	8: 5	a copy and shadow of what is in **h**.
	9: 24	he entered **h** itself, now to appear
2Pe	3: 13	we are looking forward to a new **h**
Rev	21: 1	I saw "a new **h** and a new earth,"

HEAVENLY (HEAVEN)

2Co	5: 2	clothed instead with our **h** dwelling,
Eph	1: 3	who has blessed us in the **h** realms
	1: 20	at his right hand in the **h** realms,
2Ti	4: 18	bring me safely to his **h** kingdom.
Heb	12: 22	of the living God, the **h** Jerusalem.

HEAVENS (HEAVEN)

Ge	1: 1	In the beginning God created the **h**

1Ki 8: 27 The **h**, even the highest heaven,
2Ch 2: 6 since the **h**, even the highest **h**,
Ps 8: 3 When I consider your **h**, the work
19: 1 The **h** declare the glory of God;
102: 25 the **h** are the work of your hands.
108: 4 is your love, higher than the **h**;
119: 89 it stands firm in the **h**.
139: 8 If I go up to the **h**, you are there;
Isa 51: 6 the **h** will vanish like smoke,
55: 9 "As the **h** are higher than the earth,
65: 17 will create new **h** and a new earth.
Joel 2: 30 I will show wonders in the **h**
Eph 4: 10 ascended higher than all the **h**,
2Pe 3: 10 The **h** will disappear with a roar;

HEBREW
Ge 14: 13 and reported this to Abram the **H**.

HEEDS
Pr 13: 1 A wise son **h** his father's
13: 18 whoever **h** correction is honored.
15: 5 but whoever **h** correction shows
15: 32 but the one who **h** correction gains

HEEL
Ge 3: 15 head, and you will strike his **h**."

HEIRS (INHERIT)
Ro 8: 17 **h** of God and co-heirs with Christ,
Gal 3: 29 and **h** according to the promise.
Eph 3: 6 gospel the Gentiles are **h** together
1Pe 3: 7 as **h** with you of the gracious gift

HELL
Mt 5: 22 will be in danger of the fire of **h**.
2Pe 2: 4 but sent them to **h**, putting them

HELMET
Isa 59: 17 and the **h** of salvation on his head;
Eph 6: 17 Take the **h** of salvation
1Th 5: 8 and the hope of salvation as a **h**.

HELP (HELPED HELPER HELPING HELPS)
2Sa 22: 36 You make your saving **h** my shield;
Ps 18: 6 I cried to my God for **h**.
30: 2 called to you for **h**, and you healed
46: 1 an ever-present **h** in trouble.
70: 4 long for your saving **h** always say,
79: 9 **H** us, God our Savior, for the glory
121: 1 where does my **h** come from?
Isa 41: 10 I will strengthen you and **h** you;
Jnh 2: 2 the realm of the dead I called for **h**,
Mk 9: 24 **h** me overcome my unbelief!"
Ac 16: 9 over to Macedonia and **h** us."

HELPED (HELP)
1Sa 7: 12 "Thus far the LORD has **h** us."

HELPER (HELP)
Ge 2: 18 I will make a **h** suitable for him."
Ps 10: 14 you are the **h** of the fatherless.
Heb 13: 6 confidence, "The Lord is my **h**;

HELPING (HELP)
Ac 9: 36 always doing good and **h** the poor.
1Co 12: 28 gifts of healing, of **h**, of guidance,
1Ti 5: 10 **h** those in trouble and devoting

HELPS (HELP)
Ro 8: 26 the Spirit **h** us in our weakness.

HEN
Mt 23: 37 as a **h** gathers her chicks under her

HERITAGE (INHERIT)
Ps 127: 3 Children are a **h** from the LORD,

HEROD
1. King of Judea who tried to kill Jesus (Mt 2; Lk 1:5).

2. Son of 1. Tetrarch of Galilee who arrested and beheaded John the Baptist (Mt 14:1-12; Mk 6:14-29; Lk 3:1, 19-20; 9:7-9); tried Jesus (Lk 23:6-15).

3. Grandson of 1. King of Judea who killed James (Ac 12:2); arrested Peter (Ac 12:3-19). Death (Ac 12:19-23).

HERODIAS
Wife of Herod the Tetrarch who persuaded her daughter to ask for John the Baptist's head (Mt 14:1-12; Mk 6:14-29).

HEZEKIAH
King of Judah. Restored the temple and worship (2Ch 29-31). Sought the LORD for help against Assyria (2Ki 18-19; 2Ch 32:1-23; Isa 36-37). Illness healed (2Ki 20:1-11; 2Ch 32:24-26; Isa 38). Judged for showing Babylonians his treasures (2Ki 20:12-21; 2Ch 32:31; Isa 39).

HID (HIDE)
Ge 3: 8 they **h** from the LORD God among
Ex 2: 2 child, she **h** him for three months.
Jos 6: 17 because she **h** the spies we sent.
Heb 11: 23 faith Moses' parents **h** him for

HIDDEN (HIDE)
Ps 19: 12 Forgive my **h** faults.
119: 11 I have **h** your word in my heart
Pr 2: 4 and search for it as for **h** treasure,
Isa 59: 2 your sins have **h** his face from you,
Mt 5: 14 A town built on a hill cannot be **h**.
13: 44 heaven is like treasure **h** in a field.
Col 1: 26 that has been kept **h** for ages
2: 3 in whom are **h** all the treasures
3: 3 and your life is now **h** with Christ

HIDE (HID HIDDEN)
Ps 17: 8 **h** me in the shadow of your wings
143: 9 LORD, for I **h** myself in you.

HIGH
Isa 57: 15 "I live in a **h** and holy place,

HILL (HILLS)
Mt 5: 14 town built on a **h** cannot be hidden.

HILLS (HILL)
Ps 50: 10 and the cattle on a thousand **h**.

HINDER (HINDERS)
1Sa 14: 6 Nothing can **h** the LORD
Mt 19: 14 do not **h** them, for the kingdom
1Co 9: 12 anything rather than **h** the gospel
1Pe 3: 7 so that nothing will **h** your prayers.

HINDERS (HINDER)
Heb 12: 1 let us throw off everything that **h**

HINT
Eph 5: 3 you there must not be even a **h**

HOLD
Ex 20: 7 LORD will not **h** anyone guiltless
Lev 19: 13 "'Do not **h** back the wages
Jos 22: 5 to **h** fast to him and to serve him
Ps 73: 23 you **h** me by my right hand.
Pr 4: 4 "Take **h** of my words with all your
Isa 54: 2 tent curtains wide, do not **h** back;
Mk 11: 25 if you **h** anything against anyone,
Php 2: 16 as you **h** firmly to the word of life.
3: 12 which Christ Jesus took **h** of me.
Col 1: 17 and in him all things **h** together.
1Th 5: 21 test them all; **h** on to what is good,
1Ti 6: 12 Take **h** of the eternal life
Heb 10: 23 Let us **h** unswervingly to the hope

HOLINESS (HOLY)
Ex 15: 11 majestic in **h**, awesome in glory,
Ps 29: 2 the LORD in the splendor of his **h**.

Ps 96: 9 the LORD in the splendor of his **h**;
Ro 6: 19 to righteousness leading to **h**.
2Co 7: 1 perfecting **h** out of reverence
Eph 4: 24 God in true righteousness and **h**.
Heb 12: 10 in order that we may share in his **h**.
12: 14 without **h** no one will see the Lord.

HOLY (HALLOWED HOLINESS)
Ex 19: 6 kingdom of priests and a **h** nation.'
20: 8 the Sabbath day by keeping it **h**.
Lev 11: 44 and be **h**, because I am **h**.
20: 7 yourselves and be **h**, because I am
20: 26 You are to be **h** to me because I,
21: 8 LORD am **h**—I who make you **h**.
22: 32 Do not profane my **h** name,
Ps 24: 3 Who may stand in his **h** place?
77: 13 Your ways, God, are **h**. What god is
99: 3 great and awesome name—he is **h**.
99: 5 worship at his footstool; he is **h**.
99: 9 for the LORD our God is **h**.
111: 9 **h** and awesome is his name.
Isa 5: 16 the **h** God will be proved **h** by his
6: 3 "**H, h, h** is the LORD Almighty;
40: 25 who is my equal?" says the **H** One.
57: 15 who lives forever, whose name is **h**:
Eze 28: 25 I will be proved **h** through them
Da 9: 24 and to anoint the Most **H** Place.
Hab 2: 20 The LORD is in his **h** temple;
Ac 2: 27 will not let your **h** one see decay.
Ro 7: 12 the law is **h**, and the commandment
is **h**,
12: 1 sacrifice, **h** and pleasing to God—
2Th 1: 10 to be glorified in his **h** people
2Ti 1: 9 saved us and called us to a **h** life—
3: 15 you have known the **H** Scriptures,
Titus 1: 8 upright, **h** and disciplined.
1Pe 1: 15 is **h**, so be **h** in all you do;
1: 16 "Be **h**, because I am **h**."
2: 9 a royal priesthood, a **h** nation,
2Pe 3: 11 You ought to live **h** and godly lives
Rev 4: 8 "'**H, h, h** is the Lord God

HOME (HOMES)
Dt 6: 7 Talk about them when you sit at **h**
Ps 84: 3 Even the sparrow has found a **h**,
Pr 3: 33 he blesses the **h** of the righteous.
Mk 10: 29 "no one who has left **h** or brothers
Jn 14: 23 and make our **h** with them.
Titus 2: 5 pure, to be busy at **h**, to be kind,

HOMES (HOME)
Ne 4: 14 daughters, your wives and your **h**."
1Ti 5: 14 to manage their **h** and to give

HOMOSEXUALITY
1Ti 1: 10 for those practicing **h**, for slave

HONEST
Lev 19: 36 **h** weights, an **h** ephah and an **h** hin.
Dt 25: 15 must have accurate and **h** weights
Job 31: 6 let God weigh me in **h** scales and
Pr 12: 17 An **h** witness tells the truth,

HONEY
Ex 3: 8 a land flowing with milk and **h**—
Ps 19: 10 they are sweeter than **h**, than **h**
119:103 taste, sweeter than **h** to my mouth!

HONOR (HONORABLE HONORABLY HONORED HONORS)
Ex 20: 12 "**H** your father and your mother,
Nu 25: 13 he was zealous for the **h** of his God
Dt 5: 16 "**H** your father and your mother,
1Sa 2: 30 Those who **h** me I will **h**, but those

Ps 8: 5 crowned them with glory and **h**.
Pr 3: 9 **H** the LORD with your wealth,
11: 16 A kindhearted woman gains **h**,
15: 33 and humility comes before **h**.
20: 3 It is to one's **h** to avoid strife,
31: 31 **H** her for all that her hands have
Mt 15: 4 '**H** your father and mother'
Ro 12: 10 **H** one another above yourselves.
1Co 6: 20 Therefore **h** God with your bodies.
Eph 6: 2 "**H** your father and mother"—
1Ti 5: 17 church well are worthy of double **h**,
Heb 2: 7 crowned them with glory and **h**
Rev 4: 9 **h** and thanks to him who sits

HONORABLE (HONOR)
1Th 4: 4 body in a way that is holy and **h**,

HONORABLY (HONOR)
Heb 13: 18 and desire to live **h** in every way.

HONORED (HONOR)
Ps 12: 8 what is vile is **h** by the human race.
Pr 13: 18 but whoever heeds correction is **h**.
1Co 12: 26 if one part is **h**, every part rejoices
Heb 13: 4 Marriage should be **h** by all,

HONORS (HONOR)
Ps 15: 4 but **h** those who fear the LORD;
Pr 14: 31 is kind to the needy **h** God.
3Jn : 6 their way in a manner that **h** God.

HOOKS
Isa 2: 4 and their spears into pruning **h**.
Joel 3: 10 and your pruning **h** into spears.

HOPE (HOPES)
Job 13: 15 he slay me, yet will I **h** in him;
Ps 42: 5 Put your **h** in God, for I will yet
62: 5 rest in God; my **h** comes from him.
119: 74 for I have put my **h** in your word.
130: 7 Israel, put your **h** in the LORD,
147: 11 put their **h** in his unfailing love.
Pr 13: 12 **H** deferred makes the heart sick,
Isa 40: 31 but those who **h** in the LORD will
Ro 5: 4 and character, **h**.
8: 24 But **h** that is seen is no **h** at all.
12: 12 Be joyful in **h**, patient in affliction,
15: 4 they provide us might have **h**.
1Co 13: 13 three remain: faith, **h** and love.
15: 19 for this life we have **h** in Christ,
Col 1: 27 is Christ in you, the **h** of glory.
1Th 5: 8 and the **h** of salvation as a helmet.
1Ti 6: 17 to put their **h** in God, who richly
Titus 2: 13 while we wait for the blessed **h**—
Heb 6: 19 We have this **h** as an anchor
11: 1 faith is confidence in what we **h**
1Jn 3: 3 All who have this **h** in him purify

HOPES (HOPE)
1Co 13: 7 trusts, always **h**, always perseveres.

HORSE
Ps 147: 10 is not in the strength of the **h**,
Pr 26: 3 A whip for the **h**, a bridle
Zec 1: 8 me was a man mounted on a red **h**.
Rev 6: 2 and there before me was a white **h**!
6: 4 Then another **h** came out, a fiery
6: 5 and there before me was a black **h**!
6: 8 and there before me was a pale **h**!
19: 11 and there before me was a white **h**,

HOSANNA
Mt 21: 9 shouted, "**H** to the Son of David!"

HOSHEA
Last king of Israel (2Ki 15:30; 17:1-6).

HOSPITABLE (HOSPITALITY)
1Ti 3: 2 respectable, **h**, able to teach,
Titus 1: 8 he must be **h**, one who loves what

HOSPITALITY (HOSPITABLE)
Ro 12: 13 people who are in need. Practice **h**.
1Ti 5: 10 showing **h**, washing the feet
Heb 13: 2 shown **h** to angels without knowing
1Pe 4: 9 Offer **h** to one another without

HOSTILE
Ro 8: 7 governed by the flesh is **h** to God;

HOT
1Ti 4: 2 have been seared as with a **h** iron.
Rev 3: 15 that you are neither cold nor **h**.

HOT-TEMPERED
Pr 15: 18 A **h** person stirs up conflict,
    19: 19 A **h** person must pay the penalty;
    22: 24 not make friends with a **h** person,
    29: 22 and a **h** person commits many sins.

HOTHEADED (HEAD)
Pr 14: 16 but a fool is **h** and yet feels secure.

HOUR
Ecc 9: 12 one knows when their **h** will come:
Mt 6: 27 worrying add a single **h** to your life?
Lk 12: 40 an **h** when you do not expect him."
Jn 12: 23 "The **h** has come for the Son
    12: 27 this very reason I came to this **h**.

HOUSE (HOUSEHOLD HOUSEHOLDS STOREHOUSE)
Ex 20: 17 shall not covet your neighbor's **h**.
Ps 23: 6 in the **h** of the Lord forever.
    84: 10 in the **h** of my God than dwell
  122: 1 "Let us go to the **h** of the Lord."
  127: 1 Unless the Lord builds the **h**,
Pr 7: 27 Her **h** is a highway to the grave,
    21: 9 of the roof than share a **h**
Isa 56: 7 my **h** will be called a **h** of prayer
Zec 13: 6 I was given at the **h** of my friends.'
Mt 7: 24 is like a wise man who built his **h**
    12: 29 can anyone enter a strong man's **h**
    21: 13 "'My **h** will be called a **h**
Mk 3: 25 If a **h** is divided against itself, that **h**
Lk 11: 17 a **h** divided against itself will fall.
Jn 2: 16 Stop turning my Father's **h**
    12: 3 the **h** was filled with the fragrance
    14: 2 My Father's **h** has many rooms;
Heb 3: 3 of a **h** has greater honor than the **h**

HOUSEHOLD (HOUSE)
Jos 24: 15 But as for me and my **h**, we will
Mic 7: 6 are the members of his own **h**.
Mt 10: 36 will be the members of his own **h**.'
    12: 25 or **h** divided against itself will not
1Ti 3: 12 manage his children and his **h** well.
    3: 15 to conduct themselves in God's **h**,

HOUSEHOLDS (HOUSE)
Pr 15: 27 The greedy bring ruin to their **h**,

HUMAN (HUMANITY)
Ge 9: 6 "Whoever sheds **h** blood,
1Sa 15: 29 for he is not a **h** being, that he
Ac 5: 29 obey God rather than **h** beings!
2Pe 1: 21 never had its origin in the **h** will,

HUMANITY (HUMAN)
Heb 2: 14 he too shared in their **h** so

HUMBLE (HUMBLED HUMILIATE HUMILIATING HUMILITY)
2Ch 7: 14 will **h** themselves and pray and

Ps 25: 9 He guides the **h** in what is right
Pr 3: 34 favor to the **h** and oppressed.
Isa 66: 2 those who are **h** and contrite
Mt 11: 29 for I am gentle and **h** in heart,
Eph 4: 2 Be completely **h** and gentle;
Jas 4: 10 **H** yourselves before the Lord,
1Pe 5: 6 **H** yourselves, therefore,

HUMBLED (HUMBLE)
Mt 23: 12 who exalt themselves will be **h**,
Php 2: 8 he **h** himself by becoming obedient

HUMILIATE (HUMBLE)
Pr 25: 7 for him to **h** you before his nobles.

HUMILIATING (HUMBLE)
1Co 11: 22 God by **h** those who have nothing?

HUMILITY (HUMBLE)
Pr 11: 2 but with **h** comes wisdom.
    15: 33 Lord, and **h** comes before honor.
2Co 10: 1 the **h** and gentleness of Christ,
Php 2: 3 in **h** value others above yourselves,
1Pe 5: 5 with **h** toward one another,

HUNGRY
Ps 107: 9 and fills the **h** with good things.
    146: 7 oppressed and gives food to the **h**.
Pr 25: 21 If your enemy is **h**, give him food
Eze 18: 7 his food to the **h** and provides
Mt 25: 35 For I was **h** and you gave me
Lk 1: 53 has filled the **h** with good things
Jn 6: 35 comes to me will never go **h**,
Ro 12: 20 "If your enemy is **h**, feed him;

HURT (HURTS)
Ecc 8: 9 lords it over others to his own **h**.
Mk 16: 18 it will not **h** them
Rev 2: 11 one who is victorious will not be **h**

HURTS (HURT)
Ps 15: 4 who keeps an oath even when it **h**,
Pr 26: 28 A lying tongue hates those it **h**,

HUSBAND (HUSBAND'S HUSBANDS)
1Co 7: 3 The **h** should fulfill his marital
    7: 3 and likewise the wife to her **h**.
    7: 4 her own body but yields it to her **h**.
    7: 4 the **h** does not have authority over
    7: 10 wife must not separate from her **h**.
    7: 11 And a **h** must not divorce his wife.
    7: 13 And if a woman has a **h** who is not
    7: 39 But if her **h** dies, she is free
2Co 11: 2 I promised you to one **h**, to Christ,
Eph 5: 23 For the **h** is the head of the wife as
    5: 33 and the wife must respect her **h**.

HUSBAND'S (HUSBAND)
Pr 12: 4 of noble character is her **h** crown,

HUSBANDS (HUSBAND)
Eph 5: 22 yourselves to your own **h** as you do
    5: 25 **H**, love your wives, just as Christ
Titus 2: 4 the younger women to love their **h**
1Pe 3: 1 yourselves to your own **h** so that,
    3: 7 **H**, in the same way be considerate

HYMN
1Co 14: 26 each of you has a **h**, or a word

HYPOCRISY (HYPOCRITE HYPOCRITES)
Mt 23: 28 on the inside you are full of **h**
1Pe 2: 1 of all malice and all deceit, **h**, envy,

HYPOCRITE (HYPOCRISY)
Mt 7: 5 You **h**, first take the plank

HYPOCRITES (HYPOCRISY)
Ps 26: 4 deceitful, nor do I associate with **h**.
Mt 6: 5 do not be like the **h**, for they love

HYSSOP
Ps 51: 7 Cleanse me with **h**, and I will be

IDLE (IDLENESS)
1Th 5: 14 those who are **i** and disruptive,
2Th 3: 6 away from every believer who is **i**
1Ti 5: 13 they get into the habit of being **i**

IDLENESS (IDLE)
Pr 31: 27 and does not eat the bread of **i**.

IDOL (IDOLATRY IDOLS)
Isa 44: 17 From the rest he makes a god, his **i**;
1Co 8: 4 We know that "An **i** is nothing

IDOLATRY (IDOL)
Col 3: 5 evil desires and greed, which is **i**.

IDOLS (IDOL)
1Co 8: 1 Now about food sacrificed to **i**:

IGNORANT (IGNORE)
1Co 15: 34 there are some who are **i** of God—
Heb 5: 2 to deal gently with those who are **i**
1Pe 2: 15 good you should silence the **i** talk
2Pe 3: 16 **i** and unstable people distort,

IGNORE (IGNORANT IGNORES)
Dt 22: 1 not **i** it but be sure to take it back
Ps 9: 12 he does not **i** the cries
Heb 2: 3 escape if we **i** so great a salvation?

IGNORES (IGNORE)
Pr 10: 17 whoever **i** correction leads others

ILLUMINATED
Rev 18: 1 and the earth was **i** by his splendor.

IMAGE
Ge 1: 26 "Let us make mankind in our **i**,
    1: 27 God created mankind in his own **i**, in
        the **i** of God he created them;
Ro 8: 29 to be conformed to the **i** of his Son,
1Co 11: 7 since he is the **i** and glory of God;
2Co 3: 18 into his **i** with ever-increasing glory,
Col 1: 15 The Son is the **i** of the invisible
    3: 10 in knowledge in the **i** of its Creator.

IMAGINE
Eph 3: 20 more than all we ask or **i**,

IMITATE (IMITATORS)
1Co 4: 16 Therefore I urge you to **i** me.
Heb 6: 12 but to **i** those who through faith
    13: 7 of their way of life and **i** their faith.
3Jn : 11 do not **i** what is evil but what is

IMITATORS (IMITATE)
1Th 1: 6 You became **i** of us and of the Lord,
    2: 14 became **i** of God's churches

IMMANUEL
Isa 7: 14 birth to a son, and will call him **I**.
Mt 1: 23 they will call him **I**" (which means

IMMORAL (IMMORALITY)
1Co 5: 9 to associate with sexually **i** people
    5: 10 the people of this world who are **i**,
    5: 11 or sister but is sexually **i** or greedy,
    6: 9 Neither the sexually **i** nor idolaters
Eph 5: 5 No **i**, impure or greedy person—
Heb 12: 16 See that no one is sexually **i**, or is
    13: 4 the adulterer and all the sexually **i**.
Rev 21: 8 the sexually **i**, those who practice
    22: 15 arts, the sexually **i**, the murderers,

IMMORALITY (IMMORAL)
Mt 5: 32 except for sexual **i**, makes her
    19: 9 except for sexual **i**, and marries

1Co 6: 13 is not meant for sexual **i**
    6: 18 Flee from sexual **i**. All other sins
    10: 8 We should not commit sexual **i**,
Gal 5: 19 sexual **i**, impurity and debauchery;
Eph 5: 3 must not be even a hint of sexual **i**,
1Th 4: 3 that you should avoid sexual **i**;
Jude : 4 grace of our God into a license for **i**

IMMORTAL (IMMORTALITY)
Ro 1: 23 exchanged the glory of the **i** God
1Ti 1: 17 Now to the King eternal, **i**,
    6: 16 who alone is **i** and who lives

IMMORTALITY (IMMORTAL)
Ro 2: 7 and **i**, he will give eternal life.
1Co 15: 53 and the mortal with **i**.
2Ti 1: 10 and **i** to light through the gospel.

IMPERISHABLE
1Pe 1: 23 seed, but of **i**, through the living

IMPORTANCE (IMPORTANT)
1Co 15: 3 I passed on to you as of first **i**:

IMPORTANT (IMPORTANCE)
Mt 23: 23 have neglected the more **i** matters
Mk 12: 29 "The most **i** one," answered Jesus,
    12: 33 as yourself is more **i** than all burnt
Php 1: 18 The **i** thing is that in every way,

IMPOSSIBLE
Mt 17: 20 Nothing will be **i** for you."
Lk 18: 27 "What is **i** with man is possible
Heb 6: 18 in which it is **i** for God to lie,
    11: 6 without faith it is **i** to please God,

IMPROPER
Eph 5: 3 because these are **i** for God's holy

IMPURE (IMPURITY)
Ac 10: 15 "Do not call anything **i** that God
Eph 5: 5 No immoral, **i** or greedy person—
1Th 4: 7 For God did not call us to be **i**,
Rev 21: 27 Nothing **i** will ever enter it,

IMPURITY (IMPURE)
Ro 1: 24 hearts to sexual **i** for the degrading
Eph 5: 3 or of any kind of **i**, or of greed,

INCENSE
Ex 40: 5 Place the gold altar of **i** in front
Ps 141: 2 my prayer be set before you like **i**;

INCOME
Ecc 5: 10 is never satisfied with their **i**.
1Co 16: 2 of money in keeping with your **i**,

INCOMPARABLE
Eph 2: 7 ages he might show the **i** riches

INCREASE (EVER-INCREASING INCREASED
    INCREASING)
Ge 1: 22 "Be fruitful and **i** in number and
Ps 62: 10 though your riches **i**, do not set
Lk 17: 5 said to the Lord, "**I** our faith!"
1Th 3: 12 May the Lord make your love **i**

INCREASED (INCREASE)
Ac 6: 7 of disciples in Jerusalem **i** rapidly,
Ro 5: 20 where sin **i**, grace **i** all the more,

INCREASING (INCREASE)
Ac 6: 1 the number of disciples was **i**,
2Th 1: 3 all of you have for one another is **i**.
2Pe 1: 8 these qualities in **i** measure,

INDEPENDENT
1Co 11: 11 in the Lord woman is not **i** of man, nor
        is man **i** of woman.

INDESCRIBABLE
2Co 9: 15 Thanks be to God for his **i** gift!

INDISPENSABLE
1Co 12: 22 body that seem to be weaker are **i**,

INEFFECTIVE
2Pe 1: 8 they will keep you from being **i**

INEXPRESSIBLE
2Co 12: 4 up to paradise and heard **i** things,
1Pe 1: 8 are filled with an **i** and glorious joy,

INFANTS
Mt 21: 16 the lips of children and **i** you, Lord,
1Co 14: 20 In regard to evil be **i**, but in your

INHERIT (CO-HEIRS HEIRS HERITAGE
 INHERITANCE)
Ps 37: 11 the meek will **i** the land and enjoy
 37: 29 The righteous will **i** the land
Mt 5: 5 the meek, for they will **i** the earth.
Mk 10: 17 "what must I do to **i** eternal life?"
1Co 15: 50 cannot **i** the kingdom of God,

INHERITANCE (INHERIT)
Dt 4: 20 to be the people of his **i**, as you
Pr 13: 22 A good person leaves an **i** for their
Eph 1: 14 deposit guaranteeing our **i** until
 5: 5 has any **i** in the kingdom of Christ
Heb 9: 15 receive the promised eternal **i**—
1Pe 1: 4 This **i** is kept in heaven for you,

INIQUITIES (INIQUITY)
Ps 78: 38 he forgave their **i** and did not
 103: 10 or repay us according to our **i**.
Isa 59: 2 your **i** have separated you from
Mic 7: 19 hurl all our **i** into the depths

INIQUITY (INIQUITIES)
Ps 51: 2 Wash away all my **i** and cleanse me
Isa 53: 6 has laid on him the **i** of us all.

INJUSTICE
2Ch 19: 7 the Lord our God there is no **i**

INNOCENT
Pr 17: 26 a fine on the **i** is not good,
Mt 10: 16 shrewd as snakes and as **i** as doves.
 27: 4 said, "for I have betrayed **i** blood."
1Co 4: 4 clear, but that does not make me **i**.

INSCRIPTION
Mt 22: 20 image is this? And whose **i**?"

INSOLENT
Ro 1: 30 **i**, arrogant and boastful;

INSTITUTED
Ro 13: 2 is rebelling against what God has **i**,

INSTRUCT (INSTRUCTED INSTRUCTION)
Ps 32: 8 I will **i** you and teach you
Pr 9: 9 **I** the wise and they will be wiser
Ro 15: 14 and competent to **i** one another.

INSTRUCTED (INSTRUCT)
2Ti 2: 25 Opponents must be gently **i**,

INSTRUCTION (INSTRUCT)
Pr 1: 3 for receiving **i** in prudent behavior,
 1: 7 but fools despise wisdom and **i**.
 1: 8 your father's **i** and do not forsake
 4: 1 Listen, my sons, to a father's **i**;
 4: 13 Hold on to **i**, do not let it go;
 6: 23 correction and **i** are the way to life,
 8: 10 Choose my **i** instead of silver,
 8: 33 Listen to my **i** and be wise;
 13: 1 A wise son heeds his father's **i**,
 13: 13 Whoever scorns **i** will pay for it,
 16: 20 Whoever gives heed to **i** prospers,
 16: 21 and gracious words promote **i**.

Pr 23: 12 Apply your heart to **i** and your ears
 23: 23 wisdom, **i** and insight as well.
Isa 8: 20 Consult God's **i** and the testimony
1Co 14: 6 or prophecy or word of **i**?
 14: 26 hymn, or a word of **i**, a revelation,
Eph 6: 4 in the training and **i** of the Lord.
1Th 4: 8 who rejects this **i** does not reject
2Th 3: 14 anyone who does not obey our **i**
1Ti 6: 3 sound **i** of our Lord Jesus Christ
2Ti 4: 2 with great patience and careful **i**.

INSULT (INSULTS)
Pr 12: 16 but the prudent overlook an **i**.
Mt 5: 11 are you when people **i** you,
Lk 6: 22 when they exclude you and **i** you
1Pe 3: 9 not repay evil with evil or **i** with **i**.

INSULTS (INSULT)
Pr 9: 7 corrects a mocker invites **i**;

INTEGRITY
1Ki 9: 4 walk before me faithfully with **i**
Job 2: 3 And he still maintains his **i**,
 27: 5 till I die, I will not deny my **i**.
Pr 10: 9 Whoever walks in **i** walks securely,
 11: 3 The **i** of the upright guides them,
 29: 10 The bloodthirsty hate a person of **i**
Titus 2: 7 In your teaching show **i**,

INTELLIGENCE
Isa 29: 14 the **i** of the intelligent will vanish."
1Co 1: 19 the **i** of the intelligent I will

INTELLIGIBLE
1Co 14: 19 I would rather speak five **i** words

INTERCEDE (INTERCEDES INTERCESSION)
Heb 7: 25 him, because he always lives to **i**

INTERCEDES (INTERCEDE)
Ro 8: 26 the Spirit himself **i** for us through

INTERCESSION (INTERCEDE)
Isa 53: 12 and made **i** for the transgressors.
1Ti 2: 1 **i** and thanksgiving be made for all

INTEREST
Ne 5: 10 But let us stop charging **i**!

INTERESTS
1Co 7: 34 and his **i** are divided.
Php 2: 4 not looking to your own **i** but each of
 you to the **i** of the others.
 2: 21 everyone looks out for their own **i**,

INTERMARRY (MARRY)
Dt 7: 3 Do not **i** with them. Do not give

INVESTIGATED
Lk 1: 3 I myself have carefully **i** everything

INVISIBLE
Ro 1: 20 of the world God's **i** qualities—
Col 1: 15 The Son is the image of the **i** God,
1Ti 1: 17 eternal, immortal, **i**, the only God,

INVITE (INVITED INVITES)
Lk 14: 13 you give a banquet, **i** the poor,

INVITED (INVITE)
Mt 22: 14 "For many are **i**, but few are
 25: 35 I was a stranger and you **i** me in,

INVITES (INVITE)
1Co 10: 27 If an unbeliever **i** you to a meal

IRON
1Ti 4: 2 have been seared as with a hot **i**.
Rev 2: 27 'will rule them with an **i** scepter

IRREVOCABLE
Ro 11: 29 for God's gifts and his call are **i**.

ISAAC

Son of Abraham by Sarah (Ge 17:19; 21:1-7; 1Ch 1:28). Offered up by Abraham (Ge 22; Heb 11:17-19). Rebekah taken as wife (Ge 24). Fathered Esau and Jacob (Ge 25:19-26; 1Ch 1:34). Tricked into blessing Jacob (Ge 27). Father of Israel (Ex 3:6; Dt 29:13; Ro 9:10).

ISAIAH

Prophet to Judah (Isa 1:1). Called by the LORD (Isa 6).

ISHMAEL

Son of Abraham by Hagar (Ge 16; 1Ch 1:28). Blessed, but not son of covenant (Ge 17:18-21; Gal 4:21-31). Sent away by Sarah (Ge 21:8-21).

ISRAEL (ISRAELITES)

1. Name given to Jacob (see JACOB).
2. Corporate name of Jacob's descendants; often specifically Northern Kingdom.

Dt	6: 4	Hear, O I: The LORD our God,
1Sa	4: 21	"The Glory has departed from I"—
Isa	27: 6	I will bud and blossom and fill all
Jer	31: 10	'He who scattered I will gather
Eze	39: 23	that the people of I went into exile
Mk	12: 29	'Hear, O I: The Lord our God,
Lk	22: 30	judging the twelve tribes of I.
Ro	9: 6	all who are descended from I are I.
	11: 26	and in this way all I will be saved.
Eph	3: 6	Gentiles are heirs together with I,

ISRAELITES (ISRAEL)

Ex	14: 22	the I went through the sea on dry
	16: 35	The I ate manna forty years,
Hos	1: 10	"Yet the I will be like the sand
Ro	9: 27	number of the I be like the sand

ITCHING

2Ti 4: 3 say what their i ears want to hear.

JACOB

Second son of Isaac, twin of Esau (Ge 25:21-26; 1Ch 1:34). Bought Esau's birthright (Ge 25:29-34); tricked Isaac into blessing him (Ge 27:1-37). Abrahamic covenant perpetuated through (Ge 28:13-15; Mal 1:2). Vision at Bethel (Ge 28:10-22). Wives and children (Ge 29:1—30:24; 35:16-26; 1Ch 2-9). Wrestled with God; name changed to Israel (Ge 32:22-32). Sent sons to Egypt during famine (Ge 42-43). Settled in Egypt (Ge 46). Blessed Ephraim and Manasseh (Ge 48). Blessed sons (Ge 49:1-28; Heb 11:21). Death (Ge 49:29-33). Burial (Ge 50:1-14).

JAMES

1. Apostle; brother of John (Mt 4:21-22; 10:2; Mk 3:17; Lk 5:1-10). At transfiguration (Mt 17:1-13; Mk 9:1-13; Lk 9:28-36). Killed by Herod (Ac 12:2).
2. Apostle; son of Alphaeus (Mt 10:3; Mk 3:18; Lk 6:15).
3. Brother of Jesus (Mt 13:55; Mk 6:3; Lk 24:10; Gal 1:19) and Judas (Jude 1). With believers before Pentecost (Ac 1:13). Leader of church at Jerusalem (Ac 12:17; 15; 21:18; Gal 2:9, 12). Author of epistle (Jas 1:1).

JAPHETH

Son of Noah (Ge 5:32; 1Ch 1:4-5). Blessed (Ge 9:18-28).

JARS

2Co 4: 7 we have this treasure in j of clay

JEALOUS (JEALOUSY)

Ex	20: 5	am a j God, punishing the children
	34: 14	whose name is J, is a j God.
Dt	4: 24	God is a consuming fire, a j God.
Joel	2: 18	Then the LORD was j for his land
Zec	1: 14	I am very j for Jerusalem and Zion,
2Co	11: 2	am j for you with a godly jealousy.

JEALOUSY (JEALOUS)

1Co	3: 3	For since there is j and quarreling
2Co	11: 2	I am jealous for you with a godly j.
Gal	5: 20	hatred, discord, j, fits of rage,

JEHOAHAZ

1. Son of Jehu; king of Israel (2Ki 13:1-9).
2. Son of Josiah; king of Judah (2Ki 23:31-34; 2Ch 36:1-4).

JEHOASH

Son of Jehoahaz; king of Israel (2Ki 13-14; 2Ch 25).

JEHOIACHIN

Son of Jehoiakim; king of Judah exiled by Nebuchadnezzar (2Ki 24:8-17; 2Ch 36:8-10; Jer 22:24-30; 24:1). Raised from prisoner status (2Ki 25:27-30; Jer 52:31-34).

JEHOIAKIM

Son of Josiah; king of Judah (2Ki 23:34—24:6; 2Ch 36:4-8; Jer 22:18-23; 36).

JEHORAM

Son of Jehoshaphat; king of Judah (2Ki 8:16-24).

JEHOSHAPHAT

Son of Asa; king of Judah (1Ki 22:41-50; 2Ki 3; 2Ch 17-20).

JEHU

King of Israel (1Ki 19:16-19; 2Ki 9-10).

JEPHTHAH

Judge from Gilead who delivered Israel from Ammon (Jdg 10:6—12:7). Made rash vow concerning his daughter (Jdg 11:30-40).

JEREMIAH

Prophet to Judah (Jer 1:1-3). Called by the LORD (Jer 1). Put in stocks (Jer 20:1-3). Threatened for prophesying (Jer 11:18-23; 26). Opposed by Hananiah (Jer 28). Scroll burned (Jer 36). Imprisoned (Jer 37). Thrown into cistern (Jer 38). Forced to Egypt with those fleeing Babylonians (Jer 43).

JEROBOAM

1. Official of Solomon; rebelled to become first king of Israel (1Ki 11:26-40; 12:1-20; 2Ch 10). Idolatry (1Ki 12:25-33); judgment for (1Ki 13-14; 2Ch 13).
2. Son of Jehoash; king of Israel (1Ki 14:23-29).

JERUSALEM

2Ki	23: 27	and I will reject J, the city I chose,
2Ch	6: 6	now I have chosen J for my Name
Ne	2: 17	let us rebuild the wall of J,
Ps	122: 6	Pray for the peace of J:
	125: 2	As the mountains surround J,
	137: 5	If I forget you, J, may my right
Isa	40: 9	You who bring good news to J,
	65: 18	for I will create J to be a delight
Joel	3: 17	J will be holy; never again will
Zep	3: 16	On that day they will say to J,
Zec	2: 4	man, 'J will be a city without walls
	8: 8	I will bring them back to live in J;
	14: 8	living water will flow out from J,
Mt	23: 37	"J, J, you who kill the prophets
Lk	13: 34	"J, J, you who kill the prophets
	21: 24	J will be trampled
Jn	4: 20	where we must worship is in J."
Ac	1: 8	and you will be my witnesses in J,
Gal	4: 25	to the present city of J,
Rev	21: 2	the new J, coming down

JESUS

LIFE: Genealogy (Mt 1:1-17; Lk 3:21-37). Birth announced (Mt 1:18-25; Lk 1:26-45). Birth (Mt 2:1-12; Lk 2:1-40). Escape to Egypt (Mt 2:13-23). As a boy in the

temple (Lk 2:41–52). Baptism (Mt 3:13–17; Mk 1:9–11; Lk 3:21–22; Jn 1:32–34). Temptation (Mt 4:1–11; Mk 1:12–13; Lk 4:1–13). Ministry in Galilee (Mt 4:12–18:35; Mk 1:14–9:50; Lk 4:14–13:9; Jn 1:35–2:11; 4; 6), Transfiguration (Mt 17:1–8; Mk 9:2–8; Lk 9:28–36), on the way to Jerusalem (Mt 19–20; Mk 10; Lk 13:10–19:27), in Jerusalem (Mt 21–25; Mk 11–13; Lk 19:28–21:38; Jn 2:12–3:36; 5; 7–12). Last supper (Mt 26:17–35; Mk 14:12–31; Lk 22:1–38; Jn 13–17). Arrest and trial (Mt 26:36–27:31; Mk 14:43–15:20; Lk 22:39–23:25; Jn 18:1–19:16). Crucifixion (Mt 27:32–66; Mk 15:21–47; Lk 23:26–55; Jn 19:28–42). Resurrection and appearances (Mt 28; Mk 16; Lk 24; Jn 20–21; Ac 1:1–11; 7:56; 9:3–6; 1Co 15:1–8; Rev 1:1–20).

MIRACLES. Healings: official's son (Jn 4:43–54), demoniac in Capernaum (Mk 1:23–26; Lk 4:33–35), Peter's mother-in-law (Mt 8:14–17; Mk 1:29–31; Lk 4:38–39), leper (Mt 8:2–4; Mk 1:40–45; Lk 5:12–16), paralytic (Mt 9:1–8; Mk 2:1–12; Lk 5:17–26), cripple (Jn 5:1–9), shriveled hand (Mt 12:10–13; Mk 3:1–5; Lk 6:6–11), centurion's servant (Mt 8:5–13; Lk 7:1–10), widow's son raised (Lk 7:11–17), demoniac (Mt 12:22–23; Lk 11:14), Gadarene demoniacs (Mt 8:28–34; Mk 5:1–20; Lk 8:26–39), woman's bleeding and Jairus' daughter (Mt 9:18–26; Mk 5:21–43; Lk 8:40–56), blind man (Mt 9:27–31), mute man (Mt 9:32–33), Canaanite woman's daughter (Mt 15:21–28; Mk 7:24–30), deaf man (Mk 7:31–37), blind man (Mk 8:22–26), demoniac boy (Mt 17:14–18; Mk 9:14–29; Lk 9:37–43), ten lepers (Lk 17:11–19), man born blind (Jn 9:1–7), Lazarus raised (Jn 11), crippled woman (Lk 13:11–17), man with dropsy (Lk 14:1–6), two blind men (Mt 20:29–34; Mk 10:46–52; Lk 18:35–43), Malchus' ear (Lk 22:50–51). Other Miracles: water to wine (Jn 2:1–11), catch of fish (Lk 5:1–11), storm stilled (Mt 8:23–27; Mk 4:37–41; Lk 8:22–25), 5,000 fed (Mt 14:15–21; Mk 6:35–44; Lk 9:10–17; Jn 6:1–14), walking on water (Mt 14:25–33; Mk 6:48–52; Jn 6:15–21), 4,000 fed (Mt 15:32–39; Mk 8:1–9), money from fish (Mt 17:24–27), fig tree cursed (Mt 21:18–22; Mk 11:12–14), catch of fish (Jn 21:1–14).

MAJOR TEACHING: Sermon on the Mount (Mt 5–7; Lk 6:17–49), to Nicodemus (Jn 3), to Samaritan woman (Jn 4), Bread of Life (Jn 6:22–59), at Feast of Tabernacles (Jn 7–8), woes to Pharisees (Mt 23; Lk 11:37–54), Good Shepherd (Jn 10:1–18), Olivet Discourse (Mt 24–25; Mk 13; Lk 21:5–36), Upper Room Discourse (Jn 13–16).

PARABLES: Sower (Mt 13:3–23; Mk 4:3–25; Lk 8:5–18), seed's growth (Mk 4:26–29), wheat and weeds (Mt 13:24–30, 36–43), mustard seed (Mt 13:31–32; Mk 4:30–32), yeast (Mt 13:33; Lk 13:20–21), hidden treasure (Mt 13:44), valuable pearl (Mt 13:45–46), net (Mt 13:47–51), house owner (Mt 13:52), good Samaritan (Lk 10:25–37), unmerciful servant (Mt 18:15–35), lost sheep (Mt 18:10–14; Lk 15:4–7), lost coin (Lk 15:8–10), prodigal son (Lk 15:11–32), dishonest manager (Lk 16:1–13), rich man and Lazarus (Lk 16:19–31), persistent widow (Lk 18:1–8), Pharisee and tax collector (Lk 18:9–14), payment of workers (Mt 20:1–16), tenants and the vineyard (Mt 21:28–46; Mk 12:1–12; Lk 20:9–19), wedding banquet (Mt 22:1–14), faithful servant (Mt 24:45–51), ten virgins (Mt 25:1–13), talents (Mt 25:1–30; Lk 19:12–27).

DISCIPLES see APOSTLES. Call of (Jn 1:35–51; Mt 4:18–22; 9:9; Mk 1:16–20; 2:13–14; Lk 5:1–11, 27–28). Named Apostles (Mk 3:13–19; Lk 6:12–16). Twelve sent out (Mt 10; Mk 6:7–11; Lk 9:1–5). Seventy sent out (Lk 10:1–24). Defection of (Jn 6:60–71; Mt 26:56; Mk 14:50–52). Final commission (Mt 28:16–20; Jn 21:15–23; Ac 1:3–8).

Ac	2: 32	God has raised this **J** to life, and we
	9: 5	Saul asked. "I am **J**, whom you are
	15: 11	of our Lord **J** that we are saved,
	16: 31	"Believe in the Lord **J**, and you will
Ro	3: 24	redemption that came by Christ **J**.
	5: 17	life through the one man, **J** Christ!
	8: 1	for those who are in Christ **J**,
1Co	2: 2	I was with you except **J** Christ
	8: 6	and there is but one Lord, **J** Christ,
	12: 3	and no one can say, "**J** is Lord,"
2Co	4: 5	but **J** Christ as Lord, and ourselves
Gal	2: 16	of the law, but by faith in **J** Christ.
	3: 28	for you are all one in Christ **J**.
	5: 6	in Christ **J** neither circumcision
Eph	2: 10	in Christ **J** to do good works,
	2: 20	with Christ **J** himself as the chief
Php	1: 6	until the day of Christ **J**.
	2: 5	have the same mindset as Christ **J**:
	2: 10	name of **J** every knee should bow,
Col	3: 17	do it all in the name of the Lord **J**,
2Th	2: 1	the coming of our Lord **J** Christ
1Ti	1: 15	**J** came into the world to save
2Ti	3: 12	life in Christ **J** will be persecuted,
Titus	2: 13	our great God and Savior, **J** Christ,
Heb	2: 9	But we do see **J**, who was made
	3: 1	fix your thoughts on **J**, whom we
	4: 14	into heaven, **J** the Son of God,
	7: 22	**J** has become the guarantor
	7: 24	but because **J** lives forever, he has
	12: 2	fixing our eyes on **J**, the pioneer
2Pe	1: 16	of our Lord **J** Christ in power,
1Jn	1: 7	and the blood of **J**, his Son,
	2: 1	**J** Christ, the Righteous One.
	2: 6	to live in him must live as **J** did.
	4: 15	acknowledges that **J** is the Son
Rev	22: 20	Amen. Come, Lord **J**.

JEW (JEWS JUDAISM)

Zec	8: 23	take firm hold of one **J** by the hem
Ro	1: 16	first to the **J**, then to the Gentile.
	10: 12	there is no difference between **J**
1Co	9: 20	To the Jews I became like a **J**,
Gal	3: 28	There is neither **J** nor Gentile,

JEWELRY (JEWELS)

| 1Pe | 3: 3 | wearing of gold **j** or fine clothes. |

JEWELS (JEWELRY)

| Isa | 61: 10 | as a bride adorns herself with her **j**. |
| Zec | 9: 16 | in his land like **j** in a crown. |

JEWS (JEW)

Mt	2: 2	who has been born king of the **J**?
	27: 11	him, "Are you the king of the **J**?"
Jn	4: 22	know, for salvation is from the **J**.
Ro	3: 29	Or is God the God of **J** only?
1Co	1: 22	**J** demand signs and Greeks look
	9: 20	To the **J** I became like a Jew, to win
	12: 13	whether **J** or Gentiles,
Rev	3: 9	claim to be **J** though they are not,

JEZEBEL

Sidonian wife of Ahab (1Ki 16:31). Promoted Baal worship (1Ki 16:32–33). Killed prophets of the LORD (1Ki 18:4, 13). Opposed Elijah (1Ki 19:1–2). Had Naboth killed (1Ki 21). Death prophesied (1Ki 21:17–24). Killed by Jehu (2Ki 9:30–37).

JOASH

Son of Ahaziah; king of Judah. Sheltered from Athaliah by Jehoiada (2Ki 11; 2Ch 22:10–23:21). Repaired temple (2Ki 12; 2Ch 24).

JOB

Wealthy man from Uz; feared God (Job 1:1–5). Righteousness tested by disaster (Job 1:6–22), personal affliction (Job 2). Maintained innocence in debate with

three friends (Job 3–31), Elihu (Job 32–37). Rebuked by the LORD (Job 38–41). Vindicated and restored to greater stature by the LORD (Job 42). Example of righteousness (Eze 14:14, 20).

JOHN

1. Son of Zechariah and Elizabeth (Lk 1). Called the Baptist (Mt 3:1–12; Mk 1:2–8). Witness to Jesus (Mt 3:11–12; Mk 1:7–8; Lk 3:15–18; Jn 1:6–35; 3:27–30; 5:33–36). Doubts about Jesus (Mt 11:2–6; Lk 7:18–23). Arrest (Mt 4:12; Mk 1:14). Execution (Mt 14:1–12; Mk 6:14–29; Lk 9:7–9). Ministry compared to Elijah (Mt 11:7–19; Mk 9:11–13; Lk 7:24–35).

2. Apostle; brother of James (Mt 4:21–22; 10:2; Mk 3:17; Lk 5:1–10). At transfiguration (Mt 17:1–13; Mk 9:1–13; Lk 9:28–36). Desire to be greatest (Mk 10:35–45). Leader of church at Jerusalem (Ac 4:1–3; Gal 2:9). Elder who wrote epistles (2Jn 1; 3Jn 1). Prophet who wrote Revelation (Rev 1:1; 22:8).

3. Cousin of Barnabas, co-worker with Paul, (Ac 12:12—13:13; 15:37), see MARK.

JOIN (JOINED)

Pr	23: 20	not **j** those who drink too much
	24: 21	do not **j** with rebellious officials,
Ro	15: 30	to **j** me in my struggle by praying
2Ti	1: 8	**j** with me in suffering
2Ti	2: 3	**J** with me in suffering, like a good

JOINED (JOIN)

Mt	19: 6	Therefore what God has **j** together,
Mk	10: 9	Therefore what God has **j** together,
Eph	2: 21	the whole building is **j** together
	4: 16	body, **j** and held together by every

JOINTS

Heb	4: 12	soul and spirit, **j** and marrow;

JOKING

Eph	5: 4	foolish talk or coarse **j**, which are

JONAH

Prophet in days of Jeroboam II (2Ki 14:25). Called to Nineveh; fled to Tarshish (Jnh 1:1–3). Cause of storm; thrown into sea (Jnh 1:4–16). Swallowed by fish (Jnh 1:17). Prayer (Jnh 2). Preached to Nineveh (Jnh 3). Attitude reproved by the LORD (Jnh 4). Sign of (Mt 12:39–41; Lk 11:29–32).

JONATHAN

Son of Saul (1Sa 13:16; 1Ch 8:33). Valiant warrior (1Sa 13–14). Relation to David (1Sa 18:1–4; 19–20; 23:16–18). Killed at Gilboa (1Sa 31). Mourned by David (2Sa 1).

JORAM

Son of Ahab; king of Israel (2Ki 3; 8–9; 2Ch 22).

JORDAN

Nu	34: 12	boundary will go down along the **J**
Jos	4: 22	'Israel crossed the **J** on dry ground.'
Mt	3: 6	baptized by him in the **J** River.

JOSEPH

1. Son of Jacob by Rachel (Ge 30:24; 1Ch 2:2). Favored by Jacob, hated by brothers (Ge 37:3–4). Dreams (Ge 37:5–11). Sold by brothers (Ge 37:12–36). Served Potiphar; imprisoned by false accusation (Ge 39). Interpreted dreams of Pharaoh's servants (Ge 40), of Pharaoh (Ge 41:4–40). Made greatest in Egypt (Ge 41:41–57). Sold grain to brothers (Ge 42–45). Brought Jacob and sons to Egypt (Ge 46–47). Sons Ephraim and Manasseh blessed (Ge 48). Blessed (Ge 49:22–26; Dt 33:13–17). Death (Ge 50:22–26; Ex 13:19; Heb 11:22). 12,000 from (Rev 7:8).

2. Husband of Mary, mother of Jesus (Mt 1:16–24; 2:13–19; Lk 1:27; 2; Jn 1:45).

3. Disciple from Arimathea, who gave his tomb for Jesus' burial (Mt 27:57–61; Mk 15:43–47; Lk 23:50–53).

4. Original name of Barnabas (Ac 4:36).

JOSHUA

1. Son of Nun; name changed from Hoshea (Nu 13:8, 16; 1Ch 7:27). Fought Amalekites under Moses (Ex 17:9–14). Servant of Moses on Sinai (Ex 24:13; 32:17). Spied Canaan (Nu 13). With Caleb, allowed to enter land (Nu 14:6, 30). Succeeded Moses (Dt 1:38; 31:1–8; 34:9).

Charged Israel to conquer Canaan (Jos 1). Crossed Jordan (Jos 3–4). Circumcised sons of wilderness wanderings (Jos 5). Conquered Jericho (Jos 6), Ai (Jos 7–8), five kings at Gibeon (Jos 10:1–28), southern Canaan (Jos 10:29–43), northern Canaan (Jos 11–12). Defeated at Ai (Jos 7). Deceived by Gibeonites (Jos 9). Renewed covenant (Jos 8:30–35; 24:1–27). Divided land among tribes (Jos 13–22). Last words (Jos 23). Death (Jos 24:28–31).

2. High priest during rebuilding of temple (Hag 1–2; Zec 3:1–9; 6:11).

JOSIAH

Son of Amon; king of Judah (2Ki 22–23; 2Ch 34–35).

JOTHAM

Son of Azariah (Uzziah); king of Judah (2Ki 15:32–38; 2Ch 26:21—27:9).

JOY (ENJOY ENJOYMENT JOYFUL OVERJOYED REJOICE REJOICES REJOICING)

Dt	16: 15	hands, and your **j** will be complete.
1Ch	16: 27	and **j** are in his dwelling place.
Ne	8: 10	for the **j** of the LORD is your
Est	9: 22	their sorrow was turned into **j**
Job	38: 7	and all the angels shouted for **j**?
Ps	4: 7	Fill my heart with **j** when their
	21: 6	glad with the **j** of your presence.
	30: 11	sackcloth and clothed me with **j**,
	43: 4	God, to God, my **j** and my delight.
	51: 12	to me the **j** of your salvation.
	66: 1	Shout for **j** to God, all the earth!
	96: 12	all the trees of the forest sing for **j**.
	107: 22	tell of his works with songs of **j**.
	119: 111	forever; they are the **j** of my heart.
Pr	10: 1	A wise son brings **j** to his father,
	10: 28	The prospect of the righteous is **j**,
	12: 20	those who promote peace have **j**.
	15: 30	in a messenger's eyes brings **j**
Isa	35: 10	everlasting **j** will crown their heads
	51: 11	Gladness and **j** will overtake them,
	55: 12	You will go out in **j** and be led
Lk	1: 44	the baby in my womb leaped for **j**.
	2: 10	will cause great **j** for all the people.
Jn	15: 11	and that your **j** may be complete.
	16: 20	grieve, but your grief will turn to **j**.
2Co	8: 2	trial, their overflowing **j** and their
Php	2: 2	then make my **j** complete by being
	4: 1	love and long for, my **j** and crown,
1Th	2: 19	our **j**, or the crown in which we
Phm	: 7	Your love has given me great **j**
Heb	12: 2	the **j** set before him he endured
Jas	1: 2	Consider it pure **j**, my brothers
1Pe	1: 8	an inexpressible and glorious **j**,
2Jn	: 4	It has given me great **j** to find some
3Jn	: 4	I have no greater **j** than to hear

JOYFUL (JOY)

Ps	100: 2	come before him with **j** songs.
Pr	23: 25	may she who gave you birth be **j**!
Hab	3: 18	I will be **j** in God my Savior.

JUDAH

1. Son of Jacob by Leah (Ge 29:35; 35:23; 1Ch 2:1). Tribe of blessed as ruling tribe (Ge 49:8–12; Dt 33:7).

2. Name used for people and land of Southern Kingdom.
Jer 13: 19 All **J** will be carried into exile,
Zec 10: 4 From **J** will come the cornerstone,
Heb   7: 14 that our Lord descended from **J**,

JUDAISM (JEW)
Gal   1: 13 of my previous way of life in **J**,

JUDAS
1. Apostle (Lk 6:16; Jn 14:22; Ac 1:13). Probably also called Thaddaeus (Mt 10:3; Mk 3:18).
2. Brother of James and Jesus (Mt 13:55; Mk 6:3), also called Jude (Jude 1).
3. Apostle, also called Iscariot, who betrayed Jesus (Mt 10:4; 26:14–56; Mk 3:19; 14:10–50; Lk 6:16; 22:3–53; Jn 6:71; 12:4; 13:2–30; 18:2–11). Suicide of (Mt 27:3–5; Ac 1:16–25).

JUDGE (JUDGED JUDGES JUDGING JUDGMENT)
Ge   18: 25 Will not the **J** of all the earth do
1Ch 16: 33 Lord, for he comes to **j** the earth.
Joel 3: 12 there I will sit to **j** all the nations
Mt   7: 1 "Do not **j**, or you too will be
Jn   7: 24 but instead **j** correctly."
     12: 47 For I did not come to **j** the world,
Ac   17: 31 set a day when he will **j** the world
1Co   4: 3 indeed, I do not even **j** myself.
      6: 2 the Lord's people will **j** the world?
2Ti   4: 1 who will **j** the living and the dead,
      4: 8 the righteous, **J**, will award to me
Jas   4: 12 who are you to **j** your neighbor?
Rev 20: 4 who had been given authority to **j**.

JUDGED (JUDGE)
Mt   7: 1 "Do not judge, or you too will be **j**.
Jn   5: 24 will not be **j** but has crossed over
Jas   3: 1 who teach will be **j** more strictly.
Rev 20: 12 The dead were **j** according to what

JUDGES (JUDGE)
Jdg   2: 16 Then the Lord raised up **j**,
Ps   9: 8 and **j** the peoples with equity.
     58: 11 there is a God who **j** the earth."
Ro   2: 16 God **j** people's secrets through Jesus
Heb   4: 12 it **j** the thoughts and attitudes
Rev 19: 11 With justice he **j** and wages war.

JUDGING (JUDGE)
Mt   19: 28 **j** the twelve tribes of Israel.
Jn   7: 24 Stop **j** by mere appearances,
2Co 10: 7 You are **j** by appearances.

JUDGMENT (JUDGE)
Dt   1: 17 of anyone, for **j** belongs to God.
Ps   1: 5 the wicked will not stand in the **j**,
    119: 66 Teach me knowledge and good **j**,
Ecc 12: 14 God will bring every deed into **j**,
Isa 66: 16 his sword the Lord will execute **j**
Mt   5: 21 who murders will be subject to **j**.'
     10: 15 Gomorrah on the day of **j** than
     12: 36 the day of **j** for every empty word
Jn   5: 22 but has entrusted all **j** to the Son,
     16: 8 about sin and righteousness and **j**:
Ro   14: 10 will all stand before God's **j** seat.
     14: 13 Therefore let us stop passing **j**
1Co 11: 29 eat and drink **j** on themselves.
     11: 31 we would not come under such **j**.
2Co   5: 10 we must all appear before the **j** seat
Heb   9: 27 to die once, and after that to face **j**,
     10: 27 only a fearful expectation of **j**
1Pe   4: 17 For it is time for **j** to begin
Jude : 6 everlasting chains for **j** on the great

JUST (JUSTICE JUSTIFICATION JUSTIFIED JUSTIFY
     JUSTLY)
Dt   32: 4 are perfect, and all his ways are **j**.

Ps   37: 28 For the Lord loves the **j** and will
    111: 7 of his hands are faithful and **j**;
Pr   1: 3 doing what is right and **j** and fair;
      2: 8 for he guards the course of the **j**
Da   4: 37 does is right and all his ways are **j**.
Ro   3: 26 time, so as to be **j** and the one who
Heb   2: 2 received its **j** punishment,
1Jn   1: 9 he is faithful and **j** and will forgive
Rev 16: 7 true and **j** are your judgments."

JUSTICE (JUST)
Ex   23: 2 do not pervert **j** by siding
     23: 6 "Do not deny **j** to your poor people
Job 37: 23 in his **j** and great righteousness,
Ps   9: 16 Lord is known by his acts of **j**;
     11: 7 the Lord is righteous, he loves **j**;
     45: 6 a scepter of **j** will be the scepter
    101: 1 I will sing of your love and **j**;
Pr   21: 15 When **j** is done, it brings joy
     29: 4 By **j** a king gives a country stability,
     29: 26 is from the Lord that one gets **j**.
Isa   9: 7 and upholding it with **j**
     28: 17 I will make **j** the measuring line
     30: 18 For the Lord is a God of **j**.
     42: 1 and he will bring **j** to the nations.
     42: 4 be discouraged till he establishes **j**
     56: 1 "Maintain **j** and do what is right,
     61: 8 "For I, the Lord, love **j**;
Eze 34: 16 I will shepherd the flock with **j**.
Am   5: 15 maintain **j** in the courts.
      5: 24 But let **j** roll on like a river,
Zec   7: 9 'Administer true **j**; show mercy
Lk   11: 42 you neglect **j** and the love of God.

JUSTIFICATION (JUST)
Ac   13: 39 sin, a **j** you were not able to obtain
Ro   4: 25 sins and was raised to life for our **j**.
      5: 18 one righteous act resulted in **j**

JUSTIFIED (JUST)
Ro   3: 24 all are **j** freely by his grace through
      3: 28 that a person is **j** by faith apart
      5: 1 since we have been **j** through faith,
      5: 9 Since we have now been **j** by his
      8: 30 he called, he also **j**; those he **j**,
1Co   6: 11 you were **j** in the name of the Lord
Gal   2: 16 that a person is not **j** by the works
      3: 11 relies on the law is **j** before God,
      3: 24 came that we might be **j** by faith.

JUSTIFY (JUST)
Gal   3: 8 that God would **j** the Gentiles

JUSTLY (JUST)
Ps 106: 3 Blessed are those who act **j**,
Mic   6: 8 To act **j** and to love mercy

KEEP (KEEPER KEEPING KEEPS KEPT)
Ge   31: 49 "May the Lord **k** watch between
Ex   20: 6 love me and **k** my commandments.
Nu   6: 24 Lord bless you and **k** you;
Ps   18: 28 You, Lord, **k** my lamp burning;
     19: 13 **K** your servant also from willful
    121: 7 The Lord will **k** you from all
    141: 3 **k** watch over the door of my lips.
Pr   4: 24 **K** your mouth free of perversity;
     17: 28 are thought wise if they **k** silent,
Isa 26: 3 You will **k** in perfect peace those
Am   5: 13 Therefore the prudent **k** quiet
Mt   10: 10 staff, for the worker is worth his **k**.
Lk   12: 35 service and **k** your lamps burning,
Gal   5: 25 let us **k** in step with the Spirit.
Eph   4: 3 Make every effort to **k** the unity
1Ti   5: 22 the sins of others. **K** yourself pure.

2Ti 4: 5 you, **k** your head in all situations,
Heb 13: 5 **K** your lives free from the love
Jas 1: 26 and yet do not **k** a tight rein on
2: 8 If you really **k** the royal law found
1Jn 5: 3 love for God: to **k** his commands.
Jude : 24 To him who is able to **k** you

KEEPER (KEEP)
Ge 4: 9 "Am I my brother's **k**?"

KEEPING (KEEP)
Ex 20: 8 the Sabbath day by **k** it holy.
Ps 19: 11 in **k** them there is great reward.
Mt 3: 8 Produce fruit in **k** with repentance.
Lk 2: 8 **k** watch over their flocks at night.
1Co 7: 19 **K** God's commands is what counts.
2Pe 3: 9 Lord is not slow in **k** his promise,

KEEPS (KEEP)
1Co 13: 5 angered, it **k** no record of wrongs,
Jas 2: 10 For whoever **k** the whole law

KEPT (KEEP)
Ps 130: 3 LORD, **k** a record of sins, Lord,
2Ti 4: 7 finished the race, I have **k** the faith.
1Pe 1: 4 This inheritance is **k** in heaven

KEYS
Mt 16: 19 will give you the **k** of the kingdom

KILL (KILLS)
Mt 17: 23 will **k** him, and on the third day

KILLS (KILL)
Lev 24: 21 whoever **k** a human being is to be
2Co 3: 6 for the letter **k**, but the Spirit gives

KIND (KINDNESS KINDS)
Ge 1: 24 animals, each according to its **k**."
2Ch 10: 7 "If you will be **k** to these people
Pr 11: 17 Those who are **k** benefit themselves,
12: 25 the heart, but a **k** word cheers it up.
14: 21 blessed is the one who is **k**
14: 31 whoever is **k** to the needy honors
19: 17 Whoever is **k** to the poor lends
Da 4: 27 by being **k** to the oppressed.
Lk 6: 35 because he is **k** to the ungrateful
1Co 13: 4 Love is patient, love is **k**.
15: 35 what **k** of body will they come?"
Eph 4: 32 Be **k** and compassionate to one
2Ti 2: 24 but must be **k** to everyone,
Titus 2: 5 to be **k**, and to be subject to their

KINDNESS (KIND)
Ac 14: 17 He has shown **k** by giving you rain
Ro 11: 22 but **k** to you, provided that you
continue in his **k**.
Gal 5: 22 peace, forbearance, **k**, goodness,
Eph 2: 7 expressed in his **k** to us in Christ

KINDS (KIND)
1Co 12: 4 There are different **k** of gifts,
1Ti 6: 10 of money is a root of all **k** of evil.

KING (KINGDOM KINGS)
　1. Kings of Judah and Israel: see Saul, David, Solomon.
　2. Kings of Judah: see Rehoboam, Abijah, Asa, Jehoshaphat, Jehoram, Ahaziah, Athaliah (Queen), Joash,
Amaziah, Uzziah, Jotham, Ahaz, Hezekiah, Manasseh,
Amon, Josiah, Jehoahaz, Jehoiakim, Jehoiachin, Zedekiah.
　3. Kings of Israel: see Jeroboam I, Nadab, Baasha,
Elah, Zimri, Tibni, Omri, Ahab, Ahaziah, Joram, Jehu,
Jehoahaz, Jehoash, Jeroboam II, Zechariah, Shallum,
Menahem, Pekah, Pekahiah, Hoshea.
Jdg 17: 6 In those days Israel had no **k**;
1Sa 12: 12 'No, we want a **k** to rule over us'—
12: 12 the LORD your God was your **k**.

Ps 24: 7 that the **K** of glory may come in.
Isa 32: 1 a **k** will reign in righteousness
Zec 9: 9 See, your **k** comes to you,
1Ti 6: 15 the **K** of kings and Lord of lords,
Rev 19: 16 thigh he has this name written: **K**

KINGDOM (KING)
Ex 19: 6 you will be for me a **k** of priests
1Ch 29: 11 Yours, LORD, is the **k**;
Ps 45: 6 justice will be the scepter of your **k**.
Da 4: 3 His **k** is an eternal **k**;
Mt 3: 2 for the **k** of heaven has come near."
5: 3 spirit, for theirs is the **k** of heaven.
6: 10 your **k** come, your will be done,
6: 33 But seek first his **k** and his
7: 21 Lord,' will enter the **k** of heaven,
11: 11 the **k** of heaven is greater than he.
13: 24 "The **k** of heaven is like a man who
13: 31 "The **k** of heaven is like a mustard
13: 33 "The **k** of heaven is like yeast
13: 44 "The **k** of heaven is like treasure
13: 45 the **k** of heaven is like a merchant
13: 47 the **k** of heaven is like a net that
16: 19 you the keys of the **k** of heaven;
18: 23 the **k** of heaven is like a king who
19: 24 who is rich to enter the **k** of God."
24: 7 rise against nation, and **k** against **k**.
24: 14 gospel of the **k** will be preached
25: 34 the **k** prepared for you since
Mk 9: 47 you to enter the **k** of God with one
10: 14 for the **k** of God belongs to such as
10: 23 for the rich to enter the **k** of God!"
Lk 10: 9 'The **k** of God has come near
12: 31 But seek his **k**, and these things
17: 21 is,' because the **k** of God is in your
Jn 3: 5 one can enter the **k** of God unless
18: 36 said, "My **k** is not of this world.
1Co 6: 9 wrongdoers will not inherit the **k**
15: 24 when he hands over the **k** to God
Rev 1: 6 has made us to be a **k** and priests
11: 15 "The **k** of the world has become

KINGS (KING)
Ps 2: 2 The **k** of the earth rise
72: 11 May all **k** bow down to him and all
Da 7: 24 ten horns are ten **k** who will come
1Ti 2: 2 for **k** and all those in authority,
Rev 1: 5 and the ruler of the **k** of the earth.

KISS
Ps 2: 12 **K** his son, or he will be angry
Pr 24: 26 An honest answer is like a **k**
Lk 22: 48 the Son of Man with a **k**?"

KNEE (KNEES)
Isa 45: 23 Before me every **k** will bow;
Ro 14: 11 Lord, 'every **k** will bow before me;
Php 2: 10 name of Jesus every **k** should bow,

KNEES (KNEE)
Isa 35: 3 hands, steady the **k** that give way;
Heb 12: 12 your feeble arms and weak **k**.

KNEW (KNOW)
Job 23: 3 If only I **k** where to find him;
Jnh 4: 2 I **k** that you are a gracious
Mt 7: 23 tell them plainly, 'I never **k** you.

KNOCK
Mt 7: 7 **k** and the door will be opened
Rev 3: 20 I stand at the door and **k**.

KNOW (FOREKNEW KNEW KNOWING
　　KNOWLEDGE KNOWN KNOWS)
Dt 18: 21 "How can we **k** when a message
Job 19: 25 I **k** that my redeemer lives,
42: 3 things too wonderful for me to **k**.

Ps 46: 10 says, "Be still, and **k** that I am God;
    73: 11 Does the Most High **k** anything?"
    139: 1 LORD, and you **k** me.
    139: 23 Search me, God, and **k** my heart;
Pr 27: 1   you do not **k** what a day may bring.
Jer 24: 7   I will give them a heart to **k** me,
    31: 34 because they will all **k** me,
Mt 6: 3   let your left hand **k** what your right
    24: 42 because you do not **k** on what day
Lk 1: 4   so that you may **k** the certainty
Jn 3: 11   you, we speak of what we **k**, and we
    4: 22   worship what you do not **k**;
    9: 25   One thing I do **k**. I was blind
    10: 14 I **k** my sheep and my sheep **k** me—
    17: 3   that they **k** you, the only true God,
    21: 24 We **k** that his testimony is true.
Ac 1: 7   "It is not for you to **k** the times
Ro 6: 6   we **k** that our old self was crucified
    7: 18   I **k** that good itself does not dwell
    8: 28   we **k** that in all things God works
1Co 2: 2   I resolved to **k** nothing while I was
    6: 15   Do you not **k** that your bodies are
    6: 19   Do you not **k** that your bodies are
    8: 2   do not yet **k** as they ought to **k**.
    13: 12 Now I **k** in part; then I shall **k** fully,
    15: 58 because you **k** that your labor
Php 3: 10   I want to **k** Christ—yes, to **k**
2Ti 1: 12   because I **k** whom I have believed,
Jas 4: 14   do not even **k** what will happen
1Jn 2: 4   Whoever says, "I **k** him," but does
    3: 14   We **k** that we have passed
    3: 16   This is how we **k** what love is:
    5: 2   This is how we **k** that we love
    5: 13   may **k** that you have eternal life.

KNOWING (KNOW)
Ge 3: 5   will be like God, **k** good and evil."
Php 3: 8   worth of **k** Christ Jesus my Lord,

KNOWLEDGE (KNOW)
Ge 2: 9   the tree of the **k** of good and evil.
Job 42: 3   that obscures my plans without **k**?'
Ps 19: 2   night after night they reveal **k**.
    139: 6 Such **k** is too wonderful for me,
Pr 1: 7   of the LORD is the beginning of **k**,
    10: 14 The wise store up **k**, but the mouth
    12: 1   Whoever loves discipline loves **k**,
    13: 16 All who are prudent act with **k**,
    19: 2   Desire without **k** is not good—
Isa 11: 9   the **k** of the LORD as the waters
Hab 2: 14   will be filled with the **k** of the glory
Ro 11: 33 riches of the wisdom and **k** of God!
1Co 8: 1   But **k** puffs up while love builds up.
    8: 11   Christ died, is destroyed by your **k**.
    13: 2   can fathom all mysteries and all **k**,
2Co 2: 14   aroma of the **k** of him everywhere.
    4: 6   of the **k** of God's glory displayed
Eph 3: 19   know this love that surpasses **k**—
Col 2: 3   all the treasures of wisdom and **k**.
1Ti 6: 20   ideas of what is falsely called **k**,
2Pe 3: 18   grow in the grace and **k** of our Lord

KNOWN (KNOW)
Ps 16: 11 You make **k** to me the path of life;
    105: 1 make **k** among the nations what he
Isa 46: 10 I make **k** the end
Mt 10: 26 or hidden that will not be made **k**.
Ro 1: 19   since what may be **k** about God is
    11: 34 "Who has **k** the mind of the Lord?
    15: 20 the gospel where Christ was not **k**,
2Co 3: 2   our hearts, **k** and read by everyone.
2Pe 2: 21   than to have **k** it and then to turn

KNOWS (KNOW)
1Sa 2: 3   for the LORD is a God who **k**,
Job 23: 10 But he **k** the way that I take;
Ps 44: 21 since he **k** the secrets of the heart?
    94: 11 The LORD **k** all human plans; he **k**
Ecc 8: 7   Since no one **k** the future, who can
Mt 6: 8   your Father **k** what you need
    24: 36 about that day or hour no one **k**,
Ro 8: 27   searches our hearts **k** the mind
2Ti 2: 19   "The Lord **k** those who are his,"

LABAN
Brother of Rebekah (Ge 24:29–51), father of Rachel and Leah (Ge 29–31).

LABOR
Ex 20: 9   Six days you shall **l** and do all your
Isa 55: 2   your **l** on what does not satisfy?
Mt 6: 28   They do not **l** or spin.
1Co 3: 8   rewarded according to their own **l**.
    15: 58 know that your **l** in the Lord is not

LACK (LACKING LACKS)
Pr 15: 22 Plans fail for **l** of counsel,
Col 2: 23   but they **l** any value in restraining

LACKING (LACK)
Ro 12: 11 Never be **l** in zeal, but keep your
Jas 1: 4   and complete, not **l** anything.

LACKS (LACK)
Jas 1: 5   If any of you **l** wisdom, you should

LAID (LAY)
Isa 53: 6   and the LORD has **l** on him
1Co 3: 11   other than the one already **l**,
1Jn 3: 16   Jesus Christ **l** down his life for us.

LAKE
Rev 19: 20 into the fiery **l** of burning sulfur.
    20: 14 The **l** of fire is the second death.

LAMB (LAMB'S LAMBS)
Ge 22: 8   "God himself will provide the **l**
Ex 12: 21 and slaughter the Passover **l**.
Isa 11: 6   The wolf will live with the **l**,
    53: 7   he was led like a **l** to the slaughter,
Jn 1: 29   "Look, the **L** of God, who takes
1Co 5: 7   our Passover **l**, has been sacrificed.
1Pe 1: 19   a **l** without blemish or defect.
Rev 5: 6   Then I saw a **L**, looking as if it had
    5: 12   "Worthy is the **L**, who was slain,
    14: 4   as firstfruits to God and the **L**.

LAMB'S (LAMB)
Rev 21: 27 names are written in the **L** book

LAMBS (LAMB)
Lk 10: 3   you out like **l** among wolves.
Jn 21: 15 Jesus said, "Feed my **l**."

LAMENT
2Sa 1: 17   took up this **l** concerning Saul

LAMP (LAMPS)
2Sa 22: 29 You, LORD, are my **l**;
Ps 18: 28 You, LORD, keep my **l** burning;
    119:105 Your word is a **l** to my feet
Pr 31: 18 and her **l** does not go out at night.
Lk 8: 16   "No one lights a **l** and hides it
Rev 21: 23 gives it light, and the Lamb is its **l**.

LAMPS (LAMP)
Mt 25: 1   be like ten virgins who took their **l**
Lk 12: 35 service and keep your **l** burning,

LAND
Ge 1: 10   God called the dry ground "**l**,"
    1: 11   said, "Let the **l** produce vegetation:

Ge 12: 7 your offspring I will give this **l**."
Ex 3: 8 a **l** flowing with milk and honey—
Nu 35: 33 Bloodshed pollutes the **l**,
Dt 34: 1 Lord showed him the whole **l**—
Jos 13: 2 "This is the **l** that remains:
14: 4 Levites received no share of the **l**
2Ch 7: 14 their sin and will heal their **l**.
7: 20 then I will uproot Israel from my **l**,
Eze 36: 24 bring you back into your own **l**.

LANGUAGE
Ge 11: 1 Now the whole world had one **l**
Jn 8: 44 speaks his native **l**, for he is a liar
Ac 2: 6 heard their own **l** being spoken.
Col 3: 8 slander, and filthy **l** from your lips.
Rev 5: 9 God persons from every tribe and **l**

LAST (LASTING LASTS LATTER)
2Sa 23: 1 These are the **l** words of David:
Isa 44: 6 I am the first and I am the **l**;
Mt 19: 30 But many who are first will be **l**,
Mk 10: 31 will be **l**, and the **l** first."
Jn 15: 16 fruit that will **l**—and so
Ro 1: 17 that is by faith from first to **l**,
2Ti 3: 1 will be terrible times in the **l** days.
2Pe 3: 3 in the **l** days scoffers will come,
Rev 1: 17 I am the First and the **L**.
22: 13 the First and the **L**, the Beginning

LASTING (LAST)
Ex 12: 14 to the Lord—a **l** ordinance.
Lev 24: 8 of the Israelites, as a **l** covenant.
Nu 25: 13 have a covenant of a **l** priesthood,
Heb 10: 34 had better and **l** possessions.

LASTS (LAST)
Ps 30: 5 For his anger **l** only a moment,
2Co 3: 11 greater is the glory of that which **l**!

LATTER (LAST)
Job 42: 12 The Lord blessed the **l** part

LAUGH (LAUGHS)
Ecc 3: 4 a time to weep and a time to **l**,

LAUGHS (LAUGH)
Ps 2: 4 The One enthroned in heaven **l**;
37: 13 but the Lord **l** at the wicked, for he

LAVISHED
Eph 1: 8 that he **l** on us. With all wisdom
1Jn 3: 1 See what great love the Father has **l**

LAW (LAWS)
Dt 31: 11 you shall read this **l** before them
31: 26 "Take this Book of the **L** and place
Jos 1: 8 Keep this Book of the **L** always
Ne 8: 8 from the Book of the **L** of God,
Ps 1: 2 delight is in the **l** of the Lord,
19: 7 The **l** of the Lord is perfect,
119: 18 may see wonderful things in your **l**.
119: 72 The **l** from your mouth is more
119: 97 Oh, how I love your **l**! I meditate
119: 165 peace have those who love your **l**,
Jer 31: 33 "I will put my **l** in their minds
Mt 5: 17 that I have come to abolish the **L**
7: 12 you, for this sums up the **L**
22: 40 All the **L** and the Prophets hang
Lk 16: 17 stroke of a pen to drop out of the **L**.
Jn 1: 17 For the **l** was given through Moses;
Ro 2: 12 All who sin apart from the **l** will
2: 15 requirements of the **l** are written
5: 13 account where there is no **l**.
5: 20 The **l** was brought in so
6: 14 because you are not under the **l**,
7: 6 we have been released from the **l** so

Ro 7: 12 So then, the **l** is holy,
8: 3 For what the **l** was powerless to do
10: 4 Christ is the culmination of the **l**
13: 10 love is the fulfillment of the **l**.
Gal 3: 13 curse of the **l** by becoming a curse
3: 24 So the **l** was our guardian until
5: 3 he is obligated to obey the whole **l**.
5: 4 by the **l** have been alienated
5: 14 For the entire **l** is fulfilled
Heb 7: 19 (for the **l** made nothing perfect),
10: 1 The **l** is only a shadow of the good
Jas 1: 25 the perfect **l** that gives freedom,
2: 10 For whoever keeps the whole **l**

LAWLESSNESS
2Th 2: 3 occurs and the man of **l** is revealed,
2: 7 the secret power of **l** is already
1Jn 3: 4 sins breaks the law; in fact, sin is **l**.

LAWS (LAW)
Lev 25: 18 and be careful to obey my **l**,
Ps 119: 30 I have set my heart on your **l**.
119: 120 fear of you; I stand in awe of your **l**.
Heb 8: 10 I will put my **l** in their minds
10: 16 I will put my **l** in their hearts, and I

LAY (LAID LAYING)
Job 22: 22 and **l** up his words in your heart.
Isa 28: 16 "See, I **l** a stone in Zion, a tested
Mt 8: 20 of Man has no place to **l** his head."
Jn 10: 15 and I **l** down my life for the sheep.
15: 13 to **l** down one's life for one's
1Co 3: 11 no one can **l** any foundation other
1Jn 3: 16 we ought to **l** down our lives for
Rev 4: 10 They **l** their crowns before

LAYING (LAY)
1Ti 5: 22 not be hasty in the **l** on of hands,
Heb 6: 1 not **l** again the foundation

LAZARUS
1. Poor man in Jesus' parable (Lk 16:19-31).
2. Brother of Mary and Martha whom Jesus raised from the dead (Jn 11:1—12:19).

LAZY
Pr 10: 4 **L** hands make for poverty,
Heb 6: 12 We do not want you to become **l**,

LEAD (LEADERS LEADS LED)
Ex 15: 13 love you will **l** the people you have
Ps 27: 11 **l** me in a straight path because
61: 2 **l** me to the rock that is higher than I.
139: 24 and **l** me in the way everlasting.
143: 10 may your good Spirit **l** me on level
Ecc 5: 6 Do not let your mouth **l** you
Isa 11: 6 and a little child will **l** them.
Da 12: 3 those who **l** many to righteousness,
Mt 6: 13 And **l** us not into temptation,
1Jn 3: 7 do not let anyone **l** you astray.

LEADERS (LEAD)
Heb 13: 7 Remember your **l**, who spoke
13: 17 Have confidence in your **l**

LEADS (LEAD)
Ps 23: 2 he **l** me beside quiet waters,
Pr 19: 23 The fear of the Lord **l** to life;
Isa 40: 11 he gently **l** those that have young.
Mt 7: 13 gate and broad is the road that **l**
Jn 10: 3 sheep by name and **l** them out.
Ro 14: 19 every effort to do what **l** to peace
2Co 2: 14 God, who always **l** us as captives

LEAH
Wife of Jacob (Ge 29:16-30); bore six sons and one daughter (Ge 29:31—30:21; 34:1; 35:23).

LEAN
Pr   3: 5 l not on your own understanding;

LEARN (LEARNED LEARNING)
Isa   1: 17 **L** to do right; seek justice.
Mt   11: 29 my yoke upon you and l from me,

LEARNED (LEARN)
Php   4: 11 I have l to be content whatever
2Ti   3: 14 know those from whom you l it,

LEARNING (LEARN)
Pr   1: 5 the wise listen and add to their l,
2Ti   3: 7 always l but never able to come

LED (LEAD)
Isa 53: 7 he was l like a lamb
Am   2: 10 l you forty years in the wilderness
Ro   8: 14 For those who are l by the Spirit

LEFT
Jos   1: 7 turn from it to the right or to the l,
Pr   4: 27 Do not turn to the right or the l;
Mt   6: 3 do not let your l hand know what
     25: 33 on his right and the goats on his l.

LEGION
Mk   5: 9 "My name is **L**," he replied,

LEND (LENDS)
Dt   15: 8 freely l them whatever they need.
Ps   37: 26 are always generous and l freely;
Lk   6: 34 Even sinners l to sinners,

LENDS (LEND)
Pr   19: 17 kind to the poor l to the LORD,

LENGTH (LONG)
Pr   10: 27 fear of the LORD adds l to life,

LEPROSY
2Ki   7: 3 Now there were four men with l

LETTER (LETTERS)
Mt   5: 18 not the smallest l, not the least
2Co   3: 2 You yourselves are our l,
      3: 6 not of the l but of the Spirit; for the l
                 kills,
2Th   3: 14 not obey our instruction in this l.

LETTERS (LETTER)
2Co   3: 7 which was engraved in l on stone,
     10: 10 "His l are weighty and forceful,
2Pe   3: 16 He writes the same way in all his l,

LEVEL
Ps 143: 10 good Spirit lead me on l ground.
Isa 26: 7 The path of the righteous is l;
Heb 12: 13 "Make l paths for your feet,"

LEVI (LEVITES)
  1. Son of Jacob by Leah (Ge 29:34; 46:11; 1Ch 2:1). Tribe of blessed (Ge 49:5-7; Dt 33:8-11), chosen as priests (Nu 3-4), numbered (Nu 3:39; 26:62), allotted cities, but not land (Nu 18; 35; Dt 10:9; Jos 13:14; 21), land (Eze 48:8-22), 12,000 from (Rev 7:7).
  2. See MATTHEW.

LEVITES (LEVI)
Nu   1: 53 The **L** are to be responsible
      8: 6 "Take the **L** from among all
     18: 21 "I give to the **L** all the tithes

LEWDNESS
Mk   7: 22 malice, deceit, l, envy, slander,

LIAR (LIE)
Pr   19: 22 better to be poor than a l.
Jn   8: 44 for he is a l and the father of lies.
Ro   3: 4 be true, and every human being a l.

LIBERATED
Ro   8: 21 the creation itself will be l from its

LIE (LIAR LIED LIES LYING)
Lev 19: 11 "'Do not l. "'Do not deceive
Nu   23: 19 that he should l, not a human
Dt   6: 7 when you l down and when you
Ps   23: 2 He makes me l down in green
Isa 11: 6 the leopard will l down
Eze 34: 14 There they will l down in good
Ro   1: 25 the truth about God for a l,
Col   3: 9 Do not l to each other, since you
Heb   6: 18 which it is impossible for God to l,

LIED (LIE)
Ac   5: 4 You have not l just to human

LIES (LIE)
Ps   34: 13 evil and your lips from telling l.
Jn   8: 44 for he is a liar and the father of l.

LIFE (LIVE)
Ge   2: 7 into his nostrils the breath of l,
      2: 9 of the garden were the tree of l
      9: 11 Never again will all l be destroyed
Ex   21: 23 injury, you are to take l for l,
Lev 17: 14 because the l of every creature is its
     24: 18 must make restitution—l for l.
Dt   30: 19 Now choose l, so that you and your
Ps   16: 11 make known to me the path of l;
     23: 6 will follow me all the days of my l,
     34: 12 Whoever of you loves l and desires
     39: 4 let me know how fleeting my l is.
     49: 7 one can redeem the l of another
    104: 33 I will sing to the LORD all my l;
Pr   6: 23 and instruction are the way to l,
      7: 23 little knowing it will cost him his l.
      8: 35 For those who find me find l
     11: 30 fruit of the righteous is a tree of l,
     21: 21 righteousness and love finds l,
Eze 37: 5 enter you, and you will come to l.
Da   12: 2 some to everlasting l,
Mt   6: 25 do not worry about your l,
      7: 14 and narrow the road that leads to l,
     10: 39 whoever loses their l for my sake
     16: 25 wants to save their l will lose it,
     20: 28 to give his l as a ransom for many."
Mk   10: 45 to give his l as a ransom for many."
Lk   12: 15 l does not consist in an abundance
     12: 22 do not worry about your l,
     14: 26 yes, even their own l—
Jn   1: 4 In him was l, and that l was the light
      3: 15 who believes may have eternal l
      3: 36 believes in the Son has eternal l,
      4: 14 of water welling up to eternal l."
      5: 24 has crossed over from death to l.
      6: 35 Jesus declared, "I am the bread of l.
      6: 47 the one who believes has eternal l.
      6: 68 You have the words of eternal l.
     10: 10 I have come that they may have l,
     10: 15 and I lay down my l for the sheep.
     10: 28 I give them eternal l, and they shall
     11: 25 "I am the resurrection and the l.
     14: 6 am the way and the truth and the l.
     15: 13 lay down one's l for one's friends.
     20: 31 by believing you may have l in his
Ac   13: 48 appointed for eternal l believed.
Ro   4: 25 was raised to l for our justification.
      6: 13 have been brought from death to l,
      6: 23 God is eternal l in Christ Jesus our
      8: 38 convinced that neither death nor l,
1Co 15: 19 If only for this l we have hope
2Co   3: 6 the letter kills, but the Spirit gives l.

Gal 2: 20 The l I now live in the body, I live
Eph 4: 1 to live a l worthy of the calling you
Php 2: 16 as you hold firmly to the word of l.
Col 1: 10 you may live a l worthy of the Lord
1Th 4: 12 your daily l may win the respect
1Ti 4: 8 the present l and the l to come.
 4: 16 Watch your l and doctrine closely.
 6: 19 take hold of the l that is truly l.
2Ti 3: 12 live a godly l in Christ Jesus will be
Jas 1: 12 person will receive the crown of l
 3: 13 Let them show it by their good l,
1Pe 3: 10 "Whoever would love l and see
2Pe 1: 3 a godly l through our knowledge
1Jn 3: 14 we have passed from death to l,
 5: 11 God has given us eternal l, and this l
Rev 13: 8 written in the Lamb's book of l,
 20: 12 was opened, which is the book of l.
 21: 27 are written in the Lamb's book of l.
 22: 2 side of the river stood the tree of l,

LIFT (LIFTED LIFTING)

Ps 121: 1 I l up my eyes to the mountains—
 134: 2 L up your hands in the sanctuary
La 3: 41 Let us l up our hearts and our hands

LIFTED (LIFT)

Ps 40: 2 He l me out of the slimy pit,
Jn 3: 14 so the Son of Man must be l up,
 12: 32 I, when I am l up from the earth,

LIFTING (LIFT)

1Ti 2: 8 l up holy hands without anger

LIGHT (ENLIGHTENED)

Ge 1: 3 "Let there be l," and there was l.
2Sa 22: 29 Lord turns my darkness into l.
Job 38: 19 "What is the way to the abode of l?
Ps 4: 6 Let the l of your face shine on us.
 19: 8 are radiant, giving l to the eyes.
 27: 1 The Lord is my l and my
 56: 13 walk before God in the l of life.
 76: 4 You are radiant with l,
 104: 2 The Lord wraps himself in l as
 119:105 lamp to my feet and a l for my path.
 119:130 unfolding of your words gives l;
Isa 2: 5 let us walk in the l of the Lord.
 9: 2 in darkness have seen a great l;
 49: 6 also make you a l for the Gentiles,
Mt 4: 16 shadow of death a l has dawned."
 5: 16 way, let your l shine before others,
 11: 30 yoke is easy and my burden is l."
Jn 3: 19 L has come into the world,
 8: 12 he said, "I am the l of the world.
2Co 4: 6 made his l shine in our hearts
 6: 14 Or what fellowship can l have
 11: 14 masquerades as an angel of l.
1Ti 6: 16 and who lives in unapproachable l,
1Pe 2: 9 of darkness into his wonderful l.
1Jn 1: 5 God is l; in him there is no darkness
 1: 7 But if we walk in the l, as he is
Rev 21: 23 for the glory of God gives it l,

LIGHTNING

Da 10: 6 his face like l, his eyes like flaming
Mt 24: 27 For as l that comes from the east is
 28: 3 His appearance was like l, and his

LIKENESS

Ge 1: 26 in our l, so that they may rule over
Ps 17: 15 will be satisfied with seeing your l.
Isa 52: 14 his form marred beyond human l
Ro 8: 3 his own Son in the l of sinful flesh
Php 2: 7 a servant, being made in human l.
Jas 3: 9 who have been made in God's l.

LION

Isa 11: 7 and the l will eat straw like the ox.
1Pe 5: 8 around like a roaring l looking
Rev 5: 5 See, the L of the tribe of Judah,

LIPS

Ps 34: 1 his praise will always be on my l.
 119: 171 May my l overflow with praise,
Pr 13: 3 who guard their l preserve their
 27: 2 an outsider, and not your own l.
Isa 6: 5 For I am a man of unclean l, and I
Mt 21: 16 read, "'From the l of children
Col 3: 8 and filthy language from your l.

LISTEN (LISTENING)

Dt 30: 20 Lord your God, l to his voice,
Pr 1: 5 let the wise l and add to their
 12: 15 to them, but the wise l to advice.
Jn 10: 27 My sheep l to my voice;
Jas 1: 19 Everyone should be quick to l,
 1: 22 Do not merely l to the word,

LISTENING (LISTEN)

1Sa 3: 9 Lord, for your servant is l.'"
Pr 18: 13 To answer before l—that is folly

LIVE (ALIVE LIFE LIVES LIVING)

Ex 20: 12 that you may l long in the land
 33: 20 face, for no one may see me and l."
Dt 8: 3 that man does not l on bread alone
Job 14: 14 If someone dies, will they l again?
Ps 119:175 Let me l that I may praise you,
Isa 55: 3 come to me; listen, that you may l.
Eze 37: 3 "Son of man, can these bones l?"
Hab 2: 4 the righteous person will l by his
Mt 4: 4 'Man shall not l on bread alone,
Ac 17: 24 not l in temples built by human
 17: 28 'For in him we l and move and
Ro 1: 17 "The righteous will l by faith."
2Co 5: 7 For we l by faith, not by sight.
Gal 2: 20 The life I now l in the body,
 5: 25 Since we l by the Spirit, let us keep
Php 1: 21 me, to l is Christ and to die is gain.
1Th 5: 13 L in peace with each other.
2Ti 3: 12 who wants to l a godly life
Heb 12: 14 Make every effort to l in peace
1Pe 1: 17 l out your time as foreigners here

LIVES (LIVE)

Job 19: 25 I know that my redeemer l,
Pr 11: 30 and the one who is wise saves l.
Isa 57: 15 he who l forever, whose name is
Da 3: 28 to give up their l rather than serve
Jn 14: 17 he l with you and will be in you.
Gal 2: 20 I no longer live, but Christ l in me.
Heb 13: 5 Keep your l free from the love
2Pe 3: 11 You ought to live holy and godly l
1Jn 3: 16 to lay down our l for our brothers
 4: 16 Whoever l in love l in God,

LIVING (LIVE)

Ge 2: 7 life, and the man became a l being.
Jer 2: 13 the spring of l water, and have dug
Mt 22: 32 the God of the dead but of the l."
Jn 7: 38 said, rivers of l water will flow
Ro 12: 1 to offer your bodies as a l sacrifice,
Heb 10: 31 to fall into the hands of the l God.
Rev 1: 18 I am the L One; I was dead,

LOAD

Gal 6: 5 each one should carry their own l.

LOCUSTS

Mt 3: 4 His food was l and wild honey.

LOFTY

Ps 139: 6 for me, too l for me to attain.

LONELY
Ps 68: 6 God sets the l in families, he leads

LONG (LENGTH LONGED LONGING LONGS)
1Ki 18: 21 "How l will you waver between
Jn 9: 4 As l as it is day, we must do
Eph 3: 18 to grasp how wide and l and high
1Pe 1: 12 Even angels l to look into these

LONGED (LONG)
Mt 13: 17 righteous people l to see what you
23: 37 how often I have l to gather your
2Ti 4: 8 to all who have l for his appearing.

LONGING (LONG)
Pr 13: 19 A l fulfilled is sweet to the soul,
2Co 5: 2 l to be clothed instead with our

LONGS (LONG)
Isa 30: 18 Yet the Lord l to be gracious

LOOK (LOOKING LOOKS)
Job 31: 1 my eyes not to l lustfully at a young
Ps 34: 5 Those who l to him are radiant;
Pr 4: 25 Let your eyes l straight ahead;
Isa 60: 5 Then you will l and be radiant,
Hab 1: 13 Your eyes are too pure to l on evil;
Zec 12: 10 They will l on me, the one they
Mk 13: 21 is the Messiah!' or, 'L, there he is!'
Lk 24: 39 L at my hands and my feet. It is I
Jn 1: 36 by, he said, "L, the Lamb of God!"
4: 35 open your eyes and l at the fields!
19: 37 "They will l on the one they have
Jas 1: 27 to l after orphans and widows
1Pe 1: 12 Even angels long to l into these

LOOKING (LOOK)
Rev 5: 6 a Lamb, l as if it had been slain,

LOOKS (LOOK)
1Sa 16: 7 but the Lord l at the heart."
Lk 9: 62 puts a hand to the plow and l back
Php 2: 21 everyone l out for their own interests,

LORD (LORD'S LORDING)
Ne 4: 14 Remember the L, who is great
Job 28: 28 human race, "The fear of the L—
Ps 54: 4 the L is the one who sustains me.
62: 12 and with you, L, is unfailing love";
86: 5 You, L, are forgiving and good,
110: 1 The Lord says to my l:
147: 5 Great is our L and mighty in power
Isa 6: 1 died, I saw the L, high and exalted,
Da 9: 4 "L, the great and awesome God,
Mt 3: 3 'Prepare the way for the L,
4: 7 'Do not put the L your God
7: 21 "Not everyone who says to me, 'L,
22: 37 "'Love the L your God with all
22: 44 "'The L said to my L: "Sit at my
Mk 12: 11 the L has done this, and it is
12: 29 The L our God, the L is one.
Lk 2: 9 An angel of the L appeared to
6: 46 "Why do you call me, 'L, L,'
10: 27 "'Love the L your God with all
Ac 2: 21 on the name of the L will be saved.'
16: 31 "Believe in the L Jesus, and you
Ro 10: 9 "Jesus is L," and believe in your
10: 13 the name of the L will be saved."
12: 11 your spiritual fervor, serving the L.
14: 8 we live or die, we belong to the L.
1Co 1: 31 the one who boasts boast in the L."
3: 5 as the L has assigned to each his
7: 34 to be devoted to the L in both body
11: 23 The L Jesus, on the night he was
12: 3 "Jesus is L," except by the Holy

1Co 15: 57 victory through our L Jesus Christ.
16: 22 let that person be cursed! Come, L!
2Co 3: 17 Now the L is the Spirit, and where
8: 5 gave themselves first of all to the L,
10: 17 the one who boasts boast in the L."
Gal 6: 14 in the cross of our L Jesus Christ,
Eph 4: 5 one L, one faith, one baptism;
5: 10 and find out what pleases the L.
5: 19 music from your heart to the L,
Php 2: 11 acknowledge that Jesus Christ is L,
3: 1 and sisters, rejoice in the L!
4: 4 Rejoice in the L always. I will say it
Col 2: 6 as you received Christ Jesus as L,
3: 17 do it all in the name of the L Jesus,
3: 23 working for the L, not for human
4: 17 you have received in the L."
1Th 3: 12 May the L make your love increase
5: 2 day of the L will come like a thief
5: 23 at the coming of our L Jesus Christ.
2Th 2: 1 the coming of our L Jesus Christ
2Ti 2: 19 "The L knows those who are his,"
Heb 12: 14 holiness no one will see the L.
13: 6 confidence, "The L is my helper;
Jas 4: 10 Humble yourselves before the L,
1Pe 1: 25 the word of the L endures forever."
2: 3 you have tasted that the L is good.
3: 15 in your hearts revere Christ as L.
2Pe 1: 16 the coming of our L Jesus Christ
2: 1 sovereign L who bought them—
3: 9 The L is not slow in keeping his
Jude : 14 the L is coming with thousands
Rev 4: 8 holy is the L God Almighty,'
4: 11 "You are worthy, our L and God,
17: 14 triumph over them because he is L
22: 20 Amen. Come, L Jesus.

LORD'S (LORD)
Ac 21: 14 up and said, "The L will be done."
1Co 10: 26 "The earth is the L, and everything
11: 26 you proclaim the L death until he
2Co 3: 18 faces contemplate the L glory,
2Ti 2: 24 And the L servant must not be
Jas 4: 15 "If it is the L will, we will live

LORDING (LORD)
1Pe 5: 3 not l it over those entrusted to you,

LORD* (LORD'S*; this is the proper name of God, *Yahweh*, spelled "Lord" in the NIV)
Ge 2: 4 when the L God made the earth
2: 7 the L God formed a man
3: 21 The L God made garments of skin
7: 16 Then the L shut him in.
15: 6 Abram believed the L, and he
18: 14 Is anything too hard for the L?
31: 49 "May the L keep watch between
Ex 3: 2 There the angel of the L appeared
9: 12 But the L hardened Pharaoh's heart
14: 30 That day the L saved Israel
20: 2 "I am the L your God, who
33: 11 The L would speak to Moses face
40: 34 glory of the L filled the tabernacle.
Lev 19: 2 'Be holy because I, the L your God,
Nu 8: 5 The L said to Moses:
14: 21 glory of the L fills the whole earth,
Dt 2: 7 The L your God has blessed you
5: 9 for I, the L your God, am a jealous
6: 4 The L our God, the L is one.
6: 5 Love the L your God with all your
6: 16 Do not put the L your God
10: 14 L your God belong the heavens,
10: 17 For the L your God is God of gods

Dt	11: 1	Love the **L** your God and keep his
	28: 1	If you fully obey the **L** your God
	30: 16	you today to love the **L** your God,
	30: 20	For the **L** is your life, and he will
	31: 6	for the **L** your God goes with you;
Jos	22: 5	to love the **L** your God, to walk
	24: 15	household, we will serve the **L**."
1Sa	1: 28	So now I give him to the **L**.
	2: 2	"There is no one holy like the **L**;
	7: 12	"Thus far the **L** has helped us."
	12: 22	his great name the **L** will not reject
	15: 22	as much as in obeying the **L**?
2Sa	22: 2	"The **L** is my rock, my fortress
1Ki	2: 3	and observe what the **L** your God
	8: 11	the glory of the **L** filled his temple.
	8: 61	fully committed to the **L** our God,
	18: 21	If the **L** is God, follow him;
2Ki	13: 23	But the **L** was gracious to them
1Ch	16: 8	Give praise to the **L**, proclaim his
	16: 23	Sing to the **L**, all the earth;
	28: 9	for the **L** searches every heart
	29: 11	Yours, **L**, is the kingdom;
2Ch	5: 14	the glory of the **L** filled the temple
	16: 9	the **L** range throughout the earth
	19: 6	for mere mortals but for the **L**,
	30: 9	for the **L** your God is gracious
Ne	1: 5	"**L**, the God of heaven, the great
Job	1: 21	The **L** gave and the **L** has taken
	38: 1	the **L** spoke to Job out of the storm.
	42: 9	did what the **L** told them;
Ps	1: 2	whose delight is in the law of the **L**,
	9: 9	The **L** is a refuge for the oppressed,
	12: 6	the words of the **L** are flawless,
	16: 8	I keep my eyes always on the **L**.
	19: 7	The law of the **L** is perfect,
	19: 14	heart be pleasing in your sight, **L**,
	23: 1	The **L** is my shepherd, I lack
	23: 6	dwell in the house of the **L** forever.
	27: 1	The **L** is the stronghold of my life
	27: 4	to gaze on the beauty of the **L**
	29: 1	ascribe to the **L** glory and strength.
	32: 2	one whose sin the **L** does not count
	33: 12	is the nation whose God is the **L**,
	33: 18	the eyes of the **L** are on those who
	34: 3	Glorify the **L** with me; let us exalt
	34: 7	of the **L** encamps around those
	34: 8	Taste and see that the **L** is good;
	34: 18	The **L** is close to the brokenhearted
	37: 4	Take delight in the **L**, and he will
	40: 1	I waited patiently for the **L**;
	47: 2	For the **L** Most High is awesome,
	48: 1	Great is the **L**, and most worthy
	55: 22	Cast your cares on the **L** and he
	75: 8	In the hand of the **L** is a cup full
	84: 11	For the **L** God is a sun and shield;
	86: 11	Teach me your way, **L**, that I may
	89: 5	heavens praise your wonders, **L**,
	95: 1	Come, let us sing for joy to the **L**;
	96: 1	Sing to the **L** a new song;
	98: 4	Shout for joy to the **L**, all the earth,
	100: 1	Shout for joy to the **L**, all the earth.
	103: 1	Praise the **L**, my soul; all my
	103: 8	The **L** is compassionate
	104: 1	Praise the **L**, my soul. **L** my God,
	107: 8	to the **L** for his unfailing love
	110: 1	The **L** says to my lord: "Sit at my
	113: 4	The **L** is exalted over all the nations
	115: 1	Not to us, **L**, not to us but to your
	116: 15	the sight of the **L** is the death of his
	118: 1	Give thanks to the **L**, for he is good;

Ps	118: 24	The **L** has done it this very day;
	121: 2	My help comes from the **L**,
	121: 5	The **L** watches over you—the **L** is
	125: 2	so the **L** surrounds his people both
	127: 1	Unless the **L** builds the house,
	127: 3	Children are a heritage from the **L**,
	130: 3	If you, **L**, kept a record of sins,
	135: 6	The **L** does whatever pleases him,
	136: 1	Give thanks to the **L**, for he is good.
	139: 1	You have searched me, **L**, and you
	144: 3	**L**, what are human beings that you
	145: 3	Great is the **L** and most worthy
	145: 18	The **L** is near to all who call on him,
Pr	1: 7	The fear of the **L** is the beginning
	3: 5	Trust in the **L** with all your heart
	3: 9	Honor the **L** with your wealth,
	3: 12	because the **L** disciplines those he
	3: 19	By wisdom the **L** laid the earth's
	5: 21	your ways are in full view of the **L**,
	6: 16	There are six things the **L** hates,
	10: 27	The fear of the **L** adds length to life,
	11: 1	The **L** detests dishonest scales,
	12: 22	The **L** detests lying lips, but he
	14: 26	Whoever fears the **L** has a secure
	15: 3	The eyes of the **L** are everywhere,
	16: 2	but motives are weighed by the **L**.
	16: 4	The **L** works out everything to its
	16: 9	but the **L** establishes their steps.
	16: 33	but its every decision is from the **L**.
	18: 10	name of the **L** is a fortified tower;
	18: 22	and receives favor from the **L**.
	19: 14	but a prudent wife is from the **L**.
	19: 17	is kind to the poor lends to the **L**,
	21: 3	acceptable to the **L** than sacrifice.
	21: 30	plan that can succeed against the **L**.
	21: 31	battle, but victory rests with the **L**.
	22: 2	The **L** is the Maker of them all.
	24: 18	or the **L** will see and disapprove
	31: 30	a woman who fears the **L** is to be
Isa	6: 3	holy, holy is the **L** Almighty;
	11: 2	The Spirit of the **L** will rest on him
	11: 9	of the **L** as the waters cover the sea.
	12: 2	The **L**, the **L** himself, is my strength
	24: 1	the **L** is going to lay waste the earth
	25: 8	The Sovereign **L** will wipe away
	29: 15	to hide their plans from the **L**,
	33: 6	the fear of the **L** is the key to this
	35: 10	those the **L** has rescued will return.
	40: 5	For the mouth of the **L** has spoken.
	40: 7	because the breath of the **L** blows
	40: 10	the Sovereign **L** comes with power,
	40: 28	The **L** is the everlasting God,
	40: 31	in the **L** will renew their strength.
	42: 8	"I am the **L**; that is my name!
	43: 11	I am the **L**, and apart from me
	44: 24	I am the **L**, the Maker of all things,
	45: 5	I am the **L**, and there is no other;
	45: 21	Was it not I, the **L**? And there is no
	51: 11	Those the **L** has rescued will return
	53: 6	the **L** has laid on him the iniquity
	53: 10	the will of the **L** will prosper in his
	55: 6	Seek the **L** while he may be found;
	58: 8	of the **L** will be your rear guard.
	58: 11	The **L** will guide you always;
	59: 1	the arm of the **L** is not too short
	61: 3	a planting of the **L** for the display
	61: 10	I delight greatly in the **L**;
Jer	1: 9	Then the **L** reached out his hand
	9: 24	in these I delight," declares the **L**.
	16: 19	**L**, my strength and my fortress,

Jer	17: 7	is the one who trusts in the **L**,
La	3: 40	and let us return to the **L**.
Eze	1: 28	of the likeness of the glory of the **L**.
Hos	1: 7	but I, the **L** their God, will save
	3: 5	return and seek the **L** their God
	6: 1	"Come, let us return to the **L**.
Joel	2: 1	for the day of the **L** is coming.
	2: 11	The day of the **L** is great;
	3: 14	day of the **L** is near in the valley
Am	5: 18	you who long for the day of the **L**!
Jnh	1: 3	But Jonah ran away from the **L**
Mic	4: 2	the word of the **L** from Jerusalem.
	6: 8	what does the **L** require of you?
Na	1: 2	The **L** is a jealous and avenging
	1: 3	The **L** is slow to anger but great
Hab	2: 14	of the **L** as the waters cover the sea.
	2: 20	The **L** is in his holy temple;
Zep	3: 17	The **L** your God is with you,
Zec	1: 17	and the **L** will again comfort Zion
	9: 16	The **L** their God will save his people
	14: 5	Then the **L** my God will come,
	14: 9	On that day there will be one **L**,
Mal	4: 5	and dreadful day of the **L** comes.

LORD'S* (LORD*; this is the proper name of God, *Yahweh*, spelled "LORD's" in the NIV)

Ex	34: 34	he entered the **L** presence to speak
Nu	14: 41	you disobeying the **L** command?
Dt	6: 18	is right and good in the **L** sight,
	32: 9	For the **L** portion is his people,
Jos	21: 45	all the **L** good promises to Israel
Ps	24: 1	The earth is the **L**,
	32: 10	the **L** unfailing love surrounds
	89: 1	I will sing of the **L** great love
	103: 17	the **L** love is with those who fear
Pr	3: 11	do not despise the **L** discipline,
Isa	24: 14	west they acclaim the **L** majesty.
	62: 3	a crown of splendor in the **L** hand,
Jer	48: 10	who is lax in doing the **L** work!
La	3: 22	Because of the **L** great love we are
Mic	4: 1	the mountain of the **L** temple will

LOSE (LOSES LOSS LOST)

1Sa	17: 32	"Let no one **l** heart on account
Mt	10: 39	Whoever finds their life will **l** it,
Lk	9: 25	and yet **l** or forfeit their very self?
Jn	6: 39	that I shall **l** none of all those
Heb	12: 3	will not grow weary and **l** heart.
	12: 5	not **l** heart when he rebukes you,

LOSES (LOSE)

Mt	5: 13	But if the salt **l** its saltiness,
Lk	15: 4	a hundred sheep and **l** one of them.
	15: 8	has ten silver coins and **l** one.

LOSS (LOSE)

Ro	11: 12	their **l** means riches for the Gentiles,
1Co	3: 15	the builder will suffer **l** but yet will
Php	3: 8	I consider everything a **l** because

LOST (LOSE)

Ps	73: 2	I had nearly **l** my foothold.
Jer	50: 6	"My people have been **l** sheep;
Eze	34: 4	the strays or searched for the **l**.
	34: 16	I will search for the **l** and bring
Lk	15: 4	go after the **l** sheep until he finds
	15: 6	I have found my **l** sheep.'
	15: 9	I have found my **l** coin.'
	15: 24	he was **l** and is found.'
	19: 10	came to seek and to save the **l**."
Php	3: 8	for whose sake I have **l** all things.

LOT (LOTS)

Nephew of Abraham (Ge 11:27; 12:5). Chose to live

in Sodom (Ge 13). Rescued from four kings (Ge 14). Rescued from Sodom (Ge 19:1-29; 2Pe 2:7). Fathered Moab and Ammon by his daughters (Ge 19:30-38).

Est	3: 7	the **l)** was cast in the presence
	9: 24	the **l)** for their ruin and destruction.
Pr	16: 33	The **l** is cast into the lap, but its
	18: 18	Casting the **l** settles disputes
Ecc	3: 22	their work, because that is their **l**.
Ac	1: 26	cast lots, and the **l** fell to Matthias;

LOTS (LOT)

Ps	22: 18	them and cast **l** for my garment.
Mt	27: 35	divided up his clothes by casting **l**.

LOVE (BELOVED LOVED LOVELY LOVER LOVERS LOVES LOVING)

Ge	22: 2	son, your only son, whom you **l**—
Ex	15: 13	In your unfailing **l** you will lead
	20: 6	showing **l** to a thousand generations
	34: 6	abounding in **l** and faithfulness,
Lev	19: 18	but **l** your neighbor as yourself.
	19: 34	**L** them as yourself, for you were
Nu	14: 18	abounding in **l** and forgiving sin
Dt	5: 10	showing **l** to a thousand generations
	6: 5	**L** the LORD your God with all
	7: 13	He will **l** you and bless you
	10: 12	to **l** him, to serve the LORD your
	11: 13	to **l** the LORD your God
	13: 6	or the wife you **l**, or your closest
	30: 6	you may **l** him with all your heart
Jos	22: 5	to **l** the LORD your God, to walk
1Ki	3: 3	Solomon showed his **l**
	8: 23	you who keep your covenant of **l**
2Ch	5: 13	his **l** endures forever."
Ne	1: 5	covenant of **l** with those who **l** him
Ps	18: 1	I **l** you, LORD, my strength.
	23: 6	**l** will follow me all the days of my
	25: 6	your great mercy and **l**, for they are
	31: 16	save me in your unfailing **l**.
	32: 10	LORD's unfailing **l** surrounds
	33: 5	the earth is full of his unfailing **l**.
	33: 18	whose hope is in his unfailing **l**,
	36: 5	Your **l**, LORD,
	36: 7	How priceless is your unfailing **l**,
	45: 7	You **l** righteousness and hate
	51: 1	God, according to your unfailing **l**;
	57: 10	For great is your **l**,
	63: 3	Because your **l** is better than life,
	66: 20	prayer or withheld his **l** from me!
	77: 8	his unfailing **l** vanished forever?
	85: 7	Show us your unfailing **l**, LORD,
	85: 10	**L** and faithfulness meet together;
	86: 13	For great is your **l** toward me;
	89: 1	sing of the LORD's great **l** forever;
	89: 33	but I will not take my **l** from him,
	92: 2	proclaiming your **l** in the morning
	94: 18	slipping," your unfailing **l**, LORD,
	100: 5	is good and his **l** endures forever;
	101: 1	I will sing of your **l** and justice;
	103: 4	crowns you with **l** and compassion,
	103: 8	slow to anger, abounding in **l**.
	103: 11	so great is his **l** for those who fear
	107: 8	to the LORD for his unfailing **l**
	108: 4	For great is your **l**, higher than
	116: 1	I **l** the LORD, for he heard my
	118: 1	he is good; his **l** endures forever.
	119: 47	your commands because I **l** them.
	119: 64	The earth is filled with your **l**,
	119: 76	May your unfailing **l** be my
	119: 97	Oh, how I **l** your law! I meditate
	119:119	dross; therefore I **l** your statutes.
	119:124	your servant according to your **l**

Ps 119:132 do to those who l your name.
119:159 See how I l your precepts;
119:163 detest falsehood but I l your law.
119:165 peace have those who l your law,
122: 6 "May those who l you be secure.
130: 7 for with the LORD is unfailing l
136: 1 *His l endures forever.*
143: 8 bring me word of your unfailing l,
145: 8 slow to anger and rich in l.
145: 20 LORD watches over all who l him,
147: 11 put their hope in his unfailing l.
Pr 3: 3 Let l and faithfulness never leave
4: 6 l her, and she will watch over you.
5: 19 you ever be intoxicated with her l.
8: 17 I l those who l me, and those who
9: 8 rebuke the wise and they will l you.
10: 12 but l covers over all wrongs.
14: 22 those who plan what is good find l
15: 17 with l than a fattened calf
17: 9 Whoever would foster l covers
19: 22 a person desires is unfailing l;
20: 6 Many claim to have unfailing l,
20: 13 Do not l sleep or you will grow
20: 28 L and faithfulness keep a king safe;
21: 21 righteousness and l finds life,
27: 5 is open rebuke than hidden l.
Ecc 9: 6 Their l, their hate and their
9: 9 whom you l, all the days of this
SS 2: 4 and let his banner over me be l.
8: 6 for l is as strong as death,
8: 7 Many waters cannot quench l;
Isa 5: 1 sing for the one I l a song about his
16: 5 In l a throne will be established;
38: 17 In your l you kept me from the pit
54: 10 yet my unfailing l for you will not
55: 3 my faithful l promised to David.
61: 8 "For I, the LORD, l justice;
63: 9 In his l and mercy he redeemed
Jer 5: 31 and my people l it this way.
31: 3 loved you with an everlasting l;
32: 18 You show l to thousands but bring
33: 11 his l endures forever."
La 3: 22 of the LORD's great l we are not
3: 32 so great is his unfailing l.
Eze 33: 32 more than one who sings l songs
Da 9: 4 covenant of l with those who l him
Hos 2: 19 and justice, in l and compassion.
3: 1 L her as the LORD loves
11: 4 of human kindness, with ties of l.
12: 6 maintain l and justice, and wait
Joel 2: 13 slow to anger and abounding in l,
Am 5: 15 Hate evil, l good; maintain justice
Mic 3: 2 you who hate good and l evil;
6: 8 to l mercy and to walk humbly
Zep 3: 17 his l he will no longer rebuke you,
Zec 8: 19 Therefore l truth and peace."
Mt 3: 17 said, "This is my Son, whom I l;
5: 44 l your enemies and pray for those
6: 24 will hate the one and l the other,
17: 5 said, "This is my Son, whom I l;
19: 19 l your neighbor as yourself.'"
22: 37 "'L the Lord your God with all
Lk 6: 32 "If you l those who l you,
7: 42 which of them will l him more?"
20: 13 I will send my son, whom I l;
Jn 13: 34 command I give you: L one another.
13: 35 my disciples, if you l one another."
14: 15 "If you l me, keep my commands.
15: 13 Greater l has no one than this:
15: 17 This is my command: L each other.
21: 15 do you l me more than these?"

Ro 5: 5 because God's l has been poured
5: 8 God demonstrates his own l for us
8: 28 for the good of those who l him,
8: 35 separate us from the l of Christ?
8: 39 separate us from the l of God that
12: 9 L must be sincere. Hate what is
12: 10 Be devoted to one another in l.
13: 8 continuing debt to l one another,
13: 9 "L your neighbor as yourself."
13: 10 Therefore l is the fulfillment
1Co 2: 9 prepared for those who l him—
8: 1 puffs up while l builds up.
13: 1 but do not have l, I am only
13: 2 but do not have l, I am nothing.
13: 3 but do not have l, I gain nothing.
13: 4 L is patient, l is kind. It does not
13: 6 L does not delight in evil
13: 8 L never fails. But where there are
13: 13 these three remain: faith, hope and l.
But the greatest of these is l.
14: 1 Follow the way of l and eagerly
16: 14 Do everything in l.
2Co 5: 14 For Christ's l compels us,
8: 8 sincerity of your l by comparing it
8: 24 show these men the proof of your l
Gal 5: 6 is faith expressing itself through l.
5: 13 serve one another humbly in l.
5: 22 But the fruit of the Spirit is l, joy,
Eph 1: 4 holy and blameless in his sight. In l
2: 4 But because of his great l for us,
3: 17 being rooted and established in l,
3: 18 high and deep is the l of Christ,
3: 19 and to know this l that surpasses
4: 2 bearing with one another in l.
4: 15 speaking the truth in l, we will
5: 2 and walk in the way of l, just as
5: 25 Husbands, l your wives, just as
5: 28 to l their wives as their own bodies.
5: 33 must l his wife as he loves himself.
Php 1: 9 that your l may abound more
2: 2 having the same l, being one
Col 1: 5 l that spring from the hope stored
2: 2 in heart and united in l,
3: 14 And over all these virtues put on l,
3: 19 l your wives and do not be harsh
1Th 1: 3 your labor prompted by l, and your
4: 9 been taught by God to l each other.
5: 8 on faith and l as a breastplate,
2Th 3: 5 Lord direct your hearts into God's l
1Ti 1: 5 The goal of this command is l,
2: 15 faith, l and holiness with propriety.
4: 12 conduct, in l, in faith and in purity.
6: 10 For the l of money is a root of all
6: 11 faith, l, endurance and gentleness.
2Ti 1: 7 us power, l and self-discipline.
2: 22 faith, l and peace, along with those
3: 10 faith, patience, l, endurance,
Titus 2: 4 women to l their husbands
Phm : 9 to appeal to you on the basis of l.
Heb 6: 10 the l you have shown him as you
10: 24 may spur one another on toward l
13: 5 your lives free from the l of money
Jas 1: 12 has promised to those who l him.
2: 5 he promised those who l him?
2: 8 "L your neighbor as yourself,"
1Pe 1: 22 you have sincere l for each other,
2: 17 everyone, l the family of believers,
3: 8 be sympathetic, l one another,
3: 10 For, "Whoever would l life and see
4: 8 Above all, l each other deeply,

1Pe	4: 8	because l covers over a multitude
	5: 14	Greet one another with a kiss of l.
2Pe	1: 7	and to mutual affection, l.
	1: 17	saying, "This is my Son, whom I l;
1Jn	2: 5	l for God is truly made complete
	2: 15	Do not l the world or anything
	3: 1	See what great l the Father has
	3: 10	who does not l their brother
	3: 11	We should l one another.
	3: 14	to life, because we l each other.
	3: 16	This is how we know what l is:
	3: 18	let us not l with words or speech
	3: 23	l one another as he commanded
	4: 7	one another, for l comes from God.
	4: 8	not know God, because God is l.
	4: 9	is how God showed his l among us:
	4: 10	This is l: not that we loved God,
	4: 11	us, we also ought to l one another.
	4: 12	but if we l one another, God lives
	4: 16	God is l. Whoever lives in l lives
	4: 17	This is how l is made complete
	4: 18	There is no fear in l. But perfect l
	4: 19	We l because he first loved us.
	4: 20	whoever does not l their brother
	4: 21	loves God must also l their brother
	5: 2	we know that we l the children
	5: 3	In fact, this is l for God: to keep his
2Jn	: 5	I ask that we l one another.
	: 6	his command is that you walk in l.
Jude	: 12	are blemishes at your l feasts,
	: 21	yourselves in God's l as you wait
Rev	2: 4	You have forsaken the l you had
	3: 19	Those whom I l I rebuke
	12: 11	they did not l their lives so much

LOVED (LOVE)

Ge	24: 67	she became his wife, and he l her;
	37: 3	Now Israel l Joseph more than any
Dt	7: 8	it was because the LORD l you
1Sa	1: 5	a double portion because he l her,
	20: 17	because he l him as he l himself.
Ps	44: 3	light of your face, for you l them.
Jer	2: 2	youth, how as a bride you l me
	31: 3	"I have l you with an everlasting
Hos	2: 23	to the one I called 'Not my l one.'
	3: 1	though she is l by another man
	9: 10	became as vile as the thing they l.
	11: 1	"When Israel was a child, I l him,
Mal	1: 2	"I have l you," says the LORD.
Mk	12: 6	one left to send, a son, whom he l.
Jn	3: 16	For God so l the world that he gave
	3: 19	people l darkness instead of light
	11: 5	Now Jesus l Martha and her sister
	12: 43	for they l human praise more than
	13: 1	in the world, he l them to the end.
	13: 23	the disciple whom Jesus l
	13: 34	As I have l you, so you must love
	14: 21	The one who loves me will be l
	15: 9	"As the Father has l me, so have I l
	15: 12	Love each other as I have l you.
	19: 26	disciple whom he l standing
Ro	8: 37	conquerors through him who l us.
	9: 13	"Jacob I l, but Esau I hated."
	9: 25	'my l one' who is not my l one,'"
	11: 28	they are l on account
Gal	2: 20	who l me and gave himself for me.
Eph	5: 2	just as Christ l and gave himself
	5: 25	just as Christ l the church and gave
2Th	2: 16	who l us and by his grace gave us
2Ti	4: 10	for Demas, because he l this world,
Heb	1: 9	You have l righteousness and hated

1Jn	4: 10	not that we l God, but that he l us
	4: 11	since God so l us, we also ought
	4: 19	We love because he first l us.

LOVELY (LOVE)

Ps	84: 1	How l is your dwelling place,
SS	2: 14	voice is sweet, and your face is l.
	5: 16	sweetness itself; he is altogether l.
Php	4: 8	is pure, whatever is l, whatever is

LOVER (LOVE)

1Ti	3: 3	not quarrelsome, not a l of money.

LOVERS (LOVE)

2Ti	3: 2	People will be l of themselves,
	3: 3	brutal, not l of the good,
	3: 4	l of pleasure rather than l of God—

LOVES (LOVE)

Ps	11: 7	LORD is righteous, he l justice;
	33: 5	The LORD l righteousness
	34: 12	Whoever of you l life and desires
	127: 2	for he grants sleep to those he l.
Pr	3: 12	the LORD disciplines those he l,
	12: 1	Whoever l discipline l knowledge,
	17: 17	A friend l at all times, and
	17: 19	Whoever l a quarrel l sin;
	22: 11	One who l a pure heart and who
Mt	10: 37	"Anyone who l their father
Lk	7: 47	has been forgiven little l little."
Jn	3: 35	The Father l the Son and has
	10: 17	The reason my Father l me is that I
	14: 21	The one who l me will be loved
	14: 23	"Anyone who l me will obey my
Ro	13: 8	for whoever l others has fulfilled
2Co	9: 7	for God l a cheerful giver.
Eph	5: 28	He who l his wife l himself.
	5: 33	must love his wife as he l himself,
Heb	12: 6	the Lord disciplines the one he l,
1Jn	4: 7	Everyone who l has been born
	5: 1	who l the father l his child
3Jn	: 9	but Diotrephes, who l to be first,
Rev	1: 5	To him who l us and has freed us

LOVING (LOVE)

Ps	25: 10	All the ways of the LORD are l
Heb	13: 1	Keep on l one another as brothers
1Jn	5: 2	by l God and carrying out his

LOWLY

Job	5: 11	The l he sets on high, and those
Pr	29: 23	low, but the l in spirit gain honor.
Isa	57: 15	to revive the spirit of the l
Eze	21: 26	The l will be exalted and
Mt	18: 4	whoever takes the l position
1Co	1: 28	God chose the l things of this

LUKE

Co-worker with Paul (Col 4:14; 2Ti 4:11; Phm 24).

LUKEWARM

Rev	3: 16	So, because you are l—

LUST

Pr	6: 25	Do not l in your heart after her
Col	3: 5	impurity, l, evil desires and greed,
1Th	4: 5	not in passionate l like the pagans,
1Jn	2: 16	the l of the flesh, the l of the eyes,

LYING (LIE)

Pr	6: 17	haughty eyes, a l tongue,
	26: 28	A l tongue hates those it hurts,

MACEDONIA

Ac	16: 9	a vision of a man of M standing

MADE (MAKE)

Ge	1: 16	God m two great lights—
	1: 25	God m the wild animals according
	2: 22	the LORD God m a woman
2Ki	19: 15	You have m heaven and earth.

Ps 95: 5 for he **m** it, and his hands formed
100: 3 It is he who **m** us, and we are his;
139: 14 I am fearfully and wonderfully **m**;
Ecc 3: 11 He has **m** everything beautiful in
Mk 2: 27 "The Sabbath was **m** for man,
Jn 1: 3 Through him all things were **m**;
Ac 17: 24 "The God who **m** the world
Heb 1: 2 whom also he **m** the universe,
Rev 14: 7 Worship him who **m** the heavens,

MAGI
Mt 2: 1 **M** from the east came to Jerusalem

MAGOG
Eze 38: 2 of the land of **M**, the chief prince
39: 6 I will send fire on **M** and on those
Rev 20: 8 Gog and **M**—and to gather them

MAIMED
Mt 18: 8 It is better for you to enter life **m**

MAJESTIC (MAJESTY)
Ex 15: 6 hand, LORD, was **m** in power.
15: 11 **m** in holiness, awesome in glory,
Ps 8: 1 **m** is your name in all the earth!
29: 4 the voice of the LORD is **m**.
111: 3 Glorious and **m** are his deeds,
SS 6: 10 sun, **m** as the stars in procession?
2Pe 1: 17 came to him from the **M** Glory,

MAJESTY (MAJESTIC)
Ex 15: 7 your **m** you threw down those who
Dt 33: 26 and on the clouds in his **m**.
1Ch 16: 27 Splendor and **m** are before him;
Est 1: 4 the splendor and glory of his **m**.
Job 37: 22 God comes in awesome **m**.
40: 10 clothe yourself in honor and **m**.
Ps 45: 4 In your **m** ride forth victoriously
93: 1 LORD reigns, he is robed in **m**;
145: 5 the glorious splendor of your **m**—
Isa 53: 2 beauty or **m** to attract us to him,
Eze 31: 2 can be compared with you in **m**?
2Pe 1: 16 but we were eyewitnesses of his **m**.
Jude : 25 only God our Savior be glory, **m**,

MAKE (MADE MAKER MAKES MAKING)
Ge 1: 26 "Let us **m** mankind in our image,
2: 18 I will **m** a helper suitable for him."
12: 2 "I will **m** you into a great nation,
Ex 22: 3 steals must certainly **m** restitution,
Nu 6: 25 the LORD **m** his face shine on you
Ps 108: 1 sing and **m** music with all my soul.
Isa 14: 14 I will **m** myself like the Most
29: 16 formed it, "You did not **m** me"?
Jer 31: 31 "when I will **m** a new covenant
Mt 3: 3 Lord, **m** straight paths for him.'"
28: 19 go and **m** disciples of all nations,
Lk 13: 24 "**M** every effort to enter through
Ro 14: 19 Let us therefore **m** every effort to
2Co 5: 9 So we **m** it our goal to please him,
Eph 4: 3 **M** every effort to keep the unity
Col 4: 5 **m** the most of every opportunity.
1Th 4: 11 **m** it your ambition to lead a quiet
Heb 4: 11 **m** every effort to enter that rest,
12: 14 **M** every effort to live in peace
2Pe 1: 5 **m** every effort to add to your faith
3: 14 **m** every effort to be found spotless,

MAKER (MAKE)
Job 4: 17 man be more pure than his **M**?
36: 3 I will ascribe justice to my **M**.
Ps 95: 6 us kneel before the LORD our **M**;
Pr 22: 2 The LORD is the **M** of them all.
Isa 45: 9 to those who quarrel with their **M**,
54: 5 For your **M** is your husband—
Jer 10: 16 these, for he is the **M** of all things,

MAKES (MAKE)
1Co 3: 7 but only God, who **m** things grow.

MAKING (MAKE)
Ps 19: 7 are trustworthy, **m** wise the simple.
Ecc 12: 12 Of **m** many books there is no end,
Jn 5: 18 Father, **m** himself equal with God.
Eph 5: 16 **m** the most of every opportunity,

MALE
Ge 1: 27 **m** and female he created them.
Gal 3: 28 nor free, nor is there **m** and female,

MALICE (MALICIOUS)
Ro 1: 29 envy, murder, strife, deceit and **m**.
Col 3: 8 anger, rage, **m**, slander, and filthy
1Pe 2: 1 rid yourselves of all **m** and all

MALICIOUS (MALICE)
1Ti 3: 11 not **m** talkers but temperate
6: 4 envy, strife, **m** talk, evil suspicions

MAN (MANKIND MEN WOMAN WOMEN)
Ge 2: 7 the LORD God formed a **m**
2: 18 not good for the **m** to be alone.
2: 23 for she was taken out of **m**."
Dt 8: 3 **m** does not live on bread alone
1Sa 13: 14 sought out a **m** after his own heart
Ps 127: 5 Blessed is the **m** whose quiver is
Pr 30: 19 way of a **m** with a young woman.
Isa 53: 3 by mankind, a **m** of suffering,
Mt 19: 5 this reason a **m** will leave his father
Lk 4: 4 '**M** shall not live on bread alone.'"
Ro 5: 12 entered the world through one **m**,
1Co 7: 2 **m** should have sexual relations
11: 3 that the head of every **m** is Christ,
11: 3 and the head of the woman is **m**,
13: 11 When I became a **m**, I put the ways
Php 2: 8 being found in appearance as a **m**,
1Ti 2: 5 and mankind, the **m** Christ Jesus,
2: 12 or to assume authority over a **m**;

MANAGE
Jer 12: 5 how will you **m** in the thickets
1Ti 3: 4 He must **m** his own family well
3: 12 to his wife and must **m** his children
5: 14 to **m** their homes and to give

MANASSEH
1. Firstborn of Joseph (Ge 41:51; 46:20). Blessed (Ge 48).
2. Son of Hezekiah; king of Judah (2Ki 21:1-18; 2Ch 33:1-20).

MANGER
Lk 2: 12 in cloths and lying in a **m**."

MANKIND (MAN)
Ge 1: 26 "Let us make **m** in our image,

MANNA
Ex 16: 31 people of Israel called the bread **m**.
Dt 8: 16 He gave you **m** to eat
Jn 6: 49 Your ancestors ate the **m**
Rev 2: 17 I will give some of the hidden **m**.

MANNER
1Co 11: 27 in an unworthy **m** will be guilty
Php 1: 27 conduct yourselves in a **m** worthy

MARITAL (MARRY)
Ex 21: 10 of her food, clothing and **m** rights.
1Co 7: 3 husband should fulfill his **m** duty

MARK (MARKS)
Cousin of Barnabas (Col 4:10; 2Ti 4:11; Phm 24; 1Pe 5:13), see JOHN.

Ge   4: 15 the LORD put a **m** on Cain so
Rev 13: 16 to receive a **m** on their right hands

MARKS (MARK)
Jn   20: 25 "Unless I see the nail **m** in his
Gal   6: 17 I bear on my body the **m** of Jesus.

MARRED
Isa 52: 14 and his form **m** beyond human

MARRIAGE (MARRY)
Mt   22: 30 neither marry nor be given in **m**;
      24: 38 marrying and giving in **m**,
Heb 13: 4 **M** should be honored by all,

MARRIED (MARRY)
Ro   7: 2 by law a **m** woman is bound to her
1Co   7: 33 But a **m** man is concerned
      7: 36 is not sinning. They should get **m**.

MARRIES (MARRY)
Mt   5: 32 anyone who **m** a divorced woman
      19: 9 and **m** another woman commits
Lk   16: 18 the man who **m** a divorced woman

MARRY (INTERMARRY MARITAL MARRIAGE
    MARRIED MARRIES)
Mt   22: 30 people will neither **m** nor be given
1Co   7: 9 they should **m**, for it is better to **m**
1Ti   5: 14 So I counsel younger widows to **m**,

MARTHA
    Sister of Mary and Lazarus (Lk 10:38–42; Jn 11; 12:2).

MARVELED
Lk   2: 33 mother **m** at what was said

MARY
    1. Mother of Jesus (Mt 1:16–25; Lk 1:27–56; 2:1–40).
With Jesus at temple (Lk 2:41–52), at the wedding in
Cana (Jn 2:1–5), questioning his sanity (Mk 3:21), at
the cross (Jn 19:25–27). Among disciples after Ascension (Ac 1:14).
    2. Magdalene; former demoniac (Lk 8:2). Helped
support Jesus' ministry (Lk 8:1–3). At the cross (Mt
27:56; Mk 15:40; Jn 19:25), burial (Mt 27:61; Mk 15:47).
Saw angel after resurrection (Mt 28:1–10; Mk 16:1–9;
Lk 24:1–12); also Jesus (Jn 20:1–18).
    3. Sister of Martha and Lazarus (Jn 11). Washed Jesus'
feet (Jn 12:1–8).

MASQUERADES
2Co 11: 14 for Satan himself **m** as an angel

MASTER (MASTERED MASTERS)
Mt   10: 24 teacher, nor a servant above his **m**.
      24: 46 servant whose **m** finds him doing
      25: 21 "His **m** replied, 'Well done,
Ro   6: 14 For sin shall no longer be your **m**,
      14: 4 To their own **m**, servants stand
2Ti   2: 21 useful to the **M** and prepared to do

MASTERED (MASTER)
1Co   6: 12 but I will not be **m** by anything.
2Pe   2: 19 are slaves to whatever has **m** them."

MASTERS (MASTER)
Mt   6: 24 "No one can serve two **m**.
Eph   6: 5 obey your earthly **m** with respect
      6: 9 **m**, treat your slaves in the same
Titus 2: 9 be subject to their **m** in everything,

MATTHEW
    Apostle; former tax collector (Mt 9:9–13; 10:3; Mk
3:18; Lk 6:15; Ac 1:13). Also called Levi (Mk 2:14–17;
Lk 5:27–32).

MATURE (MATURITY)
Eph   4: 13 of the Son of God and become **m**,

Php   3: 15 who are **m** should take such a view
Heb   5: 14 But solid food is for the **m**,
Jas   1: 4 its work so that you may be **m**

MATURITY (MATURE)
Heb   6: 1 Christ and be taken forward to **m**,

MEAL
1Co 10: 27 If an unbeliever invites you to a **m**
Heb 12: 16 single **m** sold his inheritance rights

MEANING
Ne   8: 8 and giving the **m** so that the people

MEANS
1Co   9: 22 by all possible **m** I might save some.

MEAT
Ro   14: 6 eats **m** does so to the Lord,
      14: 21 It is better not to eat **m** or drink

MEDIATOR
1Ti   2: 5 one God and one **m** between God
Heb   8: 6 which he is **m** is superior to the old
      9: 15 this reason Christ is the **m** of a new
      12: 24 to Jesus the **m** of a new covenant,

MEDICINE
Pr   17: 22 A cheerful heart is good **m**,

MEDITATE (MEDITATES MEDITATION)
Jos   1: 8 **m** on it day and night, so that you
Ps 119: 15 I **m** on your precepts and consider
     119: 78 but I will **m** on your precepts.
     119: 97 I **m** on it all day long.
     145: 5 I will **m** on your wonderful works.

MEDITATES (MEDITATE)
Ps   1: 2 who **m** on his law day and night.

MEDITATION (MEDITATE)
Ps   19: 14 this **m** of my heart be pleasing
     104: 34 May my **m** be pleasing to him, as I

MEDIUM
Lev 20: 27 or woman who is a **m** or spiritist

MEEK
Ps   37: 11 But the **m** will inherit the land
Mt   5: 5 Blessed are the **m**, for they will

MEET (MEETING)
Ps   85: 10 Love and faithfulness **m** together;
Am   4: 12 Israel, prepare to **m** your God."
1Th   4: 17 the clouds to **m** the Lord in the air.

MEETING (MEET)
Heb 10: 25 not giving up **m** together, as some

MELCHIZEDEK
Ge   14: 18 **M** king of Salem brought out bread
Ps 110: 4 a priest forever, in the order of **M**."
Heb   7: 11 one in the order of **M**,

MELT
2Pe   3: 12 the elements will **m** in the heat.

MEMBERS
Mic   7: 6 a man's enemies are the **m** of his
Ro   12: 4 of us has one body with many **m**,
1Co   6: 15 your bodies are **m** of Christ
Eph   4: 25 for we are all **m** of one body.
Col   3: 15 since as **m** of one body you were

MEN (MAN)
Ro   1: 27 **M** committed shameful acts with
                 other **m**,
1Ti   2: 8 Therefore I want the **m** everywhere

MENAHEM
    King of Israel (2Ki 15:17–22).

MERCIFUL (MERCY)
Dt   4: 31 the LORD your God is a **m** God;
Ne   9: 31 for you are a gracious and **m** God.
Mt   5: 7 Blessed are the **m**, for they will be
Lk   6: 36 Be **m**, just as your Father is **m**.
Heb 2: 17 in order that he might become a **m**
Jude : 22 Be **m** to those who doubt;

MERCY (MERCIFUL)
Ex 33: 19 have **m** on whom I will have **m**,
Ps 25: 6 LORD, your great **m** and love,
Isa 63: 9 his love and **m** he redeemed them;
Hos 6: 6 For I desire **m**, not sacrifice,
Mic 6: 8 to love **m** and to walk humbly
Hab 3: 2 in wrath remember **m**.
Mt 12: 7 mean, 'I desire **m**, not sacrifice,'
    23: 23 justice, **m** and faithfulness.
Ro   9: 15 "I will have **m** on whom I have **m**,
Eph 2: 4 love for us, God, who is rich in **m**,
Jas 2: 13 **M** triumphs over judgment.
1Pe 1: 3 In his great **m** he has given us new

MESSAGE
Isa 53: 1 Who has believed our **m**
Jn 12: 38 who has believed our **m**
Ro 10: 17 faith comes from hearing the **m**,
1Co 1: 18 the **m** of the cross is foolishness
2Co 5: 19 to us the **m** of reconciliation.

MESSIAH (CHRIST MESSIAHS)
Mt   1: 16 of Jesus who is called the **M**.
    16: 16 "You are the **M**, the Son
    22: 42 "What do you think about the **M**?
Jn   1: 41 "We have found the **M**" (that is,
     4: 25 that **M**" (called Christ) "is coming.
    20: 31 may believe that Jesus is the **M**,
Ac   2: 36 you crucified, both Lord and **M**."
     5: 42 the good news that Jesus is the **M**.
     9: 22 by proving that Jesus is the **M**.
    17: 3 proving that the **M** had to suffer
    18: 28 the Scriptures that Jesus was the **M**.
    26: 23 that the **M** would suffer and,

MESSIAHS (MESSIAH)
Mt 24: 24 For false **m** and false prophets will

METHUSELAH
Ge   5: 27 **M** lived a total of 969 years,

MICHAEL
  Archangel (Jude 9); warrior in angelic realm, protector of Israel (Da 10:13, 21; 12:1; Rev 12:7).

MIDWIVES
Ex   1: 17 The **m**, however, feared God

MIGHT (ALMIGHTY MIGHTY)
Jdg 16: 30 Then he pushed with all his **m**,
2Sa 6: 14 before the LORD with all his **m**,
Ps 21: 13 we will sing and praise your **m**.
Zec 4: 6 'Not by **m** nor by power, but by my
1Ti 6: 16 To him be honor and **m** forever.

MIGHTY (MIGHT)
Ex   6: 1 of my **m** hand he will let them go;
Dt   7: 8 he brought you out with a **m** hand
2Sa 1: 19 How the **m** have fallen!
    23: 8 the names of David's **m** warriors:
Ps 24: 8 and **m**, the LORD **m** in battle.
    50: 1 The **M** One, God, the LORD,
    89: 8 are **m**, and your faithfulness
   136: 12 a **m** hand and outstretched arm;
   147: 5 Great is our Lord and **m** in power;
Isa 9: 6 Wonderful Counselor, **M** God,
Zep 3: 17 you, the **M** Warrior who saves.
Eph 6: 10 in the Lord and in his **m** power.

MILE
Mt   5: 41 If anyone forces you to go one **m**,

MILK
Ex   3: 8 a land flowing with **m** and honey—
Isa 55: 1 buy wine and **m** without money
1Co 3: 2 I gave you **m**, not solid food,
Heb 5: 12 You need **m**, not solid food!
1Pe 2: 2 crave pure spiritual **m**, so that by it

MILLSTONE (STONE)
Lk 17: 2 with a **m** tied around their neck

MIND (DOUBLE-MINDED MINDFUL MINDS
      MINDSET)
1Sa 15: 29 does not lie or change his **m**;
1Ch 28: 9 devotion and with a willing **m**,
Ps 26: 2 me, examine my heart and my **m**;
Mt 22: 37 all your soul and with all your **m**.'
Ac   4: 32 believers were one in heart and **m**.
Ro   7: 25 then, I myself in my **m** am a slave
     8: 7 The **m** governed by the flesh is
    12: 2 by the renewing of your **m**.
1Co 2: 9 what no human **m** has conceived"
    14: 14 spirit prays, but my **m** is unfruitful.
2Co 13: 11 another, be of one **m**, live in peace.
Php 3: 19 Their **m** is set on earthly things.
1Th 4: 11 You should **m** your own business
Heb 7: 21 sworn and will not change his **m**:

MINDFUL (MIND)
Ps   8: 4 is mankind that you are **m** of them,
Lk   1: 48 he has been **m** of the humble state
Heb 2: 6 is mankind that you are **m** of them,

MINDS (MIND)
Ps   7: 9 the righteous God who probes **m**
Isa 26: 3 peace those whose **m** are steadfast,
Jer 31: 33 "I will put my law in their **m**
Eph 4: 23 new in the attitude of your **m**;
Col 3: 2 Set your **m** on things above,
Heb 8: 10 I will put my laws in their **m**
Rev 2: 23 he who searches hearts and **m**,

MINDSET (MIND)
Php 2: 5 have the same **m** as Christ Jesus:

MINISTERING (MINISTRY)
Heb 1: 14 Are not all angels **m** spirits sent

MINISTRY (MINISTERING)
Ac   6: 4 to prayer and the **m** of the word."
2Co 5: 18 gave us the **m** of reconciliation:
2Ti 4: 5 discharge all the duties of your **m**.

MIRACLES
1Ch 16: 12 done, his **m**, and the judgments he
Ps 77: 14 You are the God who performs **m**;
Mt 11: 20 most of his **m** had been performed,
    11: 21 the **m** that were performed in you
Mk   6: 2 What are these remarkable **m** he is
Ac   2: 22 accredited by God to you by **m**,
    19: 11 did extraordinary **m** through Paul,
1Co 12: 28 then **m**, then gifts of healing,
Heb 2: 4 wonders and various **m**, and by

MIRE
Ps 40: 2 slimy pit, out of the mud and **m**;
Isa 57: 20 whose waves cast up **m** and mud.

MIRIAM
  Sister of Moses and Aaron (Nu 26:59). Led dancing at Red Sea (Ex 15:20-21). Struck with leprosy for criticizing Moses (Nu 12). Death (Nu 20:1).

MIRROR
Jas 1: 23 who looks at his face in a **m**

MISERY

Ex	3: 7	"I have indeed seen the **m** of my
Jdg	10: 16	he could bear Israel's **m** no longer.
Hos	5: 15	in their **m** they will earnestly seek
Ro	3: 16	ruin and **m** mark their ways,
Jas	5: 1	because of the **m** that is coming

MISLED

1Co	15: 33	Do not be **m**:

MISS

Pr	19: 2	more will hasty feet **m** the way!

MIST

Hos	6: 4	Your love is like the morning **m**,
Jas	4: 14	You are a **m** that appears for a little

MISUSE

Ex	20: 7	"You shall not **m** the name
Dt	5: 11	"You shall not **m** the name
Ps	139: 20	your adversaries **m** your name.

MOCK (MOCKED MOCKER MOCKERS MOCKING)

Ps	22: 7	All who see me **m** me;
Pr	14: 9	Fools **m** at making amends for sin,
Mk	10: 34	who will **m** him and spit on him,

MOCKED (MOCK)

Mt	27: 29	knelt in front of him and **m** him.
	27: 41	of the law and the elders **m** him.
Gal	6: 7	not be deceived: God cannot be **m**.

MOCKER (MOCK)

Pr	9: 7	corrects a **m** invites insults;
	9: 12	you are a **m**, you alone will suffer.
	20: 1	Wine is a **m** and beer a brawler;
	22: 10	Drive out the **m**, and out goes

MOCKERS (MOCK)

Ps	1: 1	take or sit in the company of **m**,

MOCKING (MOCK)

Isa	50: 6	I did not hide my face from **m**

MODEL

1Th	1: 7	And so you became a **m** to all
2Th	3: 9	to offer ourselves as a **m** for you

MOMENT

Job	20: 5	the joy of the godless lasts but a **m**.
Ps	30: 5	For his anger lasts only a **m**, but his
Isa	66: 8	a nation be brought forth in a **m**?
Gal	2: 5	We did not give in to them for a **m**,

MONEY

Ecc	5: 10	loves **m** never has enough;
Isa	55: 1	and you who have no **m**, come,
Mt	6: 24	You cannot serve both God and **m**.
Lk	9: 3	bag, no bread, no **m**, no extra shirt.
1Co	16: 2	you should set aside a sum of **m**
1Ti	3: 3	not quarrelsome, not a lover of **m**.
	6: 10	the love of **m** is a root of all kinds
2Ti	3: 2	themselves, lovers of **m**, boastful,
Heb	13: 5	your lives free from the love of **m**

MOON

Ps	121: 6	you by day, nor the **m** by night.
Joel	2: 31	the **m** to blood before the coming
1Co	15: 41	the **m** another and the stars

MORNING

Ge	1: 5	was evening, and there was **m**—
Dt	28: 67	In the **m** you will say, "If only it
Ps	5: 3	In the **m**, LORD, you hear my
2Pe	1: 19	and the **m** star rises in your hearts.
Rev	22: 16	of David, and the bright **M** Star."

MORTAL

1Co	15: 53	and the **m** with immortality.

MOSES

Levite; brother of Aaron (Ex 6:20; 1Ch 6:3). Put in basket into Nile; discovered and raised by Pharaoh's daughter (Ex 2:1-10). Fled to Midian after killing Egyptian (Ex 2:11-15). Married to Zipporah, fathered Gershom (Ex 2:16-22).

Called by the LORD to deliver Israel (Ex 3-4). Pharaoh's resistance (Ex 5). Ten plagues (Ex 7-11). Passover and Exodus (Ex 12-13). Led Israel through Red Sea (Ex 14). Song of deliverance (Ex 15:1-21). Brought water from rock (Ex 17:1-7). Raised hands to defeat Amalekites (Ex 17:8-16). Delegated judges (Ex 18; Dt 1:9-18).

Received Law at Sinai (Ex 19-23; 25-31; Jn 1:17). Announced Law to Israel (Ex 19:7-8; 24; 35). Broke tablets because of golden calf (Ex 32; Dt 9). Saw glory of the LORD (Ex 33-34). Supervised building of tabernacle (Ex 36-40). Set apart Aaron and priests (Lev 8-9). Numbered tribes (Nu 1-4; 26). Opposed by Aaron and Miriam (Nu 12). Sent spies into Canaan (Nu 13). Announced forty years of wandering for failure to enter land (Nu 14). Opposed by Korah (Nu 16). Forbidden to enter land for striking rock (Nu 20:1-13; Dt 1:37). Lifted bronze snake for healing (Nu 21:4-9; Jn 3:14). Final address to Israel (Dt 1-33). Succeeded by Joshua (Nu 27:12-23; Dt 34). Death (Dt 34:5-12).

"Law of Moses" (1Ki 2:3; Ezr 3:2; Mk 12:26; Lk 24:44). "Book of Moses" (2Ch 25:12; Ne 13:1). "Song of Moses" (Ex 15:1-21; Rev 15:3). "Prayer of Moses" (Ps 90).

MOTHER (MOTHER'S)

Ge	2: 24	why a man leaves his father and **m**
	3: 20	because she would become the **m**
Ex	20: 12	"Honor your father and your **m**,
Lev	20: 9	they have cursed their father or **m**,
Dt	5: 16	"Honor your father and your **m**,
	21: 18	does not obey his father and **m**
	27: 16	who dishonors their father or **m**."
1Sa	2: 19	Each year his **m** made him a little
Ps	113: 9	her home as a happy **m** of children.
Pr	23: 25	May your father and **m** rejoice;
	29: 15	left undisciplined disgraces its **m**.
	31: 1	utterance his **m** taught him.
Isa	49: 15	"Can a **m** forget the baby at her
	66: 13	As a **m** comforts her child, so will I
Mt	10: 37	or **m** more than me is not worthy
	15: 4	said, 'Honor your father and **m**'
	19: 5	a man will leave his father and **m**
Mk	7: 10	'Honor your father and **m**,' and,
	10: 19	honor your father and **m**.'"
Jn	19: 27	to the disciple, "Here is your **m**."

MOTHER'S (MOTHER)

Job	1: 21	"Naked I came from my **m** womb,
Pr	1: 8	do not forsake your **m** teaching.

MOTHS

Mt	6: 19	where **m** and vermin destroy,

MOTIVES

Pr	16: 2	but **m** are weighed by the LORD.
1Co	4: 5	and will expose the **m** of the heart.
Php	1: 18	way, whether from false **m** or true,
1Th	2: 3	not spring from error or impure **m**,
Jas	4: 3	because you ask with wrong **m**,

MOUNTAIN (MOUNTAINS)

Mic	4: 2	let us go up to the **m** of the LORD,
Mt	17: 20	you can say to this **m**,

MOUNTAINS (MOUNTAIN)

Isa	52: 7	beautiful on the **m** are the feet
	55: 12	the **m** and hills will burst into song
1Co	13: 2	if I have a faith that can move **m**,

MOURN (MOURNING)

Ecc	3: 4	a time to **m** and a time to dance,
Isa	61: 2	of our God, to comfort all who **m**,
Mt	5: 4	Blessed are those who **m**, for they
Ro	12: 15	**m** with those who **m**.

MOURNING (MOURN)

Jer	31: 13	I will turn their **m** into gladness;
Rev	21: 4	There will be no more death' or **m**

MOUTH

Ps	19: 14	May these words of my **m** and this
	40: 3	He put a new song in my **m**,
	119:103	taste, sweeter than honey to my **m**!
Pr	27: 2	praise you, and not your own **m**;
Isa	51: 16	I have put my words in your **m**
Mt	12: 34	the **m** speaks what the heart is full
	15: 11	but what comes out of their **m**,
Ro	10: 9	If you declare with your **m**,

MUD

Ps	40: 2	slimy pit, out of the **m** and mire;
Isa	57: 20	whose waves cast up mire and **m**.
2Pe	2: 22	returns to her wallowing in the **m**."

MULTITUDE (MULTITUDES)

Isa	31: 1	who trust in the **m** of their chariots
1Pe	4: 8	because love covers over a **m**
Rev	7: 9	there before me was a great **m**

MULTITUDES (MULTITUDE)

Joel	3: 14	**M**, m in the valley of decision!

MURDER (MURDERER MURDERERS)

Ex	20: 13	"You shall not **m**.
Mt	15: 19	**m**, adultery, sexual immorality,
Ro	13: 9	"You shall not **m**," "You shall not
Jas	2: 11	commit adultery but do commit **m**,

MURDERER (MURDER)

Nu	35: 16	a **m**; the **m** is to be put to death.
Jn	8: 44	He was a **m** from the beginning,
1Jn	3: 15	hates a brother or sister is a **m**,

MURDERERS (MURDER)

1Ti	1: 9	kill their fathers or mothers, for **m**,
Rev	21: 8	vile, the **m**, the sexually immoral,

MUSIC

Ps	27: 6	sing and make **m** to the LORD.
	95: 2	and extol him with **m** and song.
	98: 4	burst into jubilant song with **m**;
	108: 1	sing and make **m** with all my soul.
Eph	5: 19	make **m** from your heart to the Lord,

MUSTARD

Mt	13: 31	kingdom of heaven is like a **m** seed,
	17: 20	you have faith as small as a **m** seed,

MUZZLE

Dt	25: 4	Do not **m** an ox while it is treading
Ps	39: 1	I will put a **m** on my mouth while
1Co	9: 9	Do not **m** an ox while it is treading

MYRRH

Mt	2: 11	gifts of gold, frankincense and **m**.
Mk	15: 23	offered him wine mixed with **m**,

MYSTERY

Ro	16: 25	the revelation of the **m** hidden
1Co	15: 51	Listen, I tell you a **m**: We will not
Eph	5: 32	This is a profound **m**—but I am
Col	1: 26	the **m** that has been kept hidden
1Ti	3: 16	the **m** from which true godliness

MYTHS

1Ti	4: 7	Have nothing to do with godless **m**

NADAB

Son of Jeroboam I; king of Israel (1Ki 15:25-32).

NAIL (NAILING)

Jn	20: 25	"Unless I see the **n** marks in his

NAILING (NAIL)

Ac	2: 23	him to death by **n** him to the cross.
Col	2: 14	has taken it away, **n** it to the cross.

NAKED

Ge	2: 25	Adam and his wife were both **n**,
Job	1: 21	womb, and **n** I will depart.
Isa	58: 7	you see the **n**, to clothe them,
2Co	5: 3	are clothed, we will not be found **n**.

NAME

Ex	3: 15	"This is my **n** forever, the **n** you
	20: 7	"You shall not misuse the **n**
Dt	5: 11	"You shall not misuse the **n**
	28: 58	this glorious and awesome **n**—
1Ki	5: 5	will build the temple for my **N**.'
2Ch	7: 14	people, who are called by my **n**,
Ps	34: 3	let us exalt his **n** together.
	103: 1	my inmost being, praise his holy **n**.
	147: 4	the stars and calls them each by **n**.
Pr	22: 1	A good **n** is more desirable than
	30: 4	What is his **n**, and what is the **n**
Isa	40: 26	and calls forth each of them by **n**.
	57: 15	who lives forever, whose **n** is holy:
Jer	14: 7	LORD, for the sake of your **n**.
Da	12: 1	everyone whose **n** is found written
Joel	2: 32	the **n** of the LORD will be saved;
Zec	14: 9	one LORD, and his **n** the only **n**.
Mt	1: 21	you are to give him the **n** Jesus,
	6: 9	in heaven, hallowed be your **n**,
	18: 20	where two or three gather in my **n**,
Jn	10: 3	He calls his own sheep by **n**
	16: 24	not asked for anything in my **n**.
Ac	4: 12	is no other **n** under heaven given
Ro	10: 13	on the **n** of the Lord will be saved."
Php	2: 9	the **n** that is above every **n**,
Col	3: 17	do it all in the **n** of the Lord Jesus,
Heb	1: 4	the angels as the **n** he has inherited
Rev	20: 15	whose **n** was not found written

NAOMI

Mother-in-law of Ruth (Ru 1). Advised Ruth to seek marriage with Boaz (Ru 2-4).

NARROW

Mt	7: 13	"Enter through the **n** gate.

NATHANAEL

Apostle (Jn 1:45-49; 21:2). Probably also called Bartholomew (Mt 10:3).

NATION (NATIONS)

Ge	12: 2	"I will make you into a great **n**,
Ps	33: 12	Blessed is the **n** whose God is
Pr	14: 34	Righteousness exalts a **n**, but sin
Isa	65: 1	a **n** that did not call on my name,
1Pe	2: 9	a holy **n**, God's special possession,
Rev	7: 9	could count, from every **n**, tribe,

NATIONS (NATION)

Ge	17: 4	You will be the father of many **n**.
	18: 18	and all **n** on earth will be blessed
Ex	19: 5	of all **n** you will be my treasured
Ne	1: 8	I will scatter you among the **n**,
Ps	96: 3	Declare his glory among the **n**,
Isa	40: 15	Surely the **n** are like a drop
Eze	36: 23	has been profaned among the **n**,
Hag	2: 7	what is desired by all **n** will come,
Zec	8: 23	**n** will take firm hold of one Jew
	14: 2	I will gather all the **n** to Jerusalem
Mt	28: 19	go and make disciples of all **n**,
Rev	21: 24	The **n** will walk by its light,

NATURAL (NATURE)
1Co 15: 44 it is sown a **n** body, it is raised

NATURE (NATURAL)
Php 2: 6 Who, being in very **n** God, did not

NAZARENE
Mt 2: 23 that he would be called a **N**.

NAZIRITE
Jdg 13: 7 because the boy will be a **N** of God

NECESSARY
Ro 13: 5 it is **n** to submit to the authorities,

NEED (NEEDS NEEDY)
Mt 6: 8 knows what you **n** before you ask
Ro 12: 13 the Lord's people who are in **n**.
1Co 12: 21 say to the hand, "I don't **n** you!"
1Jn 3: 17 sister in **n** but has no pity on them,

NEEDLE
Mt 19: 24 to go through the eye of a **n** than

NEEDS (NEED)
Isa 58: 11 he will satisfy your **n**
Php 4: 19 God will meet all your **n** according

NEEDY (NEED)
Pr 14: 21 is the one who is kind to the **n**.
14: 31 is kind to the **n** honors God.
31: 20 and extends her hands to the **n**.
Mt 6: 2 "So when you give to the **n**, do not

NEGLECT (NEGLECTED)
Ne 10: 39 "We will not **n** the house of our
Ps 119: 16 I will not **n** your word.
Ac 6: 2 for us to **n** the ministry of the word
1Ti 4: 14 not **n** your gift, which was given

NEGLECTED (NEGLECT)
Mt 23: 23 But you have **n** the more important

NEHEMIAH
Cupbearer of Artaxerxes (Ne 2:1); governor of Israel (Ne 8:9). Returned to Jerusalem to rebuild walls (Ne 2–6). With Ezra, reestablished worship (Ne 8). Prayer confessing nation's sin (Ne 9). Dedicated wall (Ne 12).

NEIGHBOR (NEIGHBOR'S)
Ex 20: 16 give false testimony against your **n**.
Lev 19: 18 people, but love your **n** as yourself.
Pr 27: 10 better a **n** nearby than a relative far
Mt 19: 19 and 'love your **n** as yourself.'"
Lk 10: 29 asked Jesus, "And who is my **n**?"
Ro 13: 10 Love does no harm to a **n**.

NEIGHBOR'S (NEIGHBOR)
Ex 20: 17 "You shall not covet your **n** house.
Dt 5: 21 "You shall not covet your **n** wife.
19: 14 not move your **n** boundary stone
Pr 25: 17 Seldom set foot in your **n** house—

NEW
Ps 40: 3 He put a **n** song in my mouth,
Ecc 1: 9 there is nothing **n** under the sun.
Isa 65: 17 I will create **n** heavens and a **n**
Jer 31: 31 I will make a **n** covenant
Eze 36: 26 I will give you a **n** heart and put a **n**
spirit in you;
Mt 9: 17 they pour **n** wine into **n** wineskins,
Lk 22: 20 "This cup is the **n** covenant in my
2Co 5: 17 in Christ, the **n** creation has come:
Eph 4: 24 and to put on the **n** self,
2Pe 3: 13 to a **n** heaven and a **n** earth,
1Jn 2: 8 Yet I am writing you a **n** command;

NEWBORN (BEAR)
1Pe 2: 2 Like **n** babies, crave pure spiritual

NEWS
Isa 52: 7 the feet of those who bring good **n**,
Mk 1: 15 Repent and believe the good **n**!"
Lk 2: 10 I bring you good **n** that will cause
Ac 5: 42 proclaiming the good **n** that Jesus
17: 18 Paul was preaching the good **n**
Ro 10: 15 feet of those who bring good **n**!"

NICODEMUS
Pharisee who visited Jesus at night (Jn 3). Argued fair treatment of Jesus (Jn 7:50-52). With Joseph, prepared Jesus for burial (Jn 19:38-42).

NIGHT
Job 35: 10 Maker, who gives songs in the **n**,
Ps 1: 2 meditates on his law day and **n**.
91: 5 You will not fear the terror of **n**,
Jn 3: 2 He came to Jesus at **n** and said,
1Th 5: 2 Lord will come like a thief in the **n**.
5: 5 We do not belong to the **n**
Rev 21: 25 shut, for there will be no **n** there.

NOAH
Righteous man (Eze 14:14, 20) called to build ark (Ge 6–8; Heb 11:7; 1Pe 3:20; 2Pe 2:5). God's covenant with (Ge 9:1–17). Drunkenness of (Ge 9:18–23). Blessed sons, cursed Canaan (Ge 9:24–27).

NOBLE
Ru 3: 11 you are a woman of **n** character.
Ps 45: 1 by a **n** theme as I recite my verses
Pr 12: 4 **n** character is her husband's crown,
31: 10 wife of **n** character who can find?
31: 29 "Many women do **n** things, but
Isa 32: 8 But the **n** make **n** plans, and by **n**
Lk 8: 15 good soil stands for those with a **n**
Php 4: 8 whatever is **n**, whatever is right,

NOTHING
Ne 9: 21 they lacked **n**, their clothes did not
Jer 32: 17 **N** is too hard for you.
Jn 15: 5 apart from me you can do **n**.

NULLIFY
Ro 3: 31 we, then, **n** the law by this faith?

OATH
Dt 7: 8 and kept the **o** he swore to your

OBEDIENCE (OBEY)
2Ch 31: 21 of God's temple and in **o** to the law
Ro 1: 5 all the Gentiles to the **o** that comes
6: 16 to death, or to **o**, which leads
2Jn : 6 that we walk in **o** to his commands.

OBEDIENT (OBEY)
Lk 2: 51 with them and was **o** to them.
Php 2: 8 himself by becoming **o** to death—
1Pe 1: 14 As **o** children, do not conform

OBEY (OBEDIENCE OBEDIENT OBEYED)
Ex 12: 24 "**O** these instructions as a lasting
Dt 6: 3 be careful to **o** so that it may go
13: 4 Keep his commands and **o** him;
21: 18 son who does not **o** his father
30: 2 God and **o** him with all your heart
32: 46 to **o** carefully all the words
1Sa 15: 22 To **o** is better than sacrifice,
Ps 119: 34 your law and **o** it with all my heart.
Mt 28: 20 to **o** everything I have commanded
Jn 14: 23 who loves me will **o** my teaching.
Ac 5: 29 must **o** God rather than human
Ro 6: 16 you are slaves of the one you **o**—
Gal 5: 3 he is obligated to **o** the whole law.
Eph 6: 1 **o** your parents in the Lord, for this
6: 5 heart, just as you would **o** Christ.

Col 3: 20 **o** your parents in everything,
1Ti 3: 4 and see that his children **o** him,

OBEYED (OBEY)
Ps 119: 4 precepts that are to be fully **o**.
Jnh 3: 3 Jonah **o** the word of the LORD
Jn 17: 6 to me and they have **o** your word.
Heb 11: 8 as his inheritance, **o** and went,
1Pe 3: 6 who **o** Abraham and called him

OBLIGATED
Ro 1: 14 I am **o** both to Greeks
Gal 5: 3 that he is **o** to obey the whole law.

OBSCENITY
Eph 5: 4 Nor should there be **o**, foolish talk

OBSOLETE
Heb 8: 13 "new," he has made the first one **o**;

OBTAINED
Ro 9: 30 not pursue righteousness, have **o** it,
Php 3: 12 Not that I have already **o** all this,

OFFENSE (OFFENSIVE)
Pr 17: 9 would foster love covers over an **o**,
19: 11 it is to one's glory to overlook an **o**.

OFFENSIVE (OFFENSE)
Ps 139: 24 See if there is any **o** way in me,

OFFER (OFFERED OFFERING OFFERINGS)
Ro 12: 1 **o** your bodies as a living sacrifice,
Heb 13: 15 let us continually **o** to God

OFFERED (OFFER)
Heb 7: 27 sins once for all when he **o** himself.

OFFERING (OFFER)
Ge 22: 8 provide the lamb for the burnt **o**,
Ps 40: 6 Sacrifice and **o** you did not desire,
Isa 53: 10 the LORD makes his life an **o**
Mt 5: 23 if you are **o** your gift at the altar
Eph 5: 2 himself up for us as a fragrant **o**
Heb 10: 5 "Sacrifice and **o** you did not desire,

OFFERINGS (OFFER)
Mal 3: 8 we robbing you?' "In tithes and **o**.
Mk 12: 33 is more important than all burnt **o**

OFFICER
2Ti 2: 4 tries to please his commanding **o**.

OFFSPRING
Ge 3: 15 and between your **o** and hers;
12: 7 "To your **o** I will give this land."

OIL
Ps 23: 5 You anoint my head with **o**;
Isa 61: 3 the **o** of joy instead of mourning,
Heb 1: 9 by anointing you with the **o** of joy."

OLIVE (OLIVES)
Zec 4: 3 Also there are two **o** trees by it,
Ro 11: 17 though a wild **o** shoot, have been
Rev 11: 4 They are "the two **o** trees"

OLIVES (OLIVE)
Jas 3: 12 can a fig tree bear **o**, or a grapevine

OMEGA
Rev 1: 8 "I am the Alpha and the **O**,"

OMRI
King of Israel (1Ki 16:21-26).

OPINIONS
1Ki 18: 21 will you waver between two **o**?
Pr 18: 2 but delight in airing their own **o**.

OPPORTUNITY
Ro 7: 11 sin, seizing the **o** afforded
Gal 6: 10 as we have **o**, let us do good to all

Eph 5: 16 making the most of every **o**,
Col 4: 5 make the most of every **o**.
1Ti 5: 14 to give the enemy no **o** for slander.

OPPOSES
Jas 4: 6 "God **o** the proud but shows favor
1Pe 5: 5 "God **o** the proud but shows favor

OPPRESS (OPPRESSED)
Ex 22: 21 "Do not mistreat or **o** a foreigner,
Zec 7: 10 Do not **o** the widow

OPPRESSED (OPPRESS)
Ps 9: 9 The LORD is a refuge for the **o**,
Isa 53: 7 He was **o** and afflicted, yet he did
Zec 10: 2 the people wander like sheep **o**

ORDERLY
1Co 14: 40 be done in a fitting and **o** way.

ORGIES
Gal 5: 21 drunkenness, **o**, and the like.
1Pe 4: 3 lust, drunkenness, **o**,

ORIGIN
2Pe 1: 21 For prophecy never had its **o**

ORPHANS
Jn 14: 18 I will not leave you as **o**;
Jas 1: 27 to look after **o** and widows in their

OUTCOME
Heb 13: 7 Consider the **o** of their way of life
1Pe 4: 17 what will the **o** be for those who do

OUTSIDERS
Col 4: 5 wise in the way you act toward **o**;
1Th 4: 12 daily life may win the respect of **o**
1Ti 3: 7 also have a good reputation with **o**,

OUTSTANDING
SS 5: 10 and ruddy, **o** among ten thousand.
Ro 13: 8 Let no debt remain **o**,

OUTSTRETCHED
Ex 6: 6 I will redeem you with an **o** arm
Jer 27: 5 power and **o** arm I made the earth
Eze 20: 33 with a mighty hand and an **o** arm

OUTWEIGHS
2Co 4: 17 an eternal glory that far **o** them all.

OVERCOME (OVERCOMES)
Mt 16: 18 and the gates of Hades will not **o** it.
Mk 9: 24 help me **o** my unbelief!"
Jn 16: 33 But take heart! I have **o** the world."
Ro 12: 21 Do not be **o** by evil, but **o** evil
1Jn 5: 4 is the victory that has **o** the world,

OVERCOMES (OVERCOME)
1Jn 5: 4 everyone born of God **o** the world.
5: 5 Who is it that **o** the world?

OVERFLOW (OVERFLOWS)
Ps 119:171 May my lips **o** with praise, for you
Ro 15: 13 so that you may **o** with hope
2Co 4: 15 may cause thanksgiving to **o**
1Th 3: 12 love increase and **o** for each other

OVERFLOWS (OVERFLOW)
Ps 23: 5 anoint my head with oil; my cup **o**.

OVERJOYED (JOY)
Da 6: 23 The king was **o** and gave orders
Mt 2: 10 they saw the star, they were **o**.
Jn 20: 20 disciples were **o** when they saw
Ac 12: 14 she was so **o** she ran back without
1Pe 4: 13 that you may be **o** when his glory

OVERSEER (OVERSEERS)
1Ti 3: 1 to be an **o** desires a noble task.
3: 2 Now the **o** is to be above reproach,
Titus 1: 7 Since an **o** manages God's

OVERSEERS (OVERSEER)
Ac 20: 28 the Holy Spirit has made you **o**.
Php   1: 1 together with the **o** and deacons:

OVERWHELMED
Ps 38: 4 My guilt has **o** me like a burden
     65: 3 When we were **o** by sins,
Mt 26: 38 "My soul is **o** with sorrow
Mk   7: 37 People were **o** with amazement.

OWE
Ro 13: 7 Give to everyone what you **o** them:
Phm   : 19 that you **o** me your very self.

OX
Dt 25: 4 Do not muzzle an **o** while it is
Isa 11: 7 the lion will eat straw like the **o**.
1Co   9: 9 "Do not muzzle an **o** while it is

PAGANS
Mt   5: 47 Do not even **p** do that?
1Pe   2: 12 such good lives among the **p** that,

PAIN (PAINFUL PAINS)
Job 33: 19 on a bed of **p** with constant distress
Jn 16: 21 to a child has **p** because her time

PAINFUL (PAIN)
Ge   3: 17 through **p** toil you will eat food
Heb 12: 11 seems pleasant at the time, but **p**.

PAINS (PAIN)
Ge   3: 16 "I will make your **p** in childbearing

PALMS
Isa 49: 16 engraved you on the **p** of my hands

PANTS
Ps 42: 1 As the deer **p** for streams of water, so
           my soul **p** for you,

PARADISE
Lk 23: 43 today you will be with me in **p**."
2Co 12: 4 was caught up to **p** and heard
Rev   2: 7 tree of life, which is in the **p** of God.

PARALYZED
Mk   2: 3 bringing to him a **p** man,

PARDON (PARDONS)
Isa 55: 7 and to our God, for he will freely **p**.

PARDONS (PARDON)
Mic   7: 18 like you, who **p** sin and forgives

PARENT (PARENT'S PARENTS)
Pr 17: 21 is no joy for the **p** of a godless fool.

PARENT'S (PARENT)
     15: 5 A fool spurns a **p** discipline,

PARENTS (PARENT)
Ex 20: 5 for the sin of the **p** to the third
Pr 17: 6 **p** are the pride of their children.
Lk 18: 29 sisters or **p** or children for the sake
     21: 16 You will be betrayed even by **p**,
Ro   1: 30 of doing evil; they disobey their **p**;
2Co 12: 14 not have to save up for their **p**,
Eph   6: 1 Children, obey your **p** in the Lord,
Col   3: 20 obey your **p** in everything,
2Ti   3: 2 disobedient to their **p**, ungrateful,

PARTIALITY
Dt 10: 17 who shows no **p** and accepts no
2Ch 19: 7 our God there is no injustice or **p**
Lk 20: 21 that you do not show **p** but teach

PARTICIPATION
1Co 10: 16 bread that we break a **p** in the body

PASS
Ex 12: 13 I see the blood, I will **p** over you.

La   1: 12 nothing to you, all you who **p** by?
Lk 21: 33 but my words will never **p** away.
1Co 13: 8 there is knowledge, it will **p** away.

PASSION (PASSIONS)
1Co   7: 9 to marry than to burn with **p**.

PASSIONS (PASSION)
Gal   5: 24 have crucified the flesh with its **p**
Titus 2: 12 to ungodliness and worldly **p**,

PASSOVER
Ex 12: 11 Eat it in haste; it is the Lord's **P**.
Dt 16: 1 celebrate the **P** of the Lord your
1Co   5: 7 For Christ, our **P** lamb, has been

PAST
Isa 43: 18 do not dwell on the **p**.
Ro 15: 4 was written in the **p** was written
Heb   1: 1 the **p** God spoke to our ancestors

PASTORS
Eph   4: 11 the evangelists, the **p** and teachers,

PASTURE (PASTURES)
Ps 37: 3 dwell in the land and enjoy safe **p**.
    100: 3 are his people, the sheep of his **p**.
Jer 50: 7 their verdant **p**, the Lord,
Eze 34: 13 I will **p** them on the mountains
Jn 10: 9 come in and go out, and find **p**.

PASTURES (PASTURE)
Ps 23: 2 He makes me lie down in green **p**,

PATCH
Mt   9: 16 No one sews a **p** of unshrunk cloth

PATH (PATHS)
Ps 27: 11 me in a straight **p** because of my
    119: 9 person stay on the **p** of purity?
    119:105 to my feet and a light for my **p**.
Pr 15: 19 the **p** of the upright is a highway.
     15: 24 The **p** of life leads upward
Isa 26: 7 The **p** of the righteous is level;
Lk   1: 79 guide our feet into the **p** of peace."
2Co   6: 3 no stumbling block in anyone's **p**,

PATHS (PATH)
Ps 23: 3 He guides me along the right **p**
     25: 4 ways, Lord, teach me your **p**.
Pr   3: 6 and he will make your **p** straight.
Ro 11: 33 and his **p** beyond tracing out!
Heb 12: 13 "Make level **p** for your feet,"

PATIENCE (PATIENT)
Pr 19: 11 A person's wisdom yields **p**; it is
2Co   6: 6 understanding, **p** and kindness;
Col   1: 11 may have great endurance and **p**,
      3: 12 humility, gentleness and **p**.

PATIENT (PATIENCE PATIENTLY)
Pr 15: 18 the one who is **p** calms a quarrel.
Ro 12: 12 Be joyful in hope, **p** in affliction,
1Co 13: 4 Love is **p**, love is kind. It does not
Eph   4: 2 be **p**, bearing with one another
1Th   5: 14 help the weak, be **p** with everyone.

PATIENTLY (PATIENT)
Ps 40: 1 I waited **p** for the Lord;
Ro   8: 25 we do not yet have, we wait for it **p**.

PATTERN
Ro   5: 14 who is a **p** of the one to come.
     12: 2 not conform to the **p** of this world,
2Ti   1: 13 keep as the **p** of sound teaching,

PAUL
Also called Saul (Ac 13:9). Pharisee from Tarsus (Ac 9:11; Php 3:5). Apostle (Gal 1). At stoning of Stephen

(Ac 8:1). Persecuted Church (Ac 9:1-2; Gal 1:13). Vision of Jesus on road to Damascus (Ac 9:4-9; 26:12-18). In Arabia (Gal 1:17). Preached in Damascus; escaped death through the wall in a basket (Ac 9:19-25). In Jerusalem; sent back to Tarsus (Ac 9:26-30).

Brought to Antioch by Barnabas (Ac 11:22-26). First missionary journey to Cyprus and Galatia (Ac 13-14). Stoned at Lystra (Ac 14:19-20). At Jerusalem council (Ac 15). Split with Barnabas over Mark (Ac 15:36-41).

Second missionary journey with Silas (Ac 16-20). Called to Macedonia (Ac 16:6-10). Freed from prison in Philippi (Ac 16:16-40). In Thessalonica (Ac 17:1-9). Speech in Athens (Ac 17:16-33). In Corinth (Ac 18). In Ephesus (Ac 19). Return to Jerusalem (Ac 20). Farewell to Ephesian elders (Ac 20:13-38). Arrival in Jerusalem (Ac 21:1-26). Arrested (Ac 21:27-36). Addressed crowds (Ac 22), Sanhedrin (Ac 23:1-11). Transferred to Caesarea (Ac 23:12-35). Trial before Felix (Ac 24), Festus (Ac 25:1-12). Before Agrippa (Ac 25:13—26:32). Voyage to Rome; shipwreck (Ac 27). Arrival in Rome (Ac 28).

PAY (REPAID REPAY)
Lev	26: 43	They will **p** for their sins because
Pr	22: 17	**P** attention and turn your ear
Mt	22: 17	Is it right to **p** the imperial tax
Ro	13: 6	This is also why you **p** taxes,
2Pe	1: 19	you will do well to **p** attention to it,

PEACE (PEACEMAKERS)
Nu	6: 26	toward you and give you **p**."'
Ps	34: 14	and do good; seek **p** and pursue it.
	85: 10	righteousness and **p** kiss each
	119:165	Great **p** have those who love your
	122: 6	Pray for the **p** of Jerusalem:
Pr	14: 30	A heart at **p** gives life to the body,
	17: 1	Better a dry crust with **p** and quiet
Isa	9: 6	Everlasting Father, Prince of **P**.
	26: 3	in perfect **p** those whose minds are
	48: 22	"There is no **p**," says the LORD,
Zec	9: 10	He will proclaim **p** to the nations.
Mt	10: 34	I did not come to bring **p**,
Lk	2: 14	and on earth **p** to those on whom
Jn	14: 27	**P** I leave with you; my **p** I give you.
	16: 33	so that in me you may have **p**.
Ro	5: 1	we have **p** with God through our
1Co	7: 15	God has called us to live in **p**.
	14: 33	is not a God of disorder but of **p**—
Gal	5: 22	Spirit is love, joy, **p**, forbearance,
Eph	2: 14	For he himself is our **p**, who has
Php	4: 7	the **p** of God, which transcends
Col	1: 20	by making **p** through his blood,
	3: 15	Let the **p** of Christ rule in your
1Th	5: 3	people are saying, "**P** and safety,"
2Th	3: 16	the Lord of **p** himself give you **p**
2Ti	2: 22	love and **p**, along with those who
1Pe	3: 11	they must seek **p** and pursue it.
Rev	6: 4	power to take **p** from the earth

PEACEMAKERS (PEACE)
Mt	5: 9	Blessed are the **p**, for they will be
Jas	3: 18	**P** who sow in peace reap a harvest

PEARL (PEARLS)
Rev	21: 21	each gate made of a single **p**.

PEARLS (PEARL)
Mt	7: 6	do not throw your **p** to pigs.
	13: 45	like a merchant looking for fine **p**.
1Ti	2: 9	or gold or **p** or expensive clothes,
Rev	21: 21	The twelve gates were twelve **p**,

PEKAH
King of Israel (2Ki 15:25-31; Isa 7:1).

PEKAHIAH
Son of Menahem; king of Israel (2Ki 15:22-26).

PEN
Mt	5: 18	not the least stroke of a **p**,

PENTECOST
Ac	2: 1	When the day of **P** came, they were

PEOPLE (PEOPLES)
Dt	32: 9	For the LORD's portion is his **p**,
Ru	1: 16	Your **p** will be my **p** and your God
2Ch	7: 14	if my **p**, who are called by my
Ps	133: 1	it is when God's **p** live together
Jer	24: 7	They will be my **p**, and I will be
Zec	2: 11	in that day and will become my **p**.
Mt	4: 19	I will send you out to fish for **p**."
Lk	2: 10	will cause great joy for all the **p**.
Jn	12: 32	earth, will draw all **p** to myself."
Ac	15: 14	to choose a **p** for his name
Ro	5: 12	and in this way death came to all **p**,
	8: 27	for God's **p** in accordance
1Co	9: 22	I have become all things to all **p** so
2Co	6: 16	their God, and they will be my **p**."
Eph	1: 18	glorious inheritance in his holy **p**,
	6: 18	keep on praying for all the Lord's **p**.
1Ti	2: 4	who wants all **p** to be saved
2Ti	2: 2	entrust to reliable **p** who will also
Titus	2: 14	himself a **p** that are his very own,
Heb	9: 27	Just as **p** are destined to die once,
1Pe	2: 9	But you are a chosen **p**, a royal
Rev	5: 8	which are the prayers of God's **p**.
	19: 8	the righteous acts of God's holy **p**.)
	21: 3	They will be his **p**, and God

PEOPLES (PEOPLE)
Da	7: 14	**p** of every language worshiped him
Mic	4: 1	the hills, and **p** will stream to it.

PERCEIVING
Isa	6: 9	be ever seeing, but never **p**.'

PERFECT (PERFECTER PERFECTION)
SS	6: 9	but my dove, my **p** one, is unique,
Isa	26: 3	in **p** peace those whose minds are
Mt	5: 48	Be **p**, therefore, as your heavenly Father is **p**.
Ro	12: 2	his good, pleasing and **p** will.
2Co	12: 9	my power is made **p** in weakness."
Col	3: 14	binds them all together in **p** unity.
Heb	9: 11	more **p** tabernacle that is not made
	10: 14	he has made **p** forever those who
Jas	1: 17	good and **p** gift is from above,
	1: 25	looks intently into the **p** law
	3: 2	never at fault in what they say is **p**,
1Jn	4: 18	But **p** love drives out fear,

PERFECTER (PERFECT)
Heb	12: 2	on Jesus, the pioneer and **p** of faith.

PERFECTION (PERFECT)
Ps	119: 96	To all **p** I see a limit, but your
Heb	7: 11	If **p** could have been attained

PERFORMS
Ps	77: 14	You are the God who **p** miracles;

PERISH (PERISHABLE)
Ps	102: 26	They will **p**, but you remain;
Lk	13: 3	you repent, you too will all **p**.
Jn	10: 28	eternal life, and they shall never **p**;
Col	2: 22	that are all destined to **p** with use,
Heb	1: 11	They will **p**, but you remain;
2Pe	3: 9	you, not wanting anyone to **p**,

PERISHABLE (PERISH)
1Co	15: 42	The body that is sown is **p**, it is

PERJURERS
1Ti	1: 10	for slave traders and liars and **p**—

PERMIT
1Ti 2: 12 I do not **p** a woman to teach

PERSECUTE (PERSECUTED PERSECUTION)
Mt 5: 11 **p** you and falsely say all kinds
Jn 15: 20 persecuted me, they will **p** you
Ac 9: 4 "Saul, Saul, why do you **p** me?"
Ro 12: 14 Bless those who **p** you; bless and

PERSECUTED (PERSECUTE)
1Co 4: 12 when we are **p**, we endure it;
2Ti 3: 12 godly life in Christ Jesus will be **p**,

PERSECUTION (PERSECUTE)
Ro 8: 35 trouble or hardship or **p** or famine

PERSEVERANCE (PERSEVERE)
Ro 5: 3 we know that suffering produces **p**;
   5: 4 **p**, character; and character, hope.
Heb 12: 1 let us run with **p** the race marked
Jas 1: 3 testing of your faith produces **p**.
2Pe 1: 6 and to self-control, **p**; and to **p**,

PERSEVERE (PERSEVERANCE PERSEVERED PERSEVERES)
1Ti 4: 16 **P** in them, because if you do,
Heb 10: 36 You need to **p** so that when you

PERSEVERED (PERSEVERE)
Heb 11: 27 he **p** because he saw him who is
Jas 5: 11 count as blessed those who have **p**.
Rev 2: 3 You have **p** and have endured

PERSEVERES (PERSEVERE)
1Co 13: 7 trusts, always hopes, always **p**.
Jas 1: 12 one who **p** under trial because,

PERSUADE
2Co 5: 11 to fear the Lord, we try to **p** others.

PERVERSION (PERVERT)
Lev 18: 23 sexual relations with it; that is a **p**.
Jude : 7 up to sexual immorality and **p**.

PERVERT (PERVERSION)
Gal 1: 7 are trying to **p** the gospel of Christ.

PESTILENCE
Ps 91: 6 the **p** that stalks in the darkness,

PETER
Apostle, brother of Andrew, also called Simon (Mt 10:2; Mk 3:16; Lk 6:14; Ac 1:13), and Cephas (Jn 1:42). Confession of Christ (Mt 16:13–20; Mk 8:27–30; Lk 9:18–27). At transfiguration (Mt 17:1–8; Mk 9:2–8; Lk 9:28–36; 2Pe 1:16–18). Caught fish with coin (Mt 17:24–27). Denial of Jesus predicted (Mt 26:31–35; Mk 14:27–31; Lk 22:31–34; Jn 13:31–38). Denied Jesus (Mt 26:69–75; Mk 14:66–72; Lk 22:54–62; Jn 18:15–27). Commissioned by Jesus to shepherd his flock (Jn 21:15–23).
Speech at Pentecost (Ac 2). Healed beggar (Ac 3:1–10). Speech at temple (Ac 3:11–26), before Sanhedrin (Ac 4:1–22). In Samaria (Ac 8:14–25). Sent by vision to Cornelius (Ac 10). Announced salvation of Gentiles in Jerusalem (Ac 11; 15). Freed from prison (Ac 12). Inconsistency at Antioch (Gal 2:11–21). At Jerusalem Council (Ac 15).

PHARISEES
Mt 5: 20 surpasses that of the **P**

PHILIP
1. Apostle (Mt 10:3; Mk 3:18; Lk 6:14; Jn 1:43–48; 14:8; Ac 1:13).
2. Deacon (Ac 6:1–7); evangelist in Samaria (Ac 8:4–25), to Ethiopian (Ac 8:26–40).

PHILOSOPHY
Col 2: 8 through hollow and deceptive **p**,

PHYLACTERIES
Mt 23: 5 They make their **p** wide

PHYSICAL
1Ti 4: 8 For **p** training is of some value,
Jas 2: 16 does nothing about their **p** needs,

PIECES
Ge 15: 17 and passed between the **p**.
Jer 34: 18 two and then walked between its **p**.

PIERCE (PIERCED)
Ps 22: 16 they **p** my hands and my feet.

PIERCED (PIERCE)
Isa 53: 5 he was **p** for our transgressions,
Zec 12: 10 the one they have **p**, and they will
Jn 19: 37 will look on the one they have **p**."

PIGS
Mt 7: 6 do not throw your pearls to **p**.

PILATE
Governor of Judea. Questioned Jesus (Mt 27:1–26; Mk 15:15; Lk 22:66—23:25; Jn 18:28—19:16); sent him to Herod (Lk 23:6–12); consented to his crucifixion when crowds chose Barabbas (Mt 27:15–26; Mk 15:6–15; Lk 23:13–25; Jn 19:1–10).

PILLAR
Ge 19: 26 back, and she became a **p** of salt.
Ex 13: 21 by night in a **p** of fire to give them
1Ti 3: 15 the **p** and foundation of the truth.

PIT
Ps 40: 2 He lifted me out of the slimy **p**,
   103: 4 who redeems your life from the **p**
Mt 15: 14 the blind, both will fall into a **p**."

PITIED
1Co 15: 19 we are of all people most to be **p**.

PLAGUE
2Ch 6: 28 famine or **p** comes to the land,

PLAIN
Ro 1: 19 God has made it **p** to them.

PLAN (PLANNED PLANS)
Pr 14: 22 those who **p** what is good find love
Eph 1: 11 to the **p** of him who works

PLANK
Mt 7: 3 attention to the **p** in your own eye?
Lk 6: 41 attention to the **p** in your own eye?

PLANNED (PLAN)
Ps 40: 5 have done, the things you **p** for us.
Isa 46: 11 what I have **p**, that I will do.
Heb 11: 40 since God had **p** something better

PLANS (PLAN)
Ps 20: 4 heart and make all your **p** succeed.
   33: 11 But the **p** of the LORD stand firm
Pr 20: 18 **P** are established by seeking advice;
Isa 32: 8 But the noble make noble **p**,

PLANTED (PLANTS)
Ps 1: 3 person is like a tree **p** by streams
Mt 15: 13 Father has not **p** will be pulled
1Co 3: 6 I **p** the seed, Apollos watered it,

PLANTS (PLANTED)
1Co 3: 7 neither the one who **p** nor the one
   9: 7 Who **p** a vineyard and does not eat

PLATTER
Mk 6: 25 head of John the Baptist on a **p**."

PLAYED
Lk 7: 32 "'We **p** the pipe for you, and you
1Co 14: 7 what tune is being **p** unless there is

PLEADED
2Co 12: 8 Three times I **p** with the Lord

PLEASANT (PLEASE)
Ps 16: 6 lines have fallen for me in **p** places;
133: 1 and **p** it is when God's people live
147: 1 how **p** and fitting to praise him!
Heb 12: 11 No discipline seems **p** at the time,

PLEASE (PLEASANT PLEASED PLEASES PLEASING
  PLEASURE PLEASURES)
Pr 20: 23 and dishonest scales do not **p** him.
Jer 6: 20 your sacrifices do not **p** me.″
Jn 5: 30 for I seek not to **p** myself but him
Ro 8: 8 realm of the flesh cannot **p** God.
15: 2 Each of us should **p** our neighbors
1Co 7: 32 how he can **p** the Lord.
10: 33 even as I try to **p** everyone in every
2Co 5: 9 So we make it our goal to **p** him,
Gal 1: 10 If I were still trying to **p** people,
1Th 4: 1 you how to live in order to **p** God,
2Ti 2: 4 tries to **p** his commanding officer.
Heb 11: 6 faith it is impossible to **p** God,

PLEASED (PLEASE)
Mt 3: 17 with him I am well **p**.″
1Co 1: 21 God was **p** through the foolishness
Col 1: 19 God was **p** to have all his fullness
Heb 11: 5 commended as one who **p** God.
2Pe 1: 17 with him I am well **p**.″

PLEASES (PLEASE)
Ps 135: 6 The LORD does whatever **p** him,
Pr 15: 8 the prayer of the upright **p** him.
Jn 3: 8 The wind blows wherever it **p**.
8: 29 alone, for I always do what **p** him.″
Col 3: 20 in everything, for this **p** the Lord.
1Ti 2: 3 is good, and **p** God our Savior,
1Jn 3: 22 his commands and do what **p** him.

PLEASING (PLEASE)
Ps 104: 34 May my meditation be **p** to him,
Ro 12: 1 living sacrifice, holy and **p** to God
Php 4: 18 an acceptable sacrifice, **p** to God.
Heb 13: 21 he work in us what is **p** to him,

PLEASURE (PLEASE)
Ps 147: 10 His **p** is not in the strength
Pr 21: 17 loves **p** will become poor;
Eze 18: 32 For I take no **p** in the death
Eph 1: 5 in accordance with his **p** and will—
1: 9 of his will according to his good **p**,
2Ti 3: 4 lovers of **p** rather than lovers

PLEASURES (PLEASE)
Ps 16: 11 with eternal **p** at your right hand.
Heb 11: 25 than to enjoy the fleeting **p** of sin.
2Pe 2: 13 reveling in their **p** while they feast

PLENTIFUL
Mt 9: 37 "The harvest is **p** but the workers

PLOW (PLOWSHARES)
Lk 9: 62 "No one who puts a hand to the **p**

PLOWSHARES (PLOW)
Isa 2: 4 They will beat their swords into **p**
Joel 3: 10 Beat your **p** into swords and your

PLUNDER
Ex 3: 22 And so you will **p** the Egyptians."

POINT
Jas 2: 10 yet stumbles at just one **p** is guilty

POISON
Mk 16: 18 *and when they drink deadly* **p**,
Jas 3: 8 It is a restless evil, full of deadly **p**.

POLLUTE (POLLUTED)
Nu 35: 33 "'Do not **p** the land where you
Jude : 8 these ungodly people **p** their own

POLLUTED (POLLUTE)
Ezr 9: 11 is a land **p** by the corruption
Pr 25: 26 a **p** well are the righteous who give
Ac 15: 20 to abstain from food **p** by idols,
Jas 1: 27 oneself from being **p** by the world.

PONDER
Ps 64: 9 of God and **p** what he has done.
119: 95 me, but I will **p** your statutes.

POOR (POVERTY)
Dt 15: 4 need be no **p** people among you,
15: 11 There will always be **p** people
Ps 34: 6 This **p** man called, and the LORD
82: 3 uphold the cause of the **p**
112: 9 freely scattered their gifts to the **p**,
Pr 13: 7 another pretends to be **p**, yet has
14: 31 oppresses the **p** shows contempt
19: 1 Better the **p** whose walk is
19: 17 Whoever is kind to the **p** lends
22: 2 Rich and **p** have this in common:
22: 9 they share their food with the **p**.
28: 6 Better the **p** whose walk is
31: 20 She opens her arms to the **p**
Isa 61: 1 to proclaim good news to the **p**.
Mt 5: 3 "Blessed are the **p** in spirit,
11: 5 good news is proclaimed to the **p**.
19: 21 your possessions and give to the **p**,
26: 11 The **p** you will always have
Mk 12: 42 a **p** widow came and put in two
Ac 10: 4 and gifts to the **p** have come up as
1Co 13: 3 If I give all I possess to the **p**
2Co 8: 9 yet for your sake he became **p**,
Jas 2: 2 and a **p** man in filthy old clothes

PORTION
Dt 32: 9 For the LORD's **p** is his people,
2Ki 2: 9 "Let me inherit a double **p** of your
La 3: 24 to myself, "The LORD is my **p**;

POSSESS (POSSESSING POSSESSION
  POSSESSIONS)
Nu 33: 53 for I have given you the land to **p**.

POSSESSING (POSSESS)
2Co 6: 10 nothing, and yet **p** everything.

POSSESSION (POSSESS)
Ge 15: 7 give you this land to take **p** of it."
Nu 13: 30 go up and take **p** of the land,
Eph 1: 14 of those who are God's **p**—

POSSESSIONS (POSSESS)
Lk 12: 15 not consist in an abundance of **p**."
2Co 12: 14 because what I want is not your **p**
1Jn 3: 17 If anyone has material **p** and sees

POSSIBLE
Mt 19: 26 but with God all things are **p**."
Mk 9: 23 "Everything is **p** for one who
10: 27 all things are **p** with God."
Ro 12: 18 If it is **p**, as far as it depends on you
1Co 9: 22 by all **p** means I might save some.

POT (POTSHERDS POTTER POTTERY)
2Ki 4: 40 of God, there is death in the **p**!"
Jer 18: 4 the potter formed it into another **p**,

POTSHERDS (POT)
Isa 45: 9 but **p** among the **p** on the ground.

POTTER (POT)
Isa 29: 16 Can the pot say to the **p**,
45: 9 Does the clay say to the **p**,
64: 8 We are the clay, you are the **p**;

Jer 18: 6 do with you, Israel, as this **p** does?"
Ro 9: 21 Does not the **p** have the right

POTTERY (POT)
Ro 9: 21 of clay some **p** for special purposes

POUR (POURED)
Ps 62: 8 **p** out your hearts to him, for God
Joel 2: 28 I will **p** out my Spirit on all people.
Mal 3: 10 **p** out so much blessing that there
Ac 2: 17 I will **p** out my Spirit on all people.

POURED (POUR)
Ac 10: 45 the Holy Spirit had been **p** out
Ro 5: 5 because God's love has been **p**

POVERTY (POOR)
Pr 14: 23 but mere talk leads only to **p**.
21: 5 profit as surely as haste leads to **p**.
30: 8 give me neither **p** nor riches,
Mk 12: 44 she, out of her **p**, put in everything
2Co 8: 2 their extreme **p** welled up in rich
8: 9 you through his **p** might become

POWER (POWERFUL POWERS)
1Ch 29: 11 greatness and the **p** and the glory
2Ch 32: 7 for there is a greater **p** with us than
Job 36: 22 "God is exalted in his **p**. Who is
Ps 63: 2 and beheld your **p** and your glory.
68: 34 Proclaim the **p** of God,
147: 5 Great is our Lord and mighty in **p**;
Pr 24: 5 The wise prevail through great **p**,
Isa 40: 10 Sovereign LORD comes with **p**,
Zec 4: 6 'Not by might nor by **p**, but by my
Mt 22: 29 the Scriptures or the **p** of God.
24: 30 of heaven, with **p** and great glory.
Ac 1: 8 you will receive **p** when the Holy
4: 33 With great **p** the apostles
10: 38 with the Holy Spirit and **p**,
Ro 1: 16 because it is the **p** of God
1Co 1: 18 us who are being saved it is the **p**
15: 56 is sin, and the **p** of sin is the law.
2Co 12: 9 so that Christ's **p** may rest on me.
Eph 1: 19 his incomparably great **p** for us
Php 3: 10 to know the **p** of his resurrection
Col 1: 11 strengthened with all **p** according
2Ti 1: 7 us timid, but gives us **p**,
Heb 7: 16 of the **p** of an indestructible life.
Rev 4: 11 to receive glory and honor and **p**,
19: 1 glory and **p** belong to our God,
20: 6 second death has no **p** over them,

POWERFUL (POWER)
Ps 29: 4 The voice of the LORD is **p**;
Lk 24: 19 **p** in word and deed before God
2Th 1: 7 in blazing fire with his **p** angels.
Heb 1: 3 sustaining all things by his **p** word.
Jas 5: 16 prayer of a righteous person is **p**

POWERLESS
Ro 5: 6 when we were still **p**, Christ died
8: 3 what the law was **p** to do because it

POWERS (POWER)
Ro 8: 38 present nor the future, nor any **p**,
1Co 12: 10 to another miraculous **p**,
Col 1: 16 whether thrones or **p** or rulers
2: 15 And having disarmed the **p**

PRACTICE
Lev 19: 26 "'Do not **p** divination or seek
Mt 23: 3 for they do not **p** what they preach.
Lk 8: 21 hear God's word and put it into **p**."
Ro 12: 13 who are in need. **P** hospitality.
1Ti 5: 4 put their religion into **p** by caring

PRAISE (PRAISED PRAISES PRAISING)
Ex 15: 2 and I will **p** him, my father's God,

Dt 32: 3 Oh, **p** the greatness of our God!
Ru 4: 14 "**P** be to the LORD, who this day
2Sa 22: 47 **P** be to my Rock!
1Ch 16: 25 the LORD and most worthy of **p**;
2Ch 20: 21 to **p** him for the splendor of his
Ps 8: 2 Through the **p** of children
33: 1 it is fitting for the upright to **p** him.
34: 1 his **p** will always be on my lips.
40: 3 mouth, a hymn of **p** to our God.
48: 1 and most worthy of **p**, in the city
68: 19 **P** be to the Lord, to God our Savior.
89: 5 The heavens **p** your wonders,
100: 4 give thanks to him and **p** his name.
105: 2 Sing to him, sing **p** to him;
106: 1 **P** the LORD. Give thanks
119:175 Let me live that I may **p** you,
139: 14 I **p** you because I am fearfully
145: 21 Let every creature **p** his holy name
146: 1 **P** the LORD. **P** the LORD, my soul.
150: 2 **p** him for his surpassing greatness.
150: 6 Let everything that has breath **p** the LORD. **P** the LORD.
Pr 27: 2 Let someone else **p** you, and not
27: 21 but people are tested by their **p**.
31: 31 let her works bring her **p** at the city
Mt 21: 16 Lord, have called forth your **p**'?"
Jn 12: 43 they loved human **p** more than **p** from God.
Eph 1: 6 to the **p** of his glorious grace,
1: 12 might be for the **p** of his glory.
1: 14 to the **p** of his glory.
Heb 13: 15 offer to God a sacrifice of **p**—
Jas 5: 13 Let them sing songs of **p**.

PRAISED (PRAISE)
1Ch 29: 10 David **p** the LORD in the presence
Ne 8: 6 Ezra **p** the LORD, the great God;
Da 2: 19 Then Daniel **p** the God of heaven
Ro 9: 5 who is God over all, forever **p**!
1Pe 4: 11 God may be **p** through Jesus Christ

PRAISES (PRAISE)
2Sa 22: 50 I will sing the **p** of your name.
Ps 47: 6 Sing **p** to God, sing **p**; sing **p**
147: 1 good it is to sing **p** to our God,
Pr 31: 28 her husband also, and he **p** her:

PRAISING (PRAISE)
Ac 10: 46 speaking in tongues and **p** God.
1Co 14: 16 when you are **p** God in the Spirit,

PRAY (PRAYED PRAYER PRAYERS PRAYING)
Dt 4: 7 our God is near us whenever we **p**
1Sa 12: 23 the LORD by failing to **p** for you.
2Ch 7: 14 will humble themselves and **p**
Job 42: 8 My servant Job will **p** for you,
Ps 122: 6 **P** for the peace of Jerusalem:
Mt 5: 44 and **p** for those who persecute you,
6: 5 for they love to **p** standing
6: 9 "This, then, is how you should **p**:
26: 36 here while I go over there and **p**."
Lk 6: 28 you, **p** for those who mistreat you.
18: 1 them that they should always **p**
22: 40 them, "**P** that you will not fall
Ro 8: 26 not know what we ought to **p** for,
1Co 14: 13 in a tongue should **p** that they may
1Th 5: 17 **p** continually,
Jas 5: 13 Let them **p**. Is anyone happy?
5: 16 **p** for each other so that you may be

PRAYED (PRAY)
1Sa 1: 27 I **p** for this child, and the LORD
Jnh 2: 1 From inside the fish Jonah **p**
Mk 14: 35 and **p** that if possible the hour

PRAYER (PRAY)
2Ch 30: 27 for their **p** reached heaven, his holy
Ezr 8: 23 about this, and he answered our **p**.
Ps   6: 9 the LORD accepts my **p**.
    86: 6 Hear my **p**, LORD; listen to my
Pr 15: 8 the **p** of the upright pleases him.
Isa 56: 7 house will be called a house of **p**
Mt 21: 13 house will be called a house of **p**,'
Mk 11: 24 whatever you ask for in **p**,
Jn 17: 15 My **p** is not that you take them
Ac   6: 4 will give our attention to **p**
Php 4: 6 every situation, by **p** and petition,
Jas   5: 15 the **p** offered in faith will make
1Pe 3: 12 and his ears are attentive to their **p**,

PRAYERS (PRAY)
1Ch 5: 20 He answered their **p**, because they
Mk 12: 40 and for a show make lengthy **p**.
1Pe 3: 7 so that nothing will hinder your **p**.
Rev 5: 8 which are the **p** of God's people.

PRAYING (PRAY)
Mk 11: 25 And when you stand **p**, if you hold
Jn 17: 9 I am not **p** for the world,
Ac 16: 25 Silas were **p** and singing hymns
Eph 6: 18 always keep on **p** for all the Lord's

PREACH (PREACHED PREACHING)
Mt 23: 3 they do not practice what they **p**.
Mk 16: 15 *and p the gospel to all creation.*
Ac   9: 20 At once he began to **p**
Ro 10: 15 how can anyone **p** unless they are
    15: 20 to **p** the gospel where Christ was
1Co 1: 17 to baptize, but to **p** the gospel—
    1: 23 but we **p** Christ crucified:
    9: 14 that those who **p** the gospel should
    9: 16 Woe to me if I do not **p** the gospel!
2Co 10: 16 so that we can **p** the gospel
Gal 1: 8 heaven should **p** a gospel other
2Ti 4: 2 **P** the word; be prepared in season

PREACHED (PREACH)
Mk 13: 10 the gospel must first be **p** to all
Ac   8: 4 who had been scattered **p** the word
1Co 9: 27 so that after I have **p** to others,
    15: 1 remind you of the gospel I **p** to you
2Co 11: 4 a Jesus other than the Jesus we **p**,
Gal 1: 8 a gospel other than the one we **p**
Php 1: 18 false motives or true, Christ is **p**.
1Ti 3: 16 angels, was **p** among the nations,

PREACHING (PREACH)
Ro 10: 14 can they hear without someone **p**
1Co 9: 18 in **p** the gospel I may offer it free
1Ti 4: 13 of Scripture, to **p** and to teaching.
    5: 17 especially those whose work is **p**

PRECEPTS
Ps 19: 8 The **p** of the LORD are right,
  111: 7 all his **p** are trustworthy.
  111: 10 all who follow his **p** have good
  119: 40 How I long for your **p**!
  119: 69 I keep your **p** with all my heart.
  119:104 I gain understanding from your **p**;
  119:159 See how I love your **p**; preserve my

PRECIOUS
Ps 19: 10 They are more **p** than gold,
  116: 15 **P** in the sight of the LORD is
Pr   8: 11 for wisdom is more **p** than rubies.
Isa 28: 16 stone, a **p** cornerstone for a sure
1Pe 1: 19 but with the **p** blood of Christ,
    2: 6 a chosen and **p** cornerstone,
2Pe 1: 4 us his very great and **p** promises,

PREDESTINED (DESTINY)
Ro   8: 29 **p** to be conformed to the image
    8: 30 And those he **p**, he also called;
Eph 1: 5 he **p** us for adoption to sonship
    1: 11 been **p** according to the plan

PREDICTION
Jer 28: 9 LORD only if his **p** comes true."

PREPARE (PREPARED)
Ps 23: 5 You **p** a table before me
Am   4: 12 to you, Israel, **p** to meet your God."
Jn 14: 2 that I am going there to **p** a place

PREPARED (PREPARE)
Mt 25: 34 the kingdom **p** for you since
1Co 2: 9 the things God has **p** for those who
Eph 2: 10 which God **p** in advance for us
2Ti 4: 2 be **p** in season and out of season;
1Pe 3: 15 Always be **p** to give an answer

PRESENCE (PRESENT)
Ex 25: 30 Put the bread of the **P** on this table
Ezr 9: 15 not one of us can stand in your **p**."
Ps 31: 20 the shelter of your **p** you hide them
    89: 15 who walk in the light of your **p**,
    90: 8 secret sins in the light of your **p**.
  139: 7 Where can I flee from your **p**?
Jer   5: 22 "Should you not tremble in my **p**?
Heb 9: 24 now to appear for us in God's **p**.
Jude   : 24 before his glorious **p** without fault

PRESENT (PRESENCE)
2Co 11: 2 that I might **p** you as a pure virgin
Eph 5: 27 and to **p** her to himself as a radiant
2Ti 2: 15 Do your best to **p** yourself to God

PRESERVES
Ps 119: 50 Your promise **p** my life.

PRESS (PRESSED PRESSURE)
Php 3: 14 I **p** on toward the goal to win

PRESSED (PRESS)
Lk   6: 38 A good measure, **p** down,

PRESSURE (PRESS)
2Co 1: 8 We were under great **p**, far beyond
    11: 28 I face daily the **p** of my concern

PREVAILS
1Sa 2: 9 "It is not by strength that one **p**;

PRICE
Job 28: 18 the **p** of wisdom is beyond rubies.
1Co 6: 20 you were bought at a **p**.
    7: 23 You were bought at a **p**;

PRIDE (PROUD)
Pr   8: 13 I hate **p** and arrogance,
    16: 18 **P** goes before destruction,
Da   4: 37 those who walk in **p** he is able
Gal 6: 4 can take **p** in themselves alone,
Jas   1: 9 to take **p** in their high position.

PRIEST (PRIESTHOOD PRIESTS)
Heb 4: 14 a great high **p** who has ascended
    4: 15 do not have a high **p** who is unable
    7: 26 Such a high **p** truly meets our need
    8: 1 We do have such a high **p**, who sat

PRIESTHOOD (PRIEST)
Heb 7: 24 lives forever, he has a permanent **p**.
1Pe 2: 5 a spiritual house to be a holy **p**,
    2: 9 people, a royal **p**, a holy nation,

PRIESTS (PRIEST)
Ex 19: 6 you will be for me a kingdom of **p**
Rev 5: 10 a kingdom and **p** to serve our God,

PRINCE
Isa   9: 6 Everlasting Father, **P** of Peace.
Jn 12: 31 now the **p** of this world will be
Ac   5: 31 him to his own right hand as **P**

PRISON (PRISONER)
Isa 42: 7 blind, to free captives from **p**
Mt 25: 36 I was in **p** and you came to visit
Rev 20: 7 Satan will be released from his **p**

PRISONER (PRISON)
Ro   7: 23 making me a **p** of the law of sin
Eph 3: 1 the **p** of Christ Jesus for the sake

PRIVILEGE
2Co 8: 4 for the **p** of sharing in this service

PRIZE
1Co 9: 24 Run in such a way as to get the **p**.
Php 3: 14 on toward the goal to win the **p**

PROCLAIM (PROCLAIMED)
1Ch 16: 23 **p** his salvation day after day.
Ps 19: 1 the skies **p** the work of his hands.
     50: 6 the heavens **p** his righteousness,
     68: 34 **P** the power of God, whose majesty
  118: 17 will **p** what the Lord has done.
Zec 9: 10 He will **p** peace to the nations.
Ac 20: 27 I have not hesitated to **p** to you
Ro 10: 8 concerning faith that we **p**:
1Co 11: 26 cup, you **p** the Lord's death until

PROCLAIMED (PROCLAIM)
Ro 15: 19 I have fully **p** the gospel of Christ.
Col 1: 23 has been **p** to every creature under

PRODUCE (PRODUCES)
Mt 3: 8 **P** fruit in keeping with repentance.
   3: 10 does not **p** good fruit will be cut

PRODUCES (PRODUCE)
Pr 30: 33 so stirring up anger **p** strife."
Ro 5: 3 that suffering **p** perseverance;
Heb 12: 11 it **p** a harvest of righteousness

PROFANE
Lev 22: 32 Do not **p** my holy name, for I must

PROFESS
1Ti 2: 10 for women who **p** to worship God.
Heb 4: 14 let us hold firmly to the faith we **p**.
  10: 23 unswervingly to the hope we **p**,

PROMISE (PROMISED PROMISES)
1Ki 8: 20 Lord has kept the **p** he made:
Ac 2: 39 The **p** is for you and your children
Gal 3: 14 faith we might receive the **p**
1Ti 4: 8 holding **p** for both the present life
2Pe 3: 9 Lord is not slow in keeping his **p**,

PROMISED (PROMISE)
Ex 3: 17 I have **p** to bring you up out of
Dt 26: 18 his treasured possession as he **p**,
Ps 119: 57 I have **p** to obey your words.
Ro 4: 21 had power to do what he had **p**.
Heb 10: 23 we profess, for he who **p** is faithful.
2Pe 3: 4 say, "Where is this 'coming' he **p**?

PROMISES (PROMISE)
Jos 21: 45 of all the Lord's good **p** to Israel
Ro 9: 4 law, the temple worship and the **p**.
2Pe 1: 4 us his very great and precious **p**,

PROMPTED
1Th 1: 3 by faith, your labor **p** by love,
2Th 1: 11 and your every deed **p** by faith.

PROPHECIES (PROPHESY)
1Co 13: 8 But where there are **p**, they will
1Th 5: 20 Do not treat **p** with contempt

PROPHECY (PROPHESY)
1Co 14: 1 gifts of the Spirit, especially **p**.
2Pe 1: 20 that no **p** of Scripture came

PROPHESY (PROPHECIES PROPHECY
    PROPHESYING PROPHET PROPHETS)
Joel 2: 28 Your sons and daughters will **p**,
Mt 7: 22 did we not **p** in your name
1Co 14: 39 be eager to **p**, and do not forbid

PROPHESYING (PROPHESY)
Ro 12: 6 If your gift is **p**, then prophesy

PROPHET (PROPHESY)
Dt 18: 18 for them a **p** like you from among
Am 7: 14 neither a **p** nor the son of a **p**,
Mt 10: 41 Whoever welcomes a **p** as a **p** will
Lk 4: 24 "no **p** is accepted in his hometown.

PROPHETS (PROPHESY)
Ps 105: 15 do my **p** no harm."
Mt 5: 17 come to abolish the Law or the **P**;
   7: 12 for this sums up the Law and the **P**.
  24: 24 messiahs and false **p** will appear
Lk 24: 25 believe all that the **p** have spoken!
Ac 10: 43 All the **p** testify about him
1Co 12: 28 apostles, second **p**, third teachers,
  14: 32 The spirits of **p** are subject
Eph 2: 20 foundation of the apostles and **p**,
Heb 1: 1 ancestors through the **p** at many
1Pe 1: 10 the **p**, who spoke of the grace

PROSPER (PROSPERITY PROSPERS)
Pr 28: 25 who trust in the Lord will **p**.

PROSPERITY (PROSPER)
Ps 73: 3 when I saw the **p** of the wicked.

PROSPERS (PROSPER)
Ps 1: 3 whatever they do **p**.

PROSTITUTE (PROSTITUTES)
1Co 6: 15 of Christ and unite them with a **p**?

PROSTITUTES (PROSTITUTE)
Mt 21: 31 **p** are entering the kingdom of God
Lk 15: 30 your property with **p** comes home,

PROSTRATE
Dt 9: 18 again I fell **p** before the Lord

PROTECT (PROTECTS)
Ps 32: 7 you will **p** me from trouble
Pr 2: 11 Discretion will **p** you,
Jn 17: 11 **p** them by the power of your name,

PROTECTS (PROTECT)
1Co 13: 7 It always **p**, always trusts,

PROUD (PRIDE)
Pr 16: 5 The Lord detests all the **p**
Ro 12: 16 Do not be **p**, but be willing
1Co 13: 4 envy, it does not boast, it is not **p**.

PROVE
1Co 4: 2 been given a trust must **p** faithful.

PROVIDE (PROVIDED PROVIDES)
Ge 22: 8 "God himself will **p** the lamb
Isa 43: 20 because I **p** water in the wilderness
1Ti 5: 8 Anyone who does not **p** for their

PROVIDED (PROVIDE)
Jnh 1: 17 Now the Lord **p** a huge fish
   4: 6 the Lord God **p** a leafy plant
   4: 7 dawn the next day God **p** a worm,
   4: 8 rose, God **p** a scorching east wind,

PROVIDES (PROVIDE)
1Ti 6: 17 who richly **p** us with everything
1Pe 4: 11 do so with the strength God **p**,

PROVOKED
Ecc 7: 9 Do not be quickly **p** in your spirit,

PRUDENT
Pr 14: 15 the **p** give thought to their steps.
    19: 14 but a **p** wife is from the LORD.
Am 5: 13 Therefore the **p** keep quiet in such

PRUNING
Isa 2: 4 and their spears into **p** hooks.
Joel 3: 10 and your **p** hooks into spears.

PSALMS
Eph 5: 19 speaking to one another with **p**,
Col 3: 16 with all wisdom through **p**,

PUBLICLY
Ac 20: 20 have taught you **p** and from house

PUFFS
1Co 8: 1 knowledge **p** up while love builds

PUNISH (PUNISHED)
Ex 32: 34 to **p**, I will **p** them for their sin."
Pr 23: 13 if you **p** them with the rod,
Isa 13: 11 I will **p** the world for its evil,
1Pe 2: 14 by him to **p** those who do wrong

PUNISHED (PUNISH)
La 3: 39 should the living complain when **p**
2Th 1: 9 They will be **p** with everlasting
Heb 10: 29 to be **p** who has trampled the Son

PURE (PURIFIES PURIFY PURITY)
2Sa 22: 27 to the **p** you show yourself **p**,
Ps 24: 4 who has clean hands and a **p** heart,
    51: 10 Create in me a **p** heart, O God,
Pr 20: 9 can say, "I have kept my heart **p**;
Isa 52: 11 Come out from it and be **p**,
Hab 1: 13 Your eyes are too **p** to look on evil;
Mt 5: 8 Blessed are the **p** in heart, for they
2Co 11: 2 I might present you as a **p** virgin
Php 4: 8 whatever is **p**, whatever is lovely,
1Ti 5: 22 the sins of others. Keep yourself **p**.
Titus 1: 15 To the **p**, all things are **p**,
    2: 5 to be self-controlled and **p**, to be
Heb 13: 4 all, and the marriage bed kept **p**,
1Jn 3: 3 purify themselves, just as he is **p**.

PURGE
Pr 20: 30 and beatings **p** the inmost being.

PURIFIES (PURE)
1Jn 1: 7 of Jesus, his Son, **p** us from all sin.

PURIFY (PURE)
Titus 2: 14 to **p** for himself a people that are
1Jn 1: 9 and **p** us from all unrighteousness.
    3: 3 this hope in him **p** themselves,

PURITY (PURE)
Ps 119: 9 person stay on the path of **p**?
2Co 6: 6 in **p**, understanding,
1Ti 4: 12 conduct, in love, in faith and in **p**.

PURPOSE
Pr 19: 21 it is the LORD's **p** that prevails.
Isa 55: 11 achieve the **p** for which I sent it.
Ro 8: 28 been called according to his **p**.

PURSES
Lk 12: 33 Provide **p** for yourselves that will

PURSUE
Ps 34: 14 and do good; seek peace and **p** it.
2Ti 2: 22 of youth and **p** righteousness, faith,
1Pe 3: 11 they must seek peace and **p** it.

QUALITIES (QUALITY)
2Pe 1: 8 if you possess these **q** in increasing

QUALITY (QUALITIES)
1Co 3: 13 and the fire will test the **q** of each

QUARREL (QUARRELSOME)
Pr 15: 18 the one who is patient calms a **q**.
    17: 14 Starting a **q** is like breaching a dam
    17: 19 Whoever loves a **q** loves sin;

QUARRELSOME (QUARREL)
Pr 19: 13 **q** wife is like the constant dripping
1Ti 3: 3 gentle, not **q**, not a lover of money.
2Ti 2: 24 the Lord's servant must not be **q**

QUENCH
1Th 5: 19 Do not **q** the Spirit.

QUICK-TEMPERED
Titus 1: 7 not **q**, not given to drunkenness,

QUIET (QUIETNESS)
Ps 23: 2 he leads me beside **q** waters,
Lk 19: 40 "if they keep **q**, the stones will cry
1Ti 2: 2 peaceful and **q** lives in all godliness
1Pe 3: 4 beauty of a gentle and **q** spirit,

QUIETNESS (QUIET)
Isa 30: 15 in **q** and trust is your strength,
    32: 17 its effect will be **q** and confidence
1Ti 2: 11 woman should learn in **q** and full

QUIVER
Ps 127: 5 Blessed is the man whose **q** is full

RACE
Ecc 9: 11 The **r** is not to the swift or
1Co 9: 24 that in a **r** all the runners run,
2Ti 4: 7 I have finished the **r**, I have kept
Heb 12: 1 with perseverance the **r** marked

RACHEL
    Daughter of Laban (Ge 29:16); wife of Jacob (Ge 29:28); bore two sons (Ge 30:22–24; 35:16–24; 46:19).

RADIANCE (RADIANT)
Heb 1: 3 The Son is the **r** of God's glory

RADIANT (RADIANCE)
Ex 34: 29 that his face was **r** because he had
Ps 34: 5 Those who look to him are **r**;
SS 5: 10 My beloved is **r** and ruddy,
Isa 60: 5 Then you will look and be **r**,
Eph 5: 27 her to himself as a **r** church,

RAIN (RAINBOW)
Mt 5: 45 and sends **r** on the righteous

RAINBOW (RAIN)
Ge 9: 13 I have set my **r** in the clouds, and it

RAISED (RISE)
Ro 4: 25 was **r** to life for our justification.
    10: 9 your heart that God **r** him
1Co 15: 4 he was **r** on the third day according

RAN (RUN)
Jnh 1: 3 But Jonah **r** away from the LORD

RANSOM
Mt 20: 28 to give his life as a **r** for many."
Heb 9: 15 he has died as a **r** to set them free

RAVENS
1Ki 17: 6 The **r** brought him bread and meat
Lk 12: 24 Consider the **r**: They do not sow

READ (READS)
Jos 8: 34 Joshua **r** all the words of the law—
Ne 8: 8 understood what was being **r**.
2Co 3: 2 hearts, known and **r** by everyone.

READS (READ)
Rev 1: 3 is the one who **r** aloud the words

REAL (REALITY)
Jn 6: 55 For my flesh is **r** food and my blood is **r** drink.

REALITY (REAL)
Col 2: 17 the **r**, however, is found in Christ.

REAP (REAPS)
Job 4: 8 evil and those who sow trouble **r** it.
2Co 9: 6 generously will also **r** generously.

REAPS (REAP)
Gal 6: 7 A man **r** what he sows.

REASON
1Pe 3: 15 asks you to give the **r** for the hope

REBEKAH
Sister of Laban, secured as bride for Isaac (Ge 24). Mother of Esau and Jacob (Ge 25:19–26). Taken by Abimelek as sister of Isaac; returned (Ge 26:1–11). Encouraged Jacob to trick Isaac out of blessing (Ge 27:1–17).

REBEL
Mt 10: 21 children will **r** against their parents

REBUKE (REBUKING)
Pr 9: 8 **r** the wise and they will love you.
27: 5 Better is open **r** than hidden love.
Lk 17: 3 or sister sins against you, **r** them;
2Ti 4: 2 correct, **r** and encourage—
Rev 3: 19 Those whom I love I **r**

REBUKING (REBUKE)
2Ti 3: 16 and is useful for teaching, **r**,

RECEIVE (RECEIVED RECEIVES)
Ac 1: 8 you will **r** power when the Holy
20: 35 more blessed to give than to **r**.'"
2Co 6: 17 no unclean thing, and I will **r** you."
Rev 4: 11 to **r** glory and honor and power,

RECEIVED (RECEIVE)
Mt 6: 2 they have **r** their reward in full.
10: 8 Freely you have **r**; freely give.
1Co 11: 23 For I **r** from the Lord what I
Col 2: 6 just as you **r** Christ Jesus as Lord,
1Pe 4: 10 should use whatever gift you have **r**

RECEIVES (RECEIVE)
Mt 7: 8 For everyone who asks **r**;
Ac 10: 43 who believes in him **r** forgiveness

RECKONING
Isa 10: 3 What will you do on the day of **r**,

RECOGNIZE (RECOGNIZED)
Mt 7: 16 By their fruit you will **r** them.

RECOGNIZED (RECOGNIZE)
Mt 12: 33 be bad, for a tree is **r** by its fruit.
Ro 7: 13 in order that sin might be **r** as sin,

RECOMPENSE
Isa 40: 10 him, and his **r** accompanies him.

RECONCILE (RECONCILED RECONCILIATION)
Eph 2: 16 and in one body to **r** both of them

RECONCILED (RECONCILE)
Mt 5: 24 First go and be **r** to them;
Ro 5: 10 were **r** to him through the death
2Co 5: 18 who **r** us to himself through Christ

RECONCILIATION (RECONCILE)
Ro 5: 11 whom we have now received **r**.
11: 15 For if their rejection brought **r**
2Co 5: 18 and gave us the ministry of **r**:
5: 19 committed to us the message of **r**.

RECORD
Ps 130: 3 you, LORD, kept a **r** of sins, Lord,

RED
Isa 1: 18 though they are **r** as crimson,

REDEEM (REDEEMED REDEEMER REDEMPTION)
2Sa 7: 23 out to **r** as a people for himself,
Ps 49: 7 No one can **r** the life of another
Gal 4: 5 to **r** those under the law, that we

REDEEMED (REDEEM)
Gal 3: 13 Christ **r** us from the curse of the law
1Pe 1: 18 you were **r** from the empty way

REDEEMER (REDEEM)
Job 19: 25 I know that my **r** lives,

REDEMPTION (REDEEM)
Ps 130: 7 love and with him is full **r**.
Lk 21: 28 because your **r** is drawing near."
Ro 8: 23 to sonship, the **r** of our bodies.
Eph 1: 7 we have **r** through his blood,
Col 1: 14 in whom we have **r**, the forgiveness
Heb 9: 12 blood, thus obtaining eternal **r**.

REFUGE
Nu 35: 11 some towns to be your cities of **r**,
Dt 33: 27 The eternal God is your **r**,
Ru 2: 12 wings you have come to take **r**."
Ps 46: 1 God is our **r** and strength,
91: 2 "He is my **r** and my fortress,

REHOBOAM
Son of Solomon (1Ki 11:43; 1Ch 3:10). Harsh treatment of subjects caused divided kingdom (1Ki 12:1–24; 14:21–31; 2Ch 10–12).

REIGN (REIGNS)
Ro 6: 12 not let sin **r** in your mortal body
1Co 15: 25 he must **r** until he has put all his
2Ti 2: 12 if we endure, we will also **r** with
Rev 20: 6 **r** with him for a thousand years.

REIGNS (REIGN)
Ex 15: 18 "The LORD **r** for ever and ever."

REJECTED (REJECTS)
Ps 118: 22 stone the builders **r** has become
Isa 53: 3 was despised and **r** by mankind,
1Ti 4: 4 nothing is to be **r** if it is received
1Pe 2: 4 **r** by humans but chosen by God
2: 7 stone the builders **r** has become

REJECTS (REJECTED)
Lk 10: 16 whoever **r** me **r** him who sent me."
Jn 3: 36 whoever **r** the Son will not see life,

REJOICE (JOY)
Ps 66: 6 come, let us **r** in him.
118: 24 let us **r** today and be glad.
Pr 5: 18 you **r** in the wife of your youth.
Lk 10: 20 but **r** that your names are written
15: 6 together and says, '**R** with me;
Ro 12: 15 **R** with those who **r**;
Php 4: 4 **R** in the Lord always. I will say it again: **R**!

REJOICES (JOY)
Isa 61: 10 my soul **r** in my God.
Lk 1: 47 and my spirit **r** in God my Savior,
1Co 12: 26 is honored, every part **r** with it.
13: 6 delight in evil but **r** with the truth.

REJOICING (JOY)
Ps 30: 5 night, but **r** comes in the morning.
Lk 15: 7 the same way there will be more **r**
Ac 5: 41 **r** because they had been counted

RELIABLE
2Ti 2: 2 entrust to **r** people who will also be

RELIGION
1Ti 5: 4 of all to put their **r** into practice
Jas 1: 27 **R** that God our Father accepts as

REMAIN (REMAINS)
Nu 33: 55 you allow to **r** will become barbs
Jn 15: 7 If you **r** in me and my words **r**
Ro 13: 8 Let no debt **r** outstanding,
1Co 13: 13 And now these three **r**:

REMAINS (REMAIN)
Ps 146: 6 he **r** faithful forever.
2Ti 2: 13 if we are faithless, he **r** faithful,
Heb 7: 3 Son of God, he **r** a priest forever.

REMEMBER (REMEMBERS REMEMBRANCE)
Ex 20: 8 "**R** the Sabbath day by keeping it
1Ch 16: 12 **R** the wonders he has done,
Ecc 12: 1 **R** your Creator in the days of your
Jer 31: 34 and will **r** their sins no more."
Gal 2: 10 we should continue to **r** the poor,
Php 1: 3 I thank my God every time I **r** you.
Heb 8: 12 and will **r** their sins no more."

REMEMBERS (REMEMBER)
Ps 103: 14 are formed, he **r** that we are dust.
111: 5 he **r** his covenant forever.
Isa 43: 25 own sake, and **r** your sins no more.

REMEMBRANCE (REMEMBER)
1Co 11: 24 is for you; do this in **r** of me."

REMIND
Jn 14: 26 will **r** you of everything I have said

REMOVED
Ps 30: 11 you **r** my sackcloth and clothed me
103: 12 so far has he **r** our transgressions
Jn 20: 1 that the stone had been **r**

RENEW (RENEWED RENEWING)
Ps 51: 10 and **r** a steadfast spirit within me.
Isa 40: 31 in the LORD will **r** their strength.

RENEWED (RENEW)
Ps 103: 5 that your youth is **r** like the eagle's.
2Co 4: 16 yet inwardly we are being **r** day

RENEWING (RENEW)
Ro 12: 2 transformed by the **r** of your mind.

RENOUNCE (RENOUNCES)
Da 4: 27 **R** your sins by doing what is right,

RENOUNCES (RENOUNCE)
Pr 28: 13 confesses and **r** them finds mercy.

RENOWN
Isa 63: 12 to gain for himself everlasting **r**,
Jer 32: 20 have gained the **r** that is still yours.

REPAID (PAY)
Lk 14: 14 you will be **r** at the resurrection
Col 3: 25 Anyone who does wrong will be **r**

REPAY (PAY)
Dt 32: 35 It is mine to avenge; I will **r**.
Ru 2: 12 May the LORD **r** you for what you
Ro 12: 19 I will **r**," says the Lord.
1Pe 3: 9 the contrary, **r** evil with blessing,

REPENT (REPENTANCE REPENTS)
Job 42: 6 I despise myself and **r** in dust
Jer 15: 19 "If you **r**, I will restore you that you
Mt 4: 17 time on Jesus began to preach, "**R**,
Lk 13: 3 But unless you **r**, you too will all
17: 3 and if they **r**, forgive them.
Ac 2: 38 Peter replied, "**R** and be baptized,
17: 30 all people everywhere to **r**.

REPENTANCE (REPENT)
Lk 3: 8 Produce fruit in keeping with **r**.

Lk 5: 32 call the righteous, but sinners to **r**."
Ac 26: 20 demonstrate their **r** by their deeds.
2Co 7: 10 Godly sorrow brings **r** that leads

REPENTS (REPENT)
Lk 15: 10 of God over one sinner who **r**."

REPROACH
1Ti 3: 2 Now the overseer is to be above **r**,

REPUTATION
1Ti 3: 7 also have a good **r** with outsiders,

REQUESTS
Ps 20: 5 May the LORD grant all your **r**.
Php 4: 6 present your **r** to God.

REQUIRE
Mic 6: 8 what does the LORD **r** of you?

RESCUE (RESCUES)
Da 6: 20 been able to **r** you from the lions?"
2Pe 2: 9 the Lord knows how to **r** the godly

RESCUES (RESCUE)
1Th 1: 10 who **r** us from the coming wrath.

RESIST
Jas 4: 7 **R** the devil, and he will flee
1Pe 5: 9 **R** him, standing firm in the faith,

RESOLVED
Da 1: 8 Daniel **r** not to defile himself
1Co 2: 2 For I **r** to know nothing while I

RESPECT (RESPECTABLE)
Lev 19: 3 of you must **r** your mother
19: 32 show **r** for the elderly and revere
Mal 1: 6 a master, where is the **r** due me?"
1Th 4: 12 that your daily life may win the **r**
1Ti 3: 4 do so in a manner worthy of full **r**.
1Pe 2: 17 Show proper **r** to everyone,
3: 7 them with **r** as the weaker partner

RESPECTABLE (RESPECT)
1Ti 3: 2 self-controlled, **r**, hospitable,

REST
Ex 31: 15 seventh day is a day of sabbath **r**,
Ps 91: 1 the Most High will **r** in the shadow
Jer 6: 16 and you will find **r** for your souls.
Mt 11: 28 burdened, and I will give you **r**.

RESTITUTION
Ex 22: 3 who steals must certainly make **r**,
Lev 6: 5 must make **r** in full, add a fifth

RESTORE
Ps 51: 12 **R** to me the joy of your salvation
Gal 6: 1 by the Spirit should **r** that person

RESURRECTION
Mt 22: 30 the **r** people will neither marry nor
Lk 14: 14 be repaid at the **r** of the righteous."
Jn 11: 25 said to her, "I am the **r** and the life.
Ro 1: 4 in power by his **r** from the dead:
1Co 15: 12 say that there is no **r** of the dead?
Php 3: 10 yes, to know the power of his **r**
Rev 20: 5 This is the first **r**.

RETRIBUTION
Jer 51: 56 For the LORD is a God of **r**;

RETURN
2Ch 30: 9 If you **r** to the LORD, then your
Ne 1: 9 but if you **r** to me and obey my
Isa 55: 11 It will not **r** to me empty, but will
Hos 6: 1 "Come, let us **r** to the LORD.
Joel 2: 12 "**r** to me with all your heart,

REVEALED (REVELATION)
Dt 29: 29 but the things **r** belong to us

Isa 40: 5 the glory of the LORD will be **r**,
Mt 11: 25 and **r** them to little children.
Ro 1: 17 the righteousness of God is **r**—
8: 18 with the glory that will be **r** in us

REVELATION (REVEALED)
Gal 1: 12 I received it by **r** from Jesus Christ.
Rev 1: 1 The **r** from Jesus Christ,

REVENGE (VENGEANCE)
Lev 19: 18 "'Do not seek **r** or bear a grudge
Ro 12: 19 Do not take **r**, my dear friends,

REVERE (REVERENCE)
Ps 33: 8 all the people of the world **r** him.

REVERENCE (REVERE)
Lev 19: 30 and have **r** for my sanctuary.
Ps 5: 7 in **r** I bow down toward your holy
Col 3: 22 of heart and **r** for the Lord.
1Pe 3: 2 see the purity and **r** of your lives.

REVIVE
Ps 85: 6 Will you not **r** us again, that your
Isa 57: 15 to **r** the spirit of the lowly and to **r**

REWARD (REWARDED)
Ps 19: 11 in keeping them there is great **r**.
127: 3 the LORD, offspring a **r** from him.
Pr 19: 17 he will **r** them for what they have
25: 22 head, and the LORD will **r** you.
Jer 17: 10 to **r** each person according to their
Mt 5: 12 because great is your **r** in heaven,
6: 5 they have received their **r** in full.
16: 27 he will **r** each person according
1Co 3: 14 the builder will receive a **r**.
Rev 22: 12 My **r** is with me, and I will give

REWARDED (REWARD)
Ru 2: 12 May you be richly **r** by the LORD,
Ps 18: 24 The LORD has **r** me according
Pr 14: 14 and the good **r** for theirs.
1Co 3: 8 and they will each be **r** according

RICH (RICHES)
Pr 23: 4 Do not wear yourself out to get **r**;
Jer 9: 23 or the **r** boast of their riches,
Mt 19: 23 for someone who is **r** to enter
2Co 6: 10 poor, yet making many **r**;
8: 9 his poverty might become **r**.
1Ti 6: 17 Command those who are **r** in this

RICHES (RICH)
Ps 119: 14 statutes as one rejoices in great **r**.
Pr 30: 8 give me neither poverty nor **r**,
Isa 10: 3 Where will you leave your **r**?
Ro 9: 23 to make the **r** of his glory known
11: 33 the depth of the **r** of the wisdom
Eph 2: 7 he might show the incomparable **r**
3: 8 to the Gentiles the boundless **r**
Col 1: 27 among the Gentiles the glorious **r**

RID
Ge 21: 10 "Get **r** of that slave woman and her
1Co 5: 7 Get **r** of the old yeast, so that you
Gal 4: 30 "Get **r** of the slave woman and her

RIGHT (RIGHTS)
Ge 18: 25 not the Judge of all the earth do **r**?"
Ex 15: 26 God and do what is **r** in his eyes,
Dt 5: 32 do not turn aside to the **r**
Ps 16: 8 With him at my **r** hand, I will not
19: 8 The precepts of the LORD are **r**,
63: 8 your **r** hand upholds me.
110: 1 "Sit at my **r** hand until I make your
Pr 4: 27 Do not turn to the **r** or the left;
14: 12 There is a way that appears to be **r**,

Isa 1: 17 Learn to do **r**; seek justice.
Jer 23: 5 do what is just and **r** in the land.
Hos 14: 9 The ways of the LORD are **r**;
Mt 6: 8 know what your **r** hand is doing,
Jn 1: 12 he gave the **r** to become children
Ro 9: 21 Does not the potter have the **r**
12: 17 careful to do what is **r** in the eyes
Eph 1: 20 and seated him at his **r** hand
Php 4: 8 whatever is **r**, whatever is pure,

RIGHTEOUS (RIGHTEOUSNESS)
Ps 34: 15 eyes of the LORD are on the **r**,
37: 25 yet I have never seen the **r** forsaken
119:137 You are **r**, LORD, and your laws
143: 2 no one living is **r** before you.
Pr 3: 33 but he blesses the home of the **r**.
11: 30 The fruit of the **r** is a tree of life,
18: 10 the **r** run to it and are safe.
Isa 64: 6 all our **r** acts are like filthy rags;
Hab 2: 4 but the **r** person will live by his
Mt 5: 45 and sends rain on the **r**
9: 13 For I have not come to call the **r**,
13: 49 and separate the wicked from the **r**
25: 46 but the **r** to eternal life."
Ro 1: 17 "The **r** will live by faith."
3: 10 "There is no one **r**, not even one;
1Ti 1: 9 that the law is made not for the **r**
Jas 2: 24 is considered **r** by what they do
1Pe 3: 18 for sins, the **r** for the unrighteous,
1Jn 3: 7 is right is **r**, just as he is **r**.
Rev 19: 8 (Fine linen stands for the **r** acts

RIGHTEOUSNESS (RIGHTEOUS)
Ge 15: 6 and he credited it to him as **r**.
1Sa 26: 23 rewards everyone for their **r**
Ps 9: 8 He rules the world in **r** and judges
45: 7 You love **r** and hate wickedness;
85: 10 **r** and peace kiss each other.
89: 14 **R** and justice are the foundation
111: 3 deeds, and his **r** endures forever.
Pr 14: 34 **R** exalts a nation, but sin
21: 21 Whoever pursues **r** and love finds
Isa 59: 17 He put on **r** as his breastplate,
Eze 18: 20 The **r** of the righteous will be
Da 9: 24 to bring in everlasting **r**, to seal
12: 3 and those who lead many to **r**,
Mal 4: 2 the sun of **r** will rise with healing
Mt 5: 6 those who hunger and thirst for **r**,
5: 20 you that unless your **r** surpasses
6: 1 practice your **r** in front of others
6: 33 seek first his kingdom and his **r**,
Ro 3: 25 He did this to demonstrate his **r**,
4: 3 and it was credited to him as **r**."
4: 9 faith was credited to him as **r**.
6: 13 to him as an instrument of **r**,
2Co 5: 21 we might become the **r** of God.
Gal 2: 21 **r** could be gained through the law,
3: 6 and it was credited to him as **r**."
Eph 6: 14 with the breastplate of **r** in place,
Php 3: 9 not having a **r** of my own
2Ti 3: 16 correcting and training in **r**,
4: 8 is in store for me the crown of **r**,
Heb 11: 7 and became heir of the **r** that is
2Pe 2: 21 not to have known the way of **r**,

RIGHTS (RIGHT)
La 3: 35 deny people their **r** before the Most

RISE (RAISED)
Isa 26: 19 their bodies will **r**—let those who
Mt 27: 63 'After three days I will **r** again.'
Jn 5: 29 who have done what is good will **r**
1Th 4: 16 and the dead in Christ will **r** first.

ROAD
Mt 7: 13 gate and broad is the **r** that leads

ROBBERS
Jer 7: 11 Name, become a den of **r** to you?
Lk 19: 46 you have made it 'a den of **r.**'"
Jn 10: 8 come before me are thieves and **r,**

ROCK
Ps 18: 2 The LORD is my **r**, my fortress
40: 2 he set my feet on a **r** and gave me
Mt 7: 24 man who built his house on the **r.**
16: 18 on this **r** I will build my church,
Ro 9: 33 and a **r** that makes them fall,
1Co 10: 4 them, and that **r** was Christ.

ROD
Ps 23: 4 your **r** and your staff, they comfort
Pr 13: 24 Whoever spares the **r** hates their
23: 13 if you punish them with the **r,**

ROOM (ROOMS)
Mt 6: 6 go into your **r**, close the door
Lk 2: 7 there was no guest **r** available
Jn 21: 25 the whole world would not have **r**

ROOMS (ROOM)
Jn 14: 2 My Father's house has many **r;**

ROOT
Isa 53: 2 and like a **r** out of dry ground.
1Ti 6: 10 the love of money is a **r** of all kinds

ROYAL
Jas 2: 8 If you really keep the **r** law found
1Pe 2: 9 are a chosen people, a **r** priesthood,

RUIN (RUINS)
Pr 18: 24 unreliable friends soon comes to **r,**
19: 3 person's own folly leads to their **r,**
1Ti 6: 9 desires that plunge people into **r**

RUINS (RUIN)
2Ti 2: 14 value, and only **r** those who listen.

RULE (RULER RULERS RULES)
1Sa 12: 12 'No, we want a king to **r** over us'—
Ps 119:133 to your word; let no sin **r** over me.
Zec 9: 10 His **r** will extend from sea to sea
Col 3: 15 peace of Christ **r** in your hearts,
Rev 2: 27 that one 'will **r** them with an iron

RULER (RULE)
Eph 2: 2 of the **r** of the kingdom of the air,
1Ti 6: 15 the blessed and only **R**, the King

RULERS (RULE)
Ps 2: 2 and the **r** band together against
8: 6 You made them **r** over the works
Col 1: 16 or powers or **r** or authorities;

RULES (RULE)
Ps 103: 19 heaven, and his kingdom **r** over all.
Lk 22: 26 and the one who **r** like the one who
2Ti 2: 5 by competing according to the **r.**

RUMORS
Mt 24: 6 You will hear of wars and **r** of wars,

RUN (RAN)
Isa 40: 31 they will **r** and not grow weary,
1Co 9: 24 **R** in such a way as to get the prize.
Heb 12: 1 let us **r** with perseverance the race

RUTH
Moabitess; widow who went to Bethlehem with mother-in-law Naomi (Ru 1). Gleaned in field of Boaz; shown favor (Ru 2). Proposed marriage to Boaz (Ru 3). Married (Ru 4:1–12); bore Obed, ancestor of David (Ru 4:13–22), Jesus (Mt 1:5).

SABBATH
Ex 20: 8 "Remember the **S** day by keeping it
Dt 5: 12 "Observe the **S** day by keeping it
Col 2: 16 New Moon celebration or a **S** day.

SACKCLOTH
Mt 11: 21 would have repented long ago in **s**

SACRED
Mt 7: 6 "Do not give dogs what is **s;**
1Co 3: 17 for God's temple is **s**, and you

SACRIFICE (SACRIFICED)
Ge 22: 2 **S** him there as a burnt offering
Ex 12: 27 'It is the Passover **s** to the LORD,
1Sa 15: 22 To obey is better than **s,**
Ps 51: 17 My **s**, O God, is a broken spirit;
Hos 6: 6 not **s**, and acknowledgment of God
Mt 9: 13 'I desire mercy, not **s.**
Ro 12: 1 to offer your bodies as a living **s,**
Heb 9: 26 away with sin by the **s** of himself.
13: 15 offer to God a **s** of praise—
1Jn 2: 2 He is the atoning **s** for our sins,

SACRIFICED (SACRIFICE)
1Co 5: 7 our Passover lamb, has been **s.**
8: 1 Now about food **s** to idols;
Heb 9: 28 so Christ was **s** once to take away

SADDUCEES
Mk 12: 18 Then the **S**, who say there is no

SAFE (SAVE)
Ps 37: 3 in the land and enjoy **s** pasture.
Pr 18: 10 the righteous run to it and are **s.**

SAFETY (SAVE)
Ps 4: 8 alone, LORD, make me dwell in **s.**
1Th 5: 3 "Peace and **s**," destruction will

SAINTS See FAITHFUL, [GOD'S] PEOPLE

SAKE
Ps 44: 22 your **s** we face death all day long;
Php 3: 7 consider loss for the **s** of Christ.
Heb 11: 26 disgrace for the **s** of Christ as

SALT
Ge 19: 26 back, and she became a pillar of **s.**
Mt 5: 13 "You are the **s** of the earth.

SALVATION (SAVE)
Ex 15: 2 he has become my **s.**
1Ch 16: 23 proclaim his **s** day after day.
Ps 27: 1 The LORD is my light and my **s**—
51: 12 Restore to me the joy of your **s**
62: 2 Truly he is my rock and my **s;**
85: 9 Surely his **s** is near those who fear
96: 2 proclaim his **s** day after day.
Isa 25: 9 let us rejoice and be glad in his **s.**"
45: 17 the LORD with an everlasting **s;**
51: 6 But my **s** will last forever,
59: 17 and the helmet of **s** on his head;
61: 10 has clothed me with garments of **s**
Jnh 2: 9 'S comes from the LORD.'"
Lk 2: 30 For my eyes have seen your **s,**
Jn 4: 22 we do know, for **s** is from the Jews.
Ac 4: 12 **S** is found in no one else, for there
13: 47 that you may bring **s** to the ends
Ro 11: 11 **s** has come to the Gentiles to make
2Co 7: 10 brings repentance that leads to **s**
Eph 6: 17 Take the helmet of **s** and the sword
Php 2: 12 to work out your **s** with fear
1Th 5: 8 and the hope of **s** as a helmet.
2Ti 3: 15 make you wise for **s** through faith
Heb 2: 3 we escape if we ignore so great a **s?**
6: 9 the things that have to do with **s.**

1Pe 1: 10 Concerning this **s**, the prophets,
2: 2 by it you may grow up in your **s**,

SAMARITAN
Lk 10: 33 But a **S**, as he traveled, came where

SAMSON
Danite judge. Birth promised (Jdg 13). Married to Philistine (Jdg 14). Vengeance on Philistines (Jdg 15). Betrayed by Delilah (Jdg 16:1–22). Death (Jdg 16:23–31). Feats of strength: killed lion (Jdg 14:6), 30 Philistines (Jdg 14:19), 1,000 Philistines with jawbone (Jdg 15:13–17), carried off gates of Gaza (Jdg 16:3), pushed down temple of Dagon (Jdg 16:25–30).

SAMUEL
Ephraimite judge and prophet (Heb 11:32). Birth prayed for (1Sa 1:10–18). Dedicated to temple by Hannah (1Sa 1:21–28). Raised by Eli (1Sa 2:11, 18–26). Called as prophet (1Sa 3). Led Israel to victory over Philistines (1Sa 7). Asked by Israel for a king (1Sa 8). Anointed Saul as king (1Sa 9–10). Farewell speech (1Sa 12). Rebuked Saul for sacrifice (1Sa 13). Announced rejection of Saul (1Sa 15). Anointed David as king (1Sa 16). Protected David from Saul (1Sa 19:18–24). Death (1Sa 25:1). Returned from dead to condemn Saul (1Sa 28).

SANCTIFIED (SANCTIFY)
Ac 20: 32 among all those who are **s**.
Ro 15: 16 to God, **s** by the Holy Spirit.
1Co 6: 11 you were **s**, you were justified
7: 14 husband has been **s** through his
Heb 10: 29 blood of the covenant that **s** them,

SANCTIFY (SANCTIFIED SANCTIFYING)
1Th 5: 23 peace, **s** you through and through.

SANCTIFYING (SANCTIFY)
2Th 2: 13 be saved through the **s** work

SANCTUARY
Ex 25: 8 "Then have them make a **s** for me,

SAND
Ge 22: 17 sky and as the **s** on the seashore.
Mt 7: 26 man who built his house on **s**.

SANDALS
Ex 3: 5 "Take off your **s**, for the place
Jos 5: 15 "Take off your **s**, for the place

SANG (SING)
Job 38: 7 while the morning stars **s** together
Rev 5: 9 And they **s** a new song, saying:

SARAH
Wife of Abraham, originally named Sarai; barren (Ge 11:29–31; 1Pe 3:6). Taken by Pharaoh as Abraham's sister; returned (Ge 12:10–20). Gave Hagar to Abraham; sent her away in pregnancy (Ge 16). Name changed; Isaac promised (Ge 17:15–21; 18:10–15; Heb 11:11). Taken by Abimelek as Abraham's sister; returned (Ge 20). Isaac born; Hagar and Ishmael sent away (Ge 21:1–21; Gal 4:21–31). Death (Ge 23).

SATAN
Job 1: 6 and **S** also came with them.
Zec 3: 2 to **S**, "The LORD rebuke you, **S**!
Mk 4: 15 **S** comes and takes away the word
2Co 11: 14 **S** himself masquerades as an angel
12: 7 a messenger of **S**, to torment me.
Rev 12: 9 or **S**, who leads the whole world
20: 2 **S**, and bound him for a thousand
20: 7 **S** will be released from his prison

SATISFIED (SATISFY)
Isa 53: 11 he will see the light of life and be **s**;

SATISFIES (SATISFY)
Ps 103: 5 **s** your desires with good things

SATISFY (SATISFIED SATISFIES)
Isa 55: 2 and your labor on what does not **s**?

SAUL
1. Benjamite; anointed by Samuel as first king of Israel (1Sa 9–10). Defeated Ammonites (1Sa 11). Rebuked for offering sacrifice (1Sa 13:1–15). Defeated Philistines (1Sa 14). Rejected as king for failing to annihilate Amalekites (1Sa 15). Soothed from evil spirit by David (1Sa 16:14–23). Sent David against Goliath (1Sa 17). Jealousy and attempted murder of David (1Sa 18:1–11). Gave David Michal as wife (1Sa 18:12–30). Second attempt to kill David (1Sa 19). Anger at Jonathan (1Sa 20:26–34). Pursued David; killed priests at Nob (1Sa 22), went to Keilah and Ziph (1Sa 23), life spared by David at En Gedi (1Sa 24) and in his tent (1Sa 26). Rebuked by Samuel's spirit for consulting witch at Endor (1Sa 28). Wounded by Philistines; took his own life (1Sa 31; 1Ch 10).
2. See PAUL

SAVE (SAFE SAFETY SALVATION SAVED SAVIOR)
Isa 63: 1 proclaiming victory, mighty to **s**."
Mt 1: 21 because he will **s** his people
16: 25 wants to **s** their life will lose it,
Lk 19: 10 came to seek and to **s** the lost."
Jn 3: 17 but to **s** the world through him.
1Ti 1: 15 came into the world to **s** sinners—
Jas 5: 20 of their way will **s** them from death

SAVED (SAVE)
Ps 34: 6 he **s** him out of all his troubles.
Isa 45: 22 "Turn to me and be **s**, all you ends
Joel 2: 32 the name of the LORD will be **s**;
Mk 13: 13 stands firm to the end will be **s**.
16: 16 *believes and is baptized will be **s**,*
Jn 10: 9 enters through me will be **s**.
Ac 4: 12 mankind by which we must be **s**."
16: 30 "Sirs, what must I do to be **s**?"
Ro 9: 27 the sea, only the remnant will be **s**.
10: 9 him from the dead, you will be **s**.
1Co 3: 15 will suffer loss but yet will be **s**—
15: 2 By this gospel you are **s**, if you hold
Eph 2: 5 it is by grace you have been **s**.
2: 8 For it is by grace you have been **s**,
1Ti 2: 4 who wants all people to be **s**

SAVIOR (SAVE)
Ps 89: 26 Father, my God, the Rock my **S**.'
Isa 43: 11 and apart from me there is no **s**.
Hos 13: 4 no God but me, no **S** except me.
Lk 1: 47 and my spirit rejoices in God my **S**,
2: 11 town of David a **S** has been born
Jn 4: 42 that this man really is the **S**
Eph 5: 23 his body, of which he is the **S**.
1Ti 4: 10 God, who is the **S** of all people,
Titus 2: 10 about God our **S** attractive.
2: 13 the glory of our great God and **S**,
3: 4 and love of God our **S** appeared,
1Jn 4: 14 his Son to be the **S** of the world.
Jude : 25 to the only God our **S** be glory,

SCALES
Lev 19: 36 Use honest **s** and honest weights,
Da 5: 27 You have been weighed on the **s**

SCAPEGOAT (GOAT)
Lev 16: 10 it into the wilderness as a **s**.

SCARLET
Isa 1: 18 "Though your sins are like **s**,

SCATTERED
Jer 31: 10 'He who **s** Israel will gather them
Ac 8: 4 who had been **s** preached the word

SCEPTER
Rev 19: 15 "He will rule them with an iron **s**."

SCHEMES
2Co 2: 11 For we are not unaware of his **s**.
Eph 6: 11 your stand against the devil's **s**.

SCOFFERS
2Pe 3: 3 that in the last days **s** will come,

SCORPION
Rev 9: 5 of the sting of a **s** when it strikes.

SCRIPTURE (SCRIPTURES)
Jn 10: 35 and **S** cannot be set aside—
1Ti 4: 13 yourself to the public reading of **S**,
2Ti 3: 16 All **S** is God-breathed and is useful
2Pe 1: 20 that no prophecy of **S** came

SCRIPTURES (SCRIPTURE)
Lk 24: 27 in all the **S** concerning himself.
Jn 5: 39 You study the **S** diligently because
Ac 17: 11 examined the **S** every day to see

SCROLL
Eze 3: 1 eat what is before you, eat this **s**;

SEA
Ex 14: 16 the Israelites can go through the **s**
Isa 57: 20 the wicked are like the tossing **s**,
Mic 7: 19 iniquities into the depths of the **s**.
Jas 1: 6 who doubts is like a wave of the **s**,
Rev 13: 1 I saw a beast coming out of the **s**.

SEAL (SEALS)
Jn 6: 27 God the Father has placed his **s**
2Co 1: 22 set his **s** of ownership on us,
Eph 1: 13 you were marked in him with a **s**,

SEALS (SEAL)
Rev 5: 2 "Who is worthy to break the **s**
6: 1 opened the first of the seven **s**.

SEARCH (SEARCHED SEARCHES SEARCHING)
Ps 4: 4 beds, **s** your hearts and be silent.
139: 23 **S** me, God, and know my heart;
Pr 2: 4 and **s** for it as for hidden treasure,
Jer 17: 10 "I the LORD **s** the heart
Eze 34: 16 I will **s** for the lost and bring back
Lk 15: 8 and **s** carefully until she finds it?

SEARCHED (SEARCH)
Ps 139: 1 You have **s** me, LORD, and you

SEARCHES (SEARCH)
Ro 8: 27 who **s** our hearts knows the mind
1Co 2: 10 The Spirit **s** all things, even the

SEARCHING (SEARCH)
Am 8: 12 east, **s** for the word of the LORD,

SEARED
1Ti 4: 2 whose consciences have been **s** as

SEASON
2Ti 4: 2 be prepared in **s** and out of **s**;

SEAT (SEATED SEATS)
Da 7: 9 and the Ancient of Days took his **s**.
2Co 5: 10 all appear before the judgment **s**

SEATED (SEAT)
Ps 47: 8 God is **s** on his holy throne.
Isa 6: 1 high and exalted, **s** on a throne;
Col 3: 1 Christ is, **s** at the right hand of God.

SEATS (SEAT)
Lk 11: 43 you love the most important **s**

SECRET (SECRETS)
Dt 29: 29 The **s** things belong to the LORD
Jdg 16: 6 "Tell me the **s** of your great
Ps 90: 8 you, our **s** sins in the light of your
Pr 11: 13 but a trustworthy person keeps a **s**.

Mt 6: 4 so that your giving may be in **s**.
2Co 4: 2 we have renounced **s** and shameful
Php 4: 12 have learned the **s** of being content

SECRETS (SECRET)
Ps 44: 21 since he knows the **s** of the heart?
1Co 14: 25 as the **s** of their hearts are laid bare.

SECURE (SECURITY)
Ps 112: 8 Their hearts are **s**, they will have
Heb 6: 19 an anchor for the soul, firm and **s**.

SECURITY (SECURE)
Job 31: 24 or said to pure gold, 'You are my **s**,'

SEED (SEEDS)
Lk 8: 11 The **s** is the word of God.
1Co 3: 6 I planted the **s**, Apollos watered it,
2Co 9: 10 he who supplies **s** to the sower
Gal 3: 29 you are Abraham's **s**, and heirs
1Pe 1: 23 again, not of perishable **s**,

SEEDS (SEED)
Jn 12: 24 But if it dies, it produces many **s**.
Gal 3: 16 Scripture does not say "and to **s**,"

SEEK (SEEKS SELF-SEEKING)
Dt 4: 29 you will find him if you **s** him
1Ch 28: 9 If you **s** him, he will be found
2Ch 7: 14 pray and **s** my face and turn
Ps 119: 10 I **s** you with all my heart; do not let
Isa 55: 6 **S** the LORD while he may be
65: 1 found by those who did not **s** me.
Mt 6: 33 But **s** first his kingdom and his
Lk 19: 10 For the Son of Man came to **s**
Ro 10: 20 found by those who did not **s** me;
1Co 7: 27 Do not **s** to be released.

SEEKS (SEEK)
Jn 4: 23 the kind of worshipers the Father **s**.

SEER
1Sa 9: 9 of today used to be called a **s**.)

SELF-CONTROL (CONTROL)
1Co 7: 5 tempt you because of your lack of **s**.
Gal 5: 23 gentleness and **s**.
2Pe 1: 6 and to knowledge, **s**; and to **s**,

SELF-CONTROLLED (CONTROL)
1Ti 3: 2 his wife, temperate, **s**, respectable,
Titus 1: 8 what is good, who is **s**, upright,
2: 2 worthy of respect, **s**, and sound
2: 5 to be **s** and pure, to be busy
2: 6 encourage the young men to be **s**.
2: 12 to live **s**, upright and godly lives

SELF-INDULGENCE
Mt 23: 25 inside they are full of greed and **s**.

SELFISH
Ps 119: 36 statutes and not toward **s** gain.
Pr 18: 1 unfriendly person pursues **s** ends
Gal 5: 20 fits of rage, **s** ambition, dissensions,
Php 1: 17 preach Christ out of **s** ambition,
2: 3 Do nothing out of **s** ambition
Jas 3: 14 envy and **s** ambition in your hearts,
3: 16 you have envy and **s** ambition,

SELF-SEEKING (SEEK)
1Co 13: 5 it is not **s**, it is not easily angered,

SEND (SENDING SENT)
Isa 6: 8 And I said, "Here am I. **S** me!"
Mt 9: 38 to **s** out workers into his harvest
Jn 16: 7 but if I go, I will **s** him to you.

SENDING (SEND)
Jn 20: 21 the Father has sent me, I am **s** you."

SENSES
Lk 15: 17 "When he came to his **s**, he said,
1Co 15: 34 Come back to your **s** as you ought,
2Ti 2: 26 that they will come to their **s**

SENSUAL
Col 2: 23 value in restraining **s** indulgence.

SENT (SEND)
Isa 55: 11 achieve the purpose for which I **s** it.
Mt 10: 40 me welcomes the one who **s** me.
Jn 4: 34 "is to do the will of him who **s** me
Ro 10: 15 anyone preach unless they are **s**?
1Jn 4: 10 **s** his Son as an atoning sacrifice

SEPARATE (SEPARATED SEPARATES)
Mt 19: 6 has joined together, let no one **s**."
Ro 8: 35 Who shall **s** us from the love
1Co 7: 10 A wife must not **s** from her
2Co 6: 17 "Come out from them and be **s**,

SEPARATED (SEPARATE)
Isa 59: 2 your iniquities have **s** you from

SEPARATES (SEPARATE)
Pr 16: 28 and a gossip **s** close friends.

SERPENT
Ge 3: 1 Now the **s** was more crafty than
Rev 12: 9 that ancient **s** called the devil,

SERVANT (SERVANTS)
1Sa 3: 10 "Speak, for your **s** is listening."
Mt 20: 26 great among you must be your **s**,
25: 21 'Well done, good and faithful **s**!
Php 2: 7 by taking the very nature of a **s**,
2Ti 2: 24 And the Lord's **s** must not be

SERVANTS (SERVANT)
Lk 17: 10 do, should say, 'We are unworthy **s**;
Jn 15: 15 I no longer call you **s**,

SERVE (SERVICE SERVING)
Dt 10: 12 to **s** the LORD your God with all
Jos 22: 5 and to **s** him with all your heart
24: 15 household, we will **s** the LORD."
Mt 4: 10 Lord your God, and **s** him only.'"
6: 24 "No one can **s** two masters.
6: 24 You cannot **s** both God and money.
20: 28 but to **s**, and to give his life as
Eph 6: 7 **S** wholeheartedly, as if you were

SERVICE (SERVE)
1Co 12: 5 There are different kinds of **s**,
Eph 4: 12 to equip his people for works of **s**,

SERVING (SERVE)
Ro 12: 11 your spiritual fervor, **s** the Lord.
Eph 6: 7 as if you were **s** the Lord,
Col 3: 24 It is the Lord Christ you are **s**.
2Ti 2: 4 No one **s** as a soldier gets entangled

SEVEN (SEVENTH)
Ge 7: 2 Take with you **s** pairs of every kind
Jos 6: 4 march around the city **s** times,
1Ki 19: 18 Yet I reserve **s** thousand in Israel—
Pr 6: 16 hates, **s** that are detestable to him:
24: 16 though the righteous fall **s** times,
Isa 4: 1 that day **s** women will take hold
Da 9: 25 comes, there will be **s** 'sevens,'
Mt 18: 21 sins against me? Up to **s** times?"
Lk 11: 26 takes **s** other spirits more wicked
Ro 11: 4 myself **s** thousand who have not
Rev 1: 4 To the **s** churches in the province
1: 4 from the **s** spirits before his throne,
6: 1 Lamb opened the first of the **s** seals.
8: 2 I saw the **s** angels who stand before

Rev 8: 2 and **s** trumpets were given to them.
10: 4 And when the **s** thunders spoke,
15: 7 to the **s** angels **s** golden bowls filled

SEVENTH (SEVEN)
Ge 2: 2 so on the **s** day he rested from all
Ex 23: 12 but on the **s** day do not work,

SEX (SEXUAL SEXUALLY)
1Co 6: 9 nor men who have **s** with men

SEXUAL (SEX)
Mt 5: 32 except for **s** immorality, makes her
19: 9 except for **s** immorality,
1Co 6: 13 is not meant for **s** immorality
6: 18 Flee from **s** immorality.
7: 1 a man not to have **s** relations
10: 8 should not commit **s** immorality,
Eph 5: 3 not be even a hint of **s** immorality,
1Th 4: 3 you should avoid **s** immorality;

SEXUALLY (SEX)
1Co 5: 9 associate with **s** immoral people—
6: 18 but whoever sins **s**, sins against

SHADOW
Ps 36: 7 take refuge in the **s** of your wings.
Heb 10: 1 The law is only a **s** of the good

SHALLUM
King of Israel (2Ki 15:10-16).

SHAME (ASHAMED)
Ps 22: 5 they trusted and were not put to **s**.
34: 5 faces are never covered with **s**.
Pr 13: 18 discipline comes to poverty and **s**,
Heb 12: 2 scorning its **s**, and sat down

SHARE (SHARED)
Ge 21: 10 that woman's son will never **s**
Lk 3: 11 who has two shirts should **s**
Gal 4: 30 the slave woman's son will never **s**
6: 6 the word should **s** all good things
Eph 4: 28 they may have something to **s**
1Ti 6: 18 to be generous and willing to **s**.
Heb 12: 10 order that we may **s** in his holiness.
13: 16 to do good and to **s** with others,

SHARED (SHARE)
Heb 2: 14 he too **s** in their humanity so

SHARON
SS 2: 1 I am a rose of **S**, a lily

SHARPER
Heb 4: 12 **S** than any double-edged sword,

SHED (SHEDDING)
Ge 9: 6 by humans shall their blood be **s**;
Col 1: 20 through his blood, **s** on the cross.

SHEDDING (SHED)
Heb 9: 22 without the **s** of blood there is no

SHEEP
Ps 100: 3 are his people, the **s** of his pasture.
119:176 I have strayed like a lost **s**.
Isa 53: 6 We all, like **s**, have gone astray,
Jer 50: 6 "My people have been lost **s**;
Eze 34: 11 I myself will search for my **s**
Mt 9: 36 helpless, like **s** without a shepherd.
Jn 10: 3 He calls his own **s** by name
10: 15 and I lay down my life for the **s**.
10: 27 My **s** listen to my voice;
21: 17 Jesus said, "Feed my **s**.
1Pe 2: 25 For "you were like **s** going astray,"

SHELTER
Ps 61: 4 take refuge in the **s** of your wings.
91: 1 in the **s** of the Most High will rest

SHEM
Son of Noah (Ge 5:32; 6:10). Blessed (Ge 9:26). Descendants (Ge 10:21-31; 11:10-32).

SHEPHERD (SHEPHERDS)
Ps	23: 1	The Lord is my **s**, I lack nothing.
Isa	40: 11	He tends his flock like a **s**:
Jer	31: 10	will watch over his flock like a **s**.'
Eze	34: 12	a **s** looks after his scattered flock
Zec	11: 17	"Woe to the worthless **s**,
Mt	9: 36	and helpless, like sheep without a **s**.
Jn	10: 11	"I am the good **s**. The good **s** lays
	10: 16	there shall be one flock and one **s**.
1Pe	5: 4	And when the Chief **S** appears,

SHEPHERDS (SHEPHERD)
Jer	23: 1	"Woe to the **s** who are destroying
Lk	2: 8	there were **s** living out in the fields
Ac	20: 28	Be **s** of the church of God,
1Pe	5: 2	Be **s** of God's flock that is under

SHIELD
Ps	28: 7	Lord is my strength and my **s**;
Eph	6: 16	take up the **s** of faith,

SHINE (SHONE)
Ps	4: 6	Let the light of your face **s** on us.
	80: 1	between the cherubim, **s** forth
Isa	60: 1	"Arise, **s**, for your light has come,
Da	12: 3	are wise will **s** like the brightness
Mt	5: 16	let your light **s** before others,
	13: 43	the righteous will **s** like the sun
2Co	4: 6	made his light **s** in our hearts
Eph	5: 14	the dead, and Christ will **s** on you."

SHIPWRECK (SHIPWRECKED)
1Ti	1: 19	so have suffered **s** with regard

SHIPWRECKED (SHIPWRECK)
2Co	11: 25	three times I was **s**, I spent a night

SHONE (SHINE)
Mt	17: 2	His face **s** like the sun, and his
Lk	2: 9	glory of the Lord **s** around them,
Rev	21: 11	It **s** with the glory of God, and its

SHORT
Isa	59: 1	of the Lord is not too **s** to save,
Ro	3: 23	and fall **s** of the glory of God,

SHOULDERS
Isa	9: 6	the government will be on his **s**.
Lk	15: 5	finds it, he joyfully puts it on his **s**

SHOWED
1Jn	4: 9	This is how God **s** his love among

SHREWD
Mt	10: 16	Therefore be as **s** as snakes and as

SHUN
Job	28: 28	and to **s** evil is understanding."
Pr	3: 7	fear the Lord and **s** evil.

SICK
Pr	13: 12	Hope deferred makes the heart **s**,
Mt	9: 12	who need a doctor, but the **s**.
	25: 36	I was **s** and you looked after me,
Jas	5: 14	Is anyone among you **s**?

SICKLE
Joel	3: 13	Swing the **s**, for the harvest is ripe.

SIDE
Ps	91: 7	A thousand may fall at your **s**,
	124: 1	the Lord had not been on our **s**—
2Ti	4: 17	Lord stood at my **s** and gave me

SIGHT
Ps	90: 4	years in your **s** are like a day
	116: 15	in the **s** of the Lord is the death

2Co	5: 7	For we live by faith, not by **s**.
1Pe	3: 4	which is of great worth in God's **s**.

SIGN (SIGNS)
Isa	7: 14	the Lord himself will give you a **s**:

SIGNS (SIGN)
Mt	24: 24	and perform great **s** and wonders
Mk	16: 17	*these **s** will accompany those who*
Jn	3: 2	could perform the **s** you are doing
	9: 16	can a sinner perform such **s**?"
	20: 30	Jesus performed many other **s**
1Co	1: 22	Jews demand **s** and Greeks look

SILENT
Pr	17: 28	are thought wise if they keep **s**,
Isa	53: 7	as a sheep before its shearers is **s**,
Hab	2: 20	let all the earth be **s** before him.
1Co	14: 34	Women should remain **s**

SILVER
Pr	25: 11	of **s** is a ruling rightly given.
Hag	2: 8	'The **s** is mine and the gold is
1Co	3: 12	on this foundation using gold, **s**,

SIMON
1. See PETER.
2. Apostle, called the Zealot (Mt 10:4; Mk 3:18; Lk 6:15; Ac 1:13).
3. Samaritan sorcerer (Ac 8:9-24).

SIN (SINFUL SINNED SINNER SINNERS SINNING SINS)
Nu	5: 7	and must confess the **s** they have
	32: 23	sure that your **s** will find you out.
Dt	24: 16	each will die for their own **s**.
1Ki	8: 46	there is no one who does not **s**—
2Ch	7: 14	I will forgive their **s** and will heal
Ps	4: 4	Tremble and do not **s**; when you
	32: 2	is the one whose **s** the Lord does
	32: 5	And you forgave the guilt of my **s**.
	51: 2	iniquity and cleanse me from my **s**.
	66: 18	If I had cherished **s** in my heart,
	119: 11	that I might not **s** against you.
	119:133	to your word; let no **s** rule over me.
Isa	6: 7	taken away and your **s** atoned for."
Mic	7: 18	you, who pardons **s** and forgives
Jn	1: 29	who takes away the **s** of the world!
	8: 34	everyone who sins is a slave to **s**.
Ro	5: 12	just as **s** entered the world through
	5: 20	But where **s** increased,
	6: 11	count yourselves dead to **s** but alive
	6: 23	For the wages of **s** is death,
	14: 23	that does not come from faith is **s**.
2Co	5: 21	God made him who had no **s** to be **s**
Gal	6: 1	if someone is caught in a **s**,
Heb	9: 26	to do away with **s** by the sacrifice
	11: 25	to enjoy the fleeting pleasures of **s**.
	12: 1	and the **s** that so easily entangles.
1Pe	2: 22	"He committed no **s**, and no deceit
1Jn	1: 8	If we claim to be without **s**,
	3: 4	in fact, **s** is lawlessness.
	3: 5	away our sins. And in him is no **s**.
	3: 9	is born of God will continue to **s**,
	5: 18	born of God does not continue to **s**;

SINCERE
Ro	12: 9	Love must be **s**. Hate what is evil;
Heb	10: 22	us draw near to God with a **s** heart

SINFUL (SIN)
Ps	51: 5	Surely I was **s** at birth,
Ro	7: 5	the **s** passions aroused by the law
1Pe	2: 11	to abstain from **s** desires,

SINFUL NATURE See FLESH

SING (SANG SINGING SONG SONGS)
Ps 30: 4 **S** the praises of the LORD, you his
47: 6 **S** praises to God, **s** praises; **s** praises
59: 16 in the morning I will **s** of your love
89: 1 I will **s** of the LORD's great love
101: 1 I will **s** of your love and justice;
Eph 5: 19 **S** and make music from your heart

SINGING (SING)
Ps 63: 5 **s** lips my mouth will praise you.
Ac 16: 25 were praying and **s** hymns to God,

SINNED (SIN)
2Sa 12: 13 "I have **s** against the LORD."
Job 1: 5 "Perhaps my children have **s**
Ps 51: 4 have I **s** and done what is evil
Da 9: 5 we have **s** and done wrong.
Mic 7: 9 Because I have **s** against him, I will
Lk 15: 18 I have **s** against heaven and against
Ro 3: 23 for all have **s** and fall short
1Jn 1: 10 If we claim we have not **s**, we make

SINNER (SIN)
Ecc 9: 18 war, but one **s** destroys much good.
Lk 15: 7 heaven over one **s** who repents
18: 13 said, 'God, have mercy on me, a **s**.'
Jas 5: 20 Whoever turns a **s** from the error
1Pe 4: 18 become of the ungodly and the **s**?"

SINNERS (SIN)
Ps 1: 1 stand in the way that **s** take or sit
Pr 23: 17 Do not let your heart envy **s**,
Mt 9: 13 come to call the righteous, but **s**."
Ro 5: 8 While we were still **s**, Christ died
1Ti 1: 15 came into the world to save **s**—

SINNING (SIN)
Ex 20: 20 be with you to keep you from **s**."
1Co 15: 34 senses as you ought, and stop **s**;
Heb 10: 26 If we deliberately keep on **s** after
1Jn 3: 6 one who lives in him keeps on **s**.
3: 9 they cannot go on **s**, because they

SINS (SIN)
Ezr 9: 6 because our **s** are higher than our
Ps 19: 13 your servant also from willful **s**;
32: 1 are forgiven, whose **s** are covered.
103: 3 who forgives all your **s** and heals
130: 3 LORD, kept a record of **s**, Lord,
Pr 28: 13 Whoever conceals their **s** does not
Isa 1: 18 "Though your **s** are like scarlet,
43: 25 and remembers your **s** no more.
59: 2 your **s** have hidden his face
Eze 18: 4 The one who **s** is the one who will
Mt 1: 21 will save his people from their **s**."
18: 15 "If your brother or sister **s**,
Lk 11: 4 Forgive us our **s**, for we also forgive
everyone who **s** against us.
17: 3 your brother or sister **s** against you,
Ac 22: 16 be baptized and wash your **s** away,
1Co 15: 3 Christ died for our **s** according
Eph 2: 1 dead in your transgressions and **s**,
Col 2: 13 He forgave us all our **s**,
Heb 1: 3 he had provided purification for **s**,
7: 27 He sacrificed for their **s** once for all
8: 12 will remember their **s** no more."
10: 12 for all time one sacrifice for **s**,
Jas 5: 16 Therefore confess your **s** to each
5: 20 and cover over a multitude of **s**.
1Pe 2: 24 so that we might die to **s** and live
3: 18 For Christ also suffered once for **s**,
1Jn 1: 9 If we confess our **s**, he is faithful
1: 9 will forgive us our **s** and purify us
Rev 1: 5 freed us from our **s** by his blood,

SITS
Ps 99: 1 he **s** enthroned between
Isa 40: 22 He **s** enthroned above the circle
Mt 19: 28 Son of Man **s** on his glorious throne,
Rev 4: 9 thanks to him who **s** on the throne

SKIN
Job 19: 20 escaped only by the **s** of my teeth.
19: 26 And after my **s** has been destroyed,
Jer 13: 23 Can an Ethiopian change his **s**

SLAIN (SLAY)
Rev 5: 12 who was **s**, to receive power

SLANDER (SLANDERED SLANDERERS)
Lev 19: 16 spreading **s** among your people.
1Ti 5: 14 the enemy no opportunity for **s**.
Titus 3: 2 to **s** no one, to be peaceable

SLANDERED (SLANDER)
1Co 4: 13 when we are **s**, we answer kindly.

SLANDERERS (SLANDER)
Ro 1: 30 **s**, God-haters, insolent,
1Co 6: 10 nor drunkards nor **s** nor swindlers
Titus 2: 3 not to be **s** or addicted to much

SLAUGHTER
Isa 53: 7 he was led like a lamb to the **s**,

SLAVE (SLAVERY SLAVES)
Ge 21: 10 "Get rid of that **s** woman and her
Mt 20: 27 wants to be first must be your **s**—
Jn 8: 34 everyone who sins is a **s** to sin.
1Co 12: 13 whether Jews or Gentiles, **s** or free
Gal 3: 28 Jew nor Gentile, neither **s** nor free,
4: 30 the **s** woman's son will never share

SLAVERY (SLAVE)
Gal 4: 3 in **s** under the elemental spiritual

SLAVES (SLAVE)
Ro 6: 6 we should no longer be **s** to sin—
6: 22 and have become **s** of God,
2Pe 2: 19 for "people are **s** to whatever has

SLAY (SLAIN)
Job 13: 15 Though he **s** me, yet will I hope

SLEEP (SLEEPING)
Ps 121: 4 Israel will neither slumber nor **s**.
1Co 15: 51 We will not all **s**, but we will all be

SLEEPING (SLEEP)
Mk 13: 36 do not let him find you **s**.

SLOW
Ex 34: 6 and gracious God, **s** to anger,
Jas 1: 19 **s** to speak and **s** to become angry,
2Pe 3: 9 The Lord is not **s** in keeping his

SLUGGARD (SLUGGARDS)
Pr 6: 6 Go to the ant, you **s**;

SLUGGARDS (SLUGGARD)
Pr 20: 4 **S** do not plow in season;

SLUMBER
Ps 121: 3 he who watches over you will not **s**;
Pr 6: 10 little **s**, a little folding of the hands
Ro 13: 11 for you to wake up from your **s**,

SNAKE (SNAKES)
Nu 21: 8 "Make a **s** and put it up on a pole;
Pr 23: 32 In the end it bites like a **s**
Jn 3: 14 lifted up the **s** in the wilderness,

SNAKES (SNAKE)
Mt 10: 16 Therefore be as shrewd as **s** and as
Mk 16: 18 *they will pick up* **s**

SNATCH (SNATCHING)
Jn 10: 28 no one will **s** them out of my hand.

SNATCHING (SNATCH)
Jude : 23 save others by **s** them from the fire;

SNOW
Ps 51: 7 me, and I will be whiter than **s**.

SOAR
Isa 40: 31 They will **s** on wings like eagles;

SODOM
Ge 19: 24 rained down burning sulfur on **S**
Ro 9: 29 we would have become like **S**,

SOIL
Ge 4: 2 kept flocks, and Cain worked the **s**.
Mt 13: 23 the seed falling on good **s** refers

SOLDIER
1Co 9: 7 Who serves as a **s** at his own
2Ti 2: 3 like a good **s** of Christ Jesus.

SOLE
Dt 28: 65 resting place for the **s** of your foot.
Isa 1: 6 From the **s** of your foot to the top

SOLID
2Ti 2: 19 God's **s** foundation stands firm,
Heb 5: 12 You need milk, not **s** food!

SOLOMON
 Son of David by Bathsheba; king of Judah (2Sa 12:24; 1Ch 3:5, 10). Appointed king by David (1Ki 1); adversaries Adonijah, Joab, Shimei killed by Benaiah (1Ki 2). Asked for wisdom (1Ki 3; 2Ch 1). Judged between two prostitutes (1Ki 3:16–28). Built temple (1Ki 5–7; 2Ch 2–5); prayer of dedication (1Ki 8; 2Ch 6). Visited by Queen of Sheba (1Ki 10; 2Ch 9). Wives turned his heart from God (1Ki 11:1–13). Jeroboam rebelled against (1Ki 11:26–40). Death (1Ki 11:41–43; 2Ch 9:29–31).
 Proverbs of (1Ki 4:32; Pr 1:1; 10:1; 25:1); psalms of (Ps 72; 127); song of (SS 1:1).

SON (SONS)
Ge 22: 2 said, "Take your **s**, your only **s**,
Ex 11: 5 Every firstborn **s** in Egypt will die,
Dt 21: 18 rebellious **s** who does not obey his
Ps 2: 7 He said to me, "You are my **s**;
 2: 12 Kiss his **s**, or he will be angry
Pr 10: 1 A wise **s** brings joy to his father,
Isa 7: 14 will conceive and give birth to a **s**,
Hos 11: 1 and out of Egypt I called my **s**.
Mt 2: 15 "Out of Egypt I called my **s**."
 3: 17 said, "This is my **S**, whom I love;
 11: 27 knows the **S** except the Father,
 11: 27 knows the Father except the **S**
 16: 16 Messiah, the **S** of the living God."
 17: 5 said, "This is my **S**, whom I love;
 20: 18 the **S** of Man will be delivered over
 24: 30 appear the sign of the **S** of Man
 24: 44 because the **S** of Man will come
 27: 54 "Surely he was the **S** of God!"
 28: 19 and of the **S** and of the Holy Spirit,
Mk 10: 45 even the **S** of Man did not come
 14: 62 you will see the **S** of Man sitting
Lk 9: 58 the **S** of Man has no place to lay his
 18: 8 when the **S** of Man comes, will he
 19: 10 For the **S** of Man came to seek
Jn 3: 14 so the **S** of Man must be lifted up,
 3: 16 that he gave his one and only **S**,
 17: 1 Glorify your **S**, that your **S** may
Ro 8: 29 conformed to the image of his **S**,
 8: 32 He who did not spare his own **S**,
1Co 15: 28 the **S** himself will be made subject
Gal 4: 30 for the slave woman's **s** will never
1Th 1: 10 and to wait for his **S** from heaven,
Heb 1: 2 days he has spoken to us by his **S**,
 10: 29 punished who has trampled the **S**

1Jn 1: 7 Jesus, his **S**, purifies us from all sin.
 4: 9 only **S** into the world that we might
 5: 5 believes that Jesus is the **S** of God.
 5: 11 eternal life, and this life is in his **S**.

SONG (SING)
Ps 40: 3 He put a new **s** in my mouth,
 96: 1 Sing to the LORD a new **s**;
 149: 1 Sing to the LORD a new **s**,
Isa 49: 13 burst into **s**, you mountains!
 55: 12 hills will burst into **s** before you,
Rev 5: 9 And they sang a new **s**, saying:
 15: 3 sang the **s** of God's servant Moses

SONGS (SING)
Job 35: 10 Maker, who gives **s** in the night,
Ps 100: 2 come before him with joyful **s**.
Eph 5: 19 hymns, and **s** from the Spirit.
Jas 5: 13 Let them sing **s** of praise.

SONS (SON)
Joel 2: 28 **s** and daughters will prophesy,
2Co 6: 18 you will be my **s** and daughters,

SORROW
Jer 31: 12 garden, and they will **s** no more.
Ro 9: 2 I have great **s** and unceasing
2Co 7: 10 Godly **s** brings repentance that

SOUL (SOULS)
Dt 6: 5 and with all your **s** and with all
 10: 12 all your heart and with all your **s**,
Jos 22: 5 all your heart and with all your **s**."
Ps 23: 3 he refreshes my **s**. He guides me
 42: 1 of water, so my **s** pants for you,
 42: 11 Why, my **s**, are you downcast?
 103: 1 Praise the LORD, my **s**;
Pr 13: 19 A longing fulfilled is sweet to the **s**,
Mt 10: 28 of the One who can destroy both **s**
 16: 26 the whole world, yet forfeit their **s**?
 22: 37 with all your **s** and with all your
Heb 4: 12 it penetrates even to dividing **s**

SOULS (SOUL)
Jer 6: 16 and you will find rest for your **s**.
Mt 11: 29 and you will find rest for your **s**.

SOUND
1Co 14: 8 the trumpet does not **s** a clear call,
 15: 52 the trumpet will **s**, the dead will
2Ti 4: 3 will not put up with **s** doctrine.

SOVEREIGN
Da 4: 25 Most High is **s** over all kingdoms

SOW (SOWS)
Job 4: 8 and those who **s** trouble reap it.
Mt 6: 26 they do not **s** or reap or store away
2Pe 2: 22 "A **s** that is washed returns to her

SOWS (SOW)
2Co 9: 6 and whoever **s** generously will

SPARE (SPARES)
Ro 8: 32 He who did not **s** his own Son,
 11: 21 God did not **s** the natural branches,

SPARES (SPARE)
Pr 13: 24 Whoever **s** the rod hates their

SPEARS
Isa 2: 4 and their **s** into pruning hooks.
Joel 3: 10 and your pruning hooks into **s**.
Mic 4: 3 and their **s** into pruning hooks.

SPECTACLE
1Co 4: 9 have been made a **s** to the whole
Col 2: 15 he made a public **s** of them,

SPIN
Mt 6: 28 They do not labor or **s**.

SPIRIT (SPIRITS SPIRITUAL)
Ge	1: 2	the **S** of God was hovering over
	6: 3	said, "My **S** will not contend
2Ki	2: 9	inherit a double portion of your **s**,"
Job	33: 4	The **S** of God has made me;
Ps	31: 5	Into your hands I commit my **s**;
	51: 10	and renew a steadfast **s** within me.
	51: 11	or take your Holy **S** from me.
	51: 17	My sacrifice, O God, is a broken **s**;
	139: 7	Where can I go from your **S**?
Isa	57: 15	to revive the spirit of the lowly
	63: 10	rebelled and grieved his Holy **S**.
Eze	11: 19	heart and put a new **s** in them;
	36: 26	a new heart and put a new **s** in you;
Joel	2: 28	I will pour out my **S** on all people.
Zec	4: 6	but by my **S**,' says the LORD
Mt	1: 18	to be pregnant through the Holy **S**.
	3: 11	He will baptize you with the Holy **S**
	3: 16	he saw the **S** of God descending
	4: 1	led by the **S** into the wilderness
	5: 3	"Blessed are the poor in **s**, for
	26: 41	The **s** is willing, but the flesh is
	28: 19	and of the Son and of the Holy **S**,
Lk	1: 80	child grew and became strong in **s**;
	11: 13	in heaven give the Holy **S** to those
Jn	4: 24	God is **s**, and his worshipers must worship in the **S**
	7: 39	that time the **S** had not been given,
	14: 26	the Holy **S**, whom the Father will
	16: 13	But when he, the **S** of truth, comes,
	20: 22	and said, "Receive the Holy **S**
Ac	1: 5	will be baptized with the Holy **S**."
	2: 4	tongues as the **S** enabled them.
	2: 38	will receive the gift of the Holy **S**.
	6: 3	who are known to be full of the **S**
	19: 2	"Did you receive the Holy **S**
Ro	8: 9	if indeed the **S** of God lives in you.
	8: 26	the **S** helps us in our weakness.
1Co	2: 10	God has revealed to us by his **S**.
	2: 10	The **S** searches all things,
	2: 14	without the **S** does not accept
	3: 1	as people who live by the **S** but as
	6: 19	bodies are temples of the Holy **S**,
	12: 1	Now about the gifts of the **S**,
	12: 13	we were all baptized by one **S**
	12: 13	and we were all given the one **S**
	14: 1	and eagerly desire gifts of the **S**,
2Co	3: 6	the letter kills, but the **S** gives life.
	5: 5	who has given us the **S** as a deposit,
Gal	5: 16	say, walk by the **S**, and you will not
	5: 22	But the fruit of the **S** is love, joy,
	5: 25	Since we live by the **S**, let us keep
Gal	6: 1	who live by the **S** should restore
Eph	1: 13	with a seal, the promised Holy **S**,
	4: 30	do not grieve the Holy **S** of God,
	5: 18	Instead, be filled with the **S**,
	5: 19	hymns, and songs from the **S**.
	6: 17	of salvation and the sword of the **S**,
1Th	5: 19	Do not quench the **S**.
2Th	2: 13	the sanctifying work of the **S**
Heb	4: 12	even to dividing soul and **s**,
1Pe	3: 4	beauty of a gentle and quiet **s**,
2Pe	1: 21	were carried along by the Holy **S**.
1Jn	4: 1	do not believe every **s**, but test

SPIRITS (SPIRIT)
1Co	12: 10	another distinguishing between **s**,
	14: 32	The **s** of prophets are subject
1Jn	4: 1	but test the **s** to see whether they

SPIRITUAL (SPIRIT)
Ro	12: 11	but keep your **s** fervor,
1Co	2: 13	the Spirit, explaining **s** realities
	15: 44	a natural body, it is raised a **s** body.

Eph	1: 3	realms with every **s** blessing
	6: 12	against the **s** forces of evil
1Pe	2: 2	crave pure **s** milk, so that by it you
	2: 5	offering **s** sacrifices acceptable

SPLENDOR
1Ch	16: 29	the LORD in the **s** of his holiness.
	29: 11	glory and the majesty and the **s**,
Job	37: 22	of the north he comes in golden **s**;
Ps	29: 2	the LORD in the **s** of his holiness.
	45: 3	clothe yourself with **s** and majesty.
	96: 6	**S** and majesty are before him;
	96: 9	the LORD in the **s** of his holiness;
	104: 1	you are clothed with **s** and majesty.
	145: 5	of the glorious **s** of your majesty—
Isa	61: 3	the LORD for the display of his **s**.
	63: 1	robed in **s**, striding forward
Lk	9: 30	Elijah, appeared in glorious **s**,
2Th	2: 8	and destroy by the **s** of his coming.

SPOIL
Ps	119:162	promise like one who finds great **s**.

SPOTLESS
2Pe	3: 14	make every effort to be found **s**,

SPREAD (SPREADING)
Ac	12: 24	the word of God continued to **s**
	19: 20	way the word of the Lord **s** widely

SPREADING (SPREAD)
1Th	3: 2	in God's service in **s** the gospel

SPRING
Jer	2: 13	forsaken me, the **s** of living water,
Jn	4: 14	in them a **s** of water welling
Jas	3: 12	can a salt **s** produce fresh water.

SPUR
Heb	10: 24	how we may **s** one another

SPURNS
Pr	15: 5	A fool **s** a parent's discipline,

STAFF
Ps	23: 4	your rod and your **s**, they comfort

STAKES
Isa	54: 2	your cords, strengthen your **s**.

STAND (STANDING STANDS)
Ex	14: 13	**S** firm and you will see
2Ch	20: 17	**s** firm and see the deliverance
Ps	1: 5	Therefore the wicked will not **s**
	40: 2	rock and gave me a firm place to **s**.
	119:120	fear of you; I **s** in awe of your laws.
Eze	22: 30	**s** before me in the gap on behalf
Zec	14: 4	day his feet will **s** on the Mount
Mt	12: 25	divided against itself will not **s**.
Ro	14: 10	we will all **s** before God's judgment
1Co	15: 58	dear brothers and sisters, **s** firm.
Eph	6: 14	**S** firm then, with the belt of truth
2Th	2: 15	firm and hold fast to the teachings
Jas	5: 8	be patient and **s** firm,
Rev	3: 20	I **s** at the door and knock.

STANDING (STAND)
Ex	3: 5	where you are **s** is holy ground."
Jos	5: 15	the place where you are **s** is holy."
1Pe	5: 9	Resist him, **s** firm in the faith,

STANDS (STAND)
Ps	89: 2	that your love **s** firm forever,
	119: 89	it **s** firm in the heavens.
2Ti	2: 19	God's solid foundation **s** firm,

STAR (STARS)
Nu	24: 17	A **s** will come out of Jacob;
Rev	22: 16	David, and the bright Morning **S**."

STARS (STAR)
Da 12: 3 like the **s** for ever and ever.
Php 2: 15 you will shine among them like **s**

STEADFAST
Ps 51: 10 and renew a **s** spirit within me.
Isa 26: 3 peace those whose minds are **s**,
1Pe 5: 10 and make you strong, firm and **s**.

STEAL
Ex 20: 15 "You shall not **s**.
Mt 19: 18 you shall not **s**, you shall not give
Eph 4: 28 has been stealing must **s** no longer,

STEP (STEPS)
Gal 5: 25 let us keep in **s** with the Spirit.

STEPS (STEP)
Pr 16: 9 but the LORD establishes their **s**.
Jer 10: 23 it is not for them to direct their **s**.
1Pe 2: 21 that you should follow in his **s**.

STICKS
Pr 18: 24 there is a friend who **s** closer than

STIFF-NECKED
Ex 34: 9 Although this is a **s** people,

STILL
Ps 46: 10 "Be **s**, and know that I am God;
Zec 2: 13 Be **s** before the LORD,

STIRS
Pr 6: 19 a person who **s** up conflict
10: 12 Hatred **s** up conflict, but love
15: 1 wrath, but a harsh word **s** up anger.
29: 22 An angry person **s** up conflict,

STONE (CORNERSTONE MILLSTONE)
1Sa 17: 50 the Philistine with a sling and a **s**;
Isa 8: 14 and Judah he will be a **s** that causes
Eze 11: 19 remove from them their heart of **s**
Mk 16: 3 "Who will roll the **s** away
Lk 4: 3 God, tell this **s** to become bread."
Jn 8: 7 *the first to throw a **s** at her."*
2Co 3: 3 not on tablets of **s** but on tablets

STORE
Pr 10: 14 The wise **s** up knowledge,
Mt 6: 19 "Do not **s** up for yourselves

STOREHOUSE (HOUSE)
Mal 3: 10 Bring the whole tithe into the **s**,

STRAIGHT
Pr 3: 6 and he will make your paths **s**.
4: 25 Let your eyes look **s** ahead;
15: 21 understanding keeps a **s** course.
Jn 1: 23 'Make **s** the way for the Lord.'"

STRAIN
Mt 23: 24 You **s** out a gnat but swallow

STRANGER
Mt 25: 35 I was a **s** and you invited me in,
Jn 10: 5 But they will never follow a **s**;

STRAPS
Mk 1: 7 **s** of whose sandals I am not worthy

STREAMS
Ps 1: 3 person is like a tree planted by **s**
46: 4 a river whose **s** make glad the city
Ecc 1: 7 All **s** flow into the sea, yet the sea is

STRENGTH (STRONG)
Ex 15: 2 "The LORD is my **s** and my
Dt 6: 5 all your soul and with all your **s**.
2Sa 22: 33 It is God who arms me with **s**
Ne 8: 10 the joy of the LORD is your **s**."

Ps 28: 7 The LORD is my **s** and my shield;
46: 1 God is our refuge and **s**,
96: 7 ascribe to the LORD glory and **s**.
118: 14 The LORD is my **s** and my
147: 10 pleasure is not in the **s** of the horse,
Isa 40: 31 in the LORD will renew their **s**.
Mk 12: 30 all your mind and with all your **s**.'
1Co 1: 25 of God is stronger than human **s**.
Php 4: 13 this through him who gives me **s**.
1Pe 4: 11 do so with the **s** God provides,

STRENGTHEN (STRONG)
2Ch 16: 9 to **s** those whose hearts are fully
Ps 119: 28 **s** me according to your word.
Isa 35: 3 **S** the feeble hands, steady the
41: 10 I will **s** you and help you;
Eph 3: 16 of his glorious riches he may **s** you
2Th 2: 17 and **s** you in every good deed
Heb 12: 12 **s** your feeble arms and weak knees.

STRIFE
Pr 20: 3 It is to one's honor to avoid **s**,
22: 10 out the mocker, and out goes **s**;

STRIKE
Ge 3: 15 your head, and you will **s** his heel."
Zec 13: 7 "**S** the shepherd, and the sheep will
Mt 26: 31 "'I will **s** the shepherd,

STRONG (STRENGTH STRENGTHEN)
Dt 31: 6 Be **s** and courageous. Do not be
1Ki 2: 2 "So be **s**, act like a man,
Pr 31: 17 her arms are **s** for her tasks.
SS 8: 6 for love is as **s** as death, its jealousy
Lk 2: 40 And the child grew and became **s**;
Ro 15: 1 We who are **s** ought to bear
1Co 1: 27 things of the world to shame the **s**.
16: 13 in the faith; be courageous; be **s**.
2Co 12: 10 For when I am weak, then I am **s**.
Eph 6: 10 be **s** in the Lord and in his mighty

STRUGGLE
Ro 15: 30 join me in my **s** by praying to God
Eph 6: 12 For our **s** is not against flesh
Heb 12: 4 In your **s** against sin, you have not

STUDY
Ezr 7: 10 Ezra had devoted himself to the **s**
Ecc 12: 12 end, and much **s** wearies the body.
Jn 5: 39 You **s** the Scriptures diligently

STUMBLE (STUMBLING)
Ps 37: 24 though he may **s**, he will not fall,
119:165 law, and nothing can make them **s**.
Isa 8: 14 be a stone that causes people to **s**
Jer 31: 9 a level path where they will not **s**,
Eze 7: 19 for it has caused them to **s** into sin.
1Co 10: 32 Do not cause anyone to **s**,
1Pe 2: 8 "A stone that causes people to **s**

STUMBLING (STUMBLE)
Ro 14: 13 your mind not to put any **s** block
1Co 8: 9 rights does not become a **s** block
2Co 6: 3 We put no **s** block in anyone's path,

SUBDUE
Ge 1: 28 fill the earth and **s** it.

SUBJECT (SUBJECTED)
1Co 14: 32 of prophets are **s** to the control
15: 28 the Son himself will be made **s**
Titus 2: 5 and to be **s** to their husbands,
2: 9 slaves to be **s** to their masters
3: 1 Remind the people to be **s** to rulers

SUBJECTED (SUBJECT)
Ro 8: 20 the creation was **s** to frustration,

SUBMISSION (SUBMIT)
1Co 14: 34 but must be in **s**, as the law says.
1Ti 2: 11 learn in quietness and full **s**.

SUBMISSIVE (SUBMIT)
Jas 3: 17 considerate, **s**, full of mercy

SUBMIT (SUBMISSION SUBMISSIVE SUBMITS)
Ro 13: 5 necessary to **s** to the authorities,
1Co 16: 16 to **s** to such people and to everyone
Eph 5: 21 **S** to one another out of reverence
Col 3: 18 **s** yourselves to your husbands, as is
Heb 12: 9 How much more should we **s**
13: 17 leaders and **s** to their authority,
Jas 4: 7 **S** yourselves, then, to God.
1Pe 2: 18 reverent fear of God **s** yourselves

SUBMITS (SUBMIT)
Eph 5: 24 Now as the church **s** to Christ,

SUCCESSFUL
Jos 1: 7 that you may be **s** wherever you go.
2Ki 18: 7 he was **s** in whatever he undertook.
2Ch 20: 20 in his prophets and you will be **s**."

SUFFER (SUFFERED SUFFERING SUFFERINGS SUFFERS)
Isa 53: 10 to crush him and cause him to **s**,
Mk 8: 31 Son of Man must **s** many things
Lk 24: 26 the Messiah have to **s** these things
24: 46 The Messiah will **s** and rise
Php 1: 29 believe in him, but also to **s** for him,
1Pe 4: 16 if you **s** as a Christian, do not be

SUFFERED (SUFFER)
Heb 2: 9 and honor because he **s** death,
2: 18 Because he himself **s** when he was
1Pe 2: 21 called, because Christ **s** for you,

SUFFERING (SUFFER)
Isa 53: 3 a man of **s**, and familiar with pain.
Ac 5: 41 been counted worthy of **s** disgrace
2Ti 1: 8 join with me in **s** for the gospel,

SUFFERINGS (SUFFER)
Ro 8: 17 if indeed we share in his **s** in order
8: 18 that our present **s** are not worth
2Co 1: 5 share abundantly in the **s** of Christ,
Php 3: 10 and participation in his **s**,

SUFFERS (SUFFER)
Pr 13: 20 for a companion of fools **s** harm.
1Co 12: 26 If one part **s**, every part **s** with it;

SUFFICIENT
2Co 12: 9 said to me, "My grace is **s** for you,

SUITABLE
Ge 2: 18 I will make a helper **s** for him."

SUN
Ecc 1: 9 there is nothing new under the **s**.
Mal 4: 2 the **s** of righteousness will rise
Mt 5: 45 He causes his **s** to rise on the evil
17: 2 His face shone like the **s**, and his
Rev 1: 16 His face was like the **s** shining in
21: 23 The city does not need the **s**

SUPERIOR
Heb 1: 4 as the name he has inherited is **s**
8: 6 he is mediator is **s** to the old one,

SUPREMACY
Col 1: 18 in everything he might have the **s**.

SURE
Nu 32: 23 you may be **s** that your sin will find
Dt 6: 17 Be **s** to keep the commands
14: 22 Be **s** to set aside a tenth of all
Isa 28: 16 cornerstone for a **s** foundation;

SURPASS (SURPASSES SURPASSING)
Pr 31: 29 noble things, but you **s** them all."

SURPASSES (SURPASS)
Mt 5: 20 that unless your righteousness **s**
Eph 3: 19 to know this love that **s** knowledge

SURPASSING (SURPASS)
Ps 150: 2 praise him for his **s** greatness.
2Co 3: 10 in comparison with the **s** glory.
9: 14 of the **s** grace God has given you.
Php 3: 8 a loss because of the **s** worth

SURROUNDED
Heb 12: 1 since we are **s** by such a great cloud

SUSPENDS
Job 26: 7 he **s** the earth over nothing.

SUSTAINING (SUSTAINS)
Heb 1: 3 **s** all things by his powerful word.

SUSTAINS (SUSTAINING)
Ps 18: 35 shield, and your right hand **s** me;
146: 9 the foreigner and **s** the fatherless
147: 6 The LORD **s** the humble but casts
Isa 50: 4 to know the word that **s** the weary.

SWALLOWED
1Co 15: 54 "Death has been **s** up in victory."
2Co 5: 4 so that what is mortal may be **s**

SWEAR
Mt 5: 34 I tell you, do not **s** an oath at all:

SWORD (SWORDS)
Ps 45: 3 Gird your **s** on your side,
Mt 10: 34 not come to bring peace, but a **s**.
26: 52 all who draw the **s** will die by the **s**.
Lk 2: 35 a **s** will pierce your own soul too."
Ro 13: 4 for rulers do not bear the **s** for no
Eph 6: 17 of salvation and the **s** of the Spirit,
Heb 4: 12 Sharper than any double-edged **s**,
Rev 1: 16 was a sharp, double-edged **s**.

SWORDS (SWORD)
Pr 12: 18 words of the reckless pierce like **s**,
Isa 2: 4 They will beat their **s**
Joel 3: 10 Beat your plowshares into **s**

SYMPATHETIC
1Pe 3: 8 be **s**, love one another,

SYNAGOGUE
Lk 4: 16 the Sabbath day he went into the **s**,
Ac 17: 2 Paul went into the **s**, and on three

TABERNACLE
Ex 40: 34 the glory of the LORD filled the **t**.

TABLE (TABLES)
Ps 23: 5 You prepare a **t** before me

TABLES (TABLE)
Ac 6: 2 word of God in order to wait on **t**.

TABLET (TABLETS)
Pr 3: 3 write them on the **t** of your heart.
7: 3 write them on the **t** of your heart.

TABLETS (TABLET)
Ex 31: 18 Sinai, he gave him the two **t**
Dt 10: 5 put the **t** in the ark I had made,
2Co 3: 3 not on **t** of stone but on **t** of human

TAKE (TAKEN TAKES TAKING TOOK)
Dt 12: 32 do not add to it or **t** away from it.
31: 26 "**T** this Book of the Law and place
Job 23: 10 But he knows the way that I **t**;
Ps 49: 17 for they will **t** nothing with them
51: 11 or **t** your Holy Spirit from me.

Mt 10: 38 Whoever does not **t** up their cross
    11: 29 **T** my yoke upon you and learn
    16: 24 deny themselves and **t** up their cross

TAKEN (TAKE)
Lev 6: 4 they have stolen or **t** by extortion,
Isa 6: 7 your guilt is **t** away and your sin
Mt 24: 40 one will be **t** and the other left.
Mk 16: 19 *them, he was **t** up into heaven*
1Ti 3: 16 on in the world, was **t** up in glory.

TAKES (TAKE)
1Ki 20: 11 not boast like one who **t** it off.'"
Jn 1: 29 who **t** away the sin of the world!
Rev 22: 19 if anyone **t** words away from this

TAKING (TAKE)
Php 2: 7 nothing by **t** the very nature

TALENT See BAGS

TAME
Jas 3: 8 no human being can **t** the tongue.

TASK
Mk 13: 34 each with their assigned **t**, and tells
Ac 20: 24 complete the **t** the Lord Jesus has
1Co 3: 5 the Lord has assigned to each his **t**.
2Co 2: 16 And who is equal to such a **t**?

TASTE (TASTED)
Ps 34: 8 **T** and see that the LORD is good;
Col 2: 21 Do not **t**! Do not touch!"?
Heb 2: 9 God he might **t** death for everyone.

TASTED (TASTE)
1Pe 2: 3 you have **t** that the Lord is good.

TAUGHT (TEACH)
Mt 7: 29 because he **t** as one who had
1Co 2: 13 but in words **t** by the Spirit,
Gal 1: 12 it from any man, nor was I **t** it;

TAX (TAXES)
Mt 22: 17 to pay the imperial **t** to Caesar

TAXES (TAX)
Ro 13: 7 you owe them: If you owe **t**, pay **t**;

TEACH (TAUGHT TEACHER TEACHERS TEACHES
    TEACHING)
Ex 33: 13 **t** me your ways so I may know you
Dt 4: 9 **T** them to your children and to
    8: 3 to **t** you that man does not live
    11: 19 **T** them to your children,
1Sa 12: 23 I will **t** you the way that is good
Ps 32: 8 **t** you in the way you should go;
    51: 13 I will **t** transgressors your ways,
    90: 12 **T** us to number our days, that we
    143: 10 **T** me to do your will, for you are
Jer 31: 34 longer will they **t** their neighbor,
Lk 11: 1 "Lord, **t** us to pray, just as John
Jn 14: 26 will **t** you all things and will
1Ti 2: 12 I do not permit a woman to **t**
    3: 2 respectable, hospitable, able to **t**,
Titus 2: 1 **t** what is appropriate to sound
Heb 8: 11 longer will they **t** their neighbor,
Jas 3: 1 that we who **t** will be judged more
1Jn 2: 27 you do not need anyone to **t** you.

TEACHER (TEACH)
Mt 10: 24 "The student is not above the **t**,
    23: 8 for you have one **T**, and you are
Jn 13: 14 your Lord and **T**, have washed

TEACHERS (TEACH)
1Co 12: 28 prophets, third **t**, then miracles,
Eph 4: 11 the evangelists, the pastors and **t**,
Heb 5: 12 by this time you ought to be **t**,

TEACHES (TEACH)
1Ti 6: 3 If anyone **t** otherwise and does not

TEACHING (TEACH)
Pr 1: 8 and do not forsake your mother's **t**.
Mt 28: 20 **t** them to obey everything I have
Jn 7: 17 out whether my **t** comes from God
    14: 23 who loves me will obey my **t**.
1Ti 4: 13 of Scripture, to preaching and to **t**.
2Ti 3: 16 is God-breathed and is useful for **t**,
Titus 2: 7 In your **t** show integrity,

TEAR (TEARS)
Rev 7: 17 God will wipe away every **t**

TEARS (TEAR)
Ps 126: 5 Those who sow with **t** will reap
Php 3: 18 and now tell you again even with **t**,

TEETH (TOOTH)
Mt 8: 12 will be weeping and gnashing of **t**."

TEMPERATE
1Ti 3: 2 reproach, faithful to his wife, **t**,
    3: 11 not malicious talkers but **t**
Titus 2: 2 Teach the older men to be **t**,

TEMPEST
Ps 55: 8 shelter, far from the **t** and storm."

TEMPLE (TEMPLES)
1Ki 8: 27 How much less this **t** I have built!
Hab 2: 20 The LORD is in his holy **t**;
1Co 3: 16 that you yourselves are God's **t**
2Co 6: 16 For we are the **t** of the living God.

TEMPLES (TEMPLE)
Ac 17: 24 does not live in **t** built by human
1Co 6: 19 your bodies are **t** of the Holy Spirit,

TEMPT (TEMPTATION TEMPTED)
1Co 7: 5 Satan will not **t** you because of

TEMPTATION (TEMPT)
Mt 6: 13 lead us not into **t**, but deliver us
    26: 41 pray so that you will not fall into **t**.
1Co 10: 13 No **t** has overtaken you except

TEMPTED (TEMPT)
Mt 4: 1 the wilderness to be **t** by the devil.
1Co 10: 13 not let you be **t** beyond what you
Heb 2: 18 he himself suffered when he was **t**,
    2: 18 able to help those who are being **t**.
    4: 15 but we have one who has been **t**
Jas 1: 13 For God cannot be **t** by evil,

TEN (TENTH TITHE TITHES)
Ex 34: 28 the **T** Commandments.
Ps 91: 7 side, **t** thousand at your right hand,
Mt 25: 28 give it to the one who has **t** bags.
Lk 15: 8 suppose a woman has **t** silver coins

TENTH (TEN)
Dt 14: 22 Be sure to set aside a **t** of all

TERRIBLE (TERROR)
2Ti 3: 1 There will be **t** times in the last

TERROR (TERRIBLE)
Ps 91: 5 You will not fear the **t** of night,
Lk 21: 26 People will faint from **t**,
Ro 13: 3 rulers hold no **t** for those who do

TEST (TESTED TESTS)
Dt 6: 16 your God to the **t** as you did
Ps 139: 23 **t** me and know my anxious
Ro 12: 2 you will be able to **t** and approve
1Co 3: 13 the fire will **t** the quality of each
1Jn 4: 1 **t** the spirits to see whether they are

TESTED (TEST)
Ge 22: 1 Some time later God **t** Abraham.

Job 23: 10 when he has **t** me, I will come forth
Pr   27: 21 but people are **t** by their praise.
1Ti   3: 10 They must first be **t**;

TESTIFY (TESTIMONY)
Jn   5: 39 These are the very Scriptures that **t**

TESTIMONY (TESTIFY)
Isa   8: 20 instruction and the **t** of warning.
Lk   18: 20 you shall not give false **t**,
2Ti   1: 8 be ashamed of the **t** about our Lord

TESTS (TEST)
Pr   17: 3 for gold, but the LORD **t** the heart.
1Th   2: 4 people but God, who **t** our hearts.

THADDAEUS
      Apostle (Mt 10:3; Mk 3:18); probably also known as
Judas son of James (Lk 6:16; Ac 1:13).

THANKFUL (THANKS)
Heb 12: 28 let us be **t**, and so worship God

THANKS (THANKFUL THANKSGIVING)
Ne   12: 31 assigned two large choirs to give **t**.
Ps 100: 4 give **t** to him and praise his name.
1Co 15: 57 But **t** be to God! He gives us
2Co   2: 14 But **t** be to God, who always leads
      9: 15 **T** be to God for his indescribable
1Th   5: 18 give **t** in all circumstances;

THANKSGIVING (THANKS)
Ps   95: 2 Let us come before him with **t**
     100: 4 Enter his gates with **t** and his
Php   4: 6 **t**, present your requests to God.
1Ti   4: 3 to be received with **t** by those who

THIEF (THIEVES)
1Th   5: 2 of the Lord will come like a **t**
Rev 16: 15 "Look, I come like a **t**!

THIEVES (THIEF)
1Co   6: 10 nor **t** nor the greedy nor drunkards

THINK (THOUGHT THOUGHTS)
Ro   12: 3 Do not **t** of yourself more highly
Php   4: 8 **t** about such things.

THIRST (THIRSTY)
Ps   69: 21 food and gave me vinegar for my **t**.
Mt   5: 6 hunger and **t** for righteousness,
Jn   4: 14 the water I give them will never **t**.

THIRSTY (THIRST)
Isa 55: 1 all you who are **t**,
Jn   7: 37 "Let anyone who is **t** come to me
Rev 22: 17 Let the one who is **t** come;

THOMAS
      Apostle (Mt 10:3; Mk 3:18; Lk 6:15; Jn 11:16; 14:5; 21:2;
Ac 1:13). Doubted resurrection (Jn 20:24–28).

THORN (THORNS)
2Co 12: 7 I was given a **t** in my flesh,

THORNS (THORN)
Nu   33: 55 in your eyes and **t** in your sides.
Mt   27: 29 twisted together a crown of **t** and
Heb   6: 8 land that produces **t** and thistles is

THOUGHT (THINK)
Pr   14: 15 the prudent give **t** to their steps.
1Co 13: 11 I talked like a child, I **t** like a child,

THOUGHTS (THINK)
Ps 139: 23 test me and know my anxious **t**.
Isa 55: 8 "For my **t** are not your **t**, neither
Heb   4: 12 it judges the **t** and attitudes

THREE
Ecc   4: 12 of **t** strands is not quickly broken.

Mt   12: 40 the Son of Man will be **t** days and **t**
             nights in the heart of the earth.
     18: 20 where two or **t** gather in my name,
     27: 63 said, 'After **t** days I will rise again.'
1Co 13: 13 And now these **t** remain:
     14: 27 or at the most **t**—should speak,
2Co 13: 1 testimony of two or **t** witnesses."

THRESHING
2Sa 24: 18 altar to the LORD on the **t** floor

THRONE (ENTHRONED)
2Sa   7: 16 your **t** will be established
Ps   45: 6 Your **t**, O God, will last for ever
     47: 8 God is seated on his holy **t**.
Isa   6: 1 high and exalted, seated on a **t**;
     66: 1 "Heaven is my **t**, and the earth is
Heb   4: 16 then approach God's **t** of grace
     12: 2 at the right hand of the **t** of God.
Rev   4: 10 They lay their crowns before the **t**
     20: 11 I saw a great white **t** and him who
     22: 3 The **t** of God and of the Lamb will

THROW
Jn   8: 7 *the first to t a stone at her."*
Heb 10: 35 So do not **t** away your confidence;
     12: 1 let us **t** off everything that hinders

THWART
Isa 14: 27 has purposed, and who can **t** him?

TIBNI
      King of Israel (1Ki 16:21–22).

TIME (TIMES)
Est   4: 14 royal position for such a **t** as this?"
Da   7: 25 be delivered into his hands for a **t**, times
             and half a **t**.
Hos 10: 12 for it is **t** to seek the LORD,
Ro   9: 9 "At the appointed **t** I will return,
Heb   9: 28 and he will appear a second **t**,
     10: 12 had offered for all **t** one sacrifice
1Pe   4: 17 For it is **t** for judgment to begin

TIMES (TIME)
Ps   9: 9 a stronghold in **t** of trouble.
     31: 15 My **t** are in your hands;
     62: 8 Trust in him at all **t**, you people;
Pr   17: 17 A friend loves at all **t**,
Am   5: 13 in such **t**, for the **t** are evil.
Mt   18: 21 sins against me? Up to seven **t**?"
Ac   1: 7 "It is not for you to know the **t**
Rev 12: 14 care of for a time, **t** and half a time,

TIMID
2Ti   1: 7 God gave us does not make us **t**,

TIMOTHY
      Believer from Lystra (Ac 16:1). Joined Paul on second
missionary journey (Ac 16–20). Sent to settle problems
at Corinth (1Co 4:17; 16:10). Led church at Ephesus
(1Ti 1:3). Co-writer with Paul (1Th 1:1; 2Th 1:1; Phm 1).

TIRE (TIRED)
2Th   3: 13 never **t** of doing what is good.

TIRED (TIRE)
Ex   17: 12 When Moses' hands grew **t**,
Isa 40: 28 He will not grow **t** or weary,

TITHE (TEN)
Lev 27: 30 "'A **t** of everything
Dt   12: 17 your own towns the **t** of your grain
Mal   3: 10 Bring the whole **t**

TITHES (TEN)
Mal   3: 8 "In **t** and offerings.

TITUS
      Gentile co-worker of Paul (Gal 2:1–3; 2Ti 4:10); sent
to Corinth (2Co 2:13; 7–8; 12:18), Crete (Titus 1:4–5).

TODAY
Mt 6: 11 Give us **t** our daily bread.
Lk 23: 43 **t** you will be with me in paradise."
Heb 3: 13 as long as it is called "**T**,"
13: 8 Christ is the same yesterday and **t**

TOIL
Ge 3: 17 through painful **t** you will eat food

TOLERATE
Hab 1: 13 then do you **t** the treacherous?
Rev 2: 2 that you cannot **t** wicked people,

TOMB
Mt 27: 65 make the **t** as secure as you know
Lk 24: 2 the stone rolled away from the **t**,

TOMORROW
Pr 27: 1 not boast about **t**, for you do not
Isa 22: 13 drink," you say, "for **t** we die!"
Mt 6: 34 do not worry about **t**, for **t**
Jas 4: 13 "Today or **t** we will go to this

TONGUE (TONGUES)
Ps 39: 1 my ways and keep my **t** from sin;
Pr 12: 18 but the **t** of the wise brings healing.
1Co 14: 2 who speaks in a **t** does not speak
14: 4 speaks in a **t** edifies themselves,
14: 13 one who speaks in a **t** should pray
14: 19 than ten thousand words in a **t**.
Php 2: 11 and every **t** acknowledge that Jesus
Jas 3: 8 no human being can tame the **t**.

TONGUES (TONGUE)
Isa 28: 11 strange **t** God will speak to this
Mk 16: 17 *they will speak in new t*;
Ac 2: 4 other **t** as the Spirit enabled them.
10: 46 For they heard them speaking in **t**
19: 6 they spoke in **t** and prophesied.
1Co 12: 30 Do all speak in **t**? Do all interpret?
14: 18 I speak in **t** more than all of you.
14: 39 and do not forbid speaking in **t**.
Jas 1: 26 rein on their **t** deceive themselves,

TOOK (TAKE)
1Co 11: 23 the night he was betrayed, **t** bread,
Php 3: 12 which Christ Jesus **t** hold of me.

TOOTH (TEETH)
Ex 21: 24 eye for eye, **t** for **t**, hand for hand,
Mt 5: 38 was said, 'Eye for eye, and **t** for **t**.'

TORMENTED
Rev 20: 10 They will be **t** day and night

TORN
Gal 4: 15 you would have **t** out your eyes
Php 1: 23 I am **t** between the two: I desire

TOUCH (TOUCHED)
Ps 105: 15 "Do not **t** my anointed ones;
Lk 24: 39 **T** me and see; a ghost does not
2Co 6: 17 **T** no unclean thing, and I will
Col 2: 21 Do not taste! Do not **t**!"?

TOUCHED (TOUCH)
1Sa 10: 26 men whose hearts God had **t**.
Mt 14: 36 cloak, and all who **t** it were healed.

TOWER
Ge 11: 4 a **t** that reaches to the heavens,
Pr 18: 10 name of the LORD is a fortified **t**;

TOWN (TOWNS)
Mt 5: 14 **t** built on a hill cannot be hidden.

TOWNS (TOWN)
Nu 35: 2 to give the Levites **t** to live
35: 15 These six **t** will be a place of refuge

TRACING
Ro 11: 33 and his paths beyond **t** out!

TRADITION
Mt 15: 6 word of God for the sake of your **t**.
Col 2: 8 which depends on human **t**

TRAINING
1Co 9: 25 in the games goes into strict **t**.
2Ti 3: 16 correcting and **t** in righteousness,

TRAMPLED
Lk 21: 24 Jerusalem will be **t**
Heb 10: 29 to be punished who has **t** the Son

TRANCE
Ac 10: 10 was being prepared, he fell into a **t**.

TRANSCENDS
Php 4: 7 God, which **t** all understanding,

TRANSFIGURED
Mt 17: 2 There he was **t** before them.

TRANSFORM (TRANSFORMED)
Php 3: 21 will **t** our lowly bodies so that they

TRANSFORMED (TRANSFORM)
Ro 12: 2 be **t** by the renewing of your mind.
2Co 3: 18 are being **t** into his image

TRANSGRESSION (TRANSGRESSIONS
TRANSGRESSORS)
Isa 53: 8 **t** of my people he was punished.
Ro 4: 15 where there is no law there is no **t**.

TRANSGRESSIONS (TRANSGRESSION)
Ps 32: 1 is the one whose **t** are forgiven,
51: 1 great compassion blot out my **t**.
103: 12 so far has he removed our **t** from
Isa 53: 5 But he was pierced for our **t**,
Eph 2: 1 you were dead in your **t** and sins,

TRANSGRESSORS (TRANSGRESSION)
Ps 51: 13 Then I will teach **t** your ways,
Isa 53: 12 and was numbered with the **t**.
53: 12 and made intercession for the **t**.

TREADING
Dt 25: 4 Do not muzzle an ox while it is **t**
1Co 9: 9 "Do not muzzle an ox while it is **t**

TREASURE (TREASURED TREASURES)
Isa 33: 6 of the LORD is the key to this **t**.
Mt 6: 21 where your **t** is, there your heart
2Co 4: 7 But we have this **t** in jars of clay

TREASURED (TREASURE)
Dt 7: 6 to be his people, his **t** possession.
Lk 2: 19 But Mary **t** up all these things

TREASURES (TREASURE)
Mt 6: 19 store up for yourselves **t** on earth,
Col 2: 3 in whom are hidden all the **t**
Heb 11: 26 of greater value than the **t** of Egypt,

TREAT
Lev 22: 2 sons to **t** with respect the sacred
1Ti 5: 1 **T** younger men as brothers,
1Pe 3: 7 **t** them with respect as the weaker

TREATY
Dt 7: 2 Make no **t** with them, and show

TREE
Ge 2: 9 of the garden were the **t** of life
2: 9 and the **t** of the knowledge of good
Ps 1: 3 is like a **t** planted by streams
Mt 3: 10 every **t** that does not produce good
12: 33 for a **t** is recognized by its fruit.
Rev 22: 14 may have the right to the **t** of life

TREMBLE (TREMBLING)
1Ch 16: 30 **T** before him, all the earth!
Ps 114: 7 **T**, earth, at the presence of the Lord,

TREMBLING (TREMBLE)
Ps 2: 11 fear and celebrate his rule with **t**.
Php 2: 12 out your salvation with fear and **t**,

TRESPASS
Ro 5: 17 if, by the **t** of the one man,

TRIALS
1Th 3: 3 one would be unsettled by these **t**.
Jas 1: 2 whenever you face **t** of many kinds,
2Pe 2: 9 how to rescue the godly from **t**

TRIBES
Ge 49: 28 All these are the twelve **t** of Israel,
Mt 19: 28 judging the twelve **t** of Israel.

TRIBULATION
Rev 7: 14 who have come out of the great **t**;

TRIUMPHAL (TRIUMPHING)
Isa 60: 11 their kings led in **t** procession.
2Co 2: 14 as captives in Christ's **t** procession

TRIUMPHING (TRIUMPHAL)
Col 2: 15 of them, **t** over them by the cross.

TROUBLE (TROUBLED TROUBLES)
Job 14: 1 are of few days and full of **t**.
Ps 46: 1 strength, an ever-present help in **t**.
107: 13 they cried to the LORD in their **t**,
Pr 24: 10 If you falter in a time of **t**,
Mt 6: 34 Each day has enough **t** of its own.
Jn 16: 33 In this world you will have **t**.
Ro 8: 35 Shall **t** or hardship or persecution

TROUBLED (TROUBLE)
Jn 14: 1 "Do not let your hearts be **t**.
14: 27 Do not let your hearts be **t** and do

TROUBLES (TROUBLE)
1Co 7: 28 those who marry will face many **t**
2Co 1: 4 who comforts us in all our **t**,
4: 17 momentary **t** are achieving for us

TRUE (TRUTH)
Dt 18: 22 does not take place or come **t**,
1Sa 9: 6 and everything he says comes **t**.
Ps 119:160 All your words are **t**; all your
Jn 17: 3 the only **t** God, and Jesus Christ,
Ro 3: 4 Let God be **t**, and every human
Php 4: 8 whatever is **t**, whatever is noble,
Rev 22: 6 These words are trustworthy and **t**.

TRUMPET
1Co 14: 8 if the **t** does not sound a clear call,
15: 52 twinkling of an eye, at the last **t**.

TRUST (ENTRUSTED TRUSTED TRUSTWORTHY)
Ps 20: 7 we **t** in the name of the LORD our
37: 3 **T** in the LORD and do good;
56: 4 in God I **t** and am not afraid.
119: 42 taunts me, for I **t** in your word.
Pr 3: 5 **T** in the LORD with all your heart
Isa 30: 15 in quietness and **t** is your strength,
1Co 4: 2 been given a **t** must prove faithful.

TRUSTED (TRUST)
Ps 26: 1 I have **t** in the LORD and have not
Isa 25: 9 we **t** in him, and he saved us.
Da 3: 28 They **t** in him and defied the king's
Lk 16: 10 "Whoever can be **t** with very little

TRUSTWORTHY (TRUST)
Ps 119:138 are righteous; they are fully **t**.
Pr 11: 13 but a **t** person keeps a secret.
Rev 22: 6 to me, "These words are **t** and true.

TRUTH (TRUE TRUTHFUL TRUTHS)
Isa 45: 19 I, the LORD, speak the **t**;
Zec 8: 16 Speak the **t** to each other,
Jn 4: 23 the Father in the Spirit and in **t**,
8: 32 Then you will know the **t**, and the **t**
14: 6 "I am the way and the **t** and the life.
16: 13 he will guide you into all the **t**.
18: 38 "What is **t**?" retorted Pilate.
Ro 1: 25 They exchanged the **t** about God
1Co 13: 6 in evil but rejoices with the **t**.
2Co 13: 8 against the **t**, but only for the **t**.
Eph 4: 15 Instead, speaking the **t** in love,
6: 14 belt of **t** buckled around your waist,
2Th 2: 10 because they refused to love the **t**
1Ti 2: 4 to come to a knowledge of the **t**.
3: 15 the pillar and foundation of the **t**.
2Ti 2: 15 correctly handles the word of **t**.
3: 7 to come to a knowledge of the **t**.
Heb 10: 26 received the knowledge of the **t**,
1Pe 1: 22 by obeying the **t** so that you have
2Pe 2: 2 and will bring the way of **t**
1Jn 1: 6 we lie and do not live out the **t**.
1: 8 ourselves and the **t** is not in us.

TRUTHFUL (TRUTH)
Jn 3: 33 it has certified that God is **t**.

TRUTHS (TRUTH)
1Ti 3: 9 keep hold of the deep **t** of the faith
Heb 5: 12 teach you the elementary **t** of God's

TRY (TRYING)
Ps 26: 2 and **t** me, examine my heart and
Isa 7: 13 Will you **t** the patience of my God
1Co 14: 12 **t** to excel in those that build
2Co 5: 11 the Lord, we **t** to persuade others.

TRYING (TRY)
2Co 5: 12 We are not **t** to commend ourselves
1Th 2: 4 We are not **t** to please people

TURN (TURNED TURNS)
Ex 32: 12 **T** from your fierce anger;
Dt 5: 32 do not **t** aside to the right
28: 14 Do not **t** aside from any
Jos 1: 7 do not **t** from it to the right
2Ch 7: 14 face and **t** from their wicked ways,
30: 9 He will not **t** his face from you
Ps 78: 6 they in **t** would tell their children.
Pr 22: 6 they are old they will not **t** from it.
Isa 29: 16 You **t** things upside down,
30: 21 Whether you **t** to the right
45: 22 "**T** to me and be saved, all you ends
55: 7 Let them **t** to the LORD, and he
Eze 33: 11 they **t** from their ways and live.
Mal 4: 6 He will **t** the hearts of the parents
Mt 5: 39 **t** to them the other cheek also.
10: 35 to **t** "'a man against his father,
Jn 12: 40 understand with their hearts, nor **t**
Ac 3: 19 and **t** to God, so that your sins may
26: 18 and **t** them from darkness to light,
1Ti 6: 20 **T** away from godless chatter
1Pe 3: 11 must **t** from evil and do good;

TURNED (TURN)
Ps 30: 11 You **t** my wailing into dancing;
40: 1 he **t** to me and heard my cry.
Isa 53: 6 each of us has **t** to our own way;
Hos 7: 8 Ephraim is a flat loaf not **t** over.
Joel 2: 31 The sun will be **t** to darkness
Ro 3: 12 All have **t** away, they have together

TURNS (TURN)
2Sa 22: 29 the LORD **t** my darkness
Pr 15: 1 A gentle answer **t** away wrath,

Isa 44: 25 of the wise and **t** it into nonsense,
Jas 5: 20 Whoever **t** a sinner from the error

TWELVE
Ge 49: 28 All these are the **t** tribes of Israel,
Mt 10: 1 Jesus called his **t** disciples to him

TWINKLING
1Co 15: 52 a flash, in the **t** of an eye, at the last

UNAPPROACHABLE
1Ti 6: 16 immortal and who lives in **u** light,

UNBELIEF (UNBELIEVER UNBELIEVERS
UNBELIEVING)
Mk 9: 24 help me overcome my **u**!"
Ro 11: 20 they were broken off because of **u**,
Heb 3: 19 able to enter, because of their **u**.

UNBELIEVER (UNBELIEF)
1Co 7: 15 But if the **u** leaves, let it be so.
10: 27 If an **u** invites you to a meal
14: 24 if an **u** or an inquirer comes in
2Co 6: 15 have in common with an **u**?
1Ti 5: 8 the faith and is worse than an **u**.

UNBELIEVERS (UNBELIEF)
1Co 6: 6 and this in front of **u**!
2Co 6: 14 Do not be yoked together with **u**.

UNBELIEVING (UNBELIEF)
1Co 7: 14 the **u** husband has been sanctified
7: 14 and the **u** wife has been sanctified
Rev 21: 8 But the cowardly, the **u**, the vile,

UNCERTAIN
1Ti 6: 17 which is so **u**, but to put their hope

UNCHANGEABLE
Heb 6: 18 that, by two **u** things in which it is

UNCIRCUMCISED
1Sa 17: 26 Who is this **u** Philistine that he
Col 3: 11 or Jew, circumcised or **u**,

UNCIRCUMCISION
1Co 7: 19 is nothing and **u** is nothing.
Gal 5: 6 neither circumcision nor **u** has any

UNCLEAN
Isa 6: 5 For I am a man of **u** lips, and I live
Ro 14: 14 Jesus, that nothing is **u** in itself.
2Co 6: 17 Touch no **u** thing, and I will

UNCONCERNED
Eze 16: 49 were arrogant, overfed and **u**;

UNCOVERED
Heb 4: 13 Everything is **u** and laid bare

UNDERSTAND (UNDERSTANDING
UNDERSTANDS)
Job 42: 3 Surely I spoke of things I did not **u**,
Ps 73: 16 When I tried to **u** all this,
119:125 that I may **u** your statutes.
Lk 24: 45 so they could **u** the Scriptures.
Ac 8: 30 "Do you **u** what you are reading?"
Ro 7: 15 I do not **u** what I do. For what I
1Co 2: 14 and cannot **u** them because they
Eph 5: 17 but **u** what the Lord's will is.
2Pe 3: 16 some things that are hard to **u**,

UNDERSTANDING (UNDERSTAND)
Ps 119: 32 for you have broadened my **u**.
119:104 I gain **u** from your precepts;
147: 5 in power; his **u** has no limit.
Pr 3: 5 heart and lean not on your own **u**;
4: 7 Though it cost all you have, get **u**.
10: 23 a person of **u** delights in wisdom.
11: 12 one who has **u** holds their tongue.
15: 21 but whoever has **u** keeps a straight
15: 32 one who heeds correction gains **u**.

Isa 40: 28 and his **u** no one can fathom.
Da 5: 12 a keen mind and knowledge and **u**,
Mk 4: 12 and ever hearing but never **u**;
12: 33 with all your **u** and with all your
Php 4: 7 which transcends all **u**, will guard

UNDERSTANDS (UNDERSTAND)
1Ch 28: 9 every heart and **u** every desire

UNDIVIDED
1Ch 12: 33 to help David with **u** loyalty—
Ps 86: 11 give me an **u** heart, that I may fear
Eze 11: 19 I will give them an **u** heart and put
1Co 7: 35 in a right way in **u** devotion

UNDOING
Pr 18: 7 The mouths of fools are their **u**,

UNDYING
Eph 6: 24 Lord Jesus Christ with an **u** love.

UNFADING
1Pe 3: 4 the **u** beauty of a gentle and quiet

UNFAILING
Ps 33: 5 the earth is full of his **u** love.
119: 76 May your **u** love be my comfort,
143: 8 bring me word of your **u** love, for I
Pr 19: 22 What a person desires is **u** love;
La 3: 32 compassion, so great is his **u** love.

UNFAITHFUL
Lev 6: 2 is **u** to the LORD by deceiving
1Ch 10: 13 Saul died because he was **u**
Pr 13: 15 but the way of the **u** leads to their

UNFOLDING
Ps 119:130 The **u** of your words gives light;

UNGODLINESS
Titus 2: 12 It teaches us to say "No" to **u**

UNITED (UNITY)
Ro 6: 5 For if we have been **u** with him
Php 2: 1 from being **u** with Christ, if any
Col 2: 2 encouraged in heart and **u** in love,

UNITY (UNITED)
Ps 133: 1 God's people live together in **u**!
Eph 4: 3 keep the **u** of the Spirit through
4: 13 until we all reach **u** in the faith
Col 3: 14 them all together in perfect **u**.

UNIVERSE
Heb 1: 2 through whom also he made the **u**.

UNKNOWN
Ac 17: 23 with this inscription: TO AN **U** GOD.

UNLEAVENED
Ex 12: 17 "Celebrate the Festival of **U** Bread,

UNPROFITABLE
Titus 3: 9 because these are **u** and useless.

UNPUNISHED
Ex 34: 7 Yet he does not leave the guilty **u**;
Pr 19: 5 A false witness will not go **u**,

UNREPENTANT
Ro 2: 5 stubbornness and your **u** heart,

UNRIGHTEOUS
Zep 3: 5 not fail, yet the **u** know no shame.
Mt 5: 45 rain on the righteous and the **u**.
1Pe 3: 18 the righteous for the **u**, to bring
2Pe 2: 9 to hold the **u** for punishment

UNSEARCHABLE
Ro 11: 33 How **u** his judgments, and his

UNSEEN
2Co 4: 18 temporary, but what is **u** is eternal.

UNSTABLE
Jas   1: 8 double-minded and **u** in all they
2Pe 2: 14 they seduce the **u**; they are experts
      3: 16 ignorant and **u** people distort,

UNTHINKABLE
Job 34: 12 It is **u** that God would do wrong,

UNVEILED
2Co 3: 18 with **u** faces contemplate the Lord's

UNWORTHY
Job 40: 4 "I am **u**—how can I reply to you?
Lk 17: 10 do, should say, 'We are **u** servants;

UPRIGHT
Job   1: 1 This man was blameless and **u**;
Pr   2: 7 He holds success in store for the **u**,
    15: 8 but the prayer of the **u** pleases him.
Titus 1: 8 who is self-controlled, **u**,
     2: 12 **u** and godly lives in this present

UPROOTED
Jude : 12 autumn trees, without fruit and **u**

USEFUL
2Ti   2: 21 **u** to the Master and prepared to do
     3: 16 God-breathed and is **u** for teaching

USELESS
1Co 15: 14 our preaching is **u** and so is your
Jas   2: 20 that faith without deeds is **u**?

UZZIAH
Son of Amaziah; king of Judah also known as Azariah (2Ki 15:1–7; 1Ch 6:24; 2Ch 26).

VAIN
Ps 33: 17 A horse is a **v** hope for deliverance;
Isa 65: 23 They will not labor in **v**, nor will
1Co 15: 2 Otherwise, you have believed in **v**.
    15: 58 your labor in the Lord is not in **v**.
2Co 6: 1 you not to receive God's grace in **v**.

VALLEY
Ps 23: 4 I walk through the darkest **v**,
Isa 40: 4 Every **v** shall be raised up,
Joel 3: 14 Lord is near in the **v** of decision.

VALUABLE (VALUE)
Lk 12: 24 how much more **v** you are than

VALUE (VALUABLE)
Mt 13: 46 When he found one of great **v**,
1Ti   4: 8 For physical training is of some **v**, but godliness has **v** for all things,
Heb 11: 26 as of greater **v** than the treasures

VEIL
Ex 34: 33 to them, he put a **v** over his face.
2Co 3: 14 to this day the same **v** remains

VENGEANCE (AVENGE REVENGE)
Isa 34: 8 For the Lord has a day of **v**,

VICTORIES (VICTORY)
Ps 18: 50 He gives his king great **v**;
    21: 1 great is his joy in the **v** you give!

VICTORIOUS (VICTORY)
Zec 9: 9 king comes to you, righteous and **v**,
Rev 2: 7 To the one who is **v**, I will give
     2: 11 The one who is **v** will not be hurt
     2: 17 To the one who is **v**, I will give
     2: 26 To the one who is **v** and does my
     3: 5 The one who is **v** will, like them,
     3: 12 The one who is **v** I will make
     3: 21 To the one who is **v**, I will give
    21: 7 Those who are **v** will inherit all

VICTORIOUSLY (VICTORY)
Ps 45: 4 In your majesty ride forth **v**

VICTORY (VICTORIES VICTORIOUS VICTORIOUSLY)
Ps 60: 12 With God we will gain the **v**,
1Co 15: 54 has been swallowed up in **v**."
    15: 57 He gives us the **v** through our Lord
1Jn 5: 4 This is the **v** that has overcome

VINDICATED
1Ti 3: 16 in the flesh, was **v** by the Spirit,

VINE
Jn 15: 1 "I am the true **v**, and my Father is

VINEGAR
Mk 15: 36 filled a sponge with wine **v**, put it

VIOLATION
Heb 2: 2 every **v** and disobedience received

VIOLENCE
Isa 60: 18 No longer will **v** be heard in your
Eze 45: 9 Give up your **v** and oppression

VIPERS
Ro   3: 13 "The poison of **v** is on their lips."

VIRGIN
Isa   7: 14 The **v** will conceive and give birth
Mt   1: 23 "The **v** will conceive and give birth
2Co 11: 2 I might present you as a pure **v**

VIRTUES
Col   3: 14 And over all these **v** put on love,

VISION
Ac 26: 19 disobedient to the **v** from heaven.

VOICE
Ps 95: 7 if only you would hear his **v**,
Isa 30: 21 your ears will hear a **v** behind you,
Jn   5: 28 are in their graves will hear his **v**
    10: 3 him, and the sheep listen to his **v**.
Heb 3: 7 "Today, if you hear his **v**,
Rev 3: 20 If anyone hears my **v** and opens

VOMIT
Pr 26: 11 As a dog returns to its **v**, so fools
2Pe 2: 22 "A dog returns to its **v**," and,

VOW
Nu 30: 2 a man makes a **v** to the Lord

WAGES
Lk 10: 7 you, for the worker deserves his **w**.
Ro   4: 4 **w** are not credited as a gift but as
     6: 23 the **w** of sin is death, but the gift

WAILING
Ps 30: 11 You turned my **w** into dancing;

WAIST
2Ki 1: 8 had a leather belt around his **w**."
Mt   3: 4 he had a leather belt around his **w**.

WAIT (WAITED WAITS)
Ps 27: 14 **W** for the Lord; be strong
 130: 5 I **w** for the Lord, my whole being
Isa 30: 18 Blessed are all who **w** for him!
Ac   1: 4 **w** for the gift my Father promised,
Ro   8: 23 groan inwardly as we **w** eagerly
1Th 1: 10 and to **w** for his Son from heaven,
Titus 2: 13 while we **w** for the blessed hope—

WAITED (WAIT)
Ps 40: 1 I **w** patiently for the Lord;

WAITS (WAIT)
Ro   8: 19 the creation **w** in eager expectation

WALK (WALKED)
Dt 11: 19 and when you **w** along the road,
Ps   1: 1 Blessed is the one who does not **w**

Ps   23: 4   though I **w** through the darkest
     89: 15   **w** in the light of your presence,
Isa   2: 5   let us **w** in the light of the LORD.
     30: 21   saying, "This is the way; **w** in it."
     40: 31   weary, they will **w** and not be faint.
Jer   6: 16   and **w** in it, and you will find rest
Da   4: 37   those who **w** in pride he is able
Am   3: 3   Do two **w** together unless they
Mic   6: 8   and to **w** humbly with your God.
Mk   2: 9   say, 'Get up, take your mat and **w**'?
Jn   8: 12   Whoever follows me will never **w**
1Jn   1: 7   But if we **w** in the light, as he is
2Jn   :   6   his command is that you **w** in love.

WALKED (WALK)
Ge   5: 24   Enoch **w** faithfully with God;
Jos 14: 9   which your feet have **w** will be
Mt   14: 29   **w** on the water and came toward

WALL
Jos   6: 20   gave a loud shout, the **w** collapsed;
Ne   2: 17   let us rebuild the **w** of Jerusalem,
Rev 21: 12   a great, high **w** with twelve gates,

WALLOWING
2Pe   2: 22   returns to her **w** in the mud."

WANT (WANTED WANTING WANTS)
1Sa   8: 19   they said. "We **w** a king over us.
Lk   19: 14   say, 'We don't **w** this man to be our
Ro   7: 15   For what I **w** to do I do not do,
Php   3: 10   I **w** to know Christ—yes, to know

WANTED (WANT)
1Co 12: 18   of them, just as he **w** them to be.

WANTING (WANT)
Da   5: 27   weighed on the scales and found **w**.
2Pe   3: 9   with you, not **w** anyone to perish,

WANTS (WANT)
Mt   20: 26   whoever **w** to become great among
Mk   8: 35   For whoever **w** to save their life
Ro   9: 18   on whom he **w** to have mercy,
      9: 18   he hardens whom he **w** to harden.
1Ti   2: 4   who **w** all people to be saved

WAR (WARS)
Isa   2: 4   nor will they train for **w** anymore.
Da   9: 26   **W** will continue until the end,
2Co 10: 3   we do not wage **w** as the world
Rev 19: 11   justice he judges and wages **w**.

WARN (WARNED WARNINGS)
Eze   3: 19   if you do **w** the wicked person
     33: 9   if you do **w** the wicked person

WARNED (WARN)
Ps   19: 11   By them your servant is **w**;

WARNINGS (WARN)
1Co 10: 11   and were written down as **w** for us,

WARS (WAR)
Ps   46: 9   He makes **w** cease to the ends
Mt   24: 6   will hear of **w** and rumors of **w**,

WASH (WASHED WASHING)
Ps   51: 7   **w** me, and I will be whiter than
Jn   13: 5   and began to **w** his disciples' feet,
Ac   22: 16   be baptized and **w** your sins away,
Rev 22: 14   are those who **w** their robes,

WASHED (WASH)
1Co   6: 11   But you were **w**, you were
Rev   7: 14   they have **w** their robes and made

WASHING (WASH)
Eph   5: 26   the **w** with water through the word,
Titus 3: 5   saved us through the **w** of rebirth

WATCH (WATCHES WATCHING WATCHMAN)
Ge   31: 49   the LORD keep **w** between you
Jer 31: 10   them and will **w** over his flock like
Mt   24: 42   "Therefore keep **w**, because you do
     26: 41   "**W** and pray so that you will not
Lk   2: 8   keeping **w** over their flocks at night
1Ti   4: 16   **W** your life and doctrine closely.

WATCHES (WATCH)
Ps   1: 6   For the LORD **w** over the way
    121: 3   he who **w** over you will not

WATCHING (WATCH)
Lk   12: 37   servants whose master finds them **w**

WATCHMAN (WATCH)
Eze   3: 17   I have made you a **w** for the people

WATER (WATERED WATERS)
Ps   1: 3   like a tree planted by streams of **w**,
     22: 14   I am poured out like **w**, and all my
Pr   25: 21   if he is thirsty, give him **w** to drink.
Isa 49: 10   and lead them beside springs of **w**.
Jer   2: 13   broken cisterns that cannot hold **w**.
Zec 14: 8   On that day living **w** will flow
Mk   9: 41   anyone who gives you a cup of **w**
Jn   4: 10   he would have given you living **w**."
      7: 38   rivers of living **w** will flow
Eph   5: 26   washing with **w** through the word,
1Pe   3: 21   this **w** symbolizes baptism that
Rev 21: 6   thirsty I will give **w** without cost

WATERED (WATER)
1Co   3: 6   I planted the seed, Apollos **w** it,

WATERS (WATER)
Ps   23: 2   he leads me beside quiet **w**,
Isa 58: 11   like a spring whose **w** never fail.
1Co   3: 7   nor the one who **w** is anything,

WAVE (WAVES)
Jas   1: 6   the one who doubts is like a **w**

WAVES (WAVE)
Isa 57: 20   whose **w** cast up mire and mud.
Mt   8: 27   the winds and the **w** obey him!"
Eph   4: 14   tossed back and forth by the **w**,

WAY (WAYS)
Dt   1: 33   to show you the **w** you should go.
2Sa 22: 31   "As for God, his **w** is perfect:
Job 23: 10   But he knows the **w** that I take;
Ps   1: 1   stand in the **w** that sinners take
     37: 5   Commit your **w** to the LORD;
    139: 24   and lead me in the **w** everlasting.
Pr   14: 12   is a **w** that appears to be right,
     22: 6   off on the **w** they should go,
Isa 30: 21   behind you, saying, "This is the **w**;
     53: 6   of us has turned to our own **w**;
Mt   3: 3   'Prepare the **w** for the Lord,
Jn   14: 6   "I am the **w** and the truth
1Co 10: 13   provide a **w** out so that you can
     12: 31   will show you the most excellent **w**.
Heb   4: 15   who has been tempted in every **w**,
      9: 8   the **w** into the Most Holy Place had
     10: 20   living **w** opened for us through

WAYS (WAY)
Ex   33: 13   teach me your **w** so I may know
Ps   25: 10   All the **w** of the LORD are loving
     51: 13   I will teach transgressors your **w**,
Pr   3: 6   in all your **w** submit to him, and he
     16: 17   who guard their **w** preserve their
Isa 55: 7   Let the wicked forsake their **w**
     55: 8   neither are your **w** my **w**,"
Jas   3: 2   We all stumble in many **w**.

WEAK (WEAKER WEAKNESS)
Mt 26: 41 spirit is willing, but the flesh is **w**."
Ro 14: 1 Accept the one whose faith is **w**,
1Co 1: 27 chose the **w** things of the world
8: 9 a stumbling block to the **w**.
9: 22 To the **w** I became **w**, to win the **w**.
2Co 12: 10 For when I am **w**, then I am strong.
Heb 12: 12 your feeble arms and **w** knees.

WEAKER (WEAK)
1Co 12: 22 seem to be **w** are indispensable,
1Pe 3: 7 them with respect as the **w** partner

WEAKNESS (WEAK)
Ro 8: 26 way, the Spirit helps us in our **w**.
1Co 1: 25 **w** of God is stronger than human
2Co 12: 9 my power is made perfect in **w**."
Heb 5: 2 since he himself is subject to **w**.

WEALTH
Pr 3: 9 Honor the LORD with your **w**,
Mk 10: 22 away sad, because he had great **w**.
Lk 15: 13 and there squandered his **w** in wild

WEAPONS
2Co 10: 4 The **w** we fight with are not the **w**

WEARIES (WEARY)
Ecc 12: 12 and much study **w** the body.

WEARY (WEARIES)
Isa 40: 31 they will run and not grow **w**,
Mt 11: 28 all you who are **w** and burdened,
Gal 6: 9 not become **w** in doing good,

WEDDING
Mt 22: 11 who was not wearing **w** clothes.
Rev 19: 7 For the **w** of the Lamb has come,

WEEP (WEEPING WEPT)
Ecc 3: 4 a time to **w** and a time to laugh,
Lk 6: 21 Blessed are you who **w** now, for

WEEPING (WEEP)
Ps 30: 5 **w** may stay for the night,
126: 6 Those who go out **w**, carrying seed
Mt 8: 12 where there will be **w** and gnashing

WELCOMES
Mt 18: 5 **w** one such child in my name **w** me.
2Jn : 11 Anyone who **w** them shares in

WELL
Lk 17: 19 your faith has made you **w**."
Jas 5: 15 faith will make the sick person **w**;

WEPT (WEEP)
Ps 137: 1 and **w** when we remembered Zion.
Jn 11: 35 Jesus **w**.

WEST
Ps 103: 12 as far as the east is from the **w**,

WHIRLWIND (WIND)
2Ki 2: 1 to take Elijah up to heaven in a **w**,
Hos 8: 7 They sow the wind and reap the **w**.
Na 1: 3 His way is in the **w** and the storm,

WHITE (WHITER)
Isa 1: 18 scarlet, they shall be as **w** as snow;
Da 7: 9 His clothing was as **w** as snow;
Rev 1: 14 hair on his head was **w** like wool,
3: 4 dressed in **w**, for they are worthy.
20: 11 I saw a great **w** throne and him

WHITER (WHITE)
Ps 51: 7 wash me, and I will be **w** than snow.

WHOLE
Mt 16: 26 for someone to gain the **w** world,
24: 14 in the **w** world as a testimony to all

Jn 13: 10 their **w** body is clean.
21: 25 even the **w** world would not have
Ac 20: 27 proclaim to you the **w** will of God.
Ro 3: 19 and the **w** world held accountable
8: 22 the **w** creation has been groaning
Gal 5: 3 he is obligated to obey the **w** law.
Eph 4: 13 attaining to the **w** measure
Jas 2: 10 For whoever keeps the **w** law
1Jn 2: 2 but also for the sins of the **w** world.

WHOLEHEARTEDLY (HEART)
Dt 1: 36 he followed the LORD **w**."
Eph 6: 7 Serve **w**, as if you were serving

WICKED (WICKEDNESS)
Ps 1: 1 does not walk in step with the **w**
1: 5 Therefore the **w** will not stand
73: 3 when I saw the prosperity of the **w**.
Pr 10: 20 the heart of the **w** is of little value.
11: 21 The **w** will not go unpunished,
Isa 53: 9 was assigned a grave with the **w**,
55: 7 Let the **w** forsake their ways
57: 20 But the **w** are like the tossing sea,
Eze 3: 18 that **w** person will die for their sin,
18: 23 any pleasure in the death of the **w**?
33: 14 And if I say to a **w** person,

WICKEDNESS (WICKED)
Eze 28: 15 you were created till **w** was found

WIDE
Isa 54: 2 stretch your tent curtains **w**, do not
Mt 7: 13 For **w** is the gate and broad is
Eph 3: 18 to grasp how **w** and long and high

WIDOW (WIDOWS)
Dt 10: 18 cause of the fatherless and the **w**,
Lk 21: 2 saw a poor **w** put in two very small

WIDOWS (WIDOW)
Jas 1: 27 orphans and **w** in their distress

WIFE (WIVES)
Ge 2: 24 and mother and is united to his **w**,
24: 67 So she became his **w**, and he loved
Ex 20: 17 shall not covet your neighbor's **w**,
Dt 5: 21 shall not covet your neighbor's **w**.
Pr 5: 18 you rejoice in the **w** of your youth.
12: 4 A **w** of noble character is her
18: 22 who finds a **w** finds what is good
19: 13 quarrelsome **w** is like the constant
31: 10 A **w** of noble character who can
Mt 19: 3 for a man to divorce his **w** for any
1Co 7: 2 sexual relations with his own **w**,
7: 33 how he can please his **w**—
Eph 5: 23 head of the **w** as Christ is the head
5: 33 must love his **w** as he loves himself,
5: 33 the **w** must respect her husband.
1Ti 3: 2 faithful to his **w**, temperate,
Rev 21: 9 you the bride, the **w** of the Lamb."

WILD
Lk 15: 13 squandered his wealth in **w** living,
Ro 11: 17 and you, though a **w** olive shoot,

WILL (WILLING WILLINGNESS)
Ps 40: 8 I desire to do your **w**, my God;
143: 10 Teach me to do your **w**, for you are
Isa 53: 10 Yet it was the LORD's **w** to crush
Mt 6: 10 kingdom come, your **w** be done,
26: 39 Yet not as I **w**, but as you **w**."
Jn 7: 17 chooses to do the **w** of God **w** find
Ac 20: 27 to you the whole **w** of God.
Ro 12: 2 test and approve what God's **w** is—
1Co 7: 37 but has control over his own **w**,
Eph 5: 17 understand what the Lord's **w** is.
Php 2: 13 for it is God who works in you to **w**

1Th	4: 3	It is God's **w** that you should be
	5: 18	for this is God's **w** for you in Christ
Heb	9: 16	In the case of a **w**, it is necessary
	10: 7	I have come to do your **w**,
Jas	4: 15	"If it is the Lord's **w**, we **w** live
1Jn	5: 14	ask anything according to his **w**,
Rev	4: 11	by your **w** they were created

WILLING (WILL)

Ps	51: 12	salvation and grant me a **w** spirit,
Da	3: 28	were **w** to give up their lives rather
Mt	18: 14	Father in heaven is not **w** that any
	23: 37	her wings, and you were not **w**.
	26: 41	The spirit is **w**, but the flesh is

WILLINGNESS (WILL)

2Co	8: 12	For if the **w** is there, the gift is

WIN

Php	3: 14	on toward the goal to **w** the prize
1Th	4: 12	your daily life may **w** the respect

WIND (WHIRLWIND)

Jas	1: 6	the sea, blown and tossed by the **w**.

WINE

Pr	20: 1	**W** is a mocker and beer a brawler;
Isa	55: 1	buy **w** and milk without money
Mt	9: 17	Neither do people pour new **w**
Lk	23: 36	They offered him **w** vinegar
Ro	14: 21	drink **w** or to do anything else
Eph	5: 18	Do not get drunk on **w**, which

WINESKINS

Mt	9: 17	people pour new wine into old **w**.

WINGS

Ru	2: 12	under whose **w** you have come
Ps	17: 8	hide me in the shadow of your **w**
Isa	40: 31	They will soar on **w** like eagles;
Lk	13: 34	gathers her chicks under her **w**,

WIPE

Rev	7: 17	God will **w** away every tear

WISDOM (WISE)

1Ki	4: 29	God gave Solomon **w** and very
Ps	111: 10	the Lord is the beginning of **w**;
Pr	31: 26	She speaks with **w**, and faithful
Jer	10: 12	he founded the world by his **w**
Mt	11: 19	**w** is proved right by her deeds."
Lk	2: 52	And Jesus grew in **w** and stature,
Ro	11: 33	the depth of the riches of the **w**
Col	2: 3	are hidden all the treasures of **w**
Jas	1: 5	If any of you lacks **w**, you should

WISE (WISDOM WISER)

1Ki	3: 12	I will give you a **w** and discerning
Job	5: 13	He catches the **w** in their craftiness,
Ps	19: 7	trustworthy, making **w** the simple.
Pr	3: 7	Do not be **w** in your own eyes;
	9: 8	rebuke the **w** and they will love
	10: 1	A **w** son brings joy to his father,
	11: 30	and the one who is **w** saves lives.
	13: 20	Walk with the **w** and become **w**,
	17: 28	Even fools are thought **w** if they
Da	12: 3	Those who are **w** will shine like
Mt	11: 25	hidden these things from the **w**
1Co	1: 27	things of the world to shame the **w**;
2Ti	3: 15	make you **w** for salvation through

WISER (WISE)

1Co	1: 25	of God is **w** than human wisdom,

WITHER (WITHERS)

Ps	1: 3	and whose leaf does not **w**—

WITHERS (WITHER)

Isa	40: 7	The grass **w** and the flowers fall,
1Pe	1: 24	the grass **w** and the flowers fall,

WITHHOLD

Ps	84: 11	no good thing does he **w** from
Pr	23: 13	Do not **w** discipline from a child;

WITNESS (WITNESSES)

Jn	1: 8	he came only as a **w** to the light.

WITNESSES (WITNESS)

Dt	19: 15	by the testimony of two or three **w**.
Ac	1: 8	and you will be my **w** in Jerusalem,

WIVES (WIFE)

Eph	5: 22	**W**, submit yourselves to your own
	5: 25	love your **w**, just as Christ loved
1Pe	3: 1	**W**, in the same way submit

WOE

Isa	6: 5	"**W** to me!" I cried. "I am ruined!

WOLF

Isa	65: 25	The **w** and the lamb will feed

WOMAN (MAN)

Ge	2: 22	the Lord God made a **w**
	3: 15	put enmity between you and the **w**,
Lev	20: 13	with a man as one does with a **w**,
Dt	22: 5	A **w** must not wear men's clothing,
Ru	3: 11	that you are a **w** of noble character.
Pr	31: 30	a **w** who fears the Lord is to be
Mt	5: 28	a **w** lustfully has already committed
Jn	8: 3	brought in a **w** caught
Ro	7: 2	by law a married **w** is bound to her
1Co	11: 3	and the head of the **w** is man,
	11: 13	Is it proper for a **w** to pray to God
1Ti	2: 11	A **w** should learn in quietness

WOMB

Job	1: 21	I came from my mother's **w**,
Jer	1: 5	I formed you in the **w** I knew you,
Lk	1: 44	the baby in my **w** leaped for joy.

WOMEN (MAN)

Lk	1: 42	"Blessed are you among **w**,
1Co	14: 34	**W** should remain silent
1Ti	2: 9	I also want the **w** to dress modestly,
Titus	2: 3	teach the older **w** to be reverent
1Pe	3: 5	the way the holy **w** of the past

WONDERFUL (WONDERS)

Job	42: 3	things too **w** for me to know.
Ps	119: 18	that I may see **w** things in your law.
	119: 27	I may meditate on your **w** deeds.
	119:129	statutes are **w**; therefore I obey
	139: 6	Such knowledge is too **w** for me,
Isa	9: 6	he will be called **W** Counselor,
1Pe	2: 9	out of darkness into his **w** light.

WONDERS (WONDERFUL)

Job	37: 14	stop and consider God's **w**.
Ps	17: 7	Show me the **w** of your great love,
	31: 21	for he showed me the **w** of his love
Joel	2: 30	I will show **w** in the heavens
Ac	2: 19	I will show **w** in the heavens

WOOD

Isa	44: 19	Shall I bow down to a block of **w**?"
1Co	3: 12	costly stones, **w**, hay or straw,

WORD (WORDS)

Dt	8: 3	but on every **w** that comes
2Sa	22: 31	The Lord's **w** is flawless;
Ps	119: 9	By living according to your **w**.
	119: 11	I have hidden your **w** in my heart
	119:105	Your **w** is a lamp to my feet
Pr	12: 25	the heart, but a kind **w** cheers it up.
	30: 5	"Every **w** of God is flawless; he is
Isa	55: 11	so is my **w** that goes out from my

Jn 1: 1 In the beginning was the **W**, and the **W** was with God, and the **W** was God.
    1: 14 The **W** became flesh and made his
2Co 2: 17 we do not peddle the **w** of God
    4: 2 nor do we distort the **w** of God.
Eph 6: 17 of the Spirit, which is the **w** of God.
Php 2: 16 as you hold firmly to the **w** of life.
2Ti 2: 15 and who correctly handles the **w**
Heb 4: 12 the **w** of God is alive and active.
Jas 1: 22 Do not merely listen to the **w**,

WORDS (WORD)
Dt 11: 18 Fix these **w** of mine in your hearts
Ps 119:103 How sweet are your **w** to my taste,
   119:130 unfolding of your **w** gives light;
   119:160 All your **w** are true; all your
Pr 30: 6 Do not add to his **w**, or he will
Jer 15: 16 When your **w** came, I ate them;
Mt 24: 35 but my **w** will never pass away.
Jn 6: 68 You have the **w** of eternal life.
    15: 7 in me and my **w** remain in you,
1Co 14: 19 rather speak five intelligible **w**
Rev 22: 19 if anyone takes **w** away from this

WORK (HANDIWORK WORKER WORKERS WORKING WORKS)
Ex 23: 12 but on the seventh day do not **w**,
Nu   8: 11 be ready to do the **w** of the Lord.
Dt   5: 14 On it you shall not do any **w**,
Jer 48: 10 who is lax in doing the Lord's **w**!
Jn   6: 27 Do not **w** for food that spoils,
     9: 4 is coming, when no one can **w**.
1Co 3: 13 test the quality of each person's **w**.
Php 1: 6 he who began a good **w** in you will
     2: 12 continue to **w** out your salvation
Col 3: 23 you do, **w** at it with all your heart,
1Th 5: 12 those who **w** hard among you,
2Th 3: 10 is unwilling to **w** shall not eat."
2Ti 3: 17 equipped for every good **w**.
Heb 6: 10 he will not forget your **w**

WORKER (WORK)
Lk 10: 7 for the **w** deserves his wages.
1Ti 5: 18 and "The **w** deserves his wages."
2Ti 2: 15 a **w** who does not need to be

WORKERS (WORK)
Mt   9: 37 is plentiful but the **w** are few.
1Co 3: 9 For we are **c** in God's service;

WORKING (WORK)
Col 3: 23 all your heart, as **w** for the Lord,

WORKS (WORK)
Pr 31: 31 her **w** bring her praise at the city
Ro   8: 28 in all things God **w** for the good
Eph 2: 9 not by **w**, so that no one can boast.
     4: 12 to equip his people for **w** of service,

WORLD (WORLDLY)
Ps 50: 12 for the **w** is mine, and all that is
Isa 13: 11 I will punish the **w** for its evil,
Mt   5: 14 "You are the light of the **w**.
    16: 26 for someone to gain the whole **w**,
Mk 16: 15 "*Go into all the **w** and preach*
Jn   1: 29 who takes away the sin of the **w**!
     3: 16 God so loved the **w** that he gave his
     8: 12 he said, "I am the light of the **w**.
    15: 19 but I have chosen you out of the **w**. That is why the **w** hates you.
    16: 33 I have overcome the **w**."
    18: 36 said, "My kingdom is not of this **w**.
Ro   3: 19 and the whole **w** held accountable
1Co 3: 19 the wisdom of this **w** is foolishness
2Co 5: 19 that God was reconciling the **w**
    10: 3 For though we live in the **w**, we do

1Ti 6: 7 For we brought nothing into the **w**,
1Jn 2: 2 but also for the sins of the whole **w**.
     2: 15 not love the **w** or anything in the **w**.
Rev 13: 8 slain from the creation of the **w**.

WORLDLY (WORLD)
Titus 2: 12 to ungodliness and **w** passions,

WORMS
Mk   9: 48 where "'the **w** that eat them do

WORRY (WORRYING)
Mt   6: 25 I tell you, do not **w** about your life,
    10: 19 do not **w** about what to say or how

WORRYING (WORRY)
Mt   6: 27 you by **w** add a single hour to your

WORSHIP
1Ch 16: 29 **W** the Lord in the splendor of his
Ps 95: 6 let us bow down in **w**, let us kneel
Mt   2: 2 it rose and have come to **w** him."
Jn   4: 24 his worshipers must **w** in the Spirit
Ro 12: 1 this is your true and proper **w**.

WORTH (WORTHY)
Job 28: 13 No mortal comprehends its **w**;
Pr 31: 10 She is far more than rubies.
Mt 10: 31 you are **w** more than many
Ro   8: 18 sufferings are not **w** comparing
1Pe 1: 7 of greater **w** than gold,
     3: 4 which is of great **w** in God's sight.

WORTHLESS
Pr 11: 4 Wealth is **w** in the day of wrath,
Jas 1: 26 themselves, and their religion is **w**.

WORTHY (WORTH)
1Ch 16: 25 is the Lord and most **w** of praise;
Eph 4: 1 live a life **w** of the calling you have
Php 1: 27 in a manner **w** of the gospel
Rev 5: 2 "Who is **w** to break the seals

WOUNDS
Pr 27: 6 **W** from a friend can be trusted,
Isa 53: 5 and by his **w** we are healed.
Zec 13: 6 'What are these **w** on your body?'
1Pe 2: 24 "by his **w** you have been healed."

WRATH
2Ch 36: 16 at his prophets until the **w**
Ps   2: 5 anger and terrifies them in his **w**,
    76: 10 Surely your **w** against mankind
Pr 15: 1 A gentle answer turns away **w**,
Jer 25: 15 cup filled with the wine of my **w**
Ro   1: 18 The **w** of God is being revealed
     5: 9 saved from God's **w** through him!
1Th 5: 9 God did not appoint us to suffer **w**
Rev 6: 16 and from the **w** of the Lamb!

WRESTLED
Ge 32: 24 a man **w** with him till daybreak.

WRITE (WRITING WRITTEN)
Dt   6: 9 **W** them on the doorframes of your
Pr   7: 3 **w** them on the tablet of your heart.
Heb 8: 10 minds and **w** them on their hearts.

WRITING (WRITE)
1Co 14: 37 what I am **w** to you is the Lord's

WRITTEN (WRITE)
Jos 1: 8 be careful to do everything **w** in it.
Da 12: 1 everyone whose name is found **w**
Lk 10: 20 that your names are **w** in heaven."
Jn 20: 31 these are **w** that you may believe
1Co 4: 6 "Do not go beyond what is **w**."
2Co 3: 3 **w** not with ink but with the Spirit
Heb 12: 23 whose names are **w** in heaven.

WRONG (WRONGDOING WRONGED WRONGS)
Ex 23: 2 not follow the crowd in doing **w**.
Nu 5: 7 restitution for the **w** they have
Job 34: 12 unthinkable that God would do **w**,
1Th 5: 15 that nobody pays back **w** for **w**,

WRONGDOING (WRONG)
Job 1: 22 not sin by charging God with **w**.

WRONGED (WRONG)
1Co 6: 7 Why not rather be **w**?

WRONGS (WRONG)
Pr 10: 12 conflict, but love covers over all **w**.
1Co 13: 5 angered, it keeps no record of **w**.

YEARS
Ps 90: 4 A thousand **y** in your sight are like
   90: 10 Our days may come to seventy **y**,
2Pe 3: 8 the Lord a day is like a thousand **y**,
Rev 20: 2 and bound him for a thousand **y**.

YESTERDAY
Heb 13: 8 Jesus Christ is the same **y** and today

YOKE (YOKED)
Mt 11: 29 Take my **y** upon you and learn

YOKED (YOKE)
2Co 6: 14 Do not be **y** together

YOUNG (YOUTH)
Ps 119: 9 can a **y** person stay on the path
1Ti 4: 12 down on you because you are **y**,

YOUTH (YOUNG)
Ps 103: 5 your **y** is renewed like the eagle's.
Ecc 12: 1 your Creator in the days of your **y**,
2Ti 2: 22 Flee the evil desires of **y** and

ZEAL
Jn 2: 17 **Z** for your house will consume me.
Ro 12: 11 Never be lacking in **z**, but keep

ZECHARIAH
   1. Son of Jeroboam II; king of Israel (2Ki 15:8–12).
   2. Post-exilic prophet who encouraged rebuilding of temple (Ezr 5:1; 6:14; Zec 1:1).
   3. Father of John the Baptist (Lk 1:13; 3:2).

ZEDEKIAH
   Mattaniah, son of Josiah (1Ch 3:15), made king of Judah by Nebuchadnezzar (2Ki 24:17—25:7; 2Ch 36:10–14; Jer 37–39; 52:1–11).

ZERUBBABEL
   Descendant of David (1Ch 3:19; Mt 1:3). Led return from exile (Ezr 2–3; Ne 7:7; Hag 1–2; Zec 4).

ZIMRI
   King of Israel (1Ki 16:9–20).

ZION
Ps 137: 3 "Sing us one of the songs of **Z**!"
Jer 50: 5 They will ask the way to **Z** and
Ro 9: 33 I lay in **Z** a stone that causes people
   11: 26 "The deliverer will come from **Z**;

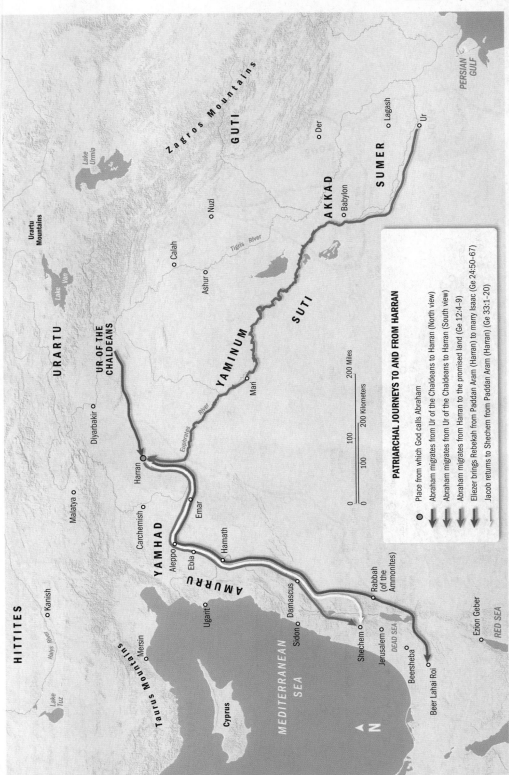

PATRIARCHAL JOURNEYS TO AND FROM HARRAN

- Place from which God calls Abraham
- Abraham migrates from Ur of the Chaldeans to Harran (North view)
- Abraham migrates from Ur of the Chaldeans to Harran (South view)
- Abraham migrates from Harran to the promised land (Ge 12:4–9)
- Eliezer brings Rebekah from Paddan Aram (Harran) to marry Isaac (Ge 24:50–67)
- Jacob returns to Shechem from Paddan Aram (Harran) (Ge 33:1–20)

200 Miles

100   200 Kilometers

0   100   200

HITTITES

URARTU

GUTI

SUMER

AKKAD

SUTI

YAMINUM

YAMHAD

AMURRU

Lake Tuz
Lake Van
Lake Urmia

Urartu Mountains

Zagros Mountains

Taurus Mountains

Halys River

Tigris River

Euphrates River

PERSIAN GULF

MEDITERRANEAN SEA

DEAD SEA

RED SEA

Cyprus

Kanish
Mersin
Malatya
Diyarbakir
Ugarit
Sidon
Carchemish
Emar
Harran
UR OF THE CHALDEANS
Aleppo
Ebla
Hamath
Damascus
Mari
Ashur
Calah
Nuzi
Der
Babylon
Lagash
Ur
Rabbah (of the Ammonites)
Shechem
Jerusalem
Beersheba
Ezion Geber
Beer Lahai Roi

N

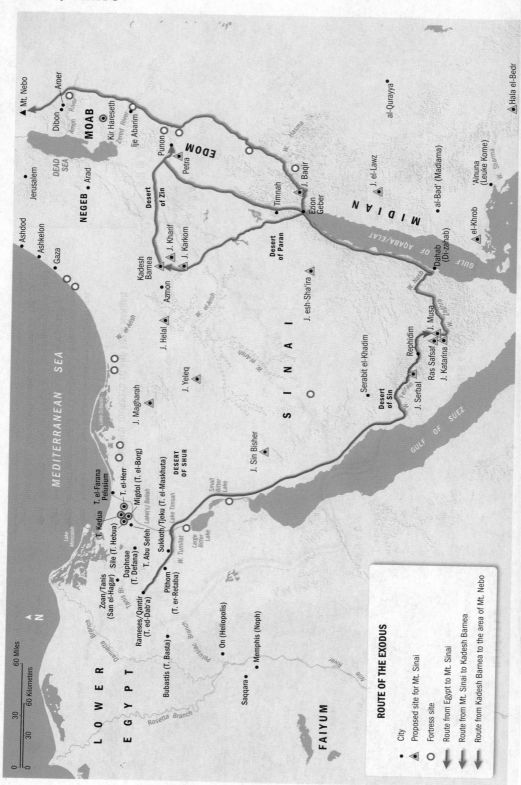

ROUTE OF THE EXODUS

- • City
- ◣ Proposed site for Mt. Sinai
- ○ Fortress site
- ↓ Route from Egypt to Mt. Sinai
- ↓ Route from Mt. Sinai to Kadesh Barnea
- ↓ Route from Kadesh Barnea to the area of Mt. Nebo

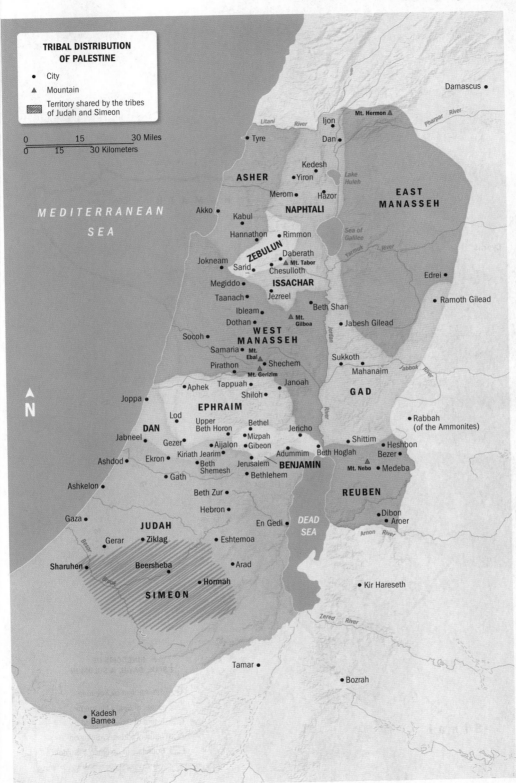

TRIBAL DISTRIBUTION
OF PALESTINE

- • City
- ▲ Mountain
- ▨ Territory shared by the tribes of Judah and Simeon

0   15   30 Miles
0   15   30 Kilometers

MEDITERRANEAN SEA

Damascus •

Litani River
Ijon
Mt. Hermon ▲
Tyre •
Dan •
Pharpar River

Kedesh
ASHER
• Yiron
Lake Huleh
EAST MANASSEH

Merom •
Hazor •

Akko •
Kabul •
NAPHTALI

Hannathon •
• Rimmon
Sea of Galilee

Jokneam •
ZEBULUN
Daberath •
Yarmuk River
Edrei •

Sarid •
▲ Mt. Tabor
Chesulloth •

Megiddo •
ISSACHAR
• Ramoth Gilead

Taanach •
Jezreel •

Ibleam •
Beth Shan •

Dothan •
▲ Mt. Gilboa
Jabesh Gilead •

Socoh •
WEST MANASSEH

Samaria •
Mt. Ebal ▲
Sukkoth •

Pirathon •
▲ Shechem
Mahanaim •

Mt. Gerizim ▲

Aphek •
Tappuah •
Janoah •
GAD

Joppa •
Shiloh •

EPHRAIM
Jordan River

Lod •
Upper Beth Horon •
Bethel •
• Rabbah (of the Ammonites)

DAN
• Mizpah •
Jericho •

Jabneel •
Aijalon •
Gibeon •
Shittim •

Gezer •
• Heshbon

Ashdod •
Ekron •
Kiriath Jearim •
Adummim •
Beth Hoglah •
Bezer •

• Beth Shemesh
Jerusalem •
BENJAMIN
Mt. Nebo ▲
• Medeba

• Gath
• Bethlehem

Ashkelon •
REUBEN

Beth Zur •
• Dibon

Hebron •
• Aroer

Gaza •
En Gedi •
DEAD SEA
Arnon River

JUDAH

Gerar •
• Ziklag
• Eshtemoa

Sharuhen •
Beersheba •
• Arad
• Kir Hareseth

Besor Brook
• Hormah

SIMEON

Zered River

Tamar •

• Bozrah

Kadesh Barnea •

N

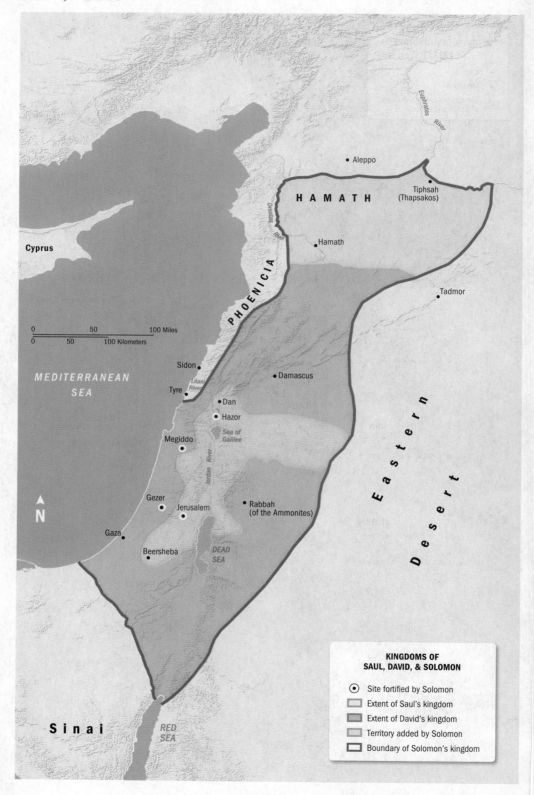

Cyprus

HAMATH

Aleppo

Tiphsah
(Thapsakos)

Euphrates River

Orontes River

Hamath

PHOENICIA

Tadmor

MEDITERRANEAN
SEA

Sidon

Damascus

Tyre

Litani River

Dan

Hazor

Sea of
Galilee

Megiddo

Jordan River

Eastern

Desert

Gezer

Jerusalem

Rabbah
(of the Ammonites)

Gaza

Beersheba

DEAD
SEA

N

Sinai

RED
SEA

**KINGDOMS OF
SAUL, DAVID, & SOLOMON**

⊙ Site fortified by Solomon
☐ Extent of Saul's kingdom
☐ Extent of David's kingdom
☐ Territory added by Solomon
☐ Boundary of Solomon's kingdom

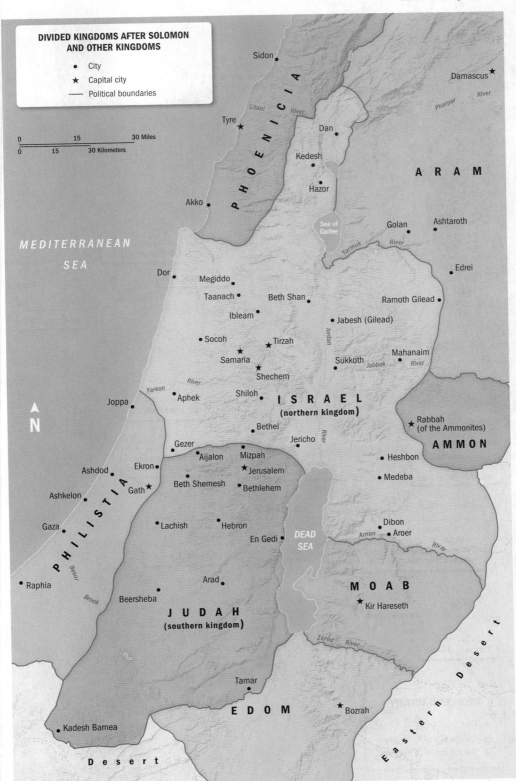

DIVIDED KINGDOMS AFTER SOLOMON AND OTHER KINGDOMS

- • City
- ★ Capital city
- — Political boundaries

0   15   30 Miles
0   15   30 Kilometers

Sidon

Damascus ★

PHOENICIA

Litani   River

Tyre ★

Dan

ARAM

Kedesh

Hazor

Akko

Sea of Galilee

Golan   Ashtaroth

Pharpar   River

Yarmuk   River

MEDITERRANEAN SEA

Dor

Megiddo

Taanach   Beth Shan

Edrei

Ibleam

Ramoth Gilead

Jabesh (Gilead)

Socoh   Tirzah

Mahanaim

Samaria ★

Sukkoth

Jabbok   River

Shechem ★

Jordan

Yarkon   River

Aphek   Shiloh

ISRAEL
(northern kingdom)

N

Joppa

Bethel

Rabbah ★
(of the Ammonites)

Gezer

Jericho

AMMON

Aijalon   Mizpah

Heshbon

Ekron

Jerusalem ★

Ashdod

Beth Shemesh   Bethlehem

Medeba

Ashkelon

Gath ★

Gaza

Lachish   Hebron

Dibon

Raphia

En Gedi   DEAD SEA

Aroer

Arnon   River

PHILISTIA

Besor

Arad

MOAB

Brook

Beersheba

Kir Haresheth ★

JUDAH
(southern kingdom)

Zered   River

Tamar

Eastern Desert

EDOM   Bozrah ★

Kadesh Barnea

Desert

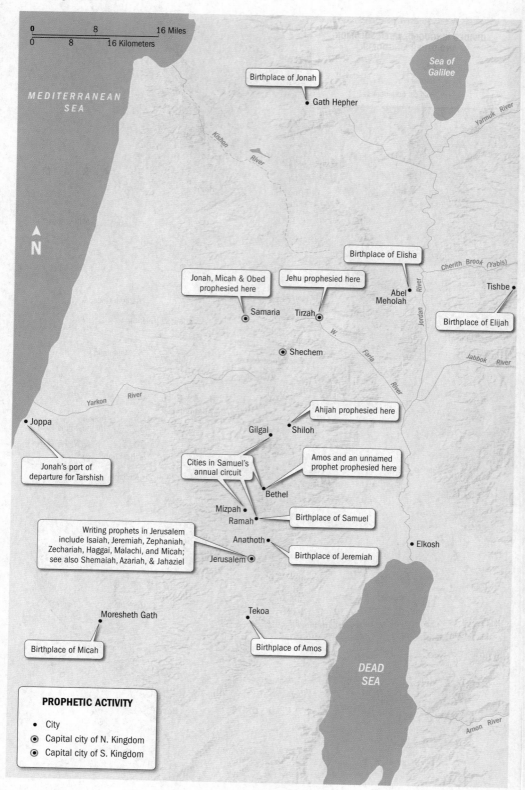

Birthplace of Jonah
Gath Hepher

Sea of Galilee

MEDITERRANEAN SEA

Kishon River

Yarmuk River

N

Birthplace of Elisha

Jonah, Micah & Obed prophesied here

Jehu prophesied here

Cherith Brook (Yabis)

Abel Meholah

Tishbe

Samaria

Tirzah

Birthplace of Elijah

Jordan River

Shechem

W. Farial River

Jabbok River

Yarkon River

Joppa

Ahijah prophesied here

Gilgal
Shiloh

Jonah's port of departure for Tarshish

Cities in Samuel's annual circuit

Amos and an unnamed prophet prophesied here

Bethel

Mizpah

Birthplace of Samuel

Ramah

Writing prophets in Jerusalem include Isaiah, Jeremiah, Zephaniah, Zechariah, Haggai, Malachi, and Micah; see also Shemaiah, Azariah, & Jahaziel

Anathoth

Elkosh

Jerusalem

Birthplace of Jeremiah

Moresheth Gath

Tekoa

Birthplace of Micah

Birthplace of Amos

DEAD SEA

PROPHETIC ACTIVITY

• City
◉ Capital city of N. Kingdom
◉ Capital city of S. Kingdom

Arnon River

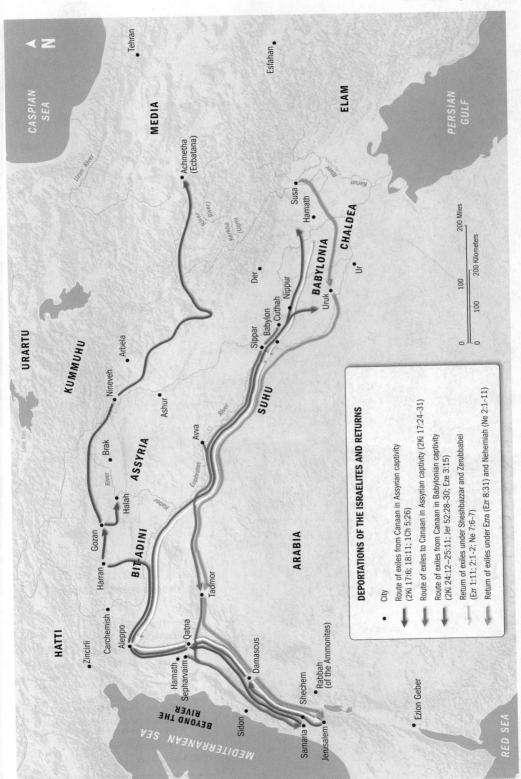

DEPORTATIONS OF THE ISRAELITES AND RETURNS

• City

Route of exiles from Canaan in Assyrian captivity (2Ki 17:6; 18:11; 1Ch 5:26)

Route of exiles to Canaan in Assyrian captivity (2Ki 17:24–31)

Route of exiles from Canaan in Babylonian captivity (2Ki 24:12–25:11; Jer 52:28–30; Eze 3:15)

Return of exiles under Sheshbazzar and Zerubbabel (Ezr 1:11; 2:1–2; Ne 7:6–7)

Return of exiles under Ezra (Ezr 8:31) and Nehemiah (Ne 2:1–11)

0   15   30 Miles
0   15   30 Kilometers

N

MEDITERRANEAN SEA

Sidon

ITUREA

Damascus

SYRIA

Tyre

Litani River

PHOENICIA

Panias
(Caesarea
Philippi)

Pharpar

River

TRACHONITIS

Kedesh

Lake Huleh

Akko

Hazor

Chorazin

Capernaum

GAULANITIS

Bethsaida

BATANEA

Raphana

Sepphoris

GALILEE

Arbela

Tiberias

Hippos

Yarmuk River

Ashtaroth

Canatha
(Kenath)

Gaba

Nazareth

*Sea of
Galilee*

Gadara

Abila

AURANITIS

Edrei

Dor

Caesarea
Maritima
(Strato's Tower)

Scythopolis
(Beth Shan)

Pella

DECAPOLIS

Dion

Gerasa
(Jerash)

Sebaste
(Samaria)

SAMARIA

Shechem

W. Far'a River

Amathus

Jabbok

River

Antipatris
(Aphek)

River

Joppa

Yarkon

Alexandrium

Jordan River

Phasaelis

Philadelphia
(Amman)

Jamnia

Gophna

PEREA

Tyrus

Azotus
(Ashdod)

Emmaus
(Nicopolis)

Cypros

Jericho

Livias

Ascalon
(Ashkelon)

Jerusalem

Esbus
(Heshbon)

Betogabris
(Beth-guvrin)

Bethlehem

Hyrcania

Medeba

Gaza

Marisa
(Mareshah)

JUDEA

Herodium

Hebron

Adora

Callirrhoe

Machaerus

**Eastern
Desert**

*DEAD
SEA*

Dibon

Arnon

River

IDUMEA

Masada

Beersheba

Malatha

Mampsis

Zered River

NABATEA

KINGDOM OF HEROD THE GREAT

- • City
- ◉ Site of Herodian fortress
- ◉ Decapolis city
- ◉ Cities Herod gave to his sister Salome
- ▬ Boundary of Herod the Great's Kingdom
- Domain given to Archelaus, son of Herod,
  by Augustus Caesar in 4 BC, when Herod died
- Domain given to Herod Antipas, son of Herod,
  by Augustus Caesar in 4 BC, when Herod died
- Domain given to Herod Philip, son of Herod,
  by Augustus Caesar in 4 BC, when Herod died
- Semi-independent municipality
- Syrian province

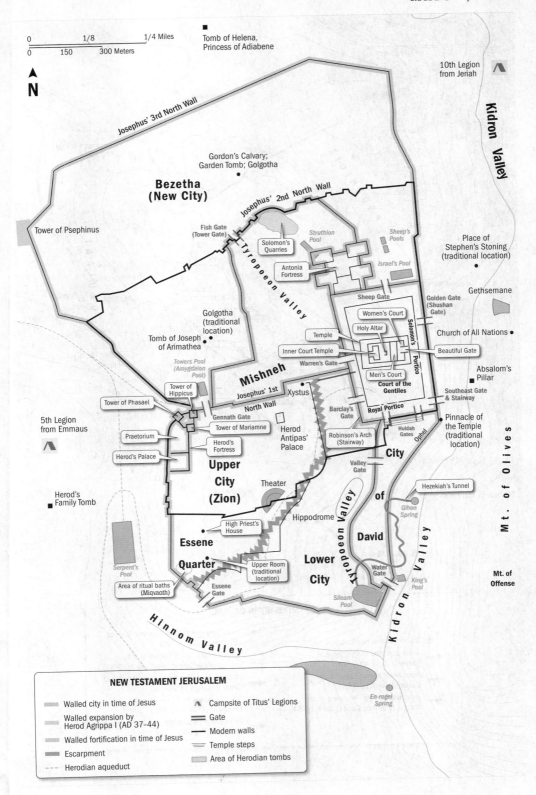

NEW TESTAMENT JERUSALEM

0 1/8 1/4 Miles
0 150 300 Meters

N

Tomb of Helena, Princess of Adiabene

10th Legion from Jeriah

Kidron Valley

Josephus' 3rd North Wall

Gordon's Calvary; Garden Tomb; Golgotha

Bezetha (New City)

Tower of Psephinus

Josephus' 2nd North Wall

Fish Gate (Tower Gate)

Solomon's Quarries

Struthion Pool

Sheep's Pools

Place of Stephen's Stoning (traditional location)

Tyropoeon Valley

Antonia Fortress

Israel's Pool

Sheep Gate

Gethsemane

Golden Gate (Shushan Gate)

Golgotha (traditional location)

Women's Court

Holy Altar

Temple

Church of All Nations

Tomb of Joseph of Arimathea

Inner Court Temple

Beautiful Gate

Solomon's Portico

Towers Pool (Amygdalon Pool)

Warren's Gate

Men's Court

Absalom's Pillar

Mishneh

Tower of Hippicus

Josephus' 1st North Wall

Xystus

Court of the Gentiles

Southeast Gate & Stairway

Tower of Phasael

Gennath Gate

Barclay's Gate

Royal Portico

Pinnacle of the Temple (traditional location)

5th Legion from Emmaus

Praetorium

Tower of Mariamne

Herod Antipas' Palace

Robinson's Arch (Stairway)

Huldah Gates

City

Mt. of Olives

Herod's Fortress

Herod's Palace

Upper City (Zion)

Theater

Valley Gate

of

Hezekiah's Tunnel

Herod's Family Tomb

High Priest's House

Hippodrome

Gihon Spring

David

Tyropoeon Valley

Kidron Valley

Mt. of Offense

Essene Quarter

Upper Room (traditional location)

Lower City

Water Gate

King's Pool

Serpent's Pool

Area of ritual baths (Miqvaoth)

Essene Gate

Siloam Pool

Hinnom Valley

En-rogel Spring

NEW TESTAMENT JERUSALEM

Walled city in time of Jesus

Campsite of Titus' Legions

Walled expansion by Herod Agrippa I (AD 37–44)

Gate

Walled fortification in time of Jesus

Modern walls

Escarpment

Temple steps

Herodian aqueduct

Area of Herodian tombs

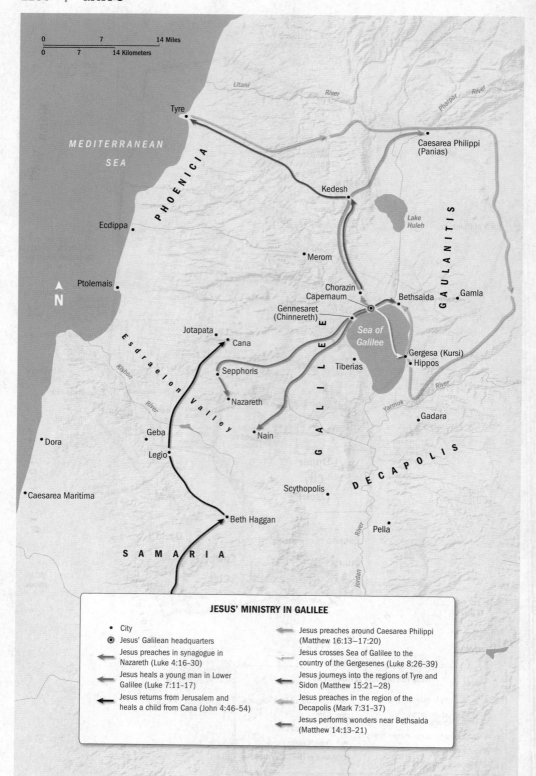

0 7 14 Miles
0 7 14 Kilometers

MEDITERRANEAN SEA

PHOENICIA

Litani River
Pharpar River

Tyre

Caesarea Philippi (Panias)

Kedesh

Ecdippa

Lake Huleh

Merom

GAULANITIS

Ptolemais

Chorazin
Capernaum
Bethsaida
Gamla

Gennesaret (Chinnereth)

Sea of Galilee

Jotapata
Cana

Gergesa (Kursi)
Hippos

Sepphoris

Tiberias

GALILEE

Nazareth

River

Yarmuk

Esdraelon Valley

Kishon

Nain

Gadara

Geba

Dora

Legio

DECAPOLIS

Caesarea Maritima

Scythopolis

Beth Haggan

Pella

River

Jordan

SAMARIA

JESUS' MINISTRY IN GALILEE

- City
- Jesus' Galilean headquarters
- Jesus preaches in synagogue in Nazareth (Luke 4:16–30)
- Jesus heals a young man in Lower Galilee (Luke 7:11–17)
- Jesus returns from Jerusalem and heals a child from Cana (John 4:46–54)
- Jesus preaches around Caesarea Philippi (Matthew 16:13—17:20)
- Jesus crosses Sea of Galilee to the country of the Gergesenes (Luke 8:26–39)
- Jesus journeys into the regions of Tyre and Sidon (Matthew 15:21–28)
- Jesus preaches in the region of the Decapolis (Mark 7:31–37)
- Jesus performs wonders near Bethsaida (Matthew 14:13–21)

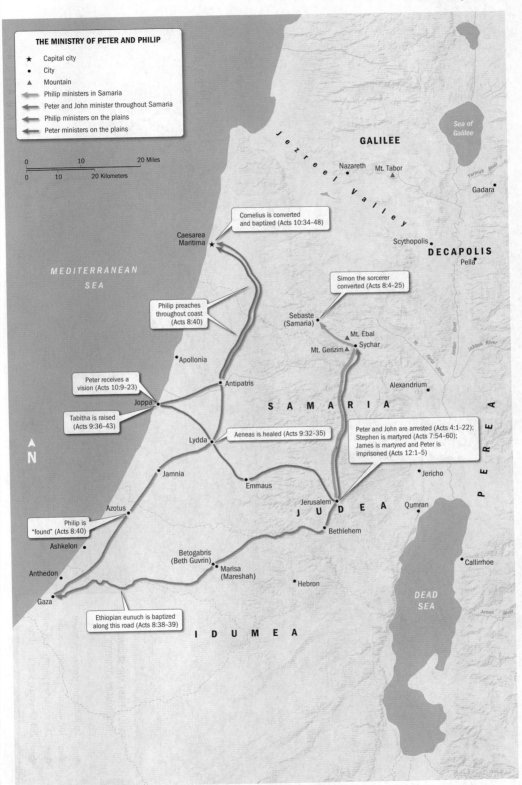

THE MINISTRY OF PETER AND PHILIP

★ Capital city
● City
▲ Mountain
⬅ Philip ministers in Samaria
⬅ Peter and John minister throughout Samaria
⬅ Philip ministers on the plains
⬅ Peter ministers on the plains

0   10   20 Miles
0   10   20 Kilometers

GALILEE

Sea of Galilee

Nazareth   Mt. Tabor
Gadara

Yarmuk River

MEDITERRANEAN SEA

Cornelius is converted and baptized (Acts 10:34–48)

Caesarea Maritima ★

Scythopolis

DECAPOLIS
Pella

Simon the sorcerer converted (Acts 8:4–25)

Philip preaches throughout coast (Acts 8:40)

Sebaste (Samaria)

Mt. Ebal
Mt. Gerizim   Sychar

Jordan River
Jabbok River

Apollonia

Peter receives a vision (Acts 10:9–23)

Antipatris

S A M A R I A

Alexandrium

Joppa

Tabitha is raised (Acts 9:36–43)

Aeneas is healed (Acts 9:32–35)

Lydda

Peter and John are arrested (Acts 4:1–22); Stephen is martyred (Acts 7:54–60); James is martyred and Peter is imprisoned (Acts 12:1–5)

P E R E A

N

Jamnia

Emmaus

Jericho

Jerusalem
J U D E A
Qumran

Azotus

Philip is "found" (Acts 8:40)

Bethlehem

Ashkelon

Betogabris (Beth Guvrin)
Marisa (Mareshah)

Hebron

Callirrhoe

Anthedon

Gaza

DEAD SEA

Arnon River

Ethiopian eunuch is baptized along this road (Acts 8:38–39)

I D U M E A

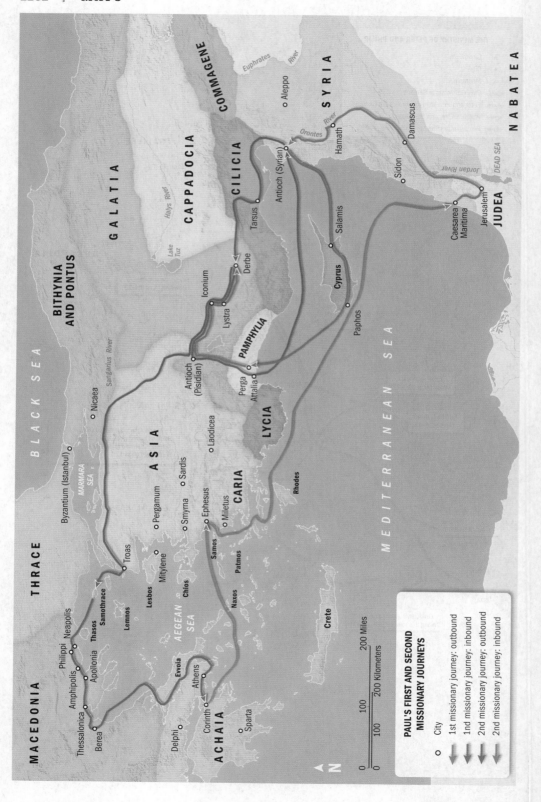

PAUL'S FIRST AND SECOND
MISSIONARY JOURNEYS

∘ City
1st missionary journey: outbound
1nd missionary journey: inbound
2nd missionary journey: outbound
2nd missionary journey: inbound

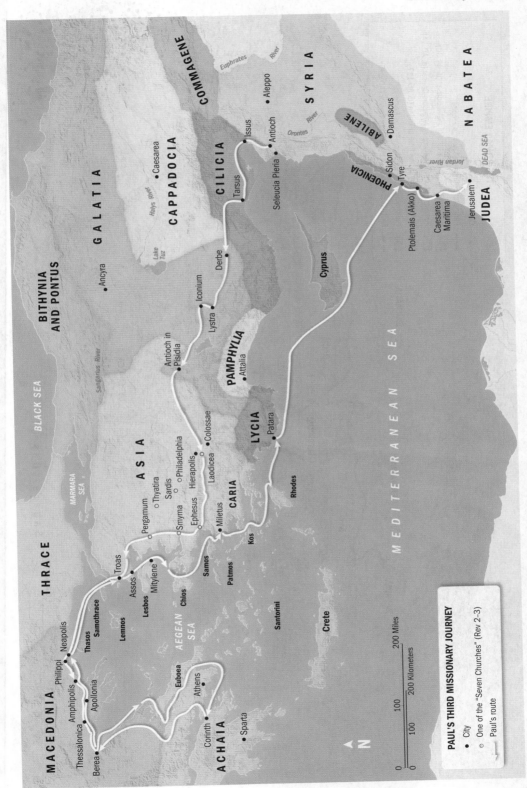

PAUL'S THIRD MISSIONARY JOURNEY

- • City
- ○ One of the "Seven Churches" (Rev 2–3)
- — Paul's route

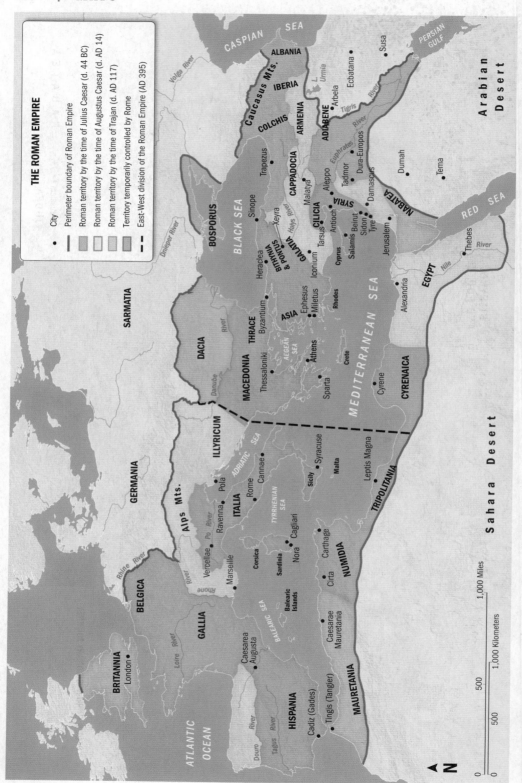

THE ROMAN EMPIRE

- • City
- | Perimeter boundary of Roman Empire
- Roman territory by the time of Julius Caesar (d. 44 BC)
- Roman territory by the time of Augustus Caesar (d. AD 14)
- Roman territory by the time of Trajan (d. AD 117)
- Territory temporarily controlled by Rome
- ‖ East-West division of the Roman Empire (AD 395)